AMERICAN

SALARIES

AND

WAGES

SURVEY

AMERICAN
SALARIES
AND
WAGES
SURVEY
Sixth Edition

Statistical Data Derived
from More Than 200
Government, Business &
News Sources

Arsen J. Darnay

GALE GROUP

Detroit
New York
San Francisco
London
Boston
Woodbridge, CT

Arsen J. Darnay, Editor

Editorial Code & Data Inc. Staff

Robert S. Lazich and Susan M. Turner, Contributing Editors
Sherae R. Carroll, Data Entry Associate
Joyce Piwowarski, Programmer

Gale Research Staff

Jason B. Baldwin, Coordinating Editor

Mary Beth Trimper, Production Director
Nekita McKee, Buyer

Kenn Zorn, Product Design Manager
Mike Logusz, Graphic Artist

This book is printed on recycled paper that meets Environmental Protection Agency Standards.

The paper used in this publication meets the minimum requirements of American National Standard for Information Sciences—Permanence Paper for Printed Library Materials, ANSI Z39.48-1984.

Copyright © 2001
Gale Group
27500 Drake Road
Farmington Hills, MI 48331-3535

ISBN 0-7876-4022-0
ISSN 1055-7628

Printed in the United States of America

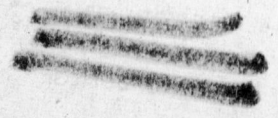

CONTENTS

INTRODUCTION

American Salaries & Wages Survey (*ASWS*), now in its sixth edition, is a compilation of 970 occupational combinations (2,835 occupations) and their corresponding salaries obtained from more than 220 federal and state government sources and various trade associations and journals.

Incorporating wage data for the period 1997 through 2000, *ASWS* provides extensive compensation information for industry, economic planners and developers, human resources professionals, employment counselors, job seekers, and job changers. Most of the data shown were collected in the last quarter of 1999 and released, for the first time, early in 2001.

Unique features of this edition include:

- More than 220 data sources.

- Significantly more salaries — 89,000 entries, up from 48,000.

- More than 970 occupational combinations, 2,835 occupations.

- Significantly improved geographical coverage than in previous editions, featuring data for every state, 3 possessions, 356 metro areas/counties, 54 cities, and 25 regions. Nationwide date are also included.

- Occupational outline of contents with numerous cross references

- Geographical outline of contents.

- Employment statistics for 1998 and 2008.

- Complete source listings for further research.

Sources

In order to provide a comprehensive data base, wage information was sought at the city level, the county or state region level, the state level, the U.S. region level, and the national level. Most Federal data are from the Occupational Employment Statistics (OES) annual survey. It samples and contacts approximately 400,00 establishments annually and about 1.2 million establishements over a three year period. Data from this program are available for 711 occupations.

A number of trade/professional associations conduct annual wage surveys of their members. Typically, these groups survey members of their professional societies to obtain data and report wages across the nation or within U.S. regions. Because the number of uniformly defined entries has significantly increased, fewer *entries* from these sources, and from trade journals, are included — but the number of *sources* has been increased to provide users of *ASWS* more points of entry for further research.

Occupational Titles

Federal data—and state data reported through the Federal government—follow the Standard Occupational Classification System (SOC). This system has now been adopted by the Occupational Employment Statistics program of the Bureau of Labor Statistics.

Occupational titles from other sources follow no particular standard. They are reproduced essentially as reported. Therefore it is possible to find both *Registered Nurse* under R and *Nurse Practitioner* under N. The Outline of Contents provides a cross-referenced alphabetical listing of all titles to help the user identify all variants of an occupation. Thus *Nurse* provides references to *Registered Nurse* and vice versa.

Wage Denominations

Wage figures presented in *ASWS* are given in the form provided by the original source—hourly, daily, weekly, monthly, or annual. A wage conversion chart is provided for your convenience in Appendix II. The denomination type is referred to by its first letter in the wage denomination column (H for hourly, W for weekly, etc.). A special code (S) is used to signal that both an hourly and an annual salary/wage are included on the same line. We chose this convention to provide more information in less space. The number of wage calculations varies from source to source; one source may provide only an average wage figure, another may report only a median. Many reports, however, give three or more calculated wage amounts — a mid-level value such as average or median, as well as a low and a high value. In some cases, ranges are provided; when the range is of such magnitude that it will not fit the space provided, abbreviations are used. A value for annual compensation such as 30-37500, for instance, means $30,000 to $37,500 per annum. Occasionally the low and high figures will be replaced by or supplemented with percentile or quartile figures. *ASWS* presents, wherever possible, three points on the wage spectrum: Low, Mid and High.

The ideal entry will show Lowest Wage Paid, Average Wage Paid, and Highest Wage Paid. But these figures are not always available; therefore, a coding system is used to specify what type of wage amount is being presented. For example,

- **FQ** stands for First Quartile and means that 25% of the workers surveyed earned less than the dollar amount shown.

- **TQ** stands for Third Quartile and means that 75% of the workers surveyed earned less than the dollar amount shown and 25% earned more than the dollar amount shown. All abbreviations of wage types are listed in alphabetical order at the bottom of every page in the data section.

Organization

Outlines of Contents

ASWS includes two outlines of contents providing access to the salaries listed. The Outline of Contents provides the reader with the means to find all listings of an occupation, despite variations in naming conventions. It lists the primary occupational classifications found in the main body of *ASWS,* in alphabetical order. In addition, the outline supplies derivations of those titles and cross-references them to their base forms. For example, the primary occupational title, Planner, can be found in the data section. The Outline of Contents provides several additional titles, including:

> *Financial Planner*
> *Meeting and Convention Planner*
> *Urban and Regional Planner*
> *Urban Planner*

The reader is advised to check the Outline of Contents when seeking wage information about a particular occupation in order to locate all available entries. The Geographic Outline is a listing of geographic locations down to the state level and the primary occupations provided for those locations. Metro areas and cities are not listed individually because the same occupations tend to be present at the state and local levels.

Main Body

The main body of *ASWS* is organized alphabetically by primary occupation first, then by secondary occupation and/or industry designation, then by geographic area. Data are presented in an eight-column table. The following is an explanation of these data columns from left to right.

Occupation/Type/Industry Column–

Lists the primary occupational title (e.g., Accountant), the secondary occupational title/type (e.g., Tax or Cost) and/or the industry designation (e.g., Transportation & Utilities or Manufacturing). In cases where both a secondary title and an industry designation are provided, the secondary title precedes the industry.

Location Column–

Specifies the geographical area to which the data refer. The column is organized by size of region in descending order: national data, U.S. regional (e.g., Southwest) data, statewide data, metropolitan statistical area (MSA) and county data, and city data. If the area is smaller than a U.S. state, the location is followed by its two-letter postal code (e.g., MI for Michigan). *Please note*: Cities appear alphabetically by state, so that California cities will appear ahead of those located in New Jersey, for instance.

Wage Denomination (Per) Column–

Specifies intervals at which the wage amount is paid to the employee. The single-letter codes are translated at the bottom of each page. Wages may be given in hourly, daily, weekly, monthly, or annual denominations. A wage conversion table is provided in Appendix II.

Low, Mid, and High Columns–

The columns list the wage figures for each entry in U.S. dollars. Each amount is followed by an explanatory code. A typical code is AHW, standing for Average Hourly Wage, or AAW, standing for Average Annual Wage. Sometimes references to "quartiles" may be found. The third quartile (TQ) wage, for instance, means that 75% of individuals earned less than the amount shown and 25% earned more.

Source Column–

Alphanumeric codes in this column refer to titles of sources from which data were obtained. A code like AZBLS means that the source is Bureau of Labor Statistics data supplied by the State of Arizona. These codes are explained in Appendix I.

Date Column–

Specifies the dates to which respective entries refer. If a particular source did not report a precise date, an approximate date ("1999") is provided.

Code Listings Block–

An explanation for all wages codes is shown at the bottom of each page. These abbreviations may also be found in the Abbreviations Table, Appendix III.

ASWS has four appendices, some of which have been mentioned above.

Appendix I - Sources

Appendix I lists 222 organizations which contributed data from one or multiple wage surveys or job banks. The appendix is organized alphabetically by source codes.

Appendix II - Wage Conversion Table

Appendix II is a table that translates an hour wage into its weekly, monthly, and annual equivalent. The reader, however, should note that these equivalencies are only approximate since wages reported in hourly formats may pertain to work weeks of different lengths.

Appendix III - Abbreviations

Appendix III lists and explains the abbreviations used throughout *ASWS*. Source abbreviations, of course, are explained in Appendix I.

Appendix IV - Employment by Occupation, 1998 and 2008

Appendix IV reproduces a portion of the BLS Occupational Matrix, a data base that lists important occupations and groupings and shows total employment in 1998 together with projections to the year 2008. The appendix provides three presentations — alphabetical, by largest employment, and by growth — to help the user gain further insight into wage trends in the United States.

Data Limitations

A number of points should be kept in mind when using *ASWS* for wage information. *ASWS* is a compilation of a large number of sources. Some are scientific surveys, some are job offers, and some are themselves compilations of other sources. No attempt was made to standardize the data from these sources. Therefore, the user should take great care drawing general conclusions. Variations and/or skewed data occur in title derivations, wage calculations, job descriptions, and methodology.

In this edition, occupational titles are generally more uniform and follow Federal naming conventions much more consistently than in the first four editions. Ambiguous titles, however, continue to exist.

The editors have made a limited effort to edit the occupational titles presented. Grammatical forms and punctuation have been made consistent whenever possible. Titles are presented in singular forms (Nurse *vs* Nurses).

It is important to bear in mind that wage variations between different entries with the same occupational title may be due to differences in job responsibilities.

ASWS provides base salary figures only. Unless otherwise specified, supplemental compensation — i.e., fringe benefits, overtime, bonuses, etc. — have not been included.

Wage figures shown are not adjusted in any way to reflect cost of living. Salaries may be significantly higher in major metropolitan areas where living costs are high.

Acknowledgments

ASWS was initially suggested to Gale by Ms. Flower L. Hund, Central Missouri State University, Warrensburg, Mo. From the start, the editors have attempted to realize, in practice, Ms. Hund's original concepts; to the extent that they have succeeded, the credit is Ms. Hund's; she is, however, in no way responsible for shortcomings in *ASWS*.

The editors would like to thank the many individuals in state government and in associations who helped in the creation of *ASWS* by providing reports, data, clarifications, and permissions.

Comments and Suggestions

Comments on *ASW*S or suggestions for improvement of its usefulness, format, and coverage are always welcome. Although we have made every effort to be as accurate and consistent as possible, errors may be noted by others; we will appreciate having these called to our attention. Please contact:

> Editor
> *American Salaries & Wages Survey*
> Gale Group
> 27500 Drake Road
> Farmington Hills, MI 48331-3535
> Phone: (248)-699-GALE

OUTLINE OF CONTENTS

GEOGRAPHICAL OUTLINE OF CONTENTS

Geographical Outline of Contents

Colorado - continued:

Desktop Publisher
Detective and Criminal Investigator
Diagnostic Medical Sonographer
Dietetic Technician
Dietitian and Nutritionist
Dining Room and Cafeteria Attendant and Bartender Helper
Director, Religious Activities and Education
Dishwasher
Dispatcher
Drilling and Boring Machine Tool Setter, Operator, and Tender
Driver/Sales Worker
Drywall and Ceiling Tile Installer
Earth Driller
Economics Teacher
Economist
Editor
Education Administrator
Education Teacher
Educational, Vocational, and School Counselor
Electric Motor, Power Tool, and Related Repairer
Electrical and Electronic Engineering Technician
Electrical and Electronic Equipment Assembler
Electrical and Electronics Drafter
Electrical and Electronics Installer and Repairer
Electrical and Electronics Repairer
Electrical Engineer
Electrician
Electro-Mechanical Technician
Electromechanical Equipment Assembler
Electronic Equipment Installer and Repairer
Electronic Home Entertainment Equipment Installer and Repairer
Electronics Engineer
Elementary School Teacher
Eligibility Interviewer
Embalmer
Emergency Medical Technician and Paramedic
Employment, Recruitment, and Placement Specialist
Engine and Other Machine Assembler
Engineering Manager
Engineering Teacher
English Language and Literature Teacher
Environmental Engineer
Environmental Engineering Technician
Environmental Science and Protection Technician, Including Health
Environmental Scientist and Specialist, Including Health
Etcher and Engraver
Excavating and Loading Machine and Dragline Operator
Executive Secretary and Administrative Assistant
Explosives Worker, Ordnance Handling Expert, and Blaster

Extruding and Drawing Machine Setter, Operator, and Tender
Extruding, Forming, Pressing, and Compacting Machine Setter, Operator, and Tender
Farm and Home Management Advisor
Farm Equipment Mechanic
Farm, Ranch, and Other Agricultural Manager
Farmworker and Laborer, Crop, Nursery, and Greenhouse
Farmworker, Farm and Ranch Animal
Fashion Designer
Fence Erector
File Clerk
Film and Video Editor
Financial Analyst
Financial Examiner
Financial Manager
Fire Fighter
First-Line Supervisor/Manager
Fish and Game Warden
Fitness Trainer and Aerobics Instructor
Floor Layer
Floor Sander and Finisher
Floral Designer
Food and Tobacco Roasting, Baking, and Drying Machine Operator and Tender
Food Batchmaker
Food Cooking Machine Operator and Tender
Food Preparation Worker
Food Server
Food Service Manager
Foreign Language and Literature Teacher
Forensic Science Technician
Forest and Conservation Technician
Forest and Conservation Worker
Forester
Forging Machine Setter, Operator, and Tender
Foundry Mold and Coremaker
Funeral Attendant
Funeral Director
Furnace, Kiln, Oven, Drier, and Kettle Operator and Tender
Furniture Finisher
Gaming Surveillance Officer and Gaming Investigator
Gas Compressor and Gas Pumping Station Operator
Gas Plant Operator
General and Operations Manager
Geography Teacher
Geological and Petroleum Technician
Geoscientist
Glazier
Grader and Sorter
Graphic Designer
Grinding and Polishing Worker
Grinding, Lapping, Polishing, and Buffing Machine Tool Setter, Operator, and Tender
Hairdresser, Hairstylist, and Cosmetologist
Hazardous Materials Removal Worker

Health and Safety Engineer
Health Educator
Health Specialties Teacher
Heat Treating Equipment Setter, Operator, and Tender
Heating, Air Conditioning, and Refrigeration Mechanic and Installer
Helper
Highway Maintenance Worker
Historian
History Teacher
Hoist and Winch Operator
Home Appliance Repairer
Home Health Aide
Host and Hostess
Hotel, Motel, and Resort Desk Clerk
Human Resources Assistant
Human Resources Manager
Hydrologist
Industrial Engineer
Industrial Engineering Technician
Industrial Production Manager
Industrial Truck and Tractor Operator
Inspector, Tester, Sorter, Sampler, and Weigher
Insulation Worker
Insurance Appraiser
Insurance Claim and Policy Processing Clerk
Insurance Sales Agent
Insurance Underwriter
Interior Designer
Interpreter and Translator
Interviewer
IT Professional
Janitor and Cleaner
Jeweler and Precious Stone and Metal Worker
Job Printer
Judge, Magistrate Judge, and Magistrate
Kindergarten Teacher
Laborer and Freight, Stock, and Material Mover
Landscape Architect
Landscaping and Groundskeeping Worker
Lathe and Turning Machine Tool Setter, Operator, and Tender
Laundry and Dry-Cleaning Worker
Law Clerk
Lawyer
Legal Secretary
Librarian
Library Assistant, Clerical
Library Technician
Licensed Practical and Licensed Vocational Nurse
Loan Counselor
Loan Interviewer and Clerk
Loan Officer
Locker Room, Coatroom, and Dressing Room Attendant
Locksmith and Safe Repairer
Locomotive Engineer
Lodging Manager
Logging Equipment Operator
Machine Feeder and Offbearer
Machinist
Maid and Housekeeping Cleaner
Mail Clerk and Mail Machine

Operator
Maintenance and Repair Worker
Management Analyst
Manicurist and Pedicurist
Manufactured Building and Mobile Home Installer
Marketing Manager
Marriage and Family Therapist
Materials Engineer
Materials Scientist
Mathematical Science Teacher
Mathematician
Meat, Poultry, and Fish Cutter and Trimmer
Mechanical Door Repairer
Mechanical Drafter
Mechanical Engineer
Mechanical Engineering Technician
Medical and Clinical Laboratory Technician
Medical and Clinical Laboratory Technologist
Medical and Health Services Manager
Medical and Public Health Social Worker
Medical Appliance Technician
Medical Assistant
Medical Equipment Preparer
Medical Equipment Repairer
Medical Scientist
Medical Secretary
Medical Transcriptionist
Meeting and Convention Planner
Mental Health and Substance Abuse Social Worker
Mental Health Counselor
Merchandise Displayer and Window Trimmer
Metal-Refining Furnace Operator and Tender
Meter Reader
Microbiologist
Middle School Teacher
Millwright
Mining and Geological Engineer
Mixing and Blending Machine Setter, Operator, and Tender
Mobile Heavy Equipment Mechanic
Model Maker
Molder, Shaper, and Caster
Molding, Coremaking, and Casting Machine Setter, Operator, and Tender
Motion Picture Projectionist
Motorboat Mechanic
Motorcycle Mechanic
Multi-Media Artist and Animator
Multiple Machine Tool Setter, Operator, and Tender
Natural Sciences Manager
Network and Computer Systems Administrator
Network System and Data Communications Analyst
New Accounts Clerk
News Analyst, Reporter and Correspondent
Nonfarm Animal Caretaker
Nuclear Engineer
Nuclear Medicine Technologist

Idaho - continued:

Grinding, Lapping, Polishing, and
　Buffing Machine Tool Setter,
　Operator, and Tender
Hairdresser, Hairstylist, and
　Cosmetologist
Hazardous Materials Removal
　Worker
Health and Safety Engineer
Health Educator
Health Specialties Teacher
Heat Treating Equipment Setter,
　Operator, and Tender
Heating, Air Conditioning, and
　Refrigeration Mechanic and
　Installer
Helper
Highway Maintenance Worker
History Teacher
Hoist and Winch Operator
Home Appliance Repairer
Home Health Aide
Host and Hostess
Hotel, Motel, and Resort Desk Clerk
Human Resources Assistant
Human Resources Manager
Hydrologist
Industrial Engineer
Industrial Machinery Mechanic
Industrial Production Manager
Industrial Truck and Tractor Operator
Industrial-Organizational
　Psychologist
Inspector, Tester, Sorter, Sampler,
　and Weigher
Insulation Worker
Insurance Claim and Policy
　Processing Clerk
Insurance Sales Agent
Insurance Underwriter
Interior Designer
Interpreter and Translator
Interviewer
Janitor and Cleaner
Jeweler and Precious Stone and Metal
　Worker
Job Printer
Judge, Magistrate Judge, and
　Magistrate
Kindergarten Teacher
Laborer and Freight, Stock, and
　Material Mover
Landscape Architect
Landscaping and Groundskeeping
　Worker
Lathe and Turning Machine Tool
　Setter, Operator, and Tender
Laundry and Dry-Cleaning Worker
Law Clerk
Lawyer
Lay-Out Worker
Legal Secretary
Legislator
Librarian
Library Assistant, Clerical
Library Technician
Licensed Practical and Licensed
　Vocational Nurse
Loan Interviewer and Clerk
Loan Officer
Locomotive Engineer
Lodging Manager

Log Grader and Scaler
Logging Equipment Operator
Machine Feeder and Offbearer
Machinist
Maid and Housekeeping Cleaner
Mail Clerk and Mail Machine
　Operator
Maintenance and Repair Worker
Maintenance Worker
Manufactured Building and Mobile
　Home Installer
Marketing Manager
Marriage and Family Therapist
Massage Therapist
Mathematical Science Teacher
Meat, Poultry, and Fish Cutter and
　Trimmer
Mechanical Drafter
Mechanical Engineer
Mechanical Engineering Technician
Medical and Clinical Laboratory
　Technician
Medical and Clinical Laboratory
　Technologist
Medical and Health Services
　Manager
Medical and Public Health Social
　Worker
Medical Appliance Technician
Medical Assistant
Medical Record and Health
　Information Technician
Medical Secretary
Medical Transcriptionist
Meeting and Convention Planner
Mental Health and Substance Abuse
　Social Worker
Mental Health Counselor
Merchandise Displayer and Window
　Trimmer
Meter Reader
Microbiologist
Milling and Planing Machine Setter,
　Operator, and Tender
Millwright
Mining and Geological Engineer
Mixing and Blending Machine Setter,
　Operator, and Tender
Mobile Heavy Equipment Mechanic
Molder, Shaper, and Caster
Molding, Coremaking, and Casting
　Machine Setter, Operator, and
　Tender
Motion Picture Projectionist
Motorboat Mechanic
Motorcycle Mechanic
Multiple Machine Tool Setter,
　Operator, and Tender
Natural Sciences Manager
Network and Computer Systems
　Administrator
Network System and Data
　Communications Analyst
New Accounts Clerk
News Analyst, Reporter and
　Correspondent
Nonfarm Animal Caretaker
Numerical Tool and Process Control
　Programmer
Nursing Aide, Orderly, and Attendant
Nursing Instructor and Teacher
Occupational Therapist

Occupational Therapist Aide
Occupational Therapist Assistant
Office Clerk
Office Machine Operator
Operating Engineer and Other
　Construction Equipment Operator
Ophthalmic Laboratory Technician
Optician, Dispensing
Optometrist
Order Clerk
Outdoor Power Equipment and Other
　Small Engine Mechanic
Packaging and Filling Machine
　Operator and Tender
Packer and Packager
Painter
Painting, Coating, and Decorating
　Worker
Paper Goods Machine Setter,
　Operator, and Tender
Paralegal and Legal Assistant
Parking Lot Attendant
Parts Salesperson
Paving, Surfacing, and Tamping
　Equipment Operator
Payroll and Timekeeping Clerk
Personal and Home Care Aide
Pest Control Worker
Pesticide Handler, Sprayer, and
　Applicator
Pharmacist
Pharmacy Aide
Pharmacy Technician
Photographer
Photographic Processing Machine
　Operator
Physical Therapist
Physical Therapist Aide
Physical Therapist Assistant
Physician Assistant
Pipelayer
Plasterer and Stucco Mason
Plating and Coating Machine Setter,
　Operator, and Tender
Plumber, Pipefitter, and Steamfitter
Police and Sheriff's Patrol Officer
Police, Fire, and Ambulance
　Dispatcher
Postal Service Clerk
Postal Service Mail Carrier
Postmaster and Mail Superintendent
Power Distributor and Dispatcher
Power Plant Operator
Prepress Technician and Worker
Preschool Teacher
Presser
Printing Machine Operator
Probation Officer and Correctional
　Treatment Specialist
Procurement Clerk
Production, Planning, and Expediting
　Clerk
Proofreader and Copy Marker
Property, Real Estate, and
　Community Association Manager
Psychiatric Aide
Psychiatric Technician
Psychology Teacher
Public Relations Manager
Public Relations Specialist
Pump Operator
Purchasing Agent

Purchasing Agent and Buyer
Purchasing Manager
Radiologic Technologist and
　Technician
Railroad Conductor and Yardmaster
Real Estate Sales Agent
Receptionist and Information Clerk
Recreation Worker
Recreational Therapist
Recreational Vehicle Service
　Technician
Refuse and Recyclable Material
　Collector
Registered Nurse
Rehabilitation Counselor
Reinforcing Iron and Rebar Worker
Reservation and Transportation
　Ticket Agent and Travel Clerk
Residential Advisor
Respiratory Therapist
Respiratory Therapy Technician
Retail Salesperson
Rigger
Roofer
Sales Engineer
Sales Manager
Sales Representative
Sawing Machine Setter, Operator,
　and Tender, Wood
Secondary School Teacher
Secretary
Securities, Commodities, and
　Financial Services Sales Agent
Security and Fire Alarm Systems
　Installer
Security Guard
Self-Enrichment Education Teacher
Semiconductor Processor
Separating, Filtering, Clarifying,
　Precipitating, and Still Machine
　Setter, Operator, and Tender
Service Station Attendant
Sewing Machine Operator
Sheet Metal Worker
Shipping, Receiving, and Traffic
　Clerk
Slaughterer and Meat Packer
Social and Community Service
　Manager
Social and Human Service Assistant
Social Work Teacher
Speech-Language Pathologist
Stationary Engineer and Boiler
　Operator
Statistical Assistant
Stock Clerk and Order Filler
Structural Iron and Steel Worker
Structural Metal Fabricator and Fitter
Substance Abuse and Behavioral
　Disorder Counselor
Surgical Technologist
Surveying and Mapping Technician
Surveyor
Switchboard Operator
Tank Car, Truck, and Ship Loader
Taper
Tax Examiner, Collector, and
　Revenue Agent
Tax Preparer
Taxi Driver and Chauffeur
Teacher Assistant
Team Assembler

Missouri - continued:

Industrial Engineer
Industrial Engineering Technician
Industrial Machinery Mechanic
Industrial Production Manager
Industrial Truck and Tractor Operator
Inspector, Tester, Sorter, Sampler, and Weigher
Instructional Coordinator
Insulation Worker
Insurance Claim and Policy Processing Clerk
Insurance Sales Agent
Insurance Underwriter
Interior Designer
Internist, General
Interpreter and Translator
Interviewer
Janitor and Cleaner
Jeweler and Precious Stone and Metal Worker
Job Printer
Kindergarten Teacher
Laborer and Freight, Stock, and Material Mover
Landscape Architect
Landscaping and Groundskeeping Worker
Lathe and Turning Machine Tool Setter, Operator, and Tender
Laundry and Dry-Cleaning Worker
Law Clerk
Lawyer
Lay-Out Worker
Legal Secretary
Legislator
Librarian
Library Assistant, Clerical
Library Science Teacher
Library Technician
Licensed Practical and Licensed Vocational Nurse
Loan Counselor
Loan Interviewer and Clerk
Loan Officer
Locker Room, Coatroom, and Dressing Room Attendant
Locksmith and Safe Repairer
Lodging Manager
Log Grader and Scaler
Logging Equipment Operator
Machine Feeder and Offbearer
Machinist
Maid and Housekeeping Cleaner
Mail Clerk and Mail Machine Operator
Maintenance and Repair Worker
Maintenance Worker
Management Analyst
Manicurist and Pedicurist
Manufactured Building and Mobile Home Installer
Market Research Analyst
Marketing Manager
Marriage and Family Therapist
Mathematical Science Teacher
Meat, Poultry, and Fish Cutter and Trimmer
Mechanical Drafter
Mechanical Engineer
Mechanical Engineering Technician
Medical and Clinical Laboratory

Technician
Medical and Clinical Laboratory Technologist
Medical and Health Services Manager
Medical and Public Health Social Worker
Medical Appliance Technician
Medical Assistant
Medical Equipment Preparer
Medical Equipment Repairer
Medical Record and Health Information Technician
Medical Secretary
Medical Transcriptionist
Meeting and Convention Planner
Mental Health and Substance Abuse Social Worker
Mental Health Counselor
Merchandise Displayer and Window Trimmer
Metal-Refining Furnace Operator and Tender
Meter Reader
Microbiologist
Middle School Teacher
Milling and Planing Machine Setter, Operator, and Tender
Millwright
Mining and Geological Engineer
Mixing and Blending Machine Setter, Operator, and Tender
Mobile Heavy Equipment Mechanic
Model Maker
Molder, Shaper, and Caster
Molding, Coremaking, and Casting Machine Setter, Operator, and Tender
Motion Picture Projectionist
Motorboat Mechanic
Motorcycle Mechanic
Multi-Media Artist and Animator
Multiple Machine Tool Setter, Operator, and Tender
Music Director and Composer
Musical Instrument Repairer and Tuner
Musician and Singer
Natural Sciences Manager
Network and Computer Systems Administrator
Network System and Data Communications Analyst
New Accounts Clerk
News Analyst, Reporter and Correspondent
Nonfarm Animal Caretaker
Nuclear Medicine Technologist
Numerical Tool and Process Control Programmer
Nursing Aide, Orderly, and Attendant
Nursing Instructor and Teacher
Obstetrician and Gynecologist
Occupational Health and Safety Specialist and Technician
Occupational Therapist
Occupational Therapist Aide
Occupational Therapist Assistant
Office Clerk
Office Machine Operator
Operating Engineer and Other Construction Equipment Operator

Operations Research Analyst
Ophthalmic Laboratory Technician
Optician, Dispensing
Optometrist
Order Clerk
Outdoor Power Equipment and Other Small Engine Mechanic
Packaging and Filling Machine Operator and Tender
Packer and Packager
Painter
Painting, Coating, and Decorating Worker
Paper Goods Machine Setter, Operator, and Tender
Paperhanger
Paralegal and Legal Assistant
Parking Enforcement Worker
Parking Lot Attendant
Parts Salesperson
Patternmaker
Paving, Surfacing, and Tamping Equipment Operator
Payroll and Timekeeping Clerk
Pediatrician
Personal and Home Care Aide
Pesticide Handler, Sprayer, and Applicator
Pharmacist
Pharmacy Aide
Pharmacy Technician
Philosophy and Religion Teacher
Photographer
Photographic Process Worker
Photographic Processing Machine Operator
Physical Therapist
Physical Therapist Aide
Physician Assistant
Physicist
Pipelayer
Plasterer and Stucco Mason
Plating and Coating Machine Setter, Operator, and Tender
Plumber, Pipefitter, and Steamfitter
Police and Sheriff's Patrol Officer
Police, Fire, and Ambulance Dispatcher
Political Science Teacher
Postal Service Clerk
Postal Service Mail Carrier
Postal Service Mail Sorter, Processor, and Processing Machine Operator
Postmaster and Mail Superintendent
Pourer and Caster
Power Distributor and Dispatcher
Power Plant Operator
Prepress Technician and Worker
Preschool Teacher
Presser
Printing Machine Operator
Private Detective and Investigator
Probation Officer and Correctional Treatment Specialist
Procurement Clerk
Producer and Director
Production, Planning, and Expediting Clerk
Proofreader and Copy Marker
Property, Real Estate, and Community Association Manager
Psychiatrist

Psychology Teacher
Public Relations Manager
Public Relations Specialist
Purchasing Agent
Purchasing Agent and Buyer
Purchasing Manager
Radiation Therapist
Radio Mechanic
Radiologic Technologist and Technician
Rail-Track Laying and Maintenance Equipment Operator
Real Estate Broker
Real Estate Sales Agent
Receptionist and Information Clerk
Recreation and Fitness Studies Teacher
Recreation Worker
Recreational Therapist
Refractory Materials Repairer
Refuse and Recyclable Material Collector
Registered Nurse
Rehabilitation Counselor
Reinforcing Iron and Rebar Worker
Reservation and Transportation Ticket Agent and Travel Clerk
Residential Advisor
Respiratory Therapist
Respiratory Therapy Technician
Retail Salesperson
Rolling Machine Setter, Operator, and Tender
Roofer
Sales Engineer
Sales Manager
Sales Representative
Sawing Machine Setter, Operator, and Tender, Wood
Schoolbus Driver
Secondary School Teacher
Secretary
Securities, Commodities, and Financial Services Sales Agent
Security Guard
Self-Enrichment Education Teacher
Separating, Filtering, Clarifying, Precipitating, and Still Machine Setter, Operator, and Tender
Septic Tank Service' and Sewer Pipe Cleaner
Service Station Attendant
Sewer, Hand
Sewing Machine Operator
Shampooer
Sheet Metal Worker
Shipping, Receiving, and Traffic Clerk
Shoe Machine Operator and Tender
Skin Care Specialist
Slaughterer and Meat Packer
Slot Key Person
Social and Community Service Manager
Social and Human Service Assistant
Social Work Teacher
Sound Engineering Technician
Special Education Teacher
Speech-Language Pathologist
Stationary Engineer and Boiler Operator
Statistical Assistant

Nevada - continued:

Computer Operator
Computer Programmer
Computer Science Teacher
Computer Software Engineer
Computer Support Specialist
Computer Systems Analyst
Computer, Automated Teller, and
  Office Machine Repairer
Computer-Controlled Machine Tool
  Operator
Concierge
Conservation Scientist
Construction and Building Inspector
Construction Laborer
Construction Manager
Conveyor Operator and Tender
Cook
Correctional Officer and Jailer
Correspondence Clerk
Cost Estimator
Costume Attendant
Counter and Rental Clerk
Counter Attendant
Courier and Messenger
Court, Municipal, and License Clerk
Crane and Tower Operator
Credit Analyst
Credit Authorizer, Checker, and
  Clerk
Crossing Guard
Crushing, Grinding, and Polishing
  Machine Setter, Operator, and
  Tender
Customer Service Representative
Cutter and Trimmer
Cutting and Slicing Machine Setter,
  Operator, and Tender
Cutting, Punching, and Press
  Machine Setter, Operator, and
  Tender
Dancer
Data Entry Keyer
Database Administrator
Demonstrator and Product Promoter
Dental Assistant
Dental Hygienist
Dental Laboratory Technician
Dentist
Desktop Publisher
Detective and Criminal Investigator
Diagnostic Medical Sonographer
Dietetic Technician
Dietitian and Nutritionist
Dining Room and Cafeteria Attendant
  and Bartender Helper
Dishwasher
Dispatcher
Door-To-Door Sales Worker, New
  and Street Vendor, and Related
  Worker
Drilling and Boring Machine Tool
  Setter, Operator, and Tender
Driver/Sales Worker
Drywall and Ceiling Tile Installer
Earth Driller
Editor
Education Administrator
Education Teacher
Educational, Vocational, and School
  Counselor
Electric Motor, Power Tool, and

Related Repairer
Electrical and Electronic Engineering
  Technician
Electrical and Electronic Equipment
  Assembler
Electrical and Electronics Drafter
Electrical and Electronics Installer
  and Repairer
Electrical and Electronics Repairer
Electrical Engineer
Electrical Power-Line Installer and
  Repairer
Electrician
Electro-Mechanical Technician
Electromechanical Equipment
  Assembler
Electronic Equipment Installer and
  Repairer
Electronic Home Entertainment
  Equipment Installer and Repairer
Electronics Engineer
Elementary School Teacher
Elevator Installer and Repairer
Embalmer
Emergency Management Specialist
Emergency Medical Technician and
  Paramedic
Employment, Recruitment, and
  Placement Specialist
Engine and Other Machine
  Assembler
Engineering Manager
English Language and Literature
  Teacher
Environmental Engineer
Environmental Engineering
  Technician
Environmental Science and
  Protection Technician, Including
  Health
Environmental Science Teacher
Environmental Scientist and
  Specialist, Including Health
Excavating and Loading Machine and
  Dragline Operator
Executive Secretary and
  Administrative Assistant
Explosives Worker, Ordnance
  Handling Expert, and Blaster
Extruding and Drawing Machine
  Setter, Operator, and Tender
Extruding, Forming, Pressing, and
  Compacting Machine Setter,
  Operator, and Tender
Family and General Practitioner
Farm Equipment Mechanic
Farm, Ranch, and Other Agricultural
  Manager
Farmworker and Laborer, Crop,
  Nursery, and Greenhouse
Fence Erector
Fiberglass Laminator and Fabricator
File Clerk
Film and Video Editor
Financial Analyst
Financial Manager
Fine Artist, Including Painter,
  Sculptor, and Illustrator
Fire Fighter
Fire Inspector and Investigator
First-Line Supervisor/Manager
Fitness Trainer and Aerobics

Instructor
Floral Designer
Food Batchmaker
Food Preparation Worker
Food Server
Food Service Manager
Foreign Language and Literature
  Teacher
Forensic Science Technician
Forest and Conservation Technician
Forest and Conservation Worker
Forester
Funeral Attendant
Funeral Director
Furnace, Kiln, Oven, Drier, and
  Kettle Operator and Tender
Furniture Finisher
Gaming and Sports Book Writer and
  Runner
Gaming Cage Worker
Gaming Change Person and Booth
  Cashier
Gaming Dealer
Gaming Manager
Gaming Supervisor
Gaming Surveillance Officer and
  Gaming Investigator
General and Operations Manager
Geography Teacher
Geological and Petroleum Technician
Geoscientist
Glazier
Grader and Sorter
Graphic Designer
Grinding and Polishing Worker
Grinding, Lapping, Polishing, and
  Buffing Machine Tool Setter,
  Operator, and Tender
Hairdresser, Hairstylist, and
  Cosmetologist
Hazardous Materials Removal
  Worker
Health and Safety Engineer
Health Educator
Heating, Air Conditioning, and
  Refrigeration Mechanic and
  Installer
Helper
Highway Maintenance Worker
History Teacher
Home Appliance Repairer
Home Health Aide
Host and Hostess
Hotel, Motel, and Resort Desk Clerk
Human Resources Assistant
Human Resources Manager
Hydrologist
Industrial Engineer
Industrial Machinery Mechanic
Industrial Production Manager
Industrial Truck and Tractor Operator
Inspector, Tester, Sorter, Sampler,
  and Weigher
Instructional Coordinator
Insulation Worker
Insurance Appraiser
Insurance Claim and Policy
  Processing Clerk
Insurance Sales Agent
Insurance Underwriter
Interior Designer
Internist, General

Interviewer
Janitor and Cleaner
Jeweler and Precious Stone and Metal
  Worker
Job Printer
Judge, Magistrate Judge, and
  Magistrate
Kindergarten Teacher
Laborer and Freight, Stock, and
  Material Mover
Landscape Architect
Landscaping and Groundskeeping
  Worker
Lathe and Turning Machine Tool
  Setter, Operator, and Tender
Laundry and Dry-Cleaning Worker
Law Clerk
Lawyer
Lay-Out Worker
Legal Secretary
Legislator
Librarian
Library Assistant, Clerical
Library Technician
Licensed Practical and Licensed
  Vocational Nurse
Loan Counselor
Loan Interviewer and Clerk
Loan Officer
Locker Room, Coatroom, and
  Dressing Room Attendant
Locksmith and Safe Repairer
Lodging Manager
Machine Feeder and Offbearer
Machinist
Maid and Housekeeping Cleaner
Mail Clerk and Mail Machine
  Operator
Maintenance and Repair Worker
Maintenance Worker
Management Analyst
Manicurist and Pedicurist
Market Research Analyst
Marketing Manager
Materials Engineer
Mathematical Science Teacher
Meat, Poultry, and Fish Cutter and
  Trimmer
Mechanical Door Repairer
Mechanical Drafter
Mechanical Engineer
Mechanical Engineering Technician
Medical and Clinical Laboratory
  Technician
Medical and Clinical Laboratory
  Technologist
Medical and Health Services
  Manager
Medical and Public Health Social
  Worker
Medical Assistant
Medical Equipment Preparer
Medical Equipment Repairer
Medical Record and Health
  Information Technician
Medical Secretary
Medical Transcriptionist
Meeting and Convention Planner
Mental Health and Substance Abuse
  Social Worker
Mental Health Counselor

New Hampshire - continued:
Veterinarian
Veterinary Assistant and Laboratory
  Animal Caretaker
Veterinary Technologist and
  Technician
Vocational Education Teacher
Waiter and Waitress
Watch Repairer
Water and Liquid Waste Treatment
  Plant and System Operator
Weigher, Measurer, Checker, and
  Sampler, Recordkeeping
Welder, Cutter, Solderer, and Brazer
Welding, Soldering, and Brazing
  Machine Setter, Operator, and
  Tender
Wholesale and Retail Buyer
Woodworking Machine Setter,
  Operator, and Tender
Word Processor and Typist
Writer and Author
Zoologist and Wildlife Biologist

New Jersey

Accountant and Auditor
Actor
Actuary
Administrative Law Judge,
  Adjudicator, and Hearing Officer
Administrative Services Manager
Adult Literacy, Remedial Education,
  and GED Teacher and Instructor
Advertising and Promotions Manager
Advertising Sales Agent
Aerospace Engineer
Aerospace Engineering and
  Operations Technician
Agricultural and Food Science
  Technician
Agricultural and Food Scientist
Agricultural Engineer
Agricultural Inspector
Agricultural Sciences Teacher
Air Traffic Controller
Aircraft Cargo Handling Supervisor
Aircraft Mechanic and Service
  Technician
Airline Pilot, Copilot, and Flight
  Engineer
Ambulance Driver and Attendant
Amusement and Recreation
  Attendant
Anesthesiologist
Animal Control Worker
Animal Trainer
Announcer
Anthropology and Archeology
  Teacher
Appraiser and Assessor of Real
  Estate
Architect
Architectural and Civil Drafter
Archivist, Curator, and Museum
  Technician
Area, Ethnic, and Cultural Studies
  Teacher
Art Director
Art, Drama, and Music Teacher
Athletic Trainer

Atmospheric and Space Scientist
Atmospheric, Earth, Marine, and
  Space Sciences Teacher
Audio-Visual Collections Specialist
Audiologist
Automotive Body and Related
  Repairer
Automotive Service Technician and
  Mechanic
Avionics Technician
Baggage Porter and Bellhop
Bailiff
Baker
Barber
Bartender
Bill and Account Collector
Billing and Posting Clerk and
  Machine Operator
Bindery Worker
Biochemist and Biophysicist
Biological Science Teacher
Biological Technician
Biomedical Engineer
Boilermaker
Bookbinder
Bookkeeping, Accounting, and
  Auditing Clerk
Brickmason and Blockmason
Bridge and Lock Tender
Broadcast Technician
Brokerage Clerk
Budget Analyst
Bus and Truck Mechanic and Diesel
  Engine Specialist
Bus Driver
Business Teacher
Butcher and Meat Cutter
Cabinetmaker and Bench Carpenter
Camera and Photographic Equipment
  Repairer
Camera Operator
Captain, Mate, and Pilot
Cardiovascular Technologist and
  Technician
Cargo and Freight Agent
Carpenter
Carpet Installer
Cashier
Cement Mason and Concrete Finisher
Cementing and Gluing Machine
  Operator and Tender
Chef and Head Cook
Chemical Engineer
Chemical Equipment Operator and
  Tender
Chemical Plant and System Operator
Chemical Technician
Chemist
Chemistry Teacher
Chief Executive
Child Care Worker
Child, Family, and School Social
  Worker
Chiropractor
Choreographer
Civil Engineer
Civil Engineering Technician
Claims Adjuster, Examiner, and
  Investigator
Cleaner of Vehicle and Equipment
Cleaning, Washing, and Metal
  Pickling Equipment Operator and

Tender
Clergy
Clinical, Counseling, and School
  Psychologist
Coach and Scout
Coating, Painting, and Spraying
  Machine Setter, Operator, and
  Tender
Coil Winder, Taper, and Finisher
Coin, Vending, and Amusement
  Machine Servicer and Repairer
Combined Food Preparation and
  Serving Worker
Commercial and Industrial Designer
Commercial Diver
Commercial Pilot
Communications Teacher
Compensation, Benefits, and Job
  Analysis Specialist
Compliance Officer
Computer and Information Scientist
Computer and Information Systems
  Manager
Computer Hardware Engineer
Computer Operator
Computer Programmer
Computer Science Teacher
Computer Software Engineer
Computer Support Specialist
Computer Systems Analyst
Computer, Automated Teller, and
  Office Machine Repairer
Computer-Controlled Machine Tool
  Operator
Concierge
Conservation Scientist
Construction and Building Inspector
Construction Laborer
Construction Manager
Control and Valve Installer and
  Repairer
Conveyor Operator and Tender
Cook
Correctional Officer and Jailer
Correspondence Clerk
Cost Estimator
Counter and Rental Clerk
Counter Attendant
Courier and Messenger
Court Reporter
Court, Municipal, and License Clerk
Crane and Tower Operator
Credit Analyst
Credit Authorizer, Checker, and
  Clerk
Criminal Justice and Law
  Enforcement Teacher
Crossing Guard
Crushing, Grinding, and Polishing
  Machine Setter, Operator, and
  Tender
Customer Service Representative
Cutter and Trimmer
Cutting and Slicing Machine Setter,
  Operator, and Tender
Cutting, Punching, and Press
  Machine Setter, Operator, and
  Tender
Dancer
Data Entry Keyer
Database Administrator
Demonstrator and Product Promoter

Dental Assistant
Dental Hygienist
Dental Laboratory Technician
Dentist
Desktop Publisher
Detective and Criminal Investigator
Diagnostic Medical Sonographer
Dietetic Technician
Dietitian and Nutritionist
Dining Room and Cafeteria Attendant
  and Bartender Helper
Director, Religious Activities and
  Education
Dishwasher
Dispatcher
Door-To-Door Sales Worker, New
  and Street Vendor, and Related
  Worker
Dredge Operator
Drilling and Boring Machine Tool
  Setter, Operator, and Tender
Driver/Sales Worker
Drywall and Ceiling Tile Installer
Earth Driller
Economics Teacher
Economist
Editor
Education Administrator
Education Teacher
Educational, Vocational, and School
  Counselor
Electric Motor, Power Tool, and
  Related Repairer
Electrical and Electronic Engineering
  Technician
Electrical and Electronic Equipment
  Assembler
Electrical and Electronics Drafter
Electrical and Electronics Installer
  and Repairer
Electrical and Electronics Repairer
Electrical Engineer
Electrical Power-Line Installer and
  Repairer
Electrician
Electro-Mechanical Technician
Electromechanical Equipment
  Assembler
Electronic Equipment Installer and
  Repairer
Electronic Home Entertainment
  Equipment Installer and Repairer
Electronics Engineer
Elementary School Teacher
Elevator Installer and Repairer
Eligibility Interviewer
Embalmer
Emergency Management Specialist
Emergency Medical Technician and
  Paramedic
Employment, Recruitment, and
  Placement Specialist
Engine and Other Machine
  Assembler
Engineer
Engineering Manager
Engineering Teacher
English Language and Literature
  Teacher
Environmental Engineer
Environmental Engineering
  Technician

Geographical Outline of Contents

Geographical Outline of Contents

cxvii

Geographical Outline of Contents

Geographical Outline of Contents

Geographical Outline of Contents

Geographical Outline of Contents

Geographical Outline of Contents

OCCUPATIONS

Occupation/Type/Industry	Location	Per	Low	Mid	High	Source	Date
Account Executive							
Advertising	East	Y		52000 AW		ADAGE1	2000
Advertising	Midwest	Y		49000 AW		ADAGE1	2000
Advertising	South	Y		45000 AW		ADAGE1	2000
Advertising	West	Y		48000 AW		ADAGE1	2000
Public Relations/Communications	United States	Y		36000 AW		COMW	1999
Accountant	United States	Y	34772 AE			CSM1	2000
Chief	United States	Y		49681 AW		SFIN	1999
Financial Industry	United States	Y		64434 AW		PENINV	2000
Accountant and Auditor	Alabama	S	18.06 MW	19.98 AW	41570 AAW	ALBLS	10//99-12//99
	Anniston MSA, AL	S	17.68 MW	15.36 AW	36760 AAW	ALBLS	10//99-12//99
	Auburn-Opelika MSA, AL	S	17.10 MW	16.16 AW	35560 AAW	ALBLS	10//99-12//99
	Birmingham MSA, AL	S	22.46 MW	20.06 AW	46710 AAW	ALBLS	10//99-12//99
	Decatur MSA, AL	S	18.29 MW	18.32 AW	38040 AAW	ALBLS	10//99-12//99
	Dothan MSA, AL	S	16.00 MW	14.67 AW	33270 AAW	ALBLS	10//99-12//99
	Florence MSA, AL	S	15.80 MW	15.04 AW	32870 AAW	ALBLS	10//99-12//99
	Gadsden MSA, AL	S	18.70 MW	17.61 AW	38900 AAW	ALBLS	10//99-12//99
	Huntsville MSA, AL	S	20.28 MW	18.50 AW	42180 AAW	ALBLS	10//99-12//99
	Mobile MSA, AL	S	17.26 MW	16.25 AW	35910 AAW	ALBLS	10//99-12//99
	Montgomery MSA, AL	S	20.87 MW	18.41 AW	43420 AAW	ALBLS	10//99-12//99
	Tuscaloosa MSA, AL	S	19.39 MW	16.03 AW	40320 AAW	ALBLS	10//99-12//99
	Alaska	S	21.56 MW	23.75 AW	49390 AAW	AKBLS	10//99-12//99
	Anchorage MSA, AK	S	23.96 MW	21.43 AW	49830 AAW	AKBLS	10//99-12//99
	Arizona	S	19.7 MW	22.19 AW	46150 AAW	AZBLS	10//99-12//99
	Flagstaff MSA, AZ-UT	S	18.25 MW	18.34 AW	37950 AAW	AZBLS	10//99-12//99
	Phoenix-Mesa MSA, AZ	S	22.97 MW	20.27 AW	47780 AAW	AZBLS	10//99-12//99
	Tucson MSA, AZ	S	18.93 MW	17.18 AW	39370 AAW	AZBLS	10//99-12//99
	Yuma MSA, AZ	S	18.10 MW	15.91 AW	37650 AAW	AZBLS	10//99-12//99
	Arkansas	S	16.88 MW	19.02 AW	39560 AAW	ARBLS	10//99-12//99
	Fayetteville-Springdale-Rogers MSA, AR	S	17.87 MW	15.19 AW	37180 AAW	ARBLS	10//99-12//99
	Fort Smith MSA, AR-OK	S	18.72 MW	16.59 AW	38930 AAW	ARBLS	10//99-12//99
	Jonesboro MSA, AR	S	21.46 MW	16.57 AW	44630 AAW	ARBLS	10//99-12//99
	Little Rock-North Little Rock MSA, AR	S	20.13 MW	17.62 AW	41870 AAW	ARBLS	10//99-12//99
	Pine Bluff MSA, AR	S	21.32 MW	18.94 AW	44340 AAW	ARBLS	10//99-12//99
	California	S	20.76 MW	23.80 AW	49510 AAW	CABLS	10//99-12//99
	Bakersfield MSA, CA	S	20.92 MW	19.64 AW	43510 AAW	CABLS	10//99-12//99
	Chico-Paradise MSA, CA	S	16.82 MW	15.30 AW	34980 AAW	CABLS	10//99-12//99
	Fresno MSA, CA	S	19.95 MW	19.28 AW	41490 AAW	CABLS	10//99-12//99
	Los Angeles-Long Beach PMSA, CA	S	25.52 MW	20.96 AW	53080 AAW	CABLS	10//99-12//99
	Merced MSA, CA	S	19.96 MW	19.18 AW	41510 AAW	CABLS	10//99-12//99
	Modesto MSA, CA	S	19.83 MW	18.90 AW	41240 AAW	CABLS	10//99-12//99
	Oakland PMSA, CA	S	22.71 MW	21.68 AW	47250 AAW	CABLS	10//99-12//99
	Orange County PMSA, CA	S	22.01 MW	20.32 AW	45790 AAW	CABLS	10//99-12//99
	Redding MSA, CA	S	19.45 MW	18.89 AW	40460 AAW	CABLS	10//99-12//99
	Riverside-San Bernardino PMSA, CA	S	19.40 MW	18.31 AW	40360 AAW	CABLS	10//99-12//99
	Salinas MSA, CA	S	21.14 MW	19.50 AW	43980 AAW	CABLS	10//99-12//99
	San Diego MSA, CA	S	20.54 MW	19.18 AW	42720 AAW	CABLS	10//99-12//99
	San Francisco PMSA, CA	S	24.48 MW	22.95 AW	50910 AAW	CABLS	10//99-12//99
	San Jose PMSA, CA	S	23.69 MW	22.32 AW	49270 AAW	CABLS	10//99-12//99
	San Luis Obispo-Atascadero-Paso Robles MSA, CA	S	22.24 MW	19.67 AW	46260 AAW	CABLS	10//99-12//99
	Santa Barbara-Santa Maria-Lompoc MSA, CA	S	21.45 MW	19.63 AW	44620 AAW	CABLS	10//99-12//99

AAW Average annual wage	**AOH** Average offered, high	**ASH** Average starting, high	**H** Hourly	**M** Monthly	**S** Special: hourly and annual
AE Average entry wage	**AOL** Average offered, low	**ASL** Average starting, low	**HI** Highest wage paid	**MTC** Median total compensation	**TQ** Third quartile wage
AEX Average experienced wage	**APH** Average pay, high range	**AW** Average wage paid	**HR** High end range	**MW** Median wage paid	**W** Weekly
AO Average offered	**APL** Average pay, low range	**FQ** First quartile wage	**LR** Low end range	**SQ** Second quartile wage	**Y** Yearly

Occupation/Type/Industry	Location	Per	Low	Mid	High	Source	Date
Accountant and Auditor	Santa Cruz-Watsonville PMSA, CA	S	21.70 MW	20.57 AW	45140 AAW	CABLS	10//99-12//99
	Santa Rosa PMSA, CA	S	21.86 MW	20.17 AW	45460 AAW	CABLS	10//99-12//99
	Stockton-Lodi MSA, CA	S	21.85 MW	20.08 AW	45440 AAW	CABLS	10//99-12//99
	Vallejo-Fairfield-Napa PMSA, CA	S	22.99 MW	21.05 AW	47830 AAW	CABLS	10//99-12//99
	Ventura PMSA, CA	S	23.31 MW	20.55 AW	48490 AAW	CABLS	10//99-12//99
	Visalia-Tulare-Porterville MSA, CA	S	20.27 MW	18.75 AW	42160 AAW	CABLS	10//99-12//99
	Yolo PMSA, CA	S	21.04 MW	19.28 AW	43770 AAW	CABLS	10//99-12//99
	Yuba City MSA, CA	S	17.41 MW	16.50 AW	36220 AAW	CABLS	10//99-12//99
	Colorado	S	19.39 MW	21.49 AW	44710 AAW	COBLS	10//99-12//99
	Boulder-Longmont PMSA, CO	S	21.30 MW	20.30 AW	44300 AAW	COBLS	10//99-12//99
	Colorado Springs MSA, CO	S	19.86 MW	18.47 AW	41300 AAW	COBLS	10//99-12//99
	Denver PMSA, CO	S	22.25 MW	19.80 AW	46290 AAW	COBLS	10//99-12//99
	Fort Collins-Loveland MSA, CO	S	16.75 MW	15.92 AW	34840 AAW	COBLS	10//99-12//99
	Grand Junction MSA, CO	S	20.43 MW	18.27 AW	42500 AAW	COBLS	10//99-12//99
	Greeley PMSA, CO	S	21.10 MW	20.03 AW	43890 AAW	COBLS	10//99-12//99
	Pueblo MSA, CO	S	17.19 MW	14.76 AW	35750 AAW	COBLS	10//99-12//99
	Connecticut	S	22 MW	24.00 AW	49920 AAW	CTBLS	10//99-12//99
	Bridgeport PMSA, CT	S	23.38 MW	21.22 AW	48630 AAW	CTBLS	10//99-12//99
	Danbury PMSA, CT	S	24.61 MW	23.66 AW	51190 AAW	CTBLS	10//99-12//99
	Hartford MSA, CT	S	22.58 MW	21.16 AW	46970 AAW	CTBLS	10//99-12//99
	New Haven-Meriden PMSA, CT	S	25.78 MW	22.80 AW	53630 AAW	CTBLS	10//99-12//99
	New London-Norwich MSA, CT-RI	S	21.29 MW	18.83 AW	44290 AAW	CTBLS	10//99-12//99
	Stamford-Norwalk PMSA, CT	S	25.75 MW	23.62 AW	53570 AAW	CTBLS	10//99-12//99
	Waterbury PMSA, CT	S	26.76 MW	22.22 AW	55660 AAW	CTBLS	10//99-12//99
	Delaware	S	19.58 MW	21.30 AW	44300 AAW	DEBLS	10//99-12//99
	Dover MSA, DE	S	18.83 MW	17.59 AW	39160 AAW	DEBLS	10//99-12//99
	Wilmington-Newark PMSA, DE-MD	S	21.15 MW	19.73 AW	44000 AAW	DEBLS	10//99-12//99
	District of Columbia	S	22.67 MW	24.61 AW	51190 AAW	DCBLS	10//99-12//99
	Washington PMSA, DC-MD-VA-WV	S	23.36 MW	21.17 AW	48580 AAW	DCBLS	10//99-12//99
	Florida	S	17.32 MW	19.70 AW	40980 AAW	FLBLS	10//99-12//99
	Daytona Beach MSA, FL	S	17.64 MW	15.70 AW	36680 AAW	FLBLS	10//99-12//99
	Fort Lauderdale PMSA, FL	S	21.17 MW	17.05 AW	44040 AAW	FLBLS	10//99-12//99
	Fort Myers-Cape Coral MSA, FL	S	21.47 MW	19.71 AW	44660 AAW	FLBLS	10//99-12//99
	Fort Pierce-Port St. Lucie MSA, FL	S	22.80 MW	20.05 AW	47430 AAW	FLBLS	10//99-12//99
	Fort Walton Beach MSA, FL	S	18.63 MW	17.19 AW	38750 AAW	FLBLS	10//99-12//99
	Gainesville MSA, FL	S	16.76 MW	15.65 AW	34860 AAW	FLBLS	10//99-12//99
	Jacksonville MSA, FL	S	18.46 MW	16.96 AW	38400 AAW	FLBLS	10//99-12//99
	Lakeland-Winter Haven MSA, FL	S	27.24 MW	19.75 AW	56670 AAW	FLBLS	10//99-12//99
	Melbourne-Titusville-Palm Bay MSA, FL	S	18.85 MW	16.55 AW	39200 AAW	FLBLS	10//99-12//99
	Miami PMSA, FL	S	21.36 MW	19.27 AW	44430 AAW	FLBLS	10//99-12//99
	Naples MSA, FL	S	19.16 MW	18.37 AW	39850 AAW	FLBLS	10//99-12//99
	Ocala MSA, FL	S	16.99 MW	15.89 AW	35330 AAW	FLBLS	10//99-12//99
	Orlando MSA, FL	S	18.77 MW	17.07 AW	39050 AAW	FLBLS	10//99-12//99
	Panama City MSA, FL	S	14.13 MW	12.07 AW	29390 AAW	FLBLS	10//99-12//99
	Pensacola MSA, FL	S	15.63 MW	14.04 AW	32520 AAW	FLBLS	10//99-12//99
	Punta Gorda MSA, FL	S	20.83 MW	16.48 AW	43320 AAW	FLBLS	10//99-12//99
	Sarasota-Bradenton MSA, FL	S	21.79 MW	18.64 AW	45320 AAW	FLBLS	10//99-12//99
	Tampa-St. Petersburg-Clearwater MSA, FL	S	18.94 MW	17.19 AW	39380 AAW	FLBLS	10//99-12//99
	West Palm Beach-Boca Raton MSA, FL	S	20.88 MW	18.33 AW	43430 AAW	FLBLS	10//99-12//99
	Georgia	S	18.36 MW	19.78 AW	41130 AAW	GABLS	10//99-12//99
	Albany MSA, GA	S	20.32 MW	18.81 AW	42260 AAW	GABLS	10//99-12//99
	Atlanta MSA, GA	S	20.45 MW	18.89 AW	42530 AAW	GABLS	10//99-12//99
	Augusta-Aiken MSA, GA-SC	S	20.38 MW	18.28 AW	42390 AAW	GABLS	10//99-12//99
	Columbus MSA, GA-AL	S	18.39 MW	17.80 AW	38250 AAW	GABLS	10//99-12//99
	Macon MSA, GA	S	17.75 MW	16.52 AW	36910 AAW	GABLS	10//99-12//99
	Savannah MSA, GA	S	18.48 MW	16.71 AW	38440 AAW	GABLS	10//99-12//99
	Hawaii	S	18.89 MW	21.21 AW	44110 AAW	HIBLS	10//99-12//99
	Honolulu MSA, HI	S	21.60 MW	19.17 AW	44930 AAW	HIBLS	10//99-12//99

AAW Average annual wage	**AOH** Average offered, high	**ASH** Average starting, high	**H** Hourly	**M** Monthly	**S** Special: hourly and annual
AE Average entry wage	**AOL** Average offered, low	**ASL** Average starting, low	**HI** Highest wage paid	**MTC** Median total compensation	**TQ** Third quartile wage
AEX Average experienced wage	**APH** Average pay, high range	**AW** Average wage paid	**HR** High end range	**MW** Median wage paid	**W** Weekly
AO Average offered	**APL** Average pay, low range	**FQ** First quartile wage	**LR** Low end range	**SQ** Second quartile wage	**Y** Yearly

Occupation/Type/Industry	Location	Per	Low	Mid	High	Source	Date
Accountant and Auditor	Idaho	S	18.14 MW	20.10 AW	41810 AAW	IDBLS	10//99-12//99
	Boise City MSA, ID	S	20.98 MW	18.75 AW	43640 AAW	IDBLS	10//99-12//99
	Pocatello MSA, ID	S	17.29 MW	17.11 AW	35960 AAW	IDBLS	10//99-12//99
	Illinois	S	18.19 MW	19.62 AW	40810 AAW	ILBLS	10//99-12//99
	Bloomington-Normal MSA, IL	S	21.81 MW	19.73 AW	45360 AAW	ILBLS	10//99-12//99
	Champaign-Urbana MSA, IL	S	18.17 MW	17.97 AW	37790 AAW	ILBLS	10//99-12//99
	Chicago PMSA, IL	S	20.11 MW	18.66 AW	41820 AAW	ILBLS	10//99-12//99
	Decatur MSA, IL	S	17.91 MW	15.40 AW	37260 AAW	ILBLS	10//99-12//99
	Kankakee PMSA, IL	S	18.39 MW	16.62 AW	38250 AAW	ILBLS	10//99-12//99
	Peoria-Pekin MSA, IL	S	17.31 MW	16.12 AW	36000 AAW	ILBLS	10//99-12//99
	Rockford MSA, IL	S	18.64 MW	17.98 AW	38780 AAW	ILBLS	10//99-12//99
	Indiana	S	17.12 MW	18.65 AW	38780 AAW	INBLS	10//99-12//99
	Bloomington MSA, IN	S	17.82 MW	16.47 AW	37070 AAW	INBLS	10//99-12//99
	Elkhart-Goshen MSA, IN	S	18.68 MW	16.52 AW	38860 AAW	INBLS	10//99-12//99
	Evansville-Henderson MSA, IN-KY	S	18.15 MW	16.39 AW	37740 AAW	INBLS	10//99-12//99
	Fort Wayne MSA, IN	S	18.51 MW	16.89 AW	38510 AAW	INBLS	10//99-12//99
	Gary PMSA, IN	S	20.53 MW	20.07 AW	42700 AAW	INBLS	10//99-12//99
	Indianapolis MSA, IN	S	18.88 MW	17.47 AW	39270 AAW	INBLS	10//99-12//99
	Kokomo MSA, IN	S	19.86 MW	18.28 AW	41320 AAW	INBLS	10//99-12//99
	Lafayette MSA, IN	S	18.07 MW	16.66 AW	37590 AAW	INBLS	10//99-12//99
	Muncie MSA, IN	S	19.84 MW	17.65 AW	41270 AAW	INBLS	10//99-12//99
	South Bend MSA, IN	S	17.31 MW	16.30 AW	36010 AAW	INBLS	10//99-12//99
	Terre Haute MSA, IN	S	16.28 MW	14.96 AW	33850 AAW	INBLS	10//99-12//99
	Iowa	S	16.76 MW	17.68 AW	36780 AAW	IABLS	10//99-12//99
	Cedar Rapids MSA, IA	S	19.87 MW	18.32 AW	41330 AAW	IABLS	10//99-12//99
	Davenport-Moline-Rock Island MSA, IA-IL	S	17.83 MW	16.42 AW	37100 AAW	IABLS	10//99-12//99
	Des Moines MSA, IA	S	18.93 MW	17.94 AW	39370 AAW	IABLS	10//99-12//99
	Dubuque MSA, IA	S	17.48 MW	17.36 AW	36350 AAW	IABLS	10//99-12//99
	Iowa City MSA, IA	S	18.57 MW	18.25 AW	38630 AAW	IABLS	10//99-12//99
	Sioux City MSA, IA-NE	S	16.19 MW	16.22 AW	33670 AAW	IABLS	10//99-12//99
	Waterloo-Cedar Falls MSA, IA	S	17.24 MW	16.43 AW	35860 AAW	IABLS	10//99-12//99
	Kansas	S	18.25 MW	19.81 AW	41210 AAW	KSBLS	10//99-12//99
	Lawrence MSA, KS	S	19.49 MW	17.28 AW	40540 AAW	KSBLS	10//99-12//99
	Topeka MSA, KS	S	19.62 MW	17.72 AW	40810 AAW	KSBLS	10//99-12//99
	Wichita MSA, KS	S	21.42 MW	18.78 AW	44560 AAW	KSBLS	10//99-12//99
	Kentucky	S	17.36 MW	19.31 AW	40170 AAW	KYBLS	10//99-12//99
	Lexington MSA, KY	S	18.63 MW	16.69 AW	38750 AAW	KYBLS	10//99-12//99
	Louisville MSA, KY-IN	S	21.04 MW	18.50 AW	43750 AAW	KYBLS	10//99-12//99
	Owensboro MSA, KY	S	20.37 MW	18.19 AW	42370 AAW	KYBLS	10//99-12//99
	Louisiana	S	16.09 MW	17.52 AW	36440 AAW	LABLS	10//99-12//99
	Alexandria MSA, LA	S	16.91 MW	15.84 AW	35170 AAW	LABLS	10//99-12//99
	Baton Rouge MSA, LA	S	16.94 MW	15.90 AW	35230 AAW	LABLS	10//99-12//99
	Houma MSA, LA	S	17.83 MW	16.39 AW	37090 AAW	LABLS	10//99-12//99
	Lafayette MSA, LA	S	18.29 MW	16.34 AW	38050 AAW	LABLS	10//99-12//99
	Lake Charles MSA, LA	S	17.02 MW	15.55 AW	35390 AAW	LABLS	10//99-12//99
	Monroe MSA, LA	S	15.04 MW	14.03 AW	31290 AAW	LABLS	10//99-12//99
	New Orleans MSA, LA	S	18.09 MW	16.39 AW	37620 AAW	LABLS	10//99-12//99
	Shreveport-Bossier City MSA, LA	S	18.67 MW	17.22 AW	38830 AAW	LABLS	10//99-12//99
	Maine	S	16.26 MW	18.26 AW	37980 AAW	MEBLS	10//99-12//99
	Bangor MSA, ME	S	17.05 MW	16.42 AW	35460 AAW	MEBLS	10//99-12//99
	Lewiston-Auburn MSA, ME	S	20.36 MW	16.53 AW	42350 AAW	MEBLS	10//99-12//99
	Portland MSA, ME	S	18.76 MW	17.33 AW	39010 AAW	MEBLS	10//99-12//99
	Maryland	S	20.06 MW	21.80 AW	45340 AAW	MDBLS	10//99-12//99
	Baltimore PMSA, MD	S	21.24 MW	19.57 AW	44180 AAW	MDBLS	10//99-12//99
	Cumberland MSA, MD-WV	S	21.13 MW	16.19 AW	43940 AAW	MDBLS	10//99-12//99
	Hagerstown PMSA, MD	S	18.18 MW	16.40 AW	37810 AAW	MDBLS	10//99-12//99
	Massachusetts	S	20.17 MW	22.02 AW	45790 AAW	MABLS	10//99-12//99
	Barnstable-Yarmouth MSA, MA	S	26.32 MW	22.78 AW	54740 AAW	MABLS	10//99-12//99
	Boston PMSA, MA-NH	S	22.23 MW	20.35 AW	46240 AAW	MABLS	10//99-12//99
	Brockton PMSA, MA	S	20.69 MW	19.84 AW	43030 AAW	MABLS	10//99-12//99
	Fitchburg-Leominster PMSA, MA	S	19.52 MW	18.30 AW	40600 AAW	MABLS	10//99-12//99
	Lawrence PMSA, MA-NH	S	20.74 MW	19.02 AW	43130 AAW	MABLS	10//99-12//99
	Lowell PMSA, MA-NH	S	20.97 MW	19.54 AW	43610 AAW	MABLS	10//99-12//99
	New Bedford PMSA, MA	S	19.59 MW	16.83 AW	40740 AAW	MABLS	10//99-12//99
	Pittsfield MSA, MA	S	21.02 MW	19.22 AW	43720 AAW	MABLS	10//99-12//99
	Springfield MSA, MA	S	20.88 MW	19.37 AW	43440 AAW	MABLS	10//99-12//99
	Worcester PMSA, MA-CT	S	21.70 MW	19.77 AW	45130 AAW	MABLS	10//99-12//99

AAW Average annual wage	**AOH** Average offered, high	**ASH** Average starting, high	**H** Hourly	**M** Monthly	**S** Special: hourly and annual
AE Average entry wage	**AOL** Average offered, low	**ASL** Average starting, low	**HI** Highest wage paid	**MTC** Median total compensation	**TQ** Third quartile wage
AEX Average experienced wage	**APH** Average pay, high range	**AW** Average wage paid	**HR** High end range	**MW** Median wage paid	**W** Weekly
AO Average offered	**APL** Average pay, low range	**FQ** First quartile wage	**LR** Low end range	**SQ** Second quartile wage	**Y** Yearly

Accountant and Auditor

Occupation/Type/Industry	Location	Per	Low	Mid	High	Source	Date
Accountant and Auditor	Michigan	S	20.04 MW	22.31 AW	46400 AAW	MIBLS	10//99-12//99
	Ann Arbor PMSA, MI	S	22.97 MW	20.00 AW	47790 AAW	MIBLS	10//99-12//99
	Benton Harbor MSA, MI	S	22.16 MW	19.41 AW	46080 AAW	MIBLS	10//99-12//99
	Detroit PMSA, MI	S	23.25 MW	20.59 AW	48360 AAW	MIBLS	10//99-12//99
	Flint PMSA, MI	S	23.99 MW	21.25 AW	49910 AAW	MIBLS	10//99-12//99
	Grand Rapids-Muskegon-Holland MSA, MI	S	20.33 MW	19.02 AW	42290 AAW	MIBLS	10//99-12//99
	Jackson MSA, MI	S	21.44 MW	21.01 AW	44580 AAW	MIBLS	10//99-12//99
	Kalamazoo-Battle Creek MSA, MI	S	19.32 MW	17.55 AW	40180 AAW	MIBLS	10//99-12//99
	Lansing-East Lansing MSA, MI	S	23.97 MW	22.28 AW	49850 AAW	MIBLS	10//99-12//99
	Saginaw-Bay City-Midland MSA, MI	S	18.92 MW	17.32 AW	39350 AAW	MIBLS	10//99-12//99
	Minnesota	S	19.04 MW	20.45 AW	42540 AAW	MNBLS	10//99-12//99
	Duluth-Superior MSA, MN-WI	S	18.72 MW	17.71 AW	38950 AAW	MNBLS	10//99-12//99
	Minneapolis-St. Paul MSA, MN-WI	S	21.17 MW	19.59 AW	44040 AAW	MNBLS	10//99-12//99
	Rochester MSA, MN	S	19.71 MW	19.54 AW	40990 AAW	MNBLS	10//99-12//99
	St. Cloud MSA, MN	S	18.10 MW	16.94 AW	37660 AAW	MNBLS	10//99-12//99
	Mississippi	S	16.82 MW	18.90 AW	39310 AAW	MSBLS	10//99-12//99
	Biloxi-Gulfport-Pascagoula MSA, MS	S	20.44 MW	17.93 AW	42510 AAW	MSBLS	10//99-12//99
	Hattiesburg MSA, MS	S	17.72 MW	15.53 AW	36850 AAW	MSBLS	10//99-12//99
	Jackson MSA, MS	S	18.93 MW	16.67 AW	39380 AAW	MSBLS	10//99-12//99
	Missouri	S	16.62 MW	18.41 AW	38290 AAW	MOBLS	10//99-12//99
	Columbia MSA, MO	S	18.18 MW	17.27 AW	37820 AAW	MOBLS	10//99-12//99
	Joplin MSA, MO	S	17.89 MW	16.59 AW	37210 AAW	MOBLS	10//99-12//99
	Kansas City MSA, MO-KS	S	18.69 MW	17.53 AW	38880 AAW	MOBLS	10//99-12//99
	St. Joseph MSA, MO	S	15.82 MW	14.75 AW	32900 AAW	MOBLS	10//99-12//99
	St. Louis MSA, MO-IL	S	18.89 MW	16.91 AW	39280 AAW	MOBLS	10//99-12//99
	Springfield MSA, MO	S	18.28 MW	15.63 AW	38020 AAW	MOBLS	10//99-12//99
	Montana	S	15.73 MW	18.14 AW	37720 AAW	MTBLS	10//99-12//99
	Billings MSA, MT	S	19.53 MW	15.74 AW	40630 AAW	MTBLS	10//99-12//99
	Great Falls MSA, MT	S	16.53 MW	15.48 AW	34390 AAW	MTBLS	10//99-12//99
	Missoula MSA, MT	S	20.98 MW	16.57 AW	43650 AAW	MTBLS	10//99-12//99
	Nebraska	S	16.84 MW	19.06 AW	39630 AAW	NEBLS	10//99-12//99
	Lincoln MSA, NE	S	18.28 MW	17.25 AW	38030 AAW	NEBLS	10//99-12//99
	Omaha MSA, NE-IA	S	19.53 MW	16.87 AW	40620 AAW	NEBLS	10//99-12//99
	Nevada	S	18.33 MW	20.64 AW	42920 AAW	NVBLS	10//99-12//99
	Las Vegas MSA, NV-AZ	S	20.83 MW	18.07 AW	43330 AAW	NVBLS	10//99-12//99
	Reno MSA, NV	S	20.56 MW	18.63 AW	42770 AAW	NVBLS	10//99-12//99
	New Hampshire	S	17.82 MW	19.59 AW	40740 AAW	NHBLS	10//99-12//99
	Manchester PMSA, NH	S	22.39 MW	19.73 AW	46570 AAW	NHBLS	10//99-12//99
	Nashua PMSA, NH	S	21.43 MW	19.09 AW	44580 AAW	NHBLS	10//99-12//99
	Portsmouth-Rochester PMSA, NH-ME	S	17.23 MW	16.52 AW	35840 AAW	NHBLS	10//99-12//99
	New Jersey	S	23.41 MW	26.00 AW	54080 AAW	NJBLS	10//99-12//99
	Atlantic-Cape May PMSA, NJ	S	22.41 MW	19.33 AW	46600 AAW	NJBLS	10//99-12//99
	Bergen-Passaic PMSA, NJ	S	26.67 MW	24.24 AW	55480 AAW	NJBLS	10//99-12//99
	Jersey City PMSA, NJ	S	24.56 MW	22.46 AW	51090 AAW	NJBLS	10//99-12//99
	Middlesex-Somerset-Hunterdon PMSA, NJ	S	25.61 MW	22.77 AW	53270 AAW	NJBLS	10//99-12//99
	Monmouth-Ocean PMSA, NJ	S	26.16 MW	23.24 AW	54420 AAW	NJBLS	10//99-12//99
	Newark PMSA, NJ	S	28.26 MW	25.12 AW	58770 AAW	NJBLS	10//99-12//99
	Trenton PMSA, NJ	S	25.80 MW	24.52 AW	53670 AAW	NJBLS	10//99-12//99
	Vineland-Millville-Bridgeton PMSA, NJ	S	21.60 MW	20.59 AW	44930 AAW	NJBLS	10//99-12//99
	New Mexico	S	15.97 MW	16.94 AW	35230 AAW	NMBLS	10//99-12//99
	Albuquerque MSA, NM	S	17.48 MW	16.55 AW	36350 AAW	NMBLS	10//99-12//99
	Las Cruces MSA, NM	S	14.32 MW	12.90 AW	29800 AAW	NMBLS	10//99-12//99
	Santa Fe MSA, NM	S	16.40 MW	15.64 AW	34110 AAW	NMBLS	10//99-12//99
	New York	S	21.44 MW	23.88 AW	49670 AAW	NYBLS	10//99-12//99
	Albany-Schenectady-Troy MSA, NY	S	21.35 MW	20.96 AW	44400 AAW	NYBLS	10//99-12//99
	Binghamton MSA, NY	S	20.61 MW	19.42 AW	42860 AAW	NYBLS	10//99-12//99
	Buffalo-Niagara Falls MSA, NY	S	18.04 MW	16.07 AW	37520 AAW	NYBLS	10//99-12//99
	Dutchess County PMSA, NY	S	21.72 MW	19.34 AW	45180 AAW	NYBLS	10//99-12//99
	Elmira MSA, NY	S	20.36 MW	17.33 AW	42350 AAW	NYBLS	10//99-12//99
	Glens Falls MSA, NY	S	19.13 MW	17.01 AW	39790 AAW	NYBLS	10//99-12//99
	Jamestown MSA, NY	S	17.30 MW	16.45 AW	35990 AAW	NYBLS	10//99-12//99
	Nassau-Suffolk PMSA, NY	S	22.90 MW	20.62 AW	47640 AAW	NYBLS	10//99-12//99

AAW Average annual wage	AOH Average offered, high	ASH Average starting, high	H Hourly	M Monthly	S Special: hourly and annual
AE Average entry wage	AOL Average offered, low	ASL Average starting, low	HI Highest wage paid	MTC Median total compensation	TQ Third quartile wage
AEX Average experienced wage	APH Average pay, high range	AW Average wage paid	HR High end range	MW Median wage paid	W Weekly
AO Average offered	APL Average pay, low range	FQ First quartile wage	LR Low end range	SQ Second quartile wage	Y Yearly

Occupation/Type/Industry	Location	Per	Low	Mid	High	Source	Date
Accountant and Auditor	New York PMSA, NY	S	25.79 MW	23.22 AW	53640 AAW	NYBLS	10//99-12//99
	Newburgh PMSA, NY-PA	S	22.17 MW	20.26 AW	46110 AAW	NYBLS	10//99-12//99
	Rochester MSA, NY	S	20.64 MW	18.44 AW	42940 AAW	NYBLS	10//99-12//99
	Syracuse MSA, NY	S	23.61 MW	20.09 AW	49120 AAW	NYBLS	10//99-12//99
	Utica-Rome MSA, NY	S	16.81 MW	14.39 AW	34970 AAW	NYBLS	10//99-12//99
	North Carolina	S	18.35 MW	19.68 AW	40930 AAW	NCBLS	10//99-12//99
	Asheville MSA, NC	S	19.05 MW	16.68 AW	39630 AAW	NCBLS	10//99-12//99
	Charlotte-Gastonia-Rock Hill MSA, NC-SC	S	20.72 MW	19.20 AW	43090 AAW	NCBLS	10//99-12//99
	Fayetteville MSA, NC	S	18.12 MW	14.50 AW	37700 AAW	NCBLS	10//99-12//99
	Goldsboro MSA, NC	S	17.85 MW	17.43 AW	37130 AAW	NCBLS	10//99-12//99
	Greensboro--Winston-Salem-- High Point MSA, NC	S	20.96 MW	19.27 AW	43600 AAW	NCBLS	10//99-12//99
	Greenville MSA, NC	S	17.84 MW	17.44 AW	37120 AAW	NCBLS	10//99-12//99
	Hickory-Morganton-Lenoir MSA, NC	S	20.48 MW	18.23 AW	42600 AAW	NCBLS	10//99-12//99
	Jacksonville MSA, NC	S	17.31 MW	15.72 AW	36010 AAW	NCBLS	10//99-12//99
	Raleigh-Durham-Chapel Hill MSA, NC	S	19.88 MW	19.14 AW	41350 AAW	NCBLS	10//99-12//99
	Rocky Mount MSA, NC	S	20.63 MW	17.37 AW	42920 AAW	NCBLS	10//99-12//99
	Wilmington MSA, NC	S	18.03 MW	16.90 AW	37500 AAW	NCBLS	10//99-12//99
	North Dakota	S	15.1 MW	16.40 AW	34100 AAW	NDBLS	10//99-12//99
	Bismarck MSA, ND	S	18.16 MW	17.26 AW	37770 AAW	NDBLS	10//99-12//99
	Fargo-Moorhead MSA, ND-MN	S	16.82 MW	15.66 AW	34980 AAW	NDBLS	10//99-12//99
	Grand Forks MSA, ND-MN	S	18.71 MW	18.22 AW	38910 AAW	NDBLS	10//99-12//99
	Ohio	S	18.38 MW	20.34 AW	42310 AAW	OHBLS	10//99-12//99
	Akron PMSA, OH	S	21.80 MW	19.65 AW	45340 AAW	OHBLS	10//99-12//99
	Canton-Massillon MSA, OH	S	18.37 MW	17.34 AW	38210 AAW	OHBLS	10//99-12//99
	Cincinnati PMSA, OH-KY-IN	S	19.80 MW	18.38 AW	41190 AAW	OHBLS	10//99-12//99
	Cleveland-Lorain-Elyria PMSA, OH	S	21.53 MW	19.57 AW	44770 AAW	OHBLS	10//99-12//99
	Columbus MSA, OH	S	20.82 MW	18.14 AW	43310 AAW	OHBLS	10//99-12//99
	Dayton-Springfield MSA, OH	S	21.38 MW	18.13 AW	44470 AAW	OHBLS	10//99-12//99
	Hamilton-Middletown PMSA, OH	S	19.70 MW	18.18 AW	40980 AAW	OHBLS	10//99-12//99
	Lima MSA, OH	S	16.22 MW	16.04 AW	33730 AAW	OHBLS	10//99-12//99
	Mansfield MSA, OH	S	19.79 MW	18.19 AW	41170 AAW	OHBLS	10//99-12//99
	Steubenville-Weirton MSA, OH-WV	S	17.05 MW	17.40 AW	35460 AAW	OHBLS	10//99-12//99
	Toledo MSA, OH	S	17.35 MW	16.89 AW	36080 AAW	OHBLS	10//99-12//99
	Youngstown-Warren MSA, OH	S	18.24 MW	17.17 AW	37940 AAW	OHBLS	10//99-12//99
	Oklahoma	S	15.7 MW	17.65 AW	36710 AAW	OKBLS	10//99-12//99
	Enid MSA, OK	S	17.66 MW	14.74 AW	36730 AAW	OKBLS	10//99-12//99
	Oklahoma City MSA, OK	S	17.24 MW	15.30 AW	35860 AAW	OKBLS	10//99-12//99
	Tulsa MSA, OK	S	19.64 MW	17.95 AW	40840 AAW	OKBLS	10//99-12//99
	Oregon	S	19.27 MW	21.80 AW	45340 AAW	ORBLS	10//99-12//99
	Corvallis MSA, OR	S	21.61 MW	20.31 AW	44950 AAW	ORBLS	10//99-12//99
	Eugene-Springfield MSA, OR	S	23.63 MW	22.40 AW	49160 AAW	ORBLS	10//99-12//99
	Medford-Ashland MSA, OR	S	17.80 MW	15.87 AW	37030 AAW	ORBLS	10//99-12//99
	Portland-Vancouver PMSA, OR-WA	S	21.71 MW	19.48 AW	45150 AAW	ORBLS	10//99-12//99
	Salem PMSA, OR	S	19.72 MW	18.63 AW	41010 AAW	ORBLS	10//99-12//99
	Pennsylvania	S	18.7 MW	20.76 AW	43190 AAW	PABLS	10//99-12//99
	Allentown-Bethlehem-Easton MSA, PA	S	21.69 MW	20.71 AW	45120 AAW	PABLS	10//99-12//99
	Altoona MSA, PA	S	19.72 MW	18.09 AW	41010 AAW	PABLS	10//99-12//99
	Erie MSA, PA	S	15.62 MW	14.63 AW	32480 AAW	PABLS	10//99-12//99
	Harrisburg-Lebanon-Carlisle MSA, PA	S	20.41 MW	18.97 AW	42450 AAW	PABLS	10//99-12//99
	Johnstown MSA, PA	S	14.82 MW	13.68 AW	30820 AAW	PABLS	10//99-12//99
	Lancaster MSA, PA	S	18.56 MW	17.77 AW	38600 AAW	PABLS	10//99-12//99
	Philadelphia PMSA, PA-NJ	S	22.79 MW	20.26 AW	47400 AAW	PABLS	10//99-12//99
	Pittsburgh MSA, PA	S	19.47 MW	17.39 AW	40510 AAW	PABLS	10//99-12//99
	Reading MSA, PA	S	21.21 MW	19.16 AW	44110 AAW	PABLS	10//99-12//99
	Scranton--Wilkes-Barre-- Hazleton MSA, PA	S	16.73 MW	15.38 AW	34800 AAW	PABLS	10//99-12//99
	Sharon MSA, PA	S	14.31 MW	13.05 AW	29760 AAW	PABLS	10//99-12//99
	State College MSA, PA	S	21.42 MW	18.47 AW	44560 AAW	PABLS	10//99-12//99
	Williamsport MSA, PA	S	15.40 MW	14.69 AW	32020 AAW	PABLS	10//99-12//99
	York MSA, PA	S	21.43 MW	19.79 AW	44560 AAW	PABLS	10//99-12//99
	Rhode Island	S	21.73 MW	23.36 AW	48580 AAW	RIBLS	10//99-12//99

AAW	Average annual wage	AOH	Average offered, high	ASH	Average starting, high	H	Hourly
AE	Average entry wage	AOL	Average offered, low	ASL	Average starting, low	HI	Highest wage paid
AEX	Average experienced wage	APH	Average pay, high range	AW	Average wage paid	HR	High end range
AO	Average offered	APL	Average pay, low range	FQ	First quartile wage	LR	Low end range

M	Monthly	S	Special: hourly and annual
MTC	Median total compensation	TQ	Third quartile wage
MW	Median wage paid	W	Weekly
SQ	Second quartile wage	Y	Yearly

Occupation/Type/Industry	Location	Per	Low	Mid	High	Source	Date
Accountant and Auditor	Providence-Fall River- Warwick MSA, RI-MA	S	23.11 MW	21.45 AW	48070 AAW	RIBLS	10//99-12//99
	South Carolina	S	16.66 MW	18.96 AW	39430 AAW	SCBLS	10//99-12//99
	Charleston-North Charleston MSA, SC	S	17.95 MW	15.78 AW	37330 AAW	SCBLS	10//99-12//99
	Columbia MSA, SC	S	17.98 MW	15.93 AW	37400 AAW	SCBLS	10//99-12//99
	Florence MSA, SC	S	20.02 MW	18.31 AW	41640 AAW	SCBLS	10//99-12//99
	Greenville-Spartanburg- Anderson MSA, SC	S	19.79 MW	17.85 AW	41170 AAW	SCBLS	10//99-12//99
	Myrtle Beach MSA, SC	S	16.89 MW	16.04 AW	35140 AAW	SCBLS	10//99-12//99
	Sumter MSA, SC	S	18.79 MW	16.78 AW	39090 AAW	SCBLS	10//99-12//99
	South Dakota	S	15.87 MW	17.21 AW	35800 AAW	SDBLS	10//99-12//99
	Rapid City MSA, SD	S	17.43 MW	15.93 AW	36250 AAW	SDBLS	10//99-12//99
	Sioux Falls MSA, SD	S	17.70 MW	16.26 AW	36820 AAW	SDBLS	10//99-12//99
	Tennessee	S	17.86 MW	19.15 AW	39820 AAW	TNBLS	10//99-12//99
	Chattanooga MSA, TN-GA	S	19.11 MW	17.89 AW	39760 AAW	TNBLS	10//99-12//99
	Clarksville-Hopkinsville MSA, TN-KY	S	17.47 MW	15.47 AW	36330 AAW	TNBLS	10//99-12//99
	Jackson MSA, TN	S	18.51 MW	16.98 AW	38500 AAW	TNBLS	10//99-12//99
	Johnson City-Kingsport-Bristol MSA, TN-VA	S	16.25 MW	15.09 AW	33800 AAW	TNBLS	10//99-12//99
	Knoxville MSA, TN	S	20.70 MW	19.05 AW	43060 AAW	TNBLS	10//99-12//99
	Memphis MSA, TN-AR-MS	S	18.39 MW	16.79 AW	38250 AAW	MSBLS	10//99-12//99
	Nashville MSA, TN	S	19.45 MW	17.84 AW	40450 AAW	TNBLS	10//99-12//99
	Texas	S	19.18 MW	20.69 AW	43030 AAW	TXBLS	10//99-12//99
	Abilene MSA, TX	S	16.47 MW	15.40 AW	34250 AAW	TXBLS	10//99-12//99
	Amarillo MSA, TX	S	18.43 MW	16.53 AW	38340 AAW	TXBLS	10//99-12//99
	Austin-San Marcos MSA, TX	S	18.49 MW	17.32 AW	38450 AAW	TXBLS	10//99-12//99
	Beaumont-Port Arthur MSA, TX	S	19.85 MW	18.15 AW	41300 AAW	TXBLS	10//99-12//99
	Brazoria PMSA, TX	S	18.70 MW	17.08 AW	38900 AAW	TXBLS	10//99-12//99
	Brownsville-Harlingen-San Benito MSA, TX	S	15.71 MW	14.10 AW	32670 AAW	TXBLS	10//99-12//99
	Bryan-College Station MSA, TX	S	18.14 MW	16.72 AW	37740 AAW	TXBLS	10//99-12//99
	Corpus Christi MSA, TX	S	17.06 MW	13.93 AW	35490 AAW	TXBLS	10//99-12//99
	Dallas PMSA, TX	S	21.42 MW	20.09 AW	44560 AAW	TXBLS	10//99-12//99
	El Paso MSA, TX	S	22.02 MW	17.99 AW	45800 AAW	TXBLS	10//99-12//99
	Fort Worth-Arlington PMSA, TX	S	20.91 MW	19.17 AW	43490 AAW	TXBLS	10//99-12//99
	Galveston-Texas City PMSA, TX	S	17.74 MW	16.34 AW	36900 AAW	TXBLS	10//99-12//99
	Houston PMSA, TX	S	22.74 MW	20.89 AW	47310 AAW	TXBLS	10//99-12//99
	Killeen-Temple MSA, TX	S	17.88 MW	16.06 AW	37200 AAW	TXBLS	10//99-12//99
	Laredo MSA, TX	S	16.74 MW	15.25 AW	34820 AAW	TXBLS	10//99-12//99
	Longview-Marshall MSA, TX	S	21.80 MW	18.56 AW	45350 AAW	TXBLS	10//99-12//99
	Lubbock MSA, TX	S	18.95 MW	16.46 AW	39410 AAW	TXBLS	10//99-12//99
	McAllen-Edinburg-Mission MSA, TX	S	18.24 MW	16.54 AW	37940 AAW	TXBLS	10//99-12//99
	Odessa-Midland MSA, TX	S	18.17 MW	17.31 AW	37800 AAW	TXBLS	10//99-12//99
	San Angelo MSA, TX	S	16.40 MW	16.56 AW	34120 AAW	TXBLS	10//99-12//99
	San Antonio MSA, TX	S	17.61 MW	16.61 AW	36620 AAW	TXBLS	10//99-12//99
	Sherman-Denison MSA, TX	S	19.77 MW	17.80 AW	41130 AAW	TXBLS	10//99-12//99
	Texarkana MSA, TX-AR	S	18.26 MW	15.49 AW	37980 AAW	TXBLS	10//99-12//99
	Tyler MSA, TX	S	20.44 MW	18.72 AW	42520 AAW	TXBLS	10//99-12//99
	Victoria MSA, TX	S	17.14 MW	17.34 AW	35650 AAW	TXBLS	10//99-12//99
	Waco MSA, TX	S	19.62 MW	17.73 AW	40800 AAW	TXBLS	10//99-12//99
	Wichita Falls MSA, TX	S	17.88 MW	16.18 AW	37190 AAW	TXBLS	10//99-12//99
	Utah	S	18.04 MW	20.21 AW	42040 AAW	UTBLS	10//99-12//99
	Provo-Orem MSA, UT	S	17.98 MW	16.18 AW	37400 AAW	UTBLS	10//99-12//99
	Salt Lake City-Ogden MSA, UT	S	20.56 MW	18.23 AW	42770 AAW	UTBLS	10//99-12//99
	Vermont	S	19.71 MW	20.83 AW	43320 AAW	VTBLS	10//99-12//99
	Burlington MSA, VT	S	21.02 MW	19.84 AW	43730 AAW	VTBLS	10//99-12//99
	Virginia	S	18.6 MW	20.60 AW	42850 AAW	VABLS	10//99-12//99
	Charlottesville MSA, VA	S	17.89 MW	16.97 AW	37220 AAW	VABLS	10//99-12//99
	Danville MSA, VA	S	16.21 MW	15.49 AW	33720 AAW	VABLS	10//99-12//99
	Lynchburg MSA, VA	S	16.98 MW	16.29 AW	35320 AAW	VABLS	10//99-12//99

	Norfolk-Virginia Beach-
	  Newport News MSA, VA-
	  NC
		S	18.12 MW	16.58 AW	37700 AAW	VABLS	10//99-12//99

AAW Average annual wage	**AOH** Average offered, high	**ASH** Average starting, high	**H** Hourly	**M** Monthly	**S** Special: hourly and annual
AE Average entry wage	**AOL** Average offered, low	**ASL** Average starting, low	**HI** Highest wage paid	**MTC** Median total compensation	**TQ** Third quartile wage
AEX Average experienced wage	**APH** Average pay, high range	**AW** Average wage paid	**HR** High end range	**MW** Median wage paid	**W** Weekly
AO Average offered	**APL** Average pay, low range	**FQ** First quartile wage	**LR** Low end range	**SQ** Second quartile wage	**Y** Yearly

Occupation/Type/Industry	Location	Per	Low	Mid	High	Source	Date
Accountant and Auditor	Richmond-Petersburg MSA, VA	S	19.83 MW	18.20 AW	41250 AAW	VABLS	10//99-12//99
	Roanoke MSA, VA	S	17.06 MW	16.59 AW	35490 AAW	VABLS	10//99-12//99
	Washington	S	20.05 MW	22.94 AW	47710 AAW	WABLS	10//99-12//99
	Bellingham MSA, WA	S	20.85 MW	18.83 AW	43370 AAW	WABLS	10//99-12//99
	Bremerton PMSA, WA	S	19.54 MW	18.37 AW	40640 AAW	WABLS	10//99-12//99
	Richland-Kennewick-Pasco MSA, WA	S	23.60 MW	22.25 AW	49080 AAW	WABLS	10//99-12//99
	Seattle-Bellevue-Everett PMSA, WA	S	24.82 MW	21.16 AW	51620 AAW	WABLS	10//99-12//99
	Spokane MSA, WA	S	20.32 MW	18.49 AW	42270 AAW	WABLS	10//99-12//99
	Tacoma PMSA, WA	S	20.39 MW	18.68 AW	42410 AAW	WABLS	10//99-12//99
	Yakima MSA, WA	S	19.82 MW	18.34 AW	41230 AAW	WABLS	10//99-12//99
	West Virginia	S	15.53 MW	17.45 AW	36290 AAW	WVBLS	10//99-12//99
	Charleston MSA, WV	S	18.92 MW	16.61 AW	39350 AAW	WVBLS	10//99-12//99
	Huntington-Ashland MSA, WV-KY-OH	S	16.92 MW	14.38 AW	35190 AAW	WVBLS	10//99-12//99
	Parkersburg-Marietta MSA, WV-OH	S	17.76 MW	15.70 AW	36950 AAW	WVBLS	10//99-12//99
	Wheeling MSA, WV-OH	S	18.89 MW	19.26 AW	39280 AAW	WVBLS	10//99-12//99
	Wisconsin	S	17.74 MW	19.48 AW	40520 AAW	WIBLS	10//99-12//99
	Appleton-Oshkosh-Neenah MSA, WI	S	18.29 MW	16.58 AW	38040 AAW	WIBLS	10//99-12//99
	Eau Claire MSA, WI	S	20.95 MW	16.57 AW	43580 AAW	WIBLS	10//99-12//99
	Green Bay MSA, WI	S	20.71 MW	18.09 AW	43080 AAW	WIBLS	10//99-12//99
	Janesville-Beloit MSA, WI	S	18.73 MW	18.02 AW	38960 AAW	WIBLS	10//99-12//99
	Kenosha PMSA, WI	S	17.66 MW	16.14 AW	36730 AAW	WIBLS	10//99-12//99
	La Crosse MSA, WI-MN	S	16.55 MW	15.46 AW	34420 AAW	WIBLS	10//99-12//99
	Madison MSA, WI	S	19.25 MW	17.96 AW	40040 AAW	WIBLS	10//99-12//99
	Milwaukee-Waukesha PMSA, WI	S	21.29 MW	18.91 AW	44290 AAW	WIBLS	10//99-12//99
	Racine PMSA, WI	S	17.52 MW	16.43 AW	36440 AAW	WIBLS	10//99-12//99
	Sheboygan MSA, WI	S	17.77 MW	16.72 AW	36960 AAW	WIBLS	10//99-12//99
	Wausau MSA, WI	S	18.34 MW	16.46 AW	38140 AAW	WIBLS	10//99-12//99
	Wyoming	S	17.11 MW	19.44 AW	40430 AAW	WYBLS	10//99-12//99
	Casper MSA, WY	S	19.99 MW	17.85 AW	41570 AAW	WYBLS	10//99-12//99
	Cheyenne MSA, WY	S	16.58 MW	15.91 AW	34480 AAW	WYBLS	10//99-12//99
	Puerto Rico	S	11.15 MW	12.36 AW	25710 AAW	PRBLS	10//99-12//99
	Aguadilla MSA, PR	S	13.09 MW	11.39 AW	27230 AAW	PRBLS	10//99-12//99
	Arecibo PMSA, PR	S	11.52 MW	9.74 AW	23960 AAW	PRBLS	10//99-12//99
	Caguas PMSA, PR	S	11.86 MW	10.56 AW	24680 AAW	PRBLS	10//99-12//99
	Mayaguez MSA, PR	S	10.50 MW	9.57 AW	21840 AAW	PRBLS	10//99-12//99
	Ponce MSA, PR	S	10.33 MW	9.75 AW	21490 AAW	PRBLS	10//99-12//99
	San Juan-Bayamon PMSA, PR	S	13.03 MW	11.75 AW	27100 AAW	PRBLS	10//99-12//99
	Virgin Islands	S	16.13 MW	17.29 AW	35960 AAW	VIBLS	10//99-12//99
	Guam	S	15.27 MW	16.30 AW	33910 AAW	GUBLS	10//99-12//99
Actor	Arizona	Y		33930 AAW		AZBLS	10//99-12//99
	Phoenix-Mesa MSA, AZ	Y		34670 AAW		AZBLS	10//99-12//99
	Arkansas	Y		13910 AAW		ARBLS	10//99-12//99
	Little Rock-North Little Rock MSA, AR	Y		13910 AAW		ARBLS	10//99-12//99
	California	Y		74730 AAW		CABLS	10//99-12//99
	Los Angeles-Long Beach PMSA, CA	Y		78950 AAW		CABLS	10//99-12//99
	Colorado	Y		47210 AAW		COBLS	10//99-12//99
	Denver PMSA, CO	Y		47820 AAW		COBLS	10//99-12//99
	Connecticut	Y		31150 AAW		CTBLS	10//99-12//99
	Washington PMSA, DC-MD-VA-WV	Y		28360 AAW		DCBLS	10//99-12//99
	Florida	Y		22590 AAW		FLBLS	10//99-12//99
	Orlando MSA, FL	Y		23060 AAW		FLBLS	10//99-12//99
	Tampa-St. Petersburg-Clearwater MSA, FL	Y		16370 AAW		FLBLS	10//99-12//99
	Georgia	Y		19780 AAW		GABLS	10//99-12//99
	Illinois	Y		30420 AAW		ILBLS	10//99-12//99
	Chicago PMSA, IL	Y		42310 AAW		ILBLS	10//99-12//99
	Indiana	Y		79370 AAW		INBLS	10//99-12//99
	Louisiana	Y		13980 AAW		LABLS	10//99-12//99
	Maryland	Y		24430 AAW		MDBLS	10//99-12//99
	Massachusetts	Y		32090 AAW		MABLS	10//99-12//99
	Boston PMSA, MA-NH	Y		32650 AAW		MABLS	10//99-12//99
	Minnesota	Y		31270 AAW		MNBLS	10//99-12//99

AAW	Average annual wage	AOH	Average offered, high	ASH	Average starting, high
AE	Average entry wage	AOL	Average offered, low	ASL	Average starting, low
AEX	Average experienced wage	APH	Average pay, high range	AW	Average wage paid
AO	Average offered	APL	Average pay, low range	FQ	First quartile wage

H	Hourly	M	Monthly
HI	Highest wage paid	MTC	Median total compensation
HR	High end range	MW	Median wage paid
LR	Low end range	SQ	Second quartile wage

S	Special: hourly and annual
TQ	Third quartile wage
W	Weekly
Y	Yearly

Occupation/Type/Industry	Location	Per	Low	Mid	High	Source	Date
Actor	Minneapolis-St. Paul MSA,						
	MN-WI	Y		31580 AAW		MNBLS	10//99-12//99
	Missouri	Y		30080 AAW		MOBLS	10//99-12//99
	Nevada	Y		46870 AAW		NVBLS	10//99-12//99
	Las Vegas MSA, NV-AZ	Y		45530 AAW		NVBLS	10//99-12//99
	New Jersey	Y		63150 AAW		NJBLS	10//99-12//99
	New York	Y		42410 AAW		NYBLS	10//99-12//99
	New York PMSA, NY	Y		43010 AAW		NYBLS	10//99-12//99
	North Carolina	Y		13780 AAW		NCBLS	10//99-12//99
	Cleveland-Lorain-Elyria						
	PMSA, OH	Y		14040 AAW		OHBLS	10//99-12//99
	Oklahoma	Y		17600 AAW		OKBLS	10//99-12//99
	Oklahoma City MSA, OK	Y		14400 AAW		OKBLS	10//99-12//99
	Pennsylvania	Y		35630 AAW		PABLS	10//99-12//99
	Philadelphia PMSA, PA-NJ	Y		31500 AAW		PABLS	10//99-12//99
	South Carolina	Y		22160 AAW		SCBLS	10//99-12//99
	Charleston-North Charleston						
	MSA, SC	Y		19670 AAW		SCBLS	10//99-12//99
	South Dakota	Y		19330 AAW		SDBLS	10//99-12//99
	Tennessee	Y		42850 AAW		TNBLS	10//99-12//99
	Nashville MSA, TN	Y		41960 AAW		TNBLS	10//99-12//99
	Texas	Y		59700 AAW		TXBLS	10//99-12//99
	Houston PMSA, TX	Y		36020 AAW		TXBLS	10//99-12//99
	Virginia	Y		27420 AAW		VABLS	10//99-12//99
	Washington	Y		63610 AAW		WABLS	10//99-12//99
	Puerto Rico	Y		12740 AAW		PRBLS	10//99-12//99
Actor, Director	United States	H		37.17 AW		NCS98	1998
Actuary	United States	H		27.38 AW		NCS98	1998
	Alabama	S	21.88 MW	24.27 AW	50480 AAW	ALBLS	10//99-12//99
	Arizona	S	20.13 MW	22.11 AW	45980 AAW	AZBLS	10//99-12//99
	California	S	37.04 MW	39.13 AW	81390 AAW	CABLS	10//99-12//99
	Colorado	S	29.79 MW	29.22 AW	60790 AAW	COBLS	10//99-12//99
	Connecticut	S	36.56 MW	37.68 AW	78370 AAW	CTBLS	10//99-12//99
	District of Columbia	S	35.45 MW	39.99 AW	83170 AAW	DCBLS	10//99-12//99
	Florida	S	23.68 MW	27.74 AW	57690 AAW	FLBLS	10//99-12//99
	Georgia	S	26.86 MW	27.91 AW	58060 AAW	GABLS	10//99-12//99
	Illinois	S	24.53 MW	27.92 AW	58080 AAW	ILBLS	10//99-12//99
	Indiana	S	29.56 MW	32.93 AW	68500 AAW	INBLS	10//99-12//99
	Iowa	S	34.38 MW	34.94 AW	72680 AAW	IABLS	10//99-12//99
	Kansas	S	26.19 MW	31.66 AW	65850 AAW	KSBLS	10//99-12//99
	Kentucky	S	33.72 MW	34.83 AW	72440 AAW	KYBLS	10//99-12//99
	Louisiana	S	30.19 MW	33.16 AW	68980 AAW	LABLS	10//99-12//99
	Maine	S	39.82 MW	38.84 AW	80790 AAW	MEBLS	10//99-12//99
	Maryland	S	32.41 MW	34.01 AW	70730 AAW	MDBLS	10//99-12//99
	Massachusetts	S	30.64 MW	32.52 AW	67650 AAW	MABLS	10//99-12//99
	Michigan	S	26.12 MW	29.48 AW	61320 AAW	MIBLS	10//99-12//99
	Minnesota	S	49.04 MW	44.29 AW	92120 AAW	MNBLS	10//99-12//99
	Missouri	S	44.21 MW	42.21 AW	87800 AAW	MOBLS	10//99-12//99
	Nebraska	S	27.5 MW	29.84 AW	62080 AAW	NEBLS	10//99-12//99
	Nevada	S	32.2 MW	34.09 AW	70910 AAW	NVBLS	10//99-12//99
	New Jersey	S	37.88 MW	39.77 AW	82730 AAW	NJBLS	10//99-12//99
	New York	S	30.64 MW	35.18 AW	73180 AAW	NYBLS	10//99-12//99
	North Carolina	S	31.41 MW	32.25 AW	67070 AAW	NCBLS	10//99-12//99
	Pennsylvania	S	37.18 MW	36.69 AW	76310 AAW	PABLS	10//99-12//99
	Tennessee	S	29.18 MW	32.49 AW	67570 AAW	TNBLS	10//99-12//99
	Texas	S	33.93 MW	34.77 AW	72320 AAW	TXBLS	10//99-12//99
	Virginia	S	34.32 MW	37.75 AW	78510 AAW	VABLS	10//99-12//99
	Washington	S	30.71 MW	33.01 AW	68660 AAW	WABLS	10//99-12//99
	Wisconsin	S	27.37 MW	32.71 AW	68050 AAW	WIBLS	10//99-12//99
Addictionologist							
Ph.D., Behavioral Health Organization	United States	Y	41300 APL	50884 AW	59547 APH	ADAW	2000
Addictions Counselor							
Certified, Behavioral Health Organization	United States	Y	24323 APL	29110 AW	35672 APH	ADAW	2000
Administrative Law Judge, Adjudicator, and Hearing Officer	Tucson MSA, AZ	S	27.74 MW	20.09 AW	57690 AAW	AZBLS	10//99-12//99
	Arkansas	S	16.65 MW	19.48 AW	40510 AAW	ARBLS	10//99-12//99

AAW	Average annual wage	AOH	Average offered, high	ASH	Average starting, high	H	Hourly	M	Monthly	S	Special: hourly and annual
AE	Average entry wage	AOL	Average offered, low	ASL	Average starting, low	HI	Highest wage paid	MTC	Median total compensation	TQ	Third quartile wage
AEX	Average experienced wage	APH	Average pay, high range	AW	Average wage paid	HR	High end range	MW	Median wage paid	W	Weekly
AO	Average offered	APL	Average pay, low range	FQ	First quartile wage	LR	Low end range	SQ	Second quartile wage	Y	Yearly

Occupation/Type/Industry	Location	Per	Low	Mid	High	Source	Date
Administrative Law Judge, Adjudicator, and Hearing Officer	California	S	26.27 MW	29.55 AW	61460 AAW	CABLS	10//99-12//99
	Los Angeles-Long Beach PMSA, CA	S	28.79 MW	25.62 AW	59880 AAW	CABLS	10//99-12//99
	Riverside-San Bernardino PMSA, CA	S	37.21 MW	36.81 AW	77410 AAW	CABLS	10//99-12//99
	Colorado	S	23.84 MW	26.20 AW	54490 AAW	COBLS	10//99-12//99
	Denver PMSA, CO	S	25.44 MW	21.47 AW	52920 AAW	COBLS	10//99-12//99
	Florida	S	21 MW	25.12 AW	52240 AAW	FLBLS	10//99-12//99
	Kansas	S	25.67 MW	30.20 AW	62820 AAW	KSBLS	10//99-12//99
	Kentucky	S	21.73 MW	24.86 AW	51700 AAW	KYBLS	10//99-12//99
	Michigan	S	31.83 MW	31.09 AW	64680 AAW	MIBLS	10//99-12//99
	Grand Rapids-Muskegon-Holland MSA, MI	S	32.83 MW	32.00 AW	68290 AAW	MIBLS	10//99-12//99
	Minnesota	S	26.43 MW	28.94 AW	60190 AAW	MNBLS	10//99-12//99
	Mississippi	S	20.9 MW	24.59 AW	51150 AAW	MSBLS	10//99-12//99
	Montana	S	18.01 MW	19.60 AW	40760 AAW	MTBLS	10//99-12//99
	Nebraska	S	21.11 MW	24.60 AW	51180 AAW	NEBLS	10//99-12//99
	New Hampshire	S	19.02 MW	21.03 AW	43730 AAW	NHBLS	10//99-12//99
	New Jersey	S	29.25 MW	30.62 AW	63690 AAW	NJBLS	10//99-12//99
	Atlantic-Cape May PMSA, NJ	S	33.05 MW	32.58 AW	68740 AAW	NJBLS	10//99-12//99
	New Mexico	S	18.03 MW	20.62 AW	42890 AAW	NMBLS	10//99-12//99
	New York	S	28.29 MW	28.77 AW	59840 AAW	NYBLS	10//99-12//99
	New York PMSA, NY	S	28.79 MW	28.77 AW	59880 AAW	NYBLS	10//99-12//99
	North Carolina	S	18.9 MW	22.10 AW	45960 AAW	NCBLS	10//99-12//99
	North Dakota	S	18.2 MW	21.18 AW	44050 AAW	NDBLS	10//99-12//99
	Dayton-Springfield MSA, OH	S	25.82 MW	20.38 AW	53700 AAW	OHBLS	10//99-12//99
	Oregon	S	20.56 MW	21.91 AW	45560 AAW	ORBLS	10//99-12//99
	Pennsylvania	S	20.67 MW	23.10 AW	48060 AAW	PABLS	10//99-12//99
	Allentown-Bethlehem-Easton MSA, PA	S	20.94 MW	21.97 AW	43550 AAW	PABLS	10//99-12//99
	Tennessee	S	17.6 MW	22.59 AW	46980 AAW	TNBLS	10//99-12//99
	Nashville MSA, TN	S	20.84 MW	17.79 AW	43360 AAW	TNBLS	10//99-12//99
	Texas	S	21.38 MW	25.45 AW	52940 AAW	TXBLS	10//99-12//99
	Utah	S	19.57 MW	21.28 AW	44250 AAW	UTBLS	10//99-12//99
	Salt Lake City-Ogden MSA, UT	S	21.82 MW	20.00 AW	45380 AAW	UTBLS	10//99-12//99
	Washington	S	27.62 MW	26.61 AW	55350 AAW	WABLS	10//99-12//99
	San Juan-Bayamon PMSA, PR	S	16.01 MW	12.99 AW	33300 AAW	PRBLS	10//99-12//99
Administrative Services Manager	Alabama	S	15.02 MW	18.72 AW	38940 AAW	ALBLS	10//99-12//99
	Anniston MSA, AL	S	19.87 MW	16.71 AW	41330 AAW	ALBLS	10//99-12//99
	Auburn-Opelika MSA, AL	S	14.01 MW	11.57 AW	29130 AAW	ALBLS	10//99-12//99
	Birmingham MSA, AL	S	20.32 MW	14.98 AW	42270 AAW	ALBLS	10//99-12//99
	Decatur MSA, AL	S	17.51 MW	13.73 AW	36410 AAW	ALBLS	10//99-12//99
	Dothan MSA, AL	S	18.75 MW	18.83 AW	38990 AAW	ALBLS	10//99-12//99
	Florence MSA, AL	S	19.21 MW	14.65 AW	39960 AAW	ALBLS	10//99-12//99
	Gadsden MSA, AL	S	17.47 MW	12.55 AW	36330 AAW	ALBLS	10//99-12//99
	Huntsville MSA, AL	S	22.84 MW	19.69 AW	47510 AAW	ALBLS	10//99-12//99
	Mobile MSA, AL	S	15.65 MW	13.04 AW	32540 AAW	ALBLS	10//99-12//99
	Montgomery MSA, AL	S	19.15 MW	15.24 AW	39820 AAW	ALBLS	10//99-12//99
	Tuscaloosa MSA, AL	S	21.95 MW	17.01 AW	45660 AAW	ALBLS	10//99-12//99
	Alaska	S	19.18 MW	20.96 AW	43600 AAW	AKBLS	10//99-12//99
	Anchorage MSA, AK	S	21.18 MW	19.60 AW	44040 AAW	AKBLS	10//99-12//99
	Arizona	S	23.27 MW	24.43 AW	50820 AAW	AZBLS	10//99-12//99
	Flagstaff MSA, AZ-UT	S	22.53 MW	22.93 AW	46870 AAW	AZBLS	10//99-12//99
	Phoenix-Mesa MSA, AZ	S	25.84 MW	24.87 AW	53740 AAW	AZBLS	10//99-12//99
	Tucson MSA, AZ	S	19.64 MW	16.25 AW	40850 AAW	AZBLS	10//99-12//99
	Yuma MSA, AZ	S	28.89 MW	22.65 AW	60090 AAW	AZBLS	10//99-12//99
	Arkansas	S	20 MW	21.33 AW	44370 AAW	ARBLS	10//99-12//99
	Fayetteville-Springdale-Rogers MSA, AR	S	17.08 MW	16.03 AW	35530 AAW	ARBLS	10//99-12//99
	Fort Smith MSA, AR-OK	S	22.04 MW	20.44 AW	45850 AAW	ARBLS	10//99-12//99
	Jonesboro MSA, AR	S	23.70 MW	21.85 AW	49310 AAW	ARBLS	10//99-12//99
	Little Rock-North Little Rock MSA, AR	S	25.37 MW	23.30 AW	52780 AAW	ARBLS	10//99-12//99
	Pine Bluff MSA, AR	S	20.30 MW	18.13 AW	42220 AAW	ARBLS	10//99-12//99
	California	S	23.18 MW	25.41 AW	52850 AAW	CABLS	10//99-12//99
	Bakersfield MSA, CA	S	23.77 MW	25.88 AW	49450 AAW	CABLS	10//99-12//99
	Chico-Paradise MSA, CA	S	18.86 MW	18.75 AW	39220 AAW	CABLS	10//99-12//99
	Fresno MSA, CA	S	23.41 MW	21.48 AW	48680 AAW	CABLS	10//99-12//99

AAW	Average annual wage	AOH	Average offered, high	ASH	Average starting, high	H	Hourly	M	Monthly	S	Special: hourly and annual
AE	Average entry wage	AOL	Average offered, low	ASL	Average starting, low	HI	Highest wage paid	MTC	Median total compensation	TQ	Third quartile wage
AEX	Average experienced wage	APH	Average pay, high range	AW	Average wage paid	HR	High end range	MW	Median wage paid	W	Weekly
AO	Average offered	APL	Average pay, low range	FQ	First quartile wage	LR	Low end range	SQ	Second quartile wage	Y	Yearly

Occupation/Type/Industry	Location	Per	Low	Mid	High	Source	Date
Administrative Services Manager	Los Angeles-Long Beach PMSA, CA	S	25.80 MW	24.02 AW	53670 AAW	CABLS	10//99-12//99
	Merced MSA, CA	S	19.11 MW	16.52 AW	39760 AAW	CABLS	10//99-12//99
	Modesto MSA, CA	S	21.68 MW	19.87 AW	45100 AAW	CABLS	10//99-12//99
	Oakland PMSA, CA	S	26.48 MW	24.36 AW	55090 AAW	CABLS	10//99-12//99
	Orange County PMSA, CA	S	27.76 MW	24.49 AW	57730 AAW	CABLS	10//99-12//99
	Redding MSA, CA	S	14.21 MW	12.72 AW	29560 AAW	CABLS	10//99-12//99
	Riverside-San Bernardino PMSA, CA	S	22.71 MW	20.96 AW	47250 AAW	CABLS	10//99-12//99
	Sacramento PMSA, CA	S	27.24 MW	25.17 AW	56660 AAW	CABLS	10//99-12//99
	Salinas MSA, CA	S	21.64 MW	18.08 AW	45020 AAW	CABLS	10//99-12//99
	San Diego MSA, CA	S	21.45 MW	19.78 AW	44620 AAW	CABLS	10//99-12//99
	San Francisco PMSA, CA	S	23.45 MW	20.08 AW	48790 AAW	CABLS	10//99-12//99
	San Jose PMSA, CA	S	31.25 MW	32.82 AW	65000 AAW	CABLS	10//99-12//99
	San Luis Obispo-Atascadero-Paso Robles MSA, CA	S	18.66 MW	15.53 AW	38820 AAW	CABLS	10//99-12//99
	Santa Barbara-Santa Maria-Lompoc MSA, CA	S	21.53 MW	18.84 AW	44790 AAW	CABLS	10//99-12//99
	Santa Cruz-Watsonville PMSA, CA	S	26.02 MW	21.44 AW	54120 AAW	CABLS	10//99-12//99
	Santa Rosa PMSA, CA	S	21.22 MW	19.11 AW	44130 AAW	CABLS	10//99-12//99
	Stockton-Lodi MSA, CA	S	23.60 MW	23.88 AW	49080 AAW	CABLS	10//99-12//99
	Vallejo-Fairfield-Napa PMSA, CA	S	24.40 MW	22.16 AW	50760 AAW	CABLS	10//99-12//99
	Ventura PMSA, CA	S	28.14 MW	23.81 AW	58540 AAW	CABLS	10//99-12//99
	Visalia-Tulare-Porterville MSA, CA	S	22.12 MW	21.43 AW	46010 AAW	CABLS	10//99-12//99
	Yolo PMSA, CA	S	15.82 MW	12.76 AW	32910 AAW	CABLS	10//99-12//99
	Colorado	S	18.2 MW	21.49 AW	44700 AAW	COBLS	10//99-12//99
	Denver PMSA, CO	S	23.87 MW	22.54 AW	49650 AAW	COBLS	10//99-12//99
	Connecticut	S	27.85 MW	29.88 AW	62160 AAW	CTBLS	10//99-12//99
	Bridgeport PMSA, CT	S	26.57 MW	23.64 AW	55260 AAW	CTBLS	10//99-12//99
	Danbury PMSA, CT	S	22.29 MW	20.72 AW	46360 AAW	CTBLS	10//99-12//99
	Hartford MSA, CT	S	33.09 MW	30.74 AW	68840 AAW	CTBLS	10//99-12//99
	New Haven-Meriden PMSA, CT	S	25.93 MW	23.98 AW	53930 AAW	CTBLS	10//99-12//99
	New London-Norwich MSA, CT-RI	S	23.50 MW	21.11 AW	48870 AAW	CTBLS	10//99-12//99
	Stamford-Norwalk PMSA, CT	S	33.15 MW	32.08 AW	68950 AAW	CTBLS	10//99-12//99
	Waterbury PMSA, CT	S	26.50 MW	22.27 AW	55120 AAW	CTBLS	10//99-12//99
	Delaware	S	21.37 MW	26.32 AW	54740 AAW	DEBLS	10//99-12//99
	Dover MSA, DE	S	23.79 MW	20.00 AW	49490 AAW	DEBLS	10//99-12//99
	Wilmington-Newark PMSA, DE-MD	S	25.14 MW	20.61 AW	52300 AAW	DEBLS	10//99-12//99
	District of Columbia	S	20.98 MW	23.15 AW	48150 AAW	DCBLS	10//99-12//99
	Washington PMSA, DC-MD-VA-WV	S	24.89 MW	23.13 AW	51770 AAW	DCBLS	10//99-12//99
	Florida	S	16.74 MW	19.52 AW	40610 AAW	FLBLS	10//99-12//99
	Daytona Beach MSA, FL	S	17.51 MW	16.49 AW	36430 AAW	FLBLS	10//99-12//99
	Fort Lauderdale PMSA, FL	S	21.34 MW	18.66 AW	44380 AAW	FLBLS	10//99-12//99
	Fort Myers-Cape Coral MSA, FL	S	16.00 MW	13.64 AW	33290 AAW	FLBLS	10//99-12//99
	Fort Pierce-Port St. Lucie MSA, FL	S	14.03 MW	12.06 AW	29170 AAW	FLBLS	10//99-12//99
	Fort Walton Beach MSA, FL	S	18.20 MW	17.95 AW	37850 AAW	FLBLS	10//99-12//99
	Gainesville MSA, FL	S	16.82 MW	14.34 AW	34980 AAW	FLBLS	10//99-12//99
	Jacksonville MSA, FL	S	23.29 MW	21.17 AW	48440 AAW	FLBLS	10//99-12//99
	Lakeland-Winter Haven MSA, FL	S	19.15 MW	18.28 AW	39820 AAW	FLBLS	10//99-12//99
	Melbourne-Titusville-Palm Bay MSA, FL	S	19.49 MW	18.05 AW	40530 AAW	FLBLS	10//99-12//99
	Miami PMSA, FL	S	20.26 MW	18.15 AW	42130 AAW	FLBLS	10//99-12//99
	Naples MSA, FL	S	18.76 MW	18.02 AW	39030 AAW	FLBLS	10//99-12//99
	Ocala MSA, FL	S	14.51 MW	14.69 AW	30180 AAW	FLBLS	10//99-12//99
	Orlando MSA, FL	S	20.51 MW	16.78 AW	42650 AAW	FLBLS	10//99-12//99
	Panama City MSA, FL	S	14.03 MW	12.42 AW	29170 AAW	FLBLS	10//99-12//99
	Pensacola MSA, FL	S	15.23 MW	12.92 AW	31690 AAW	FLBLS	10//99-12//99
	Punta Gorda MSA, FL	S	13.16 MW	13.52 AW	27380 AAW	FLBLS	10//99-12//99
	Sarasota-Bradenton MSA, FL	S	19.14 MW	16.10 AW	39810 AAW	FLBLS	10//99-12//99
	Tallahassee MSA, FL	S	20.44 MW	16.04 AW	42520 AAW	FLBLS	10//99-12//99
	Tampa-St. Petersburg-Clearwater MSA, FL	S	20.52 MW	17.32 AW	42680 AAW	FLBLS	10//99-12//99

AAW Average annual wage	**AOH** Average offered, high	**ASH** Average starting, high	**H** Hourly	**M** Monthly	**S** Special: hourly and annual
AE Average entry wage	**AOL** Average offered, low	**ASL** Average starting, low	**HI** Highest wage paid	**MTC** Median total compensation	**TQ** Third quartile wage
AEX Average experienced wage	**APH** Average pay, high range	**AW** Average wage paid	**HR** High end range	**MW** Median wage paid	**W** Weekly
AO Average offered	**APL** Average pay, low range	**FQ** First quartile wage	**LR** Low end range	**SQ** Second quartile wage	**Y** Yearly

Occupation/Type/Industry	Location	Per	Low	Mid	High	Source	Date
Administrative Services Manager	West Palm Beach-Boca Raton MSA, FL	s	19.31 MW	16.44 AW	40170 AAW	FLBLS	10//99-12//99
	Georgia	s	23.2 MW	24.42 AW	50780 AAW	GABLS	10//99-12//99
	Albany MSA, GA	s	18.29 MW	17.80 AW	38040 AAW	GABLS	10//99-12//99
	Atlanta MSA, GA	s	25.70 MW	25.07 AW	53460 AAW	GABLS	10//99-12//99
	Macon MSA, GA	s	25.01 MW	23.05 AW	52020 AAW	GABLS	10//99-12//99
	Savannah MSA, GA	s	19.46 MW	18.14 AW	40470 AAW	GABLS	10//99-12//99
	Hawaii	s	22.15 MW	23.58 AW	49040 AAW	HIBLS	10//99-12//99
	Honolulu MSA, HI	s	24.08 MW	22.65 AW	50080 AAW	HIBLS	10//99-12//99
	Idaho	s	19.2 MW	21.23 AW	44150 AAW	IDBLS	10//99-12//99
	Boise City MSA, ID	s	23.36 MW	22.03 AW	48580 AAW	IDBLS	10//99-12//99
	Illinois	s	18.59 MW	20.97 AW	43610 AAW	ILBLS	10//99-12//99
	Bloomington-Normal MSA, IL	s	19.82 MW	15.77 AW	41230 AAW	ILBLS	10//99-12//99
	Champaign-Urbana MSA, IL	s	15.58 MW	12.49 AW	32410 AAW	ILBLS	10//99-12//99
	Chicago PMSA, IL	s	22.16 MW	19.84 AW	46100 AAW	ILBLS	10//99-12//99
	Decatur MSA, IL	s.	16.72 MW	14.72 AW	34770 AAW	ILBLS	10//99-12//99
	Kankakee PMSA, IL	s	16.37 MW	16.22 AW	34040 AAW	ILBLS	10//99-12//99
	Peoria-Pekin MSA, IL	s	19.11 MW	14.22 AW	39750 AAW	ILBLS	10//99-12//99
	Rockford MSA, IL	s	16.21 MW	14.98 AW	33710 AAW	ILBLS	10//99-12//99
	Springfield MSA, IL	s	20.90 MW	19.32 AW	43460 AAW	ILBLS	10//99-12//99
	Indiana	s	21.17 MW	22.40 AW	46580 AAW	INBLS	10//99-12//99
	Elkhart-Goshen MSA, IN	s	19.76 MW	19.28 AW	41090 AAW	INBLS	10//99-12//99
	Evansville-Henderson MSA, IN-KY	s	19.17 MW	18.01 AW	39880 AAW	INBLS	10//99-12//99
	Fort Wayne MSA, IN	s	23.03 MW	22.86 AW	47890 AAW	INBLS	10//99-12//99
	Gary PMSA, IN	s	22.98 MW	18.65 AW	47790 AAW	INBLS	10//99-12//99
	Indianapolis MSA, IN	s	26.15 MW	24.88 AW	54390 AAW	INBLS	10//99-12//99
	Kokomo MSA, IN	s	23.72 MW	24.02 AW	49340 AAW	INBLS	10//99-12//99
	Lafayette MSA, IN	s	22.34 MW	24.50 AW	46460 AAW	INBLS	10//99-12//99
	Muncie MSA, IN	s	21.58 MW	16.36 AW	44880 AAW	INBLS	10//99-12//99
	South Bend MSA, IN	s	18.78 MW	18.31 AW	39060 AAW	INBLS	10//99-12//99
	Terre Haute MSA, IN	s	29.43 MW	27.74 AW	61220 AAW	INBLS	10//99-12//99
	Iowa	s	17.77 MW	19.86 AW	41320 AAW	IABLS	10//99-12//99
	Cedar Rapids MSA, IA	s	23.12 MW	21.55 AW	48090 AAW	IABLS	10//99-12//99
	Davenport-Moline-Rock Island MSA, IA-IL	s	18.98 MW	17.72 AW	39480 AAW	IABLS	10//99-12//99
	Des Moines MSA, IA	s	22.51 MW	20.46 AW	46820 AAW	IABLS	10//99-12//99
	Dubuque MSA, IA	s	15.54 MW	13.59 AW	32330 AAW	IABLS	10//99-12//99
	Iowa City MSA, IA	s	22.03 MW	18.66 AW	45830 AAW	IABLS	10//99-12//99
	Sioux City MSA, IA-NE	s	20.26 MW	19.05 AW	42140 AAW	IABLS	10//99-12//99
	Kansas	s	19.23 MW	21.12 AW	43930 AAW	KSBLS	10//99-12//99
	Lawrence MSA, KS	s	17.73 MW	17.15 AW	36890 AAW	KSBLS	10//99-12//99
	Topeka MSA, KS	s	19.53 MW	17.55 AW	40610 AAW	KSBLS	10//99-12//99
	Wichita MSA, KS	s	20.97 MW	19.67 AW	43610 AAW	KSBLS	10//99-12//99
	Kentucky	s	17.05 MW	19.39 AW	40330 AAW	KYBLS	10//99-12//99
	Lexington MSA, KY	s	19.04 MW	16.30 AW	39600 AAW	KYBLS	10//99-12//99
	Louisville MSA, KY-IN	s	19.66 MW	17.06 AW	40900 AAW	KYBLS	10//99-12//99
	Owensboro MSA, KY	s	16.48 MW	14.87 AW	34280 AAW	KYBLS	10//99-12//99
	Louisiana	s	13.84 MW	17.23 AW	35840 AAW	LABLS	10//99-12//99
	Alexandria MSA, LA	s	15.38 MW	11.54 AW	32000 AAW	LABLS	10//99-12//99
	Baton Rouge MSA, LA	s	23.91 MW	19.44 AW	49720 AAW	LABLS	10//99-12//99
	Houma MSA, LA	s	17.14 MW	15.48 AW	35660 AAW	LABLS	10//99-12//99
	Lafayette MSA, LA	s	16.15 MW	14.66 AW	33590 AAW	LABLS	10//99-12//99
	Lake Charles MSA, LA	s	20.54 MW	17.67 AW	42710 AAW	LABLS	10//99-12//99
	Monroe MSA, LA	s	23.70 MW	26.33 AW	49290 AAW	LABLS	10//99-12//99
	New Orleans MSA, LA	s	18.91 MW	17.49 AW	39340 AAW	LABLS	10//99-12//99
	Shreveport-Bossier City MSA, LA	s	16.69 MW	14.34 AW	34720 AAW	LABLS	10//99-12//99
	Maine	s	17.72 MW	19.72 AW	41020 AAW	MEBLS	10//99-12//99
	Bangor MSA, ME	s	17.02 MW	16.07 AW	35400 AAW	MEBLS	10//99-12//99
	Lewiston-Auburn MSA, ME	s	14.87 MW	13.79 AW	30920 AAW	MEBLS	10//99-12//99
	Portland MSA, ME	s	21.46 MW	21.05 AW	44640 AAW	MEBLS	10//99-12//99
	Maryland	s	19.76 MW	22.14 AW	46050 AAW	MDBLS	10//99-12//99
	Baltimore PMSA, MD	s	20.87 MW	18.55 AW	43400 AAW	MDBLS	10//99-12//99
	Cumberland MSA, MD-WV	s	15.28 MW	13.47 AW	31780 AAW	MDBLS	10//99-12//99
	Hagerstown PMSA, MD	s	20.67 MW	17.50 AW	43000 AAW	MDBLS	10//99-12//99
	Massachusetts	s	26.03 MW	27.94 AW	58120 AAW	MABLS	10//99-12//99
	Barnstable-Yarmouth MSA, MA	s	20.24 MW	18.27 AW	42110 AAW	MABLS	10//99-12//99
	Boston PMSA, MA-NH	s	29.36 MW	27.16 AW	61070 AAW	MABLS	10//99-12//99
	Brockton PMSA, MA	s	25.75 MW	24.72 AW	53570 AAW	MABLS	10//99-12//99

AAW Average annual wage	AOH Average offered, high	ASH Average starting, high	H Hourly	M Monthly	S Special: hourly and annual
AE Average entry wage	AOL Average offered, low	ASL Average starting, low	HI Highest wage paid	MTC Median total compensation	TQ Third quartile wage
AEX Average experienced wage	APH Average pay, high range	AW Average wage paid	HR High end range	MW Median wage paid	W Weekly
AO Average offered	APL Average pay, low range	FQ First quartile wage	LR Low end range	SQ Second quartile wage	Y Yearly

Occupation/Type/Industry	Location	Per	Low	Mid	High	Source	Date
Administrative Services Manager	Fitchburg-Leominster PMSA, MA	S	17.47 MW	15.78 AW	36350 AAW	MABLS	10//99-12//99
	Lawrence PMSA, MA-NH	S	26.30 MW	24.99 AW	54700 AAW	MABLS	10//99-12//99
	Lowell PMSA, MA-NH	S	36.86 MW	35.02 AW	76660 AAW	MABLS	10//99-12//99
	New Bedford PMSA, MA	S	22.78 MW	23.41 AW	47380 AAW	MABLS	10//99-12//99
	Springfield MSA, MA	S	22.23 MW	20.49 AW	46230 AAW	MABLS	10//99-12//99
	Worcester PMSA, MA-CT	S	24.36 MW	23.23 AW	50670 AAW	MABLS	10//99-12//99
	Michigan	S	25.24 MW	27.04 AW	56240 AAW	MIBLS	10//99-12//99
	Ann Arbor PMSA, MI	S	20.14 MW	18.28 AW	41880 AAW	MIBLS	10//99-12//99
	Benton Harbor MSA, MI	S	23.49 MW	21.10 AW	48870 AAW	MIBLS	10//99-12//99
	Detroit PMSA, MI	S	28.68 MW	26.23 AW	59650 AAW	MIBLS	10//99-12//99
	Flint PMSA, MI	S	24.76 MW	23.98 AW	51510 AAW	MIBLS	10//99-12//99
	Grand Rapids-Muskegon-Holland MSA, MI	S	32.93 MW	31.84 AW	68480 AAW	MIBLS	10//99-12//99
	Kalamazoo-Battle Creek MSA, MI	S	23.89 MW	24.12 AW	49700 AAW	MIBLS	10//99-12//99
	Lansing-East Lansing MSA, MI	S	22.23 MW	17.50 AW	46240 AAW	MIBLS	10//99-12//99
	Saginaw-Bay City-Midland MSA, MI	S	25.68 MW	25.08 AW	53420 AAW	MIBLS	10//99-12//99
	Minnesota	S	28.81 MW	29.27 AW	60880 AAW	MNBLS	10//99-12//99
	Duluth-Superior MSA, MN-WI	S	25.02 MW	25.62 AW	52030 AAW	MNBLS	10//99-12//99
	Minneapolis-St. Paul MSA, MN-WI	S	29.68 MW	29.17 AW	61740 AAW	MNBLS	10//99-12//99
	Rochester MSA, MN	S	29.32 MW	30.65 AW	60980 AAW	MNBLS	10//99-12//99
	St. Cloud MSA, MN	S	27.81 MW	28.26 AW	57840 AAW	MNBLS	10//99-12//99
	Mississippi	S	16.92 MW	19.66 AW	40890 AAW	MSBLS	10//99-12//99
	Biloxi-Gulfport-Pascagoula MSA, MS	S	16.97 MW	14.38 AW	35300 AAW	MSBLS	10//99-12//99
	Hattiesburg MSA, MS	S	18.25 MW	16.54 AW	37960 AAW	MSBLS	10//99-12//99
	Jackson MSA, MS	S	24.03 MW	20.61 AW	49980 AAW	MSBLS	10//99-12//99
	Missouri	S	18.01 MW	20.47 AW	42580 AAW	MOBLS	10//99-12//99
	Joplin MSA, MO	S	13.08 MW	10.48 AW	27220 AAW	MOBLS	10//99-12//99
	Kansas City MSA, MO-KS	S	22.70 MW	20.27 AW	47220 AAW	MOBLS	10//99-12//99
	St. Joseph MSA, MO	S	17.90 MW	15.21 AW	37240 AAW	MOBLS	10//99-12//99
	St. Louis MSA, MO-IL	S	20.88 MW	18.44 AW	43430 AAW	MOBLS	10//99-12//99
	Springfield MSA, MO	S	21.42 MW	18.20 AW	44560 AAW	MOBLS	10//99-12//99
	Montana	S	13.36 MW	15.76 AW	32780 AAW	MTBLS	10//99-12//99
	Billings MSA, MT	S	12.03 MW	11.46 AW	25030 AAW	MTBLS	10//99-12//99
	Great Falls MSA, MT	S	14.38 MW	13.63 AW	29920 AAW	MTBLS	10//99-12//99
	Missoula MSA, MT	S	20.28 MW	19.67 AW	42170 AAW	MTBLS	10//99-12//99
	Nebraska	S	20.24 MW	22.80 AW	47430 AAW	NEBLS	10//99-12//99
	Lincoln MSA, NE	S	21.27 MW	16.80 AW	44250 AAW	NEBLS	10//99-12//99
	Omaha MSA, NE-IA	S	24.56 MW	22.20 AW	51070 AAW	NEBLS	10//99-12//99
	Nevada	S	21.2 MW	24.75 AW	51490 AAW	NVBLS	10//99-12//99
	Las Vegas MSA, NV-AZ	S	25.98 MW	21.92 AW	54030 AAW	NVBLS	10//99-12//99
	Reno MSA, NV	S	20.58 MW	16.14 AW	42810 AAW	NVBLS	10//99-12//99
	New Hampshire	S	18.88 MW	21.10 AW	43880 AAW	NHBLS	10//99-12//99
	Manchester PMSA, NH	S	19.29 MW	18.19 AW	40120 AAW	NHBLS	10//99-12//99
	Nashua PMSA, NH	S	22.97 MW	20.23 AW	47790 AAW	NHBLS	10//99-12//99
	Portsmouth-Rochester PMSA, NH-ME	S	17.71 MW	15.94 AW	36840 AAW	NHBLS	10//99-12//99
	New Jersey	S	31.92 MW	33.47 AW	69620 AAW	NJBLS	10//99-12//99
	Atlantic-Cape May PMSA, NJ	S	27.13 MW	25.01 AW	56440 AAW	NJBLS	10//99-12//99
	Bergen-Passaic PMSA, NJ	S	33.22 MW	32.48 AW	69110 AAW	NJBLS	10//99-12//99
	Jersey City PMSA, NJ	S	34.77 MW	33.17 AW	72320 AAW	NJBLS	10//99-12//99
	Middlesex-Somerset-Hunterdon PMSA, NJ	S	35.55 MW	33.03 AW	73950 AAW	NJBLS	10//99-12//99
	Monmouth-Ocean PMSA, NJ	S	28.73 MW	26.72 AW	59760 AAW	NJBLS	10//99-12//99
	Newark PMSA, NJ	S	35.98 MW	34.13 AW	74840 AAW	NJBLS	10//99-12//99
	Trenton PMSA, NJ	S	30.91 MW	31.70 AW	64280 AAW	NJBLS	10//99-12//99
	Vineland-Millville-Bridgeton PMSA, NJ	S	25.93 MW	20.50 AW	53930 AAW	NJBLS	10//99-12//99
	New Mexico	S	18.69 MW	21.26 AW	44220 AAW	NMBLS	10//99-12//99
	Albuquerque MSA, NM	S	26.02 MW	23.63 AW	54120 AAW	NMBLS	10//99-12//99
	Las Cruces MSA, NM	S	14.79 MW	12.49 AW	30760 AAW	NMBLS	10//99-12//99
	Santa Fe MSA, NM	S	17.50 MW	15.08 AW	36410 AAW	NMBLS	10//99-12//99
	New York	S	32.54 MW	35.83 AW	74530 AAW	NYBLS	10//99-12//99
	Albany-Schenectady-Troy MSA, NY	S	35.93 MW	32.46 AW	74740 AAW	NYBLS	10//99-12//99
	Binghamton MSA, NY	S	30.57 MW	29.04 AW	63590 AAW	NYBLS	10//99-12//99
	Buffalo-Niagara Falls MSA, NY	S	28.37 MW	25.12 AW	59020 AAW	NYBLS	10//99-12//99

AAW	Average annual wage	**AOH**	Average offered, high	**ASH**	Average starting, high	**H**	Hourly
AE	Average entry wage	**AOL**	Average offered, low	**ASL**	Average starting, low	**HI**	Highest wage paid
AEX	Average experienced wage	**APH**	Average pay, high range	**AW**	Average wage paid	**HR**	High end range
AO	Average offered	**APL**	Average pay, low range	**FQ**	First quartile wage	**LR**	Low end range

M	Monthly	**S**	Special: hourly and annual
MTC	Median total compensation	**TQ**	Third quartile wage
MW	Median wage paid	**W**	Weekly
SQ	Second quartile wage	**Y**	Yearly

Occupation/Type/Industry	Location	Per	Low	Mid	High	Source	Date
Administrative Services Manager	Elmira MSA, NY	S	24.17 MW	23.97 AW	50280 AAW	NYBLS	10//99-12//99
	Jamestown MSA, NY	S	21.36 MW	15.99 AW	44430 AAW	NYBLS	10//99-12//99
	Nassau-Suffolk PMSA, NY	S	35.11 MW	31.04 AW	73040 AAW	NYBLS	10//99-12//99
	New York PMSA, NY	S	37.61 MW	34.23 AW	78240 AAW	NYBLS	10//99-12//99.
	Newburgh PMSA, NY-PA	S	32.42 MW	30.01 AW	67430 AAW	NYBLS	10//99-12//99
	Rochester MSA, NY	S	35.16 MW	32.21 AW	73140 AAW	NYBLS	10//99-12//99
	Syracuse MSA, NY	S	34.61 MW	32.06 AW	71980 AAW	NYBLS	10//99-12//99
	Utica-Rome MSA, NY	S	34.29 MW	31.46 AW	71330 AAW	NYBLS	10//99-12//99
	North Carolina	S	17.56 MW	20.60 AW	42850 AAW	NCBLS	10//99-12//99
	Asheville MSA, NC	S	18.29 MW	16.42 AW	38040 AAW	NCBLS	10//99-12//99
	Charlotte-Gastonia-Rock Hill MSA, NC-SC	S	21.48 MW	17.66 AW	44670 AAW	NCBLS	10//99-12//99
	Fayetteville MSA, NC	S	18.88 MW	17.22 AW	39260 AAW	NCBLS	10//99-12//99
	Goldsboro MSA, NC	S	22.23 MW	17.85 AW	46240 AAW	NCBLS	10//99-12//99
	Greensboro--Winston-Salem-- High Point MSA, NC	S	20.32 MW	17.95 AW	42270 AAW	NCBLS	10//99-12//99
	Greenville MSA, NC	S	19.71 MW	17.78 AW	41000 AAW	NCBLS	10//99-12//99
	Hickory-Morganton-Lenoir MSA, NC	S	19.47 MW	16.71 AW	40500 AAW	NCBLS	10//99-12//99
	Jacksonville MSA, NC	S	15.73 MW	14.56 AW	32730 AAW	NCBLS	10//99-12//99
	Raleigh-Durham-Chapel Hill MSA, NC	S	23.76 MW	22.61 AW	49410 AAW	NCBLS	10//99-12//99
	Rocky Mount MSA, NC	S	19.47 MW	17.93 AW	40490 AAW	NCBLS	10//99-12//99
	North Dakota	S	14.3 MW	15.73 AW	32720 AAW	NDBLS	10//99-12//99
	Bismarck MSA, ND	S	16.62 MW	15.55 AW	34580 AAW	NDBLS	10//99-12//99
	Fargo-Moorhead MSA, ND-MN	S	18.76 MW	16.29 AW	39030 AAW	NDBLS	10//99-12//99
	Grand Forks MSA, ND-MN	S	18.71 MW	18.99 AW	38910 AAW	NDBLS	10//99-12//99
	Ohio	S	19.15 MW	21.07 AW	43830 AAW	OHBLS	10//99-12//99
	Akron PMSA, OH	S	24.28 MW	22.93 AW	50500 AAW	OHBLS	10//99-12//99
	Canton-Massillon MSA, OH	S	17.69 MW	15.73 AW	36790 AAW	OHBLS	10//99-12//99
	Cincinnati PMSA, OH-KY-IN	S	19.53 MW	17.71 AW	40620 AAW	OHBLS	10//99-12//99
	Cleveland-Lorain-Elyria PMSA, OH	S	22.07 MW	21.14 AW	45900 AAW	OHBLS	10//99-12//99
	Columbus MSA, OH	S	22.75 MW	21.74 AW	47320 AAW	OHBLS	10//99-12//99
	Dayton-Springfield MSA, OH	S	20.65 MW	18.73 AW	42950 AAW	OHBLS	10//99-12//99
	Hamilton-Middletown PMSA, OH	S	18.70 MW	17.82 AW	38900 AAW	OHBLS	10//99-12//99
	Lima MSA, OH	S	20.05 MW	17.95 AW	41700 AAW	OHBLS	10//99-12//99
	Mansfield MSA, OH	S	18.83 MW	16.81 AW	39170 AAW	OHBLS	10//99-12//99
	Steubenville-Weirton MSA, OH-WV	S	19.48 MW	17.11 AW	40520 AAW	OHBLS	10//99-12//99
	Toledo MSA, OH	S	22.32 MW	18.83 AW	46420 AAW	OHBLS	10//99-12//99
	Youngstown-Warren MSA, OH	S	21.92 MW	21.91 AW	45590 AAW	OHBLS	10//99-12//99
	Oklahoma	S	16.86 MW	19.00 AW	39520 AAW	OKBLS	10//99-12//99
	Enid MSA, OK	S	17.76 MW	15.44 AW	36940 AAW	OKBLS	10//99-12//99
	Lawton MSA, OK	S	17.27 MW	12.09 AW	35920 AAW	OKBLS	10//99-12//99
	Oklahoma City MSA, OK	S	19.36 MW	18.79 AW	40260 AAW	OKBLS	10//99-12//99
	Tulsa MSA, OK	S	23.02 MW	19.85 AW	47880 AAW	OKBLS	10//99-12//99
	Oregon	S	23.41 MW	25.17 AW	52350 AAW	ORBLS	10//99-12//99
	Corvallis MSA, OR	S	17.63 MW	14.66 AW	36670 AAW	ORBLS	10//99-12//99
	Eugene-Springfield MSA, OR	S	20.84 MW	18.76 AW	43350 AAW	ORBLS	10//99-12//99
	Medford-Ashland MSA, OR	S	20.32 MW	18.12 AW	42260 AAW	ORBLS	10//99-12//99
	Portland-Vancouver PMSA, OR-WA	S	27.14 MW	25.36 AW	56450 AAW	ORBLS	10//99-12//99
	Salem PMSA, OR	S	21.84 MW	16.96 AW	45420 AAW	ORBLS	10//99-12//99
	Pennsylvania	S	19.79 MW	21.81 AW	45370 AAW	PABLS	10//99-12//99
	Allentown-Bethlehem-Easton MSA, PA	S	20.81 MW	18.04 AW	43280 AAW	PABLS	10//99-12//99
	Erie MSA, PA	S	20.67 MW	16.37 AW	42990 AAW	PABLS	10//99-12//99
	Harrisburg-Lebanon-Carlisle MSA, PA	S	24.16 MW	21.24 AW	50250 AAW	PABLS	10//99-12//99
	Johnstown MSA, PA	S	29.69 MW	25.59 AW	61750 AAW	PABLS	10//99-12//99
	Lancaster MSA, PA	S	20.52 MW	19.47 AW	42680 AAW	PABLS	10//99-12//99
	Philadelphia PMSA, PA-NJ	S	24.96 MW	23.43 AW	51920 AAW	PABLS	10//99-12//99
	Pittsburgh MSA, PA	S	19.87 MW	17.13 AW	41330 AAW	PABLS	10//99-12//99
	Reading MSA, PA	S	22.65 MW	21.71 AW	47100 AAW	PABLS	10//99-12//99
	Scranton--Wilkes-Barre-- Hazleton MSA, PA	S	23.13 MW	21.08 AW	48120 AAW	PABLS	10//99-12//99
	Sharon MSA, PA	S	19.05 MW	17.75 AW	39620 AAW	PABLS	10//99-12//99
	Williamsport MSA, PA	S	21.46 MW	22.68 AW	44630 AAW	PABLS	10//99-12//99
	Rhode Island	S	26.22 MW	28.25 AW	58770 AAW	RIBLS	10//99-12//99

AAW Average annual wage	**AOH** Average offered, high	**ASH** Average starting, high	**H** Hourly	**M** Monthly	**S** Special: hourly and annual
AE Average entry wage	**AOL** Average offered, low	**ASL** Average starting, low	**HI** Highest wage paid	**MTC** Median total compensation	**TQ** Third quartile wage
AEX Average experienced wage	**APH** Average pay, high range	**AW** Average wage paid	**HR** High end range	**MW** Median wage paid	**W** Weekly
AO Average offered	**APL** Average pay, low range	**FQ** First quartile wage	**LR** Low end range	**SQ** Second quartile wage	**Y** Yearly

Occupation/Type/Industry	Location	Per	Low	Mid	High	Source	Date
Administrative Services Manager	Providence-Fall River-Warwick MSA, RI-MA	S	26.81 MW	25.76 AW	55760 AAW	RIBLS	10//99-12//99
	South Carolina	S	15.36 MW	19.14 AW	39800 AAW	SCBLS	10//99-12//99
	Charleston-North Charleston MSA, SC	S	14.16 MW	12.91 AW	29450 AAW	SCBLS	10//99-12//99
	Columbia MSA, SC	S	18.98 MW	15.91 AW	39480 AAW	SCBLS	10//99-12//99
	Florence MSA, SC	S	22.87 MW	25.51 AW	47570 AAW	SCBLS	10//99-12//99
	Greenville-Spartanburg-Anderson MSA, SC	S	19.20 MW	15.94 AW	39930 AAW	SCBLS	10//99-12//99
	Myrtle Beach MSA, SC	S	12.49 MW	11.39 AW	25980 AAW	SCBLS	10//99-12//99
	Sumter MSA, SC	S	17.36 MW	12.69 AW	36110 AAW	SCBLS	10//99-12//99
	South Dakota	S	24.72 MW	27.55 AW	57310 AAW	SDBLS	10//99-12//99
	Sioux Falls MSA, SD	S	23.91 MW	23.98 AW	49730 AAW	SDBLS	10//99-12//99
	Tennessee	S	17.89 MW	19.84 AW	41280 AAW	TNBLS	10//99-12//99
	Chattanooga MSA, TN-GA	S	17.95 MW	15.86 AW	37340 AAW	TNBLS	10//99-12//99
	Clarksville-Hopkinsville MSA, TN-KY	S	18.42 MW	17.58 AW	38320 AAW	TNBLS	10//99-12//99
	Jackson MSA, TN	S	15.00 MW	10.10 AW	31190 AAW	TNBLS	10//99-12//99
	Johnson City-Kingsport-Bristol MSA, TN-VA	S	17.73 MW	16.11 AW	36870 AAW	TNBLS	10//99-12//99
	Knoxville MSA, TN	S	20.14 MW	19.30 AW	41900 AAW	TNBLS	10//99-12//99
	Memphis MSA, TN-AR-MS	S	22.69 MW	20.02 AW	47200 AAW	MSBLS	10//99-12//99
	Nashville MSA, TN	S	21.55 MW	20.71 AW	44830 AAW	TNBLS	10//99-12//99
	Texas	S	19.33 MW	21.47 AW	44660 AAW	TXBLS	10//99-12//99
	Abilene MSA, TX	S	16.48 MW	13.91 AW	34270 AAW	TXBLS	10//99-12//99
	Amarillo MSA, TX	S	24.72 MW	22.33 AW	51410 AAW	TXBLS	10//99-12//99
	Austin-San Marcos MSA, TX	S	24.00 MW	22.90 AW	49910 AAW	TXBLS	10//99-12//99
	Beaumont-Port Arthur MSA, TX	S	21.90 MW	21.21 AW	45560 AAW	TXBLS	10//99-12//99
	Brazoria PMSA, TX	S	21.24 MW	20.16 AW	44170 AAW	TXBLS	10//99-12//99
	Brownsville-Harlingen-San Benito MSA, TX	S	16.34 MW	12.95 AW	33980 AAW	TXBLS	10//99-12//99
	Bryan-College Station MSA, TX	S	24.83 MW	23.87 AW	51650 AAW	TXBLS	10//99-12//99
	Corpus Christi MSA, TX	S	16.77 MW	13.05 AW	34890 AAW	TXBLS	10//99-12//99
	Dallas PMSA, TX	S	23.68 MW	21.43 AW	49260 AAW	TXBLS	10//99-12//99
	El Paso MSA, TX	S	16.55 MW	14.70 AW	34420 AAW	TXBLS	10//99-12//99
	Fort Worth-Arlington PMSA, TX	S	23.06 MW	20.83 AW	47960 AAW	TXBLS	10//99-12//99
	Houston PMSA, TX	S	20.96 MW	18.63 AW	43590 AAW	TXBLS	10//99-12//99
	Killeen-Temple MSA, TX	S	18.81 MW	16.01 AW	39130 AAW	TXBLS	10//99-12//99
	Longview-Marshall MSA, TX	S	19.46 MW	17.10 AW	40470 AAW	TXBLS	10//99-12//99
	Lubbock MSA, TX	S	19.99 MW	15.95 AW	41580 AAW	TXBLS	10//99-12//99
	McAllen-Edinburg-Mission MSA, TX	S	16.56 MW	15.39 AW	34450 AAW	TXBLS	10//99-12//99
	Odessa-Midland MSA, TX	S	16.11 MW	10.26 AW	33500 AAW	TXBLS	10//99-12//99
	San Antonio MSA, TX	S	21.41 MW	18.61 AW	44530 AAW	TXBLS	10//99-12//99
	Sherman-Denison MSA, TX	S	16.68 MW	13.39 AW	34690 AAW	TXBLS	10//99-12//99
	Texarkana MSA, TX-Texarkana, AR	S	15.55 MW	13.30 AW	32340 AAW	TXBLS	10//99-12//99
	Tyler MSA, TX	S	14.92 MW	14.66 AW	31020 AAW	TXBLS	10//99-12//99
	Victoria MSA, TX	S	15.77 MW	13.04 AW	32810 AAW	TXBLS	10//99-12//99
	Waco MSA, TX	S	16.11 MW	15.36 AW	33510 AAW	TXBLS	10//99-12//99
	Wichita Falls MSA, TX	S	17.07 MW	14.31 AW	35500 AAW	TXBLS	10//99-12//99
	Utah	S	20.53 MW	22.96 AW	47760 AAW	UTBLS	10//99-12//99
	Provo-Orem MSA, UT	S	17.06 MW	14.71 AW	35480 AAW	UTBLS	10//99-12//99
	Salt Lake City-Ogden MSA, UT	S	21.39 MW	20.62 AW	44500 AAW	UTBLS	10//99-12//99
	Vermont	S	22.34 MW	21.94 AW	45640 AAW	VTBLS	10//99-12//99
	Burlington MSA, VT	S	18.22 MW	13.48 AW	37890 AAW	VTBLS	10//99-12//99
	Virginia	S	22.88 MW	24.45 AW	50850 AAW	VABLS	10//99-12//99
	Charlottesville MSA, VA	S	19.07 MW	15.92 AW	39660 AAW	VABLS	10//99-12//99
	Danville MSA, VA	S	27.66 MW	29.79 AW	57530 AAW	VABLS	10//99-12//99
	Lynchburg MSA, VA	S	19.47 MW	18.80 AW	40500 AAW	VABLS	10//99-12//99
	Norfolk-Virginia Beach-Newport News MSA, VA-NC	S	21.91 MW	18.74 AW	45570 AAW	VABLS	10//99-12//99
	Richmond-Petersburg MSA, VA	S	25.59 MW	23.70 AW	53220 AAW	VABLS	10//99-12//99
	Roanoke MSA, VA	S	18.98 MW	15.41 AW	39470 AAW	VABLS	10//99-12//99
	Washington	S	26.31 MW	27.84 AW	57910 AAW	WABLS	10//99-12//99
	Bellingham MSA, WA	S	22.13 MW	16.48 AW	46030 AAW	WABLS	10//99-12//99

AAW	Average annual wage	AOH	Average offered, high	ASH	Average starting, high	H	Hourly	M Monthly	S Special: hourly and annual
AE	Average entry wage	AOL	Average offered, low	ASL	Average starting, low	HI	Highest wage paid	MTC Median total compensation	TQ Third quartile wage
AEX	Average experienced wage	APH	Average pay, high range	AW	Average wage paid	HR	High end range	MW Median wage paid	W Weekly
AO	Average offered	APL	Average pay, low range	FQ	First quartile wage	LR	Low end range	SQ Second quartile wage	Y Yearly

Occupation/Type/Industry	Location	Per	Low	Mid	High	Source	Date
Administrative Services Manager	Richland-Kennewick-Pasco MSA, WA	S	27.93 MW	26.98 AW	58090 AAW	WABLS	10//99-12//99
	Seattle-Bellevue-Everett PMSA, WA	S	29.17 MW	27.44 AW	60680 AAW	WABLS	10//99-12//99
	Spokane MSA, WA	S	21.95 MW	19.79 AW	45670 AAW	WABLS	10//99-12//99
	Tacoma PMSA, WA	S	27.08 MW	26.08 AW	56330 AAW	WABLS	10//99-12//99
	Yakima MSA, WA	S	25.06 MW	26.80 AW	52120 AAW	WABLS	10//99-12//99
	West Virginia	S	14.98 MW	17.26 AW	35900 AAW	WVBLS	10//99-12//99
	Charleston MSA, WV	S	16.93 MW	14.56 AW	35220 AAW	WVBLS	10//99-12//99
	Huntington-Ashland MSA, WV-KY-OH	S	16.12 MW	13.75 AW	33540 AAW	WVBLS	10//99-12//99
	Parkersburg-Marietta MSA, WV-OH	S	13.14 MW	10.26 AW	27330 AAW	WVBLS	10//99-12//99
	Wheeling MSA, WV-OH	S	16.38 MW	14.43 AW	34080 AAW	WVBLS	10//99-12//99
	Wisconsin	S	19.33 MW	21.68 AW	45090 AAW	WIBLS	10//99-12//99
	Appleton-Oshkosh-Neenah MSA, WI	S	24.68 MW	21.35 AW	51330 AAW	WIBLS	10//99-12//99
	Eau Claire MSA, WI	S	17.63 MW	14.40 AW	36680 AAW	WIBLS	10//99-12//99
	Green Bay MSA, WI	S	22.55 MW	19.38 AW	46890 AAW	WIBLS	10//99-12//99
	Janesville-Beloit MSA, WI	S	17.04 MW	13.90 AW	35450 AAW	WIBLS	10//99-12//99
	Kenosha PMSA, WI	S	26.14 MW	26.38 AW	54380 AAW	WIBLS	10//99-12//99
	Madison MSA, WI	S	22.20 MW	19.59 AW	46170 AAW	WIBLS	10//99-12//99
	Milwaukee-Waukesha PMSA, WI	S	22.49 MW	20.55 AW	46770 AAW	WIBLS	10//99-12//99
	Racine PMSA, WI	S	23.19 MW	23.15 AW	48240 AAW	WIBLS	10//99-12//99
	Sheboygan MSA, WI	S	18.27 MW	18.29 AW	38000 AAW	WIBLS	10//99-12//99
	Wausau MSA, WI	S	18.65 MW	12.72 AW	38800 AAW	WIBLS	10//99-12//99
	Wyoming	S	16.11 MW	17.22 AW	35820 AAW	WYBLS	10//99-12//99
	Casper MSA, WY	S	17.46 MW	12.78 AW	36310 AAW	WYBLS	10//99-12//99
	Puerto Rico	S	18.08 MW	21.33 AW	44370 AAW	PRBLS	10//99-12//99
	Caguas PMSA, PR	S	15.03 MW	14.28 AW	31260 AAW	PRBLS	10//99-12//99
	Mayaguez MSA, PR	S	15.19 MW	14.28 AW	31590 AAW	PRBLS	10//99-12//99
	Ponce MSA, PR	S	13.28 MW	12.49 AW	27630 AAW	PRBLS	10//99-12//99
	San Juan-Bayamon PMSA, PR	S	22.42 MW	18.94 AW	46630 AAW	PRBLS	10//99-12//99
	Virgin Islands	S	22.63 MW	22.66 AW	47140 AAW	VIBLS	10//99-12//99
	Guam	S	15.06 MW	18.93 AW	39380 AAW	GUBLS	10//99-12//99
Administrator							
Assisted Living Facility	United States	Y		41995 MW		CHW3	1997-1998
Nursing Home	United States	Y		59849 AW		CHW2	1998
Nursing Home	United States	Y		38050 MW		CHW3	1998
Adult Literacy, Remedial Education, and GED Teacher and Instructor	Alabama	S	13.4 MW	13.93 AW	28980 AAW	ALBLS	10//99-12//99
	Alaska	S	14.7 MW	14.20 AW	29540 AAW	AKBLS	10//99-12//99
	Arizona	S	11.93 MW	12.91 AW	26840 AAW	AZBLS	10//99-12//99
	Arkansas	S	18.37 MW	19.09 AW	39710 AAW	ARBLS	10//99-12//99
	California	S	20.18 MW	21.98 AW	45710 AAW	CABLS	10//99-12//99
	Colorado	S	10.31 MW	12.16 AW	25290 AAW	COBLS	10//99-12//99
	Connecticut	S	15.96 MW	16.49 AW	34300 AAW	CTBLS	10//99-12//99
	Delaware	S	16.55 MW	18.73 AW	38950 AAW	DEBLS	10//99-12//99
	District of Columbia	S	10.31 MW	11.08 AW	23040 AAW	DCBLS	10//99-12//99
	Florida	S	12.83 MW	14.62 AW	30410 AAW	FLBLS	10//99-12//99
	Georgia	S	10.27 MW	12.38 AW	25740 AAW	GABLS	10//99-12//99
	Hawaii	S	17.2 MW	16.71 AW	34760 AAW	HIBLS	10//99-12//99
	Idaho	S	13.39 MW	13.33 AW	27730 AAW	IDBLS	10//99-12//99
	Illinois	S	11.61 MW	12.60 AW	26210 AAW	ILBLS	10//99-12//99
	Indiana	S	12.74 MW	12.97 AW	26970 AAW	INBLS	10//99-12//99
	Iowa	S	20.98 MW	22.41 AW	46620 AAW	IABLS	10//99-12//99
	Kansas	S	16.07 MW	17.53 AW	36450 AAW	KSBLS	10//99-12//99
	Kentucky	S	10.87 MW	11.97 AW	24890 AAW	KYBLS	10//99-12//99
	Louisiana	S	17.86 MW	16.51 AW	34350 AAW	LABLS	10//99-12//99
	Maine	S	15.16 MW	14.91 AW	31010 AAW	MEBLS	10//99-12//99
	Maryland	S	13.24 MW	13.88 AW	28880 AAW	MDBLS	10//99-12//99
	Massachusetts	S	17.22 MW	16.84 AW	35030 AAW	MABLS	10//99-12//99
	Michigan	S	14.63 MW	15.58 AW	32400 AAW	MIBLS	10//99-12//99
	Minnesota	S	16.55 MW	17.49 AW	36370 AAW	MNBLS	10//99-12//99
	Mississippi	S	17.8 MW	16.00 AW	33290 AAW	MSBLS	10//99-12//99
	Missouri	S	12.32 MW	12.23 AW	25430 AAW	MOBLS	10//99-12//99
	Montana	S	7.88 MW	9.35 AW	19450 AAW	MTBLS	10//99-12//99
	Nebraska	S	15.34 MW	16.32 AW	33940 AAW	NEBLS	10//99-12//99

AAW	Average annual wage	AOH	Average offered, high	ASH	Average starting, high	H	Hourly	M	Monthly	S	Special: hourly and annual
AE	Average entry wage	AOL	Average offered, low	ASL	Average starting, low	HI	Highest wage paid	MTC	Median total compensation	TQ	Third quartile wage
AEX	Average experienced wage	APH	Average pay, high range	AW	Average wage paid	HR	High end range	MW	Median wage paid	W	Weekly
AO	Average offered	APL	Average pay, low range	FQ	First quartile wage	LR	Low end range	SQ	Second quartile wage	Y	Yearly

Occupation/Type/Industry	Location	Per	Low	Mid	High	Source	Date
Adult Literacy, Remedial Education, and GED Teacher and Instructor							
	Nevada	S	18.37 MW	18.16 AW	37770 AAW	NVBLS	10//99-12//99
	New Jersey	S	17.65 MW	18.41 AW	38290 AAW	NJBLS	10//99-12//99
	New Mexico	S	13.82 MW	13.96 AW	29030 AAW	NMBLS	10//99-12//99
	New York	S	15.09 MW	16.84 AW	35020 AAW	NYBLS	10//99-12//99
	North Carolina	S	14.26 MW	14.34 AW	29830 AAW	NCBLS	10//99-12//99
	Oklahoma	S	12.47 MW	12.23 AW	25440 AAW	OKBLS	10//99-12//99
	Oregon	S	22.05 MW	21.08 AW	43850 AAW	ORBLS	10//99-12//99
	Pennsylvania	S	12.74 MW	13.34 AW	27740 AAW	PABLS	10//99-12//99
	Rhode Island	S	15.31 MW	17.93 AW	37300 AAW	RIBLS	10//99-12//99
	South Carolina	S	11.66 MW	12.86 AW	26740 AAW	SCBLS	10//99-12//99
	Tennessee	S	14.05 MW	14.75 AW	30680 AAW	TNBLS	10//99-12//99
	Texas	S	15.78 MW	15.92 AW	33110 AAW	TXBLS	10//99-12//99
	Utah	S	13.93 MW	14.58 AW	30340 AAW	UTBLS	10//99-12//99
	Vermont	S	14.03 MW	14.07 AW	29270 AAW	VTBLS	10//99-12//99
	Virginia	S	9.5 MW	10.79 AW	22440 AAW	VABLS	10//99-12//99
	Washington	S	12.99 MW	13.57 AW	28230 AAW	WABLS	10//99-12//99
	West Virginia	S	17.52 MW	17.41 AW	36220 AAW	WVBLS	10//99-12//99
	Wisconsin	S	13.33 MW	14.95 AW	31090 AAW	WIBLS	10//99-12//99
	Wyoming	S	12.79 MW	12.80 AW	26630 AAW	WYBLS	10//99-12//99
	Puerto Rico	S	14.71 MW	15.52 AW	32270 AAW	PRBLS	10//99-12//99
Advertising and Promotions Manager							
	Alabama	S	15.47 MW	18.13 AW	37710 AAW	ALBLS	10//99-12//99
	Birmingham MSA, AL	S	20.74 MW	19.03 AW	43130 AAW	ALBLS	10//99-12//99
	Decatur MSA, AL	S	11.12 MW	10.34 AW	23120 AAW	ALBLS	10//99-12//99
	Dothan MSA, AL	S	11.42 MW	11.91 AW	23750 AAW	ALBLS	10//99-12//99
	Huntsville MSA, AL	S	20.93 MW	15.70 AW	43530 AAW	ALBLS	10//99-12//99
	Mobile MSA, AL	S	19.30 MW	15.51 AW	40140 AAW	ALBLS	10//99-12//99
	Montgomery MSA, AL	S	19.60 MW	17.47 AW	40770 AAW	ALBLS	10//99-12//99
	Tuscaloosa MSA, AL	S	13.38 MW	9.33 AW	27820 AAW	ALBLS	10//99-12//99
	Alaska	S	22.46 MW	23.13 AW	48120 AAW	AKBLS	10//99-12//99
	Anchorage MSA, AK	S	22.29 MW	20.29 AW	46370 AAW	AKBLS	10//99-12//99
	Arizona	S	25.93 MW	27.19 AW	56550 AAW	AZBLS	10//99-12//99
	Phoenix-Mesa MSA, AZ	S	29.35 MW	28.71 AW	61050 AAW	AZBLS	10//99-12//99
	Tucson MSA, AZ	S	23.30 MW	19.78 AW	48470 AAW	AZBLS	10//99-12//99
	Arkansas	S	16.77 MW	20.19 AW	42000 AAW	ARBLS	10//99-12//99
	Fayetteville-Springdale-Rogers MSA, AR	S	18.77 MW	16.10 AW	39050 AAW	ARBLS	10//99-12//99
	Fort Smith MSA, AR-OK	S	25.66 MW	24.19 AW	53370 AAW	ARBLS	10//99-12//99
	Little Rock-North Little Rock MSA, AR	S	22.84 MW	18.86 AW	47510 AAW	ARBLS	10//99-12//99
	California	S	30.54 MW	32.36 AW	67320 AAW	CABLS	10//99-12//99
	Bakersfield MSA, CA	S	24.41 MW	23.78 AW	50770 AAW	CABLS	10//99-12//99
	Chico-Paradise MSA, CA	S	18.02 MW	15.45 AW	37470 AAW	CABLS	10//99-12//99
	Fresno MSA, CA	S	24.04 MW	22.96 AW	50000 AAW	CABLS	10//99-12//99
	Los Angeles-Long Beach PMSA, CA	S	37.40 MW	37.44 AW	77780 AAW	CABLS	10//99-12//99
	Modesto MSA, CA	S	19.38 MW	17.68 AW	40310 AAW	CABLS	10//99-12//99
	Oakland PMSA, CA	S	34.20 MW	31.30 AW	71130 AAW	CABLS	10//99-12//99
	Orange County PMSA, CA	S	30.61 MW	28.68 AW	63670 AAW	CABLS	10//99-12//99
	Riverside-San Bernardino PMSA, CA	S	30.38 MW	25.19 AW	63180 AAW	CABLS	10//99-12//99
	Sacramento PMSA, CA	S	21.87 MW	19.39 AW	45480 AAW	CABLS	10//99-12//99
	Salinas MSA, CA	S	25.89 MW	24.90 AW	53850 AAW	CABLS	10//99-12//99
	San Diego MSA, CA	S	27.98 MW	25.47 AW	58200 AAW	CABLS	10//99-12//99
	San Francisco PMSA, CA	S	31.07 MW	30.21 AW	64620 AAW	CABLS	10//99-12//99
	San Jose PMSA, CA	S	40.96 MW	40.95 AW	85190 AAW	CABLS	10//99-12//99
	San Luis Obispo-Atascadero-Paso Robles MSA, CA	S	21.13 MW	19.69 AW	43960 AAW	CABLS	10//99-12//99
	Santa Barbara-Santa Maria-Lompoc MSA, CA	S	28.36 MW	21.03 AW	59000 AAW	CABLS	10//99-12//99
	Santa Cruz-Watsonville PMSA, CA	S	41.97 MW	46.02 AW	87310 AAW	CABLS	10//99-12//99
	Santa Rosa PMSA, CA	S	25.80 MW	24.25 AW	53660 AAW	CABLS	10//99-12//99
	Stockton-Lodi MSA, CA	S	27.83 MW	23.48 AW	57890 AAW	CABLS	10//99-12//99
	Vallejo-Fairfield-Napa PMSA, CA	S	28.67 MW	25.68 AW	59640 AAW	CABLS	10//99-12//99
	Ventura PMSA, CA	S	30.21 MW	26.04 AW	62840 AAW	CABLS	10//99-12//99

Occupation/Type/Industry	Location	Per	Low	Mid	High	Source	Date
Advertising and Promotions Manager	Visalia-Tulare-Porterville MSA, CA	S	22.09 MW	21.29 AW	45960 AAW	CABLS	10//99-12//99
	Colorado	S	26.83 MW	29.12 AW	60560 AAW	COBLS	10//99-12//99
	Boulder-Longmont PMSA, CO	S	32.39 MW	35.34 AW	67380 AAW	COBLS	10//99-12//99
	Colorado Springs MSA, CO	S	27.21 MW	21.02 AW	56600 AAW	COBLS	10//99-12//99
	Denver PMSA, CO	S	30.75 MW	27.00 AW	63950 AAW	COBLS	10//99-12//99
	Connecticut	S	26.9 MW	29.83 AW	62040 AAW	CTBLS	10//99-12//99
	Bridgeport PMSA, CT	S	25.44 MW	17.32 AW	52920 AAW	CTBLS	10//99-12//99
	Danbury PMSA, CT	S	34.57 MW	30.91 AW	71910 AAW	CTBLS	10//99-12//99
	Hartford MSA, CT	S	28.25 MW	25.74 AW	58760 AAW	CTBLS	10//99-12//99
	New Haven-Meriden PMSA, CT	S	28.01 MW	25.70 AW	58260 AAW	CTBLS	10//99-12//99
	New London-Norwich MSA, CT-RI	S	29.10 MW	25.15 AW	60520 AAW	CTBLS	10//99-12//99
	Stamford-Norwalk PMSA, CT	S	31.34 MW	31.83 AW	65180 AAW	CTBLS	10//99-12//99
	Delaware	S	20.15 MW	28.17 AW	58590 AAW	DEBLS	10//99-12//99
	Dover MSA, DE	S	22.13 MW	19.43 AW	46020 AAW	DEBLS	10//99-12//99
	Wilmington-Newark PMSA, DE-MD	S	29.50 MW	20.54 AW	61360 AAW	DEBLS	10//99-12//99
	District of Columbia	S	23.48 MW	27.13 AW	56420 AAW	DCBLS	10//99-12//99
	Washington PMSA, DC-MD-VA-WV	S	29.00 MW	24.75 AW	60320 AAW	DCBLS	10//99-12//99
	Florida	S	22.58 MW	25.15 AW	52310 AAW	FLBLS	10//99-12//99
	Daytona Beach MSA, FL	S	28.55 MW	31.63 AW	59390 AAW	FLBLS	10//99-12//99
	Fort Lauderdale PMSA, FL	S	29.45 MW	26.22 AW	61250 AAW	FLBLS	10//99-12//99
	Fort Myers-Cape Coral MSA, FL	S	22.01 MW	17.36 AW	45790 AAW	FLBLS	10//99-12//99
	Fort Pierce-Port St. Lucie MSA, FL	S	19.28 MW	19.13 AW	40100 AAW	FLBLS	10//99-12//99
	Fort Walton Beach MSA, FL	S	24.65 MW	22.84 AW	51270 AAW	FLBLS	10//99-12//99
	Gainesville MSA, FL	S	21.06 MW	14.52 AW	43800 AAW	FLBLS	10//99-12//99
	Jacksonville MSA, FL	S	23.84 MW	21.05 AW	49590 AAW	FLBLS	10//99-12//99
	Lakeland-Winter Haven MSA, FL	S	19.15 MW	16.59 AW	39820 AAW	FLBLS	10//99-12//99
	Melbourne-Titusville-Palm Bay MSA, FL	S	19.50 MW	19.66 AW	40560 AAW	FLBLS	10//99-12//99
	Miami PMSA, FL	S	27.91 MW	29.03 AW	58060 AAW	FLBLS	10//99-12//99
	Orlando MSA, FL	S	23.55 MW	19.59 AW	48990 AAW	FLBLS	10//99-12//99
	Panama City MSA, FL	S	18.45 MW	19.22 AW	38380 AAW	FLBLS	10//99-12//99
	Pensacola MSA, FL	S	20.98 MW	20.56 AW	43640 AAW	FLBLS	10//99-12//99
	Sarasota-Bradenton MSA, FL	S	24.53 MW	20.95 AW	51030 AAW	FLBLS	10//99-12//99
	Tallahassee MSA, FL	S	25.15 MW	24.09 AW	52310 AAW	FLBLS	10//99-12//99
	Tampa-St. Petersburg-Clearwater MSA, FL	S	23.61 MW	20.26 AW	49120 AAW	FLBLS	10//99-12//99
	West Palm Beach-Boca Raton MSA, FL	S	27.43 MW	21.94 AW	57050 AAW	FLBLS	10//99-12//99
	Georgia	S	22.45 MW	26.16 AW	54400 AAW	GABLS	10//99-12//99
	Athens MSA, GA	S	18.09 MW	14.99 AW	37640 AAW	GABLS	10//99-12//99
	Atlanta MSA, GA	S	27.64 MW	23.58 AW	57490 AAW	GABLS	10//99-12//99
	Augusta-Aiken MSA, GA-SC	S	21.25 MW	19.92 AW	44200 AAW	GABLS	10//99-12//99
	Columbus MSA, GA-AL	S	21.44 MW	22.84 AW	44590 AAW	GABLS	10//99-12//99
	Macon MSA, GA	S	22.55 MW	22.38 AW	46900 AAW	GABLS	10//99-12//99
	Savannah MSA, GA	S	17.28 MW	16.14 AW	35950 AAW	GABLS	10//99-12//99
	Hawaii	S	25.61 MW	29.64 AW	61660 AAW	HIBLS	10//99-12//99
	Honolulu MSA, HI	S	29.06 MW	23.98 AW	60450 AAW	HIBLS	10//99-12//99
	Idaho	S	18.74 MW	20.41 AW	42440 AAW	IDBLS	10//99-12//99
	Boise City MSA, ID	S	21.58 MW	19.91 AW	44880 AAW	IDBLS	10//99-12//99
	Illinois	S	26.36 MW	28.96 AW	60240 AAW	ILBLS	10//99-12//99
	Bloomington-Normal MSA, IL	S	35.13 MW	25.83 AW	73060 AAW	ILBLS	10//99-12//99
	Champaign-Urbana MSA, IL	S	21.49 MW	20.64 AW	44690 AAW	ILBLS	10//99-12//99
	Chicago PMSA, IL	S	30.82 MW	28.61 AW	64100 AAW	ILBLS	10//99-12//99
	Kankakee PMSA, IL	S	18.82 MW	15.54 AW	39150 AAW	ILBLS	10//99-12//99
	Peoria-Pekin MSA, IL	S	16.36 MW	15.15 AW	34030 AAW	ILBLS	10//99-12//99
	Rockford MSA, IL	S	22.61 MW	19.89 AW	47030 AAW	ILBLS	10//99-12//99
	Springfield MSA, IL	S	20.33 MW	18.75 AW	42290 AAW	ILBLS	10//99-12//99
	Indiana	S	21.93 MW	25.17 AW	52350 AAW	INBLS	10//99-12//99
	Elkhart-Goshen MSA, IN	S	28.54 MW	34.61 AW	59350 AAW	INBLS	10//99-12//99
	Evansville-Henderson MSA, IN-KY	S	24.10 MW	24.03 AW	50130 AAW	INBLS	10//99-12//99
	Fort Wayne MSA, IN	S	23.90 MW	20.67 AW	49720 AAW	INBLS	10//99-12//99
	Gary PMSA, IN	S	19.96 MW	18.36 AW	41510 AAW	INBLS	10//99-12//99

Occupation/Type/Industry	Location	Per	Low	Mid	High	Source	Date
Advertising and Promotions Manager							
	Indianapolis MSA, IN	S	28.80 MW	24.46 AW	59900 AAW	INBLS	10//99-12//99
	South Bend MSA, IN	S	17.95 MW	16.66 AW	37340 AAW	INBLS	10//99-12//99
	Iowa	S	17.85 MW	20.98 AW	43640 AAW	IABLS	10//99-12//99
	Davenport-Moline-Rock Island MSA, IA-IL	S	18.67 MW	18.02 AW	38840 AAW	IABLS	10//99-12//99
	Des Moines MSA, IA	S	22.26 MW	19.26 AW	46290 AAW	IABLS	10//99-12//99
	Dubuque MSA, IA	S	16.94 MW	14.71 AW	35220 AAW	IABLS	10//99-12//99
	Sioux City MSA, IA-NE	S	18.19 MW	15.83 AW	37830 AAW	IABLS	10//99-12//99
	Waterloo-Cedar Falls MSA, IA	S	23.17 MW	20.91 AW	48190 AAW	IABLS	10//99-12//99
	Kansas	S	22.56 MW	23.16 AW	48180 AAW	KSBLS	10//99-12//99
	Lawrence MSA, KS	S	18.32 MW	15.85 AW	38110 AAW	KSBLS	10//99-12//99
	Topeka MSA, KS	S	21.39 MW	16.97 AW	44500 AAW	KSBLS	10//99-12//99
	Wichita MSA, KS	S	23.69 MW	19.65 AW	49270 AAW	KSBLS	10//99-12//99
	Kentucky	S	19.26 MW	21.91 AW	45580 AAW	KYBLS	10//99-12//99
	Louisville MSA, KY-IN	S	22.83 MW	19.42 AW	47480 AAW	KYBLS	10//99-12//99
	Louisiana	S	15.96 MW	19.49 AW	40540 AAW	LABLS	10//99-12//99
	Baton Rouge MSA, LA	S	18.11 MW	14.36 AW	37660 AAW	LABLS	10//99-12//99
	Houma MSA, LA	S	35.47 MW	34.54 AW	73780 AAW	LABLS	10//99-12//99
	Lafayette MSA, LA	S	20.65 MW	20.53 AW	42950 AAW	LABLS	10//99-12//99
	Lake Charles MSA, LA	S	15.86 MW	13.60 AW	32980 AAW	LABLS	10//99-12//99
	New Orleans MSA, LA	S	19.94 MW	16.14 AW	41480 AAW	LABLS	10//99-12//99
	Shreveport-Bossier City MSA, LA	S	14.97 MW	13.88 AW	31130 AAW	LABLS	10//99-12//99
	Maine	S	17.74 MW	20.37 AW	42380 AAW	MEBLS	10//99-12//99
	Bangor MSA, ME	S	19.41 MW	19.21 AW	40370 AAW	MEBLS	10//99-12//99
	Portland MSA, ME	S	26.59 MW	23.12 AW	55310 AAW	MEBLS	10//99-12//99
	Maryland	S	20.04 MW	24.41 AW	50780 AAW	MDBLS	10//99-12//99
	Baltimore PMSA, MD	S	24.84 MW	17.58 AW	51670 AAW	MDBLS	10//99-12//99
	Hagerstown PMSA, MD	S	21.20 MW	14.66 AW	44100 AAW	MDBLS	10//99-12//99
	Massachusetts	S	28.35 MW	31.26 AW	65020 AAW	MABLS	10//99-12//99
	Boston PMSA, MA-NH	S	31.92 MW	29.28 AW	66400 AAW	MABLS	10//99-12//99
	Fitchburg-Leominster PMSA, MA	S	21.00 MW	16.19 AW	43680 AAW	MABLS	10//99-12//99
	Lawrence PMSA, MA-NH	S	30.80 MW	30.67 AW	64070 AAW	MABLS	10//99-12//99
	Springfield MSA, MA	S	26.20 MW	21.00 AW	54490 AAW	MABLS	10//99-12//99
	Worcester PMSA, MA-CT	S	24.29 MW	20.91 AW	50520 AAW	MABLS	10//99-12//99
	Michigan	S	25.1 MW	29.47 AW	61290 AAW	MIBLS	10//99-12//99
	Ann Arbor PMSA, MI	S	23.39 MW	21.30 AW	48640 AAW	MIBLS	10//99-12//99
	Detroit PMSA, MI	S	34.05 MW	29.98 AW	70830 AAW	MIBLS	10//99-12//99
	Flint PMSA, MI	S	21.25 MW	20.65 AW	44200 AAW	MIBLS	10//99-12//99
	Grand Rapids-Muskegon-Holland MSA, MI	S	28.10 MW	22.88 AW	58460 AAW	MIBLS	10//99-12//99
	Kalamazoo-Battle Creek MSA, MI	S	22.46 MW	22.30 AW	46710 AAW	MIBLS	10//99-12//99
	Lansing-East Lansing MSA, MI	S	23.43 MW	20.34 AW	48740 AAW	MIBLS	10//99-12//99
	Saginaw-Bay City-Midland MSA, MI	S	30.66 MW	25.62 AW	63760 AAW	MIBLS	10//99-12//99
	Minnesota	S	28.36 MW	32.82 AW	68260 AAW	MNBLS	10//99-12//99
	Duluth-Superior MSA, MN-WI	S	22.90 MW	19.88 AW	47630 AAW	MNBLS	10//99-12//99
	Minneapolis-St. Paul MSA, MN-WI	S	33.92 MW	29.09 AW	70560 AAW	MNBLS	10//99-12//99
	St. Cloud MSA, MN	S	25.09 MW	24.78 AW	52200 AAW	MNBLS	10//99-12//99
	Mississippi	S	19.79 MW	22.51 AW	46810 AAW	MSBLS	10//99-12//99
	Biloxi-Gulfport-Pascagoula MSA, MS	S	24.23 MW	16.11 AW	50400 AAW	MSBLS	10//99-12//99
	Jackson MSA, MS	S	22.19 MW	17.48 AW	46150 AAW	MSBLS	10//99-12//99
	Missouri	S	20.34 MW	22.31 AW	46410 AAW	MOBLS	10//99-12//99
	Kansas City MSA, MO-KS	S	24.46 MW	22.86 AW	50870 AAW	MOBLS	10//99-12//99
	St. Louis MSA, MO-IL	S	23.17 MW	22.25 AW	48200 AAW	MOBLS	10//99-12//99
	Springfield MSA, MO	S	21.10 MW	22.39 AW	43890 AAW	MOBLS	10//99-12//99
	Montana	S	13.35 MW	18.56 AW	38600 AAW	MTBLS	10//99-12//99
	Great Falls MSA, MT	S	13.14 MW	11.93 AW	27340 AAW	MTBLS	10//99-12//99
	Missoula MSA, MT	S	22.49 MW	18.23 AW	46780 AAW	MTBLS	10//99-12//99
	Nebraska	S	19.09 MW	19.89 AW	41370 AAW	NEBLS	10//99-12//99
	Lincoln MSA, NE	S	16.81 MW	17.74 AW	34960 AAW	NEBLS	10//99-12//99
	Omaha MSA, NE-IA	S	24.64 MW	23.84 AW	51250 AAW	NEBLS	10//99-12//99
	Nevada	S	20.92 MW	23.82 AW	49540 AAW	NVBLS	10//99-12//99
	Las Vegas MSA, NV-AZ	S	24.60 MW	21.06 AW	51170 AAW	NVBLS	10//99-12//99
	Reno MSA, NV	S	22.38 MW	20.66 AW	46560 AAW	NVBLS	10//99-12//99
	New Hampshire	S	23.99 MW	28.64 AW	59580 AAW	NHBLS	10//99-12//99
	Manchester PMSA, NH	S	19.24 MW	19.24 AW	40030 AAW	NHBLS	10//99-12//99

AAW	Average annual wage	AOH	Average offered, high	ASH	Average starting, high	H	Hourly	M	Monthly	S	Special: hourly and annual
AE	Average entry wage	AOL	Average offered, low	ASL	Average starting, low	HI	Highest wage paid	MTC	Median total compensation	TQ	Third quartile wage
AEX	Average experienced wage	APH	Average pay, high range	AW	Average wage paid	HR	High end range	MW	Median wage paid	W	Weekly
AO	Average offered	APL	Average pay, low range	FQ	First quartile wage	LR	Low end range	SQ	Second quartile wage	Y	Yearly

Occupation/Type/Industry	Location	Per	Low	Mid	High	Source	Date
Advertising and Promotions Manager	Nashua PMSA, NH	S	26.07 MW	22.98 AW	54220 AAW	NHBLS	10//99-12//99
	Portsmouth-Rochester PMSA, NH-ME	S	24.35 MW	21.59 AW	50650 AAW	NHBLS	10//99-12//99
	New Jersey	S	29.88 MW	33.53 AW	69750 AAW	NJBLS	10//99-12//99
	Atlantic-Cape May PMSA, NJ	S	21.85 MW	20.47 AW	45450 AAW	NJBLS	10//99-12//99
	Bergen-Passaic PMSA, NJ	S	37.70 MW	36.44 AW	78410 AAW	NJBLS	10//99-12//99
	Jersey City PMSA, NJ	S	36.44 MW	35.95 AW	75800 AAW	NJBLS	10//99-12//99
	Middlesex-Somerset-Hunterdon PMSA, NJ	S	34.22 MW	35.64 AW	71180 AAW	NJBLS	10//99-12//99
	Monmouth-Ocean PMSA, NJ	S	23.77 MW	21.15 AW	49450 AAW	NJBLS	10//99-12//99
	Newark PMSA, NJ	S	35.26 MW	31.57 AW	73340 AAW	NJBLS	10//99-12//99
	Trenton PMSA, NJ	S	27.64 MW	24.70 AW	57480 AAW	NJBLS	10//99-12//99
	New Mexico	S	18.62 MW	21.18 AW	44060 AAW	NMBLS	10//99-12//99
	Albuquerque MSA, NM	S	22.27 MW	20.79 AW	46320 AAW	NMBLS	10//99-12//99
	Santa Fe MSA, NM	S	25.75 MW	16.34 AW	53560 AAW	NMBLS	10//99-12//99
	Albany-Schenectady-Troy MSA, NY	S	30.62 MW	27.27 AW	63680 AAW	NYBLS	10//99-12//99
	Binghamton MSA, NY	S	25.84 MW	19.79 AW	53740 AAW	NYBLS	10//99-12//99
	Buffalo-Niagara Falls MSA, NY	S	26.09 MW	21.14 AW	54260 AAW	NYBLS	10//99-12//99
	Nassau-Suffolk PMSA, NY	S	31.21 MW	24.81 AW	64930 AAW	NYBLS	10//99-12//99
	New York PMSA, NY	S	48.55 MW	50.74 AW	100980 AAW	NYBLS	10//99-12//99
	Newburgh PMSA, NY-PA	S	18.19 MW	15.71 AW	37820 AAW	NYBLS	10//99-12//99
	Syracuse MSA, NY	S	21.33 MW	18.14 AW	44360 AAW	NYBLS	10//99-12//99
	North Carolina	S	20.17 MW	23.84 AW	49580 AAW	NCBLS	10//99-12//99
	Asheville MSA, NC	S	16.67 MW	15.85 AW	34670 AAW	NCBLS	10//99-12//99
	Charlotte-Gastonia-Rock Hill MSA, NC-SC	S	28.23 MW	24.74 AW	58720 AAW	NCBLS	10//99-12//99
	Greensboro--Winston-Salem--High Point MSA, NC	S	23.68 MW	21.51 AW	49250 AAW	NCBLS	10//99-12//99
	Hickory-Morganton-Lenoir MSA, NC	S	23.54 MW	15.78 AW	48970 AAW	NCBLS	10//99-12//99
	Raleigh-Durham-Chapel Hill MSA, NC	S	23.26 MW	18.90 AW	48370 AAW	NCBLS	10//99-12//99
	Rocky Mount MSA, NC	S	24.73 MW	23.84 AW	51450 AAW	NCBLS	10//99-12//99
	Wilmington MSA, NC	S	17.04 MW	15.82 AW	35440 AAW	NCBLS	10//99-12//99
	North Dakota	S	15.19 MW	16.38 AW	34080 AAW	NDBLS	10//99-12//99
	Bismarck MSA, ND	S	17.00 MW	16.85 AW	35360 AAW	NDBLS	10//99-12//99
	Fargo-Moorhead MSA, ND-MN	S	19.72 MW	20.57 AW	41020 AAW	NDBLS	10//99-12//99
	Ohio	S	21.93 MW	25.69 AW	53430 AAW	OHBLS	10//99-12//99
	Akron PMSA, OH	S	30.08 MW	26.70 AW	62570 AAW	OHBLS	10//99-12//99
	Canton-Massillon MSA, OH	S	16.16 MW	14.95 AW	33600 AAW	OHBLS	10//99-12//99
	Cincinnati PMSA, OH-KY-IN	S	27.30 MW	22.40 AW	56790 AAW	OHBLS	10//99-12//99
	Cleveland-Lorain-Elyria PMSA, OH	S	25.11 MW	22.61 AW	52220 AAW	OHBLS	10//99-12//99
	Columbus MSA, OH	S	28.01 MW	24.25 AW	58260 AAW	OHBLS	10//99-12//99
	Dayton-Springfield MSA, OH	S	26.70 MW	23.22 AW	55530 AAW	OHBLS	10//99-12//99
	Hamilton-Middletown PMSA, OH	S	21.10 MW	19.14 AW	43880 AAW	OHBLS	10//99-12//99
	Lima MSA, OH	S	19.49 MW	17.19 AW	40530 AAW	OHBLS	10//99-12//99
	Mansfield MSA, OH	S	23.44 MW	21.77 AW	48760 AAW	OHBLS	10//99-12//99
	Toledo MSA, OH	S	23.05 MW	19.77 AW	47940 AAW	OHBLS	10//99-12//99
	Youngstown-Warren MSA, OH	S	22.31 MW	18.27 AW	46410 AAW	OHBLS	10//99-12//99
	Oklahoma	S	17.27 MW	19.53 AW	40630 AAW	OKBLS	10//99-12//99
	Oklahoma City MSA, OK	S	21.93 MW	19.46 AW	45610 AAW	OKBLS	10//99-12//99
	Tulsa MSA, OK	S	20.48 MW	18.27 AW	42600 AAW	OKBLS	10//99-12//99
	Oregon	S	22.55 MW	23.91 AW	49730 AAW	ORBLS	10//99-12//99
	Eugene-Springfield MSA, OR	S	25.30 MW	27.94 AW	52620 AAW	ORBLS	10//99-12//99
	Medford-Ashland MSA, OR	S	18.90 MW	15.72 AW	39310 AAW	ORBLS	10//99-12//99
	Portland-Vancouver PMSA, OR-WA	S	23.54 MW	23.05 AW	48970 AAW	ORBLS	10//99-12//99
	Salem PMSA, OR	S	34.29 MW	27.97 AW	71320 AAW	ORBLS	10//99-12//99
	Pennsylvania	S	22.32 MW	25.16 AW	52330 AAW	PABLS	10//99-12//99
	Allentown-Bethlehem-Easton MSA, PA	S	23.62 MW	21.12 AW	49140 AAW	PABLS	10//99-12//99
	Erie MSA, PA	S	19.75 MW	18.10 AW	41080 AAW	PABLS	10//99-12//99
	Harrisburg-Lebanon-Carlisle MSA, PA	S	24.78 MW	23.03 AW	51540 AAW	PABLS	10//99-12//99
	Lancaster MSA, PA	S	23.83 MW	21.36 AW	49570 AAW	PABLS	10//99-12//99
	Philadelphia PMSA, PA-NJ	S	28.17 MW	24.23 AW	58590 AAW	PABLS	10//99-12//99

Occupation/Type/Industry	Location	Per	Low	Mid	High	Source	Date
Advertising and Promotions Manager							
	Pittsburgh MSA, PA	S	25.14 MW	22.62 AW	52280 AAW	PABLS	10//99-12//99
	Reading MSA, PA	S	22.28 MW	23.01 AW	46340 AAW	PABLS	10//99-12//99
	Scranton--Wilkes-Barre-- Hazleton MSA, PA	S	20.35 MW	16.00 AW	42320 AAW	PABLS	10//99-12//99
	Rhode Island	S	21.04 MW	24.98 AW	51970 AAW	RIBLS	10//99-12//99
	Providence-Fall River- Warwick MSA, RI-MA	S	23.54 MW	18.78 AW	48960 AAW	RIBLS	10//99-12//99
	South Carolina	S	21.11 MW	24.99 AW	51980 AAW	SCBLS	10//99-12//99
	Charleston-North Charleston MSA, SC	S	23.06 MW	19.99 AW	47960 AAW	SCBLS	10//99-12//99
	Columbia MSA, SC	S	22.26 MW	18.24 AW	46290 AAW	SCBLS	10//99-12//99
	Greenville-Spartanburg- Anderson MSA, SC	S	26.13 MW	24.01 AW	54350 AAW	SCBLS	10//99-12//99
	Myrtle Beach MSA, SC	S	20.67 MW	19.48 AW	42990 AAW	SCBLS	10//99-12//99
	South Dakota	S	26.5 MW	28.50 AW	59270 AAW	SDBLS	10//99-12//99
	Sioux Falls MSA, SD	S	31.10 MW	29.36 AW	64690 AAW	SDBLS	10//99-12//99
	Tennessee	S	18.31 MW	21.46 AW	44630 AAW	TNBLS	10//99-12//99
	Chattanooga MSA, TN-GA	S	21.84 MW	20.45 AW	45420 AAW	TNBLS	10//99-12//99
	Johnson City-Kingsport-Bristol MSA, TN-VA	S	16.41 MW	16.30 AW	34140 AAW	TNBLS	10//99-12//99
	Knoxville MSA, TN	S	21.42 MW	18.52 AW	44560 AAW	TNBLS	10//99-12//99
	Memphis MSA, TN-AR-MS	S	22.84 MW	18.40 AW	47510 AAW	MSBLS	10//99-12//99
	Nashville MSA, TN	S	20.82 MW	17.73 AW	43290 AAW	TNBLS	10//99-12//99
	Texas	S	22.17 MW	25.79 AW	53640 AAW	TXBLS	10//99-12//99
	Abilene MSA, TX	S	22.04 MW	20.39 AW	45840 AAW	TXBLS	10//99-12//99
	Amarillo MSA, TX	S	18.57 MW	16.71 AW	38620 AAW	TXBLS	10//99-12//99
	Austin-San Marcos MSA, TX	S	24.68 MW	21.19 AW	51340 AAW	TXBLS	10//99-12//99
	Beaumont-Port Arthur MSA, TX	S	20.68 MW	18.65 AW	43020 AAW	TXBLS	10//99-12//99
	Corpus Christi MSA, TX	S	22.38 MW	18.73 AW	46540 AAW	TXBLS	10//99-12//99
	Dallas PMSA, TX	S	31.26 MW	29.76 AW	65030 AAW	TXBLS	10//99-12//99
	Fort Worth-Arlington PMSA, TX	S	25.00 MW	20.19 AW	52010 AAW	TXBLS	10//99-12//99
	Houston PMSA, TX	S	24.96 MW	20.64 AW	51920 AAW	TXBLS	10//99-12//99
	Killeen-Temple MSA, TX	S	18.29 MW	19.13 AW	38040 AAW	TXBLS	10//99-12//99
	Longview-Marshall MSA, TX	S	19.69 MW	19.25 AW	40960 AAW	TXBLS	10//99-12//99
	Lubbock MSA, TX	S	17.51 MW	18.42 AW	36420 AAW	TXBLS	10//99-12//99
	McAllen-Edinburg-Mission MSA, TX	S	19.28 MW	16.15 AW	40110 AAW	TXBLS	10//99-12//99
	San Antonio MSA, TX	S	26.86 MW	25.43 AW	55860 AAW	TXBLS	10//99-12//99
	Utah	S	21.29 MW	25.23 AW	52490 AAW	UTBLS	10//99-12//99
	Provo-Orem MSA, UT	S	27.31 MW	25.38 AW	56810 AAW	UTBLS	10//99-12//99
	Salt Lake City-Ogden MSA, UT	S	25.75 MW	23.12 AW	53560 AAW	UTBLS	10//99-12//99
	Vermont	S	24.59 MW	25.43 AW	52880 AAW	VTBLS	10//99-12//99
	Burlington MSA, VT	S	30.52 MW	25.82 AW	63490 AAW	VTBLS	10//99-12//99
	Virginia	S	29.76 MW	31.97 AW	66510 AAW	VABLS	10//99-12//99
	Charlottesville MSA, VA	S	22.06 MW	15.28 AW	45890 AAW	VABLS	10//99-12//99
	Lynchburg MSA, VA	S	23.06 MW	13.43 AW	47970 AAW	VABLS	10//99-12//99
	Norfolk-Virginia Beach- Newport News MSA, VA-NC	S	35.14 MW	24.81 AW	73080 AAW	VABLS	10//99-12//99
	Richmond-Petersburg MSA, VA	S	31.51 MW	34.77 AW	65550 AAW	VABLS	10//99-12//99
	Roanoke MSA, VA	S	21.97 MW	19.83 AW	45690 AAW	VABLS	10//99-12//99
	Washington	S	27.18 MW	30.09 AW	62580 AAW	WABLS	10//99-12//99
	Bremerton PMSA, WA	S	24.45 MW	24.29 AW	50860 AAW	WABLS	10//99-12//99
	Olympia PMSA, WA	S	15.42 MW	15.30 AW	32070 AAW	WABLS	10//99-12//99
	Richland-Kennewick-Pasco MSA, WA	S	26.91 MW	28.23 AW	55960 AAW	WABLS	10//99-12//99
	Seattle-Bellevue-Everett PMSA, WA	S	33.58 MW	30.70 AW	69850 AAW	WABLS	10//99-12//99
	Spokane MSA, WA	S	26.28 MW	21.39 AW	54660 AAW	WABLS	10//99-12//99
	Tacoma PMSA, WA	S	27.18 MW	25.09 AW	56530 AAW	WABLS	10//99-12//99
	Yakima MSA, WA	S	18.41 MW	16.88 AW	38290 AAW	WABLS	10//99-12//99
	West Virginia	S	16.09 MW	19.52 AW	40600 AAW	WVBLS	10//99-12//99
	Charleston MSA, WV	S	27.39 MW	24.84 AW	56980 AAW	WVBLS	10//99-12//99
	Huntington-Ashland MSA, WV-KY-OH	S	16.12 MW	14.87 AW	33530 AAW	WVBLS	10//99-12//99
	Parkersburg-Marietta MSA, WV-OH	S	21.42 MW	21.12 AW	44540 AAW	WVBLS	10//99-12//99

AAW	Average annual wage	AOH	Average offered, high	ASH	Average starting, high
AE	Average entry wage	AOL	Average offered, low	ASL	Average starting, low
AEX	Average experienced wage	APH	Average pay, high range	AW	Average wage paid
AO	Average offered	APL	Average pay, low range	FQ	First quartile wage

H	Hourly	M	Monthly
HI	Highest wage paid	MTC	Median total compensation
HR	High end range	MW	Median wage paid
LR	Low end range	SQ	Second quartile wage

S	Special: hourly and annual
TQ	Third quartile wage
W	Weekly
Y	Yearly

Occupation/Type/Industry	Location	Per	Low	Mid	High	Source	Date
Advertising and Promotions Manager							
	Wheeling MSA, WV-OH	S	18.21 MW	16.11 AW	37870 AAW	WVBLS	10//99-12//99
	Wisconsin	S	17.32 MW	20.59 AW	42820 AAW	WIBLS	10//99-12//99
	Appleton-Oshkosh-Neenah MSA, WI	S	20.43 MW	19.32 AW	42500 AAW	WIBLS	10//99-12//99
	Green Bay MSA, WI	S	19.98 MW	14.69 AW	41560 AAW	WIBLS	10//99-12//99
	Janesville-Beloit MSA, WI	S	17.66 MW	15.68 AW	36730 AAW	WIBLS	10//99-12//99
	Kenosha PMSA, WI	S	17.71 MW	15.18 AW	36830 AAW	WIBLS	10//99-12//99
	Madison MSA, WI	S	21.35 MW	17.89 AW	44400 AAW	WIBLS	10//99-12//99
	Milwaukee-Waukesha PMSA, WI	S	23.87 MW	20.66 AW	49640 AAW	WIBLS	10//99-12//99
	Racine PMSA, WI	S	25.84 MW	20.21 AW	53750 AAW	WIBLS	10//99-12//99
	Wyoming	S	14.44 MW	16.36 AW	34040 AAW	WYBLS	10//99-12//99
	Puerto Rico	S	19.74 MW	21.67 AW	45070 AAW	PRBLS	10//99-12//99
	San Juan-Bayamon PMSA, PR	S	22.19 MW	20.36 AW	46150 AAW	PRBLS	10//99-12//99
	Guam	S	15.61 MW	19.08 AW	39690 AAW	GUBLS	10//99-12//99
Advertising Sales Agent	Alabama	S	14.6 MW	16.41 AW	34130 AAW	ALBLS	10//99-12//99
	Anniston MSA, AL	S	24.39 MW	21.71 AW	50730 AAW	ALBLS	10//99-12//99
	Birmingham MSA, AL	S	19.92 MW	17.75 AW	41440 AAW	ALBLS	10//99-12//99
	Decatur MSA, AL	S	12.70 MW	12.22 AW	26410 AAW	ALBLS	10//99-12//99
	Dothan MSA, AL	S	10.67 MW	10.22 AW	22200 AAW	ALBLS	10//99-12//99
	Huntsville MSA, AL	S	15.05 MW	13.22 AW	31300 AAW	ALBLS	10//99-12//99
	Mobile MSA, AL	S	13.92 MW	12.72 AW	28960 AAW	ALBLS	10//99-12//99
	Montgomery MSA, AL	S	15.55 MW	14.45 AW	32330 AAW	ALBLS	10//99-12//99
	Tuscaloosa MSA, AL	S	16.62 MW	16.94 AW	34570 AAW	ALBLS	10//99-12//99
	Alaska	S	14.56 MW	17.08 AW	35520 AAW	AKBLS	10//99-12//99
	Anchorage MSA, AK	S	17.95 MW	15.33 AW	37330 AAW	AKBLS	10//99-12//99
	Arizona	S	14.62 MW	19.73 AW	41030 AAW	AZBLS	10//99-12//99
	Flagstaff MSA, AZ-UT	S	16.85 MW	12.82 AW	35040 AAW	AZBLS	10//99-12//99
	Phoenix-Mesa MSA, AZ	S	21.27 MW	15.75 AW	44230 AAW	AZBLS	10//99-12//99
	Tucson MSA, AZ	S	17.68 MW	12.92 AW	36780 AAW	AZBLS	10//99-12//99
	Arkansas	S	12.72 MW	15.67 AW	32600 AAW	ARBLS	10//99-12//99
	Fayetteville-Springdale-Rogers MSA, AR	S	12.63 MW	10.87 AW	26280 AAW	ARBLS	10//99-12//99
	Fort Smith MSA, AR-OK	S	14.20 MW	11.85 AW	29530 AAW	ARBLS	10//99-12//99
	Little Rock-North Little Rock MSA, AR	S	21.73 MW	19.27 AW	45200 AAW	ARBLS	10//99-12//99
	California	S	18.79 MW	22.51 AW	46830 AAW	CABLS	10//99-12//99
	Bakersfield MSA, CA	S	16.69 MW	14.71 AW	34710 AAW	CABLS	10//99-12//99
	Chico-Paradise MSA, CA	S	16.60 MW	14.33 AW	34540 AAW	CABLS	10//99-12//99
	Fresno MSA, CA	S	18.95 MW	14.80 AW	39430 AAW	CABLS	10//99-12//99
	Los Angeles-Long Beach PMSA, CA	S	24.57 MW	20.19 AW	51100 AAW	CABLS	10//99-12//99
	Modesto MSA, CA	S	20.22 MW	14.44 AW	42070 AAW	CABLS	10//99-12//99
	Oakland PMSA, CA	S	21.46 MW	17.64 AW	44640 AAW	CABLS	10//99-12//99
	Orange County PMSA, CA	S	23.75 MW	22.07 AW	49400 AAW	CABLS	10//99-12//99
	Redding MSA, CA	S	20.78 MW	18.06 AW	43220 AAW	CABLS	10//99-12//99
	Riverside-San Bernardino PMSA, CA	S	15.30 MW	11.95 AW	31820 AAW	CABLS	10//99-12//99
	Sacramento PMSA, CA	S	19.14 MW	17.15 AW	39820 AAW	CABLS	10//99-12//99
	Salinas MSA, CA	S	18.39 MW	16.50 AW	38240 AAW	CABLS	10//99-12//99
	San Diego MSA, CA	S	23.36 MW	18.87 AW	48580 AAW	CABLS	10//99-12//99
	San Francisco PMSA, CA	S	25.86 MW	22.01 AW	53790 AAW	CABLS	10//99-12//99
	San Jose PMSA, CA	S	23.74 MW	20.77 AW	49370 AAW	CABLS	10//99-12//99
	San Luis Obispo-Atascadero-Paso Robles MSA, CA	S	17.38 MW	13.07 AW	36150 AAW	CABLS	10//99-12//99
	Santa Barbara-Santa Maria-Lompoc MSA, CA	S	20.17 MW	17.80 AW	41950 AAW	CABLS	10//99-12//99
	Santa Cruz-Watsonville PMSA, CA	S	18.85 MW	19.57 AW	39200 AAW	CABLS	10//99-12//99
	Santa Rosa PMSA, CA	S	17.22 MW	13.71 AW	35810 AAW	CABLS	10//99-12//99
	Stockton-Lodi MSA, CA	S	17.10 MW	14.91 AW	35570 AAW	CABLS	10//99-12//99
	Vallejo-Fairfield-Napa PMSA, CA	S	12.61 MW	8.41 AW	26240 AAW	CABLS	10//99-12//99
	Ventura PMSA, CA	S	16.85 MW	13.57 AW	35040 AAW	CABLS	10//99-12//99
	Visalia-Tulare-Porterville MSA, CA	S	17.79 MW	12.73 AW	36990 AAW	CABLS	10//99-12//99
	Colorado	S	16.36 MW	19.29 AW	40130 AAW	COBLS	10//99-12//99
	Boulder-Longmont PMSA, CO	S	15.61 MW	13.35 AW	32470 AAW	COBLS	10//99-12//99
	Denver PMSA, CO	S	20.08 MW	17.33 AW	41780 AAW	COBLS	10//99-12//99
	Grand Junction MSA, CO	S	13.01 MW	10.88 AW	27070 AAW	COBLS	10//99-12//99

AAW Average annual wage	**AOH** Average offered, high	**ASH** Average starting, high	**H** Hourly	**M** Monthly	**S** Special: hourly and annual
AE Average entry wage	**AOL** Average offered, low	**ASL** Average starting, low	**HI** Highest wage paid	**MTC** Median total compensation	**TQ** Third quartile wage
AEX Average experienced wage	**APH** Average pay, high range	**AW** Average wage paid	**HR** High end range	**MW** Median wage paid	**W** Weekly
AO Average offered	**APL** Average pay, low range	**FQ** First quartile wage	**LR** Low end range	**SQ** Second quartile wage	**Y** Yearly

Occupation/Type/Industry	Location	Per	Low	Mid	High	Source	Date
Advertising Sales Agent	Greeley PMSA, CO	S	17.19 MW	14.73 AW	35750 AAW	COBLS	10//99-12//99
	Connecticut	S	17.3 MW	22.49 AW	46780 AAW	CTBLS	10//99-12//99
	Bridgeport PMSA, CT	S	27.08 MW	20.80 AW	56320 AAW	CTBLS	10//99-12//99
	Danbury PMSA, CT	S	20.14 MW	18.97 AW	41890 AAW	CTBLS	10//99-12//99
	Hartford MSA, CT	S	23.45 MW	19.29 AW	48780 AAW	CTBLS	10//99-12//99
	New Haven-Meriden PMSA, CT	S	19.91 MW	15.44 AW	41410 AAW	CTBLS	10//99-12//99
	New London-Norwich MSA, CT-RI	S	19.03 MW	15.45 AW	39570 AAW	CTBLS	10//99-12//99
	Stamford-Norwalk PMSA, CT	S	22.93 MW	17.77 AW	47700 AAW	CTBLS	10//99-12//99
	Waterbury PMSA, CT	S	21.06 MW	14.84 AW	43800 AAW	CTBLS	10//99-12//99
	Delaware	S	15.89 MW	20.46 AW	42550 AAW	DEBLS	10//99-12//99
	Dover MSA, DE	S	14.62 MW	14.03 AW	30400 AAW	DEBLS	10//99-12//99
	Wilmington-Newark PMSA, DE-MD	S	24.29 MW	20.68 AW	50530 AAW	DEBLS	10//99-12//99
	District of Columbia	S	19.22 MW	23.44 AW	48760 AAW	DCBLS	10//99-12//99
	Washington PMSA, DC-MD-VA-WV	S	32.78 MW	24.20 AW	68190 AAW	DCBLS	10//99-12//99
	Florida	S	15.9 MW	19.74 AW	41050 AAW	FLBLS	10//99-12//99
	Daytona Beach MSA, FL	S	16.30 MW	13.66 AW	33900 AAW	FLBLS	10//99-12//99
	Fort Lauderdale PMSA, FL	S	19.48 MW	16.44 AW	40520 AAW	FLBLS	10//99-12//99
	Fort Myers-Cape Coral MSA, FL	S	19.07 MW	15.12 AW	39660 AAW	FLBLS	10//99-12//99
	Fort Walton Beach MSA, FL	S	17.50 MW	12.60 AW	36390 AAW	FLBLS	10//99-12//99
	Gainesville MSA, FL	S	22.41 MW	16.59 AW	46620 AAW	FLBLS	10//99-12//99
	Jacksonville MSA, FL	S	25.31 MW	21.60 AW	52640 AAW	FLBLS	10//99-12//99
	Lakeland-Winter Haven MSA, FL	S	13.50 MW	10.23 AW	28070 AAW	FLBLS	10//99-12//99
	Melbourne-Titusville-Palm Bay MSA, FL	S	19.92 MW	16.98 AW	41430 AAW	FLBLS	10//99-12//99
	Miami PMSA, FL	S	22.14 MW	16.72 AW	46060 AAW	FLBLS	10//99-12//99
	Ocala MSA, FL	S	14.72 MW	12.06 AW	30610 AAW	FLBLS	10//99-12//99
	Orlando MSA, FL	S	19.08 MW	14.51 AW	39680 AAW	FLBLS	10//99-12//99
	Panama City MSA, FL	S	16.71 MW	17.39 AW	34750 AAW	FLBLS	10//99-12//99
	Pensacola MSA, FL	S	18.21 MW	17.94 AW	37880 AAW	FLBLS	10//99-12//99
	Sarasota-Bradenton MSA, FL	S	17.26 MW	15.31 AW	35900 AAW	FLBLS	10//99-12//99
	Tallahassee MSA, FL	S	16.68 MW	16.97 AW	34700 AAW	FLBLS	10//99-12//99
	Tampa-St. Petersburg-Clearwater MSA, FL	S	19.43 MW	15.91 AW	40410 AAW	FLBLS	10//99-12//99
	West Palm Beach-Boca Raton MSA, FL	S	17.13 MW	13.09 AW	35630 AAW	FLBLS	10//99-12//99
	Georgia	S	15.43 MW	17.77 AW	36970 AAW	GABLS	10//99-12//99
	Albany MSA, GA	S	14.19 MW	13.45 AW	29520 AAW	GABLS	10//99-12//99
	Athens MSA, GA	S	14.52 MW	12.53 AW	30210 AAW	GABLS	10//99-12//99
	Atlanta MSA, GA	S	19.23 MW	16.37 AW	40000 AAW	GABLS	10//99-12//99
	Augusta-Aiken MSA, GA-SC	S	16.89 MW	14.82 AW	35130 AAW	GABLS	10//99-12//99
	Columbus MSA, GA-AL	S	15.13 MW	13.77 AW	31470 AAW	GABLS	10//99-12//99
	Macon MSA, GA	S	14.47 MW	13.27 AW	30100 AAW	GABLS	10//99-12//99
	Savannah MSA, GA	S	18.34 MW	15.65 AW	38140 AAW	GABLS	10//99-12//99
	Hawaii	S	9.89 MW	14.00 AW	29120 AAW	HIBLS	10//99-12//99
	Honolulu MSA, HI	S	13.40 MW	8.42 AW	27860 AAW	HIBLS	10//99-12//99
	Idaho	S	12.21 MW	14.88 AW	30950 AAW	IDBLS	10//99-12//99
	Boise City MSA, ID	S	14.20 MW	11.36 AW	29530 AAW	IDBLS	10//99-12//99
	Pocatello MSA, ID	S	15.33 MW	13.98 AW	31880 AAW	IDBLS	10//99-12//99
	Illinois	S	15.83 MW	18.86 AW	39220 AAW	ILBLS	10//99-12//99
	Bloomington-Normal MSA, IL	S	17.16 MW	15.86 AW	35700 AAW	ILBLS	10//99-12//99
	Champaign-Urbana MSA, IL	S	14.63 MW	12.68 AW	30430 AAW	ILBLS	10//99-12//99
	Chicago PMSA, IL	S	20.73 MW	17.67 AW	43110 AAW	ILBLS	10//99-12//99
	Peoria-Pekin MSA, IL	S	14.94 MW	14.21 AW	31080 AAW	ILBLS	10//99-12//99
	Rockford MSA, IL	S	16.69 MW	12.92 AW	34720 AAW	ILBLS	10//99-12//99
	Springfield MSA, IL	S	15.09 MW	14.05 AW	31390 AAW	ILBLS	10//99-12//99
	Indiana	S	13.4 MW	16.13 AW	33550 AAW	INBLS	10//99-12//99
	Bloomington MSA, IN	S	15.85 MW	13.60 AW	32960 AAW	INBLS	10//99-12//99
	Evansville-Henderson MSA, IN-KY	S	15.23 MW	13.34 AW	31670 AAW	INBLS	10//99-12//99
	Fort Wayne MSA, IN	S	17.24 MW	15.53 AW	35860 AAW	INBLS	10//99-12//99
	Gary PMSA, IN	S	14.39 MW	12.02 AW	29920 AAW	INBLS	10//99-12//99
	Indianapolis MSA, IN	S	18.17 MW	14.35 AW	37800 AAW	INBLS	10//99-12//99
	Lafayette MSA, IN	S	15.53 MW	14.21 AW	32300 AAW	INBLS	10//99-12//99
	Muncie MSA, IN	S	17.65 MW	13.53 AW	36700 AAW	INBLS	10//99-12//99
	South Bend MSA, IN	S	19.11 MW	16.01 AW	39740 AAW	INBLS	10//99-12//99
	Iowa	S	13.08 MW	14.82 AW	30820 AAW	IABLS	10//99-12//99

AAW Average annual wage	**AOH** Average offered, high	**ASH** Average starting, high	**H** Hourly	**M** Monthly	**S** Special: hourly and annual
AE Average entry wage	**AOL** Average offered, low	**ASL** Average starting, low	**HI** Highest wage paid	**MTC** Median total compensation	**TQ** Third quartile wage
AEX Average experienced wage	**APH** Average pay, high range	**AW** Average wage paid	**HR** High end range	**MW** Median wage paid	**W** Weekly
AO Average offered	**APL** Average pay, low range	**FQ** First quartile wage	**LR** Low end range	**SQ** Second quartile wage	**Y** Yearly

Occupation/Type/Industry	Location	Per	Low	Mid	High	Source	Date
Advertising Sales Agent	Davenport-Moline-Rock Island MSA, IA-IL	S	14.08 MW	12.57 AW	29280 AAW	IABLS	10//99-12//99
	Des Moines MSA, IA	S	18.55 MW	16.76 AW	38580 AAW	IABLS	10//99-12//99
	Dubuque MSA, IA	S	12.54 MW	12.61 AW	26080 AAW	IABLS	10//99-12//99
	Iowa City MSA, IA	S	10.57 MW	10.10 AW	21980 AAW	IABLS	10//99-12//99
	Sioux City MSA, IA-NE	S	16.74 MW	16.30 AW	34810 AAW	IABLS	10//99-12//99
	Waterloo-Cedar Falls MSA, IA	S	16.63 MW	13.44 AW	34600 AAW	IABLS	10//99-12//99
	Kansas	S	13.79 MW	17.83 AW	37080 AAW	KSBLS	10//99-12//99
	Topeka MSA, KS	S	17.56 MW	17.33 AW	36510 AAW	KSBLS	10//99-12//99
	Wichita MSA, KS	S	17.12 MW	13.38 AW	35610 AAW	KSBLS	10//99-12//99
	Kentucky	S	13.2 MW	15.78 AW	32830 AAW	KYBLS	10//99-12//99
	Lexington MSA, KY	S	17.76 MW	13.68 AW	36950 AAW	KYBLS	10//99-12//99
	Louisville MSA, KY-IN	S	17.24 MW	14.21 AW	35860 AAW	KYBLS	10//99-12//99
	Owensboro MSA, KY	S	12.06 MW	11.74 AW	25080 AAW	KYBLS	10//99-12//99
	Louisiana	S	13.63 MW	15.98 AW	33230 AAW	LABLS	10//99-12//99
	Baton Rouge MSA, LA	S	14.62 MW	11.59 AW	30400 AAW	LABLS	10//99-12//99
	Houma MSA, LA	S	14.46 MW	11.93 AW	30080 AAW	LABLS	10//99-12//99
	Lafayette MSA, LA	S	14.50 MW	11.96 AW	30150 AAW	LABLS	10//99-12//99
	Lake Charles MSA, LA	S	12.06 MW	9.76 AW	25090 AAW	LABLS	10//99-12//99
	Monroe MSA, LA	S	15.37 MW	13.70 AW	31960 AAW	LABLS	10//99-12//99
	New Orleans MSA, LA	S	18.64 MW	17.22 AW	38780 AAW	LABLS	10//99-12//99
	Shreveport-Bossier City MSA, LA	S	15.10 MW	12.46 AW	31400 AAW	LABLS	10//99-12//99
	Maine	S	14.12 MW	16.23 AW	33760 AAW	MEBLS	10//99-12//99
	Bangor MSA, ME	S	18.22 MW	15.96 AW	37900 AAW	MEBLS	10//99-12//99
	Portland MSA, ME	S	20.25 MW	16.59 AW	42130 AAW	MEBLS	10//99-12//99
	Maryland	S	16.29 MW	19.56 AW	40680 AAW	MDBLS	10//99-12//99
	Baltimore PMSA, MD	S	18.99 MW	15.69 AW	39510 AAW	MDBLS	10//99-12//99
	Cumberland MSA, MD-WV	S	16.90 MW	14.92 AW	35160 AAW	MDBLS	10//99-12//99
	Hagerstown PMSA, MD	S	18.45 MW	15.58 AW	38370 AAW	MDBLS	10//99-12//99
	Massachusetts	S	17.85 MW	22.08 AW	45920 AAW	MABLS	10//99-12//99
	Boston PMSA, MA-NH	S	22.41 MW	17.86 AW	46620 AAW	MABLS	10//99-12//99
	Brockton PMSA, MA	S	19.61 MW	19.20 AW	40800 AAW	MABLS	10//99-12//99
	Lawrence PMSA, MA-NH	S	18.39 MW	16.14 AW	38250 AAW	MABLS	10//99-12//99
	Lowell PMSA, MA-NH	S	24.76 MW	17.38 AW	51490 AAW	MABLS	10//99-12//99
	New Bedford PMSA, MA	S	19.09 MW	15.66 AW	39710 AAW	MABLS	10//99-12//99
	Springfield MSA, MA	S	18.47 MW	15.25 AW	38410 AAW	MABLS	10//99-12//99
	Michigan	S	15.28 MW	21.60 AW	44930 AAW	MIBLS	10//99-12//99
	Ann Arbor PMSA, MI	S	19.37 MW	16.49 AW	40280 AAW	MIBLS	10//99-12//99
	Benton Harbor MSA, MI	S	16.36 MW	13.48 AW	34020 AAW	MIBLS	10//99-12//99
	Detroit PMSA, MI	S	22.71 MW	16.52 AW	47230 AAW	MIBLS	10//99-12//99
	Flint PMSA, MI	S	16.34 MW	13.69 AW	33990 AAW	MIBLS	10//99-12//99
	Grand Rapids-Muskegon-Holland MSA, MI	S	19.22 MW	14.56 AW	39990 AAW	MIBLS	10//99-12//99
	Kalamazoo-Battle Creek MSA, MI	S	19.12 MW	16.00 AW	39760 AAW	MIBLS	10//99-12//99
	Lansing-East Lansing MSA, MI	S	22.00 MW	18.99 AW	45760 AAW	MIBLS	10//99-12//99
	Saginaw-Bay City-Midland MSA, MI	S	19.74 MW	16.57 AW	41050 AAW	MIBLS	10//99-12//99
	Minnesota	S	17.06 MW	21.13 AW	43960 AAW	MNBLS	10//99-12//99
	Minneapolis-St. Paul MSA, MN-WI	S	22.67 MW	19.62 AW	47150 AAW	MNBLS	10//99-12//99
	Rochester MSA, MN	S	16.94 MW	13.74 AW	35240 AAW	MNBLS	10//99-12//99
	St. Cloud MSA, MN	S	15.93 MW	12.39 AW	33130 AAW	MNBLS	10//99-12//99
	Mississippi	S	12.14 MW	14.72 AW	30620 AAW	MSBLS	10//99-12//99
	Biloxi-Gulfport-Pascagoula MSA, MS	S	14.68 MW	12.50 AW	30540 AAW	MSBLS	10//99-12//99
	Jackson MSA, MS	S	20.07 MW	17.57 AW	41750 AAW	MSBLS	10//99-12//99
	Missouri	S	12.11 MW	15.35 AW	31940 AAW	MOBLS	10//99-12//99
	Columbia MSA, MO	S	14.47 MW	11.69 AW	30100 AAW	MOBLS	10//99-12//99
	Joplin MSA, MO	S	16.37 MW	12.21 AW	34060 AAW	MOBLS	10//99-12//99
	Kansas City MSA, MO-KS	S	17.71 MW	13.69 AW	36840 AAW	MOBLS	10//99-12//99
	St. Joseph MSA, MO	S	14.29 MW	13.74 AW	29720 AAW	MOBLS	10//99-12//99
	St. Louis MSA, MO-IL	S	17.83 MW	14.37 AW	37080 AAW	MOBLS	10//99-12//99
	Springfield MSA, MO	S	15.01 MW	12.72 AW	31210 AAW	MOBLS	10//99-12//99
	Montana	S	11.94 MW	14.19 AW	29510 AAW	MTBLS	10//99-12//99
	Billings MSA, MT	S	14.92 MW	12.98 AW	31040 AAW	MTBLS	10//99-12//99
	Great Falls MSA, MT	S	12.77 MW	11.59 AW	26550 AAW	MTBLS	10//99-12//99
	Missoula MSA, MT	S	14.79 MW	12.23 AW	30770 AAW	MTBLS	10//99-12//99
	Nebraska	S	14.71 MW	17.92 AW	37270 AAW	NEBLS	10//99-12//99
	Lincoln MSA, NE	S	16.82 MW	15.00 AW	34990 AAW	NEBLS	10//99-12//99
	Omaha MSA, NE-IA	S	21.65 MW	18.33 AW	45030 AAW	NEBLS	10//99-12//99

AAW	Average annual wage	AOH	Average offered, high	ASH	Average starting, high	H	Hourly	M	Monthly	S	Special: hourly and annual
AE	Average entry wage	AOL	Average offered, low	ASL	Average starting, low	HI	Highest wage paid	MTC	Median total compensation	TQ	Third quartile wage
AEX	Average experienced wage	APH	Average pay, high range	AW	Average wage paid	HR	High end range	MW	Median wage paid	W	Weekly
AO	Average offered	APL	Average pay, low range	FQ	First quartile wage	LR	Low end range	SQ	Second quartile wage	Y	Yearly

23

Occupation/Type/Industry	Location	Per	Low	Mid	High	Source	Date
Advertising Sales Agent	Nevada	S	17.86 MW	22.46 AW	46720 AAW	NVBLS	10//99-12//99
	Las Vegas MSA, NV-AZ	S	21.79 MW	15.99 AW	45330 AAW	NVBLS	10//99-12//99
	Reno MSA, NV	S	21.61 MW	18.82 AW	44950 AAW	NVBLS	10//99-12//99
	New Hampshire	S	15.19 MW	18.43 AW	38340 AAW	NHBLS	10//99-12//99
	Manchester PMSA, NH	S	19.88 MW	17.54 AW	41350 AAW	NHBLS	10//99-12//99
	Nashua PMSA, NH	S	18.21 MW	18.10 AW	37880 AAW	NHBLS	10//99-12//99
	Portsmouth-Rochester PMSA, NH-ME	S	17.44 MW	15.32 AW	36270 AAW	NHBLS	10//99-12//99
	New Jersey	S	18.63 MW	21.99 AW	45740 AAW	NJBLS	10//99-12//99
	Atlantic-Cape May PMSA, NJ	S	21.31 MW	19.61 AW	44320 AAW	NJBLS	10//99-12//99
	Bergen-Passaic PMSA, NJ	S	24.44 MW	19.76 AW	50840 AAW	NJBLS	10//99-12//99
	Jersey City PMSA, NJ	S	25.36 MW	20.25 AW	52740 AAW	NJBLS	10//99-12//99
	Middlesex-Somerset-Hunterdon PMSA, NJ	S	19.03 MW	17.34 AW	39590 AAW	NJBLS	10//99-12//99
	Monmouth-Ocean PMSA, NJ	S	19.06 MW	15.83 AW	39640 AAW	NJBLS	10//99-12//99
	Newark PMSA, NJ	S	22.53 MW	19.13 AW	46870 AAW	NJBLS	10//99-12//99
	Trenton PMSA, NJ	S	22.66 MW	20.05 AW	47120 AAW	NJBLS	10//99-12//99
	New Mexico	S	12.89 MW	15.13 AW	31470 AAW	NMBLS	10//99-12//99
	Albuquerque MSA, NM	S	17.26 MW	15.36 AW	35890 AAW	NMBLS	10//99-12//99
	Santa Fe MSA, NM	S	14.07 MW	12.96 AW	29260 AAW	NMBLS	10//99-12//99
	New York	S	22.22 MW	27.01 AW	56190 AAW	NYBLS	10//99-12//99
	Albany-Schenectady-Troy MSA, NY	S	19.98 MW	15.68 AW	41570 AAW	NYBLS	10//99-12//99
	Binghamton MSA, NY	S	15.29 MW	11.35 AW	31800 AAW	NYBLS	10//99-12//99
	Buffalo-Niagara Falls MSA, NY	S	21.80 MW	20.02 AW	45340 AAW	NYBLS	10//99-12//99
	Dutchess County PMSA, NY	S	19.71 MW	14.52 AW	41000 AAW	NYBLS	10//99-12//99
	Glens Falls MSA, NY	S	16.69 MW	12.86 AW	34710 AAW	NYBLS	10//99-12//99
	Nassau-Suffolk PMSA, NY	S	18.21 MW	14.96 AW	37880 AAW	NYBLS	10//99-12//99
	New York PMSA, NY	S	30.95 MW	27.40 AW	64380 AAW	NYBLS	10//99-12//99
	Newburgh PMSA, NY-PA	S	15.46 MW	13.39 AW	32150 AAW	NYBLS	10//99-12//99
	Rochester MSA, NY	S	21.72 MW	19.28 AW	45180 AAW	NYBLS	10//99-12//99
	Syracuse MSA, NY	S	16.88 MW	15.48 AW	35100 AAW	NYBLS	10//99-12//99
	Utica-Rome MSA, NY	S	14.28 MW	10.89 AW	29710 AAW	NYBLS	10//99-12//99
	North Carolina	S	14.52 MW	17.66 AW	36740 AAW	NCBLS	10//99-12//99
	Asheville MSA, NC	S	16.17 MW	12.43 AW	33640 AAW	NCBLS	10//99-12//99
	Charlotte-Gastonia-Rock Hill MSA, NC-SC	S	22.53 MW	20.00 AW	46860 AAW	NCBLS	10//99-12//99
	Fayetteville MSA, NC	S	17.41 MW	14.27 AW	36220 AAW	NCBLS	10//99-12//99
	Goldsboro MSA, NC	S	10.96 MW	9.75 AW	22790 AAW	NCBLS	10//99-12//99
	Greensboro--Winston-Salem--High Point MSA, NC	S	19.76 MW	16.48 AW	41110 AAW	NCBLS	10//99-12//99
	Hickory-Morganton-Lenoir MSA, NC	S	16.56 MW	15.94 AW	34450 AAW	NCBLS	10//99-12//99
	Raleigh-Durham-Chapel Hill MSA, NC	S	15.70 MW	13.05 AW	32650 AAW	NCBLS	10//99-12//99
	Wilmington MSA, NC	S	13.42 MW	12.02 AW	27920 AAW	NCBLS	10//99-12//99
	North Dakota	S	11.87 MW	13.62 AW	28330 AAW	NDBLS	10//99-12//99
	Bismarck MSA, ND	S	17.22 MW	14.93 AW	35820 AAW	NDBLS	10//99-12//99
	Fargo-Moorhead MSA, ND-MN	S	14.93 MW	12.79 AW	31050 AAW	NDBLS	10//99-12//99
	Grand Forks MSA, ND-MN	S	14.26 MW	13.87 AW	29650 AAW	NDBLS	10//99-12//99
	Ohio	S	15.69 MW	17.67 AW	36750 AAW	OHBLS	10//99-12//99
	Akron PMSA, OH	S	21.96 MW	18.73 AW	45670 AAW	OHBLS	10//99-12//99
	Canton-Massillon MSA, OH	S	10.78 MW	9.87 AW	22420 AAW	OHBLS	10//99-12//99
	Cincinnati PMSA, OH-KY-IN	S	19.61 MW	16.94 AW	40790 AAW	OHBLS	10//99-12//99
	Cleveland-Lorain-Elyria PMSA, OH	S	18.58 MW	16.91 AW	38640 AAW	OHBLS	10//99-12//99
	Columbus MSA, OH	S	20.32 MW	17.25 AW	42270 AAW	OHBLS	10//99-12//99
	Dayton-Springfield MSA, OH	S	15.71 MW	12.11 AW	32680 AAW	OHBLS	10//99-12//99
	Hamilton-Middletown PMSA, OH	S	16.19 MW	13.52 AW	33680 AAW	OHBLS	10//99-12//99
	Lima MSA, OH	S	12.22 MW	11.33 AW	25410 AAW	OHBLS	10//99-12//99
	Mansfield MSA, OH	S	21.31 MW	16.47 AW	44330 AAW	OHBLS	10//99-12//99
	Steubenville-Weirton MSA, OH-WV	S	14.66 MW	12.47 AW	30500 AAW	OHBLS	10//99-12//99
	Toledo MSA, OH	S	18.71 MW	17.08 AW	38920 AAW	OHBLS	10//99-12//99
	Youngstown-Warren MSA, OH	S	16.67 MW	14.80 AW	34680 AAW	OHBLS	10//99-12//99
	Oklahoma	S	13.82 MW	16.90 AW	35140 AAW	OKBLS	10//99-12//99
	Oklahoma City MSA, OK	S	15.85 MW	13.30 AW	32960 AAW	OKBLS	10//99-12//99
	Tulsa MSA, OK	S	19.44 MW	18.32 AW	40430 AAW	OKBLS	10//99-12//99
	Oregon	S	14.17 MW	15.86 AW	32990 AAW	ORBLS	10//99-12//99

AAW Average annual wage	AOH Average offered, high	ASH Average starting, high	H Hourly	M Monthly	S Special: hourly and annual
AE Average entry wage	AOL Average offered, low	ASL Average starting, low	HI Highest wage paid	MTC Median total compensation	TQ Third quartile wage
AEX Average experienced wage APH Average pay, high range	AW Average wage paid	HR High end range	MW Median wage paid	W Weekly
AO Average offered	APL Average pay, low range	FQ First quartile wage	LR Low end range	SQ Second quartile wage	Y Yearly

Occupation/Type/Industry	Location	Per	Low	Mid	High	Source	Date
Advertising Sales Agent	Eugene-Springfield MSA, OR	S	17.69 MW	15.89 AW	36800 AAW	ORBLS	10//99-12//99
	Portland-Vancouver PMSA, OR-WA	S	16.96 MW	16.38 AW	35270 AAW	ORBLS	10//99-12//99
	Salem PMSA, OR	S	14.30 MW	12.49 AW	29750 AAW	ORBLS	10//99-12//99
	Pennsylvania	S	13.85 MW	16.12 AW	33530 AAW	PABLS	10//99-12//99
	Allentown-Bethlehem-Easton MSA, PA	S	15.83 MW	13.91 AW	32930 AAW	PABLS	10//99-12//99
	Erie MSA, PA	S	13.43 MW	12.04 AW	27940 AAW	PABLS	10//99-12//99
	Harrisburg-Lebanon-Carlisle MSA, PA	S	15.86 MW	13.29 AW	32980 AAW	PABLS	10//99-12//99
	Johnstown MSA, PA	S	12.35 MW	9.94 AW	25700 AAW	PABLS	10//99-12//99
	Lancaster MSA, PA	S	17.83 MW	16.88 AW	37080 AAW	PABLS	10//99-12//99
	Philadelphia PMSA, PA-NJ	S	18.25 MW	15.71 AW	37960 AAW	PABLS	10//99-12//99
	Pittsburgh MSA, PA	S	16.44 MW	14.46 AW	34200 AAW	PABLS	10//99-12//99
	Reading MSA, PA	S	16.85 MW	14.77 AW	35040 AAW	PABLS	10//99-12//99
	Scranton--Wilkes-Barre--Hazleton MSA, PA	S	13.97 MW	12.97 AW	29050 AAW	PABLS	10//99-12//99
	Williamsport MSA, PA	S	16.50 MW	15.21 AW	34320 AAW	PABLS	10//99-12//99
	York MSA, PA	S	12.73 MW	11.17 AW	26470 AAW	PABLS	10//99-12//99
	Rhode Island	S	13.74 MW	17.91 AW	37250 AAW	RIBLS	10//99-12//99
	Providence-Fall River-Warwick MSA, RI-MA	S	18.22 MW	14.04 AW	37900 AAW	RIBLS	10//99-12//99
	South Carolina	S	13.16 MW	15.72 AW	32710 AAW	SCBLS	10//99-12//99
	Charleston-North Charleston MSA, SC	S	15.73 MW	13.62 AW	32730 AAW	SCBLS	10//99-12//99
	Columbia MSA, SC	S	15.55 MW	12.40 AW	32340 AAW	SCBLS	10//99-12//99
	Greenville-Spartanburg-Anderson MSA, SC	S	16.72 MW	12.86 AW	34770 AAW	SCBLS	10//99-12//99
	Myrtle Beach MSA, SC	S	14.79 MW	13.74 AW	30770 AAW	SCBLS	10//99-12//99
	South Dakota	S	13.42 MW	14.99 AW	31190 AAW	SDBLS	10//99-12//99
	Rapid City MSA, SD	S	15.40 MW	14.10 AW	32030 AAW	SDBLS	10//99-12//99
	Sioux Falls MSA, SD	S	18.19 MW	17.59 AW	37830 AAW	SDBLS	10//99-12//99
	Tennessee	S	12.66 MW	15.91 AW	33100 AAW	TNBLS	10//99-12//99
	Chattanooga MSA, TN-GA	S	18.22 MW	15.01 AW	37900 AAW	TNBLS	10//99-12//99
	Jackson MSA, TN	S	13.78 MW	10.22 AW	28660 AAW	TNBLS	10//99-12//99
	Johnson City-Kingsport-Bristol MSA, TN-VA	S	13.64 MW	10.42 AW	28370 AAW	TNBLS	10//99-12//99
	Knoxville MSA, TN	S	18.23 MW	16.06 AW	37920 AAW	TNBLS	10//99-12//99
	Memphis MSA, TN-AR-MS	S	18.89 MW	16.48 AW	39290 AAW	MSBLS	10//99-12//99
	Nashville MSA, TN	S	17.09 MW	13.47 AW	35550 AAW	TNBLS	10//99-12//99
	Texas	S	15.15 MW	18.13 AW	37710 AAW	TXBLS	10//99-12//99
	Abilene MSA, TX	S	13.80 MW	12.39 AW	28700 AAW	TXBLS	10//99-12//99
	Amarillo MSA, TX	S	16.40 MW	15.29 AW	34110 AAW	TXBLS	10//99-12//99
	Austin-San Marcos MSA, TX	S	19.81 MW	16.73 AW	41200 AAW	TXBLS	10//99-12//99
	Beaumont-Port Arthur MSA, TX	S	15.89 MW	12.61 AW	33060 AAW	TXBLS	10//99-12//99
	Brownsville-Harlingen-San Benito MSA, TX	S	15.65 MW	13.92 AW	32550 AAW	TXBLS	10//99-12//99
	Corpus Christi MSA, TX	S	20.60 MW	18.41 AW	42840 AAW	TXBLS	10//99-12//99
	Dallas PMSA, TX	S	21.06 MW	17.30 AW	43790 AAW	TXBLS	10//99-12//99
	El Paso MSA, TX	S	20.43 MW	16.91 AW	42500 AAW	TXBLS	10//99-12//99
	Fort Worth-Arlington PMSA, TX	S	15.13 MW	12.73 AW	31470 AAW	TXBLS	10//99-12//99
	Houston PMSA, TX	S	17.52 MW	14.15 AW	36450 AAW	TXBLS	10//99-12//99
	Killeen-Temple MSA, TX	S	15.61 MW	14.64 AW	32470 AAW	TXBLS	10//99-12//99
	Laredo MSA, TX	S	16.82 MW	14.59 AW	34990 AAW	TXBLS	10//99-12//99
	Lubbock MSA, TX	S	17.31 MW	15.04 AW	36010 AAW	TXBLS	10//99-12//99
	McAllen-Edinburg-Mission MSA, TX	S	16.00 MW	13.53 AW	33280 AAW	TXBLS	10//99-12//99
	Odessa-Midland MSA, TX	S	19.93 MW	16.93 AW	41460 AAW	TXBLS	10//99-12//99
	San Angelo MSA, TX	S	13.03 MW	12.00 AW	27110 AAW	TXBLS	10//99-12//99
	San Antonio MSA, TX	S	19.15 MW	16.90 AW	39840 AAW	TXBLS	10//99-12//99
	Tyler MSA, TX	S	18.18 MW	14.94 AW	37800 AAW	TXBLS	10//99-12//99
	Victoria MSA, TX	S	22.58 MW	27.59 AW	46970 AAW	TXBLS	10//99-12//99
	Wichita Falls MSA, TX	S	14.24 MW	13.24 AW	29610 AAW	TXBLS	10//99-12//99
	Utah	S	14.4 MW	17.50 AW	36390 AAW	UTBLS	10//99-12//99
	Provo-Orem MSA, UT	S	14.32 MW	12.52 AW	29790 AAW	UTBLS	10//99-12//99
	Salt Lake City-Ogden MSA, UT	S	18.52 MW	14.89 AW	38510 AAW	UTBLS	10//99-12//99
	Vermont	S	13.71 MW	15.33 AW	31890 AAW	VTBLS	10//99-12//99
	Burlington MSA, VT	S	17.63 MW	15.28 AW	36670 AAW	VTBLS	10//99-12//99
	Virginia	S	16.07 MW	26.55 AW	55220 AAW	VABLS	10//99-12//99

AAW	Average annual wage	AOH	Average offered, high	ASH	Average starting, high	H	Hourly	M	Monthly	S	Special: hourly and annual
AE	Average entry wage	AOL	Average offered, low	ASL	Average starting, low	HI	Highest wage paid	MTC	Median total compensation	TQ	Third quartile wage
AEX	Average experienced wage	APH	Average pay, high range	AW	Average wage paid	HR	High end range	MW	Median wage paid	W	Weekly
AO	Average offered	APL	Average pay, low range	FQ	First quartile wage	LR	Low end range	SQ	Second quartile wage	Y	Yearly

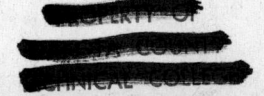

25

Occupation/Type/Industry	Location	Per	Low	Mid	High	Source	Date
Advertising Sales Agent	Lynchburg MSA, VA	S	13.80 MW	10.63 AW	28700 AAW	VABLS	10//99-12//99
	Norfolk-Virginia Beach-Newport News MSA, VA-NC	S	14.45 MW	11.31 AW	30070 AAW	VABLS	10//99-12//99
	Richmond-Petersburg MSA, VA	S	20.27 MW	15.35 AW	42170 AAW	VABLS	10//99-12//99
	Roanoke MSA, VA	S	14.55 MW	11.30 AW	30270 AAW	VABLS	10//99-12//99
	Washington	S	18.02 MW	20.73 AW	43110 AAW	WABLS	10//99-12//99
	Bellingham MSA, WA	S	18.18 MW	15.81 AW	37810 AAW	WABLS	10//99-12//99
	Bremerton PMSA, WA	S	21.14 MW	19.16 AW	43970 AAW	WABLS	10//99-12//99
	Olympia PMSA, WA	S	16.68 MW	15.57 AW	34700 AAW	WABLS	10//99-12//99
	Richland-Kennewick-Pasco MSA, WA	S	15.06 MW	14.51 AW	31320 AAW	WABLS	10//99-12//99
	Seattle-Bellevue-Everett PMSA, WA	S	23.71 MW	20.26 AW	49320 AAW	WABLS	10//99-12//99
	Spokane MSA, WA	S	15.39 MW	12.84 AW	32010 AAW	WABLS	10//99-12//99
	Tacoma PMSA, WA	S	17.94 MW	16.03 AW	37320 AAW	WABLS	10//99-12//99
	Yakima MSA, WA	S	18.83 MW	16.63 AW	39170 AAW	WABLS	10//99-12//99
	West Virginia	S	11.9 MW	14.31 AW	29770 AAW	WVBLS	10//99-12//99
	Charleston MSA, WV	S	18.46 MW	15.75 AW	38390 AAW	WVBLS	10//99-12//99
	Huntington-Ashland MSA, WV-KY-OH	S	14.04 MW	12.17 AW	29200 AAW	WVBLS	10//99-12//99
	Parkersburg-Marietta MSA, WV-OH	S	16.04 MW	14.36 AW	33360 AAW	WVBLS	10//99-12//99
	Wheeling MSA, WV-OH	S	14.41 MW	12.34 AW	29980 AAW	WVBLS	10//99-12//99
	Wisconsin	S	13.9 MW	16.52 AW	34360 AAW	WIBLS	10//99-12//99
	Appleton-Oshkosh-Neenah MSA, WI	S	17.27 MW	15.68 AW	35920 AAW	WIBLS	10//99-12//99
	Eau Claire MSA, WI	S	15.10 MW	14.51 AW	31410 AAW	WIBLS	10//99-12//99
	Green Bay MSA, WI	S	15.18 MW	11.65 AW	31560 AAW	WIBLS	10//99-12//99
	Janesville-Beloit MSA, WI	S	15.75 MW	14.44 AW	32770 AAW	WIBLS	10//99-12//99
	Kenosha PMSA, WI	S	18.06 MW	17.01 AW	37560 AAW	WIBLS	10//99-12//99
	La Crosse MSA, WI-MN	S	17.78 MW	15.26 AW	36990 AAW	WIBLS	10//99-12//99
	Madison MSA, WI	S	18.96 MW	16.89 AW	39440 AAW	WIBLS	10//99-12//99
	Milwaukee-Waukesha PMSA, WI	S	21.89 MW	19.50 AW	45530 AAW	WIBLS	10//99-12//99
	Wausau MSA, WI	S	15.17 MW	14.16 AW	31550 AAW	WIBLS	10//99-12//99
	Wyoming	S	8.72 MW	10.42 AW	21670 AAW	WYBLS	10//99-12//99
	Casper MSA, WY	S	10.29 MW	9.13 AW	21410 AAW	WYBLS	10//99-12//99
	Cheyenne MSA, WY	S	10.64 MW	8.52 AW	22130 AAW	WYBLS	10//99-12//99
	Puerto Rico	S	13.3 MW	15.99 AW	33270 AAW	PRBLS	10//99-12//99
	Caguas PMSA, PR	S	13.20 MW	11.35 AW	27450 AAW	PRBLS	10//99-12//99
	Ponce MSA, PR	S	13.08 MW	10.65 AW	27210 AAW	PRBLS	10//99-12//99
	San Juan-Bayamon PMSA, PR	S	16.55 MW	14.03 AW	34430 AAW	PRBLS	10//99-12//99
	Guam	S	11.2 MW	15.22 AW	31660 AAW	GUBLS	10//99-12//99
Advertising Sales Director Magazine	United States	Y		112000 AW		FOLIO	2000
Aerospace Engineer	Alabama	S	31.54 MW	31.33 AW	65170 AAW	ALBLS	10//99-12//99
	Huntsville MSA, AL	S	31.49 MW	31.66 AW	65510 AAW	ALBLS	10//99-12//99
	Arizona	S	23.52 MW	25.55 AW	53140 AAW	AZBLS	10//99-12//99
	Phoenix-Mesa MSA, AZ	S	27.48 MW	25.81 AW	57160 AAW	AZBLS	10//99-12//99
	Arkansas	S	28.58 MW	28.05 AW	58340 AAW	ARBLS	10//99-12//99
	California	S	33.37 MW	33.15 AW	68960 AAW	CABLS	10//99-12//99
	Los Angeles-Long Beach PMSA, CA	S	34.50 MW	32.76 AW	71770 AAW	CABLS	10//99-12//99
	Oakland PMSA, CA	S	36.47 MW	36.03 AW	75860 AAW	CABLS	10//99-12//99
	Riverside-San Bernardino PMSA, CA	S	32.43 MW	34.25 AW	67460 AAW	CABLS	10//99-12//99
	Sacramento PMSA, CA	S	29.72 MW	29.91 AW	61810 AAW	CABLS	10//99-12//99
	San Diego MSA, CA	S	31.68 MW	32.26 AW	65900 AAW	CABLS	10//99-12//99
	San Jose PMSA, CA	S	33.01 MW	35.01 AW	68660 AAW	CABLS	10//99-12//99
	Washington PMSA, DC-MD-VA-WV	S	32.70 MW	33.10 AW	68020 AAW	DCBLS	10//99-12//99
	Florida	S	24.92 MW	26.37 AW	54840 AAW	FLBLS	10//99-12//99
	Fort Lauderdale PMSA, FL	S	27.72 MW	24.86 AW	57660 AAW	FLBLS	10//99-12//99
	Melbourne-Titusville-Palm Bay MSA, FL	S	26.97 MW	24.99 AW	56090 AAW	FLBLS	10//99-12//99
	Miami PMSA, FL	S	24.88 MW	24.46 AW	51760 AAW	FLBLS	10//99-12//99
	Orlando MSA, FL	S	25.34 MW	24.24 AW	52720 AAW	FLBLS	10//99-12//99
	Tampa-St. Petersburg-Clearwater MSA, FL	S	31.23 MW	32.69 AW	64950 AAW	FLBLS	10//99-12//99

Occupation/Type/Industry	Location	Per	Low	Mid	High	Source	Date
Aerospace Engineer	West Palm Beach-Boca Raton MSA, FL	S	29.73 MW	28.46 AW	61830 AAW	FLBLS	10//99-12//99
	Georgia	S	45.15 MW	39.07 AW	81280 AAW	GABLS	10//99-12//99
	Atlanta MSA, GA	S	43.46 MW	50.26 AW	90390 AAW	GABLS	10//99-12//99
	Macon MSA, GA	S	29.24 MW	29.97 AW	60810 AAW	GABLS	10//99-12//99
	Savannah MSA, GA	S	31.65 MW	34.57 AW	65820 AAW	GABLS	10//99-12//99
	Illinois	S	24.47 MW	25.26 AW	52540 AAW	ILBLS	10//99-12//99
	Chicago PMSA, IL	S	24.85 MW	24.15 AW	51680 AAW	ILBLS	10//99-12//99
	Indiana	S	18.83 MW	20.36 AW	42350 AAW	INBLS	10//99-12//99
	Indianapolis MSA, IN	S	22.18 MW	22.42 AW	46130 AAW	INBLS	10//99-12//99
	Kansas	S	30.24 MW	32.08 AW	66730 AAW	KSBLS	10//99-12//99
	Baltimore PMSA, MD	S	31.50 MW	32.28 AW	65520 AAW	MDBLS	10//99-12//99
	Massachusetts	S	32.45 MW	33.14 AW	68940 AAW	MABLS	10//99-12//99
	Boston PMSA, MA-NH	S	34.38 MW	33.70 AW	71500 AAW	MABLS	10//99-12//99
	Michigan	S	25.1 MW	26.85 AW	55860 AAW	MIBLS	10//99-12//99
	Detroit PMSA, MI	S	26.47 MW	25.10 AW	55060 AAW	MIBLS	10//99-12//99
	Minnesota	S	32.42 MW	30.97 AW	64420 AAW	MNBLS	10//99-12//99
	Minneapolis-St. Paul MSA, MN-WI	S	30.68 MW	32.44 AW	63810 AAW	MNBLS	10//99-12//99
	Mississippi	S	32.94 MW	31.46 AW	65440 AAW	MSBLS	10//99-12//99
	Kansas City MSA, MO-KS	S	32.38 MW	35.99 AW	67350 AAW	MOBLS	10//99-12//99
	Nebraska	S	30.52 MW	28.43 AW	59140 AAW	NEBLS	10//99-12//99
	New Jersey	S	32.78 MW	31.25 AW	64990 AAW	NJBLS	10//99-12//99
	New Mexico	S	29.77 MW	28.34 AW	58940 AAW	NMBLS	10//99-12//99
	New York	S	33.91 MW	32.86 AW	68350 AAW	NYBLS	10//99-12//99
	Nassau-Suffolk PMSA, NY	S	31.95 MW	34.22 AW	66460 AAW	NYBLS	10//99-12//99
	New York PMSA, NY	S	35.92 MW	36.77 AW	74710 AAW	NYBLS	10//99-12//99
	Ohio	S	32.15 MW	31.96 AW	66470 AAW	OHBLS	10//99-12//99
	Oklahoma	S	29.64 MW	28.69 AW	59670 AAW	OKBLS	10//99-12//99
	Tulsa MSA, OK	S	28.62 MW	29.50 AW	59540 AAW	OKBLS	10//99-12//99
	Philadelphia PMSA, PA-NJ	S	28.66 MW	29.51 AW	59610 AAW	PABLS	10//99-12//99
	South Carolina	S	30.87 MW	29.94 AW	62260 AAW	SCBLS	10//99-12//99
	Tennessee	S	27.98 MW	27.45 AW	57100 AAW	TNBLS	10//99-12//99
	Memphis MSA, TN-AR-MS	S	27.09 MW	26.82 AW	56350 AAW	MSBLS	10//99-12//99
	Texas	S	30.75 MW	30.82 AW	64110 AAW	TXBLS	10//99-12//99
	Dallas PMSA, TX	S	30.93 MW	30.99 AW	64330 AAW	TXBLS	10//99-12//99
	Houston PMSA, TX	S	32.19 MW	32.17 AW	66950 AAW	TXBLS	10//99-12//99
	Waco MSA, TX	S	33.48 MW	31.20 AW	69640 AAW	TXBLS	10//99-12//99
	Virginia	S	31.8 MW	31.44 AW	65390 AAW	VABLS	10//99-12//99
	Norfolk-Virginia Beach-Newport News MSA, VA-NC	S	32.83 MW	32.69 AW	68290 AAW	VABLS	10//99-12//99
	West Virginia	S	30.18 MW	29.12 AW	60560 AAW	WVBLS	10//99-12//99
Aerospace Engineering and Operations Technician	Alabama	S	22 MW	22.90 AW	47630 AAW	ALBLS	10//99-12//99
	Huntsville MSA, AL	S	24.25 MW	25.29 AW	50440 AAW	ALBLS	10//99-12//99
	Arizona	S	21.81 MW	22.91 AW	47640 AAW	AZBLS	10//99-12//99
	Phoenix-Mesa MSA, AZ	S	23.25 MW	22.20 AW	48360 AAW	AZBLS	10//99-12//99
	California	S	26.47 MW	26.42 AW	54950 AAW	CABLS	10//99-12//99
	Los Angeles-Long Beach PMSA, CA	S	26.96 MW	27.73 AW	56080 AAW	CABLS	10//99-12//99
	Orange County PMSA, CA	S	23.29 MW	22.84 AW	48450 AAW	CABLS	10//99-12//99
	San Francisco PMSA, CA	S	43.30 MW	45.50 AW	90060 AAW	CABLS	10//99-12//99
	San Jose PMSA, CA	S	24.08 MW	23.57 AW	50090 AAW	CABLS	10//99-12//99
	Colorado	S	21.69 MW	20.69 AW	43030 AAW	COBLS	10//99-12//99
	Connecticut	S	24.22 MW	24.97 AW	51930 AAW	CTBLS	10//99-12//99
	Hartford MSA, CT	S	25.06 MW	24.28 AW	52120 AAW	CTBLS	10//99-12//99
	Washington PMSA, DC-MD-VA-WV	S	25.78 MW	25.52 AW	53630 AAW	DCBLS	10//99-12//99
	Florida	S	19.9 MW	20.34 AW	42300 AAW	FLBLS	10//99-12//99
	Tampa-St. Petersburg-Clearwater MSA, FL	S	19.62 MW	20.15 AW	40810 AAW	FLBLS	10//99-12//99
	Georgia	S	20.86 MW	23.50 AW	48880 AAW	GABLS	10//99-12//99
	Macon MSA, GA	S	20.23 MW	21.97 AW	42080 AAW	GABLS	10//99-12//99
	Illinois	S	35.75 MW	32.61 AW	67830 AAW	ILBLS	10//99-12//99
	Chicago PMSA, IL	S	32.96 MW	36.78 AW	68550 AAW	ILBLS	10//99-12//99
	Iowa	S	18.22 MW	16.49 AW	34290 AAW	IABLS	10//99-12//99
	Maryland	S	20.77 MW	22.27 AW	46330 AAW	MDBLS	10//99-12//99
	Massachusetts	S	25.66 MW	27.02 AW	56200 AAW	MABLS	10//99-12//99
	Boston PMSA, MA-NH	S	30.55 MW	29.61 AW	63530 AAW	MABLS	10//99-12//99
	Michigan	S	19.88 MW	22.03 AW	45820 AAW	MIBLS	10//99-12//99

AAW Average annual wage	AOH Average offered, high	ASH Average starting, high	H Hourly	M Monthly	S Special: hourly and annual
AE Average entry wage	AOL Average offered, low	ASL Average starting, low	HI Highest wage paid	MTC Median total compensation	TQ Third quartile wage
AEX Average experienced wage	APH Average pay, high range	AW Average wage paid	HR High end range	MW Median wage paid	W Weekly
AO Average offered	APL Average pay, low range	FQ First quartile wage	LR Low end range	SQ Second quartile wage	Y Yearly

Occupation/Type/Industry	Location	Per	Low	Mid	High	Source	Date
Aerospace Engineering and Operations Technician	Detroit PMSA, MI	S	22.11 MW	20.06 AW	46000 AAW	MIBLS	10//99-12//99
	Minnesota	S	22.27 MW	22.19 AW	46160 AAW	MNBLS	10//99-12//99
	Minneapolis-St. Paul MSA, MN-WI	S	21.54 MW	21.92 AW	44800 AAW	MNBLS	10//99-12//99
	New Jersey	S	21.12 MW	21.51 AW	44750 AAW	NJBLS	10//99-12//99
	New York	S	23.05 MW	23.48 AW	48850 AAW	NYBLS	10//99-12//99
	North Carolina	S	23.09 MW	20.66 AW	42980 AAW	NCBLS	10//99-12//99
	Ohio	S	16.83 MW	17.78 AW	36980 AAW	OHBLS	10//99-12//99
	Cleveland-Lorain-Elyria PMSA, OH	S	18.60 MW	16.49 AW	38680 AAW	OHBLS	10//99-12//99
	Columbus MSA, OH	S	16.14 MW	15.71 AW	33560 AAW	OHBLS	10//99-12//99
	Dayton-Springfield MSA, OH	S	21.40 MW	21.94 AW	44520 AAW	OHBLS	10//99-12//99
	Oklahoma	S	15.64 MW	16.94 AW	35240 AAW	OKBLS	10//99-12//99
	Tulsa MSA, OK	S	12.48 MW	9.95 AW	25960 AAW	OKBLS	10//99-12//99
	Pennsylvania	S	20.42 MW	20.96 AW	43590 AAW	PABLS	10//99-12//99
	Philadelphia PMSA, PA-NJ	S	18.84 MW	19.65 AW	39190 AAW	PABLS	10//99-12//99
	Texas	S	19 MW	19.02 AW	39550 AAW	TXBLS	10//99-12//99
	Austin-San Marcos MSA, TX	S	17.80 MW	18.26 AW	37020 AAW	TXBLS	10//99-12//99
	Dallas PMSA, TX	S	19.15 MW	19.05 AW	39830 AAW	TXBLS	10//99-12//99
	Fort Worth-Arlington PMSA, TX	S	21.60 MW	21.42 AW	44930 AAW	TXBLS	10//99-12//99
	Utah	S	14.94 MW	16.27 AW	33830 AAW	UTBLS	10//99-12//99
	Salt Lake City-Ogden MSA, UT	S	15.40 MW	13.05 AW	32020 AAW	UTBLS	10//99-12//99
	Virginia	S	24.97 MW	26.80 AW	55740 AAW	VABLS	10//99-12//99
	Norfolk-Virginia Beach-Newport News MSA, VA-NC	S	25.92 MW	25.98 AW	53920 AAW	VABLS	10//99-12//99
	Washington	S	30.21 MW	31.68 AW	65900 AAW	WABLS	10//99-12//99
	Seattle-Bellevue-Everett PMSA, WA	S	31.73 MW	30.25 AW	66000 AAW	WABLS	10//99-12//99
	West Virginia	S	19.55 MW	18.94 AW	39400 AAW	WVBLS	10//99-12//99
Agent and Business Manager							
Artists, Performers, and Athletes	Alabama	S	23.09 MW	23.25 AW	48370 AAW	ALBLS	10//99-12//99
Artists, Performers, and Athletes	Birmingham MSA, AL	S	23.25 MW	23.09 AW	48370 AAW	ALBLS	10//99-12//99
Artists, Performers, and Athletes	California	S	55.85 MW	48.44 AW	100750 AAW	CABLS	10//99-12//99
Artists, Performers, and Athletes	Los Angeles-Long Beach PMSA, CA	S	46.92 MW	52.32 AW	97600 AAW	CABLS	10//99-12//99
Artists, Performers, and Athletes	San Francisco PMSA, CA	S	54.35 MW	61.94 AW	113060 AAW	CABLS	10//99-12//99
Artists, Performers, and Athletes	Colorado	S	12.32 MW	13.46 AW	27990 AAW	COBLS	10//99-12//99
Artists, Performers, and Athletes	Connecticut	S	15.77 MW	17.50 AW	36390 AAW	CTBLS	10//99-12//99
Artists, Performers, and Athletes	Florida	S	18.51 MW	20.10 AW	41800 AAW	FLBLS	10//99-12//99
Artists, Performers, and Athletes	Hawaii	S	21.57 MW	20.41 AW	42440 AAW	HIBLS	10//99-12//99
Artists, Performers, and Athletes	Illinois	S	11.73 MW	14.55 AW	30270 AAW	ILBLS	10//99-12//99
Artists, Performers, and Athletes	Indiana	S	20.11 MW	20.32 AW	42280 AAW	INBLS	10//99-12//99
Artists, Performers, and Athletes	Iowa	S	22.55 MW	20.89 AW	43460 AAW	IABLS	10//99-12//99
Artists, Performers, and Athletes	Louisiana	S	22.6 MW	20.97 AW	43610 AAW	LABLS	10//99-12//99
Artists, Performers, and Athletes	Baton Rouge MSA, LA	S	18.64 MW	16.49 AW	38770 AAW	LABLS	10//99-12//99
Artists, Performers, and Athletes	New Orleans MSA, LA	S	19.04 MW	19.46 AW	39610 AAW	LABLS	10//99-12//99
Artists, Performers, and Athletes	Massachusetts	S	22.87 MW	24.88 AW	51750 AAW	MABLS	10//99-12//99
Artists, Performers, and Athletes	Minnesota	S	16.83 MW	26.08 AW	54240 AAW	MNBLS	10//99-12//99
Artists, Performers, and Athletes	Missouri	S	16.69 MW	21.64 AW	45010 AAW	MOBLS	10//99-12//99
Artists, Performers, and Athletes	Nevada	S	10.05 MW	12.69 AW	26390 AAW	NVBLS	10//99-12//99
Artists, Performers, and Athletes	New York	S	33.27 MW	39.21 AW	81560 AAW	NYBLS	10//99-12//99
Artists, Performers, and Athletes	New York PMSA, NY	S	39.02 MW	33.02 AW	81160 AAW	NYBLS	10//99-12//99
Artists, Performers, and Athletes	Ohio	S	22.43 MW	21.75 AW	45240 AAW	OHBLS	10//99-12//99
Artists, Performers, and Athletes	Oklahoma	S	16.69 MW	18.99 AW	39500 AAW	OKBLS	10//99-12//99
Artists, Performers, and Athletes	Pennsylvania	S	21.63 MW	18.16 AW	37760 AAW	PABLS	10//99-12//99
Artists, Performers, and Athletes	Philadelphia PMSA, PA-NJ	S	20.72 MW	22.41 AW	43100 AAW	PABLS	10//99-12//99
Artists, Performers, and Athletes	South Carolina	S	11.15 MW	11.53 AW	23990 AAW	SCBLS	10//99-12//99
Artists, Performers, and Athletes	Houston PMSA, TX	S	23.57 MW	22.08 AW	49020 AAW	TXBLS	10//99-12//99
Artists, Performers, and Athletes	Washington	S	12.2 MW	12.17 AW	25300 AAW	WABLS	10//99-12//99
Artists, Performers, and Athletes	Seattle-Bellevue-Everett PMSA, WA	S	12.20 MW	12.22 AW	25380 AAW	WABLS	10//99-12//99
Artists, Performers, and Athletes	Wisconsin	S	12.92 MW	15.33 AW	31890 AAW	WIBLS	10//99-12//99
Agricultural and Food Science Technician	Alabama	S	8.34 MW	10.97 AW	22820 AAW	ALBLS	10//99-12//99
	Arizona	S	11.04 MW	13.42 AW	27920 AAW	AZBLS	10//99-12//99
	Arkansas	S	9.78 MW	10.61 AW	22060 AAW	ARBLS	10//99-12//99

AAW Average annual wage	**AOH** Average offered, high	**ASH** Average starting, high	**H** Hourly	**M** Monthly	**S** Special: hourly and annual
AE Average entry wage	**AOL** Average offered, low	**ASL** Average starting, low	**HI** Highest wage paid	**MTC** Median total compensation	**TQ** Third quartile wage
AEX Average experienced wage	**APH** Average pay, high range	**AW** Average wage paid	**HR** High end range	**MW** Median wage paid	**W** Weekly
AO Average offered	**APL** Average pay, low range	**FQ** First quartile wage	**LR** Low end range	**SQ** Second quartile wage	**Y** Yearly

Occupation/Type/Industry	Location	Per	Low	Mid	High	Source	Date
Agricultural and Food Science Technician	California	S	12.1 MW	13.44 AW	27960 AAW	CABLS	10//99-12//99
	Connecticut	S	20.52 MW	20.19 AW	41990 AAW	CTBLS	10//99-12//99
	Florida	S	11.78 MW	12.26 AW	25510 AAW	FLBLS	10//99-12//99
	Georgia	S	12.33 MW	12.90 AW	26830 AAW	GABLS	10//99-12//99
	Hawaii	S	10.71 MW	10.81 AW	22490 AAW	HIBLS	10//99-12//99
	Idaho	S	11.1 MW	12.34 AW	25680 AAW	IDBLS	10//99-12//99
	Illinois	S	12.77 MW	14.04 AW	29210 AAW	ILBLS	10//99-12//99
	Indiana	S	12.48 MW	13.28 AW	27620 AAW	INBLS	10//99-12//99
	Iowa	S	16.81 MW	18.26 AW	37980 AAW	IABLS	10//99-12//99
	Kansas	S	11.99 MW	14.56 AW	30280 AAW	KSBLS	10//99-12//99
	Kentucky	S	14.93 MW	15.02 AW	31240 AAW	KYBLS	10//99-12//99
	Louisiana	S	12.58 MW	13.04 AW	27130 AAW	LABLS	10//99-12//99
	Maryland	S	22.09 MW	21.83 AW	45400 AAW	MDBLS	10//99-12//99
	Massachusetts	S	13.33 MW	15.12 AW	31440 AAW	MABLS	10//99-12//99
	Minnesota	S	12.68 MW	13.22 AW	27490 AAW	MNBLS	10//99-12//99
	Mississippi	S	14.4 MW	14.14 AW	29410 AAW	MSBLS	10//99-12//99
	Missouri	S	10.58 MW	13.97 AW	29060 AAW	MOBLS	10//99-12//99
	Nebraska	S	12.45 MW	12.89 AW	26820 AAW	NEBLS	10//99-12//99
	New Jersey	S	14.68 MW	15.80 AW	32870 AAW	NJBLS	10//99-12//99
	New York	S	10.51 MW	12.94 AW	26920 AAW	NYBLS	10//99-12//99
	North Carolina	S	11.98 MW	12.11 AW	25190 AAW	NCBLS	10//99-12//99
	North Dakota	S	8.36 MW	8.98 AW	18680 AAW	NDBLS	10//99-12//99
	Oklahoma	S	14.49 MW	13.99 AW	29090 AAW	OKBLS	10//99-12//99
	Oregon	S	8.59 MW	9.41 AW	19560 AAW	ORBLS	10//99-12//99
	Pennsylvania	S	14.94 MW	14.81 AW	30810 AAW	PABLS	10//99-12//99
	South Carolina	S	11.18 MW	11.96 AW	24890 AAW	SCBLS	10//99-12//99
	South Dakota	S	12.76 MW	16.11 AW	33500 AAW	SDBLS	10//99-12//99
	Tennessee	S	13.27 MW	14.04 AW	29210 AAW	TNBLS	10//99-12//99
	Texas	S	13.37 MW	14.34 AW	29830 AAW	TXBLS	10//99-12//99
	Vermont	S	17.77 MW	17.87 AW	37180 AAW	VTBLS	10//99-12//99
	Virginia	S	12.34 MW	12.55 AW	26110 AAW	VABLS	10//99-12//99
	Washington	S	14.89 MW	15.17 AW	31550 AAW	WABLS	10//99-12//99
	Wisconsin	S	12.21 MW	13.50 AW	28080 AAW	WIBLS	10//99-12//99
Agricultural and Food Scientist	Alabama	S	21.02 MW	21.38 AW	44480 AAW	ALBLS	10//99-12//99
	Alaska	S	21.51 MW	22.27 AW	46330 AAW	AKBLS	10//99-12//99
	Arizona	S	18.58 MW	18.85 AW	39210 AAW	AZBLS	10//99-12//99
	Arkansas	S	21.56 MW	22.29 AW	46350 AAW	ARBLS	10//99-12//99
	California	S	21.22 MW	22.04 AW	45840 AAW	CABLS	10//99-12//99
	Fresno MSA, CA	S	22.78 MW	22.89 AW	47380 AAW	CABLS	10//99-12//99
	Modesto MSA, CA	S	23.32 MW	23.22 AW	48500 AAW	CABLS	10//99-12//99
	Oakland PMSA, CA	S	25.63 MW	25.65 AW	53320 AAW	CABLS	10//99-12//99
	Orange County PMSA, CA	S	20.58 MW	18.51 AW	42810 AAW	CABLS	10//99-12//99
	Riverside-San Bernardino PMSA, CA	S	29.39 MW	26.83 AW	61140 AAW	CABLS	10//99-12//99
	Salinas MSA, CA	S	17.27 MW	15.85 AW	35910 AAW	CABLS	10//99-12//99
	San Francisco PMSA, CA	S	21.58 MW	20.38 AW	44890 AAW	CABLS	10//99-12//99
	San Jose PMSA, CA	S	28.25 MW	28.72 AW	58770 AAW	CABLS	10//99-12//99
	Vallejo-Fairfield-Napa PMSA, CA	S	23.22 MW	20.18 AW	48290 AAW	CABLS	10//99-12//99
	Colorado	S	20.19 MW	20.94 AW	43550 AAW	COBLS	10//99-12//99
	Denver PMSA, CO	S	19.75 MW	16.46 AW	41080 AAW	COBLS	10//99-12//99
	Connecticut	S	32.11 MW	33.43 AW	69530 AAW	CTBLS	10//99-12//99
	District of Columbia	S	22.25 MW	25.06 AW	52130 AAW	DCBLS	10//99-12//99
	Washington PMSA, DC-MD-VA-WV	S	26.98 MW	24.39 AW	56110 AAW	DCBLS	10//99-12//99
	Florida	S	19.7 MW	20.52 AW	42680 AAW	FLBLS	10//99-12//99
	West Palm Beach-Boca Raton MSA, FL	S	18.61 MW	18.04 AW	38720 AAW	FLBLS	10//99-12//99
	Georgia	S	19.55 MW	20.13 AW	41870 AAW	GABLS	10//99-12//99
	Idaho	S	23.98 MW	23.77 AW	49430 AAW	IDBLS	10//99-12//99
	Illinois	S	22.97 MW	25.63 AW	53310 AAW	ILBLS	10//99-12//99
	Indiana	S	15.69 MW	16.39 AW	34090 AAW	INBLS	10//99-12//99
	Indianapolis MSA, IN	S	20.24 MW	17.83 AW	42100 AAW	INBLS	10//99-12//99
	Iowa	S	22.56 MW	24.94 AW	51880 AAW	IABLS	10//99-12//99
	Kansas	S	17.38 MW	18.06 AW	37550 AAW	KSBLS	10//99-12//99
	Kentucky	S	22.8 MW	24.26 AW	50460 AAW	KYBLS	10//99-12//99
	Louisiana	S	18.91 MW	19.06 AW	39650 AAW	LABLS	10//99-12//99
	Maine	S	22.6 MW	23.05 AW	47950 AAW	MEBLS	10//99-12//99
	Maryland	S	23.98 MW	26.11 AW	54310 AAW	MDBLS	10//99-12//99
	Baltimore PMSA, MD	S	21.58 MW	19.82 AW	44890 AAW	MDBLS	10//99-12//99

AAW Average annual wage	AOH Average offered, high	ASH Average starting, high	H Hourly	M Monthly	S Special: hourly and annual
AE Average entry wage	AOL Average offered, low	ASL Average starting, low	HI Highest wage paid	MTC Median total compensation	TQ Third quartile wage
AEX Average experienced wage	APH Average pay, high range	AW Average wage paid	HR High end range	MW Median wage paid	W Weekly
AO Average offered	APL Average pay, low range	FQ First quartile wage	LR Low end range	SQ Second quartile wage	Y Yearly

Occupation/Type/Industry	Location	Per	Low	Mid	High	Source	Date
Agricultural and Food Scientist	Massachusetts	S	26.31 MW	26.69 AW	55520 AAW	MABLS	10//99-12//99
	Boston PMSA, MA-NH	S	26.14 MW	27.27 AW	54380 AAW	MABLS	10//99-12//99
	Michigan	S	23.77 MW	23.58 AW	49040 AAW	MIBLS	10//99-12//99
	Detroit PMSA, MI	S	22.04 MW	22.30 AW	45830 AAW	MIBLS	10//99-12//99
	Minnesota	S	20.14 MW	22.25 AW	46280 AAW	MNBLS	10//99-12//99
	Minneapolis-St. Paul MSA, MN-WI	S	27.00 MW	25.76 AW	56170 AAW	MNBLS	10//99-12//99
	Mississippi	S	21.21 MW	22.38 AW	46540 AAW	MSBLS	10//99-12//99
	Missouri	S	23.03 MW	22.50 AW	46800 AAW	MOBLS	10//99-12//99
	Kansas City MSA, MO-KS	S	18.47 MW	17.56 AW	38420 AAW	MOBLS	10//99-12//99
	St. Louis MSA, MO-IL	S	21.12 MW	21.23 AW	43930 AAW	MOBLS	10//99-12//99
	Montana	S	22.03 MW	22.06 AW	45890 AAW	MTBLS	10//99-12//99
	Nebraska	S	16.77 MW	19.72 AW	41020 AAW	NEBLS	10//99-12//99
	Nevada	S	21.1 MW	21.62 AW	44960 AAW	NVBLS	10//99-12//99
	New Hampshire	S	21.13 MW	23.58 AW	49040 AAW	NHBLS	10//99-12//99
	New Jersey	S	21.83 MW	23.81 AW	49510 AAW	NJBLS	10//99-12//99
	New Mexico	S	23.36 MW	23.22 AW	48310 AAW	NMBLS	10//99-12//99
	New York	S	20.72 MW	20.92 AW	43520 AAW	NYBLS	10//99-12//99
	North Carolina	S	20.27 MW	21.32 AW	44350 AAW	NCBLS	10//99-12//99
	Charlotte-Gastonia-Rock Hill MSA, NC-SC	S	18.31 MW	16.61 AW	38070 AAW	NCBLS	10//99-12//99
	Raleigh-Durham-Chapel Hill MSA, NC	S	21.29 MW	20.08 AW	44290 AAW	NCBLS	10//99-12//99
	North Dakota	S	23.12 MW	23.29 AW	48440 AAW	NDBLS	10//99-12//99
	Fargo-Moorhead MSA, ND-MN	S	25.42 MW	23.11 AW	52880 AAW	NDBLS	10//99-12//99
	Ohio	S	19.54 MW	21.35 AW	44410 AAW	OHBLS	10//99-12//99
	Columbus MSA, OH	S	22.03 MW	19.43 AW	45820 AAW	OHBLS	10//99-12//99
	Oklahoma	S	18.17 MW	20.22 AW	42060 AAW	OKBLS	10//99-12//99
	Oregon	S	21.61 MW	21.67 AW	45070 AAW	ORBLS	10//99-12//99
	Portland-Vancouver PMSA, OR-WA	S	23.20 MW	22.06 AW	48250 AAW	ORBLS	10//99-12//99
	Salem PMSA, OR	S	22.27 MW	20.66 AW	46320 AAW	ORBLS	10//99-12//99
	Pennsylvania	S	21.28 MW	21.79 AW	45330 AAW	PABLS	10//99-12//99
	Philadelphia PMSA, PA-NJ	S	26.03 MW	23.83 AW	54150 AAW	PABLS	10//99-12//99
	Pittsburgh MSA, PA	S	22.96 MW	21.94 AW	47760 AAW	PABLS	10//99-12//99
	South Carolina	S	22.04 MW	22.06 AW	45890 AAW	SCBLS	10//99-12//99
	Tennessee	S	21.71 MW	21.99 AW	45740 AAW	TNBLS	10//99-12//99
	Memphis MSA, TN-AR-MS	S	23.09 MW	20.63 AW	48030 AAW	MSBLS	10//99-12//99
	Nashville MSA, TN	S	18.87 MW	18.40 AW	39240 AAW	TNBLS	10//99-12//99
	Texas	S	16.91 MW	17.49 AW	36380 AAW	TXBLS	10//99-12//99
	Dallas PMSA, TX	S	23.04 MW	20.11 AW	47930 AAW	TXBLS	10//99-12//99
	San Antonio MSA, TX	S	17.59 MW	16.18 AW	36590 AAW	TXBLS	10//99-12//99
	Utah	S	18.82 MW	19.90 AW	41390 AAW	UTBLS	10//99-12//99
	Salt Lake City-Ogden MSA, UT	S	19.22 MW	18.60 AW	39980 AAW	UTBLS	10//99-12//99
	Vermont	S	24.68 MW	25.43 AW	52900 AAW	VTBLS	10//99-12//99
	Virginia	S	21.52 MW	24.41 AW	50780 AAW	VABLS	10//99-12//99
	Washington	S	20.53 MW	21.45 AW	44610 AAW	WABLS	10//99-12//99
	Seattle-Bellevue-Everett PMSA, WA	S	21.33 MW	19.86 AW	44360 AAW	WABLS	10//99-12//99
	Yakima MSA, WA	S	17.71 MW	17.21 AW	36830 AAW	WABLS	10//99-12//99
	West Virginia	S	26.05 MW	26.40 AW	54910 AAW	WVBLS	10//99-12//99
	Wisconsin	S	19.31 MW	22.31 AW	46400 AAW	WIBLS	10//99-12//99
	Madison MSA, WI	S	25.15 MW	20.84 AW	52310 AAW	WIBLS	10//99-12//99
	Milwaukee-Waukesha PMSA, WI	S	20.46 MW	19.32 AW	42570 AAW	WIBLS	10//99-12//99
	Wyoming	S	21.9 MW	20.56 AW	42760 AAW	WYBLS	10//99-12//99
Agricultural Engineer	California	S	25.57 MW	27.51 AW	57220 AAW	CABLS	10//99-12//99
	Colorado	S	25.82 MW	25.99 AW	54060 AAW	COBLS	10//99-12//99
	Florida	S	18.55 MW	20.82 AW	43300 AAW	FLBLS	10//99-12//99
	Georgia	S	21.65 MW	22.91 AW	47650 AAW	GABLS	10//99-12//99
	Indiana	S	26.5 MW	26.66 AW	55460 AAW	INBLS	10//99-12//99
	Iowa	S	20.85 MW	22.07 AW	45900 AAW	IABLS	10//99-12//99
	Michigan	S	23.71 MW	24.46 AW	50880 AAW	MIBLS	10//99-12//99
	Mississippi	S	24.88 MW	25.28 AW	52590 AAW	MSBLS	10//99-12//99
	Nebraska	S	21.88 MW	24.07 AW	50060 AAW	NEBLS	10//99-12//99
	New Jersey	S	18.67 MW	19.63 AW	40840 AAW	NJBLS	10//99-12//99
	New York	S	21.07 MW	21.94 AW	45630 AAW	NYBLS	10//99-12//99
	Oregon	S	19.46 MW	22.32 AW	46430 AAW	ORBLS	10//99-12//99
	Pennsylvania	S	29.51 MW	28.87 AW	60060 AAW	PABLS	10//99-12//99
	Tennessee	S	28.18 MW	26.59 AW	55320 AAW	TNBLS	10//99-12//99

Occupation/Type/Industry	Location	Per	Low	Mid	High	Source	Date
Agricultural Engineer	Texas	S	34.54 MW	31.46 AW	65450 AAW	TXBLS	10//99-12//99
	Washington	S	25.77 MW	26.28 AW	54660 AAW	WABLS	10//99-12//99
Agricultural Equipment Operator	Arizona	S	7.1 MW	7.50 AW	15600 AAW	AZBLS	10//99-12//99
	Arkansas	S	6.81 MW	7.66 AW	15930 AAW	ARBLS	10//99-12//99
	California	S	7.4 MW	8.54 AW	17770 AAW	CABLS	10//99-12//99
	Colorado	S	6.61 MW	7.59 AW	15790 AAW	COBLS	10//99-12//99
	Florida	S	7.74 MW	8.39 AW	17450 AAW	FLBLS	10//99-12//99
	Georgia	S	6.71 MW	7.52 AW	15640 AAW	GABLS	10//99-12//99
	Hawaii	S	10.56 MW	10.60 AW	22040 AAW	HIBLS	10//99-12//99
	Idaho	S	6.97 MW	7.81 AW	16250 AAW	IDBLS	10//99-12//99
	Illinois	S	10.41 MW	10.97 AW	22810 AAW	ILBLS	10//99-12//99
	Indiana	S	12.69 MW	12.54 AW	26080 AAW	INBLS	10//99-12//99
	Iowa	S	9.2 MW	10.10 AW	21000 AAW	IABLS	10//99-12//99
	Kansas	S	9.68 MW	9.70 AW	20170 AAW	KSBLS	10//99-12//99
	Kentucky	S	8.91 MW	9.06 AW	18850 AAW	KYBLS	10//99-12//99
	Louisiana	S	6.09 MW	7.31 AW	15200 AAW	LABLS	10//99-12//99
	Michigan	S	9.14 MW	9.62 AW	20010 AAW	MIBLS	10//99-12//99
	Minnesota	S	10.01 MW	9.87 AW	20540 AAW	MNBLS	10//99-12//99
	Mississippi	S	7.69 MW	7.85 AW	16330 AAW	MSBLS	10//99-12//99
	Missouri	S	7.05 MW	7.96 AW	16550 AAW	MOBLS	10//99-12//99
	Montana	S	8.16 MW	8.19 AW	17030 AAW	MTBLS	10//99-12//99
	Nebraska	S	7.85 MW	8.05 AW	16740 AAW	NEBLS	10//99-12//99
	New Mexico	S	8.3 MW	8.72 AW	18140 AAW	NMBLS	10//99-12//99
	New York	S	8.62 MW	8.57 AW	17820 AAW	NYBLS	10//99-12//99
	North Carolina	S	8.39 MW	9.93 AW	20650 AAW	NCBLS	10//99-12//99
	Ohio	S	11.05 MW	11.15 AW	23190 AAW	OHBLS	10//99-12//99
	Oklahoma	S	8.26 MW	8.33 AW	17330 AAW	OKBLS	10//99-12//99
	Oregon	S	9.66 MW	10.02 AW	20850 AAW	ORBLS	10//99-12//99
	South Dakota	S	8.15 MW	8.01 AW	16660 AAW	SDBLS	10//99-12//99
	Tennessee	S	8.69 MW	9.22 AW	19180 AAW	TNBLS	10//99-12//99
	Texas	S	6.93 MW	7.30 AW	15180 AAW	TXBLS	10//99-12//99
	Utah	S	10.14 MW	10.69 AW	22230 AAW	UTBLS	10//99-12//99
	Virginia	S	9.06 MW	8.72 AW	18140 AAW	VABLS	10//99-12//99
	Washington	S	7.77 MW	8.38 AW	17430 AAW	WABLS	10//99-12//99
	Wisconsin	S	9.18 MW	9.69 AW	20150 AAW	WIBLS	10//99-12//99
	Wyoming	S	9.86 MW	10.40 AW	21630 AAW	WYBLS	10//99-12//99
	Puerto Rico	S	6.9 MW	7.51 AW	15610 AAW	PRBLS	10//99-12//99
Agricultural Inspector	Alabama	S	13.65 MW	14.73 AW	30640 AAW	ALBLS	10//99-12//99
	Arkansas	S	10.84 MW	12.30 AW	25590 AAW	ARBLS	10//99-12//99
	California	S	15.5 MW	15.45 AW	32140 AAW	CABLS	10//99-12//99
	Connecticut	S	22.21 MW	20.54 AW	42730 AAW	CTBLS	10//99-12//99
	Florida	S	13.13 MW	13.63 AW	28350 AAW	FLBLS	10//99-12//99
	Georgia	S	13.12 MW	13.74 AW	28570 AAW	GABLS	10//99-12//99
	Idaho	S	13.4 MW	14.27 AW	29670 AAW	IDBLS	10//99-12//99
	Illinois	S	14.65 MW	15.07 AW	31350 AAW	ILBLS	10//99-12//99
	Indiana	S	18.23 MW	17.97 AW	37370 AAW	INBLS	10//99-12//99
	Iowa	S	13.82 MW	14.02 AW	29150 AAW	IABLS	10//99-12//99
	Louisiana	S	14.67 MW	14.62 AW	30410 AAW	LABLS	10//99-12//99
	Massachusetts	S	14.43 MW	15.76 AW	32780 AAW	MABLS	10//99-12//99
	Michigan	S	15.57 MW	16.19 AW	33670 AAW	MIBLS	10//99-12//99
	Minnesota	S	14.78 MW	14.88 AW	30940 AAW	MNBLS	10//99-12//99
	Mississippi	S	11.53 MW	11.54 AW	24000 AAW	MSBLS	10//99-12//99
	Missouri	S	13 MW	14.40 AW	29940 AAW	MOBLS	10//99-12//99
	Nebraska	S	18.41 MW	17.54 AW	36480 AAW	NEBLS	10//99-12//99
	New Jersey	S	11.69 MW	13.73 AW	28560 AAW	NJBLS	10//99-12//99
	North Carolina	S	12.75 MW	13.20 AW	27450 AAW	NCBLS	10//99-12//99
	Oregon	S	11.96 MW	12.51 AW	26030 AAW	ORBLS	10//99-12//99
	Pennsylvania	S	16.65 MW	16.24 AW	33780 AAW	PABLS	10//99-12//99
	South Carolina	S	12.13 MW	13.23 AW	27510 AAW	SCBLS	10//99-12//99
	South Dakota	S	11.27 MW	12.09 AW	25140 AAW	SDBLS	10//99-12//99
	Texas	S	13.99 MW	14.19 AW	29520 AAW	TXBLS	10//99-12//99
	Washington	S	13.31 MW	14.34 AW	29830 AAW	WABLS	10//99-12//99
	Wisconsin	S	15.51 MW	15.56 AW	32370 AAW	WIBLS	10//99-12//99
Agricultural Sciences Teacher							
Postsecondary	Alabama	Y		59280 AAW		ALBLS	10//99-12//99
Postsecondary	California	Y		58230 AAW		CABLS	10//99-12//99
Postsecondary	Colorado	Y		49540 AAW		COBLS	10//99-12//99
Postsecondary	Florida	Y		68870 AAW		FLBLS	10//99-12//99
Postsecondary	Georgia	Y		57370 AAW		GABLS	10//99-12//99
Postsecondary	Iowa	Y		66050 AAW		IABLS	10//99-12//99

AAW	Average annual wage	AOH	Average offered, high	ASH	Average starting, high	H	Hourly	M	Monthly	S	Special: hourly and annual
AE	Average entry wage	AOL	Average offered, low	ASL	Average starting, low	HI	Highest wage paid	MTC	Median total compensation	TQ	Third quartile wage
AEX	Average experienced wage	APH	Average pay, high range	AW	Average wage paid	HR	High end range	MW	Median wage paid	W	Weekly
AO	Average offered	APL	Average pay, low range	FQ	First quartile wage	LR	Low end range	SQ	Second quartile wage	Y	Yearly

Occupation/Type/Industry	Location	Per	Low	Mid	High	Source	Date
Agricultural Sciences Teacher							
Postsecondary	Kentucky	Y		62640 AAW		KYBLS	10//99-12//99
Postsecondary	Louisiana	Y		51680 AAW		LABLS	10//99-12//99
Postsecondary	Maryland	Y		66390 AAW		MDBLS	10//99-12//99
Postsecondary	Michigan	Y		64620 AAW		MIBLS	10//99-12//99
Postsecondary	Missouri	Y		53890 AAW		MOBLS	10//99-12//99
Postsecondary	New Jersey	Y		58690 AAW		NJBLS	10//99-12//99
Postsecondary	New York	Y		57660 AAW		NYBLS	10//99-12//99
Postsecondary	Ohio	Y		57400 AAW		OHBLS	10//99-12//99
Postsecondary	Pennsylvania	Y		58760 AAW		PABLS	10//99-12//99
Postsecondary	South Carolina	Y		52890 AAW		SCBLS	10//99-12//99
Postsecondary	Tennessee	Y		58300 AAW		TNBLS	10//99-12//99
Postsecondary	Texas	Y		49790 AAW		TXBLS	10//99-12//99
Postsecondary	Virginia	Y		54120 AAW		VABLS	10//99-12//99
Air Traffic Controller	United States	Y		64880 AW		DENE	1999
	Alabama	S	28.35 MW	27.00 AW	56170 AAW	ALBLS	10//99-12//99
	Arizona	S	31.23 MW	30.76 AW	63970 AAW	AZBLS	10//99-12//99
	Arkansas	S	30.2 MW	29.45 AW	61260 AAW	ARBLS	10//99-12//99
	California	S	37.64 MW	36.93 AW	76800 AAW	CABLS	10//99-12//99
	Denver PMSA, CO	S	37.58 MW	38.49 AW	78180 AAW	COBLS	10//99-12//99
	Connecticut	S	27.91 MW	26.42 AW	54960 AAW	CTBLS	10//99-12//99
	Florida	S	38.15 MW	37.20 AW	77380 AAW	FLBLS	10//99-12//99
	Iowa	S	29.04 MW	28.08 AW	58400 AAW	IABLS	10//99-12//99
	Kentucky	S	32.07 MW	31.84 AW	66220 AAW	KYBLS	10//99-12//99
	Louisiana	S	28.54 MW	27.46 AW	57120 AAW	LABLS	10//99-12//99
	Massachusetts	S	35.9 MW	34.08 AW	70880 AAW	MABLS	10//99-12//99
	Michigan	S	31.23 MW	31.94 AW	66430 AAW	MIBLS	10//99-12//99
	Mississippi	S	27.71 MW	26.76 AW	55650 AAW	MSBLS	10//99-12//99
	Missouri	S	33.5 MW	33.83 AW	70360 AAW	MOBLS	10//99-12//99
	Nebraska	S	28.78 MW	24.76 AW	51500 AAW	NEBLS	10//99-12//99
	New Jersey	S	31.31 MW	30.79 AW	64030 AAW	NJBLS	10//99-12//99
	New York	S	40.43 MW	38.55 AW	80180 AAW	NYBLS	10//99-12//99
	North Carolina	S	31.99 MW	31.49 AW	65500 AAW	NCBLS	10//99-12//99
	Oklahoma	S	32.65 MW	30.82 AW	64100 AAW	OKBLS	10//99-12//99
	Oregon	S	30.98 MW	30.49 AW	63420 AAW	ORBLS	10//99-12//99
	Pennsylvania	S	33.86 MW	35.31 AW	73450 AAW	PABLS	10//99-12//99
	South Carolina	S	28.39 MW	27.08 AW	56330 AAW	SCBLS	10//99-12//99
	South Dakota	S	23.87 MW	23.94 AW	49790 AAW	SDBLS	10//99-12//99
	Texas	S	34.5 MW	33.41 AW	69490 AAW	TXBLS	10//99-12//99
	Houston PMSA, TX	S	29.30 MW	20.87 AW	60940 AAW	TXBLS	10//99-12//99
	West Virginia	S	25.77 MW	25.64 AW	53340 AAW	WVBLS	10//99-12//99
	Wisconsin	S	21.31 MW	24.51 AW	50970 AAW	WIBLS	10//99-12//99
	Milwaukee-Waukesha PMSA, WI	S	21.68 MW	18.10 AW	45100 AAW	WIBLS	10//99-12//99
Aircraft Cargo Handling Supervisor	Alaska	S	13.21 MW	14.26 AW	29670 AAW	AKBLS	10//99-12//99
	Anchorage MSA, AK	S	11.80 MW	11.44 AW	24540 AAW	AKBLS	10//99-12//99
	Arizona	S	18.76 MW	19.53 AW	40610 AAW	AZBLS	10//99-12//99
	Arkansas	S	28.79 MW	26.01 AW	54110 AAW	ARBLS	10//99-12//99
	California	S	13.1 MW	16.74 AW	34820 AAW	CABLS	10//99-12//99
	Los Angeles-Long Beach PMSA, CA	S	15.82 MW	12.76 AW	32900 AAW	CABLS	10//99-12//99
	Riverside-San Bernardino PMSA, CA	S	17.61 MW	16.08 AW	36640 AAW	CABLS	10//99-12//99
	San Diego MSA, CA	S	18.97 MW	21.68 AW	39460 AAW	CABLS	10//99-12//99
	Denver PMSA, CO	S	15.78 MW	15.81 AW	32810 AAW	COBLS	10//99-12//99
	Connecticut	S	17.78 MW	16.18 AW	33660 AAW	CTBLS	10//99-12//99
	Washington PMSA, DC-MD-VA-WV	S	21.52 MW	20.49 AW	44750 AAW	DCBLS	10//99-12//99
	Florida	S	12.39 MW	14.05 AW	29230 AAW	FLBLS	10//99-12//99
	Fort Lauderdale PMSA, FL	S	14.95 MW	12.39 AW	31090 AAW	FLBLS	10//99-12//99
	Miami PMSA, FL	S	12.51 MW	12.26 AW	26020 AAW	FLBLS	10//99-12//99
	Tampa-St. Petersburg-Clearwater MSA, FL	S	27.72 MW	29.39 AW	57670 AAW	FLBLS	10//99-12//99
	Georgia	S	16.33 MW	17.75 AW	36930 AAW	GABLS	10//99-12//99
	Atlanta MSA, GA	S	22.67 MW	21.50 AW	47150 AAW	GABLS	10//99-12//99
	Idaho	S	13.64 MW	14.41 AW	29970 AAW	IDBLS	10//99-12//99
	Boise City MSA, ID	S	14.10 MW	13.50 AW	29330 AAW	IDBLS	10//99-12//99
	Illinois	S	23.8 MW	26.65 AW	55430 AAW	ILBLS	10//99-12//99
	Chicago PMSA, IL	S	25.82 MW	22.84 AW	53710 AAW	ILBLS	10//99-12//99

AAW	Average annual wage	AOH	Average offered, high	ASH	Average starting, high	H	Hourly	M	Monthly	S	Special: hourly and annual
AE	Average entry wage	AOL	Average offered, low	ASL	Average starting, low	HI	Highest wage paid	MTC	Median total compensation	TQ	Third quartile wage
AEX	Average experienced wage	APH	Average pay, high range	AW	Average wage paid	HR	High end range	MW	Median wage paid	W	Weekly
AO	Average offered	APL	Average pay, low range	FQ	First quartile wage	LR	Low end range	SQ	Second quartile wage	Y	Yearly

Occupation/Type/Industry	Location	Per	Low	Mid	High	Source	Date
Aircraft Cargo Handling Supervisor							
	Indiana	S	20.23 MW	20.04 AW	41690 AAW	INBLS	10//99-12//99
	Fort Wayne MSA, IN	S	18.85 MW	19.14 AW	39210 AAW	INBLS	10//99-12//99
	Indianapolis MSA, IN	S	22.96 MW	23.68 AW	47760 AAW	INBLS	10//99-12//99
	Kansas	S	16.73 MW	17.70 AW	36820 AAW	KSBLS	10//99-12//99
	Kentucky	S	21.34 MW	20.52 AW	42690 AAW	KYBLS	10//99-12//99
	Louisiana	S	16.92 MW	18.74 AW	38980 AAW	LABLS	10//99-12//99
	Maryland	S	22.07 MW	19.33 AW	40200 AAW	MDBLS	10//99-12//99
	Baltimore PMSA, MD	S	13.10 MW	12.75 AW	27250 AAW	MDBLS	10//99-12//99
	Massachusetts	S	22.07 MW	22.05 AW	45860 AAW	MABLS	10//99-12//99
	Boston PMSA, MA-NH	S	23.64 MW	23.51 AW	49160 AAW	MABLS	10//99-12//99
	Michigan	S	16.08 MW	16.87 AW	35090 AAW	MIBLS	10//99-12//99
	Detroit PMSA, MI	S	17.50 MW	16.57 AW	36400 AAW	MIBLS	10//99-12//99
	Minnesota	S	17.96 MW	17.33 AW	36050 AAW	MNBLS	10//99-12//99
	Minneapolis-St. Paul MSA, MN-WI	S	18.36 MW	18.87 AW	38180 AAW	MNBLS	10//99-12//99
	Mississippi	S	7.95 MW	9.60 AW	19970 AAW	MSBLS	10//99-12//99
	Missouri	S	14.3 MW	14.31 AW	29760 AAW	MOBLS	10//99-12//99
	Kansas City MSA, MO-KS	S	16.57 MW	16.37 AW	34470 AAW	MOBLS	10//99-12//99
	Nebraska	S	11.45 MW	10.57 AW	21990 AAW	NEBLS	10//99-12//99
	Nevada	S	16.09 MW	19.46 AW	40470 AAW	NVBLS	10//99-12//99
	Las Vegas MSA, NV-AZ	S	21.02 MW	16.63 AW	43730 AAW	NVBLS	10//99-12//99
	Reno MSA, NV	S	16.89 MW	15.35 AW	35140 AAW	NVBLS	10//99-12//99
	New Jersey	S	22.47 MW	23.06 AW	47970 AAW	NJBLS	10//99-12//99
	Bergen-Passaic PMSA, NJ	S	24.19 MW	23.99 AW	50310 AAW	NJBLS	10//99-12//99
	New Mexico	S	9.91 MW	11.80 AW	24550 AAW	NMBLS	10//99-12//99
	New York	S	15.02 MW	17.41 AW	36220 AAW	NYBLS	10//99-12//99
	Nassau-Suffolk PMSA, NY	S	19.58 MW	16.68 AW	40730 AAW	NYBLS	10//99-12//99
	New York PMSA, NY	S	17.56 MW	14.81 AW	36530 AAW	NYBLS	10//99-12//99
	North Carolina	S	12.38 MW	13.02 AW	27080 AAW	NCBLS	10//99-12//99
	Charlotte-Gastonia-Rock Hill MSA, NC-SC	S	13.58 MW	12.37 AW	28250 AAW	NCBLS	10//99-12//99
	Ohio	S	19.8 MW	19.71 AW	41000 AAW	OHBLS	10//99-12//99
	Cleveland-Lorain-Elyria PMSA, OH	S	16.98 MW	12.68 AW	35330 AAW	OHBLS	10//99-12//99
	Columbus MSA, OH	S	20.49 MW	20.06 AW	42620 AAW	OHBLS	10//99-12//99
	Oklahoma	S	13.1 MW	13.53 AW	28150 AAW	OKBLS	10//99-12//99
	Oklahoma City MSA, OK	S	13.65 MW	12.73 AW	28390 AAW	OKBLS	10//99-12//99
	Oregon	S	10.54 MW	11.34 AW	23600 AAW	ORBLS	10//99-12//99
	Portland-Vancouver PMSA, OR-WA	S	11.16 MW	10.40 AW	23210 AAW	ORBLS	10//99-12//99
	Pennsylvania	S	20.43 MW	21.37 AW	44440 AAW	PABLS	10//99-12//99
	Harrisburg-Lebanon-Carlisle MSA, PA	S	19.72 MW	19.57 AW	41010 AAW	PABLS	10//99-12//99
	Philadelphia PMSA, PA-NJ	S	22.63 MW	22.42 AW	47070 AAW	PABLS	10//99-12//99
	Pittsburgh MSA, PA	S	19.51 MW	19.45 AW	40570 AAW	PABLS	10//99-12//99
	South Carolina	S	29.08 MW	26.43 AW	54970 AAW	SCBLS	10//99-12//99
	Charleston-North Charleston MSA, SC	S	15.29 MW	15.22 AW	31810 AAW	SCBLS	10//99-12//99
	Columbia MSA, SC	S	29.69 MW	30.48 AW	61750 AAW	SCBLS	10//99-12//99
	Greenville-Spartanburg-Anderson MSA, SC	S	20.92 MW	20.87 AW	43510 AAW	SCBLS	10//99-12//99
	Tennessee	S	12.43 MW	14.01 AW	29140 AAW	TNBLS	10//99-12//99
	Nashville MSA, TN	S	12.81 MW	12.95 AW	26640 AAW	TNBLS	10//99-12//99
	Texas	S	18.35 MW	19.76 AW	41110 AAW	TXBLS	10//99-12//99
	Austin-San Marcos MSA, TX	S	18.53 MW	18.77 AW	38550 AAW	TXBLS	10//99-12//99
	Dallas PMSA, TX	S	21.05 MW	18.97 AW	43790 AAW	TXBLS	10//99-12//99
	Fort Worth-Arlington PMSA, TX	S	27.45 MW	22.96 AW	57090 AAW	TXBLS	10//99-12//99
	Houston PMSA, TX	S	22.64 MW	20.13 AW	47090 AAW	TXBLS	10//99-12//99
	Laredo MSA, TX	S	18.57 MW	19.00 AW	38630 AAW	TXBLS	10//99-12//99
	Virginia	S	19.28 MW	19.56 AW	40690 AAW	VABLS	10//99-12//99
	Washington	S	20.17 MW	20.90 AW	43460 AAW	WABLS	10//99-12//99
	Wisconsin	S	25.63 MW	24.07 AW	50060 AAW	WIBLS	10//99-12//99
	Milwaukee-Waukesha PMSA, WI	S	12.26 MW	9.25 AW	25490 AAW	WIBLS	10//99-12//99
	Puerto Rico	S	8.31 MW	11.43 AW	23770 AAW	PRBLS	10//99-12//99
	San Juan-Bayamon PMSA, PR	S	8.80 MW	8.19 AW	18300 AAW	PRBLS	10//99-12//99
Aircraft Mechanic and Service Technician							
	Alabama	S	15.08 MW	14.95 AW	31100 AAW	ALBLS	10//99-12//99
	Huntsville MSA, AL	S	17.27 MW	15.69 AW	35920 AAW	ALBLS	10//99-12//99

AAW	Average annual wage	AOH	Average offered, high	ASH	Average starting, high
AE	Average entry wage	AOL	Average offered, low	ASL	Average starting, low
AEX	Average experienced wage	APH	Average pay, high range	AW	Average wage paid
AO	Average offered	APL	Average pay, low range	FQ	First quartile wage

H	Hourly	M	Monthly	S	Special: hourly and annual
HI	Highest wage paid	MTC	Median total compensation	TQ	Third quartile wage
HR	High end range	MW	Median wage paid	W	Weekly
LR	Low end range	SQ	Second quartile wage	Y	Yearly

Occupation/Type/Industry	Location	Per	Low	Mid	High	Source	Date
Aircraft Mechanic and Service Technician	Mobile MSA, AL	S	13.64 MW	13.68 AW	28370 AAW	ALBLS	10//99-12//99
	Alaska	S	20.34 MW	20.21 AW	42040 AAW	AKBLS	10//99-12//99
	Anchorage MSA, AK	S	20.19 MW	20.20 AW	42000 AAW	AKBLS	10//99-12//99
	Arizona	S	17.43 MW	17.72 AW	36860 AAW	AZBLS	10//99-12//99
	Flagstaff MSA, AZ-UT	S	18.86 MW	18.17 AW	39230 AAW	AZBLS	10//99-12//99
	Phoenix-Mesa MSA, AZ	S	18.20 MW	17.72 AW	37850 AAW	AZBLS	10//99-12//99
	Tucson MSA, AZ	S	17.26 MW	17.34 AW	35900 AAW	AZBLS	10//99-12//99
	Yuma MSA, AZ	S	11.65 MW	7.72 AW	24230 AAW	AZBLS	10//99-12//99
	Arkansas	S	12.64 MW	12.98 AW	26990 AAW	ARBLS	10//99-12//99
	California	S	19.71 MW	19.67 AW	40920 AAW	CABLS	10//99-12//99
	Bakersfield MSA, CA	S	19.38 MW	18.90 AW	40310 AAW	CABLS	10//99-12//99
	Fresno MSA, CA	S	17.19 MW	17.37 AW	35750 AAW	CABLS	10//99-12//99
	Los Angeles-Long Beach PMSA, CA	S	21.31 MW	21.09 AW	44320 AAW	CABLS	10//99-12//99
	Oakland PMSA, CA	S	19.02 MW	18.34 AW	39560 AAW	CABLS	10//99-12//99
	Orange County PMSA, CA	S	15.72 MW	15.74 AW	32700 AAW	CABLS	10//99-12//99
	Riverside-San Bernardino PMSA, CA	S	17.28 MW	16.98 AW	35940 AAW	CABLS	10//99-12//99
	Sacramento PMSA, CA	S	17.67 MW	18.63 AW	36740 AAW	CABLS	10//99-12//99
	Salinas MSA, CA	S	19.76 MW	19.44 AW	41090 AAW	CABLS	10//99-12//99
	San Diego MSA, CA	S	18.95 MW	19.11 AW	39410 AAW	CABLS	10//99-12//99
	San Jose PMSA, CA	S	21.69 MW	21.33 AW	45120 AAW	CABLS	10//99-12//99
	Santa Barbara-Santa Maria-Lompoc MSA, CA	S	15.89 MW	12.99 AW	33050 AAW	CABLS	10//99-12//99
	Santa Rosa PMSA, CA	S	13.74 MW	14.28 AW	28570 AAW	CABLS	10//99-12//99
	Stockton-Lodi MSA, CA	S	14.77 MW	14.92 AW	30730 AAW	CABLS	10//99-12//99
	Colorado	S	18.92 MW	19.10 AW	39720 AAW	COBLS	10//99-12//99
	Denver PMSA, CO	S	19.41 MW	19.40 AW	40370 AAW	COBLS	10//99-12//99
	Connecticut	S	17.21 MW	17.70 AW	36820 AAW	CTBLS	10//99-12//99
	Bridgeport PMSA, CT	S	17.29 MW	15.99 AW	35960 AAW	CTBLS	10//99-12//99
	Hartford MSA, CT	S	21.25 MW	21.85 AW	44210 AAW	CTBLS	10//99-12//99
	Delaware	S	19.25 MW	19.45 AW	40450 AAW	DEBLS	10//99-12//99
	Wilmington-Newark PMSA, DE-MD	S	19.49 MW	18.97 AW	40530 AAW	DEBLS	10//99-12//99
	Washington PMSA, DC-MD-VA-WV	S	19.92 MW	19.93 AW	41440 AAW	DCBLS	10//99-12//99
	Florida	S	16.74 MW	17.12 AW	35620 AAW	FLBLS	10//99-12//99
	Daytona Beach MSA, FL	S	10.75 MW	9.56 AW	22360 AAW	FLBLS	10//99-12//99
	Fort Lauderdale PMSA, FL	S	16.00 MW	15.99 AW	33280 AAW	FLBLS	10//99-12//99
	Fort Pierce-Port St. Lucie MSA, FL	S	14.67 MW	15.03 AW	30510 AAW	FLBLS	10//99-12//99
	Gainesville MSA, FL	S	14.33 MW	13.02 AW	29810 AAW	FLBLS	10//99-12//99
	Jacksonville MSA, FL	S	19.84 MW	18.96 AW	41260 AAW	FLBLS	10//99-12//99
	Melbourne-Titusville-Palm Bay MSA, FL	S	17.39 MW	17.74 AW	36160 AAW	FLBLS	10//99-12//99
	Miami PMSA, FL	S	15.06 MW	14.92 AW	31320 AAW	FLBLS	10//99-12//99
	Naples MSA, FL	S	14.45 MW	14.73 AW	30050 AAW	FLBLS	10//99-12//99
	Orlando MSA, FL	S	17.57 MW	18.25 AW	36550 AAW	FLBLS	10//99-12//99
	Panama City MSA, FL	S	16.94 MW	18.06 AW	35240 AAW	FLBLS	10//99-12//99
	Sarasota-Bradenton MSA, FL	S	24.87 MW	18.78 AW	51730 AAW	FLBLS	10//99-12//99
	Tallahassee MSA, FL	S	13.02 MW	13.20 AW	27080 AAW	FLBLS	10//99-12//99
	Tampa-St. Petersburg-Clearwater MSA, FL	S	27.30 MW	29.02 AW	56790 AAW	FLBLS	10//99-12//99
	West Palm Beach-Boca Raton MSA, FL	S	15.00 MW	13.54 AW	31190 AAW	FLBLS	10//99-12//99
	Georgia	S	22.05 MW	21.44 AW	44600 AAW	GABLS	10//99-12//99
	Atlanta MSA, GA	S	22.73 MW	23.39 AW	47270 AAW	GABLS	10//99-12//99
	Hawaii	S	19.13 MW	18.99 AW	39500 AAW	HIBLS	10//99-12//99
	Honolulu MSA, HI	S	19.06 MW	19.19 AW	39650 AAW	HIBLS	10//99-12//99
	Idaho	S	16.31 MW	15.99 AW	33260 AAW	IDBLS	10//99-12//99
	Boise City MSA, ID	S	17.01 MW	17.33 AW	35380 AAW	IDBLS	10//99-12//99
	Illinois	S	22.79 MW	22.42 AW	46630 AAW	ILBLS	10//99-12//99
	Chicago PMSA, IL	S	22.62 MW	22.97 AW	47050 AAW	ILBLS	10//99-12//99
	Indiana	S	21.55 MW	20.62 AW	42880 AAW	INBLS	10//99-12//99
	Indianapolis MSA, IN	S	20.96 MW	21.98 AW	43600 AAW	INBLS	10//99-12//99
	Iowa	S	15.92 MW	15.86 AW	33000 AAW	IABLS	10//99-12//99
	Des Moines MSA, IA	S	16.82 MW	16.23 AW	34980 AAW	IABLS	10//99-12//99
	Kansas	S	17.82 MW	17.52 AW	36430 AAW	KSBLS	10//99-12//99
	Wichita MSA, KS	S	17.91 MW	18.20 AW	37250 AAW	KSBLS	10//99-12//99
	Kentucky	S	26.8 MW	24.89 AW	51770 AAW	KYBLS	10//99-12//99
	Louisville MSA, KY-IN	S	20.24 MW	19.40 AW	42090 AAW	KYBLS	10//99-12//99

AAW Average annual wage	**AOH** Average offered, high	**ASH** Average starting, high	**H** Hourly	**M** Monthly	**S** Special: hourly and annual
AE Average entry wage	**AOL** Average offered, low	**ASL** Average starting, low	**HI** Highest wage paid	**MTC** Median total compensation	**TQ** Third quartile wage
AEX Average experienced wage	**APH** Average pay, high range	**AW** Average wage paid	**HR** High end range	**MW** Median wage paid	**W** Weekly
AO Average offered	**APL** Average pay, low range	**FQ** First quartile wage	**LR** Low end range	**SQ** Second quartile wage	**Y** Yearly

Occupation/Type/Industry	Location	Per	Low	Mid	High	Source	Date
Aircraft Mechanic and Service Technician	Louisiana	S	20.27 MW	20.29 AW	42210 AAW	LABLS	10//99-12//99
	Lafayette MSA, LA	S	22.21 MW	22.50 AW	46210 AAW	LABLS	10//99-12//99
	New Orleans MSA, LA	S	19.17 MW	19.05 AW	39880 AAW	LABLS	10//99-12//99
	Maryland	S	18.66 MW	18.50 AW	38470 AAW	MDBLS	10//99-12//99
	Baltimore PMSA, MD	S	20.45 MW	19.79 AW	42540 AAW	MDBLS	10//99-12//99
	Massachusetts	S	16.44 MW	16.41 AW	34140 AAW	MABLS	10//99-12//99
	Boston PMSA, MA-NH	S	16.31 MW	16.57 AW	33920 AAW	MABLS	10//99-12//99
	Springfield MSA, MA	S	16.66 MW	15.98 AW	34650 AAW	MABLS	10//99-12//99
	Michigan	S	18.84 MW	18.17 AW	37800 AAW	MIBLS	10//99-12//99
	Ann Arbor PMSA, MI	S	17.56 MW	18.04 AW	36520 AAW	MIBLS	10//99-12//99
	Detroit PMSA, MI	S	18.47 MW	19.18 AW	38410 AAW	MIBLS	10//99-12//99
	Minnesota	S	18.09 MW	18.58 AW	38650 AAW	MNBLS	10//99-12//99
	Duluth-Superior MSA, MN-WI	S	20.00 MW	21.04 AW	41600 AAW	MNBLS	10//99-12//99
	Minneapolis-St. Paul MSA, MN-WI	S	17.59 MW	17.26 AW	36580 AAW	MNBLS	10//99-12//99
	Mississippi	S	17.18 MW	17.24 AW	35850 AAW	MSBLS	10//99-12//99
	Biloxi-Gulfport-Pascagoula MSA, MS	S	17.91 MW	18.07 AW	37260 AAW	MSBLS	10//99-12//99
	Jackson MSA, MS	S	16.87 MW	16.70 AW	35080 AAW	MSBLS	10//99-12//99
	Missouri	S	19.33 MW	19.13 AW	39800 AAW	MOBLS	10//99-12//99
	Kansas City MSA, MO-KS	S	16.11 MW	15.50 AW	33510 AAW	MOBLS	10//99-12//99
	St. Louis MSA, MO-IL	S	19.83 MW	19.70 AW	41250 AAW	MOBLS	10//99-12//99
	Montana	S	14.34 MW	14.72 AW	30630 AAW	MTBLS	10//99-12//99
	Nebraska	S	13.72 MW	13.37 AW	27800 AAW	NEBLS	10//99-12//99
	Lincoln MSA, NE	S	14.49 MW	14.30 AW	30140 AAW	NEBLS	10//99-12//99
	Omaha MSA, NE-IA	S	14.13 MW	14.58 AW	29400 AAW	NEBLS	10//99-12//99
	Nevada	S	19.52 MW	20.23 AW	42070 AAW	NVBLS	10//99-12//99
	Las Vegas MSA, NV-AZ	S	21.42 MW	22.07 AW	44540 AAW	NVBLS	10//99-12//99
	New Hampshire	S	16.97 MW	18.51 AW	38500 AAW	NHBLS	10//99-12//99
	Manchester PMSA, NH	S	22.76 MW	20.99 AW	47350 AAW	NHBLS	10//99-12//99
	Portsmouth-Rochester PMSA, NH-ME	S	19.84 MW	20.80 AW	41260 AAW	NHBLS	10//99-12//99
	New Jersey	S	19.42 MW	19.46 AW	40480 AAW	NJBLS	10//99-12//99
	Bergen-Passaic PMSA, NJ	S	18.99 MW	18.94 AW	39490 AAW	NJBLS	10//99-12//99
	Newark PMSA, NJ	S	20.15 MW	19.94 AW	41910 AAW	NJBLS	10//99-12//99
	New Mexico	S	15.37 MW	15.66 AW	32570 AAW	NMBLS	10//99-12//99
	Albuquerque MSA, NM	S	17.22 MW	16.54 AW	35820 AAW	NMBLS	10//99-12//99
	New York	S	20.64 MW	20.93 AW	43530 AAW	NYBLS	10//99-12//99
	Albany-Schenectady-Troy MSA, NY	S	15.78 MW	13.48 AW	32820 AAW	NYBLS	10//99-12//99
	Buffalo-Niagara Falls MSA, NY	S	17.94 MW	18.79 AW	37310 AAW	NYBLS	10//99-12//99
	Dutchess County PMSA, NY	S	18.56 MW	17.60 AW	38600 AAW	NYBLS	10//99-12//99
	Nassau-Suffolk PMSA, NY	S	17.99 MW	16.57 AW	37420 AAW	NYBLS	10//99-12//99
	New York PMSA, NY	S	24.45 MW	24.84 AW	50860 AAW	NYBLS	10//99-12//99
	Rochester MSA, NY	S	16.18 MW	16.78 AW	33660 AAW	NYBLS	10//99-12//99
	North Carolina	S	16.9 MW	16.66 AW	34650 AAW	NCBLS	10//99-12//99
	Charlotte-Gastonia-Rock Hill MSA, NC-SC	S	16.89 MW	17.66 AW	35140 AAW	NCBLS	10//99-12//99
	Greensboro--Winston-Salem-- High Point MSA, NC	S	15.64 MW	14.29 AW	32540 AAW	NCBLS	10//99-12//99
	Raleigh-Durham-Chapel Hill MSA, NC	S	22.07 MW	23.22 AW	45910 AAW	NCBLS	10//99-12//99
	North Dakota	S	14.96 MW	15.32 AW	31860 AAW	NDBLS	10//99-12//99
	Bismarck MSA, ND	S	15.38 MW	14.97 AW	31990 AAW	NDBLS	10//99-12//99
	Fargo-Moorhead MSA, ND-MN	S	15.43 MW	14.75 AW	32090 AAW	NDBLS	10//99-12//99
	Ohio	S	18.32 MW	17.88 AW	37190 AAW	OHBLS	10//99-12//99
	Cincinnati PMSA, OH-KY-IN	S	27.11 MW	28.91 AW	56390 AAW	OHBLS	10//99-12//99
	Cleveland-Lorain-Elyria PMSA, OH	S	17.84 MW	18.12 AW	37110 AAW	OHBLS	10//99-12//99
	Columbus MSA, OH	S	19.43 MW	20.67 AW	40410 AAW	OHBLS	10//99-12//99
	Dayton-Springfield MSA, OH	S	17.90 MW	18.73 AW	37220 AAW	OHBLS	10//99-12//99
	Oklahoma	S	16.02 MW	15.72 AW	32700 AAW	OKBLS	10//99-12//99
	Enid MSA, OK	S	13.80 MW	13.94 AW	28710 AAW	OKBLS	10//99-12//99
	Tulsa MSA, OK	S	18.00 MW	17.88 AW	37440 AAW	OKBLS	10//99-12//99
	Oregon	S	16.91 MW	16.64 AW	34620 AAW	ORBLS	10//99-12//99
	Medford-Ashland MSA, OR	S	13.82 MW	14.21 AW	28750 AAW	ORBLS	10//99-12//99
	Portland-Vancouver PMSA, OR-WA	S	16.94 MW	17.39 AW	35230 AAW	ORBLS	10//99-12//99
	Pennsylvania	S	19.11 MW	18.58 AW	38650 AAW	PABLS	10//99-12//99

AAW	Average annual wage	AOH	Average offered, high	ASH	Average starting, high	H	Hourly	M	Monthly	S	Special: hourly and annual
AE	Average entry wage	AOL	Average offered, low	ASL	Average starting, low	HI	Highest wage paid	MTC	Median total compensation	TQ	Third quartile wage
AEX	Average experienced wage	APH	Average pay, high range	AW	Average wage paid	HR	High end range	MW	Median wage paid	W	Weekly
AO	Average offered	APL	Average pay, low range	FQ	First quartile wage	LR	Low end range	SQ	Second quartile wage	Y	Yearly

Occupation/Type/Industry	Location	Per	Low	Mid	High	Source	Date
Aircraft Mechanic and Service Technician	Philadelphia PMSA, PA-NJ	S	20.96 MW	21.97 AW	43600 AAW	PABLS	10//99-12//99
	Rhode Island	S	20.26 MW	21.38 AW	44470 AAW	RIBLS	10//99-12//99
	South Carolina	S	16.46 MW	15.91 AW	33090 AAW	SCBLS	10//99-12//99
	Greenville-Spartanburg-Anderson MSA, SC	S	14.42 MW	13.08 AW	29990 AAW	SCBLS	10//99-12//99
	South Dakota	S	14.53 MW	14.37 AW	29900 AAW	SDBLS	10//99-12//99
	Tennessee	S	17.35 MW	16.12 AW	33540 AAW	TNBLS	10//99-12//99
	Chattanooga MSA, TN-GA	S	22.40 MW	23.48 AW	46590 AAW	TNBLS	10//99-12//99
	Knoxville MSA, TN	S	15.00 MW	14.78 AW	31210 AAW	TNBLS	10//99-12//99
	Memphis MSA, TN-AR-MS	S	16.16 MW	17.45 AW	33620 AAW	MSBLS	10//99-12//99
	Nashville MSA, TN	S	16.25 MW	17.14 AW	33800 AAW	TNBLS	10//99-12//99
	Texas	S	19.64 MW	19.47 AW	40490 AAW	TXBLS	10//99-12//99
	Austin-San Marcos MSA, TX	S	16.42 MW	16.21 AW	34160 AAW	TXBLS	10//99-12//99
	Brownsville-Harlingen-San Benito MSA, TX	S	9.88 MW	9.49 AW	20540 AAW	TXBLS	10//99-12//99
	Dallas PMSA, TX	S	17.51 MW	17.06 AW	36430 AAW	TXBLS	10//99-12//99
	El Paso MSA, TX	S	16.88 MW	17.88 AW	35110 AAW	TXBLS	10//99-12//99
	Fort Worth-Arlington PMSA, TX	S	21.32 MW	22.52 AW	44340 AAW	TXBLS	10//99-12//99
	Galveston-Texas City PMSA, TX	S	17.34 MW	18.54 AW	36070 AAW	TXBLS	10//99-12//99
	Texarkana MSA, TX-Texarkana, AR	S	20.33 MW	19.25 AW	42290 AAW	TXBLS	10//99-12//99
	Vermont	S	19.23 MW	18.55 AW	38590 AAW	VTBLS	10//99-12//99
	Virginia	S	19.62 MW	19.42 AW	40400 AAW	VABLS	10//99-12//99
	Norfolk-Virginia Beach-Newport News MSA, VA-NC	S	19.46 MW	18.97 AW	40480 AAW	VABLS	10//99-12//99
	Richmond-Petersburg MSA, VA	S	15.77 MW	17.03 AW	32810 AAW	VABLS	10//99-12//99
	Washington	S	21.12 MW	20.87 AW	43410 AAW	WABLS	10//99-12//99
	Seattle-Bellevue-Everett PMSA, WA	S	21.20 MW	21.61 AW	44090 AAW	WABLS	10//99-12//99
	Spokane MSA, WA	S	17.27 MW	17.07 AW	35920 AAW	WABLS	10//99-12//99
	West Virginia	S	17.48 MW	17.02 AW	35410 AAW	WVBLS	10//99-12//99
	Charleston MSA, WV	S	21.91 MW	20.04 AW	45570 AAW	WVBLS	10//99-12//99
	Wisconsin	S	17.58 MW	17.43 AW	36260 AAW	WIBLS	10//99-12//99
	Green Bay MSA, WI	S	15.72 MW	14.18 AW	32690 AAW	WIBLS	10//99-12//99
	Milwaukee-Waukesha PMSA, WI	S	19.00 MW	19.30 AW	39520 AAW	WIBLS	10//99-12//99
	Wyoming	S	14.97 MW	14.80 AW	30780 AAW	WYBLS	10//99-12//99
	Cheyenne MSA, WY	S	14.51 MW	14.93 AW	30180 AAW	WYBLS	10//99-12//99
	Puerto Rico	S	17.36 MW	17.57 AW	36550 AAW	PRBLS	10//99-12//99
	San Juan-Bayamon PMSA, PR	S	18.54 MW	20.89 AW	38560 AAW	PRBLS	10//99-12//99
	Virgin Islands	S	19.29 MW	18.84 AW	39190 AAW	VIBLS	10//99-12//99
Aircraft Structure, Surfaces, Rigging, and Systems Assembler	Alabama	S	12.96 MW	13.11 AW	27270 AAW	ALBLS	10//99-12//99
	Arizona	S	19.3 MW	18.62 AW	38720 AAW	AZBLS	10//99-12//99
	California	S	22.27 MW	20.34 AW	42300 AAW	CABLS	10//99-12//99
	Connecticut	S	20.59 MW	19.77 AW	41120 AAW	CTBLS	10//99-12//99
	Florida	S	15 MW	15.50 AW	32250 AAW	FLBLS	10//99-12//99
	Georgia	S	12.38 MW	13.36 AW	27780 AAW	GABLS	10//99-12//99
	Idaho	S	11.26 MW	14.76 AW	30690 AAW	IDBLS	10//99-12//99
	Indiana	S	17.68 MW	16.48 AW	34280 AAW	INBLS	10//99-12//99
	Louisiana	S	25.77 MW	24.17 AW	50280 AAW	LABLS	10//99-12//99
	Maryland	S	14.83 MW	14.45 AW	30060 AAW	MDBLS	10//99-12//99
	Minnesota	S	8.29 MW	9.04 AW	18790 AAW	MNBLS	10//99-12//99
	New York	S	12.97 MW	15.07 AW	31340 AAW	NYBLS	10//99-12//99
	North Carolina	S	12.86 MW	12.99 AW	27030 AAW	NCBLS	10//99-12//99
	Ohio	S	17.74 MW	17.49 AW	36390 AAW	OHBLS	10//99-12//99
	Pennsylvania	S	21.81 MW	20.28 AW	42190 AAW	PABLS	10//99-12//99
	Texas	S	17.15 MW	15.58 AW	32410 AAW	TXBLS	10//99-12//99
Airfield Operations Specialist	Alaska	S	15.66 MW	17.08 AW	35530 AAW	AKBLS	10//99-12//99
	California	S	15.52 MW	16.75 AW	34840 AAW	CABLS	10//99-12//99
	Florida	S	9.63 MW	10.32 AW	21460 AAW	FLBLS	10//99-12//99
	Georgia	S	16.01 MW	18.17 AW	37800 AAW	GABLS	10//99-12//99
	Idaho	S	18.42 MW	16.84 AW	35030 AAW	IDBLS	10//99-12//99
	Illinois	S	18.51 MW	19.41 AW	40370 AAW	ILBLS	10//99-12//99
	Louisiana	S	14.68 MW	14.88 AW	30950 AAW	LABLS	10//99-12//99

AAW Average annual wage	AOH Average offered, high	ASH Average starting, high	H Hourly	M Monthly	S Special: hourly and annual
AE Average entry wage	AOL Average offered, low	ASL Average starting, low	HI Highest wage paid	MTC Median total compensation	TQ Third quartile wage
AEX Average experienced wage	APH Average pay, high range	AW Average wage paid	HR High end range	MW Median wage paid	W Weekly
AO Average offered	APL Average pay, low range	FQ First quartile wage	LR Low end range	SQ Second quartile wage	Y Yearly

Occupation/Type/Industry	Location	Per	Low	Mid	High	Source	Date
Airfield Operations Specialist	Michigan	S	14.91 MW	14.91 AW	31020 AAW	MIBLS	10//99-12//99
	Minnesota	S	18.95 MW	19.17 AW	39880 AAW	MNBLS	10//99-12//99
	Nebraska	S	7.38 MW	7.72 AW	16050 AAW	NEBLS	10//99-12//99
	New York	S	14.09 MW	14.35 AW	29850 AAW	NYBLS	10//99-12//99
	Ohio	S	10.5 MW	12.71 AW	26440 AAW	OHBLS	10//99-12//99
	Oklahoma	S	12.53 MW	15.43 AW	32090 AAW	OKBLS	10//99-12//99
	Pennsylvania	S	12.05 MW	12.80 AW	26610 AAW	PABLS	10//99-12//99
	Texas	S	10.85 MW	14.07 AW	29270 AAW	TXBLS	10//99-12//99
	Washington	S	29.71 MW	28.72 AW	59740 AAW	WABLS	10//99-12//99
Airframe and Powerplant Mechanic	United States	H	6.00 ASL		10.00 ASH	AVWEEK	2000
	United States	H		18.00 AEX	25.00 HI	AVWEEK	2000
Airline Pilot, Copilot, and Flight Engineer	Alabama	Y		58280 AAW		ALBLS	10//99-12//99
	Birmingham MSA, AL	Y		52380 AAW		ALBLS	10//99-12//99
	Montgomery MSA, AL	Y		65800 AAW		ALBLS	10//99-12//99
	Alaska	Y		104520 AAW		AKBLS	10//99-12//99
	Anchorage MSA, AK	Y		110870 AAW		AKBLS	10//99-12//99
	Arizona	Y		88600 AAW		AZBLS	10//99-12//99
	Phoenix-Mesa MSA, AZ	Y		89380 AAW		AZBLS	10//99-12//99
	Arkansas	Y		59900 AAW		ARBLS	10//99-12//99
	California	Y		129180 AAW		CABLS	10//99-12//99
	San Jose PMSA, CA	Y		74340 AAW		CABLS	10//99-12//99
	Colorado	Y		81370 AAW		COBLS	10//99-12//99
	Denver PMSA, CO	Y		82480 AAW		COBLS	10//99-12//99
	Connecticut	Y		41310 AAW		CTBLS	10//99-12//99
	Bridgeport PMSA, CT	Y		45240 AAW		CTBLS	10//99-12//99
	Hartford MSA, CT	Y		39050 AAW		CTBLS	10//99-12//99
	Delaware	Y		71260 AAW		DEBLS	10//99-12//99
	Wilmington-Newark PMSA, DE-MD	Y		69360 AAW		DEBLS	10//99-12//99
	Washington PMSA, DC-MD-VA-WV	Y		141030 AAW		DCBLS	10//99-12//99
	Florida	Y		93630 AAW		FLBLS	10//99-12//99
	Fort Lauderdale PMSA, FL	Y		58260 AAW		FLBLS	10//99-12//99
	Fort Walton Beach MSA, FL	Y		62350 AAW		FLBLS	10//99-12//99
	Jacksonville MSA, FL	Y		59450 AAW		FLBLS	10//99-12//99
	Orlando MSA, FL	Y		118220 AAW		FLBLS	10//99-12//99
	Tampa-St. Petersburg-Clearwater MSA, FL	Y		36880 AAW		FLBLS	10//99-12//99
	Hawaii	Y		101320 AAW		HIBLS	10//99-12//99
	Honolulu MSA, HI	Y		101380 AAW		HIBLS	10//99-12//99
	Idaho	Y		46390 AAW		IDBLS	10//99-12//99
	Boise City MSA, ID	Y		45740 AAW		IDBLS	10//99-12//99
	Illinois	Y		105800 AAW		ILBLS	10//99-12//99
	Chicago PMSA, IL	Y		106480 AAW		ILBLS	10//99-12//99
	Indianapolis MSA, IN	Y		49170 AAW		INBLS	10//99-12//99
	Iowa	Y		54660 AAW		IABLS	10//99-12//99
	Cedar Rapids MSA, IA	Y		53480 AAW		IABLS	10//99-12//99
	Sioux City MSA, IA-NE	Y		56020 AAW		IABLS	10//99-12//99
	Kansas	Y		60280 AAW		KSBLS	10//99-12//99
	Wichita MSA, KS	Y		83060 AAW		KSBLS	10//99-12//99
	Louisiana	Y		58510 AAW		LABLS	10//99-12//99
	Baton Rouge MSA, LA	Y		44950 AAW		LABLS	10//99-12//99
	Lafayette MSA, LA	Y		39670 AAW		LABLS	10//99-12//99
	New Orleans MSA, LA	Y		60760 AAW		LABLS	10//99-12//99
	Shreveport-Bossier City MSA, LA	Y		50620 AAW		LABLS	10//99-12//99
	Maryland	Y		69900 AAW		MDBLS	10//99-12//99
	Baltimore PMSA, MD	Y		78830 AAW		MDBLS	10//99-12//99
	Michigan	Y		66810 AAW		MIBLS	10//99-12//99
	Detroit PMSA, MI	Y		68110 AAW		MIBLS	10//99-12//99
	Grand Rapids-Muskegon-Holland MSA, MI	Y		37020 AAW		MIBLS	10//99-12//99
	Minnesota	Y		69970 AAW		MNBLS	10//99-12//99
	Minneapolis-St. Paul MSA, MN-WI	Y		70530 AAW		MNBLS	10//99-12//99
	Mississippi	Y		59310 AAW		MSBLS	10//99-12//99
	Jackson MSA, MS	Y		42320 AAW		MSBLS	10//99-12//99
	Nebraska	Y		36020 AAW		NEBLS	10//99-12//99

AAW	Average annual wage	**AOH**	Average offered, high	**ASH**	Average starting, high	**H** Hourly
AE	Average entry wage	**AOL**	Average offered, low	**ASL**	Average starting, low	**HI** Highest wage paid
AEX	Average experienced wage	**APH**	Average pay, high range	**AW**	Average wage paid	**HR** High end range
AO	Average offered	**APL**	Average pay, low range	**FQ**	First quartile wage	**LR** Low end range

M Monthly	**S** Special: hourly and annual
MTC Median total compensation	**TQ** Third quartile wage
MW Median wage paid	**W** Weekly
SQ Second quartile wage	**Y** Yearly

Occupation/Type/Industry	Location	Per	Low	Mid	High	Source	Date
Airline Pilot, Copilot, and Flight Engineer	Lincoln MSA, NE	Y		31080 AAW		NEBLS	10//99-12//99
	Reno MSA, NV	Y		54120 AAW		NVBLS	10//99-12//99
	New Hampshire	Y		74160 AAW		NHBLS	10//99-12//99
	Newark PMSA, NJ	Y		71900 AAW		NJBLS	10//99-12//99
	New York	Y		51730 AAW		NYBLS	10//99-12//99
	Nassau-Suffolk PMSA, NY	Y		53800 AAW		NYBLS	10//99-12//99
	New York PMSA, NY	Y		51820 AAW		NYBLS	10//99-12//99
	North Carolina	Y		47650 AAW		NCBLS	10//99-12//99
	North Dakota	Y		36270 AAW		NDBLS	10//99-12//99
	Columbus MSA, OH	Y		65250 AAW		OHBLS	10//99-12//99
	Dayton-Springfield MSA, OH	Y		34770 AAW		OHBLS	10//99-12//99
	Pennsylvania	Y		89660 AAW		PABLS	10//99-12//99
	Pittsburgh MSA, PA	Y		38170 AAW		PABLS	10//99-12//99
	South Carolina	Y		50550 AAW		SCBLS	10//99-12//99
	Greenville-Spartanburg-Anderson MSA, SC	Y		40460 AAW		SCBLS	10//99-12//99
	South Dakota	Y		52020 AAW		SDBLS	10//99-12//99
	Tennessee	Y		65820 AAW		TNBLS	10//99-12//99
	Memphis MSA, TN-AR-MS	Y		66030 AAW		MSBLS	10//99-12//99
	Nashville MSA, TN	Y		57230 AAW		TNBLS	10//99-12//99
	Texas	Y		123640 AAW		TXBLS	10//99-12//99
	Austin-San Marcos MSA, TX	Y		59470 AAW		TXBLS	10//99-12//99
	Dallas PMSA, TX	Y		41110 AAW		TXBLS	10//99-12//99
	El Paso MSA, TX	Y		45860 AAW		TXBLS	10//99-12//99
	Virginia	Y		138600 AAW		VABLS	10//99-12//99
	West Virginia	Y		45740 AAW		WVBLS	10//99-12//99
	Cheyenne MSA, WY	Y		52820 AAW		WYBLS	10//99-12//99
	Virgin Islands	Y		44050 AAW		VIBLS	10//99-12//99
Airplane Pilot, Navigator	United States	H		79.31 AW		NCS98	1998
Ambulance Driver and Attendant							
Except Emergency Medical Technician	Arizona	S	7.49 MW	8.51 AW	17700 AAW	AZBLS	10//99-12//99
Except Emergency Medical Technician	Arkansas	S	9.6 MW	10.11 AW	21040 AAW	ARBLS	10//99-12//99
Except Emergency Medical Technician	California	S	13.16 MW	16.39 AW	34090 AAW	CABLS	10//99-12//99
Except Emergency Medical Technician	Bakersfield MSA, CA	S	12.97 MW	10.56 AW	26990 AAW	CABLS	10//99-12//99
Except Emergency Medical Technician	Los Angeles-Long Beach PMSA, CA	S	23.04 MW	26.46 AW	47910 AAW	CABLS	10//99-12//99
Except Emergency Medical Technician	Riverside-San Bernardino PMSA, CA	S	21.49 MW	13.71 AW	44700 AAW	CABLS	10//99-12//99
Except Emergency Medical Technician	San Diego MSA, CA	S	27.92 MW	32.29 AW	58070 AAW	CABLS	10//99-12//99
Except Emergency Medical Technician	Connecticut	S	9.63 MW	9.88 AW	20540 AAW	CTBLS	10//99-12//99
Except Emergency Medical Technician	Hartford MSA, CT	S	10.00 MW	9.76 AW	20810 AAW	CTBLS	10//99-12//99
Except Emergency Medical Technician	Delaware	S	9.38 MW	9.09 AW	18920 AAW	DEBLS	10//99-12//99
Except Emergency Medical Technician	Washington PMSA, DC-MD-VA-WV	S	9.04 MW	8.14 AW	18790 AAW	DCBLS	10//99-12//99
Except Emergency Medical Technician	Florida	S	7.74 MW	8.87 AW	18440 AAW	FLBLS	10//99-12//99
Except Emergency Medical Technician	Fort Lauderdale PMSA, FL	S	12.50 MW	8.27 AW	26010 AAW	FLBLS	10//99-12//99
Except Emergency Medical Technician	Jacksonville MSA, FL	S	9.91 MW	7.96 AW	20620 AAW	FLBLS	10//99-12//99
Except Emergency Medical Technician	Orlando MSA, FL	S	9.50 MW	8.12 AW	19760 AAW	FLBLS	10//99-12//99
Except Emergency Medical Technician	Tampa-St. Petersburg-Clearwater MSA, FL	S	7.35 MW	7.08 AW	15290 AAW	FLBLS	10//99-12//99
Except Emergency Medical Technician	Georgia	S	6.82 MW	8.27 AW	17210 AAW	GABLS	10//99-12//99
Except Emergency Medical Technician	Atlanta MSA, GA	S	10.38 MW	10.88 AW	21590 AAW	GABLS	10//99-12//99
Except Emergency Medical Technician	Idaho	S	10.15 MW	11.11 AW	23100 AAW	IDBLS	10//99-12//99
Except Emergency Medical Technician	Illinois	S	8.99 MW	10.67 AW	22200 AAW	ILBLS	10//99-12//99
Except Emergency Medical Technician	Chicago PMSA, IL	S	10.89 MW	8.95 AW	22650 AAW	ILBLS	10//99-12//99
Except Emergency Medical Technician	Indiana	S	8.33 MW	8.95 AW	18620 AAW	INBLS	10//99-12//99
Except Emergency Medical Technician	Gary PMSA, IN	S	9.63 MW	9.56 AW	20030 AAW	INBLS	10//99-12//99
Except Emergency Medical Technician	Indianapolis MSA, IN	S	10.37 MW	10.73 AW	21560 AAW	INBLS	10//99-12//99
Except Emergency Medical Technician	Iowa	S	6.98 MW	7.98 AW	16610 AAW	IABLS	10//99-12//99
Except Emergency Medical Technician	Kansas	S	8.88 MW	9.32 AW	19380 AAW	KSBLS	10//99-12//99
Except Emergency Medical Technician	Kentucky	S	7.92 MW	8.03 AW	16700 AAW	KYBLS	10//99-12//99
Except Emergency Medical Technician	Louisville MSA, KY-IN	S	8.34 MW	8.08 AW	17340 AAW	KYBLS	10//99-12//99
Except Emergency Medical Technician	Louisiana	S	6.99 MW	7.37 AW	15320 AAW	LABLS	10//99-12//99
Except Emergency Medical Technician	Baton Rouge MSA, LA	S	7.22 MW	7.01 AW	15020 AAW	LABLS	10//99-12//99
Except Emergency Medical Technician	Lafayette MSA, LA	S	6.34 MW	6.02 AW	13180 AAW	LABLS	10//99-12//99
Except Emergency Medical Technician	Maine	S	7.78 MW	8.23 AW	17110 AAW	MEBLS	10//99-12//99
Except Emergency Medical Technician	Maryland	S	7.28 MW	7.76 AW	16150 AAW	MDBLS	10//99-12//99
Except Emergency Medical Technician	Massachusetts	S	10.01 MW	11.53 AW	23990 AAW	MABLS	10//99-12//99
Except Emergency Medical Technician	Boston PMSA, MA-NH	S	10.52 MW	9.92 AW	21890 AAW	MABLS	10//99-12//99

AAW Average annual wage	**AOH** Average offered, high	**ASH** Average starting, high	**H** Hourly	**M** Monthly	**S** Special: hourly and annual
AE Average entry wage	**AOL** Average offered, low	**ASL** Average starting, low	**HI** Highest wage paid	**MTC** Median total compensation	**TQ** Third quartile wage
AEX Average experienced wage	**APH** Average pay, high range	**AW** Average wage paid	**HR** High end range	**MW** Median wage paid	**W** Weekly
AO Average offered	**APL** Average pay, low range	**FQ** First quartile wage	**LR** Low end range	**SQ** Second quartile wage	**Y** Yearly

Occupation/Type/Industry	Location	Per	Low	Mid	High	Source	Date
Ambulance Driver and Attendant							
Except Emergency Medical Technician	Michigan	S	6.72 MW	7.10 AW	14770 AAW	MIBLS	10//99-12//99
Except Emergency Medical Technician	Minnesota	S	7.69 MW	8.55 AW	17780 AAW	MNBLS	10//99-12//99
Except Emergency Medical Technician	Minneapolis-St. Paul MSA, MN-WI	S	7.70 MW	7.52 AW	16020 AAW	MNBLS	10//99-12//99
Except Emergency Medical Technician	Mississippi	S	7.28 MW	7.56 AW	15730 AAW	MSBLS	10//99-12//99
Except Emergency Medical Technician	Montana	S	6 MW	6.54 AW	13600 AAW	MTBLS	10//99-12//99
Except Emergency Medical Technician	Nebraska	S	10.43 MW	10.24 AW	21310 AAW	NEBLS	10//99-12//99
Except Emergency Medical Technician	Nevada	S	7.73 MW	7.62 AW	15850 AAW	NVBLS	10//99-12//99
Except Emergency Medical Technician	New Jersey	S	8.92 MW	10.75 AW	22360 AAW	NJBLS	10//99-12//99
Except Emergency Medical Technician	Atlantic-Cape May PMSA, NJ	S	8.49 MW	8.42 AW	17660 AAW	NJBLS	10//99-12//99
Except Emergency Medical Technician	Bergen-Passaic PMSA, NJ	S	9.23 MW	9.31 AW	19190 AAW	NJBLS	10//99-12//99
Except Emergency Medical Technician	Newark PMSA, NJ	S	7.96 MW	7.96 AW	16570 AAW	NJBLS	10//99-12//99
Except Emergency Medical Technician	New Mexico	S	8.82 MW	8.18 AW	17020 AAW	NMBLS	10//99-12//99
Except Emergency Medical Technician	New York	S	8.72 MW	9.68 AW	20130 AAW	NYBLS	10//99-12//99
Except Emergency Medical Technician	Buffalo-Niagara Falls MSA, NY	S	9.63 MW	7.72 AW	20030 AAW	NYBLS	10//99-12//99
Except Emergency Medical Technician	Nassau-Suffolk PMSA, NY	S	9.55 MW	6.57 AW	19870 AAW	NYBLS	10//99-12//99
Except Emergency Medical Technician	New York PMSA, NY	S	9.73 MW	8.67 AW	20230 AAW	NYBLS	10//99-12//99
Except Emergency Medical Technician	Syracuse MSA, NY	S	10.14 MW	9.92 AW	21080 AAW	NYBLS	10//99-12//99
Except Emergency Medical Technician	North Dakota	S	8.4 MW	9.33 AW	19410 AAW	NDBLS	10//99-12//99
Except Emergency Medical Technician	Ohio	S	8.07 MW	10.46 AW	21760 AAW	OHBLS	10//99-12//99
Except Emergency Medical Technician	Cincinnati PMSA, OH-KY-IN	S	8.39 MW	7.77 AW	17440 AAW	OHBLS	10//99-12//99
Except Emergency Medical Technician	Oklahoma	S	7.11 MW	7.14 AW	14850 AAW	OKBLS	10//99-12//99
Except Emergency Medical Technician	Pennsylvania	S	8.05 MW	8.93 AW	18560 AAW	PABLS	10//99-12//99
Except Emergency Medical Technician	Pittsburgh MSA, PA	S	9.88 MW	8.52 AW	20560 AAW	PABLS	10//99-12//99
Except Emergency Medical Technician	Rhode Island	S	11.91 MW	12.08 AW	25120 AAW	RIBLS	10//99-12//99
Except Emergency Medical Technician	Providence-Fall River-Warwick MSA, RI-MA	S	12.96 MW	11.97 AW	26960 AAW	RIBLS	10//99-12//99
Except Emergency Medical Technician	South Carolina	S	6.51 MW	7.21 AW	15000 AAW	SCBLS	10//99-12//99
Except Emergency Medical Technician	Tennessee	S	9.03 MW	9.30 AW	19350 AAW	TNBLS	10//99-12//99
Except Emergency Medical Technician	Chattanooga MSA, TN-GA	S	9.53 MW	8.86 AW	19810 AAW	TNBLS	10//99-12//99
Except Emergency Medical Technician	Johnson City-Kingsport-Bristol MSA, TN-VA	S	8.63 MW	7.95 AW	17960 AAW	TNBLS	10//99-12//99
Except Emergency Medical Technician	Memphis MSA, TN-AR-MS	S	9.07 MW	8.46 AW	18870 AAW	MSBLS	10//99-12//99
Except Emergency Medical Technician	Texas	S	7.62 MW	7.90 AW	16420 AAW	TXBLS	10//99-12//99
Except Emergency Medical Technician	Austin-San Marcos MSA, TX	S	7.74 MW	7.87 AW	16090 AAW	TXBLS	10//99-12//99
Except Emergency Medical Technician	Houston PMSA, TX	S	7.61 MW	7.41 AW	15840 AAW	TXBLS	10//99-12//99
Except Emergency Medical Technician	San Antonio MSA, TX	S	7.83 MW	7.66 AW	16280 AAW	TXBLS	10//99-12//99
Except Emergency Medical Technician	Utah	S	10.23 MW	10.25 AW	21310 AAW	UTBLS	10//99-12//99
Except Emergency Medical Technician	Virginia	S	8.78 MW	8.96 AW	18630 AAW	VABLS	10//99-12//99
Except Emergency Medical Technician	Norfolk-Virginia Beach-Newport News MSA, VA-NC	S	9.35 MW	8.39 AW	19450 AAW	VABLS	10//99-12//99
Except Emergency Medical Technician	Washington	S	9.1 MW	9.44 AW	19640 AAW	WABLS	10//99-12//99
Except Emergency Medical Technician	Seattle-Bellevue-Everett PMSA, WA	S	10.26 MW	9.85 AW	21340 AAW	WABLS	10//99-12//99
Except Emergency Medical Technician	West Virginia	S	6.45 MW	7.16 AW	14880 AAW	WVBLS	10//99-12//99
Except Emergency Medical Technician	Wisconsin	S	7.91 MW	8.53 AW	17740 AAW	WIBLS	10//99-12//99
Except Emergency Medical Technician	Milwaukee-Waukesha PMSA, WI	S	8.26 MW	8.20 AW	17190 AAW	WIBLS	10//99-12//99
Except Emergency Medical Technician	Puerto Rico	S	5.89 MW	5.77 AW	12010 AAW	PRBLS	10//99-12//99
Except Emergency Medical Technician	Mayaguez MSA, PR	S	5.78 MW	5.86 AW	12010 AAW	PRBLS	10//99-12//99
Except Emergency Medical Technician	Ponce MSA, PR	S	5.90 MW	5.95 AW	12270 AAW	PRBLS	10//99-12//99
Except Emergency Medical Technician	San Juan-Bayamon PMSA, PR	S	5.77 MW	5.89 AW	12010 AAW	PRBLS	10//99-12//99
Ambulatory Surgery Center Manager	Central	Y		57479 AW		ORMAN2	1999
	East	Y		73300 AW		ORMAN2	1999
	South	Y		54958 AW		ORMAN2	1999
	West	Y		66893 AW		ORMAN2	1999
Amusement and Recreation Attendant	Alabama	S	6.2 MW	6.59 AW	13700 AAW	ALBLS	10//99-12//99
	Alaska	S	9.65 MW	9.65 AW	20080 AAW	AKBLS	10//99-12//99
	Arizona	S	6.26 MW	6.66 AW	13840 AAW	AZBLS	10//99-12//99
	Arkansas	S	6.02 MW	5.94 AW	12360 AAW	ARBLS	10//99-12//99
	California	S	6.97 MW	7.64 AW	15900 AAW	CABLS	10//99-12//99
	Colorado	S	6.81 MW	6.97 AW	14510 AAW	COBLS	10//99-12//99
	Connecticut	S	6.71 MW	7.54 AW	15680 AAW	CTBLS	10//99-12//99
	Delaware	S	6.79 MW	7.44 AW	15470 AAW	DEBLS	10//99-12//99
	Florida	S	6.26 MW	6.58 AW	13680 AAW	FLBLS	10//99-12//99

AAW Average annual wage	**AOH** Average offered, high	**ASH** Average starting, high	**H** Hourly	**M** Monthly	**S** Special: hourly and annual
AE Average entry wage	**AOL** Average offered, low	**ASL** Average starting, low	**HI** Highest wage paid	**MTC** Median total compensation	**TQ** Third quartile wage
AEX Average experienced wage	**APH** Average pay, high range	**AW** Average wage paid	**HR** High end range	**MW** Median wage paid	**W** Weekly
AO Average offered	**APL** Average pay, low range	**FQ** First quartile wage	**LR** Low end range	**SQ** Second quartile wage	**Y** Yearly

Occupation/Type/Industry	Location	Per	Low	Mid	High	Source	Date
Amusement and Recreation Attendant	Georgia	S	6.15 MW	6.32 AW	13140 AAW	GABLS	10//99-12//99
	Hawaii	S	7.6 MW	8.32 AW	17310 AAW	HIBLS	10//99-12//99
	Idaho	S	6.39 MW	7.17 AW	14920 AAW	IDBLS	10//99-12//99
	Illinois	S	6.42 MW	6.69 AW	13910 AAW	ILBLS	10//99-12//99
	Indiana	S	6.45 MW	6.96 AW	14480 AAW	INBLS	10//99-12//99
	Iowa	S	6.11 MW	6.24 AW	12970 AAW	IABLS	10//99-12//99
	Kansas	S	6.08 MW	6.56 AW	13640 AAW	KSBLS	10//99-12//99
	Kentucky	S	6.56 MW	6.92 AW	14390 AAW	KYBLS	10//99-12//99
	Louisiana	S	6.47 MW	7.01 AW	14570 AAW	LABLS	10//99-12//99
	Maine	S	6.99 MW	7.88 AW	16380 AAW	MEBLS	10//99-12//99
	Maryland	S	6.67 MW	6.94 AW	14430 AAW	MDBLS	10//99-12//99
	Massachusetts	S	8.03 MW	8.44 AW	17560 AAW	MABLS	10//99-12//99
	Michigan	S	6.7 MW	7.12 AW	14810 AAW	MIBLS	10//99-12//99
	Minnesota	S	6.51 MW	8.26 AW	17190 AAW	MNBLS	10//99-12//99
	Mississippi	S	6.74 MW	7.26 AW	15100 AAW	MSBLS	10//99-12//99
	Missouri	S	6.36 MW	6.77 AW	14090 AAW	MOBLS	10//99-12//99
	Montana	S	6.27 MW	6.33 AW	13160 AAW	MTBLS	10//99-12//99
	Nebraska	S	6.12 MW	6.36 AW	13220 AAW	NEBLS	10//99-12//99
	Nevada	S	6.4 MW	6.72 AW	13970 AAW	NVBLS	10//99-12//99
	New Hampshire	S	7.38 MW	7.34 AW	15260 AAW	NHBLS	10//99-12//99
	New Jersey	S	7.44 MW	8.10 AW	16850 AAW	NJBLS	10//99-12//99
	New Mexico	S	8.34 MW	11.11 AW	23110 AAW	NMBLS	10//99-12//99
	New York	S	7.14 MW	7.49 AW	15580 AAW	NYBLS	10//99-12//99
	North Carolina	S	6.59 MW	7.23 AW	15040 AAW	NCBLS	10//99-12//99
	North Dakota	S	6.19 MW	6.51 AW	13550 AAW	NDBLS	10//99-12//99
	Ohio	S	6.49 MW	7.29 AW	15170 AAW	OHBLS	10//99-12//99
	Oklahoma	S	6.21 MW	6.71 AW	13950 AAW	OKBLS	10//99-12//99
	Oregon	S	6.73 MW	7.22 AW	15020 AAW	ORBLS	10//99-12//99
	Pennsylvania	S	6.19 MW	6.56 AW	13650 AAW	PABLS	10//99-12//99
	Rhode Island	S	8.66 MW	9.85 AW	20490 AAW	RIBLS	10//99-12//99
	South Carolina	S	8.86 MW	8.25 AW	17160 AAW	SCBLS	10//99-12//99
	South Dakota	S	6.15 MW	6.16 AW	12810 AAW	SDBLS	10//99-12//99
	Tennessee	S	6.67 MW	7.90 AW	16420 AAW	TNBLS	10//99-12//99
	Texas	S	6.19 MW	6.82 AW	14190 AAW	TXBLS	10//99-12//99
	Utah	S	6.36 MW	6.83 AW	14200 AAW	UTBLS	10//99-12//99
	Vermont	S	6.71 MW	7.58 AW	15770 AAW	VTBLS	10//99-12//99
	Virginia	S	6.36 MW	6.82 AW	14180 AAW	VABLS	10//99-12//99
	Washington	S	7.09 MW	7.50 AW	15590 AAW	WABLS	10//99-12//99
	West Virginia	S	6.42 MW	6.99 AW	14540 AAW	WVBLS	10//99-12//99
	Wisconsin	S	6.6 MW	6.97 AW	14490 AAW	WIBLS	10//99-12//99
	Wyoming	S	6.83 MW	7.63 AW	15870 AAW	WYBLS	10//99-12//99
	Puerto Rico	S	6.04 MW	6.13 AW	12740 AAW	PRBLS	10//99-12//99
	Guam	S	6.26 MW	6.68 AW	13900 AAW	GUBLS	10//99-12//99
Analyst Female, Logistics	United States	Y	41000 FQ	56000 SQ	66000 TQ	TRAFWD	2000
Anesthesiologist	Alabama	S	53.33 MW	56.35 AW	117210 AAW	ALBLS	10//99-12//99
	Arizona	S	17.37 MW	18.06 AW	37560 AAW	AZBLS	10//99-12//99
	California	S	42.22 MW	43.45 AW	90380 AAW	CABLS	10//99-12//99
	Georgia	S	53.02 MW	49.74 AW	103460 AAW	GABLS	10//99-12//99
	Idaho	S	42.36 MW	41.78 AW	86890 AAW	IDBLS	10//99-12//99
	Illinois	S	41.2 MW	39.39 AW	81930 AAW	ILBLS	10//99-12//99
	Indiana	S	56.12 MW	49.58 AW	103130 AAW	INBLS	10//99-12//99
	Kentucky	S		66.57 AW	138470 AAW	KYBLS	10//99-12//99
	Louisville MSA, KY-IN	S	68.29 MW		142050 AAW	KYBLS	10//99-12//99
	Louisiana	S	55.3 MW	47.55 AW	98900 AAW	LABLS	10//99-12//99
	Maine	S	38.64 MW	38.19 AW	79430 AAW	MEBLS	10//99-12//99
	Massachusetts	S		65.29 AW	135810 AAW	MABLS	10//99-12//99
	Michigan	S	63.6 MW	58.09 AW	120830 AAW	MIBLS	10//99-12//99
	Detroit PMSA, MI	S	62.14 MW		129250 AAW	MIBLS	10//99-12//99
	Missouri	S	58.99 MW	55.42 AW	115270 AAW	MOBLS	10//99-12//99
	Nebraska	S	30.75 MW	34.88 AW	72540 AAW	NEBLS	10//99-12//99
	New Jersey	S		65.82 AW	136910 AAW	NJBLS	10//99-12//99
	North Carolina	S	46.34 MW	44.55 AW	92670 AAW	NCBLS	10//99-12//99
	Charlotte-Gastonia-Rock Hill MSA, NC-SC	S	47.61 MW	49.46 AW	99030 AAW	NCBLS	10//99-12//99
	Greensboro--Winston-Salem--High Point MSA, NC	S	39.93 MW	39.76 AW	83040 AAW	NCBLS	10//99-12//99
	Ohio	S		62.29 AW	129560 AAW	OHBLS	10//99-12//99
	Oklahoma	S	54.81 MW	56.24 AW	116980 AAW	OKBLS	10//99-12//99

AAW	Average annual wage	AOH	Average offered, high	ASH	Average starting, high	H	Hourly	M	Monthly	S	Special: hourly and annual
AE	Average entry wage	AOL	Average offered, low	ASL	Average starting, low	HI	Highest wage paid	MTC	Median total compensation	TQ	Third quartile wage
AEX	Average experienced wage	APH	Average pay, high range	AW	Average wage paid	HR	High end range	MW	Median wage paid	W	Weekly
AO	Average offered	APL	Average pay, low range	FQ	First quartile wage	LR	Low end range	SQ	Second quartile wage	Y	Yearly

Occupation/Type/Industry	Location	Per	Low	Mid	High	Source	Date
Anesthesiologist	Pennsylvania	S		58.22 AW	121090 AAW	PABLS	10//99-12//99
	Philadelphia PMSA, PA-NJ	S	57.87 MW		120370 AAW	PABLS	10//99-12//99
	South Carolina	S		65.33 AW	135880 AAW	SCBLS	10//99-12//99
	Tennessee	S		69.41 AW	144370 AAW	TNBLS	10//99-12//99
	Puerto Rico	S	28.78 MW	29.74 AW	61860 AAW	PRBLS	10//99-12//99
Animal Breeder	Illinois	S	10.36 MW	15.60 AW	32450 AAW	ILBLS	10//99-12//99
	Kentucky	S	9.63 MW	9.80 AW	20380 AAW	KYBLS	10//99-12//99
	Minnesota	S	9.32 MW	9.33 AW	19400 AAW	MNBLS	10//99-12//99
	Ohio	S	10.95 MW	11.25 AW	23390 AAW	OHBLS	10//99-12//99
	Tennessee	S	9.04 MW	9.34 AW	19430 AAW	TNBLS	10//99-12//99
Animal Control Worker	Alabama	S	8.31 MW	8.78 AW	18270 AAW	ALBLS	10//99-12//99
	Alaska	S	15.98 MW	16.54 AW	34390 AAW	AKBLS	10//99-12//99
	Arizona	S	9.09 MW	9.33 AW	19400 AAW	AZBLS	10//99-12//99
	Arkansas	S	7.92 MW	8.32 AW	17300 AAW	ARBLS	10//99-12//99
	California	S	11.21 MW	11.57 AW	24070 AAW	CABLS	10//99-12//99
	Colorado	S	12.96 MW	13.34 AW	27750 AAW	COBLS	10//99-12//99
	Connecticut	S	10.71 MW	12.42 AW	25840 AAW	CTBLS	10//99-12//99
	Florida	S	10.19 MW	10.48 AW	21790 AAW	FLBLS	10//99-12//99
	Georgia	S	9.9 MW	10.05 AW	20910 AAW	GABLS	10//99-12//99
	Illinois	S	11.51 MW	11.90 AW	24740 AAW	ILBLS	10//99-12//99
	Indiana	S	11.01 MW	11.44 AW	23790 AAW	INBLS	10//99-12//99
	Iowa	S	10.16 MW	9.32 AW	19380 AAW	IABLS	10//99-12//99
	Kansas	S	9.35 MW	9.43 AW	19610 AAW	KSBLS	10//99-12//99
	Louisiana	S	9.37 MW	9.14 AW	19000 AAW	LABLS	10//99-12//99
	Maine	S	9.14 MW	9.10 AW	18940 AAW	MEBLS	10//99-12//99
	Maryland	S	12.11 MW	12.49 AW	25980 AAW	MDBLS	10//99-12//99
	Massachusetts	S	14.94 MW	14.18 AW	29500 AAW	MABLS	10//99-12//99
	Michigan	S	13.92 MW	13.74 AW	28580 AAW	MIBLS	10//99-12//99
	Minnesota	S	13.93 MW	11.18 AW	23260 AAW	MNBLS	10//99-12//99
	Montana	S	7.44 MW	8.52 AW	17730 AAW	MTBLS	10//99-12//99
	Nebraska	S	9.71 MW	10.33 AW	21480 AAW	NEBLS	10//99-12//99
	Nevada	S	15.59 MW	15.33 AW	31890 AAW	NVBLS	10//99-12//99
	New Hampshire	S	9.48 MW	10.02 AW	20850 AAW	NHBLS	10//99-12//99
	New Jersey	S	22.33 MW	20.05 AW	41710 AAW	NJBLS	10//99-12//99
	New Mexico	S	10.74 MW	10.71 AW	22280 AAW	NMBLS	10//99-12//99
	New York	S	8.26 MW	9.76 AW	20300 AAW	NYBLS	10//99-12//99
	North Carolina	S	10.33 MW	10.45 AW	21740 AAW	NCBLS	10//99-12//99
	Ohio	S	11.5 MW	11.24 AW	23380 AAW	OHBLS	10//99-12//99
	Oklahoma	S	10.23 MW	10.83 AW	22520 AAW	OKBLS	10//99-12//99
	Oregon	S	10.86 MW	10.44 AW	21720 AAW	ORBLS	10//99-12//99
	Pennsylvania	S	11.12 MW	11.48 AW	23880 AAW	PABLS	10//99-12//99
	Rhode Island	S	11.97 MW	11.79 AW	24520 AAW	RIBLS	10//99-12//99
	South Carolina	S	8.24 MW	9.01 AW	18730 AAW	SCBLS	10//99-12//99
	Tennessee	S	9.09 MW	8.72 AW	18130 AAW	TNBLS	10//99-12//99
	Texas	S	10.49 MW	10.77 AW	22400 AAW	TXBLS	10//99-12//99
	Utah	S	12.31 MW	12.47 AW	25940 AAW	UTBLS	10//99-12//99
	Vermont	S	7.65 MW	7.70 AW	16020 AAW	VTBLS	10//99-12//99
	Virginia	S	11.66 MW	12.10 AW	25160 AAW	VABLS	10//99-12//99
	Washington	S	10.42 MW	11.53 AW	23990 AAW	WABLS	10//99-12//99
	Wisconsin	S	13.62 MW	14.53 AW	30230 AAW	WIBLS	10//99-12//99
Animal Trainer	Arizona	S	10.14 MW	15.43 AW	32100 AAW	AZBLS	10//99-12//99
	California	S	10.92 MW	12.34 AW	25680 AAW	CABLS	10//99-12//99
	Connecticut	S	10.67 MW	12.38 AW	25750 AAW	CTBLS	10//99-12//99
	Florida	S	12.24 MW	12.17 AW	25320 AAW	FLBLS	10//99-12//99
	Georgia	S	8.78 MW	10.10 AW	21020 AAW	GABLS	10//99-12//99
	Idaho	S	11.65 MW	10.96 AW	22790 AAW	IDBLS	10//99-12//99
	Illinois	S	18.74 MW	17.38 AW	36150 AAW	ILBLS	10//99-12//99
	Indiana	S	7.83 MW	9.70 AW	20170 AAW	INBLS	10//99-12//99
	Kansas	S	9.99 MW	11.28 AW	23460 AAW	KSBLS	10//99-12//99
	Kentucky	S	9.38 MW	10.15 AW	21110 AAW	KYBLS	10//99-12//99
	Louisiana	S	6.4 MW	8.74 AW	18190 AAW	LABLS	10//99-12//99
	Maryland	S	12.07 MW	14.03 AW	29180 AAW	MDBLS	10//99-12//99
	Massachusetts	S	11.4 MW	14.28 AW	29700 AAW	MABLS	10//99-12//99
	Minnesota	S	17.77 MW	14.80 AW	30770 AAW	MNBLS	10//99-12//99
	Missouri	S	7.43 MW	8.53 AW	17730 AAW	MOBLS	10//99-12//99
	Nevada	S	7.71 MW	11.06 AW	23010 AAW	NVBLS	10//99-12//99
	New Jersey	S	12.37 MW	13.50 AW	28080 AAW	NJBLS	10//99-12//99
	New Mexico	S	8.57 MW	9.33 AW	19410 AAW	NMBLS	10//99-12//99
	New York	S	8.4 MW	11.23 AW	23350 AAW	NYBLS	10//99-12//99
	North Carolina	S	6.49 MW	8.31 AW	17280 AAW	NCBLS	10//99-12//99

AAW Average annual wage	**AOH** Average offered, high	**ASH** Average starting, high	**H** Hourly	**M** Monthly	**S** Special: hourly and annual
AE Average entry wage	**AOL** Average offered, low	**ASL** Average starting, low	**HI** Highest wage paid	**MTC** Median total compensation	**TQ** Third quartile wage
AEX Average experienced wage	**APH** Average pay, high range	**AW** Average wage paid	**HR** High end range	**MW** Median wage paid	**W** Weekly
AO Average offered	**APL** Average pay, low range	**FQ** First quartile wage	**LR** Low end range	**SQ** Second quartile wage	**Y** Yearly

Occupation/Type/Industry	Location	Per	Low	Mid	High	Source	Date
Animal Trainer	Ohio	S	11.49 MW	13.75 AW	28610 AAW	OHBLS	10//99-12//99
	Oklahoma	S	10.37 MW	11.60 AW	24120 AAW	OKBLS	10//99-12//99
	Oregon	S	12.09 MW	14.81 AW	30810 AAW	ORBLS	10//99-12//99
	Rhode Island	S	12.66 MW	19.84 AW	41270 AAW	RIBLS	10//99-12//99
	South Carolina	S	7.89 MW	8.63 AW	17940 AAW	SCBLS	10//99-12//99
	Tennessee	S	13.71 MW	12.93 AW	26900 AAW	TNBLS	10//99-12//99
	Texas	S	10.18 MW	11.32 AW	23550 AAW	TXBLS	10//99-12//99
	Virginia	S	7.79 MW	9.05 AW	18820 AAW	VABLS	10//99-12//99
	Wisconsin	S	13.48 MW	15.37 AW	31970 AAW	WIBLS	10//99-12//99
Announcer	United States	H		26.98 AW		NCS98	1998
	Alabama	S	6.59 MW	8.87 AW	18440 AAW	ALBLS	10//99-12//99
	Alaska	S	8.62 MW	11.91 AW	24780 AAW	AKBLS	10//99-12//99
	Arizona	S	8.39 MW	12.27 AW	25510 AAW	AZBLS	10//99-12//99
	Arkansas	S	7.83 MW	9.37 AW	19490 AAW	ARBLS	10//99-12//99
	California	S	11.98 MW	15.45 AW	32140 AAW	CABLS	10//99-12//99
	Colorado	S	10.24 MW	12.31 AW	25610 AAW	COBLS	10//99-12//99
	Connecticut	S	11.36 MW	13.60 AW	28280 AAW	CTBLS	10//99-12//99
	Delaware	S	9.98 MW	10.70 AW	22250 AAW	DEBLS	10//99-12//99
	Florida	S	10.68 MW	14.30 AW	29740 AAW	FLBLS	10//99-12//99
	Georgia	S	10.07 MW	12.18 AW	25330 AAW	GABLS	10//99-12//99
	Hawaii	S	8.22 MW	10.55 AW	21950 AAW	HIBLS	10//99-12//99
	Idaho	S	8.66 MW	10.22 AW	21250 AAW	IDBLS	10//99-12//99
	Illinois	S	10.17 MW	14.49 AW	30140 AAW	ILBLS	10//99-12//99
	Indiana	S	8.49 MW	10.41 AW	21660 AAW	INBLS	10//99-12//99
	Iowa	S	6.88 MW	8.44 AW	17550 AAW	IABLS	10//99-12//99
	Kansas	S	10.08 MW	12.05 AW	25060 AAW	KSBLS	10//99-12//99
	Kentucky	S	6.94 MW	8.20 AW	17060 AAW	KYBLS	10//99-12//99
	Louisiana	S	7.58 MW	9.51 AW	19770 AAW	LABLS	10//99-12//99
	Maine	S	8.89 MW	11.12 AW	23120 AAW	MEBLS	10//99-12//99
	Maryland	S	10.2 MW	15.30 AW	31830 AAW	MDBLS	10//99-12//99
	Massachusetts	S	11.24 MW	16.19 AW	33680 AAW	MABLS	10//99-12//99
	Michigan	S	9.37 MW	12.71 AW	26430 AAW	MIBLS	10//99-12//99
	Minnesota	S	8.41 MW	9.81 AW	20410 AAW	MNBLS	10//99-12//99
	Mississippi	S	8.63 MW	9.29 AW	19320 AAW	MSBLS	10//99-12//99
	Missouri	S	6.89 MW	9.60 AW	19970 AAW	MOBLS	10//99-12//99
	Montana	S	7.51 MW	9.13 AW	18990 AAW	MTBLS	10//99-12//99
	Nebraska	S	8.94 MW	10.78 AW	22430 AAW	NEBLS	10//99-12//99
	Nevada	S	11.66 MW	14.94 AW	31070 AAW	NVBLS	10//99-12//99
	New Hampshire	S	9.12 MW	9.61 AW	19990 AAW	NHBLS	10//99-12//99
	New Jersey	S	11.02 MW	13.63 AW	28350 AAW	NJBLS	10//99-12//99
	New Mexico	S	7.92 MW	9.67 AW	20110 AAW	NMBLS	10//99-12//99
	New York	S	10.1 MW	19.62 AW	40800 AAW	NYBLS	10//99-12//99
	North Carolina	S	8 MW	11.06 AW	23000 AAW	NCBLS	10//99-12//99
	North Dakota	S	7.61 MW	9.49 AW	19750 AAW	NDBLS	10//99-12//99
	Ohio	S	8.93 MW	12.07 AW	25100 AAW	OHBLS	10//99-12//99
	Oklahoma	S	6.82 MW	8.90 AW	18510 AAW	OKBLS	10//99-12//99
	Pennsylvania	S	8.28 MW	12.93 AW	26890 AAW	PABLS	10//99-12//99
	Rhode Island	S	11.27 MW	13.73 AW	28570 AAW	RIBLS	10//99-12//99
	South Carolina	S	8.5 MW	10.85 AW	22570 AAW	SCBLS	10//99-12//99
	South Dakota	S	8.91 MW	9.95 AW	20700 AAW	SDBLS	10//99-12//99
	Tennessee	S	8 MW	10.36 AW	21550 AAW	TNBLS	10//99-12//99
	Texas	S	8.44 MW	11.46 AW	23840 AAW	TXBLS	10//99-12//99
	Vermont	S	8.4 MW	9.68 AW	20140 AAW	VTBLS	10//99-12//99
	Virginia	S	7.53 MW	10.12 AW	21050 AAW	VABLS	10//99-12//99
	Washington	S	11.52 MW	13.26 AW	27580 AAW	WABLS	10//99-12//99
	West Virginia	S	6.56 MW	9.28 AW	19310 AAW	WVBLS	10//99-12//99
	Wisconsin	S	8.41 MW	10.58 AW	22000 AAW	WIBLS	10//99-12//99
	Wyoming	S	8.19 MW	8.42 AW	17520 AAW	WYBLS	10//99-12//99
	Puerto Rico	S	7.62 MW	9.11 AW	18950 AAW	PRBLS	10//99-12//99
	Guam	S	7.44 MW	9.79 AW	20370 AAW	GUBLS	10//99-12//99
Anthropologist and Archeologist	Alaska	S	20.05 MW	20.29 AW	42200 AAW	AKBLS	10//99-12//99
	Arizona	S	18.48 MW	19.08 AW	39690 AAW	AZBLS	10//99-12//99
	Arkansas	S	18.19 MW	16.96 AW	35280 AAW	ARBLS	10//99-12//99
	California	S	15.71 MW	17.23 AW	35840 AAW	CABLS	10//99-12//99
	Colorado	S	15.22 MW	16.88 AW	35120 AAW	COBLS	10//99-12//99
	Florida	S	18.02 MW	19.27 AW	40090 AAW	FLBLS	10//99-12//99
	Georgia	S	16.07 MW	18.30 AW	38060 AAW	GABLS	10//99-12//99
	Hawaii	S	19.79 MW	20.26 AW	42140 AAW	HIBLS	10//99-12//99
	Idaho	S	22.46 MW	22.63 AW	47070 AAW	IDBLS	10//99-12//99
	Illinois	S	13.98 MW	15.12 AW	31450 AAW	ILBLS	10//99-12//99
	Kentucky	S	18.36 MW	18.33 AW	38120 AAW	KYBLS	10//99-12//99

AAW	Average annual wage	AOH	Average offered, high	ASH	Average starting, high	H	Hourly	M	Monthly	S	Special: hourly and annual
AE	Average entry wage	AOL	Average offered, low	ASL	Average starting, low	HI	Highest wage paid	MTC	Median total compensation	TQ	Third quartile wage
AEX	Average experienced wage	APH	Average pay, high range	AW	Average wage paid	HR	High end range	MW	Median wage paid	W	Weekly
AO	Average offered	APL	Average pay, low range	FQ	First quartile wage	LR	Low end range	SQ	Second quartile wage	Y	Yearly

Occupation/Type/Industry	Location	Per	Low	Mid	High	Source	Date
Anthropologist and Archeologist	Massachusetts	S	31.47 MW	33.88 AW	70460 AAW	MABLS	10//99-12//99
	Missouri	S	20.74 MW	21.83 AW	45400 AAW	MOBLS	10//99-12//99
	Montana	S	17.04 MW	18.42 AW	38320 AAW	MTBLS	10//99-12//99
	Nevada	S	24 MW	23.71 AW	49310 AAW	NVBLS	10//99-12//99
	New Mexico	S	14.08 MW	14.81 AW	30810 AAW	NMBLS	10//99-12//99
	New York	S	24.2 MW	24.48 AW	50910 AAW	NYBLS	10//99-12//99
	Oregon	S	21.31 MW	22.34 AW	46470 AAW	ORBLS	10//99-12//99
	Pennsylvania	S	14.32 MW	14.73 AW	30650 AAW	PABLS	10//99-12//99
	Texas	S	18.07 MW	20.07 AW	41750 AAW	TXBLS	10//99-12//99
	Utah	S	23.36 MW	23.43 AW	48720 AAW	UTBLS	10//99-12//99
	Washington	S	18.47 MW	19.20 AW	39940 AAW	WABLS	10//99-12//99
	Wisconsin	S	13.59 MW	15.18 AW	31570 AAW	WIBLS	10//99-12//99
	Wyoming	S	14.77 MW	15.91 AW	33100 AAW	WYBLS	10//99-12//99
	Puerto Rico	S	11.15 MW	12.81 AW	26640 AAW	PRBLS	10//99-12//99
Anthropology and Archeology Teacher							
Postsecondary	California	Y		59590 AAW		CABLS	10//99-12//99
Postsecondary	Colorado	Y		51770 AAW		COBLS	10//99-12//99
Postsecondary	Florida	Y		71410 AAW		FLBLS	10//99-12//99
Postsecondary	Georgia	Y		44550 AAW		GABLS	10//99-12//99
Postsecondary	Illinois	Y		51360 AAW		ILBLS	10//99-12//99
Postsecondary	Massachusetts	Y		51950 AAW		MABLS	10//99-12//99
Postsecondary	Michigan	Y		56460 AAW		MIBLS	10//99-12//99
Postsecondary	Minnesota	Y		64400 AAW		MNBLS	10//99-12//99
Postsecondary	Nevada	Y		56870 AAW		NVBLS	10//99-12//99
Postsecondary	New Jersey	Y		65430 AAW		NJBLS	10//99-12//99
Postsecondary	New York	Y		57970 AAW		NYBLS	10//99-12//99
Postsecondary	North Carolina	Y		58700 AAW		NCBLS	10//99-12//99
Postsecondary	Ohio	Y		53760 AAW		OHBLS	10//99-12//99
Postsecondary	Oklahoma	Y		61110 AAW		OKBLS	10//99-12//99
Postsecondary	Oregon	Y		52950 AAW		ORBLS	10//99-12//99
Postsecondary	Pennsylvania	Y		64720 AAW		PABLS	10//99-12//99
Postsecondary	Tennessee	Y		48370 AAW		TNBLS	10//99-12//99
Postsecondary	Texas	Y		59330 AAW		TXBLS	10//99-12//99
Postsecondary	Virginia	Y		55960 AAW		VABLS	10//99-12//99
Postsecondary	Washington	Y		37970 AAW		WABLS	10//99-12//99
Appointment Secretary							
Health Care Office, Family Practice	United States	Y		18741 AW		MEDEC1	1999
Health Care Office, Internal Medicine	United States	Y		18374 AW		MEDEC1	1999
Health Care Office, Obstetrics-gynecology	United States	Y		18675 AW		MEDEC1	1999
Health Care Office, Pediatrics	United States	Y		20343 AW		MEDEC1	1999
Appraiser and Assessor of Real Estate							
	Alabama	S	14.39 MW	18.80 AW	39100 AAW	ALBLS	10//99-12//99
	Birmingham MSA, AL	S	17.40 MW	15.28 AW	36190 AAW	ALBLS	10//99-12//99
	Alaska	S	24.98 MW	26.47 AW	55060 AAW	AKBLS	10//99-12//99
	Arizona	S	20.95 MW	21.17 AW	44020 AAW	AZBLS	10//99-12//99
	Flagstaff MSA, AZ-UT	S	13.66 MW	14.44 AW	28400 AAW	AZBLS	10//99-12//99
	Phoenix-Mesa MSA, AZ	S	21.83 MW	21.34 AW	45410 AAW	AZBLS	10//99-12//99
	Tucson MSA, AZ	S	21.63 MW	22.18 AW	45000 AAW	AZBLS	10//99-12//99
	Arkansas	S	10.11 MW	11.33 AW	23570 AAW	ARBLS	10//99-12//99
	Little Rock-North Little Rock MSA, AR	S	17.01 MW	15.61 AW	35380 AAW	ARBLS	10//99-12//99
	California	S	22.63 MW	24.08 AW	50080 AAW	CABLS	10//99-12//99
	Fresno MSA, CA	S	24.28 MW	22.47 AW	50510 AAW	CABLS	10//99-12//99
	Los Angeles-Long Beach PMSA, CA	S	23.93 MW	22.43 AW	49780 AAW	CABLS	10//99-12//99
	Modesto MSA, CA	S	29.83 MW	30.95 AW	62040 AAW	CABLS	10//99-12//99
	Oakland PMSA, CA	S	25.00 MW	24.67 AW	52000 AAW	CABLS	10//99-12//99
	Orange County PMSA, CA	S	30.73 MW	33.68 AW	63920 AAW	CABLS	10//99-12//99
	Riverside-San Bernardino PMSA, CA	S	19.76 MW	19.90 AW	41090 AAW	CABLS	10//99-12//99
	Sacramento PMSA, CA	S	25.36 MW	24.99 AW	52750 AAW	CABLS	10//99-12//99
	San Diego MSA, CA	S	18.32 MW	16.58 AW	38120 AAW	CABLS	10//99-12//99
	San Francisco PMSA, CA	S	27.31 MW	25.59 AW	56810 AAW	CABLS	10//99-12//99
	San Jose PMSA, CA	S	29.80 MW	26.89 AW	61980 AAW	CABLS	10//99-12//99
	San Luis Obispo-Atascadero-Paso Robles MSA, CA	S	19.81 MW	18.89 AW	41210 AAW	CABLS	10//99-12//99
	Santa Barbara-Santa Maria-Lompoc MSA, CA	S	23.10 MW	21.52 AW	48050 AAW	CABLS	10//99-12//99

AAW	Average annual wage	AOH	Average offered, high	ASH	Average starting, high
AE	Average entry salary	AOL	Average offered, low	ASL	Average starting, low
AEX	Average experienced wage	APH	Average pay, high range	AW	Average wage paid
AO	Average offered	APL	Average pay, low range	FQ	First quartile wage

H	Hourly	M	Monthly
HI	Highest wage paid	MTC	Median total compensation
HR	High end range	MW	Median wage paid
LR	Low end range	SQ	Second quartile wage

S	Special: hourly and annual
TQ	Third quartile wage
W	Weekly
Y	Yearly

Occupation/Type/Industry	Location	Per	Low	Mid	High	Source	Date
Appraiser and Assessor of Real Estate	Santa Cruz-Watsonville						
	PMSA, CA	S	21.16 MW	20.90 AW	44020 AAW	CABLS	10//99-12//99
	Santa Rosa PMSA, CA	S	24.36 MW	23.09 AW	50660 AAW	CABLS	10//99-12//99
	Stockton-Lodi MSA, CA	S	22.48 MW	22.56 AW	46770 AAW	CABLS	10//99-12//99
	Ventura PMSA, CA	S	17.45 MW	15.88 AW	36300 AAW	CABLS	10//99-12//99
	Visalia-Tulare-Porterville MSA, CA	S	25.27 MW	23.86 AW	52550 AAW	CABLS	10//99-12//99
	Colorado	S	22.95 MW	26.50 AW	55130 AAW	COBLS	10//99-12//99
	Denver PMSA, CO	S	26.72 MW	23.37 AW	55580 AAW	COBLS	10//99-12//99
	Connecticut	S	23.27 MW	23.59 AW	49060 AAW	CTBLS	10//99-12//99
	Bridgeport PMSA, CT	S	26.20 MW	23.04 AW	54490 AAW	CTBLS	10//99-12//99
	Danbury PMSA, CT	S	23.04 MW	23.94 AW	47920 AAW	CTBLS	10//99-12//99
	Hartford MSA, CT	S	23.77 MW	23.32 AW	49450 AAW	CTBLS	10//99-12//99
	New Haven-Meriden PMSA, CT	S	25.87 MW	23.60 AW	53810 AAW	CTBLS	10//99-12//99
	New London-Norwich MSA, CT-RI	S	18.74 MW	18.99 AW	38970 AAW	CTBLS	10//99-12//99
	Stamford-Norwalk PMSA, CT	S	25.99 MW	25.98 AW	54050 AAW	CTBLS	10//99-12//99
	Waterbury PMSA, CT	S	18.23 MW	17.17 AW	37920 AAW	CTBLS	10//99-12//99
	Delaware	S	27.32 MW	28.60 AW	59490 AAW	DEBLS	10//99-12//99
	District of Columbia	S	23.51 MW	24.60 AW	51160 AAW	DCBLS	10//99-12//99
	Washington PMSA, DC-MD-VA-WV	S	19.80 MW	17.86 AW	41180 AAW	DCBLS	10//99-12//99
	Florida	S	15.97 MW	18.37 AW	38210 AAW	FLBLS	10//99-12//99
	Fort Myers-Cape Coral MSA, FL	S	24.97 MW	21.97 AW	51940 AAW	FLBLS	10//99-12//99
	Jacksonville MSA, FL	S	21.46 MW	17.63 AW	44650 AAW	FLBLS	10//99-12//99
	Miami PMSA, FL	S	20.18 MW	20.61 AW	41970 AAW	FLBLS	10//99-12//99
	Orlando MSA, FL	S	13.69 MW	11.74 AW	28480 AAW	FLBLS	10//99-12//99
	Pensacola MSA, FL	S	28.79 MW	19.53 AW	59880 AAW	FLBLS	10//99-12//99
	Tampa-St. Petersburg-Clearwater MSA, FL	S	20.42 MW	18.43 AW	42470 AAW	FLBLS	10//99-12//99
	West Palm Beach-Boca Raton MSA, FL	S	18.41 MW	17.73 AW	38290 AAW	FLBLS	10//99-12//99
	Georgia	S	17.07 MW	20.07 AW	41740 AAW	GABLS	10//99-12//99
	Atlanta MSA, GA	S	24.55 MW	25.29 AW	51050 AAW	GABLS	10//99-12//99
	Augusta-Aiken MSA, GA-SC	S	15.55 MW	13.61 AW	32350 AAW	GABLS	10//99-12//99
	Columbus MSA, GA-AL	S	15.50 MW	13.09 AW	32240 AAW	GABLS	10//99-12//99
	Macon MSA, GA	S	20.76 MW	20.25 AW	43180 AAW	GABLS	10//99-12//99
	Savannah MSA, GA	S	16.91 MW	13.42 AW	35180 AAW	GABLS	10//99-12//99
	Hawaii	S	24.66 MW	29.58 AW	61540 AAW	HIBLS	10//99-12//99
	Honolulu MSA, HI	S	30.85 MW	26.39 AW	64160 AAW	HIBLS	10//99-12//99
	Idaho	S	13.11 MW	15.08 AW	31380 AAW	IDBLS	10//99-12//99
	Boise City MSA, ID	S	23.08 MW	19.94 AW	48000 AAW	IDBLS	10//99-12//99
	Illinois	S	17.56 MW	18.56 AW	38610 AAW	ILBLS	10//99-12//99
	Champaign-Urbana MSA, IL	S	22.33 MW	18.96 AW	46440 AAW	ILBLS	10//99-12//99
	Chicago PMSA, IL	S	20.49 MW	19.20 AW	42630 AAW	ILBLS	10//99-12//99
	Peoria-Pekin MSA, IL	S	19.66 MW	16.61 AW	40900 AAW	ILBLS	10//99-12//99
	Indiana	S	11.57 MW	13.21 AW	27470 AAW	INBLS	10//99-12//99
	Evansville-Henderson MSA, IN-KY	S	16.55 MW	14.61 AW	34430 AAW	INBLS	10//99-12//99
	Fort Wayne MSA, IN	S	12.59 MW	12.65 AW	26190 AAW	INBLS	10//99-12//99
	Gary PMSA, IN	S	13.55 MW	12.26 AW	28170 AAW	INBLS	10//99-12//99
	Indianapolis MSA, IN	S	15.53 MW	13.33 AW	32300 AAW	INBLS	10//99-12//99
	Lafayette MSA, IN	S	11.59 MW	10.44 AW	24100 AAW	INBLS	10//99-12//99
	Terre Haute MSA, IN	S	15.04 MW	10.27 AW	31280 AAW	INBLS	10//99-12//99
	Iowa	S	17.33 MW	18.23 AW	37920 AAW	IABLS	10//99-12//99
	Des Moines MSA, IA	S	23.02 MW	22.33 AW	47890 AAW	IABLS	10//99-12//99
	Kansas	S	16.5 MW	19.97 AW	41530 AAW	KSBLS	10//99-12//99
	Topeka MSA, KS	S	21.37 MW	19.70 AW	44450 AAW	KSBLS	10//99-12//99
	Wichita MSA, KS	S	18.81 MW	16.64 AW	39130 AAW	KSBLS	10//99-12//99
	Kentucky	S	17 MW	19.06 AW	39650 AAW	KYBLS	10//99-12//99
	Louisville MSA, KY-IN	S	17.10 MW	14.31 AW	35570 AAW	KYBLS	10//99-12//99
	Louisiana	S	19.72 MW	22.18 AW	46120 AAW	LABLS	10//99-12//99
	New Orleans MSA, LA	S	26.76 MW	25.51 AW	55650 AAW	LABLS	10//99-12//99
	Shreveport-Bossier City MSA, LA	S	19.03 MW	18.56 AW	39590 AAW	LABLS	10//99-12//99
	Maine	S	14.75 MW	16.26 AW	33830 AAW	MEBLS	10//99-12//99
	Portland MSA, ME	S	19.11 MW	14.88 AW	39740 AAW	MEBLS	10//99-12//99
	Maryland	S	16.81 MW	17.51 AW	36420 AAW	MDBLS	10//99-12//99
	Baltimore PMSA, MD	S	16.97 MW	16.48 AW	35300 AAW	MDBLS	10//99-12//99

AAW Average annual wage; AE Average entry wage; AEX Average experienced wage; AO Average offered; AOH Average offered, high; AOL Average offered, low; APH Average pay, high range; APL Average pay, low range; ASH Average starting, high; ASL Average starting, low; AW Average wage paid; FQ First quartile wage; H Hourly; HI Highest wage paid; HR High end range; LR Low end range; M Monthly; MTC Median total compensation; MW Median wage paid; SQ Second quartile wage; S Special: hourly and annual; TQ Third quartile wage; W Weekly; Y Yearly

Appraiser and Assessor of Real Estate

Occupation/Type/Industry	Location	Per	Low	Mid	High	Source	Date
Appraiser and Assessor of Real Estate	Massachusetts	S	18.04 MW	19.01 AW	39550 AAW	MABLS	10//99-12//99
	Barnstable-Yarmouth MSA, MA	S	17.39 MW	15.62 AW	36170 AAW	MABLS	10//99-12//99
	Boston PMSA, MA-NH	S	20.99 MW	21.83 AW	43660 AAW	MABLS	10//99-12//99
	Lawrence PMSA, MA-NH	S	16.72 MW	15.79 AW	34780 AAW	MABLS	10//99-12//99
	Lowell PMSA, MA-NH	S	16.09 MW	15.49 AW	33470 AAW	MABLS	10//99-12//99
	Pittsfield MSA, MA	S	17.50 MW	16.48 AW	36400 AAW	MABLS	10//99-12//99
	Worcester PMSA, MA-CT	S	17.57 MW	18.10 AW	36550 AAW	MABLS	10//99-12//99
	Michigan	S	19.38 MW	20.85 AW	43360 AAW	MIBLS	10//99-12//99
	Ann Arbor PMSA, MI	S	19.13 MW	20.80 AW	39790 AAW	MIBLS	10//99-12//99
	Detroit PMSA, MI	S	23.55 MW	20.22 AW	48990 AAW	MIBLS	10//99-12//99
	Flint PMSA, MI	S	23.56 MW	21.27 AW	49010 AAW	MIBLS	10//99-12//99
	Grand Rapids-Muskegon-Holland MSA, MI	S	21.80 MW	19.67 AW	45340 AAW	MIBLS	10//99-12//99
	Kalamazoo-Battle Creek MSA, MI	S	23.54 MW	20.56 AW	48960 AAW	MIBLS	10//99-12//99
	Lansing-East Lansing MSA, MI	S	21.92 MW	19.03 AW	45600 AAW	MIBLS	10//99-12//99
	Saginaw-Bay City-Midland MSA, MI	S	15.90 MW	14.73 AW	33080 AAW	MIBLS	10//99-12//99
	Minnesota	S	18.8 MW	20.30 AW	42220 AAW	MNBLS	10//99-12//99
	Duluth-Superior MSA, MN-WI	S	19.89 MW	18.69 AW	41370 AAW	MNBLS	10//99-12//99
	Minneapolis-St. Paul MSA, MN-WI	S	21.20 MW	20.01 AW	44090 AAW	MNBLS	10//99-12//99
	St. Cloud MSA, MN	S	19.69 MW	19.74 AW	40950 AAW	MNBLS	10//99-12//99
	Mississippi	S	13.69 MW	14.17 AW	29470 AAW	MSBLS	10//99-12//99
	Missouri	S	16.22 MW	17.88 AW	37190 AAW	MOBLS	10//99-12//99
	Kansas City MSA, MO-KS	S	23.36 MW	20.19 AW	48590 AAW	MOBLS	10//99-12//99
	St. Louis MSA, MO-IL	S	19.96 MW	18.25 AW	41520 AAW	MOBLS	10//99-12//99
	Montana	S	14.64 MW	15.94 AW	33160 AAW	MTBLS	10//99-12//99
	Nebraska	S	15.18 MW	17.91 AW	37250 AAW	NEBLS	10//99-12//99
	Lincoln MSA, NE	S	22.52 MW	20.17 AW	46850 AAW	NEBLS	10//99-12//99
	Omaha MSA, NE-IA	S	18.90 MW	16.27 AW	39310 AAW	NEBLS	10//99-12//99
	Nevada	S	23.22 MW	25.22 AW	52460 AAW	NVBLS	10//99-12//99
	Las Vegas MSA, NV-AZ	S	24.51 MW	22.94 AW	50970 AAW	NVBLS	10//99-12//99
	Reno MSA, NV	S	29.79 MW	25.18 AW	61960 AAW	NVBLS	10//99-12//99
	New Hampshire	S	18.82 MW	20.00 AW	41590 AAW	NHBLS	10//99-12//99
	Manchester PMSA, NH	S	26.14 MW	27.95 AW	54360 AAW	NHBLS	10//99-12//99
	Portsmouth-Rochester PMSA, NH-ME	S	15.72 MW	13.55 AW	32690 AAW	NHBLS	10//99-12//99
	New Jersey	S	23.08 MW	25.65 AW	53350 AAW	NJBLS	10//99-12//99
	Atlantic-Cape May PMSA, NJ	S	19.17 MW	16.67 AW	39880 AAW	NJBLS	10//99-12//99
	Bergen-Passaic PMSA, NJ	S	21.96 MW	20.43 AW	45680 AAW	NJBLS	10//99-12//99
	Middlesex-Somerset-Hunterdon PMSA, NJ	S	23.50 MW	20.84 AW	48870 AAW	NJBLS	10//99-12//99
	Monmouth-Ocean PMSA, NJ	S	26.08 MW	26.69 AW	54250 AAW	NJBLS	10//99-12//99
	Newark PMSA, NJ	S	26.38 MW	23.58 AW	54870 AAW	NJBLS	10//99-12//99
	Trenton PMSA, NJ	S	26.72 MW	22.75 AW	55570 AAW	NJBLS	10//99-12//99
	New Mexico	S	13.02 MW	15.42 AW	32080 AAW	NMBLS	10//99-12//99
	Santa Fe MSA, NM	S	14.31 MW	13.79 AW	29760 AAW	NMBLS	10//99-12//99
	New York	S	15.3 MW	17.07 AW	35510 AAW	NYBLS	10//99-12//99
	Buffalo-Niagara Falls MSA, NY	S	11.81 MW	8.07 AW	24560 AAW	NYBLS	10//99-12//99
	Dutchess County PMSA, NY	S	17.58 MW	18.20 AW	36570 AAW	NYBLS	10//99-12//99
	Jamestown MSA, NY	S	14.45 MW	13.52 AW	30050 AAW	NYBLS	10//99-12//99
	Nassau-Suffolk PMSA, NY	S	17.99 MW	15.87 AW	37410 AAW	NYBLS	10//99-12//99
	New York PMSA, NY	S	23.22 MW	22.95 AW	48300 AAW	NYBLS	10//99-12//99
	Rochester MSA, NY	S	14.69 MW	13.55 AW	30560 AAW	NYBLS	10//99-12//99
	Syracuse MSA, NY	S	13.97 MW	13.91 AW	29060 AAW	NYBLS	10//99-12//99
	North Carolina	S	17.25 MW	19.20 AW	39930 AAW	NCBLS	10//99-12//99
	Charlotte-Gastonia-Rock Hill MSA, NC-SC	S	24.37 MW	22.19 AW	50690 AAW	NCBLS	10//99-12//99
	Greensboro--Winston-Salem--High Point MSA, NC	S	22.33 MW	20.52 AW	46440 AAW	NCBLS	10//99-12//99
	Hickory-Morganton-Lenoir MSA, NC	S	16.31 MW	15.38 AW	33920 AAW	NCBLS	10//99-12//99
	Jacksonville MSA, NC	S	14.04 MW	14.48 AW	29200 AAW	NCBLS	10//99-12//99
	Raleigh-Durham-Chapel Hill MSA, NC	S	18.75 MW	18.39 AW	39000 AAW	NCBLS	10//99-12//99
	Rocky Mount MSA, NC	S	21.04 MW	22.64 AW	43760 AAW	NCBLS	10//99-12//99
	North Dakota	S	21.33 MW	21.47 AW	44650 AAW	NDBLS	10//99-12//99
	Bismarck MSA, ND	S	19.40 MW	20.11 AW	40360 AAW	NDBLS	10//99-12//99

AAW Average annual wage	AOH Average offered, high	ASH Average starting, high	H Hourly	M Monthly	S Special: hourly and annual
AE Average entry wage	AOL Average offered, low	ASL Average starting, low	HI Highest wage paid	MTC Median total compensation	TQ Third quartile wage
AEX Average experienced wage	APH Average pay, high range	AW Average wage paid	HR High end range	MW Median wage paid	W Weekly
AO Average offered	APL Average pay, low range	FQ First quartile wage	LR Low end range	SQ Second quartile wage	Y Yearly

Occupation/Type/Industry	Location	Per	Low	Mid	High	Source	Date
Appraiser and Assessor of Real Estate	Ohio	S	19.06 MW	20.64 AW	42930 AAW	OHBLS	10//99-12//99
	Akron PMSA, OH	S	19.14 MW	17.76 AW	39810 AAW	OHBLS	10//99-12//99
	Cincinnati PMSA, OH-KY-IN	S	18.99 MW	16.04 AW	39490 AAW	OHBLS	10//99-12//99
	Cleveland-Lorain-Elyria PMSA, OH	S	22.33 MW	21.29 AW	46450 AAW	OHBLS	10//99-12//99
	Columbus MSA, OH	S	18.89 MW	17.20 AW	39300 AAW	OHBLS	10//99-12//99
	Dayton-Springfield MSA, OH	S	21.45 MW	19.75 AW	44610 AAW	OHBLS	10//99-12//99
	Steubenville-Weirton MSA, OH-WV	S	14.25 MW	9.31 AW	29640 AAW	OHBLS	10//99-12//99
	Toledo MSA, OH	S	23.85 MW	18.65 AW	49610 AAW	OHBLS	10//99-12//99
	Oklahoma	S	13.06 MW	15.42 AW	32070 AAW	OKBLS	10//99-12//99
	Lawton MSA, OK	S	15.42 MW	15.15 AW	32060 AAW	OKBLS	10//99-12//99
	Oklahoma City MSA, OK	S	20.25 MW	17.45 AW	42120 AAW	OKBLS	10//99-12//99
	Tulsa MSA, OK	S	14.18 MW	13.14 AW	29500 AAW	OKBLS	10//99-12//99
	Oregon	S	21.85 MW	21.55 AW	44820 AAW	ORBLS	10//99-12//99
	Portland-Vancouver PMSA, OR-WA	S	21.99 MW	22.32 AW	45730 AAW	ORBLS	10//99-12//99
	Salem PMSA, OR	S	27.20 MW	26.61 AW	56570 AAW	ORBLS	10//99-12//99
	Pennsylvania	S	20.17 MW	22.70 AW	47220 AAW	PABLS	10//99-12//99
	Allentown-Bethlehem-Easton MSA, PA	S	20.51 MW	16.98 AW	42660 AAW	PABLS	10//99-12//99
	Harrisburg-Lebanon-Carlisle MSA, PA	S	11.65 MW	8.84 AW	24240 AAW	PABLS	10//99-12//99
	Lancaster MSA, PA	S	18.96 MW	17.72 AW	39440 AAW	PABLS	10//99-12//99
	Philadelphia PMSA, PA-NJ	S	28.18 MW	27.95 AW	58600 AAW	PABLS	10//99-12//99
	Pittsburgh MSA, PA	S	22.95 MW	22.38 AW	47730 AAW	PABLS	10//99-12//99
	State College MSA, PA	S	15.86 MW	13.09 AW	32990 AAW	PABLS	10//99-12//99
	York MSA, PA	S	14.96 MW	9.36 AW	31110 AAW	PABLS	10//99-12//99
	Rhode Island	S	34.79 MW	27.71 AW	57630 AAW	RIBLS	10//99-12//99
	Providence-Fall River-Warwick MSA, RI-MA	S	27.21 MW	30.75 AW	56600 AAW	RIBLS	10//99-12//99
	South Carolina	S	11.9 MW	14.81 AW	30800 AAW	SCBLS	10//99-12//99
	Charleston-North Charleston MSA, SC	S	16.49 MW	15.17 AW	34300 AAW	SCBLS	10//99-12//99
	Columbia MSA, SC	S	11.57 MW	9.62 AW	24060 AAW	SCBLS	10//99-12//99
	Greenville-Spartanburg-Anderson MSA, SC	S	24.27 MW	19.52 AW	50480 AAW	SCBLS	10//99-12//99
	South Dakota	S	13.57 MW	15.64 AW	32530 AAW	SDBLS	10//99-12//99
	Tennessee	S	19.47 MW	21.26 AW	44230 AAW	TNBLS	10//99-12//99
	Chattanooga MSA, TN-GA	S	15.15 MW	12.98 AW	31520 AAW	TNBLS	10//99-12//99
	Johnson City-Kingsport-Bristol MSA, TN-VA	S	15.39 MW	13.94 AW	32000 AAW	TNBLS	10//99-12//99
	Knoxville MSA, TN	S	26.50 MW	24.56 AW	55130 AAW	TNBLS	10//99-12//99
	Texas	S	18.29 MW	21.38 AW	44460 AAW	TXBLS	10//99-12//99
	Austin-San Marcos MSA, TX	S	29.06 MW	22.88 AW	60440 AAW	TXBLS	10//99-12//99
	Beaumont-Port Arthur MSA, TX	S	21.49 MW	19.37 AW	44700 AAW	TXBLS	10//99-12//99
	Corpus Christi MSA, TX	S	17.43 MW	15.91 AW	36260 AAW	TXBLS	10//99-12//99
	Dallas PMSA, TX	S	30.39 MW	24.84 AW	63210 AAW	TXBLS	10//99-12//99
	Fort Worth-Arlington PMSA, TX	S	17.57 MW	20.93 AW	36550 AAW	TXBLS	10//99-12//99
	Houston PMSA, TX	S	15.57 MW	14.98 AW	32390 AAW	TXBLS	10//99-12//99
	San Antonio MSA, TX	S	19.84 MW	18.97 AW	41260 AAW	TXBLS	10//99-12//99
	Utah	S	18.83 MW	20.63 AW	42910 AAW	UTBLS	10//99-12//99
	Provo-Orem MSA, UT	S	33.64 MW	46.20 AW	69970 AAW	UTBLS	10//99-12//99
	Vermont	S	16.18 MW	17.78 AW	36990 AAW	VTBLS	10//99-12//99
	Virginia	S	18.49 MW	20.57 AW	42790 AAW	VABLS	10//99-12//99
	Charlottesville MSA, VA	S	19.85 MW	17.24 AW	41280 AAW	VABLS	10//99-12//99
	Lynchburg MSA, VA	S	22.44 MW	22.15 AW	46680 AAW	VABLS	10//99-12//99
	Norfolk-Virginia Beach-Newport News MSA, VA-NC	S	27.49 MW	29.26 AW	57170 AAW	VABLS	10//99-12//99
	Richmond-Petersburg MSA, VA	S	19.81 MW	18.08 AW	41200 AAW	VABLS	10//99-12//99
	Roanoke MSA, VA	S	17.49 MW	16.66 AW	36380 AAW	VABLS	10//99-12//99
	Washington	S	19.85 MW	21.34 AW	44390 AAW	WABLS	10//99-12//99
	Richland-Kennewick-Pasco MSA, WA	S	18.12 MW	18.37 AW	37690 AAW	WABLS	10//99-12//99
	Seattle-Bellevue-Everett PMSA, WA	S	22.65 MW	21.21 AW	47110 AAW	WABLS	10//99-12//99
	Spokane MSA, WA	S	21.69 MW	20.52 AW	45120 AAW	WABLS	10//99-12//99

AAW	Average annual wage	AOH	Average offered, high	ASH	Average starting, high
AE	Average entry wage	AOL	Average offered, low	ASL	Average starting, low
AEX	Average experienced wage	APH	Average pay, high range	AW	Average wage paid
AO	Average offered	APL	Average pay, low range	FQ	First quartile wage

H	Hourly	M	Monthly
HI	Highest wage paid	MTC	Median total compensation
HR	High end range	MW	Median wage paid
LR	Low end range	SQ	Second quartile wage

S	Special: hourly and annual
TQ	Third quartile wage
W	Weekly
Y	Yearly

Occupation/Type/Industry	Location	Per	Low	Mid	High	Source	Date
Appraiser and Assessor of Real Estate	West Virginia	S	11.46 MW	15.21 AW	31630 AAW	WVBLS	10//99-12//99
	Huntington-Ashland MSA, WV-KY-OH	S	12.46 MW	9.71 AW	25920 AAW	WVBLS	10//99-12//99
	Parkersburg-Marietta MSA, WV-OH	S	11.43 MW	10.40 AW	23770 AAW	WVBLS	10//99-12//99
	Wisconsin	S	14.58 MW	15.48 AW	32210 AAW	WIBLS	10//99-12//99
	Appleton-Oshkosh-Neenah MSA, WI	S	17.71 MW	15.69 AW	36830 AAW	WIBLS	10//99-12//99
	Green Bay MSA, WI	S	19.28 MW	20.89 AW	40100 AAW	WIBLS	10//99-12//99
	Janesville-Beloit MSA, WI	S	22.11 MW	18.53 AW	45980 AAW	WIBLS	10//99-12//99
	Madison MSA, WI	S	17.99 MW	16.83 AW	37430 AAW	WIBLS	10//99-12//99
	Milwaukee-Waukesha PMSA, WI	S	18.40 MW	16.74 AW	38260 AAW	WIBLS	10//99-12//99
	Racine PMSA, WI	S	20.06 MW	19.27 AW	41720 AAW	WIBLS	10//99-12//99
	Wausau MSA, WI	S	12.00 MW	11.80 AW	24960 AAW	WIBLS	10//99-12//99
	Wyoming	S	14.37 MW	14.53 AW	30220 AAW	WYBLS	10//99-12//99
	Cheyenne MSA, WY	S	16.43 MW	15.80 AW	34170 AAW	WYBLS	10//99-12//99
Arbitrator, Mediator, and Conciliator	California	S	25.89 MW	24.90 AW	51790 AAW	CABLS	10//99-12//99
	Colorado	S	16.03 MW	19.10 AW	39720 AAW	COBLS	10//99-12//99
	District of Columbia	S	20.9 MW	22.80 AW	47410 AAW	DCBLS	10//99-12//99
	Georgia	S	19.56 MW	19.94 AW	41480 AAW	GABLS	10//99-12//99
	Indiana	S	19.89 MW	20.86 AW	43380 AAW	INBLS	10//99-12//99
	Maryland	S	23.59 MW	22.87 AW	47570 AAW	MDBLS	10//99-12//99
	Michigan	S	18.93 MW	20.16 AW	41930 AAW	MIBLS	10//99-12//99
	Minnesota	S	22.24 MW	24.07 AW	50060 AAW	MNBLS	10//99-12//99
	Mississippi	S	11.92 MW	11.19 AW	23280 AAW	MSBLS	10//99-12//99
	New York	S	27.95 MW	28.85 AW	60010 AAW	NYBLS	10//99-12//99
	North Carolina	S	17.41 MW	18.45 AW	38370 AAW	NCBLS	10//99-12//99
	Ohio	S	21.94 MW	20.96 AW	43600 AAW	OHBLS	10//99-12//99
	Pennsylvania	S	18.36 MW	18.34 AW	38150 AAW	PABLS	10//99-12//99
	Texas	S	17.4 MW	20.60 AW	42840 AAW	TXBLS	10//99-12//99
	Virginia	S	8.21 MW	11.54 AW	23990 AAW	VABLS	10//99-12//99
	Washington	S	20.4 MW	20.57 AW	42780 AAW	WABLS	10//99-12//99
Architect	United States	H		25.83 AW		NCS98	1998
Except Landscape and Naval	Alabama	S	22.29 MW	25.16 AW	52340 AAW	ALBLS	10//99-12//99
Except Landscape and Naval	Birmingham MSA, AL	S	24.27 MW	19.86 AW	50470 AAW	ALBLS	10//99-12//99
Except Landscape and Naval	Montgomery MSA, AL	S	28.60 MW	24.74 AW	59490 AAW	ALBLS	10//99-12//99
Except Landscape and Naval	Alaska	S	30.42 MW	29.84 AW	62070 AAW	AKBLS	10//99-12//99
Except Landscape and Naval	Anchorage MSA, AK	S	29.74 MW	30.15 AW	61850 AAW	AKBLS	10//99-12//99
Except Landscape and Naval	Arizona	S	25.87 MW	27.81 AW	57840 AAW	AZBLS	10//99-12//99
Except Landscape and Naval	Phoenix-Mesa MSA, AZ	S	28.76 MW	26.91 AW	59810 AAW	AZBLS	10//99-12//99
Except Landscape and Naval	Tucson MSA, AZ	S	23.66 MW	22.72 AW	49220 AAW	AZBLS	10//99-12//99
Except Landscape and Naval	Arkansas	S	21.54 MW	21.15 AW	43990 AAW	ARBLS	10//99-12//99
Except Landscape and Naval	Fayetteville-Springdale-Rogers MSA, AR	S	18.92 MW	20.58 AW	39350 AAW	ARBLS	10//99-12//99
Except Landscape and Naval	Little Rock-North Little Rock MSA, AR	S	23.68 MW	23.30 AW	49260 AAW	ARBLS	10//99-12//99
Except Landscape and Naval	California	S	28.43 MW	29.68 AW	61730 AAW	CABLS	10//99-12//99
Except Landscape and Naval	Fresno MSA, CA	S	26.86 MW	25.81 AW	55860 AAW	CABLS	10//99-12//99
Except Landscape and Naval	Los Angeles-Long Beach PMSA, CA	S	30.80 MW	30.69 AW	64060 AAW	CABLS	10//99-12//99
Except Landscape and Naval	Oakland PMSA, CA	S	28.87 MW	27.38 AW	60050 AAW	CABLS	10//99-12//99
Except Landscape and Naval	Orange County PMSA, CA	S	36.15 MW	33.85 AW	75190 AAW	CABLS	10//99-12//99
Except Landscape and Naval	Riverside-San Bernardino PMSA, CA	S	25.15 MW	24.12 AW	52310 AAW	CABLS	10//99-12//99
Except Landscape and Naval	Sacramento PMSA, CA	S	24.94 MW	24.27 AW	51880 AAW	CABLS	10//99-12//99
Except Landscape and Naval	San Diego MSA, CA	S	32.66 MW	27.06 AW	67940 AAW	CABLS	10//99-12//99
Except Landscape and Naval	San Francisco PMSA, CA	S	28.01 MW	26.25 AW	58270 AAW	CABLS	10//99-12//99
Except Landscape and Naval	San Jose PMSA, CA	S	31.85 MW	34.01 AW	66250 AAW	CABLS	10//99-12//99
Except Landscape and Naval	San Luis Obispo-Atascadero-Paso Robles MSA, CA	S	27.57 MW	30.44 AW	57340 AAW	CABLS	10//99-12//99
Except Landscape and Naval	Santa Rosa PMSA, CA	S	26.56 MW	25.85 AW	55240 AAW	CABLS	10//99-12//99
Except Landscape and Naval	Colorado	S	23.9 MW	25.53 AW	53100 AAW	COBLS	10//99-12//99
Except Landscape and Naval	Boulder-Longmont PMSA, CO	S	27.67 MW	23.84 AW	57560 AAW	COBLS	10//99-12//99
Except Landscape and Naval	Colorado Springs MSA, CO	S	25.61 MW	25.03 AW	53270 AAW	COBLS	10//99-12//99
Except Landscape and Naval	Denver PMSA, CO	S	24.51 MW	23.30 AW	50980 AAW	COBLS	10//99-12//99
Except Landscape and Naval	Fort Collins-Loveland MSA, CO	S	25.61 MW	25.51 AW	53270 AAW	COBLS	10//99-12//99

AAW Average annual wage | AOH Average offered, high | ASH Average starting, high | H Hourly | M Monthly | S Special: hourly and annual
AE Average entry wage | AOL Average offered, low | ASL Average starting, low | HI Highest wage paid | MTC Median total compensation | TQ Third quartile wage
AEX Average experienced wage | APH Average pay, high range | AW Average wage paid | HR High end range | MW Median wage paid | W Weekly
AO Average offered | APL Average pay, low range | FQ First quartile wage | LR Low end range | SQ Second quartile wage | Y Yearly

47

Architect

Occupation/Type/Industry	Location	Per	Low	Mid	High	Source	Date
Architect							
Except Landscape and Naval	Connecticut	S	27.53 MW	27.47 AW	57140 AAW	CTBLS	10//99-12//99
Except Landscape and Naval	Bridgeport PMSA, CT	S	33.92 MW	32.92 AW	70560 AAW	CTBLS	10//99-12//99
Except Landscape and Naval	Hartford MSA, CT	S	24.92 MW	24.06 AW	51830 AAW	CTBLS	10//99-12//99
Except Landscape and Naval	New Haven-Meriden PMSA, CT	S	26.83 MW	23.99 AW	55810 AAW	CTBLS	10//99-12//99
Except Landscape and Naval	Stamford-Norwalk PMSA, CT	S	30.73 MW	33.03 AW	63920 AAW	CTBLS	10//99-12//99
Except Landscape and Naval	Delaware	S	24.21 MW	24.58 AW	51130 AAW	DEBLS	10//99-12//99
Except Landscape and Naval	Wilmington-Newark PMSA, DE-MD	S	28.03 MW	25.83 AW	58310 AAW	DEBLS	10//99-12//99
Except Landscape and Naval	District of Columbia	S	15.7 MW	19.54 AW	40640 AAW	DCBLS	10//99-12//99
Except Landscape and Naval	Washington PMSA, DC-MD-VA-WV	S	21.71 MW	17.49 AW	45170 AAW	DCBLS	10//99-12//99
Except Landscape and Naval	Florida	S	23.66 MW	24.84 AW	51670 AAW	FLBLS	10//99-12//99
Except Landscape and Naval	Fort Lauderdale PMSA, FL	S	27.99 MW	27.94 AW	58230 AAW	FLBLS	10//99-12//99
Except Landscape and Naval	Fort Myers-Cape Coral MSA, FL	S	26.75 MW	26.46 AW	55650 AAW	FLBLS	10//99-12//99
Except Landscape and Naval	Gainesville MSA, FL	S	19.60 MW	19.92 AW	40760 AAW	FLBLS	10//99-12//99
Except Landscape and Naval	Jacksonville MSA, FL	S	23.14 MW	20.98 AW	48140 AAW	FLBLS	10//99-12//99
Except Landscape and Naval	Melbourne-Titusville-Palm Bay MSA, FL	S	24.03 MW	24.03 AW	49990 AAW	FLBLS	10//99-12//99
Except Landscape and Naval	Miami PMSA, FL	S	24.98 MW	23.89 AW	51960 AAW	FLBLS	10//99-12//99
Except Landscape and Naval	Orlando MSA, FL	S	26.44 MW	25.05 AW	55010 AAW	FLBLS	10//99-12//99
Except Landscape and Naval	Pensacola MSA, FL	S	23.44 MW	22.07 AW	48760 AAW	FLBLS	10//99-12//99
Except Landscape and Naval	Sarasota-Bradenton MSA, FL	S	22.00 MW	19.52 AW	45750 AAW	FLBLS	10//99-12//99
Except Landscape and Naval	Tallahassee MSA, FL	S	24.22 MW	22.27 AW	50380 AAW	FLBLS	10//99-12//99
Except Landscape and Naval	Tampa-St. Petersburg-Clearwater MSA, FL	S	24.82 MW	23.77 AW	51630 AAW	FLBLS	10//99-12//99
Except Landscape and Naval	West Palm Beach-Boca Raton MSA, FL	S	29.21 MW	29.19 AW	60750 AAW	FLBLS	10//99-12//99
Except Landscape and Naval	Georgia	S	22.73 MW	24.97 AW	51940 AAW	GABLS	10//99-12//99
Except Landscape and Naval	Atlanta MSA, GA	S	24.92 MW	22.71 AW	51830 AAW	GABLS	10//99-12//99
Except Landscape and Naval	Augusta-Aiken MSA, GA-SC	S	22.58 MW	17.93 AW	46970 AAW	GABLS	10//99-12//99
Except Landscape and Naval	Savannah MSA, GA	S	26.82 MW	25.86 AW	55790 AAW	GABLS	10//99-12//99
Except Landscape and Naval	Hawaii	S	23.6 MW	25.84 AW	53750 AAW	HIBLS	10//99-12//99
Except Landscape and Naval	Honolulu MSA, HI	S	27.51 MW	24.30 AW	57220 AAW	HIBLS	10//99-12//99
Except Landscape and Naval	Idaho	S	19.63 MW	21.64 AW	45020 AAW	IDBLS	10//99-12//99
Except Landscape and Naval	Boise City MSA, ID	S	21.88 MW	19.68 AW	45510 AAW	IDBLS	10//99-12//99
Except Landscape and Naval	Illinois	S	24.69 MW	27.48 AW	57170 AAW	ILBLS	10//99-12//99
Except Landscape and Naval	Chicago PMSA, IL	S	27.68 MW	24.78 AW	57580 AAW	ILBLS	10//99-12//99
Except Landscape and Naval	Rockford MSA, IL	S	31.00 MW	30.07 AW	64480 AAW	ILBLS	10//99-12//99
Except Landscape and Naval	Indiana	S	23.75 MW	24.47 AW	50900 AAW	INBLS	10//99-12//99
Except Landscape and Naval	Evansville-Henderson MSA, IN-KY	S	24.88 MW	23.79 AW	51740 AAW	INBLS	10//99-12//99
Except Landscape and Naval	Fort Wayne MSA, IN	S	25.33 MW	24.21 AW	52690 AAW	INBLS	10//99-12//99
Except Landscape and Naval	Indianapolis MSA, IN	S	26.46 MW	25.30 AW	55030 AAW	INBLS	10//99-12//99
Except Landscape and Naval	South Bend MSA, IN	S	26.36 MW	24.52 AW	54830 AAW	INBLS	10//99-12//99
Except Landscape and Naval	Iowa	S	20.32 MW	22.54 AW	46880 AAW	IABLS	10//99-12//99
Except Landscape and Naval	Des Moines MSA, IA	S	21.59 MW	21.10 AW	44900 AAW	IABLS	10//99-12//99
Except Landscape and Naval	Dubuque MSA, IA	S	18.21 MW	15.66 AW	37870 AAW	IABLS	10//99-12//99
Except Landscape and Naval	Kansas	S	20.55 MW	25.67 AW	53380 AAW	KSBLS	10//99-12//99
Except Landscape and Naval	Topeka MSA, KS	S	21.88 MW	20.92 AW	45500 AAW	KSBLS	10//99-12//99
Except Landscape and Naval	Wichita MSA, KS	S	24.15 MW	21.71 AW	50230 AAW	KSBLS	10//99-12//99
Except Landscape and Naval	Kentucky	S	22.88 MW	26.70 AW	55540 AAW	KYBLS	10//99-12//99
Except Landscape and Naval	Lexington MSA, KY	S	23.81 MW	22.66 AW	49530 AAW	KYBLS	10//99-12//99
Except Landscape and Naval	Louisville MSA, KY-IN	S	27.96 MW	23.40 AW	58150 AAW	KYBLS	10//99-12//99
Except Landscape and Naval	Louisiana	S	21.96 MW	24.09 AW	50110 AAW	LABLS	10//99-12//99
Except Landscape and Naval	Baton Rouge MSA, LA	S	27.21 MW	24.27 AW	56600 AAW	LABLS	10//99-12//99
Except Landscape and Naval	New Orleans MSA, LA	S	21.30 MW	19.79 AW	44300 AAW	LABLS	10//99-12//99
Except Landscape and Naval	Maine	S	22.97 MW	23.43 AW	48730 AAW	MEBLS	10//99-12//99
Except Landscape and Naval	Portland MSA, ME	S	21.72 MW	22.23 AW	45180 AAW	MEBLS	10//99-12//99
Except Landscape and Naval	Maryland	S	25.37 MW	27.29 AW	56760 AAW	MDBLS	10//99-12//99
Except Landscape and Naval	Baltimore PMSA, MD	S	31.15 MW	25.75 AW	64790 AAW	MDBLS	10//99-12//99
Except Landscape and Naval	Massachusetts	S	22.69 MW	24.86 AW	51720 AAW	MABLS	10//99-12//99
Except Landscape and Naval	Boston PMSA, MA-NH	S	24.49 MW	22.45 AW	50940 AAW	MABLS	10//99-12//99
Except Landscape and Naval	Springfield MSA, MA	S	26.40 MW	23.31 AW	54910 AAW	MABLS	10//99-12//99
Except Landscape and Naval	Michigan	S	24.07 MW	25.13 AW	52280 AAW	MIBLS	10//99-12//99
Except Landscape and Naval	Detroit PMSA, MI	S	26.34 MW	25.64 AW	54790 AAW	MIBLS	10//99-12//99
Except Landscape and Naval	Flint PMSA, MI	S	23.43 MW	22.64 AW	48740 AAW	MIBLS	10//99-12//99
Except Landscape and Naval	Grand Rapids-Muskegon-Holland MSA, MI	S	27.30 MW	25.90 AW	56770 AAW	MIBLS	10//99-12//99

Occupation/Type/Industry	Location	Per	Low	Mid	High	Source	Date
Architect							
Except Landscape and Naval	Kalamazoo-Battle Creek MSA, MI	S	25.89 MW	24.65 AW	53850 AAW	MIBLS	10//99-12//99
Except Landscape and Naval	Lansing-East Lansing MSA, MI	S	27.77 MW	27.17 AW	57750 AAW	MIBLS	10//99-12//99
Except Landscape and Naval	Saginaw-Bay City-Midland MSA, MI	S	28.14 MW	30.55 AW	58540 AAW	MIBLS	10//99-12//99
Except Landscape and Naval	Minnesota	S	23.24 MW	25.32 AW	52670 AAW	MNBLS	10//99-12//99
Except Landscape and Naval	Duluth-Superior MSA, MN-WI	S	21.55 MW	18.31 AW	44820 AAW	MNBLS	10//99-12//99
Except Landscape and Naval	Minneapolis-St. Paul MSA, MN-WI	S	25.62 MW	23.36 AW	53280 AAW	MNBLS	10//99-12//99
Except Landscape and Naval	St. Cloud MSA, MN	S	20.39 MW	18.19 AW	42410 AAW	MNBLS	10//99-12//99
Except Landscape and Naval	Mississippi	S	30.56 MW	31.38 AW	65270 AAW	MSBLS	10//99-12//99
Except Landscape and Naval	Jackson MSA, MS	S	29.44 MW	29.28 AW	61240 AAW	MSBLS	10//99-12//99
Except Landscape and Naval	Missouri	S	23.51 MW	26.82 AW	55780 AAW	MOBLS	10//99-12//99
Except Landscape and Naval	Kansas City MSA, MO-KS	S	27.27 MW	24.49 AW	56720 AAW	MOBLS	10//99-12//99
Except Landscape and Naval	St. Louis MSA, MO-IL	S	28.50 MW	23.87 AW	59280 AAW	MOBLS	10//99-12//99
Except Landscape and Naval	Montana	S	20.09 MW	21.05 AW	43790 AAW	MTBLS	10//99-12//99
Except Landscape and Naval	Nebraska	S	21.47 MW	23.82 AW	49550 AAW	NEBLS	10//99-12//99
Except Landscape and Naval	Lincoln MSA, NE	S	21.85 MW	19.62 AW	45440 AAW	NEBLS	10//99-12//99
Except Landscape and Naval	Omaha MSA, NE-IA	S	24.25 MW	21.78 AW	50440 AAW	NEBLS	10//99-12//99
Except Landscape and Naval	Nevada	S	30.65 MW	29.36 AW	61080 AAW	NVBLS	10//99-12//99
Except Landscape and Naval	Las Vegas MSA, NV-AZ	S	27.56 MW	29.20 AW	57330 AAW	NVBLS	10//99-12//99
Except Landscape and Naval	Reno MSA, NV	S	34.90 MW	36.28 AW	72590 AAW	NVBLS	10//99-12//99
Except Landscape and Naval	New Hampshire	S	24.88 MW	25.07 AW	52140 AAW	NHBLS	10//99-12//99
Except Landscape and Naval	Manchester PMSA, NH	S	25.72 MW	25.26 AW	53490 AAW	NHBLS	10//99-12//99
Except Landscape and Naval	Portsmouth-Rochester PMSA, NH-ME	S	27.16 MW	27.38 AW	56500 AAW	NHBLS	10//99-12//99
Except Landscape and Naval	New Jersey	S	23.6 MW	26.33 AW	54760 AAW	NJBLS	10//99-12//99
Except Landscape and Naval	Atlantic-Cape May PMSA, NJ	S	24.68 MW	23.90 AW	51340 AAW	NJBLS	10//99-12//99
Except Landscape and Naval	Bergen-Passaic PMSA, NJ	S	23.88 MW	19.73 AW	49660 AAW	NJBLS	10//99-12//99
Except Landscape and Naval	Jersey City PMSA, NJ	S	27.22 MW	27.74 AW	56620 AAW	NJBLS	10//99-12//99
Except Landscape and Naval	Newark PMSA, NJ	S	28.19 MW	24.37 AW	58640 AAW	NJBLS	10//99-12//99
Except Landscape and Naval	Trenton PMSA, NJ	S	28.96 MW	27.37 AW	60230 AAW	NJBLS	10//99-12//99
Except Landscape and Naval	New Mexico	S	18.01 MW	19.92 AW	41440 AAW	NMBLS	10//99-12//99
Except Landscape and Naval	Albuquerque MSA, NM	S	19.62 MW	17.69 AW	40810 AAW	NMBLS	10//99-12//99
Except Landscape and Naval	Las Cruces MSA, NM	S	22.97 MW	23.62 AW	47780 AAW	NMBLS	10//99-12//99
Except Landscape and Naval	New York	S	25.28 MW	28.19 AW	58630 AAW	NYBLS	10//99-12//99
Except Landscape and Naval	Albany-Schenectady-Troy MSA, NY	S	24.39 MW	23.99 AW	50740 AAW	NYBLS	10//99-12//99
Except Landscape and Naval	Buffalo-Niagara Falls MSA, NY	S	23.27 MW	21.08 AW	48400 AAW	NYBLS	10//99-12//99
Except Landscape and Naval	Dutchess County PMSA, NY	S	24.82 MW	19.72 AW	51630 AAW	NYBLS	10//99-12//99
Except Landscape and Naval	Nassau-Suffolk PMSA, NY	S	31.27 MW	32.78 AW	65030 AAW	NYBLS	10//99-12//99
Except Landscape and Naval	New York PMSA, NY	S	28.94 MW	25.45 AW	60190 AAW	NYBLS	10//99-12//99
Except Landscape and Naval	Rochester MSA, NY	S	25.78 MW	25.16 AW	53630 AAW	NYBLS	10//99-12//99
Except Landscape and Naval	Syracuse MSA, NY	S	26.37 MW	23.46 AW	54850 AAW	NYBLS	10//99-12//99
Except Landscape and Naval	Utica-Rome MSA, NY	S	14.69 MW	11.49 AW	30560 AAW	NYBLS	10//99-12//99
Except Landscape and Naval	North Carolina	S	22.21 MW	23.49 AW	48860 AAW	NCBLS	10//99-12//99
Except Landscape and Naval	Asheville MSA, NC	S	21.29 MW	19.87 AW	44290 AAW	NCBLS	10//99-12//99
Except Landscape and Naval	Charlotte-Gastonia-Rock Hill MSA, NC-SC	S	23.43 MW	22.67 AW	48740 AAW	NCBLS	10//99-12//99
Except Landscape and Naval	Greensboro--Winston-Salem--High Point MSA, NC	S	21.54 MW	20.58 AW	44810 AAW	NCBLS	10//99-12//99
Except Landscape and Naval	Raleigh-Durham-Chapel Hill MSA, NC	S	25.76 MW	23.11 AW	53580 AAW	NCBLS	10//99-12//99
Except Landscape and Naval	Wilmington MSA, NC	S	24.66 MW	23.81 AW	51300 AAW	NCBLS	10//99-12//99
Except Landscape and Naval	Ohio	S	23.68 MW	25.21 AW	52430 AAW	OHBLS	10//99-12//99
Except Landscape and Naval	Akron PMSA, OH	S	22.30 MW	22.22 AW	46370 AAW	OHBLS	10//99-12//99
Except Landscape and Naval	Canton-Massillon MSA, OH	S	26.35 MW	28.77 AW	54820 AAW	OHBLS	10//99-12//99
Except Landscape and Naval	Cincinnati PMSA, OH-KY-IN	S	23.87 MW	21.51 AW	49650 AAW	OHBLS	10//99-12//99
Except Landscape and Naval	Cleveland-Lorain-Elyria PMSA, OH	S	30.26 MW	31.18 AW	62930 AAW	OHBLS	10//99-12//99
Except Landscape and Naval	Columbus MSA, OH	S	21.47 MW	20.48 AW	44660 AAW	OHBLS	10//99-12//99
Except Landscape and Naval	Dayton-Springfield MSA, OH	S	24.71 MW	21.67 AW	51390 AAW	OHBLS	10//99-12//99
Except Landscape and Naval	Hamilton-Middletown PMSA, OH	S	32.53 MW	28.03 AW	67660 AAW	OHBLS	10//99-12//99
Except Landscape and Naval	Mansfield MSA, OH	S	19.99 MW	19.37 AW	41590 AAW	OHBLS	10//99-12//99
Except Landscape and Naval	Oklahoma	S	21.57 MW	23.04 AW	47930 AAW	OKBLS	10//99-12//99
Except Landscape and Naval	Oklahoma City MSA, OK	S	23.67 MW	23.51 AW	49220 AAW	OKBLS	10//99-12//99
Except Landscape and Naval	Oregon	S	22.09 MW	23.80 AW	49500 AAW	ORBLS	10//99-12//99
Except Landscape and Naval	Eugene-Springfield MSA, OR	S	22.75 MW	20.87 AW	47310 AAW	ORBLS	10//99-12//99

Architect

Occupation/Type/Industry	Location	Per	Low	Mid	High	Source	Date
Except Landscape and Naval	Portland-Vancouver PMSA, OR-WA	S	23.73 MW	21.92 AW	49350 AAW	ORBLS	10//99-12//99
Except Landscape and Naval	Salem PMSA, OR	S	25.62 MW	22.79 AW	53290 AAW	ORBLS	10//99-12//99
Except Landscape and Naval	Pennsylvania	S	24.41 MW	25.10 AW	52200 AAW	PABLS	10//99-12//99
Except Landscape and Naval	Allentown-Bethlehem-Easton MSA, PA	S	27.12 MW	24.86 AW	56420 AAW	PABLS	10//99-12//99
Except Landscape and Naval	Harrisburg-Lebanon-Carlisle MSA, PA	S	27.40 MW	27.69 AW	56990 AAW	PABLS	10//99-12//99
Except Landscape and Naval	Lancaster MSA, PA	S	25.24 MW	24.02 AW	52500 AAW	PABLS	10//99-12//99
Except Landscape and Naval	Philadelphia PMSA, PA-NJ	S	25.34 MW	25.17 AW	52710 AAW	PABLS	10//99-12//99
Except Landscape and Naval	Pittsburgh MSA, PA	S	22.91 MW	22.32 AW	47650 AAW	PABLS	10//99-12//99
Except Landscape and Naval	Scranton--Wilkes-Barre--Hazleton MSA, PA	S	26.15 MW	25.19 AW	54390 AAW	PABLS	10//99-12//99
Except Landscape and Naval	York MSA, PA	S	26.29 MW	26.45 AW	54680 AAW	PABLS	10//99-12//99
Except Landscape and Naval	Rhode Island	S	25.25 MW	27.24 AW	56660 AAW	RIBLS	10//99-12//99
Except Landscape and Naval	Providence-Fall River-Warwick MSA, RI-MA	S	26.27 MW	24.37 AW	54630 AAW	RIBLS	10//99-12//99
Except Landscape and Naval	South Carolina	S	21.4 MW	23.16 AW	48170 AAW	SCBLS	10//99-12//99
Except Landscape and Naval	Charleston-North Charleston MSA, SC	S	24.24 MW	23.53 AW	50410 AAW	SCBLS	10//99-12//99
Except Landscape and Naval	Columbia MSA, SC	S	27.41 MW	27.79 AW	57010 AAW	SCBLS	10//99-12//99
Except Landscape and Naval	Greenville-Spartanburg-Anderson MSA, SC	S	23.82 MW	21.09 AW	49540 AAW	SCBLS	10//99-12//99
Except Landscape and Naval	South Dakota	S	21.51 MW	21.09 AW	43870 AAW	SDBLS	10//99-12//99
Except Landscape and Naval	Rapid City MSA, SD	S	20.83 MW	21.43 AW	43330 AAW	SDBLS	10//99-12//99
Except Landscape and Naval	Tennessee	S	23.18 MW	24.41 AW	50780 AAW	TNBLS	10//99-12//99
Except Landscape and Naval	Chattanooga MSA, TN-GA	S	32.72 MW	27.99 AW	68060 AAW	TNBLS	10//99-12//99
Except Landscape and Naval	Knoxville MSA, TN	S	21.15 MW	21.24 AW	43990 AAW	TNBLS	10//99-12//99
Except Landscape and Naval	Memphis MSA, TN-AR-MS	S	22.40 MW	21.52 AW	46590 AAW	MSBLS	10//99-12//99
Except Landscape and Naval	Nashville MSA, TN	S	27.07 MW	25.87 AW	56300 AAW	TNBLS	10//99-12//99
Except Landscape and Naval	Texas	S	22.39 MW	24.70 AW	51380 AAW	TXBLS	10//99-12//99
Except Landscape and Naval	Austin-San Marcos MSA, TX	S	24.37 MW	24.01 AW	50690 AAW	TXBLS	10//99-12//99
Except Landscape and Naval	Dallas PMSA, TX	S	27.14 MW	22.90 AW	56460 AAW	TXBLS	10//99-12//99
Except Landscape and Naval	El Paso MSA, TX	S	22.34 MW	18.50 AW	46470 AAW	TXBLS	10//99-12//99
Except Landscape and Naval	Fort Worth-Arlington PMSA, TX	S	25.85 MW	23.79 AW	53780 AAW	TXBLS	10//99-12//99
Except Landscape and Naval	Galveston-Texas City PMSA, TX	S	17.23 MW	13.19 AW	35840 AAW	TXBLS	10//99-12//99
Except Landscape and Naval	Houston PMSA, TX	S	23.87 MW	22.40 AW	49640 AAW	TXBLS	10//99-12//99
Except Landscape and Naval	Lubbock MSA, TX	S	17.11 MW	18.01 AW	35590 AAW	TXBLS	10//99-12//99
Except Landscape and Naval	Odessa-Midland MSA, TX	S	25.75 MW	22.22 AW	53560 AAW	TXBLS	10//99-12//99
Except Landscape and Naval	San Antonio MSA, TX	S	20.62 MW	18.85 AW	42890 AAW	TXBLS	10//99-12//99
Except Landscape and Naval	Tyler MSA, TX	S	22.58 MW	22.54 AW	46970 AAW	TXBLS	10//99-12//99
Except Landscape and Naval	Utah	S	19.77 MW	23.81 AW	49530 AAW	UTBLS	10//99-12//99
Except Landscape and Naval	Vermont	S	21.22 MW	22.62 AW	47060 AAW	VTBLS	10//99-12//99
Except Landscape and Naval	Burlington MSA, VT	S	21.99 MW	21.40 AW	45750 AAW	VTBLS	10//99-12//99
Except Landscape and Naval	Virginia	S	23.54 MW	25.83 AW	53720 AAW	VABLS	10//99-12//99
Except Landscape and Naval	Norfolk-Virginia Beach-Newport News MSA, VA-NC	S	25.55 MW	24.96 AW	53130 AAW	VABLS	10//99-12//99
Except Landscape and Naval	Richmond-Petersburg MSA, VA	S	23.09 MW	22.07 AW	48030 AAW	VABLS	10//99-12//99
Except Landscape and Naval	Washington	S	22.92 MW	23.56 AW	49010 AAW	WABLS	10//99-12//99
Except Landscape and Naval	Seattle-Bellevue-Everett PMSA, WA	S	23.21 MW	22.75 AW	48270 AAW	WABLS	10//99-12//99
Except Landscape and Naval	Spokane MSA, WA	S	22.12 MW	22.19 AW	46020 AAW	WABLS	10//99-12//99
Except Landscape and Naval	Tacoma PMSA, WA	S	24.38 MW	23.53 AW	50700 AAW	WABLS	10//99-12//99
Except Landscape and Naval	West Virginia	S	30.93 MW	32.26 AW	67100 AAW	WVBLS	10//99-12//99
Except Landscape and Naval	Charleston MSA, WV	S	34.24 MW	32.85 AW	71220 AAW	WVBLS	10//99-12//99
Except Landscape and Naval	Wisconsin	S	24.57 MW	25.08 AW	52170 AAW	WIBLS	10//99-12//99
Except Landscape and Naval	Appleton-Oshkosh-Neenah MSA, WI	S	26.24 MW	26.14 AW	54570 AAW	WIBLS	10//99-12//99
Except Landscape and Naval	Green Bay MSA, WI	S	29.00 MW	30.07 AW	60330 AAW	WIBLS	10//99-12//99
Except Landscape and Naval	Kenosha PMSA, WI	S	16.47 MW	14.78 AW	34260 AAW	WIBLS	10//99-12//99
Except Landscape and Naval	Madison MSA, WI	S	24.21 MW	22.88 AW	50350 AAW	WIBLS	10//99-12//99
Except Landscape and Naval	Milwaukee-Waukesha PMSA, WI	S	26.10 MW	26.47 AW	54290 AAW	WIBLS	10//99-12//99
Except Landscape and Naval	Wyoming	S	19.91 MW	21.80 AW	45350 AAW	WYBLS	10//99-12//99
Except Landscape and Naval	Puerto Rico	S	17.93 MW	21.73 AW	45190 AAW	PRBLS	10//99-12//99
Except Landscape and Naval	San Juan-Bayamon PMSA, PR	S	22.36 MW	19.01 AW	46510 AAW	PRBLS	10//99-12//99
Except Landscape and Naval	Guam	S	22.4 MW	23.56 AW	49000 AAW	GUBLS	10//99-12//99

AAW Average annual wage	**AOH** Average offered, high	**ASH** Average starting, high	**H** Hourly	**M** Monthly	**S** Special: hourly and annual
AE Average entry wage	**AOL** Average offered, low	**ASL** Average starting, low	**HI** Highest wage paid	**MTC** Median total compensation	**TQ** Third quartile wage
AEX Average experienced wage	**APH** Average pay, high range	**AW** Average wage paid	**HR** High end range	**MW** Median wage paid	**W** Weekly
AO Average offered	**APL** Average pay, low range	**FQ** First quartile wage	**LR** Low end range	**SQ** Second quartile wage	**Y** Yearly

Occupation/Type/Industry	Location	Per	Low	Mid	High	Source	Date
Architectural and Civil Drafter	Alabama	S	14.45 MW	14.58 AW	30340 AAW	ALBLS	10//99-12//99
	Birmingham MSA, AL	S	15.15 MW	14.94 AW	31520 AAW	ALBLS	10//99-12//99
	Florence MSA, AL	S	12.90 MW	13.52 AW	26830 AAW	ALBLS	10//99-12//99
	Mobile MSA, AL	S	15.54 MW	15.08 AW	32320 AAW	ALBLS	10//99-12//99
	Montgomery MSA, AL	S	13.40 MW	12.91 AW	27880 AAW	ALBLS	10//99-12//99
	Alaska	S	18.01 MW	18.35 AW	38170 AAW	AKBLS	10//99-12//99
	Anchorage MSA, AK	S	17.49 MW	16.68 AW	36380 AAW	AKBLS	10//99-12//99
	Arizona	S	16.18 MW	17.18 AW	35740 AAW	AZBLS	10//99-12//99
	Phoenix-Mesa MSA, AZ	S	17.83 MW	16.67 AW	37080 AAW	AZBLS	10//99-12//99
	Tucson MSA, AZ	S	14.91 MW	14.83 AW	31000 AAW	AZBLS	10//99-12//99
	Arkansas	S	14.55 MW	14.60 AW	30370 AAW	ARBLS	10//99-12//99
	Fayetteville-Springdale-Rogers MSA, AR	S	13.46 MW	13.23 AW	28000 AAW	ARBLS	10//99-12//99
	Fort Smith MSA, AR-OK	S	13.96 MW	13.26 AW	29050 AAW	ARBLS	10//99-12//99
	Jonesboro MSA, AR	S	9.35 MW	9.45 AW	19450 AAW	ARBLS	10//99-12//99
	Little Rock-North Little Rock MSA, AR	S	14.97 MW	15.13 AW	31150 AAW	ARBLS	10//99-12//99
	California	S	20.6 MW	21.07 AW	43820 AAW	CABLS	10//99-12//99
	Bakersfield MSA, CA	S	21.89 MW	20.29 AW	45540 AAW	CABLS	10//99-12//99
	Fresno MSA, CA	S	15.35 MW	14.75 AW	31920 AAW	CABLS	10//99-12//99
	Los Angeles-Long Beach PMSA, CA	S	20.70 MW	19.82 AW	43060 AAW	CABLS	10//99-12//99
	Modesto MSA, CA	S	22.95 MW	26.18 AW	47740 AAW	CABLS	10//99-12//99
	Oakland PMSA, CA	S	20.57 MW	22.05 AW	42780 AAW	CABLS	10//99-12//99
	Orange County PMSA, CA	S	22.71 MW	22.96 AW	47240 AAW	CABLS	10//99-12//99
	Redding MSA, CA	S	13.98 MW	12.66 AW	29090 AAW	CABLS	10//99-12//99
	Riverside-San Bernardino PMSA, CA	S	19.87 MW	19.10 AW	41340 AAW	CABLS	10//99-12//99
	Sacramento PMSA, CA	S	23.54 MW	23.33 AW	48960 AAW	CABLS	10//99-12//99
	Salinas MSA, CA	S	19.77 MW	19.86 AW	41120 AAW	CABLS	10//99-12//99
	San Diego MSA, CA	S	16.32 MW	15.98 AW	33940 AAW	CABLS	10//99-12//99
	San Francisco PMSA, CA	S	24.09 MW	23.60 AW	50110 AAW	CABLS	10//99-12//99
	San Jose PMSA, CA	S	20.83 MW	19.90 AW	43330 AAW	CABLS	10//99-12//99
	San Luis Obispo-Atascadero-Paso Robles MSA, CA	S	17.32 MW	15.45 AW	36040 AAW	CABLS	10//99-12//99
	Santa Barbara-Santa Maria-Lompoc MSA, CA	S	17.20 MW	16.60 AW	35770 AAW	CABLS	10//99-12//99
	Santa Rosa PMSA, CA	S	20.14 MW	19.45 AW	41900 AAW	CABLS	10//99-12//99
	Stockton-Lodi MSA, CA	S	19.25 MW	18.68 AW	40050 AAW	CABLS	10//99-12//99
	Vallejo-Fairfield-Napa PMSA, CA	S	21.83 MW	19.50 AW	45400 AAW	CABLS	10//99-12//99
	Ventura PMSA, CA	S	21.93 MW	21.45 AW	45620 AAW	CABLS	10//99-12//99
	Visalia-Tulare-Porterville MSA, CA	S	12.76 MW	10.76 AW	26540 AAW	CABLS	10//99-12//99
	Colorado	S	17.4 MW	17.85 AW	37140 AAW	COBLS	10//99-12//99
	Boulder-Longmont PMSA, CO	S	17.52 MW	17.46 AW	36430 AAW	COBLS	10//99-12//99
	Denver PMSA, CO	S	19.62 MW	19.73 AW	40810 AAW	COBLS	10//99-12//99
	Grand Junction MSA, CO	S	17.85 MW	17.42 AW	37130 AAW	COBLS	10//99-12//99
	Connecticut	S	19.24 MW	20.05 AW	41700 AAW	CTBLS	10//99-12//99
	Bridgeport PMSA, CT	S	16.58 MW	15.96 AW	34490 AAW	CTBLS	10//99-12//99
	Hartford MSA, CT	S	17.52 MW	17.92 AW	36440 AAW	CTBLS	10//99-12//99
	New Haven-Meriden PMSA, CT	S	16.34 MW	15.79 AW	33990 AAW	CTBLS	10//99-12//99
	New London-Norwich MSA, CT-RI	S	15.61 MW	15.38 AW	32460 AAW	CTBLS	10//99-12//99
	Stamford-Norwalk PMSA, CT	S	25.49 MW	26.88 AW	53010 AAW	CTBLS	10//99-12//99
	Delaware	S	14.24 MW	14.02 AW	29170 AAW	DEBLS	10//99-12//99
	Wilmington-Newark PMSA, DE-MD	S	13.92 MW	14.00 AW	28960 AAW	DEBLS	10//99-12//99
	District of Columbia	S	21.3 MW	21.06 AW	43790 AAW	DCBLS	10//99-12//99
	Washington PMSA, DC-MD-VA-WV	S	16.81 MW	16.07 AW	34970 AAW	DCBLS	10//99-12//99
	Florida	S	16.02 MW	16.73 AW	34800 AAW	FLBLS	10//99-12//99
	Daytona Beach MSA, FL	S	17.46 MW	15.55 AW	36310 AAW	FLBLS	10//99-12//99
	Fort Lauderdale PMSA, FL	S	16.28 MW	15.80 AW	33860 AAW	FLBLS	10//99-12//99
	Fort Myers-Cape Coral MSA, FL	S	17.25 MW	16.78 AW	35880 AAW	FLBLS	10//99-12//99
	Fort Walton Beach MSA, FL	S	11.45 MW	11.19 AW	23820 AAW	FLBLS	10//99-12//99
	Gainesville MSA, FL	S	12.51 MW	12.31 AW	26020 AAW	FLBLS	10//99-12//99
	Jacksonville MSA, FL	S	15.55 MW	15.12 AW	32340 AAW	FLBLS	10//99-12//99
	Lakeland-Winter Haven MSA, FL	S	16.70 MW	17.44 AW	34730 AAW	FLBLS	10//99-12//99

AAW Average annual wage	AOH Average offered, high	ASH Average starting, high	H Hourly	M Monthly	S Special: hourly and annual
AE Average entry wage	AOL Average offered, low	ASL Average starting, low	HI Highest wage paid	MTC Median total compensation	TQ Third quartile wage
AEX Average experienced wage	APH Average pay, high range	AW Average wage paid	HR High end range	MW Median wage paid	W Weekly
AO Average offered	APL Average pay, low range	FQ First quartile wage	LR Low end range	SQ Second quartile wage	Y Yearly

Occupation/Type/Industry	Location	Per	Low	Mid	High	Source	Date
Architectural and Civil Drafter	Melbourne-Titusville-Palm Bay MSA, FL	S	17.98 MW	17.82 AW	37390 AAW	FLBLS	10//99-12//99
	Miami PMSA, FL	S	17.32 MW	16.64 AW	36020 AAW	FLBLS	10//99-12//99
	Ocala MSA, FL	S	16.46 MW	16.13 AW	34240 AAW	FLBLS	10//99-12//99
	Orlando MSA, FL	S	17.37 MW	16.78 AW	36120 AAW	FLBLS	10//99-12//99
	Panama City MSA, FL	S	12.56 MW	13.46 AW	26120 AAW	FLBLS	10//99-12//99
	Pensacola MSA, FL	S	10.39 MW	10.17 AW	21610 AAW	FLBLS	10//99-12//99
	Punta Gorda MSA, FL	S	14.25 MW	13.35 AW	29650 AAW	FLBLS	10//99-12//99
	Sarasota-Bradenton MSA, FL	S	16.02 MW	15.40 AW	33320 AAW	FLBLS	10//99-12//99
	Tallahassee MSA, FL	S	13.67 MW	12.94 AW	28440 AAW	FLBLS	10//99-12//99
	Tampa-St. Petersburg-Clearwater MSA, FL	S	17.20 MW	16.59 AW	35780 AAW	FLBLS	10//99-12//99
	West Palm Beach-Boca Raton MSA, FL	S	18.84 MW	16.41 AW	39180 AAW	FLBLS	10//99-12//99
	Georgia	S	16.51 MW	16.79 AW	34920 AAW	GABLS	10//99-12//99
	Atlanta MSA, GA	S	17.10 MW	17.22 AW	35570 AAW	GABLS	10//99-12//99
	Augusta-Aiken MSA, GA-SC	S	15.14 MW	15.29 AW	31490 AAW	GABLS	10//99-12//99
	Macon MSA, GA	S	21.05 MW	20.57 AW	43790 AAW	GABLS	10//99-12//99
	Hawaii	S	14.14 MW	14.20 AW	29540 AAW	HIBLS	10//99-12//99
	Honolulu MSA, HI	S	14.14 MW	14.10 AW	29400 AAW	HIBLS	10//99-12//99
	Idaho	S	13.1 MW	14.40 AW	29960 AAW	IDBLS	10//99-12//99
	Boise City MSA, ID	S	14.37 MW	14.31 AW	29900 AAW	IDBLS	10//99-12//99
	Illinois	S	15.49 MW	15.99 AW	33250 AAW	ILBLS	10//99-12//99
	Bloomington-Normal MSA, IL	S	14.85 MW	14.99 AW	30890 AAW	ILBLS	10//99-12//99
	Champaign-Urbana MSA, IL	S	13.32 MW	13.07 AW	27700 AAW	ILBLS	10//99-12//99
	Chicago PMSA, IL	S	15.83 MW	15.31 AW	32930 AAW	ILBLS	10//99-12//99
	Peoria-Pekin MSA, IL	S	15.62 MW	15.45 AW	32500 AAW	ILBLS	10//99-12//99
	Rockford MSA, IL	S	16.10 MW	15.55 AW	33490 AAW	ILBLS	10//99-12//99
	Indiana	S	15.62 MW	16.64 AW	34610 AAW	INBLS	10//99-12//99
	Elkhart-Goshen MSA, IN	S	14.87 MW	15.10 AW	30920 AAW	INBLS	10//99-12//99
	Evansville-Henderson MSA, IN-KY	S	21.74 MW	23.48 AW	45210 AAW	INBLS	10//99-12//99
	Fort Wayne MSA, IN	S	14.92 MW	13.69 AW	31030 AAW	INBLS	10//99-12//99
	Gary PMSA, IN	S	17.17 MW	16.81 AW	35720 AAW	INBLS	10//99-12//99
	Indianapolis MSA, IN	S	16.63 MW	15.88 AW	34580 AAW	INBLS	10//99-12//99
	South Bend MSA, IN	S	16.26 MW	15.24 AW	33830 AAW	INBLS	10//99-12//99
	Iowa	S	14.24 MW	14.86 AW	30900 AAW	IABLS	10//99-12//99
	Cedar Rapids MSA, IA	S	12.32 MW	11.97 AW	25630 AAW	IABLS	10//99-12//99
	Davenport-Moline-Rock Island MSA, IA-IL	S	12.50 MW	11.69 AW	25990 AAW	IABLS	10//99-12//99
	Des Moines MSA, IA	S	16.02 MW	14.88 AW	33310 AAW	IABLS	10//99-12//99
	Kansas	S	15.5 MW	16.33 AW	33970 AAW	KSBLS	10//99-12//99
	Wichita MSA, KS	S	13.12 MW	13.58 AW	27280 AAW	KSBLS	10//99-12//99
	Kentucky	S	13.2 MW	13.92 AW	28960 AAW	KYBLS	10//99-12//99
	Lexington MSA, KY	S	13.09 MW	12.46 AW	27230 AAW	KYBLS	10//99-12//99
	Louisville MSA, KY-IN	S	14.21 MW	13.85 AW	29560 AAW	KYBLS	10//99-12//99
	Owensboro MSA, KY	S	12.76 MW	12.41 AW	26540 AAW	KYBLS	10//99-12//99
	Louisiana	S	14.57 MW	15.12 AW	31460 AAW	LABLS	10//99-12//99
	Baton Rouge MSA, LA	S	14.32 MW	14.09 AW	29800 AAW	LABLS	10//99-12//99
	Lafayette MSA, LA	S	8.07 MW	6.49 AW	16790 AAW	LABLS	10//99-12//99
	Lake Charles MSA, LA	S	11.26 MW	10.80 AW	23420 AAW	LABLS	10//99-12//99
	Monroe MSA, LA	S	17.14 MW	15.75 AW	35660 AAW	LABLS	10//99-12//99
	New Orleans MSA, LA	S	17.95 MW	16.98 AW	37330 AAW	LABLS	10//99-12//99
	Shreveport-Bossier City MSA, LA	S	14.85 MW	14.85 AW	30880 AAW	LABLS	10//99-12//99
	Maine	S	14.51 MW	14.57 AW	30300 AAW	MEBLS	10//99-12//99
	Portland MSA, ME	S	15.10 MW	14.81 AW	31410 AAW	MEBLS	10//99-12//99
	Maryland	S	15.66 MW	16.41 AW	34120 AAW	MDBLS	10//99-12//99
	Baltimore PMSA, MD	S	14.69 MW	13.96 AW	30550 AAW	MDBLS	10//99-12//99
	Massachusetts	S	18.62 MW	19.00 AW	39520 AAW	MABLS	10//99-12//99
	Boston PMSA, MA-NH	S	19.11 MW	18.60 AW	39750 AAW	MABLS	10//99-12//99
	Brockton PMSA, MA	S	17.59 MW	18.36 AW	36590 AAW	MABLS	10//99-12//99
	Lawrence PMSA, MA-NH	S	17.07 MW	14.90 AW	35510 AAW	MABLS	10//99-12//99
	Lowell PMSA, MA-NH	S	22.99 MW	20.82 AW	47830 AAW	MABLS	10//99-12//99
	Worcester PMSA, MA-CT	S	17.82 MW	18.63 AW	37070 AAW	MABLS	10//99-12//99
	Michigan	S	18.2 MW	19.61 AW	40780 AAW	MIBLS	10//99-12//99
	Ann Arbor PMSA, MI	S	17.91 MW	18.23 AW	37250 AAW	MIBLS	10//99-12//99
	Detroit PMSA, MI	S	21.49 MW	20.21 AW	44700 AAW	MIBLS	10//99-12//99
	Grand Rapids-Muskegon-Holland MSA, MI	S	18.11 MW	17.84 AW	37670 AAW	MIBLS	10//99-12//99
	Lansing-East Lansing MSA, MI	S	15.76 MW	15.36 AW	32780 AAW	MIBLS	10//99-12//99

AAW	Average annual wage	AOH	Average offered, high	ASH	Average starting, high	H	Hourly	M	Monthly	S	Special: hourly and annual
AE	Average entry wage	AOL	Average offered, low	ASL	Average starting, low	HI	Highest wage paid	MTC	Median total compensation	TQ	Third quartile wage
AEX	Average experienced wage	APH	Average pay, high range	AW	Average wage paid	HR	High end range	MW	Median wage paid	W	Weekly
AO	Average offered	APL	Average pay, low range	FQ	First quartile wage	LR	Low end range	SQ	Second quartile wage	Y	Yearly

Occupation/Type/Industry	Location	Per	Low	Mid	High	Source	Date
Architectural and Civil Drafter	Saginaw-Bay City-Midland MSA, MI	S	14.71 MW	14.74 AW	30600 AAW	MIBLS	10//99-12//99
	Minnesota	S	16.54 MW	17.37 AW	36130 AAW	MNBLS	10//99-12//99
	Minneapolis-St. Paul MSA, MN-WI	S	18.11 MW	17.22 AW	37670 AAW	MNBLS	10//99-12//99
	St. Cloud MSA, MN	S	14.73 MW	15.10 AW	30640 AAW	MNBLS	10//99-12//99
	Mississippi	S	13.97 MW	14.93 AW	31060 AAW	MSBLS	10//99-12//99
	Biloxi-Gulfport-Pascagoula MSA, MS	S	16.41 MW	15.61 AW	34140 AAW	MSBLS	10//99-12//99
	Hattiesburg MSA, MS	S	20.20 MW	19.55 AW	42010 AAW	MSBLS	10//99-12//99
	Jackson MSA, MS	S	17.11 MW	15.77 AW	35590 AAW	MSBLS	10//99-12//99
	Missouri	S	15.49 MW	15.77 AW	32790 AAW	MOBLS	10//99-12//99
	Kansas City MSA, MO-KS	S	15.47 MW	14.81 AW	32170 AAW	MOBLS	10//99-12//99
	St. Louis MSA, MO-IL	S	17.14 MW	17.67 AW	35640 AAW	MOBLS	10//99-12//99
	Springfield MSA, MO	S	14.38 MW	13.81 AW	29910 AAW	MOBLS	10//99-12//99
	Montana	S	13.26 MW	14.76 AW	30700 AAW	MTBLS	10//99-12//99
	Billings MSA, MT	S	16.64 MW	15.18 AW	34610 AAW	MTBLS	10//99-12//99
	Nebraska	S	13.94 MW	14.42 AW	30000 AAW	NEBLS	10//99-12//99
	Lincoln MSA, NE	S	14.28 MW	14.09 AW	29700 AAW	NEBLS	10//99-12//99
	Omaha MSA, NE-IA	S	15.31 MW	14.52 AW	31840 AAW	NEBLS	10//99-12//99
	Nevada	S	18.4 MW	18.61 AW	38720 AAW	NVBLS	10//99-12//99
	Las Vegas MSA, NV-AZ	S	18.51 MW	18.44 AW	38510 AAW	NVBLS	10//99-12//99
	Reno MSA, NV	S	20.29 MW	18.90 AW	42200 AAW	NVBLS	10//99-12//99
	New Hampshire	S	15.76 MW	16.61 AW	34550 AAW	NHBLS	10//99-12//99
	Manchester PMSA, NH	S	16.00 MW	15.55 AW	33270 AAW	NHBLS	10//99-12//99
	New Jersey	S	16.92 MW	18.67 AW	38830 AAW	NJBLS	10//99-12//99
	Atlantic-Cape May PMSA, NJ	S	16.86 MW	14.30 AW	35070 AAW	NJBLS	10//99-12//99
	Jersey City PMSA, NJ	S	19.92 MW	19.04 AW	41430 AAW	NJBLS	10//99-12//99
	Middlesex-Somerset-Hunterdon PMSA, NJ	S	18.42 MW	17.86 AW	38320 AAW	NJBLS	10//99-12//99
	Monmouth-Ocean PMSA, NJ	S	18.18 MW	16.99 AW	37800 AAW	NJBLS	10//99-12//99
	Newark PMSA, NJ	S	17.56 MW	15.78 AW	36520 AAW	NJBLS	10//99-12//99
	Trenton PMSA, NJ	S	21.48 MW	20.08 AW	44670 AAW	NJBLS	10//99-12//99
	Vineland-Millville-Bridgeton PMSA, NJ	S	18.90 MW	16.90 AW	39320 AAW	NJBLS	10//99-12//99
	New Mexico	S	13.18 MW	13.46 AW	28010 AAW	NMBLS	10//99-12//99
	Albuquerque MSA, NM	S	13.56 MW	13.34 AW	28200 AAW	NMBLS	10//99-12//99
	Las Cruces MSA, NM	S	13.97 MW	13.17 AW	29050 AAW	NMBLS	10//99-12//99
	Santa Fe MSA, NM	S	13.83 MW	13.34 AW	28760 AAW	NMBLS	10//99-12//99
	New York	S	18.71 MW	18.70 AW	38890 AAW	NYBLS	10//99-12//99
	Albany-Schenectady-Troy MSA, NY	S	16.67 MW	15.76 AW	34670 AAW	NYBLS	10//99-12//99
	Binghamton MSA, NY	S	16.07 MW	16.44 AW	33430 AAW	NYBLS	10//99-12//99
	Buffalo-Niagara Falls MSA, NY	S	15.41 MW	12.80 AW	32050 AAW	NYBLS	10//99-12//99
	Dutchess County PMSA, NY	S	19.25 MW	15.89 AW	40040 AAW	NYBLS	10//99-12//99
	Jamestown MSA, NY	S	15.16 MW	14.86 AW	31540 AAW	NYBLS	10//99-12//99
	Nassau-Suffolk PMSA, NY	S	19.30 MW	19.30 AW	40150 AAW	NYBLS	10//99-12//99
	New York PMSA, NY	S	19.48 MW	18.46 AW	40510 AAW	NYBLS	10//99-12//99
	Rochester MSA, NY	S	16.81 MW	16.66 AW	34960 AAW	NYBLS	10//99-12//99
	Syracuse MSA, NY	S	17.37 MW	17.87 AW	36120 AAW	NYBLS	10//99-12//99
	Utica-Rome MSA, NY	S	14.31 MW	13.67 AW	29760 AAW	NYBLS	10//99-12//99
	North Carolina	S	16.43 MW	17.31 AW	36010 AAW	NCBLS	10//99-12//99
	Charlotte-Gastonia-Rock Hill MSA, NC-SC	S	18.14 MW	17.07 AW	37740 AAW	NCBLS	10//99-12//99
	Fayetteville MSA, NC	S	15.45 MW	15.42 AW	32130 AAW	NCBLS	10//99-12//99
	Greensboro--Winston-Salem--High Point MSA, NC	S	16.79 MW	16.57 AW	34930 AAW	NCBLS	10//99-12//99
	Greenville MSA, NC	S	18.70 MW	16.48 AW	38910 AAW	NCBLS	10//99-12//99
	Hickory-Morganton-Lenoir MSA, NC	S	11.91 MW	12.13 AW	24770 AAW	NCBLS	10//99-12//99
	Raleigh-Durham-Chapel Hill MSA, NC	S	17.17 MW	16.67 AW	35720 AAW	NCBLS	10//99-12//99
	North Dakota	S	12.33 MW	13.14 AW	27330 AAW	NDBLS	10//99-12//99
	Bismarck MSA, ND	S	12.12 MW	12.06 AW	25210 AAW	NDBLS	10//99-12//99
	Fargo-Moorhead MSA, ND-MN	S	13.29 MW	12.61 AW	27650 AAW	NDBLS	10//99-12//99
	Grand Forks MSA, ND-MN	S	13.31 MW	11.66 AW	27680 AAW	NDBLS	10//99-12//99
	Ohio	S	14.98 MW	15.32 AW	31860 AAW	OHBLS	10//99-12//99
	Akron PMSA, OH	S	14.54 MW	14.64 AW	30250 AAW	OHBLS	10//99-12//99
	Canton-Massillon MSA, OH	S	14.57 MW	14.10 AW	30310 AAW	OHBLS	10//99-12//99
	Cincinnati PMSA, OH-KY-IN	S	15.92 MW	14.65 AW	33110 AAW	OHBLS	10//99-12//99

AAW Average annual wage	AOH Average offered, high	ASH Average starting, high	H Hourly	M Monthly	S Special: hourly and annual
AE Average entry wage	AOL Average offered, low	ASL Average starting, low	HI Highest wage paid	MTC Median total compensation	TQ Third quartile wage
AEX Average experienced wage	APH Average pay, high range	AW Average wage paid	HR High end range	MW Median wage paid	W Weekly
AO Average offered	APL Average pay, low range	FQ First quartile wage	LR Low end range	SQ Second quartile wage	Y Yearly

Occupation/Type/Industry	Location	Per	Low	Mid	High	Source	Date
Architectural and Civil Drafter	Cleveland-Lorain-Elyria PMSA, OH	S	15.85 MW	15.46 AW	32970 AAW	OHBLS	10//99-12//99
	Columbus MSA, OH	S	15.19 MW	14.75 AW	31600 AAW	OHBLS	10//99-12//99
	Dayton-Springfield MSA, OH	S	17.50 MW	16.12 AW	36400 AAW	OHBLS	10//99-12//99
	Hamilton-Middletown PMSA, OH	S	16.16 MW	15.49 AW	33610 AAW	OHBLS	10//99-12//99
	Lima MSA, OH	S	12.80 MW	12.31 AW	26630 AAW	OHBLS	10//99-12//99
	Toledo MSA, OH	S	15.40 MW	15.62 AW	32030 AAW	OHBLS	10//99-12//99
	Youngstown-Warren MSA, OH	S	16.24 MW	16.72 AW	33790 AAW	OHBLS	10//99-12//99
	Oklahoma	S	15.71 MW	17.37 AW	36120 AAW	OKBLS	10//99-12//99
	Oklahoma City MSA, OK	S	16.21 MW	15.28 AW	33720 AAW	OKBLS	10//99-12//99
	Tulsa MSA, OK	S	19.35 MW	16.58 AW	40240 AAW	OKBLS	10//99-12//99
	Oregon	S	15.94 MW	16.43 AW	34180 AAW	ORBLS	10//99-12//99
	Eugene-Springfield MSA, OR	S	15.95 MW	12.94 AW	33170 AAW	ORBLS	10//99-12//99
	Portland-Vancouver PMSA, OR-WA	S	17.05 MW	16.69 AW	35460 AAW	ORBLS	10//99-12//99
	Salem PMSA, OR	S	16.12 MW	15.94 AW	33540 AAW	ORBLS	10//99-12//99
	Pennsylvania	S	15.61 MW	16.11 AW	33500 AAW	PABLS	10//99-12//99
	Allentown-Bethlehem-Easton MSA, PA	S	15.17 MW	13.49 AW	31550 AAW	PABLS	10//99-12//99
	Altoona MSA, PA	S	15.02 MW	14.18 AW	31250 AAW	PABLS	10//99-12//99
	Erie MSA, PA	S	13.82 MW	13.72 AW	28750 AAW	PABLS	10//99-12//99
	Harrisburg-Lebanon-Carlisle MSA, PA	S	15.71 MW	15.40 AW	32670 AAW	PABLS	10//99-12//99
	Johnstown MSA, PA	S	15.94 MW	15.62 AW	33150 AAW	PABLS	10//99-12//99
	Lancaster MSA, PA	S	16.21 MW	15.71 AW	33710 AAW	PABLS	10//99-12//99
	Philadelphia PMSA, PA-NJ	S	17.49 MW	17.31 AW	36370 AAW	PABLS	10//99-12//99
	Pittsburgh MSA, PA	S	16.91 MW	16.46 AW	35160 AAW	PABLS	10//99-12//99
	Reading MSA, PA	S	17.20 MW	17.72 AW	35770 AAW	PABLS	10//99-12//99
	Scranton--Wilkes-Barre--Hazleton MSA, PA	S	12.83 MW	12.14 AW	26680 AAW	PABLS	10//99-12//99
	Sharon MSA, PA	S	13.82 MW	13.58 AW	28740 AAW	PABLS	10//99-12//99
	State College MSA, PA	S	15.32 MW	15.89 AW	31860 AAW	PABLS	10//99-12//99
	York MSA, PA	S	15.30 MW	15.11 AW	31820 AAW	PABLS	10//99-12//99
	Rhode Island	S	29.47 MW	26.57 AW	55260 AAW	RIBLS	10//99-12//99
	Providence-Fall River-Warwick MSA, RI-MA	S	26.73 MW	29.40 AW	55590 AAW	RIBLS	10//99-12//99
	South Carolina	S	14.41 MW	16.81 AW	34970 AAW	SCBLS	10//99-12//99
	Charleston-North Charleston MSA, SC	S	14.72 MW	13.25 AW	30630 AAW	SCBLS	10//99-12//99
	Columbia MSA, SC	S	18.14 MW	14.49 AW	37740 AAW	SCBLS	10//99-12//99
	Greenville-Spartanburg-Anderson MSA, SC	S	16.62 MW	14.23 AW	34580 AAW	SCBLS	10//99-12//99
	South Dakota	S	13.97 MW	13.74 AW	28580 AAW	SDBLS	10//99-12//99
	Sioux Falls MSA, SD	S	14.05 MW	13.46 AW	29220 AAW	SDBLS	10//99-12//99
	Tennessee	S	15.21 MW	15.94 AW	33150 AAW	TNBLS	10//99-12//99
	Chattanooga MSA, TN-GA	S	12.88 MW	12.39 AW	26790 AAW	TNBLS	10//99-12//99
	Clarksville-Hopkinsville MSA, TN-KY	S	12.21 MW	11.42 AW	25390 AAW	TNBLS	10//99-12//99
	Jackson MSA, TN	S	13.71 MW	13.78 AW	28520 AAW	TNBLS	10//99-12//99
	Johnson City-Kingsport-Bristol MSA, TN-VA	S	15.58 MW	15.03 AW	32400 AAW	TNBLS	10//99-12//99
	Knoxville MSA, TN	S	17.02 MW	15.83 AW	35410 AAW	TNBLS	10//99-12//99
	Memphis MSA, TN-AR-MS	S	15.28 MW	14.82 AW	31780 AAW	MSBLS	10//99-12//99
	Nashville MSA, TN	S	16.46 MW	15.47 AW	34240 AAW	TNBLS	10//99-12//99
	Texas	S	16.08 MW	17.94 AW	37310 AAW	TXBLS	10//99-12//99
	Austin-San Marcos MSA, TX	S	14.64 MW	14.52 AW	30450 AAW	TXBLS	10//99-12//99
	Beaumont-Port Arthur MSA, TX	S	17.02 MW	17.19 AW	35400 AAW	TXBLS	10//99-12//99
	Brazoria PMSA, TX	S	17.61 MW	18.18 AW	36630 AAW	TXBLS	10//99-12//99
	Brownsville-Harlingen-San Benito MSA, TX	S	14.46 MW	14.79 AW	30070 AAW	TXBLS	10//99-12//99
	Corpus Christi MSA, TX	S	13.99 MW	14.36 AW	29100 AAW	TXBLS	10//99-12//99
	Dallas PMSA, TX	S	17.31 MW	16.86 AW	36000 AAW	TXBLS	10//99-12//99
	El Paso MSA, TX	S	15.54 MW	12.29 AW	32330 AAW	TXBLS	10//99-12//99
	Fort Worth-Arlington PMSA, TX	S	14.82 MW	15.60 AW	30820 AAW	TXBLS	10//99-12//99
	Galveston-Texas City PMSA, TX	S	18.02 MW	16.91 AW	37490 AAW	TXBLS	10//99-12//99
	Houston PMSA, TX	S	25.42 MW	22.21 AW	52870 AAW	TXBLS	10//99-12//99
	Longview-Marshall MSA, TX	S	15.33 MW	13.55 AW	31890 AAW	TXBLS	10//99-12//99
	Lubbock MSA, TX	S	11.07 MW	10.16 AW	23030 AAW	TXBLS	10//99-12//99

Occupation/Type/Industry	Location	Per	Low	Mid	High	Source	Date
Architectural and Civil Drafter	McAllen-Edinburg-Mission MSA, TX	S	10.66 MW	10.46 AW	22170 AAW	TXBLS	10//99-12//99
	San Angelo MSA, TX	S	10.75 MW	10.67 AW	22350 AAW	TXBLS	10//99-12//99
	San Antonio MSA, TX	S	13.69 MW	14.29 AW	28480 AAW	TXBLS	10//99-12//99
	Sherman-Denison MSA, TX	S	12.70 MW	13.90 AW	26420 AAW	TXBLS	10//99-12//99
	Tyler MSA, TX	S	13.70 MW	13.93 AW	28490 AAW	TXBLS	10//99-12//99
	Utah	S	14.71 MW	15.21 AW	31640 AAW	UTBLS	10//99-12//99
	Provo-Orem MSA, UT	S	13.46 MW	13.52 AW	28000 AAW	UTBLS	10//99-12//99
	Salt Lake City-Ogden MSA, UT	S	15.99 MW	15.22 AW	33260 AAW	UTBLS	10//99-12//99
	Vermont	S	14.3 MW	14.37 AW	29900 AAW	VTBLS	10//99-12//99
	Burlington MSA, VT	S	14.88 MW	14.99 AW	30940 AAW	VTBLS	10//99-12//99
	Virginia	S	15.12 MW	15.32 AW	31860 AAW	VABLS	10//99-12//99
	Charlottesville MSA, VA	S	13.63 MW	12.86 AW	28350 AAW	VABLS	10//99-12//99
	Norfolk-Virginia Beach-Newport News MSA, VA-NC	S	16.43 MW	17.26 AW	34170 AAW	VABLS	10//99-12//99
	Richmond-Petersburg MSA, VA	S	16.39 MW	15.93 AW	34080 AAW	VABLS	10//99-12//99
	Roanoke MSA, VA	S	12.35 MW	12.44 AW	25680 AAW	VABLS	10//99-12//99
	Washington	S	20.12 MW	21.24 AW	44170 AAW	WABLS	10//99-12//99
	Olympia PMSA, WA	S	17.95 MW	16.45 AW	37340 AAW	WABLS	10//99-12//99
	Seattle-Bellevue-Everett PMSA, WA	S	23.28 MW	24.05 AW	48410 AAW	WABLS	10//99-12//99
	Spokane MSA, WA	S	13.60 MW	13.84 AW	28290 AAW	WABLS	10//99-12//99
	Tacoma PMSA, WA	S	18.26 MW	17.97 AW	37980 AAW	WABLS	10//99-12//99
	Yakima MSA, WA	S	18.48 MW	18.84 AW	38440 AAW	WABLS	10//99-12//99
	West Virginia	S	14.47 MW	15.25 AW	31710 AAW	WVBLS	10//99-12//99
	Charleston MSA, WV	S	15.16 MW	14.79 AW	31530 AAW	WVBLS	10//99-12//99
	Wisconsin	S	14.76 MW	15.37 AW	31970 AAW	WIBLS	10//99-12//99
	Appleton-Oshkosh-Neenah MSA, WI	S	15.88 MW	13.18 AW	33030 AAW	WIBLS	10//99-12//99
	Eau Claire MSA, WI	S	15.15 MW	14.91 AW	31510 AAW	WIBLS	10//99-12//99
	Green Bay MSA, WI	S	16.10 MW	15.88 AW	33480 AAW	WIBLS	10//99-12//99
	Madison MSA, WI	S	14.23 MW	13.56 AW	29590 AAW	WIBLS	10//99-12//99
	Milwaukee-Waukesha PMSA, WI	S	16.29 MW	15.65 AW	33880 AAW	WIBLS	10//99-12//99
	Sheboygan MSA, WI	S	13.96 MW	14.59 AW	29040 AAW	WIBLS	10//99-12//99
	Wausau MSA, WI	S	15.44 MW	14.91 AW	32110 AAW	WIBLS	10//99-12//99
	Wyoming	S	10.73 MW	11.36 AW	23620 AAW	WYBLS	10//99-12//99
	Casper MSA, WY	S	11.00 MW	10.82 AW	22890 AAW	WYBLS	10//99-12//99
	Puerto Rico	S	9.54 MW	10.21 AW	21230 AAW	PRBLS	10//99-12//99
	Ponce MSA, PR	S	10.37 MW	7.99 AW	21580 AAW	PRBLS	10//99-12//99
	San Juan-Bayamon PMSA, PR	S	10.65 MW	10.15 AW	22150 AAW	PRBLS	10//99-12//99
	Guam	S	16.45 MW	16.97 AW	35290 AAW	GUBLS	10//99-12//99
Architecture Teacher							
Postsecondary	California	Y		56630 AAW		CABLS	10//99-12//99
Postsecondary	San Diego MSA, CA	Y		57210 AAW		CABLS	10//99-12//99
Postsecondary	San Francisco PMSA, CA	Y		44980 AAW		CABLS	10//99-12//99
Postsecondary	Washington PMSA, DC-MD-VA-WV	Y		56840 AAW		DCBLS	10//99-12//99
Postsecondary	Florida	Y		69740 AAW		FLBLS	10//99-12//99
Postsecondary	Georgia	Y		48180 AAW		GABLS	10//99-12//99
Postsecondary	Illinois	Y		49710 AAW		ILBLS	10//99-12//99
Postsecondary	Chicago PMSA, IL	Y		49530 AAW		ILBLS	10//99-12//99
Postsecondary	Louisiana	Y		45540 AAW		LABLS	10//99-12//99
Postsecondary	Michigan	Y		60050 AAW		MIBLS	10//99-12//99
Postsecondary	Detroit PMSA, MI	Y		57800 AAW		MIBLS	10//99-12//99
Postsecondary	Nevada	Y		58160 AAW		NVBLS	10//99-12//99
Postsecondary	New York	Y		45720 AAW		NYBLS	10//99-12//99
Postsecondary	New York PMSA, NY	Y		42830 AAW		NYBLS	10//99-12//99
Postsecondary	North Carolina	Y		44400 AAW		NCBLS	10//99-12//99
Postsecondary	Pennsylvania	Y		65880 AAW		PABLS	10//99-12//99
Postsecondary	Rhode Island	Y		60990 AAW		RIBLS	10//99-12//99
Postsecondary	Providence-Fall River-Warwick MSA, RI-MA	Y		60990 AAW		RIBLS	10//99-12//99
Postsecondary	South Carolina	Y		51210 AAW		SCBLS	10//99-12//99
Postsecondary	Texas	Y		52860 AAW		TXBLS	10//99-12//99
Postsecondary	Washington	Y		51610 AAW		WABLS	10//99-12//99
Postsecondary	Wisconsin	Y		55200 AAW		WIBLS	10//99-12//99
Postsecondary	Puerto Rico	Y		35820 AAW		PRBLS	10//99-12//99
Postsecondary	San Juan-Bayamon PMSA, PR	Y		35550 AAW		PRBLS	10//99-12//99

AAW	Average annual wage	AOH	Average offered, high	ASH	Average starting, high	H	Hourly	M	Monthly	S	Special: hourly and annual
AE	Average entry wage	AOL	Average offered, low	ASL	Average starting, low	HI	Highest wage paid	MTC	Median total compensation	TQ	Third quartile wage
AEX	Average experienced wage	APH	Average pay, high range	AW	Average wage paid	HR	High end range	MW	Median wage paid	W	Weekly
AO	Average offered	APL	Average pay, low range	FQ	First quartile wage	LR	Low end range	SQ	Second quartile wage	Y	Yearly

Occupation/Type/Industry	Location	Per	Low	Mid	High	Source	Date
Archivist, Curator	United States	H		20.43 AW		NCS98	1998
Archivist, Curator, and Museum Technician	Alabama	S	16.23 MW	16.06 AW	33410 AAW	ALBLS	10//99-12//99
	Alaska	S	17.89 MW	17.75 AW	36920 AAW	AKBLS	10//99-12//99
	Arizona	S	16.34 MW	17.58 AW	36570 AAW	AZBLS	10//99-12//99
	Phoenix-Mesa MSA, AZ	S	19.69 MW	18.15 AW	40960 AAW	AZBLS	10//99-12//99
	Arkansas	S	11.6 MW	12.16 AW	25290 AAW	ARBLS	10//99-12//99
	California	S	16.55 MW	18.20 AW	37860 AAW	CABLS	10//99-12//99
	Los Angeles-Long Beach PMSA, CA	S	21.79 MW	20.01 AW	45330 AAW	CABLS	10//99-12//99
	Riverside-San Bernardino PMSA, CA	S	15.37 MW	13.99 AW	31970 AAW	CABLS	10//99-12//99
	Sacramento PMSA, CA	S	20.01 MW	19.95 AW	41620 AAW	CABLS	10//99-12//99
	Salinas MSA, CA	S	17.33 MW	15.62 AW	36040 AAW	CABLS	10//99-12//99
	San Diego MSA, CA	S	13.44 MW	12.86 AW	27960 AAW	CABLS	10//99-12//99
	San Francisco PMSA, CA	S	18.65 MW	16.38 AW	38800 AAW	CABLS	10//99-12//99
	San Jose PMSA, CA	S	16.11 MW	14.36 AW	33500 AAW	CABLS	10//99-12//99
	Santa Barbara-Santa Maria-Lompoc MSA, CA	S	19.27 MW	17.49 AW	40090 AAW	CABLS	10//99-12//99
	Visalia-Tulare-Porterville MSA, CA	S	19.49 MW	18.56 AW	40530 AAW	CABLS	10//99-12//99
	Colorado	S	15.16 MW	16.40 AW	34100 AAW	COBLS	10//99-12//99
	Denver PMSA, CO	S	17.32 MW	15.71 AW	36030 AAW	COBLS	10//99-12//99
	Connecticut	S	16.62 MW	17.53 AW	36470 AAW	CTBLS	10//99-12//99
	New Haven-Meriden PMSA, CT	S	17.48 MW	18.99 AW	36360 AAW	CTBLS	10//99-12//99
	Florida	S	13.55 MW	15.80 AW	32870 AAW	FLBLS	10//99-12//99
	Fort Lauderdale PMSA, FL	S	14.25 MW	10.67 AW	29640 AAW	FLBLS	10//99-12//99
	Jacksonville MSA, FL	S	12.39 MW	10.29 AW	25760 AAW	FLBLS	10//99-12//99
	Orlando MSA, FL	S	18.33 MW	20.83 AW	38120 AAW	FLBLS	10//99-12//99
	West Palm Beach-Boca Raton MSA, FL	S	15.38 MW	15.36 AW	31990 AAW	FLBLS	10//99-12//99
	Georgia	S	13.96 MW	14.41 AW	29970 AAW	GABLS	10//99-12//99
	Atlanta MSA, GA	S	14.55 MW	14.32 AW	30270 AAW	GABLS	10//99-12//99
	Hawaii	S	13.4 MW	14.72 AW	30620 AAW	HIBLS	10//99-12//99
	Honolulu MSA, HI	S	14.83 MW	13.53 AW	30840 AAW	HIBLS	10//99-12//99
	Idaho	S	15.73 MW	16.50 AW	34310 AAW	IDBLS	10//99-12//99
	Illinois	S	13.87 MW	16.27 AW	33840 AAW	ILBLS	10//99-12//99
	Chicago PMSA, IL	S	17.23 MW	14.64 AW	35840 AAW	ILBLS	10//99-12//99
	Indiana	S	14.51 MW	15.01 AW	31220 AAW	INBLS	10//99-12//99
	Indianapolis MSA, IN	S	16.89 MW	15.97 AW	35140 AAW	INBLS	10//99-12//99
	Iowa	S	14.74 MW	14.25 AW	29640 AAW	IABLS	10//99-12//99
	Cedar Rapids MSA, IA	S	10.56 MW	9.08 AW	21960 AAW	IABLS	10//99-12//99
	Kansas	S	9.95 MW	11.16 AW	23210 AAW	KSBLS	10//99-12//99
	Kentucky	S	13.06 MW	14.29 AW	29720 AAW	KYBLS	10//99-12//99
	Lexington MSA, KY	S	14.94 MW	12.95 AW	31080 AAW	KYBLS	10//99-12//99
	Louisiana	S	12.34 MW	12.24 AW	25450 AAW	LABLS	10//99-12//99
	Baton Rouge MSA, LA	S	12.10 MW	11.89 AW	25160 AAW	LABLS	10//99-12//99
	Lafayette MSA, LA	S	13.09 MW	13.39 AW	27220 AAW	LABLS	10//99-12//99
	New Orleans MSA, LA	S	13.57 MW	13.07 AW	28220 AAW	LABLS	10//99-12//99
	Maine	S	14.86 MW	15.45 AW	32130 AAW	MEBLS	10//99-12//99
	Baltimore PMSA, MD	S	14.04 MW	12.83 AW	29200 AAW	MDBLS	10//99-12//99
	Massachusetts	S	13.44 MW	15.16 AW	31540 AAW	MABLS	10//99-12//99
	Boston PMSA, MA-NH	S	15.42 MW	13.72 AW	32070 AAW	MABLS	10//99-12//99
	Pittsfield MSA, MA	S	14.03 MW	12.34 AW	29190 AAW	MABLS	10//99-12//99
	Worcester PMSA, MA-CT	S	14.29 MW	14.42 AW	29730 AAW	MABLS	10//99-12//99
	Michigan	S	16.66 MW	18.18 AW	37810 AAW	MIBLS	10//99-12//99
	Detroit PMSA, MI	S	16.06 MW	17.03 AW	33390 AAW	MIBLS	10//99-12//99
	Minnesota	S	16.9 MW	17.82 AW	37060 AAW	MNBLS	10//99-12//99
	Minneapolis-St. Paul MSA, MN-WI	S	20.09 MW	18.74 AW	41780 AAW	MNBLS	10//99-12//99
	Mississippi	S	11.76 MW	13.03 AW	27110 AAW	MSBLS	10//99-12//99
	Missouri	S	11.31 MW	12.03 AW	25030 AAW	MOBLS	10//99-12//99
	Montana	S	12.83 MW	12.83 AW	26680 AAW	MTBLS	10//99-12//99
	Nebraska	S	14.24 MW	15.51 AW	32260 AAW	NEBLS	10//99-12//99
	Nevada	S	14.67 MW	15.36 AW	31940 AAW	NVBLS	10//99-12//99
	Las Vegas MSA, NV-AZ	S	13.94 MW	12.28 AW	29000 AAW	NVBLS	10//99-12//99
	New Hampshire	S	11.47 MW	11.65 AW	24230 AAW	NHBLS	10//99-12//99
	New Jersey	S	17.99 MW	18.40 AW	38270 AAW	NJBLS	10//99-12//99
	Bergen-Passaic PMSA, NJ	S	17.74 MW	16.10 AW	36900 AAW	NJBLS	10//99-12//99

AAW Average annual wage	**AOH** Average offered, high	**ASH** Average starting, high	**H** Hourly	**M** Monthly	**S** Special: hourly and annual
AE Average entry wage	**AOL** Average offered, low	**ASL** Average starting, low	**HI** Highest wage paid	**MTC** Median total compensation	**TQ** Third quartile wage
AEX Average experienced wage	**APH** Average pay, high range	**AW** Average wage paid	**HR** High end range	**MW** Median wage paid	**W** Weekly
AO Average offered	**APL** Average pay, low range	**FQ** First quartile wage	**LR** Low end range	**SQ** Second quartile wage	**Y** Yearly

Occupation/Type/Industry	Location	Per	Low	Mid	High	Source	Date
Archivist, Curator, and Museum Technician	Middlesex-Somerset-Hunterdon PMSA, NJ	S	15.20 MW	14.09 AW	31620 AAW	NJBLS	10//99-12//99
	Newark PMSA, NJ	S	17.43 MW	17.53 AW	36250 AAW	NJBLS	10//99-12//99
	New Mexico	S	15.63 MW	15.63 AW	32500 AAW	NMBLS	10//99-12//99
	Albuquerque MSA, NM	S	16.41 MW	16.65 AW	34130 AAW	NMBLS	10//99-12//99
	New York	S	17.6 MW	19.77 AW	41130 AAW	NYBLS	10//99-12//99
	Buffalo-Niagara Falls MSA, NY	S	13.83 MW	12.37 AW	28760 AAW	NYBLS	10//99-12//99
	Nassau-Suffolk PMSA, NY	S	20.50 MW	18.34 AW	42630 AAW	NYBLS	10//99-12//99
	New York PMSA, NY	S	21.77 MW	19.23 AW	45270 AAW	NYBLS	10//99-12//99
	Newburgh PMSA, NY-PA	S	15.68 MW	14.61 AW	32610 AAW	NYBLS	10//99-12//99
	Rochester MSA, NY	S	14.68 MW	13.31 AW	30530 AAW	NYBLS	10//99-12//99
	Syracuse MSA, NY	S	15.88 MW	14.88 AW	33030 AAW	NYBLS	10//99-12//99
	North Carolina	S	14.52 MW	15.20 AW	31620 AAW	NCBLS	10//99-12//99
	Charlotte-Gastonia-Rock Hill MSA, NC-SC	S	14.92 MW	15.11 AW	31030 AAW	NCBLS	10//99-12//99
	Greensboro--Winston-Salem--High Point MSA, NC	S	12.97 MW	12.07 AW	26980 AAW	NCBLS	10//99-12//99
	Wilmington MSA, NC	S	11.96 MW	12.18 AW	24880 AAW	NCBLS	10//99-12//99
	North Dakota	S	10.18 MW	11.04 AW	22970 AAW	NDBLS	10//99-12//99
	Ohio	S	13.64 MW	15.18 AW	31580 AAW	OHBLS	10//99-12//99
	Cincinnati PMSA, OH-KY-IN	S	17.74 MW	15.74 AW	36890 AAW	OHBLS	10//99-12//99
	Cleveland-Lorain-Elyria PMSA, OH	S	16.81 MW	14.65 AW	34960 AAW	OHBLS	10//99-12//99
	Columbus MSA, OH	S	15.36 MW	14.41 AW	31960 AAW	OHBLS	10//99-12//99
	Toledo MSA, OH	S	16.51 MW	14.15 AW	34340 AAW	OHBLS	10//99-12//99
	Oklahoma	S	11.98 MW	12.86 AW	26740 AAW	OKBLS	10//99-12//99
	Oklahoma City MSA, OK	S	12.69 MW	11.74 AW	26390 AAW	OKBLS	10//99-12//99
	Oregon	S	13.45 MW	15.49 AW	32230 AAW	ORBLS	10//99-12//99
	Portland-Vancouver PMSA, OR-WA	S	16.08 MW	14.34 AW	33440 AAW	ORBLS	10//99-12//99
	Pennsylvania	S	12.97 MW	14.67 AW	30510 AAW	PABLS	10//99-12//99
	Philadelphia PMSA, PA-NJ	S	15.17 MW	13.10 AW	31560 AAW	PABLS	10//99-12//99
	Pittsburgh MSA, PA	S	15.25 MW	13.78 AW	31720 AAW	PABLS	10//99-12//99
	Rhode Island	S	17.59 MW	18.21 AW	37870 AAW	RIBLS	10//99-12//99
	Providence-Fall River-Warwick MSA, RI-MA	S	17.81 MW	17.30 AW	37030 AAW	RIBLS	10//99-12//99
	South Carolina	S	14.6 MW	14.83 AW	30850 AAW	SCBLS	10//99-12//99
	Charleston-North Charleston MSA, SC	S	9.67 MW	8.90 AW	20110 AAW	SCBLS	10//99-12//99
	South Dakota	S	12.75 MW	13.58 AW	28250 AAW	SDBLS	10//99-12//99
	Tennessee	S	12.96 MW	14.03 AW	29180 AAW	TNBLS	10//99-12//99
	Memphis MSA, TN-AR-MS	S	14.86 MW	13.54 AW	30920 AAW	MSBLS	10//99-12//99
	Texas	S	13.99 MW	16.44 AW	34200 AAW	TXBLS	10//99-12//99
	Austin-San Marcos MSA, TX	S	12.89 MW	12.28 AW	26800 AAW	TXBLS	10//99-12//99
	Dallas PMSA, TX	S	15.60 MW	15.20 AW	32450 AAW	TXBLS	10//99-12//99
	Fort Worth-Arlington PMSA, TX	S	16.80 MW	14.13 AW	34940 AAW	TXBLS	10//99-12//99
	Houston PMSA, TX	S	22.61 MW	17.18 AW	47030 AAW	TXBLS	10//99-12//99
	Utah	S	16.12 MW	16.26 AW	33810 AAW	UTBLS	10//99-12//99
	Salt Lake City-Ogden MSA, UT	S	15.03 MW	14.00 AW	31270 AAW	UTBLS	10//99-12//99
	Vermont	S	14.19 MW	14.99 AW	31190 AAW	VTBLS	10//99-12//99
	Virginia	S	13.38 MW	15.24 AW	31700 AAW	VABLS	10//99-12//99
	Norfolk-Virginia Beach-Newport News MSA, VA-NC	S	13.99 MW	12.58 AW	29090 AAW	VABLS	10//99-12//99
	Washington	S	13.98 MW	15.41 AW	32040 AAW	WABLS	10//99-12//99
	Seattle-Bellevue-Everett PMSA, WA	S	16.90 MW	15.10 AW	35150 AAW	WABLS	10//99-12//99
	Tacoma PMSA, WA	S	15.85 MW	15.50 AW	32960 AAW	WABLS	10//99-12//99
	West Virginia	S	13.78 MW	16.91 AW	35170 AAW	WVBLS	10//99-12//99
	Wisconsin	S	14.78 MW	15.30 AW	31830 AAW	WIBLS	10//99-12//99
	Wyoming	S	12.96 MW	13.90 AW	28910 AAW	WYBLS	10//99-12//99
Area, Ethnic, and Cultural Studies Teacher							
Postsecondary	California	Y		59380 AAW		CABLS	10//99-12//99
Postsecondary	Colorado	Y		45520 AAW		COBLS	10//99-12//99
Postsecondary	Florida	Y		61050 AAW		FLBLS	10//99-12//99
Postsecondary	Illinois	Y		47460 AAW		ILBLS	10//99-12//99

AAW	Average annual wage	AOH	Average offered, high	ASH	Average starting, high	H	Hourly			M	Monthly	S	Special: hourly and annual
AE	Average entry wage	AOL	Average offered, low	ASL	Average starting, low	HI	Highest wage paid	MTC	Median total compensation	TQ	Third quartile wage
AEX	Average experienced wage	APH	Average pay, high range	AW	Average wage paid	HR	High end range	MW	Median wage paid	W	Weekly
AO	Average offered	APL	Average pay, low range	FQ	First quartile wage	LR	Low end range	SQ	Second quartile wage	Y	Yearly

Occupation/Type/Industry	Location	Per	Low	Mid	High	Source	Date
Area, Ethnic, and Cultural							
Studies Teacher							
Postsecondary	Maryland	Y		58390 AAW		MDBLS	10//99-12//99
Postsecondary	Massachusetts	Y		51440 AAW		MABLS	10//99-12//99
Postsecondary	Minnesota	Y		50920 AAW		MNBLS	10//99-12//99
Postsecondary	New Jersey	Y		60210 AAW		NJBLS	10//99-12//99
Postsecondary	New York	Y		55680 AAW		NYBLS	10//99-12//99
Postsecondary	North Carolina	Y		40230 AAW		NCBLS	10//99-12//99
Postsecondary	Ohio	Y		50150 AAW		OHBLS	10//99-12//99
Postsecondary	Pennsylvania	Y		55210 AAW		PABLS	10//99-12//99
Postsecondary	Tennessee	Y		49840 AAW		TNBLS	10//99-12//99
Postsecondary	Texas	Y		48790 AAW		TXBLS	10//99-12//99
Postsecondary	Vermont	Y		50680 AAW		VTBLS	10//99-12//99
Postsecondary	Virginia	Y		57870 AAW		VABLS	10//99-12//99
Postsecondary	Washington	Y		45130 AAW		WABLS	10//99-12//99
Art Director	Alabama	S	18.07 MW	21.99 AW	45730 AAW	ALBLS	10//99-12//99
	Alaska	S	19.06 MW	18.94 AW	39390 AAW	AKBLS	10//99-12//99
	Arizona	S	19.77 MW	21.41 AW	44540 AAW	AZBLS	10//99-12//99
	Arkansas	S	13.44 MW	17.62 AW	36650 AAW	ARBLS	10//99-12//99
	California	S	32.29 MW	34.12 AW	70960 AAW	CABLS	10//99-12//99
	Colorado	S	17.85 MW	19.65 AW	40880 AAW	COBLS	10//99-12//99
	Connecticut	S	30.9 MW	32.22 AW	67020 AAW	CTBLS	10//99-12//99
	Delaware	S	22.48 MW	24.93 AW	51860 AAW	DEBLS	10//99-12//99
	District of Columbia	S	30.9 MW	30.80 AW	64070 AAW	DCBLS	10//99-12//99
	Florida	S	19.22 MW	22.06 AW	45880 AAW	FLBLS	10//99-12//99
	Georgia	S	24.27 MW	27.27 AW	56710 AAW	GABLS	10//99-12//99
	Hawaii	S	18.33 MW	18.98 AW	39490 AAW	HIBLS	10//99-12//99
	Illinois	S	21.07 MW	23.52 AW	48910 AAW	ILBLS	10//99-12//99
	Indiana	S	26.89 MW	27.57 AW	57350 AAW	INBLS	10//99-12//99
	Iowa	S	11.44 MW	12.71 AW	26430 AAW	IABLS	10//99-12//99
	Kansas	S	20.68 MW	20.74 AW	43150 AAW	KSBLS	10//99-12//99
	Louisiana	S	19.67 MW	20.46 AW	42560 AAW	LABLS	10//99-12//99
	Maryland	S	27.64 MW	27.90 AW	58040 AAW	MDBLS	10//99-12//99
	Massachusetts	S	23.56 MW	27.17 AW	56510 AAW	MABLS	10//99-12//99
	Minnesota	S	24.83 MW	27.66 AW	57540 AAW	MNBLS	10//99-12//99
	Mississippi	S	17.23 MW	23.25 AW	48370 AAW	MSBLS	10//99-12//99
	Missouri	S	25.59 MW	28.17 AW	58590 AAW	MOBLS	10//99-12//99
	Nebraska	S	12.14 MW	14.58 AW	30330 AAW	NEBLS	10//99-12//99
	Nevada	S	22.45 MW	21.48 AW	44670 AAW	NVBLS	10//99-12//99
	New Hampshire	S	24.65 MW	29.03 AW	60370 AAW	NHBLS	10//99-12//99
	New Jersey	S	26.42 MW	33.46 AW	69590 AAW	NJBLS	10//99-12//99
	New York	S	38.32 MW	38.73 AW	80560 AAW	NYBLS	10//99-12//99
	North Carolina	S	22.98 MW	29.51 AW	61380 AAW	NCBLS	10//99-12//99
	Ohio	S	26.07 MW	27.07 AW	56310 AAW	OHBLS	10//99-12//99
	Oklahoma	S	17.31 MW	16.99 AW	35340 AAW	OKBLS	10//99-12//99
	Oregon	S	19.08 MW	21.31 AW	44310 AAW	ORBLS	10//99-12//99
	Pennsylvania	S	19.43 MW	22.65 AW	47110 AAW	PABLS	10//99-12//99
	Rhode Island	S	29.88 MW	31.91 AW	66380 AAW	RIBLS	10//99-12//99
	South Carolina	S	19.03 MW	20.08 AW	41770 AAW	SCBLS	10//99-12//99
	South Dakota	S	21.07 MW	24.92 AW	51840 AAW	SDBLS	10//99-12//99
	Tennessee	S	16.51 MW	17.19 AW	35750 AAW	TNBLS	10//99-12//99
	Texas	S	18.98 MW	24.08 AW	50080 AAW	TXBLS	10//99-12//99
	Utah	S	20.29 MW	24.62 AW	51210 AAW	UTBLS	10//99-12//99
	Vermont	S	26.69 MW	25.63 AW	53310 AAW	VTBLS	10//99-12//99
	Virginia	S	23.84 MW	25.29 AW	52600 AAW	VABLS	10//99-12//99
	Washington	S	34.08 MW	40.91 AW	85100 AAW	WABLS	10//99-12//99
	West Virginia	S	18.25 MW	19.08 AW	39680 AAW	WVBLS	10//99-12//99
	Wisconsin	S	22.59 MW	23.94 AW	49800 AAW	WIBLS	10//99-12//99
	Puerto Rico	S	25.21 MW	25.69 AW	53430 AAW	PRBLS	10//99-12//99
Advertising	East	Y		57000 AW		ADAGE1	2000
Advertising	Midwest	Y		53000 AW		ADAGE1	2000
Advertising	South	Y		50000 AW		ADAGE1	2000
Advertising	West	Y		56000 AW		ADAGE1	2000
Art, Drama, and Music Teacher							
Postsecondary	Alabama	Y		39320 AAW		ALBLS	10//99-12//99
Postsecondary	Birmingham MSA, AL	Y		40550 AAW		ALBLS	10//99-12//99
Postsecondary	Montgomery MSA, AL	Y		42270 AAW		ALBLS	10//99-12//99
Postsecondary	Arizona	Y		32860 AAW		AZBLS	10//99-12//99
Postsecondary	Arkansas	Y		45900 AAW		ARBLS	10//99-12//99
Postsecondary	California	Y		50460 AAW		CABLS	10//99-12//99

AAW Average annual wage	AOH Average offered, high	ASH Average starting, high	H Hourly	M Monthly	S Special: hourly and annual
AE Average entry wage	AOL Average offered, low	ASL Average starting, low	HI Highest wage paid	MTC Median total compensation	TQ Third quartile wage
AEX Average experienced wage	APH Average pay, high range	AW Average wage paid	HR High end range	MW Median wage paid	W Weekly
AO Average offered	APL Average pay, low range	FQ First quartile wage	LR Low end range	SQ Second quartile wage	Y Yearly

Occupation/Type/Industry	Location	Per	Low	Mid	High	Source	Date
Art, Drama, and Music Teacher							
Postsecondary	Fresno MSA, CA	Y		46540 AAW		CABLS	10//99-12//99
Postsecondary	Los Angeles-Long Beach PMSA, CA	Y		47830 AAW		CABLS	10//99-12//99
Postsecondary	Riverside-San Bernardino PMSA, CA	Y		50180 AAW		CABLS	10//99-12//99
Postsecondary	Sacramento PMSA, CA	Y		42530 AAW		CABLS	10//99-12//99
Postsecondary	San Diego MSA, CA	Y		51140 AAW		CABLS	10//99-12//99
Postsecondary	San Francisco PMSA, CA	Y		62000 AAW		CABLS	10//99-12//99
Postsecondary	Colorado	Y		47230 AAW		COBLS	10//99-12//99
Postsecondary	Colorado Springs MSA, CO	Y		55000 AAW		COBLS	10//99-12//99
Postsecondary	Denver PMSA, CO	Y		47610 AAW		COBLS	10//99-12//99
Postsecondary	Connecticut	Y		58550 AAW		CTBLS	10//99-12//99
Postsecondary	Hartford MSA, CT	Y		62120 AAW		CTBLS	10//99-12//99
Postsecondary	New Haven-Meriden PMSA, CT	Y		58190 AAW		CTBLS	10//99-12//99
Postsecondary	Delaware	Y		50020 AAW		DEBLS	10//99-12//99
Postsecondary	Wilmington-Newark PMSA, DE-MD	Y		50300 AAW		DEBLS	10//99-12//99
Postsecondary	District of Columbia	Y		46830 AAW		DCBLS	10//99-12//99
Postsecondary	Washington PMSA, DC-MD-VA-WV	Y		46870 AAW		DCBLS	10//99-12//99
Postsecondary	Florida	Y		53110 AAW		FLBLS	10//99-12//99
Postsecondary	Miami PMSA, FL	Y		60540 AAW		FLBLS	10//99-12//99
Postsecondary	Orlando MSA, FL	Y		46480 AAW		FLBLS	10//99-12//99
Postsecondary	Pensacola MSA, FL	Y		45460 AAW		FLBLS	10//99-12//99
Postsecondary	Tampa-St. Petersburg-Clearwater MSA, FL	Y		48000 AAW		FLBLS	10//99-12//99
Postsecondary	West Palm Beach-Boca Raton MSA, FL	Y		45330 AAW		FLBLS	10//99-12//99
Postsecondary	Georgia	Y		41930 AAW		GABLS	10//99-12//99
Postsecondary	Atlanta MSA, GA	Y		43650 AAW		GABLS	10//99-12//99
Postsecondary	Savannah MSA, GA	Y		44020 AAW		GABLS	10//99-12//99
Postsecondary	Idaho	Y		42370 AAW		IDBLS	10//99-12//99
Postsecondary	Illinois	Y		45850 AAW		ILBLS	10//99-12//99
Postsecondary	Chicago PMSA, IL	Y		46240 AAW		ILBLS	10//99-12//99
Postsecondary	Indiana	Y		49080 AAW		INBLS	10//99-12//99
Postsecondary	Fort Wayne MSA, IN	Y		51100 AAW		INBLS	10//99-12//99
Postsecondary	Indianapolis MSA, IN	Y		43730 AAW		INBLS	10//99-12//99
Postsecondary	Iowa	Y		41310 AAW		IABLS	10//99-12//99
Postsecondary	Des Moines MSA, IA	Y		46290 AAW		IABLS	10//99-12//99
Postsecondary	Kansas	Y		34190 AAW		KSBLS	10//99-12//99
Postsecondary	Wichita MSA, KS	Y		36820 AAW		KSBLS	10//99-12//99
Postsecondary	Kentucky	Y		41820 AAW		KYBLS	10//99-12//99
Postsecondary	Louisiana	Y		35930 AAW		LABLS	10//99-12//99
Postsecondary	New Orleans MSA, LA	Y		42140 AAW		LABLS	10//99-12//99
Postsecondary	Maryland	Y		47150 AAW		MDBLS	10//99-12//99
Postsecondary	Baltimore PMSA, MD	Y		48540 AAW		MDBLS	10//99-12//99
Postsecondary	Massachusetts	Y		44640 AAW		MABLS	10//99-12//99
Postsecondary	Boston PMSA, MA-NH	Y		43890 AAW		MABLS	10//99-12//99
Postsecondary	Brockton PMSA, MA	Y		44060 AAW		MABLS	10//99-12//99
Postsecondary	Springfield MSA, MA	Y		50990 AAW		MABLS	10//99-12//99
Postsecondary	Worcester PMSA, MA-CT	Y		47280 AAW		MABLS	10//99-12//99
Postsecondary	Michigan	Y		47140 AAW		MIBLS	10//99-12//99
Postsecondary	Detroit PMSA, MI	Y		51270 AAW		MIBLS	10//99-12//99
Postsecondary	Grand Rapids-Muskegon-Holland MSA, MI	Y		37050 AAW		MIBLS	10//99-12//99
Postsecondary	Minnesota	Y		50210 AAW		MNBLS	10//99-12//99
Postsecondary	Minneapolis-St. Paul MSA, MN-WI	Y		52340 AAW		MNBLS	10//99-12//99
Postsecondary	St. Cloud MSA, MN	Y		46660 AAW		MNBLS	10//99-12//99
Postsecondary	Mississippi	Y		40760 AAW		MSBLS	10//99-12//99
Postsecondary	Jackson MSA, MS	Y		36040 AAW		MSBLS	10//99-12//99
Postsecondary	Missouri	Y		36140 AAW		MOBLS	10//99-12//99
Postsecondary	St. Louis MSA, MO-IL	Y		33660 AAW		MOBLS	10//99-12//99
Postsecondary	Montana	Y		51560 AAW		MTBLS	10//99-12//99
Postsecondary	Nebraska	Y		43850 AAW		NEBLS	10//99-12//99
Postsecondary	Omaha MSA, NE-IA	Y		42800 AAW		NEBLS	10//99-12//99
Postsecondary	Nevada	Y		41390 AAW		NVBLS	10//99-12//99
Postsecondary	Las Vegas MSA, NV-AZ	Y		49890 AAW		NVBLS	10//99-12//99
Postsecondary	New Hampshire	Y		52360 AAW		NHBLS	10//99-12//99
Postsecondary	Manchester PMSA, NH	Y		42300 AAW		NHBLS	10//99-12//99

AAW	Average annual wage	AOH	Average offered, high	ASH	Average starting, high	H	Hourly	M	Monthly	S	Special: hourly and annual
AE	Average entry wage	AOL	Average offered, low	ASL	Average starting, low	HI	Highest wage paid	MTC	Median total compensation	TQ	Third quartile wage
AEX	Average experienced wage	APH	Average pay, high range	AW	Average wage paid	HR	High end range	MW	Median wage paid	W	Weekly
AO	Average offered	APL	Average pay, low range	FQ	First quartile wage	LR	Low end range	SQ	Second quartile wage	Y	Yearly

Occupation/Type/Industry	Location	Per	Low	Mid	High	Source	Date
Art, Drama, and Music Teacher							
Postsecondary	New Jersey	Y		53660 AAW		NJBLS	10//99-12//99
Postsecondary	Bergen-Passaic PMSA, NJ	Y		53570 AAW		NJBLS	10//99-12//99
Postsecondary	Monmouth-Ocean PMSA, NJ	Y		47950 AAW		NJBLS	10//99-12//99
Postsecondary	Newark PMSA, NJ	Y		55140 AAW		NJBLS	10//99-12//99
Postsecondary	Trenton PMSA, NJ	Y		39000 AAW		NJBLS	10//99-12//99
Postsecondary	New Mexico	Y		39200 AAW		NMBLS	10//99-12//99
Postsecondary	New York	Y		58280 AAW		NYBLS	10//99-12//99
Postsecondary	Albany-Schenectady-Troy MSA, NY	Y		53780 AAW		NYBLS	10//99-12//99
Postsecondary	New York PMSA, NY	Y		63110 AAW		NYBLS	10//99-12//99
Postsecondary	Utica-Rome MSA, NY	Y		46650 AAW		NYBLS	10//99-12//99
Postsecondary	North Carolina	Y		42800 AAW		NCBLS	10//99-12//99
Postsecondary	Asheville MSA, NC	Y		33760 AAW		NCBLS	10//99-12//99
Postsecondary	Charlotte-Gastonia-Rock Hill MSA, NC-SC	Y		40260 AAW		NCBLS	10//99-12//99
Postsecondary	Greensboro--Winston-Salem-- High Point MSA, NC	Y		42580 AAW		NCBLS	10//99-12//99
Postsecondary	Hickory-Morganton-Lenoir MSA, NC	Y		40300 AAW		NCBLS	10//99-12//99
Postsecondary	Raleigh-Durham-Chapel Hill MSA, NC	Y		45000 AAW		NCBLS	10//99-12//99
Postsecondary	Wilmington MSA, NC	Y		54090 AAW		NCBLS	10//99-12//99
Postsecondary	Ohio	Y		41960 AAW		OHBLS	10//99-12//99
Postsecondary	Canton-Massillon MSA, OH	Y		38780 AAW		OHBLS	10//99-12//99
Postsecondary	Cincinnati PMSA, OH-KY-IN	Y		41320 AAW		OHBLS	10//99-12//99
Postsecondary	Cleveland-Lorain-Elyria PMSA, OH	Y		42490 AAW		OHBLS	10//99-12//99
Postsecondary	Columbus MSA, OH	Y		40820 AAW		OHBLS	10//99-12//99
Postsecondary	Dayton-Springfield MSA, OH	Y		40590 AAW		OHBLS	10//99-12//99
Postsecondary	Toledo MSA, OH	Y		40890 AAW		OHBLS	10//99-12//99
Postsecondary	Oklahoma	Y		40500 AAW		OKBLS	10//99-12//99
Postsecondary	Oklahoma City MSA, OK	Y		38630 AAW		OKBLS	10//99-12//99
Postsecondary	Oregon	Y		44360 AAW		ORBLS	10//99-12//99
Postsecondary	Eugene-Springfield MSA, OR	Y		47930 AAW		ORBLS	10//99-12//99
Postsecondary	Portland-Vancouver PMSA, OR-WA	Y		40950 AAW		ORBLS	10//99-12//99
Postsecondary	Pennsylvania	Y		52210 AAW		PABLS	10//99-12//99
Postsecondary	Allentown-Bethlehem-Easton MSA, PA	Y		37410 AAW		PABLS	10//99-12//99
Postsecondary	Harrisburg-Lebanon-Carlisle MSA, PA	Y		45380 AAW		PABLS	10//99-12//99
Postsecondary	Philadelphia PMSA, PA-NJ	Y		56310 AAW		PABLS	10//99-12//99
Postsecondary	Pittsburgh MSA, PA	Y		50660 AAW		PABLS	10//99-12//99
Postsecondary	Reading MSA, PA	Y		33590 AAW		PABLS	10//99-12//99
Postsecondary	Scranton--Wilkes-Barre-- Hazleton MSA, PA	Y		36750 AAW		PABLS	10//99-12//99
Postsecondary	Rhode Island	Y		41930 AAW		RIBLS	10//99-12//99
Postsecondary	Providence-Fall River- Warwick MSA, RI-MA	Y		41770 AAW		RIBLS	10//99-12//99
Postsecondary	South Carolina	Y		45780 AAW		SCBLS	10//99-12//99
Postsecondary	Greenville-Spartanburg- Anderson MSA, SC	Y		43310 AAW		SCBLS	10//99-12//99
Postsecondary	South Dakota	Y		39150 AAW		SDBLS	10//99-12//99
Postsecondary	Tennessee	Y		41840 AAW		TNBLS	10//99-12//99
Postsecondary	Johnson City-Kingsport-Bristol MSA, TN-VA	Y		38660 AAW		TNBLS	10//99-12//99
Postsecondary	Memphis MSA, TN-AR-MS	Y		38320 AAW		MSBLS	10//99-12//99
Postsecondary	Nashville MSA, TN	Y		49680 AAW		TNBLS	10//99-12//99
Postsecondary	Texas	Y		43670 AAW		TXBLS	10//99-12//99
Postsecondary	Dallas PMSA, TX	Y		49990 AAW		TXBLS	10//99-12//99
Postsecondary	Houston PMSA, TX	Y		45790 AAW		TXBLS	10//99-12//99
Postsecondary	Killeen-Temple MSA, TX	Y		29460 AAW		TXBLS	10//99-12//99
Postsecondary	Longview-Marshall MSA, TX	Y		33790 AAW		TXBLS	10//99-12//99
Postsecondary	Odessa-Midland MSA, TX	Y		43110 AAW		TXBLS	10//99-12//99
Postsecondary	San Antonio MSA, TX	Y		45160 AAW		TXBLS	10//99-12//99
Postsecondary	Vermont	Y		48100 AAW		VTBLS	10//99-12//99
Postsecondary	Burlington MSA, VT	Y		47200 AAW		VTBLS	10//99-12//99
Postsecondary	Virginia	Y		43630 AAW		VABLS	10//99-12//99
Postsecondary	Norfolk-Virginia Beach- Newport News MSA, VA- NC	Y		45670 AAW		VABLS	10//99-12//99

AAW Average annual wage	**AOH** Average offered, high	**ASH** Average starting, high	**H** Hourly	**M** Monthly	**S** Special: hourly and annual
AE Average entry wage	**AOL** Average offered, low	**ASL** Average starting, low	**HI** Highest wage paid	**MTC** Median total compensation	**TQ** Third quartile wage
AEX Average experienced wage	**APH** Average pay, high range	**AW** Average wage paid	**HR** High end range	**MW** Median wage paid	**W** Weekly
AO Average offered	**APL** Average pay, low range	**FQ** First quartile wage	**LR** Low end range	**SQ** Second quartile wage	**Y** Yearly

Occupation/Type/Industry	Location	Per	Low	Mid	High	Source	Date
Art, Drama, and Music Teacher							
Postsecondary	Richmond-Petersburg MSA, VA	Y		44290 AAW		VABLS	10//99-12//99
Postsecondary	Washington	Y		40460 AAW		WABLS	10//99-12//99
Postsecondary	Seattle-Bellevue-Everett PMSA, WA	Y		41660 AAW		WABLS	10//99-12//99
Postsecondary	Tacoma PMSA, WA	Y		50290 AAW		WABLS	10//99-12//99
Postsecondary	West Virginia	Y		52500 AAW		WVBLS	10//99-12//99
Postsecondary	Wisconsin	Y		40550 AAW		WIBLS	10//99-12//99
Postsecondary	Milwaukee-Waukesha PMSA, WI	Y		36190 AAW		WIBLS	10//99-12//99
Postsecondary	Wyoming	Y		40750 AAW		WYBLS	10//99-12//99
Postsecondary	Puerto Rico	Y		37140 AAW		PRBLS	10//99-12//99
Postsecondary	San Juan-Bayamon PMSA, PR	Y		36920 AAW		PRBLS	10//99-12//99
Artist							
Comic Book	United States	Y		44000 AW		MENHEL	1999
Assistant Vice President							
Finance	United States	Y		130047 AW		PENINV	2000
Associate Editor							
Publishing, Revenues $10-99.9 million	United States	Y		58000 AW		PUBWK	1999
Publishing, Revenues under $10 million	United States	Y		36380 AW		PUBWK	1999
Associate Professor							
Medical Technology	United States	Y	43020 APL	59569 AW	97362 APH	LABMED	1999
Astronomer	Arizona	S	31.03 MW	31.32 AW	65150 AAW	AZBLS	10//99-12//99
	California	S	32.93 MW	34.70 AW	72170 AAW	CABLS	10//99-12//99
Athlete	United States	H		40.88 AW		NCS98	1998
Athlete and Sports Competitor	California	Y		110230 AAW		CABLS	10//99-12//99
	Connecticut	Y		26950 AAW		CTBLS	10//99-12//99
	Hartford MSA, CT	Y		21360 AAW		CTBLS	10//99-12//99
	Florida	Y		44850 AAW		FLBLS	10//99-12//99
	Fort Lauderdale PMSA, FL	Y		54850 AAW		FLBLS	10//99-12//99
	Georgia	Y		27330 AAW		GABLS	10//99-12//99
	Iowa	Y		65040 AAW		IABLS	10//99-12//99
	Kentucky	Y		36040 AAW		KYBLS	10//99-12//99
	Massachusetts	Y		47190 AAW		MABLS	10//99-12//99
	Springfield MSA, MA	Y		52470 AAW		MABLS	10//99-12//99
	Nebraska	Y		19860 AAW		NEBLS	10//99-12//99
	Ohio	Y		26640 AAW		OHBLS	10//99-12//99
	Cincinnati PMSA, OH-KY-IN	Y		23280 AAW		OHBLS	10//99-12//99
	Cleveland-Lorain-Elyria PMSA, OH	Y		26920 AAW		OHBLS	10//99-12//99
	Columbus MSA, OH	Y		35070 AAW		OHBLS	10//99-12//99
	Oklahoma	Y		36430 AAW		OKBLS	10//99-12//99
	Pennsylvania	Y		109490 AAW		PABLS	10//99-12//99
	Philadelphia PMSA, PA-NJ	Y		136330 AAW		PABLS	10//99-12//99
	South Carolina	Y		26050 AAW		SCBLS	10//99-12//99
	Utah	Y		39040 AAW		UTBLS	10//99-12//99
	Salt Lake City-Ogden MSA, UT	Y		39030 AAW		UTBLS	10//99-12//99
	Virginia	Y		37620 AAW		VABLS	10//99-12//99
	Washington	Y		29190 AAW		WABLS	10//99-12//99
Athletic Trainer	Alabama	Y		25310 AAW		ALBLS	10//99-12//99
	Arizona	Y		36970 AAW		AZBLS	10//99-12//99
	Arkansas	Y		31700 AAW		ARBLS	10//99-12//99
	California	Y		25600 AAW		CABLS	10//99-12//99
	Colorado	Y		30020 AAW		COBLS	10//99-12//99
	Connecticut	Y		37160 AAW		CTBLS	10//99-12//99
	Florida	Y		35090 AAW		FLBLS	10//99-12//99
	Georgia	Y		43230 AAW		GABLS	10//99-12//99
	Hawaii	Y		29850 AAW		HIBLS	10//99-12//99
	Illinois	Y		27590 AAW		ILBLS	10//99-12//99
	Indiana	Y		31860 AAW		INBLS	10//99-12//99
	Iowa	Y		32060 AAW		IABLS	10//99-12//99
	Kansas	Y		34340 AAW		KSBLS	10//99-12//99
	Kentucky	Y		27610 AAW		KYBLS	10//99-12//99
	Louisiana	Y		38040 AAW		LABLS	10//99-12//99

AAW Average annual wage	**AOH** Average offered, high	**ASH** Average starting, high	**H** Hourly	**M** Monthly	**S** Special: hourly and annual
AE Average entry wage	**AOL** Average offered, low	**ASL** Average starting, low	**HI** Highest wage paid	**MTC** Median total compensation	**TQ** Third quartile wage
AEX Average experienced wage	**APH** Average pay, high range	**AW** Average wage paid	**HR** High end range	**MW** Median wage paid	**W** Weekly
AO Average offered	**APL** Average pay, low range	**FQ** First quartile wage	**LR** Low end range	**SQ** Second quartile wage	**Y** Yearly

Occupation/Type/Industry	Location	Per	Low	Mid	High	Source	Date
Athletic Trainer	Maryland	Y		34430 AAW		MDBLS	10//99-12//99
	Massachusetts	Y		32510 AAW		MABLS	10//99-12//99
	Michigan	Y		38780 AAW		MIBLS	10//99-12//99
	Minnesota	Y		34240 AAW		MNBLS	10//99-12//99
	Mississippi	Y		30470 AAW		MSBLS	10//99-12//99
	Missouri	Y		32090 AAW		MOBLS	10//99-12//99
	Montana	Y		28620 AAW		MTBLS	10//99-12//99
	Nebraska	Y		34520 AAW		NEBLS	10//99-12//99
	Nevada	Y		39640 AAW		NVBLS	10//99-12//99
	New Hampshire	Y		22940 AAW		NHBLS	10//99-12//99
	New Jersey	Y		35550 AAW		NJBLS	10//99-12//99
	New York	Y		36730 AAW		NYBLS	10//99-12//99
	North Carolina	Y		29680 AAW		NCBLS	10//99-12//99
	Ohio	Y		32350 AAW		OHBLS	10//99-12//99
	Oklahoma	Y		30660 AAW		OKBLS	10//99-12//99
	Oregon	Y		35660 AAW		ORBLS	10//99-12//99
	Pennsylvania	Y		29150 AAW		PABLS	10//99-12//99
	South Carolina	Y		55040 AAW		SCBLS	10//99-12//99
	South Dakota	Y		23580 AAW		SDBLS	10//99-12//99
	Tennessee	Y		30790 AAW		TNBLS	10//99-12//99
	Texas	Y		34520 AAW		TXBLS	10//99-12//99
	Vermont	Y		27820 AAW		VTBLS	10//99-12//99
	Virginia	Y		21010 AAW		VABLS	10//99-12//99
	Washington	Y		30730 AAW		WABLS	10//99-12//99
Atmospheric and Space Scientist	Alabama	S	22.6 MW	22.48 AW	46760 AAW	ALBLS	10//99-12//99
	Arizona	S	28.27 MW	26.89 AW	55920 AAW	AZBLS	10//99-12//99
	Arkansas	S	18.51 MW	19.96 AW	41520 AAW	ARBLS	10//99-12//99
	California	S	25.87 MW	25.99 AW	54060 AAW	CABLS	10//99-12//99
	Colorado	S	21.3 MW	24.65 AW	51270 AAW	COBLS	10//99-12//99
	Connecticut	S	28.16 MW	32.46 AW	67510 AAW	CTBLS	10//99-12//99
	Florida	S	27.49 MW	26.50 AW	55120 AAW	FLBLS	10//99-12//99
	Georgia	S	23.61 MW	25.91 AW	53900 AAW	GABLS	10//99-12//99
	Illinois	S	23.55 MW	23.32 AW	48490 AAW	ILBLS	10//99-12//99
	Indiana	S	22.82 MW	22.42 AW	46630 AAW	INBLS	10//99-12//99
	Kansas	S	22.35 MW	21.47 AW	44650 AAW	KSBLS	10//99-12//99
	Kentucky	S	24.47 MW	23.95 AW	49820 AAW	KYBLS	10//99-12//99
	Louisiana	S	24.3 MW	24.65 AW	51280 AAW	LABLS	10//99-12//99
	Maryland	S	30.76 MW	30.44 AW	63310 AAW	MDBLS	10//99-12//99
	Massachusetts	S	19.03 MW	21.33 AW	44360 AAW	MABLS	10//99-12//99
	Michigan	S	23.4 MW	22.69 AW	47190 AAW	MIBLS	10//99-12//99
	Mississippi	S	23.36 MW	22.73 AW	47280 AAW	MSBLS	10//99-12//99
	Missouri	S	25.47 MW	25.32 AW	52660 AAW	MOBLS	10//99-12//99
	Montana	S	27.64 MW	26.55 AW	55220 AAW	MTBLS	10//99-12//99
	Nebraska	S	23.71 MW	22.25 AW	46270 AAW	NEBLS	10//99-12//99
	Nevada	S	29.58 MW	28.32 AW	58900 AAW	NVBLS	10//99-12//99
	New Jersey	S	30.81 MW	29.92 AW	62240 AAW	NJBLS	10//99-12//99
	New Mexico	S	30.23 MW	30.95 AW	64370 AAW	NMBLS	10//99-12//99
	New York	S	22.38 MW	23.77 AW	49440 AAW	NYBLS	10//99-12//99
	North Carolina	S	26.79 MW	26.31 AW	54720 AAW	NCBLS	10//99-12//99
	Ohio	S	25.33 MW	24.20 AW	50340 AAW	OHBLS	10//99-12//99
	Oklahoma	S	27.59 MW	24.25 AW	50450 AAW	OKBLS	10//99-12//99
	Oregon	S	27.87 MW	25.86 AW	53780 AAW	ORBLS	10//99-12//99
	Pennsylvania	S	26.08 MW	25.68 AW	53410 AAW	PABLS	10//99-12//99
	South Carolina	S	25.68 MW	25.37 AW	52760 AAW	SCBLS	10//99-12//99
	South Dakota	S	26.24 MW	24.26 AW	50450 AAW	SDBLS	10//99-12//99
	Tennessee	S	26.75 MW	24.95 AW	51890 AAW	TNBLS	10//99-12//99
	Texas	S	27.54 MW	25.97 AW	54020 AAW	TXBLS	10//99-12//99
	Virginia	S	26.96 MW	28.45 AW	59190 AAW	VABLS	10//99-12//99
	West Virginia	S	20.61 MW	23.07 AW	47990 AAW	WVBLS	10//99-12//99
	Wisconsin	S	23.53 MW	21.91 AW	45580 AAW	WIBLS	10//99-12//99
	Wyoming	S	25.58 MW	23.08 AW	48000 AAW	WYBLS	10//99-12//99
Atmospheric, Earth, Marine, and Space Sciences Teacher							
Postsecondary	Alabama	Y		33480 AAW		ALBLS	10//99-12//99
Postsecondary	Arkansas	Y		46360 AAW		ARBLS	10//99-12//99
Postsecondary	California	Y		63870 AAW		CABLS	10//99-12//99
Postsecondary	Colorado	Y		49120 AAW		COBLS	10//99-12//99
Postsecondary	Florida	Y		60270 AAW		FLBLS	10//99-12//99
Postsecondary	Georgia	Y		47370 AAW		GABLS	10//99-12//99
Postsecondary	Illinois	Y		55100 AAW		ILBLS	10//99-12//99

AAW	Average annual wage	AOH	Average offered, high	ASH	Average starting, high	H	Hourly	M	Monthly	S	Special: hourly and annual
AE	Average entry wage	AOL	Average offered, low	ASL	Average starting, low	HI	Highest wage paid	MTC	Median total compensation	TQ	Third quartile wage
AEX	Average experienced wage	APH	Average pay, high range	AW	Average wage paid	HR	High end range	MW	Median wage paid	W	Weekly
AO	Average offered	APL	Average pay, low range	FQ	First quartile wage	LR	Low end range	SQ	Second quartile wage	Y	Yearly

Occupation/Type/Industry	Location	Per	Low	Mid	High	Source	Date
Atmospheric, Earth, Marine, and Space Sciences Teacher							
Postsecondary	Iowa	Y		58370 AAW		IABLS	10//99-12//99
Postsecondary	Maryland	Y		71050 AAW		MDBLS	10//99-12//99
Postsecondary	Massachusetts	Y		64100 AAW		MABLS	10//99-12//99
Postsecondary	Michigan	Y		51810 AAW		MIBLS	10//99-12//99
Postsecondary	Minnesota	Y		70830 AAW		MNBLS	10//99-12//99
Postsecondary	Mississippi	Y		34420 AAW		MSBLS	10//99-12//99
Postsecondary	New Hampshire	Y		39580 AAW		NHBLS	10//99-12//99
Postsecondary	New Jersey	Y		61950 AAW		NJBLS	10//99-12//99
Postsecondary	New York	Y		63790 AAW		NYBLS	10//99-12//99
Postsecondary	North Carolina	Y		49120 AAW		NCBLS	10//99-12//99
Postsecondary	Ohio	Y		44710 AAW		OHBLS	10//99-12//99
Postsecondary	Pennsylvania	Y		61800 AAW		PABLS	10//99-12//99
Postsecondary	South Carolina	Y		58950 AAW		SCBLS	10//99-12//99
Postsecondary	Texas	Y		51800 AAW		TXBLS	10//99-12//99
Postsecondary	Virginia	Y		55340 AAW		VABLS	10//99-12//99
Postsecondary	Washington	Y		41560 AAW		WABLS	10//99-12//99
Attorney							
Associate, Fifth Year	United States	Y		87000 AW		BUS1COL	4//99
Associate, First Year	United States	Y		70000 AW		BUS1COL	4//99
Associate, First Year	San Diego, CA	Y	67000 ASLO	110000 MW	125000 HI	SDBUSJ	4//00
Associate, First Year	Boston, MA	Y		85000 AW		BOSBUS	2000
Associate, Fourth Year	United States	Y		82000 AW		BUS1COL	4//99
Associate, Fourth Year	Los Angeles, CA	Y		155000 MW		SDBUSJ	4//00
Associate, Fourth Year	San Diego, CA	Y		125000 MW		SDBUSJ	4//00
Associate, Second Year	United States	Y		75000 AW		BUS1COL	4//99
Associate, Seventh Year	United States	Y		100000 AW		BUS1COL	4//99
Associate, Seventh Year	Boston, MA	Y		130000 AW		BOSBUS	2000
Associate, Sixth Year	United States	Y		93250 AW		BUS1COL	4//99
Associate, Third Year	United States	Y		77900 AW		BUS1COL	4//99
Associate, Third Year	Boston, MA	Y		104000 AW		BOSBUS	2000
Audio and Video Equipment Technician							
	Alabama	S	10.31 MW	11.43 AW	23770 AAW	ALBLS	10//99-12//99
	Alaska	S	11.35 MW	12.71 AW	26440 AAW	AKBLS	10//99-12//99
	Arizona	S	8.77 MW	9.69 AW	20160 AAW	AZBLS	10//99-12//99
	Arkansas	S	8.22 MW	9.26 AW	19260 AAW	ARBLS	10//99-12//99
	California	S	14.12 MW	17.60 AW	36610 AAW	CABLS	10//99-12//99
	Colorado	S	16.56 MW	16.80 AW	34950 AAW	COBLS	10//99-12//99
	Connecticut	S	16.59 MW	17.46 AW	36320 AAW	CTBLS	10//99-12//99
	Delaware	S	14.66 MW	15.19 AW	31590 AAW	DEBLS	10//99-12//99
	District of Columbia	S	19.51 MW	22.94 AW	47720 AAW	DCBLS	10//99-12//99
	Florida	S	12.59 MW	13.83 AW	28770 AAW	FLBLS	10//99-12//99
	Georgia	S	9.19 MW	11.60 AW	24130 AAW	GABLS	10//99-12//99
	Hawaii	S	14.09 MW	13.61 AW	28310 AAW	HIBLS	10//99-12//99
	Idaho	S	6.51 MW	7.73 AW	16070 AAW	IDBLS	10//99-12//99
	Illinois	S	11.76 MW	12.49 AW	25990 AAW	ILBLS	10//99-12//99
	Indiana	S	10.21 MW	10.98 AW	22840 AAW	INBLS	10//99-12//99
	Iowa	S	13.77 MW	13.92 AW	28950 AAW	IABLS	10//99-12//99
	Kansas	S	6.97 MW	9.27 AW	19280 AAW	KSBLS	10//99-12//99
	Kentucky	S	11.16 MW	11.88 AW	24710 AAW	KYBLS	10//99-12//99
	Louisiana	S	11.45 MW	11.68 AW	24300 AAW	LABLS	10//99-12//99
	Maine	S	9.8 MW	10.19 AW	21190 AAW	MEBLS	10//99-12//99
	Maryland	S	11.54 MW	11.64 AW	24210 AAW	MDBLS	10//99-12//99
	Massachusetts	S	13.2 MW	14.53 AW	30220 AAW	MABLS	10//99-12//99
	Michigan	S	12.79 MW	14.82 AW	30820 AAW	MIBLS	10//99-12//99
	Minnesota	S	16.98 MW	15.89 AW	33050 AAW	MNBLS	10//99-12//99
	Mississippi	S	13.85 MW	15.33 AW	31890 AAW	MSBLS	10//99-12//99
	Missouri	S	19.14 MW	20.58 AW	42820 AAW	MOBLS	10//99-12//99
	Montana	S	9.16 MW	9.14 AW	19010 AAW	MTBLS	10//99-12//99
	Nebraska	S	10.74 MW	16.80 AW	34950 AAW	NEBLS	10//99-12//99
	Nevada	S	15.85 MW	15.90 AW	33080 AAW	NVBLS	10//99-12//99
	New Mexico	S	10.63 MW	10.85 AW	22570 AAW	NMBLS	10//99-12//99
	North Carolina	S	12.05 MW	13.22 AW	27490 AAW	NCBLS	10//99-12//99
	North Dakota	S	14.23 MW	18.42 AW	38310 AAW	NDBLS	10//99-12//99
	Ohio	S	11.58 MW	12.06 AW	25080 AAW	OHBLS	10//99-12//99
	Oklahoma	S	10.28 MW	11.77 AW	24470 AAW	OKBLS	10//99-12//99
	Oregon	S	14.06 MW	15.81 AW	32870 AAW	ORBLS	10//99-12//99
	Pennsylvania	S	13.23 MW	14.69 AW	30550 AAW	PABLS	10//99-12//99
	Rhode Island	S	15.84 MW	16.50 AW	34310 AAW	RIBLS	10//99-12//99

AAW	Average annual wage	AOH	Average offered, high	ASH	Average starting, high	H	Hourly	M	Monthly	S	Special: hourly and annual
AE	Average entry wage	AOL	Average offered, low	ASL	Average starting, low	HI	Highest wage paid	MTC	Median total compensation	TQ	Third quartile wage
AEX	Average experienced wage	APH	Average pay, high range	AW	Average wage paid	HR	High end range	MW	Median wage paid	W	Weekly
AO	Average offered	APL	Average pay, low range	FQ	First quartile wage	LR	Low end range	SQ	Second quartile wage	Y	Yearly

Occupation/Type/Industry	Location	Per	Low	Mid	High	Source	Date
Audio and Video Equipment Technician	South Carolina	S	13.59 MW	13.26 AW	27590 AAW	SCBLS	10//99-12//99
	Tennessee	S	11.85 MW	12.66 AW	26330 AAW	TNBLS	10//99-12//99
	Texas	S	12.12 MW	12.29 AW	25570 AAW	TXBLS	10//99-12//99
	Virginia	S	12.23 MW	14.94 AW	31080 AAW	VABLS	10//99-12//99
	Washington	S	17.1 MW	17.99 AW	37420 AAW	WABLS	10//99-12//99
	West Virginia	S	13.83 MW	13.66 AW	28410 AAW	WVBLS	10//99-12//99
	Wisconsin	S	11.35 MW	12.14 AW	25250 AAW	WIBLS	10//99-12//99
	Puerto Rico	S	9.98 MW	10.28 AW	21380 AAW	PRBLS	10//99-12//99
	Guam	S	6.55 MW	7.46 AW	15510 AAW	GUBLS	10//99-12//99
Audio-Visual Collections Specialist	Alabama	S	8.74 MW	9.45 AW	19660 AAW	ALBLS	10//99-12//99
	Arizona	S	9.42 MW	11.34 AW	23580 AAW	AZBLS	10//99-12//99
	Arkansas	S	7.53 MW	8.84 AW	18380 AAW	ARBLS	10//99-12//99
	California	S	15.34 MW	16.56 AW	34440 AAW	CABLS	10//99-12//99
	Colorado	S	10.38 MW	13.31 AW	27680 AAW	COBLS	10//99-12//99
	Connecticut	S	14.55 MW	16.33 AW	33960 AAW	CTBLS	10//99-12//99
	Florida	S	20.1 MW	20.35 AW	42330 AAW	FLBLS	10//99-12//99
	Idaho	S	12.79 MW	14.26 AW	29660 AAW	IDBLS	10//99-12//99
	Illinois	S	14.41 MW	19.13 AW	39790 AAW	ILBLS	10//99-12//99
	Indiana	S	21.89 MW	21.12 AW	43920 AAW	INBLS	10//99-12//99
	Iowa	S	14.89 MW	14.33 AW	29810 AAW	IABLS	10//99-12//99
	Kansas	S	18.17 MW	17.45 AW	36290 AAW	KSBLS	10//99-12//99
	Kentucky	S	14.04 MW	13.38 AW	27820 AAW	KYBLS	10//99-12//99
	Louisiana	S	13.03 MW	14.44 AW	30040 AAW	LABLS	10//99-12//99
	Massachusetts	S	14.85 MW	18.29 AW	38040 AAW	MABLS	10//99-12//99
	Minnesota	S	18.83 MW	18.18 AW	37810 AAW	MNBLS	10//99-12//99
	Nebraska	S	8.1 MW	10.33 AW	21480 AAW	NEBLS	10//99-12//99
	New Hampshire	S	14.54 MW	14.68 AW	30530 AAW	NHBLS	10//99-12//99
	New Jersey	S	15.72 MW	16.51 AW	34350 AAW	NJBLS	10//99-12//99
	New Mexico	S	12.76 MW	13.42 AW	27920 AAW	NMBLS	10//99-12//99
	New York	S	15.23 MW	16.67 AW	34680 AAW	NYBLS	10//99-12//99
	North Carolina	S	15.76 MW	15.78 AW	32820 AAW	NCBLS	10//99-12//99
	Ohio	S	11.13 MW	11.35 AW	23610 AAW	OHBLS	10//99-12//99
	Oklahoma	S	12.18 MW	13.15 AW	27350 AAW	OKBLS	10//99-12//99
	Oregon	S	15.57 MW	15.73 AW	32720 AAW	ORBLS	10//99-12//99
	Pennsylvania	S	13.22 MW	15.54 AW	32330 AAW	PABLS	10//99-12//99
	South Carolina	S	14.57 MW	14.06 AW	29240 AAW	SCBLS	10//99-12//99
	Texas	S	10.95 MW	13.97 AW	29050 AAW	TXBLS	10//99-12//99
	Utah	S	21.46 MW	22.11 AW	45980 AAW	UTBLS	10//99-12//99
	Vermont	S	10.64 MW	10.76 AW	22370 AAW	VTBLS	10//99-12//99
	Virginia	S	6.19 MW	8.06 AW	16770 AAW	VABLS	10//99-12//99
	Washington	S	6.73 MW	8.96 AW	18630 AAW	WABLS	10//99-12//99
	Wisconsin	S	19.73 MW	18.55 AW	38580 AAW	WIBLS	10//99-12//99
	Puerto Rico	S	11.5 MW	11.55 AW	24020 AAW	PRBLS	10//99-12//99
Audiologist	Alabama	S	17.5 MW	17.62 AW	36650 AAW	ALBLS	10//99-12//99
	Alaska	S	20.78 MW	24.12 AW	50160 AAW	AKBLS	10//99-12//99
	Arizona	S	16.94 MW	18.32 AW	38110 AAW	AZBLS	10//99-12//99
	Arkansas	S	18.37 MW	18.69 AW	38880 AAW	ARBLS	10//99-12//99
	California	S	22.26 MW	21.65 AW	45040 AAW	CABLS	10//99-12//99
	Colorado	S	19.52 MW	19.31 AW	40170 AAW	COBLS	10//99-12//99
	Connecticut	S	15.25 MW	20.53 AW	42690 AAW	CTBLS	10//99-12//99
	Florida	S	20.71 MW	20.60 AW	42860 AAW	FLBLS	10//99-12//99
	Georgia	S	19.87 MW	21.03 AW	43740 AAW	GABLS	10//99-12//99
	Hawaii	S	22.07 MW	22.24 AW	46260 AAW	HIBLS	10//99-12//99
	Illinois	S	21.18 MW	20.61 AW	42870 AAW	ILBLS	10//99-12//99
	Indiana	S	20.58 MW	19.73 AW	41040 AAW	INBLS	10//99-12//99
	Iowa	S	19.28 MW	18.63 AW	38750 AAW	IABLS	10//99-12//99
	Kansas	S	22.35 MW	22.76 AW	47340 AAW	KSBLS	10//99-12//99
	Kentucky	S	18.67 MW	19.34 AW	40240 AAW	KYBLS	10//99-12//99
	Louisiana	S	14.95 MW	16.26 AW	33820 AAW	LABLS	10//99-12//99
	Maine	S	19.33 MW	19.26 AW	40060 AAW	MEBLS	10//99-12//99
	Maryland	S	21.29 MW	29.81 AW	62000 AAW	MDBLS	10//99-12//99
	Massachusetts	S	21.99 MW	22.92 AW	47670 AAW	MABLS	10//99-12//99
	Michigan	S	21.21 MW	24.17 AW	50260 AAW	MIBLS	10//99-12//99
	Minnesota	S	19.66 MW	19.08 AW	39690 AAW	MNBLS	10//99-12//99
	Mississippi	S	20.53 MW	19.54 AW	40630 AAW	MSBLS	10//99-12//99
	Missouri	S	20.63 MW	20.69 AW	43040 AAW	MOBLS	10//99-12//99
	New Jersey	S	23.62 MW	23.27 AW	48400 AAW	NJBLS	10//99-12//99
	New Mexico	S	17.72 MW	16.51 AW	34340 AAW	NMBLS	10//99-12//99

AAW Average annual wage	**AOH** Average offered, high	**ASH** Average starting, high	**H** Hourly	**M** Monthly	**S** Special: hourly and annual
AE Average entry wage	**AOL** Average offered, low	**ASL** Average starting, low	**HI** Highest wage paid	**MTC** Median total compensation	**TQ** Third quartile wage
AEX Average experienced wage	**APH** Average pay, high range	**AW** Average wage paid	**HR** High end range	**MW** Median wage paid	**W** Weekly
AO Average offered	**APL** Average pay, low range	**FQ** First quartile wage	**LR** Low end range	**SQ** Second quartile wage	**Y** Yearly

Occupation/Type/Industry	Location	Per	Low	Mid	High	Source	Date
Audiologist	New York	S	23.6 MW	25.87 AW	53800 AAW	NYBLS	10//99-12//99
	North Carolina	S	20.99 MW	22.15 AW	46060 AAW	NCBLS	10//99-12//99
	Ohio	S	20.88 MW	22.09 AW	45950 AAW	OHBLS	10//99-12//99
	Oklahoma	S	23.77 MW	25.49 AW	53020 AAW	OKBLS	10//99-12//99
	Oregon	S	22.02 MW	21.05 AW	43780 AAW	ORBLS	10//99-12//99
	Pennsylvania	S	20.18 MW	20.39 AW	42410 AAW	PABLS	10//99-12//99
	South Carolina	S	31.17 MW	33.85 AW	70400 AAW	SCBLS	10//99-12//99
	Tennessee	S	16.13 MW	16.68 AW	34700 AAW	TNBLS	10//99-12//99
	Texas	S	20.25 MW	22.41 AW	46610 AAW	TXBLS	10//99-12//99
	Utah	S	21.17 MW	21.73 AW	45190 AAW	UTBLS	10//99-12//99
	Virginia	S	18.4 MW	18.29 AW	38040 AAW	VABLS	10//99-12//99
	Washington	S	19.42 MW	20.05 AW	41700 AAW	WABLS	10//99-12//99
	Wisconsin	S	19.63 MW	19.83 AW	41240 AAW	WIBLS	10//99-12//99
Automotive Body and Related Repairer	Alabama	S	11.56 MW	12.91 AW	26860 AAW	ALBLS	10//99-12//99
	Anniston MSA, AL	S	10.93 MW	9.74 AW	22730 AAW	ALBLS	10//99-12//99
	Birmingham MSA, AL	S	13.52 MW	10.76 AW	28120 AAW	ALBLS	10//99-12//99
	Dothan MSA, AL	S	11.07 MW	10.51 AW	23020 AAW	ALBLS	10//99-12//99
	Huntsville MSA, AL	S	15.88 MW	12.75 AW	33030 AAW	ALBLS	10//99-12//99
	Mobile MSA, AL	S	12.59 MW	11.83 AW	26180 AAW	ALBLS	10//99-12//99
	Montgomery MSA, AL	S	13.41 MW	12.44 AW	27900 AAW	ALBLS	10//99-12//99
	Alaska	S	16.46 MW	17.44 AW	36280 AAW	AKBLS	10//99-12//99
	Anchorage MSA, AK	S	16.81 MW	15.55 AW	34950 AAW	AKBLS	10//99-12//99
	Arizona	S	13.93 MW	14.71 AW	30600 AAW	AZBLS	10//99-12//99
	Phoenix-Mesa MSA, AZ	S	14.67 MW	14.76 AW	30520 AAW	AZBLS	10//99-12//99
	Yuma MSA, AZ	S	21.45 MW	23.24 AW	44620 AAW	AZBLS	10//99-12//99
	Arkansas	S	10.94 MW	11.87 AW	24690 AAW	ARBLS	10//99-12//99
	Fayetteville-Springdale-Rogers MSA, AR	S	9.98 MW	9.71 AW	20770 AAW	ARBLS	10//99-12//99
	Fort Smith MSA, AR-OK	S	12.62 MW	12.59 AW	26250 AAW	ARBLS	10//99-12//99
	Little Rock-North Little Rock MSA, AR	S	15.87 MW	13.03 AW	33000 AAW	ARBLS	10//99-12//99
	California	S	16.54 MW	16.62 AW	34560 AAW	CABLS	10//99-12//99
	Bakersfield MSA, CA	S	12.72 MW	13.87 AW	26460 AAW	CABLS	10//99-12//99
	Fresno MSA, CA	S	12.91 MW	12.39 AW	26860 AAW	CABLS	10//99-12//99
	Los Angeles-Long Beach PMSA, CA	S	10.95 MW	10.47 AW	22780 AAW	CABLS	10//99-12//99
	Modesto MSA, CA	S	14.17 MW	13.67 AW	29480 AAW	CABLS	10//99-12//99
	Oakland PMSA, CA	S	18.74 MW	19.09 AW	38970 AAW	CABLS	10//99-12//99
	Orange County PMSA, CA	S	21.91 MW	22.88 AW	45570 AAW	CABLS	10//99-12//99
	Redding MSA, CA	S	13.83 MW	12.87 AW	28770 AAW	CABLS	10//99-12//99
	Riverside-San Bernardino PMSA, CA	S	10.47 MW	9.36 AW	21770 AAW	CABLS	10//99-12//99
	Sacramento PMSA, CA	S	26.35 MW	29.08 AW	54800 AAW	CABLS	10//99-12//99
	Salinas MSA, CA	S	17.06 MW	18.35 AW	35480 AAW	CABLS	10//99-12//99
	San Diego MSA, CA	S	17.39 MW	14.98 AW	36170 AAW	CABLS	10//99-12//99
	San Jose PMSA, CA	S	18.10 MW	19.40 AW	37650 AAW	CABLS	10//99-12//99
	San Luis Obispo-Atascadero-Paso Robles MSA, CA	S	12.88 MW	10.57 AW	26790 AAW	CABLS	10//99-12//99
	Santa Cruz-Watsonville PMSA, CA	S	16.14 MW	14.28 AW	33580 AAW	CABLS	10//99-12//99
	Santa Rosa PMSA, CA	S	20.27 MW	22.16 AW	42160 AAW	CABLS	10//99-12//99
	Stockton-Lodi MSA, CA	S	14.75 MW	14.90 AW	30670 AAW	CABLS	10//99-12//99
	Ventura PMSA, CA	S	10.69 MW	9.20 AW	22240 AAW	CABLS	10//99-12//99
	Visalia-Tulare-Porterville MSA, CA	S	17.94 MW	17.71 AW	37310 AAW	CABLS	10//99-12//99
	Colorado	S	16.03 MW	16.43 AW	34180 AAW	COBLS	10//99-12//99
	Denver PMSA, CO	S	16.47 MW	15.81 AW	34260 AAW	COBLS	10//99-12//99
	Connecticut	S	15.96 MW	16.31 AW	33920 AAW	CTBLS	10//99-12//99
	Bridgeport PMSA, CT	S	18.65 MW	18.24 AW	38800 AAW	CTBLS	10//99-12//99
	Hartford MSA, CT	S	15.96 MW	16.01 AW	33200 AAW	CTBLS	10//99-12//99
	New Haven-Meriden PMSA, CT	S	13.34 MW	13.77 AW	27740 AAW	CTBLS	10//99-12//99
	New London-Norwich MSA, CT-RI	S	14.62 MW	15.06 AW	30400 AAW	CTBLS	10//99-12//99
	Waterbury PMSA, CT	S	15.38 MW	13.12 AW	32000 AAW	CTBLS	10//99-12//99
	Delaware	S	13.31 MW	15.56 AW	32360 AAW	DEBLS	10//99-12//99
	Wilmington-Newark PMSA, DE-MD	S	15.36 MW	13.44 AW	31940 AAW	DEBLS	10//99-12//99
	District of Columbia	S	10.17 MW	13.52 AW	28130 AAW	DCBLS	10//99-12//99

AAW Average annual wage	AOH Average offered, high	ASH Average starting, high	H Hourly	M Monthly	S Special: hourly and annual
AE Average entry wage	AOL Average offered, low	ASL Average starting, low	HI Highest wage paid	MTC Median total compensation	TQ Third quartile wage
AEX Average experienced wage	APH Average pay, high range	AW Average wage paid	HR High end range	MW Median wage paid	W Weekly
AO Average offered	APL Average pay, low range	FQ First quartile wage	LR Low end range	SQ Second quartile wage	Y Yearly

Occupation/Type/Industry	Location	Per	Low	Mid	High	Source	Date
Automotive Body and Related Repairer	Washington PMSA, DC-MD-VA-WV	S	20.10 MW	18.82 AW	41800 AAW	DCBLS	10//99-12//99
	Florida	S	13.07 MW	17.05 AW	35470 AAW	FLBLS	10//99-12//99
	Daytona Beach MSA, FL	S	13.09 MW	12.30 AW	27220 AAW	FLBLS	10//99-12//99
	Fort Myers-Cape Coral MSA, FL	S	17.82 MW	13.07 AW	37070 AAW	FLBLS	10//99-12//99
	Fort Pierce-Port St. Lucie MSA, FL	S	16.53 MW	15.70 AW	34380 AAW	FLBLS	10//99-12//99
	Gainesville MSA, FL	S	21.67 MW	23.50 AW	45070 AAW	FLBLS	10//99-12//99
	Jacksonville MSA, FL	S	26.74 MW	20.36 AW	55620 AAW	FLBLS	10//99-12//99
	Lakeland-Winter Haven MSA, FL	S	17.85 MW	18.90 AW	37130 AAW	FLBLS	10//99-12//99
	Melbourne-Titusville-Palm Bay MSA, FL	S	13.32 MW	12.71 AW	27700 AAW	FLBLS	10//99-12//99
	Ocala MSA, FL	S	15.34 MW	12.71 AW	31900 AAW	FLBLS	10//99-12//99
	Orlando MSA, FL	S	17.12 MW	13.22 AW	35600 AAW	FLBLS	10//99-12//99
	Panama City MSA, FL	S	15.04 MW	12.85 AW	31290 AAW	FLBLS	10//99-12//99
	Pensacola MSA, FL	S	11.96 MW	10.97 AW	24870 AAW	FLBLS	10//99-12//99
	Punta Gorda MSA, FL	S	18.44 MW	19.08 AW	38360 AAW	FLBLS	10//99-12//99
	Sarasota-Bradenton MSA, FL	S	17.73 MW	16.45 AW	36870 AAW	FLBLS	10//99-12//99
	Tampa-St. Petersburg-Clearwater MSA, FL	S	16.49 MW	12.97 AW	34310 AAW	FLBLS	10//99-12//99
	West Palm Beach-Boca Raton MSA, FL	S	29.25 MW	30.46 AW	60830 AAW	FLBLS	10//99-12//99
	Georgia	S	16.97 MW	17.33 AW	36040 AAW	GABLS	10//99-12//99
	Albany MSA, GA	S	17.71 MW	17.17 AW	36840 AAW	GABLS	10//99-12//99
	Athens MSA, GA	S	19.14 MW	18.66 AW	39810 AAW	GABLS	10//99-12//99
	Atlanta MSA, GA	S	18.61 MW	18.90 AW	38710 AAW	GABLS	10//99-12//99
	Augusta-Aiken MSA, GA-SC	S	16.13 MW	13.66 AW	33540 AAW	GABLS	10//99-12//99
	Columbus MSA, GA-AL	S	14.69 MW	13.10 AW	30550 AAW	GABLS	10//99-12//99
	Macon MSA, GA	S	16.17 MW	15.98 AW	33630 AAW	GABLS	10//99-12//99
	Savannah MSA, GA	S	16.17 MW	15.35 AW	33640 AAW	GABLS	10//99-12//99
	Hawaii	S	17.15 MW	16.39 AW	34080 AAW	HIBLS	10//99-12//99
	Honolulu MSA, HI	S	17.04 MW	17.57 AW	35450 AAW	HIBLS	10//99-12//99
	Idaho	S	14.04 MW	14.96 AW	31120 AAW	IDBLS	10//99-12//99
	Boise City MSA, ID	S	17.45 MW	16.34 AW	36300 AAW	IDBLS	10//99-12//99
	Pocatello MSA, ID	S	12.28 MW	11.64 AW	25530 AAW	IDBLS	10//99-12//99
	Illinois	S	16.42 MW	17.27 AW	35930 AAW	ILBLS	10//99-12//99
	Bloomington-Normal MSA, IL	S	13.57 MW	11.84 AW	28220 AAW	ILBLS	10//99-12//99
	Chicago PMSA, IL	S	17.68 MW	16.08 AW	36770 AAW	ILBLS	10//99-12//99
	Peoria-Pekin MSA, IL	S	10.45 MW	10.96 AW	21730 AAW	ILBLS	10//99-12//99
	Rockford MSA, IL	S	18.90 MW	16.93 AW	39300 AAW	ILBLS	10//99-12//99
	Springfield MSA, IL	S	17.13 MW	16.55 AW	35620 AAW	ILBLS	10//99-12//99
	Indiana	S	15.14 MW	15.53 AW	32310 AAW	INBLS	10//99-12//99
	Elkhart-Goshen MSA, IN	S	11.19 MW	7.98 AW	23270 AAW	INBLS	10//99-12//99
	Evansville-Henderson MSA, IN-KY	S	12.08 MW	12.13 AW	25130 AAW	INBLS	10//99-12//99
	Fort Wayne MSA, IN	S	17.60 MW	15.88 AW	36610 AAW	INBLS	10//99-12//99
	Gary PMSA, IN	S	17.21 MW	18.12 AW	35790 AAW	INBLS	10//99-12//99
	Indianapolis MSA, IN	S	16.18 MW	17.16 AW	33660 AAW	INBLS	10//99-12//99
	Kokomo MSA, IN	S	16.41 MW	17.09 AW	34130 AAW	INBLS	10//99-12//99
	Lafayette MSA, IN	S	17.96 MW	16.42 AW	37350 AAW	INBLS	10//99-12//99
	South Bend MSA, IN	S	16.03 MW	15.98 AW	33340 AAW	INBLS	10//99-12//99
	Terre Haute MSA, IN	S	15.02 MW	15.09 AW	31230 AAW	INBLS	10//99-12//99
	Iowa	S	13.78 MW	14.00 AW	29130 AAW	IABLS	10//99-12//99
	Cedar Rapids MSA, IA	S	13.76 MW	13.77 AW	28620 AAW	IABLS	10//99-12//99
	Davenport-Moline-Rock Island MSA, IA-IL	S	16.38 MW	17.82 AW	34070 AAW	IABLS	10//99-12//99
	Des Moines MSA, IA	S	14.57 MW	14.75 AW	30300 AAW	IABLS	10//99-12//99
	Dubuque MSA, IA	S	12.88 MW	13.16 AW	26790 AAW	IABLS	10//99-12//99
	Sioux City MSA, IA-NE	S	15.58 MW	14.88 AW	32400 AAW	IABLS	10//99-12//99
	Waterloo-Cedar Falls MSA, IA	S	11.72 MW	10.49 AW	24380 AAW	IABLS	10//99-12//99
	Kansas	S	12.49 MW	12.65 AW	26300 AAW	KSBLS	10//99-12//99
	Topeka MSA, KS	S	10.76 MW	11.28 AW	22380 AAW	KSBLS	10//99-12//99
	Wichita MSA, KS	S	14.01 MW	13.10 AW	29140 AAW	KSBLS	10//99-12//99
	Kentucky	S	10.99 MW	12.06 AW	25080 AAW	KYBLS	10//99-12//99
	Lexington MSA, KY	S	11.02 MW	9.75 AW	22930 AAW	KYBLS	10//99-12//99
	Louisville MSA, KY-IN	S	15.76 MW	14.92 AW	32790 AAW	KYBLS	10//99-12//99
	Owensboro MSA, KY	S	12.45 MW	11.85 AW	25890 AAW	KYBLS	10//99-12//99
	Louisiana	S	13.37 MW	13.89 AW	28890 AAW	LABLS	10//99-12//99
	Alexandria MSA, LA	S	8.64 MW	6.53 AW	17970 AAW	LABLS	10//99-12//99

AAW Average annual wage	**AOH** Average offered, high	**ASH** Average starting, high	**H** Hourly	**M** Monthly	**S** Special: hourly and annual
AE Average entry wage	**AOL** Average offered, low	**ASL** Average starting, low	**HI** Highest wage paid	**MTC** Median total compensation	**TQ** Third quartile wage
AEX Average experienced wage	**APH** Average pay, high range	**AW** Average wage paid	**HR** High end range	**MW** Median wage paid	**W** Weekly
AO Average offered	**APL** Average pay, low range	**FQ** First quartile wage	**LR** Low end range	**SQ** Second quartile wage	**Y** Yearly

Occupation/Type/Industry	Location	Per	Low	Mid	High	Source	Date
Automotive Body and Related Repairer							
	Baton Rouge MSA, LA	S	13.86 MW	13.64 AW	28830 AAW	LABLS	10//99-12//99
	Lafayette MSA, LA	S	13.05 MW	13.82 AW	27130 AAW	LABLS	10//99-12//99
	Maine	S	14.91 MW	14.48 AW	30120 AAW	MEBLS	10//99-12//99
	Portland MSA, ME	S	14.50 MW	14.94 AW	30160 AAW	MEBLS	10//99-12//99
	Maryland	S	19.24 MW	20.36 AW	42350 AAW	MDBLS	10//99-12//99
	Baltimore PMSA, MD	S	18.28 MW	16.79 AW	38020 AAW	MDBLS	10//99-12//99
	Hagerstown PMSA, MD	S	15.03 MW	14.60 AW	31260 AAW	MDBLS	10//99-12//99
	Massachusetts	S	14.35 MW	14.93 AW	31060 AAW	MABLS	10//99-12//99
	Barnstable-Yarmouth MSA, MA	S	13.21 MW	13.08 AW	27470 AAW	MABLS	10//99-12//99
	Boston PMSA, MA-NH	S	18.72 MW	18.85 AW	38940 AAW	MABLS	10//99-12//99
	Fitchburg-Leominster PMSA, MA	S	9.65 MW	9.69 AW	20070 AAW	MABLS	10//99-12//99
	Lawrence PMSA, MA-NH	S	17.07 MW	17.15 AW	35500 AAW	MABLS	10//99-12//99
	Lowell PMSA, MA-NH	S	15.96 MW	15.90 AW	33210 AAW	MABLS	10//99-12//99
	New Bedford PMSA, MA	S	13.26 MW	12.32 AW	27570 AAW	MABLS	10//99-12//99
	Springfield MSA, MA	S	13.32 MW	13.85 AW	27700 AAW	MABLS	10//99-12//99
	Worcester PMSA, MA-CT	S	17.62 MW	16.88 AW	36650 AAW	MABLS	10//99-12//99
	Michigan	S	19.13 MW	18.61 AW	38710 AAW	MIBLS	10//99-12//99
	Ann Arbor PMSA, MI	S	17.71 MW	18.45 AW	36840 AAW	MIBLS	10//99-12//99
	Benton Harbor MSA, MI	S	15.95 MW	13.23 AW	33170 AAW	MIBLS	10//99-12//99
	Detroit PMSA, MI	S	18.89 MW	19.28 AW	39290 AAW	MIBLS	10//99-12//99
	Flint PMSA, MI	S	17.73 MW	18.80 AW	36870 AAW	MIBLS	10//99-12//99
	Grand Rapids-Muskegon-Holland MSA, MI	S	21.07 MW	21.06 AW	43820 AAW	MIBLS	10//99-12//99
	Jackson MSA, MI	S	19.10 MW	19.64 AW	39720 AAW	MIBLS	10//99-12//99
	Kalamazoo-Battle Creek MSA, MI	S	12.92 MW	12.95 AW	26870 AAW	MIBLS	10//99-12//99
	Lansing-East Lansing MSA, MI	S	16.53 MW	16.34 AW	34390 AAW	MIBLS	10//99-12//99
	Saginaw-Bay City-Midland MSA, MI	S	15.32 MW	15.17 AW	31870 AAW	MIBLS	10//99-12//99
	Minnesota	S	21.14 MW	21.89 AW	45530 AAW	MNBLS	10//99-12//99
	Duluth-Superior MSA, MN-WI	S	17.14 MW	15.72 AW	35650 AAW	MNBLS	10//99-12//99
	Minneapolis-St. Paul MSA, MN-WI	S	24.94 MW	24.65 AW	51880 AAW	MNBLS	10//99-12//99
	St. Cloud MSA, MN	S	14.07 MW	14.78 AW	29270 AAW	MNBLS	10//99-12//99
	Mississippi	S	13.38 MW	14.09 AW	29310 AAW	MSBLS	10//99-12//99
	Biloxi-Gulfport-Pascagoula MSA, MS	S	15.42 MW	13.19 AW	32070 AAW	MSBLS	10//99-12//99
	Hattiesburg MSA, MS	S	12.50 MW	8.31 AW	26000 AAW	MSBLS	10//99-12//99
	Jackson MSA, MS	S	14.21 MW	14.12 AW	29550 AAW	MSBLS	10//99-12//99
	Missouri	S	18.04 MW	19.21 AW	39960 AAW	MOBLS	10//99-12//99
	Kansas City MSA, MO-KS	S	16.27 MW	15.15 AW	33850 AAW	MOBLS	10//99-12//99
	St. Louis MSA, MO-IL	S	20.33 MW	19.33 AW	42280 AAW	MOBLS	10//99-12//99
	Springfield MSA, MO	S	12.25 MW	12.02 AW	25480 AAW	MOBLS	10//99-12//99
	Montana	S	15.21 MW	15.23 AW	31680 AAW	MTBLS	10//99-12//99
	Great Falls MSA, MT	S	14.58 MW	13.44 AW	30330 AAW	MTBLS	10//99-12//99
	Nebraska	S	16.43 MW	16.04 AW	33360 AAW	NEBLS	10//99-12//99
	Lincoln MSA, NE	S	17.26 MW	17.30 AW	35900 AAW	NEBLS	10//99-12//99
	Omaha MSA, NE-IA	S	14.93 MW	13.21 AW	31050 AAW	NEBLS	10//99-12//99
	Nevada	S	12.58 MW	14.77 AW	30730 AAW	NVBLS	10//99-12//99
	Reno MSA, NV	S	21.02 MW	16.81 AW	43730 AAW	NVBLS	10//99-12//99
	New Hampshire	S	13.53 MW	13.26 AW	27590 AAW	NHBLS	10//99-12//99
	Nashua PMSA, NH	S	12.86 MW	13.65 AW	26740 AAW	NHBLS	10//99-12//99
	New Jersey	S	22.58 MW	23.50 AW	48880 AAW	NJBLS	10//99-12//99
	Atlantic-Cape May PMSA, NJ	S	16.11 MW	15.47 AW	33510 AAW	NJBLS	10//99-12//99
	Bergen-Passaic PMSA, NJ	S	18.33 MW	18.19 AW	38120 AAW	NJBLS	10//99-12//99
	Middlesex-Somerset-Hunterdon PMSA, NJ	S	18.08 MW	18.27 AW	37600 AAW	NJBLS	10//99-12//99
	Monmouth-Ocean PMSA, NJ	S	21.17 MW	21.53 AW	44020 AAW	NJBLS	10//99-12//99
	Newark PMSA, NJ	S	22.38 MW	19.29 AW	46550 AAW	NJBLS	10//99-12//99
	Trenton PMSA, NJ	S	17.00 MW	14.91 AW	35360 AAW	NJBLS	10//99-12//99
	New Mexico	S	14.12 MW	14.44 AW	30040 AAW	NMBLS	10//99-12//99
	Albuquerque MSA, NM	S	12.54 MW	11.37 AW	26080 AAW	NMBLS	10//99-12//99
	New York	S	14.52 MW	14.55 AW	30250 AAW	NYBLS	10//99-12//99
	Albany-Schenectady-Troy MSA, NY	S	14.30 MW	13.98 AW	29750 AAW	NYBLS	10//99-12//99
	Binghamton MSA, NY	S	11.99 MW	11.88 AW	24930 AAW	NYBLS	10//99-12//99
	Buffalo-Niagara Falls MSA, NY	S	11.68 MW	12.80 AW	24300 AAW	NYBLS	10//99-12//99
	Elmira MSA, NY	S	12.04 MW	10.31 AW	25050 AAW	NYBLS	10//99-12//99

AAW	Average annual wage	AOH	Average offered, high	ASH	Average starting, high
AE	Average entry wage	AOL	Average offered, low	ASL	Average starting, low
AEX	Average experienced wage	APH	Average pay, high range	AW	Average wage paid
AO	Average offered	APL	Average pay, low range	FQ	First quartile wage

H	Hourly	M	Monthly
HI	Highest wage paid	MTC	Median total compensation
HR	High end range	MW	Median wage paid
LR	Low end range	SQ	Second quartile wage

S	Special: hourly and annual
TQ	Third quartile wage
W	Weekly
Y	Yearly

Occupation/Type/Industry	Location	Per	Low	Mid	High	Source	Date
Automotive Body and Related Repairer	Glens Falls MSA, NY	S	12.89 MW	13.16 AW	26810 AAW	NYBLS	10//99-12//99
	Jamestown MSA, NY	S	10.74 MW	9.63 AW	22330 AAW	NYBLS	10//99-12//99
	New York PMSA, NY	S	15.55 MW	16.06 AW	32350 AAW	NYBLS	10//99-12//99
	Newburgh PMSA, NY-PA	S	15.49 MW	15.40 AW	32220 AAW	NYBLS	10//99-12//99
	Syracuse MSA, NY	S	13.49 MW	13.44 AW	28060 AAW	NYBLS	10//99-12//99
	Utica-Rome MSA, NY	S	14.28 MW	12.26 AW	29690 AAW	NYBLS	10//99-12//99
	North Carolina	S	14.69 MW	17.35 AW	36080 AAW	NCBLS	10//99-12//99
	Asheville MSA, NC	S	15.15 MW	13.57 AW	31500 AAW	NCBLS	10//99-12//99
	Charlotte-Gastonia-Rock Hill MSA, NC-SC	S	25.01 MW	26.53 AW	52020 AAW	NCBLS	10//99-12//99
	Greensboro--Winston-Salem-- High Point MSA, NC	S	14.61 MW	14.07 AW	30390 AAW	NCBLS	10//99-12//99
	Greenville MSA, NC	S	14.47 MW	13.41 AW	30090 AAW	NCBLS	10//99-12//99
	Hickory-Morganton-Lenoir MSA, NC	S	12.27 MW	13.02 AW	25510 AAW	NCBLS	10//99-12//99
	Jacksonville MSA, NC	S	23.77 MW	23.47 AW	49440 AAW	NCBLS	10//99-12//99
	Raleigh-Durham-Chapel Hill MSA, NC	S	13.65 MW	11.25 AW	28380 AAW	NCBLS	10//99-12//99
	Wilmington MSA, NC	S	11.93 MW	14.22 AW	24820 AAW	NCBLS	10//99-12//99
	North Dakota	S	15.39 MW	15.67 AW	32600 AAW	NDBLS	10//99-12//99
	Bismarck MSA, ND	S	17.66 MW	18.64 AW	36740 AAW	NDBLS	10//99-12//99
	Fargo-Moorhead MSA, ND-MN	S	18.64 MW	17.46 AW	38770 AAW	NDBLS	10//99-12//99
	Ohio	S	12.7 MW	13.61 AW	28300 AAW	OHBLS	10//99-12//99
	Akron PMSA, OH	S	12.84 MW	12.68 AW	26710 AAW	OHBLS	10//99-12//99
	Canton-Massillon MSA, OH	S	11.08 MW	11.54 AW	23050 AAW	OHBLS	10//99-12//99
	Cincinnati PMSA, OH-KY-IN	S	14.39 MW	14.63 AW	29940 AAW	OHBLS	10//99-12//99
	Cleveland-Lorain-Elyria PMSA, OH	S	12.45 MW	12.37 AW	25890 AAW	OHBLS	10//99-12//99
	Columbus MSA, OH	S	13.94 MW	12.48 AW	29000 AAW	OHBLS	10//99-12//99
	Dayton-Springfield MSA, OH	S	18.94 MW	18.59 AW	39390 AAW	OHBLS	10//99-12//99
	Lima MSA, OH	S	13.54 MW	14.72 AW	28160 AAW	OHBLS	10//99-12//99
	Mansfield MSA, OH	S	12.61 MW	12.19 AW	26230 AAW	OHBLS	10//99-12//99
	Toledo MSA, OH	S	16.73 MW	15.91 AW	34790 AAW	OHBLS	10//99-12//99
	Youngstown-Warren MSA, OH	S	13.78 MW	13.36 AW	28660 AAW	OHBLS	10//99-12//99
	Oklahoma	S	13.13 MW	13.53 AW	28140 AAW	OKBLS	10//99-12//99
	Oklahoma City MSA, OK	S	12.45 MW	12.09 AW	25900 AAW	OKBLS	10//99-12//99
	Tulsa MSA, OK	S	12.60 MW	12.26 AW	26210 AAW	OKBLS	10//99-12//99
	Oregon	S	14.37 MW	14.41 AW	29970 AAW	ORBLS	10//99-12//99
	Eugene-Springfield MSA, OR	S	14.13 MW	13.59 AW	29380 AAW	ORBLS	10//99-12//99
	Portland-Vancouver PMSA, OR-WA	S	15.58 MW	15.59 AW	32400 AAW	ORBLS	10//99-12//99
	Salem PMSA, OR	S	18.91 MW	20.66 AW	39330 AAW	ORBLS	10//99-12//99
	Pennsylvania	S	13.53 MW	14.01 AW	29140 AAW	PABLS	10//99-12//99
	Allentown-Bethlehem-Easton MSA, PA	S	13.18 MW	12.34 AW	27410 AAW	PABLS	10//99-12//99
	Altoona MSA, PA	S	10.54 MW	10.02 AW	21930 AAW	PABLS	10//99-12//99
	Erie MSA, PA	S	15.79 MW	16.52 AW	32830 AAW	PABLS	10//99-12//99
	Harrisburg-Lebanon-Carlisle MSA, PA	S	13.07 MW	12.56 AW	27180 AAW	PABLS	10//99-12//99
	Johnstown MSA, PA	S	12.69 MW	12.37 AW	26400 AAW	PABLS	10//99-12//99
	Lancaster MSA, PA	S	14.60 MW	14.14 AW	30380 AAW	PABLS	10//99-12//99
	Philadelphia PMSA, PA-NJ	S	22.15 MW	21.65 AW	46080 AAW	PABLS	10//99-12//99
	Pittsburgh MSA, PA	S	15.92 MW	13.52 AW	33110 AAW	PABLS	10//99-12//99
	Reading MSA, PA	S	15.10 MW	15.16 AW	31400 AAW	PABLS	10//99-12//99
	Scranton--Wilkes-Barre--Hazleton MSA, PA	S	13.86 MW	14.04 AW	28830 AAW	PABLS	10//99-12//99
	Sharon MSA, PA	S	12.92 MW	14.11 AW	26870 AAW	PABLS	10//99-12//99
	State College MSA, PA	S	13.87 MW	12.49 AW	28840 AAW	PABLS	10//99-12//99
	Williamsport MSA, PA	S	12.77 MW	12.59 AW	26560 AAW	PABLS	10//99-12//99
	York MSA, PA	S	15.07 MW	14.45 AW	31340 AAW	PABLS	10//99-12//99
	Rhode Island	S	13.74 MW	13.62 AW	28330 AAW	RIBLS	10//99-12//99
	Providence-Fall River-Warwick MSA, RI-MA	S	13.74 MW	13.76 AW	28580 AAW	RIBLS	10//99-12//99
	South Carolina	S	12.19 MW	13.51 AW	28090 AAW	SCBLS	10//99-12//99
	Charleston-North Charleston MSA, SC	S	9.84 MW	6.51 AW	20480 AAW	SCBLS	10//99-12//99
	Columbia MSA, SC	S	15.60 MW	15.00 AW	32440 AAW	SCBLS	10//99-12//99
	Greenville-Spartanburg-Anderson MSA, SC	S	14.58 MW	14.38 AW	30320 AAW	SCBLS	10//99-12//99
	Myrtle Beach MSA, SC	S	14.54 MW	11.09 AW	30240 AAW	SCBLS	10//99-12//99

AAW Average annual wage	**AOH** Average offered, high	**ASH** Average starting, high	**H** Hourly	**M** Monthly	**S** Special: hourly and annual
AE Average entry wage	**AOL** Average offered, low	**ASL** Average starting, low	**HI** Highest wage paid	**MTC** Median total compensation	**TQ** Third quartile wage
AEX Average experienced wage	**APH** Average pay, high range	**AW** Average wage paid	**HR** High end range	**MW** Median wage paid	**W** Weekly
AO Average offered	**APL** Average pay, low range	**FQ** First quartile wage	**LR** Low end range	**SQ** Second quartile wage	**Y** Yearly

Occupation/Type/Industry	Location	Per	Low	Mid	High	Source	Date
Automotive Body and Related Repairer							
	South Dakota	S	12.18 MW	12.20 AW	25380 AAW	SDBLS	10//99-12//99
	Sioux Falls MSA, SD	S	12.93 MW	12.08 AW	26890 AAW	SDBLS	10//99-12//99
	Tennessee	S	15.51 MW	15.52 AW	32290 AAW	TNBLS	10//99-12//99
	Chattanooga MSA, TN-GA	S	16.30 MW	16.44 AW	33900 AAW	TNBLS	10//99-12//99
	Jackson MSA, TN	S	16.84 MW	16.53 AW	35020 AAW	TNBLS	10//99-12//99
	Johnson City-Kingsport-Bristol MSA, TN-VA	S	16.94 MW	17.80 AW	35230 AAW	TNBLS	10//99-12//99
	Knoxville MSA, TN	S	17.88 MW	18.36 AW	37190 AAW	TNBLS	10//99-12//99
	Memphis MSA, TN-AR-MS	S	13.85 MW	12.60 AW	28810 AAW	MSBLS	10//99-12//99
	Nashville MSA, TN	S	18.36 MW	18.52 AW	38190 AAW	TNBLS	10//99-12//99
	Texas	S	13.22 MW	15.88 AW	33040 AAW	TXBLS	10//99-12//99
	Abilene MSA, TX	S	11.39 MW	12.07 AW	23700 AAW	TXBLS	10//99-12//99
	Amarillo MSA, TX	S	20.33 MW	23.18 AW	42290 AAW	TXBLS	10//99-12//99
	Austin-San Marcos MSA, TX	S	14.36 MW	12.28 AW	29870 AAW	TXBLS	10//99-12//99
	Beaumont-Port Arthur MSA, TX	S	17.86 MW	15.17 AW	37150 AAW	TXBLS	10//99-12//99
	Brazoria PMSA, TX	S	13.75 MW	13.84 AW	28590 AAW	TXBLS	10//99-12//99
	Brownsville-Harlingen-San Benito MSA, TX	S	9.01 MW	7.63 AW	18730 AAW	TXBLS	10//99-12//99
	Bryan-College Station MSA, TX	S	16.92 MW	13.49 AW	35190 AAW	TXBLS	10//99-12//99
	El Paso MSA, TX	S	10.73 MW	9.25 AW	22320 AAW	TXBLS	10//99-12//99
	Fort Worth-Arlington PMSA, TX	S	16.93 MW	14.42 AW	35210 AAW	TXBLS	10//99-12//99
	Galveston-Texas City PMSA, TX	S	14.91 MW	13.33 AW	31000 AAW	TXBLS	10//99-12//99
	Houston PMSA, TX	S	19.33 MW	13.43 AW	40210 AAW	TXBLS	10//99-12//99
	Killeen-Temple MSA, TX	S	13.46 MW	14.21 AW	28000 AAW	TXBLS	10//99-12//99
	Laredo MSA, TX	S	10.81 MW	9.69 AW	22490 AAW	TXBLS	10//99-12//99
	Longview-Marshall MSA, TX	S	15.34 MW	14.66 AW	31910 AAW	TXBLS	10//99-12//99
	Lubbock MSA, TX	S	21.01 MW	19.47 AW	43700 AAW	TXBLS	10//99-12//99
	Odessa-Midland MSA, TX	S	15.04 MW	12.20 AW	31290 AAW	TXBLS	10//99-12//99
	San Angelo MSA, TX	S	15.41 MW	17.30 AW	32040 AAW	TXBLS	10//99-12//99
	San Antonio MSA, TX	S	15.78 MW	12.86 AW	32820 AAW	TXBLS	10//99-12//99
	Sherman-Denison MSA, TX	S	11.49 MW	10.59 AW	23900 AAW	TXBLS	10//99-12//99
	Texarkana MSA, TX-Texarkana, AR	S	12.65 MW	13.49 AW	26310 AAW	TXBLS	10//99-12//99
	Waco MSA, TX	S	13.24 MW	11.54 AW	27540 AAW	TXBLS	10//99-12//99
	Utah	S	13.69 MW	12.62 AW	26250 AAW	UTBLS	10//99-12//99
	Provo-Orem MSA, UT	S	14.21 MW	14.31 AW	29550 AAW	UTBLS	10//99-12//99
	Vermont	S	17.85 MW	16.55 AW	34420 AAW	VTBLS	10//99-12//99
	Burlington MSA, VT	S	18.69 MW	19.05 AW	38870 AAW	VTBLS	10//99-12//99
	Virginia	S	13.84 MW	15.94 AW	33150 AAW	VABLS	10//99-12//99
	Danville MSA, VA	S	11.32 MW	10.72 AW	23540 AAW	VABLS	10//99-12//99
	Lynchburg MSA, VA	S	13.65 MW	11.51 AW	28390 AAW	VABLS	10//99-12//99
	Norfolk-Virginia Beach-Newport News MSA, VA-NC	S	16.13 MW	14.66 AW	33540 AAW	VABLS	10//99-12//99
	Richmond-Petersburg MSA, VA	S	13.88 MW	12.85 AW	28880 AAW	VABLS	10//99-12//99
	Roanoke MSA, VA	S	17.56 MW	16.34 AW	36520 AAW	VABLS	10//99-12//99
	Washington	S	14.52 MW	14.75 AW	30680 AAW	WABLS	10//99-12//99
	Bremerton PMSA, WA	S	14.39 MW	14.11 AW	29940 AAW	WABLS	10//99-12//99
	Seattle-Bellevue-Everett PMSA, WA	S	17.85 MW	16.55 AW	37130 AAW	WABLS	10//99-12//99
	Spokane MSA, WA	S	14.07 MW	11.80 AW	29260 AAW	WABLS	10//99-12//99
	Tacoma PMSA, WA	S	11.54 MW	10.12 AW	24000 AAW	WABLS	10//99-12//99
	West Virginia	S	7.9 MW	8.92 AW	18560 AAW	WVBLS	10//99-12//99
	Charleston MSA, WV	S	10.58 MW	11.01 AW	22010 AAW	WVBLS	10//99-12//99
	Huntington-Ashland MSA, WV-KY-OH	S	10.33 MW	9.79 AW	21490 AAW	WVBLS	10//99-12//99
	Parkersburg-Marietta MSA, WV-OH	S	12.85 MW	12.98 AW	26720 AAW	WVBLS	10//99-12//99
	Wheeling MSA, WV-OH	S	12.13 MW	12.10 AW	25230 AAW	WVBLS	10//99-12//99
	Wisconsin	S	15.72 MW	16.71 AW	34760 AAW	WIBLS	10//99-12//99
	Appleton-Oshkosh-Neenah MSA, WI	S	13.74 MW	12.64 AW	28570 AAW	WIBLS	10//99-12//99
	Eau Claire MSA, WI	S	15.50 MW	15.78 AW	32230 AAW	WIBLS	10//99-12//99
	Green Bay MSA, WI	S	17.84 MW	17.84 AW	37110 AAW	WIBLS	10//99-12//99
	Janesville-Beloit MSA, WI	S	12.52 MW	12.44 AW	26050 AAW	WIBLS	10//99-12//99
	La Crosse MSA, WI-MN	S	12.76 MW	13.71 AW	26540 AAW	WIBLS	10//99-12//99

AAW Average annual wage	**AOH** Average offered, high	**ASH** Average starting, high	**H** Hourly	**M** Monthly	**S** Special: hourly and annual
AE Average entry wage	**AOL** Average offered, low	**ASL** Average starting, low	**HI** Highest wage paid	**MTC** Median total compensation	**TQ** Third quartile wage
AEX Average experienced wage	**APH** Average pay, high range	**AW** Average wage paid	**HR** High end range	**MW** Median wage paid	**W** Weekly
AO Average offered	**APL** Average pay, low range	**FQ** First quartile wage	**LR** Low end range	**SQ** Second quartile wage	**Y** Yearly

Occupation/Type/Industry	Location	Per	Low	Mid	High	Source	Date
Automotive Body and Related Repairer	Madison MSA, WI	S	15.32 MW	14.56 AW	31870 AAW	WIBLS	10//99-12//99
	Milwaukee-Waukesha PMSA, WI	S	20.96 MW	20.75 AW	43590 AAW	WIBLS	10//99-12//99
	Racine PMSA, WI	S	13.90 MW	13.99 AW	28910 AAW	WIBLS	10//99-12//99
	Wyoming	S	14.59 MW	14.52 AW	30200 AAW	WYBLS	10//99-12//99
	Casper MSA, WY	S	11.05 MW	8.29 AW	22980 AAW	WYBLS	10//99-12//99
	Cheyenne MSA, WY	S	15.53 MW	15.30 AW	32310 AAW	WYBLS	10//99-12//99
	Puerto Rico	S	6.68 MW	7.50 AW	15610 AAW	PRBLS	10//99-12//99
	Aguadilla MSA, PR	S	5.75 MW	5.95 AW	11960 AAW	PRBLS	10//99-12//99
	Arecibo PMSA, PR	S	6.50 MW	6.54 AW	13530 AAW	PRBLS	10//99-12//99
	San Juan-Bayamon PMSA, PR	S	7.63 MW	7.13 AW	15860 AAW	PRBLS	10//99-12//99
	Virgin Islands	S	12.67 MW	13.32 AW	27700 AAW	VIBLS	10//99-12//99
	Guam	S	10.08 MW	11.09 AW	23080 AAW	GUBLS	10//99-12//99
Automotive Glass Installer and Repairer	Alabama	S	11.28 MW	10.97 AW	22810 AAW	ALBLS	10//99-12//99
	Arizona	S	14.29 MW	13.67 AW	28430 AAW	AZBLS	10//99-12//99
	Arkansas	S	6.51 MW	8.76 AW	18230 AAW	ARBLS	10//99-12//99
	California	S	15.53 MW	15.50 AW	32240 AAW	CABLS	10//99-12//99
	Colorado	S	12.72 MW	12.16 AW	25280 AAW	COBLS	10//99-12//99
	Florida	S	23.17 MW	20.43 AW	42500 AAW	FLBLS	10//99-12//99
	Georgia	S	12.86 MW	13.16 AW	27380 AAW	GABLS	10//99-12//99
	Idaho	S	11.82 MW	11.41 AW	23740 AAW	IDBLS	10//99-12//99
	Illinois	S	10.92 MW	10.68 AW	22210 AAW	ILBLS	10//99-12//99
	Indiana	S	12.94 MW	12.94 AW	26910 AAW	INBLS	10//99-12//99
	Kansas	S	15.23 MW	15.12 AW	31450 AAW	KSBLS	10//99-12//99
	Kentucky	S	13.58 MW	13.64 AW	28370 AAW	KYBLS	10//99-12//99
	Louisiana	S	9.7 MW	9.96 AW	20720 AAW	LABLS	10//99-12//99
	Maryland	S	12.42 MW	12.50 AW	26010 AAW	MDBLS	10//99-12//99
	Massachusetts	S	16.1 MW	16.40 AW	34110 AAW	MABLS	10//99-12//99
	Michigan	S	13.14 MW	13.10 AW	27240 AAW	MIBLS	10//99-12//99
	Minnesota	S	14.66 MW	15.02 AW	31230 AAW	MNBLS	10//99-12//99
	Mississippi	S	12.43 MW	11.76 AW	24460 AAW	MSBLS	10//99-12//99
	Missouri	S	12.6 MW	14.61 AW	30390 AAW	MOBLS	10//99-12//99
	Montana	S	7.78 MW	8.44 AW	17550 AAW	MTBLS	10//99-12//99
	Nebraska	S	14.37 MW	13.63 AW	28350 AAW	NEBLS	10//99-12//99
	New Hampshire	S	13.27 MW	13.53 AW	28140 AAW	NHBLS	10//99-12//99
	New Mexico	S	6.31 MW	7.07 AW	14710 AAW	NMBLS	10//99-12//99
	North Carolina	S	11.54 MW	13.11 AW	27280 AAW	NCBLS	10//99-12//99
	Ohio	S	12.04 MW	11.79 AW	24510 AAW	OHBLS	10//99-12//99
	Oklahoma	S	10.83 MW	11.68 AW	24300 AAW	OKBLS	10//99-12//99
	Oregon	S	18.06 MW	17.00 AW	35360 AAW	ORBLS	10//99-12//99
	Pennsylvania	S	11.41 MW	11.27 AW	23450 AAW	PABLS	10//99-12//99
	South Carolina	S	12.15 MW	12.80 AW	26620 AAW	SCBLS	10//99-12//99
	South Dakota	S	10.12 MW	10.41 AW	21650 AAW	SDBLS	10//99-12//99
	Texas	S	9.5 MW	9.59 AW	19960 AAW	TXBLS	10//99-12//99
	Utah	S	12.17 MW	13.84 AW	28800 AAW	UTBLS	10//99-12//99
	Virginia	S	10.54 MW	11.47 AW	23860 AAW	VABLS	10//99-12//99
	Washington	S	14.19 MW	13.84 AW	28790 AAW	WABLS	10//99-12//99
	Wisconsin	S	14.74 MW	14.66 AW	30490 AAW	WIBLS	10//99-12//99
Automotive Service Technician and Mechanic	Alabama	S	11.46 MW	12.63 AW	26270 AAW	ALBLS	10//99-12//99
	Anniston MSA, AL	S	11.41 MW	9.78 AW	23740 AAW	ALBLS	10//99-12//99
	Auburn-Opelika MSA, AL	S	13.78 MW	12.33 AW	28660 AAW	ALBLS	10//99-12//99
	Birmingham MSA, AL	S	13.56 MW	12.65 AW	28210 AAW	ALBLS	10//99-12//99
	Decatur MSA, AL	S	11.51 MW	10.24 AW	23950 AAW	ALBLS	10//99-12//99
	Dothan MSA, AL	S	12.38 MW	11.55 AW	25760 AAW	ALBLS	10//99-12//99
	Florence MSA, AL	S	13.32 MW	12.96 AW	27710 AAW	ALBLS	10//99-12//99
	Gadsden MSA, AL	S	12.62 MW	10.79 AW	26250 AAW	ALBLS	10//99-12//99
	Huntsville MSA, AL	S	13.31 MW	11.82 AW	27690 AAW	ALBLS	10//99-12//99
	Mobile MSA, AL	S	12.46 MW	10.80 AW	25920 AAW	ALBLS	10//99-12//99
	Montgomery MSA, AL	S	12.25 MW	11.43 AW	25490 AAW	ALBLS	10//99-12//99
	Tuscaloosa MSA, AL	S	11.26 MW	11.01 AW	23430 AAW	ALBLS	10//99-12//99
	Alaska	S	17.13 MW	18.41 AW	38280 AAW	AKBLS	10//99-12//99
	Anchorage MSA, AK	S	17.50 MW	16.31 AW	36410 AAW	AKBLS	10//99-12//99
	Arizona	S	13.43 MW	14.72 AW	30620 AAW	AZBLS	10//99-12//99
	Flagstaff MSA, AZ-UT	S	14.95 MW	14.88 AW	31100 AAW	AZBLS	10//99-12//99
	Phoenix-Mesa MSA, AZ	S	15.50 MW	13.82 AW	32230 AAW	AZBLS	10//99-12//99
	Tucson MSA, AZ	S	12.20 MW	11.19 AW	25380 AAW	AZBLS	10//99-12//99
	Yuma MSA, AZ	S	12.96 MW	11.41 AW	26950 AAW	AZBLS	10//99-12//99

Occupation/Type/Industry	Location	Per	Low	Mid	High	Source	Date
Automotive Service Technician and Mechanic	Arkansas	S	11.99 MW	12.89 AW	26820 AAW	ARBLS	10//99-12//99
	Fayetteville-Springdale-Rogers MSA, AR	S	12.99 MW	11.90 AW	27020 AAW	ARBLS	10//99-12//99
	Fort Smith MSA, AR-OK	S	11.70 MW	11.07 AW	24330 AAW	ARBLS	10//99-12//99
	Jonesboro MSA, AR	S	12.44 MW	11.78 AW	25870 AAW	ARBLS	10//99-12//99
	Little Rock-North Little Rock MSA, AR	S	14.87 MW	14.81 AW	30920 AAW	ARBLS	10//99-12//99
	Pine Bluff MSA, AR	S	12.34 MW	12.25 AW	25660 AAW	ARBLS	10//99-12//99
	California	S	15.59 MW	16.39 AW	34090 AAW	CABLS	10//99-12//99
	Bakersfield MSA, CA	S	13.56 MW	13.26 AW	28210 AAW	CABLS	10//99-12//99
	Chico-Paradise MSA, CA	S	15.18 MW	14.94 AW	31570 AAW	CABLS	10//99-12//99
	Fresno MSA, CA	S	13.93 MW	13.32 AW	28970 AAW	CABLS	10//99-12//99
	Los Angeles-Long Beach PMSA, CA	S	16.21 MW	15.09 AW	33710 AAW	CABLS	10//99-12//99
	Merced MSA, CA	S	14.01 MW	14.35 AW	29140 AAW	CABLS	10//99-12//99
	Modesto MSA, CA	S	13.51 MW	11.54 AW	28100 AAW	CABLS	10//99-12//99
	Oakland PMSA, CA	S	17.72 MW	16.41 AW	36860 AAW	CABLS	10//99-12//99
	Orange County PMSA, CA	S	17.41 MW	15.88 AW	36210 AAW	CABLS	10//99-12//99
	Redding MSA, CA	S	13.25 MW	12.84 AW	27560 AAW	CABLS	10//99-12//99
	Riverside-San Bernardino PMSA, CA	S	15.58 MW	15.28 AW	32400 AAW	CABLS	10//99-12//99
	Sacramento PMSA, CA	S	17.73 MW	16.46 AW	36890 AAW	CABLS	10//99-12//99
	Salinas MSA, CA	S	19.77 MW	18.80 AW	41120 AAW	CABLS	10//99-12//99
	San Diego MSA, CA	S	15.83 MW	15.20 AW	32920 AAW	CABLS	10//99-12//99
	San Francisco PMSA, CA	S	17.04 MW	17.05 AW	35450 AAW	CABLS	10//99-12//99
	San Jose PMSA, CA	S	18.73 MW	18.71 AW	38960 AAW	CABLS	10//99-12//99
	San Luis Obispo-Atascadero-Paso Robles MSA, CA	S	16.65 MW	17.23 AW	34640 AAW	CABLS	10//99-12//99
	Santa Barbara-Santa Maria-Lompoc MSA, CA	S	14.07 MW	11.53 AW	29270 AAW	CABLS	10//99-12//99
	Santa Cruz-Watsonville PMSA, CA	S	16.40 MW	15.84 AW	34110 AAW	CABLS	10//99-12//99
	Santa Rosa PMSA, CA	S	17.68 MW	16.21 AW	36770 AAW	CABLS	10//99-12//99
	Stockton-Lodi MSA, CA	S	15.19 MW	13.36 AW	31590 AAW	CABLS	10//99-12//99
	Vallejo-Fairfield-Napa PMSA, CA	S	16.39 MW	16.55 AW	34080 AAW	CABLS	10//99-12//99
	Ventura PMSA, CA	S	16.60 MW	16.05 AW	34530 AAW	CABLS	10//99-12//99
	Visalia-Tulare-Porterville MSA, CA	S	13.97 MW	13.35 AW	29060 AAW	CABLS	10//99-12//99
	Yolo PMSA, CA	S	14.86 MW	14.32 AW	30910 AAW	CABLS	10//99-12//99
	Yuba City MSA, CA	S	12.40 MW	11.35 AW	25800 AAW	CABLS	10//99-12//99
	Colorado	S	14.82 MW	15.55 AW	32340 AAW	COBLS	10//99-12//99
	Boulder-Longmont PMSA, CO	S	16.28 MW	14.47 AW	33870 AAW	COBLS	10//99-12//99
	Colorado Springs MSA, CO	S	16.21 MW	15.81 AW	33720 AAW	COBLS	10//99-12//99
	Denver PMSA, CO	S	16.24 MW	15.41 AW	33770 AAW	COBLS	10//99-12//99
	Fort Collins-Loveland MSA, CO	S	14.43 MW	12.52 AW	30020 AAW	COBLS	10//99-12//99
	Grand Junction MSA, CO	S	13.41 MW	13.50 AW	27890 AAW	COBLS	10//99-12//99
	Greeley PMSA, CO	S	14.53 MW	13.19 AW	30220 AAW	COBLS	10//99-12//99
	Pueblo MSA, CO	S	14.95 MW	14.85 AW	31100 AAW	COBLS	10//99-12//99
	Connecticut	S	14.96 MW	15.22 AW	31660 AAW	CTBLS	10//99-12//99
	Bridgeport PMSA, CT	S	14.88 MW	14.33 AW	30960 AAW	CTBLS	10//99-12//99
	Danbury PMSA, CT	S	17.43 MW	17.48 AW	36250 AAW	CTBLS	10//99-12//99
	Hartford MSA, CT	S	15.46 MW	15.45 AW	32150 AAW	CTBLS	10//99-12//99
	New Haven-Meriden PMSA, CT	S	13.86 MW	12.82 AW	28820 AAW	CTBLS	10//99-12//99
	New London-Norwich MSA, CT-RI	S	13.93 MW	14.21 AW	28980 AAW	CTBLS	10//99-12//99
	Stamford-Norwalk PMSA, CT	S	16.68 MW	16.67 AW	34700 AAW	CTBLS	10//99-12//99
	Waterbury PMSA, CT	S	15.16 MW	14.04 AW	31530 AAW	CTBLS	10//99-12//99
	Delaware	S	13.7 MW	14.30 AW	29740 AAW	DEBLS	10//99-12//99
	Dover MSA, DE	S	12.92 MW	12.47 AW	26880 AAW	DEBLS	10//99-12//99
	Wilmington-Newark PMSA, DE-MD	S	15.51 MW	14.99 AW	32250 AAW	DEBLS	10//99-12//99
	District of Columbia	S	16.87 MW	15.89 AW	33040 AAW	DCBLS	10//99-12//99
	Washington PMSA, DC-MD-VA-WV	S	17.35 MW	15.95 AW	36080 AAW	DCBLS	10//99-12//99
	Florida	S	13.2 MW	14.28 AW	29710 AAW	FLBLS	10//99-12//99
	Daytona Beach MSA, FL	S	11.21 MW	10.08 AW	23330 AAW	FLBLS	10//99-12//99
	Fort Lauderdale PMSA, FL	S	15.06 MW	13.25 AW	31330 AAW	FLBLS	10//99-12//99

AAW	Average annual wage	AOH	Average offered, high	ASH	Average starting, high	H	Hourly	M	Monthly	S	Special: hourly and annual
AE	Average entry wage	AOL	Average offered, low	ASL	Average starting, low	HI	Highest wage paid	MTC	Median total compensation	TQ	Third quartile wage
AEX	Average experienced wage	APH	Average pay, high range	AW	Average wage paid	HR	High end range	MW	Median wage paid	W	Weekly
AO	Average offered	APL	Average pay, low range	FQ	First quartile wage	LR	Low end range	SQ	Second quartile wage	Y	Yearly

Occupation/Type/Industry	Location	Per	Low	Mid	High	Source	Date
Automotive Service Technician and Mechanic	Fort Myers-Cape Coral MSA, FL	S	15.40 MW	16.42 AW	32040 AAW	FLBLS	10//99-12//99
	Fort Pierce-Port St. Lucie MSA, FL	S	13.77 MW	12.06 AW	28640 AAW	FLBLS	10//99-12//99
	Fort Walton Beach MSA, FL	S	11.10 MW	11.06 AW	23100 AAW	FLBLS	10//99-12//99
	Gainesville MSA, FL	S	14.38 MW	14.65 AW	29910 AAW	FLBLS	10//99-12//99
	Jacksonville MSA, FL	S	15.93 MW	14.89 AW	33130 AAW	FLBLS	10//99-12//99
	Lakeland-Winter Haven MSA, FL	S	13.12 MW	13.22 AW	27290 AAW	FLBLS	10//99-12//99
	Melbourne-Titusville-Palm Bay MSA, FL	S	12.97 MW	12.16 AW	26970 AAW	FLBLS	10//99-12//99
	Miami PMSA, FL	S	14.44 MW	14.12 AW	30030 AAW	FLBLS	10//99-12//99
	Naples MSA, FL	S	15.77 MW	15.66 AW	32810 AAW	FLBLS	10//99-12//99
	Ocala MSA, FL	S	13.17 MW	11.73 AW	27390 AAW	FLBLS	10//99-12//99
	Orlando MSA, FL	S	15.38 MW	13.68 AW	32000 AAW	FLBLS	10//99-12//99
	Panama City MSA, FL	S	13.26 MW	12.28 AW	27580 AAW	FLBLS	10//99-12//99
	Pensacola MSA, FL	S	13.64 MW	11.45 AW	28380 AAW	FLBLS	10//99-12//99
	Punta Gorda MSA, FL	S	15.57 MW	14.38 AW	32380 AAW	FLBLS	10//99-12//99
	Sarasota-Bradenton MSA, FL	S	15.26 MW	14.39 AW	31750 AAW	FLBLS	10//99-12//99
	Tallahassee MSA, FL	S	13.26 MW	12.70 AW	27580 AAW	FLBLS	10//99-12//99
	Tampa-St. Petersburg-Clearwater MSA, FL	S	13.44 MW	11.85 AW	27950 AAW	FLBLS	10//99-12//99
	West Palm Beach-Boca Raton MSA, FL	S	15.49 MW	13.87 AW	32220 AAW	FLBLS	10//99-12//99
	Georgia	S	13.61 MW	14.43 AW	30010 AAW	GABLS	10//99-12//99
	Albany MSA, GA	S	12.96 MW	12.79 AW	26950 AAW	GABLS	10//99-12//99
	Athens MSA, GA	S	14.18 MW	11.51 AW	29500 AAW	GABLS	10//99-12//99
	Atlanta MSA, GA	S	15.50 MW	14.86 AW	32240 AAW	GABLS	10//99-12//99
	Augusta-Aiken MSA, GA-SC	S	13.00 MW	12.78 AW	27040 AAW	GABLS	10//99-12//99
	Columbus MSA, GA-AL	S	12.70 MW	12.35 AW	26420 AAW	GABLS	10//99-12//99
	Macon MSA, GA	S	14.32 MW	14.16 AW	29790 AAW	GABLS	10//99-12//99
	Savannah MSA, GA	S	12.20 MW	12.09 AW	25380 AAW	GABLS	10//99-12//99
	Hawaii	S	15.94 MW	15.48 AW	32190 AAW	HIBLS	10//99-12//99
	Honolulu MSA, HI	S	16.56 MW	16.94 AW	34450 AAW	HIBLS	10//99-12//99
	Idaho	S	12.18 MW	12.86 AW	26750 AAW	IDBLS	10//99-12//99
	Boise City MSA, ID	S	13.31 MW	12.62 AW	27680 AAW	IDBLS	10//99-12//99
	Pocatello MSA, ID	S	12.48 MW	10.12 AW	25950 AAW	IDBLS	10//99-12//99
	Illinois	S	14.6 MW	15.45 AW	32140 AAW	ILBLS	10//99-12//99
	Bloomington-Normal MSA, IL	S	14.13 MW	14.25 AW	29390 AAW	ILBLS	10//99-12//99
	Champaign-Urbana MSA, IL	S	16.26 MW	15.34 AW	33810 AAW	ILBLS	10//99-12//99
	Chicago PMSA, IL	S	16.52 MW	15.53 AW	34360 AAW	ILBLS	10//99-12//99
	Decatur MSA, IL	S	12.47 MW	12.22 AW	25940 AAW	ILBLS	10//99-12//99
	Kankakee PMSA, IL	S	15.77 MW	13.64 AW	32800 AAW	ILBLS	10//99-12//99
	Peoria-Pekin MSA, IL	S	13.94 MW	13.05 AW	29000 AAW	ILBLS	10//99-12//99
	Rockford MSA, IL	S	12.47 MW	11.12 AW	25950 AAW	ILBLS	10//99-12//99
	Springfield MSA, IL	S	14.24 MW	13.68 AW	29620 AAW	ILBLS	10//99-12//99
	Indiana	S	13.1 MW	13.83 AW	28760 AAW	INBLS	10//99-12//99
	Bloomington MSA, IN	S	13.51 MW	13.19 AW	28090 AAW	INBLS	10//99-12//99
	Elkhart-Goshen MSA, IN	S	15.05 MW	14.67 AW	31300 AAW	INBLS	10//99-12//99
	Evansville-Henderson MSA, IN-KY	S	12.67 MW	11.88 AW	26360 AAW	INBLS	10//99-12//99
	Fort Wayne MSA, IN	S	14.75 MW	13.98 AW	30670 AAW	INBLS	10//99-12//99
	Gary PMSA, IN	S	14.36 MW	13.45 AW	29860 AAW	INBLS	10//99-12//99
	Indianapolis MSA, IN	S	15.96 MW	15.58 AW	33200 AAW	INBLS	10//99-12//99
	Kokomo MSA, IN	S	14.64 MW	14.34 AW	30460 AAW	INBLS	10//99-12//99
	Lafayette MSA, IN	S	13.94 MW	12.42 AW	29000 AAW	INBLS	10//99-12//99
	Muncie MSA, IN	S	12.78 MW	12.23 AW	26570 AAW	INBLS	10//99-12//99
	South Bend MSA, IN	S	13.81 MW	13.02 AW	28720 AAW	INBLS	10//99-12//99
	Terre Haute MSA, IN	S	13.10 MW	12.79 AW	27250 AAW	INBLS	10//99-12//99
	Iowa	S	11.63 MW	12.57 AW	26140 AAW	IABLS	10//99-12//99
	Cedar Rapids MSA, IA	S	12.98 MW	12.44 AW	27010 AAW	IABLS	10//99-12//99
	Davenport-Moline-Rock Island MSA, IA-IL	S	13.30 MW	12.47 AW	27660 AAW	IABLS	10//99-12//99
	Des Moines MSA, IA	S	13.81 MW	13.20 AW	28720 AAW	IABLS	10//99-12//99
	Dubuque MSA, IA	S	14.46 MW	14.07 AW	30090 AAW	IABLS	10//99-12//99
	Iowa City MSA, IA	S	12.72 MW	12.82 AW	26450 AAW	IABLS	10//99-12//99
	Sioux City MSA, IA-NE	S	14.97 MW	13.10 AW	31130 AAW	IABLS	10//99-12//99
	Waterloo-Cedar Falls MSA, IA	S	13.50 MW	13.48 AW	28080 AAW	IABLS	10//99-12//99
	Kansas	S	12.07 MW	13.08 AW	27210 AAW	KSBLS	10//99-12//99
	Lawrence MSA, KS	S	13.79 MW	12.98 AW	28690 AAW	KSBLS	10//99-12//99
	Topeka MSA, KS	S	13.07 MW	13.21 AW	27190 AAW	KSBLS	10//99-12//99

AAW Average annual wage	**AOH** Average offered, high	**ASH** Average starting, high	**H** Hourly	**M** Monthly	**S** Special: hourly and annual
AE Average entry wage	**AOL** Average offered, low	**ASL** Average starting, low	**HI** Highest wage paid	**MTC** Median total compensation	**TQ** Third quartile wage
AEX Average experienced wage	**APH** Average pay, high range	**AW** Average wage paid	**HR** High end range	**MW** Median wage paid	**W** Weekly
AO Average offered	**APL** Average pay, low range	**FQ** First quartile wage	**LR** Low end range	**SQ** Second quartile wage	**Y** Yearly

Occupation/Type/Industry	Location	Per	Low	Mid	High	Source	Date
Automotive Service Technician and Mechanic	Wichita MSA, KS	S	12.21 MW	10.46 AW	25390 AAW	KSBLS	10//99-12//99
	Kentucky	S	11.7 MW	12.50 AW	26000 AAW	KYBLS	10//99-12//99
	Lexington MSA, KY	S	14.19 MW	13.52 AW	29510 AAW	KYBLS	10//99-12//99
	Louisville MSA, KY-IN	S	13.71 MW	12.88 AW	28510 AAW	KYBLS	10//99-12//99
	Owensboro MSA, KY	S	11.61 MW	11.27 AW	24140 AAW	KYBLS	10//99-12//99
	Louisiana	S	12.5 MW	13.49 AW	28050 AAW	LABLS	10//99-12//99
	Alexandria MSA, LA	S	13.84 MW	13.71 AW	28780 AAW	LABLS	10//99-12//99
	Baton Rouge MSA, LA	S	13.83 MW	13.08 AW	28760 AAW	LABLS	10//99-12//99
	Houma MSA, LA	S	14.20 MW	14.14 AW	29540 AAW	LABLS	10//99-12//99
	Lafayette MSA, LA	S	13.62 MW	12.90 AW	28340 AAW	LABLS	10//99-12//99
	Lake Charles MSA, LA	S	14.17 MW	12.74 AW	29480 AAW	LABLS	10//99-12//99
	Monroe MSA, LA	S	12.14 MW	12.36 AW	25240 AAW	LABLS	10//99-12//99
	New Orleans MSA, LA	S	14.03 MW	12.25 AW	29180 AAW	LABLS	10//99-12//99
	Shreveport-Bossier City MSA, LA	S	13.06 MW	12.86 AW	27150 AAW	LABLS	10//99-12//99
	Maine	S	11.8 MW	12.69 AW	26390 AAW	MEBLS	10//99-12//99
	Bangor MSA, ME	S	11.80 MW	11.33 AW	24540 AAW	MEBLS	10//99-12//99
	Portland MSA, ME	S	12.90 MW	12.65 AW	26840 AAW	MEBLS	10//99-12//99
	Maryland	S	16.01 MW	16.97 AW	35290 AAW	MDBLS	10//99-12//99
	Baltimore PMSA, MD	S	17.20 MW	16.79 AW	35780 AAW	MDBLS	10//99-12//99
	Cumberland MSA, MD-WV	S	11.43 MW	10.25 AW	23770 AAW	MDBLS	10//99-12//99
	Hagerstown PMSA, MD	S	14.61 MW	13.67 AW	30390 AAW	MDBLS	10//99-12//99
	Massachusetts	S	14.94 MW	15.50 AW	32240 AAW	MABLS	10//99-12//99
	Barnstable-Yarmouth MSA, MA	S	14.98 MW	14.68 AW	31150 AAW	MABLS	10//99-12//99
	Boston PMSA, MA-NH	S	16.36 MW	15.56 AW	34030 AAW	MABLS	10//99-12//99
	Brockton PMSA, MA	S	14.61 MW	13.92 AW	30390 AAW	MABLS	10//99-12//99
	Fitchburg-Leominster PMSA, MA	S	13.46 MW	12.81 AW	27990 AAW	MABLS	10//99-12//99
	Lawrence PMSA, MA-NH	S	13.63 MW	13.25 AW	28360 AAW	MABLS	10//99-12//99
	Lowell PMSA, MA-NH	S	14.61 MW	14.04 AW	30400 AAW	MABLS	10//99-12//99
	New Bedford PMSA, MA	S	12.87 MW	12.34 AW	26780 AAW	MABLS	10//99-12//99
	Pittsfield MSA, MA	S	14.44 MW	13.88 AW	30030 AAW	MABLS	10//99-12//99
	Springfield MSA, MA	S	14.70 MW	14.32 AW	30570 AAW	MABLS	10//99-12//99
	Worcester PMSA, MA-CT	S	16.26 MW	15.45 AW	33810 AAW	MABLS	10//99-12//99
	Michigan	S	15.46 MW	16.28 AW	33860 AAW	MIBLS	10//99-12//99
	Ann Arbor PMSA, MI	S	20.51 MW	18.35 AW	42650 AAW	MIBLS	10//99-12//99
	Benton Harbor MSA, MI	S	13.07 MW	13.12 AW	27180 AAW	MIBLS	10//99-12//99
	Detroit PMSA, MI	S	17.92 MW	17.81 AW	37270 AAW	MIBLS	10//99-12//99
	Flint PMSA, MI	S	17.43 MW	17.58 AW	36250 AAW	MIBLS	10//99-12//99
	Grand Rapids-Muskegon-Holland MSA, MI	S	14.27 MW	12.84 AW	29670 AAW	MIBLS	10//99-12//99
	Jackson MSA, MI	S	15.27 MW	14.54 AW	31760 AAW	MIBLS	10//99-12//99
	Kalamazoo-Battle Creek MSA, MI	S	13.11 MW	12.46 AW	27260 AAW	MIBLS	10//99-12//99
	Lansing-East Lansing MSA, MI	S	15.69 MW	15.40 AW	32640 AAW	MIBLS	10//99-12//99
	Saginaw-Bay City-Midland MSA, MI	S	13.01 MW	11.73 AW	27050 AAW	MIBLS	10//99-12//99
	Minnesota	S	13.74 MW	14.37 AW	29880 AAW	MNBLS	10//99-12//99
	Duluth-Superior MSA, MN-WI	S	12.89 MW	13.09 AW	26820 AAW	MNBLS	10//99-12//99
	Minneapolis-St. Paul MSA, MN-WI	S	15.99 MW	16.26 AW	33250 AAW	MNBLS	10//99-12//99
	Rochester MSA, MN	S	13.11 MW	12.40 AW	27260 AAW	MNBLS	10//99-12//99
	St. Cloud MSA, MN	S	14.41 MW	14.64 AW	29970 AAW	MNBLS	10//99-12//99
	Mississippi	S	11.98 MW	12.68 AW	26370 AAW	MSBLS	10//99-12//99
	Biloxi-Gulfport-Pascagoula MSA, MS	S	12.90 MW	11.86 AW	26820 AAW	MSBLS	10//99-12//99
	Hattiesburg MSA, MS	S	11.22 MW	10.20 AW	23330 AAW	MSBLS	10//99-12//99
	Jackson MSA, MS	S	12.35 MW	11.46 AW	25690 AAW	MSBLS	10//99-12//99
	Missouri	S	14.08 MW	14.33 AW	29810 AAW	MOBLS	10//99-12//99
	Columbia MSA, MO	S	14.09 MW	14.54 AW	29320 AAW	MOBLS	10//99-12//99
	Joplin MSA, MO	S	12.57 MW	11.44 AW	26140 AAW	MOBLS	10//99-12//99
	Kansas City MSA, MO-KS	S	15.43 MW	16.03 AW	32090 AAW	MOBLS	10//99-12//99
	St. Louis MSA, MO-IL	S	15.40 MW	15.33 AW	32030 AAW	MOBLS	10//99-12//99
	Springfield MSA, MO	S	12.09 MW	11.02 AW	25150 AAW	MOBLS	10//99-12//99
	Montana	S	12.39 MW	12.72 AW	26470 AAW	MTBLS	10//99-12//99
	Billings MSA, MT	S	13.60 MW	13.31 AW	28290 AAW	MTBLS	10//99-12//99
	Great Falls MSA, MT	S	11.27 MW	10.16 AW	23450 AAW	MTBLS	10//99-12//99
	Missoula MSA, MT	S	15.65 MW	15.00 AW	32550 AAW	MTBLS	10//99-12//99
	Nebraska	S	11.81 MW	12.82 AW	26670 AAW	NEBLS	10//99-12//99
	Lincoln MSA, NE	S	11.76 MW	11.11 AW	24470 AAW	NEBLS	10//99-12//99

AAW	Average annual wage	AOH	Average offered, high	ASH	Average starting, high	H	Hourly	M	Monthly		Special: hourly and annual
AE	Average entry wage	AOL	Average offered, low	ASL	Average starting, low	HI	Highest wage paid	MTC	Median total compensation	TQ	Third quartile wage
AEX	Average experienced wage	APH	Average pay, high range	AW	Average wage paid	HR	High end range	MW	Median wage paid	W	Weekly
AO	Average offered	APL	Average pay, low range	FQ	First quartile wage	LR	Low end range	SQ	Second quartile wage	Y	Yearly

Occupation/Type/Industry	Location	Per	Low	Mid	High	Source	Date
Automotive Service Technician and Mechanic	Omaha MSA, NE-IA	S	14.39 MW	13.09 AW	29930 AAW	NEBLS	10//99-12//99
	Nevada	S	15.95 MW	16.68 AW	34680 AAW	NVBLS	10//99-12//99
	Las Vegas MSA, NV-AZ	S	16.53 MW	15.43 AW	34390 AAW	NVBLS	10//99-12//99
	Reno MSA, NV	S	16.78 MW	16.29 AW	34900 AAW	NVBLS	10//99-12//99
	New Hampshire	S	13.87 MW	14.50 AW	30150 AAW	NHBLS	10//99-12//99
	Manchester PMSA, NH	S	15.16 MW	14.05 AW	31540 AAW	NHBLS	10//99-12//99
	Nashua PMSA, NH	S	16.73 MW	16.05 AW	34800 AAW	NHBLS	10//99-12//99
	Portsmouth-Rochester PMSA, NH-ME	S	13.84 MW	12.94 AW	28800 AAW	NHBLS	10//99-12//99
	New Jersey	S	15.46 MW	16.15 AW	33600 AAW	NJBLS	10//99-12//99
	Atlantic-Cape May PMSA, NJ	S	15.75 MW	14.61 AW	32770 AAW	NJBLS	10//99-12//99
	Bergen-Passaic PMSA, NJ	S	15.37 MW	12.43 AW	31970 AAW	NJBLS	10//99-12//99
	Jersey City PMSA, NJ	S	14.22 MW	12.87 AW	29570 AAW	NJBLS	10//99-12//99
	Middlesex-Somerset-Hunterdon PMSA, NJ	S	16.07 MW	15.75 AW	33420 AAW	NJBLS	10//99-12//99
	Monmouth-Ocean PMSA, NJ	S	16.82 MW	16.20 AW	34990 AAW	NJBLS	10//99-12//99
	Newark PMSA, NJ	S	16.79 MW	15.76 AW	34930 AAW	NJBLS	10//99-12//99
	Trenton PMSA, NJ	S	17.86 MW	17.88 AW	37140 AAW	NJBLS	10//99-12//99
	Vineland-Millville-Bridgeton PMSA, NJ	S	13.16 MW	11.54 AW	27380 AAW	NJBLS	10//99-12//99
	New Mexico	S	12.9 MW	13.35 AW	27760 AAW	NMBLS	10//99-12//99
	Albuquerque MSA, NM	S	14.94 MW	14.46 AW	31080 AAW	NMBLS	10//99-12//99
	Las Cruces MSA, NM	S	12.52 MW	11.33 AW	26030 AAW	NMBLS	10//99-12//99
	Santa Fe MSA, NM	S	14.99 MW	15.28 AW	31180 AAW	NMBLS	10//99-12//99
	New York	S	12.9 MW	13.80 AW	28700 AAW	NYBLS	10//99-12//99
	Albany-Schenectady-Troy MSA, NY	S	12.34 MW	12.07 AW	25670 AAW	NYBLS	10//99-12//99
	Binghamton MSA, NY	S	11.86 MW	11.43 AW	24680 AAW	NYBLS	10//99-12//99
	Buffalo-Niagara Falls MSA, NY	S	14.34 MW	14.52 AW	29840 AAW	NYBLS	10//99-12//99
	Dutchess County PMSA, NY	S	13.97 MW	13.33 AW	29060 AAW	NYBLS	10//99-12//99
	Elmira MSA, NY	S	12.00 MW	11.83 AW	24970 AAW	NYBLS	10//99-12//99
	Glens Falls MSA, NY	S	12.12 MW	11.27 AW	25210 AAW	NYBLS	10//99-12//99
	Jamestown MSA, NY	S	13.04 MW	12.58 AW	27130 AAW	NYBLS	10//99-12//99
	Nassau-Suffolk PMSA, NY	S	16.39 MW	15.14 AW	34080 AAW	NYBLS	10//99-12//99
	New York PMSA, NY	S	13.56 MW	12.17 AW	28200 AAW	NYBLS	10//99-12//99
	Newburgh PMSA, NY-PA	S	15.52 MW	15.89 AW	32270 AAW	NYBLS	10//99-12//99
	Rochester MSA, NY	S	12.88 MW	12.15 AW	26780 AAW	NYBLS	10//99-12//99
	Syracuse MSA, NY	S	13.39 MW	12.95 AW	27860 AAW	NYBLS	10//99-12//99
	Utica-Rome MSA, NY	S	11.00 MW	10.71 AW	22880 AAW	NYBLS	10//99-12//99
	North Carolina	S	13.01 MW	14.33 AW	29800 AAW	NCBLS	10//99-12//99
	Asheville MSA, NC	S	11.83 MW	10.97 AW	24600 AAW	NCBLS	10//99-12//99
	Charlotte-Gastonia-Rock Hill MSA, NC-SC	S	15.91 MW	14.48 AW	33100 AAW	NCBLS	10//99-12//99
	Fayetteville MSA, NC	S	12.88 MW	12.49 AW	26780 AAW	NCBLS	10//99-12//99
	Goldsboro MSA, NC	S	12.38 MW	12.16 AW	25750 AAW	NCBLS	10//99-12//99
	Greensboro--Winston-Salem--High Point MSA, NC	S	15.65 MW	14.46 AW	32540 AAW	NCBLS	10//99-12//99
	Greenville MSA, NC	S	12.15 MW	11.00 AW	25270 AAW	NCBLS	10//99-12//99
	Hickory-Morganton-Lenoir MSA, NC	S	12.75 MW	12.11 AW	26530 AAW	NCBLS	10//99-12//99
	Jacksonville MSA, NC	S	13.65 MW	13.09 AW	28380 AAW	NCBLS	10//99-12//99
	Raleigh-Durham-Chapel Hill MSA, NC	S	16.07 MW	15.17 AW	33420 AAW	NCBLS	10//99-12//99
	Rocky Mount MSA, NC	S	12.25 MW	12.12 AW	25470 AAW	NCBLS	10//99-12//99
	Wilmington MSA, NC	S	13.44 MW	12.08 AW	27950 AAW	NCBLS	10//99-12//99
	North Dakota	S	11.21 MW	12.07 AW	25110 AAW	NDBLS	10//99-12//99
	Bismarck MSA, ND	S	12.52 MW	11.96 AW	26050 AAW	NDBLS	10//99-12//99
	Fargo-Moorhead MSA, ND-MN	S	12.29 MW	10.92 AW	25550 AAW	NDBLS	10//99-12//99
	Grand Forks MSA, ND-MN	S	12.14 MW	11.27 AW	25250 AAW	NDBLS	10//99-12//99
	Ohio	S	13.17 MW	13.69 AW	28480 AAW	OHBLS	10//99-12//99
	Akron PMSA, OH	S	14.47 MW	13.83 AW	30100 AAW	OHBLS	10//99-12//99
	Canton-Massillon MSA, OH	S	12.54 MW	12.23 AW	26090 AAW	OHBLS	10//99-12//99
	Cincinnati PMSA, OH-KY-IN	S	15.11 MW	14.67 AW	31430 AAW	OHBLS	10//99-12//99
	Cleveland-Lorain-Elyria PMSA, OH	S	14.48 MW	14.15 AW	30110 AAW	OHBLS	10//99-12//99
	Columbus MSA, OH	S	15.12 MW	14.75 AW	31450 AAW	OHBLS	10//99-12//99
	Dayton-Springfield MSA, OH	S	13.74 MW	13.12 AW	28570 AAW	OHBLS	10//99-12//99
	Hamilton-Middletown PMSA, OH	S	14.73 MW	13.90 AW	30640 AAW	OHBLS	10//99-12//99

AAW	Average annual wage	**AOH**	Average offered, high	**ASH**	Average starting, high	**H**	Hourly	
AE	Average entry wage	**AOL**	Average offered, low	**ASL**	Average starting, low	**HI**	Highest wage paid	
AEX	Average experienced wage	**APH**	Average pay, high range	**AW**	Average wage paid	**HR**	High end range	
AO	Average offered	**APL**	Average pay, low range	**FQ**	First quartile wage	**LR**	Low end range	

M	Monthly	**S**	Special: hourly and annual
MTC	Median total compensation	**TQ**	Third quartile wage
MW	Median wage paid	**W**	Weekly
SQ	Second quartile wage	**Y**	Yearly

Occupation/Type/Industry	Location	Per	Low	Mid	High	Source	Date
Automotive Service Technician and Mechanic							
	Lima MSA, OH	S	12.86 MW	12.65 AW	26740 AAW	OHBLS	10//99-12//99
	Mansfield MSA, OH	S	13.09 MW	12.18 AW	27230 AAW	OHBLS	10//99-12//99
	Steubenville-Weirton MSA, OH-WV	S	10.41 MW	10.06 AW	21650 AAW	OHBLS	10//99-12//99
	Toledo MSA, OH	S	13.36 MW	11.62 AW	27780 AAW	OHBLS	10//99-12//99
	Youngstown-Warren MSA, OH	S	11.61 MW	10.25 AW	24150 AAW	OHBLS	10//99-12//99
	Oklahoma	S	13.1 MW	13.54 AW	28170 AAW	OKBLS	10//99-12//99
	Enid MSA, OK	S	11.47 MW	10.57 AW	23860 AAW	OKBLS	10//99-12//99
	Lawton MSA, OK	S	13.20 MW	13.16 AW	27460 AAW	OKBLS	10//99-12//99
	Oklahoma City MSA, OK	S	13.57 MW	13.55 AW	28210 AAW	OKBLS	10//99-12//99
	Tulsa MSA, OK	S	15.13 MW	13.58 AW	31480 AAW	OKBLS	10//99-12//99
	Oregon	S	14.8 MW	15.36 AW	31950 AAW	ORBLS	10//99-12//99
	Corvallis MSA, OR	S	14.63 MW	13.09 AW	30420 AAW	ORBLS	10//99-12//99
	Eugene-Springfield MSA, OR	S	14.38 MW	13.57 AW	29920 AAW	ORBLS	10//99-12//99
	Medford-Ashland MSA, OR	S	12.92 MW	10.41 AW	26860 AAW	ORBLS	10//99-12//99
	Portland-Vancouver PMSA, OR-WA	S	16.45 MW	16.07 AW	34220 AAW	ORBLS	10//99-12//99
	Salem PMSA, OR	S	14.29 MW	13.41 AW	29730 AAW	ORBLS	10//99-12//99
	Pennsylvania	S	12.03 MW	13.15 AW	27340 AAW	PABLS	10//99-12//99
	Allentown-Bethlehem-Easton MSA, PA	S	13.64 MW	13.45 AW	28370 AAW	PABLS	10//99-12//99
	Altoona MSA, PA	S	12.44 MW	11.61 AW	25870 AAW	PABLS	10//99-12//99
	Erie MSA, PA	S	12.66 MW	11.78 AW	26330 AAW	PABLS	10//99-12//99
	Harrisburg-Lebanon-Carlisle MSA, PA	S	13.30 MW	12.15 AW	27670 AAW	PABLS	10//99-12//99
	Johnstown MSA, PA	S	10.57 MW	9.96 AW	21990 AAW	PABLS	10//99-12//99
	Lancaster MSA, PA	S	13.99 MW	12.89 AW	29110 AAW	PABLS	10//99-12//99
	Philadelphia PMSA, PA-NJ	S	15.24 MW	14.95 AW	31700 AAW	PABLS	10//99-12//99
	Pittsburgh MSA, PA	S	12.94 MW	12.08 AW	26920 AAW	PABLS	10//99-12//99
	Reading MSA, PA	S	13.50 MW	14.06 AW	28080 AAW	PABLS	10//99-12//99
	Scranton--Wilkes-Barre--Hazleton MSA, PA	S	10.42 MW	10.02 AW	21670 AAW	PABLS	10//99-12//99
	Sharon MSA, PA	S	11.22 MW	10.35 AW	23340 AAW	PABLS	10//99-12//99
	State College MSA, PA	S	11.29 MW	10.72 AW	23480 AAW	PABLS	10//99-12//99
	Williamsport MSA, PA	S	11.05 MW	10.94 AW	22980 AAW	PABLS	10//99-12//99
	York MSA, PA	S	13.09 MW	12.50 AW	27230 AAW	PABLS	10//99-12//99
	Rhode Island	S	13.19 MW	13.96 AW	29030 AAW	RIBLS	10//99-12//99
	Providence-Fall River-Warwick MSA, RI-MA	S	13.93 MW	13.01 AW	28970 AAW	RIBLS	10//99-12//99
	South Carolina	S	11.44 MW	12.54 AW	26080 AAW	SCBLS	10//99-12//99
	Charleston-North Charleston MSA, SC	S	14.23 MW	12.25 AW	29590 AAW	SCBLS	10//99-12//99
	Columbia MSA, SC	S	13.20 MW	12.01 AW	27460 AAW	SCBLS	10//99-12//99
	Florence MSA, SC	S	12.09 MW	12.03 AW	25140 AAW	SCBLS	10//99-12//99
	Greenville-Spartanburg-Anderson MSA, SC	S	12.72 MW	11.89 AW	26450 AAW	SCBLS	10//99-12//99
	Myrtle Beach MSA, SC	S	14.15 MW	12.90 AW	29420 AAW	SCBLS	10//99-12//99
	Sumter MSA, SC	S	11.08 MW	10.66 AW	23050 AAW	SCBLS	10//99-12//99
	South Dakota	S	11.77 MW	12.37 AW	25730 AAW	SDBLS	10//99-12//99
	Rapid City MSA, SD	S	12.59 MW	11.92 AW	26190 AAW	SDBLS	10//99-12//99
	Sioux Falls MSA, SD	S	11.93 MW	11.32 AW	24810 AAW	SDBLS	10//99-12//99
	Tennessee	S	13.01 MW	13.74 AW	28580 AAW	TNBLS	10//99-12//99
	Chattanooga MSA, TN-GA	S	14.54 MW	14.87 AW	30250 AAW	TNBLS	10//99-12//99
	Clarksville-Hopkinsville MSA, TN-KY	S	12.25 MW	11.05 AW	25480 AAW	TNBLS	10//99-12//99
	Jackson MSA, TN	S	13.69 MW	13.15 AW	28480 AAW	TNBLS	10//99-12//99
	Johnson City-Kingsport-Bristol MSA, TN-VA	S	10.58 MW	9.91 AW	22000 AAW	TNBLS	10//99-12//99
	Knoxville MSA, TN	S	12.79 MW	11.58 AW	26610 AAW	TNBLS	10//99-12//99
	Memphis MSA, TN-AR-MS	S	15.41 MW	14.18 AW	32040 AAW	MSBLS	10//99-12//99
	Nashville MSA, TN	S	15.30 MW	15.17 AW	31830 AAW	TNBLS	10//99-12//99
	Texas	S	13.17 MW	14.04 AW	29210 AAW	TXBLS	10//99-12//99
	Abilene MSA, TX	S	13.90 MW	14.34 AW	28910 AAW	TXBLS	10//99-12//99
	Amarillo MSA, TX	S	11.62 MW	10.79 AW	24160 AAW	TXBLS	10//99-12//99
	Austin-San Marcos MSA, TX	S	14.19 MW	13.28 AW	29520 AAW	TXBLS	10//99-12//99
	Beaumont-Port Arthur MSA, TX	S	13.49 MW	12.80 AW	28070 AAW	TXBLS	10//99-12//99
	Brazoria PMSA, TX	S	11.57 MW	10.59 AW	24060 AAW	TXBLS	10//99-12//99
	Brownsville-Harlingen-San Benito MSA, TX	S	11.05 MW	11.12 AW	22980 AAW	TXBLS	10//99-12//99

AAW Average annual wage	AOH Average offered, high	ASH Average starting, high	H Hourly	M Monthly	S Special: hourly and annual
AE Average entry wage	AOL Average offered, low	ASL Average starting, low	HI Highest wage paid	MTC Median total compensation	TQ Third quartile wage
AEX Average experienced wage	APH Average pay, high range	AW Average wage paid	HR High end range	MW Median wage paid	W Weekly
AO Average offered	APL Average pay, low range	FQ First quartile wage	LR Low end range	SQ Second quartile wage	Y Yearly

Occupation/Type/Industry	Location	Per	Low	Mid	High	Source	Date
Automotive Service Technician and Mechanic	Bryan-College Station MSA, TX	S	11.96 MW	11.35 AW	24880 AAW	TXBLS	10//99-12//99
	Corpus Christi MSA, TX	S	12.08 MW	10.86 AW	25120 AAW	TXBLS	10//99-12//99
	Dallas PMSA, TX	S	15.20 MW	14.54 AW	31620 AAW	TXBLS	10//99-12//99
	El Paso MSA, TX	S	11.24 MW	10.20 AW	23370 AAW	TXBLS	10//99-12//99
	Fort Worth-Arlington PMSA, TX	S	15.25 MW	14.54 AW	31730 AAW	TXBLS	10//99-12//99
	Galveston-Texas City PMSA, TX	S	16.03 MW	14.88 AW	33350 AAW	TXBLS	10//99-12//99
	Houston PMSA, TX	S	15.87 MW	15.09 AW	33000 AAW	TXBLS	10//99-12//99
	Killeen-Temple MSA, TX	S	12.06 MW	11.36 AW	25090 AAW	TXBLS	10//99-12//99
	Laredo MSA, TX	S	11.05 MW	10.38 AW	22980 AAW	TXBLS	10//99-12//99
	Longview-Marshall MSA, TX	S	13.96 MW	12.34 AW	29030 AAW	TXBLS	10//99-12//99
	Lubbock MSA, TX	S	12.28 MW	11.51 AW	25550 AAW	TXBLS	10//99-12//99
	McAllen-Edinburg-Mission MSA, TX	S	9.22 MW	9.03 AW	19180 AAW	TXBLS	10//99-12//99
	Odessa-Midland MSA, TX	S	12.83 MW	12.34 AW	26680 AAW	TXBLS	10//99-12//99
	San Angelo MSA, TX	S	11.72 MW	11.05 AW	24380 AAW	TXBLS	10//99-12//99
	San Antonio MSA, TX	S	13.00 MW	12.03 AW	27040 AAW	TXBLS	10//99-12//99
	Sherman-Denison MSA, TX	S	12.51 MW	11.59 AW	26020 AAW	TXBLS	10//99-12//99
	Texarkana MSA, TX-Texarkana, AR	S	11.81 MW	10.93 AW	24570 AAW	TXBLS	10//99-12//99
	Tyler MSA, TX	S	14.00 MW	13.35 AW	29120 AAW	TXBLS	10//99-12//99
	Victoria MSA, TX	S	13.84 MW	13.68 AW	28790 AAW	TXBLS	10//99-12//99
	Waco MSA, TX	S	13.61 MW	12.37 AW	28310 AAW	TXBLS	10//99-12//99
	Wichita Falls MSA, TX	S	13.17 MW	11.47 AW	27390 AAW	TXBLS	10//99-12//99
	Utah	S	13.42 MW	13.95 AW	29020 AAW	UTBLS	10//99-12//99
	Provo-Orem MSA, UT	S	14.78 MW	13.77 AW	30740 AAW	UTBLS	10//99-12//99
	Salt Lake City-Ogden MSA, UT	S	13.92 MW	13.34 AW	28960 AAW	UTBLS	10//99-12//99
	Vermont	S	11.4 MW	12.60 AW	26210 AAW	VTBLS	10//99-12//99
	Burlington MSA, VT	S	12.85 MW	12.53 AW	26740 AAW	VTBLS	10//99-12//99
	Virginia	S	13.55 MW	14.63 AW	30420 AAW	VABLS	10//99-12//99
	Charlottesville MSA, VA	S	14.93 MW	13.89 AW	31060 AAW	VABLS	10//99-12//99
	Danville MSA, VA	S	11.86 MW	11.57 AW	24670 AAW	VABLS	10//99-12//99
	Lynchburg MSA, VA	S	12.41 MW	12.09 AW	25820 AAW	VABLS	10//99-12//99
	Norfolk-Virginia Beach-Newport News MSA, VA-NC	S	12.98 MW	12.68 AW	26990 AAW	VABLS	10//99-12//99
	Richmond-Petersburg MSA, VA	S	15.86 MW	15.16 AW	32980 AAW	VABLS	10//99-12//99
	Roanoke MSA, VA	S	12.98 MW	11.76 AW	27000 AAW	VABLS	10//99-12//99
	Washington	S	13.85 MW	14.91 AW	31010 AAW	WABLS	10//99-12//99
	Bellingham MSA, WA	S	13.57 MW	13.52 AW	28220 AAW	WABLS	10//99-12//99
	Bremerton PMSA, WA	S	15.99 MW	15.58 AW	33270 AAW	WABLS	10//99-12//99
	Olympia PMSA, WA	S	14.23 MW	13.32 AW	29600 AAW	WABLS	10//99-12//99
	Richland-Kennewick-Pasco MSA, WA	S	14.10 MW	13.36 AW	29330 AAW	WABLS	10//99-12//99
	Seattle-Bellevue-Everett PMSA, WA	S	15.33 MW	13.91 AW	31890 AAW	WABLS	10//99-12//99
	Spokane MSA, WA	S	14.99 MW	14.15 AW	31180 AAW	WABLS	10//99-12//99
	Tacoma PMSA, WA	S	15.39 MW	14.71 AW	32010 AAW	WABLS	10//99-12//99
	Yakima MSA, WA	S	12.92 MW	12.26 AW	26880 AAW	WABLS	10//99-12//99
	West Virginia	S	10.23 MW	10.82 AW	22510 AAW	WVBLS	10//99-12//99
	Charleston MSA, WV	S	11.98 MW	11.17 AW	24920 AAW	WVBLS	10//99-12//99
	Huntington-Ashland MSA, WV-KY-OH	S	10.65 MW	9.88 AW	22150 AAW	WVBLS	10//99-12//99
	Parkersburg-Marietta MSA, WV-OH	S	10.47 MW	9.94 AW	21780 AAW	WVBLS	10//99-12//99
	Wheeling MSA, WV-OH	S	10.19 MW	9.58 AW	21190 AAW	WVBLS	10//99-12//99
	Wisconsin	S	12.89 MW	13.62 AW	28320 AAW	WIBLS	10//99-12//99
	Appleton-Oshkosh-Neenah MSA, WI	S	12.46 MW	11.92 AW	25910 AAW	WIBLS	10//99-12//99
	Eau Claire MSA, WI	S	10.84 MW	11.11 AW	22550 AAW	WIBLS	10//99-12//99
	Green Bay MSA, WI	S	14.27 MW	13.83 AW	29690 AAW	WIBLS	10//99-12//99
	Janesville-Beloit MSA, WI	S	13.14 MW	12.29 AW	27330 AAW	WIBLS	10//99-12//99
	Kenosha PMSA, WI	S	12.96 MW	11.97 AW	26950 AAW	WIBLS	10//99-12//99
	La Crosse MSA, WI-MN	S	10.51 MW	8.68 AW	21850 AAW	WIBLS	10//99-12//99
	Madison MSA, WI	S	15.13 MW	14.81 AW	31460 AAW	WIBLS	10//99-12//99
	Milwaukee-Waukesha PMSA, WI	S	15.55 MW	14.25 AW	32340 AAW	WIBLS	10//99-12//99

AAW Average annual wage	**AOH** Average offered, high	**ASH** Average starting, high	**H** Hourly	**M** Monthly	**S** Special: hourly and annual
AE Average entry wage	**AOL** Average offered, low	**ASL** Average starting, low	**HI** Highest wage paid	**MTC** Median total compensation	**TQ** Third quartile wage
AEX Average experienced wage	**APH** Average pay, high range	**AW** Average wage paid	**HR** High end range	**MW** Median wage paid	**W** Weekly
AO Average offered	**APL** Average pay, low range	**FQ** First quartile wage	**LR** Low end range	**SQ** Second quartile wage	**Y** Yearly

Occupation/Type/Industry	Location	Per	Low	Mid	High	Source	Date
Automotive Service Technician and Mechanic	Racine PMSA, WI	S	13.06 MW	11.22 AW	27170 AAW	WIBLS	10//99-12//99
	Sheboygan MSA, WI	S	14.10 MW	14.25 AW	29330 AAW	WIBLS	10//99-12//99
	Wausau MSA, WI	S	13.48 MW	14.24 AW	28030 AAW	WIBLS	10//99-12//99
	Wyoming	S	10.84 MW	11.34 AW	23590 AAW	WYBLS	10//99-12//99
	Casper MSA, WY	S	11.82 MW	11.42 AW	24580 AAW	WYBLS	10//99-12//99
	Cheyenne MSA, WY	S	13.64 MW	13.58 AW	28370 AAW	WYBLS	10//99-12//99
	Puerto Rico	S	6.63 MW	7.45 AW	15500 AAW	PRBLS	10//99-12//99
	Aguadilla MSA, PR	S	6.69 MW	6.08 AW	13910 AAW	PRBLS	10//99-12//99
	Arecibo PMSA, PR	S	6.85 MW	6.38 AW	14240 AAW	PRBLS	10//99-12//99
	Caguas PMSA, PR	S	6.84 MW	6.31 AW	14220 AAW	PRBLS	10//99-12//99
	Mayaguez MSA, PR	S	6.35 MW	6.25 AW	13210 AAW	PRBLS	10//99-12//99
	Ponce MSA, PR	S	6.72 MW	6.24 AW	13980 AAW	PRBLS	10//99-12//99
	San Juan-Bayamon PMSA, PR	S	7.76 MW	6.94 AW	16140 AAW	PRBLS	10//99-12//99
	Virgin Islands	S	12.21 MW	12.82 AW	26670 AAW	VIBLS	10//99-12//99
	Guam	S	12.36 MW	12.73 AW	26470 AAW	GUBLS	10//99-12//99
Avionics Technician	Alabama	S	16.59 MW	16.51 AW	34330 AAW	ALBLS	10//99-12//99
	Alaska	S	18.79 MW	18.61 AW	38710 AAW	AKBLS	10//99-12//99
	Anchorage MSA, AK	S	18.50 MW	18.71 AW	38480 AAW	AKBLS	10//99-12//99
	Arizona	S	20.06 MW	21.21 AW	44120 AAW	AZBLS	10//99-12//99
	Phoenix-Mesa MSA, AZ	S	21.68 MW	20.67 AW	45100 AAW	AZBLS	10//99-12//99
	Arkansas	S	11.72 MW	12.58 AW	26170 AAW	ARBLS	10//99-12//99
	California	S	20.42 MW	21.10 AW	43890 AAW	CABLS	10//99-12//99
	Los Angeles-Long Beach PMSA, CA	S	22.16 MW	22.34 AW	46100 AAW	CABLS	10//99-12//99
	Orange County PMSA, CA	S	23.83 MW	24.23 AW	49560 AAW	CABLS	10//99-12//99
	Connecticut	S	22.9 MW	22.13 AW	46030 AAW	CTBLS	10//99-12//99
	Hartford MSA, CT	S	22.67 MW	23.48 AW	47150 AAW	CTBLS	10//99-12//99
	Delaware	S	17.42 MW	15.51 AW	32250 AAW	DEBLS	10//99-12//99
	Washington PMSA, DC-MD-VA-WV	S	20.68 MW	19.12 AW	43010 AAW	DCBLS	10//99-12//99
	Florida	S	19.95 MW	20.17 AW	41950 AAW	FLBLS	10//99-12//99
	Melbourne-Titusville-Palm Bay MSA, FL	S	19.78 MW	19.55 AW	41150 AAW	FLBLS	10//99-12//99
	Miami PMSA, FL	S	21.07 MW	22.38 AW	43830 AAW	FLBLS	10//99-12//99
	Orlando MSA, FL	S	19.19 MW	19.21 AW	39910 AAW	FLBLS	10//99-12//99
	Pensacola MSA, FL	S	18.32 MW	18.85 AW	38110 AAW	FLBLS	10//99-12//99
	Georgia	S	21.27 MW	21.33 AW	44360 AAW	GABLS	10//99-12//99
	Atlanta MSA, GA	S	23.92 MW	24.23 AW	49760 AAW	GABLS	10//99-12//99
	Illinois	S	23.84 MW	22.90 AW	47640 AAW	ILBLS	10//99-12//99
	Chicago PMSA, IL	S	22.99 MW	23.91 AW	47820 AAW	ILBLS	10//99-12//99
	Indiana	S	16.79 MW	16.87 AW	35090 AAW	INBLS	10//99-12//99
	Indianapolis MSA, IN	S	16.62 MW	16.41 AW	34560 AAW	INBLS	10//99-12//99
	Iowa	S	18.89 MW	18.91 AW	39330 AAW	IABLS	10//99-12//99
	Kansas	S	16.4 MW	16.74 AW	34830 AAW	KSBLS	10//99-12//99
	Wichita MSA, KS	S	16.76 MW	16.43 AW	34860 AAW	KSBLS	10//99-12//99
	Kentucky	S	17.61 MW	18.44 AW	38350 AAW	KYBLS	10//99-12//99
	Louisville MSA, KY-IN	S	16.97 MW	16.17 AW	35290 AAW	KYBLS	10//99-12//99
	Louisiana	S	19.06 MW	18.61 AW	38700 AAW	LABLS	10//99-12//99
	Maryland	S	18.22 MW	18.82 AW	39140 AAW	MDBLS	10//99-12//99
	Baltimore PMSA, MD	S	20.64 MW	20.20 AW	42930 AAW	MDBLS	10//99-12//99
	Massachusetts	S	15.52 MW	15.97 AW	33210 AAW	MABLS	10//99-12//99
	Michigan	S	18.48 MW	18.40 AW	38260 AAW	MIBLS	10//99-12//99
	Minnesota	S	22.28 MW	19.88 AW	41340 AAW	MNBLS	10//99-12//99
	Minneapolis-St. Paul MSA, MN-WI	S	22.69 MW	23.49 AW	47200 AAW	MNBLS	10//99-12//99
	Mississippi	S	18.24 MW	18.67 AW	38820 AAW	MSBLS	10//99-12//99
	Biloxi-Gulfport-Pascagoula MSA, MS	S	21.81 MW	23.34 AW	45360 AAW	MSBLS	10//99-12//99
	Nevada	S	29.1 MW	27.44 AW	57080 AAW	NVBLS	10//99-12//99
	Las Vegas MSA, NV-AZ	S	29.78 MW	30.58 AW	61940 AAW	NVBLS	10//99-12//99
	New Jersey	S	19.91 MW	21.29 AW	44270 AAW	NJBLS	10//99-12//99
	Newark PMSA, NJ	S	17.53 MW	17.34 AW	36460 AAW	NJBLS	10//99-12//99
	New Mexico	S	12.87 MW	13.37 AW	27800 AAW	NMBLS	10//99-12//99
	Albuquerque MSA, NM	S	13.34 MW	12.83 AW	27740 AAW	NMBLS	10//99-12//99
	New York	S	17.03 MW	17.77 AW	36950 AAW	NYBLS	10//99-12//99
	New York PMSA, NY	S	18.18 MW	17.29 AW	37820 AAW	NYBLS	10//99-12//99
	North Carolina	S	18.63 MW	18.43 AW	38330 AAW	NCBLS	10//99-12//99
	Charlotte-Gastonia-Rock Hill MSA, NC-SC	S	19.74 MW	19.52 AW	41070 AAW	NCBLS	10//99-12//99

AAW Average annual wage	AOH Average offered, high	ASH Average starting, high	**H** Hourly	**M** Monthly	**S** Special: hourly and annual
AE Average entry wage	AOL Average offered, low	ASL Average starting, low	**HI** Highest wage paid	MTC Median total compensation	TQ Third quartile wage
AEX Average experienced wage	APH Average pay, high range	AW Average wage paid	**HR** High end range	MW Median wage paid	**W** Weekly
AO Average offered	APL Average pay, low range	FQ First quartile wage	**LR** Low end range	SQ Second quartile wage	**Y** Yearly

Occupation/Type/Industry	Location	Per	Low	Mid	High	Source	Date
Avionics Technician	Raleigh-Durham-Chapel Hill MSA, NC	S	18.83 MW	14.43 AW	39160 AAW	NCBLS	10//99-12//99
	Ohio	S	18.78 MW	18.58 AW	38660 AAW	OHBLS	10//99-12//99
	Dayton-Springfield MSA, OH	S	19.00 MW	19.06 AW	39530 AAW	OHBLS	10//99-12//99
	Oregon	S	15.25 MW	15.10 AW	31410 AAW	ORBLS	10//99-12//99
	Pennsylvania	S	17.45 MW	17.83 AW	37090 AAW	PABLS	10//99-12//99
	Philadelphia PMSA, PA-NJ	S	17.06 MW	17.72 AW	35480 AAW	PABLS	10//99-12//99
	South Carolina	S	18.92 MW	18.85 AW	39200 AAW	SCBLS	10//99-12//99
	Charleston-North Charleston MSA, SC	S	21.28 MW	20.03 AW	44260 AAW	SCBLS	10//99-12//99
	Columbia MSA, SC	S	17.47 MW	17.99 AW	36330 AAW	SCBLS	10//99-12//99
	Greenville-Spartanburg-Anderson MSA, SC	S	17.48 MW	18.41 AW	36360 AAW	SCBLS	10//99-12//99
	Tennessee	S	18.63 MW	18.24 AW	37940 AAW	TNBLS	10//99-12//99
	Memphis MSA, TN-AR-MS	S	13.85 MW	13.48 AW	28810 AAW	MSBLS	10//99-12//99
	Nashville MSA, TN	S	22.42 MW	23.32 AW	46640 AAW	TNBLS	10//99-12//99
	Texas	S	19.22 MW	19.14 AW	39810 AAW	TXBLS	10//99-12//99
	Dallas PMSA, TX	S	18.96 MW	18.97 AW	39430 AAW	TXBLS	10//99-12//99
	Fort Worth-Arlington PMSA, TX	S	22.54 MW	23.25 AW	46880 AAW	TXBLS	10//99-12//99
	Houston PMSA, TX	S	15.35 MW	13.34 AW	31920 AAW	TXBLS	10//99-12//99
	Virginia	S	15.7 MW	16.24 AW	33770 AAW	VABLS	10//99-12//99
	Norfolk-Virginia Beach-Newport News MSA, VA-NC	S	16.02 MW	15.57 AW	33330 AAW	VABLS	10//99-12//99
	Washington	S	24.52 MW	24.10 AW	50120 AAW	WABLS	10//99-12//99
	Seattle-Bellevue-Everett PMSA, WA	S	24.14 MW	24.56 AW	50220 AAW	WABLS	10//99-12//99
	Wisconsin	S	16.2 MW	16.71 AW	34760 AAW	WIBLS	10//99-12//99
Baggage Porter and Bellhop	Alabama	S	6.08 MW	6.16 AW	12810 AAW	ALBLS	10//99-12//99
	Birmingham MSA, AL	S	6.52 MW	6.41 AW	13560 AAW	ALBLS	10//99-12//99
	Huntsville MSA, AL	S	5.79 MW	5.97 AW	12050 AAW	ALBLS	10//99-12//99
	Mobile MSA, AL	S	5.99 MW	6.01 AW	12450 AAW	ALBLS	10//99-12//99
	Alaska	S	8.4 MW	10.66 AW	22170 AAW	AKBLS	10//99-12//99
	Anchorage MSA, AK	S	11.41 MW	8.77 AW	23720 AAW	AKBLS	10//99-12//99
	Arizona	S	6.33 MW	6.68 AW	13900 AAW	AZBLS	10//99-12//99
	Flagstaff MSA, AZ-UT	S	7.14 MW	6.42 AW	14860 AAW	AZBLS	10//99-12//99
	Phoenix-Mesa MSA, AZ	S	6.84 MW	6.45 AW	14230 AAW	AZBLS	10//99-12//99
	Tucson MSA, AZ	S	6.33 MW	6.11 AW	13160 AAW	AZBLS	10//99-12//99
	Arkansas	S	5.97 MW	6.07 AW	12630 AAW	ARBLS	10//99-12//99
	Little Rock-North Little Rock MSA, AR	S	6.19 MW	6.10 AW	12860 AAW	ARBLS	10//99-12//99
	California	S	6.73 MW	7.73 AW	16080 AAW	CABLS	10//99-12//99
	Los Angeles-Long Beach PMSA, CA	S	7.56 MW	6.68 AW	15730 AAW	CABLS	10//99-12//99
	Oakland PMSA, CA	S	7.03 MW	6.70 AW	14620 AAW	CABLS	10//99-12//99
	Orange County PMSA, CA	S	6.99 MW	6.57 AW	14540 AAW	CABLS	10//99-12//99
	Riverside-San Bernardino PMSA, CA	S	6.71 MW	6.45 AW	13960 AAW	CABLS	10//99-12//99
	Sacramento PMSA, CA	S	7.41 MW	6.79 AW	15410 AAW	CABLS	10//99-12//99
	Salinas MSA, CA	S	7.10 MW	6.73 AW	14760 AAW	CABLS	10//99-12//99
	San Diego MSA, CA	S	6.80 MW	6.45 AW	14140 AAW	CABLS	10//99-12//99
	San Francisco PMSA, CA	S	9.72 MW	8.05 AW	20220 AAW	CABLS	10//99-12//99
	San Jose PMSA, CA	S	7.88 MW	7.51 AW	16390 AAW	CABLS	10//99-12//99
	Santa Barbara-Santa Maria-Lompoc MSA, CA	S	6.35 MW	6.09 AW	13210 AAW	CABLS	10//99-12//99
	Vallejo-Fairfield-Napa PMSA, CA	S	7.21 MW	6.58 AW	14990 AAW	CABLS	10//99-12//99
	Ventura PMSA, CA	S	7.27 MW	6.67 AW	15110 AAW	CABLS	10//99-12//99
	Colorado	S	6.64 MW	7.65 AW	15910 AAW	COBLS	10//99-12//99
	Boulder-Longmont PMSA, CO	S	6.39 MW	6.36 AW	13290 AAW	COBLS	10//99-12//99
	Colorado Springs MSA, CO	S	6.08 MW	6.14 AW	12640 AAW	COBLS	10//99-12//99
	Denver PMSA, CO	S	8.13 MW	7.24 AW	16910 AAW	COBLS	10//99-12//99
	Connecticut	S	8.22 MW	8.67 AW	18020 AAW	CTBLS	10//99-12//99
	Hartford MSA, CT	S	7.68 MW	7.31 AW	15970 AAW	CTBLS	10//99-12//99
	New London-Norwich MSA, CT-RI	S	7.22 MW	6.68 AW	15020 AAW	CTBLS	10//99-12//99
	Stamford-Norwalk PMSA, CT	S	9.70 MW	10.54 AW	20180 AAW	CTBLS	10//99-12//99
	District of Columbia	S	11.16 MW	10.59 AW	22020 AAW	DCBLS	10//99-12//99
	Washington PMSA, DC-MD-VA-WV	S	9.82 MW	8.87 AW	20430 AAW	DCBLS	10//99-12//99
	Florida	S	6.55 MW	7.65 AW	15900 AAW	FLBLS	10//99-12//99

AAW Average annual wage	**AOH** Average offered, high	**ASH** Average starting, high	**H** Hourly	**M** Monthly	**S** Special: hourly and annual
AE Average entry wage	**AOL** Average offered, low	**ASL** Average starting, low	**HI** Highest wage paid	**MTC** Median total compensation	**TQ** Third quartile wage
AEX Average experienced wage	**APH** Average pay, high range	**AW** Average wage paid	**HR** High end range	**MW** Median wage paid	**W** Weekly
AO Average offered	**APL** Average pay, low range	**FQ** First quartile wage	**LR** Low end range	**SQ** Second quartile wage	**Y** Yearly

Occupation/Type/Industry	Location	Per	Low	Mid	High	Source	Date
Baggage Porter and Bellhop	Daytona Beach MSA, FL	S	6.16 MW	5.98 AW	12810 AAW	FLBLS	10//99-12//99
	Fort Lauderdale PMSA, FL	S	6.32 MW	6.30 AW	13140 AAW	FLBLS	10//99-12//99
	Fort Myers-Cape Coral MSA, FL	S	6.15 MW	6.06 AW	12780 AAW	FLBLS	10//99-12//99
	Fort Pierce-Port St. Lucie MSA, FL	S	6.32 MW	6.11 AW	13160 AAW	FLBLS	10//99-12//99
	Jacksonville MSA, FL	S	6.72 MW	6.58 AW	13980 AAW	FLBLS	10//99-12//99
	Miami PMSA, FL	S	8.48 MW	7.57 AW	17630 AAW	FLBLS	10//99-12//99
	Naples MSA, FL	S	6.87 MW	6.68 AW	14290 AAW	FLBLS	10//99-12//99
	Orlando MSA, FL	S	7.49 MW	6.41 AW	15570 AAW	FLBLS	10//99-12//99
	Sarasota-Bradenton MSA, FL	S	6.53 MW	6.30 AW	13580 AAW	FLBLS	10//99-12//99
	Tampa-St. Petersburg-Clearwater MSA, FL	S	7.22 MW	5.94 AW	15010 AAW	FLBLS	10//99-12//99
	West Palm Beach-Boca Raton MSA, FL	S	7.29 MW	7.17 AW	15150 AAW	FLBLS	10//99-12//99
	Atlanta MSA, GA	S	8.77 MW	7.17 AW	18240 AAW	GABLS	10//99-12//99
	Hawaii	S	6.2 MW	6.81 AW	14170 AAW	HIBLS	10//99-12//99
	Honolulu MSA, HI	S	6.69 MW	6.19 AW	13910 AAW	HIBLS	10//99-12//99
	Idaho	S	6.39 MW	6.84 AW	14230 AAW	IDBLS	10//99-12//99
	Illinois	S	6.53 MW	7.39 AW	15380 AAW	ILBLS	10//99-12//99
	Chicago PMSA, IL	S	6.86 MW	6.48 AW	14260 AAW	ILBLS	10//99-12//99
	Peoria-Pekin MSA, IL	S	6.14 MW	6.04 AW	12770 AAW	ILBLS	10//99-12//99
	Springfield MSA, IL	S	5.94 MW	5.98 AW	12360 AAW	ILBLS	10//99-12//99
	Indiana	S	6.62 MW	8.17 AW	16990 AAW	INBLS	10//99-12//99
	Indianapolis MSA, IN	S	6.35 MW	6.25 AW	13210 AAW	INBLS	10//99-12//99
	South Bend MSA, IN	S	5.98 MW	6.10 AW	12430 AAW	INBLS	10//99-12//99
	Iowa	S	7.58 MW	9.94 AW	20670 AAW	IABLS	10//99-12//99
	Kansas	S	6.84 MW	8.59 AW	17870 AAW	KSBLS	10//99-12//99
	Wichita MSA, KS	S	6.96 MW	6.15 AW	14470 AAW	KSBLS	10//99-12//99
	Kentucky	S	6.47 MW	6.65 AW	13830 AAW	KYBLS	10//99-12//99
	Lexington MSA, KY	S	6.42 MW	6.14 AW	13350 AAW	KYBLS	10//99-12//99
	Louisville MSA, KY-IN	S	6.75 MW	6.51 AW	14030 AAW	KYBLS	10//99-12//99
	Louisiana	S	6.33 MW	6.95 AW	14450 AAW	LABLS	10//99-12//99
	New Orleans MSA, LA	S	6.98 MW	6.38 AW	14520 AAW	LABLS	10//99-12//99
	Shreveport-Bossier City MSA, LA	S	6.38 MW	6.26 AW	13280 AAW	LABLS	10//99-12//99
	Maine	S	7.92 MW	8.37 AW	17400 AAW	MEBLS	10//99-12//99
	Portland MSA, ME	S	8.36 MW	8.24 AW	17400 AAW	MEBLS	10//99-12//99
	Maryland	S	7.13 MW	8.94 AW	18600 AAW	MDBLS	10//99-12//99
	Baltimore PMSA, MD	S	8.59 MW	7.68 AW	17860 AAW	MDBLS	10//99-12//99
	Massachusetts	S	7.29 MW	9.33 AW	19410 AAW	MABLS	10//99-12//99
	Barnstable-Yarmouth MSA, MA	S	7.14 MW	6.48 AW	14860 AAW	MABLS	10//99-12//99
	Boston PMSA, MA-NH	S	9.66 MW	7.47 AW	20100 AAW	MABLS	10//99-12//99
	Pittsfield MSA, MA	S	7.85 MW	6.98 AW	16320 AAW	MABLS	10//99-12//99
	Minnesota	S	6.19 MW	6.78 AW	14100 AAW	MNBLS	10//99-12//99
	Minneapolis-St. Paul MSA, MN-WI	S	6.72 MW	6.10 AW	13980 AAW	MNBLS	10//99-12//99
	Mississippi	S	6.25 MW	6.32 AW	13140 AAW	MSBLS	10//99-12//99
	Biloxi-Gulfport-Pascagoula MSA, MS	S	6.25 MW	6.10 AW	13010 AAW	MSBLS	10//99-12//99
	Missouri	S	7.11 MW	7.81 AW	16250 AAW	MOBLS	10//99-12//99
	St. Louis MSA, MO-IL	S	6.91 MW	6.73 AW	14380 AAW	MOBLS	10//99-12//99
	Montana	S	8.06 MW	10.26 AW	21350 AAW	MTBLS	10//99-12//99
	Billings MSA, MT	S	6.08 MW	5.88 AW	12640 AAW	MTBLS	10//99-12//99
	Nebraska	S	6.7 MW	6.88 AW	14320 AAW	NEBLS	10//99-12//99
	Lincoln MSA, NE	S	7.04 MW	6.78 AW	14650 AAW	NEBLS	10//99-12//99
	Omaha MSA, NE-IA	S	6.57 MW	6.63 AW	13670 AAW	NEBLS	10//99-12//99
	Nevada	S	8.38 MW	8.25 AW	17170 AAW	NVBLS	10//99-12//99
	Las Vegas MSA, NV-AZ	S	8.47 MW	8.63 AW	17610 AAW	NVBLS	10//99-12//99
	Reno MSA, NV	S	6.45 MW	6.26 AW	13420 AAW	NVBLS	10//99-12//99
	New Hampshire	S	6.54 MW	6.72 AW	13970 AAW	NHBLS	10//99-12//99
	New Jersey	S	7.93 MW	9.19 AW	19120 AAW	NJBLS	10//99-12//99
	Atlantic-Cape May PMSA, NJ	S	6.89 MW	6.93 AW	14340 AAW	NJBLS	10//99-12//99
	Bergen-Passaic PMSA, NJ	S	11.54 MW	10.81 AW	24010 AAW	NJBLS	10//99-12//99
	Middlesex-Somerset-Hunterdon PMSA, NJ	S	9.18 MW	8.36 AW	19100 AAW	NJBLS	10//99-12//99
	Newark PMSA, NJ	S	11.18 MW	9.81 AW	23260 AAW	NJBLS	10//99-12//99
	New Mexico	S	6.03 MW	6.19 AW	12870 AAW	NMBLS	10//99-12//99
	Albuquerque MSA, NM	S	6.19 MW	6.11 AW	12870 AAW	NMBLS	10//99-12//99
	Santa Fe MSA, NM	S	6.21 MW	6.02 AW	12920 AAW	NMBLS	10//99-12//99
	New York	S	9.08 MW	10.39 AW	21620 AAW	NYBLS	10//99-12//99

AAW Average annual wage	AOH Average offered, high	ASH Average starting, high	H Hourly	M Monthly	S Special: hourly and annual
AE Average entry wage	AOL Average offered, low	ASL Average starting, low	HI Highest wage paid	MTC Median total compensation	TQ Third quartile wage
AEX Average experienced wage	APH Average pay, high range	AW Average wage paid	HR High end range	MW Median wage paid	W Weekly
AO Average offered	APL Average pay, low range	FQ First quartile wage	LR Low end range	SQ Second quartile wage	Y Yearly

Occupation/Type/Industry	Location	Per	Low	Mid	High	Source	Date
Baggage Porter and Bellhop	Albany-Schenectady-Troy MSA, NY	S	7.28 MW	6.95 AW	15140 AAW	NYBLS	10//99-12//99
	Buffalo-Niagara Falls MSA, NY	S	9.67 MW	6.94 AW	20120 AAW	NYBLS	10//99-12//99
	Nassau-Suffolk PMSA, NY	S	7.61 MW	6.49 AW	15820 AAW	NYBLS	10//99-12//99
	New York PMSA, NY	S	10.97 MW	9.71 AW	22820 AAW	NYBLS	10//99-12//99
	Rochester MSA, NY	S	6.16 MW	6.12 AW	12800 AAW	NYBLS	10//99-12//99
	Syracuse MSA, NY	S	5.82 MW	5.88 AW	12100 AAW	NYBLS	10//99-12//99
	North Carolina	S	6.27 MW	7.17 AW	14920 AAW	NCBLS	10//99-12//99
	Asheville MSA, NC	S	6.21 MW	6.14 AW	12920 AAW	NCBLS	10//99-12//99
	Charlotte-Gastonia-Rock Hill MSA, NC-SC	S	6.16 MW	6.02 AW	12800 AAW	NCBLS	10//99-12//99
	Greensboro--Winston-Salem--High Point MSA, NC	S	6.82 MW	6.16 AW	14180 AAW	NCBLS	10//99-12//99
	North Dakota	S	6.44 MW	7.93 AW	16500 AAW	NDBLS	10//99-12//99
	Ohio	S	6.5 MW	7.07 AW	14720 AAW	OHBLS	10//99-12//99
	Cincinnati PMSA, OH-KY-IN	S	6.45 MW	6.34 AW	13420 AAW	OHBLS	10//99-12//99
	Cleveland-Lorain-Elyria PMSA, OH	S	7.26 MW	7.11 AW	15090 AAW	OHBLS	10//99-12//99
	Columbus MSA, OH	S	8.10 MW	7.15 AW	16840 AAW	OHBLS	10//99-12//99
	Oklahoma	S	6.17 MW	6.29 AW	13090 AAW	OKBLS	10//99-12//99
	Tulsa MSA, OK	S	6.19 MW	6.06 AW	12870 AAW	OKBLS	10//99-12//99
	Oregon	S	6.87 MW	8.58 AW	17850 AAW	ORBLS	10//99-12//99
	Portland-Vancouver PMSA, OR-WA	S	7.34 MW	6.65 AW	15260 AAW	ORBLS	10//99-12//99
	Pennsylvania	S	6.37 MW	7.62 AW	15850 AAW	PABLS	10//99-12//99
	Allentown-Bethlehem-Easton MSA, PA	S	5.96 MW	6.02 AW	12400 AAW	PABLS	10//99-12//99
	Harrisburg-Lebanon-Carlisle MSA, PA	S	5.97 MW	6.03 AW	12430 AAW	PABLS	10//99-12//99
	Philadelphia PMSA, PA-NJ	S	7.48 MW	6.48 AW	15560 AAW	PABLS	10//99-12//99
	Pittsburgh MSA, PA	S	6.12 MW	6.04 AW	12730 AAW	PABLS	10//99-12//99
	Rhode Island	S	6.31 MW	7.59 AW	15790 AAW	RIBLS	10//99-12//99
	South Carolina	S	6.27 MW	6.51 AW	13540 AAW	SCBLS	10//99-12//99
	Charleston-North Charleston MSA, SC	S	6.68 MW	6.31 AW	13890 AAW	SCBLS	10//99-12//99
	Greenville-Spartanburg-Anderson MSA, SC	S	6.18 MW	6.22 AW	12860 AAW	SCBLS	10//99-12//99
	Myrtle Beach MSA, SC	S	6.15 MW	6.12 AW	12780 AAW	SCBLS	10//99-12//99
	South Dakota	S	6.11 MW	6.36 AW	13230 AAW	SDBLS	10//99-12//99
	Tennessee	S	6.3 MW	8.13 AW	16910 AAW	TNBLS	10//99-12//99
	Knoxville MSA, TN	S	6.02 MW	6.10 AW	12520 AAW	TNBLS	10//99-12//99
	Memphis MSA, TN-AR-MS	S	6.55 MW	6.07 AW	13630 AAW	MSBLS	10//99-12//99
	Texas	S	6.49 MW	6.94 AW	14430 AAW	TXBLS	10//99-12//99
	Austin-San Marcos MSA, TX	S	6.37 MW	6.22 AW	13260 AAW	TXBLS	10//99-12//99
	Brownsville-Harlingen-San Benito MSA, TX	S	6.29 MW	6.14 AW	13080 AAW	TXBLS	10//99-12//99
	Dallas PMSA, TX	S	6.91 MW	6.64 AW	14370 AAW	TXBLS	10//99-12//99
	Fort Worth-Arlington PMSA, TX	S	9.28 MW	7.21 AW	19300 AAW	TXBLS	10//99-12//99
	Galveston-Texas City PMSA, TX	S	6.01 MW	6.11 AW	12500 AAW	TXBLS	10//99-12//99
	Houston PMSA, TX	S	6.35 MW	6.11 AW	13210 AAW	TXBLS	10//99-12//99
	San Antonio MSA, TX	S	7.03 MW	7.09 AW	14620 AAW	TXBLS	10//99-12//99
	Utah	S	6.64 MW	7.33 AW	15240 AAW	UTBLS	10//99-12//99
	Vermont	S	6.36 MW	6.62 AW	13760 AAW	VTBLS	10//99-12//99
	Burlington MSA, VT	S	6.96 MW	6.68 AW	14470 AAW	VTBLS	10//99-12//99
	Virginia	S	6.96 MW	9.10 AW	18930 AAW	VABLS	10//99-12//99
	Charlottesville MSA, VA	S	6.77 MW	6.57 AW	14080 AAW	VABLS	10//99-12//99
	Norfolk-Virginia Beach-Newport News MSA, VA-NC	S	6.94 MW	6.22 AW	14440 AAW	VABLS	10//99-12//99
	Richmond-Petersburg MSA, VA	S	8.34 MW	6.40 AW	17360 AAW	VABLS	10//99-12//99
	Roanoke MSA, VA	S	6.10 MW	5.96 AW	12690 AAW	VABLS	10//99-12//99
	Washington	S	6.52 MW	7.32 AW	15230 AAW	WABLS	10//99-12//99
	Seattle-Bellevue-Everett PMSA, WA	S	7.49 MW	6.54 AW	15580 AAW	WABLS	10//99-12//99
	Spokane MSA, WA	S	6.61 MW	6.42 AW	13760 AAW	WABLS	10//99-12//99
	Tacoma PMSA, WA	S	6.35 MW	6.13 AW	13210 AAW	WABLS	10//99-12//99
	West Virginia	S	6.64 MW	6.77 AW	14070 AAW	WVBLS	10//99-12//99
	Wisconsin	S	7.08 MW	9.25 AW	19240 AAW	WIBLS	10//99-12//99

AAW	Average annual wage	AOH	Average offered, high	ASH	Average starting, high	H	Hourly	M	Monthly	S	Special: hourly and annual
AE	Average entry wage	AOL	Average offered, low	ASL	Average starting, low	HI	Highest wage paid	MTC	Median total compensation	TQ	Third quartile wage
AEX	Average experienced wage	APH	Average pay, high range	AW	Average wage paid	HR	High end range	MW	Median wage paid	W	Weekly
AO	Average offered	APL	Average pay, low range	FQ	First quartile wage	LR	Low end range	SQ	Second quartile wage	Y	Yearly

Occupation/Type/Industry	Location	Per	Low	Mid	High	Source	Date
Baggage Porter and Bellhop	Milwaukee-Waukesha PMSA, WI	S	10.88 MW	7.99 AW	22630 AAW	WIBLS	10//99-12//99
	Wyoming	S	6.37 MW	6.94 AW	14440 AAW	WYBLS	10//99-12//99
	Puerto Rico	S	6.25 MW	6.99 AW	14550 AAW	PRBLS	10//99-12//99
	San Juan-Bayamon PMSA, PR	S	6.35 MW	6.14 AW	13220 AAW	PRBLS	10//99-12//99
	Virgin Islands	S	6.08 MW	6.02 AW	12520 AAW	VIBLS	10//99-12//99
	Guam	S	6.38 MW	6.48 AW	13470 AAW	GUBLS	10//99-12//99
Bailiff	Alabama	S	12.04 MW	11.74 AW	24420 AAW	ALBLS	10//99-12//99
	Birmingham MSA, AL	S	12.46 MW	12.75 AW	25920 AAW	ALBLS	10//99-12//99
	Arizona	S	11.22 MW	12.42 AW	25830 AAW	AZBLS	10//99-12//99
	Arkansas	S	9.84 MW	10.67 AW	22190 AAW	ARBLS	10//99-12//99
	Fayetteville-Springdale-Rogers MSA, AR	S	10.71 MW	10.50 AW	22270 AAW	ARBLS	10//99-12//99
	California	S	13.1 MW	13.73 AW	28560 AAW	CABLS	10//99-12//99
	Connecticut	S	20.72 MW	20.90 AW	43480 AAW	CTBLS	10//99-12//99
	Florida	S	16.02 MW	15.91 AW	33090 AAW	FLBLS	10//99-12//99
	Orlando MSA, FL	S	13.32 MW	11.49 AW	27700 AAW	FLBLS	10//99-12//99
	Georgia	S	7.67 MW	7.80 AW	16220 AAW	GABLS	10//99-12//99
	Atlanta MSA, GA	S	8.45 MW	8.37 AW	17590 AAW	GABLS	10//99-12//99
	Idaho	S	10.95 MW	11.13 AW	23140 AAW	IDBLS	10//99-12//99
	Illinois	S	12.3 MW	12.29 AW	25560 AAW	ILBLS	10//99-12//99
	Chicago PMSA, IL	S	13.95 MW	14.62 AW	29020 AAW	ILBLS	10//99-12//99
	Indiana	S	10.2 MW	10.10 AW	21010 AAW	INBLS	10//99-12//99
	Fort Wayne MSA, IN	S	10.78 MW	10.38 AW	22430 AAW	INBLS	10//99-12//99
	Indianapolis MSA, IN	S	10.94 MW	11.65 AW	22760 AAW	INBLS	10//99-12//99
	Lafayette MSA, IN	S	10.92 MW	11.16 AW	22710 AAW	INBLS	10//99-12//99
	Kansas	S	6.71 MW	8.36 AW	17380 AAW	KSBLS	10//99-12//99
	Kentucky	S	8.42 MW	9.74 AW	20260 AAW	KYBLS	10//99-12//99
	Louisiana	S	6.92 MW	9.15 AW	19030 AAW	LABLS	10//99-12//99
	Maine	S	9.85 MW	10.48 AW	21790 AAW	MEBLS	10//99-12//99
	Massachusetts	S	19.3 MW	19.36 AW	40260 AAW	MABLS	10//99-12//99
	Michigan	S	13.34 MW	14.43 AW	30000 AAW	MIBLS	10//99-12//99
	Detroit PMSA, MI	S	12.74 MW	12.54 AW	26490 AAW	MIBLS	10//99-12//99
	Minnesota	S	10.82 MW	14.75 AW	30690 AAW	MNBLS	10//99-12//99
	Mississippi	S	8.66 MW	8.89 AW	18480 AAW	MSBLS	10//99-12//99
	Missouri	S	12.71 MW	13.37 AW	27810 AAW	MOBLS	10//99-12//99
	St. Louis MSA, MO-IL	S	13.56 MW	13.23 AW	28200 AAW	MOBLS	10//99-12//99
	Montana	S	6.59 MW	7.75 AW	16110 AAW	MTBLS	10//99-12//99
	Nebraska	S	15.04 MW	15.18 AW	31570 AAW	NEBLS	10//99-12//99
	New Hampshire	S	9.3 MW	9.09 AW	18910 AAW	NHBLS	10//99-12//99
	New Jersey	S	10.97 MW	11.03 AW	22940 AAW	NJBLS	10//99-12//99
	New Mexico	S	9.63 MW	9.54 AW	19840 AAW	NMBLS	10//99-12//99
	New York	S	18.6 MW	18.23 AW	37910 AAW	NYBLS	10//99-12//99
	Buffalo-Niagara Falls MSA, NY	S	11.48 MW	10.93 AW	23890 AAW	NYBLS	10//99-12//99
	New York PMSA, NY	S	18.88 MW	18.83 AW	39280 AAW	NYBLS	10//99-12//99
	Rochester MSA, NY	S	9.85 MW	10.03 AW	20490 AAW	NYBLS	10//99-12//99
	North Carolina	S	10.95 MW	10.72 AW	22300 AAW	NCBLS	10//99-12//99
	Ohio	S	14.21 MW	14.67 AW	30510 AAW	OHBLS	10//99-12//99
	Cleveland-Lorain-Elyria PMSA, OH	S	15.47 MW	14.60 AW	32170 AAW	OHBLS	10//99-12//99
	Dayton-Springfield MSA, OH	S	16.27 MW	15.93 AW	33850 AAW	OHBLS	10//99-12//99
	Toledo MSA, OH	S	11.87 MW	11.64 AW	24680 AAW	OHBLS	10//99-12//99
	Youngstown-Warren MSA, OH	S	14.44 MW	13.75 AW	30030 AAW	OHBLS	10//99-12//99
	Oklahoma	S	13.15 MW	12.59 AW	26190 AAW	OKBLS	10//99-12//99
	Pennsylvania	S	9.3 MW	9.90 AW	20600 AAW	PABLS	10//99-12//99
	Allentown-Bethlehem-Easton MSA, PA	S	8.56 MW	8.65 AW	17810 AAW	PABLS	10//99-12//99
	Philadelphia PMSA, PA-NJ	S	10.99 MW	9.93 AW	22870 AAW	PABLS	10//99-12//99
	South Carolina	S	7.07 MW	7.63 AW	15870 AAW	SCBLS	10//99-12//99
	Charleston-North Charleston MSA, SC	S	7.96 MW	7.84 AW	16560 AAW	SCBLS	10//99-12//99
	Tennessee	S	9.28 MW	10.06 AW	20930 AAW	TNBLS	10//99-12//99
	Texas	S	12.39 MW	12.96 AW	26950 AAW	TXBLS	10//99-12//99
	Austin-San Marcos MSA, TX	S	10.83 MW	10.64 AW	22530 AAW	TXBLS	10//99-12//99
	Dallas PMSA, TX	S	17.60 MW	18.01 AW	36610 AAW	TXBLS	10//99-12//99
	Fort Worth-Arlington PMSA, TX	S	14.23 MW	14.87 AW	29600 AAW	TXBLS	10//99-12//99
	Houston PMSA, TX	S	15.68 MW	15.83 AW	32610 AAW	TXBLS	10//99-12//99
	Utah	S	12.04 MW	11.57 AW	24060 AAW	UTBLS	10//99-12//99
	Virginia	S	18.46 MW	18.06 AW	37570 AAW	VABLS	10//99-12//99

AAW	Average annual wage	AOH	Average offered, high	ASH	Average starting, high	H	Hourly	M	Monthly	S	Special: hourly and annual
AE	Average entry wage	AOL	Average offered, low	ASL	Average starting, low	HI	Highest wage paid	MTC	Median total compensation	TQ	Third quartile wage
AEX	Average experienced wage	APH	Average pay, high range	AW	Average wage paid	HR	High end range	MW	Median wage paid	W	Weekly
AO	Average offered	APL	Average pay, low range	FQ	First quartile wage	LR	Low end range	SQ	Second quartile wage	Y	Yearly

Occupation/Type/Industry	Location	Per	Low	Mid	High	Source	Date
Bailiff	Norfolk-Virginia Beach-Newport News MSA, VA-NC	S	18.91 MW	19.18 AW	39330 AAW	VABLS	10//99-12//99
	Washington	S	15.41 MW	15.44 AW	32110 AAW	WABLS	10//99-12//99
	West Virginia	S	10.24 MW	10.85 AW	22570 AAW	WVBLS	10//99-12//99
	Wisconsin	S	20.84 MW	17.21 AW	35810 AAW	WIBLS	10//99-12//99
Baker	Alabama	S	8.58 MW	8.65 AW	18000 AAW	ALBLS	10//99-12//99
	Auburn-Opelika MSA, AL	S	10.07 MW	9.91 AW	20940 AAW	ALBLS	10//99-12//99
	Birmingham MSA, AL	S	8.89 MW	8.96 AW	18490 AAW	ALBLS	10//99-12//99
	Dothan MSA, AL	S	8.09 MW	7.73 AW	16820 AAW	ALBLS	10//99-12//99
	Gadsden MSA, AL	S	7.32 MW	6.96 AW	15230 AAW	ALBLS	10//99-12//99
	Huntsville MSA, AL	S	8.38 MW	7.94 AW	17440 AAW	ALBLS	10//99-12//99
	Mobile MSA, AL	S	8.77 MW	9.06 AW	18250 AAW	ALBLS	10//99-12//99
	Montgomery MSA, AL	S	8.33 MW	7.83 AW	17340 AAW	ALBLS	10//99-12//99
	Tuscaloosa MSA, AL	S	9.75 MW	10.61 AW	20290 AAW	ALBLS	10//99-12//99
	Alaska	S	11.62 MW	12.29 AW	25570 AAW	AKBLS	10//99-12//99
	Anchorage MSA, AK	S	13.57 MW	12.71 AW	28220 AAW	AKBLS	10//99-12//99
	Arizona	S	9.5 MW	9.71 AW	20190 AAW	AZBLS	10//99-12//99
	Flagstaff MSA, AZ-UT	S	8.62 MW	8.31 AW	17930 AAW	AZBLS	10//99-12//99
	Phoenix-Mesa MSA, AZ	S	9.92 MW	9.75 AW	20630 AAW	AZBLS	10//99-12//99
	Tucson MSA, AZ	S	9.29 MW	8.84 AW	19330 AAW	AZBLS	10//99-12//99
	Yuma MSA, AZ	S	8.64 MW	8.62 AW	17970 AAW	AZBLS	10//99-12//99
	Arkansas	S	7.7 MW	8.05 AW	16750 AAW	ARBLS	10//99-12//99
	Fayetteville-Springdale-Rogers MSA, AR	S	8.77 MW	8.12 AW	18250 AAW	ARBLS	10//99-12//99
	Fort Smith MSA, AR-OK	S	8.79 MW	8.13 AW	18280 AAW	ARBLS	10//99-12//99
	Little Rock-North Little Rock MSA, AR	S	8.23 MW	7.95 AW	17110 AAW	ARBLS	10//99-12//99
	California	S	9.47 MW	10.22 AW	21250 AAW	CABLS	10//99-12//99
	Bakersfield MSA, CA	S	9.84 MW	8.76 AW	20470 AAW	CABLS	10//99-12//99
	Chico-Paradise MSA, CA	S	9.37 MW	8.41 AW	19490 AAW	CABLS	10//99-12//99
	Fresno MSA, CA	S	9.99 MW	8.01 AW	20770 AAW	CABLS	10//99-12//99
	Los Angeles-Long Beach PMSA, CA	S	9.61 MW	8.90 AW	19990 AAW	CABLS	10//99-12//99
	Merced MSA, CA	S	8.96 MW	7.22 AW	18650 AAW	CABLS	10//99-12//99
	Modesto MSA, CA	S	8.42 MW	7.44 AW	17520 AAW	CABLS	10//99-12//99
	Oakland PMSA, CA	S	11.17 MW	10.99 AW	23240 AAW	CABLS	10//99-12//99
	Orange County PMSA, CA	S	9.62 MW	8.81 AW	20010 AAW	CABLS	10//99-12//99
	Redding MSA, CA	S	10.40 MW	10.32 AW	21630 AAW	CABLS	10//99-12//99
	Riverside-San Bernardino PMSA, CA	S	9.90 MW	9.32 AW	20590 AAW	CABLS	10//99-12//99
	Sacramento PMSA, CA	S	11.94 MW	11.26 AW	24830 AAW	CABLS	10//99-12//99
	Salinas MSA, CA	S	11.16 MW	10.07 AW	23210 AAW	CABLS	10//99-12//99
	San Diego MSA, CA	S	9.74 MW	8.46 AW	20250 AAW	CABLS	10//99-12//99
	San Francisco PMSA, CA	S	10.60 MW	9.72 AW	22060 AAW	CABLS	10//99-12//99
	San Jose PMSA, CA	S	11.66 MW	10.84 AW	24240 AAW	CABLS	10//99-12//99
	San Luis Obispo-Atascadero-Paso Robles MSA, CA	S	8.81 MW	8.03 AW	18320 AAW	CABLS	10//99-12//99
	Santa Barbara-Santa Maria-Lompoc MSA, CA	S	9.52 MW	8.46 AW	19800 AAW	CABLS	10//99-12//99
	Santa Cruz-Watsonville PMSA, CA	S	9.85 MW	9.32 AW	20480 AAW	CABLS	10//99-12//99
	Santa Rosa PMSA, CA	S	11.42 MW	10.49 AW	23750 AAW	CABLS	10//99-12//99
	Stockton-Lodi MSA, CA	S	14.35 MW	14.95 AW	29850 AAW	CABLS	10//99-12//99
	Vallejo-Fairfield-Napa PMSA, CA	S	11.39 MW	11.04 AW	23700 AAW	CABLS	10//99-12//99
	Ventura PMSA, CA	S	9.96 MW	8.81 AW	20720 AAW	CABLS	10//99-12//99
	Visalia-Tulare-Porterville MSA, CA	S	9.15 MW	7.95 AW	19040 AAW	CABLS	10//99-12//99
	Yolo PMSA, CA	S	11.09 MW	10.95 AW	23070 AAW	CABLS	10//99-12//99
	Yuba City MSA, CA	S	7.87 MW	6.90 AW	16370 AAW	CABLS	10//99-12//99
	Colorado	S	10.97 MW	11.37 AW	23660 AAW	COBLS	10//99-12//99
	Boulder-Longmont PMSA, CO	S	10.14 MW	9.70 AW	21080 AAW	COBLS	10//99-12//99
	Colorado Springs MSA, CO	S	10.42 MW	10.21 AW	21670 AAW	COBLS	10//99-12//99
	Denver PMSA, CO	S	12.53 MW	11.77 AW	26050 AAW	COBLS	10//99-12//99
	Fort Collins-Loveland MSA, CO	S	9.10 MW	8.40 AW	18920 AAW	COBLS	10//99-12//99
	Grand Junction MSA, CO	S	11.72 MW	12.01 AW	24370 AAW	COBLS	10//99-12//99
	Greeley PMSA, CO	S	9.31 MW	8.77 AW	19360 AAW	COBLS	10//99-12//99
	Pueblo MSA, CO	S	8.76 MW	7.02 AW	18210 AAW	COBLS	10//99-12//99
	Connecticut	S	9.24 MW	9.94 AW	20680 AAW	CTBLS	10//99-12//99
	Bridgeport PMSA, CT	S	9.96 MW	9.81 AW	20730 AAW	CTBLS	10//99-12//99

AAW Average annual wage	AOH Average offered, high	ASH Average starting, high	H Hourly	M Monthly	S Special: hourly and annual
AE Average entry wage	AOL Average offered, low	ASL Average starting, low	HI Highest wage paid	MTC Median total compensation	TQ Third quartile wage
AEX Average experienced wage	APH Average pay, high range	AW Average wage paid	HR High end range	MW Median wage paid	W Weekly
AO Average offered	APL Average pay, low range	FQ First quartile wage	LR Low end range	SQ Second quartile wage	Y Yearly

Occupation/Type/Industry	Location	Per	Low	Mid	High	Source	Date
Baker	Danbury PMSA, CT	S	9.80 MW	8.66 AW	20370 AAW	CTBLS	10//99-12//99
	Hartford MSA, CT	S	9.40 MW	8.78 AW	19550 AAW	CTBLS	10//99-12//99
	New Haven-Meriden PMSA, CT	S	10.38 MW	8.93 AW	21590 AAW	CTBLS	10//99-12//99
	New London-Norwich MSA, CT-RI	S	9.86 MW	9.49 AW	20500 AAW	CTBLS	10//99-12//99
	Stamford-Norwalk PMSA, CT	S	11.97 MW	10.67 AW	24910 AAW	CTBLS	10//99-12//99
	Waterbury PMSA, CT	S	10.02 MW	9.71 AW	20840 AAW	CTBLS	10//99-12//99
	Delaware	S	8.1 MW	8.72 AW	18140 AAW	DEBLS	10//99-12//99
	Dover MSA, DE	S	7.68 MW	6.30 AW	15970 AAW	DEBLS	10//99-12//99
	Wilmington-Newark PMSA, DE-MD	S	8.97 MW	8.24 AW	18650 AAW	DEBLS	10//99-12//99
	District of Columbia	S	10.11 MW	10.90 AW	22670 AAW	DCBLS	10//99-12//99
	Washington PMSA, DC-MD-VA-WV	S	10.94 MW	10.32 AW	22740 AAW	DCBLS	10//99-12//99
	Florida	S	8.45 MW	8.95 AW	18620 AAW	FLBLS	10//99-12//99
	Daytona Beach MSA, FL	S	8.49 MW	8.37 AW	17650 AAW	FLBLS	10//99-12//99
	Fort Lauderdale PMSA, FL	S	8.76 MW	8.29 AW	18220 AAW	FLBLS	10//99-12//99
	Fort Myers-Cape Coral MSA, FL	S	9.39 MW	9.26 AW	19530 AAW	FLBLS	10//99-12//99
	Fort Pierce-Port St. Lucie MSA, FL	S	8.45 MW	8.00 AW	17570 AAW	FLBLS	10//99-12//99
	Fort Walton Beach MSA, FL	S	8.05 MW	7.34 AW	16740 AAW	FLBLS	10//99-12//99
	Gainesville MSA, FL	S	8.84 MW	8.36 AW	18390 AAW	FLBLS	10//99-12//99
	Jacksonville MSA, FL	S	9.31 MW	9.30 AW	19360 AAW	FLBLS	10//99-12//99
	Lakeland-Winter Haven MSA, FL	S	8.58 MW	8.21 AW	17840 AAW	FLBLS	10//99-12//99
	Melbourne-Titusville-Palm Bay MSA, FL	S	8.00 MW	7.67 AW	16640 AAW	FLBLS	10//99-12//99
	Miami PMSA, FL	S	8.83 MW	8.40 AW	18370 AAW	FLBLS	10//99-12//99
	Naples MSA, FL	S	9.42 MW	8.46 AW	19600 AAW	FLBLS	10//99-12//99
	Ocala MSA, FL	S	8.36 MW	8.18 AW	17400 AAW	FLBLS	10//99-12//99
	Orlando MSA, FL	S	9.14 MW	8.37 AW	19020 AAW	FLBLS	10//99-12//99
	Panama City MSA, FL	S	8.19 MW	7.97 AW	17040 AAW	FLBLS	10//99-12//99
	Pensacola MSA, FL	S	7.83 MW	7.39 AW	16290 AAW	FLBLS	10//99-12//99
	Sarasota-Bradenton MSA, FL	S	8.96 MW	8.53 AW	18630 AAW	FLBLS	10//99-12//99
	Tallahassee MSA, FL	S	8.41 MW	8.06 AW	17480 AAW	FLBLS	10//99-12//99
	Tampa-St. Petersburg-Clearwater MSA, FL	S	9.20 MW	8.61 AW	19130 AAW	FLBLS	10//99-12//99
	West Palm Beach-Boca Raton MSA, FL	S	9.84 MW	9.66 AW	20460 AAW	FLBLS	10//99-12//99
	Georgia	S	8.89 MW	9.32 AW	19390 AAW	GABLS	10//99-12//99
	Albany MSA, GA	S	8.30 MW	8.02 AW	17270 AAW	GABLS	10//99-12//99
	Athens MSA, GA	S	9.13 MW	9.31 AW	18990 AAW	GABLS	10//99-12//99
	Atlanta MSA, GA	S	9.60 MW	9.29 AW	19960 AAW	GABLS	10//99-12//99
	Augusta-Aiken MSA, GA-SC	S	8.12 MW	7.20 AW	16890 AAW	GABLS	10//99-12//99
	Macon MSA, GA	S	9.32 MW	9.48 AW	19380 AAW	GABLS	10//99-12//99
	Savannah MSA, GA	S	9.64 MW	9.41 AW	20060 AAW	GABLS	10//99-12//99
	Hawaii	S	9.55 MW	10.20 AW	21220 AAW	HIBLS	10//99-12//99
	Honolulu MSA, HI	S	9.79 MW	9.37 AW	20350 AAW	HIBLS	10//99-12//99
	Idaho	S	7.75 MW	8.47 AW	17620 AAW	IDBLS	10//99-12//99
	Boise City MSA, ID	S	8.92 MW	8.59 AW	18550 AAW	IDBLS	10//99-12//99
	Pocatello MSA, ID	S	7.32 MW	7.16 AW	15220 AAW	IDBLS	10//99-12//99
	Illinois	S	8.56 MW	10.01 AW	20830 AAW	ILBLS	10//99-12//99
	Bloomington-Normal MSA, IL	S	8.09 MW	8.01 AW	16820 AAW	ILBLS	10//99-12//99
	Champaign-Urbana MSA, IL	S	7.06 MW	6.56 AW	14680 AAW	ILBLS	10//99-12//99
	Chicago PMSA, IL	S	10.81 MW	9.35 AW	22470 AAW	ILBLS	10//99-12//99
	Kankakee PMSA, IL	S	10.19 MW	6.80 AW	21190 AAW	ILBLS	10//99-12//99
	Peoria-Pekin MSA, IL	S	8.89 MW	7.80 AW	18500 AAW	ILBLS	10//99-12//99
	Rockford MSA, IL	S	8.33 MW	8.10 AW	17320 AAW	ILBLS	10//99-12//99
	Springfield MSA, IL	S	8.88 MW	8.16 AW	18470 AAW	ILBLS	10//99-12//99
	Indiana	S	8.62 MW	9.88 AW	20550 AAW	INBLS	10//99-12//99
	Bloomington MSA, IN	S	7.59 MW	7.50 AW	15790 AAW	INBLS	10//99-12//99
	Elkhart-Goshen MSA, IN	S	8.64 MW	8.01 AW	17960 AAW	INBLS	10//99-12//99
	Evansville-Henderson MSA, IN-KY	S	9.76 MW	9.29 AW	20300 AAW	INBLS	10//99-12//99
	Fort Wayne MSA, IN	S	9.39 MW	8.51 AW	19530 AAW	INBLS	10//99-12//99
	Gary PMSA, IN	S	7.99 MW	7.45 AW	16610 AAW	INBLS	10//99-12//99
	Indianapolis MSA, IN	S	10.71 MW	9.54 AW	22270 AAW	INBLS	10//99-12//99
	Kokomo MSA, IN	S	8.18 MW	7.86 AW	17010 AAW	INBLS	10//99-12//99
	Lafayette MSA, IN	S	8.33 MW	7.99 AW	17330 AAW	INBLS	10//99-12//99
	South Bend MSA, IN	S	9.53 MW	8.79 AW	19830 AAW	INBLS	10//99-12//99

Occupation/Type/Industry	Location	Per	Low	Mid	High	Source	Date
Baker	Iowa	S	9.48 MW	9.61 AW	19980 AAW	IABLS	10//99-12//99
	Cedar Rapids MSA, IA	S	9.69 MW	10.34 AW	20160 AAW	IABLS	10//99-12//99
	Davenport-Moline-Rock Island MSA, IA-IL	S	7.83 MW	7.15 AW	16280 AAW	IABLS	10//99-12//99
	Des Moines MSA, IA	S	10.04 MW	10.46 AW	20880 AAW	IABLS	10//99-12//99
	Dubuque MSA, IA	S	9.65 MW	9.76 AW	20080 AAW	IABLS	10//99-12//99
	Iowa City MSA, IA	S	8.92 MW	8.37 AW	18550 AAW	IABLS	10//99-12//99
	Sioux City MSA, IA-NE	S	10.74 MW	10.94 AW	22330 AAW	IABLS	10//99-12//99
	Waterloo-Cedar Falls MSA, IA	S	10.43 MW	11.01 AW	21700 AAW	IABLS	10//99-12//99
	Kansas	S	7.62 MW	8.18 AW	17010 AAW	KSBLS	10//99-12//99
	Lawrence MSA, KS	S	7.89 MW	7.83 AW	16420 AAW	KSBLS	10//99-12//99
	Topeka MSA, KS	S	7.80 MW	7.64 AW	16220 AAW	KSBLS	10//99-12//99
	Wichita MSA, KS	S	7.59 MW	7.14 AW	15790 AAW	KSBLS	10//99-12//99
	Kentucky	S	8.32 MW	8.60 AW	17880 AAW	KYBLS	10//99-12//99
	Lexington MSA, KY	S	8.00 MW	7.95 AW	16640 AAW	KYBLS	10//99-12//99
	Louisville MSA, KY-IN	S	8.43 MW	8.25 AW	17540 AAW	KYBLS	10//99-12//99
	Owensboro MSA, KY	S	9.84 MW	10.81 AW	20470 AAW	KYBLS	10//99-12//99
	Louisiana	S	7.35 MW	8.03 AW	16690 AAW	LABLS	10//99-12//99
	Alexandria MSA, LA	S	11.30 MW	12.11 AW	23510 AAW	LABLS	10//99-12//99
	Baton Rouge MSA, LA	S	8.23 MW	7.17 AW	17120 AAW	LABLS	10//99-12//99
	Houma MSA, LA	S	6.84 MW	6.18 AW	14230 AAW	LABLS	10//99-12//99
	Lafayette MSA, LA	S	7.93 MW	7.76 AW	16500 AAW	LABLS	10//99-12//99
	Lake Charles MSA, LA	S	7.97 MW	7.76 AW	16580 AAW	LABLS	10//99-12//99
	Monroe MSA, LA	S	7.84 MW	7.49 AW	16300 AAW	LABLS	10//99-12//99
	New Orleans MSA, LA	S	8.09 MW	7.21 AW	16820 AAW	LABLS	10//99-12//99
	Shreveport-Bossier City MSA, LA	S	7.85 MW	7.70 AW	16330 AAW	LABLS	10//99-12//99
	Maine	S	8.35 MW	8.62 AW	17930 AAW	MEBLS	10//99-12//99
	Bangor MSA, ME	S	7.90 MW	7.60 AW	16420 AAW	MEBLS	10//99-12//99
	Lewiston-Auburn MSA, ME	S	8.18 MW	8.10 AW	17010 AAW	MEBLS	10//99-12//99
	Portland MSA, ME	S	9.11 MW	8.83 AW	18950 AAW	MEBLS	10//99-12//99
	Maryland	S	10.53 MW	11.52 AW	23960 AAW	MDBLS	10//99-12//99
	Baltimore PMSA, MD	S	11.82 MW	10.40 AW	24590 AAW	MDBLS	10//99-12//99
	Hagerstown PMSA, MD	S	9.65 MW	8.98 AW	20060 AAW	MDBLS	10//99-12//99
	Massachusetts	S	10.1 MW	10.43 AW	21700 AAW	MABLS	10//99-12//99
	Barnstable-Yarmouth MSA, MA	S	9.81 MW	9.19 AW	20410 AAW	MABLS	10//99-12//99
	Boston PMSA, MA-NH	S	10.75 MW	10.50 AW	22360 AAW	MABLS	10//99-12//99
	Brockton PMSA, MA	S	11.35 MW	10.60 AW	23600 AAW	MABLS	10//99-12//99
	Fitchburg-Leominster PMSA, MA	S	10.64 MW	9.65 AW	22130 AAW	MABLS	10//99-12//99
	Lawrence PMSA, MA-NH	S	9.94 MW	9.61 AW	20670 AAW	MABLS	10//99-12//99
	Lowell PMSA, MA-NH	S	10.00 MW	9.30 AW	20800 AAW	MABLS	10//99-12//99
	New Bedford PMSA, MA	S	10.78 MW	10.90 AW	22430 AAW	MABLS	10//99-12//99
	Pittsfield MSA, MA	S	9.28 MW	8.20 AW	19310 AAW	MABLS	10//99-12//99
	Springfield MSA, MA	S	10.08 MW	9.53 AW	20970 AAW	MABLS	10//99-12//99
	Worcester PMSA, MA-CT	S	11.41 MW	10.66 AW	23730 AAW	MABLS	10//99-12//99
	Michigan	S	9.1 MW	9.98 AW	20760 AAW	MIBLS	10//99-12//99
	Ann Arbor PMSA, MI	S	10.85 MW	10.82 AW	22570 AAW	MIBLS	10//99-12//99
	Benton Harbor MSA, MI	S	8.51 MW	8.30 AW	17690 AAW	MIBLS	10//99-12//99
	Detroit PMSA, MI	S	10.27 MW	9.47 AW	21360 AAW	MIBLS	10//99-12//99
	Flint PMSA, MI	S	8.30 MW	8.08 AW	17270 AAW	MIBLS	10//99-12//99
	Grand Rapids-Muskegon-Holland MSA, MI	S	10.54 MW	9.86 AW	21920 AAW	MIBLS	10//99-12//99
	Jackson MSA, MI	S	8.39 MW	8.21 AW	17460 AAW	MIBLS	10//99-12//99
	Kalamazoo-Battle Creek MSA, MI	S	12.99 MW	11.24 AW	27010 AAW	MIBLS	10//99-12//99
	Lansing-East Lansing MSA, MI	S	8.88 MW	8.13 AW	18460 AAW	MIBLS	10//99-12//99
	Saginaw-Bay City-Midland MSA, MI	S	7.65 MW	6.67 AW	15910 AAW	MIBLS	10//99-12//99
	Minnesota	S	9.66 MW	10.36 AW	21550 AAW	MNBLS	10//99-12//99
	Duluth-Superior MSA, MN-WI	S	8.51 MW	7.96 AW	17710 AAW	MNBLS	10//99-12//99
	Minneapolis-St. Paul MSA, MN-WI	S	11.30 MW	10.71 AW	23500 AAW	MNBLS	10//99-12//99
	Rochester MSA, MN	S	9.19 MW	8.51 AW	19110 AAW	MNBLS	10//99-12//99
	St. Cloud MSA, MN	S	10.20 MW	9.60 AW	21220 AAW	MNBLS	10//99-12//99
	Mississippi	S	7.49 MW	7.75 AW	16120 AAW	MSBLS	10//99-12//99
	Biloxi-Gulfport-Pascagoula MSA, MS	S	8.64 MW	8.19 AW	17980 AAW	MSBLS	10//99-12//99
	Hattiesburg MSA, MS	S	7.34 MW	7.14 AW	15260 AAW	MSBLS	10//99-12//99
	Jackson MSA, MS	S	9.15 MW	8.87 AW	19020 AAW	MSBLS	10//99-12//99
	Missouri	S	7.94 MW	8.49 AW	17670 AAW	MOBLS	10//99-12//99

Occupation/Type/Industry	Location	Per	Low	Mid	High	Source	Date
Baker	Joplin MSA, MO	S	7.34 MW	6.87 AW	15270 AAW	MOBLS	10//99-12//99
	Kansas City MSA, MO-KS	S	8.59 MW	8.26 AW	17860 AAW	MOBLS	10//99-12//99
	St. Louis MSA, MO-IL	S	8.62 MW	8.02 AW	17930 AAW	MOBLS	10//99-12//99
	Springfield MSA, MO	S	10.18 MW	10.02 AW	21180 AAW	MOBLS	10//99-12//99
	Montana	S	8.35 MW	8.57 AW	17830 AAW	MTBLS	10//99-12//99
	Billings MSA, MT	S	7.97 MW	6.94 AW	16570 AAW	MTBLS	10//99-12//99
	Missoula MSA, MT	S	9.22 MW	9.60 AW	19180 AAW	MTBLS	10//99-12//99
	Nebraska	S	8.57 MW	8.94 AW	18600 AAW	NEBLS	10//99-12//99
	Lincoln MSA, NE	S	9.14 MW	9.46 AW	19010 AAW	NEBLS	10//99-12//99
	Omaha MSA, NE-IA	S	9.40 MW	8.93 AW	19550 AAW	NEBLS	10//99-12//99
	Nevada	S	11.51 MW	11.28 AW	23450 AAW	NVBLS	10//99-12//99
	Las Vegas MSA, NV-AZ	S	11.32 MW	11.66 AW	23550 AAW	NVBLS	10//99-12//99
	Reno MSA, NV	S	11.06 MW	10.91 AW	22990 AAW	NVBLS	10//99-12//99
	New Hampshire	S	9.02 MW	9.47 AW	19700 AAW	NHBLS	10//99-12//99
	Manchester PMSA, NH	S	8.53 MW	8.40 AW	17750 AAW	NHBLS	10//99-12//99
	Nashua PMSA, NH	S	8.81 MW	8.69 AW	18330 AAW	NHBLS	10//99-12//99
	Portsmouth-Rochester PMSA, NH-ME	S	9.25 MW	9.15 AW	19240 AAW	NHBLS	10//99-12//99
	New Jersey	S	11.11 MW	11.68 AW	24300 AAW	NJBLS	10//99-12//99
	Atlantic-Cape May PMSA, NJ	S	11.09 MW	10.58 AW	23060 AAW	NJBLS	10//99-12//99
	Bergen-Passaic PMSA, NJ	S	11.52 MW	10.88 AW	23960 AAW	NJBLS	10//99-12//99
	Jersey City PMSA, NJ	S	12.57 MW	13.77 AW	26140 AAW	NJBLS	10//99-12//99
	Middlesex-Somerset-Hunterdon PMSA, NJ	S	13.53 MW	13.31 AW	28150 AAW	NJBLS	10//99-12//99
	Monmouth-Ocean PMSA, NJ	S	10.43 MW	9.37 AW	21700 AAW	NJBLS	10//99-12//99
	Newark PMSA, NJ	S	11.63 MW	11.51 AW	24190 AAW	NJBLS	10//99-12//99
	Trenton PMSA, NJ	S	9.89 MW	9.95 AW	20570 AAW	NJBLS	10//99-12//99
	Vineland-Millville-Bridgeton PMSA, NJ	S	11.27 MW	9.46 AW	23440 AAW	NJBLS	10//99-12//99
	New Mexico	S	7.64 MW	8.13 AW	16910 AAW	NMBLS	10//99-12//99
	Albuquerque MSA, NM	S	8.50 MW	8.08 AW	17690 AAW	NMBLS	10//99-12//99
	Las Cruces MSA, NM	S	7.15 MW	6.10 AW	14860 AAW	NMBLS	10//99-12//99
	Santa Fe MSA, NM	S	9.51 MW	9.66 AW	19780 AAW	NMBLS	10//99-12//99
	New York	S	8.78 MW	9.94 AW	20680 AAW	NYBLS	10//99-12//99
	Albany-Schenectady-Troy MSA, NY	S	10.07 MW	8.87 AW	20940 AAW	NYBLS	10//99-12//99
	Binghamton MSA, NY	S	8.46 MW	8.22 AW	17590 AAW	NYBLS	10//99-12//99
	Buffalo-Niagara Falls MSA, NY	S	9.94 MW	9.21 AW	20670 AAW	NYBLS	10//99-12//99
	Dutchess County PMSA, NY	S	10.64 MW	8.91 AW	22140 AAW	NYBLS	10//99-12//99
	Elmira MSA, NY	S	8.82 MW	8.91 AW	18350 AAW	NYBLS	10//99-12//99
	Glens Falls MSA, NY	S	9.85 MW	8.92 AW	20480 AAW	NYBLS	10//99-12//99
	Jamestown MSA, NY	S	8.18 MW	7.50 AW	17020 AAW	NYBLS	10//99-12//99
	Nassau-Suffolk PMSA, NY	S	11.46 MW	9.70 AW	23840 AAW	NYBLS	10//99-12//99
	New York PMSA, NY	S	10.45 MW	9.62 AW	21730 AAW	NYBLS	10//99-12//99
	Newburgh PMSA, NY-PA	S	9.02 MW	8.02 AW	18750 AAW	NYBLS	10//99-12//99
	Rochester MSA, NY	S	9.30 MW	8.98 AW	19340 AAW	NYBLS	10//99-12//99
	Syracuse MSA, NY	S	9.11 MW	8.24 AW	18960 AAW	NYBLS	10//99-12//99
	Utica-Rome MSA, NY	S	8.16 MW	7.74 AW	16960 AAW	NYBLS	10//99-12//99
	North Carolina	S	7.95 MW	8.17 AW	17000 AAW	NCBLS	10//99-12//99
	Asheville MSA, NC	S	8.93 MW	8.40 AW	18580 AAW	NCBLS	10//99-12//99
	Charlotte-Gastonia-Rock Hill MSA, NC-SC	S	8.34 MW	8.18 AW	17350 AAW	NCBLS	10//99-12//99
	Fayetteville MSA, NC	S	8.05 MW	7.77 AW	16750 AAW	NCBLS	10//99-12//99
	Greensboro--Winston-Salem--High Point MSA, NC	S	8.40 MW	8.06 AW	17480 AAW	NCBLS	10//99-12//99
	Greenville MSA, NC	S	9.26 MW	9.20 AW	19250 AAW	NCBLS	10//99-12//99
	Hickory-Morganton-Lenoir MSA, NC	S	7.87 MW	7.61 AW	16370 AAW	NCBLS	10//99-12//99
	Raleigh-Durham-Chapel Hill MSA, NC	S	8.54 MW	8.31 AW	17760 AAW	NCBLS	10//99-12//99
	Wilmington MSA, NC	S	7.88 MW	7.62 AW	16390 AAW	NCBLS	10//99-12//99
	North Dakota	S	8.2 MW	8.95 AW	18620 AAW	NDBLS	10//99-12//99
	Bismarck MSA, ND	S	8.44 MW	7.70 AW	17560 AAW	NDBLS	10//99-12//99
	Fargo-Moorhead MSA, ND-MN	S	10.15 MW	10.39 AW	21100 AAW	NDBLS	10//99-12//99
	Ohio	S	8.27 MW	9.10 AW	18930 AAW	OHBLS	10//99-12//99
	Akron PMSA, OH	S	10.04 MW	8.72 AW	20890 AAW	OHBLS	10//99-12//99
	Canton-Massillon MSA, OH	S	9.11 MW	8.15 AW	18950 AAW	OHBLS	10//99-12//99
	Cincinnati PMSA, OH-KY-IN	S	10.61 MW	10.56 AW	22070 AAW	OHBLS	10//99-12//99
	Cleveland-Lorain-Elyria PMSA, OH	S	9.15 MW	8.31 AW	19030 AAW	OHBLS	10//99-12//99

AAW Average annual wage	**AOH** Average offered, high	**ASH** Average starting, high	**H** Hourly	**M** Monthly	**S** Special: hourly and annual
AE Average entry wage	**AOL** Average offered, low	**ASL** Average starting, low	**HI** Highest wage paid	**MTC** Median total compensation	**TQ** Third quartile wage
AEX Average experienced wage	**APH** Average pay, high range	**AW** Average wage paid	**HR** High end range	**MW** Median wage paid	**W** Weekly
AO Average offered	**APL** Average pay, low range	**FQ** First quartile wage	**LR** Low end range	**SQ** Second quartile wage	**Y** Yearly

Occupation/Type/Industry	Location	Per	Low	Mid	High	Source	Date
Baker	Columbus MSA, OH	S	8.20 MW	7.17 AW	17060 AAW	OHBLS	10//99-12//99
	Dayton-Springfield MSA, OH	S	8.13 MW	7.79 AW	16920 AAW	OHBLS	10//99-12//99
	Hamilton-Middletown PMSA, OH	S	8.16 MW	7.72 AW	16970 AAW	OHBLS	10//99-12//99
	Lima MSA, OH	S	8.26 MW	7.70 AW	17180 AAW	OHBLS	10//99-12//99
	Mansfield MSA, OH	S	7.61 MW	7.58 AW	15830 AAW	OHBLS	10//99-12//99
	Steubenville-Weirton MSA, OH-WV	S	7.09 MW	6.25 AW	14750 AAW	OHBLS	10//99-12//99
	Toledo MSA, OH	S	8.52 MW	8.06 AW	17720 AAW	OHBLS	10//99-12//99
	Youngstown-Warren MSA, OH	S	9.50 MW	9.50 AW	19760 AAW	OHBLS	10//99-12//99
	Oklahoma	S	7.25 MW	8.05 AW	16750 AAW	OKBLS	10//99-12//99
	Enid MSA, OK	S	7.06 MW	6.68 AW	14690 AAW	OKBLS	10//99-12//99
	Lawton MSA, OK	S	6.82 MW	6.84 AW	14180 AAW	OKBLS	10//99-12//99
	Oklahoma City MSA, OK	S	8.41 MW	7.67 AW	17500 AAW	OKBLS	10//99-12//99
	Tulsa MSA, OK	S	9.84 MW	10.15 AW	20470 AAW	OKBLS	10//99-12//99
	Oregon	S	9.57 MW	10.43 AW	21700 AAW	ORBLS	10//99-12//99
	Corvallis MSA, OR	S	8.79 MW	8.23 AW	18280 AAW	ORBLS	10//99-12//99
	Eugene-Springfield MSA, OR	S	9.54 MW	8.53 AW	19850 AAW	ORBLS	10//99-12//99
	Medford-Ashland MSA, OR	S	10.29 MW	9.64 AW	21400 AAW	ORBLS	10//99-12//99
	Portland-Vancouver PMSA, OR-WA	S	11.21 MW	10.73 AW	23320 AAW	ORBLS	10//99-12//99
	Salem PMSA, OR	S	10.38 MW	9.59 AW	21580 AAW	ORBLS	10//99-12//99
	Pennsylvania	S	8.71 MW	9.08 AW	18890 AAW	PABLS	10//99-12//99
	Allentown-Bethlehem-Easton MSA, PA	S	10.34 MW	9.67 AW	21510 AAW	PABLS	10//99-12//99
	Erie MSA, PA	S	8.50 MW	8.09 AW	17680 AAW	PABLS	10//99-12//99
	Harrisburg-Lebanon-Carlisle MSA, PA	S	10.07 MW	9.91 AW	20950 AAW	PABLS	10//99-12//99
	Johnstown MSA, PA	S	7.44 MW	6.92 AW	15470 AAW	PABLS	10//99-12//99
	Lancaster MSA, PA	S	9.50 MW	8.78 AW	19760 AAW	PABLS	10//99-12//99
	Philadelphia PMSA, PA-NJ	S	10.65 MW	10.70 AW	22160 AAW	PABLS	10//99-12//99
	Pittsburgh MSA, PA	S	8.15 MW	7.86 AW	16960 AAW	PABLS	10//99-12//99
	Reading MSA, PA	S	9.37 MW	9.53 AW	19490 AAW	PABLS	10//99-12//99
	Scranton--Wilkes-Barre--Hazleton MSA, PA	S	7.44 MW	6.78 AW	15480 AAW	PABLS	10//99-12//99
	State College MSA, PA	S	9.37 MW	9.57 AW	19490 AAW	PABLS	10//99-12//99
	Williamsport MSA, PA	S	14.51 MW	11.11 AW	30190 AAW	PABLS	10//99-12//99
	York MSA, PA	S	10.64 MW	10.77 AW	22140 AAW	PABLS	10//99-12//99
	Rhode Island	S	9.8 MW	9.99 AW	20780 AAW	RIBLS	10//99-12//99
	Providence-Fall River-Warwick MSA, RI-MA	S	9.50 MW	9.34 AW	19760 AAW	RIBLS	10//99-12//99
	South Carolina	S	7.84 MW	8.08 AW	16800 AAW	SCBLS	10//99-12//99
	Charleston-North Charleston MSA, SC	S	8.33 MW	7.86 AW	17330 AAW	SCBLS	10//99-12//99
	Columbia MSA, SC	S	8.08 MW	8.32 AW	16810 AAW	SCBLS	10//99-12//99
	Greenville-Spartanburg-Anderson MSA, SC	S	8.42 MW	8.14 AW	17500 AAW	SCBLS	10//99-12//99
	Myrtle Beach MSA, SC	S	7.68 MW	7.61 AW	15970 AAW	SCBLS	10//99-12//99
	Sumter MSA, SC	S	6.68 MW	6.35 AW	13890 AAW	SCBLS	10//99-12//99
	South Dakota	S	8.25 MW	8.40 AW	17480 AAW	SDBLS	10//99-12//99
	Rapid City MSA, SD	S	7.49 MW	7.60 AW	15580 AAW	SDBLS	10//99-12//99
	Sioux Falls MSA, SD	S	8.90 MW	8.87 AW	18510 AAW	SDBLS	10//99-12//99
	Tennessee	S	8.68 MW	9.46 AW	19680 AAW	TNBLS	10//99-12//99
	Chattanooga MSA, TN-GA	S	9.47 MW	8.64 AW	19710 AAW	TNBLS	10//99-12//99
	Clarksville-Hopkinsville MSA, TN-KY	S	7.86 MW	7.49 AW	16360 AAW	TNBLS	10//99-12//99
	Jackson MSA, TN	S	7.83 MW	7.87 AW	16280 AAW	TNBLS	10//99-12//99
	Johnson City-Kingsport-Bristol MSA, TN-VA	S	7.66 MW	7.64 AW	15940 AAW	TNBLS	10//99-12//99
	Knoxville MSA, TN	S	8.73 MW	8.43 AW	18170 AAW	TNBLS	10//99-12//99
	Memphis MSA, TN-AR-MS	S	10.16 MW	8.88 AW	21140 AAW	MSBLS	10//99-12//99
	Nashville MSA, TN	S	9.88 MW	9.33 AW	20540 AAW	TNBLS	10//99-12//99
	Texas	S	7.9 MW	8.40 AW	17470 AAW	TXBLS	10//99-12//99
	Abilene MSA, TX	S	9.45 MW	9.83 AW	19650 AAW	TXBLS	10//99-12//99
	Amarillo MSA, TX	S	7.73 MW	7.43 AW	16080 AAW	TXBLS	10//99-12//99
	Austin-San Marcos MSA, TX	S	8.44 MW	8.22 AW	17550 AAW	TXBLS	10//99-12//99
	Beaumont-Port Arthur MSA, TX	S	7.38 MW	7.34 AW	15350 AAW	TXBLS	10//99-12//99
	Brazoria PMSA, TX	S	7.53 MW	7.35 AW	15660 AAW	TXBLS	10//99-12//99
	Brownsville-Harlingen-San Benito MSA, TX	S	6.97 MW	6.70 AW	14500 AAW	TXBLS	10//99-12//99

AAW	Average annual wage	**AOH**	Average offered, high	**ASH**	Average starting, high	**H**	Hourly	**M**	Monthly	**S**	Special: hourly and annual
AE	Average entry wage	**AOL**	Average offered, low	**ASL**	Average starting, low	**HI**	Highest wage paid	**MTC**	Median total compensation	**TQ**	Third quartile wage
AEX	Average experienced wage	**APH**	Average pay, high range	**AW**	Average wage paid	**HR**	High end range	**MW**	Median wage paid	**W**	Weekly
AO	Average offered	**APL**	Average pay, low range	**FQ**	First quartile wage	**LR**	Low end range	**SQ**	Second quartile wage	**Y**	Yearly

Occupation/Type/Industry	Location	Per	Low	Mid	High	Source	Date
Baker	Bryan-College Station MSA, TX	S	9.68 MW	10.83 AW	20130 AAW	TXBLS	10//99-12//99
	Corpus Christi MSA, TX	S	6.93 MW	6.17 AW	14420 AAW	TXBLS	10//99-12//99
	Dallas PMSA, TX	S	9.36 MW	9.27 AW	19460 AAW	TXBLS	10//99-12//99
	El Paso MSA, TX	S	7.93 MW	7.24 AW	16500 AAW	TXBLS	10//99-12//99
	Fort Worth-Arlington PMSA, TX	S	9.00 MW	8.43 AW	18720 AAW	TXBLS	10//99-12//99
	Galveston-Texas City PMSA, TX	S	10.09 MW	10.08 AW	20980 AAW	TXBLS	10//99-12//99
	Houston PMSA, TX	S	8.49 MW	7.82 AW	17660 AAW	TXBLS	10//99-12//99
	Laredo MSA, TX	S	6.78 MW	6.61 AW	14110 AAW	TXBLS	10//99-12//99
	Longview-Marshall MSA, TX	S	7.65 MW	7.60 AW	15900 AAW	TXBLS	10//99-12//99
	Lubbock MSA, TX	S	7.88 MW	7.55 AW	16400 AAW	TXBLS	10//99-12//99
	McAllen-Edinburg-Mission MSA, TX	S	7.25 MW	7.12 AW	15070 AAW	TXBLS	10//99-12//99
	Odessa-Midland MSA, TX	S	8.07 MW	7.85 AW	16780 AAW	TXBLS	10//99-12//99
	San Angelo MSA, TX	S	7.87 MW	7.77 AW	16380 AAW	TXBLS	10//99-12//99
	San Antonio MSA, TX	S	7.76 MW	7.40 AW	16140 AAW	TXBLS	10//99-12//99
	Sherman-Denison MSA, TX	S	6.51 MW	6.25 AW	13550 AAW	TXBLS	10//99-12//99
	Texarkana MSA, TX-Texarkana, AR	S	8.04 MW	7.40 AW	16730 AAW	TXBLS	10//99-12//99
	Tyler MSA, TX	S	8.36 MW	8.08 AW	17390 AAW	TXBLS	10//99-12//99
	Victoria MSA, TX	S	6.07 MW	5.96 AW	12630 AAW	TXBLS	10//99-12//99
	Waco MSA, TX	S	8.64 MW	8.36 AW	17960 AAW	TXBLS	10//99-12//99
	Wichita Falls MSA, TX	S	8.31 MW	7.90 AW	17290 AAW	TXBLS	10//99-12//99
	Utah	S	9.39 MW	10.08 AW	20960 AAW	UTBLS	10//99-12//99
	Provo-Orem MSA, UT	S	8.28 MW	7.99 AW	17230 AAW	UTBLS	10//99-12//99
	Salt Lake City-Ogden MSA, UT	S	10.60 MW	10.36 AW	22050 AAW	UTBLS	10//99-12//99
	Vermont	S	8.38 MW	8.76 AW	18210 AAW	VTBLS	10//99-12//99
	Burlington MSA, VT	S	8.68 MW	8.12 AW	18050 AAW	VTBLS	10//99-12//99
	Virginia	S	8.43 MW	9.07 AW	18860 AAW	VABLS	10//99-12//99
	Danville MSA, VA	S	7.31 MW	6.69 AW	15210 AAW	VABLS	10//99-12//99
	Norfolk-Virginia Beach-Newport News MSA, VA-NC	S	7.58 MW	7.34 AW	15770 AAW	VABLS	10//99-12//99
	Richmond-Petersburg MSA, VA	S	9.33 MW	8.61 AW	19410 AAW	VABLS	10//99-12//99
	Roanoke MSA, VA	S	8.56 MW	8.59 AW	17800 AAW	VABLS	10//99-12//99
	Washington	S	10.58 MW	11.10 AW	23090 AAW	WABLS	10//99-12//99
	Bellingham MSA, WA	S	9.81 MW	9.59 AW	20400 AAW	WABLS	10//99-12//99
	Bremerton PMSA, WA	S	10.51 MW	11.10 AW	21870 AAW	WABLS	10//99-12//99
	Olympia PMSA, WA	S	10.32 MW	10.50 AW	21470 AAW	WABLS	10//99-12//99
	Richland-Kennewick-Pasco MSA, WA	S	9.57 MW	8.82 AW	19900 AAW	WABLS	10//99-12//99
	Seattle-Bellevue-Everett PMSA, WA	S	11.38 MW	10.69 AW	23670 AAW	WABLS	10//99-12//99
	Spokane MSA, WA	S	12.41 MW	11.69 AW	25810 AAW	WABLS	10//99-12//99
	Tacoma PMSA, WA	S	10.71 MW	10.68 AW	22280 AAW	WABLS	10//99-12//99
	Yakima MSA, WA	S	10.06 MW	9.91 AW	20930 AAW	WABLS	10//99-12//99
	West Virginia	S	6.89 MW	7.77 AW	16160 AAW	WVBLS	10//99-12//99
	Charleston MSA, WV	S	7.06 MW	6.84 AW	14690 AAW	WVBLS	10//99-12//99
	Parkersburg-Marietta MSA, WV-OH	S	9.21 MW	8.39 AW	19150 AAW	WVBLS	10//99-12//99
	Wheeling MSA, WV-OH	S	8.65 MW	7.93 AW	17990 AAW	WVBLS	10//99-12//99
	Wisconsin	S	8.61 MW	8.95 AW	18620 AAW	WIBLS	10//99-12//99
	Appleton-Oshkosh-Neenah MSA, WI	S	10.37 MW	9.78 AW	21570 AAW	WIBLS	10//99-12//99
	Eau Claire MSA, WI	S	8.55 MW	8.47 AW	17790 AAW	WIBLS	10//99-12//99
	Green Bay MSA, WI	S	8.76 MW	8.10 AW	18230 AAW	WIBLS	10//99-12//99
	Janesville-Beloit MSA, WI	S	8.71 MW	8.40 AW	18120 AAW	WIBLS	10//99-12//99
	Kenosha PMSA, WI	S	9.26 MW	8.86 AW	19270 AAW	WIBLS	10//99-12//99
	La Crosse MSA, WI-MN	S	9.21 MW	9.11 AW	19150 AAW	WIBLS	10//99-12//99
	Madison MSA, WI	S	9.47 MW	9.53 AW	19690 AAW	WIBLS	10//99-12//99
	Milwaukee-Waukesha PMSA, WI	S	9.06 MW	8.67 AW	18850 AAW	WIBLS	10//99-12//99
	Racine PMSA, WI	S	11.47 MW	10.41 AW	23860 AAW	WIBLS	10//99-12//99
	Sheboygan MSA, WI	S	7.71 MW	7.31 AW	16030 AAW	WIBLS	10//99-12//99
	Wausau MSA, WI	S	8.89 MW	8.92 AW	18490 AAW	WIBLS	10//99-12//99
	Wyoming	S	8.21 MW	8.71 AW	18120 AAW	WYBLS	10//99-12//99
	Cheyenne MSA, WY	S	8.20 MW	7.90 AW	17060 AAW	WYBLS	10//99-12//99
	Puerto Rico	S	6.02 MW	6.37 AW	13260 AAW	PRBLS	10//99-12//99

AAW	Average annual wage	AOH	Average offered, high	ASH	Average starting, high	H	Hourly	M	Monthly	S	Special: hourly and annual
AE	Average entry wage	AOL	Average offered, low	ASL	Average starting, low	HI	Highest wage paid	MTC	Median total compensation	TQ	Third quartile wage
AEX	Average experienced wage	APH	Average pay, high range	AW	Average wage paid	HR	High end range	MW	Median wage paid	W	Weekly
AO	Average offered	APL	Average pay, low range	FQ	First quartile wage	LR	Low end range	SQ	Second quartile wage	Y	Yearly

Occupation/Type/Industry	Location	Per	Low	Mid	High	Source	Date
Baker	Aguadilla MSA, PR	S	6.24 MW	6.00 AW	12970 AAW	PRBLS	10//99-12//99
	Arecibo PMSA, PR	S	5.92 MW	5.91 AW	12320 AAW	PRBLS	10//99-12//99
	Caguas PMSA, PR	S	7.73 MW	6.19 AW	16080 AAW	PRBLS	10//99-12//99
	Mayaguez MSA, PR	S	5.85 MW	5.98 AW	12160 AAW	PRBLS	10//99-12//99
	Ponce MSA, PR	S	6.23 MW	5.99 AW	12960 AAW	PRBLS	10//99-12//99
	San Juan-Bayamon PMSA, PR	S	6.29 MW	6.00 AW	13080 AAW	PRBLS	10//99-12//99
	Virgin Islands	S	10.37 MW	10.37 AW	21560 AAW	VIBLS	10//99-12//99
	Guam	S	7.54 MW	8.21 AW	17090 AAW	GUBLS	10//99-12//99
Barber	Alabama	S	6.55 MW	8.36 AW	17380 AAW	ALBLS	10//99-12//99
	Alaska	S	16.75 MW	17.36 AW	36100 AAW	AKBLS	10//99-12//99
	Arizona	S	8.24 MW	8.94 AW	18590 AAW	AZBLS	10//99-12//99
	Phoenix-Mesa MSA, AZ	S	8.85 MW	8.22 AW	18410 AAW	AZBLS	10//99-12//99
	Tucson MSA, AZ	S	10.69 MW	10.15 AW	22230 AAW	AZBLS	10//99-12//99
	Arkansas	S	13.96 MW	14.60 AW	30360 AAW	ARBLS	10//99-12//99
	California	S	7.61 MW	8.77 AW	18230 AAW	CABLS	10//99-12//99
	Los Angeles-Long Beach PMSA, CA	S	7.78 MW	7.16 AW	16180 AAW	CABLS	10//99-12//99
	Orange County PMSA, CA	S	8.83 MW	7.62 AW	18370 AAW	CABLS	10//99-12//99
	Riverside-San Bernardino PMSA, CA	S	8.16 MW	7.80 AW	16970 AAW	CABLS	10//99-12//99
	San Francisco PMSA, CA	S	11.41 MW	9.15 AW	23730 AAW	CABLS	10//99-12//99
	San Jose PMSA, CA	S	8.12 MW	6.97 AW	16900 AAW	CABLS	10//99-12//99
	Colorado	S	15.36 MW	15.22 AW	31660 AAW	COBLS	10//99-12//99
	Denver PMSA, CO	S	15.91 MW	17.72 AW	33090 AAW	COBLS	10//99-12//99
	Connecticut	S	10.91 MW	12.30 AW	25590 AAW	CTBLS	10//99-12//99
	Bridgeport PMSA, CT	S	7.89 MW	6.88 AW	16400 AAW	CTBLS	10//99-12//99
	Hartford MSA, CT	S	10.79 MW	10.77 AW	22450 AAW	CTBLS	10//99-12//99
	New London-Norwich MSA, CT-RI	S	11.35 MW	10.45 AW	23620 AAW	CTBLS	10//99-12//99
	Delaware	S	9.92 MW	10.64 AW	22120 AAW	DEBLS	10//99-12//99
	Wilmington-Newark PMSA, DE-MD	S	11.56 MW	10.61 AW	24050 AAW	DEBLS	10//99-12//99
	District of Columbia	S	9.02 MW	8.73 AW	18160 AAW	DCBLS	10//99-12//99
	Washington PMSA, DC-MD-VA-WV	S	10.49 MW	9.99 AW	21820 AAW	DCBLS	10//99-12//99
	Florida	S	7.45 MW	8.04 AW	16730 AAW	FLBLS	10//99-12//99
	Fort Lauderdale PMSA, FL	S	6.51 MW	6.08 AW	13540 AAW	FLBLS	10//99-12//99
	Miami PMSA, FL	S	7.19 MW	6.79 AW	14960 AAW	FLBLS	10//99-12//99
	Georgia	S	9.81 MW	10.31 AW	21440 AAW	GABLS	10//99-12//99
	Atlanta MSA, GA	S	10.49 MW	9.89 AW	21810 AAW	GABLS	10//99-12//99
	Hawaii	S	8.28 MW	10.13 AW	21070 AAW	HIBLS	10//99-12//99
	Honolulu MSA, HI	S	10.13 MW	8.28 AW	21070 AAW	HIBLS	10//99-12//99
	Illinois	S	12.31 MW	12.26 AW	25490 AAW	ILBLS	10//99-12//99
	Champaign-Urbana MSA, IL	S	10.00 MW	8.67 AW	20800 AAW	ILBLS	10//99-12//99
	Chicago PMSA, IL	S	13.14 MW	13.28 AW	27320 AAW	ILBLS	10//99-12//99
	Indiana	S	9.46 MW	10.58 AW	22000 AAW	INBLS	10//99-12//99
	Iowa	S	11.54 MW	11.81 AW	24570 AAW	IABLS	10//99-12//99
	Kansas	S	13 MW	13.72 AW	28540 AAW	KSBLS	10//99-12//99
	Wichita MSA, KS	S	16.27 MW	16.25 AW	33830 AAW	KSBLS	10//99-12//99
	Kentucky	S	12.02 MW	12.04 AW	25040 AAW	KYBLS	10//99-12//99
	Louisville MSA, KY-IN	S	10.96 MW	10.70 AW	22790 AAW	KYBLS	10//99-12//99
	Louisiana	S	6.1 MW	6.66 AW	13860 AAW	LABLS	10//99-12//99
	Baton Rouge MSA, LA	S	6.22 MW	5.98 AW	12940 AAW	LABLS	10//99-12//99
	Maryland	S	9.31 MW	9.60 AW	19970 AAW	MDBLS	10//99-12//99
	Baltimore PMSA, MD	S	10.88 MW	9.86 AW	22620 AAW	MDBLS	10//99-12//99
	Massachusetts	S	12.48 MW	13.25 AW	27570 AAW	MABLS	10//99-12//99
	Boston PMSA, MA-NH	S	13.54 MW	14.45 AW	28160 AAW	MABLS	10//99-12//99
	Springfield MSA, MA	S	13.55 MW	12.23 AW	28180 AAW	MABLS	10//99-12//99
	Michigan	S	8.16 MW	9.03 AW	18770 AAW	MIBLS	10//99-12//99
	Detroit PMSA, MI	S	9.70 MW	8.71 AW	20190 AAW	MIBLS	10//99-12//99
	Grand Rapids-Muskegon-Holland MSA, MI	S	8.97 MW	8.21 AW	18660 AAW	MIBLS	10//99-12//99
	Minnesota	S	12.55 MW	12.26 AW	25510 AAW	MNBLS	10//99-12//99
	Minneapolis-St. Paul MSA, MN-WI	S	13.15 MW	13.26 AW	27360 AAW	MNBLS	10//99-12//99
	Mississippi	S	13.97 MW	12.55 AW	26110 AAW	MSBLS	10//99-12//99
	Missouri	S	8.9 MW	10.46 AW	21750 AAW	MOBLS	10//99-12//99
	Kansas City MSA, MO-KS	S	12.06 MW	10.70 AW	25080 AAW	MOBLS	10//99-12//99
	Montana	S	9.61 MW	9.18 AW	19100 AAW	MTBLS	10//99-12//99
	Great Falls MSA, MT	S	9.86 MW	10.10 AW	20510 AAW	MTBLS	10//99-12//99
	Nebraska	S	9.61 MW	10.18 AW	21160 AAW	NEBLS	10//99-12//99
	Omaha MSA, NE-IA	S	9.33 MW	8.69 AW	19410 AAW	NEBLS	10//99-12//99

AAW Average annual wage	AOH Average offered, high	ASH Average starting, high	H Hourly	M Monthly	S Special: hourly and annual
AE Average entry wage	AOL Average offered, low	ASL Average starting, low	HI Highest wage paid	MTC Median total compensation	TQ Third quartile wage
AEX Average experienced wage	APH Average pay, high range	AW Average wage paid	HR High end range	MW Median wage paid	W Weekly
AO Average offered	APL Average pay, low range	FQ First quartile wage	LR Low end range	SQ Second quartile wage	Y Yearly

Occupation/Type/Industry	Location	Per	Low	Mid	High	Source	Date
Barber	New Hampshire	S	11.04 MW	11.34 AW	23580 AAW	NHBLS	10//99-12//99
	New Jersey	S	9.59 MW	10.11 AW	21020 AAW	NJBLS	10//99-12//99
	Bergen-Passaic PMSA, NJ	S	11.22 MW	10.84 AW	23350 AAW	NJBLS	10//99-12//99
	Jersey City PMSA, NJ	S	8.51 MW	8.09 AW	17710 AAW	NJBLS	10//99-12//99
	Middlesex-Somerset- Hunterdon PMSA, NJ	S	10.70 MW	9.97 AW	22260 AAW	NJBLS	10//99-12//99
	Monmouth-Ocean PMSA, NJ	S	9.80 MW	8.36 AW	20370 AAW	NJBLS	10//99-12//99
	Newark PMSA, NJ	S	9.21 MW	9.07 AW	19160 AAW	NJBLS	10//99-12//99
	New Mexico	S	7.92 MW	8.72 AW	18140 AAW	NMBLS	10//99-12//99
	New York	S	6.73 MW	9.20 AW	19130 AAW	NYBLS	10//99-12//99
	Nassau-Suffolk PMSA, NY	S	9.29 MW	6.74 AW	19320 AAW	NYBLS	10//99-12//99
	New York PMSA, NY	S	9.29 MW	6.54 AW	19320 AAW	NYBLS	10//99-12//99
	Newburgh PMSA, NY-PA	S	12.92 MW	13.55 AW	26870 AAW	NYBLS	10//99-12//99
	Rochester MSA, NY	S	6.81 MW	6.22 AW	14170 AAW	NYBLS	10//99-12//99
	North Carolina	S	10.97 MW	10.87 AW	22610 AAW	NCBLS	10//99-12//99
	Charlotte-Gastonia-Rock Hill MSA, NC-SC	S	11.08 MW	11.31 AW	23050 AAW	NCBLS	10//99-12//99
	Greensboro--Winston-Salem-- High Point MSA, NC	S	9.46 MW	9.84 AW	19670 AAW	NCBLS	10//99-12//99
	Raleigh-Durham-Chapel Hill MSA, NC	S	12.23 MW	11.98 AW	25430 AAW	NCBLS	10//99-12//99
	Ohio	S	9.84 MW	10.85 AW	22570 AAW	OHBLS	10//99-12//99
	Cincinnati PMSA, OH-KY-IN	S	10.82 MW	11.16 AW	22500 AAW	OHBLS	10//99-12//99
	Cleveland-Lorain-Elyria PMSA, OH	S	14.48 MW	13.31 AW	30110 AAW	OHBLS	10//99-12//99
	Oklahoma	S	7.55 MW	8.73 AW	18160 AAW	OKBLS	10//99-12//99
	Oklahoma City MSA, OK	S	9.44 MW	7.36 AW	19640 AAW	OKBLS	10//99-12//99
	Tulsa MSA, OK	S	7.80 MW	7.68 AW	16230 AAW	OKBLS	10//99-12//99
	Oregon	S	13.93 MW	13.69 AW	28470 AAW	ORBLS	10//99-12//99
	Pennsylvania	S	8.12 MW	9.36 AW	19480 AAW	PABLS	10//99-12//99
	Harrisburg-Lebanon-Carlisle MSA, PA	S	9.55 MW	8.16 AW	19860 AAW	PABLS	10//99-12//99
	Lancaster MSA, PA	S	11.80 MW	10.66 AW	24550 AAW	PABLS	10//99-12//99
	Philadelphia PMSA, PA-NJ	S	8.89 MW	8.12 AW	18480 AAW	PABLS	10//99-12//99
	Pittsburgh MSA, PA	S	7.48 MW	7.15 AW	15570 AAW	PABLS	10//99-12//99
	Rhode Island	S	8.28 MW	9.66 AW	20090 AAW	RIBLS	10//99-12//99
	Providence-Fall River- Warwick MSA, RI-MA	S	10.00 MW	8.43 AW	20810 AAW	RIBLS	10//99-12//99
	South Carolina	S	6.47 MW	7.93 AW	16480 AAW	SCBLS	10//99-12//99
	Tennessee	S	7.77 MW	9.21 AW	19150 AAW	TNBLS	10//99-12//99
	Memphis MSA, TN-AR-MS	S	8.20 MW	7.84 AW	17060 AAW	MSBLS	10//99-12//99
	Texas	S	8.28 MW	10.07 AW	20950 AAW	TXBLS	10//99-12//99
	Dallas PMSA, TX	S	15.68 MW	17.37 AW	32620 AAW	TXBLS	10//99-12//99
	El Paso MSA, TX	S	7.19 MW	7.42 AW	14950 AAW	TXBLS	10//99-12//99
	Fort Worth-Arlington PMSA, TX	S	8.17 MW	8.01 AW	16980 AAW	TXBLS	10//99-12//99
	Houston PMSA, TX	S	10.32 MW	9.01 AW	21460 AAW	TXBLS	10//99-12//99
	Lubbock MSA, TX	S	9.11 MW	9.46 AW	18950 AAW	TXBLS	10//99-12//99
	San Antonio MSA, TX	S	7.28 MW	6.14 AW	15140 AAW	TXBLS	10//99-12//99
	Virginia	S	10.74 MW	10.95 AW	22770 AAW	VABLS	10//99-12//99
	Norfolk-Virginia Beach- Newport News MSA, VA- NC	S	8.19 MW	6.11 AW	17030 AAW	VABLS	10//99-12//99
	Washington	S	9.73 MW	10.29 AW	21400 AAW	WABLS	10//99-12//99
	Seattle-Bellevue-Everett PMSA, WA	S	10.92 MW	10.65 AW	22710 AAW	WABLS	10//99-12//99
	West Virginia	S	6.65 MW	8.40 AW	17470 AAW	WVBLS	10//99-12//99
	Wisconsin	S	7.86 MW	8.80 AW	18310 AAW	WIBLS	10//99-12//99
	Janesville-Beloit MSA, WI	S	5.79 MW	5.97 AW	12040 AAW	WIBLS	10//99-12//99
	Madison MSA, WI	S	14.02 MW	14.83 AW	29160 AAW	WIBLS	10//99-12//99
	Milwaukee-Waukesha PMSA, WI	S	8.78 MW	6.10 AW	18260 AAW	WIBLS	10//99-12//99
	Puerto Rico	S	5.98 MW	6.53 AW	13570 AAW	PRBLS	10//99-12//99
	San Juan-Bayamon PMSA, PR	S	6.51 MW	5.96 AW	13550 AAW	PRBLS	10//99-12//99
	Guam	S	12.23 MW	11.02 AW	22930 AAW	GUBLS	10//99-12//99
Bartender	Alabama	S	6.11 MW	6.41 AW	13340 AAW	ALBLS	10//99-12//99
	Anniston MSA, AL	S	6.16 MW	6.18 AW	12810 AAW	ALBLS	10//99-12//99
	Auburn-Opelika MSA, AL	S	6.11 MW	5.95 AW	12710 AAW	ALBLS	10//99-12//99
	Birmingham MSA, AL	S	6.52 MW	6.14 AW	13560 AAW	ALBLS	10//99-12//99
	Decatur MSA, AL	S	6.35 MW	5.99 AW	13210 AAW	ALBLS	10//99-12//99
	Dothan MSA, AL	S	6.05 MW	5.95 AW	12580 AAW	ALBLS	10//99-12//99
	Gadsden MSA, AL	S	6.00 MW	6.15 AW	12470 AAW	ALBLS	10//99-12//99

Occupation/Type/Industry	Location	Per	Low	Mid	High	Source	Date
Bartender	Huntsville MSA, AL	S	6.89 MW	6.17 AW	14330 AAW	ALBLS	10//99-12//99
	Mobile MSA, AL	S	6.57 MW	6.14 AW	13660 AAW	ALBLS	10//99-12//99
	Montgomery MSA, AL	S	6.36 MW	6.19 AW	13220 AAW	ALBLS	10//99-12//99
	Tuscaloosa MSA, AL	S	6.55 MW	6.17 AW	13630 AAW	ALBLS	10//99-12//99
	Alaska	S	10.05 MW	9.92 AW	20630 AAW	AKBLS	10//99-12//99
	Anchorage MSA, AK	S	9.25 MW	9.34 AW	19240 AAW	AKBLS	10//99-12//99
	Arizona	S	6.01 MW	6.09 AW	12660 AAW	AZBLS	10//99-12//99
	Flagstaff MSA, AZ-UT	S	6.00 MW	5.95 AW	12480 AAW	AZBLS	10//99-12//99
	Phoenix-Mesa MSA, AZ	S	6.03 MW	6.00 AW	12550 AAW	AZBLS	10//99-12//99
	Tucson MSA, AZ	S	6.24 MW	5.96 AW	12980 AAW	AZBLS	10//99-12//99
	Yuma MSA, AZ	S	6.39 MW	6.40 AW	13290 AAW	AZBLS	10//99-12//99
	Arkansas	S	6.09 MW	6.46 AW	13430 AAW	ARBLS	10//99-12//99
	Fayetteville-Springdale-Rogers MSA, AR	S	6.24 MW	5.95 AW	12980 AAW	ARBLS	10//99-12//99
	Fort Smith MSA, AR-OK	S	6.34 MW	6.00 AW	13190 AAW	ARBLS	10//99-12//99
	Little Rock-North Little Rock MSA, AR	S	6.37 MW	6.11 AW	13250 AAW	ARBLS	10//99-12//99
	California	S	6.92 MW	7.75 AW	16120 AAW	CABLS	10//99-12//99
	Bakersfield MSA, CA	S	6.96 MW	6.51 AW	14470 AAW	CABLS	10//99-12//99
	Chico-Paradise MSA, CA	S	6.85 MW	6.44 AW	14260 AAW	CABLS	10//99-12//99
	Fresno MSA, CA	S	6.63 MW	6.45 AW	13790 AAW	CABLS	10//99-12//99
	Los Angeles County, CA	Y		19356 AW		LABJ	1999
	Los Angeles-Long Beach PMSA, CA	S	7.81 MW	6.84 AW	16250 AAW	CABLS	10//99-12//99
	Merced MSA, CA	S	7.29 MW	7.03 AW	15160 AAW	CABLS	10//99-12//99
	Modesto MSA, CA	S	6.77 MW	6.08 AW	14070 AAW	CABLS	10//99-12//99
	Oakland PMSA, CA	S	8.71 MW	8.69 AW	18110 AAW	CABLS	10//99-12//99
	Orange County PMSA, CA	S	6.99 MW	6.48 AW	14540 AAW	CABLS	10//99-12//99
	Redding MSA, CA	S	7.40 MW	6.80 AW	15380 AAW	CABLS	10//99-12//99
	Riverside-San Bernardino PMSA, CA	S	7.22 MW	6.67 AW	15020 AAW	CABLS	10//99-12//99
	Sacramento PMSA, CA	S	7.19 MW	6.67 AW	14960 AAW	CABLS	10//99-12//99
	Salinas MSA, CA	S	8.09 MW	7.17 AW	16820 AAW	CABLS	10//99-12//99
	San Diego MSA, CA	S	7.10 MW	6.55 AW	14770 AAW	CABLS	10//99-12//99
	San Francisco PMSA, CA	S	9.35 MW	8.26 AW	19440 AAW	CABLS	10//99-12//99
	San Jose PMSA, CA	S	7.92 MW	7.54 AW	16460 AAW	CABLS	10//99-12//99
	San Luis Obispo-Atascadero-Paso Robles MSA, CA	S	7.89 MW	6.70 AW	16410 AAW	CABLS	10//99-12//99
	Santa Barbara-Santa Maria-Lompoc MSA, CA	S	7.70 MW	6.74 AW	16020 AAW	CABLS	10//99-12//99
	Santa Cruz-Watsonville PMSA, CA	S	8.01 MW	7.15 AW	16660 AAW	CABLS	10//99-12//99
	Santa Rosa PMSA, CA	S	8.45 MW	8.38 AW	17580 AAW	CABLS	10//99-12//99
	Stockton-Lodi MSA, CA	S	7.49 MW	6.99 AW	15570 AAW	CABLS	10//99-12//99
	Vallejo-Fairfield-Napa PMSA, CA	S	8.26 MW	8.12 AW	17180 AAW	CABLS	10//99-12//99
	Ventura PMSA, CA	S	8.49 MW	7.17 AW	17670 AAW	CABLS	10//99-12//99
	Visalia-Tulare-Porterville MSA, CA	S	7.88 MW	7.78 AW	16380 AAW	CABLS	10//99-12//99
	Yolo PMSA, CA	S	6.98 MW	6.67 AW	14530 AAW	CABLS	10//99-12//99
	Yuba City MSA, CA	S	6.93 MW	6.69 AW	14410 AAW	CABLS	10//99-12//99
	Colorado	S	6.38 MW	6.70 AW	13930 AAW	COBLS	10//99-12//99
	Boulder-Longmont PMSA, CO	S	6.89 MW	6.56 AW	14330 AAW	COBLS	10//99-12//99
	Colorado Springs MSA, CO	S	6.51 MW	6.10 AW	13540 AAW	COBLS	10//99-12//99
	Denver PMSA, CO	S	6.71 MW	6.42 AW	13960 AAW	COBLS	10//99-12//99
	Fort Collins-Loveland MSA, CO	S	6.66 MW	6.31 AW	13850 AAW	COBLS	10//99-12//99
	Grand Junction MSA, CO	S	6.42 MW	6.34 AW	13350 AAW	COBLS	10//99-12//99
	Greeley PMSA, CO	S	6.17 MW	6.16 AW	12840 AAW	COBLS	10//99-12//99
	Pueblo MSA, CO	S	6.26 MW	6.01 AW	13020 AAW	COBLS	10//99-12//99
	Connecticut	S	6.63 MW	7.59 AW	15790 AAW	CTBLS	10//99-12//99
	Bridgeport PMSA, CT	S	7.47 MW	6.57 AW	15540 AAW	CTBLS	10//99-12//99
	Danbury PMSA, CT	S	7.58 MW	6.70 AW	15760 AAW	CTBLS	10//99-12//99
	Hartford MSA, CT	S	7.64 MW	7.04 AW	15880 AAW	CTBLS	10//99-12//99
	New Haven-Meriden PMSA, CT	S	7.23 MW	6.56 AW	15040 AAW	CTBLS	10//99-12//99
	New London-Norwich MSA, CT-RI	S	6.68 MW	6.14 AW	13890 AAW	CTBLS	10//99-12//99
	Stamford-Norwalk PMSA, CT	S	10.03 MW	7.63 AW	20860 AAW	CTBLS	10//99-12//99
	Waterbury PMSA, CT	S	7.34 MW	6.53 AW	15260 AAW	CTBLS	10//99-12//99
	Delaware	S	6.12 MW	6.97 AW	14510 AAW	DEBLS	10//99-12//99
	Dover MSA, DE	S	6.94 MW	6.06 AW	14430 AAW	DEBLS	10//99-12//99

AAW Average annual wage	**AOH** Average offered, high	**ASH** Average starting, high	**H** Hourly	**M** Monthly	**S** Special: hourly and annual
AE Average entry wage	**AOL** Average offered, low	**ASL** Average starting, low	**HI** Highest wage paid	**MTC** Median total compensation	**TQ** Third quartile wage
AEX Average experienced wage	**APH** Average pay, high range	**AW** Average wage paid	**HR** High end range	**MW** Median wage paid	**W** Weekly
AO Average offered	**APL** Average pay, low range	**FQ** First quartile wage	**LR** Low end range	**SQ** Second quartile wage	**Y** Yearly

Occupation/Type/Industry	Location	Per	Low	Mid	High	Source	Date
Bartender	Wilmington-Newark PMSA, DE-MD	S	7.15 MW	6.28 AW	14860 AAW	DEBLS	10//99-12//99
	District of Columbia	S	8.36 MW	8.84 AW	18390 AAW	DCBLS	10//99-12//99
	Washington PMSA, DC-MD-VA-WV	S	7.29 MW	6.58 AW	15170 AAW	DCBLS	10//99-12//99
	Florida	S	6.11 MW	6.71 AW	13960 AAW	FLBLS	10//99-12//99
	Daytona Beach MSA, FL	S	6.20 MW	6.09 AW	12900 AAW	FLBLS	10//99-12//99
	Fort Lauderdale PMSA, FL	S	7.24 MW	6.56 AW	15060 AAW	FLBLS	10//99-12//99
	Fort Myers-Cape Coral MSA, FL	S	6.99 MW	6.19 AW	14540 AAW	FLBLS	10//99-12//99
	Fort Pierce-Port St. Lucie MSA, FL	S	6.68 MW	6.19 AW	13890 AAW	FLBLS	10//99-12//99
	Fort Walton Beach MSA, FL	S	7.24 MW	6.24 AW	15050 AAW	FLBLS	10//99-12//99
	Gainesville MSA, FL	S	7.73 MW	6.35 AW	16070 AAW	FLBLS	10//99-12//99
	Jacksonville MSA, FL	S	7.17 MW	6.32 AW	14920 AAW	FLBLS	10//99-12//99
	Lakeland-Winter Haven MSA, FL	S	6.42 MW	5.97 AW	13360 AAW	FLBLS	10//99-12//99
	Melbourne-Titusville-Palm Bay MSA, FL	S	6.16 MW	5.93 AW	12810 AAW	FLBLS	10//99-12//99
	Miami PMSA, FL	S	7.00 MW	6.29 AW	14550 AAW	FLBLS	10//99-12//99
	Naples MSA, FL	S	7.73 MW	6.75 AW	16080 AAW	FLBLS	10//99-12//99
	Ocala MSA, FL	S	6.09 MW	5.91 AW	12670 AAW	FLBLS	10//99-12//99
	Orlando MSA, FL	S	6.21 MW	6.03 AW	12920 AAW	FLBLS	10//99-12//99
	Panama City MSA, FL	S	6.62 MW	6.10 AW	13760 AAW	FLBLS	10//99-12//99
	Pensacola MSA, FL	S	5.98 MW	6.05 AW	12440 AAW	FLBLS	10//99-12//99
	Punta Gorda MSA, FL	S	6.39 MW	5.88 AW	13280 AAW	FLBLS	10//99-12//99
	Sarasota-Bradenton MSA, FL	S	6.37 MW	6.09 AW	13260 AAW	FLBLS	10//99-12//99
	Tallahassee MSA, FL	S	6.71 MW	6.23 AW	13960 AAW	FLBLS	10//99-12//99
	Tampa-St. Petersburg-Clearwater MSA, FL	S	6.69 MW	6.12 AW	13920 AAW	FLBLS	10//99-12//99
	West Palm Beach-Boca Raton MSA, FL	S	7.15 MW	6.08 AW	14870 AAW	FLBLS	10//99-12//99
	Georgia	S	6.23 MW	7.35 AW	15290 AAW	GABLS	10//99-12//99
	Albany MSA, GA	S	6.04 MW	5.98 AW	12560 AAW	GABLS	10//99-12//99
	Athens MSA, GA	S	7.32 MW	7.27 AW	15230 AAW	GABLS	10//99-12//99
	Atlanta MSA, GA	S	7.60 MW	6.26 AW	15810 AAW	GABLS	10//99-12//99
	Augusta-Aiken MSA, GA-SC	S	6.54 MW	6.24 AW	13600 AAW	GABLS	10//99-12//99
	Columbus MSA, GA-AL	S	6.25 MW	5.94 AW	13000 AAW	GABLS	10//99-12//99
	Macon MSA, GA	S	6.66 MW	6.21 AW	13840 AAW	GABLS	10//99-12//99
	Savannah MSA, GA	S	6.40 MW	6.14 AW	13320 AAW	GABLS	10//99-12//99
	Hawaii	S	8.56 MW	10.52 AW	21880 AAW	HIBLS	10//99-12//99
	Honolulu MSA, HI	S	9.74 MW	8.09 AW	20250 AAW	HIBLS	10//99-12//99
	Idaho	S	6.33 MW	6.45 AW	13420 AAW	IDBLS	10//99-12//99
	Boise City MSA, ID	S	6.45 MW	6.39 AW	13420 AAW	IDBLS	10//99-12//99
	Pocatello MSA, ID	S	6.45 MW	6.48 AW	13410 AAW	IDBLS	10//99-12//99
	Illinois	S	6.95 MW	7.44 AW	15480 AAW	ILBLS	10//99-12//99
	Bloomington-Normal MSA, IL	S	6.46 MW	6.32 AW	13440 AAW	ILBLS	10//99-12//99
	Champaign-Urbana MSA, IL	S	6.55 MW	6.05 AW	13620 AAW	ILBLS	10//99-12//99
	Chicago PMSA, IL	S	8.04 MW	7.81 AW	16720 AAW	ILBLS	10//99-12//99
	Decatur MSA, IL	S	7.31 MW	7.28 AW	15200 AAW	ILBLS	10//99-12//99
	Kankakee PMSA, IL	S	6.45 MW	6.39 AW	13420 AAW	ILBLS	10//99-12//99
	Peoria-Pekin MSA, IL	S	6.25 MW	6.24 AW	13000 AAW	ILBLS	10//99-12//99
	Rockford MSA, IL	S	6.99 MW	6.56 AW	14530 AAW	ILBLS	10//99-12//99
	Springfield MSA, IL	S	6.30 MW	6.27 AW	13110 AAW	ILBLS	10//99-12//99
	Indiana	S	6.67 MW	7.06 AW	14690 AAW	INBLS	10//99-12//99
	Bloomington MSA, IN	S	6.82 MW	6.45 AW	14180 AAW	INBLS	10//99-12//99
	Elkhart-Goshen MSA, IN	S	7.26 MW	6.80 AW	15090 AAW	INBLS	10//99-12//99
	Evansville-Henderson MSA, IN-KY	S	6.89 MW	6.72 AW	14320 AAW	INBLS	10//99-12//99
	Fort Wayne MSA, IN	S	7.44 MW	7.45 AW	15470 AAW	INBLS	10//99-12//99
	Gary PMSA, IN	S	6.76 MW	6.12 AW	14060 AAW	INBLS	10//99-12//99
	Indianapolis MSA, IN	S	7.00 MW	6.70 AW	14560 AAW	INBLS	10//99-12//99
	Kokomo MSA, IN	S	5.97 MW	5.87 AW	12420 AAW	INBLS	10//99-12//99
	Lafayette MSA, IN	S	6.44 MW	6.19 AW	13390 AAW	INBLS	10//99-12//99
	Muncie MSA, IN	S	6.46 MW	6.05 AW	13440 AAW	INBLS	10//99-12//99
	South Bend MSA, IN	S	7.19 MW	6.72 AW	14950 AAW	INBLS	10//99-12//99
	Terre Haute MSA, IN	S	6.72 MW	6.58 AW	13980 AAW	INBLS	10//99-12//99
	Iowa	S	6.52 MW	6.73 AW	14000 AAW	IABLS	10//99-12//99
	Cedar Rapids MSA, IA	S	7.11 MW	6.99 AW	14790 AAW	IABLS	10//99-12//99
	Davenport-Moline-Rock Island MSA, IA-IL	S	6.71 MW	6.42 AW	13960 AAW	IABLS	10//99-12//99
	Des Moines MSA, IA	S	7.65 MW	7.75 AW	15910 AAW	IABLS	10//99-12//99

AAW Average annual wage	**AOH** Average offered, high	**ASH** Average starting, high	**H** Hourly	**M** Monthly	**S** Special: hourly and annual
AE Average entry wage	**AOL** Average offered, low	**ASL** Average starting, low	**HI** Highest wage paid	**MTC** Median total compensation	**TQ** Third quartile wage
AEX Average experienced wage	**APH** Average pay, high range	**AW** Average wage paid	**HR** High end range	**MW** Median wage paid	**W** Weekly
AO Average offered	**APL** Average pay, low range	**FQ** First quartile wage	**LR** Low end range	**SQ** Second quartile wage	**Y** Yearly

Occupation/Type/Industry	Location	Per	Low	Mid	High	Source	Date
Bartender	Dubuque MSA, IA	S	6.13 MW	6.00 AW	12750 AAW	IABLS	10//99-12//99
	Iowa City MSA, IA	S	6.89 MW	6.84 AW	14340 AAW	IABLS	10//99-12//99
	Sioux City MSA, IA-NE	S	7.06 MW	7.03 AW	14690 AAW	IABLS	10//99-12//99
	Waterloo-Cedar Falls MSA, IA	S	5.99 MW	5.89 AW	12470 AAW	IABLS	10//99-12//99
	Kansas	S	6.49 MW	6.78 AW	14110 AAW	KSBLS	10//99-12//99
	Lawrence MSA, KS	S	7.48 MW	7.34 AW	15570 AAW	KSBLS	10//99-12//99
	Topeka MSA, KS	S	6.70 MW	6.11 AW	13930 AAW	KSBLS	10//99-12//99
	Wichita MSA, KS	S	6.68 MW	6.38 AW	13900 AAW	KSBLS	10//99-12//99
	Kentucky	S	6.35 MW	6.64 AW	13800 AAW	KYBLS	10//99-12//99
	Lexington MSA, KY	S	6.55 MW	6.03 AW	13630 AAW	KYBLS	10//99-12//99
	Louisville MSA, KY-IN	S	7.19 MW	6.98 AW	14950 AAW	KYBLS	10//99-12//99
	Owensboro MSA, KY	S	6.66 MW	6.41 AW	13840 AAW	KYBLS	10//99-12//99
	Louisiana	S	6.29 MW	7.02 AW	14600 AAW	LABLS	10//99-12//99
	Alexandria MSA, LA	S	6.60 MW	6.34 AW	13730 AAW	LABLS	10//99-12//99
	Baton Rouge MSA, LA	S	6.19 MW	6.05 AW	12880 AAW	LABLS	10//99-12//99
	Houma MSA, LA	S	6.23 MW	5.98 AW	12970 AAW	LABLS	10//99-12//99
	Lafayette MSA, LA	S	6.44 MW	6.05 AW	13380 AAW	LABLS	10//99-12//99
	Lake Charles MSA, LA	S	6.21 MW	6.02 AW	12910 AAW	LABLS	10//99-12//99
	Monroe MSA, LA	S	6.74 MW	6.59 AW	14020 AAW	LABLS	10//99-12//99
	New Orleans MSA, LA	S	7.88 MW	6.94 AW	16390 AAW	LABLS	10//99-12//99
	Shreveport-Bossier City MSA, LA	S	6.49 MW	6.09 AW	13500 AAW	LABLS	10//99-12//99
	Maine	S	6.45 MW	6.94 AW	14440 AAW	MEBLS	10//99-12//99
	Bangor MSA, ME	S	8.10 MW	6.78 AW	16850 AAW	MEBLS	10//99-12//99
	Lewiston-Auburn MSA, ME	S	6.66 MW	6.62 AW	13860 AAW	MEBLS	10//99-12//99
	Portland MSA, ME	S	7.14 MW	6.41 AW	14860 AAW	MEBLS	10//99-12//99
	Maryland	S	6.07 MW	6.54 AW	13610 AAW	MDBLS	10//99-12//99
	Baltimore PMSA, MD	S	6.47 MW	5.98 AW	13450 AAW	MDBLS	10//99-12//99
	Cumberland MSA, MD-WV	S	6.49 MW	6.06 AW	13510 AAW	MDBLS	10//99-12//99
	Hagerstown PMSA, MD	S	6.00 MW	6.10 AW	12470 AAW	MDBLS	10//99-12//99
	Massachusetts	S	6.68 MW	7.50 AW	15600 AAW	MABLS	10//99-12//99
	Barnstable-Yarmouth MSA, MA	S	7.04 MW	6.44 AW	14640 AAW	MABLS	10//99-12//99
	Boston PMSA, MA-NH	S	7.91 MW	6.99 AW	16440 AAW	MABLS	10//99-12//99
	Brockton PMSA, MA	S	6.63 MW	6.26 AW	13790 AAW	MABLS	10//99-12//99
	Fitchburg-Leominster PMSA, MA	S	7.00 MW	6.54 AW	14570 AAW	MABLS	10//99-12//99
	Lawrence PMSA, MA-NH	S	6.83 MW	6.41 AW	14210 AAW	MABLS	10//99-12//99
	Lowell PMSA, MA-NH	S	7.14 MW	6.68 AW	14840 AAW	MABLS	10//99-12//99
	New Bedford PMSA, MA	S	7.39 MW	6.60 AW	15380 AAW	MABLS	10//99-12//99
	Pittsfield MSA, MA	S	6.84 MW	6.62 AW	14230 AAW	MABLS	10//99-12//99
	Springfield MSA, MA	S	7.06 MW	6.36 AW	14690 AAW	MABLS	10//99-12//99
	Worcester PMSA, MA-CT	S	6.84 MW	6.25 AW	14240 AAW	MABLS	10//99-12//99
	Michigan	S	6.35 MW	6.74 AW	14030 AAW	MIBLS	10//99-12//99
	Ann Arbor PMSA, MI	S	6.75 MW	6.58 AW	14040 AAW	MIBLS	10//99-12//99
	Benton Harbor MSA, MI	S	7.44 MW	6.82 AW	15470 AAW	MIBLS	10//99-12//99
	Detroit PMSA, MI	S	7.27 MW	6.77 AW	15120 AAW	MIBLS	10//99-12//99
	Flint PMSA, MI	S	6.33 MW	6.32 AW	13160 AAW	MIBLS	10//99-12//99
	Grand Rapids-Muskegon-Holland MSA, MI	S	6.79 MW	6.52 AW	14130 AAW	MIBLS	10//99-12//99
	Jackson MSA, MI	S	9.65 MW	8.20 AW	20060 AAW	MIBLS	10//99-12//99
	Kalamazoo-Battle Creek MSA, MI	S	6.41 MW	6.34 AW	13340 AAW	MIBLS	10//99-12//99
	Lansing-East Lansing MSA, MI	S	6.36 MW	6.09 AW	13230 AAW	MIBLS	10//99-12//99
	Saginaw-Bay City-Midland MSA, MI	S	6.86 MW	6.06 AW	14260 AAW	MIBLS	10//99-12//99
	Minnesota	S	6.76 MW	7.04 AW	14640 AAW	MNBLS	10//99-12//99
	Duluth-Superior MSA, MN-WI	S	6.55 MW	6.45 AW	13630 AAW	MNBLS	10//99-12//99
	Minneapolis-St. Paul MSA, MN-WI	S	7.21 MW	6.95 AW	15010 AAW	MNBLS	10//99-12//99
	Rochester MSA, MN	S	8.45 MW	8.51 AW	17570 AAW	MNBLS	10//99-12//99
	St. Cloud MSA, MN	S	6.65 MW	6.51 AW	13840 AAW	MNBLS	10//99-12//99
	Mississippi	S	6.32 MW	6.35 AW	13210 AAW	MSBLS	10//99-12//99
	Biloxi-Gulfport-Pascagoula MSA, MS	S	6.14 MW	6.24 AW	12770 AAW	MSBLS	10//99-12//99
	Hattiesburg MSA, MS	S	6.20 MW	6.12 AW	12890 AAW	MSBLS	10//99-12//99
	Jackson MSA, MS	S	6.69 MW	6.33 AW	13910 AAW	MSBLS	10//99-12//99
	Missouri	S	6.45 MW	6.85 AW	14250 AAW	MOBLS	10//99-12//99
	Joplin MSA, MO	S	6.41 MW	6.34 AW	13330 AAW	MOBLS	10//99-12//99
	Kansas City MSA, MO-KS	S	7.11 MW	6.57 AW	14790 AAW	MOBLS	10//99-12//99
	St. Joseph MSA, MO	S	6.16 MW	6.21 AW	12820 AAW	MOBLS	10//99-12//99
	St. Louis MSA, MO-IL	S	6.73 MW	6.45 AW	14010 AAW	MOBLS	10//99-12//99

AAW Average annual wage	**AOH** Average offered, high	**ASH** Average starting, high	**H** Hourly	**M** Monthly	**S** Special: hourly and annual
AE Average entry wage	**AOL** Average offered, low	**ASL** Average starting, low	**HI** Highest wage paid	**MTC** Median total compensation	**TQ** Third quartile wage
AEX Average experienced wage	**APH** Average pay, high range	**AW** Average wage paid	**HR** High end range	**MW** Median wage paid	**W** Weekly
AO Average offered	**APL** Average pay, low range	**FQ** First quartile wage	**LR** Low end range	**SQ** Second quartile wage	**Y** Yearly

Bartender

Occupation/Type/Industry	Location	Per	Low	Mid	High	Source	Date
Bartender	Montana	S	6.41 MW	6.51 AW	13540 AAW	MTBLS	10//99-12//99
	Billings MSA, MT	S	6.66 MW	6.21 AW	13850 AAW	MTBLS	10//99-12//99
	Great Falls MSA, MT	S	6.77 MW	6.71 AW	14080 AAW	MTBLS	10//99-12//99
	Missoula MSA, MT	S	6.90 MW	6.90 AW	14350 AAW	MTBLS	10//99-12//99
	Nebraska	S	6.65 MW	6.79 AW	14120 AAW	NEBLS	10//99-12//99
	Lincoln MSA, NE	S	6.53 MW	6.11 AW	13590 AAW	NEBLS	10//99-12//99
	Omaha MSA, NE-IA	S	6.87 MW	6.71 AW	14290 AAW	NEBLS	10//99-12//99
	Nevada	S	7.7 MW	8.37 AW	17400 AAW	NVBLS	10//99-12//99
	Las Vegas MSA, NV-AZ	S	8.80 MW	8.25 AW	18300 AAW	NVBLS	10//99-12//99
	Reno MSA, NV	S	7.17 MW	6.95 AW	14910 AAW	NVBLS	10//99-12//99
	New Hampshire	S	6.72 MW	7.20 AW	14980 AAW	NHBLS	10//99-12//99
	Manchester PMSA, NH	S	8.29 MW	7.88 AW	17230 AAW	NHBLS	10//99-12//99
	Nashua PMSA, NH	S	7.25 MW	6.81 AW	15070 AAW	NHBLS	10//99-12//99
	Portsmouth-Rochester PMSA, NH-ME	S	7.02 MW	6.49 AW	14590 AAW	NHBLS	10//99-12//99
	New Jersey	S	6.57 MW	7.53 AW	15660 AAW	NJBLS	10//99-12//99
	Atlantic-Cape May PMSA, NJ	S	8.95 MW	7.16 AW	18620 AAW	NJBLS	10//99-12//99
	Bergen-Passaic PMSA, NJ	S	7.80 MW	7.68 AW	16220 AAW	NJBLS	10//99-12//99
	Jersey City PMSA, NJ	S	6.97 MW	6.20 AW	14500 AAW	NJBLS	10//99-12//99
	Middlesex-Somerset-Hunterdon PMSA, NJ	S	8.94 MW	6.53 AW	18600 AAW	NJBLS	10//99-12//99
	Monmouth-Ocean PMSA, NJ	S	6.90 MW	6.05 AW	14360 AAW	NJBLS	10//99-12//99
	Newark PMSA, NJ	S	7.50 MW	6.69 AW	15590 AAW	NJBLS	10//99-12//99
	Trenton PMSA, NJ	S	6.85 MW	6.38 AW	14240 AAW	NJBLS	10//99-12//99
	Vineland-Millville-Bridgeton PMSA, NJ	S	8.57 MW	9.01 AW	17820 AAW	NJBLS	10//99-12//99
	New Mexico	S	6.02 MW	6.35 AW	13210 AAW	NMBLS	10//99-12//99
	Albuquerque MSA, NM	S	6.16 MW	5.91 AW	12820 AAW	NMBLS	10//99-12//99
	Las Cruces MSA, NM	S	6.10 MW	6.09 AW	12680 AAW	NMBLS	10//99-12//99
	Santa Fe MSA, NM	S	8.38 MW	8.21 AW	17440 AAW	NMBLS	10//99-12//99
	New York	S	6.3 MW	7.04 AW	14650 AAW	NYBLS	10//99-12//99
	Albany-Schenectady-Troy MSA, NY	S	6.18 MW	6.05 AW	12850 AAW	NYBLS	10//99-12//99
	Binghamton MSA, NY	S	6.64 MW	6.42 AW	13820 AAW	NYBLS	10//99-12//99
	Buffalo-Niagara Falls MSA, NY	S	6.23 MW	6.11 AW	12950 AAW	NYBLS	10//99-12//99
	Dutchess County PMSA, NY	S	7.30 MW	6.08 AW	15190 AAW	NYBLS	10//99-12//99
	Elmira MSA, NY	S	6.12 MW	6.18 AW	12730 AAW	NYBLS	10//99-12//99
	Glens Falls MSA, NY	S	6.21 MW	5.99 AW	12920 AAW	NYBLS	10//99-12//99
	Jamestown MSA, NY	S	6.49 MW	6.20 AW	13490 AAW	NYBLS	10//99-12//99
	Nassau-Suffolk PMSA, NY	S	6.95 MW	6.39 AW	14460 AAW	NYBLS	10//99-12//99
	New York PMSA, NY	S	8.21 MW	6.73 AW	17090 AAW	NYBLS	10//99-12//99
	Newburgh PMSA, NY-PA	S	6.99 MW	6.50 AW	14540 AAW	NYBLS	10//99-12//99
	Rochester MSA, NY	S	6.51 MW	6.12 AW	13540 AAW	NYBLS	10//99-12//99
	Syracuse MSA, NY	S	6.24 MW	6.07 AW	12970 AAW	NYBLS	10//99-12//99
	Utica-Rome MSA, NY	S	6.47 MW	6.10 AW	13460 AAW	NYBLS	10//99-12//99
	North Carolina	S	6.14 MW	6.53 AW	13590 AAW	NCBLS	10//99-12//99
	Asheville MSA, NC	S	6.82 MW	6.62 AW	14190 AAW	NCBLS	10//99-12//99
	Charlotte-Gastonia-Rock Hill MSA, NC-SC	S	6.82 MW	6.31 AW	14180 AAW	NCBLS	10//99-12//99
	Fayetteville MSA, NC	S	6.37 MW	6.04 AW	13250 AAW	NCBLS	10//99-12//99
	Greensboro--Winston-Salem--High Point MSA, NC	S	6.84 MW	6.45 AW	14220 AAW	NCBLS	10//99-12//99
	Greenville MSA, NC	S	6.00 MW	5.90 AW	12480 AAW	NCBLS	10//99-12//99
	Jacksonville MSA, NC	S	5.83 MW	6.02 AW	12130 AAW	NCBLS	10//99-12//99
	Raleigh-Durham-Chapel Hill MSA, NC	S	6.54 MW	6.10 AW	13610 AAW	NCBLS	10//99-12//99
	Wilmington MSA, NC	S	6.18 MW	5.99 AW	12850 AAW	NCBLS	10//99-12//99
	North Dakota	S	6.17 MW	6.25 AW	13000 AAW	NDBLS	10//99-12//99
	Bismarck MSA, ND	S	6.39 MW	6.38 AW	13300 AAW	NDBLS	10//99-12//99
	Fargo-Moorhead MSA, ND-MN	S	6.43 MW	6.25 AW	13370 AAW	NDBLS	10//99-12//99
	Grand Forks MSA, ND-MN	S	6.68 MW	6.48 AW	13890 AAW	NDBLS	10//99-12//99
	Ohio	S	6.32 MW	6.73 AW	14010 AAW	OHBLS	10//99-12//99
	Akron PMSA, OH	S	6.19 MW	5.97 AW	12880 AAW	OHBLS	10//99-12//99
	Canton-Massillon MSA, OH	S	6.31 MW	6.13 AW	13120 AAW	OHBLS	10//99-12//99
	Cincinnati PMSA, OH-KY-IN	S	6.96 MW	6.53 AW	14480 AAW	OHBLS	10//99-12//99
	Cleveland-Lorain-Elyria PMSA, OH	S	7.05 MW	6.50 AW	14660 AAW	OHBLS	10//99-12//99
	Columbus MSA, OH	S	6.61 MW	6.32 AW	13760 AAW	OHBLS	10//99-12//99
	Dayton-Springfield MSA, OH	S	6.84 MW	6.41 AW	14220 AAW	OHBLS	10//99-12//99

AAW Average annual wage	AOH Average offered, high	ASH Average starting, high	H Hourly	M Monthly	S Special: hourly and annual
AE Average entry wage	AOL Average offered, low	ASL Average starting, low	HI Highest wage paid	MTC Median total compensation	TQ Third quartile wage
AEX Average experienced wage	APH Average pay, high range	AW Average wage paid	HR High end range	MW Median wage paid	W Weekly
AO Average offered	APL Average pay, low range	FQ First quartile wage	LR Low end range	SQ Second quartile wage	Y Yearly

Occupation/Type/Industry	Location	Per	Low	Mid	High	Source	Date
Bartender	Hamilton-Middletown PMSA, OH	S	6.51 MW	6.37 AW	13530 AAW	OHBLS	10//99-12//99
	Lima MSA, OH	S	6.54 MW	6.29 AW	13610 AAW	OHBLS	10//99-12//99
	Mansfield MSA, OH	S	7.56 MW	7.41 AW	15720 AAW	OHBLS	10//99-12//99
	Steubenville-Weirton MSA, OH-WV	S	5.94 MW	5.99 AW	12360 AAW	OHBLS	10//99-12//99
	Toledo MSA, OH	S	6.38 MW	6.06 AW	13260 AAW	OHBLS	10//99-12//99
	Youngstown-Warren MSA, OH	S	6.84 MW	6.10 AW	14230 AAW	OHBLS	10//99-12//99
	Oklahoma	S	6.02 MW	6.20 AW	12890 AAW	OKBLS	10//99-12//99
	Oklahoma City MSA, OK	S	6.34 MW	6.08 AW	13190 AAW	OKBLS	10//99-12//99
	Tulsa MSA, OK	S	6.32 MW	6.23 AW	13150 AAW	OKBLS	10//99-12//99
	Oregon	S	7.55 MW	7.66 AW	15940 AAW	ORBLS	10//99-12//99
	Corvallis MSA, OR	S	7.58 MW	7.51 AW	15760 AAW	ORBLS	10//99-12//99
	Eugene-Springfield MSA, OR	S	8.01 MW	7.87 AW	16660 AAW	ORBLS	10//99-12//99
	Medford-Ashland MSA, OR	S	7.46 MW	7.48 AW	15510 AAW	ORBLS	10//99-12//99
	Portland-Vancouver PMSA, OR-WA	S	7.69 MW	7.55 AW	16000 AAW	ORBLS	10//99-12//99
	Salem PMSA, OR	S	7.61 MW	7.52 AW	15830 AAW	ORBLS	10//99-12//99
	Pennsylvania	S	6.35 MW	6.79 AW	14120 AAW	PABLS	10//99-12//99
	Allentown-Bethlehem-Easton MSA, PA	S	7.69 MW	7.27 AW	16000 AAW	PABLS	10//99-12//99
	Altoona MSA, PA	S	7.71 MW	7.17 AW	16030 AAW	PABLS	10//99-12//99
	Erie MSA, PA	S	7.03 MW	6.51 AW	14620 AAW	PABLS	10//99-12//99
	Harrisburg-Lebanon-Carlisle MSA, PA	S	6.60 MW	6.31 AW	13730 AAW	PABLS	10//99-12//99
	Johnstown MSA, PA	S	6.94 MW	6.09 AW	14430 AAW	PABLS	10//99-12//99
	Lancaster MSA, PA	S	7.79 MW	6.84 AW	16200 AAW	PABLS	10//99-12//99
	Philadelphia PMSA, PA-NJ	S	6.96 MW	6.33 AW	14480 AAW	PABLS	10//99-12//99
	Pittsburgh MSA, PA	S	6.42 MW	6.25 AW	13340 AAW	PABLS	10//99-12//99
	Reading MSA, PA	S	7.65 MW	7.46 AW	15910 AAW	PABLS	10//99-12//99
	Scranton--Wilkes-Barre--Hazleton MSA, PA	S	6.20 MW	6.05 AW	12890 AAW	PABLS	10//99-12//99
	Sharon MSA, PA	S	6.10 MW	6.06 AW	12690 AAW	PABLS	10//99-12//99
	State College MSA, PA	S	6.49 MW	6.33 AW	13500 AAW	PABLS	10//99-12//99
	Williamsport MSA, PA	S	7.70 MW	7.42 AW	16030 AAW	PABLS	10//99-12//99
	York MSA, PA	S	6.44 MW	6.19 AW	13390 AAW	PABLS	10//99-12//99
	Rhode Island	S	6.22 MW	6.71 AW	13960 AAW	RIBLS	10//99-12//99
	Providence-Fall River-Warwick MSA, RI-MA	S	7.01 MW	6.35 AW	14580 AAW	RIBLS	10//99-12//99
	South Carolina	S	6.14 MW	6.83 AW	14210 AAW	SCBLS	10//99-12//99
	Charleston-North Charleston MSA, SC	S	6.08 MW	5.93 AW	12640 AAW	SCBLS	10//99-12//99
	Columbia MSA, SC	S	6.58 MW	6.11 AW	13690 AAW	SCBLS	10//99-12//99
	Greenville-Spartanburg-Anderson MSA, SC	S	7.56 MW	6.18 AW	15730 AAW	SCBLS	10//99-12//99
	Myrtle Beach MSA, SC	S	7.02 MW	6.50 AW	14600 AAW	SCBLS	10//99-12//99
	South Dakota	S	6.34 MW	6.56 AW	13640 AAW	SDBLS	10//99-12//99
	Rapid City MSA, SD	S	6.52 MW	6.50 AW	13570 AAW	SDBLS	10//99-12//99
	Sioux Falls MSA, SD	S	6.77 MW	6.78 AW	14080 AAW	SDBLS	10//99-12//99
	Tennessee	S	6.3 MW	6.72 AW	13980 AAW	TNBLS	10//99-12//99
	Chattanooga MSA, TN-GA	S	7.85 MW	6.73 AW	16320 AAW	TNBLS	10//99-12//99
	Clarksville-Hopkinsville MSA, TN-KY	S	6.50 MW	6.30 AW	13520 AAW	TNBLS	10//99-12//99
	Jackson MSA, TN	S	7.22 MW	7.11 AW	15020 AAW	TNBLS	10//99-12//99
	Johnson City-Kingsport-Bristol MSA, TN-VA	S	6.32 MW	6.10 AW	13140 AAW	TNBLS	10//99-12//99
	Knoxville MSA, TN	S	6.52 MW	6.21 AW	13550 AAW	TNBLS	10//99-12//99
	Memphis MSA, TN-AR-MS	S	7.08 MW	6.37 AW	14740 AAW	MSBLS	10//99-12//99
	Nashville MSA, TN	S	6.69 MW	6.32 AW	13910 AAW	TNBLS	10//99-12//99
	Texas	S	6.08 MW	6.47 AW	13460 AAW	TXBLS	10//99-12//99
	Abilene MSA, TX	S	6.05 MW	5.95 AW	12590 AAW	TXBLS	10//99-12//99
	Amarillo MSA, TX	S	7.31 MW	6.45 AW	15200 AAW	TXBLS	10//99-12//99
	Austin-San Marcos MSA, TX	S	6.62 MW	6.04 AW	13760 AAW	TXBLS	10//99-12//99
	Beaumont-Port Arthur MSA, TX	S	6.96 MW	6.70 AW	14470 AAW	TXBLS	10//99-12//99
	Brazoria PMSA, TX	S	6.93 MW	6.76 AW	14400 AAW	TXBLS	10//99-12//99
	Brownsville-Harlingen-San Benito MSA, TX	S	5.98 MW	6.00 AW	12430 AAW	TXBLS	10//99-12//99
	Bryan-College Station MSA, TX	S	6.00 MW	6.03 AW	12470 AAW	TXBLS	10//99-12//99
	Corpus Christi MSA, TX	S	6.73 MW	6.21 AW	13990 AAW	TXBLS	10//99-12//99
	Dallas PMSA, TX	S	6.51 MW	6.33 AW	13550 AAW	TXBLS	10//99-12//99

AAW Average annual wage	**AOH** Average offered, high	**ASH** Average starting, high	**H** Hourly	**M** Monthly	**S** Special: hourly and annual
AE Average entry wage	**AOL** Average offered, low	**ASL** Average starting, low	**HI** Highest wage paid	**MTC** Median total compensation	**TQ** Third quartile wage
AEX Average experienced wage	**APH** Average pay, high range	**AW** Average wage paid	**HR** High end range	**MW** Median wage paid	**W** Weekly
AO Average offered	**APL** Average pay, low range	**FQ** First quartile wage	**LR** Low end range	**SQ** Second quartile wage	**Y** Yearly

Bartender

Occupation/Type/Industry	Location	Per	Low	Mid	High	Source	Date
Bartender	El Paso MSA, TX	S	6.36 MW	6.04 AW	13220 AAW	TXBLS	10//99-12//99
	Fort Worth-Arlington PMSA, TX	S	6.58 MW	6.03 AW	13680 AAW	TXBLS	10//99-12//99
	Galveston-Texas City PMSA, TX	S	6.15 MW	6.13 AW	12780 AAW	TXBLS	10//99-12//99
	Houston PMSA, TX	S	6.81 MW	6.20 AW	14170 AAW	TXBLS	10//99-12//99
	Killeen-Temple MSA, TX	S	6.04 MW	6.05 AW	12560 AAW	TXBLS	10//99-12//99
	Laredo MSA, TX	S	6.67 MW	6.12 AW	13870 AAW	TXBLS	10//99-12//99
	Longview-Marshall MSA, TX	S	7.05 MW	7.03 AW	14670 AAW	TXBLS	10//99-12//99
	Lubbock MSA, TX	S	6.62 MW	6.33 AW	13770 AAW	TXBLS	10//99-12//99
	McAllen-Edinburg-Mission MSA, TX	S	6.32 MW	6.28 AW	13140 AAW	TXBLS	10//99-12//99
	Odessa-Midland MSA, TX	S	7.75 MW	7.86 AW	16110 AAW	TXBLS	10//99-12//99
	San Antonio MSA, TX	S	6.10 MW	5.87 AW	12680 AAW	TXBLS	10//99-12//99
	Sherman-Denison MSA, TX	S	6.92 MW	6.31 AW	14400 AAW	TXBLS	10//99-12//99
	Texarkana MSA, TX-Texarkana, AR	S	6.25 MW	5.99 AW	13000 AAW	TXBLS	10//99-12//99
	Tyler MSA, TX	S	6.45 MW	6.12 AW	13420 AAW	TXBLS	10//99-12//99
	Victoria MSA, TX	S	5.91 MW	5.92 AW	12300 AAW	TXBLS	10//99-12//99
	Waco MSA, TX	S	5.83 MW	5.92 AW	12120 AAW	TXBLS	10//99-12//99
	Wichita Falls MSA, TX	S	6.83 MW	6.79 AW	14210 AAW	TXBLS	10//99-12//99
	Utah	S	6.52 MW	7.06 AW	14680 AAW	UTBLS	10//99-12//99
	Provo-Orem MSA, UT	S	7.36 MW	6.73 AW	15310 AAW	UTBLS	10//99-12//99
	Salt Lake City-Ogden MSA, UT	S	7.01 MW	6.47 AW	14580 AAW	UTBLS	10//99-12//99
	Vermont	S	6.58 MW	7.15 AW	14880 AAW	VTBLS	10//99-12//99
	Burlington MSA, VT	S	6.80 MW	6.13 AW	14130 AAW	VTBLS	10//99-12//99
	Virginia	S	6.09 MW	6.57 AW	13660 AAW	VABLS	10//99-12//99
	Charlottesville MSA, VA	S	6.63 MW	6.25 AW	13780 AAW	VABLS	10//99-12//99
	Lynchburg MSA, VA	S	6.30 MW	6.08 AW	13100 AAW	VABLS	10//99-12//99
	Norfolk-Virginia Beach-Newport News MSA, VA-NC	S	6.12 MW	5.99 AW	12730 AAW	VABLS	10//99-12//99
	Richmond-Petersburg MSA, VA	S	6.55 MW	6.05 AW	13620 AAW	VABLS	10//99-12//99
	Roanoke MSA, VA	S	6.75 MW	6.19 AW	14040 AAW	VABLS	10//99-12//99
	Washington	S	7.5 MW	7.69 AW	16000 AAW	WABLS	10//99-12//99
	Bellingham MSA, WA	S	7.70 MW	7.56 AW	16010 AAW	WABLS	10//99-12//99
	Bremerton PMSA, WA	S	7.32 MW	7.16 AW	15240 AAW	WABLS	10//99-12//99
	Olympia PMSA, WA	S	7.30 MW	7.22 AW	15190 AAW	WABLS	10//99-12//99
	Richland-Kennewick-Pasco MSA, WA	S	7.49 MW	7.36 AW	15580 AAW	WABLS	10//99-12//99
	Seattle-Bellevue-Everett PMSA, WA	S	7.92 MW	7.72 AW	16470 AAW	WABLS	10//99-12//99
	Spokane MSA, WA	S	7.51 MW	6.92 AW	15620 AAW	WABLS	10//99-12//99
	Tacoma PMSA, WA	S	7.66 MW	7.59 AW	15920 AAW	WABLS	10//99-12//99
	Yakima MSA, WA	S	7.45 MW	7.21 AW	15490 AAW	WABLS	10//99-12//99
	West Virginia	S	6.15 MW	6.25 AW	13010 AAW	WVBLS	10//99-12//99
	Charleston MSA, WV	S	6.28 MW	6.23 AW	13060 AAW	WVBLS	10//99-12//99
	Huntington-Ashland MSA, WV-KY-OH	S	6.52 MW	6.39 AW	13560 AAW	WVBLS	10//99-12//99
	Parkersburg-Marietta MSA, WV-OH	S	6.35 MW	6.24 AW	13200 AAW	WVBLS	10//99-12//99
	Wheeling MSA, WV-OH	S	6.48 MW	6.40 AW	13480 AAW	WVBLS	10//99-12//99
	Wisconsin	S	7.05 MW	7.33 AW	15250 AAW	WIBLS	10//99-12//99
	Appleton-Oshkosh-Neenah MSA, WI	S	7.44 MW	7.59 AW	15470 AAW	WIBLS	10//99-12//99
	Eau Claire MSA, WI	S	6.12 MW	5.94 AW	12730 AAW	WIBLS	10//99-12//99
	Green Bay MSA, WI	S	7.58 MW	7.60 AW	15760 AAW	WIBLS	10//99-12//99
	Janesville-Beloit MSA, WI	S	6.70 MW	6.54 AW	13940 AAW	WIBLS	10//99-12//99
	Kenosha PMSA, WI	S	7.14 MW	7.29 AW	14860 AAW	WIBLS	10//99-12//99
	La Crosse MSA, WI-MN	S	6.33 MW	6.10 AW	13170 AAW	WIBLS	10//99-12//99
	Madison MSA, WI	S	7.03 MW	6.91 AW	14620 AAW	WIBLS	10//99-12//99
	Milwaukee-Waukesha PMSA, WI	S	8.30 MW	7.59 AW	17260 AAW	WIBLS	10//99-12//99
	Racine PMSA, WI	S	6.68 MW	6.37 AW	13900 AAW	WIBLS	10//99-12//99
	Sheboygan MSA, WI	S	6.78 MW	6.08 AW	14100 AAW	WIBLS	10//99-12//99
	Wausau MSA, WI	S	7.62 MW	7.46 AW	15860 AAW	WIBLS	10//99-12//99
	Wyoming	S	6.57 MW	6.74 AW	14010 AAW	WYBLS	10//99-12//99
	Casper MSA, WY	S	6.55 MW	6.38 AW	13620 AAW	WYBLS	10//99-12//99
	Cheyenne MSA, WY	S	7.27 MW	7.23 AW	15120 AAW	WYBLS	10//99-12//99
	Puerto Rico	S	6.07 MW	6.61 AW	13740 AAW	PRBLS	10//99-12//99

AAW Average annual wage · AE Average entry wage · AEX Average experienced wage · AO Average offered · AOH Average offered, high · AOL Average offered, low · APH Average pay, high range · APL Average pay, low range · ASH Average starting, high · ASL Average starting, low · AW Average wage paid · FQ First quartile wage · H Hourly · HI Highest wage paid · HR High end range · LR Low end range · M Monthly · MTC Median total compensation · MW Median wage paid · SQ Second quartile wage · S Special: hourly and annual · TQ Third quartile wage · W Weekly · Y Yearly

Occupation/Type/Industry	Location	Per	Low	Mid	High	Source	Date
Bartender	Aguadilla MSA, PR	S	5.73 MW	5.87 AW	11910 AAW	PRBLS	10//99-12//99
	Mayaguez MSA, PR	S	5.87 MW	6.12 AW	12200 AAW	PRBLS	10//99-12//99
	Ponce MSA, PR	S	5.86 MW	6.04 AW	12190 AAW	PRBLS	10//99-12//99
	San Juan-Bayamon PMSA, PR	S	7.02 MW	6.23 AW	14600 AAW	PRBLS	10//99-12//99
	Virgin Islands	S	6.09 MW	6.04 AW	12560 AAW	VIBLS	10//99-12//99
	Guam	S	7.37 MW	7.47 AW	15550 AAW	GUBLS	10//99-12//99
Baseball Player Professional	United States	Y	200000 APL	1720049 AW	11949794 APH	SPORTS	1999
Basketball Player Professional	United States	Y	301875 APL	3522134 AW	20170000 APH	SPORTS	1999
Beautician	Louisiana	H	7.98 MW	10.61 AW		STLA	1998
Beef Manager Beef Herd, Agriculture	United States	Y	24000 APL	26833 AW	35000 APL	FAJO	1998
Benefits Specialist Human Resources	United States	Y		55600 AW		HRMAG	1999
Bicycle Repairer	Alabama	S	8.52 MW	8.65 AW	18000 AAW	ALBLS	10//99-12//99
	California	S	7.66 MW	7.97 AW	16580 AAW	CABLS	10//99-12//99
	Los Angeles-Long Beach PMSA, CA	S	7.16 MW	7.09 AW	14880 AAW	CABLS	10//99-12//99
	Sacramento PMSA, CA	S	7.78 MW	7.63 AW	16180 AAW	CABLS	10//99-12//99
	Salinas MSA, CA	S	6.92 MW	6.82 AW	14390 AAW	CABLS	10//99-12//99
	San Diego MSA, CA	S	8.33 MW	7.93 AW	17320 AAW	CABLS	10//99-12//99
	San Francisco PMSA, CA	S	9.35 MW	8.94 AW	19450 AAW	CABLS	10//99-12//99
	Ventura PMSA, CA	S	7.75 MW	7.83 AW	16130 AAW	CABLS	10//99-12//99
	Colorado	S	8.59 MW	8.79 AW	18280 AAW	COBLS	10//99-12//99
	Colorado Springs MSA, CO	S	9.03 MW	8.23 AW	18780 AAW	COBLS	10//99-12//99
	Denver PMSA, CO	S	8.93 MW	8.27 AW	18570 AAW	COBLS	10//99-12//99
	Connecticut	S	7.96 MW	8.39 AW	17450 AAW	CTBLS	10//99-12//99
	Washington PMSA, DC-MD-VA-WV	S	8.78 MW	8.76 AW	18250 AAW	DCBLS	10//99-12//99
	Florida	S	7.01 MW	7.40 AW	15400 AAW	FLBLS	10//99-12//99
	Melbourne-Titusville-Palm Bay MSA, FL	S	6.02 MW	6.09 AW	12520 AAW	FLBLS	10//99-12//99
	Georgia	S	5.86 MW	5.93 AW	12340 AAW	GABLS	10//99-12//99
	Hawaii	S	11.05 MW	10.33 AW	21480 AAW	HIBLS	10//99-12//99
	Idaho	S	7.39 MW	7.52 AW	15650 AAW	IDBLS	10//99-12//99
	Boise City MSA, ID	S	7.48 MW	7.26 AW	15550 AAW	IDBLS	10//99-12//99
	Illinois	S	7.25 MW	8.78 AW	18270 AAW	ILBLS	10//99-12//99
	Indiana	S	7.92 MW	8.24 AW	17130 AAW	INBLS	10//99-12//99
	Iowa	S	6.61 MW	7.19 AW	14950 AAW	IABLS	10//99-12//99
	Kansas	S	7.14 MW	7.21 AW	15000 AAW	KSBLS	10//99-12//99
	Louisiana	S	6.48 MW	6.92 AW	14390 AAW	LABLS	10//99-12//99
	Maryland	S	8.62 MW	9.05 AW	18810 AAW	MDBLS	10//99-12//99
	Massachusetts	S	8.4 MW	8.68 AW	18050 AAW	MABLS	10//99-12//99
	Boston PMSA, MA-NH	S	9.15 MW	9.00 AW	19040 AAW	MABLS	10//99-12//99
	Michigan	S	6.98 MW	7.53 AW	15670 AAW	MIBLS	10//99-12//99
	Minnesota	S	8.89 MW	8.54 AW	17770 AAW	MNBLS	10//99-12//99
	Minneapolis-St. Paul MSA, MN-WI	S	9.24 MW	8.98 AW	19210 AAW	MNBLS	10//99-12//99
	Nevada	S	10.26 MW	10.29 AW	21390 AAW	NVBLS	10//99-12//99
	New Hampshire	S	8.67 MW	8.76 AW	18210 AAW	NHBLS	10//99-12//99
	Portsmouth-Rochester PMSA, NH-ME	S	8.82 MW	9.03 AW	18350 AAW	NHBLS	10//99-12//99
	New York	S	7.18 MW	8.27 AW	17200 AAW	NYBLS	10//99-12//99
	Nassau-Suffolk PMSA, NY	S	11.90 MW	12.73 AW	24750 AAW	NYBLS	10//99-12//99
	New York PMSA, NY	S	9.59 MW	9.59 AW	19940 AAW	NYBLS	10//99-12//99
	North Carolina	S	7.47 MW	8.43 AW	17530 AAW	NCBLS	10//99-12//99
	Raleigh-Durham-Chapel Hill MSA, NC	S	8.84 MW	8.36 AW	18380 AAW	NCBLS	10//99-12//99
	Ohio	S	6.4 MW	6.81 AW	14160 AAW	OHBLS	10//99-12//99
	Oregon	S	8.29 MW	8.61 AW	17910 AAW	ORBLS	10//99-12//99
	Eugene-Springfield MSA, OR	S	9.39 MW	9.36 AW	19540 AAW	ORBLS	10//99-12//99
	Portland-Vancouver PMSA, OR-WA	S	9.90 MW	9.81 AW	20590 AAW	ORBLS	10//99-12//99
	Pennsylvania	S	6.59 MW	6.61 AW	13760 AAW	PABLS	10//99-12//99
	Rhode Island	S	6.78 MW	7.75 AW	16110 AAW	RIBLS	10//99-12//99

AAW Average annual wage	**AOH** Average offered, high	**ASH** Average starting, high	**H** Hourly	**M** Monthly	**S** Special: hourly and annual
AE Average entry wage	**AOL** Average offered, low	**ASL** Average starting, low	**HI** Highest wage paid	**MTC** Median total compensation	**TQ** Third quartile wage
AEX Average experienced wage	**APH** Average pay, high range	**AW** Average wage paid	**HR** High end range	**MW** Median wage paid	**W** Weekly
AO Average offered	**APL** Average pay, low range	**FQ** First quartile wage	**LR** Low end range	**SQ** Second quartile wage	**Y** Yearly

Occupation/Type/Industry	Location	Per	Low	Mid	High	Source	Date
Bicycle Repairer	Providence-Fall River-						
	Warwick MSA, RI-MA	S	8.68 MW	9.13 AW	18060 AAW	RIBLS	10//99-12//99
	Texas	S	8.8 MW	9.09 AW	18920 AAW	TXBLS	10//99-12//99
	Dallas PMSA, TX	S	8.15 MW	7.89 AW	16950 AAW	TXBLS	10//99-12//99
	Houston PMSA, TX	S	9.45 MW	9.37 AW	19660 AAW	TXBLS	10//99-12//99
	Utah	S	7.59 MW	7.46 AW	15520 AAW	UTBLS	10//99-12//99
	Virginia	S	8.22 MW	8.39 AW	17450	VABLS	10//99-12//99
	Washington	S	8.16 MW	8.49 AW	17660 AAW	WABLS	10//99-12//99
	Seattle-Bellevue-Everett						
	PMSA, WA	S	8.68 MW	8.25 AW	18060 AAW	WABLS	10//99-12//99
	Wisconsin	S	7.61 MW	7.96 AW	16560 AAW	WIBLS	10//99-12//99
	Milwaukee-Waukesha PMSA,						
	WI	S	7.93 MW	7.89 AW	16500 AAW	WIBLS	10//99-12//99
	Wyoming	S	8.21 MW	8.07 AW	16780 AAW	WYBLS	10//99-12//99
Bike Mechanic							
Sales	United States	H	5.85 APL		12.00 APH	BICRET	2000
Bill and Account Collector	Alabama	S	9.66 MW	10.63 AW	22100 AAW	ALBLS	10//99-12//99
	Anniston MSA, AL	S	9.66 MW	9.37 AW	20090 AAW	ALBLS	10//99-12//99
	Auburn-Opelika MSA, AL	S	9.50 MW	9.34 AW	19760 AAW	ALBLS	10//99-12//99
	Birmingham MSA, AL	S	11.93 MW	10.47 AW	24810 AAW	ALBLS	10//99-12//99
	Decatur MSA, AL	S	9.29 MW	9.02 AW	19330 AAW	ALBLS	10//99-12//99
	Dothan MSA, AL	S	9.88 MW	9.43 AW	20540 AAW	ALBLS	10//99-12//99
	Florence MSA, AL	S	10.24 MW	11.00 AW	21300 AAW	ALBLS	10//99-12//99
	Gadsden MSA, AL	S	9.76 MW	8.91 AW	20290 AAW	ALBLS	10//99-12//99
	Huntsville MSA, AL	S	12.00 MW	10.63 AW	24960 AAW	ALBLS	10//99-12//99
	Mobile MSA, AL	S	9.01 MW	8.28 AW	18730 AAW	ALBLS	10//99-12//99
	Montgomery MSA, AL	S	11.64 MW	10.74 AW	24210 AAW	ALBLS	10//99-12//99
	Tuscaloosa MSA, AL	S	8.75 MW	7.67 AW	18200 AAW	ALBLS	10//99-12//99
	Alaska	S	13.05 MW	13.46 AW	27990 AAW	AKBLS	10//99-12//99
	Anchorage MSA, AK	S	13.28 MW	12.70 AW	27620 AAW	AKBLS	10//99-12//99
	Arizona	S	10.61 MW	11.18 AW	23260 AAW	AZBLS	10//99-12//99
	Flagstaff MSA, AZ-UT	S	12.32 MW	11.19 AW	25620 AAW	AZBLS	10//99-12//99
	Phoenix-Mesa MSA, AZ	S	11.18 MW	10.65 AW	23260 AAW	AZBLS	10//99-12//99
	Tucson MSA, AZ	S	11.54 MW	10.71 AW	24010 AAW	AZBLS	10//99-12//99
	Yuma MSA, AZ	S	9.62 MW	9.78 AW	20000 AAW	AZBLS	10//99-12//99
	Arkansas	S	9.44 MW	10.32 AW	21470 AAW	ARBLS	10//99-12//99
	Fayetteville-Springdale-Rogers						
	MSA, AR	S	11.85 MW	10.73 AW	24650 AAW	ARBLS	10//99-12//99
	Fort Smith MSA, AR-OK	S	10.44 MW	9.86 AW	21720 AAW	ARBLS	10//99-12//99
	Jonesboro MSA, AR	S	7.73 MW	7.35 AW	16080 AAW	ARBLS	10//99-12//99
	Little Rock-North Little Rock						
	MSA, AR	S	10.00 MW	9.71 AW	20790 AAW	ARBLS	10//99-12//99
	Pine Bluff MSA, AR	S	9.48 MW	8.72 AW	19720 AAW	ARBLS	10//99-12//99
	California	S	12.5 MW	13.00 AW	27030 AAW	CABLS	10//99-12//99
	Bakersfield MSA, CA	S	10.85 MW	10.35 AW	22570 AAW	CABLS	10//99-12//99
	Chico-Paradise MSA, CA	S	12.84 MW	12.16 AW	26710 AAW	CABLS	10//99-12//99
	Fresno MSA, CA	S	11.57 MW	11.10 AW	24070 AAW	CABLS	10//99-12//99
	Los Angeles-Long Beach						
	PMSA, CA	S	13.33 MW	12.83 AW	27720 AAW	CABLS	10//99-12//99
	Merced MSA, CA	S	10.75 MW	10.41 AW	22370 AAW	CABLS	10//99-12//99
	Modesto MSA, CA	S	11.52 MW	11.24 AW	23960 AAW	CABLS	10//99-12//99
	Oakland PMSA, CA	S	14.32 MW	14.22 AW	29780 AAW	CABLS	10//99-12//99
	Orange County PMSA, CA	S	13.12 MW	12.75 AW	27300 AAW	CABLS	10//99-12//99
	Redding MSA, CA	S	10.50 MW	10.12 AW	21840 AAW	CABLS	10//99-12//99
	Riverside-San Bernardino						
	PMSA, CA	S	11.96 MW	11.67 AW	24870 AAW	CABLS	10//99-12//99
	Sacramento PMSA, CA	S	12.37 MW	12.13 AW	25730 AAW	CABLS	10//99-12//99
	Salinas MSA, CA	S	13.21 MW	12.72 AW	27470 AAW	CABLS	10//99-12//99
	San Diego MSA, CA	S	11.55 MW	10.74 AW	24020 AAW	CABLS	10//99-12//99
	San Francisco PMSA, CA	S	14.66 MW	14.75 AW	30490 AAW	CABLS	10//99-12//99
	San Jose PMSA, CA	S	14.03 MW	13.84 AW	29180 AAW	CABLS	10//99-12//99
	San Luis Obispo-Atascadero-						
	Paso Robles MSA, CA	S	10.67 MW	10.93 AW	22190 AAW	CABLS	10//99-12//99
	Santa Barbara-Santa Maria-						
	Lompoc MSA, CA	S	11.07 MW	10.46 AW	23030 AAW	CABLS	10//99-12//99
	Santa Cruz-Watsonville						
	PMSA, CA	S	11.98 MW	11.41 AW	24920 AAW	CABLS	10//99-12//99
	Santa Rosa PMSA, CA	S	12.68 MW	12.30 AW	26380 AAW	CABLS	10//99-12//99
	Stockton-Lodi MSA, CA	S	12.34 MW	11.68 AW	25670 AAW	CABLS	10//99-12//99
	Vallejo-Fairfield-Napa PMSA,						
	CA	S	10.24 MW	9.81 AW	21300 AAW	CABLS	10//99-12//99

AAW	Average annual wage	AOH	Average offered, high	ASH	Average starting, high	H	Hourly	M	Monthly	S	Special: hourly and annual
AE	Average entry wage	AOL	Average offered, low	ASL	Average starting, low	HI	Highest wage paid	MTC	Median total compensation	TQ	Third quartile wage
AEX	Average experienced wage	APH	Average pay, high range	AW	Average wage paid	HR	High end range	MW	Median wage paid	W	Weekly
AO	Average offered	APL	Average pay, low range	FQ	First quartile wage	LR	Low end range	SQ	Second quartile wage	Y	Yearly

Occupation/Type/Industry	Location	Per	Low	Mid	High	Source	Date
Bill and Account Collector	Ventura PMSA, CA	S	12.97 MW	12.34 AW	26970 AAW	CABLS	10//99-12//99
	Visalia-Tulare-Porterville MSA, CA	S	11.07 MW	10.07 AW	23020 AAW	CABLS	10//99-12//99
	Yolo PMSA, CA	S	12.92 MW	11.80 AW	26870 AAW	CABLS	10//99-12//99
	Yuba City MSA, CA	S	10.51 MW	10.38 AW	21870 AAW	CABLS	10//99-12//99
	Colorado	S	11.62 MW	12.00 AW	24970 AAW	COBLS	10//99-12//99
	Boulder-Longmont PMSA, CO	S	11.18 MW	10.31 AW	23260 AAW	COBLS	10//99-12//99
	Colorado Springs MSA, CO	S	11.34 MW	11.30 AW	23590 AAW	COBLS	10//99-12//99
	Denver PMSA, CO	S	12.35 MW	11.81 AW	25680 AAW	COBLS	10//99-12//99
	Fort Collins-Loveland MSA, CO	S	10.94 MW	10.59 AW	22750 AAW	COBLS	10//99-12//99
	Grand Junction MSA, CO	S	11.43 MW	11.59 AW	23770 AAW	COBLS	10//99-12//99
	Greeley PMSA, CO	S	10.95 MW	10.39 AW	22780 AAW	COBLS	10//99-12//99
	Pueblo MSA, CO	S	10.66 MW	10.77 AW	22170 AAW	COBLS	10//99-12//99
	Connecticut	S	14.03 MW	14.53 AW	30220 AAW	CTBLS	10//99-12//99
	Bridgeport PMSA, CT	S	15.39 MW	14.48 AW	32010 AAW	CTBLS	10//99-12//99
	Danbury PMSA, CT	S	16.06 MW	15.73 AW	33400 AAW	CTBLS	10//99-12//99
	Hartford MSA, CT	S	13.99 MW	13.50 AW	29100 AAW	CTBLS	10//99-12//99
	New Haven-Meriden PMSA, CT	S	13.70 MW	13.25 AW	28500 AAW	CTBLS	10//99-12//99
	New London-Norwich MSA, CT-RI	S	14.17 MW	13.81 AW	29470 AAW	CTBLS	10//99-12//99
	Stamford-Norwalk PMSA, CT	S	15.64 MW	15.41 AW	32520 AAW	CTBLS	10//99-12//99
	Waterbury PMSA, CT	S	13.44 MW	13.80 AW	27950 AAW	CTBLS	10//99-12//99
	Delaware	S	10.15 MW	10.64 AW	22120 AAW	DEBLS	10//99-12//99
	Dover MSA, DE	S	9.88 MW	9.32 AW	20550 AAW	DEBLS	10//99-12//99
	Wilmington-Newark PMSA, DE-MD	S	10.64 MW	10.08 AW	22130 AAW	DEBLS	10//99-12//99
	District of Columbia	S	12.18 MW	12.59 AW	26190 AAW	DCBLS	10//99-12//99
	Washington PMSA, DC-MD-VA-WV	S	13.25 MW	12.48 AW	27560 AAW	DCBLS	10//99-12//99
	Florida	S	10.91 MW	11.28 AW	23470 AAW	FLBLS	10//99-12//99
	Daytona Beach MSA, FL	S	10.83 MW	10.14 AW	22520 AAW	FLBLS	10//99-12//99
	Fort Lauderdale PMSA, FL	S	12.16 MW	11.74 AW	25300 AAW	FLBLS	10//99-12//99
	Fort Myers-Cape Coral MSA, FL	S	9.98 MW	9.84 AW	20750 AAW	FLBLS	10//99-12//99
	Fort Pierce-Port St. Lucie MSA, FL	S	10.11 MW	9.85 AW	21030 AAW	FLBLS	10//99-12//99
	Fort Walton Beach MSA, FL	S	8.81 MW	8.51 AW	18320 AAW	FLBLS	10//99-12//99
	Gainesville MSA, FL	S	10.69 MW	10.24 AW	22230 AAW	FLBLS	10//99-12//99
	Jacksonville MSA, FL	S	11.52 MW	11.06 AW	23960 AAW	FLBLS	10//99-12//99
	Lakeland-Winter Haven MSA, FL	S	10.17 MW	9.83 AW	21160 AAW	FLBLS	10//99-12//99
	Melbourne-Titusville-Palm Bay MSA, FL	S	9.57 MW	9.63 AW	19910 AAW	FLBLS	10//99-12//99
	Miami PMSA, FL	S	12.92 MW	12.48 AW	26880 AAW	FLBLS	10//99-12//99
	Naples MSA, FL	S	11.38 MW	10.81 AW	23670 AAW	FLBLS	10//99-12//99
	Ocala MSA, FL	S	9.15 MW	9.02 AW	19040 AAW	FLBLS	10//99-12//99
	Orlando MSA, FL	S	11.12 MW	10.95 AW	23140 AAW	FLBLS	10//99-12//99
	Panama City MSA, FL	S	10.62 MW	10.65 AW	22090 AAW	FLBLS	10//99-12//99
	Pensacola MSA, FL	S	10.59 MW	11.05 AW	22030 AAW	FLBLS	10//99-12//99
	Punta Gorda MSA, FL	S	11.03 MW	10.52 AW	22950 AAW	FLBLS	10//99-12//99
	Sarasota-Bradenton MSA, FL	S	9.50 MW	9.30 AW	19760 AAW	FLBLS	10//99-12//99
	Tallahassee MSA, FL	S	12.28 MW	11.41 AW	25540 AAW	FLBLS	10//99-12//99
	Tampa-St. Petersburg-Clearwater MSA, FL	S	10.64 MW	10.27 AW	22120 AAW	FLBLS	10//99-12//99
	West Palm Beach-Boca Raton MSA, FL	S	11.75 MW	11.32 AW	24450 AAW	FLBLS	10//99-12//99
	Georgia	S	11.16 MW	11.38 AW	23670 AAW	GABLS	10//99-12//99
	Albany MSA, GA	S	8.77 MW	8.66 AW	18250 AAW	GABLS	10//99-12//99
	Athens MSA, GA	S	8.98 MW	8.48 AW	18670 AAW	GABLS	10//99-12//99
	Atlanta MSA, GA	S	11.93 MW	11.60 AW	24810 AAW	GABLS	10//99-12//99
	Augusta-Aiken MSA, GA-SC	S	8.90 MW	8.81 AW	18510 AAW	GABLS	10//99-12//99
	Columbus MSA, GA-AL	S	9.89 MW	9.94 AW	20570 AAW	GABLS	10//99-12//99
	Macon MSA, GA	S	9.84 MW	8.97 AW	20460 AAW	GABLS	10//99-12//99
	Savannah MSA, GA	S	11.15 MW	10.90 AW	23190 AAW	GABLS	10//99-12//99
	Hawaii	S	12.53 MW	13.30 AW	27660 AAW	HIBLS	10//99-12//99
	Honolulu MSA, HI	S	13.43 MW	12.76 AW	27940 AAW	HIBLS	10//99-12//99
	Idaho	S	9.63 MW	9.84 AW	20480 AAW	IDBLS	10//99-12//99
	Boise City MSA, ID	S	9.71 MW	9.71 AW	20200 AAW	IDBLS	10//99-12//99
	Illinois	S	11.95 MW	12.31 AW	25610 AAW	ILBLS	10//99-12//99
	Bloomington-Normal MSA, IL	S	12.87 MW	11.44 AW	26770 AAW	ILBLS	10//99-12//99

Occupation/Type/Industry	Location	Per	Low	Mid	High	Source	Date
Bill and Account Collector	Champaign-Urbana MSA, IL	s	11.28 MW	10.43 AW	23470 AAW	ILBLS	10//99-12//99
	Chicago PMSA, IL	s	12.73 MW	12.47 AW	26480 AAW	ILBLS	10//99-12//99
	Decatur MSA, IL	s	10.45 MW	9.67 AW	21740 AAW	ILBLS	10//99-12//99
	Kankakee PMSA, IL	s	10.69 MW	10.23 AW	22240 AAW	ILBLS	10//99-12//99
	Peoria-Pekin MSA, IL	s	10.94 MW	10.83 AW	22750 AAW	ILBLS	10//99-12//99
	Rockford MSA, IL	s	11.22 MW	11.12 AW	23340 AAW	ILBLS	10//99-12//99
	Springfield MSA, IL	s	10.18 MW	10.32 AW	21170 AAW	ILBLS	10//99-12//99
	Indiana	s	9.91 MW	10.20 AW	21210 AAW	INBLS	10//99-12//99
	Bloomington MSA, IN	s	11.47 MW	10.41 AW	23860 AAW	INBLS	10//99-12//99
	Elkhart-Goshen MSA, IN	s	11.03 MW	10.71 AW	22930 AAW	INBLS	10//99-12//99
	Evansville-Henderson MSA, IN-KY	s	9.44 MW	9.20 AW	19640 AAW	INBLS	10//99-12//99
	Fort Wayne MSA, IN	s	9.91 MW	9.62 AW	20620 AAW	INBLS	10//99-12//99
	Gary PMSA, IN	s	10.63 MW	10.66 AW	22100 AAW	INBLS	10//99-12//99
	Indianapolis MSA, IN	s	10.36 MW	10.14 AW	21550 AAW	INBLS	10//99-12//99
	Kokomo MSA, IN	s	9.66 MW	9.71 AW	20100 AAW	INBLS	10//99-12//99
	Lafayette MSA, IN	s	9.89 MW	9.90 AW	20570 AAW	INBLS	10//99-12//99
	Muncie MSA, IN	s	10.11 MW	9.98 AW	21020 AAW	INBLS	10//99-12//99
	South Bend MSA, IN	s	9.56 MW	9.55 AW	19890 AAW	INBLS	10//99-12//99
	Terre Haute MSA, IN	s	10.69 MW	10.14 AW	22220 AAW	INBLS	10//99-12//99
	Iowa	s	10.28 MW	11.04 AW	22960 AAW	IABLS	10//99-12//99
	Cedar Rapids MSA, IA	s	11.76 MW	11.56 AW	24460 AAW	IABLS	10//99-12//99
	Davenport-Moline-Rock Island MSA, IA-IL	s	10.79 MW	10.40 AW	22440 AAW	IABLS	10//99-12//99
	Des Moines MSA, IA	s	10.97 MW	10.28 AW	22820 AAW	IABLS	10//99-12//99
	Dubuque MSA, IA	s	11.11 MW	10.24 AW	23100 AAW	IABLS	10//99-12//99
	Sioux City MSA, IA-NE	s	9.85 MW	9.74 AW	20480 AAW	IABLS	10//99-12//99
	Waterloo-Cedar Falls MSA, IA	s	10.85 MW	10.42 AW	22560 AAW	IABLS	10//99-12//99
	Kansas	s	10.37 MW	10.61 AW	22070 AAW	KSBLS	10//99-12//99
	Wichita MSA, KS	s	9.96 MW	9.70 AW	20720 AAW	KSBLS	10//99-12//99
	Kentucky	s	10.25 MW	11.12 AW	23120 AAW	KYBLS	10//99-12//99
	Lexington MSA, KY	s	11.30 MW	10.86 AW	23500 AAW	KYBLS	10//99-12//99
	Louisville MSA, KY-IN	s	12.51 MW	10.91 AW	26010 AAW	KYBLS	10//99-12//99
	Owensboro MSA, KY	s	11.01 MW	10.03 AW	22910 AAW	KYBLS	10//99-12//99
	Louisiana	s	9.44 MW	9.97 AW	20750 AAW	LABLS	10//99-12//99
	Alexandria MSA, LA	s	8.63 MW	8.45 AW	17950 AAW	LABLS	10//99-12//99
	Baton Rouge MSA, LA	s	10.14 MW	9.72 AW	21080 AAW	LABLS	10//99-12//99
	Houma MSA, LA	s	9.61 MW	9.41 AW	19990 AAW	LABLS	10//99-12//99
	Lafayette MSA, LA	s	9.21 MW	9.01 AW	19170 AAW	LABLS	10//99-12//99
	Lake Charles MSA, LA	s	9.75 MW	9.02 AW	20270 AAW	LABLS	10//99-12//99
	Monroe MSA, LA	s	9.75 MW	9.31 AW	20280 AAW	LABLS	10//99-12//99
	New Orleans MSA, LA	s	10.77 MW	10.11 AW	22400 AAW	LABLS	10//99-12//99
	Shreveport-Bossier City MSA, LA	s	9.99 MW	9.68 AW	20780 AAW	LABLS	10//99-12//99
	Maine	s	12.24 MW	12.07 AW	25100 AAW	MEBLS	10//99-12//99
	Bangor MSA, ME	s	10.50 MW	10.16 AW	21830 AAW	MEBLS	10//99-12//99
	Lewiston-Auburn MSA, ME	s	10.46 MW	9.57 AW	21760 AAW	MEBLS	10//99-12//99
	Portland MSA, ME	s	12.21 MW	11.82 AW	25400 AAW	MEBLS	10//99-12//99
	Maryland	s	11.91 MW	12.47 AW	25930 AAW	MDBLS	10//99-12//99
	Baltimore PMSA, MD	s	12.06 MW	11.86 AW	25080 AAW	MDBLS	10//99-12//99
	Cumberland MSA, MD-WV	s	10.40 MW	9.55 AW	21630 AAW	MDBLS	10//99-12//99
	Hagerstown PMSA, MD	s	10.90 MW	10.50 AW	22660 AAW	MDBLS	10//99-12//99
	Massachusetts	s	12.82 MW	13.18 AW	27410 AAW	MABLS	10//99-12//99
	Barnstable-Yarmouth MSA, MA	s	13.29 MW	12.57 AW	27630 AAW	MABLS	10//99-12//99
	Boston PMSA, MA-NH	s	13.25 MW	12.89 AW	27560 AAW	MABLS	10//99-12//99
	Brockton PMSA, MA	s	13.23 MW	12.76 AW	27510 AAW	MABLS	10//99-12//99
	Fitchburg-Leominster PMSA, MA	s	12.90 MW	12.35 AW	26830 AAW	MABLS	10//99-12//99
	Lawrence PMSA, MA-NH	s	12.61 MW	12.37 AW	26220 AAW	MABLS	10//99-12//99
	Lowell PMSA, MA-NH	s	13.95 MW	13.97 AW	29010 AAW	MABLS	10//99-12//99
	New Bedford PMSA, MA	s	11.50 MW	10.67 AW	23910 AAW	MABLS	10//99-12//99
	Pittsfield MSA, MA	s	11.85 MW	11.45 AW	24650 AAW	MABLS	10//99-12//99
	Springfield MSA, MA	s	12.99 MW	12.44 AW	27020 AAW	MABLS	10//99-12//99
	Worcester PMSA, MA-CT	s	13.03 MW	12.75 AW	27110 AAW	MABLS	10//99-12//99
	Michigan	s	11.52 MW	12.07 AW	25110 AAW	MIBLS	10//99-12//99
	Ann Arbor PMSA, MI	s	12.52 MW	12.09 AW	26040 AAW	MIBLS	10//99-12//99
	Benton Harbor MSA, MI	s	11.12 MW	10.70 AW	23140 AAW	MIBLS	10//99-12//99
	Detroit PMSA, MI	s	12.82 MW	12.19 AW	26650 AAW	MIBLS	10//99-12//99
	Flint PMSA, MI	s	11.51 MW	10.82 AW	23940 AAW	MIBLS	10//99-12//99
	Grand Rapids-Muskegon-Holland MSA, MI	s	11.03 MW	10.75 AW	22950 AAW	MIBLS	10//99-12//99

AAW	Average annual wage	AOH	Average offered, high	ASH	Average starting, high
AE	Average entry wage	AOL	Average offered, low	ASL	Average starting, low
AEX	Average experienced wage	APH	Average pay, high range	AW	Average wage paid
AO	Average offered	APL	Average pay, low range	FQ	First quartile wage

H	Hourly	M	Monthly
HI	Highest wage paid	MTC	Median total compensation
HR	High end range	MW	Median wage paid
LR	Low end range	SQ	Second quartile wage

S	Special: hourly and annual
TQ	Third quartile wage
W	Weekly
Y	Yearly

Occupation/Type/Industry	Location	Per	Low	Mid	High	Source	Date
Bill and Account Collector	Jackson MSA, MI	S	12.00 MW	11.48 AW	24960 AAW	MIBLS	10//99-12//99
	Kalamazoo-Battle Creek MSA, MI	S	10.33 MW	10.05 AW	21480 AAW	MIBLS	10//99-12//99
	Lansing-East Lansing MSA, MI	S	11.02 MW	10.37 AW	22930 AAW	MIBLS	10//99-12//99
	Saginaw-Bay City-Midland MSA, MI	S	12.05 MW	11.07 AW	25070 AAW	MIBLS	10//99-12//99
	Minnesota	S	11.99 MW	12.64 AW	26290 AAW	MNBLS	10//99-12//99
	Duluth-Superior MSA, MN-WI	S	12.29 MW	12.44 AW	25560 AAW	MNBLS	10//99-12//99
	Minneapolis-St. Paul MSA, MN-WI	S	13.25 MW	12.64 AW	27550 AAW	MNBLS	10//99-12//99
	Mississippi	S	9.86 MW	10.27 AW	21360 AAW	MSBLS	10//99-12//99
	Biloxi-Gulfport-Pascagoula MSA, MS	S	9.73 MW	8.88 AW	20250 AAW	MSBLS	10//99-12//99
	Hattiesburg MSA, MS	S	9.89 MW	9.67 AW	20580 AAW	MSBLS	10//99-12//99
	Jackson MSA, MS	S	11.47 MW	10.45 AW	23860 AAW	MSBLS	10//99-12//99
	Missouri	S	10.62 MW	11.10 AW	23090 AAW	MOBLS	10//99-12//99
	Columbia MSA, MO	S	9.15 MW	8.36 AW	19040 AAW	MOBLS	10//99-12//99
	Joplin MSA, MO	S	9.09 MW	8.13 AW	18900 AAW	MOBLS	10//99-12//99
	Kansas City MSA, MO-KS	S	11.60 MW	11.13 AW	24130 AAW	MOBLS	10//99-12//99
	St. Joseph MSA, MO	S	12.46 MW	13.55 AW	25920 AAW	MOBLS	10//99-12//99
	St. Louis MSA, MO-IL	S	10.96 MW	10.45 AW	22810 AAW	MOBLS	10//99-12//99
	Springfield MSA, MO	S	10.30 MW	9.65 AW	21430 AAW	MOBLS	10//99-12//99
	Montana	S	9.46 MW	10.41 AW	21650 AAW	MTBLS	10//99-12//99
	Billings MSA, MT	S	10.78 MW	10.12 AW	22430 AAW	MTBLS	10//99-12//99
	Great Falls MSA, MT	S	10.06 MW	9.40 AW	20930 AAW	MTBLS	10//99-12//99
	Missoula MSA, MT	S	10.01 MW	9.58 AW	20820 AAW	MTBLS	10//99-12//99
	Nebraska	S	9.77 MW	10.14 AW	21090 AAW	NEBLS	10//99-12//99
	Lincoln MSA, NE	S	10.32 MW	9.77 AW	21450 AAW	NEBLS	10//99-12//99
	Omaha MSA, NE-IA	S	10.43 MW	10.14 AW	21690 AAW	NEBLS	10//99-12//99
	Nevada	S	10.44 MW	11.34 AW	23580 AAW	NVBLS	10//99-12//99
	Las Vegas MSA, NV-AZ	S	11.01 MW	10.30 AW	22890 AAW	NVBLS	10//99-12//99
	Reno MSA, NV	S	12.94 MW	12.34 AW	26910 AAW	NVBLS	10//99-12//99
	New Hampshire	S	11 MW	11.46 AW	23830 AAW	NHBLS	10//99-12//99
	Manchester PMSA, NH	S	11.11 MW	11.53 AW	23100 AAW	NHBLS	10//99-12//99
	Nashua PMSA, NH	S	13.45 MW	12.58 AW	27970 AAW	NHBLS	10//99-12//99
	New Jersey	S	12.65 MW	13.18 AW	27410 AAW	NJBLS	10//99-12//99
	Atlantic-Cape May PMSA, NJ	S	13.30 MW	12.48 AW	27670 AAW	NJBLS	10//99-12//99
	Bergen-Passaic PMSA, NJ	S	14.21 MW	13.82 AW	29550 AAW	NJBLS	10//99-12//99
	Jersey City PMSA, NJ	S	13.74 MW	13.62 AW	28590 AAW	NJBLS	10//99-12//99
	Middlesex-Somerset-Hunterdon PMSA, NJ	S	12.91 MW	12.29 AW	26840 AAW	NJBLS	10//99-12//99
	Monmouth-Ocean PMSA, NJ	S	11.57 MW	10.92 AW	24070 AAW	NJBLS	10//99-12//99
	Newark PMSA, NJ	S	14.04 MW	13.74 AW	29200 AAW	NJBLS	10//99-12//99
	Trenton PMSA, NJ	S	11.89 MW	11.29 AW	24730 AAW	NJBLS	10//99-12//99
	New Mexico	S	9.77 MW	10.08 AW	20970 AAW	NMBLS	10//99-12//99
	Albuquerque MSA, NM	S	10.36 MW	10.11 AW	21540 AAW	NMBLS	10//99-12//99
	Las Cruces MSA, NM	S	9.58 MW	9.32 AW	19930 AAW	NMBLS	10//99-12//99
	New York	S	12.37 MW	13.90 AW	28910 AAW	NYBLS	10//99-12//99
	Albany-Schenectady-Troy MSA, NY	S	12.06 MW	11.55 AW	25080 AAW	NYBLS	10//99-12//99
	Binghamton MSA, NY	S	10.24 MW	9.75 AW	21300 AAW	NYBLS	10//99-12//99
	Buffalo-Niagara Falls MSA, NY	S	10.99 MW	10.27 AW	22860 AAW	NYBLS	10//99-12//99
	Dutchess County PMSA, NY	S	12.90 MW	11.90 AW	26830 AAW	NYBLS	10//99-12//99
	Elmira MSA, NY	S	11.59 MW	10.94 AW	24110 AAW	NYBLS	10//99-12//99
	Glens Falls MSA, NY	S	11.32 MW	10.40 AW	23550 AAW	NYBLS	10//99-12//99
	Jamestown MSA, NY	S	10.91 MW	10.40 AW	22690 AAW	NYBLS	10//99-12//99
	Nassau-Suffolk PMSA, NY	S	12.52 MW	11.67 AW	26050 AAW	NYBLS	10//99-12//99
	New York PMSA, NY	S	17.14 MW	14.91 AW	35640 AAW	NYBLS	10//99-12//99
	Newburgh PMSA, NY-PA	S	12.90 MW	12.97 AW	26820 AAW	NYBLS	10//99-12//99
	Rochester MSA, NY	S	11.75 MW	11.02 AW	24450 AAW	NYBLS	10//99-12//99
	Syracuse MSA, NY	S	10.62 MW	10.02 AW	22080 AAW	NYBLS	10//99-12//99
	Utica-Rome MSA, NY	S	9.32 MW	8.09 AW	19390 AAW	NYBLS	10//99-12//99
	North Carolina	S	10.95 MW	11.45 AW	23810 AAW	NCBLS	10//99-12//99
	Asheville MSA, NC	S	11.82 MW	10.86 AW	24580 AAW	NCBLS	10//99-12//99
	Charlotte-Gastonia-Rock Hill MSA, NC-SC	S	12.89 MW	12.05 AW	26820 AAW	NCBLS	10//99-12//99
	Fayetteville MSA, NC	S	9.92 MW	9.68 AW	20640 AAW	NCBLS	10//99-12//99
	Goldsboro MSA, NC	S	10.63 MW	10.89 AW	22110 AAW	NCBLS	10//99-12//99
	Greensboro--Winston-Salem--High Point MSA, NC	S	11.65 MW	11.18 AW	24230 AAW	NCBLS	10//99-12//99
	Greenville MSA, NC	S	8.44 MW	7.95 AW	17560 AAW	NCBLS	10//99-12//99

AAW Average annual wage	**AOH** Average offered, high	**ASH** Average starting, high	**H** Hourly	**M** Monthly	**S** Special: hourly and annual
AE Average entry wage	**AOL** Average offered, low	**ASL** Average starting, low	**HI** Highest wage paid	**MTC** Median total compensation	**TQ** Third quartile wage
AEX Average experienced wage	**APH** Average pay, high range	**AW** Average wage paid	**HR** High end range	**MW** Median wage paid	**W** Weekly
AO Average offered	**APL** Average pay, low range	**FQ** First quartile wage	**LR** Low end range	**SQ** Second quartile wage	**Y** Yearly

Occupation/Type/Industry	Location	Per	Low	Mid	High	Source	Date
Bill and Account Collector	Hickory-Morganton-Lenoir MSA, NC	S	11.75 MW	10.56 AW	24440 AAW	NCBLS	10//99-12//99
	Jacksonville MSA, NC	S	8.39 MW	8.25 AW	17450 AAW	NCBLS	10//99-12//99
	Raleigh-Durham-Chapel Hill MSA, NC	S	11.34 MW	11.07 AW	23590 AAW	NCBLS	10//99-12//99
	Rocky Mount MSA, NC	S	9.50 MW	9.30 AW	19770 AAW	NCBLS	10//99-12//99
	Wilmington MSA, NC	S	9.45 MW	9.25 AW	19650 AAW	NCBLS	10//99-12//99
	North Dakota	S	10.22 MW	10.94 AW	22750 AAW	NDBLS	10//99-12//99
	Bismarck MSA, ND	S	10.69 MW	9.81 AW	22240 AAW	NDBLS	10//99-12//99
	Fargo-Moorhead MSA, ND-MN	S	11.92 MW	10.84 AW	24790 AAW	NDBLS	10//99-12//99
	Grand Forks MSA, ND-MN	S	11.87 MW	10.92 AW	24700 AAW	NDBLS	10//99-12//99
	Ohio	S	10.94 MW	11.36 AW	23630 AAW	OHBLS	10//99-12//99
	Akron PMSA, OH	S	10.38 MW	10.14 AW	21590 AAW	OHBLS	10//99-12//99
	Canton-Massillon MSA, OH	S	10.56 MW	10.30 AW	21970 AAW	OHBLS	10//99-12//99
	Cincinnati PMSA, OH-KY-IN	S	11.52 MW	11.20 AW	23970 AAW	OHBLS	10//99-12//99
	Cleveland-Lorain-Elyria PMSA, OH	S	11.65 MW	11.14 AW	24240 AAW	OHBLS	10//99-12//99
	Columbus MSA, OH	S	11.35 MW	10.88 AW	23610 AAW	OHBLS	10//99-12//99
	Dayton-Springfield MSA, OH	S	10.90 MW	10.55 AW	22680 AAW	OHBLS	10//99-12//99
	Hamilton-Middletown PMSA, OH	S	11.86 MW	10.97 AW	24670 AAW	OHBLS	10//99-12//99
	Lima MSA, OH	S	11.02 MW	11.03 AW	22930 AAW	OHBLS	10//99-12//99
	Mansfield MSA, OH	S	10.32 MW	10.83 AW	21460 AAW	OHBLS	10//99-12//99
	Toledo MSA, OH	S	11.12 MW	10.58 AW	23130 AAW	OHBLS	10//99-12//99
	Youngstown-Warren MSA, OH	S	11.57 MW	10.83 AW	24060 AAW	OHBLS	10//99-12//99
	Oklahoma	S	10.28 MW	11.03 AW	22940 AAW	OKBLS	10//99-12//99
	Enid MSA, OK	S	11.12 MW	10.39 AW	23120 AAW	OKBLS	10//99-12//99
	Lawton MSA, OK	S	7.96 MW	6.99 AW	16550 AAW	OKBLS	10//99-12//99
	Oklahoma City MSA, OK	S	11.15 MW	10.05 AW	23200 AAW	OKBLS	10//99-12//99
	Tulsa MSA, OK	S	11.42 MW	11.12 AW	23740 AAW	OKBLS	10//99-12//99
	Oregon	S	12.48 MW	12.97 AW	26980 AAW	ORBLS	10//99-12//99
	Eugene-Springfield MSA, OR	S	12.04 MW	11.84 AW	25030 AAW	ORBLS	10//99-12//99
	Medford-Ashland MSA, OR	S	12.48 MW	12.44 AW	25970 AAW	ORBLS	10//99-12//99
	Portland-Vancouver PMSA, OR-WA	S	13.28 MW	12.69 AW	27620 AAW	ORBLS	10//99-12//99
	Salem PMSA, OR	S	12.72 MW	10.85 AW	26450 AAW	ORBLS	10//99-12//99
	Pennsylvania	S	11.29 MW	11.75 AW	24450 AAW	PABLS	10//99-12//99
	Allentown-Bethlehem-Easton MSA, PA	S	11.68 MW	11.62 AW	24290 AAW	PABLS	10//99-12//99
	Altoona MSA, PA	S	10.99 MW	10.87 AW	22860 AAW	PABLS	10//99-12//99
	Erie MSA, PA	S	10.50 MW	10.17 AW	21850 AAW	PABLS	10//99-12//99
	Harrisburg-Lebanon-Carlisle MSA, PA	S	12.52 MW	12.36 AW	26030 AAW	PABLS	10//99-12//99
	Johnstown MSA, PA	S	11.19 MW	11.02 AW	23280 AAW	PABLS	10//99-12//99
	Lancaster MSA, PA	S	12.70 MW	11.28 AW	26420 AAW	PABLS	10//99-12//99
	Philadelphia PMSA, PA-NJ	S	12.11 MW	11.34 AW	25200 AAW	PABLS	10//99-12//99
	Pittsburgh MSA, PA	S	11.34 MW	11.30 AW	23580 AAW	PABLS	10//99-12//99
	Reading MSA, PA	S	12.15 MW	11.78 AW	25270 AAW	PABLS	10//99-12//99
	Scranton--Wilkes-Barre--Hazleton MSA, PA	S	10.49 MW	10.33 AW	21820 AAW	PABLS	10//99-12//99
	Sharon MSA, PA	S	10.97 MW	10.79 AW	22820 AAW	PABLS	10//99-12//99
	Williamsport MSA, PA	S	9.52 MW	9.58 AW	19800 AAW	PABLS	10//99-12//99
	York MSA, PA	S	10.75 MW	10.93 AW	22370 AAW	PABLS	10//99-12//99
	Rhode Island	S	13.24 MW	13.56 AW	28210 AAW	RIBLS	10//99-12//99
	Providence-Fall River-Warwick MSA, RI-MA	S	13.33 MW	13.06 AW	27730 AAW	RIBLS	10//99-12//99
	South Carolina	S	9.69 MW	10.24 AW	21290 AAW	SCBLS	10//99-12//99
	Charleston-North Charleston MSA, SC	S	10.19 MW	10.05 AW	21200 AAW	SCBLS	10//99-12//99
	Columbia MSA, SC	S	9.98 MW	9.86 AW	20760 AAW	SCBLS	10//99-12//99
	Florence MSA, SC	S	9.11 MW	9.22 AW	18950 AAW	SCBLS	10//99-12//99
	Greenville-Spartanburg-Anderson MSA, SC	S	11.05 MW	10.51 AW	22980 AAW	SCBLS	10//99-12//99
	Myrtle Beach MSA, SC	S	11.18 MW	10.13 AW	23260 AAW	SCBLS	10//99-12//99
	Sumter MSA, SC	S	9.41 MW	8.44 AW	19570 AAW	SCBLS	10//99-12//99
	South Dakota	S	9.94 MW	10.70 AW	22260 AAW	SDBLS	10//99-12//99
	Sioux Falls MSA, SD	S	11.82 MW	11.31 AW	24590 AAW	SDBLS	10//99-12//99
	Tennessee	S	10.88 MW	11.45 AW	23810 AAW	TNBLS	10//99-12//99
	Chattanooga MSA, TN-GA	S	9.67 MW	9.62 AW	20120 AAW	TNBLS	10//99-12//99
	Clarksville-Hopkinsville MSA, TN-KY	S	11.46 MW	10.87 AW	23840 AAW	TNBLS	10//99-12//99

AAW Average annual wage	**AOH** Average offered, high	**ASH** Average starting, high	**H** Hourly	**M** Monthly	**S** Special: hourly and annual
AE Average entry wage	**AOL** Average offered, low	**ASL** Average starting, low	**HI** Highest wage paid	**MTC** Median total compensation	**TQ** Third quartile wage
AEX Average experienced wage	**APH** Average pay, high range	**AW** Average wage paid	**HR** High end range	**MW** Median wage paid	**W** Weekly
AO Average offered	**APL** Average pay, low range	**FQ** First quartile wage	**LR** Low end range	**SQ** Second quartile wage	**Y** Yearly

Occupation/Type/Industry	Location	Per	Low	Mid	High	Source	Date
Bill and Account Collector	Jackson MSA, TN	S	9.93 MW	9.74 AW	20660 AAW	TNBLS	10//99-12//99
	Knoxville MSA, TN	S	11.09 MW	11.05 AW	23080 AAW	TNBLS	10//99-12//99
	Memphis MSA, TN-AR-MS	S	10.56 MW	10.14 AW	21960 AAW	MSBLS	10//99-12//99
	Nashville MSA, TN	S	13.06 MW	11.40 AW	27160 AAW	TNBLS	10//99-12//99
	Texas	S	11.1 MW	11.58 AW	24090 AAW	TXBLS	10//99-12//99
	Abilene MSA, TX	S	10.65 MW	10.03 AW	22150 AAW	TXBLS	10//99-12//99
	Amarillo MSA, TX	S	9.14 MW	8.76 AW	19010 AAW	TXBLS	10//99-12//99
	Austin-San Marcos MSA, TX	S	10.58 MW	10.24 AW	22000 AAW	TXBLS	10//99-12//99
	Beaumont-Port Arthur MSA, TX	S	9.41 MW	9.27 AW	19580 AAW	TXBLS	10//99-12//99
	Brazoria PMSA, TX	S	10.50 MW	10.58 AW	21850 AAW	TXBLS	10//99-12//99
	Brownsville-Harlingen-San Benito MSA, TX	S	9.48 MW	8.51 AW	19720 AAW	TXBLS	10//99-12//99
	Bryan-College Station MSA, TX	S	11.01 MW	11.20 AW	22900 AAW	TXBLS	10//99-12//99
	Corpus Christi MSA, TX	S	9.23 MW	9.10 AW	19190 AAW	TXBLS	10//99-12//99
	Dallas PMSA, TX	S	13.66 MW	12.69 AW	28420 AAW	TXBLS	10//99-12//99
	El Paso MSA, TX	S	9.75 MW	9.63 AW	20270 AAW	TXBLS	10//99-12//99
	Fort Worth-Arlington PMSA, TX	S	11.70 MW	11.60 AW	24340 AAW	TXBLS	10//99-12//99
	Galveston-Texas City PMSA, TX	S	10.00 MW	10.18 AW	20810 AAW	TXBLS	10//99-12//99
	Houston PMSA, TX	S	11.39 MW	11.16 AW	23680 AAW	TXBLS	10//99-12//99
	Killeen-Temple MSA, TX	S	10.60 MW	9.73 AW	22060 AAW	TXBLS	10//99-12//99
	Laredo MSA, TX	S	9.13 MW	9.11 AW	18980 AAW	TXBLS	10//99-12//99
	Longview-Marshall MSA, TX	S	11.32 MW	10.15 AW	23540 AAW	TXBLS	10//99-12//99
	Lubbock MSA, TX	S	8.95 MW	8.48 AW	18620 AAW	TXBLS	10//99-12//99
	McAllen-Edinburg-Mission MSA, TX	S	8.87 MW	8.79 AW	18450 AAW	TXBLS	10//99-12//99
	Odessa-Midland MSA, TX	S	9.90 MW	9.37 AW	20580 AAW	TXBLS	10//99-12//99
	San Angelo MSA, TX	S	8.92 MW	8.40 AW	18550 AAW	TXBLS	10//99-12//99
	San Antonio MSA, TX	S	10.17 MW	9.93 AW	21160 AAW	TXBLS	10//99-12//99
	Sherman-Denison MSA, TX	S	9.70 MW	9.30 AW	20170 AAW	TXBLS	10//99-12//99
	Texarkana MSA, TX-Texarkana, AR	S	9.51 MW	9.19 AW	19780 AAW	TXBLS	10//99-12//99
	Tyler MSA, TX	S	11.16 MW	11.14 AW	23210 AAW	TXBLS	10//99-12//99
	Victoria MSA, TX	S	11.52 MW	10.51 AW	23960 AAW	TXBLS	10//99-12//99
	Waco MSA, TX	S	9.94 MW	9.77 AW	20680 AAW	TXBLS	10//99-12//99
	Wichita Falls MSA, TX	S	9.12 MW	8.11 AW	18970 AAW	TXBLS	10//99-12//99
	Provo-Orem MSA, UT	S	11.78 MW	10.66 AW	24490 AAW	UTBLS	10//99-12//99
	Vermont	S	10.7 MW	11.81 AW	24570 AAW	VTBLS	10//99-12//99
	Burlington MSA, VT	S	12.99 MW	11.88 AW	27010 AAW	VTBLS	10//99-12//99
	Virginia	S	11.75 MW	11.94 AW	24840 AAW	VABLS	10//99-12//99
	Charlottesville MSA, VA	S	12.24 MW	12.48 AW	25460 AAW	VABLS	10//99-12//99
	Danville MSA, VA	S	10.67 MW	10.52 AW	22190 AAW	VABLS	10//99-12//99
	Lynchburg MSA, VA	S	10.88 MW	10.24 AW	22630 AAW	VABLS	10//99-12//99
	Norfolk-Virginia Beach-Newport News MSA, VA-NC	S	11.39 MW	10.93 AW	23700 AAW	VABLS	10//99-12//99
	Richmond-Petersburg MSA, VA	S	12.00 MW	12.00 AW	24960 AAW	VABLS	10//99-12//99
	Roanoke MSA, VA	S	11.16 MW	11.33 AW	23210 AAW	VABLS	10//99-12//99
	Washington	S	11.86 MW	12.45 AW	25890 AAW	WABLS	10//99-12//99
	Bellingham MSA, WA	S	11.45 MW	11.26 AW	23830 AAW	WABLS	10//99-12//99
	Bremerton PMSA, WA	S	10.94 MW	10.45 AW	22760 AAW	WABLS	10//99-12//99
	Olympia PMSA, WA	S	14.77 MW	14.24 AW	30710 AAW	WABLS	10//99-12//99
	Richland-Kennewick-Pasco MSA, WA	S	11.29 MW	10.97 AW	23480 AAW	WABLS	10//99-12//99
	Seattle-Bellevue-Everett PMSA, WA	S	12.71 MW	12.17 AW	26440 AAW	WABLS	10//99-12//99
	Spokane MSA, WA	S	11.40 MW	11.11 AW	23700 AAW	WABLS	10//99-12//99
	Tacoma PMSA, WA	S	14.47 MW	12.49 AW	30090 AAW	WABLS	10//99-12//99
	Yakima MSA, WA	S	11.55 MW	11.16 AW	24030 AAW	WABLS	10//99-12//99
	West Virginia	S	9.7 MW	10.26 AW	21350 AAW	WVBLS	10//99-12//99
	Charleston MSA, WV	S	9.47 MW	8.85 AW	19700 AAW	WVBLS	10//99-12//99
	Huntington-Ashland MSA, WV-KY-OH	S	11.64 MW	11.94 AW	24210 AAW	WVBLS	10//99-12//99
	Parkersburg-Marietta MSA, WV-OH	S	10.89 MW	9.91 AW	22660 AAW	WVBLS	10//99-12//99
	Wheeling MSA, WV-OH	S	10.07 MW	10.02 AW	20940 AAW	WVBLS	10//99-12//99
	Wisconsin	S	10.69 MW	11.16 AW	23210 AAW	WIBLS	10//99-12//99

AAW Average annual wage	**AOH** Average offered, high	**ASH** Average starting, high	**H** Hourly	**M** Monthly	**S** Special: hourly and annual
AE Average entry wage	**AOL** Average offered, low	**ASL** Average starting, low	**HI** Highest wage paid	**MTC** Median total compensation	**TQ** Third quartile wage
AEX Average experienced wage	**APH** Average pay, high range	**AW** Average wage paid	**HR** High end range	**MW** Median wage paid	**W** Weekly
AO Average offered	**APL** Average pay, low range	**FQ** First quartile wage	**LR** Low end range	**SQ** Second quartile wage	**Y** Yearly

Occupation/Type/Industry	Location	Per	Low	Mid	High	Source	Date
Bill and Account Collector	Appleton-Oshkosh-Neenah						
	MSA, WI	S	11.23 MW	11.23 AW	23370 AAW	WIBLS	10//99-12//99
	Eau Claire MSA, WI	S	10.16 MW	10.43 AW	21130 AAW	WIBLS	10//99-12//99
	Green Bay MSA, WI	S	12.22 MW	11.57 AW	25420 AAW	WIBLS	10//99-12//99
	Janesville-Beloit MSA, WI	S	11.97 MW	11.54 AW	24900 AAW	WIBLS	10//99-12//99
	Kenosha PMSA, WI	S	11.15 MW	10.76 AW	23200 AAW	WIBLS	10//99-12//99
	La Crosse MSA, WI-MN	S	11.54 MW	10.96 AW	24010 AAW	WIBLS	10//99-12//99
	Madison MSA, WI	S	11.72 MW	11.27 AW	24380 AAW	WIBLS	10//99-12//99
	Milwaukee-Waukesha PMSA,						
	WI	S	10.79 MW	10.34 AW	22440 AAW	WIBLS	10//99-12//99
	Racine PMSA, WI	S	10.30 MW	9.68 AW	21420 AAW	WIBLS	10//99-12//99
	Sheboygan MSA, WI	S	11.68 MW	9.84 AW	24290 AAW	WIBLS	10//99-12//99
	Wausau MSA, WI	S	12.64 MW	11.79 AW	26280 AAW	WIBLS	10//99-12//99
	Wyoming	S	10.02 MW	11.58 AW	24090 AAW	WYBLS	10//99-12//99
	Casper MSA, WY	S	13.81 MW	10.26 AW	28730 AAW	WYBLS	10//99-12//99
	Cheyenne MSA, WY	S	10.56 MW	10.15 AW	21960 AAW	WYBLS	10//99-12//99
	Puerto Rico	S	6.74 MW	7.84 AW	16310 AAW	PRBLS	10//99-12//99
	Arecibo PMSA, PR	S	6.81 MW	6.33 AW	14170 AAW	PRBLS	10//99-12//99
	Caguas PMSA, PR	S	7.83 MW	6.63 AW	16290 AAW	PRBLS	10//99-12//99
	Mayaguez MSA, PR	S	6.48 MW	6.10 AW	13470 AAW	PRBLS	10//99-12//99
	Ponce MSA, PR	S	7.20 MW	6.47 AW	14980 AAW	PRBLS	10//99-12//99
	San Juan-Bayamon PMSA, PR	S	8.08 MW	6.97 AW	16810 AAW	PRBLS	10//99-12//99
	Virgin Islands	S	10.34 MW	11.15 AW	23190 AAW	VIBLS	10//99-12//99
	Guam	S	9.39 MW	9.72 AW	20210 AAW	GUBLS	10//99-12//99
Billing and Posting Clerk and							
Machine Operator	Alabama	S	9.88 MW	10.09 AW	21000 AAW	ALBLS	10//99-12//99
	Alaska	S	13.29 MW	13.85 AW	28800 AAW	AKBLS	10//99-12//99
	Arizona	S	10.25 MW	10.65 AW	22160 AAW	AZBLS	10//99-12//99
	Arkansas	S	9.41 MW	9.63 AW	20030 AAW	ARBLS	10//99-12//99
	California	S	12.1 MW	12.67 AW	26360 AAW	CABLS	10//99-12//99
	Colorado	S	11.27 MW	11.49 AW	23890 AAW	COBLS	10//99-12//99
	Connecticut	S	12.43 MW	12.98 AW	26990 AAW	CTBLS	10//99-12//99
	Delaware	S	12.02 MW	12.56 AW	26120 AAW	DEBLS	10//99-12//99
	District of Columbia	S	12.59 MW	13.55 AW	28190 AAW	DCBLS	10//99-12//99
	Florida	S	10.14 MW	10.73 AW	22310 AAW	FLBLS	10//99-12//99
	Georgia	S	10.85 MW	11.11 AW	23110 AAW	GABLS	10//99-12//99
	Hawaii	S	11.78 MW	12.18 AW	25320 AAW	HIBLS	10//99-12//99
	Idaho	S	10.48 MW	10.69 AW	22240 AAW	IDBLS	10//99-12//99
	Illinois	S	11.29 MW	11.77 AW	24470 AAW	ILBLS	10//99-12//99
	Indiana	S	10.5 MW	10.87 AW	22610 AAW	INBLS	10//99-12//99
	Iowa	S	10.24 MW	10.59 AW	22040 AAW	IABLS	10//99-12//99
	Kansas	S	9.86 MW	10.51 AW	21870 AAW	KSBLS	10//99-12//99
	Kentucky	S	10.5 MW	10.62 AW	22080 AAW	KYBLS	10//99-12//99
	Louisiana	S	9.37 MW	9.88 AW	20540 AAW	LABLS	10//99-12//99
	Maine	S	10.35 MW	10.53 AW	21900 AAW	MEBLS	10//99-12//99
	Maryland	S	11.57 MW	12.03 AW	25020 AAW	MDBLS	10//99-12//99
	Massachusetts	S	12.45 MW	12.63 AW	26260 AAW	MABLS	10//99-12//99
	Michigan	S	11.4 MW	11.91 AW	24780 AAW	MIBLS	10//99-12//99
	Minnesota	S	11.55 MW	11.84 AW	24620 AAW	MNBLS	10//99-12//99
	Mississippi	S	9.49 MW	9.84 AW	20460 AAW	MSBLS	10//99-12//99
	Missouri	S	10.32 MW	10.67 AW	22200 AAW	MOBLS	10//99-12//99
	Montana	S	9.5 MW	9.74 AW	20270 AAW	MTBLS	10//99-12//99
	Nebraska	S	9.94 MW	10.18 AW	21180 AAW	NEBLS	10//99-12//99
	Nevada	S	11.13 MW	11.43 AW	23770 AAW	NVBLS	10//99-12//99
	New Hampshire	S	10.68 MW	10.89 AW	22650 AAW	NHBLS	10//99-12//99
	New Jersey	S	12.31 MW	12.65 AW	26320 AAW	NJBLS	10//99-12//99
	New Mexico	S	9.78 MW	9.98 AW	20750 AAW	NMBLS	10//99-12//99
	New York	S	11.94 MW	12.56 AW	26120 AAW	NYBLS	10//99-12//99
	North Carolina	S	10.65 MW	11.17 AW	23240 AAW	NCBLS	10//99-12//99
	North Dakota	S	9.35 MW	9.59 AW	19940 AAW	NDBLS	10//99-12//99
	Ohio	S	10.76 MW	11.14 AW	23170 AAW	OHBLS	10//99-12//99
	Oklahoma	S	9.83 MW	10.14 AW	21080 AAW	OKBLS	10//99-12//99
	Oregon	S	11.45 MW	11.64 AW	24210 AAW	ORBLS	10//99-12//99
	Pennsylvania	S	11.17 MW	11.54 AW	24010 AAW	PABLS	10//99-12//99
	Rhode Island	S	12.08 MW	12.48 AW	25960 AAW	RIBLS	10//99-12//99
	South Carolina	S	10.06 MW	10.48 AW	21800 AAW	SCBLS	10//99-12//99
	South Dakota	S	9.72 MW	9.68 AW	20140 AAW	SDBLS	10//99-12//99
	Tennessee	S	10.26 MW	10.52 AW	21890 AAW	TNBLS	10//99-12//99
	Texas	S	10.5 MW	11.08 AW	23040 AAW	TXBLS	10//99-12//99
	Utah	S	9.82 MW	10.05 AW	20910 AAW	UTBLS	10//99-12//99
	Vermont	S	10.66 MW	11.01 AW	22890 AAW	VTBLS	10//99-12//99

AAW Average annual wage	**AOH** Average offered, high	**ASH** Average starting, high	**H** Hourly	**M** Monthly	**S** Special: hourly and annual
AE Average entry wage	**AOL** Average offered, low	**ASL** Average starting, low	**HI** Highest wage paid	**MTC** Median total compensation	**TQ** Third quartile wage
AEX Average experienced wage	**APH** Average pay, high range	**AW** Average wage paid	**HR** High end range	**MW** Median wage paid	**W** Weekly
AO Average offered	**APL** Average pay, low range	**FQ** First quartile wage	**LR** Low end range	**SQ** Second quartile wage	**Y** Yearly

Occupation/Type/Industry	Location	Per	Low	Mid	High	Source	Date
Billing and Posting Clerk and Machine Operator	Virginia	S	10.78 MW	11.18 AW	23250 AAW	VABLS	10//99-12//99
	Washington	S	11.91 MW	12.30 AW	25580 AAW	WABLS	10//99-12//99
	West Virginia	S	8.66 MW	8.98 AW	18670 AAW	WVBLS	10//99-12//99
	Wisconsin	S	10.59 MW	10.94 AW	22750 AAW	WIBLS	10//99-12//99
	Wyoming	S	9.57 MW	9.96 AW	20720 AAW	WYBLS	10//99-12//99
	Puerto Rico	S	6.69 MW	7.36 AW	15320 AAW	PRBLS	10//99-12//99
	Virgin Islands	S	9.59 MW	9.70 AW	20180 AAW	VIBLS	10//99-12//99
	Guam	S	9.08 MW	9.64 AW	20050 AAW	GUBLS	10//99-12//99
Billing Coordinator Medical Doctor's Office	United States	H		13.65 AEX		MEDEC	2000
Bindery Worker	Alabama	S	9.4 MW	9.95 AW	20690 AAW	ALBLS	10//99-12//99
	Alaska	S	16.33 MW	15.34 AW	31900 AAW	AKBLS	10//99-12//99
	Arizona	S	10.24 MW	10.92 AW	22710 AAW	AZBLS	10//99-12//99
	Arkansas	S	8.81 MW	9.00 AW	18720 AAW	ARBLS	10//99-12//99
	California	S	8.76 MW	10.17 AW	21150 AAW	CABLS	10//99-12//99
	Colorado	S	8.44 MW	9.55 AW	19860 AAW	COBLS	10//99-12//99
	Connecticut	S	11.2 MW	11.87 AW	24680 AAW	CTBLS	10//99-12//99
	Florida	S	9.76 MW	10.28 AW	21390 AAW	FLBLS	10//99-12//99
	Georgia	S	12.08 MW	13.04 AW	27110 AAW	GABLS	10//99-12//99
	Idaho	S	10.98 MW	10.92 AW	22710 AAW	IDBLS	10//99-12//99
	Illinois	S	9.24 MW	10.51 AW	21850 AAW	ILBLS	10//99-12//99
	Indiana	S	10.2 MW	10.87 AW	22620 AAW	INBLS	10//99-12//99
	Iowa	S	9.8 MW	10.53 AW	21910 AAW	IABLS	10//99-12//99
	Kansas	S	9.36 MW	9.36 AW	19480 AAW	KSBLS	10//99-12//99
	Kentucky	S	10.13 MW	10.66 AW	22180 AAW	KYBLS	10//99-12//99
	Louisiana	S	7.94 MW	8.32 AW	17300 AAW	LABLS	10//99-12//99
	Maine	S	7.98 MW	8.27 AW	17200 AAW	MEBLS	10//99-12//99
	Maryland	S	10.79 MW	11.82 AW	24580 AAW	MDBLS	10//99-12//99
	Massachusetts	S	11.18 MW	12.30 AW	25590 AAW	MABLS	10//99-12//99
	Michigan	S	10.06 MW	11.07 AW	23020 AAW	MIBLS	10//99-12//99
	Minnesota	S	11.39 MW	12.41 AW	25820 AAW	MNBLS	10//99-12//99
	Mississippi	S	9.21 MW	9.44 AW	19630 AAW	MSBLS	10//99-12//99
	Missouri	S	9.78 MW	11.23 AW	23360 AAW	MOBLS	10//99-12//99
	Montana	S	7.61 MW	7.64 AW	15890 AAW	MTBLS	10//99-12//99
	Nebraska	S	8.46 MW	8.97 AW	18660 AAW	NEBLS	10//99-12//99
	Nevada	S	8.21 MW	8.84 AW	18380 AAW	NVBLS	10//99-12//99
	New Hampshire	S	10.07 MW	10.60 AW	22040 AAW	NHBLS	10//99-12//99
	New Jersey	S	9.29 MW	10.73 AW	22330 AAW	NJBLS	10//99-12//99
	New York	S	10.16 MW	12.87 AW	26770 AAW	NYBLS	10//99-12//99
	North Carolina	S	9.62 MW	10.24 AW	21290 AAW	NCBLS	10//99-12//99
	North Dakota	S	6.61 MW	7.16 AW	14890 AAW	NDBLS	10//99-12//99
	Ohio	S	9.37 MW	9.99 AW	20790 AAW	OHBLS	10//99-12//99
	Oklahoma	S	6.24 MW	6.85 AW	14250 AAW	OKBLS	10//99-12//99
	Oregon	S	13.33 MW	13.34 AW	27750 AAW	ORBLS	10//99-12//99
	Pennsylvania	S	10.78 MW	12.09 AW	25150 AAW	PABLS	10//99-12//99
	Rhode Island	S	6.56 MW	8.57 AW	17830 AAW	RIBLS	10//99-12//99
	South Carolina	S	8.22 MW	9.50 AW	19770 AAW	SCBLS	10//99-12//99
	South Dakota	S	8.16 MW	8.89 AW	18490 AAW	SDBLS	10//99-12//99
	Tennessee	S	10.85 MW	10.66 AW	22160 AAW	TNBLS	10//99-12//99
	Texas	S	9.06 MW	9.50 AW	19760 AAW	TXBLS	10//99-12//99
	Utah	S	8.93 MW	9.25 AW	19240 AAW	UTBLS	10//99-12//99
	Vermont	S	11.57 MW	12.93 AW	26890 AAW	VTBLS	10//99-12//99
	Virginia	S	9.96 MW	10.70 AW	22250 AAW	VABLS	10//99-12//99
	Washington	S	9.2 MW	9.92 AW	20640 AAW	WABLS	10//99-12//99
	West Virginia	S	7.68 MW	8.03 AW	16690 AAW	WVBLS	10//99-12//99
	Wisconsin	S	10.61 MW	11.38 AW	23670 AAW	WIBLS	10//99-12//99
	Wyoming	S	7.34 MW	7.41 AW	15400 AAW	WYBLS	10//99-12//99
	Puerto Rico	S	6.67 MW	8.32 AEX	17310 AAW	PRBLS	10//99-12//99
Biochemist and Biophysicist	Arizona	S	21.5 MW	28.74 AW	59780 AAW	AZBLS	10//99-12//99
	Phoenix-Mesa MSA, AZ	S	20.11 MW	18.31 AW	41830 AAW	AZBLS	10//99-12//99
	California	S	27.19 MW	27.22 AW	56620 AAW	CABLS	10//99-12//99
	Los Angeles-Long Beach PMSA, CA	S	27.77 MW	25.95 AW	57750 AAW	CABLS	10//99-12//99
	Oakland PMSA, CA	S	29.52 MW	29.82 AW	61400 AAW	CABLS	10//99-12//99
	San Diego MSA, CA	S	20.56 MW	18.18 AW	42760 AAW	CABLS	10//99-12//99
	San Francisco PMSA, CA	S	25.79 MW	24.98 AW	53640 AAW	CABLS	10//99-12//99
	San Jose PMSA, CA	S	32.51 MW	31.76 AW	67630 AAW	CABLS	10//99-12//99
	Colorado	S	36.02 MW	31.16 AW	64810 AAW	COBLS	10//99-12//99

AAW Average annual wage	**AOH** Average offered, high	**ASH** Average starting, high	**H** Hourly	**M** Monthly	**S** Special: hourly and annual
AE Average entry wage	**AOL** Average offered, low	**ASL** Average starting, low	**HI** Highest wage paid	**MTC** Median total compensation	**TQ** Third quartile wage
AEX Average experienced wage	**APH** Average pay, high range	**AW** Average wage paid	**HR** High end range	**MW** Median wage paid	**W** Weekly
AO Average offered	**APL** Average pay, low range	**FQ** First quartile wage	**LR** Low end range	**SQ** Second quartile wage	**Y** Yearly

Occupation/Type/Industry	Location	Per	Low	Mid	High	Source	Date
Biochemist and Biophysicist	Connecticut	S	25.78 MW	27.41 AW	57010 AAW	CTBLS	10//99-12//99
	New Haven-Meriden PMSA, CT	S	27.26 MW	25.56 AW	56690 AAW	CTBLS	10//99-12//99
	Delaware	S	33.89 MW	35.23 AW	73270 AAW	DEBLS	10//99-12//99
	Wilmington-Newark PMSA, DE-MD	S	35.23 MW	33.89 AW	73270 AAW	DEBLS	10//99-12//99
	Washington PMSA, DC-MD-VA-WV	S	28.88 MW	28.70 AW	60080 AAW	DCBLS	10//99-12//99
	Florida	S	19.03 MW	20.77 AW	43200 AAW	FLBLS	10//99-12//99
	Tampa-St. Petersburg-Clearwater MSA, FL	S	19.91 MW	18.86 AW	41420 AAW	FLBLS	10//99-12//99
	Georgia	S	38.52 MW	36.15 AW	75180 AAW	GABLS	10//99-12//99
	Illinois	S	25.45 MW	26.98 AW	56110 AAW	ILBLS	10//99-12//99
	Chicago PMSA, IL	S	27.28 MW	26.02 AW	56750 AAW	ILBLS	10//99-12//99
	Indiana	S	20.54 MW	22.36 AW	46510 AAW	INBLS	10//99-12//99
	Indianapolis MSA, IN	S	23.47 MW	21.25 AW	48830 AAW	INBLS	10//99-12//99
	Kansas	S	18.11 MW	18.19 AW	37840 AAW	KSBLS	10//99-12//99
	Maine	S	29.38 MW	27.23 AW	56630 AAW	MEBLS	10//99-12//99
	Massachusetts	S	31.65 MW	30.95 AW	64380 AAW	MABLS	10//99-12//99
	Boston PMSA, MA-NH	S	30.42 MW	30.05 AW	63280 AAW	MABLS	10//99-12//99
	Minnesota	S	24.56 MW	25.83 AW	53730 AAW	MNBLS	10//99-12//99
	Minneapolis-St. Paul MSA, MN-WI	S	26.86 MW	25.39 AW	55860 AAW	MNBLS	10//99-12//99
	Missouri	S	17.18 MW	23.96 AW	49830 AAW	MOBLS	10//99-12//99
	New Jersey	S	23.74 MW	28.82 AW	59950 AAW	NJBLS	10//99-12//99
	Monmouth-Ocean PMSA, NJ	S	29.35 MW	28.30 AW	61040 AAW	NJBLS	10//99-12//99
	Newark PMSA, NJ	S	29.59 MW	24.22 AW	61550 AAW	NJBLS	10//99-12//99
	Trenton PMSA, NJ	S	27.78 MW	17.18 AW	57790 AAW	NJBLS	10//99-12//99
	New York	S	24.23 MW	26.80 AW	55750 AAW	NYBLS	10//99-12//99
	Buffalo-Niagara Falls MSA, NY	S	24.21 MW	22.56 AW	50350 AAW	NYBLS	10//99-12//99
	North Carolina	S	34.12 MW	33.55 AW	69790 AAW	NCBLS	10//99-12//99
	Raleigh-Durham-Chapel Hill MSA, NC	S	33.42 MW	34.08 AW	69510 AAW	NCBLS	10//99-12//99
	Ohio	S	27.49 MW	27.82 AW	57860 AAW	OHBLS	10//99-12//99
	Oklahoma	S	21.72 MW	21.43 AW	44570 AAW	OKBLS	10//99-12//99
	Oklahoma City MSA, OK	S	19.70 MW	19.58 AW	40980 AAW	OKBLS	10//99-12//99
	Pennsylvania	S	20.35 MW	23.67 AW	49230 AAW	PABLS	10//99-12//99
	Philadelphia PMSA, PA-NJ	S	22.37 MW	19.52 AW	46540 AAW	PABLS	10//99-12//99
	Texas	S	25.6 MW	27.95 AW	58130 AAW	TXBLS	10//99-12//99
	Utah	S	23.68 MW	24.00 AW	49910 AAW	UTBLS	10//99-12//99
	Salt Lake City-Ogden MSA, UT	S	24.00 MW	23.68 AW	49910 AAW	UTBLS	10//99-12//99
	Washington	S	31.74 MW	38.18 AW	79410 AAW	WABLS	10//99-12//99
	Seattle-Bellevue-Everett PMSA, WA	S	38.18 MW	31.74 AW	79410 AAW	WABLS	10//99-12//99
	Wisconsin	S	21.77 MW	24.60 AW	51170 AAW	WIBLS	10//99-12//99
	Milwaukee-Waukesha PMSA, WI	S	24.58 MW	21.32 AW	51130 AAW	WIBLS	10//99-12//99
Biological Science Teacher							
Postsecondary	Alabama	Y		33610 AAW		ALBLS	10//99-12//99
Postsecondary	Arizona	Y		40640 AAW		AZBLS	10//99-12//99
Postsecondary	Phoenix-Mesa MSA, AZ	Y		48110 AAW		AZBLS	10//99-12//99
Postsecondary	Arkansas	Y		44410 AAW		ARBLS	10//99-12//99
Postsecondary	California	Y		61730 AAW		CABLS	10//99-12//99
Postsecondary	San Francisco PMSA, CA	Y		75990 AAW		CABLS	10//99-12//99
Postsecondary	Colorado	Y		56890 AAW		COBLS	10//99-12//99
Postsecondary	New Haven-Meriden PMSA, CT	Y		47500 AAW		CTBLS	10//99-12//99
Postsecondary	Washington PMSA, DC-MD-VA-WV	Y		58160 AAW		DCBLS	10//99-12//99
Postsecondary	Florida	Y		60750 AAW		FLBLS	10//99-12//99
Postsecondary	Miami PMSA, FL	Y		72810 AAW		FLBLS	10//99-12//99
Postsecondary	Orlando MSA, FL	Y		57890 AAW		FLBLS	10//99-12//99
Postsecondary	Tallahassee MSA, FL	Y		63410 AAW		FLBLS	10//99-12//99
Postsecondary	Tampa-St. Petersburg-Clearwater MSA, FL	Y		50770 AAW		FLBLS	10//99-12//99
Postsecondary	Georgia	Y		47330 AAW		GABLS	10//99-12//99
Postsecondary	Atlanta MSA, GA	Y		50830 AAW		GABLS	10//99-12//99
Postsecondary	Illinois	Y		46480 AAW		ILBLS	10//99-12//99
Postsecondary	Chicago PMSA, IL	Y		45840 AAW		ILBLS	10//99-12//99
Postsecondary	Indiana	Y		49070 AAW		INBLS	10//99-12//99

AAW	Average annual wage	AOH	Average offered, high	ASH	Average starting, high	H	Hourly	M	Monthly	S	Special: hourly and annual
AE	Average entry wage	AOL	Average offered, low	ASL	Average starting, low	HI	Highest wage paid	MTC	Median total compensation	TQ	Third quartile wage
AEX	Average experienced wage	APH	Average pay, high range	AW	Average wage paid	HR	High end range	MW	Median wage paid	W	Weekly
AO	Average offered	APL	Average pay, low range	FQ	First quartile wage	LR	Low end range	SQ	Second quartile wage	Y	Yearly

Occupation/Type/Industry	Location	Per	Low	Mid	High	Source	Date
Biological Science Teacher							
Postsecondary	Iowa	Y		57090 AAW		IABLS	10//99-12//99
Postsecondary	Kansas	Y		41400 AAW		KSBLS	10//99-12//99
Postsecondary	Kentucky	Y		40810 AAW		KYBLS	10//99-12//99
Postsecondary	Louisiana	Y		54600 AAW		LABLS	10//99-12//99
Postsecondary	Maryland	Y		54220 AAW		MDBLS	10//99-12//99
Postsecondary	Baltimore PMSA, MD	Y		47240 AAW		MDBLS	10//99-12//99
Postsecondary	Massachusetts	Y		55560 AAW		MABLS	10//99-12//99
Postsecondary	Boston PMSA, MA-NH	Y		54500 AAW		MABLS	10//99-12//99
Postsecondary	Springfield MSA, MA	Y		57890 AAW		MABLS	10//99-12//99
Postsecondary	Michigan	Y		54390 AAW		MIBLS	10//99-12//99
Postsecondary	Detroit PMSA, MI	Y		59230 AAW		MIBLS	10//99-12//99
Postsecondary	Minnesota	Y		68020 AAW		MNBLS	10//99-12//99
Postsecondary	Minneapolis-St. Paul MSA, MN-WI	Y		76390 AAW		MNBLS	10//99-12//99
Postsecondary	Mississippi	Y		44160 AAW		MSBLS	10//99-12//99
Postsecondary	Jackson MSA, MS	Y		42890 AAW		MSBLS	10//99-12//99
Postsecondary	Missouri	Y		42010 AAW		MOBLS	10//99-12//99
Postsecondary	St. Louis MSA, MO-IL	Y		41150 AAW		MOBLS	10//99-12//99
Postsecondary	Montana	Y		65510 AAW		MTBLS	10//99-12//99
Postsecondary	Nebraska	Y		42960 AAW		NEBLS	10//99-12//99
Postsecondary	Nevada	Y		43570 AAW		NVBLS	10//99-12//99
Postsecondary	New Hampshire	Y		44550 AAW		NHBLS	10//99-12//99
Postsecondary	New Jersey	Y		64300 AAW		NJBLS	10//99-12//99
Postsecondary	Newark PMSA, NJ	Y		62590 AAW		NJBLS	10//99-12//99
Postsecondary	New Mexico	Y		50100 AAW		NMBLS	10//99-12//99
Postsecondary	New York	Y		73560 AAW		NYBLS	10//99-12//99
Postsecondary	Buffalo-Niagara Falls MSA, NY	Y		57880 AAW		NYBLS	10//99-12//99
Postsecondary	New York PMSA, NY	Y		80980 AAW		NYBLS	10//99-12//99
Postsecondary	North Carolina	Y		47300 AAW		NCBLS	10//99-12//99
Postsecondary	Asheville MSA, NC	Y		45600 AAW		NCBLS	10//99-12//99
Postsecondary	Charlotte-Gastonia-Rock Hill MSA, NC-SC	Y		55470 AAW		NCBLS	10//99-12//99
Postsecondary	Fayetteville MSA, NC	Y		44170 AAW		NCBLS	10//99-12//99
Postsecondary	Greensboro--Winston-Salem--High Point MSA, NC	Y		49370 AAW		NCBLS	10//99-12//99
Postsecondary	Raleigh-Durham-Chapel Hill MSA, NC	Y		47050 AAW		NCBLS	10//99-12//99
Postsecondary	North Dakota	Y		30020 AAW		NDBLS	10//99-12//99
Postsecondary	Ohio	Y		43690 AAW		OHBLS	10//99-12//99
Postsecondary	Cleveland-Lorain-Elyria PMSA, OH	Y		55010 AAW		OHBLS	10//99-12//99
Postsecondary	Columbus MSA, OH	Y		39620 AAW		OHBLS	10//99-12//99
Postsecondary	Dayton-Springfield MSA, OH	Y		41610 AAW		OHBLS	10//99-12//99
Postsecondary	Oklahoma	Y		45640 AAW		OKBLS	10//99-12//99
Postsecondary	Oklahoma City MSA, OK	Y		39250 AAW		OKBLS	10//99-12//99
Postsecondary	Oregon	Y		50220 AAW		ORBLS	10//99-12//99
Postsecondary	Portland-Vancouver PMSA, OR-WA	Y		50400 AAW		ORBLS	10//99-12//99
Postsecondary	Pennsylvania	Y		55280 AAW		PABLS	10//99-12//99
Postsecondary	Allentown-Bethlehem-Easton MSA, PA	Y		46640 AAW		PABLS	10//99-12//99
Postsecondary	Philadelphia PMSA, PA-NJ	Y		56420 AAW		PABLS	10//99-12//99
Postsecondary	Pittsburgh MSA, PA	Y		54980 AAW		PABLS	10//99-12//99
Postsecondary	Scranton--Wilkes-Barre--Hazleton MSA, PA	Y		51300 AAW		PABLS	10//99-12//99
Postsecondary	South Carolina	Y		52000 AAW		SCBLS	10//99-12//99
Postsecondary	Greenville-Spartanburg-Anderson MSA, SC	Y		57860 AAW		SCBLS	10//99-12//99
Postsecondary	South Dakota	Y		48510 AAW		SDBLS	10//99-12//99
Postsecondary	Tennessee	Y		53470 AAW		TNBLS	10//99-12//99
Postsecondary	Johnson City-Kingsport-Bristol MSA, TN-VA	Y		52820 AAW		TNBLS	10//99-12//99
Postsecondary	Texas	Y		70530 AAW		TXBLS	10//99-12//99
Postsecondary	Dallas PMSA, TX	Y		73980 AAW		TXBLS	10//99-12//99
Postsecondary	El Paso MSA, TX	Y		52800 AAW		TXBLS	10//99-12//99
Postsecondary	Fort Worth-Arlington PMSA, TX	Y		68700 AAW		TXBLS	10//99-12//99
Postsecondary	Houston PMSA, TX	Y		71020 AAW		TXBLS	10//99-12//99
Postsecondary	Vermont	Y		60800 AAW		VTBLS	10//99-12//99
Postsecondary	Virginia	Y		47150 AAW		VABLS	10//99-12//99

AAW	Average annual wage	**AOH**	Average offered, high	**ASH**	Average starting, high	**H**	Hourly	**M**	Monthly
AE	Average entry wage	**AOL**	Average offered, low	**ASL**	Average starting, low	**HI**	Highest wage paid	**MTC**	Median total compensation
AEX	Average experienced wage	**APH**	Average pay, high range	**AW**	Average wage paid	**HR**	High end range	**MW**	Median wage paid
AO	Average offered	**APL**	Average pay, low range	**FQ**	First quartile wage	**LR**	Low end range	**SQ**	Second quartile wage

(continued legend:) **S** Special: hourly and annual   **TQ** Third quartile wage   **W** Weekly   **Y** Yearly

Occupation/Type/Industry	Location	Per	Low	Mid	High	Source	Date
Biological Science Teacher							
Postsecondary	Washington	Y		41600 ᴀᴀᴡ		WABLS	10//99-12//99
Postsecondary	Seattle-Bellevue-Everett PMSA, WA	Y		41180 ᴀᴀᴡ		WABLS	10//99-12//99
Postsecondary	West Virginia	Y		57580 ᴀᴀᴡ		WVBLS	10//99-12//99
Postsecondary	Wisconsin	Y		40740 ᴀᴀᴡ		WIBLS	10//99-12//99
Postsecondary	Wyoming	Y		60210 ᴀᴀᴡ		WYBLS	10//99-12//99
Postsecondary	Puerto Rico	Y		45210 ᴀᴀᴡ		PRBLS	10//99-12//99
Postsecondary	San Juan-Bayamon PMSA, PR	Y		44840 ᴀᴀᴡ		PRBLS	10//99-12//99
Biological Technician	United States	H		15.53 ᴀᴡ		NCS98	1998
	Alabama	S	13.14 ᴍᴡ	13.94 ᴀᴡ	28990 ᴀᴀᴡ	ALBLS	10//99-12//99
	Huntsville MSA, AL	S	14.49 ᴍᴡ	13.42 ᴀᴡ	30130 ᴀᴀᴡ	ALBLS	10//99-12//99
	Alaska	S	11.82 ᴍᴡ	11.87 ᴀᴡ	24690 ᴀᴀᴡ	AKBLS	10//99-12//99
	Arizona	S	11.6 ᴍᴡ	12.54 ᴀᴡ	26080 ᴀᴀᴡ	AZBLS	10//99-12//99
	Phoenix-Mesa MSA, AZ	S	12.77 ᴍᴡ	11.69 ᴀᴡ	26550 ᴀᴀᴡ	AZBLS	10//99-12//99
	Arkansas	S	14.43 ᴍᴡ	14.63 ᴀᴡ	30420 ᴀᴀᴡ	ARBLS	10//99-12//99
	California	S	15.67 ᴍᴡ	16.51 ᴀᴡ	34340 ᴀᴀᴡ	CABLS	10//99-12//99
	Los Angeles-Long Beach PMSA, CA	S	15.98 ᴍᴡ	14.69 ᴀᴡ	33240 ᴀᴀᴡ	CABLS	10//99-12//99
	Oakland PMSA, CA	S	20.08 ᴍᴡ	19.40 ᴀᴡ	41760 ᴀᴀᴡ	CABLS	10//99-12//99
	Orange County PMSA, CA	S	12.99 ᴍᴡ	12.27 ᴀᴡ	27020 ᴀᴀᴡ	CABLS	10//99-12//99
	Riverside-San Bernardino PMSA, CA	S	19.33 ᴍᴡ	17.38 ᴀᴡ	40210 ᴀᴀᴡ	CABLS	10//99-12//99
	Sacramento PMSA, CA	S	12.82 ᴍᴡ	12.37 ᴀᴡ	26670 ᴀᴀᴡ	CABLS	10//99-12//99
	San Diego MSA, CA	S	16.03 ᴍᴡ	15.01 ᴀᴡ	33350 ᴀᴀᴡ	CABLS	10//99-12//99
	San Francisco PMSA, CA	S	16.33 ᴍᴡ	15.22 ᴀᴡ	33970 ᴀᴀᴡ	CABLS	10//99-12//99
	San Jose PMSA, CA	S	18.84 ᴍᴡ	18.00 ᴀᴡ	39180 ᴀᴀᴡ	CABLS	10//99-12//99
	Santa Barbara-Santa Maria-Lompoc MSA, CA	S	13.31 ᴍᴡ	14.46 ᴀᴡ	27690 ᴀᴀᴡ	CABLS	10//99-12//99
	Stockton-Lodi MSA, CA	S	12.37 ᴍᴡ	12.35 ᴀᴡ	25730 ᴀᴀᴡ	CABLS	10//99-12//99
	Ventura PMSA, CA	S	11.03 ᴍᴡ	11.70 ᴀᴡ	22940 ᴀᴀᴡ	CABLS	10//99-12//99
	Yolo PMSA, CA	S	13.46 ᴍᴡ	12.66 ᴀᴡ	27990 ᴀᴀᴡ	CABLS	10//99-12//99
	Colorado	S	13.98 ᴍᴡ	14.63 ᴀᴡ	30440 ᴀᴀᴡ	COBLS	10//99-12//99
	Colorado Springs MSA, CO	S	14.14 ᴍᴡ	13.48 ᴀᴡ	29410 ᴀᴀᴡ	COBLS	10//99-12//99
	Denver PMSA, CO	S	14.74 ᴍᴡ	14.17 ᴀᴡ	30660 ᴀᴀᴡ	COBLS	10//99-12//99
	Connecticut	S	19.76 ᴍᴡ	20.13 ᴀᴡ	41880 ᴀᴀᴡ	CTBLS	10//99-12//99
	New Haven-Meriden PMSA, CT	S	20.83 ᴍᴡ	20.37 ᴀᴡ	43320 ᴀᴀᴡ	CTBLS	10//99-12//99
	Washington PMSA, DC-MD-VA-WV	S	16.06 ᴍᴡ	16.99 ᴀᴡ	33400 ᴀᴀᴡ	DCBLS	10//99-12//99
	Florida	S	11.98 ᴍᴡ	12.36 ᴀᴡ	25700 ᴀᴀᴡ	FLBLS	10//99-12//99
	Fort Lauderdale PMSA, FL	S	17.04 ᴍᴡ	15.87 ᴀᴡ	35450 ᴀᴀᴡ	FLBLS	10//99-12//99
	Fort Pierce-Port St. Lucie MSA, FL	S	10.30 ᴍᴡ	8.44 ᴀᴡ	21420 ᴀᴀᴡ	FLBLS	10//99-12//99
	Jacksonville MSA, FL	S	12.22 ᴍᴡ	11.78 ᴀᴡ	25410 ᴀᴀᴡ	FLBLS	10//99-12//99
	Melbourne-Titusville-Palm Bay MSA, FL	S	14.38 ᴍᴡ	12.45 ᴀᴡ	29910 ᴀᴀᴡ	FLBLS	10//99-12//99
	Miami PMSA, FL	S	11.13 ᴍᴡ	10.61 ᴀᴡ	23150 ᴀᴀᴡ	FLBLS	10//99-12//99
	Orlando MSA, FL	S	11.86 ᴍᴡ	11.08 ᴀᴡ	24660 ᴀᴀᴡ	FLBLS	10//99-12//99
	Tampa-St. Petersburg-Clearwater MSA, FL	S	14.12 ᴍᴡ	13.95 ᴀᴡ	29370 ᴀᴀᴡ	FLBLS	10//99-12//99
	Georgia	S	13.24 ᴍᴡ	13.99 ᴀᴡ	29110 ᴀᴀᴡ	GABLS	10//99-12//99
	Atlanta MSA, GA	S	14.14 ᴍᴡ	13.96 ᴀᴡ	29410 ᴀᴀᴡ	GABLS	10//99-12//99
	Idaho	S	11.32 ᴍᴡ	11.93 ᴀᴡ	24810 ᴀᴀᴡ	IDBLS	10//99-12//99
	Illinois	S	11.91 ᴍᴡ	13.14 ᴀᴡ	27330 ᴀᴀᴡ	ILBLS	10//99-12//99
	Chicago PMSA, IL	S	12.37 ᴍᴡ	10.73 ᴀᴡ	25740 ᴀᴀᴡ	ILBLS	10//99-12//99
	Indiana	S	16.67 ᴍᴡ	18.26 ᴀᴡ	37980 ᴀᴀᴡ	INBLS	10//99-12//99
	Iowa	S	16.04 ᴍᴡ	15.87 ᴀᴡ	33000 ᴀᴀᴡ	IABLS	10//99-12//99
	Des Moines MSA, IA	S	18.85 ᴍᴡ	18.95 ᴀᴡ	39200 ᴀᴀᴡ	IABLS	10//99-12//99
	Kansas	S	12.73 ᴍᴡ	13.56 ᴀᴡ	28200 ᴀᴀᴡ	KSBLS	10//99-12//99
	Kentucky	S	11.98 ᴍᴡ	12.22 ᴀᴡ	25410 ᴀᴀᴡ	KYBLS	10//99-12//99
	Louisiana	S	12.88 ᴍᴡ	13.29 ᴀᴡ	27630 ᴀᴀᴡ	LABLS	10//99-12//99
	New Orleans MSA, LA	S	13.25 ᴍᴡ	12.84 ᴀᴡ	27560 ᴀᴀᴡ	LABLS	10//99-12//99
	Maine	S	13.49 ᴍᴡ	14.47 ᴀᴡ	30110 ᴀᴀᴡ	MEBLS	10//99-12//99
	Maryland	S	17.46 ᴍᴡ	16.79 ᴀᴡ	34920 ᴀᴀᴡ	MDBLS	10//99-12//99
	Baltimore PMSA, MD	S	15.54 ᴍᴡ	15.54 ᴀᴡ	32320 ᴀᴀᴡ	MDBLS	10//99-12//99
	Massachusetts	S	16.88 ᴍᴡ	18.59 ᴀᴡ	38660 ᴀᴀᴡ	MABLS	10//99-12//99
	Boston PMSA, MA-NH	S	18.57 ᴍᴡ	16.56 ᴀᴡ	38620 ᴀᴀᴡ	MABLS	10//99-12//99
	Minnesota	S	14.18 ᴍᴡ	14.47 ᴀᴡ	30090 ᴀᴀᴡ	MNBLS	10//99-12//99
	Duluth-Superior MSA, MN-WI	S	9.60 ᴍᴡ	9.08 ᴀᴡ	19960 ᴀᴀᴡ	MNBLS	10//99-12//99
	Minneapolis-St. Paul MSA, MN-WI	S	15.33 ᴍᴡ	14.60 ᴀᴡ	31890 ᴀᴀᴡ	MNBLS	10//99-12//99

AAW Average annual wage	**AOH** Average offered, high	**ASH** Average starting, high	**H** Hourly	**M** Monthly	**S** Special: hourly and annual
AE Average entry wage	**AOL** Average offered, low	**ASL** Average starting, low	**HI** Highest wage paid	**MTC** Median total compensation	**TQ** Third quartile wage
AEX Average experienced wage	**APH** Average pay, high range	**AW** Average wage paid	**HR** High end range	**MW** Median wage paid	**W** Weekly
AO Average offered	**APL** Average pay, low range	**FQ** First quartile wage	**LR** Low end range	**SQ** Second quartile wage	**Y** Yearly

Occupation/Type/Industry	Location	Per	Low	Mid	High	Source	Date
Biological Technician	Mississippi	S	13.23 MW	13.45 AW	27970 AAW	MSBLS	10//99-12//99
	Missouri	S	13.37 MW	13.85 AW	28810 AAW	MOBLS	10//99-12//99
	Kansas City MSA, MO-KS	S	13.62 MW	12.77 AW	28330 AAW	MOBLS	10//99-12//99
	St. Louis MSA, MO-IL	S	15.60 MW	15.35 AW	32450 AAW	MOBLS	10//99-12//99
	Montana	S	12.49 MW	13.66 AW	28410 AAW	MTBLS	10//99-12//99
	Nebraska	S	11.61 MW	12.18 AW	25330 AAW	NEBLS	10//99-12//99
	Lincoln MSA, NE	S	9.51 MW	8.99 AW	19790 AAW	NEBLS	10//99-12//99
	Omaha MSA, NE-IA	S	16.69 MW	17.66 AW	34720 AAW	NEBLS	10//99-12//99
	New Hampshire	S	14.89 MW	15.71 AW	32680 AAW	NHBLS	10//99-12//99
	New Jersey	S	14.94 MW	15.53 AW	32310 AAW	NJBLS	10//99-12//99
	Middlesex-Somerset-Hunterdon PMSA, NJ	S	15.05 MW	14.27 AW	31300 AAW	NJBLS	10//99-12//99
	Monmouth-Ocean PMSA, NJ	S	15.60 MW	15.10 AW	32450 AAW	NJBLS	10//99-12//99
	Newark PMSA, NJ	S	16.17 MW	16.41 AW	33640 AAW	NJBLS	10//99-12//99
	Trenton PMSA, NJ	S	16.35 MW	15.85 AW	34000 AAW	NJBLS	10//99-12//99
	New Mexico	S	13.48 MW	13.39 AW	27840 AAW	NMBLS	10//99-12//99
	New York	S	15.16 MW	15.87 AW	33000 AAW	NYBLS	10//99-12//99
	Albany-Schenectady-Troy MSA, NY	S	14.89 MW	14.54 AW	30970 AAW	NYBLS	10//99-12//99
	Buffalo-Niagara Falls MSA, NY	S	15.98 MW	15.70 AW	33250 AAW	NYBLS	10//99-12//99
	Nassau-Suffolk PMSA, NY	S	19.01 MW	18.80 AW	39540 AAW	NYBLS	10//99-12//99
	New York PMSA, NY	S	16.53 MW	15.46 AW	34380 AAW	NYBLS	10//99-12//99
	Rochester MSA, NY	S	15.33 MW	15.24 AW	31890 AAW	NYBLS	10//99-12//99
	North Carolina	S	14.63 MW	15.38 AW	31990 AAW	NCBLS	10//99-12//99
	Greensboro--Winston-Salem--High Point MSA, NC	S	9.97 MW	9.88 AW	20750 AAW	NCBLS	10//99-12//99
	Raleigh-Durham-Chapel Hill MSA, NC	S	15.27 MW	14.76 AW	31760 AAW	NCBLS	10//99-12//99
	Wilmington MSA, NC	S	19.56 MW	19.24 AW	40680 AAW	NCBLS	10//99-12//99
	North Dakota	S	12.26 MW	12.79 AW	26590 AAW	NDBLS	10//99-12//99
	Bismarck MSA, ND	S	13.14 MW	12.44 AW	27320 AAW	NDBLS	10//99-12//99
	Ohio	S	15.39 MW	15.80 AW	32860 AAW	OHBLS	10//99-12//99
	Cincinnati PMSA, OH-KY-IN	S	14.93 MW	14.69 AW	31050 AAW	OHBLS	10//99-12//99
	Cleveland-Lorain-Elyria PMSA, OH	S	18.45 MW	17.90 AW	38370 AAW	OHBLS	10//99-12//99
	Oklahoma	S	11.5 MW	12.01 AW	24990 AAW	OKBLS	10//99-12//99
	Tulsa MSA, OK	S	10.89 MW	10.30 AW	22650 AAW	OKBLS	10//99-12//99
	Oregon	S	11.45 MW	11.90 AW	24740 AAW	ORBLS	10//99-12//99
	Eugene-Springfield MSA, OR	S	10.76 MW	10.23 AW	22370 AAW	ORBLS	10//99-12//99
	Portland-Vancouver PMSA, OR-WA	S	12.76 MW	12.26 AW	26550 AAW	ORBLS	10//99-12//99
	Pennsylvania	S	16.06 MW	16.18 AW	33650 AAW	PABLS	10//99-12//99
	Philadelphia PMSA, PA-NJ	S	15.83 MW	15.84 AW	32930 AAW	PABLS	10//99-12//99
	Pittsburgh MSA, PA	S	19.17 MW	21.05 AW	39880 AAW	PABLS	10//99-12//99
	Rhode Island	S	14.11 MW	14.11 AW	29350 AAW	RIBLS	10//99-12//99
	Providence-Fall River-Warwick MSA, RI-MA	S	14.15 MW	14.17 AW	29430 AAW	RIBLS	10//99-12//99
	South Carolina	S	13.31 MW	14.16 AW	29450 AAW	SCBLS	10//99-12//99
	South Dakota	S	10.5 MW	11.09 AW	23070 AAW	SDBLS	10//99-12//99
	Tennessee	S	11.85 MW	12.08 AW	25130 AAW	TNBLS	10//99-12//99
	Knoxville MSA, TN	S	11.66 MW	10.63 AW	24260 AAW	TNBLS	10//99-12//99
	Memphis MSA, TN-AR-MS	S	14.11 MW	12.80 AW	29360 AAW	MSBLS	10//99-12//99
	Nashville MSA, TN	S	10.22 MW	9.73 AW	21260 AAW	TNBLS	10//99-12//99
	Texas	S	13.1 MW	13.94 AW	29000 AAW	TXBLS	10//99-12//99
	Austin-San Marcos MSA, TX	S	12.75 MW	12.85 AW	26520 AAW	TXBLS	10//99-12//99
	Brazoria PMSA, TX	S	13.18 MW	12.76 AW	27420 AAW	TXBLS	10//99-12//99
	Corpus Christi MSA, TX	S	13.28 MW	12.32 AW	27630 AAW	TXBLS	10//99-12//99
	Dallas PMSA, TX	S	14.31 MW	12.77 AW	29760 AAW	TXBLS	10//99-12//99
	Houston PMSA, TX	S	14.81 MW	13.38 AW	30810 AAW	TXBLS	10//99-12//99
	San Antonio MSA, TX	S	15.66 MW	15.23 AW	32580 AAW	TXBLS	10//99-12//99
	Utah	S	12.85 MW	13.59 AW	28260 AAW	UTBLS	10//99-12//99
	Provo-Orem MSA, UT	S	13.44 MW	14.29 AW	27950 AAW	UTBLS	10//99-12//99
	Salt Lake City-Ogden MSA, UT	S	14.30 MW	13.65 AW	29750 AAW	UTBLS	10//99-12//99
	Virginia	S	13.18 MW	14.24 AW	29610 AAW	VABLS	10//99-12//99
	Norfolk-Virginia Beach-Newport News MSA, VA-NC	S	15.16 MW	13.82 AW	31530 AAW	VABLS	10//99-12//99
	Richmond-Petersburg MSA, VA	S	14.26 MW	13.30 AW	29650 AAW	VABLS	10//99-12//99
	Washington	S	16.5 MW	17.89 AW	37220 AAW	WABLS	10//99-12//99

AAW Average annual wage	**AOH** Average offered, high	**ASH** Average starting, high	**H** Hourly	**M** Monthly	**S** Special: hourly and annual
AE Average entry wage	**AOL** Average offered, low	**ASL** Average starting, low	**HI** Highest wage paid	**MTC** Median total compensation	**TQ** Third quartile wage
AEX Average experienced wage	**APH** Average pay, high range	**AW** Average wage paid	**HR** High end range	**MW** Median wage paid	**W** Weekly
AO Average offered	**APL** Average pay, low range	**FQ** First quartile wage	**LR** Low end range	**SQ** Second quartile wage	**Y** Yearly

Occupation/Type/Industry	Location	Per	Low	Mid	High	Source	Date
Biological Technician	Seattle-Bellevue-Everett						
	PMSA, WA	S	19.24 MW	17.90 AW	40030 AAW	WABLS	10//99-12//99
	West Virginia	S	12.35 MW	12.83 AW	26690 AAW	WVBLS	10//99-12//99
	Wisconsin	S	11.9 MW	13.09 AW	27220 AAW	WIBLS	10//99-12//99
	Madison MSA, WI	S	14.59 MW	13.58 AW	30350 AAW	WIBLS	10//99-12//99
	Milwaukee-Waukesha PMSA, WI	S	11.56 MW	10.22 AW	24040 AAW	WIBLS	10//99-12//99
	Wyoming	S	11.35 MW	11.70 AW	24330 AAW	WYBLS	10//99-12//99
	Puerto Rico	S	11.1 MW	11.63 AW	24190 AAW	PRBLS	10//99-12//99
Biomedical Engineer	Alabama	S	14.52 MW	16.53 AW	34380 AAW	ALBLS	10//99-12//99
	Arizona	S	23.3 MW	24.45 AW	50860 AAW	AZBLS	10//99-12//99
	Tucson MSA, AZ	S	20.87 MW	20.87 AW	43420 AAW	AZBLS	10//99-12//99
	California	S	27.65 MW	29.75 AW	61880 AAW	CABLS	10//99-12//99
	Los Angeles-Long Beach PMSA, CA	S	25.90 MW	24.58 AW	53860 AAW	CABLS	10//99-12//99
	Oakland PMSA, CA	S	32.30 MW	31.58 AW	67180 AAW	CABLS	10//99-12//99
	Orange County PMSA, CA	S	35.49 MW	31.91 AW	73810 AAW	CABLS	10//99-12//99
	San Diego MSA, CA	S	23.21 MW	21.49 AW	48290 AAW	CABLS	10//99-12//99
	San Francisco PMSA, CA	S	26.70 MW	25.38 AW	55530 AAW	CABLS	10//99-12//99
	San Jose PMSA, CA	S	32.51 MW	31.16 AW	67630 AAW	CABLS	10//99-12//99
	Santa Barbara-Santa Maria-Lompoc MSA, CA	S	24.96 MW	24.38 AW	51910 AAW	CABLS	10//99-12//99
	Connecticut	S	27.26 MW	26.08 AW	54240 AAW	CTBLS	10//99-12//99
	Hartford MSA, CT	S	26.95 MW	28.44 AW	56050 AAW	CTBLS	10//99-12//99
	Florida	S	22.93 MW	21.90 AW	45550 AAW	FLBLS	10//99-12//99
	Miami PMSA, FL	S	23.95 MW	24.50 AW	49820 AAW	FLBLS	10//99-12//99
	Georgia	S	20.72 MW	21.91 AW	45580 AAW	GABLS	10//99-12//99
	Atlanta MSA, GA	S	21.89 MW	20.65 AW	45540 AAW	GABLS	10//99-12//99
	Illinois	S	24.72 MW	24.65 AW	51270 AAW	ILBLS	10//99-12//99
	Chicago PMSA, IL	S	24.98 MW	24.90 AW	51960 AAW	ILBLS	10//99-12//99
	Indiana	S	21.22 MW	21.51 AW	44740 AAW	INBLS	10//99-12//99
	Kentucky	S	19.26 MW	18.70 AW	38900 AAW	KYBLS	10//99-12//99
	Louisiana	S	19.18 MW	19.44 AW	40430 AAW	LABLS	10//99-12//99
	Maryland	S	22.69 MW	24.82 AW	51620 AAW	MDBLS	10//99-12//99
	Baltimore PMSA, MD	S	20.52 MW	19.45 AW	42690 AAW	MDBLS	10//99-12//99
	Massachusetts	S	32.11 MW	31.87 AW	66300 AAW	MABLS	10//99-12//99
	Boston PMSA, MA-NH	S	32.28 MW	32.53 AW	67130 AAW	MABLS	10//99-12//99
	Minnesota	S	24.49 MW	24.52 AW	51000 AAW	MNBLS	10//99-12//99
	Minneapolis-St. Paul MSA, MN-WI	S	26.32 MW	26.06 AW	54740 AAW	MNBLS	10//99-12//99
	Missouri	S	23.74 MW	25.86 AW	53790 AAW	MOBLS	10//99-12//99
	Nebraska	S	18.97 MW	21.71 AW	45150 AAW	NEBLS	10//99-12//99
	New Hampshire	S	29.07 MW	27.52 AW	57230 AAW	NHBLS	10//99-12//99
	New Jersey	S	20.01 MW	21.91 AW	45580 AAW	NJBLS	10//99-12//99
	New York	S	25.16 MW	25.59 AW	53230 AAW	NYBLS	10//99-12//99
	New York PMSA, NY	S	22.74 MW	22.04 AW	47310 AAW	NYBLS	10//99-12//99
	North Carolina	S	16.94 MW	18.38 AW	38230 AAW	NCBLS	10//99-12//99
	Charlotte-Gastonia-Rock Hill MSA, NC-SC	S	26.94 MW	29.15 AW	56030 AAW	NCBLS	10//99-12//99
	Raleigh-Durham-Chapel Hill MSA, NC	S	17.64 MW	16.32 AW	36700 AAW	NCBLS	10//99-12//99
	Ohio	S	24.72 MW	25.47 AW	52970 AAW	OHBLS	10//99-12//99
	Cincinnati PMSA, OH-KY-IN	S	23.01 MW	20.05 AW	47870 AAW	OHBLS	10//99-12//99
	Cleveland-Lorain-Elyria PMSA, OH	S	26.69 MW	25.63 AW	55510 AAW	OHBLS	10//99-12//99
	Columbus MSA, OH	S	26.97 MW	25.79 AW	56100 AAW	OHBLS	10//99-12//99
	Pennsylvania	S	28.83 MW	28.37 AW	59010 AAW	PABLS	10//99-12//99
	Philadelphia PMSA, PA-NJ	S	28.99 MW	28.73 AW	60310 AAW	PABLS	10//99-12//99
	Pittsburgh MSA, PA	S	29.24 MW	30.07 AW	60820 AAW	PABLS	10//99-12//99
	Texas	S	23.35 MW	23.72 AW	49340 AAW	TXBLS	10//99-12//99
	Dallas PMSA, TX	S	24.23 MW	24.51 AW	50410 AAW	TXBLS	10//99-12//99
	Fort Worth-Arlington PMSA, TX	S	18.44 MW	18.39 AW	38350 AAW	TXBLS	10//99-12//99
	Houston PMSA, TX	S	21.43 MW	21.03 AW	44580 AAW	TXBLS	10//99-12//99
	Washington	S	24.19 MW	25.30 AW	52630 AAW	WABLS	10//99-12//99
	Wisconsin	S	19.88 MW	20.29 AW	42200 AAW	WIBLS	10//99-12//99
Body Shop Manager Auto Dealership	United States	Y		48158 MW		WARD2	1999
Boilermaker	Alabama	S	16.9 MW	15.30 AW	31820 AAW	ALBLS	10//99-12//99
	Arkansas	S	19.02 MW	19.08 AW	39690 AAW	ARBLS	10//99-12//99

AAW Average annual wage	AOH Average offered, high	ASH Average starting, high	H Hourly	M Monthly	S Special: hourly and annual
AE Average entry wage	AOL Average offered, low	ASL Average starting, low	HI Highest wage paid	MTC Median total compensation	TQ Third quartile wage
AEX Average experienced wage	APH Average pay, high range	AW Average wage paid	HR High end range	MW Median wage paid	W Weekly
AO Average offered	APL Average pay, low range	FQ First quartile wage	LR Low end range	SQ Second quartile wage	Y Yearly

Boilermaker

Occupation/Type/Industry	Location	Per	Low	Mid	High	Source	Date
Boilermaker	California	S	21.06 MW	22.49 AW	46780 AAW	CABLS	10//99-12//99
	Los Angeles-Long Beach PMSA, CA	S	21.86 MW	22.35 AW	45470 AAW	CABLS	10//99-12//99
	Riverside-San Bernardino PMSA, CA	S	24.89 MW	25.84 AW	51780 AAW	CABLS	10//99-12//99
	San Diego MSA, CA	S	15.60 MW	14.88 AW	32440 AAW	CABLS	10//99-12//99
	Stamford-Norwalk PMSA, CT	S	13.91 MW	13.47 AW	28930 AAW	CTBLS	10//99-12//99
	Washington PMSA, DC-MD-VA-WV	S	20.47 MW	21.60 AW	42570 AAW	DCBLS	10//99-12//99
	Florida	S	14.76 MW	14.47 AW	30100 AAW	FLBLS	10//99-12//99
	Tampa-St. Petersburg-Clearwater MSA, FL	S	15.45 MW	15.81 AW	32130 AAW	FLBLS	10//99-12//99
	Georgia	S	22.17 MW	20.13 AW	41880 AAW	GABLS	10//99-12//99
	Idaho	S	11.31 MW	13.47 AW	28020 AAW	IDBLS	10//99-12//99
	Illinois	S	21.93 MW	21.91 AW	45570 AAW	ILBLS	10//99-12//99
	Chicago PMSA, IL	S	22.80 MW	24.78 AW	47420 AAW	ILBLS	10//99-12//99
	Indiana	S	23.58 MW	22.71 AW	47230 AAW	INBLS	10//99-12//99
	Iowa	S	16.09 MW	17.23 AW	35830 AAW	IABLS	10//99-12//99
	Davenport-Moline-Rock Island MSA, IA-IL	S	19.16 MW	17.86 AW	39850 AAW	IABLS	10//99-12//99
	Lexington MSA, KY	S	17.20 MW	16.99 AW	35780 AAW	KYBLS	10//99-12//99
	Louisiana	S	17.14 MW	17.98 AW	37390 AAW	LABLS	10//99-12//99
	Baton Rouge MSA, LA	S	18.70 MW	17.95 AW	38890 AAW	LABLS	10//99-12//99
	New Orleans MSA, LA	S	16.90 MW	16.40 AW	35140 AAW	LABLS	10//99-12//99
	Maine	S	14.86 MW	14.98 AW	31150 AAW	MEBLS	10//99-12//99
	Maryland	S	20.52 MW	20.11 AW	41830 AAW	MDBLS	10//99-12//99
	Baltimore PMSA, MD	S	20.24 MW	20.19 AW	42090 AAW	MDBLS	10//99-12//99
	Massachusetts	S	11.24 MW	14.54 AW	30240 AAW	MABLS	10//99-12//99
	Boston PMSA, MA-NH	S	16.17 MW	15.24 AW	33630 AAW	MABLS	10//99-12//99
	Michigan	S	23.42 MW	22.58 AW	46970 AAW	MIBLS	10//99-12//99
	Detroit PMSA, MI	S	23.22 MW	23.87 AW	48290 AAW	MIBLS	10//99-12//99
	Grand Rapids-Muskegon-Holland MSA, MI	S	18.62 MW	17.97 AW	38720 AAW	MIBLS	10//99-12//99
	Minnesota	S	22.47 MW	21.05 AW	43790 AAW	MNBLS	10//99-12//99
	Minneapolis-St. Paul MSA, MN-WI	S	21.25 MW	23.01 AW	44200 AAW	MNBLS	10//99-12//99
	Mississippi	S	11.32 MW	13.55 AW	28190 AAW	MSBLS	10//99-12//99
	Montana	S	19.48 MW	19.69 AW	40960 AAW	MTBLS	10//99-12//99
	New Hampshire	S	19.06 MW	19.41 AW	40380 AAW	NHBLS	10//99-12//99
	New Jersey	S	18.87 MW	19.93 AW	41460 AAW	NJBLS	10//99-12//99
	New York	S	18.32 MW	18.05 AW	37530 AAW	NYBLS	10//99-12//99
	Buffalo-Niagara Falls MSA, NY	S	20.99 MW	22.26 AW	43660 AAW	NYBLS	10//99-12//99
	New York PMSA, NY	S	17.41 MW	18.02 AW	36210 AAW	NYBLS	10//99-12//99
	North Carolina	S	14.11 MW	14.59 AW	30360 AAW	NCBLS	10//99-12//99
	Charlotte-Gastonia-Rock Hill MSA, NC-SC	S	13.86 MW	11.81 AW	28840 AAW	NCBLS	10//99-12//99
	Cleveland-Lorain-Elyria PMSA, OH	S	25.65 MW	24.40 AW	53360 AAW	OHBLS	10//99-12//99
	Oklahoma	S	10.38 MW	11.23 AW	23360 AAW	OKBLS	10//99-12//99
	Oklahoma City MSA, OK	S	9.41 MW	7.72 AW	19580 AAW	OKBLS	10//99-12//99
	Tulsa MSA, OK	S	13.53 MW	14.73 AW	28140 AAW	OKBLS	10//99-12//99
	Oregon	S	19.89 MW	19.68 AW	40930 AAW	ORBLS	10//99-12//99
	Portland-Vancouver PMSA, OR-WA	S	17.88 MW	17.59 AW	37200 AAW	ORBLS	10//99-12//99
	Pennsylvania	S	22.38 MW	21.36 AW	44440 AAW	PABLS	10//99-12//99
	Philadelphia PMSA, PA-NJ	S	21.81 MW	21.42 AW	45370 AAW	PABLS	10//99-12//99
	Providence-Fall River-Warwick MSA, RI-MA	S	19.27 MW	18.32 AW	40090 AAW	RIBLS	10//99-12//99
	South Carolina	S	17.63 MW	18.58 AW	38640 AAW	SCBLS	10//99-12//99
	Tennessee	S	22.19 MW	20.24 AW	42100 AAW	TNBLS	10//99-12//99
	Chattanooga MSA, TN-GA	S	19.31 MW	20.55 AW	40160 AAW	TNBLS	10//99-12//99
	Johnson City-Kingsport-Bristol MSA, TN-VA	S	16.98 MW	15.72 AW	35320 AAW	TNBLS	10//99-12//99
	Knoxville MSA, TN	S	22.36 MW	22.83 AW	46500 AAW	TNBLS	10//99-12//99
	Texas	S	14.26 MW	14.37 AW	29880 AAW	TXBLS	10//99-12//99
	Houston PMSA, TX	S	15.71 MW	14.88 AW	32670 AAW	TXBLS	10//99-12//99
	Utah	S	18.54 MW	17.99 AW	37410 AAW	UTBLS	10//99-12//99
	Virginia	S	16.95 MW	18.14 AW	37730 AAW	VABLS	10//99-12//99
	Richmond-Petersburg MSA, VA	S	21.89 MW	22.10 AW	45540 AAW	VABLS	10//99-12//99
	Washington	S	19.33 MW	19.43 AW	40400 AAW	WABLS	10//99-12//99

AAW Average annual wage	AOH Average offered, high	ASH Average starting, high	H Hourly	M Monthly	S Special: hourly and annual
AE Average entry wage	AOL Average offered, low	ASL Average starting, low	HI Highest wage paid	MTC Median total compensation	TQ Third quartile wage
AEX Average experienced wage	APH Average pay, high range	AW Average wage paid	HR High end range	MW Median wage paid	W Weekly
AO Average offered	APL Average pay, low range	FQ First quartile wage	LR Low end range	SQ Second quartile wage	Y Yearly

Occupation/Type/Industry	Location	Per	Low	Mid	High	Source	Date
Boilermaker	Seattle-Bellevue-Everett						
	PMSA, WA	S	17.77 MW	17.80 AW	36950 AAW	WABLS	10//99-12//99
	West Virginia	S	18.91 MW	19.36 AW	40260 AAW	WVBLS	10//99-12//99
	Wisconsin	S	22.82 MW	21.17 AW	44030 AAW	WIBLS	10//99-12//99
	Milwaukee-Waukesha PMSA, WI	S	21.97 MW	23.51 AW	45700 AAW	WIBLS	10//99-12//99
	Puerto Rico	S	8.02 MW	12.37 AW	25740 AAW	PRBLS	10//99-12//99
	San Juan-Bayamon PMSA, PR	S	12.59 MW	7.85 AW	26190 AAW	PRBLS	10//99-12//99
Bookbinder	Alabama	S	8.37 MW	10.78 AW	22410 AAW	ALBLS	10//99-12//99
	Birmingham MSA, AL	S	10.97 MW	8.03 AW	22810 AAW	ALBLS	10//99-12//99
	California	S	8.89 MW	11.35 AW	23600 AAW	CABLS	10//99-12//99
	Los Angeles-Long Beach PMSA, CA	S	9.68 MW	8.54 AW	20140 AAW	CABLS	10//99-12//99
	Connecticut	S	10.94 MW	11.74 AW	24430 AAW	CTBLS	10//99-12//99
	New Haven-Meriden PMSA, CT	S	15.15 MW	12.28 AW	31510 AAW	CTBLS	10//99-12//99
	Washington PMSA, DC-MD-VA-WV	S	17.79 MW	17.88 AW	37000 AAW	DCBLS	10//99-12//99
	Florida	S	9.67 MW	10.24 AW	21290 AAW	FLBLS	10//99-12//99
	Miami PMSA, FL	S	9.56 MW	8.58 AW	19890 AAW	FLBLS	10//99-12//99
	Tampa-St. Petersburg-Clearwater MSA, FL	S	11.27 MW	11.33 AW	23440 AAW	FLBLS	10//99-12//99
	Georgia	S	7.83 MW	8.31 AW	17280 AAW	GABLS	10//99-12//99
	Illinois	S	9.35 MW	11.08 AW	23040 AAW	ILBLS	10//99-12//99
	Chicago PMSA, IL	S	10.96 MW	9.25 AW	22800 AAW	ILBLS	10//99-12//99
	Indiana	S	8.94 MW	10.61 AW	22080 AAW	INBLS	10//99-12//99
	Iowa	S	12.66 MW	13.74 AW	28570 AAW	IABLS	10//99-12//99
	Kansas	S	11.84 MW	12.86 AW	26750 AAW	KSBLS	10//99-12//99
	Wichita MSA, KS	S	15.17 MW	14.39 AW	31560 AAW	KSBLS	10//99-12//99
	Kentucky	S	12.57 MW	13.03 AW	27100 AAW	KYBLS	10//99-12//99
	Maryland	S	10.34 MW	12.01 AW	24970 AAW	MDBLS	10//99-12//99
	Massachusetts	S	10.46 MW	11.79 AW	24530 AAW	MABLS	10//99-12//99
	Boston PMSA, MA-NH	S	11.86 MW	10.33 AW	24670 AAW	MABLS	10//99-12//99
	Minnesota	S	16.52 MW	14.82 AW	30820 AAW	MNBLS	10//99-12//99
	Minneapolis-St. Paul MSA, MN-WI	S	15.15 MW	16.57 AW	31500 AAW	MNBLS	10//99-12//99
	New Jersey	S	11.85 MW	12.61 AW	26230 AAW	NJBLS	10//99-12//99
	New York	S	8.89 MW	9.49 AW	19750 AAW	NYBLS	10//99-12//99
	New York PMSA, NY	S	10.21 MW	9.59 AW	21240 AAW	NYBLS	10//99-12//99
	North Carolina	S	7.99 MW	9.30 AW	19340 AAW	NCBLS	10//99-12//99
	Greensboro--Winston-Salem--High Point MSA, NC	S	8.35 MW	7.10 AW	17360 AAW	NCBLS	10//99-12//99
	Ohio	S	11.29 MW	12.39 AW	25770 AAW	OHBLS	10//99-12//99
	Akron PMSA, OH	S	13.64 MW	12.36 AW	28370 AAW	OHBLS	10//99-12//99
	Cincinnati PMSA, OH-KY-IN	S	10.59 MW	9.80 AW	22030 AAW	OHBLS	10//99-12//99
	Cleveland-Lorain-Elyria PMSA, OH	S	12.47 MW	11.73 AW	25950 AAW	OHBLS	10//99-12//99
	Columbus MSA, OH	S	11.21 MW	10.18 AW	23310 AAW	OHBLS	10//99-12//99
	Pennsylvania	S	13.21 MW	13.36 AW	27790 AAW	PABLS	10//99-12//99
	Lancaster MSA, PA	S	14.10 MW	14.18 AW	29330 AAW	PABLS	10//99-12//99
	Philadelphia PMSA, PA-NJ	S	12.88 MW	11.56 AW	26790 AAW	PABLS	10//99-12//99
	Tennessee	S	9.48 MW	9.75 AW	20290 AAW	TNBLS	10//99-12//99
	Nashville MSA, TN	S	10.17 MW	9.86 AW	21150 AAW	TNBLS	10//99-12//99
	Texas	S	9.78 MW	11.95 AW	24850 AAW	TXBLS	10//99-12//99
	Austin-San Marcos MSA, TX	S	11.18 MW	11.67 AW	23250 AAW	TXBLS	10//99-12//99
	Dallas PMSA, TX	S	9.89 MW	9.57 AW	20570 AAW	TXBLS	10//99-12//99
	Vermont	S	11.92 MW	12.51 AW	26020 AAW	VTBLS	10//99-12//99
	Virginia	S	10.46 MW	10.41 AW	21650 AAW	VABLS	10//99-12//99
	Richmond-Petersburg MSA, VA	S	10.51 MW	10.90 AW	21860 AAW	VABLS	10//99-12//99
	Washington	S	11.43 MW	12.88 AW	26790 AAW	WABLS	10//99-12//99
	Seattle-Bellevue-Everett PMSA, WA	S	14.19 MW	13.09 AW	29510 AAW	WABLS	10//99-12//99
	Wisconsin	S	9.61 MW	10.36 AW	21560 AAW	WIBLS	10//99-12//99
	Appleton-Oshkosh-Neenah MSA, WI	S	12.86 MW	12.86 AW	26750 AAW	WIBLS	10//99-12//99
	Milwaukee-Waukesha PMSA, WI	S	10.28 MW	9.56 AW	21380 AAW	WIBLS	10//99-12//99
Bookkeeper							
Medical Doctor's Office	United States	H		13.45 AEX		MEDEC	2000

AAW	Average annual wage	AOH	Average offered, high	ASH	Average starting, high	H	Hourly	M	Monthly	S	Special: hourly and annual
AE	Average entry wage	AOL	Average offered, low	ASL	Average starting, low	HI	Highest wage paid	MTC	Median total compensation	TQ	Third quartile wage
AEX	Average experienced wage	APH	Average pay, high range	AW	Average wage paid	HR	High end range	MW	Median wage paid	W	Weekly
AO	Average offered	APL	Average pay, low range	FQ	First quartile wage	LR	Low end range	SQ	Second quartile wage	Y	Yearly

111

Occupation/Type/Industry	Location	Per	Low	Mid	High	Source	Date
Bookkeeping, Accounting, and Auditing Clerk							
	Alabama	S	10.24 MW	10.72 AW	22300 AAW	ALBLS	10//99-12//99
	Anniston MSA, AL	S	10.35 MW	9.51 AW	21540 AAW	ALBLS	10//99-12//99
	Auburn-Opelika MSA, AL	S	10.02 MW	9.92 AW	20840 AAW	ALBLS	10//99-12//99
	Birmingham MSA, AL	S	11.94 MW	11.44 AW	24840 AAW	ALBLS	10//99-12//99
	Decatur MSA, AL	S	10.69 MW	10.52 AW	22240 AAW	ALBLS	10//99-12//99
	Dothan MSA, AL	S	10.05 MW	9.70 AW	20900 AAW	ALBLS	10//99-12//99
	Florence MSA, AL	S	10.99 MW	10.74 AW	22860 AAW	ALBLS	10//99-12//99
	Gadsden MSA, AL	S	10.33 MW	10.09 AW	21480 AAW	ALBLS	10//99-12//99
	Huntsville MSA, AL	S	11.09 MW	10.79 AW	23070 AAW	ALBLS	10//99-12//99
	Mobile MSA, AL	S	10.46 MW	9.84 AW	21750 AAW	ALBLS	10//99-12//99
	Montgomery MSA, AL	S	10.91 MW	10.51 AW	22690 AAW	ALBLS	10//99-12//99
	Tuscaloosa MSA, AL	S	10.72 MW	10.84 AW	22300 AAW	ALBLS	10//99-12//99
	Alaska	S	13.49 MW	14.55 AW	30260 AAW	AKBLS	10//99-12//99
	Anchorage MSA, AK	S	15.05 MW	13.63 AW	31300 AAW	AKBLS	10//99-12//99
	Arizona	S	11.24 MW	11.58 AW	24080 AAW	AZBLS	10//99-12//99
	Flagstaff MSA, AZ-UT	S	10.61 MW	10.19 AW	22070 AAW	AZBLS	10//99-12//99
	Phoenix-Mesa MSA, AZ	S	11.90 MW	11.48 AW	24760 AAW	AZBLS	10//99-12//99
	Tucson MSA, AZ	S	11.02 MW	10.73 AW	22910 AAW	AZBLS	10//99-12//99
	Yuma MSA, AZ	S	10.57 MW	10.18 AW	21980 AAW	AZBLS	10//99-12//99
	Arkansas	S	9.68 MW	10.12 AW	21060 AAW	ARBLS	10//99-12//99
	Fayetteville-Springdale-Rogers MSA, AR	S	10.24 MW	9.71 AW	21300 AAW	ARBLS	10//99-12//99
	Fort Smith MSA, AR-OK	S	10.16 MW	9.74 AW	21130 AAW	ARBLS	10//99-12//99
	Jonesboro MSA, AR	S	9.77 MW	9.52 AW	20320 AAW	ARBLS	10//99-12//99
	Little Rock-North Little Rock MSA, AR	S	10.98 MW	10.42 AW	22830 AAW	ARBLS	10//99-12//99
	Pine Bluff MSA, AR	S	9.85 MW	9.59 AW	20490 AAW	ARBLS	10//99-12//99
	California	S	13.25 MW	13.78 AW	28670 AAW	CABLS	10//99-12//99
	Bakersfield MSA, CA	S	12.63 MW	11.87 AW	26260 AAW	CABLS	10//99-12//99
	Chico-Paradise MSA, CA	S	11.13 MW	10.71 AW	23150 AAW	CABLS	10//99-12//99
	Fresno MSA, CA	S	11.80 MW	11.33 AW	24540 AAW	CABLS	10//99-12//99
	Los Angeles-Long Beach PMSA, CA	S	14.08 MW	13.41 AW	29280 AAW	CABLS	10//99-12//99
	Merced MSA, CA	S	11.00 MW	10.14 AW	22880 AAW	CABLS	10//99-12//99
	Modesto MSA, CA	S	11.46 MW	11.26 AW	23840 AAW	CABLS	10//99-12//99
	Oakland PMSA, CA	S	15.37 MW	14.86 AW	31960 AAW	CABLS	10//99-12//99
	Orange County PMSA, CA	S	14.15 MW	13.73 AW	29440 AAW	CABLS	10//99-12//99
	Redding MSA, CA	S	11.26 MW	10.74 AW	23420 AAW	CABLS	10//99-12//99
	Riverside-San Bernardino PMSA, CA	S	12.37 MW	11.98 AW	25730 AAW	CABLS	10//99-12//99
	Sacramento PMSA, CA	S	13.16 MW	12.96 AW	27380 AAW	CABLS	10//99-12//99
	Salinas MSA, CA	S	13.33 MW	13.25 AW	27720 AAW	CABLS	10//99-12//99
	San Diego MSA, CA	S	13.17 MW	12.60 AW	27390 AAW	CABLS	10//99-12//99
	San Francisco PMSA, CA	S	15.49 MW	15.12 AW	32220 AAW	CABLS	10//99-12//99
	San Jose PMSA, CA	S	15.12 MW	14.85 AW	31440 AAW	CABLS	10//99-12//99
	San Luis Obispo-Atascadero-Paso Robles MSA, CA	S	12.08 MW	11.25 AW	25130 AAW	CABLS	10//99-12//99
	Santa Barbara-Santa Maria-Lompoc MSA, CA	S	13.48 MW	12.82 AW	28050 AAW	CABLS	10//99-12//99
	Santa Cruz-Watsonville PMSA, CA	S	13.75 MW	13.25 AW	28590 AAW	CABLS	10//99-12//99
	Santa Rosa PMSA, CA	S	13.11 MW	12.94 AW	27260 AAW	CABLS	10//99-12//99
	Stockton-Lodi MSA, CA	S	12.04 MW	11.90 AW	25040 AAW	CABLS	10//99-12//99
	Vallejo-Fairfield-Napa PMSA, CA	S	12.66 MW	12.15 AW	26320 AAW	CABLS	10//99-12//99
	Ventura PMSA, CA	S	14.06 MW	13.57 AW	29250 AAW	CABLS	10//99-12//99
	Visalia-Tulare-Porterville MSA, CA	S	11.51 MW	11.28 AW	23940 AAW	CABLS	10//99-12//99
	Yolo PMSA, CA	S	12.82 MW	12.58 AW	26670 AAW	CABLS	10//99-12//99
	Yuba City MSA, CA	S	11.89 MW	11.55 AW	24720 AAW	CABLS	10//99-12//99
	Colorado	S	11.99 MW	12.31 AW	25610 AAW	COBLS	10//99-12//99
	Boulder-Longmont PMSA, CO	S	13.43 MW	12.88 AW	27940 AAW	COBLS	10//99-12//99
	Colorado Springs MSA, CO	S	11.55 MW	11.06 AW	24030 AAW	COBLS	10//99-12//99
	Denver PMSA, CO	S	12.73 MW	12.41 AW	26470 AAW	COBLS	10//99-12//99
	Fort Collins-Loveland MSA, CO	S	11.63 MW	11.49 AW	24200 AAW	COBLS	10//99-12//99
	Grand Junction MSA, CO	S	11.04 MW	10.76 AW	22960 AAW	COBLS	10//99-12//99
	Greeley PMSA, CO	S	11.17 MW	10.52 AW	23240 AAW	COBLS	10//99-12//99
	Pueblo MSA, CO	S	10.57 MW	10.20 AW	21970 AAW	COBLS	10//99-12//99
	Connecticut	S	13.38 MW	13.74 AW	28580 AAW	CTBLS	10//99-12//99
	Bridgeport PMSA, CT	S	14.17 MW	13.56 AW	29470 AAW	CTBLS	10//99-12//99

AAW	Average annual wage	AOH	Average offered, high	ASH	Average starting, high	H	Hourly	M	Monthly	S	Special: hourly and annual
AE	Average entry wage	AOL	Average offered, low	ASL	Average starting, low	HI	Highest wage paid	MTC	Median total compensation	TQ	Third quartile wage
AEX	Average experienced wage	APH	Average pay, high range	AW	Average wage paid	HR	High end range	MW	Median wage paid	W	Weekly
AO	Average offered	APL	Average pay, low range	FQ	First quartile wage	LR	Low end range	SQ	Second quartile wage	Y	Yearly

Occupation/Type/Industry	Location	Per	Low	Mid	High	Source	Date
Bookkeeping, Accounting, and Auditing Clerk							
	Danbury PMSA, CT	S	14.34 MW	14.16 AW	29830 AAW	CTBLS	10//99-12//99
	Hartford MSA, CT	S	14.08 MW	13.87 AW	29290 AAW	CTBLS	10//99-12//99
	New Haven-Meriden PMSA, CT	S	12.88 MW	12.46 AW	26790 AAW	CTBLS	10//99-12//99
	New London-Norwich MSA, CT-RI	S	11.43 MW	11.06 AW	23770 AAW	CTBLS	10//99-12//99
	Stamford-Norwalk PMSA, CT	S	14.99 MW	14.92 AW	31170 AAW	CTBLS	10//99-12//99
	Waterbury PMSA, CT	S	13.04 MW	12.78 AW	27120 AAW	CTBLS	10//99-12//99
	Delaware	S	11.92 MW	12.75 AW	26520 AAW	DEBLS	10//99-12//99
	Dover MSA, DE	S	11.51 MW	11.36 AW	23940 AAW	DEBLS	10//99-12//99
	Wilmington-Newark PMSA, DE-MD	S	13.08 MW	12.24 AW	27200 AAW	DEBLS	10//99-12//99
	District of Columbia	S	14.89 MW	15.83 AW	32930 AAW	DCBLS	10//99-12//99
	Washington PMSA, DC-MD-VA-WV	S	13.75 MW	13.30 AW	28600 AAW	DCBLS	10//99-12//99
	Florida	S	10.9 MW	11.43 AW	23760 AAW	FLBLS	10//99-12//99
	Daytona Beach MSA, FL	S	10.76 MW	10.18 AW	22380 AAW	FLBLS	10//99-12//99
	Fort Lauderdale PMSA, FL	S	12.37 MW	11.97 AW	25730 AAW	FLBLS	10//99-12//99
	Fort Myers-Cape Coral MSA, FL	S	11.11 MW	10.90 AW	23110 AAW	FLBLS	10//99-12//99
	Fort Pierce-Port St. Lucie MSA, FL	S	10.97 MW	10.50 AW	22810 AAW	FLBLS	10//99-12//99
	Fort Walton Beach MSA, FL	S	9.90 MW	9.41 AW	20600 AAW	FLBLS	10//99-12//99
	Gainesville MSA, FL	S	10.60 MW	10.45 AW	22040 AAW	FLBLS	10//99-12//99
	Jacksonville MSA, FL	S	11.92 MW	11.00 AW	24800 AAW	FLBLS	10//99-12//99
	Lakeland-Winter Haven MSA, FL	S	10.59 MW	10.17 AW	22030 AAW	FLBLS	10//99-12//99
	Melbourne-Titusville-Palm Bay MSA, FL	S	10.41 MW	10.06 AW	21660 AAW	FLBLS	10//99-12//99
	Miami PMSA, FL	S	12.13 MW	11.73 AW	25230 AAW	FLBLS	10//99-12//99
	Naples MSA, FL	S	11.93 MW	11.44 AW	24810 AAW	FLBLS	10//99-12//99
	Ocala MSA, FL	S	10.90 MW	10.51 AW	22660 AAW	FLBLS	10//99-12//99
	Orlando MSA, FL	S	10.84 MW	10.45 AW	22540 AAW	FLBLS	10//99-12//99
	Panama City MSA, FL	S	9.80 MW	9.62 AW	20390 AAW	FLBLS	10//99-12//99
	Pensacola MSA, FL	S	9.85 MW	9.49 AW	20480 AAW	FLBLS	10//99-12//99
	Punta Gorda MSA, FL	S	9.94 MW	9.59 AW	20660 AAW	FLBLS	10//99-12//99
	Sarasota-Bradenton MSA, FL	S	10.90 MW	10.56 AW	22670 AAW	FLBLS	10//99-12//99
	Tallahassee MSA, FL	S	10.50 MW	10.03 AW	21850 AAW	FLBLS	10//99-12//99
	Tampa-St. Petersburg-Clearwater MSA, FL	S	11.22 MW	10.69 AW	23340 AAW	FLBLS	10//99-12//99
	West Palm Beach-Boca Raton MSA, FL	S	12.41 MW	11.84 AW	25820 AAW	FLBLS	10//99-12//99
	Georgia	S	11.29 MW	11.50 AW	23910 AAW	GABLS	10//99-12//99
	Albany MSA, GA	S	10.62 MW	10.32 AW	22080 AAW	GABLS	10//99-12//99
	Athens MSA, GA	S	10.90 MW	10.99 AW	22660 AAW	GABLS	10//99-12//99
	Atlanta MSA, GA	S	12.33 MW	12.07 AW	25640 AAW	GABLS	10//99-12//99
	Augusta-Aiken MSA, GA-SC	S	10.52 MW	10.16 AW	21890 AAW	GABLS	10//99-12//99
	Columbus MSA, GA-AL	S	10.79 MW	10.79 AW	22440 AAW	GABLS	10//99-12//99
	Macon MSA, GA	S	10.92 MW	10.67 AW	22720 AAW	GABLS	10//99-12//99
	Savannah MSA, GA	S	10.81 MW	10.40 AW	22490 AAW	GABLS	10//99-12//99
	Hawaii	S	12.47 MW	12.89 AW	26800 AAW	HIBLS	10//99-12//99
	Honolulu MSA, HI	S	13.12 MW	12.68 AW	27290 AAW	HIBLS	10//99-12//99
	Idaho	S	10.2 MW	10.49 AW	21820 AAW	IDBLS	10//99-12//99
	Boise City MSA, ID	S	10.85 MW	10.55 AW	22570 AAW	IDBLS	10//99-12//99
	Pocatello MSA, ID	S	9.46 MW	9.09 AW	19670 AAW	IDBLS	10//99-12//99
	Illinois	S	11.79 MW	12.44 AW	25870 AAW	ILBLS	10//99-12//99
	Bloomington-Normal MSA, IL	S	13.72 MW	14.28 AW	28530 AAW	ILBLS	10//99-12//99
	Champaign-Urbana MSA, IL	S	11.52 MW	11.25 AW	23970 AAW	ILBLS	10//99-12//99
	Chicago PMSA, IL	S	13.18 MW	12.43 AW	27410 AAW	ILBLS	10//99-12//99
	Decatur MSA, IL	S	11.32 MW	10.95 AW	23540 AAW	ILBLS	10//99-12//99
	Kankakee PMSA, IL	S	11.36 MW	11.40 AW	23620 AAW	ILBLS	10//99-12//99
	Peoria-Pekin MSA, IL	S	10.95 MW	10.48 AW	22770 AAW	ILBLS	10//99-12//99
	Rockford MSA, IL	S	11.34 MW	11.25 AW	23590 AAW	ILBLS	10//99-12//99
	Springfield MSA, IL	S	11.03 MW	10.23 AW	22950 AAW	ILBLS	10//99-12//99
	Indiana	S	10.75 MW	11.01 AW	22910 AAW	INBLS	10//99-12//99
	Bloomington MSA, IN	S	10.38 MW	10.33 AW	21590 AAW	INBLS	10//99-12//99
	Elkhart-Goshen MSA, IN	S	11.30 MW	10.80 AW	23500 AAW	INBLS	10//99-12//99
	Evansville-Henderson MSA, IN-KY	S	10.34 MW	10.07 AW	21510 AAW	INBLS	10//99-12//99
	Fort Wayne MSA, IN	S	10.95 MW	10.58 AW	22780 AAW	INBLS	10//99-12//99
	Gary PMSA, IN	S	11.02 MW	10.70 AW	22910 AAW	INBLS	10//99-12//99

AAW Average annual wage	**AOH** Average offered, high	**ASH** Average starting, high	**H** Hourly	**M** Monthly	**S** Special: hourly and annual
AE Average entry wage	**AOL** Average offered, low	**ASL** Average starting, low	**HI** Highest wage paid	**MTC** Median total compensation	**TQ** Third quartile wage
AEX Average experienced wage	**APH** Average pay, high range	**AW** Average wage paid	**HR** High end range	**MW** Median wage paid	**W** Weekly
AO Average offered	**APL** Average pay, low range	**FQ** First quartile wage	**LR** Low end range	**SQ** Second quartile wage	**Y** Yearly

Occupation/Type/Industry	Location	Per	Low	Mid	High	Source	Date
Bookkeeping, Accounting, and Auditing Clerk							
	Indianapolis MSA, IN	S	11.72 MW	11.34 AW	24390 AAW	INBLS	10//99-12//99
	Kokomo MSA, IN	S	10.16 MW	9.86 AW	21130 AAW	INBLS	10//99-12//99
	Lafayette MSA, IN	S	10.24 MW	10.28 AW	21290 AAW	INBLS	10//99-12//99
	Muncie MSA, IN	S	10.64 MW	10.03 AW	22120 AAW	INBLS	10//99-12//99
	South Bend MSA, IN	S	11.12 MW	10.65 AW	23140 AAW	INBLS	10//99-12//99
	Terre Haute MSA, IN	S	10.45 MW	9.94 AW	21730 AAW	INBLS	10//99-12//99
	Iowa	S	9.98 MW	10.62 AW	22090 AAW	IABLS	10//99-12//99
	Cedar Rapids MSA, IA	S	11.25 MW	10.78 AW	23400 AAW	IABLS	10//99-12//99
	Davenport-Moline-Rock Island MSA, IA-IL	S	10.37 MW	10.12 AW	21570 AAW	IABLS	10//99-12//99
	Des Moines MSA, IA	S	11.74 MW	11.21 AW	24420 AAW	IABLS	10//99-12//99
	Dubuque MSA, IA	S	10.45 MW	10.20 AW	21730 AAW	IABLS	10//99-12//99
	Iowa City MSA, IA	S	10.67 MW	10.32 AW	22180 AAW	IABLS	10//99-12//99
	Sioux City MSA, IA-NE	S	10.37 MW	9.79 AW	21560 AAW	IABLS	10//99-12//99
	Waterloo-Cedar Falls MSA, IA	S	10.55 MW	10.27 AW	21950 AAW	IABLS	10//99-12//99
	Kansas	S	10.09 MW	10.47 AW	21780 AAW	KSBLS	10//99-12//99
	Lawrence MSA, KS	S	10.52 MW	10.14 AW	21890 AAW	KSBLS	10//99-12//99
	Topeka MSA, KS	S	10.46 MW	10.36 AW	21750 AAW	KSBLS	10//99-12//99
	Wichita MSA, KS	S	10.51 MW	10.20 AW	21870 AAW	KSBLS	10//99-12//99
	Kentucky	S	10.13 MW	10.54 AW	21920 AAW	KYBLS	10//99-12//99
	Lexington MSA, KY	S	10.89 MW	10.73 AW	22650 AAW	KYBLS	10//99-12//99
	Louisville MSA, KY-IN	S	11.18 MW	10.72 AW	23260 AAW	KYBLS	10//99-12//99
	Owensboro MSA, KY	S	10.40 MW	9.67 AW	21630 AAW	KYBLS	10//99-12//99
	Louisiana	S	9.88 MW	10.40 AW	21640 AAW	LABLS	10//99-12//99
	Alexandria MSA, LA	S	9.87 MW	9.35 AW	20540 AAW	LABLS	10//99-12//99
	Baton Rouge MSA, LA	S	10.73 MW	10.32 AW	22330 AAW	LABLS	10//99-12//99
	Houma MSA, LA	S	9.19 MW	8.40 AW	19120 AAW	LABLS	10//99-12//99
	Lafayette MSA, LA	S	10.16 MW	9.49 AW	21120 AAW	LABLS	10//99-12//99
	Lake Charles MSA, LA	S	9.95 MW	9.51 AW	20700 AAW	LABLS	10//99-12//99
	Monroe MSA, LA	S	10.40 MW	9.89 AW	21630 AAW	LABLS	10//99-12//99
	New Orleans MSA, LA	S	11.02 MW	10.44 AW	22920 AAW	LABLS	10//99-12//99
	Shreveport-Bossier City MSA, LA	S	10.40 MW	9.93 AW	21630 AAW	LABLS	10//99-12//99
	Maine	S	10.6 MW	10.81 AW	22490 AAW	MEBLS	10//99-12//99
	Bangor MSA, ME	S	10.69 MW	10.51 AW	22230 AAW	MEBLS	10//99-12//99
	Lewiston-Auburn MSA, ME	S	10.70 MW	10.58 AW	22260 AAW	MEBLS	10//99-12//99
	Portland MSA, ME	S	11.44 MW	11.23 AW	23810 AAW	MEBLS	10//99-12//99
	Maryland	S	12.55 MW	12.91 AW	26850 AAW	MDBLS	10//99-12//99
	Baltimore PMSA, MD	S	12.62 MW	12.20 AW	26260 AAW	MDBLS	10//99-12//99
	Cumberland MSA, MD-WV	S	9.60 MW	9.06 AW	19960 AAW	MDBLS	10//99-12//99
	Hagerstown PMSA, MD	S	10.66 MW	10.47 AW	22180 AAW	MDBLS	10//99-12//99
	Massachusetts	S	12.91 MW	13.35 AW	27760 AAW	MABLS	10//99-12//99
	Barnstable-Yarmouth MSA, MA	S	12.54 MW	12.53 AW	26090 AAW	MABLS	10//99-12//99
	Boston PMSA, MA-NH	S	13.79 MW	13.45 AW	28690 AAW	MABLS	10//99-12//99
	Brockton PMSA, MA	S	12.73 MW	12.40 AW	26470 AAW	MABLS	10//99-12//99
	Fitchburg-Leominster PMSA, MA	S	12.51 MW	12.35 AW	26020 AAW	MABLS	10//99-12//99
	Lawrence PMSA, MA-NH	S	13.02 MW	12.58 AW	27080 AAW	MABLS	10//99-12//99
	Lowell PMSA, MA-NH	S	13.47 MW	13.15 AW	28020 AAW	MABLS	10//99-12//99
	New Bedford PMSA, MA	S	12.25 MW	11.69 AW	25480 AAW	MABLS	10//99-12//99
	Pittsfield MSA, MA	S	11.75 MW	11.54 AW	24440 AAW	MABLS	10//99-12//99
	Springfield MSA, MA	S	12.75 MW	12.14 AW	26510 AAW	MABLS	10//99-12//99
	Worcester PMSA, MA-CT	S	12.45 MW	11.94 AW	25900 AAW	MABLS	10//99-12//99
	Michigan	S	11.7 MW	12.17 AW	25310 AAW	MIBLS	10//99-12//99
	Ann Arbor PMSA, MI	S	12.32 MW	12.06 AW	25620 AAW	MIBLS	10//99-12//99
	Benton Harbor MSA, MI	S	11.41 MW	10.50 AW	23740 AAW	MIBLS	10//99-12//99
	Detroit PMSA, MI	S	12.86 MW	12.32 AW	26740 AAW	MIBLS	10//99-12//99
	Flint PMSA, MI	S	11.57 MW	10.97 AW	24070 AAW	MIBLS	10//99-12//99
	Grand Rapids-Muskegon-Holland MSA, MI	S	12.12 MW	11.75 AW	25200 AAW	MIBLS	10//99-12//99
	Jackson MSA, MI	S	11.56 MW	11.20 AW	24050 AAW	MIBLS	10//99-12//99
	Kalamazoo-Battle Creek MSA, MI	S	11.53 MW	11.14 AW	23980 AAW	MIBLS	10//99-12//99
	Lansing-East Lansing MSA, MI	S	13.05 MW	12.59 AW	27150 AAW	MIBLS	10//99-12//99
	Saginaw-Bay City-Midland MSA, MI	S	10.97 MW	10.25 AW	22820 AAW	MIBLS	10//99-12//99
	Minnesota	S	11.73 MW	12.13 AW	25220 AAW	MNBLS	10//99-12//99
	Duluth-Superior MSA, MN-WI	S	10.36 MW	10.20 AW	21540 AAW	MNBLS	10//99-12//99
	Minneapolis-St. Paul MSA, MN-WI	S	13.11 MW	12.65 AW	27260 AAW	MNBLS	10//99-12//99

AAW	Average annual wage	**AOH**	Average offered, high	**ASH**	Average starting, high	**H**	Hourly	**M**	Monthly	**S**	Special: hourly and annual
AE	Average entry wage	**AOL**	Average offered, low	**ASL**	Average starting, low	**HI**	Highest wage paid	**MTC**	Median total compensation	**TQ**	Third quartile wage
AEX	Average experienced wage	**APH**	Average pay, high range	**AW**	Average wage paid	**HR**	High end range	**MW**	Median wage paid	**W**	Weekly
AO	Average offered	**APL**	Average pay, low range	**FQ**	First quartile wage	**LR**	Low end range	**SQ**	Second quartile wage	**Y**	Yearly

114

Occupation/Type/Industry	Location	Per	Low	Mid	High	Source	Date
Bookkeeping, Accounting, and Auditing Clerk							
	Rochester MSA, MN	S	11.72 MW	11.41 AW	24370 AAW	MNBLS	10//99-12//99
	St. Cloud MSA, MN	S	10.62 MW	10.27 AW	22090 AAW	MNBLS	10//99-12//99
	Mississippi	S	10.07 MW	10.49 AW	21820 AAW	MSBLS	10//99-12//99
	Biloxi-Gulfport-Pascagoula MSA, MS	S	10.88 MW	10.22 AW	22620 AAW	MSBLS	10//99-12//99
	Hattiesburg MSA, MS	S	9.49 MW	9.24 AW	19750 AAW	MSBLS	10//99-12//99
	Jackson MSA, MS	S	11.30 MW	10.65 AW	23510 AAW	MSBLS	10//99-12//99
	Missouri	S	10.42 MW	10.83 AW	22530 AAW	MOBLS	10//99-12//99
	Columbia MSA, MO	S	10.25 MW	9.92 AW	21320 AAW	MOBLS	10//99-12//99
	Joplin MSA, MO	S	9.57 MW	9.17 AW	19900 AAW	MOBLS	10//99-12//99
	Kansas City MSA, MO-KS	S	11.81 MW	11.33 AW	24570 AAW	MOBLS	10//99-12//99
	St. Joseph MSA, MO	S	9.45 MW	9.37 AW	19660 AAW	MOBLS	10//99-12//99
	St. Louis MSA, MO-IL	S	11.66 MW	11.16 AW	24260 AAW	MOBLS	10//99-12//99
	Springfield MSA, MO	S	9.66 MW	9.46 AW	20090 AAW	MOBLS	10//99-12//99
	Montana	S	9.53 MW	9.81 AW	20400 AAW	MTBLS	10//99-12//99
	Billings MSA, MT	S	10.44 MW	10.18 AW	21710 AAW	MTBLS	10//99-12//99
	Great Falls MSA, MT	S	9.99 MW	9.59 AW	20790 AAW	MTBLS	10//99-12//99
	Missoula MSA, MT	S	10.45 MW	10.32 AW	21730 AAW	MTBLS	10//99-12//99
	Nebraska	S	9.85 MW	10.22 AW	21260 AAW	NEBLS	10//99-12//99
	Lincoln MSA, NE	S	10.82 MW	10.47 AW	22510 AAW	NEBLS	10//99-12//99
	Omaha MSA, NE-IA	S	11.23 MW	10.89 AW	23350 AAW	NEBLS	10//99-12//99
	Nevada	S	11.63 MW	12.18 AW	25320 AAW	NVBLS	10//99-12//99
	Las Vegas MSA, NV-AZ	S	12.12 MW	11.48 AW	25210 AAW	NVBLS	10//99-12//99
	Reno MSA, NV	S	12.56 MW	12.46 AW	26130 AAW	NVBLS	10//99-12//99
	New Hampshire	S	11.68 MW	12.04 AW	25050 AAW	NHBLS	10//99-12//99
	Manchester PMSA, NH	S	12.17 MW	11.96 AW	25310 AAW	NHBLS	10//99-12//99
	Nashua PMSA, NH	S	12.12 MW	11.72 AW	25200 AAW	NHBLS	10//99-12//99
	Portsmouth-Rochester PMSA, NH-ME	S	11.56 MW	11.42 AW	24050 AAW	NHBLS	10//99-12//99
	New Jersey	S	13.5 MW	14.10 AW	29330 AAW	NJBLS	10//99-12//99
	Atlantic-Cape May PMSA, NJ	S	12.61 MW	12.16 AW	26230 AAW	NJBLS	10//99-12//99
	Bergen-Passaic PMSA, NJ	S	14.83 MW	14.28 AW	30840 AAW	NJBLS	10//99-12//99
	Jersey City PMSA, NJ	S	14.77 MW	13.67 AW	30730 AAW	NJBLS	10//99-12//99
	Middlesex-Somerset-Hunterdon PMSA, NJ	S	14.15 MW	13.41 AW	29420 AAW	NJBLS	10//99-12//99
	Monmouth-Ocean PMSA, NJ	S	13.05 MW	12.43 AW	27150 AAW	NJBLS	10//99-12//99
	Newark PMSA, NJ	S	14.54 MW	14.20 AW	30240 AAW	NJBLS	10//99-12//99
	Trenton PMSA, NJ	S	14.50 MW	14.40 AW	30170 AAW	NJBLS	10//99-12//99
	Vineland-Millville-Bridgeton PMSA, NJ	S	12.39 MW	11.95 AW	25770 AAW	NJBLS	10//99-12//99
	New Mexico	S	10.14 MW	10.78 AW	22430 AAW	NMBLS	10//99-12//99
	Albuquerque MSA, NM	S	10.80 MW	10.34 AW	22470 AAW	NMBLS	10//99-12//99
	Las Cruces MSA, NM	S	9.74 MW	9.20 AW	20260 AAW	NMBLS	10//99-12//99
	Santa Fe MSA, NM	S	13.49 MW	12.12 AW	28060 AAW	NMBLS	10//99-12//99
	New York	S	12.96 MW	14.05 AW	29220 AAW	NYBLS	10//99-12//99
	Albany-Schenectady-Troy MSA, NY	S	12.40 MW	12.16 AW	25790 AAW	NYBLS	10//99-12//99
	Binghamton MSA, NY	S	10.48 MW	10.11 AW	21800 AAW	NYBLS	10//99-12//99
	Buffalo-Niagara Falls MSA, NY	S	11.49 MW	11.22 AW	23900 AAW	NYBLS	10//99-12//99
	Dutchess County PMSA, NY	S	13.00 MW	12.52 AW	27030 AAW	NYBLS	10//99-12//99
	Elmira MSA, NY	S	10.88 MW	10.98 AW	22630 AAW	NYBLS	10//99-12//99
	Glens Falls MSA, NY	S	10.96 MW	10.97 AW	22810 AAW	NYBLS	10//99-12//99
	Jamestown MSA, NY	S	10.03 MW	9.85 AW	20870 AAW	NYBLS	10//99-12//99
	Nassau-Suffolk PMSA, NY	S	14.27 MW	13.88 AW	29670 AAW	NYBLS	10//99-12//99
	New York PMSA, NY	S	15.92 MW	14.38 AW	33120 AAW	NYBLS	10//99-12//99
	Newburgh PMSA, NY-PA	S	12.02 MW	11.84 AW	25000 AAW	NYBLS	10//99-12//99
	Rochester MSA, NY	S	11.70 MW	11.31 AW	24330 AAW	NYBLS	10//99-12//99
	Syracuse MSA, NY	S	11.15 MW	10.91 AW	23180 AAW	NYBLS	10//99-12//99
	Utica-Rome MSA, NY	S	10.71 MW	10.44 AW	22270 AAW	NYBLS	10//99-12//99
	North Carolina	S	11.12 MW	11.41 AW	23740 AAW	NCBLS	10//99-12//99
	Asheville MSA, NC	S	10.54 MW	10.18 AW	21920 AAW	NCBLS	10//99-12//99
	Charlotte-Gastonia-Rock Hill MSA, NC-SC	S	12.24 MW	11.80 AW	25460 AAW	NCBLS	10//99-12//99
	Fayetteville MSA, NC	S	10.17 MW	9.90 AW	21160 AAW	NCBLS	10//99-12//99
	Goldsboro MSA, NC	S	10.28 MW	9.99 AW	21390 AAW	NCBLS	10//99-12//99
	Greensboro--Winston-Salem--High Point MSA, NC	S	11.66 MW	11.43 AW	24260 AAW	NCBLS	10//99-12//99
	Greenville MSA, NC	S	10.56 MW	10.46 AW	21970 AAW	NCBLS	10//99-12//99
	Hickory-Morganton-Lenoir MSA, NC	S	11.15 MW	11.01 AW	23190 AAW	NCBLS	10//99-12//99

AAW	Average annual wage	AOH	Average offered, high	ASH	Average starting, high	H	Hourly
AE	Average entry wage	AOL	Average offered, low	ASL	Average starting, low	HI	Highest wage paid
AEX	Average experienced wage	APH	Average pay, high range	AW	Average wage paid	HR	High end range
AO	Average offered	APL	Average pay, low range	FQ	First quartile wage	LR	Low end range

M	Monthly	S	Special: hourly and annual
MTC	Median total compensation	TQ	Third quartile wage
MW	Median wage paid	W	Weekly
SQ	Second quartile wage	Y	Yearly

Occupation/Type/Industry	Location	Per	Low	Mid	High	Source	Date
Bookkeeping, Accounting, and Auditing Clerk	Jacksonville MSA, NC	S	9.68 MW	8.82 AW	20120 AAW	NCBLS	10//99-12//99
	Raleigh-Durham-Chapel Hill MSA, NC	S	12.47 MW	12.12 AW	25930 AAW	NCBLS	10//99-12//99
	Rocky Mount MSA, NC	S	11.54 MW	11.29 AW	24010 AAW	NCBLS	10//99-12//99
	Wilmington MSA, NC	S	10.78 MW	10.71 AW	22430 AAW	NCBLS	10//99-12//99
	North Dakota	S	9.3 MW	9.65 AW	20070 AAW	NDBLS	10//99-12//99
	Bismarck MSA, ND	S	9.55 MW	9.46 AW	19860 AAW	NDBLS	10//99-12//99
	Fargo-Moorhead MSA, ND-MN	S	10.53 MW	10.20 AW	21900 AAW	NDBLS	10//99-12//99
	Grand Forks MSA, ND-MN	S	10.29 MW	10.02 AW	21410 AAW	NDBLS	10//99-12//99
	Ohio	S	11.18 MW	11.54 AW	24010 AAW	OHBLS	10//99-12//99
	Akron PMSA, OH	S	11.49 MW	11.26 AW	23900 AAW	OHBLS	10//99-12//99
	Canton-Massillon MSA, OH	S	10.80 MW	10.34 AW	22470 AAW	OHBLS	10//99-12//99
	Cincinnati PMSA, OH-KY-IN	S	11.55 MW	11.21 AW	24030 AAW	OHBLS	10//99-12//99
	Cleveland-Lorain-Elyria PMSA, OH	S	11.89 MW	11.54 AW	24730 AAW	OHBLS	10//99-12//99
	Columbus MSA, OH	S	12.21 MW	11.79 AW	25400 AAW	OHBLS	10//99-12//99
	Dayton-Springfield MSA, OH	S	11.70 MW	11.28 AW	24340 AAW	OHBLS	10//99-12//99
	Hamilton-Middletown PMSA, OH	S	12.07 MW	11.59 AW	25100 AAW	OHBLS	10//99-12//99
	Lima MSA, OH	S	10.73 MW	10.43 AW	22320 AAW	OHBLS	10//99-12//99
	Mansfield MSA, OH	S	11.02 MW	10.87 AW	22910 AAW	OHBLS	10//99-12//99
	Steubenville-Weirton MSA, OH-WV	S	10.15 MW	9.04 AW	21110 AAW	OHBLS	10//99-12//99
	Toledo MSA, OH	S	11.70 MW	11.11 AW	24350 AAW	OHBLS	10//99-12//99
	Youngstown-Warren MSA, OH	S	10.74 MW	10.25 AW	22330 AAW	OHBLS	10//99-12//99
	Oklahoma	S	9.98 MW	10.49 AW	21820 AAW	OKBLS	10//99-12//99
	Enid MSA, OK	S	10.31 MW	9.35 AW	21450 AAW	OKBLS	10//99-12//99
	Lawton MSA, OK	S	9.42 MW	9.07 AW	19590 AAW	OKBLS	10//99-12//99
	Oklahoma City MSA, OK	S	10.89 MW	10.43 AW	22650 AAW	OKBLS	10//99-12//99
	Tulsa MSA, OK	S	11.28 MW	10.84 AW	23460 AAW	OKBLS	10//99-12//99
	Oregon	S	11.57 MW	12.01 AW	24970 AAW	ORBLS	10//99-12//99
	Corvallis MSA, OR	S	11.87 MW	11.32 AW	24690 AAW	ORBLS	10//99-12//99
	Eugene-Springfield MSA, OR	S	11.36 MW	11.03 AW	23630 AAW	ORBLS	10//99-12//99
	Medford-Ashland MSA, OR	S	11.12 MW	10.53 AW	23130 AAW	ORBLS	10//99-12//99
	Portland-Vancouver PMSA, OR-WA	S	12.73 MW	12.26 AW	26490 AAW	ORBLS	10//99-12//99
	Salem PMSA, OR	S	12.21 MW	11.97 AW	25390 AAW	ORBLS	10//99-12//99
	Pennsylvania	S	11.24 MW	11.83 AW	24600 AAW	PABLS	10//99-12//99
	Allentown-Bethlehem-Easton MSA, PA	S	11.60 MW	11.03 AW	24120 AAW	PABLS	10//99-12//99
	Altoona MSA, PA	S	9.56 MW	9.31 AW	19880 AAW	PABLS	10//99-12//99
	Erie MSA, PA	S	10.59 MW	10.13 AW	22030 AAW	PABLS	10//99-12//99
	Harrisburg-Lebanon-Carlisle MSA, PA	S	11.69 MW	11.26 AW	24310 AAW	PABLS	10//99-12//99
	Johnstown MSA, PA	S	9.48 MW	8.82 AW	19720 AAW	PABLS	10//99-12//99
	Lancaster MSA, PA	S	11.65 MW	11.22 AW	24230 AAW	PABLS	10//99-12//99
	Philadelphia PMSA, PA-NJ	S	13.46 MW	12.76 AW	27990 AAW	PABLS	10//99-12//99
	Pittsburgh MSA, PA	S	10.90 MW	10.47 AW	22660 AAW	PABLS	10//99-12//99
	Reading MSA, PA	S	11.52 MW	11.35 AW	23970 AAW	PABLS	10//99-12//99
	Scranton--Wilkes-Barre--Hazleton MSA, PA	S	10.29 MW	9.96 AW	21390 AAW	PABLS	10//99-12//99
	Sharon MSA, PA	S	9.41 MW	8.86 AW	19580 AAW	PABLS	10//99-12//99
	State College MSA, PA	S	10.41 MW	10.05 AW	21650 AAW	PABLS	10//99-12//99
	Williamsport MSA, PA	S	10.50 MW	9.91 AW	21830 AAW	PABLS	10//99-12//99
	York MSA, PA	S	11.29 MW	10.72 AW	23470 AAW	PABLS	10//99-12//99
	Rhode Island	S	12.2 MW	12.40 AW	25800 AAW	RIBLS	10//99-12//99
	Providence-Fall River-Warwick MSA, RI-MA	S	12.34 MW	12.06 AW	25670 AAW	RIBLS	10//99-12//99
	South Carolina	S	10.38 MW	10.77 AW	22400 AAW	SCBLS	10//99-12//99
	Charleston-North Charleston MSA, SC	S	10.51 MW	10.23 AW	21850 AAW	SCBLS	10//99-12//99
	Columbia MSA, SC	S	10.97 MW	10.66 AW	22810 AAW	SCBLS	10//99-12//99
	Florence MSA, SC	S	10.66 MW	10.47 AW	22170 AAW	SCBLS	10//99-12//99
	Greenville-Spartanburg-Anderson MSA, SC	S	10.85 MW	10.37 AW	22560 AAW	SCBLS	10//99-12//99
	Myrtle Beach MSA, SC	S	11.03 MW	10.52 AW	22940 AAW	SCBLS	10//99-12//99
	Sumter MSA, SC	S	10.02 MW	9.78 AW	20840 AAW	SCBLS	10//99-12//99
	South Dakota	S	9.34 MW	9.22 AW	19180 AAW	SDBLS	10//99-12//99
	Rapid City MSA, SD	S	9.35 MW	9.47 AW	19450 AAW	SDBLS	10//99-12//99
	Sioux Falls MSA, SD	S	9.67 MW	9.78 AW	20110 AAW	SDBLS	10//99-12//99

AAW Average annual wage	AOH Average offered, high	ASH Average starting, high	H Hourly	M Monthly	S Special: hourly and annual
AE Average entry wage	AOL Average offered, low	ASL Average starting, low	HI Highest wage paid	MTC Median total compensation	TQ Third quartile wage
AEX Average experienced wage	APH Average pay, high range	AW Average wage paid	HR High end range	MW Median wage paid	W Weekly
AO Average offered	APL Average pay, low range	FQ First quartile wage	LR Low end range	SQ Second quartile wage	Y Yearly

Occupation/Type/Industry	Location	Per	Low	Mid	High	Source	Date
Bookkeeping, Accounting, and Auditing Clerk	Tennessee	S	10.86 MW	11.29 AW	23470 AAW	TNBLS	10//99-12//99
	Chattanooga MSA, TN-GA	S	11.12 MW	10.78 AW	23120 AAW	TNBLS	10//99-12//99
	Clarksville-Hopkinsville MSA, TN-KY	S	10.29 MW	9.72 AW	21400 AAW	TNBLS	10//99-12//99
	Jackson MSA, TN	S	10.40 MW	9.99 AW	21630 AAW	TNBLS	10//99-12//99
	Johnson City-Kingsport-Bristol MSA, TN-VA	S	10.18 MW	9.91 AW	21170 AAW	TNBLS	10//99-12//99
	Knoxville MSA, TN	S	11.33 MW	10.89 AW	23560 AAW	TNBLS	10//99-12//99
	Memphis MSA, TN-AR-MS	S	11.97 MW	11.34 AW	24890 AAW	MSBLS	10//99-12//99
	Nashville MSA, TN	S	11.90 MW	11.57 AW	24750 AAW	TNBLS	10//99-12//99
	Texas	S	11.09 MW	11.63 AW	24190 AAW	TXBLS	10//99-12//99
	Abilene MSA, TX	S	9.99 MW	9.37 AW	20770 AAW	TXBLS	10//99-12//99
	Amarillo MSA, TX	S	10.74 MW	10.06 AW	22330 AAW	TXBLS	10//99-12//99
	Austin-San Marcos MSA, TX	S	11.49 MW	11.28 AW	23890 AAW	TXBLS	10//99-12//99
	Beaumont-Port Arthur MSA, TX	S	11.32 MW	10.49 AW	23550 AAW	TXBLS	10//99-12//99
	Brazoria PMSA, TX	S	11.98 MW	11.69 AW	24910 AAW	TXBLS	10//99-12//99
	Brownsville-Harlingen-San Benito MSA, TX	S	9.42 MW	9.01 AW	19600 AAW	TXBLS	10//99-12//99
	Bryan-College Station MSA, TX	S	10.20 MW	9.94 AW	21220 AAW	TXBLS	10//99-12//99
	Corpus Christi MSA, TX	S	10.51 MW	10.27 AW	21860 AAW	TXBLS	10//99-12//99
	Dallas PMSA, TX	S	12.80 MW	12.30 AW	26620 AAW	TXBLS	10//99-12//99
	El Paso MSA, TX	S	10.24 MW	10.42 AW	21300 AAW	TXBLS	10//99-12//99
	Fort Worth-Arlington PMSA, TX	S	11.94 MW	11.39 AW	24840 AAW	TXBLS	10//99-12//99
	Galveston-Texas City PMSA, TX	S	10.92 MW	10.73 AW	22710 AAW	TXBLS	10//99-12//99
	Houston PMSA, TX	S	12.93 MW	12.23 AW	26900 AAW	TXBLS	10//99-12//99
	Killeen-Temple MSA, TX	S	9.47 MW	9.32 AW	19700 AAW	TXBLS	10//99-12//99
	Laredo MSA, TX	S	9.02 MW	8.45 AW	18760 AAW	TXBLS	10//99-12//99
	Longview-Marshall MSA, TX	S	11.03 MW	10.37 AW	22940 AAW	TXBLS	10//99-12//99
	Lubbock MSA, TX	S	10.19 MW	9.70 AW	21200 AAW	TXBLS	10//99-12//99
	McAllen-Edinburg-Mission MSA, TX	S	9.32 MW	8.71 AW	19390 AAW	TXBLS	10//99-12//99
	Odessa-Midland MSA, TX	S	10.26 MW	9.56 AW	21340 AAW	TXBLS	10//99-12//99
	San Angelo MSA, TX	S	9.90 MW	9.06 AW	20580 AAW	TXBLS	10//99-12//99
	San Antonio MSA, TX	S	11.15 MW	10.52 AW	23180 AAW	TXBLS	10//99-12//99
	Sherman-Denison MSA, TX	S	10.67 MW	10.22 AW	22180 AAW	TXBLS	10//99-12//99
	Texarkana MSA, TX-Texarkana, AR	S	9.10 MW	8.87 AW	18930 AAW	TXBLS	10//99-12//99
	Tyler MSA, TX	S	9.87 MW	8.53 AW	20530 AAW	TXBLS	10//99-12//99
	Victoria MSA, TX	S	9.69 MW	9.53 AW	20160 AAW	TXBLS	10//99-12//99
	Waco MSA, TX	S	10.41 MW	9.99 AW	21660 AAW	TXBLS	10//99-12//99
	Wichita Falls MSA, TX	S	11.60 MW	10.90 AW	24120 AAW	TXBLS	10//99-12//99
	Utah	S	10.27 MW	10.75 AW	22360 AAW	UTBLS	10//99-12//99
	Provo-Orem MSA, UT	S	10.42 MW	9.94 AW	21670 AAW	UTBLS	10//99-12//99
	Salt Lake City-Ogden MSA, UT	S	10.96 MW	10.51 AW	22790 AAW	UTBLS	10//99-12//99
	Vermont	S	11.18 MW	11.53 AW	23970 AAW	VTBLS	10//99-12//99
	Burlington MSA, VT	S	12.18 MW	11.77 AW	25330 AAW	VTBLS	10//99-12//99
	Virginia	S	11.18 MW	11.54 AW	24010 AAW	VABLS	10//99-12//99
	Charlottesville MSA, VA	S	11.03 MW	10.91 AW	22950 AAW	VABLS	10//99-12//99
	Danville MSA, VA	S	9.62 MW	9.36 AW	20010 AAW	VABLS	10//99-12//99
	Lynchburg MSA, VA	S	10.60 MW	10.42 AW	22040 AAW	VABLS	10//99-12//99
	Norfolk-Virginia Beach-Newport News MSA, VA-NC	S	11.09 MW	10.74 AW	23070 AAW	VABLS	10//99-12//99
	Richmond-Petersburg MSA, VA	S	11.95 MW	11.58 AW	24850 AAW	VABLS	10//99-12//99
	Roanoke MSA, VA	S	10.64 MW	10.26 AW	22130 AAW	VABLS	10//99-12//99
	Washington	S	12.46 MW	12.83 AW	26690 AAW	WABLS	10//99-12//99
	Bellingham MSA, WA	S	11.89 MW	11.59 AW	24730 AAW	WABLS	10//99-12//99
	Bremerton PMSA, WA	S	12.14 MW	12.14 AW	25250 AAW	WABLS	10//99-12//99
	Olympia PMSA, WA	S	12.83 MW	12.33 AW	26680 AAW	WABLS	10//99-12//99
	Richland-Kennewick-Pasco MSA, WA	S	11.68 MW	11.17 AW	24290 AAW	WABLS	10//99-12//99
	Seattle-Bellevue-Everett PMSA, WA	S	13.58 MW	13.28 AW	28240 AAW	WABLS	10//99-12//99
	Spokane MSA, WA	S	11.36 MW	11.11 AW	23630 AAW	WABLS	10//99-12//99
	Tacoma PMSA, WA	S	13.34 MW	12.84 AW	27750 AAW	WABLS	10//99-12//99

AAW Average annual wage
AE   Average entry wage
AEX Average experienced wage
AO   Average offered
AOH Average offered, high
AOL Average offered, low
APH Average pay, high range
APL Average pay, low range
ASH Average starting, high
ASL Average starting, low
AW   Average wage paid
FQ   First quartile wage
H   Hourly
HI   Highest wage paid
HR   High end range
LR   Low end range
M   Monthly
MTC Median total compensation
MW   Median wage paid
SQ   Second quartile wage
S   Special: hourly and annual
TQ   Third quartile wage
W   Weekly
Y   Yearly

Occupation/Type/Industry	Location	Per	Low	Mid	High	Source	Date
Bookkeeping, Accounting, and Auditing Clerk	Yakima MSA, WA	S	11.39 MW	11.23 AW	23700 AAW	WABLS	10//99-12//99
	West Virginia	S	9.47 MW	9.92 AW	20630 AAW	WVBLS	10//99-12//99
	Charleston MSA, WV	S	10.28 MW	9.91 AW	21380 AAW	WVBLS	10//99-12//99
	Huntington-Ashland MSA, WV-KY-OH	S	9.80 MW	9.27 AW	20380 AAW	WVBLS	10//99-12//99
	Parkersburg-Marietta MSA, WV-OH	S	9.66 MW	9.44 AW	20100 AAW	WVBLS	10//99-12//99
	Wheeling MSA, WV-OH	S	8.85 MW	8.26 AW	18400 AAW	WVBLS	10//99-12//99
	Wisconsin	S	10.9 MW	11.27 AW	23440 AAW	WIBLS	10//99-12//99
	Appleton-Oshkosh-Neenah MSA, WI	S	11.05 MW	10.58 AW	22990 AAW	WIBLS	10//99-12//99
	Eau Claire MSA, WI	S	9.64 MW	9.46 AW	20050 AAW	WIBLS	10//99-12//99
	Green Bay MSA, WI	S	11.48 MW	11.19 AW	23880 AAW	WIBLS	10//99-12//99
	Janesville-Beloit MSA, WI	S	10.57 MW	10.48 AW	21990 AAW	WIBLS	10//99-12//99
	Kenosha PMSA, WI	S	11.77 MW	11.30 AW	24480 AAW	WIBLS	10//99-12//99
	La Crosse MSA, WI-MN	S	10.13 MW	9.76 AW	21070 AAW	WIBLS	10//99-12//99
	Madison MSA, WI	S	12.18 MW	11.59 AW	25330 AAW	WIBLS	10//99-12//99
	Milwaukee-Waukesha PMSA, WI	S	12.44 MW	12.00 AW	25880 AAW	WIBLS	10//99-12//99
	Racine PMSA, WI	S	10.81 MW	10.51 AW	22490 AAW	WIBLS	10//99-12//99
	Sheboygan MSA, WI	S	9.67 MW	9.50 AW	20120 AAW	WIBLS	10//99-12//99
	Wausau MSA, WI	S	10.69 MW	10.69 AW	22250 AAW	WIBLS	10//99-12//99
	Wyoming	S	9.56 MW	9.95 AW	20690 AAW	WYBLS	10//99-12//99
	Casper MSA, WY	S	10.20 MW	9.93 AW	21230 AAW	WYBLS	10//99-12//99
	Cheyenne MSA, WY	S	10.17 MW	9.74 AW	21140 AAW	WYBLS	10//99-12//99
	Puerto Rico	S	7.51 MW	7.99 AW	16620 AAW	PRBLS	10//99-12//99
	Aguadilla MSA, PR	S	7.53 MW	7.19 AW	15670 AAW	PRBLS	10//99-12//99
	Arecibo PMSA, PR	S	6.87 MW	6.20 AW	14280 AAW	PRBLS	10//99-12//99
	Caguas PMSA, PR	S	7.33 MW	6.64 AW	15250 AAW	PRBLS	10//99-12//99
	Mayaguez MSA, PR	S	7.51 MW	7.10 AW	15630 AAW	PRBLS	10//99-12//99
	Ponce MSA, PR	S	7.26 MW	6.98 AW	15100 AAW	PRBLS	10//99-12//99
	San Juan-Bayamon PMSA, PR	S	8.18 MW	7.73 AW	17020 AAW	PRBLS	10//99-12//99
	Virgin Islands	S	10.49 MW	11.01 AW	22910 AAW	VIBLS	10//99-12//99
	Guam	S	10.26 MW	10.58 AW	22000 AAW	GUBLS	10//99-12//99
Brand Manager Beer Wholesaling	United States	Y	53196 MW	67081 AW		BEVW	1999
Bricklayer Nonunion, Construction	United States	H		33.08 AW		ENR1	2000
Nonunion, Construction	Central	H		18.35 AW		ENR3	2000
Nonunion, Construction	Middle Atlantic	H		17.77 AW		ENR3	2000
Nonunion, Construction	New England	H		16.15 AW		ENR3	2000
Nonunion, Construction	Southeast	H		16.78 AW		ENR3	2000
Nonunion, Construction	West	H		19.38 AW		ENR3	2000
Brickmason and Blockmason	Alabama	S	16.04 MW	15.84 AW	32940 AAW	ALBLS	10//99-12//99
	Birmingham MSA, AL	S	17.89 MW	18.49 AW	37200 AAW	ALBLS	10//99-12//99
	Mobile MSA, AL	S	14.13 MW	14.45 AW	29400 AAW	ALBLS	10//99-12//99
	Montgomery MSA, AL	S	15.98 MW	15.64 AW	33240 AAW	ALBLS	10//99-12//99
	Alaska	S	20.52 MW	21.81 AW	45360 AAW	AKBLS	10//99-12//99
	Anchorage MSA, AK	S	21.79 MW	20.40 AW	45320 AAW	AKBLS	10//99-12//99
	Arizona	S	14.57 MW	14.53 AW	30220 AAW	AZBLS	10//99-12//99
	Flagstaff MSA, AZ-UT	S	14.57 MW	14.85 AW	30290 AAW	AZBLS	10//99-12//99
	Phoenix-Mesa MSA, AZ	S	14.77 MW	15.05 AW	30710 AAW	AZBLS	10//99-12//99
	Tucson MSA, AZ	S	12.42 MW	12.35 AW	25840 AAW	AZBLS	10//99-12//99
	Arkansas	S	15.57 MW	15.58 AW	32410 AAW	ARBLS	10//99-12//99
	Little Rock-North Little Rock MSA, AR	S	18.41 MW	18.66 AW	38280 AAW	ARBLS	10//99-12//99
	California	S	20.64 MW	21.65 AW	45030 AAW	CABLS	10//99-12//99
	Bakersfield MSA, CA	S	20.91 MW	20.24 AW	43480 AAW	CABLS	10//99-12//99
	Los Angeles-Long Beach PMSA, CA	S	18.33 MW	16.54 AW	38120 AAW	CABLS	10//99-12//99
	Oakland PMSA, CA	S	27.18 MW	27.44 AW	56530 AAW	CABLS	10//99-12//99
	Riverside-San Bernardino PMSA, CA	S	18.92 MW	18.26 AW	39360 AAW	CABLS	10//99-12//99
	San Diego MSA, CA	S	15.54 MW	17.32 AW	32320 AAW	CABLS	10//99-12//99
	San Jose PMSA, CA	S	25.65 MW	25.60 AW	53350 AAW	CABLS	10//99-12//99
	Santa Rosa PMSA, CA	S	17.59 MW	18.28 AW	36580 AAW	CABLS	10//99-12//99
	Ventura PMSA, CA	S	18.01 MW	16.09 AW	37460 AAW	CABLS	10//99-12//99
	Colorado	S	19.55 MW	21.04 AW	43770 AAW	COBLS	10//99-12//99
	Denver PMSA, CO	S	22.60 MW	20.39 AW	47000 AAW	COBLS	10//99-12//99

AAW Average annual wage	**AOH** Average offered, high	**ASH** Average starting, high	**H** Hourly	**M** Monthly	**S** Special: hourly and annual
AE Average entry wage	**AOL** Average offered, low	**ASL** Average starting, low	**HI** Highest wage paid	**MTC** Median total compensation	**TQ** Third quartile wage
AEX Average experienced wage	**APH** Average pay, high range	**AW** Average wage paid	**HR** High end range	**MW** Median wage paid	**W** Weekly
AO Average offered	**APL** Average pay, low range	**FQ** First quartile wage	**LR** Low end range	**SQ** Second quartile wage	**Y** Yearly

Occupation/Type/Industry	Location	Per	Low	Mid	High	Source	Date
Brickmason and Blockmason	Pueblo MSA, CO	S	18.23 MW	18.25 AW	37910 AAW	COBLS	10//99-12//99
	Connecticut	S	17.09 MW	18.16 AW	37780 AAW	CTBLS	10//99-12//99
	Bridgeport PMSA, CT	S	15.72 MW	15.36 AW	32690 AAW	CTBLS	10//99-12//99
	Danbury PMSA, CT	S	15.66 MW	14.90 AW	32580 AAW	CTBLS	10//99-12//99
	Hartford MSA, CT	S	19.61 MW	19.69 AW	40800 AAW	CTBLS	10//99-12//99
	Stamford-Norwalk PMSA, CT	S	24.27 MW	24.42 AW	50480 AAW	CTBLS	10//99-12//99
	Waterbury PMSA, CT	S	12.31 MW	12.16 AW	25610 AAW	CTBLS	10//99-12//99
	Delaware	S	20.04 MW	20.28 AW	42180 AAW	DEBLS	10//99-12//99
	Wilmington-Newark PMSA, DE-MD	S	20.60 MW	20.57 AW	42850 AAW	DEBLS	10//99-12//99
	District of Columbia	S	18.83 MW	18.70 AW	38890 AAW	DCBLS	10//99-12//99
	Washington PMSA, DC-MD-VA-WV		17.71 MW	18.30 AW	36830 AAW	DCBLS	10//99-12//99
	Florida	S	14.78 MW	15.23 AW	31670 AAW	FLBLS	10//99-12//99
	Fort Pierce-Port St. Lucie MSA, FL	S	14.93 MW	14.74 AW	31060 AAW	FLBLS	10//99-12//99
	Gainesville MSA, FL	S	14.63 MW	14.92 AW	30430 AAW	FLBLS	10//99-12//99
	Jacksonville MSA, FL	S	12.14 MW	12.16 AW	25250 AAW	FLBLS	10//99-12//99
	Miami PMSA, FL	S	15.67 MW	16.91 AW	32590 AAW	FLBLS	10//99-12//99
	Orlando MSA, FL	S	18.13 MW	18.63 AW	37710 AAW	FLBLS	10//99-12//99
	Pensacola MSA, FL	S	16.92 MW	17.10 AW	35200 AAW	FLBLS	10//99-12//99
	Sarasota-Bradenton MSA, FL	S	15.26 MW	14.87 AW	31740 AAW	FLBLS	10//99-12//99
	Tallahassee MSA, FL	S	14.72 MW	14.97 AW	30620 AAW	FLBLS	10//99-12//99
	Tampa-St. Petersburg-Clearwater MSA, FL	S	16.17 MW	15.01 AW	33640 AAW	FLBLS	10//99-12//99
	West Palm Beach-Boca Raton MSA, FL	S	19.34 MW	19.31 AW	40230 AAW	FLBLS	10//99-12//99
	Georgia	S	15.06 MW	15.00 AW	31200 AAW	GABLS	10//99-12//99
	Albany MSA, GA	S	12.56 MW	12.86 AW	26130 AAW	GABLS	10//99-12//99
	Atlanta MSA, GA	S	15.40 MW	15.36 AW	32030 AAW	GABLS	10//99-12//99
	Augusta-Aiken MSA, GA-SC	S	18.19 MW	18.87 AW	37840 AAW	GABLS	10//99-12//99
	Columbus MSA, GA-AL	S	13.44 MW	13.29 AW	27950 AAW	GABLS	10//99-12//99
	Savannah MSA, GA	S	15.08 MW	15.07 AW	31370 AAW	GABLS	10//99-12//99
	Hawaii	S	24.14 MW	23.29 AW	48450 AAW	HIBLS	10//99-12//99
	Honolulu MSA, HI	S	23.24 MW	24.13 AW	48350 AAW	HIBLS	10//99-12//99
	Idaho	S	18.81 MW	18.12 AW	37680 AAW	IDBLS	10//99-12//99
	Boise City MSA, ID	S	18.43 MW	20.48 AW	38330 AAW	IDBLS	10//99-12//99
	Illinois	S	29.19 MW	27.52 AW	57230 AAW	ILBLS	10//99-12//99
	Bloomington-Normal MSA, IL	S	22.10 MW	22.40 AW	45970 AAW	ILBLS	10//99-12//99
	Chicago PMSA, IL	S	28.31 MW	29.88 AW	58890 AAW	ILBLS	10//99-12//99
	Rockford MSA, IL	S	23.92 MW	24.38 AW	49760 AAW	ILBLS	10//99-12//99
	Indiana	S	20.98 MW	20.92 AW	43520 AAW	INBLS	10//99-12//99
	Elkhart-Goshen MSA, IN	S	16.43 MW	15.45 AW	34180 AAW	INBLS	10//99-12//99
	Evansville-Henderson MSA, IN-KY	S	18.22 MW	17.91 AW	37890 AAW	INBLS	10//99-12//99
	Gary PMSA, IN	S	21.38 MW	22.62 AW	44480 AAW	INBLS	10//99-12//99
	Indianapolis MSA, IN	S	23.30 MW	22.73 AW	48460 AAW	INBLS	10//99-12//99
	Lafayette MSA, IN	S	21.99 MW	21.64 AW	45740 AAW	INBLS	10//99-12//99
	Terre Haute MSA, IN	S	20.83 MW	21.26 AW	43330 AAW	INBLS	10//99-12//99
	Iowa	S	21.29 MW	20.14 AW	41890 AAW	IABLS	10//99-12//99
	Davenport-Moline-Rock Island MSA, IA-IL	S	20.20 MW	19.95 AW	42010 AAW	IABLS	10//99-12//99
	Des Moines MSA, IA	S	22.56 MW	23.84 AW	46930 AAW	IABLS	10//99-12//99
	Waterloo-Cedar Falls MSA, IA	S	17.29 MW	18.13 AW	35970 AAW	IABLS	10//99-12//99
	Kansas	S	17 MW	15.93 AW	33140 AAW	KSBLS	10//99-12//99
	Wichita MSA, KS	S	19.36 MW	19.31 AW	40280 AAW	KSBLS	10//99-12//99
	Kentucky	S	18.38 MW	17.65 AW	36700 AAW	KYBLS	10//99-12//99
	Lexington MSA, KY	S	15.81 MW	15.83 AW	32880 AAW	KYBLS	10//99-12//99
	Louisville MSA, KY-IN	S	17.62 MW	18.50 AW	36640 AAW	KYBLS	10//99-12//99
	Louisiana	S	14.25 MW	14.32 AW	29790 AAW	LABLS	10//99-12//99
	Baton Rouge MSA, LA	S	16.63 MW	16.23 AW	34590 AAW	LABLS	10//99-12//99
	New Orleans MSA, LA	S	12.39 MW	12.41 AW	25760 AAW	LABLS	10//99-12//99
	Maine	S	13.11 MW	13.27 AW	27610 AAW	MEBLS	10//99-12//99
	Maryland	S	17.5 MW	16.45 AW	34210 AAW	MDBLS	10//99-12//99
	Baltimore PMSA, MD	S	16.58 MW	17.98 AW	34490 AAW	MDBLS	10//99-12//99
	Hagerstown PMSA, MD	S	18.74 MW	18.93 AW	38990 AAW	MDBLS	10//99-12//99
	Massachusetts	S	26.2 MW	25.06 AW	52130 AAW	MABLS	10//99-12//99
	Boston PMSA, MA-NH	S	25.53 MW	27.66 AW	53100 AAW	MABLS	10//99-12//99
	Lawrence PMSA, MA-NH	S	19.06 MW	19.09 AW	39650 AAW	MABLS	10//99-12//99
	New Bedford PMSA, MA	S	25.50 MW	25.78 AW	53040 AAW	MABLS	10//99-12//99
	Worcester PMSA, MA-CT	S	23.15 MW	23.94 AW	48160 AAW	MABLS	10//99-12//99
	Michigan	S	21.44 MW	20.92 AW	43520 AAW	MIBLS	10//99-12//99

AAW Average annual wage	AOH Average offered, high	ASH Average starting, high	H Hourly	M Monthly	S Special: hourly and annual
AE Average entry wage	AOL Average offered, low	ASL Average starting, low	HI Highest wage paid	MTC Median total compensation	TQ Third quartile wage
AEX Average experienced wage	APH Average pay, high range	AW Average wage paid	HR High end range	MW Median wage paid	W Weekly
AO Average offered	APL Average pay, low range	FQ First quartile wage	LR Low end range	SQ Second quartile wage	Y Yearly

Occupation/Type/Industry	Location	Per	Low	Mid	High	Source	Date
Brickmason and Blockmason	Detroit PMSA, MI	S	22.41 MW	23.59 AW	46600 AAW	MIBLS	10//99-12//99
	Grand Rapids-Muskegon-						
	Holland MSA, MI	S	17.04 MW	17.83 AW	35450 AAW	MIBLS	10//99-12//99
	Minnesota	S	23.93 MW	23.17 AW	48190 AAW	MNBLS	10//99-12//99
	Duluth-Superior MSA, MN-WI	S	21.14 MW	21.11 AW	43980 AAW	MNBLS	10//99-12//99
	Minneapolis-St. Paul MSA,						
	MN-WI	S	22.28 MW	23.63 AW	46340 AAW	MNBLS	10//99-12//99
	St. Cloud MSA, MN	S	26.29 MW	26.45 AW	54690 AAW	MNBLS	10//99-12//99
	Mississippi	S	10.79 MW	11.66 AW	24250 AAW	MSBLS	10//99-12//99
	Jackson MSA, MS	S	14.60 MW	14.31 AW	30370 AAW	MSBLS	10//99-12//99
	Missouri	S	22.8 MW	21.38 AW	44460 AAW	MOBLS	10//99-12//99
	Kansas City MSA, MO-KS	S	20.23 MW	21.92 AW	42080 AAW	MOBLS	10//99-12//99
	St. Louis MSA, MO-IL	S	23.92 MW	24.46 AW	49750 AAW	MOBLS	10//99-12//99
	Montana	S	23.37 MW	22.24 AW	46260 AAW	MTBLS	10//99-12//99
	Nebraska	S	16.36 MW	16.34 AW	33980 AAW	NEBLS	10//99-12//99
	Omaha MSA, NE-IA	S	16.79 MW	16.63 AW	34930 AAW	NEBLS	10//99-12//99
	Nevada	S	21.98 MW	20.60 AW	42850 AAW	NVBLS	10//99-12//99
	Las Vegas MSA, NV-AZ	S	19.67 MW	21.49 AW	40910 AAW	NVBLS	10//99-12//99
	New Hampshire	S	17.98 MW	18.54 AW	38570 AAW	NHBLS	10//99-12//99
	Nashua PMSA, NH	S	16.08 MW	15.90 AW	33440 AAW	NHBLS	10//99-12//99
	New Jersey	S	21.4 MW	20.60 AW	42850 AAW	NJBLS	10//99-12//99
	Atlantic-Cape May PMSA, NJ	S	23.33 MW	20.89 AW	48530 AAW	NJBLS	10//99-12//99
	Bergen-Passaic PMSA, NJ	S	23.76 MW	24.35 AW	49420 AAW	NJBLS	10//99-12//99
	Jersey City PMSA, NJ	S	28.01 MW	28.81 AW	58270 AAW	NJBLS	10//99-12//99
	Middlesex-Somerset-						
	Hunterdon PMSA, NJ	S	23.60 MW	24.23 AW	49080 AAW	NJBLS	10//99-12//99
	Monmouth-Ocean PMSA, NJ	S	18.72 MW	18.32 AW	38940 AAW	NJBLS	10//99-12//99
	Newark PMSA, NJ	S	19.42 MW	18.32 AW	40390 AAW	NJBLS	10//99-12//99
	Vineland-Millville-Bridgeton						
	PMSA, NJ	S	26.53 MW	28.11 AW	55190 AAW	NJBLS	10//99-12//99
	New Mexico	S	11.38 MW	11.60 AW	24130 AAW	NMBLS	10//99-12//99
	New York	S	27.02 MW	25.17 AW	52360 AAW	NYBLS	10//99-12//99
	Albany-Schenectady-Troy						
	MSA, NY	S	18.15 MW	18.25 AW	37750 AAW	NYBLS	10//99-12//99
	Buffalo-Niagara Falls MSA,						
	NY	S	22.07 MW	22.94 AW	45900 AAW	NYBLS	10//99-12//99
	Glens Falls MSA, NY	S	13.11 MW	13.01 AW	27270 AAW	NYBLS	10//99-12//99
	Nassau-Suffolk PMSA, NY	S	28.60 MW	30.24 AW	59490 AAW	NYBLS	10//99-12//99
	New York PMSA, NY	S	28.59 MW	30.16 AW	59460 AAW	NYBLS	10//99-12//99
	Rochester MSA, NY	S	18.88 MW	19.07 AW	39260 AAW	NYBLS	10//99-12//99
	Syracuse MSA, NY	S	19.23 MW	19.22 AW	40000 AAW	NYBLS	10//99-12//99
	Utica-Rome MSA, NY	S	17.71 MW	17.89 AW	36840 AAW	NYBLS	10//99-12//99
	North Carolina	S	15.45 MW	15.49 AW	32220 AAW	NCBLS	10//99-12//99
	Charlotte-Gastonia-Rock Hill						
	MSA, NC-SC	S	13.73 MW	13.61 AW	28560 AAW	NCBLS	10//99-12//99
	Fayetteville MSA, NC	S	18.82 MW	19.01 AW	39140 AAW	NCBLS	10//99-12//99
	Greensboro--Winston-Salem--						
	High Point MSA, NC	Per	15.31 MW	15.32 AW	31850 AAW	NCBLS	10//99-12//99
	Hickory-Morganton-Lenoir						
	MSA, NC	S	16.54 MW	17.36 AW	34390 AAW	NCBLS	10//99-12//99
	Raleigh-Durham-Chapel Hill						
	MSA, NC	S	17.30 MW	18.06 AW	35980 AAW	NCBLS	10//99-12//99
	North Dakota	S	18.96 MW	19.02 AW	39560 AAW	NDBLS	10//99-12//99
	Fargo-Moorhead MSA, ND-						
	MN	S	22.80 MW	23.71 AW	47430 AAW	NDBLS	10//99-12//99
	Grand Forks MSA, ND-MN	S	18.40 MW	18.19 AW	38270 AAW	NDBLS	10//99-12//99
	Ohio	S	22.04 MW	20.63 AW	42920 AAW	OHBLS	10//99-12//99
	Akron PMSA, OH	S	20.68 MW	21.00 AW	43010 AAW	OHBLS	10//99-12//99
	Canton-Massillon MSA, OH	S	20.81 MW	20.99 AW	43280 AAW	OHBLS	10//99-12//99
	Cincinnati PMSA, OH-KY-IN	S	16.83 MW	17.99 AW	35000 AAW	OHBLS	10//99-12//99
	Cleveland-Lorain-Elyria						
	PMSA, OH	S	22.64 MW	23.70 AW	47090 AAW	OHBLS	10//99-12//99
	Columbus MSA, OH	S	21.45 MW	23.07 AW	44620 AAW	OHBLS	10//99-12//99
	Dayton-Springfield MSA, OH	S	16.21 MW	17.46 AW	33720 AAW	OHBLS	10//99-12//99
	Hamilton-Middletown PMSA,						
	OH	S	19.32 MW	19.61 AW	40190 AAW	OHBLS	10//99-12//99
	Mansfield MSA, OH	S	22.00 MW	23.36 AW	45770 AAW	OHBLS	10//99-12//99
	Steubenville-Weirton MSA,						
	OH-WV	S	17.24 MW	16.79 AW	35870 AAW	OHBLS	10//99-12//99
	Toledo MSA, OH	S	22.71 MW	23.49 AW	47230 AAW	OHBLS	10//99-12//99
	Youngstown-Warren MSA, OH	S	21.78 MW	22.42 AW	45300 AAW	OHBLS	10//99-12//99
	Oklahoma	S	13.74 MW	13.84 AW	28790 AAW	OKBLS	10//99-12//99

AAW Average annual wage	**AOH** Average offered, high	**ASH** Average starting, high	**H** Hourly	**M** Monthly	**S** Special: hourly and annual
AE Average entry wage	**AOL** Average offered, low	**ASL** Average starting, low	**HI** Highest wage paid	**MTC** Median total compensation	**TQ** Third quartile wage
AEX Average experienced wage	**APH** Average pay, high range	**AW** Average wage paid	**HR** High end range	**MW** Median wage paid	**W** Weekly
AO Average offered	**APL** Average pay, low range	**FQ** First quartile wage	**LR** Low end range	**SQ** Second quartile wage	**Y** Yearly

Occupation/Type/Industry	Location	Per	Low	Mid	High	Source	Date
Brickmason and Blockmason	Oklahoma City MSA, OK	S	18.53 MW	18.75 AW	38540 AAW	OKBLS	10//99-12//99
	Tulsa MSA, OK	S	18.71 MW	18.66 AW	38910 AAW	OKBLS	10//99-12//99
	Oregon	S	23.83 MW	23.22 AW	48290 AAW	ORBLS	10//99-12//99
	Salem PMSA, OR	S	24.04 MW	24.22 AW	50000 AAW	ORBLS	10//99-12//99
	Pennsylvania	S	19.52 MW	20.57 AW	42780 AAW	PABLS	10//99-12//99
	Altoona MSA, PA	S	13.38 MW	13.02 AW	27820 AAW	PABLS	10//99-12//99
	Erie MSA, PA	S	13.58 MW	12.94 AW	28240 AAW	PABLS	10//99-12//99
	Harrisburg-Lebanon-Carlisle MSA, PA	S	15.94 MW	15.69 AW	33160 AAW	PABLS	10//99-12//99
	Lancaster MSA, PA	S	16.15 MW	15.88 AW	33590 AAW	PABLS	10//99-12//99
	Philadelphia PMSA, PA-NJ	S	22.84 MW	22.93 AW	47510 AAW	PABLS	10//99-12//99
	Pittsburgh MSA, PA	S	19.47 MW	19.44 AW	40510 AAW	PABLS	10//99-12//99
	Reading MSA, PA	S	27.60 MW	29.91 AW	57400 AAW	PABLS	10//99-12//99
	Scranton--Wilkes-Barre--Hazleton MSA, PA	S	18.27 MW	16.19 AW	38000 AAW	PABLS	10//99-12//99
	State College MSA, PA	S	14.79 MW	12.98 AW	30760 AAW	PABLS	10//99-12//99
	Rhode Island	S	21.18 MW	21.09 AW	43860 AAW	RIBLS	10//99-12//99
	Providence-Fall River-Warwick MSA, RI-MA	S	21.89 MW	19.87 AW	45530 AAW	RIBLS	10//99-12//99
	South Carolina	S	14.97 MW	14.60 AW	30370 AAW	SCBLS	10//99-12//99
	Charleston-North Charleston MSA, SC	S	11.81 MW	11.79 AW	24570 AAW	SCBLS	10//99-12//99
	Columbia MSA, SC	S	13.89 MW	13.79 AW	28880 AAW	SCBLS	10//99-12//99
	Myrtle Beach MSA, SC	S	16.71 MW	17.12 AW	34750 AAW	SCBLS	10//99-12//99
	South Dakota	S	19.17 MW	19.21 AW	39960 AAW	SDBLS	10//99-12//99
	Sioux Falls MSA, SD	S	18.27 MW	18.73 AW	38000 AAW	SDBLS	10//99-12//99
	Tennessee	S	17.82 MW	17.30 AW	35980 AAW	TNBLS	10//99-12//99
	Chattanooga MSA, TN-GA	S	14.93 MW	15.03 AW	31060 AAW	TNBLS	10//99-12//99
	Clarksville-Hopkinsville MSA, TN-KY	S	12.24 MW	12.17 AW	25460 AAW	TNBLS	10//99-12//99
	Memphis MSA, TN-AR-MS	S	15.76 MW	15.03 AW	32790 AAW	MSBLS	10//99-12//99
	Nashville MSA, TN	S	16.36 MW	17.45 AW	34040 AAW	TNBLS	10//99-12//99
	Texas	S	17.12 MW	16.35 AW	34020 AAW	TXBLS	10//99-12//99
	Amarillo MSA, TX	S	16.93 MW	17.85 AW	35210 AAW	TXBLS	10//99-12//99
	Corpus Christi MSA, TX	S	12.54 MW	13.66 AW	26080 AAW	TXBLS	10//99-12//99
	Dallas PMSA, TX	S	17.42 MW	17.83 AW	36220 AQW	TXBLS	10//99-12//99
	El Paso MSA, TX	S	18.71 MW	19.11 AW	38920 AAW	TXBLS	10//99-12//99
	Fort Worth-Arlington PMSA, TX	S	17.50 MW	17.87 AW	36390 AAW	TXBLS	10//99-12//99
	Houston PMSA, TX	S	17.77 MW	16.72 AW	36960 AAW	TXBLS	10//99-12//99
	Odessa-Midland MSA, TX	S	19.02 MW	19.09 AW	39570 AAW	TXBLS	10//99-12//99
	San Antonio MSA, TX	S	11.27 MW	10.59 AW	23440 AAW	TXBLS	10//99-12//99
	Waco MSA, TX	S	19.14 MW	19.13 AW	39820 AAW	TXBLS	10//99-12//99
	Vermont	S	15.55 MW	15.74 AW	32740 AAW	VTBLS	10//99-12//99
	Virginia	S	18.74 MW	18.33 AW	38120 AAW	VABLS	10//99-12//99
	Norfolk-Virginia Beach-Newport News MSA, VA-NC	S	16.15 MW	17.06 AW	33590 AAW	VABLS	10//99-12//99
	Richmond-Petersburg MSA, VA	S	19.52 MW	19.53 AW	40590 AAW	VABLS	10//99-12//99
	Roanoke MSA, VA	S	17.71 MW	18.07 AW	36850 AAW	VABLS	10//99-12//99
	Washington	S	25.28 MW	24.78 AW	51550 AAW	WABLS	10//99-12//99
	Seattle-Bellevue-Everett PMSA, WA	S	24.87 MW	25.42 AW	51740 AAW	WABLS	10//99-12//99
	West Virginia	S	15.46 MW	15.45 AW	32130 AAW	WVBLS	10//99-12//99
	Parkersburg-Marietta MSA, WV-OH	S	12.05 MW	11.73 AW	25050 AAW	WVBLS	10//99-12//99
	Wisconsin	S	20.28 MW	20.05 AW	41700 AAW	WIBLS	10//99-12//99
	Appleton-Oshkosh-Neenah MSA, WI	S	20.82 MW	21.39 AW	43310 AAW	WIBLS	10//99-12//99
	Eau Claire MSA, WI	S	21.19 MW	22.68 AW	44070 AAW	WIBLS	10//99-12//99
	Janesville-Beloit MSA, WI	S	11.93 MW	12.08 AW	24810 AAW	WIBLS	10//99-12//99
	La Crosse MSA, WI-MN	S	14.48 MW	12.22 AW	30120 AAW	WIBLS	10//99-12//99
	Milwaukee-Waukesha PMSA, WI	S	23.11 MW	24.21 AW	48080 AAW	WIBLS	10//99-12//99
	Racine PMSA, WI	S	20.89 MW	22.00 AW	43450 AAW	WIBLS	10//99-12//99
	Wyoming	S	12.64 MW	13.44 AW	27960 AAW	WYBLS	10//99-12//99
	Puerto Rico	S	7.05 MW	7.08 AW	14720 AAW	PRBLS	10//99-12//99
	San Juan-Bayamon PMSA, PR	S	6.82 MW	6.66 AW	14200 AAW	PRBLS	10//99-12//99
	Guam	S	12.83 MW	14.18 AW	29500 AAW	GUBLS	10//99-12//99
Bridge and Lock Tender	Alabama	S	17.45 MW	17.29 AW	35960 AAW	ALBLS	10//99-12//99
	Arkansas	S	15 MW	14.56 AW	30290 AAW	ARBLS	10//99-12//99

AAW Average annual wage	**AOH** Average offered, high	**ASH** Average starting, high	**H** Hourly	**M** Monthly	**S** Special: hourly and annual
AE Average entry wage	**AOL** Average offered, low	**ASL** Average starting, low	**HI** Highest wage paid	**MTC** Median total compensation	**TQ** Third quartile wage
AEX Average experienced wage	**APH** Average pay, high range	**AW** Average wage paid	**HR** High end range	**MW** Median wage paid	**W** Weekly
AO Average offered	**APL** Average pay, low range	**FQ** First quartile wage	**LR** Low end range	**SQ** Second quartile wage	**Y** Yearly

Occupation/Type/Industry	Location	Per	Low	Mid	High	Source	Date
Bridge and Lock Tender	California	S	15.45 MW	15.58 AW	32410 AAW	CABLS	10//99-12//99
	Connecticut	S	14.88 MW	14.59 AW	30350 AAW	CTBLS	10//99-12//99
	Florida	S	8.37 MW	10.26 AW	21340 AAW	FLBLS	10//99-12//99
	West Palm Beach-Boca Raton MSA, FL	S	10.12 MW	8.04 AW	21060 AAW	FLBLS	10//99-12//99
	Georgia	S	12.57 MW	14.16 AW	29450 AAW	GABLS	10//99-12//99
	Illinois	S	18.27 MW	18.02 AW	37490 AAW	ILBLS	10//99-12//99
	Peoria-Pekin MSA, IL	S	18.94 MW	19.06 AW	39390 AAW	ILBLS	10//99-12//99
	Indiana	S	17.15 MW	16.23 AW	33760 AAW	INBLS	10//99-12//99
	Iowa	S	19.09 MW	18.99 AW	39490 AAW	IABLS	10//99-12//99
	Kentucky	S	17.68 MW	17.27 AW	35920 AAW	KYBLS	10//99-12//99
	Louisiana	S	9.47 MW	10.53 AW	21900 AAW	LABLS	10//99-12//99
	Lake Charles MSA, LA	S	13.63 MW	14.57 AW	28340 AAW	LABLS	10//99-12//99
	Michigan	S	14.91 MW	14.45 AW	30060 AAW	MIBLS	10//99-12//99
	Detroit PMSA, MI	S	10.37 MW	9.91 AW	21570 AAW	MIBLS	10//99-12//99
	Minnesota	S	18.13 MW	17.84 AW	37120 AAW	MNBLS	10//99-12//99
	Mississippi	S	11.43 MW	13.32 AW	27710 AAW	MSBLS	10//99-12//99
	Missouri	S	19.03 MW	18.66 AW	38810 AAW	MOBLS	10//99-12//99
	St. Louis MSA, MO-IL	S	18.85 MW	19.04 AW	39220 AAW	MOBLS	10//99-12//99
	New Jersey	S	15.1 MW	14.87 AW	30940 AAW	NJBLS	10//99-12//99
	Monmouth-Ocean PMSA, NJ	S	14.27 MW	14.61 AW	29690 AAW	NJBLS	10//99-12//99
	New York	S	13.46 MW	13.33 AW	27720 AAW	NYBLS	10//99-12//99
	New York PMSA, NY	S	13.44 MW	14.02 AW	27950 AAW	NYBLS	10//99-12//99
	Ohio	S	16.07 MW	15.83 AW	32920 AAW	OHBLS	10//99-12//99
	Oklahoma	S	19.25 MW	19.26 AW	40060 AAW	OKBLS	10//99-12//99
	Pennsylvania	S	18.78 MW	18.29 AW	38040 AAW	PABLS	10//99-12//99
	Tennessee	S	15.37 MW	15.38 AW	31980 AAW	TNBLS	10//99-12//99
	Texas	S	14.62 MW	13.92 AW	28960 AAW	TXBLS	10//99-12//99
	Washington	S	18.08 MW	17.69 AW	36800 AAW	WABLS	10//99-12//99
	Seattle-Bellevue-Everett PMSA, WA	S	17.94 MW	18.38 AW	37320 AAW	WABLS	10//99-12//99
	West Virginia	S	18.51 MW	18.23 AW	37920 AAW	WVBLS	10//99-12//99
	Wisconsin	S	16.44 MW	16.66 AW	34650 AAW	WIBLS	10//99-12//99
Broadcast Equipment Operator	United States	H		19.37 AW		NCS98	1998
Broadcast Technician	Alabama	S	8.28 MW	9.66 AW	20100 AAW	ALBLS	10//99-12//99
	Birmingham MSA, AL	S	10.91 MW	10.90 AW	22690 AAW	ALBLS	10//99-12//99
	Mobile MSA, AL	S	8.48 MW	7.71 AW	17640 AAW	ALBLS	10//99-12//99
	Montgomery MSA, AL	S	9.38 MW	8.01 AW	19500 AAW	ALBLS	10//99-12//99
	Arizona	S	12.25 MW	16.59 AW	34510 AAW	AZBLS	10//99-12//99
	Phoenix-Mesa MSA, AZ	S	17.51 MW	15.21 AW	36430 AAW	AZBLS	10//99-12//99
	Tucson MSA, AZ	S	15.31 MW	10.79 AW	31840 AAW	AZBLS	10//99-12//99
	Arkansas	S	6.47 MW	7.99 AW	16620 AAW	ARBLS	10//99-12//99
	California	S	7.99 MW	10.79 AW	22440 AAW	CABLS	10//99-12//99
	Fresno MSA, CA	S	7.70 MW	7.66 AW	16010 AAW	CABLS	10//99-12//99
	Los Angeles-Long Beach PMSA, CA	S	11.08 MW	8.17 AW	23040 AAW	CABLS	10//99-12//99
	San Diego MSA, CA	S	10.43 MW	7.83 AW	21700 AAW	CABLS	10//99-12//99
	San Francisco PMSA, CA	S	12.90 MW	8.56 AW	26830 AAW	CABLS	10//99-12//99
	Colorado	S	12.85 MW	18.98 AW	39480 AAW	COBLS	10//99-12//99
	Denver PMSA, CO	S	20.48 MW	13.16 AW	42600 AAW	COBLS	10//99-12//99
	Connecticut	S	12.63 MW	14.58 AW	30330 AAW	CTBLS	10//99-12//99
	Hartford MSA, CT	S	14.76 MW	12.57 AW	30690 AAW	CTBLS	10//99-12//99
	District of Columbia	S	19.49 MW	21.13 AW	43940 AAW	DCBLS	10//99-12//99
	Washington PMSA, DC-MD-VA-WV	S	19.47 MW	17.97 AW	40500 AAW	DCBLS	10//99-12//99
	Florida	S	10.92 MW	11.86 AW	24670 AAW	FLBLS	10//99-12//99
	Fort Lauderdale PMSA, FL	S	10.74 MW	9.32 AW	22340 AAW	FLBLS	10//99-12//99
	Fort Myers-Cape Coral MSA, FL	S	16.68 MW	15.99 AW	34700 AAW	FLBLS	10//99-12//99
	Jacksonville MSA, FL	S	12.54 MW	10.71 AW	26090 AAW	FLBLS	10//99-12//99
	Miami PMSA, FL	S	11.88 MW	10.91 AW	24710 AAW	FLBLS	10//99-12//99
	Orlando MSA, FL	S	13.19 MW	13.61 AW	27440 AAW	FLBLS	10//99-12//99
	Pensacola MSA, FL	S	11.84 MW	11.97 AW	24630 AAW	FLBLS	10//99-12//99
	Tallahassee MSA, FL	S	10.31 MW	9.73 AW	21440 AAW	FLBLS	10//99-12//99
	Tampa-St. Petersburg-Clearwater MSA, FL	S	11.30 MW	10.13 AW	23510 AAW	FLBLS	10//99-12//99
	West Palm Beach-Boca Raton MSA, FL	S	10.75 MW	10.49 AW	22350 AAW	FLBLS	10//99-12//99
	Georgia	S	13.62 MW	14.58 AW	30330 AAW	GABLS	10//99-12//99
	Augusta-Aiken MSA, GA-SC	S	15.63 MW	15.05 AW	32510 AAW	GABLS	10//99-12//99
	Idaho	S	6.6 MW	7.46 AW	15520 AAW	IDBLS	10//99-12//99

AAW Average annual wage	**AOH** Average offered, high	**ASH** Average starting, high	**H** Hourly	**M** Monthly	**S** Special: hourly and annual
AE Average entry wage	**AOL** Average offered, low	**ASL** Average starting, low	**HI** Highest wage paid	**MTC** Median total compensation	**TQ** Third quartile wage
AEX Average experienced wage	**APH** Average pay, high range	**AW** Average wage paid	**HR** High end range	**MW** Median wage paid	**W** Weekly
AO Average offered	**APL** Average pay, low range	**FQ** First quartile wage	**LR** Low end range	**SQ** Second quartile wage	**Y** Yearly

Occupation/Type/Industry	Location	Per	Low	Mid	High	Source	Date
Broadcast Technician	Illinois	S	10.9 MW	10.46 AW	21750 AAW	ILBLS	10//99-12//99
	Chicago PMSA, IL	S	10.65 MW	11.35 AW	22160 AAW	ILBLS	10//99-12//99
	Indiana	S	10.27 MW	11.75 AW	24430 AAW	INBLS	10//99-12//99
	Fort Wayne MSA, IN	S	10.00 MW	9.20 AW	20810 AAW	INBLS	10//99-12//99
	Indianapolis MSA, IN	S	13.67 MW	14.10 AW	28420 AAW	INBLS	10//99-12//99
	Iowa	S	11.02 MW	14.16 AW	29460 AAW	IABLS	10//99-12//99
	Kansas	S	13.01 MW	14.42 AW	29990 AAW	KSBLS	10//99-12//99
	Kentucky	S	13.37 MW	14.72 AW	30610 AAW	KYBLS	10//99-12//99
	Louisville MSA, KY-IN	S	15.26 MW	14.84 AW	31730 AAW	KYBLS	10//99-12//99
	Louisiana	S	8.94 MW	11.02 AW	22930 AAW	LABLS	10//99-12//99
	Maryland	S	13.59 MW	15.75 AW	32750 AAW	MDBLS	10//99-12//99
	Massachusetts	S	12.66 MW	14.08 AW	29300 AAW	MABLS	10//99-12//99
	Boston PMSA, MA-NH	S	14.34 MW	12.80 AW	29830 AAW	MABLS	10//99-12//99
	Michigan	S	16.77 MW	19.18 AW	39890 AAW	MIBLS	10//99-12//99
	Detroit PMSA, MI	S	19.52 MW	16.83 AW	40600 AAW	MIBLS	10//99-12//99
	Kalamazoo-Battle Creek MSA, MI	S	19.18 MW	19.21 AW	39900 AAW	MIBLS	10//99-12//99
	Minnesota	S	11.39 MW	13.49 AW	28060 AAW	MNBLS	10//99-12//99
	Minneapolis-St. Paul MSA, MN-WI	S	15.09 MW	13.19 AW	31400 AAW	MNBLS	10//99-12//99
	Mississippi	S	9.41 MW	10.31 AW	21450 AAW	MSBLS	10//99-12//99
	Missouri	S	6.69 MW	9.48 AW	19710 AAW	MOBLS	10//99-12//99
	Springfield MSA, MO	S	8.62 MW	6.57 AW	17930 AAW	MOBLS	10//99-12//99
	Montana	S	9.62 MW	10.05 AW	20900 AAW	MTBLS	10//99-12//99
	Nebraska	S	14.66 MW	14.61 AW	30380 AAW	NEBLS	10//99-12//99
	Omaha MSA, NE-IA	S	14.59 MW	14.65 AW	30340 AAW	NEBLS	10//99-12//99
	Nevada	S	9.82 MW	11.08 AW	23050 AAW	NVBLS	10//99-12//99
	Las Vegas MSA, NV-AZ	S	10.92 MW	9.41 AW	22720 AAW	NVBLS	10//99-12//99
	New Jersey	S	13.43 MW	14.86 AW	30910 AAW	NJBLS	10//99-12//99
	Newark PMSA, NJ	S	13.13 MW	13.65 AW	27300 AAW	NJBLS	10//99-12//99
	New Mexico	S	8.56 MW	8.64 AW	17980 AAW	NMBLS	10//99-12//99
	New York	S	14.26 MW	15.56 AW	32370 AAW	NYBLS	10//99-12//99
	Buffalo-Niagara Falls MSA, NY	S	15.63 MW	14.76 AW	32500 AAW	NYBLS	10//99-12//99
	Nassau-Suffolk PMSA, NY	S	15.36 MW	10.54 AW	31940 AAW	NYBLS	10//99-12//99
	New York PMSA, NY	S	15.67 MW	14.33 AW	32590 AAW	NYBLS	10//99-12//99
	Rochester MSA, NY	S	15.01 MW	14.22 AW	31230 AAW	NYBLS	10//99-12//99
	Syracuse MSA, NY	S	15.62 MW	15.38 AW	32490 AAW	NYBLS	10//99-12//99
	Utica-Rome MSA, NY	S	14.69 MW	12.15 AW	30550 AAW	NYBLS	10//99-12//99
	North Carolina	S	14.77 MW	15.70 AW	32650 AAW	NCBLS	10//99-12//99
	Charlotte-Gastonia-Rock Hill MSA, NC-SC	S	15.85 MW	13.90 AW	32970 AAW	NCBLS	10//99-12//99
	Greensboro--Winston-Salem--High Point MSA, NC	S	14.25 MW	14.52 AW	29640 AAW	NCBLS	10//99-12//99
	Raleigh-Durham-Chapel Hill MSA, NC	S	16.14 MW	14.89 AW	33580 AAW	NCBLS	10//99-12//99
	Ohio	S	12.88 MW	13.71 AW	28510 AAW	OHBLS	10//99-12//99
	Cleveland-Lorain-Elyria PMSA, OH	S	16.16 MW	15.43 AW	33600 AAW	OHBLS	10//99-12//99
	Columbus MSA, OH	S	13.79 MW	12.90 AW	28690 AAW	OHBLS	10//99-12//99
	Youngstown-Warren MSA, OH	S	13.12 MW	12.45 AW	27280 AAW	OHBLS	10//99-12//99
	Oklahoma	S	11.63 MW	13.43 AW	27940 AAW	OKBLS	10//99-12//99
	Pennsylvania	S	8.13 MW	12.97 AW	26970 AAW	PABLS	10//99-12//99
	Erie MSA, PA	S	11.07 MW	9.40 AW	23030 AAW	PABLS	10//99-12//99
	Johnstown MSA, PA	S	7.31 MW	6.33 AW	15200 AAW	PABLS	10//99-12//99
	Philadelphia PMSA, PA-NJ	S	22.09 MW	24.98 AW	45950 AAW	PABLS	10//99-12//99
	Pittsburgh MSA, PA	S	8.79 MW	8.12 AW	18280 AAW	PABLS	10//99-12//99
	Scranton--Wilkes-Barre--Hazleton MSA, PA	S	7.55 MW	7.57 AW	15710 AAW	PABLS	10//99-12//99
	Rhode Island	S	12.86 MW	14.23 AW	29610 AAW	RIBLS	10//99-12//99
	Providence-Fall River-Warwick MSA, RI-MA	S	14.23 MW	12.86 AW	29610 AAW	RIBLS	10//99-12//99
	South Carolina	S	13.33 MW	15.01 AW	31220 AAW	SCBLS	10//99-12//99
	South Dakota	S	9.74 MW	11.03 AW	22940 AAW	SDBLS	10//99-12//99
	Memphis MSA, TN-AR-MS	S	8.13 MW	7.55 AW	16910 AAW	MSBLS	10//99-12//99
	Texas	S	9.84 MW	11.40 AW	23710 AAW	TXBLS	10//99-12//99
	Austin-San Marcos MSA, TX	S	10.28 MW	8.15 AW	21380 AAW	TXBLS	10//99-12//99
	Dallas PMSA, TX	S	11.54 MW	11.28 AW	24000 AAW	TXBLS	10//99-12//99
	El Paso MSA, TX	S	8.67 MW	7.81 AW	18030 AAW	TXBLS	10//99-12//99
	Houston PMSA, TX	S	11.17 MW	9.66 AW	23230 AAW	TXBLS	10//99-12//99
	San Antonio MSA, TX	S	16.80 MW	18.75 AW	34950 AAW	TXBLS	10//99-12//99
	Utah	S	12.66 MW	13.71 AW	28510 AAW	UTBLS	10//99-12//99

AAW Average annual wage	AOH Average offered, high	ASH Average starting, high	H Hourly	M Monthly	S Special: hourly and annual
AE Average entry wage	AOL Average offered, low	ASL Average starting, low	HI Highest wage paid	MTC Median total compensation	TQ Third quartile wage
AEX Average experienced wage	APH Average pay, high range	AW Average wage paid	HR High end range	MW Median wage paid	W Weekly
AO Average offered	APL Average pay, low range	FQ First quartile wage	LR Low end range	SQ Second quartile wage	Y Yearly

Occupation/Type/Industry	Location	Per	Low	Mid	High	Source	Date
Broadcast Technician	Salt Lake City-Ogden MSA, UT	S	13.82 MW	12.73 AW	28750 AAW	UTBLS	10//99-12//99
	Virginia	S	10.62 MW	12.57 AW	26140 AAW	VABLS	10//99-12//99
	Washington	S	17.42 MW	16.46 AW	34240 AAW	WABLS	10//99-12//99
	Seattle-Bellevue-Everett PMSA, WA	S	17.48 MW	18.47 AW	36360 AAW	WABLS	10//99-12//99
	Huntington-Ashland MSA, WV-KY-OH	S	15.80 MW	14.26 AW	32860 AAW	WVBLS	10//99-12//99
	Wisconsin	S	16.53 MW	16.30 AW	33900 AAW	WIBLS	10//99-12//99
	Green Bay MSA, WI	S	10.48 MW	9.65 AW	21810 AAW	WIBLS	10//99-12//99
	Madison MSA, WI	S	12.78 MW	10.24 AW	26570 AAW	WIBLS	10//99-12//99
	Milwaukee-Waukesha PMSA, WI	S	21.09 MW	22.96 AW	43880 AAW	WIBLS	10//99-12//99
	Puerto Rico	S	9.99 MW	10.35 AW	21520 AAW	PRBLS	10//99-12//99
	San Juan-Bayamon PMSA, PR	S	10.41 MW	10.08 AW	21650 AAW	PRBLS	10//99-12//99
	Guam	S	7.94 MW	8.61 AW	17900 AAW	GUBLS	10//99-12//99
Broker							
Real Estate	United States	Y		59000 MW		REALM	4//99
Brokerage Clerk	Alabama	S	12.08 MW	11.57 AW	24060 AAW	ALBLS	10//99-12//99
	Arizona	S	13.84 MW	13.68 AW	28460 AAW	AZBLS	10//99-12//99
	Arkansas	S	10.24 MW	10.71 AW	22270 AAW	ARBLS	10//99-12//99
	California	S	15.54 MW	16.60 AW	34520 AAW	CABLS	10//99-12//99
	Connecticut	S	13.77 MW	14.39 AW	29930 AAW	CTBLS	10//99-12//99
	Delaware	S	15.69 MW	15.44 AW	32110 AAW	DEBLS	10//99-12//99
	District of Columbia	S	13.26 MW	14.40 AW	29960 AAW	DCBLS	10//99-12//99
	Florida	S	11.99 MW	12.55 AW	26100 AAW	FLBLS	10//99-12//99
	Georgia	S	14.16 MW	13.52 AW	28120 AAW	GABLS	10//99-12//99
	Idaho	S	10.27 MW	10.40 AW	21630 AAW	IDBLS	10//99-12//99
	Illinois	S	12.83 MW	13.90 AW	28910 AAW	ILBLS	10//99-12//99
	Indiana	S	12.11 MW	12.08 AW	25130 AAW	INBLS	10//99-12//99
	Iowa	S	11.52 MW	11.73 AW	24400 AAW	IABLS	10//99-12//99
	Kansas	S	12.79 MW	13.77 AW	28640 AAW	KSBLS	10//99-12//99
	Kentucky	S	11.18 MW	11.70 AW	24340 AAW	KYBLS	10//99-12//99
	Louisiana	S	12.75 MW	13.59 AW	28260 AAW	LABLS	10//99-12//99
	Maine	S	12.87 MW	14.06 AW	29240 AAW	MEBLS	10//99-12//99
	Maryland	S	13.4 MW	13.11 AW	27280 AAW	MDBLS	10//99-12//99
	Massachusetts	S	14.46 MW	15.35 AW	31930 AAW	MABLS	10//99-12//99
	Michigan	S	12.92 MW	13.09 AW	27230 AAW	MIBLS	10//99-12//99
	Minnesota	S	13.84 MW	14.21 AW	29560 AAW	MNBLS	10//99-12//99
	Mississippi	S	11.38 MW	11.69 AW	24320 AAW	MSBLS	10//99-12//99
	Montana	S	12.1 MW	12.38 AW	25750 AAW	MTBLS	10//99-12//99
	Nebraska	S	12.21 MW	11.76 AW	24450 AAW	NEBLS	10//99-12//99
	Nevada	S	13.78 MW	14.56 AW	30280 AAW	NVBLS	10//99-12//99
	New Hampshire	S	13.31 MW	14.32 AW	29800 AAW	NHBLS	10//99-12//99
	New Jersey	S	16.46 MW	16.93 AW	35210 AAW	NJBLS	10//99-12//99
	New Mexico	S	14.68 MW	14.36 AW	29870 AAW	NMBLS	10//99-12//99
	New York	S	16.42 MW	17.82 AW	37070 AAW	NYBLS	10//99 12//99
	North Carolina	S	12.61 MW	12.96 AW	26960 AAW	NCBLS	10//99-12//99
	Ohio	S	12.38 MW	14.88 AW	30940 AAW	OHBLS	10//99-12//99
	Oklahoma	S	10.31 MW	10.66 AW	22180 AAW	OKBLS	10//99-12//99
	Pennsylvania	S	12.34 MW	12.50 AW	25990 AAW	PABLS	10//99-12//99
	Rhode Island	S	13.6 MW	14.25 AW	29640 AAW	RIBLS	10//99-12//99
	South Carolina	S	11.47 MW	12.08 AW	25120 AAW	SCBLS	10//99-12//99
	South Dakota	S	11.67 MW	11.86 AW	24670 AAW	SDBLS	10//99-12//99
	Tennessee	S	13.24 MW	14.55 AW	30260 AAW	TNBLS	10//99-12//99
	Texas	S	11.4 MW	12.29 AW	25560 AAW	TXBLS	10//99-12//99
	Utah	S	13.47 MW	13.32 AW	27700 AAW	UTBLS	10//99-12//99
	Virginia	S	11.25 MW	11.95 AW	24850 AAW	VABLS	10//99-12//99
	Washington	S	13.43 MW	14.16 AW	29450 AAW	WABLS	10//99-12//99
	West Virginia	S	12.21 MW	13.36 AW	27790 AAW	WVBLS	10//99-12//99
	Wisconsin	S	11.57 MW	12.22 AW	25410 AAW	WIBLS	10//99-12//99
	Puerto Rico	S	12.9 MW	13.17 AW	27400 AAW	PRBLS	10//99-12//99
Budget Analyst	Alabama	S	21.86 MW	23.04 AW	47920 AAW	ALBLS	10//99-12//99
	Alaska	S	20.93 MW	22.03 AW	45820 AAW	AKBLS	10//99-12//99
	Arizona	S	21.96 MW	23.46 AW	48790 AAW	AZBLS	10//99-12//99
	Arkansas	S	19.55 MW	19.91 AW	41420 AAW	ARBLS	10//99-12//99
	California	S	24.65 MW	25.96 AW	54010 AAW	CABLS	10//99-12//99
	Colorado	S	22.2 MW	23.66 AW	49220 AAW	COBLS	10//99-12//99
	Connecticut	S	25.74 MW	26.46 AW	55040 AAW	CTBLS	10//99-12//99
	Delaware	S	26.05 MW	27.26 AW	56710 AAW	DEBLS	10//99-12//99

AAW	Average annual wage	AOH	Average offered, high	ASH	Average starting, high
AE	Average entry wage	AOL	Average offered, low	ASL	Average starting, low
AEX	Average experienced wage	APH	Average pay, high range	AW	Average wage paid
AO	Average offered	APL	Average pay, low range	FQ	First quartile wage

H	Hourly	M	Monthly	S	Special: hourly and annual
HI	Highest wage paid	MTC	Median total compensation	TQ	Third quartile wage
HR	High end range	MW	Median wage paid	W	Weekly
LR	Low end range	SQ	Second quartile wage	Y	Yearly

Occupation/Type/Industry	Location	Per	Low	Mid	High	Source	Date
Budget Analyst	Florida	S	21.05 MW	22.00 AW	45750 AAW	FLBLS	10//99-12//99
	Georgia	S	20.91 MW	21.72 AW	45170 AAW	GABLS	10//99-12//99
	Hawaii	S	21.44 MW	22.29 AW	46360 AAW	HIBLS	10//99-12//99
	Idaho	S	20.51 MW	22.25 AW	46270 AAW	IDBLS	10//99-12//99
	Illinois	S	18.24 MW	20.54 AW	42720 AAW	ILBLS	10//99-12//99
	Indiana	S	20.26 MW	20.90 AW	43470 AAW	INBLS	10//99-12//99
	Iowa	S	19.99 MW	20.83 AW	43330 AAW	IABLS	10//99-12//99
	Kansas	S	21.38 MW	22.53 AW	46870 AAW	KSBLS	10//99-12//99
	Kentucky	S	21.44 MW	22.07 AW	45900 AAW	KYBLS	10//99-12//99
	Louisiana	S	21.7 MW	23.23 AW	48330 AAW	LABLS	10//99-12//99
	Maine	S	19.95 MW	19.94 AW	41480 AAW	MEBLS	10//99-12//99
	Maryland	S	23.24 MW	24.24 AW	50420 AAW	MDBLS	10//99-12//99
	Massachusetts	S	24.87 MW	26.93 AW	56010 AAW	MABLS	10//99-12//99
	Michigan	S	23.13 MW	24.04 AW	50010 AAW	MIBLS	10//99-12//99
	Minnesota	S	22.76 MW	24.05 AW	50030 AAW	MNBLS	10//99-12//99
	Mississippi	S	18.86 MW	19.80 AW	41190 AAW	MSBLS	10//99-12//99
	Missouri	S	21.94 MW	23.64 AW	49180 AAW	MOBLS	10//99-12//99
	Montana	S	18.52 MW	19.14 AW	39800 AAW	MTBLS	10//99-12//99
	Nebraska	S	19.96 MW	20.47 AW	42570 AAW	NEBLS	10//99-12//99
	Nevada	S	21.61 MW	22.49 AW	46780 AAW	NVBLS	10//99-12//99
	New Hampshire	S	21.63 MW	21.67 AW	45070 AAW	NHBLS	10//99-12//99
	New Jersey	S	24.81 MW	25.98 AW	54040 AAW	NJBLS	10//99-12//99
	New Mexico	S	15.83 MW	17.33 AW	36060 AAW	NMBLS	10//99-12//99
	New York	S	24 MW	25.45 AW	52930 AAW	NYBLS	10//99-12//99
	North Carolina	S	21.83 MW	23.18 AW	48210 AAW	NCBLS	10//99-12//99
	North Dakota	S	16.77 MW	17.96 AW	37350 AAW	NDBLS	10//99-12//99
	Ohio	S	22.02 MW	23.19 AW	48230 AAW	OHBLS	10//99-12//99
	Oklahoma	S	19.78 MW	20.45 AW	42530 AAW	OKBLS	10//99-12//99
	Oregon	S	20.75 MW	21.42 AW	44540 AAW	ORBLS	10//99-12//99
	Pennsylvania	S	21.94 MW	23.20 AW	48250 AAW	PABLS	10//99-12//99
	Rhode Island	S	23.2 MW	24.40 AW	50750 AAW	RIBLS	10//99-12//99
	South Carolina	S	22.6 MW	24.63 AW	51220 AAW	SCBLS	10//99-12//99
	South Dakota	S	18.61 MW	19.22 AW	39980 AAW	SDBLS	10//99-12//99
	Tennessee	S	19.49 MW	20.34 AW	42300 AAW	TNBLS	10//99-12//99
	Texas	S	20.74 MW	22.50 AW	46790 AAW	TXBLS	10//99-12//99
	Utah	S	21.51 MW	22.71 AW	47230 AAW	UTBLS	10//99-12//99
	Vermont	S	23.08 MW	22.99 AW	47830 AAW	VTBLS	10//99-12//99
	Virginia	S	24.12 MW	25.01 AW	52010 AAW	VABLS	10//99-12//99
	Washington	S	22.44 MW	22.82 AW	47470 AAW	WABLS	10//99-12//99
	West Virginia	S	25.9 MW	26.52 AW	55160 AAW	WVBLS	10//99-12//99
	Wisconsin	S	20.49 MW	21.77 AW	45270 AAW	WIBLS	10//99-12//99
	Wyoming	S	20.28 MW	21.80 AW	45340 AAW	WYBLS	10//99-12//99
	Puerto Rico	S	12.6 MW	14.70 AW	30570 AAW	PRBLS	10//99-12//99
Bus and Truck Mechanic and Diesel Engine Specialist	Alabama	S	12.46 MW	12.84 AW	26700 AAW	ALBLS	10//99-12//99
	Anniston MSA, AL	S	13.18 MW	12.79 AW	27410 AAW	ALBLS	10//99-12//99
	Auburn-Opelika MSA, AL	S	12.32 MW	11.76 AW	25620 AAW	ALBLS	10//99-12//99
	Birmingham MSA, AL	S	14.18 MW	14.00 AW	29480 AAW	ALBLS	10//99-12//99
	Decatur MSA, AL	S	12.70 MW	12.77 AW	26420 AAW	ALBLS	10//99-12//99
	Dothan MSA, AL	S	13.01 MW	12.69 AW	27060 AAW	ALBLS	10//99-12//99
	Florence MSA, AL	S	12.36 MW	12.32 AW	25710 AAW	ALBLS	10//99-12//99
	Huntsville MSA, AL	S	12.77 MW	11.77 AW	26550 AAW	ALBLS	10//99-12//99
	Mobile MSA, AL	S	11.50 MW	11.39 AW	23920 AAW	ALBLS	10//99-12//99
	Montgomery MSA, AL	S	13.62 MW	13.34 AW	28320 AAW	ALBLS	10//99-12//99
	Tuscaloosa MSA, AL	S	12.73 MW	12.47 AW	26480 AAW	ALBLS	10//99-12//99
	Alaska	S	20.82 MW	21.24 AW	44180 AAW	AKBLS	10//99-12//99
	Anchorage MSA, AK	S	20.83 MW	21.19 AW	43320 AAW	AKBLS	10//99-12//99
	Arizona	S	15.08 MW	15.48 AW	32200 AAW	AZBLS	10//99-12//99
	Flagstaff MSA, AZ-UT	S	15.20 MW	15.02 AW	31620 AAW	AZBLS	10//99-12//99
	Phoenix-Mesa MSA, AZ	S	15.90 MW	15.50 AW	33080 AAW	AZBLS	10//99-12//99
	Tucson MSA, AZ	S	15.54 MW	15.10 AW	32330 AAW	AZBLS	10//99-12//99
	Yuma MSA, AZ	S	13.82 MW	13.25 AW	28750 AAW	AZBLS	10//99-12//99
	Arkansas	S	11.79 MW	12.26 AW	25490 AAW	ARBLS	10//99-12//99
	Fayetteville-Springdale-Rogers MSA, AR	S	12.53 MW	12.27 AW	26060 AAW	ARBLS	10//99-12//99
	Fort Smith MSA, AR-OK	S	12.01 MW	11.49 AW	24970 AAW	ARBLS	10//99-12//99
	Jonesboro MSA, AR	S	12.00 MW	11.94 AW	24960 AAW	ARBLS	10//99-12//99
	Little Rock-North Little Rock MSA, AR	S	13.64 MW	13.26 AW	28380 AAW	ARBLS	10//99-12//99
	Pine Bluff MSA, AR	S	12.19 MW	11.90 AW	25360 AAW	ARBLS	10//99-12//99
	California	S	17.16 MW	17.16 AW	35700 AAW	CABLS	10//99-12//99

Occupation/Type/Industry	Location	Per	Low	Mid	High	Source	Date
Bus and Truck Mechanic and Diesel Engine Specialist	Bakersfield MSA, CA	S	15.32 MW	15.53 AW	31870 AAW	CABLS	10//99-12//99
	Chico-Paradise MSA, CA	S	13.26 MW	13.21 AW	27580 AAW	CABLS	10//99-12//99
	Fresno MSA, CA	S	15.46 MW	15.97 AW	32160 AAW	CABLS	10//99-12//99
	Los Angeles-Long Beach PMSA, CA	S	17.28 MW	17.25 AW	35940 AAW	CABLS	10//99-12//99
	Merced MSA, CA	S	14.24 MW	13.82 AW	29620 AAW	CABLS	10//99-12//99
	Modesto MSA, CA	S	17.32 MW	17.44 AW	36030 AAW	CABLS	10//99-12//99
	Oakland PMSA, CA	S	20.50 MW	19.88 AW	42630 AAW	CABLS	10//99-12//99
	Orange County PMSA, CA	S	16.97 MW	17.25 AW	35290 AAW	CABLS	10//99-12//99
	Redding MSA, CA	S	15.83 MW	15.46 AW	32930 AAW	CABLS	10//99-12//99
	Riverside-San Bernardino PMSA, CA	S	13.99 MW	12.32 AW	29090 AAW	CABLS	10//99-12//99
	Sacramento PMSA, CA	S	17.15 MW	17.00 AW	35670 AAW	CABLS	10//99-12//99
	Salinas MSA, CA	S	16.82 MW	16.04 AW	34990 AAW	CABLS	10//99-12//99
	San Diego MSA, CA	S	19.58 MW	18.43 AW	40740 AAW	CABLS	10//99-12//99
	San Francisco PMSA, CA	S	17.78 MW	17.86 AW	36990 AAW	CABLS	10//99-12//99
	San Jose PMSA, CA	S	20.31 MW	20.47 AW	42240 AAW	CABLS	10//99-12//99
	San Luis Obispo-Atascadero-Paso Robles MSA, CA	S	15.64 MW	15.57 AW	32540 AAW	CABLS	10//99-12//99
	Santa Barbara-Santa Maria-Lompoc MSA, CA	S	15.41 MW	15.82 AW	32050 AAW	CABLS	10//99-12//99
	Santa Cruz-Watsonville PMSA, CA	S	16.36 MW	17.05 AW	34040 AAW	CABLS	10//99-12//99
	Santa Rosa PMSA, CA	S	16.60 MW	16.55 AW	34540 AAW	CABLS	10//99-12//99
	Stockton-Lodi MSA, CA	S	16.14 MW	16.85 AW	33570 AAW	CABLS	10//99-12//99
	Vallejo-Fairfield-Napa PMSA, CA	S	19.25 MW	18.50 AW	40050 AAW	CABLS	10//99-12//99
	Ventura PMSA, CA	S	18.78 MW	19.03 AW	39060 AAW	CABLS	10//99-12//99
	Visalia-Tulare-Porterville MSA, CA	S	14.16 MW	14.54 AW	29450 AAW	CABLS	10//99-12//99
	Yolo PMSA, CA	S	19.36 MW	20.72 AW	40270 AAW	CABLS	10//99-12//99
	Yuba City MSA, CA	S	14.99 MW	13.90 AW	31190 AAW	CABLS	10//99-12//99
	Colorado	S	16.04 MW	16.15 AW	33590 AAW	COBLS	10//99-12//99
	Boulder-Longmont PMSA, CO	S	15.21 MW	15.03 AW	31630 AAW	COBLS	10//99-12//99
	Colorado Springs MSA, CO	S	15.01 MW	14.93 AW	31220 AAW	COBLS	10//99-12//99
	Denver PMSA, CO	S	16.67 MW	16.64 AW	34670 AAW	COBLS	10//99-12//99
	Fort Collins-Loveland MSA, CO	S	16.78 MW	16.46 AW	34910 AAW	COBLS	10//99-12//99
	Grand Junction MSA, CO	S	15.02 MW	15.07 AW	31230 AAW	COBLS	10//99-12//99
	Greeley PMSA, CO	S	14.43 MW	14.31 AW	30010 AAW	COBLS	10//99-12//99
	Pueblo MSA, CO	S	14.46 MW	14.21 AW	30080 AAW	COBLS	10//99-12//99
	Connecticut	S	17.67 MW	17.75 AW	36930 AAW	CTBLS	10//99-12//99
	Bridgeport PMSA, CT	S	17.98 MW	17.75 AW	37390 AAW	CTBLS	10//99-12//99
	Danbury PMSA, CT	S	17.88 MW	17.88 AW	37200 AAW	CTBLS	10//99-12//99
	Hartford MSA, CT	S	17.55 MW	17.49 AW	36500 AAW	CTBLS	10//99-12//99
	New Haven-Meriden PMSA, CT	S	19.31 MW	18.76 AW	40160 AAW	CTBLS	10//99-12//99
	New London-Norwich MSA, CT-RI	S	15.58 MW	15.22 AW	32400 AAW	CTBLS	10//99-12//99
	Stamford-Norwalk PMSA, CT	S	19.28 MW	18.99 AW	40090 AAW	CTBLS	10//99-12//99
	Waterbury PMSA, CT	S	17.14 MW	17.02 AW	35640 AAW	CTBLS	10//99-12//99
	Delaware	S	13.51 MW	14.49 AW	30140 AAW	DEBLS	10//99-12//99
	Dover MSA, DE	S	12.95 MW	12.53 AW	26940 AAW	DEBLS	10//99-12//99
	Wilmington-Newark PMSA, DE-MD	S	15.14 MW	14.69 AW	31480 AAW	DEBLS	10//99-12//99
	District of Columbia	S	13.19 MW	15.27 AW	31760 AAW	DCBLS	10//99-12//99
	Washington PMSA, DC-MD-VA-WV	S	16.04 MW	15.66 AW	33360 AAW	DCBLS	10//99-12//99
	Florida	S	13.68 MW	14.34 AW	29830 AAW	FLBLS	10//99-12//99
	Daytona Beach MSA, FL	S	11.41 MW	11.48 AW	23730 AAW	FLBLS	10//99-12//99
	Fort Lauderdale PMSA, FL	S	16.65 MW	16.06 AW	34620 AAW	FLBLS	10//99-12//99
	Fort Myers-Cape Coral MSA, FL	S	14.32 MW	13.23 AW	29790 AAW	FLBLS	10//99-12//99
	Fort Pierce-Port St. Lucie MSA, FL	S	14.67 MW	14.06 AW	30510 AAW	FLBLS	10//99-12//99
	Gainesville MSA, FL	S	13.11 MW	12.38 AW	27270 AAW	FLBLS	10//99-12//99
	Jacksonville MSA, FL	S	13.98 MW	13.38 AW	29070 AAW	FLBLS	10//99-12//99
	Lakeland-Winter Haven MSA, FL	S	13.18 MW	12.90 AW	27420 AAW	FLBLS	10//99-12//99
	Melbourne-Titusville-Palm Bay MSA, FL	S	14.06 MW	12.09 AW	29240 AAW	FLBLS	10//99-12//99

AAW Average annual wage	AOH Average offered, high	ASH Average starting, high	H Hourly	M Monthly	S Special: hourly and annual
AE Average entry wage	AOL Average offered, low	ASL Average starting, low	HI Highest wage paid	MTC Median total compensation	TQ Third quartile wage
AEX Average experienced wage	APH Average pay, high range	AW Average wage paid	HR High end range	MW Median wage paid	W Weekly
AO Average offered	APL Average pay, low range	FQ First quartile wage	LR Low end range	SQ Second quartile wage	Y Yearly

Occupation/Type/Industry	Location	Per	Low	Mid	High	Source	Date
Bus and Truck Mechanic and Diesel Engine Specialist	Miami PMSA, FL	S	16.95 MW	16.95 AW	35250 AAW	FLBLS	10//99-12//99
	Naples MSA, FL	S	14.11 MW	13.75 AW	29350 AAW	FLBLS	10//99-12//99
	Ocala MSA, FL	S	13.05 MW	13.35 AW	27140 AAW	FLBLS	10//99-12//99
	Orlando MSA, FL	S	14.23 MW	13.67 AW	29610 AAW	FLBLS	10//99-12//99
	Panama City MSA, FL	S	13.12 MW	12.53 AW	27290 AAW	FLBLS	10//99-12//99
	Pensacola MSA, FL	S	13.80 MW	13.85 AW	28690 AAW	FLBLS	10//99-12//99
	Sarasota-Bradenton MSA, FL	S	13.84 MW	13.27 AW	28780 AAW	FLBLS	10//99-12//99
	Tallahassee MSA, FL	S	12.66 MW	12.65 AW	26320 AAW	FLBLS	10//99-12//99
	Tampa-St. Petersburg-Clearwater MSA, FL	S	13.67 MW	13.42 AW	28440 AAW	FLBLS	10//99-12//99
	West Palm Beach-Boca Raton MSA, FL	S	15.11 MW	15.00 AW	31440 AAW	FLBLS	10//99-12//99
	Georgia	S	14.5 MW	15.59 AW	32430 AAW	GABLS	10//99-12//99
	Albany MSA, GA	S	13.79 MW	14.08 AW	28680 AAW	GABLS	10//99-12//99
	Athens MSA, GA	S	12.84 MW	12.48 AW	26720 AAW	GABLS	10//99-12//99
	Atlanta MSA, GA	S	16.76 MW	15.30 AW	34860 AAW	GABLS	10//99-12//99
	Augusta-Aiken MSA, GA-SC	S	16.36 MW	14.78 AW	34040 AAW	GABLS	10//99-12//99
	Columbus MSA, GA-AL	S	13.31 MW	12.94 AW	27680 AAW	GABLS	10//99-12//99
	Macon MSA, GA	S	14.47 MW	14.52 AW	30090 AAW	GABLS	10//99-12//99
	Savannah MSA, GA	S	14.78 MW	14.62 AW	30730 AAW	GABLS	10//99-12//99
	Hawaii	S	18.08 MW	18.86 AW	39230 AAW	HIBLS	10//99-12//99
	Honolulu MSA, HI	S	19.03 MW	18.53 AW	39570 AAW	HIBLS	10//99-12//99
	Idaho	S	14.4 MW	14.05 AW	29230 AAW	IDBLS	10//99-12//99
	Boise City MSA, ID	S	14.74 MW	14.85 AW	30660 AAW	IDBLS	10//99-12//99
	Illinois	S	16.71 MW	17.32 AW	36020 AAW	ILBLS	10//99-12//99
	Bloomington-Normal MSA, IL	S	14.35 MW	14.01 AW	29840 AAW	ILBLS	10//99-12//99
	Champaign-Urbana MSA, IL	S	13.98 MW	13.22 AW	29080 AAW	ILBLS	10//99-12//99
	Chicago PMSA, IL	S	18.79 MW	18.80 AW	39080 AAW	ILBLS	10//99-12//99
	Decatur MSA, IL	S	15.41 MW	13.85 AW	32060 AAW	ILBLS	10//99-12//99
	Kankakee PMSA, IL	S	15.02 MW	16.14 AW	31240 AAW	ILBLS	10//99-12//99
	Peoria-Pekin MSA, IL	S	16.93 MW	16.10 AW	35220 AAW	ILBLS	10//99-12//99
	Rockford MSA, IL	S	17.30 MW	16.98 AW	35980 AAW	ILBLS	10//99-12//99
	Springfield MSA, IL	S	18.02 MW	15.53 AW	37490 AAW	ILBLS	10//99-12//99
	Indiana	S	14.23 MW	14.47 AW	30100 AAW	INBLS	10//99-12//99
	Bloomington MSA, IN	S	13.65 MW	13.09 AW	28400 AAW	INBLS	10//99-12//99
	Elkhart-Goshen MSA, IN	S	14.16 MW	14.06 AW	29460 AAW	INBLS	10//99-12//99
	Evansville-Henderson MSA, IN-KY	S	12.89 MW	12.33 AW	26810 AAW	INBLS	10//99-12//99
	Fort Wayne MSA, IN	S	14.72 MW	14.58 AW	30620 AAW	INBLS	10//99-12//99
	Gary PMSA, IN	S	15.34 MW	15.07 AW	31910 AAW	INBLS	10//99-12//99
	Indianapolis MSA, IN	S	15.71 MW	15.90 AW	32680 AAW	INBLS	10//99-12//99
	Kokomo MSA, IN	S	14.43 MW	14.83 AW	30020 AAW	INBLS	10//99-12//99
	Lafayette MSA, IN	S	15.50 MW	15.11 AW	32250 AAW	INBLS	10//99-12//99
	South Bend MSA, IN	S	14.31 MW	14.35 AW	29770 AAW	INBLS	10//99-12//99
	Terre Haute MSA, IN	S	14.82 MW	14.25 AW	30820 AAW	INBLS	10//99-12//99
	Iowa	S	13.39 MW	13.75 AW	28590 AAW	IABLS	10//99-12//99
	Cedar Rapids MSA, IA	S	14.17 MW	14.43 AW	29480 AAW	IABLS	10//99-12//99
	Davenport-Moline-Rock Island MSA, IA-IL	S	13.11 MW	12.57 AW	27270 AAW	IABLS	10//99-12//99
	Des Moines MSA, IA	S	14.36 MW	14.01 AW	29870 AAW	IABLS	10//99-12//99
	Dubuque MSA, IA	S	14.44 MW	14.51 AW	30040 AAW	IABLS	10//99-12//99
	Iowa City MSA, IA	S	14.05 MW	13.69 AW	29230 AAW	IABLS	10//99-12//99
	Sioux City MSA, IA-NE	S	12.87 MW	12.77 AW	26770 AAW	IABLS	10//99-12//99
	Waterloo-Cedar Falls MSA, IA	S	13.29 MW	13.22 AW	27640 AAW	IABLS	10//99-12//99
	Kansas	S	13.34 MW	13.78 AW	28650 AAW	KSBLS	10//99-12//99
	Topeka MSA, KS	S	14.31 MW	13.60 AW	29760 AAW	KSBLS	10//99-12//99
	Wichita MSA, KS	S	13.79 MW	13.09 AW	28690 AAW	KSBLS	10//99-12//99
	Kentucky	S	12.92 MW	13.37 AW	27800 AAW	KYBLS	10//99-12//99
	Lexington MSA, KY	S	14.01 MW	13.86 AW	29140 AAW	KYBLS	10//99-12//99
	Louisville MSA, KY-IN	S	14.57 MW	14.25 AW	30300 AAW	KYBLS	10//99-12//99
	Owensboro MSA, KY	S	12.69 MW	12.55 AW	26390 AAW	KYBLS	10//99-12//99
	Louisiana	S	13.01 MW	13.59 AW	28280 AAW	LABLS	10//99-12//99
	Alexandria MSA, LA	S	13.60 MW	13.32 AW	28280 AAW	LABLS	10//99-12//99
	Baton Rouge MSA, LA	S	14.29 MW	13.43 AW	29730 AAW	LABLS	10//99-12//99
	Houma MSA, LA	S	13.28 MW	12.98 AW	27610 AAW	LABLS	10//99-12//99
	Lafayette MSA, LA	S	13.29 MW	12.63 AW	27640 AAW	LABLS	10//99-12//99
	Lake Charles MSA, LA	S	12.86 MW	12.12 AW	26750 AAW	LABLS	10//99-12//99
	Monroe MSA, LA	S	12.27 MW	12.37 AW	25510 AAW	LABLS	10//99-12//99
	New Orleans MSA, LA	S	14.87 MW	13.91 AW	30930 AAW	LABLS	10//99-12//99
	Shreveport-Bossier City MSA, LA	S	12.72 MW	12.27 AW	26450 AAW	LABLS	10//99-12//99

AAW Average annual wage	**AOH** Average offered, high	**ASH** Average starting, high	**H** Hourly	**M** Monthly	**S** Special: hourly and annual
AE Average entry wage	**AOL** Average offered, low	**ASL** Average starting, low	**HI** Highest wage paid	**MTC** Median total compensation	**TQ** Third quartile wage
AEX Average experienced wage	**APH** Average pay, high range	**AW** Average wage paid	**HR** High end range	**MW** Median wage paid	**W** Weekly
AO Average offered	**APL** Average pay, low range	**FQ** First quartile wage	**LR** Low end range	**SQ** Second quartile wage	**Y** Yearly

Occupation/Type/Industry	Location	Per	Low	Mid	High	Source	Date
Bus and Truck Mechanic and Diesel Engine Specialist	Maine	S	12.74 MW	12.98 AW	27000 AAW	MEBLS	10//99-12//99
	Bangor MSA, ME	S	13.26 MW	13.34 AW	27570 AAW	MEBLS	10//99-12//99
	Lewiston-Auburn MSA, ME	S	12.87 MW	12.62 AW	26770 AAW	MEBLS	10//99-12//99
	Portland MSA, ME	S	14.02 MW	13.82 AW	29160 AAW	MEBLS	10//99-12//99
	Maryland	S	14.86 MW	15.26 AW	31740 AAW	MDBLS	10//99-12//99
	Baltimore PMSA, MD	S	15.74 MW	15.32 AW	32740 AAW	MDBLS	10//99-12//99
	Cumberland MSA, MD-WV	S	11.68 MW	11.76 AW	24300 AAW	MDBLS	10//99-12//99
	Hagerstown PMSA, MD	S	13.55 MW	13.16 AW	28190 AAW	MDBLS	10//99-12//99
	Massachusetts	S	16.52 MW	16.76 AW	34860 AAW	MABLS	10//99-12//99
	Barnstable-Yarmouth MSA, MA	S	17.11 MW	16.51 AW	35600 AAW	MABLS	10//99-12//99
	Boston PMSA, MA-NH	S	17.36 MW	17.13 AW	36110 AAW	MABLS	10//99-12//99
	Brockton PMSA, MA	S	16.35 MW	15.60 AW	34020 AAW	MABLS	10//99-12//99
	Fitchburg-Leominster PMSA, MA	S	15.83 MW	15.27 AW	32920 AAW	MABLS	10//99-12//99
	Lawrence PMSA, MA-NH	S	16.01 MW	15.32 AW	33310 AAW	MABLS	10//99-12//99
	Lowell PMSA, MA-NH	S	17.71 MW	17.82 AW	36840 AAW	MABLS	10//99-12//99
	New Bedford PMSA, MA	S	15.72 MW	15.56 AW	32700 AAW	MABLS	10//99-12//99
	Pittsfield MSA, MA	S	15.67 MW	15.12 AW	32590 AAW	MABLS	10//99-12//99
	Springfield MSA, MA	S	15.02 MW	14.92 AW	31240 AAW	MABLS	10//99-12//99
	Worcester PMSA, MA-CT	S	16.92 MW	16.72 AW	35200 AAW	MABLS	10//99-12//99
	Michigan	S	15.9 MW	16.33 AW	33960 AAW	MIBLS	10//99-12//99
	Ann Arbor PMSA, MI	S	16.82 MW	16.87 AW	34990 AAW	MIBLS	10//99-12//99
	Benton Harbor MSA, MI	S	15.76 MW	15.25 AW	32770 AAW	MIBLS	10//99-12//99
	Detroit PMSA, MI	S	17.79 MW	17.76 AW	37000 AAW	MIBLS	10//99-12//99
	Flint PMSA, MI	S	18.82 MW	19.03 AW	39150 AAW	MIBLS	10//99-12//99
	Grand Rapids-Muskegon-Holland MSA, MI	S	16.04 MW	16.12 AW	33370 AAW	MIBLS	10//99-12//99
	Jackson MSA, MI	S	14.27 MW	14.59 AW	29690 AAW	MIBLS	10//99-12//99
	Kalamazoo-Battle Creek MSA, MI	S	13.66 MW	13.54 AW	28420 AAW	MIBLS	10//99-12//99
	Lansing-East Lansing MSA, MI	S	15.36 MW	14.82 AW	31950 AAW	MIBLS	10//99-12//99
	Saginaw-Bay City-Midland MSA, MI	S	16.61 MW	15.24 AW	34550 AAW	MIBLS	10//99-12//99
	Minnesota	S	16.61 MW	16.51 AW	34330 AAW	MNBLS	10//99-12//99
	Duluth-Superior MSA, MN-WI	S	14.10 MW	13.98 AW	29320 AAW	MNBLS	10//99-12//99
	Minneapolis-St. Paul MSA, MN-WI	S	17.75 MW	18.00 AW	36910 AAW	MNBLS	10//99-12//99
	Rochester MSA, MN	S	14.22 MW	13.36 AW	29580 AAW	MNBLS	10//99-12//99
	St. Cloud MSA, MN	S	14.44 MW	13.87 AW	30040 AAW	MNBLS	10//99-12//99
	Mississippi	S	12.5 MW	12.74 AW	26500 AAW	MSBLS	10//99-12//99
	Biloxi-Gulfport-Pascagoula MSA, MS	S	14.35 MW	14.31 AW	29850 AAW	MSBLS	10//99-12//99
	Hattiesburg MSA, MS	S	12.40 MW	11.67 AW	25790 AAW	MSBLS	10//99-12//99
	Jackson MSA, MS	S	13.88 MW	13.75 AW	28870 AAW	MSBLS	10//99-12//99
	Missouri	S	14.2 MW	14.63 AW	30420 AAW	MOBLS	10//99-12//99
	Joplin MSA, MO	S	14.12 MW	12.85 AW	29370 AAW	MOBLS	10//99-12//99
	Kansas City MSA, MO-KS	S	14.86 MW	14.63 AW	30900 AAW	MOBLS	10//99-12//99
	St. Joseph MSA, MO	S	14.21 MW	13.08 AW	29570 AAW	MOBLS	10//99-12//99
	St. Louis MSA, MO-IL	S	16.11 MW	15.96 AW	33510 AAW	MOBLS	10//99-12//99
	Springfield MSA, MO	S	14.27 MW	13.87 AW	29680 AAW	MOBLS	10//99-12//99
	Montana	S	14.11 MW	14.16 AW	29450 AAW	MTBLS	10//99-12//99
	Billings MSA, MT	S	14.84 MW	14.64 AW	30860 AAW	MTBLS	10//99-12//99
	Great Falls MSA, MT	S	13.63 MW	14.25 AW	28340 AAW	MTBLS	10//99-12//99
	Missoula MSA, MT	S	13.97 MW	14.55 AW	29050 AAW	MTBLS	10//99-12//99
	Nebraska	S	12.5 MW	12.87 AW	26770 AAW	NEBLS	10//99-12//99
	Lincoln MSA, NE	S	13.21 MW	12.86 AW	27480 AAW	NEBLS	10//99-12//99
	Omaha MSA, NE-IA	S	14.03 MW	13.93 AW	29170 AAW	NEBLS	10//99-12//99
	Nevada	S	17.4 MW	17.64 AW	36680 AAW	NVBLS	10//99-12//99
	Las Vegas MSA, NV-AZ	S	17.02 MW	16.85 AW	35410 AAW	NVBLS	10//99-12//99
	Reno MSA, NV	S	18.36 MW	18.28 AW	38190 AAW	NVBLS	10//99-12//99
	New Hampshire	S	15.25 MW	15.32 AW	31870 AAW	NHBLS	10//99-12//99
	Manchester PMSA, NH	S	15.59 MW	15.35 AW	32430 AAW	NHBLS	10//99-12//99
	Nashua PMSA, NH	S	14.97 MW	14.88 AW	31140 AAW	NHBLS	10//99-12//99
	Portsmouth-Rochester PMSA, NH-ME	S	14.14 MW	14.49 AW	29410 AAW	NHBLS	10//99-12//99
	New Jersey	S	17.23 MW	17.51 AW	36410 AAW	NJBLS	10//99-12//99
	Atlantic-Cape May PMSA, NJ	S	15.10 MW	15.23 AW	31400 AAW	NJBLS	10//99-12//99
	Bergen-Passaic PMSA, NJ	S	18.83 MW	18.28 AW	39170 AAW	NJBLS	10//99-12//99
	Jersey City PMSA, NJ	S	18.19 MW	17.64 AW	37840 AAW	NJBLS	10//99-12//99

AAW	Average annual wage	AOH	Average offered, high	ASH	Average starting, high	H	Hourly	M	Monthly	S	Special: hourly and annual
AE	Average entry wage	AOL	Average offered, low	ASL	Average starting, low	HI	Highest wage paid	MTC	Median total compensation	TQ	Third quartile wage
AEX	Average experienced wage	APH	Average pay, high range	AW	Average wage paid	HR	High end range	MW	Median wage paid	W	Weekly
AO	Average offered	APL	Average pay, low range	FQ	First quartile wage	LR	Low end range	SQ	Second quartile wage	Y	Yearly

Occupation/Type/Industry	Location	Per	Low	Mid	High	Source	Date
Bus and Truck Mechanic and Diesel Engine Specialist							
	Middlesex-Somerset-Hunterdon PMSA, NJ	S	17.53 MW	17.88 AW	36460 AAW	NJBLS	10//99-12//99
	Monmouth-Ocean PMSA, NJ	S	17.73 MW	17.06 AW	36880 AAW	NJBLS	10//99-12//99
	Newark PMSA, NJ	S	18.76 MW	18.45 AW	39020 AAW	NJBLS	10//99-12//99
	Trenton PMSA, NJ	S	17.23 MW	17.34 AW	35840 AAW	NJBLS	10//99-12//99
	Vineland-Millville-Bridgeton PMSA, NJ	S	15.09 MW	14.17 AW	31390 AAW	NJBLS	10//99-12//99
	New Mexico	S	13.29 MW	13.63 AW	28340 AAW	NMBLS	10//99-12//99
	Albuquerque MSA, NM	S	14.21 MW	13.98 AW	29560 AAW	NMBLS	10//99-12//99
	Las Cruces MSA, NM	S	12.63 MW	12.51 AW	26270 AAW	NMBLS	10//99-12//99
	New York	S	16.14 MW	16.97 AW	35290 AAW	NYBLS	10//99-12//99
	Albany-Schenectady-Troy MSA, NY	S	16.29 MW	16.13 AW	33890 AAW	NYBLS	10//99-12//99
	Binghamton MSA, NY	S	13.55 MW	13.21 AW	28190 AAW	NYBLS	10//99-12//99
	Buffalo-Niagara Falls MSA, NY	S	15.67 MW	15.79 AW	32600 AAW	NYBLS	10//99-12//99
	Dutchess County PMSA, NY	S	16.00 MW	16.01 AW	33290 AAW	NYBLS	10//99-12//99
	Elmira MSA, NY	S	15.12 MW	14.18 AW	31450 AAW	NYBLS	10//99-12//99
	Glens Falls MSA, NY	S	17.52 MW	16.18 AW	36450 AAW	NYBLS	10//99-12//99
	Jamestown MSA, NY	S	14.02 MW	13.62 AW	29160 AAW	NYBLS	10//99-12//99
	Nassau-Suffolk PMSA, NY	S	18.69 MW	18.12 AW	38870 AAW	NYBLS	10//99-12//99
	New York PMSA, NY	S	19.73 MW	19.55 AW	41040 AAW	NYBLS	10//99-12//99
	Newburgh PMSA, NY-PA	S	16.44 MW	16.65 AW	34190 AAW	NYBLS	10//99-12//99
	Rochester MSA, NY	S	15.27 MW	14.77 AW	31760 AAW	NYBLS	10//99-12//99
	Syracuse MSA, NY	S	14.39 MW	13.63 AW	29930 AAW	NYBLS	10//99-12//99
	Utica-Rome MSA, NY	S	15.14 MW	13.61 AW	31490 AAW	NYBLS	10//99-12//99
	North Carolina	S	13.64 MW	14.03 AW	29180 AAW	NCBLS	10//99-12//99
	Asheville MSA, NC	S	14.39 MW	14.55 AW	29930 AAW	NCBLS	10//99-12//99
	Charlotte-Gastonia-Rock Hill MSA, NC-SC	S	15.48 MW	15.16 AW	32200 AAW	NCBLS	10//99-12//99
	Fayetteville MSA, NC	S	12.42 MW	12.26 AW	25830 AAW	NCBLS	10//99-12//99
	Goldsboro MSA, NC	S	11.64 MW	10.48 AW	24210 AAW	NCBLS	10//99-12//99
	Greensboro--Winston-Salem--High Point MSA, NC	S	14.93 MW	14.56 AW	31060 AAW	NCBLS	10//99-12//99
	Greenville MSA, NC	S	13.25 MW	13.67 AW	27550 AAW	NCBLS	10//99-12//99
	Hickory-Morganton-Lenoir MSA, NC	S	13.49 MW	13.11 AW	28060 AAW	NCBLS	10//99-12//99
	Jacksonville MSA, NC	S	11.35 MW	11.08 AW	23620 AAW	NCBLS	10//99-12//99
	Raleigh-Durham-Chapel Hill MSA, NC	S	14.41 MW	14.48 AW	29970 AAW	NCBLS	10//99-12//99
	Rocky Mount MSA, NC	S	13.46 MW	13.05 AW	28000 AAW	NCBLS	10//99-12//99
	Wilmington MSA, NC	S	12.90 MW	12.36 AW	26840 AAW	NCBLS	10//99-12//99
	North Dakota	S	13.23 MW	13.05 AW	27130 AAW	NDBLS	10//99-12//99
	Bismarck MSA, ND	S	13.75 MW	13.08 AW	28590 AAW	NDBLS	10//99-12//99
	Fargo-Moorhead MSA, ND-MN	S	12.82 MW	13.02 AW	26670 AAW	NDBLS	10//99-12//99
	Grand Forks MSA, ND-MN	S	13.86 MW	14.35 AW	28820 AAW	NDBLS	10//99-12//99
	Ohio	S	14.41 MW	14.99 AW	31170 AAW	OHBLS	10//99-12//99
	Akron PMSA, OH	S	16.54 MW	16.16 AW	34410 AAW	OHBLS	10//99-12//99
	Canton-Massillon MSA, OH	S	14.67 MW	14.39 AW	30510 AAW	OHBLS	10//99-12//99
	Cincinnati PMSA, OH-KY-IN	S	14.91 MW	14.72 AW	31010 AAW	OHBLS	10//99-12//99
	Cleveland-Lorain-Elyria PMSA, OH	S	16.69 MW	16.52 AW	34710 AAW	OHBLS	10//99-12//99
	Columbus MSA, OH	S	14.82 MW	14.01 AW	30820 AAW	OHBLS	10//99-12//99
	Dayton-Springfield MSA, OH	S	15.23 MW	14.99 AW	31670 AAW	OHBLS	10//99-12//99
	Hamilton-Middletown PMSA, OH	S	16.15 MW	15.98 AW	33600 AAW	OHBLS	10//99-12//99
	Lima MSA, OH	S	14.10 MW	14.19 AW	29320 AAW	OHBLS	10//99-12//99
	Mansfield MSA, OH	S	14.91 MW	12.89 AW	31010 AAW	OHBLS	10//99-12//99
	Steubenville-Weirton MSA, OH-WV	S	14.99 MW	15.98 AW	31170 AAW	OHBLS	10//99-12//99
	Toledo MSA, OH	S	15.77 MW	15.63 AW	32800 AAW	OHBLS	10//99-12//99
	Youngstown-Warren MSA, OH	S	13.75 MW	13.31 AW	28600 AAW	OHBLS	10//99-12//99
	Oklahoma	S	12.52 MW	13.18 AW	27410 AAW	OKBLS	10//99-12//99
	Lawton MSA, OK	S	12.17 MW	12.09 AW	25320 AAW	OKBLS	10//99-12//99
	Oklahoma City MSA, OK	S	13.53 MW	12.59 AW	28130 AAW	OKBLS	10//99-12//99
	Tulsa MSA, OK	S	13.75 MW	13.49 AW	28590 AAW	OKBLS	10//99-12//99
	Oregon	S	16.26 MW	16.09 AW	33470 AAW	ORBLS	10//99-12//99
	Eugene-Springfield MSA, OR	S	15.00 MW	14.89 AW	31190 AAW	ORBLS	10//99-12//99
	Medford-Ashland MSA, OR	S	15.64 MW	16.29 AW	32530 AAW	ORBLS	10//99-12//99

AAW	Average annual wage	AOH	Average offered, high	ASH	Average starting, high
AE	Average entry wage	AOL	Average offered, low	ASL	Average starting, low
AEX	Average experienced wage	APH	Average pay, high range	AW	Average wage paid
AO	Average offered	APL	Average pay, low range	FQ	First quartile wage

H	Hourly	M	Monthly	S	Special: hourly and annual
HI	Highest wage paid	MTC	Median total compensation	TQ	Third quartile wage
HR	High end range	MW	Median wage paid	W	Weekly
LR	Low end range	SQ	Second quartile wage	Y	Yearly

Bus and Truck Mechanic and Diesel Engine Specialist

Occupation/Type/Industry	Location	Per	Low	Mid	High	Source	Date
	Portland-Vancouver PMSA, OR-WA	S	17.16 MW	17.65 AW	35690 AAW	ORBLS	10//99-12//99
	Salem PMSA, OR	S	15.66 MW	15.64 AW	32580 AAW	ORBLS	10//99-12//99
	Pennsylvania	S	14.92 MW	15.20 AW	31620 AAW	PABLS	10//99-12//99
	Allentown-Bethlehem-Easton MSA, PA	S	14.92 MW	14.84 AW	31040 AAW	PABLS	10//99-12//99
	Altoona MSA, PA	S	12.85 MW	12.37 AW	26720 AAW	PABLS	10//99-12//99
	Erie MSA, PA	S	15.38 MW	15.05 AW	32000 AAW	PABLS	10//99-12//99
	Harrisburg-Lebanon-Carlisle MSA, PA	S	16.48 MW	16.06 AW	34280 AAW	PABLS	10//99-12//99
	Johnstown MSA, PA	S	12.60 MW	12.13 AW	26200 AAW	PABLS	10//99-12//99
	Lancaster MSA, PA	S	14.47 MW	14.43 AW	30090 AAW	PABLS	10//99-12//99
	Philadelphia PMSA, PA-NJ	S	16.79 MW	16.53 AW	34930 AAW	PABLS	10//99-12//99
	Pittsburgh MSA, PA	S	14.94 MW	14.65 AW	31070 AAW	PABLS	10//99-12//99
	Reading MSA, PA	S	15.13 MW	14.92 AW	31480 AAW	PABLS	10//99-12//99
	Scranton--Wilkes-Barre--Hazleton MSA, PA	S	13.31 MW	12.98 AW	27680 AAW	PABLS	10//99-12//99
	Sharon MSA, PA	S	12.46 MW	12.27 AW	25920 AAW	PABLS	10//99-12//99
	State College MSA, PA	S	12.90 MW	12.33 AW	26820 AAW	PABLS	10//99-12//99
	Williamsport MSA, PA	S	14.00 MW	13.71 AW	29110 AAW	PABLS	10//99-12//99
	York MSA, PA	S	13.85 MW	13.21 AW	28810 AAW	PABLS	10//99-12//99
	Rhode Island	S	15.72 MW	16.37 AW	34050 AAW	RIBLS	10//99-12//99
	Providence-Fall River-Warwick MSA, RI-MA	S	16.24 MW	15.65 AW	33770 AAW	RIBLS	10//99-12//99
	South Carolina	S	13.9 MW	14.56 AW	30280 AAW	SCBLS	10//99-12//99
	Charleston-North Charleston MSA, SC	S	13.52 MW	12.93 AW	28120 AAW	SCBLS	10//99-12//99
	Columbia MSA, SC	S	16.17 MW	14.99 AW	33630 AAW	SCBLS	10//99-12//99
	Florence MSA, SC	S	11.73 MW	11.53 AW	24400 AAW	SCBLS	10//99-12//99
	Greenville-Spartanburg-Anderson MSA, SC	S	14.62 MW	14.69 AW	30410 AAW	SCBLS	10//99-12//99
	Myrtle Beach MSA, SC	S	13.53 MW	14.22 AW	28140 AAW	SCBLS	10//99-12//99
	South Dakota	S	12.06 MW	12.45 AW	25900 AAW	SDBLS	10//99-12//99
	Rapid City MSA, SD	S	12.31 MW	12.13 AW	25610 AAW	SDBLS	10//99-12//99
	Sioux Falls MSA, SD	S	12.59 MW	12.12 AW	26180 AAW	SDBLS	10//99-12//99
	Tennessee	S	12.76 MW	13.21 AW	27470 AAW	TNBLS	10//99-12//99
	Chattanooga MSA, TN-GA	S	13.63 MW	13.34 AW	28340 AAW	TNBLS	10//99-12//99
	Clarksville-Hopkinsville MSA, TN-KY	S	12.67 MW	11.98 AW	26350 AAW	TNBLS	10//99-12//99
	Jackson MSA, TN	S	12.92 MW	12.68 AW	26880 AAW	TNBLS	10//99-12//99
	Johnson City-Kingsport-Bristol MSA, TN-VA	S	11.61 MW	11.21 AW	24160 AAW	TNBLS	10//99-12//99
	Knoxville MSA, TN	S	13.01 MW	12.05 AW	27050 AAW	TNBLS	10//99-12//99
	Memphis MSA, TN-AR-MS	S	13.75 MW	13.57 AW	28600 AAW	MSBLS	10//99-12//99
	Nashville MSA, TN	S	13.70 MW	13.15 AW	28500 AAW	TNBLS	10//99-12//99
	Texas	S	13.7 MW	13.97 AW	29050 AAW	TXBLS	10//99-12//99
	Abilene MSA, TX	S	13.02 MW	12.80 AW	27080 AAW	TXBLS	10//99-12//99
	Amarillo MSA, TX	S	13.83 MW	13.05 AW	28760 AAW	TXBLS	10//99-12//99
	Austin-San Marcos MSA, TX	S	14.97 MW	14.57 AW	31150 AAW	TXBLS	10//99-12//99
	Beaumont-Port Arthur MSA, TX	S	13.13 MW	12.00 AW	27310 AAW	TXBLS	10//99-12//99
	Brazoria PMSA, TX	S	12.82 MW	12.59 AW	26660 AAW	TXBLS	10//99-12//99
	Brownsville-Harlingen-San Benito MSA, TX	S	9.92 MW	9.32 AW	20630 AAW	TXBLS	10//99-12//99
	Bryan-College Station MSA, TX	S	13.75 MW	13.45 AW	28590 AAW	TXBLS	10//99-12//99
	Corpus Christi MSA, TX	S	12.41 MW	12.31 AW	25810 AAW	TXBLS	10//99-12//99
	Dallas PMSA, TX	S	14.06 MW	13.98 AW	29250 AAW	TXBLS	10//99-12//99
	El Paso MSA, TX	S	13.43 MW	12.58 AW	27930 AAW	TXBLS	10//99-12//99
	Fort Worth-Arlington PMSA, TX	S	14.78 MW	14.54 AW	30740 AAW	TXBLS	10//99-12//99
	Galveston-Texas City PMSA, TX	S	13.55 MW	12.94 AW	28180 AAW	TXBLS	10//99-12//99
	Houston PMSA, TX	S	15.14 MW	15.00 AW	31490 AAW	TXBLS	10//99-12//99
	Killeen-Temple MSA, TX	S	13.45 MW	12.15 AW	27970 AAW	TXBLS	10//99-12//99
	Laredo MSA, TX	S	11.29 MW	11.13 AW	23470 AAW	TXBLS	10//99-12//99
	Longview-Marshall MSA, TX	S	13.96 MW	13.69 AW	29030 AAW	TXBLS	10//99-12//99
	Lubbock MSA, TX	S	12.75 MW	11.96 AW	26520 AAW	TXBLS	10//99-12//99
	McAllen-Edinburg-Mission MSA, TX	S	11.12 MW	10.93 AW	23130 AAW	TXBLS	10//99-12//99
	Odessa-Midland MSA, TX	S	13.61 MW	14.31 AW	28300 AAW	TXBLS	10//99-12//99

Occupation/Type/Industry	Location	Per	Low	Mid	High	Source	Date
Bus and Truck Mechanic and Diesel Engine Specialist	San Angelo MSA, TX	S	11.62 MW	10.91 AW	24170 AAW	TXBLS	10//99-12//99
	San Antonio MSA, TX	S	14.59 MW	14.41 AW	30340 AAW	TXBLS	10//99-12//99
	Sherman-Denison MSA, TX	S	12.47 MW	12.54 AW	25940 AAW	TXBLS	10//99-12//99
	Texarkana MSA, TX- Texarkana, AR	S	11.43 MW	11.00 AW	23780 AAW	TXBLS	10//99-12//99
	Tyler MSA, TX	S	13.78 MW	13.20 AW	28660 AAW	TXBLS	10//99-12//99
	Victoria MSA, TX	S	13.91 MW	13.75 AW	28930 AAW	TXBLS	10//99-12//99
	Waco MSA, TX	S	15.49 MW	15.79 AW	32220 AAW	TXBLS	10//99-12//99
	Wichita Falls MSA, TX	S	12.17 MW	10.44 AW	25320 AAW	TXBLS	10//99-12//99
	Utah	S	15.12 MW	15.22 AW	31650 AAW	UTBLS	10//99-12//99
	Provo-Orem MSA, UT	S	15.67 MW	15.83 AW	32590 AAW	UTBLS	10//99-12//99
	Salt Lake City-Ogden MSA, UT	S	15.21 MW	15.16 AW	31630 AAW	UTBLS	10//99-12//99
	Vermont	S	12.28 MW	13.11 AW	27260 AAW	VTBLS	10//99-12//99
	Burlington MSA, VT	S	13.62 MW	12.97 AW	28330 AAW	VTBLS	10//99-12//99
	Virginia	S	14.1 MW	14.41 AW	29980 AAW	VABLS	10//99-12//99
	Charlottesville MSA, VA	S	13.51 MW	13.10 AW	28100 AAW	VABLS	10//99-12//99
	Danville MSA, VA	S	13.10 MW	12.97 AW	27240 AAW	VABLS	10//99-12//99
	Lynchburg MSA, VA	S	12.00 MW	11.77 AW	24960 AAW	VABLS	10//99-12//99
	Norfolk-Virginia Beach- Newport News MSA, VA-NC	S	13.93 MW	13.49 AW	28960 AAW	VABLS	10//99-12//99
	Richmond-Petersburg MSA, VA	S	15.40 MW	15.33 AW	32040 AAW	VABLS	10//99-12//99
	Roanoke MSA, VA	S	14.03 MW	13.25 AW	29180 AAW	VABLS	10//99-12//99
	Washington	S	17.98 MW	18.30 AW	38070 AAW	WABLS	10//99-12//99
	Bellingham MSA, WA	S	17.23 MW	16.99 AW	35850 AAW	WABLS	10//99-12//99
	Bremerton PMSA, WA	S	18.76 MW	18.72 AW	39020 AAW	WABLS	10//99-12//99
	Olympia PMSA, WA	S	18.62 MW	18.60 AW	38720 AAW	WABLS	10//99-12//99
	Richland-Kennewick-Pasco MSA, WA	S	18.46 MW	17.99 AW	38400 AAW	WABLS	10//99-12//99
	Seattle-Bellevue-Everett PMSA, WA	S	20.00 MW	19.73 AW	41590 AAW	WABLS	10//99-12//99
	Spokane MSA, WA	S	15.40 MW	15.15 AW	32020 AAW	WABLS	10//99-12//99
	Tacoma PMSA, WA	S	17.51 MW	17.92 AW	36420 AAW	WABLS	10//99-12//99
	Yakima MSA, WA	S	14.04 MW	14.04 AW	29200 AAW	WABLS	10//99-12//99
	West Virginia	S	11.64 MW	12.42 AW	25840 AAW	WVBLS	10//99-12//99
	Charleston MSA, WV	S	13.17 MW	12.28 AW	27390 AAW	WVBLS	10//99-12//99
	Huntington-Ashland MSA, WV-KY-OH	S	11.57 MW	11.52 AW	24060 AAW	WVBLS	10//99-12//99
	Parkersburg-Marietta MSA, WV-OH	S	13.79 MW	13.42 AW	28680 AAW	WVBLS	10//99-12//99
	Wheeling MSA, WV-OH	S	11.52 MW	11.35 AW	23960 AAW	WVBLS	10//99-12//99
	Wisconsin	S	14.39 MW	14.66 AW	30490 AAW	WIBLS	10//99-12//99
	Appleton-Oshkosh-Neenah MSA, WI	S	14.39 MW	14.35 AW	29920 AAW	WIBLS	10//99-12//99
	Eau Claire MSA, WI	S	13.91 MW	13.76 AW	28930 AAW	WIBLS	10//99-12//99
	Green Bay MSA, WI	S	14.68 MW	14.74 AW	30530 AAW	WIBLS	10//99-12//99
	Janesville-Beloit MSA, WI	S	16.74 MW	15.34 AW	34820 AAW	WIBLS	10//99-12//99
	Kenosha PMSA, WI	S	16.12 MW	15.41 AW	33530 AAW	WIBLS	10//99-12//99
	La Crosse MSA, WI-MN	S	14.09 MW	14.21 AW	29300 AAW	WIBLS	10//99-12//99
	Madison MSA, WI	S	14.31 MW	14.10 AW	29770 AAW	WIBLS	10//99-12//99
	Milwaukee-Waukesha PMSA, WI	S	15.49 MW	14.95 AW	32230 AAW	WIBLS	10//99-12//99
	Racine PMSA, WI	S	15.77 MW	15.36 AW	32790 AAW	WIBLS	10//99-12//99
	Sheboygan MSA, WI	S	14.55 MW	14.97 AW	30250 AAW	WIBLS	10//99-12//99
	Wausau MSA, WI	S	14.54 MW	14.48 AW	30250 AAW	WIBLS	10//99-12//99
	Wyoming	S	13.55 MW	14.52 AW	30210 AAW	WYBLS	10//99-12//99
	Casper MSA, WY	S	15.19 MW	14.77 AW	31600 AAW	WYBLS	10//99-12//99
	Cheyenne MSA, WY	S	14.66 MW	13.41 AW	30490 AAW	WYBLS	10//99-12//99
	Puerto Rico	S	7.89 MW	8.98 AW	18680 AAW	PRBLS	10//99-12//99
	Aguadilla MSA, PR	S	8.50 MW	6.45 AW	17680 AAW	PRBLS	10//99-12//99
	Arecibo PMSA, PR	S	7.49 MW	6.57 AW	15570 AAW	PRBLS	10//99-12//99
	Caguas PMSA, PR	S	8.29 MW	7.72 AW	17240 AAW	PRBLS	10//99-12//99
	Mayaguez MSA, PR	S	8.66 MW	9.17 AW	18020 AAW	PRBLS	10//99-12//99
	Ponce MSA, PR	S	7.46 MW	7.04 AW	15510 AAW	PRBLS	10//99-12//99
	San Juan-Bayamon PMSA, PR	S	9.43 MW	8.11 AW	19610 AAW	PRBLS	10//99-12//99
	Guam	S	13.15 MW	14.36 AW	29880 AAW	GUBLS	10//99-12//99
Bus Driver School	Alabama	S	6.09 MW	6.42 AW	13350 AAW	ALBLS	10//99-12//99

AAW Average annual wage	AOH Average offered, high	ASH Average starting, high	H Hourly	M Monthly	S Special: hourly and annual
AE Average entry wage	AOL Average offered, low	ASL Average starting, low	HI Highest wage paid	MTC Median total compensation	TQ Third quartile wage
AEX Average experienced wage	APH Average pay, high range	AW Average wage paid	HR High end range	MW Median wage paid	W Weekly
AO Average offered	APL Average pay, low range	FQ First quartile wage	LR Low end range	SQ Second quartile wage	Y Yearly

Occupation/Type/Industry	Location	Per	Low	Mid	High	Source	Date
Bus Driver							
School	Anniston MSA, AL	S	6.89 MW	6.50 AW	14330 AAW	ALBLS	10//99-12//99
School	Auburn-Opelika MSA, AL	S	5.86 MW	6.09 AW	12180 AAW	ALBLS	10//99-12//99
School	Birmingham MSA, AL	S	6.50 MW	6.14 AW	13520 AAW	ALBLS	10//99-12//99
School	Dothan MSA, AL	S	7.56 MW	7.43 AW	15720 AAW	ALBLS	10//99-12//99
School	Florence MSA, AL	S	5.76 MW	5.85 AW	11980 AAW	ALBLS	10//99-12//99
School	Huntsville MSA, AL	S	6.08 MW	6.00 AW	12650 AAW	ALBLS	10//99-12//99
School	Mobile MSA, AL	S	5.92 MW	6.16 AW	12320 AAW	ALBLS	10//99-12//99
School	Alaska	S	11.44 MW	11.61 AW	24150 AAW	AKBLS	10//99-12//99
School	Anchorage MSA, AK	S	11.43 MW	11.27 AW	23780 AAW	AKBLS	10//99-12//99
School	Arizona	S	9.47 MW	9.26 AW	19250 AAW	AZBLS	10//99-12//99
School	Flagstaff MSA, AZ-UT	S	8.60 MW	7.73 AW	17880 AAW	AZBLS	10//99-12//99
School	Phoenix-Mesa MSA, AZ	S	9.43 MW	9.67 AW	19610 AAW	AZBLS	10//99-12//99
School	Tucson MSA, AZ	S	9.83 MW	9.54 AW	20450 AAW	AZBLS	10//99-12//99
School	Yuma MSA, AZ	S	8.96 MW	9.27 AW	18630 AAW	AZBLS	10//99-12//99
School	Arkansas	S	6.09 MW	6.74 AW	14020 AAW	ARBLS	10//99-12//99
School	Fayetteville-Springdale-Rogers MSA, AR	S	6.54 MW	5.95 AW	13600 AAW	ARBLS	10//99-12//99
School	Fort Smith MSA, AR-OK	S	5.80 MW	5.96 AW	12070 AAW	ARBLS	10//99-12//99
School	Jonesboro MSA, AR	S	6.32 MW	6.25 AW	13150 AAW	ARBLS	10//99-12//99
School	Little Rock-North Little Rock MSA, AR	S	7.12 MW	6.30 AW	14820 AAW	ARBLS	10//99-12//99
School	California	S	11.54 MW	11.71 AW	24350 AAW	CABLS	10//99-12//99
School	Bakersfield MSA, CA	S	12.51 MW	12.58 AW	26020 AAW	CABLS	10//99-12//99
School	Chico-Paradise MSA, CA	S	9.83 MW	8.28 AW	20440 AAW	CABLS	10//99-12//99
School	Fresno MSA, CA	S	11.99 MW	12.19 AW	24930 AAW	CABLS	10//99-12//99
School	Los Angeles-Long Beach PMSA, CA	S	11.19 MW	10.73 AW	23280 AAW	CABLS	10//99-12//99
School	Merced MSA, CA	S	10.43 MW	10.64 AW	21700 AAW	CABLS	10//99-12//99
School	Modesto MSA, CA	S	11.23 MW	11.17 AW	23370 AAW	CABLS	10//99-12//99
School	Oakland PMSA, CA	S	11.28 MW	11.22 AW	23470 AAW	CABLS	10//99-12//99
School	Orange County PMSA, CA	S	12.43 MW	12.31 AW	25850 AAW	CABLS	10//99-12//99
School	Redding MSA, CA	S	11.40 MW	11.75 AW	23720 AAW	CABLS	10//99-12//99
School	Riverside-San Bernardino PMSA, CA	S	11.51 MW	11.52 AW	23940 AAW	CABLS	10//99-12//99
School	Sacramento PMSA, CA	S	11.78 MW	11.72 AW	24500 AAW	CABLS	10//99-12//99
School	Salinas MSA, CA	S	12.30 MW	12.50 AW	25580 AAW	CABLS	10//99-12//99
School	San Diego MSA, CA	S	11.12 MW	11.13 AW	23120 AAW	CABLS	10//99-12//99
School	San Francisco PMSA, CA	S	11.89 MW	11.73 AW	24740 AAW	CABLS	10//99-12//99
School	San Jose PMSA, CA	S	13.29 MW	13.60 AW	27640 AAW	CABLS	10//99-12//99
School	San Luis Obispo-Atascadero-Paso Robles MSA, CA	S	13.81 MW	13.37 AW	28720 AAW	CABLS	10//99-12//99
School	Stockton-Lodi MSA, CA	S	11.51 MW	11.79 AW	23950 AAW	CABLS	10//99-12//99
School	Vallejo-Fairfield-Napa PMSA, CA	S	10.32 MW	10.43 AW	21470 AAW	CABLS	10//99-12//99
School	Ventura PMSA, CA	S	11.99 MW	12.08 AW	24930 AAW	CABLS	10//99-12//99
School	Visalia-Tulare-Porterville MSA, CA	S	10.97 MW	11.35 AW	22810 AAW	CABLS	10//99-12//99
School	Yolo PMSA, CA	S	10.38 MW	10.18 AW	21600 AAW	CABLS	10//99-12//99
School	Yuba City MSA, CA	S	9.22 MW	8.42 AW	19170 AAW	CABLS	10//99-12//99
School	Colorado	S	9.82 MW	9.93 AW	20650 AAW	COBLS	10//99-12//99
School	Boulder-Longmont PMSA, CO	S	9.16 MW	9.26 AW	19050 AAW	COBLS	10//99-12//99
School	Colorado Springs MSA, CO	S	9.53 MW	9.43 AW	19820 AAW	COBLS	10//99-12//99
School	Denver PMSA, CO	S	10.28 MW	9.97 AW	21390 AAW	COBLS	10//99-12//99
School	Fort Collins-Loveland MSA, CO	S	10.25 MW	10.19 AW	21330 AAW	COBLS	10//99-12//99
School	Greeley PMSA, CO	S	9.70 MW	9.89 AW	20170 AAW	COBLS	10//99-12//99
School	Pueblo MSA, CO	S	9.42 MW	9.64 AW	19600 AAW	COBLS	10//99-12//99
School	Connecticut	S	10.6 MW	10.68 AW	22210 AAW	CTBLS	10//99-12//99
School	Bridgeport PMSA, CT	S	11.52 MW	11.49 AW	23950 AAW	CTBLS	10//99-12//99
School	Hartford MSA, CT	S	10.62 MW	10.34 AW	22090 AAW	CTBLS	10//99-12//99
School	New Haven-Meriden PMSA, CT	S	9.87 MW	9.96 AW	20530 AAW	CTBLS	10//99-12//99
School	New London-Norwich MSA, CT-RI	S	10.43 MW	10.15 AW	21700 AAW	CTBLS	10//99-12//99
School	Waterbury PMSA, CT	S	10.33 MW	10.68 AW	21490 AAW	CTBLS	10//99-12//99
School	Delaware	S	9.85 MW	9.85 AW	20490 AAW	DEBLS	10//99-12//99
School	Dover MSA, DE	S	10.04 MW	8.98 AW	20870 AAW	DEBLS	10//99-12//99
School	Wilmington-Newark PMSA, DE-MD	S	9.91 MW	10.16 AW	20600 AAW	DEBLS	10//99-12//99
School	District of Columbia	S	10.97 MW	10.78 AW	22420 AAW	DCBLS	10//99-12//99

AAW Average annual wage	**AOH** Average offered, high	**ASH** Average starting, high	**H** Hourly	**M** Monthly	**S** Special: hourly and annual
AE Average entry wage	**AOL** Average offered, low	**ASL** Average starting, low	**HI** Highest wage paid	**MTC** Median total compensation	**TQ** Third quartile wage
AEX Average experienced wage	**APH** Average pay, high range	**AW** Average wage paid	**HR** High end range	**MW** Median wage paid	**W** Weekly
AO Average offered	**APL** Average pay, low range	**FQ** First quartile wage	**LR** Low end range	**SQ** Second quartile wage	**Y** Yearly

Occupation/Type/Industry	Location	Per	Low	Mid	High	Source	Date
Bus Driver							
School	Washington PMSA, DC-MD-VA-WV	S	8.76 MW	8.27 AW	18230 AAW	DCBLS	10//99-12//99
School	Florida	S	9.2 MW	9.17 AW	19080 AAW	FLBLS	10//99-12//99
School	Fort Pierce-Port St. Lucie MSA, FL	S	9.62 MW	9.75 AW	20010 AAW	FLBLS	10//99-12//99
School	Jacksonville MSA, FL	S	8.73 MW	8.64 AW	18160 AAW	FLBLS	10//99-12//99
School	Miami PMSA, FL	S	7.68 MW	7.48 AW	15980 AAW	FLBLS	10//99-12//99
School	Orlando MSA, FL	S	10.05 MW	10.19 AW	20900 AAW	FLBLS	10//99-12//99
School	Pensacola MSA, FL	S	7.83 MW	6.15 AW	16300 AAW	FLBLS	10//99-12//99
School	Sarasota-Bradenton MSA, FL	S	7.60 MW	7.46 AW	15800 AAW	FLBLS	10//99-12//99
School	Tampa-St. Petersburg-Clearwater MSA, FL	S	9.65 MW	9.66 AW	20070 AAW	FLBLS	10//99-12//99
School	West Palm Beach-Boca Raton MSA, FL	S	7.89 MW	7.78 AW	16410 AAW	FLBLS	10//99-12//99
School	Georgia	S	6.66 MW	8.47 AW	17610 AAW	GABLS	10//99-12//99
School	Albany MSA, GA	S	6.02 MW	6.05 AW	12520 AAW	GABLS	10//99-12//99
School	Atlanta MSA, GA	S	10.17 MW	11.01 AW	21150 AAW	GABLS	10//99-12//99
School	Augusta-Aiken MSA, GA-SC	S	8.73 MW	8.59 AW	18160 AAW	GABLS	10//99-12//99
School	Columbus MSA, GA-AL	S	8.25 MW	8.08 AW	17160 AAW	GABLS	10//99-12//99
School	Savannah MSA, GA	S	5.96 MW	5.92 AW	12400 AAW	GABLS	10//99-12//99
School	Hawaii	S	11.27 MW	11.03 AW	22940 AAW	HIBLS	10//99-12//99
School	Honolulu MSA, HI	S	10.42 MW	10.19 AW	21680 AAW	HIBLS	10//99-12//99
School	Idaho	S	8.65 MW	8.57 AW	17820 AAW	IDBLS	10//99-12//99
School	Boise City MSA, ID	S	8.80 MW	9.19 AW	18310 AAW	IDBLS	10//99-12//99
School	Illinois	S	9.43 MW	9.93 AW	20650 AAW	ILBLS	10//99-12//99
School	Bloomington-Normal MSA, IL	S	12.10 MW	11.92 AW	25170 AAW	ILBLS	10//99-12//99
School	Champaign-Urbana MSA, IL	S	14.27 MW	9.49 AW	29680 AAW	ILBLS	10//99-12//99
School	Chicago PMSA, IL	S	10.31 MW	9.96 AW	21440 AAW	ILBLS	10//99-12//99
School	Kankakee PMSA, IL	S	8.25 MW	7.86 AW	17150 AAW	ILBLS	10//99-12//99
School	Peoria-Pekin MSA, IL	S	9.74 MW	8.28 AW	20270 AAW	ILBLS	10//99-12//99
School	Rockford MSA, IL	S	10.83 MW	10.95 AW	22520 AAW	ILBLS	10//99-12//99
School	Springfield MSA, IL	S	7.73 MW	6.21 AW	16080 AAW	ILBLS	10//99-12//99
School	Indiana	S	10.11 MW	10.55 AW	21940 AAW	INBLS	10//99-12//99
School	Elkhart-Goshen MSA, IN	S	13.07 MW	14.46 AW	27190 AAW	INBLS	10//99-12//99
School	Fort Wayne MSA, IN	S	8.74 MW	7.54 AW	18180 AAW	INBLS	10//99-12//99
School	Gary PMSA, IN	S	10.51 MW	10.29 AW	21860 AAW	INBLS	10//99-12//99
School	Indianapolis MSA, IN	S	10.83 MW	11.24 AW	22520 AAW	INBLS	10//99-12//99
School	Kokomo MSA, IN	S	9.21 MW	8.09 AW	19150 AAW	INBLS	10//99-12//99
School	Lafayette MSA, IN	S	10.54 MW	10.37 AW	21920 AAW	INBLS	10//99-12//99
School	Muncie MSA, IN	S	7.58 MW	6.63 AW	15770 AAW	INBLS	10//99-12//99
School	Iowa	S	10.77 MW	11.00 AW	22880 AAW	IABLS	10//99-12//99
School	Cedar Rapids MSA, IA	S	10.73 MW	12.23 AW	22310 AAW	IABLS	10//99-12//99
School	Davenport-Moline-Rock Island MSA, IA-IL	S	10.67 MW	11.16 AW	22200 AAW	IABLS	10//99-12//99
School	Des Moines MSA, IA	S	10.97 MW	11.68 AW	22810 AAW	IABLS	10//99-12//99
School	Sioux City MSA, IA-NE	S	6.63 MW	6.08 AW	13790 AAW	IABLS	10//99-12//99
School	Waterloo-Cedar Falls MSA, IA	S	12.73 MW	11.40 AW	26470 AAW	IABLS	10//99-12//99
School	Kansas	S	9.06 MW	9.24 AW	19230 AAW	KSBLS	10//99-12//99
School	Topeka MSA, KS	S	10.06 MW	10.00 AW	20920 AAW	KSBLS	10//99-12//99
School	Wichita MSA, KS	S	9.73 MW	9.18 AW	20250 AAW	KSBLS	10//99-12//99
School	Kentucky	S	9.47 MW	9.55 AW	19860 AAW	KYBLS	10//99-12//99
School	Lexington MSA, KY	S	10.52 MW	10.45 AW	21880 AAW	KYBLS	10//99-12//99
School	Louisiana	S	6.67 MW	8.43 AW	17530 AAW	LABLS	10//99-12//99
School	Houma MSA, LA	S	8.05 MW	7.22 AW	16740 AAW	LABLS	10//99-12//99
School	Lafayette MSA, LA	S	10.81 MW	10.44 AW	22480 AAW	LABLS	10//99-12//99
School	New Orleans MSA, LA	S	8.83 MW	7.33 AW	18360 AAW	LABLS	10//99-12//99
School	Shreveport-Bossier City MSA, LA	S	10.88 MW	9.75 AW	22640 AAW	LABLS	10//99-12//99
School	Maine	S	10.44 MW	10.06 AW	20920 AAW	MEBLS	10//99-12//99
School	Lewiston-Auburn MSA, ME	S	9.69 MW	9.62 AW	20150 AAW	MEBLS	10//99-12//99
School	Portland MSA, ME	S	11.13 MW	11.30 AW	23140 AAW	MEBLS	10//99-12//99
School	Maryland	S	9.24 MW	9.22 AW	19170 AAW	MDBLS	10//99-12//99
School	Baltimore PMSA, MD	S	8.95 MW	9.21 AW	18620 AAW	MDBLS	10//99-12//99
School	Cumberland MSA, MD-WV	S	9.21 MW	9.00 AW	19160 AAW	MDBLS	10//99-12//99
School	Massachusetts	S	10.7 MW	10.69 AW	22230 AAW	MABLS	10//99-12//99
School	Barnstable-Yarmouth MSA, MA	S	9.86 MW	9.80 AW	20520 AAW	MABLS	10//99-12//99
School	Boston PMSA, MA-NH	S	10.61 MW	10.46 AW	22060 AAW	MABLS	10//99-12//99
School	Brockton PMSA, MA	S	10.18 MW	10.80 AW	21170 AAW	MABLS	10//99-12//99
School	Fitchburg-Leominster PMSA, MA	S	10.87 MW	11.31 AW	22600 AAW	MABLS	10//99-12//99

AAW	Average annual wage	AOH	Average offered, high	ASH	Average starting, high	H	Hourly	M	Monthly	S	Special: hourly and annual
AE	Average entry wage	AOL	Average offered, low	ASL	Average starting, low	HI	Highest wage paid	MTC	Median total compensation	TQ	Third quartile wage
AEX	Average experienced wage	APH	Average pay, high range	AW	Average wage paid	HR	High end range	MW	Median wage paid	W	Weekly
AO	Average offered	APL	Average pay, low range	FQ	First quartile wage	LR	Low end range	SQ	Second quartile wage	Y	Yearly

Occupation/Type/Industry	Location	Per	Low	Mid	High	Source	Date
Bus Driver							
School	Lawrence PMSA, MA-NH	S	9.83 MW	9.79 AW	20450 AAW	MABLS	10//99-12//99
School	Lowell PMSA, MA-NH	S	8.50 MW	6.56 AW	17680 AAW	MABLS	10//99-12//99
School	New Bedford PMSA, MA	S	13.30 MW	14.13 AW	27660 AAW	MABLS	10//99-12//99
School	Pittsfield MSA, MA	S	10.47 MW	10.60 AW	21780 AAW	MABLS	10//99-12//99
School	Springfield MSA, MA	S	11.51 MW	12.06 AW	23940 AAW	MABLS	10//99-12//99
School	Worcester PMSA, MA-CT	S	11.55 MW	11.57 AW	24020 AAW	MABLS	10//99-12//99
School	Michigan	S	12.84 MW	12.41 AW	25820 AAW	MIBLS	10//99-12//99
School	Ann Arbor PMSA, MI	S	11.06 MW	10.91 AW	23000 AAW	MIBLS	10//99-12//99
School	Benton Harbor MSA, MI	S	11.72 MW	12.29 AW	24370 AAW	MIBLS	10//99-12//99
School	Detroit PMSA, MI	S	12.97 MW	14.09 AW	26980 AAW	MIBLS	10//99-12//99
School	Flint PMSA, MI	S	11.91 MW	12.17 AW	24770 AAW	MIBLS	10//99-12//99
School	Grand Rapids-Muskegon-Holland MSA, MI	S	13.70 MW	14.09 AW	28500 AAW	MIBLS	10//99-12//99
School	Jackson MSA, MI	S	11.22 MW	11.47 AW	23330 AAW	MIBLS	10//99-12//99
School	Kalamazoo-Battle Creek MSA, MI	S	11.26 MW	11.34 AW	23430 AAW	MIBLS	10//99-12//99
School	Lansing-East Lansing MSA, MI	S	12.49 MW	12.92 AW	25980 AAW	MIBLS	10//99-12//99
School	Saginaw-Bay City-Midland MSA, MI	S	10.04 MW	9.77 AW	20870 AAW	MIBLS	10//99-12//99
School	Minnesota	S	11.2 MW	10.94 AW	22760 AAW	MNBLS	10//99-12//99
School	Duluth-Superior MSA, MN-WI	S	11.40 MW	10.37 AW	23710 AAW	MNBLS	10//99-12//99
School	Minneapolis-St. Paul MSA, MN-WI	S	11.56 MW	11.61 AW	24050 AAW	MNBLS	10//99-12//99
School	Rochester MSA, MN	S	11.72 MW	10.75 AW	24380 AAW	MNBLS	10//99-12//99
School	St. Cloud MSA, MN	S	8.57 MW	7.87 AW	17830 AAW	MNBLS	10//99-12//99
School	Mississippi	S	6.1 MW	6.45 AW	13410 AAW	MSBLS	10//99-12//99
School	Biloxi-Gulfport-Pascagoula MSA, MS	S	6.49 MW	6.36 AW	13500 AAW	MSBLS	10//99-12//99
School	Hattiesburg MSA, MS	S	6.03 MW	5.95 AW	12550 AAW	MSBLS	10//99-12//99
School	Jackson MSA, MS	S	7.77 MW	7.41 AW	16170 AAW	MSBLS	10//99-12//99
School	Missouri	S	8.8 MW	8.85 AW	18410 AAW	MOBLS	10//99-12//99
School	Joplin MSA, MO	S	8.65 MW	8.01 AW	17990 AAW	MOBLS	10//99-12//99
School	Kansas City MSA, MO-KS	S	9.28 MW	9.46 AW	19310 AAW	MOBLS	10//99-12//99
School	St. Louis MSA, MO-IL	S	9.23 MW	9.38 AW	19190 AAW	MOBLS	10//99-12//99
School	Springfield MSA, MO	S	6.98 MW	6.08 AW	14520 AAW	MOBLS	10//99-12//99
School	Montana	S	9.59 MW	9.72 AW	20220 AAW	MTBLS	10//99-12//99
School	Missoula MSA, MT	S	10.70 MW	10.18 AW	22260 AAW	MTBLS	10//99-12//99
School	Nebraska	S	7.97 MW	8.86 AW	18430 AAW	NEBLS	10//99-12//99
School	Omaha MSA, NE-IA	S	8.63 MW	8.56 AW	17960 AAW	NEBLS	10//99-12//99
School	Nevada	S	13.59 MW	13.77 AW	28640 AAW	NVBLS	10//99-12//99
School	New Hampshire	S	9.74 MW	9.53 AW	19810 AAW	NHBLS	10//99-12//99
School	Manchester PMSA, NH	S	7.48 MW	6.83 AW	15560 AAW	NHBLS	10//99-12//99
School	Nashua PMSA, NH	S	9.64 MW	9.72 AW	20050 AAW	NHBLS	10//99-12//99
School	Portsmouth-Rochester PMSA, NH-ME	S	9.75 MW	9.81 AW	20290 AAW	NHBLS	10//99-12//99
School	New Jersey	S	10.42 MW	10.43 AW	21690 AAW	NJBLS	10//99-12//99
School	Bergen-Passaic PMSA, NJ	S	10.97 MW	10.90 AW	22820 AAW	NJBLS	10//99-12//99
School	Jersey City PMSA, NJ	S	11.08 MW	10.60 AW	23040 AAW	NJBLS	10//99-12//99
School	Middlesex-Somerset-Hunterdon PMSA, NJ	S	10.44 MW	10.49 AW	21720 AAW	NJBLS	10//99-12//99
School	Monmouth-Ocean PMSA, NJ	S	9.54 MW	9.07 AW	19850 AAW	NJBLS	10//99-12//99
School	Newark PMSA, NJ	S	11.41 MW	11.25 AW	23730 AAW	NJBLS	10//99-12//99
School	Trenton PMSA, NJ	S	11.80 MW	11.28 AW	24530 AAW	NJBLS	10//99-12//99
School	Vineland-Millville-Bridgeton PMSA, NJ	S	9.80 MW	10.75 AW	20380 AAW	NJBLS	10//99-12//99
School	New Mexico	S	8.04 MW	8.17 AW	16990 AAW	NMBLS	10//99-12//99
School	Albuquerque MSA, NM	S	9.08 MW	9.27 AW	18890 AAW	NMBLS	10//99-12//99
School	New York	S	10.84 MW	11.50 AW	23920 AAW	NYBLS	10//99-12//99
School	Albany-Schenectady-Troy MSA, NY	S	10.94 MW	11.37 AW	22760 AAW	NYBLS	10//99-12//99
School	Binghamton MSA, NY	S	10.58 MW	10.84 AW	22010 AAW	NYBLS	10//99-12//99
School	Buffalo-Niagara Falls MSA, NY	S	10.50 MW	9.20 AW	21830 AAW	NYBLS	10//99-12//99
School	Dutchess County PMSA, NY	S	12.91 MW	14.32 AW	26850 AAW	NYBLS	10//99-12//99
School	Glens Falls MSA, NY	S	9.54 MW	8.54 AW	19840 AAW	NYBLS	10//99-12//99
School	Jamestown MSA, NY	S	12.01 MW	12.57 AW	24980 AAW	NYBLS	10//99-12//99
School	Nassau-Suffolk PMSA, NY	S	11.25 MW	10.98 AW	23390 AAW	NYBLS	10//99-12//99
School	New York PMSA, NY	S	12.54 MW	12.12 AW	26080 AAW	NYBLS	10//99-12//99
School	Newburgh PMSA, NY-PA	S	9.29 MW	9.67 AW	19320 AAW	NYBLS	10//99-12//99
School	Rochester MSA, NY	S	9.74 MW	8.75 AW	20260 AAW	NYBLS	10//99-12//99
School	Syracuse MSA, NY	S	11.66 MW	10.74 AW	24260 AAW	NYBLS	10//99-12//99

Bus Driver

Occupation/Type/Industry	Location	Per	Low	Mid	High	Source	Date
School	Utica-Rome MSA, NY	S	10.85 MW	10.31 AW	22560 AAW	NYBLS	10//99-12//99
School	North Carolina	S	9.15 MW	8.86 AW	18420 AAW	NCBLS	10//99-12//99
School	Asheville MSA, NC	S	6.94 MW	6.77 AW	14440 AAW	NCBLS	10//99-12//99
School	Charlotte-Gastonia-Rock Hill MSA, NC-SC	S	9.21 MW	9.62 AW	19150 AAW	NCBLS	10//99-12//99
School	Greensboro--Winston-Salem--High Point MSA, NC	S	9.91 MW	10.32 AW	20600 AAW	NCBLS	10//99-12//99
School	Hickory-Morganton-Lenoir MSA, NC	S	7.83 MW	7.51 AW	16280 AAW	NCBLS	10//99-12//99
School	Raleigh-Durham-Chapel Hill MSA, NC	S	8.99 MW	8.48 AW	18700 AAW	NCBLS	10//99-12//99
School	North Dakota	S	10.57 MW	10.54 AW	21930 AAW	NDBLS	10//99-12//99
School	Bismarck MSA, ND	S	11.03 MW	10.35 AW	22930 AAW	NDBLS	10//99-12//99
School	Fargo-Moorhead MSA, ND-MN	S	8.79 MW	8.75 AW	18280 AAW	NDBLS	10//99-12//99
School	Grand Forks MSA, ND-MN	S	11.09 MW	11.36 AW	23070 AAW	NDBLS	10//99-12//99
School	Ohio	S	9.84 MW	10.04 AW	20880 AAW	OHBLS	10//99-12//99
School	Akron PMSA, OH	S	10.39 MW	10.61 AW	21620 AAW	OHBLS	10//99-12//99
School	Canton-Massillon MSA, OH	S	11.55 MW	12.26 AW	24010 AAW	OHBLS	10//99-12//99
School	Cincinnati PMSA, OH-KY-IN	S	10.65 MW	10.16 AW	22150 AAW	OHBLS	10//99-12//99
School	Cleveland-Lorain-Elyria PMSA, OH	S	10.70 MW	10.44 AW	22260 AAW	OHBLS	10//99-12//99
School	Columbus MSA, OH	S	11.50 MW	11.82 AW	23920 AAW	OHBLS	10//99-12//99
School	Dayton-Springfield MSA, OH	S	9.36 MW	9.09 AW	19470 AAW	OHBLS	10//99-12//99
School	Hamilton-Middletown PMSA, OH	S	9.47 MW	9.38 AW	19700 AAW	OHBLS	10//99-12//99
School	Lima MSA, OH	S	8.85 MW	6.91 AW	18400 AAW	OHBLS	10//99-12//99
School	Mansfield MSA, OH	S	10.54 MW	10.94 AW	21930 AAW	OHBLS	10//99-12//99
School	Steubenville-Weirton MSA, OH-WV	S	9.04 MW	8.63 AW	18810 AAW	OHBLS	10//99-12//99
School	Toledo MSA, OH	S	12.00 MW	12.84 AW	24960 AAW	OHBLS	10//99-12//99
School	Youngstown-Warren MSA, OH	S	9.06 MW	8.52 AW	18830 AAW	OHBLS	10//99-12//99
School	Oklahoma	S	6.48 MW	7.00 AW	14550 AAW	OKBLS	10//99-12//99
School	Enid MSA, OK	S	6.70 MW	6.07 AW	13940 AAW	OKBLS	10//99-12//99
School	Oklahoma City MSA, OK	S	7.02 MW	6.51 AW	14610 AAW	OKBLS	10//99-12//99
School	Tulsa MSA, OK	S	7.97 MW	7.78 AW	16570 AAW	OKBLS	10//99-12//99
School	Oregon	S	10.3 MW	10.46 AW	21760 AAW	ORBLS	10//99-12//99
School	Corvallis MSA, OR	S	8.59 MW	8.24 AW	17870 AAW	ORBLS	10//99-12//99
School	Portland-Vancouver PMSA, OR-WA	S	11.19 MW	10.94 AW	23270 AAW	ORBLS	10//99-12//99
School	Salem PMSA, OR	S	10.35 MW	10.31 AW	21520 AAW	ORBLS	10//99-12//99
School	Pennsylvania	S	9.26 MW	9.61 AW	19980 AAW	PABLS	10//99-12//99
School	Allentown-Bethlehem-Easton MSA, PA	S	10.80 MW	10.65 AW	22470 AAW	PABLS	10//99-12//99
School	Altoona MSA, PA	S	10.04 MW	10.10 AW	20890 AAW	PABLS	10//99-12//99
School	Harrisburg-Lebanon-Carlisle MSA, PA	S	9.41 MW	9.15 AW	19580 AAW	PABLS	10//99-12//99
School	Johnstown MSA, PA	S	7.97 MW	7.88 AW	16590 AAW	PABLS	10//99-12//99
School	Lancaster MSA, PA	S	10.10 MW	9.89 AW	21020 AAW	PABLS	10//99-12//99
School	Philadelphia PMSA, PA-NJ	S	10.79 MW	10.93 AW	22450 AAW	PABLS	10//99-12//99
School	Pittsburgh MSA, PA	S	8.58 MW	8.05 AW	17850 AAW	PABLS	10//99-12//99
School	Reading MSA, PA	S	11.01 MW	11.18 AW	22900 AAW	PABLS	10//99-12//99
School	Scranton--Wilkes-Barre--Hazleton MSA, PA	S	7.97 MW	6.75 AW	16580 AAW	PABLS	10//99-12//99
School	Sharon MSA, PA	S	8.50 MW	8.08 AW	17680 AAW	PABLS	10//99-12//99
School	State College MSA, PA	S	9.55 MW	10.23 AW	19860 AAW	PABLS	10//99-12//99
School	Williamsport MSA, PA	S	7.87 MW	7.61 AW	16370 AAW	PABLS	10//99-12//99
School	York MSA, PA	S	10.18 MW	7.40 AW	21170 AAW	PABLS	10//99-12//99
School	Rhode Island	S	10.34 MW	10.45 AW	21730 AAW	RIBLS	10//99-12//99
School	Providence-Fall River-Warwick MSA, RI-MA	S	10.47 MW	10.36 AW	21770 AAW	RIBLS	10//99-12//99
School	South Carolina	S	7.1 MW	7.14 AW	14850 AAW	SCBLS	10//99-12//99
School	Charleston-North Charleston MSA, SC	S	6.82 MW	6.67 AW	14180 AAW	SCBLS	10//99-12//99
School	Columbia MSA, SC	S	7.38 MW	7.17 AW	15360 AAW	SCBLS	10//99-12//99
School	Greenville-Spartanburg-Anderson MSA, SC	S	7.67 MW	7.72 AW	15960 AAW	SCBLS	10//99-12//99
School	South Dakota	S	9.2 MW	8.95 AW	18620 AAW	SDBLS	10//99-12//99
School	Sioux Falls MSA, SD	S	11.29 MW	10.16 AW	23470 AAW	SDBLS	10//99-12//99
School	Tennessee	S	6.14 MW	6.58 AW	13680 AAW	TNBLS	10//99-12//99
School	Chattanooga MSA, TN-GA	S	6.17 MW	5.97 AW	12840 AAW	TNBLS	10//99-12//99

AAW	Average annual wage	AOH	Average offered, high	ASH	Average starting, high	H	Hourly	M	Monthly	S	Special: hourly and annual
AE	Average entry wage	AOL	Average offered, low	ASL	Average starting, low	HI	Highest wage paid	MTC	Median total compensation	TQ	Third quartile wage
AEX	Average experienced wage	APH	Average pay, high range	AW	Average wage paid	HR	High end range	MW	Median wage paid	W	Weekly
AO	Average offered	APL	Average pay, low range	FQ	First quartile wage	LR	Low end range	SQ	Second quartile wage	Y	Yearly

Occupation/Type/Industry	Location	Per	Low	Mid	High	Source	Date
Bus Driver							
School	Johnson City-Kingsport-Bristol MSA, TN-VA	S	6.34 MW	6.04 AW	13190 AAW	TNBLS	10//99-12//99
School	Knoxville MSA, TN	S	7.52 MW	6.42 AW	15630 AAW	TNBLS	10//99-12//99
School	Memphis MSA, TN-AR-MS	S	7.04 MW	7.09 AW	14640 AAW	MSBLS	10//99-12//99
School	Nashville MSA, TN	S	6.82 MW	6.33 AW	14180 AAW	TNBLS	10//99-12//99
School	Texas	S	8.59 MW	8.88 AW	18470 AAW	TXBLS	10//99-12//99
School	Austin-San Marcos MSA, TX	S	9.50 MW	9.77 AW	19750 AAW	TXBLS	10//99-12//99
School	Brazoria PMSA, TX	S	8.11 MW	6.95 AW	16870 AAW	TXBLS	10//99-12//99
School	Brownsville-Harlingen-San Benito MSA, TX	S	7.48 MW	7.16 AW	15570 AAW	TXBLS	10//99-12//99
School	Dallas PMSA, TX	S	9.84 MW	9.97 AW	20470 AAW	TXBLS	10//99-12//99
School	El Paso MSA, TX	S	8.40 MW	8.05 AW	17470 AAW	TXBLS	10//99-12//99
School	Fort Worth-Arlington PMSA, TX	S	8.70 MW	8.46 AW	18100 AAW	TXBLS	10//99-12//99
School	Galveston-Texas City PMSA, TX	S	9.56 MW	9.61 AW	19890 AAW	TXBLS	10//99-12//99
School	Houston PMSA, TX	S	9.58 MW	9.53 AW	19930 AAW	TXBLS	10//99-12//99
School	Killeen-Temple MSA, TX	S	7.33 MW	6.92 AW	15250 AAW	TXBLS	10//99-12//99
School	Longview-Marshall MSA, TX	S	9.89 MW	10.09 AW	20580 AAW	TXBLS	10//99-12//99
School	McAllen-Edinburg-Mission MSA, TX	S	8.23 MW	8.23 AW	17110 AAW	TXBLS	10//99-12//99
School	Odessa-Midland MSA, TX	S	7.65 MW	7.38 AW	15920 AAW	TXBLS	10//99-12//99
School	San Angelo MSA, TX	S	7.78 MW	7.76 AW	16180 AAW	TXBLS	10//99-12//99
School	San Antonio MSA, TX	S	9.38 MW	9.35 AW	19500 AAW	TXBLS	10//99-12//99
School	Sherman-Denison MSA, TX	S	10.27 MW	11.32 AW	21350 AAW	TXBLS	10//99-12//99
School	Texarkana MSA, TX-Texarkana, AR	S	5.85 MW	5.94 AW	12180 AAW	TXBLS	10//99-12//99
School	Tyler MSA, TX	S	8.22 MW	7.83 AW	17090 AAW	TXBLS	10//99-12//99
School	Victoria MSA, TX	S	8.23 MW	7.54 AW	17120 AAW	TXBLS	10//99-12//99
School	Waco MSA, TX	S	7.14 MW	7.14 AW	14850 AAW	TXBLS	10//99-12//99
School	Wichita Falls MSA, TX	S	7.55 MW	7.45 AW	15710 AAW	TXBLS	10//99-12//99
School	Utah	S	12.75 MW	12.20 AW	25370 AAW	UTBLS	10//99-12//99
School	Salt Lake City-Ogden MSA, UT	S	11.61 MW	12.25 AW	24150 AAW	UTBLS	10//99-12//99
School	Vermont	S	9.96 MW	10.06 AW	20920 AAW	VTBLS	10//99-12//99
School	Burlington MSA, VT	S	11.87 MW	11.61 AW	24680 AAW	VTBLS	10//99-12//99
School	Virginia	S	6.77 MW	7.70 AW	16020 AAW	VABLS	10//99-12//99
School	Charlottesville MSA, VA	S	8.85 MW	8.87 AW	18410 AAW	VABLS	10//99-12//99
School	Lynchburg MSA, VA	S	7.49 MW	7.36 AW	15570 AAW	VABLS	10//99-12//99
School	Norfolk-Virginia Beach-Newport News MSA, VA-NC	S	8.68 MW	8.99 AW	18060 AAW	VABLS	10//99-12//99
School	Richmond-Petersburg MSA, VA	S	7.61 MW	6.90 AW	15830 AAW	VABLS	10//99-12//99
School	Roanoke MSA, VA	S	5.94 MW	6.08 AW	12360 AAW	VABLS	10//99-12//99
School	Washington	S	12.76 MW	12.62 AW	26240 AAW	WABLS	10//99-12//99
School	Bellingham MSA, WA	S	12.87 MW	12.75 AW	26770 AAW	WABLS	10//99-12//99
School	Bremerton PMSA, WA	S	13.72 MW	14.32 AW	28540 AAW	WABLS	10//99-12//99
School	Olympia PMSA, WA	S	11.76 MW	12.40 AW	24460 AAW	WABLS	10//99-12//99
School	Richland-Kennewick-Pasco MSA, WA	S	12.17 MW	12.40 AW	25320 AAW	WABLS	10//99-12//99
School	Seattle-Bellevue-Everett PMSA, WA	S	12.68 MW	12.96 AW	26370 AAW	WABLS	10//99-12//99
School	Spokane MSA, WA	S	12.93 MW	12.85 AW	26890 AAW	WABLS	10//99-12//99
School	Tacoma PMSA, WA	S	12.41 MW	12.51 AW	25820 AAW	WABLS	10//99-12//99
School	Yakima MSA, WA	S	12.79 MW	12.83 AW	26610 AAW	WABLS	10//99-12//99
School	West Virginia	S	8.16 MW	8.27 AW	17200 AAW	WVBLS	10//99-12//99
School	Huntington-Ashland MSA, WV-KY-OH	S	8.49 MW	8.12 AW	17660 AAW	WVBLS	10//99-12//99
School	Parkersburg-Marietta MSA, WV-OH	S	9.30 MW	9.22 AW	19340 AAW	WVBLS	10//99-12//99
School	Wheeling MSA, WV-OH	S	8.56 MW	8.35 AW	17810 AAW	WVBLS	10//99-12//99
School	Wisconsin	S	9.66 MW	9.66 AW	20090 AAW	WIBLS	10//99-12//99
School	Appleton-Oshkosh-Neenah MSA, WI	S	10.34 MW	10.07 AW	21500 AAW	WIBLS	10//99-12//99
School	Eau Claire MSA, WI	S	9.57 MW	10.26 AW	19910 AAW	WIBLS	10//99-12//99
School	Green Bay MSA, WI	S	9.45 MW	9.63 AW	19660 AAW	WIBLS	10//99-12//99
School	Janesville-Beloit MSA, WI	S	7.96 MW	7.93 AW	16560 AAW	WIBLS	10//99-12//99
School	Kenosha PMSA, WI	S	12.19 MW	13.63 AW	25350 AAW	WIBLS	10//99-12//99
School	La Crosse MSA, WI-MN	S	10.78 MW	11.41 AW	22420 AAW	WIBLS	10//99-12//99
School	Madison MSA, WI	S	9.99 MW	10.16 AW	20780 AAW	WIBLS	10//99-12//99

AAW	Average annual wage	**AOH**	Average offered, high	**ASH**	Average starting, high	**H**	Hourly	**M**	Monthly	**S**	Special: hourly and annual
AE	Average entry wage	**AOL**	Average offered, low	**ASL**	Average starting, low	**HI**	Highest wage paid	**MTC**	Median total compensation	**TQ**	Third quartile wage
AEX	Average experienced wage	**APH**	Average pay, high range	**AW**	Average wage paid	**HR**	High end range	**MW**	Median wage paid	**W**	Weekly
AO	Average offered	**APL**	Average pay, low range	**FQ**	First quartile wage	**LR**	Low end range	**SQ**	Second quartile wage	**Y**	Yearly

Occupation/Type/Industry	Location	Per	Low	Mid	High	Source	Date
Bus Driver							
School	Milwaukee-Waukesha PMSA, WI	S	9.80 MW	9.81 AW	20390 AAW	WIBLS	10//99-12//99
School	Sheboygan MSA, WI	S	8.66 MW	8.71 AW	18010 AAW	WIBLS	10//99-12//99
School	Wyoming	S	9.4 MW	9.30 AW	19340 AAW	WYBLS	10//99-12//99
School	Puerto Rico	S	6.03 MW	6.07 AW	12620 AAW	PRBLS	10//99-12//99
School	Ponce MSA, PR	S	5.86 MW	5.94 AW	12200 AAW	PRBLS	10//99-12//99
School	San Juan-Bayamon PMSA, PR	S	6.11 MW	6.04 AW	12700 AAW	PRBLS	10//99-12//99
Transit and Intercity	Alabama	S	8.15 MW	9.06 AW	18850 AAW	ALBLS	10//99-12//99
Transit and Intercity	Huntsville MSA, AL	S	7.70 MW	6.99 AW	16010 AAW	ALBLS	10//99-12//99
Transit and Intercity	Mobile MSA, AL	S	8.46 MW	7.75 AW	17590 AAW	ALBLS	10//99-12//99
Transit and Intercity	Alaska	S	11.1 MW	12.95 AW	26940 AAW	AKBLS	10//99-12//99
Transit and Intercity	Arizona	S	10.08 MW	14.29 AW	29730 AAW	AZBLS	10//99-12//99
Transit and Intercity	Phoenix-Mesa MSA, AZ	S	15.71 MW	10.10 AW	32670 AAW	AZBLS	10//99-12//99
Transit and Intercity	Arkansas	S	7.91 MW	8.63 AW	17960 AAW	ARBLS	10//99-12//99
Transit and Intercity	Little Rock-North Little Rock MSA, AR	S	9.95 MW	10.32 AW	20690 AAW	ARBLS	10//99-12//99
Transit and Intercity	California	S	13.06 MW	13.02 AW	27090 AAW	CABLS	10//99-12//99
Transit and Intercity	Los Angeles-Long Beach PMSA, CA	S	12.50 MW	11.20 AW	26000 AAW	CABLS	10//99-12//99
Transit and Intercity	Modesto MSA, CA	S	9.64 MW	9.12 AW	20060 AAW	CABLS	10//99-12//99
Transit and Intercity	Oakland PMSA, CA	S	12.82 MW	13.05 AW	26670 AAW	CABLS	10//99-12//99
Transit and Intercity	Orange County PMSA, CA	S	14.10 MW	15.08 AW	29330 AAW	CABLS	10//99-12//99
Transit and Intercity	Riverside-San Bernardino PMSA, CA	S	10.65 MW	9.79 AW	22160 AAW	CABLS	10//99-12//99
Transit and Intercity	Sacramento PMSA, CA	S	13.80 MW	14.68 AW	28700 AAW	CABLS	10//99-12//99
Transit and Intercity	Salinas MSA, CA	S	13.86 MW	14.18 AW	28840 AAW	CABLS	10//99-12//99
Transit and Intercity	San Diego MSA, CA	S	11.85 MW	11.04 AW	24640 AAW	CABLS	10//99-12//99
Transit and Intercity	San Francisco PMSA, CA	S	14.14 MW	14.38 AW	29400 AAW	CABLS	10//99-12//99
Transit and Intercity	San Jose PMSA, CA	S	14.26 MW	14.69 AW	29650 AAW	CABLS	10//99-12//99
Transit and Intercity	San Luis Obispo-Atascadero-Paso Robles MSA, CA	S	13.41 MW	14.14 AW	27900 AAW	CABLS	10//99-12//99
Transit and Intercity	Santa Barbara-Santa Maria-Lompoc MSA, CA	S	14.05 MW	13.99 AW	29220 AAW	CABLS	10//99-12//99
Transit and Intercity	Santa Rosa PMSA, CA	S	11.24 MW	11.19 AW	23380 AAW	CABLS	10//99-12//99
Transit and Intercity	Stockton-Lodi MSA, CA	S	15.04 MW	17.10 AW	31280 AAW	CABLS	10//99-12//99
Transit and Intercity	Vallejo-Fairfield-Napa PMSA, CA	S	13.44 MW	14.16 AW	27950 AAW	CABLS	10//99-12//99
Transit and Intercity	Ventura PMSA, CA	S	14.76 MW	17.05 AW	30700 AAW	CABLS	10//99-12//99
Transit and Intercity	Visalia-Tulare-Porterville MSA, CA	S	12.29 MW	11.75 AW	25560 AAW	CABLS	10//99-12//99
Transit and Intercity	Colorado	S	11.21 MW	11.25 AW	23400 AAW	COBLS	10//99-12//99
Transit and Intercity	Colorado Springs MSA, CO	S	10.18 MW	10.20 AW	21180 AAW	COBLS	10//99-12//99
Transit and Intercity	Denver PMSA, CO	S	11.95 MW	11.97 AW	24860 AAW	COBLS	10//99-12//99
Transit and Intercity	Connecticut	S	11.77 MW	13.04 AW	27120 AAW	CTBLS	10//99-12//99
Transit and Intercity	Danbury PMSA, CT	S	13.02 MW	12.76 AW	27080 AAW	CTBLS	10//99-12//99
Transit and Intercity	Hartford MSA, CT	S	13.07 MW	11.59 AW	27180 AAW	CTBLS	10//99-12//99
Transit and Intercity	New Haven-Meriden PMSA, CT	S	13.82 MW	10.38 AW	28750 AAW	CTBLS	10//99-12//99
Transit and Intercity	New London-Norwich MSA, CT-RI	S	10.84 MW	10.79 AW	22540 AAW	CTBLS	10//99-12//99
Transit and Intercity	Stamford-Norwalk PMSA, CT	S	14.39 MW	14.25 AW	29930 AAW	CTBLS	10//99-12//99
Transit and Intercity	Waterbury PMSA, CT	S	12.90 MW	14.27 AW	26820 AAW	CTBLS	10//99-12//99
Transit and Intercity	Delaware	S	9.17 MW	9.19 AW	19120 AAW	DEBLS	10//99-12//99
Transit and Intercity	Wilmington-Newark PMSA, DE-MD	S	9.43 MW	9.33 AW	19620 AAW	DEBLS	10//99-12//99
Transit and Intercity	Washington PMSA, DC-MD-VA-WV	S	12.06 MW	11.79 AW	25080 AAW	DCBLS	10//99-12//99
Transit and Intercity	Florida	S	10.14 MW	10.96 AW	22800 AAW	FLBLS	10//99-12//99
Transit and Intercity	Jacksonville MSA, FL	S	13.03 MW	14.43 AW	27090 AAW	FLBLS	10//99-12//99
Transit and Intercity	Lakeland-Winter Haven MSA, FL	S	9.74 MW	9.74 AW	20270 AAW	FLBLS	10//99-12//99
Transit and Intercity	Melbourne-Titusville-Palm Bay MSA, FL	S	13.83 MW	14.74 AW	28770 AAW	FLBLS	10//99-12//99
Transit and Intercity	Miami PMSA, FL	S	8.76 MW	8.25 AW	18220 AAW	FLBLS	10//99-12//99
Transit and Intercity	Ocala MSA, FL	S	7.69 MW	7.71 AW	15990 AAW	FLBLS	10//99-12//99
Transit and Intercity	Orlando MSA, FL	S	10.52 MW	8.95 AW	21870 AAW	FLBLS	10//99-12//99
Transit and Intercity	Pensacola MSA, FL	S	9.44 MW	8.74 AW	19640 AAW	FLBLS	10//99-12//99
Transit and Intercity	Sarasota-Bradenton MSA, FL	S	9.23 MW	9.41 AW	19200 AAW	FLBLS	10//99-12//99
Transit and Intercity	Tampa-St. Petersburg-Clearwater MSA, FL	S	11.32 MW	10.71 AW	23540 AAW	FLBLS	10//99-12//99
Transit and Intercity	Hawaii	S	13.37 MW	14.65 AW	30470 AAW	HIBLS	10//99-12//99

AAW	Average annual wage	AOH	Average offered, high	ASH	Average starting, high
AE	Average entry wage	AOL	Average offered, low	ASL	Average starting, low
AEX	Average experienced wage	APH	Average pay, high range	AW	Average wage paid
AO	Average offered	APL	Average pay, low range	FQ	First quartile wage

H	Hourly	M	Monthly
HI	Highest wage paid	MTC	Median total compensation
HR	High end range	MW	Median wage paid
LR	Low end range	SQ	Second quartile wage

S	Special: hourly and annual
TQ	Third quartile wage
W	Weekly
Y	Yearly

Occupation/Type/Industry	Location	Per	Low	Mid	High	Source	Date
Bus Driver							
Transit and Intercity	Idaho	S	8.74 MW	10.70 AW	22250 AAW	IDBLS	10//99-12//99
Transit and Intercity	Boise City MSA, ID	S	11.27 MW	10.73 AW	23450 AAW	IDBLS	10//99-12//99
Transit and Intercity	Illinois	S	14.7 MW	13.73 AW	28560 AAW	ILBLS	10//99-12//99
Transit and Intercity	Indiana	S	10.46 MW	10.76 AW	22370 AAW	INBLS	10//99-12//99
Transit and Intercity	Bloomington MSA, IN	S	9.28 MW	9.04 AW	19300 AAW	INBLS	10//99-12//99
Transit and Intercity	Evansville-Henderson MSA, IN-KY	S	7.71 MW	7.29 AW	16040 AAW	INBLS	10//99-12//99
Transit and Intercity	Fort Wayne MSA, IN	S	10.67 MW	9.76 AW	22190 AAW	INBLS	10//99-12//99
Transit and Intercity	Gary PMSA, IN	S	10.42 MW	10.26 AW	21670 AAW	INBLS	10//99-12//99
Transit and Intercity	Indianapolis MSA, IN	S	11.43 MW	11.27 AW	23770 AAW	INBLS	10//99-12//99
Transit and Intercity	Terre Haute MSA, IN	S	12.04 MW	13.02 AW	25030 AAW	INBLS	10//99-12//99
Transit and Intercity	Iowa	S	9.26 MW	10.03 AW	20870 AAW	IABLS	10//99-12//99
Transit and Intercity	Cedar Rapids MSA, IA	S	13.45 MW	14.13 AW	27970 AAW	IABLS	10//99-12//99
Transit and Intercity	Davenport-Moline-Rock Island MSA, IA-IL	S	12.57 MW	12.72 AW	26140 AAW	IABLS	10//99-12//99
Transit and Intercity	Des Moines MSA, IA	S	12.58 MW	12.17 AW	26170 AAW	IABLS	10//99-12//99
Transit and Intercity	Iowa City MSA, IA	S	12.93 MW	13.28 AW	26900 AAW	IABLS	10//99-12//99
Transit and Intercity	Sioux City MSA, IA-NE	S	11.10 MW	10.62 AW	23080 AAW	IABLS	10//99-12//99
Transit and Intercity	Kansas	S	9.06 MW	9.79 AW	20360 AAW	KSBLS	10//99-12//99
Transit and Intercity	Wichita MSA, KS	S	10.20 MW	11.27 AW	21210 AAW	KSBLS	10//99-12//99
Transit and Intercity	Kentucky	S	9.77 MW	10.47 AW	21780 AAW	KYBLS	10//99-12//99
Transit and Intercity	Lexington MSA, KY	S	8.99 MW	8.34 AW	18700 AAW	KYBLS	10//99-12//99
Transit and Intercity	Louisville MSA, KY-IN	S	12.36 MW	13.89 AW	25710 AAW	KYBLS	10//99-12//99
Transit and Intercity	Louisiana	S	10.25 MW	10.79 AW	22450 AAW	LABLS	10//99-12//99
Transit and Intercity	Baton Rouge MSA, LA	S	10.53 MW	10.75 AW	21900 AAW	LABLS	10//99-12//99
Transit and Intercity	Houma MSA, LA	S	7.87 MW	8.07 AW	16360 AAW	LABLS	10//99-12//99
Transit and Intercity	Lake Charles MSA, LA	S	7.51 MW	6.86 AW	15610 AAW	LABLS	10//99-12//99
Transit and Intercity	New Orleans MSA, LA	S	11.62 MW	10.94 AW	24180 AAW	LABLS	10//99-12//99
Transit and Intercity	Shreveport-Bossier City MSA, LA	S	9.41 MW	8.03 AW	19580 AAW	LABLS	10//99-12//99
Transit and Intercity	Maine	S	13.61 MW	12.28 AW	25540 AAW	MEBLS	10//99-12//99
Transit and Intercity	Maryland	S	10.57 MW	11.58 AW	24080 AAW	MDBLS	10//99-12//99
Transit and Intercity	Baltimore PMSA, MD	S	11.42 MW	10.15 AW	23750 AAW	MDBLS	10//99-12//99
Transit and Intercity	Massachusetts	S	12.02 MW	13.18 AW	27420 AAW	MABLS	10//99-12//99
Transit and Intercity	Barnstable-Yarmouth MSA, MA	S	9.03 MW	8.27 AW	18780 AAW	MABLS	10//99-12//99
Transit and Intercity	Boston PMSA, MA-NH	S	11.65 MW	11.37 AW	24230 AAW	MABLS	10//99-12//99
Transit and Intercity	Lawrence PMSA, MA-NH	S	12.13 MW	12.22 AW	25240 AAW	MABLS	10//99-12//99
Transit and Intercity	Lowell PMSA, MA-NH	S	12.26 MW	12.77 AW	25500 AAW	MABLS	10//99-12//99
Transit and Intercity	Springfield MSA, MA	S	11.49 MW	12.01 AW	23900 AAW	MABLS	10//99-12//99
Transit and Intercity	Worcester PMSA, MA-CT	S	13.06 MW	11.93 AW	27170 AAW	MABLS	10//99-12//99
Transit and Intercity	Michigan	S	11.32 MW	11.79 AW	24510 AAW	MIBLS	10//99-12//99
Transit and Intercity	Detroit PMSA, MI	S	12.19 MW	12.50 AW	25360 AAW	MIBLS	10//99-12//99
Transit and Intercity	Grand Rapids-Muskegon-Holland MSA, MI	S	11.20 MW	12.00 AW	23290 AAW	MIBLS	10//99-12//99
Transit and Intercity	Minnesota	S	12.63 MW	13.63 AW	28350 AAW	MNBLS	10//99-12//99
Transit and Intercity	Minneapolis-St. Paul MSA, MN-WI	S	15.18 MW	17.04 AW	31580 AAW	MNBLS	10//99-12//99
Transit and Intercity	Mississippi	S	8.09 MW	8.43 AW	17540 AAW	MSBLS	10//99-12//99
Transit and Intercity	Biloxi-Gulfport-Pascagoula MSA, MS	S	8.30 MW	8.17 AW	17250 AAW	MSBLS	10//99-12//99
Transit and Intercity	Jackson MSA, MS	S	10.55 MW	9.82 AW	21940 AAW	MSBLS	10//99-12//99
Transit and Intercity	Missouri	S	9.13 MW	9.70 AW	20180 AAW	MOBLS	10//99-12//99
Transit and Intercity	St. Louis MSA, MO-IL	S	10.16 MW	9.23 AW	21130 AAW	MOBLS	10//99-12//99
Transit and Intercity	Montana	S	8.73 MW	9.81 AW	20410 AAW	MTBLS	10//99-12//99
Transit and Intercity	Nebraska	S	10.18 MW	10.59 AW	22020 AAW	NEBLS	10//99-12//99
Transit and Intercity	Omaha MSA, NE-IA	S	11.78 MW	11.64 AW	24510 AAW	NEBLS	10//99-12//99
Transit and Intercity	Nevada	S	10.11 MW	10.17 AW	21150 AAW	NVBLS	10//99-12//99
Transit and Intercity	Las Vegas MSA, NV-AZ	S	10.09 MW	10.18 AW	20990 AAW	NVBLS	10//99-12//99
Transit and Intercity	Reno MSA, NV	S	11.12 MW	10.66 AW	23140 AAW	NVBLS	10//99-12//99
Transit and Intercity	New Hampshire	S	9.89 MW	10.27 AW	21360 AAW	NHBLS	10//99-12//99
Transit and Intercity	New Jersey	S	12.29 MW	13.12 AW	27280 AAW	NJBLS	10//99-12//99
Transit and Intercity	Atlantic-Cape May PMSA, NJ	S	13.98 MW	13.41 AW	29070 AAW	NJBLS	10//99-12//99
Transit and Intercity	Bergen-Passaic PMSA, NJ	S	13.58 MW	12.72 AW	28240 AAW	NJBLS	10//99-12//99
Transit and Intercity	Jersey City PMSA, NJ	S	12.08 MW	11.46 AW	25120 AAW	NJBLS	10//99-12//99
Transit and Intercity	Middlesex-Somerset-Hunterdon PMSA, NJ	S	11.73 MW	11.81 AW	24390 AAW	NJBLS	10//99-12//99
Transit and Intercity	Monmouth-Ocean PMSA, NJ	S	13.04 MW	11.68 AW	27120 AAW	NJBLS	10//99-12//99
Transit and Intercity	Newark PMSA, NJ	S	13.50 MW	12.81 AW	28070 AAW	NJBLS	10//99-12//99
Transit and Intercity	New Mexico	S	10.24 MW	10.62 AW	22080 AAW	NMBLS	10//99-12//99
Transit and Intercity	New York	S	19.33 MW	17.64 AW	36700 AAW	NYBLS	10//99-12//99

AAW Average annual wage	**AOH** Average offered, high	**ASH** Average starting, high	**H** Hourly	**M** Monthly	**S** Special: hourly and annual
AE Average entry wage	**AOL** Average offered, low	**ASL** Average starting, low	**HI** Highest wage paid	**MTC** Median total compensation	**TQ** Third quartile wage
AEX Average experienced wage	**APH** Average pay, high range	**AW** Average wage paid	**HR** High end range	**MW** Median wage paid	**W** Weekly
AO Average offered	**APL** Average pay, low range	**FQ** First quartile wage	**LR** Low end range	**SQ** Second quartile wage	**Y** Yearly

Occupation/Type/Industry	Location	Per	Low	Mid	High	Source	Date
Bus Driver							
Transit and Intercity	Albany-Schenectady-Troy MSA, NY	S	10.25 MW	9.47 AW	21320 AAW	NYBLS	10//99-12//99
Transit and Intercity	Binghamton MSA, NY	S	11.03 MW	10.14 AW	22950 AAW	NYBLS	10//99-12//99
Transit and Intercity	Buffalo-Niagara Falls MSA, NY	S	10.08 MW	8.94 AW	20960 AAW	NYBLS	10//99-12//99
Transit and Intercity	Dutchess County PMSA, NY	S	12.61 MW	11.78 AW	26220 AAW	NYBLS	10//99-12//99
Transit and Intercity	Elmira MSA, NY	S	11.16 MW	8.41 AW	23210 AAW	NYBLS	10//99-12//99
Transit and Intercity	Glens Falls MSA, NY	S	8.48 MW	7.95 AW	17640 AAW	NYBLS	10//99-12//99
Transit and Intercity	Nassau-Suffolk PMSA, NY	S	12.24 MW	11.92 AW	25450 AAW	NYBLS	10//99-12//99
Transit and Intercity	New York PMSA, NY	S	19.25 MW	20.57 AW	40050 AAW	NYBLS	10//99-12//99
Transit and Intercity	Newburgh PMSA, NY-PA	S	11.64 MW	9.84 AW	24200 AAW	NYBLS	10//99-12//99
Transit and Intercity	Rochester MSA, NY	S	19.40 MW	21.20 AW	40340 AAW	NYBLS	10//99-12//99
Transit and Intercity	Syracuse MSA, NY	S	9.25 MW	7.94 AW	19240 AAW	NYBLS	10//99-12//99
Transit and Intercity	Utica-Rome MSA, NY	S	9.40 MW	9.58 AW	19550 AAW	NYBLS	10//99-12//99
Transit and Intercity	North Carolina	S	9.58 MW	10.30 AW	21430 AAW	NCBLS	10//99-12//99
Transit and Intercity	Charlotte-Gastonia-Rock Hill MSA, NC-SC	S	12.32 MW	12.65 AW	25630 AAW	NCBLS	10//99-12//99
Transit and Intercity	Greensboro--Winston-Salem--High Point MSA, NC	S	10.32 MW	10.81 AW	21450 AAW	NCBLS	10//99-12//99
Transit and Intercity	Raleigh-Durham-Chapel Hill MSA, NC	S	10.15 MW	9.55 AW	21100 AAW	NCBLS	10//99-12//99
Transit and Intercity	North Dakota	S	7.41 MW	7.65 AW	15910 AAW	NDBLS	10//99-12//99
Transit and Intercity	Bismarck MSA, ND	S	6.84 MW	6.86 AW	14220 AAW	NDBLS	10//99-12//99
Transit and Intercity	Ohio	S	14.06 MW	14.92 AW	31040 AAW	OHBLS	10//99-12//99
Transit and Intercity	Cincinnati PMSA, OH-KY-IN	S	10.40 MW	9.59 AW	21620 AAW	OHBLS	10//99-12//99
Transit and Intercity	Steubenville-Weirton MSA, OH-WV	S	7.69 MW	6.40 AW	15990 AAW	OHBLS	10//99-12//99
Transit and Intercity	Toledo MSA, OH	S	10.83 MW	10.91 AW	22520 AAW	OHBLS	10//99-12//99
Transit and Intercity	Oklahoma	S	10.3 MW	9.90 AW	20600 AAW	OKBLS	10//99-12//99
Transit and Intercity	Oklahoma City MSA, OK	S	10.85 MW	12.03 AW	22570 AAW	OKBLS	10//99-12//99
Transit and Intercity	Tulsa MSA, OK	S	10.09 MW	10.81 AW	20990 AAW	OKBLS	10//99-12//99
Transit and Intercity	Pennsylvania	S	11.17 MW	11.85 AW	24640 AAW	PABLS	10//99-12//99
Transit and Intercity	Allentown-Bethlehem-Easton MSA, PA	S	13.61 MW	13.98 AW	28300 AAW	PABLS	10//99-12//99
Transit and Intercity	Harrisburg-Lebanon-Carlisle MSA, PA	S	10.69 MW	9.06 AW	22220 AAW	PABLS	10//99-12//99
Transit and Intercity	Johnstown MSA, PA	S	10.32 MW	8.68 AW	21460 AAW	PABLS	10//99-12//99
Transit and Intercity	Lancaster MSA, PA	S	11.93 MW	9.63 AW	24820 AAW	PABLS	10//99-12//99
Transit and Intercity	Philadelphia PMSA, PA-NJ	S	11.93 MW	11.57 AW	24810 AAW	PABLS	10//99-12//99
Transit and Intercity	Reading MSA, PA	S	11.36 MW	11.20 AW	23630 AAW	PABLS	10//99-12//99
Transit and Intercity	Scranton--Wilkes-Barre--Hazleton MSA, PA	S	12.16 MW	12.78 AW	25300 AAW	PABLS	10//99-12//99
Transit and Intercity	Rhode Island	S	10.18 MW	11.39 AW	23690 AAW	RIBLS	10//99-12//99
Transit and Intercity	Providence-Fall River-Warwick MSA, RI-MA	S	11.49 MW	10.33 AW	23900 AAW	RIBLS	10//99-12//99
Transit and Intercity	South Carolina	S	8.67 MW	9.10 AW	18930 AAW	SCBLS	10//99-12//99
Transit and Intercity	Charleston-North Charleston MSA, SC	S	7.72 MW	7.39 AW	16060 AAW	SCBLS	10//99-12//99
Transit and Intercity	Columbia MSA, SC	S	9.89 MW	8.63 AW	20580 AAW	SCBLS	10//99-12//99
Transit and Intercity	Greenville-Spartanburg-Anderson MSA, SC	S	8.10 MW	7.50 AW	16840 AAW	SCBLS	10//99-12//99
Transit and Intercity	South Dakota	S	8.61 MW	9.17 AW	19060 AAW	SDBLS	10//99-12//99
Transit and Intercity	Rapid City MSA, SD	S	8.19 MW	8.00 AW	17030 AAW	SDBLS	10//99-12//99
Transit and Intercity	Tennessee	S	8.03 MW	9.78 AW	20340 AAW	TNBLS	10//99-12//99
Transit and Intercity	Clarksville-Hopkinsville MSA, TN-KY	S	7.99 MW	7.29 AW	16610 AAW	TNBLS	10//99-12//99
Transit and Intercity	Johnson City-Kingsport-Bristol MSA, TN-VA	S	8.40 MW	7.86 AW	17470 AAW	TNBLS	10//99-12//99
Transit and Intercity	Knoxville MSA, TN	S	10.30 MW	8.46 AW	21430 AAW	TNBLS	10//99-12//99
Transit and Intercity	Memphis MSA, TN-AR-MS	S	9.91 MW	7.89 AW	20620 AAW	MSBLS	10//99-12//99
Transit and Intercity	Nashville MSA, TN	S	11.09 MW	8.57 AW	23070 AAW	TNBLS	10//99-12//99
Transit and Intercity	Texas	S	10.83 MW	11.08 AW	23050 AAW	TXBLS	10//99-12//99
Transit and Intercity	Abilene MSA, TX	S	8.30 MW	6.92 AW	17250 AAW	TXBLS	10//99-12//99
Transit and Intercity	Amarillo MSA, TX	S	14.55 MW	14.97 AW	30270 AAW	TXBLS	10//99-12//99
Transit and Intercity	Brownsville-Harlingen-San Benito MSA, TX	S	10.36 MW	9.41 AW	21540 AAW	TXBLS	10//99-12//99
Transit and Intercity	Dallas PMSA, TX	S	10.59 MW	9.50 AW	22030 AAW	TXBLS	10//99-12//99
Transit and Intercity	El Paso MSA, TX	S	10.97 MW	11.60 AW	22820 AAW	TXBLS	10//99-12//99
Transit and Intercity	Fort Worth-Arlington PMSA, TX	S	10.94 MW	10.58 AW	22760 AAW	TXBLS	10//99-12//99
Transit and Intercity	Houston PMSA, TX	S	11.72 MW	11.70 AW	24370 AAW	TXBLS	10//99-12//99

AAW Average annual wage	**AOH** Average offered, high	**ASH** Average starting, high	**H** Hourly	**M** Monthly	**S** Special: hourly and annual
AE Average entry wage	**AOL** Average offered, low	**ASL** Average starting, low	**HI** Highest wage paid	**MTC** Median total compensation	**TQ** Third quartile wage
AEX Average experienced wage	**APH** Average pay, high range	**AW** Average wage paid	**HR** High end range	**MW** Median wage paid	**W** Weekly
AO Average offered	**APL** Average pay, low range	**FQ** First quartile wage	**LR** Low end range	**SQ** Second quartile wage	**Y** Yearly

Occupation/Type/Industry	Location	Per	Low	Mid	High	Source	Date
Bus Driver							
Transit and Intercity	Laredo MSA, TX	S	11.84 MW	11.13 AW	24620 AAW	TXBLS	10//99-12//99
Transit and Intercity	McAllen-Edinburg-Mission MSA, TX	S	6.43 MW	6.35 AW	13370 AAW	TXBLS	10//99-12//99
Transit and Intercity	San Antonio MSA, TX	S	10.49 MW	10.38 AW	21820 AAW	TXBLS	10//99-12//99
Transit and Intercity	Tyler MSA, TX	S	9.50 MW	9.28 AW	19760 AAW	TXBLS	10//99-12//99
Transit and Intercity	Waco MSA, TX	S	12.39 MW	12.36 AW	25770 AAW	TXBLS	10//99-12//99
Transit and Intercity	Utah	S	13.28 MW	12.38 AW	25750 AAW	UTBLS	10//99-12//99
Transit and Intercity	Vermont	S	9.64 MW	9.69 AW	20150 AAW	VTBLS	10//99-12//99
Transit and Intercity	Virginia	S	10.21 MW	10.33 AW	21490 AAW	VABLS	10//99-12//99
Transit and Intercity	Charlottesville MSA, VA	S	9.09 MW	8.74 AW	18900 AAW	VABLS	10//99-12//99
Transit and Intercity	Lynchburg MSA, VA	S	11.38 MW	11.82 AW	23670 AAW	VABLS	10//99-12//99
Transit and Intercity	Norfolk-Virginia Beach-Newport News MSA, VA-NC	S	8.26 MW	7.54 AW	17180 AAW	VABLS	10//99-12//99
Transit and Intercity	Richmond-Petersburg MSA, VA	S	12.39 MW	13.70 AW	25770 AAW	VABLS	10//99-12//99
Transit and Intercity	Roanoke MSA, VA	S	9.67 MW	9.62 AW	20120 AAW	VABLS	10//99-12//99
Transit and Intercity	Washington	S	13.07 MW	13.72 AW	28550 AAW	WABLS	10//99-12//99
Transit and Intercity	Olympia PMSA, WA	S	11.38 MW	11.70 AW	23670 AAW	WABLS	10//99-12//99
Transit and Intercity	Seattle-Bellevue-Everett PMSA, WA	S	13.50 MW	11.28 AW	28090 AAW	WABLS	10//99-12//99
Transit and Intercity	Tacoma PMSA, WA	S	15.30 MW	17.57 AW	31830 AAW	WABLS	10//99-12//99
Transit and Intercity	West Virginia	S	8.06 MW	8.75 AW	18210 AAW	WVBLS	10//99-12//99
Transit and Intercity	Huntington-Ashland MSA, WV-KY-OH	S	7.91 MW	7.09 AW	16450 AAW	WVBLS	10//99-12//99
Transit and Intercity	Parkersburg-Marietta MSA, WV-OH	S	10.82 MW	11.41 AW	22510 AAW	WVBLS	10//99-12//99
Transit and Intercity	Wisconsin	S	11.55 MW	12.54 AW	26080 AAW	WIBLS	10//99-12//99
Transit and Intercity	Eau Claire MSA, WI	S	9.67 MW	9.17 AW	20110 AAW	WIBLS	10//99-12//99
Transit and Intercity	Janesville-Beloit MSA, WI	S	10.24 MW	8.89 AW	21300 AAW	WIBLS	10//99-12//99
Transit and Intercity	Wausau MSA, WI	S	11.32 MW	10.28 AW	23550 AAW	WIBLS	10//99-12//99
Transit and Intercity	Wyoming	S	9.57 MW	9.99 AW	20780 AAW	WYBLS	10//99-12//99
Transit and Intercity	Mayaguez MSA, PR	S	5.78 MW	5.99 AW	12030 AAW	PRBLS	10//99-12//99
Transit and Intercity	Guam	S	7.95 MW	8.30 AW	17250 AAW	GUBLS	10//99-12//99
Business Analyst							
Information Technology	Atlanta, GA	Y		76986 AW		ATBUS	3//00
Business Teacher							
Postsecondary	Alabama	Y		44180 AAW		ALBLS	10//99-12//99
Postsecondary	Birmingham MSA, AL	Y		48100 AAW		ALBLS	10//99-12//99
Postsecondary	Mobile MSA, AL	Y		31480 AAW		ALBLS	10//99-12//99
Postsecondary	Montgomery MSA, AL	Y		42090 AAW		ALBLS	10//99-12//99
Postsecondary	Tuscaloosa MSA, AL	Y		43510 AAW		ALBLS	10//99-12//99
Postsecondary	Arizona	Y		41180 AAW		AZBLS	10//99-12//99
Postsecondary	Phoenix-Mesa MSA, AZ	Y		38260 AAW		AZBLS	10//99-12//99
Postsecondary	Arkansas	Y		47100 AAW		ARBLS	10//99-12//99
Postsecondary	California	Y		56500 AAW		CABLS	10//99-12//99
Postsecondary	Fresno MSA, CA	Y		51810 AAW		CABLS	10//99-12//99
Postsecondary	Los Angeles-Long Beach PMSA, CA	Y		53670 AAW		CABLS	10//99-12//99
Postsecondary	Riverside-San Bernardino PMSA, CA	Y		51810 AAW		CABLS	10//99-12//99
Postsecondary	Sacramento PMSA, CA	Y		54170 AAW		CABLS	10//99-12//99
Postsecondary	Salinas MSA, CA	Y		57670 AAW		CABLS	10//99-12//99
Postsecondary	San Diego MSA, CA	Y		55340 AAW		CABLS	10//99-12//99
Postsecondary	San Francisco PMSA, CA	Y		70900 AAW		CABLS	10//99-12//99
Postsecondary	Colorado	Y		44710 AAW		COBLS	10//99-12//99
Postsecondary	Denver PMSA, CO	Y		43630 AAW		COBLS	10//99-12//99
Postsecondary	Connecticut	Y		73330 AAW		CTBLS	10//99-12//99
Postsecondary	Hartford MSA, CT	Y		86800 AAW		CTBLS	10//99-12//99
Postsecondary	New Haven-Meriden PMSA, CT	Y		51500 AAW		CTBLS	10//99-12//99
Postsecondary	District of Columbia	Y		48600 AAW		DCBLS	10//99-12//99
Postsecondary	Washington PMSA, DC-MD-VA-WV	Y		50840 AAW		DCBLS	10//99-12//99
Postsecondary	Florida	Y		60740 AAW		FLBLS	10//99-12//99
Postsecondary	Jacksonville MSA, FL	Y		46770 AAW		FLBLS	10//99-12//99
Postsecondary	Melbourne-Titusville-Palm Bay MSA, FL	Y		52130 AAW		FLBLS	10//99-12//99
Postsecondary	Miami PMSA, FL	Y		72400 AAW		FLBLS	10//99-12//99
Postsecondary	Orlando MSA, FL	Y		60990 AAW		FLBLS	10//99-12//99

AAW	Average annual wage	AOH	Average offered, high	ASH	Average starting, high	H	Hourly	M	Monthly	S	Special: hourly and annual
AE	Average entry wage	AOL	Average offered, low	ASL	Average starting, low	HI	Highest wage paid	MTC	Median total compensation	TQ	Third quartile wage
AEX	Average experienced wage	APH	Average pay, high range	AW	Average wage paid	HR	High end range	MW	Median wage paid	W	Weekly
AO	Average offered	APL	Average pay, low range	FQ	First quartile wage	LR	Low end range	SQ	Second quartile wage	Y	Yearly

Occupation/Type/Industry	Location	Per	Low	Mid	High	Source	Date
Business Teacher							
Postsecondary	Pensacola MSA, FL	Y		57390 AAW		FLBLS	10//99-12//99
Postsecondary	Tampa-St. Petersburg-Clearwater MSA, FL	Y		59740 AAW		FLBLS	10//99-12//99
Postsecondary	Georgia	Y		48430 AAW		GABLS	10//99-12//99
Postsecondary	Atlanta MSA, GA	Y		46030 AAW		GABLS	10//99-12//99
Postsecondary	Savannah MSA, GA	Y		47210 AAW		GABLS	10//99-12//99
Postsecondary	Idaho	Y		50900 AAW		IDBLS	10//99-12//99
Postsecondary	Illinois	Y		50300 AAW		ILBLS	10//99-12//99
Postsecondary	Chicago PMSA, IL	Y		51740 AAW		ILBLS	10//99-12//99
Postsecondary	Indiana	Y		49580 AAW		INBLS	10//99-12//99
Postsecondary	Fort Wayne MSA, IN	Y		75190 AAW		INBLS	10//99-12//99
Postsecondary	Gary PMSA, IN	Y		53300 AAW		INBLS	10//99-12//99
Postsecondary	Indianapolis MSA, IN	Y		39490 AAW		INBLS	10//99-12//99
Postsecondary	South Bend MSA, IN	Y		43110 AAW		INBLS	10//99-12//99
Postsecondary	Iowa	Y		58040 AAW		IABLS	10//99-12//99
Postsecondary	Des Moines MSA, IA	Y		58290 AAW		IABLS	10//99-12//99
Postsecondary	Kansas	Y		38880 AAW		KSBLS	10//99-12//99
Postsecondary	Kentucky	Y		47660 AAW		KYBLS	10//99-12//99
Postsecondary	Louisiana	Y		54580 AAW		LABLS	10//99-12//99
Postsecondary	New Orleans MSA, LA	Y		55870 AAW		LABLS	10//99-12//99
Postsecondary	Maine	Y		44580 AAW		MEBLS	10//99-12//99
Postsecondary	Portland MSA, ME	Y		47620 AAW		MEBLS	10//99-12//99
Postsecondary	Maryland	Y		60090 AAW		MDBLS	10//99-12//99
Postsecondary	Baltimore PMSA, MD	Y		55240 AAW		MDBLS	10//99-12//99
Postsecondary	Massachusetts	Y		58630 AAW		MABLS	10//99-12//99
Postsecondary	Boston PMSA, MA-NH	Y		59830 AAW		MABLS	10//99-12//99
Postsecondary	Brockton PMSA, MA	Y		50460 AAW		MABLS	10//99-12//99
Postsecondary	Fitchburg-Leominster PMSA, MA	Y		50710 AAW		MABLS	10//99-12//99
Postsecondary	Lawrence PMSA, MA-NH	Y		48550 AAW		MABLS	10//99-12//99
Postsecondary	Springfield MSA, MA	Y		61110 AAW		MABLS	10//99-12//99
Postsecondary	Worcester PMSA, MA-CT	Y		51460 AAW		MABLS	10//99-12//99
Postsecondary	Michigan	Y		67730 AAW		MIBLS	10//99-12//99
Postsecondary	Ann Arbor PMSA, MI	Y		85340 AAW		MIBLS	10//99-12//99
Postsecondary	Detroit PMSA, MI	Y		70490 AAW		MIBLS	10//99-12//99
Postsecondary	Flint PMSA, MI	Y		67840 AAW		MIBLS	10//99-12//99
Postsecondary	Saginaw-Bay City-Midland MSA, MI	Y		59150 AAW		MIBLS	10//99-12//99
Postsecondary	Minnesota	Y		58550 AAW		MNBLS	10//99-12//99
Postsecondary	Minneapolis-St. Paul MSA, MN-WI	Y		58820 AAW		MNBLS	10//99-12//99
Postsecondary	Mississippi	Y		50440 AAW		MSBLS	10//99-12//99
Postsecondary	Jackson MSA, MS	Y		44270 AAW		MSBLS	10//99-12//99
Postsecondary	Missouri	Y		46920 AAW		MOBLS	10//99-12//99
Postsecondary	Kansas City MSA, MO-KS	Y		45490 AAW		MOBLS	10//99-12//99
Postsecondary	Montana	Y		65880 AAW		MTBLS	10//99-12//99
Postsecondary	Nebraska	Y		58760 AAW		NEBLS	10//99-12//99
Postsecondary	Omaha MSA, NE-IA	Y		50050 AAW		NEBLS	10//99-12//99
Postsecondary	Nevada	Y		48570 AAW		NVBLS	10//99-12//99
Postsecondary	Las Vegas MSA, NV-AZ	Y		58390 AAW		NVBLS	10//99-12//99
Postsecondary	New Hampshire	Y		59590 AAW		NHBLS	10//99-12//99
Postsecondary	Nashua PMSA, NH	Y		50970 AAW		NHBLS	10//99-12//99
Postsecondary	New Jersey	Y		64350 AAW		NJBLS	10//99-12//99
Postsecondary	Bergen-Passaic PMSA, NJ	Y		61600 AAW		NJBLS	10//99-12//99
Postsecondary	Jersey City PMSA, NJ	Y		75120 AAW		NJBLS	10//99-12//99
Postsecondary	Newark PMSA, NJ	Y		60780 AAW		NJBLS	10//99-12//99
Postsecondary	New Mexico	Y		47470 AAW		NMBLS	10//99-12//99
Postsecondary	New York	Y		53450 AAW		NYBLS	10//99-12//99
Postsecondary	Albany-Schenectady-Troy MSA, NY	Y		53490 AAW		NYBLS	10//99-12//99
Postsecondary	Buffalo-Niagara Falls MSA, NY	Y		45160 AAW		NYBLS	10//99-12//99
Postsecondary	Nassau-Suffolk PMSA, NY	Y		56150 AAW		NYBLS	10//99-12//99
Postsecondary	New York PMSA, NY	Y		56540 AAW		NYBLS	10//99-12//99
Postsecondary	Utica-Rome MSA, NY	Y		44690 AAW		NYBLS	10//99-12//99
Postsecondary	North Carolina	Y		47610 AAW		NCBLS	10//99-12//99
Postsecondary	Asheville MSA, NC	Y		47110 AAW		NCBLS	10//99-12//99
Postsecondary	Charlotte-Gastonia-Rock Hill MSA, NC-SC	Y		46960 AAW		NCBLS	10//99-12//99
Postsecondary	Greensboro--Winston-Salem--High Point MSA, NC	Y		58020 AAW		NCBLS	10//99-12//99

AAW	Average annual wage	AOH	Average offered, high	ASH	Average starting, high
AE	Average entry wage	AOL	Average offered, low	ASL	Average starting, low
AEX	Average experienced wage	APH	Average pay, high range	AW	Average wage paid
AO	Average offered	APL	Average pay, low range	FQ	First quartile wage

H	Hourly	M	Monthly
HI	Highest wage paid	MTC	Median total compensation
HR	High end range	MW	Median wage paid
LR	Low end range	SQ	Second quartile wage

S	Special: hourly and annual
TQ	Third quartile wage
W	Weekly
Y	Yearly

Occupation/Type/Industry	Location	Per	Low	Mid	High	Source	Date
Business Teacher							
Postsecondary	Hickory-Morganton-Lenoir MSA, NC	Y		39770 AAW		NCBLS	10//99-12//99
Postsecondary	Raleigh-Durham-Chapel Hill MSA, NC	Y		48630 AAW		NCBLS	10//99-12//99
Postsecondary	Rocky Mount MSA, NC	Y		40230 AAW		NCBLS	10//99-12//99
Postsecondary	Wilmington MSA, NC	Y		55280 AAW		NCBLS	10//99-12//99
Postsecondary	North Dakota	Y		45620 AAW		NDBLS	10//99-12//99
Postsecondary	Grand Forks MSA, ND-MN	Y		53610 AAW		NDBLS	10//99-12//99
Postsecondary	Ohio	Y		44230 AAW		OHBLS	10//99-12//99
Postsecondary	Canton-Massillon MSA, OH	Y		40630 AAW		OHBLS	10//99-12//99
Postsecondary	Cleveland-Lorain-Elyria PMSA, OH	Y		55120 AAW		OHBLS	10//99-12//99
Postsecondary	Columbus MSA, OH	Y		42980 AAW		OHBLS	10//99-12//99
Postsecondary	Dayton-Springfield MSA, OH	Y		28320 AAW		OHBLS	10//99-12//99
Postsecondary	Lima MSA, OH	Y		44030 AAW		OHBLS	10//99-12//99
Postsecondary	Toledo MSA, OH	Y		44410 AAW		OHBLS	10//99-12//99
Postsecondary	Oklahoma	Y		54980 AAW		OKBLS	10//99-12//99
Postsecondary	Oklahoma City MSA, OK	Y		49060 AAW		OKBLS	10//99-12//99
Postsecondary	Tulsa MSA, OK	Y		50920 AAW		OKBLS	10//99-12//99
Postsecondary	Oregon	Y		53340 AAW		ORBLS	10//99-12//99
Postsecondary	Portland-Vancouver PMSA, OR-WA	Y		52560 AAW		ORBLS	10//99-12//99
Postsecondary	Pennsylvania	Y		60800 AAW		PABLS	10//99-12//99
Postsecondary	Allentown-Bethlehem-Easton MSA, PA	Y		44540 AAW		PABLS	10//99-12//99
Postsecondary	Erie MSA, PA	Y		48730 AAW		PABLS	10//99-12//99
Postsecondary	Harrisburg-Lebanon-Carlisle MSA, PA	Y		57180 AAW		PABLS	10//99-12//99
Postsecondary	Philadelphia PMSA, PA-NJ	Y		60060 AAW		PABLS	10//99-12//99
Postsecondary	Pittsburgh MSA, PA	Y		66890 AAW		PABLS	10//99-12//99
Postsecondary	Reading MSA, PA	Y		49390 AAW		PABLS	10//99-12//99
Postsecondary	Scranton--Wilkes-Barre--Hazleton MSA, PA	Y		53840 AAW		PABLS	10//99-12//99
Postsecondary	Rhode Island	Y		68410 AAW		RIBLS	10//99-12//99
Postsecondary	Providence-Fall River-Warwick MSA, RI-MA	Y		68730 AAW		RIBLS	10//99-12//99
Postsecondary	South Carolina	Y		51050 AAW		SCBLS	10//99-12//99
Postsecondary	Greenville-Spartanburg-Anderson MSA, SC	Y		51180 AAW		SCBLS	10//99-12//99
Postsecondary	South Dakota	Y		42720 AAW		SDBLS	10//99-12//99
Postsecondary	Sioux Falls MSA, SD	Y		35150 AAW		SDBLS	10//99-12//99
Postsecondary	Tennessee	Y		51890 AAW		TNBLS	10//99-12//99
Postsecondary	Chattanooga MSA, TN-GA	Y		46450 AAW		TNBLS	10//99-12//99
Postsecondary	Johnson City-Kingsport-Bristol MSA, TN-VA	Y		47170 AAW		TNBLS	10//99-12//99
Postsecondary	Memphis MSA, TN-AR-MS	Y		58250 AAW		MSBLS	10//99-12//99
Postsecondary	Nashville MSA, TN	Y		56810 AAW		TNBLS	10//99-12//99
Postsecondary	Texas	Y		47770 AAW		TXBLS	10//99-12//99
Postsecondary	Dallas PMSA, TX	Y		51380 AAW		TXBLS	10//99-12//99
Postsecondary	El Paso MSA, TX	Y		38820 AAW		TXBLS	10//99-12//99
Postsecondary	Houston PMSA, TX	Y		52280 AAW		TXBLS	10//99-12//99
Postsecondary	Killeen-Temple MSA, TX	Y		35380 AAW		TXBLS	10//99-12//99
Postsecondary	Longview-Marshall MSA, TX	Y		34820 AAW		TXBLS	10//99-12//99
Postsecondary	Odessa-Midland MSA, TX	Y		42190 AAW		TXBLS	10//99-12//99
Postsecondary	San Antonio MSA, TX	Y		48200 AAW		TXBLS	10//99-12//99
Postsecondary	Vermont	Y		52170 AAW		VTBLS	10//99-12//99
Postsecondary	Burlington MSA, VT	Y		55100 AAW		VTBLS	10//99-12//99
Postsecondary	Virginia	Y		49460 AAW		VABLS	10//99-12//99
Postsecondary	Richmond-Petersburg MSA, VA	Y		55580 AAW		VABLS	10//99-12//99
Postsecondary	Washington	Y		44680 AAW		WABLS	10//99-12//99
Postsecondary	Seattle-Bellevue-Everett PMSA, WA	Y		56360 AAW		WABLS	10//99-12//99
Postsecondary	Spokane MSA, WA	Y		34720 AAW		WABLS	10//99-12//99
Postsecondary	Tacoma PMSA, WA	Y		42480 AAW		WABLS	10//99-12//99
Postsecondary	West Virginia	Y		53140 AAW		WVBLS	10//99-12//99
Postsecondary	Wisconsin	Y		49980 AAW		WIBLS	10//99-12//99
Postsecondary	Green Bay MSA, WI	Y		42760 AAW		WIBLS	10//99-12//99
Postsecondary	Kenosha PMSA, WI	Y		54510 AAW		WIBLS	10//99-12//99
Postsecondary	Milwaukee-Waukesha PMSA, WI	Y		33530 AAW		WIBLS	10//99-12//99

AAW	Average annual wage	AOH	Average offered, high	ASH	Average starting, high	H	Hourly	M	Monthly	S	Special: hourly and annual
AE	Average entry wage	AOL	Average offered, low	ASL	Average starting, low	HI	Highest wage paid	MTC	Median total compensation	TQ	Third quartile wage
AEX	Average experienced wage	APH	Average pay, high range	AW	Average wage paid	HR	High end range	MW	Median wage paid	W	Weekly
AO	Average offered	APL	Average pay, low range	FQ	First quartile wage	LR	Low end range	SQ	Second quartile wage	Y	Yearly

Occupation/Type/Industry	Location	Per	Low	Mid	High	Source	Date
Business Teacher							
Postsecondary	Wyoming	Y		53830 AAW		WYBLS	10//99-12//99
Postsecondary	Puerto Rico	Y		29550 AAW		PRBLS	10//99-12//99
Postsecondary	Arecibo PMSA, PR	Y		31970 AAW		PRBLS	10//99-12//99
Postsecondary	Mayaguez MSA, PR	Y		25870 AAW		PRBLS	10//99-12//99
Postsecondary	San Juan-Bayamon PMSA, PR	Y		29800 AAW		PRBLS	10//99-12//99
Butcher	United States	Y		20420 AW		DENE	1999
Butcher and Meat Cutter	Alabama	S	9.05 MW	9.13 AW	18990 AAW	ALBLS	10//99-12//99
	Anniston MSA, AL	S	9.28 MW	8.80 AW	19310 AAW	ALBLS	10//99-12//99
	Auburn-Opelika MSA, AL	S	9.35 MW	9.68 AW	19460 AAW	ALBLS	10//99-12//99
	Birmingham MSA, AL	S	9.91 MW	9.71 AW	20610 AAW	ALBLS	10//99-12//99
	Decatur MSA, AL	S	11.92 MW	12.20 AW	24800 AAW	ALBLS	10//99-12//99
	Dothan MSA, AL	S	9.30 MW	8.56 AW	19350 AAW	ALBLS	10//99-12//99
	Florence MSA, AL	S	7.82 MW	7.23 AW	16270 AAW	ALBLS	10//99-12//99
	Gadsden MSA, AL	S	8.67 MW	8.39 AW	18040 AAW	ALBLS	10//99-12//99
	Huntsville MSA, AL	S	10.17 MW	10.03 AW	21150 AAW	ALBLS	10//99-12//99
	Mobile MSA, AL	S	8.04 MW	7.78 AW	16730 AAW	ALBLS	10//99-12//99
	Montgomery MSA, AL	S	10.07 MW	10.04 AW	20940 AAW	ALBLS	10//99-12//99
	Tuscaloosa MSA, AL	S	9.45 MW	9.46 AW	19660 AAW	ALBLS	10//99-12//99
	Alaska	S	12.77 MW	13.26 AW	27570 AAW	AKBLS	10//99-12//99
	Anchorage MSA, AK	S	13.57 MW	13.07 AW	28220 AAW	AKBLS	10//99-12//99
	Arizona	S	12.65 MW	12.06 AW	25080 AAW	AZBLS	10//99-12//99
	Phoenix-Mesa MSA, AZ	S	11.03 MW	11.35 AW	22930 AAW	AZBLS	10//99-12//99
	Tucson MSA, AZ	S	12.84 MW	13.99 AW	26710 AAW	AZBLS	10//99-12//99
	Arkansas	S	8.77 MW	8.79 AW	18290 AAW	ARBLS	10//99-12//99
	Fayetteville-Springdale-Rogers MSA, AR	S	8.97 MW	8.91 AW	18660 AAW	ARBLS	10//99-12//99
	Fort Smith MSA, AR-OK	S	10.61 MW	10.64 AW	22060 AAW	ARBLS	10//99-12//99
	Little Rock-North Little Rock MSA, AR	S	10.67 MW	10.96 AW	22190 AAW	ARBLS	10//99-12//99
	California	S	14.46 MW	14.05 AW	29220 AAW	CABLS	10//99-12//99
	Bakersfield MSA, CA	S	12.26 MW	10.14 AW	25500 AAW	CABLS	10//99-12//99
	Chico-Paradise MSA, CA	S	16.53 MW	17.13 AW	34380 AAW	CABLS	10//99-12//99
	Fresno MSA, CA	S	8.39 MW	7.02 AW	17450 AAW	CABLS	10//99-12//99
	Los Angeles-Long Beach PMSA, CA	S	12.84 MW	11.08 AW	26710 AAW	CABLS	10//99-12//99
	Merced MSA, CA	S	9.08 MW	8.80 AW	18890 AAW	CABLS	10//99-12//99
	Modesto MSA, CA	S	11.63 MW	11.78 AW	24190 AAW	CABLS	10//99-12//99
	Oakland PMSA, CA	S	15.80 MW	15.62 AW	32870 AAW	CABLS	10//99-12//99
	Orange County PMSA, CA	S	18.04 MW	18.52 AW	37530 AAW	CABLS	10//99-12//99
	Redding MSA, CA	S	14.06 MW	13.89 AW	29250 AAW	CABLS	10//99-12//99
	Riverside-San Bernardino PMSA, CA	S	11.48 MW	10.78 AW	23880 AAW	CABLS	10//99-12//99
	Sacramento PMSA, CA	S	17.80 MW	18.58 AW	37010 AAW	CABLS	10//99-12//99
	Salinas MSA, CA	S	15.84 MW	15.72 AW	32960 AAW	CABLS	10//99-12//99
	San Diego MSA, CA	S	14.74 MW	14.98 AW	30660 AAW	CABLS	10//99-12//99
	San Francisco PMSA, CA	S	16.34 MW	17.47 AW	33990 AAW	CABLS	10//99-12//99
	San Jose PMSA, CA	S	18.17 MW	18.72 AW	37790 AAW	CABLS	10//99-12//99
	San Luis Obispo-Atascadero-Paso Robles MSA, CA	S	14.13 MW	14.93 AW	29390 AAW	CABLS	10//99-12//99
	Santa Barbara-Santa Maria-Lompoc MSA, CA	S	16.85 MW	17.43 AW	35040 AAW	CABLS	10//99-12//99
	Santa Rosa PMSA, CA	S	15.45 MW	15.79 AW	32150 AAW	CABLS	10//99-12//99
	Stockton-Lodi MSA, CA	S	12.95 MW	12.22 AW	26940 AAW	CABLS	10//99-12//99
	Vallejo-Fairfield-Napa PMSA, CA	S	16.37 MW	17.38 AW	34060 AAW	CABLS	10//99-12//99
	Ventura PMSA, CA	S	13.94 MW	12.69 AW	28990 AAW	CABLS	10//99-12//99
	Visalia-Tulare-Porterville MSA, CA	S	8.30 MW	8.02 AW	17270 AAW	CABLS	10//99-12//99
	Yolo PMSA, CA	S	17.57 MW	18.64 AW	36550 AAW	CABLS	10//99-12//99
	Yuba City MSA, CA	S	12.15 MW	9.97 AW	25270 AAW	CABLS	10//99-12//99
	Colorado	S	13.93 MW	12.87 AW	26760 AAW	COBLS	10//99-12//99
	Boulder-Longmont PMSA, CO	S	13.72 MW	14.29 AW	28530 AAW	COBLS	10//99-12//99
	Colorado Springs MSA, CO	S	13.91 MW	14.64 AW	28940 AAW	COBLS	10//99-12//99
	Denver PMSA, CO	S	14.01 MW	14.54 AW	29140 AAW	COBLS	10//99-12//99
	Fort Collins-Loveland MSA, CO	S	13.20 MW	14.13 AW	27460 AAW	COBLS	10//99-12//99
	Greeley PMSA, CO	S	11.66 MW	12.50 AW	24260 AAW	COBLS	10//99-12//99
	Pueblo MSA, CO	S	13.87 MW	14.87 AW	28850 AAW	COBLS	10//99-12//99
	Connecticut	S	17.45 MW	16.75 AW	34850 AAW	CTBLS	10//99-12//99
	Bridgeport PMSA, CT	S	18.95 MW	19.45 AW	39420 AAW	CTBLS	10//99-12//99

AAW	Average annual wage	AOH	Average offered, high	ASH	Average starting, high	H	Hourly	M	Monthly	S	Special: hourly and annual
AE	Average entry wage	AOL	Average offered, low	ASL	Average starting, low	HI	Highest wage paid	MTC	Median total compensation	TQ	Third quartile wage
AEX	Average experienced wage	APH	Average pay, high range	AW	Average wage paid	HR	High end range	MW	Median wage paid	W	Weekly
AO	Average offered	APL	Average pay, low range	FQ	First quartile wage	LR	Low end range	SQ	Second quartile wage	Y	Yearly

Occupation/Type/Industry	Location	Per	Low	Mid	High	Source	Date
Butcher and Meat Cutter	Danbury PMSA, CT	S	16.21 MW	17.08 AW	33720 AAW	CTBLS	10//99-12//99
	Hartford MSA, CT	S	15.00 MW	13.37 AW	31200 AAW	CTBLS	10//99-12//99
	New Haven-Meriden PMSA, CT	S	17.13 MW	22.11 AW	35630 AAW	CTBLS	10//99-12//99
	Stamford-Norwalk PMSA, CT	S	17.62 MW	16.32 AW	36650 AAW	CTBLS	10//99-12//99
	Waterbury PMSA, CT	S	18.86 MW	21.98 AW	39230 AAW	CTBLS	10//99-12//99
	Delaware	S	14.73 MW	14.57 AW	30310 AAW	DEBLS	10//99-12//99
	Dover MSA, DE	S	13.61 MW	14.06 AW	28320 AAW	DEBLS	10//99-12//99
	Wilmington-Newark PMSA, DE-MD	S	14.93 MW	15.13 AW	31050 AAW	DEBLS	10//99-12//99
	District of Columbia	S	11.6 MW	12.16 AW	25300 AAW	DCBLS	10//99-12//99
	Washington PMSA, DC-MD-VA-WV	S	15.30 MW	15.47 AW	31820 AAW	DCBLS	10//99-12//99
	Florida	S	9.13 MW	9.47 AW	19690 AAW	FLBLS	10//99-12//99
	Daytona Beach MSA, FL	S	9.02 MW	8.82 AW	18750 AAW	FLBLS	10//99-12//99
	Fort Lauderdale PMSA, FL	S	9.26 MW	9.15 AW	19260 AAW	FLBLS	10//99-12//99
	Fort Pierce-Port St. Lucie MSA, FL	S	8.94 MW	8.49 AW	18590 AAW	FLBLS	10//99-12//99
	Fort Walton Beach MSA, FL	S	10.96 MW	10.62 AW	22800 AAW	FLBLS	10//99-12//99
	Jacksonville MSA, FL	S	8.93 MW	8.46 AW	18580 AAW	FLBLS	10//99-12//99
	Lakeland-Winter Haven MSA, FL	S	9.52 MW	9.49 AW	19810 AAW	FLBLS	10//99-12//99
	Melbourne-Titusville-Palm Bay MSA, FL	S	10.96 MW	11.09 AW	22800 AAW	FLBLS	10//99-12//99
	Miami PMSA, FL	S	9.15 MW	8.45 AW	19040 AAW	FLBLS	10//99-12//99
	Ocala MSA, FL	S	9.48 MW	9.54 AW	19720 AAW	FLBLS	10//99-12//99
	Orlando MSA, FL	S	10.19 MW	9.88 AW	21190 AAW	FLBLS	10//99-12//99
	Panama City MSA, FL	S	10.04 MW	9.91 AW	20880 AAW	FLBLS	10//99-12//99
	Pensacola MSA, FL	S	11.89 MW	11.39 AW	24740 AAW	FLBLS	10//99-12//99
	Punta Gorda MSA, FL	S	9.47 MW	9.59 AW	19690 AAW	FLBLS	10//99-12//99
	Sarasota-Bradenton MSA, FL	S	9.15 MW	8.97 AW	19020 AAW	FLBLS	10//99-12//99
	Tallahassee MSA, FL	S	9.24 MW	9.07 AW	19230 AAW	FLBLS	10//99-12//99
	Tampa-St. Petersburg-Clearwater MSA, FL	S	9.87 MW	9.60 AW	20530 AAW	FLBLS	10//99-12//99
	West Palm Beach-Boca Raton MSA, FL	S	9.09 MW	8.45 AW	18910 AAW	FLBLS	10//99-12//99
	Georgia	S	9.92 MW	10.44 AW	21720 AAW	GABLS	10//99-12//99
	Albany MSA, GA	S	11.39 MW	10.94 AW	23700 AAW	GABLS	10//99-12//99
	Athens MSA, GA	S	11.67 MW	11.68 AW	24270 AAW	GABLS	10//99-12//99
	Atlanta MSA, GA	S	10.49 MW	10.00 AW	21810 AAW	GABLS	10//99-12//99
	Augusta-Aiken MSA, GA-SC	S	11.34 MW	11.52 AW	23590 AAW	GABLS	10//99-12//99
	Columbus MSA, GA-AL	S	9.63 MW	9.59 AW	20020 AAW	GABLS	10//99-12//99
	Macon MSA, GA	S	10.23 MW	9.69 AW	21280 AAW	GABLS	10//99-12//99
	Hawaii	S	13.71 MW	12.92 AW	26870 AAW	HIBLS	10//99-12//99
	Honolulu MSA, HI	S	12.25 MW	13.63 AW	25480 AAW	HIBLS	10//99-12//99
	Idaho	S	8.13 MW	9.62 AW	20020 AAW	IDBLS	10//99-12//99
	Illinois	S	11.22 MW	11.04 AW	22970 AAW	ILBLS	10//99-12//99
	Bloomington-Normal MSA, IL	S	11.06 MW	10.92 AW	23010 AAW	ILBLS	10//99-12//99
	Champaign-Urbana MSA, IL	S	9.77 MW	9.95 AW	20310 AAW	ILBLS	10//99-12//99
	Chicago PMSA, IL	S	11.67 MW	11.82 AW	24270 AAW	ILBLS	10//99-12//99
	Peoria-Pekin MSA, IL	S	12.40 MW	12.53 AW	25790 AAW	ILBLS	10//99-12//99
	Rockford MSA, IL	S	9.34 MW	8.36 AW	19430 AAW	ILBLS	10//99-12//99
	Springfield MSA, IL	S	13.09 MW	13.07 AW	27220 AAW	ILBLS	10//99-12//99
	Indiana	S	10.71 MW	10.35 AW	21520 AAW	INBLS	10//99-12//99
	Bloomington MSA, IN	S	10.87 MW	10.83 AW	22600 AAW	INBLS	10//99-12//99
	Elkhart-Goshen MSA, IN	S	8.64 MW	8.54 AW	17980 AAW	INBLS	10//99-12//99
	Evansville-Henderson MSA, IN-KY	S	10.29 MW	10.58 AW	21410 AAW	INBLS	10//99-12//99
	Fort Wayne MSA, IN	S	10.36 MW	11.13 AW	21550 AAW	INBLS	10//99-12//99
	Gary PMSA, IN	S	11.62 MW	10.43 AW	24170 AAW	INBLS	10//99-12//99
	Indianapolis MSA, IN	S	11.13 MW	11.59 AW	23150 AAW	INBLS	10//99-12//99
	Kokomo MSA, IN	S	10.50 MW	10.56 AW	21850 AAW	INBLS	10//99-12//99
	Lafayette MSA, IN	S	10.29 MW	10.87 AW	21390 AAW	INBLS	10//99-12//99
	South Bend MSA, IN	S	11.16 MW	11.54 AW	23210 AAW	INBLS	10//99-12//99
	Terre Haute MSA, IN	S	9.13 MW	9.54 AW	18990 AAW	INBLS	10//99-12//99
	Iowa	S	9.65 MW	9.98 AW	20760 AAW	IABLS	10//99-12//99
	Cedar Rapids MSA, IA	S	11.08 MW	10.61 AW	23050 AAW	IABLS	10//99-12//99
	Davenport-Moline-Rock Island MSA, IA-IL	S	11.53 MW	10.54 AW	23980 AAW	IABLS	10//99-12//99
	Dubuque MSA, IA	S	10.39 MW	8.59 AW	21610 AAW	IABLS	10//99-12//99
	Sioux City MSA, IA-NE	S	9.69 MW	9.67 AW	20160 AAW	IABLS	10//99-12//99
	Waterloo-Cedar Falls MSA, IA	S	11.95 MW	13.76 AW	24860 AAW	IABLS	10//99-12//99

AAW Average annual wage	**AOH** Average offered, high	**ASH** Average starting, high	**H** Hourly	**M** Monthly	**S** Special: hourly and annual
AE Average entry wage	**AOL** Average offered, low	**ASL** Average starting, low	**HI** Highest wage paid	**MTC** Median total compensation	**TQ** Third quartile wage
AEX Average experienced wage	**APH** Average pay, high range	**AW** Average wage paid	**HR** High end range	**MW** Median wage paid	**W** Weekly
AO Average offered	**APL** Average pay, low range	**FQ** First quartile wage	**LR** Low end range	**SQ** Second quartile wage	**Y** Yearly

Occupation/Type/Industry	Location	Per	Low	Mid	High	Source	Date
Butcher and Meat Cutter	Kansas	S	9.1 MW	9.77 AW	20320 AAW	KSBLS	10//99-12//99
	Wichita MSA, KS	S	11.03 MW	10.66 AW	22950 AAW	KSBLS	10//99-12//99
	Kentucky	S	10.49 MW	10.82 AW	22510 AAW	KYBLS	10//99-12//99
	Lexington MSA, KY	S	10.62 MW	9.87 AW	22090 AAW	KYBLS	10//99-12//99
	Louisville MSA, KY-IN	S	11.65 MW	12.84 AW	24230 AAW	KYBLS	10//99-12//99
	Louisiana	S	9.72 MW	9.81 AW	20400 AAW	LABLS	10//99-12//99
	Alexandria MSA, LA	S	9.64 MW	9.29 AW	20050 AAW	LABLS	10//99-12//99
	Baton Rouge MSA, LA	S	10.74 MW	10.21 AW	22340 AAW	LABLS	10//99-12//99
	Houma MSA, LA	S	9.66 MW	9.63 AW	20080 AAW	LABLS	10//99-12//99
	Lafayette MSA, LA	S	9.56 MW	9.60 AW	19880 AAW	LABLS	10//99-12//99
	Lake Charles MSA, LA	S	11.26 MW	10.94 AW	23420 AAW	LABLS	10//99-12//99
	New Orleans MSA, LA	S	9.09 MW	9.10 AW	18910 AAW	LABLS	10//99-12//99
	Shreveport-Bossier City MSA, LA	S	12.03 MW	11.08 AW	25030 AAW	LABLS	10//99-12//99
	Maine	S	15.77 MW	15.52 AW	32290 AAW	MEBLS	10//99-12//99
	Portland MSA, ME	S	15.35 MW	14.94 AW	31920 AAW	MEBLS	10//99-12//99
	Maryland	S	14.94 MW	14.72 AW	30630 AAW	MDBLS	10//99-12//99
	Baltimore PMSA, MD	S	14.52 MW	14.86 AW	30200 AAW	MDBLS	10//99-12//99
	Massachusetts	S	17.72 MW	16.07 AW	33430 AAW	MABLS	10//99-12//99
	Boston PMSA, MA-NH	S	17.19 MW	18.23 AW	35760 AAW	MABLS	10//99-12//99
	Brockton PMSA, MA	S	11.08 MW	10.03 AW	23040 AAW	MABLS	10//99-12//99
	Fitchburg-Leominster PMSA, MA	S	16.62 MW	17.82 AW	34580 AAW	MABLS	10//99-12//99
	Lawrence PMSA, MA-NH	S	18.29 MW	18.44 AW	38050 AAW	MABLS	10//99-12//99
	Pittsfield MSA, MA	S	11.71 MW	8.36 AW	24360 AAW	MABLS	10//99-12//99
	Springfield MSA, MA	S	16.52 MW	18.16 AW	34360 AAW	MABLS	10//99-12//99
	Worcester PMSA, MA-CT	S	18.24 MW	19.11 AW	37940 AAW	MABLS	10//99-12//99
	Michigan	S	11.77 MW	11.75 AW	24430 AAW	MIBLS	10//99-12//99
	Ann Arbor PMSA, MI	S	11.62 MW	12.06 AW	24180 AAW	MIBLS	10//99-12//99
	Benton Harbor MSA, MI	S	11.38 MW	11.66 AW	23680 AAW	MIBLS	10//99-12//99
	Detroit PMSA, MI	S	12.07 MW	12.33 AW	25100 AAW	MIBLS	10//99-12//99
	Flint PMSA, MI	S	10.83 MW	11.22 AW	22520 AAW	MIBLS	10//99-12//99
	Grand Rapids-Muskegon-Holland MSA, MI	S	14.12 MW	14.63 AW	29360 AAW	MIBLS	10//99-12//99
	Jackson MSA, MI	S	9.83 MW	9.55 AW	20440 AAW	MIBLS	10//99-12//99
	Kalamazoo-Battle Creek MSA, MI	S	13.28 MW	12.68 AW	27630 AAW	MIBLS	10//99-12//99
	Lansing-East Lansing MSA, MI	S	13.95 MW	14.37 AW	29020 AAW	MIBLS	10//99-12//99
	Saginaw-Bay City-Midland MSA, MI	S	10.58 MW	9.94 AW	22010 AAW	MIBLS	10//99-12//99
	Minnesota	S	10.21 MW	12.04 AW	25040 AAW	MNBLS	10//99-12//99
	Duluth-Superior MSA, MN-WI	S	13.82 MW	14.27 AW	28740 AAW	MNBLS	10//99-12//99
	Minneapolis-St. Paul MSA, MN-WI	S	17.17 MW	18.21 AW	35710 AAW	MNBLS	10//99-12//99
	Rochester MSA, MN	S	12.79 MW	12.61 AW	26600 AAW	MNBLS	10//99-12//99
	St. Cloud MSA, MN	S	12.36 MW	12.95 AW	25700 AAW	MNBLS	10//99-12//99
	Mississippi	S	11.09 MW	10.66 AW	22170 AAW	MSBLS	10//99-12//99
	Biloxi-Gulfport-Pascagoula MSA, MS	S	10.82 MW	10.60 AW	22500 AAW	MSBLS	10//99-12//99
	Hattiesburg MSA, MS	S	13.18 MW	12.99 AW	27410 AAW	MSBLS	10//99-12//99
	Jackson MSA, MS	S	11.48 MW	11.55 AW	23880 AAW	MSBLS	10//99-12//99
	Missouri	S	9.91 MW	10.34 AW	21510 AAW	MOBLS	10//99-12//99
	Joplin MSA, MO	S	12.31 MW	12.60 AW	25610 AAW	MOBLS	10//99-12//99
	Kansas City MSA, MO-KS	S	11.10 MW	10.78 AW	23080 AAW	MOBLS	10//99-12//99
	St. Louis MSA, MO-IL	S	9.62 MW	9.07 AW	20000 AAW	MOBLS	10//99-12//99
	Springfield MSA, MO	S	11.43 MW	10.37 AW	23770 AAW	MOBLS	10//99-12//99
	Montana	S	11.65 MW	11.73 AW	24400 AAW	MTBLS	10//99-12//99
	Billings MSA, MT	S	11.37 MW	11.21 AW	23640 AAW	MTBLS	10//99-12//99
	Missoula MSA, MT	S	13.40 MW	12.46 AW	27880 AAW	MTBLS	10//99-12//99
	Nebraska	S	9.76 MW	10.06 AW	20920 AAW	NEBLS	10//99-12//99
	Lincoln MSA, NE	S	10.68 MW	10.43 AW	22210 AAW	NEBLS	10//99-12//99
	Omaha MSA, NE-IA	S	10.52 MW	9.94 AW	21880 AAW	NEBLS	10//99-12//99
	Nevada	S	17.04 MW	15.43 AW	32100 AAW	NVBLS	10//99-12//99
	Las Vegas MSA, NV-AZ	S	14.29 MW	13.81 AW	29730 AAW	NVBLS	10//99-12//99
	Reno MSA, NV	S	17.46 MW	18.47 AW	36310 AAW	NVBLS	10//99-12//99
	New Hampshire	S	14.22 MW	13.12 AW	27280 AAW	NHBLS	10//99-12//99
	Portsmouth-Rochester PMSA, NH-ME	S	13.10 MW	14.05 AW	27250 AAW	NHBLS	10//99-12//99
	New Jersey	S	17.95 MW	16.52 AW	34370 AAW	NJBLS	10//99-12//99
	Bergen-Passaic PMSA, NJ	S	17.53 MW	18.11 AW	36450 AAW	NJBLS	10//99-12//99
	Jersey City PMSA, NJ	S	16.57 MW	18.07 AW	34470 AAW	NJBLS	10//99-12//99

AAW Average annual wage	**AOH** Average offered, high	**ASH** Average starting, high	**H** Hourly	**M** Monthly	**S** Special: hourly and annual
AE Average entry wage	**AOL** Average offered, low	**ASL** Average starting, low	**HI** Highest wage paid	**MTC** Median total compensation	**TQ** Third quartile wage
AEX Average experienced wage	**APH** Average pay, high range	**AW** Average wage paid	**HR** High end range	**MW** Median wage paid	**W** Weekly
AO Average offered	**APL** Average pay, low range	**FQ** First quartile wage	**LR** Low end range	**SQ** Second quartile wage	**Y** Yearly

Butcher and Meat Cutter

Occupation/Type/Industry	Location	Per	Low	Mid	High	Source	Date
Butcher and Meat Cutter	Middlesex-Somerset-						
	Hunterdon PMSA, NJ	S	17.57 MW	18.61 AW	36540 AAW	NJBLS	10//99-12//99
	Monmouth-Ocean PMSA, NJ	S	14.87 MW	15.14 AW	30930 AAW	NJBLS	10//99-12//99
	Newark PMSA, NJ	S	17.05 MW	18.17 AW	35460 AAW	NJBLS	10//99-12//99
	Trenton PMSA, NJ	S	16.72 MW	17.07 AW	34770 AAW	NJBLS	10//99-12//99
	New Mexico	S	8.16 MW	9.62 AW	20020 AAW	NMBLS	10//99-12//99
	Albuquerque MSA, NM	S	11.97 MW	11.40 AW	24900 AAW	NMBLS	10//99-12//99
	Las Cruces MSA, NM	S	11.92 MW	11.00 AW	24780 AAW	NMBLS	10//99-12//99
	Santa Fe MSA, NM	S	11.12 MW	10.03 AW	23140 AAW	NMBLS	10//99-12//99
	New York	S	15.26 MW	15.74 AW	32730 AAW	NYBLS	10//99-12//99
	Albany-Schenectady-Troy						
	MSA, NY	S	14.00 MW	14.35 AW	29110 AAW	NYBLS	10//99-12//99
	Binghamton MSA, NY	S	12.62 MW	13.88 AW	26250 AAW	NYBLS	10//99-12//99
	Buffalo-Niagara Falls MSA,						
	NY	S	11.12 MW	10.75 AW	23130 AAW	NYBLS	10//99-12//99
	Dutchess County PMSA, NY	S	14.87 MW	15.31 AW	30930 AAW	NYBLS	10//99-12//99
	Glens Falls MSA, NY	S	12.87 MW	14.00 AW	26770 AAW	NYBLS	10//99-12//99
	Jamestown MSA, NY	S	7.12 MW	6.12 AW	14810 AAW	NYBLS	10//99-12//99
	Nassau-Suffolk PMSA, NY	S	20.50 MW	21.12 AW	42630 AAW	NYBLS	10//99-12//99
	New York PMSA, NY	S	18.28 MW	20.37 AW	38030 AAW	NYBLS	10//99-12//99
	Newburgh PMSA, NY-PA	S	12.74 MW	12.05 AW	26500 AAW	NYBLS	10//99-12//99
	Rochester MSA, NY	S	10.18 MW	10.01 AW	21170 AAW	NYBLS	10//99-12//99
	Syracuse MSA, NY	S	9.88 MW	6.74 AW	20550 AAW	NYBLS	10//99-12//99
	Utica-Rome MSA, NY	S	13.38 MW	14.66 AW	27820 AAW	NYBLS	10//99-12//99
	North Carolina	S	10.47 MW	10.34 AW	21500 AAW	NCBLS	10//99-12//99
	Charlotte-Gastonia-Rock Hill						
	MSA, NC-SC	S	10.70 MW	10.46 AW	22260 AAW	NCBLS	10//99-12//99
	Fayetteville MSA, NC	S	11.57 MW	11.62 AW	24060 AAW	NCBLS	10//99-12//99
	Goldsboro MSA, NC	S	10.00 MW	8.49 AW	20800 AAW	NCBLS	10//99-12//99
	Greensboro--Winston-Salem--						
	High Point MSA, NC	S	11.16 MW	11.32 AW	23210 AAW	NCBLS	10//99-12//99
	Greenville MSA, NC	S	10.38 MW	10.45 AW	21590 AAW	NCBLS	10//99-12//99
	Hickory-Morganton-Lenoir						
	MSA, NC	S	10.37 MW	10.48 AW	21570 AAW	NCBLS	10//99-12//99
	Jacksonville MSA, NC	S	9.77 MW	10.00 AW	20330 AAW	NCBLS	10//99-12//99
	Raleigh-Durham-Chapel Hill						
	MSA, NC	S	9.67 MW	9.34 AW	20110 AAW	NCBLS	10//99-12//99
	Rocky Mount MSA, NC	S	7.47 MW	7.60 AW	15540 AAW	NCBLS	10//99-12//99
	North Dakota	S	9.3 MW	9.62 AW	20010 AAW	NDBLS	10//99-12//99
	Bismarck MSA, ND	S	10.40 MW	11.48 AW	21630 AAW	NDBLS	10//99-12//99
	Fargo-Moorhead MSA, ND-						
	MN	S	11.02 MW	10.83 AW	22910 AAW	NDBLS	10//99-12//99
	Grand Forks MSA, ND-MN	S	10.38 MW	10.23 AW	21590 AAW	NDBLS	10//99-12//99
	Ohio	S	11.87 MW	11.72 AW	24380 AAW	OHBLS	10//99-12//99
	Akron PMSA, OH	S	12.95 MW	12.89 AW	26940 AAW	OHBLS	10//99-12//99
	Canton-Massillon MSA, OH	S	11.24 MW	10.74 AW	23380 AAW	OHBLS	10//99-12//99
	Cincinnati PMSA, OH-KY-IN	S	11.77 MW	12.16 AW	24480 AAW	OHBLS	10//99-12//99
	Cleveland-Lorain-Elyria						
	PMSA, OH	S	13.28 MW	13.64 AW	27630 AAW	OHBLS	10//99-12//99
	Columbus MSA, OH	S	11.70 MW	12.05 AW	24330 AAW	OHBLS	10//99-12//99
	Dayton-Springfield MSA, OH	S	11.59 MW	11.28 AW	24110 AAW	OHBLS	10//99-12//99
	Hamilton-Middletown PMSA,						
	OH	S	11.80 MW	12.27 AW	24540 AAW	OHBLS	10//99-12//99
	Lima MSA, OH	S	12.48 MW	11.73 AW	25960 AAW	OHBLS	10//99-12//99
	Mansfield MSA, OH	S	11.60 MW	11.97 AW	24130 AAW	OHBLS	10//99-12//99
	Toledo MSA, OH	S	13.45 MW	14.08 AW	27970 AAW	OHBLS	10//99-12//99
	Youngstown-Warren MSA, OH	S	11.81 MW	12.38 AW	24570 AAW	OHBLS	10//99-12//99
	Oklahoma	S	8.3 MW	9.00 AW	18720 AAW	OKBLS	10//99-12//99
	Enid MSA, OK	S	7.74 MW	7.15 AW	16090 AAW	OKBLS	10//99-12//99
	Lawton MSA, OK	S	10.51 MW	8.41 AW	21860 AAW	OKBLS	10//99-12//99
	Oklahoma City MSA, OK	S	11.21 MW	10.67 AW	23310 AAW	OKBLS	10//99-12//99
	Tulsa MSA, OK	S	10.01 MW	9.25 AW	20820 AAW	OKBLS	10//99-12//99
	Oregon	S	15.29 MW	14.72 AW	30610 AAW	ORBLS	10//99-12//99
	Corvallis MSA, OR	S	12.23 MW	13.78 AW	25450 AAW	ORBLS	10//99-12//99
	Eugene-Springfield MSA, OR	S	18.44 MW	18.98 AW	38350 AAW	ORBLS	10//99-12//99
	Medford-Ashland MSA, OR	S	15.72 MW	15.93 AW	32700 AAW	ORBLS	10//99-12//99
	Portland-Vancouver PMSA,						
	OR-WA	S	15.89 MW	16.01 AW	33050 AAW	ORBLS	10//99-12//99
	Salem PMSA, OR	S	14.22 MW	14.50 AW	29570 AAW	ORBLS	10//99-12//99
	Pennsylvania	S	10.84 MW	11.97 AW	24890 AAW	PABLS	10//99-12//99
	Erie MSA, PA	S	9.87 MW	10.88 AW	20530 AAW	PABLS	10//99-12//99

Occupation/Type/Industry	Location	Per	Low	Mid	High	Source	Date
Butcher and Meat Cutter	Harrisburg-Lebanon-Carlisle MSA, PA	S	12.45 MW	12.87 AW	25890 AAW	PABLS	10//99-12//99
	Johnstown MSA, PA	S	8.42 MW	8.54 AW	17520 AAW	PABLS	10//99-12//99
	Lancaster MSA, PA	S	11.56 MW	11.86 AW	24040 AAW	PABLS	10//99-12//99
	Philadelphia PMSA, PA-NJ	S	13.37 MW	12.44 AW	27800 AAW	PABLS	10//99-12//99
	Pittsburgh MSA, PA	S	10.58 MW	10.56 AW	22010 AAW	PABLS	10//99-12//99
	Reading MSA, PA	S	16.15 MW	17.82 AW	33580 AAW	PABLS	10//99-12//99
	Scranton--Wilkes-Barre--Hazleton MSA, PA	S	8.61 MW	7.87 AW	17900 AAW	PABLS	10//99-12//99
	Williamsport MSA, PA	S	12.96 MW	10.24 AW	26960 AAW	PABLS	10//99-12//99
	York MSA, PA	S	12.89 MW	13.07 AW	26810 AAW	PABLS	10//99-12//99
	Rhode Island	S	14.24 MW	13.88 AW	28860 AAW	RIBLS	10//99-12//99
	Providence-Fall River-Warwick MSA, RI-MA	S	14.28 MW	15.53 AW	29700 AAW	RIBLS	10//99-12//99
	South Carolina	S	9.13 MW	9.33 AW	19410 AAW	SCBLS	10//99-12//99
	Charleston-North Charleston MSA, SC	S	10.14 MW	9.60 AW	21090 AAW	SCBLS	10//99-12//99
	Columbia MSA, SC	S	10.80 MW	11.43 AW	22460 AAW	SCBLS	10//99-12//99
	Florence MSA, SC	S	9.36 MW	8.16 AW	19470 AAW	SCBLS	10//99-12//99
	Greenville-Spartanburg-Anderson MSA, SC	S	11.19 MW	10.30 AW	23270 AAW	SCBLS	10//99-12//99
	Sumter MSA, SC	S	12.61 MW	12.77 AW	26220 AAW	SCBLS	10//99-12//99
	South Dakota	S	8.33 MW	8.88 AW	18460 AAW	SDBLS	10//99-12//99
	Rapid City MSA, SD	S	9.94 MW	9.43 AW	20670 AAW	SDBLS	10//99-12//99
	Sioux Falls MSA, SD	S	10.94 MW	11.04 AW	22760 AAW	SDBLS	10//99-12//99
	Tennessee	S	10.09 MW	10.26 AW	21330 AAW	TNBLS	10//99-12//99
	Chattanooga MSA, TN-GA	S	10.39 MW	10.31 AW	21620 AAW	TNBLS	10//99-12//99
	Clarksville-Hopkinsville MSA, TN-KY	S	10.67 MW	10.49 AW	22200 AAW	TNBLS	
	Johnson City-Kingsport-Bristol MSA, TN-VA	S	9.64 MW	10.20 AW	20050 AAW	TNBLS	10//99-12//99
	Knoxville MSA, TN	S	10.06 MW	9.93 AW	20930 AAW	TNBLS	10//99-12//99
	Memphis MSA, TN-AR-MS	S	11.84 MW	12.13 AW	24630 AAW	MSBLS	10//99-12//99
	Nashville MSA, TN	S	9.67 MW	9.65 AW	20120 AAW	TNBLS	10//99-12//99
	Texas	S	11.27 MW	11.21 AW	23320 AAW	TXBLS	10//99-12//99
	Abilene MSA, TX	S	10.23 MW	10.23 AW	21290 AAW	TXBLS	10//99-12//99
	Amarillo MSA, TX	S	11.84 MW	11.35 AW	24620 AAW	TXBLS	10//99-12//99
	Austin-San Marcos MSA, TX	S	12.47 MW	12.50 AW	25930 AAW	TXBLS	10//99-12//99
	Beaumont-Port Arthur MSA, TX	S	10.73 MW	10.53 AW	22310 AAW	TXBLS	10//99-12//99
	Brazoria PMSA, TX	S	11.57 MW	11.02 AW	24070 AAW	TXBLS	10//99-12//99
	Brownsville-Harlingen-San Benito MSA, TX	S	10.11 MW	10.77 AW	21040 AAW	TXBLS	10//99-12//99
	Bryan-College Station MSA, TX	S	11.17 MW	11.33 AW	23240 AAW	TXBLS	10//99-12//99
	Corpus Christi MSA, TX	S	12.64 MW	12.62 AW	26290 AAW	TXBLS	10//99-12//99
	Dallas PMSA, TX	S	10.72 MW	10.46 AW	22290 AAW	TXBLS	10//99-12//99
	El Paso MSA, TX	S	8.75 MW	8.03 AW	18190 AAW	TXBLS	10//99-12//99
	Fort Worth-Arlington PMSA, TX	S	12.30 MW	12.74 AW	25580 AAW	TXBLS	10//99-12//99
	Galveston-Texas City PMSA, TX	S	11.88 MW	12.07 AW	24710 AAW	TXBLS	10//99-12//99
	Houston PMSA, TX	S	11.88 MW	12.22 AW	24700 AAW	TXBLS	10//99-12//99
	Killeen-Temple MSA, TX	S	12.43 MW	12.37 AW	25850 AAW	TXBLS	10//99-12//99
	Laredo MSA, TX	S	8.70 MW	7.72 AW	18090 AAW	TXBLS	10//99-12//99
	Longview-Marshall MSA, TX	S	10.64 MW	9.93 AW	22140 AAW	TXBLS	10//99-12//99
	Lubbock MSA, TX	S	10.81 MW	8.88 AW	22490 AAW	TXBLS	10//99-12//99
	McAllen-Edinburg-Mission MSA, TX	S	10.70 MW	10.32 AW	22260 AAW	TXBLS	10//99-12//99
	Odessa-Midland MSA, TX	S	11.75 MW	10.60 AW	24440 AAW	TXBLS	10//99-12//99
	San Angelo MSA, TX	S	11.10 MW	10.82 AW	23080 AAW	TXBLS	10//99-12//99
	San Antonio MSA, TX	S	11.74 MW	11.99 AW	24410 AAW	TXBLS	10//99-12//99
	Tyler MSA, TX	S	10.65 MW	8.85 AW	22160 AAW	TXBLS	10//99-12//99
	Waco MSA, TX	S	10.82 MW	11.15 AW	22510 AAW	TXBLS	10//99-12//99
	Wichita Falls MSA, TX	S	10.87 MW	9.65 AW	22620 AAW	TXBLS	10//99-12//99
	Utah	S	14.26 MW	13.56 AW	28200 AAW	UTBLS	10//99-12//99
	Provo-Orem MSA, UT	S	12.93 MW	13.84 AW	26890 AAW	UTBLS	10//99-12//99
	Salt Lake City-Ogden MSA, UT	S	13.46 MW	14.04 AW	28000 AAW	UTBLS	10//99-12//99
	Vermont	S	14.31 MW	13.02 AW	27090 AAW	VTBLS	10//99-12//99
	Burlington MSA, VT	S	11.50 MW	10.60 AW	23910 AAW	VTBLS	10//99-12//99
	Virginia	S	12.27 MW	12.28 AW	25540 AAW	VABLS	10//99-12//99

AAW	Average annual wage	AOH	Average offered, high	ASH	Average starting, high	H	Hourly	M	Monthly	S	Special: hourly and annual
AE	Average entry wage	AOL	Average offered, low	ASL	Average starting, low	HI	Highest wage paid	MTC	Median total compensation	TQ	Third quartile wage
AEX	Average experienced wage	APH	Average pay, high range	AW	Average wage paid	HR	High end range	MW	Median wage paid	W	Weekly
AO	Average offered	APL	Average pay, low range	FQ	First quartile wage	LR	Low end range	SQ	Second quartile wage	Y	Yearly

Occupation/Type/Industry	Location	Per	Low	Mid	High	Source	Date
Butcher and Meat Cutter	Charlottesville MSA, VA	S	8.22 MW	8.13 AW	17090 AAW	VABLS	10//99-12//99
	Lynchburg MSA, VA	S	10.36 MW	11.18 AW	21550 AAW	VABLS	10//99-12//99
	Norfolk-Virginia Beach-Newport News MSA, VA-NC	S	11.54 MW	11.82 AW	24010 AAW	VABLS	10//99-12//99
	Richmond-Petersburg MSA, VA	S	15.63 MW	15.48 AW	32520 AAW	VABLS	10//99-12//99
	Roanoke MSA, VA	S	10.57 MW	11.12 AW	21980 AAW	VABLS	10//99-12//99
	Washington	S	15.31 MW	14.89 AW	30970 AAW	WABLS	10//99-12//99
	Bellingham MSA, WA	S	17.75 MW	17.94 AW	36920 AAW	WABLS	10//99-12//99
	Bremerton PMSA, WA	S	12.89 MW	13.20 AW	26820 AAW	WABLS	10//99-12//99
	Olympia PMSA, WA	S	14.60 MW	16.74 AW	30360 AAW	WABLS	10//99-12//99
	Seattle-Bellevue-Everett PMSA, WA	S	15.40 MW	15.71 AW	32030 AAW	WABLS	10//99-12//99
	Spokane MSA, WA	S	12.00 MW	10.96 AW	24950 AAW	WABLS	10//99-12//99
	Tacoma PMSA, WA	S	17.11 MW	18.09 AW	35590 AAW	WABLS	10//99-12//99
	Yakima MSA, WA	S	11.99 MW	13.60 AW	24940 AAW	WABLS	10//99-12//99
	West Virginia	S	10.3 MW	10.05 AW	20900 AAW	WVBLS	10//99-12//99
	Charleston MSA, WV	S	10.84 MW	11.53 AW	22550 AAW	WVBLS	10//99-12//99
	Huntington-Ashland MSA, WV-KY-OH	S	8.34 MW	7.89 AW	17350 AAW	WVBLS	10//99-12//99
	Parkersburg-Marietta MSA, WV-OH	S	10.65 MW	11.29 AW	22140 AAW	WVBLS	10//99-12//99
	Wheeling MSA, WV-OH	S	8.92 MW	9.47 AW	18560 AAW	WVBLS	10//99-12//99
	Wisconsin	S	9.43 MW	10.52 AW	21880 AAW	WIBLS	10//99-12//99
	Appleton-Oshkosh-Neenah MSA, WI	S	13.20 MW	12.85 AW	27460 AAW	WIBLS	10//99-12//99
	Eau Claire MSA, WI	S	10.92 MW	10.17 AW	22700 AAW	WIBLS	10//99-12//99
	Green Bay MSA, WI	S	10.86 MW	11.88 AW	22590 AAW	WIBLS	10//99-12//99
	Janesville-Beloit MSA, WI	S	12.37 MW	12.03 AW	25730 AAW	WIBLS	10//99-12//99
	Kenosha PMSA, WI	S	16.27 MW	17.31 AW	33850 AAW	WIBLS	10//99-12//99
	La Crosse MSA, WI-MN	S	10.81 MW	11.20 AW	22480 AAW	WIBLS	10//99-12//99
	Madison MSA, WI	S	13.20 MW	13.58 AW	27450 AAW	WIBLS	10//99-12//99
	Milwaukee-Waukesha PMSA, WI	S	14.05 MW	13.88 AW	29220 AAW	WIBLS	10//99-12//99
	Racine PMSA, WI	S	13.44 MW	13.41 AW	27950 AAW	WIBLS	10//99-12//99
	Sheboygan MSA, WI	S	13.09 MW	12.49 AW	27240 AAW	WIBLS	10//99-12//99
	Wausau MSA, WI	S	9.99 MW	10.75 AW	20790 AAW	WIBLS	10//99-12//99
	Wyoming	S	11.67 MW	11.59 AW	24100 AAW	WYBLS	10//99-12//99
	Casper MSA, WY	S	10.24 MW	9.41 AW	21290 AAW	WYBLS	10//99-12//99
	Cheyenne MSA, WY	S	12.20 MW	12.20 AW	25390 AAW	WYBLS	10//99-12//99
	Puerto Rico	S	6.45 MW	6.67 AW	13880 AAW	PRBLS	10//99-12//99
	Aguadilla MSA, PR	S	6.97 MW	6.40 AW	14490 AAW	PRBLS	10//99-12//99
	Arecibo PMSA, PR	S	6.49 MW	6.53 AW	13500 AAW	PRBLS	10//99-12//99
	Caguas PMSA, PR	S	6.76 MW	6.64 AW	14070 AAW	PRBLS	10//99-12//99
	Mayaguez MSA, PR	S	5.77 MW	5.96 AW	12000 AAW	PRBLS	10//99-12//99
	Ponce MSA, PR	S	6.77 MW	6.69 AW	14080 AAW	PRBLS	10//99-12//99
	San Juan-Bayamon PMSA, PR	S	6.71 MW	6.43 AW	13970 AAW	PRBLS	10//99-12//99
	Virgin Islands	S	11.43 MW	11.97 AW	24900 AAW	VIBLS	10//99-12//99
	Guam	S	9.31 MW	9.74 AW	20270 AAW	GUBLS	10//99-12//99
Buyer							
Apparel & Accessories Retailer	United States	Y		75400 MW		STORES	2000
Gas/Convenience Retailer	United States	Y		55900 MW		STORES	2000
Junior, Manufacturing	United States	Y		32756 MW		WARD3	1998
Restaurant	United States	Y		56900 MW		STORES	2000
Specialty Store	United States	Y		59600 MW		STORES	2000
Supermarket	United States	Y		55000 MW		STORES	2000
Cabinetmaker and Bench Carpenter	Alabama	S	8.3 MW	8.55 AW	17790 AAW	ALBLS	10//99-12//99
	Auburn-Opelika MSA, AL	S	8.54 MW	8.55 AW	17760 AAW	ALBLS	10//99-12//99
	Birmingham MSA, AL	S	9.95 MW	9.91 AW	20700 AAW	ALBLS	10//99-12//99
	Huntsville MSA, AL	S	10.90 MW	10.92 AW	22660 AAW	ALBLS	10//99-12//99
	Mobile MSA, AL	S	8.17 MW	8.14 AW	16980 AAW	ALBLS	10//99-12//99
	Tuscaloosa MSA, AL	S	12.06 MW	10.48 AW	25080 AAW	ALBLS	10//99-12//99
	Alaska	S	12.62 MW	13.87 AW	28840 AAW	AKBLS	10//99-12//99
	Anchorage MSA, AK	S	12.08 MW	11.73 AW	25130 AAW	AKBLS	10//99-12//99
	Arizona	S	9.64 MW	10.21 AW	21230 AAW	AZBLS	10//99-12//99
	Phoenix-Mesa MSA, AZ	S	10.69 MW	9.88 AW	22240 AAW	AZBLS	10//99-12//99
	Tucson MSA, AZ	S	9.86 MW	9.77 AW	20500 AAW	AZBLS	10//99-12//99
	Yuma MSA, AZ	S	10.26 MW	9.53 AW	21340 AAW	AZBLS	10//99-12//99

Occupation/Type/Industry	Location	Per	Low	Mid	High	Source	Date
Cabinetmaker and Bench Carpenter	Arkansas	S	8.88 MW	9.06 AW	18840 AAW	ARBLS	10//99-12//99
	Fayetteville-Springdale-Rogers MSA, AR	S	9.58 MW	9.44 AW	19920 AAW	ARBLS	10//99-12//99
	Fort Smith MSA, AR-OK	S	8.64 MW	8.76 AW	17980 AAW	ARBLS	10//99-12//99
	Little Rock-North Little Rock MSA, AR	S	10.96 MW	10.49 AW	22800 AAW	ARBLS	10//99-12//99
	California	S	9.43 MW	10.79 AW	22440 AAW	CABLS	10//99-12//99
	Bakersfield MSA, CA	S	10.76 MW	9.81 AW	22380 AAW	CABLS	10//99-12//99
	Chico-Paradise MSA, CA	S	8.90 MW	8.22 AW	18500 AAW	CABLS	10//99-12//99
	Fresno MSA, CA	S	8.06 MW	6.58 AW	16760 AAW	CABLS	10//99-12//99
	Los Angeles-Long Beach PMSA, CA	S	9.14 MW	8.36 AW	19020 AAW	CABLS	10//99-12//99
	Modesto MSA, CA	S	8.35 MW	8.88 AW	17370 AAW	CABLS	10//99-12//99
	Oakland PMSA, CA	S	15.42 MW	13.55 AW	32070 AAW	CABLS	10//99-12//99
	Orange County PMSA, CA	S	9.07 MW	8.07 AW	18870 AAW	CABLS	10//99-12//99
	Riverside-San Bernardino PMSA, CA	S	12.25 MW	11.91 AW	25480 AAW	CABLS	10//99-12//99
	Sacramento PMSA, CA	S	9.17 MW	8.35 AW	19070 AAW	CABLS	10//99-12//99
	Salinas MSA, CA	S	11.00 MW	9.25 AW	22870 AAW	CABLS	10//99-12//99
	San Diego MSA, CA	S	12.38 MW	12.15 AW	25740 AAW	CABLS	10//99-12//99
	San Francisco PMSA, CA	S	15.57 MW	14.46 AW	32390 AAW	CABLS	10//99-12//99
	San Jose PMSA, CA	S	14.91 MW	13.67 AW	31010 AAW	CABLS	10//99-12//99
	San Luis Obispo-Atascadero-Paso Robles MSA, CA	S	10.70 MW	10.76 AW	22250 AAW	CABLS	10//99-12//99
	Santa Barbara-Santa Maria-Lompoc MSA, CA	S	13.92 MW	10.71 AW	28960 AAW	CABLS	10//99-12//99
	Santa Cruz-Watsonville PMSA, CA	S	13.58 MW	14.07 AW	28250 AAW	CABLS	10//99-12//99
	Santa Rosa PMSA, CA	S	12.70 MW	13.95 AW	26420 AAW	CABLS	10//99-12//99
	Stockton-Lodi MSA, CA	S	11.72 MW	10.31 AW	24370 AAW	CABLS	10//99-12//99
	Vallejo-Fairfield-Napa PMSA, CA	S	13.81 MW	12.64 AW	28720 AAW	CABLS	10//99-12//99
	Ventura PMSA, CA	S	12.05 MW	11.84 AW	25050 AAW	CABLS	10//99-12//99
	Yolo PMSA, CA	S	9.54 MW	8.69 AW	19840 AAW	CABLS	10//99-12//99
	Colorado	S	10.06 MW	10.92 AW	22710 AAW	COBLS	10//99-12//99
	Boulder-Longmont PMSA, CO	S	12.75 MW	12.68 AW	26520 AAW	COBLS	10//99-12//99
	Colorado Springs MSA, CO	S	9.76 MW	8.43 AW	20310 AAW	COBLS	10//99-12//99
	Denver PMSA, CO	S	11.87 MW	10.68 AW	24690 AAW	COBLS	10//99-12//99
	Fort Collins-Loveland MSA, CO	S	7.19 MW	6.50 AW	14960 AAW	COBLS	10//99-12//99
	Connecticut	S	14.63 MW	14.52 AW	30190 AAW	CTBLS	10//99-12//99
	Bridgeport PMSA, CT	S	17.30 MW	18.08 AW	35990 AAW	CTBLS	10//99-12//99
	Hartford MSA, CT	S	15.13 MW	15.23 AW	31470 AAW	CTBLS	10//99-12//99
	New Haven-Meriden PMSA, CT	S	11.00 MW	10.51 AW	22880 AAW	CTBLS	10//99-12//99
	New London-Norwich MSA, CT-RI	S	10.22 MW	9.83 AW	21250 AAW	CTBLS	10//99-12//99
	Stamford-Norwalk PMSA, CT	S	19.16 MW	17.97 AW	39850 AAW	CTBLS	10//99-12//99
	Waterbury PMSA, CT	S	14.76 MW	14.85 AW	30710 AAW	CTBLS	10//99-12//99
	Washington PMSA, DC-MD-VA-WV	S	14.12 MW	13.40 AW	29360 AAW	DCBLS	10//99-12//99
	Florida	S	9.29 MW	10.02 AW	20840 AAW	FLBLS	10//99-12//99
	Daytona Beach MSA, FL	S	7.45 MW	6.45 AW	15490 AAW	FLBLS	10//99-12//99
	Fort Lauderdale PMSA, FL	S	11.47 MW	10.98 AW	23850 AAW	FLBLS	10//99-12//99
	Fort Myers-Cape Coral MSA, FL	S	9.32 MW	8.64 AW	19390 AAW	FLBLS	10//99-12//99
	Fort Pierce-Port St. Lucie MSA, FL	S	15.42 MW	16.28 AW	32070 AAW	FLBLS	10//99-12//99
	Fort Walton Beach MSA, FL	S	8.73 MW	8.01 AW	18150 AAW	FLBLS	10//99-12//99
	Gainesville MSA, FL	S	11.48 MW	11.38 AW	23890 AAW	FLBLS	10//99-12//99
	Jacksonville MSA, FL	S	12.56 MW	11.88 AW	26120 AAW	FLBLS	10//99-12//99
	Melbourne-Titusville-Palm Bay MSA, FL	S	9.61 MW	9.80 AW	20000 AAW	FLBLS	10//99-12//99
	Miami PMSA, FL	S	8.13 MW	7.67 AW	16910 AAW	FLBLS	10//99-12//99
	Naples MSA, FL	S	14.65 MW	13.57 AW	30470 AAW	FLBLS	10//99-12//99
	Orlando MSA, FL	S	11.82 MW	11.48 AW	24600 AAW	FLBLS	10//99-12//99
	Pensacola MSA, FL	S	10.97 MW	10.84 AW	22830 AAW	FLBLS	10//99-12//99
	Punta Gorda MSA, FL	S	9.31 MW	9.10 AW	19370 AAW	FLBLS	10//99-12//99
	Sarasota-Bradenton MSA, FL	S	11.49 MW	11.29 AW	23900 AAW	FLBLS	10//99-12//99
	Tampa-St. Petersburg-Clearwater MSA, FL	S	9.30 MW	9.24 AW	19340 AAW	FLBLS	10//99-12//99

AAW Average annual wage	**AOH** Average offered, high	**ASH** Average starting, high	**H** Hourly	**M** Monthly	**S** Special: hourly and annual
AE Average entry wage	**AOL** Average offered, low	**ASL** Average starting, low	**HI** Highest wage paid	**MTC** Median total compensation	**TQ** Third quartile wage
AEX Average experienced wage	**APH** Average pay, high range	**AW** Average wage paid	**HR** High end range	**MW** Median wage paid	**W** Weekly
AO Average offered	**APL** Average pay, low range	**FQ** First quartile wage	**LR** Low end range	**SQ** Second quartile wage	**Y** Yearly

Occupation/Type/Industry	Location	Per	Low	Mid	High	Source	Date
Cabinetmaker and Bench Carpenter							
	West Palm Beach-Boca Raton MSA, FL	S	11.36 MW	11.52 AW	23630 AAW	FLBLS	10//99-12//99
	Georgia	S	9.24 MW	10.25 AW	21320 AAW	GABLS	10//99-12//99
	Atlanta MSA, GA	S	11.26 MW	10.00 AW	23420 AAW	GABLS	10//99-12//99
	Augusta-Aiken MSA, GA-SC	S	8.81 MW	8.30 AW	18330 AAW	GABLS	10//99-12//99
	Columbus MSA, GA-AL	S	9.76 MW	9.43 AW	20300 AAW	GABLS	10//99-12//99
	Macon MSA, GA	S	9.93 MW	8.91 AW	20660 AAW	GABLS	10//99-12//99
	Hawaii	S	16.72 MW	16.27 AW	33830 AAW	HIBLS	10//99-12//99
	Honolulu MSA, HI	S	16.12 MW	16.74 AW	33520 AAW	HIBLS	10//99-12//99
	Idaho	S	9.61 MW	9.97 AW	20740 AAW	IDBLS	10//99-12//99
	Boise City MSA, ID	S	10.91 MW	10.05 AW	22690 AAW	IDBLS	10//99-12//99
	Illinois	S	12.98 MW	13.27 AW	27600 AAW	ILBLS	10//99-12//99
	Chicago PMSA, IL	S	14.38 MW	14.45 AW	29910 AAW	ILBLS	10//99-12//99
	Rockford MSA, IL	S	11.24 MW	10.36 AW	23380 AAW	ILBLS	10//99-12//99
	Springfield MSA, IL	S	12.00 MW	12.12 AW	24950 AAW	ILBLS	10//99-12//99
	Indiana	S	12.83 MW	13.63 AW	28340 AAW	INBLS	10//99-12//99
	Elkhart-Goshen MSA, IN	S	15.25 MW	15.42 AW	31710 AAW	INBLS	10//99-12//99
	Fort Wayne MSA, IN	S	10.08 MW	8.94 AW	20970 AAW	INBLS	10//99-12//99
	Gary PMSA, IN	S	9.80 MW	9.67 AW	20380 AAW	INBLS	10//99-12//99
	Indianapolis MSA, IN	S	12.00 MW	11.55 AW	24950 AAW	INBLS	10//99-12//99
	Iowa	S	11.79 MW	11.99 AW	24940 AAW	IABLS	10//99-12//99
	Davenport-Moline-Rock Island MSA, IA-IL	S	11.21 MW	10.59 AW	23330 AAW	IABLS	10//99-12//99
	Des Moines MSA, IA	S	13.31 MW	13.71 AW	27680 AAW	IABLS	10//99-12//99
	Waterloo-Cedar Falls MSA, IA	S	11.83 MW	11.74 AW	24620 AAW	IABLS	10//99-12//99
	Kansas	S	9.82 MW	9.97 AW	20730 AAW	KSBLS	10//99-12//99
	Wichita MSA, KS	S	10.41 MW	10.05 AW	21660 AAW	KSBLS	10//99-12//99
	Kentucky	S	9.39 MW	9.54 AW	19850 AAW	KYBLS	10//99-12//99
	Lexington MSA, KY	S	10.81 MW	10.85 AW	22490 AAW	KYBLS	10//99-12//99
	Louisville MSA, KY-IN	S	15.85 MW	17.94 AW	32970 AAW	KYBLS	10//99-12//99
	Louisiana	S	9.33 MW	9.68 AW	20130 AAW	LABLS	10//99-12//99
	Baton Rouge MSA, LA	S	9.37 MW	9.50 AW	19490 AAW	LABLS	10//99-12//99
	New Orleans MSA, LA	S	9.09 MW	8.11 AW	18900 AAW	LABLS	10//99-12//99
	Shreveport-Bossier City MSA, LA	S	10.03 MW	9.68 AW	20860 AAW	LABLS	10//99-12//99
	Maine	S	10.06 MW	10.88 AW	22630 AAW	MEBLS	10//99-12//99
	Portland MSA, ME	S	12.53 MW	12.72 AW	26060 AAW	MEBLS	10//99-12//99
	Maryland	S	14.57 MW	14.33 AW	29800 AAW	MDBLS	10//99-12//99
	Baltimore PMSA, MD	S	13.48 MW	13.51 AW	28030 AAW	MDBLS	10//99-12//99
	Massachusetts	S	13.09 MW	13.29 AW	27640 AAW	MABLS	10//99-12//99
	Barnstable-Yarmouth MSA, MA	S	10.28 MW	9.70 AW	21380 AAW	MABLS	10//99-12//99
	Boston PMSA, MA-NH	S	13.47 MW	13.08 AW	28020 AAW	MABLS	10//99-12//99
	Brockton PMSA, MA	S	14.79 MW	14.84 AW	30770 AAW	MABLS	10//99-12//99
	Lawrence PMSA, MA-NH	S	13.09 MW	13.44 AW	27230 AAW	MABLS	10//99-12//99
	Springfield MSA, MA	S	12.75 MW	13.24 AW	26520 AAW	MABLS	10//99-12//99
	Worcester PMSA, MA-CT	S	12.43 MW	12.48 AW	25860 AAW	MABLS	10//99-12//99
	Michigan	S	12.05 MW	12.62 AW	26250 AAW	MIBLS	10//99-12//99
	Ann Arbor PMSA, MI	S	17.81 MW	17.58 AW	37050 AAW	MIBLS	10//99-12//99
	Detroit PMSA, MI	S	12.22 MW	11.71 AW	25430 AAW	MIBLS	10//99-12//99
	Grand Rapids-Muskegon-Holland MSA, MI	S	14.33 MW	13.23 AW	29810 AAW	MIBLS	10//99-12//99
	Kalamazoo-Battle Creek MSA, MI	S	9.59 MW	8.98 AW	19940 AAW	MIBLS	10//99-12//99
	Saginaw-Bay City-Midland MSA, MI	S	10.95 MW	11.56 AW	22770 AAW	MIBLS	10//99-12//99
	Minnesota	S	11.52 MW	11.40 AW	23720 AAW	MNBLS	10//99-12//99
	Minneapolis-St. Paul MSA, MN-WI	S	12.35 MW	12.17 AW	25690 AAW	MNBLS	10//99-12//99
	St. Cloud MSA, MN	S	11.32 MW	11.17 AW	23540 AAW	MNBLS	10//99-12//99
	Mississippi	S	11.08 MW	11.22 AW	23350 AAW	MSBLS	10//99-12//99
	Biloxi-Gulfport-Pascagoula MSA, MS	S	11.66 MW	11.40 AW	24260 AAW	MSBLS	10//99-12//99
	Jackson MSA, MS	S	10.33 MW	10.04 AW	21490 AAW	MSBLS	10//99-12//99
	Missouri	S	10.13 MW	10.56 AW	21960 AAW	MOBLS	10//99-12//99
	Kansas City MSA, MO-KS	S	10.72 MW	10.24 AW	22290 AAW	MOBLS	10//99-12//99
	St. Louis MSA, MO-IL	S	11.94 MW	12.00 AW	24830 AAW	MOBLS	10//99-12//99
	Springfield MSA, MO	S	8.58 MW	8.65 AW	17840 AAW	MOBLS	10//99-12//99
	Montana	S	9.8 MW	10.12 AW	21050 AAW	MTBLS	10//99-12//99
	Nebraska	S	11.48 MW	11.43 AW	23770 AAW	NEBLS	10//99-12//99
	Lincoln MSA, NE	S	9.34 MW	9.34 AW	19430 AAW	NEBLS	10//99-12//99

AAW Average annual wage	**AOH** Average offered, high	**ASH** Average starting, high	**H** Hourly	**M** Monthly	**S** Special: hourly and annual
AE Average entry wage	**AOL** Average offered, low	**ASL** Average starting, low	**HI** Highest wage paid	**MTC** Median total compensation	**TQ** Third quartile wage
AEX Average experienced wage	**APH** Average pay, high range	**AW** Average wage paid	**HR** High end range	**MW** Median wage paid	**W** Weekly
AO Average offered	**APL** Average pay, low range	**FQ** First quartile wage	**LR** Low end range	**SQ** Second quartile wage	**Y** Yearly

Occupation/Type/Industry	Location	Per	Low	Mid	High	Source	Date
Cabinetmaker and Bench Carpenter	Omaha MSA, NE-IA	S	11.77 MW	11.91 AW	24490 AAW	NEBLS	10//99-12//99
	Nevada	S	14.21 MW	14.41 AW	29980 AAW	NVBLS	10//99-12//99
	Las Vegas MSA, NV-AZ	S	14.14 MW	14.93 AW	29410 AAW	NVBLS	10//99-12//99
	Reno MSA, NV	S	14.28 MW	12.95 AW	29710 AAW	NVBLS	10//99-12//99
	New Hampshire	S	14.24 MW	14.28 AW	29710 AAW	NHBLS	10//99-12//99
	Nashua PMSA, NH	S	11.37 MW	8.27 AW	23640 AAW	NHBLS	10//99-12//99
	New Jersey	S	14.26 MW	15.06 AW	31330 AAW	NJBLS	10//99-12//99
	Bergen-Passaic PMSA, NJ	S	14.90 MW	13.29 AW	31000 AAW	NJBLS	10//99-12//99
	Monmouth-Ocean PMSA, NJ	S	15.91 MW	15.24 AW	33100 AAW	NJBLS	10//99-12//99
	Newark PMSA, NJ	S	15.77 MW	14.71 AW	32810 AAW	NJBLS	10//99-12//99
	New Mexico	S	10.48 MW	11.57 AW	24060 AAW	NMBLS	10//99-12//99
	Albuquerque MSA, NM	S	11.18 MW	10.17 AW	23260 AAW	NMBLS	10//99-12//99
	Santa Fe MSA, NM	S	14.45 MW	14.90 AW	30060 AAW	NMBLS	10//99-12//99
	New York	S	10.64 MW	12.21 AW	25400 AAW	NYBLS	10//99-12//99
	Binghamton MSA, NY	S	11.12 MW	8.97 AW	23130 AAW	NYBLS	10//99-12//99
	Buffalo-Niagara Falls MSA, NY	S	12.68 MW	12.37 AW	26370 AAW	NYBLS	10//99-12//99
	Dutchess County PMSA, NY	S	12.21 MW	10.44 AW	25390 AAW	NYBLS	10//99-12//99
	Jamestown MSA, NY	S	8.54 MW	8.11 AW	17770 AAW	NYBLS	10//99-12//99
	Nassau-Suffolk PMSA, NY	S	16.32 MW	16.12 AW	33950 AAW	NYBLS	10//99-12//99
	New York PMSA, NY	S	12.71 MW	10.87 AW	26440 AAW	NYBLS	10//99-12//99
	Newburgh PMSA, NY-PA	S	15.68 MW	16.26 AW	32610 AAW	NYBLS	10//99-12//99
	Rochester MSA, NY	S	12.04 MW	10.74 AW	25040 AAW	NYBLS	10//99-12//99
	Syracuse MSA, NY	S	10.33 MW	10.17 AW	21480 AAW	NYBLS	10//99-12//99
	Utica-Rome MSA, NY	S	10.57 MW	9.57 AW	21980 AAW	NYBLS	10//99-12//99
	North Carolina	S	10.02 MW	10.31 AW	21440 AAW	NCBLS	10//99-12//99
	Charlotte-Gastonia-Rock Hill MSA, NC-SC	S	9.79 MW	8.50 AW	20360 AAW	NCBLS	10//99-12//99
	Greensboro--Winston-Salem--High Point MSA, NC	S	10.39 MW	10.46 AW	21620 AAW	NCBLS	10//99-12//99
	Hickory-Morganton-Lenoir MSA, NC	S	10.58 MW	10.49 AW	22000 AAW	NCBLS	10//99-12//99
	Raleigh-Durham-Chapel Hill MSA, NC	S	10.77 MW	10.09 AW	22410 AAW	NCBLS	10//99-12//99
	Rocky Mount MSA, NC	S	7.55 MW	6.21 AW	15700 AAW	NCBLS	10//99-12//99
	North Dakota	S	10.62 MW	10.91 AW	22700 AAW	NDBLS	10//99-12//99
	Fargo-Moorhead MSA, ND-MN	S	10.10 MW	10.04 AW	21010 AAW	NDBLS	10//99-12//99
	Ohio	S	10.6 MW	11.44 AW	23790 AAW	OHBLS	10//99-12//99
	Akron PMSA, OH	S	10.80 MW	10.94 AW	22470 AAW	OHBLS	10//99-12//99
	Cincinnati PMSA, OH-KY-IN	S	11.75 MW	11.44 AW	24440 AAW	OHBLS	10//99-12//99
	Cleveland-Lorain-Elyria PMSA, OH	S	14.69 MW	14.34 AW	30560 AAW	OHBLS	10//99-12//99
	Columbus MSA, OH	S	12.51 MW	12.61 AW	26020 AAW	OHBLS	10//99-12//99
	Dayton-Springfield MSA, OH	S	12.23 MW	11.68 AW	25430 AAW	OHBLS	10//99-12//99
	Lima MSA, OH	S	8.34 MW	8.12 AW	17350 AAW	OHBLS	10//99-12//99
	Toledo MSA, OH	S	10.84 MW	10.28 AW	22540 AAW	OHBLS	10//99-12//99
	Youngstown-Warren MSA, OH	S	12.90 MW	12.80 AW	26840 AAW	OHBLS	10//99-12//99
	Oklahoma	S	10.64 MW	10.36 AW	21550 AAW	OKBLS	10//99-12//99
	Oklahoma City MSA, OK	S	11.24 MW	11.52 AW	23390 AAW	OKBLS	10//99-12//99
	Oregon	S	11.68 MW	12.28 AW	25550 AAW	ORBLS	10//99-12//99
	Eugene-Springfield MSA, OR	S	12.89 MW	12.22 AW	26820 AAW	ORBLS	10//99-12//99
	Medford-Ashland MSA, OR	S	12.44 MW	10.41 AW	25880 AAW	ORBLS	10//99-12//99
	Portland-Vancouver PMSA, OR-WA	S	10.82 MW	10.47 AW	22510 AAW	ORBLS	10//99-12//99
	Salem PMSA, OR	S	14.38 MW	15.07 AW	29910 AAW	ORBLS	10//99-12//99
	Pennsylvania	S	11.9 MW	12.02 AW	25000 AAW	PABLS	10//99-12//99
	Allentown-Bethlehem-Easton MSA, PA	S	14.33 MW	14.82 AW	29810 AAW	PABLS	10//99-12//99
	Harrisburg-Lebanon-Carlisle MSA, PA	S	10.29 MW	10.02 AW	21400 AAW	PABLS	10//99-12//99
	Lancaster MSA, PA	S	11.27 MW	11.46 AW	23450 AAW	PABLS	10//99-12//99
	Philadelphia PMSA, PA-NJ	S	14.72 MW	14.79 AW	30620 AAW	PABLS	10//99-12//99
	Pittsburgh MSA, PA	S	13.72 MW	14.43 AW	28540 AAW	PABLS	10//99-12//99
	Reading MSA, PA	S	13.98 MW	12.64 AW	29080 AAW	PABLS	10//99-12//99
	Williamsport MSA, PA	S	9.04 MW	8.68 AW	18800 AAW	PABLS	10//99-12//99
	Rhode Island	S	14.68 MW	14.29 AW	29730 AAW	RIBLS	10//99-12//99
	Providence-Fall River-Warwick MSA, RI-MA	S	14.57 MW	14.91 AW	30300 AAW	RIBLS	10//99-12//99
	South Carolina	S	8.69 MW	8.96 AW	18640 AAW	SCBLS	10//99-12//99

Occupation/Type/Industry	Location	Per	Low	Mid	High	Source	Date
Cabinetmaker and Bench Carpenter							
	Charleston-North Charleston MSA, SC	S	11.23 MW	10.39 AW	23360 AAW	SCBLS	10//99-12//99
	Columbia MSA, SC	S	12.39 MW	12.08 AW	25780 AAW	SCBLS	10//99-12//99
	Greenville-Spartanburg-Anderson MSA, SC	S	9.97 MW	9.42 AW	20740 AAW	SCBLS	10//99-12//99
	Sumter MSA, SC	S	7.96 MW	8.29 AW	16560 AAW	SCBLS	10//99-12//99
	South Dakota	S	9.64 MW	9.64 AW	20050 AAW	SDBLS	10//99-12//99
	Sioux Falls MSA, SD	S	9.74 MW	9.73 AW	20260 AAW	SDBLS	10//99-12//99
	Tennessee	S	9.52 MW	9.63 AW	20040 AAW	TNBLS	10//99-12//99
	Chattanooga MSA, TN-GA	S	9.66 MW	9.67 AW	20080 AAW	TNBLS	10//99-12//99
	Johnson City-Kingsport-Bristol MSA, TN-VA	S	9.74 MW	9.69 AW	20260 AAW	TNBLS	10//99-12//99
	Knoxville MSA, TN	S	9.31 MW	8.96 AW	19370 AAW	TNBLS	10//99-12//99
	Memphis MSA, TN-AR-MS	S	12.76 MW	12.53 AW	26540 AAW	MSBLS	10//99-12//99
	Nashville MSA, TN	S	11.55 MW	10.91 AW	24030 AAW	TNBLS	10//99-12//99
	Texas	S	9.17 MW	9.56 AW	19880 AAW	TXBLS	10//99-12//99
	Austin-San Marcos MSA, TX	S	10.27 MW	10.33 AW	21350 AAW	TXBLS	10//99-12//99
	Beaumont-Port Arthur MSA, TX	S	8.85 MW	7.75 AW	18400 AAW	TXBLS	10//99-12//99
	Corpus Christi MSA, TX	S	8.28 MW	7.91 AW	17230 AAW	TXBLS	10//99-12//99
	Dallas PMSA, TX	S	9.55 MW	9.56 AW	19870 AAW	TXBLS	10//99-12//99
	El Paso MSA, TX	S	7.00 MW	6.53 AW	14550 AAW	TXBLS	10//99-12//99
	Fort Worth-Arlington PMSA, TX	S	9.84 MW	9.77 AW	20470 AAW	TXBLS	10//99-12//99
	Houston PMSA, TX	S	11.13 MW	10.07 AW	23140 AAW	TXBLS	10//99-12//99
	Killeen-Temple MSA, TX	S	9.40 MW	8.34 AW	19560 AAW	TXBLS	10//99-12//99
	Longview-Marshall MSA, TX	S	9.42 MW	9.38 AW	19590 AAW	TXBLS	10//99-12//99
	Lubbock MSA, TX	S	7.75 MW	7.77 AW	16130 AAW	TXBLS	10//99-12//99
	McAllen-Edinburg-Mission MSA, TX	S	8.08 MW	7.74 AW	16800 AAW	TXBLS	10//99-12//99
	Odessa-Midland MSA, TX	S	7.79 MW	6.55 AW	16190 AAW	TXBLS	10//99-12//99
	San Antonio MSA, TX	S	9.01 MW	8.03 AW	18740 AAW	TXBLS	10//99-12//99
	Sherman-Denison MSA, TX	S	10.48 MW	9.56 AW	21800 AAW	TXBLS	10//99-12//99
	Tyler MSA, TX	S	9.91 MW	9.43 AW	20620 AAW	TXBLS	10//99-12//99
	Utah	S	10.09 MW	10.77 AW	22410 AAW	UTBLS	10//99-12//99
	Provo-Orem MSA, UT	S	9.52 MW	9.38 AW	19800 AAW	UTBLS	10//99-12//99
	Salt Lake City-Ogden MSA, UT	S	11.92 MW	11.19 AW	24790 AAW	UTBLS	10//99-12//99
	Vermont	S	9.88 MW	10.32 AW	21460 AAW	VTBLS	10//99-12//99
	Burlington MSA, VT	S	11.83 MW	11.72 AW	24610 AAW	VTBLS	10//99-12//99
	Virginia	S	10.28 MW	10.88 AW	22640 AAW	VABLS	10//99-12//99
	Lynchburg MSA, VA	S	10.81 MW	10.49 AW	22480 AAW	VABLS	10//99-12//99
	Norfolk-Virginia Beach-Newport News MSA, VA-NC	S	12.24 MW	12.55 AW	25450 AAW	VABLS	10//99-12//99
	Richmond-Petersburg MSA, VA	S	11.05 MW	11.32 AW	22990 AAW	VABLS	10//99-12//99
	Roanoke MSA, VA	S	9.92 MW	9.88 AW	20630 AAW	VABLS	10//99-12//99
	Washington	S	12.63 MW	12.76 AW	26540 AAW	WABLS	10//99-12//99
	Bremerton PMSA, WA	S	15.48 MW	15.06 AW	32200 AAW	WABLS	10//99-12//99
	Seattle-Bellevue-Everett PMSA, WA	S	12.70 MW	12.51 AW	26410 AAW	WABLS	10//99-12//99
	Spokane MSA, WA	S	14.25 MW	14.78 AW	29630 AAW	WABLS	10//99-12//99
	Tacoma PMSA, WA	S	12.22 MW	11.90 AW	25410 AAW	WABLS	10//99-12//99
	West Virginia	S	8.99 MW	9.32 AW	19380 AAW	WVBLS	10//99-12//99
	Parkersburg-Marietta MSA, WV-OH	S	10.09 MW	8.46 AW	20990 AAW	WVBLS	10//99-12//99
	Wisconsin	S	12.18 MW	12.37 AW	25730 AAW	WIBLS	10//99-12//99
	Appleton-Oshkosh-Neenah MSA, WI	S	12.35 MW	12.41 AW	25690 AAW	WIBLS	10//99-12//99
	Green Bay MSA, WI	S	8.92 MW	8.08 AW	18550 AAW	WIBLS	10//99-12//99
	Kenosha PMSA, WI	S	14.79 MW	13.22 AW	30760 AAW	WIBLS	10//99-12//99
	La Crosse MSA, WI-MN	S	10.97 MW	11.20 AW	22810 AAW	WIBLS	10//99-12//99
	Madison MSA, WI	S	13.57 MW	13.28 AW	28230 AAW	WIBLS	10//99-12//99
	Milwaukee-Waukesha PMSA, WI	S	13.64 MW	13.92 AW	28380 AAW	WIBLS	10//99-12//99
	Sheboygan MSA, WI	S	9.99 MW	9.90 AW	20780 AAW	WIBLS	10//99-12//99
	Wyoming	S	13.15 MW	12.33 AW	25650 AAW	WYBLS	10//99-12//99
	Puerto Rico	S	6.04 MW	6.03 AW	12550 AAW	PRBLS	10//99-12//99
	Caguas PMSA, PR	S	5.88 MW	6.00 AW	12220 AAW	PRBLS	10//99-12//99
	Mayaguez MSA, PR	S	5.85 MW	5.97 AW	12170 AAW	PRBLS	10//99-12//99

AAW	Average annual wage	AOH	Average offered, high	ASH	Average starting, high	H	Hourly	M	Monthly	S	Special: hourly and annual
AE	Average entry wage	AOL	Average offered, low	ASL	Average starting, low	HI	Highest wage paid	MTC	Median total compensation	TQ	Third quartile wage
AEX	Average experienced wage	APH	Average pay, high range	AW	Average wage paid	HR	High end range	MW	Median wage paid	W	Weekly
AO	Average offered	APL	Average pay, low range	FQ	First quartile wage	LR	Low end range	SQ	Second quartile wage	Y	Yearly

Occupation/Type/Industry	Location	Per	Low	Mid	High	Source	Date
Cabinetmaker and Bench Carpenter	Ponce MSA, PR	S	5.75 MW	5.95 AW	11960 AAW	PRBLS	10//99-12//99
	San Juan-Bayamon PMSA, PR	S	6.25 MW	6.12 AW	13010 AAW	PRBLS	10//99-12//99
Camera and Photographic Equipment Repairer	Alabama	S	13.73 MW	14.14 AW	29420 AAW	ALBLS	10//99-12//99
	Alaska	S	15.13 MW	14.95 AW	31090 AAW	AKBLS	10//99-12//99
	Arizona	S	10.23 MW	10.34 AW	21500 AAW	AZBLS	10//99-12//99
	Phoenix-Mesa MSA, AZ	S	10.46 MW	10.31 AW	21760 AAW	AZBLS	10//99-12//99
	California	S	17.52 MW	18.74 AW	38980 AAW	CABLS	10//99-12//99
	Connecticut	S	14.6 MW	16.36 AW	34030 AAW	CTBLS	10//99-12//99
	Washington PMSA, DC-MD-VA-WV	S	12.54 MW	12.46 AW	26080 AAW	DCBLS	10//99-12//99
	Florida	S	13.42 MW	14.05 AW	29220 AAW	FLBLS	10//99-12//99
	Georgia	S	17.9 MW	18.28 AW	38030 AAW	GABLS	10//99-12//99
	Atlanta MSA, GA	S	18.43 MW	18.37 AW	38330 AAW	GABLS	10//99-12//99
	Illinois	S	8.44 MW	12.12 AW	25200 AAW	ILBLS	10//99-12//99
	Chicago PMSA, IL	S	11.52 MW	6.05 AW	23950 AAW	ILBLS	10//99-12//99
	Indiana	S	13.25 MW	14.72 AW	30610 AAW	INBLS	10//99-12//99
	Kentucky	S	17.37 MW	16.60 AW	34530 AAW	KYBLS	10//99-12//99
	Louisville MSA, KY-IN	S	16.78 MW	17.84 AW	34900 AAW	KYBLS	10//99-12//99
	Louisiana	S	6.67 MW	8.94 AW	18590 AAW	LABLS	10//99-12//99
	Lafayette MSA, LA	S	6.14 MW	6.21 AW	12780 AAW	LABLS	10//99-12//99
	New Orleans MSA, LA	S	14.58 MW	10.68 AW	30330 AAW	LABLS	10//99-12//99
	Maryland	S	13.69 MW	12.99 AW	27030 AAW	MDBLS	10//99-12//99
	Baltimore PMSA, MD	S	14.75 MW	15.06 AW	30680 AAW	MDBLS	10//99-12//99
	Massachusetts	S	17.73 MW	17.00 AW	35360 AAW	MABLS	10//99-12//99
	Boston PMSA, MA-NH	S	13.25 MW	12.78 AW	27570 AAW	MABLS	10//99-12//99
	Michigan	S	28.32 MW	22.85 AW	47530 AAW	MIBLS	10//99-12//99
	Minnesota	S	21.45 MW	20.81 AW	43280 AAW	MNBLS	10//99-12//99
	Minneapolis-St. Paul MSA, MN-WI	S	20.81 MW	21.01 AW	43280 AAW	MNBLS	10//99-12//99
	Nebraska	S	9.42 MW	10.02 AW	20840 AAW	NEBLS	10//99-12//99
	New Hampshire	S	13.82 MW	16.26 AW	33830 AAW	NHBLS	10//99-12//99
	New Jersey	S	15.27 MW	15.23 AW	31670 AAW	NJBLS	10//99-12//99
	Bergen-Passaic PMSA, NJ	S	16.54 MW	16.02 AW	34400 AAW	NJBLS	10//99-12//99
	Jersey City PMSA, NJ	S	13.48 MW	13.78 AW	28030 AAW	NJBLS	10//99-12//99
	Monmouth-Ocean PMSA, NJ	S	7.92 MW	6.51 AW	16460 AAW	NJBLS	10//99-12//99
	New York	S	14.7 MW	15.02 AW	31240 AAW	NYBLS	10//99-12//99
	Nassau-Suffolk PMSA, NY	S	16.39 MW	16.83 AW	34090 AAW	NYBLS	10//99-12//99
	New York PMSA, NY	S	15.06 MW	14.78 AW	31320 AAW	NYBLS	10//99-12//99
	Ohio	S	14.55 MW	15.06 AW	31330 AAW	OHBLS	10//99-12//99
	Oklahoma	S	16.94 MW	18.34 AW	38140 AAW	OKBLS	10//99-12//99
	Pennsylvania	S	9.42 MW	13.51 AW	28090 AAW	PABLS	10//99-12//99
	Philadelphia PMSA, PA-NJ	S	13.99 MW	13.78 AW	29110 AAW	PABLS	10//99-12//99
	South Carolina	S	9.76 MW	10.37 AW	21570 AAW	SCBLS	10//99-12//99
	Texas	S	13.28 MW	13.49 AW	28060 AAW	TXBLS	10//99-12//99
	Virginia	S	11.77 MW	13.10 AW	27240 AAW	VABLS	10//99-12//99
	Wisconsin	S	12.27 MW	13.95 AW	29020 AAW	WIBLS	10//99-12//99
Camera Operator							
Television, Video, and Motion Picture	Alabama	S	10.23 MW	11.28 AW	23460 AAW	ALBLS	10//99-12//99
Television, Video, and Motion Picture	Birmingham MSA, AL	S	12.61 MW	11.20 AW	26230 AAW	ALBLS	10//99-12//99
Television, Video, and Motion Picture	Huntsville MSA, AL	S	12.61 MW	10.98 AW	26220 AAW	ALBLS	10//99-12//99
Television, Video, and Motion Picture	Alaska	S	9.48 MW	10.80 AW	22460 AAW	AKBLS	10//99-12//99
Television, Video, and Motion Picture	Anchorage MSA, AK	S	10.46 MW	9.12 AW	21750 AAW	AKBLS	10//99-12//99
Television, Video, and Motion Picture	Arizona	S	12.17 MW	15.02 AW	31250 AAW	AZBLS	10//99-12//99
Television, Video, and Motion Picture	Phoenix-Mesa MSA, AZ	S	18.46 MW	15.53 AW	38390 AAW	AZBLS	10//99-12//99
Television, Video, and Motion Picture	Tucson MSA, AZ	S	11.31 MW	9.76 AW	23530 AAW	AZBLS	10//99-12//99
Television, Video, and Motion Picture	Arkansas	S	8.31 MW	10.73 AW	22330 AAW	ARBLS	10//99-12//99
Television, Video, and Motion Picture	Fort Smith MSA, AR-OK	S	7.01 MW	6.85 AW	14570 AAW	ARBLS	10//99-12//99
Television, Video, and Motion Picture	California	S	22.36 MW	22.34 AW	46460 AAW	CABLS	10//99-12//99
Television, Video, and Motion Picture	Bakersfield MSA, CA	S	21.50 MW	23.10 AW	44730 AAW	CABLS	10//99-12//99
Television, Video, and Motion Picture	Los Angeles-Long Beach PMSA, CA	S	25.34 MW	26.60 AW	52700 AAW	CABLS	10//99-12//99
Television, Video, and Motion Picture	Orange County PMSA, CA	S	23.99 MW	23.35 AW	49900 AAW	CABLS	10//99-12//99
Television, Video, and Motion Picture	Riverside-San Bernardino PMSA, CA	S	16.47 MW	15.62 AW	34260 AAW	CABLS	10//99-12//99
Television, Video, and Motion Picture	San Diego MSA, CA	S	21.47 MW	19.98 AW	44660 AAW	CABLS	10//99-12//99
Television, Video, and Motion Picture	San Francisco PMSA, CA	S	17.78 MW	17.88 AW	36970 AAW	CABLS	10//99-12//99
Television, Video, and Motion Picture	San Jose PMSA, CA	S	22.93 MW	21.53 AW	47700 AAW	CABLS	10//99-12//99

AAW Average annual wage	**AOH** Average offered, high	**ASH** Average starting, high	**H** Hourly	**M** Monthly	**S** Special: hourly and annual
AE Average entry wage	**AOL** Average offered, low	**ASL** Average starting, low	**HI** Highest wage paid	**MTC** Median total compensation	**TQ** Third quartile wage
AEX Average experienced wage	**APH** Average pay, high range	**AW** Average wage paid	**HR** High end range	**MW** Median wage paid	**W** Weekly
AO Average offered	**APL** Average pay, low range	**FQ** First quartile wage	**LR** Low end range	**SQ** Second quartile wage	**Y** Yearly

Occupation/Type/Industry	Location	Per	Low	Mid	High	Source	Date
Camera Operator							
Television, Video, and Motion Picture	Santa Barbara-Santa Maria-Lompoc MSA, CA	S	19.29 MW	19.65 AW	40110 AAW	CABLS	10//99-12//99
Television, Video, and Motion Picture	Colorado	S	14.7 MW	16.73 AW	34800 AAW	COBLS	10//99-12//99
Television, Video, and Motion Picture	Denver PMSA, CO	S	18.42 MW	19.07 AW	38310 AAW	COBLS	10//99-12//99
Television, Video, and Motion Picture	Connecticut	S	13.82 MW	14.56 AW	30280 AAW	CTBLS	10//99-12//99
Television, Video, and Motion Picture	Bridgeport PMSA, CT	S	13.56 MW	12.87 AW	28200 AAW	CTBLS	10//99-12//99
Television, Video, and Motion Picture	Hartford MSA, CT	S	14.90 MW	14.02 AW	31000 AAW	CTBLS	10//99-12//99
Television, Video, and Motion Picture	District of Columbia	S	19.69 MW	18.83 AW	39170 AAW	DCBLS	10//99-12//99
Television, Video, and Motion Picture	Washington PMSA, DC-MD-VA-WV	S	18.72 MW	19.28 AW	38940 AAW	DCBLS	10//99-12//99
Television, Video, and Motion Picture	Florida	S	10.3 MW	11.80 AW	24550 AAW	FLBLS	10//99-12//99
Television, Video, and Motion Picture	Daytona Beach MSA, FL	S	11.48 MW	10.44 AW	23870 AAW	FLBLS	10//99-12//99
Television, Video, and Motion Picture	Fort Lauderdale PMSA, FL	S	11.48 MW	10.32 AW	23880 AAW	FLBLS	10//99-12//99
Television, Video, and Motion Picture	Jacksonville MSA, FL	S	10.13 MW	8.47 AW	21070 AAW	FLBLS	10//99-12//99
Television, Video, and Motion Picture	Miami PMSA, FL	S	11.60 MW	10.52 AW	24130 AAW	FLBLS	10//99-12//99
Television, Video, and Motion Picture	Orlando MSA, FL	S	13.72 MW	14.24 AW	28550 AAW	FLBLS	10//99-12//99
Television, Video, and Motion Picture	Tampa-St. Petersburg-Clearwater MSA, FL	S	12.17 MW	9.74 AW	25310 AAW	FLBLS	10//99-12//99
Television, Video, and Motion Picture	West Palm Beach-Boca Raton MSA, FL	S	13.69 MW	14.17 AW	28470 AAW	FLBLS	10//99-12//99
Television, Video, and Motion Picture	Georgia	S	12.86 MW	15.80 AW	32860 AAW	GABLS	10//99-12//99
Television, Video, and Motion Picture	Atlanta MSA, GA	S	15.88 MW	12.87 AW	33030 AAW	GABLS	10//99-12//99
Television, Video, and Motion Picture	Augusta-Aiken MSA, GA-SC	S	9.96 MW	9.39 AW	20720 AAW	GABLS	10//99-12//99
Television, Video, and Motion Picture	Hawaii	S	11.48 MW	13.09 AW	27230 AAW	HIBLS	10//99-12//99
Television, Video, and Motion Picture	Honolulu MSA, HI	S	15.11 MW	14.01 AW	31430 AAW	HIBLS	10//99-12//99
Television, Video, and Motion Picture	Idaho	S	8.52 MW	10.10 AW	21020 AAW	IDBLS	10//99-12//99
Television, Video, and Motion Picture	Boise City MSA, ID	S	11.13 MW	9.51 AW	23140 AAW	IDBLS	10//99-12//99
Television, Video, and Motion Picture	Illinois	S	8.97 MW	18.00 AW	37430 AAW	ILBLS	10//99-12//99
Television, Video, and Motion Picture	Chicago PMSA, IL	S	19.19 MW	10.34 AW	39920 AAW	ILBLS	10//99-12//99
Television, Video, and Motion Picture	Rockford MSA, IL	S	9.71 MW	7.57 AW	20200 AAW	ILBLS	10//99-12//99
Television, Video, and Motion Picture	Indiana	S	10.69 MW	13.36 AW	27780 AAW	INBLS	10//99-12//99
Television, Video, and Motion Picture	Evansville-Henderson MSA, IN-KY	S	9.71 MW	9.09 AW	20190 AAW	INBLS	10//99-12//99
Television, Video, and Motion Picture	Fort Wayne MSA, IN	S	12.77 MW	11.70 AW	26550 AAW	INBLS	10//99-12//99
Television, Video, and Motion Picture	Indianapolis MSA, IN	S	16.38 MW	16.45 AW	34060 AAW	INBLS	10//99-12//99
Television, Video, and Motion Picture	Iowa	S	10.46 MW	11.97 AW	24910 AAW	IABLS	10//99-12//99
Television, Video, and Motion Picture	Davenport-Moline-Rock Island MSA, IA-IL	S	14.12 MW	13.68 AW	29360 AAW	IABLS	10//99-12//99
Television, Video, and Motion Picture	Des Moines MSA, IA	S	14.71 MW	12.45 AW	30600 AAW	IABLS	10//99-12//99
Television, Video, and Motion Picture	Kansas	S	10.68 MW	12.63 AW	26260 AAW	KSBLS	10//99-12//99
Television, Video, and Motion Picture	Topeka MSA, KS	S	9.15 MW	6.59 AW	19030 AAW	KSBLS	10//99-12//99
Television, Video, and Motion Picture	Wichita MSA, KS	S	12.14 MW	9.38 AW	25250 AAW	KSBLS	10//99-12//99
Television, Video, and Motion Picture	Kentucky	S	10.54 MW	11.51 AW	23940 AAW	KYBLS	10//99-12//99
Television, Video, and Motion Picture	Lexington MSA, KY	S	10.59 MW	10.31 AW	22020 AAW	KYBLS	10//99-12//99
Television, Video, and Motion Picture	Louisville MSA, KY-IN	S	12.60 MW	11.35 AW	26210 AAW	KYBLS	10//99-12//99
Television, Video, and Motion Picture	Louisiana	S	8.88 MW	10.61 AW	22060 AAW	LABLS	10//99-12//99
Television, Video, and Motion Picture	New Orleans MSA, LA	S	10.67 MW	8.55 AW	22200 AAW	LABLS	10//99-12//99
Television, Video, and Motion Picture	Maine	S	6.79 MW	9.48 AW	19710 AAW	MEBLS	10//99-12//99
Television, Video, and Motion Picture	Portland MSA, ME	S	12.30 MW	9.96 AW	25580 AAW	MEBLS	10//99-12//99
Television, Video, and Motion Picture	Maryland	S	18.58 MW	18.45 AW	38380 AAW	MDBLS	10//99-12//99
Television, Video, and Motion Picture	Baltimore PMSA, MD	S	19.96 MW	19.26 AW	41510 AAW	MDBLS	10//99-12//99
Television, Video, and Motion Picture	Massachusetts	S	15.4 MW	16.67 AW	34680 AAW	MABLS	10//99-12//99
Television, Video, and Motion Picture	Boston PMSA, MA-NH	S	17.80 MW	16.12 AW	37020 AAW	MABLS	10//99-12//99
Television, Video, and Motion Picture	Michigan	S	18.77 MW	18.69 AW	38870 AAW	MIBLS	10//99-12//99
Television, Video, and Motion Picture	Detroit PMSA, MI	S	22.29 MW	23.11 AW	46360 AAW	MIBLS	10//99-12//99
Television, Video, and Motion Picture	Minnesota	S	14.25 MW	15.46 AW	32150 AAW	MNBLS	10//99-12//99
Television, Video, and Motion Picture	Minneapolis-St. Paul MSA, MN-WI	S	16.76 MW	17.29 AW	34860 AAW	MNBLS	10//99-12//99
Television, Video, and Motion Picture	Mississippi	S	9.42 MW	9.69 AW	20160 AAW	MSBLS	10//99-12//99
Television, Video, and Motion Picture	Missouri	S	12.73 MW	13.68 AW	28460 AAW	MOBLS	10//99-12//99
Television, Video, and Motion Picture	St. Louis MSA, MO-IL	S	14.55 MW	13.32 AW	30270 AAW	MOBLS	10//99-12//99
Television, Video, and Motion Picture	Montana	S	6.37 MW	8.27 AW	17200 AAW	MTBLS	10//99-12//99
Television, Video, and Motion Picture	Nebraska	S	11.08 MW	11.03 AW	22940 AAW	NEBLS	10//99-12//99
Television, Video, and Motion Picture	Nevada	S	11.38 MW	15.07 AW	31340 AAW	NVBLS	10//99-12//99
Television, Video, and Motion Picture	Las Vegas MSA, NV-AZ	S	14.12 MW	10.83 AW	29370 AAW	NVBLS	10//99-12//99
Television, Video, and Motion Picture	Reno MSA, NV	S	13.23 MW	11.10 AW	27510 AAW	NVBLS	10//99-12//99
Television, Video, and Motion Picture	New Hampshire	S	13.3 MW	17.70 AW	36820 AAW	NHBLS	10//99-12//99
Television, Video, and Motion Picture	New Jersey	S	13.83 MW	16.09 AW	33470 AAW	NJBLS	10//99-12//99
Television, Video, and Motion Picture	Atlantic-Cape May PMSA, NJ	S	10.92 MW	9.94 AW	22710 AAW	NJBLS	10//99-12//99
Television, Video, and Motion Picture	Bergen-Passaic PMSA, NJ	S	15.04 MW	14.64 AW	31290 AAW	NJBLS	10//99-12//99
Television, Video, and Motion Picture	New Mexico	S	10.58 MW	12.73 AW	26470 AAW	NMBLS	10//99-12//99

AAW Average annual wage	**AOH** Average offered, high	**ASH** Average starting, high	**H** Hourly	**M** Monthly	**S** Special: hourly and annual
AE Average entry wage	**AOL** Average offered, low	**ASL** Average starting, low	**HI** Highest wage paid	**MTC** Median total compensation	**TQ** Third quartile wage
AEX Average experienced wage	**APH** Average pay, high range	**AW** Average wage paid	**HR** High end range	**MW** Median wage paid	**W** Weekly
AO Average offered	**APL** Average pay, low range	**FQ** First quartile wage	**LR** Low end range	**SQ** Second quartile wage	**Y** Yearly

Camera Operator

Occupation/Type/Industry	Location	Per	Low	Mid	High	Source	Date
Camera Operator							
Television, Video, and Motion Picture	Nassau-Suffolk PMSA, NY	s	15.38 MW	11.45 AW	32000 AAW	NYBLS	10//99-12//99
Television, Video, and Motion Picture	New York PMSA, NY	s	21.74 MW	19.50 AW	45230 AAW	NYBLS	10//99-12//99
Television, Video, and Motion Picture	Rochester MSA, NY	s	15.04 MW	11.79 AW	31280 AAW	NYBLS	10//99-12//99
Television, Video, and Motion Picture	Syracuse MSA, NY	s	18.53 MW	16.58 AW	38530 AAW	NYBLS	10//99-12//99
Television, Video, and Motion Picture	North Carolina	s	9.93 MW	12.15 AW	25260 AAW	NCBLS	10//99-12//99
Television, Video, and Motion Picture	Charlotte-Gastonia-Rock Hill MSA, NC-SC	s	13.16 MW	12.78 AW	27380 AAW	NCBLS	10//99-12//99
Television, Video, and Motion Picture	Greensboro--Winston-Salem--High Point MSA, NC	s	9.05 MW	9.35 AW	18820 AAW	NCBLS	10//99-12//99
Television, Video, and Motion Picture	Raleigh-Durham-Chapel Hill MSA, NC	s	12.89 MW	11.08 AW	26800 AAW	NCBLS	10//99-12//99
Television, Video, and Motion Picture	Ohio	s	10.43 MW	13.61 AW	28300 AAW	OHBLS	10//99-12//99
Television, Video, and Motion Picture	Akron PMSA, OH	s	11.52 MW	10.19 AW	23950 AAW	OHBLS	10//99-12//99
Television, Video, and Motion Picture	Cincinnati PMSA, OH-KY-IN	s	10.98 MW	10.04 AW	22850 AAW	OHBLS	10//99-12//99
Television, Video, and Motion Picture	Columbus MSA, OH	s	13.50 MW	13.35 AW	28080 AAW	OHBLS	10//99-12//99
Television, Video, and Motion Picture	Dayton-Springfield MSA, OH	s	15.87 MW	16.70 AW	33000 AAW	OHBLS	10//99-12//99
Television, Video, and Motion Picture	Toledo MSA, OH	s	12.26 MW	12.31 AW	25490 AAW	OHBLS	10//99-12//99
Television, Video, and Motion Picture	Oklahoma	s	9.13 MW	10.01 AW	20810 AAW	OKBLS	10//99-12//99
Television, Video, and Motion Picture	Oklahoma City MSA, OK	s	10.89 MW	10.02 AW	22650 AAW	OKBLS	10//99-12//99
Television, Video, and Motion Picture	Tulsa MSA, OK	s	8.97 MW	8.09 AW	18660 AAW	OKBLS	10//99-12//99
Television, Video, and Motion Picture	Pennsylvania	s	8.9 MW	12.22 AW	25410 AAW	PABLS	10//99-12//99
Television, Video, and Motion Picture	Allentown-Bethlehem-Easton MSA, PA	s	10.43 MW	8.73 AW	21690 AAW	PABLS	10//99-12//99
Television, Video, and Motion Picture	Erie MSA, PA	s	9.00 MW	7.15 AW	18730 AAW	PABLS	10//99-12//99
Television, Video, and Motion Picture	Harrisburg-Lebanon-Carlisle MSA, PA	s	9.09 MW	8.16 AW	18920 AAW	PABLS	10//99-12//99
Television, Video, and Motion Picture	Philadelphia PMSA, PA-NJ	s	19.77 MW	16.71 AW	41130 AAW	PABLS	10//99-12//99
Television, Video, and Motion Picture	Pittsburgh MSA, PA	s	10.78 MW	8.45 AW	22420 AAW	PABLS	10//99-12//99
Television, Video, and Motion Picture	Reading MSA, PA	s	9.29 MW	9.92 AW	19330 AAW	PABLS	10//99-12//99
Television, Video, and Motion Picture	South Carolina	s	8.67 MW	10.17 AW	21150 AAW	SCBLS	10//99-12//99
Television, Video, and Motion Picture	Columbia MSA, SC	s	12.34 MW	10.26 AW	25660 AAW	SCBLS	10//99-12//99
Television, Video, and Motion Picture	Greenville-Spartanburg-Anderson MSA, SC	s	9.71 MW	9.15 AW	20210 AAW	SCBLS	10//99-12//99
Television, Video, and Motion Picture	South Dakota	s	8.37 MW	8.84 AW	18400 AAW	SDBLS	10//99-12//99
Television, Video, and Motion Picture	Tennessee	s	13.57 MW	13.67 AW	28440 AAW	TNBLS	10//99-12//99
Television, Video, and Motion Picture	Chattanooga MSA, TN-GA	s	11.68 MW	10.27 AW	24290 AAW	TNBLS	10//99-12//99
Television, Video, and Motion Picture	Johnson City-Kingsport-Bristol MSA, TN-VA	s	10.85 MW	10.75 AW	22570 AAW	TNBLS	10//99-12//99
Television, Video, and Motion Picture	Knoxville MSA, TN	s	15.02 MW	14.25 AW	31240 AAW	TNBLS	10//99-12//99
Television, Video, and Motion Picture	Memphis MSA, TN-AR-MS	s	14.82 MW	14.75 AW	30830 AAW	MSBLS	10//99-12//99
Television, Video, and Motion Picture	Nashville MSA, TN	s	12.91 MW	12.83 AW	26860 AAW	TNBLS	10//99-12//99
Television, Video, and Motion Picture	Texas	s	10.45 MW	11.72 AW	24390 AAW	TXBLS	10//99-12//99
Television, Video, and Motion Picture	Amarillo MSA, TX	s	7.33 MW	6.45 AW	15250 AAW	TXBLS	10//99-12//99
Television, Video, and Motion Picture	Austin-San Marcos MSA, TX	s	15.51 MW	11.08 AW	32260 AAW	TXBLS	10//99-12//99
Television, Video, and Motion Picture	Beaumont-Port Arthur MSA, TX	s	8.12 MW	6.42 AW	16900 AAW	TXBLS	10//99-12//99
Television, Video, and Motion Picture	Dallas PMSA, TX	s	10.88 MW	7.90 AW	22630 AAW	TXBLS	10//99-12//99
Television, Video, and Motion Picture	Fort Worth-Arlington PMSA, TX	s	14.35 MW	10.81 AW	29860 AAW	TXBLS	10//99-12//99
Television, Video, and Motion Picture	Houston PMSA, TX	s	13.56 MW	11.23 AW	28200 AAW	TXBLS	10//99-12//99
Television, Video, and Motion Picture	San Antonio MSA, TX	s	11.12 MW	10.68 AW	23120 AAW	TXBLS	10//99-12//99
Television, Video, and Motion Picture	Salt Lake City-Ogden MSA, UT	s	11.65 MW	9.86 AW	24230 AAW	UTBLS	10//99-12//99
Television, Video, and Motion Picture	Vermont	s	9.73 MW	12.43 AW	25840 AAW	VTBLS	10//99-12//99
Television, Video, and Motion Picture	Burlington MSA, VT	s	11.81 MW	9.91 AW	24570 AAW	VTBLS	10//99-12//99
Television, Video, and Motion Picture	Virginia	s	12 MW	13.93 AW	28970 AAW	VABLS	10//99-12//99
Television, Video, and Motion Picture	Norfolk-Virginia Beach-Newport News MSA, VA-NC	s	12.17 MW	9.29 AW	25320 AAW	VABLS	10//99-12//99
Television, Video, and Motion Picture	Roanoke MSA, VA	s	14.81 MW	11.48 AW	30800 AAW	VABLS	10//99-12//99
Television, Video, and Motion Picture	Washington	s	12.3 MW	13.10 AW	27240 AAW	WABLS	10//99-12//99
Television, Video, and Motion Picture	Seattle-Bellevue-Everett PMSA, WA	s	14.31 MW	14.90 AW	29760 AAW	WABLS	10//99-12//99
Television, Video, and Motion Picture	Spokane MSA, WA	s	9.82 MW	6.79 AW	20420 AAW	WABLS	10//99-12//99
Television, Video, and Motion Picture	West Virginia	s	8.29 MW	10.28 AW	21380 AAW	WVBLS	10//99-12//99
Television, Video, and Motion Picture	Huntington-Ashland MSA, WV-KY-OH	s	9.89 MW	7.85 AW	20580 AAW	WVBLS	10//99-12//99
Television, Video, and Motion Picture	Wisconsin	s	9.15 MW	12.38 AW	25760 AAW	WIBLS	10//99-12//99
Television, Video, and Motion Picture	Madison MSA, WI	s	12.82 MW	8.88 AW	26660 AAW	WIBLS	10//99-12//99
Television, Video, and Motion Picture	Milwaukee-Waukesha PMSA, WI	s	15.30 MW	12.11 AW	31830 AAW	WIBLS	10//99-12//99

AAW	Average annual wage	AOH	Average offered, high	ASH	Average starting, high
AE	Average entry wage	AOL	Average offered, low	ASL	Average starting, low
AEX	Average experienced wage	APH	Average pay, high range	AW	Average wage paid
AO	Average offered	APL	Average pay, low range	FQ	First quartile wage

H	Hourly	M	Monthly	S	Special: hourly and annual
HI	Highest wage paid	MTC	Median total compensation	TQ	Third quartile wage
HR	High end range	MW	Median wage paid	W	Weekly
LR	Low end range	SQ	Second quartile wage	Y	Yearly

Occupation/Type/Industry	Location	Per	Low	Mid	High	Source	Date
Camera Operator							
Television, Video, and Motion Picture	Puerto Rico	S	9.67 MW	10.07 AW	20950 AAW	PRBLS	10//99-12//99
Television, Video, and Motion Picture	San Juan-Bayamon PMSA, PR	S	9.73 MW	9.64 AW	20230 AAW	PRBLS	10//99-12//99
Captain, Mate, and Pilot							
Water Vessel	Alaska	S	24.34 MW	24.13 AW	50180 AAW	AKBLS	10//99-12//99
Water Vessel	Arkansas	S	18.11 MW	21.90 AW	45560 AAW	ARBLS	10//99-12//99
Water Vessel	California	S	18.36 MW	19.16 AW	39840 AAW	CABLS	10//99-12//99
Water Vessel	Connecticut	S	20.75 MW	24.06 AW	50050 AAW	CTBLS	10//99-12//99
Water Vessel	Florida	S	15.05 MW	17.39 AW	36170 AAW	FLBLS	10//99-12//99
Water Vessel	Georgia	S	15.87 MW	17.47 AW	36340 AAW	GABLS	10//99-12//99
Water Vessel	Hawaii	S	15.56 MW	17.02 AW	35410 AAW	HIBLS	10//99-12//99
Water Vessel	Illinois	S	16.55 MW	16.70 AW	34730 AAW	ILBLS	10//99-12//99
Water Vessel	Indiana	S	25.06 MW	24.58 AW	51120 AAW	INBLS	10//99-12//99
Water Vessel	Iowa	S	18.99 MW	20.89 AW	43460 AAW	IABLS	10//99-12//99
Water Vessel	Kentucky	S	18.94 MW	20.20 AW	42020 AAW	KYBLS	10//99-12//99
Water Vessel	Louisiana	S	18.02 MW	18.46 AW	38390 AAW	LABLS	10//99-12//99
Water Vessel	Maine	S	15.01 MW	16.25 AW	33790 AAW	MEBLS	10//99-12//99
Water Vessel	Maryland	S	13.23 MW	16.86 AW	35070 AAW	MDBLS	10//99-12//99
Water Vessel	Massachusetts	S	9.63 MW	11.60 AW	24130 AAW	MABLS	10//99-12//99
Water Vessel	Michigan	S	15.68 MW	19.04 AW	39610 AAW	MIBLS	10//99-12//99
Water Vessel	Minnesota	S	18.83 MW	18.46 AW	38390 AAW	MNBLS	10//99-12//99
Water Vessel	Mississippi	S	23.15 MW	23.22 AW	48290 AAW	MSBLS	10//99-12//99
Water Vessel	Missouri	S	6.69 MW	10.94 AW	22740 AAW	MOBLS	10//99-12//99
Water Vessel	New Hampshire	S	20.28 MW	26.44 AW	55000 AAW	NHBLS	10//99-12//99
Water Vessel	New Jersey	S	20.72 MW	21.73 AW	45200 AAW	NJBLS	10//99-12//99
Water Vessel	New York	S	23.03 MW	24.50 AW	50950 AAW	NYBLS	10//99-12//99
Water Vessel	North Carolina	S	13.21 MW	13.98 AW	29080 AAW	NCBLS	10//99-12//99
Water Vessel	Ohio	S	23.64 MW	26.31 AW	54720 AAW	OHBLS	10//99-12//99
Water Vessel	Oregon	S	23.53 MW	26.95 AW	56050 AAW	ORBLS	10//99-12//99
Water Vessel	Pennsylvania	S	20.85 MW	22.81 AW	47450 AAW	PABLS	10//99-12//99
Water Vessel	Rhode Island	S	13.66 MW	14.57 AW	30300 AAW	RIBLS	10//99-12//99
Water Vessel	South Carolina	S	11.3 MW	15.61 AW	32480 AAW	SCBLS	10//99-12//99
Water Vessel	Tennessee	S	14.24 MW	15.66 AW	32570 AAW	TNBLS	10//99-12//99
Water Vessel	Texas	S	21.79 MW	23.24 AW	48340 AAW	TXBLS	10//99-12//99
Water Vessel	Virginia	S	20.06 MW	22.24 AW	46260 AAW	VABLS	10//99-12//99
Water Vessel	Washington	S	25.72 MW	27.07 AW	56310 AAW	WABLS	10//99-12//99
Water Vessel	West Virginia	S	22.58 MW	22.90 AW	47640 AAW	WVBLS	10//99-12//99
Water Vessel	Wisconsin	S	18.88 MW	20.12 AW	41840 AAW	WIBLS	10//99-12//99
Water Vessel	Puerto Rico	S	14.8 MW	17.46 AW	36310 AAW	PRBLS	10//99-12//99
Water Vessel	Virgin Islands	S	14.92 MW	17.41 AW	36200 AAW	VIBLS	10//99-12//99
Cardiovascular Technologist and Technician	Alabama	S	13.99 MW	14.24 AW	29610 AAW	ALBLS	10//99-12//99
	Anniston MSA, AL	S	12.50 MW	12.00 AW	26010 AAW	ALBLS	10//99-12//99
	Birmingham MSA, AL	S	14.33 MW	14.60 AW	29800 AAW	ALBLS	10//99-12//99
	Dothan MSA, AL	S	13.46 MW	12.91 AW	28000 AAW	ALBLS	10//99-12//99
	Mobile MSA, AL	S	10.87 MW	9.16 AW	22600 AAW	ALBLS	10//99-12//99
	Montgomery MSA, AL	S	14.99 MW	15.07 AW	31180 AAW	ALBLS	10//99-12//99
	Alaska	S	20.76 MW	18.63 AW	38740 AAW	AKBLS	10//99-12//99
	Anchorage MSA, AK	S	18.65 MW	21.00 AW	38780 AAW	AKBLS	10//99-12//99
	Arizona	S	17.27 MW	16.72 AW	34780 AAW	AZBLS	10//99-12//99
	Tucson MSA, AZ	S	17.20 MW	18.31 AW	35780 AAW	AZBLS	10//99-12//99
	Arkansas	S	15.87 MW	15.69 AW	32640 AAW	ARBLS	10//99-12//99
	Fayetteville-Springdale-Rogers MSA, AR	S	15.04 MW	15.16 AW	31280 AAW	ARBLS	10//99-12//99
	Little Rock-North Little Rock MSA, AR	S	18.30 MW	17.84 AW	38070 AAW	ARBLS	10//99-12//99
	California	S	18.16 MW	18.52 AW	38510 AAW	CABLS	10//99-12//99
	Fresno MSA, CA	S	18.40 MW	18.55 AW	38280 AAW	CABLS	10//99-12//99
	Los Angeles-Long Beach PMSA, CA	S	17.99 MW	17.64 AW	37420 AAW	CABLS	10//99-12//99
	Oakland PMSA, CA	S	18.83 MW	18.86 AW	39160 AAW	CABLS	10//99-12//99
	Orange County PMSA, CA	S	18.84 MW	18.05 AW	39190 AAW	CABLS	10//99-12//99
	Riverside-San Bernardino PMSA, CA	S	19.09 MW	18.59 AW	39710 AAW	CABLS	10//99-12//99
	Sacramento PMSA, CA	S	17.10 MW	17.40 AW	35570 AAW	CABLS	10//99-12//99
	Salinas MSA, CA	S	15.10 MW	14.78 AW	31400 AAW	CABLS	10//99-12//99
	San Diego MSA, CA	S	17.37 MW	16.80 AW	36130 AAW	CABLS	10//99-12//99
	San Francisco PMSA, CA	S	21.65 MW	19.70 AW	45040 AAW	CABLS	10//99-12//99
	San Jose PMSA, CA	S	19.04 MW	17.97 AW	39600 AAW	CABLS	10//99-12//99

AAW Average annual wage	**AOH** Average offered, high	**ASH** Average starting, high	**H** Hourly	**M** Monthly	**S** Special: hourly and annual
AE Average entry wage	**AOL** Average offered, low	**ASL** Average starting, low	**HI** Highest wage paid	**MTC** Median total compensation	**TQ** Third quartile wage
AEX Average experienced wage	**APH** Average pay, high range	**AW** Average wage paid	**HR** High end range	**MW** Median wage paid	**W** Weekly
AO Average offered	**APL** Average pay, low range	**FQ** First quartile wage	**LR** Low end range	**SQ** Second quartile wage	**Y** Yearly

Occupation/Type/Industry	Location	Per	Low	Mid	High	Source	Date
Cardiovascular Technologist and Technician	San Luis Obispo-Atascadero-Paso Robles MSA, CA	S	17.68 MW	17.43 AW	36770 AAW	CABLS	10//99-12//99
	Vallejo-Fairfield-Napa PMSA, CA	S	23.43 MW	22.81 AW	48730 AAW	CABLS	10//99-12//99
	Ventura PMSA, CA	S	17.15 MW	17.10 AW	35670 AAW	CABLS	10//99-12//99
	Colorado	S	15.66 MW	16.15 AW	33590 AAW	COBLS	10//99-12//99
	Denver PMSA, CO	S	16.19 MW	15.54 AW	33680 AAW	COBLS	10//99-12//99
	Connecticut	S	17.89 MW	18.85 AW	39200 AAW	CTBLS	10//99-12//99
	Hartford MSA, CT	S	17.94 MW	17.46 AW	37310 AAW	CTBLS	10//99-12//99
	New Haven-Meriden PMSA, CT	S	21.57 MW	20.20 AW	44860 AAW	CTBLS	10//99-12//99
	Delaware	S	14.87 MW	15.94 AW	33160 AAW	DEBLS	10//99-12//99
	Wilmington-Newark PMSA, DE-MD	S	15.99 MW	14.88 AW	33260 AAW	DEBLS	10//99-12//99
	Washington PMSA, DC-MD-VA-WV		18.77 MW	18.62 AW	39040 AAW	DCBLS	10//99-12//99
	Florida	S	15.04 MW	14.94 AW	31080 AAW	FLBLS	10//99-12//99
	Fort Lauderdale PMSA, FL	S	15.91 MW	16.01 AW	33090 AAW	FLBLS	10//99-12//99
	Gainesville MSA, FL	S	14.60 MW	13.89 AW	30360 AAW	FLBLS	10//99-12//99
	Jacksonville MSA, FL	S	14.08 MW	14.42 AW	29300 AAW	FLBLS	10//99-12//99
	Lakeland-Winter Haven MSA, FL	S	16.73 MW	17.63 AW	34800 AAW	FLBLS	10//99-12//99
	Melbourne-Titusville-Palm Bay MSA, FL	S	15.45 MW	16.03 AW	32140 AAW	FLBLS	10//99-12//99
	Miami PMSA, FL	S	14.48 MW	14.49 AW	30120 AAW	FLBLS	10//99-12//99
	Orlando MSA, FL	S	15.00 MW	15.23 AW	31210 AAW	FLBLS	10//99-12//99
	Pensacola MSA, FL	S	14.34 MW	14.18 AW	29820 AAW	FLBLS	10//99-12//99
	Sarasota-Bradenton MSA, FL	S	13.24 MW	10.01 AW	27530 AAW	FLBLS	10//99-12//99
	Tampa-St. Petersburg-Clearwater MSA, FL	S	14.49 MW	14.84 AW	30140 AAW	FLBLS	10//99-12//99
	West Palm Beach-Boca Raton MSA, FL	S	17.00 MW	17.18 AW	35350 AAW	FLBLS	10//99-12//99
	Georgia	S	15.02 MW	15.45 AW	32130 AAW	GABLS	10//99-12//99
	Atlanta MSA, GA	S	16.51 MW	16.06 AW	34340 AAW	GABLS	10//99-12//99
	Columbus MSA, GA-AL	S	13.75 MW	12.94 AW	28590 AAW	GABLS	10//99-12//99
	Macon MSA, GA	S	14.35 MW	13.49 AW	29850 AAW	GABLS	10//99-12//99
	Hawaii	S	14.93 MW	16.80 AW	34940 AAW	HIBLS	10//99-12//99
	Honolulu MSA, HI	S	16.81 MW	14.93 AW	34960 AAW	HIBLS	10//99-12//99
	Idaho	S	13.59 MW	14.46 AW	30070 AAW	IDBLS	10//99-12//99
	Illinois	S	14.81 MW	15.94 AW	33150 AAW	ILBLS	10//99-12//99
	Chicago PMSA, IL	S	15.49 MW	15.10 AW	32230 AAW	ILBLS	10//99-12//99
	Peoria-Pekin MSA, IL	S	13.57 MW	12.85 AW	28230 AAW	ILBLS	10//99-12//99
	Indiana	S	13.86 MW	14.60 AW	30360 AAW	INBLS	10//99-12//99
	Evansville-Henderson MSA, IN-KY	S	13.29 MW	12.72 AW	27630 AAW	INBLS	10//99-12//99
	Fort Wayne MSA, IN	S	15.46 MW	14.42 AW	32160 AAW	INBLS	10//99-12//99
	Gary PMSA, IN	S	14.23 MW	13.68 AW	29600 AAW	INBLS	10//99-12//99
	Indianapolis MSA, IN	S	15.73 MW	15.91 AW	32710 AAW	INBLS	10//99-12//99
	South Bend MSA, IN	S	13.94 MW	12.69 AW	29000 AAW	INBLS	10//99-12//99
	Terre Haute MSA, IN	S	14.13 MW	13.41 AW	29390 AAW	INBLS	10//99-12//99
	Iowa	S	13.92 MW	14.15 AW	29430 AAW	IABLS	10//99-12//99
	Kansas	S	15.24 MW	15.23 AW	31680 AAW	KSBLS	10//99-12//99
	Kentucky	S	13.28 MW	15.43 AW	32100 AAW	KYBLS	10//99-12//99
	Lexington MSA, KY	S	21.73 MW	14.12 AW	45210 AAW	KYBLS	10//99-12//99
	Louisville MSA, KY-IN	S	13.74 MW	12.69 AW	28580 AAW	KYBLS	10//99-12//99
	Louisiana	S	11.87 MW	13.67 AW	28430 AAW	LABLS	10//99-12//99
	Lafayette MSA, LA	S	13.90 MW	12.13 AW	28900 AAW	LABLS	10//99-12//99
	New Orleans MSA, LA	S	14.96 MW	13.31 AW	31120 AAW	LABLS	10//99-12//99
	Shreveport-Bossier City MSA, LA	S	11.64 MW	10.51 AW	24210 AAW	LABLS	10//99-12//99
	Maine	S	12.87 MW	13.79 AW	28680 AAW	MEBLS	10//99-12//99
	Maryland	S	17.65 MW	17.19 AW	35740 AAW	MDBLS	10//99-12//99
	Baltimore PMSA, MD	S	18.11 MW	18.64 AW	37670 AAW	MDBLS	10//99-12//99
	Massachusetts	S	16.01 MW	16.92 AW	35190 AAW	MABLS	10//99-12//99
	Boston PMSA, MA-NH	S	16.38 MW	15.69 AW	34070 AAW	MABLS	10//99-12//99
	Brockton PMSA, MA	S	17.65 MW	17.61 AW	36700 AAW	MABLS	10//99-12//99
	Springfield MSA, MA	S	18.63 MW	16.78 AW	38750 AAW	MABLS	10//99-12//99
	Worcester PMSA, MA-CT	S	15.85 MW	15.49 AW	32960 AAW	MABLS	10//99-12//99
	Michigan	S	14.92 MW	15.18 AW	31570 AAW	MIBLS	10//99-12//99
	Ann Arbor PMSA, MI	S	15.89 MW	15.84 AW	33050 AAW	MIBLS	10//99-12//99
	Detroit PMSA, MI	S	15.14 MW	14.81 AW	31500 AAW	MIBLS	10//99-12//99

AAW	Average annual wage	AOH	Average offered, high	ASH	Average starting, high	H	Hourly	M	Monthly	S	Special: hourly and annual
AE	Average entry wage	AOL	Average offered, low	ASL	Average starting, low	HI	Highest wage paid	MTC	Median total compensation	TQ	Third quartile wage
AEX	Average experienced wage	APH	Average pay, high range	AW	Average wage paid	HR	High end range	MW	Median wage paid	W	Weekly
AO	Average offered	APL	Average pay, low range	FQ	First quartile wage	LR	Low end range	SQ	Second quartile wage	Y	Yearly

Cardiovascular Technologist and Technician

Occupation/Type/Industry	Location	Per	Low	Mid	High	Source	Date
Cardiovascular Technologist and Technician	Grand Rapids-Muskegon-Holland MSA, MI	S	14.17 MW	13.13 AW	29470 AAW	MIBLS	10//99-12//99
	Kalamazoo-Battle Creek MSA, MI	S	17.12 MW	17.51 AW	35620 AAW	MIBLS	10//99-12//99
	Lansing-East Lansing MSA, MI	S	16.01 MW	16.29 AW	33290 AAW	MIBLS	10//99-12//99
	Saginaw-Bay City-Midland MSA, MI	S	15.12 MW	15.14 AW	31460 AAW	MIBLS	10//99-12//99
	Minnesota	S	17.53 MW	17.07 AW	35500 AAW	MNBLS	10//99-12//99
	Minneapolis-St. Paul MSA, MN-WI	S	17.37 MW	17.77 AW	36140 AAW	MNBLS	10//99-12//99
	Mississippi	S	13.61 MW	14.25 AW	29640 AAW	MSBLS	10//99-12//99
	Hattiesburg MSA, MS	S	12.48 MW	10.23 AW	25950 AAW	MSBLS	10//99-12//99
	Missouri	S	14.97 MW	15.25 AW	31710 AAW	MOBLS	10//99-12//99
	Kansas City MSA, MO-KS	S	15.07 MW	14.87 AW	31350 AAW	MOBLS	10//99-12//99
	St. Louis MSA, MO-IL	S	14.83 MW	14.37 AW	30850 AAW	MOBLS	10//99-12//99
	Montana	S	16.26 MW	16.41 AW	34140 AAW	MTBLS	10//99-12//99
	Great Falls MSA, MT	S	16.78 MW	17.02 AW	34900 AAW	MTBLS	10//99-12//99
	Nebraska	S	16.27 MW	15.81 AW	32890 AAW	NEBLS	10//99-12//99
	Omaha MSA, NE-IA	S	14.27 MW	13.56 AW	29680 AAW	NEBLS	10//99-12//99
	Nevada	S	15.49 MW	16.05 AW	33380 AAW	NVBLS	10//99-12//99
	Las Vegas MSA, NV-AZ	S	14.48 MW	13.50 AW	30120 AAW	NVBLS	10//99-12//99
	Reno MSA, NV	S	17.98 MW	17.96 AW	37400 AAW	NVBLS	10//99-12//99
	New Hampshire	S	18.22 MW	17.88 AW	37190 AAW	NHBLS	10//99-12//99
	Portsmouth-Rochester PMSA, NH-ME	S	17.40 MW	18.69 AW	36200 AAW	NHBLS	10//99-12//99
	New Jersey	S	18.19 MW	18.98 AW	39470 AAW	NJBLS	10//99-12//99
	Bergen-Passaic PMSA, NJ	S	20.57 MW	18.90 AW	42780 AAW	NJBLS	10//99-12//99
	Middlesex-Somerset-Hunterdon PMSA, NJ	S	20.65 MW	20.32 AW	42950 AAW	NJBLS	10//99-12//99
	Monmouth-Ocean PMSA, NJ	S	17.46 MW	17.42 AW	36310 AAW	NJBLS	10//99-12//99
	Newark PMSA, NJ	S	19.43 MW	18.82 AW	40410 AAW	NJBLS	10//99-12//99
	New Mexico	S	14 MW	15.01 AW	31210 AAW	NMBLS	10//99-12//99
	New York	S	16.97 MW	18.63 AW	38750 AAW	NYBLS	10//99-12//99
	Albany-Schenectady-Troy MSA, NY	S	15.27 MW	14.65 AW	31770 AAW	NYBLS	10//99-12//99
	Buffalo-Niagara Falls MSA, NY	S	17.75 MW	16.69 AW	36910 AAW	NYBLS	10//99-12//99
	Elmira MSA, NY	S	16.78 MW	17.55 AW	34910 AAW	NYBLS	10//99-12//99
	Nassau-Suffolk PMSA, NY	S	19.82 MW	19.04 AW	41220 AAW	NYBLS	10//99-12//99
	New York PMSA, NY	S	19.92 MW	18.02 AW	41440 AAW	NYBLS	10//99-12//99
	Newburgh PMSA, NY-PA	S	20.77 MW	17.74 AW	43190 AAW	NYBLS	10//99-12//99
	Rochester MSA, NY	S	16.34 MW	14.56 AW	33980 AAW	NYBLS	10//99-12//99
	Syracuse MSA, NY	S	21.15 MW	18.43 AW	43990 AAW	NYBLS	10//99-12//99
	Utica-Rome MSA, NY	S	16.16 MW	14.49 AW	33620 AAW	NYBLS	10//99-12//99
	North Carolina	S	15.6 MW	15.89 AW	33060 AAW	NCBLS	10//99-12//99
	Charlotte-Gastonia-Rock Hill MSA, NC-SC	S	18.97 MW	19.07 AW	39450 AAW	NCBLS	10//99-12//99
	Fayetteville MSA, NC	S	13.69 MW	12.59 AW	28480 AAW	NCBLS	10//99-12//99
	Greensboro--Winston-Salem--High Point MSA, NC	S	15.23 MW	14.65 AW	31670 AAW	NCBLS	10//99-12//99
	Raleigh-Durham-Chapel Hill MSA, NC	S	15.20 MW	14.90 AW	31610 AAW	NCBLS	10//99-12//99
	North Dakota	S	11.97 MW	12.65 AW	26310 AAW	NDBLS	10//99-12//99
	Ohio	S	15.25 MW	15.51 AW	32250 AAW	OHBLS	10//99-12//99
	Cincinnati PMSA, OH-KY-IN	S	15.10 MW	14.76 AW	31410 AAW	OHBLS	10//99-12//99
	Cleveland-Lorain-Elyria PMSA, OH	S	16.62 MW	16.38 AW	34570 AAW	OHBLS	10//99-12//99
	Columbus MSA, OH	S	14.37 MW	13.56 AW	29900 AAW	OHBLS	10//99-12//99
	Dayton-Springfield MSA, OH	S	13.99 MW	13.33 AW	29100 AAW	OHBLS	10//99-12//99
	Toledo MSA, OH	S	16.03 MW	16.12 AW	33340 AAW	OHBLS	10//99-12//99
	Youngstown-Warren MSA, OH	S	15.68 MW	14.30 AW	32610 AAW	OHBLS	10//99-12//99
	Oklahoma	S	12.39 MW	14.50 AW	30160 AAW	OKBLS	10//99-12//99
	Oklahoma City MSA, OK	S	15.21 MW	12.73 AW	31640 AAW	OKBLS	10//99-12//99
	Tulsa MSA, OK	S	14.83 MW	16.47 AW	30850 AAW	OKBLS	10//99-12//99
	Oregon	S	16.11 MW	16.45 AW	34210 AAW	ORBLS	10//99-12//99
	Portland-Vancouver PMSA, OR-WA	S	16.52 MW	16.21 AW	34350 AAW	ORBLS	10//99-12//99
	Salem PMSA, OR	S	16.92 MW	13.40 AW	35180 AAW	ORBLS	10//99-12//99
	Pennsylvania	S	13.96 MW	14.70 AW	30580 AAW	PABLS	10//99-12//99
	Allentown-Bethlehem-Easton MSA, PA	S	14.71 MW	13.58 AW	30600 AAW	PABLS	10//99-12//99

AAW Average annual wage	**AOH** Average offered, high	**ASH** Average starting, high	**H** Hourly	**M** Monthly	**S** Special: hourly and annual
AE Average entry wage	**AOL** Average offered, low	**ASL** Average starting, low	**HI** Highest wage paid	**MTC** Median total compensation	**TQ** Third quartile wage
AEX Average experienced wage	**APH** Average pay, high range	**AW** Average wage paid	**HR** High end range	**MW** Median wage paid	**W** Weekly
AO Average offered	**APL** Average pay, low range	**FQ** First quartile wage	**LR** Low end range	**SQ** Second quartile wage	**Y** Yearly

Occupation/Type/Industry	Location	Per	Low	Mid	High	Source	Date
Cardiovascular Technologist and Technician	Altoona MSA, PA	S	15.34 MW	13.30 AW	31910 AAW	PABLS	10//99-12//99
	Harrisburg-Lebanon-Carlisle MSA, PA	S	16.25 MW	15.21 AW	33790 AAW	PABLS	10//99-12//99
	Philadelphia PMSA, PA-NJ	S	16.54 MW	14.98 AW	34400 AAW	PABLS	10//99-12//99
	Pittsburgh MSA, PA	S	13.19 MW	13.45 AW	27430 AAW	PABLS	10//99-12//99
	Scranton--Wilkes-Barre--Hazleton MSA, PA	S	16.77 MW	13.84 AW	34890 AAW	PABLS	10//99-12//99
	Rhode Island	S	13.59 MW	14.74 AW	30670 AAW	RIBLS	10//99-12//99
	Providence-Fall River-Warwick MSA, RI-MA	S	16.64 MW	15.19 AW	34620 AAW	RIBLS	10//99-12//99
	South Carolina	S	11.89 MW	14.01 AW	29150 AAW	SCBLS	10//99-12//99
	Charleston-North Charleston MSA, SC	S	16.70 MW	15.39 AW	34750 AAW	SCBLS	10//99-12//99
	Columbia MSA, SC	S	13.87 MW	11.35 AW	28850 AAW	SCBLS	10//99-12//99
	Greenville-Spartanburg-Anderson MSA, SC	S	13.36 MW	11.57 AW	27780 AAW	SCBLS	10//99-12//99
	South Dakota	S	15.33 MW	15.77 AW	32800 AAW	SDBLS	10//99-12//99
	Sioux Falls MSA, SD	S	15.50 MW	15.12 AW	32250 AAW	SDBLS	10//99-12//99
	Tennessee	S	14.05 MW	14.06 AW	29240 AAW	TNBLS	10//99-12//99
	Jackson MSA, TN	S	15.76 MW	17.43 AW	32780 AAW	TNBLS	10//99-12//99
	Johnson City-Kingsport-Bristol MSA, TN-VA	S	16.06 MW	17.47 AW	33400 AAW	TNBLS	10//99-12//99
	Knoxville MSA, TN	S	12.14 MW	10.46 AW	25240 AAW	TNBLS	10//99-12//99
	Nashville MSA, TN	S	13.35 MW	13.35 AW	27760 AAW	TNBLS	10//99-12//99
	Texas	S	14.04 MW	14.39 AW	29930 AAW	TXBLS	10//99-12//99
	Austin-San Marcos MSA, TX	S	14.19 MW	14.26 AW	29520 AAW	TXBLS	10//99-12//99
	Beaumont-Port Arthur MSA, TX	S	13.90 MW	13.55 AW	28910 AAW	TXBLS	10//99-12//99
	Corpus Christi MSA, TX	S	11.63 MW	10.85 AW	24190 AAW	TXBLS	10//99-12//99
	Dallas PMSA, TX	S	14.60 MW	14.34 AW	30370 AAW	TXBLS	10//99-12//99
	El Paso MSA, TX	S	15.22 MW	15.37 AW	31670 AAW	TXBLS	10//99-12//99
	Fort Worth-Arlington PMSA, TX	S	14.00 MW	13.88 AW	29120 AAW	TXBLS	10//99-12//99
	Houston PMSA, TX	S	15.35 MW	15.26 AW	31930 AAW	TXBLS	10//99-12//99
	Lubbock MSA, TX	S	10.78 MW	9.92 AW	22410 AAW	TXBLS	10//99-12//99
	McAllen-Edinburg-Mission MSA, TX	S	14.23 MW	14.62 AW	29600 AAW	TXBLS	10//99-12//99
	San Antonio MSA, TX	S	15.23 MW	15.10 AW	31680 AAW	TXBLS	10//99-12//99
	Tyler MSA, TX	S	13.52 MW	12.14 AW	28130 AAW	TXBLS	10//99-12//99
	Salt Lake City-Ogden MSA, UT	S	14.22 MW	14.24 AW	29580 AAW	UTBLS	10//99-12//99
	Vermont	S	15.18 MW	16.24 AW	33780 AAW	VTBLS	10//99-12//99
	Virginia	S	17.63 MW	17.68 AW	36780 AAW	VABLS	10//99-12//99
	Norfolk-Virginia Beach-Newport News MSA, VA-NC	S	16.25 MW	16.67 AW	33790 AAW	VABLS	10//99-12//99
	Richmond-Petersburg MSA, VA	S	16.62 MW	16.98 AW	34580 AAW	VABLS	10//99-12//99
	Washington	S	18.87 MW	18.72 AW	38930 AAW	WABLS	10//99-12//99
	Olympia PMSA, WA	S	16.45 MW	16.10 AW	34220 AAW	WABLS	10//99-12//99
	Richland-Kennewick-Pasco MSA, WA	S	17.74 MW	16.82 AW	36910 AAW	WABLS	10//99-12//99
	Seattle-Bellevue-Everett PMSA, WA	S	19.66 MW	20.24 AW	40900 AAW	WABLS	10//99-12//99
	Spokane MSA, WA	S	18.55 MW	19.23 AW	38570 AAW	WABLS	10//99-12//99
	Yakima MSA, WA	S	14.41 MW	14.19 AW	29980 AAW	WABLS	10//99-12//99
	West Virginia	S	13.9 MW	13.86 AW	28830 AAW	WVBLS	10//99-12//99
	Huntington-Ashland MSA, WV-KY-OH	S	13.50 MW	12.85 AW	28070 AAW	WVBLS	10//99-12//99
	Wisconsin	S	14.45 MW	15.12 AW	31450 AAW	WIBLS	10//99-12//99
	Janesville-Beloit MSA, WI	S	15.63 MW	15.52 AW	32520 AAW	WIBLS	10//99-12//99
	Madison MSA, WI	S	14.92 MW	13.64 AW	31020 AAW	WIBLS	10//99-12//99
	Milwaukee-Waukesha PMSA, WI	S	14.82 MW	13.72 AW	30810 AAW	WIBLS	10//99-12//99
	Puerto Rico	S	7.5 MW	8.15 AW	16960 AAW	PRBLS	10//99-12//99
	Mayaguez MSA, PR	S	7.37 MW	7.55 AW	15340 AAW	PRBLS	10//99-12//99
	San Juan-Bayamon PMSA, PR	S	8.64 MW	8.00 AW	17960 AAW	PRBLS	10//99-12//99
Cargo and Freight Agent	Alabama	S	10.91 MW	11.25 AW	23390 AAW	ALBLS	10//99-12//99
	Birmingham MSA, AL	S	11.34 MW	11.61 AW	23590 AAW	ALBLS	10//99-12//99
	Mobile MSA, AL	S	10.93 MW	10.53 AW	22730 AAW	ALBLS	10//99-12//99

AAW	Average annual wage	AOH	Average offered, high	ASH	Average starting, high
AE	Average entry wage	AOL	Average offered, low	ASL	Average starting, low
AEX	Average experienced wage	APH	Average pay, high range	AW	Average wage paid
AO	Average offered	APL	Average pay, low range	FQ	First quartile wage

H	Hourly	M	Monthly	S	Special: hourly and annual
HI	Highest wage paid	MTC	Median total compensation	TQ	Third quartile wage
HR	High end range	MW	Median wage paid	W	Weekly
LR	Low end range	SQ	Second quartile wage	Y	Yearly

Occupation/Type/Industry	Location	Per	Low	Mid	High	Source	Date
Cargo and Freight Agent	Alaska	S	11.44 MW	11.92 AW	24800 AAW	AKBLS	10//99-12//99
	Anchorage MSA, AK	S	11.27 MW	11.36 AW	23440 AAW	AKBLS	10//99-12//99
	Arizona	S	16.46 MW	16.41 AW	34120 AAW	AZBLS	10//99-12//99
	Phoenix-Mesa MSA, AZ	S	16.61 MW	16.57 AW	34550 AAW	AZBLS	10//99-12//99
	Tucson MSA, AZ	S	11.06 MW	9.27 AW	23000 AAW	AZBLS	10//99-12//99
	Arkansas	S	10.94 MW	13.04 AW	27120 AAW	ARBLS	10//99-12//99
	Fayetteville-Springdale-Rogers MSA, AR	S	14.36 MW	12.74 AW	29870 AAW	ARBLS	10//99-12//99
	California	S	11.06 MW	12.46 AW	25910 AAW	CABLS	10//99-12//99
	Los Angeles-Long Beach PMSA, CA	S	11.29 MW	9.97 AW	23480 AAW	CABLS	10//99-12//99
	Orange County PMSA, CA	S	14.28 MW	11.96 AW	29700 AAW	CABLS	10//99-12//99
	Riverside-San Bernardino PMSA, CA	S	13.91 MW	14.21 AW	28940 AAW	CABLS	10//99-12//99
	Salinas MSA, CA	S	14.61 MW	13.48 AW	30380 AAW	CABLS	10//99-12//99
	San Diego MSA, CA	S	15.55 MW	16.97 AW	32350 AAW	CABLS	10//99-12//99
	San Francisco PMSA, CA	S	14.44 MW	12.66 AW	30030 AAW	CABLS	10//99-12//99
	Ventura PMSA, CA	S	14.46 MW	15.10 AW	30070 AAW	CABLS	10//99-12//99
	Visalia-Tulare-Porterville MSA, CA	S	12.62 MW	12.98 AW	26250 AAW	CABLS	10//99-12//99
	Colorado	S	10.94 MW	11.51 AW	23940 AAW	COBLS	10//99-12//99
	Denver PMSA, CO	S	15.64 MW	17.44 AW	32540 AAW	COBLS	10//99-12//99
	Connecticut	S	16.96 MW	14.91 AW	31010 AAW	CTBLS	10//99-12//99
	Hartford MSA, CT	S	14.44 MW	17.08 AW	30030 AAW	CTBLS	10//99-12//99
	New Haven-Meriden PMSA, CT	S	17.08 MW	17.62 AW	35530 AAW	CTBLS	10//99-12//99
	New London-Norwich MSA, CT-RI	S	11.04 MW	9.91 AW	22950 AAW	CTBLS	10//99-12//99
	Delaware	S	10.36 MW	11.74 AW	24420 AAW	DEBLS	10//99-12//99
	Wilmington-Newark PMSA, DE-MD	S	13.20 MW	12.01 AW	27450 AAW	DEBLS	10//99-12//99
	Washington PMSA, DC-MD-VA-WV	S	17.04 MW	16.77 AW	35430 AAW	DCBLS	10//99-12//99
	Florida	S	11.45 MW	12.52 AW	26040 AAW	FLBLS	10//99-12//99
	Fort Lauderdale PMSA, FL	S	16.20 MW	15.89 AW	33690 AAW	FLBLS	10//99-12//99
	Fort Myers-Cape Coral MSA, FL	S	14.65 MW	13.63 AW	30480 AAW	FLBLS	10//99-12//99
	Miami PMSA, FL	S	11.85 MW	10.83 AW	24650 AAW	FLBLS	10//99-12//99
	Orlando MSA, FL	S	11.89 MW	10.10 AW	24740 AAW	FLBLS	10//99-12//99
	Pensacola MSA, FL	S	15.95 MW	15.32 AW	33170 AAW	FLBLS	10//99-12//99
	Tampa-St. Petersburg-Clearwater MSA, FL	S	14.57 MW	14.76 AW	30300 AAW	FLBLS	10//99-12//99
	West Palm Beach-Boca Raton MSA, FL	S	11.33 MW	11.80 AW	23560 AAW	FLBLS	10//99-12//99
	Georgia	S	12.04 MW	13.03 AW	27090 AAW	GABLS	10//99-12//99
	Atlanta MSA, GA	S	12.85 MW	12.07 AW	26730 AAW	GABLS	10//99-12//99
	Hawaii	S	13.37 MW	14.03 AW	29180 AAW	HIBLS	10//99-12//99
	Honolulu MSA, HI	S	13.60 MW	12.52 AW	28300 AAW	HIBLS	10//99-12//99
	Idaho	S	9.53 MW	10.83 AW	22520 AAW	IDBLS	10//99-12//99
	Boise City MSA, ID	S	10.27 MW	9.35 AW	21370 AAW	IDBLS	10//99-12//99
	Illinois	S	13.09 MW	13.27 AW	27600 AAW	ILBLS	10//99-12//99
	Bloomington-Normal MSA, IL	S	9.50 MW	9.79 AW	19760 AAW	ILBLS	10//99-12//99
	Chicago PMSA, IL	S	14.28 MW	14.45 AW	29710 AAW	ILBLS	10//99-12//99
	Rockford MSA, IL	S	15.03 MW	15.18 AW	31260 AAW	ILBLS	10//99-12//99
	Indiana	S	10.27 MW	11.83 AW	24610 AAW	INBLS	10//99-12//99
	Gary PMSA, IN	S	12.31 MW	11.47 AW	25610 AAW	INBLS	10//99-12//99
	Indianapolis MSA, IN	S	13.62 MW	12.86 AW	28320 AAW	INBLS	10//99-12//99
	Iowa	S	9.32 MW	10.35 AW	21530 AAW	IABLS	10//99-12//99
	Cedar Rapids MSA, IA	S	11.90 MW	12.37 AW	24750 AAW	IABLS	10//99-12//99
	Des Moines MSA, IA	S	11.34 MW	9.76 AW	23580 AAW	IABLS	10//99-12//99
	Kansas	S	12.32 MW	13.39 AW	27850 AAW	KSBLS	10//99-12//99
	Kentucky	S	11.63 MW	12.23 AW	25430 AAW	KYBLS	10//99-12//99
	Louisville MSA, KY-IN	S	12.14 MW	11.49 AW	25260 AAW	KYBLS	10//99-12//99
	Louisiana	S	11.79 MW	12.28 AW	25550 AAW	LABLS	10//99-12//99
	New Orleans MSA, LA	S	13.59 MW	12.71 AW	28280 AAW	LABLS	10//99-12//99
	Maine	S	15.68 MW	15.69 AW	32640 AAW	MEBLS	10//99-12//99
	Baltimore PMSA, MD	S	13.55 MW	11.77 AW	28180 AAW	MDBLS	10//99-12//99
	Massachusetts	S	14.24 MW	14.59 AW	30340 AAW	MABLS	10//99-12//99
	Boston PMSA, MA-NH	S	14.40 MW	13.90 AW	29940 AAW	MABLS	10//99-12//99
	Michigan	S	13.55 MW	14.11 AW	29350 AAW	MIBLS	10//99-12//99
	Detroit PMSA, MI	S	16.42 MW	16.39 AW	34150 AAW	MIBLS	10//99-12//99

AAW Average annual wage	AOH Average offered, high	ASH Average starting, high	H Hourly	M Monthly	S Special: hourly and annual
AE Average entry wage	AOL Average offered, low	ASL Average starting, low	HI Highest wage paid	MTC Median total compensation	TQ Third quartile wage
AEX Average experienced wage	APH Average pay, high range	AW Average wage paid	HR High end range	MW Median wage paid	W Weekly
AO Average offered	APL Average pay, low range	FQ First quartile wage	LR Low end range	SQ Second quartile wage	Y Yearly

Occupation/Type/Industry	Location	Per	Low	Mid	High	Source	Date
Cargo and Freight Agent	Grand Rapids-Muskegon-Holland MSA, MI	S	12.31 MW	11.63 AW	25610 AAW	MIBLS	10//99-12//99
	Minnesota	S	14.37 MW	13.90 AW	28920 AAW	MNBLS	10//99-12//99
	Minneapolis-St. Paul MSA, MN-WI	S	14.18 MW	14.51 AW	29500 AAW	MNBLS	10//99-12//99
	Mississippi	S	8.7 MW	9.40 AW	19550 AAW	MSBLS	10//99-12//99
	Kansas City MSA, MO-KS	S	13.55 MW	12.44 AW	28180 AAW	MOBLS	10//99-12//99
	Nebraska	S	11.73 MW	13.18 AW	27410 AAW	NEBLS	10//99-12//99
	Omaha MSA, NE-IA	S	13.18 MW	11.55 AW	27420 AAW	NEBLS	10//99-12//99
	Nevada	S	15.11 MW	14.44 AW	30040 AAW	NVBLS	10//99-12//99
	Reno MSA, NV	S	15.68 MW	15.51 AW	32620 AAW	NVBLS	10//99-12//99
	New Jersey	S	12 MW	13.34 AW	27740 AAW	NJBLS	10//99-12//99
	Bergen-Passaic PMSA, NJ	S	11.92 MW	11.75 AW	24790 AAW	NJBLS	10//99-12//99
	Jersey City PMSA, NJ	S	10.67 MW	9.74 AW	22200 AAW	NJBLS	10//99-12//99
	Newark PMSA, NJ	S	12.73 MW	11.64 AW	26480 AAW	NJBLS	10//99-12//99
	New Mexico	S	11.76 MW	12.39 AW	25760 AAW	NMBLS	10//99-12//99
	New York	S	15.43 MW	15.91 AW	33080 AAW	NYBLS	10//99-12//99
	Buffalo-Niagara Falls MSA, NY	S	13.37 MW	12.56 AW	27810 AAW	NYBLS	10//99-12//99
	Jamestown MSA, NY	S	10.80 MW	10.01 AW	22460 AAW	NYBLS	10//99-12//99
	Nassau-Suffolk PMSA, NY	S	17.68 MW	17.67 AW	36770 AAW	NYBLS	10//99-12//99
	New York PMSA, NY	S	15.82 MW	15.17 AW	32900 AAW	NYBLS	10//99-12//99
	Rochester MSA, NY	S	13.26 MW	13.17 AW	27570 AAW	NYBLS	10//99-12//99
	North Carolina	S	8.67 MW	10.78 AW	22420 AAW	NCBLS	10//99-12//99
	Charlotte-Gastonia-Rock Hill MSA, NC-SC	S	15.31 MW	14.92 AW	31830 AAW	NCBLS	10//99-12//99
	North Dakota	S	10.61 MW	10.75 AW	22360 AAW	NDBLS	10//99-12//99
	Ohio	S	9.11 MW	10.75 AW	22370 AAW	OHBLS	10//99-12//99
	Akron PMSA, OH	S	8.48 MW	7.44 AW	17640 AAW	OHBLS	10//99-12//99
	Cincinnati PMSA, OH-KY-IN	S	9.76 MW	8.45 AW	20300 AAW	OHBLS	10//99-12//99
	Cleveland-Lorain-Elyria PMSA, OH	S	11.16 MW	10.33 AW	23220 AAW	OHBLS	10//99-12//99
	Dayton-Springfield MSA, OH	S	10.68 MW	9.09 AW	22210 AAW	OHBLS	10//99-12//99
	Youngstown-Warren MSA, OH	S	8.41 MW	6.88 AW	17490 AAW	OHBLS	10//99-12//99
	Oklahoma	S	11.48 MW	12.06 AW	25080 AAW	OKBLS	10//99-12//99
	Oklahoma City MSA, OK	S	13.50 MW	12.90 AW	28080 AAW	OKBLS	10//99-12//99
	Tulsa MSA, OK	S	11.28 MW	10.94 AW	23470 AAW	OKBLS	10//99-12//99
	Oregon	S	13.66 MW	15.81 AW	32880 AAW	ORBLS	10//99-12//99
	Portland-Vancouver PMSA, OR-WA	S	15.66 MW	13.11 AW	32570 AAW	ORBLS	10//99-12//99
	Pennsylvania	S	12.49 MW	13.64 AW	28360 AAW	PABLS	10//99-12//99
	Harrisburg-Lebanon-Carlisle MSA, PA	S	12.40 MW	10.47 AW	25800 AAW	PABLS	10//99-12//99
	Philadelphia PMSA, PA-NJ	S	14.52 MW	14.61 AW	30200 AAW	PABLS	10//99-12//99
	Pittsburgh MSA, PA	S	13.31 MW	11.26 AW	27670 AAW	PABLS	10//99-12//99
	Rhode Island	S	10.47 MW	11.59 AW	24110 AAW	RIBLS	10//99-12//99
	Providence-Fall River-Warwick MSA, RI-MA	S	11.62 MW	10.80 AW	24160 AAW	RIBLS	10//99-12//99
	Charleston-North Charleston MSA, SC	S	15.05 MW	15.07 AW	31310 AAW	SCBLS	10//99-12//99
	South Dakota	S	15.46 MW	15.33 AW	31880 AAW	SDBLS	10//99-12//99
	Sioux Falls MSA, SD	S	16.52 MW	15.78 AW	34370 AAW	SDBLS	10//99-12//99
	Tennessee	S	10.76 MW	13.56 AW	28210 AAW	TNBLS	10//99-12//99
	Memphis MSA, TN-AR-MS	S	10.96 MW	9.99 AW	22800 AAW	MSBLS	10//99-12//99
	Texas	S	13.92 MW	14.68 AW	30530 AAW	TXBLS	10//99-12//99
	Austin-San Marcos MSA, TX	S	16.12 MW	17.04 AW	33520 AAW	TXBLS	10//99-12//99
	Beaumont-Port Arthur MSA, TX	S	10.01 MW	8.51 AW	20820 AAW	TXBLS	10//99-12//99
	Dallas PMSA, TX	S	15.86 MW	15.43 AW	32990 AAW	TXBLS	10//99-12//99
	Fort Worth-Arlington PMSA, TX	S	17.57 MW	18.33 AW	36540 AAW	TXBLS	10//99-12//99
	Houston PMSA, TX	S	12.72 MW	12.20 AW	26470 AAW	TXBLS	10//99-12//99
	Laredo MSA, TX	S	10.45 MW	9.85 AW	21740 AAW	TXBLS	10//99-12//99
	Lubbock MSA, TX	S	13.03 MW	11.57 AW	27090 AAW	TXBLS	10//99-12//99
	McAllen-Edinburg-Mission MSA, TX	S	11.81 MW	11.98 AW	24560 AAW	TXBLS	10//99-12//99
	Utah	S	11.09 MW	11.72 AW	24370 AAW	UTBLS	10//99-12//99
	Salt Lake City-Ogden MSA, UT	S	11.72 MW	11.08 AW	24380 AAW	UTBLS	10//99-12//99
	Vermont	S	11.33 MW	12.29 AW	25570 AAW	VTBLS	10//99-12//99
	Virginia	S	13.91 MW	13.74 AW	28570 AAW	VABLS	10//99-12//99

AAW Average annual wage	AOH Average offered, high	ASH Average starting, high	H Hourly	M Monthly	S Special: hourly and annual
AE Average entry wage	AOL Average offered, low	ASL Average starting, low	HI Highest wage paid	MTC Median total compensation	TQ Third quartile wage
AEX Average experienced wage	APH Average pay, high range	AW Average wage paid	HR High end range	MW Median wage paid	W Weekly
AO Average offered	APL Average pay, low range	FQ First quartile wage	LR Low end range	SQ Second quartile wage	Y Yearly

Occupation/Type/Industry	Location	Per	Low	Mid	High	Source	Date
Cargo and Freight Agent	Norfolk-Virginia Beach-Newport News MSA, VA-NC	S	12.96 MW	12.85 AW	26960 AAW	VABLS	10//99-12//99
	Washington	S	11.94 MW	13.02 AW	27070 AAW	WABLS	10//99-12//99
	Seattle-Bellevue-Everett PMSA, WA	S	12.75 MW	11.78 AW	26530 AAW	WABLS	10//99-12//99
	Spokane MSA, WA	S	16.03 MW	17.34 AW	33340 AAW	WABLS	10//99-12//99
	West Virginia	S	9.46 MW	10.52 AW	21880 AAW	WVBLS	10//99-12//99
	Charleston MSA, WV	S	12.77 MW	11.54 AW	26560 AAW	WVBLS	10//99-12//99
	Huntington-Ashland MSA, WV-KY-OH	S	10.15 MW	9.69 AW	21110 AAW	WVBLS	10//99-12//99
	Wisconsin	S	14.24 MW	14.70 AW	30570 AAW	WIBLS	10//99-12//99
	Green Bay MSA, WI	S	13.53 MW	14.09 AW	28140 AAW	WIBLS	10//99-12//99
	Milwaukee-Waukesha PMSA, WI	S	16.11 MW	14.10 AW	33520 AAW	WIBLS	10//99-12//99
	Virgin Islands	S	16.21 MW	16.49 AW	34310 AAW	VIBLS	10//99-12//99
Carpenter	Alabama	S	11.01 MW	11.57 AW	24060 AAW	ALBLS	10//99-12//99
	Anniston MSA, AL	S	12.26 MW	12.52 AW	25500 AAW	ALBLS	10//99-12//99
	Auburn-Opelika MSA, AL	S	10.95 MW	10.41 AW	22780 AAW	ALBLS	10//99-12//99
	Birmingham MSA, AL	S	12.35 MW	12.16 AW	25700 AAW	ALBLS	10//99-12//99
	Decatur MSA, AL	S	12.55 MW	12.55 AW	26100 AAW	ALBLS	10//99-12//99
	Dothan MSA, AL	S	12.11 MW	11.02 AW	25180 AAW	ALBLS	10//99-12//99
	Florence MSA, AL	S	13.98 MW	14.18 AW	29070 AAW	ALBLS	10//99-12//99
	Gadsden MSA, AL	S	12.97 MW	13.18 AW	26980 AAW	ALBLS	10//99-12//99
	Huntsville MSA, AL	S	11.28 MW	11.21 AW	23470 AAW	ALBLS	10//99-12//99
	Mobile MSA, AL	S	10.51 MW	9.93 AW	21850 AAW	ALBLS	10//99-12//99
	Montgomery MSA, AL	S	12.43 MW	12.44 AW	25860 AAW	ALBLS	10//99-12//99
	Tuscaloosa MSA, AL	S	12.33 MW	12.20 AW	25640 AAW	ALBLS	10//99-12//99
	Alaska	S	20.92 MW	20.71 AW	43080 AAW	AKBLS	10//99-12//99
	Arizona	S	14.37 MW	14.93 AW	31050 AAW	AZBLS	10//99-12//99
	Flagstaff MSA, AZ-UT	S	18.15 MW	13.28 AW	37760 AAW	AZBLS	10//99-12//99
	Phoenix-Mesa MSA, AZ	S	15.17 MW	14.87 AW	31540 AAW	AZBLS	10//99-12//99
	Tucson MSA, AZ	S	14.09 MW	13.61 AW	29320 AAW	AZBLS	10//99-12//99
	Yuma MSA, AZ	S	12.72 MW	10.77 AW	26460 AAW	AZBLS	10//99-12//99
	Arkansas	S	12.04 MW	12.03 AW	25030 AAW	ARBLS	10//99-12//99
	Fayetteville-Springdale-Rogers MSA, AR	S	11.65 MW	11.66 AW	24240 AAW	ARBLS	10//99-12//99
	Fort Smith MSA, AR-OK	S	12.26 MW	12.45 AW	25490 AAW	ARBLS	10//99-12//99
	Jonesboro MSA, AR	S	11.40 MW	11.67 AW	23720 AAW	ARBLS	10//99-12//99
	Little Rock-North Little Rock MSA, AR	S	13.21 MW	13.07 AW	27480 AAW	ARBLS	10//99-12//99
	Pine Bluff MSA, AR	S	10.74 MW	11.91 AW	22340 AAW	ARBLS	10//99-12//99
	California	S	19.82 MW	19.87 AW	41330 AAW	CABLS	10//99-12//99
	Bakersfield MSA, CA	S	15.97 MW	15.61 AW	33220 AAW	CABLS	10//99-12//99
	Chico-Paradise MSA, CA	S	13.84 MW	12.97 AW	28790 AAW	CABLS	10//99-12//99
	Fresno MSA, CA	S	16.59 MW	17.07 AW	34520 AAW	CABLS	10//99-12//99
	Los Angeles-Long Beach PMSA, CA	S	21.42 MW	22.29 AW	44560 AAW	CABLS	10//99-12//99
	Merced MSA, CA	S	15.53 MW	14.46 AW	32300 AAW	CABLS	10//99-12//99
	Modesto MSA, CA	S	15.40 MW	14.71 AW	32030 AAW	CABLS	10//99-12//99
	Oakland PMSA, CA	S	19.44 MW	19.47 AW	40430 AAW	CABLS	10//99-12//99
	Orange County PMSA, CA	S	22.13 MW	21.21 AW	46030 AAW	CABLS	10//99-12//99
	Redding MSA, CA	S	18.47 MW	17.23 AW	38420 AAW	CABLS	10//99-12//99
	Riverside-San Bernardino PMSA, CA	S	18.30 MW	18.72 AW	38060 AAW	CABLS	10//99-12//99
	Sacramento PMSA, CA	S	17.26 MW	16.56 AW	35910 AAW	CABLS	10//99-12//99
	Salinas MSA, CA	S	22.12 MW	22.09 AW	46010 AAW	CABLS	10//99-12//99
	San Diego MSA, CA	S	19.54 MW	19.27 AW	40650 AAW	CABLS	10//99-12//99
	San Francisco PMSA, CA	S	27.24 MW	27.95 AW	56660 AAW	CABLS	10//99-12//99
	San Jose PMSA, CA	S	20.79 MW	21.33 AW	43250 AAW	CABLS	10//99-12//99
	San Luis Obispo-Atascadero-Paso Robles MSA, CA	S	17.78 MW	17.78 AW	36970 AAW	CABLS	10//99-12//99
	Santa Barbara-Santa Maria-Lompoc MSA, CA	S	21.23 MW	22.40 AW	44160 AAW	CABLS	10//99-12//99
	Santa Cruz-Watsonville PMSA, CA	S	21.48 MW	21.97 AW	44690 AAW	CABLS	10//99-12//99
	Santa Rosa PMSA, CA	S	20.75 MW	21.02 AW	43150 AAW	CABLS	10//99-12//99
	Stockton-Lodi MSA, CA	S	21.90 MW	22.61 AW	45550 AAW	CABLS	10//99-12//99
	Vallejo-Fairfield-Napa PMSA, CA	S	20.95 MW	19.59 AW	43570 AAW	CABLS	10//99-12//99
	Ventura PMSA, CA	S	14.92 MW	13.49 AW	31040 AAW	CABLS	10//99-12//99

AAW Average annual wage	**AOH** Average offered, high	**ASH** Average starting, high	**H** Hourly	**M** Monthly	**S** Special: hourly and annual
AE Average entry wage	**AOL** Average offered, low	**ASL** Average starting, low	**HI** Highest wage paid	**MTC** Median total compensation	**TQ** Third quartile wage
AEX Average experienced wage	**APH** Average pay, high range	**AW** Average wage paid	**HR** High end range	**MW** Median wage paid	**W** Weekly
AO Average offered	**APL** Average pay, low range	**FQ** First quartile wage	**LR** Low end range	**SQ** Second quartile wage	**Y** Yearly

Occupation/Type/Industry	Location	Per	Low	Mid	High	Source	Date
Carpenter	Visalia-Tulare-Porterville MSA, CA	S	14.34 MW	13.10 AW	29820 AAW	CABLS	10//99-12//99
	Yolo PMSA, CA	S	22.71 MW	23.15 AW	47240 AAW	CABLS	10//99-12//99
	Yuba City MSA, CA	S	16.40 MW	17.16 AW	34110 AAW	CABLS	10//99-12//99
	Colorado	S	15.57 MW	15.68 AW	32600 AAW	COBLS	10//99-12//99
	Boulder-Longmont PMSA, CO	S	16.64 MW	17.51 AW	34610 AAW	COBLS	10//99-12//99
	Denver PMSA, CO	S	16.29 MW	15.94 AW	33890 AAW	COBLS	10//99-12//99
	Fort Collins-Loveland MSA, CO	S	13.90 MW	14.10 AW	28920 AAW	COBLS	10//99-12//99
	Grand Junction MSA, CO	S	13.75 MW	13.14 AW	28600 AAW	COBLS	10//99-12//99
	Greeley PMSA, CO	S	15.76 MW	15.07 AW	32790 AAW	COBLS	10//99-12//99
	Pueblo MSA, CO	S	13.21 MW	13.06 AW	27480 AAW	COBLS	10//99-12//99
	Connecticut	S	17.48 MW	17.52 AW	36450 AAW	CTBLS	10//99-12//99
	Bridgeport PMSA, CT	S	16.16 MW	17.31 AW	33620 AAW	CTBLS	10//99-12//99
	Danbury PMSA, CT	S	18.67 MW	18.37 AW	38830 AAW	CTBLS	10//99-12//99
	Hartford MSA, CT	S	17.06 MW	17.49 AW	35480 AAW	CTBLS	10//99-12//99
	New Haven-Meriden PMSA, CT	S	16.57 MW	15.81 AW	34470 AAW	CTBLS	10//99-12//99
	New London-Norwich MSA, CT-RI	S	16.71 MW	16.83 AW	34760 AAW	CTBLS	10//99-12//99
	Stamford-Norwalk PMSA, CT	S	20.08 MW	19.79 AW	41770 AAW	CTBLS	10//99-12//99
	Waterbury PMSA, CT	S	15.81 MW	15.30 AW	32880 AAW	CTBLS	10//99-12//99
	Delaware	S	14.48 MW	16.17 AW	33640 AAW	DEBLS	10//99-12//99
	Dover MSA, DE	S	14.01 MW	12.98 AW	29130 AAW	DEBLS	10//99-12//99
	Wilmington-Newark PMSA, DE-MD	S	17.76 MW	16.64 AW	36950 AAW	DEBLS	10//99-12//99
	District of Columbia	S	18.5 MW	18.01 AW	37460 AAW	DCBLS	10//99-12//99
	Washington PMSA, DC-MD-VA-WV	S	15.85 MW	15.83 AW	32980 AAW	DCBLS	10//99-12//99
	Florida	S	12.23 MW	12.40 AW	25800 AAW	FLBLS	10//99-12//99
	Daytona Beach MSA, FL	S	10.08 MW	9.52 AW	20970 AAW	FLBLS	10//99-12//99
	Fort Lauderdale PMSA, FL	S	14.06 MW	14.25 AW	29230 AAW	FLBLS	10//99-12//99
	Fort Myers-Cape Coral MSA, FL	S	12.69 MW	12.40 AW	26390 AAW	FLBLS	10//99-12//99
	Fort Pierce-Port St. Lucie MSA, FL	S	15.06 MW	14.69 AW	31320 AAW	FLBLS	10//99-12//99
	Fort Walton Beach MSA, FL	S	11.89 MW	10.67 AW	24720 AAW	FLBLS	10//99-12//99
	Gainesville MSA, FL	S	12.52 MW	12.44 AW	26040 AAW	FLBLS	10//99-12//99
	Jacksonville MSA, FL	S	12.20 MW	11.97 AW	25370 AAW	FLBLS	10//99-12//99
	Lakeland-Winter Haven MSA, FL	S	9.68 MW	9.10 AW	20140 AAW	FLBLS	10//99-12//99
	Melbourne-Titusville-Palm Bay MSA, FL	S	13.19 MW	12.15 AW	27440 AAW	FLBLS	10//99-12//99
	Miami PMSA, FL	S	12.25 MW	12.57 AW	25480 AAW	FLBLS	10//99-12//99
	Naples MSA, FL	S	15.45 MW	15.86 AW	32140 AAW	FLBLS	10//99-12//99
	Ocala MSA, FL	S	9.24 MW	8.98 AW	19220 AAW	FLBLS	10//99-12//99
	Orlando MSA, FL	S	12.42 MW	12.35 AW	25840 AAW	FLBLS	10//99-12//99
	Panama City MSA, FL	S	10.33 MW	10.04 AW	21480 AAW	FLBLS	10//99-12//99
	Pensacola MSA, FL	S	10.00 MW	9.72 AW	20800 AAW	FLBLS	10//99-12//99
	Punta Gorda MSA, FL	S	11.29 MW	11.46 AW	23490 AAW	FLBLS	10//99-12//99
	Sarasota-Bradenton MSA, FL	S	11.59 MW	10.87 AW	24110 AAW	FLBLS	10//99-12//99
	Tallahassee MSA, FL	S	13.98 MW	14.58 AW	29070 AAW	FLBLS	10//99-12//99
	Tampa-St. Petersburg-Clearwater MSA, FL	S	12.43 MW	12.27 AW	25850 AAW	FLBLS	10//99-12//99
	West Palm Beach-Boca Raton MSA, FL	S	13.64 MW	13.12 AW	28370 AAW	FLBLS	10//99-12//99
	Georgia	S	12.66 MW	12.83 AW	26680 AAW	GABLS	10//99-12//99
	Albany MSA, GA	S	11.57 MW	11.41 AW	24070 AAW	GABLS	10//99-12//99
	Athens MSA, GA	S	12.69 MW	12.53 AW	26400 AAW	GABLS	10//99-12//99
	Atlanta MSA, GA	S	12.81 MW	12.67 AW	26650 AAW	GABLS	10//99-12//99
	Augusta-Aiken MSA, GA-SC	S	12.83 MW	11.90 AW	26680 AAW	GABLS	10//99-12//99
	Columbus MSA, GA-AL	S	11.10 MW	10.60 AW	23090 AAW	GABLS	10//99-12//99
	Macon MSA, GA	S	12.31 MW	11.96 AW	25600 AAW	GABLS	10//99-12//99
	Savannah MSA, GA	S	14.35 MW	14.11 AW	29840 AAW	GABLS	10//99-12//99
	Hawaii	S	25.7 MW	24.44 AW	50830 AAW	HIBLS	10//99-12//99
	Honolulu MSA, HI	S	24.40 MW	25.38 AW	50750 AAW	HIBLS	10//99-12//99
	Idaho	S	12.12 MW	12.65 AW	26300 AAW	IDBLS	10//99-12//99
	Boise City MSA, ID	S	14.87 MW	14.78 AW	30940 AAW	IDBLS	10//99-12//99
	Pocatello MSA, ID	S	11.51 MW	11.33 AW	23950 AAW	IDBLS	10//99-12//99
	Illinois	S	21.97 MW	21.48 AW	44670 AAW	ILBLS	10//99-12//99
	Bloomington-Normal MSA, IL	S	16.83 MW	15.57 AW	35010 AAW	ILBLS	10//99-12//99
	Chicago PMSA, IL	S	22.80 MW	23.15 AW	47430 AAW	ILBLS	10//99-12//99

Occupation/Type/Industry	Location	Per	Low	Mid	High	Source	Date
Carpenter	Decatur MSA, IL	S	14.78 MW	14.04 AW	30740 AAW	ILBLS	10//99-12//99
	Kankakee PMSA, IL	S	24.58 MW	24.75 AW	51120 AAW	ILBLS	10//99-12//99
	Peoria-Pekin MSA, IL	S	18.64 MW	19.03 AW	38760 AAW	ILBLS	10//99-12//99
	Rockford MSA, IL	S	20.65 MW	21.89 AW	42960 AAW	ILBLS	10//99-12//99
	Springfield MSA, IL	S	13.08 MW	12.07 AW	27220 AAW	ILBLS	10//99-12//99
	Indiana	S	16.43 MW	16.87 AW	35090 AAW	INBLS	10//99-12//99
	Bloomington MSA, IN	S	12.40 MW	11.23 AW	25800 AAW	INBLS	10//99-12//99
	Elkhart-Goshen MSA, IN	S	13.91 MW	14.50 AW	28930 AAW	INBLS	10//99-12//99
	Evansville-Henderson MSA, IN-KY	S	17.19 MW	18.40 AW	35740 AAW	INBLS	10//99-12//99
	Fort Wayne MSA, IN	S	16.56 MW	15.74 AW	34430 AAW	INBLS	10//99-12//99
	Gary PMSA, IN	S	21.49 MW	23.65 AW	44690 AAW	INBLS	10//99-12//99
	Indianapolis MSA, IN	S	17.94 MW	18.14 AW	37320 AAW	INBLS	10//99-12//99
	Kokomo MSA, IN	S	17.52 MW	18.66 AW	36440 AAW	INBLS	10//99-12//99
	Lafayette MSA, IN	S	16.04 MW	17.77 AW	33360 AAW	INBLS	10//99-12//99
	South Bend MSA, IN	S	15.65 MW	15.83 AW	32560 AAW	INBLS	10//99-12//99
	Terre Haute MSA, IN	S	17.15 MW	17.71 AW	35670 AAW	INBLS	10//99-12//99
	Iowa	S	13.13 MW	13.88 AW	28870 AAW	IABLS	10//99-12//99
	Cedar Rapids MSA, IA	S	17.49 MW	18.15 AW	36390 AAW	IABLS	10//99-12//99
	Davenport-Moline-Rock Island MSA, IA-IL	S	16.66 MW	17.14 AW	34650 AAW	IABLS	10//99-12//99
	Des Moines MSA, IA	S	14.07 MW	13.20 AW	29260 AAW	IABLS	10//99-12//99
	Dubuque MSA, IA	S	14.27 MW	13.88 AW	29670 AAW	IABLS	10//99-12//99
	Iowa City MSA, IA	S	12.93 MW	12.42 AW	26900 AAW	IABLS	10//99-12//99
	Sioux City MSA, IA-NE	S	14.72 MW	13.95 AW	30610 AAW	IABLS	10//99-12//99
	Waterloo-Cedar Falls MSA, IA	S	11.96 MW	12.02 AW	24870 AAW	IABLS	10//99-12//99
	Kansas	S	13.65 MW	14.62 AW	30400 AAW	KSBLS	10//99-12//99
	Lawrence MSA, KS	S	12.27 MW	12.02 AW	25530 AAW	KSBLS	10//99-12//99
	Topeka MSA, KS	S	15.11 MW	14.75 AW	31440 AAW	KSBLS	10//99-12//99
	Wichita MSA, KS	S	14.40 MW	14.47 AW	29960 AAW	KSBLS	10//99-12//99
	Kentucky	S	12.6 MW	13.50 AW	28080 AAW	KYBLS	10//99-12//99
	Lexington MSA, KY	S	13.16 MW	12.57 AW	27380 AAW	KYBLS	10//99-12//99
	Louisville MSA, KY-IN	S	13.90 MW	13.48 AW	28900 AAW	KYBLS	10//99-12//99
	Owensboro MSA, KY	S	11.57 MW	11.46 AW	24070 AAW	KYBLS	10//99-12//99
	Louisiana	S	13.4 MW	13.25 AW	27550 AAW	LABLS	10//99-12//99
	Alexandria MSA, LA	S	12.72 MW	12.81 AW	26470 AAW	LABLS	10//99-12//99
	Baton Rouge MSA, LA	S	14.58 MW	14.45 AW	30330 AAW	LABLS	10//99-12//99
	Houma MSA, LA	S	10.16 MW	10.28 AW	21130 AAW	LABLS	10//99-12//99
	Lafayette MSA, LA	S	12.84 MW	12.72 AW	26710 AAW	LABLS	10//99-12//99
	Lake Charles MSA, LA	S	14.73 MW	14.86 AW	30640 AAW	LABLS	10//99-12//99
	Monroe MSA, LA	S	13.16 MW	12.89 AW	27370 AAW	LABLS	10//99-12//99
	New Orleans MSA, LA	S	12.97 MW	13.23 AW	26980 AAW	LABLS	10//99-12//99
	Shreveport-Bossier City MSA, LA	S	12.03 MW	12.12 AW	25020 AAW	LABLS	10//99-12//99
	Maine	S	11.69 MW	12.02 AW	25000 AAW	MEBLS	10//99-12//99
	Bangor MSA, ME	S	11.89 MW	11.27 AW	24740 AAW	MEBLS	10//99-12//99
	Lewiston-Auburn MSA, ME	S	11.29 MW	11.57 AW	23490 AAW	MEBLS	10//99-12//99
	Portland MSA, ME	S	12.47 MW	11.90 AW	25930 AAW	MEBLS	10//99-12//99
	Maryland	S	14.98 MW	15.05 AW	31300 AAW	MDBLS	10//99-12//99
	Baltimore PMSA, MD	S	14.00 MW	13.83 AW	29120 AAW	MDBLS	10//99-12//99
	Cumberland MSA, MD-WV	S	11.45 MW	10.38 AW	23810 AAW	MDBLS	10//99-12//99
	Hagerstown PMSA, MD	S	12.93 MW	12.20 AW	26900 AAW	MDBLS	10//99-12//99
	Massachusetts	S	19.27 MW	19.40 AW	40350 AAW	MABLS	10//99-12//99
	Barnstable-Yarmouth MSA, MA	S	21.04 MW	17.61 AW	43770 AAW	MABLS	10//99-12//99
	Boston PMSA, MA-NH	S	21.08 MW	22.08 AW	43850 AAW	MABLS	10//99-12//99
	Brockton PMSA, MA	S	17.31 MW	17.20 AW	36000 AAW	MABLS	10//99-12//99
	Fitchburg-Leominster PMSA, MA	S	19.63 MW	17.76 AW	40820 AAW	MABLS	10//99-12//99
	Lawrence PMSA, MA-NH	S	21.18 MW	22.03 AW	44060 AAW	MABLS	10//99-12//99
	Lowell PMSA, MA-NH	S	19.45 MW	18.33 AW	40450 AAW	MABLS	10//99-12//99
	New Bedford PMSA, MA	S	14.52 MW	13.30 AW	30190 AAW	MABLS	10//99-12//99
	Pittsfield MSA, MA	S	14.30 MW	14.16 AW	29740 AAW	MABLS	10//99-12//99
	Springfield MSA, MA	S	17.89 MW	17.83 AW	37220 AAW	MABLS	10//99-12//99
	Worcester PMSA, MA-CT	S	15.21 MW	15.12 AW	31630 AAW	MABLS	10//99-12//99
	Michigan	S	16.37 MW	17.64 AW	36690 AAW	MIBLS	10//99-12//99
	Ann Arbor PMSA, MI	S	14.35 MW	14.32 AW	29840 AAW	MIBLS	10//99-12//99
	Benton Harbor MSA, MI	S	12.71 MW	12.34 AW	26430 AAW	MIBLS	10//99-12//99
	Detroit PMSA, MI	S	20.79 MW	22.75 AW	43240 AAW	MIBLS	10//99-12//99
	Flint PMSA, MI	S	19.72 MW	20.99 AW	41020 AAW	MIBLS	10//99-12//99
	Grand Rapids-Muskegon-Holland MSA, MI	S	15.83 MW	15.87 AW	32930 AAW	MIBLS	10//99-12//99

AAW Average annual wage	**AOH** Average offered, high	**ASH** Average starting, high	**H** Hourly	**M** Monthly	**S** Special: hourly and annual
AE Average entry wage	**AOL** Average offered, low	**ASL** Average starting, low	**HI** Highest wage paid	**MTC** Median total compensation	**TQ** Third quartile wage
AEX Average experienced wage	**APH** Average pay, high range	**AW** Average wage paid	**HR** High end range	**MW** Median wage paid	**W** Weekly
AO Average offered	**APL** Average pay, low range	**FQ** First quartile wage	**LR** Low end range	**SQ** Second quartile wage	**Y** Yearly

Carpenter

Occupation/Type/Industry	Location	Per	Low	Mid	High	Source	Date
Carpenter	Jackson MSA, MI	S	14.85 MW	14.73 AW	30880 AAW	MIBLS	10//99-12//99
	Kalamazoo-Battle Creek MSA, MI	S	13.73 MW	13.50 AW	28550 AAW	MIBLS	10//99-12//99
	Lansing-East Lansing MSA, MI	S	19.67 MW	21.42 AW	40920 AAW	MIBLS	10//99-12//99
	Saginaw-Bay City-Midland MSA, MI	S	15.37 MW	12.83 AW	31960 AAW	MIBLS	10//99-12//99
	Minnesota	S	16.82 MW	17.17 AW	35720 AAW	MNBLS	10//99-12//99
	Duluth-Superior MSA, MN-WI	S	16.28 MW	16.91 AW	33860 AAW	MNBLS	10//99-12//99
	Minneapolis-St. Paul MSA, MN-WI	S	18.48 MW	18.58 AW	38440 AAW	MNBLS	10//99-12//99
	Rochester MSA, MN	S	16.92 MW	17.51 AW	35200 AAW	MNBLS	10//99-12//99
	St. Cloud MSA, MN	S	14.08 MW	13.24 AW	29280 AAW	MNBLS	10//99-12//99
	Mississippi	S	12.38 MW	12.91 AW	26860 AAW	MSBLS	10//99-12//99
	Biloxi-Gulfport-Pascagoula MSA, MS	S	14.26 MW	14.57 AW	29660 AAW	MSBLS	10//99-12//99
	Hattiesburg MSA, MS	S	11.98 MW	11.89 AW	24920 AAW	MSBLS	10//99-12//99
	Jackson MSA, MS	S	15.98 MW	14.77 AW	33240 AAW	MSBLS	10//99-12//99
	Missouri	S	16.41 MW	17.28 AW	35940 AAW	MOBLS	10//99-12//99
	Columbia MSA, MO	S	13.86 MW	13.66 AW	28820 AAW	MOBLS	10//99-12//99
	Joplin MSA, MO	S	11.63 MW	10.97 AW	24200 AAW	MOBLS	10//99-12//99
	Kansas City MSA, MO-KS	S	18.47 MW	18.68 AW	38430 AAW	MOBLS	10//99-12//99
	St. Joseph MSA, MO	S	14.43 MW	14.71 AW	30020 AAW	MOBLS	10//99-12//99
	St. Louis MSA, MO-IL	S	19.68 MW	19.89 AW	40930 AAW	MOBLS	10//99-12//99
	Springfield MSA, MO	S	12.64 MW	12.11 AW	26290 AAW	MOBLS	10//99-12//99
	Montana	S	14.1 MW	13.40 AW	27860 AAW	MTBLS	10//99-12//99
	Billings MSA, MT	S	13.27 MW	13.83 AW	27590 AAW	MTBLS	10//99-12//99
	Great Falls MSA, MT	S	13.62 MW	14.56 AW	28330 AAW	MTBLS	10//99-12//99
	Missoula MSA, MT	S	15.06 MW	15.21 AW	31320 AAW	MTBLS	10//99-12//99
	Nebraska	S	13.94 MW	14.16 AW	29450 AAW	NEBLS	10//99-12//99
	Lincoln MSA, NE	S	13.27 MW	13.96 AW	27610 AAW	NEBLS	10//99-12//99
	Omaha MSA, NE-IA	S	15.38 MW	15.48 AW	31990 AAW	NEBLS	10//99-12//99
	Nevada	S	19.42 MW	19.17 AW	39880 AAW	NVBLS	10//99-12//99
	Las Vegas MSA, NV-AZ	S	19.19 MW	20.17 AW	39910 AAW	NVBLS	10//99-12//99
	Reno MSA, NV	S	19.11 MW	18.76 AW	39750 AAW	NVBLS	10//99-12//99
	New Hampshire	S	13.2 MW	13.39 AW	27850 AAW	NHBLS	10//99-12//99
	Manchester PMSA, NH	S	15.43 MW	15.11 AW	32100 AAW	NHBLS	10//99-12//99
	Nashua PMSA, NH	S	14.91 MW	13.39 AW	31020 AAW	NHBLS	10//99-12//99
	Portsmouth-Rochester PMSA, NH-ME	S	12.54 MW	12.21 AW	26080 AAW	NHBLS	10//99-12//99
	New Jersey	S	22.47 MW	22.31 AW	46400 AAW	NJBLS	10//99-12//99
	Atlantic-Cape May PMSA, NJ	S	23.06 MW	25.50 AW	47970 AAW	NJBLS	10//99-12//99
	Bergen-Passaic PMSA, NJ	S	22.58 MW	25.30 AW	46970 AAW	NJBLS	10//99-12//99
	Jersey City PMSA, NJ	S	21.54 MW	20.42 AW	44810 AAW	NJBLS	10//99-12//99
	Middlesex-Somerset-Hunterdon PMSA, NJ	S	20.50 MW	19.98 AW	42650 AAW	NJBLS	10//99-12//99
	Monmouth-Ocean PMSA, NJ	S	22.08 MW	21.98 AW	45920 AAW	NJBLS	10//99-12//99
	Newark PMSA, NJ	S	21.74 MW	21.93 AW	45230 AAW	NJBLS	10//99-12//99
	Vineland-Millville-Bridgeton PMSA, NJ	S	20.13 MW	19.12 AW	41870 AAW	NJBLS	10//99-12//99
	New Mexico	S	12.5 MW	13.16 AW	27380 AAW	NMBLS	10//99-12//99
	Albuquerque MSA, NM	S	13.86 MW	13.35 AW	28820 AAW	NMBLS	10//99-12//99
	Las Cruces MSA, NM	S	11.70 MW	10.22 AW	24330 AAW	NMBLS	10//99-12//99
	Santa Fe MSA, NM	S	13.75 MW	12.91 AW	28600 AAW	NMBLS	10//99-12//99
	New York	S	19.32 MW	21.38 AW	44470 AAW	NYBLS	10//99-12//99
	Albany-Schenectady-Troy MSA, NY	S	17.52 MW	18.16 AW	36430 AAW	NYBLS	10//99-12//99
	Binghamton MSA, NY	S	13.29 MW	13.39 AW	27640 AAW	NYBLS	10//99-12//99
	Buffalo-Niagara Falls MSA, NY	S	18.04 MW	16.83 AW	37520 AAW	NYBLS	10//99-12//99
	Dutchess County PMSA, NY	S	20.23 MW	19.75 AW	42080 AAW	NYBLS	10//99-12//99
	Elmira MSA, NY	S	17.37 MW	18.50 AW	36140 AAW	NYBLS	10//99-12//99
	Glens Falls MSA, NY	S	12.84 MW	13.72 AW	26720 AAW	NYBLS	10//99-12//99
	Jamestown MSA, NY	S	11.92 MW	11.84 AW	24800 AAW	NYBLS	10//99-12//99
	Nassau-Suffolk PMSA, NY	S	23.14 MW	23.66 AW	48130 AAW	NYBLS	10//99-12//99
	New York PMSA, NY	S	25.86 MW	27.62 AW	53780 AAW	NYBLS	10//99-12//99
	Newburgh PMSA, NY-PA	S	15.64 MW	15.25 AW	32530 AAW	NYBLS	10//99-12//99
	Rochester MSA, NY	S	15.25 MW	15.01 AW	31710 AAW	NYBLS	10//99-12//99
	Syracuse MSA, NY	S	14.82 MW	14.12 AW	30830 AAW	NYBLS	10//99-12//99
	North Carolina	S	12.07 MW	12.84 AW	26700 AAW	NCBLS	10//99-12//99
	Asheville MSA, NC	S	11.64 MW	11.57 AW	24210 AAW	NCBLS	10//99-12//99
	Charlotte-Gastonia-Rock Hill MSA, NC-SC	S	14.95 MW	13.51 AW	31100 AAW	NCBLS	10//99-12//99

Occupation/Type/Industry	Location	Per	Low	Mid	High	Source	Date
Carpenter	Fayetteville MSA, NC	S	11.50 MW	10.36 AW	23920 AAW	NCBLS	10//99-12//99
	Goldsboro MSA, NC	S	13.33 MW	14.02 AW	27730 AAW	NCBLS	10//99-12//99
	Greensboro--Winston-Salem-- High Point MSA, NC	S	12.26 MW	11.84 AW	25510 AAW	NCBLS	10//99-12//99
	Greenville MSA, NC	S	10.15 MW	10.12 AW	21110 AAW	NCBLS	10//99-12//99
	Hickory-Morganton-Lenoir MSA, NC	S	13.76 MW	12.36 AW	28630 AAW	NCBLS	10//99-12//99
	Jacksonville MSA, NC	S	11.53 MW	10.81 AW	23980 AAW	NCBLS	10//99-12//99
	Raleigh-Durham-Chapel Hill MSA, NC	S	13.06 MW	12.67 AW	27170 AAW	NCBLS	10//99-12//99
	Rocky Mount MSA, NC	S	11.17 MW	10.51 AW	23240 AAW	NCBLS	10//99-12//99
	Wilmington MSA, NC	S	12.22 MW	12.01 AW	25410 AAW	NCBLS	10//99-12//99
	North Dakota	S	11.38 MW	11.84 AW	24630 AAW	NDBLS	10//99-12//99
	Bismarck MSA, ND	S	12.69 MW	12.17 AW	26390 AAW	NDBLS	10//99-12//99
	Fargo-Moorhead MSA, ND-MN	S	13.98 MW	14.15 AW	29070 AAW	NDBLS	10//99-12//99
	Grand Forks MSA, ND-MN	S	14.14 MW	13.43 AW	29410 AAW	NDBLS	10//99-12//99
	Ohio	S	15.87 MW	16.08 AW	33450 AAW	OHBLS	10//99-12//99
	Cincinnati PMSA, OH-KY-IN	S	15.14 MW	15.39 AW	31490 AAW	OHBLS	10//99-12//99
	Columbus MSA, OH	S	14.25 MW	13.83 AW	29640 AAW	OHBLS	10//99-12//99
	Dayton-Springfield MSA, OH	S	13.22 MW	12.72 AW	27490 AAW	OHBLS	10//99-12//99
	Hamilton-Middletown PMSA, OH	S	13.84 MW	12.76 AW	28800 AAW	OHBLS	10//99-12//99
	Mansfield MSA, OH	S	13.28 MW	11.80 AW	27620 AAW	OHBLS	10//99-12//99
	Steubenville-Weirton MSA, OH-WV	S	11.24 MW	10.68 AW	23370 AAW	OHBLS	10//99-12//99
	Youngstown-Warren MSA, OH	S	15.32 MW	14.61 AW	31870 AAW	OHBLS	10//99-12//99
	Oklahoma	S	12.42 MW	13.09 AW	27230 AAW	OKBLS	10//99-12//99
	Enid MSA, OK	S	9.30 MW	10.99 AW	19340 AAW	OKBLS	10//99-12//99
	Lawton MSA, OK	S	14.50 MW	14.71 AW	30150 AAW	OKBLS	10//99-12//99
	Oklahoma City MSA, OK	S	14.95 MW	13.17 AW	31090 AAW	OKBLS	10//99-12//99
	Tulsa MSA, OK	S	12.37 MW	12.37 AW	25720 AAW	OKBLS	10//99-12//99
	Oregon	S	16.87 MW	17.22 AW	35810 AAW	ORBLS	10//99-12//99
	Corvallis MSA, OR	S	14.90 MW	14.09 AW	30990 AAW	ORBLS	10//99-12//99
	Eugene-Springfield MSA, OR	S	13.07 MW	12.44 AW	27190 AAW	ORBLS	10//99-12//99
	Medford-Ashland MSA, OR	S	16.88 MW	17.17 AW	35120 AAW	ORBLS	10//99-12//99
	Portland-Vancouver PMSA, OR-WA	S	18.10 MW	17.93 AW	37660 AAW	ORBLS	10//99-12//99
	Salem PMSA, OR	S	19.09 MW	19.58 AW	39700 AAW	ORBLS	10//99-12//99
	Pennsylvania	S	15.47 MW	16.36 AW	34030 AAW	PABLS	10//99-12//99
	Allentown-Bethlehem-Easton MSA, PA	S	15.93 MW	15.23 AW	33130 AAW	PABLS	10//99-12//99
	Altoona MSA, PA	S	11.03 MW	11.41 AW	22930 AAW	PABLS	10//99-12//99
	Erie MSA, PA	S	19.97 MW	16.19 AW	41540 AAW	PABLS	10//99-12//99
	Harrisburg-Lebanon-Carlisle MSA, PA	S	17.60 MW	17.82 AW	36620 AAW	PABLS	10//99-12//99
	Johnstown MSA, PA	S	10.71 MW	9.92 AW	22280 AAW	PABLS	10//99-12//99
	Lancaster MSA, PA	S	14.17 MW	13.88 AW	29470 AAW	PABLS	10//99-12//99
	Philadelphia PMSA, PA-NJ	S	19.78 MW	19.17 AW	41140 AAW	PABLS	10//99-12//99
	Pittsburgh MSA, PA	S	19.16 MW	19.46 AW	39850 AAW	PABLS	10//99-12//99
	Reading MSA, PA	S	15.32 MW	14.23 AW	31870 AAW	PABLS	10//99-12//99
	Scranton--Wilkes-Barre-- Hazleton MSA, PA	S	15.98 MW	15.62 AW	33250 AAW	PABLS	10//99-12//99
	Sharon MSA, PA	S	13.71 MW	12.34 AW	28520 AAW	PABLS	10//99-12//99
	State College MSA, PA	S	14.49 MW	12.83 AW	30130 AAW	PABLS	10//99-12//99
	Williamsport MSA, PA	S	12.60 MW	12.12 AW	26200 AAW	PABLS	10//99-12//99
	York MSA, PA	S	15.20 MW	13.94 AW	31610 AAW	PABLS	10//99-12//99
	Rhode Island	S	17.29 MW	17.04 AW	35440 AAW	RIBLS	10//99-12//99
	Providence-Fall River- Warwick MSA, RI-MA	S	17.66 MW	17.20 AW	36730 AAW	RIBLS	10//99-12//99
	South Carolina	S	12.48 MW	13.03 AW	27100 AAW	SCBLS	10//99-12//99
	Charleston-North Charleston MSA, SC	S	12.23 MW	11.87 AW	25430 AAW	SCBLS	10//99-12//99
	Columbia MSA, SC	S	13.14 MW	13.00 AW	27320 AAW	SCBLS	10//99-12//99
	Florence MSA, SC	S	10.29 MW	9.82 AW	21400 AAW	SCBLS	10//99-12//99
	Greenville-Spartanburg- Anderson MSA, SC	S	14.10 MW	13.30 AW	29340 AAW	SCBLS	10//99-12//99
	Myrtle Beach MSA, SC	S	13.10 MW	12.08 AW	27250 AAW	SCBLS	10//99-12//99
	Sumter MSA, SC	S	10.19 MW	9.84 AW	21190 AAW	SCBLS	10//99-12//99
	South Dakota	S	10.78 MW	11.14 AW	23180 AAW	SDBLS	10//99-12//99
	Rapid City MSA, SD	S	12.34 MW	12.17 AW	25670 AAW	SDBLS	10//99-12//99
	Sioux Falls MSA, SD	S	12.29 MW	12.05 AW	25560 AAW	SDBLS	10//99-12//99

AAW Average annual wage	**AOH** Average offered, high	**ASH** Average starting, high	**H** Hourly	**M** Monthly	**S** Special: hourly and annual
AE Average entry wage	**AOL** Average offered, low	**ASL** Average starting, low	**HI** Highest wage paid	**MTC** Median total compensation	**TQ** Third quartile wage
AEX Average experienced wage	**APH** Average pay, high range	**AW** Average wage paid	**HR** High end range	**MW** Median wage paid	**W** Weekly
AO Average offered	**APL** Average pay, low range	**FQ** First quartile wage	**LR** Low end range	**SQ** Second quartile wage	**Y** Yearly

Carpenter

Occupation/Type/Industry	Location	Per	Low	Mid	High	Source	Date
Carpenter	Tennessee	S	13 MW	12.90 AW	26820 AAW	TNBLS	10//99-12//99
	Chattanooga MSA, TN-GA	S	14.01 MW	14.62 AW	29140 AAW	TNBLS	10//99-12//99
	Clarksville-Hopkinsville MSA, TN-KY	S	11.09 MW	10.67 AW	23070 AAW	TNBLS	10//99-12//99
	Jackson MSA, TN	S	12.29 MW	12.12 AW	25560 AAW	TNBLS	10//99-12//99
	Johnson City-Kingsport-Bristol MSA, TN-VA	S	10.52 MW	10.23 AW	21890 AAW	TNBLS	10//99-12//99
	Knoxville MSA, TN	S	13.59 MW	14.05 AW	28260 AAW	TNBLS	10//99-12//99
	Memphis MSA, TN-AR-MS	S	13.64 MW	13.96 AW	28370 AAW	MSBLS	10//99-12//99
	Nashville MSA, TN	S	13.44 MW	13.54 AW	27950 AAW	TNBLS	10//99-12//99
	Texas	S	12.21 MW	12.36 AW	25710 AAW	TXBLS	10//99-12//99
	Abilene MSA, TX	S	9.55 MW	9.04 AW	19860 AAW	TXBLS	10//99-12//99
	Amarillo MSA, TX	S	15.84 MW	13.15 AW	32940 AAW	TXBLS	10//99-12//99
	Austin-San Marcos MSA, TX	S	10.61 MW	10.61 AW	22060 AAW	TXBLS	10//99-12//99
	Beaumont-Port Arthur MSA, TX	S	14.03 MW	13.32 AW	29180 AAW	TXBLS	10//99-12//99
	Brazoria PMSA, TX	S	13.77 MW	12.54 AW	28640 AAW	TXBLS	10//99-12//99
	Brownsville-Harlingen-San Benito MSA, TX	S	9.52 MW	8.50 AW	19800 AAW	TXBLS	10//99-12//99
	Bryan-College Station MSA, TX	S	11.93 MW	10.67 AW	24820 AAW	TXBLS	10//99-12//99
	Corpus Christi MSA, TX	S	10.23 MW	8.43 AW	21280 AAW	TXBLS	10//99-12//99
	Dallas PMSA, TX	S	11.96 MW	11.90 AW	24870 AAW	TXBLS	10//99-12//99
	El Paso MSA, TX	S	10.06 MW	9.84 AW	20920 AAW	TXBLS	10//99-12//99
	Fort Worth-Arlington PMSA, TX	S	11.12 MW	10.09 AW	23120 AAW	TXBLS	10//99-12//99
	Galveston-Texas City PMSA, TX	S	10.24 MW	8.62 AW	21290 AAW	TXBLS	10//99-12//99
	Houston PMSA, TX	S	13.96 MW	14.05 AW	29040 AAW	TXBLS	10//99-12//99
	Killeen-Temple MSA, TX	S	12.78 MW	13.04 AW	26570 AAW	TXBLS	10//99-12//99
	Laredo MSA, TX	S	10.21 MW	9.86 AW	21250 AAW	TXBLS	10//99-12//99
	Longview-Marshall MSA, TX	S	12.44 MW	12.55 AW	25880 AAW	TXBLS	10//99-12//99
	Lubbock MSA, TX	S	11.93 MW	12.07 AW	24820 AAW	TXBLS	10//99-12//99
	McAllen-Edinburg-Mission MSA, TX	S	7.69 MW	7.26 AW	16000 AAW	TXBLS	10//99-12//99
	Odessa-Midland MSA, TX	S	12.57 MW	12.24 AW	26150 AAW	TXBLS	10//99-12//99
	San Angelo MSA, TX	S	10.74 MW	10.62 AW	22340 AAW	TXBLS	10//99-12//99
	San Antonio MSA, TX	S	11.34 MW	10.73 AW	23600 AAW	TXBLS	10//99-12//99
	Sherman-Denison MSA, TX	S	12.06 MW	12.02 AW	25080 AAW	TXBLS	10//99-12//99
	Texarkana MSA, TX-Texarkana, AR	S	12.48 MW	12.41 AW	25950 AAW	TXBLS	10//99-12//99
	Tyler MSA, TX	S	11.67 MW	11.29 AW	24270 AAW	TXBLS	10//99-12//99
	Victoria MSA, TX	S	11.28 MW	10.76 AW	23460 AAW	TXBLS	10//99-12//99
	Waco MSA, TX	S	10.26 MW	9.73 AW	21350 AAW	TXBLS	10//99-12//99
	Wichita Falls MSA, TX	S	12.38 MW	13.31 AW	25760 AAW	TXBLS	10//99-12//99
	Utah	S	12.84 MW	13.04 AW	27130 AAW	UTBLS	10//99-12//99
	Provo-Orem MSA, UT	S	13.51 MW	12.52 AW	28100 AAW	UTBLS	10//99-12//99
	Salt Lake City-Ogden MSA, UT	S	13.15 MW	13.12 AW	27350 AAW	UTBLS	10//99-12//99
	Vermont	S	13.12 MW	13.24 AW	27540 AAW	VTBLS	10//99-12//99
	Burlington MSA, VT	S	14.09 MW	14.04 AW	29320 AAW	VTBLS	10//99-12//99
	Virginia	S	12.97 MW	13.06 AW	27160 AAW	VABLS	10//99-12//99
	Charlottesville MSA, VA	S	12.32 MW	12.25 AW	25620 AAW	VABLS	10//99-12//99
	Danville MSA, VA	S	8.66 MW	8.26 AW	18000 AAW	VABLS	10//99-12//99
	Lynchburg MSA, VA	S	10.55 MW	10.02 AW	21940 AAW	VABLS	10//99-12//99
	Norfolk-Virginia Beach-Newport News MSA, VA-NC	S	13.17 MW	13.52 AW	27400 AAW	VABLS	10//99-12//99
	Richmond-Petersburg MSA, VA	S	14.39 MW	14.65 AW	29940 AAW	VABLS	10//99-12//99
	Roanoke MSA, VA	S	13.95 MW	12.84 AW	29020 AAW	VABLS	10//99-12//99
	Washington	S	19.74 MW	19.22 AW	39990 AAW	WABLS	10//99-12//99
	Bellingham MSA, WA	S	15.55 MW	14.54 AW	32330 AAW	WABLS	10//99-12//99
	Bremerton PMSA, WA	S	17.78 MW	17.71 AW	36980 AAW	WABLS	10//99-12//99
	Olympia PMSA, WA	S	15.44 MW	15.03 AW	32120 AAW	WABLS	10//99-12//99
	Richland-Kennewick-Pasco MSA, WA	S	11.69 MW	11.31 AW	24320 AAW	WABLS	10//99-12//99
	Seattle-Bellevue-Everett PMSA, WA	S	20.88 MW	22.00 AW	43430 AAW	WABLS	10//99-12//99
	Spokane MSA, WA	S	17.09 MW	15.62 AW	35550 AAW	WABLS	10//99-12//99
	Tacoma PMSA, WA	S	18.83 MW	17.85 AW	39170 AAW	WABLS	10//99-12//99
	Yakima MSA, WA	S	15.23 MW	15.05 AW	31680 AAW	WABLS	10//99-12//99

AAW	Average annual wage	AOH	Average offered, high	ASH	Average starting, high
AE	Average entry wage	AOL	Average offered, low	ASL	Average starting, low
AEX	Average experienced wage	APH	Average pay, high range	AW	Average wage paid
AO	Average offered	APL	Average pay, low range	FQ	First quartile wage

H	Hourly	M	Monthly
HI	Highest wage paid	MTC	Median total compensation
HR	High end range	MW	Median wage paid
LR	Low end range	SQ	Second quartile wage

S	Special: hourly and annual
TQ	Third quartile wage
W	Weekly
Y	Yearly

Occupation/Type/Industry	Location	Per	Low	Mid	High	Source	Date
Carpenter	West Virginia	S	12.95 MW	14.93 AW	31040 AAW	WVBLS	10//99-12//99
	Charleston MSA, WV	S	14.51 MW	13.44 AW	30170 AAW	WVBLS	10//99-12//99
	Huntington-Ashland MSA, WV-KY-OH	S	12.08 MW	10.92 AW	25120 AAW	WVBLS	10//99-12//99
	Parkersburg-Marietta MSA, WV-OH	S	12.88 MW	12.18 AW	26790 AAW	WVBLS	10//99-12//99
	Wheeling MSA, WV-OH	S	11.74 MW	11.65 AW	24410 AAW	WVBLS	10//99-12//99
	Wisconsin	S	15.75 MW	16.79 AW	34920 AAW	WIBLS	10//99-12//99
	Appleton-Oshkosh-Neenah MSA, WI	S	15.28 MW	15.21 AW	31780 AAW	WIBLS	10//99-12//99
	Eau Claire MSA, WI	S	13.21 MW	12.77 AW	27480 AAW	WIBLS	10//99-12//99
	Green Bay MSA, WI	S	15.76 MW	15.15 AW	32790 AAW	WIBLS	10//99-12//99
	Janesville-Beloit MSA, WI	S	15.91 MW	16.20 AW	33090 AAW	WIBLS	10//99-12//99
	Kenosha PMSA, WI	S	17.75 MW	16.00 AW	36910 AAW	WIBLS	10//99-12//99
	La Crosse MSA, WI-MN	S	15.78 MW	15.17 AW	32830 AAW	WIBLS	10//99-12//99
	Madison MSA, WI	S	14.72 MW	14.13 AW	30610 AAW	WIBLS	10//99-12//99
	Milwaukee-Waukesha PMSA, WI	S	21.87 MW	22.95 AW	45500 AAW	WIBLS	10//99-12//99
	Racine PMSA, WI	S	16.89 MW	17.91 AW	35130 AAW	WIBLS	10//99-12//99
	Sheboygan MSA, WI	S	15.47 MW	14.83 AW	32170 AAW	WIBLS	10//99-12//99
	Wausau MSA, WI	S	12.51 MW	12.63 AW	26020 AAW	WIBLS	10//99-12//99
	Wyoming	S	14.89 MW	15.24 AW	31690 AAW	WYBLS	10//99-12//99
	Casper MSA, WY	S	13.65 MW	12.35 AW	28400 AAW	WYBLS	10//99-12//99
	Cheyenne MSA, WY	S	15.62 MW	15.24 AW	32480 AAW	WYBLS	10//99-12//99
	Puerto Rico	S	7.04 MW	7.06 AW	14680 AAW	PRBLS	10//99-12//99
	Aguadilla MSA, PR	S	5.78 MW	5.97 AW	12030 AAW	PRBLS	10//99-12//99
	Arecibo PMSA, PR	S	6.54 MW	6.60 AW	13600 AAW	PRBLS	10//99-12//99
	Caguas PMSA, PR	S	6.63 MW	6.53 AW	13790 AAW	PRBLS	10//99-12//99
	Mayaguez MSA, PR	S	6.64 MW	6.52 AW	13800 AAW	PRBLS	10//99-12//99
	Ponce MSA, PR	S	6.72 MW	6.83 AW	13990 AAW	PRBLS	10//99-12//99
	San Juan-Bayamon PMSA, PR	S	7.40 MW	7.42 AW	15390 AAW	PRBLS	10//99-12//99
	Virgin Islands	S	13.36 MW	13.84 AW	28780 AAW	VIBLS	10//99-12//99
	Guam	S	12.16 MW	12.20 AW	25370 AAW	GUBLS	10//99-12//99
General Maintenance	Los Angeles County, CA	Y		36093 AW		LABJ	1999
Nonunion, Construction	Central	H		15.04 AW		ENR3	2000
Nonunion, Construction	Middle Atlantic	H		15.54 AW		ENR3	2000
Nonunion, Construction	New England	H		16.99 AW		ENR3	2000
Nonunion, Construction	Southeast	H		14.48 AW		ENR3	2000
Nonunion, Construction	West	H		17.51 AW		ENR3	2000
Carpet Installer	Alabama	S	11.82 MW	11.71 AW	24360 AAW	ALBLS	10//99-12//99
	Alaska	S	17.73 MW	15.25 AW	31720 AAW	AKBLS	10//99-12//99
	Arizona	S	11.61 MW	12.57 AW	26150 AAW	AZBLS	10//99-12//99
	Arkansas	S	8.94 MW	9.90 AW	20590 AAW	ARBLS	10//99-12//99
	California	S	13.67 MW	15.08 AW	31360 AAW	CABLS	10//99-12//99
	Connecticut	S	16.69 MW	16.53 AW	34380 AAW	CTBLS	10//99-12//99
	Delaware	S	14.13 MW	13.86 AW	28820 AAW	DEBLS	10//99-12//99
	Florida	S	12.12 MW	12.92 AW	26880 AAW	FLBLS	10//99-12//99
	Georgia	S	11.41 MW	12.48 AW	25960 AAW	GABLS	10//99-12//99
	Hawaii	S	13.07 MW	14.53 AW	30210 AAW	HIBLS	10//99-12//99
	Idaho	S	12.36 MW	12.71 AW	26440 AAW	IDBLS	10//99-12//99
	Illinois	S	18.7 MW	24.88 AW	51750 AAW	ILBLS	10//99-12//99
	Indiana	S	11.24 MW	12.58 AW	26170 AAW	INBLS	10//99-12//99
	Iowa	S	11.87 MW	12.09 AW	25150 AAW	IABLS	10//99-12//99
	Kansas	S	16.4 MW	16.67 AW	34680 AAW	KSBLS	10//99-12//99
	Kentucky	S	11.58 MW	11.81 AW	24560 AAW	KYBLS	10//99-12//99
	Louisiana	S	11.1 MW	11.65 AW	24240 AAW	LABLS	10//99-12//99
	Maine	S	11.63 MW	12.19 AW	25350 AAW	MEBLS	10//99-12//99
	Maryland	S	14.38 MW	15.27 AW	31750 AAW	MDBLS	10//99-12//99
	Massachusetts	S	17.51 MW	17.19 AW	35750 AAW	MABLS	10//99-12//99
	Michigan	S	11.14 MW	12.13 AW	25240 AAW	MIBLS	10//99-12//99
	Minnesota	S	21.67 MW	20.34 AW	42300 AAW	MNBLS	10//99-12//99
	Mississippi	S	9.19 MW	9.80 AW	20390 AAW	MSBLS	10//99-12//99
	Missouri	S	21.41 MW	18.64 AW	38760 AAW	MOBLS	10//99-12//99
	Nebraska	S	11.23 MW	12.13 AW	25240 AAW	NEBLS	10//99-12//99
	Nevada	S	25.2 MW	24.86 AW	51710 AAW	NVBLS	10//99-12//99
	New Hampshire	S	12.47 MW	13.61 AW	28300 AAW	NHBLS	10//99-12//99
	New Jersey	S	15.59 MW	18.00 AW	37430 AAW	NJBLS	10//99-12//99
	New Mexico	S	11.62 MW	12.10 AW	25170 AAW	NMBLS	10//99-12//99
	New York	S	15.06 MW	17.56 AW	36520 AAW	NYBLS	10//99-12//99
	North Carolina	S	9.17 MW	10.31 AW	21450 AAW	NCBLS	10//99-12//99
	North Dakota	S	9.23 MW	10.37 AW	21570 AAW	NDBLS	10//99-12//99
	Ohio	S	12.72 MW	14.37 AW	29880 AAW	OHBLS	10//99-12//99

AAW	Average annual wage	**AOH**	Average offered, high	**ASH**	Average starting, high	**H**	Hourly	**M**	Monthly	**S** Special: hourly and annual
AE	Average entry wage	**AOL**	Average offered, low	**ASL**	Average starting, low	**HI**	Highest wage paid	**MTC**	Median total compensation	**TQ** Third quartile wage
AEX	Average experienced wage	**APH**	Average pay, high range	**AW**	Average wage paid	**HR**	High end range	**MW**	Median wage paid	**W** Weekly
AO	Average offered	**APL**	Average pay, low range	**FQ**	First quartile wage	**LR**	Low end range	**SQ**	Second quartile wage	**Y** Yearly

Occupation/Type/Industry	Location	Per	Low	Mid	High	Source	Date
Carpet Installer	Oklahoma	S	10.41 MW	11.43 AW	23780 AAW	OKBLS	10//99-12//99
	Oregon	S	13.28 MW	15.11 AW	31440 AAW	ORBLS	10//99-12//99
	Pennsylvania	S	11.96 MW	14.62 AW	30410 AAW	PABLS	10//99-12//99
	South Carolina	S	9.71 MW	10.02 AW	20850 AAW	SCBLS	10//99-12//99
	Tennessee	S	11.47 MW	11.69 AW	24320 AAW	TNBLS	10//99-12//99
	Texas	S	11.24 MW	11.61 AW	24160 AAW	TXBLS	10//99-12//99
	Vermont	S	11.19 MW	11.04 AW	22970 AAW	VTBLS	10//99-12//99
	Virginia	S	12.43 MW	13.58 AW	28250 AAW	VABLS	10//99-12//99
	Washington	S	16.7 MW	17.69 AW	36790 AAW	WABLS	10//99-12//99
	West Virginia	S	7.39 MW	9.13 AW	18990 AAW	WVBLS	10//99-12//99
	Wisconsin	S	14.89 MW	15.57 AW	32390 AAW	WIBLS	10//99-12//99
	Wyoming	S	11.91 MW	12.28 AW	25540 AAW	WYBLS	10//99-12//99
Cartographer and Photogrammetrist	Alabama	S	16.96 MW	16.70 AW	34740 AAW	ALBLS	10//99-12//99
	Alaska	S	21.22 MW	21.36 AW	44440 AAW	AKBLS	10//99-12//99
	Arizona	S	20.33 MW	19.90 AW	41400 AAW	AZBLS	10//99-12//99
	Arkansas	S	12.2 MW	13.40 AW	27870 AAW	ARBLS	10//99-12//99
	California	S	21.27 MW	23.12 AW	48080 AAW	CABLS	10//99-12//99
	Connecticut	S	23.34 MW	22.27 AW	46330 AAW	CTBLS	10//99-12//99
	Florida	S	18.26 MW	18.20 AW	37850 AAW	FLBLS	10//99-12//99
	Georgia	S	16.81 MW	18.45 AW	38370 AAW	GABLS	10//99-12//99
	Idaho	S	14.43 MW	14.46 AW	30070 AAW	IDBLS	10//99-12//99
	Illinois	S	35.55 MW	30.05 AW	62500 AAW	ILBLS	10//99-12//99
	Indiana	S	12.37 MW	13.98 AW	29080 AAW	INBLS	10//99-12//99
	Kansas	S	10.71 MW	13.58 AW	28240 AAW	KSBLS	10//99-12//99
	Kentucky	S	12.98 MW	14.02 AW	29160 AAW	KYBLS	10//99-12//99
	Louisiana	S	16.41 MW	17.39 AW	36170 AAW	LABLS	10//99-12//99
	Maine	S	13.69 MW	16.03 AW	33340 AAW	MEBLS	10//99-12//99
	Massachusetts	S	25.02 MW	24.88 AW	51760 AAW	MABLS	10//99-12//99
	Minnesota	S	19.14 MW	19.27 AW	40070 AAW	MNBLS	10//99-12//99
	Missouri	S	18.55 MW	19.44 AW	40440 AAW	MOBLS	10//99-12//99
	Montana	S	15.4 MW	16.33 AW	33970 AAW	MTBLS	10//99-12//99
	Nebraska	S	17.26 MW	18.25 AW	37950 AAW	NEBLS	10//99-12//99
	New Mexico	S	17.95 MW	17.62 AW	36650 AAW	NMBLS	10//99-12//99
	New York	S	20.33 MW	21.47 AW	44660 AAW	NYBLS	10//99-12//99
	North Carolina	S	22.69 MW	22.89 AW	47600 AAW	NCBLS	10//99-12//99
	Ohio	S	21.93 MW	21.25 AW	44210 AAW	OHBLS	10//99-12//99
	Oklahoma	S	11.23 MW	16.04 AW	33370 AAW	OKBLS	10//99-12//99
	Oregon	S	20.04 MW	21.60 AW	44930 AAW	ORBLS	10//99-12//99
	Pennsylvania	S	15.26 MW	16.45 AW	34220 AAW	PABLS	10//99-12//99
	South Carolina	S	21.27 MW	22.10 AW	45970 AAW	SCBLS	10//99-12//99
	Texas	S	12.38 MW	13.64 AW	28370 AAW	TXBLS	10//99-12//99
	Utah	S	18.56 MW	19.72 AW	41030 AAW	UTBLS	10//99-12//99
	Virginia	S	25.89 MW	25.60 AW	53240 AAW	VABLS	10//99-12//99
	Washington	S	22.72 MW	21.63 AW	45000 AAW	WABLS	10//99-12//99
	Wisconsin	S	15.05 MW	15.62 AW	32500 AAW	WIBLS	10//99-12//99
Cashier	Alabama	S	6.19 MW	6.48 AW	13470 AAW	ALBLS	10//99-12//99
	Anniston MSA, AL	S	6.47 MW	6.22 AW	13460 AAW	ALBLS	10//99-12//99
	Auburn-Opelika MSA, AL	S	6.33 MW	6.16 AW	13170 AAW	ALBLS	10//99-12//99
	Birmingham MSA, AL	S	6.59 MW	6.28 AW	13710 AAW	ALBLS	10//99-12//99
	Decatur MSA, AL	S	6.53 MW	6.24 AW	13580 AAW	ALBLS	10//99-12//99
	Dothan MSA, AL	S	6.38 MW	6.17 AW	13260 AAW	ALBLS	10//99-12//99
	Florence MSA, AL	S	6.42 MW	6.16 AW	13350 AAW	ALBLS	10//99-12//99
	Gadsden MSA, AL	S	6.43 MW	6.18 AW	13370 AAW	ALBLS	10//99-12//99
	Huntsville MSA, AL	S	6.52 MW	6.18 AW	13570 AAW	ALBLS	10//99-12//99
	Mobile MSA, AL	S	6.53 MW	6.23 AW	13580 AAW	ALBLS	10//99-12//99
	Montgomery MSA, AL	S	6.45 MW	6.17 AW	13410 AAW	ALBLS	10//99-12//99
	Tuscaloosa MSA, AL	S	6.34 MW	6.11 AW	13190 AAW	ALBLS	10//99-12//99
	Alaska	S	8.21 MW	9.11 AW	18950 AAW	AKBLS	10//99-12//99
	Anchorage MSA, AK	S	8.70 MW	8.03 AW	18090 AAW	AKBLS	10//99-12//99
	Arizona	S	7.29 MW	7.92 AW	16480 AAW	AZBLS	10//99-12//99
	Flagstaff MSA, AZ-UT	S	7.08 MW	6.76 AW	14720 AAW	AZBLS	10//99-12//99
	Phoenix-Mesa MSA, AZ	S	7.99 MW	7.37 AW	16620 AAW	AZBLS	10//99-12//99
	Tucson MSA, AZ	S	8.06 MW	7.45 AW	16760 AAW	AZBLS	10//99-12//99
	Yuma MSA, AZ	S	7.21 MW	6.59 AW	15010 AAW	AZBLS	10//99-12//99
	Arkansas	S	6.32 MW	6.67 AW	13880 AAW	ARBLS	10//99-12//99
	Fayetteville-Springdale-Rogers MSA, AR	S	7.00 MW	6.80 AW	14550 AAW	ARBLS	10//99-12//99
	Fort Smith MSA, AR-OK	S	6.46 MW	6.23 AW	13440 AAW	ARBLS	10//99-12//99
	Jonesboro MSA, AR	S	6.87 MW	6.49 AW	14290 AAW	ARBLS	10//99-12//99

AAW Average annual wage	**AOH** Average offered, high	**ASH** Average starting, high	**H** Hourly	**M** Monthly	**S** Special: hourly and annual
AE Average entry wage	**AOL** Average offered, low	**ASL** Average starting, low	**HI** Highest wage paid	**MTC** Median total compensation	**TQ** Third quartile wage
AEX Average experienced wage	**APH** Average pay, high range	**AW** Average wage paid	**HR** High end range	**MW** Median wage paid	**W** Weekly
AO Average offered	**APL** Average pay, low range	**FQ** First quartile wage	**LR** Low end range	**SQ** Second quartile wage	**Y** Yearly

Cashier

Occupation/Type/Industry	Location	Per	Low	Mid	High	Source	Date
Cashier	Little Rock-North Little Rock MSA, AR	S	7.03 MW	6.68 AW	14630 AAW	ARBLS	10//99-12//99
	Pine Bluff MSA, AR	S	6.28 MW	6.10 AW	13060 AAW	ARBLS	10//99-12//99
	California	S	7.3 MW	8.76 AW	18230 AAW	CABLS	10//99-12//99
	Bakersfield MSA, CA	S	8.05 MW	6.66 AW	16740 AAW	CABLS	10//99-12//99
	Chico-Paradise MSA, CA	S	8.42 MW	6.90 AW	17520 AAW	CABLS	10//99-12//99
	Fresno MSA, CA	S	7.84 MW	6.71 AW	16300 AAW	CABLS	10//99-12//99
	Los Angeles-Long Beach PMSA, CA	S	8.73 MW	7.16 AW	18150 AAW	CABLS	10//99-12//99
	Merced MSA, CA	S	7.63 MW	6.73 AW	15860 AAW	CABLS	10//99-12//99
	Modesto MSA, CA	S	8.21 MW	7.22 AW	17070 AAW	CABLS	10//99-12//99
	Oakland PMSA, CA	S	9.27 MW	7.77 AW	19280 AAW	CABLS	10//99-12//99
	Orange County PMSA, CA	S	8.80 MW	7.28 AW	18300 AAW	CABLS	10//99-12//99
	Redding MSA, CA	S	8.46 MW	7.20 AW	17600 AAW	CABLS	10//99-12//99
	Riverside-San Bernardino PMSA, CA	S	8.58 MW	6.81 AW	17860 AAW	CABLS	10//99-12//99
	Sacramento PMSA, CA	S	9.27 MW	7.59 AW	19280 AAW	CABLS	10//99-12//99
	Salinas MSA, CA	S	8.53 MW	7.49 AW	17740 AAW	CABLS	10//99-12//99
	San Diego MSA, CA	S	9.08 MW	7.41 AW	18890 AAW	CABLS	10//99-12//99
	San Francisco PMSA, CA	S	9.28 MW	8.11 AW	19290 AAW	CABLS	10//99-12//99
	San Jose PMSA, CA	S	8.89 MW	7.64 AW	18500 AAW	CABLS	10//99-12//99
	San Luis Obispo-Atascadero-Paso Robles MSA, CA	S	8.89 MW	7.22 AW	18480 AAW	CABLS	10//99-12//99
	Santa Barbara-Santa Maria-Lompoc MSA, CA	S	8.77 MW	7.29 AW	18230 AAW	CABLS	10//99-12//99
	Santa Cruz-Watsonville PMSA, CA	S	8.58 MW	7.57 AW	17850 AAW	CABLS	10//99-12//99
	Santa Rosa PMSA, CA	S	9.03 MW	7.82 AW	18770 AAW	CABLS	10//99-12//99
	Stockton-Lodi MSA, CA	S	7.90 MW	6.95 AW	16440 AAW	CABLS	10//99-12//99
	Vallejo-Fairfield-Napa PMSA, CA	S	8.37 MW	6.96 AW	17410 AAW	CABLS	10//99-12//99
	Ventura PMSA, CA	S	9.00 MW	7.34 AW	18710 AAW	CABLS	10//99-12//99
	Visalia-Tulare-Porterville MSA, CA	S	7.83 MW	6.95 AW	16290 AAW	CABLS	10//99-12//99
	Yolo PMSA, CA	S	10.12 MW	8.12 AW	21060 AAW	CABLS	10//99-12//99
	Yuba City MSA, CA	S	7.82 MW	6.66 AW	16260 AAW	CABLS	10//99-12//99
	Colorado	S	7.75 MW	8.54 AW	17760 AAW	COBLS	10//99-12//99
	Boulder-Longmont PMSA, CO	S	8.76 MW	8.05 AW	18220 AAW	COBLS	10//99-12//99
	Colorado Springs MSA, CO	S	8.38 MW	7.58 AW	17420 AAW	COBLS	10//99-12//99
	Denver PMSA, CO	S	8.76 MW	7.92 AW	18230 AAW	COBLS	10//99-12//99
	Fort Collins-Loveland MSA, CO	S	8.64 MW	7.73 AW	17970 AAW	COBLS	10//99-12//99
	Grand Junction MSA, CO	S	8.06 MW	7.42 AW	16770 AAW	COBLS	10//99-12//99
	Greeley PMSA, CO	S	8.73 MW	7.56 AW	18150 AAW	COBLS	10//99-12//99
	Pueblo MSA, CO	S	7.93 MW	6.66 AW	16490 AAW	COBLS	10//99-12//99
	Connecticut	S	7.12 MW	7.74 AW	16110 AAW	CTBLS	10//99-12//99
	Bridgeport PMSA, CT	S	7.52 MW	6.92 AW	15650 AAW	CTBLS	10//99-12//99
	Danbury PMSA, CT	S	8.09 MW	7.43 AW	16840 AAW	CTBLS	10//99-12//99
	Hartford MSA, CT	S	7.60 MW	6.92 AW	15800 AAW	CTBLS	10//99-12//99
	New Haven-Meriden PMSA, CT	S	7.74 MW	7.16 AW	16100 AAW	CTBLS	10//99-12//99
	New London-Norwich MSA, CT-RI	S	7.41 MW	6.89 AW	15410 AAW	CTBLS	10//99-12//99
	Stamford-Norwalk PMSA, CT	S	8.41 MW	7.79 AW	17490 AAW	CTBLS	10//99-12//99
	Waterbury PMSA, CT	S	7.48 MW	6.69 AW	15560 AAW	CTBLS	10//99-12//99
	Delaware	S	6.74 MW	7.36 AW	15310 AAW	DEBLS	10//99-12//99
	Dover MSA, DE	S	6.84 MW	6.25 AW	14230 AAW	DEBLS	10//99-12//99
	Wilmington-Newark PMSA, DE-MD	S	7.47 MW	6.81 AW	15550 AAW	DEBLS	10//99-12//99
	District of Columbia	S	7.59 MW	8.59 AW	17870 AAW	DCBLS	10//99-12//99
	Washington PMSA, DC-MD-VA-WV	S	8.20 MW	7.26 AW	17050 AAW	DCBLS	10//99-12//99
	Florida	S	6.8 MW	7.11 AW	14790 AAW	FLBLS	10//99-12//99
	Daytona Beach MSA, FL	S	7.02 MW	6.92 AW	14610 AAW	FLBLS	10//99-12//99
	Fort Lauderdale PMSA, FL	S	7.06 MW	6.74 AW	14680 AAW	FLBLS	10//99-12//99
	Fort Myers-Cape Coral MSA, FL	S	7.18 MW	7.02 AW	14940 AAW	FLBLS	10//99-12//99
	Fort Pierce-Port St. Lucie MSA, FL	S	7.04 MW	6.68 AW	14650 AAW	FLBLS	10//99-12//99
	Fort Walton Beach MSA, FL	S	6.74 MW	6.54 AW	14020 AAW	FLBLS	10//99-12//99
	Gainesville MSA, FL	S	6.82 MW	6.46 AW	14190 AAW	FLBLS	10//99-12//99
	Jacksonville MSA, FL	S	7.03 MW	6.69 AW	14620 AAW	FLBLS	10//99-12//99

AAW	Average annual wage	AOH	Average offered, high	ASH	Average starting, high
AE	Average entry wage	AOL	Average offered, low	ASL	Average starting, low
AEX	Average experienced wage	APH	Average pay, high range	AW	Average wage paid
AO	Average offered	APL	Average pay, low range	FQ	First quartile wage

H	Hourly	M	Monthly
HI	Highest wage paid	MTC	Median total compensation
HR	High end range	MW	Median wage paid
LR	Low end range	SQ	Second quartile wage

S	Special: hourly and annual
TQ	Third quartile wage
W	Weekly
Y	Yearly

Occupation/Type/Industry	Location	Per	Low	Mid	High	Source	Date
Cashier	Lakeland-Winter Haven MSA, FL	s	7.06 MW	6.89 AW	14670 AAW	FLBLS	10//99-12//99
	Melbourne-Titusville-Palm Bay MSA, FL	s	6.93 MW	6.57 AW	14420 AAW	FLBLS	10//99-12//99
	Miami PMSA, FL	s	7.23 MW	6.83 AW	15040 AAW	FLBLS	10//99-12//99
	Naples MSA, FL	s	7.25 MW	6.92 AW	15080 AAW	FLBLS	10//99-12//99
	Ocala MSA, FL	s	7.09 MW	6.76 AW	14750 AAW	FLBLS	10//99-12//99
	Orlando MSA, FL	s	7.18 MW	6.86 AW	14930 AAW	FLBLS	10//99-12//99
	Panama City MSA, FL	s	7.20 MW	7.02 AW	14980 AAW	FLBLS	10//99-12//99
	Pensacola MSA, FL	s	6.85 MW	6.57 AW	14250 AAW	FLBLS	10//99-12//99
	Punta Gorda MSA, FL	s	7.29 MW	7.13 AW	15150 AAW	FLBLS	10//99-12//99
	Sarasota-Bradenton MSA, FL	s	7.12 MW	6.95 AW	14820 AAW	FLBLS	10//99-12//99
	Tallahassee MSA, FL	s	7.01 MW	6.81 AW	14590 AAW	FLBLS	10//99-12//99
	Tampa-St. Petersburg-Clearwater MSA, FL	s	7.13 MW	6.84 AW	14820 AAW	FLBLS	10//99-12//99
	West Palm Beach-Boca Raton MSA, FL	s	7.31 MW	6.89 AW	15210 AAW	FLBLS	10//99-12//99
	Georgia	s	6.46 MW	6.90 AW	14340 AAW	GABLS	10//99-12//99
	Albany MSA, GA	s	6.67 MW	6.46 AW	13870 AAW	GABLS	10//99-12//99
	Athens MSA, GA	s	6.86 MW	6.35 AW	14260 AAW	GABLS	10//99-12//99
	Atlanta MSA, GA	s	7.24 MW	6.94 AW	15060 AAW	GABLS	10//99-12//99
	Augusta-Aiken MSA, GA-SC	s	6.46 MW	6.18 AW	13430 AAW	GABLS	10//99-12//99
	Columbus MSA, GA-AL	s	6.54 MW	6.24 AW	13610 AAW	GABLS	10//99-12//99
	Macon MSA, GA	s	6.51 MW	6.17 AW	13530 AAW	GABLS	10//99-12//99
	Savannah MSA, GA	s	6.60 MW	6.22 AW	13720 AAW	GABLS	10//99-12//99
	Hawaii	s	8.03 MW	8.85 AW	18410 AAW	HIBLS	10//99-12//99
	Honolulu MSA, HI	s	9.10 MW	8.15 AW	18920 AAW	HIBLS	10//99-12//99
	Idaho	s	6.54 MW	7.19 AW	14960 AAW	IDBLS	10//99-12//99
	Boise City MSA, ID	s	7.58 MW	6.89 AW	15760 AAW	IDBLS	10//99-12//99
	Pocatello MSA, ID	s	6.85 MW	6.31 AW	14250 AAW	IDBLS	10//99-12//99
	Illinois	s	6.82 MW	7.37 AW	15320 AAW	ILBLS	10//99-12//99
	Bloomington-Normal MSA, IL	s	6.98 MW	6.69 AW	14510 AAW	ILBLS	10//99-12//99
	Champaign-Urbana MSA, IL	s	7.11 MW	6.75 AW	14790 AAW	ILBLS	10//99-12//99
	Chicago PMSA, IL	s	7.62 MW	7.12 AW	15860 AAW	ILBLS	10//99-12//99
	Decatur MSA, IL	s	7.20 MW	6.88 AW	14970 AAW	ILBLS	10//99-12//99
	Kankakee PMSA, IL	s	6.77 MW	6.35 AW	14080 AAW	ILBLS	10//99-12//99
	Peoria-Pekin MSA, IL	s	6.81 MW	6.41 AW	14160 AAW	ILBLS	10//99-12//99
	Rockford MSA, IL	s	7.43 MW	7.00 AW	15450 AAW	ILBLS	10//99-12//99
	Springfield MSA, IL	s	7.15 MW	6.73 AW	14880 AAW	ILBLS	10//99-12//99
	Indiana	s	6.55 MW	6.88 AW	14310 AAW	INBLS	10//99-12//99
	Bloomington MSA, IN	s	7.14 MW	6.72 AW	14840 AAW	INBLS	10//99-12//99
	Elkhart-Goshen MSA, IN	s	7.11 MW	6.89 AW	14790 AAW	INBLS	10//99-12//99
	Evansville-Henderson MSA, IN-KY	s	7.02 MW	6.32 AW	14590 AAW	INBLS	10//99-12//99
	Fort Wayne MSA, IN	s	6.92 MW	6.62 AW	14390 AAW	INBLS	10//99-12//99
	Gary PMSA, IN	s	6.50 MW	6.21 AW	13520 AAW	INBLS	10//99-12//99
	Indianapolis MSA, IN	s	7.28 MW	7.03 AW	15150 AAW	INBLS	10//99-12//99
	Kokomo MSA, IN	s	6.64 MW	6.32 AW	13810 AAW	INBLS	10//99-12//99
	Lafayette MSA, IN	s	6.59 MW	6.34 AW	13700 AAW	INBLS	10//99-12//99
	Muncie MSA, IN	s	6.42 MW	6.24 AW	13360 AAW	INBLS	10//99-12//99
	South Bend MSA, IN	s	7.06 MW	6.78 AW	14690 AAW	INBLS	10//99-12//99
	Terre Haute MSA, IN	s	6.80 MW	6.40 AW	14130 AAW	INBLS	10//99-12//99
	Iowa	s	6.32 MW	6.73 AW	14000 AAW	IABLS	10//99-12//99
	Cedar Rapids MSA, IA	s	7.02 MW	6.69 AW	14610 AAW	IABLS	10//99-12//99
	Davenport-Moline-Rock Island MSA, IA-IL	s	6.86 MW	6.34 AW	14280 AAW	IABLS	10//99-12//99
	Des Moines MSA, IA	s	7.34 MW	7.08 AW	15260 AAW	IABLS	10//99-12//99
	Dubuque MSA, IA	s	6.52 MW	6.25 AW	13570 AAW	IABLS	10//99-12//99
	Iowa City MSA, IA	s	7.29 MW	6.94 AW	15160 AAW	IABLS	10//99-12//99
	Sioux City MSA, IA-NE	s	6.69 MW	6.24 AW	13920 AAW	IABLS	10//99-12//99
	Waterloo-Cedar Falls MSA, IA	s	6.80 MW	6.31 AW	14140 AAW	IABLS	10//99-12//99
	Kansas	s	6.38 MW	6.76 AW	14060 AAW	KSBLS	10//99-12//99
	Lawrence MSA, KS	s	6.98 MW	6.46 AW	14510 AAW	KSBLS	10//99-12//99
	Topeka MSA, KS	s	6.95 MW	6.48 AW	14460 AAW	KSBLS	10//99-12//99
	Wichita MSA, KS	s	7.34 MW	6.93 AW	15260 AAW	KSBLS	10//99-12//99
	Kentucky	s	6.43 MW	6.90 AW	14350 AAW	KYBLS	10//99-12//99
	Lexington MSA, KY	s	7.67 MW	7.02 AW	15940 AAW	KYBLS	10//99-12//99
	Louisville MSA, KY-IN	s	7.11 MW	6.86 AW	14790 AAW	KYBLS	10//99-12//99
	Owensboro MSA, KY	s	6.54 MW	6.16 AW	13610 AAW	KYBLS	10//99-12//99
	Louisiana	s	6.16 MW	6.43 AW	13380 AAW	LABLS	10//99-12//99
	Alexandria MSA, LA	s	6.69 MW	6.34 AW	13920 AAW	LABLS	10//99-12//99
	Baton Rouge MSA, LA	s	6.48 MW	6.15 AW	13490 AAW	LABLS	10//99-12//99

Occupation/Type/Industry	Location	Per	Low	Mid	High	Source	Date
Cashier	Houma MSA, LA	S	6.32 MW	6.12 AW	13150 AAW	LABLS	10//99-12//99
	Lafayette MSA, LA	S	6.21 MW	6.11 AW	12930 AAW	LABLS	10//99-12//99
	Lake Charles MSA, LA	S	6.44 MW	6.21 AW	13400 AAW	LABLS	10//99-12//99
	Monroe MSA, LA	S	6.50 MW	6.19 AW	13510 AAW	LABLS	10//99-12//99
	New Orleans MSA, LA	S	6.52 MW	6.17 AW	13550 AAW	LABLS	10//99-12//99
	Shreveport-Bossier City MSA, LA	S	6.67 MW	6.21 AW	13880 AAW	LABLS	10//99-12//99
	Maine	S	6.83 MW	7.20 AW	14970 AAW	MEBLS	10//99-12//99
	Bangor MSA, ME	S	6.87 MW	6.64 AW	14300 AAW	MEBLS	10//99-12//99
	Lewiston-Auburn MSA, ME	S	6.89 MW	6.52 AW	14330 AAW	MEBLS	10//99-12//99
	Portland MSA, ME	S	7.56 MW	7.49 AW	15720 AAW	MEBLS	10//99-12//99
	Maryland	S	7.02 MW	8.10 AW	16850 AAW	MDBLS	10//99-12//99
	Baltimore PMSA, MD	S	7.94 MW	7.05 AW	16520 AAW	MDBLS	10//99-12//99
	Cumberland MSA, MD-WV	S	6.47 MW	6.19 AW	13460 AAW	MDBLS	10//99-12//99
	Hagerstown PMSA, MD	S	6.38 MW	6.15 AW	13270 AAW	MDBLS	10//99-12//99
	Massachusetts	S	7.06 MW	7.46 AW	15510 AAW	MABLS	10//99-12//99
	Barnstable-Yarmouth MSA, MA	S	7.45 MW	7.19 AW	15490 AAW	MABLS	10//99-12//99
	Boston PMSA, MA-NH	S	7.58 MW	7.22 AW	15760 AAW	MABLS	10//99-12//99
	Brockton PMSA, MA	S	7.37 MW	7.01 AW	15330 AAW	MABLS	10//99-12//99
	Fitchburg-Leominster PMSA, MA	S	7.24 MW	6.73 AW	15060 AAW	MABLS	10//99-12//99
	Lawrence PMSA, MA-NH	S	7.34 MW	7.02 AW	15260 AAW	MABLS	10//99-12//99
	Lowell PMSA, MA-NH	S	7.20 MW	6.76 AW	14970 AAW	MABLS	10//99-12//99
	New Bedford PMSA, MA	S	7.32 MW	7.03 AW	15220 AAW	MABLS	10//99-12//99
	Pittsfield MSA, MA	S	7.38 MW	7.03 AW	15340 AAW	MABLS	10//99-12//99
	Springfield MSA, MA	S	7.20 MW	6.74 AW	14980 AAW	MABLS	10//99-12//99
	Worcester PMSA, MA-CT	S	7.16 MW	6.74 AW	14890 AAW	MABLS	10//99-12//99
	Michigan	S	6.9 MW	7.47 AW	15540 AAW	MIBLS	10//99-12//99
	Ann Arbor PMSA, MI	S	8.06 MW	7.68 AW	16770 AAW	MIBLS	10//99-12//99
	Benton Harbor MSA, MI	S	7.55 MW	7.07 AW	15710 AAW	MIBLS	10//99-12//99
	Detroit PMSA, MI	S	7.75 MW	7.22 AW	16120 AAW	MIBLS	10//99-12//99
	Flint PMSA, MI	S	7.63 MW	6.93 AW	15870 AAW	MIBLS	10//99-12//99
	Grand Rapids-Muskegon-Holland MSA, MI	S	7.49 MW	6.99 AW	15580 AAW	MIBLS	10//99-12//99
	Jackson MSA, MI	S	7.56 MW	6.73 AW	15730 AAW	MIBLS	10//99-12//99
	Kalamazoo-Battle Creek MSA, MI	S	7.36 MW	6.97 AW	15300 AAW	MIBLS	10//99-12//99
	Lansing-East Lansing MSA, MI	S	7.16 MW	6.51 AW	14900 AAW	MIBLS	10//99-12//99
	Saginaw-Bay City-Midland MSA, MI	S	6.96 MW	6.26 AW	14480 AAW	MIBLS	10//99-12//99
	Minnesota	S	7.11 MW	7.43 AW	15450 AAW	MNBLS	10//99-12//99
	Duluth-Superior MSA, MN-WI	S	6.98 MW	6.43 AW	14530 AAW	MNBLS	10//99-12//99
	Minneapolis-St. Paul MSA, MN-WI	S	7.85 MW	7.63 AW	16320 AAW	MNBLS	10//99-12//99
	Rochester MSA, MN	S	7.18 MW	6.99 AW	14930 AAW	MNBLS	10//99-12//99
	St. Cloud MSA, MN	S	6.70 MW	6.44 AW	13930 AAW	MNBLS	10//99-12//99
	Mississippi	S	6.23 MW	6.59 AW	13700 AAW	MSBLS	10//99-12//99
	Biloxi-Gulfport-Pascagoula MSA, MS	S	6.68 MW	6.27 AW	13890 AAW	MSBLS	10//99-12//99
	Hattiesburg MSA, MS	S	6.65 MW	6.31 AW	13830 AAW	MSBLS	10//99-12//99
	Jackson MSA, MS	S	6.82 MW	6.39 AW	14190 AAW	MSBLS	10//99-12//99
	Missouri	S	6.48 MW	6.87 AW	14300 AAW	MOBLS	10//99-12//99
	Columbia MSA, MO	S	6.51 MW	6.18 AW	13550 AAW	MOBLS	10//99-12//99
	Joplin MSA, MO	S	6.89 MW	6.45 AW	14330 AAW	MOBLS	10//99-12//99
	Kansas City MSA, MO-KS	S	7.09 MW	6.87 AW	14750 AAW	MOBLS	10//99-12//99
	St. Joseph MSA, MO	S	6.55 MW	6.21 AW	13630 AAW	MOBLS	10//99-12//99
	St. Louis MSA, MO-IL	S	7.02 MW	6.63 AW	14610 AAW	MOBLS	10//99-12//99
	Springfield MSA, MO	S	7.04 MW	6.58 AW	14650 AAW	MOBLS	10//99-12//99
	Montana	S	6.41 MW	7.07 AW	14700 AAW	MTBLS	10//99-12//99
	Billings MSA, MT	S	7.17 MW	6.36 AW	14920 AAW	MTBLS	10//99-12//99
	Great Falls MSA, MT	S	7.07 MW	6.32 AW	14710 AAW	MTBLS	10//99-12//99
	Missoula MSA, MT	S	7.01 MW	6.23 AW	14580 AAW	MTBLS	10//99-12//99
	Nebraska	S	6.74 MW	7.04 AW	14650 AAW	NEBLS	10//99-12//99
	Lincoln MSA, NE	S	7.28 MW	6.84 AW	15150 AAW	NEBLS	10//99-12//99
	Omaha MSA, NE-IA	S	7.25 MW	7.18 AW	15090 AAW	NEBLS	10//99-12//99
	Nevada	S	7.54 MW	8.35 AW	17370 AAW	NVBLS	10//99-12//99
	Las Vegas MSA, NV-AZ	S	8.38 MW	7.53 AW	17420 AAW	NVBLS	10//99-12//99
	Reno MSA, NV	S	8.52 MW	7.79 AW	17720 AAW	NVBLS	10//99-12//99
	New Hampshire	S	7.11 MW	7.30 AW	15180 AAW	NHBLS	10//99-12//99
	Manchester PMSA, NH	S	7.29 MW	7.19 AW	15170 AAW	NHBLS	10//99-12//99
	Nashua PMSA, NH	S	7.65 MW	7.54 AW	15900 AAW	NHBLS	10//99-12//99

AAW Average annual wage	**AOH** Average offered, high	**ASH** Average starting, high	**H** Hourly	**M** Monthly	**S** Special: hourly and annual
AE Average entry wage	**AOL** Average offered, low	**ASL** Average starting, low	**HI** Highest wage paid	**MTC** Median total compensation	**TQ** Third quartile wage
AEX Average experienced wage	**APH** Average pay, high range	**AW** Average wage paid	**HR** High end range	**MW** Median wage paid	**W** Weekly
AO Average offered	**APL** Average pay, low range	**FQ** First quartile wage	**LR** Low end range	**SQ** Second quartile wage	**Y** Yearly

Occupation/Type/Industry	Location	Per	Low	Mid	High	Source	Date
Cashier							
	Portsmouth-Rochester PMSA, NH-ME	S	7.34 MW	7.21 AW	15270 AAW	NHBLS	10//99-12//99
	New Jersey	S	6.93 MW	7.62 AW	15850 AAW	NJBLS	10//99-12//99
	Atlantic-Cape May PMSA, NJ	S	7.62 MW	7.07 AW	15850 AAW	NJBLS	10//99-12//99
	Bergen-Passaic PMSA, NJ	S	7.53 MW	6.87 AW	15660 AAW	NJBLS	10//99-12//99
	Jersey City PMSA, NJ	S	7.46 MW	6.80 AW	15510 AAW	NJBLS	10//99-12//99
	Middlesex-Somerset-Hunterdon PMSA, NJ	S	7.83 MW	7.13 AW	16290 AAW	NJBLS	10//99-12//99
	Monmouth-Ocean PMSA, NJ	S	7.64 MW	6.82 AW	15880 AAW	NJBLS	10//99-12//99
	Newark PMSA, NJ	S	7.60 MW	6.92 AW	15800 AAW	NJBLS	10//99-12//99
	Trenton PMSA, NJ	S	7.77 MW	7.26 AW	16170 AAW	NJBLS	10//99-12//99
	Vineland-Millville-Bridgeton PMSA, NJ	S	6.97 MW	6.47 AW	14500 AAW	NJBLS	10//99-12//99
	New Mexico	S	6.56 MW	7.16 AW	14880 AAW	NMBLS	10//99-12//99
	Albuquerque MSA, NM	S	7.48 MW	6.83 AW	15550 AAW	NMBLS	10//99-12//99
	Las Cruces MSA, NM	S	7.22 MW	7.02 AW	15020 AAW	NMBLS	10//99-12//99
	Santa Fe MSA, NM	S	8.40 MW	7.76 AW	17480 AAW	NMBLS	10//99-12//99
	New York	S	6.38 MW	7.19 AW	14940 AAW	NYBLS	10//99-12//99
	Albany-Schenectady-Troy MSA, NY	S	7.26 MW	6.55 AW	15110 AAW	NYBLS	10//99-12//99
	Binghamton MSA, NY	S	6.43 MW	6.17 AW	13370 AAW	NYBLS	10//99-12//99
	Buffalo-Niagara Falls MSA, NY	S	6.67 MW	6.17 AW	13870 AAW	NYBLS	10//99-12//99
	Dutchess County PMSA, NY	S	6.99 MW	6.43 AW	14540 AAW	NYBLS	10//99-12//99
	Elmira MSA, NY	S	6.63 MW	6.20 AW	13780 AAW	NYBLS	10//99-12//99
	Glens Falls MSA, NY	S	6.70 MW	6.38 AW	13940 AAW	NYBLS	10//99-12//99
	Jamestown MSA, NY	S	6.46 MW	6.11 AW	13440 AAW	NYBLS	10//99-12//99
	Nassau-Suffolk PMSA, NY	S	7.59 MW	6.74 AW	15780 AAW	NYBLS	10//99-12//99
	New York PMSA, NY	S	7.60 MW	6.54 AW	15800 AAW	NYBLS	10//99-12//99
	Newburgh PMSA, NY-PA	S	6.94 MW	6.40 AW	14430 AAW	NYBLS	10//99-12//99
	Rochester MSA, NY	S	6.65 MW	6.21 AW	13840 AAW	NYBLS	10//99-12//99
	Syracuse MSA, NY	S	6.71 MW	6.20 AW	13960 AAW	NYBLS	10//99-12//99
	Utica-Rome MSA, NY	S	6.63 MW	6.24 AW	13780 AAW	NYBLS	10//99-12//99
	North Carolina	S	6.52 MW	6.86 AW	14260 AAW	NCBLS	10//99-12//99
	Asheville MSA, NC	S	6.99 MW	6.77 AW	14550 AAW	NCBLS	10//99-12//99
	Charlotte-Gastonia-Rock Hill MSA, NC-SC	S	7.07 MW	6.82 AW	14710 AAW	NCBLS	10//99-12//99
	Fayetteville MSA, NC	S	6.55 MW	6.27 AW	13620 AAW	NCBLS	10//99-12//99
	Goldsboro MSA, NC	S	6.63 MW	6.22 AW	13790 AAW	NCBLS	10//99-12//99
	Greensboro--Winston-Salem--High Point MSA, NC	S	6.98 MW	6.63 AW	14510 AAW	NCBLS	10//99-12//99
	Greenville MSA, NC	S	6.73 MW	6.22 AW	14000 AAW	NCBLS	10//99-12//99
	Hickory-Morganton-Lenoir MSA, NC	S	6.80 MW	6.42 AW	14150 AAW	NCBLS	10//99-12//99
	Jacksonville MSA, NC	S	6.56 MW	6.35 AW	13650 AAW	NCBLS	10//99-12//99
	Raleigh-Durham-Chapel Hill MSA, NC	S	7.13 MW	6.82 AW	14830 AAW	NCBLS	10//99-12//99
	Rocky Mount MSA, NC	S	6.50 MW	6.20 AW	13530 AAW	NCBLS	10//99-12//99
	Wilmington MSA, NC	S	6.72 MW	6.30 AW	13980 AAW	NCBLS	10//99-12//99
	North Dakota	S	6.39 MW	6.68 AW	13900 AAW	NDBLS	10//99-12//99
	Bismarck MSA, ND	S	6.56 MW	6.25 AW	13650 AAW	NDBLS	10//99-12//99
	Fargo-Moorhead MSA, ND-MN	S	6.90 MW	6.76 AW	14350 AAW	NDBLS	10//99-12//99
	Grand Forks MSA, ND-MN	S	7.16 MW	6.98 AW	14900 AAW	NDBLS	10//99-12//99
	Ohio	S	6.49 MW	6.95 AW	14450 AAW	OHBLS	10//99-12//99
	Akron PMSA, OH	S	7.06 MW	6.41 AW	14690 AAW	OHBLS	10//99-12//99
	Canton-Massillon MSA, OH	S	6.72 MW	6.34 AW	13990 AAW	OHBLS	10//99-12//99
	Cincinnati PMSA, OH-KY-IN	S	7.03 MW	6.56 AW	14620 AAW	OHBLS	10//99-12//99
	Cleveland-Lorain-Elyria PMSA, OH	S	6.95 MW	6.50 AW	14450 AAW	OHBLS	10//99-12//99
	Columbus MSA, OH	S	7.12 MW	6.73 AW	14820 AAW	OHBLS	10//99-12//99
	Dayton-Springfield MSA, OH	S	6.91 MW	6.46 AW	14360 AAW	OHBLS	10//99-12//99
	Hamilton-Middletown PMSA, OH	S	7.09 MW	6.68 AW	14750 AAW	OHBLS	10//99-12//99
	Lima MSA, OH	S	6.48 MW	6.21 AW	13470 AAW	OHBLS	10//99-12//99
	Mansfield MSA, OH	S	6.72 MW	6.31 AW	13970 AAW	OHBLS	10//99-12//99
	Steubenville-Weirton MSA, OH-WV	S	6.35 MW	6.14 AW	13210 AAW	OHBLS	10//99-12//99
	Toledo MSA, OH	S	7.32 MW	6.65 AW	15230 AAW	OHBLS	10//99-12//99
	Youngstown-Warren MSA, OH	S	6.48 MW	6.17 AW	13480 AAW	OHBLS	10//99-12//99
	Oklahoma	S	6.4 MW	6.79 AW	14130 AAW	OKBLS	10//99-12//99
	Enid MSA, OK	S	6.35 MW	6.10 AW	13210 AAW	OKBLS	10//99-12//99

AAW Average annual wage	AOH Average offered, high	ASH Average starting, high	H Hourly	M Monthly	S Special: hourly and annual
AE Average entry wage	AOL Average offered, low	ASL Average starting, low	HI Highest wage paid	MTC Median total compensation	TQ Third quartile wage
AEX Average experienced wage	APH Average pay, high range	AW Average wage paid	HR High end range	MW Median wage paid	W Weekly
AO Average offered	APL Average pay, low range	FQ First quartile wage	LR Low end range	SQ Second quartile wage	Y Yearly

Occupation/Type/Industry	Location	Per	Low	Mid	High	Source	Date
Cashier	Lawton MSA, OK	S	6.82 MW	6.53 AW	14180 AAW	OKBLS	10//99-12//99
	Oklahoma City MSA, OK	S	6.98 MW	6.63 AW	14510 AAW	OKBLS	10//99-12//99
	Tulsa MSA, OK	S	7.06 MW	6.66 AW	14690 AAW	OKBLS	10//99-12//99
	Oregon	S	7.75 MW	8.62 AW	17920 AAW	ORBLS	10//99-12//99
	Corvallis MSA, OR	S	8.05 MW	7.51 AW	16740 AAW	ORBLS	10//99-12//99
	Eugene-Springfield MSA, OR	S	8.40 MW	7.58 AW	17480 AAW	ORBLS	10//99-12//99
	Medford-Ashland MSA, OR	S	8.35 MW	7.47 AW	17380 AAW	ORBLS	10//99-12//99
	Portland-Vancouver PMSA, OR-WA	S	9.01 MW	7.97 AW	18740 AAW	ORBLS	10//99-12//99
	Salem PMSA, OR	S	8.52 MW	7.79 AW	17730 AAW	ORBLS	10//99-12//99
	Pennsylvania	S	6.45 MW	7.01 AW	14590 AAW	PABLS	10//99-12//99
	Allentown-Bethlehem-Easton MSA, PA	S	7.05 MW	6.59 AW	14670 AAW	PABLS	10//99-12//99
	Altoona MSA, PA	S	6.29 MW	6.10 AW	13090 AAW	PABLS	10//99-12//99
	Erie MSA, PA	S	6.41 MW	6.17 AW	13330 AAW	PABLS	10//99-12//99
	Harrisburg-Lebanon-Carlisle MSA, PA	S	6.71 MW	6.33 AW	13950 AAW	PABLS	10//99-12//99
	Johnstown MSA, PA	S	6.29 MW	6.13 AW	13090 AAW	PABLS	10//99-12//99
	Lancaster MSA, PA	S	7.08 MW	6.63 AW	14730 AAW	PABLS	10//99-12//99
	Philadelphia PMSA, PA-NJ	S	7.76 MW	7.01 AW	16150 AAW	PABLS	10//99-12//99
	Pittsburgh MSA, PA	S	6.68 MW	6.26 AW	13900 AAW	PABLS	10//99-12//99
	Reading MSA, PA	S	6.52 MW	6.24 AW	13570 AAW	PABLS	10//99-12//99
	Scranton--Wilkes-Barre--Hazleton MSA, PA	S	6.65 MW	6.26 AW	13840 AAW	PABLS	10//99-12//99
	Sharon MSA, PA	S	6.62 MW	6.20 AW	13760 AAW	PABLS	10//99-12//99
	State College MSA, PA	S	6.70 MW	6.30 AW	13940 AAW	PABLS	10//99-12//99
	Williamsport MSA, PA	S	6.33 MW	6.15 AW	13160 AAW	PABLS	10//99-12//99
	York MSA, PA	S	6.79 MW	6.57 AW	14120 AAW	PABLS	10//99-12//99
	Rhode Island	S	6.73 MW	7.48 AW	15560 AAW	RIBLS	10//99-12//99
	Providence-Fall River-Warwick MSA, RI-MA	S	7.40 MW	6.69 AW	15400 AAW	RIBLS	10//99-12//99
	South Carolina	S	6.27 MW	6.57 AW	13670 AAW	SCBLS	10//99-12//99
	Charleston-North Charleston MSA, SC	S	6.49 MW	6.21 AW	13490 AAW	SCBLS	10//99-12//99
	Columbia MSA, SC	S	6.60 MW	6.29 AW	13730 AAW	SCBLS	10//99-12//99
	Florence MSA, SC	S	6.32 MW	6.13 AW	13140 AAW	SCBLS	10//99-12//99
	Greenville-Spartanburg-Anderson MSA, SC	S	6.75 MW	6.51 AW	14040 AAW	SCBLS	10//99-12//99
	Myrtle Beach MSA, SC	S	6.96 MW	6.76 AW	14470 AAW	SCBLS	10//99-12//99
	Sumter MSA, SC	S	6.30 MW	6.10 AW	13110 AAW	SCBLS	10//99-12//99
	South Dakota	S	6.53 MW	6.75 AW	14040 AAW	SDBLS	10//99-12//99
	Rapid City MSA, SD	S	6.70 MW	6.51 AW	13930 AAW	SDBLS	10//99-12//99
	Sioux Falls MSA, SD	S	7.14 MW	7.06 AW	14850 AAW	SDBLS	10//99-12//99
	Tennessee	S	6.65 MW	7.04 AW	14640 AAW	TNBLS	10//99-12//99
	Chattanooga MSA, TN-GA	S	6.73 MW	6.34 AW	14000 AAW	TNBLS	10//99-12//99
	Clarksville-Hopkinsville MSA, TN-KY	S	6.63 MW	6.43 AW	13800 AAW	TNBLS	10//99-12//99
	Jackson MSA, TN	S	6.97 MW	6.69 AW	14500 AAW	TNBLS	10//99-12//99
	Johnson City-Kingsport-Bristol MSA, TN-VA	S	6.59 MW	6.26 AW	13710 AAW	TNBLS	10//99-12//99
	Knoxville MSA, TN	S	7.08 MW	6.85 AW	14740 AAW	TNBLS	10//99-12//99
	Memphis MSA, TN-AR-MS	S	7.22 MW	6.79 AW	15010 AAW	MSBLS	10//99-12//99
	Nashville MSA, TN	S	7.23 MW	7.04 AW	15040 AAW	TNBLS	10//99-12//99
	Texas	S	6.55 MW	6.96 AW	14480 AAW	TXBLS	10//99-12//99
	Abilene MSA, TX	S	6.94 MW	6.58 AW	14430 AAW	TXBLS	10//99-12//99
	Amarillo MSA, TX	S	6.79 MW	6.42 AW	14130 AAW	TXBLS	10//99-12//99
	Austin-San Marcos MSA, TX	S	7.47 MW	7.38 AW	15530 AAW	TXBLS	10//99-12//99
	Beaumont-Port Arthur MSA, TX	S	6.52 MW	6.21 AW	13550 AAW	TXBLS	10//99-12//99
	Brazoria PMSA, TX	S	7.05 MW	6.66 AW	14660 AAW	TXBLS	10//99-12//99
	Brownsville-Harlingen-San Benito MSA, TX	S	6.72 MW	6.26 AW	13980 AAW	TXBLS	10//99-12//99
	Bryan-College Station MSA, TX	S	6.83 MW	6.48 AW	14210 AAW	TXBLS	10//99-12//99
	Corpus Christi MSA, TX	S	7.12 MW	6.51 AW	14810 AAW	TXBLS	10//99-12//99
	Dallas PMSA, TX	S	7.25 MW	6.84 AW	15070 AAW	TXBLS	10//99-12//99
	El Paso MSA, TX	S	6.75 MW	6.30 AW	14050 AAW	TXBLS	10//99-12//99
	Fort Worth-Arlington PMSA, TX	S	7.29 MW	6.96 AW	15170 AAW	TXBLS	10//99-12//99
	Galveston-Texas City PMSA, TX	S	6.83 MW	6.37 AW	14200 AAW	TXBLS	10//99-12//99
	Houston PMSA, TX	S	6.84 MW	6.37 AW	14230 AAW	TXBLS	10//99-12//99

AAW Average annual wage	**AOH** Average offered, high	**ASH** Average starting, high	**H** Hourly	**M** Monthly	**S** Special: hourly and annual
AE Average entry wage	**AOL** Average offered, low	**ASL** Average starting, low	**HI** Highest wage paid	**MTC** Median total compensation	**TQ** Third quartile wage
AEX Average experienced wage	**APH** Average pay, high range	**AW** Average wage paid	**HR** High end range	**MW** Median wage paid	**W** Weekly
AO Average offered	**APL** Average pay, low range	**FQ** First quartile wage	**LR** Low end range	**SQ** Second quartile wage	**Y** Yearly

Occupation/Type/Industry	Location	Per	Low	Mid	High	Source	Date
Cashier	Killeen-Temple MSA, TX	S	6.69 MW	6.38 AW	13920 AAW	TXBLS	10//99-12//99
	Laredo MSA, TX	S	6.86 MW	6.47 AW	14280 AAW	TXBLS	10//99-12//99
	Longview-Marshall MSA, TX	S	6.73 MW	6.29 AW	14000 AAW	TXBLS	10//99-12//99
	Lubbock MSA, TX	S	6.50 MW	6.14 AW	13510 AAW	TXBLS	10//99-12//99
	McAllen-Edinburg-Mission MSA, TX	S	6.86 MW	6.40 AW	14260 AAW	TXBLS	10//99-12//99
	Odessa-Midland MSA, TX	S	7.15 MW	6.73 AW	14870 AAW	TXBLS	10//99-12//99
	San Angelo MSA, TX	S	7.13 MW	6.60 AW	14820 AAW	TXBLS	10//99-12//99
	San Antonio MSA, TX	S	7.19 MW	7.03 AW	14950 AAW	TXBLS	10//99-12//99
	Sherman-Denison MSA, TX	S	7.09 MW	6.68 AW	14750 AAW	TXBLS	10//99-12//99
	Texarkana MSA, TX-Texarkana, AR	S	6.65 MW	6.29 AW	13840 AAW	TXBLS	10//99-12//99
	Tyler MSA, TX	S	7.05 MW	6.61 AW	14660 AAW	TXBLS	10//99-12//99
	Victoria MSA, TX	S	6.73 MW	6.40 AW	13990 AAW	TXBLS	10//99-12//99
	Waco MSA, TX	S	7.04 MW	6.71 AW	14650 AAW	TXBLS	10//99-12//99
	Wichita Falls MSA, TX	S	6.92 MW	6.30 AW	14390 AAW	TXBLS	10//99-12//99
	Utah	S	6.99 MW	7.24 AW	15060 AAW	UTBLS	10//99-12//99
	Provo-Orem MSA, UT	S	6.89 MW	6.57 AW	14320 AAW	UTBLS	10//99-12//99
	Salt Lake City-Ogden MSA, UT	S	7.55 MW	7.44 AW	15710 AAW	UTBLS	10//99-12//99
	Vermont	S	6.61 MW	7.02 AW	14610 AAW	VTBLS	10//99-12//99
	Burlington MSA, VT	S	7.36 MW	7.11 AW	15310 AAW	VTBLS	10//99-12//99
	Virginia	S	6.42 MW	6.89 AW	14330 AAW	VABLS	10//99-12//99
	Charlottesville MSA, VA	S	7.03 MW	6.68 AW	14620 AAW	VABLS	10//99-12//99
	Danville MSA, VA	S	6.57 MW	6.28 AW	13670 AAW	VABLS	10//99-12//99
	Lynchburg MSA, VA	S	6.59 MW	6.21 AW	13700 AAW	VABLS	10//99-12//99
	Norfolk-Virginia Beach-Newport News MSA, VA-NC	S	6.37 MW	6.14 AW	13240 AAW	VABLS	10//99-12//99
	Richmond-Petersburg MSA, VA	S	6.98 MW	6.70 AW	14520 AAW	VABLS	10//99-12//99
	Roanoke MSA, VA	S	6.73 MW	6.33 AW	13990 AAW	VABLS	10//99-12//99
	Washington	S	7.98 MW	9.09 AW	18910 AAW	WABLS	10//99-12//99
	Bellingham MSA, WA	S	9.02 MW	8.06 AW	18760 AAW	WABLS	10//99-12//99
	Bremerton PMSA, WA	S	9.55 MW	8.10 AW	19860 AAW	WABLS	10//99-12//99
	Olympia PMSA, WA	S	8.92 MW	7.91 AW	18550 AAW	WABLS	10//99-12//99
	Richland-Kennewick-Pasco MSA, WA	S	8.25 MW	7.40 AW	17160 AAW	WABLS	10//99-12//99
	Seattle-Bellevue-Everett PMSA, WA	S	9.54 MW	8.27 AW	19850 AAW	WABLS	10//99-12//99
	Spokane MSA, WA	S	8.45 MW	7.60 AW	17580 AAW	WABLS	10//99-12//99
	Tacoma PMSA, WA	S	9.21 MW	8.13 AW	19160 AAW	WABLS	10//99-12//99
	Yakima MSA, WA	S	8.22 MW	6.99 AW	17100 AAW	WABLS	10//99-12//99
	West Virginia	S	6.11 MW	6.38 AW	13270 AAW	WVBLS	10//99-12//99
	Charleston MSA, WV	S	6.73 MW	6.15 AW	14000 AAW	WVBLS	10//99-12//99
	Huntington-Ashland MSA, WV-KY-OH	S	6.29 MW	6.12 AW	13090 AAW	WVBLS	10//99-12//99
	Parkersburg-Marietta MSA, WV-OH	S	6.41 MW	6.13 AW	13330 AAW	WVBLS	10//99-12//99
	Wheeling MSA, WV-OH	S	6.42 MW	6.20 AW	13340 AAW	WVBLS	10//99-12//99
	Wisconsin	S	6.67 MW	7.02 AW	14610 AAW	WIBLS	10//99-12//99
	Appleton-Oshkosh-Neenah MSA, WI	S	7.47 MW	7.16 AW	15530 AAW	WIBLS	10//99-12//99
	Eau Claire MSA, WI	S	6.56 MW	6.33 AW	13650 AAW	WIBLS	10//99-12//99
	Green Bay MSA, WI	S	6.84 MW	6.67 AW	14230 AAW	WIBLS	10//99-12//99
	Janesville-Beloit MSA, WI	S	7.38 MW	7.01 AW	15360 AAW	WIBLS	10//99-12//99
	Kenosha PMSA, WI	S	7.24 MW	7.13 AW	15050 AAW	WIBLS	10//99-12//99
	La Crosse MSA, WI-MN	S	7.17 MW	6.81 AW	14910 AAW	WIBLS	10//99-12//99
	Madison MSA, WI	S	7.66 MW	7.47 AW	15940 AAW	WIBLS	10//99-12//99
	Milwaukee-Waukesha PMSA, WI	S	7.12 MW	6.76 AW	14810 AAW	WIBLS	10//99-12//99
	Racine PMSA, WI	S	7.20 MW	6.84 AW	14990 AAW	WIBLS	10//99-12//99
	Sheboygan MSA, WI	S	7.01 MW	7.00 AW	14590 AAW	WIBLS	10//99-12//99
	Wausau MSA, WI	S	7.02 MW	6.74 AW	14600 AAW	WIBLS	10//99-12//99
	Wyoming	S	6.66 MW	7.23 AW	15050 AAW	WYBLS	10//99-12//99
	Casper MSA, WY	S	7.02 MW	6.44 AW	14600 AAW	WYBLS	10//99-12//99
	Cheyenne MSA, WY	S	7.59 MW	7.29 AW	15790 AAW	WYBLS	10//99-12//99
	Puerto Rico	S	6 MW	5.98 AW	12440 AAW	PRBLS	10//99-12//99
	Aguadilla MSA, PR	S	5.80 MW	5.98 AW	12070 AAW	PRBLS	10//99-12//99
	Arecibo PMSA, PR	S	5.88 MW	6.00 AW	12240 AAW	PRBLS	10//99-12//99
	Caguas PMSA, PR	S	5.90 MW	6.00 AW	12260 AAW	PRBLS	10//99-12//99
	Mayaguez MSA, PR	S	5.83 MW	5.99 AW	12120 AAW	PRBLS	10//99-12//99

AAW	Average annual wage	AOH	Average offered, high	ASH	Average starting, high	H	Hourly	M	Monthly	S	Special: hourly and annual
AE	Average entry wage	AOL	Average offered, low	ASL	Average starting, low	HI	Highest wage paid	MTC	Median total compensation	TQ	Third quartile wage
AEX	Average experienced wage	APH	Average pay, high range	AW	Average wage paid	HR	High end range	MW	Median wage paid	W	Weekly
AO	Average offered	APL	Average pay, low range	FQ	First quartile wage	LR	Low end range	SQ	Second quartile wage	Y	Yearly

Occupation/Type/Industry	Location	Per	Low	Mid	High	Source	Date
Cashier	Ponce MSA, PR	S	5.88 MW	5.98 AW	12220 AAW	PRBLS	10//99-12//99
	San Juan-Bayamon PMSA, PR	S	6.01 MW	6.01 AW	12510 AAW	PRBLS	10//99-12//99
	Virgin Islands	S	6.41 MW	6.94 AW	14430 AAW	VIBLS	10//99-12//99
	Guam	S	6.49 MW	7.06 AW	14680 AAW	GUBLS	10//99-12//99
Cellar Master							
Winery/Vineyard, Over 150K Cases/Year	United States	Y	25500 MW	25584 AW		PWV	1999
Cement Mason	United States	H		31.63 AW		ENR1	2000
Nonunion, Construction	Central	H		15.92 AW		ENR3	2000
Nonunion, Construction	Middle Atlantic	H		16.97 AW		ENR3	2000
Nonunion, Construction	New England	H		17.60 AW		ENR3	2000
Nonunion, Construction	Southeast	H		14.46 AW		ENR3	2000
Nonunion, Construction	West	H		16.23 AW		ENR3	2000
Cement Mason and Concrete Finisher	Alabama	S	10.09 MW	10.74 AW	22330 AAW	ALBLS	10//99-12//99
	Anniston MSA, AL	S	12.81 MW	13.22 AW	26650 AAW	ALBLS	10//99-12//99
	Decatur MSA, AL	S	11.98 MW	12.08 AW	24920 AAW	ALBLS	10//99-12//99
	Dothan MSA, AL	S	10.39 MW	9.79 AW	21610 AAW	ALBLS	10//99-12//99
	Florence MSA, AL	S	19.86 MW	16.06 AW	41300 AAW	ALBLS	10//99-12//99
	Huntsville MSA, AL	S	11.79 MW	11.77 AW	24520 AAW	ALBLS	10//99-12//99
	Mobile MSA, AL	S	10.73 MW	11.01 AW	22310 AAW	ALBLS	10//99-12//99
	Montgomery MSA, AL	S	9.62 MW	9.65 AW	20010 AAW	ALBLS	10//99-12//99
	Tuscaloosa MSA, AL	S	9.63 MW	9.68 AW	20040 AAW	ALBLS	10//99-12//99
	Alaska	S	29.19 MW	28.62 AW	59530 AAW	AKBLS	10//99-12//99
	Anchorage MSA, AK	S	31.16 MW	36.23 AW	64820 AAW	AKBLS	10//99-12//99
	Arizona	S	13.07 MW	13.32 AW	27700 AAW	AZBLS	10//99-12//99
	Flagstaff MSA, AZ-UT	S	12.78 MW	12.84 AW	26580 AAW	AZBLS	10//99-12//99
	Phoenix-Mesa MSA, AZ	S	13.55 MW	13.29 AW	28180 AAW	AZBLS	10//99-12//99
	Tucson MSA, AZ	S	12.12 MW	11.97 AW	25220 AAW	AZBLS	10//99-12//99
	Yuma MSA, AZ	S	11.14 MW	11.51 AW	23180 AAW	AZBLS	10//99-12//99
	Arkansas	S	11.8 MW	11.74 AW	24410 AAW	ARBLS	10//99-12//99
	Fayetteville-Springdale-Rogers MSA, AR	S	11.51 MW	11.83 AW	23940 AAW	ARBLS	10//99-12//99
	Fort Smith MSA, AR-OK	S	12.92 MW	12.73 AW	26870 AAW	ARBLS	10//99-12//99
	Little Rock-North Little Rock MSA, AR	S	13.94 MW	14.33 AW	29000 AAW	ARBLS	10//99-12//99
	California	S	17.49 MW	17.75 AW	36920 AAW	CABLS	10//99-12//99
	Bakersfield MSA, CA	S	13.40 MW	13.64 AW	27860 AAW	CABLS	10//99-12//99
	Chico-Paradise MSA, CA	S	14.46 MW	14.27 AW	30070 AAW	CABLS	10//99-12//99
	Fresno MSA, CA	S	16.19 MW	15.51 AW	33680 AAW	CABLS	10//99-12//99
	Los Angeles-Long Beach PMSA, CA	S	20.16 MW	21.17 AW	41940 AAW	CABLS	10//99-12//99
	Merced MSA, CA	S	11.88 MW	10.79 AW	24710 AAW	CABLS	10//99-12//99
	Modesto MSA, CA	S	16.70 MW	16.82 AW	34750 AAW	CABLS	10//99-12//99
	Oakland PMSA, CA	S	18.58 MW	17.52 AW	38650 AAW	CABLS	10//99-12//99
	Orange County PMSA, CA	S	17.83 MW	17.43 AW	37100 AAW	CABLS	10//99-12//99
	Redding MSA, CA	S	15.30 MW	15.92 AW	31820 AAW	CABLS	10//99-12//99
	Riverside-San Bernardino PMSA, CA	S	17.67 MW	17.52 AW	36760 AAW	CABLS	10//99-12//99
	Sacramento PMSA, CA	S	17.55 MW	17.78 AW	36510 AAW	CABLS	10//99-12//99
	Salinas MSA, CA	S	22.20 MW	20.72 AW	46170 AAW	CABLS	10//99-12//99
	San Diego MSA, CA	S	20.18 MW	21.04 AW	41970 AAW	CABLS	10//99-12//99
	San Francisco PMSA, CA	S	18.32 MW	15.87 AW	38110 AAW	CABLS	10//99-12//99
	San Jose PMSA, CA	S	16.40 MW	15.21 AW	34100 AAW	CABLS	10//99-12//99
	San Luis Obispo-Atascadero-Paso Robles MSA, CA	S	17.90 MW	17.30 AW	37230 AAW	CABLS	10//99-12//99
	Santa Barbara-Santa Maria-Lompoc MSA, CA	S	17.18 MW	18.34 AW	35740 AAW	CABLS	10//99-12//99
	Santa Cruz-Watsonville PMSA, CA	S	16.46 MW	17.28 AW	34240 AAW	CABLS	10//99-12//99
	Santa Rosa PMSA, CA	S	15.07 MW	15.05 AW	31340 AAW	CABLS	10//99-12//99
	Stockton-Lodi MSA, CA	S	19.45 MW	19.54 AW	40460 AAW	CABLS	10//99-12//99
	Vallejo-Fairfield-Napa PMSA, CA	S	15.09 MW	14.31 AW	31380 AAW	CABLS	10//99-12//99
	Ventura PMSA, CA	S	21.19 MW	19.99 AW	44070 AAW	CABLS	10//99-12//99
	Visalia-Tulare-Porterville MSA, CA	S	15.51 MW	14.24 AW	32250 AAW	CABLS	10//99-12//99
	Yolo PMSA, CA	S	17.41 MW	17.71 AW	36210 AAW	CABLS	10//99-12//99
	Yuba City MSA, CA	S	12.49 MW	10.43 AW	25990 AAW	CABLS	10//99-12//99
	Connecticut	S	18.7 MW	18.49 AW	38460 AAW	CTBLS	10//99-12//99

AAW Average annual wage	**AOH** Average offered, high	**ASH** Average starting, high	**H** Hourly	**M** Monthly	**S** Special: hourly and annual
AE Average entry wage	**AOL** Average offered, low	**ASL** Average starting, low	**HI** Highest wage paid	**MTC** Median total compensation	**TQ** Third quartile wage
AEX Average experienced wage	**APH** Average pay, high range	**AW** Average wage paid	**HR** High end range	**MW** Median wage paid	**W** Weekly
AO Average offered	**APL** Average pay, low range	**FQ** First quartile wage	**LR** Low end range	**SQ** Second quartile wage	**Y** Yearly

Occupation/Type/Industry	Location	Per	Low	Mid	High	Source	Date
Cement Mason and Concrete Finisher							
	Bridgeport PMSA, CT	S	23.81 MW	23.61 AW	49530 AAW	CTBLS	10//99-12//99
	Hartford MSA, CT	S	17.91 MW	18.71 AW	37250 AAW	CTBLS	10//99-12//99
	Delaware	S	14.88 MW	15.20 AW	31610 AAW	DEBLS	10//99-12//99
	Wilmington-Newark PMSA, DE-MD	S	15.94 MW	15.45 AW	33150 AAW	DEBLS	10//99-12//99
	Washington PMSA, DC-MD-VA-WV	S	16.34 MW	16.40 AW	33990 AAW	DCBLS	10//99-12//99
	Florida	S	10.97 MW	11.49 AW	23900 AAW	FLBLS	10//99-12//99
	Daytona Beach MSA, FL	S	12.53 MW	12.40 AW	26070 AAW	FLBLS	10//99-12//99
	Fort Lauderdale PMSA, FL	S	12.15 MW	11.38 AW	25270 AAW	FLBLS	10//99-12//99
	Fort Myers-Cape Coral MSA, FL	S	13.08 MW	13.10 AW	27200 AAW	FLBLS	10//99-12//99
	Fort Pierce-Port St. Lucie MSA, FL	S	15.73 MW	15.40 AW	32730 AAW	FLBLS	10//99-12//99
	Jacksonville MSA, FL	S	11.01 MW	10.48 AW	22900 AAW	FLBLS	10//99-12//99
	Lakeland-Winter Haven MSA, FL	S	12.18 MW	11.58 AW	25340 AAW	FLBLS	10//99-12//99
	Melbourne-Titusville-Palm Bay MSA, FL	S	11.29 MW	10.93 AW	23470 AAW	FLBLS	10//99-12//99
	Miami PMSA, FL	S	11.13 MW	8.81 AW	23160 AAW	FLBLS	10//99-12//99
	Naples MSA, FL	S	12.10 MW	12.13 AW	25170 AAW	FLBLS	10//99-12//99
	Ocala MSA, FL	S	11.22 MW	11.63 AW	23340 AAW	FLBLS	10//99-12//99
	Orlando MSA, FL	S	10.29 MW	10.01 AW	21410 AAW	FLBLS	10//99-12//99
	Panama City MSA, FL	S	9.51 MW	9.08 AW	19780 AAW	FLBLS	10//99-12//99
	Pensacola MSA, FL	S	8.84 MW	9.09 AW	18380 AAW	FLBLS	10//99-12//99
	Punta Gorda MSA, FL	S	12.54 MW	12.46 AW	26090 AAW	FLBLS	10//99-12//99
	Sarasota-Bradenton MSA, FL	S	11.33 MW	10.55 AW	23580 AAW	FLBLS	10//99-12//99
	Tallahassee MSA, FL	S	12.10 MW	9.55 AW	25160 AAW	FLBLS	10//99-12//99
	Tampa-St. Petersburg-Clearwater MSA, FL	S	11.47 MW	10.98 AW	23850 AAW	FLBLS	10//99-12//99
	West Palm Beach-Boca Raton MSA, FL	S	13.84 MW	14.56 AW	28780 AAW	FLBLS	10//99-12//99
	Georgia	S	10.53 MW	11.13 AW	23150 AAW	GABLS	10//99-12//99
	Albany MSA, GA	S	11.97 MW	10.17 AW	24910 AAW	GABLS	10//99-12//99
	Athens MSA, GA	S	10.92 MW	10.41 AW	22720 AAW	GABLS	10//99-12//99
	Atlanta MSA, GA	S	11.40 MW	10.61 AW	23710 AAW	GABLS	10//99-12//99
	Augusta-Aiken MSA, GA-SC	S	13.91 MW	14.40 AW	28940 AAW	GABLS	10//99-12//99
	Columbus MSA, GA-AL	S	11.45 MW	11.60 AW	23810 AAW	GABLS	10//99-12//99
	Macon MSA, GA	S	11.84 MW	10.88 AW	24620 AAW	GABLS	10//99-12//99
	Hawaii	S	22.86 MW	22.02 AW	45790 AAW	HIBLS	10//99-12//99
	Honolulu MSA, HI	S	21.18 MW	21.99 AW	44060 AAW	HIBLS	10//99-12//99
	Idaho	S	13.33 MW	13.00 AW	27040 AAW	IDBLS	10//99-12//99
	Boise City MSA, ID	S	13.70 MW	14.18 AW	28500 AAW	IDBLS	10//99-12//99
	Illinois	S	23.64 MW	22.25 AW	46280 AAW	ILBLS	10//99-12//99
	Bloomington-Normal MSA, IL	S	12.22 MW	10.27 AW	25430 AAW	ILBLS	10//99-12//99
	Champaign-Urbana MSA, IL	S	22.48 MW	23.52 AW	46750 AAW	ILBLS	10//99-12//99
	Chicago PMSA, IL	S	24.01 MW	24.41 AW	49950 AAW	ILBLS	10//99-12//99
	Decatur MSA, IL	S	23.74 MW	22.70 AW	49380 AAW	ILBLS	10//99-12//99
	Peoria-Pekin MSA, IL	S	19.80 MW	21.60 AW	41180 AAW	ILBLS	10//99-12//99
	Rockford MSA, IL	S	24.05 MW	24.38 AW	50030 AAW	ILBLS	10//99-12//99
	Springfield MSA, IL	S	14.73 MW	15.04 AW	30630 AAW	ILBLS	10//99-12//99
	Indiana	S	14.96 MW	15.61 AW	32460 AAW	INBLS	10//99-12//99
	Bloomington MSA, IN	S	11.40 MW	11.70 AW	23720 AAW	INBLS	10//99-12//99
	Elkhart-Goshen MSA, IN	S	14.91 MW	13.97 AW	31020 AAW	INBLS	10//99-12//99
	Evansville-Henderson MSA, IN-KY	S	16.96 MW	17.76 AW	35270 AAW	INBLS	10//99-12//99
	Fort Wayne MSA, IN	S	14.20 MW	13.02 AW	29530 AAW	INBLS	10//99-12//99
	Gary PMSA, IN	S	22.15 MW	23.20 AW	46070 AAW	INBLS	10//99-12//99
	Indianapolis MSA, IN	S	15.41 MW	13.82 AW	32050 AAW	INBLS	10//99-12//99
	Kokomo MSA, IN	S	15.63 MW	15.47 AW	32500 AAW	INBLS	10//99-12//99
	Lafayette MSA, IN	S	18.40 MW	18.65 AW	38280 AAW	INBLS	10//99-12//99
	South Bend MSA, IN	S	19.47 MW	19.33 AW	40490 AAW	INBLS	10//99-12//99
	Terre Haute MSA, IN	S	15.46 MW	16.92 AW	32160 AAW	INBLS	10//99-12//99
	Iowa	S	11.39 MW	12.49 AW	25970 AAW	IABLS	10//99-12//99
	Cedar Rapids MSA, IA	S	18.02 MW	17.36 AW	37470 AAW	IABLS	10//99-12//99
	Davenport-Moline-Rock Island MSA, IA-IL	S	13.10 MW	10.45 AW	27240 AAW	IABLS	10//99-12//99
	Des Moines MSA, IA	S	11.02 MW	10.23 AW	22930 AAW	IABLS	10//99-12//99
	Iowa City MSA, IA	S	9.83 MW	9.25 AW	20440 AAW	IABLS	10//99-12//99
	Sioux City MSA, IA-NE	S	12.86 MW	13.02 AW	26750 AAW	IABLS	10//99-12//99
	Waterloo-Cedar Falls MSA, IA	S	10.71 MW	10.24 AW	22280 AAW	IABLS	10//99-12//99

AAW Average annual wage	**AOH** Average offered, high	**ASH** Average starting, high	**H** Hourly	**M** Monthly	**S** Special: hourly and annual
AE Average entry wage	**AOL** Average offered, low	**ASL** Average starting, low	**HI** Highest wage paid	**MTC** Median total compensation	**TQ** Third quartile wage
AEX Average experienced wage	**APH** Average pay, high range	**AW** Average wage paid	**HR** High end range	**MW** Median wage paid	**W** Weekly
AO Average offered	**APL** Average pay, low range	**FQ** First quartile wage	**LR** Low end range	**SQ** Second quartile wage	**Y** Yearly

Occupation/Type/Industry	Location	Per	Low	Mid	High	Source	Date
Cement Mason and Concrete Finisher							
	Kansas	S	11.94 MW	12.41 AW	25810 AAW	KSBLS	10//99-12//99
	Topeka MSA, KS	S	15.60 MW	15.43 AW	32450 AAW	KSBLS	10//99-12//99
	Wichita MSA, KS	S	12.17 MW	11.96 AW	25320 AAW	KSBLS	10//99-12//99
	Kentucky	S	14.06 MW	14.51 AW	30170 AAW	KYBLS	10//99-12//99
	Lexington MSA, KY	S	12.90 MW	12.78 AW	26840 AAW	KYBLS	10//99-12//99
	Louisville MSA, KY-IN	S	11.31 MW	10.34 AW	23510 AAW	KYBLS	10//99-12//99
	Owensboro MSA, KY	S	12.38 MW	12.32 AW	25760 AAW	KYBLS	10//99-12//99
	Louisiana	S	11.74 MW	11.83 AW	24610 AAW	LABLS	10//99-12//99
	Baton Rouge MSA, LA	S	12.94 MW	13.02 AW	26920 AAW	LABLS	10//99-12//99
	Houma MSA, LA	S	7.72 MW	6.25 AW	16050 AAW	LABLS	10//99-12//99
	Lafayette MSA, LA	S	10.54 MW	9.72 AW	21920 AAW	LABLS	10//99-12//99
	Monroe MSA, LA	S	10.06 MW	9.94 AW	20930 AAW	LABLS	10//99-12//99
	New Orleans MSA, LA	S	11.08 MW	11.51 AW	23040 AAW	LABLS	10//99-12//99
	Shreveport-Bossier City MSA, LA	S	13.11 MW	12.50 AW	27270 AAW	LABLS	10//99-12//99
	Maine	S	10.9 MW	11.32 AW	23540 AAW	MEBLS	10//99-12//99
	Lewiston-Auburn MSA, ME	S	10.09 MW	9.86 AW	20990 AAW	MEBLS	10//99-12//99
	Portland MSA, ME	S	12.72 MW	12.37 AW	26470 AAW	MEBLS	10//99-12//99
	Maryland	S	14.81 MW	14.96 AW	31120 AAW	MDBLS	10//99-12//99
	Baltimore PMSA, MD	S	13.82 MW	14.18 AW	28760 AAW	MDBLS	10//99-12//99
	Hagerstown PMSA, MD	S	12.75 MW	12.04 AW	26520 AAW	MDBLS	10//99-12//99
	Massachusetts	S	19.6 MW	20.41 AW	42440 AAW	MABLS	10//99-12//99
	Boston PMSA, MA-NH	S	18.65 MW	19.11 AW	38780 AAW	MABLS	10//99-12//99
	Lowell PMSA, MA-NH	S	19.26 MW	19.25 AW	40060 AAW	MABLS	10//99-12//99
	Springfield MSA, MA	S	23.62 MW	24.23 AW	49140 AAW	MABLS	10//99-12//99
	Michigan	S	18.36 MW	17.69 AW	36790 AAW	MIBLS	10//99-12//99
	Ann Arbor PMSA, MI	S	22.39 MW	23.04 AW	46580 AAW	MIBLS	10//99-12//99
	Benton Harbor MSA, MI	S	22.93 MW	23.63 AW	47690 AAW	MIBLS	10//99-12//99
	Detroit PMSA, MI	S	19.61 MW	19.81 AW	40790 AAW	MIBLS	10//99-12//99
	Flint PMSA, MI	S	17.65 MW	18.55 AW	36720 AAW	MIBLS	10//99-12//99
	Grand Rapids-Muskegon-Holland MSA, MI	S	15.10 MW	15.48 AW	31400 AAW	MIBLS	10//99-12//99
	Jackson MSA, MI	S	14.99 MW	15.07 AW	31180 AAW	MIBLS	10//99-12//99
	Kalamazoo-Battle Creek MSA, MI	S	13.09 MW	11.78 AW	27230 AAW	MIBLS	10//99-12//99
	Saginaw-Bay City-Midland MSA, MI	S	17.66 MW	18.23 AW	36730 AAW	MIBLS	10//99-12//99
	Minnesota	S	17.19 MW	17.14 AW	35650 AAW	MNBLS	10//99-12//99
	Duluth-Superior MSA, MN-WI	S	16.42 MW	16.86 AW	34140 AAW	MNBLS	10//99-12//99
	Minneapolis-St. Paul MSA, MN-WI	S	18.53 MW	18.75 AW	38540 AAW	MNBLS	10//99-12//99
	Rochester MSA, MN	S	21.57 MW	21.43 AW	44870 AAW	MNBLS	10//99-12//99
	St. Cloud MSA, MN	S	17.72 MW	17.54 AW	36850 AAW	MNBLS	10//99-12//99
	Mississippi	S	10.84 MW	11.78 AW	24500 AAW	MSBLS	10//99-12//99
	Biloxi-Gulfport-Pascagoula MSA, MS	S	10.98 MW	11.36 AW	22850 AAW	MSBLS	10//99-12//99
	Jackson MSA, MS	S	11.42 MW	10.32 AW	23740 AAW	MSBLS	10//99-12//99
	Missouri	S	13.41 MW	15.44 AW	32110 AAW	MOBLS	10//99-12//99
	Columbia MSA, MO	S	11.95 MW	11.05 AW	24850 AAW	MOBLS	10//99-12//99
	Kansas City MSA, MO-KS	S	16.01 MW	16.60 AW	33300 AAW	MOBLS	10//99-12//99
	St. Joseph MSA, MO	S	22.20 MW	22.74 AW	46170 AAW	MOBLS	10//99-12//99
	St. Louis MSA, MO-IL	S	19.29 MW	21.29 AW	40130 AAW	MOBLS	10//99-12//99
	Montana	S	13.96 MW	13.83 AW	28760 AAW	MTBLS	10//99-12//99
	Billings MSA, MT	S	12.34 MW	12.29 AW	25660 AAW	MTBLS	10//99-12//99
	Nebraska	S	12.84 MW	13.09 AW	27220 AAW	NEBLS	10//99-12//99
	Lincoln MSA, NE	S	13.15 MW	14.15 AW	27350 AAW	NEBLS	10//99-12//99
	Omaha MSA, NE-IA	S	14.42 MW	14.52 AW	29990 AAW	NEBLS	10//99-12//99
	Nevada	S	19.16 MW	18.51 AW	38500 AAW	NVBLS	10//99-12//99
	Las Vegas MSA, NV-AZ	S	19.21 MW	19.78 AW	39960 AAW	NVBLS	10//99-12//99
	Reno MSA, NV	S	15.22 MW	14.45 AW	31650 AAW	NVBLS	10//99-12//99
	New Hampshire	S	10.51 MW	12.21 AW	25390 AAW	NHBLS	10//99-12//99
	Nashua PMSA, NH	S	14.47 MW	14.20 AW	30090 AAW	NHBLS	10//99-12//99
	New Jersey	S	19.41 MW	19.45 AW	40460 AAW	NJBLS	10//99-12//99
	Monmouth-Ocean PMSA, NJ	S	18.57 MW	18.68 AW	38630 AAW	NJBLS	10//99-12//99
	Vineland-Millville-Bridgeton PMSA, NJ	S	19.31 MW	22.40 AW	40170 AAW	NJBLS	10//99-12//99
	New Mexico	S	11.82 MW	11.55 AW	24030 AAW	NMBLS	10//99-12//99
	Albuquerque MSA, NM	S	11.67 MW	11.89 AW	24280 AAW	NMBLS	10//99-12//99
	Las Cruces MSA, NM	S	9.68 MW	9.04 AW	20140 AAW	NMBLS	10//99-12//99
	New York	S	20.54 MW	21.27 AW	44250 AAW	NYBLS	10//99-12//99

AAW Average annual wage	**AOH** Average offered, high	**ASH** Average starting, high	**H** Hourly	**M** Monthly	**S** Special: hourly and annual
AE Average entry wage	**AOL** Average offered, low	**ASL** Average starting, low	**HI** Highest wage paid	**MTC** Median total compensation	**TQ** Third quartile wage
AEX Average experienced wage	**APH** Average pay, high range	**AW** Average wage paid	**HR** High end range	**MW** Median wage paid	**W** Weekly
AO Average offered	**APL** Average pay, low range	**FQ** First quartile wage	**LR** Low end range	**SQ** Second quartile wage	**Y** Yearly

Occupation/Type/Industry	Location	Per	Low	Mid	High	Source	Date
Cement Mason and Concrete Finisher							
	Albany-Schenectady-Troy MSA, NY	S	19.10 MW	19.09 AW	39740 AAW	NYBLS	10//99-12//99
	Binghamton MSA, NY	S	13.51 MW	12.75 AW	28090 AAW	NYBLS	10//99-12//99
	Buffalo-Niagara Falls MSA, NY	S	20.12 MW	21.65 AW	41860 AAW	NYBLS	10//99-12//99
	Nassau-Suffolk PMSA, NY	S	23.27 MW	24.58 AW	48410 AAW	NYBLS	10//99-12//99
	New York PMSA, NY	S	31.92 MW	34.86 AW	66390 AAW	NYBLS	10//99-12//99
	Newburgh PMSA, NY-PA	S	19.31 MW	17.45 AW	40170 AAW	NYBLS	10//99-12//99
	Rochester MSA, NY	S	14.24 MW	12.82 AW	29620 AAW	NYBLS	10//99-12//99
	Syracuse MSA, NY	S	18.95 MW	19.22 AW	39420 AAW	NYBLS	10//99-12//99
	North Carolina	S	11.34 MW	11.78 AW	24500 AAW	NCBLS	10//99-12//99
	Asheville MSA, NC	S	13.05 MW	13.03 AW	27150 AAW	NCBLS	10//99-12//99
	Charlotte-Gastonia-Rock Hill MSA, NC-SC	S	11.95 MW	12.01 AW	24860 AAW	NCBLS	10//99-12//99
	Fayetteville MSA, NC	S	18.14 MW	18.78 AW	37730 AAW	NCBLS	10//99-12//99
	Greensboro--Winston-Salem--High Point MSA, NC	S	13.87 MW	13.87 AW	28840 AAW	NCBLS	10//99-12//99
	Hickory-Morganton-Lenoir MSA, NC	S	15.64 MW	15.57 AW	32530 AAW	NCBLS	10//99-12//99
	Raleigh-Durham-Chapel Hill MSA, NC	S	11.79 MW	11.12 AW	24530 AAW	NCBLS	10//99-12//99
	Rocky Mount MSA, NC	S	8.86 MW	7.85 AW	18420 AAW	NCBLS	10//99-12//99
	North Dakota	S	11.32 MW	11.89 AW	24730 AAW	NDBLS	10//99-12//99
	Fargo-Moorhead MSA, ND-MN	S	12.25 MW	12.05 AW	25480 AAW	NDBLS	10//99-12//99
	Grand Forks MSA, ND-MN	S	13.47 MW	14.01 AW	28020 AAW	NDBLS	10//99-12//99
	Ohio	S	18.21 MW	17.99 AW	37420 AAW	OHBLS	10//99-12//99
	Cincinnati PMSA, OH-KY-IN	S	15.88 MW	14.89 AW	33020 AAW	OHBLS	10//99-12//99
	Cleveland-Lorain-Elyria PMSA, OH	S	20.18 MW	21.89 AW	41980 AAW	OHBLS	10//99-12//99
	Columbus MSA, OH	S	15.21 MW	14.28 AW	31640 AAW	OHBLS	10//99-12//99
	Dayton-Springfield MSA, OH	S	13.29 MW	13.14 AW	27650 AAW	OHBLS	10//99-12//99
	Toledo MSA, OH	S	14.14 MW	14.35 AW	29410 AAW	OHBLS	10//99-12//99
	Youngstown-Warren MSA, OH	S	20.40 MW	22.21 AW	42430 AAW	OHBLS	10//99-12//99
	Oklahoma	S	11.23 MW	11.63 AW	24200 AAW	OKBLS	10//99-12//99
	Lawton MSA, OK	S	10.55 MW	10.38 AW	21950 AAW	OKBLS	10//99-12//99
	Oklahoma City MSA, OK	S	10.22 MW	9.92 AW	21260 AAW	OKBLS	10//99-12//99
	Tulsa MSA, OK	S	14.73 MW	14.64 AW	30640 AAW	OKBLS	10//99-12//99
	Oregon	S	16.73 MW	17.66 AW	36740 AAW	ORBLS	10//99-12//99
	Eugene-Springfield MSA, OR	S	15.23 MW	15.09 AW	31680 AAW	ORBLS	10//99-12//99
	Medford-Ashland MSA, OR	S	16.31 MW	15.51 AW	33920 AAW	ORBLS	10//99-12//99
	Portland-Vancouver PMSA, OR-WA	S	19.54 MW	19.96 AW	40640 AAW	ORBLS	10//99-12//99
	Pennsylvania	S	18.36 MW	18.20 AW	37850 AAW	PABLS	10//99-12//99
	Allentown-Bethlehem-Easton MSA, PA	S	12.64 MW	12.63 AW	26290 AAW	PABLS	10//99-12//99
	Altoona MSA, PA	S	10.66 MW	11.11 AW	22170 AAW	PABLS	10//99-12//99
	Erie MSA, PA	S	14.61 MW	14.86 AW	30380 AAW	PABLS	10//99-12//99
	Harrisburg-Lebanon-Carlisle MSA, PA	S	18.90 MW	18.87 AW	39300 AAW	PABLS	10//99-12//99
	Johnstown MSA, PA	S	10.47 MW	10.08 AW	21770 AAW	PABLS	10//99-12//99
	Lancaster MSA, PA	S	12.90 MW	13.31 AW	26840 AAW	PABLS	10//99-12//99
	Philadelphia PMSA, PA-NJ	S	19.32 MW	19.95 AW	40190 AAW	PABLS	10//99-12//99
	Pittsburgh MSA, PA	S	18.05 MW	18.84 AW	37550 AAW	PABLS	10//99-12//99
	Reading MSA, PA	S	15.38 MW	14.56 AW	31980 AAW	PABLS	10//99-12//99
	Scranton--Wilkes-Barre--Hazleton MSA, PA	S	15.01 MW	15.56 AW	31220 AAW	PABLS	10//99-12//99
	York MSA, PA	S	16.18 MW	15.06 AW	33650 AAW	PABLS	10//99-12//99
	Rhode Island	S	10.67 MW	15.22 AW	31650 AAW	RIBLS	10//99-12//99
	Providence-Fall River-Warwick MSA, RI-MA	S	15.59 MW	10.67 AW	32440 AAW	RIBLS	10//99-12//99
	South Carolina	S	11.35 MW	11.23 AW	23360 AAW	SCBLS	10//99-12//99
	Charleston-North Charleston MSA, SC	S	11.58 MW	11.69 AW	24080 AAW	SCBLS	10//99-12//99
	Columbia MSA, SC	S	10.36 MW	9.93 AW	21560 AAW	SCBLS	10//99-12//99
	Greenville-Spartanburg-Anderson MSA, SC	S	11.70 MW	11.90 AW	24330 AAW	SCBLS	10//99-12//99
	Myrtle Beach MSA, SC	S	11.32 MW	11.42 AW	23550 AAW	SCBLS	10//99-12//99
	Sumter MSA, SC	S	14.46 MW	15.00 AW	30070 AAW	SCBLS	10//99-12//99
	South Dakota	S	11.96 MW	12.19 AW	25360 AAW	SDBLS	10//99-12//99
	Rapid City MSA, SD	S	13.94 MW	14.26 AW	29000 AAW	SDBLS	10//99-12//99

AAW	Average annual wage	AOH	Average offered, high	ASH	Average starting, high	H	Hourly	M	Monthly	S	Special: hourly and annual
AE	Average entry wage	AOL	Average offered, low	ASL	Average starting, low	HI	Highest wage paid	MTC	Median total compensation	TQ	Third quartile wage
AEX	Average experienced wage	APH	Average pay, high range	AW	Average wage paid	HR	High end range	MW	Median wage paid	W	Weekly
AO	Average offered	APL	Average pay, low range	FQ	First quartile wage	LR	Low end range	SQ	Second quartile wage	Y	Yearly

Cement Mason and Concrete Finisher

Occupation/Type/Industry	Location	Per	Low	Mid	High	Source	Date
Cement Mason and Concrete Finisher	Sioux Falls MSA, SD	S	11.84 MW	11.63 AW	24630 AAW	SDBLS	10//99-12//99
	Tennessee	S	12.34 MW	12.48 AW	25970 AAW	TNBLS	10//99-12//99
	Chattanooga MSA, TN-GA	S	12.78 MW	12.14 AW	26580 AAW	TNBLS	10//99-12//99
	Jackson MSA, TN	S	11.66 MW	11.65 AW	24250 AAW	TNBLS	10//99-12//99
	Johnson City-Kingsport-Bristol MSA, TN-VA	S	11.19 MW	11.26 AW	23270 AAW	TNBLS	10//99-12//99
	Knoxville MSA, TN	S	12.42 MW	12.35 AW	25840 AAW	TNBLS	10//99-12//99
	Memphis MSA, TN-AR-MS	S	12.70 MW	12.21 AW	26420 AAW	MSBLS	10//99-12//99
	Nashville MSA, TN	S	11.60 MW	11.08 AW	24120 AAW	TNBLS	10//99-12//99
	Texas	S	10.11 MW	10.44 AW	21710 AAW	TXBLS	10//99-12//99
	Amarillo MSA, TX	S	11.94 MW	12.24 AW	24830 AAW	TXBLS	10//99-12//99
	Austin-San Marcos MSA, TX	S	11.38 MW	11.19 AW	23670 AAW	TXBLS	10//99-12//99
	Beaumont-Port Arthur MSA, TX	S	11.57 MW	11.41 AW	24070 AAW	TXBLS	10//99-12//99
	Brownsville-Harlingen-San Benito MSA, TX	S	8.14 MW	8.09 AW	16940 AAW	TXBLS	10//99-12//99
	Bryan-College Station MSA, TX	S	8.59 MW	8.50 AW	17870 AAW	TXBLS	10//99-12//99
	Corpus Christi MSA, TX	S	10.68 MW	10.27 AW	22210 AAW	TXBLS	10//99-12//99
	Dallas PMSA, TX	S	10.54 MW	10.32 AW	21910 AAW	TXBLS	10//99-12//99
	El Paso MSA, TX	S	9.04 MW	8.93 AW	18810 AAW	TXBLS	10//99-12//99
	Fort Worth-Arlington PMSA, TX	S	9.94 MW	9.74 AW	20670 AAW	TXBLS	10//99-12//99
	Galveston-Texas City PMSA, TX	S	11.17 MW	10.74 AW	23240 AAW	TXBLS	10//99-12//99
	Houston PMSA, TX	S	10.21 MW	9.94 AW	21250 AAW	TXBLS	10//99-12//99
	Killeen-Temple MSA, TX	S	10.81 MW	11.11 AW	22490 AAW	TXBLS	10//99-12//99
	Laredo MSA, TX	S	8.03 MW	7.81 AW	16700 AAW	TXBLS	10//99-12//99
	Longview-Marshall MSA, TX	S	9.46 MW	9.49 AW	19670 AAW	TXBLS	10//99-12//99
	McAllen-Edinburg-Mission MSA, TX	S	7.31 MW	7.26 AW	15210 AAW	TXBLS	10//99-12//99
	Odessa-Midland MSA, TX	S	8.59 MW	8.49 AW	17860 AAW	TXBLS	10//99-12//99
	San Antonio MSA, TX	S	11.38 MW	10.51 AW	23670 AAW	TXBLS	10//99-12//99
	Texarkana MSA, TX-Texarkana, AR	S	10.39 MW	9.70 AW	21600 AAW	TXBLS	10//99-12//99
	Waco MSA, TX	S	8.16 MW	7.82 AW	16970 AAW	TXBLS	10//99-12//99
	Wichita Falls MSA, TX	S	11.67 MW	11.34 AW	24280 AAW	TXBLS	10//99-12//99
	Utah	S	12.66 MW	13.00 AW	27050 AAW	UTBLS	10//99-12//99
	Provo-Orem MSA, UT	S	12.52 MW	12.16 AW	26040 AAW	UTBLS	10//99-12//99
	Salt Lake City-Ogden MSA, UT	S	12.65 MW	12.42 AW	26320 AAW	UTBLS	10//99-12//99
	Vermont	S	11.02 MW	11.29 AW	23480 AAW	VTBLS	10//99-12//99
	Virginia	S	12.67 MW	13.23 AW	27520 AAW	VABLS	10//99-12//99
	Charlottesville MSA, VA	S	9.25 MW	8.15 AW	19250 AAW	VABLS	10//99-12//99
	Danville MSA, VA	S	8.45 MW	8.18 AW	17590 AAW	VABLS	10//99-12//99
	Lynchburg MSA, VA	S	9.65 MW	9.68 AW	20080 AAW	VABLS	10//99-12//99
	Norfolk-Virginia Beach-Newport News MSA, VA-NC	S	12.36 MW	12.39 AW	25700 AAW	VABLS	10//99-12//99
	Richmond-Petersburg MSA, VA	S	11.00 MW	10.78 AW	22880 AAW	VABLS	10//99-12//99
	Roanoke MSA, VA	S	11.02 MW	10.17 AW	22920 AAW	VABLS	10//99-12//99
	Washington	S	19.49 MW	19.10 AW	39730 AAW	WABLS	10//99-12//99
	Bellingham MSA, WA	S	24.76 MW	28.60 AW	51490 AAW	WABLS	10//99-12//99
	Olympia PMSA, WA	S	19.26 MW	19.25 AW	40060 AAW	WABLS	10//99-12//99
	Richland-Kennewick-Pasco MSA, WA	S	19.27 MW	19.19 AW	40080 AAW	WABLS	10//99-12//99
	Seattle-Bellevue-Everett PMSA, WA	S	22.11 MW	23.63 AW	45990 AAW	WABLS	10//99-12//99
	Spokane MSA, WA	S	19.80 MW	19.58 AW	41190 AAW	WABLS	10//99-12//99
	Tacoma PMSA, WA	S	16.90 MW	15.95 AW	35150 AAW	WABLS	10//99-12//99
	Yakima MSA, WA	S	15.25 MW	15.19 AW	31710 AAW	WABLS	10//99-12//99
	West Virginia	S	17.48 MW	17.08 AW	35520 AAW	WVBLS	10//99-12//99
	Charleston MSA, WV	S	13.44 MW	13.09 AW	27940 AAW	WVBLS	10//99-12//99
	Huntington-Ashland MSA, WV-KY-OH	S	12.77 MW	12.74 AW	26560 AAW	WVBLS	10//99-12//99
	Parkersburg-Marietta MSA, WV-OH	S	20.73 MW	19.61 AW	43110 AAW	WVBLS	10//99-12//99
	Wheeling MSA, WV-OH	S	15.28 MW	15.42 AW	31790 AAW	WVBLS	10//99-12//99
	Wisconsin	S	16.01 MW	16.61 AW	34540 AAW	WIBLS	10//99-12//99

AAW Average annual wage	**AOH** Average offered, high	**ASH** Average starting, high	**H** Hourly	**M** Monthly	**S** Special: hourly and annual
AE Average entry wage	**AOL** Average offered, low	**ASL** Average starting, low	**HI** Highest wage paid	**MTC** Median total compensation	**TQ** Third quartile wage
AEX Average experienced wage	**APH** Average pay, high range	**AW** Average wage paid	**HR** High end range	**MW** Median wage paid	**W** Weekly
AO Average offered	**APL** Average pay, low range	**FQ** First quartile wage	**LR** Low end range	**SQ** Second quartile wage	**Y** Yearly

Occupation/Type/Industry	Location	Per	Low	Mid	High	Source	Date
Cement Mason and Concrete Finisher							
	Appleton-Oshkosh-Neenah MSA, WI	S	16.24 MW	15.78 AW	33770 AAW	WIBLS	10//99-12//99
	Eau Claire MSA, WI	S	16.62 MW	15.72 AW	34580 AAW	WIBLS	10//99-12//99
	Green Bay MSA, WI	S	15.45 MW	14.42 AW	32130 AAW	WIBLS	10//99-12//99
	Janesville-Beloit MSA, WI	S	15.56 MW	16.13 AW	32370 AAW	WIBLS	10//99-12//99
	La Crosse MSA, WI-MN	S	15.58 MW	13.47 AW	32410 AAW	WIBLS	10//99-12//99
	Madison MSA, WI	S	18.73 MW	19.46 AW	38960 AAW	WIBLS	10//99-12//99
	Milwaukee-Waukesha PMSA, WI	S	19.15 MW	20.33 AW	39830 AAW	WIBLS	10//99-12//99
	Racine PMSA, WI	S	17.00 MW	16.56 AW	35350 AAW	WIBLS	10//99-12//99
	Sheboygan MSA, WI	S	14.60 MW	13.47 AW	30360 AAW	WIBLS	10//99-12//99
	Wyoming	S	12.03 MW	12.08 AW	25140 AAW	WYBLS	10//99-12//99
	Casper MSA, WY	S	11.70 MW	11.39 AW	24330 AAW	WYBLS	10//99-12//99
	Puerto Rico	S	6.98 MW	6.83 AW	14210 AAW	PRBLS	10//99-12//99
	Aguadilla MSA, PR	S	5.75 MW	5.95 AW	11960 AAW	PRBLS	10//99-12//99
	Arecibo PMSA, PR	S	7.40 MW	7.57 AW	15400 AAW	PRBLS	10//99-12//99
	Caguas PMSA, PR	S	6.03 MW	6.10 AW	12550 AAW	PRBLS	10//99-12//99
	Mayaguez MSA, PR	S	6.92 MW	7.16 AW	14400 AAW	PRBLS	10//99-12//99
	Ponce MSA, PR	S	6.19 MW	6.22 AW	12880 AAW	PRBLS	10//99-12//99
	San Juan-Bayamon PMSA, PR	S	7.06 MW	7.26 AW	14690 AAW	PRBLS	10//99-12//99
	Virgin Islands	S	12.14 MW	12.09 AW	25140 AAW	VIBLS	10//99-12//99
	Guam	S	12.1 MW	11.95 AW	24860 AAW	GUBLS	10//99-12//99
Cementing and Gluing Machine Operator and Tender							
	Alabama	S	12.6 MW	12.38 AW	25750 AAW	ALBLS	10//99-12//99
	Arizona	S	9.69 MW	9.49 AW	19740 AAW	AZBLS	10//99-12//99
	Arkansas	S	9.62 MW	10.00 AW	20800 AAW	ARBLS	10//99-12//99
	California	S	8.35 MW	9.56 AW	19890 AAW	CABLS	10//99-12//99
	Colorado	S	10.78 MW	11.53 AW	23990 AAW	COBLS	10//99-12//99
	Connecticut	S	11.13 MW	11.66 AW	24240 AAW	CTBLS	10//99-12//99
	Georgia	S	8.11 MW	9.26 AW	19250 AAW	GABLS	10//99-12//99
	Idaho	S	12 MW	11.64 AW	24210 AAW	IDBLS	10//99-12//99
	Illinois	S	10.63 MW	11.09 AW	23080 AAW	ILBLS	10//99-12//99
	Indiana	S	11.14 MW	11.09 AW	23060 AAW	INBLS	10//99-12//99
	Iowa	S	11.09 MW	11.57 AW	24060 AAW	IABLS	10//99-12//99
	Kansas	S	9.5 MW	9.61 AW	19990 AAW	KSBLS	10//99-12//99
	Kentucky	S	8.7 MW	9.81 AW	20400 AAW	KYBLS	10//99-12//99
	Louisiana	S	11.26 MW	10.66 AW	22160 AAW	LABLS	10//99-12//99
	Maine	S	8.34 MW	9.26 AW	19260 AAW	MEBLS	10//99-12//99
	Maryland	S	11.39 MW	11.71 AW	24360 AAW	MDBLS	10//99-12//99
	Massachusetts	S	10.88 MW	11.18 AW	23250 AAW	MABLS	10//99-12//99
	Michigan	S	10.08 MW	10.39 AW	21610 AAW	MIBLS	10//99-12//99
	Minnesota	S	12.32 MW	12.39 AW	25770 AAW	MNBLS	10//99-12//99
	Mississippi	S	9.41 MW	9.71 AW	20200 AAW	MSBLS	10//99-12//99
	Missouri	S	9.73 MW	10.08 AW	20970 AAW	MOBLS	10//99-12//99
	Montana	S	12.49 MW	12.23 AW	25440 AAW	MTBLS	10//99-12//99
	Nebraska	S	11.89 MW	11.61 AW	24140 AAW	NEBLS	10//99-12//99
	New Jersey	S	10.82 MW	10.92 AW	22710 AAW	NJBLS	10//99-12//99
	New York	S	9.85 MW	10.09 AW	20990 AAW	NYBLS	10//99-12//99
	North Carolina	S	10.44 MW	10.58 AW	22010 AAW	NCBLS	10//99-12//99
	Ohio	S	11.24 MW	11.56 AW	24040 AAW	OHBLS	10//99-12//99
	Oregon	S	14.29 MW	13.71 AW	28530 AAW	ORBLS	10//99-12//99
	Pennsylvania	S	10.95 MW	11.18 AW	23260 AAW	PABLS	10//99-12//99
	Rhode Island	S	11.19 MW	10.81 AW	22490 AAW	RIBLS	10//99-12//99
	South Carolina	S	13.16 MW	15.36 AW	31950 AAW	SCBLS	10//99-12//99
	South Dakota	S	10.11 MW	9.62 AW	20000 AAW	SDBLS	10//99-12//99
	Tennessee	S	9.77 MW	9.91 AW	20610 AAW	TNBLS	10//99-12//99
	Texas	S	8.64 MW	8.98 AW	18690 AAW	TXBLS	10//99-12//99
	Utah	S	10.36 MW	10.60 AW	22050 AAW	UTBLS	10//99-12//99
	Vermont	S	9.57 MW	9.67 AW	20120 AAW	VTBLS	10//99-12//99
	Virginia	S	9.74 MW	9.71 AW	20190 AAW	VABLS	10//99-12//99
	Washington	S	11.27 MW	11.45 AW	23810 AAW	WABLS	10//99-12//99
	Wisconsin	S	10.27 MW	10.70 AW	22250 AAW	WIBLS	10//99-12//99
	Puerto Rico	S	6.51 MW	6.99 AW	14530 AAW	PRBLS	10//99-12//99
CEO							
Financial Planning Firm	United States	Y		146439 AW		INVNEWS	2000
CEO/President							
Financial Industry	United States	Y		210039 AW		PENINV	2000

AAW	Average annual wage	AOH	Average offered, high	ASH	Average starting, high	H	Hourly	M	Monthly	S	Special: hourly and annual
AE	Average entry wage	AOL	Average offered, low	ASL	Average starting, low	HI	Highest wage paid	MTC	Median total compensation	TQ	Third quartile wage
AEX	Average experienced wage	APH	Average pay, high range	AW	Average wage paid	HR	High end range	MW	Median wage paid	W	Weekly
AO	Average offered	APL	Average pay, low range	FQ	First quartile wage	LR	Low end range	SQ	Second quartile wage	Y	Yearly

Occupation/Type/Industry	Location	Per	Low	Mid	High	Source	Date
Chef							
Executive	United States	Y		38000 AW		TQUES	1999
Household	United States	Y	35000 LR		300000 HR	COLBIZ	2000
Chef and Head Cook	Alabama	S	11.45 MW	12.09 AW	25140 AAW	ALBLS	10//99-12//99
	Birmingham MSA, AL	S	14.29 MW	12.27 AW	29710 AAW	ALBLS	10//99-12//99
	Dothan MSA, AL	S	7.76 MW	6.42 AW	16130 AAW	ALBLS	10//99-12//99
	Huntsville MSA, AL	S	10.27 MW	9.44 AW	21370 AAW	ALBLS	10//99-12//99
	Mobile MSA, AL	S	14.22 MW	12.75 AW	29580 AAW	ALBLS	10//99-12//99
	Montgomery MSA, AL	S	9.88 MW	7.96 AW	20550 AAW	ALBLS	10//99-12//99
	Alaska	S	12.97 MW	14.73 AW	30640 AAW	AKBLS	10//99-12//99
	Anchorage MSA, AK	S	18.36 MW	16.43 AW	38190 AAW	AKBLS	10//99-12//99
	Arizona	S	13.86 MW	13.81 AW	28730 AAW	AZBLS	10//99-12//99
	Flagstaff MSA, AZ-UT	S	10.50 MW	9.91 AW	21840 AAW	AZBLS	10//99-12//99
	Phoenix-Mesa MSA, AZ	S	15.77 MW	14.68 AW	32800 AAW	AZBLS	10//99-12//99
	Tucson MSA, AZ	S	15.28 MW	14.77 AW	31770 AAW	AZBLS	10//99-12//99
	Yuma MSA, AZ	S	8.42 MW	8.25 AW	17510 AAW	AZBLS	10//99-12//99
	Arkansas	S	10.42 MW	12.60 AW	26210 AAW	ARBLS	10//99-12//99
	Fayetteville-Springdale-Rogers MSA, AR	S	10.07 MW	9.29 AW	20950 AAW	ARBLS	10//99-12//99
	Fort Smith MSA, AR-OK	S	8.28 MW	7.85 AW	17220 AAW	ARBLS	10//99-12//99
	Little Rock-North Little Rock MSA, AR	S	17.45 MW	15.84 AW	36300 AAW	ARBLS	10//99-12//99
	California	S	13.04 MW	14.62 AW	30420 AAW	CABLS	10//99-12//99
	Bakersfield MSA, CA	S	12.26 MW	10.48 AW	25510 AAW	CABLS	10//99-12//99
	Chico-Paradise MSA, CA	S	11.13 MW	11.22 AW	23150 AAW	CABLS	10//99-12//99
	Fresno MSA, CA	S	12.45 MW	12.68 AW	25890 AAW	CABLS	10//99-12//99
	Los Angeles-Long Beach PMSA, CA	S	17.65 MW	15.76 AW	36720 AAW	CABLS	10//99-12//99
	Modesto MSA, CA	S	13.74 MW	13.68 AW	28580 AAW	CABLS	10//99-12//99
	Oakland PMSA, CA	S	19.11 MW	19.15 AW	39750 AAW	CABLS	10//99-12//99
	Orange County PMSA, CA	S	15.93 MW	14.83 AW	33140 AAW	CABLS	10//99-12//99
	Redding MSA, CA	S	11.55 MW	11.77 AW	24030 AAW	CABLS	10//99-12//99
	Riverside-San Bernardino PMSA, CA	S	15.52 MW	14.39 AW	32280 AAW	CABLS	10//99-12//99
	Sacramento PMSA, CA	S	14.90 MW	13.76 AW	31000 AAW	CABLS	10//99-12//99
	San Diego MSA, CA	S	12.96 MW	10.67 AW	26960 AAW	CABLS	10//99-12//99
	San Francisco PMSA, CA	S	15.41 MW	13.38 AW	32040 AAW	CABLS	10//99-12//99
	San Jose PMSA, CA	S	18.44 MW	16.23 AW	38360 AAW	CABLS	10//99-12//99
	San Luis Obispo-Atascadero-Paso Robles MSA, CA	S	11.37 MW	11.66 AW	23640 AAW	CABLS	10//99-12//99
	Santa Barbara-Santa Maria-Lompoc MSA, CA	S	9.69 MW	8.17 AW	20160 AAW	CABLS	10//99-12//99
	Santa Cruz-Watsonville PMSA, CA	S	11.50 MW	11.02 AW	23920 AAW	CABLS	10//99-12//99
	Santa Rosa PMSA, CA	S	15.71 MW	15.66 AW	32680 AAW	CABLS	10//99-12//99
	Stockton-Lodi MSA, CA	S	10.18 MW	8.16 AW	21180 AAW	CABLS	10//99-12//99
	Vallejo-Fairfield-Napa PMSA, CA	S	17.29 MW	14.65 AW	35960 AAW	CABLS	10//99-12//99
	Ventura PMSA, CA	S	11.63 MW	10.61 AW	24190 AAW	CABLS	10//99-12//99
	Visalia-Tulare-Porterville MSA, CA	S	9.61 MW	8.97 AW	19990 AAW	CABLS	10//99-12//99
	Yolo PMSA, CA	S	8.21 MW	7.34 AW	17080 AAW	CABLS	10//99-12//99
	Yuba City MSA, CA	S	15.16 MW	15.25 AW	31530 AAW	CABLS	10//99-12//99
	Colorado	S	16.61 MW	17.30 AW	35990 AAW	COBLS	10//99-12//99
	Colorado Springs MSA, CO	S	15.04 MW	12.96 AW	31290 AAW	COBLS	10//99-12//99
	Denver PMSA, CO	S	16.21 MW	15.05 AW	33710 AAW	COBLS	10//99-12//99
	Connecticut	S	16.31 MW	22.40 AW	46590 AAW	CTBLS	10//99-12//99
	Danbury PMSA, CT	S	24.51 MW	22.34 AW	50980 AAW	CTBLS	10//99-12//99
	Hartford MSA, CT	S	25.55 MW	16.85 AW	53150 AAW	CTBLS	10//99-12//99
	New London-Norwich MSA, CT-RI	S	17.10 MW	14.37 AW	35560 AAW	CTBLS	10//99-12//99
	Stamford-Norwalk PMSA, CT	S	33.88 MW	25.98 AW	70470 AAW	CTBLS	10//99-12//99
	Waterbury PMSA, CT	S	16.81 MW	12.87 AW	34960 AAW	CTBLS	10//99-12//99
	Delaware	S	11.52 MW	11.36 AW	23620 AAW	DEBLS	10//99-12//99
	Dover MSA, DE	S	16.43 MW	17.70 AW	34180 AAW	DEBLS	10//99-12//99
	District of Columbia	S	18.83 MW	19.42 AW	40390 AAW	DCBLS	10//99-12//99
	Washington PMSA, DC-MD-VA-WV	S	18.49 MW	16.87 AW	38460 AAW	DCBLS	10//99-12//99
	Florida	S	12.85 MW	14.67 AW	30510 AAW	FLBLS	10//99-12//99
	Daytona Beach MSA, FL	S	12.88 MW	11.86 AW	26780 AAW	FLBLS	10//99-12//99
	Fort Lauderdale PMSA, FL	S	11.92 MW	11.56 AW	24780 AAW	FLBLS	10//99-12//99

AAW	Average annual wage	AOH	Average offered, high	ASH	Average starting, high	H	Hourly	
AE	Average entry wage	AOL	Average offered, low	ASL	Average starting, low	HI	Highest wage paid	
AEX	Average experienced wage	APH	Average pay, high range	AW	Average wage paid	HR	High end range	
AO	Average offered	APL	Average pay, low range	FQ	First quartile wage	LR	Low end range	

M	Monthly	S	Special: hourly and annual
MTC	Median total compensation	TQ	Third quartile wage
MW	Median wage paid	W	Weekly
SQ	Second quartile wage	Y	Yearly

Occupation/Type/Industry	Location	Per	Low	Mid	High	Source	Date
Chef and Head Cook	Fort Myers-Cape Coral MSA, FL	S	14.86 MW	13.16 AW	30910 AAW	FLBLS	10//99-12//99
	Fort Pierce-Port St. Lucie MSA, FL	S	16.05 MW	15.91 AW	33390 AAW	FLBLS	10//99-12//99
	Fort Walton Beach MSA, FL	S	12.10 MW	11.72 AW	25170 AAW	FLBLS	10//99-12//99
	Jacksonville MSA, FL	S	15.22 MW	13.25 AW	31650 AAW	FLBLS	10//99-12//99
	Lakeland-Winter Haven MSA, FL	S	14.69 MW	13.81 AW	30550 AAW	FLBLS	10//99-12//99
	Melbourne-Titusville-Palm Bay MSA, FL	S	11.71 MW	11.85 AW	24360 AAW	FLBLS	10//99-12//99
	Miami PMSA, FL	S	16.50 MW	15.71 AW	34330 AAW	FLBLS	10//99-12//99
	Naples MSA, FL	S	16.11 MW	12.94 AW	33500 AAW	FLBLS	10//99-12//99
	Orlando MSA, FL	S	15.45 MW	13.10 AW	32140 AAW	FLBLS	10//99-12//99
	Panama City MSA, FL	S	14.01 MW	13.63 AW	29140 AAW	FLBLS	10//99-12//99
	Pensacola MSA, FL	S	13.59 MW	12.57 AW	28260 AAW	FLBLS	10//99-12//99
	Sarasota-Bradenton MSA, FL	S	13.10 MW	10.57 AW	27250 AAW	FLBLS	10//99-12//99
	Tallahassee MSA, FL	S	14.59 MW	12.95 AW	30350 AAW	FLBLS	10//99-12//99
	Tampa-St. Petersburg-Clearwater MSA, FL	S	13.02 MW	10.61 AW	27080 AAW	FLBLS	10//99-12//99
	West Palm Beach-Boca Raton MSA, FL	S	16.29 MW	14.80 AW	33880 AAW	FLBLS	10//99-12//99
	Georgia	S	13.26 MW	13.89 AW	28890 AAW	GABLS	10//99-12//99
	Albany MSA, GA	S	16.34 MW	14.94 AW	33980 AAW	GABLS	10//99-12//99
	Athens MSA, GA	S	12.17 MW	10.73 AW	25320 AAW	GABLS	10//99-12//99
	Atlanta MSA, GA	S	15.28 MW	14.90 AW	31780 AAW	GABLS	10//99-12//99
	Augusta-Aiken MSA, GA-SC	S	13.65 MW	12.48 AW	28390 AAW	GABLS	10//99-12//99
	Columbus MSA, GA-AL	S	12.50 MW	12.27 AW	25990 AAW	GABLS	10//99-12//99
	Macon MSA, GA	S	12.37 MW	12.40 AW	25720 AAW	GABLS	10//99-12//99
	Savannah MSA, GA	S	13.77 MW	12.53 AW	28640 AAW	GABLS	10//99-12//99
	Hawaii	S	17.68 MW	19.73 AW	41050 AAW	HIBLS	10//99-12//99
	Honolulu MSA, HI	S	20.49 MW	18.43 AW	42630 AAW	HIBLS	10//99-12//99
	Idaho	S	10.29 MW	12.10 AW	25160 AAW	IDBLS	10//99-12//99
	Illinois	S	14.08 MW	14.29 AW	29720 AAW	ILBLS	10//99-12//99
	Bloomington-Normal MSA, IL	S	10.83 MW	9.94 AW	22520 AAW	ILBLS	10//99-12//99
	Chicago PMSA, IL	S	18.70 MW	16.45 AW	38890 AAW	ILBLS	10//99-12//99
	Rockford MSA, IL	S	15.89 MW	15.10 AW	33050 AAW	ILBLS	10//99-12//99
	Springfield MSA, IL	S	13.17 MW	12.45 AW	27400 AAW	ILBLS	10//99-12//99
	Indiana	S	12.05 MW	13.55 AW	28180 AAW	INBLS	10//99-12//99
	Bloomington MSA, IN	S	9.09 MW	8.37 AW	18900 AAW	INBLS	10//99-12//99
	Elkhart-Goshen MSA, IN	S	10.76 MW	8.25 AW	22380 AAW	INBLS	10//99-12//99
	Evansville-Henderson MSA, IN-KY	S	10.20 MW	9.05 AW	21210 AAW	INBLS	10//99-12//99
	Fort Wayne MSA, IN	S	8.16 MW	6.31 AW	16980 AAW	INBLS	10//99-12//99
	Gary PMSA, IN	S	21.39 MW	19.76 AW	44500 AAW	INBLS	10//99-12//99
	Indianapolis MSA, IN	S	15.15 MW	13.07 AW	31500 AAW	INBLS	10//99-12//99
	South Bend MSA, IN	S	10.09 MW	9.70 AW	20980 AAW	INBLS	10//99-12//99
	Iowa	S	10.68 MW	11.66 AW	24250 AAW	IABLS	10//99-12//99
	Cedar Rapids MSA, IA	S	12.84 MW	12.63 AW	26700 AAW	IABLS	10//99-12//99
	Davenport-Moline-Rock Island MSA, IA-IL	S	12.52 MW	10.84 AW	26040 AAW	IABLS	10//99-12//99
	Des Moines MSA, IA	S	13.33 MW	13.80 AW	27740 AAW	IABLS	10//99-12//99
	Sioux City MSA, IA-NE	S	11.00 MW	10.07 AW	22880 AAW	IABLS	10//99-12//99
	Kansas	S	10.72 MW	11.73 AW	24410 AAW	KSBLS	10//99-12//99
	Lawrence MSA, KS	S	11.80 MW	11.48 AW	24540 AAW	KSBLS	10//99-12//99
	Topeka MSA, KS	S	11.05 MW	9.69 AW	22980 AAW	KSBLS	10//99-12//99
	Wichita MSA, KS	S	12.28 MW	11.98 AW	25550 AAW	KSBLS	10//99-12//99
	Kentucky	S	9.92 MW	11.14 AW	23180 AAW	KYBLS	10//99-12//99
	Lexington MSA, KY	S	17.05 MW	17.35 AW	35470 AAW	KYBLS	10//99-12//99
	Louisville MSA, KY-IN	S	12.24 MW	11.54 AW	25470 AAW	KYBLS	10//99-12//99
	Louisiana	S	12.61 MW	13.43 AW	27940 AAW	LABLS	10//99-12//99
	Baton Rouge MSA, LA	S	14.59 MW	14.36 AW	30340 AAW	LABLS	10//99-12//99
	Lafayette MSA, LA	S	12.53 MW	12.30 AW	26070 AAW	LABLS	10//99-12//99
	Lake Charles MSA, LA	S	10.05 MW	7.92 AW	20910 AAW	LABLS	10//99-12//99
	New Orleans MSA, LA	S	13.90 MW	12.52 AW	28920 AAW	LABLS	10//99-12//99
	Shreveport-Bossier City MSA, LA	S	14.31 MW	14.35 AW	29770 AAW	LABLS	10//99-12//99
	Maine	S	11.16 MW	12.46 AW	25910 AAW	MEBLS	10//99-12//99
	Bangor MSA, ME	S	13.54 MW	12.84 AW	28160 AAW	MEBLS	10//99-12//99
	Portland MSA, ME	S	12.94 MW	12.77 AW	26920 AAW	MEBLS	10//99-12//99
	Maryland	S	15.49 MW	17.12 AW	35600 AAW	MDBLS	10//99-12//99
	Baltimore PMSA, MD	S	18.91 MW	17.87 AW	39330 AAW	MDBLS	10//99-12//99
	Cumberland MSA, MD-WV	S	17.79 MW	18.12 AW	37010 AAW	MDBLS	10//99-12//99

AAW	Average annual wage	AOH	Average offered, high	ASH	Average starting, high
AE	Average entry wage	AOL	Average offered, low	ASL	Average starting, low
AEX	Average experienced wage	APH	Average pay, high range	AW	Average wage paid
AO	Average offered	APL	Average pay, low range	FQ	First quartile wage

H	Hourly	M	Monthly	S	Special: hourly and annual
HI	Highest wage paid	MTC	Median total compensation	TQ	Third quartile wage
HR	High end range	MW	Median wage paid	W	Weekly
LR	Low end range	SQ	Second quartile wage	Y	Yearly

Occupation/Type/Industry	Location	Per	Low	Mid	High	Source	Date
Chef and Head Cook	Hagerstown PMSA, MD	S	11.54 MW	11.77 AW	24000 AAW	MDBLS	10//99-12//99
	Massachusetts	S	14 MW	15.41 AW	32050 AAW	MABLS	10//99-12//99
	Barnstable-Yarmouth MSA, MA	S	14.93 MW	12.71 AW	31060 AAW	MABLS	10//99-12//99
	Boston PMSA, MA-NH	S	17.74 MW	16.71 AW	36890 AAW	MABLS	10//99-12//99
	Brockton PMSA, MA	S	24.28 MW	24.95 AW	50500 AAW	MABLS	10//99-12//99
	Fitchburg-Leominster PMSA, MA	S	21.00 MW	19.04 AW	43680 AAW	MABLS	10//99-12//99
	Lawrence PMSA, MA-NH	S	17.15 MW	15.70 AW	35670 AAW	MABLS	10//99-12//99
	Lowell PMSA, MA-NH	S	9.96 MW	9.49 AW	20720 AAW	MABLS	10//99-12//99
	New Bedford PMSA, MA	S	12.23 MW	12.17 AW	25440 AAW	MABLS	10//99-12//99
	Pittsfield MSA, MA	S	11.81 MW	10.44 AW	24570 AAW	MABLS	10//99-12//99
	Springfield MSA, MA	S	17.36 MW	15.26 AW	36110 AAW	MABLS	10//99-12//99
	Worcester PMSA, MA-CT	S	11.93 MW	10.26 AW	24820 AAW	MABLS	10//99-12//99
	Michigan	S	14.19 MW	14.47 AW	30100 AAW	MIBLS	10//99-12//99
	Ann Arbor PMSA, MI	S	15.14 MW	13.16 AW	31490 AAW	MIBLS	10//99-12//99
	Benton Harbor MSA, MI	S	13.09 MW	12.62 AW	27220 AAW	MIBLS	10//99-12//99
	Detroit PMSA, MI	S	16.50 MW	15.41 AW	34310 AAW	MIBLS	10//99-12//99
	Flint PMSA, MI	S	13.03 MW	12.90 AW	27100 AAW	MIBLS	10//99-12//99
	Grand Rapids-Muskegon-Holland MSA, MI	S	14.35 MW	13.25 AW	29860 AAW	MIBLS	10//99-12//99
	Jackson MSA, MI	S	14.20 MW	13.57 AW	29530 AAW	MIBLS	10//99-12//99
	Kalamazoo-Battle Creek MSA, MI	S	15.64 MW	14.70 AW	32520 AAW	MIBLS	10//99-12//99
	Lansing-East Lansing MSA, MI	S	14.16 MW	14.63 AW	29460 AAW	MIBLS	10//99-12//99
	Saginaw-Bay City-Midland MSA, MI	S	12.78 MW	11.98 AW	26580 AAW	MIBLS	10//99-12//99
	Minnesota	S	11.87 MW	12.80 AW	26620 AAW	MNBLS	10//99-12//99
	Duluth-Superior MSA, MN-WI	S	11.44 MW	9.88 AW	23800 AAW	MNBLS	10//99-12//99
	Minneapolis-St. Paul MSA, MN-WI	S	13.78 MW	12.45 AW	28660 AAW	MNBLS	10//99-12//99
	Rochester MSA, MN	S	15.49 MW	10.61 AW	32230 AAW	MNBLS	10//99-12//99
	St. Cloud MSA, MN	S	11.10 MW	11.95 AW	23090 AAW	MNBLS	10//99-12//99
	Mississippi	S	12.54 MW	13.48 AW	28040 AAW	MSBLS	10//99-12//99
	Biloxi-Gulfport-Pascagoula MSA, MS	S	14.66 MW	13.50 AW	30500 AAW	MSBLS	10//99-12//99
	Hattiesburg MSA, MS	S	9.66 MW	9.65 AW	20100 AAW	MSBLS	10//99-12//99
	Jackson MSA, MS	S	10.66 MW	8.90 AW	22180 AAW	MSBLS	10//99-12//99
	Missouri	S	8.27 MW	10.90 AW	22670 AAW	MOBLS	10//99-12//99
	Columbia MSA, MO	S	9.65 MW	7.96 AW	20060 AAW	MOBLS	10//99-12//99
	Kansas City MSA, MO-KS	S	12.71 MW	11.59 AW	26430 AAW	MOBLS	10//99-12//99
	St. Louis MSA, MO-IL	S	10.97 MW	8.11 AW	22810 AAW	MOBLS	10//99-12//99
	Springfield MSA, MO	S	10.78 MW	11.02 AW	22430 AAW	MOBLS	10//99-12//99
	Montana	S	10.65 MW	12.57 AW	26130 AAW	MTBLS	10//99-12//99
	Billings MSA, MT	S	11.14 MW	11.57 AW	23170 AAW	MTBLS	10//99-12//99
	Nebraska	S	11.33 MW	11.90 AW	24750 AAW	NEBLS	10//99-12//99
	Lincoln MSA, NE	S	11.71 MW	11.61 AW	24350 AAW	NEBLS	10//99-12//99
	Omaha MSA, NE-IA	S	12.00 MW	11.13 AW	24970 AAW	NEBLS	10//99-12//99
	Nevada	S	13.72 MW	14.38 AW	29920 AAW	NVBLS	10//99-12//99
	Las Vegas MSA, NV-AZ	S	14.41 MW	13.94 AW	29980 AAW	NVBLS	10//99-12//99
	Reno MSA, NV	S	14.96 MW	13.70 AW	31110 AAW	NVBLS	10//99-12//99
	New Hampshire	S	17.68 MW	15.49 AW	32220 AAW	NHBLS	10//99-12//99
	Manchester PMSA, NH	S	9.23 MW	6.41 AW	19190 AAW	NHBLS	10//99-12//99
	New Jersey	S	18.05 MW	19.50 AW	40550 AAW	NJBLS	10//99-12//99
	Atlantic-Cape May PMSA, NJ	S	23.61 MW	23.58 AW	49100 AAW	NJBLS	10//99-12//99
	Bergen-Passaic PMSA, NJ	S	18.15 MW	16.73 AW	37760 AAW	NJBLS	10//99-12//99
	Middlesex-Somerset-Hunterdon PMSA, NJ	S	18.83 MW	17.46 AW	39160 AAW	NJBLS	10//99-12//99
	Monmouth-Ocean PMSA, NJ	S	18.36 MW	16.62 AW	38180 AAW	NJBLS	10//99-12//99
	Newark PMSA, NJ	S	22.04 MW	20.97 AW	45840 AAW	NJBLS	10//99-12//99
	Trenton PMSA, NJ	S	21.53 MW	21.34 AW	44780 AAW	NJBLS	10//99-12//99
	New Mexico	S	13.11 MW	13.55 AW	28190 AAW	NMBLS	10//99-12//99
	Albuquerque MSA, NM	S	15.51 MW	14.58 AW	32270 AAW	NMBLS	10//99-12//99
	Santa Fe MSA, NM	S	12.75 MW	11.63 AW	26520 AAW	NMBLS	10//99-12//99
	New York	S	11.71 MW	13.48 AW	28040 AAW	NYBLS	10//99-12//99
	Albany-Schenectady-Troy MSA, NY	S	12.05 MW	12.10 AW	25060 AAW	NYBLS	10//99-12//99
	Binghamton MSA, NY	S	10.56 MW	10.07 AW	21970 AAW	NYBLS	10//99-12//99
	Buffalo-Niagara Falls MSA, NY	S	11.53 MW	11.07 AW	23980 AAW	NYBLS	10//99-12//99
	Glens Falls MSA, NY	S	11.50 MW	8.24 AW	23920 AAW	NYBLS	10//99-12//99
	Jamestown MSA, NY	S	9.47 MW	8.70 AW	19710 AAW	NYBLS	10//99-12//99

AAW	Average annual wage	**AOH**	Average offered, high	**ASH**	Average starting, high	**H**	Hourly	**M**	Monthly	**S**	Special: hourly and annual
AE	Average entry wage	**AOL**	Average offered, low	**ASL**	Average starting, low	**HI**	Highest wage paid	**MTC**	Median total compensation	**TQ**	Third quartile wage
AEX	Average experienced wage	**APH**	Average pay, high range	**AW**	Average wage paid	**HR**	High end range	**MW**	Median wage paid	**W**	Weekly
AO	Average offered	**APL**	Average pay, low range	**FQ**	First quartile wage	**LR**	Low end range	**SQ**	Second quartile wage	**Y**	Yearly

Occupation/Type/Industry	Location	Per	Low	Mid	High	Source	Date
Chef and Head Cook	Nassau-Suffolk PMSA, NY	S	12.22 MW	10.02 AW	25410 AAW	NYBLS	10//99-12//99
	Newburgh PMSA, NY-PA	S	14.92 MW	12.89 AW	31040 AAW	NYBLS	10//99-12//99
	Rochester MSA, NY	S	12.59 MW	11.16 AW	26190 AAW	NYBLS	10//99-12//99
	Syracuse MSA, NY	S	13.12 MW	12.66 AW	27290 AAW	NYBLS	10//99-12//99
	Utica-Rome MSA, NY	S	9.80 MW	9.66 AW	20390 AAW	NYBLS	10//99-12//99
	North Carolina	S	10.95 MW	12.93 AW	26900 AAW	NCBLS	10//99-12//99
	Asheville MSA, NC	S	11.87 MW	11.26 AW	24690 AAW	NCBLS	10//99-12//99
	Charlotte-Gastonia-Rock Hill MSA, NC-SC	S	12.80 MW	8.42 AW	26630 AAW	NCBLS	10//99-12//99
	Fayetteville MSA, NC	S	12.37 MW	10.17 AW	25740 AAW	NCBLS	10//99-12//99
	Goldsboro MSA, NC	S	7.90 MW	7.40 AW	16430 AAW	NCBLS	10//99-12//99
	Greensboro--Winston-Salem--High Point MSA, NC	S	15.82 MW	14.55 AW	32900 AAW	NCBLS	10//99-12//99
	Hickory-Morganton-Lenoir MSA, NC	S	9.89 MW	9.64 AW	20560 AAW	NCBLS	10//99-12//99
	Jacksonville MSA, NC	S	10.59 MW	7.74 AW	22020 AAW	NCBLS	10//99-12//99
	Wilmington MSA, NC	S	12.76 MW	14.22 AW	26540 AAW	NCBLS	10//99-12//99
	North Dakota	S	7.84 MW	8.18 AW	17020 AAW	NDBLS	10//99-12//99
	Bismarck MSA, ND	S	7.95 MW	7.78 AW	16530 AAW	NDBLS	10//99-12//99
	Fargo-Moorhead MSA, ND-MN	S	8.27 MW	7.67 AW	17210 AAW	NDBLS	10//99-12//99
	Grand Forks MSA, ND-MN	S	8.85 MW	8.20 AW	18400 AAW	NDBLS	10//99-12//99
	Akron PMSA, OH	S	11.35 MW	9.88 AW	23610 AAW	OHBLS	10//99-12//99
	Canton-Massillon MSA, OH	S	9.91 MW	6.42 AW	20610 AAW	OHBLS	10//99-12//99
	Cincinnati PMSA, OH-KY-IN	S	10.85 MW	8.91 AW	22560 AAW	OHBLS	10//99-12//99
	Columbus MSA, OH	S	13.43 MW	12.12 AW	27930 AAW	OHBLS	10//99-12//99
	Lima MSA, OH	S	9.77 MW	9.17 AW	20330 AAW	OHBLS	10//99-12//99
	Oklahoma	S	8.11 MW	8.88 AW	18480 AAW	OKBLS	10//99-12//99
	Lawton MSA, OK	S	6.24 MW	6.15 AW	12980 AAW	OKBLS	10//99-12//99
	Oklahoma City MSA, OK	S	9.63 MW	8.45 AW	20020 AAW	OKBLS	10//99-12//99
	Tulsa MSA, OK	S	9.58 MW	9.19 AW	19930 AAW	OKBLS	10//99-12//99
	Oregon	S	12.55 MW	14.97 AW	31140 AAW	ORBLS	10//99-12//99
	Eugene-Springfield MSA, OR	S	14.53 MW	12.61 AW	30230 AAW	ORBLS	10//99-12//99
	Medford-Ashland MSA, OR	S	10.60 MW	9.90 AW	22060 AAW	ORBLS	10//99-12//99
	Portland-Vancouver PMSA, OR-WA	S	13.04 MW	10.30 AW	27130 AAW	ORBLS	10//99-12//99
	Pennsylvania	S	12.85 MW	15.87 AW	33010 AAW	PABLS	10//99-12//99
	Allentown-Bethlehem-Easton MSA, PA	S	20.60 MW	20.11 AW	42840 AAW	PABLS	10//99-12//99
	Erie MSA, PA	S	11.00 MW	11.67 AW	22870 AAW	PABLS	10//99-12//99
	Johnstown MSA, PA	S	8.64 MW	8.14 AW	17960 AAW	PABLS	10//99-12//99
	Lancaster MSA, PA	S	17.20 MW	14.67 AW	35770 AAW	PABLS	10//99-12//99
	Philadelphia PMSA, PA-NJ	S	22.20 MW	22.01 AW	46170 AAW	PABLS	10//99-12//99
	Pittsburgh MSA, PA	S	14.31 MW	11.52 AW	29770 AAW	PABLS	10//99-12//99
	Reading MSA, PA	S	23.52 MW	22.86 AW	48920 AAW	PABLS	10//99-12//99
	Scranton--Wilkes-Barre--Hazleton MSA, PA	S	13.76 MW	12.93 AW	28630 AAW	PABLS	10//99-12//99
	Sharon MSA, PA	S	12.43 MW	12.41 AW	25860 AAW	PABLS	10//99-12//99
	State College MSA, PA	S	9.90 MW	8.27 AW	20590 AAW	PABLS	10//99-12//99
	Williamsport MSA, PA	S	12.71 MW	10.04 AW	26440 AAW	PABLS	10//99-12//99
	York MSA, PA	S	19.26 MW	16.93 AW	40050 AAW	PABLS	10//99-12//99
	Rhode Island	S	19.26 MW	19.43 AW	40420 AAW	RIBLS	10//99-12//99
	Providence-Fall River-Warwick MSA, RI-MA	S	15.40 MW	13.30 AW	32030 AAW	RIBLS	10//99-12//99
	South Carolina	S	12.84 MW	13.91 AW	28940 AAW	SCBLS	10//99-12//99
	Charleston-North Charleston MSA, SC	S	15.02 MW	14.99 AW	31250 AAW	SCBLS	10//99-12//99
	Greenville-Spartanburg-Anderson MSA, SC	S	14.93 MW	13.23 AW	31050 AAW	SCBLS	10//99-12//99
	Myrtle Beach MSA, SC	S	13.21 MW	13.30 AW	27470 AAW	SCBLS	10//99-12//99
	South Dakota	S	10.59 MW	12.01 AW	24980 AAW	SDBLS	10//99-12//99
	Tennessee	S	8.11 MW	8.86 AW	18430 AAW	TNBLS	10//99-12//99
	Chattanooga MSA, TN-GA	S	10.70 MW	9.32 AW	22250 AAW	TNBLS	10//99-12//99
	Clarksville-Hopkinsville MSA, TN-KY	S	7.78 MW	6.18 AW	16180 AAW	TNBLS	10//99-12//99
	Knoxville MSA, TN	S	8.49 MW	8.29 AW	17670 AAW	TNBLS	10//99-12//99
	Memphis MSA, TN-AR-MS	S	10.49 MW	9.74 AW	21820 AAW	MSBLS	10//99-12//99
	Nashville MSA, TN	S	22.09 MW	22.36 AW	45950 AAW	TNBLS	10//99-12//99
	Texas	S	9.66 MW	10.47 AW	21790 AAW	TXBLS	10//99-12//99
	Abilene MSA, TX	S	7.94 MW	7.86 AW	16510 AAW	TXBLS	10//99-12//99
	Austin-San Marcos MSA, TX	S	10.57 MW	9.73 AW	21990 AAW	TXBLS	10//99-12//99

AAW	Average annual wage	AOH	Average offered, high	ASH	Average starting, high	H	Hourly	M	Monthly	S	Special: hourly and annual
AE	Average entry wage	AOL	Average offered, low	ASL	Average starting, low	HI	Highest wage paid	MTC	Median total compensation	TQ	Third quartile wage
AEX	Average experienced wage	APH	Average pay, high range	AW	Average wage paid	HR	High end range	MW	Median wage paid	W	Weekly
AO	Average offered	APL	Average pay, low range	FQ	First quartile wage	LR	Low end range	SQ	Second quartile wage	Y	Yearly

Occupation/Type/Industry	Location	Per	Low	Mid	High	Source	Date
Chef and Head Cook	Brownsville-Harlingen-San Benito MSA, TX	S	8.93 MW	9.10 AW	18580 AAW	TXBLS	10//99-12//99
	Dallas PMSA, TX	S	11.09 MW	9.48 AW	23070 AAW	TXBLS	10//99-12//99
	El Paso MSA, TX	S	11.14 MW	10.21 AW	23170 AAW	TXBLS	10//99-12//99
	Fort Worth-Arlington PMSA, TX	S	13.16 MW	10.69 AW	27370 AAW	TXBLS	10//99-12//99
	Galveston-Texas City PMSA, TX	S	13.39 MW	10.16 AW	27850 AAW	TXBLS	10//99-12//99
	Houston PMSA, TX	S	10.04 MW	9.71 AW	20880 AAW	TXBLS	10//99-12//99
	Killeen-Temple MSA, TX	S	10.66 MW	9.35 AW	22180 AAW	TXBLS	10//99-12//99
	Longview-Marshall MSA, TX	S	9.78 MW	9.16 AW	20340 AAW	TXBLS	10//99-12//99
	Lubbock MSA, TX	S	7.81 MW	7.71 AW	16250 AAW	TXBLS	10//99-12//99
	San Antonio MSA, TX	S	12.39 MW	11.11 AW	25770 AAW	TXBLS	10//99-12//99
	Texarkana MSA, TX-Texarkana, AR	S	9.52 MW	8.04 AW	19800 AAW	TXBLS	10//99-12//99
	Tyler MSA, TX	S	13.16 MW	10.63 AW	27370 AAW	TXBLS	10//99-12//99
	Waco MSA, TX	S	8.44 MW	7.73 AW	17550 AAW	TXBLS	10//99-12//99
	Provo-Orem MSA, UT	S	11.93 MW	10.79 AW	24820 AAW	UTBLS	10//99-12//99
	Salt Lake City-Ogden MSA, UT	S	15.90 MW	16.32 AW	33060 AAW	UTBLS	10//99-12//99
	Vermont	S	16.52 MW	18.50 AW	38490 AAW	VTBLS	10//99-12//99
	Burlington MSA, VT	S	20.22 MW	21.61 AW	42050 AAW	VTBLS	10//99-12//99
	Virginia	S	12.61 MW	14.07 AW	29270 AAW	VABLS	10//99-12//99
	Charlottesville MSA, VA	S	17.13 MW	16.46 AW	35640 AAW	VABLS	10//99-12//99
	Lynchburg MSA, VA	S	12.63 MW	12.79 AW	26260 AAW	VABLS	10//99-12//99
	Norfolk-Virginia Beach-Newport News MSA, VA-NC	S	11.71 MW	10.47 AW	24350 AAW	VABLS	10//99-12//99
	Richmond-Petersburg MSA, VA	S	14.34 MW	13.92 AW	29830 AAW	VABLS	10//99-12//99
	Roanoke MSA, VA	S	15.43 MW	15.19 AW	32090 AAW	VABLS	10//99-12//99
	Washington	S	11.18 MW	12.14 AW	25260 AAW	WABLS	10//99-12//99
	Bellingham MSA, WA	S	12.77 MW	12.19 AW	26550 AAW	WABLS	10//99-12//99
	Bremerton PMSA, WA	S	12.51 MW	12.03 AW	26020 AAW	WABLS	10//99-12//99
	Olympia PMSA, WA	S	10.07 MW	10.54 AW	20940 AAW	WABLS	10//99-12//99
	Seattle-Bellevue-Everett PMSA, WA	S	13.44 MW	13.29 AW	27950 AAW	WABLS	10//99-12//99
	Spokane MSA, WA	S	15.00 MW	13.27 AW	31200 AAW	WABLS	10//99-12//99
	Tacoma PMSA, WA	S	18.24 MW	16.43 AW	37950 AAW	WABLS	10//99-12//99
	Yakima MSA, WA	S	9.03 MW	8.39 AW	18780 AAW	WABLS	10//99-12//99
	West Virginia	S	8.27 MW	10.30 AW	21430 AAW	WVBLS	10//99-12//99
	Charleston MSA, WV	S	10.24 MW	9.38 AW	21300 AAW	WVBLS	10//99-12//99
	Huntington-Ashland MSA, WV-KY-OH	S	10.74 MW	9.59 AW	22340 AAW	WVBLS	10//99-12//99
	Parkersburg-Marietta MSA, WV-OH	S	10.76 MW	7.60 AW	22390 AAW	WVBLS	10//99-12//99
	Wheeling MSA, WV-OH	S	8.40 MW	7.68 AW	17480 AAW	WVBLS	10//99-12//99
	Wisconsin	S	10.48 MW	11.58 AW	24080 AAW	WIBLS	10//99-12//99
	Appleton-Oshkosh-Neenah MSA, WI	S	10.31 MW	9.96 AW	21440 AAW	WIBLS	10//99-12//99
	Eau Claire MSA, WI	S	9.20 MW	7.82 AW	19130 AAW	WIBLS	10//99-12//99
	Green Bay MSA, WI	S	12.49 MW	11.82 AW	25990 AAW	WIBLS	10//99-12//99
	Janesville-Beloit MSA, WI	S	8.95 MW	9.18 AW	18610 AAW	WIBLS	10//99-12//99
	Kenosha PMSA, WI	S	8.81 MW	7.59 AW	18320 AAW	WIBLS	10//99-12//99
	La Crosse MSA, WI-MN	S	11.30 MW	10.04 AW	23490 AAW	WIBLS	10//99-12//99
	Madison MSA, WI	S	12.95 MW	12.17 AW	26940 AAW	WIBLS	10//99-12//99
	Milwaukee-Waukesha PMSA, WI	S	11.07 MW	10.26 AW	23030 AAW	WIBLS	10//99-12//99
	Racine PMSA, WI	S	14.16 MW	14.78 AW	29440 AAW	WIBLS	10//99-12//99
	Sheboygan MSA, WI	S	13.17 MW	14.15 AW	27380 AAW	WIBLS	10//99-12//99
	Wausau MSA, WI	S	10.15 MW	8.55 AW	21120 AAW	WIBLS	10//99-12//99
	Wyoming	S	8.32 MW	10.01 AW	20810 AAW	WYBLS	10//99-12//99
	Casper MSA, WY	S	9.77 MW	9.76 AW	20330 AAW	WYBLS	10//99-12//99
	Puerto Rico	S	11.36 MW	13.76 AW	28610 AAW	PRBLS	10//99-12//99
	San Juan-Bayamon PMSA, PR	S	18.50 MW	15.17 AW	38470 AAW	PRBLS	10//99-12//99
	Virgin Islands	S	16.51 MW	18.60 AW	38700 AAW	VIBLS	10//99-12//99
	Guam	S	11.36 MW	12.46 AW	25930 AAW	GUBLS	10//99-12//99
Chemical Engineer	Alabama	S	31.85 MW	30.47 AW	63380 AAW	ALBLS	10//99-12//99
	Huntsville MSA, AL	S	29.59 MW	30.07 AW	61550 AAW	ALBLS	10//99-12//99
	Mobile MSA, AL	S	32.58 MW	33.91 AW	67770 AAW	ALBLS	10//99-12//99
	Arizona	S	24.83 MW	27.66 AW	57530 AAW	AZBLS	10//99-12//99
	Phoenix-Mesa MSA, AZ	S	27.83 MW	25.09 AW	57890 AAW	AZBLS	10//99-12//99

AAW	Average annual wage	AOH	Average offered, high	ASH	Average starting, high	H	Hourly
AE	Average entry wage	AOL	Average offered, low	ASL	Average starting, low	HI	Highest wage paid
AEX	Average experienced wage	APH	Average pay, high range	AW	Average wage paid	HR	High end range
AO	Average offered	APL	Average pay, low range	FQ	First quartile wage	LR	Low end range

M Monthly · MTC Median total compensation · MW Median wage paid · SQ Second quartile wage · S Special: hourly and annual · TQ Third quartile wage · W Weekly · Y Yearly

Occupation/Type/Industry	Location	Per	Low	Mid	High	Source	Date
Chemical Engineer	Arkansas	S	27.59 MW	28.33 AW	58920 AAW	ARBLS	10//99-12//99
	Little Rock-North Little Rock MSA, AR	S	24.87 MW	23.86 AW	51730 AAW	ARBLS	10//99-12//99
	California	S	35.02 MW	33.49 AW	69660 AAW	CABLS	10//99-12//99
	Bakersfield MSA, CA	S	31.60 MW	34.14 AW	65730 AAW	CABLS	10//99-12//99
	Oakland PMSA, CA	S	34.29 MW	35.03 AW	71330 AAW	CABLS	10//99-12//99
	Orange County PMSA, CA	S	33.11 MW	33.45 AW	68860 AAW	CABLS	10//99-12//99
	Sacramento PMSA, CA	S	31.14 MW	31.41 AW	64780 AAW	CABLS	10//99-12//99
	San Diego MSA, CA	S	31.36 MW	29.66 AW	65230 AAW	CABLS	10//99-12//99
	San Francisco PMSA, CA	S	42.65 MW	47.25 AW	88720 AAW	CABLS	10//99-12//99
	San Jose PMSA, CA	S	32.67 MW	34.73 AW	67950 AAW	CABLS	10//99-12//99
	Ventura PMSA, CA	S	34.45 MW	34.71 AW	71660 AAW	CABLS	10//99-12//99
	Colorado	S	32.18 MW	31.29 AW	65090 AAW	COBLS	10//99-12//99
	Boulder-Longmont PMSA, CO	S	31.69 MW	31.60 AW	65910 AAW	COBLS	10//99-12//99
	Denver PMSA, CO	S	31.72 MW	33.26 AW	65980 AAW	COBLS	10//99-12//99
	Connecticut	S	31.07 MW	30.46 AW	63360 AAW	CTBLS	10//99-12//99
	Hartford MSA, CT	S	28.43 MW	28.37 AW	59140 AAW	CTBLS	10//99-12//99
	Delaware	S	32.83 MW	32.31 AW	67210 AAW	DEBLS	10//99-12//99
	Wilmington-Newark PMSA, DE-MD	S	32.23 MW	32.78 AW	67040 AAW	DEBLS	10//99-12//99
	Washington PMSA, DC-MD-VA-WV	S	30.68 MW	31.51 AW	63820 AAW	DCBLS	10//99-12//99
	Florida	S	29.89 MW	28.98 AW	60280 AAW	FLBLS	10//99-12//99
	Tampa-St. Petersburg-Clearwater MSA, FL	S	25.89 MW	24.34 AW	53840 AAW	FLBLS	10//99-12//99
	Georgia	S	30.9 MW	30.39 AW	63200 AAW	GABLS	10//99-12//99
	Atlanta MSA, GA	S	32.58 MW	32.31 AW	67780 AAW	GABLS	10//99-12//99
	Columbus MSA, GA-AL	S	28.81 MW	30.42 AW	59930 AAW	GABLS	10//99-12//99
	Idaho	S	32.17 MW	29.90 AW	62190 AAW	IDBLS	10//99-12//99
	Illinois	S	29.85 MW	28.65 AW	59590 AAW	ILBLS	10//99-12//99
	Chicago PMSA, IL	S	28.61 MW	29.88 AW	59500 AAW	ILBLS	10//99-12//99
	Kankakee PMSA, IL	S	27.96 MW	26.39 AW	58160 AAW	ILBLS	10//99-12//99
	Peoria-Pekin MSA, IL	S	30.70 MW	32.63 AW	63860 AAW	ILBLS	10//99-12//99
	Rockford MSA, IL	S	27.95 MW	26.47 AW	58130 AAW	ILBLS	10//99-12//99
	Indiana	S	29.13 MW	29.45 AW	61260 AAW	INBLS	10//99-12//99
	Fort Wayne MSA, IN	S	25.02 MW	25.65 AW	52050 AAW	INBLS	10//99-12//99
	Gary PMSA, IN	S	32.74 MW	32.28 AW	68100 AAW	INBLS	10//99-12//99
	Indianapolis MSA, IN	S	30.30 MW	27.20 AW	63030 AAW	INBLS	10//99-12//99
	Terre Haute MSA, IN	S	31.87 MW	30.38 AW	66290 AAW	INBLS	10//99-12//99
	Iowa	S	26.84 MW	26.29 AW	54680 AAW	IABLS	10//99-12//99
	Kansas	S	30.66 MW	29.79 AW	61970 AAW	KSBLS	10//99-12//99
	Kentucky	S	31.2 MW	29.93 AW	62250 AAW	KYBLS	10//99-12//99
	Louisville MSA, KY-IN	S	29.13 MW	29.27 AW	60580 AAW	KYBLS	10//99-12//99
	Louisiana	S	31.99 MW	31.75 AW	66030 AAW	LABLS	10//99-12//99
	Baton Rouge MSA, LA	S	32.25 MW	32.31 AW	67070 AAW	LABLS	10//99-12//99
	New Orleans MSA, LA	S	33.15 MW	33.70 AW	68960 AAW	LABLS	10//99-12//99
	Shreveport-Bossier City MSA, LA	S	34.54 MW	33.19 AW	71840 AAW	LABLS	10//99-12//99
	Maine	S	29.46 MW	28.73 AW	59760 AAW	MEBLS	10//99-12//99
	Maryland	S	32.01 MW	30.74 AW	63950 AAW	MDBLS	10//99-12//99
	Baltimore PMSA, MD	S	30.63 MW	31.95 AW	63710 AAW	MDBLS	10//99-12//99
	Massachusetts	S	33.76 MW	31.66 AW	65860 AAW	MABLS	10//99-12//99
	Boston PMSA, MA-NH	S	31.82 MW	33.98 AW	66180 AAW	MABLS	10//99-12//99
	Lowell PMSA, MA-NH	S	36.05 MW	37.11 AW	74980 AAW	MABLS	10//99-12//99
	Michigan	S	30.91 MW	29.55 AW	61460 AAW	MIBLS	10//99-12//99
	Ann Arbor PMSA, MI	S	29.71 MW	28.84 AW	61810 AAW	MIBLS	10//99-12//99
	Detroit PMSA, MI	S	29.95 MW	31.01 AW	62300 AAW	MIBLS	10//99-12//99
	Grand Rapids-Muskegon-Holland MSA, MI	S	25.64 MW	26.27 AW	53330 AAW	MIBLS	10//99-12//99
	Kalamazoo-Battle Creek MSA, MI	S	26.29 MW	25.73 AW	54690 AAW	MIBLS	10//99-12//99
	Lansing-East Lansing MSA, MI	S	29.80 MW	31.55 AW	61990 AAW	MIBLS	10//99-12//99
	Minnesota	S	28.9 MW	28.97 AW	60260 AAW	MNBLS	10//99-12//99
	Minneapolis-St. Paul MSA, MN-WI	S	28.92 MW	27.88 AW	60160 AAW	MNBLS	10//99-12//99
	Mississippi	S	30.14 MW	29.40 AW	61150 AAW	MSBLS	10//99-12//99
	Biloxi-Gulfport-Pascagoula MSA, MS	S	32.15 MW	34.64 AW	66860 AAW	MSBLS	10//99-12//99
	Jackson MSA, MS	S	27.44 MW	29.61 AW	57070 AAW	MSBLS	10//99-12//99
	Missouri	S	28.67 MW	28.75 AW	59800 AAW	MOBLS	10//99-12//99
	Kansas City MSA, MO-KS	S	26.32 MW	25.64 AW	54740 AAW	MOBLS	10//99-12//99
	St. Louis MSA, MO-IL	S	30.70 MW	31.66 AW	63850 AAW	MOBLS	10//99-12//99

AAW	Average annual wage	**AOH**	Average offered, high	**ASH**	Average starting, high	**H**	Hourly	**M**	Monthly	**S**	Special: hourly and annual
AE	Average entry wage	**AOL**	Average offered, low	**ASL**	Average starting, low	**HI**	Highest wage paid	**MTC**	Median total compensation	**TQ**	Third quartile wage
AEX	Average experienced wage	**APH**	Average pay, high range	**AW**	Average wage paid	**HR**	High end range	**MW**	Median wage paid	**W**	Weekly
AO	Average offered	**APL**	Average pay, low range	**FQ**	First quartile wage	**LR**	Low end range	**SQ**	Second quartile wage	**Y**	Yearly

Occupation/Type/Industry	Location	Per	Low	Mid	High	Source	Date
Chemical Engineer	Montana	S	31.48 MW	30.11 AW	62620 AAW	MTBLS	10//99-12//99
	Billings MSA, MT	S	31.02 MW	32.50 AW	64520 AAW	MTBLS	10//99-12//99
	Nebraska	S	27.66 MW	26.92 AW	55990 AAW	NEBLS	10//99-12//99
	Omaha MSA, NE-IA	S	27.26 MW	27.98 AW	56700 AAW	NEBLS	10//99-12//99
	Nevada	S	28.62 MW	31.62 AW	65780 AAW	NVBLS	10//99-12//99
	Las Vegas MSA, NV-AZ	S	31.80 MW	29.89 AW	66130 AAW	NVBLS	10//99-12//99
	New Hampshire	S	27.94 MW	27.66 AW	57530 AAW	NHBLS	10//99-12//99
	New Jersey	S	34.78 MW	33.14 AW	68920 AAW	NJBLS	10//99-12//99
	Bergen-Passaic PMSA, NJ	S	32.81 MW	34.25 AW	68250 AAW	NJBLS	10//99-12//99
	Jersey City PMSA, NJ	S	31.59 MW	33.86 AW	65710 AAW	NJBLS	10//99-12//99
	Middlesex-Somerset- Hunterdon PMSA, NJ	S	34.89 MW	36.68 AW	72580 AAW	NJBLS	10//99-12//99
	Monmouth-Ocean PMSA, NJ	S	33.11 MW	34.96 AW	68870 AAW	NJBLS	10//99-12//99
	Newark PMSA, NJ	S	32.74 MW	34.19 AW	68100 AAW	NJBLS	10//99-12//99
	Trenton PMSA, NJ	S	32.75 MW	34.70 AW	68130 AAW	NJBLS	10//99-12//99
	New York	S	33.09 MW	32.61 AW	67830 AAW	NYBLS	10//99-12//99
	Buffalo-Niagara Falls MSA, NY	S	30.65 MW	31.95 AW	63760 AAW	NYBLS	10//99-12//99
	Nassau-Suffolk PMSA, NY	S	42.37 MW	48.91 AW	88130 AAW	NYBLS	10//99-12//99
	New York PMSA, NY	S	31.54 MW	31.52 AW	65610 AAW	NYBLS	10//99-12//99
	Rochester MSA, NY	S	34.37 MW	35.68 AW	71500 AAW	NYBLS	10//99-12//99
	North Carolina	S	31.79 MW	30.71 AW	63870 AAW	NCBLS	10//99-12//99
	Charlotte-Gastonia-Rock Hill MSA, NC-SC	S	31.65 MW	34.40 AW	65840 AAW	NCBLS	10//99-12//99
	Greensboro--Winston-Salem-- High Point MSA, NC	S	27.24 MW	28.05 AW	56670 AAW	NCBLS	10//99-12//99
	Raleigh-Durham-Chapel Hill MSA, NC	S	29.16 MW	28.68 AW	60660 AAW	NCBLS	10//99-12//99
	Wilmington MSA, NC	S	32.84 MW	33.46 AW	68300 AAW	NCBLS	10//99-12//99
	Ohio	S	29.5 MW	29.53 AW	61420 AAW	OHBLS	10//99-12//99
	Cincinnati PMSA, OH-KY-IN	S	29.91 MW	30.31 AW	62210 AAW	OHBLS	10//99-12//99
	Cleveland-Lorain-Elyria PMSA, OH	S	28.70 MW	29.30 AW	59700 AAW	OHBLS	10//99-12//99
	Columbus MSA, OH	S	30.27 MW	30.66 AW	62950 AAW	OHBLS	10//99-12//99
	Dayton-Springfield MSA, OH	S	27.93 MW	29.44 AW	58100 AAW	OHBLS	10//99-12//99
	Oklahoma	S	32.58 MW	31.25 AW	64990 AAW	OKBLS	10//99-12//99
	Oklahoma City MSA, OK	S	31.34 MW	29.81 AW	65190 AAW	OKBLS	10//99-12//99
	Tulsa MSA, OK	S	32.32 MW	34.30 AW	67230 AAW	OKBLS	10//99-12//99
	Oregon	S	31.13 MW	30.84 AW	64140 AAW	ORBLS	10//99-12//99
	Portland-Vancouver PMSA, OR-WA	S	31.49 MW	33.87 AW	65510 AAW	ORBLS	10//99-12//99
	Pennsylvania	S	27.18 MW	27.73 AW	57690 AAW	PABLS	10//99-12//99
	Allentown-Bethlehem-Easton MSA, PA	S	27.30 MW	25.34 AW	56780 AAW	PABLS	10//99-12//99
	Philadelphia PMSA, PA-NJ	S	29.35 MW	29.86 AW	61050 AAW	PABLS	10//99-12//99
	Pittsburgh MSA, PA	S	26.41 MW	25.22 AW	54940 AAW	PABLS	10//99-12//99
	Rhode Island	S	27.02 MW	29.26 AW	60860 AAW	RIBLS	10//99-12//99
	Providence-Fall River- Warwick MSA, RI-MA	S	29.40 MW	27.16 AW	61150 AAW	RIBLS	10//99-12//99
	South Carolina	S	32.17 MW	31.29 AW	65080 AAW	SCBLS	10//99-12//99
	Greenville-Spartanburg- Anderson MSA, SC	S	32.86 MW	34.03 AW	68350 AAW	SCBLS	10//99-12//99
	Tennessee	S	29.54 MW	30.37 AW	63180 AAW	TNBLS	10//99-12//99
	Johnson City-Kingsport-Bristol MSA, TN-VA	S	36.56 MW	37.94 AW	76040 AAW	TNBLS	10//99-12//99
	Memphis MSA, TN-AR-MS	S	25.56 MW	23.49 AW	53170 AAW	MSBLS	10//99-12//99
	Nashville MSA, TN	S	36.41 MW	37.48 AW	75730 AAW	TNBLS	10//99-12//99
	Texas	S	33.62 MW	31.79 AW	66120 AAW	TXBLS	10//99-12//99
	Austin-San Marcos MSA, TX	S	27.72 MW	26.98 AW	57660 AAW	TXBLS	10//99-12//99
	Beaumont-Port Arthur MSA, TX	S	32.60 MW	33.80 AW	67800 AAW	TXBLS	10//99-12//99
	Brazoria PMSA, TX	S	32.15 MW	34.71 AW	66860 AAW	TXBLS	10//99-12//99
	Corpus Christi MSA, TX	S	31.08 MW	32.81 AW	64640 AAW	TXBLS	10//99-12//99
	Dallas PMSA, TX	S	30.79 MW	30.02 AW	64050 AAW	TXBLS	10//99-12//99
	Fort Worth-Arlington PMSA, TX	S	24.76 MW	21.87 AW	51500 AAW	TXBLS	10//99-12//99
	Galveston-Texas City PMSA, TX	S	29.97 MW	32.01 AW	62340 AAW	TXBLS	10//99-12//99
	Houston PMSA, TX	S	32.56 MW	34.74 AW	67720 AAW	TXBLS	10//99-12//99
	Odessa-Midland MSA, TX	S	35.96 MW	36.26 AW	74790 AAW	TXBLS	10//99-12//99
	San Antonio MSA, TX	S	32.96 MW	33.26 AW	68550 AAW	TXBLS	10//99-12//99
	Virginia	S	28.47 MW	27.97 AW	58180 AAW	VABLS	10//99-12//99

AAW	Average annual wage	AOH	Average offered, high	ASH	Average starting, high	H	Hourly		M	Monthly		S	Special: hourly and annual
AE	Average entry wage	AOL	Average offered, low	ASL	Average starting, low	HI	Highest wage paid		MTC	Median total compensation	TQ	Third quartile wage
AEX	Average experienced wage	APH	Average pay, high range	AW	Average wage paid	HR	High end range		MW	Median wage paid		W	Weekly
AO	Average offered	APL	Average pay, low range	FQ	First quartile wage	LR	Low end range		SQ	Second quartile wage		Y	Yearly

Occupation/Type/Industry	Location	Per	Low	Mid	High	Source	Date
Chemical Engineer	Norfolk-Virginia Beach-Newport News MSA, VA-NC	S	29.02 MW	28.36 AW	60370 AAW	VABLS	10//99-12//99
	Richmond-Petersburg MSA, VA	S	27.57 MW	28.60 AW	57340 AAW	VABLS	10//99-12//99
	Washington	S	35.03 MW	33.37 AW	69410 AAW	WABLS	10//99-12//99
	Bellingham MSA, WA	S	32.80 MW	35.16 AW	68230 AAW	WABLS	10//99-12//99
	Seattle-Bellevue-Everett PMSA, WA	S	32.38 MW	33.82 AW	67350 AAW	WABLS	10//99-12//99
	West Virginia	S	32.67 MW	31.24 AW	64990 AAW	WVBLS	10//99-12//99
	Charleston MSA, WV	S	31.08 MW	32.51 AW	64640 AAW	WVBLS	10//99-12//99
	Huntington-Ashland MSA, WV-KY-OH	S	29.48 MW	30.37 AW	61310 AAW	WVBLS	10//99-12//99
	Parkersburg-Marietta MSA, WV-OH	S	32.47 MW	33.04 AW	67540 AAW	WVBLS	10//99-12//99
	Wisconsin	S	31.58 MW	30.26 AW	62950 AAW	WIBLS	10//99-12//99
	Appleton-Oshkosh-Neenah MSA, WI	S	30.54 MW	31.50 AW	63530 AAW	WIBLS	10//99-12//99
	Milwaukee-Waukesha PMSA, WI	S	29.03 MW	31.11 AW	60380 AAW	WIBLS	10//99-12//99
	Puerto Rico	S	23.09 MW	23.76 AW	49420 AAW	PRBLS	10//99-12//99
	San Juan-Bayamon PMSA, PR	S	24.38 MW	23.73 AW	50720 AAW	PRBLS	10//99-12//99
Recent Graduate	United States	Y		68000 MW		C&EN2	1999
Chemical Equipment Operator and Tender	Alabama	S	16.43 MW	16.48 AW	34270 AAW	ALBLS	10//99-12//99
	Birmingham MSA, AL	S	14.72 MW	13.86 AW	30610 AAW	ALBLS	10//99-12//99
	Decatur MSA, AL	S	18.32 MW	18.58 AW	38110 AAW	ALBLS	10//99-12//99
	Huntsville MSA, AL	S	14.40 MW	14.43 AW	29950 AAW	ALBLS	10//99-12//99
	Mobile MSA, AL	S	16.34 MW	16.05 AW	34000 AAW	ALBLS	10//99-12//99
	Arizona	S	14.6 MW	14.36 AW	29860 AAW	AZBLS	10//99-12//99
	Phoenix-Mesa MSA, AZ	S	14.79 MW	15.06 AW	30760 AAW	AZBLS	10//99-12//99
	Arkansas	S	16.52 MW	16.01 AW	33310 AAW	ARBLS	10//99-12//99
	California	S	13.18 MW	14.27 AW	29690 AAW	CABLS	10//99-12//99
	Los Angeles-Long Beach PMSA, CA	S	12.67 MW	11.52 AW	26360 AAW	CABLS	10//99-12//99
	Oakland PMSA, CA	S	17.36 MW	17.60 AW	36100 AAW	CABLS	10//99-12//99
	Orange County PMSA, CA	S	14.31 MW	13.39 AW	29760 AAW	CABLS	10//99-12//99
	Riverside-San Bernardino PMSA, CA	S	11.93 MW	12.50 AW	24810 AAW	CABLS	10//99-12//99
	San Diego MSA, CA	S	15.44 MW	16.99 AW	32110 AAW	CABLS	10//99-12//99
	San Jose PMSA, CA	S	19.78 MW	20.95 AW	41150 AAW	CABLS	10//99-12//99
	Santa Rosa PMSA, CA	S	16.20 MW	16.55 AW	33690 AAW	CABLS	10//99-12//99
	Connecticut	S	15.24 MW	15.38 AW	31980 AAW	CTBLS	10//99-12//99
	Bridgeport PMSA, CT	S	14.20 MW	13.46 AW	29530 AAW	CTBLS	10//99-12//99
	Danbury PMSA, CT	S	15.35 MW	15.47 AW	31930 AAW	CTBLS	10//99-12//99
	Hartford MSA, CT	S	15.08 MW	14.15 AW	31370 AAW	CTBLS	10//99-12//99
	New Haven-Meriden PMSA, CT	S	15.16 MW	14.52 AW	31530 AAW	CTBLS	10//99-12//99
	New London-Norwich MSA, CT-RI	S	12.96 MW	13.19 AW	26970 AAW	CTBLS	10//99-12//99
	Delaware	S	20.86 MW	20.25 AW	42120 AAW	DEBLS	10//99-12//99
	Wilmington-Newark PMSA, DE-MD	S	20.54 MW	21.52 AW	42720 AAW	DEBLS	10//99-12//99
	Washington PMSA, DC-MD-VA-WV	S	16.90 MW	16.26 AW	35150 AAW	DCBLS	10//99-12//99
	Florida	S	15.01 MW	14.87 AW	30930 AAW	FLBLS	10//99-12//99
	Jacksonville MSA, FL	S	15.96 MW	16.16 AW	33190 AAW	FLBLS	10//99-12//99
	Lakeland-Winter Haven MSA, FL	S	13.34 MW	14.38 AW	27740 AAW	FLBLS	10//99-12//99
	Miami PMSA, FL	S	13.83 MW	14.58 AW	28770 AAW	FLBLS	10//99-12//99
	Georgia	S	15.27 MW	15.62 AW	32480 AAW	GABLS	10//99-12//99
	Atlanta MSA, GA	S	16.14 MW	15.90 AW	33570 AAW	GABLS	10//99-12//99
	Savannah MSA, GA	S	15.37 MW	15.43 AW	31970 AAW	GABLS	10//99-12//99
	Idaho	S	18.66 MW	18.67 AW	38830 AAW	IDBLS	10//99-12//99
	Illinois	S	16.1 MW	16.58 AW	34490 AAW	ILBLS	10//99-12//99
	Chicago PMSA, IL	S	16.29 MW	15.65 AW	33870 AAW	ILBLS	10//99-12//99
	Kankakee PMSA, IL	S	14.60 MW	14.64 AW	30370 AAW	ILBLS	10//99-12//99
	Indiana	S	15.89 MW	16.05 AW	33390 AAW	INBLS	10//99-12//99
	Evansville-Henderson MSA, IN-KY	S	17.45 MW	16.70 AW	36290 AAW	INBLS	10//99-12//99
	Gary PMSA, IN	S	14.68 MW	15.80 AW	30540 AAW	INBLS	10//99-12//99

AAW	Average annual wage	AOH	Average offered, high	ASH	Average starting, high	H	Hourly			M	Monthly	S	Special: hourly and annual
AE	Average entry wage	AOL	Average offered, low	ASL	Average starting, low	HI	Highest wage paid			MTC	Median total compensation	TQ	Third quartile wage
AEX	Average experienced wage	APH	Average pay, high range	AW	Average wage paid	HR	High end range			MW	Median wage paid	W	Weekly
AO	Average offered	APL	Average pay, low range	FQ	First quartile wage	LR	Low end range			SQ	Second quartile wage	Y	Yearly

Occupation/Type/Industry	Location	Per	Low	Mid	High	Source	Date
Chemical Equipment Operator and Tender	Indianapolis MSA, IN	S	14.36 MW	14.15 AW	29880 AAW	INBLS	10//99-12//99
	Kansas	S	14.57 MW	14.44 AW	30040 AAW	KSBLS	10//99-12//99
	Wichita MSA, KS	S	13.13 MW	11.90 AW	27310 AAW	KSBLS	10//99-12//99
	Kentucky	S	18.16 MW	18.03 AW	37490 AAW	KYBLS	10//99-12//99
	Louisville MSA, KY-IN	S	16.67 MW	17.16 AW	34680 AAW	KYBLS	10//99-12//99
	Louisiana	S	21.73 MW	20.81 AW	43280 AAW	LABLS	10//99-12//99
	Baton Rouge MSA, LA	S	20.23 MW	20.38 AW	42080 AAW	LABLS	10//99-12//99
	New Orleans MSA, LA	S	21.82 MW	22.49 AW	45390 AAW	LABLS	10//99-12//99
	Maine	S	14.45 MW	14.66 AW	30490 AAW	MEBLS	10//99-12//99
	Maryland	S	19.99 MW	19.05 AW	39620 AAW	MDBLS	10//99-12//99
	Baltimore PMSA, MD	S	19.52 MW	20.43 AW	40590 AAW	MDBLS	10//99-12//99
	Massachusetts	S	14.45 MW	14.49 AW	30140 AAW	MABLS	10//99-12//99
	Boston PMSA, MA-NH	S	14.62 MW	14.52 AW	30410 AAW	MABLS	10//99-12//99
	Worcester PMSA, MA-CT	S	14.24 MW	14.67 AW	29610 AAW	MABLS	10//99-12//99
	Michigan	S	15.75 MW	16.47 AW	34260 AAW	MIBLS	10//99-12//99
	Detroit PMSA, MI	S	17.58 MW	17.61 AW	36570 AAW	MIBLS	10//99-12//99
	Grand Rapids-Muskegon-Holland MSA, MI	S	16.08 MW	15.52 AW	33450 AAW	MIBLS	10//99-12//99
	Kalamazoo-Battle Creek MSA, MI	S	19.85 MW	19.75 AW	41280 AAW	MIBLS	10//99-12//99
	Minnesota	S	14.98 MW	15.40 AW	32040 AAW	MNBLS	10//99-12//99
	Minneapolis-St. Paul MSA, MN-WI	S	16.29 MW	16.00 AW	33890 AAW	MNBLS	10//99-12//99
	Mississippi	S	15.6 MW	15.55 AW	32340 AAW	MSBLS	10//99-12//99
	Biloxi-Gulfport-Pascagoula MSA, MS	S	16.54 MW	16.40 AW	34410 AAW	MSBLS	10//99-12//99
	Missouri	S	16.76 MW	16.14 AW	33570 AAW	MOBLS	10//99-12//99
	Kansas City MSA, MO-KS	S	15.24 MW	15.81 AW	31710 AAW	MOBLS	10//99-12//99
	Nebraska	S	11.54 MW	11.75 AW	24440 AAW	NEBLS	10//99-12//99
	Omaha MSA, NE-IA	S	15.76 MW	15.80 AW	32780 AAW	NEBLS	10//99-12//99
	New Hampshire	S	15.67 MW	15.39 AW	32020 AAW	NHBLS	10//99-12//99
	Portsmouth-Rochester PMSA, NH-ME	S	16.39 MW	16.81 AW	34080 AAW	NHBLS	10//99-12//99
	New Jersey	S	16.53 MW	16.53 AW	34380 AAW	NJBLS	10//99-12//99
	Bergen-Passaic PMSA, NJ	S	15.95 MW	16.22 AW	33180 AAW	NJBLS	10//99-12//99
	Jersey City PMSA, NJ	S	17.38 MW	18.20 AW	36160 AAW	NJBLS	10//99-12//99
	Middlesex-Somerset-Hunterdon PMSA, NJ	S	16.84 MW	17.37 AW	35030 AAW	NJBLS	10//99-12//99
	Monmouth-Ocean PMSA, NJ	S	12.97 MW	12.12 AW	26990 AAW	NJBLS	10//99-12//99
	Newark PMSA, NJ	S	16.20 MW	16.11 AW	33690 AAW	NJBLS	10//99-12//99
	Trenton PMSA, NJ	S	16.34 MW	15.83 AW	33990 AAW	NJBLS	10//99-12//99
	New York	S	15.02 MW	14.31 AW	29770 AAW	NYBLS	10//99-12//99
	Buffalo-Niagara Falls MSA, NY	S	16.15 MW	16.67 AW	33580 AAW	NYBLS	10//99-12//99
	Nassau-Suffolk PMSA, NY	S	14.00 MW	13.51 AW	29120 AAW	NYBLS	10//99-12//99
	New York PMSA, NY	S	12.91 MW	14.18 AW	26850 AAW	NYBLS	10//99-12//99
	Newburgh PMSA, NY-PA	S	14.52 MW	14.47 AW	30200 AAW	NYBLS	10//99-12//99
	Rochester MSA, NY	S	16.16 MW	16.60 AW	33620 AAW	NYBLS	10//99-12//99
	North Carolina	S	17.12 MW	16.62 AW	34560 AAW	NCBLS	10//99-12//99
	Charlotte-Gastonia-Rock Hill MSA, NC-SC	S	16.11 MW	16.21 AW	33510 AAW	NCBLS	10//99-12//99
	Greensboro--Winston-Salem--High Point MSA, NC	S	13.66 MW	13.03 AW	28420 AAW	NCBLS	10//99-12//99
	Hickory-Morganton-Lenoir MSA, NC	S	14.35 MW	14.95 AW	29850 AAW	NCBLS	10//99-12//99
	Raleigh-Durham-Chapel Hill MSA, NC	S	16.90 MW	17.41 AW	35160 AAW	NCBLS	10//99-12//99
	Ohio	S	17.72 MW	17.48 AW	36360 AAW	OHBLS	10//99-12//99
	Akron PMSA, OH	S	16.42 MW	17.19 AW	34150 AAW	OHBLS	10//99-12//99
	Cincinnati PMSA, OH-KY-IN	S	17.56 MW	17.80 AW	36520 AAW	OHBLS	10//99-12//99
	Cleveland-Lorain-Elyria PMSA, OH	S	15.48 MW	15.75 AW	32190 AAW	OHBLS	10//99-12//99
	Oklahoma	S	17.56 MW	16.16 AW	33610 AAW	OKBLS	10//99-12//99
	Oregon	S	18.6 MW	18.74 AW	38990 AAW	ORBLS	10//99-12//99
	Portland-Vancouver PMSA, OR-WA	S	18.04 MW	18.17 AW	37530 AAW	ORBLS	10//99-12//99
	Pennsylvania	S	17.4 MW	17.28 AW	35940 AAW	PABLS	10//99-12//99
	Allentown-Bethlehem-Easton MSA, PA	S	16.25 MW	16.33 AW	33800 AAW	PABLS	10//99-12//99
	Altoona MSA, PA	S	16.02 MW	15.72 AW	33310 AAW	PABLS	10//99-12//99
	Philadelphia PMSA, PA-NJ	S	18.54 MW	17.88 AW	38570 AAW	PABLS	10//99-12//99

AAW Average annual wage	**AOH** Average offered, high	**ASH** Average starting, high	**H** Hourly	**M** Monthly	**S** Special: hourly and annual
AE Average entry wage	**AOL** Average offered, low	**ASL** Average starting, low	**HI** Highest wage paid	**MTC** Median total compensation	**TQ** Third quartile wage
AEX Average experienced wage	**APH** Average pay, high range	**AW** Average wage paid	**HR** High end range	**MW** Median wage paid	**W** Weekly
AO Average offered	**APL** Average pay, low range	**FQ** First quartile wage	**LR** Low end range	**SQ** Second quartile wage	**Y** Yearly

Occupation/Type/Industry	Location	Per	Low	Mid	High	Source	Date
Chemical Equipment Operator and Tender							
	Pittsburgh MSA, PA	S	16.92 MW	17.75 AW	35200 AAW	PABLS	10//99-12//99
	Reading MSA, PA	S	16.53 MW	16.37 AW	34380 AAW	PABLS	10//99-12//99
	Providence-Fall River-Warwick MSA, RI-MA	S	15.33 MW	15.54 AW	31880 AAW	RIBLS	10//99-12//99
	South Carolina	S	17.81 MW	18.78 AW	39060 AAW	SCBLS	10//99-12//99
	Greenville-Spartanburg-Anderson MSA, SC	S	16.09 MW	16.58 AW	33460 AAW	SCBLS	10//99-12//99
	Tennessee	S	16.38 MW	15.86 AW	33000 AAW	TNBLS	10//99-12//99
	Johnson City-Kingsport-Bristol MSA, TN-VA	S	17.25 MW	17.12 AW	35870 AAW	TNBLS	10//99-12//99
	Memphis MSA, TN-AR-MS	S	17.05 MW	17.81 AW	35470 AAW	MSBLS	10//99-12//99
	Nashville MSA, TN	S	11.61 MW	10.20 AW	24150 AAW	TNBLS	10//99-12//99
	Texas	S	18.14 MW	17.41 AW	36220 AAW	TXBLS	10//99-12//99
	Austin-San Marcos MSA, TX	S	11.94 MW	9.82 AW	24840 AAW	TXBLS	10//99-12//99
	Beaumont-Port Arthur MSA, TX	S	20.76 MW	21.82 AW	43180 AAW	TXBLS	10//99-12//99
	Dallas PMSA, TX	S	13.28 MW	12.47 AW	27620 AAW	TXBLS	10//99-12//99
	Fort Worth-Arlington PMSA, TX	S	13.79 MW	12.75 AW	28680 AAW	TXBLS	10//99-12//99
	Houston PMSA, TX	S	16.73 MW	17.06 AW	34790 AAW	TXBLS	10//99-12//99
	San Antonio MSA, TX	S	15.62 MW	14.93 AW	32500 AAW	TXBLS	10//99-12//99
	Utah	S	14.14 MW	13.28 AW	27620 AAW	UTBLS	10//99-12//99
	Salt Lake City-Ogden MSA, UT	S	11.44 MW	11.04 AW	23790 AAW	UTBLS	10//99-12//99
	Virginia	S	15.99 MW	16.81 AW	34970 AAW	VABLS	10//99-12//99
	Norfolk-Virginia Beach-Newport News MSA, VA-NC	S	14.97 MW	13.17 AW	31130 AAW	VABLS	10//99-12//99
	Richmond-Petersburg MSA, VA	S	20.67 MW	21.93 AW	43000 AAW	VABLS	10//99-12//99
	Washington	S	20.2 MW	19.59 AW	40740 AAW	WABLS	10//99-12//99
	Seattle-Bellevue-Everett PMSA, WA	S	18.60 MW	17.53 AW	38700 AAW	WABLS	10//99-12//99
	Spokane MSA, WA	S	17.57 MW	16.45 AW	36550 AAW	WABLS	10//99-12//99
	West Virginia	S	18.48 MW	18.18 AW	37820 AAW	WVBLS	10//99-12//99
	Wisconsin	S	15.02 MW	15.40 AW	32030 AAW	WIBLS	10//99-12//99
	Appleton-Oshkosh-Neenah MSA, WI	S	17.29 MW	18.11 AW	35960 AAW	WIBLS	10//99-12//99
	Madison MSA, WI	S	11.17 MW	11.50 AW	23240 AAW	WIBLS	10//99-12//99
	Milwaukee-Waukesha PMSA, WI	S	13.59 MW	12.89 AW	28270 AAW	WIBLS	10//99-12//99
	Puerto Rico	S	13.19 MW	12.75 AW	26510 AAW	PRBLS	10//99-12//99
	San Juan-Bayamon PMSA, PR	S	13.39 MW	14.05 AW	27850 AAW	PRBLS	10//99-12//99
Chemical Plant and System Operator							
	Alabama	S	18.08 MW	18.66 AW	38810 AAW	ALBLS	10//99-12//99
	Arizona	S	15.52 MW	16.39 AW	34100 AAW	AZBLS	10//99-12//99
	Arkansas	S	18.84 MW	18.74 AW	38980 AAW	ARBLS	10//99-12//99
	California	S	19.16 MW	19.45 AW	40460 AAW	CABLS	10//99-12//99
	Colorado	S	13.07 MW	14.23 AW	29610 AAW	COBLS	10//99-12//99
	Delaware	S	18.81 MW	18.92 AW	39340 AAW	DEBLS	10//99-12//99
	Florida	S	14.94 MW	15.25 AW	31710 AAW	FLBLS	10//99-12//99
	Georgia	S	17.5 MW	17.05 AW	35460 AAW	GABLS	10//99-12//99
	Idaho	S	19.32 MW	19.31 AW	40160 AAW	IDBLS	10//99-12//99
	Illinois	S	18.39 MW	18.21 AW	37880 AAW	ILBLS	10//99-12//99
	Indiana	S	19.42 MW	19.26 AW	40070 AAW	INBLS	10//99-12//99
	Iowa	S	18.78 MW	18.73 AW	38960 AAW	IABLS	10//99-12//99
	Kentucky	S	19.79 MW	18.85 AW	39200 AAW	KYBLS	10//99-12//99
	Louisiana	S	22.95 MW	22.72 AW	47250 AAW	LABLS	10//99-12//99
	Maine	S	13.41 MW	14.51 AW	30180 AAW	MEBLS	10//99-12//99
	Maryland	S	17.54 MW	16.67 AW	34680 AAW	MDBLS	10//99-12//99
	Michigan	S	21.43 MW	20.14 AW	41890 AAW	MIBLS	10//99-12//99
	Minnesota	S	22.83 MW	21.43 AW	44570 AAW	MNBLS	10//99-12//99
	Mississippi	S	17.7 MW	16.95 AW	35260 AAW	MSBLS	10//99-12//99
	Missouri	S	18.15 MW	18.41 AW	38290 AAW	MOBLS	10//99-12//99
	Nevada	S	18.92 MW	18.94 AW	39400 AAW	NVBLS	10//99-12//99
	New Jersey	S	20.92 MW	20.09 AW	41780 AAW	NJBLS	10//99-12//99
	New Mexico	S	16.2 MW	16.92 AW	35190 AAW	NMBLS	10//99-12//99
	New York	S	17.97 MW	17.79 AW	36990 AAW	NYBLS	10//99-12//99
	North Carolina	S	16.71 MW	16.50 AW	34320 AAW	NCBLS	10//99-12//99
	Ohio	S	16.68 MW	16.94 AW	35230 AAW	OHBLS	10//99-12//99

AAW Average annual wage	AOH Average offered, high	ASH Average starting, high	H Hourly	M Monthly	S Special: hourly and annual
AE Average entry wage	AOL Average offered, low	ASL Average starting, low	HI Highest wage paid	MTC Median total compensation	TQ Third quartile wage
AEX Average experienced wage	APH Average pay, high range	AW Average wage paid	HR High end range	MW Median wage paid	W Weekly
AO Average offered	APL Average pay, low range	FQ First quartile wage	LR Low end range	SQ Second quartile wage	Y Yearly

Occupation/Type/Industry	Location	Per	Low	Mid	High	Source	Date
Chemical Plant and System Operator	Oklahoma	S	18.4 MW	17.97 AW	37380 AAW	OKBLS	10//99-12//99
	Pennsylvania	S	17.94 MW	17.53 AW	36450 AAW	PABLS	10//99-12//99
	South Carolina	S	14.82 MW	14.93 AW	31060 AAW	SCBLS	10//99-12//99
	Tennessee	S	16.76 MW	16.92 AW	35200 AAW	TNBLS	10//99-12//99
	Texas	S	22.95 MW	22.55 AW	46910 AAW	TXBLS	10//99-12//99
	Utah	S	17.73 MW	18.24 AW	37930 AAW	UTBLS	10//99-12//99
	Virginia	S	18.35 MW	18.20 AW	37860 AAW	VABLS	10//99-12//99
	Washington	S	20.79 MW	19.98 AW	41550 AAW	WABLS	10//99-12//99
	West Virginia	S	20.74 MW	20.57 AW	42790 AAW	WVBLS	10//99-12//99
	Wisconsin	S	15.74 MW	16.23 AW	33760 AAW	WIBLS	10//99-12//99
	Puerto Rico	S	12.92 MW	12.52 AW	26040 AAW	PRBLS	10//99-12//99
Chemical Technician	United States	H		17.15 AW		NCS98	1998
	Alabama	S	14.71 MW	15.72 AW	32700 AAW	ALBLS	10//99-12//99
	Birmingham MSA, AL	S	15.91 MW	16.12 AW	33090 AAW	ALBLS	10//99-12//99
	Decatur MSA, AL	S	16.89 MW	15.02 AW	35130 AAW	ALBLS	10//99-12//99
	Florence MSA, AL	S	11.82 MW	12.02 AW	24580 AAW	ALBLS	10//99-12//99
	Mobile MSA, AL	S	16.45 MW	15.40 AW	34230 AAW	ALBLS	10//99-12//99
	Alaska	S	15.55 MW	15.84 AW	32950 AAW	AKBLS	10//99-12//99
	Arizona	S	18.73 MW	21.32 AW	44340 AAW	AZBLS	10//99-12//99
	Phoenix-Mesa MSA, AZ	S	24.63 MW	22.70 AW	51230 AAW	AZBLS	10//99-12//99
	Tucson MSA, AZ	S	13.67 MW	14.07 AW	28430 AAW	AZBLS	10//99-12//99
	Yuma MSA, AZ	S	14.78 MW	12.73 AW	30750 AAW	AZBLS	10//99-12//99
	Arkansas	S	11.72 MW	12.68 AW	26370 AAW	ARBLS	10//99-12//99
	Little Rock-North Little Rock MSA, AR	S	12.68 MW	12.56 AW	26380 AAW	ARBLS	10//99-12//99
	California	S	16.59 MW	17.53 AW	36460 AAW	CABLS	10//99-12//99
	Los Angeles-Long Beach PMSA, CA	S	17.82 MW	17.50 AW	37070 AAW	CABLS	10//99-12//99
	Modesto MSA, CA	S	10.14 MW	9.76 AW	21090 AAW	CABLS	10//99-12//99
	Oakland PMSA, CA	S	17.55 MW	17.61 AW	36510 AAW	CABLS	10//99-12//99
	Orange County PMSA, CA	S	17.31 MW	13.09 AW	36000 AAW	CABLS	10//99-12//99
	Riverside-San Bernardino PMSA, CA	S	20.46 MW	19.11 AW	42550 AAW	CABLS	10//99-12//99
	Sacramento PMSA, CA	S	17.49 MW	16.73 AW	36380 AAW	CABLS	10//99-12//99
	San Diego MSA, CA	S	21.06 MW	22.22 AW	43810 AAW	CABLS	10//99-12//99
	San Francisco PMSA, CA	S	26.77 MW	22.81 AW	55670 AAW	CABLS	10//99-12//99
	San Jose PMSA, CA	S	16.86 MW	17.18 AW	35060 AAW	CABLS	10//99-12//99
	Santa Barbara-Santa Maria-Lompoc MSA, CA	S	14.52 MW	14.94 AW	30190 AAW	CABLS	10//99-12//99
	Santa Rosa PMSA, CA	S	11.15 MW	9.98 AW	23190 AAW	CABLS	10//99-12//99
	Colorado	S	15.59 MW	16.00 AW	33280 AAW	COBLS	10//99-12//99
	Boulder-Longmont PMSA, CO	S	15.75 MW	15.53 AW	32770 AAW	COBLS	10//99-12//99
	Denver PMSA, CO	S	16.92 MW	16.15 AW	35190 AAW	COBLS	10//99-12//99
	Connecticut	S	16.59 MW	16.97 AW	35310 AAW	CTBLS	10//99-12//99
	Bridgeport PMSA, CT	S	17.32 MW	18.50 AW	36020 AAW	CTBLS	10//99-12//99
	Hartford MSA, CT	S	18.85 MW	16.75 AW	39200 AAW	CTBLS	10//99-12//99
	New Haven-Meriden PMSA, CT	S	16.79 MW	15.56 AW	34910 AAW	CTBLS	10//99-12//99
	New London-Norwich MSA, CT-RI	S	13.28 MW	12.34 AW	27620 AAW	CTBLS	10//99-12//99
	Stamford-Norwalk PMSA, CT	S	19.13 MW	19.23 AW	39800 AAW	CTBLS	10//99-12//99
	Waterbury PMSA, CT	S	17.38 MW	16.91 AW	36150 AAW	CTBLS	10//99-12//99
	Delaware	S	23.47 MW	22.30 AW	46390 AAW	DEBLS	10//99-12//99
	Dover MSA, DE	S	13.22 MW	13.62 AW	27500 AAW	DEBLS	10//99-12//99
	Wilmington-Newark PMSA, DE-MD	S	22.70 MW	23.63 AW	47210 AAW	DEBLS	10//99-12//99
	Washington PMSA, DC-MD-VA-WV	S	18.46 MW	18.47 AW	38390 AAW	DCBLS	10//99-12//99
	Florida	S	13.02 MW	14.29 AW	29720 AAW	FLBLS	10//99-12//99
	Daytona Beach MSA, FL	S	12.03 MW	11.90 AW	25010 AAW	FLBLS	10//99-12//99
	Jacksonville MSA, FL	S	12.36 MW	10.52 AW	25710 AAW	FLBLS	10//99-12//99
	Lakeland-Winter Haven MSA, FL	S	11.55 MW	10.13 AW	24030 AAW	FLBLS	10//99-12//99
	Melbourne-Titusville-Palm Bay MSA, FL	S	18.20 MW	18.82 AW	37850 AAW	FLBLS	10//99-12//99
	Miami PMSA, FL	S	12.73 MW	11.72 AW	26480 AAW	FLBLS	10//99-12//99
	Orlando MSA, FL	S	12.73 MW	11.16 AW	26480 AAW	FLBLS	10//99-12//99
	Tampa-St. Petersburg-Clearwater MSA, FL	S	15.45 MW	15.87 AW	32140 AAW	FLBLS	10//99-12//99

AAW Average annual wage	AOH Average offered, high	ASH Average starting, high	H Hourly	M Monthly	S Special: hourly and annual
AE Average entry wage	AOL Average offered, low	ASL Average starting, low	HI Highest wage paid	MTC Median total compensation	TQ Third quartile wage
AEX Average experienced wage	APH Average pay, high range	AW Average wage paid	HR High end range	MW Median wage paid	W Weekly
AO Average offered	APL Average pay, low range	FQ First quartile wage	LR Low end range	SQ Second quartile wage	Y Yearly

Occupation/Type/Industry	Location	Per	Low	Mid	High	Source	Date
Chemical Technician	West Palm Beach-Boca Raton MSA, FL	s	11.29 MW	10.61 AW	23490 AAW	FLBLS	10//99-12//99
	Georgia	s	12.65 MW	13.41 AW	27900 AAW	GABLS	10//99-12//99
	Albany MSA, GA	s	12.61 MW	13.78 AW	26230 AAW	GABLS	10//99-12//99
	Athens MSA, GA	s	10.73 MW	10.87 AW	22320 AAW	GABLS	10//99-12//99
	Atlanta MSA, GA	s	12.53 MW	10.45 AW	26060 AAW	GABLS	10//99-12//99
	Augusta-Aiken MSA, GA-SC	s	14.51 MW	14.29 AW	30190 AAW	GABLS	10//99-12//99
	Columbus MSA, GA-AL	s	12.63 MW	12.67 AW	26280 AAW	GABLS	10//99-12//99
	Savannah MSA, GA	s	18.41 MW	17.58 AW	38300 AAW	GABLS	10//99-12//99
	Idaho	s	12.16 MW	13.34 AW	27740 AAW	IDBLS	10//99-12//99
	Boise City MSA, ID	s	12.35 MW	12.24 AW	25690 AAW	IDBLS	10//99-12//99
	Illinois	s	15.34 MW	15.61 AW	32480 AAW	ILBLS	10//99-12//99
	Chicago PMSA, IL	s	15.49 MW	15.31 AW	32220 AAW	ILBLS	10//99-12//99
	Rockford MSA, IL	s	14.33 MW	14.88 AW	29800 AAW	ILBLS	10//99-12//99
	Indiana	s	15.23 MW	15.19 AW	31600 AAW	INBLS	10//99-12//99
	Elkhart-Goshen MSA, IN	s	12.15 MW	11.96 AW	25260 AAW	INBLS	10//99-12//99
	Evansville-Henderson MSA, IN-KY	s	17.05 MW	18.32 AW	35460 AAW	INBLS	10//99-12//99
	Fort Wayne MSA, IN	s	12.00 MW	10.38 AW	24970 AAW	INBLS	10//99-12//99
	Gary PMSA, IN	s	17.09 MW	16.21 AW	35550 AAW	INBLS	10//99-12//99
	Indianapolis MSA, IN	s	15.18 MW	15.21 AW	31580 AAW	INBLS	10//99-12//99
	Lafayette MSA, IN	s	15.98 MW	15.03 AW	33250 AAW	INBLS	10//99-12//99
	Terre Haute MSA, IN	s	18.52 MW	18.88 AW	38510 AAW	INBLS	10//99-12//99
	Iowa	s	15.91 MW	16.91 AW	35170 AAW	IABLS	10//99-12//99
	Des Moines MSA, IA	s	10.68 MW	9.62 AW	22220 AAW	IABLS	10//99-12//99
	Kansas	s	11.94 MW	13.23 AW	27520 AAW	KSBLS	10//99-12//99
	Wichita MSA, KS	s	11.58 MW	10.20 AW	24090 AAW	KSBLS	10//99-12//99
	Kentucky	s	15.9 MW	16.78 AW	34900 AAW	KYBLS	10//99-12//99
	Lexington MSA, KY	s	14.49 MW	14.08 AW	30150 AAW	KYBLS	10//99-12//99
	Louisville MSA, KY-IN	s	13.89 MW	13.29 AW	28900 AAW	KYBLS	10//99-12//99
	Louisiana	s	22.99 MW	21.39 AW	44500 AAW	LABLS	10//99-12//99
	Baton Rouge MSA, LA	s	23.23 MW	23.74 AW	48320 AAW	LABLS	10//99-12//99
	Lake Charles MSA, LA	s	20.93 MW	23.06 AW	43540 AAW	LABLS	10//99-12//99
	New Orleans MSA, LA	s	14.42 MW	13.34 AW	30000 AAW	LABLS	10//99-12//99
	Shreveport-Bossier City MSA, LA	s	23.40 MW	23.99 AW	48670 AAW	LABLS	10//99-12//99
	Maine	s	12.28 MW	12.90 AW	26830 AAW	MEBLS	10//99-12//99
	Maryland	s	18.62 MW	18.52 AW	38530 AAW	MDBLS	10//99-12//99
	Baltimore PMSA, MD	s	18.48 MW	18.62 AW	38440 AAW	MDBLS	10//99-12//99
	Massachusetts	s	16.34 MW	17.57 AW	36560 AAW	MABLS	10//99-12//99
	Boston PMSA, MA-NH	s	17.63 MW	16.25 AW	36680 AAW	MABLS	10//99-12//99
	Lawrence PMSA, MA-NH	s	15.24 MW	15.03 AW	31690 AAW	MABLS	10//99-12//99
	Lowell PMSA, MA-NH	s	18.58 MW	18.29 AW	38650 AAW	MABLS	10//99-12//99
	Worcester PMSA, MA-CT	s	15.37 MW	15.43 AW	31970 AAW	MABLS	10//99-12//99
	Michigan	s	18.89 MW	19.79 AW	41160 AAW	MIBLS	10//99-12//99
	Ann Arbor PMSA, MI	s	14.86 MW	14.01 AW	30900 AAW	MIBLS	10//99-12//99
	Detroit PMSA, MI	s	19.45 MW	18.57 AW	40460 AAW	MIBLS	10//99-12//99
	Grand Rapids-Muskegon-Holland MSA, MI	s	21.78 MW	21.64 AW	45300 AAW	MIBLS	10//99-12//99
	Jackson MSA, MI	s	14.36 MW	14.64 AW	29870 AAW	MIBLS	10//99-12//99
	Kalamazoo-Battle Creek MSA, MI	s	20.27 MW	21.20 AW	42160 AAW	MIBLS	10//99-12//99
	Lansing-East Lansing MSA, MI	s	22.02 MW	21.10 AW	45810 AAW	MIBLS	10//99-12//99
	Minnesota	s	16.46 MW	16.83 AW	35000 AAW	MNBLS	10//99-12//99
	Minneapolis-St. Paul MSA, MN-WI	s	17.02 MW	16.49 AW	35390 AAW	MNBLS	10//99-12//99
	Mississippi	s	14.66 MW	15.54 AW	32330 AAW	MSBLS	10//99-12//99
	Biloxi-Gulfport-Pascagoula MSA, MS	s	14.83 MW	14.11 AW	30840 AAW	MSBLS	10//99-12//99
	Jackson MSA, MS	s	13.57 MW	12.00 AW	28220 AAW	MSBLS	10//99-12//99
	Missouri	s	18.42 MW	19.67 AW	40910 AAW	MOBLS	10//99-12//99
	Kansas City MSA, MO-KS	s	16.83 MW	16.74 AW	35010 AAW	MOBLS	10//99-12//99
	St. Louis MSA, MO-IL	s	19.12 MW	17.93 AW	39770 AAW	MOBLS	10//99-12//99
	Nebraska	s	12.51 MW	12.77 AW	26560 AAW	NEBLS	10//99-12//99
	Omaha MSA, NE-IA	s	12.78 MW	12.71 AW	26590 AAW	NEBLS	10//99-12//99
	Nevada	s	18.18 MW	18.23 AW	37920 AAW	NVBLS	10//99-12//99
	Las Vegas MSA, NV-AZ	s	17.93 MW	15.94 AW	37290 AAW	NVBLS	10//99-12//99
	New Hampshire	s	16.85 MW	18.17 AW	37800 AAW	NHBLS	10//99-12//99
	Nashua PMSA, NH	s	19.26 MW	21.71 AW	40070 AAW	NHBLS	10//99-12//99
	Portsmouth-Rochester PMSA, NH-ME	s	17.36 MW	16.73 AW	36110 AAW	NHBLS	10//99-12//99
	New Jersey	s	15.73 MW	16.59 AW	34510 AAW	NJBLS	10//99-12//99

AAW Average annual wage	**AOH** Average offered, high	**ASH** Average starting, high	**H** Hourly	**M** Monthly	**S** Special: hourly and annual
AE Average entry wage	**AOL** Average offered, low	**ASL** Average starting, low	**HI** Highest wage paid	**MTC** Median total compensation	**TQ** Third quartile wage
AEX Average experienced wage	**APH** Average pay, high range	**AW** Average wage paid	**HR** High end range	**MW** Median wage paid	**W** Weekly
AO Average offered	**APL** Average pay, low range	**FQ** First quartile wage	**LR** Low end range	**SQ** Second quartile wage	**Y** Yearly

Occupation/Type/Industry	Location	Per	Low	Mid	High	Source	Date
Chemical Technician	Bergen-Passaic PMSA, NJ	S	19.05 MW	16.63 AW	39620 AAW	NJBLS	10//99-12//99
	Middlesex-Somerset-Hunterdon PMSA, NJ	S	18.26 MW	17.88 AW	37970 AAW	NJBLS	10//99-12//99
	Monmouth-Ocean PMSA, NJ	S	18.60 MW	18.46 AW	38690 AAW	NJBLS	10//99-12//99
	Newark PMSA, NJ	S	14.07 MW	12.62 AW	29270 AAW	NJBLS	10//99-12//99
	Trenton PMSA, NJ	S	17.44 MW	17.16 AW	36280 AAW	NJBLS	10//99-12//99
	New York	S	15.9 MW	16.09 AW	33460 AAW	NYBLS	10//99-12//99
	Albany-Schenectady-Troy MSA, NY	S	14.97 MW	14.72 AW	31130 AAW	NYBLS	10//99-12//99
	Buffalo-Niagara Falls MSA, NY	S	18.01 MW	18.14 AW	37470 AAW	NYBLS	10//99-12//99
	Glens Falls MSA, NY	S	16.73 MW	15.48 AW	34790 AAW	NYBLS	10//99-12//99
	Nassau-Suffolk PMSA, NY	S	14.40 MW	12.52 AW	29950 AAW	NYBLS	10//99-12//99
	New York PMSA, NY	S	12.00 MW	10.69 AW	24970 AAW	NYBLS	10//99-12//99
	Newburgh PMSA, NY-PA	S	10.91 MW	9.96 AW	22690 AAW	NYBLS	10//99-12//99
	Rochester MSA, NY	S	20.14 MW	20.44 AW	41900 AAW	NYBLS	10//99-12//99
	Syracuse MSA, NY	S	12.03 MW	10.54 AW	25010 AAW	NYBLS	10//99-12//99
	North Carolina	S	15.29 MW	16.02 AW	33330 AAW	NCBLS	10//99-12//99
	Charlotte-Gastonia-Rock Hill MSA, NC-SC	S	17.78 MW	17.29 AW	36990 AAW	NCBLS	10//99-12//99
	Greensboro--Winston-Salem--High Point MSA, NC	S	13.81 MW	13.10 AW	28720 AAW	NCBLS	10//99-12//99
	Hickory-Morganton-Lenoir MSA, NC	S	15.93 MW	15.58 AW	33130 AAW	NCBLS	10//99-12//99
	Raleigh-Durham-Chapel Hill MSA, NC	S	15.41 MW	15.28 AW	32060 AAW	NCBLS	10//99-12//99
	Wilmington MSA, NC	S	22.63 MW	22.44 AW	47070 AAW	NCBLS	10//99-12//99
	Ohio	S	14.55 MW	15.23 AW	31670 AAW	OHBLS	10//99-12//99
	Akron PMSA, OH	S	14.36 MW	14.37 AW	29860 AAW	OHBLS	10//99-12//99
	Cincinnati PMSA, OH-KY-IN	S	17.06 MW	15.53 AW	35480 AAW	OHBLS	10//99-12//99
	Cleveland-Lorain-Elyria PMSA, OH	S	14.95 MW	14.32 AW	31090 AAW	OHBLS	10//99-12//99
	Columbus MSA, OH	S	15.01 MW	14.65 AW	31220 AAW	OHBLS	10//99-12//99
	Hamilton-Middletown PMSA, OH	S	15.83 MW	15.86 AW	32940 AAW	OHBLS	10//99-12//99
	Steubenville-Weirton MSA, OH-WV	S	16.23 MW	13.01 AW	33750 AAW	OHBLS	10//99-12//99
	Toledo MSA, OH	S	17.55 MW	16.73 AW	36500 AAW	OHBLS	10//99-12//99
	Oklahoma	S	17.87 MW	17.99 AW	37420 AAW	OKBLS	10//99-12//99
	Oklahoma City MSA, OK	S	17.55 MW	17.74 AW	36510 AAW	OKBLS	10//99-12//99
	Tulsa MSA, OK	S	19.40 MW	19.31 AW	40350 AAW	OKBLS	10//99-12//99
	Oregon	S	16.64 MW	16.90 AW	35150 AAW	ORBLS	10//99-12//99
	Portland-Vancouver PMSA, OR-WA	S	17.18 MW	16.78 AW	35740 AAW	ORBLS	10//99-12//99
	Pennsylvania	S	16.81 MW	18.21 AW	37880 AAW	PABLS	10//99-12//99
	Allentown-Bethlehem-Easton MSA, PA	S	18.84 MW	17.99 AW	39190 AAW	PABLS	10//99-12//99
	Erie MSA, PA	S	13.93 MW	13.42 AW	28970 AAW	PABLS	10//99-12//99
	Harrisburg-Lebanon-Carlisle MSA, PA	S	17.22 MW	16.02 AW	35810 AAW	PABLS	10//99-12//99
	Philadelphia PMSA, PA-NJ	S	22.05 MW	20.24 AW	45860 AAW	PABLS	10//99-12//99
	Pittsburgh MSA, PA	S	14.73 MW	14.61 AW	30650 AAW	PABLS	10//99-12//99
	Reading MSA, PA	S	17.53 MW	17.54 AW	36470 AAW	PABLS	10//99-12//99
	Scranton--Wilkes-Barre--Hazleton MSA, PA	S	23.20 MW	25.15 AW	48260 AAW	PABLS	10//99-12//99
	Rhode Island	S	15.35 MW	16.11 AW	33510 AAW	RIBLS	10//99-12//99
	Providence-Fall River-Warwick MSA, RI-MA	S	16.04 MW	15.33 AW	33360 AAW	RIBLS	10//99-12//99
	South Carolina	S	16.31 MW	16.41 AW	34130 AAW	SCBLS	10//99-12//99
	Charleston-North Charleston MSA, SC	S	19.18 MW	18.63 AW	39890 AAW	SCBLS	10//99-12//99
	Greenville-Spartanburg-Anderson MSA, SC	S	16.12 MW	16.06 AW	33540 AAW	SCBLS	10//99-12//99
	South Dakota	S	12.86 MW	12.64 AW	26290 AAW	SDBLS	10//99-12//99
	Tennessee	S	18.38 MW	17.65 AW	36710 AAW	TNBLS	10//99-12//99
	Chattanooga MSA, TN-GA	S	13.88 MW	13.01 AW	28880 AAW	TNBLS	10//99-12//99
	Johnson City-Kingsport-Bristol MSA, TN-VA	S	21.61 MW	22.29 AW	44940 AAW	TNBLS	10//99-12//99
	Knoxville MSA, TN	S	12.49 MW	12.26 AW	25990 AAW	TNBLS	10//99-12//99
	Memphis MSA, TN-AR-MS	S	14.89 MW	13.07 AW	30970 AAW	MSBLS	10//99-12//99
	Texas	S	22.43 MW	21.07 AW	43830 AAW	TXBLS	10//99-12//99
	Austin-San Marcos MSA, TX	S	15.88 MW	15.26 AW	33030 AAW	TXBLS	10//99-12//99

AAW Average annual wage	AOH Average offered, high	ASH Average starting, high	H Hourly	M Monthly	S Special: hourly and annual
AE Average entry wage	AOL Average offered, low	ASL Average starting, low	HI Highest wage paid	MTC Median total compensation	TQ Third quartile wage
AEX Average experienced wage	APH Average pay, high range	AW Average wage paid	HR High end range	MW Median wage paid	W Weekly
AO Average offered	APL Average pay, low range	FQ First quartile wage	LR Low end range	SQ Second quartile wage	Y Yearly

Occupation/Type/Industry	Location	Per	Low	Mid	High	Source	Date
Chemical Technician	Beaumont-Port Arthur MSA, TX	s	21.11 MW	20.69 AW	43910 AAW	TXBLS	10//99-12//99
	Brazoria PMSA, TX	s	24.32 MW	24.45 AW	50590 AAW	TXBLS	10//99-12//99
	Corpus Christi MSA, TX	s	21.88 MW	22.57 AW	45510 AAW	TXBLS	10//99-12//99
	Dallas PMSA, TX	s	18.32 MW	18.91 AW	38110 AAW	TXBLS	10//99-12//99
	El Paso MSA, TX	s	15.39 MW	15.38 AW	32010 AAW	TXBLS	10//99-12//99
	Fort Worth-Arlington PMSA, TX	s	13.04 MW	12.57 AW	27120 AAW	TXBLS	10//99-12//99
	Houston PMSA, TX	s	22.81 MW	23.51 AW	47440 AAW	TXBLS	10//99-12//99
	San Antonio MSA, TX	s	17.41 MW	17.80 AW	36200 AAW	TXBLS	10//99-12//99
	Utah	s	13.18 MW	15.44 AW	32110 AAW	UTBLS	10//99-12//99
	Salt Lake City-Ogden MSA, UT	s	14.74 MW	12.85 AW	30660 AAW	UTBLS	10//99-12//99
	Vermont	s	14.18 MW	16.18 AW	33650 AAW	VTBLS	10//99-12//99
	Virginia	s	17.56 MW	15.97 AW	33230 AAW	VABLS	10//99-12//99
	Norfolk-Virginia Beach-Newport News MSA, VA-NC	s	16.14 MW	16.36 AW	33580 AAW	VABLS	10//99-12//99
	Richmond-Petersburg MSA, VA	s	16.62 MW	18.25 AW	34580 AAW	VABLS	10//99-12//99
	Roanoke MSA, VA	s	17.80 MW	18.92 AW	37030 AAW	VABLS	10//99-12//99
	Washington	s	18.7 MW	19.90 AW	41400 AAW	WABLS	10//99-12//99
	Bellingham MSA, WA	s	19.82 MW	18.76 AW	41230 AAW	WABLS	10//99-12//99
	Seattle-Bellevue-Everett PMSA, WA	s	20.16 MW	18.91 AW	41930 AAW	WABLS	10//99-12//99
	Spokane MSA, WA	s	20.58 MW	20.14 AW	42800 AAW	WABLS	10//99-12//99
	Tacoma PMSA, WA	s	15.49 MW	15.79 AW	32220 AAW	WABLS	10//99-12//99
	West Virginia	s	20.27 MW	19.73 AW	41040 AAW	WVBLS	10//99-12//99
	Huntington-Ashland MSA, WV-KY-OH	s	18.79 MW	18.58 AW	39080 AAW	WVBLS	10//99-12//99
	Parkersburg-Marietta MSA, WV-OH	s	18.69 MW	19.07 AW	38870 AAW	WVBLS	10//99-12//99
	Wisconsin	s	13.18 MW	14.67 AW	30520 AAW	WIBLS	10//99-12//99
	Appleton-Oshkosh-Neenah MSA, WI	s	11.42 MW	12.25 AW	23760 AAW	WIBLS	10//99-12//99
	Madison MSA, WI	s	12.99 MW	13.16 AW	27020 AAW	WIBLS	10//99-12//99
	Milwaukee-Waukesha PMSA, WI	s	15.87 MW	14.64 AW	33000 AAW	WIBLS	10//99-12//99
	Racine PMSA, WI	s	15.72 MW	15.32 AW	32700 AAW	WIBLS	10//99-12//99
	Wyoming	s	10.57 MW	13.21 AW	27480 AAW	WYBLS	10//99-12//99
	Puerto Rico	s	12.85 MW	12.56 AW	26120 AAW	PRBLS	10//99-12//99
	Mayaguez MSA, PR	s	9.92 MW	9.98 AW	20630 AAW	PRBLS	10//99-12//99
	Ponce MSA, PR	s	9.65 MW	8.30 AW	20080 AAW	PRBLS	10//99-12//99
	San Juan-Bayamon PMSA, PR	s	12.74 MW	13.13 AW	26490 AAW	PRBLS	10//99-12//99
Chemist	Alabama	s	22.77 MW	24.19 AW	50300 AAW	ALBLS	10//99-12//99
	Birmingham MSA, AL	s	22.21 MW	20.26 AW	46200 AAW	ALBLS	10//99-12//99
	Decatur MSA, AL	s	23.75 MW	22.37 AW	49400 AAW	ALBLS	10//99-12//99
	Huntsville MSA, AL	s	27.15 MW	29.29 AW	56480 AAW	ALBLS	10//99-12//99
	Mobile MSA, AL	s	26.73 MW	27.89 AW	55600 AAW	ALBLS	10//99-12//99
	Montgomery MSA, AL	s	21.84 MW	19.59 AW	45430 AAW	ALBLS	10//99-12//99
	Tuscaloosa MSA, AL	s	26.01 MW	24.14 AW	54100 AAW	ALBLS	10//99-12//99
	Alaska	s	21.45 MW	21.73 AW	45190 AAW	AKBLS	10//99-12//99
	Anchorage MSA, AK	s	20.39 MW	19.60 AW	42410 AAW	AKBLS	10//99-12//99
	Arizona	s	19.71 MW	21.51 AW	44740 AAW	AZBLS	10//99-12//99
	Phoenix-Mesa MSA, AZ	s	22.07 MW	19.96 AW	45910 AAW	AZBLS	10//99-12//99
	Arkansas	s	21.41 MW	22.15 AW	46070 AAW	ARBLS	10//99-12//99
	Fayetteville-Springdale-Rogers MSA, AR	s	19.64 MW	17.57 AW	40860 AAW	ARBLS	10//99-12//99
	Little Rock-North Little Rock MSA, AR	s	19.48 MW	18.08 AW	40510 AAW	ARBLS	10//99-12//99
	California	s	22.26 MW	24.00 AW	49920 AAW	CABLS	10//99-12//99
	Bakersfield MSA, CA	s	27.91 MW	28.14 AW	58050 AAW	CABLS	10//99-12//99
	Fresno MSA, CA	s	20.87 MW	21.02 AW	43410 AAW	CABLS	10//99-12//99
	Los Angeles-Long Beach PMSA, CA	s	24.61 MW	22.30 AW	51190 AAW	CABLS	10//99-12//99
	Modesto MSA, CA	s	19.46 MW	16.88 AW	40470 AAW	CABLS	10//99-12//99
	Oakland PMSA, CA	s	25.48 MW	24.42 AW	52990 AAW	CABLS	10//99-12//99
	Orange County PMSA, CA	s	22.01 MW	21.05 AW	45780 AAW	CABLS	10//99-12//99
	Riverside-San Bernardino PMSA, CA	s	20.86 MW	19.51 AW	43380 AAW	CABLS	10//99-12//99
	Sacramento PMSA, CA	s	25.35 MW	24.80 AW	52720 AAW	CABLS	10//99-12//99
	San Diego MSA, CA	s	23.12 MW	20.28 AW	48080 AAW	CABLS	10//99-12//99

AAW	Average annual wage	AOH	Average offered, high	ASH	Average starting, high	H	Hourly	M	Monthly	S	Special: hourly and annual
AE	Average entry wage	AOL	Average offered, low	ASL	Average starting, low	HI	Highest wage paid	MTC	Median total compensation	TQ	Third quartile wage
AEX	Average experienced wage	APH	Average pay, high range	AW	Average wage paid	HR	High end range	MW	Median wage paid	W	Weekly
AO	Average offered	APL	Average pay, low range	FQ	First quartile wage	LR	Low end range	SQ	Second quartile wage	Y	Yearly

Occupation/Type/Industry	Location	Per	Low	Mid	High	Source	Date
Chemist	San Francisco PMSA, CA	S	24.92 MW	23.08 AW	51840 AAW	CABLS	10//99-12//99
	San Jose PMSA, CA	S	26.31 MW	25.56 AW	54720 AAW	CABLS	10//99-12//99
	Santa Barbara-Santa Maria-Lompoc MSA, CA	S	21.35 MW	20.67 AW	44400 AAW	CABLS	10//99-12//99
	Santa Cruz-Watsonville PMSA, CA	S	22.90 MW	21.40 AW	47630 AAW	CABLS	10//99-12//99
	Santa Rosa PMSA, CA	S	16.96 MW	16.08 AW	35290 AAW	CABLS	10//99-12//99
	Vallejo-Fairfield-Napa PMSA, CA	S	23.21 MW	21.39 AW	48270 AAW	CABLS	10//99-12//99
	Ventura PMSA, CA	S	26.62 MW	26.37 AW	55370 AAW	CABLS	10//99-12//99
	Visalia-Tulare-Porterville MSA, CA	S	18.63 MW	14.85 AW	38760 AAW	CABLS	10//99-12//99
	Colorado	S	23.25 MW	24.36 AW	50660 AAW	COBLS	10//99-12//99
	Boulder-Longmont PMSA, CO	S	28.15 MW	29.02 AW	58560 AAW	COBLS	10//99-12//99
	Denver PMSA, CO	S	22.81 MW	21.72 AW	47440 AAW	COBLS	10//99-12//99
	Connecticut	S	26.71 MW	27.18 AW	56540 AAW	CTBLS	10//99-12//99
	Bridgeport PMSA, CT	S	28.73 MW	29.16 AW	59760 AAW	CTBLS	10//99-12//99
	Hartford MSA, CT	S	26.46 MW	27.15 AW	55040 AAW	CTBLS	10//99-12//99
	New Haven-Meriden PMSA, CT	S	28.17 MW	26.34 AW	58590 AAW	CTBLS	10//99-12//99
	Stamford-Norwalk PMSA, CT	S	25.09 MW	23.37 AW	52180 AAW	CTBLS	10//99-12//99
	Delaware	S	35.36 MW	33.67 AW	70030 AAW	DEBLS	10//99-12//99
	Wilmington-Newark PMSA, DE-MD	S	33.75 MW	35.57 AW	70200 AAW	DEBLS	10//99-12//99
	Washington PMSA, DC-MD-VA-WV	S	31.57 MW	31.60 AW	65660 AAW	DCBLS	10//99-12//99
	Florida	S	17.82 MW	19.23 AW	40000 AAW	FLBLS	10//99-12//99
	Daytona Beach MSA, FL	S	17.50 MW	16.64 AW	36400 AAW	FLBLS	10//99-12//99
	Fort Lauderdale PMSA, FL	S	19.45 MW	17.47 AW	40460 AAW	FLBLS	10//99-12//99
	Gainesville MSA, FL	S	19.27 MW	15.35 AW	40090 AAW	FLBLS	10//99-12//99
	Jacksonville MSA, FL	S	19.09 MW	17.49 AW	39710 AAW	FLBLS	10//99-12//99
	Lakeland-Winter Haven MSA, FL	S	22.53 MW	19.83 AW	46870 AAW	FLBLS	10//99-12//99
	Melbourne-Titusville-Palm Bay MSA, FL	S	23.97 MW	23.64 AW	49850 AAW	FLBLS	10//99-12//99
	Miami PMSA, FL	S	19.71 MW	18.44 AW	41000 AAW	FLBLS	10//99-12//99
	Orlando MSA, FL	S	18.70 MW	16.79 AW	38890 AAW	FLBLS	10//99-12//99
	Pensacola MSA, FL	S	15.72 MW	12.80 AW	32690 AAW	FLBLS	10//99-12//99
	Tampa-St. Petersburg-Clearwater MSA, FL	S	20.03 MW	18.55 AW	41660 AAW	FLBLS	10//99-12//99
	West Palm Beach-Boca Raton MSA, FL	S	19.66 MW	17.93 AW	40900 AAW	FLBLS	10//99-12//99
	Georgia	S	24.42 MW	24.75 AW	51490 AAW	GABLS	10//99-12//99
	Atlanta MSA, GA	S	25.18 MW	24.83 AW	52380 AAW	GABLS	10//99-12//99
	Savannah MSA, GA	S	20.14 MW	19.51 AW	41880 AAW	GABLS	10//99-12//99
	Hawaii	S	19.85 MW	20.62 AW	42880 AAW	HIBLS	10//99-12//99
	Honolulu MSA, HI	S	20.38 MW	19.67 AW	42400 AAW	HIBLS	10//99-12//99
	Idaho	S	21.51 MW	21.54 AW	44810 AAW	IDBLS	10//99-12//99
	Boise City MSA, ID	S	20.14 MW	20.17 AW	41900 AAW	IDBLS	10//99-12//99
	Illinois	S	24.17 MW	26.44 AW	55000 AAW	ILBLS	10//99-12//99
	Champaign-Urbana MSA, IL	S	18.74 MW	17.57 AW	38970 AAW	ILBLS	10//99-12//99
	Chicago PMSA, IL	S	27.33 MW	24.84 AW	56850 AAW	ILBLS	10//99-12//99
	Kankakee PMSA, IL	S	24.31 MW	24.90 AW	50560 AAW	ILBLS	10//99-12//99
	Peoria-Pekin MSA, IL	S	26.43 MW	25.24 AW	54980 AAW	ILBLS	10//99-12//99
	Indiana	S	21.03 MW	22.95 AW	47740 AAW	INBLS	10//99-12//99
	Elkhart-Goshen MSA, IN	S	21.16 MW	19.74 AW	44010 AAW	INBLS	10//99-12//99
	Evansville-Henderson MSA, IN-KY	S	21.67 MW	21.32 AW	45080 AAW	INBLS	10//99-12//99
	Fort Wayne MSA, IN	S	24.62 MW	22.50 AW	51200 AAW	INBLS	10//99-12//99
	Gary PMSA, IN	S	27.36 MW	25.72 AW	56900 AAW	INBLS	10//99-12//99
	Indianapolis MSA, IN	S	22.46 MW	20.81 AW	46710 AAW	INBLS	10//99-12//99
	Terre Haute MSA, IN	S	23.19 MW	21.56 AW	48230 AAW	INBLS	10//99-12//99
	Iowa	S	19.73 MW	20.89 AW	43450 AAW	IABLS	10//99-12//99
	Davenport-Moline-Rock Island MSA, IA-IL	S	23.86 MW	22.68 AW	49640 AAW	IABLS	10//99-12//99
	Kansas	S	20.86 MW	21.62 AW	44970 AAW	KSBLS	10//99-12//99
	Wichita MSA, KS	S	23.63 MW	23.12 AW	49160 AAW	KSBLS	10//99-12//99
	Kentucky	S	21.03 MW	21.97 AW	45690 AAW	KYBLS	10//99-12//99
	Lexington MSA, KY	S	24.54 MW	23.84 AW	51050 AAW	KYBLS	10//99-12//99
	Louisville MSA, KY-IN	S	23.10 MW	21.81 AW	48040 AAW	KYBLS	10//99-12//99
	Louisiana	S	26.2 MW	25.03 AW	52050 AAW	LABLS	10//99-12//99
	Baton Rouge MSA, LA	S	26.45 MW	28.86 AW	55010 AAW	LABLS	10//99-12//99

AAW	Average annual wage	**AOH**	Average offered, high	**ASH**	Average starting, high	**H**	Hourly	**M**	Monthly	**S**	Special: hourly and annual
AE	Average entry wage	**AOL**	Average offered, low	**ASL**	Average starting, low	**HI**	Highest wage paid	**MTC**	Median total compensation	**TQ**	Third quartile wage
AEX	Average experienced wage	**APH**	Average pay, high range	**AW**	Average wage paid	**HR**	High end range	**MW**	Median wage paid	**W**	Weekly
AO	Average offered	**APL**	Average pay, low range	**FQ**	First quartile wage	**LR**	Low end range	**SQ**	Second quartile wage	**Y**	Yearly

Occupation/Type/Industry	Location	Per	Low	Mid	High	Source	Date
Chemist	Lafayette MSA, LA	S	19.93 MW	19.71 AW	41460 AAW	LABLS	10//99-12//99
	Lake Charles MSA, LA	S	30.99 MW	32.97 AW	64460 AAW	LABLS	10//99-12//99
	New Orleans MSA, LA	S	23.26 MW	22.17 AW	48380 AAW	LABLS	10//99-12//99
	Shreveport-Bossier City MSA, LA	S	17.66 MW	17.77 AW	36740 AAW	LABLS	10//99-12//99
	Maine	S	20.02 MW	22.51 AW	46820 AAW	MEBLS	10//99-12//99
	Maryland	S	29.66 MW	29.66 AW	61700 AAW	MDBLS	10//99-12//99
	Baltimore PMSA, MD	S	27.49 MW	27.40 AW	57180 AAW	MDBLS	10//99-12//99
	Massachusetts	S	24.13 MW	26.54 AW	55200 AAW	MABLS	10//99-12//99
	Boston PMSA, MA-NH	S	24.18 MW	22.97 AW	50290 AAW	MABLS	10//99-12//99
	Lowell PMSA, MA-NH	S	28.95 MW	26.00 AW	60220 AAW	MABLS	10//99-12//99
	Springfield MSA, MA	S	23.21 MW	21.34 AW	48270 AAW	MABLS	10//99-12//99
	Worcester PMSA, MA-CT	S	25.57 MW	26.23 AW	53190 AAW	MABLS	10//99-12//99
	Michigan	S	24.1 MW	25.52 AW	53080 AAW	MIBLS	10//99-12//99
	Ann Arbor PMSA, MI	S	23.91 MW	22.91 AW	49740 AAW	MIBLS	10//99-12//99
	Benton Harbor MSA, MI	S	27.18 MW	26.65 AW	56530 AAW	MIBLS	10//99-12//99
	Detroit PMSA, MI	S	24.64 MW	22.93 AW	51260 AAW	MIBLS	10//99-12//99
	Grand Rapids-Muskegon-Holland MSA, MI	S	23.43 MW	22.93 AW	48730 AAW	MIBLS	10//99-12//99
	Kalamazoo-Battle Creek MSA, MI	S	26.13 MW	27.74 AW	54340 AAW	MIBLS	10//99-12//99
	Minnesota	S	23.52 MW	24.04 AW	50000 AAW	MNBLS	10//99-12//99
	Duluth-Superior MSA, MN-WI	S	21.33 MW	20.02 AW	44370 AAW	MNBLS	10//99-12//99
	Minneapolis-St. Paul MSA, MN-WI	S	24.18 MW	23.74 AW	50290 AAW	MNBLS	10//99-12//99
	Mississippi	S	19.34 MW	20.73 AW	43120 AAW	MSBLS	10//99-12//99
	Biloxi-Gulfport-Pascagoula MSA, MS	S	18.82 MW	17.66 AW	39140 AAW	MSBLS	10//99-12//99
	Missouri	S	19.78 MW	21.34 AW	44380 AAW	MOBLS	10//99-12//99
	Kansas City MSA, MO-KS	S	23.65 MW	23.16 AW	49200 AAW	MOBLS	10//99-12//99
	St. Louis MSA, MO-IL	S	21.68 MW	19.95 AW	45090 AAW	MOBLS	10//99-12//99
	Montana	S	16.81 MW	20.13 AW	41870 AAW	MTBLS	10//99-12//99
	Nebraska	S	19.06 MW	20.05 AW	41710 AAW	NEBLS	10//99-12//99
	Lincoln MSA, NE	S	19.58 MW	16.89 AW	40720 AAW	NEBLS	10//99-12//99
	Omaha MSA, NE-IA	S	19.93 MW	19.47 AW	41460 AAW	NEBLS	10//99-12//99
	Nevada	S	22.65 MW	23.18 AW	48210 AAW	NVBLS	10//99-12//99
	Las Vegas MSA, NV-AZ	S	27.52 MW	28.19 AW	57230 AAW	NVBLS	10//99-12//99
	New Hampshire	S	21.43 MW	23.57 AW	49030 AAW	NHBLS	10//99-12//99
	Nashua PMSA, NH	S	24.49 MW	19.51 AW	50940 AAW	NHBLS	10//99-12//99
	New Jersey	S	24.16 MW	26.25 AW	54610 AAW	NJBLS	10//99-12//99
	Bergen-Passaic PMSA, NJ	S	28.71 MW	25.05 AW	59720 AAW	NJBLS	10//99-12//99
	Jersey City PMSA, NJ	S	24.81 MW	23.01 AW	51600 AAW	NJBLS	10//99-12//99
	Middlesex-Somerset-Hunterdon PMSA, NJ	S	28.07 MW	27.19 AW	58380 AAW	NJBLS	10//99-12//99
	Monmouth-Ocean PMSA, NJ	S	25.98 MW	24.74 AW	54030 AAW	NJBLS	10//99-12//99
	Newark PMSA, NJ	S	24.11 MW	22.05 AW	50140 AAW	NJBLS	10//99-12//99
	Trenton PMSA, NJ	S	25.50 MW	25.22 AW	53040 AAW	NJBLS	10//99-12//99
	New York	S	23.56 MW	24.93 AW	51850 AAW	NYBLS	10//99-12//99
	Albany-Schenectady-Troy MSA, NY	S	23.61 MW	23.61 AW	49110 AAW	NYBLS	10//99-12//99
	Buffalo-Niagara Falls MSA, NY	S	26.47 MW	26.92 AW	55060 AAW	NYBLS	10//99-12//99
	Nassau-Suffolk PMSA, NY	S	24.94 MW	23.62 AW	51870 AAW	NYBLS	10//99-12//99
	New York PMSA, NY	S	25.68 MW	23.62 AW	53410 AAW	NYBLS	10//99-12//99
	Rochester MSA, NY	S	26.08 MW	25.51 AW	54250 AAW	NYBLS	10//99-12//99
	Syracuse MSA, NY	S	22.95 MW	22.56 AW	47740 AAW	NYBLS	10//99-12//99
	North Carolina	S	21.28 MW	23.48 AW	48840 AAW	NCBLS	10//99-12//99
	Charlotte-Gastonia-Rock Hill MSA, NC-SC	S	25.34 MW	24.16 AW	52720 AAW	NCBLS	10//99-12//99
	Greensboro--Winston-Salem--High Point MSA, NC	S	26.96 MW	24.39 AW	56080 AAW	NCBLS	10//99-12//99
	Greenville MSA, NC	S	18.01 MW	17.14 AW	37470 AAW	NCBLS	10//99-12//99
	Hickory-Morganton-Lenoir MSA, NC	S	24.79 MW	23.86 AW	51570 AAW	NCBLS	10//99-12//99
	Raleigh-Durham-Chapel Hill MSA, NC	S	22.48 MW	19.56 AW	46750 AAW	NCBLS	10//99-12//99
	North Dakota	S	17.03 MW	18.47 AW	38410 AAW	NDBLS	10//99-12//99
	Fargo-Moorhead MSA, ND-MN	S	19.17 MW	13.38 AW	39860 AAW	NDBLS	10//99-12//99
	Ohio	S	23.41 MW	25.22 AW	52450 AAW	OHBLS	10//99-12//99
	Akron PMSA, OH	S	22.56 MW	20.95 AW	46920 AAW	OHBLS	10//99-12//99
	Cincinnati PMSA, OH-KY-IN	S	25.02 MW	24.70 AW	52030 AAW	OHBLS	10//99-12//99

AAW	Average annual wage	AOH	Average offered, high	ASH	Average starting, high	H	Hourly
AE	Average entry wage	AOL	Average offered, low	ASL	Average starting, low	HI	Highest wage paid
AEX	Average experienced wage	APH	Average pay, high range	AW	Average wage paid	HR	High end range
AO	Average offered	APL	Average pay, low range	FQ	First quartile wage	LR	Low end range

M	Monthly	S	Special: hourly and annual
MTC	Median total compensation	TQ	Third quartile wage
MW	Median wage paid	W	Weekly
SQ	Second quartile wage	Y	Yearly

Occupation/Type/Industry	Location	Per	Low	Mid	High	Source	Date
Chemist	Cleveland-Lorain-Elyria						
	PMSA, OH	S	27.26 MW	25.79 AW	56700 AAW	OHBLS	10//99-12//99
	Columbus MSA, OH	S	23.19 MW	20.88 AW	48230 AAW	OHBLS	10//99-12//99
	Dayton-Springfield MSA, OH	S	24.31 MW	21.44 AW	50570 AAW	OHBLS	10//99-12//99
	Hamilton-Middletown PMSA,						
	OH	S	23.29 MW	22.21 AW	48440 AAW	OHBLS	10//99-12//99
	Toledo MSA, OH	S	23.27 MW	21.29 AW	48400 AAW	OHBLS	10//99-12//99
	Youngstown-Warren MSA, OH	S	17.92 MW	18.16 AW	37270 AAW	OHBLS	10//99-12//99
	Oklahoma	S	20.42 MW	23.77 AW	49450 AAW	OKBLS	10//99-12//99
	Oklahoma City MSA, OK	S	18.18 MW	17.00 AW	37810 AAW	OKBLS	10//99-12//99
	Oregon	S	22.32 MW	23.44 AW	48760 AAW	ORBLS	10//99-12//99
	Corvallis MSA, OR	S	23.03 MW	21.92 AW	47890 AAW	ORBLS	10//99-12//99
	Eugene-Springfield MSA, OR	S	24.76 MW	23.74 AW	51510 AAW	ORBLS	10//99-12//99
	Portland-Vancouver PMSA,						
	OR-WA	S	23.37 MW	22.17 AW	48610 AAW	ORBLS	10//99-12//99
	Pennsylvania	S	19.32 MW	21.24 AW	44180 AAW	PABLS	10//99-12//99
	Allentown-Bethlehem-Easton						
	MSA, PA	S	23.27 MW	20.28 AW	48400 AAW	PABLS	10//99-12//99
	Erie MSA, PA	S	21.86 MW	19.62 AW	45470 AAW	PABLS	10//99-12//99
	Philadelphia PMSA, PA-NJ	S	23.67 MW	20.97 AW	49240 AAW	PABLS	10//99-12//99
	Pittsburgh MSA, PA	S	20.14 MW	18.53 AW	41900 AAW	PABLS	10//99-12//99
	Reading MSA, PA	S	24.08 MW	22.20 AW	50080 AAW	PABLS	10//99-12//99
	Scranton--Wilkes-Barre--						
	Hazleton MSA, PA	S	21.57 MW	17.99 AW	44870 AAW	PABLS	10//99-12//99
	York MSA, PA	S	21.55 MW	19.04 AW	44830 AAW	PABLS	10//99-12//99
	Rhode Island	S	21.09 MW	22.78 AW	47380 AAW	RIBLS	10//99-12//99
	Providence-Fall River-						
	Warwick MSA, RI-MA	S	23.15 MW	21.35 AW	48160 AAW	RIBLS	10//99-12//99
	South Carolina	S	27.37 MW	28.09 AW	58420 AAW	SCBLS	10//99-12//99
	Charleston-North Charleston						
	MSA, SC	S	23.93 MW	23.61 AW	49770 AAW	SCBLS	10//99-12//99
	Greenville-Spartanburg-						
	Anderson MSA, SC	S	26.68 MW	24.63 AW	55500 AAW	SCBLS	10//99-12//99
	South Dakota	S	18.1 MW	18.52 AW	38520 AAW	SDBLS	10//99-12//99
	Tennessee	S	22.77 MW	24.83 AW	51640 AAW	TNBLS	10//99-12//99
	Chattanooga MSA, TN-GA	S	23.81 MW	23.35 AW	49520 AAW	TNBLS	10//99-12//99
	Johnson City-Kingsport-Bristol						
	MSA, TN-VA	S	34.05 MW	35.55 AW	70830 AAW	TNBLS	10//99-12//99
	Knoxville MSA, TN	S	21.46 MW	18.31 AW	44630 AAW	TNBLS	10//99-12//99
	Memphis MSA, TN-AR-MS	S	20.44 MW	18.73 AW	42510 AAW	MSBLS	10//99-12//99
	Nashville MSA, TN	S	19.43 MW	16.90 AW	40410 AAW	TNBLS	10//99-12//99
	Texas	S	22.67 MW	24.07 AW	50070 AAW	TXBLS	10//99-12//99
	Austin-San Marcos MSA, TX	S	21.26 MW	20.03 AW	44210 AAW	TXBLS	10//99-12//99
	Beaumont-Port Arthur MSA,						
	TX	S	27.85 MW	29.24 AW	57940 AAW	TXBLS	10//99-12//99
	Brazoria PMSA, TX	S	29.13 MW	29.15 AW	60590 AAW	TXBLS	10//99-12//99
	Bryan-College Station MSA,						
	TX	S	26.26 MW	19.64 AW	54630 AAW	TXBLS	10//99-12//99
	Corpus Christi MSA, TX	S	22.64 MW	22.48 AW	47090 AAW	TXBLS	10//99-12//99
	Dallas PMSA, TX	S	19.80 MW	18.86 AW	41180 AAW	TXBLS	10//99-12//99
	El Paso MSA, TX	S	22.10 MW	17.90 AW	45970 AAW	TXBLS	10//99-12//99
	Fort Worth-Arlington PMSA,						
	TX	S	23.71 MW	23.06 AW	49310 AAW	TXBLS	10//99-12//99
	Galveston-Texas City PMSA,						
	TX	S	19.70 MW	16.48 AW	40980 AAW	TXBLS	10//99-12//99
	Houston PMSA, TX	S	25.34 MW	24.18 AW	52700 AAW	TXBLS	10//99-12//99
	Odessa-Midland MSA, TX	S	26.37 MW	24.50 AW	54850 AAW	TXBLS	10//99-12//99
	San Antonio MSA, TX	S	20.97 MW	18.97 AW	43610 AAW	TXBLS	10//99-12//99
	Utah	S	19.29 MW	21.29 AW	44280 AAW	UTBLS	10//99-12//99
	Salt Lake City-Ogden MSA,						
	UT	S	21.47 MW	19.34 AW	44650 AAW	UTBLS	10//99-12//99
	Vermont	S	19.04 MW	19.94 AW	41470 AAW	VTBLS	10//99-12//99
	Virginia	S	22.1 MW	24.41 AW	50770 AAW	VABLS	10//99-12//99
	Norfolk-Virginia Beach-						
	Newport News MSA, VA-						
	NC	S	21.28 MW	19.41 AW	44260 AAW	VABLS	10//99-12//99
	Richmond-Petersburg MSA,						
	VA	S	21.86 MW	20.05 AW	45460 AAW	VABLS	10//99-12//99
	Washington	S	29.31 MW	29.97 AW	62340 AAW	WABLS	10//99-12//99
	Olympia PMSA, WA	S	22.53 MW	23.40 AW	46860 AAW	WABLS	10//99-12//99
	Seattle-Bellevue-Everett						
	PMSA, WA	S	27.17 MW	28.19 AW	56500 AAW	WABLS	10//99-12//99

AAW	Average annual wage	AOH	Average offered, high	ASH	Average starting, high
AE	Average entry wage	AOL	Average offered, low	ASL	Average starting, low
AEX	Average experienced wage	APH	Average pay, high range	AW	Average wage paid
AO	Average offered	APL	Average pay, low range	FQ	First quartile wage

H	Hourly
HI	Highest wage paid
HR	High end range
LR	Low end range

M	Monthly
MTC	Median total compensation
MW	Median wage paid
SQ	Second quartile wage

S	Special: hourly and annual
TQ	Third quartile wage
W	Weekly
Y	Yearly

Occupation/Type/Industry	Location	Per	Low	Mid	High	Source	Date
Chemist							
	Spokane MSA, WA	S	19.36 MW	20.11 AW	40260 AAW	WABLS	10//99-12//99
	Tacoma PMSA, WA	S	20.26 MW	21.10 AW	42130 AAW	WABLS	10//99-12//99
	West Virginia	S	27.85 MW	27.88 AW	57990 AAW	WVBLS	10//99-12//99
	Charleston MSA, WV	S	28.30 MW	27.52 AW	58860 AAW	WVBLS	10//99-12//99
	Parkersburg-Marietta MSA, WV-OH	S	28.25 MW	29.02 AW	58760 AAW	WVBLS	10//99-12//99
	Wisconsin	S	19.74 MW	21.75 AW	45230 AAW	WIBLS	10//99-12//99
	Appleton-Oshkosh-Neenah MSA, WI	S	21.00 MW	18.35 AW	43680 AAW	WIBLS	10//99-12//99
	Madison MSA, WI	S	22.63 MW	21.10 AW	47060 AAW	WIBLS	10//99-12//99
	Milwaukee-Waukesha PMSA, WI	S	21.03 MW	18.88 AW	43750 AAW	WIBLS	10//99-12//99
	Wyoming	S	18.27 MW	21.11 AW	43910 AAW	WYBLS	10//99-12//99
	Puerto Rico	S	15.15 MW	15.75 AW	32760 AAW	PRBLS	10//99-12//99
	Caguas PMSA, PR	S	14.92 MW	14.49 AW	31030 AAW	PRBLS	10//99-12//99
	Mayaguez MSA, PR	S	16.03 MW	15.72 AW	33340 AAW	PRBLS	10//99-12//99
	Ponce MSA, PR	S	13.64 MW	12.48 AW	28360 AAW	PRBLS	10//99-12//99
	San Juan-Bayamon PMSA, PR	S	15.95 MW	15.24 AW	33170 AAW	PRBLS	10//99-12//99
	Virgin Islands	S	20.28 MW	21.60 AW	44930 AAW	VIBLS	10//99-12//99
Academia	United States	Y		58000 MW		C&EN1	2000
Government	United States	Y		70000 MW		C&EN1	2000
Industry	United States	Y		74500 MW		C&EN1	2000
Recent Graduate	United States	Y		60500 MW		C&EN2	1999
Chemistry Teacher							
Postsecondary	Alabama	Y		49720 AAW		ALBLS	10//99-12//99
Postsecondary	Phoenix-Mesa MSA, AZ	Y		35190 AAW		AZBLS	10//99-12//99
Postsecondary	Arkansas	Y		54180 AAW		ARBLS	10//99-12//99
Postsecondary	California	Y		54990 AAW		CABLS	10//99-12//99
Postsecondary	Los Angeles-Long Beach PMSA, CA	Y		52660 AAW		CABLS	10//99-12//99
Postsecondary	Riverside-San Bernardino PMSA, CA	Y		52420 AAW		CABLS	10//99-12//99
Postsecondary	San Diego MSA, CA	Y		58920 AAW		CABLS	10//99-12//99
Postsecondary	San Francisco PMSA, CA	Y		60960 AAW		CABLS	10//99-12//99
Postsecondary	Colorado	Y		59420 AAW		COBLS	10//99-12//99
Postsecondary	Connecticut	Y		54220 AAW		CTBLS	10//99-12//99
Postsecondary	Hartford MSA, CT	Y		63880 AAW		CTBLS	10//99-12//99
Postsecondary	District of Columbia	Y		54360 AAW		DCBLS	10//99-12//99
Postsecondary	Washington PMSA, DC-MD-VA-WV	Y		55600 AAW		DCBLS	10//99-12//99
Postsecondary	Florida	Y		61880 AAW		FLBLS	10//99-12//99
Postsecondary	Miami PMSA, FL	Y		68630 AAW		FLBLS	10//99-12//99
Postsecondary	Tampa-St. Petersburg-Clearwater MSA, FL	Y		54260 AAW		FLBLS	10//99-12//99
Postsecondary	West Palm Beach-Boca Raton MSA, FL	Y		58170 AAW		FLBLS	10//99-12//99
Postsecondary	Georgia	Y		49590 AAW		GABLS	10//99-12//99
Postsecondary	Atlanta MSA, GA	Y		52550 AAW		GABLS	10//99-12//99
Postsecondary	Savannah MSA, GA	Y		47300 AAW		GABLS	10//99-12//99
Postsecondary	Hawaii	Y		57310 AAW		HIBLS	10//99-12//99
Postsecondary	Honolulu MSA, HI	Y		55450 AAW		HIBLS	10//99-12//99
Postsecondary	Idaho	Y		44550 AAW		IDBLS	10//99-12//99
Postsecondary	Illinois	Y		42720 AAW		ILBLS	10//99-12//99
Postsecondary	Chicago PMSA, IL	Y		43420 AAW		ILBLS	10//99-12//99
Postsecondary	Indiana	Y		48850 AAW		INBLS	10//99-12//99
Postsecondary	Gary PMSA, IN	Y		50170 AAW		INBLS	10//99-12//99
Postsecondary	Indianapolis MSA, IN	Y		45460 AAW		INBLS	10//99-12//99
Postsecondary	Iowa	Y		59040 AAW		IABLS	10//99-12//99
Postsecondary	Kansas	Y		47590 AAW		KSBLS	10//99-12//99
Postsecondary	Kentucky	Y		45860 AAW		KYBLS	10//99-12//99
Postsecondary	Louisiana	Y		45940 AAW		LABLS	10//99-12//99
Postsecondary	Maryland	Y		54290 AAW		MDBLS	10//99-12//99
Postsecondary	Baltimore PMSA, MD	Y		54490 AAW		MDBLS	10//99-12//99
Postsecondary	Massachusetts	Y		56080 AAW		MABLS	10//99-12//99
Postsecondary	Boston PMSA, MA-NH	Y		52710 AAW		MABLS	10//99-12//99
Postsecondary	Springfield MSA, MA	Y		59810 AAW		MABLS	10//99-12//99
Postsecondary	Michigan	Y		54440 AAW		MIBLS	10//99-12//99
Postsecondary	Detroit PMSA, MI	Y		57740 AAW		MIBLS	10//99-12//99
Postsecondary	Kalamazoo-Battle Creek MSA, MI	Y		56760 AAW		MIBLS	10//99-12//99
Postsecondary	Minnesota	Y		58020 AAW		MNBLS	10//99-12//99

AAW	Average annual wage	AOH	Average offered, high	ASH	Average starting, high	H	Hourly		M	Monthly		S	Special: hourly and annual
AE	Average entry wage	AOL	Average offered, low	ASL	Average starting, low	HI	Highest wage paid	MTC	Median total compensation	TQ	Third quartile wage
AEX	Average experienced wage	APH	Average pay, high range	AW	Average wage paid	HR	High end range	MW	Median wage paid	W	Weekly
AO	Average offered	APL	Average pay, low range	FQ	First quartile wage	LR	Low end range	SQ	Second quartile wage	Y	Yearly

Occupation/Type/Industry	Location	Per	Low	Mid	High	Source	Date
Chemistry Teacher							
Postsecondary	Minneapolis-St. Paul MSA, MN-WI	Y		64800 AAW		MNBLS	10//99-12//99
Postsecondary	St. Cloud MSA, MN	Y		50390 AAW		MNBLS	10//99-12//99
Postsecondary	Mississippi	Y		46580 AAW		MSBLS	10//99-12//99
Postsecondary	Jackson MSA, MS	Y		45150 AAW		MSBLS	10//99-12//99
Postsecondary	Missouri	Y		47220 AAW		MOBLS	10//99-12//99
Postsecondary	St. Louis MSA, MO-IL	Y		46710 AAW		MOBLS	10//99-12//99
Postsecondary	Montana	Y		65280 AAW		MTBLS	10//99-12//99
Postsecondary	Nevada	Y		51800 AAW		NVBLS	10//99-12//99
Postsecondary	Las Vegas MSA, NV-AZ	Y		50430 AAW		NVBLS	10//99-12//99
Postsecondary	New Hampshire	Y		72410 AAW		NHBLS	10//99-12//99
Postsecondary	New Jersey	Y		64330 AAW		NJBLS	10//99-12//99
Postsecondary	Jersey City PMSA, NJ	Y		67380 AAW		NJBLS	10//99-12//99
Postsecondary	Newark PMSA, NJ	Y		66310 AAW		NJBLS	10//99-12//99
Postsecondary	New Mexico	Y		52360 AAW		NMBLS	10//99-12//99
Postsecondary	New York	Y		58220 AAW		NYBLS	10//99-12//99
Postsecondary	Albany-Schenectady-Troy MSA, NY	Y		57570 AAW		NYBLS	10//99-12//99
Postsecondary	Nassau-Suffolk PMSA, NY	Y		64670 AAW		NYBLS	10//99-12//99
Postsecondary	New York PMSA, NY	Y		60450 AAW		NYBLS	10//99-12//99
Postsecondary	North Carolina	Y		49330 AAW		NCBLS	10//99-12//99
Postsecondary	Charlotte-Gastonia-Rock Hill MSA, NC-SC	Y		47090 AAW		NCBLS	10//99-12//99
Postsecondary	Greensboro--Winston-Salem-- High Point MSA, NC	Y		47040 AAW		NCBLS	10//99-12//99
Postsecondary	Raleigh-Durham-Chapel Hill MSA, NC	Y		50930 AAW		NCBLS	10//99-12//99
Postsecondary	North Dakota	Y		49610 AAW		NDBLS	10//99-12//99
Postsecondary	Ohio	Y		49120 AAW		OHBLS	10//99-12//99
Postsecondary	Cincinnati PMSA, OH-KY-IN	Y		43890 AAW		OHBLS	10//99-12//99
Postsecondary	Cleveland-Lorain-Elyria PMSA, OH	Y		49140 AAW		OHBLS	10//99-12//99
Postsecondary	Columbus MSA, OH	Y		50660 AAW		OHBLS	10//99-12//99
Postsecondary	Toledo MSA, OH	Y		46430 AAW		OHBLS	10//99-12//99
Postsecondary	Oklahoma	Y		50280 AAW		OKBLS	10//99-12//99
Postsecondary	Oregon	Y		52330 AAW		ORBLS	10//99-12//99
Postsecondary	Portland-Vancouver PMSA, OR-WA	Y		51880 AAW		ORBLS	10//99-12//99
Postsecondary	Pennsylvania	Y		57720 AAW		PABLS	10//99-12//99
Postsecondary	Allentown-Bethlehem-Easton MSA, PA	Y		48370 AAW		PABLS	10//99-12//99
Postsecondary	Harrisburg-Lebanon-Carlisle MSA, PA	Y		57190 AAW		PABLS	10//99-12//99
Postsecondary	Philadelphia PMSA, PA-NJ	Y		60210 AAW		PABLS	10//99-12//99
Postsecondary	Reading MSA, PA	Y		57200 AAW		PABLS	10//99-12//99
Postsecondary	Scranton--Wilkes-Barre-- Hazleton MSA, PA	Y		53530 AAW		PABLS	10//99-12//99
Postsecondary	Rhode Island	Y		70200 AAW		RIBLS	10//99-12//99
Postsecondary	Providence-Fall River- Warwick MSA, RI-MA	Y		70620 AAW		RIBLS	10//99-12//99
Postsecondary	South Carolina	Y		49250 AAW		SCBLS	10//99-12//99
Postsecondary	Greenville-Spartanburg- Anderson MSA, SC	Y		48480 AAW		SCBLS	10//99-12//99
Postsecondary	South Dakota	Y		44680 AAW		SDBLS	10//99-12//99
Postsecondary	Tennessee	Y		51860 AAW		TNBLS	10//99-12//99
Postsecondary	Johnson City-Kingsport-Bristol MSA, TN-VA	Y		53120 AAW		TNBLS	10//99-12//99
Postsecondary	Memphis MSA, TN-AR-MS	Y		50290 AAW		MSBLS	10//99-12//99
Postsecondary	Nashville MSA, TN	Y		52200 AAW		TNBLS	10//99-12//99
Postsecondary	Texas	Y		52070 AAW		TXBLS	10//99-12//99
Postsecondary	Dallas PMSA, TX	Y		48570 AAW		TXBLS	10//99-12//99
Postsecondary	El Paso MSA, TX	Y		41620 AAW		TXBLS	10//99-12//99
Postsecondary	Fort Worth-Arlington PMSA, TX	Y		51620 AAW		TXBLS	10//99-12//99
Postsecondary	Houston PMSA, TX	Y		64170 AAW		TXBLS	10//99-12//99
Postsecondary	San Antonio MSA, TX	Y		56490 AAW		TXBLS	10//99-12//99
Postsecondary	Vermont	Y		55740 AAW		VTBLS	10//99-12//99
Postsecondary	Virginia	Y		52900 AAW		VABLS	10//99-12//99
Postsecondary	Norfolk-Virginia Beach- Newport News MSA, VA- NC	Y		52180 AAW		VABLS	10//99-12//99

AAW	Average annual wage	AOH	Average offered, high	ASH	Average starting, high	H	Hourly
AE	Average entry wage	AOL	Average offered, low	ASL	Average starting, low	HI	Highest wage paid
AEX	Average experienced wage	APH	Average pay, high range	AW	Average wage paid	HR	High end range
AO	Average offered	APL	Average pay, low range	FQ	First quartile wage	LR	Low end range

M   Monthly   S   Special: hourly and annual
MTC   Median total compensation   TQ   Third quartile wage
MW   Median wage paid   W   Weekly
SQ   Second quartile wage   Y   Yearly

Occupation/Type/Industry	Location	Per	Low	Mid	High	Source	Date
Chemistry Teacher							
Postsecondary	Washington	Y		48670 AAW		WABLS	10//99-12//99
Postsecondary	Seattle-Bellevue-Everett PMSA, WA	Y		57090 AAW		WABLS	10//99-12//99
Postsecondary	Tacoma PMSA, WA	Y		46640 AAW		WABLS	10//99-12//99
Postsecondary	West Virginia	Y		53810 AAW		WVBLS	10//99-12//99
Postsecondary	Milwaukee-Waukesha PMSA, WI	Y		42530 AAW		WIBLS	10//99-12//99
Postsecondary	Wyoming	Y		55340 AAW		WYBLS	10//99-12//99
Postsecondary	Puerto Rico	Y		33340 AAW		PRBLS	10//99-12//99
Postsecondary	San Juan-Bayamon PMSA, PR	Y		33560 AAW		PRBLS	10//99-12//99
Chief Estimator							
Mechanical Contracting Firm	United States	Y		51800 AW		CONTR	1998
Chief Executive	Alabama	S	44.77 MW	44.21 AW	91960 AAW	ALBLS	10//99-12//99
	Anniston MSA, AL	S	39.18 MW	43.19 AW	81490 AAW	ALBLS	10//99-12//99
	Auburn-Opelika MSA, AL	S	34.18 MW	29.78 AW	71100 AAW	ALBLS	10//99-12//99
	Birmingham MSA, AL	S	46.07 MW	45.96 AW	95820 AAW	ALBLS	10//99-12//99
	Decatur MSA, AL	S	38.28 MW	32.93 AW	79620 AAW	ALBLS	10//99-12//99
	Dothan MSA, AL	S	37.30 MW	29.32 AW	77580 AAW	ALBLS	10//99-12//99
	Florence MSA, AL	S	48.02 MW	51.91 AW	99880 AAW	ALBLS	10//99-12//99
	Gadsden MSA, AL	S	36.17 MW	36.55 AW	75230 AAW	ALBLS	10//99-12//99
	Huntsville MSA, AL	S	40.65 MW	44.97 AW	84540 AAW	ALBLS	10//99-12//99
	Mobile MSA, AL	S	46.52 MW	46.20 AW	96750 AAW	ALBLS	10//99-12//99
	Montgomery MSA, AL	S	50.47 MW	57.36 AW	104980 AAW	ALBLS	10//99-12//99
	Tuscaloosa MSA, AL	S	35.53 MW	28.79 AW	73900 AAW	ALBLS	10//99-12//99
	Alaska	S	40.86 MW	44.35 AW	92250 AAW	AKBLS	10//99-12//99
	Anchorage MSA, AK	S	48.07 MW	42.44 AW	99980 AAW	AKBLS	10//99-12//99
	Arizona	S	50.68 MW	48.35 AW	100570 AAW	AZBLS	10//99-12//99
	Flagstaff MSA, AZ-UT	S	38.81 MW	39.36 AW	80730 AAW	AZBLS	10//99-12//99
	Phoenix-Mesa MSA, AZ	S	50.35 MW	54.50 AW	104730 AAW	AZBLS	10//99-12//99
	Tucson MSA, AZ	S	44.24 MW	43.34 AW	92020 AAW	AZBLS	10//99-12//99
	Yuma MSA, AZ	S	37.44 MW	37.82 AW	77880 AAW	AZBLS	10//99-12//99
	Arkansas	S	46.87 MW	44.98 AW	93560 AAW	ARBLS	10//99-12//99
	Fayetteville-Springdale-Rogers MSA, AR	S	44.95 MW	43.13 AW	93500 AAW	ARBLS	10//99-12//99
	Fort Smith MSA, AR-OK	S	43.03 MW	45.97 AW	89510 AAW	ARBLS	10//99-12//99
	Jonesboro MSA, AR	S	44.66 MW	42.44 AW	92900 AAW	ARBLS	10//99-12//99
	Little Rock-North Little Rock MSA, AR	S	47.75 MW	47.93 AW	99310 AAW	ARBLS	10//99-12//99
	California	S	57.66 MW	52.66 AW	109530 AAW	CABLS	10//99-12//99
	Bakersfield MSA, CA	S	50.92 MW	54.14 AW	105920 AAW	CABLS	10//99-12//99
	Chico-Paradise MSA, CA	S	39.85 MW	35.20 AW	82890 AAW	CABLS	10//99-12//99
	Fresno MSA, CA	S	43.29 MW	44.78 AW	90040 AAW	CABLS	10//99-12//99
	Los Angeles-Long Beach PMSA, CA	S	54.10 MW	60.48 AW	112520 AAW	CABLS	10//99-12//99
	Merced MSA, CA	S	43.76 MW	39.94 AW	91020 AAW	CABLS	10//99-12//99
	Modesto MSA, CA	S	40.94 MW	40.37 AW	85160 AAW	CABLS	10//99-12//99
	Oakland PMSA, CA	S	53.04 MW	58.21 AW	110320 AAW	CABLS	10//99-12//99
	Orange County PMSA, CA	S	57.44 MW	69.82 AW	119480 AAW	CABLS	10//99-12//99
	Redding MSA, CA	S	49.82 MW	49.81 AW	103620 AAW	CABLS	10//99-12//99
	Riverside-San Bernardino PMSA, CA	S	43.36 MW	41.77 AW	90200 AAW	CABLS	10//99-12//99
	Sacramento PMSA, CA	S	51.35 MW	51.65 AW	106800 AAW	CABLS	10//99-12//99
	Salinas MSA, CA	S	43.33 MW	42.77 AW	90130 AAW	CABLS	10//99-12//99
	San Diego MSA, CA	S	49.65 MW	52.51 AW	103270 AAW	CABLS	10//99-12//99
	San Francisco PMSA, CA	S	57.29 MW		119160 AAW	CABLS	10//99-12//99
	San Jose PMSA, CA	S	58.64 MW		121960 AAW	CABLS	10//99-12//99
	San Luis Obispo-Atascadero-Paso Robles MSA, CA	S	43.50 MW	42.33 AW	90480 AAW	CABLS	10//99-12//99
	Santa Barbara-Santa Maria-Lompoc MSA, CA	S	46.69 MW	44.62 AW	97120 AAW	CABLS	10//99-12//99
	Santa Cruz-Watsonville PMSA, CA	S	52.24 MW	60.99 AW	108660 AAW	CABLS	10//99-12//99
	Santa Rosa PMSA, CA	S	45.99 MW	45.18 AW	95660 AAW	CABLS	10//99-12//99
	Stockton-Lodi MSA, CA	S	50.33 MW	54.06 AW	104680 AAW	CABLS	10//99-12//99
	Vallejo-Fairfield-Napa PMSA, CA	S	43.16 MW	39.70 AW	89780 AAW	CABLS	10//99-12//99
	Ventura PMSA, CA	S	57.45 MW		119500 AAW	CABLS	10//99-12//99
	Visalia-Tulare-Porterville MSA, CA	S	49.81 MW	49.17 AW	103600 AAW	CABLS	10//99-12//99
	Yolo PMSA, CA	S	49.45 MW	53.26 AW	102860 AAW	CABLS	10//99-12//99

AAW Average annual wage	AOH Average offered, high	ASH Average starting, high	H Hourly	M Monthly	S Special: hourly and annual
AE Average entry wage	AOL Average offered, low	ASL Average starting, low	HI Highest wage paid	MTC Median total compensation	TQ Third quartile wage
AEX Average experienced wage	APH Average pay, high range	AW Average wage paid	HR High end range	MW Median wage paid	W Weekly
AO Average offered	APL Average pay, low range	FQ First quartile wage	LR Low end range	SQ Second quartile wage	Y Yearly

Occupation/Type/Industry	Location	Per	Low	Mid	High	Source	Date
Chief Executive	Yuba City MSA, CA	S	39.71 MW	38.41 AW	82590 AAW	CABLS	10//99-12//99
	Colorado	S	58.15 MW	52.40 AW	108980 AAW	COBLS	10//99-12//99
	Boulder-Longmont PMSA, CO	S	59.01 MW		122740 AAW	COBLS	10//99-12//99
	Colorado Springs MSA, CO	S	47.91 MW	48.61 AW	99650 AAW	COBLS	10//99-12//99
	Denver PMSA, CO	S	55.74 MW	65.37 AW	115950 AAW	COBLS	10//99-12//99
	Fort Collins-Loveland MSA, CO	S	54.69 MW	62.42 AW	113760 AAW	COBLS	10//99-12//99
	Grand Junction MSA, CO	S	37.97 MW	33.73 AW	78970 AAW	COBLS	10//99-12//99
	Greeley PMSA, CO	S	38.55 MW	36.41 AW	80190 AAW	COBLS	10//99-12//99
	Pueblo MSA, CO	S	34.43 MW	29.01 AW	71610 AAW	COBLS	10//99-12//99
	Connecticut	S	66.1 MW	54.01 AW	112350 AAW	CTBLS	10//99-12//99
	Bridgeport PMSA, CT	S	47.87 MW	48.83 AW	99570 AAW	CTBLS	10//99-12//99
	Danbury PMSA, CT	S	41.92 MW	35.69 AW	87200 AAW	CTBLS	10//99-12//99
	Hartford MSA, CT	S	57.77 MW		120160 AAW	CTBLS	10//99-12//99
	New Haven-Meriden PMSA, CT	S	55.07 MW	58.41 AW	114550 AAW	CTBLS	10//99-12//99
	New London-Norwich MSA, CT-RI	S	41.50 MW	35.39 AW	86330 AAW	CTBLS	10//99-12//99
	Stamford-Norwalk PMSA, CT	S	58.95 MW		122620 AAW	CTBLS	10//99-12//99
	Waterbury PMSA, CT	S	57.17 MW		118910 AAW	CTBLS	10//99-12//99
	Delaware	S	51.53 MW	48.07 AW	99990 AAW	DEBLS	10//99-12//99
	Dover MSA, DE	S	38.11 MW	29.55 AW	79270 AAW	DEBLS	10//99-12//99
	Wilmington-Newark PMSA, DE-MD	S	48.29 MW	50.94 AW	100450 AAW	DEBLS	10//99-12//99
	District of Columbia	S	45.78 MW	43.72 AW	90940 AAW	DCBLS	10//99-12//99
	Washington PMSA, DC-MD-VA-WV	S	49.64 MW	54.22 AW	103250 AAW	DCBLS	10//99-12//99
	Florida	S	53.05 MW	49.53 AW	103020 AAW	FLBLS	10//99-12//99
	Daytona Beach MSA, FL	S	36.96 MW	37.44 AW	76880 AAW	FLBLS	10//99-12//99
	Fort Lauderdale PMSA, FL	S	50.23 MW	53.32 AW	104490 AAW	FLBLS	10//99-12//99
	Fort Myers-Cape Coral MSA, FL	S	50.07 MW	66.83 AW	104140 AAW	FLBLS	10//99-12//99
	Fort Pierce-Port St. Lucie MSA, FL	S	36.78 MW	34.50 AW	76510 AAW	FLBLS	10//99-12//99
	Fort Walton Beach MSA, FL	S	44.87 MW	41.34 AW	93340 AAW	FLBLS	10//99-12//99
	Gainesville MSA, FL	S	51.96 MW		108080 AAW	FLBLS	10//99-12//99
	Jacksonville MSA, FL	S	46.74 MW	49.59 AW	97220 AAW	FLBLS	10//99-12//99
	Lakeland-Winter Haven MSA, FL	S	42.88 MW	42.39 AW	89200 AAW	FLBLS	10//99-12//99
	Melbourne-Titusville-Palm Bay MSA, FL	S	46.38 MW	46.43 AW	96470 AAW	FLBLS	10//99-12//99
	Miami PMSA, FL	S	57.91 MW		120460 AAW	FLBLS	10//99-12//99
	Naples MSA, FL	S	45.34 MW	48.76 AW	94320 AAW	FLBLS	10//99-12//99
	Ocala MSA, FL	S	30.92 MW	23.75 AW	64310 AAW	FLBLS	10//99-12//99
	Orlando MSA, FL	S	48.18 MW	56.08 AW	100220 AAW	FLBLS	10//99-12//99
	Panama City MSA, FL	S	51.33 MW	67.23 AW	106770 AAW	FLBLS	10//99-12//99
	Pensacola MSA, FL	S	47.71 MW	48.93 AW	99240 AAW	FLBLS	10//99-12//99
	Punta Gorda MSA, FL	S	54.36 MW	61.77 AW	113070 AAW	FLBLS	10//99-12//99
	Sarasota-Bradenton MSA, FL	S	44.75 MW	41.48 AW	93070 AAW	FLBLS	10//99-12//99
	Tallahassee MSA, FL	S	48.09 MW	48.69 AW	100030 AAW	FLBLS	10//99-12//99
	Tampa-St. Petersburg-Clearwater MSA, FL	S	47.55 MW	47.96 AW	98890 AAW	FLBLS	10//99-12//99
	West Palm Beach-Boca Raton MSA, FL	S	49.58 MW	52.64 AW	103140 AAW	FLBLS	10//99-12//99
	Georgia	S	49.34 MW	47.60 AW	99000 AAW	GABLS	10//99-12//99
	Albany MSA, GA	S	43.30 MW	43.94 AW	90070 AAW	GABLS	10//99-12//99
	Athens MSA, GA	S	35.29 MW	31.82 AW	73400 AAW	GABLS	10//99-12//99
	Atlanta MSA, GA	S	53.34 MW	60.10 AW	110940 AAW	GABLS	10//99-12//99
	Augusta-Aiken MSA, GA-SC	S	36.26 MW	34.44 AW	75420 AAW	GABLS	10//99-12//99
	Columbus MSA, GA-AL	S	40.40 MW	40.40 AW	84040 AAW	GABLS	10//99-12//99
	Macon MSA, GA	S	36.98 MW	32.35 AW	76920 AAW	GABLS	10//99-12//99
	Savannah MSA, GA	S	31.54 MW	23.84 AW	65610 AAW	GABLS	10//99-12//99
	Hawaii	S	52.37 MW	50.43 AW	104890 AAW	HIBLS	10//99-12//99
	Honolulu MSA, HI	S	52.41 MW	57.33 AW	109020 AAW	HIBLS	10//99-12//99
	Idaho	S	38.97 MW	40.96 AW	85210 AAW	IDBLS	10//99-12//99
	Boise City MSA, ID	S	49.21 MW	50.08 AW	102360 AAW	IDBLS	10//99-12//99
	Pocatello MSA, ID	S	36.33 MW	37.76 AW	75580 AAW	IDBLS	10//99-12//99
	Illinois	S	48.22 MW	46.24 AW	96170 AAW	ILBLS	10//99-12//99
	Bloomington-Normal MSA, IL	S	42.55 MW	42.91 AW	88500 AAW	ILBLS	10//99-12//99
	Champaign-Urbana MSA, IL	S	30.51 MW	24.77 AW	63470 AAW	ILBLS	10//99-12//99
	Chicago PMSA, IL	S	52.41 MW	58.62 AW	109010 AAW	ILBLS	10//99-12//99
	Decatur MSA, IL	S	40.67 MW	38.95 AW	84600 AAW	ILBLS	10//99-12//99

Occupation/Type/Industry	Location	Per	Low	Mid	High	Source	Date
Chief Executive	Peoria-Pekin MSA, IL	s	40.18 MW	36.26 AW	83580 AAW	ILBLS	10//99-12//99
	Rockford MSA, IL	s	31.17 MW	27.20 AW	64820 AAW	ILBLS	10//99-12//99
	Indiana	s	57.78 MW	51.30 AW	106690 AAW	INBLS	10//99-12//99
	Bloomington MSA, IN	s	60.32 MW		125460 AAW	INBLS	10//99-12//99
	Evansville-Henderson MSA, IN-KY	s	45.34 MW	43.08 AW	94320 AAW	INBLS	10//99-12//99
	Fort Wayne MSA, IN	s	46.88 MW	46.72 AW	97500 AAW	INBLS	10//99-12//99
	Gary PMSA, IN	s	54.29 MW	61.33 AW	112920 AAW	INBLS	10//99-12//99
	Indianapolis MSA, IN	s	59.99 MW		124770 AAW	INBLS	10//99-12//99
	Kokomo MSA, IN	s	56.03 MW	63.86 AW	116530 AAW	INBLS	10//99-12//99
	Lafayette MSA, IN	s	50.90 MW	56.81 AW	105870 AAW	INBLS	10//99-12//99
	Muncie MSA, IN	s	49.81 MW		103610 AAW	INBLS	10//99-12//99
	South Bend MSA, IN	s	47.40 MW	43.99 AW	98600 AAW	INBLS	10//99-12//99
	Terre Haute MSA, IN	s	39.25 MW	30.50 AW	81650 AAW	INBLS	10//99-12//99
	Iowa	s	35.36 MW	37.26 AW	77500 AAW	IABLS	10//99-12//99
	Cedar Rapids MSA, IA	s	34.68 MW	35.35 AW	72140 AAW	IABLS	10//99-12//99
	Davenport-Moline-Rock Island MSA, IA-IL	s	34.04 MW	31.34 AW	70800 AAW	IABLS	10//99-12//99
	Des Moines MSA, IA	s	43.94 MW	45.28 AW	91390 AAW	IABLS	10//99-12//99
	Dubuque MSA, IA	s	35.31 MW	33.48 AW	73440 AAW	IABLS	10//99-12//99
	Iowa City MSA, IA	s	39.37 MW	28.05 AW	81880 AAW	IABLS	10//99-12//99
	Sioux City MSA, IA-NE	s	32.37 MW	29.26 AW	67320 AAW	IABLS	10//99-12//99
	Waterloo-Cedar Falls MSA, IA	s	41.17 MW	40.99 AW	85620 AAW	IABLS	10//99-12//99
	Kansas	s	50.23 MW	47.76 AW	99340 AAW	KSBLS	10//99-12//99
	Lawrence MSA, KS	s	60.50 MW	66.09 AW	125850 AAW	KSBLS	10//99-12//99
	Wichita MSA, KS	s	45.90 MW	45.65 AW	95480 AAW	KSBLS	10//99-12//99
	Kentucky	s	47.31 MW	46.28 AW	96260 AAW	KYBLS	10//99-12//99
	Lexington MSA, KY	s	47.75 MW	48.56 AW	99320 AAW	KYBLS	10//99-12//99
	Louisville MSA, KY-IN	s	50.83 MW	53.88 AW	105730 AAW	KYBLS	10//99-12//99
	Owensboro MSA, KY	s	40.44 MW	30.60 AW	84110 AAW	KYBLS	10//99-12//99
	Louisiana	s	40.29 MW	42.22 AW	87820 AAW	LABLS	10//99-12//99
	Alexandria MSA, LA	s	28.80 MW	23.08 AW	59900 AAW	LABLS	10//99-12//99
	Baton Rouge MSA, LA	s	48.26 MW	48.81 AW	100380 AAW	LABLS	10//99-12//99
	Houma MSA, LA	s	39.75 MW	30.49 AW	82690 AAW	LABLS	10//99-12//99
	Lafayette MSA, LA	s	42.76 MW	40.89 AW	88940 AAW	LABLS	10//99-12//99
	Lake Charles MSA, LA	s	30.75 MW	20.82 AW	63960 AAW	LABLS	10//99-12//99
	Monroe MSA, LA	s	33.58 MW	29.38 AW	69840 AAW	LABLS	10//99-12//99
	New Orleans MSA, LA	s	44.96 MW	42.27 AW	93520 AAW	LABLS	10//99-12//99
	Shreveport-Bossier City MSA, LA	s	38.23 MW	38.04 AW	79520 AAW	LABLS	10//99-12//99
	Maine	s	41.8 MW	43.67 AW	90820 AAW	MEBLS	10//99-12//99
	Bangor MSA, ME	s	50.53 MW	54.58 AW	105090 AAW	MEBLS	10//99-12//99
	Lewiston-Auburn MSA, ME	s	39.15 MW	39.16 AW	81430 AAW	MEBLS	10//99-12//99
	Portland MSA, ME	s	49.00 MW	49.50 AW	101920 AAW	MEBLS	10//99-12//99
	Maryland	s	52.84 MW	50.23 AW	104480 AAW	MDBLS	10//99-12//99
	Baltimore PMSA, MD	s	50.04 MW	53.87 AW	104090 AAW	MDBLS	10//99-12//99
	Cumberland MSA, MD-WV	s	37.58 MW	32.44 AW	78160 AAW	MDBLS	10//99-12//99
	Hagerstown PMSA, MD	s	42.29 MW	39.14 AW	87960 AAW	MDBLS	10//99-12//99
	Massachusetts	s	65.39 MW	54.69 AW	113760 AAW	MABLS	10//99-12//99
	Barnstable-Yarmouth MSA, MA	s	42.38 MW	42.82 AW	88140 AAW	MABLS	10//99-12//99
	Boston PMSA, MA-NH	s	58.46 MW		121600 AAW	MABLS	10//99-12//99
	Brockton PMSA, MA	s	47.93 MW	46.04 AW	99690 AAW	MABLS	10//99-12//99
	Fitchburg-Leominster PMSA, MA	s	40.53 MW	38.67 AW	84300 AAW	MABLS	10//99-12//99
	Lawrence PMSA, MA-NH	s	53.48 MW	55.00 AW	111240 AAW	MABLS	10//99-12//99
	Lowell PMSA, MA-NH	s	54.49 MW	64.56 AW	113340 AAW	MABLS	10//99-12//99
	New Bedford PMSA, MA	s	46.05 MW	46.88 AW	95790 AAW	MABLS	10//99-12//99
	Pittsfield MSA, MA	s	33.36 MW	30.60 AW	69380 AAW	MABLS	10//99-12//99
	Springfield MSA, MA	s	50.30 MW	46.35 AW	104620 AAW	MABLS	10//99-12//99
	Worcester PMSA, MA-CT	s	45.71 MW	42.44 AW	95080 AAW	MABLS	10//99-12//99
	Michigan	s	63.96 MW	55.30 AW	115030 AAW	MIBLS	10//99-12//99
	Ann Arbor PMSA, MI	s	50.26 MW	53.38 AW	104530 AAW	MIBLS	10//99-12//99
	Benton Harbor MSA, MI	s	49.06 MW	53.11 AW	102030 AAW	MIBLS	10//99-12//99
	Detroit PMSA, MI	s	58.99 MW		122700 AAW	MIBLS	10//99-12//99
	Flint PMSA, MI	s	48.70 MW	50.01 AW	101300 AAW	MIBLS	10//99-12//99
	Grand Rapids-Muskegon-Holland MSA, MI	s	55.26 MW	62.73 AW	114940 AAW	MIBLS	10//99-12//99
	Jackson MSA, MI	s	45.38 MW	45.52 AW	94400 AAW	MIBLS	10//99-12//99
	Kalamazoo-Battle Creek MSA, MI	s	49.53 MW	51.53 AW	103030 AAW	MIBLS	10//99-12//99
	Lansing-East Lansing MSA, MI	s	53.84 MW	60.87 AW	111990 AAW	MIBLS	10//99-12//99

Occupation/Type/Industry	Location	Per	Low	Mid	High	Source	Date
Chief Executive	Saginaw-Bay City-Midland						
	MSA, MI	S	53.94 MW		112200 AAW	MIBLS	10//99-12//99
	Minnesota	S	64.11 MW	55.56 AW	115560 AAW	MNBLS	10//99-12//99
	Duluth-Superior MSA, MN-WI	S	44.96 MW	41.30 AW	93510 AAW	MNBLS	10//99-12//99
	Minneapolis-St. Paul MSA,						
	MN-WI	S	58.26 MW	67.83 AW	121180 AAW	MNBLS	10//99-12//99
	Rochester MSA, MN	S	45.62 MW	46.79 AW	94900 AAW	MNBLS	10//99-12//99
	St. Cloud MSA, MN	S	43.17 MW	40.89 AW	89800 AAW	MNBLS	10//99-12//99
	Mississippi	S	36.82 MW	41.39 AW	86090 AAW	MSBLS	10//99-12//99
	Biloxi-Gulfport-Pascagoula						
	MSA, MS	S	50.61 MW	67.20 AW	105280 AAW	MSBLS	10//99-12//99
	Hattiesburg MSA, MS	S	31.14 MW	29.74 AW	64770 AAW	MSBLS	10//99-12//99
	Jackson MSA, MS	S	38.65 MW	31.99 AW	80400 AAW	MSBLS	10//99-12//99
	Missouri	S	50.42 MW	47.25 AW	98290 AAW	MOBLS	10//99-12//99
	Columbia MSA, MO	S	37.63 MW	31.89 AW	78270 AAW	MOBLS	10//99-12//99
	Joplin MSA, MO	S	30.87 MW	25.74 AW	64220 AAW	MOBLS	10//99-12//99
	Kansas City MSA, MO-KS	S	52.25 MW	60.02 AW	108680 AAW	MOBLS	10//99-12//99
	St. Joseph MSA, MO	S	34.93 MW	30.35 AW	72660 AAW	MOBLS	10//99-12//99
	St. Louis MSA, MO-IL	S	46.33 MW	49.55 AW	96370 AAW	MOBLS	10//99-12//99
	Springfield MSA, MO	S	40.08 MW	35.13 AW	83370 AAW	MOBLS	10//99-12//99
	Montana	S	34.57 MW	40.89 AW	85050 AAW	MTBLS	10//99-12//99
	Billings MSA, MT	S	32.56 MW	27.48 AW	67730 AAW	MTBLS	10//99-12//99
	Great Falls MSA, MT	S	37.40 MW	31.46 AW	77790 AAW	MTBLS	10//99-12//99
	Missoula MSA, MT	S	43.20 MW	42.25 AW	89850 AAW	MTBLS	10//99-12//99
	Nebraska	S	30.3 MW	35.25 AW	73320 AAW	NEBLS	10//99-12//99
	Lincoln MSA, NE	S	39.40 MW	34.58 AW	81960 AAW	NEBLS	10//99-12//99
	Omaha MSA, NE-IA	S	41.40 MW	40.59 AW	86120 AAW	NEBLS	10//99-12//99
	Nevada	S	56.76 MW	50.64 AW	105330 AAW	NVBLS	10//99-12//99
	Las Vegas MSA, NV-AZ	S	53.62 MW	59.95 AW	111530 AAW	NVBLS	10//99-12//99
	Reno MSA, NV	S	42.78 MW	39.93 AW	88980 AAW	NVBLS	10//99-12//99
	New Hampshire	S	44.94 MW	44.36 AW	92270 AAW	NHBLS	10//99-12//99
	Manchester PMSA, NH	S	46.41 MW	47.08 AW	96530 AAW	NHBLS	10//99-12//99
	Nashua PMSA, NH	S	57.12 MW		118800 AAW	NHBLS	10//99-12//99
	Portsmouth-Rochester PMSA,						
	NH-ME	S	45.24 MW	42.56 AW	94110 AAW	NHBLS	10//99-12//99
	New Jersey	S		61.47 AW	127850 AAW	NJBLS	10//99-12//99
	Atlantic-Cape May PMSA, NJ	S	60.66 MW		126170 AAW	NJBLS	10//99-12//99
	Bergen-Passaic PMSA, NJ	S	64.80 MW		134790 AAW	NJBLS	10//99-12//99
	Jersey City PMSA, NJ	S	62.64 MW		130300 AAW	NJBLS	10//99-12//99
	Middlesex-Somerset-						
	Hunterdon PMSA, NJ	S	57.12 MW		118820 AAW	NJBLS	10//99-12//99
	Newark PMSA, NJ	S	62.75 MW		130510 AAW	NJBLS	10//99-12//99
	Trenton PMSA, NJ	S	56.70 MW	67.79 AW	117930 AAW	NJBLS	10//99-12//99
	Vineland-Millville-Bridgeton						
	PMSA, NJ	S	64.44 MW		134030 AAW	NJBLS	10//99-12//99
	New Mexico	S	56.42 MW	49.82 AW	103630 AAW	NMBLS	10//99-12//99
	Albuquerque MSA, NM	S	53.58 MW		111450 AAW	NMBLS	10//99-12//99
	Santa Fe MSA, NM	S	48.27 MW	56.65 AW	100400 AAW	NMBLS	10//99-12//99
	New York	S		58.65 AW	121990 AAW	NYBLS	10//99-12//99
	Albany-Schenectady-Troy						
	MSA, NY	S	48.21 MW	49.38 AW	100280 AAW	NYBLS	10//99-12//99
	Binghamton MSA, NY	S	48.52 MW	49.88 AW	100920 AAW	NYBLS	10//99-12//99
	Buffalo-Niagara Falls MSA,						
	NY	S	53.61 MW	55.38 AW	111500 AAW	NYBLS	10//99-12//99
	Dutchess County PMSA, NY	S	52.35 MW	52.15 AW	108890 AAW	NYBLS	10//99-12//99
	Elmira MSA, NY	S	65.00 MW		135200 AAW	NYBLS	10//99-12//99
	Glens Falls MSA, NY	S	51.35 MW	51.37 AW	106800 AAW	NYBLS	10//99-12//99
	Jamestown MSA, NY	S	42.65 MW	37.16 AW	88700 AAW	NYBLS	10//99-12//99
	Nassau-Suffolk PMSA, NY	S	58.84 MW		122380 AAW	NYBLS	10//99-12//99
	New York PMSA, NY	S	62.56 MW		130130 AAW	NYBLS	10//99-12//99
	Newburgh PMSA, NY-PA	S	42.55 MW	42.23 AW	88500 AAW	NYBLS	10//99-12//99
	Rochester MSA, NY	S	53.95 MW	53.89 AW	112220 AAW	NYBLS	10//99-12//99
	Syracuse MSA, NY	S	53.37 MW	63.63 AW	111010 AAW	NYBLS	10//99-12//99
	Utica-Rome MSA, NY	S	45.97 MW	47.58 AW	95630 AAW	NYBLS	10//99-12//99
	North Carolina	S	52.66 MW	48.22 AW	100300 AAW	NCBLS	10//99-12//99
	Asheville MSA, NC	S	39.03 MW	38.95 AW	81190 AAW	NCBLS	10//99-12//99
	Charlotte-Gastonia-Rock Hill						
	MSA, NC-SC	S	48.19 MW	52.49 AW	100230 AAW	NCBLS	10//99-12//99
	Fayetteville MSA, NC	S	38.84 MW	37.29 AW	80790 AAW	NCBLS	10//99-12//99
	Goldsboro MSA, NC	S	36.60 MW	31.20 AW	76140 AAW	NCBLS	10//99-12//99
	Greensboro--Winston-Salem--						
	High Point MSA, NC	S	55.46 MW	66.59 AW	115360 AAW	NCBLS	10//99-12//99

AAW	Average annual wage	AOH	Average offered, high	ASH	Average starting, high	H	Hourly	M	Monthly	S	Special: hourly and annual
AE	Average entry wage	AOL	Average offered, low	ASL	Average starting, low	HI	Highest wage paid	MTC	Median total compensation	TQ	Third quartile wage
AEX	Average experienced wage	APH	Average pay, high range	AW	Average wage paid	HR	High end range	MW	Median wage paid	W	Weekly
AO	Average offered	APL	Average pay, low range	FQ	First quartile wage	LR	Low end range	SQ	Second quartile wage	Y	Yearly

Occupation/Type/Industry	Location	Per	Low	Mid	High	Source	Date
Chief Executive	Greenville MSA, NC	S	44.67 MW	42.97 AW	92920 AAW	NCBLS	10//99-12//99
	Hickory-Morganton-Lenoir MSA, NC	S	38.92 MW	41.02 AW	80960 AAW	NCBLS	10//99-12//99
	Jacksonville MSA, NC	S	32.12 MW	23.43 AW	66810 AAW	NCBLS	10//99-12//99
	Raleigh-Durham-Chapel Hill MSA, NC	S	53.08 MW	60.31 AW	110410 AAW	NCBLS	10//99-12//99
	Rocky Mount MSA, NC	S	44.54 MW	47.82 AW	92650 AAW	NCBLS	10//99-12//99
	Wilmington MSA, NC	S	41.41 MW	41.56 AW	86130 AAW	NCBLS	10//99-12//99
	North Dakota	S	34.64 MW	37.77 AW	78560 AAW	NDBLS	10//99-12//99
	Bismarck MSA, ND	S	39.67 MW	38.58 AW	82500 AAW	NDBLS	10//99-12//99
	Fargo-Moorhead MSA, ND-MN	S	48.12 MW	49.26 AW	100080 AAW	NDBLS	10//99-12//99
	Grand Forks MSA, ND-MN	S	35.77 MW	31.37 AW	74410 AAW	NDBLS	10//99-12//99
	Ohio	S	52.81 MW	49.62 AW	103210 AAW	OHBLS	10//99-12//99
	Akron PMSA, OH	S	51.71 MW	58.93 AW	107550 AAW	OHBLS	10//99-12//99
	Canton-Massillon MSA, OH	S	43.30 MW	41.26 AW	90070 AAW	OHBLS	10//99-12//99
	Cincinnati PMSA, OH-KY-IN	S	49.43 MW	51.26 AW	102810 AAW	OHBLS	10//99-12//99
	Cleveland-Lorain-Elyria PMSA, OH	S	55.20 MW	68.96 AW	114830 AAW	OHBLS	10//99-12//99
	Columbus MSA, OH	S	47.94 MW	49.52 AW	99720 AAW	OHBLS	10//99-12//99
	Dayton-Springfield MSA, OH	S	50.87 MW	54.33 AW	105810 AAW	OHBLS	10//99-12//99
	Hamilton-Middletown PMSA, OH	S	44.20 MW	40.28 AW	91940 AAW	OHBLS	10//99-12//99
	Lima MSA, OH	S	42.07 MW	43.19 AW	87500 AAW	OHBLS	10//99-12//99
	Mansfield MSA, OH	S	40.69 MW	39.36 AW	84630 AAW	OHBLS	10//99-12//99
	Steubenville-Weirton MSA, OH-WV	S	33.58 MW	25.78 AW	69850 AAW	OHBLS	10//99-12//99
	Toledo MSA, OH	S	52.08 MW	60.62 AW	108320 AAW	OHBLS	10//99-12//99
	Youngstown-Warren MSA, OH	S	45.92 MW	49.34 AW	95520 AAW	OHBLS	10//99-12//99
	Oklahoma	S	36.34 MW	38.37 AW	79810 AAW	OKBLS	10//99-12//99
	Enid MSA, OK	S	46.57 MW	55.72 AW	96860 AAW	OKBLS	10//99-12//99
	Oklahoma City MSA, OK	S	37.65 MW	38.13 AW	78310 AAW	OKBLS	10//99-12//99
	Tulsa MSA, OK	S	44.35 MW	43.13 AW	92250 AAW	OKBLS	10//99-12//99
	Oregon	S	55.68 MW	52.35 AW	108880 AAW	ORBLS	10//99-12//99
	Corvallis MSA, OR	S	42.81 MW	38.88 AW	89050 AAW	ORBLS	10//99-12//99
	Eugene-Springfield MSA, OR	S	49.42 MW	48.28 AW	102800 AAW	ORBLS	10//99-12//99
	Medford-Ashland MSA, OR	S	56.00 MW	65.09 AW	116480 AAW	ORBLS	10//99-12//99
	Portland-Vancouver PMSA, OR-WA	S	54.41 MW	63.90 AW	113180 AAW	ORBLS	10//99-12//99
	Salem PMSA, OR	S	51.72 MW	48.57 AW	107580 AAW	ORBLS	10//99-12//99
	Pennsylvania	S	47.47 MW	46.00 AW	95680 AAW	PABLS	10//99-12//99
	Allentown-Bethlehem-Easton MSA, PA	S	33.90 MW	25.01 AW	70510 AAW	PABLS	10//99-12//99
	Altoona MSA, PA	S	42.73 MW	43.95 AW	88880 AAW	PABLS	10//99-12//99
	Erie MSA, PA	S	41.25 MW	39.59 AW	85800 AAW	PABLS	10//99-12//99
	Harrisburg-Lebanon-Carlisle MSA, PA	S	43.67 MW	42.02 AW	90830 AAW	PABLS	10//99-12//99
	Johnstown MSA, PA	S	41.66 MW	33.82 AW	86660 AAW	PABLS	10//99-12//99
	Lancaster MSA, PA	S	47.47 MW	50.53 AW	98740 AAW	PABLS	10//99-12//99
	Philadelphia PMSA, PA-NJ	S	51.56 MW	54.69 AW	107240 AAW	PABLS	10//99-12//99
	Pittsburgh MSA, PA	S	46.70 MW	50.74 AW	97130 AAW	PABLS	10//99-12//99
	Reading MSA, PA	S	43.37 MW	42.05 AW	90210 AAW	PABLS	10//99-12//99
	Scranton--Wilkes-Barre--Hazleton MSA, PA	S	38.75 MW	35.25 AW	80600 AAW	PABLS	10//99-12//99
	Sharon MSA, PA	S	29.47 MW	23.98 AW	61300 AAW	PABLS	10//99-12//99
	State College MSA, PA	S	37.09 MW	32.68 AW	77140 AAW	PABLS	10//99-12//99
	Williamsport MSA, PA	S	31.10 MW	26.29 AW	64690 AAW	PABLS	10//99-12//99
	York MSA, PA	S	40.03 MW	37.97 AW	83250 AAW	PABLS	10//99-12//99
	Rhode Island	S		62.75 AW	130520 AAW	RIBLS	10//99-12//99
	Providence-Fall River-Warwick MSA, RI-MA	S	54.27 MW	66.84 AW	112890 AAW	RIBLS	10//99-12//99
	South Carolina	S	37.31 MW	39.11 AW	81340 AAW	SCBLS	10//99-12//99
	Charleston-North Charleston MSA, SC	S	38.44 MW	36.77 AW	79960 AAW	SCBLS	10//99-12//99
	Columbia MSA, SC	S	40.34 MW	38.89 AW	83910 AAW	SCBLS	10//99-12//99
	Florence MSA, SC	S	28.54 MW	16.73 AW	59370 AAW	SCBLS	10//99-12//99
	Greenville-Spartanburg-Anderson MSA, SC	S	41.73 MW	39.40 AW	86800 AAW	SCBLS	10//99-12//99
	Myrtle Beach MSA, SC	S	36.74 MW	34.41 AW	76410 AAW	SCBLS	10//99-12//99
	Sumter MSA, SC	S	41.70 MW	40.06 AW	86740 AAW	SCBLS	10//99-12//99
	Rapid City MSA, SD	S	49.62 MW	50.91 AW	103220 AAW	SDBLS	10//99-12//99
	Sioux Falls MSA, SD	S	46.19 MW	44.17 AW	96080 AAW	SDBLS	10//99-12//99

Occupation/Type/Industry	Location	Per	Low	Mid	High	Source	Date
Chief Executive	Tennessee	S	51.33 MW	48.15 AW	100160 AAW	TNBLS	10//99-12//99
	Chattanooga MSA, TN-GA	S	46.42 MW	44.78 AW	96560 AAW	TNBLS	10//99-12//99
	Clarksville-Hopkinsville MSA, TN-KY	S	33.89 MW	25.69 AW	70500 AAW	TNBLS	10//99-12//99
	Jackson MSA, TN	S	43.73 MW	40.60 AW	90950 AAW	TNBLS	10//99-12//99
	Johnson City-Kingsport-Bristol MSA, TN-VA	S	35.92 MW	29.59 AW	74710 AAW	TNBLS	10//99-12//99
	Knoxville MSA, TN	S	47.49 MW	49.92 AW	98770 AAW	TNBLS	10//99-12//99
	Memphis MSA, TN-AR-MS	S	53.11 MW	57.23 AW	110470 AAW	MSBLS	10//99-12//99
	Nashville MSA, TN	S	52.66 MW	59.57 AW	109540 AAW	TNBLS	10//99-12//99
	Texas	S	45.88 MW	44.75 AW	93080 AAW	TXBLS	10//99-12//99
	Abilene MSA, TX	S	38.84 MW	39.32 AW	80780 AAW	TXBLS	10//99-12//99
	Amarillo MSA, TX	S	40.28 MW	34.45 AW	83790 AAW	TXBLS	10//99-12//99
	Austin-San Marcos MSA, TX	S	45.61 MW	46.77 AW	94860 AAW	TXBLS	10//99-12//99
	Beaumont-Port Arthur MSA, TX	S	36.68 MW	33.04 AW	76300 AAW	TXBLS	10//99-12//99
	Brazoria PMSA, TX	S	39.64 MW	44.61 AW	82440 AAW	TXBLS	10//99-12//99
	Dallas PMSA, TX	S	51.62 MW	60.61 AW	107360 AAW	TXBLS	10//99-12//99
	El Paso MSA, TX	S	36.45 MW	36.72 AW	75810 AAW	TXBLS	10//99-12//99
	Fort Worth-Arlington PMSA, TX	S	49.26 MW	56.08 AW	102460 AAW	TXBLS	10//99-12//99
	Galveston-Texas City PMSA, TX	S	32.69 MW	28.82 AW	68000 AAW	TXBLS	10//99-12//99
	Houston PMSA, TX	S	47.34 MW	49.49 AW	98480 AAW	TXBLS	10//99-12//99
	Killeen-Temple MSA, TX	S	36.87 MW	32.98 AW	76700 AAW	TXBLS	10//99-12//99
	Laredo MSA, TX	S	45.14 MW	52.85 AW	93900 AAW	TXBLS	10//99-12//99
	Longview-Marshall MSA, TX	S	32.96 MW	32.20 AW	68560 AAW	TXBLS	10//99-12//99
	Lubbock MSA, TX	S	33.88 MW	28.29 AW	70470 AAW	TXBLS	10//99-12//99
	McAllen-Edinburg-Mission MSA, TX	S	42.45 MW	40.09 AW	88290 AAW	TXBLS	10//99-12//99
	Odessa-Midland MSA, TX	S	39.67 MW	35.43 AW	82500 AAW	TXBLS	10//99-12//99
	San Angelo MSA, TX	S	39.67 MW	45.19 AW	82510 AAW	TXBLS	10//99-12//99
	San Antonio MSA, TX	S	44.86 MW	47.73 AW	93310 AAW	TXBLS	10//99-12//99
	Sherman-Denison MSA, TX	S	32.49 MW	31.79 AW	67580 AAW	TXBLS	10//99-12//99
	Texarkana MSA, TX-Texarkana, AR	S	43.55 MW	40.50 AW	90590 AAW	TXBLS	10//99-12//99
	Tyler MSA, TX	S	42.07 MW	40.90 AW	87510 AAW	TXBLS	10//99-12//99
	Victoria MSA, TX	S	32.57 MW	35.75 AW	67740 AAW	TXBLS	10//99-12//99
	Waco MSA, TX	S	37.76 MW	36.92 AW	78540 AAW	TXBLS	10//99-12//99
	Wichita Falls MSA, TX	S	32.04 MW	30.22 AW	66650 AAW	TXBLS	10//99-12//99
	Utah	S	41.42 MW	43.04 AW	89530 AAW	UTBLS	10//99-12//99
	Provo-Orem MSA, UT	S	35.27 MW	35.18 AW	73350 AAW	UTBLS	10//99-12//99
	Vermont	S	38.48 MW	38.64 AW	80380 AAW	VTBLS	10//99-12//99
	Burlington MSA, VT	S	33.42 MW	31.84 AW	69520 AAW	VTBLS	10//99-12//99
	Virginia	S	57.64 MW	51.62 AW	107370 AAW	VABLS	10//99-12//99
	Charlottesville MSA, VA	S	45.14 MW	45.62 AW	93890 AAW	VABLS	10//99-12//99
	Danville MSA, VA	S	31.17 MW	29.32 AW	64830 AAW	VABLS	10//99-12//99
	Lynchburg MSA, VA	S	37.92 MW	29.92 AW	78870 AAW	VABLS	10//99-12//99
	Norfolk-Virginia Beach-Newport News MSA, VA-NC	S	47.60 MW	47.41 AW	99020 AAW	VABLS	10//99-12//99
	Richmond-Petersburg MSA, VA	S	52.26 MW	58.97 AW	108710 AAW	VABLS	10//99-12//99
	Roanoke MSA, VA	S	39.74 MW	33.98 AW	82660 AAW	VABLS	10//99-12//99
	Washington	S	65.51 MW	56.06 AW	116610 AAW	WABLS	10//99-12//99
	Bellingham MSA, WA	S	54.57 MW	54.76 AW	113500 AAW	WABLS	10//99-12//99
	Bremerton PMSA, WA	S	61.30 MW		127490 AAW	WABLS	10//99-12//99
	Olympia PMSA, WA	S	50.28 MW	52.84 AW	104590 AAW	WABLS	10//99-12//99
	Richland-Kennewick-Pasco MSA, WA	S	50.71 MW	52.50 AW	105480 AAW	WABLS	10//99-12//99
	Seattle-Bellevue-Everett PMSA, WA	S	58.91 MW		122520 AAW	WABLS	10//99-12//99
	Spokane MSA, WA	S	54.10 MW	61.66 AW	112530 AAW	WABLS	10//99-12//99
	Tacoma PMSA, WA	S	49.84 MW	48.06 AW	103670 AAW	WABLS	10//99-12//99
	Yakima MSA, WA	S	46.60 MW	48.17 AW	96920 AAW	WABLS	10//99-12//99
	West Virginia	S	27.48 MW	33.53 AW	69750 AAW	WVBLS	10//99-12//99
	Charleston MSA, WV	S	36.50 MW	30.98 AW	75930 AAW	WVBLS	10//99-12//99
	Huntington-Ashland MSA, WV-KY-OH	S	37.03 MW	34.87 AW	77020 AAW	WVBLS	10//99-12//99
	Parkersburg-Marietta MSA, WV-OH	S	39.99 MW	40.99 AW	83170 AAW	WVBLS	10//99-12//99
	Wheeling MSA, WV-OH	S	28.68 MW	23.39 AW	59650 AAW	WVBLS	10//99-12//99

Occupation/Type/Industry	Location	Per	Low	Mid	High	Source	Date
Chief Executive	Wisconsin	S	45.15 MW	45.21 AW	94030 AAW	WIBLS	10//99-12//99
	Appleton-Oshkosh-Neenah MSA, WI	S	44.94 MW	45.47 AW	93470 AAW	WIBLS	10//99-12//99
	Eau Claire MSA, WI	S	35.90 MW	34.60 AW	74680 AAW	WIBLS	10//99-12//99
	Green Bay MSA, WI	S	42.15 MW	45.24 AW	87670 AAW	WIBLS	10//99-12//99
	Janesville-Beloit MSA, WI	S	40.27 MW	35.70 AW	83760 AAW	WIBLS	10//99-12//99
	Kenosha PMSA, WI	S	39.70 MW	40.05 AW	82580 AAW	WIBLS	10//99-12//99
	La Crosse MSA, WI-MN	S	35.62 MW	34.16 AW	74080 AAW	WIBLS	10//99-12//99
	Madison MSA, WI	S	48.38 MW	47.14 AW	100620 AAW	WIBLS	10//99-12//99
	Milwaukee-Waukesha PMSA, WI	S	48.93 MW	51.80 AW	101760 AAW	WIBLS	10//99-12//99
	Racine PMSA, WI	S	47.92 MW	45.26 AW	99670 AAW	WIBLS	10//99-12//99
	Sheboygan MSA, WI	S	45.98 MW	57.95 AW	95640 AAW	WIBLS	10//99-12//99
	Wausau MSA, WI	S	44.20 MW	44.12 AW	91930 AAW	WIBLS	10//99-12//99
	Wyoming	S	35.01 MW	34.47 AW	71700 AAW	WYBLS	10//99-12//99
	Casper MSA, WY	S	39.59 MW	45.04 AW	82350 AAW	WYBLS	10//99-12//99
	Cheyenne MSA, WY	S	33.00 MW	31.01 AW	68630 AAW	WYBLS	10//99-12//99
	Puerto Rico	S	34.7 MW	38.20 AW	79470 AAW	PRBLS	10//99-12//99
	Aguadilla MSA, PR	S	45.99 MW	48.38 AW	95670 AAW	PRBLS	10//99-12//99
	Arecibo PMSA, PR	S	25.28 MW	22.57 AW	52590 AAW	PRBLS	10//99-12//99
	Caguas PMSA, PR	S	36.92 MW	30.71 AW	76800 AAW	PRBLS	10//99-12//99
	Mayaguez MSA, PR	S	34.94 MW	27.24 AW	72680 AAW	PRBLS	10//99-12//99
	Ponce MSA, PR	S	33.67 MW	26.91 AW	70040 AAW	PRBLS	10//99-12//99
	San Juan-Bayamon PMSA, PR	S	39.95 MW	36.39 AW	83090 AAW	PRBLS	10//99-12//99
	Guam	S	34.56 MW	35.77 AW	74400 AAW	GUBLS	10//99-12//99
Chief Executive Officer							
Advertising	East	Y		168000 AW		ADAGE1	2000
Advertising	Midwest	Y		170000 AW		ADAGE1	2000
Advertising	South	Y		220000 AW		ADAGE1	2000
Advertising	West	Y		170000 AW		ADAGE1	2000
Association	United States	Y		117100 MW		ASMA	1998
Beer Wholesaling	United States	Y	150000 MW	215055 AW		BEVW	1999
Behavioral Health Organization	United States	Y	65021 APL	89171 AW	96122 APH	ADAW	2000
Continuing Care Retirement Community	United States	Y		91181 AW		CHW2	1998
Health System/Integrated Delivery System	United States	Y		202500 AW		HFM3	1999
Home Care Organization	United States	Y		66599 AW		CHW1	1998
Hospice	United States	Y		58259 AW		CHW1	1998
Hospital	United States	Y		216600 MW		HHN	2000
Hospital	United States	Y		173448 AW		HFM3	1999
Mechanical Contracting Firm	United States	Y		102000 AW		CONTR	1998
Nursing Home	United States	Y		61901 AW		CHW1	1998
Physicians Group	United States	Y		180000 AW		HFM3	1999
Teaching Hospital	United States	Y		376667 AW		HFM3	1999
Chief Financial Officer	United States	Y		175870 AW		PENINV	2000
Beer Wholesaling	United States	Y	96000 MW	113174 AW		BEVW	1999
Health Care Organization	Midwest	Y		96788 AW		HFM	1999
Health Care Organization	Northeast	Y		145022 AW		HFM	1999
Health Care Organization	South	Y		98932 AW		HFM	1999
Health Care Organization	West	Y		119117 AW		HFM	1999
Hospital	United States	Y		129500 MW		HHN	2000
Chief Information Officer							
Health Care Organization	Middle Atlantic	Y		147100 AW		HEMAT	1999
Health Care Organization	Mountain	Y		137300 AW		HEMAT	1999
Health Care Organization	New England	Y		152500 AW		HEMAT	1999
Health Care Organization	North Central	Y		126000 AW		HEMAT	1999
Health Care Organization	Pacific	Y		128500 AW		HEMAT	1999
Health Care Organization	South Atlantic	Y		132600 AW		HEMAT	1999
Health Care Organization	South Central	Y		116000 AW		HEMAT	1999
Chief Medical Officer							
Hospital	United States	Y		209000 MW		HHN	2000
Child Care Worker	Alabama	S	6.12 MW	6.56 AW	13640 AAW	ALBLS	10//99-12//99
	Anniston MSA, AL	S	6.68 MW	6.40 AW	13890 AAW	ALBLS	10//99-12//99
	Auburn-Opelika MSA, AL	S	6.47 MW	5.95 AW	13460 AAW	ALBLS	10//99-12//99
	Birmingham MSA, AL	S	6.76 MW	6.29 AW	14050 AAW	ALBLS	10//99-12//99
	Decatur MSA, AL	S	6.01 MW	5.95 AW	12490 AAW	ALBLS	10//99-12//99
	Dothan MSA, AL	S	5.98 MW	5.89 AW	12430 AAW	ALBLS	10//99-12//99
	Florence MSA, AL	S	6.17 MW	5.90 AW	12830 AAW	ALBLS	10//99-12//99
	Gadsden MSA, AL	S	6.01 MW	5.91 AW	12500 AAW	ALBLS	10//99-12//99

AAW Average annual wage	AOH Average offered, high	ASH Average starting, high	H Hourly	M Monthly	S Special: hourly and annual
AE Average entry wage	AOL Average offered, low	ASL Average starting, low	HI Highest wage paid	MTC Median total compensation	TQ Third quartile wage
AEX Average experienced wage	APH Average pay, high range	AW Average wage paid	HR High end range	MW Median wage paid	W Weekly
AO Average offered	APL Average pay, low range	FQ First quartile wage	LR Low end range	SQ Second quartile wage	Y Yearly

Child Care Worker

Occupation/Type/Industry	Location	Per	Low	Mid	High	Source	Date
Child Care Worker	Huntsville MSA, AL	S	6.65 MW	6.45 AW	13830 AAW	ALBLS	10//99-12//99
	Mobile MSA, AL	S	6.56 MW	6.34 AW	13640 AAW	ALBLS	10//99-12//99
	Montgomery MSA, AL	S	7.08 MW	6.38 AW	14730 AAW	ALBLS	10//99-12//99
	Alaska	S	8.14 MW	8.64 AW	17970 AAW	AKBLS	10//99-12//99
	Anchorage MSA, AK	S	8.71 MW	8.29 AW	18120 AAW	AKBLS	10//99-12//99
	Arizona	S	6.78 MW	6.92 AW	14390 AAW	AZBLS	10//99-12//99
	Flagstaff MSA, AZ-UT	S	6.62 MW	6.14 AW	13770 AAW	AZBLS	10//99-12//99
	Phoenix-Mesa MSA, AZ	S	6.73 MW	6.59 AW	14000 AAW	AZBLS	10//99-12//99
	Tucson MSA, AZ	S	6.74 MW	6.42 AW	14010 AAW	AZBLS	10//99-12//99
	Yuma MSA, AZ	S	6.06 MW	6.04 AW	12600 AAW	AZBLS	10//99-12//99
	Arkansas	S	6.09 MW	6.32 AW	13150 AAW	ARBLS	10//99-12//99
	Fayetteville-Springdale-Rogers MSA, AR	S	6.60 MW	6.51 AW	13720 AAW	ARBLS	10//99-12//99
	Fort Smith MSA, AR-OK	S	6.22 MW	6.09 AW	12940 AAW	ARBLS	10//99-12//99
	Jonesboro MSA, AR	S	6.50 MW	6.05 AW	13510 AAW	ARBLS	10//99-12//99
	Little Rock-North Little Rock MSA, AR	S	6.27 MW	6.06 AW	13040 AAW	ARBLS	10//99-12//99
	Pine Bluff MSA, AR	S	7.95 MW	6.55 AW	16530 AAW	ARBLS	10//99-12//99
	California	S	7.89 MW	8.38 AW	17420 AAW	CABLS	10//99-12//99
	Bakersfield MSA, CA	S	8.56 MW	8.42 AW	17810 AAW	CABLS	10//99-12//99
	Chico-Paradise MSA, CA	S	7.36 MW	6.77 AW	15300 AAW	CABLS	10//99-12//99
	Fresno MSA, CA	S	7.48 MW	7.01 AW	15560 AAW	CABLS	10//99-12//99
	Los Angeles-Long Beach PMSA, CA	S	8.38 MW	7.84 AW	17430 AAW	CABLS	10//99-12//99
	Merced MSA, CA	S	7.71 MW	7.30 AW	16040 AAW	CABLS	10//99-12//99
	Modesto MSA, CA	S	7.58 MW	7.05 AW	15760 AAW	CABLS	10//99-12//99
	Oakland PMSA, CA	S	9.06 MW	8.74 AW	18830 AAW	CABLS	10//99-12//99
	Orange County PMSA, CA	S	8.41 MW	8.08 AW	17500 AAW	CABLS	10//99-12//99
	Redding MSA, CA	S	7.96 MW	7.33 AW	16560 AAW	CABLS	10//99-12//99
	Riverside-San Bernardino PMSA, CA	S	7.94 MW	7.61 AW	16500 AAW	CABLS	10//99-12//99
	Sacramento PMSA, CA	S	7.58 MW	7.38 AW	15780 AAW	CABLS	10//99-12//99
	San Diego MSA, CA	S	8.59 MW	8.23 AW	17870 AAW	CABLS	10//99-12//99
	San Francisco PMSA, CA	S	9.43 MW	8.45 AW	19610 AAW	CABLS	10//99-12//99
	San Jose PMSA, CA	S	8.66 MW	8.13 AW	18010 AAW	CABLS	10//99-12//99
	San Luis Obispo-Atascadero-Paso Robles MSA, CA	S	7.80 MW	7.55 AW	16210 AAW	CABLS	10//99-12//99
	Santa Barbara-Santa Maria-Lompoc MSA, CA	S	7.75 MW	7.21 AW	16120 AAW	CABLS	10//99-12//99
	Santa Cruz-Watsonville PMSA, CA	S	8.12 MW	7.98 AW	16880 AAW	CABLS	10//99-12//99
	Santa Rosa PMSA, CA	S	9.19 MW	9.20 AW	19120 AAW	CABLS	10//99-12//99
	Stockton-Lodi MSA, CA	S	8.00 MW	7.25 AW	16650 AAW	CABLS	10//99-12//99
	Vallejo-Fairfield-Napa PMSA, CA	S	7.63 MW	6.93 AW	15880 AAW	CABLS	10//99-12//99
	Ventura PMSA, CA	S	8.65 MW	8.01 AW	18000 AAW	CABLS	10//99-12//99
	Visalia-Tulare-Porterville MSA, CA	S	8.06 MW	7.76 AW	16760 AAW	CABLS	10//99-12//99
	Yolo PMSA, CA	S	8.24 MW	7.83 AW	17130 AAW	CABLS	10//99-12//99
	Yuba City MSA, CA	S	8.55 MW	7.82 AW	17780 AAW	CABLS	10//99-12//99
	Colorado	S	7.15 MW	7.24 AW	15060 AAW	COBLS	10//99-12//99
	Boulder-Longmont PMSA, CO	S	7.59 MW	7.33 AW	15790 AAW	COBLS	10//99-12//99
	Colorado Springs MSA, CO	S	6.87 MW	6.83 AW	14280 AAW	COBLS	10//99-12//99
	Denver PMSA, CO	S	7.50 MW	7.47 AW	15590 AAW	COBLS	10//99-12//99
	Fort Collins-Loveland MSA, CO	S	6.55 MW	6.51 AW	13620 AAW	COBLS	10//99-12//99
	Grand Junction MSA, CO	S	5.90 MW	5.90 AW	12270 AAW	COBLS	10//99-12//99
	Greeley PMSA, CO	S	7.01 MW	6.78 AW	14590 AAW	COBLS	10//99-12//99
	Pueblo MSA, CO	S	6.83 MW	6.41 AW	14200 AAW	COBLS	10//99-12//99
	Connecticut	S	7.99 MW	8.51 AW	17710 AAW	CTBLS	10//99-12//99
	Bridgeport PMSA, CT	S	7.54 MW	7.57 AW	15670 AAW	CTBLS	10//99-12//99
	Danbury PMSA, CT	S	7.94 MW	7.66 AW	16520 AAW	CTBLS	10//99-12//99
	Hartford MSA, CT	S	8.35 MW	7.89 AW	17370 AAW	CTBLS	10//99-12//99
	New Haven-Meriden PMSA, CT	S	9.15 MW	8.52 AW	19040 AAW	CTBLS	10//99-12//99
	New London-Norwich MSA, CT-RI	S	7.89 MW	7.57 AW	16400 AAW	CTBLS	10//99-12//99
	Stamford-Norwalk PMSA, CT	S	9.95 MW	9.31 AW	20690 AAW	CTBLS	10//99-12//99
	Waterbury PMSA, CT	S	7.59 MW	7.45 AW	15800 AAW	CTBLS	10//99-12//99
	Delaware	S	6.79 MW	7.24 AW	15060 AAW	DEBLS	10//99-12//99
	Dover MSA, DE	S	7.00 MW	6.46 AW	14560 AAW	DEBLS	10//99-12//99

AAW	Average annual wage	AOH	Average offered, high	ASH	Average starting, high	H	Hourly	M	Monthly	S	Special: hourly and annual
AE	Average entry wage	AOL	Average offered, low	ASL	Average starting, low	HI	Highest wage paid	MTC	Median total compensation	TQ	Third quartile wage
AEX	Average experienced wage	APH	Average pay, high range	AW	Average wage paid	HR	High end range	MW	Median wage paid	W	Weekly
AO	Average offered	APL	Average pay, low range	FQ	First quartile wage	LR	Low end range	SQ	Second quartile wage	Y	Yearly

Occupation/Type/Industry	Location	Per	Low	Mid	High	Source	Date
Child Care Worker	Wilmington-Newark PMSA, DE-MD	S	7.32 MW	6.94 AW	15230 AAW	DEBLS	10//99-12//99
	District of Columbia	S	9.57 MW	10.62 AW	22090 AAW	DCBLS	10//99-12//99
	Washington PMSA, DC-MD-VA-WV	S	8.53 MW	7.66 AW	17740 AAW	DCBLS	10//99-12//99
	Florida	S	6.61 MW	6.95 AW	14460 AAW	FLBLS	10//99-12//99
	Daytona Beach MSA, FL	S	7.01 MW	6.95 AW	14570 AAW	FLBLS	10//99-12//99
	Fort Lauderdale PMSA, FL	S	7.14 MW	6.67 AW	14850 AAW	FLBLS	10//99-12//99
	Fort Myers-Cape Coral MSA, FL	S	7.33 MW	7.34 AW	15250 AAW	FLBLS	10//99-12//99
	Fort Pierce-Port St. Lucie MSA, FL	S	7.11 MW	7.29 AW	14790 AAW	FLBLS	10//99-12//99
	Fort Walton Beach MSA, FL	S	6.63 MW	6.49 AW	13790 AAW	FLBLS	10//99-12//99
	Gainesville MSA, FL	S	7.42 MW	6.66 AW	15420 AAW	FLBLS	10//99-12//99
	Jacksonville MSA, FL	S	6.50 MW	6.26 AW	13520 AAW	FLBLS	10//99-12//99
	Lakeland-Winter Haven MSA, FL	S	6.15 MW	5.94 AW	12780 AAW	FLBLS	10//99-12//99
	Melbourne-Titusville-Palm Bay MSA, FL	S	7.82 MW	7.37 AW	16270 AAW	FLBLS	10//99-12//99
	Miami PMSA, FL	S	6.45 MW	6.27 AW	13410 AAW	FLBLS	10//99-12//99
	Orlando MSA, FL	S	6.85 MW	6.59 AW	14250 AAW	FLBLS	10//99-12//99
	Panama City MSA, FL	S	6.94 MW	6.97 AW	14440 AAW	FLBLS	10//99-12//99
	Pensacola MSA, FL	S	6.43 MW	6.38 AW	13380 AAW	FLBLS	10//99-12//99
	Sarasota-Bradenton MSA, FL	S	6.96 MW	6.60 AW	14480 AAW	FLBLS	10//99-12//99
	Tallahassee MSA, FL	S	6.61 MW	6.57 AW	13740 AAW	FLBLS	10//99-12//99
	Tampa-St. Petersburg-Clearwater MSA, FL	S	7.48 MW	7.07 AW	15560 AAW	FLBLS	10//99-12//99
	West Palm Beach-Boca Raton MSA, FL	S	7.74 MW	7.60 AW	16100 AAW	FLBLS	10//99-12//99
	Georgia	S	6.49 MW	6.71 AW	13950 AAW	GABLS	10//99-12//99
	Athens MSA, GA	S	6.82 MW	6.78 AW	14200 AAW	GABLS	10//99-12//99
	Atlanta MSA, GA	S	6.84 MW	6.69 AW	14230 AAW	GABLS	10//99-12//99
	Augusta-Aiken MSA, GA-SC	S	6.84 MW	6.40 AW	14230 AAW	GABLS	10//99-12//99
	Columbus MSA, GA-AL	S	6.33 MW	6.11 AW	13160 AAW	GABLS	10//99-12//99
	Macon MSA, GA	S	6.14 MW	6.06 AW	12760 AAW	GABLS	10//99-12//99
	Savannah MSA, GA	S	6.79 MW	6.60 AW	14130 AAW	GABLS	10//99-12//99
	Hawaii	S	6.63 MW	6.97 AW	14500 AAW	HIBLS	10//99-12//99
	Idaho	S	6.32 MW	6.50 AW	13520 AAW	IDBLS	10//99-12//99
	Boise City MSA, ID	S	6.24 MW	6.32 AW	12980 AAW	IDBLS	10//99-12//99
	Illinois	S	7.71 MW	8.75 AW	18210 AAW	ILBLS	10//99-12//99
	Bloomington-Normal MSA, IL	S	7.93 MW	7.26 AW	16500 AAW	ILBLS	10//99-12//99
	Champaign-Urbana MSA, IL	S	9.12 MW	7.32 AW	18970 AAW	ILBLS	10//99-12//99
	Chicago PMSA, IL	S	9.11 MW	8.02 AW	18940 AAW	ILBLS	10//99-12//99
	Decatur MSA, IL	S	8.68 MW	7.80 AW	18060 AAW	ILBLS	10//99-12//99
	Kankakee PMSA, IL	S	8.14 MW	7.43 AW	16940 AAW	ILBLS	10//99-12//99
	Peoria-Pekin MSA, IL	S	8.01 MW	7.42 AW	16660 AAW	ILBLS	10//99-12//99
	Rockford MSA, IL	S	7.62 MW	6.64 AW	15840 AAW	ILBLS	10//99-12//99
	Springfield MSA, IL	S	8.77 MW	7.86 AW	18250 AAW	ILBLS	10//99-12//99
	Indiana	S	6.89 MW	7.11 AW	14780 AAW	INBLS	10//99-12//99
	Bloomington MSA, IN	S	6.53 MW	6.33 AW	13580 AAW	INBLS	10//99-12//99
	Elkhart-Goshen MSA, IN	S	6.76 MW	6.40 AW	14060 AAW	INBLS	10//99-12//99
	Evansville-Henderson MSA, IN-KY	S	6.42 MW	6.21 AW	13350 AAW	INBLS	10//99-12//99
	Fort Wayne MSA, IN	S	7.21 MW	7.19 AW	15000 AAW	INBLS	10//99-12//99
	Gary PMSA, IN	S	6.79 MW	6.27 AW	14120 AAW	INBLS	10//99-12//99
	Indianapolis MSA, IN	S	7.52 MW	7.48 AW	15650 AAW	INBLS	10//99-12//99
	Kokomo MSA, IN	S	6.77 MW	6.34 AW	14080 AAW	INBLS	10//99-12//99
	Lafayette MSA, IN	S	6.90 MW	6.33 AW	14350 AAW	INBLS	10//99-12//99
	South Bend MSA, IN	S	7.90 MW	7.84 AW	16430 AAW	INBLS	10//99-12//99
	Terre Haute MSA, IN	S	6.91 MW	6.63 AW	14380 AAW	INBLS	10//99-12//99
	Iowa	S	6.45 MW	6.78 AW	14100 AAW	IABLS	10//99-12//99
	Cedar Rapids MSA, IA	S	7.13 MW	7.29 AW	14830 AAW	IABLS	10//99-12//99
	Davenport-Moline-Rock Island MSA, IA-IL	S	8.07 MW	7.07 AW	16790 AAW	IABLS	10//99-12//99
	Des Moines MSA, IA	S	7.54 MW	7.47 AW	15670 AAW	IABLS	10//99-12//99
	Dubuque MSA, IA	S	7.58 MW	7.54 AW	15760 AAW	IABLS	10//99-12//99
	Iowa City MSA, IA	S	6.86 MW	6.67 AW	14270 AAW	IABLS	10//99-12//99
	Sioux City MSA, IA-NE	S	6.87 MW	6.58 AW	14290 AAW	IABLS	10//99-12//99
	Waterloo-Cedar Falls MSA, IA	S	6.08 MW	5.87 AW	12640 AAW	IABLS	10//99-12//99
	Kansas	S	6.74 MW	6.88 AW	14310 AAW	KSBLS	10//99-12//99
	Lawrence MSA, KS	S	6.74 MW	6.77 AW	14030 AAW	KSBLS	10//99-12//99
	Topeka MSA, KS	S	6.60 MW	6.44 AW	13730 AAW	KSBLS	10//99-12//99

AAW Average annual wage	AOH Average offered, high	ASH Average starting, high	H Hourly	M Monthly	S Special: hourly and annual
AE Average entry wage	AOL Average offered, low	ASL Average starting, low	HI Highest wage paid	MTC Median total compensation	TQ Third quartile wage
AEX Average experienced wage	APH Average pay, high range	AW Average wage paid	HR High end range	MW Median wage paid	W Weekly
AO Average offered	APL Average pay, low range	FQ First quartile wage	LR Low end range	SQ Second quartile wage	Y Yearly

Occupation/Type/Industry	Location	Per	Low	Mid	High	Source	Date
Child Care Worker	Wichita MSA, KS	S	6.92 MW	6.83 AW	14390 AAW	KSBLS	10//99-12//99
	Kentucky	S	6.29 MW	6.49 AW	13490 AAW	KYBLS	10//99-12//99
	Lexington MSA, KY	S	6.56 MW	6.33 AW	13640 AAW	KYBLS	10//99-12//99
	Louisville MSA, KY-IN	S	6.63 MW	6.51 AW	13780 AAW	KYBLS	10//99-12//99
	Owensboro MSA, KY	S	6.46 MW	6.35 AW	13440 AAW	KYBLS	10//99-12//99
	Louisiana	S	6.08 MW	6.38 AW	13280 AAW	LABLS	10//99-12//99
	Baton Rouge MSA, LA	S	6.20 MW	6.02 AW	12900 AAW	LABLS	10//99-12//99
	Houma MSA, LA	S	6.09 MW	5.91 AW	12670 AAW	LABLS	10//99-12//99
	Lafayette MSA, LA	S	6.41 MW	6.30 AW	13320 AAW	LABLS	10//99-12//99
	Lake Charles MSA, LA	S	6.58 MW	6.31 AW	13690 AAW	LABLS	10//99-12//99
	Monroe MSA, LA	S	6.85 MW	6.29 AW	14240 AAW	LABLS	10//99-12//99
	New Orleans MSA, LA	S	6.26 MW	6.01 AW	13010 AAW	LABLS	10//99-12//99
	Shreveport-Bossier City MSA, LA	S	6.73 MW	6.35 AW	14000 AAW	LABLS	10//99-12//99
	Maine	S	7.49 MW	7.80 AW	16230 AAW	MEBLS	10//99-12//99
	Bangor MSA, ME	S	6.82 MW	6.73 AW	14190 AAW	MEBLS	10//99-12//99
	Portland MSA, ME	S	8.08 MW	7.84 AW	16800 AAW	MEBLS	10//99-12//99
	Maryland	S	7.78 MW	7.97 AW	16570 AAW	MDBLS	10//99-12//99
	Baltimore PMSA, MD	S	8.12 MW	8.06 AW	16890 AAW	MDBLS	10//99-12//99
	Hagerstown PMSA, MD	S	7.34 MW	7.28 AW	15270 AAW	MDBLS	10//99-12//99
	Massachusetts	S	8.93 MW	8.96 AW	18640 AAW	MABLS	10//99-12//99
	Boston PMSA, MA-NH	S	9.36 MW	9.32 AW	19480 AAW	MABLS	10//99-12//99
	Brockton PMSA, MA	S	9.17 MW	8.84 AW	19080 AAW	MABLS	10//99-12//99
	Fitchburg-Leominster PMSA, MA	S	7.86 MW	7.23 AW	16340 AAW	MABLS	10//99-12//99
	Lawrence PMSA, MA-NH	S	8.64 MW	8.38 AW	17980 AAW	MABLS	10//99-12//99
	Lowell PMSA, MA-NH	S	8.17 MW	8.12 AW	17000 AAW	MABLS	10//99-12//99
	New Bedford PMSA, MA	S	8.57 MW	8.23 AW	17830 AAW	MABLS	10//99-12//99
	Springfield MSA, MA	S	8.08 MW	7.94 AW	16800 AAW	MABLS	10//99-12//99
	Worcester PMSA, MA-CT	S	7.72 MW	7.52 AW	16050 AAW	MABLS	10//99-12//99
	Michigan	S	7.4 MW	7.74 AW	16090 AAW	MIBLS	10//99-12//99
	Ann Arbor PMSA, MI	S	7.31 MW	7.26 AW	15200 AAW	MIBLS	10//99-12//99
	Benton Harbor MSA, MI	S	6.55 MW	6.16 AW	13630 AAW	MIBLS	10//99-12//99
	Detroit PMSA, MI	S	8.17 MW	7.85 AW	17000 AAW	MIBLS	10//99-12//99
	Flint PMSA, MI	S	6.50 MW	6.07 AW	13530 AAW	MIBLS	10//99-12//99
	Grand Rapids-Muskegon-Holland MSA, MI	S	8.25 MW	7.57 AW	17160 AAW	MIBLS	10//99-12//99
	Jackson MSA, MI	S	6.29 MW	6.19 AW	13080 AAW	MIBLS	10//99-12//99
	Kalamazoo-Battle Creek MSA, MI	S	7.28 MW	6.82 AW	15150 AAW	MIBLS	10//99-12//99
	Lansing-East Lansing MSA, MI	S	7.09 MW	6.63 AW	14740 AAW	MIBLS	10//99-12//99
	Saginaw-Bay City-Midland MSA, MI	S	6.99 MW	6.42 AW	14530 AAW	MIBLS	10//99-12//99
	Minnesota	S	7.38 MW	7.58 AW	15770 AAW	MNBLS	10//99-12//99
	Duluth-Superior MSA, MN-WI	S	6.23 MW	6.00 AW	12970 AAW	MNBLS	10//99-12//99
	Minneapolis-St. Paul MSA, MN-WI	S	7.59 MW	7.41 AW	15790 AAW	MNBLS	10//99-12//99
	Rochester MSA, MN	S	7.69 MW	7.55 AW	16000 AAW	MNBLS	10//99-12//99
	St. Cloud MSA, MN	S	7.16 MW	6.85 AW	14890 AAW	MNBLS	10//99-12//99
	Mississippi	S	5.94 MW	6.19 AW	12870 AAW	MSBLS	10//99-12//99
	Biloxi-Gulfport-Pascagoula MSA, MS	S	7.48 MW	6.28 AW	15570 AAW	MSBLS	10//99-12//99
	Hattiesburg MSA, MS	S	6.12 MW	5.94 AW	12720 AAW	MSBLS	10//99-12//99
	Jackson MSA, MS	S	5.93 MW	5.94 AW	12340 AAW	MSBLS	10//99-12//99
	Missouri	S	6.61 MW	7.02 AW	14610 AAW	MOBLS	10//99-12//99
	Joplin MSA, MO	S	6.28 MW	6.06 AW	13050 AAW	MOBLS	10//99-12//99
	Kansas City MSA, MO-KS	S	7.01 MW	6.63 AW	14580 AAW	MOBLS	10//99-12//99
	St. Louis MSA, MO-IL	S	7.85 MW	7.40 AW	16320 AAW	MOBLS	10//99-12//99
	Montana	S	6.16 MW	6.34 AW	13180 AAW	MTBLS	10//99-12//99
	Billings MSA, MT	S	6.00 MW	5.96 AW	12480 AAW	MTBLS	10//99-12//99
	Great Falls MSA, MT	S	6.44 MW	6.29 AW	13390 AAW	MTBLS	10//99-12//99
	Missoula MSA, MT	S	6.60 MW	6.31 AW	13730 AAW	MTBLS	10//99-12//99
	Nebraska	S	6.41 MW	6.67 AW	13880 AAW	NEBLS	10//99-12//99
	Lincoln MSA, NE	S	7.24 MW	6.84 AW	15050 AAW	NEBLS	10//99-12//99
	Omaha MSA, NE-IA	S	6.93 MW	6.85 AW	14420 AAW	NEBLS	10//99-12//99
	Nevada	S	6.7 MW	7.07 AW	14710 AAW	NVBLS	10//99-12//99
	Las Vegas MSA, NV-AZ	S	7.06 MW	6.70 AW	14680 AAW	NVBLS	10//99-12//99
	Reno MSA, NV	S	7.48 MW	7.05 AW	15560 AAW	NVBLS	10//99-12//99
	New Hampshire	S	7.55 MW	7.64 AW	15900 AAW	NHBLS	10//99-12//99
	Manchester PMSA, NH	S	7.67 MW	7.62 AW	15960 AAW	NHBLS	10//99-12//99
	Nashua PMSA, NH	S	7.52 MW	7.35 AW	15650 AAW	NHBLS	10//99-12//99

AAW Average annual wage	AOH Average offered, high	ASH Average starting, high	H Hourly	M Monthly	S Special: hourly and annual
AE Average entry wage	AOL Average offered, low	ASL Average starting, low	HI Highest wage paid	MTC Median total compensation	TQ Third quartile wage
AEX Average experienced wage	APH Average pay, high range	AW Average wage paid	HR High end range	MW Median wage paid	W Weekly
AO Average offered	APL Average pay, low range	FQ First quartile wage	LR Low end range	SQ Second quartile wage	Y Yearly

Child Care Worker

Occupation/Type/Industry	Location	Per	Low	Mid	High	Source	Date
Child Care Worker	Portsmouth-Rochester PMSA, NH-ME	S	7.67 MW	7.46 AW	15940 AAW	NHBLS	10//99-12//99
	New Jersey	S	7.47 MW	7.84 AW	16320 AAW	NJBLS	10//99-12//99
	Atlantic-Cape May PMSA, NJ	S	8.60 MW	8.20 AW	17900 AAW	NJBLS	10//99-12//99
	Bergen-Passaic PMSA, NJ	S	8.27 MW	7.83 AW	17200 AAW	NJBLS	10//99-12//99
	Jersey City PMSA, NJ	S	7.04 MW	6.59 AW	14650 AAW	NJBLS	10//99-12//99
	Middlesex-Somerset-Hunterdon PMSA, NJ	S	7.57 MW	7.29 AW	15750 AAW	NJBLS	10//99-12//99
	Monmouth-Ocean PMSA, NJ	S	7.85 MW	7.53 AW	16320 AAW	NJBLS	10//99-12//99
	Newark PMSA, NJ	S	8.19 MW	7.83 AW	17030 AAW	NJBLS	10//99-12//99
	Trenton PMSA, NJ	S	8.12 MW	7.90 AW	16890 AAW	NJBLS	10//99-12//99
	Vineland-Millville-Bridgeton PMSA, NJ	S	7.90 MW	7.26 AW	16440 AAW	NJBLS	10//99-12//99
	New Mexico	S	6.24 MW	6.60 AW	13730 AAW	NMBLS	10//99-12//99
	Albuquerque MSA, NM	S	6.48 MW	6.15 AW	13470 AAW	NMBLS	10//99-12//99
	Santa Fe MSA, NM	S	7.65 MW	6.55 AW	15910 AAW	NMBLS	10//99-12//99
	New York	S	7.97 MW	8.37 AW	17400 AAW	NYBLS	10//99-12//99
	Albany-Schenectady-Troy MSA, NY	S	8.68 MW	8.29 AW	18050 AAW	NYBLS	10//99-12//99
	Binghamton MSA, NY	S	6.86 MW	6.45 AW	14260 AAW	NYBLS	10//99-12//99
	Buffalo-Niagara Falls MSA, NY	S	7.19 MW	6.47 AW	14960 AAW	NYBLS	10//99-12//99
	Dutchess County PMSA, NY	S	7.58 MW	7.02 AW	15770 AAW	NYBLS	10//99-12//99
	Elmira MSA, NY	S	6.66 MW	6.54 AW	13850 AAW	NYBLS	10//99-12//99
	Glens Falls MSA, NY	S	7.02 MW	6.47 AW	14600 AAW	NYBLS	10//99-12//99
	Jamestown MSA, NY	S	7.15 MW	6.90 AW	14870 AAW	NYBLS	10//99-12//99
	Nassau-Suffolk PMSA, NY	S	8.84 MW	8.71 AW	18380 AAW	NYBLS	10//99-12//99
	New York PMSA, NY	S	9.65 MW	9.66 AW	20070 AAW	NYBLS	10//99-12//99
	Newburgh PMSA, NY-PA	S	8.53 MW	8.19 AW	17740 AAW	NYBLS	10//99-12//99
	Rochester MSA, NY	S	6.62 MW	6.26 AW	13760 AAW	NYBLS	10//99-12//99
	Syracuse MSA, NY	S	7.03 MW	6.56 AW	14630 AAW	NYBLS	10//99-12//99
	Utica-Rome MSA, NY	S	7.88 MW	6.67 AW	16380 AAW	NYBLS	10//99-12//99
	North Carolina	S	6.63 MW	6.95 AW	14460 AAW	NCBLS	10//99-12//99
	Asheville MSA, NC	S	7.36 MW	7.45 AW	15310 AAW	NCBLS	10//99-12//99
	Charlotte-Gastonia-Rock Hill MSA, NC-SC	S	7.28 MW	7.08 AW	15150 AAW	NCBLS	10//99-12//99
	Fayetteville MSA, NC	S	5.94 MW	6.02 AW	12350 AAW	NCBLS	10//99-12//99
	Goldsboro MSA, NC	S	6.76 MW	6.41 AW	14070 AAW	NCBLS	10//99-12//99
	Greensboro--Winston-Salem--High Point MSA, NC	S	7.11 MW	6.87 AW	14780 AAW	NCBLS	10//99-12//99
	Greenville MSA, NC	S	6.19 MW	6.06 AW	12880 AAW	NCBLS	10//99-12//99
	Hickory-Morganton-Lenoir MSA, NC	S	6.92 MW	6.66 AW	14400 AAW	NCBLS	10//99-12//99
	Jacksonville MSA, NC	S	6.28 MW	6.22 AW	13070 AAW	NCBLS	10//99-12//99
	Raleigh-Durham-Chapel Hill MSA, NC	S	7.87 MW	7.34 AW	16370 AAW	NCBLS	10//99-12//99
	Rocky Mount MSA, NC	S	6.31 MW	6.04 AW	13120 AAW	NCBLS	10//99-12//99
	Wilmington MSA, NC	S	6.28 MW	6.09 AW	13050 AAW	NCBLS	10//99-12//99
	North Dakota	S	6.23 MW	6.46 AW	13450 AAW	NDBLS	10//99-12//99
	Bismarck MSA, ND	S	5.82 MW	6.04 AW	12100 AAW	NDBLS	10//99-12//99
	Fargo-Moorhead MSA, ND-MN	S	6.50 MW	6.22 AW	13520 AAW	NDBLS	10//99-12//99
	Grand Forks MSA, ND-MN	S	7.34 MW	7.19 AW	15270 AAW	NDBLS	10//99-12//99
	Ohio	S	6.9 MW	7.39 AW	15370 AAW	OHBLS	10//99-12//99
	Akron PMSA, OH	S	6.96 MW	6.55 AW	14480 AAW	OHBLS	10//99-12//99
	Canton-Massillon MSA, OH	S	6.77 MW	6.28 AW	14070 AAW	OHBLS	10//99-12//99
	Cincinnati PMSA, OH-KY-IN	S	7.01 MW	6.73 AW	14570 AAW	OHBLS	10//99-12//99
	Cleveland-Lorain-Elyria PMSA, OH	S	7.21 MW	6.98 AW	14990 AAW	OHBLS	10//99-12//99
	Columbus MSA, OH	S	8.26 MW	8.31 AW	17180 AAW	OHBLS	10//99-12//99
	Dayton-Springfield MSA, OH	S	7.53 MW	7.33 AW	15660 AAW	OHBLS	10//99-12//99
	Hamilton-Middletown PMSA, OH	S	7.26 MW	7.23 AW	15090 AAW	OHBLS	10//99-12//99
	Mansfield MSA, OH	S	6.11 MW	6.19 AW	12720 AAW	OHBLS	10//99-12//99
	Steubenville-Weirton MSA, OH-WV	S	6.21 MW	6.03 AW	12920 AAW	OHBLS	10//99-12//99
	Toledo MSA, OH	S	7.86 MW	7.16 AW	16340 AAW	OHBLS	10//99-12//99
	Youngstown-Warren MSA, OH	S	7.24 MW	6.68 AW	15050 AAW	OHBLS	10//99-12//99
	Oklahoma	S	6.39 MW	6.58 AW	13690 AAW	OKBLS	10//99-12//99
	Enid MSA, OK	S	6.83 MW	6.54 AW	14200 AAW	OKBLS	10//99-12//99
	Lawton MSA, OK	S	6.22 MW	6.25 AW	12940 AAW	OKBLS	10//99-12//99
	Oklahoma City MSA, OK	S	6.43 MW	6.35 AW	13370 AAW	OKBLS	10//99-12//99

AAW	Average annual wage	AOH	Average offered, high	ASH	Average starting, high
AE	Average entry wage	AOL	Average offered, low	ASL	Average starting, low
AEX	Average experienced wage	APH	Average pay, high range	AW	Average wage paid
AO	Average offered	APL	Average pay, low range	FQ	First quartile wage

H	Hourly
HI	Highest wage paid
HR	High end range
LR	Low end range

M	Monthly
MTC	Median total compensation
MW	Median wage paid
SQ	Second quartile wage

S	Special: hourly and annual
TQ	Third quartile wage
W	Weekly
Y	Yearly

Occupation/Type/Industry	Location	Per	Low	Mid	High	Source	Date
Child Care Worker	Tulsa MSA, OK	S	7.25 MW	7.08 AW	15080 AAW	OKBLS	10//99-12//99
	Oregon	S	6.94 MW	7.44 AW	15470 AAW	ORBLS	10//99-12//99
	Eugene-Springfield MSA, OR	S	7.42 MW	7.10 AW	15430 AAW	ORBLS	10//99-12//99
	Portland-Vancouver PMSA, OR-WA	S	7.55 MW	7.09 AW	15690 AAW	ORBLS	10//99-12//99
	Salem PMSA, OR	S	7.33 MW	6.86 AW	15250 AAW	ORBLS	10//99-12//99
	Pennsylvania	S	6.96 MW	7.55 AW	15710 AAW	PABLS	10//99-12//99
	Allentown-Bethlehem-Easton MSA, PA	S	7.04 MW	6.61 AW	14640 AAW	PABLS	10//99-12//99
	Altoona MSA, PA	S	6.61 MW	6.48 AW	13760 AAW	PABLS	10//99-12//99
	Erie MSA, PA	S	6.32 MW	6.02 AW	13140 AAW	PABLS	10//99-12//99
	Harrisburg-Lebanon-Carlisle MSA, PA	S	7.28 MW	6.77 AW	15130 AAW	PABLS	10//99-12//99
	Johnstown MSA, PA	S	6.04 MW	5.97 AW	12570 AAW	PABLS	10//99-12//99
	Lancaster MSA, PA	S	7.11 MW	6.83 AW	14790 AAW	PABLS	10//99-12//99
	Philadelphia PMSA, PA-NJ	S	8.00 MW	7.66 AW	16630 AAW	PABLS	10//99-12//99
	Pittsburgh MSA, PA	S	7.07 MW	6.66 AW	14720 AAW	PABLS	10//99-12//99
	Reading MSA, PA	S	7.70 MW	7.51 AW	16010 AAW	PABLS	10//99-12//99
	Scranton--Wilkes-Barre--Hazleton MSA, PA	S	6.79 MW	6.44 AW	14120 AAW	PABLS	10//99-12//99
	State College MSA, PA	S	6.74 MW	6.55 AW	14020 AAW	PABLS	10//99-12//99
	Williamsport MSA, PA	S	6.56 MW	6.04 AW	13650 AAW	PABLS	10//99-12//99
	York MSA, PA	S	6.54 MW	6.22 AW	13590 AAW	PABLS	10//99-12//99
	Rhode Island	S	7.49 MW	8.09 AW	16820 AAW	RIBLS	10//99-12//99
	Providence-Fall River-Warwick MSA, RI-MA	S	8.19 MW	7.71 AW	17040 AAW	RIBLS	10//99-12//99
	South Carolina	S	6.22 MW	6.47 AW	13460 AAW	SCBLS	10//99-12//99
	Charleston-North Charleston MSA, SC	S	6.09 MW	5.99 AW	12660 AAW	SCBLS	10//99-12//99
	Columbia MSA, SC	S	6.69 MW	6.47 AW	13910 AAW	SCBLS	10//99-12//99
	Florence MSA, SC	S	6.56 MW	6.32 AW	13640 AAW	SCBLS	10//99-12//99
	Greenville-Spartanburg-Anderson MSA, SC	S	6.68 MW	6.50 AW	13890 AAW	SCBLS	10//99-12//99
	Myrtle Beach MSA, SC	S	6.09 MW	6.01 AW	12670 AAW	SCBLS	10//99-12//99
	Sumter MSA, SC	S	6.98 MW	6.20 AW	14510 AAW	SCBLS	10//99-12//99
	South Dakota	S	6.84 MW	6.96 AW	14480 AAW	SDBLS	10//99-12//99
	Rapid City MSA, SD	S	7.01 MW	6.94 AW	14590 AAW	SDBLS	10//99-12//99
	Sioux Falls MSA, SD	S	7.36 MW	7.34 AW	15320 AAW	SDBLS	10//99-12//99
	Tennessee	S	6.24 MW	6.45 AW	13410 AAW	TNBLS	10//99-12//99
	Chattanooga MSA, TN-GA	S	6.36 MW	6.23 AW	13240 AAW	TNBLS	10//99-12//99
	Clarksville-Hopkinsville MSA, TN-KY	S	6.38 MW	6.06 AW	13270 AAW	TNBLS	10//99-12//99
	Jackson MSA, TN	S	6.57 MW	6.41 AW	13660 AAW	TNBLS	10//99-12//99
	Johnson City-Kingsport-Bristol MSA, TN-VA	S	6.20 MW	6.00 AW	12890 AAW	TNBLS	10//99-12//99
	Knoxville MSA, TN	S	6.32 MW	6.02 AW	13140 AAW	TNBLS	10//99-12//99
	Memphis MSA, TN-AR-MS	S	6.41 MW	6.29 AW	13340 AAW	MSBLS	10//99-12//99
	Nashville MSA, TN	S	6.43 MW	6.37 AW	13380 AAW	TNBLS	10//99-12//99
	Texas	S	6.43 MW	6.64 AW	13820 AAW	TXBLS	10//99-12//99
	Abilene MSA, TX	S	6.02 MW	6.09 AW	12530 AAW	TXBLS	10//99-12//99
	Amarillo MSA, TX	S	6.83 MW	6.35 AW	14200 AAW	TXBLS	10//99-12//99
	Austin-San Marcos MSA, TX	S	7.22 MW	7.18 AW	15030 AAW	TXBLS	10//99-12//99
	Beaumont-Port Arthur MSA, TX	S	6.46 MW	6.22 AW	13440 AAW	TXBLS	10//99-12//99
	Brazoria PMSA, TX	S	6.36 MW	6.16 AW	13230 AAW	TXBLS	10//99-12//99
	Brownsville-Harlingen-San Benito MSA, TX	S	6.18 MW	6.12 AW	12860 AAW	TXBLS	10//99-12//99
	Bryan-College Station MSA, TX	S	6.26 MW	6.22 AW	13010 AAW	TXBLS	10//99-12//99
	Corpus Christi MSA, TX	S	6.40 MW	6.24 AW	13320 AAW	TXBLS	10//99-12//99
	Dallas PMSA, TX	S	6.86 MW	6.64 AW	14270 AAW	TXBLS	10//99-12//99
	El Paso MSA, TX	S	6.30 MW	6.21 AW	13110 AAW	TXBLS	10//99-12//99
	Fort Worth-Arlington PMSA, TX	S	6.63 MW	6.55 AW	13800 AAW	TXBLS	10//99-12//99
	Galveston-Texas City PMSA, TX	S	6.66 MW	6.26 AW	13840 AAW	TXBLS	10//99-12//99
	Houston PMSA, TX	S	6.48 MW	6.34 AW	13480 AAW	TXBLS	10//99-12//99
	Killeen-Temple MSA, TX	S	6.09 MW	6.18 AW	12670 AAW	TXBLS	10//99-12//99
	Laredo MSA, TX	S	6.15 MW	6.04 AW	12780 AAW	TXBLS	10//99-12//99
	Longview-Marshall MSA, TX	S	6.00 MW	6.11 AW	12470 AAW	TXBLS	10//99-12//99
	Lubbock MSA, TX	S	6.17 MW	6.22 AW	12830 AAW	TXBLS	10//99-12//99

Occupation/Type/Industry	Location	Per	Low	Mid	High	Source	Date
Child Care Worker	McAllen-Edinburg-Mission MSA, TX	S	5.90 MW	6.06 AW	12270 AAW	TXBLS	10//99-12//99
	Odessa-Midland MSA, TX	S	6.00 MW	6.09 AW	12490 AAW	TXBLS	10//99-12//99
	San Angelo MSA, TX	S	6.12 MW	6.00 AW	12740 AAW	TXBLS	10//99-12//99
	San Antonio MSA, TX	S	6.26 MW	6.26 AW	13010 AAW	TXBLS	10//99-12//99
	Sherman-Denison MSA, TX	S	6.10 MW	6.03 AW	12700 AAW	TXBLS	10//99-12//99
	Texarkana MSA, TX-Texarkana, AR	S	6.02 MW	6.01 AW	12510 AAW	TXBLS	10//99-12//99
	Tyler MSA, TX	S	6.30 MW	6.14 AW	13100 AAW	TXBLS	10//99-12//99
	Victoria MSA, TX	S	7.07 MW	7.26 AW	14700 AAW	TXBLS	10//99-12//99
	Waco MSA, TX	S	6.71 MW	6.14 AW	13970 AAW	TXBLS	10//99-12//99
	Wichita Falls MSA, TX	S	6.44 MW	6.17 AW	13400 AAW	TXBLS	10//99-12//99
	Utah	S	7.06 MW	7.17 AW	14910 AAW	UTBLS	10//99-12//99
	Provo-Orem MSA, UT	S	6.55 MW	6.47 AW	13620 AAW	UTBLS	10//99-12//99
	Salt Lake City-Ogden MSA, UT	S	7.16 MW	7.11 AW	14890 AAW	UTBLS	10//99-12//99
	Vermont	S	7.12 MW	7.53 AW	15670 AAW	VTBLS	10//99-12//99
	Burlington MSA, VT	S	7.34 MW	6.88 AW	15260 AAW	VTBLS	10//99-12//99
	Virginia	S	6.49 MW	7.04 AW	14640 AAW	VABLS	10//99-12//99
	Charlottesville MSA, VA	S	6.45 MW	6.41 AW	13420 AAW	VABLS	10//99-12//99
	Lynchburg MSA, VA	S	6.54 MW	5.99 AW	13600 AAW	VABLS	10//99-12//99
	Norfolk-Virginia Beach-Newport News MSA, VA-NC	S	6.63 MW	6.29 AW	13800 AAW	VABLS	10//99-12//99
	Richmond-Petersburg MSA, VA	S	6.84 MW	6.72 AW	14240 AAW	VABLS	10//99-12//99
	Roanoke MSA, VA	S	6.26 MW	6.24 AW	13030 AAW	VABLS	10//99-12//99
	Washington	S	7.6 MW	7.86 AW	16350 AAW	WABLS	10//99-12//99
	Bellingham MSA, WA	S	7.50 MW	6.76 AW	15610 AAW	WABLS	10//99-12//99
	Bremerton PMSA, WA	S	7.29 MW	7.19 AW	15170 AAW	WABLS	10//99-12//99
	Olympia PMSA, WA	S	7.97 MW	7.56 AW	16590 AAW	WABLS	10//99-12//99
	Richland-Kennewick-Pasco MSA, WA	S	7.32 MW	6.70 AW	15230 AAW	WABLS	10//99-12//99
	Seattle-Bellevue-Everett PMSA, WA	S	8.03 MW	7.86 AW	16700 AAW	WABLS	10//99-12//99
	Spokane MSA, WA	S	7.05 MW	6.63 AW	14660 AAW	WABLS	10//99-12//99
	Tacoma PMSA, WA	S	7.78 MW	6.83 AW	16180 AAW	WABLS	10//99-12//99
	Yakima MSA, WA	S	7.37 MW	7.02 AW	15330 AAW	WABLS	10//99-12//99
	West Virginia	S	6.07 MW	6.44 AW	13400 AAW	WVBLS	10//99-12//99
	Charleston MSA, WV	S	6.77 MW	6.48 AW	14080 AAW	WVBLS	10//99-12//99
	Huntington-Ashland MSA, WV-KY-OH	S	7.05 MW	6.60 AW	14670 AAW	WVBLS	10//99-12//99
	Parkersburg-Marietta MSA, WV-OH	S	5.97 MW	5.90 AW	12410 AAW	WVBLS	10//99-12//99
	Wheeling MSA, WV-OH	S	6.16 MW	6.11 AW	12810 AAW	WVBLS	10//99-12//99
	Wisconsin	S	7.27 MW	7.35 AW	15290 AAW	WIBLS	10//99-12//99
	Appleton-Oshkosh-Neenah MSA, WI	S	7.25 MW	7.35 AW	15090 AAW	WIBLS	10//99-12//99
	Eau Claire MSA, WI	S	7.12 MW	6.84 AW	14810 AAW	WIBLS	10//99-12//99
	Green Bay MSA, WI	S	7.46 MW	7.57 AW	15510 AAW	WIBLS	10//99-12//99
	Janesville-Beloit MSA, WI	S	6.31 MW	6.04 AW	13130 AAW	WIBLS	10//99-12//99
	Kenosha PMSA, WI	S	7.28 MW	7.29 AW	15150 AAW	WIBLS	10//99-12//99
	La Crosse MSA, WI-MN	S	7.07 MW	6.89 AW	14710 AAW	WIBLS	10//99-12//99
	Madison MSA, WI	S	7.65 MW	7.57 AW	15910 AAW	WIBLS	10//99-12//99
	Milwaukee-Waukesha PMSA, WI	S	7.46 MW	7.39 AW	15510 AAW	WIBLS	10//99-12//99
	Racine PMSA, WI	S	7.82 MW	7.55 AW	16270 AAW	WIBLS	10//99-12//99
	Sheboygan MSA, WI	S	7.12 MW	7.23 AW	14800 AAW	WIBLS	10//99-12//99
	Wyoming	S	6.26 MW	6.35 AW	13200 AAW	WYBLS	10//99-12//99
	Cheyenne MSA, WY	S	6.32 MW	6.07 AW	13150 AAW	WYBLS	10//99-12//99
	Puerto Rico	S	6.09 MW	6.21 AW	12910 AAW	PRBLS	10//99-12//99
	Mayaguez MSA, PR	S	5.82 MW	5.92 AW	12110 AAW	PRBLS	10//99-12//99
	Ponce MSA, PR	S	6.87 MW	6.70 AW	14290 AAW	PRBLS	10//99-12//99
	San Juan-Bayamon PMSA, PR	S	6.31 MW	6.15 AW	13130 AAW	PRBLS	10//99-12//99
	Virgin Islands	S	6.19 MW	6.27 AW	13050 AAW	VIBLS	10//99-12//99
	Guam	S	7.03 MW	7.21 AW	15000 AAW	GUBLS	10//99-12//99
Child, Family, and School Social Worker	Alabama	S	13.14 MW	13.70 AW	28500 AAW	ALBLS	10//99-12//99
	Anniston MSA, AL	S	9.02 MW	8.75 AW	18760 AAW	ALBLS	10//99-12//99
	Auburn-Opelika MSA, AL	S	11.54 MW	10.80 AW	24010 AAW	ALBLS	10//99-12//99
	Birmingham MSA, AL	S	13.22 MW	12.90 AW	27500 AAW	ALBLS	10//99-12//99

AAW	Average annual wage	AOH	Average offered, high	ASH	Average starting, high	H	Hourly
AE	Average entry wage	AOL	Average offered, low	ASL	Average starting, low	HI	Highest wage paid
AEX	Average experienced wage	APH	Average pay, high range	AW	Average wage paid	HR	High end range
AO	Average offered	APL	Average pay, low range	FQ	First quartile wage	LR	Low end range

M	Monthly	S	Special: hourly and annual
MTC	Median total compensation	TQ	Third quartile wage
MW	Median wage paid	W	Weekly
SQ	Second quartile wage	Y	Yearly

Occupation/Type/Industry	Location	Per	Low	Mid	High	Source	Date
Child, Family, and School Social Worker							
	Dothan MSA, AL	S	13.23 MW	13.29 AW	27530 AAW	ALBLS	10//99-12//99
	Huntsville MSA, AL	S	18.64 MW	19.15 AW	38760 AAW	ALBLS	10//99-12//99
	Mobile MSA, AL	S	15.10 MW	15.05 AW	31410 AAW	ALBLS	10//99-12//99
	Montgomery MSA, AL	S	19.26 MW	19.72 AW	40060 AAW	ALBLS	10//99-12//99
	Alaska	S	15.44 MW	16.12 AW	33520 AAW	AKBLS	10//99-12//99
	Arizona	S	13.61 MW	14.93 AW	31060 AAW	AZBLS	10//99-12//99
	Phoenix-Mesa MSA, AZ	S	14.52 MW	13.30 AW	30190 AAW	AZBLS	10//99-12//99
	Tucson MSA, AZ	S	16.21 MW	15.49 AW	33710 AAW	AZBLS	10//99-12//99
	Arkansas	S	11.95 MW	12.45 AW	25890 AAW	ARBLS	10//99-12//99
	Fayetteville-Springdale-Rogers MSA, AR	S	9.90 MW	9.25 AW	20580 AAW	ARBLS	10//99-12//99
	Fort Smith MSA, AR-OK	S	11.19 MW	10.43 AW	23280 AAW	ARBLS	10//99-12//99
	Little Rock-North Little Rock MSA, AR	S	15.57 MW	15.04 AW	32380 AAW	ARBLS	10//99-12//99
	Pine Bluff MSA, AR	S	13.11 MW	11.68 AW	27280 AAW	ARBLS	10//99-12//99
	California	S	16.3 MW	16.22 AW	33740 AAW	CABLS	10//99-12//99
	Bakersfield MSA, CA	S	12.11 MW	10.97 AW	25180 AAW	CABLS	10//99-12//99
	Chico-Paradise MSA, CA	S	12.31 MW	12.09 AW	25610 AAW	CABLS	10//99-12//99
	Fresno MSA, CA	S	16.65 MW	17.69 AW	34630 AAW	CABLS	10//99-12//99
	Los Angeles-Long Beach PMSA, CA	S	17.74 MW	17.90 AW	36890 AAW	CABLS	10//99-12//99
	Modesto MSA, CA	S	14.29 MW	13.27 AW	29720 AAW	CABLS	10//99-12//99
	Oakland PMSA, CA	S	14.59 MW	14.66 AW	30350 AAW	CABLS	10//99-12//99
	Orange County PMSA, CA	S	15.87 MW	16.41 AW	33010 AAW	CABLS	10//99-12//99
	Redding MSA, CA	S	17.30 MW	17.45 AW	35990 AAW	CABLS	10//99-12//99
	Riverside-San Bernardino PMSA, CA	S	13.12 MW	9.98 AW	27300 AAW	CABLS	10//99-12//99
	Sacramento PMSA, CA	S	14.80 MW	14.54 AW	30790 AAW	CABLS	10//99-12//99
	Salinas MSA, CA	S	12.55 MW	12.34 AW	26100 AAW	CABLS	10//99-12//99
	San Diego MSA, CA	S	11.00 MW	10.92 AW	22870 AAW	CABLS	10//99-12//99
	San Francisco PMSA, CA	S	16.03 MW	13.11 AW	33350 AAW	CABLS	10//99-12//99
	San Jose PMSA, CA	S	12.04 MW	10.38 AW	25050 AAW	CABLS	10//99-12//99
	Santa Cruz-Watsonville PMSA, CA	S	15.47 MW	14.97 AW	32180 AAW	CABLS	10//99-12//99
	Santa Rosa PMSA, CA	S	15.38 MW	14.29 AW	31990 AAW	CABLS	10//99-12//99
	Stockton-Lodi MSA, CA	S	21.00 MW	21.81 AW	43690 AAW	CABLS	10//99-12//99
	Vallejo-Fairfield-Napa PMSA, CA	S	15.84 MW	15.08 AW	32940 AAW	CABLS	10//99-12//99
	Ventura PMSA, CA	S	17.66 MW	16.67 AW	36740 AAW	CABLS	10//99-12//99
	Visalia-Tulare-Porterville MSA, CA	S	12.36 MW	8.24 AW	25710 AAW	CABLS	10//99-12//99
	Yolo PMSA, CA	S	17.45 MW	16.73 AW	36290 AAW	CABLS	10//99-12//99
	Yuba City MSA, CA	S	25.03 MW	20.19 AW	52070 AAW	CABLS	10//99-12//99
	Colorado	S	15.98 MW	16.60 AW	34530 AAW	COBLS	10//99-12//99
	Colorado Springs MSA, CO	S	20.12 MW	16.89 AW	41850 AAW	COBLS	10//99-12//99
	Denver PMSA, CO	S	16.80 MW	16.65 AW	34940 AAW	COBLS	10//99-12//99
	Fort Collins-Loveland MSA, CO	S	15.10 MW	14.12 AW	31400 AAW	COBLS	10//99-12//99
	Connecticut	S	21.56 MW	21.29 AW	44280 AAW	CTBLS	10//99-12//99
	Bridgeport PMSA, CT	S	21.14 MW	20.74 AW	43980 AAW	CTBLS	10//99-12//99
	Hartford MSA, CT	S	21.28 MW	21.68 AW	44270 AAW	CTBLS	10//99-12//99
	New Haven-Meriden PMSA, CT	S	21.26 MW	21.14 AW	44220 AAW	CTBLS	10//99-12//99
	Stamford-Norwalk PMSA, CT	S	21.83 MW	21.30 AW	45410 AAW	CTBLS	10//99-12//99
	Waterbury PMSA, CT	S	18.88 MW	18.53 AW	39270 AAW	CTBLS	10//99-12//99
	District of Columbia	S	14.41 MW	16.07 AW	33420 AAW	DCBLS	10//99-12//99
	Washington PMSA, DC-MD-VA-WV	S	18.61 MW	18.17 AW	38710 AAW	DCBLS	10//99-12//99
	Florida	S	13.51 MW	14.15 AW	29440 AAW	FLBLS	10//99-12//99
	Daytona Beach MSA, FL	S	15.38 MW	13.09 AW	31980 AAW	FLBLS	10//99-12//99
	Fort Lauderdale PMSA, FL	S	14.01 MW	13.21 AW	29130 AAW	FLBLS	10//99-12//99
	Fort Myers-Cape Coral MSA, FL	S	12.34 MW	12.09 AW	25670 AAW	FLBLS	10//99-12//99
	Fort Pierce-Port St. Lucie MSA, FL	S	13.27 MW	12.41 AW	27590 AAW	FLBLS	10//99-12//99
	Gainesville MSA, FL	S	13.95 MW	14.04 AW	29020 AAW	FLBLS	10//99-12//99
	Jacksonville MSA, FL	S	14.49 MW	13.40 AW	30140 AAW	FLBLS	10//99-12//99
	Lakeland-Winter Haven MSA, FL	S	11.98 MW	11.63 AW	24920 AAW	FLBLS	10//99-12//99
	Melbourne-Titusville-Palm Bay MSA, FL	S	11.62 MW	11.88 AW	24160 AAW	FLBLS	10//99-12//99

AAW Average annual wage	**AOH** Average offered, high	**ASH** Average starting, high	**H** Hourly	**M** Monthly	**S** Special: hourly and annual
AE Average entry wage	**AOL** Average offered, low	**ASL** Average starting, low	**HI** Highest wage paid	**MTC** Median total compensation	**TQ** Third quartile wage
AEX Average experienced wage	**APH** Average pay, high range	**AW** Average wage paid	**HR** High end range	**MW** Median wage paid	**W** Weekly
AO Average offered	**APL** Average pay, low range	**FQ** First quartile wage	**LR** Low end range	**SQ** Second quartile wage	**Y** Yearly

Occupation/Type/Industry	Location	Per	Low	Mid	High	Source	Date
Child, Family, and School Social Worker	Naples MSA, FL	S	14.96 MW	14.44 AW	31120 AAW	FLBLS	10//99-12//99
	Orlando MSA, FL	S	15.26 MW	14.52 AW	31740 AAW	FLBLS	10//99-12//99
	Panama City MSA, FL	S	12.59 MW	12.45 AW	26190 AAW	FLBLS	10//99-12//99
	Pensacola MSA, FL	S	13.31 MW	13.05 AW	27690 AAW	FLBLS	10//99-12//99
	Sarasota-Bradenton MSA, FL	S	13.47 MW	14.17 AW	28020 AAW	FLBLS	10//99-12//99
	Tallahassee MSA, FL	S	14.14 MW	13.36 AW	29400 AAW	FLBLS	10//99-12//99
	Tampa-St. Petersburg-Clearwater MSA, FL	S	14.53 MW	14.33 AW	30220 AAW	FLBLS	10//99-12//99
	Georgia	S	13.34 MW	14.10 AW	29330 AAW	GABLS	10//99-12//99
	Albany MSA, GA	S	16.31 MW	16.67 AW	33920 AAW	GABLS	10//99-12//99
	Atlanta MSA, GA	S	13.40 MW	13.30 AW	27870 AAW	GABLS	10//99-12//99
	Augusta-Aiken MSA, GA-SC	S	12.13 MW	10.55 AW	25240 AAW	GABLS	10//99-12//99
	Macon MSA, GA	S	16.90 MW	16.99 AW	35160 AAW	GABLS	10//99-12//99
	Savannah MSA, GA	S	12.75 MW	12.41 AW	26520 AAW	GABLS	10//99-12//99
	Idaho	S	16.38 MW	16.50 AW	34310 AAW	IDBLS	10//99-12//99
	Boise City MSA, ID	S	18.29 MW	19.16 AW	38050 AAW	IDBLS	10//99-12//99
	Illinois	S	15.02 MW	15.57 AW	32390 AAW	ILBLS	10//99-12//99
	Bloomington-Normal MSA, IL	S	11.89 MW	11.17 AW	24740 AAW	ILBLS	10//99-12//99
	Chicago PMSA, IL	S	16.34 MW	15.40 AW	33980 AAW	ILBLS	10//99-12//99
	Decatur MSA, IL	S	13.40 MW	12.95 AW	27880 AAW	ILBLS	10//99-12//99
	Kankakee PMSA, IL	S	13.83 MW	13.89 AW	28770 AAW	ILBLS	10//99-12//99
	Peoria-Pekin MSA, IL	S	12.02 MW	11.19 AW	25000 AAW	ILBLS	10//99-12//99
	Rockford MSA, IL	S	14.11 MW	15.15 AW	29350 AAW	ILBLS	10//99-12//99
	Springfield MSA, IL	S	14.07 MW	14.62 AW	29270 AAW	ILBLS	10//99-12//99
	Indiana	S	12.92 MW	13.20 AW	27450 AAW	INBLS	10//99-12//99
	Evansville-Henderson MSA, IN-KY	S	11.79 MW	12.09 AW	24530 AAW	INBLS	10//99-12//99
	Fort Wayne MSA, IN	S	13.57 MW	12.55 AW	28220 AAW	INBLS	10//99-12//99
	Gary PMSA, IN	S	14.15 MW	13.98 AW	29430 AAW	INBLS	10//99-12//99
	Indianapolis MSA, IN	S	13.56 MW	13.52 AW	28190 AAW	INBLS	10//99-12//99
	Kokomo MSA, IN	S	10.10 MW	9.95 AW	21020 AAW	INBLS	10//99-12//99
	Lafayette MSA, IN	S	12.15 MW	12.13 AW	25280 AAW	INBLS	10//99-12//99
	South Bend MSA, IN	S	13.23 MW	13.03 AW	27510 AAW	INBLS	10//99-12//99
	Terre Haute MSA, IN	S	11.97 MW	11.14 AW	24890 AAW	INBLS	10//99-12//99
	Iowa	S	16.02 MW	15.95 AW	33170 AAW	IABLS	10//99-12//99
	Cedar Rapids MSA, IA	S	17.77 MW	17.92 AW	36970 AAW	IABLS	10//99-12//99
	Davenport-Moline-Rock Island MSA, IA-IL	S	14.50 MW	13.49 AW	30160 AAW	IABLS	10//99-12//99
	Des Moines MSA, IA	S	17.97 MW	18.32 AW	37370 AAW	IABLS	10//99-12//99
	Iowa City MSA, IA	S	15.28 MW	14.45 AW	31780 AAW	IABLS	10//99-12//99
	Sioux City MSA, IA-NE	S	14.82 MW	14.33 AW	30830 AAW	IABLS	10//99-12//99
	Waterloo-Cedar Falls MSA, IA	S	15.99 MW	17.13 AW	33270 AAW	IABLS	10//99-12//99
	Kansas	S	11.77 MW	12.77 AW	26550 AAW	KSBLS	10//99-12//99
	Lawrence MSA, KS	S	11.40 MW	11.49 AW	23710 AAW	KSBLS	10//99-12//99
	Topeka MSA, KS	S	13.54 MW	13.63 AW	28170 AAW	KSBLS	10//99-12//99
	Wichita MSA, KS	S	13.14 MW	12.72 AW	27330 AAW	KSBLS	10//99-12//99
	Lexington MSA, KY	S	13.42 MW	12.59 AW	27910 AAW	KYBLS	10//99-12//99
	Louisiana	S	13.32 MW	13.90 AW	28910 AAW	LABLS	10//99-12//99
	Baton Rouge MSA, LA	S	17.05 MW	16.32 AW	35470 AAW	LABLS	10//99-12//99
	Houma MSA, LA	S	14.24 MW	13.32 AW	29620 AAW	LABLS	10//99-12//99
	Lafayette MSA, LA	S	16.20 MW	15.69 AW	33690 AAW	LABLS	10//99-12//99
	Lake Charles MSA, LA	S	12.92 MW	12.52 AW	26860 AAW	LABLS	10//99-12//99
	Monroe MSA, LA	S	13.63 MW	13.15 AW	28350 AAW	LABLS	10//99-12//99
	New Orleans MSA, LA	S	13.64 MW	13.03 AW	28360 AAW	LABLS	10//99-12//99
	Shreveport-Bossier City MSA, LA	S	12.94 MW	11.45 AW	26910 AAW	LABLS	10//99-12//99
	Maine	S	13.04 MW	13.80 AW	28710 AAW	MEBLS	10//99-12//99
	Bangor MSA, ME	S	13.95 MW	13.74 AW	29010 AAW	MEBLS	10//99-12//99
	Lewiston-Auburn MSA, ME	S	15.86 MW	15.45 AW	32990 AAW	MEBLS	10//99-12//99
	Portland MSA, ME	S	13.91 MW	12.98 AW	28930 AAW	MEBLS	10//99-12//99
	Maryland	S	17.08 MW	17.20 AW	35770 AAW	MDBLS	10//99-12//99
	Baltimore PMSA, MD	S	16.93 MW	17.45 AW	35220 AAW	MDBLS	10//99-12//99
	Hagerstown PMSA, MD	S	14.51 MW	13.60 AW	30170 AAW	MDBLS	10//99-12//99
	Massachusetts	S	16.39 MW	17.06 AW	35490 AAW	MABLS	10//99-12//99
	Barnstable-Yarmouth MSA, MA	S	17.03 MW	15.84 AW	35420 AAW	MABLS	10//99-12//99
	Boston PMSA, MA-NH	S	16.97 MW	16.18 AW	35300 AAW	MABLS	10//99-12//99
	Lawrence PMSA, MA-NH	S	14.20 MW	13.20 AW	29550 AAW	MABLS	10//99-12//99
	Lowell PMSA, MA-NH	S	16.68 MW	15.94 AW	34690 AAW	MABLS	10//99-12//99
	New Bedford PMSA, MA	S	16.17 MW	15.36 AW	33630 AAW	MABLS	10//99-12//99
	Springfield MSA, MA	S	17.39 MW	17.21 AW	36160 AAW	MABLS	10//99-12//99

AAW	Average annual wage	AOH	Average offered, high	ASH	Average starting, high
AE	Average entry wage	AOL	Average offered, low	ASL	Average starting, low
AEX	Average experienced wage	APH	Average pay, high range	AW	Average wage paid
AO	Average offered	APL	Average pay, low range	FQ	First quartile wage

H	Hourly
HI	Highest wage paid
HR	High end range
LR	Low end range

M	Monthly	S	Special: hourly and annual
MTC	Median total compensation	TQ	Third quartile wage
MW	Median wage paid	W	Weekly
SQ	Second quartile wage	Y	Yearly

Occupation/Type/Industry	Location	Per	Low	Mid	High	Source	Date
Child, Family, and School Social Worker							
	Michigan	S	18.09 MW	18.06 AW	37560 AAW	MIBLS	10//99-12//99
	Ann Arbor PMSA, MI	S	19.62 MW	18.80 AW	40810 AAW	MIBLS	10//99-12//99
	Detroit PMSA, MI	S	18.23 MW	17.90 AW	37930 AAW	MIBLS	10//99-12//99
	Grand Rapids-Muskegon-Holland MSA, MI	S	16.82 MW	17.26 AW	34990 AAW	MIBLS	10//99-12//99
	Kalamazoo-Battle Creek MSA, MI	S	17.50 MW	18.52 AW	36390 AAW	MIBLS	10//99-12//99
	Saginaw-Bay City-Midland MSA, MI	S	16.93 MW	17.65 AW	35210 AAW	MIBLS	10//99-12//99
	Minnesota	S	14.8 MW	16.40 AW	34100 AAW	MNBLS	10//99-12//99
	Duluth-Superior MSA, MN-WI	S	22.56 MW	23.33 AW	46920 AAW	MNBLS	10//99-12//99
	Minneapolis-St. Paul MSA, MN-WI	S	16.17 MW	13.44 AW	33640 AAW	MNBLS	10//99-12//99
	Rochester MSA, MN	S	19.08 MW	19.09 AW	39690 AAW	MNBLS	10//99-12//99
	St. Cloud MSA, MN	S	19.61 MW	20.77 AW	40800 AAW	MNBLS	10//99-12//99
	Mississippi	S	12.8 MW	13.12 AW	27290 AAW	MSBLS	10//99-12//99
	Biloxi-Gulfport-Pascagoula MSA, MS	S	12.20 MW	12.23 AW	25380 AAW	MSBLS	10//99-12//99
	Jackson MSA, MS	S	14.42 MW	13.61 AW	29980 AAW	MSBLS	10//99-12//99
	Kansas City MSA, MO-KS	S	11.27 MW	11.13 AW	23440 AAW	MOBLS	10//99-12//99
	St. Louis MSA, MO-IL	S	12.73 MW	12.89 AW	26490 AAW	MOBLS	10//99-12//99
	Springfield MSA, MO	S	17.82 MW	17.90 AW	37070 AAW	MOBLS	10//99-12//99
	Montana	S	10.62 MW	10.70 AW	22270 AAW	MTBLS	10//99-12//99
	Billings MSA, MT	S	10.36 MW	9.52 AW	21550 AAW	MTBLS	10//99-12//99
	Great Falls MSA, MT	S	9.73 MW	8.82 AW	20230 AAW	MTBLS	10//99-12//99
	Missoula MSA, MT	S	12.38 MW	12.20 AW	25750 AAW	MTBLS	10//99-12//99
	Nebraska	S	10.17 MW	11.44 AW	23790 AAW	NEBLS	10//99-12//99
	Lincoln MSA, NE	S	11.91 MW	10.15 AW	24770 AAW	NEBLS	10//99-12//99
	Omaha MSA, NE-IA	S	12.99 MW	12.36 AW	27020 AAW	NEBLS	10//99-12//99
	Nevada	S	17.04 MW	17.66 AW	36740 AAW	NVBLS	10//99-12//99
	Las Vegas MSA, NV-AZ	S	18.44 MW	17.99 AW	38350 AAW	NVBLS	10//99-12//99
	Reno MSA, NV	S	15.33 MW	14.78 AW	31890 AAW	NVBLS	10//99-12//99
	New Hampshire	S	12.72 MW	15.60 AW	32440 AAW	NHBLS	10//99-12//99
	Manchester PMSA, NH	S	13.63 MW	13.04 AW	28350 AAW	NHBLS	10//99-12//99
	Portsmouth-Rochester PMSA, NH-ME	S	11.39 MW	9.63 AW	23690 AAW	NHBLS	10//99-12//99
	New Jersey	S	19.26 MW	20.81 AW	43280 AAW	NJBLS	10//99-12//99
	Atlantic-Cape May PMSA, NJ	S	16.90 MW	15.45 AW	35160 AAW	NJBLS	10//99-12//99
	Bergen-Passaic PMSA, NJ	S	19.64 MW	19.54 AW	40860 AAW	NJBLS	10//99-12//99
	Jersey City PMSA, NJ	S	24.82 MW	21.97 AW	51620 AAW	NJBLS	10//99-12//99
	Middlesex-Somerset-Hunterdon PMSA, NJ	S	23.24 MW	22.55 AW	48330 AAW	NJBLS	10//99-12//99
	Monmouth-Ocean PMSA, NJ	S	21.30 MW	19.12 AW	44300 AAW	NJBLS	10//99-12//99
	Newark PMSA, NJ	S	20.56 MW	17.32 AW	42760 AAW	NJBLS	10//99-12//99
	Trenton PMSA, NJ	S	19.56 MW	18.55 AW	40680 AAW	NJBLS	10//99-12//99
	Vineland-Millville-Bridgeton PMSA, NJ	S	18.45 MW	16.99 AW	38370 AAW	NJBLS	10//99-12//99
	New Mexico	S	14.65 MW	14.80 AW	30780 AAW	NMBLS	10//99-12//99
	Albuquerque MSA, NM	S	16.29 MW	16.33 AW	33880 AAW	NMBLS	10//99-12//99
	Las Cruces MSA, NM	S	13.85 MW	13.56 AW	28810 AAW	NMBLS	10//99-12//99
	Santa Fe MSA, NM	S	14.13 MW	14.91 AW	29400 AAW	NMBLS	10//99-12//99
	New York	S	15.97 MW	16.75 AW	34850 AAW	NYBLS	10//99-12//99
	Albany-Schenectady-Troy MSA, NY	S	18.36 MW	17.35 AW	38200 AAW	NYBLS	10//99-12//99
	Binghamton MSA, NY	S	13.75 MW	12.37 AW	28600 AAW	NYBLS	10//99-12//99
	Buffalo-Niagara Falls MSA, NY	S	15.87 MW	14.04 AW	33010 AAW	NYBLS	10//99-12//99
	Dutchess County PMSA, NY	S	16.77 MW	16.48 AW	34880 AAW	NYBLS	10//99-12//99
	Elmira MSA, NY	S	15.82 MW	17.18 AW	32900 AAW	NYBLS	10//99-12//99
	Glens Falls MSA, NY	S	12.99 MW	13.12 AW	27010 AAW	NYBLS	10//99-12//99
	Jamestown MSA, NY	S	13.17 MW	12.83 AW	27390 AAW	NYBLS	10//99-12//99
	Nassau-Suffolk PMSA, NY	S	19.49 MW	18.87 AW	40540 AAW	NYBLS	10//99-12//99
	New York PMSA, NY	S	17.10 MW	16.20 AW	35580 AAW	NYBLS	10//99-12//99
	Newburgh PMSA, NY-PA	S	16.85 MW	13.32 AW	35050 AAW	NYBLS	10//99-12//99
	Rochester MSA, NY	S	15.65 MW	13.56 AW	32540 AAW	NYBLS	10//99-12//99
	Syracuse MSA, NY	S	15.69 MW	15.86 AW	32640 AAW	NYBLS	10//99-12//99
	Utica-Rome MSA, NY	S	9.82 MW	8.39 AW	20420 AAW	NYBLS	10//99-12//99
	North Carolina	S	14.65 MW	14.87 AW	30930 AAW	NCBLS	10//99-12//99
	Asheville MSA, NC	S	15.21 MW	15.20 AW	31630 AAW	NCBLS	10//99-12//99
	Charlotte-Gastonia-Rock Hill MSA, NC-SC	S	16.76 MW	16.08 AW	34870 AAW	NCBLS	10//99-12//99

AAW Average annual wage	AOH Average offered, high	ASH Average starting, high	H Hourly	M Monthly	S Special: hourly and annual
AE Average entry wage	AOL Average offered, low	ASL Average starting, low	HI Highest wage paid	MTC Median total compensation	TQ Third quartile wage
AEX Average experienced wage	APH Average pay, high range	AW Average wage paid	HR High end range	MW Median wage paid	W Weekly
AO Average offered	APL Average pay, low range	FQ First quartile wage	LR Low end range	SQ Second quartile wage	Y Yearly

Occupation/Type/Industry	Location	Per	Low	Mid	High	Source	Date
Child, Family, and School Social Worker							
	Fayetteville MSA, NC	S	16.70 MW	15.37 AW	34730 AAW	NCBLS	10//99-12//99
	Greensboro--Winston-Salem-- High Point MSA, NC	S	12.60 MW	12.54 AW	26210 AAW	NCBLS	10//99-12//99
	Hickory-Morganton-Lenoir MSA, NC	S	16.60 MW	16.24 AW	34530 AAW	NCBLS	10//99-12//99
	Raleigh-Durham-Chapel Hill MSA, NC	S	17.34 MW	16.55 AW	36070 AAW	NCBLS	10//99-12//99
	Rocky Mount MSA, NC	S	16.56 MW	16.29 AW	34430 AAW	NCBLS	10//99-12//99
	Wilmington MSA, NC	S	13.02 MW	12.84 AW	27070 AAW	NCBLS	10//99-12//99
	North Dakota	S	14.27 MW	14.21 AW	29560 AAW	NDBLS	10//99-12//99
	Fargo-Moorhead MSA, ND-MN	S	16.65 MW	17.13 AW	34640 AAW	NDBLS	10//99-12//99
	Grand Forks MSA, ND-MN	S	13.09 MW	12.42 AW	27230 AAW	NDBLS	10//99-12//99
	Ohio	S	13.51 MW	14.75 AW	30680 AAW	OHBLS	10//99-12//99
	Akron PMSA, OH	S	13.96 MW	12.66 AW	29050 AAW	OHBLS	10//99-12//99
	Canton-Massillon MSA, OH	S	13.91 MW	13.12 AW	28930 AAW	OHBLS	10//99-12//99
	Cincinnati PMSA, OH-KY-IN	S	13.34 MW	13.25 AW	27750 AAW	OHBLS	10//99-12//99
	Cleveland-Lorain-Elyria PMSA, OH	S	14.82 MW	13.46 AW	30830 AAW	OHBLS	10//99-12//99
	Columbus MSA, OH	S	17.03 MW	15.48 AW	35410 AAW	OHBLS	10//99-12//99
	Lima MSA, OH	S	13.09 MW	13.20 AW	27220 AAW	OHBLS	10//99-12//99
	Toledo MSA, OH	S	16.33 MW	15.87 AW	33960 AAW	OHBLS	10//99-12//99
	Youngstown-Warren MSA, OH	S	11.93 MW	11.09 AW	24820 AAW	OHBLS	10//99-12//99
	Oregon	S	15.68 MW	15.79 AW	32850 AAW	ORBLS	10//99-12//99
	Portland-Vancouver PMSA, OR-WA	S	14.90 MW	14.48 AW	30980 AAW	ORBLS	10//99-12//99
	Pennsylvania	S	12.54 MW	13.79 AW	28690 AAW	PABLS	10//99-12//99
	Allentown-Bethlehem-Easton MSA, PA	S	13.88 MW	12.35 AW	28860 AAW	PABLS	10//99-12//99
	Altoona MSA, PA	S	10.29 MW	9.17 AW	21400 AAW	PABLS	10//99-12//99
	Erie MSA, PA	S	11.69 MW	11.30 AW	24320 AAW	PABLS	10//99-12//99
	Harrisburg-Lebanon-Carlisle MSA, PA	S	12.81 MW	12.17 AW	26650 AAW	PABLS	10//99-12//99
	Johnstown MSA, PA	S	15.15 MW	14.22 AW	31510 AAW	PABLS	10//99-12//99
	Lancaster MSA, PA	S	16.31 MW	13.87 AW	33930 AAW	PABLS	10//99-12//99
	Philadelphia PMSA, PA-NJ	S	17.62 MW	15.86 AW	36650 AAW	PABLS	10//99-12//99
	Pittsburgh MSA, PA	S	11.78 MW	11.34 AW	24490 AAW	PABLS	10//99-12//99
	Reading MSA, PA	S	13.87 MW	13.70 AW	28850 AAW	PABLS	10//99-12//99
	Scranton--Wilkes-Barre-- Hazleton MSA, PA	S	18.08 MW	16.59 AW	37610 AAW	PABLS	10//99-12//99
	Sharon MSA, PA	S	11.24 MW	10.29 AW	23380 AAW	PABLS	10//99-12//99
	Williamsport MSA, PA	S	12.28 MW	12.19 AW	25530 AAW	PABLS	10//99-12//99
	York MSA, PA	S	12.33 MW	10.97 AW	25650 AAW	PABLS	10//99-12//99
	Rhode Island	S	20.05 MW	19.82 AW	41230 AAW	RIBLS	10//99-12//99
	Providence-Fall River- Warwick MSA, RI-MA	S	19.64 MW	19.41 AW	40860 AAW	RIBLS	10//99-12//99
	South Carolina	S	13.41 MW	13.96 AW	29030 AAW	SCBLS	10//99-12//99
	Charleston-North Charleston MSA, SC	S	13.91 MW	12.92 AW	28920 AAW	SCBLS	10//99-12//99
	Columbia MSA, SC	S	13.93 MW	13.04 AW	28980 AAW	SCBLS	10//99-12//99
	Florence MSA, SC	S	13.43 MW	12.94 AW	27940 AAW	SCBLS	10//99-12//99
	South Dakota	S	12.97 MW	13.09 AW	27230 AAW	SDBLS	10//99-12//99
	Rapid City MSA, SD	S	12.70 MW	12.22 AW	26420 AAW	SDBLS	10//99-12//99
	Sioux Falls MSA, SD	S	12.74 MW	12.71 AW	26500 AAW	SDBLS	10//99-12//99
	Tennessee	S	11.12 MW	12.06 AW	25080 AAW	TNBLS	10//99-12//99
	Chattanooga MSA, TN-GA	S	12.06 MW	11.93 AW	25090 AAW	TNBLS	10//99-12//99
	Johnson City-Kingsport-Bristol MSA, TN-VA	S	12.38 MW	11.92 AW	25750 AAW	TNBLS	10//99-12//99
	Knoxville MSA, TN	S	11.40 MW	10.77 AW	23710 AAW	TNBLS	10//99-12//99
	Memphis MSA, TN-AR-MS	S	11.73 MW	9.89 AW	24400 AAW	MSBLS	10//99-12//99
	Nashville MSA, TN	S	12.14 MW	11.54 AW	25260 AAW	TNBLS	10//99-12//99
	Texas	S	13.55 MW	13.85 AW	28810 AAW	TXBLS	10//99-12//99
	Abilene MSA, TX	S	10.69 MW	10.34 AW	22240 AAW	TXBLS	10//99-12//99
	Amarillo MSA, TX	S	13.06 MW	14.15 AW	27170 AAW	TXBLS	10//99-12//99
	Austin-San Marcos MSA, TX	S	14.11 MW	13.51 AW	29340 AAW	TXBLS	10//99-12//99
	Beaumont-Port Arthur MSA, TX	S	12.06 MW	12.01 AW	25080 AAW	TXBLS	10//99-12//99
	Brownsville-Harlingen-San Benito MSA, TX	S	12.11 MW	11.56 AW	25200 AAW	TXBLS	10//99-12//99
	Corpus Christi MSA, TX	S	9.75 MW	9.61 AW	20280 AAW	TXBLS	10//99-12//99
	Dallas PMSA, TX	S	14.64 MW	13.77 AW	30440 AAW	TXBLS	10//99-12//99

AAW	Average annual wage	AOH	Average offered, high	ASH	Average starting, high	H	Hourly	M	Monthly	S	Special: hourly and annual
AE	Average entry wage	AOL	Average offered, low	ASL	Average starting, low	HI	Highest wage paid	MTC	Median total compensation	TQ	Third quartile wage
AEX	Average experienced wage	APH	Average pay, high range	AW	Average wage paid	HR	High end range	MW	Median wage paid	W	Weekly
AO	Average offered	APL	Average pay, low range	FQ	First quartile wage	LR	Low end range	SQ	Second quartile wage	Y	Yearly

Occupation/Type/Industry	Location	Per	Low	Mid	High	Source	Date
Child, Family, and School Social Worker	Fort Worth-Arlington PMSA, TX	S	13.62 MW	13.27 AW	28330 AAW	TXBLS	10//99-12//99
	Houston PMSA, TX	S	14.09 MW	13.85 AW	29320 AAW	TXBLS	10//99-12//99
	Killeen-Temple MSA, TX	S	11.45 MW	10.31 AW	23810 AAW	TXBLS	10//99-12//99
	Longview-Marshall MSA, TX	S	8.30 MW	6.67 AW	17270 AAW	TXBLS	10//99-12//99
	Lubbock MSA, TX	S	12.86 MW	12.68 AW	26750 AAW	TXBLS	10//99-12//99
	McAllen-Edinburg-Mission MSA, TX	S	12.39 MW	12.65 AW	25760 AAW	TXBLS	10//99-12//99
	San Angelo MSA, TX	S	13.45 MW	13.75 AW	27980 AAW	TXBLS	10//99-12//99
	San Antonio MSA, TX	S	16.13 MW	14.90 AW	33540 AAW	TXBLS	10//99-12//99
	Sherman-Denison MSA, TX	S	11.22 MW	10.89 AW	23340 AAW	TXBLS	10//99-12//99
	Texarkana MSA, TX-Texarkana, AR	S	14.30 MW	13.39 AW	29750 AAW	TXBLS	10//99-12//99
	Tyler MSA, TX	S	13.86 MW	10.62 AW	28830 AAW	TXBLS	10//99-12//99
	Utah	S	13.15 MW	13.64 AW	28360 AAW	UTBLS	10//99-12//99
	Provo-Orem MSA, UT	S	15.90 MW	15.46 AW	33080 AAW	UTBLS	10//99-12//99
	Salt Lake City-Ogden MSA, UT	S	13.24 MW	13.05 AW	27550 AAW	UTBLS	10//99-12//99
	Vermont	S	10.51 MW	11.60 AW	24120 AAW	VTBLS	10//99-12//99
	Burlington MSA, VT	S	17.87 MW	18.43 AW	37170 AAW	VTBLS	10//99-12//99
	Virginia	S	15.91 MW	16.44 AW	34200 AAW	VABLS	10//99-12//99
	Charlottesville MSA, VA	S	16.23 MW	15.71 AW	33770 AAW	VABLS	10//99-12//99
	Danville MSA, VA	S	18.66 MW	18.28 AW	38820 AAW	VABLS	10//99-12//99
	Lynchburg MSA, VA	S	14.28 MW	13.22 AW	29700 AAW	VABLS	10//99-12//99
	Norfolk-Virginia Beach-Newport News MSA, VA-NC	S	17.08 MW	16.55 AW	35520 AAW	VABLS	10//99-12//99
	Richmond-Petersburg MSA, VA	S	15.16 MW	14.14 AW	31540 AAW	VABLS	10//99-12//99
	Roanoke MSA, VA	S	13.40 MW	12.91 AW	27880 AAW	VABLS	10//99-12//99
	Washington	S	13.06 MW	13.55 AW	28170 AAW	WABLS	10//99-12//99
	Bellingham MSA, WA	S	11.89 MW	11.07 AW	24730 AAW	WABLS	10//99-12//99
	Bremerton PMSA, WA	S	12.67 MW	13.82 AW	26350 AAW	WABLS	10//99-12//99
	Olympia PMSA, WA	S	12.09 MW	12.12 AW	25140 AAW	WABLS	10//99-12//99
	Richland-Kennewick-Pasco MSA, WA	S	13.29 MW	13.57 AW	27630 AAW	WABLS	10//99-12//99
	Seattle-Bellevue-Everett PMSA, WA	S	13.63 MW	13.20 AW	28350 AAW	WABLS	10//99-12//99
	Spokane MSA, WA	S	10.58 MW	9.93 AW	22010 AAW	WABLS	10//99-12//99
	Tacoma PMSA, WA	S	16.03 MW	14.77 AW	33350 AAW	WABLS	10//99-12//99
	Yakima MSA, WA	S	16.69 MW	15.96 AW	34720 AAW	WABLS	10//99-12//99
	West Virginia	S	11.11 MW	10.97 AW	22820 AAW	WVBLS	10//99-12//99
	Charleston MSA, WV	S	12.14 MW	11.62 AW	25260 AAW	WVBLS	10//99-12//99
	Huntington-Ashland MSA, WV-KY-OH	S	12.34 MW	11.94 AW	25660 AAW	WVBLS	10//99-12//99
	Parkersburg-Marietta MSA, WV-OH	S	10.53 MW	10.37 AW	21900 AAW	WVBLS	10//99-12//99
	Wheeling MSA, WV-OH	S	12.79 MW	12.21 AW	26600 AAW	WVBLS	10//99-12//99
	Wisconsin	S	13.83 MW	14.79 AW	30770 AAW	WIBLS	10//99-12//99
	Eau Claire MSA, WI	S	15.30 MW	15.37 AW	31820 AAW	WIBLS	10//99-12//99
	Green Bay MSA, WI	S	14.19 MW	13.31 AW	29510 AAW	WIBLS	10//99-12//99
	Janesville-Beloit MSA, WI	S	14.03 MW	12.22 AW	29190 AAW	WIBLS	10//99-12//99
	Kenosha PMSA, WI	S	13.01 MW	10.45 AW	27060 AAW	WIBLS	10//99-12//99
	La Crosse MSA, WI-MN	S	15.90 MW	15.93 AW	33080 AAW	WIBLS	10//99-12//99
	Madison MSA, WI	S	14.49 MW	12.68 AW	30130 AAW	WIBLS	10//99-12//99
	Milwaukee-Waukesha PMSA, WI	S	16.47 MW	14.48 AW	34260 AAW	WIBLS	10//99-12//99
	Wyoming	S	11 MW	11.99 AW	24940 AAW	WYBLS	10//99-12//99
	Puerto Rico	S	9.52 MW	10.09 AW	20980 AAW	PRBLS	10//99-12//99
	Caguas PMSA, PR	S	9.32 MW	9.52 AW	19390 AAW	PRBLS	10//99-12//99
	Ponce MSA, PR	S	9.08 MW	9.38 AW	18890 AAW	PRBLS	10//99-12//99
	San Juan-Bayamon PMSA, PR	S	10.10 MW	9.40 AW	21020 AAW	PRBLS	10//99-12//99
	Guam	S	6.61 MW	8.57 AW	17830 AAW	GUBLS	10//99-12//99
Chiropractor	California	S	24.8 MW	27.87 AW	57960 AAW	CABLS	10//99-12//99
	Los Angeles County, CA	Y		90370 AW		LABJ	1999
	Connecticut	S	31.48 MW	34.68 AW	72130 AAW	CTBLS	10//99-12//99
	Florida	S	28.54 MW	34.52 AW	71800 AAW	FLBLS	10//99-12//99
	Idaho	S	24.87 MW	25.97 AW	54020 AAW	IDBLS	10//99-12//99
	Illinois	S	45.09 MW	39.89 AW	82980 AAW	ILBLS	10//99-12//99
	Indiana	S	24.08 MW	23.61 AW	49100 AAW	INBLS	10//99-12//99

Occupation/Type/Industry	Location	Per	Low	Mid	High	Source	Date
Chiropractor	Kansas	S	39.81 MW	39.61 AW	82400 AAW	KSBLS	10//99-12//99
	Louisiana	S	36.26 MW	35.40 AW	73630 AAW	LABLS	10//99-12//99
	Minnesota	S	37.38 MW	37.86 AW	78750 AAW	MNBLS	10//99-12//99
	Nevada	S	46.69 MW	39.03 AW	81180 AAW	NVBLS	10//99-12//99
	New Jersey	S	63.1 MW	58.05 AW	120750 AAW	NJBLS	10//99-12//99
	North Carolina	S	43.32 MW	49.80 AW	103590 AAW	NCBLS	10//99-12//99
	Oregon	S	49.34 MW	47.05 AW	97860 AAW	ORBLS	10//99-12//99
	Pennsylvania	S	35.61 MW	34.82 AW	72430 AAW	PABLS	10//99-12//99
	South Carolina	S	10.12 MW	12.69 AW	26390 AAW	SCBLS	10//99-12//99
	Texas	S	21.66 MW	21.43 AW	44570 AAW	TXBLS	10//99-12//99
	Washington	S	24.85 MW	27.68 AW	57560 AAW	WABLS	10//99-12//99
	West Virginia	S	18.91 MW	21.22 AW	44140 AAW	WVBLS	10//99-12//99
	Wisconsin	S	30.21 MW	37.69 AW	78400 AAW	WIBLS	10//99-12//99
Choreographer	Alabama	S	15.03 MW	14.51 AW	30170 AAW	ALBLS	10//99-12//99
	Arizona	S	18.77 MW	18.50 AW	38470 AAW	AZBLS	10//99-12//99
	Arkansas	S	12.27 MW	13.63 AW	28360 AAW	ARBLS	10//99-12//99
	California	S	14.7 MW	18.72 AW	38930 AAW	CABLS	10//99-12//99
	Colorado	S	17.11 MW	17.01 AW	35380 AAW	COBLS	10//99-12//99
	Connecticut	S	15.51 MW	17.51 AW	36410 AAW	CTBLS	10//99-12//99
	Florida	S	12.19 MW	12.83 AW	26680 AAW	FLBLS	10//99-12//99
	Georgia	S	6.43 MW	10.82 AW	22510 AAW	GABLS	10//99-12//99
	Illinois	S	18.08 MW	16.38 AW	34070 AAW	ILBLS	10//99-12//99
	Indiana	S	12.67 MW	14.34 AW	29830 AAW	INBLS	10//99-12//99
	Kansas	S	13.59 MW	11.47 AW	23850 AAW	KSBLS	10//99-12//99
	Kentucky	S	10.02 MW	12.27 AW	25520 AAW	KYBLS	10//99-12//99
	Louisiana	S	10.17 MW	11.70 AW	24340 AAW	LABLS	10//99-12//99
	Maryland	S	15.96 MW	18.79 AW	39080 AAW	MDBLS	10//99-12//99
	Massachusetts	S	21.04 MW	20.60 AW	42850 AAW	MABLS	10//99-12//99
	Minnesota	S	14.61 MW	16.63 AW	34600 AAW	MNBLS	10//99-12//99
	Mississippi	S	8.48 MW	9.24 AW	19210 AAW	MSBLS	10//99-12//99
	Missouri	S	10.64 MW	13.52 AW	28120 AAW	MOBLS	10//99-12//99
	New Jersey	S	16.59 MW	16.88 AW	35100 AAW	NJBLS	10//99-12//99
	New Mexico	S	11.78 MW	12.43 AW	25850 AAW	NMBLS	10//99-12//99
	New York	S	12.41 MW	16.18 AW	33650 AAW	NYBLS	10//99-12//99
	North Carolina	S	10.91 MW	13.84 AW	28780 AAW	NCBLS	10//99-12//99
	Oklahoma	S	13.6 MW	13.01 AW	27070 AAW	OKBLS	10//99-12//99
	Pennsylvania	S	9.58 MW	13.49 AW	28060 AAW	PABLS	10//99-12//99
	South Carolina	S	11.79 MW	13.47 AW	28030 AAW	SCBLS	10//99-12//99
	Tennessee	S	36.38 MW	31.16 AW	64810 AAW	TNBLS	10//99-12//99
	Texas	S	9.86 MW	10.07 AW	20950 AAW	TXBLS	10//99-12//99
	Utah	S	12.91 MW	14.09 AW	29300 AAW	UTBLS	10//99-12//99
	Vermont	S	15.18 MW	15.37 AW	31980 AAW	VTBLS	10//99-12//99
	Virginia	S	17.12 MW	16.82 AW	34980 AAW	VABLS	10//99-12//99
	Washington	S	21.97 MW	30.33 AW	63080 AAW	WABLS	10//99-12//99
	West Virginia	S	11.13 MW	11.61 AW	24150 AAW	WVBLS	10//99-12//99
Circulation Director Magazine	United States	Y		75300 AW		FOLIO	2000
City Manager	Midwest	Y		64136 AW		PUBMAN	1998
	Mountain	Y		66187 AW		PUBMAN	1998
	Northeast	Y		61902 AW		PUBMAN	1998
	Southeast	Y		66882 AW		PUBMAN	1998
	West Coast	Y		91838 AW		PUBMAN	1998
Civil Engineer	Alabama	S	24.15 MW	24.94 AW	51870 AAW	ALBLS	10//99-12//99
	Anniston MSA, AL	S	21.23 MW	20.98 AW	44160 AAW	ALBLS	10//99-12//99
	Birmingham MSA, AL	S	24.83 MW	23.41 AW	51640 AAW	ALBLS	10//99-12//99
	Decatur MSA, AL	S	24.39 MW	24.13 AW	50740 AAW	ALBLS	10//99-12//99
	Huntsville MSA, AL	S	27.71 MW	29.72 AW	57640 AAW	ALBLS	10//99-12//99
	Mobile MSA, AL	S	26.06 MW	26.01 AW	54210 AAW	ALBLS	10//99-12//99
	Tuscaloosa MSA, AL	S	20.12 MW	18.88 AW	41840 AAW	ALBLS	10//99-12//99
	Alaska	S	27.21 MW	27.31 AW	56810 AAW	AKBLS	10//99-12//99
	Anchorage MSA, AK	S	27.64 MW	28.56 AW	57490 AAW	AKBLS	10//99-12//99
	Arizona	S	25.75 MW	26.99 AW	56130 AAW	AZBLS	10//99-12//99
	Flagstaff MSA, AZ-UT	S	22.93 MW	22.31 AW	47690 AAW	AZBLS	10//99-12//99
	Phoenix-Mesa MSA, AZ	S	28.09 MW	26.76 AW	58420 AAW	AZBLS	10//99-12//99
	Tucson MSA, AZ	S	23.47 MW	23.18 AW	48810 AAW	AZBLS	10//99-12//99
	Yuma MSA, AZ	S	24.95 MW	23.68 AW	51890 AAW	AZBLS	10//99-12//99
	Arkansas	S	24.71 MW	25.54 AW	53110 AAW	ARBLS	10//99-12//99
	Fayetteville-Springdale-Rogers MSA, AR	S	21.26 MW	19.32 AW	44210 AAW	ARBLS	10//99-12//99

AAW	Average annual wage	AOH	Average offered, high	ASH	Average starting, high	H	Hourly	M	Monthly	S	Special: hourly and annual
AE	Average entry wage	AOL	Average offered, low	ASL	Average starting, low	HI	Highest wage paid	MTC	Median total compensation	TQ	Third quartile wage
AEX	Average experienced wage	APH	Average pay, high range	AW	Average wage paid	HR	High end range	MW	Median wage paid	W	Weekly
AO	Average offered	APL	Average pay, low range	FQ	First quartile wage	LR	Low end range	SQ	Second quartile wage	Y	Yearly

Occupation/Type/Industry	Location	Per	Low	Mid	High	Source	Date
Civil Engineer	Fort Smith MSA, AR-OK	S	23.64 MW	23.71 AW	49160 AAW	ARBLS	10//99-12//99
	Little Rock-North Little Rock MSA, AR	S	26.08 MW	25.62 AW	54240 AAW	ARBLS	10//99-12//99
	California	S	28.62 MW	29.14 AW	60610 AAW	CABLS	10//99-12//99
	Bakersfield MSA, CA	S	30.61 MW	32.07 AW	63680 AAW	CABLS	10//99-12//99
	Chico-Paradise MSA, CA	S	26.34 MW	24.57 AW	54780 AAW	CABLS	10//99-12//99
	Los Angeles-Long Beach PMSA, CA	S	27.96 MW	26.47 AW	58160 AAW	CABLS	10//99-12//99
	Merced MSA, CA	S	28.48 MW	29.29 AW	59250 AAW	CABLS	10//99-12//99
	Modesto MSA, CA	S	27.39 MW	27.76 AW	56970 AAW	CABLS	10//99-12//99
	Oakland PMSA, CA	S	30.92 MW	31.08 AW	64310 AAW	CABLS	10//99-12//99
	Orange County PMSA, CA	S	30.34 MW	30.27 AW	63100 AAW	CABLS	10//99-12//99
	Riverside-San Bernardino PMSA, CA	S	27.60 MW	27.44 AW	57420 AAW	CABLS	10//99-12//99
	Salinas MSA, CA	S	29.03 MW	31.45 AW	60380 AAW	CABLS	10//99-12//99
	San Diego MSA, CA	S	28.41 MW	27.78 AW	59100 AAW	CABLS	10//99-12//99
	San Francisco PMSA, CA	S	30.41 MW	30.28 AW	63250 AAW	CABLS	10//99-12//99
	San Jose PMSA, CA	S	31.27 MW	31.37 AW	65030 AAW	CABLS	10//99-12//99
	Santa Barbara-Santa Maria-Lompoc MSA, CA	S	31.17 MW	29.80 AW	64840 AAW	CABLS	
	Santa Cruz-Watsonville PMSA, CA	S	31.43 MW	28.85 AW	65380 AAW	CABLS	10//99-12//99
	Santa Rosa PMSA, CA	S	31.01 MW	29.47 AW	64500 AAW	CABLS	10//99-12//99
	Vallejo-Fairfield-Napa PMSA, CA	S	30.56 MW	31.05 AW	63570 AAW	CABLS	10//99-12//99
	Ventura PMSA, CA	S	29.88 MW	30.59 AW	62150 AAW	CABLS	10//99-12//99
	Visalia-Tulare-Porterville MSA, CA	S	24.71 MW	23.52 AW	51400 AAW	CABLS	10//99-12//99
	Yolo PMSA, CA	S	28.45 MW	26.23 AW	59170 AAW	CABLS	10//99-12//99
	Colorado	S	25.66 MW	26.86 AW	55870 AAW	COBLS	10//99-12//99
	Boulder-Longmont PMSA, CO	S	25.23 MW	23.29 AW	52470 AAW	COBLS	10//99-12//99
	Colorado Springs MSA, CO	S	24.93 MW	23.02 AW	51860 AAW	COBLS	10//99-12//99
	Denver PMSA, CO	S	27.59 MW	26.70 AW	57390 AAW	COBLS	10//99-12//99
	Fort Collins-Loveland MSA, CO	S	23.97 MW	21.99 AW	49850 AAW	COBLS	10//99-12//99
	Grand Junction MSA, CO	S	25.77 MW	24.77 AW	53590 AAW	COBLS	10//99-12//99
	Greeley PMSA, CO	S	24.34 MW	24.03 AW	50620 AAW	COBLS	10//99-12//99
	Pueblo MSA, CO	S	27.41 MW	28.44 AW	57000 AAW	COBLS	10//99-12//99
	Connecticut	S	26.1 MW	27.07 AW	56310 AAW	CTBLS	10//99-12//99
	Bridgeport PMSA, CT	S	24.95 MW	23.27 AW	51890 AAW	CTBLS	10//99-12//99
	Danbury PMSA, CT	S	30.92 MW	30.58 AW	64320 AAW	CTBLS	10//99-12//99
	New Haven-Meriden PMSA, CT	S	25.71 MW	24.78 AW	53470 AAW	CTBLS	10//99-12//99
	New London-Norwich MSA, CT-RI	S	27.35 MW	25.67 AW	56890 AAW	CTBLS	10//99-12//99
	Stamford-Norwalk PMSA, CT	S	30.75 MW	29.13 AW	63960 AAW	CTBLS	10//99-12//99
	Delaware	S	25.09 MW	25.98 AW	54030 AAW	DEBLS	10//99-12//99
	Wilmington-Newark PMSA, DE-MD	S	27.55 MW	26.81 AW	57300 AAW	DEBLS	10//99-12//99
	District of Columbia	S	31.02 MW	30.40 AW	63240 AAW	DCBLS	10//99-12//99
	Washington PMSA, DC-MD-VA-WV	S	27.94 MW	27.39 AW	58110 AAW	DCBLS	10//99-12//99
	Florida	S	26.12 MW	27.06 AW	56280 AAW	FLBLS	10//99-12//99
	Fort Lauderdale PMSA, FL	S	27.96 MW	26.73 AW	58150 AAW	FLBLS	10//99-12//99
	Fort Myers-Cape Coral MSA, FL	S	30.47 MW	29.76 AW	63380 AAW	FLBLS	10//99-12//99
	Fort Walton Beach MSA, FL	S	25.38 MW	25.99 AW	52790 AAW	FLBLS	10//99-12//99
	Gainesville MSA, FL	S	23.37 MW	22.72 AW	48610 AAW	FLBLS	10//99-12//99
	Jacksonville MSA, FL	S	28.94 MW	29.42 AW	60190 AAW	FLBLS	10//99-12//99
	Lakeland-Winter Haven MSA, FL	S	27.23 MW	26.42 AW	56650 AAW	FLBLS	10//99-12//99
	Melbourne-Titusville-Palm Bay MSA, FL	S	25.36 MW	24.88 AW	52740 AAW	FLBLS	10//99-12//99
	Miami PMSA, FL	S	26.47 MW	24.72 AW	55050 AAW	FLBLS	10//99-12//99
	Naples MSA, FL	S	31.62 MW	34.40 AW	65760 AAW	FLBLS	10//99-12//99
	Orlando MSA, FL	S	25.93 MW	24.94 AW	53940 AAW	FLBLS	10//99-12//99
	Panama City MSA, FL	S	28.99 MW	28.44 AW	60300 AAW	FLBLS	10//99-12//99
	Pensacola MSA, FL	S	23.86 MW	23.33 AW	49620 AAW	FLBLS	10//99-12//99
	Punta Gorda MSA, FL	S	27.38 MW	23.55 AW	56940 AAW	FLBLS	10//99-12//99
	Sarasota-Bradenton MSA, FL	S	23.23 MW	21.88 AW	48330 AAW	FLBLS	10//99-12//99
	Tallahassee MSA, FL	S	30.94 MW	30.13 AW	64340 AAW	FLBLS	10//99-12//99

AAW Average annual wage	AOH Average offered, high	ASH Average starting, high	H Hourly	M Monthly	S Special: hourly and annual
AE Average entry wage	AOL Average offered, low	ASL Average starting, low	HI Highest wage paid	MTC Median total compensation	TQ Third quartile wage
AEX Average experienced wage	APH Average pay, high range	AW Average wage paid	HR High end range	MW Median wage paid	W Weekly
AO Average offered	APL Average pay, low range	FQ First quartile wage	LR Low end range	SQ Second quartile wage	Y Yearly

Occupation/Type/Industry	Location	Per	Low	Mid	High	Source	Date
Civil Engineer	Tampa-St. Petersburg-Clearwater MSA, FL	S	26.23 MW	25.09 AW	54550 AAW	FLBLS	10//99-12//99
	West Palm Beach-Boca Raton MSA, FL	S	26.98 MW	27.10 AW	56110 AAW	FLBLS	10//99-12//99
	Georgia	S	25.11 MW	26.38 AW	54870 AAW	GABLS	10//99-12//99
	Athens MSA, GA	S	21.83 MW	20.12 AW	45400 AAW	GABLS	10//99-12//99
	Atlanta MSA, GA	S	25.95 MW	24.40 AW	53980 AAW	GABLS	10//99-12//99
	Columbus MSA, GA-AL	S	24.02 MW	23.77 AW	49960 AAW	GABLS	10//99-12//99
	Macon MSA, GA	S	23.64 MW	23.36 AW	49160 AAW	GABLS	10//99-12//99
	Hawaii	S	25.85 MW	26.66 AW	55450 AAW	HIBLS	10//99-12//99
	Honolulu MSA, HI	S	25.99 MW	25.89 AW	54060 AAW	HIBLS	10//99-12//99
	Idaho	S	23.54 MW	23.83 AW	49560 AAW	IDBLS	10//99-12//99
	Boise City MSA, ID	S	24.74 MW	24.35 AW	51460 AAW	IDBLS	10//99-12//99
	Illinois	S	26.99 MW	26.68 AW	55490 AAW	ILBLS	10//99-12//99
	Bloomington-Normal MSA, IL	S	24.53 MW	23.20 AW	51020 AAW	ILBLS	10//99-12//99
	Champaign-Urbana MSA, IL	S	25.75 MW	24.69 AW	53570 AAW	ILBLS	10//99-12//99
	Chicago PMSA, IL	S	26.91 MW	27.43 AW	55980 AAW	ILBLS	10//99-12//99
	Peoria-Pekin MSA, IL	S	28.62 MW	28.14 AW	59520 AAW	ILBLS	10//99-12//99
	Rockford MSA, IL	S	26.70 MW	27.57 AW	55540 AAW	ILBLS	10//99-12//99
	Springfield MSA, IL	S	24.21 MW	24.04 AW	50370 AAW	ILBLS	10//99-12//99
	Indiana	S	24.6 MW	25.27 AW	52560 AAW	INBLS	10//99-12//99
	Bloomington MSA, IN	S	25.00 MW	23.77 AW	52000 AAW	INBLS	10//99-12//99
	Evansville-Henderson MSA, IN-KY	S	23.02 MW	22.21 AW	47870 AAW	INBLS	10//99-12//99
	Fort Wayne MSA, IN	S	26.91 MW	28.11 AW	55970 AAW	INBLS	10//99-12//99
	Gary PMSA, IN	S	27.63 MW	25.47 AW	57470 AAW	INBLS	10//99-12//99
	Indianapolis MSA, IN	S	24.71 MW	23.67 AW	51400 AAW	INBLS	10//99-12//99
	Lafayette MSA, IN	S	23.74 MW	21.95 AW	49380 AAW	INBLS	10//99-12//99
	South Bend MSA, IN	S	23.57 MW	22.15 AW	49030 AAW	INBLS	10//99-12//99
	Terre Haute MSA, IN	S	25.61 MW	22.52 AW	53270 AAW	INBLS	10//99-12//99
	Iowa	S	25.74 MW	25.47 AW	52980 AAW	IABLS	10//99-12//99
	Cedar Rapids MSA, IA	S	23.05 MW	21.67 AW	47950 AAW	IABLS	10//99-12//99
	Davenport-Moline-Rock Island MSA, IA-IL	S	26.39 MW	26.44 AW	54880 AAW	IABLS	10//99-12//99
	Des Moines MSA, IA	S	25.54 MW	25.43 AW	53120 AAW	IABLS	10//99-12//99
	Iowa City MSA, IA	S	24.96 MW	24.18 AW	51920 AAW	IABLS	10//99-12//99
	Sioux City MSA, IA-NE	S	25.50 MW	25.02 AW	53050 AAW	IABLS	10//99-12//99
	Waterloo-Cedar Falls MSA, IA	S	23.44 MW	23.56 AW	48750 AAW	IABLS	10//99-12//99
	Kansas	S	24.68 MW	26.07 AW	54220 AAW	KSBLS	10//99-12//99
	Lawrence MSA, KS	S	29.11 MW	26.46 AW	60540 AAW	KSBLS	10//99-12//99
	Wichita MSA, KS	S	29.67 MW	26.11 AW	61720 AAW	KSBLS	10//99-12//99
	Kentucky	S	24.72 MW	25.95 AW	53980 AAW	KYBLS	10//99-12//99
	Lexington MSA, KY	S	25.97 MW	23.72 AW	54020 AAW	KYBLS	10//99-12//99
	Louisville MSA, KY-IN	S	26.60 MW	27.17 AW	55330 AAW	KYBLS	10//99-12//99
	Louisiana	S	25.41 MW	26.20 AW	54500 AAW	LABLS	10//99-12//99
	Alexandria MSA, LA	S	25.46 MW	23.61 AW	52950 AAW	LABLS	10//99-12//99
	Baton Rouge MSA, LA	S	23.17 MW	22.22 AW	48190 AAW	LABLS	10//99-12//99
	Houma MSA, LA	S	28.21 MW	28.99 AW	58690 AAW	LABLS	10//99-12//99
	Lafayette MSA, LA	S	28.77 MW	24.02 AW	59830 AAW	LABLS	10//99-12//99
	Lake Charles MSA, LA	S	23.59 MW	23.28 AW	49070 AAW	LABLS	10//99-12//99
	Monroe MSA, LA	S	24.97 MW	23.32 AW	51950 AAW	LABLS	10//99-12//99
	New Orleans MSA, LA	S	29.59 MW	29.48 AW	61560 AAW	LABLS	10//99-12//99
	Shreveport-Bossier City MSA, LA	S	26.22 MW	26.03 AW	54530 AAW	LABLS	10//99-12//99
	Maine	S	23.82 MW	24.45 AW	50850 AAW	MEBLS	10//99-12//99
	Bangor MSA, ME	S	24.43 MW	23.79 AW	50820 AAW	MEBLS	10//99-12//99
	Portland MSA, ME	S	24.67 MW	23.46 AW	51310 AAW	MEBLS	10//99-12//99
	Maryland	S	23.55 MW	24.48 AW	50920 AAW	MDBLS	10//99-12//99
	Baltimore PMSA, MD	S	22.37 MW	21.94 AW	46530 AAW	MDBLS	10//99-12//99
	Massachusetts	S	25.23 MW	26.86 AW	55880 AAW	MABLS	10//99-12//99
	Barnstable-Yarmouth MSA, MA	S	23.14 MW	21.82 AW	48140 AAW	MABLS	10//99-12//99
	Boston PMSA, MA-NH	S	27.41 MW	25.74 AW	57020 AAW	MABLS	10//99-12//99
	Brockton PMSA, MA	S	22.18 MW	22.23 AW	46140 AAW	MABLS	10//99-12//99
	Lawrence PMSA, MA-NH	S	26.08 MW	23.93 AW	54250 AAW	MABLS	10//99-12//99
	Lowell PMSA, MA-NH	S	24.31 MW	23.42 AW	50570 AAW	MABLS	10//99-12//99
	New Bedford PMSA, MA	S	22.99 MW	20.60 AW	47820 AAW	MABLS	10//99-12//99
	Pittsfield MSA, MA	S	23.92 MW	23.60 AW	49750 AAW	MABLS	10//99-12//99
	Springfield MSA, MA	S	25.80 MW	24.28 AW	53670 AAW	MABLS	10//99-12//99
	Worcester PMSA, MA-CT	S	25.07 MW	24.37 AW	52140 AAW	MABLS	10//99-12//99
	Michigan	S	23.52 MW	24.76 AW	51500 AAW	MIBLS	10//99-12//99
	Ann Arbor PMSA, MI	S	25.66 MW	24.81 AW	53380 AAW	MIBLS	10//99-12//99

Occupation/Type/Industry	Location	Per	Low	Mid	High	Source	Date
Civil Engineer	Benton Harbor MSA, MI	S	27.38 MW	29.04 AW	56940 AAW	MIBLS	10//99-12//99
	Detroit PMSA, MI	S	25.10 MW	23.77 AW	52210 AAW	MIBLS	10//99-12//99
	Flint PMSA, MI	S	23.66 MW	21.74 AW	49200 AAW	MIBLS	10//99-12//99
	Grand Rapids-Muskegon-Holland MSA, MI	S	23.32 MW	21.88 AW	48500 AAW	MIBLS	10//99-12//99
	Kalamazoo-Battle Creek MSA, MI	S	21.57 MW	19.32 AW	44870 AAW	MIBLS	10//99-12//99
	Lansing-East Lansing MSA, MI	S	24.99 MW	24.13 AW	51990 AAW	MIBLS	10//99-12//99
	Saginaw-Bay City-Midland MSA, MI	S	22.90 MW	22.17 AW	47620 AAW	MIBLS	10//99-12//99
	Minnesota	S	24.17 MW	24.55 AW	51070 AAW	MNBLS	10//99-12//99
	Duluth-Superior MSA, MN-WI	S	23.73 MW	22.71 AW	49350 AAW	MNBLS	10//99-12//99
	Minneapolis-St. Paul MSA, MN-WI	S	25.09 MW	24.93 AW	52190 AAW	MNBLS	10//99-12//99
	Rochester MSA, MN	S	23.30 MW	23.06 AW	48460 AAW	MNBLS	10//99-12//99
	St. Cloud MSA, MN	S	23.44 MW	23.06 AW	48750 AAW	MNBLS	10//99-12//99
	Mississippi	S	25.4 MW	25.27 AW	52560 AAW	MSBLS	10//99-12//99
	Biloxi-Gulfport-Pascagoula MSA, MS	S	21.23 MW	17.18 AW	44160 AAW	MSBLS	10//99-12//99
	Jackson MSA, MS	S	26.16 MW	26.70 AW	54400 AAW	MSBLS	10//99-12//99
	Missouri	S	24.82 MW	25.76 AW	53570 AAW	MOBLS	10//99-12//99
	Kansas City MSA, MO-KS	S	25.52 MW	23.86 AW	53070 AAW	MOBLS	10//99-12//99
	St. Louis MSA, MO-IL	S	25.83 MW	24.76 AW	53720 AAW	MOBLS	10//99-12//99
	Springfield MSA, MO	S	27.07 MW	26.34 AW	56310 AAW	MOBLS	10//99-12//99
	Montana	S	21.56 MW	22.56 AW	46920 AAW	MTBLS	10//99-12//99
	Billings MSA, MT	S	28.02 MW	29.08 AW	58280 AAW	MTBLS	10//99-12//99
	Great Falls MSA, MT	S	22.05 MW	22.24 AW	45870 AAW	MTBLS	10//99-12//99
	Nebraska	S	27.2 MW	26.98 AW	56110 AAW	NEBLS	10//99-12//99
	Lincoln MSA, NE	S	24.20 MW	23.51 AW	50340 AAW	NEBLS	10//99-12//99
	Omaha MSA, NE-IA	S	29.10 MW	30.13 AW	60540 AAW	NEBLS	10//99-12//99
	Nevada	S	29.32 MW	28.84 AW	59990 AAW	NVBLS	10//99-12//99
	Las Vegas MSA, NV-AZ	S	30.65 MW	32.15 AW	63760 AAW	NVBLS	10//99-12//99
	Reno MSA, NV	S	24.33 MW	23.57 AW	50610 AAW	NVBLS	10//99-12//99
	New Hampshire	S	24.38 MW	25.09 AW	52190 AAW	NHBLS	10//99-12//99
	Manchester PMSA, NH	S	23.85 MW	22.30 AW	49600 AAW	NHBLS	10//99-12//99
	Portsmouth-Rochester PMSA, NH-ME	S	19.88 MW	20.49 AW	41350 AAW	NHBLS	10//99-12//99
	New Jersey	S	29.35 MW	29.59 AW	61550 AAW	NJBLS	10//99-12//99
	Atlantic-Cape May PMSA, NJ	S	30.39 MW	31.31 AW	63200 AAW	NJBLS	10//99-12//99
	Bergen-Passaic PMSA, NJ	S	30.46 MW	28.11 AW	63350 AAW	NJBLS	10//99-12//99
	Jersey City PMSA, NJ	S	29.44 MW	27.53 AW	61230 AAW	NJBLS	10//99-12//99
	Middlesex-Somerset-Hunterdon PMSA, NJ	S	27.49 MW	26.33 AW	57170 AAW	NJBLS	10//99-12//99
	Monmouth-Ocean PMSA, NJ	S	29.27 MW	29.29 AW	60880 AAW	NJBLS	10//99-12//99
	Newark PMSA, NJ	S	31.49 MW	31.52 AW	65500 AAW	NJBLS	10//99-12//99
	New Mexico	S	25.38 MW	25.77 AW	53600 AAW	NMBLS	10//99-12//99
	Albuquerque MSA, NM	S	26.18 MW	25.64 AW	54450 AAW	NMBLS	10//99-12//99
	Las Cruces MSA, NM	S	23.73 MW	23.56 AW	49350 AAW	NMBLS	10//99-12//99
	Santa Fe MSA, NM	S	26.66 MW	25.81 AW	55450 AAW	NMBLS	10//99-12//99
	New York	S	25.3 MW	26.38 AW	54870 AAW	NYBLS	10//99-12//99
	Albany-Schenectady-Troy MSA, NY	S	27.35 MW	26.29 AW	56890 AAW	NYBLS	10//99-12//99
	Buffalo-Niagara Falls MSA, NY	S	25.27 MW	24.36 AW	52560 AAW	NYBLS	10//99-12//99
	Nassau-Suffolk PMSA, NY	S	26.04 MW	25.77 AW	54160 AAW	NYBLS	10//99-12//99
	New York PMSA, NY	S	27.09 MW	25.87 AW	56340 AAW	NYBLS	10//99-12//99
	Newburgh PMSA, NY-PA	S	26.68 MW	24.90 AW	55500 AAW	NYBLS	10//99-12//99
	Rochester MSA, NY	S	24.97 MW	24.52 AW	51940 AAW	NYBLS	10//99-12//99
	Syracuse MSA, NY	S	23.41 MW	22.36 AW	48690 AAW	NYBLS	10//99-12//99
	North Carolina	S	24.21 MW	25.14 AW	52300 AAW	NCBLS	10//99-12//99
	Asheville MSA, NC	S	25.02 MW	24.79 AW	52040 AAW	NCBLS	10//99-12//99
	Charlotte-Gastonia-Rock Hill MSA, NC-SC	S	27.23 MW	26.53 AW	56640 AAW	NCBLS	10//99-12//99
	Fayetteville MSA, NC	S	24.34 MW	24.42 AW	50630 AAW	NCBLS	10//99-12//99
	Goldsboro MSA, NC	S	24.20 MW	24.07 AW	50330 AAW	NCBLS	10//99-12//99
	Greensboro--Winston-Salem--High Point MSA, NC	S	24.71 MW	23.77 AW	51400 AAW	NCBLS	10//99-12//99
	Greenville MSA, NC	S	25.39 MW	23.80 AW	52810 AAW	NCBLS	10//99-12//99
	Raleigh-Durham-Chapel Hill MSA, NC	S	24.39 MW	23.39 AW	50740 AAW	NCBLS	10//99-12//99
	Rocky Mount MSA, NC	S	25.82 MW	25.97 AW	53700 AAW	NCBLS	10//99-12//99
	Wilmington MSA, NC	S	25.91 MW	27.31 AW	53880 AAW	NCBLS	10//99-12//99

AAW	Average annual wage	AOH	Average offered, high	ASH	Average starting, high	H	Hourly	M	Monthly	S	Special: hourly and annual
AE	Average entry wage	AOL	Average offered, low	ASL	Average starting, low	HI	Highest wage paid	MTC	Median total compensation	TQ	Third quartile wage
AEX	Average experienced wage	APH	Average pay, high range	AW	Average wage paid	HR	High end range	MW	Median wage paid	W	Weekly
AO	Average offered	APL	Average pay, low range	FQ	First quartile wage	LR	Low end range	SQ	Second quartile wage	Y	Yearly

Occupation/Type/Industry	Location	Per	Low	Mid	High	Source	Date
Civil Engineer	North Dakota	S	19.94 MW	21.34 AW	44380 AAW	NDBLS	10//99-12//99
	Fargo-Moorhead MSA, ND-MN	S	23.19 MW	19.83 AW	48230 AAW	NDBLS	10//99-12//99
	Grand Forks MSA, ND-MN	S	22.50 MW	20.57 AW	46790 AAW	NDBLS	10//99-12//99
	Ohio	S	24.32 MW	25.04 AW	52080 AAW	OHBLS	10//99-12//99
	Akron PMSA, QH	S	26.41 MW	25.72 AW	54930 AAW	OHBLS	10//99-12//99
	Cincinnati PMSA, OH-KY-IN	S	27.19 MW	27.20 AW	56550 AAW	OHBLS	10//99-12//99
	Cleveland-Lorain-Elyria PMSA, OH	S	24.47 MW	23.84 AW	50890 AAW	OHBLS	10//99-12//99
	Columbus MSA, OH	S	23.84 MW	22.93 AW	49600 AAW	OHBLS	10//99-12//99
	Dayton-Springfield MSA, OH	S	25.57 MW	24.46 AW	53190 AAW	OHBLS	10//99-12//99
	Hamilton-Middletown PMSA, OH	S	20.07 MW	20.38 AW	41740 AAW	OHBLS	10//99-12//99
	Mansfield MSA, OH	S	25.81 MW	25.84 AW	53690 AAW	OHBLS	10//99-12//99
	Toledo MSA, OH	S	23.18 MW	21.15 AW	48220 AAW	OHBLS	10//99-12//99
	Youngstown-Warren MSA, OH	S	23.57 MW	23.11 AW	49030 AAW	OHBLS	10//99-12//99
	Oklahoma	S	25.74 MW	25.28 AW	52570 AAW	OKBLS	10//99-12//99
	Oklahoma City MSA, OK	S	24.14 MW	23.31 AW	50220 AAW	OKBLS	10//99-12//99
	Tulsa MSA, OK	S	27.91 MW	30.00 AW	58060 AAW	OKBLS	10//99-12//99
	Oregon	S	26.06 MW	26.38 AW	54870 AAW	ORBLS	10//99-12//99
	Corvallis MSA, OR	S	24.54 MW	22.27 AW	51040 AAW	ORBLS	10//99-12//99
	Eugene-Springfield MSA, OR	S	26.87 MW	26.67 AW	55890 AAW	ORBLS	10//99-12//99
	Medford-Ashland MSA, OR	S	21.65 MW	21.91 AW	45030 AAW	ORBLS	10//99-12//99
	Portland-Vancouver PMSA, OR-WA	S	27.37 MW	27.28 AW	56930 AAW	ORBLS	10//99-12//99
	Pennsylvania	S	24.78 MW	25.69 AW	53430 AAW	PABLS	10//99-12//99
	Allentown-Bethlehem-Easton MSA, PA	S	25.30 MW	24.31 AW	52630 AAW	PABLS	10//99-12//99
	Altoona MSA, PA	S	23.93 MW	22.09 AW	49770 AAW	PABLS	10//99-12//99
	Erie MSA, PA	S	21.52 MW	20.26 AW	44750 AAW	PABLS	10//99-12//99
	Harrisburg-Lebanon-Carlisle MSA, PA	S	25.44 MW	24.87 AW	52920 AAW	PABLS	10//99-12//99
	Lancaster MSA, PA	S	31.39 MW	33.48 AW	65290 AAW	PABLS	10//99-12//99
	Philadelphia PMSA, PA-NJ	S	27.45 MW	26.97 AW	57100 AAW	PABLS	10//99-12//99
	Pittsburgh MSA, PA	S	25.87 MW	25.02 AW	53810 AAW	PABLS	10//99-12//99
	Reading MSA, PA	S	23.65 MW	22.21 AW	49190 AAW	PABLS	10//99-12//99
	Scranton--Wilkes-Barre--Hazleton MSA, PA	S	21.76 MW	21.03 AW	45270 AAW	PABLS	10//99-12//99
	State College MSA, PA	S	22.52 MW	22.77 AW	46850 AAW	PABLS	10//99-12//99
	York MSA, PA	S	24.79 MW	23.19 AW	51570 AAW	PABLS	10//99-12//99
	Rhode Island	S	27.34 MW	26.54 AW	55200 AAW	RIBLS	10//99-12//99
	Providence-Fall River-Warwick MSA, RI-MA	S	27.03 MW	28.03 AW	56210 AAW	RIBLS	10//99-12//99
	South Carolina	S	24.82 MW	26.43 AW	54980 AAW	SCBLS	10//99-12//99
	Charleston-North Charleston MSA, SC	S	25.59 MW	25.12 AW	53230 AAW	SCBLS	10//99-12//99
	Florence MSA, SC	S	27.69 MW	25.42 AW	57590 AAW	SCBLS	10//99-12//99
	Greenville-Spartanburg-Anderson MSA, SC	S	25.89 MW	23.68 AW	53850 AAW	SCBLS	10//99-12//99
	Myrtle Beach MSA, SC	S	22.83 MW	19.44 AW	47480 AAW	SCBLS	10//99-12//99
	Sumter MSA, SC	S	19.53 MW	21.93 AW	40630 AAW	SCBLS	10//99-12//99
	South Dakota	S	21.06 MW	22.33 AW	46460 AAW	SDBLS	10//99-12//99
	Rapid City MSA, SD	S	26.33 MW	25.28 AW	54760 AAW	SDBLS	10//99-12//99
	Sioux Falls MSA, SD	S	23.89 MW	21.77 AW	49690 AAW	SDBLS	10//99-12//99
	Tennessee	S	23.64 MW	24.78 AW	51530 AAW	TNBLS	10//99-12//99
	Chattanooga MSA, TN-GA	S	25.88 MW	27.03 AW	53840 AAW	TNBLS	10//99-12//99
	Jackson MSA, TN	S	27.40 MW	26.31 AW	57000 AAW	TNBLS	10//99-12//99
	Knoxville MSA, TN	S	26.27 MW	23.99 AW	54630 AAW	TNBLS	10//99-12//99
	Memphis MSA, TN-AR-MS	S	24.88 MW	24.74 AW	51760 AAW	MSBLS	10//99-12//99
	Nashville MSA, TN	S	22.99 MW	21.14 AW	47820 AAW	TNBLS	10//99-12//99
	Texas	S	28.72 MW	29.24 AW	60830 AAW	TXBLS	10//99-12//99
	Abilene MSA, TX	S	26.08 MW	25.39 AW	54250 AAW	TXBLS	10//99-12//99
	Austin-San Marcos MSA, TX	S	25.12 MW	24.22 AW	52250 AAW	TXBLS	10//99-12//99
	Beaumont-Port Arthur MSA, TX	S	31.29 MW	33.43 AW	65080 AAW	TXBLS	10//99-12//99
	Brazoria PMSA, TX	S	30.33 MW	33.39 AW	63080 AAW	TXBLS	10//99-12//99
	Brownsville-Harlingen-San Benito MSA, TX	S	24.54 MW	23.83 AW	51040 AAW	TXBLS	10//99-12//99
	Corpus Christi MSA, TX	S	31.96 MW	31.55 AW	66480 AAW	TXBLS	10//99-12//99
	Dallas PMSA, TX	S	25.69 MW	24.85 AW	53440 AAW	TXBLS	10//99-12//99
	El Paso MSA, TX	S	21.36 MW	22.15 AW	44430 AAW	TXBLS	10//99-12//99

AAW	Average annual wage	AOH	Average offered, high	ASH	Average starting, high	H	Hourly	M	Monthly	S	Special: hourly and annual
AE	Average entry wage	AOL	Average offered, low	ASL	Average starting, low	HI	Highest wage paid	MTC	Median total compensation	TQ	Third quartile wage
AEX	Average experienced wage	APH	Average pay, high range	AW	Average wage paid	HR	High end range	MW	Median wage paid	W	Weekly
AO	Average offered	APL	Average pay, low range	FQ	First quartile wage	LR	Low end range	SQ	Second quartile wage	Y	Yearly

Occupation/Type/Industry	Location	Per	Low	Mid	High	Source	Date
Civil Engineer	Fort Worth-Arlington PMSA, TX	S	25.16 MW	23.81 AW	52330 AAW	TXBLS	10//99-12//99
	Houston PMSA, TX	S	32.67 MW	33.25 AW	67950 AAW	TXBLS	10//99-12//99
	Killeen-Temple MSA, TX	S	26.39 MW	25.09 AW	54890 AAW	TXBLS	10//99-12//99
	Laredo MSA, TX	S	23.63 MW	21.72 AW	49150 AAW	TXBLS	10//99-12//99
	Longview-Marshall MSA, TX	S	21.03 MW	19.34 AW	43740 AAW	TXBLS	10//99-12//99
	Lubbock MSA, TX	S	24.90 MW	23.45 AW	51790 AAW	TXBLS	10//99-12//99
	McAllen-Edinburg-Mission MSA, TX	S	33.44 MW	35.72 AW	69550 AAW	TXBLS	10//99-12//99
	Odessa-Midland MSA, TX	S	34.28 MW	35.84 AW	71310 AAW	TXBLS	10//99-12//99
	San Antonio MSA, TX	S	24.67 MW	22.20 AW	51300 AAW	TXBLS	10//99-12//99
	Tyler MSA, TX	S	24.09 MW	23.54 AW	50100 AAW	TXBLS	10//99-12//99
	Waco MSA, TX	S	29.82 MW	31.18 AW	62020 AAW	TXBLS	10//99-12//99
	Wichita Falls MSA, TX	S	28.47 MW	25.33 AW	59210 AAW	TXBLS	10//99-12//99
	Utah	S	22.82 MW	23.72 AW	49330 AAW	UTBLS	10//99-12//99
	Provo-Orem MSA, UT	S	22.96 MW	22.66 AW	47750 AAW	UTBLS	10//99-12//99
	Salt Lake City-Ogden MSA, UT	S	23.91 MW	23.03 AW	49740 AAW	UTBLS	10//99-12//99
	Vermont	S	24.87 MW	25.63 AW	53310 AAW	VTBLS	10//99-12//99
	Burlington MSA, VT	S	25.64 MW	23.90 AW	53320 AAW	VTBLS	10//99-12//99
	Virginia	S	25.2 MW	25.99 AW	54060 AAW	VABLS	10//99-12//99
	Charlottesville MSA, VA	S	25.37 MW	24.76 AW	52780 AAW	VABLS	10//99-12//99
	Norfolk-Virginia Beach-Newport News MSA, VA-NC	S	25.76 MW	25.02 AW	53580 AAW	VABLS	10//99-12//99
	Richmond-Petersburg MSA, VA	S	24.71 MW	24.32 AW	51400 AAW	VABLS	10//99-12//99
	Roanoke MSA, VA	S	22.96 MW	21.99 AW	47750 AAW	VABLS	10//99-12//99
	Washington	S	26.07 MW	26.94 AW	56040 AAW	WABLS	10//99-12//99
	Bellingham MSA, WA	S	25.76 MW	25.62 AW	53590 AAW	WABLS	10//99-12//99
	Bremerton PMSA, WA	S	29.42 MW	27.87 AW	61200 AAW	WABLS	10//99-12//99
	Richland-Kennewick-Pasco MSA, WA	S	31.19 MW	31.10 AW	64870 AAW	WABLS	10//99-12//99
	Seattle-Bellevue-Everett PMSA, WA	S	27.71 MW	27.42 AW	57630 AAW	WABLS	10//99-12//99
	Spokane MSA, WA	S	22.65 MW	22.44 AW	47120 AAW	WABLS	10//99-12//99
	Tacoma PMSA, WA	S	26.43 MW	25.44 AW	54970 AAW	WABLS	10//99-12//99
	West Virginia	S	21.56 MW	22.54 AW	46890 AAW	WVBLS	10//99-12//99
	Parkersburg-Marietta MSA, WV-OH	S	22.96 MW	22.50 AW	47760 AAW	WVBLS	10//99-12//99
	Wisconsin	S	23.17 MW	24.44 AW	50840 AAW	WIBLS	10//99-12//99
	Appleton-Oshkosh-Neenah MSA, WI	S	24.95 MW	23.78 AW	51890 AAW	WIBLS	10//99-12//99
	Eau Claire MSA, WI	S	24.13 MW	22.81 AW	50200 AAW	WIBLS	10//99-12//99
	Green Bay MSA, WI	S	23.97 MW	23.25 AW	49860 AAW	WIBLS	10//99-12//99
	Janesville-Beloit MSA, WI	S	21.27 MW	21.45 AW	44230 AAW	WIBLS	10//99-12//99
	Kenosha PMSA, WI	S	32.19 MW	27.26 AW	66950 AAW	WIBLS	10//99-12//99
	La Crosse MSA, WI-MN	S	31.64 MW	27.13 AW	65810 AAW	WIBLS	10//99-12//99
	Madison MSA, WI	S	24.66 MW	23.73 AW	51290 AAW	WIBLS	10//99-12//99
	Milwaukee-Waukesha PMSA, WI	S	23.89 MW	22.44 AW	49690 AAW	WIBLS	10//99-12//99
	Racine PMSA, WI	S	28.47 MW	31.32 AW	59210 AAW	WIBLS	10//99-12//99
	Wausau MSA, WI	S	21.85 MW	20.46 AW	45460 AAW	WIBLS	10//99-12//99
	Wyoming	S	19.97 MW	21.84 AW	45420 AAW	WYBLS	10//99-12//99
	Casper MSA, WY	S	23.98 MW	23.94 AW	49880 AAW	WYBLS	10//99-12//99
	Cheyenne MSA, WY	S	21.01 MW	22.11 AW	43710 AAW	WYBLS	10//99-12//99
	Puerto Rico	S	16.64 MW	18.53 AW	38530 AAW	PRBLS	10//99-12//99
	Caguas PMSA, PR	S	15.67 MW	13.07 AW	32600 AAW	PRBLS	10//99-12//99
	Mayaguez MSA, PR	S	20.98 MW	20.28 AW	43640 AAW	PRBLS	10//99-12//99
	Ponce MSA, PR	S	15.99 MW	13.83 AW	33260 AAW	PRBLS	10//99-12//99
	San Juan-Bayamon PMSA, PR	S	18.44 MW	16.64 AW	38350 AAW	PRBLS	10//99-12//99
	Guam	S	18.29 MW	18.90 AW	39310 AAW	GUBLS	10//99-12//99
Civil Engineering Technician	Alabama	S	13.87 MW	14.41 AW	29980 AAW	ALBLS	10//99-12//99
	Alaska	S	22.65 MW	22.59 AW	46990 AAW	AKBLS	10//99-12//99
	Arizona	S	17.28 MW	18.10 AW	37650 AAW	AZBLS	10//99-12//99
	Arkansas	S	16.08 MW	17.13 AW	35620 AAW	ARBLS	10//99-12//99
	California	S	21.54 MW	22.25 AW	46270 AAW	CABLS	10//99-12//99
	Colorado	S	16.62 MW	17.79 AW	37010 AAW	COBLS	10//99-12//99
	Connecticut	S	19.34 MW	19.86 AW	41310 AAW	CTBLS	10//99-12//99
	Delaware	S	17.38 MW	18.06 AW	37560 AAW	DEBLS	10//99-12//99
	District of Columbia	S	14.7 MW	15.40 AW	32040 AAW	DCBLS	10//99-12//99
	Florida	S	15.79 MW	16.26 AW	33830 AAW	FLBLS	10//99-12//99

AAW	Average annual wage	**AOH**	Average offered, high	**ASH**	Average starting, high	**H**	Hourly	**M**	Monthly	**S**	Special: hourly and annual
AE	Average entry wage	**AOL**	Average offered, low	**ASL**	Average starting, low	**HI**	Highest wage paid	**MTC**	Median total compensation	**TQ**	Third quartile wage
AEX	Average experienced wage	**APH**	Average pay, high range	**AW**	Average wage paid	**HR**	High end range	**MW**	Median wage paid	**W**	Weekly
AO	Average offered	**APL**	Average pay, low range	**FQ**	First quartile wage	**LR**	Low end range	**SQ**	Second quartile wage	**Y**	Yearly

Occupation/Type/Industry	Location	Per	Low	Mid	High	Source	Date
Civil Engineering Technician	Georgia	S	14.54 MW	15.91 AW	33090 AAW	GABLS	10//99-12//99
	Hawaii	S	16.27 MW	17.89 AW	37220 AAW	HIBLS	10//99-12//99
	Idaho	S	15.38 MW	15.53 AW	32290 AAW	IDBLS	10//99-12//99
	Illinois	S	16.1 MW	17.21 AW	35800 AAW	ILBLS	10//99-12//99
	Indiana	S	13.43 MW	14.48 AW	30110 AAW	INBLS	10//99-12//99
	Iowa	S	15.64 MW	15.95 AW	33170 AAW	IABLS	10//99-12//99
	Kansas	S	15.1 MW	15.98 AW	33230 AAW	KSBLS	10//99-12//99
	Kentucky	S	15.7 MW	16.14 AW	33580 AAW	KYBLS	10//99-12//99
	Louisiana	S	12.52 MW	13.39 AW	27860 AAW	LABLS	10//99-12//99
	Maine	S	15.88 MW	16.05 AW	33390 AAW	MEBLS	10//99-12//99
	Maryland	S	16.1 MW	16.23 AW	33750 AAW	MDBLS	10//99-12//99
	Massachusetts	S	16.91 MW	17.97 AW	37380 AAW	MABLS	10//99-12//99
	Michigan	S	17.03 MW	17.44 AW	36280 AAW	MIBLS	10//99-12//99
	Minnesota	S	19.46 MW	19.51 AW	40590 AAW	MNBLS	10//99-12//99
	Mississippi	S	12.82 MW	13.48 AW	28040 AAW	MSBLS	10//99-12//99
	Missouri	S	17.06 MW	17.53 AW	36470 AAW	MOBLS	10//99-12//99
	Nebraska	S	14.89 MW	15.55 AW	32350 AAW	NEBLS	10//99-12//99
	Nevada	S	18.34 MW	19.46 AW	40470 AAW	NVBLS	10//99-12//99
	New Hampshire	S	10.59 MW	13.21 AW	27470 AAW	NHBLS	10//99-12//99
	New Jersey	S	20.53 MW	20.87 AW	43400 AAW	NJBLS	10//99-12//99
	New Mexico	S	14.85 MW	15.55 AW	32350 AAW	NMBLS	10//99-12//99
	New York	S	20.3 MW	20.39 AW	42410 AAW	NYBLS	10//99-12//99
	North Carolina	S	14.95 MW	15.37 AW	31960 AAW	NCBLS	10//99-12//99
	North Dakota	S	13.49 MW	13.97 AW	29060 AAW	NDBLS	10//99-12//99
	Ohio	S	16.74 MW	17.54 AW	36490 AAW	OHBLS	10//99-12//99
	Oklahoma	S	17.44 MW	18.42 AW	38300 AAW	OKBLS	10//99-12//99
	Oregon	S	18.48 MW	18.95 AW	39420 AAW	ORBLS	10//99-12//99
	Pennsylvania	S	17.66 MW	18.20 AW	37860 AAW	PABLS	10//99-12//99
	South Carolina	S	17.73 MW	18.54 AW	38570 AAW	SCBLS	10//99-12//99
	South Dakota	S	12.83 MW	13.06 AW	27160 AAW	SDBLS	10//99-12//99
	Tennessee	S	14.73 MW	15.93 AW	33130 AAW	TNBLS	10//99-12//99
	Texas	S	13.68 MW	13.75 AW	28590 AAW	TXBLS	10//99-12//99
	Utah	S	15.99 MW	16.12 AW	33530 AAW	UTBLS	10//99-12//99
	Vermont	S	18.64 MW	18.79 AW	39090 AAW	VTBLS	10//99-12//99
	Virginia	S	14.96 MW	15.40 AW	32040 AAW	VABLS	10//99-12//99
	Washington	S	19.45 MW	20.16 AW	41940 AAW	WABLS	10//99-12//99
	West Virginia	S	13.92 MW	14.64 AW	30440 AAW	WVBLS	10//99-12//99
	Wisconsin	S	17.01 MW	17.56 AW	36520 AAW	WIBLS	10//99-12//99
	Wyoming	S	13.83 MW	14.85 AW	30890 AAW	WYBLS	10//99-12//99
	Guam	S	15.48 MW	16.50 AW	34310 AAW	GUBLS	10//99-12//99
Claims Adjuster, Examiner, and Investigator	Alabama	S	17.01 MW	17.95 AW	37330 AAW	ALBLS	10//99-12//99
	Birmingham MSA, AL	S	19.64 MW	18.47 AW	40860 AAW	ALBLS	10//99-12//99
	Gadsden MSA, AL	S	18.08 MW	17.66 AW	37600 AAW	ALBLS	10//99-12//99
	Huntsville MSA, AL	S	20.75 MW	21.69 AW	43160 AAW	ALBLS	10//99-12//99
	Mobile MSA, AL	S	16.66 MW	15.63 AW	34660 AAW	ALBLS	10//99-12//99
	Montgomery MSA, AL	S	18.19 MW	17.88 AW	37840 AAW	ALBLS	10//99-12//99
	Arizona	S	19.2 MW	20.09 AW	41790 AAW	AZBLS	10//99-12//99
	Flagstaff MSA, AZ-UT	S	18.23 MW	17.83 AW	37930 AAW	AZBLS	10//99-12//99
	Phoenix-Mesa MSA, AZ	S	20.11 MW	19.22 AW	41820 AAW	AZBLS	10//99-12//99
	Tucson MSA, AZ	S	21.00 MW	19.86 AW	43670 AAW	AZBLS	10//99-12//99
	Arkansas	S	16.64 MW	17.85 AW	37140 AAW	ARBLS	10//99-12//99
	Fort Smith MSA, AR-OK	S	12.86 MW	11.79 AW	26760 AAW	ARBLS	10//99-12//99
	Jonesboro MSA, AR	S	21.23 MW	21.17 AW	44170 AAW	ARBLS	10//99-12//99
	Little Rock-North Little Rock MSA, AR	S	17.36 MW	16.61 AW	36120 AAW	ARBLS	10//99-12//99
	California	S	21.8 MW	22.59 AW	46980 AAW	CABLS	10//99-12//99
	Chico-Paradise MSA, CA	S	16.47 MW	15.82 AW	34260 AAW	CABLS	10//99-12//99
	Fresno MSA, CA	S	21.69 MW	22.55 AW	45110 AAW	CABLS	10//99-12//99
	Los Angeles-Long Beach PMSA, CA	S	22.74 MW	21.56 AW	47290 AAW	CABLS	10//99-12//99
	Oakland PMSA, CA	S	22.04 MW	21.33 AW	45830 AAW	CABLS	10//99-12//99
	Orange County PMSA, CA	S	19.33 MW	16.91 AW	40200 AAW	CABLS	10//99-12//99
	Redding MSA, CA	S	21.76 MW	23.87 AW	45270 AAW	CABLS	10//99-12//99
	Riverside-San Bernardino PMSA, CA	S	26.57 MW	26.79 AW	55270 AAW	CABLS	10//99-12//99
	Sacramento PMSA, CA	S	24.73 MW	24.62 AW	51430 AAW	CABLS	10//99-12//99
	San Diego MSA, CA	S	22.44 MW	20.46 AW	46670 AAW	CABLS	10//99-12//99
	San Francisco PMSA, CA	S	25.64 MW	27.84 AW	53340 AAW	CABLS	10//99-12//99
	San Jose PMSA, CA	S	18.40 MW	17.98 AW	38270 AAW	CABLS	10//99-12//99
	Santa Rosa PMSA, CA	S	21.45 MW	20.93 AW	44620 AAW	CABLS	10//99-12//99

AAW Average annual wage	AOH Average offered, high	ASH Average starting, high	H Hourly	M Monthly	S Special: hourly and annual
AE Average entry wage	AOL Average offered, low	ASL Average starting, low	HI Highest wage paid	MTC Median total compensation	TQ Third quartile wage
AEX Average experienced wage	APH Average pay, high range	AW Average wage paid	HR High end range	MW Median wage paid	W Weekly
AO Average offered	APL Average pay, low range	FQ First quartile wage	LR Low end range	SQ Second quartile wage	Y Yearly

Occupation/Type/Industry	Location	Per	Low	Mid	High	Source	Date
Claims Adjuster, Examiner, and Investigator	Stockton-Lodi MSA, CA	S	20.96 MW	19.32 AW	43590 AAW	CABLS	10//99-12//99
	Ventura PMSA, CA	S	28.03 MW	25.82 AW	58310 AAW	CABLS	10//99-12//99
	Colorado	S	17.81 MW	18.50 AW	38490 AAW	COBLS	10//99-12//99
	Boulder-Longmont PMSA, CO	S	17.49 MW	17.39 AW	36380 AAW	COBLS	10//99-12//99
	Colorado Springs MSA, CO	S	18.77 MW	18.66 AW	39050 AAW	COBLS	10//99-12//99
	Denver PMSA, CO	S	18.37 MW	17.27 AW	38210 AAW	COBLS	10//99-12//99
	Connecticut	S	20.5 MW	21.56 AW	44840 AAW	CTBLS	10//99-12//99
	Bridgeport PMSA, CT	S	24.68 MW	20.38 AW	51340 AAW	CTBLS	10//99-12//99
	Hartford MSA, CT	S	21.07 MW	20.14 AW	43820 AAW	CTBLS	10//99-12//99
	New Haven-Meriden PMSA, CT	S	19.87 MW	19.66 AW	41330 AAW	CTBLS	10//99-12//99
	Stamford-Norwalk PMSA, CT	S	26.36 MW	23.85 AW	54820 AAW	CTBLS	10//99-12//99
	Delaware	S	15.24 MW	15.62 AW	32490 AAW	DEBLS	10//99-12//99
	Dover MSA, DE	S	14.64 MW	12.80 AW	30450 AAW	DEBLS	10//99-12//99
	Wilmington-Newark PMSA, DE-MD	S	15.91 MW	15.46 AW	33090 AAW	DEBLS	10//99-12//99
	District of Columbia	S	17.31 MW	19.56 AW	40690 AAW	DCBLS	10//99-12//99
	Washington PMSA, DC-MD-VA-WV	S	18.04 MW	16.96 AW	37520 AAW	DCBLS	10//99-12//99
	Florida	S	18.31 MW	19.07 AW	39660 AAW	FLBLS	10//99-12//99
	Fort Lauderdale PMSA, FL	S	23.48 MW	21.15 AW	48840 AAW	FLBLS	10//99-12//99
	Jacksonville MSA, FL	S	19.46 MW	18.73 AW	40470 AAW	FLBLS	10//99-12//99
	Lakeland-Winter Haven MSA, FL	S	19.04 MW	18.50 AW	39610 AAW	FLBLS	10//99-12//99
	Miami PMSA, FL	S	15.98 MW	15.90 AW	33240 AAW	FLBLS	10//99-12//99
	Ocala MSA, FL	S	20.90 MW	22.00 AW	43480 AAW	FLBLS	10//99-12//99
	Orlando MSA, FL	S	22.30 MW	20.20 AW	46380 AAW	FLBLS	10//99-12//99
	Pensacola MSA, FL	S	17.26 MW	15.65 AW	35900 AAW	FLBLS	10//99-12//99
	Sarasota-Bradenton MSA, FL	S	20.73 MW	20.29 AW	43120 AAW	FLBLS	10//99-12//99
	Tampa-St. Petersburg-Clearwater MSA, FL	S	19.00 MW	18.46 AW	39520 AAW	FLBLS	10//99-12//99
	West Palm Beach-Boca Raton MSA, FL	S	25.22 MW	21.19 AW	52460 AAW	FLBLS	10//99-12//99
	Georgia	S	16.34 MW	17.41 AW	36220 AAW	GABLS	10//99-12//99
	Albany MSA, GA	S	19.64 MW	19.46 AW	40860 AAW	GABLS	10//99-12//99
	Atlanta MSA, GA	S	17.11 MW	15.93 AW	35590 AAW	GABLS	10//99-12//99
	Augusta-Aiken MSA, GA-SC	S	20.48 MW	19.42 AW	42610 AAW	GABLS	10//99-12//99
	Macon MSA, GA	S	20.08 MW	19.40 AW	41760 AAW	GABLS	10//99-12//99
	Savannah MSA, GA	S	16.87 MW	16.51 AW	35090 AAW	GABLS	10//99-12//99
	Idaho	S	16.15 MW	16.57 AW	34470 AAW	IDBLS	10//99-12//99
	Boise City MSA, ID	S	16.05 MW	15.81 AW	33380 AAW	IDBLS	10//99-12//99
	Illinois	S	16.94 MW	20.11 AW	41820 AAW	ILBLS	10//99-12//99
	Bloomington-Normal MSA, IL	S	21.21 MW	18.11 AW	44130 AAW	ILBLS	10//99-12//99
	Chicago PMSA, IL	S	20.05 MW	16.85 AW	41700 AAW	ILBLS	10//99-12//99
	Peoria-Pekin MSA, IL	S	18.97 MW	16.41 AW	39460 AAW	ILBLS	10//99-12//99
	Rockford MSA, IL	S	22.94 MW	21.38 AW	47720 AAW	ILBLS	10//99-12//99
	Springfield MSA, IL	S	14.58 MW	11.85 AW	30330 AAW	ILBLS	10//99-12//99
	Indiana	S	16.63 MW	18.12 AW	37680 AAW	INBLS	10//99-12//99
	Evansville-Henderson MSA, IN-KY	S	16.41 MW	17.54 AW	34140 AAW	INBLS	10//99-12//99
	Fort Wayne MSA, IN	S	17.60 MW	16.17 AW	36610 AAW	INBLS	10//99-12//99
	Gary PMSA, IN	S	15.66 MW	15.72 AW	32570 AAW	INBLS	10//99-12//99
	Indianapolis MSA, IN	S	18.12 MW	16.64 AW	37690 AAW	INBLS	10//99-12//99
	Iowa	S	14.45 MW	16.67 AW	34670 AAW	IABLS	10//99-12//99
	Cedar Rapids MSA, IA	S	14.93 MW	13.45 AW	31060 AAW	IABLS	10//99-12//99
	Davenport-Moline-Rock Island MSA, IA-IL	S	20.61 MW	18.44 AW	42870 AAW	IABLS	10//99-12//99
	Des Moines MSA, IA	S	16.82 MW	13.23 AW	34990 AAW	IABLS	10//99-12//99
	Waterloo-Cedar Falls MSA, IA	S	17.85 MW	18.71 AW	37130 AAW	IABLS	10//99-12//99
	Kansas	S	19.95 MW	21.77 AW	45280 AAW	KSBLS	10//99-12//99
	Topeka MSA, KS	S	19.74 MW	18.85 AW	41060 AAW	KSBLS	10//99-12//99
	Wichita MSA, KS	S	21.56 MW	20.07 AW	44850 AAW	KSBLS	10//99-12//99
	Kentucky	S	22.95 MW	23.32 AW	48510 AAW	KYBLS	10//99-12//99
	Lexington MSA, KY	S	24.19 MW	25.38 AW	50320 AAW	KYBLS	10//99-12//99
	Louisville MSA, KY-IN	S	23.88 MW	21.92 AW	49660 AAW	KYBLS	10//99-12//99
	Louisiana	S	18.07 MW	20.66 AW	42970 AAW	LABLS	10//99-12//99
	Alexandria MSA, LA	S	19.96 MW	19.31 AW	41510 AAW	LABLS	10//99-12//99
	Baton Rouge MSA, LA	S	17.37 MW	15.37 AW	36120 AAW	LABLS	10//99-12//99
	Lafayette MSA, LA	S	19.34 MW	17.88 AW	40220 AAW	LABLS	10//99-12//99
	Monroe MSA, LA	S	15.93 MW	15.49 AW	33130 AAW	LABLS	10//99-12//99
	New Orleans MSA, LA	S	25.95 MW	26.60 AW	53980 AAW	LABLS	10//99-12//99

AAW Average annual wage	**AOH** Average offered, high	**ASH** Average starting, high	**H** Hourly	**M** Monthly	**S** Special: hourly and annual
AE Average entry wage	**AOL** Average offered, low	**ASL** Average starting, low	**HI** Highest wage paid	**MTC** Median total compensation	**TQ** Third quartile wage
AEX Average experienced wage	**APH** Average pay, high range	**AW** Average wage paid	**HR** High end range	**MW** Median wage paid	**W** Weekly
AO Average offered	**APL** Average pay, low range	**FQ** First quartile wage	**LR** Low end range	**SQ** Second quartile wage	**Y** Yearly

Occupation/Type/Industry	Location	Per	Low	Mid	High	Source	Date
Claims Adjuster, Examiner, and Investigator							
	Shreveport-Bossier City MSA, LA	S	18.99 MW	16.46 AW	39500 AAW	LABLS	10//99-12//99
	Maine	S	17.54 MW	18.47 AW	38420 AAW	MEBLS	10//99-12//99
	Portland MSA, ME	S	18.47 MW	17.28 AW	38420 AAW	MEBLS	10//99-12//99
	Maryland	S	15.44 MW	16.39 AW	34100 AAW	MDBLS	10//99-12//99
	Baltimore PMSA, MD	S	15.76 MW	14.70 AW	32780 AAW	MDBLS	10//99-12//99
	Hagerstown PMSA, MD	S	16.51 MW	16.05 AW	34340 AAW	MDBLS	10//99-12//99
	Massachusetts	S	19.26 MW	19.52 AW	40610 AAW	MABLS	10//99-12//99
	Boston PMSA, MA-NH	S	21.66 MW	21.49 AW	45060 AAW	MABLS	10//99-12//99
	Lawrence PMSA, MA-NH	S	16.44 MW	13.20 AW	34200 AAW	MABLS	10//99-12//99
	Worcester PMSA, MA-CT	S	16.48 MW	15.09 AW	34290 AAW	MABLS	10//99-12//99
	Michigan	S	23.22 MW	24.56 AW	51090 AAW	MIBLS	10//99-12//99
	Grand Rapids-Muskegon-Holland MSA, MI	S	16.51 MW	13.50 AW	34330 AAW	MIBLS	10//99-12//99
	Kalamazoo-Battle Creek MSA, MI	S	15.33 MW	15.05 AW	31890 AAW	MIBLS	10//99-12//99
	Lansing-East Lansing MSA, MI	S	20.61 MW	21.00 AW	42870 AAW	MIBLS	10//99-12//99
	Minnesota	S	23.24 MW	25.61 AW	53260 AAW	MNBLS	10//99-12//99
	Duluth-Superior MSA, MN-WI	S	19.63 MW	19.01 AW	40830 AAW	MNBLS	10//99-12//99
	Minneapolis-St. Paul MSA, MN-WI	S	26.55 MW	24.16 AW	55230 AAW	MNBLS	10//99-12//99
	St. Cloud MSA, MN	S	17.51 MW	16.03 AW	36420 AAW	MNBLS	10//99-12//99
	Mississippi	S	15.97 MW	17.28 AW	35950 AAW	MSBLS	10//99-12//99
	Biloxi-Gulfport-Pascagoula MSA, MS	S	16.86 MW	14.85 AW	35070 AAW	MSBLS	10//99-12//99
	Hattiesburg MSA, MS	S	25.30 MW	25.18 AW	52610 AAW	MSBLS	10//99-12//99
	Jackson MSA, MS	S	14.78 MW	14.06 AW	30740 AAW	MSBLS	10//99-12//99
	Missouri	S	17.16 MW	18.39 AW	38240 AAW	MOBLS	10//99-12//99
	Kansas City MSA, MO-KS	S	20.41 MW	19.29 AW	42450 AAW	MOBLS	10//99-12//99
	St. Louis MSA, MO-IL	S	19.71 MW	18.28 AW	41000 AAW	MOBLS	10//99-12//99
	Montana	S	17.17 MW	17.03 AW	35420 AAW	MTBLS	10//99-12//99
	Great Falls MSA, MT	S	18.49 MW	18.96 AW	38470 AAW	MTBLS	10//99-12//99
	Nebraska	S	14.95 MW	15.62 AW	32480 AAW	NEBLS	10//99-12//99
	Lincoln MSA, NE	S	18.59 MW	17.45 AW	38660 AAW	NEBLS	10//99-12//99
	Omaha MSA, NE-IA	S	15.05 MW	14.43 AW	31290 AAW	NEBLS	10//99-12//99
	Nevada	S	18.38 MW	18.16 AW	37780 AAW	NVBLS	10//99-12//99
	Las Vegas MSA, NV-AZ	S	19.21 MW	19.09 AW	39950 AAW	NVBLS	10//99-12//99
	Reno MSA, NV	S	15.33 MW	13.24 AW	31900 AAW	NVBLS	10//99-12//99
	New Hampshire	S	31.06 MW	32.09 AW	66740 AAW	NHBLS	10//99-12//99
	Manchester PMSA, NH	S	26.03 MW	21.46 AW	54140 AAW	NHBLS	10//99-12//99
	New Jersey	S	20.28 MW	22.00 AW	45760 AAW	NJBLS	10//99-12//99
	Bergen-Passaic PMSA, NJ	S	20.97 MW	19.82 AW	43620 AAW	NJBLS	10//99-12//99
	Jersey City PMSA, NJ	S	24.00 MW	23.32 AW	49920 AAW	NJBLS	10//99-12//99
	Middlesex-Somerset-Hunterdon PMSA, NJ	S	26.14 MW	23.37 AW	54360 AAW	NJBLS	10//99-12//99
	Monmouth-Ocean PMSA, NJ	S	20.86 MW	18.95 AW	43390 AAW	NJBLS	10//99-12//99
	Newark PMSA, NJ	S	21.34 MW	19.59 AW	44390 AAW	NJBLS	10//99-12//99
	Trenton PMSA, NJ	S	22.05 MW	22.32 AW	45860 AAW	NJBLS	10//99-12//99
	New Mexico	S	18.9 MW	18.41 AW	38280 AAW	NMBLS	10//99-12//99
	Albuquerque MSA, NM	S	18.73 MW	19.26 AW	38970 AAW	NMBLS	10//99-12//99
	New York	S	21.45 MW	24.21 AW	50350 AAW	NYBLS	10//99-12//99
	Binghamton MSA, NY	S	21.70 MW	21.77 AW	45140 AAW	NYBLS	10//99-12//99
	Buffalo-Niagara Falls MSA, NY	S	18.27 MW	17.21 AW	38000 AAW	NYBLS	10//99-12//99
	Nassau-Suffolk PMSA, NY	S	21.81 MW	18.15 AW	45350 AAW	NYBLS	10//99-12//99
	New York PMSA, NY	S	27.47 MW	27.74 AW	57140 AAW	NYBLS	10//99-12//99
	Rochester MSA, NY	S	18.62 MW	18.12 AW	38740 AAW	NYBLS	10//99-12//99
	North Carolina	S	17.34 MW	18.40 AW	38280 AAW	NCBLS	10//99-12//99
	Charlotte-Gastonia-Rock Hill MSA, NC-SC	S	19.72 MW	19.41 AW	41010 AAW	NCBLS	10//99-12//99
	Fayetteville MSA, NC	S	20.26 MW	19.80 AW	42130 AAW	NCBLS	10//99-12//99
	Greensboro--Winston-Salem--High Point MSA, NC	S	17.66 MW	17.70 AW	36720 AAW	NCBLS	10//99-12//99
	Raleigh-Durham-Chapel Hill MSA, NC	S	17.58 MW	16.19 AW	36560 AAW	NCBLS	10//99-12//99
	North Dakota	S	16.02 MW	16.58 AW	34490 AAW	NDBLS	10//99-12//99
	Bismarck MSA, ND	S	16.09 MW	15.43 AW	33470 AAW	NDBLS	10//99-12//99
	Fargo-Moorhead MSA, ND-MN	S	16.25 MW	15.73 AW	33810 AAW	NDBLS	10//99-12//99
	Ohio	S	19.29 MW	20.37 AW	42360 AAW	OHBLS	10//99-12//99
	Canton-Massillon MSA, OH	S	19.92 MW	19.85 AW	41420 AAW	OHBLS	10//99-12//99

AAW Average annual wage	AOH Average offered, high	ASH Average starting, high	H Hourly	M Monthly	S Special: hourly and annual
AE Average entry wage	AOL Average offered, low	ASL Average starting, low	HI Highest wage paid	MTC Median total compensation	TQ Third quartile wage
AEX Average experienced wage	APH Average pay, high range	AW Average wage paid	HR High end range	MW Median wage paid	W Weekly
AO Average offered	APL Average pay, low range	FQ First quartile wage	LR Low end range	SQ Second quartile wage	Y Yearly

Occupation/Type/Industry	Location	Per	Low	Mid	High	Source	Date
Claims Adjuster, Examiner, and Investigator	Cincinnati PMSA, OH-KY-IN	S	20.47 MW	19.34 AW	42590 AAW	OHBLS	10//99-12//99
	Cleveland-Lorain-Elyria PMSA, OH	S	21.62 MW	20.46 AW	44970 AAW	OHBLS	10//99-12//99
	Columbus MSA, OH	S	18.95 MW	19.01 AW	39430 AAW	OHBLS	10//99-12//99
	Hamilton-Middletown PMSA, OH	S	22.14 MW	21.14 AW	46060 AAW	OHBLS	10//99-12//99
	Toledo MSA, OH	S	21.99 MW	19.92 AW	45740 AAW	OHBLS	10//99-12//99
	Youngstown-Warren MSA, OH	S	19.13 MW	19.22 AW	39790 AAW	OHBLS	10//99-12//99
	Oklahoma	S	15.74 MW	16.73 AW	34800 AAW	OKBLS	10//99-12//99
	Oklahoma City MSA, OK	S	17.11 MW	16.17 AW	35590 AAW	OKBLS	10//99-12//99
	Tulsa MSA, OK	S	16.17 MW	14.83 AW	33630 AAW	OKBLS	10//99-12//99
	Oregon	S	20.14 MW	20.46 AW	42570 AAW	ORBLS	10//99-12//99
	Eugene-Springfield MSA, OR	S	21.36 MW	21.06 AW	44420 AAW	ORBLS	10//99-12//99
	Portland-Vancouver PMSA, OR-WA	S	20.46 MW	20.09 AW	42560 AAW	ORBLS	10//99-12//99
	Salem PMSA, OR	S	20.32 MW	19.97 AW	42270 AAW	ORBLS	10//99-12//99
	Pennsylvania	S	19.27 MW	19.70 AW	40970 AAW	PABLS	10//99-12//99
	Allentown-Bethlehem-Easton MSA, PA	S	19.25 MW	18.24 AW	40040 AAW	PABLS	10//99-12//99
	Harrisburg-Lebanon-Carlisle MSA, PA	S	17.35 MW	16.74 AW	36090 AAW	PABLS	10//99-12//99
	Lancaster MSA, PA	S	12.24 MW	11.14 AW	25460 AAW	PABLS	10//99-12//99
	Philadelphia PMSA, PA-NJ	S	20.18 MW	19.32 AW	41970 AAW	PABLS	10//99-12//99
	Pittsburgh MSA, PA	S	18.06 MW	17.84 AW	37570 AAW	PABLS	10//99-12//99
	Reading MSA, PA	S	13.64 MW	13.63 AW	28370 AAW	PABLS	10//99-12//99
	Scranton--Wilkes-Barre--Hazleton MSA, PA	S	16.78 MW	15.72 AW	34910 AAW	PABLS	10//99-12//99
	Rhode Island	S	13.17 MW	16.50 AW	34330 AAW	RIBLS	10//99-12//99
	Providence-Fall River-Warwick MSA, RI-MA	S	16.53 MW	13.20 AW	34380 AAW	RIBLS	10//99-12//99
	South Carolina	S	19.35 MW	21.08 AW	43840 AAW	SCBLS	10//99-12//99
	Charleston-North Charleston MSA, SC	S	19.52 MW	18.68 AW	40610 AAW	SCBLS	10//99-12//99
	Columbia MSA, SC	S	18.95 MW	16.50 AW	39410 AAW	SCBLS	10//99-12//99
	Greenville-Spartanburg-Anderson MSA, SC	S	23.65 MW	22.83 AW	49200 AAW	SCBLS	10//99-12//99
	Myrtle Beach MSA, SC	S	28.24 MW	25.63 AW	58740 AAW	SCBLS	10//99-12//99
	South Dakota	S	18.38 MW	18.59 AW	38660 AAW	SDBLS	10//99-12//99
	Sioux Falls MSA, SD	S	18.94 MW	18.56 AW	39390 AAW	SDBLS	10//99-12//99
	Tennessee	S	17.3 MW	19.06 AW	39640 AAW	TNBLS	10//99-12//99
	Chattanooga MSA, TN-GA	S	18.79 MW	21.27 AW	39080 AAW	TNBLS	10//99-12//99
	Jackson MSA, TN	S	29.68 MW	31.17 AW	61730 AAW	TNBLS	10//99-12//99
	Knoxville MSA, TN	S	19.25 MW	17.21 AW	40040 AAW	TNBLS	10//99-12//99
	Memphis MSA, TN-AR-MS	S	16.73 MW	15.53 AW	34800 AAW	MSBLS	10//99-12//99
	Nashville MSA, TN	S	19.26 MW	18.14 AW	40070 AAW	TNBLS	10//99-12//99
	Texas	S	17.42 MW	19.05 AW	39620 AAW	TXBLS	10//99-12//99
	Amarillo MSA, TX	S	23.08 MW	21.99 AW	48000 AAW	TXBLS	10//99-12//99
	Austin-San Marcos MSA, TX	S	18.24 MW	16.62 AW	37940 AAW	TXBLS	10//99-12//99
	Beaumont-Port Arthur MSA, TX	S	17.41 MW	15.27 AW	36220 AAW	TXBLS	10//99-12//99
	Brownsville-Harlingen-San Benito MSA, TX	S	17.68 MW	13.11 AW	36770 AAW	TXBLS	10//99-12//99
	Corpus Christi MSA, TX	S	19.37 MW	16.57 AW	40280 AAW	TXBLS	10//99-12//99
	Dallas PMSA, TX	S	18.28 MW	16.58 AW	38010 AAW	TXBLS	10//99-12//99
	Fort Worth-Arlington PMSA, TX	S	17.74 MW	15.92 AW	36900 AAW	TXBLS	10//99-12//99
	Houston PMSA, TX	S	21.71 MW	19.68 AW	45150 AAW	TXBLS	10//99-12//99
	McAllen-Edinburg-Mission MSA, TX	S	17.19 MW	16.21 AW	35750 AAW	TXBLS	10//99-12//99
	Odessa-Midland MSA, TX	S	21.93 MW	21.26 AW	45610 AAW	TXBLS	10//99-12//99
	San Antonio MSA, TX	S	21.47 MW	23.03 AW	44650 AAW	TXBLS	10//99-12//99
	Sherman-Denison MSA, TX	S	15.48 MW	15.36 AW	32200 AAW	TXBLS	10//99-12//99
	Tyler MSA, TX	S	14.68 MW	14.68 AW	30540 AAW	TXBLS	10//99-12//99
	Waco MSA, TX	S	16.95 MW	15.89 AW	35250 AAW	TXBLS	10//99-12//99
	Utah	S	18.51 MW	19.67 AW	40920 AAW	UTBLS	10//99-12//99
	Salt Lake City-Ogden MSA, UT	S	19.40 MW	18.26 AW	40350 AAW	UTBLS	10//99-12//99
	Vermont	S	18.31 MW	21.26 AW	44220 AAW	VTBLS	10//99-12//99
	Burlington MSA, VT	S	22.63 MW	19.52 AW	47070 AAW	VTBLS	10//99-12//99
	Virginia	S	18.2 MW	18.48 AW	38430 AAW	VABLS	10//99-12//99
	Lynchburg MSA, VA	S	18.41 MW	18.47 AW	38280 AAW	VABLS	10//99-12//99

AAW Average annual wage	AOH Average offered, high	ASH Average starting, high	H Hourly
AE Average entry wage	AOL Average offered, low	ASL Average starting, low	HI Highest wage paid
AEX Average experienced wage	APH Average pay, high range	AW Average wage paid	HR High end range
AO Average offered	APL Average pay, low range	FQ First quartile wage	LR Low end range

M Monthly	S Special: hourly and annual	
MTC Median total compensation	TQ Third quartile wage	
MW Median wage paid	W Weekly	
SQ Second quartile wage	Y Yearly	

Occupation/Type/Industry	Location	Per	Low	Mid	High	Source	Date
Claims Adjuster, Examiner, and Investigator							
	Roanoke MSA, VA	S	19.31 MW	18.98 AW	40170 AAW	VABLS	10//99-12//99
	Washington	S	20.6 MW	21.66 AW	45060 AAW	WABLS	10//99-12//99
	Richland-Kennewick-Pasco MSA, WA	S	29.45 MW	30.63 AW	61260 AAW	WABLS	10//99-12//99
	Seattle-Bellevue-Everett PMSA, WA	S	21.68 MW	20.63 AW	45090 AAW	WABLS	10//99-12//99
	Spokane MSA, WA	S	22.11 MW	22.20 AW	45980 AAW	WABLS	10//99-12//99
	Tacoma PMSA, WA	S	23.27 MW	23.26 AW	48400 AAW	WABLS	10//99-12//99
	Yakima MSA, WA	S	26.33 MW	27.76 AW	54770 AAW	WABLS	10//99-12//99
	West Virginia	S	11.12 MW	13.30 AW	27670 AAW	WVBLS	10//99-12//99
	Parkersburg-Marietta MSA, WV-OH	S	17.79 MW	16.65 AW	37010 AAW	WVBLS	10//99-12//99
	Wisconsin	S	14.49 MW	15.83 AW	32930 AAW	WIBLS	10//99-12//99
	Appleton-Oshkosh-Neenah MSA, WI	S	16.35 MW	15.87 AW	34000 AAW	WIBLS	10//99-12//99
	Eau Claire MSA, WI	S	13.63 MW	13.22 AW	28360 AAW	WIBLS	10//99-12//99
	Janesville-Beloit MSA, WI	S	13.61 MW	12.83 AW	28300 AAW	WIBLS	10//99-12//99
	La Crosse MSA, WI-MN	S	13.52 MW	12.71 AW	28120 AAW	WIBLS	10//99-12//99
	Madison MSA, WI	S	14.00 MW	11.34 AW	29120 AAW	WIBLS	10//99-12//99
	Milwaukee-Waukesha PMSA, WI	S	20.07 MW	18.47 AW	41750 AAW	WIBLS	10//99-12//99
	Wausau MSA, WI	S	17.67 MW	16.63 AW	36760 AAW	WIBLS	10//99-12//99
	Wyoming	S	16.55 MW	17.60 AW	36610 AAW	WYBLS	10//99-12//99
	Puerto Rico	S	11.71 MW	12.39 AW	25770 AAW	PRBLS	10//99-12//99
	San Juan-Bayamon PMSA, PR	S	12.39 MW	11.70 AW	25760 AAW	PRBLS	10//99-12//99
	Guam	S	16.89 MW	16.07 AW	33430 AAW	GUBLS	10//99-12//99
Cleaner of Vehicle and Equipment							
	Alabama	S	6.65 MW	7.19 AW	14960 AAW	ALBLS	10//99-12//99
	Alaska	S	7.99 MW	8.21 AW	17070 AAW	AKBLS	10//99-12//99
	Arizona	S	6.85 MW	7.18 AW	14930 AAW	AZBLS	10//99-12//99
	Arkansas	S	7.74 MW	7.78 AW	16180 AAW	ARBLS	10//99-12//99
	California	S	6.77 MW	7.79 AW	16200 AAW	CABLS	10//99-12//99
	Colorado	S	7.87 MW	8.55 AW	17790 AAW	COBLS	10//99-12//99
	Connecticut	S	7.91 MW	8.45 AW	17570 AAW	CTBLS	10//99-12//99
	Delaware	S	8.18 MW	9.54 AW	19840 AAW	DEBLS	10//99-12//99
	District of Columbia	S	10 MW	10.54 AW	21930 AAW	DCBLS	10//99-12//99
	Florida	S	7.09 MW	7.63 AW	15860 AAW	FLBLS	10//99-12//99
	Georgia	S	7.22 MW	7.69 AW	16000 AAW	GABLS	10//99-12//99
	Hawaii	S	8.13 MW	8.94 AW	18600 AAW	HIBLS	10//99-12//99
	Idaho	S	6.4 MW	6.84 AW	14230 AAW	IDBLS	10//99-12//99
	Illinois	S	7.09 MW	7.92 AW	16470 AAW	ILBLS	10//99-12//99
	Indiana	S	7.75 MW	8.45 AW	17580 AAW	INBLS	10//99-12//99
	Iowa	S	7.29 MW	7.78 AW	16190 AAW	IABLS	10//99-12//99
	Kansas	S	7.23 MW	7.50 AW	15610 AAW	KSBLS	10//99-12//99
	Kentucky	S	7.35 MW	7.88 AW	16390 AAW	KYBLS	10//99-12//99
	Louisiana	S	6.5 MW	7.05 AW	14660 AAW	LABLS	10//99-12//99
	Maine	S	7.37 MW	7.72 AW	16060 AAW	MEBLS	10//99-12//99
	Maryland	S	7.81 MW	9.06 AW	18850 AAW	MDBLS	10//99-12//99
	Massachusetts	S	8.06 MW	8.88 AW	18470 AAW	MABLS	10//99-12//99
	Michigan	S	7.66 MW	8.89 AW	18500 AAW	MIBLS	10//99-12//99
	Minnesota	S	7.83 MW	8.68 AW	18060 AAW	MNBLS	10//99-12//99
	Mississippi	S	7.11 MW	7.22 AW	15010 AAW	MSBLS	10//99-12//99
	Missouri	S	7.26 MW	7.88 AW	16400 AAW	MOBLS	10//99-12//99
	Montana	S	6.32 MW	7.33 AW	15250 AAW	MTBLS	10//99-12//99
	Nebraska	S	7.87 MW	8.11 AW	16870 AAW	NEBLS	10//99-12//99
	Nevada	S	6.96 MW	7.72 AW	16050 AAW	NVBLS	10//99-12//99
	New Hampshire	S	8.18 MW	8.67 AW	18020 AAW	NHBLS	10//99-12//99
	New Jersey	S	7.8 MW	8.53 AW	17740 AAW	NJBLS	10//99-12//99
	New Mexico	S	6.55 MW	6.96 AW	14470 AAW	NMBLS	10//99-12//99
	New York	S	7.44 MW	8.57 AW	17830 AAW	NYBLS	10//99-12//99
	North Carolina	S	7.24 MW	7.83 AW	16290 AAW	NCBLS	10//99-12//99
	North Dakota	S	6.65 MW	7.23 AW	15030 AAW	NDBLS	10//99-12//99
	Ohio	S	7.6 MW	8.56 AW	17810 AAW	OHBLS	10//99-12//99
	Oklahoma	S	6.84 MW	7.57 AW	15740 AAW	OKBLS	10//99-12//99
	Oregon	S	8.24 MW	9.60 AW	19960 AAW	ORBLS	10//99-12//99
	Pennsylvania	S	7.61 MW	8.21 AW	17070 AAW	PABLS	10//99-12//99
	Rhode Island	S	8.27 MW	8.94 AW	18600 AAW	RIBLS	10//99-12//99
	South Carolina	S	6.97 MW	7.40 AW	15400 AAW	SCBLS	10//99-12//99
	South Dakota	S	6.74 MW	6.99 AW	14530 AAW	SDBLS	10//99-12//99
	Tennessee	S	7.81 MW	8.23 AW	17120 AAW	TNBLS	10//99-12//99

AAW Average annual wage	**AOH** Average offered, high	**ASH** Average starting, high	**H** Hourly
AE Average entry wage	**AOL** Average offered, low	**ASL** Average starting, low	**HI** Highest wage paid
AEX Average experienced wage	**APH** Average pay, high range	**AW** Average wage paid	**HR** High end range
AO Average offered	**APL** Average pay, low range	**FQ** First quartile wage	**LR** Low end range

M Monthly	**S** Special: hourly and annual
MTC Median total compensation	**TQ** Third quartile wage
MW Median wage paid	**W** Weekly
SQ Second quartile wage	**Y** Yearly

Occupation/Type/Industry	Location	Per	Low	Mid	High	Source	Date
Cleaner of Vehicle and Equipment	Texas	S	6.76 MW	7.44 AW	15480 AAW	TXBLS	10//99-12//99
	Utah	S	7.18 MW	7.51 AW	15630 AAW	UTBLS	10//99-12//99
	Vermont	S	7.82 MW	8.12 AW	16900 AAW	VTBLS	10//99-12//99
	Virginia	S	7.4 MW	7.89 AW	16400 AAW	VABLS	10//99-12//99
	Washington	S	7.96 MW	8.84 AW	18380 AAW	WABLS	10//99-12//99
	West Virginia	S	6.59 MW	7.38 AW	15360 AAW	WVBLS	10//99-12//99
	Wisconsin	S	7.73 MW	8.01 AW	16660 AAW	WIBLS	10//99-12//99
	Wyoming	S	6.51 MW	7.25 AW	15080 AAW	WYBLS	10//99-12//99
	Puerto Rico	S	6.01 MW	6.12 AW	12730 AAW	PRBLS	10//99-12//99
	Virgin Islands	S	7.42 MW	8.95 AW	18630 AAW	VIBLS	10//99-12//99
	Guam	S	6.39 MW	6.54 AW	13610 AAW	GUBLS	10//99-12//99
Cleaning, Washing, and Metal Pickling Equipment Operator and Tender	Alabama	S	8.39 MW	10.64 AW	22130 AAW	ALBLS	10//99-12//99
	Arizona	S	6.2 MW	6.87 AW	14280 AAW	AZBLS	10//99-12//99
	Arkansas	S	10.83 MW	15.21 AW	31640 AAW	ARBLS	10//99-12//99
	California	S	8.95 MW	9.81 AW	20400 AAW	CABLS	10//99-12//99
	Colorado	S	7.84 MW	8.50 AW	17680 AAW	COBLS	10//99-12//99
	Connecticut	S	12.17 MW	11.99 AW	24950 AAW	CTBLS	10//99-12//99
	Florida	S	7.65 MW	8.48 AW	17630 AAW	FLBLS	10//99-12//99
	Georgia	S	7.88 MW	8.11 AW	16870 AAW	GABLS	10//99-12//99
	Illinois	S	7.91 MW	9.01 AW	18750 AAW	ILBLS	10//99-12//99
	Indiana	S	12.16 MW	12.11 AW	25190 AAW	INBLS	10//99-12//99
	Iowa	S	8.64 MW	9.42 AW	19590 AAW	IABLS	10//99-12//99
	Kansas	S	11.63 MW	11.20 AW	23300 AAW	KSBLS	10//99-12//99
	Kentucky	S	10.97 MW	11.57 AW	24060 AAW	KYBLS	10//99-12//99
	Louisiana	S	10.14 MW	10.21 AW	21230 AAW	LABLS	10//99-12//99
	Maine	S	9.54 MW	9.37 AW	19490 AAW	MEBLS	10//99-12//99
	Maryland	S	7.73 MW	8.04 AW	16720 AAW	MDBLS	10//99-12//99
	Massachusetts	S	8.76 MW	9.37 AW	19490 AAW	MABLS	10//99-12//99
	Michigan	S	12.42 MW	12.21 AW	25410 AAW	MIBLS	10//99-12//99
	Minnesota	S	11.79 MW	11.24 AW	23390 AAW	MNBLS	10//99-12//99
	Mississippi	S	9.38 MW	10.33 AW	21480 AAW	MSBLS	10//99-12//99
	Missouri	S	10.67 MW	11.02 AW	22920 AAW	MOBLS	10//99-12//99
	Nebraska	S	10.14 MW	10.09 AW	20990 AAW	NEBLS	10//99-12//99
	New Hampshire	S	9.67 MW	9.66 AW	20090 AAW	NHBLS	10//99-12//99
	New Jersey	S	8.25 MW	9.49 AW	19740 AAW	NJBLS	10//99-12//99
	New York	S	9.84 MW	10.08 AW	20970 AAW	NYBLS	10//99-12//99
	North Carolina	S	10.07 MW	10.68 AW	22210 AAW	NCBLS	10//99-12//99
	Ohio	S	12.44 MW	12.63 AW	26270 AAW	OHBLS	10//99-12//99
	Oklahoma	S	8.46 MW	9.29 AW	19320 AAW	OKBLS	10//99-12//99
	Oregon	S	9.38 MW	10.65 AW	22160 AAW	ORBLS	10//99-12//99
	Pennsylvania	S	12.78 MW	13.72 AW	28530 AAW	PABLS	10//99-12//99
	Rhode Island	S	9.35 MW	9.23 AW	19200 AAW	RIBLS	10//99-12//99
	South Carolina	S	7.8 MW	8.56 AW	17800 AAW	SCBLS	10//99-12//99
	South Dakota	S	7.84 MW	8.29 AW	17240 AAW	SDBLS	10//99-12//99
	Tennessee	S	12.56 MW	14.63 AW	30430 AAW	TNBLS	10//99-12//99
	Texas	S	6.79 MW	7.77 AW	16160 AAW	TXBLS	10//99-12//99
	Utah	S	11.15 MW	11.19 AW	23270 AAW	UTBLS	10//99-12//99
	Vermont	S	11.48 MW	11.55 AW	24030 AAW	VTBLS	10//99-12//99
	Virginia	S	18.86 MW	16.94 AW	35230 AAW	VABLS	10//99-12//99
	Washington	S	9.76 MW	10.08 AW	20960 AAW	WABLS	10//99-12//99
	Wisconsin	S	8.28 MW	8.88 AW	18460 AAW	WIBLS	10//99-12//99
	Puerto Rico	S	6.42 MW	6.41 AW	13320 AAW	PRBLS	10//99-12//99
Clergy	United States	H		15.25 AW		NCS98	1998
	Alabama	S	14.55 MW	15.72 AW	32710 AAW	ALBLS	10//99-12//99
	Birmingham MSA, AL	S	15.16 MW	12.82 AW	31530 AAW	ALBLS	10//99-12//99
	Mobile MSA, AL	S	14.40 MW	14.26 AW	29950 AAW	ALBLS	10//99-12//99
	Montgomery MSA, AL	S	17.13 MW	15.19 AW	35640 AAW	ALBLS	10//99-12//99
	Alaska	S	12.8 MW	12.36 AW	25710 AAW	AKBLS	10//99-12//99
	Anchorage MSA, AK	S	13.18 MW	12.86 AW	27420 AAW	AKBLS	10//99-12//99
	Arizona	S	16.68 MW	16.23 AW	33770 AAW	AZBLS	10//99-12//99
	Phoenix-Mesa MSA, AZ	S	15.64 MW	15.84 AW	32530 AAW	AZBLS	10//99-12//99
	Tucson MSA, AZ	S	18.46 MW	18.24 AW	38390 AAW	AZBLS	10//99-12//99
	Arkansas	S	14.84 MW	15.91 AW	33090 AAW	ARBLS	10//99-12//99
	Little Rock-North Little Rock MSA, AR	S	15.35 MW	14.56 AW	31940 AAW	ARBLS	10//99-12//99
	California	S	18 MW	18.92 AW	39350 AAW	CABLS	10//99-12//99
	Bakersfield MSA, CA	S	20.86 MW	19.85 AW	43390 AAW	CABLS	10//99-12//99

AAW Average annual wage	**AOH** Average offered, high	**ASH** Average starting, high	**H** Hourly	**M** Monthly	**S** Special: hourly and annual
AE Average entry wage	**AOL** Average offered, low	**ASL** Average starting, low	**HI** Highest wage paid	**MTC** Median total compensation	**TQ** Third quartile wage
AEX Average experienced wage	**APH** Average pay, high range	**AW** Average wage paid	**HR** High end range	**MW** Median wage paid	**W** Weekly
AO Average offered	**APL** Average pay, low range	**FQ** First quartile wage	**LR** Low end range	**SQ** Second quartile wage	**Y** Yearly

Occupation/Type/Industry	Location	Per	Low	Mid	High	Source	Date
Clergy	Chico-Paradise MSA, CA	S	14.75 MW	13.43 AW	30680 AAW	CABLS	10//99-12//99
	Fresno MSA, CA	S	20.42 MW	20.33 AW	42470 AAW	CABLS	10//99-12//99
	Los Angeles-Long Beach PMSA, CA	S	23.37 MW	21.75 AW	48610 AAW	CABLS	10//99-12//99
	Modesto MSA, CA	S	14.38 MW	12.96 AW	29910 AAW	CABLS	10//99-12//99
	Oakland PMSA, CA	S	21.88 MW	19.43 AW	45500 AAW	CABLS	10//99-12//99
	Orange County PMSA, CA	S	15.99 MW	15.07 AW	33260 AAW	CABLS	10//99-12//99
	Riverside-San Bernardino PMSA, CA	S	17.27 MW	17.91 AW	35920 AAW	CABLS	10//99-12//99
	Sacramento PMSA, CA	S	14.98 MW	13.57 AW	31160 AAW	CABLS	10//99-12//99
	San Diego MSA, CA	S	9.10 MW	6.89 AW	18920 AAW	CABLS	10//99-12//99
	San Francisco PMSA, CA	S	19.19 MW	17.81 AW	39920 AAW	CABLS	10//99-12//99
	San Jose PMSA, CA	S	25.23 MW	18.09 AW	52480 AAW	CABLS	10//99-12//99
	Santa Barbara-Santa Maria-Lompoc MSA, CA	S	23.91 MW	25.09 AW	49720 AAW	CABLS	10//99-12//99
	Stockton-Lodi MSA, CA	S	18.36 MW	20.73 AW	38190 AAW	CABLS	10//99-12//99
	Vallejo-Fairfield-Napa PMSA, CA	S	18.10 MW	18.99 AW	37660 AAW	CABLS	10//99-12//99
	Visalia-Tulare-Porterville MSA, CA	S	20.24 MW	21.28 AW	42090 AAW	CABLS	10//99-12//99
	Connecticut	S	15.45 MW	17.79 AW	37010 AAW	CTBLS	10//99-12//99
	Hartford MSA, CT	S	17.08 MW	14.07 AW	35520 AAW	CTBLS	10//99-12//99
	New Haven-Meriden PMSA, CT	S	18.62 MW	16.17 AW	38730 AAW	CTBLS	10//99-12//99
	Stamford-Norwalk PMSA, CT	S	21.97 MW	18.21 AW	45710 AAW	CTBLS	10//99-12//99
	Waterbury PMSA, CT	S	16.33 MW	14.79 AW	33970 AAW	CTBLS	10//99-12//99
	Delaware	S	16.12 MW	17.21 AW	35800 AAW	DEBLS	10//99-12//99
	Wilmington-Newark PMSA, DE-MD	S	17.27 MW	15.91 AW	35920 AAW	DEBLS	10//99-12//99
	District of Columbia	S	18.43 MW	19.23 AW	40000 AAW	DCBLS	10//99-12//99
	Washington PMSA, DC-MD-VA-WV	S	12.62 MW	9.48 AW	26250 AAW	DCBLS	10//99-12//99
	Florida	S	11.48 MW	13.07 AW	27190 AAW	FLBLS	10//99-12//99
	Daytona Beach MSA, FL	S	12.95 MW	10.00 AW	26930 AAW	FLBLS	10//99-12//99
	Fort Lauderdale PMSA, FL	S	15.74 MW	15.18 AW	32730 AAW	FLBLS	10//99-12//99
	Fort Pierce-Port St. Lucie MSA, FL	S	14.93 MW	15.02 AW	31040 AAW	FLBLS	10//99-12//99
	Gainesville MSA, FL	S	16.12 MW	15.63 AW	33540 AAW	FLBLS	10//99-12//99
	Jacksonville MSA, FL	S	11.45 MW	9.84 AW	23820 AAW	FLBLS	10//99-12//99
	Lakeland-Winter Haven MSA, FL	S	11.61 MW	10.81 AW	24160 AAW	FLBLS	10//99-12//99
	Miami PMSA, FL	S	13.13 MW	9.98 AW	27310 AAW	FLBLS	10//99-12//99
	Orlando MSA, FL	S	11.07 MW	9.86 AW	23020 AAW	FLBLS	10//99-12//99
	Sarasota-Bradenton MSA, FL	S	17.06 MW	16.12 AW	35480 AAW	FLBLS	10//99-12//99
	Tallahassee MSA, FL	S	13.94 MW	13.66 AW	29000 AAW	FLBLS	10//99-12//99
	Tampa-St. Petersburg-Clearwater MSA, FL	S	12.56 MW	10.14 AW	26120 AAW	FLBLS	10//99-12//99
	West Palm Beach-Boca Raton MSA, FL	S	14.14 MW	11.25 AW	29410 AAW	FLBLS	10//99-12//99
	Georgia	S	18.43 MW	18.51 AW	38500 AAW	GABLS	10//99-12//99
	Athens MSA, GA	S	16.54 MW	17.00 AW	34400 AAW	GABLS	10//99-12//99
	Atlanta MSA, GA	S	19.66 MW	21.57 AW	40890 AAW	GABLS	10//99-12//99
	Macon MSA, GA	S	18.13 MW	18.54 AW	37720 AAW	GABLS	10//99-12//99
	Savannah MSA, GA	S	15.00 MW	12.84 AW	31190 AAW	GABLS	10//99-12//99
	Hawaii	S	16.03 MW	16.97 AW	35310 AAW	HIBLS	10//99-12//99
	Honolulu MSA, HI	S	18.46 MW	18.24 AW	38400 AAW	HIBLS	10//99-12//99
	Idaho	S	17.51 MW	16.70 AW	34730 AAW	IDBLS	10//99-12//99
	Boise City MSA, ID	S	17.78 MW	17.75 AW	36990 AAW	IDBLS	10//99-12//99
	Illinois	S	14.9 MW	15.29 AW	31810 AAW	ILBLS	10//99-12//99
	Chicago PMSA, IL	S	15.98 MW	15.44 AW	33240 AAW	ILBLS	10//99-12//99
	Indiana	S	13.02 MW	14.73 AW	30630 AAW	INBLS	10//99-12//99
	Evansville-Henderson MSA, IN-KY	S	12.88 MW	11.86 AW	26780 AAW	INBLS	10//99-12//99
	Fort Wayne MSA, IN	S	14.45 MW	13.87 AW	30050 AAW	INBLS	10//99-12//99
	Gary PMSA, IN	S	12.62 MW	10.87 AW	26240 AAW	INBLS	10//99-12//99
	Indianapolis MSA, IN	S	16.10 MW	12.80 AW	33490 AAW	INBLS	10//99-12//99
	South Bend MSA, IN	S	16.35 MW	16.85 AW	34010 AAW	INBLS	10//99-12//99
	Iowa	S	14.41 MW	14.48 AW	30120 AAW	IABLS	10//99-12//99
	Cedar Rapids MSA, IA	S	10.64 MW	6.84 AW	22140 AAW	IABLS	10//99-12//99
	Davenport-Moline-Rock Island MSA, IA-IL	S	17.19 MW	16.50 AW	35750 AAW	IABLS	10//99-12//99
	Kansas	S	15.23 MW	15.64 AW	32520 AAW	KSBLS	10//99-12//99

AAW Average annual wage	AOH Average offered, high	ASH Average starting, high	H Hourly	M Monthly	S Special: hourly and annual
AE Average entry wage	AOL Average offered, low	ASL Average starting, low	HI Highest wage paid	MTC Median total compensation	TQ Third quartile wage
AEX Average experienced wage	APH Average pay, high range	AW Average wage paid	HR High end range	MW Median wage paid	W Weekly
AO Average offered	APL Average pay, low range	FQ First quartile wage	LR Low end range	SQ Second quartile wage	Y Yearly

Clergy

Occupation/Type/Industry	Location	Per	Low	Mid	High	Source	Date
Clergy	Wichita MSA, KS	S	15.48 MW	15.99 AW	32210 AAW	KSBLS	10//99-12//99
	Kentucky	S	15.33 MW	16.52 AW	34350 AAW	KYBLS	10//99-12//99
	Lexington MSA, KY	S	20.54 MW	15.03 AW	42720 AAW	KYBLS	10//99-12//99
	Louisville MSA, KY-IN	S	15.84 MW	15.41 AW	32960 AAW	KYBLS	10//99-12//99
	Louisiana	S	15.61 MW	15.69 AW	32640 AAW	LABLS	10//99-12//99
	New Orleans MSA, LA	S	17.05 MW	16.13 AW	35470 AAW	LABLS	10//99-12//99
	Maine	S	17.41 MW	17.16 AW	35700 AAW	MEBLS	10//99-12//99
	Maryland	S	14.67 MW	15.07 AW	31350 AAW	MDBLS	10//99-12//99
	Baltimore PMSA, MD	S	15.39 MW	15.36 AW	32000 AAW	MDBLS	10//99-12//99
	Massachusetts	S	15.39 MW	16.00 AW	33280 AAW	MABLS	10//99-12//99
	Boston PMSA, MA-NH	S	15.52 MW	15.44 AW	32290 AAW	MABLS	10//99-12//99
	Springfield MSA, MA	S	13.21 MW	13.76 AW	27470 AAW	MABLS	10//99-12//99
	Michigan	S	11.4 MW	12.55 AW	26110 AAW	MIBLS	10//99-12//99
	Ann Arbor PMSA, MI	S	14.29 MW	13.48 AW	29720 AAW	MIBLS	10//99-12//99
	Detroit PMSA, MI	S	12.09 MW	11.11 AW	25150 AAW	MIBLS	10//99-12//99
	Flint PMSA, MI	S	13.25 MW	13.44 AW	27560 AAW	MIBLS	10//99-12//99
	Grand Rapids-Muskegon-Holland MSA, MI	S	11.60 MW	10.62 AW	24130 AAW	MIBLS	10//99-12//99
	Kalamazoo-Battle Creek MSA, MI	S	10.76 MW	8.24 AW	22380 AAW	MIBLS	10//99-12//99
	Lansing-East Lansing MSA, MI	S	13.22 MW	12.01 AW	27500 AAW	MIBLS	10//99-12//99
	Saginaw-Bay City-Midland MSA, MI	S	11.44 MW	9.98 AW	23800 AAW	MIBLS	10//99-12//99
	Minnesota	S	15.08 MW	14.94 AW	31080 AAW	MNBLS	10//99-12//99
	Duluth-Superior MSA, MN-WI	S	15.90 MW	15.63 AW	33070 AAW	MNBLS	10//99-12//99
	Minneapolis-St. Paul MSA, MN-WI	S	14.68 MW	14.91 AW	30540 AAW	MNBLS	10//99-12//99
	St. Cloud MSA, MN	S	15.14 MW	15.20 AW	31490 AAW	MNBLS	10//99-12//99
	Mississippi	S	13.18 MW	14.77 AW	30720 AAW	MSBLS	10//99-12//99
	Jackson MSA, MS	S	14.14 MW	12.38 AW	29410 AAW	MSBLS	10//99-12//99
	Missouri	S	15.98 MW	17.11 AW	35590 AAW	MOBLS	10//99-12//99
	Columbia MSA, MO	S	16.79 MW	16.25 AW	34920 AAW	MOBLS	10//99-12//99
	Kansas City MSA, MO-KS	S	17.55 MW	16.70 AW	36500 AAW	MOBLS	10//99-12//99
	St. Louis MSA, MO-IL	S	17.59 MW	16.09 AW	36590 AAW	MOBLS	10//99-12//99
	Montana	S	12.53 MW	13.95 AW	29020 AAW	MTBLS	10//99-12//99
	Billings MSA, MT	S	19.80 MW	20.06 AW	41190 AAW	MTBLS	10//99-12//99
	Great Falls MSA, MT	S	14.05 MW	14.67 AW	29230 AAW	MTBLS	10//99-12//99
	Nebraska	S	15.8 MW	16.40 AW	34110 AAW	NEBLS	10//99-12//99
	Lincoln MSA, NE	S	14.84 MW	15.25 AW	30870 AAW	NEBLS	10//99-12//99
	Omaha MSA, NE-IA	S	18.64 MW	17.32 AW	38770 AAW	NEBLS	10//99-12//99
	Nevada	S	23.17 MW	26.01 AW	54100 AAW	NVBLS	10//99-12//99
	Las Vegas MSA, NV-AZ	S	26.93 MW	25.83 AW	56020 AAW	NVBLS	10//99-12//99
	New Hampshire	S	18.14 MW	17.77 AW	36950 AAW	NHBLS	10//99-12//99
	New Jersey	S	18.24 MW	19.03 AW	39580 AAW	NJBLS	10//99-12//99
	Bergen-Passaic PMSA, NJ	S	18.97 MW	18.10 AW	39450 AAW	NJBLS	10//99-12//99
	Middlesex-Somerset-Hunterdon PMSA, NJ	S	21.89 MW	20.36 AW	45540 AAW	NJBLS	10//99-12//99
	Monmouth-Ocean PMSA, NJ	S	15.45 MW	14.44 AW	32130 AAW	NJBLS	10//99-12//99
	Newark PMSA, NJ	S	20.31 MW	19.08 AW	42250 AAW	NJBLS	10//99-12//99
	Vineland-Millville-Bridgeton PMSA, NJ	S	13.42 MW	13.69 AW	27920 AAW	NJBLS	10//99-12//99
	New York	S	16.2 MW	16.40 AW	34120 AAW	NYBLS	10//99-12//99
	Binghamton MSA, NY	S	11.82 MW	11.36 AW	24580 AAW	NYBLS	10//99-12//99
	Buffalo-Niagara Falls MSA, NY	S	15.83 MW	11.48 AW	32940 AAW	NYBLS	10//99-12//99
	Dutchess County PMSA, NY	S	16.73 MW	16.73 AW	34810 AAW	NYBLS	10//99-12//99
	Elmira MSA, NY	S	15.13 MW	13.98 AW	31470 AAW	NYBLS	10//99-12//99
	Jamestown MSA, NY	S	14.16 MW	14.81 AW	29440 AAW	NYBLS	10//99-12//99
	Nassau-Suffolk PMSA, NY	S	19.38 MW	18.44 AW	40300 AAW	NYBLS	10//99-12//99
	New York PMSA, NY	S	16.59 MW	15.76 AW	34510 AAW	NYBLS	10//99-12//99
	Newburgh PMSA, NY-PA	S	17.51 MW	10.30 AW	36410 AAW	NYBLS	10//99-12//99
	Rochester MSA, NY	S	18.42 MW	18.26 AW	38310 AAW	NYBLS	10//99-12//99
	Syracuse MSA, NY	S	15.99 MW	16.81 AW	33260 AAW	NYBLS	10//99-12//99
	Utica-Rome MSA, NY	S	12.45 MW	12.15 AW	25900 AAW	NYBLS	10//99-12//99
	North Carolina	S	16.61 MW	17.28 AW	35950 AAW	NCBLS	10//99-12//99
	Charlotte-Gastonia-Rock Hill MSA, NC-SC	S	19.21 MW	18.82 AW	39960 AAW	NCBLS	10//99-12//99
	Greensboro--Winston-Salem--High Point MSA, NC	S	19.25 MW	19.15 AW	40040 AAW	NCBLS	10//99-12//99
	Raleigh-Durham-Chapel Hill MSA, NC	S	14.93 MW	14.01 AW	31060 AAW	NCBLS	10//99-12//99
	North Dakota	S	11.71 MW	13.17 AW	27380 AAW	NDBLS	10//99-12//99

AAW Average annual wage	**AOH** Average offered, high	**ASH** Average starting, high	**H** Hourly	**M** Monthly	**S** Special: hourly and annual
AE Average entry wage	**AOL** Average offered, low	**ASL** Average starting, low	**HI** Highest wage paid	**MTC** Median total compensation	**TQ** Third quartile wage
AEX Average experienced wage	**APH** Average pay, high range	**AW** Average wage paid	**HR** High end range	**MW** Median wage paid	**W** Weekly
AO Average offered	**APL** Average pay, low range	**FQ** First quartile wage	**LR** Low end range	**SQ** Second quartile wage	**Y** Yearly

Occupation/Type/Industry	Location	Per	Low	Mid	High	Source	Date
Clergy	Fargo-Moorhead MSA, ND-MN	S	14.33 MW	15.50 AW	29800 AAW	NDBLS	10//99-12//99
	Ohio	S	9.63 MW	11.62 AW	24170 AAW	OHBLS	10//99-12//99
	Canton-Massillon MSA, OH	S	10.18 MW	8.75 AW	21170 AAW	OHBLS	10//99-12//99
	Cleveland-Lorain-Elyria PMSA, OH	S	12.89 MW	11.54 AW	26810 AAW	OHBLS	10//99-12//99
	Dayton-Springfield MSA, OH	S	12.31 MW	9.83 AW	25610 AAW	OHBLS	10//99-12//99
	Toledo MSA, OH	S	11.40 MW	9.41 AW	23720 AAW	OHBLS	10//99-12//99
	Oklahoma	S	21.33 MW	21.14 AW	43980 AAW	OKBLS	10//99-12//99
	Oklahoma City MSA, OK	S	16.41 MW	15.13 AW	34130 AAW	OKBLS	10//99-12//99
	Tulsa MSA, OK	S	24.23 MW	23.35 AW	50390 AAW	OKBLS	10//99-12//99
	Oregon	S	11.27 MW	12.95 AW	26940 AAW	ORBLS	10//99-12//99
	Corvallis MSA, OR	S	14.16 MW	14.85 AW	29450 AAW	ORBLS	10//99-12//99
	Eugene-Springfield MSA, OR	S	13.13 MW	11.24 AW	27310 AAW	ORBLS	10//99-12//99
	Medford-Ashland MSA, OR	S	11.78 MW	10.98 AW	24500 AAW	ORBLS	10//99-12//99
	Portland-Vancouver PMSA, OR-WA	S	13.37 MW	11.97 AW	27800 AAW	ORBLS	10//99-12//99
	Salem PMSA, OR	S	15.59 MW	17.07 AW	32430 AAW	ORBLS	10//99-12//99
	Pennsylvania	S	12.69 MW	13.76 AW	28620 AAW	PABLS	10//99-12//99
	Allentown-Bethlehem-Easton MSA, PA	S	14.33 MW	13.57 AW	29810 AAW	PABLS	10//99-12//99
	Harrisburg-Lebanon-Carlisle MSA, PA	S	19.00 MW	18.73 AW	39520 AAW	PABLS	10//99-12//99
	Lancaster MSA, PA	S	14.48 MW	14.84 AW	30110 AAW	PABLS	10//99-12//99
	Philadelphia PMSA, PA-NJ	S	16.11 MW	14.98 AW	33510 AAW	PABLS	10//99-12//99
	Pittsburgh MSA, PA	S	12.16 MW	8.69 AW	25290 AAW	PABLS	10//99-12//99
	Scranton--Wilkes-Barre--Hazleton MSA, PA	S	12.68 MW	12.44 AW	26370 AAW	PABLS	10//99-12//99
	York MSA, PA	S	13.30 MW	12.48 AW	27670 AAW	PABLS	10//99-12//99
	South Carolina	S	14.07 MW	13.98 AW	29070 AAW	SCBLS	10//99-12//99
	Columbia MSA, SC	S	19.48 MW	18.62 AW	40510 AAW	SCBLS	10//99-12//99
	Greenville-Spartanburg-Anderson MSA, SC	S	19.60 MW	18.06 AW	40760 AAW	SCBLS	10//99-12//99
	South Dakota	S	13.79 MW	15.02 AW	31250 AAW	SDBLS	10//99-12//99
	Sioux Falls MSA, SD	S	17.00 MW	15.20 AW	35370 AAW	SDBLS	10//99-12//99
	Tennessee	S	15.45 MW	16.92 AW	35200 AAW	TNBLS	10//99-12//99
	Knoxville MSA, TN	S	17.04 MW	16.33 AW	35440 AAW	TNBLS	10//99-12//99
	Memphis MSA, TN-AR-MS	S	20.18 MW	18.72 AW	41980 AAW	MSBLS	10//99-12//99
	Nashville MSA, TN	S	17.24 MW	14.89 AW	35850 AAW	TNBLS	10//99-12//99
	Texas	S	14.89 MW	15.57 AW	32380 AAW	TXBLS	10//99-12//99
	Austin-San Marcos MSA, TX	S	16.77 MW	15.68 AW	34890 AAW	TXBLS	10//99-12//99
	Beaumont-Port Arthur MSA, TX	S	17.32 MW	16.46 AW	36030 AAW	TXBLS	10//99-12//99
	Dallas PMSA, TX	S	15.86 MW	15.33 AW	32980 AAW	TXBLS	10//99-12//99
	Fort Worth-Arlington PMSA, TX	S	17.02 MW	15.68 AW	35410 AAW	TXBLS	10//99-12//99
	Houston PMSA, TX	S	15.46 MW	14.45 AW	32150 AAW	TXBLS	10//99-12//99
	Killeen-Temple MSA, TX	S	16.12 MW	15.42 AW	33530 AAW	TXBLS	10//99-12//99
	Lubbock MSA, TX	S	14.70 MW	14.97 AW	30580 AAW	TXBLS	10//99-12//99
	San Antonio MSA, TX	S	14.58 MW	14.46 AW	30320 AAW	TXBLS	10//99-12//99
	Utah	S	11.95 MW	12.84 AW	26720 AAW	UTBLS	10//99-12//99
	Virginia	S	9.64 MW	12.25 AW	25480 AAW	VABLS	10//99-12//99
	Norfolk-Virginia Beach-Newport News MSA, VA-NC	S	15.59 MW	15.35 AW	32420 AAW	VABLS	10//99-12//99
	Richmond-Petersburg MSA, VA	S	13.37 MW	12.26 AW	27810 AAW	VABLS	10//99-12//99
	Washington	S	18.47 MW	18.40 AW	38270 AAW	WABLS	10//99-12//99
	Seattle-Bellevue-Everett PMSA, WA	S	17.97 MW	18.18 AW	37390 AAW	WABLS	10//99-12//99
	West Virginia	S	15.46 MW	16.11 AW	33510 AAW	WVBLS	10//99-12//99
	Wisconsin	S	17.47 MW	17.72 AW	36850 AAW	WIBLS	10//99-12//99
	Appleton-Oshkosh-Neenah MSA, WI	S	15.50 MW	15.07 AW	32250 AAW	WIBLS	10//99-12//99
	Green Bay MSA, WI	S	16.32 MW	15.88 AW	33940 AAW	WIBLS	10//99-12//99
	La Crosse MSA, WI-MN	S	15.34 MW	15.89 AW	31910 AAW	WIBLS	10//99-12//99
	Milwaukee-Waukesha PMSA, WI	S	19.75 MW	19.12 AW	41070 AAW	WIBLS	10//99-12//99
	Puerto Rico	S	9.89 MW	11.49 AW	23890 AAW	PRBLS	10//99-12//99
	San Juan-Bayamon PMSA, PR	S	10.77 MW	10.34 AW	22400 AAW	PRBLS	10//99-12//99
Baptist Pastor	Louisville, KY	Y		50600 AW		LOUMAG	1999-2000
Catholic Priest	United States	Y		15483 AW		USCAT	1999

AAW Average annual wage	**AOH** Average offered, high	**ASH** Average starting, high	**H** Hourly	**M** Monthly	**S** Special: hourly and annual
AE Average entry wage	**AOL** Average offered, low	**ASL** Average starting, low	**HI** Highest wage paid	**MTC** Median total compensation	**TQ** Third quartile wage
AEX Average experienced wage	**APH** Average pay, high range	**AW** Average wage paid	**HR** High end range	**MW** Median wage paid	**W** Weekly
AO Average offered	**APL** Average pay, low range	**FQ** First quartile wage	**LR** Low end range	**SQ** Second quartile wage	**Y** Yearly

Occupation/Type/Industry	Location	Per	Low	Mid	High	Source	Date
Clergy							
Diocesan Prist, First Level	Louisville, KY	Y		22800 AW		LOUMAG	1999-2000
Female	United States	Y		31772 MW		WOWO1	1999
Female	United States	Y		24856 MW		WOWO2	1998
Male	United States	Y		35152 MW		WOWO1	1999
Male	United States	Y		31356 MW		WOWO2	1998
Client Server Developer							
Information Technology	Atlanta, GA	Y		73842 AW		ATBUS	3//00
Clinical, Counseling, and School							
Psychologist	Alabama	S	16.04 MW	18.13 AW	37710 AAW	ALBLS	10//99-12//99
	Alaska	S	25.25 MW	26.38 AW	54860 AAW	AKBLS	10//99-12//99
	Arizona	S	21.25 MW	21.62 AW	44970 AAW	AZBLS	10//99-12//99
	Arkansas	S	18.94 MW	19.04 AW	39600 AAW	ARBLS	10//99-12//99
	California	S	26.18 MW	25.71 AW	53490 AAW	CABLS	10//99-12//99
	Colorado	S	18.49 MW	19.91 AW	41420 AAW	COBLS	10//99-12//99
	Connecticut	S	23.07 MW	23.38 AW	48630 AAW	CTBLS	10//99-12//99
	Delaware	S	23.91 MW	24.95 AW	51900 AAW	DEBLS	10//99-12//99
	District of Columbia	S	23.74 MW	24.38 AW	50710 AAW	DCBLS	10//99-12//99
	Florida	S	21.92 MW	25.94 AW	53940 AAW	FLBLS	10//99-12//99
	Georgia	S	22.39 MW	22.99 AW	47810 AAW	GABLS	10//99-12//99
	Hawaii	S	25.26 MW	27.16 AW	56500 AAW	HIBLS	10//99-12//99
	Idaho	S	15.54 MW	16.50 AW	34310 AAW	IDBLS	10//99-12//99
	Illinois	S	20.43 MW	22.01 AW	45780 AAW	ILBLS	10//99-12//99
	Indiana	S	22.02 MW	22.67 AW	47150 AAW	INBLS	10//99-12//99
	Iowa	S	22.47 MW	21.81 AW	45360 AAW	IABLS	10//99-12//99
	Kansas	S	18.54 MW	19.44 AW	40440 AAW	KSBLS	10//99-12//99
	Kentucky	S	17.82 MW	18.99 AW	39500 AAW	KYBLS	10//99-12//99
	Louisiana	S	13.49 MW	17.36 AW	36110 AAW	LABLS	10//99-12//99
	Maine	S	21.24 MW	30.51 AW	63460 AAW	MEBLS	10//99-12//99
	Maryland	S	23.78 MW	23.40 AW	48680 AAW	MDBLS	10//99-12//99
	Massachusetts	S	22.59 MW	22.39 AW	46580 AAW	MABLS	10//99-12//99
	Michigan	S	24.1 MW	24.84 AW	51670 AAW	MIBLS	10//99-12//99
	Minnesota	S	19.77 MW	20.72 AW	43100 AAW	MNBLS	10//99-12//99
	Mississippi	S	18.43 MW	18.11 AW	37660 AAW	MSBLS	10//99-12//99
	Missouri	S	19.56 MW	21.27 AW	44230 AAW	MOBLS	10//99-12//99
	Montana	S	17.54 MW	18.75 AW	39000 AAW	MTBLS	10//99-12//99
	Nebraska	S	18.87 MW	21.78 AW	45290 AAW	NEBLS	10//99-12//99
	Nevada	S	25.96 MW	25.56 AW	53170 AAW	NVBLS	10//99-12//99
	New Hampshire	S	19.87 MW	22.55 AW	46910 AAW	NHBLS	10//99-12//99
	New Jersey	S	25.71 MW	26.26 AW	54620 AAW	NJBLS	10//99-12//99
	New Mexico	S	15.85 MW	17.02 AW	35410 AAW	NMBLS	10//99-12//99
	New York	S	26.31 MW	28.30 AW	58860 AAW	NYBLS	10//99-12//99
	North Carolina	S	25.07 MW	25.33 AW	52680 AAW	NCBLS	10//99-12//99
	North Dakota	S	19 MW	21.74 AW	45210 AAW	NDBLS	10//99-12//99
	Ohio	S	22.75 MW	23.25 AW	48360 AAW	OHBLS	10//99-12//99
	Oklahoma	S	16.95 MW	18.79 AW	39080 AAW	OKBLS	10//99-12//99
	Oregon	S	22.74 MW	22.90 AW	47630 AAW	ORBLS	10//99-12//99
	Pennsylvania	S	21.96 MW	23.47 AW	48810 AAW	PABLS	10//99-12//99
	Rhode Island	S	24.19 MW	24.15 AW	50220 AAW	RIBLS	10//99-12//99
	South Carolina	S	16.66 MW	18.43 AW	38340 AAW	SCBLS	10//99-12//99
	South Dakota	S	24.58 MW	26.31 AW	54730 AAW	SDBLS	10//99-12//99
	Tennessee	S	16.53 MW	17.47 AW	36340 AAW	TNBLS	10//99-12//99
	Texas	S	20.72 MW	21.26 AW	44210 AAW	TXBLS	10//99-12//99
	Utah	S	19.77 MW	20.68 AW	43010 AAW	UTBLS	10//99-12//99
	Virginia	S	23.72 MW	24.17 AW	50280 AAW	VABLS	10//99-12//99
	Washington	S	26.37 MW	27.09 AW	56340 AAW	WABLS	10//99-12//99
	West Virginia	S	14.81 MW	15.73 AW	32730 AAW	WVBLS	10//99-12//99
	Wisconsin	S	22.13 MW	27.70 AW	57620 AAW	WIBLS	10//99-12//99
	Wyoming	S	19.33 MW	19.45 AW	40460 AAW	WYBLS	10//99-12//99
	Puerto Rico	S	17.92 MW	17.76 AW	36950 AAW	PRBLS	10//99-12//99
Clinical Director							
Non-M.D., Behavioral Health Organization	United States	Y	44447 APL	57301 AW	65707 APH	ADAW	2000
Clinical Laboratory Technician	United States	H		15.41 AW		NCS98	1998
Clown	Louisville, KY	H	50.00 APL		100.00 APH	LOUMAG	1999-2000
Coach and Scout	Alabama	Y		29440 AAW		ALBLS	10//99-12//99
	Birmingham MSA, AL	Y		26130 AAW		ALBLS	10//99-12//99
	Mobile MSA, AL	Y		34460 AAW		ALBLS	10//99-12//99

AAW	Average annual wage	AOH	Average offered, high	ASH	Average starting, high	H	Hourly	M	Monthly	S	Special: hourly and annual
AE	Average entry wage	AOL	Average offered, low	ASL	Average starting, low	HI	Highest wage paid	MTC	Median total compensation	TQ	Third quartile wage
AEX	Average experienced wage	APH	Average pay, high range	AW	Average wage paid	HR	High end range	MW	Median wage paid	W	Weekly
AO	Average offered	APL	Average pay, low range	FQ	First quartile wage	LR	Low end range	SQ	Second quartile wage	Y	Yearly

Occupation/Type/Industry	Location	Per	Low	Mid	High	Source	Date
Coach and Scout	Montgomery MSA, AL	Y		32560 AAW		ALBLS	10//99-12//99
	Tuscaloosa MSA, AL	Y		30020 AAW		ALBLS	10//99-12//99
	Arizona	Y		30850 AAW		AZBLS	10//99-12//99
	Phoenix-Mesa MSA, AZ	Y		38150 AAW		AZBLS	10//99-12//99
	Tucson MSA, AZ	Y		24220 AAW		AZBLS	10//99-12//99
	Arkansas	Y		43620 AAW		ARBLS	10//99-12//99
	Little Rock-North Little Rock MSA, AR	Y		37650 AAW		ARBLS	10//99-12//99
	California	Y		36500 AAW		CABLS	10//99-12//99
	Chico-Paradise MSA, CA	Y		21980 AAW		CABLS	10//99-12//99
	Fresno MSA, CA	Y		30250 AAW		CABLS	10//99-12//99
	Los Angeles-Long Beach PMSA, CA	Y		50760 AAW		CABLS	10//99-12//99
	Modesto MSA, CA	Y		29920 AAW		CABLS	10//99-12//99
	Oakland PMSA, CA	Y		33040 AAW		CABLS	10//99-12//99
	Orange County PMSA, CA	Y		49030 AAW		CABLS	10//99-12//99
	Riverside-San Bernardino PMSA, CA	Y		23940 AAW		CABLS	10//99-12//99
	Sacramento PMSA, CA	Y		27480 AAW		CABLS	10//99-12//99
	San Diego MSA, CA	Y		53250 AAW		CABLS	10//99-12//99
	San Francisco PMSA, CA	Y		47120 AAW		CABLS	10//99-12//99
	San Jose PMSA, CA	Y		54410 AAW		CABLS	10//99-12//99
	San Luis Obispo-Atascadero-Paso Robles MSA, CA	Y		19920 AAW		CABLS	10//99-12//99
	Santa Barbara-Santa Maria-Lompoc MSA, CA	Y		27880 AAW		CABLS	10//99-12//99
	Santa Rosa PMSA, CA	Y		30350 AAW		CABLS	10//99-12//99
	Colorado	Y		33530 AAW		COBLS	10//99-12//99
	Boulder-Longmont PMSA, CO	Y		43040 AAW		COBLS	10//99-12//99
	Colorado Springs MSA, CO	Y		40580 AAW		COBLS	10//99-12//99
	Connecticut	Y		41280 AAW		CTBLS	10//99-12//99
	Bridgeport PMSA, CT	Y		36660 AAW		CTBLS	10//99-12//99
	Hartford MSA, CT	Y		40660 AAW		CTBLS	10//99-12//99
	Stamford-Norwalk PMSA, CT	Y		42530 AAW		CTBLS	10//99-12//99
	District of Columbia	Y		39320 AAW		DCBLS	10//99-12//99
	Washington PMSA, DC-MD-VA-WV	Y		33510 AAW		DCBLS	10//99-12//99
	Florida	Y		33540 AAW		FLBLS	10//99-12//99
	Daytona Beach MSA, FL	Y		30030 AAW		FLBLS	10//99-12//99
	Fort Lauderdale PMSA, FL	Y		35930 AAW		FLBLS	10//99-12//99
	Fort Myers-Cape Coral MSA, FL	Y		36430 AAW		FLBLS	10//99-12//99
	Fort Pierce-Port St. Lucie MSA, FL	Y		27740 AAW		FLBLS	10//99-12//99
	Gainesville MSA, FL	Y		49220 AAW		FLBLS	10//99-12//99
	Jacksonville MSA, FL	Y		22720 AAW		FLBLS	10//99-12//99
	Lakeland-Winter Haven MSA, FL	Y		28150 AAW		FLBLS	10//99-12//99
	Miami PMSA, FL	Y		26940 AAW		FLBLS	10//99-12//99
	Naples MSA, FL	Y		27530 AAW		FLBLS	10//99-12//99
	Orlando MSA, FL	Y		40100 AAW		FLBLS	10//99-12//99
	Pensacola MSA, FL	Y		34370 AAW		FLBLS	10//99-12//99
	Sarasota-Bradenton MSA, FL	Y		33830 AAW		FLBLS	10//99-12//99
	Tallahassee MSA, FL	Y		42780 AAW		FLBLS	10//99-12//99
	Tampa-St. Petersburg-Clearwater MSA, FL	Y		41090 AAW		FLBLS	10//99-12//99
	West Palm Beach-Boca Raton MSA, FL	Y		39400 AAW		FLBLS	10//99-12//99
	Georgia	Y		30670 AAW		GABLS	10//99-12//99
	Atlanta MSA, GA	Y		26950 AAW		GABLS	10//99-12//99
	Augusta-Aiken MSA, GA-SC	Y		30190 AAW		GABLS	10//99-12//99
	Hawaii	Y		40940 AAW		HIBLS	10//99-12//99
	Idaho	Y		30810 AAW		IDBLS	10//99-12//99
	Illinois	Y		28390 AAW		ILBLS	10//99-12//99
	Champaign-Urbana MSA, IL	Y		19920 AAW		ILBLS	10//99-12//99
	Chicago PMSA, IL	Y		31920 AAW		ILBLS	10//99-12//99
	Indiana	Y		25890 AAW		INBLS	10//99-12//99
	Gary PMSA, IN	Y		28150 AAW		INBLS	10//99-12//99
	Indianapolis MSA, IN	Y		24190 AAW		INBLS	10//99-12//99
	Muncie MSA, IN	Y		17400 AAW		INBLS	10//99-12//99
	Iowa	Y		28570 AAW		IABLS	10//99-12//99
	Kansas	Y		22240 AAW		KSBLS	10//99-12//99

AAW	Average annual wage	AOH	Average offered, high	ASH	Average starting, high	H	Hourly	M	Monthly	S	Special: hourly and annual
AE	Average entry wage	AOL	Average offered, low	ASL	Average starting, low	HI	Highest wage paid	MTC	Median total compensation	TQ	Third quartile wage
AEX	Average experienced wage	APH	Average pay, high range	AW	Average wage paid	HR	High end range	MW	Median wage paid	W	Weekly
AO	Average offered	APL	Average pay, low range	FQ	First quartile wage	LR	Low end range	SQ	Second quartile wage	Y	Yearly

Occupation/Type/Industry	Location	Per	Low	Mid	High	Source	Date
Coach and Scout	Wichita MSA, KS	Y		23990 AAW		KSBLS	10//99-12//99
	Kentucky	Y		18490 AAW		KYBLS	10//99-12//99
	Louisiana	Y		46550 AAW		LABLS	10//99-12//99
	New Orleans MSA, LA	Y		58430 AAW		LABLS	10//99-12//99
	Maine	Y		37670 AAW		MEBLS	10//99-12//99
	Maryland	Y		21190 AAW		MDBLS	10//99-12//99
	Massachusetts	Y		26870 AAW		MABLS	10//99-12//99
	Boston PMSA, MA-NH	Y		26560 AAW		MABLS	10//99-12//99
	Worcester PMSA, MA-CT	Y		38920 AAW		MABLS	10//99-12//99
	Lansing-East Lansing MSA, MI	Y		17630 AAW		MIBLS	10//99-12//99
	Minnesota	Y		27780 AAW		MNBLS	10//99-12//99
	Duluth-Superior MSA, MN-WI	Y		39850 AAW		MNBLS	10//99-12//99
	Minneapolis-St. Paul MSA, MN-WI	Y		28600 AAW		MNBLS	10//99-12//99
	St. Cloud MSA, MN	Y		23010 AAW		MNBLS	10//99-12//99
	Mississippi	Y		35880 AAW		MSBLS	10//99-12//99
	Jackson MSA, MS	Y		30690 AAW		MSBLS	10//99-12//99
	Missouri	Y		34630 AAW		MOBLS	10//99-12//99
	Joplin MSA, MO	Y		24560 AAW		MOBLS	10//99-12//99
	Kansas City MSA, MO-KS	Y		39990 AAW		MOBLS	10//99-12//99
	St. Louis MSA, MO-IL	Y		37310 AAW		MOBLS	10//99-12//99
	Springfield MSA, MO	Y		35380 AAW		MOBLS	10//99-12//99
	Montana	Y		34970 AAW		MTBLS	10//99-12//99
	Nebraska	Y		24460 AAW		NEBLS	10//99-12//99
	Lincoln MSA, NE	Y		22420 AAW		NEBLS	10//99-12//99
	Omaha MSA, NE-IA	Y		30470 AAW		NEBLS	10//99-12//99
	Nevada	Y		47240 AAW		NVBLS	10//99-12//99
	Las Vegas MSA, NV-AZ	Y		49110 AAW		NVBLS	10//99-12//99
	New Hampshire	Y		24010 AAW		NHBLS	10//99-12//99
	Portsmouth-Rochester PMSA, NH-ME	Y		25280 AAW		NHBLS	10//99-12//99
	New Jersey	Y		36920 AAW		NJBLS	10//99-12//99
	Bergen-Passaic PMSA, NJ	Y		34290 AAW		NJBLS	10//99-12//99
	Middlesex-Somerset-Hunterdon PMSA, NJ	Y		45020 AAW		NJBLS	10//99-12//99
	Monmouth-Ocean PMSA, NJ	Y		41090 AAW		NJBLS	10//99-12//99
	Newark PMSA, NJ	Y		39290 AAW		NJBLS	10//99-12//99
	Trenton PMSA, NJ	Y		43840 AAW		NJBLS	10//99-12//99
	Vineland-Millville-Bridgeton PMSA, NJ	Y		26640 AAW		NJBLS	10//99-12//99
	New Mexico	Y		21920 AAW		NMBLS	10//99-12//99
	New York	Y		30110 AAW		NYBLS	10//99-12//99
	Albany-Schenectady-Troy MSA, NY	Y		22360 AAW		NYBLS	10//99-12//99
	Buffalo-Niagara Falls MSA, NY	Y		28720 AAW		NYBLS	10//99-12//99
	Nassau-Suffolk PMSA, NY	Y		24640 AAW		NYBLS	10//99-12//99
	New York PMSA, NY	Y		33580 AAW		NYBLS	10//99-12//99
	Rochester MSA, NY	Y		20790 AAW		NYBLS	10//99-12//99
	Syracuse MSA, NY	Y		21640 AAW		NYBLS	10//99-12//99
	North Carolina	Y		30020 AAW		NCBLS	10//99-12//99
	Asheville MSA, NC	Y		30560 AAW		NCBLS	10//99-12//99
	Charlotte-Gastonia-Rock Hill MSA, NC-SC	Y		31650 AAW		NCBLS	10//99-12//99
	Greensboro--Winston-Salem--High Point MSA, NC	Y		24580 AAW		NCBLS	10//99-12//99
	Raleigh-Durham-Chapel Hill MSA, NC	Y		42270 AAW		NCBLS	10//99-12//99
	North Dakota	Y		20810 AAW		NDBLS	10//99-12//99
	Grand Forks MSA, ND-MN	Y		27980 AAW		NDBLS	10//99-12//99
	Ohio	Y		25010 AAW		OHBLS	10//99-12//99
	Cleveland-Lorain-Elyria PMSA, OH	Y		35010 AAW		OHBLS	10//99-12//99
	Dayton-Springfield MSA, OH	Y		29730 AAW		OHBLS	10//99-12//99
	Oklahoma	Y		35960 AAW		OKBLS	10//99-12//99
	Oklahoma City MSA, OK	Y		29250 AAW		OKBLS	10//99-12//99
	Tulsa MSA, OK	Y		42000 AAW		OKBLS	10//99-12//99
	Oregon	Y		28030 AAW		ORBLS	10//99-12//99
	Portland-Vancouver PMSA, OR-WA	Y		25520 AAW		ORBLS	10//99-12//99
	Pennsylvania	Y		34710 AAW		PABLS	10//99-12//99

AAW Average annual wage	**AOH** Average offered, high	**ASH** Average starting, high	**H** Hourly	**M** Monthly	**S** Special: hourly and annual
AE Average entry wage	**AOL** Average offered, low	**ASL** Average starting, low	**HI** Highest wage paid	**MTC** Median total compensation	**TQ** Third quartile wage
AEX Average experienced wage	**APH** Average pay, high range	**AW** Average wage paid	**HR** High end range	**MW** Median wage paid	**W** Weekly
AO Average offered	**APL** Average pay, low range	**FQ** First quartile wage	**LR** Low end range	**SQ** Second quartile wage	**Y** Yearly

Occupation/Type/Industry	Location	Per	Low	Mid	High	Source	Date
Coach and Scout	Allentown-Bethlehem-Easton MSA, PA	Y		30720 AAW		PABLS	10//99-12//99
	Harrisburg-Lebanon-Carlisle MSA, PA	Y		26900 AAW		PABLS	10//99-12//99
	Johnstown MSA, PA	Y		29230 AAW		PABLS	10//99-12//99
	Lancaster MSA, PA	Y		23630 AAW		PABLS	10//99-12//99
	Philadelphia PMSA, PA-NJ	Y		42920 AAW		PABLS	10//99-12//99
	Pittsburgh MSA, PA	Y		32820 AAW		PABLS	10//99-12//99
	Scranton--Wilkes-Barre--Hazleton MSA, PA	Y		27210 AAW		PABLS	10//99-12//99
	Rhode Island	Y		31770 AAW		RIBLS	10//99-12//99
	Providence-Fall River-Warwick MSA, RI-MA	Y		31300 AAW		RIBLS	10//99-12//99
	South Carolina	Y		34240 AAW		SCBLS	10//99-12//99
	Greenville-Spartanburg-Anderson MSA, SC	Y		47440 AAW		SCBLS	10//99-12//99
	South Dakota	Y		23690 AAW		SDBLS	10//99-12//99
	Tennessee	Y		56370 AAW		TNBLS	10//99-12//99
	Memphis MSA, TN-AR-MS	Y		60630 AAW		MSBLS	10//99-12//99
	Nashville MSA, TN	Y		69510 AAW		TNBLS	10//99-12//99
	Texas	Y		33800 AAW		TXBLS	10//99-12//99
	Austin-San Marcos MSA, TX	Y		26160 AAW		TXBLS	10//99-12//99
	Corpus Christi MSA, TX	Y		30320 AAW		TXBLS	10//99-12//99
	Dallas PMSA, TX	Y		35800 AAW		TXBLS	10//99-12//99
	Houston PMSA, TX	Y		39710 AAW		TXBLS	10//99-12//99
	Killeen-Temple MSA, TX	Y		29430 AAW		TXBLS	10//99-12//99
	Utah	Y		40170 AAW		UTBLS	10//99-12//99
	Vermont	Y		35260 AAW		VTBLS	10//99-12//99
	Burlington MSA, VT	Y		17660 AAW		VTBLS	10//99-12//99
	Virginia	Y		29920 AAW		VABLS	10//99-12//99
	Norfolk-Virginia Beach-Newport News MSA, VA-NC	Y		28220 AAW		VABLS	10//99-12//99
	Richmond-Petersburg MSA, VA	Y		33540 AAW		VABLS	10//99-12//99
	Washington	Y		27750 AAW		WABLS	10//99-12//99
	Bellingham MSA, WA	Y		25780 AAW		WABLS	10//99-12//99
	Bremerton PMSA, WA	Y		23460 AAW		WABLS	10//99-12//99
	Olympia PMSA, WA	Y		22350 AAW		WABLS	10//99-12//99
	Spokane MSA, WA	Y		31050 AAW		WABLS	10//99-12//99
	Tacoma PMSA, WA	Y		25740 AAW		WABLS	10//99-12//99
	Yakima MSA, WA	Y		28800 AAW		WABLS	10//99-12//99
	West Virginia	Y		32570 AAW		WVBLS	10//99-12//99
	Wisconsin	Y		31500 AAW		WIBLS	10//99-12//99
	Appleton-Oshkosh-Neenah MSA, WI	Y		27710 AAW		WIBLS	10//99-12//99
	Milwaukee-Waukesha PMSA, WI	Y		34940 AAW		WIBLS	10//99-12//99
	Wyoming	Y		17100 AAW		WYBLS	10//99-12//99
	Puerto Rico	Y		31950 AAW		PRBLS	10//99-12//99
	Virgin Islands	Y		37470 AAW		VIBLS	10//99-12//99
Coating, Painting, and Spraying Machine Setter, Operator, and Tender							
	Alabama	S	9.85 MW	10.39 AW	21610 AAW	ALBLS	10//99-12//99
	Alaska	S	17.57 MW	17.37 AW	36130 AAW	AKBLS	10//99-12//99
	Arizona	S	10.07 MW	10.41 AW	21650 AAW	AZBLS	10//99-12//99
	Arkansas	S	9.59 MW	9.79 AW	20370 AAW	ARBLS	10//99-12//99
	California	S	9.97 MW	10.77 AW	22410 AAW	CABLS	10//99-12//99
	Colorado	S	10.35 MW	10.58 AW	22000 AAW	COBLS	10//99-12//99
	Connecticut	S	12.28 MW	12.79 AW	26600 AAW	CTBLS	10//99-12//99
	Delaware	S	13.86 MW	13.56 AW	28200 AAW	DEBLS	10//99-12//99
	Florida	S	10.48 MW	10.49 AW	21820 AAW	FLBLS	10//99-12//99
	Georgia	S	10.86 MW	11.21 AW	23320 AAW	GABLS	10//99-12//99
	Hawaii	S	10.65 MW	12.28 AW	25550 AAW	HIBLS	10//99-12//99
	Idaho	S	9.9 MW	10.05 AW	20900 AAW	IDBLS	10//99-12//99
	Illinois	S	11.32 MW	12.01 AW	24990 AAW	ILBLS	10//99-12//99
	Indiana	S	10.33 MW	10.71 AW	22270 AAW	INBLS	10//99-12//99
	Iowa	S	11.84 MW	12.48 AW	25960 AAW	IABLS	10//99-12//99
	Kansas	S	9.61 MW	10.52 AW	21880 AAW	KSBLS	10//99-12//99
	Kentucky	S	10.74 MW	10.91 AW	22690 AAW	KYBLS	10//99-12//99
	Louisiana	S	11.1 MW	11.17 AW	23240 AAW	LABLS	10//99-12//99

AAW	Average annual wage	AOH	Average offered, high	ASH	Average starting, high	H	Hourly	M	Monthly	S	Special: hourly and annual
AE	Average entry wage	AOL	Average offered, low	ASL	Average starting, low	HI	Highest wage paid	MTC	Median total compensation	TQ	Third quartile wage
AEX	Average experienced wage	APH	Average pay, high range	AW	Average wage paid	HR	High end range	MW	Median wage paid	W	Weekly
AO	Average offered	APL	Average pay, low range	FQ	First quartile wage	LR	Low end range	SQ	Second quartile wage	Y	Yearly

Occupation/Type/Industry	Location	Per	Low	Mid	High	Source	Date
Coating, Painting, and Spraying Machine Setter, Operator, and Tender	Maine	S	14.86 MW	15.39 AW	32000 AAW	MEBLS	10//99-12//99
	Maryland	S	11.95 MW	12.61 AW	26230 AAW	MDBLS	10//99-12//99
	Massachusetts	S	11.95 MW	12.39 AW	25760 AAW	MABLS	10//99-12//99
	Michigan	S	10.9 MW	11.92 AW	24800 AAW	MIBLS	10//99-12//99
	Minnesota	S	12.58 MW	13.00 AW	27040 AAW	MNBLS	10//99-12//99
	Mississippi	S	10.25 MW	10.83 AW	22530 AAW	MSBLS	10//99-12//99
	Missouri	S	10.73 MW	11.71 AW	24360 AAW	MOBLS	10//99-12//99
	Montana	S	8.37 MW	10.03 AW	20870 AAW	MTBLS	10//99-12//99
	Nebraska	S	10.16 MW	11.01 AW	22900 AAW	NEBLS	10//99-12//99
	Nevada	S	10.71 MW	11.27 AW	23440 AAW	NVBLS	10//99-12//99
	New Hampshire	S	11.37 MW	11.83 AW	24610 AAW	NHBLS	10//99-12//99
	New Jersey	S	10.81 MW	11.65 AW	24230 AAW	NJBLS	10//99-12//99
	New Mexico	S	8.91 MW	9.30 AW	19350 AAW	NMBLS	10//99-12//99
	New York	S	11.93 MW	12.49 AW	25970 AAW	NYBLS	10//99-12//99
	North Carolina	S	10.18 MW	10.69 AW	22230 AAW	NCBLS	10//99-12//99
	North Dakota	S	11.19 MW	10.96 AW	22800 AAW	NDBLS	10//99-12//99
	Ohio	S	11.26 MW	11.75 AW	24440 AAW	OHBLS	10//99-12//99
	Oklahoma	S	11.09 MW	11.05 AW	22990 AAW	OKBLS	10//99-12//99
	Oregon	S	11.13 MW	12.04 AW	25040 AAW	ORBLS	10//99-12//99
	Pennsylvania	S	11.81 MW	12.05 AW	25060 AAW	PABLS	10//99-12//99
	Rhode Island	S	10.27 MW	10.72 AW	22290 AAW	RIBLS	10//99-12//99
	South Carolina	S	11.93 MW	12.93 AW	26890 AAW	SCBLS	10//99-12//99
	South Dakota	S	9.97 MW	10.23 AW	21270 AAW	SDBLS	10//99-12//99
	Tennessee	S	9.69 MW	9.93 AW	20650 AAW	TNBLS	10//99-12//99
	Texas	S	9.56 MW	10.26 AW	21340 AAW	TXBLS	10//99-12//99
	Utah	S	10.9 MW	11.23 AW	23350 AAW	UTBLS	10//99-12//99
	Vermont	S	11.63 MW	11.49 AW	23910 AAW	VTBLS	10//99-12//99
	Virginia	S	11.3 MW	13.15 AW	27340 AAW	VABLS	10//99-12//99
	Washington	S	11.31 MW	12.01 AW	24980 AAW	WABLS	10//99-12//99
	West Virginia	S	10.55 MW	11.27 AW	23440 AAW	WVBLS	10//99-12//99
	Wisconsin	S	11.73 MW	12.21 AW	25390 AAW	WIBLS	10//99-12//99
	Puerto Rico	S	6.06 MW	6.36 AW	13220 AAW	PRBLS	10//99-12//99
Coil Winder, Taper, and Finisher	Alabama	S	7.96 MW	8.75 AW	18210 AAW	ALBLS	10//99-12//99
	Birmingham MSA, AL	S	8.06 MW	7.67 AW	16770 AAW	ALBLS	10//99-12//99
	Arizona	S	8.8 MW	9.12 AW	18970 AAW	AZBLS	10//99-12//99
	Phoenix-Mesa MSA, AZ	S	9.09 MW	8.82 AW	18900 AAW	AZBLS	10//99-12//99
	Tucson MSA, AZ	S	8.72 MW	8.25 AW	18130 AAW	AZBLS	10//99-12//99
	Arkansas	S	10.63 MW	11.12 AW	23120 AAW	ARBLS	10//99-12//99
	California	S	8.78 MW	10.04 AW	20890 AAW	CABLS	10//99-12//99
	Los Angeles-Long Beach PMSA, CA	S	8.59 MW	7.90 AW	17870 AAW	CABLS	10//99-12//99
	Oakland PMSA, CA	S	12.84 MW	11.19 AW	26710 AAW	CABLS	10//99-12//99
	Orange County PMSA, CA	S	9.99 MW	8.88 AW	20770 AAW	CABLS	10//99-12//99
	Riverside-San Bernardino PMSA, CA	S	10.20 MW	9.69 AW	21210 AAW	CABLS	10//99-12//99
	San Diego MSA, CA	S	8.78 MW	8.35 AW	18270 AAW	CABLS	10//99-12//99
	San Francisco PMSA, CA	S	16.95 MW	18.54 AW	35260 AAW	CABLS	10//99-12//99
	San Jose PMSA, CA	S	9.11 MW	8.46 AW	18940 AAW	CABLS	10//99-12//99
	Colorado	S	7.98 MW	8.37 AW	17420 AAW	COBLS	10//99-12//99
	Denver PMSA, CO	S	8.48 MW	8.02 AW	17640 AAW	COBLS	10//99-12//99
	Connecticut	S	13.81 MW	11.92 AW	24790 AAW	CTBLS	10//99-12//99
	Hartford MSA, CT	S	11.67 MW	13.82 AW	24280 AAW	CTBLS	10//99-12//99
	Waterbury PMSA, CT	S	9.69 MW	9.07 AW	20140 AAW	CTBLS	10//99-12//99
	Delaware	S	9.3 MW	10.83 AW	22530 AAW	DEBLS	10//99-12//99
	Washington PMSA, DC-MD-VA-WV	S	10.00 MW	9.72 AW	20800 AAW	DCBLS	10//99-12//99
	Florida	S	9.09 MW	10.61 AW	22060 AAW	FLBLS	10//99-12//99
	Melbourne-Titusville-Palm Bay MSA, FL	S	9.42 MW	7.87 AW	19590 AAW	FLBLS	10//99-12//99
	Miami PMSA, FL	S	8.78 MW	8.16 AW	18260 AAW	FLBLS	10//99-12//99
	Orlando MSA, FL	S	11.46 MW	9.61 AW	23840 AAW	FLBLS	10//99-12//99
	Tampa-St. Petersburg-Clearwater MSA, FL	S	8.54 MW	8.11 AW	17750 AAW	FLBLS	10//99-12//99
	West Palm Beach-Boca Raton MSA, FL	S	14.30 MW	12.67 AW	29740 AAW	FLBLS	10//99-12//99
	Georgia	S	9.03 MW	9.33 AW	19410 AAW	GABLS	10//99-12//99
	Atlanta MSA, GA	S	8.98 MW	8.93 AW	18680 AAW	GABLS	10//99-12//99
	Illinois	S	8 MW	8.73 AW	18150 AAW	ILBLS	10//99-12//99
	Chicago PMSA, IL	S	8.49 MW	7.91 AW	17650 AAW	ILBLS	10//99-12//99

AAW	Average annual wage	AOH	Average offered, high	ASH	Average starting, high	H	Hourly	M	Monthly	S	Special: hourly and annual
AE	Average entry wage	AOL	Average offered, low	ASL	Average starting, low	HI	Highest wage paid	MTC	Median total compensation	TQ	Third quartile wage
AEX	Average experienced wage	APH	Average pay, high range	AW	Average wage paid	HR	High end range	MW	Median wage paid	W	Weekly
AO	Average offered	APL	Average pay, low range	FQ	First quartile wage	LR	Low end range	SQ	Second quartile wage	Y	Yearly

Occupation/Type/Industry	Location	Per	Low	Mid	High	Source	Date
Coil Winder, Taper, and Finisher	Indiana	S	8.31 MW	9.27 AW	19290 AAW	INBLS	10//99-12//99
	Evansville-Henderson MSA, IN-KY	S	9.71 MW	9.69 AW	20190 AAW	INBLS	10//99-12//99
	Fort Wayne MSA, IN	S	9.39 MW	9.43 AW	19520 AAW	INBLS	10//99-12//99
	Indianapolis MSA, IN	S	14.50 MW	12.67 AW	30170 AAW	INBLS	10//99-12//99
	Iowa	S	10.42 MW	11.06 AW	23000 AAW	IABLS	10//99-12//99
	Kansas	S	8.08 MW	8.93 AW	18580 AAW	KSBLS	10//99-12//99
	Wichita MSA, KS	S	12.11 MW	12.29 AW	25190 AAW	KSBLS	10//99-12//99
	Kentucky	S	10.18 MW	10.42 AW	21670 AAW	KYBLS	10//99-12//99
	Maryland	S	9.09 MW	9.69 AW	20160 AAW	MDBLS	10//99-12//99
	Baltimore PMSA, MD	S	10.42 MW	9.88 AW	21670 AAW	MDBLS	10//99-12//99
	Massachusetts	S	10.53 MW	10.95 AW	22780 AAW	MABLS	10//99-12//99
	Boston PMSA, MA-NH	S	9.58 MW	10.07 AW	19920 AAW	MABLS	10//99-12//99
	Lowell PMSA, MA-NH	S	10.19 MW	10.14 AW	21190 AAW	MABLS	10//99-12//99
	Springfield MSA, MA	S	17.57 MW	13.33 AW	36540 AAW	MABLS	10//99-12//99
	Worcester PMSA, MA-CT	S	13.98 MW	12.80 AW	29070 AAW	MABLS	10//99-12//99
	Michigan	S	14.03 MW	13.64 AW	28360 AAW	MIBLS	10//99-12//99
	Detroit PMSA, MI	S	12.22 MW	10.82 AW	25410 AAW	MIBLS	10//99-12//99
	Grand Rapids-Muskegon-Holland MSA, MI	S	14.94 MW	15.16 AW	31070 AAW	MIBLS	10//99-12//99
	Minnesota	S	10.45 MW	11.96 AW	24870 AAW	MNBLS	10//99-12//99
	Minneapolis-St. Paul MSA, MN-WI	S	13.01 MW	10.21 AW	27070 AAW	MNBLS	10//99-12//99
	Mississippi	S	8.27 MW	9.34 AW	19430 AAW	MSBLS	10//99-12//99
	Missouri	S	9.95 MW	10.09 AW	21000 AAW	MOBLS	10//99-12//99
	Montana	S	8.38 MW	8.36 AW	17380 AAW	MTBLS	10//99-12//99
	Nevada	S	9.17 MW	9.79 AW	20370 AAW	NVBLS	10//99-12//99
	New Hampshire	S	11 MW	11.73 AW	24400 AAW	NHBLS	10//99-12//99
	New Jersey	S	11.47 MW	11.72 AW	24390 AAW	NJBLS	10//99-12//99
	Bergen-Passaic PMSA, NJ	S	10.47 MW	9.62 AW	21780 AAW	NJBLS	10//99-12//99
	Middlesex-Somerset-Hunterdon PMSA, NJ	S	11.46 MW	11.14 AW	23830 AAW	NJBLS	10//99-12//99
	Monmouth-Ocean PMSA, NJ	S	12.68 MW	12.82 AW	26380 AAW	NJBLS	10//99-12//99
	Newark PMSA, NJ	S	11.39 MW	11.15 AW	23690 AAW	NJBLS	10//99-12//99
	New Mexico	S	6.62 MW	7.98 AW	16590 AAW	NMBLS	10//99-12//99
	New York	S	8.58 MW	9.03 AW	18790 AAW	NYBLS	10//99-12//99
	Buffalo-Niagara Falls MSA, NY	S	13.44 MW	13.86 AW	27960 AAW	NYBLS	10//99-12//99
	Dutchess County PMSA, NY	S	9.85 MW	9.86 AW	20490 AAW	NYBLS	10//99-12//99
	Nassau-Suffolk PMSA, NY	S	10.70 MW	9.12 AW	22250 AAW	NYBLS	10//99-12//99
	New York PMSA, NY	S	8.70 MW	8.22 AW	18100 AAW	NYBLS	10//99-12//99
	Rochester MSA, NY	S	8.91 MW	8.44 AW	18530 AAW	NYBLS	10//99-12//99
	Syracuse MSA, NY	S	6.99 MW	6.55 AW	14530 AAW	NYBLS	10//99-12//99
	Utica-Rome MSA, NY	S	9.16 MW	9.38 AW	19040 AAW	NYBLS	10//99-12//99
	North Carolina	S	10.73 MW	11.17 AW	23240 AAW	NCBLS	10//99-12//99
	Raleigh-Durham-Chapel Hill MSA, NC	S	8.34 MW	7.94 AW	17340 AAW	NCBLS	10//99-12//99
	Ohio	S	12.34 MW	12.33 AW	25650 AAW	OHBLS	10//99-12//99
	Akron PMSA, OH	S	9.12 MW	8.37 AW	18960 AAW	OHBLS	10//99-12//99
	Cincinnati PMSA, OH-KY-IN	S	11.75 MW	11.83 AW	24430 AAW	OHBLS	10//99-12//99
	Cleveland-Lorain-Elyria PMSA, OH	S	12.60 MW	12.64 AW	26210 AAW	OHBLS	10//99-12//99
	Dayton-Springfield MSA, OH	S	11.14 MW	10.50 AW	23170 AAW	OHBLS	10//99-12//99
	Oklahoma	S	10.83 MW	11.32 AW	23540 AAW	OKBLS	10//99-12//99
	Oklahoma City MSA, OK	S	11.64 MW	11.09 AW	24220 AAW	OKBLS	10//99-12//99
	Tulsa MSA, OK	S	9.92 MW	9.72 AW	20640 AAW	OKBLS	10//99-12//99
	Oregon	S	10.63 MW	10.51 AW	21860 AAW	ORBLS	10//99-12//99
	Portland-Vancouver PMSA, OR-WA	S	10.63 MW	11.25 AW	22110 AAW	ORBLS	10//99-12//99
	Pennsylvania	S	9.99 MW	10.88 AW	22630 AAW	PABLS	10//99-12//99
	Philadelphia PMSA, PA-NJ	S	9.99 MW	9.06 AW	20790 AAW	PABLS	10//99-12//99
	Pittsburgh MSA, PA	S	12.86 MW	11.38 AW	26740 AAW	PABLS	10//99-12//99
	Scranton--Wilkes-Barre--Hazleton MSA, PA	S	8.52 MW	7.83 AW	17710 AAW	PABLS	10//99-12//99
	Sharon MSA, PA	S	15.31 MW	15.75 AW	31850 AAW	PABLS	10//99-12//99
	Rhode Island	S	8.84 MW	9.21 AW	19160 AAW	RIBLS	10//99-12//99
	Providence-Fall River-Warwick MSA, RI-MA	S	9.30 MW	8.83 AW	19340 AAW	RIBLS	10//99-12//99
	South Carolina	S	12.92 MW	12.60 AW	26210 AAW	SCBLS	10//99-12//99
	Greenville-Spartanburg-Anderson MSA, SC	S	10.64 MW	9.71 AW	22120 AAW	SCBLS	10//99-12//99
	Tennessee	S	9.73 MW	9.67 AW	20110 AAW	TNBLS	10//99-12//99

AAW	Average annual wage	AOH	Average offered, high	ASH	Average starting, high
AE	Average entry wage	AOL	Average offered, low	ASL	Average starting, low
AEX	Average experienced wage	APH	Average pay, high range	AW	Average wage paid
AO	Average offered	APL	Average pay, low range	FQ	First quartile wage

H	Hourly	M	Monthly	S	Special: hourly and annual
HI	Highest wage paid	MTC	Median total compensation	TQ	Third quartile wage
HR	High end range	MW	Median wage paid	W	Weekly
LR	Low end range	SQ	Second quartile wage	Y	Yearly

Occupation/Type/Industry	Location	Per	Low	Mid	High	Source	Date
Coil Winder, Taper, and Finisher	Memphis MSA, TN-AR-MS	S	10.21 MW	9.86 AW	21230 AAW	MSBLS	10//99-12//99
	Nashville MSA, TN	S	8.29 MW	8.41 AW	17240 AAW	TNBLS	10//99-12//99
	Texas	S	8.23 MW	8.94 AW	18600 AAW	TXBLS	10//99-12//99
	Dallas PMSA, TX	S	9.16 MW	8.61 AW	19060 AAW	TXBLS	10//99-12//99
	Houston PMSA, TX	S	8.54 MW	8.17 AW	17760 AAW	TXBLS	10//99-12//99
	Virginia	S	9.4 MW	10.21 AW	21230 AAW	VABLS	10//99-12//99
	Washington	S	9.69 MW	10.18 AW	21170 AAW	WABLS	10//99-12//99
	Seattle-Bellevue-Everett PMSA, WA	S	10.06 MW	9.58 AW	20910 AAW	WABLS	10//99-12//99
	West Virginia	S	9.42 MW	9.84 AW	20460 AAW	WVBLS	10//99-12//99
	Wisconsin	S	10.12 MW	12.45 AW	25900 AAW	WIBLS	10//99-12//99
	Milwaukee-Waukesha PMSA, WI	S	13.79 MW	13.21 AW	28690 AAW	WIBLS	10//99-12//99
	Racine PMSA, WI	S	11.67 MW	9.97 AW	24260 AAW	WIBLS	10//99-12//99
Coin, Vending, and Amusement Machine Servicer and Repairer	Alabama	S	11.55 MW	11.34 AW	23590 AAW	ALBLS	10//99-12//99
	Arizona	S	14.15 MW	13.47 AW	28020 AAW	AZBLS	10//99-12//99
	Arkansas	S	10.57 MW	10.53 AW	21900 AAW	ARBLS	10//99-12//99
	California	S	11.92 MW	12.61 AW	26230 AAW	CABLS	10//99-12//99
	Colorado	S	11.76 MW	11.42 AW	23750 AAW	COBLS	10//99-12//99
	Connecticut	S	10.91 MW	11.12 AW	23130 AAW	CTBLS	10//99-12//99
	Delaware	S	11.72 MW	11.78 AW	24490 AAW	DEBLS	10//99-12//99
	Florida	S	13.3 MW	13.03 AW	27100 AAW	FLBLS	10//99-12//99
	Georgia	S	11.42 MW	11.19 AW	23270 AAW	GABLS	10//99-12//99
	Idaho	S	11.2 MW	9.81 AW	20400 AAW	IDBLS	10//99-12//99
	Illinois	S	12.83 MW	12.79 AW	26600 AAW	ILBLS	10//99-12//99
	Indiana	S	11.41 MW	11.86 AW	24660 AAW	INBLS	10//99-12//99
	Iowa	S	13.05 MW	13.09 AW	27220 AAW	IABLS	10//99-12//99
	Kansas	S	8.45 MW	10.11 AW	21030 AAW	KSBLS	10//99-12//99
	Kentucky	S	8.27 MW	10.01 AW	20810 AAW	KYBLS	10//99-12//99
	Louisiana	S	12.74 MW	12.35 AW	25700 AAW	LABLS	10//99-12//99
	Maryland	S	12.51 MW	12.65 AW	26320 AAW	MDBLS	10//99-12//99
	Massachusetts	S	12.27 MW	12.09 AW	25150 AAW	MABLS	10//99-12//99
	Michigan	S	12.59 MW	12.86 AW	26750 AAW	MIBLS	10//99-12//99
	Minnesota	S	11.6 MW	12.17 AW	25310 AAW	MNBLS	10//99-12//99
	Mississippi	S	12.26 MW	12.48 AW	25950 AAW	MSBLS	10//99-12//99
	Missouri	S	6.74 MW	9.72 AW	20220 AAW	MOBLS	10//99-12//99
	Montana	S	11.63 MW	11.22 AW	23330 AAW	MTBLS	10//99-12//99
	Nebraska	S	13.71 MW	13.42 AW	27920 AAW	NEBLS	10//99-12//99
	Nevada	S	13.47 MW	14.54 AW	30240 AAW	NVBLS	10//99-12//99
	New Hampshire	S	9.94 MW	10.42 AW	21670 AAW	NHBLS	10//99-12//99
	New Jersey	S	12.86 MW	12.66 AW	26330 AAW	NJBLS	10//99-12//99
	New Mexico	S	8.91 MW	9.16 AW	19050 AAW	NMBLS	10//99-12//99
	New York	S	14.87 MW	16.30 AW	33910 AAW	NYBLS	10//99-12//99
	North Carolina	S	10.62 MW	10.70 AW	22250 AAW	NCBLS	10//99-12//99
	North Dakota	S	10.94 MW	11.07 AW	23020 AAW	NDBLS	10//99-12//99
	Ohio	S	13.79 MW	13.86 AW	28830 AAW	OHBLS	10//99-12//99
	Oklahoma	S	18.09 MW	17.91 AW	37260 AAW	OKBLS	10//99-12//99
	Oregon	S	14.35 MW	14.23 AW	29600 AAW	ORBLS	10//99-12//99
	Pennsylvania	S	13.17 MW	14.60 AW	30370 AAW	PABLS	10//99-12//99
	Rhode Island	S	10.46 MW	11.21 AW	23320 AAW	RIBLS	10//99-12//99
	South Carolina	S	8.09 MW	9.53 AW	19820 AAW	SCBLS	10//99-12//99
	South Dakota	S	9.83 MW	9.85 AW	20480 AAW	SDBLS	10//99-12//99
	Tennessee	S	11 MW	10.77 AW	22400 AAW	TNBLS	10//99-12//99
	Texas	S	11.13 MW	11.54 AW	24010 AAW	TXBLS	10//99-12//99
	Virginia	S	10.94 MW	10.95 AW	22770 AAW	VABLS	10//99-12//99
	Washington	S	15.22 MW	15.37 AW	31970 AAW	WABLS	10//99-12//99
	West Virginia	S	9.12 MW	10.04 AW	20890 AAW	WVBLS	10//99-12//99
	Wisconsin	S	14.63 MW	14.15 AW	29430 AAW	WIBLS	10//99-12//99
	Wyoming	S	11.5 MW	11.78 AW	24490 AAW	WYBLS	10//99-12//99
	Puerto Rico	S	8.8 MW	9.92 AW	20640 AAW	PRBLS	10//99-12//99
Collision Repair Technician	United States	Y		37189 AW		TECHD	1998
Combined Food Preparation and Serving Worker							
Including Fast Food	Alabama	S	6.01 MW	6.18 AW	12850 AAW	ALBLS	10//99-12//99
Including Fast Food	Alaska	S	6.86 MW	7.25 AW	15070 AAW	AKBLS	10//99-12//99
Including Fast Food	Arizona	S	6.05 MW	6.35 AW	13220 AAW	AZBLS	10//99-12//99
Including Fast Food	Arkansas	S	6.06 MW	6.16 AW	12810 AAW	ARBLS	10//99-12//99
Including Fast Food	California	S	6.51 MW	7.20 AW	14980 AAW	CABLS	10//99-12//99

AAW	Average annual wage	AOH	Average offered, high	ASH	Average starting, high
AE	Average entry wage	AOL	Average offered, low	ASL	Average starting, low
AEX	Average experienced wage	APH	Average pay, high range	AW	Average wage paid
AO	Average offered	APL	Average pay, low range	FQ	First quartile wage

H	Hourly	M	Monthly
HI	Highest wage paid	MTC	Median total compensation
HR	High end range	MW	Median wage paid
LR	Low end range	SQ	Second quartile wage

S	Special: hourly and annual
TQ	Third quartile wage
W	Weekly
Y	Yearly

Occupation/Type/Industry	Location	Per	Low	Mid	High	Source	Date
Combined Food Preparation and Serving Worker							
Including Fast Food	Colorado	S	6.33 MW	6.65 AW	13840 AAW	COBLS	10//99-12//99
Including Fast Food	Connecticut	S	6.98 MW	7.64 AW	15890 AAW	CTBLS	10//99-12//99
Including Fast Food	Delaware	S	6.56 MW	7.13 AW	14830 AAW	DEBLS	10//99-12//99
Including Fast Food	District of Columbia	S	8.09 MW	8.92 AW	18560 AAW	DCBLS	10//99-12//99
Including Fast Food	Florida	S	6.32 MW	6.57 AW	13670 AAW	FLBLS	10//99-12//99
Including Fast Food	Georgia	S	6.21 MW	6.44 AW	13400 AAW	GABLS	10//99-12//99
Including Fast Food	Hawaii	S	6.31 MW	6.71 AW	13960 AAW	HIBLS	10//99-12//99
Including Fast Food	Idaho	S	6.12 MW	6.33 AW	13160 AAW	IDBLS	10//99-12//99
Including Fast Food	Illinois	S	6.2 MW	6.73 AW	14000 AAW	ILBLS	10//99-12//99
Including Fast Food	Indiana	S	6.18 MW	6.35 AW	13200 AAW	INBLS	10//99-12//99
Including Fast Food	Iowa	S	6.29 MW	6.62 AW	13770 AAW	IABLS	10//99-12//99
Including Fast Food	Kansas	S	6.14 MW	6.33 AW	13160 AAW	KSBLS	10//99-12//99
Including Fast Food	Kentucky	S	6.22 MW	6.37 AW	13240 AAW	KYBLS	10//99-12//99
Including Fast Food	Louisiana	S	6.03 MW	6.18 AW	12860 AAW	LABLS	10//99-12//99
Including Fast Food	Maine	S	6.73 MW	6.97 AW	14490 AAW	MEBLS	10//99-12//99
Including Fast Food	Maryland	S	6.46 MW	6.85 AW	14260 AAW	MDBLS	10//99-12//99
Including Fast Food	Massachusetts	S	6.82 MW	7.29 AW	15160 AAW	MABLS	10//99-12//99
Including Fast Food	Michigan	S	6.35 MW	6.63 AW	13790 AAW	MIBLS	10//99-12//99
Including Fast Food	Minnesota	S	6.5 MW	6.79 AW	14130 AAW	MNBLS	10//99-12//99
Including Fast Food	Mississippi	S	6.01 MW	6.11 AW	12700 AAW	MSBLS	10//99-12//99
Including Fast Food	Missouri	S	6.17 MW	6.32 AW	13130 AAW	MOBLS	10//99-12//99
Including Fast Food	Montana	S	6.02 MW	6.14 AW	12770 AAW	MTBLS	10//99-12//99
Including Fast Food	Nebraska	S	6.51 MW	6.66 AW	13850 AAW	NEBLS	10//99-12//99
Including Fast Food	Nevada	S	6.68 MW	7.05 AW	14660 AAW	NVBLS	10//99-12//99
Including Fast Food	New Hampshire	S	6.74 MW	7.19 AW	14950 AAW	NHBLS	10//99-12//99
Including Fast Food	New Jersey	S	6.54 MW	7.07 AW	14710 AAW	NJBLS	10//99-12//99
Including Fast Food	New Mexico	S	5.98 MW	6.17 AW	12840 AAW	NMBLS	10//99-12//99
Including Fast Food	New York	S	6.24 MW	6.81 AW	14170 AAW	NYBLS	10//99-12//99
Including Fast Food	North Carolina	S	6.35 MW	6.56 AW	13640 AAW	NCBLS	10//99-12//99
Including Fast Food	North Dakota	S	6.04 MW	6.50 AW	13510 AAW	NDBLS	10//99-12//99
Including Fast Food	Ohio	S	6.12 MW	6.39 AW	13280 AAW	OHBLS	10//99-12//99
Including Fast Food	Oklahoma	S	6.06 MW	6.20 AW	12900 AAW	OKBLS	10//99-12//99
Including Fast Food	Oregon	S	6.9 MW	7.36 AW	15310 AAW	ORBLS	10//99-12//99
Including Fast Food	Pennsylvania	S	6.1 MW	6.54 AW	13610 AAW	PABLS	10//99-12//99
Including Fast Food	Rhode Island	S	6.26 MW	6.70 AW	13930 AAW	RIBLS	10//99-12//99
Including Fast Food	South Carolina	S	6.09 MW	6.33 AW	13170 AAW	SCBLS	10//99-12//99
Including Fast Food	South Dakota	S	6.03 MW	6.13 AW	12750 AAW	SDBLS	10//99-12//99
Including Fast Food	Tennessee	S	6.31 MW	6.48 AW	13470 AAW	TNBLS	10//99-12//99
Including Fast Food	Texas	S	6.06 MW	6.22 AW	12950 AAW	TXBLS	10//99-12//99
Including Fast Food	Utah	S	6.25 MW	6.59 AW	13710 AAW	UTBLS	10//99-12//99
Including Fast Food	Vermont	S	6.53 MW	7.01 AW	14580 AAW	VTBLS	10//99-12//99
Including Fast Food	Virginia	S	6.3 MW	6.70 AW	13940 AAW	VABLS	10//99-12//99
Including Fast Food	Washington	S	6.49 MW	6.94 AW	14430 AAW	WABLS	10//99-12//99
Including Fast Food	West Virginia	S	5.96 MW	6.07 AW	12610 AAW	WVBLS	10//99-12//99
Including Fast Food	Wisconsin	S	6.53 MW	6.76 AW	14050 AAW	WIBLS	10//99-12//99
Including Fast Food	Wyoming	S	5.98 MW	5.98 AW	12440 AAW	WYBLS	10//99-12//99
Including Fast Food	Puerto Rico	S	5.91 MW	5.77 AW	11990 AAW	PRBLS	10//99-12//99
Including Fast Food	Virgin Islands	S	6.06 MW	6.10 AW	12690 AAW	VIBLS	10//99-12//99
Including Fast Food	Guam	S	6.63 MW	6.66 AW	13850 AAW	GUBLS	10//99-12//99
Commercial and Industrial Designer							
	Alabama	S	23.43 MW	22.19 AW	46150 AAW	ALBLS	10//99-12//99
	Birmingham MSA, AL	S	22.26 MW	23.62 AW	46300 AAW	ALBLS	10//99-12//99
	Arizona	S	20 MW	20.17 AW	41960 AAW	AZBLS	10//99-12//99
	Phoenix-Mesa MSA, AZ	S	20.57 MW	20.39 AW	42780 AAW	AZBLS	10//99-12//99
	Tucson MSA, AZ	S	18.80 MW	18.44 AW	39100 AAW	AZBLS	10//99-12//99
	Arkansas	S	18.56 MW	18.84 AW	39190 AAW	ARBLS	10//99-12//99
	Little Rock-North Little Rock MSA, AR	S	19.10 MW	19.36 AW	39730 AAW	ARBLS	10//99-12//99
	California	S	24.44 MW	25.25 AW	52520 AAW	CABLS	10//99-12//99
	Los Angeles-Long Beach PMSA, CA	S	22.11 MW	20.97 AW	45980 AAW	CABLS	10//99-12//99
	Oakland PMSA, CA	S	23.79 MW	21.42 AW	49490 AAW	CABLS	10//99-12//99
	Orange County PMSA, CA	S	28.68 MW	26.58 AW	59660 AAW	CABLS	10//99-12//99
	San Diego MSA, CA	S	17.40 MW	13.39 AW	36190 AAW	CABLS	10//99-12//99
	San Francisco PMSA, CA	S	25.47 MW	24.45 AW	52970 AAW	CABLS	10//99-12//99
	San Jose PMSA, CA	S	28.90 MW	27.52 AW	60120 AAW	CABLS	10//99-12//99
	Santa Rosa PMSA, CA	S	19.44 MW	19.50 AW	40440 AAW	CABLS	10//99-12//99
	Ventura PMSA, CA	S	16.81 MW	14.01 AW	34970 AAW	CABLS	10//99-12//99
	Colorado	S	16.02 MW	17.79 AW	37000 AAW	COBLS	10//99-12//99

AAW Average annual wage	**AOH** Average offered, high	**ASH** Average starting, high	**H** Hourly	**M** Monthly	**S** Special: hourly and annual
AE Average entry wage	**AOL** Average offered, low	**ASL** Average starting, low	**HI** Highest wage paid	**MTC** Median total compensation	**TQ** Third quartile wage
AEX Average experienced wage	**APH** Average pay, high range	**AW** Average wage paid	**HR** High end range	**MW** Median wage paid	**W** Weekly
AO Average offered	**APL** Average pay, low range	**FQ** First quartile wage	**LR** Low end range	**SQ** Second quartile wage	**Y** Yearly

Occupation/Type/Industry	Location	Per	Low	Mid	High	Source	Date
Commercial and Industrial Designer							
	Boulder-Longmont PMSA, CO	S	21.31 MW	21.13 AW	44330 AAW	COBLS	10//99-12//99
	Denver PMSA, CO	S	16.33 MW	15.41 AW	33970 AAW	COBLS	10//99-12//99
	Connecticut	S	20.42 MW	24.59 AW	51150 AAW	CTBLS	10//99-12//99
	Bridgeport PMSA, CT	S	32.12 MW	30.51 AW	66810 AAW	CTBLS	10//99-12//99
	Hartford MSA, CT	S	25.56 MW	20.28 AW	53170 AAW	CTBLS	10//99-12//99
	New Haven-Meriden PMSA, CT	S	16.76 MW	16.37 AW	34850 AAW	CTBLS	10//99-12//99
	New London-Norwich MSA, CT-RI	S	21.92 MW	21.00 AW	45590 AAW	CTBLS	10//99-12//99
	Stamford-Norwalk PMSA, CT	S	18.87 MW	18.52 AW	39250 AAW	CTBLS	10//99-12//99
	Delaware	S	25.66 MW	26.15 AW	54390 AAW	DEBLS	10//99-12//99
	Wilmington-Newark PMSA, DE-MD	S	26.80 MW	26.01 AW	55740 AAW	DEBLS	10//99-12//99
	District of Columbia	S	22.28 MW	22.21 AW	46200 AAW	DCBLS	10//99-12//99
	Washington PMSA, DC-MD-VA-WV	S	20.61 MW	19.55 AW	42860 AAW	DCBLS	10//99-12//99
	Florida	S	15.49 MW	17.66 AW	36730 AAW	FLBLS	10//99-12//99
	Fort Lauderdale PMSA, FL	S	18.36 MW	19.10 AW	38190 AAW	FLBLS	10//99-12//99
	Jacksonville MSA, FL	S	19.41 MW	19.21 AW	40380 AAW	FLBLS	10//99-12//99
	Miami PMSA, FL	S	20.07 MW	19.27 AW	41750 AAW	FLBLS	10//99-12//99
	Sarasota-Bradenton MSA, FL	S	20.10 MW	19.73 AW	41810 AAW	FLBLS	10//99-12//99
	Tampa-St. Petersburg-Clearwater MSA, FL	S	12.82 MW	13.01 AW	26670 AAW	FLBLS	10//99-12//99
	Georgia	S	15.69 MW	17.34 AW	36060 AAW	GABLS	10//99-12//99
	Atlanta MSA, GA	S	16.42 MW	15.34 AW	34150 AAW	GABLS	10//99-12//99
	Idaho	S	19.3 MW	19.99 AW	41570 AAW	IDBLS	10//99-12//99
	Boise City MSA, ID	S	20.15 MW	19.45 AW	41910 AAW	IDBLS	10//99-12//99
	Illinois	S	19.87 MW	19.60 AW	40760 AAW	ILBLS	10//99-12//99
	Chicago PMSA, IL	S	19.49 MW	19.89 AW	40530 AAW	ILBLS	10//99-12//99
	Peoria-Pekin MSA, IL	S	23.51 MW	24.12 AW	48910 AAW	ILBLS	10//99-12//99
	Indiana	S	22.67 MW	22.27 AW	46330 AAW	INBLS	10//99-12//99
	Evansville-Henderson MSA, IN-KY	S	16.28 MW	15.99 AW	33860 AAW	INBLS	10//99-12//99
	Indianapolis MSA, IN	S	20.86 MW	20.26 AW	43380 AAW	INBLS	10//99-12//99
	Iowa	S	17.9 MW	17.99 AW	37410 AAW	IABLS	10//99-12//99
	Cedar Rapids MSA, IA	S	18.50 MW	18.96 AW	38470 AAW	IABLS	10//99-12//99
	Des Moines MSA, IA	S	16.47 MW	16.63 AW	34260 AAW	IABLS	10//99-12//99
	Dubuque MSA, IA	S	17.73 MW	17.05 AW	36880 AAW	IABLS	10//99-12//99
	Waterloo-Cedar Falls MSA, IA	S	21.07 MW	21.21 AW	43820 AAW	IABLS	10//99-12//99
	Kansas	S	16.49 MW	18.91 AW	39330 AAW	KSBLS	10//99-12//99
	Wichita MSA, KS	S	13.29 MW	12.08 AW	27640 AAW	KSBLS	10//99-12//99
	Kentucky	S	31.06 MW	29.93 AW	62250 AAW	KYBLS	10//99-12//99
	Louisville MSA, KY-IN	S	29.28 MW	27.99 AW	60900 AAW	KYBLS	10//99-12//99
	Louisiana	S	18.85 MW	18.76 AW	39020 AAW	LABLS	10//99-12//99
	New Orleans MSA, LA	S	18.68 MW	18.83 AW	38860 AAW	LABLS	10//99-12//99
	Maryland	S	20.17 MW	23.50 AW	48880 AAW	MDBLS	10//99-12//99
	Baltimore PMSA, MD	S	21.75 MW	19.73 AW	45240 AAW	MDBLS	10//99-12//99
	Massachusetts	S	24.93 MW	25.25 AW	52520 AAW	MABLS	10//99-12//99
	Boston PMSA, MA-NH	S	26.51 MW	26.08 AW	55130 AAW	MABLS	10//99-12//99
	Lowell PMSA, MA-NH	S	21.37 MW	20.16 AW	44440 AAW	MABLS	10//99-12//99
	Springfield MSA, MA	S	18.50 MW	17.16 AW	38490 AAW	MABLS	10//99-12//99
	Michigan	S	28.8 MW	27.77 AW	57750 AAW	MIBLS	10//99-12//99
	Ann Arbor PMSA, MI	S	26.56 MW	27.44 AW	55230 AAW	MIBLS	10//99-12//99
	Detroit PMSA, MI	S	28.90 MW	29.49 AW	60110 AAW	MIBLS	10//99-12//99
	Flint PMSA, MI	S	29.80 MW	30.58 AW	61970 AAW	MIBLS	10//99-12//99
	Grand Rapids-Muskegon-Holland MSA, MI	S	25.55 MW	27.25 AW	53140 AAW	MIBLS	10//99-12//99
	Kalamazoo-Battle Creek MSA, MI	S	20.71 MW	18.80 AW	43080 AAW	MIBLS	10//99-12//99
	Minnesota	S	19.54 MW	21.17 AW	44030 AAW	MNBLS	10//99-12//99
	Minneapolis-St. Paul MSA, MN-WI	S	21.90 MW	21.57 AW	45560 AAW	MNBLS	10//99-12//99
	Mississippi	S	14.5 MW	16.52 AW	34360 AAW	MSBLS	10//99-12//99
	Jackson MSA, MS	S	12.88 MW	13.50 AW	26780 AAW	MSBLS	10//99-12//99
	Missouri	S	20.83 MW	22.91 AW	47650 AAW	MOBLS	10//99-12//99
	Kansas City MSA, MO-KS	S	24.49 MW	22.24 AW	50930 AAW	MOBLS	10//99-12//99
	Nebraska	S	18.23 MW	18.71 AW	38910 AAW	NEBLS	10//99-12//99
	Omaha MSA, NE-IA	S	17.18 MW	18.25 AW	35740 AAW	NEBLS	10//99-12//99
	Nevada	S	19.95 MW	20.55 AW	42750 AAW	NVBLS	10//99-12//99
	Las Vegas MSA, NV-AZ	S	20.27 MW	19.98 AW	42170 AAW	NVBLS	10//99-12//99
	Reno MSA, NV	S	21.53 MW	19.64 AW	44780 AAW	NVBLS	10//99-12//99

AAW Average annual wage	**AOH** Average offered, high	**ASH** Average starting, high	**H** Hourly	**M** Monthly	**S** Special: hourly and annual
AE Average entry wage	**AOL** Average offered, low	**ASL** Average starting, low	**HI** Highest wage paid	**MTC** Median total compensation	**TQ** Third quartile wage
AEX Average experienced wage	**APH** Average pay, high range	**AW** Average wage paid	**HR** High end range	**MW** Median wage paid	**W** Weekly
AO Average offered	**APL** Average pay, low range	**FQ** First quartile wage	**LR** Low end range	**SQ** Second quartile wage	**Y** Yearly

Occupation/Type/Industry	Location	Per	Low	Mid	High	Source	Date
Commercial and Industrial Designer	New Hampshire	S	16.57 MW	18.39 AW	38260 AAW	NHBLS	10//99-12//99
	Nashua PMSA, NH	S	19.52 MW	16.55 AW	40610 AAW	NHBLS	10//99-12//99
	Portsmouth-Rochester PMSA, NH-ME	S	17.78 MW	15.73 AW	36990 AAW	NHBLS	10//99-12//99
	New Jersey	S	21.4 MW	23.44 AW	48750 AAW	NJBLS	10//99-12//99
	Bergen-Passaic PMSA, NJ	S	23.19 MW	23.19 AW	48230 AAW	NJBLS	10//99-12//99
	Middlesex-Somerset-Hunterdon PMSA, NJ	S	30.05 MW	29.97 AW	62500 AAW	NJBLS	10//99-12//99
	Newark PMSA, NJ	S	27.46 MW	28.88 AW	57110 AAW	NJBLS	10//99-12//99
	New York	S	24.73 MW	25.11 AW	52220 AAW	NYBLS	10//99-12//99
	Albany-Schenectady-Troy MSA, NY	S	18.07 MW	15.73 AW	37580 AAW	NYBLS	10//99-12//99
	Buffalo-Niagara Falls MSA, NY	S	20.36 MW	18.57 AW	42340 AAW	NYBLS	10//99-12//99
	Nassau-Suffolk PMSA, NY	S	26.92 MW	28.29 AW	55990 AAW	NYBLS	10//99-12//99
	New York PMSA, NY	S	25.58 MW	24.70 AW	53200 AAW	NYBLS	10//99-12//99
	Rochester MSA, NY	S	26.97 MW	26.63 AW	56100 AAW	NYBLS	10//99-12//99
	Syracuse MSA, NY	S	20.40 MW	16.33 AW	42430 AAW	NYBLS	10//99-12//99
	North Carolina	S	19.19 MW	20.30 AW	42220 AAW	NCBLS	10//99-12//99
	Charlotte-Gastonia-Rock Hill MSA, NC-SC	S	17.97 MW	17.87 AW	37380 AAW	NCBLS	10//99-12//99
	Greensboro--Winston-Salem--High Point MSA, NC	S	22.57 MW	20.85 AW	46950 AAW	NCBLS	10//99-12//99
	Hickory-Morganton-Lenoir MSA, NC	S	22.55 MW	20.08 AW	46900 AAW	NCBLS	10//99-12//99
	North Dakota	S	15.25 MW	26.02 AW	54120 AAW	NDBLS	10//99-12//99
	Ohio	S	23.49 MW	24.24 AW	50410 AAW	OHBLS	10//99-12//99
	Akron PMSA, OH	S	29.12 MW	29.11 AW	60560 AAW	OHBLS	10//99-12//99
	Cincinnati PMSA, OH-KY-IN	S	22.50 MW	17.66 AW	46790 AAW	OHBLS	10//99-12//99
	Cleveland-Lorain-Elyria PMSA, OH	S	26.69 MW	24.82 AW	55510 AAW	OHBLS	10//99-12//99
	Columbus MSA, OH	S	25.70 MW	25.90 AW	53450 AAW	OHBLS	10//99-12//99
	Dayton-Springfield MSA, OH	S	22.19 MW	24.34 AW	46150 AAW	OHBLS	10//99-12//99
	Oklahoma	S	18.06 MW	19.16 AW	39860 AAW	OKBLS	10//99-12//99
	Oklahoma City MSA, OK	S	14.71 MW	14.14 AW	30600 AAW	OKBLS	10//99-12//99
	Tulsa MSA, OK	S	16.62 MW	15.49 AW	34570 AAW	OKBLS	10//99-12//99
	Oregon	S	24.57 MW	24.84 AW	51660 AAW	ORBLS	10//99-12//99
	Portland-Vancouver PMSA, OR-WA	S	25.09 MW	24.69 AW	52190 AAW	ORBLS	10//99-12//99
	Pennsylvania	S	19.12 MW	20.54 AW	42720 AAW	PABLS	10//99-12//99
	Philadelphia PMSA, PA-NJ	S	23.71 MW	22.36 AW	49330 AAW	PABLS	10//99-12//99
	Pittsburgh MSA, PA	S	12.75 MW	8.47 AW	26510 AAW	PABLS	10//99-12//99
	Reading MSA, PA	S	20.06 MW	22.35 AW	41730 AAW	PABLS	10//99-12//99
	Scranton--Wilkes-Barre--Hazleton MSA, PA	S	19.74 MW	18.97 AW	41050 AAW	PABLS	10//99-12//99
	York MSA, PA	S	19.74 MW	18.86 AW	41060 AAW	PABLS	10//99-12//99
	Rhode Island	S	25.99 MW	29.52 AW	61400 AAW	RIBLS	10//99-12//99
	Providence-Fall River-Warwick MSA, RI-MA	S	28.75 MW	24.53 AW	59800 AAW	RIBLS	10//99-12//99
	South Carolina	S	16.85 MW	20.22 AW	42060 AAW	SCBLS	10//99-12//99
	Charleston-North Charleston MSA, SC	S	20.73 MW	17.27 AW	43120 AAW	SCBLS	10//99-12//99
	Columbia MSA, SC	S	10.70 MW	9.65 AW	22260 AAW	SCBLS	10//99-12//99
	Greenville-Spartanburg-Anderson MSA, SC	S	18.90 MW	16.22 AW	39310 AAW	SCBLS	10//99-12//99
	South Dakota	S	13.23 MW	13.23 AW	27520 AAW	SDBLS	10//99-12//99
	Sioux Falls MSA, SD	S	13.39 MW	13.23 AW	27860 AAW	SDBLS	10//99-12//99
	Tennessee	S	23.2 MW	22.27 AW	46330 AAW	TNBLS	10//99-12//99
	Knoxville MSA, TN	S	15.71 MW	12.76 AW	32680 AAW	TNBLS	10//99-12//99
	Nashville MSA, TN	S	23.39 MW	23.43 AW	48650 AAW	TNBLS	10//99-12//99
	Texas	S	28.47 MW	27.95 AW	58140 AAW	TXBLS	10//99-12//99
	Austin-San Marcos MSA, TX	S	33.40 MW	36.38 AW	69480 AAW	TXBLS	10//99-12//99
	Dallas PMSA, TX	S	29.95 MW	30.92 AW	62300 AAW	TXBLS	10//99-12//99
	El Paso MSA, TX	S	18.42 MW	18.67 AW	38300 AAW	TXBLS	10//99-12//99
	Fort Worth-Arlington PMSA, TX	S	20.97 MW	18.34 AW	43620 AAW	TXBLS	10//99-12//99
	Houston PMSA, TX	S	29.55 MW	29.71 AW	61460 AAW	TXBLS	10//99-12//99
	San Antonio MSA, TX	S	22.54 MW	20.77 AW	46880 AAW	TXBLS	10//99-12//99
	Utah	S	16.58 MW	18.33 AW	38120 AAW	UTBLS	10//99-12//99
	Provo-Orem MSA, UT	S	16.96 MW	14.93 AW	35270 AAW	UTBLS	10//99-12//99

AAW	Average annual wage	AOH	Average offered, high	ASH	Average starting, high	H	Hourly	M	Monthly	S	Special: hourly and annual
AE	Average entry wage	AOL	Average offered, low	ASL	Average starting, low	HI	Highest wage paid	MTC	Median total compensation	TQ	Third quartile wage
AEX	Average experienced wage	APH	Average pay, high range	AW	Average wage paid	HR	High end range	MW	Median wage paid	W	Weekly
AO	Average offered	APL	Average pay, low range	FQ	First quartile wage	LR	Low end range	SQ	Second quartile wage	Y	Yearly

Occupation/Type/Industry	Location	Per	Low	Mid	High	Source	Date
Commercial and Industrial Designer	Salt Lake City-Ogden MSA, UT	S	18.65 MW	16.75 AW	38780 AAW	UTBLS	10//99-12//99
	Vermont	S	22.98 MW	21.85 AW	45440 AAW	VTBLS	10//99-12//99
	Virginia	S	19.65 MW	20.69 AW	43040 AAW	VABLS	10//99-12//99
	Norfolk-Virginia Beach-Newport News MSA, VA-NC	S	16.75 MW	18.40 AW	34840 AAW	VABLS	10//99-12//99
	Richmond-Petersburg MSA, VA	S	19.65 MW	18.91 AW	40870 AAW	VABLS	10//99-12//99
	Roanoke MSA, VA	S	27.77 MW	29.54 AW	57760 AAW	VABLS	10//99-12//99
	Washington	S	18.87 MW	19.74 AW	41050 AAW	WABLS	10//99-12//99
	Seattle-Bellevue-Everett PMSA, WA	S	20.66 MW	19.32 AW	42980 AAW	WABLS	10//99-12//99
	Spokane MSA, WA	S	14.62 MW	12.90 AW	30410 AAW	WABLS	10//99-12//99
	Wisconsin	S	21.31 MW	21.11 AW	43910 AAW	WIBLS	10//99-12//99
	Appleton-Oshkosh-Neenah MSA, WI	S	25.35 MW	25.22 AW	52720 AAW	WIBLS	10//99-12//99
	Milwaukee-Waukesha PMSA, WI	S	21.70 MW	21.61 AW	45130 AAW	WIBLS	10//99-12//99
	Puerto Rico	S	17.18 MW	17.21 AW	35800 AAW	PRBLS	10//99-12//99
	San Juan-Bayamon PMSA, PR	S	17.21 MW	17.18 AW	35800 AAW	PRBLS	10//99-12//99
Commercial Diver	Hawaii	S	16.95 MW	15.97 AW	33210 AAW	HIBLS	10//99-12//99
	Illinois	S	23.29 MW	20.95 AW	43590 AAW	ILBLS	10//99-12//99
	New Jersey	S	36.02 MW	30.55 AW	63540 AAW	NJBLS	10//99-12//99
	Washington	S	54.66 MW	53.64 AW	111570 AAW	WABLS	10//99-12//99
Commercial Pilot	Alabama	Y		51750 AAW		ALBLS	10//99-12//99
	Alaska	Y		43290 AAW		AKBLS	10//99-12//99
	Arizona	Y		46880 AAW		AZBLS	10//99-12//99
	Arkansas	Y		67310 AAW		ARBLS	10//99-12//99
	California	Y		78660 AAW		CABLS	10//99-12//99
	Colorado	Y		46900 AAW		COBLS	10//99-12//99
	Connecticut	Y		42790 AAW		CTBLS	10//99-12//99
	Florida	Y		44200 AAW		FLBLS	10//99-12//99
	Georgia	Y		49280 AAW		GABLS	10//99-12//99
	Hawaii	Y		66670 AAW		HIBLS	10//99-12//99
	Idaho	Y		60550 AAW		IDBLS	10//99-12//99
	Illinois	Y		51010 AAW		ILBLS	10//99-12//99
	Indiana	Y		34560 AAW		INBLS	10//99-12//99
	Iowa	Y		44890 AAW		IABLS	10//99-12//99
	Kentucky	Y		41660 AAW		KYBLS	10//99-12//99
	Louisiana	Y		56950 AAW		LABLS	10//99-12//99
	Maine	Y		32000 AAW		MEBLS	10//99-12//99
	Massachusetts	Y		42480 AAW		MABLS	10//99-12//99
	Michigan	Y		31950 AAW		MIBLS	10//99-12//99
	Minnesota	Y		46040 AAW		MNBLS	10//99-12//99
	Mississippi	Y		69390 AAW		MSBLS	10//99-12//99
	Missouri	Y		32200 AAW		MOBLS	10//99-12//99
	Montana	Y		34530 AAW		MTBLS	10//99-12//99
	Nebraska	Y		29380 AAW		NEBLS	10//99-12//99
	Nevada	Y		38380 AAW		NVBLS	10//99-12//99
	New Hampshire	Y		35870 AAW		NHBLS	10//99-12//99
	New Jersey	Y		42340 AAW		NJBLS	10//99-12//99
	New Mexico	Y		49670 AAW		NMBLS	10//99-12//99
	North Carolina	Y		33890 AAW		NCBLS	10//99-12//99
	Oklahoma	Y		42440 AAW		OKBLS	10//99-12//99
	Oregon	Y		46810 AAW		ORBLS	10//99-12//99
	Pennsylvania	Y		41500 AAW		PABLS	10//99-12//99
	South Carolina	Y		45710 AAW		SCBLS	10//99-12//99
	South Dakota	Y		32720 AAW		SDBLS	10//99-12//99
	Tennessee	Y		46420 AAW		TNBLS	10//99-12//99
	Texas	Y		44250 AAW		TXBLS	10//99-12//99
	Virginia	Y		40660 AAW		VABLS	10//99-12//99
	Washington	Y		38650 AAW		WABLS	10//99-12//99
	Wisconsin	Y		43900 AAW		WIBLS	10//99-12//99
	Wyoming	Y		40430 AAW		WYBLS	10//99-12//99
	Puerto Rico	Y		30790 AAW		PRBLS	10//99-12//99
Communications Teacher Postsecondary	Alabama	Y		33520 AAW		ALBLS	10//99-12//99

AAW	Average annual wage	AOH	Average offered, high	ASH	Average starting, high	H	Hourly	M	Monthly	S	Special: hourly and annual
AE	Average entry wage	AOL	Average offered, low	ASL	Average starting, low	HI	Highest wage paid	MTC	Median total compensation	TQ	Third quartile wage
AEX	Average experienced wage	APH	Average pay, high range	AW	Average wage paid	HR	High end range	MW	Median wage paid	W	Weekly
AO	Average offered	APL	Average pay, low range	FQ	First quartile wage	LR	Low end range	SQ	Second quartile wage	Y	Yearly

Occupation/Type/Industry	Location	Per	Low	Mid	High	Source	Date
Communications Teacher							
Postsecondary	Arizona	Y		43970 AAW		AZBLS	10//99-12//99
Postsecondary	Arkansas	Y		41930 AAW		ARBLS	10//99-12//99
Postsecondary	California	Y		48860 AAW		CABLS	10//99-12//99
Postsecondary	Colorado	Y		45300 AAW		COBLS	10//99-12//99
Postsecondary	Connecticut	Y		50240 AAW		CTBLS	10//99-12//99
Postsecondary	District of Columbia	Y		45320 AAW		DCBLS	10//99-12//99
Postsecondary	Florida	Y		62290 AAW		FLBLS	10//99-12//99
Postsecondary	Georgia	Y		46940 AAW		GABLS	10//99-12//99
Postsecondary	Illinois	Y		47790 AAW		ILBLS	10//99-12//99
Postsecondary	Indiana	Y		41580 AAW		INBLS	10//99-12//99
Postsecondary	Iowa	Y		46440 AAW		IABLS	10//99-12//99
Postsecondary	Kansas	Y		41840 AAW		KSBLS	10//99-12//99
Postsecondary	Kentucky	Y		38610 AAW		KYBLS	10//99-12//99
Postsecondary	Louisiana	Y		43880 AAW		LABLS	10//99-12//99
Postsecondary	Maryland	Y		60810 AAW		MDBLS	10//99-12//99
Postsecondary	Massachusetts	Y		45670 AAW		MABLS	10//99-12//99
Postsecondary	Michigan	Y		45370 AAW		MIBLS	10//99-12//99
Postsecondary	Minnesota	Y		46590 AAW		MNBLS	10//99-12//99
Postsecondary	Mississippi	Y		36210 AAW		MSBLS	10//99-12//99
Postsecondary	Missouri	Y		38020 AAW		MOBLS	10//99-12//99
Postsecondary	Montana	Y		58010 AAW		MTBLS	10//99-12//99
Postsecondary	Nebraska	Y		48960 AAW		NEBLS	10//99-12//99
Postsecondary	Nevada	Y		47940 AAW		NVBLS	10//99-12//99
Postsecondary	New Hampshire	Y		46310 AAW		NHBLS	10//99-12//99
Postsecondary	New Jersey	Y		54280 AAW		NJBLS	10//99-12//99
Postsecondary	New Mexico	Y		46280 AAW		NMBLS	10//99-12//99
Postsecondary	New York	Y		50590 AAW		NYBLS	10//99-12//99
Postsecondary	North Carolina	Y		41690 AAW		NCBLS	10//99-12//99
Postsecondary	North Dakota	Y		40720 AAW		NDBLS	10//99-12//99
Postsecondary	Ohio	Y		39910 AAW		OHBLS	10//99-12//99
Postsecondary	Oklahoma	Y		42550 AAW		OKBLS	10//99-12//99
Postsecondary	Oregon	Y		45020 AAW		ORBLS	10//99-12//99
Postsecondary	Pennsylvania	Y		51230 AAW		PABLS	10//99-12//99
Postsecondary	South Carolina	Y		41790 AAW		SCBLS	10//99-12//99
Postsecondary	South Dakota	Y		41730 AAW		SDBLS	10//99-12//99
Postsecondary	Tennessee	Y		45270 AAW		TNBLS	10//99-12//99
Postsecondary	Texas	Y		38390 AAW		TXBLS	10//99-12//99
Postsecondary	Vermont	Y		51290 AAW		VTBLS	10//99-12//99
Postsecondary	Virginia	Y		46090 AAW		VABLS	10//99-12//99
Postsecondary	Washington	Y		41680 AAW		WABLS	10//99-12//99
Postsecondary	West Virginia	Y		48450 AAW		WVBLS	10//99-12//99
Postsecondary	Wyoming	Y		43190 AAW		WYBLS	10//99-12//99
Postsecondary	Puerto Rico	Y		35320 AAW		PRBLS	10//99-12//99
Compensation and Benefits Manager	United States	Y		77800 AW		TRAVWK2	1999
Compensation, Benefits, and Job Analysis Specialist	Alabama	S	17.96 MW	18.51 AW	38500 AAW	ALBLS	10//99-12//99
	Birmingham MSA, AL	S	18.06 MW	18.19 AW	37570 AAW	ALBLS	10//99-12//99
	Huntsville MSA, AL	S	20.61 MW	19.39 AW	42860 AAW	ALBLS	10//99-12//99
	Mobile MSA, AL	S	20.92 MW	19.25 AW	43510 AAW	ALBLS	10//99-12//99
	Alaska	S	34.67 MW	30.70 AW	63850 AAW	AKBLS	10//99-12//99
	Anchorage MSA, AK	S	30.77 MW	34.82 AW	64010 AAW	AKBLS	10//99-12//99
	Arizona	S	18.94 MW	19.37 AW	40290 AAW	AZBLS	10//99-12//99
	Phoenix-Mesa MSA, AZ	S	20.44 MW	19.91 AW	42520 AAW	AZBLS	10//99-12//99
	Tucson MSA, AZ	S	15.38 MW	15.23 AW	31990 AAW	AZBLS	10//99-12//99
	Arkansas	S	12.79 MW	14.56 AW	30280 AAW	ARBLS	10//99-12//99
	Fayetteville-Springdale-Rogers MSA, AR	S	11.49 MW	11.22 AW	23900 AAW	ARBLS	10//99-12//99
	Little Rock-North Little Rock MSA, AR	S	16.86 MW	15.52 AW	35070 AAW	ARBLS	10//99-12//99
	California	S	20.55 MW	21.95 AW	45650 AAW	CABLS	10//99-12//99
	Bakersfield MSA, CA	S	21.29 MW	23.01 AW	44270 AAW	CABLS	10//99-12//99
	Fresno MSA, CA	S	22.45 MW	22.45 AW	46690 AAW	CABLS	10//99-12//99
	Los Angeles-Long Beach PMSA, CA	S	20.34 MW	19.56 AW	42310 AAW	CABLS	10//99-12//99
	Modesto MSA, CA	S	18.72 MW	18.44 AW	38940 AAW	CABLS	10//99-12//99
	Oakland PMSA, CA	S	24.21 MW	23.63 AW	50350 AAW	CABLS	10//99-12//99
	Orange County PMSA, CA	S	21.89 MW	20.90 AW	45530 AAW	CABLS	10//99-12//99

AAW	Average annual wage	AOH	Average offered, high	ASH	Average starting, high	H	Hourly
AE	Average entry wage	AOL	Average offered, low	ASL	Average starting, low	HI	Highest wage paid
AEX	Average experienced wage	APH	Average pay, high range	AW	Average wage paid	HR	High end range
AO	Average offered	APL	Average pay, low range	FQ	First quartile wage	LR	Low end range

M	Monthly	S	Special: hourly and annual
MTC	Median total compensation	TQ	Third quartile wage
MW	Median wage paid	W	Weekly
SQ	Second quartile wage	Y	Yearly

Occupation/Type/Industry	Location	Per	Low	Mid	High	Source	Date
Compensation, Benefits, and Job Analysis Specialist							
	Riverside-San Bernardino PMSA, CA	S	21.49 MW	20.40 AW	44690 AAW	CABLS	10//99-12//99
	Sacramento PMSA, CA	S	21.88 MW	21.34 AW	45520 AAW	CABLS	10//99-12//99
	Salinas MSA, CA	S	17.08 MW	17.21 AW	35530 AAW	CABLS	10//99-12//99
	San Diego MSA, CA	S	21.70 MW	20.68 AW	45140 AAW	CABLS	10//99-12//99
	San Francisco PMSA, CA	S	24.03 MW	23.62 AW	49980 AAW	CABLS	10//99-12//99
	San Jose PMSA, CA	S	24.64 MW	21.99 AW	51250 AAW	CABLS	10//99-12//99
	San Luis Obispo-Atascadero-Paso Robles MSA, CA	S	23.67 MW	20.56 AW	49240 AAW	CABLS	10//99-12//99
	Santa Barbara-Santa Maria-Lompoc MSA, CA	S	23.33 MW	22.02 AW	48520 AAW	CABLS	10//99-12//99
	Santa Rosa PMSA, CA	S	23.04 MW	22.78 AW	47910 AAW	CABLS	10//99-12//99
	Stockton-Lodi MSA, CA	S	21.96 MW	21.84 AW	45670 AAW	CABLS	10//99-12//99
	Vallejo-Fairfield-Napa PMSA, CA	S	20.93 MW	20.41 AW	43540 AAW	CABLS	10//99-12//99
	Ventura PMSA, CA	S	23.30 MW	23.02 AW	48470 AAW	CABLS	10//99-12//99
	Visalia-Tulare-Porterville MSA, CA	S	18.70 MW	18.93 AW	38900 AAW	CABLS	10//99-12//99
	Colorado	S	19.41 MW	22.80 AW	47420 AAW	COBLS	10//99-12//99
	Connecticut	S	22.78 MW	23.47 AW	48820 AAW	CTBLS	10//99-12//99
	Bridgeport PMSA, CT	S	28.16 MW	24.68 AW	58580 AAW	CTBLS	10//99-12//99
	Hartford MSA, CT	S	23.62 MW	21.01 AW	49130 AAW	CTBLS	10//99-12//99
	New Haven-Meriden PMSA, CT	S	23.34 MW	23.89 AW	48540 AAW	CTBLS	10//99-12//99
	New London-Norwich MSA, CT-RI	S	18.15 MW	16.21 AW	37750 AAW	CTBLS	10//99-12//99
	Stamford-Norwalk PMSA, CT	S	22.41 MW	20.71 AW	46610 AAW	CTBLS	10//99-12//99
	Delaware	S	21.79 MW	23.19 AW	48230 AAW	DEBLS	10//99-12//99
	Wilmington-Newark PMSA, DE-MD	S	24.22 MW	23.39 AW	50370 AAW	DEBLS	10//99-12//99
	Washington PMSA, DC-MD-VA-WV	S	23.77 MW	23.27 AW	49450 AAW	DCBLS	10//99-12//99
	Florida	S	16.26 MW	17.31 AW	36000 AAW	FLBLS	10//99-12//99
	Daytona Beach MSA, FL	S	15.29 MW	13.98 AW	31800 AAW	FLBLS	10//99-12//99
	Fort Lauderdale PMSA, FL	S	18.93 MW	17.67 AW	39380 AAW	FLBLS	10//99-12//99
	Fort Myers-Cape Coral MSA, FL	S	15.89 MW	15.53 AW	33040 AAW	FLBLS	10//99-12//99
	Fort Pierce-Port St. Lucie MSA, FL	S	16.55 MW	15.77 AW	34430 AAW	FLBLS	10//99-12//99
	Gainesville MSA, FL	S	15.72 MW	14.68 AW	32690 AAW	FLBLS	10//99-12//99
	Jacksonville MSA, FL	S	16.61 MW	16.91 AW	34550 AAW	FLBLS	10//99-12//99
	Lakeland-Winter Haven MSA, FL	S	15.40 MW	17.15 AW	32020 AAW	FLBLS	10//99-12//99
	Melbourne-Titusville-Palm Bay MSA, FL	S	17.67 MW	15.51 AW	36760 AAW	FLBLS	10//99-12//99
	Miami PMSA, FL	S	16.57 MW	15.96 AW	34470 AAW	FLBLS	10//99-12//99
	Ocala MSA, FL	S	25.33 MW	24.42 AW	52680 AAW	FLBLS	10//99-12//99
	Orlando MSA, FL	S	19.29 MW	18.25 AW	40120 AAW	FLBLS	10//99-12//99
	Pensacola MSA, FL	S	16.45 MW	17.17 AW	34210 AAW	FLBLS	10//99-12//99
	Sarasota-Bradenton MSA, FL	S	15.25 MW	14.72 AW	31710 AAW	FLBLS	10//99-12//99
	Tampa-St. Petersburg-Clearwater MSA, FL	S	19.94 MW	18.01 AW	41470 AAW	FLBLS	10//99-12//99
	West Palm Beach-Boca Raton MSA, FL	S	19.07 MW	17.31 AW	39670 AAW	FLBLS	10//99-12//99
	Georgia	S	16.68 MW	18.93 AW	39370 AAW	GABLS	10//99-12//99
	Atlanta MSA, GA	S	20.09 MW	17.92 AW	41780 AAW	GABLS	10//99-12//99
	Augusta-Aiken MSA, GA-SC	S	29.97 MW	33.92 AW	62340 AAW	GABLS	10//99-12//99
	Columbus MSA, GA-AL	S	18.38 MW	16.59 AW	38230 AAW	GABLS	10//99-12//99
	Macon MSA, GA	S	18.29 MW	17.32 AW	38040 AAW	GABLS	10//99-12//99
	Savannah MSA, GA	S	18.11 MW	16.90 AW	37660 AAW	GABLS	10//99-12//99
	Hawaii	S	19.27 MW	19.16 AW	39860 AAW	HIBLS	10//99-12//99
	Honolulu MSA, HI	S	19.43 MW	19.58 AW	40410 AAW	HIBLS	10//99-12//99
	Idaho	S	19.7 MW	22.17 AW	46110 AAW	IDBLS	10//99-12//99
	Boise City MSA, ID	S	17.56 MW	18.01 AW	36530 AAW	IDBLS	10//99-12//99
	Illinois	S	20.74 MW	23.54 AW	48970 AAW	ILBLS	10//99-12//99
	Champaign-Urbana MSA, IL	S	18.47 MW	13.48 AW	38410 AAW	ILBLS	10//99-12//99
	Chicago PMSA, IL	S	23.97 MW	21.10 AW	49860 AAW	ILBLS	10//99-12//99
	Peoria-Pekin MSA, IL	S	19.17 MW	19.23 AW	39860 AAW	ILBLS	10//99-12//99
	Rockford MSA, IL	S	21.51 MW	17.76 AW	44740 AAW	ILBLS	10//99-12//99
	Springfield MSA, IL	S	18.58 MW	16.91 AW	38650 AAW	ILBLS	10//99-12//99
	Indiana	S	17.6 MW	17.45 AW	36300 AAW	INBLS	10//99-12//99

AAW Average annual wage	**AOH** Average offered, high	**ASH** Average starting, high	**H** Hourly	**M** Monthly	**S** Special: hourly and annual	
AE Average entry wage	**AOL** Average offered, low	**ASL** Average starting, low	**HI** Highest wage paid	**MTC** Median total compensation	**TQ** Third quartile wage	
AEX Average experienced wage	**APH** Average pay, high range	**AW** Average wage paid	**HR** High end range	**MW** Median wage paid	**W** Weekly	
AO Average offered	**APL** Average pay, low range	**FQ** First quartile wage	**LR** Low end range	**SQ** Second quartile wage	**Y** Yearly	

Occupation/Type/Industry	Location	Per	Low	Mid	High	Source	Date
Compensation, Benefits, and Job Analysis Specialist	Elkhart-Goshen MSA, IN	S	12.39 MW	10.44 AW	25770 AAW	INBLS	10//99-12//99
	Evansville-Henderson MSA, IN-KY	S	8.22 MW	6.24 AW	17100 AAW	INBLS	10//99-12//99
	Fort Wayne MSA, IN	S	14.91 MW	13.90 AW	31020 AAW	INBLS	10//99-12//99
	Gary PMSA, IN	S	20.38 MW	20.43 AW	42380 AAW	INBLS	10//99-12//99
	Indianapolis MSA, IN	S	16.36 MW	15.30 AW	34030 AAW	INBLS	10//99-12//99
	Kokomo MSA, IN	S	21.04 MW	20.71 AW	43760 AAW	INBLS	10//99-12//99
	Lafayette MSA, IN	S	18.33 MW	18.28 AW	38130 AAW	INBLS	10//99-12//99
	South Bend MSA, IN	S	22.94 MW	19.29 AW	47710 AAW	INBLS	10//99-12//99
	Terre Haute MSA, IN	S	26.83 MW	26.25 AW	55800 AAW	INBLS	10//99-12//99
	Iowa	S	14.91 MW	16.24 AW	33790 AAW	IABLS	10//99-12//99
	Cedar Rapids MSA, IA	S	13.06 MW	11.83 AW	27170 AAW	IABLS	10//99-12//99
	Davenport-Moline-Rock Island MSA, IA-IL	S	18.45 MW	18.47 AW	38370 AAW	IABLS	10//99-12//99
	Des Moines MSA, IA	S	18.57 MW	16.92 AW	38630 AAW	IABLS	10//99-12//99
	Sioux City MSA, IA-NE	S	17.45 MW	15.49 AW	36290 AAW	IABLS	10//99-12//99
	Waterloo-Cedar Falls MSA, IA	S	17.69 MW	15.24 AW	36790 AAW	IABLS	10//99-12//99
	Kansas	S	16.64 MW	17.92 AW	37280 AAW	KSBLS	10//99-12//99
	Topeka MSA, KS	S	17.23 MW	15.86 AW	35840 AAW	KSBLS	10//99-12//99
	Wichita MSA, KS	S	18.52 MW	16.65 AW	38520 AAW	KSBLS	10//99-12//99
	Kentucky	S	16.14 MW	18.52 AW	38520 AAW	KYBLS	10//99-12//99
	Lexington MSA, KY	S	17.60 MW	15.76 AW	36600 AAW	KYBLS	10//99-12//99
	Louisville MSA, KY-IN	S	18.74 MW	17.13 AW	38990 AAW	KYBLS	10//99-12//99
	Louisiana	S	13.59 MW	14.65 AW	30470 AAW	LABLS	10//99-12//99
	Lafayette MSA, LA	S	13.97 MW	12.32 AW	29050 AAW	LABLS	10//99-12//99
	Lake Charles MSA, LA	S	13.92 MW	12.68 AW	28960 AAW	LABLS	10//99-12//99
	New Orleans MSA, LA	S	15.42 MW	13.45 AW	32070 AAW	LABLS	10//99-12//99
	Shreveport-Bossier City MSA, LA	S	15.16 MW	12.73 AW	31530 AAW	LABLS	10//99-12//99
	Maine	S	17.94 MW	18.75 AW	38990 AAW	MEBLS	10//99-12//99
	Bangor MSA, ME	S	18.34 MW	16.64 AW	38160 AAW	MEBLS	10//99-12//99
	Portland MSA, ME	S	21.01 MW	19.81 AW	43710 AAW	MEBLS	10//99-12//99
	Maryland	S	19.72 MW	20.56 AW	42760 AAW	MDBLS	10//99-12//99
	Baltimore PMSA, MD	S	19.66 MW	19.45 AW	40890 AAW	MDBLS	10//99-12//99
	Massachusetts	S	20.64 MW	21.91 AW	45570 AAW	MABLS	10//99-12//99
	Boston PMSA, MA-NH	S	22.66 MW	21.22 AW	47130 AAW	MABLS	10//99-12//99
	Brockton PMSA, MA	S	17.42 MW	16.54 AW	36240 AAW	MABLS	10//99-12//99
	Lowell PMSA, MA-NH	S	23.15 MW	22.72 AW	48140 AAW	MABLS	10//99-12//99
	New Bedford PMSA, MA	S	14.82 MW	14.49 AW	30820 AAW	MABLS	10//99-12//99
	Pittsfield MSA, MA	S	17.54 MW	16.27 AW	36470 AAW	MABLS	10//99-12//99
	Springfield MSA, MA	S	20.09 MW	18.97 AW	41800 AAW	MABLS	10//99-12//99
	Worcester PMSA, MA-CT	S	20.78 MW	19.58 AW	43220 AAW	MABLS	10//99-12//99
	Michigan	S	20.38 MW	20.99 AW	43670 AAW	MIBLS	10//99-12//99
	Ann Arbor PMSA, MI	S	19.52 MW	19.71 AW	40590 AAW	MIBLS	10//99-12//99
	Detroit PMSA, MI	S	21.30 MW	21.20 AW	44310 AAW	MIBLS	10//99-12//99
	Flint PMSA, MI	S	26.43 MW	28.67 AW	54960 AAW	MIBLS	10//99-12//99
	Grand Rapids-Muskegon-Holland MSA, MI	S	20.50 MW	19.33 AW	42640 AAW	MIBLS	10//99-12//99
	Saginaw-Bay City-Midland MSA, MI	S	21.84 MW	22.95 AW	45420 AAW	MIBLS	10//99-12//99
	Minnesota	S	16.86 MW	19.12 AW	39770 AAW	MNBLS	10//99-12//99
	Duluth-Superior MSA, MN-WI	S	18.04 MW	18.32 AW	37530 AAW	MNBLS	10//99-12//99
	Minneapolis-St. Paul MSA, MN-WI	S	19.28 MW	16.90 AW	40090 AAW	MNBLS	10//99-12//99
	Mississippi	S	13.99 MW	15.46 AW	32160 AAW	MSBLS	10//99-12//99
	Biloxi-Gulfport-Pascagoula MSA, MS	S	12.70 MW	11.75 AW	26430 AAW	MSBLS	10//99-12//99
	Jackson MSA, MS	S	16.99 MW	15.98 AW	35340 AAW	MSBLS	10//99-12//99
	Missouri	S	17.38 MW	18.44 AW	38350 AAW	MOBLS	10//99-12//99
	Columbia MSA, MO	S	21.11 MW	19.54 AW	43910 AAW	MOBLS	10//99-12//99
	Kansas City MSA, MO-KS	S	22.72 MW	21.44 AW	47260 AAW	MOBLS	10//99-12//99
	St. Joseph MSA, MO	S	16.40 MW	15.45 AW	34100 AAW	MOBLS	10//99-12//99
	St. Louis MSA, MO-IL	S	16.14 MW	14.00 AW	33570 AAW	MOBLS	10//99-12//99
	Springfield MSA, MO	S	17.49 MW	18.59 AW	36370 AAW	MOBLS	10//99-12//99
	Montana	S	15.23 MW	17.19 AW	35750 AAW	MTBLS	10//99-12//99
	Billings MSA, MT	S	13.78 MW	14.27 AW	28670 AAW	MTBLS	10//99-12//99
	Nebraska	S	16.43 MW	18.53 AW	38540 AAW	NEBLS	10//99-12//99
	Lincoln MSA, NE	S	17.84 MW	14.55 AW	37110 AAW	NEBLS	10//99-12//99
	Omaha MSA, NE-IA	S	15.88 MW	14.83 AW	33040 AAW	NEBLS	10//99-12//99
	Nevada	S	19.64 MW	20.02 AW	41650 AAW	NVBLS	10//99-12//99
	Las Vegas MSA, NV-AZ	S	19.40 MW	19.15 AW	40350 AAW	NVBLS	10//99-12//99

AAW	Average annual wage	AOH	Average offered, high	ASH	Average starting, high	H	Hourly	M	Monthly	S	Special: hourly and annual
AE	Average entry wage	AOL	Average offered, low	ASL	Average starting, low	HI	Highest wage paid	MTC	Median total compensation	TQ	Third quartile wage
AEX	Average experienced wage	APH	Average pay, high range	AW	Average wage paid	HR	High end range	MW	Median wage paid	W	Weekly
AO	Average offered	APL	Average pay, low range	FQ	First quartile wage	LR	Low end range	SQ	Second quartile wage	Y	Yearly

Occupation/Type/Industry	Location	Per	Low	Mid	High	Source	Date
Compensation, Benefits, and Job Analysis Specialist	Reno MSA, NV	S	25.85 MW	23.97 AW	53770 AAW	NVBLS	10//99-12//99
	New Hampshire	S	18.84 MW	19.15 AW	39830 AAW	NHBLS	10//99-12//99
	Manchester PMSA, NH	S	19.20 MW	19.37 AW	39940 AAW	NHBLS	10//99-12//99
	Portsmouth-Rochester PMSA, NH-ME	S	19.10 MW	19.06 AW	39730 AAW	NHBLS	10//99-12//99
	New Jersey	S	17.57 MW	18.90 AW	39320 AAW	NJBLS	10//99-12//99
	Bergen-Passaic PMSA, NJ	S	20.54 MW	18.86 AW	42720 AAW	NJBLS	10//99-12//99
	Jersey City PMSA, NJ	S	20.30 MW	19.30 AW	42220 AAW	NJBLS	10//99-12//99
	Middlesex-Somerset-Hunterdon PMSA, NJ	S	23.33 MW	20.72 AW	48520 AAW	NJBLS	10//99-12//99
	Newark PMSA, NJ	S	18.67 MW	18.71 AW	38840 AAW	NJBLS	10//99-12//99
	Trenton PMSA, NJ	S	13.48 MW	10.55 AW	28030 AAW	NJBLS	10//99-12//99
	Vineland-Millville-Bridgeton PMSA, NJ	S	23.30 MW	22.88 AW	48460 AAW	NJBLS	10//99-12//99
	New Mexico	S	13.23 MW	15.21 AW	31630 AAW	NMBLS	10//99-12//99
	Albuquerque MSA, NM	S	15.59 MW	13.41 AW	32440 AAW	NMBLS	10//99-12//99
	New York	S	23.02 MW	23.36 AW	48590 AAW	NYBLS	10//99-12//99
	Albany-Schenectady-Troy MSA, NY	S	19.39 MW	18.48 AW	40340 AAW	NYBLS	10//99-12//99
	Buffalo-Niagara Falls MSA, NY	S	19.40 MW	18.82 AW	40360 AAW	NYBLS	10//99-12//99
	Nassau-Suffolk PMSA, NY	S	23.32 MW	21.69 AW	48510 AAW	NYBLS	10//99-12//99
	Newburgh PMSA, NY-PA	S	17.98 MW	17.86 AW	37390 AAW	NYBLS	10//99-12//99
	Rochester MSA, NY	S	25.14 MW	24.29 AW	52280 AAW	NYBLS	10//99-12//99
	Syracuse MSA, NY	S	20.07 MW	19.52 AW	41750 AAW	NYBLS	10//99-12//99
	Utica-Rome MSA, NY	S	17.07 MW	17.66 AW	35500 AAW	NYBLS	10//99-12//99
	North Carolina	S	19.39 MW	20.50 AW	42630 AAW	NCBLS	10//99-12//99
	Asheville MSA, NC	S	27.96 MW	30.11 AW	58160 AAW	NCBLS	10//99-12//99
	Charlotte-Gastonia-Rock Hill MSA, NC-SC	S	19.79 MW	18.48 AW	41160 AAW	NCBLS	10//99-12//99
	Greensboro--Winston-Salem--High Point MSA, NC	S	21.57 MW	19.34 AW	44870 AAW	NCBLS	10//99-12//99
	Greenville MSA, NC	S	17.37 MW	15.91 AW	36130 AAW	NCBLS	10//99-12//99
	Hickory-Morganton-Lenoir MSA, NC	S	19.42 MW	17.44 AW	40390 AAW	NCBLS	10//99-12//99
	Raleigh-Durham-Chapel Hill MSA, NC	S	21.57 MW	20.99 AW	44870 AAW	NCBLS	10//99-12//99
	North Dakota	S	14.59 MW	16.65 AW	34630 AAW	NDBLS	10//99-12//99
	Fargo-Moorhead MSA, ND-MN	S	16.23 MW	13.68 AW	33760 AAW	NDBLS	10//99-12//99
	Ohio	S	18.04 MW	19.75 AW	41080 AAW	OHBLS	10//99-12//99
	Akron PMSA, OH	S	19.14 MW	16.90 AW	39800 AAW	OHBLS	10//99-12//99
	Canton-Massillon MSA, OH	S	14.76 MW	14.86 AW	30700 AAW	OHBLS	10//99-12//99
	Cincinnati PMSA, OH-KY-IN	S	20.48 MW	16.54 AW	42600 AAW	OHBLS	10//99-12//99
	Cleveland-Lorain-Elyria PMSA, OH	S	21.71 MW	20.07 AW	45160 AAW	OHBLS	10//99-12//99
	Columbus MSA, OH	S	18.50 MW	17.27 AW	38480 AAW	OHBLS	10//99-12//99
	Dayton-Springfield MSA, OH	S	18.30 MW	18.26 AW	38060 AAW	OHBLS	10//99-12//99
	Hamilton-Middletown PMSA, OH	S	17.93 MW	16.80 AW	37300 AAW	OHBLS	10//99-12//99
	Mansfield MSA, OH	S	19.26 MW	18.75 AW	40070 AAW	OHBLS	10//99-12//99
	Toledo MSA, OH	S	18.76 MW	18.43 AW	39020 AAW	OHBLS	10//99-12//99
	Youngstown-Warren MSA, OH	S	15.54 MW	15.14 AW	32320 AAW	OHBLS	10//99-12//99
	Oklahoma	S	15.14 MW	16.61 AW	34540 AAW	OKBLS	10//99-12//99
	Oklahoma City MSA, OK	S	16.67 MW	15.67 AW	34670 AAW	OKBLS	10//99-12//99
	Tulsa MSA, OK	S	18.66 MW	16.10 AW	38820 AAW	OKBLS	10//99-12//99
	Oregon	S	17.95 MW	19.02 AW	39560 AAW	ORBLS	10//99-12//99
	Eugene-Springfield MSA, OR	S	22.23 MW	22.39 AW	46240 AAW	ORBLS	10//99-12//99
	Portland-Vancouver PMSA, OR-WA	S	18.76 MW	17.66 AW	39020 AAW	ORBLS	10//99-12//99
	Pennsylvania	S	18.35 MW	19.72 AW	41010 AAW	PABLS	10//99-12//99
	Allentown-Bethlehem-Easton MSA, PA	S	19.42 MW	16.79 AW	40400 AAW	PABLS	10//99-12//99
	Harrisburg-Lebanon-Carlisle MSA, PA	S	18.93 MW	17.27 AW	39380 AAW	PABLS	10//99-12//99
	Lancaster MSA, PA	S	22.47 MW	22.12 AW	46740 AAW	PABLS	10//99-12//99
	Philadelphia PMSA, PA-NJ	S	20.20 MW	18.97 AW	42010 AAW	PABLS	10//99-12//99
	Pittsburgh MSA, PA	S	20.94 MW	19.46 AW	43550 AAW	PABLS	10//99-12//99
	Reading MSA, PA	S	15.31 MW	14.75 AW	31850 AAW	PABLS	10//99-12//99
	Scranton--Wilkes-Barre--Hazleton MSA, PA	S	17.32 MW	17.03 AW	36020 AAW	PABLS	10//99-12//99

AAW	Average annual wage	AOH	Average offered, high	ASH	Average starting, high	H	Hourly
AE	Average entry wage	AOL	Average offered, low	ASL	Average starting, low	HI	Highest wage paid
AEX	Average experienced wage	APH	Average pay, high range	AW	Average wage paid	HR	High end range
AO	Average offered	APL	Average pay, low range	FQ	First quartile wage	LR	Low end range

M	Monthly	S	Special: hourly and annual
MTC	Median total compensation	TQ	Third quartile wage
MW	Median wage paid	W	Weekly
SQ	Second quartile wage	Y	Yearly

Occupation/Type/Industry	Location	Per	Low	Mid	High	Source	Date
Compensation, Benefits, and Job Analysis Specialist	York MSA, PA	S	14.34 MW	14.06 AW	29820 AAW	PABLS	10//99-12//99
	Rhode Island	S	19.49 MW	20.51 AW	42650 AAW	RIBLS	10//99-12//99
	Providence-Fall River-Warwick MSA, RI-MA	S	20.32 MW	19.32 AW	42270 AAW	RIBLS	10//99-12//99
	South Carolina	S	18.23 MW	21.17 AW	44020 AAW	SCBLS	10//99-12//99
	Charleston-North Charleston MSA, SC	S	18.22 MW	21.60 AW	37900 AAW	SCBLS	10//99-12//99
	Columbia MSA, SC	S	15.86 MW	16.20 AW	32990 AAW	SCBLS	10//99-12//99
	Greenville-Spartanburg-Anderson MSA, SC	S	17.92 MW	17.07 AW	37280 AAW	SCBLS	10//99-12//99
	South Dakota	S	18.67 MW	20.31 AW	42250 AAW	SDBLS	10//99-12//99
	Sioux Falls MSA, SD	S	17.10 MW	16.55 AW	35560 AAW	SDBLS	10//99-12//99
	Tennessee	S	15.2 MW	15.99 AW	33250 AAW	TNBLS	10//99-12//99
	Chattanooga MSA, TN-GA	S	15.85 MW	15.23 AW	32970 AAW	TNBLS	10//99-12//99
	Johnson City-Kingsport-Bristol MSA, TN-VA	S	18.30 MW	17.22 AW	38050 AAW	TNBLS	10//99-12//99
	Knoxville MSA, TN	S	15.96 MW	15.23 AW	33200 AAW	TNBLS	10//99-12//99
	Memphis MSA, TN-AR-MS	S	19.33 MW	17.68 AW	40220 AAW	MSBLS	10//99-12//99
	Nashville MSA, TN	S	16.24 MW	15.74 AW	33780 AAW	TNBLS	10//99-12//99
	Texas	S	19.23 MW	20.45 AW	42530 AAW	TXBLS	10//99-12//99
	Austin-San Marcos MSA, TX	S	18.54 MW	18.14 AW	38560 AAW	TXBLS	10//99-12//99
	Beaumont-Port Arthur MSA, TX	S	20.30 MW	17.46 AW	42220 AAW	TXBLS	10//99-12//99
	Brazoria PMSA, TX	S	21.44 MW	20.42 AW	44600 AAW	TXBLS	10//99-12//99
	Brownsville-Harlingen-San Benito MSA, TX	S	14.60 MW	12.43 AW	30370 AAW	TXBLS	10//99-12//99
	Corpus Christi MSA, TX	S	17.19 MW	16.67 AW	35760 AAW	TXBLS	10//99-12//99
	Dallas PMSA, TX	S	20.01 MW	18.80 AW	41620 AAW	TXBLS	10//99-12//99
	El Paso MSA, TX	S	19.28 MW	18.74 AW	40100 AAW	TXBLS	10//99-12//99
	Fort Worth-Arlington PMSA, TX	S	22.41 MW	21.94 AW	46620 AAW	TXBLS	10//99-12//99
	Houston PMSA, TX	S	22.91 MW	21.48 AW	47650 AAW	TXBLS	10//99-12//99
	Killeen-Temple MSA, TX	S	12.69 MW	11.93 AW	26390 AAW	TXBLS	10//99-12//99
	Lubbock MSA, TX	S	15.94 MW	15.08 AW	33150 AAW	TXBLS	10//99-12//99
	San Antonio MSA, TX	S	19.62 MW	18.64 AW	40800 AAW	TXBLS	10//99-12//99
	Tyler MSA, TX	S	16.82 MW	18.04 AW	34980 AAW	TXBLS	10//99-12//99
	Waco MSA, TX	S	18.29 MW	16.11 AW	38040 AAW	TXBLS	10//99-12//99
	Utah	S	17.2 MW	18.10 AW	37650 AAW	UTBLS	10//99-12//99
	Provo-Orem MSA, UT	S	16.55 MW	16.55 AW	34420 AAW	UTBLS	10//99-12//99
	Salt Lake City-Ogden MSA, UT	S	18.35 MW	17.39 AW	38170 AAW	UTBLS	10//99-12//99
	Vermont	S	18.16 MW	20.77 AW	43190 AAW	VTBLS	10//99-12//99
	Burlington MSA, VT	S	21.02 MW	19.80 AW	43720 AAW	VTBLS	10//99-12//99
	Virginia	S	20.67 MW	21.68 AW	45090 AAW	VABLS	10//99-12//99
	Lynchburg MSA, VA	S	16.48 MW	14.99 AW	34280 AAW	VABLS	10//99-12//99
	Norfolk-Virginia Beach-Newport News MSA, VA-NC	S	17.43 MW	16.20 AW	36250 AAW	VABLS	
	Richmond-Petersburg MSA, VA	S	19.84 MW	19.14 AW	41270 AAW	VABLS	10//99-12//99
	Washington	S	20.86 MW	21.13 AW	43960 AAW	WABLS	10//99-12//99
	Bellingham MSA, WA	S	20.50 MW	19.37 AW	42630 AAW	WABLS	10//99-12//99
	Seattle-Bellevue-Everett PMSA, WA	S	23.09 MW	23.08 AW	48030 AAW	WABLS	10//99-12//99
	Spokane MSA, WA	S	19.21 MW	18.10 AW	39950 AAW	WABLS	10//99-12//99
	Tacoma PMSA, WA	S	17.39 MW	16.37 AW	36160 AAW	WABLS	10//99-12//99
	Yakima MSA, WA	S	17.06 MW	15.75 AW	35480 AAW	WABLS	10//99-12//99
	West Virginia	S	14.47 MW	16.03 AW	33340 AAW	WVBLS	10//99-12//99
	Huntington-Ashland MSA, WV-KY-OH	S	19.42 MW	15.51 AW	40390 AAW	WVBLS	10//99-12//99
	Wisconsin	S	15.45 MW	16.53 AW	34380 AAW	WIBLS	10//99-12//99
	Appleton-Oshkosh-Neenah MSA, WI	S	15.75 MW	15.17 AW	32770 AAW	WIBLS	10//99-12//99
	Eau Claire MSA, WI	S	12.35 MW	11.98 AW	25700 AAW	WIBLS	10//99-12//99
	Green Bay MSA, WI	S	16.47 MW	16.82 AW	34270 AAW	WIBLS	10//99-12//99
	Milwaukee-Waukesha PMSA, WI	S	18.31 MW	16.55 AW	38090 AAW	WIBLS	10//99-12//99
	Wausau MSA, WI	S	15.87 MW	15.65 AW	33010 AAW	WIBLS	10//99-12//99
	Puerto Rico	S	12.92 MW	14.51 AW	30180 AAW	PRBLS	10//99-12//99
	San Juan-Bayamon PMSA, PR	S	15.82 MW	14.33 AW	32910 AAW	PRBLS	10//99-12//99

Occupation/Type/Industry	Location	Per	Low	Mid	High	Source	Date
Compensation Specialist							
Human Resources	United States	Y		54600 AW		HRMAG	1999
Compliance Officer							
Except Agriculture, Construction, Health and Safety, and Transportation	Alabama	S	16.21 MW	17.77 AW	36960 AAW	ALBLS	10//99-12//99
Except Agriculture, Construction, Health and Safety, and Transportation	Alaska	S	20.42 MW	21.65 AW	45040 AAW	AKBLS	10//99-12//99
Except Agriculture, Construction, Health and Safety, and Transportation	Arizona	S	18.44 MW	20.54 AW	42730 AAW	AZBLS	10//99-12//99
Except Agriculture, Construction, Health and Safety, and Transportation	Arkansas	S	14.55 MW	14.69 AW	30550 AAW	ARBLS	10//99-12//99
Except Agriculture, Construction, Health and Safety, and Transportation	California	S	17.73 MW	20.06 AW	41720 AAW	CABLS	10//99-12//99
Except Agriculture, Construction, Health and Safety, and Transportation	Colorado	S	19.72 MW	20.73 AW	43120 AAW	COBLS	10//99-12//99
Except Agriculture, Construction, Health and Safety, and Transportation	Connecticut	S	25.03 MW	25.64 AW	53330 AAW	CTBLS	10//99-12//99
Except Agriculture, Construction, Health and Safety, and Transportation	Delaware	S	18.37 MW	21.39 AW	44490 AAW	DEBLS	10//99-12//99
Except Agriculture, Construction, Health and Safety, and Transportation	Florida	S	16.24 MW	17.96 AW	37350 AAW	FLBLS	10//99-12//99
Except Agriculture, Construction, Health and Safety, and Transportation	Georgia	S	17.84 MW	19.55 AW	40660 AAW	GABLS	10//99-12//99
Except Agriculture, Construction, Health and Safety, and Transportation	Hawaii	S	18.67 MW	19.19 AW	39920 AAW	HIBLS	10//99-12//99
Except Agriculture, Construction, Health and Safety, and Transportation	Idaho	S	16.74 MW	18.45 AW	38370 AAW	IDBLS	10//99-12//99
Except Agriculture, Construction, Health and Safety, and Transportation	Illinois	S	19.13 MW	19.92 AW	41430 AAW	ILBLS	10//99-12//99
Except Agriculture, Construction, Health and Safety, and Transportation	Indiana	S	17.58 MW	19.89 AW	41360 AAW	INBLS	10//99-12//99
Except Agriculture, Construction, Health and Safety, and Transportation	Iowa	S	14.76 MW	14.79 AW	30760 AAW	IABLS	10//99-12//99
Except Agriculture, Construction, Health and Safety, and Transportation	Kansas	S	16.63 MW	19.57 AW	40690 AAW	KSBLS	10//99-12//99
Except Agriculture, Construction, Health and Safety, and Transportation	Kentucky	S	18.81 MW	19.49 AW	40550 AAW	KYBLS	10//99-12//99
Except Agriculture, Construction, Health and Safety, and Transportation	Louisiana	S	17.38 MW	19.16 AW	39850 AAW	LABLS	10//99-12//99
Except Agriculture, Construction, Health and Safety, and Transportation	Maine	S	16.36 MW	17.32 AW	36020 AAW	MEBLS	10//99-12//99
Except Agriculture, Construction, Health and Safety, and Transportation	Maryland	S	18.43 MW	19.72 AW	41030 AAW	MDBLS	10//99-12//99
Except Agriculture, Construction, Health and Safety, and Transportation	Massachusetts	S	21.23 MW	23.89 AW	49680 AAW	MABLS	10//99-12//99
Except Agriculture, Construction, Health and Safety, and Transportation	Michigan	S	20.64 MW	21.51 AW	44750 AAW	MIBLS	10//99-12//99
Except Agriculture, Construction, Health and Safety, and Transportation	Minnesota	S	22.06 MW	22.73 AW	47280 AAW	MNBLS	10//99-12//99
Except Agriculture, Construction, Health and Safety, and Transportation	Mississippi	S	14.06 MW	14.22 AW	29590 AAW	MSBLS	10//99-12//99
Except Agriculture, Construction, Health and Safety, and Transportation	Missouri	S	18.56 MW	21.35 AW	44420 AAW	MOBLS	10//99-12//99
Except Agriculture, Construction, Health and Safety, and Transportation	Montana	S	14.84 MW	15.12 AW	31460 AAW	MTBLS	10//99-12//99
Except Agriculture, Construction, Health and Safety, and Transportation	Nebraska	S	15.75 MW	17.21 AW	35790 AAW	NEBLS	10//99-12//99
Except Agriculture, Construction, Health and Safety, and Transportation	Nevada	S	21.2 MW	22.09 AW	45950 AAW	NVBLS	10//99-12//99
Except Agriculture, Construction, Health and Safety, and Transportation	New Hampshire	S	16.15 MW	19.24 AW	40010 AAW	NHBLS	10//99-12//99
Except Agriculture, Construction, Health and Safety, and Transportation	New Jersey	S	21.69 MW	23.72 AW	49340 AAW	NJBLS	10//99-12//99
Except Agriculture, Construction, Health and Safety, and Transportation	New Mexico	S	17.4 MW	18.55 AW	38590 AAW	NMBLS	10//99-12//99
Except Agriculture, Construction, Health and Safety, and Transportation	New York	S	20.73 MW	22.91 AW	47650 AAW	NYBLS	10//99-12//99
Except Agriculture, Construction, Health and Safety, and Transportation	North Carolina	S	16.08 MW	17.91 AW	37240 AAW	NCBLS	10//99-12//99
Except Agriculture, Construction, Health and Safety, and Transportation	North Dakota	S	17.79 MW	17.94 AW	37310 AAW	NDBLS	10//99-12//99

AAW Average annual wage	**AOH** Average offered, high	**ASH** Average starting, high	**H** Hourly	**M** Monthly	**S** Special: hourly and annual
AE Average entry wage	**AOL** Average offered, low	**ASL** Average starting, low	**HI** Highest wage paid	**MTC** Median total compensation	**TQ** Third quartile wage
AEX Average experienced wage	**APH** Average pay, high range	**AW** Average wage paid	**HR** High end range	**MW** Median wage paid	**W** Weekly
AO Average offered	**APL** Average pay, low range	**FQ** First quartile wage	**LR** Low end range	**SQ** Second quartile wage	**Y** Yearly

Occupation/Type/Industry	Location	Per	Low	Mid	High	Source	Date
Compliance Officer							
Except Agriculture, Construction, Health and Safety, and Transportation	Ohio	S	18.46 MW	19.36 AW	40260 AAW	OHBLS	10//99-12//99
Except Agriculture, Construction, Health and Safety, and Transportation	Oklahoma	S	17.17 MW	19.58 AW	40720 AAW	OKBLS	10//99-12//99
Except Agriculture, Construction, Health and Safety, and Transportation	Oregon	S	19.6 MW	20.71 AW	43070 AAW	ORBLS	10//99-12//99
Except Agriculture, Construction, Health and Safety, and Transportation	Pennsylvania	S	19.55 MW	19.92 AW	41420 AAW	PABLS	10//99-12//99
Except Agriculture, Construction, Health and Safety, and Transportation	Rhode Island	S	21.2 MW	21.07 AW	43820 AAW	RIBLS	10//99-12//99
Except Agriculture, Construction, Health and Safety, and Transportation	South Dakota	S	15.22 MW	15.80 AW	32870 AAW	SDBLS	10//99-12//99
Except Agriculture, Construction, Health and Safety, and Transportation	Texas	S	18.26 MW	20.92 AW	43520 AAW	TXBLS	10//99-12//99
Except Agriculture, Construction, Health and Safety, and Transportation	Utah	S	15.77 MW	16.76 AW	34850 AAW	UTBLS	10//99-12//99
Except Agriculture, Construction, Health and Safety, and Transportation	Vermont	S	21.21 MW	20.84 AW	43350 AAW	VTBLS	10//99-12//99
Except Agriculture, Construction, Health and Safety, and Transportation	Virginia	S	18.15 MW	19.82 AW	41230 AAW	VABLS	10//99-12//99
Except Agriculture, Construction, Health and Safety, and Transportation	Washington	S	20.37 MW	21.34 AW	44400 AAW	WABLS	10//99-12//99
Except Agriculture, Construction, Health and Safety, and Transportation	West Virginia	S	14.43 MW	15.62 AW	32490 AAW	WVBLS	10//99-12//99
Except Agriculture, Construction, Health and Safety, and Transportation	Wisconsin	S	18.89 MW	19.30 AW	40150 AAW	WIBLS	10//99-12//99
Except Agriculture, Construction, Health and Safety, and Transportation	Wyoming	S	22.28 MW	21.09 AW	43860 AAW	WYBLS	10//99-12//99
Except Agriculture, Construction, Health and Safety, and Transportation	Puerto Rico	S	12.17 MW	13.62 AW	28320 AAW	PRBLS	10//99-12//99
Component Evaluator							
Purchasing, Electronics	United States	Y		70400 AW		ELBUY	2000
Computer and Information Scientist							
Research	Alabama	S	28.85 MW	28.30 AW	58850 AAW	ALBLS	10//99-12//99
Research	Arizona	S	30.81 MW	31.62 AW	65770 AAW	AZBLS	10//99-12//99
Research	California	S	33.27 MW	35.26 AW	73330 AAW	CABLS	10//99-12//99
Research	Colorado	S	36.16 MW	38.35 AW	79770 AAW	COBLS	10//99-12//99
Research	Connecticut	S	37.74 MW	36.38 AW	75680 AAW	CTBLS	10//99-12//99
Research	Delaware	S	31.98 MW	31.40 AW	65310 AAW	DEBLS	10//99-12//99
Research	District of Columbia	S	30.8 MW	31.31 AW	65130 AAW	DCBLS	10//99-12//99
Research	Florida	S	30.09 MW	30.90 AW	64270 AAW	FLBLS	10//99-12//99
Research	Georgia	S	29.65 MW	29.48 AW	61320 AAW	GABLS	10//99-12//99
Research	Hawaii	S	28.87 MW	28.08 AW	58410 AAW	HIBLS	10//99-12//99
Research	Idaho	S	31.35 MW	30.26 AW	62950 AAW	IDBLS	10//99-12//99
Research	Illinois	S	28.56 MW	29.72 AW	61820 AAW	ILBLS	10//99-12//99
Research	Indiana	S	24.58 MW	25.17 AW	52360 AAW	INBLS	10//99-12//99
Research	Iowa	S	24.95 MW	25.70 AW	53460 AAW	IABLS	10//99-12//99
Research	Kansas	S	31.59 MW	31.57 AW	65650 AAW	KSBLS	10//99-12//99
Research	Kentucky	S	31.08 MW	32.26 AW	67110 AAW	KYBLS	10//99-12//99
Research	Louisiana	S	23.77 MW	26.43 AW	54960 AAW	LABLS	10//99-12//99
Research	Maryland	S	31.35 MW	32.69 AW	68000 AAW	MDBLS	10//99-12//99
Research	Massachusetts	S	27.95 MW	33.85 AW	70410 AAW	MABLS	10//99-12//99
Research	Michigan	S	25.47 MW	29.71 AW	61790 AAW	MIBLS	10//99-12//99
Research	Minnesota	S	34.98 MW	33.69 AW	70080 AAW	MNBLS	10//99-12//99
Research	Missouri	S	36.74 MW	35.60 AW	74050 AAW	MOBLS	10//99-12//99
Research	Nebraska	S	16.34 MW	19.75 AW	41080 AAW	NEBLS	10//99-12//99
Research	New Hampshire	S	31.95 MW	33.78 AW	70250 AAW	NHBLS	10//99-12//99
Research	New Jersey	S	35.15 MW	35.48 AW	73790 AAW	NJBLS	10//99-12//99
Research	New Mexico	S	30.71 MW	29.06 AW	60450 AAW	NMBLS	10//99-12//99
Research	New York	S	27.49 MW	30.48 AW	63400 AAW	NYBLS	10//99-12//99
Research	North Carolina	S	34.9 MW	34.62 AW	72000 AAW	NCBLS	10//99-12//99
Research	Ohio	S	30.6 MW	31.70 AW	65930 AAW	OHBLS	10//99-12//99
Research	Oklahoma	S	24.46 MW	24.12 AW	50180 AAW	OKBLS	10//99-12//99
Research	Pennsylvania	S	30.84 MW	34.84 AW	72460 AAW	PABLS	10//99-12//99
Research	South Carolina	S	16.86 MW	22.75 AW	47310 AAW	SCBLS	10//99-12//99
Research	Tennessee	S	23.87 MW	23.94 AW	49790 AAW	TNBLS	10//99-12//99
Research	Texas	S	33.68 MW	32.72 AW	68060 AAW	TXBLS	10//99-12//99
Research	Utah	S	29.81 MW	28.25 AW	58750 AAW	UTBLS	10//99-12//99

AAW	Average annual wage	AOH	Average offered, high	ASH	Average starting, high	H	Hourly	M	Monthly	S	Special: hourly and annual
AE	Average entry wage	AOL	Average offered, low	ASL	Average starting, low	HI	Highest wage paid	MTC	Median total compensation	TQ	Third quartile wage
AEX	Average experienced wage	APH	Average pay, high range	AW	Average wage paid	HR	High end range	MW	Median wage paid	W	Weekly
AO	Average offered	APL	Average pay, low range	FQ	First quartile wage	LR	Low end range	SQ	Second quartile wage	Y	Yearly

Occupation/Type/Industry	Location	Per	Low	Mid	High	Source	Date
Computer and Information Scientist							
Research	Virginia	S	30.17 MW	31.23 AW	64970 AAW	VABLS	10//99-12//99
Research	Washington	S	31.21 MW	32.05 AW	66670 AAW	WABLS	10//99-12//99
Research	Wisconsin	S	29.86 MW	30.46 AW	63350 AAW	WIBLS	10//99-12//99
Computer and Information Systems Manager	Alabama	S	27.18 MW	27.17 AW	56510 AAW	ALBLS	10//99-12//99
	Anniston MSA, AL	S	27.24 MW	28.05 AW	56660 AAW	ALBLS	10//99-12//99
	Auburn-Opelika MSA, AL	S	19.76 MW	16.55 AW	41110 AAW	ALBLS	10//99-12//99
	Birmingham MSA, AL	S	27.51 MW	27.59 AW	57220 AAW	ALBLS	10//99-12//99
	Decatur MSA, AL	S	21.60 MW	20.12 AW	44930 AAW	ALBLS	10//99-12//99
	Dothan MSA, AL	S	29.57 MW	25.89 AW	61500 AAW	ALBLS	10//99-12//99
	Florence MSA, AL	S	22.72 MW	24.11 AW	47260 AAW	ALBLS	10//99-12//99
	Huntsville MSA, AL	S	26.82 MW	27.97 AW	55790 AAW	ALBLS	10//99-12//99
	Mobile MSA, AL	S	27.53 MW	26.65 AW	57250 AAW	ALBLS	10//99-12//99
	Montgomery MSA, AL	S	28.74 MW	29.35 AW	59780 AAW	ALBLS	10//99-12//99
	Tuscaloosa MSA, AL	S	22.93 MW	22.85 AW	47700 AAW	ALBLS	10//99-12//99
	Alaska	S	29.38 MW	30.12 AW	62650 AAW	AKBLS	10//99-12//99
	Anchorage MSA, AK	S	26.50 MW	26.67 AW	55120 AAW	AKBLS	10//99-12//99
	Arizona	S	31.33 MW	33.04 AW	68720 AAW	AZBLS	10//99-12//99
	Flagstaff MSA, AZ-UT	S	28.76 MW	28.79 AW	59830 AAW	AZBLS	10//99-12//99
	Phoenix-Mesa MSA, AZ	S	34.76 MW	32.99 AW	72300 AAW	AZBLS	10//99-12//99
	Tucson MSA, AZ	S	26.04 MW	22.08 AW	54170 AAW	AZBLS	10//99-12//99
	Arkansas	S	29.87 MW	30.55 AW	63540 AAW	ARBLS	10//99-12//99
	Fayetteville-Springdale-Rogers MSA, AR	S	29.84 MW	28.96 AW	62070 AAW	ARBLS	10//99-12//99
	Fort Smith MSA, AR-OK	S	25.83 MW	25.77 AW	53720 AAW	ARBLS	10//99-12//99
	Little Rock-North Little Rock MSA, AR	S	33.33 MW	33.14 AW	69330 AAW	ARBLS	10//99-12//99
	California	S	37.39 MW	38.00 AW	79030 AAW	CABLS	10//99-12//99
	Bakersfield MSA, CA	S	29.28 MW	30.13 AW	60900 AAW	CABLS	10//99-12//99
	Chico-Paradise MSA, CA	S	23.70 MW	22.85 AW	49290 AAW	CABLS	10//99-12//99
	Fresno MSA, CA	S	30.88 MW	30.57 AW	64240 AAW	CABLS	10//99-12//99
	Los Angeles-Long Beach PMSA, CA	S	35.80 MW	35.32 AW	74470 AAW	CABLS	10//99-12//99
	Modesto MSA, CA	S	27.44 MW	25.61 AW	57080 AAW	CABLS	10//99-12//99
	Oakland PMSA, CA	S	37.16 MW	35.80 AW	77290 AAW	CABLS	10//99-12//99
	Orange County PMSA, CA	S	40.18 MW	39.58 AW	83580 AAW	CABLS	10//99-12//99
	Redding MSA, CA	S	27.92 MW	29.25 AW	58070 AAW	CABLS	10//99-12//99
	Riverside-San Bernardino PMSA, CA	S	29.41 MW	29.68 AW	61170 AAW	CABLS	10//99-12//99
	Sacramento PMSA, CA	S	34.00 MW	34.55 AW	70730 AAW	CABLS	10//99-12//99
	Salinas MSA, CA	S	37.45 MW	38.07 AW	77890 AAW	CABLS	10//99-12//99
	San Diego MSA, CA	S	34.60 MW	33.98 AW	71970 AAW	CABLS	10//99-12//99
	San Francisco PMSA, CA	S	41.40 MW	40.14 AW	86110 AAW	CABLS	10//99-12//99
	San Jose PMSA, CA	S	44.35 MW	47.65 AW	92240 AAW	CABLS	10//99-12//99
	San Luis Obispo-Atascadero-Paso Robles MSA, CA	S	26.45 MW	26.30 AW	55010 AAW	CABLS	10//99-12//99
	Santa Barbara-Santa Maria-Lompoc MSA, CA	S	32.48 MW	34.03 AW	67560 AAW	CABLS	10//99-12//99
	Santa Cruz-Watsonville PMSA, CA	S	31.75 MW	30.71 AW	66030 AAW	CABLS	10//99-12//99
	Santa Rosa PMSA, CA	S	32.56 MW	33.90 AW	67720 AAW	CABLS	10//99-12//99
	Stockton-Lodi MSA, CA	S	26.85 MW	27.16 AW	55840 AAW	CABLS	10//99-12//99
	Vallejo-Fairfield-Napa PMSA, CA	S	33.61 MW	32.51 AW	69910 AAW	CABLS	10//99-12//99
	Ventura PMSA, CA	S	37.09 MW	35.48 AW	77140 AAW	CABLS	10//99-12//99
	Visalia-Tulare-Porterville MSA, CA	S	26.66 MW	23.40 AW	55450 AAW	CABLS	10//99-12//99
	Yolo PMSA, CA	S	32.67 MW	28.94 AW	67950 AAW	CABLS	10//99-12//99
	Colorado	S	38.5 MW	38.76 AW	80630 AAW	COBLS	10//99-12//99
	Boulder-Longmont PMSA, CO	S	43.13 MW	41.40 AW	89700 AAW	COBLS	10//99-12//99
	Denver PMSA, CO	S	40.23 MW	39.61 AW	83670 AAW	COBLS	10//99-12//99
	Fort Collins-Loveland MSA, CO	S	34.86 MW	33.70 AW	72500 AAW	COBLS	10//99-12//99
	Connecticut	S	38.93 MW	39.89 AW	82970 AAW	CTBLS	10//99-12//99
	Bridgeport PMSA, CT	S	40.05 MW	39.69 AW	83300 AAW	CTBLS	10//99-12//99
	Danbury PMSA, CT	S	34.21 MW	31.78 AW	71150 AAW	CTBLS	10//99-12//99
	Hartford MSA, CT	S	38.44 MW	38.06 AW	79950 AAW	CTBLS	10//99-12//99
	New Haven-Meriden PMSA, CT	S	32.47 MW	32.78 AW	67530 AAW	CTBLS	10//99-12//99

AAW	Average annual wage	AOH	Average offered, high	ASH	Average starting, high
AE	Average entry wage	AOL	Average offered, low	ASL	Average starting, low
AEX	Average experienced wage	APH	Average pay, high range	AW	Average wage paid
AO	Average offered	APL	Average pay, low range	FQ	First quartile wage

H	Hourly	M	Monthly	S	Special: hourly and annual
HI	Highest wage paid	MTC	Median total compensation	TQ	Third quartile wage
HR	High end range	MW	Median wage paid	W	Weekly
LR	Low end range	SQ	Second quartile wage	Y	Yearly

Occupation/Type/Industry	Location	Per	Low	Mid	High	Source	Date
Computer and Information Systems Manager	New London-Norwich MSA, CT-RI	S	37.66 MW	39.86 AW	78330 AAW	CTBLS	10//99-12//99
	Stamford-Norwalk PMSA, CT	S	46.51 MW	47.03 AW	96740 AAW	CTBLS	10//99-12//99
	Delaware	S	34.21 MW	32.40 AW	67390 AAW	DEBLS	10//99-12//99
	Wilmington-Newark PMSA, DE-MD	S	32.58 MW	34.15 AW	67760 AAW	DEBLS	10//99-12//99
	District of Columbia	S	36.81 MW	36.47 AW	75850 AAW	DCBLS	10//99-12//99
	Washington PMSA, DC-MD-VA-WV	S	39.75 MW	39.38 AW	82690 AAW	DCBLS	10//99-12//99
	Florida	S	31.79 MW	32.65 AW	67900 AAW	FLBLS	10//99-12//99
	Daytona Beach MSA, FL	S	29.84 MW	27.14 AW	62070 AAW	FLBLS	10//99-12//99
	Fort Lauderdale PMSA, FL	S	32.38 MW	31.89 AW	67340 AAW	FLBLS	10//99-12//99
	Fort Myers-Cape Coral MSA, FL	S	23.92 MW	23.89 AW	49750 AAW	FLBLS	10//99-12//99
	Fort Pierce-Port St. Lucie MSA, FL	S	31.02 MW	27.91 AW	64510 AAW	FLBLS	10//99-12//99
	Fort Walton Beach MSA, FL	S	32.45 MW	33.10 AW	67500 AAW	FLBLS	10//99-12//99
	Gainesville MSA, FL	S	30.04 MW	30.68 AW	62480 AAW	FLBLS	10//99-12//99
	Jacksonville MSA, FL	S	37.24 MW	36.41 AW	77460 AAW	FLBLS	10//99-12//99
	Lakeland-Winter Haven MSA, FL	S	22.85 MW	21.45 AW	47530 AAW	FLBLS	10//99-12//99
	Melbourne-Titusville-Palm Bay MSA, FL	S	29.04 MW	26.66 AW	60390 AAW	FLBLS	10//99-12//99
	Miami PMSA, FL	S	31.91 MW	30.00 AW	66380 AAW	FLBLS	10//99-12//99
	Naples MSA, FL	S	29.50 MW	28.91 AW	61370 AAW	FLBLS	10//99-12//99
	Ocala MSA, FL	S	17.53 MW	13.61 AW	36470 AAW	FLBLS	10//99-12//99
	Orlando MSA, FL	S	32.93 MW	31.84 AW	68490 AAW	FLBLS	10//99-12//99
	Panama City MSA, FL	S	23.58 MW	23.19 AW	49040 AAW	FLBLS	10//99-12//99
	Pensacola MSA, FL	S	27.74 MW	26.94 AW	57700 AAW	FLBLS	10//99-12//99
	Sarasota-Bradenton MSA, FL	S	28.18 MW	26.80 AW	58610 AAW	FLBLS	10//99-12//99
	Tallahassee MSA, FL	S	30.77 MW	29.92 AW	64000 AAW	FLBLS	10//99-12//99
	Tampa-St. Petersburg-Clearwater MSA, FL	S	34.77 MW	34.84 AW	72330 AAW	FLBLS	10//99-12//99
	West Palm Beach-Boca Raton MSA, FL	S	34.14 MW	32.44 AW	71000 AAW	FLBLS	10//99-12//99
	Georgia	S	35.09 MW	36.19 AW	75270 AAW	GABLS	10//99-12//99
	Albany MSA, GA	S	28.32 MW	28.31 AW	58910 AAW	GABLS	10//99-12//99
	Athens MSA, GA	S	25.54 MW	24.75 AW	53120 AAW	GABLS	10//99-12//99
	Atlanta MSA, GA	S	38.42 MW	37.97 AW	79920 AAW	GABLS	10//99-12//99
	Columbus MSA, GA-AL	S	26.89 MW	26.17 AW	55930 AAW	GABLS	10//99-12//99
	Macon MSA, GA	S	33.67 MW	32.40 AW	70030 AAW	GABLS	10//99-12//99
	Savannah MSA, GA	S	27.60 MW	28.29 AW	57410 AAW	GABLS	10//99-12//99
	Hawaii	S	33.06 MW	35.63 AW	74100 AAW	HIBLS	10//99-12//99
	Honolulu MSA, HI	S	36.24 MW	33.83 AW	75370 AAW	HIBLS	10//99-12//99
	Idaho	S	32.11 MW	32.49 AW	67590 AAW	IDBLS	10//99-12//99
	Boise City MSA, ID	S	34.78 MW	34.77 AW	72350 AAW	IDBLS	10//99-12//99
	Illinois	S	34.16 MW	35.20 AW	73220 AAW	ILBLS	10//99-12//99
	Bloomington-Normal MSA, IL	S	42.35 MW	39.49 AW	88090 AAW	ILBLS	10//99-12//99
	Champaign-Urbana MSA, IL	S	27.57 MW	26.05 AW	57350 AAW	ILBLS	10//99-12//99
	Chicago PMSA, IL	S	35.58 MW	34.74 AW	74000 AAW	ILBLS	10//99-12//99
	Peoria-Pekin MSA, IL	S	31.71 MW	31.05 AW	65950 AAW	ILBLS	10//99-12//99
	Rockford MSA, IL	S	28.36 MW	29.40 AW	59000 AAW	ILBLS	10//99-12//99
	Springfield MSA, IL	S	37.48 MW	30.77 AW	77950 AAW	ILBLS	10//99-12//99
	Indiana	S	31.11 MW	32.07 AW	66700 AAW	INBLS	10//99-12//99
	Bloomington MSA, IN	S	34.66 MW	36.21 AW	72090 AAW	INBLS	10//99-12//99
	Elkhart-Goshen MSA, IN	S	29.23 MW	30.72 AW	60790 AAW	INBLS	10//99-12//99
	Evansville-Henderson MSA, IN-KY	S	24.74 MW	25.17 AW	51470 AAW	INBLS	10//99-12//99
	Fort Wayne MSA, IN	S	28.64 MW	26.89 AW	59560 AAW	INBLS	10//99-12//99
	Gary PMSA, IN	S	38.97 MW	34.35 AW	81070 AAW	INBLS	10//99-12//99
	Indianapolis MSA, IN	S	34.99 MW	33.29 AW	72780 AAW	INBLS	10//99-12//99
	Kokomo MSA, IN	S	34.94 MW	36.84 AW	72670 AAW	INBLS	10//99-12//99
	Lafayette MSA, IN	S	30.06 MW	27.80 AW	62530 AAW	INBLS	10//99-12//99
	Muncie MSA, IN	S	32.77 MW	28.24 AW	68160 AAW	INBLS	10//99-12//99
	South Bend MSA, IN	S	33.39 MW	28.09 AW	69440 AAW	INBLS	10//99-12//99
	Terre Haute MSA, IN	S	31.28 MW	30.03 AW	65060 AAW	INBLS	10//99-12//99
	Iowa	S	30.44 MW	31.21 AW	64920 AAW	IABLS	10//99-12//99
	Cedar Rapids MSA, IA	S	29.58 MW	29.13 AW	61540 AAW	IABLS	10//99-12//99
	Davenport-Moline-Rock Island MSA, IA-IL	S	26.02 MW	24.71 AW	54120 AAW	IABLS	10//99-12//99
	Des Moines MSA, IA	S	33.54 MW	34.04 AW	69760 AAW	IABLS	10//99-12//99

AAW Average annual wage	AOH Average offered, high	ASH Average starting, high	H Hourly	M Monthly	S Special: hourly and annual
AE Average entry wage	AOL Average offered, low	ASL Average starting, low	HI Highest wage paid	MTC Median total compensation	TQ Third quartile wage
AEX Average experienced wage	APH Average pay, high range	AW Average wage paid	HR High end range	MW Median wage paid	W Weekly
AO Average offered	APL Average pay, low range	FQ First quartile wage	LR Low end range	SQ Second quartile wage	Y Yearly

Occupation/Type/Industry	Location	Per	Low	Mid	High	Source	Date
Computer and Information Systems Manager							
	Dubuque MSA, IA	S	27.67 MW	23.14 AW	57560 AAW	IABLS	10//99-12//99
	Waterloo-Cedar Falls MSA, IA	S	26.26 MW	27.70 AW	54610 AAW	IABLS	10//99-12//99
	Kansas	S	32.62 MW	32.85 AW	68330 AAW	KSBLS	10//99-12//99
	Lawrence MSA, KS	S	24.25 MW	24.07 AW	50440 AAW	KSBLS	10//99-12//99
	Topeka MSA, KS	S	27.19 MW	27.53 AW	56560 AAW	KSBLS	10//99-12//99
	Wichita MSA, KS	S	32.96 MW	33.50 AW	68560 AAW	KSBLS	10//99-12//99
	Kentucky	S	27.66 MW	27.59 AW	57390 AAW	KYBLS	10//99-12//99
	Lexington MSA, KY	S	29.08 MW	28.22 AW	60490 AAW	KYBLS	10//99-12//99
	Louisville MSA, KY-IN	S	29.04 MW	29.46 AW	60410 AAW	KYBLS	10//99-12//99
	Owensboro MSA, KY	S	20.87 MW	19.96 AW	43420 AAW	KYBLS	10//99-12//99
	Louisiana	S	29 MW	28.22 AW	58690 AAW	LABLS	10//99-12//99
	Alexandria MSA, LA	S	16.56 MW	10.61 AW	34440 AAW	LABLS	10//99-12//99
	Baton Rouge MSA, LA	S	26.80 MW	26.62 AW	55750 AAW	LABLS	10//99-12//99
	Houma MSA, LA	S	22.88 MW	20.72 AW	47600 AAW	LABLS	10//99-12//99
	Lafayette MSA, LA	S	22.31 MW	22.81 AW	46400 AAW	LABLS	10//99-12//99
	Lake Charles MSA, LA	S	27.18 MW	27.52 AW	56530 AAW	LABLS	10//99-12//99
	Monroe MSA, LA	S	22.86 MW	28.10 AW	47540 AAW	LABLS	10//99-12//99
	New Orleans MSA, LA	S	30.53 MW	31.22 AW	63500 AAW	LABLS	10//99-12//99
	Shreveport-Bossier City MSA, LA	S	26.59 MW	29.09 AW	55320 AAW	LABLS	10//99-12//99
	Maine	S	26.46 MW	27.57 AW	57340 AAW	MEBLS	10//99-12//99
	Bangor MSA, ME	S	26.68 MW	25.94 AW	55500 AAW	MEBLS	10//99-12//99
	Lewiston-Auburn MSA, ME	S	29.34 MW	29.80 AW	61030 AAW	MEBLS	10//99-12//99
	Portland MSA, ME	S	31.36 MW	31.33 AW	65230 AAW	MEBLS	10//99-12//99
	Maryland	S	37.53 MW	37.28 AW	77530 AAW	MDBLS	10//99-12//99
	Baltimore PMSA, MD	S	36.74 MW	36.30 AW	76420 AAW	MDBLS	10//99-12//99
	Massachusetts	S	36.74 MW	37.64 AW	78290 AAW	MABLS	10//99-12//99
	Barnstable-Yarmouth MSA, MA	S	35.03 MW	32.97 AW	72860 AAW	MABLS	10//99-12//99
	Boston PMSA, MA-NH	S	37.97 MW	37.35 AW	78980 AAW	MABLS	10//99-12//99
	Brockton PMSA, MA	S	34.26 MW	32.82 AW	71260 AAW	MABLS	10//99-12//99
	Fitchburg-Leominster PMSA, MA	S	32.40 MW	35.14 AW	67390 AAW	MABLS	10//99-12//99
	Lowell PMSA, MA-NH	S	37.57 MW	37.67 AW	78150 AAW	MABLS	10//99-12//99
	New Bedford PMSA, MA	S	29.00 MW	28.57 AW	60330 AAW	MABLS	10//99-12//99
	Springfield MSA, MA	S	29.64 MW	28.83 AW	61650 AAW	MABLS	10//99-12//99
	Worcester PMSA, MA-CT	S	32.49 MW	31.97 AW	67580 AAW	MABLS	10//99-12//99
	Michigan	S	34.2 MW	35.40 AW	73630 AAW	MIBLS	10//99-12//99
	Ann Arbor PMSA, MI	S	32.73 MW	32.03 AW	68080 AAW	MIBLS	10//99-12//99
	Benton Harbor MSA, MI	S	25.67 MW	24.06 AW	53400 AAW	MIBLS	10//99-12//99
	Detroit PMSA, MI	S	36.86 MW	36.72 AW	76670 AAW	MIBLS	10//99-12//99
	Flint PMSA, MI	S	32.89 MW	32.12 AW	68410 AAW	MIBLS	10//99-12//99
	Grand Rapids-Muskegon-Holland MSA, MI	S	37.01 MW	33.27 AW	76990 AAW	MIBLS	10//99-12//99
	Kalamazoo-Battle Creek MSA, MI	S	35.35 MW	33.36 AW	73530 AAW	MIBLS	10//99-12//99
	Lansing-East Lansing MSA, MI	S	31.52 MW	31.28 AW	65560 AAW	MIBLS	10//99-12//99
	Saginaw-Bay City-Midland MSA, MI	S	32.78 MW	32.80 AW	68190 AAW	MIBLS	10//99-12//99
	Minnesota	S	38.76 MW	38.98 AW	81070 AAW	MNBLS	10//99-12//99
	Duluth-Superior MSA, MN-WI	S	36.66 MW	34.92 AW	76260 AAW	MNBLS	10//99-12//99
	Minneapolis-St. Paul MSA, MN-WI	S	39.79 MW	39.52 AW	82770 AAW	MNBLS	10//99-12//99
	Rochester MSA, MN	S	43.06 MW	41.58 AW	89570 AAW	MNBLS	10//99-12//99
	St. Cloud MSA, MN	S	32.86 MW	34.58 AW	68340 AAW	MNBLS	10//99-12//99
	Mississippi	S	25.94 MW	27.24 AW	56660 AAW	MSBLS	10//99-12//99
	Biloxi-Gulfport-Pascagoula MSA, MS	S	28.28 MW	27.87 AW	58830 AAW	MSBLS	10//99-12//99
	Jackson MSA, MS	S	28.45 MW	27.82 AW	59180 AAW	MSBLS	10//99-12//99
	Missouri	S	31.61 MW	32.70 AW	68020 AAW	MOBLS	10//99-12//99
	Columbia MSA, MO	S	28.79 MW	27.83 AW	59890 AAW	MOBLS	10//99-12//99
	Joplin MSA, MO	S	28.60 MW	28.91 AW	59500 AAW	MOBLS	10//99-12//99
	Kansas City MSA, MO-KS	S	33.41 MW	32.84 AW	69480 AAW	MOBLS	10//99-12//99
	St. Joseph MSA, MO	S	26.31 MW	20.87 AW	54730 AAW	MOBLS	10//99-12//99
	St. Louis MSA, MO-IL	S	34.92 MW	33.59 AW	72630 AAW	MOBLS	10//99-12//99
	Springfield MSA, MO	S	30.86 MW	29.71 AW	64190 AAW	MOBLS	10//99-12//99
	Montana	S	24.21 MW	24.68 AW	51340 AAW	MTBLS	10//99-12//99
	Billings MSA, MT	S	21.76 MW	19.22 AW	45260 AAW	MTBLS	10//99-12//99
	Great Falls MSA, MT	S	25.45 MW	24.17 AW	52940 AAW	MTBLS	10//99-12//99
	Missoula MSA, MT	S	27.66 MW	29.20 AW	57520 AAW	MTBLS	10//99-12//99
	Nebraska	S	30.03 MW	30.56 AW	63560 AAW	NEBLS	10//99-12//99

AAW	Average annual wage	AOH	Average offered, high	ASH	Average starting, high	H	Hourly	M	Monthly	S	Special: hourly and annual
AE	Average entry wage	AOL	Average offered, low	ASL	Average starting, low	HI	Highest wage paid	MTC	Median total compensation	TQ	Third quartile wage
AEX	Average experienced wage	APH	Average pay, high range	AW	Average wage paid	HR	High end range	MW	Median wage paid	W	Weekly
AO	Average offered	APL	Average pay, low range	FQ	First quartile wage	LR	Low end range	SQ	Second quartile wage	Y	Yearly

Occupation/Type/Industry	Location	Per	Low	Mid	High	Source	Date
Computer and Information Systems Manager	Lincoln MSA, NE	S	28.36 MW	27.95 AW	58990 AAW	NEBLS	10//99-12//99
	Omaha MSA, NE-IA	S	30.95 MW	30.44 AW	64390 AAW	NEBLS	10//99-12//99
	Nevada	S	29.81 MW	31.01 AW	64500 AAW	NVBLS	10//99-12//99
	Las Vegas MSA, NV-AZ	S	31.04 MW	29.78 AW	64570 AAW	NVBLS	10//99-12//99
	Reno MSA, NV	S	31.98 MW	29.90 AW	66520 AAW	NVBLS	10//99-12//99
	New Hampshire	S	30.47 MW	32.03 AW	66620 AAW	NHBLS	10//99-12//99
	Manchester PMSA, NH	S	29.79 MW	28.06 AW	61950 AAW	NHBLS	10//99-12//99
	Nashua PMSA, NH	S	34.87 MW	31.76 AW	72530 AAW	NHBLS	10//99-12//99
	Portsmouth-Rochester PMSA, NH-ME	S	32.27 MW	34.91 AW	67120 AAW	NHBLS	10//99-12//99
	New Jersey	S	44.43 MW	43.67 AW	90830 AAW	NJBLS	10//99-12//99
	Atlantic-Cape May PMSA, NJ	S	48.42 MW	48.45 AW	100710 AAW	NJBLS	10//99-12//99
	Bergen-Passaic PMSA, NJ	S	36.27 MW	36.68 AW	75440 AAW	NJBLS	10//99-12//99
	Jersey City PMSA, NJ	S	44.65 MW	45.78 AW	92880 AAW	NJBLS	10//99-12//99
	Middlesex-Somerset-Hunterdon PMSA, NJ	S	50.43 MW	51.15 AW	104880 AAW	NJBLS	10//99-12//99
	Monmouth-Ocean PMSA, NJ	S	39.15 MW	39.14 AW	81420 AAW	NJBLS	10//99-12//99
	Newark PMSA, NJ	S	40.76 MW	39.38 AW	84770 AAW	NJBLS	10//99-12//99
	Trenton PMSA, NJ	S	35.54 MW	35.50 AW	73920 AAW	NJBLS	10//99-12//99
	Vineland-Millville-Bridgeton PMSA, NJ	S	33.10 MW	35.46 AW	68850 AAW	NJBLS	10//99-12//99
	New Mexico	S	27.84 MW	28.98 AW	60280 AAW	NMBLS	10//99-12//99
	Albuquerque MSA, NM	S	30.28 MW	29.48 AW	62990 AAW	NMBLS	10//99-12//99
	New York	S	41.35 MW	42.52 AW	88430 AAW	NYBLS	10//99-12//99
	Albany-Schenectady-Troy MSA, NY	S	37.61 MW	34.48 AW	78230 AAW	NYBLS	10//99-12//99
	Binghamton MSA, NY	S	36.93 MW	36.54 AW	76810 AAW	NYBLS	10//99-12//99
	Buffalo-Niagara Falls MSA, NY	S	31.39 MW	31.04 AW	65290 AAW	NYBLS	10//99-12//99
	Dutchess County PMSA, NY	S	33.08 MW	32.11 AW	68800 AAW	NYBLS	10//99-12//99
	Nassau-Suffolk PMSA, NY	S	46.20 MW	44.50 AW	96100 AAW	NYBLS	10//99-12//99
	New York PMSA, NY	S	44.51 MW	43.58 AW	92570 AAW	NYBLS	10//99-12//99
	Newburgh PMSA, NY-PA	S	39.54 MW	37.61 AW	82250 AAW	NYBLS	10//99-12//99
	Rochester MSA, NY	S	32.75 MW	30.54 AW	68110 AAW	NYBLS	10//99-12//99
	Syracuse MSA, NY	S	36.24 MW	34.69 AW	75370 AAW	NYBLS	10//99-12//99
	Utica-Rome MSA, NY	S	36.54 MW	40.85 AW	75990 AAW	NYBLS	10//99-12//99
	North Carolina	S	36.27 MW	35.93 AW	74730 AAW	NCBLS	10//99-12//99
	Asheville MSA, NC	S	28.86 MW	29.34 AW	60020 AAW	NCBLS	10//99-12//99
	Charlotte-Gastonia-Rock Hill MSA, NC-SC	S	37.81 MW	37.09 AW	78650 AAW	NCBLS	10//99-12//99
	Fayetteville MSA, NC	S	27.05 MW	26.21 AW	56270 AAW	NCBLS	10//99-12//99
	Greensboro--Winston-Salem--High Point MSA, NC	S	37.13 MW	36.84 AW	77240 AAW	NCBLS	10//99-12//99
	Greenville MSA, NC	S	37.56 MW	36.44 AW	78130 AAW	NCBLS	10//99-12//99
	Hickory-Morganton-Lenoir MSA, NC	S	27.79 MW	25.22 AW	57800 AAW	NCBLS	10//99-12//99
	Raleigh-Durham-Chapel Hill MSA, NC	S	39.14 MW	39.52 AW	81410 AAW	NCBLS	10//99-12//99
	Rocky Mount MSA, NC	S	24.16 MW	21.61 AW	50250 AAW	NCBLS	10//99-12//99
	Wilmington MSA, NC	S	24.30 MW	22.38 AW	50540 AAW	NCBLS	10//99-12//99
	North Dakota	S	24.37 MW	26.83 AW	55810 AAW	NDBLS	10//99-12//99
	Ohio	S	30.67 MW	31.45 AW	65420 AAW	OHBLS	10//99-12//99
	Akron PMSA, OH	S	31.01 MW	27.99 AW	64500 AAW	OHBLS	10//99-12//99
	Canton-Massillon MSA, OH	S	25.47 MW	22.26 AW	52990 AAW	OHBLS	10//99-12//99
	Cincinnati PMSA, OH-KY-IN	S	33.86 MW	32.82 AW	70440 AAW	OHBLS	10//99-12//99
	Cleveland-Lorain-Elyria PMSA, OH	S	32.80 MW	31.72 AW	68230 AAW	OHBLS	10//99-12//99
	Columbus MSA, OH	S	33.27 MW	32.78 AW	69200 AAW	OHBLS	10//99-12//99
	Dayton-Springfield MSA, OH	S	31.64 MW	31.85 AW	65820 AAW	OHBLS	10//99-12//99
	Hamilton-Middletown PMSA, OH	S	29.11 MW	28.48 AW	60550 AAW	OHBLS	10//99-12//99
	Youngstown-Warren MSA, OH	S	28.35 MW	28.64 AW	58970 AAW	OHBLS	10//99-12//99
	Oklahoma	S	27.73 MW	28.87 AW	60050 AAW	OKBLS	10//99-12//99
	Oklahoma City MSA, OK	S	30.60 MW	30.14 AW	63650 AAW	OKBLS	10//99-12//99
	Tulsa MSA, OK	S	30.35 MW	30.14 AW	63120 AAW	OKBLS	10//99-12//99
	Oregon	S	31.71 MW	32.66 AW	67930 AAW	ORBLS	10//99-12//99
	Eugene-Springfield MSA, OR	S	33.09 MW	32.43 AW	68830 AAW	ORBLS	10//99-12//99
	Medford-Ashland MSA, OR	S	27.98 MW	25.99 AW	58190 AAW	ORBLS	10//99-12//99
	Portland-Vancouver PMSA, OR-WA	S	37.62 MW	35.68 AW	78240 AAW	ORBLS	10//99-12//99
	Salem PMSA, OR	S	31.69 MW	31.40 AW	65900 AAW	ORBLS	10//99-12//99

AAW Average annual wage	AOH Average offered, high	ASH Average starting, high	H Hourly	M Monthly	S Special: hourly and annual
AE Average entry wage	AOL Average offered, low	ASL Average starting, low	HI Highest wage paid	MTC Median total compensation	TQ Third quartile wage
AEX Average experienced wage	APH Average pay, high range	AW Average wage paid	HR High end range	MW Median wage paid	W Weekly
AO Average offered	APL Average pay, low range	FQ First quartile wage	LR Low end range	SQ Second quartile wage	Y Yearly

Occupation/Type/Industry	Location	Per	Low	Mid	High	Source	Date
Computer and Information Systems Manager	Pennsylvania	S	34.4 MW	34.90 AW	72590 AAW	PABLS	10//99-12//99
	Allentown-Bethlehem-Easton MSA, PA	S	34.08 MW	32.76 AW	70890 AAW	PABLS	10//99-12//99
	Altoona MSA, PA	S	28.38 MW	25.70 AW	59040 AAW	PABLS	10//99-12//99
	Erie MSA, PA	S	24.79 MW	23.33 AW	51550 AAW	PABLS	10//99-12//99
	Harrisburg-Lebanon-Carlisle MSA, PA	S	30.92 MW	29.34 AW	64320 AAW	PABLS	10//99-12//99
	Johnstown MSA, PA	S	29.34 MW	29.51 AW	61030 AAW	PABLS	10//99-12//99
	Lancaster MSA, PA	S	27.87 MW	24.55 AW	57980 AAW	PABLS	10//99-12//99
	Philadelphia PMSA, PA-NJ	S	38.42 MW	37.82 AW	79920 AAW	PABLS	10//99-12//99
	Pittsburgh MSA, PA	S	37.37 MW	37.38 AW	77730 AAW	PABLS	10//99-12//99
	Reading MSA, PA	S	27.28 MW	26.89 AW	56750 AAW	PABLS	10//99-12//99
	Scranton--Wilkes-Barre--Hazleton MSA, PA	S	29.48 MW	29.78 AW	61320 AAW	PABLS	10//99-12//99
	Sharon MSA, PA	S	24.62 MW	22.94 AW	51210 AAW	PABLS	10//99-12//99
	State College MSA, PA	S	44.61 MW	41.77 AW	92780 AAW	PABLS	10//99-12//99
	Williamsport MSA, PA	S	28.86 MW	29.91 AW	60040 AAW	PABLS	10//99-12//99
	York MSA, PA	S	27.75 MW	26.38 AW	57730 AAW	PABLS	10//99-12//99
	Rhode Island	S	41.85 MW	41.46 AW	86230 AAW	RIBLS	10//99-12//99
	Providence-Fall River-Warwick MSA, RI-MA	S	40.79 MW	41.29 AW	84840 AAW	RIBLS	10//99-12//99
	South Carolina	S	31.93 MW	30.71 AW	63880 AAW	SCBLS	10//99-12//99
	Charleston-North Charleston MSA, SC	S	27.69 MW	27.86 AW	57590 AAW	SCBLS	10//99-12//99
	Columbia MSA, SC	S	29.41 MW	28.38 AW	61180 AAW	SCBLS	10//99-12//99
	Florence MSA, SC	S	22.68 MW	20.30 AW	47170 AAW	SCBLS	10//99-12//99
	Greenville-Spartanburg-Anderson MSA, SC	S	30.96 MW	32.51 AW	64410 AAW	SCBLS	10//99-12//99
	Myrtle Beach MSA, SC	S	23.51 MW	21.66 AW	48900 AAW	SCBLS	10//99-12//99
	Sumter MSA, SC	S	25.14 MW	24.72 AW	52290 AAW	SCBLS	10//99-12//99
	South Dakota	S	32.99 MW	36.91 AW	76770 AAW	SDBLS	10//99-12//99
	Sioux Falls MSA, SD	S	43.04 MW	37.53 AW	89520 AAW	SDBLS	10//99-12//99
	Tennessee	S	28.8 MW	29.99 AW	62380 AAW	TNBLS	10//99-12//99
	Chattanooga MSA, TN-GA	S	27.04 MW	25.42 AW	56250 AAW	TNBLS	10//99-12//99
	Clarksville-Hopkinsville MSA, TN-KY	S	24.14 MW	23.93 AW	50200 AAW	TNBLS	10//99-12//99
	Jackson MSA, TN	S	25.54 MW	25.78 AW	53110 AAW	TNBLS	10//99-12//99
	Johnson City-Kingsport-Bristol MSA, TN-VA	S	30.71 MW	31.41 AW	63880 AAW	TNBLS	10//99-12//99
	Knoxville MSA, TN	S	26.22 MW	25.63 AW	54550 AAW	TNBLS	10//99-12//99
	Memphis MSA, TN-AR-MS	S	32.19 MW	30.28 AW	66960 AAW	MSBLS	10//99-12//99
	Nashville MSA, TN	S	31.42 MW	29.78 AW	65340 AAW	TNBLS	10//99-12//99
	Texas	S	34.85 MW	35.12 AW	73040 AAW	TXBLS	10//99-12//99
	Abilene MSA, TX	S	26.42 MW	29.11 AW	54950 AAW	TXBLS	10//99-12//99
	Amarillo MSA, TX	S	26.78 MW	28.72 AW	55700 AAW	TXBLS	10//99-12//99
	Austin-San Marcos MSA, TX	S	38.27 MW	38.61 AW	79600 AAW	TXBLS	10//99-12//99
	Beaumont-Port Arthur MSA, TX	S	31.60 MW	25.71 AW	65730 AAW	TXBLS	10//99-12//99
	Brazoria PMSA, TX	S	31.04 MW	30.79 AW	64570 AAW	TXBLS	10//99-12//99
	Brownsville-Harlingen-San Benito MSA, TX	S	25.76 MW	27.08 AW	53580 AAW	TXBLS	10//99-12//99
	Bryan-College Station MSA, TX	S	29.84 MW	28.55 AW	62080 AAW	TXBLS	10//99-12//99
	Corpus Christi MSA, TX	S	23.84 MW	20.09 AW	49580 AAW	TXBLS	10//99-12//99
	Dallas PMSA, TX	S	38.61 MW	38.57 AW	80300 AAW	TXBLS	10//99-12//99
	El Paso MSA, TX	S	23.87 MW	19.81 AW	49640 AAW	TXBLS	10//99-12//99
	Fort Worth-Arlington PMSA, TX	S	32.59 MW	30.19 AW	67790 AAW	TXBLS	10//99-12//99
	Houston PMSA, TX	S	35.94 MW	35.36 AW	74750 AAW	TXBLS	10//99-12//99
	Killeen-Temple MSA, TX	S	28.01 MW	26.08 AW	58260 AAW	TXBLS	10//99-12//99
	Laredo MSA, TX	S	26.82 MW	25.10 AW	55780 AAW	TXBLS	10//99-12//99
	Longview-Marshall MSA, TX	S	21.50 MW	19.20 AW	44720 AAW	TXBLS	10//99-12//99
	Lubbock MSA, TX	S	27.71 MW	25.61 AW	57640 AAW	TXBLS	10//99-12//99
	McAllen-Edinburg-Mission MSA, TX	S	27.77 MW	26.97 AW	57750 AAW	TXBLS	10//99-12//99
	Odessa-Midland MSA, TX	S	28.42 MW	28.07 AW	59120 AAW	TXBLS	10//99-12//99
	San Angelo MSA, TX	S	25.08 MW	24.42 AW	52170 AAW	TXBLS	10//99-12//99
	San Antonio MSA, TX	S	30.02 MW	30.35 AW	62430 AAW	TXBLS	10//99-12//99
	Sherman-Denison MSA, TX	S	35.61 MW	26.21 AW	74070 AAW	TXBLS	10//99-12//99
	Tyler MSA, TX	S	27.50 MW	23.98 AW	57200 AAW	TXBLS	10//99-12//99
	Victoria MSA, TX	S	28.77 MW	21.43 AW	59850 AAW	TXBLS	10//99-12//99

Occupation/Type/Industry	Location	Per	Low	Mid	High	Source	Date
Computer and Information Systems Manager	Waco MSA, TX	S	25.37 MW	25.64 AW	52780 AAW	TXBLS	10//99-12//99
	Utah	S	30.36 MW	31.25 AW	65000 AAW	UTBLS	10//99-12//99
	Provo-Orem MSA, UT	S	30.82 MW	30.56 AW	64120 AAW	UTBLS	10//99-12//99
	Salt Lake City-Ogden MSA, UT	S	31.94 MW	30.82 AW	66430 AAW	UTBLS	10//99-12//99
	Vermont	S	33.56 MW	36.38 AW	75680 AAW	VTBLS	10//99-12//99
	Burlington MSA, VT	S	39.08 MW	34.18 AW	81290 AAW	VTBLS	10//99-12//99
	Virginia	S	38.99 MW	39.59 AW	82350 AAW	VABLS	10//99-12//99
	Charlottesville MSA, VA	S	43.19 MW	44.62 AW	89830 AAW	VABLS	10//99-12//99
	Lynchburg MSA, VA	S	31.90 MW	35.17 AW	66340 AAW	VABLS	10//99-12//99
	Norfolk-Virginia Beach-Newport News MSA, VA-NC	S	31.73 MW	31.26 AW	66000 AAW	VABLS	10//99-12//99
	Richmond-Petersburg MSA, VA	S	35.37 MW	35.20 AW	73580 AAW	VABLS	10//99-12//99
	Roanoke MSA, VA	S	36.77 MW	37.03 AW	76480 AAW	VABLS	10//99-12//99
	Washington	S	37.57 MW	36.97 AW	76890 AAW	WABLS	10//99-12//99
	Bellingham MSA, WA	S	26.62 MW	25.78 AW	55360 AAW	WABLS	10//99-12//99
	Bremerton PMSA, WA	S	31.74 MW	31.54 AW	66020 AAW	WABLS	10//99-12//99
	Olympia PMSA, WA	S	32.64 MW	30.67 AW	67900 AAW	WABLS	10//99-12//99
	Richland-Kennewick-Pasco MSA, WA	S	41.56 MW	43.93 AW	86450 AAW	WABLS	10//99-12//99
	Seattle-Bellevue-Everett PMSA, WA	S	38.40 MW	38.65 AW	79870 AAW	WABLS	10//99-12//99
	Spokane MSA, WA	S	28.07 MW	28.41 AW	58390 AAW	WABLS	10//99-12//99
	Tacoma PMSA, WA	S	26.48 MW	24.77 AW	55070 AAW	WABLS	10//99-12//99
	Yakima MSA, WA	S	19.91 MW	18.28 AW	41420 AAW	WABLS	10//99-12//99
	West Virginia	S	24.71 MW	26.36 AW	54840 AAW	WVBLS	10//99-12//99
	Charleston MSA, WV	S	23.74 MW	23.47 AW	49380 AAW	WVBLS	10//99-12//99
	Huntington-Ashland MSA, WV-KY-OH	S	23.98 MW	23.26 AW	49880 AAW	WVBLS	10//99-12//99
	Parkersburg-Marietta MSA, WV-OH	S	26.88 MW	27.14 AW	55910 AAW	WVBLS	10//99-12//99
	Wheeling MSA, WV-OH	S	19.07 MW	17.57 AW	39660 AAW	WVBLS	10//99-12//99
	Wisconsin	S	30.06 MW	30.96 AW	64390 AAW	WIBLS	10//99-12//99
	Appleton-Oshkosh-Neenah MSA, WI	S	28.42 MW	28.13 AW	59120 AAW	WIBLS	10//99-12//99
	Green Bay MSA, WI	S	24.95 MW	20.23 AW	51890 AAW	WIBLS	10//99-12//99
	Janesville-Beloit MSA, WI	S	25.50 MW	25.72 AW	53040 AAW	WIBLS	10//99-12//99
	La Crosse MSA, WI-MN	S	24.24 MW	23.44 AW	50420 AAW	WIBLS	10//99-12//99
	Madison MSA, WI	S	32.33 MW	31.33 AW	67260 AAW	WIBLS	10//99-12//99
	Milwaukee-Waukesha PMSA, WI	S	35.33 MW	35.00 AW	73490 AAW	WIBLS	10//99-12//99
	Racine PMSA, WI	S	29.73 MW	28.82 AW	61840 AAW	WIBLS	10//99-12//99
	Sheboygan MSA, WI	S	25.40 MW	24.69 AW	52830 AAW	WIBLS	10//99-12//99
	Wausau MSA, WI	S	29.16 MW	27.06 AW	60660 AAW	WIBLS	10//99-12//99
	Wyoming	S	20.35 MW	22.28 AW	46340 AAW	WYBLS	10//99-12//99
	Puerto Rico	S	23.91 MW	25.41 AW	52860 AAW	PRBLS	10//99-12//99
	Caguas PMSA, PR	S	28.26 MW	29.74 AW	58790 AAW	PRBLS	10//99-12//99
	Mayaguez MSA, PR	S	15.88 MW	12.90 AW	33020 AAW	PRBLS	10//99-12//99
	San Juan-Bayamon PMSA, PR	S	26.01 MW	24.46 AW	54110 AAW	PRBLS	10//99-12//99
	Guam	S	26.17 MW	31.43 AW	65380 AAW	GUBLS	10//99-12//99
Computer, Automated Teller, and Office Machine Repairer	Alabama	S	14.19 MW	14.80 AW	30790 AAW	ALBLS	10//99-12//99
	Alaska	S	15.84 MW	16.61 AW	34550 AAW	AKBLS	10//99-12//99
	Arizona	S	12.75 MW	13.89 AW	28890 AAW	AZBLS	10//99-12//99
	Arkansas	S	13.03 MW	14.01 AW	29130 AAW	ARBLS	10//99-12//99
	California	S	16.67 MW	17.25 AW	35890 AAW	CABLS	10//99-12//99
	Colorado	S	14.8 MW	15.12 AW	31450 AAW	COBLS	10//99-12//99
	Connecticut	S	17.64 MW	18.01 AW	37470 AAW	CTBLS	10//99-12//99
	District of Columbia	S	18.68 MW	18.23 AW	37920 AAW	DCBLS	10//99-12//99
	Florida	S	12.88 MW	13.82 AW	28750 AAW	FLBLS	10//99-12//99
	Georgia	S	16.58 MW	17.14 AW	35660 AAW	GABLS	10//99-12//99
	Hawaii	S	15.46 MW	15.06 AW	31320 AAW	HIBLS	10//99-12//99
	Idaho	S	15.13 MW	15.24 AW	31700 AAW	IDBLS	10//99-12//99
	Illinois	S	14.6 MW	15.68 AW	32620 AAW	ILBLS	10//99-12//99
	Indiana	S	13.14 MW	14.01 AW	29140 AAW	INBLS	10//99-12//99
	Iowa	S	13.51 MW	13.86 AW	28820 AAW	IABLS	10//99-12//99
	Kansas	S	12.45 MW	13.86 AW	28830 AAW	KSBLS	10//99-12//99
	Kentucky	S	12.34 MW	13.50 AW	28090 AAW	KYBLS	10//99-12//99

Occupation/Type/Industry	Location	Per	Low	Mid	High	Source	Date
Computer, Automated Teller, and Office Machine Repairer	Louisiana	S	12.28 MW	13.31 AW	27680 AAW	LABLS	10//99-12//99
	Maine	S	12.13 MW	14.59 AW	30340 AAW	MEBLS	10//99-12//99
	Maryland	S	17.36 MW	17.60 AW	36610 AAW	MDBLS	10//99-12//99
	Massachusetts	S	14.89 MW	15.59 AW	32420 AAW	MABLS	10//99-12//99
	Michigan	S	12.65 MW	13.24 AW	27540 AAW	MIBLS	10//99-12//99
	Minnesota	S	14.62 MW	15.42 AW	32060 AAW	MNBLS	10//99-12//99
	Mississippi	S	14.74 MW	14.85 AW	30890 AAW	MSBLS	10//99-12//99
	Missouri	S	12.76 MW	13.30 AW	27660 AAW	MOBLS	10//99-12//99
	Montana	S	11.33 MW	12.00 AW	24950 AAW	MTBLS	10//99-12//99
	Nebraska	S	10.78 MW	12.15 AW	25270 AAW	NEBLS	10//99-12//99
	Nevada	S	13.3 MW	16.18 AW	33640 AAW	NVBLS	10//99-12//99
	New Hampshire	S	13.87 MW	14.10 AW	29330 AAW	NHBLS	10//99-12//99
	New Jersey	S	16.19 MW	16.76 AW	34860 AAW	NJBLS	10//99-12//99
	New Mexico	S	16.39 MW	15.97 AW	33220 AAW	NMBLS	10//99-12//99
	New York	S	14.76 MW	15.58 AW	32410 AAW	NYBLS	10//99-12//99
	North Carolina	S	13.57 MW	14.42 AW	29990 AAW	NCBLS	10//99-12//99
	North Dakota	S	11.69 MW	12.00 AW	24970 AAW	NDBLS	10//99-12//99
	Ohio	S	14.51 MW	14.82 AW	30820 AAW	OHBLS	10//99-12//99
	Oklahoma	S	8.35 MW	10.06 AW	20930 AAW	OKBLS	10//99-12//99
	Oregon	S	13.7 MW	15.31 AW	31840 AAW	ORBLS	10//99-12//99
	Pennsylvania	S	15.71 MW	16.09 AW	33460 AAW	PABLS	10//99-12//99
	Rhode Island	S	14.13 MW	15.22 AW	31650 AAW	RIBLS	10//99-12//99
	South Carolina	S	13.95 MW	15.41 AW	32060 AAW	SCBLS	10//99-12//99
	South Dakota	S	13.19 MW	14.69 AW	30560 AAW	SDBLS	10//99-12//99
	Tennessee	S	13.68 MW	13.89 AW	28900 AAW	TNBLS	10//99-12//99
	Texas	S	12.24 MW	12.99 AW	27020 AAW	TXBLS	10//99-12//99
	Utah	S	19.71 MW	18.98 AW	39480 AAW	UTBLS	10//99-12//99
	Vermont	S	13.25 MW	14.65 AW	30470 AAW	VTBLS	10//99-12//99
	Virginia	S	12.83 MW	13.34 AW	27750 AAW	VABLS	10//99-12//99
	Washington	S	13.25 MW	14.13 AW	29400 AAW	WABLS	10//99-12//99
	West Virginia	S	12.45 MW	12.48 AW	25950 AAW	WVBLS	10//99-12//99
	Wisconsin	S	16.66 MW	16.27 AW	33850 AAW	WIBLS	10//99-12//99
	Wyoming	S	6.56 MW	11.20 AW	23290 AAW	WYBLS	10//99-12//99
	Puerto Rico	S	8.19 MW	10.06 AW	20930 AAW	PRBLS	10//99-12//99
	Virgin Islands	S	12.03 MW	11.95 AW	24860 AAW	VIBLS	10//99-12//99
	Guam	S	12.1 MW	12.04 AW	25040 AAW	GUBLS	10//99-12//99
Computer Consultant	Phoenix, AZ	Y		99621 AW		PBJI	2000
Computer-Controlled Machine Tool Operator							
Metals and Plastics	Alabama	S	12.06 MW	12.17 AW	25310 AAW	ALBLS	10//99-12//99
Metals and Plastics	Arizona	S	13.55 MW	14.02 AW	29170 AAW	AZBLS	10//99-12//99
Metals and Plastics	Arkansas	S	10.41 MW	11.99 AW	24930 AAW	ARBLS	10//99-12//99
Metals and Plastics	California	S	13.49 MW	14.50 AW	30150 AAW	CABLS	10//99-12//99
Metals and Plastics	Colorado	S	15.49 MW	15.52 AW	32280 AAW	COBLS	10//99-12//99
Metals and Plastics	Connecticut	S	15.48 MW	15.70 AW	32650 AAW	CTBLS	10//99-12//99
Metals and Plastics	Delaware	S	14.71 MW	14.25 AW	29640 AAW	DEBLS	10//99-12//99
Metals and Plastics	Florida	S	12.09 MW	12.22 AW	25410 AAW	FLBLS	10//99-12//99
Metals and Plastics	Georgia	S	12.53 MW	12.80 AW	26630 AAW	GABLS	10//99-12//99
Metals and Plastics	Idaho	S	9.14 MW	10.31 AW	21450 AAW	IDBLS	10//99-12//99
Metals and Plastics	Illinois	S	12.33 MW	13.32 AW	27700 AAW	ILBLS	10//99-12//99
Metals and Plastics	Indiana	S	12.09 MW	12.92 AW	26880 AAW	INBLS	10//99-12//99
Metals and Plastics	Iowa	S	12.34 MW	12.45 AW	25900 AAW	IABLS	10//99-12//99
Metals and Plastics	Kansas	S	14.23 MW	14.98 AW	31150 AAW	KSBLS	10//99-12//99
Metals and Plastics	Kentucky	S	12.95 MW	12.98 AW	27000 AAW	KYBLS	10//99-12//99
Metals and Plastics	Louisiana	S	12.05 MW	12.00 AW	24960 AAW	LABLS	10//99-12//99
Metals and Plastics	Maine	S	12.04 MW	12.26 AW	25500 AAW	MEBLS	10//99-12//99
Metals and Plastics	Maryland	S	15.86 MW	15.44 AW	32120 AAW	MDBLS	10//99-12//99
Metals and Plastics	Massachusetts	S	16.85 MW	16.12 AW	33540 AAW	MABLS	10//99-12//99
Metals and Plastics	Michigan	S	13.7 MW	14.14 AW	29420 AAW	MIBLS	10//99-12//99
Metals and Plastics	Minnesota	S	14.88 MW	15.25 AW	31720 AAW	MNBLS	10//99-12//99
Metals and Plastics	Mississippi	S	11.26 MW	11.20 AW	23290 AAW	MSBLS	10//99-12//99
Metals and Plastics	Missouri	S	10.7 MW	12.60 AW	26210 AAW	MOBLS	10//99-12//99
Metals and Plastics	Nebraska	S	11.76 MW	11.73 AW	24400 AAW	NEBLS	10//99-12//99
Metals and Plastics	Nevada	S	10.25 MW	11.28 AW	23460 AAW	NVBLS	10//99-12//99
Metals and Plastics	New Hampshire	S	14.59 MW	15.59 AW	32430 AAW	NHBLS	10//99-12//99
Metals and Plastics	New Jersey	S	16.24 MW	15.21 AW	31640 AAW	NJBLS	10//99-12//99
Metals and Plastics	New Mexico	S	11.58 MW	11.15 AW	23190 AAW	NMBLS	10//99-12//99
Metals and Plastics	New York	S	12.82 MW	13.50 AW	28080 AAW	NYBLS	10//99-12//99
Metals and Plastics	North Carolina	S	13.09 MW	13.42 AW	27910 AAW	NCBLS	10//99-12//99

AAW Average annual wage	**AOH** Average offered, high	**ASH** Average starting, high	**H** Hourly	**M** Monthly	**S** Special: hourly and annual
AE Average entry wage	**AOL** Average offered, low	**ASL** Average starting, low	**HI** Highest wage paid	**MTC** Median total compensation	**TQ** Third quartile wage
AEX Average experienced wage	**APH** Average pay, high range	**AW** Average wage paid	**HR** High end range	**MW** Median wage paid	**W** Weekly
AO Average offered	**APL** Average pay, low range	**FQ** First quartile wage	**LR** Low end range	**SQ** Second quartile wage	**Y** Yearly

Occupation/Type/Industry	Location	Per	Low	Mid	High	Source	Date
Computer-Controlled Machine							
Tool Operator							
Metals and Plastics	North Dakota	S	8.46 MW	9.85 AW	20500 AAW	NDBLS	10//99-12//99
Metals and Plastics	Ohio	S	13.43 MW	13.64 AW	28370 AAW	OHBLS	10//99-12//99
Metals and Plastics	Oklahoma	S	12.7 MW	12.74 AW	26510 AAW	OKBLS	10//99-12//99
Metals and Plastics	Oregon	S	14.08 MW	14.53 AW	30210 AAW	ORBLS	10//99-12//99
Metals and Plastics	Pennsylvania	S	12.8 MW	12.93 AW	26900 AAW	PABLS	10//99-12//99
Metals and Plastics	Rhode Island	S	14.48 MW	14.80 AW	30780 AAW	RIBLS	10//99-12//99
Metals and Plastics	South Carolina	S	11.42 MW	12.53 AW	26050 AAW	SCBLS	10//99-12//99
Metals and Plastics	South Dakota	S	12.04 MW	12.06 AW	25080 AAW	SDBLS	10//99-12//99
Metals and Plastics	Tennessee	S	10.83 MW	11.53 AW	23980 AAW	TNBLS	10//99-12//99
Metals and Plastics	Texas	S	11.87 MW	12.62 AW	26250 AAW	TXBLS	10//99-12//99
Metals and Plastics	Vermont	S	10.67 MW	11.42 AW	23760 AAW	VTBLS	10//99-12//99
Metals and Plastics	Virginia	S	15.05 MW	15.97 AW	33230 AAW	VABLS	10//99-12//99
Metals and Plastics	Washington	S	13.67 MW	14.38 AW	29910 AAW	WABLS	10//99-12//99
Metals and Plastics	West Virginia	S	12.42 MW	12.56 AW	26120 AAW	WVBLS	10//99-12//99
Metals and Plastics	Wisconsin	S	14.41 MW	14.63 AW	30430 AAW	WIBLS	10//99-12//99
Metals and Plastics	Puerto Rico	S	6.51 MW	6.50 AW	13520 AAW	PRBLS	10//99-12//99
Computer Engineer	United States	Y	48280 AE			ELENTI	2000
Computer Hardware Engineer	Alabama	S	32.35 MW	31.88 AW	66310 AAW	ALBLS	10//99-12//99
	Arizona	S	31.57 MW	33.55 AW	69780 AAW	AZBLS	10//99-12//99
	Arkansas	S	25.65 MW	28.95 AW	60210 AAW	ARBLS	10//99-12//99
	California	S	34.75 MW	36.46 AW	75840 AAW	CABLS	10//99-12//99
	Colorado	S	33.38 MW	35.09 AW	72980 AAW	COBLS	10//99-12//99
	Connecticut	S	30.21 MW	30.07 AW	62550 AAW	CTBLS	10//99-12//99
	District of Columbia	S	30.33 MW	31.85 AW	66240 AAW	DCBLS	10//99-12//99
	Florida	S	27.19 MW	27.72 AW	57660 AAW	FLBLS	10//99-12//99
	Georgia	S	35.65 MW	33.57 AW	69820 AAW	GABLS	10//99-12//99
	Idaho	S	30.55 MW	31.51 AW	65550 AAW	IDBLS	10//99-12//99
	Illinois	S	26.87 MW	27.45 AW	57090 AAW	ILBLS	10//99-12//99
	Indiana	S	15.48 MW	19.52 AW	40600 AAW	INBLS	10//99-12//99
	Kansas	S	28.56 MW	28.57 AW	59420 AAW	KSBLS	10//99-12//99
	Kentucky	S	30.53 MW	33.21 AW	69080 AAW	KYBLS	10//99-12//99
	Louisiana	S	24.14 MW	26.09 AW	54270 AAW	LABLS	10//99-12//99
	Maryland	S	30.81 MW	30.83 AW	64120 AAW	MDBLS	10//99-12//99
	Massachusetts	S	37.48 MW	37.07 AW	77100 AAW	MABLS	10//99-12//99
	Michigan	S	34.88 MW	35.23 AW	73270 AAW	MIBLS	10//99-12//99
	Minnesota	S	29.36 MW	31.85 AW	66240 AAW	MNBLS	10//99-12//99
	Mississippi	S	21.43 MW	21.60 AW	44930 AAW	MSBLS	10//99-12//99
	Missouri	S	30.01 MW	30.66 AW	63780 AAW	MOBLS	10//99-12//99
	New Hampshire	S	30.89 MW	29.91 AW	62220 AAW	NHBLS	10//99-12//99
	New Jersey	S	32.17 MW	33.20 AW	69050 AAW	NJBLS	10//99-12//99
	New Mexico	S	28.45 MW	29.89 AW	62160 AAW	NMBLS	10//99-12//99
	New York	S	32.2 MW	36.17 AW	75240 AAW	NYBLS	10//99-12//99
	North Carolina	S	27.58 MW	28.10 AW	58440 AAW	NCBLS	10//99-12//99
	Ohio	S	21.43 MW	23.62 AW	49130 AAW	OHBLS	10//99-12//99
	Oklahoma	S	32.37 MW	33.48 AW	69630 AAW	OKBLS	10//99-12//99
	Pennsylvania	S	29.44 MW	29.16 AW	60660 AAW	PABLS	10//99-12//99
	Rhode Island	S	28.11 MW	29.10 AW	60530 AAW	RIBLS	10//99-12//99
	South Carolina	S	31.52 MW	31.84 AW	66230 AAW	SCBLS	10//99-12//99
	Tennessee	S	26.37 MW	24.40 AW	50750 AAW	TNBLS	10//99-12//99
	Texas	S	30.37 MW	31.43 AW	65380 AAW	TXBLS	10//99-12//99
	Utah	S	32.19 MW	32.24 AW	67050 AAW	UTBLS	10//99-12//99
	Virginia	S	32.57 MW	32.94 AW	68510 AAW	VABLS	10//99-12//99
	Washington	S	30.92 MW	30.63 AW	63710 AAW	WABLS	10//99-12//99
	Wisconsin	S	30.53 MW	30.52 AW	63480 AAW	WIBLS	10//99-12//99
Computer Network							
Administrator	Los Angeles County, CA	Y		71914 AW		LABJ	1999
Computer Operator	Alabama	S	11.48 MW	12.42 AW	25820 AAW	ALBLS	10//99-12//99
	Alaska	S	15.61 MW	17.26 AW	35900 AAW	AKBLS	10//99-12//99
	Arizona	S	12.15 MW	13.88 AW	28860 AAW	AZBLS	10//99-12//99
	Phoenix, AZ	Y		32800 AW		COMWO	1/99-2/99
	Arkansas	S	9.91 MW	10.68 AW	22210 AAW	ARBLS	10//99-12//99
	California	S	14.31 MW	15.13 AW	31470 AAW	CABLS	10//99-12//99
	Los Angeles, CA	Y		36300 AW		COMWO	1/99-2/99
	San Diego, CA	Y		33200 AW		COMWO	1/99-2/99
	San Francisco, CA	Y		35500 AW		COMWO	1/99-2/99
	Colorado	S	14.18 MW	14.56 AW	30290 AAW	COBLS	10//99-12//99

AAW	Average annual wage	AOH	Average offered, high	ASH	Average starting, high	H	Hourly			M	Monthly		S	Special: hourly and annual
AE	Average entry wage	AOL	Average offered, low	ASL	Average starting, low	HI	Highest wage paid			MTC	Median total compensation	TQ	Third quartile wage
AEX	Average experienced wage	APH	Average pay, high range	AW	Average wage paid	HR	High end range			MW	Median wage paid		W	Weekly
AO	Average offered	APL	Average pay, low range	FQ	First quartile wage	LR	Low end range			SQ	Second quartile wage		Y	Yearly

Occupation/Type/Industry	Location	Per	Low	Mid	High	Source	Date
Computer Operator	Denver, CO	Y		33200 AW		COMWO	1//99-2//99
	Connecticut	S	15.19 MW	15.93 AW	33130 AAW	CTBLS	10//99-12//99
	Delaware	S	13.6 MW	13.78 AW	28650 AAW	DEBLS	10//99-12//99
	District of Columbia	S	14.71 MW	14.71 AW	30600 AAW	DCBLS	10//99-12//99
	Washington, DC	Y		37200 AW		COMWO	1//99-2//99
	Florida	S	11.11 MW	11.87 AW	24680 AAW	FLBLS	10//99-12//99
	Miami, FL	Y		37100 AW		COMWO	1//99-2//99
	Georgia	S	12.52 MW	13.10 AW	27250 AAW	GABLS	10//99-12//99
	Atlanta, GA	Y		33000 AW		COMWO	1//99-2//99
	Hawaii	S	14.47 MW	14.85 AW	30890 AAW	HIBLS	10//99-12//99
	Idaho	S	11.6 MW	12.03 AW	25030 AAW	IDBLS	10//99-12//99
	Illinois	S	11.68 MW	13.03 AW	27110 AAW	ILBLS	10//99-12//99
	Chicago, IL	Y		33600 AW		COMWO	1//99-2//99
	Indiana	S	12.17 MW	12.80 AW	26620 AAW	INBLS	10//99-12//99
	Iowa	S	11.63 MW	12.05 AW	25070 AAW	IABLS	10//99-12//99
	Kansas	S	10.95 MW	11.78 AW	24500 AAW	KSBLS	10//99-12//99
	Kentucky	S	11.06 MW	11.90 AW	24750 AAW	KYBLS	10//99-12//99
	Louisiana	S	10.43 MW	11.39 AW	23690 AAW	LABLS	10//99-12//99
	Maine	S	12.24 MW	13.29 AW	27650 AAW	MEBLS	10//99-12//99
	Maryland	S	13.96 MW	14.04 AW	29210 AAW	MDBLS	10//99-12//99
	Massachusetts	S	15.59 MW	16.31 AW	33930 AAW	MABLS	10//99-12//99
	Boston, MA	Y		32700 AW		COMWO	1//99-2//99
	Michigan	S	12.43 MW	13.33 AW	27730 AAW	MIBLS	10//99-12//99
	Detroit, MI	Y		33800 AW		COMWO	1//99-2//99
	Minnesota	S	13.77 MW	14.06 AW	29250 AAW	MNBLS	10//99-12//99
	Minneapolis/St. Paul, MN	Y		31100 AW		COMWO	1//99-2//99
	Mississippi	S	10.4 MW	10.93 AW	22730 AAW	MSBLS	10//99-12//99
	Missouri	S	11.52 MW	12.34 AW	25670 AAW	MOBLS	10//99-12//99
	St. Louis, MO	Y		31800 AW		COMWO	1//99-2//99
	Montana	S	11.08 MW	11.53 AW	23970 AAW	MTBLS	10//99-12//99
	Nebraska	S	11.3 MW	11.87 AW	24680 AAW	NEBLS	10//99-12//99
	Nevada	S	13.17 MW	14.11 AW	29360 AAW	NVBLS	10//99-12//99
	New Hampshire	S	14.53 MW	14.85 AW	30890 AAW	NHBLS	10//99-12//99
	New Jersey	S	15.25 MW	15.79 AW	32850 AAW	NJBLS	10//99-12//99
	New Mexico	S	11.37 MW	11.87 AW	24680 AAW	NMBLS	10//99-12//99
	New York	S	15.16 MW	16.22 AW	33730 AAW	NYBLS	10//99-12//99
	New York, NY	Y		40700 AW		COMWO	1//99-2//99
	North Carolina	S	12.13 MW	12.77 AW	26560 AAW	NCBLS	10//99-12//99
	North Dakota	S	10.5 MW	11.39 AW	23700 AAW	NDBLS	10//99-12//99
	Ohio	S	12.4 MW	12.83 AW	26690 AAW	OHBLS	10//99-12//99
	Cleveland, OH	Y		34200 AW		COMWO	1//99-2//99
	Oklahoma	S	11.1 MW	12.06 AW	25090 AAW	OKBLS	10//99-12//99
	Oregon	S	12.82 MW	13.65 AW	28380 AAW	ORBLS	10//99-12//99
	Pennsylvania	S	12.52 MW	13.38 AW	27830 AAW	PABLS	10//99-12//99
	Philadelphia, PA	Y		33800 AW		COMWO	1//99-2//99
	Rhode Island	S	13.4 MW	13.88 AW	28870 AAW	RIBLS	10//99-12//99
	South Carolina	S	11.98 MW	12.74 AW	26500 AAW	SCBLS	10//99-12//99
	South Dakota	S	10.28 MW	10.57 AW	21990 AAW	SDBLS	10//99-12//99
	Tennessee	S	12.29 MW	13.22 AW	27490 AAW	TNBLS	10//99-12//99
	Texas	S	11.54 MW	12.36 AW	25710 AAW	TXBLS	10//99-12//99
	Austin, TX	Y		35900 AW		COMWO	1//99-2//99
	Dallas, TX	Y		33500 AW		COMWO	1//99-2//99
	Houston, TX	Y		30300 AW		COMWO	1//99-2//99
	Utah	S	9.36 MW	10.31 AW	21440 AAW	UTBLS	10//99-12//99
	Vermont	S	11.78 MW	12.96 AW	26960 AAW	VTBLS	10//99-12//99
	Virginia	S	12.41 MW	12.88 AW	26800 AAW	VABLS	10//99-12//99
	Washington	S	13.87 MW	14.19 AW	29520 AAW	WABLS	10//99-12//99
	Seattle, WA	Y		34500 AW		COMWO	1//99-2//99
	West Virginia	S	10.79 MW	11.45 AW	23830 AAW	WVBLS	10//99-12//99
	Wisconsin	S	11.91 MW	12.52 AW	26030 AAW	WIBLS	10//99-12//99
	Wyoming	S	10.5 MW	10.99 AW	22860 AAW	WYBLS	10//99-12//99
	Puerto Rico	S	8.37 MW	9.35 AW	19440 AAW	PRBLS	10//99-12//99
	Virgin Islands	S	11.68 MW	12.33 AW	25650 AAW	VIBLS	10//99-12//99
	Guam	S	12.59 MW	12.56 AW	26120 AAW	GUBLS	10//99-12//99
Computer Programmer	United States	H		22.12 AW		NCS98	1998
	Alabama	S	19.33 MW	21.58 AW	44890 AAW	ALBLS	10//99-12//99
	Anniston MSA, AL	S	21.21 MW	20.16 AW	44120 AAW	ALBLS	10//99-12//99
	Birmingham MSA, AL	S	23.67 MW	20.34 AW	49230 AAW	ALBLS	10//99-12//99
	Decatur MSA, AL	S	18.94 MW	16.27 AW	39400 AAW	ALBLS	10//99-12//99
	Dothan MSA, AL	S	20.08 MW	19.15 AW	41770 AAW	ALBLS	10//99-12//99
	Florence MSA, AL	S	18.78 MW	17.15 AW	39070 AAW	ALBLS	10//99-12//99
	Huntsville MSA, AL	S	21.86 MW	19.98 AW	45470 AAW	ALBLS	10//99-12//99

AAW Average annual wage	**AOH** Average offered, high	**ASH** Average starting, high	**H** Hourly	**M** Monthly	**S** Special: hourly and annual
AE Average entry wage	**AOL** Average offered, low	**ASL** Average starting, low	**HI** Highest wage paid	**MTC** Median total compensation	**TQ** Third quartile wage
AEX Average experienced wage	**APH** Average pay, high range	**AW** Average wage paid	**HR** High end range	**MW** Median wage paid	**W** Weekly
AO Average offered	**APL** Average pay, low range	**FQ** First quartile wage	**LR** Low end range	**SQ** Second quartile wage	**Y** Yearly

Occupation/Type/Industry	Location	Per	Low	Mid	High	Source	Date
Computer Programmer	Mobile MSA, AL	S	20.42 MW	18.57 AW	42470 AAW	ALBLS	10//99-12//99
	Montgomery MSA, AL	S	19.43 MW	18.21 AW	40410 AAW	ALBLS	10//99-12//99
	Alaska	S	25.26 MW	25.95 AW	53970 AAW	AKBLS	10//99-12//99
	Anchorage MSA, AK	S	25.88 MW	24.99 AW	53830 AAW	AKBLS	10//99-12//99
	Arizona	S	24.45 MW	27.11 AW	56400 AAW	AZBLS	10//99-12//99
	Flagstaff MSA, AZ-UT	S	17.00 MW	15.32 AW	35350 AAW	AZBLS	10//99-12//99
	Phoenix-Mesa MSA, AZ	S	28.00 MW	25.57 AW	58230 AAW	AZBLS	10//99-12//99
	Tucson MSA, AZ	S	22.14 MW	20.00 AW	46060 AAW	AZBLS	10//99-12//99
	Arkansas	S	20.91 MW	23.15 AW	48160 AAW	ARBLS	10//99-12//99
	Fayetteville-Springdale-Rogers MSA, AR	S	22.17 MW	21.05 AW	46120 AAW	ARBLS	10//99-12//99
	Little Rock-North Little Rock MSA, AR	S	21.66 MW	20.68 AW	45040 AAW	ARBLS	10//99-12//99
	California	S	28.16 MW	29.22 AW	60770 AAW	CABLS	10//99-12//99
	Bakersfield MSA, CA	S	26.03 MW	27.78 AW	54140 AAW	CABLS	10//99-12//99
	Chico-Paradise MSA, CA	S	18.89 MW	16.53 AW	39300 AAW	CABLS	10//99-12//99
	Fresno MSA, CA	S	22.79 MW	21.77 AW	47400 AAW	CABLS	10//99-12//99
	Los Angeles County, CA	Y		49548 AW		LABJ	1999
	Los Angeles-Long Beach PMSA, CA	S	26.67 MW	25.79 AW	55460 AAW	CABLS	10//99-12//99
	Merced MSA, CA	S	22.28 MW	21.85 AW	46330 AAW	CABLS	10//99-12//99
	Modesto MSA, CA	S	24.23 MW	24.51 AW	50390 AAW	CABLS	10//99-12//99
	Oakland PMSA, CA	S	31.53 MW	27.76 AW	65580 AAW	CABLS	10//99-12//99
	Orange County PMSA, CA	S	27.23 MW	26.69 AW	56640 AAW	CABLS	10//99-12//99
	Redding MSA, CA	S	25.02 MW	23.34 AW	52050 AAW	CABLS	10//99-12//99
	Riverside-San Bernardino PMSA, CA	S	23.39 MW	22.30 AW	48660 AAW	CABLS	10//99-12//99
	Sacramento PMSA, CA	S	25.22 MW	24.37 AW	52470 AAW	CABLS	10//99-12//99
	Salinas MSA, CA	S	22.80 MW	21.46 AW	47420 AAW	CABLS	10//99-12//99
	San Diego MSA, CA	S	26.10 MW	24.85 AW	54290 AAW	CABLS	10//99-12//99
	San Francisco PMSA, CA	S	31.86 MW	31.27 AW	66270 AAW	CABLS	10//99-12//99
	San Jose PMSA, CA	S	33.03 MW	33.46 AW	68700 AAW	CABLS	10//99-12//99
	Santa Barbara-Santa Maria-Lompoc MSA, CA	S	28.69 MW	28.31 AW	59670 AAW	CABLS	10//99-12//99
	Santa Cruz-Watsonville PMSA, CA	S	26.91 MW	24.96 AW	55980 AAW	CABLS	10//99-12//99
	Santa Rosa PMSA, CA	S	36.85 MW	40.03 AW	76650 AAW	CABLS	10//99-12//99
	Stockton-Lodi MSA, CA	S	22.22 MW	21.92 AW	46220 AAW	CABLS	10//99-12//99
	Vallejo-Fairfield-Napa PMSA, CA	S	23.57 MW	22.35 AW	49030 AAW	CABLS	10//99-12//99
	Ventura PMSA, CA	S	32.44 MW	30.30 AW	67470 AAW	CABLS	10//99-12//99
	Visalia-Tulare-Porterville MSA, CA	S	24.34 MW	24.56 AW	50630 AAW	CABLS	10//99-12//99
	Yolo PMSA, CA	S	20.32 MW	20.59 AW	42260 AAW	CABLS	10//99-12//99
	Yuba City MSA, CA	S	21.42 MW	21.69 AW	44540 AAW	CABLS	10//99-12//99
	Colorado	S	27.02 MW	26.88 AW	55920 AAW	COBLS	10//99-12//99
	Boulder-Longmont PMSA, CO	S	28.84 MW	29.03 AW	59990 AAW	COBLS	10//99-12//99
	Denver PMSA, CO	S	27.22 MW	27.89 AW	56630 AAW	COBLS	10//99-12//99
	Connecticut	S	27.8 MW	28.43 AW	59140 AAW	CTBLS	10//99-12//99
	Bridgeport PMSA, CT	S	27.81 MW	28.80 AW	57850 AAW	CTBLS	10//99-12//99
	Danbury PMSA, CT	S	31.57 MW	31.18 AW	65670 AAW	CTBLS	10//99-12//99
	Hartford MSA, CT	S	28.42 MW	27.48 AW	59120 AAW	CTBLS	10//99-12//99
	New Haven-Meriden PMSA, CT	S	26.17 MW	26.19 AW	54430 AAW	CTBLS	10//99-12//99
	New London-Norwich MSA, CT-RI	S	26.04 MW	24.54 AW	54160 AAW	CTBLS	10//99-12//99
	Stamford-Norwalk PMSA, CT	S	28.34 MW	27.06 AW	58940 AAW	CTBLS	10//99-12//99
	Delaware	S	26.5 MW	27.19 AW	56550 AAW	DEBLS	10//99-12//99
	Dover MSA, DE	S	19.46 MW	17.95 AW	40480 AAW	DEBLS	10//99-12//99
	Wilmington-Newark PMSA, DE-MD	S	28.00 MW	27.75 AW	58250 AAW	DEBLS	10//99-12//99
	District of Columbia	S	20.87 MW	23.75 AW	49400 AAW	DCBLS	10//99-12//99
	Washington PMSA, DC-MD-VA-WV	S	24.88 MW	23.18 AW	51740 AAW	DCBLS	10//99-12//99
	Florida	S	21.88 MW	23.22 AW	48300 AAW	FLBLS	10//99-12//99
	Daytona Beach MSA, FL	S	16.61 MW	16.79 AW	34560 AAW	FLBLS	10//99-12//99
	Fort Lauderdale PMSA, FL	S	22.61 MW	20.57 AW	47030 AAW	FLBLS	10//99-12//99
	Fort Myers-Cape Coral MSA, FL	S	22.14 MW	21.15 AW	46040 AAW	FLBLS	10//99-12//99
	Fort Pierce-Port St. Lucie MSA, FL	S	17.78 MW	15.40 AW	36990 AAW	FLBLS	10//99-12//99
	Fort Walton Beach MSA, FL	S	24.10 MW	23.27 AW	50120 AAW	FLBLS	10//99-12//99

AAW Average annual wage	**AOH** Average offered, high	**ASH** Average starting, high	**H** Hourly	**M** Monthly	**S** Special: hourly and annual
AE Average entry wage	**AOL** Average offered, low	**ASL** Average starting, low	**HI** Highest wage paid	**MTC** Median total compensation	**TQ** Third quartile wage
AEX Average experienced wage	**APH** Average pay, high range	**AW** Average wage paid	**HR** High end range	**MW** Median wage paid	**W** Weekly
AO Average offered	**APL** Average pay, low range	**FQ** First quartile wage	**LR** Low end range	**SQ** Second quartile wage	**Y** Yearly

Occupation/Type/Industry	Location	Per	Low	Mid	High	Source	Date
Computer Programmer	Gainesville MSA, FL	S	20.94 MW	19.97 AW	43550 AAW	FLBLS	10//99-12//99
	Jacksonville MSA, FL	S	25.45 MW	24.54 AW	52940 AAW	FLBLS	10//99-12//99
	Lakeland-Winter Haven MSA, FL	S	22.19 MW	20.15 AW	46140 AAW	FLBLS	10//99-12//99
	Melbourne-Titusville-Palm Bay MSA, FL	S	23.39 MW	19.87 AW	48650 AAW	FLBLS	10//99-12//99
	Miami PMSA, FL	S	22.83 MW	22.11 AW	47480 AAW	FLBLS	10//99-12//99
	Naples MSA, FL	S	25.89 MW	22.62 AW	53850 AAW	FLBLS	10//99-12//99
	Ocala MSA, FL	S	21.38 MW	21.25 AW	44470 AAW	FLBLS	10//99-12//99
	Orlando MSA, FL	S	23.10 MW	22.13 AW	48050 AAW	FLBLS	10//99-12//99
	Panama City MSA, FL	S	26.60 MW	23.67 AW	55330 AAW	FLBLS	10//99-12//99
	Pensacola MSA, FL	S	15.73 MW	13.21 AW	32710 AAW	FLBLS	10//99-12//99
	Punta Gorda MSA, FL	S	14.38 MW	15.11 AW	29910 AAW	FLBLS	10//99-12//99
	Sarasota-Bradenton MSA, FL	S	24.78 MW	19.86 AW	51540 AAW	FLBLS	10//99-12//99
	Tallahassee MSA, FL	S	19.75 MW	20.04 AW	41080 AAW	FLBLS	10//99-12//99
	Tampa-St. Petersburg-Clearwater MSA, FL	S	23.63 MW	22.14 AW	49160 AAW	FLBLS	10//99-12//99
	West Palm Beach-Boca Raton MSA, FL	S	27.41 MW	27.41 AW	57010 AAW	FLBLS	10//99-12//99
	Georgia	S	23.56 MW	25.93 AW	53930 AAW	GABLS	10//99-12//99
	Albany MSA, GA	S	20.63 MW	19.28 AW	42900 AAW	GABLS	10//99-12//99
	Athens MSA, GA	S	22.31 MW	18.57 AW	46400 AAW	GABLS	10//99-12//99
	Atlanta MSA, GA	S	26.87 MW	24.60 AW	55890 AAW	GABLS	10//99-12//99
	Augusta-Aiken MSA, GA-SC	S	28.28 MW	29.72 AW	58830 AAW	GABLS	10//99-12//99
	Columbus MSA, GA-AL	S	18.91 MW	16.17 AW	39320 AAW	GABLS	10//99-12//99
	Macon MSA, GA	S	22.76 MW	22.13 AW	47350 AAW	GABLS	10//99-12//99
	Savannah MSA, GA	S	22.24 MW	19.90 AW	46250 AAW	GABLS	10//99-12//99
	Hawaii	S	19.81 MW	20.37 AW	42380 AAW	HIBLS	10//99-12//99
	Honolulu MSA, HI	S	20.34 MW	19.80 AW	42320 AAW	HIBLS	10//99-12//99
	Idaho	S	21.16 MW	23.29 AW	48440 AAW	IDBLS	10//99-12//99
	Boise City MSA, ID	S	23.76 MW	20.62 AW	49430 AAW	IDBLS	10//99-12//99
	Illinois	S	22.55 MW	24.16 AW	50260 AAW	ILBLS	10//99-12//99
	Bloomington-Normal MSA, IL	S	27.45 MW	26.07 AW	57100 AAW	ILBLS	10//99-12//99
	Champaign-Urbana MSA, IL	S	22.97 MW	22.37 AW	47780 AAW	ILBLS	10//99-12//99
	Chicago PMSA, IL	S	24.15 MW	22.63 AW	50230 AAW	ILBLS	10//99-12//99
	Kankakee PMSA, IL	S	18.03 MW	18.79 AW	37510 AAW	ILBLS	10//99-12//99
	Peoria-Pekin MSA, IL	S	19.75 MW	19.59 AW	41070 AAW	ILBLS	10//99-12//99
	Rockford MSA, IL	S	23.36 MW	24.06 AW	48590 AAW	ILBLS	10//99-12//99
	Springfield MSA, IL	S	19.52 MW	18.06 AW	40610 AAW	ILBLS	10//99-12//99
	Indiana	S	20.84 MW	21.56 AW	44850 AAW	INBLS	10//99-12//99
	Bloomington MSA, IN	S	18.75 MW	18.09 AW	39010 AAW	INBLS	10//99-12//99
	Elkhart-Goshen MSA, IN	S	21.45 MW	20.97 AW	44610 AAW	INBLS	10//99-12//99
	Evansville-Henderson MSA, IN-KY	S	20.05 MW	19.43 AW	41700 AAW	INBLS	10//99-12//99
	Fort Wayne MSA, IN	S	21.04 MW	20.00 AW	43760 AAW	INBLS	10//99-12//99
	Gary PMSA, IN	S	21.17 MW	20.29 AW	44030 AAW	INBLS	10//99-12//99
	Indianapolis MSA, IN	S	22.51 MW	21.76 AW	46820 AAW	INBLS	10//99-12//99
	Kokomo MSA, IN	S	19.24 MW	21.00 AW	40010 AAW	INBLS	10//99-12//99
	Lafayette MSA, IN	S	17.26 MW	16.32 AW	35910 AAW	INBLS	10//99-12//99
	Muncie MSA, IN	S	17.03 MW	15.96 AW	35430 AAW	INBLS	10//99-12//99
	South Bend MSA, IN	S	22.33 MW	21.96 AW	46450 AAW	INBLS	10//99-12//99
	Terre Haute MSA, IN	S	17.42 MW	16.81 AW	36230 AAW	INBLS	10//99-12//99
	Iowa	S	21.39 MW	22.25 AW	46290 AAW	IABLS	10//99-12//99
	Cedar Rapids MSA, IA	S	23.01 MW	22.25 AW	47860 AAW	IABLS	10//99-12//99
	Davenport-Moline-Rock Island MSA, IA-IL	S	20.70 MW	18.74 AW	43050 AAW	IABLS	10//99-12//99
	Dubuque MSA, IA	S	18.87 MW	17.72 AW	39240 AAW	IABLS	10//99-12//99
	Iowa City MSA, IA	S	19.46 MW	19.98 AW	40470 AAW	IABLS	10//99-12//99
	Sioux City MSA, IA-NE	S	20.36 MW	19.97 AW	42340 AAW	IABLS	10//99-12//99
	Waterloo-Cedar Falls MSA, IA	S	17.85 MW	16.89 AW	37120 AAW	IABLS	10//99-12//99
	Kansas	S	22.96 MW	24.01 AW	49930 AAW	KSBLS	10//99-12//99
	Lawrence MSA, KS	S	20.02 MW	18.87 AW	41650 AAW	KSBLS	10//99-12//99
	Topeka MSA, KS	S	20.33 MW	19.38 AW	42280 AAW	KSBLS	10//99-12//99
	Wichita MSA, KS	S	23.69 MW	22.89 AW	49280 AAW	KSBLS	10//99-12//99
	Kentucky	S	20 MW	21.44 AW	44600 AAW	KYBLS	10//99-12//99
	Lexington MSA, KY	S	23.27 MW	22.34 AW	48410 AAW	KYBLS	10//99-12//99
	Louisville MSA, KY-IN	S	21.05 MW	19.55 AW	43780 AAW	KYBLS	10//99-12//99
	Louisiana	S	20.12 MW	21.26 AW	44210 AAW	LABLS	10//99-12//99
	Alexandria MSA, LA	S	19.87 MW	18.59 AW	41340 AAW	LABLS	10//99-12//99
	Baton Rouge MSA, LA	S	20.66 MW	18.97 AW	42980 AAW	LABLS	10//99-12//99
	Lafayette MSA, LA	S	21.33 MW	20.98 AW	44360 AAW	LABLS	10//99-12//99
	Lake Charles MSA, LA	S	18.59 MW	17.20 AW	38670 AAW	LABLS	10//99-12//99

AAW	Average annual wage	AOH	Average offered, high	ASH	Average starting, high
AE	Average entry wage	AOL	Average offered, low	ASL	Average starting, low
AEX	Average experienced wage	APH	Average pay, high range	AW	Average wage paid
AO	Average offered	APL	Average pay, low range	FQ	First quartile wage

H	Hourly	M	Monthly
HI	Highest wage paid	MTC	Median total compensation
HR	High end range	MW	Median wage paid
LR	Low end range	SQ	Second quartile wage

S	Special: hourly and annual
TQ	Third quartile wage
W	Weekly
Y	Yearly

Occupation/Type/Industry	Location	Per	Low	Mid	High	Source	Date
Computer Programmer	Monroe MSA, LA	S	17.30 mw	17.81 aw	35970 aaw	LABLS	10//99-12//99
	New Orleans MSA, LA	S	23.04 mw	22.51 aw	47920 aaw	LABLS	10//99-12//99
	Shreveport-Bossier City MSA, LA	S	21.14 mw	18.72 aw	43980 aaw	LABLS	10//99-12//99
	Maine	S	20.93 mw	21.86 aw	45470 aaw	MEBLS	10//99-12//99
	Bangor MSA, ME	S	19.50 mw	17.08 aw	40570 aaw	MEBLS	10//99-12//99
	Lewiston-Auburn MSA, ME	S	19.47 mw	19.24 aw	40490 aaw	MEBLS	10//99-12//99
	Portland MSA, ME	S	23.82 mw	23.15 aw	49550 aaw	MEBLS	10//99-12//99
	Maryland	S	25.86 mw	27.96 aw	58160 aaw	MDBLS	10//99-12//99
	Baltimore PMSA, MD	S	30.73 mw	28.74 aw	63930 aaw	MDBLS	10//99-12//99
	Massachusetts	S	28.62 mw	29.24 aw	60810 aaw	MABLS	10//99-12//99
	Barnstable-Yarmouth MSA, MA	S	22.00 mw	21.43 aw	45760 aaw	MABLS	10//99-12//99
	Boston PMSA, MA-NH	S	29.43 mw	28.63 aw	61220 aaw	MABLS	10//99-12//99
	Brockton PMSA, MA	S	25.93 mw	25.08 aw	53930 aaw	MABLS	10//99-12//99
	Fitchburg-Leominster PMSA, MA	S	25.01 mw	24.44 aw	52020 aaw	MABLS	10//99-12//99
	Lawrence PMSA, MA-NH	S	29.22 mw	29.73 aw	60780 aaw	MABLS	10//99-12//99
	New Bedford PMSA, MA	S	25.80 mw	24.71 aw	53670 aaw	MABLS	10//99-12//99
	Pittsfield MSA, MA	S	26.80 mw	27.81 aw	55740 aaw	MABLS	10//99-12//99
	Springfield MSA, MA	S	29.98 mw	29.25 aw	62360 aaw	MABLS	10//99-12//99
	Worcester PMSA, MA-CT	S	27.20 mw	27.01 aw	56590 aaw	MABLS	10//99-12//99
	Michigan	S	24.55 mw	25.35 aw	52740 aaw	MIBLS	10//99-12//99
	Ann Arbor PMSA, MI	S	22.12 mw	21.62 aw	46010 aaw	MIBLS	10//99-12//99
	Detroit PMSA, MI	S	26.80 mw	26.52 aw	55740 aaw	MIBLS	10//99-12//99
	Flint PMSA, MI	S	26.50 mw	26.64 aw	55110 aaw	MIBLS	10//99-12//99
	Grand Rapids-Muskegon-Holland MSA, MI	S	24.23 mw	23.73 aw	50410 aaw	MIBLS	10//99-12//99
	Jackson MSA, MI	S	18.54 mw	16.96 aw	38560 aaw	MIBLS	10//99-12//99
	Kalamazoo-Battle Creek MSA, MI	S	23.70 mw	23.38 aw	49300 aaw	MIBLS	10//99-12//99
	Lansing-East Lansing MSA, MI	S	21.99 mw	20.70 aw	45740 aaw	MIBLS	10//99-12//99
	Saginaw-Bay City-Midland MSA, MI	S	18.81 mw	17.36 aw	39120 aaw	MIBLS	10//99-12//99
	Minnesota	S	23.99 mw	25.58 aw	53220 aaw	MNBLS	10//99-12//99
	Duluth-Superior MSA, MN-WI	S	18.09 mw	18.12 aw	37630 aaw	MNBLS	10//99-12//99
	Minneapolis-St. Paul MSA, MN-WI	S	25.59 mw	24.18 aw	53220 aaw	MNBLS	10//99-12//99
	St. Cloud MSA, MN	S	19.56 mw	17.99 aw	40690 aaw	MNBLS	10//99-12//99
	Mississippi	S	17.71 mw	19.39 aw	40340 aaw	MSBLS	10//99-12//99
	Biloxi-Gulfport-Pascagoula MSA, MS	S	19.18 mw	16.22 aw	39890 aaw	MSBLS	10//99-12//99
	Jackson MSA, MS	S	19.49 mw	17.91 aw	40540 aaw	MSBLS	10//99-12//99
	Missouri	S	23.84 mw	24.82 aw	51630 aaw	MOBLS	10//99-12//99
	Columbia MSA, MO	S	20.90 mw	19.36 aw	43460 aaw	MOBLS	10//99-12//99
	Joplin MSA, MO	S	18.73 mw	17.65 aw	38950 aaw	MOBLS	10//99-12//99
	Kansas City MSA, MO-KS	S	25.63 mw	24.54 aw	53310 aaw	MOBLS	10//99-12//99
	St. Joseph MSA, MO	S	22.56 mw	22.67 aw	46920 aaw	MOBLS	10//99-12//99
	St. Louis MSA, MO-IL	S	25.54 mw	24.33 aw	53110 aaw	MOBLS	10//99-12//99
	Springfield MSA, MO	S	20.64 mw	19.19 aw	42940 aaw	MOBLS	10//99-12//99
	Montana	S	17.73 mw	18.59 aw	38660 aaw	MTBLS	10//99-12//99
	Great Falls MSA, MT	S	17.36 mw	16.94 aw	36110 aaw	MTBLS	10//99-12//99
	Missoula MSA, MT	S	16.29 mw	15.45 aw	33880 aaw	MTBLS	10//99-12//99
	Nebraska	S	20.4 mw	21.79 aw	45330 aaw	NEBLS	10//99-12//99
	Lincoln MSA, NE	S	21.04 mw	20.69 aw	43760 aaw	NEBLS	10//99-12//99
	Omaha MSA, NE-IA	S	22.13 mw	20.43 aw	46020 aaw	NEBLS	10//99-12//99
	Nevada	S	23.43 mw	24.44 aw	50840 aaw	NVBLS	10//99-12//99
	Las Vegas MSA, NV-AZ	S	24.18 mw	22.91 aw	50300 aaw	NVBLS	10//99-12//99
	Reno MSA, NV	S	26.29 mw	24.84 aw	54670 aaw	NVBLS	10//99-12//99
	New Hampshire	S	23.78 mw	24.86 aw	51710 aaw	NHBLS	10//99-12//99
	Manchester PMSA, NH	S	23.84 mw	23.81 aw	49590 aaw	NHBLS	10//99-12//99
	Nashua PMSA, NH	S	27.97 mw	28.48 aw	58170 aaw	NHBLS	10//99-12//99
	Portsmouth-Rochester PMSA, NH-ME	S	22.40 mw	21.05 aw	46600 aaw	NHBLS	10//99-12//99
	New Jersey	S	31.69 mw	31.73 aw	66000 aaw	NJBLS	10//99-12//99
	Atlantic-Cape May PMSA, NJ	S	27.67 mw	26.44 aw	57560 aaw	NJBLS	10//99-12//99
	Bergen-Passaic PMSA, NJ	S	28.01 mw	26.89 aw	58270 aaw	NJBLS	10//99-12//99
	Jersey City PMSA, NJ	S	30.02 mw	31.05 aw	62440 aaw	NJBLS	10//99-12//99
	Monmouth-Ocean PMSA, NJ	S	28.41 mw	27.73 aw	59100 aaw	NJBLS	10//99-12//99
	Newark PMSA, NJ	S	33.06 mw	32.94 aw	68770 aaw	NJBLS	10//99-12//99
	Trenton PMSA, NJ	S	29.48 mw	28.87 aw	61320 aaw	NJBLS	10//99-12//99

AAW Average annual wage	AOH Average offered, high	ASH Average starting, high	H Hourly	M Monthly	S Special: hourly and annual
AE Average entry wage	AOL Average offered, low	ASL Average starting, low	HI Highest wage paid	MTC Median total compensation	TQ Third quartile wage
AEX Average experienced wage	APH Average pay, high range	AW Average wage paid	HR High end range	MW Median wage paid	W Weekly
AO Average offered	APL Average pay, low range	FQ First quartile wage	LR Low end range	SQ Second quartile wage	Y Yearly

Occupation/Type/Industry	Location	Per	Low	Mid	High	Source	Date
Computer Programmer	Vineland-Millville-Bridgeton PMSA, NJ	S	26.76 MW	25.96 AW	55660 AAW	NJBLS	10//99-12//99
	New Mexico	S	20.02 MW	22.16 AW	46100 AAW	NMBLS	10//99-12//99
	Albuquerque MSA, NM	S	23.06 MW	20.88 AW	47970 AAW	NMBLS	10//99-12//99
	Santa Fe MSA, NM	S	23.90 MW	22.93 AW	49720 AAW	NMBLS	10//99-12//99
	New York	S	26.55 MW	28.64 AW	59560 AAW	NYBLS	10//99-12//99
	Albany-Schenectady-Troy MSA, NY	S	25.31 MW	24.59 AW	52650 AAW	NYBLS	10//99-12//99
	Binghamton MSA, NY	S	22.15 MW	16.03 AW	46070 AAW	NYBLS	10//99-12//99
	Buffalo-Niagara Falls MSA, NY	S	23.10 MW	22.08 AW	48050 AAW	NYBLS	10//99-12//99
	Elmira MSA, NY	S	23.97 MW	22.38 AW	49860 AAW	NYBLS	10//99-12//99
	Glens Falls MSA, NY	S	20.99 MW	20.62 AW	43650 AAW	NYBLS	10//99-12//99
	Jamestown MSA, NY	S	19.70 MW	18.67 AW	40970 AAW	NYBLS	10//99-12//99
	Nassau-Suffolk PMSA, NY	S	31.20 MW	29.70 AW	64890 AAW	NYBLS	10//99-12//99
	New York PMSA, NY	S	29.85 MW	27.77 AW	62090 AAW	NYBLS	10//99-12//99
	Rochester MSA, NY	S	26.00 MW	24.46 AW	54080 AAW	NYBLS	10//99-12//99
	Syracuse MSA, NY	S	27.88 MW	28.57 AW	58000 AAW	NYBLS	10//99-12//99
	Utica-Rome MSA, NY	S	21.92 MW	21.77 AW	45580 AAW	NYBLS	10//99-12//99
	North Carolina	S	27.46 MW	28.01 AW	58260 AAW	NCBLS	10//99-12//99
	Asheville MSA, NC	S	20.39 MW	18.32 AW	42410 AAW	NCBLS	10//99-12//99
	Charlotte-Gastonia-Rock Hill MSA, NC-SC	S	27.81 MW	26.95 AW	57830 AAW	NCBLS	10//99-12//99
	Fayetteville MSA, NC	S	14.89 MW	14.71 AW	30980 AAW	NCBLS	10//99-12//99
	Greensboro--Winston-Salem--High Point MSA, NC	S	23.94 MW	22.95 AW	49800 AAW	NCBLS	10//99-12//99
	Greenville MSA, NC	S	18.38 MW	18.97 AW	38240 AAW	NCBLS	10//99-12//99
	Hickory-Morganton-Lenoir MSA, NC	S	21.76 MW	20.06 AW	45260 AAW	NCBLS	10//99-12//99
	Raleigh-Durham-Chapel Hill MSA, NC	S	30.39 MW	30.78 AW	63210 AAW	NCBLS	10//99-12//99
	Wilmington MSA, NC	S	20.68 MW	19.91 AW	43020 AAW	NCBLS	10//99-12//99
	North Dakota	S	17.69 MW	18.85 AW	39210 AAW	NDBLS	10//99-12//99
	Fargo-Moorhead MSA, ND-MN	S	19.78 MW	18.08 AW	41130 AAW	NDBLS	10//99-12//99
	Ohio	S	23.06 MW	24.16 AW	50240 AAW	OHBLS	10//99-12//99
	Akron PMSA, OH	S	24.81 MW	23.17 AW	51610 AAW	OHBLS	10//99-12//99
	Canton-Massillon MSA, OH	S	18.29 MW	15.27 AW	38040 AAW	OHBLS	10//99-12//99
	Cincinnati PMSA, OH-KY-IN	S	23.39 MW	22.54 AW	48660 AAW	OHBLS	10//99-12//99
	Cleveland-Lorain-Elyria PMSA, OH	S	24.78 MW	23.16 AW	51550 AAW	OHBLS	10//99-12//99
	Columbus MSA, OH	S	25.82 MW	25.11 AW	53710 AAW	OHBLS	10//99-12//99
	Dayton-Springfield MSA, OH	S	22.99 MW	21.69 AW	47830 AAW	OHBLS	10//99-12//99
	Hamilton-Middletown PMSA, OH	S	23.87 MW	23.27 AW	49650 AAW	OHBLS	10//99-12//99
	Lima MSA, OH	S	25.26 MW	23.16 AW	52540 AAW	OHBLS	10//99-12//99
	Mansfield MSA, OH	S	20.14 MW	19.88 AW	41890 AAW	OHBLS	10//99-12//99
	Steubenville-Weirton MSA, OH-WV	S	19.92 MW	18.56 AW	41420 AAW	OHBLS	10//99-12//99
	Toledo MSA, OH	S	20.38 MW	20.44 AW	42380 AAW	OHBLS	10//99-12//99
	Youngstown-Warren MSA, OH	S	19.10 MW	17.51 AW	39790 AAW	OHBLS	10//99-12//99
	Oklahoma	S	22.35 MW	24.30 AW	50540 AAW	OKBLS	10//99-12//99
	Oklahoma City MSA, OK	S	21.00 MW	20.68 AW	43690 AAW	OKBLS	10//99-12//99
	Tulsa MSA, OK	S	26.74 MW	24.23 AW	55620 AAW	OKBLS	10//99-12//99
	Oregon	S	24.23 MW	25.43 AW	52900 AAW	ORBLS	10//99-12//99
	Corvallis MSA, OR	S	21.19 MW	19.87 AW	44070 AAW	ORBLS	10//99-12//99
	Eugene-Springfield MSA, OR	S	25.28 MW	22.07 AW	52580 AAW	ORBLS	10//99-12//99
	Medford-Ashland MSA, OR	S	18.27 MW	16.86 AW	37990 AAW	ORBLS	10//99-12//99
	Portland-Vancouver PMSA, OR-WA	S	27.76 MW	25.84 AW	57740 AAW	ORBLS	10//99-12//99
	Salem PMSA, OR	S	22.04 MW	21.64 AW	45840 AAW	ORBLS	10//99-12//99
	Pennsylvania	S	23.72 MW	25.47 AW	52970 AAW	PABLS	10//99-12//99
	Allentown-Bethlehem-Easton MSA, PA	S	23.12 MW	22.21 AW	48100 AAW	PABLS	10//99-12//99
	Altoona MSA, PA	S	19.40 MW	18.19 AW	40350 AAW	PABLS	10//99-12//99
	Erie MSA, PA	S	19.04 MW	18.35 AW	39610 AAW	PABLS	10//99-12//99
	Harrisburg-Lebanon-Carlisle MSA, PA	S	23.49 MW	22.26 AW	48860 AAW	PABLS	10//99-12//99
	Johnstown MSA, PA	S	18.90 MW	17.73 AW	39300 AAW	PABLS	10//99-12//99
	Lancaster MSA, PA	S	22.27 MW	21.47 AW	46320 AAW	PABLS	10//99-12//99
	Philadelphia PMSA, PA-NJ	S	27.29 MW	25.27 AW	56760 AAW	PABLS	10//99-12//99
	Pittsburgh MSA, PA	S	25.02 MW	23.62 AW	52030 AAW	PABLS	10//99-12//99

Occupation/Type/Industry	Location	Per	Low	Mid	High	Source	Date
Computer Programmer	Reading MSA, PA	S	22.70 MW	21.45 AW	47210 AAW	PABLS	10//99-12//99
	Scranton--Wilkes-Barre-- Hazleton MSA, PA	S	21.92 MW	21.29 AW	45580 AAW	PABLS	10//99-12//99
	Williamsport MSA, PA	S	21.79 MW	19.29 AW	45320 AAW	PABLS	10//99-12//99
	York MSA, PA	S	18.75 MW	18.66 AW	39000 AAW	PABLS	10//99-12//99
	Rhode Island	S	23.06 MW	24.17 AW	50260 AAW	RIBLS	10//99-12//99
	Providence-Fall River- Warwick MSA, RI-MA	S	22.95 MW	22.40 AW	47730 AAW	RIBLS	10//99-12//99
	South Carolina	S	23.75 MW	24.85 AW	51680 AAW	SCBLS	10//99-12//99
	Charleston-North Charleston MSA, SC	S	22.84 MW	20.60 AW	47500 AAW	SCBLS	10//99-12//99
	Columbia MSA, SC	S	25.22 MW	24.51 AW	52460 AAW	SCBLS	10//99-12//99
	Florence MSA, SC	S	20.50 MW	19.32 AW	42640 AAW	SCBLS	10//99-12//99
	Greenville-Spartanburg- Anderson MSA, SC	S	22.16 MW	19.82 AW	46080 AAW	SCBLS	10//99-12//99
	Myrtle Beach MSA, SC	S	22.08 MW	20.69 AW	45920 AAW	SCBLS	10//99-12//99
	South Dakota	S	18.75 MW	19.39 AW	40320 AAW	SDBLS	10//99-12//99
	Rapid City MSA, SD	S	18.88 MW	18.89 AW	39270 AAW	SDBLS	10//99-12//99
	Sioux Falls MSA, SD	S	19.94 MW	19.22 AW	41470 AAW	SDBLS	10//99-12//99
	Tennessee	S	23.68 MW	24.77 AW	51530 AAW	TNBLS	10//99-12//99
	Chattanooga MSA, TN-GA	S	20.57 MW	19.26 AW	42790 AAW	TNBLS	10//99-12//99
	Jackson MSA, TN	S	18.25 MW	16.15 AW	37960 AAW	TNBLS	10//99-12//99
	Johnson City-Kingsport-Bristol MSA, TN-VA	S	17.74 MW	15.51 AW	36900 AAW	TNBLS	10//99-12//99
	Knoxville MSA, TN	S	25.04 MW	24.16 AW	52090 AAW	TNBLS	10//99-12//99
	Memphis MSA, TN-AR-MS	S	23.93 MW	23.16 AW	49780 AAW	MSBLS	10//99-12//99
	Nashville MSA, TN	S	26.65 MW	26.29 AW	55430 AAW	TNBLS	10//99-12//99
	Texas	S	26.41 MW	28.02 AW	58290 AAW	TXBLS	10//99-12//99
	Abilene MSA, TX	S	23.35 MW	22.02 AW	48570 AAW	TXBLS	10//99-12//99
	Amarillo MSA, TX	S	23.81 MW	23.26 AW	49530 AAW	TXBLS	10//99-12//99
	Austin-San Marcos MSA, TX	S	30.00 MW	28.43 AW	62390 AAW	TXBLS	10//99-12//99
	Beaumont-Port Arthur MSA, TX	S	21.99 MW	20.69 AW	45740 AAW	TXBLS	10//99-12//99
	Brazoria PMSA, TX	S	25.18 MW	27.56 AW	52370 AAW	TXBLS	10//99-12//99
	Brownsville-Harlingen-San Benito MSA, TX	S	18.35 MW	17.79 AW	38170 AAW	TXBLS	10//99-12//99
	Bryan-College Station MSA, TX	S	21.12 MW	21.35 AW	43920 AAW	TXBLS	10//99-12//99
	Corpus Christi MSA, TX	S	23.40 MW	21.66 AW	48660 AAW	TXBLS	10//99-12//99
	Dallas PMSA, TX	S	27.51 MW	26.13 AW	57230 AAW	TXBLS	10//99-12//99
	El Paso MSA, TX	S	28.71 MW	23.61 AW	59710 AAW	TXBLS	10//99-12//99
	Fort Worth-Arlington PMSA, TX	S	27.43 MW	25.09 AW	57060 AAW	TXBLS	10//99-12//99
	Houston PMSA, TX	S	29.89 MW	29.02 AW	62160 AAW	TXBLS	10//99-12//99
	Killeen-Temple MSA, TX	S	22.68 MW	20.09 AW	47170 AAW	TXBLS	10//99-12//99
	Laredo MSA, TX	S	19.12 MW	15.46 AW	39780 AAW	TXBLS	10//99-12//99
	Longview-Marshall MSA, TX	S	22.09 MW	21.25 AW	45940 AAW	TXBLS	10//99-12//99
	Lubbock MSA, TX	S	18.55 MW	18.24 AW	38580 AAW	TXBLS	10//99-12//99
	McAllen-Edinburg-Mission MSA, TX	S	18.41 MW	18.55 AW	38300 AAW	TXBLS	10//99-12//99
	Odessa-Midland MSA, TX	S	24.90 MW	23.39 AW	51790 AAW	TXBLS	10//99-12//99
	San Angelo MSA, TX	S	16.97 MW	16.31 AW	35300 AAW	TXBLS	10//99-12//99
	San Antonio MSA, TX	S	22.17 MW	21.00 AW	46110 AAW	TXBLS	10//99-12//99
	Sherman-Denison MSA, TX	S	21.51 MW	20.37 AW	44750 AAW	TXBLS	10//99-12//99
	Tyler MSA, TX	S	23.03 MW	22.38 AW	47900 AAW	TXBLS	10//99-12//99
	Victoria MSA, TX	S	20.56 MW	19.13 AW	42770 AAW	TXBLS	10//99-12//99
	Waco MSA, TX	S	19.29 MW	18.88 AW	40120 AAW	TXBLS	10//99-12//99
	Utah	S	21.69 MW	23.24 AW	48340 AAW	UTBLS	10//99-12//99
	Provo-Orem MSA, UT	S	23.30 MW	21.82 AW	48470 AAW	UTBLS	10//99-12//99
	Vermont	S	20.15 MW	22.95 AW	47730 AAW	VTBLS	10//99-12//99
	Burlington MSA, VT	S	24.41 MW	22.02 AW	50770 AAW	VTBLS	10//99-12//99
	Virginia	S	22.87 MW	24.40 AW	50750 AAW	VABLS	10//99-12//99
	Charlottesville MSA, VA	S	23.30 MW	22.50 AW	48470 AAW	VABLS	10//99-12//99
	Danville MSA, VA	S	21.31 MW	19.24 AW	44320 AAW	VABLS	10//99-12//99
	Lynchburg MSA, VA	S	24.28 MW	24.07 AW	50500 AAW	VABLS	10//99-12//99
	Norfolk-Virginia Beach- Newport News MSA, VA- NC	S	20.73 MW	19.11 AW	43110 AAW	VABLS	10//99-12//99
	Richmond-Petersburg MSA, VA	S	24.90 MW	23.34 AW	51780 AAW	VABLS	10//99-12//99
	Roanoke MSA, VA	S	20.36 MW	20.04 AW	42340 AAW	VABLS	10//99-12//99
	Washington	S	23.16 MW	25.81 AW	53690 AAW	WABLS	10//99-12//99

Occupation/Type/Industry	Location	Per	Low	Mid	High	Source	Date
Computer Programmer	Bellingham MSA, WA	S	24.96 MW	23.95 AW	51920 AAW	WABLS	10//99-12//99
	Bremerton PMSA, WA	S	23.01 MW	22.15 AW	47860 AAW	WABLS	10//99-12//99
	Seattle-Bellevue-Everett PMSA, WA	S	25.42 MW	22.96 AW	52870 AAW	WABLS	10//99-12//99
	Spokane MSA, WA	S	20.38 MW	19.11 AW	42390 AAW	WABLS	10//99-12//99
	Tacoma PMSA, WA	S	25.67 MW	22.90 AW	53390 AAW	WABLS	10//99-12//99
	Yakima MSA, WA	S	18.92 MW	18.38 AW	39360 AAW	WABLS	10//99-12//99
	West Virginia	S	19.17 MW	20.42 AW	42460 AAW	WVBLS	10//99-12//99
	Charleston MSA, WV	S	19.96 MW	19.35 AW	41520 AAW	WVBLS	10//99-12//99
	Huntington-Ashland MSA, WV-KY-OH	S	17.13 MW	15.77 AW	35620 AAW	WVBLS	10//99-12//99
	Parkersburg-Marietta MSA, WV-OH	S	18.94 MW	18.79 AW	39390 AAW	WVBLS	10//99-12//99
	Wheeling MSA, WV-OH	S	17.10 MW	17.36 AW	35560 AAW	WVBLS	10//99-12//99
	Wisconsin	S	21.73 MW	23.18 AW	48220 AAW	WIBLS	10//99-12//99
	Appleton-Oshkosh-Neenah MSA, WI	S	22.56 MW	20.39 AW	46920 AAW	WIBLS	10//99-12//99
	Eau Claire MSA, WI	S	21.98 MW	21.43 AW	45720 AAW	WIBLS	10//99-12//99
	Green Bay MSA, WI	S	20.84 MW	19.86 AW	43340 AAW	WIBLS	10//99-12//99
	Janesville-Beloit MSA, WI	S	22.03 MW	21.48 AW	45820 AAW	WIBLS	10//99-12//99
	Kenosha PMSA, WI	S	21.30 MW	19.70 AW	44300 AAW	WIBLS	10//99-12//99
	La Crosse MSA, WI-MN	S	17.08 MW	17.04 AW	35520 AAW	WIBLS	10//99-12//99
	Madison MSA, WI	S	23.54 MW	22.39 AW	48960 AAW	WIBLS	10//99-12//99
	Milwaukee-Waukesha PMSA, WI	S	24.08 MW	22.35 AW	50090 AAW	WIBLS	10//99-12//99
	Racine PMSA, WI	S	22.13 MW	22.12 AW	46040 AAW	WIBLS	10//99-12//99
	Wausau MSA, WI	S	20.42 MW	20.45 AW	42480 AAW	WIBLS	10//99-12//99
	Wyoming	S	16.8 MW	16.90 AW	35160 AAW	WYBLS	10//99-12//99
	Puerto Rico	S	13.5 MW	14.93 AW	31060 AAW	PRBLS	10//99-12//99
	Caguas PMSA, PR	S	14.57 MW	12.69 AW	30300 AAW	PRBLS	10//99-12//99
	Mayaguez MSA, PR	S	12.75 MW	10.45 AW	26520 AAW	PRBLS	10//99-12//99
	Ponce MSA, PR	S	9.91 MW	8.73 AW	20620 AAW	PRBLS	10//99-12//99
	San Juan-Bayamon PMSA, PR	S	15.63 MW	14.18 AW	32520 AAW	PRBLS	10//99-12//99
	Virgin Islands	S	15.53 MW	18.18 AW	37810 AAW	VIBLS	10//99-12//99
	Guam	S	20.4 MW	20.43 AW	42500 AAW	GUBLS	10//99-12//99
Computer Science Teacher							
Postsecondary	Alabama	Y		38580 AAW		ALBLS	10//99-12//99
Postsecondary	Huntsville MSA, AL	Y		33820 AAW		ALBLS	10//99-12//99
Postsecondary	Montgomery MSA, AL	Y		38340 AAW		ALBLS	10//99-12//99
Postsecondary	Alaska	Y		55230 AAW		AKBLS	10//99-12//99
Postsecondary	Arizona	Y		45310 AAW		AZBLS	10//99-12//99
Postsecondary	Phoenix-Mesa MSA, AZ	Y		39880 AAW		AZBLS	10//99-12//99
Postsecondary	Arkansas	Y		48150 AAW		ARBLS	10//99-12//99
Postsecondary	California	Y		51890 AAW		CABLS	10//99-12//99
Postsecondary	Fresno MSA, CA	Y		51610 AAW		CABLS	10//99-12//99
Postsecondary	Los Angeles-Long Beach PMSA, CA	Y		51000 AAW		CABLS	10//99-12//99
Postsecondary	Orange County PMSA, CA	Y		53610 AAW		CABLS	10//99-12//99
Postsecondary	Riverside-San Bernardino PMSA, CA	Y		51390 AAW		CABLS	10//99-12//99
Postsecondary	San Diego MSA, CA	Y		55700 AAW		CABLS	10//99-12//99
Postsecondary	San Francisco PMSA, CA	Y		49710 AAW		CABLS	10//99-12//99
Postsecondary	Denver PMSA, CO	Y		46530 AAW		COBLS	10//99-12//99
Postsecondary	Connecticut	Y		64470 AAW		CTBLS	10//99-12//99
Postsecondary	New Haven-Meriden PMSA, CT	Y		54130 AAW		CTBLS	10//99-12//99
Postsecondary	Wilmington-Newark PMSA, DE-MD	Y		52370 AAW		DEBLS	10//99-12//99
Postsecondary	District of Columbia	Y		46440 AAW		DCBLS	10//99-12//99
Postsecondary	Washington PMSA, DC-MD-VA-WV	Y		47060 AAW		DCBLS	10//99-12//99
Postsecondary	Florida	Y		53400 AAW		FLBLS	10//99-12//99
Postsecondary	Fort Lauderdale PMSA, FL	Y		37440 AAW		FLBLS	10//99-12//99
Postsecondary	Jacksonville MSA, FL	Y		60940 AAW		FLBLS	10//99-12//99
Postsecondary	Miami PMSA, FL	Y		62360 AAW		FLBLS	10//99-12//99
Postsecondary	Orlando MSA, FL	Y		46650 AAW		FLBLS	10//99-12//99
Postsecondary	Pensacola MSA, FL	Y		55920 AAW		FLBLS	10//99-12//99
Postsecondary	Tampa-St. Petersburg-Clearwater MSA, FL	Y		48820 AAW		FLBLS	10//99-12//99
Postsecondary	Georgia	Y		45250 AAW		GABLS	10//99-12//99
Postsecondary	Atlanta MSA, GA	Y		47300 AAW		GABLS	10//99-12//99
Postsecondary	Savannah MSA, GA	Y		49920 AAW		GABLS	10//99-12//99

AAW Average annual wage	AOH Average offered, high	ASH Average starting, high	H Hourly	M Monthly	S Special: hourly and annual
AE Average entry wage	AOL Average offered, low	ASL Average starting, low	HI Highest wage paid	MTC Median total compensation	TQ Third quartile wage
AEX Average experienced wage	APH Average pay, high range	AW Average wage paid	HR High end range	MW Median wage paid	W Weekly
AO Average offered	APL Average pay, low range	FQ First quartile wage	LR Low end range	SQ Second quartile wage	Y Yearly

Occupation/Type/Industry	Location	Per	Low	Mid	High	Source	Date
Computer Science Teacher							
Postsecondary	Hawaii	Y		60870 AAW		HIBLS	10//99-12//99
Postsecondary	Honolulu MSA, HI	Y		56680 AAW		HIBLS	10//99-12//99
Postsecondary	Idaho	Y		38820 AAW		IDBLS	10//99-12//99
Postsecondary	Illinois	Y		48450 AAW		ILBLS	10//99-12//99
Postsecondary	Chicago PMSA, IL	Y		48030 AAW		ILBLS	10//99-12//99
Postsecondary	Indiana	Y		42460 AAW		INBLS	10//99-12//99
Postsecondary	South Bend MSA, IN	Y		41160 AAW		INBLS	10//99-12//99
Postsecondary	Iowa	Y		54990 AAW		IABLS	10//99-12//99
Postsecondary	Davenport-Moline-Rock Island MSA, IA-IL	Y		47470 AAW		IABLS	10//99-12//99
Postsecondary	Des Moines MSA, IA	Y		46260 AAW		IABLS	10//99-12//99
Postsecondary	Kansas	Y		38460 AAW		KSBLS	10//99-12//99
Postsecondary	Kentucky	Y		37000 AAW		KYBLS	10//99-12//99
Postsecondary	Louisiana	Y		42940 AAW		LABLS	10//99-12//99
Postsecondary	Maine	Y		43570 AAW		MEBLS	10//99-12//99
Postsecondary	Portland MSA, ME	Y		42700 AAW		MEBLS	10//99-12//99
Postsecondary	Maryland	Y		52880 AAW		MDBLS	10//99-12//99
Postsecondary	Baltimore PMSA, MD	Y		55500 AAW		MDBLS	10//99-12//99
Postsecondary	Massachusetts	Y		52050 AAW		MABLS	10//99-12//99
Postsecondary	Boston PMSA, MA-NH	Y		51630 AAW		MABLS	10//99-12//99
Postsecondary	Brockton PMSA, MA	Y		43930 AAW		MABLS	10//99-12//99
Postsecondary	Springfield MSA, MA	Y		57990 AAW		MABLS	10//99-12//99
Postsecondary	Michigan	Y		47540 AAW		MIBLS	10//99-12//99
Postsecondary	Detroit PMSA, MI	Y		49910 AAW		MIBLS	10//99-12//99
Postsecondary	Grand Rapids-Muskegon-Holland MSA, MI	Y		44100 AAW		MIBLS	10//99-12//99
Postsecondary	Kalamazoo-Battle Creek MSA, MI	Y		66140 AAW		MIBLS	10//99-12//99
Postsecondary	Lansing-East Lansing MSA, MI	Y		44660 AAW		MIBLS	10//99-12//99
Postsecondary	Minnesota	Y		54650 AAW		MNBLS	10//99-12//99
Postsecondary	Duluth-Superior MSA, MN-WI	Y		55880 AAW		MNBLS	10//99-12//99
Postsecondary	Minneapolis-St. Paul MSA, MN-WI	Y		55840 AAW		MNBLS	10//99-12//99
Postsecondary	Mississippi	Y		47840 AAW		MSBLS	10//99-12//99
Postsecondary	Jackson MSA, MS	Y		47460 AAW		MSBLS	10//99-12//99
Postsecondary	Missouri	Y		40530 AAW		MOBLS	10//99-12//99
Postsecondary	Kansas City MSA, MO-KS	Y		44430 AAW		MOBLS	10//99-12//99
Postsecondary	St. Louis MSA, MO-IL	Y		33220 AAW		MOBLS	10//99-12//99
Postsecondary	Montana	Y		51520 AAW		MTBLS	10//99-12//99
Postsecondary	Nebraska	Y		56810 AAW		NEBLS	10//99-12//99
Postsecondary	Omaha MSA, NE-IA	Y		50920 AAW		NEBLS	10//99-12//99
Postsecondary	Nevada	Y		41640 AAW		NVBLS	10//99-12//99
Postsecondary	Las Vegas MSA, NV-AZ	Y		49420 AAW		NVBLS	10//99-12//99
Postsecondary	New Hampshire	Y		48340 AAW		NHBLS	10//99-12//99
Postsecondary	Nashua PMSA, NH	Y		52110 AAW		NHBLS	10//99-12//99
Postsecondary	New Jersey	Y		60910 AAW		NJBLS	10//99-12//99
Postsecondary	Bergen-Passaic PMSA, NJ	Y		64930 AAW		NJBLS	10//99-12//99
Postsecondary	Jersey City PMSA, NJ	Y		66500 AAW		NJBLS	10//99-12//99
Postsecondary	Middlesex-Somerset-Hunterdon PMSA, NJ	Y		59640 AAW		NJBLS	10//99-12//99
Postsecondary	Monmouth-Ocean PMSA, NJ	Y		51540 AAW		NJBLS	10//99-12//99
Postsecondary	Newark PMSA, NJ	Y		66160 AAW		NJBLS	10//99-12//99
Postsecondary	New Mexico	Y		49990 AAW		NMBLS	10//99-12//99
Postsecondary	New York	Y		48510 AAW		NYBLS	10//99-12//99
Postsecondary	Dutchess County PMSA, NY	Y		53310 AAW		NYBLS	10//99-12//99
Postsecondary	Nassau-Suffolk PMSA, NY	Y		53540 AAW		NYBLS	10//99-12//99
Postsecondary	New York PMSA, NY	Y		49990 AAW		NYBLS	10//99-12//99
Postsecondary	Utica-Rome MSA, NY	Y		43930 AAW		NYBLS	10//99-12//99
Postsecondary	North Carolina	Y		43670 AAW		NCBLS	10//99-12//99
Postsecondary	Charlotte-Gastonia-Rock Hill MSA, NC-SC	Y		45870 AAW		NCBLS	10//99-12//99
Postsecondary	Greensboro--Winston-Salem--High Point MSA, NC	Y		43510 AAW		NCBLS	10//99-12//99
Postsecondary	Hickory-Morganton-Lenoir MSA, NC	Y		37010 AAW		NCBLS	10//99-12//99
Postsecondary	Raleigh-Durham-Chapel Hill MSA, NC	Y		48260 AAW		NCBLS	10//99-12//99
Postsecondary	North Dakota	Y		48570 AAW		NDBLS	10//99-12//99
Postsecondary	Grand Forks MSA, ND-MN	Y		51960 AAW		NDBLS	10//99-12//99
Postsecondary	Ohio	Y		37640 AAW		OHBLS	10//99-12//99
Postsecondary	Cincinnati PMSA, OH-KY-IN	Y		33340 AAW		OHBLS	10//99-12//99

AAW	Average annual wage	AOH	Average offered, high	ASH	Average starting, high	H	Hourly
AE	Average entry wage	AOL	Average offered, low	ASL	Average starting, low	HI	Highest wage paid
AEX	Average experienced wage	APH	Average pay, high range	AW	Average wage paid	HR	High end range
AO	Average offered	APL	Average pay, low range	FQ	First quartile wage	LR	Low end range

M	Monthly	S	Special: hourly and annual
MTC	Median total compensation	TQ	Third quartile wage
MW	Median wage paid	W	Weekly
SQ	Second quartile wage	Y	Yearly

Occupation/Type/Industry	Location	Per	Low	Mid	High	Source	Date
Computer Science Teacher							
Postsecondary	Cleveland-Lorain-Elyria PMSA, OH	Y		40150 ᴀᴀᴡ		OHBLS	10//99-12//99
Postsecondary	Columbus MSA, OH	Y		37700 ᴀᴀᴡ		OHBLS	10//99-12//99
Postsecondary	Oklahoma	Y		46780 ᴀᴀᴡ		OKBLS	10//99-12//99
Postsecondary	Oklahoma City MSA, OK	Y		44460 ᴀᴀᴡ		OKBLS	10//99-12//99
Postsecondary	Tulsa MSA, OK	Y		48550 ᴀᴀᴡ		OKBLS	10//99-12//99
Postsecondary	Oregon	Y		48780 ᴀᴀᴡ		ORBLS	10//99-12//99
Postsecondary	Portland-Vancouver PMSA, OR-WA	Y		45730 ᴀᴀᴡ		ORBLS	10//99-12//99
Postsecondary	Pennsylvania	Y		61090 ᴀᴀᴡ		PABLS	10//99-12//99
Postsecondary	Allentown-Bethlehem-Easton MSA, PA	Y		45500 ᴀᴀᴡ		PABLS	10//99-12//99
Postsecondary	Lancaster MSA, PA	Y		61170 ᴀᴀᴡ		PABLS	10//99-12//99
Postsecondary	Philadelphia PMSA, PA-NJ	Y		62670 ᴀᴀᴡ		PABLS	10//99-12//99
Postsecondary	Pittsburgh MSA, PA	Y		61280 ᴀᴀᴡ		PABLS	10//99-12//99
Postsecondary	Reading MSA, PA	Y		60830 ᴀᴀᴡ		PABLS	10//99-12//99
Postsecondary	Scranton--Wilkes-Barre--Hazleton MSA, PA	Y		48390 ᴀᴀᴡ		PABLS	10//99-12//99
Postsecondary	South Carolina	Y		44600 ᴀᴀᴡ		SCBLS	10//99-12//99
Postsecondary	Charleston-North Charleston MSA, SC	Y		42760 ᴀᴀᴡ		SCBLS	10//99-12//99
Postsecondary	Greenville-Spartanburg-Anderson MSA, SC	Y		44730 ᴀᴀᴡ		SCBLS	10//99-12//99
Postsecondary	South Dakota	Y		43660 ᴀᴀᴡ		SDBLS	10//99-12//99
Postsecondary	Rapid City MSA, SD	Y		50410 ᴀᴀᴡ		SDBLS	10//99-12//99
Postsecondary	Tennessee	Y		45390 ᴀᴀᴡ		TNBLS	10//99-12//99
Postsecondary	Johnson City-Kingsport-Bristol MSA, TN-VA	Y		42840 ᴀᴀᴡ		TNBLS	10//99-12//99
Postsecondary	Memphis MSA, TN-AR-MS	Y		38480 ᴀᴀᴡ		MSBLS	10//99-12//99
Postsecondary	Nashville MSA, TN	Y		50920 ᴀᴀᴡ		TNBLS	10//99-12//99
Postsecondary	Texas	Y		43560 ᴀᴀᴡ		TXBLS	10//99-12//99
Postsecondary	Dallas PMSA, TX	Y		45290 ᴀᴀᴡ		TXBLS	10//99-12//99
Postsecondary	El Paso MSA, TX	Y		37690 ᴀᴀᴡ		TXBLS	10//99-12//99
Postsecondary	Fort Worth-Arlington PMSA, TX	Y		43940 ᴀᴀᴡ		TXBLS	10//99-12//99
Postsecondary	Houston PMSA, TX	Y		50180 ᴀᴀᴡ		TXBLS	10//99-12//99
Postsecondary	Killeen-Temple MSA, TX	Y		33580 ᴀᴀᴡ		TXBLS	10//99-12//99
Postsecondary	Longview-Marshall MSA, TX	Y		37550 ᴀᴀᴡ		TXBLS	10//99-12//99
Postsecondary	Odessa-Midland MSA, TX	Y		39860 ᴀᴀᴡ		TXBLS	10//99-12//99
Postsecondary	San Antonio MSA, TX	Y		54220 ᴀᴀᴡ		TXBLS	10//99-12//99
Postsecondary	Vermont	Y		55140 ᴀᴀᴡ		VTBLS	10//99-12//99
Postsecondary	Burlington MSA, VT	Y		56230 ᴀᴀᴡ		VTBLS	10//99-12//99
Postsecondary	Virginia	Y		45560 ᴀᴀᴡ		VABLS	10//99-12//99
Postsecondary	Norfolk-Virginia Beach-Newport News MSA, VA-NC	Y		59030 ᴀᴀᴡ		VABLS	10//99-12//99
Postsecondary	Richmond-Petersburg MSA, VA	Y		43240 ᴀᴀᴡ		VABLS	10//99-12//99
Postsecondary	Washington	Y		44510 ᴀᴀᴡ		WABLS	10//99-12//99
Postsecondary	Seattle-Bellevue-Everett PMSA, WA	Y		49580 ᴀᴀᴡ		WABLS	10//99-12//99
Postsecondary	Spokane MSA, WA	Y		31850 ᴀᴀᴡ		WABLS	10//99-12//99
Postsecondary	Tacoma PMSA, WA	Y		38780 ᴀᴀᴡ		WABLS	10//99-12//99
Postsecondary	West Virginia	Y		52870 ᴀᴀᴡ		WVBLS	10//99-12//99
Postsecondary	Wisconsin	Y		50530 ᴀᴀᴡ		WIBLS	10//99-12//99
Postsecondary	Milwaukee-Waukesha PMSA, WI	Y		46760 ᴀᴀᴡ		WIBLS	10//99-12//99
Postsecondary	Puerto Rico	Y		27770 ᴀᴀᴡ		PRBLS	10//99-12//99
Postsecondary	Aguadilla MSA, PR	Y		27050 ᴀᴀᴡ		PRBLS	10//99-12//99
Postsecondary	Arecibo PMSA, PR	Y		28550 ᴀᴀᴡ		PRBLS	10//99-12//99
Postsecondary	Caguas PMSA, PR	Y		26550 ᴀᴀᴡ		PRBLS	10//99-12//99
Postsecondary	Mayaguez MSA, PR	Y		22230 ᴀᴀᴡ		PRBLS	10//99-12//99
Postsecondary	San Juan-Bayamon PMSA, PR	Y		28900 ᴀᴀᴡ		PRBLS	10//99-12//99
Computer Scientist	United States	Y	48468 ᴀᴇ			ELENTI	2000
Computer Software Engineer							
Applications	Alabama	S	27.02 ᴍᴡ	27.30 ᴀᴡ	56790 ᴀᴀᴡ	ALBLS	10//99-12//99
Applications	Birmingham MSA, AL	S	28.31 ᴍᴡ	27.07 ᴀᴡ	58890 ᴀᴀᴡ	ALBLS	10//99-12//99
Applications	Huntsville MSA, AL	S	27.25 ᴍᴡ	28.06 ᴀᴡ	56670 ᴀᴀᴡ	ALBLS	10//99-12//99
Applications	Mobile MSA, AL	S	25.09 ᴍᴡ	24.53 ᴀᴡ	52190 ᴀᴀᴡ	ALBLS	10//99-12//99
Applications	Alaska	S	27.71 ᴍᴡ	28.43 ᴀᴡ	59140 ᴀᴀᴡ	AKBLS	10//99-12//99

AAW	Average annual wage	AOH	Average offered, high	ASH	Average starting, high	H	Hourly	M	Monthly	S	Special: hourly and annual
AE	Average entry wage	AOL	Average offered, low	ASL	Average starting, low	HI	Highest wage paid	MTC	Median total compensation	TQ	Third quartile wage
AEX	Average experienced wage	APH	Average pay, high range	AW	Average wage paid	HR	High end range	MW	Median wage paid	W	Weekly
AO	Average offered	APL	Average pay, low range	FQ	First quartile wage	LR	Low end range	SQ	Second quartile wage	Y	Yearly

Occupation/Type/Industry	Location	Per	Low	Mid	High	Source	Date
Computer Software Engineer							
Applications	Anchorage MSA, AK	S	29.64 MW	30.05 AW	61650 AAW	AKBLS	10//99-12//99
Applications	Arizona	S	32.84 MW	33.07 AW	68780 AAW	AZBLS	10//99-12//99
Applications	Phoenix-Mesa MSA, AZ	S	34.08 MW	32.82 AW	70890 AAW	AZBLS	10//99-12//99
Applications	Tucson MSA, AZ	S	31.53 MW	36.05 AW	65570 AAW	AZBLS	10//99-12//99
Applications	California	S	34.3 MW	35.73 AW	74310 AAW	CABLS	10//99-12//99
Applications	Bakersfield MSA, CA	S	27.53 MW	26.87 AW	57270 AAW	CABLS	10//99-12//99
Applications	Fresno MSA, CA	S	28.71 MW	29.20 AW	59720 AAW	CABLS	10//99-12//99
Applications	Los Angeles-Long Beach PMSA, CA	S	39.10 MW	34.62 AW	81320 AAW	CABLS	10//99-12//99
Applications	Oakland PMSA, CA	S	40.24 MW	40.19 AW	83700 AAW	CABLS	10//99-12//99
Applications	Orange County PMSA, CA	S	31.75 MW	30.65 AW	66040 AAW	CABLS	10//99-12//99
Applications	Riverside-San Bernardino PMSA, CA	S	32.72 MW	35.02 AW	68070 AAW	CABLS	10//99-12//99
Applications	Sacramento PMSA, CA	S	34.40 MW	33.45 AW	71560 AAW	CABLS	10//99-12//99
Applications	Salinas MSA, CA	S	24.96 MW	24.82 AW	51920 AAW	CABLS	10//99-12//99
Applications	San Diego MSA, CA	S	28.93 MW	28.75 AW	60180 AAW	CABLS	10//99-12//99
Applications	San Francisco PMSA, CA	S	37.35 MW	36.06 AW	77680 AAW	CABLS	10//99-12//99
Applications	San Jose PMSA, CA	S	37.05 MW	37.18 AW	77070 AAW	CABLS	10//99-12//99
Applications	Santa Barbara-Santa Maria-Lompoc MSA, CA	S	31.16 MW	32.57 AW	64800 AAW	CABLS	10//99-12//99
Applications	Santa Cruz-Watsonville PMSA, CA	S	42.94 MW	45.61 AW	89320 AAW	CABLS	10//99-12//99
Applications	Santa Rosa PMSA, CA	S	31.20 MW	29.62 AW	64900 AAW	CABLS	10//99-12//99
Applications	Stockton-Lodi MSA, CA	S	21.82 MW	19.76 AW	45380 AAW	CABLS	10//99-12//99
Applications	Vallejo-Fairfield-Napa PMSA, CA	S	33.19 MW	31.84 AW	69040 AAW	CABLS	10//99-12//99
Applications	Ventura PMSA, CA	S	31.54 MW	30.37 AW	65600 AAW	CABLS	10//99-12//99
Applications	Visalia-Tulare-Porterville MSA, CA	S	23.78 MW	22.15 AW	49470 AAW	CABLS	10//99-12//99
Applications	Colorado	S	30.78 MW	31.60 AW	65730 AAW	COBLS	10//99-12//99
Applications	Boulder-Longmont PMSA, CO	S	32.38 MW	31.36 AW	67340 AAW	COBLS	10//99-12//99
Applications	Colorado Springs MSA, CO	S	27.84 MW	26.53 AW	57900 AAW	COBLS	10//99-12//99
Applications	Denver PMSA, CO	S	32.59 MW	32.12 AW	67790 AAW	COBLS	10//99-12//99
Applications	Fort Collins-Loveland MSA, CO	S	26.95 MW	24.22 AW	56060 AAW	COBLS	10//99-12//99
Applications	Connecticut	S	31.83 MW	32.69 AW	67980 AAW	CTBLS	10//99-12//99
Applications	Bridgeport PMSA, CT	S	39.68 MW	42.01 AW	82530 AAW	CTBLS	10//99-12//99
Applications	Danbury PMSA, CT	S	29.96 MW	26.19 AW	62320 AAW	CTBLS	10//99-12//99
Applications	Hartford MSA, CT	S	31.10 MW	30.71 AW	64690 AAW	CTBLS	10//99-12//99
Applications	New Haven-Meriden PMSA, CT	S	30.64 MW	30.50 AW	63740 AAW	CTBLS	10//99-12//99
Applications	New London-Norwich MSA, CT-RI	S	30.60 MW	29.88 AW	63640 AAW	CTBLS	10//99-12//99
Applications	Stamford-Norwalk PMSA, CT	S	35.29 MW	34.47 AW	73400 AAW	CTBLS	10//99-12//99
Applications	Waterbury PMSA, CT	S	31.44 MW	30.73 AW	65390 AAW	CTBLS	10//99-12//99
Applications	Delaware	S	31.4 MW	31.23 AW	64960 AAW	DEBLS	10//99-12//99
Applications	Dover MSA, DE	S	24.28 MW	26.24 AW	50500 AAW	DEBLS	10//99-12//99
Applications	Wilmington-Newark PMSA, DE-MD	S	32.92 MW	33.91 AW	68480 AAW	DEBLS	10//99-12//99
Applications	District of Columbia	S	27.92 MW	29.33 AW	61010 AAW	DCBLS	10//99-12//99
Applications	Washington PMSA, DC-MD-VA-WV	S	30.52 MW	30.77 AW	63480 AAW	DCBLS	10//99-12//99
Applications	Florida	S	25.14 MW	26.66 AW	55440 AAW	FLBLS	10//99-12//99
Applications	Fort Lauderdale PMSA, FL	S	27.25 MW	24.43 AW	56690 AAW	FLBLS	10//99-12//99
Applications	Fort Myers-Cape Coral MSA, FL	S	24.76 MW	25.53 AW	51500 AAW	FLBLS	10//99-12//99
Applications	Fort Pierce-Port St. Lucie MSA, FL	S	25.52 MW	20.78 AW	53090 AAW	FLBLS	10//99-12//99
Applications	Gainesville MSA, FL	S	24.35 MW	25.14 AW	50660 AAW	FLBLS	10//99-12//99
Applications	Jacksonville MSA, FL	S	28.51 MW	26.10 AW	59300 AAW	FLBLS	10//99-12//99
Applications	Melbourne-Titusville-Palm Bay MSA, FL	S	33.03 MW	33.62 AW	68700 AAW	FLBLS	10//99-12//99
Applications	Miami PMSA, FL	S	22.97 MW	23.53 AW	47780 AAW	FLBLS	10//99-12//99
Applications	Orlando MSA, FL	S	28.14 MW	26.25 AW	58540 AAW	FLBLS	10//99-12//99
Applications	Panama City MSA, FL	S	17.95 MW	18.43 AW	37330 AAW	FLBLS	10//99-12//99
Applications	Pensacola MSA, FL	S	25.30 MW	24.10 AW	52620 AAW	FLBLS	10//99-12//99
Applications	Sarasota-Bradenton MSA, FL	S	29.39 MW	30.48 AW	61140 AAW	FLBLS	10//99-12//99
Applications	Tallahassee MSA, FL	S	25.19 MW	24.16 AW	52390 AAW	FLBLS	10//99-12//99
Applications	Tampa-St. Petersburg-Clearwater MSA, FL	S	26.67 MW	24.91 AW	55480 AAW	FLBLS	10//99-12//99

Computer Software Engineer

Occupation/Type/Industry	Location	Per	Low	Mid	High	Source	Date
Applications	West Palm Beach-Boca Raton MSA, FL	S	31.58 MW	30.09 AW	65690 AAW	FLBLS	10//99-12//99
Applications	Georgia	S	36.45 MW	39.49 AW	82130 AAW	GABLS	10//99-12//99
Applications	Athens MSA, GA	S	24.76 MW	23.34 AW	51500 AAW	GABLS	10//99-12//99
Applications	Atlanta MSA, GA	S	42.36 MW	42.90 AW	88110 AAW	GABLS	10//99-12//99
Applications	Columbus MSA, GA-AL	S	21.00 MW	19.72 AW	43680 AAW	GABLS	10//99-12//99
Applications	Macon MSA, GA	S	25.94 MW	24.05 AW	53960 AAW	GABLS	10//99-12//99
Applications	Hawaii	S	27.29 MW	27.60 AW	57400 AAW	HIBLS	10//99-12//99
Applications	Honolulu MSA, HI	S	28.06 MW	26.82 AW	58370 AAW	HIBLS	10//99-12//99
Applications	Idaho	S	32.68 MW	35.93 AW	74730 AAW	IDBLS	10//99-12//99
Applications	Boise City MSA, ID	S	33.18 MW	30.56 AW	69020 AAW	IDBLS	10//99-12//99
Applications	Illinois	S	30.41 MW	30.71 AW	63880 AAW	ILBLS	10//99-12//99
Applications	Bloomington-Normal MSA, IL	S	26.85 MW	26.74 AW	55840 AAW	ILBLS	10//99-12//99
Applications	Champaign-Urbana MSA, IL	S	30.70 MW	29.75 AW	63860 AAW	ILBLS	10//99-12//99
Applications	Chicago PMSA, IL	S	31.62 MW	31.14 AW	65760 AAW	ILBLS	10//99-12//99
Applications	Peoria-Pekin MSA, IL	S	22.30 MW	21.46 AW	46390 AAW	ILBLS	10//99-12//99
Applications	Rockford MSA, IL	S	30.02 MW	28.63 AW	62440 AAW	ILBLS	10//99-12//99
Applications	Indiana	S	24.36 MW	24.98 AW	51970 AAW	INBLS	10//99-12//99
Applications	Elkhart-Goshen MSA, IN	S	23.74 MW	23.27 AW	49380 AAW	INBLS	10//99-12//99
Applications	Evansville-Henderson MSA, IN-KY	S	19.79 MW	21.69 AW	41150 AAW	INBLS	10//99-12//99
Applications	Fort Wayne MSA, IN	S	29.18 MW	27.96 AW	60690 AAW	INBLS	10//99-12//99
Applications	Gary PMSA, IN	S	27.30 MW	25.46 AW	56780 AAW	INBLS	10//99-12//99
Applications	Indianapolis MSA, IN	S	24.81 MW	24.85 AW	51610 AAW	INBLS	10//99-12//99
Applications	Lafayette MSA, IN	S	22.82 MW	23.46 AW	47460 AAW	INBLS	10//99-12//99
Applications	South Bend MSA, IN	S	24.11 MW	23.61 AW	50150 AAW	INBLS	10//99-12//99
Applications	Terre Haute MSA, IN	S	20.20 MW	19.20 AW	42020 AAW	INBLS	10//99-12//99
Applications	Iowa	S	27.15 MW	29.55 AW	61460 AAW	IABLS	10//99-12//99
Applications	Waterloo-Cedar Falls MSA, IA	S	22.55 MW	21.94 AW	46900 AAW	IABLS	10//99-12//99
Applications	Kansas	S	22.44 MW	23.42 AW	48720 AAW	KSBLS	10//99-12//99
Applications	Wichita MSA, KS	S	24.30 MW	24.21 AW	50550 AAW	KSBLS	10//99-12//99
Applications	Kentucky	S	24.1 MW	26.59 AW	55310 AAW	KYBLS	10//99-12//99
Applications	Lexington MSA, KY	S	36.31 MW	38.41 AW	75520 AAW	KYBLS	10//99-12//99
Applications	Louisville MSA, KY-IN	S	22.80 MW	20.79 AW	47420 AAW	KYBLS	10//99-12//99
Applications	Louisiana	S	26.62 MW	26.52 AW	55170 AAW	LABLS	10//99-12//99
Applications	Baton Rouge MSA, LA	S	26.87 MW	26.45 AW	55900 AAW	LABLS	10//99-12//99
Applications	Lafayette MSA, LA	S	19.08 MW	14.60 AW	39680 AAW	LABLS	10//99-12//99
Applications	New Orleans MSA, LA	S	27.31 MW	27.36 AW	56800 AAW	LABLS	10//99-12//99
Applications	Maine	S	24.2 MW	24.50 AW	50950 AAW	MEBLS	10//99-12//99
Applications	Portland MSA, ME	S	23.74 MW	23.60 AW	49380 AAW	MEBLS	10//99-12//99
Applications	Maryland	S	31 MW	31.29 AW	65090 AAW	MDBLS	10//99-12//99
Applications	Baltimore PMSA, MD	S	29.92 MW	28.86 AW	62240 AAW	MDBLS	10//99-12//99
Applications	Hagerstown PMSA, MD	S	31.04 MW	31.70 AW	64560 AAW	MDBLS	10//99-12//99
Applications	Massachusetts	S	35.17 MW	36.07 AW	75020 AAW	MABLS	10//99-12//99
Applications	Boston PMSA, MA-NH	S	36.44 MW	35.91 AW	75800 AAW	MABLS	10//99-12//99
Applications	Fitchburg-Leominster PMSA, MA	S	37.07 MW	39.61 AW	77100 AAW	MABLS	10//99-12//99
Applications	Lawrence PMSA, MA-NH	S	39.94 MW	39.46 AW	83080 AAW	MABLS	10//99-12//99
Applications	Lowell PMSA, MA-NH	S	38.89 MW	38.89 AW	80900 AAW	MABLS	10//99-12//99
Applications	Springfield MSA, MA	S	28.62 MW	28.28 AW	59540 AAW	MABLS	10//99-12//99
Applications	Worcester PMSA, MA-CT	S	26.02 MW	24.90 AW	54110 AAW	MABLS	10//99-12//99
Applications	Michigan	S	29.34 MW	30.05 AW	62500 AAW	MIBLS	10//99-12//99
Applications	Ann Arbor PMSA, MI	S	26.81 MW	28.55 AW	55770 AAW	MIBLS	10//99-12//99
Applications	Benton Harbor MSA, MI	S	31.43 MW	32.55 AW	65370 AAW	MIBLS	10//99-12//99
Applications	Detroit PMSA, MI	S	32.44 MW	31.79 AW	67480 AAW	MIBLS	10//99-12//99
Applications	Flint PMSA, MI	S	28.06 MW	27.64 AW	58370 AAW	MIBLS	10//99-12//99
Applications	Grand Rapids-Muskegon-Holland MSA, MI	S	23.97 MW	21.87 AW	49860 AAW	MIBLS	10//99-12//99
Applications	Kalamazoo-Battle Creek MSA, MI	S	27.60 MW	29.24 AW	57400 AAW	MIBLS	10//99-12//99
Applications	Lansing-East Lansing MSA, MI	S	25.07 MW	24.14 AW	52150 AAW	MIBLS	10//99-12//99
Applications	Minnesota	S	27.6 MW	29.13 AW	60580 AAW	MNBLS	10//99-12//99
Applications	Duluth-Superior MSA, MN-WI	S	22.20 MW	20.75 AW	46180 AAW	MNBLS	10//99-12//99
Applications	Minneapolis-St. Paul MSA, MN-WI	S	28.42 MW	27.03 AW	59110 AAW	MNBLS	10//99-12//99
Applications	St. Cloud MSA, MN	S	24.39 MW	24.26 AW	50740 AAW	MNBLS	10//99-12//99
Applications	Mississippi	S	21.36 MW	22.20 AW	46180 AAW	MSBLS	10//99-12//99
Applications	Biloxi-Gulfport-Pascagoula MSA, MS	S	23.58 MW	24.11 AW	49040 AAW	MSBLS	10//99-12//99
Applications	Jackson MSA, MS	S	21.96 MW	20.78 AW	45680 AAW	MSBLS	10//99-12//99
Applications	Missouri	S	30.94 MW	31.06 AW	64600 AAW	MOBLS	10//99-12//99

AAW	Average annual wage	**AOH**	Average offered, high	**ASH**	Average starting, high	**H**	Hourly	**M** Monthly
AE	Average entry wage	**AOL**	Average offered, low	**ASL**	Average starting, low	**HI**	Highest wage paid	**MTC** Median total compensation
AEX	Average experienced wage	**APH**	Average pay, high range	**AW**	Average wage paid	**HR**	High end range	**MW** Median wage paid
AO	Average offered	**APL**	Average pay, low range	**FQ**	First quartile wage	**LR**	Low end range	**SQ** Second quartile wage

S	Special: hourly and annual
TQ	Third quartile wage
W	Weekly
Y	Yearly

Occupation/Type/Industry	Location	Per	Low	Mid	High	Source	Date
Computer Software Engineer							
Applications	Kansas City MSA, MO-KS	S	23.58 MW	22.65 AW	49050 AAW	MOBLS	10//99-12//99
Applications	St. Louis MSA, MO-IL	S	31.47 MW	31.29 AW	65460 AAW	MOBLS	10//99-12//99
Applications	Montana	S	22.87 MW	22.58 AW	46960 AAW	MTBLS	10//99-12//99
Applications	Nebraska	S	28.4 MW	27.19 AW	56550 AAW	NEBLS	10//99-12//99
Applications	Lincoln MSA, NE	S	25.65 MW	21.16 AW	53360 AAW	NEBLS	10//99-12//99
Applications	Omaha MSA, NE-IA	S	27.28 MW	28.49 AW	56750 AAW	NEBLS	10//99-12//99
Applications	Nevada	S	24.24 MW	28.23 AW	58720 AAW	NVBLS	10//99-12//99
Applications	Las Vegas MSA, NV-AZ	S	25.77 MW	24.95 AW	53600 AAW	NVBLS	10//99-12//99
Applications	Reno MSA, NV	S	21.20 MW	17.84 AW	44100 AAW	NVBLS	10//99-12//99
Applications	New Hampshire	S	32.25 MW	31.55 AW	65630 AAW	NHBLS	10//99-12//99
Applications	Manchester PMSA, NH	S	31.68 MW	29.73 AW	65890 AAW	NHBLS	10//99-12//99
Applications	Nashua PMSA, NH	S	33.52 MW	35.23 AW	69730 AAW	NHBLS	10//99-12//99
Applications	Portsmouth-Rochester PMSA, NH-ME	S	28.82 MW	29.21 AW	59940 AAW	NHBLS	10//99-12//99
Applications	New Jersey	S	34.78 MW	33.46 AW	69600 AAW	NJBLS	10//99-12//99
Applications	Atlantic-Cape May PMSA, NJ	S	33.16 MW	34.77 AW	68980 AAW	NJBLS	10//99-12//99
Applications	Bergen-Passaic PMSA, NJ	S	33.77 MW	35.10 AW	70240 AAW	NJBLS	10//99-12//99
Applications	Jersey City PMSA, NJ	S	34.17 MW	32.56 AW	71080 AAW	NJBLS	10//99-12//99
Applications	Middlesex-Somerset-Hunterdon PMSA, NJ	S	34.11 MW	35.66 AW	70960 AAW	NJBLS	10//99-12//99
Applications	Monmouth-Ocean PMSA, NJ	S	29.50 MW	28.77 AW	61370 AAW	NJBLS	10//99-12//99
Applications	Newark PMSA, NJ	S	32.54 MW	31.82 AW	67670 AAW	NJBLS	10//99-12//99
Applications	Trenton PMSA, NJ	S	33.74 MW	35.34 AW	70180 AAW	NJBLS	10//99-12//99
Applications	New Mexico	S	30.27 MW	29.94 AW	62270 AAW	NMBLS	10//99-12//99
Applications	Albuquerque MSA, NM	S	29.94 MW	30.20 AW	62270 AAW	NMBLS	10//99-12//99
Applications	Santa Fe MSA, NM	S	30.74 MW	30.81 AW	63950 AAW	NMBLS	10//99-12//99
Applications	New York	S	27.19 MW	28.54 AW	59370 AAW	NYBLS	10//99-12//99
Applications	Binghamton MSA, NY	S	34.29 MW	37.06 AW	71330 AAW	NYBLS	10//99-12//99
Applications	Buffalo-Niagara Falls MSA, NY	S	22.76 MW	22.33 AW	47330 AAW	NYBLS	10//99-12//99
Applications	Elmira MSA, NY	S	21.30 MW	18.43 AW	44300 AAW	NYBLS	10//99-12//99
Applications	Nassau-Suffolk PMSA, NY	S	32.63 MW	26.87 AW	67870 AAW	NYBLS	10//99-12//99
Applications	New York PMSA, NY	S	29.60 MW	29.04 AW	61570 AAW	NYBLS	10//99-12//99
Applications	Rochester MSA, NY	S	26.23 MW	25.82 AW	54560 AAW	NYBLS	10//99-12//99
Applications	Syracuse MSA, NY	S	27.80 MW	25.87 AW	57830 AAW	NYBLS	10//99-12//99
Applications	Utica-Rome MSA, NY	S	28.46 MW	26.28 AW	59200 AAW	NYBLS	10//99-12//99
Applications	North Carolina	S	28.83 MW	31.60 AW	65720 AAW	NCBLS	10//99-12//99
Applications	Charlotte-Gastonia-Rock Hill MSA, NC-SC	S	32.38 MW	30.58 AW	67340 AAW	NCBLS	10//99-12//99
Applications	Greensboro--Winston-Salem--High Point MSA, NC	S	29.00 MW	28.59 AW	60330 AAW	NCBLS	10//99-12//99
Applications	Raleigh-Durham-Chapel Hill MSA, NC	S	29.29 MW	27.77 AW	60930 AAW	NCBLS	10//99-12//99
Applications	Wilmington MSA, NC	S	24.14 MW	27.74 AW	50210 AAW	NCBLS	10//99-12//99
Applications	North Dakota	S	23.33 MW	23.79 AW	49470 AAW	NDBLS	10//99-12//99
Applications	Fargo-Moorhead MSA, ND-MN	S	24.20 MW	23.49 AW	50340 AAW	NDBLS	10//99-12//99
Applications	Ohio	S	26.51 MW	27.57 AW	57340 AAW	OHBLS	10//99-12//99
Applications	Akron PMSA, OH	S	24.78 MW	23.43 AW	51540 AAW	OHBLS	10//99-12//99
Applications	Canton-Massillon MSA, OH	S	21.24 MW	21.34 AW	44180 AAW	OHBLS	10//99-12//99
Applications	Cincinnati PMSA, OH-KY-IN	S	27.08 MW	26.45 AW	56330 AAW	OHBLS	10//99-12//99
Applications	Cleveland-Lorain-Elyria PMSA, OH	S	26.63 MW	25.22 AW	55400 AAW	OHBLS	10//99-12//99
Applications	Columbus MSA, OH	S	30.21 MW	29.96 AW	62830 AAW	OHBLS	10//99-12//99
Applications	Dayton-Springfield MSA, OH	S	25.87 MW	26.57 AW	53810 AAW	OHBLS	10//99-12//99
Applications	Hamilton-Middletown PMSA, OH	S	26.07 MW	22.91 AW	54230 AAW	OHBLS	10//99-12//99
Applications	Toledo MSA, OH	S	24.02 MW	22.21 AW	49950 AAW	OHBLS	10//99-12//99
Applications	Oklahoma	S	27.44 MW	25.98 AW	54030 AAW	OKBLS	10//99-12//99
Applications	Oklahoma City MSA, OK	S	24.85 MW	27.18 AW	51680 AAW	OKBLS	10//99-12//99
Applications	Tulsa MSA, OK	S	28.32 MW	29.07 AW	58900 AAW	OKBLS	10//99-12//99
Applications	Oregon	S	35.03 MW	35.19 AW	73200 AAW	ORBLS	10//99-12//99
Applications	Eugene-Springfield MSA, OR	S	25.78 MW	25.61 AW	53620 AAW	ORBLS	10//99-12//99
Applications	Portland-Vancouver PMSA, OR-WA	S	37.03 MW	37.15 AW	77020 AAW	ORBLS	10//99-12//99
Applications	Salem PMSA, OR	S	35.22 MW	32.83 AW	73260 AAW	ORBLS	10//99-12//99
Applications	Pennsylvania	S	29.31 MW	29.93 AW	62260 AAW	PABLS	10//99-12//99
Applications	Allentown-Bethlehem-Easton MSA, PA	S	30.92 MW	30.49 AW	64310 AAW	PABLS	10//99-12//99
Applications	Erie MSA, PA	S	20.12 MW	16.42 AW	41850 AAW	PABLS	10//99-12//99

AAW	Average annual wage	AOH	Average offered, high	ASH	Average starting, high	H	Hourly	M	Monthly	S	Special: hourly and annual
AE	Average entry wage	AOL	Average offered, low	ASL	Average starting, low	HI	Highest wage paid	MTC	Median total compensation	TQ	Third quartile wage
AEX	Average experienced wage	APH	Average pay, high range	AW	Average wage paid	HR	High end range	MW	Median wage paid	W	Weekly
AO	Average offered	APL	Average pay, low range	FQ	First quartile wage	LR	Low end range	SQ	Second quartile wage	Y	Yearly

Occupation/Type/Industry	Location	Per	Low	Mid	High	Source	Date
Computer Software Engineer							
Applications	Harrisburg-Lebanon-Carlisle MSA, PA	S	30.83 MW	29.94 AW	64120 AAW	PABLS	10//99-12//99
Applications	Philadelphia PMSA, PA-NJ	S	33.69 MW	33.41 AW	70070 AAW	PABLS	10//99-12//99
Applications	Pittsburgh MSA, PA	S	28.08 MW	28.26 AW	58400 AAW	PABLS	10//99-12//99
Applications	Reading MSA, PA	S	32.52 MW	37.42 AW	67640 AAW	PABLS	10//99-12//99
Applications	Scranton--Wilkes-Barre--Hazleton MSA, PA	S	31.56 MW	30.74 AW	65650 AAW	PABLS	10//99-12//99
Applications	York MSA, PA	S	26.02 MW	24.60 AW	54130 AAW	PABLS	10//99-12//99
Applications	Rhode Island	S	28.06 MW	27.73 AW	57670 AAW	RIBLS	10//99-12//99
Applications	Providence-Fall River-Warwick MSA, RI-MA	S	24.37 MW	24.62 AW	50700 AAW	RIBLS	10//99-12//99
Applications	South Carolina	S	27.54 MW	27.86 AW	57940 AAW	SCBLS	10//99-12//99
Applications	Charleston-North Charleston MSA, SC	S	24.90 MW	25.38 AW	51790 AAW	SCBLS	10//99-12//99
Applications	Greenville-Spartanburg-Anderson MSA, SC	S	25.90 MW	25.86 AW	53870 AAW	SCBLS	10//99-12//99
Applications	Sumter MSA, SC	S	29.24 MW	29.71 AW	60810 AAW	SCBLS	10//99-12//99
Applications	South Dakota	S	16.8 MW	19.28 AW	40090 AAW	SDBLS	10//99-12//99
Applications	Tennessee	S	23.72 MW	24.54 AW	51050 AAW	TNBLS	10//99-12//99
Applications	Chattanooga MSA, TN-GA	S	23.29 MW	24.24 AW	48440 AAW	TNBLS	10//99-12//99
Applications	Johnson City-Kingsport-Bristol MSA, TN-VA	S	21.13 MW	20.12 AW	43950 AAW	TNBLS	10//99-12//99
Applications	Knoxville MSA, TN	S	24.66 MW	22.60 AW	51300 AAW	TNBLS	10//99-12//99
Applications	Memphis MSA, TN-AR-MS	S	26.27 MW	23.71 AW	54650 AAW	MSBLS	10//99-12//99
Applications	Nashville MSA, TN	S	24.10 MW	24.16 AW	50120 AAW	TNBLS	10//99-12//99
Applications	Texas	S	30.52 MW	31.21 AW	64920 AAW	TXBLS	10//99-12//99
Applications	Amarillo MSA, TX	S	30.35 MW	30.36 AW	63130 AAW	TXBLS	10//99-12//99
Applications	Austin-San Marcos MSA, TX	S	33.15 MW	33.32 AW	68940 AAW	TXBLS	10//99-12//99
Applications	Dallas PMSA, TX	S	31.72 MW	30.77 AW	65980 AAW	TXBLS	10//99-12//99
Applications	Fort Worth-Arlington PMSA, TX	S	30.19 MW	30.87 AW	62790 AAW	TXBLS	10//99-12//99
Applications	Galveston-Texas City PMSA, TX	S	24.82 MW	25.50 AW	51630 AAW	TXBLS	10//99-12//99
Applications	Houston PMSA, TX	S	31.39 MW	30.22 AW	65300 AAW	TXBLS	10//99-12//99
Applications	Killeen-Temple MSA, TX	S	21.60 MW	21.94 AW	44940 AAW	TXBLS	10//99-12//99
Applications	Lubbock MSA, TX	S	21.26 MW	16.52 AW	44210 AAW	TXBLS	10//99-12//99
Applications	San Angelo MSA, TX	S	24.42 MW	24.13 AW	50800 AAW	TXBLS	10//99-12//99
Applications	San Antonio MSA, TX	S	23.89 MW	23.94 AW	49690 AAW	TXBLS	10//99-12//99
Applications	Utah	S	29.02 MW	29.11 AW	60540 AAW	UTBLS	10//99-12//99
Applications	Provo-Orem MSA, UT	S	28.75 MW	29.29 AW	59790 AAW	UTBLS	10//99-12//99
Applications	Salt Lake City-Ogden MSA, UT	S	29.56 MW	29.55 AW	61480 AAW	UTBLS	10//99-12//99
Applications	Vermont	S	23.31 MW	24.34 AW	50620 AAW	VTBLS	10//99-12//99
Applications	Burlington MSA, VT	S	22.90 MW	21.90 AW	47620 AAW	VTBLS	10//99-12//99
Applications	Virginia	S	28.69 MW	28.89 AW	60090 AAW	VABLS	10//99-12//99
Applications	Charlottesville MSA, VA	S	26.20 MW	25.41 AW	54500 AAW	VABLS	10//99-12//99
Applications	Norfolk-Virginia Beach-Newport News MSA, VA-NC	S	23.31 MW	22.37 AW	48490 AAW	VABLS	10//99-12//99
Applications	Richmond-Petersburg MSA, VA	S	27.45 MW	26.81 AW	57100 AAW	VABLS	10//99-12//99
Applications	Roanoke MSA, VA	S	27.69 MW	26.03 AW	57590 AAW	VABLS	10//99-12//99
Applications	Washington	S	25.56 MW	26.81 AW	55770 AAW	WABLS	10//99-12//99
Applications	Bremerton PMSA, WA	S	30.29 MW	30.75 AW	63000 AAW	WABLS	10//99-12//99
Applications	Olympia PMSA, WA	S	27.47 MW	27.00 AW	57140 AAW	WABLS	10//99-12//99
Applications	Richland-Kennewick-Pasco MSA, WA	S	29.81 MW	27.46 AW	62000 AAW	WABLS	10//99-12//99
Applications	Seattle-Bellevue-Everett PMSA, WA	S	26.93 MW	25.73 AW	56020 AAW	WABLS	10//99-12//99
Applications	Spokane MSA, WA	S	22.74 MW	20.73 AW	47300 AAW	WABLS	10//99-12//99
Applications	Tacoma PMSA, WA	S	27.74 MW	25.11 AW	57700 AAW	WABLS	10//99-12//99
Applications	West Virginia	S	26.13 MW	25.22 AW	52460 AAW	WVBLS	10//99-12//99
Applications	Wisconsin	S	26.3 MW	27.70 AW	57620 AAW	WIBLS	10//99-12//99
Applications	Eau Claire MSA, WI	S	27.71 MW	26.43 AW	57650 AAW	WIBLS	10//99-12//99
Applications	Green Bay MSA, WI	S	25.74 MW	24.45 AW	53540 AAW	WIBLS	10//99-12//99
Applications	Madison MSA, WI	S	29.17 MW	27.41 AW	60680 AAW	WIBLS	10//99-12//99
Applications	Milwaukee-Waukesha PMSA, WI	S	26.74 MW	25.52 AW	55610 AAW	WIBLS	10//99-12//99
Applications	Wausau MSA, WI	S	28.50 MW	26.96 AW	59270 AAW	WIBLS	10//99-12//99
Applications	Wyoming	S	20.15 MW	22.50 AW	46800 AAW	WYBLS	10//99-12//99
Applications	Puerto Rico	S	27.94 MW	29.41 AW	61160 AAW	PRBLS	f0//99-12//99

AAW Average annual wage	**AOH** Average offered, high	**ASH** Average starting, high	**H** Hourly	**M** Monthly	**S** Special: hourly and annual
AE Average entry wage	**AOL** Average offered, low	**ASL** Average starting, low	**HI** Highest wage paid	**MTC** Median total compensation	**TQ** Third quartile wage
AEX Average experienced wage	**APH** Average pay, high range	**AW** Average wage paid	**HR** High end range	**MW** Median wage paid	**W** Weekly
AO Average offered	**APL** Average pay, low range	**FQ** First quartile wage	**LR** Low end range	**SQ** Second quartile wage	**Y** Yearly

Occupation/Type/Industry	Location	Per	Low	Mid	High	Source	Date
Computer Software Engineer							
Applications	San Juan-Bayamon PMSA, PR	S	29.65 MW	28.37 AW	61670 AAW	PRBLS	10//99-12//99
Systems Software	Alabama	S	27.99 MW	28.84 AW	59980 AAW	ALBLS	10//99-12//99
Systems Software	Birmingham MSA, AL	S	26.14 MW	24.50 AW	54370 AAW	ALBLS	10//99-12//99
Systems Software	Huntsville MSA, AL	S	31.21 MW	33.00 AW	64910 AAW	ALBLS	10//99-12//99
Systems Software	Montgomery MSA, AL	S	22.64 MW	22.73 AW	47100 AAW	ALBLS	10//99-12//99
Systems Software	Arizona	S	31.78 MW	31.95 AW	66450 AAW	AZBLS	10//99-12//99
Systems Software	Phoenix-Mesa MSA, AZ	S	30.96 MW	31.21 AW	64390 AAW	AZBLS	10//99-12//99
Systems Software	Tucson MSA, AZ	S	33.92 MW	33.03 AW	70560 AAW	AZBLS	10//99-12//99
Systems Software	Arkansas	S	22.53 MW	24.56 AW	51080 AAW	ARBLS	10//99-12//99
Systems Software	Fayetteville-Springdale-Rogers MSA, AR	S	23.43 MW	19.25 AW	48740 AAW	ARBLS	10//99-12//99
Systems Software	Little Rock-North Little Rock MSA, AR	S	24.34 MW	24.18 AW	50630 AAW	ARBLS	10//99-12//99
Systems Software	California	S	33.88 MW	34.88 AW	72560 AAW	CABLS	10//99-12//99
Systems Software	Los Angeles-Long Beach PMSA, CA	S	31.81 MW	30.06 AW	66150 AAW	CABLS	10//99-12//99
Systems Software	Oakland PMSA, CA	S	34.99 MW	33.45 AW	72780 AAW	CABLS	10//99-12//99
Systems Software	Orange County PMSA, CA	S	31.25 MW	32.70 AW	65000 AAW	CABLS	10//99-12//99
Systems Software	Riverside-San Bernardino PMSA, CA	S	26.64 MW	25.03 AW	55420 AAW	CABLS	10//99-12//99
Systems Software	Sacramento PMSA, CA	S	33.09 MW	32.03 AW	68820 AAW	CABLS	10//99-12//99
Systems Software	San Diego MSA, CA	S	30.13 MW	30.18 AW	62670 AAW	CABLS	10//99-12//99
Systems Software	San Francisco PMSA, CA	S	29.77 MW	26.28 AW	61920 AAW	CABLS	10//99-12//99
Systems Software	San Jose PMSA, CA	S	39.23 MW	38.97 AW	81590 AAW	CABLS	10//99-12//99
Systems Software	Santa Barbara-Santa Maria-Lompoc MSA, CA	S	23.72 MW	23.21 AW	49330 AAW	CABLS	10//99-12//99
Systems Software	Santa Cruz-Watsonville PMSA, CA	S	39.92 MW	41.93 AW	83030 AAW	CABLS	10//99-12//99
Systems Software	Santa Rosa PMSA, CA	S	31.42 MW	30.34 AW	65350 AAW	CABLS	10//99-12//99
Systems Software	Colorado	S	31.04 MW	31.04 AW	64570 AAW	COBLS	10//99-12//99
Systems Software	Boulder-Longmont PMSA, CO	S	31.85 MW	31.77 AW	66250 AAW	COBLS	10//99-12//99
Systems Software	Colorado Springs MSA, CO	S	30.47 MW	30.72 AW	63380 AAW	COBLS	10//99-12//99
Systems Software	Denver PMSA, CO	S	31.56 MW	31.30 AW	65640 AAW	COBLS	10//99-12//99
Systems Software	Fort Collins-Loveland MSA, CO	S	30.18 MW	30.82 AW	62770 AAW	COBLS	10//99-12//99
Systems Software	Connecticut	S	28.86 MW	30.93 AW	64340 AAW	CTBLS	10//99-12//99
Systems Software	Bridgeport PMSA, CT	S	27.77 MW	26.65 AW	57770 AAW	CTBLS	10//99-12//99
Systems Software	Hartford MSA, CT	S	31.11 MW	29.54 AW	64710 AAW	CTBLS	10//99-12//99
Systems Software	New Haven-Meriden PMSA, CT	S	34.90 MW	30.69 AW	72600 AAW	CTBLS	10//99-12//99
Systems Software	Stamford-Norwalk PMSA, CT	S	29.10 MW	27.12 AW	60520 AAW	CTBLS	10//99-12//99
Systems Software	Delaware	S	38.55 MW	37.74 AW	78490 AAW	DEBLS	10//99-12//99
Systems Software	Wilmington-Newark PMSA, DE-MD	S	37.62 MW	38.47 AW	78250 AAW	DEBLS	10//99-12//99
Systems Software	District of Columbia	S	31.86 MW	34.92 AW	72640 AAW	DCBLS	10//99-12//99
Systems Software	Washington PMSA, DC-MD-VA-WV	S	31.89 MW	31.38 AW	66340 AAW	DCBLS	10//99-12//99
Systems Software	Florida	S	29.77 MW	30.68 AW	63810 AAW	FLBLS	10//99-12//99
Systems Software	Daytona Beach MSA, FL	S	28.68 MW	28.29 AW	59650 AAW	FLBLS	10//99-12//99
Systems Software	Fort Lauderdale PMSA, FL	S	36.80 MW	38.16 AW	76530 AAW	FLBLS	10//99-12//99
Systems Software	Fort Walton Beach MSA, FL	S	27.47 MW	27.26 AW	57140 AAW	FLBLS	10//99-12//99
Systems Software	Gainesville MSA, FL	S	34.99 MW	35.24 AW	72770 AAW	FLBLS	10//99-12//99
Systems Software	Jacksonville MSA, FL	S	30.12 MW	30.42 AW	62660 AAW	FLBLS	10//99-12//99
Systems Software	Melbourne-Titusville-Palm Bay MSA, FL	S	26.45 MW	25.40 AW	55010 AAW	FLBLS	10//99-12//99
Systems Software	Miami PMSA, FL	S	26.83 MW	24.49 AW	55800 AAW	FLBLS	10//99-12//99
Systems Software	Orlando MSA, FL	S	31.22 MW	34.20 AW	64930 AAW	FLBLS	10//99-12//99
Systems Software	Pensacola MSA, FL	S	17.40 MW	15.82 AW	36180 AAW	FLBLS	10//99-12//99
Systems Software	Tampa-St. Petersburg-Clearwater MSA, FL	S	28.89 MW	28.77 AW	60090 AAW	FLBLS	10//99-12//99
Systems Software	West Palm Beach-Boca Raton MSA, FL	S	29.29 MW	30.11 AW	60920 AAW	FLBLS	10//99-12//99
Systems Software	Georgia	S	29.37 MW	29.43 AW	61210 AAW	GABLS	10//99-12//99
Systems Software	Atlanta MSA, GA	S	29.47 MW	29.41 AW	61300 AAW	GABLS	10//99-12//99
Systems Software	Macon MSA, GA	S	31.64 MW	31.49 AW	65810 AAW	GABLS	10//99-12//99
Systems Software	Hawaii	S	25.38 MW	25.56 AW	53160 AAW	HIBLS	10//99-12//99
Systems Software	Honolulu MSA, HI	S	25.24 MW	24.93 AW	52490 AAW	HIBLS	10//99-12//99
Systems Software	Idaho	S	32.85 MW	32.81 AW	68250 AAW	IDBLS	10//99-12//99
Systems Software	Boise City MSA, ID	S	33.21 MW	33.30 AW	69090 AAW	IDBLS	10//99-12//99
Systems Software	Illinois	S	35.9 MW	34.35 AW	71450 AAW	ILBLS	10//99-12//99
Systems Software	Chicago PMSA, IL	S	34.75 MW	36.23 AW	72290 AAW	ILBLS	10//99-12//99

AAW	Average annual wage	AOH	Average offered, high	ASH	Average starting, high
AE	Average entry wage	AOL	Average offered, low	ASL	Average starting, low
AEX	Average experienced wage	APH	Average pay, high range	AW	Average wage paid
AO	Average offered	APL	Average pay, low range	FQ	First quartile wage

H	Hourly	M	Monthly
HI	Highest wage paid	MTC	Median total compensation
HR	High end range	MW	Median wage paid
LR	Low end range	SQ	Second quartile wage

S	Special: hourly and annual
TQ	Third quartile wage
W	Weekly
Y	Yearly

Occupation/Type/Industry	Location	Per	Low	Mid	High	Source	Date
Computer Software Engineer							
Systems Software	Rockford MSA, IL	S	29.97 MW	29.09 AW	62350 AAW	ILBLS	10//99-12//99
Systems Software	Indiana	S	32.49 MW	30.43 AW	63300 AAW	INBLS	10//99-12//99
Systems Software	Elkhart-Goshen MSA, IN	S	20.30 MW	17.27 AW	42230 AAW	INBLS	10//99-12//99
Systems Software	Fort Wayne MSA, IN	S	23.64 MW	16.42 AW	49160 AAW	INBLS	10//99-12//99
Systems Software	Indianapolis MSA, IN	S	31.99 MW	35.73 AW	66550 AAW	INBLS	10//99-12//99
Systems Software	Lafayette MSA, IN	S	27.79 MW	26.16 AW	57800 AAW	INBLS	10//99-12//99
Systems Software	Iowa	S	26.96 MW	27.01 AW	56180 AAW	IABLS	10//99-12//99
Systems Software	Davenport-Moline-Rock Island MSA, IA-IL	S	22.49 MW	20.06 AW	46780 AAW	IABLS	10//99-12//99
Systems Software	Des Moines MSA, IA	S	26.74 MW	27.28 AW	55620 AAW	IABLS	10//99-12//99
Systems Software	Kansas	S	25.61 MW	31.38 AW	65270 AAW	KSBLS	10//99-12//99
Systems Software	Wichita MSA, KS	S	23.87 MW	20.52 AW	49650 AAW	KSBLS	10//99-12//99
Systems Software	Kentucky	S	28.58 MW	27.42 AW	57030 AAW	KYBLS	10//99-12//99
Systems Software	Lexington MSA, KY	S	31.76 MW	32.60 AW	66050 AAW	KYBLS	10//99-12//99
Systems Software	Louisville MSA, KY-IN	S	27.21 MW	27.98 AW	56590 AAW	KYBLS	10//99-12//99
Systems Software	Louisiana	S	25.38 MW	26.85 AW	55840 AAW	LABLS	10//99-12//99
Systems Software	Baton Rouge MSA, LA	S	21.74 MW	16.97 AW	45210 AAW	LABLS	10//99-12//99
Systems Software	New Orleans MSA, LA	S	29.93 MW	28.53 AW	62260 AAW	LABLS	10//99-12//99
Systems Software	Maine	S	26.17 MW	25.82 AW	53710 AAW	MEBLS	10//99-12//99
Systems Software	Portland MSA, ME	S	24.33 MW	24.26 AW	50610 AAW	MEBLS	10//99-12//99
Systems Software	Maryland	S	31.7 MW	31.92 AW	66400 AAW	MDBLS	10//99-12//99
Systems Software	Baltimore PMSA, MD	S	36.66 MW	36.74 AW	76250 AAW	MDBLS	10//99-12//99
Systems Software	Massachusetts	S	36.08 MW	36.22 AW	75330 AAW	MABLS	10//99-12//99
Systems Software	Boston PMSA, MA-NH	S	36.25 MW	36.04 AW	75400 AAW	MABLS	10//99-12//99
Systems Software	Lawrence PMSA, MA-NH	S	36.50 MW	33.63 AW	75930 AAW	MABLS	10//99-12//99
Systems Software	Lowell PMSA, MA-NH	S	36.03 MW	36.72 AW	74940 AAW	MABLS	10//99-12//99
Systems Software	Springfield MSA, MA	S	36.25 MW	35.75 AW	75400 AAW	MABLS	10//99-12//99
Systems Software	Worcester PMSA, MA-CT	S	31.95 MW	35.29 AW	66450 AAW	MABLS	10//99-12//99
Systems Software	Michigan	S	33.17 MW	33.38 AW	69430 AAW	MIBLS	10//99-12//99
Systems Software	Ann Arbor PMSA, MI	S	31.92 MW	31.58 AW	66390 AAW	MIBLS	10//99-12//99
Systems Software	Detroit PMSA, MI	S	34.15 MW	34.22 AW	71040 AAW	MIBLS	10//99-12//99
Systems Software	Grand Rapids-Muskegon-Holland MSA, MI	S	31.02 MW	32.02 AW	64520 AAW	MIBLS	10//99-12//99
Systems Software	Kalamazoo-Battle Creek MSA, MI	S	25.36 MW	24.57 AW	52750 AAW	MIBLS	10//99-12//99
Systems Software	Lansing-East Lansing MSA, MI	S	25.10 MW	25.83 AW	52210 AAW	MIBLS	10//99-12//99
Systems Software	Minnesota	S	29.87 MW	30.50 AW	63440 AAW	MNBLS	10//99-12//99
Systems Software	Minneapolis-St. Paul MSA, MN-WI	S	29.96 MW	29.42 AW	62320 AAW	MNBLS	10//99-12//99
Systems Software	Mississippi	S	23.44 MW	25.49 AW	53020 AAW	MSBLS	10//99-12//99
Systems Software	Biloxi-Gulfport-Pascagoula MSA, MS	S	34.48 MW	37.59 AW	71710 AAW	MSBLS	10//99-12//99
Systems Software	Jackson MSA, MS	S	22.41 MW	20.83 AW	46610 AAW	MSBLS	10//99-12//99
Systems Software	Missouri	S	27.65 MW	28.32 AW	58900 AAW	MOBLS	10//99-12//99
Systems Software	Kansas City MSA, MO-KS	S	32.86 MW	27.22 AW	68360 AAW	MOBLS	10//99-12//99
Systems Software	St. Louis MSA, MO-IL	S	28.04 MW	27.24 AW	58320 AAW	MOBLS	10//99-12//99
Systems Software	Montana	S	25.87 MW	26.43 AW	54970 AAW	MTBLS	10//99-12//99
Systems Software	Nebraska	S	25.68 MW	27.37 AW	56930 AAW	NEBLS	10//99-12//99
Systems Software	Omaha MSA, NE-IA	S	27.36 MW	25.67 AW	56900 AAW	NEBLS	10//99-12//99
Systems Software	Nevada	S	25.1 MW	25.71 AW	53480 AAW	NVBLS	10//99-12//99
Systems Software	Las Vegas MSA, NV-AZ	S	25.29 MW	24.95 AW	52610 AAW	NVBLS	10//99-12//99
Systems Software	New Hampshire	S	30.03 MW	29.07 AW	60470 AAW	NHBLS	10//99-12//99
Systems Software	Manchester PMSA, NH	S	25.96 MW	26.16 AW	54000 AAW	NHBLS	10//99-12//99
Systems Software	Nashua PMSA, NH	S	30.69 MW	31.66 AW	63830 AAW	NHBLS	10//99-12//99
Systems Software	New Jersey	S	33.97 MW	34.25 AW	71250 AAW	NJBLS	10//99-12//99
Systems Software	Bergen-Passaic PMSA, NJ	S	32.37 MW	33.46 AW	67330 AAW	NJBLS	10//99-12//99
Systems Software	Jersey City PMSA, NJ	S	35.63 MW	35.38 AW	74110 AAW	NJBLS	10//99-12//99
Systems Software	Middlesex-Somerset-Hunterdon PMSA, NJ	S	34.86 MW	33.25 AW	72510 AAW	NJBLS	10//99-12//99
Systems Software	Monmouth-Ocean PMSA, NJ	S	29.40 MW	26.90 AW	61160 AAW	NJBLS	10//99-12//99
Systems Software	Newark PMSA, NJ	S	35.03 MW	32.96 AW	72860 AAW	NJBLS	10//99-12//99
Systems Software	Trenton PMSA, NJ	S	30.21 MW	26.85 AW	62840 AAW	NJBLS	10//99-12//99
Systems Software	New Mexico	S	28.96 MW	29.18 AW	60690 AAW	NMBLS	10//99-12//99
Systems Software	Albuquerque MSA, NM	S	29.91 MW	29.45 AW	62220 AAW	NMBLS	10//99-12//99
Systems Software	New York	S	32.27 MW	33.07 AW	68780 AAW	NYBLS	10//99-12//99
Systems Software	Buffalo-Niagara Falls MSA, NY	S	24.40 MW	23.87 AW	50750 AAW	NYBLS	10//99-12//99
Systems Software	Dutchess County PMSA, NY	S	32.43 MW	32.27 AW	67450 AAW	NYBLS	10//99-12//99
Systems Software	Nassau-Suffolk PMSA, NY	S	28.71 MW	27.40 AW	59720 AAW	NYBLS	10//99-12//99
Systems Software	New York PMSA, NY	S	35.80 MW	34.00 AW	74470 AAW	NYBLS	10//99-12//99
Systems Software	Rochester MSA, NY	S	31.92 MW	31.84 AW	66390 AAW	NYBLS	10//99-12//99

AAW Average annual wage	**AOH** Average offered, high	**ASH** Average starting, high	**H** Hourly	**M** Monthly	**S** Special: hourly and annual
AE Average entry wage	**AOL** Average offered, low	**ASL** Average starting, low	**HI** Highest wage paid	**MTC** Median total compensation	**TQ** Third quartile wage
AEX Average experienced wage	**APH** Average pay, high range	**AW** Average wage paid	**HR** High end range	**MW** Median wage paid	**W** Weekly
AO Average offered	**APL** Average pay, low range	**FQ** First quartile wage	**LR** Low end range	**SQ** Second quartile wage	**Y** Yearly

Occupation/Type/Industry	Location	Per	Low	Mid	High	Source	Date
Computer Software Engineer							
Systems Software	Syracuse MSA, NY	S	27.76 MW	26.20 AW	57740 AAW	NYBLS	10//99-12//99
Systems Software	Utica-Rome MSA, NY	S	28.83 MW	30.02 AW	59970 AAW	NYBLS	10//99-12//99
Systems Software	North Carolina	S	29.24 MW	29.37 AW	61090 AAW	NCBLS	10//99-12//99
Systems Software	Charlotte-Gastonia-Rock Hill MSA, NC-SC	S	32.05 MW	32.15 AW	66670 AAW	NCBLS	10//99-12//99
Systems Software	Fayetteville MSA, NC	S	18.26 MW	17.56 AW	37980 AAW	NCBLS	10//99-12//99
Systems Software	Greensboro--Winston-Salem-- High Point MSA, NC	S	23.03 MW	21.56 AW	47890 AAW	NCBLS	10//99-12//99
Systems Software	Raleigh-Durham-Chapel Hill MSA, NC	S	30.93 MW	31.55 AW	64340 AAW	NCBLS	10//99-12//99
Systems Software	North Dakota	S	19.88 MW	21.86 AW	45480 AAW	NDBLS	10//99-12//99
Systems Software	Ohio	S	28.97 MW	30.32 AW	63070 AAW	OHBLS	10//99-12//99
Systems Software	Akron PMSA, OH	S	29.95 MW	30.42 AW	62300 AAW	OHBLS	10//99-12//99
Systems Software	Cincinnati PMSA, OH-KY-IN	S	27.47 MW	28.27 AW	57150 AAW	OHBLS	10//99-12//99
Systems Software	Cleveland-Lorain-Elyria PMSA, OH	S	28.34 MW	28.09 AW	58950 AAW	OHBLS	10//99-12//99
Systems Software	Columbus MSA, OH	S	29.00 MW	28.17 AW	60330 AAW	OHBLS	10//99-12//99
Systems Software	Dayton-Springfield MSA, OH	S	24.21 MW	24.04 AW	50360 AAW	OHBLS	10//99-12//99
Systems Software	Lima MSA, OH	S	28.94 MW	30.19 AW	60190 AAW	OHBLS	10//99-12//99
Systems Software	Toledo MSA, OH	S	25.42 MW	25.81 AW	52880 AAW	OHBLS	10//99-12//99
Systems Software	Youngstown-Warren MSA, OH	S	24.54 MW	26.12 AW	51040 AAW	OHBLS	10//99-12//99
Systems Software	Oklahoma	S	26.84 MW	26.71 AW	55560 AAW	OKBLS	10//99-12//99
Systems Software	Oklahoma City MSA, OK	S	28.11 MW	28.50 AW	58470 AAW	OKBLS	10//99-12//99
Systems Software	Tulsa MSA, OK	S	24.78 MW	23.90 AW	51550 AAW	OKBLS	10//99-12//99
Systems Software	Oregon	S	28.29 MW	32.10 AW	66770 AAW	ORBLS	10//99-12//99
Systems Software	Portland-Vancouver PMSA, OR-WA	S	31.77 MW	28.17 AW	66090 AAW	ORBLS	10//99-12//99
Systems Software	Pennsylvania	S	29.78 MW	29.60 AW	61560 AAW	PABLS	10//99-12//99
Systems Software	Harrisburg-Lebanon-Carlisle MSA, PA	S	30.74 MW	30.21 AW	63930 AAW	PABLS	10//99-12//99
Systems Software	Philadelphia PMSA, PA-NJ	S	30.72 MW	30.90 AW	63890 AAW	PABLS	10//99-12//99
Systems Software	Pittsburgh MSA, PA	S	29.47 MW	29.88 AW	61300 AAW	PABLS	10//99-12//99
Systems Software	Reading MSA, PA	S	30.77 MW	30.79 AW	64010 AAW	PABLS	10//99-12//99
Systems Software	Rhode Island	S	31.54 MW	32.22 AW	67010 AAW	RIBLS	10//99-12//99
Systems Software	Providence-Fall River- Warwick MSA, RI-MA	S	31.56 MW	31.33 AW	65630 AAW	RIBLS	10//99-12//99
Systems Software	South Carolina	S	26.24 MW	27.31 AW	56800 AAW	SCBLS	10//99-12//99
Systems Software	Charleston-North Charleston MSA, SC	S	26.03 MW	25.58 AW	54150 AAW	SCBLS	10//99-12//99
Systems Software	Columbia MSA, SC	S	33.28 MW	33.86 AW	69220 AAW	SCBLS	10//99-12//99
Systems Software	Greenville-Spartanburg- Anderson MSA, SC	S	26.36 MW	25.01 AW	54830 AAW	SCBLS	10//99-12//99
Systems Software	South Dakota	S	22.8 MW	23.37 AW	48610 AAW	SDBLS	10//99-12//99
Systems Software	Tennessee	S	24.07 MW	25.31 AW	52650 AAW	TNBLS	10//99-12//99
Systems Software	Chattanooga MSA, TN-GA	S	25.08 MW	28.55 AW	52160 AAW	TNBLS	10//99-12//99
Systems Software	Knoxville MSA, TN	S	25.68 MW	26.97 AW	53410 AAW	TNBLS	10//99-12//99
Systems Software	Memphis MSA, TN-AR-MS	S	25.60 MW	25.24 AW	53250 AAW	MSBLS	10//99-12//99
Systems Software	Nashville MSA, TN	S	27.00 MW	23.52 AW	56160 AAW	TNBLS	10//99-12//99
Systems Software	Texas	S	30.7 MW	31.76 AW	66060 AAW	TXBLS	10//99-12//99
Systems Software	Austin-San Marcos MSA, TX	S	33.47 MW	32.59 AW	69620 AAW	TXBLS	10//99-12//99
Systems Software	Dallas PMSA, TX	S	32.44 MW	31.28 AW	67480 AAW	TXBLS	10//99-12//99
Systems Software	Fort Worth-Arlington PMSA, TX	S	30.03 MW	29.80 AW	62460 AAW	TXBLS	10//99-12//99
Systems Software	Galveston-Texas City PMSA, TX	S	26.64 MW	27.93 AW	55400 AAW	TXBLS	10//99-12//99
Systems Software	Houston PMSA, TX	S	31.52 MW	30.07 AW	65560 AAW	TXBLS	10//99-12//99
Systems Software	Killeen-Temple MSA, TX	S	35.87 MW	37.99 AW	74610 AAW	TXBLS	10//99-12//99
Systems Software	San Antonio MSA, TX	S	29.09 MW	28.20 AW	60500 AAW	TXBLS	10//99-12//99
Systems Software	Sherman-Denison MSA, TX	S	34.87 MW	35.37 AW	72530 AAW	TXBLS	10//99-12//99
Systems Software	Waco MSA, TX	S	23.85 MW	20.34 AW	49610 AAW	TXBLS	10//99-12//99
Systems Software	Utah	S	26.21 MW	26.53 AW	55180 AAW	UTBLS	10//99-12//99
Systems Software	Provo-Orem MSA, UT	S	28.39 MW	28.74 AW	59050 AAW	UTBLS	10//99-12//99
Systems Software	Salt Lake City-Ogden MSA, UT	S	25.15 MW	24.04 AW	52310 AAW	UTBLS	10//99-12//99
Systems Software	Vermont	S	35.54 MW	34.92 AW	72630 AAW	VTBLS	10//99-12//99
Systems Software	Burlington MSA, VT	S	29.41 MW	27.48 AW	61170 AAW	VTBLS	10//99-12//99
Systems Software	Virginia	S	29.74 MW	29.73 AW	61840 AAW	VABLS	10//99-12//99
Systems Software	Norfolk-Virginia Beach- Newport News MSA, VA-NC	S	27.53 MW	26.66 AW	57270 AAW	VABLS	10//99-12//99

AAW	Average annual wage	AOH Average offered, high	ASH Average starting, high	H Hourly	M Monthly	S Special: hourly and annual
AE	Average entry wage	AOL Average offered, low	ASL Average starting, low	HI Highest wage paid	MTC Median total compensation TQ Third quartile wage	
AEX	Average experienced wage	APH Average pay, high range	AW Average wage paid	HR High end range	MW Median wage paid	W Weekly
AO	Average offered	APL Average pay, low range	FQ First quartile wage	LR Low end range	SQ Second quartile wage	Y Yearly

Occupation/Type/Industry	Location	Per	Low	Mid	High	Source	Date
Computer Software Engineer							
Systems Software	Richmond-Petersburg MSA, VA	S	29.40 MW	29.72 AW	61150 AAW	VABLS	10//99-12//99
Systems Software	Roanoke MSA, VA	S	41.93 MW	38.39 AW	87210 AAW	VABLS	10//99-12//99
Systems Software	Washington	S	30.88 MW	31.62 AW	65780 AAW	WABLS	10//99-12//99
Systems Software	Olympia PMSA, WA	S	26.50 MW	26.46 AW	55110 AAW	WABLS	10//99-12//99
Systems Software	Seattle-Bellevue-Everett PMSA, WA	S	31.78 MW	30.95 AW	66110 AAW	WABLS	10//99-12//99
Systems Software	West Virginia	S	24.37 MW	25.64 AW	53340 AAW	WVBLS	10//99-12//99
Systems Software	Charleston MSA, WV	S	31.93 MW	32.53 AW	66420 AAW	WVBLS	10//99-12//99
Systems Software	Wisconsin	S	26.27 MW	26.65 AW	55430 AAW	WIBLS	10//99-12//99
Systems Software	Green Bay MSA, WI	S	23.04 MW	23.60 AW	47920 AAW	WIBLS	10//99-12//99
Systems Software	Madison MSA, WI	S	25.84 MW	25.97 AW	53740 AAW	WIBLS	10//99-12//99
Systems Software	Milwaukee-Waukesha PMSA, WI	S	25.94 MW	25.94 AW	53960 AAW	WIBLS	10//99-12//99
Systems Software	Puerto Rico	S	29.29 MW	29.78 AW	61930 AAW	PRBLS	10//99-12//99
Systems Software	San Juan-Bayamon PMSA, PR	S	30.01 MW	29.89 AW	62420 AAW	PRBLS	10//99-12//99
Computer Support Specialist	Alabama	S	14.83 MW	15.74 AW	32750 AAW	ALBLS	10//99-12//99
	Alaska	S	17.52 MW	17.99 AW	37420 AAW	AKBLS	10//99-12//99
	Arizona	S	18.47 MW	19.43 AW	40420 AAW	AZBLS	10//99-12//99
	Arkansas	S	11.27 MW	12.41 AW	25810 AAW	ARBLS	10//99-12//99
	California	S	20.19 MW	21.91 AW	45570 AAW	CABLS	10//99-12//99
	Colorado	S	15.26 MW	15.87 AW	33010 AAW	COBLS	10//99-12//99
	Connecticut	S	20.89 MW	21.37 AW	44450 AAW	CTBLS	10//99-12//99
	District of Columbia	S	20.07 MW	20.34 AW	42300 AAW	DCBLS	10//99-12//99
	Florida	S	15.42 MW	16.55 AW	34420 AAW	FLBLS	10//99-12//99
	Georgia	S	14.78 MW	16.73 AW	34800 AAW	GABLS	10//99-12//99
	Hawaii	S	19.2 MW	19.83 AW	41240 AAW	HIBLS	10//99-12//99
	Idaho	S	16.08 MW	17.18 AW	35730 AAW	IDBLS	10//99-12//99
	Illinois	S	18.99 MW	19.99 AW	41580 AAW	ILBLS	10//99-12//99
	Indiana	S	15.29 MW	15.70 AW	32650 AAW	INBLS	10//99-12//99
	Iowa	S	16.06 MW	17.30 AW	35990 AAW	IABLS	10//99-12//99
	Kansas	S	19.35 MW	19.70 AW	40970 AAW	KSBLS	10//99-12//99
	Kentucky	S	13.41 MW	15.27 AW	31760 AAW	KYBLS	10//99-12//99
	Louisiana	S	16.38 MW	17.86 AW	37150 AAW	LABLS	10//99-12//99
	Maine	S	14.65 MW	15.00 AW	31210 AAW	MEBLS	10//99-12//99
	Maryland	S	18.84 MW	19.77 AW	41130 AAW	MDBLS	10//99-12//99
	Massachusetts	S	19.45 MW	20.94 AW	43550 AAW	MABLS	10//99-12//99
	Michigan	S	18.72 MW	19.87 AW	41330 AAW	MIBLS	10//99-12//99
	Minnesota	S	18.01 MW	18.83 AW	39160 AAW	MNBLS	10//99-12//99
	Mississippi	S	14.74 MW	16.41 AW	34130 AAW	MSBLS	10//99-12//99
	Missouri	S	17.2 MW	18.98 AW	39480 AAW	MOBLS	10//99-12//99
	Montana	S	13.12 MW	13.33 AW	27720 AAW	MTBLS	10//99-12//99
	Nebraska	S	16.01 MW	17.28 AW	35940 AAW	NEBLS	10//99-12//99
	Nevada	S	15.66 MW	16.71 AW	34760 AAW	NVBLS	10//99-12//99
	New Hampshire	S	15.96 MW	16.65 AW	34640 AAW	NHBLS	10//99-12//99
	New Jersey	S	20.09 MW	22.05 AW	45870 AAW	NJBLS	10//99-12//99
	New Mexico	S	14.32 MW	15.29 AW	31810 AAW	NMBLS	10//99-12//99
	New York	S	18.59 MW	19.64 AW	40860 AAW	NYBLS	10//99-12//99
	North Carolina	S	19.1 MW	20.40 AW	42440 AAW	NCBLS	10//99-12//99
	North Dakota	S	8.88 MW	10.60 AW	22040 AAW	NDBLS	10//99-12//99
	Ohio	S	18.37 MW	19.10 AW	39720 AAW	OHBLS	10//99-12//99
	Oklahoma	S	12.81 MW	14.18 AW	29500 AAW	OKBLS	10//99-12//99
	Oregon	S	16.44 MW	17.76 AW	36950 AAW	ORBLS	10//99-12//99
	Pennsylvania	S	17.63 MW	18.60 AW	38680 AAW	PABLS	10//99-12//99
	Rhode Island	S	21.18 MW	23.33 AW	48520 AAW	RIBLS	10//99-12//99
	South Carolina	S	16.87 MW	17.86 AW	37150 AAW	SCBLS	10//99-12//99
	South Dakota	S	11.82 MW	12.23 AW	25450 AAW	SDBLS	10//99-12//99
	Tennessee	S	13.31 MW	14.49 AW	30130 AAW	TNBLS	10//99-12//99
	Texas	S	17.49 MW	19.82 AW	41230 AAW	TXBLS	10//99-12//99
	Utah	S	13.45 MW	14.37 AW	29880 AAW	UTBLS	10//99-12//99
	Vermont	S	15.56 MW	17.31 AW	36010 AAW	VTBLS	10//99-12//99
	Virginia	S	15.92 MW	17.51 AW	36420 AAW	VABLS	10//99-12//99
	Washington	S	17.42 MW	18.11 AW	37660 AAW	WABLS	10//99-12//99
	West Virginia	S	12.3 MW	13.35 AW	27770 AAW	WVBLS	10//99-12//99
	Wisconsin	S	17.71 MW	17.90 AW	37230 AAW	WIBLS	10//99-12//99
	Wyoming	S	8.04 MW	9.77 AW	20320 AAW	WYBLS	10//99-12//99
	Puerto Rico	S	10.64 MW	11.21 AW	23310 AAW	PRBLS	10//99-12//99
	Guam	S	15.12 MW	15.50 AW	32230 AAW	GUBLS	10//99-12//99
Computer Systems Analyst	United States	H		27.90 AW		NCS98	1998
	Alabama	S	24.4 MW	24.89 AW	51770 AAW	ALBLS	10//99-12//99

AAW	Average annual wage	AOH	Average offered, high	ASH	Average starting, high	H	Hourly	M	Monthly	S	Special: hourly and annual
AE	Average entry wage	AOL	Average offered, low	ASL	Average starting, low	HI	Highest wage paid	MTC	Median total compensation	TQ	Third quartile wage
AEX	Average experienced wage	APH	Average pay, high range	AW	Average wage paid	HR	High end range	MW	Median wage paid	W	Weekly
AO	Average offered	APL	Average pay, low range	FQ	First quartile wage	LR	Low end range	SQ	Second quartile wage	Y	Yearly

Occupation/Type/Industry	Location	Per	Low	Mid	High	Source	Date
Computer Systems Analyst	Birmingham MSA, AL	S	25.53 MW	24.80 AW	53100 AAW	ALBLS	10//99-12//99
	Florence MSA, AL	S	23.14 MW	23.09 AW	48130 AAW	ALBLS	10//99-12//99
	Huntsville MSA, AL	S	24.64 MW	24.26 AW	51240 AAW	ALBLS	10//99-12//99
	Mobile MSA, AL	S	25.92 MW	25.68 AW	53920 AAW	ALBLS	10//99-12//99
	Montgomery MSA, AL	S	24.30 MW	24.37 AW	50530 AAW	ALBLS	10//99-12//99
	Arizona	S	25.64 MW	26.36 AW	54840 AAW	AZBLS	10//99-12//99
	Flagstaff MSA, AZ-UT	S	21.45 MW	20.61 AW	44610 AAW	AZBLS	10//99-12//99
	Phoenix-Mesa MSA, AZ	S	27.20 MW	26.02 AW	56580 AAW	AZBLS	10//99-12//99
	Tucson MSA, AZ	S	22.27 MW	21.79 AW	46320 AAW	AZBLS	10//99-12//99
	Yuma MSA, AZ	S	20.45 MW	18.41 AW	42540 AAW	AZBLS	10//99-12//99
	Arkansas	S	20.07 MW	20.72 AW	43110 AAW	ARBLS	10//99-12//99
	Fayetteville-Springdale-Rogers MSA, AR	S	19.10 MW	18.65 AW	39730 AAW	ARBLS	10//99-12//99
	Fort Smith MSA, AR-OK	S	21.11 MW	20.76 AW	43900 AAW	ARBLS	10//99-12//99
	Little Rock-North Little Rock MSA, AR	S	20.88 MW	20.42 AW	43430 AAW	ARBLS	10//99-12//99
	California	S	27.43 MW	29.20 AW	60740 AAW	CABLS	10//99-12//99
	Chico-Paradise MSA, CA	S	22.58 MW	20.33 AW	46960 AAW	CABLS	10//99-12//99
	Fresno MSA, CA	S	23.59 MW	23.94 AW	49060 AAW	CABLS	10//99-12//99
	Los Angeles-Long Beach PMSA, CA	S	25.74 MW	24.84 AW	53540 AAW	CABLS	10//99-12//99
	Modesto MSA, CA	S	21.31 MW	21.93 AW	44330 AAW	CABLS	10//99-12//99
	Oakland PMSA, CA	S	31.16 MW	29.60 AW	64810 AAW	CABLS	10//99-12//99
	Orange County PMSA, CA	S	26.59 MW	24.89 AW	55310 AAW	CABLS	10//99-12//99
	Redding MSA, CA	S	20.73 MW	20.64 AW	43130 AAW	CABLS	10//99-12//99
	Riverside-San Bernardino PMSA, CA	S	23.54 MW	22.50 AW	48960 AAW	CABLS	10//99-12//99
	Sacramento PMSA, CA	S	25.51 MW	25.14 AW	53060 AAW	CABLS	10//99-12//99
	San Diego MSA, CA	S	24.91 MW	24.22 AW	51820 AAW	CABLS	10//99-12//99
	San Francisco PMSA, CA	S	33.20 MW	33.31 AW	69050 AAW	CABLS	10//99-12//99
	San Jose PMSA, CA	S	35.28 MW	34.65 AW	73380 AAW	CABLS	10//99-12//99
	San Luis Obispo-Atascadero-Paso Robles MSA, CA	S	24.34 MW	24.93 AW	50630 AAW	CABLS	10//99-12//99
	Santa Barbara-Santa Maria-Lompoc MSA, CA	S	28.12 MW	27.00 AW	58500 AAW	CABLS	10//99-12//99
	Santa Cruz-Watsonville PMSA, CA	S	24.61 MW	24.15 AW	51200 AAW	CABLS	10//99-12//99
	Santa Rosa PMSA, CA	S	26.91 MW	23.22 AW	55960 AAW	CABLS	10//99-12//99
	Stockton-Lodi MSA, CA	S	21.65 MW	21.28 AW	45030 AAW	CABLS	10//99-12//99
	Vallejo-Fairfield-Napa PMSA, CA	S	21.72 MW	20.74 AW	45170 AAW	CABLS	10//99-12//99
	Ventura PMSA, CA	S	28.44 MW	26.95 AW	59160 AAW	CABLS	10//99-12//99
	Visalia-Tulare-Porterville MSA, CA	S	23.57 MW	22.56 AW	49020 AAW	CABLS	10//99-12//99
	Colorado	S	28.58 MW	28.42 AW	59120 AAW	COBLS	10//99-12//99
	Boulder-Longmont PMSA, CO	S	30.46 MW	30.47 AW	63360 AAW	COBLS	10//99-12//99
	Denver PMSA, CO	S	29.67 MW	29.70 AW	61710 AAW	COBLS	10//99-12//99
	Fort Collins-Loveland MSA, CO	S	31.58 MW	31.38 AW	65680 AAW	COBLS	10//99-12//99
	Connecticut	S	27.36 MW	28.56 AW	59400 AAW	CTBLS	10//99-12//99
	Bridgeport PMSA, CT	S	29.28 MW	29.47 AW	60890 AAW	CTBLS	10//99-12//99
	Danbury PMSA, CT	S	36.51 MW	34.16 AW	75930 AAW	CTBLS	10//99-12//99
	Hartford MSA, CT	S	28.37 MW	26.75 AW	59000 AAW	CTBLS	10//99-12//99
	New Haven-Meriden PMSA, CT	S	31.23 MW	31.58 AW	64960 AAW	CTBLS	10//99-12//99
	New London-Norwich MSA, CT-RI	S	25.25 MW	24.51 AW	52510 AAW	CTBLS	10//99-12//99
	Stamford-Norwalk PMSA, CT	S	29.30 MW	28.54 AW	60950 AAW	CTBLS	10//99-12//99
	Delaware	S	28.6 MW	28.18 AW	58610 AAW	DEBLS	10//99-12//99
	Wilmington-Newark PMSA, DE-MD	S	28.09 MW	28.42 AW	58430 AAW	DEBLS	10//99-12//99
	Washington PMSA, DC-MD-VA-WV	S	29.83 MW	29.75 AW	62060 AAW	DCBLS	10//99-12//99
	Florida	S	24.56 MW	25.27 AW	52570 AAW	FLBLS	10//99-12//99
	Daytona Beach MSA, FL	S	21.27 MW	21.71 AW	44240 AAW	FLBLS	10//99-12//99
	Fort Lauderdale PMSA, FL	S	28.08 MW	28.36 AW	58400 AAW	FLBLS	10//99-12//99
	Fort Myers-Cape Coral MSA, FL	S	21.13 MW	22.26 AW	43960 AAW	FLBLS	10//99-12//99
	Fort Pierce-Port St. Lucie MSA, FL	S	19.95 MW	19.47 AW	41490 AAW	FLBLS	10//99-12//99
	Fort Walton Beach MSA, FL	S	25.32 MW	24.05 AW	52670 AAW	FLBLS	10//99-12//99
	Gainesville MSA, FL	S	18.47 MW	17.57 AW	38410 AAW	FLBLS	10//99-12//99

Occupation/Type/Industry	Location	Per	Low	Mid	High	Source	Date
Computer Systems Analyst	Jacksonville MSA, FL	S	26.82 MW	26.16 AW	55770 AAW	FLBLS	10//99-12//99
	Lakeland-Winter Haven MSA, FL	S	22.81 MW	23.28 AW	47440 AAW	FLBLS	10//99-12//99
	Melbourne-Titusville-Palm Bay MSA, FL	S	22.68 MW	22.47 AW	47170 AAW	FLBLS	10//99-12//99
	Miami PMSA, FL	S	25.63 MW	25.59 AW	53320 AAW	FLBLS	10//99-12//99
	Naples MSA, FL	S	21.57 MW	21.67 AW	44860 AAW	FLBLS	10//99-12//99
	Orlando MSA, FL	S	24.30 MW	23.88 AW	50550 AAW	FLBLS	10//99-12//99
	Panama City MSA, FL	S	22.46 MW	22.40 AW	46720 AAW	FLBLS	10//99-12//99
	Sarasota-Bradenton MSA, FL	S	24.16 MW	19.73 AW	50250 AAW	FLBLS	10//99-12//99
	Tampa-St. Petersburg-Clearwater MSA, FL	S	26.63 MW	25.95 AW	55400 AAW	FLBLS	10//99-12//99
	West Palm Beach-Boca Raton MSA, FL	S	26.42 MW	25.50 AW	54950 AAW	FLBLS	10//99-12//99
	Georgia	S	28.06 MW	28.27 AW	58800 AAW	GABLS	10//99-12//99
	Albany MSA, GA	S	23.99 MW	23.21 AW	49890 AAW	GABLS	10//99-12//99
	Atlanta MSA, GA	S	29.97 MW	29.84 AW	62340 AAW	GABLS	10//99-12//99
	Augusta-Aiken MSA, GA-SC	S	26.24 MW	24.99 AW	54580 AAW	GABLS	10//99-12//99
	Columbus MSA, GA-AL	S	24.03 MW	24.27 AW	49980 AAW	GABLS	10//99-12//99
	Macon MSA, GA	S	25.63 MW	25.47 AW	53310 AAW	GABLS	10//99-12//99
	Savannah MSA, GA	S	20.11 MW	17.95 AW	41830 AAW	GABLS	10//99-12//99
	Hawaii	S	22.17 MW	22.52 AW	46850 AAW	HIBLS	10//99-12//99
	Honolulu MSA, HI	S	22.57 MW	22.30 AW	46940 AAW	HIBLS	10//99-12//99
	Idaho	S	26.11 MW	27.14 AW	56460 AAW	IDBLS	10//99-12//99
	Boise City MSA, ID	S	28.38 MW	27.10 AW	59030 AAW	IDBLS	10//99-12//99
	Illinois	S	28.78 MW	30.29 AW	63000 AAW	ILBLS	10//99-12//99
	Bloomington-Normal MSA, IL	S	38.09 MW	39.74 AW	79230 AAW	ILBLS	10//99-12//99
	Champaign-Urbana MSA, IL	S	26.83 MW	26.02 AW	55800 AAW	ILBLS	10//99-12//99
	Chicago PMSA, IL	S	30.39 MW	28.85 AW	63210 AAW	ILBLS	10//99-12//99
	Peoria-Pekin MSA, IL	S	25.94 MW	25.90 AW	53950 AAW	ILBLS	10//99-12//99
	Rockford MSA, IL	S	25.39 MW	25.14 AW	52800 AAW	ILBLS	10//99-12//99
	Springfield MSA, IL	S	26.03 MW	26.48 AW	54150 AAW	ILBLS	10//99-12//99
	Indiana	S	22.95 MW	23.67 AW	49230 AAW	INBLS	10//99-12//99
	Bloomington MSA, IN	S	21.96 MW	21.90 AW	45670 AAW	INBLS	10//99-12//99
	Elkhart-Goshen MSA, IN	S	20.96 MW	22.83 AW	43590 AAW	INBLS	10//99-12//99
	Evansville-Henderson MSA, IN-KY	S	19.52 MW	16.51 AW	40610 AAW	INBLS	10//99-12//99
	Fort Wayne MSA, IN	S	23.84 MW	23.75 AW	49590 AAW	INBLS	10//99-12//99
	Gary PMSA, IN	S	23.59 MW	23.53 AW	49070 AAW	INBLS	10//99-12//99
	Indianapolis MSA, IN	S	23.64 MW	22.65 AW	49180 AAW	INBLS	10//99-12//99
	Lafayette MSA, IN	S	20.71 MW	21.85 AW	43070 AAW	INBLS	10//99-12//99
	South Bend MSA, IN	S	22.86 MW	20.80 AW	47550 AAW	INBLS	10//99-12//99
	Terre Haute MSA, IN	S	37.08 MW	39.74 AW	77120 AAW	INBLS	10//99-12//99
	Iowa	S	23.7 MW	23.76 AW	49430 AAW	IABLS	10//99-12//99
	Cedar Rapids MSA, IA	S	23.61 MW	23.10 AW	49100 AAW	IABLS	10//99-12//99
	Des Moines MSA, IA	S	24.65 MW	24.71 AW	51260 AAW	IABLS	10//99-12//99
	Iowa City MSA, IA	S	24.85 MW	24.00 AW	51680 AAW	IABLS	10//99-12//99
	Kansas	S	24.62 MW	26.53 AW	55180 AAW	KSBLS	10//99-12//99
	Wichita MSA, KS	S	26.12 MW	24.83 AW	54330 AAW	KSBLS	10//99-12//99
	Kentucky	S	24.63 MW	24.75 AW	51470 AAW	KYBLS	10//99-12//99
	Lexington MSA, KY	S	24.99 MW	24.36 AW	51990 AAW	KYBLS	10//99-12//99
	Louisville MSA, KY-IN	S	25.12 MW	25.46 AW	52250 AAW	KYBLS	10//99-12//99
	Louisiana	S	23.11 MW	23.82 AW	49540 AAW	LABLS	10//99-12//99
	Alexandria MSA, LA	S	21.76 MW	21.19 AW	45260 AAW	LABLS	10//99-12//99
	Baton Rouge MSA, LA	S	20.45 MW	20.14 AW	42540 AAW	LABLS	10//99-12//99
	Houma MSA, LA	S	20.69 MW	20.24 AW	43020 AAW	LABLS	10//99-12//99
	Lafayette MSA, LA	S	25.37 MW	26.67 AW	52770 AAW	LABLS	10//99-12//99
	Lake Charles MSA, LA	S	22.43 MW	20.79 AW	46650 AAW	LABLS	10//99-12//99
	Monroe MSA, LA	S	20.91 MW	20.10 AW	43500 AAW	LABLS	10//99-12//99
	New Orleans MSA, LA	S	25.02 MW	24.28 AW	52040 AAW	LABLS	10//99-12//99
	Shreveport-Bossier City MSA, LA	S	21.72 MW	21.37 AW	45180 AAW	LABLS	10//99-12//99
	Maine	S	23.2 MW	23.29 AW	48440 AAW	MEBLS	10//99-12//99
	Bangor MSA, ME	S	18.17 MW	15.89 AW	37780 AAW	MEBLS	10//99-12//99
	Portland MSA, ME	S	24.50 MW	24.53 AW	50970 AAW	MEBLS	10//99-12//99
	Maryland	S	28.82 MW	28.44 AW	59150 AAW	MDBLS	10//99-12//99
	Baltimore PMSA, MD	S	28.44 MW	28.82 AW	59150 AAW	MDBLS	10//99-12//99
	Hagerstown PMSA, MD	S	26.73 MW	26.87 AW	55590 AAW	MDBLS	10//99-12//99
	Massachusetts	S	29.46 MW	30.13 AW	62680 AAW	MABLS	10//99-12//99
	Boston PMSA, MA-NH	S	30.31 MW	29.64 AW	63050 AAW	MABLS	10//99-12//99
	Brockton PMSA, MA	S	26.13 MW	27.15 AW	54360 AAW	MABLS	10//99-12//99
	Lawrence PMSA, MA-NH	S	31.78 MW	31.43 AW	66100 AAW	MABLS	10//99-12//99

AAW Average annual wage	AOH Average offered, high	ASH Average starting, high	H Hourly	M Monthly	S Special: hourly and annual
AE Average entry wage	AOL Average offered, low	ASL Average starting, low	HI Highest wage paid	MTC Median total compensation	TQ Third quartile wage
AEX Average experienced wage	APH Average pay, high range	AW Average wage paid	HR High end range	MW Median wage paid	W Weekly
AO Average offered	APL Average pay, low range	FQ First quartile wage	LR Low end range	SQ Second quartile wage	Y Yearly

Occupation/Type/Industry	Location	Per	Low	Mid	High	Source	Date
Computer Systems Analyst	Lowell PMSA, MA-NH	S	35.02 MW	32.74 AW	72850 AAW	MABLS	10//99-12//99
	New Bedford PMSA, MA	S	25.95 MW	24.77 AW	53980 AAW	MABLS	10//99-12//99
	Pittsfield MSA, MA	S	31.95 MW	30.68 AW	66450 AAW	MABLS	10//99-12//99
	Worcester PMSA, MA-CT	S	27.99 MW	28.08 AW	58210 AAW	MABLS	10//99-12//99
	Michigan	S	26.55 MW	26.57 AW	55270 AAW	MIBLS	10//99-12//99
	Ann Arbor PMSA, MI	S	25.96 MW	26.17 AW	54000 AAW	MIBLS	10//99-12//99
	Benton Harbor MSA, MI	S	22.20 MW	19.68 AW	46170 AAW	MIBLS	10//99-12//99
	Detroit PMSA, MI	S	27.35 MW	27.90 AW	56880 AAW	MIBLS	10//99-12//99
	Flint PMSA, MI	S	26.98 MW	26.83 AW	56120 AAW	MIBLS	10//99-12//99
	Grand Rapids-Muskegon-Holland MSA, MI	S	24.71 MW	24.35 AW	51400 AAW	MIBLS	
	Kalamazoo-Battle Creek MSA, MI	S	25.24 MW	25.76 AW	52500 AAW	MIBLS	10//99-12//99
	Lansing-East Lansing MSA, MI	S	25.13 MW	24.93 AW	52270 AAW	MIBLS	10//99-12//99
	Saginaw-Bay City-Midland MSA, MI	S	26.08 MW	25.63 AW	54240 AAW	MIBLS	10//99-12//99
	Minnesota	S	27.73 MW	28.92 AW	60160 AAW	MNBLS	10//99-12//99
	Duluth-Superior MSA, MN-WI	S	26.13 MW	24.28 AW	54360 AAW	MNBLS	10//99-12//99
	Minneapolis-St. Paul MSA, MN-WI	S	29.17 MW	27.94 AW	60680 AAW	MNBLS	10//99-12//99
	St. Cloud MSA, MN	S	24.67 MW	24.87 AW	51320 AAW	MNBLS	10//99-12//99
	Mississippi	S	22.24 MW	22.61 AW	47020 AAW	MSBLS	10//99-12//99
	Biloxi-Gulfport-Pascagoula MSA, MS	S	22.13 MW	21.92 AW	46030 AAW	MSBLS	10//99-12//99
	Hattiesburg MSA, MS	S	22.48 MW	23.64 AW	46750 AAW	MSBLS	10//99-12//99
	Jackson MSA, MS	S	22.93 MW	22.20 AW	47700 AAW	MSBLS	10//99-12//99
	Missouri	S	25.62 MW	25.48 AW	52990 AAW	MOBLS	10//99-12//99
	Columbia MSA, MO	S	19.69 MW	19.28 AW	40960 AAW	MOBLS	10//99-12//99
	Kansas City MSA, MO-KS	S	24.94 MW	23.96 AW	51880 AAW	MOBLS	10//99-12//99
	St. Louis MSA, MO-IL	S	26.84 MW	27.26 AW	55830 AAW	MOBLS	10//99-12//99
	Springfield MSA, MO	S	24.71 MW	24.76 AW	51390 AAW	MOBLS	10//99-12//99
	Montana	S	23.7 MW	24.30 AW	50550 AAW	MTBLS	10//99-12//99
	Missoula MSA, MT	S	21.67 MW	20.82 AW	45080 AAW	MTBLS	10//99-12//99
	Nebraska	S	25.24 MW	24.98 AW	51950 AAW	NEBLS	10//99-12//99
	Lincoln MSA, NE	S	24.57 MW	22.93 AW	51100 AAW	NEBLS	10//99-12//99
	Omaha MSA, NE-IA	S	25.24 MW	26.13 AW	52500 AAW	NEBLS	10//99-12//99
	Nevada	S	24.66 MW	25.52 AW	53090 AAW	NVBLS	10//99-12//99
	Las Vegas MSA, NV-AZ	S	26.04 MW	25.00 AW	54150 AAW	NVBLS	10//99-12//99
	Reno MSA, NV	S	23.33 MW	23.65 AW	48520 AAW	NVBLS	10//99-12//99
	New Hampshire	S	26.2 MW	27.94 AW	58110 AAW	NHBLS	10//99-12//99
	Manchester PMSA, NH	S	24.67 MW	24.49 AW	51320 AAW	NHBLS	10//99-12//99
	Nashua PMSA, NH	S	28.41 MW	26.44 AW	59100 AAW	NHBLS	10//99-12//99
	Portsmouth-Rochester PMSA, NH-ME	S	27.52 MW	28.38 AW	57250 AAW	NHBLS	
	New Jersey	S	29.69 MW	32.03 AW	66620 AAW	NJBLS	10//99-12//99
	Jersey City PMSA, NJ	S	32.41 MW	31.13 AW	67410 AAW	NJBLS	
	Middlesex-Somerset-Hunterdon PMSA, NJ	S	30.22 MW	28.87 AW	62860 AAW	NJBLS	10//99-12//99
	Monmouth-Ocean PMSA, NJ	S	30.68 MW	29.01 AW	63820 AAW	NJBLS	10//99-12//99
	Trenton PMSA, NJ	S	23.40 MW	21.11 AW	48670 AAW	NJBLS	10//99-12//99
	Vineland-Millville-Bridgeton PMSA, NJ	S	27.79 MW	29.06 AW	57800 AAW	NJBLS	10//99-12//99
	New Mexico	S	23.54 MW	24.07 AW	50070 AAW	NMBLS	10//99-12//99
	Albuquerque MSA, NM	S	25.08 MW	24.46 AW	52170 AAW	NMBLS	10//99-12//99
	New York	S	29.53 MW	30.80 AW	64060 AAW	NYBLS	10//99-12//99
	Albany-Schenectady-Troy MSA, NY	S	30.18 MW	26.64 AW	62770 AAW	NYBLS	10//99-12//99
	Binghamton MSA, NY	S	26.72 MW	25.66 AW	55570 AAW	NYBLS	10//99-12//99
	Buffalo-Niagara Falls MSA, NY	S	20.66 MW	19.68 AW	42970 AAW	NYBLS	10//99-12//99
	Dutchess County PMSA, NY	S	31.64 MW	26.47 AW	65810 AAW	NYBLS	10//99-12//99
	Glens Falls MSA, NY	S	29.83 MW	30.30 AW	62040 AAW	NYBLS	10//99-12//99
	Nassau-Suffolk PMSA, NY	S	26.37 MW	25.33 AW	54860 AAW	NYBLS	10//99-12//99
	New York PMSA, NY	S	32.77 MW	31.68 AW	68160 AAW	NYBLS	10//99-12//99
	Newburgh PMSA, NY-PA	S	24.64 MW	24.29 AW	51250 AAW	NYBLS	10//99-12//99
	Rochester MSA, NY	S	30.59 MW	29.05 AW	63620 AAW	NYBLS	10//99-12//99
	Syracuse MSA, NY	S	24.45 MW	25.76 AW	50860 AAW	NYBLS	10//99-12//99
	Utica-Rome MSA, NY	S	25.35 MW	24.94 AW	52720 AAW	NYBLS	10//99-12//99
	North Carolina	S	26.48 MW	26.16 AW	54410 AAW	NCBLS	10//99-12//99
	Asheville MSA, NC	S	20.56 MW	20.28 AW	42770 AAW	NCBLS	10//99-12//99
	Charlotte-Gastonia-Rock Hill MSA, NC-SC	S	26.59 MW	25.64 AW	55310 AAW	NCBLS	10//99-12//99

AAW Average annual wage	AOH Average offered, high	ASH Average starting, high	H Hourly	M Monthly	S Special: hourly and annual
AE Average entry wage	AOL Average offered, low	ASL Average starting, low	HI Highest wage paid	MTC Median total compensation	TQ Third quartile wage
AEX Average experienced wage	APH Average pay, high range	AW Average wage paid	HR High end range	MW Median wage paid	W Weekly
AO Average offered	APL Average pay, low range	FQ First quartile wage	LR Low end range	SQ Second quartile wage	Y Yearly

Occupation/Type/Industry	Location	Per	Low	Mid	High	Source	Date
Computer Systems Analyst	Fayetteville MSA, NC	S	15.89 MW	14.74 AW	33060 AAW	NCBLS	10//99-12//99
	Greensboro--Winston-Salem-- High Point MSA, NC	S	29.29 MW	29.72 AW	60910 AAW	NCBLS	10//99-12//99
	Hickory-Morganton-Lenoir MSA, NC	S	19.82 MW	18.29 AW	41230 AAW	NCBLS	10//99-12//99
	Raleigh-Durham-Chapel Hill MSA, NC	S	24.64 MW	23.95 AW	51260 AAW	NCBLS	10//99-12//99
	Wilmington MSA, NC	S	22.21 MW	22.27 AW	46200 AAW	NCBLS	10//99-12//99
	North Dakota	S	21.3 MW	21.71 AW	45160 AAW	NDBLS	10//99-12//99
	Bismarck MSA, ND	S	21.98 MW	21.46 AW	45710 AAW	NDBLS	10//99-12//99
	Fargo-Moorhead MSA, ND-MN	S	23.71 MW	23.54 AW	49310 AAW	NDBLS	10//99-12//99
	Ohio	S	25.78 MW	26.62 AW	55360 AAW	OHBLS	10//99-12//99
	Akron PMSA, OH	S	24.41 MW	24.37 AW	50780 AAW	OHBLS	10//99-12//99
	Canton-Massillon MSA, OH	S	24.08 MW	24.71 AW	50080 AAW	OHBLS	10//99-12//99
	Cincinnati PMSA, OH-KY-IN	S	28.10 MW	26.52 AW	58440 AAW	OHBLS	10//99-12//99
	Cleveland-Lorain-Elyria PMSA, OH	S	28.16 MW	28.40 AW	58570 AAW	OHBLS	10//99-12//99
	Columbus MSA, OH	S	25.81 MW	24.17 AW	53690 AAW	OHBLS	10//99-12//99
	Dayton-Springfield MSA, OH	S	25.08 MW	24.79 AW	52170 AAW	OHBLS	10//99-12//99
	Hamilton-Middletown PMSA, OH	S	24.80 MW	23.74 AW	51590 AAW	OHBLS	10//99-12//99
	Lima MSA, OH	S	25.44 MW	25.39 AW	52910 AAW	OHBLS	10//99-12//99
	Mansfield MSA, OH	S	21.17 MW	21.57 AW	44030 AAW	OHBLS	10//99-12//99
	Steubenville-Weirton MSA, OH-WV	S	25.97 MW	23.38 AW	54010 AAW	OHBLS	10//99-12//99
	Toledo MSA, OH	S	25.62 MW	24.51 AW	53300 AAW	OHBLS	10//99-12//99
	Youngstown-Warren MSA, OH	S	24.43 MW	23.96 AW	50810 AAW	OHBLS	10//99-12//99
	Oklahoma	S	21.33 MW	22.12 AW	46000 AAW	OKBLS	10//99-12//99
	Oklahoma City MSA, OK	S	21.80 MW	21.34 AW	45350 AAW	OKBLS	10//99-12//99
	Tulsa MSA, OK	S	23.41 MW	23.32 AW	48700 AAW	OKBLS	10//99-12//99
	Oregon	S	26.7 MW	27.07 AW	56300 AAW	ORBLS	10//99-12//99
	Corvallis MSA, OR	S	24.07 MW	24.23 AW	50070 AAW	ORBLS	10//99-12//99
	Eugene-Springfield MSA, OR	S	26.26 MW	25.29 AW	54620 AAW	ORBLS	10//99-12//99
	Medford-Ashland MSA, OR	S	22.04 MW	22.03 AW	45850 AAW	ORBLS	10//99-12//99
	Portland-Vancouver PMSA, OR-WA	S	27.48 MW	27.06 AW	57150 AAW	ORBLS	10//99-12//99
	Salem PMSA, OR	S	26.37 MW	27.01 AW	54860 AAW	ORBLS	10//99-12//99
	Pennsylvania	S	26.57 MW	27.40 AW	56990 AAW	PABLS	10//99-12//99
	Allentown-Bethlehem-Easton MSA, PA	S	24.51 MW	24.73 AW	50990 AAW	PABLS	10//99-12//99
	Altoona MSA, PA	S	26.73 MW	28.14 AW	55610 AAW	PABLS	10//99-12//99
	Erie MSA, PA	S	24.53 MW	24.65 AW	51020 AAW	PABLS	10//99-12//99
	Harrisburg-Lebanon-Carlisle MSA, PA	S	25.21 MW	24.98 AW	52430 AAW	PABLS	10//99-12//99
	Lancaster MSA, PA	S	28.30 MW	27.74 AW	58860 AAW	PABLS	10//99-12//99
	Philadelphia PMSA, PA-NJ	S	28.99 MW	27.34 AW	60300 AAW	PABLS	10//99-12//99
	Pittsburgh MSA, PA	S	29.22 MW	29.05 AW	60790 AAW	PABLS	10//99-12//99
	Reading MSA, PA	S	24.19 MW	24.41 AW	50320 AAW	PABLS	10//99-12//99
	Scranton--Wilkes-Barre--Hazleton MSA, PA	S	24.10 MW	24.33 AW	50130 AAW	PABLS	10//99-12//99
	York MSA, PA	S	24.94 MW	24.80 AW	51870 AAW	PABLS	10//99-12//99
	Rhode Island	S	25.96 MW	25.88 AW	53830 AAW	RIBLS	10//99-12//99
	Providence-Fall River-Warwick MSA, RI-MA	S	25.89 MW	25.83 AW	53850 AAW	RIBLS	10//99-12//99
	South Carolina	S	23.84 MW	24.35 AW	50640 AAW	SCBLS	10//99-12//99
	Charleston-North Charleston MSA, SC	S	23.06 MW	21.14 AW	47960 AAW	SCBLS	10//99-12//99
	Columbia MSA, SC	S	25.49 MW	24.72 AW	53010 AAW	SCBLS	10//99-12//99
	Florence MSA, SC	S	22.01 MW	22.89 AW	45780 AAW	SCBLS	10//99-12//99
	Greenville-Spartanburg-Anderson MSA, SC	S	24.24 MW	24.12 AW	50410 AAW	SCBLS	10//99-12//99
	Myrtle Beach MSA, SC	S	22.42 MW	21.18 AW	46630 AAW	SCBLS	10//99-12//99
	South Dakota	S	23.68 MW	23.77 AW	49450 AAW	SDBLS	10//99-12//99
	Rapid City MSA, SD	S	23.14 MW	23.22 AW	48130 AAW	SDBLS	10//99-12//99
	Sioux Falls MSA, SD	S	25.43 MW	25.29 AW	52890 AAW	SDBLS	10//99-12//99
	Tennessee	S	23.57 MW	23.85 AW	49620 AAW	TNBLS	10//99-12//99
	Jackson MSA, TN	S	29.38 MW	29.64 AW	61110 AAW	TNBLS	10//99-12//99
	Johnson City-Kingsport-Bristol MSA, TN-VA	S	22.88 MW	21.63 AW	47600 AAW	TNBLS	10//99-12//99
	Knoxville MSA, TN	S	25.78 MW	25.54 AW	53610 AAW	TNBLS	10//99-12//99
	Memphis MSA, TN-AR-MS	S	24.26 MW	23.59 AW	50460 AAW	MSBLS	10//99-12//99

AAW	Average annual wage	AOH	Average offered, high	ASH	Average starting, high	H	Hourly	M	Monthly	S	Special: hourly and annual
AE	Average entry wage	AOL	Average offered, low	ASL	Average starting, low	HI	Highest wage paid	MTC	Median total compensation	TQ	Third quartile wage
AEX	Average experienced wage	APH	Average pay, high range	AW	Average wage paid	HR	High end range	MW	Median wage paid	W	Weekly
AO	Average offered	APL	Average pay, low range	FQ	First quartile wage	LR	Low end range	SQ	Second quartile wage	Y	Yearly

280

Occupation/Type/Industry	Location	Per	Low	Mid	High	Source	Date
Computer Systems Analyst	Nashville MSA, TN	S	21.95 MW	21.24 AW	45660 AAW	TNBLS	10//99-12//99
	Texas	S	25.55 MW	26.28 AW	54670 AAW	TXBLS	10//99-12//99
	Amarillo MSA, TX	S	23.24 MW	22.82 AW	48340 AAW	TXBLS	10//99-12//99
	Austin-San Marcos MSA, TX	S	24.63 MW	23.93 AW	51230 AAW	TXBLS	10//99-12//99
	Beaumont-Port Arthur MSA, TX	S	25.50 MW	25.16 AW	53040 AAW	TXBLS	10//99-12//99
	Brazoria PMSA, TX	S	21.95 MW	16.70 AW	45650 AAW	TXBLS	10//99-12//99
	Brownsville-Harlingen-San Benito MSA, TX	S	21.78 MW	22.13 AW	45310 AAW	TXBLS	10//99-12//99
	Bryan-College Station MSA, TX	S	21.96 MW	21.22 AW	45670 AAW	TXBLS	10//99-12//99
	Corpus Christi MSA, TX	S	25.04 MW	24.34 AW	52090 AAW	TXBLS	10//99-12//99
	Dallas PMSA, TX	S	29.74 MW	29.50 AW	61860 AAW	TXBLS	10//99-12//99
	El Paso MSA, TX	S	18.68 MW	18.24 AW	38850 AAW	TXBLS	10//99-12//99
	Fort Worth-Arlington PMSA, TX	S	25.14 MW	23.70 AW	52280 AAW	TXBLS	10//99-12//99
	Galveston-Texas City PMSA, TX	S	28.19 MW	27.19 AW	58630 AAW	TXBLS	10//99-12//99
	Houston PMSA, TX	S	27.88 MW	27.14 AW	57990 AAW	TXBLS	10//99-12//99
	Laredo MSA, TX	S	17.79 MW	13.30 AW	37000 AAW	TXBLS	10//99-12//99
	Lubbock MSA, TX	S	20.84 MW	20.45 AW	43340 AAW	TXBLS	10//99-12//99
	McAllen-Edinburg-Mission MSA, TX	S	23.73 MW	23.44 AW	49350 AAW	TXBLS	10//99-12//99
	Odessa-Midland MSA, TX	S	26.57 MW	28.20 AW	55270 AAW	TXBLS	10//99-12//99
	San Angelo MSA, TX	S	15.16 MW	12.85 AW	31540 AAW	TXBLS	10//99-12//99
	San Antonio MSA, TX	S	17.72 MW	15.86 AW	36850 AAW	TXBLS	10//99-12//99
	Texarkana MSA, TX-Texarkana, AR	S	27.82 MW	26.11 AW	57870 AAW	TXBLS	10//99-12//99
	Tyler MSA, TX	S	19.30 MW	20.29 AW	40150 AAW	TXBLS	10//99-12//99
	Waco MSA, TX	S	22.60 MW	19.83 AW	47010 AAW	TXBLS	10//99-12//99
	Wichita Falls MSA, TX	S	17.89 MW	18.80 AW	37200 AAW	TXBLS	10//99-12//99
	Utah	S	23.79 MW	23.65 AW	49180 AAW	UTBLS	10//99-12//99
	Provo-Orem MSA, UT	S	17.52 MW	17.53 AW	36440 AAW	UTBLS	10//99-12//99
	Salt Lake City-Ogden MSA, UT	S	24.24 MW	24.28 AW	50410 AAW	UTBLS	10//99-12//99
	Vermont	S	18.89 MW	19.69 AW	40960 AAW	VTBLS	10//99-12//99
	Burlington MSA, VT	S	20.51 MW	22.04 AW	42670 AAW	VTBLS	10//99-12//99
	Virginia	S	29.33 MW	29.69 AW	61750 AAW	VABLS	10//99-12//99
	Charlottesville MSA, VA	S	29.44 MW	30.03 AW	61230 AAW	VABLS	10//99-12//99
	Lynchburg MSA, VA	S	30.81 MW	31.25 AW	64080 AAW	VABLS	10//99-12//99
	Norfolk-Virginia Beach-Newport News MSA, VA-NC	S	24.34 MW	24.20 AW	50630 AAW	VABLS	10//99-12//99
	Richmond-Petersburg MSA, VA	S	25.97 MW	25.16 AW	54020 AAW	VABLS	10//99-12//99
	Roanoke MSA, VA	S	26.69 MW	27.23 AW	55510 AAW	VABLS	10//99-12//99
	Washington	S	29.69 MW	29.70 AW	61780 AAW	WABLS	10//99-12//99
	Olympia PMSA, WA	S	20.60 MW	19.11 AW	42850 AAW	WABLS	10//99-12//99
	Richland-Kennewick-Pasco MSA, WA	S	29.49 MW	28.75 AW	61340 AAW	WABLS	10//99-12//99
	Seattle-Bellevue-Everett PMSA, WA	S	30.38 MW	30.37 AW	63190 AAW	WABLS	10//99-12//99
	Spokane MSA, WA	S	27.07 MW	27.39 AW	56300 AAW	WABLS	10//99-12//99
	Tacoma PMSA, WA	S	22.59 MW	22.87 AW	46990 AAW	WABLS	10//99-12//99
	West Virginia	S	27.04 MW	28.91 AW	60130 AAW	WVBLS	10//99-12//99
	Charleston MSA, WV	S	25.39 MW	24.63 AW	52820 AAW	WVBLS	10//99-12//99
	Huntington-Ashland MSA, WV-KY-OH	S	26.15 MW	22.96 AW	54390 AAW	WVBLS	10//99-12//99
	Wisconsin	S	23.34 MW	23.83 AW	49570 AAW	WIBLS	10//99-12//99
	Appleton-Oshkosh-Neenah MSA, WI	S	23.49 MW	23.08 AW	48850 AAW	WIBLS	10//99-12//99
	Eau Claire MSA, WI	S	20.85 MW	20.30 AW	43360 AAW	WIBLS	10//99-12//99
	Green Bay MSA, WI	S	25.03 MW	24.98 AW	52060 AAW	WIBLS	10//99-12//99
	Janesville-Beloit MSA, WI	S	26.17 MW	25.45 AW	54430 AAW	WIBLS	10//99-12//99
	Kenosha PMSA, WI	S	20.44 MW	20.23 AW	42510 AAW	WIBLS	10//99-12//99
	La Crosse MSA, WI-MN	S	22.07 MW	22.12 AW	45910 AAW	WIBLS	10//99-12//99
	Madison MSA, WI	S	22.43 MW	22.14 AW	46660 AAW	WIBLS	10//99-12//99
	Milwaukee-Waukesha PMSA, WI	S	25.47 MW	24.80 AW	52980 AAW	WIBLS	10//99-12//99
	Racine PMSA, WI	S	24.36 MW	24.16 AW	50670 AAW	WIBLS	10//99-12//99
	Sheboygan MSA, WI	S	23.68 MW	23.42 AW	49250 AAW	WIBLS	10//99-12//99
	Wyoming	S	20.15 MW	20.95 AW	43570 AAW	WYBLS	10//99-12//99

Occupation/Type/Industry	Location	Per	Low	Mid	High	Source	Date
Computer Systems Analyst	Puerto Rico	S	18.44 MW	18.72 AW	38940 AAW	PRBLS	10//99-12//99
	Mayaguez MSA, PR	S	12.20 MW	12.13 AW	25380 AAW	PRBLS	10//99-12//99
	San Juan-Bayamon PMSA, PR	S	18.55 MW	18.34 AW	38580 AAW	PRBLS	10//99-12//99
	Guam	S	19.72 MW	19.53 AW	40620 AAW	GUBLS	10//99-12//99
Computer Technician	United States	Y		58000 MW		CORES4	2000
A+ Certification	United States	Y		50000 MW		CORES4	2000
CNE Certification	United States	Y		56000 MW		CORES4	2000
MCP and A+ Certification	United States	Y		66750 MW		CORES4	2000
MCP Certification	United States	Y		52500 MW		CORES4	2000
MCSE and CCNA Certification	United States	Y		65000 MW		CORES4	2000
MCSE and CNE Certification	United States	Y		60500 MW		CORES4	2000
MCSE Certification	United States	Y		58700 MW		CORES4	2000
Concierge	Arizona	S	8.08 MW	8.64 AW	17970 AAW	AZBLS	10//99-12//99
	California	S	11.93 MW	13.41 AW	27890 AAW	CABLS	10//99-12//99
	Colorado	S	9.54 MW	9.62 AW	20010 AAW	COBLS	10//99-12//99
	Connecticut	S	10.24 MW	10.55 AW	21940 AAW	CTBLS	10//99-12//99
	District of Columbia	S	14.19 MW	13.87 AW	28850 AAW	DCBLS	10//99-12//99
	Florida	S	7.87 MW	8.13 AW	16920 AAW	FLBLS	10//99-12//99
	Georgia	S	9.74 MW	9.90 AW	20580 AAW	GABLS	10//99-12//99
	Hawaii	S	16.76 MW	18.17 AW	37800 AAW	HIBLS	10//99-12//99
	Illinois	S	9.6 MW	9.61 AW	19990 AAW	ILBLS	10//99-12//99
	Indiana	S	8.37 MW	8.44 AW	17550 AAW	INBLS	10//99-12//99
	Iowa	S	6.91 MW	6.88 AW	14320 AAW	IABLS	10//99-12//99
	Kansas	S	6.35 MW	6.33 AW	13170 AAW	KSBLS	10//99-12//99
	Kentucky	S	7.73 MW	7.72 AW	16050 AAW	KYBLS	10//99-12//99
	Louisiana	S	6.66 MW	7.10 AW	14770 AAW	LABLS	10//99-12//99
	Maryland	S	8.38 MW	9.53 AW	19820 AAW	MDBLS	10//99-12//99
	Massachusetts	S	10.37 MW	10.61 AW	22070 AAW	MABLS	10//99-12//99
	Michigan	S	7.48 MW	7.67 AW	15960 AAW	MIBLS	10//99-12//99
	Minnesota	S	9.9 MW	10.36 AW	21540 AAW	MNBLS	10//99-12//99
	Mississippi	S	9.18 MW	9.18 AW	19100 AAW	MSBLS	10//99-12//99
	Nevada	S	9.78 MW	11.31 AW	23530 AAW	NVBLS	10//99-12//99
	New Hampshire	S	9.04 MW	8.99 AW	18700 AAW	NHBLS	10//99-12//99
	New Jersey	S	10.03 MW	10.18 AW	21180 AAW	NJBLS	10//99-12//99
	New Mexico	S	9.16 MW	9.04 AW	18810 AAW	NMBLS	10//99-12//99
	New York	S	14.87 MW	14.02 AW	29170 AAW	NYBLS	10//99-12//99
	North Carolina	S	8.22 MW	9.14 AW	19010 AAW	NCBLS	10//99-12//99
	Ohio	S	7.93 MW	8.45 AW	17580 AAW	OHBLS	10//99-12//99
	Oklahoma	S	7.61 MW	7.94 AW	16510 AAW	OKBLS	10//99-12//99
	Oregon	S	11.86 MW	11.88 AW	24700 AAW	ORBLS	10//99-12//99
	Pennsylvania	S	7.51 MW	7.89 AW	16410 AAW	PABLS	10//99-12//99
	Rhode Island	S	9.73 MW	10.54 AW	21920 AAW	RIBLS	10//99-12//99
	South Carolina	S	8.03 MW	8.06 AW	16770 AAW	SCBLS	10//99-12//99
	Tennessee	S	7.52 MW	7.55 AW	15700 AAW	TNBLS	10//99-12//99
	Texas	S	9.06 MW	10.37 AW	21560 AAW	TXBLS	10//99-12//99
	Utah	S	7.99 MW	8.25 AW	17160 AAW	UTBLS	10//99-12//99
	Vermont	S	8.56 MW	8.44 AW	17560 AAW	VTBLS	10//99-12//99
	Virginia	S	7.85 MW	7.94 AW	16510 AAW	VABLS	10//99-12//99
	Washington	S	9.27 MW	9.41 AW	19580 AAW	WABLS	10//99-12//99
	Wisconsin	S	7.9 MW	8.63 AW	17950 AAW	WIBLS	10//99-12//99
	Puerto Rico	S	7.46 MW	7.45 AW	15490 AAW	PRBLS	10//99-12//99
	Virgin Islands	S	9.13 MW	8.90 AW	18520 AAW	VIBLS	10//99-12//99
Conservation Scientist	Alabama	S	22.8 MW	22.81 AW	47440 AAW	ALBLS	10//99-12//99
	Alaska	S	21.37 MW	21.88 AW	45510 AAW	AKBLS	10//99-12//99
	Arizona	S	21.79 MW	21.28 AW	44270 AAW	AZBLS	10//99-12//99
	Arkansas	S	23.85 MW	23.45 AW	48780 AAW	ARBLS	10//99-12//99
	California	S	24.05 MW	24.08 AW	50090 AAW	CABLS	10//99-12//99
	Colorado	S	23.04 MW	23.19 AW	48230 AAW	COBLS	10//99-12//99
	Connecticut	S	29.33 MW	33.01 AW	68670 AAW	CTBLS	10//99-12//99
	Florida	S	21.98 MW	21.70 AW	45140 AAW	FLBLS	10//99-12//99
	Georgia	S	22.46 MW	22.38 AW	46550 AAW	GABLS	10//99-12//99
	Idaho	S	21.83 MW	22.09 AW	45940 AAW	IDBLS	10//99-12//99
	Illinois	S	23.63 MW	23.12 AW	48090 AAW	ILBLS	10//99-12//99
	Indiana	S	20.66 MW	19.59 AW	40740 AAW	INBLS	10//99-12//99
	Iowa	S	18.88 MW	18.84 AW	39190 AAW	IABLS	10//99-12//99
	Kansas	S	23.51 MW	23.03 AW	47900 AAW	KSBLS	10//99-12//99
	Kentucky	S	22.87 MW	22.80 AW	47420 AAW	KYBLS	10//99-12//99
	Louisiana	S	23.74 MW	23.48 AW	48830 AAW	LABLS	10//99-12//99
	Maine	S	20.96 MW	21.34 AW	44380 AAW	MEBLS	10//99-12//99
	Massachusetts	S	23.68 MW	24.73 AW	51430 AAW	MABLS	10//99-12//99

AAW	Average annual wage	AOH	Average offered, high	ASH	Average starting, high
AE	Average entry wage	AOL	Average offered, low	ASL	Average starting, low
AEX	Average experienced wage	APH	Average pay, high range	AW	Average wage paid
AO	Average offered	APL	Average pay, low range	FQ	First quartile wage

H	Hourly	M	Monthly	S	Special: hourly and annual
HI	Highest wage paid	MTC	Median total compensation	TQ	Third quartile wage
HR	High end range	MW	Median wage paid	W	Weekly
LR	Low end range	SQ	Second quartile wage	Y	Yearly

Occupation/Type/Industry	Location	Per	Low	Mid	High	Source	Date
Conservation Scientist	Michigan	S	23.77 MW	23.45 AW	48780 AAW	MIBLS	10//99-12//99
	Minnesota	S	22.73 MW	21.91 AW	45570 AAW	MNBLS	10//99-12//99
	Mississippi	S	18.12 MW	19.10 AW	39740 AAW	MSBLS	10//99-12//99
	Missouri	S	20.15 MW	20.42 AW	42480 AAW	MOBLS	10//99-12//99
	Montana	S	19.71 MW	20.03 AW	41670 AAW	MTBLS	10//99-12//99
	Nebraska	S	21.34 MW	21.86 AW	45460 AAW	NEBLS	10//99-12//99
	Nevada	S	21.01 MW	21.16 AW	44010 AAW	NVBLS	10//99-12//99
	New Hampshire	S	16.26 MW	18.60 AW	38680 AAW	NHBLS	10//99-12//99
	New Jersey	S	24.25 MW	24.38 AW	50720 AAW	NJBLS	10//99-12//99
	New Mexico	S	21.57 MW	22.20 AW	46170 AAW	NMBLS	10//99-12//99
	North Carolina	S	18.54 MW	19.19 AW	39920 AAW	NCBLS	10//99-12//99
	North Dakota	S	20.11 MW	20.59 AW	42820 AAW	NDBLS	10//99-12//99
	Ohio	S	21.42 MW	20.24 AW	42110 AAW	OHBLS	10//99-12//99
	Oklahoma	S	21.53 MW	20.49 AW	42620 AAW	OKBLS	10//99-12//99
	Oregon	S	22.7 MW	23.26 AW	48380 AAW	ORBLS	10//99-12//99
	Pennsylvania	S	22.56 MW	21.76 AW	45250 AAW	PABLS	10//99-12//99
	South Carolina	S	23.63 MW	23.12 AW	48090 AAW	SCBLS	10//99-12//99
	South Dakota	S	21.53 MW	21.16 AW	44000 AAW	SDBLS	10//99-12//99
	Tennessee	S	22.82 MW	22.88 AW	47590 AAW	TNBLS	10//99-12//99
	Texas	S	20.33 MW	21.10 AW	43880 AAW	TXBLS	10//99-12//99
	Utah	S	21.07 MW	20.97 AW	43610 AAW	UTBLS	10//99-12//99
	Vermont	S	25.25 MW	24.87 AW	51730 AAW	VTBLS	10//99-12//99
	Virginia	S	25.9 MW	25.67 AW	53390 AAW	VABLS	10//99-12//99
	Washington	S	23.01 MW	22.85 AW	47520 AAW	WABLS	10//99-12//99
	West Virginia	S	19.34 MW	20.61 AW	42870 AAW	WVBLS	10//99-12//99
	Wisconsin	S	19.8 MW	20.09 AW	41790 AAW	WIBLS	10//99-12//99
	Wyoming	S	19.5 MW	19.75 AW	41070 AAW	WYBLS	10//99-12//99
Construction and Building Inspector	Alabama	S	16.41 MW	16.97 AW	35290 AAW	ALBLS	10//99-12//99
	Birmingham MSA, AL	S	19.02 MW	18.89 AW	39560 AAW	ALBLS	10//99-12//99
	Huntsville MSA, AL	S	16.58 MW	16.91 AW	34490 AAW	ALBLS	10//99-12//99
	Mobile MSA, AL	S	15.89 MW	14.33 AW	33050 AAW	ALBLS	10//99-12//99
	Montgomery MSA, AL	S	16.72 MW	15.74 AW	34770 AAW	ALBLS	10//99-12//99
	Tuscaloosa MSA, AL	S	19.26 MW	18.64 AW	40060 AAW	ALBLS	10//99-12//99
	Alaska	S	18.32 MW	20.69 AW	43040 AAW	AKBLS	10//99-12//99
	Anchorage MSA, AK	S	19.91 MW	16.95 AW	41410 AAW	AKBLS	10//99-12//99
	Arizona	S	18.68 MW	18.94 AW	39400 AAW	AZBLS	10//99-12//99
	Flagstaff MSA, AZ-UT	S	15.77 MW	15.59 AW	32800 AAW	AZBLS	10//99-12//99
	Phoenix-Mesa MSA, AZ	S	20.22 MW	20.15 AW	42060 AAW	AZBLS	10//99-12//99
	Tucson MSA, AZ	S	15.58 MW	15.24 AW	32400 AAW	AZBLS	10//99-12//99
	Yuma MSA, AZ	S	19.50 MW	19.18 AW	40550 AAW	AZBLS	10//99-12//99
	Arkansas	S	12.92 MW	13.68 AW	28460 AAW	ARBLS	10//99-12//99
	Fayetteville-Springdale-Rogers MSA, AR	S	15.10 MW	13.26 AW	31410 AAW	ARBLS	10//99-12//99
	California	S	25.06 MW	25.45 AW	52940 AAW	CABLS	10//99-12//99
	Fresno MSA, CA	S	19.46 MW	19.29 AW	40480 AAW	CABLS	10//99-12//99
	Los Angeles-Long Beach PMSA, CA	S	27.21 MW	26.59 AW	56590 AAW	CABLS	10//99-12//99
	Merced MSA, CA	S	23.51 MW	23.69 AW	48900 AAW	CABLS	10//99-12//99
	Oakland PMSA, CA	S	27.46 MW	27.33 AW	57120 AAW	CABLS	10//99-12//99
	Orange County PMSA, CA	S	25.92 MW	25.16 AW	53900 AAW	CABLS	10//99-12//99
	Riverside-San Bernardino PMSA, CA	S	21.11 MW	20.46 AW	43910 AAW	CABLS	10//99-12//99
	Sacramento PMSA, CA	S	25.33 MW	24.74 AW	52680 AAW	CABLS	10//99-12//99
	San Diego MSA, CA	S	24.50 MW	24.07 AW	50950 AAW	CABLS	10//99-12//99
	San Francisco PMSA, CA	S	28.59 MW	28.86 AW	59460 AAW	CABLS	10//99-12//99
	San Jose PMSA, CA	S	25.29 MW	25.03 AW	52610 AAW	CABLS	10//99-12//99
	San Luis Obispo-Atascadero-Paso Robles MSA, CA	S	23.11 MW	22.28 AW	48060 AAW	CABLS	10//99-12//99
	Santa Barbara-Santa Maria-Lompoc MSA, CA	S	23.76 MW	23.67 AW	49430 AAW	CABLS	10//99-12//99
	Santa Rosa PMSA, CA	S	21.86 MW	22.93 AW	45470 AAW	CABLS	10//99-12//99
	Vallejo-Fairfield-Napa PMSA, CA	S	25.15 MW	25.61 AW	52320 AAW	CABLS	10//99-12//99
	Ventura PMSA, CA	S	22.88 MW	22.95 AW	47580 AAW	CABLS	10//99-12//99
	Visalia-Tulare-Porterville MSA, CA	S	22.47 MW	22.26 AW	46740 AAW	CABLS	10//99-12//99
	Colorado	S	18.96 MW	18.90 AW	39310 AAW	COBLS	10//99-12//99
	Boulder-Longmont PMSA, CO	S	15.41 MW	14.55 AW	32050 AAW	COBLS	10//99-12//99
	Colorado Springs MSA, CO	S	18.97 MW	18.78 AW	39460 AAW	COBLS	10//99-12//99
	Denver PMSA, CO	S	22.37 MW	22.03 AW	46530 AAW	COBLS	10//99-12//99

AAW Average annual wage	AOH Average offered, high	ASH Average starting, high	H Hourly	M Monthly	S Special: hourly and annual
AE Average entry wage	AOL Average offered, low	ASL Average starting, low	HI Highest wage paid	MTC Median total compensation	TQ Third quartile wage
AEX Average experienced wage	APH Average pay, high range	AW Average wage paid	HR High end range	MW Median wage paid	W Weekly
AO Average offered	APL Average pay, low range	FQ First quartile wage	LR Low end range	SQ Second quartile wage	Y Yearly

Occupation/Type/Industry	Location	Per	Low	Mid	High	Source	Date
Construction and Building Inspector							
	Fort Collins-Loveland MSA, CO	S	20.27 MW	20.00 AW	42170 AAW	COBLS	10//99-12//99
	Grand Junction MSA, CO	S	17.84 MW	17.49 AW	37100 AAW	COBLS	10//99-12//99
	Greeley PMSA, CO	S	20.54 MW	19.89 AW	42720 AAW	COBLS	10//99-12//99
	Pueblo MSA, CO	S	18.21 MW	20.34 AW	37880 AAW	COBLS	10//99-12//99
	Connecticut	S	22.25 MW	22.47 AW	46740 AAW	CTBLS	10//99-12//99
	Bridgeport PMSA, CT	S	21.52 MW	21.72 AW	44760 AAW	CTBLS	10//99-12//99
	Danbury PMSA, CT	S	21.32 MW	20.91 AW	44340 AAW	CTBLS	10//99-12//99
	Hartford MSA, CT	S	23.16 MW	22.82 AW	48170 AAW	CTBLS	10//99-12//99
	New Haven-Meriden PMSA, CT	S	22.45 MW	20.42 AW	46700 AAW	CTBLS	10//99-12//99
	New London-Norwich MSA, CT-RI	S	20.32 MW	21.33 AW	42270 AAW	CTBLS	10//99-12//99
	Stamford-Norwalk PMSA, CT	S	23.72 MW	23.49 AW	49340 AAW	CTBLS	10//99-12//99
	Delaware	S	16.99 MW	19.38 AW	40300 AAW	DEBLS	10//99-12//99
	Wilmington-Newark PMSA, DE-MD	S	19.74 MW	16.81 AW	41060 AAW	DEBLS	10//99-12//99
	District of Columbia	S	22.23 MW	21.88 AW	45510 AAW	DCBLS	10//99-12//99
	Washington PMSA, DC-MD-VA-WV	S	19.87 MW	19.43 AW	41330 AAW	DCBLS	10//99-12//99
	Florida	S	17.87 MW	18.58 AW	38650 AAW	FLBLS	10//99-12//99
	Daytona Beach MSA, FL	S	16.56 MW	17.83 AW	34430 AAW	FLBLS	10//99-12//99
	Fort Lauderdale PMSA, FL	S	19.39 MW	19.07 AW	40330 AAW	FLBLS	10//99-12//99
	Fort Myers-Cape Coral MSA, FL	S	17.41 MW	17.15 AW	36210 AAW	FLBLS	10//99-12//99
	Gainesville MSA, FL	S	16.99 MW	17.07 AW	35330 AAW	FLBLS	10//99-12//99
	Jacksonville MSA, FL	S	17.41 MW	17.02 AW	36210 AAW	FLBLS	10//99-12//99
	Lakeland-Winter Haven MSA, FL	S	15.27 MW	14.52 AW	31770 AAW	FLBLS	10//99-12//99
	Melbourne-Titusville-Palm Bay MSA, FL	S	17.46 MW	17.55 AW	36310 AAW	FLBLS	10//99-12//99
	Miami PMSA, FL	S	20.33 MW	19.48 AW	42280 AAW	FLBLS	10//99-12//99
	Naples MSA, FL	S	18.83 MW	18.33 AW	39160 AAW	FLBLS	10//99-12//99
	Orlando MSA, FL	S	17.58 MW	16.82 AW	36570 AAW	FLBLS	10//99-12//99
	Pensacola MSA, FL	S	18.42 MW	14.28 AW	38320 AAW	FLBLS	10//99-12//99
	Sarasota-Bradenton MSA, FL	S	18.57 MW	17.18 AW	38630 AAW	FLBLS	10//99-12//99
	Tallahassee MSA, FL	S	18.18 MW	17.12 AW	37810 AAW	FLBLS	10//99-12//99
	Tampa-St. Petersburg-Clearwater MSA, FL	S	17.92 MW	17.78 AW	37270 AAW	FLBLS	10//99-12//99
	West Palm Beach-Boca Raton MSA, FL	S	21.44 MW	22.37 AW	44590 AAW	FLBLS	10//99-12//99
	Georgia	S	15.99 MW	16.42 AW	34160 AAW	GABLS	10//99-12//99
	Atlanta MSA, GA	S	18.34 MW	18.21 AW	38140 AAW	GABLS	10//99-12//99
	Augusta-Aiken MSA, GA-SC	S	17.26 MW	16.23 AW	35900 AAW	GABLS	10//99-12//99
	Macon MSA, GA	S	13.78 MW	14.06 AW	28650 AAW	GABLS	10//99-12//99
	Savannah MSA, GA	S	15.20 MW	15.33 AW	31620 AAW	GABLS	10//99-12//99
	Hawaii	S	19.62 MW	20.13 AW	41880 AAW	HIBLS	10//99-12//99
	Honolulu MSA, HI	S	20.46 MW	19.76 AW	42550 AAW	HIBLS	10//99-12//99
	Idaho	S	15.89 MW	16.40 AW	34120 AAW	IDBLS	10//99-12//99
	Boise City MSA, ID	S	15.40 MW	15.23 AW	32030 AAW	IDBLS	10//99-12//99
	Illinois	S	19.42 MW	19.28 AW	40100 AAW	ILBLS	10//99-12//99
	Champaign-Urbana MSA, IL	S	19.65 MW	20.19 AW	40880 AAW	ILBLS	10//99-12//99
	Chicago PMSA, IL	S	19.60 MW	19.41 AW	40770 AAW	ILBLS	10//99-12//99
	Peoria-Pekin MSA, IL	S	17.75 MW	19.08 AW	36930 AAW	ILBLS	10//99-12//99
	Rockford MSA, IL	S	21.12 MW	19.75 AW	43940 AAW	ILBLS	10//99-12//99
	Springfield MSA, IL	S	20.91 MW	20.50 AW	43480 AAW	ILBLS	10//99-12//99
	Indiana	S	16.51 MW	17.13 AW	35640 AAW	INBLS	10//99-12//99
	Fort Wayne MSA, IN	S	15.36 MW	15.12 AW	31960 AAW	INBLS	10//99-12//99
	Gary PMSA, IN	S	14.33 MW	13.25 AW	29800 AAW	INBLS	10//99-12//99
	Indianapolis MSA, IN	S	19.15 MW	20.41 AW	39830 AAW	INBLS	10//99-12//99
	South Bend MSA, IN	S	15.64 MW	15.70 AW	32540 AAW	INBLS	10//99-12//99
	Iowa	S	17.08 MW	17.47 AW	36340 AAW	IABLS	10//99-12//99
	Cedar Rapids MSA, IA	S	17.37 MW	16.77 AW	36130 AAW	IABLS	10//99-12//99
	Davenport-Moline-Rock Island MSA, IA-IL	S	17.91 MW	17.80 AW	37250 AAW	IABLS	10//99-12//99
	Des Moines MSA, IA	S	18.82 MW	19.04 AW	39140 AAW	IABLS	10//99-12//99
	Sioux City MSA, IA-NE	S	17.47 MW	18.09 AW	36330 AAW	IABLS	10//99-12//99
	Waterloo-Cedar Falls MSA, IA	S	17.13 MW	17.63 AW	35630 AAW	IABLS	10//99-12//99
	Kansas	S	16.6 MW	16.98 AW	35310 AAW	KSBLS	10//99-12//99
	Wichita MSA, KS	S	15.79 MW	15.42 AW	32840 AAW	KSBLS	10//99-12//99
	Kentucky	S	15.14 MW	15.41 AW	32050 AAW	KYBLS	10//99-12//99

AAW Average annual wage	**AOH** Average offered, high	**ASH** Average starting, high	**H** Hourly	**M** Monthly	**S** Special: hourly and annual
AE Average entry wage	**AOL** Average offered, low	**ASL** Average starting, low	**HI** Highest wage paid	**MTC** Median total compensation	**TQ** Third quartile wage
AEX Average experienced wage	**APH** Average pay, high range	**AW** Average wage paid	**HR** High end range	**MW** Median wage paid	**W** Weekly
AO Average offered	**APL** Average pay, low range	**FQ** First quartile wage	**LR** Low end range	**SQ** Second quartile wage	**Y** Yearly

Occupation/Type/Industry	Location	Per	Low	Mid	High	Source	Date
Construction and Building Inspector	Lexington MSA, KY	S	15.60 MW	15.32 AW	32440 AAW	KYBLS	10//99-12//99
	Louisville MSA, KY-IN	S	16.80 MW	16.13 AW	34950 AAW	KYBLS	10//99-12//99
	Louisiana	S	14.53 MW	16.65 AW	34630 AAW	LABLS	10//99-12//99
	Baton Rouge MSA, LA	S	17.01 MW	16.41 AW	35380 AAW	LABLS	10//99-12//99
	Lake Charles MSA, LA	S	17.95 MW	17.03 AW	37340 AAW	LABLS	10//99-12//99
	New Orleans MSA, LA	S	16.92 MW	14.46 AW	35200 AAW	LABLS	10//99-12//99
	Shreveport-Bossier City MSA, LA	S	15.11 MW	12.43 AW	31420 AAW	LABLS	10//99-12//99
	Maine	S	10.14 MW	12.81 AW	26640 AAW	MEBLS	10//99-12//99
	Lewiston-Auburn MSA, ME	S	14.15 MW	13.71 AW	29440 AAW	MEBLS	10//99-12//99
	Maryland	S	18.15 MW	18.83 AW	39170 AAW	MDBLS	10//99-12//99
	Baltimore PMSA, MD	S	17.69 MW	16.92 AW	36800 AAW	MDBLS	10//99-12//99
	Massachusetts	S	20.03 MW	20.54 AW	42730 AAW	MABLS	10//99-12//99
	Barnstable-Yarmouth MSA, MA	S	15.24 MW	15.48 AW	31700 AAW	MABLS	10//99-12//99
	Boston PMSA, MA-NH	S	21.22 MW	21.06 AW	44140 AAW	MABLS	10//99-12//99
	Brockton PMSA, MA	S	16.66 MW	15.94 AW	34660 AAW	MABLS	10//99-12//99
	Lawrence PMSA, MA-NH	S	15.79 MW	15.43 AW	32840 AAW	MABLS	10//99-12//99
	Lowell PMSA, MA-NH	S	18.56 MW	19.17 AW	38610 AAW	MABLS	10//99-12//99
	Springfield MSA, MA	S	21.83 MW	19.97 AW	45410 AAW	MABLS	10//99-12//99
	Worcester PMSA, MA-CT	S	15.40 MW	14.33 AW	32030 AAW	MABLS	10//99-12//99
	Michigan	S	19.09 MW	19.13 AW	39800 AAW	MIBLS	10//99-12//99
	Ann Arbor PMSA, MI	S	21.10 MW	20.99 AW	43890 AAW	MIBLS	10//99-12//99
	Benton Harbor MSA, MI	S	17.15 MW	16.95 AW	35680 AAW	MIBLS	10//99-12//99
	Detroit PMSA, MI	S	19.94 MW	20.06 AW	41480 AAW	MIBLS	10//99-12//99
	Flint PMSA, MI	S	20.69 MW	18.98 AW	43040 AAW	MIBLS	10//99-12//99
	Grand Rapids-Muskegon-Holland MSA, MI	S	19.01 MW	18.46 AW	39540 AAW	MIBLS	
	Kalamazoo-Battle Creek MSA, MI	S	17.73 MW	17.61 AW	36890 AAW	MIBLS	10//99-12//99
	Lansing-East Lansing MSA, MI	S	21.11 MW	21.00 AW	43900 AAW	MIBLS	10//99-12//99
	Saginaw-Bay City-Midland MSA, MI	S	15.77 MW	15.17 AW	32800 AAW	MIBLS	10//99-12//99
	Minnesota	S	20.5 MW	21.12 AW	43930 AAW	MNBLS	10//99-12//99
	Minneapolis-St. Paul MSA, MN-WI	S	21.78 MW	21.64 AW	45300 AAW	MNBLS	10//99-12//99
	Mississippi	S	12.92 MW	14.29 AW	29710 AAW	MSBLS	10//99-12//99
	Biloxi-Gulfport-Pascagoula MSA, MS	S	12.61 MW	12.30 AW	26230 AAW	MSBLS	10//99-12//99
	Jackson MSA, MS	S	17.61 MW	16.34 AW	36630 AAW	MSBLS	10//99-12//99
	Missouri	S	18.51 MW	19.48 AW	40510 AAW	MOBLS	10//99-12//99
	Kansas City MSA, MO-KS	S	18.45 MW	17.85 AW	38380 AAW	MOBLS	10//99-12//99
	St. Louis MSA, MO-IL	S	18.69 MW	18.45 AW	38870 AAW	MOBLS	10//99-12//99
	Montana	S	15.14 MW	15.66 AW	32580 AAW	MTBLS	10//99-12//99
	Great Falls MSA, MT	S	17.22 MW	16.81 AW	35820 AAW	MTBLS	10//99-12//99
	Nebraska	S	17.22 MW	17.04 AW	35450 AAW	NEBLS	10//99-12//99
	Lincoln MSA, NE	S	16.94 MW	17.25 AW	35240 AAW	NEBLS	10//99-12//99
	Omaha MSA, NE-IA	S	18.58 MW	18.21 AW	38650 AAW	NEBLS	10//99-12//99
	Nevada	S	22.73 MW	22.86 AW	47540 AAW	NVBLS	10//99-12//99
	Las Vegas MSA, NV-AZ	S	23.26 MW	23.32 AW	48370 AAW	NVBLS	10//99-12//99
	Reno MSA, NV	S	20.74 MW	21.26 AW	43130 AAW	NVBLS	10//99-12//99
	New Hampshire	S	17.17 MW	17.32 AW	36030 AAW	NHBLS	10//99-12//99
	Nashua PMSA, NH	S	17.39 MW	17.76 AW	36160 AAW	NHBLS	10//99-12//99
	Portsmouth-Rochester PMSA, NH-ME	S	15.88 MW	15.92 AW	33020 AAW	NHBLS	10//99-12//99
	New Jersey	S	20.98 MW	21.16 AW	44010 AAW	NJBLS	10//99-12//99
	Atlantic-Cape May PMSA, NJ	S	18.02 MW	16.04 AW	37480 AAW	NJBLS	10//99-12//99
	Bergen-Passaic PMSA, NJ	S	18.36 MW	18.19 AW	38180 AAW	NJBLS	10//99-12//99
	Jersey City PMSA, NJ	S	21.68 MW	21.50 AW	45090 AAW	NJBLS	10//99-12//99
	Middlesex-Somerset-Hunterdon PMSA, NJ	S	20.28 MW	21.52 AW	42180 AAW	NJBLS	10//99-12//99
	Monmouth-Ocean PMSA, NJ	S	21.04 MW	20.85 AW	43770 AAW	NJBLS	10//99-12//99
	Newark PMSA, NJ	S	24.44 MW	24.10 AW	50840 AAW	NJBLS	10//99-12//99
	Trenton PMSA, NJ	S	25.28 MW	24.99 AW	52590 AAW	NJBLS	10//99-12//99
	Vineland-Millville-Bridgeton PMSA, NJ	S	18.72 MW	16.41 AW	38950 AAW	NJBLS	10//99-12//99
	New Mexico	S	17.21 MW	17.38 AW	36140 AAW	NMBLS	10//99-12//99
	Albuquerque MSA, NM	S	18.67 MW	18.83 AW	38830 AAW	NMBLS	10//99-12//99
	New York	S	20.18 MW	20.52 AW	42690 AAW	NYBLS	10//99-12//99
	Albany-Schenectady-Troy MSA, NY	S	17.74 MW	18.57 AW	36900 AAW	NYBLS	10//99-12//99

AAW	Average annual wage	AOH	Average offered, high	ASH	Average starting, high
AE	Average entry wage	AOL	Average offered, low	ASL	Average starting, low
AEX	Average experienced wage	APH	Average pay, high range	AW	Average wage paid
AO	Average offered	APL	Average pay, low range	FQ	First quartile wage

H	Hourly	M	Monthly	S	Special: hourly and annual
HI	Highest wage paid	MTC	Median total compensation	TQ	Third quartile wage
HR	High end range	MW	Median wage paid	W	Weekly
LR	Low end range	SQ	Second quartile wage	Y	Yearly

Occupation/Type/Industry	Location	Per	Low	Mid	High	Source	Date
Construction and Building Inspector	Binghamton MSA, NY	S	17.43 MW	17.29 AW	36250 AAW	NYBLS	10//99-12//99
	Buffalo-Niagara Falls MSA, NY	S	18.71 MW	19.03 AW	38920 AAW	NYBLS	10//99-12//99
	Dutchess County PMSA, NY	S	21.03 MW	21.10 AW	43730 AAW	NYBLS	10//99-12//99
	Jamestown MSA, NY	S	15.77 MW	15.28 AW	32800 AAW	NYBLS	10//99-12//99
	Nassau-Suffolk PMSA, NY	S	22.97 MW	23.10 AW	47770 AAW	NYBLS	10//99-12//99
	New York PMSA, NY	S	22.63 MW	21.16 AW	47080 AAW	NYBLS	10//99-12//99
	Newburgh PMSA, NY-PA	S	19.87 MW	20.03 AW	41340 AAW	NYBLS	10//99-12//99
	Rochester MSA, NY	S	18.26 MW	18.42 AW	37980 AAW	NYBLS	10//99-12//99
	Utica-Rome MSA, NY	S	10.62 MW	8.69 AW	22090 AAW	NYBLS	10//99-12//99
	North Carolina	S	17 MW	17.61 AW	36630 AAW	NCBLS	10//99-12//99
	Asheville MSA, NC	S	18.45 MW	16.63 AW	38380 AAW	NCBLS	10//99-12//99
	Charlotte-Gastonia-Rock Hill MSA, NC-SC	S	18.40 MW	17.94 AW	38280 AAW	NCBLS	10//99-12//99
	Fayetteville MSA, NC	S	15.35 MW	15.12 AW	31930 AAW	NCBLS	10//99-12//99
	Greensboro--Winston-Salem-- High Point MSA, NC	S	18.05 MW	17.42 AW	37540 AAW	NCBLS	10//99-12//99
	Hickory-Morganton-Lenoir MSA, NC	S	15.54 MW	15.19 AW	32310 AAW	NCBLS	10//99-12//99
	Raleigh-Durham-Chapel Hill MSA, NC	S	19.35 MW	18.75 AW	40240 AAW	NCBLS	10//99-12//99
	Fargo-Moorhead MSA, ND-MN	S	14.67 MW	13.94 AW	30510 AAW	NDBLS	10//99-12//99
	Grand Forks MSA, ND-MN	S	21.74 MW	20.62 AW	45230 AAW	NDBLS	10//99-12//99
	Ohio	S	17.77 MW	17.55 AW	36500 AAW	OHBLS	10//99-12//99
	Akron PMSA, OH	S	16.96 MW	17.52 AW	35280 AAW	OHBLS	10//99-12//99
	Cincinnati PMSA, OH-KY-IN	S	18.44 MW	18.60 AW	38350 AAW	OHBLS	10//99-12//99
	Cleveland-Lorain-Elyria PMSA, OH	S	18.36 MW	18.44 AW	38190 AAW	OHBLS	10//99-12//99
	Columbus MSA, OH	S	17.16 MW	16.56 AW	35680 AAW	OHBLS	10//99-12//99
	Dayton-Springfield MSA, OH	S	17.56 MW	16.58 AW	36520 AAW	OHBLS	10//99-12//99
	Hamilton-Middletown PMSA, OH	S	17.83 MW	18.29 AW	37080 AAW	OHBLS	10//99-12//99
	Toledo MSA, OH	S	18.25 MW	17.98 AW	37960 AAW	OHBLS	10//99-12//99
	Oklahoma	S	15.09 MW	15.17 AW	31560 AAW	OKBLS	10//99-12//99
	Oklahoma City MSA, OK	S	16.59 MW	17.32 AW	34520 AAW	OKBLS	10//99-12//99
	Tulsa MSA, OK	S	14.54 MW	14.49 AW	30240 AAW	OKBLS	10//99-12//99
	Oregon	S	20.51 MW	21.23 AW	44170 AAW	ORBLS	10//99-12//99
	Eugene-Springfield MSA, OR	S	22.14 MW	21.98 AW	46060 AAW	ORBLS	10//99-12//99
	Portland-Vancouver PMSA, OR-WA	S	22.06 MW	20.98 AW	45880 AAW	ORBLS	10//99-12//99
	Salem PMSA, OR	S	21.85 MW	21.18 AW	45450 AAW	ORBLS	10//99-12//99
	Pennsylvania	S	16.27 MW	16.42 AW	34150 AAW	PABLS	10//99-12//99
	Allentown-Bethlehem-Easton MSA, PA	S	16.74 MW	16.90 AW	34830 AAW	PABLS	10//99-12//99
	Harrisburg-Lebanon-Carlisle MSA, PA	S	17.55 MW	17.21 AW	36510 AAW	PABLS	10//99-12//99
	Lancaster MSA, PA	S	18.01 MW	15.91 AW	37460 AAW	PABLS	10//99-12//99
	Philadelphia PMSA, PA-NJ	S	19.00 MW	18.03 AW	39530 AAW	PABLS	10//99-12//99
	Pittsburgh MSA, PA	S	16.05 MW	15.86 AW	33390 AAW	PABLS	10//99-12//99
	Reading MSA, PA	S	16.91 MW	16.65 AW	35170 AAW	PABLS	10//99-12//99
	Scranton--Wilkes-Barre-- Hazleton MSA, PA	S	14.00 MW	14.23 AW	29120 AAW	PABLS	10//99-12//99
	State College MSA, PA	S	14.53 MW	15.50 AW	30220 AAW	PABLS	10//99-12//99
	York MSA, PA	S	13.85 MW	13.56 AW	28810 AAW	PABLS	10//99-12//99
	Rhode Island	S	18.03 MW	18.34 AW	38140 AAW	RIBLS	10//99-12//99
	Providence-Fall River- Warwick MSA, RI-MA	S	19.33 MW	18.98 AW	40200 AAW	RIBLS	10//99-12//99
	South Carolina	S	15.17 MW	15.80 AW	32870 AAW	SCBLS	10//99-12//99
	Charleston-North Charleston MSA, SC	S	13.83 MW	14.37 AW	28760 AAW	SCBLS	10//99-12//99
	Columbia MSA, SC	S	16.74 MW	15.40 AW	34830 AAW	SCBLS	10//99-12//99
	Greenville-Spartanburg- Anderson MSA, SC	S	15.68 MW	15.13 AW	32600 AAW	SCBLS	10//99-12//99
	Myrtle Beach MSA, SC	S	14.29 MW	14.28 AW	29730 AAW	SCBLS	10//99-12//99
	South Dakota	S	14.76 MW	15.17 AW	31560 AAW	SDBLS	10//99-12//99
	Tennessee	S	14.97 MW	15.95 AW	33180 AAW	TNBLS	10//99-12//99
	Chattanooga MSA, TN-GA	S	15.00 MW	14.79 AW	31200 AAW	TNBLS	10//99-12//99
	Clarksville-Hopkinsville MSA, TN-KY	S	13.22 MW	12.43 AW	27490 AAW	TNBLS	10//99-12//99
	Jackson MSA, TN	S	18.23 MW	16.57 AW	37910 AAW	TNBLS	10//99-12//99

AAW Average annual wage	**AOH** Average offered, high	**ASH** Average starting, high	**H** Hourly	**M** Monthly	**S** Special: hourly and annual
AE Average entry wage	**AOL** Average offered, low	**ASL** Average starting, low	**HI** Highest wage paid	**MTC** Median total compensation	**TQ** Third quartile wage
AEX Average experienced wage	**APH** Average pay, high range	**AW** Average wage paid	**HR** High end range	**MW** Median wage paid	**W** Weekly
AO Average offered	**APL** Average pay, low range	**FQ** First quartile wage	**LR** Low end range	**SQ** Second quartile wage	**Y** Yearly

Occupation/Type/Industry	Location	Per	Low	Mid	High	Source	Date
Construction and Building Inspector	Johnson City-Kingsport-Bristol MSA, TN-VA	s	14.37 MW	13.63 AW	29900 AAW	TNBLS	10//99-12//99
	Knoxville MSA, TN	s	16.78 MW	15.93 AW	34900 AAW	TNBLS	10//99-12//99
	Memphis MSA, TN-AR-MS	s	15.24 MW	14.28 AW	31690	MSBLS	10//99-12//99
	Nashville MSA, TN	s	17.11 MW	16.21 AW	35590 AAW	TNBLS	10//99-12//99
	Texas	s	16.77 MW	18.06 AW	37560 AAW	TXBLS	10//99-12//99
	Austin-San Marcos MSA, TX	s	18.38 MW	17.31 AW	38220 AAW	TXBLS	10//99-12//99
	Beaumont-Port Arthur MSA, TX	s	14.39 MW	14.56 AW	29930 AAW	TXBLS	10//99-12//99
	Brownsville-Harlingen-San Benito MSA, TX	s	10.80 MW	9.41 AW	22470	TXBLS	10//99-12//99
	Bryan-College Station MSA, TX	s	18.30 MW	17.03 AW	38060 AAW	TXBLS	10//99-12//99
	Corpus Christi MSA, TX	s	14.55 MW	14.09 AW	30250 AAW	TXBLS	10//99-12//99
	Dallas PMSA, TX	s	17.72 MW	17.32 AW	36870 AAW	TXBLS	10//99-12//99
	El Paso MSA, TX	s	13.93 MW	14.27 AW	28980 AAW	TXBLS	10//99-12//99
	Fort Worth-Arlington PMSA, TX	s	23.61 MW	21.77 AW	49110 AAW	TXBLS	10//99-12//99
	Houston PMSA, TX	s	20.18 MW	18.87 AW	41970 AAW	TXBLS	10//99-12//99
	Killeen-Temple MSA, TX	s	12.82 MW	12.45 AW	26670 AAW	TXBLS	10//99-12//99
	Lubbock MSA, TX	s	16.21 MW	15.54 AW	33720 AAW	TXBLS	10//99-12//99
	McAllen-Edinburg-Mission MSA, TX	s	12.47 MW	11.30 AW	25940 AAW	TXBLS	10//99-12//99
	Odessa-Midland MSA, TX	s	13.20 MW	12.67 AW	27450 AAW	TXBLS	10//99-12//99
	San Antonio MSA, TX	s	14.18 MW	13.31 AW	29490 AAW	TXBLS	10//99-12//99
	Utah	s	17.99 MW	18.12 AW	37690 AAW	UTBLS	10//99-12//99
	Provo-Orem MSA, UT	s	18.79 MW	18.48 AW	39080 AAW	UTBLS	10//99-12//99
	Salt Lake City-Ogden MSA, UT	s	19.25 MW	18.70 AW	40030 AAW	UTBLS	10//99-12//99
	Vermont	s	11.78 MW	15.08 AW	31360 AAW	VTBLS	10//99-12//99
	Burlington MSA, VT	s	18.73 MW	17.45 AW	38960 AAW	VTBLS	10//99-12//99
	Virginia	s	16.61 MW	17.00 AW	35350 AAW	VABLS	10//99-12//99
	Charlottesville MSA, VA	s	16.11 MW	15.66 AW	33500 AAW	VABLS	10//99-12//99
	Danville MSA, VA	s	13.02 MW	12.62 AW	27080 AAW	VABLS	10//99-12//99
	Lynchburg MSA, VA	s	14.71 MW	14.05 AW	30600 AAW	VABLS	10//99-12//99
	Norfolk-Virginia Beach-Newport News MSA, VA-NC	s	16.78 MW	16.87 AW	34910 AAW	VABLS	10//99-12//99
	Richmond-Petersburg MSA, VA	s	17.98 MW	17.70 AW	37390 AAW	VABLS	10//99-12//99
	Roanoke MSA, VA	s	12.18 MW	11.04 AW	25330 AAW	VABLS	10//99-12//99
	Washington	s	22.74 MW	23.18 AW	48210 AAW	WABLS	10//99-12//99
	Bellingham MSA, WA	s	30.17 MW	19.42 AW	62750 AAW	WABLS	10//99-12//99
	Bremerton PMSA, WA	s	22.60 MW	23.18 AW	47010 AAW	WABLS	10//99-12//99
	Olympia PMSA, WA	s	21.16 MW	22.19 AW	44000 AAW	WABLS	10//99-12//99
	Richland-Kennewick-Pasco MSA, WA	s	21.08 MW	21.73 AW	43840 AAW	WABLS	10//99-12//99
	Seattle-Bellevue-Everett PMSA, WA	s	24.13 MW	23.82 AW	50180 AAW	WABLS	10//99-12//99
	Spokane MSA, WA	s	20.96 MW	21.21 AW	43600 AAW	WABLS	10//99-12//99
	Tacoma PMSA, WA	s	21.57 MW	22.77 AW	44870 AAW	WABLS	10//99-12//99
	Yakima MSA, WA	s	18.66 MW	18.76 AW	38810 AAW	WABLS	10//99-12//99
	West Virginia	s	12.05 MW	13.91 AW	28930 AAW	WVBLS	10//99-12//99
	Charleston MSA, WV	s	17.21 MW	13.28 AW	35790 AAW	WVBLS	10//99-12//99
	Wisconsin	s	16.92 MW	16.49 AW	34310 AAW	WIBLS	10//99-12//99
	Appleton-Oshkosh-Neenah MSA, WI	s	20.08 MW	22.28 AW	41770 AAW	WIBLS	10//99-12//99
	Janesville-Beloit MSA, WI	s	22.58 MW	23.04 AW	46970 AAW	WIBLS	10//99-12//99
	Kenosha PMSA, WI	s	19.27 MW	19.24 AW	40080 AAW	WIBLS	10//99-12//99
	Madison MSA, WI	s	16.60 MW	18.10 AW	34530 AAW	WIBLS	10//99-12//99
	Milwaukee-Waukesha PMSA, WI	s	17.43 MW	17.74 AW	36250 AAW	WIBLS	10//99-12//99
	Wausau MSA, WI	s	13.90 MW	12.04 AW	28920 AAW	WIBLS	10//99-12//99
	Wyoming	s	16.24 MW	16.48 AW	34290 AAW	WYBLS	10//99-12//99
	Puerto Rico	s	10.99 MW	11.50 AW	23930 AAW	PRBLS	10//99-12//99
	Mayaguez MSA, PR	s	9.44 MW	10.76 AW	19630 AAW	PRBLS	10//99-12//99
	San Juan-Bayamon PMSA, PR	s	12.13 MW	11.77 AW	25230 AAW	PRBLS	10//99-12//99
Construction Laborer	Alabama	s	7.78 MW	8.27 AW	17190 AAW	ALBLS	10//99-12//99
	Anniston MSA, AL	s	7.50 MW	7.34 AW	15610 AAW	ALBLS	10//99-12//99
	Auburn-Opelika MSA, AL	s	8.29 MW	7.90 AW	17230 AAW	ALBLS	10//99-12//99

AAW	Average annual wage	AOH	Average offered, high	ASH	Average starting, high	H	Hourly	M	Monthly	S	Special: hourly and annual
AE	Average entry wage	AOL	Average offered, low	ASL	Average starting, low	HI	Highest wage paid	MTC	Median total compensation	TQ	Third quartile wage
AEX	Average experienced wage	APH	Average pay, high range	AW	Average wage paid	HR	High end range	MW	Median wage paid	W	Weekly
AO	Average offered	APL	Average pay, low range	FQ	First quartile wage	LR	Low end range	SQ	Second quartile wage	Y	Yearly

Construction Laborer

Occupation/Type/Industry	Location	Per	Low	Mid	High	Source	Date
Construction Laborer	Birmingham MSA, AL	S	8.62 MW	7.80 AW	17930 AAW	ALBLS	10//99-12//99
	Decatur MSA, AL	S	10.31 MW	9.95 AW	21440 AAW	ALBLS	10//99-12//99
	Dothan MSA, AL	S	6.72 MW	6.73 AW	13980 AAW	ALBLS	10//99-12//99
	Florence MSA, AL	S	10.35 MW	10.30 AW	21520 AAW	ALBLS	10//99-12//99
	Gadsden MSA, AL	S	8.34 MW	8.18 AW	17340 AAW	ALBLS	10//99-12//99
	Huntsville MSA, AL	S	8.65 MW	8.64 AW	17980 AAW	ALBLS	10//99-12//99
	Mobile MSA, AL	S	7.72 MW	7.50 AW	16050 AAW	ALBLS	10//99-12//99
	Montgomery MSA, AL	S	7.88 MW	7.66 AW	16400 AAW	ALBLS	10//99-12//99
	Tuscaloosa MSA, AL	S	8.91 MW	8.31 AW	18540 AAW	ALBLS	10//99-12//99
	Alaska	S	18.02 MW	18.73 AW	38950 AAW	AKBLS	10//99-12//99
	Anchorage MSA, AK	S	17.85 MW	16.86 AW	37140 AAW	AKBLS	10//99-12//99
	Arizona	S	9.2 MW	9.78 AW	20350 AAW	AZBLS	10//99-12//99
	Flagstaff MSA, AZ-UT	S	8.54 MW	8.26 AW	17770 AAW	AZBLS	10//99-12//99
	Phoenix-Mesa MSA, AZ	S	10.11 MW	9.59 AW	21020 AAW	AZBLS	10//99-12//99
	Tucson MSA, AZ	S	7.86 MW	7.67 AW	16350 AAW	AZBLS	10//99-12//99
	Yuma MSA, AZ	S	8.29 MW	7.52 AW	17250 AAW	AZBLS	10//99-12//99
	Arkansas	S	8.59 MW	8.94 AW	18600 AAW	ARBLS	10//99-12//99
	Fayetteville-Springdale-Rogers MSA, AR	S	9.18 MW	9.32 AW	19100 AAW	ARBLS	10//99-12//99
	Fort Smith MSA, AR-OK	S	8.39 MW	8.71 AW	17450 AAW	ARBLS	10//99-12//99
	Little Rock-North Little Rock MSA, AR	S	8.69 MW	8.52 AW	18070 AAW	ARBLS	10//99-12//99
	California	S	13.02 MW	14.64 AW	30440 AAW	CABLS	10//99-12//99
	Bakersfield MSA, CA	S	11.28 MW	10.32 AW	23450 AAW	CABLS	10//99-12//99
	Chico-Paradise MSA, CA	S	11.99 MW	10.46 AW	24940 AAW	CABLS	10//99-12//99
	Fresno MSA, CA	S	10.94 MW	9.03 AW	22760 AAW	CABLS	10//99-12//99
	Los Angeles-Long Beach PMSA, CA	S	13.81 MW	12.36 AW	28730 AAW	CABLS	10//99-12//99
	Merced MSA, CA	S	12.16 MW	10.63 AW	25300 AAW	CABLS	10//99-12//99
	Modesto MSA, CA	S	13.75 MW	12.50 AW	28590 AAW	CABLS	10//99-12//99
	Oakland PMSA, CA	S	18.52 MW	19.51 AW	38530 AAW	CABLS	10//99-12//99
	Orange County PMSA, CA	S	14.90 MW	13.21 AW	30980 AAW	CABLS	10//99-12//99
	Redding MSA, CA	S	13.13 MW	11.81 AW	27310 AAW	CABLS	10//99-12//99
	Riverside-San Bernardino PMSA, CA	S	13.83 MW	11.78 AW	28760 AAW	CABLS	10//99-12//99
	Sacramento PMSA, CA	S	13.70 MW	13.19 AW	28500 AAW	CABLS	10//99-12//99
	Salinas MSA, CA	S	12.53 MW	12.10 AW	26060 AAW	CABLS	10//99-12//99
	San Diego MSA, CA	S	15.53 MW	13.74 AW	32310 AAW	CABLS	10//99-12//99
	San Francisco PMSA, CA	S	17.75 MW	18.96 AW	36930 AAW	CABLS	10//99-12//99
	San José PMSA, CA	S	18.81 MW	17.91 AW	39120 AAW	CABLS	10//99-12//99
	San Luis Obispo-Atascadero-Paso Robles MSA, CA	S	13.94 MW	13.22 AW	29000 AAW	CABLS	10//99-12//99
	Santa Barbara-Santa Maria-Lompoc MSA, CA	S	11.92 MW	10.11 AW	24790 AAW	CABLS	10//99-12//99
	Santa Cruz-Watsonville PMSA, CA	S	9.97 MW	8.98 AW	20730 AAW	CABLS	10//99-12//99
	Santa Rosa PMSA, CA	S	11.18 MW	10.03 AW	23250 AAW	CABLS	10//99-12//99
	Stockton-Lodi MSA, CA	S	14.18 MW	13.24 AW	29490 AAW	CABLS	10//99-12//99
	Vallejo-Fairfield-Napa PMSA, CA	S	17.23 MW	14.62 AW	35830 AAW	CABLS	10//99-12//99
	Ventura PMSA, CA	S	14.66 MW	13.49 AW	30500 AAW	CABLS	10//99-12//99
	Visalia-Tulare-Porterville MSA, CA	S	11.29 MW	9.74 AW	23490 AAW	CABLS	10//99-12//99
	Yolo PMSA, CA	S	16.08 MW	17.76 AW	33440 AAW	CABLS	10//99-12//99
	Yuba City MSA, CA	S	10.71 MW	9.51 AW	22280 AAW	CABLS	10//99-12//99
	Colorado	S	10.47 MW	10.66 AW	22170 AAW	COBLS	10//99-12//99
	Boulder-Longmont PMSA, CO	S	9.66 MW	9.61 AW	20100 AAW	COBLS	10//99-12//99
	Colorado Springs MSA, CO	S	11.23 MW	11.31 AW	23360 AAW	COBLS	10//99-12//99
	Denver PMSA, CO	S	10.92 MW	10.70 AW	22720 AAW	COBLS	10//99-12//99
	Fort Collins-Loveland MSA, CO	S	10.05 MW	9.82 AW	20910 AAW	COBLS	10//99-12//99
	Grand Junction MSA, CO	S	11.01 MW	10.82 AW	22900 AAW	COBLS	10//99-12//99
	Greeley PMSA, CO	S	9.97 MW	9.68 AW	20750 AAW	COBLS	10//99-12//99
	Pueblo MSA, CO	S	9.30 MW	9.39 AW	19340 AAW	COBLS	10//99-12//99
	Connecticut	S	14.4 MW	14.93 AW	31050 AAW	CTBLS	10//99-12//99
	Danbury PMSA, CT	S	13.45 MW	12.85 AW	27980 AAW	CTBLS	10//99-12//99
	Hartford MSA, CT	S	15.41 MW	15.17 AW	32050 AAW	CTBLS	10//99-12//99
	New Haven-Meriden PMSA, CT	S	13.94 MW	13.25 AW	28990 AAW	CTBLS	10//99-12//99
	New London-Norwich MSA, CT-RI	S	11.99 MW	11.60 AW	24940 AAW	CTBLS	10//99-12//99
	Stamford-Norwalk PMSA, CT	S	15.95 MW	17.28 AW	33180 AAW	CTBLS	10//99-12//99

AAW Average annual wage	**AOH** Average offered, high	**ASH** Average starting, high	**H** Hourly	**M** Monthly	**S** Special: hourly and annual
AE Average entry wage	**AOL** Average offered, low	**ASL** Average starting, low	**HI** Highest wage paid	**MTC** Median total compensation	**TQ** Third quartile wage
AEX Average experienced wage	**APH** Average pay, high range	**AW** Average wage paid	**HR** High end range	**MW** Median wage paid	**W** Weekly
AO Average offered	**APL** Average pay, low range	**FQ** First quartile wage	**LR** Low end range	**SQ** Second quartile wage	**Y** Yearly

Construction Laborer

Occupation/Type/Industry	Location	Per	Low	Mid	High	Source	Date
Construction Laborer	Waterbury PMSA, CT	S	13.86 MW	12.65 AW	28820 AAW	CTBLS	10//99-12//99
	Delaware	S	11.53 MW	11.62 AW	24170 AAW	DEBLS	10//99-12//99
	Dover MSA, DE	S	10.98 MW	9.90 AW	22840 AAW	DEBLS	10//99-12//99
	Wilmington-Newark PMSA, DE-MD	S	11.86 MW	11.75 AW	24670 AAW	DEBLS	10//99-12//99
	District of Columbia	S	13.42 MW	14.12 AW	29370 AAW	DCBLS	10//99-12//99
	Washington PMSA, DC-MD-VA-WV	S	10.91 MW	10.48 AW	22690 AAW	DCBLS	10//99-12//99
	Florida	S	9.36 MW	9.83 AW	20440 AAW	FLBLS	10//99-12//99
	Daytona Beach MSA, FL	S	9.68 MW	9.67 AW	20120 AAW	FLBLS	10//99-12//99
	Fort Lauderdale PMSA, FL	S	9.69 MW	9.51 AW	20150 AAW	FLBLS	10//99-12//99
	Fort Myers-Cape Coral MSA, FL	S	10.08 MW	9.38 AW	20960 AAW	FLBLS	10//99-12//99
	Fort Pierce-Port St. Lucie MSA, FL	S	9.23 MW	9.31 AW	19210 AAW	FLBLS	10//99-12//99
	Fort Walton Beach MSA, FL	S	8.58 MW	7.74 AW	17840 AAW	FLBLS	10//99-12//99
	Gainesville MSA, FL	S	7.26 MW	6.96 AW	15110 AAW	FLBLS	10//99-12//99
	Jacksonville MSA, FL	S	9.51 MW	9.21 AW	19790 AAW	FLBLS	10//99-12//99
	Lakeland-Winter Haven MSA, FL	S	10.76 MW	9.79 AW	22380 AAW	FLBLS	10//99-12//99
	Melbourne-Titusville-Palm Bay MSA, FL	S	9.70 MW	9.74 AW	20170 AAW	FLBLS	10//99-12//99
	Miami PMSA, FL	S	12.06 MW	11.08 AW	25090 AAW	FLBLS	10//99-12//99
	Naples MSA, FL	S	9.74 MW	9.16 AW	20250 AAW	FLBLS	10//99-12//99
	Ocala MSA, FL	S	8.37 MW	8.11 AW	17400 AAW	FLBLS	10//99-12//99
	Orlando MSA, FL	S	9.82 MW	9.50 AW	20420 AAW	FLBLS	10//99-12//99
	Panama City MSA, FL	S	9.43 MW	8.81 AW	19610 AAW	FLBLS	10//99-12//99
	Pensacola MSA, FL	S	7.99 MW	7.78 AW	16630 AAW	FLBLS	10//99-12//99
	Punta Gorda MSA, FL	S	9.13 MW	9.22 AW	19000 AAW	FLBLS	10//99-12//99
	Sarasota-Bradenton MSA, FL	S	9.91 MW	9.53 AW	20600 AAW	FLBLS	10//99-12//99
	Tallahassee MSA, FL	S	11.95 MW	11.93 AW	24860 AAW	FLBLS	10//99-12//99
	Tampa-St. Petersburg-Clearwater MSA, FL	S	9.63 MW	9.33 AW	20040 AAW	FLBLS	10//99-12//99
	West Palm Beach-Boca Raton MSA, FL	S	9.48 MW	9.22 AW	19720 AAW	FLBLS	10//99-12//99
	Georgia	S	9.52 MW	9.63 AW	20030 AAW	GABLS	10//99-12//99
	Albany MSA, GA	S	7.36 MW	7.46 AW	15310 AAW	GABLS	10//99-12//99
	Athens MSA, GA	S	8.50 MW	8.90 AW	17680 AAW	GABLS	10//99-12//99
	Atlanta MSA, GA	S	10.12 MW	9.87 AW	21050 AAW	GABLS	10//99-12//99
	Augusta-Aiken MSA, GA-SC	S	9.22 MW	9.18 AW	19180 AAW	GABLS	10//99-12//99
	Columbus MSA, GA-AL	S	7.22 MW	7.20 AW	15010 AAW	GABLS	10//99-12//99
	Macon MSA, GA	S	8.23 MW	7.87 AW	17130 AAW	GABLS	10//99-12//99
	Savannah MSA, GA	S	9.46 MW	9.58 AW	19680 AAW	GABLS	10//99-12//99
	Hawaii	S	14.62 MW	15.76 AW	32770 AAW	HIBLS	10//99-12//99
	Honolulu MSA, HI	S	15.63 MW	14.40 AW	32500 AAW	HIBLS	10//99-12//99
	Idaho	S	10.39 MW	10.75 AW	22360 AAW	IDBLS	10//99-12//99
	Boise City MSA, ID	S	11.37 MW	11.35 AW	23650 AAW	IDBLS	10//99-12//99
	Pocatello MSA, ID	S	10.92 MW	10.34 AW	22720 AAW	IDBLS	10//99-12//99
	Illinois	S	20.76 MW	19.66 AW	40890 AAW	ILBLS	10//99-12//99
	Bloomington-Normal MSA, IL	S	18.31 MW	19.03 AW	38090 AAW	ILBLS	10//99-12//99
	Champaign-Urbana MSA, IL	S	17.89 MW	18.86 AW	37200 AAW	ILBLS	10//99-12//99
	Chicago PMSA, IL	S	20.99 MW	22.65 AW	43660 AAW	ILBLS	10//99-12//99
	Decatur MSA, IL	S	18.86 MW	21.50 AW	39230 AAW	ILBLS	10//99-12//99
	Kankakee PMSA, IL	S	15.16 MW	15.28 AW	31530 AAW	ILBLS	10//99-12//99
	Peoria-Pekin MSA, IL	S	18.82 MW	19.14 AW	39140 AAW	ILBLS	10//99-12//99
	Rockford MSA, IL	S	20.39 MW	19.87 AW	42420 AAW	ILBLS	10//99-12//99
	Springfield MSA, IL	S	17.38 MW	18.28 AW	36140 AAW	ILBLS	10//99-12//99
	Indiana	S	14.34 MW	14.38 AW	29920 AAW	INBLS	10//99-12//99
	Bloomington MSA, IN	S	10.92 MW	10.57 AW	22710 AAW	INBLS	10//99-12//99
	Elkhart-Goshen MSA, IN	S	13.05 MW	12.88 AW	27150 AAW	INBLS	10//99-12//99
	Evansville-Henderson MSA, IN-KY	S	12.48 MW	12.16 AW	25960 AAW	INBLS	10//99-12//99
	Fort Wayne MSA, IN	S	14.65 MW	15.00 AW	30470 AAW	INBLS	10//99-12//99
	Gary PMSA, IN	S	17.43 MW	19.06 AW	36260 AAW	INBLS	10//99-12//99
	Indianapolis MSA, IN	S	15.77 MW	16.47 AW	32790 AAW	INBLS	10//99-12//99
	Kokomo MSA, IN	S	11.17 MW	11.14 AW	23230 AAW	INBLS	10//99-12//99
	Lafayette MSA, IN	S	11.51 MW	10.77 AW	23930 AAW	INBLS	10//99-12//99
	Muncie MSA, IN	S	13.58 MW	13.07 AW	28240 AAW	INBLS	10//99-12//99
	South Bend MSA, IN	S	15.89 MW	16.28 AW	33060 AAW	INBLS	10//99-12//99
	Terre Haute MSA, IN	S	8.97 MW	8.00 AW	18660 AAW	INBLS	10//99-12//99
	Iowa	S	10.5 MW	11.36 AW	23620 AAW	IABLS	10//99-12//99
	Cedar Rapids MSA, IA	S	13.88 MW	14.62 AW	28860 AAW	IABLS	10//99-12//99

AAW Average annual wage	AOH Average offered, high	ASH Average starting, high	H Hourly	M Monthly	S Special: hourly and annual
AE Average entry wage	AOL Average offered, low	ASL Average starting, low	HI Highest wage paid	MTC Median total compensation	TQ Third quartile wage
AEX Average experienced wage	APH Average pay, high range	AW Average wage paid	HR High end range	MW Median wage paid	W Weekly
AO Average offered	APL Average pay, low range	FQ First quartile wage	LR Low end range	SQ Second quartile wage	Y Yearly

Occupation/Type/Industry	Location	Per	Low	Mid	High	Source	Date
Construction Laborer	Davenport-Moline-Rock Island						
	MSA, IA-IL	S	14.81 MW	14.82 AW	30810 AAW	IABLS	10//99-12//99
	Des Moines MSA, IA	S	12.55 MW	11.92 AW	26110 AAW	IABLS	10//99-12//99
	Dubuque MSA, IA	S	10.98 MW	11.11 AW	22840 AAW	IABLS	10//99-12//99
	Iowa City MSA, IA	S	12.76 MW	11.32 AW	26540 AAW	IABLS	10//99-12//99
	Sioux City MSA, IA-NE	S	9.64 MW	9.20 AW	20060 AAW	IABLS	10//99-12//99
	Waterloo-Cedar Falls MSA, IA	S	9.57 MW	8.88 AW	19900 AAW	IABLS	10//99-12//99
	Kansas	S	10.4 MW	11.28 AW	23460 AAW	KSBLS	10//99-12//99
	Topeka MSA, KS	S	10.32 MW	10.03 AW	21460 AAW	KSBLS	10//99-12//99
	Wichita MSA, KS	S	9.33 MW	9.35 AW	19400 AAW	KSBLS	10//99-12//99
	Kentucky	S	10.36 MW	11.10 AW	23090 AAW	KYBLS	10//99-12//99
	Lexington MSA, KY	S	10.07 MW	9.73 AW	20950 AAW	KYBLS	10//99-12//99
	Louisville MSA, KY-IN	S	10.36 MW	10.59 AW	21550 AAW	KYBLS	10//99-12//99
	Owensboro MSA, KY	S	9.66 MW	9.63 AW	20090 AAW	KYBLS	10//99-12//99
	Louisiana	S	8.74 MW	8.96 AW	18640 AAW	LABLS	10//99-12//99
	Alexandria MSA, LA	S	8.68 MW	8.61 AW	18060 AAW	LABLS	10//99-12//99
	Baton Rouge MSA, LA	S	8.95 MW	9.14 AW	18610 AAW	LABLS	10//99-12//99
	Houma MSA, LA	S	7.48 MW	6.85 AW	15550 AAW	LABLS	10//99-12//99
	Lafayette MSA, LA	S	8.12 MW	8.18 AW	16890 AAW	LABLS	10//99-12//99
	Lake Charles MSA, LA	S	9.47 MW	8.97 AW	19700 AAW	LABLS	10//99-12//99
	Monroe MSA, LA	S	9.17 MW	8.67 AW	19070 AAW	LABLS	10//99-12//99
	New Orleans MSA, LA	S	9.38 MW	8.88 AW	19510 AAW	LABLS	10//99-12//99
	Shreveport-Bossier City MSA,						
	LA	S	8.32 MW	8.19 AW	17300 AAW	LABLS	10//99-12//99
	Maine	S	9.01 MW	9.08 AW	18890 AAW	MEBLS	10//99-12//99
	Bangor MSA, ME	S	8.45 MW	8.42 AW	17580 AAW	MEBLS	10//99-12//99
	Lewiston-Auburn MSA, ME	S	8.39 MW	8.11 AW	17460 AAW	MEBLS	10//99-12//99
	Portland MSA, ME	S	9.87 MW	9.80 AW	20530 AAW	MEBLS	10//99-12//99
	Maryland	S	10.4 MW	10.86 AW	22580 AAW	MDBLS	10//99-12//99
	Baltimore PMSA, MD	S	11.36 MW	10.86 AW	23620 AAW	MDBLS	10//99-12//99
	Cumberland MSA, MD-WV	S	10.71 MW	10.49 AW	22270 AAW	MDBLS	10//99-12//99
	Hagerstown PMSA, MD	S	9.65 MW	9.67 AW	20080 AAW	MDBLS	10//99-12//99
	Barnstable-Yarmouth MSA,						
	MA	S	14.55 MW	14.62 AW	30270 AAW	MABLS	10//99-12//99
	Boston PMSA, MA-NH	S	20.23 MW	20.81 AW	42080 AAW	MABLS	10//99-12//99
	Brockton PMSA, MA	S	14.75 MW	14.50 AW	30690 AAW	MABLS	10//99-12//99
	Fitchburg-Leominster PMSA,						
	MA	S	15.41 MW	15.39 AW	32050 AAW	MABLS	10//99-12//99
	Lawrence PMSA, MA-NH	S	15.53 MW	15.47 AW	32300 AAW	MABLS	10//99-12//99
	Lowell PMSA, MA-NH	S	12.75 MW	13.01 AW	26520 AAW	MABLS	10//99-12//99
	New Bedford PMSA, MA	S	16.20 MW	17.35 AW	33690 AAW	MABLS	10//99-12//99
	Pittsfield MSA, MA	S	14.30 MW	14.27 AW	29740 AAW	MABLS	10//99-12//99
	Springfield MSA, MA	S	15.07 MW	15.16 AW	31340 AAW	MABLS	10//99-12//99
	Worcester PMSA, MA-CT	S	15.92 MW	15.18 AW	33110 AAW	MABLS	10//99-12//99
	Michigan	S	13.18 MW	13.22 AW	27490 AAW	MIBLS	10//99-12//99
	Ann Arbor PMSA, MI	S	18.50 MW	18.57 AW	38470 AAW	MIBLS	10//99-12//99
	Benton Harbor MSA, MI	S	13.38 MW	12.22 AW	27830 AAW	MIBLS	10//99-12//99
	Detroit PMSA, MI	S	16.08 MW	16.55 AW	33450 AAW	MIBLS	10//99-12//99
	Flint PMSA, MI	S	16.68 MW	17.85 AW	34690 AAW	MIBLS	10//99-12//99
	Jackson MSA, MI	S	11.81 MW	11.50 AW	24560 AAW	MIBLS	10//99-12//99
	Kalamazoo-Battle Creek MSA,						
	MI	S	11.18 MW	10.57 AW	23250 AAW	MIBLS	10//99-12//99
	Lansing-East Lansing MSA, MI	S	15.67 MW	15.87 AW	32600 AAW	MIBLS	10//99-12//99
	Saginaw-Bay City-Midland						
	MSA, MI	S	11.42 MW	10.38 AW	23760 AAW	MIBLS	10//99-12//99
	Minnesota	S	16.44 MW	16.11 AW	33510 AAW	MNBLS	10//99-12//99
	Duluth-Superior MSA, MN-WI	S	13.57 MW	12.46 AW	28230 AAW	MNBLS	10//99-12//99
	Minneapolis-St. Paul MSA,						
	MN-WI	S	17.86 MW	19.16 AW	37150 AAW	MNBLS	10//99-12//99
	Rochester MSA, MN	S	14.32 MW	13.95 AW	29780 AAW	MNBLS	10//99-12//99
	St. Cloud MSA, MN	S	11.86 MW	11.96 AW	24660 AAW	MNBLS	10//99-12//99
	Mississippi	S	8.1 MW	8.55 AW	17790 AAW	MSBLS	10//99-12//99
	Biloxi-Gulfport-Pascagoula						
	MSA, MS	S	8.91 MW	8.77 AW	18540 AAW	MSBLS	10//99-12//99
	Hattiesburg MSA, MS	S	7.96 MW	8.00 AW	16560 AAW	MSBLS	10//99-12//99
	Jackson MSA, MS	S	10.86 MW	10.43 AW	22590 AAW	MSBLS	10//99-12//99
	Missouri	S	14.11 MW	15.18 AW	31580 AAW	MOBLS	10//99-12//99
	Joplin MSA, MO	S	10.15 MW	9.55 AW	21120 AAW	MOBLS	10//99-12//99
	Kansas City MSA, MO-KS	S	14.59 MW	14.40 AW	30340 AAW	MOBLS	10//99-12//99
	St. Joseph MSA, MO	S	13.73 MW	13.37 AW	28550 AAW	MOBLS	10//99-12//99
	Springfield MSA, MO	S	12.29 MW	11.15 AW	25560 AAW	MOBLS	10//99-12//99
	Montana	S	10.42 MW	11.60 AW	24140 AAW	MTBLS	10//99-12//99

AAW	Average annual wage	AOH	Average offered, high	ASH	Average starting, high
AE	Average entry wage	AOL	Average offered, low	ASL	Average starting, low
AEX	Average experienced wage	APH	Average pay, high range	AW	Average wage paid
AO	Average offered	APL	Average pay, low range	FQ	First quartile wage

H	Hourly
HI	Highest wage paid
HR	High end range
LR	Low end range

M	Monthly
MTC	Median total compensation
MW	Median wage paid
SQ	Second quartile wage

S	Special: hourly and annual
TQ	Third quartile wage
W	Weekly
Y	Yearly

Occupation/Type/Industry	Location	Per	Low	Mid	High	Source	Date
Construction Laborer	Billings MSA, MT	S	14.08 MW	14.61 AW	29280 AAW	MTBLS	10//99-12//99
	Great Falls MSA, MT	S	10.86 MW	10.26 AW	22600 AAW	MTBLS	10//99-12//99
	Missoula MSA, MT	S	12.28 MW	12.49 AW	25550 AAW	MTBLS	10//99-12//99
	Nebraska	S	10.18 MW	10.78 AW	22410 AAW	NEBLS	10//99-12//99
	Lincoln MSA, NE	S	9.81 MW	9.75 AW	20400 AAW	NEBLS	10//99-12//99
	Omaha MSA, NE-IA	S	10.69 MW	10.23 AW	22240 AAW	NEBLS	10//99-12//99
	Nevada	S	10.56 MW	12.78 AW	26590 AAW	NVBLS	10//99-12//99
	Las Vegas MSA, NV-AZ	S	12.76 MW	10.54 AW	26530 AAW	NVBLS	10//99-12//99
	Reno MSA, NV	S	15.01 MW	14.00 AW	31220 AAW	NVBLS	10//99-12//99
	New Hampshire	S	11.23 MW	11.61 AW	24160 AAW	NHBLS	10//99-12//99
	Manchester PMSA, NH	S	11.44 MW	11.25 AW	23800 AAW	NHBLS	10//99-12//99
	Nashua PMSA, NH	S	13.45 MW	13.01 AW	27970 AAW	NHBLS	10//99-12//99
	Portsmouth-Rochester PMSA, NH-ME	S	11.94 MW	11.14 AW	24840 AAW	NHBLS	10//99-12//99
	New Jersey	S	16.95 MW	17.06 AW	35490 AAW	NJBLS	10//99-12//99
	Atlantic-Cape May PMSA, NJ	S	20.25 MW	22.76 AW	42110 AAW	NJBLS	10//99-12//99
	Bergen-Passaic PMSA, NJ	S	18.09 MW	18.56 AW	37620 AAW	NJBLS	10//99-12//99
	Jersey City PMSA, NJ	S	14.66 MW	14.13 AW	30490 AAW	NJBLS	10//99-12//99
	Middlesex-Somerset-Hunterdon PMSA, NJ	S	15.08 MW	14.94 AW	31370 AAW	NJBLS	10//99-12//99
	Monmouth-Ocean PMSA, NJ	S	17.70 MW	17.99 AW	36810 AAW	NJBLS	10//99-12//99
	Newark PMSA, NJ	S	19.08 MW	19.81 AW	39700 AAW	NJBLS	10//99-12//99
	Trenton PMSA, NJ	S	18.94 MW	17.83 AW	39390 AAW	NJBLS	10//99-12//99
	Vineland-Millville-Bridgeton PMSA, NJ	S	19.13 MW	20.23 AW	39790 AAW	NJBLS	10//99-12//99
	New Mexico	S	8.48 MW	9.18 AW	19090 AAW	NMBLS	10//99-12//99
	Albuquerque MSA, NM	S	9.04 MW	8.80 AW	18800 AAW	NMBLS	10//99-12//99
	Las Cruces MSA, NM	S	9.32 MW	9.33 AW	19390 AAW	NMBLS	10//99-12//99
	Santa Fe MSA, NM	S	9.83 MW	9.80 AW	20440 AAW	NMBLS	10//99-12//99
	New York	S	18.76 MW	18.47 AW	38420 AAW	NYBLS	10//99-12//99
	Albany-Schenectady-Troy MSA, NY	S	14.32 MW	14.75 AW	29780 AAW	NYBLS	10//99-12//99
	Binghamton MSA, NY	S	15.07 MW	13.09 AW	31350 AAW	NYBLS	10//99-12//99
	Buffalo-Niagara Falls MSA, NY	S	13.10 MW	11.46 AW	27260 AAW	NYBLS	10//99-12//99
	Dutchess County PMSA, NY	S	14.19 MW	14.49 AW	29520 AAW	NYBLS	10//99-12//99
	Elmira MSA, NY	S	11.68 MW	10.77 AW	24290 AAW	NYBLS	10//99-12//99
	Glens Falls MSA, NY	S	13.82 MW	13.28 AW	28750 AAW	NYBLS	10//99-12//99
	Jamestown MSA, NY	S	9.26 MW	8.28 AW	19260 AAW	NYBLS	10//99-12//99
	Nassau-Suffolk PMSA, NY	S	18.73 MW	20.23 AW	38970 AAW	NYBLS	10//99-12//99
	Newburgh PMSA, NY-PA	S	14.11 MW	13.33 AW	29360 AAW	NYBLS	10//99-12//99
	Rochester MSA, NY	S	14.07 MW	14.57 AW	29260 AAW	NYBLS	10//99-12//99
	Syracuse MSA, NY	S	13.67 MW	12.85 AW	28440 AAW	NYBLS	10//99-12//99
	Utica-Rome MSA, NY	S	15.95 MW	17.15 AW	33170 AAW	NYBLS	10//99-12//99
	North Carolina	S	9.43 MW	9.97 AW	20730 AAW	NCBLS	10//99-12//99
	Asheville MSA, NC	S	8.58 MW	8.50 AW	17840 AAW	NCBLS	10//99-12//99
	Charlotte-Gastonia-Rock Hill MSA, NC-SC	S	10.44 MW	10.13 AW	21710 AAW	NCBLS	10//99-12//99
	Fayetteville MSA, NC	S	9.27 MW	8.03 AW	19270 AAW	NCBLS	10//99-12//99
	Goldsboro MSA, NC	S	7.67 MW	7.70 AW	15950 AAW	NCBLS	10//99-12//99
	Greensboro--Winston-Salem--High Point MSA, NC	S	10.76 MW	9.84 AW	22390 AAW	NCBLS	10//99-12//99
	Greenville MSA, NC	S	7.77 MW	7.51 AW	16170 AAW	NCBLS	10//99-12//99
	Hickory-Morganton-Lenoir MSA, NC	S	11.26 MW	10.97 AW	23410 AAW	NCBLS	10//99-12//99
	Jacksonville MSA, NC	S	8.51 MW	8.31 AW	17700 AAW	NCBLS	10//99-12//99
	Raleigh-Durham-Chapel Hill MSA, NC	S	10.80 MW	10.10 AW	22460 AAW	NCBLS	10//99-12//99
	Rocky Mount MSA, NC	S	7.96 MW	8.22 AW	16570 AAW	NCBLS	10//99-12//99
	Wilmington MSA, NC	S	9.28 MW	9.01 AW	19300 AAW	NCBLS	10//99-12//99
	North Dakota	S	9.59 MW	9.65 AW	20060 AAW	NDBLS	10//99-12//99
	Bismarck MSA, ND	S	9.68 MW	9.34 AW	20130 AAW	NDBLS	10//99-12//99
	Fargo-Moorhead MSA, ND-MN	S	9.86 MW	9.75 AW	20500 AAW	NDBLS	10//99-12//99
	Grand Forks MSA, ND-MN	S	10.00 MW	9.75 AW	20800 AAW	NDBLS	10//99-12//99
	Ohio	S	16.13 MW	15.33 AW	31890 AAW	OHBLS	10//99-12//99
	Akron PMSA, OH	S	16.15 MW	17.30 AW	33600 AAW	OHBLS	10//99-12//99
	Canton-Massillon MSA, OH	S	15.44 MW	15.87 AW	32100 AAW	OHBLS	10//99-12//99
	Cincinnati PMSA, OH-KY-IN	S	13.80 MW	13.27 AW	28700 AAW	OHBLS	10//99-12//99
	Cleveland-Lorain-Elyria PMSA, OH	S	17.09 MW	18.04 AW	35540 AAW	OHBLS	10//99-12//99
	Dayton-Springfield MSA, OH	S	13.99 MW	13.22 AW	29100 AAW	OHBLS	10//99-12//99

AAW Average annual wage	AOH Average offered, high	ASH Average starting, high	H Hourly	M Monthly	S Special: hourly and annual
AE Average entry wage	AOL Average offered, low	ASL Average starting, low	HI Highest wage paid	MTC Median total compensation	TQ Third quartile wage
AEX Average experienced wage	APH Average pay, high range	AW Average wage paid	HR High end range	MW Median wage paid	W Weekly
AO Average offered	APL Average pay, low range	FQ First quartile wage	LR Low end range	SQ Second quartile wage	Y Yearly

Occupation/Type/Industry	Location	Per	Low	Mid	High	Source	Date
Construction Laborer	Hamilton-Middletown PMSA, OH	S	13.82 mw	12.57 aw	28730 aaw	OHBLS	10//99-12//99
	Lima MSA, OH	S	12.74 mw	12.35 aw	26500 aaw	OHBLS	10//99-12//99
	Mansfield MSA, OH	S	12.90 mw	12.87 aw	26830 aaw	OHBLS	10//99-12//99
	Toledo MSA, OH	S	14.62 mw	13.48 aw	30400 aaw	OHBLS	10//99-12//99
	Youngstown-Warren MSA, OH	S	16.26 mw	18.08 aw	33830 aaw	OHBLS	10//99-12//99
	Oklahoma	S	9.41 mw	9.85 aw	20490 aaw	OKBLS	10//99-12//99
	Lawton MSA, OK	S	9.07 mw	9.26 aw	18870 aaw	OKBLS	10//99-12//99
	Oklahoma City MSA, OK	S	10.36 mw	9.64 aw	21550 aaw	OKBLS	10//99-12//99
	Tulsa MSA, OK	S	9.80 mw	9.59 aw	20390 aaw	OKBLS	10//99-12//99
	Oregon	S	13.2 mw	14.32 aw	29780 aaw	ORBLS	10//99-12//99
	Corvallis MSA, OR	S	11.00 mw	10.60 aw	22880 aaw	ORBLS	10//99-12//99
	Eugene-Springfield MSA, OR	S	11.60 mw	11.71 aw	24120 aaw	ORBLS	10//99-12//99
	Medford-Ashland MSA, OR	S	12.88 mw	11.83 aw	26780 aaw	ORBLS	10//99-12//99
	Portland-Vancouver PMSA, OR-WA	S	16.02 mw	15.85 aw	33330 aaw	ORBLS	10//99-12//99
	Salem PMSA, OR	S	15.62 mw	14.78 aw	32490 aaw	ORBLS	10//99-12//99
	Pennsylvania	S	14.24 mw	14.77 aw	30720 aaw	PABLS	10//99-12//99
	Allentown-Bethlehem-Easton MSA, PA	S	11.16 mw	10.69 aw	23220 aaw	PABLS	10//99-12//99
	Altoona MSA, PA	S	10.34 mw	9.44 aw	21520 aaw	PABLS	10//99-12//99
	Erie MSA, PA	S	12.38 mw	11.43 aw	25750 aaw	PABLS	10//99-12//99
	Harrisburg-Lebanon-Carlisle MSA, PA	S	13.13 mw	13.28 aw	27310 aaw	PABLS	10//99-12//99
	Johnstown MSA, PA	S	12.86 mw	11.98 aw	26760 aaw	PABLS	10//99-12//99
	Lancaster MSA, PA	S	11.98 mw	10.93 aw	24910 aaw	PABLS	10//99-12//99
	Philadelphia PMSA, PA-NJ	S	16.48 mw	17.09 aw	34280 aaw	PABLS	10//99-12//99
	Pittsburgh MSA, PA	S	16.64 mw	16.15 aw	34620 aaw	PABLS	10//99-12//99
	Reading MSA, PA	S	13.08 mw	13.87 aw	27200 aaw	PABLS	10//99-12//99
	Scranton--Wilkes-Barre--Hazleton MSA, PA	S	12.15 mw	11.53 aw	25280 aaw	PABLS	10//99-12//99
	Sharon MSA, PA	S	12.71 mw	13.77 aw	26430 aaw	PABLS	10//99-12//99
	State College MSA, PA	S	11.50 mw	11.05 aw	23920 aaw	PABLS	10//99-12//99
	Williamsport MSA, PA	S	9.80 mw	9.36 aw	20390 aaw	PABLS	10//99-12//99
	York MSA, PA	S	12.33 mw	11.39 aw	25650 aaw	PABLS	10//99-12//99
	Rhode Island	S	12.63 mw	14.17 aw	29480 aaw	RIBLS	10//99-12//99
	Providence-Fall River-Warwick MSA, RI-MA	S	14.38 mw	13.22 aw	29900 aaw	RIBLS	10//99-12//99
	South Carolina	S	8.73 mw	8.82 aw	18350 aaw	SCBLS	10//99-12//99
	Charleston-North Charleston MSA, SC	S	7.83 mw	7.78 aw	16290 aaw	SCBLS	10//99-12//99
	Columbia MSA, SC	S	8.39 mw	8.09 aw	17440 aaw	SCBLS	10//99-12//99
	Florence MSA, SC	S	8.56 mw	8.76 aw	17800 aaw	SCBLS	10//99-12//99
	Greenville-Spartanburg-Anderson MSA, SC	S	8.58 mw	8.73 aw	17850 aaw	SCBLS	10//99-12//99
	Myrtle Beach MSA, SC	S	9.25 mw	9.29 aw	19240 aaw	SCBLS	10//99-12//99
	Sumter MSA, SC	S	8.70 mw	8.71 aw	18100 aaw	SCBLS	10//99-12//99
	South Dakota	S	9.61 mw	9.61 aw	19990 aaw	SDBLS	10//99-12//99
	Rapid City MSA, SD	S	9.91 mw	9.91 aw	20610 aaw	SDBLS	10//99-12//99
	Sioux Falls MSA, SD	S	9.65 mw	9.67 aw	20060 aaw	SDBLS	10//99-12//99
	Tennessee	S	9.65 mw	9.94 aw	20670 aaw	TNBLS	10//99-12//99
	Chattanooga MSA, TN-GA	S	9.95 mw	9.88 aw	20700 aaw	TNBLS	10//99-12//99
	Clarksville-Hopkinsville MSA, TN-KY	S	8.80 mw	8.84 aw	18310 aaw	TNBLS	10//99-12//99
	Jackson MSA, TN	S	9.09 mw	8.44 aw	18920 aaw	TNBLS	10//99-12//99
	Johnson City-Kingsport-Bristol MSA, TN-VA	S	9.34 mw	9.46 aw	19420 aaw	TNBLS	10//99-12//99
	Knoxville MSA, TN	S	10.14 mw	9.93 aw	21090 aaw	TNBLS	10//99-12//99
	Memphis MSA, TN-AR-MS	S	10.11 mw	9.71 aw	21020 aaw	MSBLS	10//99-12//99
	Nashville MSA, TN	S	10.37 mw	9.97 aw	21570 aaw	TNBLS	10//99-12//99
	Texas	S	8.37 mw	8.89 aw	18490 aaw	TXBLS	10//99-12//99
	Abilene MSA, TX	S	7.92 mw	7.71 aw	16470 aaw	TXBLS	10//99-12//99
	Amarillo MSA, TX	S	8.59 mw	8.55 aw	17870 aaw	TXBLS	10//99-12//99
	Austin-San Marcos MSA, TX	S	9.39 mw	9.27 aw	19530 aaw	TXBLS	10//99-12//99
	Beaumont-Port Arthur MSA, TX	S	8.45 mw	8.04 aw	17570 aaw	TXBLS	10//99-12//99
	Brazoria PMSA, TX	S	9.08 mw	9.05 aw	18890 aaw	TXBLS	10//99-12//99
	Brownsville-Harlingen-San Benito MSA, TX	S	6.43 mw	6.34 aw	13370 aaw	TXBLS	10//99-12//99
	Bryan-College Station MSA, TX	S	7.04 mw	7.26 aw	14640 aaw	TXBLS	10//99-12//99
	Corpus Christi MSA, TX	S	7.44 mw	7.27 aw	15470 aaw	TXBLS	10//99-12//99

Occupation/Type/Industry	Location	Per	Low	Mid	High	Source	Date
Construction Laborer	Dallas PMSA, TX	s	8.93 MW	8.36 AW	18570 AAW	TXBLS	10//99-12//99
	El Paso MSA, TX	s	7.92 MW	7.73 AW	16470 AAW	TXBLS	10//99-12//99
	Fort Worth-Arlington PMSA, TX	s	9.52 MW	8.56 AW	19800 AAW	TXBLS	10//99-12//99
	Galveston-Texas City PMSA, TX	s	10.81 MW	10.00 AW	22490 AAW	TXBLS	10//99-12//99
	Houston PMSA, TX	s	9.52 MW	9.19 AW	19800 AAW	TXBLS	10//99-12//99
	Killeen-Temple MSA, TX	s	7.80 MW	7.65 AW	16230 AAW	TXBLS	10//99-12//99
	Laredo MSA, TX	s	7.08 MW	7.28 AW	14720 AAW	TXBLS	10//99-12//99
	Longview-Marshall MSA, TX	s	8.57 MW	8.18 AW	17820 AAW	TXBLS	10//99-12//99
	Lubbock MSA, TX	s	8.99 MW	8.78 AW	18710 AAW	TXBLS	10//99-12//99
	McAllen-Edinburg-Mission MSA, TX	s	6.07 MW	6.08 AW	12620 AAW	TXBLS	10//99-12//99
	Odessa-Midland MSA, TX	s	7.86 MW	7.76 AW	16350 AAW	TXBLS	10//99-12//99
	San Angelo MSA, TX	s	8.31 MW	7.48 AW	17270 AAW	TXBLS	10//99-12//99
	San Antonio MSA, TX	s	8.06 MW	7.90 AW	16770 AAW	TXBLS	10//99-12//99
	Sherman-Denison MSA, TX	s	8.85 MW	8.34 AW	18410 AAW	TXBLS	10//99-12//99
	Texarkana MSA, TX-Texarkana, AR	s	7.76 MW	7.70 AW	16150 AAW	TXBLS	10//99-12//99
	Tyler MSA, TX	s	9.64 MW	8.32 AW	20050 AAW	TXBLS	10//99-12//99
	Victoria MSA, TX	s	7.24 MW	6.51 AW	15050 AAW	TXBLS	10//99-12//99
	Waco MSA, TX	s	8.30 MW	8.12 AW	17270 AAW	TXBLS	10//99-12//99
	Wichita Falls MSA, TX	s	7.41 MW	7.31 AW	15410 AAW	TXBLS	10//99-12//99
	Utah	s	10.43 MW	10.95 AW	22780 AAW	UTBLS	10//99-12//99
	Salt Lake City-Ogden MSA, UT	s	11.46 MW	10.75 AW	23840 AAW	UTBLS	10//99-12//99
	Vermont	s	9.57 MW	9.81 AW	20400 AAW	VTBLS	10//99-12//99
	Burlington MSA, VT	s	9.90 MW	9.86 AW	20600 AAW	VTBLS	10//99-12//99
	Virginia	s	9.1 MW	9.22 AW	19180 AAW	VABLS	10//99-12//99
	Charlottesville MSA, VA	s	8.56 MW	8.92 AW	17810 AAW	VABLS	10//99-12//99
	Danville MSA, VA	s	8.70 MW	7.97 AW	18090 AAW	VABLS	10//99-12//99
	Lynchburg MSA, VA	s	8.00 MW	8.03 AW	16640 AAW	VABLS	10//99-12//99
	Norfolk-Virginia Beach-Newport News MSA, VA-NC	s	8.49 MW	8.38 AW	17650 AAW	VABLS	
	Richmond-Petersburg MSA, VA	s	8.87 MW	8.93 AW	18450 AAW	VABLS	10//99-12//99
	Roanoke MSA, VA	s	8.62 MW	8.72 AW	17940 AAW	VABLS	10//99-12//99
	Washington	s	17.41 MW	17.31 AW	36010 AAW	WABLS	10//99-12//99
	Bellingham MSA, WA	s	14.04 MW	14.07 AW	29200 AAW	WABLS	10//99-12//99
	Bremerton PMSA, WA	s	11.99 MW	10.31 AW	24940 AAW	WABLS	10//99-12//99
	Olympia PMSA, WA	s	15.84 MW	15.15 AW	32950 AAW	WABLS	10//99-12//99
	Richland-Kennewick-Pasco MSA, WA	s	11.83 MW	11.02 AW	24610 AAW	WABLS	10//99-12//99
	Seattle-Bellevue-Everett PMSA, WA	s	19.18 MW	19.82 AW	39890 AAW	WABLS	10//99-12//99
	Spokane MSA, WA	s	13.36 MW	12.29 AW	27800 AAW	WABLS	10//99-12//99
	Tacoma PMSA, WA	s	14.71 MW	14.44 AW	30600 AAW	WABLS	10//99-12//99
	Yakima MSA, WA	s	10.88 MW	11.11 AW	22620 AAW	WABLS	10//99-12//99
	West Virginia	s	10.75 MW	12.56 AW	26130 AAW	WVBLS	10//99-12//99
	Charleston MSA, WV	s	11.45 MW	9.93 AW	23820 AAW	WVBLS	10//99-12//99
	Huntington-Ashland MSA, WV-KY-OH	s	10.44 MW	9.05 AW	21710 AAW	WVBLS	10//99-12//99
	Parkersburg-Marietta MSA, WV-OH	s	14.49 MW	14.26 AW	30150 AAW	WVBLS	10//99-12//99
	Wheeling PMSA, WV-OH	s	8.48 MW	7.02 AW	17640 AAW	WVBLS	10//99-12//99
	Wisconsin	s	14.65 MW	15.21 AW	31630 AAW	WIBLS	10//99-12//99
	Appleton-Oshkosh-Neenah MSA, WI	s	12.60 MW	12.71 AW	26210 AAW	WIBLS	10//99-12//99
	Eau Claire MSA, WI	s	21.13 MW	22.35 AW	43960 AAW	WIBLS	10//99-12//99
	Green Bay MSA, WI	s	18.19 MW	16.73 AW	37830 AAW	WIBLS	10//99-12//99
	Janesville-Beloit MSA, WI	s	13.41 MW	13.55 AW	27890 AAW	WIBLS	10//99-12//99
	Kenosha PMSA, WI	s	17.78 MW	16.69 AW	36970 AAW	WIBLS	10//99-12//99
	La Crosse MSA, WI-MN	s	10.43 MW	9.72 AW	21690 AAW	WIBLS	10//99-12//99
	Madison MSA, WI	s	16.21 MW	16.44 AW	33710 AAW	WIBLS	10//99-12//99
	Milwaukee-Waukesha PMSA, WI	s	16.99 MW	17.08 AW	35330 AAW	WIBLS	10//99-12//99
	Racine PMSA, WI	s	10.60 MW	8.44 AW	22050 AAW	WIBLS	10//99-12//99
	Sheboygan MSA, WI	s	10.60 MW	10.35 AW	22040 AAW	WIBLS	10//99-12//99
	Wausau MSA, WI	s	13.44 MW	13.73 AW	27960 AAW	WIBLS	10//99-12//99
	Wyoming	s	10.39 MW	10.65 AW	22160 AAW	WYBLS	10//99-12//99
	Casper MSA, WY	s	10.10 MW	9.94 AW	21010 AAW	WYBLS	10//99-12//99

AAW	Average annual wage	AOH	Average offered, high	ASH	Average starting, high
AE	Average entry wage	AOL	Average offered, low	ASL	Average starting, low
AEX	Average experienced wage	APH	Average pay, high range	AW	Average wage paid
AO	Average offered	APL	Average pay, low range	FQ	First quartile wage

H	Hourly	M	Monthly	S	Special: hourly and annual
HI	Highest wage paid	MTC	Median total compensation	TQ	Third quartile wage
HR	High end range	MW	Median wage paid	W	Weekly
LR	Low end range	SQ	Second quartile wage	Y	Yearly

Occupation/Type/Industry	Location	Per	Low	Mid	High	Source	Date
Construction Laborer	Cheyenne MSA, WY	S	11.43 MW	11.63 AW	23760 AAW	WYBLS	10//99-12//99
	Puerto Rico	S	6.08 MW	6.06 AW	12610 AAW	PRBLS	10//99-12//99
	Aguadilla MSA, PR	S	5.76 MW	5.96 AW	11980 AAW	PRBLS	10//99-12//99
	Arecibo PMSA, PR	S	5.79 MW	5.97 AW	12040 AAW	PRBLS	10//99-12//99
	Caguas PMSA, PR	S	5.78 MW	5.97 AW	12030 AAW	PRBLS	10//99-12//99
	Mayaguez MSA, PR	S	6.07 MW	6.13 AW	12620 AAW	PRBLS	10//99-12//99
	Ponce MSA, PR	S	6.10 MW	6.09 AW	12690 AAW	PRBLS	10//99-12//99
	San Juan-Bayamon PMSA, PR	S	6.10 MW	6.09 AW	12690 AAW	PRBLS	10//99-12//99
	Virgin Islands	S	8.42 MW	8.93 AW	18580 AAW	VIBLS	10//99-12//99
	Guam	S	7.96 MW	8.11 AW	16870 AAW	GUBLS	10//99-12//99
Construction Manager	Alabama	S	22.48 MW	24.31 AW	50560 AAW	ALBLS	10//99-12//99
	Anniston MSA, AL	S	19.37 MW	19.14 AW	40300 AAW	ALBLS	10//99-12//99
	Auburn-Opelika MSA, AL	S	22.99 MW	20.89 AW	47810 AAW	ALBLS	10//99-12//99
	Birmingham MSA, AL	S	25.98 MW	24.26 AW	54030 AAW	ALBLS	10//99-12//99
	Decatur MSA, AL	S	25.65 MW	23.41 AW	53350 AAW	ALBLS	10//99-12//99
	Dothan MSA, AL	S	26.65 MW	27.06 AW	55430 AAW	ALBLS	10//99-12//99
	Florence MSA, AL	S	20.12 MW	20.65 AW	41850 AAW	ALBLS	10//99-12//99
	Gadsden MSA, AL	S	27.01 MW	23.16 AW	56170 AAW	ALBLS	10//99-12//99
	Huntsville MSA, AL	S	21.34 MW	21.64 AW	44390 AAW	ALBLS	10//99-12//99
	Mobile MSA, AL	S	24.68 MW	23.10 AW	51330 AAW	ALBLS	10//99-12//99
	Montgomery MSA, AL	S	27.98 MW	22.89 AW	58190 AAW	ALBLS	10//99-12//99
	Tuscaloosa MSA, AL	S	16.83 MW	15.65 AW	35010 AAW	ALBLS	10//99-12//99
	Alaska	S	31.61 MW	33.07 AW	68780 AAW	AKBLS	10//99-12//99
	Anchorage MSA, AK	S	36.19 MW	34.73 AW	75280 AAW	AKBLS	10//99-12//99
	Arizona	S	31.35 MW	32.72 AW	68070 AAW	AZBLS	10//99-12//99
	Flagstaff MSA, AZ-UT	S	24.20 MW	20.98 AW	50340 AAW	AZBLS	10//99-12//99
	Phoenix-Mesa MSA, AZ	S	32.77 MW	31.47 AW	68160 AAW	AZBLS	10//99-12//99
	Tucson MSA, AZ	S	32.93 MW	31.46 AW	68500 AAW	AZBLS	10//99-12//99
	Arkansas	S	18.48 MW	20.99 AW	43660 AAW	ARBLS	
	Fayetteville-Springdale-Rogers MSA, AR	S	26.34 MW	21.27 AW	54790 AAW	ARBLS	10//99-12//99
	Fort Smith MSA, AR-OK	S	18.66 MW	16.63 AW	38820 AAW	ARBLS	10//99-12//99
	Little Rock-North Little Rock MSA, AR	S	19.43 MW	16.38 AW	40410 AAW	ARBLS	10//99-12//99
	Pine Bluff MSA, AR	S	19.89 MW	19.08 AW	41370 AAW	ARBLS	10//99-12//99
	California	S	33.18 MW	34.54 AW	71830 AAW	CABLS	10//99-12//99
	Bakersfield MSA, CA	S	28.15 MW	27.16 AW	58540 AAW	CABLS	10//99-12//99
	Chico-Paradise MSA, CA	S	22.20 MW	22.22 AW	46180 AAW	CABLS	10//99-12//99
	Fresno MSA, CA	S	26.90 MW	26.45 AW	55950 AAW	CABLS	10//99-12//99
	Los Angeles-Long Beach PMSA, CA	S	33.54 MW	32.88 AW	69760 AAW	CABLS	10//99-12//99
	Merced MSA, CA	S	24.72 MW	24.62 AW	51420 AAW	CABLS	10//99-12//99
	Modesto MSA, CA	S	28.67 MW	28.29 AW	59630 AAW	CABLS	10//99-12//99
	Oakland PMSA, CA	S	41.54 MW	39.87 AW	86410 AAW	CABLS	10//99-12//99
	Orange County PMSA, CA	S	39.30 MW	39.23 AW	81740 AAW	CABLS	10//99-12//99
	Redding MSA, CA	S	21.22 MW	19.50 AW	44130 AAW	CABLS	10//99-12//99
	Riverside-San Bernardino PMSA, CA	S	31.78 MW	31.33 AW	66090 AAW	CABLS	10//99-12//99
	Sacramento PMSA, CA	S	34.04 MW	31.22 AW	70790 AAW	CABLS	10//99-12//99
	Salinas MSA, CA	S	34.37 MW	30.79 AW	71490 AAW	CABLS	10//99-12//99
	San Diego MSA, CA	S	33.59 MW	33.31 AW	69870 AAW	CABLS	10//99-12//99
	San Francisco PMSA, CA	S	38.69 MW	38.30 AW	80470 AAW	CABLS	10//99-12//99
	San Jose PMSA, CA	S	36.07 MW	34.58 AW	75030 AAW	CABLS	10//99-12//99
	San Luis Obispo-Atascadero-Paso Robles MSA, CA	S	27.77 MW	24.72 AW	57750 AAW	CABLS	10//99-12//99
	Santa Barbara-Santa Maria-Lompoc MSA, CA	S	40.39 MW	36.28 AW	84020 AAW	CABLS	10//99-12//99
	Santa Cruz-Watsonville PMSA, CA	S	30.20 MW	31.21 AW	62820 AAW	CABLS	10//99-12//99
	Santa Rosa PMSA, CA	S	26.50 MW	22.89 AW	55130 AAW	CABLS	10//99-12//99
	Stockton-Lodi MSA, CA	S	31.26 MW	31.11 AW	65020 AAW	CABLS	10//99-12//99
	Vallejo-Fairfield-Napa PMSA, CA	S	36.05 MW	33.17 AW	74990 AAW	CABLS	10//99-12//99
	Ventura PMSA, CA	S	33.41 MW	33.11 AW	69490 AAW	CABLS	10//99-12//99
	Visalia-Tulare-Porterville MSA, CA	S	28.89 MW	28.84 AW	60100 AAW	CABLS	10//99-12//99
	Yolo PMSA, CA	S	29.60 MW	30.06 AW	61570 AAW	CABLS	10//99-12//99
	Yuba City MSA, CA	S	18.64 MW	16.76 AW	38770 AAW	CABLS	10//99-12//99
	Colorado	S	27.11 MW	28.12 AW	58480 AAW	COBLS	10//99-12//99
	Colorado Springs MSA, CO	S	29.73 MW	29.02 AW	61840 AAW	COBLS	10//99-12//99
	Denver PMSA, CO	S	29.92 MW	28.56 AW	62240 AAW	COBLS	10//99-12//99

Occupation/Type/Industry	Location	Per	Low	Mid	High	Source	Date
Construction Manager	Fort Collins-Loveland MSA, CO	S	28.78 MW	26.32 AW	59850 AAW	COBLS	10//99-12//99
	Grand Junction MSA, CO	S	25.63 MW	27.33 AW	53310 AAW	COBLS	10//99-12//99
	Greeley PMSA, €O	S	29.24 MW	29.02 AW	60820 AAW	COBLS	10//99-12//99
	Connecticut	S	34.6 MW	36.37 AW	75640 AAW	CTBLS	10//99-12//99
	Bridgeport PMSA, CT	S	29.79 MW	25.23 AW	61970 AAW	CTBLS	10//99-12//99
	Danbury PMSA, CT	S	42.43 MW	38.46 AW	88260 AAW	CTBLS	10//99-12//99
	Hartford MSA, CT	S	36.73 MW	33.71 AW	76390 AAW	CTBLS	10//99-12//99
	New Haven-Meriden PMSA, CT	S	37.59 MW	35.96 AW	78190 AAW	CTBLS	10//99-12//99
	New London-Norwich MSA, CT-RI	S	24.58 MW	24.16 AW	51120 AAW	CTBLS	10//99-12//99
	Stamford-Norwalk PMSA, CT	S	43.82 MW	45.93 AW	91150 AAW	CTBLS	10//99-12//99
	Waterbury PMSA, CT	S	34.49 MW	29.82 AW	71740 AAW	CTBLS	10//99-12//99
	District of Columbia	S	31.74 MW	35.55 AW	73940 AAW	DCBLS	10//99-12//99
	Washington PMSA, DC-MD-VA-WV	S	28.99 MW	26.19 AW	60300 AAW	DCBLS	10//99-12//99
	Florida	S	23.74 MW	25.72 AW	53500 AAW	FLBLS	10//99-12//99
	Daytona Beach MSA, FL	S	16.73 MW	12.80 AW	34800 AAW	FLBLS	10//99-12//99
	Fort Lauderdale PMSA, FL	S	30.35 MW	29.56 AW	63120 AAW	FLBLS	10//99-12//99
	Fort Pierce-Port St. Lucie MSA, FL	S	18.18 MW	16.20 AW	37820 AAW	FLBLS	10//99-12//99
	Fort Walton Beach MSA, FL	S	22.20 MW	19.27 AW	46180 AAW	FLBLS	10//99-12//99
	Gainesville MSA, FL	S	24.82 MW	23.57 AW	51630 AAW	FLBLS	10//99-12//99
	Lakeland-Winter Haven MSA, FL	S	25.01 MW	21.42 AW	52020 AAW	FLBLS	10//99-12//99
	Melbourne-Titusville-Palm Bay MSA, FL	S	22.34 MW	20.49 AW	46480 AAW	FLBLS	10//99-12//99
	Miami PMSA, FL	S	26.67 MW	24.48 AW	55470 AAW	FLBLS	10//99-12//99
	Ocala MSA, FL	S	18.16 MW	18.59 AW	37780 AAW	FLBLS	10//99-12//99
	Orlando MSA, FL	S	25.13 MW	22.86 AW	52270 AAW	FLBLS	10//99-12//99
	Panama City MSA, FL	S	19.61 MW	16.43 AW	40790 AAW	FLBLS	10//99-12//99
	Pensacola MSA, FL	S	23.67 MW	21.29 AW	49240 AAW	FLBLS	10//99-12//99
	Punta Gorda MSA, FL	S	18.81 MW	16.14 AW	39120 AAW	FLBLS	10//99-12//99
	Sarasota-Bradenton MSA, FL	S	24.29 MW	24.74 AW	50510 AAW	FLBLS	10//99-12//99
	Tallahassee MSA, FL	S	26.92 MW	27.40 AW	56000 AAW	FLBLS	10//99-12//99
	Tampa-St. Petersburg-Clearwater MSA, FL	S	26.07 MW	24.23 AW	54230 AAW	FLBLS	10//99-12//99
	West Palm Beach-Boca Raton MSA, FL	S	23.23 MW	21.41 AW	48310 AAW	FLBLS	10//99-12//99
	Georgia	S	23.39 MW	25.46 AW	52960 AAW	GABLS	10//99-12//99
	Athens MSA, GA	S	21.56 MW	20.84 AW	44850 AAW	GABLS	10//99-12//99
	Atlanta MSA, GA	S	27.41 MW	25.79 AW	57000 AAW	GABLS	10//99-12//99
	Augusta-Aiken MSA, GA-SC	S	28.61 MW	24.79 AW	59500 AAW	GABLS	10//99-12//99
	Columbus MSA, GA-AL	S	22.06 MW	18.37 AW	45890 AAW	GABLS	10//99-12//99
	Macon MSA, GA	S	23.01 MW	23.05 AW	47860 AAW	GABLS	10//99-12//99
	Savannah MSA, GA	S	19.57 MW	15.77 AW	40710 AAW	GABLS	10//99-12//99
	Hawaii	S	32.63 MW	36.81 AW	76570 AAW	HIBLS	10//99-12//99
	Honolulu MSA, HI	S	42.59 MW	45.53 AW	88590 AAW	HIBLS	10//99-12//99
	Idaho	S	24.17 MW	24.44 AW	50820 AAW	IDBLS	10//99-12//99
	Boise City MSA, ID	S	25.81 MW	26.01 AW	53690 AAW	IDBLS	10//99-12//99
	Illinois	S	29.21 MW	30.19 AW	62780 AAW	ILBLS	10//99-12//99
	Bloomington-Normal MSA, IL	S	28.82 MW	28.05 AW	59950 AAW	ILBLS	10//99-12//99
	Champaign-Urbana MSA, IL	S	26.71 MW	25.44 AW	55560 AAW	ILBLS	10//99-12//99
	Chicago PMSA, IL	S	31.49 MW	30.70 AW	65490 AAW	ILBLS	10//99-12//99
	Decatur MSA, IL	S	24.13 MW	23.43 AW	50190 AAW	ILBLS	10//99-12//99
	Peoria-Pekin MSA, IL	S	24.81 MW	23.11 AW	51600 AAW	ILBLS	10//99-12//99
	Rockford MSA, IL	S	37.29 MW	36.44 AW	77550 AAW	ILBLS	10//99-12//99
	Springfield MSA, IL	S	24.80 MW	25.03 AW	51590 AAW	ILBLS	10//99-12//99
	Indiana	S	27.7 MW	29.26 AW	60860 AAW	INBLS	10//99-12//99
	Bloomington MSA, IN	S	33.20 MW	27.96 AW	69050 AAW	INBLS	10//99-12//99
	Elkhart-Goshen MSA, IN	S	29.73 MW	25.28 AW	61840 AAW	INBLS	10//99-12//99
	Evansville-Henderson MSA, IN-KY	S	19.11 MW	19.70 AW	39750 AAW	INBLS	10//99-12//99
	Fort Wayne MSA, IN	S	25.41 MW	24.58 AW	52840 AAW	INBLS	10//99-12//99
	Gary PMSA, IN	S	29.66 MW	28.13 AW	61690 AAW	INBLS	10//99-12//99
	Indianapolis MSA, IN	S	33.57 MW	32.45 AW	69830 AAW	INBLS	10//99-12//99
	South Bend MSA, IN	S	29.21 MW	26.03 AW	60760 AAW	INBLS	10//99-12//99
	Terre Haute MSA, IN	S	27.74 MW	29.88 AW	57690 AAW	INBLS	10//99-12//99
	Iowa	S	21.51 MW	24.20 AW	50340 AAW	IABLS	10//99-12//99
	Cedar Rapids MSA, IA	S	23.06 MW	23.08 AW	47960 AAW	IABLS	10//99-12//99

AAW	Average annual wage	AOH	Average offered, high	ASH	Average starting, high	H	Hourly	M	Monthly	S	Special: hourly and annual
AE	Average entry wage	AOL	Average offered, low	ASL	Average starting, low	HI	Highest wage paid	MTC	Median total compensation	TQ	Third quartile wage
AEX	Average experienced wage	APH	Average pay, high range	AW	Average wage paid	HR	High end range	MW	Median wage paid	W	Weekly
AO	Average offered	APL	Average pay, low range	FQ	First quartile wage	LR	Low end range	SQ	Second quartile wage	Y	Yearly

Occupation/Type/Industry	Location	Per	Low	Mid	High	Source	Date
Construction Manager	Davenport-Moline-Rock Island MSA, IA-IL	S	23.72 MW	23.37 AW	49330 AAW	IABLS	10//99-12//99
	Des Moines MSA, IA	S	27.14 MW	24.71 AW	56440 AAW	IABLS	10//99-12//99
	Iowa City MSA, IA	S	23.91 MW	22.45 AW	49720 AAW	IABLS	10//99-12//99
	Sioux City MSA, IA-NE	S	19.88 MW	19.08 AW	41350 AAW	IABLS	10//99-12//99
	Waterloo-Cedar Falls MSA, IA	S	18.32 MW	18.59 AW	38110 AAW	IABLS	10//99-12//99
	Kansas	S	23.06 MW	24.94 AW	51870 AAW	KSBLS	10//99-12//99
	Lawrence MSA, KS	S	32.12 MW	25.85 AW	66800 AAW	KSBLS	10//99-12//99
	Topeka MSA, KS	S	25.43 MW	25.31 AW	52890 AAW	KSBLS	10//99-12//99
	Wichita MSA, KS	S	25.82 MW	24.47 AW	53710 AAW	KSBLS	10//99-12//99
	Kentucky	S	23.25 MW	23.78 AW	49470 AAW	KYBLS	10//99-12//99
	Lexington MSA, KY	S	27.27 MW	24.94 AW	56720 AAW	KYBLS	10//99-12//99
	Louisville MSA, KY-IN	S	25.60 MW	24.41 AW	53240 AAW	KYBLS	10//99-12//99
	Owensboro MSA, KY	S	23.73 MW	20.66 AW	49350 AAW	KYBLS	10//99-12//99
	Louisiana	S	23.4 MW	24.22 AW	50370 AAW	LABLS	10//99-12//99
	Alexandria MSA, LA	S	20.50 MW	18.20 AW	42640 AAW	LABLS	10//99-12//99
	Baton Rouge MSA, LA	S	27.08 MW	27.95 AW	56320 AAW	LABLS	10//99-12//99
	Houma MSA, LA	S	23.37 MW	21.52 AW	48620 AAW	LABLS	10//99-12//99
	Lafayette MSA, LA	S	21.49 MW	20.05 AW	44700 AAW	LABLS	10//99-12//99
	Lake Charles MSA, LA	S	20.62 MW	15.62 AW	42890 AAW	LABLS	10//99-12//99
	Monroe MSA, LA	S	26.78 MW	27.83 AW	55700 AAW	LABLS	10//99-12//99
	New Orleans MSA, LA	S	25.04 MW	23.53 AW	52080 AAW	LABLS	10//99-12//99
	Shreveport-Bossier City MSA, LA	S	24.42 MW	23.15 AW	50800 AAW	LABLS	10//99-12//99
	Maine	S	21.95 MW	23.78 AW	49470 AAW	MEBLS	10//99-12//99
	Portland MSA, ME	S	23.16 MW	20.00 AW	48160 AAW	MEBLS	10//99-12//99
	Maryland	S	35.22 MW	35.17 AW	73150 AAW	MDBLS	10//99-12//99
	Baltimore PMSA, MD	S	38.09 MW	37.45 AW	79220 AAW	MDBLS	10//99-12//99
	Hagerstown PMSA, MD	S	19.86 MW	18.62 AW	41320 AAW	MDBLS	10//99-12//99
	Massachusetts	S	30.45 MW	30.98 AW	64440 AAW	MABLS	10//99-12//99
	Barnstable-Yarmouth MSA, MA	S	29.09 MW	29.30 AW	60500 AAW	MABLS	10//99-12//99
	Boston PMSA, MA-NH	S	32.89 MW	32.82 AW	68410 AAW	MABLS	10//99-12//99
	Brockton PMSA, MA	S	26.31 MW	25.56 AW	54710 AAW	MABLS	10//99-12//99
	Fitchburg-Leominster PMSA, MA	S	28.53 MW	29.78 AW	59340 AAW	MABLS	10//99-12//99
	Lawrence PMSA, MA-NH	S	29.36 MW	26.80 AW	61060 AAW	MABLS	10//99-12//99
	Lowell PMSA, MA-NH	S	22.65 MW	21.54 AW	47100 AAW	MABLS	10//99-12//99
	New Bedford PMSA, MA	S	28.48 MW	22.24 AW	59230 AAW	MABLS	10//99-12//99
	Pittsfield MSA, MA	S	24.06 MW	20.97 AW	50050 AAW	MABLS	10//99-12//99
	Springfield MSA, MA	S	26.40 MW	26.53 AW	54910 AAW	MABLS	10//99-12//99
	Worcester PMSA, MA-CT	S	22.89 MW	19.95 AW	47610 AAW	MABLS	10//99-12//99
	Michigan	S	30.42 MW	34.28 AW	71300 AAW	MIBLS	10//99-12//99
	Ann Arbor PMSA, MI	S	36.27 MW	26.00 AW	75430 AAW	MIBLS	10//99-12//99
	Benton Harbor MSA, MI	S	26.22 MW	25.31 AW	54550 AAW	MIBLS	10//99-12//99
	Detroit PMSA, MI	S	38.01 MW	34.20 AW	79070 AAW	MIBLS	10//99-12//99
	Flint PMSA, MI	S	35.45 MW	27.14 AW	73740 AAW	MIBLS	10//99-12//99
	Grand Rapids-Muskegon-Holland MSA, MI	S	29.65 MW	29.01 AW	61670 AAW	MIBLS	10//99-12//99
	Kalamazoo-Battle Creek MSA, MI	S	25.48 MW	26.01 AW	53000 AAW	MIBLS	10//99-12//99
	Lansing-East Lansing MSA, MI	S	26.90 MW	25.87 AW	55940 AAW	MIBLS	10//99-12//99
	Minnesota	S	28.72 MW	31.59 AW	65710 AAW	MNBLS	10//99-12//99
	Duluth-Superior MSA, MN-WI	S	25.09 MW	25.63 AW	52190 AAW	MNBLS	10//99-12//99
	Minneapolis-St. Paul MSA, MN-WI	S	33.95 MW	31.16 AW	70610 AAW	MNBLS	10//99-12//99
	Rochester MSA, MN	S	24.61 MW	24.13 AW	51190 AAW	MNBLS	10//99-12//99
	St. Cloud MSA, MN	S	28.28 MW	28.99 AW	58820 AAW	MNBLS	10//99-12//99
	Mississippi	S	21.38 MW	24.64 AW	51250 AAW	MSBLS	10//99-12//99
	Biloxi-Gulfport-Pascagoula MSA, MS	S	24.77 MW	22.38 AW	51530 AAW	MSBLS	10//99-12//99
	Hattiesburg MSA, MS	S	19.89 MW	18.98 AW	41370 AAW	MSBLS	10//99-12//99
	Jackson MSA, MS	S	23.98 MW	22.56 AW	49870 AAW	MSBLS	10//99-12//99
	Missouri	S	25.13 MW	26.50 AW	55120 AAW	MOBLS	10//99-12//99
	Columbia MSA, MO	S	20.01 MW	19.80 AW	41620 AAW	MOBLS	10//99-12//99
	Joplin MSA, MO	S	23.68 MW	22.49 AW	49250 AAW	MOBLS	10//99-12//99
	Kansas City MSA, MO-KS	S	28.60 MW	27.95 AW	59490 AAW	MOBLS	10//99-12//99
	St. Joseph MSA, MO	S	23.54 MW	20.61 AW	48950 AAW	MOBLS	10//99-12//99
	St. Louis MSA, MO-IL	S	28.62 MW	26.37 AW	59530 AAW	MOBLS	10//99-12//99
	Springfield MSA, MO	S	25.58 MW	24.47 AW	53200 AAW	MOBLS	10//99-12//99
	Montana	S	18.72 MW	23.91 AW	49730 AAW	MTBLS	10//99-12//99
	Billings MSA, MT	S	22.35 MW	19.35 AW	46490 AAW	MTBLS	10//99-12//99

AAW Average annual wage	AOH Average offered, high	ASH Average starting, high	H Hourly	M Monthly	S Special: hourly and annual
AE Average entry wage	AOL Average offered, low	ASL Average starting, low	HI Highest wage paid	MTC Median total compensation	TQ Third quartile wage
AEX Average experienced wage	APH Average pay, high range	AW Average wage paid	HR High end range	MW Median wage paid	W Weekly
AO Average offered	APL Average pay, low range	FQ First quartile wage	LR Low end range	SQ Second quartile wage	Y Yearly

Occupation/Type/Industry	Location	Per	Low	Mid	High	Source	Date
Construction Manager	Nebraska	S	25.91 MW	32.56 AW	67730 AAW	NEBLS	10//99-12//99
	Lincoln MSA, NE	S	25.05 MW	20.83 AW	52110 AAW	NEBLS	10//99-12//99
	Omaha MSA, NE-IA	S	36.71 MW	29.02 AW	76360 AAW	NEBLS	10//99-12//99
	Nevada	S	26.52 MW	29.51 AW	61380 AAW	NVBLS	10//99-12//99
	Las Vegas MSA, NV-AZ	S	29.75 MW	26.44 AW	61880 AAW	NVBLS	10//99-12//99
	Reno MSA, NV	S	30.66 MW	30.17 AW	63780 AAW	NVBLS	10//99-12//99
	New Hampshire	S	23.85 MW	26.53 AW	55170 AAW	NHBLS	10//99-12//99
	Manchester PMSA, NH	S	29.56 MW	26.97 AW	61480 AAW	NHBLS	10//99-12//99
	Nashua PMSA, NH	S	26.37 MW	25.52 AW	54860 AAW	NHBLS	10//99-12//99
	Portsmouth-Rochester PMSA, NH-ME	S	27.11 MW	26.77 AW	56380 AAW	NHBLS	10//99-12//99
	New Jersey	S	34.04 MW	37.49 AW	77980 AAW	NJBLS	10//99-12//99
	Atlantic-Cape May PMSA, NJ	S	43.71 MW	40.26 AW	90910 AAW	NJBLS	10//99-12//99
	Jersey City PMSA, NJ	S	35.77 MW	36.00 AW	74400 AAW	NJBLS	10//99-12//99
	Middlesex-Somerset-Hunterdon PMSA, NJ	S	35.25 MW	32.33 AW	73330 AAW	NJBLS	10//99-12//99
	Monmouth-Ocean PMSA, NJ	S	40.13 MW	39.39 AW	83470 AAW	NJBLS	10//99-12//99
	Newark PMSA, NJ	S	36.04 MW	32.57 AW	74960 AAW	NJBLS	10//99-12//99
	Trenton PMSA, NJ	S	34.05 MW	31.42 AW	70830 AAW	NJBLS	10//99-12//99
	Vineland-Millville-Bridgeton PMSA, NJ	S	23.97 MW	20.11 AW	49850 AAW	NJBLS	10//99-12//99
	New Mexico	S	23.05 MW	24.47 AW	50890 AAW	NMBLS	10//99-12//99
	Albuquerque MSA, NM	S	24.57 MW	24.03 AW	51100 AAW	NMBLS	10//99-12//99
	Las Cruces MSA, NM	S	18.89 MW	18.35 AW	39290 AAW	NMBLS	10//99-12//99
	Santa Fe MSA, NM	S	28.85 MW	29.45 AW	60010 AAW	NMBLS	10//99-12//99
	New York	S	35.77 MW	39.33 AW	81810 AAW	NYBLS	10//99-12//99
	Albany-Schenectady-Troy MSA, NY	S	36.17 MW	33.85 AW	75220 AAW	NYBLS	10//99-12//99
	Buffalo-Niagara Falls MSA, NY	S	38.15 MW	33.38 AW	79360 AAW	NYBLS	10//99-12//99
	Glens Falls MSA, NY	S	35.34 MW	33.87 AW	73510 AAW	NYBLS	10//99-12//99
	New York PMSA, NY	S	39.97 MW	36.41 AW	83150 AAW	NYBLS	10//99-12//99
	Newburgh PMSA, NY-PA	S	27.18 MW	23.09 AW	56530 AAW	NYBLS	10//99-12//99
	North Carolina	S	21.7 MW	23.22 AW	48300 AAW	NCBLS	10//99-12//99
	Asheville MSA, NC	S	22.73 MW	21.00 AW	47280 AAW	NCBLS	10//99-12//99
	Charlotte-Gastonia-Rock Hill MSA, NC-SC	S	24.47 MW	22.32 AW	50900 AAW	NCBLS	10//99-12//99
	Fayetteville MSA, NC	S	23.47 MW	23.40 AW	48820 AAW	NCBLS	10//99-12//99
	Greensboro--Winston-Salem--High Point MSA, NC	S	25.57 MW	24.97 AW	53180 AAW	NCBLS	10//99-12//99
	Greenville MSA, NC	S	21.16 MW	16.31 AW	44010 AAW	NCBLS	10//99-12//99
	Hickory-Morganton-Lenoir MSA, NC	S	18.22 MW	15.34 AW	37900 AAW	NCBLS	10//99-12//99
	Jacksonville MSA, NC	S	17.85 MW	12.97 AW	37120 AAW	NCBLS	10//99-12//99
	Raleigh-Durham-Chapel Hill MSA, NC	S	23.14 MW	22.51 AW	48130 AAW	NCBLS	10//99-12//99
	Rocky Mount MSA, NC	S	17.97 MW	16.28 AW	37380 AAW	NCBLS	10//99-12//99
	Wilmington MSA, NC	S	22.14 MW	22.10 AW	46060 AAW	NCBLS	10//99-12//99
	North Dakota	S	20.07 MW	23.46 AW	48800 AAW	NDBLS	10//99-12//99
	Fargo-Moorhead MSA, ND-MN	S	25.54 MW	23.75 AW	53130 AAW	NDBLS	10//99-12//99
	Grand Forks MSA, ND-MN	S	37.67 MW	30.35 AW	78340 AAW	NDBLS	10//99-12//99
	Ohio	S	24.24 MW	26.22 AW	54540 AAW	OHBLS	10//99-12//99
	Akron PMSA, OH	S	24.43 MW	24.33 AW	50820 AAW	OHBLS	10//99-12//99
	Canton-Massillon MSA, OH	S	23.52 MW	21.90 AW	48920 AAW	OHBLS	10//99-12//99
	Cincinnati PMSA, OH-KY-IN	S	25.74 MW	24.83 AW	53550 AAW	OHBLS	10//99-12//99
	Cleveland-Lorain-Elyria PMSA, OH	S	27.30 MW	25.15 AW	56790 AAW	OHBLS	10//99-12//99
	Columbus MSA, OH	S	24.10 MW	22.69 AW	50130 AAW	OHBLS	10//99-12//99
	Dayton-Springfield MSA, OH	S	25.44 MW	24.72 AW	52920 AAW	OHBLS	10//99-12//99
	Lima MSA, OH	S	23.09 MW	18.72 AW	48030 AAW	OHBLS	10//99-12//99
	Youngstown-Warren MSA, OH	S	21.58 MW	21.51 AW	44890 AAW	OHBLS	10//99-12//99
	Oklahoma	S	21.03 MW	22.80 AW	47430 AAW	OKBLS	10//99-12//99
	Lawton MSA, OK	S	22.96 MW	21.32 AW	47760 AAW	OKBLS	10//99-12//99
	Oklahoma City MSA, OK	S	19.27 MW	16.84 AW	40090 AAW	OKBLS	10//99-12//99
	Tulsa MSA, OK	S	25.51 MW	25.55 AW	53050 AAW	OKBLS	10//99-12//99
	Oregon	S	30.68 MW	33.18 AW	69020 AAW	ORBLS	10//99-12//99
	Corvallis MSA, OR	S	36.87 MW	26.19 AW	76680 AAW	ORBLS	10//99-12//99
	Eugene-Springfield MSA, OR	S	29.24 MW	25.74 AW	60820 AAW	ORBLS	10//99-12//99
	Medford-Ashland MSA, OR	S	33.03 MW	29.61 AW	68710 AAW	ORBLS	10//99-12//99
	Portland-Vancouver PMSA, OR-WA	S	37.70 MW	34.73 AW	78430 AAW	ORBLS	10//99-12//99

AAW Average annual wage	**AOH** Average offered, high	**ASH** Average starting, high	**H** Hourly	**M** Monthly	**S** Special: hourly and annual
AE Average entry wage	**AOL** Average offered, low	**ASL** Average starting, low	**HI** Highest wage paid	**MTC** Median total compensation	**TQ** Third quartile wage
AEX Average experienced wage	**APH** Average pay, high range	**AW** Average wage paid	**HR** High end range	**MW** Median wage paid	**W** Weekly
AO Average offered	**APL** Average pay, low range	**FQ** First quartile wage	**LR** Low end range	**SQ** Second quartile wage	**Y** Yearly

Occupation/Type/Industry	Location	Per	Low	Mid	High	Source	Date
Construction Manager	Salem PMSA, OR	S	29.67 MW	28.66 AW	61710 AAW	ORBLS	10//99-12//99
	Pennsylvania	S	29.35 MW	29.95 AW	62300 AAW	PABLS	10//99-12//99
	Allentown-Bethlehem-Easton MSA, PA	S	25.05 MW	24.12 AW	52100 AAW	PABLS	10//99-12//99
	Altoona MSA, PA	S	34.38 MW	23.61 AW	71510 AAW	PABLS	10//99-12//99
	Erie MSA, PA	S	22.41 MW	21.60 AW	46620 AAW	PABLS	10//99-12//99
	Harrisburg-Lebanon-Carlisle MSA, PA	S	25.88 MW	25.44 AW	53840 AAW	PABLS	10//99-12//99
	Johnstown MSA, PA	S	22.48 MW	22.02 AW	46760 AAW	PABLS	10//99-12//99
	Lancaster MSA, PA	S	25.91 MW	25.50 AW	53900 AAW	PABLS	10//99-12//99
	Philadelphia PMSA, PA-NJ	S	33.85 MW	33.08 AW	70410 AAW	PABLS	10//99-12//99
	Pittsburgh MSA, PA	S	26.87 MW	27.55 AW	55890 AAW	PABLS	10//99-12//99
	Reading MSA, PA	S	29.73 MW	28.74 AW	61840 AAW	PABLS	10//99-12//99
	Scranton--Wilkes-Barre-- Hazleton MSA, PA	S	24.64 MW	22.18 AW	51260 AAW	PABLS	10//99-12//99
	Sharon MSA, PA	S	25.70 MW	25.08 AW	53450 AAW	PABLS	10//99-12//99
	State College MSA, PA	S	27.36 MW	25.56 AW	56900 AAW	PABLS	10//99-12//99
	York MSA, PA	S	27.46 MW	25.89 AW	57120 AAW	PABLS	10//99-12//99
	South Carolina	S	20.06 MW	22.47 AW	46730 AAW	SCBLS	10//99-12//99
	Columbia MSA, SC	S	24.29 MW	22.31 AW	50530 AAW	SCBLS	10//99-12//99
	Florence MSA, SC	S	22.27 MW	20.99 AW	46320 AAW	SCBLS	10//99-12//99
	Greenville-Spartanburg- Anderson MSA, SC	S	25.09 MW	23.40 AW	52180 AAW	SCBLS	10//99-12//99
	Myrtle Beach MSA, SC	S	21.43 MW	21.29 AW	44580 AAW	SCBLS	10//99-12//99
	Sumter MSA, SC	S	27.75 MW	23.25 AW	57720 AAW	SCBLS	10//99-12//99
	South Dakota	S	28.29 MW	28.13 AW	58510 AAW	SDBLS	10//99-12//99
	Rapid City MSA, SD	S	29.24 MW	29.77 AW	60810 AAW	SDBLS	10//99-12//99
	Sioux Falls MSA, SD	S	28.36 MW	26.55 AW	58980 AAW	SDBLS	10//99-12//99
	Tennessee	S	26.28 MW	27.24 AW	56660 AAW	TNBLS	10//99-12//99
	Chattanooga MSA, TN-GA	S	24.81 MW	24.87 AW	51610 AAW	TNBLS	10//99-12//99
	Clarksville-Hopkinsville MSA, TN-KY	S	25.89 MW	26.01 AW	53850 AAW	TNBLS	10//99-12//99
	Jackson MSA, TN	S	24.49 MW	22.49 AW	50950 AAW	TNBLS	10//99-12//99
	Johnson City-Kingsport-Bristol MSA, TN-VA	S	22.21 MW	19.76 AW	46200 AAW	TNBLS	10//99-12//99
	Knoxville MSA, TN	S	24.88 MW	23.98 AW	51760 AAW	TNBLS	10//99-12//99
	Memphis MSA, TN-AR-MS	S	29.66 MW	25.72 AW	61700 AAW	MSBLS	10//99-12//99
	Nashville MSA, TN	S	27.86 MW	27.93 AW	57940 AAW	TNBLS	10//99-12//99
	Texas	S	24.63 MW	26.31 AW	54720 AAW	TXBLS	10//99-12//99
	Abilene MSA, TX	S	26.40 MW	26.77 AW	54900 AAW	TXBLS	10//99-12//99
	Amarillo MSA, TX	S	17.84 MW	15.70 AW	37100 AAW	TXBLS	10//99-12//99
	Austin-San Marcos MSA, TX	S	25.24 MW	24.28 AW	52500 AAW	TXBLS	10//99-12//99
	Beaumont-Port Arthur MSA, TX	S	25.93 MW	27.84 AW	53930 AAW	TXBLS	10//99-12//99
	Brazoria PMSA, TX	S	22.07 MW	21.29 AW	45900 AAW	TXBLS	10//99-12//99
	Brownsville-Harlingen-San Benito MSA, TX	S	19.03 MW	16.82 AW	39590 AAW	TXBLS	10//99-12//99
	Bryan-College Station MSA, TX	S	20.83 MW	19.80 AW	43330 AAW	TXBLS	10//99-12//99
	Corpus Christi MSA, TX	S	19.19 MW	18.39 AW	39920 AAW	TXBLS	10//99-12//99
	Dallas PMSA, TX	S	30.61 MW	29.43 AW	63660 AAW	TXBLS	10//99-12//99
	El Paso MSA, TX	S	19.27 MW	18.63 AW	40070 AAW	TXBLS	10//99-12//99
	Fort Worth-Arlington PMSA, TX	S	34.20 MW	31.85 AW	71140 AAW	TXBLS	10//99-12//99
	Galveston-Texas City PMSA, TX	S	19.52 MW	21.71 AW	40590 AAW	TXBLS	10//99-12//99
	Houston PMSA, TX	S	26.49 MW	24.91 AW	55090 AAW	TXBLS	10//99-12//99
	Killeen-Temple MSA, TX	S	21.17 MW	19.72 AW	44040 AAW	TXBLS	10//99-12//99
	Laredo MSA, TX	S	28.38 MW	16.32 AW	59030 AAW	TXBLS	10//99-12//99
	Longview-Marshall MSA, TX	S	28.18 MW	21.99 AW	58620 AAW	TXBLS	10//99-12//99
	Lubbock MSA, TX	S	20.38 MW	20.41 AW	42380 AAW	TXBLS	10//99-12//99
	McAllen-Edinburg-Mission MSA, TX	S	24.20 MW	17.72 AW	50330 AAW	TXBLS	10//99-12//99
	Odessa-Midland MSA, TX	S	18.84 MW	19.88 AW	39180 AAW	TXBLS	10//99-12//99
	San Antonio MSA, TX	S	23.46 MW	20.98 AW	48790 AAW	TXBLS	10//99-12//99
	Sherman-Denison MSA, TX	S	19.26 MW	18.99 AW	40070 AAW	TXBLS	10//99-12//99
	Texarkana MSA, TX- Texarkana, AR	S	18.62 MW	19.18 AW	38730 AAW	TXBLS	10//99-12//99
	Tyler MSA, TX	S	26.54 MW	23.48 AW	55200 AAW	TXBLS	10//99-12//99
	Waco MSA, TX	S	19.82 MW	17.41 AW	41230 AAW	TXBLS	10//99-12//99
	Wichita Falls MSA, TX	S	17.52 MW	14.61 AW	36430 AAW	TXBLS	10//99-12//99
	Utah	S	24.23 MW	26.12 AW	54330 AAW	UTBLS	10//99-12//99

AAW	Average annual wage	AOH	Average offered, high	ASH	Average starting, high	H	Hourly	M	Monthly	S	Special: hourly and annual
AE	Average entry wage	AOL	Average offered, low	ASL	Average starting, low	HI	Highest wage paid	MTC	Median total compensation	TQ	Third quartile wage
AEX	Average experienced wage	APH	Average pay, high range	AW	Average wage paid	HR	High end range	MW	Median wage paid	W	Weekly
AO	Average offered	APL	Average pay, low range	FQ	First quartile wage	LR	Low end range	SQ	Second quartile wage	Y	Yearly

Occupation/Type/Industry	Location	Per	Low	Mid	High	Source	Date
Construction Manager	Provo-Orem MSA, UT	S	19.96 MW	19.64 AW	41520 AAW	UTBLS	10//99-12//99
	Salt Lake City-Ogden MSA, UT	S	27.46 MW	24.55 AW	57120 AAW	UTBLS	10//99-12//99
	Vermont	S	24.71 MW	29.49 AW	61330 AAW	VTBLS	10//99-12//99
	Burlington MSA, VT	S	26.16 MW	22.63 AW	54410 AAW	VTBLS	10//99-12//99
	Virginia	S	24.45 MW	26.79 AW	55720 AAW	VABLS	10//99-12//99
	Charlottesville MSA, VA	S	23.18 MW	23.85 AW	48220 AAW	VABLS	10//99-12//99
	Danville MSA, VA	S	22.77 MW	23.93 AW	47370 AAW	VABLS	10//99-12//99
	Lynchburg MSA, VA	S	28.55 MW	23.92 AW	59390 AAW	VABLS	10//99-12//99
	Norfolk-Virginia Beach-Newport News MSA, VA-NC	S	28.66 MW	25.48 AW	59620 AAW	VABLS	10//99-12//99
	Richmond-Petersburg MSA, VA	S	24.37 MW	21.89 AW	50680 AAW	VABLS	10//99-12//99
	Roanoke MSA, VA	S	24.26 MW	21.59 AW	50470 AAW	VABLS	10//99-12//99
	Washington	S	31.09 MW	33.55 AW	69770 AAW	WABLS	10//99-12//99
	Bellingham MSA, WA	S	24.42 MW	23.10 AW	50790 AAW	WABLS	10//99-12//99
	Bremerton PMSA, WA	S	28.11 MW	28.80 AW	58470 AAW	WABLS	10//99-12//99
	Olympia PMSA, WA	S	27.61 MW	25.40 AW	57440 AAW	WABLS	10//99-12//99
	Richland-Kennewick-Pasco MSA, WA	S	32.48 MW	28.17 AW	67570 AAW	WABLS	10//99-12//99
	Seattle-Bellevue-Everett PMSA, WA	S	37.35 MW	34.88 AW	77680 AAW	WABLS	10//99-12//99
	Spokane MSA, WA	S	32.93 MW	30.04 AW	68490 AAW	WABLS	10//99-12//99
	Tacoma PMSA, WA	S	31.80 MW	26.31 AW	66140 AAW	WABLS	10//99-12//99
	Yakima MSA, WA	S	22.57 MW	20.26 AW	46950 AAW	WABLS	10//99-12//99
	West Virginia	S	12.4 MW	13.59 AW	28270 AAW	WVBLS	10//99-12//99
	Charleston MSA, WV	S	19.42 MW	19.22 AW	40390 AAW	WVBLS	10//99-12//99
	Huntington-Ashland MSA, WV-KY-OH	S	19.41 MW	16.75 AW	40380 AAW	WVBLS	10//99-12//99
	Parkersburg-Marietta MSA, WV-OH	S	20.08 MW	16.61 AW	41760 AAW	WVBLS	10//99-12//99
	Wheeling MSA, WV-OH	S	29.54 MW	28.80 AW	61440 AAW	WVBLS	10//99-12//99
	Wisconsin	S	24.9 MW	27.85 AW	57920 AAW	WIBLS	10//99-12//99
	Appleton-Oshkosh-Neenah MSA, WI	S	34.56 MW	27.36 AW	71890 AAW	WIBLS	10//99-12//99
	Eau Claire MSA, WI	S	19.58 MW	16.08 AW	40740 AAW	WIBLS	10//99-12//99
	Kenosha PMSA, WI	S	21.12 MW	19.52 AW	43930 AAW	WIBLS	10//99-12//99
	La Crosse MSA, WI-MN	S	22.45 MW	16.36 AW	46700 AAW	WIBLS	10//99-12//99
	Madison MSA, WI	S	24.76 MW	23.41 AW	51500 AAW	WIBLS	10//99-12//99
	Milwaukee-Waukesha PMSA, WI	S	32.38 MW	31.18 AW	67340 AAW	WIBLS	10//99-12//99
	Racine PMSA, WI	S	35.31 MW	34.90 AW	73450 AAW	WIBLS	10//99-12//99
	Wausau MSA, WI	S	26.43 MW	20.27 AW	54970 AAW	WIBLS	10//99-12//99
	Wyoming	S	21.23 MW	24.50 AW	50960 AAW	WYBLS	10//99-12//99
	Casper MSA, WY	S	17.64 MW	18.24 AW	36690 AAW	WYBLS	10//99-12//99
	Cheyenne MSA, WY	S	22.67 MW	19.75 AW	47150 AAW	WYBLS	10//99-12//99
	Puerto Rico	S	21.16 MW	27.54 AW	57290 AAW	PRBLS	10//99-12//99
	Caguas PMSA, PR	S	23.18 MW	19.52 AW	48220 AAW	PRBLS	10//99-12//99
	Mayaguez MSA, PR	S	24.07 MW	24.51 AW	50060 AAW	PRBLS	10//99-12//99
	Ponce MSA, PR	S	14.04 MW	12.59 AW	29210 AAW	PRBLS	10//99-12//99
	San Juan-Bayamon PMSA, PR	S	30.33 MW	26.22 AW	63080 AAW	PRBLS	10//99-12//99
	Virgin Islands	S	28.55 MW	28.07 AW	58380 AAW	VIBLS	10//99-12//99
Consultant	United States	Y		46600 MW		TRAVWK5	2000
Content Developer Internet	United States	Y		52501 MW		BUS2	2000
Continuous Mining Machine Operator	Alabama	S	16.93 MW	15.68 AW	32620 AAW	ALBLS	10//99-12//99
	California	S	15.01 MW	15.16 AW	31530 AAW	CABLS	10//99-12//99
	Florida	S	12.79 MW	12.28 AW	25540 AAW	FLBLS	10//99-12//99
	Georgia	S	14.73 MW	14.96 AW	31110 AAW	GABLS	10//99-12//99
	Illinois	S	18.89 MW	19.09 AW	39720 AAW	ILBLS	10//99-12//99
	Indiana	S	25.53 MW	24.15 AW	50240 AAW	INBLS	10//99-12//99
	Kentucky	S	15.08 MW	15.32 AW	31860 AAW	KYBLS	10//99-12//99
	Maryland	S	11.38 MW	13.19 AW	27440 AAW	MDBLS	10//99-12//99
	Michigan	S	15.33 MW	15.29 AW	31810 AAW	MIBLS	10//99-12//99
	Missouri	S	11.39 MW	11.59 AW	24110 AAW	MOBLS	10//99-12//99
	New Mexico	S	17.27 MW	15.36 AW	31940 AAW	NMBLS	10//99-12//99
	North Carolina	S	12.52 MW	12.80 AW	26630 AAW	NCBLS	10//99-12//99

AAW	Average annual wage	AOH	Average offered, high	ASH	Average starting, high	H	Hourly	M	Monthly	S	Special: hourly and annual
AE	Average entry wage	AOL	Average offered, low	ASL	Average starting, low	HI	Highest wage paid	MTC	Median total compensation	TQ	Third quartile wage
AEX	Average experienced wage	APH	Average pay, high range	AW	Average wage paid	HR	High end range	MW	Median wage paid	W	Weekly
AO	Average offered	APL	Average pay, low range	FQ	First quartile wage	LR	Low end range	SQ	Second quartile wage	Y	Yearly

Occupation/Type/Industry	Location	Per	Low	Mid	High	Source	Date
Continuous Mining Machine							
Operator	Oklahoma	S	9.82 MW	10.08 AW	20960 AAW	OKBLS	10//99-12//99
	Pennsylvania	S	17.36 MW	16.90 AW	35150 AAW	PABLS	10//99-12//99
	South Carolina	S	13.58 MW	13.43 AW	27940 AAW	SCBLS	10//99-12//99
	Tennessee	S	11.6 MW	11.91 AW	24760 AAW	TNBLS	10//99-12//99
	Texas	S	12.15 MW	12.13 AW	25230 AAW	TXBLS	10//99-12//99
	Virginia	S	13 MW	13.61 AW	28300 AAW	VABLS	10//99-12//99
	West Virginia	S	17.87 MW	20.60 AW	42850 AAW	WVBLS	10//99-12//99
	Wyoming	S	23.1 MW	21.53 AW	44790 AAW	WYBLS	10//99-12//99
	Puerto Rico	S	8.42 MW	9.79 AW	20350 AAW	PRBLS	10//99-12//99
Control and Valve Installer and							
Repairer							
Except Mechanical Door	Alabama	S	22.92 MW	21.87 AW	45490 AAW	ALBLS	10//99-12//99
Except Mechanical Door	Alaska	S	24.37 MW	29.32 AW	60990 AAW	AKBLS	10//99-12//99
Except Mechanical Door	Arizona	S	19.52 MW	19.94 AW	41480 AAW	AZBLS	10//99-12//99
Except Mechanical Door	Arkansas	S	18.12 MW	17.82 AW	37070 AAW	ARBLS	10//99-12//99
Except Mechanical Door	California	S	22.41 MW	22.49 AW	46780 AAW	CABLS	10//99-12//99
Except Mechanical Door	Colorado	S	17.59 MW	18.31 AW	38090 AAW	COBLS	10//99-12//99
Except Mechanical Door	Connecticut	S	22.69 MW	22.45 AW	46700 AAW	CTBLS	10//99-12//99
Except Mechanical Door	Delaware	S	16.18 MW	17.74 AW	36900 AAW	DEBLS	10//99-12//99
Except Mechanical Door	Florida	S	12.94 MW	14.26 AW	29660 AAW	FLBLS	10//99-12//99
Except Mechanical Door	Georgia	S	18.1 MW	16.82 AW	34990 AAW	GABLS	10//99-12//99
Except Mechanical Door	Hawaii	S	15.74 MW	18.87 AW	39260 AAW	HIBLS	10//99-12//99
Except Mechanical Door	Idaho	S	22.72 MW	22.10 AW	45960 AAW	IDBLS	10//99-12//99
Except Mechanical Door	Illinois	S	34.68 MW	29.64 AW	61650 AAW	ILBLS	10//99-12//99
Except Mechanical Door	Indiana	S	20.67 MW	19.35 AW	40240 AAW	INBLS	10//99-12//99
Except Mechanical Door	Iowa	S	18.18 MW	17.95 AW	37330 AAW	IABLS	10//99-12//99
Except Mechanical Door	Kansas	S	18.73 MW	17.92 AW	37270 AAW	KSBLS	10//99-12//99
Except Mechanical Door	Kentucky	S	10.77 MW	12.35 AW	25690 AAW	KYBLS	10//99-12//99
Except Mechanical Door	Louisiana	S	17.95 MW	18.08 AW	37600 AAW	LABLS	10//99-12//99
Except Mechanical Door	Maine	S	23.71 MW	22.57 AW	46950 AAW	MEBLS	10//99-12//99
Except Mechanical Door	Maryland	S	23.26 MW	22.94 AW	47710 AAW	MDBLS	10//99-12//99
Except Mechanical Door	Massachusetts	S	19.38 MW	19.80 AW	41190 AAW	MABLS	10//99-12//99
Except Mechanical Door	Michigan	S	21.33 MW	21.10 AW	43890 AAW	MIBLS	10//99-12//99
Except Mechanical Door	Minnesota	S	22.11 MW	19.92 AW	41430 AAW	MNBLS	10//99-12//99
Except Mechanical Door	Mississippi	S	14.78 MW	14.80 AW	30780 AAW	MSBLS	10//99-12//99
Except Mechanical Door	Nebraska	S	22.65 MW	20.42 AW	42470 AAW	NEBLS	10//99-12//99
Except Mechanical Door	New Hampshire	S	15.91 MW	16.41 AW	34140 AAW	NHBLS	10//99-12//99
Except Mechanical Door	New Jersey	S	21.87 MW	20.69 AW	43040 AAW	NJBLS	10//99-12//99
Except Mechanical Door	New Mexico	S	22 MW	20.89 AW	43460 AAW	NMBLS	10//99-12//99
Except Mechanical Door	New York	S	24.48 MW	24.26 AW	50460 AAW	NYBLS	10//99-12//99
Except Mechanical Door	North Carolina	S	16.91 MW	16.96 AW	35270 AAW	NCBLS	10//99-12//99
Except Mechanical Door	North Dakota	S	19.25 MW	19.26 AW	40060 AAW	NDBLS	10//99-12//99
Except Mechanical Door	Ohio	S	18.69 MW	18.66 AW	38820 AAW	OHBLS	10//99-12//99
Except Mechanical Door	Oklahoma	S	17.85 MW	16.75 AW	34830 AAW	OKBLS	10//99-12//99
Except Mechanical Door	Pennsylvania	S	23.14 MW	22.28 AW	46350 AAW	PABLS	10//99-12//99
Except Mechanical Door	Rhode Island	S	14.8 MW	14.82 AW	30830 AAW	RIBLS	10//99-12//99
Except Mechanical Door	South Carolina	S	21.18 MW	21.55 AW	44820 AAW	SCBLS	10//99-12//99
Except Mechanical Door	South Dakota	S	18.69 MW	19.13 AW	39790 AAW	SDBLS	10//99-12//99
Except Mechanical Door	Tennessee	S	15.6 MW	16.33 AW	33970 AAW	TNBLS	10//99-12//99
Except Mechanical Door	Texas	S	16.19 MW	16.82 AW	34980 AAW	TXBLS	10//99-12//99
Except Mechanical Door	Utah	S	18.92 MW	18.94 AW	39400 AAW	UTBLS	10//99-12//99
Except Mechanical Door	Virginia	S	18.5 MW	17.41 AW	36220 AAW	VABLS	10//99-12//99
Except Mechanical Door	Washington	S	21.11 MW	20.89 AW	43460 AAW	WABLS	10//99-12//99
Except Mechanical Door	West Virginia	S	22.95 MW	22.23 AW	46230 AAW	WVBLS	10//99-12//99
Except Mechanical Door	Wisconsin	S	19.01 MW	18.29 AW	38030 AAW	WIBLS	10//99-12//99
Except Mechanical Door	Wyoming	S	23.06 MW	20.46 AW	42550 AAW	WYBLS	10//99-12//99
Controller							
Beer Wholesaling	United States	Y	53350 MW	57436 AW		BEVW	1999
Divisional	United States	Y		75444 AW		SFIN	1999
Plant Level	United States	Y		64839 AW		SFIN	1999
Conveyor Operator and Tender	Alabama	S	11.24 MW	12.17 AW	25320 AAW	ALBLS	10//99-12//99
	Arizona	S	12.32 MW	12.46 AW	25930 AAW	AZBLS	10//99-12//99
	Arkansas	S	9.74 MW	9.77 AW	20330 AAW	ARBLS	10//99-12//99
	California	S	11.25 MW	11.72 AW	24370 AAW	CABLS	10//99-12//99
	Colorado	S	13.16 MW	13.40 AW	27870 AAW	COBLS	10//99-12//99
	Connecticut	S	11.05 MW	10.90 AW	22660 AAW	CTBLS	10//99-12//99
	Delaware	S	12.5 MW	12.26 AW	25500 AAW	DEBLS	10//99-12//99
	Florida	S	8.77 MW	9.56 AW	19880 AAW	FLBLS	10//99-12//99

AAW	Average annual wage	AOH	Average offered, high	ASH	Average starting, high	H	Hourly	M	Monthly	S	Special: hourly and annual
AE	Average entry wage	AOL	Average offered, low	ASL	Average starting, low	HI	Highest wage paid	MTC	Median total compensation	TQ	Third quartile wage
AEX	Average experienced wage	APH	Average pay, high range	AW	Average wage paid	HR	High end range	MW	Median wage paid	W	Weekly
AO	Average offered	APL	Average pay, low range	FQ	First quartile wage	LR	Low end range	SQ	Second quartile wage	Y	Yearly

Occupation/Type/Industry	Location	Per	Low	Mid	High	Source	Date
Conveyor Operator and Tender	Georgia	S	9.91 MW	10.26 AW	21350 AAW	GABLS	10//99-12//99
	Hawaii	S	11.83 MW	12.50 AW	26000 AAW	HIBLS	10//99-12//99
	Idaho	S	9.93 MW	10.49 AW	21810 AAW	IDBLS	10//99-12//99
	Illinois	S	13.34 MW	14.28 AW	29700 AAW	ILBLS	10//99-12//99
	Indiana	S	11.61 MW	12.49 AW	25990 AAW	INBLS	10//99-12//99
	Iowa	S	11.86 MW	12.23 AW	25430 AAW	IABLS	10//99-12//99
	Kansas	S	10.13 MW	10.42 AW	21680 AAW	KSBLS	10//99-12//99
	Kentucky	S	11.66 MW	12.64 AW	26290 AAW	KYBLS	10//99-12//99
	Louisiana	S	9.53 MW	10.21 AW	21240 AAW	LABLS	10//99-12//99
	Maine	S	10.46 MW	10.09 AW	20990 AAW	MEBLS	10//99-12//99
	Maryland	S	13.2 MW	12.98 AW	27010 AAW	MDBLS	10//99-12//99
	Massachusetts	S	11.69 MW	12.60 AW	26220 AAW	MABLS	10//99-12//99
	Michigan	S	11.78 MW	12.04 AW	25050 AAW	MIBLS	10//99-12//99
	Minnesota	S	10.74 MW	11.35 AW	23610 AAW	MNBLS	10//99-12//99
	Mississippi	S	9.17 MW	9.91 AW	20620 AAW	MSBLS	10//99-12//99
	Montana	S	9.77 MW	10.21 AW	21230 AAW	MTBLS	10//99-12//99
	Nebraska	S	10.06 MW	10.48 AW	21810 AAW	NEBLS	10//99-12//99
	Nevada	S	14.15 MW	13.41 AW	27880 AAW	NVBLS	10//99-12//99
	New Hampshire	S	9.21 MW	10.01 AW	20830 AAW	NHBLS	10//99-12//99
	New Jersey	S	12.11 MW	12.32 AW	25620 AAW	NJBLS	10//99-12//99
	New Mexico	S	10.12 MW	10.05 AW	20910 AAW	NMBLS	10//99-12//99
	New York	S	11.26 MW	11.78 AW	24500 AAW	NYBLS	10//99-12//99
	North Carolina	S	9.46 MW	10.02 AW	20850 AAW	NCBLS	10//99-12//99
	North Dakota	S	9.52 MW	10.21 AW	21230 AAW	NDBLS	10//99-12//99
	Ohio	S	11.99 MW	12.40 AW	25790 AAW	OHBLS	10//99-12//99
	Oklahoma	S	9.49 MW	10.94 AW	22750 AAW	OKBLS	10//99-12//99
	Oregon	S	11.16 MW	11.66 AW	24250 AAW	ORBLS	10//99-12//99
	Pennsylvania	S	12.05 MW	12.15 AW	25260 AAW	PABLS	10//99-12//99
	South Carolina	S	9.91 MW	10.81 AW	22480 AAW	SCBLS	10//99-12//99
	South Dakota	S	10.33 MW	10.37 AW	21580 AAW	SDBLS	10//99-12//99
	Tennessee	S	11.45 MW	11.89 AW	24730 AAW	TNBLS	10//99-12//99
	Texas	S	10.02 MW	10.24 AW	21300 AAW	TXBLS	10//99-12//99
	Vermont	S	9.74 MW	9.80 AW	20390 AAW	VTBLS	10//99-12//99
	Virginia	S	10.99 MW	11.14 AW	23160 AAW	VABLS	10//99-12//99
	Washington	S	12.75 MW	13.25 AW	27560 AAW	WABLS	10//99-12//99
	West Virginia	S	17.82 MW	16.49 AW	34300 AAW	WVBLS	10//99-12//99
	Wisconsin	S	10.78 MW	11.07 AW	23030 AAW	WIBLS	10//99-12//99
	Wyoming	S	19.28 MW	17.23 AW	35840 AAW	WYBLS	10//99-12//99
	Puerto Rico	S	9.61 MW	9.68 AW	20140 AAW	PRBLS	10//99-12//99
Cook							
Fast Food	Alabama	S	6 MW	5.90 AW	12280 AAW	ALBLS	10//99-12//99
Fast Food	Anniston MSA, AL	S	5.79 MW	5.97 AW	12040 AAW	ALBLS	10//99-12//99
Fast Food	Auburn-Opelika MSA, AL	S	5.99 MW	5.98 AW	12470 AAW	ALBLS	10//99-12//99
Fast Food	Birmingham MSA, AL	S	6.03 MW	6.07 AW	12530 AAW	ALBLS	10//99-12//99
Fast Food	Decatur MSA, AL	S	5.91 MW	6.09 AW	12290 AAW	ALBLS	10//99-12//99
Fast Food	Dothan MSA, AL	S	5.81 MW	5.97 AW	12090 AAW	ALBLS	10//99-12//99
Fast Food	Florence MSA, AL	S	5.96 MW	5.97 AW	12400 AAW	ALBLS	10//99-12//99
Fast Food	Gadsden MSA, AL	S	5.83 MW	5.97 AW	12130 AAW	ALBLS	10//99-12//99
Fast Food	Huntsville MSA, AL	S	5.84 MW	5.94 AW	12150 AAW	ALBLS	10//99-12//99
Fast Food	Mobile MSA, AL	S	5.93 MW	6.06 AW	12330 AAW	ALBLS	10//99-12//99
Fast Food	Montgomery MSA, AL	S	5.85 MW	5.99 AW	12170 AAW	ALBLS	10//99-12//99
Fast Food	Tuscaloosa MSA, AL	S	5.92 MW	6.01 AW	12320 AAW	ALBLS	10//99-12//99
Fast Food	Alaska	S	8.36 MW	9.05 AW	18830 AAW	AKBLS	10//99-12//99
Fast Food	Anchorage MSA, AK	S	10.80 MW	10.17 AW	22470 AAW	AKBLS	10//99-12//99
Fast Food	Arizona	S	6.23 MW	6.39 AW	13290 AAW	AZBLS	10//99-12//99
Fast Food	Flagstaff MSA, AZ-UT	S	6.33 MW	6.09 AW	13160 AAW	AZBLS	10//99-12//99
Fast Food	Phoenix-Mesa MSA, AZ	S	6.49 MW	6.34 AW	13500 AAW	AZBLS	10//99-12//99
Fast Food	Tucson MSA, AZ	S	6.22 MW	6.12 AW	12940 AAW	AZBLS	10//99-12//99
Fast Food	Yuma MSA, AZ	S	6.09 MW	5.96 AW	12680 AAW	AZBLS	10//99-12//99
Fast Food	Arkansas	S	6.04 MW	6.09 AW	12660 AAW	ARBLS	10//99-12//99
Fast Food	Fort Smith MSA, AR-OK	S	6.74 MW	6.43 AW	14020 AAW	ARBLS	10//99-12//99
Fast Food	Little Rock-North Little Rock MSA, AR	S	6.23 MW	6.24 AW	12960 AAW	ARBLS	10//99-12//99
Fast Food	Pine Bluff MSA, AR	S	5.76 MW	5.90 AW	11980 AAW	ARBLS	10//99-12//99
Fast Food	California	S	6.39 MW	6.86 AW	14270 AAW	CABLS	10//99-12//99
Fast Food	Bakersfield MSA, CA	S	6.50 MW	6.12 AW	13510 AAW	CABLS	10//99-12//99
Fast Food	Chico-Paradise MSA, CA	S	6.47 MW	6.26 AW	13470 AAW	CABLS	10//99-12//99
Fast Food	Fresno MSA, CA	S	6.71 MW	6.24 AW	13960 AAW	CABLS	10//99-12//99
Fast Food	Los Angeles-Long Beach PMSA, CA	S	7.10 MW	6.48 AW	14770 AAW	CABLS	10//99-12//99
Fast Food	Merced MSA, CA	S	6.71 MW	6.50 AW	13950 AAW	CABLS	10//99-12//99
Fast Food	Modesto MSA, CA	S	6.74 MW	6.32 AW	14020 AAW	CABLS	10//99-12//99

AAW	Average annual wage	AOH	Average offered, high	ASH	Average starting, high	H	Hourly	M	Monthly	S	Special: hourly and annual
AE	Average entry wage	AOL	Average offered, low	ASL	Average starting, low	HI	Highest wage paid	MTC	Median total compensation	TQ	Third quartile wage
AEX	Average experienced wage	APH	Average pay, high range	AW	Average wage paid	HR	High end range	MW	Median wage paid	W	Weekly
AO	Average offered	APL	Average pay, low range	FQ	First quartile wage	LR	Low end range	SQ	Second quartile wage	Y	Yearly

Occupation/Type/Industry	Location	Per	Low	Mid	High	Source	Date
Cook							
Fast Food	Oakland PMSA, CA	S	7.06 MW	6.61 AW	14690 AAW	CABLS	10//99-12//99
Fast Food	Orange County PMSA, CA	S	7.01 MW	6.64 AW	14580 AAW	CABLS	10//99-12//99
Fast Food	Redding MSA, CA	S	6.61 MW	6.31 AW	13750 AAW	CABLS	10//99-12//99
Fast Food	Riverside-San Bernardino PMSA, CA	S	6.65 MW	6.41 AW	13820 AAW	CABLS	10//99-12//99
Fast Food	Sacramento PMSA, CA	S	6.83 MW	6.11 AW	14210 AAW	CABLS	10//99-12//99
Fast Food	Salinas MSA, CA	S	6.59 MW	6.10 AW	13710 AAW	CABLS	10//99-12//99
Fast Food	San Diego MSA, CA	S	6.60 MW	6.15 AW	13720 AAW	CABLS	10//99-12//99
Fast Food	San Francisco PMSA, CA	S	7.03 MW	6.46 AW	14620 AAW	CABLS	10//99-12//99
Fast Food	San Jose PMSA, CA	S	6.65 MW	6.37 AW	13830 AAW	CABLS	10//99-12//99
Fast Food	Santa Barbara-Santa Maria-Lompoc MSA, CA	S	6.57 MW	6.29 AW	13660 AAW	CABLS	10//99-12//99
Fast Food	Santa Cruz-Watsonville PMSA, CA	S	7.14 MW	6.63 AW	14840 AAW	CABLS	10//99-12//99
Fast Food	Santa Rosa PMSA, CA	S	6.90 MW	6.51 AW	14350 AAW	CABLS	10//99-12//99
Fast Food	Stockton-Lodi MSA, CA	S	6.54 MW	6.11 AW	13610 AAW	CABLS	10//99-12//99
Fast Food	Vallejo-Fairfield-Napa PMSA, CA	S	6.85 MW	6.64 AW	14250 AAW	CABLS	10//99-12//99
Fast Food	Ventura PMSA, CA	S	6.96 MW	6.53 AW	14480 AAW	CABLS	10//99-12//99
Fast Food	Visalia-Tulare-Porterville MSA, CA	S	6.47 MW	6.10 AW	13450 AAW	CABLS	10//99-12//99
Fast Food	Colorado	S	6.05 MW	6.40 AW	13300 AAW	COBLS	10//99-12//99
Fast Food	Boulder-Longmont PMSA, CO	S	6.37 MW	6.07 AW	13250 AAW	COBLS	10//99-12//99
Fast Food	Colorado Springs MSA, CO	S	6.15 MW	5.97 AW	12800 AAW	COBLS	10//99-12//99
Fast Food	Denver PMSA, CO	S	6.61 MW	6.19 AW	13750 AAW	COBLS	10//99-12//99
Fast Food	Fort Collins-Loveland MSA, CO	S	6.59 MW	6.48 AW	13710 AAW	COBLS	10//99-12//99
Fast Food	Greeley PMSA, CO	S	6.88 MW	6.51 AW	14310 AAW	COBLS	10//99-12//99
Fast Food	Pueblo MSA, CO	S	5.95 MW	6.02 AW	12370 AAW	COBLS	10//99-12//99
Fast Food	Connecticut	S	6.76 MW	7.14 AW	14850 AAW	CTBLS	10//99-12//99
Fast Food	Bridgeport PMSA, CT	S	6.86 MW	6.36 AW	14270 AAW	CTBLS	10//99-12//99
Fast Food	Danbury PMSA, CT	S	6.49 MW	6.34 AW	13500 AAW	CTBLS	10//99-12//99
Fast Food	Hartford MSA, CT	S	7.06 MW	6.60 AW	14680 AAW	CTBLS	10//99-12//99
Fast Food	New Haven-Meriden PMSA, CT	S	7.47 MW	6.69 AW	15540 AAW	CTBLS	10//99-12//99
Fast Food	New London-Norwich MSA, CT-RI	S	7.03 MW	6.53 AW	14610 AAW	CTBLS	10//99-12//99
Fast Food	Stamford-Norwalk PMSA, CT	S	8.05 MW	7.96 AW	16740 AAW	CTBLS	10//99-12//99
Fast Food	Waterbury PMSA, CT	S	7.14 MW	6.44 AW	14840 AAW	CTBLS	10//99-12//99
Fast Food	Delaware	S	6.3 MW	6.81 AW	14170 AAW	DEBLS	10//99-12//99
Fast Food	Dover MSA, DE	S	6.43 MW	6.03 AW	13380 AAW	DEBLS	10//99-12//99
Fast Food	Wilmington-Newark PMSA, DE-MD	S	6.85 MW	6.06 AW	14250 AAW	DEBLS	10//99-12//99
Fast Food	District of Columbia	S	7.53 MW	7.54 AW	15680 AAW	DCBLS	10//99-12//99
Fast Food	Washington PMSA, DC-MD-VA-WV	S	6.87 MW	6.78 AW	14290 AAW	DCBLS	10//99-12//99
Fast Food	Florida	S	6.66 MW	6.90 AW	14340 AAW	FLBLS	10//99-12//99
Fast Food	Daytona Beach MSA, FL	S	7.23 MW	7.04 AW	15040 AAW	FLBLS	10//99-12//99
Fast Food	Fort Lauderdale PMSA, FL	S	6.79 MW	6.67 AW	14120 AAW	FLBLS	10//99-12//99
Fast Food	Fort Myers-Cape Coral MSA, FL	S	6.69 MW	6.53 AW	13920 AAW	FLBLS	10//99-12//99
Fast Food	Gainesville MSA, FL	S	6.12 MW	6.08 AW	12730 AAW	FLBLS	10//99-12//99
Fast Food	Jacksonville MSA, FL	S	6.54 MW	6.38 AW	13610 AAW	FLBLS	10//99-12//99
Fast Food	Lakeland-Winter Haven MSA, FL	S	7.43 MW	6.59 AW	15440 AAW	FLBLS	10//99-12//99
Fast Food	Melbourne-Titusville-Palm Bay MSA, FL	S	7.15 MW	7.17 AW	14870 AAW	FLBLS	10//99-12//99
Fast Food	Miami PMSA, FL	S	6.88 MW	7.03 AW	14310 AAW	FLBLS	10//99-12//99
Fast Food	Naples MSA, FL	S	6.78 MW	6.45 AW	14090 AAW	FLBLS	10//99-12//99
Fast Food	Ocala MSA, FL	S	7.31 MW	7.34 AW	15210 AAW	FLBLS	10//99-12//99
Fast Food	Orlando MSA, FL	S	7.67 MW	7.66 AW	15960 AAW	FLBLS	10//99-12//99
Fast Food	Panama City MSA, FL	S	6.31 MW	6.37 AW	13120 AAW	FLBLS	10//99-12//99
Fast Food	Pensacola MSA, FL	S	7.34 MW	7.26 AW	15270 AAW	FLBLS	10//99-12//99
Fast Food	Sarasota-Bradenton MSA, FL	S	6.69 MW	6.10 AW	13910 AAW	FLBLS	10//99-12//99
Fast Food	Tallahassee MSA, FL	S	6.16 MW	6.15 AW	12820 AAW	FLBLS	10//99-12//99
Fast Food	Tampa-St. Petersburg-Clearwater MSA, FL	S	7.00 MW	6.60 AW	14570 AAW	FLBLS	10//99-12//99
Fast Food	West Palm Beach-Boca Raton MSA, FL	S	6.72 MW	6.56 AW	13990 AAW	FLBLS	10//99-12//99
Fast Food	Georgia	S	6.28 MW	6.56 AW	13640 AAW	GABLS	10//99-12//99
Fast Food	Albany MSA, GA	S	5.93 MW	6.05 AW	12330 AAW	GABLS	10//99-12//99

AAW	Average annual wage	AOH	Average offered, high	ASH	Average starting, high	H	Hourly	M	Monthly	S	Special: hourly and annual
AE	Average entry wage	AOL	Average offered, low	ASL	Average starting, low	HI	Highest wage paid	MTC	Median total compensation	TQ	Third quartile wage
AEX	Average experienced wage	APH	Average pay, high range	AW	Average wage paid	HR	High end range	MW	Median wage paid	W	Weekly
AO	Average offered	APL	Average pay, low range	FQ	First quartile wage	LR	Low end range	SQ	Second quartile wage	Y	Yearly

Cook

Occupation/Type/Industry	Location	Per	Low	Mid	High	Source	Date
Fast Food	Athens MSA, GA	S	6.00 MW	6.01 AW	12480 AAW	GABLS	10//99-12//99
Fast Food	Atlanta MSA, GA	S	7.37 MW	7.36 AW	15330 AAW	GABLS	10//99-12//99
Fast Food	Augusta-Aiken MSA, GA-SC	S	5.92 MW	5.94 AW	12320 AAW	GABLS	10//99-12//99
Fast Food	Columbus MSA, GA-AL	S	6.23 MW	6.10 AW	12960 AAW	GABLS	10//99-12//99
Fast Food	Macon MSA, GA	S	6.10 MW	6.11 AW	12680 AAW	GABLS	10//99-12//99
Fast Food	Savannah MSA, GA	S	6.65 MW	6.28 AW	13830 AAW	GABLS	10//99-12//99
Fast Food	Hawaii	S	6.83 MW	7.60 AW	15800 AAW	HIBLS	10//99-12//99
Fast Food	Honolulu MSA, HI	S	7.43 MW	6.88 AW	15460 AAW	HIBLS	10//99-12//99
Fast Food	Idaho	S	6.09 MW	6.40 AW	13310 AAW	IDBLS	10//99-12//99
Fast Food	Boise City MSA, ID	S	6.78 MW	6.54 AW	14110 AAW	IDBLS	10//99-12//99
Fast Food	Pocatello MSA, ID	S	6.25 MW	6.16 AW	13010 AAW	IDBLS	10//99-12//99
Fast Food	Illinois	S	6.39 MW	6.74 AW	14020 AAW	ILBLS	10//99-12//99
Fast Food	Bloomington-Normal MSA, IL	S	6.94 MW	6.71 AW	14440 AAW	ILBLS	10//99-12//99
Fast Food	Champaign-Urbana MSA, IL	S	6.94 MW	6.79 AW	14430 AAW	ILBLS	10//99-12//99
Fast Food	Chicago PMSA, IL	S	7.06 MW	6.64 AW	14680 AAW	ILBLS	10//99-12//99
Fast Food	Decatur MSA, IL	S	6.96 MW	6.97 AW	14470 AAW	ILBLS	10//99-12//99
Fast Food	Kankakee PMSA, IL	S	8.30 MW	7.65 AW	17250 AAW	ILBLS	10//99-12//99
Fast Food	Peoria-Pekin MSA, IL	S	6.41 MW	6.14 AW	13340 AAW	ILBLS	10//99-12//99
Fast Food	Rockford MSA, IL	S	6.23 MW	6.04 AW	12960 AAW	ILBLS	10//99-12//99
Fast Food	Indiana	S	6.41 MW	6.59 AW	13700 AAW	INBLS	10//99-12//99
Fast Food	Bloomington MSA, IN	S	6.46 MW	6.34 AW	13440 AAW	INBLS	10//99-12//99
Fast Food	Elkhart-Goshen MSA, IN	S	6.43 MW	6.37 AW	13370 AAW	INBLS	10//99-12//99
Fast Food	Evansville-Henderson MSA, IN-KY	S	6.42 MW	6.25 AW	13340 AAW	INBLS	10//99-12//99
Fast Food	Fort Wayne MSA, IN	S	7.03 MW	7.00 AW	14610 AAW	INBLS	10//99-12//99
Fast Food	Gary PMSA, IN	S	6.33 MW	6.20 AW	13170 AAW	INBLS	10//99-12//99
Fast Food	Indianapolis MSA, IN	S	6.82 MW	6.51 AW	14180 AAW	INBLS	10//99-12//99
Fast Food	Kokomo MSA, IN	S	6.46 MW	6.44 AW	13430 AAW	INBLS	10//99-12//99
Fast Food	Lafayette MSA, IN	S	6.51 MW	6.43 AW	13540 AAW	INBLS	10//99-12//99
Fast Food	South Bend MSA, IN	S	6.73 MW	6.67 AW	14000 AAW	INBLS	10//99-12//99
Fast Food	Terre Haute MSA, IN	S	6.29 MW	6.17 AW	13080 AAW	INBLS	10//99-12//99
Fast Food	Iowa	S	6.32 MW	6.65 AW	13830 AAW	IABLS	10//99-12//99
Fast Food	Davenport-Moline-Rock Island MSA, IA-IL	S	6.39 MW	6.23 AW	13280 AAW	IABLS	10//99-12//99
Fast Food	Des Moines MSA, IA	S	6.69 MW	6.73 AW	13910 AAW	IABLS	10//99-12//99
Fast Food	Dubuque MSA, IA	S	6.15 MW	6.01 AW	12800 AAW	IABLS	10//99-12//99
Fast Food	Waterloo-Cedar Falls MSA, IA	S	6.61 MW	6.63 AW	13750 AAW	IABLS	10//99-12//99
Fast Food	Kansas	S	6.43 MW	6.70 AW	13950 AAW	KSBLS	10//99-12//99
Fast Food	Lawrence MSA, KS	S	6.62 MW	6.41 AW	13770 AAW	KSBLS	10//99-12//99
Fast Food	Wichita MSA, KS	S	6.78 MW	6.68 AW	14090 AAW	KSBLS	10//99-12//99
Fast Food	Kentucky	S	6.03 MW	6.25 AW	13000 AAW	KYBLS	10//99-12//99
Fast Food	Lexington MSA, KY	S	6.47 MW	6.08 AW	13460 AAW	KYBLS	10//99-12//99
Fast Food	Louisville MSA, KY-IN	S	6.66 MW	6.20 AW	13850 AAW	KYBLS	10//99-12//99
Fast Food	Owensboro MSA, KY	S	5.99 MW	6.00 AW	12460 AAW	KYBLS	10//99-12//99
Fast Food	Louisiana	S	5.97 MW	5.96 AW	12390 AAW	LABLS	10//99-12//99
Fast Food	Alexandria MSA, LA	S	5.82 MW	6.00 AW	12100 AAW	LABLS	10//99-12//99
Fast Food	Baton Rouge MSA, LA	S	5.83 MW	5.94 AW	12120 AAW	LABLS	10//99-12//99
Fast Food	Houma MSA, LA	S	5.78 MW	5.92 AW	12030 AAW	LABLS	10//99-12//99
Fast Food	Lafayette MSA, LA	S	5.97 MW	6.04 AW	12410 AAW	LABLS	10//99-12//99
Fast Food	Lake Charles MSA, LA	S	5.96 MW	6.03 AW	12400 AAW	LABLS	10//99-12//99
Fast Food	Monroe MSA, LA	S	5.95 MW	6.09 AW	12380 AAW	LABLS	10//99-12//99
Fast Food	New Orleans MSA, LA	S	6.04 MW	5.95 AW	12560 AAW	LABLS	10//99-12//99
Fast Food	Shreveport-Bossier City MSA, LA	S	5.95 MW	5.88 AW	12370 AAW	LABLS	10//99-12//99
Fast Food	Maine	S	6.71 MW	6.78 AW	14090 AAW	MEBLS	10//99-12//99
Fast Food	Portland MSA, ME	S	7.06 MW	7.14 AW	14680 AAW	MEBLS	10//99-12//99
Fast Food	Maryland	S	6.39 MW	6.50 AW	13530 AAW	MDBLS	10//99-12//99
Fast Food	Baltimore PMSA, MD	S	6.62 MW	6.48 AW	13760 AAW	MDBLS	10//99-12//99
Fast Food	Cumberland MSA, MD-WV	S	6.40 MW	6.35 AW	13310 AAW	MDBLS	10//99-12//99
Fast Food	Hagerstown PMSA, MD	S	6.69 MW	6.59 AW	13920 AAW	MDBLS	10//99-12//99
Fast Food	Massachusetts	S	6.95 MW	7.71 AW	16030 AAW	MABLS	10//99-12//99
Fast Food	Boston PMSA, MA-NH	S	7.85 MW	7.24 AW	16330 AAW	MABLS	10//99-12//99
Fast Food	Brockton PMSA, MA	S	7.59 MW	7.20 AW	15790 AAW	MABLS	10//99-12//99
Fast Food	Lawrence PMSA, MA-NH	S	8.66 MW	8.19 AW	18010 AAW	MABLS	10//99-12//99
Fast Food	Springfield MSA, MA	S	7.18 MW	6.67 AW	14930 AAW	MABLS	10//99-12//99
Fast Food	Worcester PMSA, MA-CT	S	7.05 MW	6.81 AW	14660 AAW	MABLS	10//99-12//99
Fast Food	Michigan	S	6.34 MW	6.55 AW	13610 AAW	MIBLS	10//99-12//99
Fast Food	Ann Arbor PMSA, MI	S	6.67 MW	6.46 AW	13870 AAW	MIBLS	10//99-12//99
Fast Food	Benton Harbor MSA, MI	S	6.40 MW	6.27 AW	13300 AAW	MIBLS	10//99-12//99
Fast Food	Detroit PMSA, MI	S	6.69 MW	6.49 AW	13920 AAW	MIBLS	10//99-12//99
Fast Food	Flint PMSA, MI	S	6.68 MW	6.56 AW	13890 AAW	MIBLS	10//99-12//99

AAW	Average annual wage	AOH	Average offered, high	ASH	Average starting, high	H	Hourly	M	Monthly	S	Special: hourly and annual
AE	Average entry wage	AOL	Average offered, low	ASL	Average starting, low	HI	Highest wage paid	MTC	Median total compensation	TQ	Third quartile wage
AEX	Average experienced wage	APH	Average pay, high range	AW	Average wage paid	HR	High end range	MW	Median wage paid	W	Weekly
AO	Average offered	APL	Average pay, low range	FQ	First quartile wage	LR	Low end range	SQ	Second quartile wage	Y	Yearly

Occupation/Type/Industry	Location	Per	Low	Mid	High	Source	Date
Cook							
Fast Food	Grand Rapids-Muskegon-Holland MSA, MI	S	6.24 MW	6.24 AW	12980 AAW	MIBLS	10//99-12//99
Fast Food	Kalamazoo-Battle Creek MSA, MI	S	6.52 MW	6.21 AW	13570 AAW	MIBLS	10//99-12//99
Fast Food	Lansing-East Lansing MSA, MI	S	6.61 MW	6.45 AW	13740 AAW	MIBLS	10//99-12//99
Fast Food	Saginaw-Bay City-Midland MSA, MI	S	6.12 MW	6.13 AW	12740 AAW	MIBLS	10//99-12//99
Fast Food	Minnesota	S	6.49 MW	6.82 AW	14190 AAW	MNBLS	10//99-12//99
Fast Food	Duluth-Superior MSA, MN-WI	S	6.43 MW	6.41 AW	13380 AAW	MNBLS	10//99-12//99
Fast Food	Minneapolis-St. Paul MSA, MN-WI	S	6.97 MW	6.63 AW	14500 AAW	MNBLS	10//99-12//99
Fast Food	Rochester MSA, MN	S	7.01 MW	6.90 AW	14570 AAW	MNBLS	10//99-12//99
Fast Food	St. Cloud MSA, MN	S	6.26 MW	6.10 AW	13020 AAW	MNBLS	10//99-12//99
Fast Food	Mississippi	S	6.08 MW	6.32 AW	13150 AAW	MSBLS	10//99-12//99
Fast Food	Biloxi-Gulfport-Pascagoula MSA, MS	S	7.04 MW	6.79 AW	14650 AAW	MSBLS	10//99-12//99
Fast Food	Hattiesburg MSA, MS	S	6.29 MW	6.28 AW	13080 AAW	MSBLS	10//99-12//99
Fast Food	Jackson MSA, MS	S	6.45 MW	6.16 AW	13410 AAW	MSBLS	10//99-12//99
Fast Food	Missouri	S	6.09 MW	6.35 AW	13220 AAW	MOBLS	10//99-12//99
Fast Food	Kansas City MSA, MO-KS	S	6.98 MW	6.67 AW	14520 AAW	MOBLS	10//99-12//99
Fast Food	St. Louis MSA, MO-IL	S	6.35 MW	6.07 AW	13210 AAW	MOBLS	10//99-12//99
Fast Food	Montana	S	5.97 MW	5.93 AW	12340 AAW	MTBLS	10//99-12//99
Fast Food	Billings MSA, MT	S	5.88 MW	6.04 AW	12220 AAW	MTBLS	10//99-12//99
Fast Food	Great Falls MSA, MT	S	6.11 MW	6.02 AW	12710 AAW	MTBLS	10//99-12//99
Fast Food	Nebraska	S	7.16 MW	7.02 AW	14610 AAW	NEBLS	10//99-12//99
Fast Food	Lincoln MSA, NE	S	6.88 MW	7.06 AW	14310 AAW	NEBLS	10//99-12//99
Fast Food	Omaha MSA, NE-IA	S	7.18 MW	7.33 AW	14930 AAW	NEBLS	10//99-12//99
Fast Food	Nevada	S	6.42 MW	6.62 AW	13770 AAW	NVBLS	10//99-12//99
Fast Food	Las Vegas MSA, NV-AZ	S	6.65 MW	6.44 AW	13830 AAW	NVBLS	10//99-12//99
Fast Food	Reno MSA, NV	S	6.67 MW	6.46 AW	13870 AAW	NVBLS	10//99-12//99
Fast Food	New Hampshire	S	6.96 MW	7.21 AW	14990 AAW	NHBLS	10//99-12//99
Fast Food	Manchester PMSA, NH	S	7.29 MW	7.18 AW	15160 AAW	NHBLS	10//99-12//99
Fast Food	Nashua PMSA, NH	S	6.91 MW	7.13 AW	14360 AAW	NHBLS	10//99-12//99
Fast Food	Portsmouth-Rochester PMSA, NH-ME	S	8.59 MW	8.35 AW	17870 AAW	NHBLS	10//99-12//99
Fast Food	New Jersey	S	6.58 MW	6.83 AW	14200 AAW	NJBLS	10//99-12//99
Fast Food	Atlantic-Cape May PMSA, NJ	S	7.19 MW	6.55 AW	14960 AAW	NJBLS	10//99-12//99
Fast Food	Bergen-Passaic PMSA, NJ	S	6.86 MW	6.82 AW	14270 AAW	NJBLS	10//99-12//99
Fast Food	Middlesex-Somerset-Hunterdon PMSA, NJ	S	6.55 MW	6.06 AW	13620 AAW	NJBLS	10//99-12//99
Fast Food	Monmouth-Ocean PMSA, NJ	S	7.28 MW	7.05 AW	15150 AAW	NJBLS	10//99-12//99
Fast Food	Newark PMSA, NJ	S	6.61 MW	6.45 AW	13750 AAW	NJBLS	10//99-12//99
Fast Food	Trenton PMSA, NJ	S	6.68 MW	6.51 AW	13890 AAW	NJBLS	10//99-12//99
Fast Food	New Mexico	S	6.02 MW	6.09 AW	12680 AAW	NMBLS	10//99-12//99
Fast Food	Albuquerque MSA, NM	S	6.16 MW	6.01 AW	12820 AAW	NMBLS	10//99-12//99
Fast Food	Las Cruces MSA, NM	S	6.30 MW	6.32 AW	13100 AAW	NMBLS	10//99-12//99
Fast Food	Santa Fe MSA, NM	S	6.53 MW	6.46 AW	13580 AAW	NMBLS	10//99-12//99
Fast Food	New York	S	6.33 MW	6.69 AW	13910 AAW	NYBLS	10//99-12//99
Fast Food	Albany-Schenectady-Troy MSA, NY	S	7.35 MW	6.79 AW	15290 AAW	NYBLS	10//99-12//99
Fast Food	Binghamton MSA, NY	S	6.04 MW	6.07 AW	12550 AAW	NYBLS	10//99-12//99
Fast Food	Buffalo-Niagara Falls MSA, NY	S	6.52 MW	6.21 AW	13560 AAW	NYBLS	10//99-12//99
Fast Food	Dutchess County PMSA, NY	S	5.94 MW	6.04 AW	12350 AAW	NYBLS	10//99-12//99
Fast Food	Elmira MSA, NY	S	5.87 MW	5.90 AW	12210 AAW	NYBLS	10//99-12//99
Fast Food	Glens Falls MSA, NY	S	6.38 MW	6.06 AW	13270 AAW	NYBLS	10//99-12//99
Fast Food	Jamestown MSA, NY	S	6.34 MW	5.98 AW	13180 AAW	NYBLS	10//99-12//99
Fast Food	Nassau-Suffolk PMSA, NY	S	6.97 MW	6.79 AW	14510 AAW	NYBLS	10//99-12//99
Fast Food	New York PMSA, NY	S	6.59 MW	6.28 AW	13710 AAW	NYBLS	10//99-12//99
Fast Food	Newburgh PMSA, NY-PA	S	7.38 MW	6.64 AW	15350 AAW	NYBLS	10//99-12//99
Fast Food	Rochester MSA, NY	S	6.72 MW	6.29 AW	13980 AAW	NYBLS	10//99-12//99
Fast Food	Syracuse MSA, NY	S	7.01 MW	6.62 AW	14590 AAW	NYBLS	10//99-12//99
Fast Food	Utica-Rome MSA, NY	S	7.09 MW	6.72 AW	14750 AAW	NYBLS	10//99-12//99
Fast Food	North Carolina	S	6.08 MW	6.38 AW	13260 AAW	NCBLS	10//99-12//99
Fast Food	Asheville MSA, NC	S	6.99 MW	6.87 AW	14530 AAW	NCBLS	10//99-12//99
Fast Food	Charlotte-Gastonia-Rock Hill MSA, NC-SC	S	6.39 MW	6.01 AW	13300 AAW	NCBLS	10//99-12//99
Fast Food	Fayetteville MSA, NC	S	6.42 MW	6.30 AW	13360 AAW	NCBLS	10//99-12//99
Fast Food	Goldsboro MSA, NC	S	5.98 MW	5.99 AW	12430 AAW	NCBLS	10//99-12//99
Fast Food	Greensboro--Winston-Salem--High Point MSA, NC	S	6.34 MW	6.09 AW	13200 AAW	NCBLS	10//99-12//99

AAW Average annual wage	**AOH** Average offered, high	**ASH** Average starting, high	**H** Hourly	**M** Monthly	**S** Special: hourly and annual
AE Average entry wage	**AOL** Average offered, low	**ASL** Average starting, low	**HI** Highest wage paid	**MTC** Median total compensation	**TQ** Third quartile wage
AEX Average experienced wage	**APH** Average pay, high range	**AW** Average wage paid	**HR** High end range	**MW** Median wage paid	**W** Weekly
AO Average offered	**APL** Average pay, low range	**FQ** First quartile wage	**LR** Low end range	**SQ** Second quartile wage	**Y** Yearly

Occupation/Type/Industry	Location	Per	Low	Mid	High	Source	Date
Cook							
Fast Food	Hickory-Morganton-Lenoir MSA, NC	S	6.31 MW	6.01 AW	13120 AAW	NCBLS	10//99-12//99
Fast Food	Jacksonville MSA, NC	S	6.13 MW	6.04 AW	12760 AAW	NCBLS	10//99-12//99
Fast Food	Raleigh-Durham-Chapel Hill MSA, NC	S	6.56 MW	6.37 AW	13650 AAW	NCBLS	10//99-12//99
Fast Food	Rocky Mount MSA, NC	S	6.15 MW	5.98 AW	12790 AAW	NCBLS	10//99-12//99
Fast Food	Wilmington MSA, NC	S	6.28 MW	6.17 AW	13060 AAW	NCBLS	10//99-12//99
Fast Food	North Dakota	S	6.29 MW	6.40 AW	13320 AAW	NDBLS	10//99-12//99
Fast Food	Bismarck MSA, ND	S	6.33 MW	6.36 AW	13160 AAW	NDBLS	10//99-12//99
Fast Food	Fargo-Moorhead MSA, ND-MN	S	6.62 MW	6.33 AW	13770 AAW	NDBLS	10//99-12//99
Fast Food	Grand Forks MSA, ND-MN	S	6.64 MW	6.53 AW	13800 AAW	NDBLS	10//99-12//99
Fast Food	Ohio	S	6.14 MW	6.52 AW	13560 AAW	OHBLS	10//99-12//99
Fast Food	Akron PMSA, OH	S	6.13 MW	6.04 AW	12760 AAW	OHBLS	10//99-12//99
Fast Food	Canton-Massillon MSA, OH	S	6.23 MW	6.00 AW	12960 AAW	OHBLS	10//99-12//99
Fast Food	Cincinnati PMSA, OH-KY-IN	S	6.83 MW	6.65 AW	14210 AAW	OHBLS	10//99-12//99
Fast Food	Cleveland-Lorain-Elyria PMSA, OH	S	6.38 MW	5.99 AW	13270 AAW	OHBLS	10//99-12//99
Fast Food	Columbus MSA, OH	S	7.00 MW	7.17 AW	14550 AAW	OHBLS	10//99-12//99
Fast Food	Dayton-Springfield MSA, OH	S	7.03 MW	6.54 AW	14630 AAW	OHBLS	10//99-12//99
Fast Food	Hamilton-Middletown PMSA, OH	S	6.67 MW	6.38 AW	13880 AAW	OHBLS	10//99-12//99
Fast Food	Lima MSA, OH	S	6.14 MW	5.91 AW	12770 AAW	OHBLS	10//99-12//99
Fast Food	Mansfield MSA, OH	S	6.14 MW	5.95 AW	12770 AAW	OHBLS	10//99-12//99
Fast Food	Steubenville-Weirton MSA, OH-WV	S	5.91 MW	5.99 AW	12290 AAW	OHBLS	10//99-12//99
Fast Food	Toledo MSA, OH	S	6.91 MW	6.21 AW	14380 AAW	OHBLS	10//99-12//99
Fast Food	Youngstown-Warren MSA, OH	S	5.86 MW	5.95 AW	12180 AAW	OHBLS	10//99-12//99
Fast Food	Oklahoma	S	5.98 MW	6.08 AW	12660 AAW	OKBLS	10//99-12//99
Fast Food	Enid MSA, OK	S	6.05 MW	5.98 AW	12590 AAW	OKBLS	10//99-12//99
Fast Food	Oklahoma City MSA, OK	S	5.99 MW	5.97 AW	12450 AAW	OKBLS	10//99-12//99
Fast Food	Tulsa MSA, OK	S	6.21 MW	6.05 AW	12910 AAW	OKBLS	10//99-12//99
Fast Food	Oregon	S	6.86 MW	7.23 AW	15050 AAW	ORBLS	10//99-12//99
Fast Food	Salem PMSA, OR	S	7.46 MW	7.44 AW	15510 AAW	ORBLS	10//99-12//99
Fast Food	Pennsylvania	S	6.07 MW	6.34 AW	13180 AAW	PABLS	10//99-12//99
Fast Food	Allentown-Bethlehem-Easton MSA, PA	S	6.55 MW	6.17 AW	13610 AAW	PABLS	10//99-12//99
Fast Food	Altoona MSA, PA	S	6.10 MW	6.08 AW	12680 AAW	PABLS	10//99-12//99
Fast Food	Erie MSA, PA	S	6.03 MW	5.96 AW	12540 AAW	PABLS	10//99-12//99
Fast Food	Harrisburg-Lebanon-Carlisle MSA, PA	S	6.36 MW	6.12 AW	13240 AAW	PABLS	10//99-12//99
Fast Food	Johnstown MSA, PA	S	6.13 MW	6.11 AW	12740 AAW	PABLS	10//99-12//99
Fast Food	Philadelphia PMSA, PA-NJ	S	6.62 MW	6.15 AW	13770 AAW	PABLS	10//99-12//99
Fast Food	Pittsburgh MSA, PA	S	6.18 MW	6.00 AW	12860 AAW	PABLS	10//99-12//99
Fast Food	Reading MSA, PA	S	6.24 MW	5.92 AW	12980 AAW	PABLS	10//99-12//99
Fast Food	Scranton--Wilkes-Barre--Hazleton MSA, PA	S	6.00 MW	6.08 AW	12470 AAW	PABLS	10//99-12//99
Fast Food	Sharon MSA, PA	S	6.03 MW	6.01 AW	12540 AAW	PABLS	10//99-12//99
Fast Food	State College MSA, PA	S	6.30 MW	6.12 AW	13110 AAW	PABLS	10//99-12//99
Fast Food	Williamsport MSA, PA	S	6.28 MW	6.07 AW	13060 AAW	PABLS	10//99-12//99
Fast Food	York MSA, PA	S	6.28 MW	6.29 AW	13060 AAW	PABLS	10//99-12//99
Fast Food	Rhode Island	S	6.39 MW	6.84 AW	14230 AAW	RIBLS	10//99-12//99
Fast Food	Providence-Fall River-Warwick MSA, RI-MA	S	6.77 MW	6.31 AW	14070 AAW	RIBLS	10//99-12//99
Fast Food	South Carolina	S	6.23 MW	6.39 AW	13280 AAW	SCBLS	10//99-12//99
Fast Food	Charleston-North Charleston MSA, SC	S	6.65 MW	6.24 AW	13820 AAW	SCBLS	10//99-12//99
Fast Food	Columbia MSA, SC	S	6.11 MW	6.13 AW	12710 AAW	SCBLS	10//99-12//99
Fast Food	Florence MSA, SC	S	5.87 MW	5.94 AW	12210 AAW	SCBLS	10//99-12//99
Fast Food	Greenville-Spartanburg-Anderson MSA, SC	S	6.97 MW	6.79 AW	14510 AAW	SCBLS	10//99-12//99
Fast Food	Myrtle Beach MSA, SC	S	6.70 MW	6.60 AW	13950 AAW	SCBLS	10//99-12//99
Fast Food	Sumter MSA, SC	S	5.78 MW	5.90 AW	12020 AAW	SCBLS	10//99-12//99
Fast Food	South Dakota	S	6.29 MW	6.42 AW	13350 AAW	SDBLS	10//99-12//99
Fast Food	Rapid City MSA, SD	S	6.13 MW	6.02 AW	12750 AAW	SDBLS	10//99-12//99
Fast Food	Sioux Falls MSA, SD	S	6.54 MW	6.47 AW	13600 AAW	SDBLS	10//99-12//99
Fast Food	Tennessee	S	6.38 MW	6.53 AW	13590 AAW	TNBLS	10//99-12//99
Fast Food	Chattanooga MSA, TN-GA	S	6.24 MW	6.17 AW	12970 AAW	TNBLS	10//99-12//99
Fast Food	Clarksville-Hopkinsville MSA, TN-KY	S	5.99 MW	5.97 AW	12470 AAW	TNBLS	10//99-12//99

AAW	Average annual wage	AOH	Average offered, high	ASH	Average starting, high
AE	Average entry wage	AOL	Average offered, low	ASL	Average starting, low
AEX	Average experienced wage	APH	Average pay, high range	AW	Average wage paid
AO	Average offered	APL	Average pay, low range	FQ	First quartile wage

H Hourly
HI Highest wage paid
HR High end range
LR Low end range

M Monthly
MTC Median total compensation
MW Median wage paid
SQ Second quartile wage

S Special: hourly and annual
TQ Third quartile wage
W Weekly
Y Yearly

Cook

Occupation/Type/Industry	Location	Per	Low	Mid	High	Source	Date
Fast Food	Johnson City-Kingsport-Bristol MSA, TN-VA	S	6.26 MW	5.99 AW	13020 AAW	TNBLS	10//99-12//99
Fast Food	Knoxville MSA, TN	S	6.61 MW	6.47 AW	13750 AAW	TNBLS	10//99-12//99
Fast Food	Memphis MSA, TN-AR-MS	S	6.23 MW	6.17 AW	12960 AAW	MSBLS	10//99-12//99
Fast Food	Nashville MSA, TN	S	6.87 MW	6.83 AW	14280 AAW	TNBLS	10//99-12//99
Fast Food	Texas	S	6.05 MW	6.24 AW	12980 AAW	TXBLS	10//99-12//99
Fast Food	Abilene MSA, TX	S	6.50 MW	6.42 AW	13520 AAW	TXBLS	10//99-12//99
Fast Food	Amarillo MSA, TX	S	5.80 MW	5.90 AW	12060 AAW	TXBLS	10//99-12//99
Fast Food	Austin-San Marcos MSA, TX	S	7.16 MW	7.03 AW	14900 AAW	TXBLS	10//99-12//99
Fast Food	Brazoria PMSA, TX	S	6.22 MW	6.24 AW	12930 AAW	TXBLS	10//99-12//99
Fast Food	Brownsville-Harlingen-San Benito MSA, TX	S	5.70 MW	5.85 AW	11850 AAW	TXBLS	10//99-12//99
Fast Food	Bryan-College Station MSA, TX	S	6.65 MW	6.56 AW	13840 AAW	TXBLS	10//99-12//99
Fast Food	Corpus Christi MSA, TX	S	6.06 MW	6.20 AW	12600 AAW	TXBLS	10//99-12//99
Fast Food	Dallas PMSA, TX	S	6.30 MW	6.01 AW	13110 AAW	TXBLS	10//99-12//99
Fast Food	El Paso MSA, TX	S	5.86 MW	5.92 AW	12180 AAW	TXBLS	10//99-12//99
Fast Food	Fort Worth-Arlington PMSA, TX	S	6.09 MW	5.98 AW	12660 AAW	TXBLS	10//99-12//99
Fast Food	Galveston-Texas City PMSA, TX	S	6.49 MW	6.34 AW	13500 AAW	TXBLS	10//99-12//99
Fast Food	Houston PMSA, TX	S	6.08 MW	5.99 AW	12650 AAW	TXBLS	10//99-12//99
Fast Food	Killeen-Temple MSA, TX	S	6.28 MW	6.17 AW	13060 AAW	TXBLS	10//99-12//99
Fast Food	Laredo MSA, TX	S	5.99 MW	5.99 AW	12460 AAW	TXBLS	10//99-12//99
Fast Food	Longview-Marshall MSA, TX	S	5.99 MW	5.92 AW	12460 AAW	TXBLS	10//99-12//99
Fast Food	Lubbock MSA, TX	S	5.72 MW	5.83 AW	11890 AAW	TXBLS	10//99-12//99
Fast Food	McAllen-Edinburg-Mission MSA, TX	S	6.01 MW	6.04 AW	12500 AAW	TXBLS	10//99-12//99
Fast Food	Odessa-Midland MSA, TX	S	6.13 MW	6.06 AW	12750 AAW	TXBLS	10//99-12//99
Fast Food	San Antonio MSA, TX	S	7.07 MW	6.86 AW	14710 AAW	TXBLS	10//99-12//99
Fast Food	Sherman-Denison MSA, TX	S	7.33 MW	7.06 AW	15250 AAW	TXBLS	10//99-12//99
Fast Food	Texarkana MSA, TX-Texarkana, AR	S	5.88 MW	6.06 AW	12240 AAW	TXBLS	10//99-12//99
Fast Food	Tyler MSA, TX	S	5.85 MW	5.92 AW	12170 AAW	TXBLS	10//99-12//99
Fast Food	Waco MSA, TX	S	6.23 MW	6.06 AW	12970 AAW	TXBLS	10//99-12//99
Fast Food	Wichita Falls MSA, TX	S	6.02 MW	6.00 AW	12520 AAW	TXBLS	10//99-12//99
Fast Food	Utah	S	6.47 MW	6.70 AW	13940 AAW	UTBLS	10//99-12//99
Fast Food	Vermont	S	6.75 MW	7.52 AW	15650 AAW	VTBLS	10//99-12//99
Fast Food	Burlington MSA, VT	S	7.26 MW	6.63 AW	15100 AAW	VTBLS	10//99-12//99
Fast Food	Virginia	S	6.03 MW	6.26 AW	13020 AAW	VABLS	10//99-12//99
Fast Food	Charlottesville MSA, VA	S	6.19 MW	5.97 AW	12880 AAW	VABLS	10//99-12//99
Fast Food	Danville MSA, VA	S	6.00 MW	5.91 AW	12480 AAW	VABLS	10//99-12//99
Fast Food	Norfolk-Virginia Beach-Newport News MSA, VA-NC	S	6.04 MW	5.97 AW	12560 AAW	VABLS	10//99-12//99
Fast Food	Richmond-Petersburg MSA, VA	S	6.51 MW	6.27 AW	13540 AAW	VABLS	10//99-12//99
Fast Food	Washington	S	6.33 MW	6.74 AW	14010 AAW	WABLS	10//99-12//99
Fast Food	Bellingham MSA, WA	S	6.55 MW	6.33 AW	13620 AAW	WABLS	10//99-12//99
Fast Food	Bremerton PMSA, WA	S	7.11 MW	6.90 AW	14780 AAW	WABLS	10//99-12//99
Fast Food	Olympia PMSA, WA	S	6.45 MW	6.33 AW	13420 AAW	WABLS	10//99-12//99
Fast Food	Richland-Kennewick-Pasco MSA, WA	S	7.08 MW	6.53 AW	14730 AAW	WABLS	10//99-12//99
Fast Food	Seattle-Bellevue-Everett PMSA, WA	S	6.88 MW	6.31 AW	14310 AAW	WABLS	10//99-12//99
Fast Food	Spokane MSA, WA	S	6.92 MW	6.48 AW	14400 AAW	WABLS	10//99-12//99
Fast Food	Tacoma PMSA, WA	S	6.78 MW	6.44 AW	14100 AAW	WABLS	10//99-12//99
Fast Food	Yakima MSA, WA	S	6.31 MW	6.20 AW	13130 AAW	WABLS	10//99-12//99
Fast Food	West Virginia	S	6.02 MW	5.99 AW	12450 AAW	WVBLS	10//99-12//99
Fast Food	Charleston MSA, WV	S	5.93 MW	5.98 AW	12340 AAW	WVBLS	10//99-12//99
Fast Food	Huntington-Ashland MSA, WV-KY-OH	S	6.06 MW	6.09 AW	12600 AAW	WVBLS	10//99-12//99
Fast Food	Parkersburg-Marietta MSA, WV-OH	S	5.82 MW	5.97 AW	12100 AAW	WVBLS	10//99-12//99
Fast Food	Wheeling MSA, WV-OH	S	5.85 MW	5.99 AW	12170 AAW	WVBLS	10//99-12//99
Fast Food	Wisconsin	S	6.44 MW	6.59 AW	13720 AAW	WIBLS	10//99-12//99
Fast Food	Appleton-Oshkosh-Neenah MSA, WI	S	6.87 MW	6.62 AW	14280 AAW	WIBLS	10//99-12//99
Fast Food	Eau Claire MSA, WI	S	6.25 MW	6.30 AW	13000 AAW	WIBLS	10//99-12//99
Fast Food	Green Bay MSA, WI	S	6.34 MW	6.33 AW	13180 AAW	WIBLS	10//99-12//99
Fast Food	Janesville-Beloit MSA, WI	S	6.43 MW	6.38 AW	13360 AAW	WIBLS	10//99-12//99

AAW	Average annual wage	AOH	Average offered, high	ASH	Average starting, high	H	Hourly	M	Monthly	S	Special: hourly and annual
AE	Average entry wage	AOL	Average offered, low	ASL	Average starting, low	HI	Highest wage paid	MTC	Median total compensation	TQ	Third quartile wage
AEX	Average experienced wage	APH	Average pay, high range	AW	Average wage paid	HR	High end range	MW	Median wage paid	W	Weekly
AO	Average offered	APL	Average pay, low range	FQ	First quartile wage	LR	Low end range	SQ	Second quartile wage	Y	Yearly

Occupation/Type/Industry	Location	Per	Low	Mid	High	Source	Date
Cook							
Fast Food	Kenosha PMSA, WI	S	6.57 MW	6.47 AW	13660 AAW	WIBLS	10//99-12//99
Fast Food	La Crosse MSA, WI-MN	S	6.39 MW	6.28 AW	13300 AAW	WIBLS	10//99-12//99
Fast Food	Madison MSA, WI	S	6.87 MW	6.69 AW	14300 AAW	WIBLS	10//99-12//99
Fast Food	Milwaukee-Waukesha PMSA, WI	S	6.76 MW	6.63 AW	14070 AAW	WIBLS	10//99-12//99
Fast Food	Racine PMSA, WI	S	6.27 MW	6.33 AW	13040 AAW	WIBLS	10//99-12//99
Fast Food	Sheboygan MSA, WI	S	6.61 MW	6.47 AW	13740 AAW	WIBLS	10//99-12//99
Fast Food	Wausau MSA, WI	S	6.23 MW	6.18 AW	12950 AAW	WIBLS	10//99-12//99
Fast Food	Wyoming	S	6.05 MW	6.34 AW	13180 AAW	WYBLS	10//99-12//99
Fast Food	Casper MSA, WY	S	5.94 MW	6.00 AW	12350 AAW	WYBLS	10//99-12//99
Fast Food	Cheyenne MSA, WY	S	6.01 MW	5.97 AW	12500 AAW	WYBLS	10//99-12//99
Fast Food	Puerto Rico	S	5.95 MW	5.77 AW	12010 AAW	PRBLS	10//99-12//99
Fast Food	Aguadilla MSA, PR	S	5.74 MW	5.91 AW	11930 AAW	PRBLS	10//99-12//99
Fast Food	Arecibo PMSA, PR	S	6.02 MW	5.95 AW	12530 AAW	PRBLS	10//99-12//99
Fast Food	Caguas PMSA, PR	S	5.75 MW	5.93 AW	11960 AAW	PRBLS	10//99-12//99
Fast Food	Mayaguez MSA, PR	S	5.71 MW	5.87 AW	11870 AAW	PRBLS	10//99-12//99
Fast Food	Ponce MSA, PR	S	5.75 MW	5.94 AW	11960 AAW	PRBLS	10//99-12//99
Fast Food	San Juan-Bayamon PMSA, PR	S	5.78 MW	5.96 AW	12030 AAW	PRBLS	10//99-12//99
Fast Food	Virgin Islands	S	6.57 MW	6.91 AW	14370 AAW	VIBLS	10//99-12//99
Fast Food	Guam	S	6.16 MW	6.23 AW	12960 AAW	GUBLS	10//99-12//99
Institution and Cafeteria	Alabama	S	6.34 MW	6.78 AW	14100 AAW	ALBLS	10//99-12//99
Institution and Cafeteria	Anniston MSA, AL	S	6.48 MW	6.29 AW	13470 AAW	ALBLS	10//99-12//99
Institution and Cafeteria	Auburn-Opelika MSA, AL	S	6.52 MW	6.11 AW	13570 AAW	ALBLS	10//99-12//99
Institution and Cafeteria	Birmingham MSA, AL	S	6.61 MW	6.22 AW	13750 AAW	ALBLS	10//99-12//99
Institution and Cafeteria	Decatur MSA, AL	S	6.62 MW	6.49 AW	13780 AAW	ALBLS	10//99-12//99
Institution and Cafeteria	Dothan MSA, AL	S	6.21 MW	6.13 AW	12910 AAW	ALBLS	10//99-12//99
Institution and Cafeteria	Florence MSA, AL	S	6.40 MW	6.30 AW	13320 AAW	ALBLS	10//99-12//99
Institution and Cafeteria	Gadsden MSA, AL	S	6.50 MW	6.12 AW	13530 AAW	ALBLS	10//99-12//99
Institution and Cafeteria	Huntsville MSA, AL	S	7.40 MW	6.34 AW	15380 AAW	ALBLS	10//99-12//99
Institution and Cafeteria	Mobile MSA, AL	S	7.13 MW	6.71 AW	14820 AAW	ALBLS	10//99-12//99
Institution and Cafeteria	Montgomery MSA, AL	S	7.76 MW	6.84 AW	16140 AAW	ALBLS	10//99-12//99
Institution and Cafeteria	Tuscaloosa MSA, AL	S	8.17 MW	8.14 AW	16990 AAW	ALBLS	10//99-12//99
Institution and Cafeteria	Alaska	S	13.39 MW	13.90 AW	28910 AAW	AKBLS	10//99-12//99
Institution and Cafeteria	Anchorage MSA, AK	S	12.36 MW	11.58 AW	25710 AAW	AKBLS	10//99-12//99
Institution and Cafeteria	Arizona	S	8.32 MW	8.57 AW	17810 AAW	AZBLS	10//99-12//99
Institution and Cafeteria	Flagstaff MSA, AZ-UT	S	9.12 MW	8.41 AW	18960 AAW	AZBLS	10//99-12//99
Institution and Cafeteria	Phoenix-Mesa MSA, AZ	S	8.67 MW	8.46 AW	18030 AAW	AZBLS	10//99-12//99
Institution and Cafeteria	Tucson MSA, AZ	S	8.48 MW	8.42 AW	17640 AAW	AZBLS	10//99-12//99
Institution and Cafeteria	Yuma MSA, AZ	S	7.80 MW	7.57 AW	16220 AAW	AZBLS	10//99-12//99
Institution and Cafeteria	Arkansas	S	6.25 MW	6.53 AW	13570 AAW	ARBLS	10//99-12//99
Institution and Cafeteria	Fayetteville-Springdale-Rogers MSA, AR	S	7.31 MW	7.03 AW	15210 AAW	ARBLS	10//99-12//99
Institution and Cafeteria	Fort Smith MSA, AR-OK	S	6.59 MW	6.29 AW	13700 AAW	ARBLS	10//99-12//99
Institution and Cafeteria	Jonesboro MSA, AR	S	6.31 MW	6.16 AW	13110 AAW	ARBLS	10//99-12//99
Institution and Cafeteria	Little Rock-North Little Rock MSA, AR	S	7.04 MW	6.73 AW	14640 AAW	ARBLS	10//99-12//99
Institution and Cafeteria	Pine Bluff MSA, AR	S	5.98 MW	5.99 AW	12430 AAW	ARBLS	10//99-12//99
Institution and Cafeteria	California	S	9.74 MW	10.23 AW	21270 AAW	CABLS	10//99-12//99
Institution and Cafeteria	Bakersfield MSA, CA	S	11.09 MW	10.03 AW	23070 AAW	CABLS	10//99-12//99
Institution and Cafeteria	Chico-Paradise MSA, CA	S	8.91 MW	8.06 AW	18530 AAW	CABLS	10//99-12//99
Institution and Cafeteria	Fresno MSA, CA	S	9.34 MW	8.83 AW	19440 AAW	CABLS	10//99-12//99
Institution and Cafeteria	Los Angeles-Long Beach PMSA, CA	S	9.75 MW	9.31 AW	20270 AAW	CABLS	10//99-12//99
Institution and Cafeteria	Merced MSA, CA	S	8.33 MW	7.48 AW	17330 AAW	CABLS	10//99-12//99
Institution and Cafeteria	Modesto MSA, CA	S	9.27 MW	8.50 AW	19280 AAW	CABLS	10//99-12//99
Institution and Cafeteria	Oakland PMSA, CA	S	10.20 MW	10.16 AW	21210 AAW	CABLS	10//99-12//99
Institution and Cafeteria	Orange County PMSA, CA	S	10.99 MW	10.32 AW	22860 AAW	CABLS	10//99-12//99
Institution and Cafeteria	Redding MSA, CA	S	9.02 MW	8.71 AW	18760 AAW	CABLS	10//99-12//99
Institution and Cafeteria	Riverside-San Bernardino PMSA, CA	S	10.06 MW	9.36 AW	20920 AAW	CABLS	10//99-12//99
Institution and Cafeteria	Sacramento PMSA, CA	S	9.76 MW	9.69 AW	20310 AAW	CABLS	10//99-12//99
Institution and Cafeteria	Salinas MSA, CA	S	12.02 MW	11.25 AW	25010 AAW	CABLS	10//99-12//99
Institution and Cafeteria	San Diego MSA, CA	S	10.04 MW	9.78 AW	20890 AAW	CABLS	10//99-12//99
Institution and Cafeteria	San Francisco PMSA, CA	S	10.30 MW	9.59 AW	21410 AAW	CABLS	10//99-12//99
Institution and Cafeteria	San Jose PMSA, CA	S	11.14 MW	10.50 AW	23170 AAW	CABLS	10//99-12//99
Institution and Cafeteria	San Luis Obispo-Atascadero-Paso Robles MSA, CA	S	11.98 MW	10.86 AW	24910 AAW	CABLS	10//99-12//99
Institution and Cafeteria	Santa Barbara-Santa Maria-Lompoc MSA, CA	S	9.75 MW	9.70 AW	20280 AAW	CABLS	10//99-12//99
Institution and Cafeteria	Santa Cruz-Watsonville PMSA, CA	S	10.49 MW	10.02 AW	21820 AAW	CABLS	10//99-12//99

AAW	Average annual wage	AOH	Average offered, high	ASH	Average starting, high
AE	Average entry wage	AOL	Average offered, low	ASL	Average starting, low
AEX	Average experienced wage	APH	Average pay, high range	AW	Average wage paid
AO	Average offered	APL	Average pay, low range	FQ	First quartile wage

H	Hourly	M	Monthly
HI	Highest wage paid	MTC	Median total compensation
HR	High end range	MW	Median wage paid
LR	Low end range	SQ	Second quartile wage

S	Special: hourly and annual
TQ	Third quartile wage
W	Weekly
Y	Yearly

Occupation/Type/Industry	Location	Per	Low	Mid	High	Source	Date
Cook							
Institution and Cafeteria	Santa Rosa PMSA, CA	S	10.15 MW	9.66 AW	21110 AAW	CABLS	10//99-12//99
Institution and Cafeteria	Stockton-Lodi MSA, CA	S	11.65 MW	11.26 AW	24230 AAW	CABLS	10//99-12//99
Institution and Cafeteria	Vallejo-Fairfield-Napa PMSA, CA	S	12.52 MW	11.43 AW	26050 AAW	CABLS	10//99-12//99
Institution and Cafeteria	Ventura PMSA, CA	S	9.95 MW	9.81 AW	20700 AAW	CABLS	10//99-12//99
Institution and Cafeteria	Visalia-Tulare-Porterville MSA, CA	S	9.96 MW	9.41 AW	20710 AAW	CABLS	10//99-12//99
Institution and Cafeteria	Yolo PMSA, CA	S	10.28 MW	9.84 AW	21380 AAW	CABLS	10//99-12//99
Institution and Cafeteria	Yuba City MSA, CA	S	10.64 MW	10.67 AW	22140 AAW	CABLS	10//99-12//99
Institution and Cafeteria	Colorado	S	8.14 MW	8.43 AW	17520 AAW	COBLS	10//99-12//99
Institution and Cafeteria	Boulder-Longmont PMSA, CO	S	8.77 MW	8.48 AW	18250 AAW	COBLS	10//99-12//99
Institution and Cafeteria	Colorado Springs MSA, CO	S	8.67 MW	8.27 AW	18040 AAW	COBLS	10//99-12//99
Institution and Cafeteria	Denver PMSA, CO	S	8.83 MW	8.51 AW	18370 AAW	COBLS	10//99-12//99
Institution and Cafeteria	Fort Collins-Loveland MSA, CO	S	8.09 MW	7.85 AW	16820 AAW	COBLS	10//99-12//99
Institution and Cafeteria	Grand Junction MSA, CO	S	8.90 MW	8.28 AW	18500 AAW	COBLS	10//99-12//99
Institution and Cafeteria	Greeley PMSA, CO	S	7.27 MW	6.99 AW	15120 AAW	COBLS	10//99-12//99
Institution and Cafeteria	Pueblo MSA, CO	S	8.74 MW	8.60 AW	18180 AAW	COBLS	10//99-12//99
Institution and Cafeteria	Connecticut	S	11.26 MW	11.57 AW	24070 AAW	CTBLS	10//99-12//99
Institution and Cafeteria	Bridgeport PMSA, CT	S	13.06 MW	12.96 AW	27160 AAW	CTBLS	10//99-12//99
Institution and Cafeteria	Danbury PMSA, CT	S	12.14 MW	11.29 AW	25250 AAW	CTBLS	10//99-12//99
Institution and Cafeteria	Hartford MSA, CT	S	11.53 MW	11.08 AW	23980 AAW	CTBLS	10//99-12//99
Institution and Cafeteria	New Haven-Meriden PMSA, CT	S	12.33 MW	11.93 AW	25650 AAW	CTBLS	10//99-12//99
Institution and Cafeteria	New London-Norwich MSA, CT-RI	S	9.36 MW	8.90 AW	19470 AAW	CTBLS	10//99-12//99
Institution and Cafeteria	Stamford-Norwalk PMSA, CT	S	12.01 MW	11.56 AW	24990 AAW	CTBLS	10//99-12//99
Institution and Cafeteria	Waterbury PMSA, CT	S	11.47 MW	11.09 AW	23860 AAW	CTBLS	10//99-12//99
Institution and Cafeteria	Delaware	S	9.18 MW	9.41 AW	19570 AAW	DEBLS	10//99-12//99
Institution and Cafeteria	Dover MSA, DE	S	8.08 MW	6.70 AW	16810 AAW	DEBLS	10//99-12//99
Institution and Cafeteria	Wilmington-Newark PMSA, DE-MD	S	9.90 MW	9.56 AW	20580 AAW	DEBLS	10//99-12//99
Institution and Cafeteria	District of Columbia	S	9.18 MW	9.90 AW	20590 AAW	DCBLS	10//99-12//99
Institution and Cafeteria	Washington PMSA, DC-MD-VA-WV	S	10.38 MW	9.85 AW	21590 AAW	DCBLS	10//99-12//99
Institution and Cafeteria	Florida	S	7.91 MW	8.17 AW	16990 AAW	FLBLS	10//99-12//99
Institution and Cafeteria	Fort Lauderdale PMSA, FL	S	9.23 MW	9.31 AW	19190 AAW	FLBLS	10//99-12//99
Institution and Cafeteria	Fort Myers-Cape Coral MSA, FL	S	9.34 MW	8.94 AW	19430 AAW	FLBLS	10//99-12//99
Institution and Cafeteria	Fort Pierce-Port St. Lucie MSA, FL	S	8.29 MW	7.98 AW	17230 AAW	FLBLS	10//99-12//99
Institution and Cafeteria	Fort Walton Beach MSA, FL	S	8.16 MW	7.37 AW	16970 AAW	FLBLS	10//99-12//99
Institution and Cafeteria	Gainesville MSA, FL	S	7.75 MW	7.64 AW	16120 AAW	FLBLS	10//99-12//99
Institution and Cafeteria	Jacksonville MSA, FL	S	8.11 MW	7.94 AW	16870 AAW	FLBLS	10//99-12//99
Institution and Cafeteria	Melbourne-Titusville-Palm Bay MSA, FL	S	8.13 MW	8.06 AW	16900 AAW	FLBLS	10//99-12//99
Institution and Cafeteria	Miami PMSA, FL	S	9.06 MW	8.85 AW	18840 AAW	FLBLS	10//99-12//99
Institution and Cafeteria	Naples MSA, FL	S	9.28 MW	8.85 AW	19310 AAW	FLBLS	10//99-12//99
Institution and Cafeteria	Ocala MSA, FL	S	7.94 MW	7.76 AW	16510 AAW	FLBLS	10//99-12//99
Institution and Cafeteria	Orlando MSA, FL	S	8.41 MW	8.31 AW	17500 AAW	FLBLS	10//99-12//99
Institution and Cafeteria	Pensacola MSA, FL	S	7.83 MW	7.67 AW	16280 AAW	FLBLS	10//99-12//99
Institution and Cafeteria	Punta Gorda MSA, FL	S	6.54 MW	5.97 AW	13600 AAW	FLBLS	10//99-12//99
Institution and Cafeteria	Sarasota-Bradenton MSA, FL	S	7.61 MW	7.16 AW	15820 AAW	FLBLS	10//99-12//99
Institution and Cafeteria	Tallahassee MSA, FL	S	8.72 MW	8.41 AW	18130 AAW	FLBLS	10//99-12//99
Institution and Cafeteria	Tampa-St. Petersburg-Clearwater MSA, FL	S	8.48 MW	7.90 AW	17640 AAW	FLBLS	10//99-12//99
Institution and Cafeteria	West Palm Beach-Boca Raton MSA, FL	S	8.98 MW	9.06 AW	18670 AAW	FLBLS	10//99-12//99
Institution and Cafeteria	Georgia	S	7 MW	7.24 AW	15060 AAW	GABLS	10//99-12//99
Institution and Cafeteria	Albany MSA, GA	S	7.46 MW	7.49 AW	15510 AAW	GABLS	10//99-12//99
Institution and Cafeteria	Athens MSA, GA	S	7.66 MW	7.57 AW	15940 AAW	GABLS	10//99-12//99
Institution and Cafeteria	Atlanta MSA, GA	S	7.73 MW	7.61 AW	16070 AAW	GABLS	10//99-12//99
Institution and Cafeteria	Augusta-Aiken MSA, GA-SC	S	7.69 MW	7.07 AW	15990 AAW	GABLS	10//99-12//99
Institution and Cafeteria	Columbus MSA, GA-AL	S	6.85 MW	6.53 AW	14250 AAW	GABLS	10//99-12//99
Institution and Cafeteria	Macon MSA, GA	S	6.68 MW	6.20 AW	13890 AAW	GABLS	10//99-12//99
Institution and Cafeteria	Savannah MSA, GA	S	6.28 MW	6.23 AW	13070 AAW	GABLS	10//99-12//99
Institution and Cafeteria	Hawaii	S	11.58 MW	12.34 AW	25670 AAW	HIBLS	10//99-12//99
Institution and Cafeteria	Honolulu MSA, HI	S	12.07 MW	11.39 AW	25100 AAW	HIBLS	10//99-12//99
Institution and Cafeteria	Idaho	S	7.52 MW	7.70 AW	16010 AAW	IDBLS	10//99-12//99
Institution and Cafeteria	Boise City MSA, ID	S	7.92 MW	7.73 AW	16470 AAW	IDBLS	10//99-12//99
Institution and Cafeteria	Pocatello MSA, ID	S	7.45 MW	7.21 AW	15490 AAW	IDBLS	10//99-12//99

AAW	Average annual wage	AOH	Average offered, high	ASH	Average starting, high	H	Hourly	M	Monthly	S	Special: hourly and annual
AE	Average entry wage	AOL	Average offered, low	ASL	Average starting, low	HI	Highest wage paid	MTC	Median total compensation	TQ	Third quartile wage
AEX	Average experienced wage	APH	Average pay, high range	AW	Average wage paid	HR	High end range	MW	Median wage paid	W	Weekly
AO	Average offered	APL	Average pay, low range	FQ	First quartile wage	LR	Low end range	SQ	Second quartile wage	Y	Yearly

Cook

Occupation/Type/Industry	Location	Per	Low	Mid	High	Source	Date
Institution and Cafeteria	Illinois	S	8.21 MW	8.56 AW	17810 AAW	ILBLS	10//99-12//99
Institution and Cafeteria	Bloomington-Normal MSA, IL	S	10.71 MW	8.97 AW	22270 AAW	ILBLS	10//99-12//99
Institution and Cafeteria	Chicago PMSA, IL	S	9.24 MW	8.80 AW	19220 AAW	ILBLS	10//99-12//99
Institution and Cafeteria	Decatur MSA, IL	S	7.24 MW	6.98 AW	15060 AAW	ILBLS	10//99-12//99
Institution and Cafeteria	Kankakee PMSA, IL	S	9.31 MW	9.25 AW	19360 AAW	ILBLS	10//99-12//99
Institution and Cafeteria	Peoria-Pekin MSA, IL	S	7.88 MW	7.86 AW	16400 AAW	ILBLS	10//99-12//99
Institution and Cafeteria	Rockford MSA, IL	S	8.10 MW	8.02 AW	16840 AAW	ILBLS	10//99-12//99
Institution and Cafeteria	Springfield MSA, IL	S	7.78 MW	7.39 AW	16180 AAW	ILBLS	10//99-12//99
Institution and Cafeteria	Indiana	S	8.09 MW	8.18 AW	17020 AAW	INBLS	10//99-12//99
Institution and Cafeteria	Bloomington MSA, IN	S	8.99 MW	8.76 AW	18710 AAW	INBLS	10//99-12//99
Institution and Cafeteria	Elkhart-Goshen MSA, IN	S	7.94 MW.	7.30 AW	16520 AAW	INBLS	10//99-12//99
Institution and Cafeteria	Evansville-Henderson MSA, IN-KY	S	8.48 MW	8.70 AW	17630 AAW	INBLS	10//99-12//99
Institution and Cafeteria	Fort Wayne MSA, IN	S	8.60 MW	8.73 AW	17880 AAW	INBLS	10//99-12//99
Institution and Cafeteria	Gary PMSA, IN	S	8.38 MW	8.33 AW	17420 AAW	INBLS	10//99-12//99
Institution and Cafeteria	Indianapolis MSA, IN	S	8.46 MW	8.34 AW	17590 AAW	INBLS	10//99-12//99
Institution and Cafeteria	Kokomo MSA, IN	S	7.66 MW	7.48 AW	15930 AAW	INBLS	10//99-12//99
Institution and Cafeteria	Lafayette MSA, IN	S	8.46 MW	8.77 AW	17600 AAW	INBLS	10//99-12//99
Institution and Cafeteria	Muncie MSA, IN	S	7.82 MW	7.80 AW	16270 AAW	INBLS	10//99-12//99
Institution and Cafeteria	South Bend MSA, IN	S	8.60 MW	8.52 AW	17890 AAW	INBLS	10//99-12//99
Institution and Cafeteria	Terre Haute MSA, IN	S	8.61 MW	8.14 AW	17910 AAW	INBLS	10//99-12//99
Institution and Cafeteria	Iowa	S	7.52 MW	7.69 AW	16000 AAW	IABLS	10//99-12//99
Institution and Cafeteria	Cedar Rapids MSA, IA	S	7.49 MW	7.39 AW	15580 AAW	IABLS	10//99-12//99
Institution and Cafeteria	Davenport-Moline-Rock Island MSA, IA-IL	S	7.31 MW	6.92 AW	15210 AAW	IABLS	10//99-12//99
Institution and Cafeteria	Des Moines MSA, IA	S	8.75 MW	8.86 AW	18200 AAW	IABLS	10//99-12//99
Institution and Cafeteria	Dubuque MSA, IA	S	7.72 MW	7.74 AW	16060 AAW	IABLS	10//99-12//99
Institution and Cafeteria	Iowa City MSA, IA	S	8.69 MW	8.46 AW	18080 AAW	IABLS	10//99-12//99
Institution and Cafeteria	Sioux City MSA, IA-NE	S	7.57 MW	7.58 AW	15740 AAW	IABLS	10//99-12//99
Institution and Cafeteria	Waterloo-Cedar Falls MSA, IA	S	7.84 MW	7.72 AW	16310 AAW	IABLS	10//99-12//99
Institution and Cafeteria	Kansas	S	7.57 MW	7.74 AW	16100 AAW	KSBLS	10//99-12//99
Institution and Cafeteria	Lawrence MSA, KS	S	8.33 MW	8.14 AW	17320 AAW	KSBLS	10//99-12//99
Institution and Cafeteria	Topeka MSA, KS	S	8.47 MW	8.09 AW	17620 AAW	KSBLS	10//99-12//99
Institution and Cafeteria	Wichita MSA, KS	S	8.24 MW	8.12 AW	17130 AAW	KSBLS	10//99-12//99
Institution and Cafeteria	Kentucky	S	7.46 MW	7.54 AW	15680 AAW	KYBLS	10//99-12//99
Institution and Cafeteria	Lexington MSA, KY	S	7.77 MW	7.65 AW	16150 AAW	KYBLS	10//99-12//99
Institution and Cafeteria	Louisville MSA, KY-IN	S	8.37 MW	8.35 AW	17400 AAW	KYBLS	10//99-12//99
Institution and Cafeteria	Owensboro MSA, KY	S	7.38 MW	7.49 AW	15350 AAW	KYBLS	10//99-12//99
Institution and Cafeteria	Louisiana	S	6.28 MW	6.66 AW	13860 AAW	LABLS	10//99-12//99
Institution and Cafeteria	Alexandria MSA, LA	S	6.33 MW	6.09 AW	13170 AAW	LABLS	10//99-12//99
Institution and Cafeteria	Baton Rouge MSA, LA	S	6.76 MW	6.42 AW	14070 AAW	LABLS	10//99-12//99
Institution and Cafeteria	Houma MSA, LA	S	7.82 MW	6.70 AW	16270 AAW	LABLS	10//99-12//99
Institution and Cafeteria	Lafayette MSA, LA	S	6.73 MW	6.28 AW	14000 AAW	LABLS	10//99-12//99
Institution and Cafeteria	Lake Charles MSA, LA	S	6.33 MW	6.21 AW	13160 AAW	LABLS	10//99-12//99
Institution and Cafeteria	Monroe MSA, LA	S	6.29 MW	6.06 AW	13080 AAW	LABLS	10//99-12//99
Institution and Cafeteria	New Orleans MSA, LA	S	7.20 MW	6.82 AW	14980 AAW	LABLS	10//99-12//99
Institution and Cafeteria	Shreveport-Bossier City MSA, LA	S	6.61 MW	6.31 AW	13750 AAW	LABLS	10//99-12//99
Institution and Cafeteria	Maine	S	9.12 MW	8.97 AW	18670 AAW	MEBLS	10//99-12//99
Institution and Cafeteria	Bangor MSA, ME	S	9.47 MW	9.38 AW	19700 AAW	MEBLS	10//99-12//99
Institution and Cafeteria	Lewiston-Auburn MSA, ME	S	9.01 MW	9.25 AW	18740 AAW	MEBLS	10//99-12//99
Institution and Cafeteria	Portland MSA, ME	S	9.06 MW	9.07 AW	18850 AAW	MEBLS	10//99-12//99
Institution and Cafeteria	Maryland	S	9.88 MW	10.37 AW	21570 AAW	MDBLS	10//99-12//99
Institution and Cafeteria	Baltimore PMSA, MD	S	9.61 MW.	9.36 AW	19990 AAW	MDBLS	10//99-12//99
Institution and Cafeteria	Cumberland MSA, MD-WV	S	8.28 MW	8.01 AW	17210 AAW	MDBLS	10//99-12//99
Institution and Cafeteria	Hagerstown PMSA, MD	S	9.30 MW	9.52 AW	19350 AAW	MDBLS	10//99-12//99
Institution and Cafeteria	Massachusetts	S	10.46 MW	10.65 AW	22140 AAW	MABLS	10//99-12//99
Institution and Cafeteria	Barnstable-Yarmouth MSA, MA	S	10.04 MW	9.87 AW	20880 AAW	MABLS	10//99-12//99
Institution and Cafeteria	Boston PMSA, MA-NH	S	10.94 MW	10.72 AW	22750 AAW	MABLS	10//99-12//99
Institution and Cafeteria	Brockton PMSA, MA	S	11.17 MW	11.76 AW	23230 AAW	MABLS	10//99-12//99
Institution and Cafeteria	Fitchburg-Leominster PMSA, MA	S	9.76 MW	8.97 AW	20290 AAW	MABLS	10//99-12//99
Institution and Cafeteria	Lawrence PMSA, MA-NH	S	10.28 MW	10.04 AW	21380 AAW	MABLS	10//99-12//99
Institution and Cafeteria	Lowell PMSA, MA-NH	S	10.01 MW	9.91 AW	20810 AAW	MABLS	10//99-12//99
Institution and Cafeteria	New Bedford PMSA, MA	S	9.36 MW	9.23 AW	19470 AAW	MABLS	10//99-12//99
Institution and Cafeteria	Pittsfield MSA, MA	S	9.70 MW	9.71 AW	20190 AAW	MABLS	10//99-12//99
Institution and Cafeteria	Springfield MSA, MA	S	10.05 MW	9.93 AW	20900 AAW	MABLS	10//99-12//99
Institution and Cafeteria	Worcester PMSA, MA-CT	S	10.58 MW	10.30 AW	22010 AAW	MABLS	10//99-12//99
Institution and Cafeteria	Michigan	S	9.31 MW	9.32 AW	19390 AAW	MIBLS	10//99-12//99
Institution and Cafeteria	Ann Arbor PMSA, MI	S	8.88 MW	8.50 AW	18470 AAW	MIBLS	10//99-12//99

AAW	Average annual wage	AOH	Average offered, high	ASH	Average starting, high
AE	Average entry wage	AOL	Average offered, low	ASL	Average starting, low
AEX	Average experienced wage	APH	Average pay, high range	AW	Average wage paid
AO	Average offered	APL	Average pay, low range	FQ	First quartile wage

H	Hourly	M	Monthly
HI	Highest wage paid	MTC	Median total compensation
HR	High end range	MW	Median wage paid
LR	Low end range	SQ	Second quartile wage

S	Special: hourly and annual
TQ	Third quartile wage
W	Weekly
Y	Yearly

Occupation/Type/Industry	Location	Per	Low	Mid	High	Source	Date
Cook							
Institution and Cafeteria	Benton Harbor MSA, MI	S	8.63 MW	8.98 AW	17960 AAW	MIBLS	10//99-12//99
Institution and Cafeteria	Detroit PMSA, MI	S	9.76 MW	9.83 AW	20300 AAW	MIBLS	10//99-12//99
Institution and Cafeteria	Flint PMSA, MI	S	9.27 MW	9.21 AW	19290 AAW	MIBLS	10//99-12//99
Institution and Cafeteria	Grand Rapids-Muskegon-Holland MSA, MI	S	9.19 MW	8.93 AW	19120 AAW	MIBLS	10//99-12//99
Institution and Cafeteria	Jackson MSA, MI	S	9.02 MW	9.13 AW	18760 AAW	MIBLS	10//99-12//99
Institution and Cafeteria	Kalamazoo-Battle Creek MSA, MI	S	9.21 MW	9.20 AW	19160 AAW	MIBLS	10//99-12//99
Institution and Cafeteria	Lansing-East Lansing MSA, MI	S	10.46 MW	9.75 AW	21750 AAW	MIBLS	10//99-12//99
Institution and Cafeteria	Saginaw-Bay City-Midland MSA, MI	S	8.67 MW	8.62 AW	18030 AAW	MIBLS	10//99-12//99
Institution and Cafeteria	Minnesota	S	9.53 MW	9.71 AW	20200 AAW	MNBLS	10//99-12//99
Institution and Cafeteria	Duluth-Superior MSA, MN-WI	S	9.16 MW	8.72 AW	19060 AAW	MNBLS	10//99-12//99
Institution and Cafeteria	Minneapolis-St. Paul MSA, MN-WI	S	10.52 MW	10.17 AW	21890 AAW	MNBLS	10//99-12//99
Institution and Cafeteria	Rochester MSA, MN	S	9.24 MW	9.48 AW	19210 AAW	MNBLS	10//99-12//99
Institution and Cafeteria	St. Cloud MSA, MN	S	9.36 MW	9.30 AW	19480 AAW	MNBLS	10//99-12//99
Institution and Cafeteria	Mississippi	S	6.27 MW	6.59 AW	13700 AAW	MSBLS	10//99-12//99
Institution and Cafeteria	Biloxi-Gulfport-Pascagoula MSA, MS	S	7.11 MW	6.64 AW	14790 AAW	MSBLS	10//99-12//99
Institution and Cafeteria	Hattiesburg MSA, MS	S	6.90 MW	6.41 AW	14350 AAW	MSBLS	10//99-12//99
Institution and Cafeteria	Jackson MSA, MS	S	6.95 MW	6.78 AW	14460 AAW	MSBLS	10//99-12//99
Institution and Cafeteria	Missouri	S	6.97 MW	7.40 AW	15400 AAW	MOBLS	10//99-12//99
Institution and Cafeteria	Columbia MSA, MO	S	7.31 MW	6.88 AW	15210 AAW	MOBLS	10//99-12//99
Institution and Cafeteria	Joplin MSA, MO	S	6.97 MW	6.78 AW	14500 AAW	MOBLS	10//99-12//99
Institution and Cafeteria	Kansas City MSA, MO-KS	S	7.77 MW	7.55 AW	16170 AAW	MOBLS	10//99-12//99
Institution and Cafeteria	St. Joseph MSA, MO	S	6.53 MW	6.25 AW	13590 AAW	MOBLS	10//99-12//99
Institution and Cafeteria	St. Louis MSA, MO-IL	S	8.08 MW	7.71 AW	16800 AAW	MOBLS	10//99-12//99
Institution and Cafeteria	Springfield MSA, MO	S	7.07 MW	6.78 AW	14700 AAW	MOBLS	10//99-12//99
Institution and Cafeteria	Montana	S	7.83 MW	8.06 AW	16770 AAW	MTBLS	10//99-12//99
Institution and Cafeteria	Billings MSA, MT	S	7.82 MW	7.73 AW	16270 AAW	MTBLS	10//99-12//99
Institution and Cafeteria	Great Falls MSA, MT	S	8.35 MW	8.22 AW	17370 AAW	MTBLS	10//99-12//99
Institution and Cafeteria	Missoula MSA, MT	S	8.00 MW	7.90 AW	16630 AAW	MTBLS	10//99-12//99
Institution and Cafeteria	Nebraska	S	7.34 MW	7.43 AW	15460 AAW	NEBLS	10//99-12//99
Institution and Cafeteria	Lincoln MSA, NE	S	8.18 MW	7.98 AW	17010 AAW	NEBLS	10//99-12//99
Institution and Cafeteria	Omaha MSA, NE-IA	S	7.98 MW	7.78 AW	16600 AAW	NEBLS	10//99-12//99
Institution and Cafeteria	Nevada	S	8.92 MW	9.28 AW	19290 AAW	NVBLS	10//99-12//99
Institution and Cafeteria	Las Vegas MSA, NV-AZ	S	9.37 MW	8.93 AW	19490 AAW	NVBLS	10//99-12//99
Institution and Cafeteria	Reno MSA, NV	S	9.82 MW	9.29 AW	20430 AAW	NVBLS	10//99-12//99
Institution and Cafeteria	New Hampshire	S	9.94 MW	10.03 AW	20850 AAW	NHBLS	10//99-12//99
Institution and Cafeteria	Manchester PMSA, NH	S	10.36 MW	10.15 AW	21550 AAW	NHBLS	10//99-12//99
Institution and Cafeteria	Nashua PMSA, NH	S	9.66 MW	9.61 AW	20080 AAW	NHBLS	10//99-12//99
Institution and Cafeteria	Portsmouth-Rochester PMSA, NH-ME	S	9.54 MW	9.55 AW	19840 AAW	NHBLS	10//99-12//99
Institution and Cafeteria	New Jersey	S	10.72 MW	11.10 AW	23090 AAW	NJBLS	10//99-12//99
Institution and Cafeteria	Atlantic-Cape May PMSA, NJ	S	12.91 MW	14.40 AW	26850 AAW	NJBLS	10//99-12//99
Institution and Cafeteria	Bergen-Passaic PMSA, NJ	S	11.54 MW	10.83 AW	24010 AAW	NJBLS	10//99-12//99
Institution and Cafeteria	Jersey City PMSA, NJ	S	10.96 MW	10.34 AW	22790 AAW	NJBLS	10//99-12//99
Institution and Cafeteria	Middlesex-Somerset-Hunterdon PMSA, NJ	S	11.51 MW	11.33 AW	23940 AAW	NJBLS	10//99-12//99
Institution and Cafeteria	Monmouth-Ocean PMSA, NJ	S	10.01 MW	9.77 AW	20810 AAW	NJBLS	10//99-12//99
Institution and Cafeteria	Newark PMSA, NJ	S	11.23 MW	11.04 AW	23360 AAW	NJBLS	10//99-12//99
Institution and Cafeteria	Trenton PMSA, NJ	S	11.24 MW	11.29 AW	23380 AAW	NJBLS	10//99-12//99
Institution and Cafeteria	Vineland-Millville-Bridgeton PMSA, NJ	S	11.73 MW	11.66 AW	24400 AAW	NJBLS	10//99-12//99
Institution and Cafeteria	New Mexico	S	7.29 MW	7.66 AW	15940 AAW	NMBLS	10//99-12//99
Institution and Cafeteria	Albuquerque MSA, NM	S	8.37 MW	8.44 AW	17410 AAW	NMBLS	10//99-12//99
Institution and Cafeteria	Las Cruces MSA, NM	S	6.62 MW	6.49 AW	13760 AAW	NMBLS	10//99-12//99
Institution and Cafeteria	Santa Fe MSA, NM	S	7.15 MW	6.95 AW	14880 AAW	NMBLS	10//99-12//99
Institution and Cafeteria	New York	S	9.87 MW	10.66 AW	22160 AAW	NYBLS	10//99-12//99
Institution and Cafeteria	Albany-Schenectady-Troy MSA, NY	S	8.87 MW	8.19 AW	18450 AAW	NYBLS	10//99-12//99
Institution and Cafeteria	Binghamton MSA, NY	S	9.34 MW	8.33 AW	19430 AAW	NYBLS	10//99-12//99
Institution and Cafeteria	Buffalo-Niagara Falls MSA, NY	S	8.75 MW	8.65 AW	18200 AAW	NYBLS	10//99-12//99
Institution and Cafeteria	Dutchess County PMSA, NY	S	10.58 MW	10.13 AW	22000 AAW	NYBLS	10//99-12//99
Institution and Cafeteria	Elmira MSA, NY	S	9.55 MW	8.97 AW	19860 AAW	NYBLS	10//99-12//99
Institution and Cafeteria	Glens Falls MSA, NY	S	8.25 MW	7.85 AW	17150 AAW	NYBLS	10//99-12//99
Institution and Cafeteria	Jamestown MSA, NY	S	8.97 MW	8.62 AW	18660 AAW	NYBLS	10//99-12//99
Institution and Cafeteria	Nassau-Suffolk PMSA, NY	S	11.65 MW	10.23 AW	24240 AAW	NYBLS	10//99-12//99
Institution and Cafeteria	New York PMSA, NY	S	11.77 MW	10.71 AW	24490 AAW	NYBLS	10//99-12//99

AAW	Average annual wage	AOH	Average offered, high	ASH	Average starting, high
AE	Average entry wage	AOL	Average offered, low	ASL	Average starting, low
AEX	Average experienced wage	APH	Average pay, high range	AW	Average wage paid
AO	Average offered	APL	Average pay, low range	FQ	First quartile wage

H	Hourly	M	Monthly	S	Special: hourly and annual
HI	Highest wage paid	MTC	Median total compensation	TQ	Third quartile wage
HR	High end range	MW	Median wage paid	W	Weekly
LR	Low end range	SQ	Second quartile wage	Y	Yearly

Cook

Occupation/Type/Industry	Location	Per	Low	Mid	High	Source	Date
Institution and Cafeteria	Newburgh PMSA, NY-PA	s	9.98 MW	10.44 AW	20770 AAW	NYBLS	10//99-12//99
Institution and Cafeteria	Rochester MSA, NY	s	9.38 MW	8.49 AW	19520 AAW	NYBLS	10//99-12//99
Institution and Cafeteria	Syracuse MSA, NY	s	9.07 MW	8.92 AW	18870 AAW	NYBLS	10//99-12//99
Institution and Cafeteria	Utica-Rome MSA, NY	s	9.09 MW	8.68 AW	18910 AAW	NYBLS	10//99-12//99
Institution and Cafeteria	North Carolina	s	7.52 MW	7.66 AW	15930 AAW	NCBLS	10//99-12//99
Institution and Cafeteria	Asheville MSA, NC	s	7.88 MW	7.79 AW	16390 AAW	NCBLS	10//99-12//99
Institution and Cafeteria	Charlotte-Gastonia-Rock Hill MSA, NC-SC	s	8.21 MW	7.96 AW	17080 AAW	NCBLS	10//99-12//99
Institution and Cafeteria	Fayetteville MSA, NC	s	8.55 MW	8.33 AW	17780 AAW	NCBLS	10//99-12//99
Institution and Cafeteria	Goldsboro MSA, NC	s	7.87 MW	7.73 AW	16360 AAW	NCBLS	10//99-12//99
Institution and Cafeteria	Greensboro--Winston-Salem--High Point MSA, NC	s	8.08 MW	7.95 AW	16810 AAW	NCBLS	10//99-12//99
Institution and Cafeteria	Greenville MSA, NC	s	7.16 MW	7.02 AW	14890 AAW	NCBLS	10//99-12//99
Institution and Cafeteria	Hickory-Morganton-Lenoir MSA, NC	s	7.19 MW	6.98 AW	14950 AAW	NCBLS	10//99-12//99
Institution and Cafeteria	Raleigh-Durham-Chapel Hill MSA, NC	s	8.31 MW	8.15 AW	17290 AAW	NCBLS	10//99-12//99
Institution and Cafeteria	Rocky Mount MSA, NC	s	6.59 MW	6.20 AW	13700 AAW	NCBLS	10//99-12//99
Institution and Cafeteria	Wilmington MSA, NC	s	7.18 MW	6.85 AW	14930 AAW	NCBLS	10//99-12//99
Institution and Cafeteria	North Dakota	s	7.84 MW	7.99 AW	16620 AAW	NDBLS	10//99-12//99
Institution and Cafeteria	Bismarck MSA, ND	s	8.60 MW	8.56 AW	17880 AAW	NDBLS	10//99-12//99
Institution and Cafeteria	Fargo-Moorhead MSA, ND-MN	s	8.45 MW	8.29 AW	17570 AAW	NDBLS	10//99-12//99
Institution and Cafeteria	Grand Forks MSA, ND-MN	s	8.76 MW	8.78 AW	18220 AAW	NDBLS	10//99-12//99
Institution and Cafeteria	Ohio	s	7.99 MW	8.19 AW	17040 AAW	OHBLS	10//99-12//99
Institution and Cafeteria	Akron PMSA, OH	s	8.48 MW	8.49 AW	17630 AAW	OHBLS	10//99-12//99
Institution and Cafeteria	Canton-Massillon MSA, OH	s	8.37 MW	8.37 AW	17410 AAW	OHBLS	10//99-12//99
Institution and Cafeteria	Cincinnati PMSA, OH-KY-IN	s	8.04 MW	7.88 AW	16720 AAW	OHBLS	10//99-12//99
Institution and Cafeteria	Cleveland-Lorain-Elyria PMSA, OH	s	8.93 MW	8.87 AW	18580 AAW	OHBLS	10//99-12//99
Institution and Cafeteria	Columbus MSA, OH	s	8.58 MW	8.17 AW	17850 AAW	OHBLS	10//99-12//99
Institution and Cafeteria	Dayton-Springfield MSA, OH	s	8.25 MW	8.03 AW	17160 AAW	OHBLS	10//99-12//99
Institution and Cafeteria	Hamilton-Middletown PMSA, OH	s	8.25 MW	7.90 AW	17160 AAW	OHBLS	10//99-12//99
Institution and Cafeteria	Lima MSA, OH	s	7.89 MW	7.48 AW	16420 AAW	OHBLS	10//99-12//99
Institution and Cafeteria	Mansfield MSA, OH	s	6.97 MW	6.41 AW	14500 AAW	OHBLS	10//99-12//99
Institution and Cafeteria	Steubenville-Weirton MSA, OH-WV	s	6.86 MW	6.46 AW	14260 AAW	OHBLS	10//99-12//99
Institution and Cafeteria	Toledo MSA, OH	s	9.22 MW	9.32 AW	19190 AAW	OHBLS	10//99-12//99
Institution and Cafeteria	Youngstown-Warren MSA, OH	s	7.19 MW	6.77 AW	14950 AAW	OHBLS	10//99-12//99
Institution and Cafeteria	Oklahoma	s	6.53 MW	6.89 AW	14330 AAW	OKBLS	10//99-12//99
Institution and Cafeteria	Enid MSA, OK	s	7.29 MW	6.93 AW	15170 AAW	OKBLS	10//99-12//99
Institution and Cafeteria	Lawton MSA, OK	s	8.49 MW	8.54 AW	17650 AAW	OKBLS	10//99-12//99
Institution and Cafeteria	Oklahoma City MSA, OK	s	7.16 MW	6.70 AW	14890 AAW	OKBLS	10//99-12//99
Institution and Cafeteria	Tulsa MSA, OK	s	7.23 MW	7.21 AW	15030 AAW	OKBLS	10//99-12//99
Institution and Cafeteria	Oregon	s	9.03 MW	9.31 AW	19370 AAW	ORBLS	10//99-12//99
Institution and Cafeteria	Corvallis MSA, OR	s	10.40 MW	10.74 AW	21630 AAW	ORBLS	10//99-12//99
Institution and Cafeteria	Eugene-Springfield MSA, OR	s	9.23 MW	9.13 AW	19190 AAW	ORBLS	10//99-12//99
Institution and Cafeteria	Medford-Ashland MSA, OR	s	8.88 MW	8.30 AW	18460 AAW	ORBLS	10//99-12//99
Institution and Cafeteria	Portland-Vancouver PMSA, OR-WA	s	9.39 MW	9.14 AW	19530 AAW	ORBLS	10//99-12//99
Institution and Cafeteria	Salem PMSA, OR	s	9.48 MW	9.02 AW	19720 AAW	ORBLS	10//99-12//99
Institution and Cafeteria	Pennsylvania	s	8.83 MW	9.17 AW	19060 AAW	PABLS	10//99-12//99
Institution and Cafeteria	Allentown-Bethlehem-Easton MSA, PA	s	9.64 MW	9.63 AW	20060 AAW	PABLS	10//99-12//99
Institution and Cafeteria	Altoona MSA, PA	s	8.58 MW	8.09 AW	17840 AAW	PABLS	10//99-12//99
Institution and Cafeteria	Erie MSA, PA	s	8.59 MW	8.24 AW	17880 AAW	PABLS	10//99-12//99
Institution and Cafeteria	Harrisburg-Lebanon-Carlisle MSA, PA	s	8.51 MW	8.20 AW	17710 AAW	PABLS	10//99-12//99
Institution and Cafeteria	Johnstown MSA, PA	s	7.27 MW	7.24 AW	15130 AAW	PABLS	10//99-12//99
Institution and Cafeteria	Lancaster MSA, PA	s	9.13 MW	8.80 AW	18980 AAW	PABLS	10//99-12//99
Institution and Cafeteria	Philadelphia PMSA, PA-NJ	s	10.38 MW	9.82 AW	21600 AAW	PABLS	10//99-12//99
Institution and Cafeteria	Pittsburgh MSA, PA	s	9.16 MW	8.87 AW	19050 AAW	PABLS	10//99-12//99
Institution and Cafeteria	Reading MSA, PA	s	9.48 MW	9.28 AW	19730 AAW	PABLS	10//99-12//99
Institution and Cafeteria	Scranton--Wilkes-Barre--Hazleton MSA, PA	s	7.87 MW	7.33 AW	16370 AAW	PABLS	10//99-12//99
Institution and Cafeteria	Sharon MSA, PA	s	8.02 MW	7.98 AW	16690 AAW	PABLS	10//99-12//99
Institution and Cafeteria	State College MSA, PA	s	8.96 MW	9.09 AW	18640 AAW	PABLS	10//99-12//99
Institution and Cafeteria	Williamsport MSA, PA	s	8.81 MW	9.13 AW	18320 AAW	PABLS	10//99-12//99
Institution and Cafeteria	York MSA, PA	s	8.98 MW	9.11 AW	18680 AAW	PABLS	10//99-12//99
Institution and Cafeteria	Rhode Island	s	9.94 MW	10.32 AW	21470 AAW	RIBLS	10//99-12//99

AAW	Average annual wage	AOH	Average offered, high	ASH	Average starting, high	H	Hourly	M	Monthly	S	Special: hourly and annual
AE	Average entry wage	AOL	Average offered, low	ASL	Average starting, low	HI	Highest wage paid	MTC	Median total compensation	TQ	Third quartile wage
AEX	Average experienced wage	APH	Average pay, high range	AW	Average wage paid	HR	High end range	MW	Median wage paid	W	Weekly
AO	Average offered	APL	Average pay, low range	FQ	First quartile wage	LR	Low end range	SQ	Second quartile wage	Y	Yearly

Cook

Occupation/Type/Industry	Location	Per	Low	Mid	High	Source	Date
Institution and Cafeteria	Providence-Fall River-Warwick MSA, RI-MA	S	10.16 MW	9.77 AW	21140 AAW	RIBLS	10//99-12//99
Institution and Cafeteria	South Carolina	S	6.87 MW	7.25 AW	15080 AAW	SCBLS	10//99-12//99
Institution and Cafeteria	Charleston-North Charleston MSA, SC	S	7.69 MW	7.56 AW	16000 AAW	SCBLS	10//99-12//99
Institution and Cafeteria	Columbia MSA, SC	S	7.79 MW	7.21 AW	16190 AAW	SCBLS	10//99-12//99
Institution and Cafeteria	Florence MSA, SC	S	6.52 MW	6.08 AW	13560 AAW	SCBLS	10//99-12//99
Institution and Cafeteria	Greenville-Spartanburg-Anderson MSA, SC	S	7.38 MW	7.33 AW	15360 AAW	SCBLS	10//99-12//99
Institution and Cafeteria	Myrtle Beach MSA, SC	S	7.47 MW	7.17 AW	15540 AAW	SCBLS	10//99-12//99
Institution and Cafeteria	Sumter MSA, SC	S	6.88 MW	6.63 AW	14300 AAW	SCBLS	10//99-12//99
Institution and Cafeteria	South Dakota	S	8.02 MW	8.23 AW	17120 AAW	SDBLS	10//99-12//99
Institution and Cafeteria	Rapid City MSA, SD	S	8.18 MW	8.01 AW	17020 AAW	SDBLS	10//99-12//99
Institution and Cafeteria	Sioux Falls MSA, SD	S	9.01 MW	9.06 AW	18740 AAW	SDBLS	10//99-12//99
Institution and Cafeteria	Tennessee	S	6.78 MW	7.05 AW	14670 AAW	TNBLS	10//99-12//99
Institution and Cafeteria	Chattanooga MSA, TN-GA	S	6.71 MW	6.50 AW	13950 AAW	TNBLS	10//99-12//99
Institution and Cafeteria	Clarksville-Hopkinsville MSA, TN-KY	S	7.76 MW	7.66 AW	16140 AAW	TNBLS	10//99-12//99
Institution and Cafeteria	Jackson MSA, TN	S	7.03 MW	6.88 AW	14630 AAW	TNBLS	10//99-12//99
Institution and Cafeteria	Johnson City-Kingsport-Bristol MSA, TN-VA	S	7.34 MW	6.90 AW	15260 AAW	TNBLS	10//99-12//99
Institution and Cafeteria	Knoxville MSA, TN	S	6.76 MW	6.12 AW	14060 AAW	TNBLS	10//99-12//99
Institution and Cafeteria	Memphis MSA, TN-AR-MS	S	7.41 MW	7.30 AW	15410 AAW	MSBLS	10//99-12//99
Institution and Cafeteria	Nashville MSA, TN	S	7.47 MW	7.13 AW	15530 AAW	TNBLS	10//99-12//99
Institution and Cafeteria	Texas	S	6.97 MW	7.25 AW	15080 AAW	TXBLS	10//99-12//99
Institution and Cafeteria	Abilene MSA, TX	S	7.58 MW	7.40 AW	15760 AAW	TXBLS	10//99-12//99
Institution and Cafeteria	Amarillo MSA, TX	S	6.89 MW	6.59 AW	14320 AAW	TXBLS	10//99-12//99
Institution and Cafeteria	Austin-San Marcos MSA, TX	S	7.56 MW	7.40 AW	15720 AAW	TXBLS	10//99-12//99
Institution and Cafeteria	Beaumont-Port Arthur MSA, TX	S	6.76 MW	6.53 AW	14070 AAW	TXBLS	10//99-12//99
Institution and Cafeteria	Brazoria PMSA, TX	S	6.83 MW	6.73 AW	14200 AAW	TXBLS	10//99-12//99
Institution and Cafeteria	Brownsville-Harlingen-San Benito MSA, TX	S	7.22 MW	7.04 AW	15020 AAW	TXBLS	10//99-12//99
Institution and Cafeteria	Bryan-College Station MSA, TX	S	7.05 MW	6.92 AW	14660 AAW	TXBLS	10//99-12//99
Institution and Cafeteria	Corpus Christi MSA, TX	S	7.31 MW	7.16 AW	15210 AAW	TXBLS	10//99-12//99
Institution and Cafeteria	Dallas PMSA, TX	S	7.46 MW	7.21 AW	15510 AAW	TXBLS	10//99-12//99
Institution and Cafeteria	El Paso MSA, TX	S	7.09 MW	6.63 AW	14750 AAW	TXBLS	10//99-12//99
Institution and Cafeteria	Fort Worth-Arlington PMSA, TX	S	7.26 MW	7.08 AW	15090 AAW	TXBLS	10//99-12//99
Institution and Cafeteria	Galveston-Texas City PMSA, TX	S	7.44 MW	7.40 AW	15470 AAW	TXBLS	10//99-12//99
Institution and Cafeteria	Houston PMSA, TX	S	7.61 MW	7.32 AW	15830 AAW	TXBLS	10//99-12//99
Institution and Cafeteria	Killeen-Temple MSA, TX	S	6.62 MW	6.12 AW	13780 AAW	TXBLS	10//99-12//99
Institution and Cafeteria	Laredo MSA, TX	S	6.76 MW	6.64 AW	14060 AAW	TXBLS	10//99-12//99
Institution and Cafeteria	Longview-Marshall MSA, TX	S	7.01 MW	7.13 AW	14580 AAW	TXBLS	10//99-12//99
Institution and Cafeteria	Lubbock MSA, TX	S	7.76 MW	7.55 AW	16150 AAW	TXBLS	10//99-12//99
Institution and Cafeteria	McAllen-Edinburg-Mission MSA, TX	S	6.80 MW	6.66 AW	14140 AAW	TXBLS	10//99-12//99
Institution and Cafeteria	San Angelo MSA, TX	S	7.39 MW	6.72 AW	15360 AAW	TXBLS	10//99-12//99
Institution and Cafeteria	San Antonio MSA, TX	S	7.66 MW	7.56 AW	15930 AAW	TXBLS	10//99-12//99
Institution and Cafeteria	Sherman-Denison MSA, TX	S	7.09 MW	7.20 AW	14750 AAW	TXBLS	10//99-12//99
Institution and Cafeteria	Texarkana, MSA, TX-Texarkana, AR	S	6.42 MW	6.12 AW	13340 AAW	TXBLS	10//99-12//99
Institution and Cafeteria	Tyler MSA, TX	S	6.40 MW	6.03 AW	13320 AAW	TXBLS	10//99-12//99
Institution and Cafeteria	Victoria MSA, TX	S	7.02 MW	6.66 AW	14610 AAW	TXBLS	10//99-12//99
Institution and Cafeteria	Waco MSA, TX	S	6.77 MW	6.18 AW	14090 AAW	TXBLS	10//99-12//99
Institution and Cafeteria	Wichita Falls MSA, TX	S	7.07 MW	6.70 AW	14710 AAW	TXBLS	10//99-12//99
Institution and Cafeteria	Utah	S	8.22 MW	8.50 AW	17670 AAW	UTBLS	10//99-12//99
Institution and Cafeteria	Provo-Orem MSA, UT	S	7.75 MW	7.44 AW	16120 AAW	UTBLS	10//99-12//99
Institution and Cafeteria	Salt Lake City-Ogden MSA, UT	S	8.45 MW	8.09 AW	17570 AAW	UTBLS	10//99-12//99
Institution and Cafeteria	Vermont	S	8.54 MW	8.79 AW	18290 AAW	VTBLS	10//99-12//99
Institution and Cafeteria	Burlington MSA, VT	S	8.64 MW	8.75 AW	17980 AAW	VTBLS	10//99-12//99
Institution and Cafeteria	Virginia	S	7.83 MW	8.34 AW	17340 AAW	VABLS	10//99-12//99
Institution and Cafeteria	Charlottesville MSA, VA	S	8.39 MW	8.20 AW	17450 AAW	VABLS	10//99-12//99
Institution and Cafeteria	Lynchburg MSA, VA	S	8.18 MW	7.98 AW	17000 AAW	VABLS	10//99-12//99
Institution and Cafeteria	Norfolk-Virginia Beach-Newport News MSA, VA-NC	S	9.28 MW	8.40 AW	19290 AAW	VABLS	10//99-12//99

AAW Average annual wage	**AOH** Average offered, high	**ASH** Average starting, high	**H** Hourly	**M** Monthly	**S** Special: hourly and annual
AE Average entry wage	**AOL** Average offered, low	**ASL** Average starting, low	**HI** Highest wage paid	**MTC** Median total compensation	**TQ** Third quartile wage
AEX Average experienced wage	**APH** Average pay, high range	**AW** Average wage paid	**HR** High end range	**MW** Median wage paid	**W** Weekly
AO Average offered	**APL** Average pay, low range	**FQ** First quartile wage	**LR** Low end range	**SQ** Second quartile wage	**Y** Yearly

Occupation/Type/Industry	Location	Per	Low	Mid	High	Source	Date
Cook							
Institution and Cafeteria	Richmond-Petersburg MSA, VA	S	8.05 MW	7.90 AW	16740 AAW	VABLS	10//99-12//99
Institution and Cafeteria	Roanoke MSA, VA	S	8.09 MW	7.96 AW	16830 AAW	VABLS	10//99-12//99
Institution and Cafeteria	Washington	S	9.77 MW	10.09 AW	20980 AAW	WABLS	10//99-12//99
Institution and Cafeteria	Bellingham MSA, WA	S	9.34 MW	9.39 AW	19430 AAW	WABLS	10//99-12//99
Institution and Cafeteria	Bremerton PMSA, WA	S	10.48 MW	10.12 AW	21790 AAW	WABLS	10//99-12//99
Institution and Cafeteria	Olympia PMSA, WA	S	9.95 MW	9.61 AW	20690 AAW	WABLS	10//99-12//99
Institution and Cafeteria	Richland-Kennewick-Pasco MSA, WA	S	10.11 MW	10.05 AW	21030 AAW	WABLS	10//99-12//99
Institution and Cafeteria	Seattle-Bellevue-Everett PMSA, WA	S	10.51 MW	10.08 AW	21860 AAW	WABLS	10//99-12//99
Institution and Cafeteria	Spokane MSA, WA	S	9.51 MW	9.25 AW	19790 AAW	WABLS	10//99-12//99
Institution and Cafeteria	Tacoma PMSA, WA	S	10.43 MW	9.59 AW	21700 AAW	WABLS	10//99-12//99
Institution and Cafeteria	Yakima MSA, WA	S	9.92 MW	9.95 AW	20630 AAW	WABLS	10//99-12//99
Institution and Cafeteria	West Virginia	S	7.58 MW	7.62 AW	15850 AAW	WVBLS	10//99-12//99
Institution and Cafeteria	Charleston MSA, WV	S	7.80 MW	7.72 AW	16220 AAW	WVBLS	10//99-12//99
Institution and Cafeteria	Huntington-Ashland MSA, WV-KY-OH	S	7.23 MW	7.16 AW	15040 AAW	WVBLS	10//99-12//99
Institution and Cafeteria	Parkersburg-Marietta MSA, WV-OH	S	7.80 MW	7.74 AW	16230 AAW	WVBLS	10//99-12//99
Institution and Cafeteria	Wheeling MSA, WV-OH	S	7.65 MW	7.42 AW	15910 AAW	WVBLS	10//99-12//99
Institution and Cafeteria	Wisconsin	S	8.79 MW	8.91 AW	18540 AAW	WIBLS	10//99-12//99
Institution and Cafeteria	Appleton-Oshkosh-Neenah MSA, WI	S	8.79 MW	9.05 AW	18290 AAW	WIBLS	10//99-12//99
Institution and Cafeteria	Eau Claire MSA, WI	S	8.68 MW	8.59 AW	18060 AAW	WIBLS	10//99-12//99
Institution and Cafeteria	Green Bay MSA, WI	S	8.85 MW	8.87 AW	18410 AAW	WIBLS	10//99-12//99
Institution and Cafeteria	Janesville-Beloit MSA, WI	S	8.10 MW	8.08 AW	16850 AAW	WIBLS	10//99-12//99
Institution and Cafeteria	Kenosha PMSA, WI	S	9.00 MW	8.53 AW	18720 AAW	WIBLS	10//99-12//99
Institution and Cafeteria	La Crosse MSA, WI-MN	S	9.76 MW	9.86 AW	20310 AAW	WIBLS	10//99-12//99
Institution and Cafeteria	Madison MSA, WI	S	9.40 MW	9.19 AW	19560 AAW	WIBLS	10//99-12//99
Institution and Cafeteria	Milwaukee-Waukesha PMSA, WI	S	9.70 MW	9.57 AW	20170 AAW	WIBLS	10//99-12//99
Institution and Cafeteria	Racine PMSA, WI	S	8.59 MW	8.28 AW	17860 AAW	WIBLS	10//99-12//99
Institution and Cafeteria	Sheboygan MSA, WI	S	9.07 MW	9.19 AW	18870 AAW	WIBLS	10//99-12//99
Institution and Cafeteria	Wausau MSA, WI	S	8.57 MW	8.92 AW	17820 AAW	WIBLS	10//99-12//99
Institution and Cafeteria	Wyoming	S	7.72 MW	7.81 AW	16240 AAW	WYBLS	10//99-12//99
Institution and Cafeteria	Casper MSA, WY	S	7.82 MW	7.81 AW	16270 AAW	WYBLS	10//99-12//99
Institution and Cafeteria	Cheyenne MSA, WY	S	8.41 MW	7.86 AW	17490 AAW	WYBLS	10//99-12//99
Institution and Cafeteria	Aguadilla MSA, PR	S	5.86 MW	6.08 AW	12200 AAW	PRBLS	10//99-12//99
Institution and Cafeteria	Arecibo PMSA, PR	S	5.74 MW	5.92 AW	11950 AAW	PRBLS	10//99-12//99
Institution and Cafeteria	Caguas PMSA, PR	S	5.77 MW	5.95 AW	11990 AAW	PRBLS	10//99-12//99
Institution and Cafeteria	Mayaguez MSA, PR	S	5.75 MW	5.89 AW	11950 AAW	PRBLS	10//99-12//99
Institution and Cafeteria	Ponce MSA, PR	S	6.30 MW	6.16 AW	13110 AAW	PRBLS	10//99-12//99
Institution and Cafeteria	Virgin Islands	S	8.29 MW	8.21 AW	17080 AAW	VIBLS	10//99-12//99
Institution and Cafeteria	Guam	S	9.13 MW	9.68 AW	20130 AAW	GUBLS	10//99-12//99
Restaurant	Alabama	S	6.74 MW	7.16 AW	14890 AAW	ALBLS	10//99-12//99
Restaurant	Anniston MSA, AL	S	6.75 MW	6.43 AW	14030 AAW	ALBLS	10//99-12//99
Restaurant	Auburn-Opelika MSA, AL	S	7.34 MW	7.30 AW	15280 AAW	ALBLS	10//99-12//99
Restaurant	Birmingham MSA, AL	S	7.80 MW	7.36 AW	16230 AAW	ALBLS	10//99-12//99
Restaurant	Decatur MSA, AL	S	7.48 MW	6.80 AW	15570 AAW	ALBLS	10//99-12//99
Restaurant	Dothan MSA, AL	S	6.57 MW	6.45 AW	13660 AAW	ALBLS	10//99-12//99
Restaurant	Florence MSA, AL	S	7.48 MW	7.26 AW	15560 AAW	ALBLS	10//99-12//99
Restaurant	Gadsden MSA, AL	S	6.82 MW	6.27 AW	14190 AAW	ALBLS	10//99-12//99
Restaurant	Huntsville MSA, AL	S	7.38 MW	7.25 AW	15360 AAW	ALBLS	10//99-12//99
Restaurant	Mobile MSA, AL	S	7.38 MW	6.92 AW	15360 AAW	ALBLS	10//99-12//99
Restaurant	Montgomery MSA, AL	S	7.49 MW	7.42 AW	15580 AAW	ALBLS	10//99-12//99
Restaurant	Tuscaloosa MSA, AL	S	7.37 MW	7.30 AW	15330 AAW	ALBLS	10//99-12//99
Restaurant	Alaska	S	10.17 MW	10.15 AW	21120 AAW	AKBLS	10//99-12//99
Restaurant	Anchorage MSA, AK	S	9.91 MW	9.85 AW	20610 AAW	AKBLS	10//99-12//99
Restaurant	Arizona	S	8.14 MW	8.44 AW	17550 AAW	AZBLS	10//99-12//99
Restaurant	Flagstaff MSA, AZ-UT	S	8.17 MW	7.78 AW	17000 AAW	AZBLS	10//99-12//99
Restaurant	Phoenix-Mesa MSA, AZ	S	8.70 MW	8.45 AW	18090 AAW	AZBLS	10//99-12//99
Restaurant	Tucson MSA, AZ	S	8.09 MW	7.72 AW	16820 AAW	AZBLS	10//99-12//99
Restaurant	Yuma MSA, AZ	S	7.51 MW	7.46 AW	15620 AAW	AZBLS	10//99-12//99
Restaurant	Arkansas	S	7.12 MW	7.27 AW	15130 AAW	ARBLS	10//99-12//99
Restaurant	Fayetteville-Springdale-Rogers MSA, AR	S	7.92 MW	7.98 AW	16480 AAW	ARBLS	10//99-12//99
Restaurant	Fort Smith MSA, AR-OK	S	7.70 MW	7.57 AW	16010 AAW	ARBLS	10//99-12//99
Restaurant	Jonesboro MSA, AR	S	7.25 MW	7.24 AW	15090 AAW	ARBLS	10//99-12//99
Restaurant	Little Rock-North Little Rock MSA, AR	S	7.61 MW	7.54 AW	15820 AAW	ARBLS	10//99-12//99

AAW	Average annual wage	AOH	Average offered, high	ASH	Average starting, high
AE	Average entry wage	AOL	Average offered, low	ASL	Average starting, low
AEX	Average experienced wage	APH	Average pay, high range	AW	Average wage paid
AO	Average offered	APL	Average pay, low range	FQ	First quartile wage

H	Hourly
HI	Highest wage paid
HR	High end range
LR	Low end range

M	Monthly
MTC	Median total compensation
MW	Median wage paid
SQ	Second quartile wage

S	Special: hourly and annual
TQ	Third quartile wage
W	Weekly
Y	Yearly

Occupation/Type/Industry	Location	Per	Low	Mid	High	Source	Date
Cook							
Restaurant	Pine Bluff MSA, AR	S	6.86 MW	6.28 AW	14260 AAW	ARBLS	10//99-12//99
Restaurant	California	S	8.22 MW	8.76 AW	18230 AAW	CABLS	10//99-12//99
Restaurant	Bakersfield MSA, CA	S	7.36 MW	6.78 AW	15300 AAW	CABLS	10//99-12//99
Restaurant	Chico-Paradise MSA, CA	S	8.82 MW	8.56 AW	18330 AAW	CABLS	10//99-12//99
Restaurant	Fresno MSA, CA	S	7.62 MW	7.39 AW	15850 AAW	CABLS	10//99-12//99
Restaurant	Los Angeles-Long Beach PMSA, CA	S	8.97 MW	8.29 AW	18660 AAW	CABLS	10//99-12//99
Restaurant	Merced MSA, CA	S	6.92 MW	6.12 AW	14390 AAW	CABLS	10//99-12//99
Restaurant	Modesto MSA, CA	S	8.24 MW	7.99 AW	17140 AAW	CABLS	10//99-12//99
Restaurant	Oakland PMSA, CA	S	9.47 MW	9.07 AW	19710 AAW	CABLS	10//99-12//99
Restaurant	Orange County PMSA, CA	S	8.59 MW	8.41 AW	17880 AAW	CABLS	10//99-12//99
Restaurant	Redding MSA, CA	S	7.65 MW	7.30 AW	15920 AAW	CABLS	10//99-12//99
Restaurant	Riverside-San Bernardino PMSA, CA	S	7.67 MW	7.03 AW	15960 AAW	CABLS	10//99-12//99
Restaurant	Sacramento PMSA, CA	S	8.14 MW	7.56 AW	16930 AAW	CABLS	10//99-12//99
Restaurant	Salinas MSA, CA	S	10.04 MW	9.88 AW	20880 AAW	CABLS	10//99-12//99
Restaurant	San Diego MSA, CA	S	8.16 MW	7.61 AW	16980 AAW	CABLS	10//99-12//99
Restaurant	San Francisco PMSA, CA	S	10.20 MW	9.49 AW	21210 AAW	CABLS	10//99-12//99
Restaurant	San Jose PMSA, CA	S	9.08 MW	8.39 AW	18880 AAW	CABLS	10//99-12//99
Restaurant	San Luis Obispo-Atascadero-Paso Robles MSA, CA	S	8.78 MW	8.77 AW	18270 AAW	CABLS	10//99-12//99
Restaurant	Santa Barbara-Santa Maria-Lompoc MSA, CA	S	9.18 MW	8.78 AW	19080 AAW	CABLS	10//99-12//99
Restaurant	Santa Cruz-Watsonville PMSA, CA	S	9.27 MW	9.38 AW	19290 AAW	CABLS	10//99-12//99
Restaurant	Santa Rosa PMSA, CA	S	8.90 MW	8.49 AW	18520 AAW	CABLS	10//99-12//99
Restaurant	Stockton-Lodi MSA, CA	S	7.64 MW	7.06 AW	15890 AAW	CABLS	10//99-12//99
Restaurant	Vallejo-Fairfield-Napa PMSA, CA	S	8.97 MW	8.94 AW	18650 AAW	CABLS	10//99-12//99
Restaurant	Ventura PMSA, CA	S	8.71 MW	8.39 AW	18110 AAW	CABLS	10//99-12//99
Restaurant	Visalia-Tulare-Porterville MSA, CA	S	7.39 MW	7.19 AW	15380 AAW	CABLS	10//99-12//99
Restaurant	Yolo PMSA, CA	S	8.40 MW	8.08 AW	17470 AAW	CABLS	10//99-12//99
Restaurant	Yuba City MSA, CA	S	7.26 MW	7.10 AW	15110 AAW	CABLS	10//99-12//99
Restaurant	Colorado	S	8.43 MW	8.70 AW	18110 AAW	COBLS	10//99-12//99
Restaurant	Boulder-Longmont PMSA, CO	S	8.48 MW	8.41 AW	17650 AAW	COBLS	10//99-12//99
Restaurant	Colorado Springs MSA, CO	S	8.09 MW	7.92 AW	16820 AAW	COBLS	10//99-12//99
Restaurant	Denver PMSA, CO	S	8.79 MW	8.61 AW	18280 AAW	COBLS	10//99-12//99
Restaurant	Fort Collins-Loveland MSA, CO	S	8.50 MW	8.34 AW	17670 AAW	COBLS	10//99-12//99
Restaurant	Grand Junction MSA, CO	S	7.42 MW	7.35 AW	15440 AAW	COBLS	10//99-12//99
Restaurant	Greeley PMSA, CO	S	7.20 MW	6.96 AW	14970 AAW	COBLS	10//99-12//99
Restaurant	Pueblo MSA, CO	S	7.73 MW	7.48 AW	16070 AAW	COBLS	10//99-12//99
Restaurant	Connecticut	S	9.91 MW	10.58 AW	22010 AAW	CTBLS	10//99-12//99
Restaurant	Bridgeport PMSA, CT	S	10.82 MW	9.79 AW	22510 AAW	CTBLS	10//99-12//99
Restaurant	Danbury PMSA, CT	S	10.53 MW	10.53 AW	21900 AAW	CTBLS	10//99-12//99
Restaurant	Hartford MSA, CT	S	10.48 MW	9.94 AW	21790 AAW	CTBLS	10//99-12//99
Restaurant	New Haven-Meriden PMSA, CT	S	10.69 MW	10.37 AW	22230 AAW	CTBLS	10//99-12//99
Restaurant	New London-Norwich MSA, CT-RI	S	9.99 MW	9.46 AW	20770 AAW	CTBLS	10//99-12//99
Restaurant	Stamford-Norwalk PMSA, CT	S	11.13 MW	9.13 AW	23150 AAW	CTBLS	10//99-12//99
Restaurant	Waterbury PMSA, CT	S	11.30 MW	10.63 AW	23510 AAW	CTBLS	10//99-12//99
Restaurant	Delaware	S	8.62 MW	8.87 AW	18450 AAW	DEBLS	10//99-12//99
Restaurant	Dover MSA, DE	S	8.32 MW	7.95 AW	17310 AAW	DEBLS	10//99-12//99
Restaurant	Wilmington-Newark PMSA, DE-MD	S	9.27 MW	9.19 AW	19280 AAW	DEBLS	10//99-12//99
Restaurant	District of Columbia	S	10.58 MW	11.02 AW	22930 AAW	DCBLS	10//99-12//99
Restaurant	Washington PMSA, DC-MD-VA-WV	S	9.85 MW	9.57 AW	20490 AAW	DCBLS	10//99-12//99
Restaurant	Florida	S	8.47 MW	8.82 AW	18350 AAW	FLBLS	10//99-12//99
Restaurant	Daytona Beach MSA, FL	S	8.19 MW	7.94 AW	17030 AAW	FLBLS	10//99-12//99
Restaurant	Fort Lauderdale PMSA, FL	S	8.75 MW	8.66 AW	18200 AAW	FLBLS	10//99-12//99
Restaurant	Fort Myers-Cape Coral MSA, FL	S	8.30 MW	7.93 AW	17270 AAW	FLBLS	10//99-12//99
Restaurant	Fort Pierce-Port St. Lucie MSA, FL	S	8.91 MW	8.42 AW	18520 AAW	FLBLS	10//99-12//99
Restaurant	Fort Walton Beach MSA, FL	S	7.56 MW	7.43 AW	15730 AAW	FLBLS	10//99-12//99
Restaurant	Gainesville MSA, FL	S	7.57 MW	7.54 AW	15740 AAW	FLBLS	10//99-12//99
Restaurant	Jacksonville MSA, FL	S	8.64 MW	8.33 AW	17960 AAW	FLBLS	10//99-12//99

AAW	Average annual wage	AOH	Average offered, high	ASH	Average starting, high
AE	Average entry wage	AOL	Average offered, low	ASL	Average starting, low
AEX	Average experienced wage	APH	Average pay, high range	AW	Average wage paid
AO	Average offered	APL	Average pay, low range	FQ	First quartile wage

H	Hourly	M	Monthly	S	Special: hourly and annual
HI	Highest wage paid	MTC	Median total compensation	TQ	Third quartile wage
HR	High end range	MW	Median wage paid	W	Weekly
LR	Low end range	SQ	Second quartile wage	Y	Yearly

Cook

Occupation/Type/Industry	Location	Per	Low	Mid	High	Source	Date
Restaurant	Lakeland-Winter Haven MSA, FL	S	8.40 MW	8.11 AW	17480 AAW	FLBLS	10//99-12//99
Restaurant	Melbourne-Titusville-Palm Bay MSA, FL	S	8.32 MW	7.89 AW	17310 AAW	FLBLS	10//99-12//99
Restaurant	Miami PMSA, FL	S	9.33 MW	8.75 AW	19420 AAW	FLBLS	10//99-12//99
Restaurant	Naples MSA, FL	S	10.62 MW	10.32 AW	22080 AAW	FLBLS	10//99-12//99
Restaurant	Ocala MSA, FL	S	7.73 MW	7.65 AW	16080 AAW	FLBLS	10//99-12//99
Restaurant	Orlando MSA, FL	S	9.22 MW	9.09 AW	19180 AAW	FLBLS	10//99-12//99
Restaurant	Panama City MSA, FL	S	7.59 MW	7.59 AW	15790 AAW	FLBLS	10//99-12//99
Restaurant	Pensacola MSA, FL	S	8.04 MW	7.94 AW	16720 AAW	FLBLS	10//99-12//99
Restaurant	Punta Gorda MSA, FL	S	8.42 MW	8.23 AW	17510 AAW	FLBLS	10//99-12//99
Restaurant	Sarasota-Bradenton MSA, FL	S	8.96 MW	8.73 AW	18630 AAW	FLBLS	10//99-12//99
Restaurant	Tallahassee MSA, FL	S	8.15 MW	7.91 AW	16950 AAW	FLBLS	10//99-12//99
Restaurant	Tampa-St. Petersburg-Clearwater MSA, FL	S	8.41 MW	8.23 AW	17500 AAW	FLBLS	10//99-12//99
Restaurant	West Palm Beach-Boca Raton MSA, FL	S	9.67 MW	9.54 AW	20100 AAW	FLBLS	10//99-12//99
Restaurant	Georgia	S	7.91 MW	8.19 AW	17040 AAW	GABLS	10//99-12//99
Restaurant	Albany MSA, GA	S	7.09 MW	6.64 AW	14740 AAW	GABLS	10//99-12//99
Restaurant	Athens MSA, GA	S	8.12 MW	8.05 AW	16890 AAW	GABLS	10//99-12//99
Restaurant	Atlanta MSA, GA	S	9.06 MW	8.82 AW	18840 AAW	GABLS	10//99-12//99
Restaurant	Augusta-Aiken MSA, GA-SC	S	7.01 MW	6.61 AW	14570 AAW	GABLS	10//99-12//99
Restaurant	Columbus MSA, GA-AL	S	6.92 MW	6.54 AW	14390 AAW	GABLS	10//99-12//99
Restaurant	Macon MSA, GA	S	6.49 MW	6.31 AW	13510 AAW	GABLS	10//99-12//99
Restaurant	Savannah MSA, GA	S	7.07 MW	6.67 AW	14710 AAW	GABLS	10//99-12//99
Restaurant	Hawaii	S	9.76 MW	10.60 AW	22040 AAW	HIBLS	10//99-12//99
Restaurant	Honolulu MSA, HI	S	10.08 MW	9.00 AW	20970 AAW	HIBLS	10//99-12//99
Restaurant	Idaho	S	7.18 MW	7.47 AW	15530 AAW	IDBLS	10//99-12//99
Restaurant	Boise City MSA, ID	S	7.51 MW	7.13 AW	15630 AAW	IDBLS	10//99-12//99
Restaurant	Pocatello MSA, ID	S	7.76 MW	7.63 AW	16150 AAW	IDBLS	10//99-12//99
Restaurant	Illinois	S	8.25 MW	8.64 AW	17970 AAW	ILBLS	10//99-12//99
Restaurant	Bloomington-Normal MSA, IL	S	8.75 MW	8.65 AW	18200 AAW	ILBLS	10//99-12//99
Restaurant	Champaign-Urbana MSA, IL	S	8.52 MW	8.26 AW	17730 AAW	ILBLS	10//99-12//99
Restaurant	Chicago PMSA, IL	S	8.99 MW	8.57 AW	18690 AAW	ILBLS	10//99-12//99
Restaurant	Decatur MSA, IL	S	8.25 MW	8.04 AW	17160 AAW	ILBLS	10//99-12//99
Restaurant	Kankakee PMSA, IL	S	8.97 MW	9.26 AW	18660 AAW	ILBLS	10//99-12//99
Restaurant	Peoria-Pekin MSA, IL	S	8.08 MW	7.97 AW	16820 AAW	ILBLS	10//99-12//99
Restaurant	Rockford MSA, IL	S	8.07 MW	7.91 AW	16780 AAW	ILBLS	10//99-12//99
Restaurant	Springfield MSA, IL	S	8.27 MW	8.12 AW	17190 AAW	ILBLS	10//99-12//99
Restaurant	Indiana	S	7.95 MW	8.15 AW	16940 AAW	INBLS	10//99-12//99
Restaurant	Bloomington MSA, IN	S	7.59 MW	7.47 AW	15780 AAW	INBLS	10//99-12//99
Restaurant	Elkhart-Goshen MSA, IN	S	8.19 MW	8.15 AW	17030 AAW	INBLS	10//99-12//99
Restaurant	Evansville-Henderson MSA, IN-KY	S	7.80 MW	7.45 AW	16220 AAW	INBLS	10//99-12//99
Restaurant	Fort Wayne MSA, IN	S	7.90 MW	7.70 AW	16430 AAW	INBLS	10//99-12//99
Restaurant	Gary PMSA, IN	S	8.27 MW	8.06 AW	17210 AAW	INBLS	10//99-12//99
Restaurant	Indianapolis MSA, IN	S	8.35 MW	8.19 AW	17360 AAW	INBLS	10//99-12//99
Restaurant	Kokomo MSA, IN	S	7.78 MW	7.56 AW	16190 AAW	INBLS	10//99-12//99
Restaurant	Lafayette MSA, IN	S	8.56 MW	8.26 AW	17810 AAW	INBLS	10//99-12//99
Restaurant	Muncie MSA, IN	S	7.54 MW	7.49 AW	15690 AAW	INBLS	10//99-12//99
Restaurant	South Bend MSA, IN	S	8.09 MW	7.91 AW	16830 AAW	INBLS	10//99-12//99
Restaurant	Terre Haute MSA, IN	S	7.71 MW	7.57 AW	16030 AAW	INBLS	10//99-12//99
Restaurant	Iowa	S	7.24 MW	7.41 AW	15410 AAW	IABLS	10//99-12//99
Restaurant	Cedar Rapids MSA, IA	S	8.38 MW	8.44 AW	17430 AAW	IABLS	10//99-12//99
Restaurant	Davenport-Moline-Rock Island MSA, IA-IL	S	7.12 MW	6.95 AW	14810 AAW	IABLS	10//99-12//99
Restaurant	Des Moines MSA, IA	S	8.26 MW	8.03 AW	17180 AAW	IABLS	10//99-12//99
Restaurant	Dubuque MSA, IA	S	7.43 MW	7.30 AW	15450 AAW	IABLS	10//99-12//99
Restaurant	Iowa City MSA, IA	S	8.13 MW	8.15 AW	16910 AAW	IABLS	10//99-12//99
Restaurant	Sioux City MSA, IA-NE	S	8.02 MW	7.84 AW	16670 AAW	IABLS	10//99-12//99
Restaurant	Waterloo-Cedar Falls MSA, IA	S	7.74 MW	7.35 AW	16100 AAW	IABLS	10//99-12//99
Restaurant	Kansas	S	7.51 MW	7.66 AW	15920 AAW	KSBLS	10//99-12//99
Restaurant	Lawrence MSA, KS	S	7.81 MW	7.75 AW	16240 AAW	KSBLS	10//99-12//99
Restaurant	Topeka MSA, KS	S	7.45 MW	7.29 AW	15490 AAW	KSBLS	10//99-12//99
Restaurant	Wichita MSA, KS	S	8.02 MW	7.88 AW	16680 AAW	KSBLS	10//99-12//99
Restaurant	Kentucky	S	7.81 MW	7.98 AW	16600 AAW	KYBLS	10//99-12//99
Restaurant	Lexington MSA, KY	S	8.11 MW	8.05 AW	16870 AAW	KYBLS	10//99-12//99
Restaurant	Louisville MSA, KY-IN	S	8.58 MW	8.46 AW	17850 AAW	KYBLS	10//99-12//99
Restaurant	Owensboro MSA, KY	S	7.19 MW	7.04 AW	14960 AAW	KYBLS	10//99-12//99
Restaurant	Louisiana	S	7.28 MW	7.48 AW	15550 AAW	LABLS	10//99-12//99
Restaurant	Alexandria MSA, LA	S	7.37 MW	6.97 AW	15320 AAW	LABLS	10//99-12//99

AAW Average annual wage	AOH Average offered, high	ASH Average starting, high	H Hourly	M Monthly	S Special: hourly and annual
AE Average entry wage	AOL Average offered, low	ASL Average starting, low	HI Highest wage paid	MTC Median total compensation	TQ Third quartile wage
AEX Average experienced wage	APH Average pay, high range	AW Average wage paid	HR High end range	MW Median wage paid	W Weekly
AO Average offered	APL Average pay, low range	FQ First quartile wage	LR Low end range	SQ Second quartile wage	Y Yearly

Occupation/Type/Industry	Location	Per	Low	Mid	High	Source	Date
Cook							
Restaurant	Baton Rouge MSA, LA	S	7.43 MW	7.44 AW	15450 AAW	LABLS	10//99-12//99
Restaurant	Houma MSA, LA	S	7.26 MW	7.06 AW	15090 AAW	LABLS	10//99-12//99
Restaurant	Lafayette MSA, LA	S	6.35 MW	6.00 AW	13200 AAW	LABLS	10//99-12//99
Restaurant	Lake Charles MSA, LA	S	7.60 MW	7.50 AW	15810 AAW	LABLS	10//99-12//99
Restaurant	Monroe MSA, LA	S	7.25 MW	7.25 AW	15080 AAW	LABLS	10//99-12//99
Restaurant	New Orleans MSA, LA	S	8.19 MW	7.83 AW	17040 AAW	LABLS	10//99-12//99
Restaurant	Shreveport-Bossier City MSA, LA	S	7.35 MW	7.12 AW	15300 AAW	LABLS	10//99-12//99
Restaurant	Maine	S	8.55 MW	8.98 AW	18690 AAW	MEBLS	10//99-12//99
Restaurant	Bangor MSA, ME	S	8.12 MW	7.93 AW	16890 AAW	MEBLS	10//99-12//99
Restaurant	Lewiston-Auburn MSA, ME	S	8.80 MW	8.00 AW	18300 AAW	MEBLS	10//99-12//99
Restaurant	Portland MSA, ME	S	9.16 MW	9.15 AW	19060 AAW	MEBLS	10//99-12//99
Restaurant	Maryland	S	8.47 MW	8.99 AW	18700 AAW	MDBLS	10//99-12//99
Restaurant	Baltimore PMSA, MD	S	9.02 MW	8.42 AW	18760 AAW	MDBLS	10//99-12//99
Restaurant	Cumberland MSA, MD-WV	S	6.70 MW	6.39 AW	13940 AAW	MDBLS	10//99-12//99
Restaurant	Hagerstown PMSA, MD	S	8.70 MW	7.96 AW	18090 AAW	MDBLS	10//99-12//99
Restaurant	Massachusetts	S	10.01 MW	10.27 AW	21370 AAW	MABLS	10//99-12//99
Restaurant	Barnstable-Yarmouth MSA, MA	S	10.57 MW	10.20 AW	21980 AAW	MABLS	10//99-12//99
Restaurant	Boston PMSA, MA-NH	S	10.41 MW	10.25 AW	21650 AAW	MABLS	10//99-12//99
Restaurant	Brockton PMSA, MA	S	10.51 MW	10.03 AW	21870 AAW	MABLS	10//99-12//99
Restaurant	Fitchburg-Leominster PMSA, MA	S	8.71 MW	8.93 AW	18120 AAW	MABLS	10//99-12//99
Restaurant	Lawrence PMSA, MA-NH	S	10.07 MW	9.92 AW	20950 AAW	MABLS	10//99-12//99
Restaurant	Lowell PMSA, MA-NH	S	10.39 MW	10.24 AW	21620 AAW	MABLS	10//99-12//99
Restaurant	New Bedford PMSA, MA	S	8.32 MW	7.83 AW	17290 AAW	MABLS	10//99-12//99
Restaurant	Pittsfield MSA, MA	S	9.65 MW	9.49 AW	20070 AAW	MABLS	10//99-12//99
Restaurant	Springfield MSA, MA	S	9.96 MW	8.94 AW	20720 AAW	MABLS	10//99-12//99
Restaurant	Worcester PMSA, MA-CT	S	10.21 MW	9.92 AW	21230 AAW	MABLS	10//99-12//99
Restaurant	Michigan	S	7.85 MW	8.15 AW	16950 AAW	MIBLS	10//99-12//99
Restaurant	Ann Arbor PMSA, MI	S	9.29 MW	9.39 AW	19310 AAW	MIBLS	10//99-12//99
Restaurant	Benton Harbor MSA, MI	S	9.35 MW	9.55 AW	19440 AAW	MIBLS	10//99-12//99
Restaurant	Detroit PMSA, MI	S	8.57 MW	8.23 AW	17820 AAW	MIBLS	10//99-12//99
Restaurant	Flint PMSA, MI	S	8.13 MW	7.93 AW	16910 AAW	MIBLS	10//99-12//99
Restaurant	Grand Rapids-Muskegon-Holland MSA, MI	S	8.25 MW	8.05 AW	17160 AAW	MIBLS	10//99-12//99
Restaurant	Jackson MSA, MI	S	8.61 MW	8.43 AW	17900 AAW	MIBLS	10//99-12//99
Restaurant	Kalamazoo-Battle Creek MSA, MI	S	7.68 MW	7.50 AW	15970 AAW	MIBLS	10//99-12//99
Restaurant	Lansing-East Lansing MSA, MI	S	8.09 MW	7.90 AW	16830 AAW	MIBLS	10//99-12//99
Restaurant	Saginaw-Bay City-Midland MSA, MI	S	6.75 MW	6.46 AW	14030 AAW	MIBLS	10//99-12//99
Restaurant	Minnesota	S	8.51 MW	8.56 AW	17800 AAW	MNBLS	10//99-12//99
Restaurant	Duluth-Superior MSA, MN-WI	S	6.99 MW	6.71 AW	14550 AAW	MNBLS	10//99-12//99
Restaurant	Minneapolis-St. Paul MSA, MN-WI	S	9.26 MW	9.33 AW	19250 AAW	MNBLS	10//99-12//99
Restaurant	Rochester MSA, MN	S	9.52 MW	9.43 AW	19790 AAW	MNBLS	10//99-12//99
Restaurant	St. Cloud MSA, MN	S	7.90 MW	7.82 AW	16420 AAW	MNBLS	10//99-12//99
Restaurant	Mississippi	S	7.11 MW	7.36 AW	15300 AAW	MSBLS	10//99-12//99
Restaurant	Biloxi-Gulfport-Pascagoula MSA, MS	S	8.06 MW	7.95 AW	16770 AAW	MSBLS	10//99-12//99
Restaurant	Hattiesburg MSA, MS	S	7.26 MW	7.20 AW	15100 AAW	MSBLS	10//99-12//99
Restaurant	Jackson MSA, MS	S	7.90 MW	7.69 AW	16430 AAW	MSBLS	10//99-12//99
Restaurant	Missouri	S	7.52 MW	8.03 AW	16690 AAW	MOBLS	10//99-12//99
Restaurant	Joplin MSA, MO	S	7.59 MW	7.46 AW	15800 AAW	MOBLS	10//99-12//99
Restaurant	Kansas City MSA, MO-KS	S	8.55 MW	8.14 AW	17780 AAW	MOBLS	10//99-12//99
Restaurant	St. Joseph MSA, MO	S	7.28 MW	6.91 AW	15150 AAW	MOBLS	10//99-12//99
Restaurant	St. Louis MSA, MO-IL	S	8.57 MW	7.98 AW	17820 AAW	MOBLS	10//99-12//99
Restaurant	Springfield MSA, MO	S	7.64 MW	7.45 AW	15900 AAW	MOBLS	10//99-12//99
Restaurant	Montana	S	7.26 MW	7.41 AW	15400 AAW	MTBLS	10//99-12//99
Restaurant	Billings MSA, MT	S	7.60 MW	7.56 AW	15810 AAW	MTBLS	10//99-12//99
Restaurant	Great Falls MSA, MT	S	6.95 MW	6.78 AW	14460 AAW	MTBLS	10//99-12//99
Restaurant	Missoula MSA, MT	S	7.40 MW	7.41 AW	15400 AAW	MTBLS	10//99-12//99
Restaurant	Nebraska	S	8.12 MW	8.32 AW	17310 AAW	NEBLS	10//99-12//99
Restaurant	Lincoln MSA, NE	S	7.76 MW	7.37 AW	16140 AAW	NEBLS	10//99-12//99
Restaurant	Omaha MSA, NE-IA	S	9.27 MW	9.02 AW	19280 AAW	NEBLS	10//99-12//99
Restaurant	Nevada	S	10.32 MW	10.33 AW	21480 AAW	NVBLS	10//99-12//99
Restaurant	Las Vegas MSA, NV-AZ	S	10.63 MW	10.80 AW	22100 AAW	NVBLS	10//99-12//99
Restaurant	Reno MSA, NV	S	9.51 MW	9.46 AW	19770 AAW	NVBLS	10//99-12//99
Restaurant	New Hampshire	S	9.79 MW	10.04 AW	20880 AAW	NHBLS	10//99-12//99
Restaurant	Manchester PMSA, NH	S	9.98 MW	10.28 AW	20750 AAW	NHBLS	10//99-12//99

AAW Average annual wage	AOH Average offered, high	ASH Average starting, high	H Hourly	M Monthly
AE Average entry wage	AOL Average offered, low	ASL Average starting, low	HI Highest wage paid	MTC Median total compensation
AEX Average experienced wage	APH Average pay, high range	AW Average wage paid	HR High end range	MW Median wage paid
AO Average offered	APL Average pay, low range	FQ First quartile wage	LR Low end range	SQ Second quartile wage

Key continued:
- S   Special: hourly and annual
- TQ   Third quartile wage
- W   Weekly
- Y   Yearly

Cook

Occupation/Type/Industry	Location	Per	Low	Mid	High	Source	Date
Restaurant	Nashua PMSA, NH	S	9.93 MW	9.90 AW	20650 AAW	NHBLS	10//99-12//99
Restaurant	Portsmouth-Rochester PMSA, NH-ME	S	8.99 MW	9.08 AW	18690 AAW	NHBLS	10//99-12//99
Restaurant	New Jersey	S	9.78 MW	10.26 AW	21350 AAW	NJBLS	10//99-12//99
Restaurant	Atlantic-Cape May PMSA, NJ	S	10.89 MW	10.06 AW	22640 AAW	NJBLS	10//99-12//99
Restaurant	Bergen-Passaic PMSA, NJ	S	10.13 MW	9.78 AW	21080 AAW	NJBLS	10//99-12//99
Restaurant	Middlesex-Somerset-Hunterdon PMSA, NJ	S	9.40 MW	9.18 AW	19550 AAW	NJBLS	10//99-12//99
Restaurant	Monmouth-Ocean PMSA, NJ	S	10.41 MW	10.16 AW	21650 AAW	NJBLS	10//99-12//99
Restaurant	Newark PMSA, NJ	S	10.34 MW	9.69 AW	21500 AAW	NJBLS	10//99-12//99
Restaurant	Trenton PMSA, NJ	S	9.97 MW	9.38 AW	20740 AAW	NJBLS	10//99-12//99
Restaurant	Vineland-Millville-Bridgeton PMSA, NJ	S	8.77 MW	8.83 AW	18240 AAW	NJBLS	10//99-12//99
Restaurant	New Mexico	S	7.47 MW	7.64 AW	15890 AAW	NMBLS	10//99-12//99
Restaurant	Albuquerque MSA, NM	S	7.79 MW	7.69 AW	16210 AAW	NMBLS	10//99-12//99
Restaurant	Las Cruces MSA, NM	S	6.92 MW	6.77 AW	14400 AAW	NMBLS	10//99-12//99
Restaurant	Santa Fe MSA, NM	S	8.32 MW	8.13 AW	17300 AAW	NMBLS	10//99-12//99
Restaurant	New York	S	9.12 MW	10.40 AW	21620 AAW	NYBLS	10//99-12//99
Restaurant	Albany-Schenectady-Troy MSA, NY	S	8.40 MW	8.23 AW	17480 AAW	NYBLS	10//99-12//99
Restaurant	Binghamton MSA, NY	S	7.86 MW	7.72 AW	16360 AAW	NYBLS	10//99-12//99
Restaurant	Buffalo-Niagara Falls MSA, NY	S	8.40 MW	8.03 AW	17470 AAW	NYBLS	10//99-12//99
Restaurant	Dutchess County PMSA, NY	S	8.56 MW	8.15 AW	17800 AAW	NYBLS	10//99-12//99
Restaurant	Elmira MSA, NY	S	8.64 MW	8.92 AW	17960 AAW	NYBLS	10//99-12//99
Restaurant	Glens Falls MSA, NY	S	8.65 MW	8.15 AW	17980 AAW	NYBLS	10//99-12//99
Restaurant	Jamestown MSA, NY	S	7.71 MW	7.52 AW	16030 AAW	NYBLS	10//99-12//99
Restaurant	Nassau-Suffolk PMSA, NY	S	11.40 MW	10.18 AW	23710 AAW	NYBLS	10//99-12//99
Restaurant	New York PMSA, NY	S	11.35 MW	10.16 AW	23610 AAW	NYBLS	10//99-12//99
Restaurant	Newburgh PMSA, NY-PA	S	8.55 MW	7.41 AW	17780 AAW	NYBLS	10//99-12//99
Restaurant	Rochester MSA, NY	S	9.02 MW	8.42 AW	18770 AAW	NYBLS	10//99-12//99
Restaurant	Syracuse MSA, NY	S	9.03 MW	8.82 AW	18780 AAW	NYBLS	10//99-12//99
Restaurant	Utica-Rome MSA, NY	S	8.16 MW	7.81 AW	16960 AAW	NYBLS	10//99-12//99
Restaurant	North Carolina	S	7.8 MW	8.09 AW	16820 AAW	NCBLS	10//99-12//99
Restaurant	Asheville MSA, NC	S	7.93 MW	7.83 AW	16500 AAW	NCBLS	10//99-12//99
Restaurant	Charlotte-Gastonia-Rock Hill MSA, NC-SC	S	8.98 MW	8.82 AW	18670 AAW	NCBLS	10//99-12//99
Restaurant	Fayetteville MSA, NC	S	7.70 MW	7.29 AW	16010 AAW	NCBLS	10//99-12//99
Restaurant	Goldsboro MSA, NC	S	7.30 MW	7.17 AW	15180 AAW	NCBLS	10//99-12//99
Restaurant	Greensboro--Winston-Salem--High Point MSA, NC	S	8.17 MW	7.82 AW	16990 AAW	NCBLS	10//99-12//99
Restaurant	Greenville MSA, NC	S	6.73 MW	6.39 AW	13990 AAW	NCBLS	10//99-12//99
Restaurant	Hickory-Morganton-Lenoir MSA, NC	S	8.02 MW	7.65 AW	16670 AAW	NCBLS	10//99-12//99
Restaurant	Jacksonville MSA, NC	S	7.15 MW	6.91 AW	14870 AAW	NCBLS	10//99-12//99
Restaurant	Raleigh-Durham-Chapel Hill MSA, NC	S	8.89 MW	8.69 AW	18490 AAW	NCBLS	10//99-12//99
Restaurant	Rocky Mount MSA, NC	S	7.25 MW	7.17 AW	15080 AAW	NCBLS	10//99-12//99
Restaurant	Wilmington MSA, NC	S	7.64 MW	7.45 AW	15890 AAW	NCBLS	10//99-12//99
Restaurant	North Dakota	S	7.14 MW	7.25 AW	15080 AAW	NDBLS	10//99-12//99
Restaurant	Bismarck MSA, ND	S	7.31 MW	7.24 AW	15200 AAW	NDBLS	10//99-12//99
Restaurant	Fargo-Moorhead MSA, ND-MN	S	7.75 MW	7.69 AW	16110 AAW	NDBLS	10//99-12//99
Restaurant	Grand Forks MSA, ND-MN	S	7.48 MW	7.53 AW	15560 AAW	NDBLS	10//99-12//99
Restaurant	Ohio	S	7.57 MW	7.92 AW	16460 AAW	OHBLS	10//99-12//99
Restaurant	Akron PMSA, OH	S	8.17 MW	7.92 AW	17000 AAW	OHBLS	10//99-12//99
Restaurant	Canton-Massillon MSA, OH	S	6.91 MW	6.67 AW	14360 AAW	OHBLS	10//99-12//99
Restaurant	Cincinnati PMSA, OH-KY-IN	S	8.50 MW	8.16 AW	17680 AAW	OHBLS	10//99-12//99
Restaurant	Cleveland-Lorain-Elyria PMSA, OH	S	8.41 MW	8.10 AW	17490 AAW	OHBLS	10//99-12//99
Restaurant	Columbus MSA, OH	S	8.98 MW	8.80 AW	18670 AAW	OHBLS	10//99-12//99
Restaurant	Dayton-Springfield MSA, OH	S	7.74 MW	7.51 AW	16090 AAW	OHBLS	10//99-12//99
Restaurant	Hamilton-Middletown PMSA, OH	S	7.40 MW	6.77 AW	15390 AAW	OHBLS	10//99-12//99
Restaurant	Lima MSA, OH	S	6.97 MW	6.65 AW	14500 AAW	OHBLS	10//99-12//99
Restaurant	Mansfield MSA, OH	S	7.11 MW	6.55 AW	14790 AAW	OHBLS	10//99-12//99
Restaurant	Steubenville-Weirton MSA, OH-WV	S	7.71 MW	7.29 AW	16040 AAW	OHBLS	10//99-12//99
Restaurant	Toledo MSA, OH	S	7.93 MW	7.89 AW	16500 AAW	OHBLS	10//99-12//99
Restaurant	Youngstown-Warren MSA, OH	S	6.72 MW	6.37 AW	13980 AAW	OHBLS	10//99-12//99
Restaurant	Oklahoma	S	7.05 MW	7.29 AW	15160 AAW	OKBLS	10//99-12//99

AAW	Average annual wage	AOH	Average offered, high	ASH	Average starting, high	H	Hourly
AE	Average entry wage	AOL	Average offered, low	ASL	Average starting, low	HI	Highest wage paid
AEX	Average experienced wage	APH	Average pay, high range	AW	Average wage paid	HR	High end range
AO	Average offered	APL	Average pay, low range	FQ	First quartile wage	LR	Low end range

M	Monthly	S	Special: hourly and annual
MTC	Median total compensation	TQ	Third quartile wage
MW	Median wage paid	W	Weekly
SQ	Second quartile wage	Y	Yearly

Occupation/Type/Industry	Location	Per	Low	Mid	High	Source	Date
Cook							
Restaurant	Enid MSA, OK	S	6.20 MW	6.26 AW	12890 AAW	OKBLS	10//99-12//99
Restaurant	Lawton MSA, OK	S	6.33 MW	6.07 AW	13160 AAW	OKBLS	10//99-12//99
Restaurant	Oklahoma City MSA, OK	S	8.01 MW	7.79 AW	16650 AAW	OKBLS	10//99-12//99
Restaurant	Tulsa MSA, OK	S	7.51 MW	7.47 AW	15630 AAW	OKBLS	10//99-12//99
Restaurant	Oregon	S	8.24 MW	8.48 AW	17630 AAW	ORBLS	10//99-12//99
Restaurant	Corvallis MSA, OR	S	7.93 MW	7.89 AW	16500 AAW	ORBLS	10//99-12//99
Restaurant	Eugene-Springfield MSA, OR	S	8.33 MW	8.15 AW	17320 AAW	ORBLS	10//99-12//99
Restaurant	Medford-Ashland MSA, OR	S	8.68 MW	8.58 AW	18060 AAW	ORBLS	10//99-12//99
Restaurant	Portland-Vancouver PMSA, OR-WA	S	8.71 MW	8.50 AW	18120 AAW	ORBLS	10//99-12//99
Restaurant	Salem PMSA, OR	S	8.68 MW	8.30 AW	18060 AAW	ORBLS	10//99-12//99
Restaurant	Pennsylvania	S	7.69 MW	8.07 AW	16790 AAW	PABLS	10//99-12//99
Restaurant	Allentown-Bethlehem-Easton MSA, PA	S	7.98 MW	7.79 AW	16600 AAW	PABLS	10//99-12//99
Restaurant	Altoona MSA, PA	S	7.51 MW	7.36 AW	15620 AAW	PABLS	10//99-12//99
Restaurant	Erie MSA, PA	S	6.81 MW	6.55 AW	14170 AAW	PABLS	10//99-12//99
Restaurant	Harrisburg-Lebanon-Carlisle MSA, PA	S	8.67 MW	8.17 AW	18030 AAW	PABLS	10//99-12//99
Restaurant	Johnstown MSA, PA	S	6.80 MW	6.21 AW	14140 AAW	PABLS	10//99-12//99
Restaurant	Lancaster MSA, PA	S	7.95 MW	7.62 AW	16550 AAW	PABLS	10//99-12//99
Restaurant	Philadelphia PMSA, PA-NJ	S	9.17 MW	8.88 AW	19080 AAW	PABLS	10//99-12//99
Restaurant	Pittsburgh MSA, PA	S	7.64 MW	7.45 AW	15900 AAW	PABLS	10//99-12//99
Restaurant	Reading MSA, PA	S	8.52 MW	8.21 AW	17720 AAW	PABLS	10//99-12//99
Restaurant	Scranton--Wilkes-Barre--Hazleton MSA, PA	S	8.39 MW	7.99 AW	17450 AAW	PABLS	10//99-12//99
Restaurant	Sharon MSA, PA	S	7.28 MW	7.16 AW	15140 AAW	PABLS	10//99-12//99
Restaurant	State College MSA, PA	S	7.51 MW	7.26 AW	15610 AAW	PABLS	10//99-12//99
Restaurant	Williamsport MSA, PA	S	7.47 MW	7.30 AW	15530 AAW	PABLS	10//99-12//99
Restaurant	York MSA, PA	S	7.72 MW	7.60 AW	16060 AAW	PABLS	10//99-12//99
Restaurant	Rhode Island	S	8.51 MW	9.11 AW	18950 AAW	RIBLS	10//99-12//99
Restaurant	Providence-Fall River-Warwick MSA, RI-MA	S	9.02 MW	8.41 AW	18760 AAW	RIBLS	10//99-12//99
Restaurant	South Carolina	S	7.9 MW	8.22 AW	17110 AAW	SCBLS	10//99-12//99
Restaurant	Charleston-North Charleston MSA, SC	S	8.26 MW	7.85 AW	17190 AAW	SCBLS	10//99-12//99
Restaurant	Columbia MSA, SC	S	7.92 MW	7.67 AW	16470 AAW	SCBLS	10//99-12//99
Restaurant	Florence MSA, SC	S	7.36 MW	7.46 AW	15310 AAW	SCBLS	10//99-12//99
Restaurant	Greenville-Spartanburg-Anderson MSA, SC	S	7.92 MW	7.90 AW	16480 AAW	SCBLS	10//99-12//99
Restaurant	Myrtle Beach MSA, SC	S	8.43 MW	8.16 AW	17530 AAW	SCBLS	10//99-12//99
Restaurant	Sumter MSA, SC	S	7.81 MW	7.75 AW	16240 AAW	SCBLS	10//99-12//99
Restaurant	South Dakota	S	7.8 MW	7.81 AW	16240 AAW	SDBLS	10//99-12//99
Restaurant	Rapid City MSA, SD	S	7.71 MW	7.64 AW	16040 AAW	SDBLS	10//99-12//99
Restaurant	Sioux Falls MSA, SD	S	8.40 MW	8.41 AW	17460 AAW	SDBLS	10//99-12//99
Restaurant	Tennessee	S	7.49 MW	7.77 AW	16160 AAW	TNBLS	10//99-12//99
Restaurant	Chattanooga MSA, TN-GA	S	7.62 MW	7.35 AW	15860 AAW	TNBLS	10//99-12//99
Restaurant	Clarksville-Hopkinsville MSA, TN-KY	S	8.38 MW	8.15 AW	17420 AAW	TNBLS	10//99-12//99
Restaurant	Jackson MSA, TN	S	8.02 MW	7.92 AW	16670 AAW	TNBLS	10//99-12//99
Restaurant	Johnson City-Kingsport-Bristol MSA, TN-VA	S	7.92 MW	7.88 AW	16480 AAW	TNBLS	10//99-12//99
Restaurant	Knoxville MSA, TN	S	7.21 MW	6.72 AW	15000 AAW	TNBLS	10//99-12//99
Restaurant	Memphis MSA, TN-AR-MS	S	8.51 MW	8.15 AW	17690 AAW	MSBLS	10//99-12//99
Restaurant	Nashville MSA, TN	S	8.54 MW	8.28 AW	17760 AAW	TNBLS	10//99-12//99
Restaurant	Texas	S	7.14 MW	7.42 AW	15430 AAW	TXBLS	10//99-12//99
Restaurant	Abilene MSA, TX	S	6.38 MW	6.18 AW	13280 AAW	TXBLS	10//99-12//99
Restaurant	Amarillo MSA, TX	S	8.22 MW	8.25 AW	17090 AAW	TXBLS	10//99-12//99
Restaurant	Austin-San Marcos MSA, TX	S	8.26 MW	8.01 AW	17190 AAW	TXBLS	10//99-12//99
Restaurant	Beaumont-Port Arthur MSA, TX	S	6.99 MW	6.65 AW	14540 AAW	TXBLS	10//99-12//99
Restaurant	Brazoria PMSA, TX	S	6.54 MW	6.34 AW	13610 AAW	TXBLS	10//99-12//99
Restaurant	Brownsville-Harlingen-San Benito MSA, TX	S	6.33 MW	6.09 AW	13160 AAW	TXBLS	10//99-12//99
Restaurant	Bryan-College Station MSA, TX	S	7.16 MW	6.86 AW	14900 AAW	TXBLS	10//99-12//99
Restaurant	Corpus Christi MSA, TX	S	6.67 MW	6.44 AW	13870 AAW	TXBLS	10//99-12//99
Restaurant	Dallas PMSA, TX	S	8.01 MW	7.67 AW	16650 AAW	TXBLS	10//99-12//99
Restaurant	El Paso MSA, TX	S	7.06 MW	6.82 AW	14680 AAW	TXBLS	10//99-12//99
Restaurant	Fort Worth-Arlington PMSA, TX	S	7.57 MW	7.32 AW	15750 AAW	TXBLS	10//99-12//99

AAW Average annual wage	AOH Average offered, high	ASH Average starting, high	H Hourly	M Monthly	S Special: hourly and annual
AE Average entry wage	AOL Average offered, low	ASL Average starting, low	HI Highest wage paid	MTC Median total compensation	TQ Third quartile wage
AEX Average experienced wage	APH Average pay, high range	AW Average wage paid	HR High end range	MW Median wage paid	W Weekly
AO Average offered	APL Average pay, low range	FQ First quartile wage	LR Low end range	SQ Second quartile wage	Y Yearly

Occupation/Type/Industry	Location	Per	Low	Mid	High	Source	Date
Cook							
Restaurant	Galveston-Texas City PMSA, TX	S	7.12 MW	6.83 AW	14820 AAW	TXBLS	10//99-12//99
Restaurant	Houston PMSA, TX	S	7.55 MW	7.28 AW	15700 AAW	TXBLS	10//99-12//99
Restaurant	Killeen-Temple MSA, TX	S	7.74 MW	7.56 AW	16100 AAW	TXBLS	10//99-12//99
Restaurant	Laredo MSA, TX	S	6.54 MW	6.46 AW	13600 AAW	TXBLS	10//99-12//99
Restaurant	Longview-Marshall MSA, TX	S	7.10 MW	6.67 AW	14770 AAW	TXBLS	10//99-12//99
Restaurant	Lubbock MSA, TX	S	6.62 MW	6.47 AW	13770 AAW	TXBLS	10//99-12//99
Restaurant	McAllen-Edinburg-Mission MSA, TX	S	6.64 MW	6.50 AW	13820 AAW	TXBLS	10//99-12//99
Restaurant	Odessa-Midland MSA, TX	S	7.41 MW	7.31 AW	15420 AAW	TXBLS	10//99-12//99
Restaurant	San Angelo MSA, TX	S	7.50 MW	7.43 AW	15600 AAW	TXBLS	10//99-12//99
Restaurant	San Antonio MSA, TX	S	7.42 MW	7.34 AW	15440 AAW	TXBLS	10//99-12//99
Restaurant	Sherman-Denison MSA, TX	S	7.32 MW	6.75 AW	15220 AAW	TXBLS	10//99-12//99
Restaurant	Texarkana MSA, TX-Texarkana, AR	S	7.13 MW	7.01 AW	14830 AAW	TXBLS	10//99-12//99
Restaurant	Tyler MSA, TX	S	7.09 MW	7.00 AW	14750 AAW	TXBLS	10//99-12//99
Restaurant	Victoria MSA, TX	S	7.37 MW	7.10 AW	15330 AAW	TXBLS	10//99-12//99
Restaurant	Waco MSA, TX	S	7.46 MW	7.46 AW	15520 AAW	TXBLS	10//99-12//99
Restaurant	Wichita Falls MSA, TX	S	7.39 MW	7.27 AW	15370 AAW	TXBLS	10//99-12//99
Restaurant	Utah	S	7.94 MW	8.27 AW	17200 AAW	UTBLS	10//99-12//99
Restaurant	Provo-Orem MSA, UT	S	9.45 MW	8.18 AW	19650 AAW	UTBLS	10//99-12//99
Restaurant	Salt Lake City-Ogden MSA, UT	S	8.15 MW	7.92 AW	16950 AAW	UTBLS	10//99-12//99
Restaurant	Vermont	S	9.47 MW	9.88 AW	20550 AAW	VTBLS	10//99-12//99
Restaurant	Burlington MSA, VT	S	9.30 MW	8.97 AW	19340 AAW	VTBLS	10//99-12//99
Restaurant	Virginia	S	7.93 MW	8.33 AW	17340 AAW	VABLS	10//99-12//99
Restaurant	Charlottesville MSA, VA	S	7.83 MW	7.74 AW	16290 AAW	VABLS	10//99-12//99
Restaurant	Danville MSA, VA	S	7.64 MW	7.69 AW	15900 AAW	VABLS	10//99-12//99
Restaurant	Lynchburg MSA, VA	S	7.39 MW	7.10 AW	15380 AAW	VABLS	10//99-12//99
Restaurant	Norfolk-Virginia Beach-Newport News MSA, VA-NC	S	7.55 MW	7.34 AW	15690 AAW	VABLS	10//99-12//99
Restaurant	Richmond-Petersburg MSA, VA	S	8.38 MW	8.13 AW	17430 AAW	VABLS	10//99-12//99
Restaurant	Roanoke MSA, VA	S	7.40 MW	7.31 AW	15400 AAW	VABLS	10//99-12//99
Restaurant	Washington	S	8.83 MW	9.06 AW	18840 AAW	WABLS	10//99-12//99
Restaurant	Bellingham MSA, WA	S	8.36 MW	8.05 AW	17390 AAW	WABLS	10//99-12//99
Restaurant	Bremerton PMSA, WA	S	8.25 MW	8.18 AW	17160 AAW	WABLS	10//99-12//99
Restaurant	Olympia PMSA, WA	S	8.40 MW	8.07 AW	17460 AAW	WABLS	10//99-12//99
Restaurant	Richland-Kennewick-Pasco MSA, WA	S	7.96 MW	7.85 AW	16560 AAW	WABLS	10//99-12//99
Restaurant	Seattle-Bellevue-Everett PMSA, WA	S	9.70 MW	9.55 AW	20170 AAW	WABLS	10//99-12//99
Restaurant	Spokane MSA, WA	S	8.02 MW	7.82 AW	16690 AAW	WABLS	10//99-12//99
Restaurant	Tacoma PMSA, WA	S	8.97 MW	8.84 AW	18650 AAW	WABLS	10//99-12//99
Restaurant	Yakima MSA, WA	S	7.37 MW	7.12 AW	15320 AAW	WABLS	10//99-12//99
Restaurant	West Virginia	S	6.49 MW	6.78 AW	14100 AAW	WVBLS	10//99-12//99
Restaurant	Charleston MSA, WV	S	6.89 MW	6.64 AW	14340 AAW	WVBLS	10//99-12//99
Restaurant	Huntington-Ashland MSA, WV-KY-OH	S	6.86 MW	6.42 AW	14270 AAW	WVBLS	10//99-12//99
Restaurant	Parkersburg-Marietta MSA, WV-OH	S	7.41 MW	7.16 AW	15410 AAW	WVBLS	10//99-12//99
Restaurant	Wheeling MSA, WV-OH	S	6.42 MW	6.25 AW	13360 AAW	WVBLS	10//99-12//99
Restaurant	Wisconsin	S	8 MW	8.35 AW	17370 AAW	WIBLS	10//99-12//99
Restaurant	Appleton-Oshkosh-Neenah MSA, WI	S	8.36 MW	8.11 AW	17390 AAW	WIBLS	10//99-12//99
Restaurant	Eau Claire MSA, WI	S	7.66 MW	7.56 AW	15930 AAW	WIBLS	10//99-12//99
Restaurant	Green Bay MSA, WI	S	8.83 MW	8.48 AW	18360 AAW	WIBLS	10//99-12//99
Restaurant	Janesville-Beloit MSA, WI	S	8.03 MW	7.86 AW	16700 AAW	WIBLS	10//99-12//99
Restaurant	Kenosha PMSA, WI	S	8.29 MW	8.07 AW	17250 AAW	WIBLS	10//99-12//99
Restaurant	La Crosse MSA, WI-MN	S	8.29 MW	8.13 AW	17250 AAW	WIBLS	10//99-12//99
Restaurant	Madison MSA, WI	S	8.45 MW	8.26 AW	17580 AAW	WIBLS	10//99-12//99
Restaurant	Milwaukee-Waukesha PMSA, WI	S	8.98 MW	8.79 AW	18690 AAW	WIBLS	10//99-12//99
Restaurant	Racine PMSA, WI	S	8.06 MW	7.35 AW	16760 AAW	WIBLS	10//99-12//99
Restaurant	Sheboygan MSA, WI	S	8.01 MW	7.80 AW	16660 AAW	WIBLS	10//99-12//99
Restaurant	Wausau MSA, WI	S	8.56 MW	8.57 AW	17810 AAW	WIBLS	10//99-12//99
Restaurant	Wyoming	S	7.23 MW	7.81 AW	16240 AAW	WYBLS	10//99-12//99
Restaurant	Casper MSA, WY	S	7.13 MW	6.73 AW	14820 AAW	WYBLS	10//99-12//99
Restaurant	Cheyenne MSA, WY	S	8.09 MW	8.05 AW	16830 AAW	WYBLS	10//99-12//99
Restaurant	Puerto Rico	S	6.44 MW	7.00 AW	14560 AAW	PRBLS	10//99-12//99

Occupation/Type/Industry	Location	Per	Low	Mid	High	Source	Date
Cook							
Restaurant	Aguadilla MSA, PR	S	5.76 MW	5.86 AW	11980 AAW	PRBLS	10//99-12//99
Restaurant	Mayaguez MSA, PR	S	6.19 MW	6.16 AW	12880 AAW	PRBLS	10//99-12//99
Restaurant	Ponce MSA, PR	S	6.91 MW	6.33 AW	14370 AAW	PRBLS	10//99-12//99
Restaurant	San Juan-Bayamon PMSA, PR	S	7.17 MW	6.63 AW	14920 AAW	PRBLS	10//99-12//99
Restaurant	Virgin Islands	S	10.14 MW	10.55 AW	21950 AAW	VIBLS	10//99-12//99
Restaurant	Guam	S	7.87 MW	8.76 AW	18220 AAW	GUBLS	10//99-12//99
Short Order	Alabama	S	6.58 MW	6.67 AW	13880 AAW	ALBLS	10//99-12//99
Short Order	Anniston MSA, AL	S	7.76 MW	7.81 AW	16150 AAW	ALBLS	10//99-12//99
Short Order	Auburn-Opelika MSA, AL	S	7.37 MW	7.52 AW	15340 AAW	ALBLS	10//99-12//99
Short Order	Birmingham MSA, AL	S	6.24 MW	6.22 AW	12980 AAW	ALBLS	10//99-12//99
Short Order	Decatur MSA, AL	S	8.55 MW	8.58 AW	17790 AAW	ALBLS	10//99-12//99
Short Order	Dothan MSA, AL	S	6.20 MW	6.13 AW	12890 AAW	ALBLS	10//99-12//99
Short Order	Florence MSA, AL	S	6.74 MW	6.68 AW	14020 AAW	ALBLS	10//99-12//99
Short Order	Huntsville MSA, AL	S	7.16 MW	7.16 AW	14890 AAW	ALBLS	10//99-12//99
Short Order	Mobile MSA, AL	S	7.39 MW	7.25 AW	15380 AAW	ALBLS	10//99-12//99
Short Order	Montgomery MSA, AL	S	6.83 MW	6.74 AW	14200 AAW	ALBLS	10//99-12//99
Short Order	Tuscaloosa MSA, AL	S	6.93 MW	7.01 AW	14420 AAW	ALBLS	10//99-12//99
Short Order	Alaska	S	8.33 MW	9.08 AW	18880 AAW	AKBLS	10//99-12//99
Short Order	Anchorage MSA, AK	S	9.76 MW	9.08 AW	20290 AAW	AKBLS	10//99-12//99
Short Order	Arizona	S	7.26 MW	7.28 AW	15140 AAW	AZBLS	10//99-12//99
Short Order	Flagstaff MSA, AZ-UT	S	6.79 MW	6.72 AW	14130 AAW	AZBLS	10//99-12//99
Short Order	Phoenix-Mesa MSA, AZ	S	7.61 MW	7.68 AW	15830 AAW	AZBLS	10//99-12//99
Short Order	Tucson MSA, AZ	S	7.05 MW	6.88 AW	14670 AAW	AZBLS	10//99-12//99
Short Order	Yuma MSA, AZ	S	6.31 MW	6.39 AW	13130 AAW	AZBLS	10//99-12//99
Short Order	Arkansas	S	6.11 MW	6.27 AW	13040 AAW	ARBLS	10//99-12//99
Short Order	Fort Smith MSA, AR-OK	S	6.10 MW	6.05 AW	12690 AAW	ARBLS	10//99-12//99
Short Order	Little Rock-North Little Rock MSA, AR	S	6.32 MW	6.38 AW	13150 AAW	ARBLS	10//99-12//99
Short Order	Pine Bluff MSA, AR	S	6.04 MW	5.92 AW	12570 AAW	ARBLS	10//99-12//99
Short Order	California	S	7.72 MW	8.18 AW	17010 AAW	CABLS	10//99-12//99
Short Order	Bakersfield MSA, CA	S	7.40 MW	7.16 AW	15400 AAW	CABLS	10//99-12//99
Short Order	Chico-Paradise MSA, CA	S	7.06 MW	6.70 AW	14680 AAW	CABLS	10//99-12//99
Short Order	Fresno MSA, CA	S	7.23 MW	6.72 AW	15030 AAW	CABLS	10//99-12//99
Short Order	Los Angeles-Long Beach PMSA, CA	S	8.65 MW	8.36 AW	18000 AAW	CABLS	10//99-12//99
Short Order	Merced MSA, CA	S	8.70 MW	9.05 AW	18110 AAW	CABLS	10//99-12//99
Short Order	Oakland PMSA, CA	S	8.47 MW	8.27 AW	17610 AAW	CABLS	10//99-12//99
Short Order	Orange County PMSA, CA	S	7.58 MW	7.03 AW	15760 AAW	CABLS	10//99-12//99
Short Order	Riverside-San Bernardino PMSA, CA	S	7.79 MW	6.87 AW	16210 AAW	CABLS	10//99-12//99
Short Order	Sacramento PMSA, CA	S	7.93 MW	6.87 AW	16500 AAW	CABLS	10//99-12//99
Short Order	Salinas MSA, CA	S	8.31 MW	7.87 AW	17290 AAW	CABLS	10//99-12//99
Short Order	San Diego MSA, CA	S	7.72 MW	6.83 AW	16060 AAW	CABLS	10//99-12//99
Short Order	San Francisco PMSA, CA	S	8.31 MW	7.76 AW	17290 AAW	CABLS	10//99-12//99
Short Order	San Jose PMSA, CA	S	9.28 MW	8.51 AW	19310 AAW	CABLS	10//99-12//99
Short Order	San Luis Obispo-Atascadero-Paso Robles MSA, CA	S	7.63 MW	7.69 AW	15880 AAW	CABLS	10//99-12//99
Short Order	Santa Barbara-Santa Maria-Lompoc MSA, CA	S	8.83 MW	8.68 AW	18370 AAW	CABLS	10//99-12//99
Short Order	Santa Cruz-Watsonville PMSA, CA	S	9.16 MW	9.25 AW	19050 AAW	CABLS	10//99-12//99
Short Order	Santa Rosa PMSA, CA	S	7.96 MW	7.72 AW	16550 AAW	CABLS	10//99-12//99
Short Order	Stockton-Lodi MSA, CA	S	7.89 MW	6.74 AW	16400 AAW	CABLS	10//99-12//99
Short Order	Vallejo-Fairfield-Napa PMSA, CA	S	8.77 MW	8.56 AW	18250 AAW	CABLS	10//99-12//99
Short Order	Ventura PMSA, CA	S	8.86 MW	8.57 AW	18430 AAW	CABLS	10//99-12//99
Short Order	Visalia-Tulare-Porterville MSA, CA	S	7.36 MW	6.80 AW	15300 AAW	CABLS	10//99-12//99
Short Order	Yolo PMSA, CA	S	8.81 MW	9.10 AW	18330 AAW	CABLS	10//99-12//99
Short Order	Yuba City MSA, CA	S	7.48 MW	6.65 AW	15550 AAW	CABLS	10//99-12//99
Short Order	Colorado	S	7.9 MW	7.99 AW	16620 AAW	COBLS	10//99-12//99
Short Order	Colorado Springs MSA, CO	S	7.45 MW	7.68 AW	15500 AAW	COBLS	10//99-12//99
Short Order	Denver PMSA, CO	S	8.18 MW	8.10 AW	17020 AAW	COBLS	10//99-12//99
Short Order	Grand Junction MSA, CO	S	7.72 MW	7.82 AW	16050 AAW	COBLS	10//99-12//99
Short Order	Greeley PMSA, CO	S	8.07 MW	8.12 AW	16790 AAW	COBLS	10//99-12//99
Short Order	Pueblo MSA, CO	S	7.34 MW	7.25 AW	15260 AAW	COBLS	10//99-12//99
Short Order	Connecticut	S	8.24 MW	8.69 AW	18080 AAW	CTBLS	10//99-12//99
Short Order	Bridgeport PMSA, CT	S	8.08 MW	7.67 AW	16810 AAW	CTBLS	10//99-12//99
Short Order	Danbury PMSA, CT	S	7.79 MW	6.77 AW	16210 AAW	CTBLS	10//99-12//99
Short Order	Hartford MSA, CT	S	8.94 MW	8.38 AW	18600 AAW	CTBLS	10//99-12//99

AAW	Average annual wage	**AOH**	Average offered, high	**ASH**	Average starting, high	**H**	Hourly	**M**	Monthly	**S**	Special: hourly and annual
AE	Average entry wage	**AOL**	Average offered, low	**ASL**	Average starting, low	**HI**	Highest wage paid	**MTC**	Median total compensation	**TQ**	Third quartile wage
AEX	Average experienced wage	**APH**	Average pay, high range	**AW**	Average wage paid	**HR**	High end range	**MW**	Median wage paid	**W**	Weekly
AO	Average offered	**APL**	Average pay, low range	**FQ**	First quartile wage	**LR**	Low end range	**SQ**	Second quartile wage	**Y**	Yearly

Occupation/Type/Industry	Location	Per	Low	Mid	High	Source	Date
Cook							
Short Order	New Haven-Meriden PMSA, CT	S	9.59 MW	8.97 AW	19940 AAW	CTBLS	10//99-12//99
Short Order	New London-Norwich MSA, CT-RI	S	9.59 MW	9.35 AW	19950 AAW	CTBLS	10//99-12//99
Short Order	Stamford-Norwalk PMSA, CT	S	8.38 MW	8.72 AW	17430 AAW	CTBLS	10//99-12//99
Short Order	Waterbury PMSA, CT	S	8.76 MW	8.33 AW	18220 AAW	CTBLS	10//99-12//99
Short Order	Delaware	S	7.41 MW	8.04 AW	16720 AAW	DEBLS	10//99-12//99
Short Order	Dover MSA, DE	S	7.68 MW	7.00 AW	15970 AAW	DEBLS	10//99-12//99
Short Order	Wilmington-Newark PMSA, DE-MD	S	7.91 MW	7.44 AW	16440 AAW	DEBLS	10//99-12//99
Short Order	District of Columbia	S	9.18 MW	9.70 AW	20170 AAW	DCBLS	10//99-12//99
Short Order	Washington PMSA, DC-MD-VA-WV	S	8.75 MW	8.26 AW	18190 AAW	DCBLS	10//99-12//99
Short Order	Florida	S	7.83 MW	8.02 AW	16690 AAW	FLBLS	10//99-12//99
Short Order	Daytona Beach MSA, FL	S	6.79 MW	6.87 AW	14120 AAW	FLBLS	10//99-12//99
Short Order	Fort Lauderdale PMSA, FL	S	7.76 MW	7.50 AW	16140 AAW	FLBLS	10//99-12//99
Short Order	Fort Myers-Cape Coral MSA, FL	S	10.49 MW	11.10 AW	21820 AAW	FLBLS	10//99-12//99
Short Order	Fort Pierce-Port St. Lucie MSA, FL	S	8.08 MW	7.85 AW	16810 AAW	FLBLS	10//99-12//99
Short Order	Gainesville MSA, FL	S	6.39 MW	6.10 AW	13280 AAW	FLBLS	10//99-12//99
Short Order	Jacksonville MSA, FL	S	7.56 MW	7.60 AW	15730 AAW	FLBLS	10//99-12//99
Short Order	Lakeland-Winter Haven MSA, FL	S	6.76 MW	6.49 AW	14050 AAW	FLBLS	10//99-12//99
Short Order	Melbourne-Titusville-Palm Bay MSA, FL	S	7.46 MW	7.55 AW	15520 AAW	FLBLS	10//99-12//99
Short Order	Miami PMSA, FL	S	7.62 MW	7.52 AW	15840 AAW	FLBLS	10//99-12//99
Short Order	Naples MSA, FL	S	9.32 MW	9.33 AW	19390 AAW	FLBLS	10//99-12//99
Short Order	Ocala MSA, FL	S	8.21 MW	7.79 AW	17080 AAW	FLBLS	10//99-12//99
Short Order	Orlando MSA, FL	S	8.48 MW	8.19 AW	17640 AAW	FLBLS	10//99-12//99
Short Order	Panama City MSA, FL	S	8.12 MW	7.30 AW	16890 AAW	FLBLS	10//99-12//99
Short Order	Pensacola MSA, FL	S	6.48 MW	6.32 AW	13470 AAW	FLBLS	10//99-12//99
Short Order	Punta Gorda MSA, FL	S	7.37 MW	7.40 AW	15330 AAW	FLBLS	10//99-12//99
Short Order	Sarasota-Bradenton MSA, FL	S	8.56 MW	9.21 AW	17810 AAW	FLBLS	10//99-12//99
Short Order	Tallahassee MSA, FL	S	7.75 MW	8.60 AW	16130 AAW	FLBLS	10//99-12//99
Short Order	Tampa-St. Petersburg-Clearwater MSA, FL	S	8.15 MW	8.04 AW	16960 AAW	FLBLS	10//99-12//99
Short Order	West Palm Beach-Boca Raton MSA, FL	S	9.06 MW	8.84 AW	18850 AAW	FLBLS	10//99-12//99
Short Order	Georgia	S	7.43 MW	7.63 AW	15870 AAW	GABLS	10//99-12//99
Short Order	Albany MSA, GA	S	6.84 MW	6.64 AW	14220 AAW	GABLS	10//99-12//99
Short Order	Athens MSA, GA	S	7.25 MW	7.13 AW	15080 AAW	GABLS	10//99-12//99
Short Order	Atlanta MSA, GA	S	8.36 MW	8.10 AW	17380 AAW	GABLS	10//99-12//99
Short Order	Augusta-Aiken MSA, GA-SC	S	6.49 MW	6.07 AW	13500 AAW	GABLS	10//99-12//99
Short Order	Columbus MSA, GA-AL	S	6.95 MW	6.56 AW	14450 AAW	GABLS	10//99-12//99
Short Order	Macon MSA, GA	S	7.58 MW	7.56 AW	15760 AAW	GABLS	10//99-12//99
Short Order	Savannah MSA, GA	S	6.89 MW	6.81 AW	14320 AAW	GABLS	10//99-12//99
Short Order	Hawaii	S	9.02 MW	9.32 AW	19390 AAW	HIBLS	10//99-12//99
Short Order	Honolulu MSA, HI	S	9.12 MW	8.85 AW	18960 AAW	HIBLS	10//99-12//99
Short Order	Idaho	S	7.4 MW	7.62 AW	15860 AAW	IDBLS	10//99-12//99
Short Order	Boise City MSA, ID	S	8.11 MW	8.15 AW	16860 AAW	IDBLS	10//99-12//99
Short Order	Pocatello MSA, ID	S	6.88 MW	6.86 AW	14300 AAW	IDBLS	10//99-12//99
Short Order	Illinois	S	6.52 MW	6.93 AW	14420 AAW	ILBLS	10//99-12//99
Short Order	Bloomington-Normal MSA, IL	S	6.90 MW	6.33 AW	14350 AAW	ILBLS	10//99-12//99
Short Order	Champaign-Urbana MSA, IL	S	6.26 MW	6.30 AW	13030 AAW	ILBLS	10//99-12//99
Short Order	Chicago PMSA, IL	S	7.29 MW	6.92 AW	15170 AAW	ILBLS	10//99-12//99
Short Order	Decatur MSA, IL	S	6.52 MW	6.43 AW	13550 AAW	ILBLS	10//99-12//99
Short Order	Kankakee PMSA, IL	S	6.82 MW	6.08 AW	14180 AAW	ILBLS	10//99-12//99
Short Order	Peoria-Pekin MSA, IL	S	6.23 MW	6.02 AW	12950 AAW	ILBLS	10//99-12//99
Short Order	Rockford MSA, IL	S	6.44 MW	5.94 AW	13390 AAW	ILBLS	10//99-12//99
Short Order	Springfield MSA, IL	S	6.80 MW	6.74 AW	14150 AAW	ILBLS	10//99-12//99
Short Order	Indiana	S	6.6 MW	6.85 AW	14260 AAW	INBLS	10//99-12//99
Short Order	Bloomington MSA, IN	S	6.50 MW	6.39 AW	13520 AAW	INBLS	10//99-12//99
Short Order	Elkhart-Goshen MSA, IN	S	10.00 MW	8.31 AW	20800 AAW	INBLS	10//99-12//99
Short Order	Evansville-Henderson MSA, IN-KY	S	6.08 MW	5.98 AW	12650 AAW	INBLS	10//99-12//99
Short Order	Fort Wayne MSA, IN	S	7.70 MW	7.13 AW	16030 AAW	INBLS	10//99-12//99
Short Order	Gary PMSA, IN	S	6.51 MW	6.24 AW	13530 AAW	INBLS	10//99-12//99
Short Order	Indianapolis MSA, IN	S	6.97 MW	6.80 AW	14500 AAW	INBLS	10//99-12//99
Short Order	Kokomo MSA, IN	S	8.04 MW	7.92 AW	16720 AAW	INBLS	10//99-12//99
Short Order	Muncie MSA, IN	S	6.47 MW	6.28 AW	13470 AAW	INBLS	10//99-12//99

Cook

Occupation/Type/Industry	Location	Per	Low	Mid	High	Source	Date
Cook							
Short Order	South Bend MSA, IN	S	6.20 MW	6.31 AW	12900 AAW	INBLS	10//99-12//99
Short Order	Terre Haute MSA, IN	S	6.91 MW	6.85 AW	14380 AAW	INBLS	10//99-12//99
Short Order	Iowa	S	6.46 MW	6.87 AW	14280 AAW	IABLS	10//99-12//99
Short Order	Cedar Rapids MSA, IA	S	6.63 MW	6.15 AW	13780 AAW	IABLS	10//99-12//99
Short Order	Davenport-Moline-Rock Island MSA, IA-IL	S	7.16 MW	7.13 AW	14890 AAW	IABLS	10//99-12//99
Short Order	Des Moines MSA, IA	S	8.13 MW	7.29 AW	16910 AAW	IABLS	10//99-12//99
Short Order	Dubuque MSA, IA	S	8.11 MW	7.90 AW	16880 AAW	IABLS	10//99-12//99
Short Order	Sioux City MSA, IA-NE	S	6.72 MW	6.47 AW	13980 AAW	IABLS	10//99-12//99
Short Order	Kansas	S	7.3 MW	7.45 AW	15490 AAW	KSBLS	10//99-12//99
Short Order	Lawrence MSA, KS	S	8.05 MW	8.17 AW	16740 AAW	KSBLS	10//99-12//99
Short Order	Wichita MSA, KS	S	7.17 MW	7.11 AW	14910 AAW	KSBLS	10//99-12//99
Short Order	Kentucky	S	6.95 MW	7.21 AW	14990 AAW	KYBLS	10//99-12//99
Short Order	Lexington MSA, KY	S	7.62 MW	7.54 AW	15860 AAW	KYBLS	10//99-12//99
Short Order	Louisville MSA, KY-IN	S	6.86 MW	6.56 AW	14270 AAW	KYBLS	10//99-12//99
Short Order	Louisiana	S	6.19 MW	6.61 AW	13750 AAW	LABLS	10//99-12//99
Short Order	Alexandria MSA, LA	S	6.57 MW	6.32 AW	13670 AAW	LABLS	10//99-12//99
Short Order	Baton Rouge MSA, LA	S	6.84 MW	6.87 AW	14230 AAW	LABLS	10//99-12//99
Short Order	Houma MSA, LA	S	5.90 MW	6.10 AW	12270 AAW	LABLS	10//99-12//99
Short Order	Lafayette MSA, LA	S	5.99 MW	5.85 AW	12460 AAW	LABLS	10//99-12//99
Short Order	Lake Charles MSA, LA	S	6.37 MW	6.07 AW	13260 AAW	LABLS	10//99-12//99
Short Order	Monroe MSA, LA	S	6.37 MW	6.13 AW	13250 AAW	LABLS	10//99-12//99
Short Order	New Orleans MSA, LA	S	7.83 MW	7.85 AW	16290 AAW	LABLS	10//99-12//99
Short Order	Shreveport-Bossier City MSA, LA	S	6.74 MW	6.62 AW	14030 AAW	LABLS	10//99-12//99
Short Order	Maine	S	7.13 MW	7.30 AW	15190 AAW	MEBLS	10//99-12//99
Short Order	Bangor MSA, ME	S	7.09 MW	6.94 AW	14750 AAW	MEBLS	10//99-12//99
Short Order	Lewiston-Auburn MSA, ME	S	7.08 MW	7.00 AW	14730 AAW	MEBLS	10//99-12//99
Short Order	Portland MSA, ME	S	8.03 MW	7.99 AW	16690 AAW	MEBLS	10//99-12//99
Short Order	Maryland	S	7.53 MW	7.56 AW	15720 AAW	MDBLS	10//99-12//99
Short Order	Baltimore PMSA, MD	S	7.73 MW	7.67 AW	16090 AAW	MDBLS	10//99-12//99
Short Order	Cumberland MSA, MD-WV	S	6.09 MW	6.20 AW	12660 AAW	MDBLS	10//99-12//99
Short Order	Hagerstown PMSA, MD	S	6.95 MW	6.69 AW	14460 AAW	MDBLS	10//99-12//99
Short Order	Massachusetts	S	8.5 MW	8.78 AW	18250 AAW	MABLS	10//99-12//99
Short Order	Barnstable-Yarmouth MSA, MA	S	10.52 MW	10.35 AW	21890 AAW	MABLS	10//99-12//99
Short Order	Boston PMSA, MA-NH	S	8.80 MW	8.64 AW	18290 AAW	MABLS	10//99-12//99
Short Order	Brockton PMSA, MA	S	9.52 MW	9.77 AW	19810 AAW	MABLS	10//99-12//99
Short Order	Lawrence PMSA, MA-NH	S	7.92 MW	7.11 AW	16470 AAW	MABLS	10//99-12//99
Short Order	Lowell PMSA, MA-NH	S	9.73 MW	9.72 AW	20230 AAW	MABLS	10//99-12//99
Short Order	New Bedford PMSA, MA	S	9.53 MW	8.87 AW	19820 AAW	MABLS	10//99-12//99
Short Order	Pittsfield MSA, MA	S	8.50 MW	8.41 AW	17670 AAW	MABLS	10//99-12//99
Short Order	Springfield MSA, MA	S	9.26 MW	8.47 AW	19260 AAW	MABLS	10//99-12//99
Short Order	Worcester PMSA, MA-CT	S	8.42 MW	7.90 AW	17510 AAW	MABLS	10//99-12//99
Short Order	Michigan	S	7.42 MW	7.75 AW	16110 AAW	MIBLS	10//99-12//99
Short Order	Ann Arbor PMSA, MI	S	8.06 MW	8.35 AW	16770 AAW	MIBLS	10//99-12//99
Short Order	Benton Harbor MSA, MI	S	7.58 MW	6.94 AW	15760 AAW	MIBLS	10//99-12//99
Short Order	Detroit PMSA, MI	S	8.51 MW	8.19 AW	17710 AAW	MIBLS	10//99-12//99
Short Order	Flint PMSA, MI	S	7.81 MW	7.39 AW	16250 AAW	MIBLS	10//99-12//99
Short Order	Grand Rapids-Muskegon-Holland MSA, MI	S	7.11 MW	6.72 AW	14790 AAW	MIBLS	10//99-12//99
Short Order	Jackson MSA, MI	S	7.39 MW	7.25 AW	15380 AAW	MIBLS	10//99-12//99
Short Order	Kalamazoo-Battle Creek MSA, MI	S	7.12 MW	7.17 AW	14810 AAW	MIBLS	10//99-12//99
Short Order	Lansing-East Lansing MSA, MI	S	6.43 MW	5.92 AW	13380 AAW	MIBLS	10//99-12//99
Short Order	Saginaw-Bay City-Midland MSA, MI	S	7.06 MW	6.81 AW	14680 AAW	MIBLS	10//99-12//99
Short Order	Minnesota	S	7.87 MW	8.03 AW	16690 AAW	MNBLS	10//99-12//99
Short Order	Duluth-Superior MSA, MN-WI	S	7.16 MW	6.96 AW	14880 AAW	MNBLS	10//99-12//99
Short Order	Minneapolis-St. Paul MSA, MN-WI	S	8.73 MW	8.77 AW	18150 AAW	MNBLS	10//99-12//99
Short Order	Rochester MSA, MN	S	7.59 MW	7.66 AW	15780 AAW	MNBLS	10//99-12//99
Short Order	St. Cloud MSA, MN	S	7.44 MW	7.25 AW	15470 AAW	MNBLS	10//99-12//99
Short Order	Mississippi	S	6.64 MW	6.79 AW	14120 AAW	MSBLS	10//99-12//99
Short Order	Biloxi-Gulfport-Pascagoula MSA, MS	S	7.21 MW	7.22 AW	15000 AAW	MSBLS	10//99-12//99
Short Order	Hattiesburg MSA, MS	S	6.13 MW	6.03 AW	12760 AAW	MSBLS	10//99-12//99
Short Order	Jackson MSA, MS	S	7.36 MW	7.19 AW	15300 AAW	MSBLS	10//99-12//99
Short Order	Missouri	S	6.85 MW	6.94 AW	14440 AAW	MOBLS	10//99-12//99
Short Order	Joplin MSA, MO	S	6.70 MW	6.52 AW	13930 AAW	MOBLS	10//99-12//99
Short Order	Kansas City MSA, MO-KS	S	7.59 MW	7.66 AW	15800 AAW	MOBLS	10//99-12//99

AAW	Average annual wage	AOH	Average offered, high	ASH	Average starting, high	H	Hourly	M	Monthly	S	Special: hourly and annual
AE	Average entry wage	AOL	Average offered, low	ASL	Average starting, low	HI	Highest wage paid	MTC	Median total compensation	TQ	Third quartile wage
AEX	Average experienced wage	APH	Average pay, high range	AW	Average wage paid	HR	High end range	MW	Median wage paid	W	Weekly
AO	Average offered	APL	Average pay, low range	FQ	First quartile wage	LR	Low end range	SQ	Second quartile wage	Y	Yearly

322

Cook

Occupation/Type/Industry	Location	Per	Low	Mid	High	Source	Date
Short Order	Montana	S	6.49 MW	6.59 AW	13710 AAW	MTBLS	10//99-12//99
Short Order	Billings MSA, MT	S	7.28 MW	7.35 AW	15130 AAW	MTBLS	10//99-12//99
Short Order	Great Falls MSA, MT	S	6.44 MW	6.47 AW	13390 AAW	MTBLS	10//99-12//99
Short Order	Nebraska	S	6.31 MW	6.42 AW	13350 AAW	NEBLS	10//99-12//99
Short Order	Lincoln MSA, NE	S	7.23 MW	7.38 AW	15050 AAW	NEBLS	10//99-12//99
Short Order	Omaha MSA, NE-IA	S	6.52 MW	6.38 AW	13570 AAW	NEBLS	10//99-12//99
Short Order	Nevada	S	8.71 MW	9.08 AW	18890 AAW	NVBLS	10//99-12//99
Short Order	Las Vegas MSA, NV-AZ	S	9.18 MW	8.90 AW	19100 AAW	NVBLS	10//99-12//99
Short Order	Reno MSA, NV	S	8.30 MW	8.13 AW	17260 AAW	NVBLS	10//99-12//99
Short Order	New Hampshire	S	7.41 MW	7.53 AW	15660 AAW	NHBLS	10//99-12//99
Short Order	Manchester PMSA, NH	S	7.62 MW	7.44 AW	15860 AAW	NHBLS	10//99-12//99
Short Order	Nashua PMSA, NH	S	7.10 MW	7.15 AW	14770 AAW	NHBLS	10//99-12//99
Short Order	Portsmouth-Rochester PMSA, NH-ME	S	8.64 MW	8.65 AW	17970 AAW	NHBLS	10//99-12//99
Short Order	New Jersey	S	6.91 MW	7.71 AW	16040 AAW	NJBLS	10//99-12//99
Short Order	Atlantic-Cape May PMSA, NJ	S	8.48 MW	7.95 AW	17640 AAW	NJBLS	10//99-12//99
Short Order	Bergen-Passaic PMSA, NJ	S	7.48 MW	6.84 AW	15570 AAW	NJBLS	10//99-12//99
Short Order	Jersey City PMSA, NJ	S	8.24 MW	8.10 AW	17140 AAW	NJBLS	10//99-12//99
Short Order	Middlesex-Somerset-Hunterdon PMSA, NJ	S	7.93 MW	7.53 AW	16490 AAW	NJBLS	10//99-12//99
Short Order	Monmouth-Ocean PMSA, NJ	S	7.66 MW	7.25 AW	15940 AAW	NJBLS	10//99-12//99
Short Order	Newark PMSA, NJ	S	7.78 MW	6.86 AW	16190 AAW	NJBLS	10//99-12//99
Short Order	Vineland-Millville-Bridgeton PMSA, NJ	S	6.89 MW	6.73 AW	14340 AAW	NJBLS	10//99-12//99
Short Order	New Mexico	S	6.57 MW	6.84 AW	14230 AAW	NMBLS	10//99-12//99
Short Order	Albuquerque MSA, NM	S	6.95 MW	6.78 AW	14450 AAW	NMBLS	10//99-12//99
Short Order	Las Cruces MSA, NM	S	6.92 MW	6.37 AW	14400 AAW	NMBLS	10//99-12//99
Short Order	Santa Fe MSA, NM	S	8.06 MW	8.03 AW	16760 AAW	NMBLS	10//99-12//99
Short Order	New York	S	7.26 MW	7.68 AW	15980 AAW	NYBLS	10//99-12//99
Short Order	Albany-Schenectady-Troy MSA, NY	S	8.28 MW	8.48 AW	17220 AAW	NYBLS	10//99-12//99
Short Order	Binghamton MSA, NY	S	6.93 MW	6.74 AW	14410 AAW	NYBLS	10//99-12//99
Short Order	Buffalo-Niagara Falls MSA, NY	S	6.46 MW	6.38 AW	13430 AAW	NYBLS	10//99-12//99
Short Order	Dutchess County PMSA, NY	S	7.73 MW	7.27 AW	16070 AAW	NYBLS	10//99-12//99
Short Order	Elmira MSA, NY	S	8.54 MW	8.33 AW	17770 AAW	NYBLS	10//99-12//99
Short Order	Glens Falls MSA, NY	S	6.78 MW	6.74 AW	14100 AAW	NYBLS	10//99-12//99
Short Order	Jamestown MSA, NY	S	7.26 MW	7.26 AW	15110 AAW	NYBLS	10//99-12//99
Short Order	Nassau-Suffolk PMSA, NY	S	7.13 MW	6.53 AW	14840 AAW	NYBLS	10//99-12//99
Short Order	New York PMSA, NY	S	8.55 MW	8.11 AW	17780 AAW	NYBLS	10//99-12//99
Short Order	Newburgh PMSA, NY-PA	S	8.01 MW	6.86 AW	16660 AAW	NYBLS	10//99-12//99
Short Order	Rochester MSA, NY	S	7.60 MW	7.54 AW	15800 AAW	NYBLS	10//99-12//99
Short Order	Syracuse MSA, NY	S	6.47 MW	6.17 AW	13450 AAW	NYBLS	10//99-12//99
Short Order	Utica-Rome MSA, NY	S	6.82 MW	6.50 AW	14180 AAW	NYBLS	10//99-12//99
Short Order	North Carolina	S	6.96 MW	7.09 AW	14740 AAW	NCBLS	10//99-12//99
Short Order	Asheville MSA, NC	S	7.38 MW	7.33 AW	15340 AAW	NCBLS	10//99-12//99
Short Order	Charlotte-Gastonia-Rock Hill MSA, NC-SC	S	6.87 MW	6.80 AW	14280 AAW	NCBLS	10//99-12//99
Short Order	Fayetteville MSA, NC	S	7.06 MW	7.15 AW	14690 AAW	NCBLS	10//99-12//99
Short Order	Greensboro--Winston-Salem--High Point MSA, NC	S	8.97 MW	8.44 AW	18650 AAW	NCBLS	10//99-12//99
Short Order	Greenville MSA, NC	S	7.17 MW	7.44 AW	14920 AAW	NCBLS	10//99-12//99
Short Order	Hickory-Morganton-Lenoir MSA, NC	S	7.69 MW	7.68 AW	15990 AAW	NCBLS	10//99-12//99
Short Order	Jacksonville MSA, NC	S	5.70 MW	5.82 AW	11860 AAW	NCBLS	10//99-12//99
Short Order	Raleigh-Durham-Chapel Hill MSA, NC	S	7.56 MW	7.70 AW	15730 AAW	NCBLS	10//99-12//99
Short Order	Wilmington MSA, NC	S	6.92 MW	6.70 AW	14400 AAW	NCBLS	10//99-12//99
Short Order	North Dakota	S	6.75 MW	6.98 AW	14530 AAW	NDBLS	10//99-12//99
Short Order	Bismarck MSA, ND	S	7.06 MW	6.97 AW	14690 AAW	NDBLS	10//99-12//99
Short Order	Fargo-Moorhead MSA, ND-MN	S	7.66 MW	7.45 AW	15940 AAW	NDBLS	10//99-12//99
Short Order	Grand Forks MSA, ND-MN	S	7.40 MW	7.02 AW	15400 AAW	NDBLS	10//99-12//99
Short Order	Ohio	S	7.01 MW	7.36 AW	15310 AAW	OHBLS	10//99-12//99
Short Order	Akron PMSA, OH	S	7.37 MW	7.41 AW	15330 AAW	OHBLS	10//99-12//99
Short Order	Canton-Massillon MSA, OH	S	6.55 MW	6.41 AW	13620 AAW	OHBLS	10//99-12//99
Short Order	Cincinnati PMSA, OH-KY-IN	S	7.87 MW	7.68 AW	16360 AAW	OHBLS	10//99-12//99
Short Order	Cleveland-Lorain-Elyria PMSA, OH	S	8.11 MW	7.82 AW	16870 AAW	OHBLS	10//99-12//99
Short Order	Columbus MSA, OH	S	7.52 MW	7.06 AW	15630 AAW	OHBLS	10//99-12//99
Short Order	Dayton-Springfield MSA, OH	S	7.07 MW	6.63 AW	14700 AAW	OHBLS	10//99-12//99

AAW Average annual wage	**AOH** Average offered, high	**ASH** Average starting, high	**H** Hourly	**M** Monthly	**S** Special: hourly and annual
AE Average entry wage	**AOL** Average offered, low	**ASL** Average starting, low	**HI** Highest wage paid	**MTC** Median total compensation	**TQ** Third quartile wage
AEX Average experienced wage	**APH** Average pay, high range	**AW** Average wage paid	**HR** High end range	**MW** Median wage paid	**W** Weekly
AO Average offered	**APL** Average pay, low range	**FQ** First quartile wage	**LR** Low end range	**SQ** Second quartile wage	**Y** Yearly

Cook

Occupation/Type/Industry	Location	Per	Low	Mid	High	Source	Date
Short Order	Hamilton-Middletown PMSA, OH	S	6.91 MW	6.91 AW	14370 AAW	OHBLS	10//99-12//99
Short Order	Mansfield MSA, OH	S	7.36 MW	6.65 AW	15300 AAW	OHBLS	10//99-12//99
Short Order	Steubenville-Weirton MSA, OH-WV	S	6.51 MW	6.44 AW	13540 AAW	OHBLS	10//99-12//99
Short Order	Toledo MSA, OH	S	6.66 MW	6.42 AW	13850 AAW	OHBLS	10//99-12//99
Short Order	Youngstown-Warren MSA, OH	S	6.56 MW	6.40 AW	13650 AAW	OHBLS	10//99-12//99
Short Order	Oklahoma	S	6.35 MW	6.66 AW	13850 AAW	OKBLS	10//99-12//99
Short Order	Enid MSA, OK	S	6.83 MW	6.48 AW	14210 AAW	OKBLS	10//99-12//99
Short Order	Lawton MSA, OK	S	6.72 MW	6.04 AW	13970 AAW	OKBLS	10//99-12//99
Short Order	Oklahoma City MSA, OK	S	6.53 MW	6.42 AW	13580 AAW	OKBLS	10//99-12//99
Short Order	Tulsa MSA, OK	S	7.16 MW	6.91 AW	14900 AAW	OKBLS	10//99-12//99
Short Order	Oregon	S	8.02 MW	8.16 AW	16970 AAW	ORBLS	10//99-12//99
Short Order	Eugene-Springfield MSA, OR	S	8.00 MW	7.83 AW	16650 AAW	ORBLS	10//99-12//99
Short Order	Portland-Vancouver PMSA, OR-WA	S	8.24 MW	8.10 AW	17150 AAW	ORBLS	10//99-12//99
Short Order	Pennsylvania	S	7.16 MW	7.38 AW	15350 AAW	PABLS	10//99-12//99
Short Order	Allentown-Bethlehem-Easton MSA, PA	S	7.56 MW	7.51 AW	15730 AAW	PABLS	10//99-12//99
Short Order	Altoona MSA, PA	S	6.72 MW	6.73 AW	13980 AAW	PABLS	10//99-12//99
Short Order	Erie MSA, PA	S	8.33 MW	8.02 AW	17330 AAW	PABLS	10//99-12//99
Short Order	Harrisburg-Lebanon-Carlisle MSA, PA	S	7.22 MW	7.12 AW	15020 AAW	PABLS	10//99-12//99
Short Order	Johnstown MSA, PA	S	6.11 MW	5.94 AW	12720 AAW	PABLS	10//99-12//99
Short Order	Lancaster MSA, PA	S	7.61 MW	7.21 AW	15840 AAW	PABLS	10//99-12//99
Short Order	Philadelphia PMSA, PA-NJ	S	7.97 MW	7.59 AW	16580 AAW	PABLS	10//99-12//99
Short Order	Pittsburgh MSA, PA	S	6.70 MW	6.49 AW	13940 AAW	PABLS	10//99-12//99
Short Order	Reading MSA, PA	S	7.64 MW	7.68 AW	15880 AAW	PABLS	10//99-12//99
Short Order	Scranton--Wilkes-Barre--Hazleton MSA, PA	S	7.10 MW	6.93 AW	14760 AAW	PABLS	10//99-12//99
Short Order	State College MSA, PA	S	7.70 MW	7.87 AW	16020 AAW	PABLS	10//99-12//99
Short Order	Williamsport MSA, PA	S	8.39 MW	7.92 AW	17440 AAW	PABLS	10//99-12//99
Short Order	York MSA, PA	S	7.39 MW	7.29 AW	15380 AAW	PABLS	10//99-12//99
Short Order	Rhode Island	S	6.79 MW	7.61 AW	15820 AAW	RIBLS	10//99-12//99
Short Order	Providence-Fall River-Warwick MSA, RI-MA	S	7.13 MW	6.59 AW	14840 AAW	RIBLS	10//99-12//99
Short Order	South Carolina	S	7.09 MW	7.18 AW	14940 AAW	SCBLS	10//99-12//99
Short Order	Charleston-North Charleston MSA, SC	S	8.12 MW	7.77 AW	16890 AAW	SCBLS	10//99-12//99
Short Order	Columbia MSA, SC	S	7.06 MW	6.99 AW	14680 AAW	SCBLS	10//99-12//99
Short Order	Florence MSA, SC	S	6.59 MW	6.57 AW	13700 AAW	SCBLS	10//99-12//99
Short Order	Greenville-Spartanburg-Anderson MSA, SC	S	7.18 MW	7.19 AW	14940 AAW	SCBLS	10//99-12//99
Short Order	Myrtle Beach MSA, SC	S	7.40 MW	7.25 AW	15400 AAW	SCBLS	10//99-12//99
Short Order	Sumter MSA, SC	S	6.11 MW	5.90 AW	12700 AAW	SCBLS	10//99-12//99
Short Order	South Dakota	S	6.85 MW	6.96 AW	14480 AAW	SDBLS	10//99-12//99
Short Order	Sioux Falls MSA, SD	S	7.67 MW	7.70 AW	15960 AAW	SDBLS	10//99-12//99
Short Order	Tennessee	S	6.94 MW	7.11 AW	14790 AAW	TNBLS	10//99-12//99
Short Order	Chattanooga MSA, TN-GA	S	6.67 MW	6.63 AW	13870 AAW	TNBLS	10//99-12//99
Short Order	Clarksville-Hopkinsville MSA, TN-KY	S	6.39 MW	6.35 AW	13280 AAW	TNBLS	10//99-12//99
Short Order	Jackson MSA, TN	S	7.47 MW	7.45 AW	15530 AAW	TNBLS	10//99-12//99
Short Order	Johnson City-Kingsport-Bristol MSA, TN-VA	S	7.24 MW	7.23 AW	15050 AAW	TNBLS	10//99-12//99
Short Order	Knoxville MSA, TN	S	7.63 MW	7.62 AW	15860 AAW	TNBLS	10//99-12//99
Short Order	Memphis MSA, TN-AR-MS	S	6.77 MW	6.54 AW	14070 AAW	MSBLS	10//99-12//99
Short Order	Nashville MSA, TN	S	7.39 MW	7.05 AW	15380 AAW	TNBLS	10//99-12//99
Short Order	Texas	S	6.97 MW	7.23 AW	15040 AAW	TXBLS	10//99-12//99
Short Order	Abilene MSA, TX	S	7.75 MW	7.48 AW	16110 AAW	TXBLS	10//99-12//99
Short Order	Amarillo MSA, TX	S	7.00 MW	6.74 AW	14550 AAW	TXBLS	10//99-12//99
Short Order	Austin-San Marcos MSA, TX	S	7.87 MW	7.61 AW	16370 AAW	TXBLS	10//99-12//99
Short Order	Beaumont-Port Arthur MSA, TX	S	6.63 MW	6.00 AW	13790 AAW	TXBLS	10//99-12//99
Short Order	Brazoria PMSA, TX	S	6.84 MW	6.75 AW	14230 AAW	TXBLS	10//99-12//99
Short Order	Brownsville-Harlingen-San Benito MSA, TX	S	7.35 MW	7.47 AW	15300 AAW	TXBLS	10//99-12//99
Short Order	Corpus Christi MSA, TX	S	7.70 MW	7.60 AW	16020 AAW	TXBLS	10//99-12//99
Short Order	Dallas PMSA, TX	S	7.88 MW	7.63 AW	16390 AAW	TXBLS	10//99-12//99
Short Order	El Paso MSA, TX	S	7.31 MW	6.89 AW	15190 AAW	TXBLS	10//99-12//99
Short Order	Fort Worth-Arlington PMSA, TX	S	7.69 MW	7.34 AW	15990 AAW	TXBLS	10//99-12//99

Occupation/Type/Industry	Location	Per	Low	Mid	High	Source	Date
Cook							
Short Order	Galveston-Texas City PMSA, TX	S	7.29 MW	7.03 AW	15160 AAW	TXBLS	10//99-12//99
Short Order	Houston PMSA, TX	S	7.06 MW	7.05 AW	14690 AAW	TXBLS	10//99-12//99
Short Order	Killeen-Temple MSA, TX	S	7.69 MW	7.13 AW	15990 AAW	TXBLS	10//99-12//99
Short Order	Laredo MSA, TX	S	6.37 MW	5.96 AW	13250 AAW	TXBLS	10//99-12//99
Short Order	Lubbock MSA, TX	S	6.76 MW	6.60 AW	14060 AAW	TXBLS	10//99-12//99
Short Order	McAllen-Edinburg-Mission MSA, TX	S	6.83 MW	6.65 AW	14210 AAW	TXBLS	10//99-12//99
Short Order	Odessa-Midland MSA, TX	S	7.65 MW	7.31 AW	15910 AAW	TXBLS	10//99-12//99
Short Order	San Angelo MSA, TX	S	6.17 MW	6.26 AW	12820 AAW	TXBLS	10//99-12//99
Short Order	San Antonio MSA, TX	S	7.05 MW	6.83 AW	14670 AAW	TXBLS	10//99-12//99
Short Order	Sherman-Denison MSA, TX	S	6.13 MW	6.01 AW	12750 AAW	TXBLS	10//99-12//99
Short Order	Tyler MSA, TX	S	6.36 MW	6.36 AW	13230 AAW	TXBLS	10//99-12//99
Short Order	Waco MSA, TX	S	7.43 MW	7.40 AW	15450 AAW	TXBLS	10//99-12//99
Short Order	Wichita Falls MSA, TX	S	7.24 MW	7.44 AW	15050 AAW	TXBLS	10//99-12//99
Short Order	Provo-Orem MSA, UT	S	6.79 MW	6.68 AW	14120 AAW	UTBLS	10//99-12//99
Short Order	Salt Lake City-Ogden MSA, UT	S	6.63 MW	6.57 AW	13780 AAW	UTBLS	10//99-12//99
Short Order	Vermont	S	7.53 MW	7.77 AW	16150 AAW	VTBLS	10//99-12//99
Short Order	Burlington MSA, VT	S	8.68 MW	8.24 AW	18060 AAW	VTBLS	10//99-12//99
Short Order	Virginia	S	6.79 MW	7.28 AW	15140 AAW	VABLS	10//99-12//99
Short Order	Charlottesville MSA, VA	S	7.25 MW	7.44 AW	15070 AAW	VABLS	10//99-12//99
Short Order	Danville MSA, VA	S	6.23 MW	6.01 AW	12950 AAW	VABLS	10//99-12//99
Short Order	Lynchburg MSA, VA	S	6.83 MW	6.50 AW	14210 AAW	VABLS	10//99-12//99
Short Order	Norfolk-Virginia Beach-Newport News MSA, VA-NC	S	6.52 MW	6.06 AW	13560 AAW	VABLS	10//99-12//99
Short Order	Richmond-Petersburg MSA, VA	S	7.42 MW	7.07 AW	15430 AAW	VABLS	10//99-12//99
Short Order	Roanoke MSA, VA	S	7.14 MW	7.24 AW	14850 AAW	VABLS	10//99-12//99
Short Order	Washington	S	7.99 MW	8.12 AW	16890 AAW	WABLS	10//99-12//99
Short Order	Bellingham MSA, WA	S	7.43 MW	7.11 AW	15450 AAW	WABLS	10//99-12//99
Short Order	Bremerton PMSA, WA	S	7.22 MW	6.67 AW	15010 AAW	WABLS	10//99-12//99
Short Order	Olympia PMSA, WA	S	7.55 MW	7.27 AW	15710 AAW	WABLS	10//99-12//99
Short Order	Richland-Kennewick-Pasco MSA, WA	S	7.58 MW	7.48 AW	15760 AAW	WABLS	10//99-12//99
Short Order	Seattle-Bellevue-Everett PMSA, WA	S	9.34 MW	9.41 AW	19420 AAW	WABLS	10//99-12//99
Short Order	Spokane MSA, WA	S	7.69 MW	7.47 AW	15990 AAW	WABLS	10//99-12//99
Short Order	Tacoma PMSA, WA	S	8.21 MW	8.15 AW	17070 AAW	WABLS	10//99-12//99
Short Order	West Virginia	S	5.98 MW	6.15 AW	12790 AAW	WVBLS	10//99-12//99
Short Order	Charleston MSA, WV	S	6.39 MW	6.19 AW	13280 AAW	WVBLS	10//99-12//99
Short Order	Huntington-Ashland MSA, WV-KY-OH	S	6.18 MW	5.99 AW	12860 AAW	WVBLS	10//99-12//99
Short Order	Parkersburg-Marietta MSA, WV-OH	S	6.18 MW	5.96 AW	12850 AAW	WVBLS	10//99-12//99
Short Order	Wheeling MSA, WV-OH	S	6.42 MW	6.13 AW	13340 AAW	WVBLS	10//99-12//99
Short Order	Wisconsin	S	7.37 MW	7.56 AW	15720 AAW	WIBLS	10//99-12//99
Short Order	Appleton-Oshkosh-Neenah MSA, WI	S	7.78 MW	7.70 AW	16180 AAW	WIBLS	10//99-12//99
Short Order	Eau Claire MSA, WI	S	7.04 MW	7.00 AW	14640 AAW	WIBLS	10//99-12//99
Short Order	Green Bay MSA, WI	S	7.77 MW	7.75 AW	16160 AAW	WIBLS	10//99-12//99
Short Order	Janesville-Beloit MSA, WI	S	8.28 MW	8.41 AW	17220 AAW	WIBLS	10//99-12//99
Short Order	La Crosse MSA, WI-MN	S	7.40 MW	7.46 AW	15400 AAW	WIBLS	10//99-12//99
Short Order	Madison MSA, WI	S	7.58 MW	6.97 AW	15770 AAW	WIBLS	10//99-12//99
Short Order	Milwaukee-Waukesha PMSA, WI	S	7.28 MW	7.08 AW	15150 AAW	WIBLS	10//99-12//99
Short Order	Racine PMSA, WI	S	7.66 MW	7.69 AW	15930 AAW	WIBLS	10//99-12//99
Short Order	Sheboygan MSA, WI	S	7.20 MW	7.15 AW	14980 AAW	WIBLS	10//99-12//99
Short Order	Wausau MSA, WI	S	7.21 MW	7.09 AW	14990 AAW	WIBLS	10//99-12//99
Short Order	Wyoming	S	7.16 MW	7.29 AW	15160 AAW	WYBLS	10//99-12//99
Short Order	Casper MSA, WY	S	6.55 MW	6.70 AW	13630 AAW	WYBLS	10//99-12//99
Short Order	Cheyenne MSA, WY	S	7.59 MW	7.53 AW	15780 AAW	WYBLS	10//99-12//99
Short Order	Puerto Rico	S	5.96 MW	6.00 AW	12480 AAW	PRBLS	10//99-12//99
Short Order	Caguas PMSA, PR	S	6.11 MW	6.04 AW	12710 AAW	PRBLS	10//99-12//99
Short Order	Mayaguez MSA, PR	S	5.85 MW	6.02 AW	12170 AAW	PRBLS	10//99-12//99
Short Order	Ponce MSA, PR	S	5.75 MW	5.83 AW	11950 AAW	PRBLS	10//99-12//99
Short Order	San Juan-Bayamon PMSA, PR	S	6.10 MW	6.03 AW	12690 AAW	PRBLS	10//99-12//99
Short Order	Guam	S	7.45 MW	7.46 AW	15510 AAW	GUBLS	10//99-12//99

AAW Average annual wage	**AOH** Average offered, high	**ASH** Average starting, high	**H** Hourly	**M** Monthly	**S** Special: hourly and annual
AE Average entry wage	**AOL** Average offered, low	**ASL** Average starting, low	**HI** Highest wage paid	**MTC** Median total compensation	**TQ** Third quartile wage
AEX Average experienced wage	**APH** Average pay, high range	**AW** Average wage paid	**HR** High end range	**MW** Median wage paid	**W** Weekly
AO Average offered	**APL** Average pay, low range	**FQ** First quartile wage	**LR** Low end range	**SQ** Second quartile wage	**Y** Yearly

Occupation/Type/Industry	Location	Per	Low	Mid	High	Source	Date
Cooling and Freezing Equipment Operator and Tender	Alaska	S	11.31 MW	11.64 AW	24220 AAW	AKBLS	10//99-12//99
	Arkansas	S	8.52 MW	8.69 AW	18080 AAW	ARBLS	10//99-12//99
	Fayetteville-Springdale-Rogers MSA, AR	S	8.89 MW	8.77 AW	18480 AAW	ARBLS	10//99-12//99
	California	S	14.08 MW	12.74 AW	26500 AAW	CABLS	10//99-12//99
	Los Angeles-Long Beach PMSA, CA	S	14.01 MW	15.09 AW	29140 AAW	CABLS	10//99-12//99
	Orange County PMSA, CA	S	12.76 MW	14.02 AW	26530 AAW	CABLS	10//99-12//99
	Sacramento PMSA, CA	S	9.42 MW	9.22 AW	19580 AAW	CABLS	10//99-12//99
	Santa Barbara-Santa Maria-Lompoc MSA, CA	S	10.65 MW	10.57 AW	22150 AAW	CABLS	10//99-12//99
	Colorado	S	10.12 MW	10.53 AW	21910 AAW	COBLS	10//99-12//99
	Florida	S	10.93 MW	10.90 AW	22680 AAW	FLBLS	10//99-12//99
	Lakeland-Winter Haven MSA, FL	S	10.58 MW	10.53 AW	22000 AAW	FLBLS	10//99-12//99
	Illinois	S	11.9 MW	12.35 AW	25680 AAW	ILBLS	10//99-12//99
	Chicago PMSA, IL	S	13.08 MW	13.94 AW	27200 AAW	ILBLS	10//99-12//99
	Indiana	S	10.5 MW	12.86 AW	26750 AAW	INBLS	10//99-12//99
	Indianapolis MSA, IN	S	13.39 MW	10.76 AW	27850 AAW	INBLS	10//99-12//99
	Kansas	S	8.3 MW	8.77 AW	18230 AAW	KSBLS	10//99-12//99
	Kentucky	S	8.12 MW	8.32 AW	17300 AAW	KYBLS	10//99-12//99
	Louisiana	S	7.28 MW	8.54 AW	17760 AAW	LABLS	10//99-12//99
	Maine	S	9.76 MW	9.78 AW	20330 AAW	MEBLS	10//99-12//99
	Michigan	S	13.63 MW	13.19 AW	27440 AAW	MIBLS	10//99-12//99
	Minnesota	S	10.9 MW	12.12 AW	25210 AAW	MNBLS	10//99-12//99
	Mississippi	S	6.92 MW	7.29 AW	15160 AAW	MSBLS	10//99-12//99
	Nebraska	S	8.9 MW	9.60 AW	19960 AAW	NEBLS	10//99-12//99
	Omaha MSA, NE-IA	S	9.93 MW	10.12 AW	20660 AAW	NEBLS	10//99-12//99
	New York	S	10.55 MW	11.80 AW	24540 AAW	NYBLS	10//99-12//99
	North Carolina	S	8.43 MW	8.47 AW	17610 AAW	NCBLS	10//99-12//99
	Ohio	S	12.74 MW	12.79 AW	26590 AAW	OHBLS	10//99-12//99
	Cleveland-Lorain-Elyria PMSA, OH	S	12.14 MW	12.12 AW	25250 AAW	OHBLS	10//99-12//99
	Oklahoma	S	10.69 MW	11.32 AW	23540 AAW	OKBLS	10//99-12//99
	Oregon	S	8.42 MW	10.78 AW	22430 AAW	ORBLS	10//99-12//99
	Pennsylvania	S	12.75 MW	14.32 AW	29790 AAW	PABLS	10//99-12//99
	Lancaster MSA, PA	S	15.88 MW	13.84 AW	33030 AAW	PABLS	10//99-12//99
	Philadelphia PMSA, PA-NJ	S	12.55 MW	11.94 AW	26100 AAW	PABLS	10//99-12//99
	South Dakota	S	10.09 MW	10.03 AW	20870 AAW	SDBLS	10//99-12//99
	Tennessee	S	11.03 MW	10.23 AW	21270 AAW	TNBLS	10//99-12//99
	Memphis MSA, TN-AR-MS	S	11.41 MW	11.44 AW	23740 AAW	MSBLS	10//99-12//99
	Texas	S	7.4 MW	7.83 AW	16280 AAW	TXBLS	10//99-12//99
	Virginia	S	8.15 MW	9.40 AW	19560 AAW	VABLS	10//99-12//99
	Washington	S	17.31 MW	15.96 AW	33190 AAW	WABLS	10//99-12//99
	Wisconsin	S	10.39 MW	10.61 AW	22060 AAW	WIBLS	10//99-12//99
	Puerto Rico	S	6.34 MW	6.76 AW	14060 AAW	PRBLS	10//99-12//99
	San Juan-Bayamon PMSA, PR	S	7.05 MW	6.43 AW	14660 AAW	PRBLS	10//99-12//99
Copywriter							
Advertising	East	Y		60000 AW		ADAGE1	2000
Advertising	Midwest	Y		55000 AW		ADAGE1	2000
Advertising	South	Y		52000 AW		ADAGE1	2000
Advertising	West	Y		59000 AW		ADAGE1	2000
Correctional Officer	United States	H		14.19 AW		NCS98	1998
Correctional Officer and Jailer	Alabama	S	12.56 MW	12.58 AW	26160 AAW	ALBLS	10//99-12//99
	Anniston MSA, AL	S	10.50 MW	9.88 AW	21830 AAW	ALBLS	10//99-12//99
	Decatur MSA, AL	S	12.96 MW	12.67 AW	26950 AAW	ALBLS	10//99-12//99
	Mobile MSA, AL	S	10.77 MW	10.15 AW	22410 AAW	ALBLS	10//99-12//99
	Arizona	S	12.94 MW	13.33 AW	27730 AAW	AZBLS	10//99-12//99
	Phoenix-Mesa MSA, AZ	S	13.45 MW	13.06 AW	27970 AAW	AZBLS	10//99-12//99
	Arkansas	S	10.02 MW	10.53 AW	21910 AAW	ARBLS	10//99-12//99
	Fayetteville-Springdale-Rogers MSA, AR	S	10.18 MW	10.06 AW	21170 AAW	ARBLS	10//99-12//99
	California	S	22.13 MW	21.06 AW	43800 AAW	CABLS	10//99-12//99
	Los Angeles-Long Beach PMSA, CA	S	21.01 MW	21.29 RW	43700 AAW	CABLS	10//99-12//99
	Oakland PMSA, CA	S	19.60 MW	19.40 AW	40770 AAW	CABLS	10//99-12//99
	Colorado	S	16.14 MW	16.28 AW	33860 AAW	COBLS	10//99-12//99
	Denver PMSA, CO	S	16.09 MW	16.40 AW	33460 AAW	COBLS	10//99-12//99

AAW	Average annual wage	AOH	Average offered, high	ASH	Average starting, high	H	Hourly	M	Monthly	S	Special: hourly and annual
AE	Average entry wage	AOL	Average offered, low	ASL	Average starting, low	HI	Highest wage paid	MTC	Median total compensation	TQ	Third quartile wage
AEX	Average experienced wage	APH	Average pay, high range	AW	Average wage paid	HR	High end range	MW	Median wage paid	W	Weekly
AO	Average offered	APL	Average pay, low range	FQ	First quartile wage	LR	Low end range	SQ	Second quartile wage	Y	Yearly

Occupation/Type/Industry	Location	Per	Low	Mid	High	Source	Date
Correctional Officer and Jailer	Connecticut	S	18.38 MW	17.95 AW	37330 AAW	CTBLS	10//99-12//99
	Delaware	S	13.11 MW	13.71 AW	28520 AAW	DEBLS	10//99-12//99
	Washington PMSA, DC-MD-VA-WV	S	15.44 MW	14.22 AW	32120 AAW	DCBLS	10//99-12//99
	Florida	S	13.08 MW	13.83 AW	28770 AAW	FLBLS	10//99-12//99
	Fort Pierce-Port St. Lucie MSA, FL	S	13.18 MW	12.75 AW	27410 AAW	FLBLS	10//99-12//99
	Gainesville MSA, FL	S	13.34 MW	12.66 AW	27750 AAW	FLBLS	10//99-12//99
	Jacksonville MSA, FL	S	10.57 MW	10.32 AW	21980 AAW	FLBLS	10//99-12//99
	Miami PMSA, FL	S	12.86 MW	11.80 AW	26760 AAW	FLBLS	10//99-12//99
	Ocala MSA, FL	S	15.74 MW	14.78 AW	32750 AAW	FLBLS	10//99-12//99
	Orlando MSA, FL	S	13.39 MW	13.01 AW	27860 AAW	FLBLS	10//99-12//99
	Pensacola MSA, FL	S	13.11 MW	12.71 AW	27270 AAW	FLBLS	10//99-12//99
	Sarasota-Bradenton MSA, FL	S	12.49 MW	10.30 AW	25980 AAW	FLBLS	10//99-12//99
	Tallahassee MSA, FL	S	12.32 MW	12.24 AW	25620 AAW	FLBLS	10//99-12//99
	Tampa-St. Petersburg-Clearwater MSA, FL	S	15.18 MW	14.83 AW	31570 AAW	FLBLS	10//99-12//99
	West Palm Beach-Boca Raton MSA, FL	S	17.07 MW	16.49 AW	35500 AAW	FLBLS	10//99-12//99
	Georgia	S	11.5 MW	11.57 AW	24070 AAW	GABLS	10//99-12//99
	Athens MSA, GA	S	10.76 MW	10.20 AW	22380 AAW	GABLS	10//99-12//99
	Atlanta MSA, GA	S	13.40 MW	12.67 AW	27860 AAW	GABLS	10//99-12//99
	Idaho	S	11.95 MW	11.81 AW	24560 AAW	IDBLS	10//99-12//99
	Illinois	S	14.52 MW	14.41 AW	29970 AAW	ILBLS	10//99-12//99
	Chicago PMSA, IL	S	14.67 MW	14.61 AW	30520 AAW	ILBLS	10//99-12//99
	Peoria-Pekin MSA, IL	S	15.16 MW	15.07 AW	31530 AAW	ILBLS	10//99-12//99
	Rockford MSA, IL	S	15.32 MW	15.06 AW	31860 AAW	ILBLS	10//99-12//99
	Indiana	S	11.36 MW	11.37 AW	23650 AAW	INBLS	10//99-12//99
	Evansville-Henderson MSA, IN-KY	S	11.14 MW	11.43 AW	23160 AAW	INBLS	10//99-12//99
	Fort Wayne MSA, IN	S	11.25 MW	11.33 AW	23400 AAW	INBLS	10//99-12//99
	Iowa	S	14.68 MW	14.10 AW	29320 AAW	IABLS	10//99-12//99
	Des Moines MSA, IA	S	16.22 MW	15.89 AW	33740 AAW	IABLS	10//99-12//99
	Kansas	S	11.95 MW	12.07 AW	25100 AAW	KSBLS	10//99-12//99
	Kentucky	S	9.79 MW	10.49 AW	21810 AAW	KYBLS	10//99-12//99
	Lexington MSA, KY	S	13.43 MW	12.15 AW	27940 AAW	KYBLS	10//99-12//99
	Louisiana	S	9.17 MW	9.59 AW	19950 AAW	LABLS	10//99-12//99
	Alexandria MSA, LA	S	9.97 MW	9.92 AW	20740 AAW	LABLS	10//99-12//99
	Baton Rouge MSA, LA	S	11.65 MW	12.26 AW	24220 AAW	LABLS	10//99-12//99
	Lafayette MSA, LA	S	9.00 MW	8.69 AW	18710 AAW	LABLS	10//99-12//99
	New Orleans MSA, LA	S	7.95 MW	6.77 AW	16530 AAW	LABLS	10//99-12//99
	Maine	S	11.27 MW	11.18 AW	23260 AAW	MEBLS	10//99-12//99
	Maryland	S	14.85 MW	15.10 AW	31420 AAW	MDBLS	10//99-12//99
	Baltimore PMSA, MD	S	14.68 MW	14.58 AW	30540 AAW	MDBLS	10//99-12//99
	Michigan	S	18.09 MW	17.40 AW	36190 AAW	MIBLS	10//99-12//99
	Ann Arbor PMSA, MI	S	17.03 MW	17.81 AW	35420 AAW	MIBLS	10//99-12//99
	Kalamazoo-Battle Creek MSA, MI	S	18.05 MW	17.93 AW	37530 AAW	MIBLS	10//99-12//99
	Lansing-East Lansing MSA, MI	S	17.31 MW	17.82 AW	36000 AAW	MIBLS	10//99-12//99
	Minnesota	S	14.5 MW	14.70 AW	30580 AAW	MNBLS	10//99-12//99
	Duluth-Superior MSA, MN-WI	S	15.70 MW	15.74 AW	32650 AAW	MNBLS	10//99-12//99
	Minneapolis-St. Paul MSA, MN-WI	S	15.33 MW	15.47 AW	31890 AAW	MNBLS	10//99-12//99
	Rochester MSA, MN	S	16.11 MW	16.13 AW	33510 AAW	MNBLS	10//99-12//99
	St. Cloud MSA, MN	S	14.74 MW	14.62 AW	30650 AAW	MNBLS	10//99-12//99
	Mississippi	S	9.29 MW	9.58 AW	19930 AAW	MSBLS	10//99-12//99
	Jackson MSA, MS	S	9.75 MW	9.66 AW	20270 AAW	MSBLS	10//99-12//99
	St. Louis MSA, MO-IL	S	14.01 MW	13.82 AW	29140 AAW	MOBLS	10//99-12//99
	Montana	S	10.25 MW	10.39 AW	21620 AAW	MTBLS	10//99-12//99
	Nebraska	S	12.21 MW	12.15 AW	25270 AAW	NEBLS	10//99-12//99
	Omaha MSA, NE-IA	S	12.60 MW	12.45 AW	26210 AAW	NEBLS	10//99-12//99
	Nevada	S	16.73 MW	17.96 AW	37350 AAW	NVBLS	10//99-12//99
	Las Vegas MSA, NV-AZ	S	20.45 MW	20.09 AW	42540 AAW	NVBLS	10//99-12//99
	New Hampshire	S	12.45 MW	12.71 AW	26430 AAW	NHBLS	10//99-12//99
	New Jersey	S	22.28 MW	21.54 AW	44800 AAW	NJBLS	10//99-12//99
	Middlesex-Somerset-Hunterdon PMSA, NJ	S	23.02 MW	23.47 AW	47890 AAW	NJBLS	10//99-12//99
	Newark PMSA, NJ	S	21.29 MW	22.18 AW	44280 AAW	NJBLS	10//99-12//99
	New Mexico	S	9.75 MW	9.94 AW	20670 AAW	NMBLS	10//99-12//99
	Albany-Schenectady-Troy MSA, NY	S	19.29 MW	19.47 AW	40120 AAW	NYBLS	10//99-12//99
	North Carolina	S	12.09 MW	12.14 AW	25250 AAW	NCBLS	10//99-12//99

AAW Average annual wage	AOH Average offered, high	ASH Average starting, high	H Hourly	M Monthly	S Special: hourly and annual
AE Average entry wage	AOL Average offered, low	ASL Average starting, low	HI Highest wage paid	MTC Median total compensation	TQ Third quartile wage
AEX Average experienced wage	APH Average pay, high range	AW Average wage paid	HR High end range	MW Median wage paid	W Weekly
AO Average offered	APL Average pay, low range	FQ First quartile wage	LR Low end range	SQ Second quartile wage	Y Yearly

Occupation/Type/Industry	Location	Per	Low	Mid	High	Source	Date
Correctional Officer and Jailer	Greensboro--Winston-Salem-- High Point MSA, NC	S	13.46 MW	13.25 AW	27990 AAW	NCBLS	10//99-12//99
	North Dakota	S	11.59 MW	11.68 AW	24290 AAW	NDBLS	10//99-12//99
	Cleveland-Lorain-Elyria PMSA, OH	S	11.91 MW	11.67 AW	24770 AAW	OHBLS	10//99-12//99
	Dayton-Springfield MSA, OH	S	12.90 MW	12.47 AW	26830 AAW	OHBLS	10//99-12//99
	Mansfield MSA, OH	S	11.98 MW	12.15 AW	24920 AAW	OHBLS	10//99-12//99
	Steubenville-Weirton MSA, OH-WV	S	11.20 MW	10.90 AW	23290 AAW	OHBLS	10//99-12//99
	Toledo MSA, OH	S	12.78 MW	12.72 AW	26580 AAW	OHBLS	10//99-12//99
	Oklahoma	S	10.09 MW	10.60 AW	22040 AAW	OKBLS	10//99-12//99
	Oregon	S	17.36 MW	17.51 AW	36420 AAW	ORBLS	10//99-12//99
	Portland-Vancouver PMSA, OR-WA	S	18.83 MW	19.30 AW	39160 AAW	ORBLS	10//99-12//99
	Pennsylvania	S	15.94 MW	16.43 AW	34180 AAW	PABLS	10//99-12//99
	Allentown-Bethlehem-Easton MSA, PA	S	15.14 MW	15.06 AW	31490 AAW	PABLS	10//99-12//99
	Philadelphia PMSA, PA-NJ	S	19.44 MW	19.36 AW	40430 AAW	PABLS	10//99-12//99
	South Carolina	S	10.72 MW	11.23 AW	23370 AAW	SCBLS	10//99-12//99
	South Dakota	S	11.35 MW	11.76 AW	24460 AAW	SDBLS	10//99-12//99
	Chattanooga MSA, TN-GA	S	9.96 MW	9.49 AW	20730 AAW	TNBLS	10//99-12//99
	Johnson City-Kingsport-Bristol MSA, TN-VA	S	10.84 MW	10.35 AW	22540 AAW	TNBLS	10//99-12//99
	Memphis MSA, TN-AR-MS	S	12.39 MW	10.74 AW	25770 AAW	MSBLS	10//99-12//99
	Texas	S	11.77 MW	11.62 AW	24170 AAW	TXBLS	10//99-12//99
	Austin-San Marcos MSA, TX	S	10.23 MW	9.64 AW	21290 AAW	TXBLS	10//99-12//99
	Brownsville-Harlingen-San Benito MSA, TX	S	11.03 MW	11.02 AW	22950 AAW	TXBLS	10//99-12//99
	Dallas PMSA, TX	S	12.08 MW	12.11 AW	25130 AAW	TXBLS	10//99-12//99
	Fort Worth-Arlington PMSA, TX	S	14.38 MW	14.08 AW	29920 AAW	TXBLS	10//99-12//99
	Houston PMSA, TX	S	11.93 MW	11.86 AW	24820 AAW	TXBLS	10//99-12//99
	Utah	S	13.66 MW	13.80 AW	28710 AAW	UTBLS	10//99-12//99
	Salt Lake City-Ogden MSA, UT	S	14.03 MW	13.79 AW	29180 AAW	UTBLS	10//99-12//99
	Virginia	S	12.47 MW	12.90 AW	26820 AAW	VABLS	10//99-12//99
	Lynchburg MSA, VA	S	13.10 MW	12.73 AW	27250 AAW	VABLS	10//99-12//99
	Norfolk-Virginia Beach-Newport News MSA, VA-NC	S	12.52 MW	12.32 AW	26040 AAW	VABLS	10//99-12//99
	Washington	S	15.33 MW	15.66 AW	32580 AAW	WABLS	10//99-12//99
	Seattle-Bellevue-Everett PMSA, WA	S	16.99 MW	16.27 AW	35350 AAW	WABLS	10//99-12//99
	West Virginia	S	10.13 MW	10.97 AW	22830 AAW	WVBLS	10//99-12//99
	Huntington-Ashland MSA, WV-KY-OH	S	13.06 MW	11.49 AW	27170 AAW	WVBLS	10//99-12//99
	Wisconsin	S	14.6 MW	14.25 AW	29650 AAW	WIBLS	10//99-12//99
	Eau Claire MSA, WI	S	13.93 MW	14.48 AW	28970 AAW	WIBLS	10//99-12//99
Correspondence Clerk	Alabama	S	9.92 MW	10.79 AW	22430 AAW	ALBLS	10//99-12//99
	Arizona	S	11.69 MW	11.53 AW	23990 AAW	AZBLS	10//99-12//99
	Arkansas	S	9.76 MW	10.31 AW	21450 AAW	ARBLS	10//99-12//99
	California	S	11.87 MW	12.14 AW	25250 AAW	CABLS	10//99-12//99
	Colorado	S	10.51 MW	11.15 AW	23200 AAW	COBLS	10//99-12//99
	Connecticut	S	11.42 MW	11.48 AW	23880 AAW	CTBLS	10//99-12//99
	Delaware	S	11.71 MW	12.17 AW	25320 AAW	DEBLS	10//99-12//99
	District of Columbia	S	12.26 MW	13.64 AW	28360 AAW	DCBLS	10//99-12//99
	Florida	S	10.15 MW	10.35 AW	21530 AAW	FLBLS	10//99-12//99
	Georgia	S	10.73 MW	11.03 AW	22940 AAW	GABLS	10//99-12//99
	Illinois	S	10.49 MW	10.68 AW	22210 AAW	ILBLS	10//99-12//99
	Indiana	S	10.36 MW	10.79 AW	22450 AAW	INBLS	10//99-12//99
	Iowa	S	9.02 MW	9.62 AW	20020 AAW	IABLS	10//99-12//99
	Kansas	S	10.56 MW	11.20 AW	23290 AAW	KSBLS	10//99-12//99
	Kentucky	S	11.13 MW	11.40 AW	23710 AAW	KYBLS	10//99-12//99
	Louisiana	S	11.43 MW	11.32 AW	23540 AAW	LABLS	10//99-12//99
	Maine	S	11.9 MW	11.75 AW	24430 AAW	MEBLS	10//99-12//99
	Maryland	S	10.4 MW	12.86 AW	26740 AAW	MDBLS	10//99-12//99
	Massachusetts	S	11.79 MW	12.81 AW	26640 AAW	MABLS	10//99-12//99
	Michigan	S	11.49 MW	11.68 AW	24300 AAW	MIBLS	10//99-12//99
	Minnesota	S	11.75 MW	11.55 AW	24030 AAW	MNBLS	10//99-12//99
	Mississippi	S	10.11 MW	10.28 AW	21390 AAW	MSBLS	10//99-12//99
	Missouri	S	9.73 MW	10.58 AW	22010 AAW	MOBLS	10//99-12//99
	Montana	S	11.33 MW	11.42 AW	23750 AAW	MTBLS	10//99-12//99

AAW Average annual wage	**AOH** Average offered, high	**ASH** Average starting, high	**H** Hourly	**M** Monthly	**S** Special: hourly and annual
AE Average entry wage	**AOL** Average offered, low	**ASL** Average starting, low	**HI** Highest wage paid	**MTC** Median total compensation	**TQ** Third quartile wage
AEX Average experienced wage	**APH** Average pay, high range	**AW** Average wage paid	**HR** High end range	**MW** Median wage paid	**W** Weekly
AO Average offered	**APL** Average pay, low range	**FQ** First quartile wage	**LR** Low end range	**SQ** Second quartile wage	**Y** Yearly

Occupation/Type/Industry	Location	Per	Low	Mid	High	Source	Date
Correspondence Clerk	Nebraska	S	9.84 MW	9.95 AW	20700 AAW	NEBLS	10//99-12//99
	Nevada	S	13.99 MW	13.81 AW	28710 AAW	NVBLS	10//99-12//99
	New Hampshire	S	10.21 MW	10.85 AW	22570 AAW	NHBLS	10//99-12//99
	New Jersey	S	12.36 MW	12.79 AW	26590 AAW	NJBLS	10//99-12//99
	New Mexico	S	9.89 MW	9.58 AW	19930 AAW	NMBLS	10//99-12//99
	New York	S	10.75 MW	11.93 AW	24810 AAW	NYBLS	10//99-12//99
	North Carolina	S	12.14 MW	12.05 AW	25060 AAW	NCBLS	10//99-12//99
	Ohio	S	11.23 MW	11.23 AW	23360 AAW	OHBLS	10//99-12//99
	Oklahoma	S	9.73 MW	9.95 AW	20690 AAW	OKBLS	10//99-12//99
	Oregon	S	10.61 MW	11.53 AW	23990 AAW	ORBLS	10//99-12//99
	Pennsylvania	S	10.59 MW	11.18 AW	23260 AAW	PABLS	10//99-12//99
	Rhode Island	S	12.21 MW	12.64 AW	26290 AAW	RIBLS	10//99-12//99
	South Carolina	S	10 MW	10.46 AW	21770 AAW	SCBLS	10//99-12//99
	South Dakota	S	9.24 MW	9.08 AW	18880 AAW	SDBLS	10//99-12//99
	Tennessee	S	11.94 MW	12.25 AW	25470 AAW	TNBLS	10//99-12//99
	Texas	S	10.33 MW	11.05 AW	22990 AAW	TXBLS	10//99-12//99
	Utah	S	11.71 MW	12.02 AW	25000 AAW	UTBLS	10//99-12//99
	Vermont	S	12.6 MW	13.63 AW	28340 AAW	VTBLS	10//99-12//99
	Virginia	S	11.86 MW	12.28 AW	25540 AAW	VABLS	10//99-12//99
	Washington	S	11.26 MW	12.78 AW	26580 AAW	WABLS	10//99-12//99
	West Virginia	S	10.83 MW	11.21 AW	23310 AAW	WVBLS	10//99-12//99
	Wisconsin	S	12.87 MW	13.24 AW	27550 AAW	WIBLS	10//99-12//99
	Puerto Rico	S	8.5 MW	9.09 AW	18900 AAW	PRBLS	10//99-12//99
Cost Estimator	Alabama	S	19.17 MW	20.74 AW	43130 AAW	ALBLS	10//99-12//99
	Anniston MSA, AL	S	19.32 MW	17.08 AW	40180 AAW	ALBLS	10//99-12//99
	Auburn-Opelika MSA, AL	S	20.74 MW	19.81 AW	43130 AAW	ALBLS	10//99-12//99
	Birmingham MSA, AL	S	22.47 MW	20.61 AW	46750 AAW	ALBLS	10//99-12//99
	Decatur MSA, AL	S	22.10 MW	20.41 AW	45970 AAW	ALBLS	10//99-12//99
	Dothan MSA, AL	S	15.93 MW	14.76 AW	33130 AAW	ALBLS	10//99-12//99
	Florence MSA, AL	S	18.87 MW	13.76 AW	39260 AAW	ALBLS	10//99-12//99
	Gadsden MSA, AL	S	17.32 MW	18.41 AW	36030 AAW	ALBLS	10//99-12//99
	Huntsville MSA, AL	S	20.88 MW	19.30 AW	43430 AAW	ALBLS	10//99-12//99
	Mobile MSA, AL	S	20.84 MW	19.10 AW	43350 AAW	ALBLS	10//99-12//99
	Montgomery MSA, AL	S	19.20 MW	16.66 AW	39940 AAW	ALBLS	10//99-12//99
	Tuscaloosa MSA, AL	S	20.41 MW	20.67 AW	42460 AAW	ALBLS	10//99-12//99
	Alaska	S	29.19 MW	29.83 AW	62050 AAW	AKBLS	10//99-12//99
	Anchorage MSA, AK	S	30.63 MW	29.76 AW	63700 AAW	AKBLS	10//99-12//99
	Arizona	S	20.46 MW	22.48 AW	46760 AAW	AZBLS	10//99-12//99
	Flagstaff MSA, AZ-UT	S	16.49 MW	16.28 AW	34300 AAW	AZBLS	10//99-12//99
	Phoenix-Mesa MSA, AZ	S	23.61 MW	21.58 AW	49100 AAW	AZBLS	10//99-12//99
	Tucson MSA, AZ	S	17.50 MW	16.30 AW	36400 AAW	AZBLS	10//99-12//99
	Yuma MSA, AZ	S	23.99 MW	20.74 AW	49900 AAW	AZBLS	10//99-12//99
	Arkansas	S	17.75 MW	19.97 AW	41530 AAW	ARBLS	10//99-12//99
	Fayetteville-Springdale-Rogers MSA, AR	S	16.00 MW	14.79 AW	33280 AAW	ARBLS	10//99-12//99
	Fort Smith MSA, AR-OK	S	19.64 MW	18.35 AW	40860 AAW	ARBLS	10//99-12//99
	Jonesboro MSA, AR	S	16.16 MW	15.11 AW	33620 AAW	ARBLS	10//99-12//99
	Little Rock-North Little Rock MSA, AR	S	20.52 MW	19.52 AW	42670 AAW	ARBLS	10//99-12//99
	California	S	22.72 MW	24.28 AW	50510 AAW	CABLS	10//99-12//99
	Bakersfield MSA, CA	S	20.81 MW	21.37 AW	43290 AAW	CABLS	10//99-12//99
	Chico-Paradise MSA, CA	S	20.60 MW	18.93 AW	42840 AAW	CABLS	10//99-12//99
	Fresno MSA, CA	S	21.00 MW	20.46 AW	43670 AAW	CABLS	10//99-12//99
	Los Angeles-Long Beach PMSA, CA	S	23.35 MW	21.56 AW	48570 AAW	CABLS	10//99-12//99
	Merced MSA, CA	S	20.56 MW	19.90 AW	42770 AAW	CABLS	10//99-12//99
	Modesto MSA, CA	S	24.24 MW	23.90 AW	50420 AAW	CABLS	10//99-12//99
	Oakland PMSA, CA	S	27.76 MW	28.37 AW	57730 AAW	CABLS	10//99-12//99
	Orange County PMSA, CA	S	23.57 MW	22.45 AW	49030 AAW	CABLS	10//99-12//99
	Redding MSA, CA	S	21.69 MW	17.77 AW	45120 AAW	CABLS	10//99-12//99
	Riverside-San Bernardino PMSA, CA	S	25.02 MW	22.76 AW	52040 AAW	CABLS	10//99-12//99
	Sacramento PMSA, CA	S	22.19 MW	19.40 AW	46160 AAW	CABLS	10//99-12//99
	Salinas MSA, CA	S	23.03 MW	21.09 AW	47900 AAW	CABLS	10//99-12//99
	San Diego MSA, CA	S	23.79 MW	21.42 AW	49470 AAW	CABLS	10//99-12//99
	San Francisco PMSA, CA	S	26.10 MW	24.66 AW	54280 AAW	CABLS	10//99-12//99
	San Jose PMSA, CA	S	27.62 MW	26.81 AW	57450 AAW	CABLS	10//99-12//99
	San Luis Obispo-Atascadero-Paso Robles MSA, CA	S	21.88 MW	20.83 AW	45500 AAW	CABLS	10//99-12//99
	Santa Barbara-Santa Maria-Lompoc MSA, CA	S	23.66 MW	22.08 AW	49210 AAW	CABLS	10//99-12//99

Cost Estimator

Occupation/Type/Industry	Location	Per	Low	Mid	High	Source	Date
Cost Estimator	Santa Cruz-Watsonville PMSA, CA	S	23.78 MW	22.13 AW	49460 AAW	CABLS	10//99-12//99
	Santa Rosa PMSA, CA	S	23.39 MW	22.07 AW	48640 AAW	CABLS	10//99-12//99
	Stockton-Lodi MSA, CA	S	23.21 MW	21.66 AW	48280 AAW	CABLS	10//99-12//99
	Vallejo-Fairfield-Napa PMSA, CA	S	23.51 MW	23.07 AW	48900 AAW	CABLS	10//99-12//99
	Ventura PMSA, CA	S	24.11 MW	22.52 AW	50140 AAW	CABLS	10//99-12//99
	Visalia-Tulare-Porterville MSA, CA	S	20.30 MW	19.71 AW	42220 AAW	CABLS	10//99-12//99
	Yolo PMSA, CA	S	23.06 MW	21.54 AW	47960 AAW	CABLS	10//99-12//99
	Yuba City MSA, CA	S	22.65 MW	18.58 AW	47120 AAW	CABLS	10//99-12//99
	Colorado	S	21.15 MW	22.23 AW	46250 AAW	COBLS	10//99-12//99
	Boulder-Longmont PMSA, CO	S	19.59 MW	18.45 AW	40750 AAW	COBLS	10//99-12//99
	Colorado Springs MSA, CO	S	20.79 MW	19.36 AW	43240 AAW	COBLS	10//99-12//99
	Denver PMSA, CO	S	23.55 MW	21.83 AW	48990 AAW	COBLS	10//99-12//99
	Fort Collins-Loveland MSA, CO	S	21.19 MW	20.78 AW	44070 AAW	COBLS	10//99-12//99
	Grand Junction MSA, CO	S	22.49 MW	20.96 AW	46780 AAW	COBLS	10//99-12//99
	Greeley PMSA, CO	S	22.72 MW	21.74 AW	47260 AAW	COBLS	10//99-12//99
	Pueblo MSA, CO	S	20.39 MW	20.15 AW	42400 AAW	COBLS	10//99-12//99
	Connecticut	S	24.28 MW	25.74 AW	53530 AAW	CTBLS	10//99-12//99
	Bridgeport PMSA, CT	S	23.33 MW	20.63 AW	48530 AAW	CTBLS	10//99-12//99
	Danbury PMSA, CT	S	23.47 MW	22.06 AW	48820 AAW	CTBLS	10//99-12//99
	Hartford MSA, CT	S	26.77 MW	24.75 AW	55690 AAW	CTBLS	10//99-12//99
	New Haven-Meriden PMSA, CT	S	25.50 MW	27.26 AW	53040 AAW	CTBLS	10//99-12//99
	New London-Norwich MSA, CT-RI	S	22.38 MW	22.05 AW	46550 AAW	CTBLS	10//99-12//99
	Stamford-Norwalk PMSA, CT	S	27.63 MW	24.25 AW	57480 AAW	CTBLS	10//99-12//99
	Waterbury PMSA, CT	S	26.22 MW	23.65 AW	54530 AAW	CTBLS	10//99-12//99
	Delaware	S	23.45 MW	24.31 AW	50560 AAW	DEBLS	10//99-12//99
	Dover MSA, DE	S	16.61 MW	14.41 AW	34540 AAW	DEBLS	10//99-12//99
	Wilmington-Newark PMSA, DE-MD	S	25.64 MW	24.87 AW	53340 AAW	DEBLS	10//99-12//99
	District of Columbia	S	21.59 MW	23.40 AW	48670 AAW	DCBLS	10//99-12//99
	Washington PMSA, DC-MD-VA-WV	S	25.07 MW	23.17 AW	52140 AAW	DCBLS	10//99-12//99
	Florida	S	18.37 MW	19.67 AW	40900 AAW	FLBLS	10//99-12//99
	Daytona Beach MSA, FL	S	17.22 MW	17.28 AW	35820 AAW	FLBLS	10//99-12//99
	Fort Lauderdale PMSA, FL	S	19.58 MW	17.61 AW	40740 AAW	FLBLS	10//99-12//99
	Fort Myers-Cape Coral MSA, FL	S	20.18 MW	18.78 AW	41980 AAW	FLBLS	10//99-12//99
	Fort Pierce-Port St. Lucie MSA, FL	S	16.47 MW	16.96 AW	34260 AAW	FLBLS	10//99-12//99
	Gainesville MSA, FL	S	16.53 MW	15.77 AW	34390 AAW	FLBLS	10//99-12//99
	Jacksonville MSA, FL	S	20.39 MW	17.92 AW	42410 AAW	FLBLS	10//99-12//99
	Lakeland-Winter Haven MSA, FL	S	22.40 MW	20.69 AW	46590 AAW	FLBLS	10//99-12//99
	Melbourne-Titusville-Palm Bay MSA, FL	S	17.75 MW	16.61 AW	36920 AAW	FLBLS	10//99-12//99
	Miami PMSA, FL	S	20.31 MW	19.39 AW	42250 AAW	FLBLS	10//99-12//99
	Naples MSA, FL	S	18.88 MW	17.68 AW	39260 AAW	FLBLS	10//99-12//99
	Ocala MSA, FL	S	17.19 MW	16.49 AW	35740 AAW	FLBLS	10//99-12//99
	Orlando MSA, FL	S	20.63 MW	19.16 AW	42910 AAW	FLBLS	10//99-12//99
	Panama City MSA, FL	S	14.24 MW	13.35 AW	29620 AAW	FLBLS	10//99-12//99
	Pensacola MSA, FL	S	17.02 MW	17.20 AW	35390 AAW	FLBLS	10//99-12//99
	Sarasota-Bradenton MSA, FL	S	20.54 MW	19.09 AW	42730 AAW	FLBLS	10//99-12//99
	Tallahassee MSA, FL	S	19.17 MW	20.42 AW	39870 AAW	FLBLS	10//99-12//99
	Tampa-St. Petersburg-Clearwater MSA, FL	S	19.17 MW	18.23 AW	39870 AAW	FLBLS	10//99-12//99
	West Palm Beach-Boca Raton MSA, FL	S	23.24 MW	21.36 AW	48340 AAW	FLBLS	10//99-12//99
	Georgia	S	19.33 MW	21.42 AW	44550 AAW	GABLS	10//99-12//99
	Albany MSA, GA	S	18.79 MW	17.31 AW	39080 AAW	GABLS	10//99-12//99
	Athens MSA, GA	S	22.22 MW	23.09 AW	46210 AAW	GABLS	10//99-12//99
	Atlanta MSA, GA	S	22.15 MW	19.72 AW	46070 AAW	GABLS	10//99-12//99
	Augusta-Aiken MSA, GA-SC	S	23.35 MW	22.32 AW	48580 AAW	GABLS	10//99-12//99
	Columbus MSA, GA-AL	S	20.75 MW	19.37 AW	43160 AAW	GABLS	10//99-12//99
	Macon MSA, GA	S	23.84 MW	18.86 AW	49580 AAW	GABLS	10//99-12//99
	Savannah MSA, GA	S	18.78 MW	18.01 AW	39070 AAW	GABLS	10//99-12//99
	Hawaii	S	22.75 MW	23.84 AW	49580 AAW	HIBLS	10//99-12//99
	Honolulu MSA, HI	S	23.84 MW	22.78 AW	49580 AAW	HIBLS	10//99-12//99

AAW	Average annual wage	AOH	Average offered, high	ASH	Average starting, high
AE	Average entry wage	AOL	Average offered, low	ASL	Average starting, low
AEX	Average experienced wage	APH	Average pay, high range	AW	Average wage paid
AO	Average offered	APL	Average pay, low range	FQ	First quartile wage

H	Hourly	M	Monthly
HI	Highest wage paid	MTC	Median total compensation
HR	High end range	MW	Median wage paid
LR	Low end range	SQ	Second quartile wage

S	Special: hourly and annual
TQ	Third quartile wage
W	Weekly
Y	Yearly

Occupation/Type/Industry	Location	Per	Low	Mid	High	Source	Date
Cost Estimator	Idaho	S	18.84 MW	19.55 AW	40660 AAW	IDBLS	10//99-12//99
	Boise City MSA, ID	S	19.29 MW	18.97 AW	40110 AAW	IDBLS	10//99-12//99
	Pocatello MSA, ID	S	19.27 MW	17.63 AW	40070 AAW	IDBLS	10//99-12//99
	Illinois	S	20.03 MW	21.69 AW	45110 AAW	ILBLS	10//99-12//99
	Bloomington-Normal MSA, IL	S	21.56 MW	20.95 AW	44850 AAW	ILBLS	10//99-12//99
	Champaign-Urbana MSA, IL	S	20.00 MW	17.50 AW	41590 AAW	ILBLS	10//99-12//99
	Chicago PMSA, IL	S	21.86 MW	20.22 AW	45470 AAW	ILBLS	10//99-12//99
	Decatur MSA, IL	S	25.35 MW	26.23 AW	52730 AAW	ILBLS	10//99-12//99
	Peoria-Pekin MSA, IL	S	21.57 MW	19.57 AW	44870 AAW	ILBLS	10//99-12//99
	Rockford MSA, IL	S	22.14 MW	19.92 AW	46040 AAW	ILBLS	10//99-12//99
	Springfield MSA, IL	S	20.63 MW	17.39 AW	42910 AAW	ILBLS	10//99-12//99
	Indiana	S	19.67 MW	21.10 AW	43880 AAW	INBLS	10//99-12//99
	Bloomington MSA, IN	S	22.29 MW	20.80 AW	46350 AAW	INBLS	10//99-12//99
	Elkhart-Goshen MSA, IN	S	20.51 MW	19.91 AW	42660 AAW	INBLS	10//99-12//99
	Evansville-Henderson MSA, IN-KY	S	19.56 MW	17.98 AW	40680 AAW	INBLS	10//99-12//99
	Fort Wayne MSA, IN	S	21.71 MW	20.34 AW	45150 AAW	INBLS	10//99-12//99
	Gary PMSA, IN	S	23.05 MW	21.65 AW	47940 AAW	INBLS	10//99-12//99
	Indianapolis MSA, IN	S	21.89 MW	20.79 AW	45520 AAW	INBLS	10//99-12//99
	Kokomo MSA, IN	S	19.45 MW	16.43 AW	40450 AAW	INBLS	10//99-12//99
	Lafayette MSA, IN	S	24.38 MW	24.53 AW	50710 AAW	INBLS	10//99-12//99
	Muncie MSA, IN	S	20.85 MW	19.54 AW	43370 AAW	INBLS	10//99-12//99
	South Bend MSA, IN	S	20.93 MW	19.69 AW	43540 AAW	INBLS	10//99-12//99.
	Terre Haute MSA, IN	S	20.62 MW	18.84 AW	42900 AAW	INBLS	10//99-12//99
	Iowa	S	17.94 MW	19.76 AW	41100 AAW	IABLS	10//99-12//99
	Davenport-Moline-Rock Island MSA, IA-IL	S	20.54 MW	19.36 AW	42720 AAW	IABLS	10//99-12//99
	Des Moines MSA, IA	S	19.51 MW	17.10 AW	40570 AAW	IABLS	10//99-12//99
	Dubuque MSA, IA	S	17.81 MW	18.65 AW	37040 AAW	IABLS	10//99-12//99
	Iowa City MSA, IA	S	20.37 MW	17.20 AW	42370 AAW	IABLS	10//99-12//99
	Sioux City MSA, IA-NE	S	19.34 MW	20.50 AW	40220 AAW	IABLS	10//99-12//99
	Waterloo-Cedar Falls MSA, IA	S	18.85 MW	17.70 AW	39220 AAW	IABLS	10//99-12//99
	Kansas	S	18.58 MW	19.45 AW	40450 AAW	KSBLS	10//99-12//99
	Lawrence MSA, KS	S	17.55 MW	15.89 AW	36500 AAW	KSBLS	10//99-12//99
	Topeka MSA, KS	S	20.38 MW	19.22 AW	42400 AAW	KSBLS	10//99-12//99
	Wichita MSA, KS	S	20.80 MW	18.82 AW	43270 AAW	KSBLS	10//99-12//99
	Kentucky	S	18.17 MW	19.13 AW	39790 AAW	KYBLS	10//99-12//99
	Lexington MSA, KY	S	21.04 MW	19.97 AW	43770 AAW	KYBLS	10//99-12//99
	Louisville MSA, KY-IN	S	19.91 MW	18.94 AW	41420 AAW	KYBLS	10//99-12//99
	Owensboro MSA, KY	S	16.82 MW	15.84 AW	34990 AAW	KYBLS	10//99-12//99
	Louisiana	S	19.23 MW	21.15 AW	43990 AAW	LABLS	10//99-12//99
	Alexandria MSA, LA	S	19.05 MW	17.82 AW	39620 AAW	LABLS	10//99-12//99
	Baton Rouge MSA, LA	S	21.73 MW	19.80 AW	45190 AAW	LABLS	10//99-12//99
	Houma MSA, LA	S	22.62 MW	21.01 AW	47050 AAW	LABLS	10//99-12//99
	Lafayette MSA, LA	S	20.16 MW	18.19 AW	41920 AAW	LABLS	10//99-12//99
	Lake Charles MSA, LA	S	20.91 MW	19.17 AW	43480 AAW	LABLS	10//99-12//99
	Monroe MSA, LA	S	17.57 MW	17.07 AW	36530 AAW	LABLS	10//99-12//99
	New Orleans MSA, LA	S	22.50 MW	20.17 AW	46800 AAW	LABLS	10//99-12//99
	Shreveport-Bossier City MSA, LA	S	16.76 MW	15.91 AW	34860 AAW	LABLS	10//99-12//99
	Maine	S	17.52 MW	18.28 AW	38020 AAW	MEBLS	10//99-12//99
	Lewiston-Auburn MSA, ME	S	18.50 MW	18.09 AW	38470 AAW	MEBLS	10//99-12//99
	Portland MSA, ME	S	18.47 MW	18.10 AW	38430 AAW	MEBLS	10//99-12//99
	Maryland	S	21.35 MW	24.08 AW	50080 AAW	MDBLS	10//99-12//99
	Baltimore PMSA, MD	S	22.34 MW	20.86 AW	46470 AAW	MDBLS	10//99-12//99
	Hagerstown PMSA, MD	S	20.16 MW	18.24 AW	41920 AAW	MDBLS	10//99-12//99
	Massachusetts	S	22.68 MW	23.88 AW	49680 AAW	MABLS	10//99-12//99
	Boston PMSA, MA-NH	S	24.99 MW	23.48 AW	51980 AAW	MABLS	10//99-12//99
	Brockton PMSA, MA	S	23.70 MW	21.46 AW	49290 AAW	MABLS	10//99-12//99
	Fitchburg-Leominster PMSA, MA	S	22.65 MW	20.87 AW	47110 AAW	MABLS	10//99-12//99
	Lawrence PMSA, MA-NH	S	24.78 MW	25.15 AW	51540 AAW	MABLS	10//99-12//99
	Lowell PMSA, MA-NH	S	22.47 MW	21.93 AW	46730 AAW	MABLS	10//99-12//99
	New Bedford PMSA, MA	S	23.74 MW	23.16 AW	49380 AAW	MABLS	10//99-12//99
	Pittsfield MSA, MA	S	19.71 MW	18.55 AW	40990 AAW	MABLS	10//99-12//99
	Springfield MSA, MA	S	20.80 MW	19.56 AW	43270 AAW	MABLS	10//99-12//99
	Worcester PMSA, MA-CT	S	22.27 MW	20.91 AW	46310 AAW	MABLS	10//99-12//99
	Michigan	S	22.89 MW	24.09 AW	50110 AAW	MIBLS	10//99-12//99
	Ann Arbor PMSA, MI	S	22.73 MW	21.11 AW	47270 AAW	MIBLS	10//99-12//99
	Benton Harbor MSA, MI	S	21.42 MW	18.64 AW	44550 AAW	MIBLS	10//99-12//99
	Detroit PMSA, MI	S	26.10 MW	25.71 AW	54290 AAW	MIBLS	10//99-12//99
	Flint PMSA, MI	S	25.65 MW	23.69 AW	53350 AAW	MIBLS	10//99-12//99

AAW	Average annual wage	AOH	Average offered, high	ASH	Average starting, high	H	Hourly	M	Monthly	S	Special: hourly and annual
AE	Average entry wage	AOL	Average offered, low	ASL	Average starting, low	HI	Highest wage paid	MTC	Median total compensation	TQ	Third quartile wage
AEX	Average experienced wage	APH	Average pay, high range	AW	Average wage paid	HR	High end range	MW	Median wage paid	W	Weekly
AO	Average offered	APL	Average pay, low range	FQ	First quartile wage	LR	Low end range	SQ	Second quartile wage	Y	Yearly

331

Occupation/Type/Industry	Location	Per	Low	Mid	High	Source	Date
Cost Estimator							
	Grand Rapids-Muskegon-Holland MSA, MI	S	23.08 MW	22.74 AW	48000 AAW	MIBLS	10//99-12//99
	Jackson MSA, MI	S	18.85 MW	18.32 AW	39210 AAW	MIBLS	10//99-12//99
	Kalamazoo-Battle Creek MSA, MI	S	20.91 MW	19.93 AW	43480 AAW	MIBLS	10//99-12//99
	Lansing-East Lansing MSA, MI	S	21.54 MW	19.14 AW	44800 AAW	MIBLS	10//99-12//99
	Saginaw-Bay City-Midland MSA, MI	S	23.42 MW	22.03 AW	48710 AAW	MIBLS	10//99-12//99
	Minnesota	S	20.3 MW	21.55 AW	44830 AAW	MNBLS	10//99-12//99
	Duluth-Superior MSA, MN-WI	S	18.59 MW	17.50 AW	38680 AAW	MNBLS	10//99-12//99
	Minneapolis-St. Paul MSA, MN-WI	S	22.98 MW	21.56 AW	47800 AAW	MNBLS	10//99-12//99
	Rochester MSA, MN	S	21.00 MW	18.04 AW	43670 AAW	MNBLS	10//99-12//99
	St. Cloud MSA, MN	S	17.85 MW	16.29 AW	37120 AAW	MNBLS	10//99-12//99
	Mississippi	S	17.24 MW	18.90 AW	39320 AAW	MSBLS	10//99-12//99
	Biloxi-Gulfport-Pascagoula MSA, MS	S	17.58 MW	16.67 AW	36560 AAW	MSBLS	10//99-12//99
	Hattiesburg MSA, MS	S	19.11 MW	17.59 AW	39750 AAW	MSBLS	10//99-12//99
	Jackson MSA, MS	S	19.16 MW	17.64 AW	39860 AAW	MSBLS	10//99-12//99
	Missouri	S	19.93 MW	21.80 AW	45350 AAW	MOBLS	10//99-12//99
	Columbia MSA, MO	S	18.22 MW	16.93 AW	37910 AAW	MOBLS	10//99-12//99
	Joplin MSA, MO	S	15.24 MW	14.86 AW	31700 AAW	MOBLS	10//99-12//99
	Kansas City MSA, MO-KS	S	22.59 MW	20.98 AW	46980 AAW	MOBLS	10//99-12//99
	St. Joseph MSA, MO	S	20.62 MW	17.79 AW	42890 AAW	MOBLS	10//99-12//99
	St. Louis MSA, MO-IL	S	22.92 MW	21.29 AW	47680 AAW	MOBLS	10//99-12//99
	Springfield MSA, MO	S	16.38 MW	15.14 AW	34070 AAW	MOBLS	10//99-12//99
	Montana	S	15.99 MW	16.90 AW	35160 AAW	MTBLS	10//99-12//99
	Billings MSA, MT	S	18.93 MW	18.43 AW	39370 AAW	MTBLS	10//99-12//99
	Great Falls MSA, MT	S	16.98 MW	16.73 AW	35310 AAW	MTBLS	10//99-12//99
	Missoula MSA, MT	S	16.83 MW	15.39 AW	35000 AAW	MTBLS	10//99-12//99
	Nebraska	S	16.22 MW	17.88 AW	37190 AAW	NEBLS	10//99-12//99
	Lincoln MSA, NE	S	13.91 MW	12.87 AW	28930 AAW	NEBLS	10//99-12//99
	Omaha MSA, NE-IA	S	20.69 MW	18.39 AW	43030 AAW	NEBLS	10//99-12//99
	Nevada	S	22.19 MW	24.12 AW	50170 AAW	NVBLS	10//99-12//99
	Las Vegas MSA, NV-AZ	S	24.08 MW	22.63 AW	50090 AAW	NVBLS	10//99-12//99
	Reno MSA, NV	S	24.92 MW	19.48 AW	51840 AAW	NVBLS	10//99-12//99
	New Hampshire	S	20.4 MW	22.24 AW	46250 AAW	NHBLS	10//99-12//99
	Manchester PMSA, NH	S	24.40 MW	22.06 AW	50750 AAW	NHBLS	10//99-12//99
	Nashua PMSA, NH	S	24.51 MW	21.50 AW	50980 AAW	NHBLS	10//99-12//99
	Portsmouth-Rochester PMSA, NH-ME	S	20.34 MW	19.08 AW	42310 AAW	NHBLS	10//99-12//99
	New Jersey	S	24.35 MW	25.33 AW	52690 AAW	NJBLS	10//99-12//99
	Atlantic-Cape May PMSA, NJ	S	23.70 MW	22.98 AW	49300 AAW	NJBLS	10//99-12//99
	Bergen-Passaic PMSA, NJ	S	25.34 MW	24.72 AW	52710 AAW	NJBLS	10//99-12//99
	Jersey City PMSA, NJ	S	27.53 MW	27.11 AW	57260 AAW	NJBLS	10//99-12//99
	Middlesex-Somerset-Hunterdon PMSA, NJ	S	25.90 MW	24.46 AW	53860 AAW	NJBLS	10//99-12//99
	Monmouth-Ocean PMSA, NJ	S	22.98 MW	20.54 AW	47800 AAW	NJBLS	10//99-12//99
	Newark PMSA, NJ	S	25.92 MW	24.97 AW	53910 AAW	NJBLS	10//99-12//99
	Trenton PMSA, NJ	S	25.10 MW	24.35 AW	52200 AAW	NJBLS	10//99-12//99
	Vineland-Millville-Bridgeton PMSA, NJ	S	21.17 MW	20.76 AW	44040 AAW	NJBLS	10//99-12//99
	New Mexico	S	17.35 MW	18.29 AW	38040 AAW	NMBLS	10//99-12//99
	Albuquerque MSA, NM	S	18.73 MW	17.77 AW	38970 AAW	NMBLS	10//99-12//99
	Las Cruces MSA, NM	S	13.01 MW	12.56 AW	27060 AAW	NMBLS	10//99-12//99
	Santa Fe MSA, NM	S	19.18 MW	19.96 AW	39900 AAW	NMBLS	10//99-12//99
	New York	S	22.48 MW	24.77 AW	51520 AAW	NYBLS	10//99-12//99
	Albany-Schenectady-Troy MSA, NY	S	20.46 MW	18.75 AW	42560 AAW	NYBLS	10//99-12//99
	Binghamton MSA, NY	S	18.91 MW	18.32 AW	39340 AAW	NYBLS	10//99-12//99
	Buffalo-Niagara Falls MSA, NY	S	21.09 MW	20.43 AW	43880 AAW	NYBLS	10//99-12//99
	Dutchess County PMSA, NY	S	20.42 MW	18.77 AW	42460 AAW	NYBLS	10//99-12//99
	Jamestown MSA, NY	S	18.71 MW	17.93 AW	38920 AAW	NYBLS	10//99-12//99
	Nassau-Suffolk PMSA, NY	S	25.78 MW	25.60 AW	53630 AAW	NYBLS	10//99-12//99
	New York PMSA, NY	S	29.13 MW	27.92 AW	60580 AAW	NYBLS	10//99-12//99
	Newburgh PMSA, NY-PA	S	24.37 MW	22.71 AW	50690 AAW	NYBLS	10//99-12//99
	Rochester MSA, NY	S	20.23 MW	18.13 AW	42080 AAW	NYBLS	10//99-12//99
	Syracuse MSA, NY	S	19.74 MW	18.98 AW	41060 AAW	NYBLS	10//99-12//99
	Utica-Rome MSA, NY	S	16.53 MW	15.83 AW	34380 AAW	NYBLS	10//99-12//99
	North Carolina	S	19.24 MW	20.78 AW	43220 AAW	NCBLS	10//99-12//99
	Asheville MSA, NC	S	16.61 MW	16.61 AW	34550 AAW	NCBLS	10//99-12//99

AAW Average annual wage	AOH Average offered, high	ASH Average starting, high	H Hourly	M Monthly	S Special: hourly and annual
AE Average entry wage	AOL Average offered, low	ASL Average starting, low	HI Highest wage paid	MTC Median total compensation	TQ Third quartile wage
AEX Average experienced wage	APH Average pay, high range	AW Average wage paid	HR High end range	MW Median wage paid	W Weekly
AO Average offered	APL Average pay, low range	FQ First quartile wage	LR Low end range	SQ Second quartile wage	Y Yearly

Occupation/Type/Industry	Location	Per	Low	Mid	High	Source	Date
Cost Estimator	Charlotte-Gastonia-Rock Hill						
	MSA, NC-SC	S	22.08 MW	20.21 AW	45920 AAW	NCBLS	10//99-12//99
	Fayetteville MSA, NC	S	18.22 MW	17.06 AW	37910 AAW	NCBLS	10//99-12//99
	Goldsboro MSA, NC	S	19.38 MW	18.78 AW	40300 AAW	NCBLS	10//99-12//99
	Greensboro--Winston-Salem--						
	High Point MSA, NC	S	20.20 MW	18.47 AW	42020 AAW	NCBLS	10//99-12//99
	Greenville MSA, NC	S	19.25 MW	19.31 AW	40030 AAW	NCBLS	10//99-12//99
	Hickory-Morganton-Lenoir						
	MSA, NC	S	19.54 MW	18.74 AW	40640 AAW	NCBLS	10//99-12//99
	Jacksonville MSA, NC	S	14.54 MW	14.19 AW	30250 AAW	NCBLS	10//99-12//99
	Raleigh-Durham-Chapel Hill						
	MSA, NC	S	22.32 MW	21.06 AW	46430 AAW	NCBLS	10//99-12//99
	Rocky Mount MSA, NC	S	18.67 MW	16.74 AW	38840 AAW	NCBLS	10//99-12//99
	Wilmington MSA, NC	S	20.05 MW	18.32 AW	41710 AAW	NCBLS	10//99-12//99
	North Dakota	S	15.68 MW	16.90 AW	35150 AAW	NDBLS	10//99-12//99
	Bismarck MSA, ND	S	16.09 MW	15.53 AW	33460 AAW	NDBLS	10//99-12//99
	Fargo-Moorhead MSA, ND-						
	MN	S	17.21 MW	16.53 AW	35800 AAW	NDBLS	10//99-12//99
	Grand Forks MSA, ND-MN	S	18.72 MW	16.80 AW	38940 AAW	NDBLS	10//99-12//99
	Ohio	S	19.63 MW	20.88 AW	43430 AAW	OHBLS	10//99-12//99
	Akron PMSA, OH	S	21.33 MW	20.37 AW	44370 AAW	OHBLS	10//99-12//99
	Canton-Massillon MSA, OH	S	18.37 MW	17.27 AW	38200 AAW	OHBLS	10//99-12//99
	Cincinnati PMSA, OH-KY-IN	S	20.69 MW	19.50 AW	43030 AAW	OHBLS	10//99-12//99
	Cleveland-Lorain-Elyria						
	PMSA, OH	S	22.25 MW	20.44 AW	46280 AAW	OHBLS	10//99-12//99
	Columbus MSA, OH	S	20.93 MW	19.52 AW	43520 AAW	OHBLS	10//99-12//99
	Dayton-Springfield MSA, OH	S	21.43 MW	20.23 AW	44570 AAW	OHBLS	10//99-12//99
	Hamilton-Middletown PMSA,						
	OH	S	22.44 MW	21.94 AW	46670 AAW	OHBLS	10//99-12//99
	Lima MSA, OH	S	19.62 MW	18.95 AW	40800 AAW	OHBLS	10//99-12//99
	Mansfield MSA, OH	S	17.85 MW	17.12 AW	37130 AAW	OHBLS	10//99-12//99
	Steubenville-Weirton MSA,						
	OH-WV	S	18.89 MW	18.50 AW	39300 AAW	OHBLS	10//99-12//99
	Toledo MSA, OH	S	20.56 MW	19.19 AW	42760 AAW	OHBLS	10//99-12//99
	Youngstown-Warren MSA, OH	S	19.33 MW	18.90 AW	40200 AAW	OHBLS	10//99-12//99
	Oklahoma	S	17.79 MW	19.78 AW	41150 AAW	OKBLS	10//99-12//99
	Oklahoma City MSA, OK	S	20.13 MW	18.29 AW	41860 AAW	OKBLS	10//99-12//99
	Tulsa MSA, OK	S	19.67 MW	17.81 AW	40910 AAW	OKBLS	10//99-12//99
	Oregon	S	20.58 MW	22.33 AW	46450 AAW	ORBLS	10//99-12//99
	Corvallis MSA, OR	S	19.81 MW	19.24 AW	41210 AAW	ORBLS	10//99-12//99
	Eugene-Springfield MSA, OR	S	19.61 MW	17.22 AW	40790 AAW	ORBLS	10//99-12//99
	Medford-Ashland MSA, OR	S	19.71 MW	17.29 AW	40990 AAW	ORBLS	10//99-12//99
	Portland-Vancouver PMSA,						
	OR-WA	S	22.75 MW	20.92 AW	47330 AAW	ORBLS	10//99-12//99
	Salem PMSA, OR	S	22.98 MW	20.34 AW	47800 AAW	ORBLS	10//99-12//99
	Pennsylvania	S	18.8 MW	20.14 AW	41890 AAW	PABLS	10//99-12//99
	Allentown-Bethlehem-Easton						
	MSA, PA	S	19.68 MW	18.50 AW	40930 AAW	PABLS	10//99-12//99
	Altoona MSA, PA	S	18.05 MW	16.86 AW	37540 AAW	PABLS	10//99-12//99
	Erie MSA, PA	S	16.61 MW	15.74 AW	34550 AAW	PABLS	10//99-12//99
	Harrisburg-Lebanon-Carlisle						
	MSA, PA	S	20.17 MW	18.01 AW	41950 AAW	PABLS	10//99-12//99
	Johnstown MSA, PA	S	17.18 MW	16.45 AW	35730 AAW	PABLS	10//99-12//99
	Lancaster MSA, PA	S	19.67 MW	18.51 AW	40910 AAW	PABLS	10//99-12//99
	Philadelphia PMSA, PA-NJ	S	22.76 MW	21.27 AW	47340 AAW	PABLS	10//99-12//99
	Pittsburgh MSA, PA	S	19.67 MW	18.69 AW	40910 AAW	PABLS	10//99-12//99
	Reading MSA, PA	S	21.54 MW	19.69 AW	44810 AAW	PABLS	10//99-12//99
	Scranton--Wilkes-Barre--						
	Hazleton MSA, PA	S	17.67 MW	15.94 AW	36760 AAW	PABLS	10//99-12//99
	Sharon MSA, PA	S	19.03 MW	17.50 AW	39590 AAW	PABLS	10//99-12//99
	State College MSA, PA	S	18.33 MW	16.40 AW	38130 AAW	PABLS	10//99-12//99
	Williamsport MSA, PA	S	17.50 MW	16.94 AW	36390 AAW	PABLS	10//99-12//99
	York MSA, PA	S	19.82 MW	18.69 AW	41230 AAW	PABLS	10//99-12//99
	Rhode Island	S	21.04 MW	23.67 AW	49240 AAW	RIBLS	10//99-12//99
	Providence-Fall River-						
	Warwick MSA, RI-MA	S	22.70 MW	20.32 AW	47210 AAW	RIBLS	10//99-12//99
	South Carolina	S	18.05 MW	19.94 AW	41470 AAW	SCBLS	10//99-12//99
	Charleston-North Charleston						
	MSA, SC	S	18.49 MW	16.51 AW	38460 AAW	SCBLS	10//99-12//99
	Columbia MSA, SC	S	17.63 MW	15.64 AW	36670 AAW	SCBLS	10//99-12//99
	Florence MSA, SC	S	16.24 MW	14.05 AW	33770 AAW	SCBLS	10//99-12//99

AAW	Average annual wage	AOH	Average offered, high	ASH	Average starting, high	H	Hourly	M	Monthly	S	Special: hourly and annual
AE	Average entry wage	AOL	Average offered, low	ASL	Average starting, low	HI	Highest wage paid	MTC	Median total compensation	TQ	Third quartile wage
AEX	Average experienced wage	APH	Average pay, high range	AW	Average wage paid	HR	High end range	MW	Median wage paid	W	Weekly
AO	Average offered	APL	Average pay, low range	FQ	First quartile wage	LR	Low end range	SQ	Second quartile wage	Y	Yearly

Occupation/Type/Industry	Location	Per	Low	Mid	High	Source	Date
Cost Estimator							
Cost Estimator	Greenville-Spartanburg-Anderson MSA, SC	S	22.15 MW	21.37 AW	46060 AAW	SCBLS	10//99-12//99
	Myrtle Beach MSA, SC	S	20.11 MW	18.34 AW	41830 AAW	SCBLS	10//99-12//99
	South Dakota	S	17.23 MW	17.48 AW	36360 AAW	SDBLS	10//99-12//99
	Rapid City MSA, SD	S	18.02 MW	17.87 AW	37490 AAW	SDBLS	10//99-12//99
	Sioux Falls MSA, SD	S	17.36 MW	16.61 AW	36110 AAW	SDBLS	10//99-12//99
	Tennessee	S	19.09 MW	20.82 AW	43300 AAW	TNBLS	10//99-12//99
	Chattanooga MSA, TN-GA	S	21.35 MW	18.89 AW	44400 AAW	TNBLS	10//99-12//99
	Clarksville-Hopkinsville MSA, TN-KY	S	16.97 MW	16.20 AW	35300 AAW	TNBLS	10//99-12//99
	Jackson MSA, TN	S	18.92 MW	17.69 AW	39350 AAW	TNBLS	10//99-12//99
	Johnson City-Kingsport-Bristol MSA, TN-VA	S	16.45 MW	15.85 AW	34230 AAW	TNBLS	10//99-12//99
	Knoxville MSA, TN	S	20.65 MW	19.28 AW	42960 AAW	TNBLS	10//99-12//99
	Memphis MSA, TN-AR-MS	S	23.45 MW	20.93 AW	48770 AAW	MSBLS	10//99-12//99
	Nashville MSA, TN	S	21.43 MW	19.94 AW	44570 AAW	TNBLS	10//99-12//99
	Texas	S	21.01 MW	22.54 AW	46870 AAW	TXBLS	10//99-12//99
	Abilene MSA, TX	S	17.52 MW	16.55 AW	36430 AAW	TXBLS	10//99-12//99
	Amarillo MSA, TX	S	19.33 MW	17.18 AW	40210 AAW	TXBLS	10//99-12//99
	Austin-San Marcos MSA, TX	S	20.24 MW	18.99 AW	42100 AAW	TXBLS	10//99-12//99
	Beaumont-Port Arthur MSA, TX	S	23.12 MW	22.31 AW	48100 AAW	TXBLS	10//99-12//99
	Brazoria PMSA, TX	S	20.17 MW	21.39 AW	41950 AAW	TXBLS	10//99-12//99
	Brownsville-Harlingen-San Benito MSA, TX	S	15.38 MW	13.36 AW	31990 AAW	TXBLQ	10//99-12//99
	Bryan-College Station MSA, TX	S	19.55 MW	18.63 AW	40660 AAW	TXBLS	10//99-12//99
	Corpus Christi MSA, TX	S	20.57 MW	19.80 AW	42790 AAW	TXBLS	10//99-12//99
	Dallas PMSA, TX	S	23.83 MW	22.33 AW	49560 AAW	TXBLS	10//99-12//99
	El Paso MSA, TX	S	16.98 MW	15.28 AW	35310 AAW	TXBLS	10//99-12//99
	Fort Worth-Arlington PMSA, TX	S	20.94 MW	19.10 AW	43550 AAW	TXBLS	10//99-12//99
	Galveston-Texas City PMSA, TX	S	23.92 MW	23.11 AW	49740 AAW	TXBLS	10//99-12//99
	Houston PMSA, TX	S	25.48 MW	25.66 AW	53000 AAW	TXBLS	10//99-12//99
	Killeen-Temple MSA, TX	S	19.20 MW	17.17 AW	39930 AAW	TXBLS	10//99-12//99
	Longview-Marshall MSA, TX	S	19.82 MW	18.97 AW	41230 AAW	TXBLS	10//99-12//99
	Lubbock MSA, TX	S	21.90 MW	20.09 AW	45550 AAW	TXBLS	10//99-12//99
	McAllen-Edinburg-Mission MSA, TX	S	14.95 MW	14.80 AW	31100 AAW	TXBLS	10//99-12//99
	Odessa-Midland MSA, TX	S	19.07 MW	18.95 AW	39660 AAW	TXBLS	10//99-12//99
	San Angelo MSA, TX	S	15.15 MW	14.63 AW	31500 AAW	TXBLS	10//99-12//99
	San Antonio MSA, TX	S	18.08 MW	16.46 AW	37610 AAW	TXBLS	10//99-12//99
	Sherman-Denison MSA, TX	S	22.91 MW	20.29 AW	47640 AAW	TXBLS	10//99-12//99
	Tyler MSA, TX	S	18.30 MW	17.37 AW	38070 AAW	TXBLS	10//99-12//99
	Victoria MSA, TX	S	17.26 MW	16.86 AW	35900 AAW	TXBLS	10//99-12//99
	Waco MSA, TX	S	16.95 MW	16.10 AW	35260 AAW	TXBLS	10//99-12//99
	Wichita Falls MSA, TX	S	16.61 MW	16.59 AW	34540 AAW	TXBLS	10//99-12//99
	Utah	S	18.58 MW	20.41 AW	42450 AAW	UTBLS	10//99-12//99
	Salt Lake City-Ogden MSA, UT	S	20.96 MW	19.39 AW	43600 AAW	UTBLS	10//99-12//99
	Vermont	S	17.63 MW	19.28 AW	40090 AAW	VTBLS	10//99-12//99
	Burlington MSA, VT	S	19.79 MW	18.09 AW	41160 AAW	VTBLS	10//99-12//99
	Virginia	S	19.97 MW	21.21 AW	44120 AAW	VABLS	10//99-12//99
	Charlottesville MSA, VA	S	18.90 MW	17.68 AW	39300 AAW	VABLS	10//99-12//99
	Lynchburg MSA, VA	S	20.71 MW	16.80 AW	43070 AAW	VABLS	10//99-12//99
	Norfolk-Virginia Beach-Newport News MSA, VA-NC	S	18.65 MW	18.20 AW	38790 AAW	VABLS	10//99-12//99
	Richmond-Petersburg MSA, VA	S	19.37 MW	18.39 AW	40290 AAW	VABLS	10//99-12//99
	Roanoke MSA, VA	S	19.43 MW	17.68 AW	40420 AAW	VABLS	10//99-12//99
	Washington	S	21.41 MW	23.02 AW	47880 AAW	WABLS	10//99-12//99
	Bellingham MSA, WA	S	21.61 MW	20.88 AW	44960 AAW	WABLS	10//99-12//99
	Bremerton PMSA, WA	S	17.85 MW	16.75 AW	37130 AAW	WABLS	10//99-12//99
	Olympia PMSA, WA	S	22.49 MW	19.87 AW	46780 AAW	WABLS	10//99-12//99
	Richland-Kennewick-Pasco MSA, WA	S	23.79 MW	22.90 AW	49490 AAW	WABLS	10//99-12//99
	Seattle-Bellevue-Everett PMSA, WA	S	24.44 MW	23.29 AW	50830 AAW	WABLS	10//99-12//99
	Spokane MSA, WA	S	20.85 MW	18.62 AW	43360 AAW	WABLS	10//99-12//99
	Tacoma PMSA, WA	S	22.20 MW	21.71 AW	46180 AAW	WABLS	10//99-12//99

AAW Average annual wage; AE Average entry wage; AEX Average experienced wage; AO Average offered; AOH Average offered, high; AOL Average offered, low; APH Average pay, high range; APL Average pay, low range; ASH Average starting, high; ASL Average starting, low; AW Average wage paid; FQ First quartile wage; H Hourly; HI Highest wage paid; HR High end range; LR Low end range; M Monthly; MTC Median total compensation; MW Median wage paid; SQ Second quartile wage; S Special: hourly and annual; TQ Third quartile wage; W Weekly; Y Yearly

Occupation/Type/Industry	Location	Per	Low	Mid	High	Source	Date
Cost Estimator	Yakima MSA, WA	S	20.76 MW	20.76 AW	43180 AAW	WABLS	10//99-12//99
	West Virginia	S	16.69 MW	18.58 AW	38640 AAW	WVBLS	10//99-12//99
	Charleston MSA, WV	S	17.64 MW	15.90 AW	36690 AAW	WVBLS	10//99-12//99
	Huntington-Ashland MSA, WV-KY-OH	S	19.59 MW	16.78 AW	40740 AAW	WVBLS	10//99-12//99
	Parkersburg-Marietta MSA, WV-OH	S	20.70 MW	20.73 AW	43050 AAW	WVBLS	10//99-12//99
	Wheeling MSA, WV-OH	S	19.58 MW	17.71 AW	40730 AAW	WVBLS	10//99-12//99
	Wisconsin	S	17.63 MW	18.79 AW	39090 AAW	WIBLS	10//99-12//99
	Appleton-Oshkosh-Neenah MSA, WI	S	20.51 MW	18.84 AW	42660 AAW	WIBLS	10//99-12//99
	Eau Claire MSA, WI	S	16.85 MW	16.46 AW	35040 AAW	WIBLS	10//99-12//99
	Green Bay MSA, WI	S	20.63 MW	19.53 AW	42910 AAW	WIBLS	10//99-12//99
	Janesville-Beloit MSA, WI	S	19.70 MW	19.99 AW	40980 AAW	WIBLS	10//99-12//99
	Kenosha PMSA, WI	S	22.43 MW	19.69 AW	46650 AAW	WIBLS	10//99-12//99
	La Crosse MSA, WI-MN	S	18.03 MW	17.45 AW	37500 AAW	WIBLS	10//99-12//99
	Madison MSA, WI	S	20.33 MW	19.49 AW	42290 AAW	WIBLS	10//99-12//99
	Milwaukee-Waukesha PMSA, WI	S	18.37 MW	17.52 AW	38200 AAW	WIBLS	10//99-12//99
	Racine PMSA, WI	S	18.97 MW	17.41 AW	39460 AAW	WIBLS	10//99-12//99
	Sheboygan MSA, WI	S	20.12 MW	18.61 AW	41860 AAW	WIBLS	10//99-12//99
	Wausau MSA, WI	S	16.34 MW	15.09 AW	33990 AAW	WIBLS	10//99-12//99
	Wyoming	S	19.31 MW	21.61 AW	44940 AAW	WYBLS	10//99-12//99
	Casper MSA, WY	S	16.21 MW	15.81 AW	33720 AAW	WYBLS	10//99-12//99
	Cheyenne MSA, WY	S	18.59 MW	16.48 AW	38670 AAW	WYBLS	10//99-12//99
	Puerto Rico	S	13.32 MW	14.23 AW	29600 AAW	PRBLS	10//99-12//99
	Caguas PMSA, PR	S	16.12 MW	17.57 AW	33520 AAW	PRBLS	10//99-12//99
	San Juan-Bayamon PMSA, PR	S	14.30 MW	13.54 AW	29750 AAW	PRBLS	10//99-12//99
	Guam	S	16.43 MW	16.83 AW	35000 AAW	GUBLS	10//99-12//99
Costume Attendant	Arizona	S	9.6 MW	10.22 AW	21260 AAW	AZBLS	10//99-12//99
	California	S	11.7 MW	12.93 AW	26890 AAW	CABLS	10//99-12//99
	Florida	S	7.26 MW	7.90 AW	16430 AAW	FLBLS	10//99-12//99
	Illinois	S	9.81 MW	10.00 AW	20800 AAW	ILBLS	10//99-12//99
	Minnesota	S	12.63 MW	12.84 AW	26710 AAW	MNBLS	10//99-12//99
	Mississippi	S	7.53 MW	7.57 AW	15750 AAW	MSBLS	10//99-12//99
	Missouri	S	10.72 MW	12.46 AW	25920 AAW	MOBLS	10//99-12//99
	Nevada	S	10.73 MW	10.36 AW	21550 AAW	NVBLS	10//99-12//99
	Ohio	S	9.6 MW	9.43 AW	19610 AAW	OHBLS	10//99-12//99
	Pennsylvania	S	6.71 MW	8.30 AW	17260 AAW	PABLS	10//99-12//99
	South Carolina	S	7.69 MW	7.65 AW	15910 AAW	SCBLS	10//99-12//99
	Texas	S	6.54 MW	9.21 AW	19150 AAW	TXBLS	10//99-12//99
	Washington	S	12.13 MW	12.50 AW	25990 AAW	WABLS	10//99-12//99
Counselor							
Bachelors, Behavioral Health Organization	United States	Y	21838 APL	25269 AW	30950 APH	ADAW	2000
Counter and Rental Clerk	Alabama	S	6.55 MW	7.22 AW	15020 AAW	ALBLS	10//99-12//99
	Anniston MSA, AL	S	8.28 MW	6.80 AW	17220 AAW	ALBLS	10//99-12//99
	Auburn-Opelika MSA, AL	S	7.69 MW	6.60 AW	16000 AAW	ALBLS	10//99-12//99
	Birmingham MSA, AL	S	7.59 MW	7.31 AW	15780 AAW	ALBLS	10//99-12//99
	Decatur MSA, AL	S	7.00 MW	6.54 AW	14560 AAW	ALBLS	10//99-12//99
	Dothan MSA, AL	S	7.03 MW	6.40 AW	14610 AAW	ALBLS	10//99-12//99
	Florence MSA, AL	S	6.47 MW	6.10 AW	13450 AAW	ALBLS	10//99-12//99
	Gadsden MSA, AL	S	7.71 MW	6.98 AW	16040 AAW	ALBLS	10//99-12//99
	Huntsville MSA, AL	S	7.37 MW	6.95 AW	15320 AAW	ALBLS	10//99-12//99
	Mobile MSA, AL	S	7.69 MW	6.53 AW	16000 AAW	ALBLS	10//99-12//99
	Montgomery MSA, AL	S	7.10 MW	6.54 AW	14760 AAW	ALBLS	10//99-12//99
	Tuscaloosa MSA, AL	S	7.32 MW	6.44 AW	15230 AAW	ALBLS	10//99-12//99
	Alaska	S	8.55 MW	9.39 AW	19540 AAW	AKBLS	10//99-12//99
	Anchorage MSA, AK	S	9.88 MW	9.01 AW	20550 AAW	AKBLS	10//99-12//99
	Arizona	S	7.73 MW	8.60 AW	17890 AAW	AZBLS	10//99-12//99
	Flagstaff MSA, AZ-UT	S	6.77 MW	6.32 AW	14080 AAW	AZBLS	10//99-12//99
	Phoenix-Mesa MSA, AZ	S	8.81 MW	7.89 AW	18320 AAW	AZBLS	10//99-12//99
	Tucson MSA, AZ	S	8.05 MW	7.62 AW	16750 AAW	AZBLS	10//99-12//99
	Yuma MSA, AZ	S	7.64 MW	6.44 AW	15890 AAW	AZBLS	10//99-12//99
	Arkansas	S	6.45 MW	7.01 AW	14580 AAW	ARBLS	10//99-12//99
	Fayetteville-Springdale-Rogers MSA, AR	S	7.63 MW	7.08 AW	15860 AAW	ARBLS	10//99-12//99
	Fort Smith MSA, AR-OK	S	6.54 MW	6.22 AW	13610 AAW	ARBLS	10//99-12//99
	Jonesboro MSA, AR	S	6.49 MW	6.13 AW	13500 AAW	ARBLS	10//99-12//99
	Little Rock-North Little Rock MSA, AR	S	7.55 MW	6.97 AW	15710 AAW	ARBLS	10//99-12//99

AAW	Average annual wage	AOH	Average offered, high	ASH	Average starting, high
AE	Average entry wage	AOL	Average offered, low	ASL	Average starting, low
AEX	Average experienced wage	APH	Average pay, high range	AW	Average wage paid
AO	Average offered	APL	Average pay, low range	FQ	First quartile wage

H	Hourly	M	Monthly
HI	Highest wage paid	MTC	Median total compensation
HR	High end range	MW	Median wage paid
LR	Low end range	SQ	Second quartile wage

S	Special: hourly and annual
TQ	Third quartile wage
W	Weekly
Y	Yearly

Counter and Rental Clerk

Occupation/Type/Industry	Location	Per	Low	Mid	High	Source	Date
Counter and Rental Clerk	Pine Bluff MSA, AR	S	6.57 MW	6.15 AW	13670 AAW	ARBLS	10//99-12//99
	California	S	7.6 MW	8.58 AW	17840 AAW	CABLS	10//99-12//99
	Bakersfield MSA, CA	S	8.27 MW	7.09 AW	17210 AAW	CABLS	10//99-12//99
	Chico-Paradise MSA, CA	S	7.68 MW	6.62 AW	15970 AAW	CABLS	10//99-12//99
	Fresno MSA, CA	S	8.53 MW	7.56 AW	17740 AAW	CABLS	10//99-12//99
	Los Angeles-Long Beach PMSA, CA	S	8.63 MW	7.79 AW	17960 AAW	CABLS	10//99-12//99
	Merced MSA, CA	S	7.57 MW	6.43 AW	15750 AAW	CABLS	10//99-12//99
	Modesto MSA, CA	S	7.90 MW	6.62 AW	16440 AAW	CABLS	10//99-12//99
	Oakland PMSA, CA	S	8.64 MW	7.84 AW	17960 AAW	CABLS	10//99-12//99
	Orange County PMSA, CA	S	8.46 MW	7.22 AW	17600 AAW	CABLS	10//99-12//99
	Redding MSA, CA	S	7.49 MW	6.66 AW	15580 AAW	CABLS	10//99-12//99
	Riverside-San Bernardino PMSA, CA	S	8.62 MW	7.64 AW	17920 AAW	CABLS	10//99-12//99
	Sacramento PMSA, CA	S	8.60 MW	7.20 AW	17890 AAW	CABLS	10//99-12//99
	Salinas MSA, CA	S	9.37 MW	8.22 AW	19480 AAW	CABLS	10//99-12//99
	San Diego MSA, CA	S	8.27 MW	7.33 AW	17200 AAW	CABLS	10//99-12//99
	San Francisco PMSA, CA	S	8.84 MW	8.36 AW	18390 AAW	CABLS	10//99-12//99
	San Jose PMSA, CA	S	9.49 MW	8.17 AW	19750 AAW	CABLS	10//99-12//99
	San Luis Obispo-Atascadero-Paso Robles MSA, CA	S	8.20 MW	6.72 AW	17060 AAW	CABLS	10//99-12//99
	Santa Barbara-Santa Maria-Lompoc MSA, CA	S	7.56 MW	6.84 AW	15730 AAW	CABLS	10//99-12//99
	Santa Cruz-Watsonville PMSA, CA	S	8.83 MW	7.44 AW	18370 AAW	CABLS	10//99-12//99
	Santa Rosa PMSA, CA	S	8.56 MW	7.10 AW	17810 AAW	CABLS	10//99-12//99
	Stockton-Lodi MSA, CA	S	7.97 MW	7.07 AW	16570 AAW	CABLS	10//99-12//99
	Vallejo-Fairfield-Napa PMSA, CA	S	8.06 MW	6.73 AW	16760 AAW	CABLS	10//99-12//99
	Ventura PMSA, CA	S	8.36 MW	6.86 AW	17400 AAW	CABLS	10//99-12//99
	Visalia-Tulare-Porterville MSA, CA	S	7.34 MW	6.64 AW	15270 AAW	CABLS	10//99-12//99
	Yolo PMSA, CA	S	9.34 MW	7.87 AW	19420 AAW	CABLS	10//99-12//99
	Yuba City MSA, CA	S	8.30 MW	7.87 AW	17270 AAW	CABLS	10//99-12//99
	Colorado	S	7.56 MW	8.22 AW	17090 AAW	COBLS	10//99-12//99
	Boulder-Longmont PMSA, CO	S	8.25 MW	7.54 AW	17160 AAW	COBLS	10//99-12//99
	Colorado Springs MSA, CO	S	8.04 MW	7.58 AW	16730 AAW	COBLS	10//99-12//99
	Denver PMSA, CO	S	8.53 MW	7.65 AW	17740 AAW	COBLS	10//99-12//99
	Fort Collins-Loveland MSA, CO	S	7.57 MW	7.21 AW	15740 AAW	COBLS	10//99-12//99
	Grand Junction MSA, CO	S	8.11 MW	7.20 AW	16870 AAW	COBLS	10//99-12//99
	Greeley PMSA, CO	S	7.50 MW	6.49 AW	15590 AAW	COBLS	10//99-12//99
	Pueblo MSA, CO	S	8.11 MW	6.86 AW	16870 AAW	COBLS	10//99-12//99
	Connecticut	S	7.29 MW	8.22 AW	17090 AAW	CTBLS	10//99-12//99
	Bridgeport PMSA, CT	S	8.03 MW	6.83 AW	16700 AAW	CTBLS	10//99-12//99
	Danbury PMSA, CT	S	8.81 MW	7.86 AW	18320 AAW	CTBLS	10//99-12//99
	Hartford MSA, CT	S	8.27 MW	7.29 AW	17200 AAW	CTBLS	10//99-12//99
	New Haven-Meriden PMSA, CT	S	8.20 MW	7.53 AW	17060 AAW	CTBLS	10//99-12//99
	New London-Norwich MSA, CT-RI	S	8.17 MW	7.60 AW	17000 AAW	CTBLS	10//99-12//99
	Stamford-Norwalk PMSA, CT	S	9.24 MW	8.04 AW	19220 AAW	CTBLS	10//99-12//99
	Waterbury PMSA, CT	S	7.09 MW	6.46 AW	14740 AAW	CTBLS	10//99-12//99
	Delaware	S	7.38 MW	8.69 AW	18080 AAW	DEBLS	10//99-12//99
	Dover MSA, DE	S	8.31 MW	6.38 AW	17280 AAW	DEBLS	10//99-12//99
	Wilmington-Newark PMSA, DE-MD	S	8.76 MW	7.68 AW	18220 AAW	DEBLS	10//99-12//99
	District of Columbia	S	8.04 MW	8.60 AW	17890 AAW	DCBLS	10//99-12//99
	Washington PMSA, DC-MD-VA-WV	S	8.38 MW	7.46 AW	17440 AAW	DCBLS	10//99-12//99
	Florida	S	7.71 MW	8.44 AW	17540 AAW	FLBLS	10//99-12//99
	Daytona Beach MSA, FL	S	8.14 MW	7.99 AW	16930 AAW	FLBLS	10//99-12//99
	Fort Lauderdale PMSA, FL	S	9.27 MW	8.67 AW	19290 AAW	FLBLS	10//99-12//99
	Fort Myers-Cape Coral MSA, FL	S	8.02 MW	7.38 AW	16690 AAW	FLBLS	10//99-12//99
	Fort Pierce-Port St. Lucie MSA, FL	S	7.94 MW	7.07 AW	16510 AAW	FLBLS	10//99-12//99
	Fort Walton Beach MSA, FL	S	7.53 MW	6.75 AW	15650 AAW	FLBLS	10//99-12//99
	Gainesville MSA, FL	S	7.26 MW	6.55 AW	15090 AAW	FLBLS	10//99-12//99
	Jacksonville MSA, FL	S	7.75 MW	7.25 AW	16120 AAW	FLBLS	10//99-12//99
	Lakeland-Winter Haven MSA, FL	S	7.43 MW	6.43 AW	15450 AAW	FLBLS	10//99-12//99

AAW Average annual wage	AOH Average offered, high	ASH Average starting, high	H Hourly	M Monthly	S Special: hourly and annual
AE Average entry wage	AOL Average offered, low	ASL Average starting, low	HI Highest wage paid	MTC Median total compensation	TQ Third quartile wage
AEX Average experienced wage	APH Average pay, high range	AW Average wage paid	HR High end range	MW Median wage paid	W Weekly
AO Average offered	APL Average pay, low range	FQ First quartile wage	LR Low end range	SQ Second quartile wage	Y Yearly

Occupation/Type/Industry	Location	Per	Low	Mid	High	Source	Date
Counter and Rental Clerk	Melbourne-Titusville-Palm						
	Bay MSA, FL	S	7.84 MW	6.84 AW	16310 AAW	FLBLS	10//99-12//99
	Miami PMSA, FL	S	9.18 MW	8.05 AW	19090 AAW	FLBLS	10//99-12//99
	Naples MSA, FL	S	8.15 MW	7.84 AW	16950 AAW	FLBLS	10//99-12//99
	Ocala MSA, FL	S	6.91 MW	6.14 AW	14380 AAW	FLBLS	10//99-12//99
	Orlando MSA, FL	S	8.94 MW	8.48 AW	18590 AAW	FLBLS	10//99-12//99
	Panama City MSA, FL	S	7.50 MW	7.11 AW	15590 AAW	FLBLS	10//99-12//99
	Pensacola MSA, FL	S	7.99 MW	7.21 AW	16630 AAW	FLBLS	10//99-12//99
	Punta Gorda MSA, FL	S	7.75 MW	7.12 AW	16120 AAW	FLBLS	10//99-12//99
	Sarasota-Bradenton MSA, FL	S	8.94 MW	7.81 AW	18590 AAW	FLBLS	10//99-12//99
	Tallahassee MSA, FL	S	7.04 MW	6.32 AW	14650 AAW	FLBLS	10//99-12//99
	Tampa-St. Petersburg-						
	Clearwater MSA, FL	S	8.59 MW	7.92 AW	17860 AAW	FLBLS	10//99-12//99
	West Palm Beach-Boca Raton						
	MSA, FL	S	7.89 MW	7.14 AW	16400 AAW	FLBLS	10//99-12//99
	Georgia	S	7.4 MW	7.93 AW	16500 AAW	GABLS	10//99-12//99
	Albany MSA, GA	S	7.19 MW	6.40 AW	14950 AAW	GABLS	10//99-12//99
	Athens MSA, GA	S	7.03 MW	6.32 AW	14630 AAW	GABLS	10//99-12//99
	Atlanta MSA, GA	S	8.30 MW	7.91 AW	17260 AAW	GABLS	10//99-12//99
	Augusta-Aiken MSA, GA-SC	S	7.58 MW	6.75 AW	15760 AAW	GABLS	10//99-12//99
	Columbus MSA, GA-AL	S	7.05 MW	6.50 AW	14660 AAW	GABLS	10//99-12//99
	Macon MSA, GA	S	7.17 MW	6.41 AW	14920 AAW	GABLS	10//99-12//99
	Savannah MSA, GA	S	7.31 MW	6.73 AW	15210 AAW	GABLS	10//99-12//99
	Hawaii	S	8.49 MW	9.06 AW	18850 AAW	HIBLS	10//99-12//99
	Honolulu MSA, HI	S	9.23 MW	8.63 AW	19190 AAW	HIBLS	10//99-12//99
	Idaho	S	6.82 MW	7.41 AW	15410 AAW	IDBLS	10//99-12//99
	Boise City MSA, ID	S	7.96 MW	7.38 AW	16560 AAW	IDBLS	10//99-12//99
	Pocatello MSA, ID	S	6.88 MW	6.25 AW	14310 AAW	IDBLS	10//99-12//99
	Illinois	S	7.29 MW	8.09 AW	16820 AAW	ILBLS	10//99-12//99
	Bloomington-Normal MSA, IL	S	7.38 MW	6.80 AW	15340 AAW	ILBLS	10//99-12//99
	Champaign-Urbana MSA, IL	S	7.65 MW	6.60 AW	15910 AAW	ILBLS	10//99-12//99
	Chicago PMSA, IL	S	8.27 MW	7.49 AW	17200 AAW	ILBLS	10//99-12//99
	Decatur MSA, IL	S	7.49 MW	6.33 AW	15580 AAW	ILBLS	10//99-12//99
	Kankakee PMSA, IL	S	7.45 MW	7.04 AW	15490 AAW	ILBLS	10//99-12//99
	Peoria-Pekin MSA, IL	S	7.59 MW	6.80 AW	15800 AAW	ILBLS	10//99-12//99
	Rockford MSA, IL	S	7.45 MW	6.80 AW	15500 AAW	ILBLS	10//99-12//99
	Springfield MSA, IL	S	6.92 MW	6.45 AW	14390 AAW	ILBLS	10//99-12//99
	Indiana	S	7 MW	7.61 AW	15830 AAW	INBLS	10//99-12//99
	Bloomington MSA, IN	S	8.06 MW	6.81 AW	16760 AAW	INBLS	10//99-12//99
	Elkhart-Goshen MSA, IN	S	7.58 MW	7.19 AW	15760 AAW	INBLS	10//99-12//99
	Evansville-Henderson MSA,						
	IN-KY	S	7.27 MW	6.68 AW	15110 AAW	INBLS	10//99-12//99
	Fort Wayne MSA, IN	S	8.05 MW	7.04 AW	16740 AAW	INBLS	10//99-12//99
	Gary PMSA, IN	S	7.76 MW	6.54 AW	16150 AAW	INBLS	10//99-12//99
	Indianapolis MSA, IN	S	7.61 MW	7.28 AW	15830 AAW	INBLS	10//99-12//99
	Kokomo MSA, IN	S	7.20 MW	6.59 AW	14980 AAW	INBLS	10//99-12//99
	Lafayette MSA, IN	S	7.27 MW	6.63 AW	15120 AAW	INBLS	10//99-12//99
	Muncie MSA, IN	S	6.92 MW	6.21 AW	14390 AAW	INBLS	10//99-12//99
	South Bend MSA, IN	S	8.18 MW	8.02 AW	17010 AAW	INBLS	10//99-12//99
	Terre Haute MSA, IN	S	7.43 MW	6.62 AW	15440 AAW	INBLS	10//99-12//99
	Iowa	S	6.39 MW	6.95 AW	14450 AAW	IABLS	10//99-12//99
	Cedar Rapids MSA, IA	S	7.32 MW	7.05 AW	15220 AAW	IABLS	10//99-12//99
	Davenport-Moline-Rock Island						
	MSA, IA-IL	S	7.57 MW	6.74 AW	15750 AAW	IABLS	10//99-12//99
	Des Moines MSA, IA	S	7.11 MW	6.50 AW	14790 AAW	IABLS	10//99-12//99
	Dubuque MSA, IA	S	7.93 MW	6.95 AW	16500 AAW	IABLS	10//99-12//99
	Iowa City MSA, IA	S	7.07 MW	6.27 AW	14710 AAW	IABLS	10//99-12//99
	Sioux City MSA, IA-NE	S	6.76 MW	6.50 AW	14050 AAW	IABLS	10//99-12//99
	Waterloo-Cedar Falls MSA, IA	S	6.53 MW	6.13 AW	13590 AAW	IABLS	10//99-12//99
	Kansas	S	6.61 MW	7.36 AW	15300 AAW	KSBLS	10//99-12//99
	Lawrence MSA, KS	S	7.03 MW	6.69 AW	14620 AAW	KSBLS	10//99-12//99
	Topeka MSA, KS	S	7.44 MW	6.67 AW	15470 AAW	KSBLS	10//99-12//99
	Wichita MSA, KS	S	7.13 MW	6.29 AW	14840 AAW	KSBLS	10//99-12//99
	Kentucky	S	6.38 MW	7.03 AW	14630 AAW	KYBLS	10//99-12//99
	Lexington MSA, KY	S	7.24 MW	6.50 AW	15070 AAW	KYBLS	10//99-12//99
	Louisville MSA, KY-IN	S	7.32 MW	6.68 AW	15220 AAW	KYBLS	10//99-12//99
	Owensboro MSA, KY	S	6.44 MW	6.18 AW	13400 AAW	KYBLS	10//99-12//99
	Louisiana	S	6.71 MW	7.92 AW	16480 AAW	LABLS	10//99-12//99
	Alexandria MSA, LA	S	6.63 MW	6.26 AW	13780 AAW	LABLS	10//99-12//99
	Baton Rouge MSA, LA	S	7.61 MW	6.56 AW	15830 AAW	LABLS	10//99-12//99
	Houma MSA, LA	S	7.99 MW	6.88 AW	16620 AAW	LABLS	10//99-12//99
	Lafayette MSA, LA	S	8.60 MW	7.11 AW	17890 AAW	LABLS	10//99-12//99

AAW Average annual wage	AOH Average offered, high	ASH Average starting, high	H Hourly	M Monthly	S Special: hourly and annual
AE Average entry wage	AOL Average offered, low	ASL Average starting, low	HI Highest wage paid	MTC Median total compensation	TQ Third quartile wage
AEX Average experienced wage	APH Average pay, high range	AW Average wage paid	HR High end range	MW Median wage paid	W Weekly
AO Average offered	APL Average pay, low range	FQ First quartile wage	LR Low end range	SQ Second quartile wage	Y Yearly

Occupation/Type/Industry	Location	Per	Low	Mid	High	Source	Date
Counter and Rental Clerk	Lake Charles MSA, LA	S	6.95 MW	6.43 AW	14460 AAW	LABLS	10//99-12//99
	Monroe MSA, LA	S	7.23 MW	7.00 AW	15040 AAW	LABLS	10//99-12//99
	New Orleans MSA, LA	S	8.82 MW	6.70 AW	18360 AAW	LABLS	10//99-12//99
	Shreveport-Bossier City MSA, LA	S	7.12 MW	7.09 AW	14820 AAW	LABLS	10//99-12//99
	Maine	S	6.87 MW	7.44 AW	15470 AAW	MEBLS	10//99-12//99
	Bangor MSA, ME	S	7.10 MW	6.11 AW	14780 AAW	MEBLS	10//99-12//99
	Lewiston-Auburn MSA, ME	S	7.38 MW	6.66 AW	15360 AAW	MEBLS	10//99-12//99
	Portland MSA, ME	S	8.00 MW	7.69 AW	16630 AAW	MEBLS	10//99-12//99
	Maryland	S	7.47 MW	8.57 AW	17840 AAW	MDBLS	10//99-12//99
	Baltimore PMSA, MD	S	8.62 MW	7.57 AW	17930 AAW	MDBLS	10//99-12//99
	Cumberland MSA, MD-WV	S	7.73 MW	6.20 AW	16080 AAW	MDBLS	10//99-12//99
	Hagerstown PMSA, MD	S	7.41 MW	6.90 AW	15420 AAW	MDBLS	10//99-12//99
	Massachusetts	S	7.67 MW	8.34 AW	17350 AAW	MABLS	10//99-12//99
	Barnstable-Yarmouth MSA, MA	S	8.49 MW	7.35 AW	17670 AAW	MABLS	10//99-12//99
	Boston PMSA, MA-NH	S	8.46 MW	7.93 AW	17590 AAW	MABLS	10//99-12//99
	Brockton PMSA, MA	S	7.87 MW	7.36 AW	16380 AAW	MABLS	10//99-12//99
	Fitchburg-Leominster PMSA, MA	S	8.14 MW	7.09 AW	16940 AAW	MABLS	10//99-12//99
	Lawrence PMSA, MA-NH	S	7.86 MW	6.68 AW	16350 AAW	MABLS	10//99-12//99
	Lowell PMSA, MA-NH	S	7.87 MW	7.05 AW	16380 AAW	MABLS	10//99-12//99
	New Bedford PMSA, MA	S	6.92 MW	6.44 AW	14400 AAW	MABLS	10//99-12//99
	Pittsfield MSA, MA	S	7.77 MW	6.93 AW	16160 AAW	MABLS	10//99-12//99
	Springfield MSA, MA	S	8.12 MW	7.29 AW	16890 AAW	MABLS	10//99-12//99
	Worcester PMSA, MA-CT	S	8.90 MW	7.68 AW	18510 AAW	MABLS	10//99-12//99
	Michigan	S	7.06 MW	7.89 AW	16410 AAW	MIBLS	10//99-12//99
	Ann Arbor PMSA, MI	S	8.84 MW	7.70 AW	18390 AAW	MIBLS	10//99-12//99
	Benton Harbor MSA, MI	S	7.53 MW	6.24 AW	15660 AAW	MIBLS	10//99-12//99
	Detroit PMSA, MI	S	7.87 MW	7.16 AW	16370 AAW	MIBLS	10//99-12//99
	Flint PMSA, MI	S	7.83 MW	7.35 AW	16300 AAW	MIBLS	10//99-12//99
	Grand Rapids-Muskegon-Holland MSA, MI	S	8.87 MW	8.00 AW	18440 AAW	MIBLS	10//99-12//99
	Jackson MSA, MI	S	7.10 MW	6.22 AW	14780 AAW	MIBLS	10//99-12//99
	Kalamazoo-Battle Creek MSA, MI	S	7.43 MW	6.74 AW	15450 AAW	MIBLS	10//99-12//99
	Lansing-East Lansing MSA, MI	S	7.71 MW	6.79 AW	16030 AAW	MIBLS	10//99-12//99
	Saginaw-Bay City-Midland MSA, MI	S	8.01 MW	7.64 AW	16670 AAW	MIBLS	10//99-12//99
	Minnesota	S	6.85 MW	7.58 AW	15770 AAW	MNBLS	10//99-12//99
	Duluth-Superior MSA, MN-WI	S	6.63 MW	6.16 AW	13790 AAW	MNBLS	10//99-12//99
	Minneapolis-St. Paul MSA, MN-WI	S	7.88 MW	7.18 AW	16380 AAW	MNBLS	10//99-12//99
	Rochester MSA, MN	S	7.35 MW	6.27 AW	15300 AAW	MNBLS	10//99-12//99
	St. Cloud MSA, MN	S	7.84 MW	7.40 AW	16310 AAW	MNBLS	10//99-12//99
	Mississippi	S	6.38 MW	7.06 AW	14690 AAW	MSBLS	10//99-12//99
	Biloxi-Gulfport-Pascagoula MSA, MS	S	7.35 MW	6.97 AW	15290 AAW	MSBLS	10//99-12//99
	Hattiesburg MSA, MS	S	6.17 MW	6.12 AW	12840 AAW	MSBLS	10//99-12//99
	Jackson MSA, MS	S	7.80 MW	7.33 AW	16220 AAW	MSBLS	10//99-12//99
	Missouri	S	6.69 MW	7.59 AW	15790 AAW	MOBLS	10//99-12//99
	Columbia MSA, MO	S	7.78 MW	6.25 AW	16180 AAW	MOBLS	10//99-12//99
	Joplin MSA, MO	S	7.36 MW	6.47 AW	15310 AAW	MOBLS	10//99-12//99
	Kansas City MSA, MO-KS	S	7.73 MW	6.77 AW	16080 AAW	MOBLS	10//99-12//99
	St. Joseph MSA, MO	S	6.68 MW	6.21 AW	13890 AAW	MOBLS	10//99-12//99
	St. Louis MSA, MO-IL	S	7.77 MW	7.03 AW	16150 AAW	MOBLS	10//99-12//99
	Springfield MSA, MO	S	7.23 MW	6.39 AW	15040 AAW	MOBLS	10//99-12//99
	Montana	S	6.26 MW	6.85 AW	14250 AAW	MTBLS	10//99-12//99
	Billings MSA, MT	S	6.94 MW	6.31 AW	14430 AAW	MTBLS	10//99-12//99
	Great Falls MSA, MT	S	7.52 MW	6.25 AW	15650 AAW	MTBLS	10//99-12//99
	Missoula MSA, MT	S	6.55 MW	6.13 AW	13620 AAW	MTBLS	10//99-12//99
	Nebraska	S	7.04 MW	7.56 AW	15730 AAW	NEBLS	10//99-12//99
	Lincoln MSA, NE	S	8.13 MW	7.54 AW	16900 AAW	NEBLS	10//99-12//99
	Omaha MSA, NE-IA	S	8.24 MW	7.53 AW	17130 AAW	NEBLS	10//99-12//99
	Nevada	S	7.81 MW	8.57 AW	17830 AAW	NVBLS	10//99-12//99
	Las Vegas MSA, NV-AZ	S	8.89 MW	8.06 AW	18490 AAW	NVBLS	10//99-12//99
	Reno MSA, NV	S	7.54 MW	6.95 AW	15680 AAW	NVBLS	10//99-12//99
	New Hampshire	S	7.53 MW	8.25 AW	17170 AAW	NHBLS	10//99-12//99
	Manchester PMSA, NH	S	8.38 MW	7.38 AW	17440 AAW	NHBLS	10//99-12//99
	Nashua PMSA, NH	S	8.53 MW	7.73 AW	17750 AAW	NHBLS	10//99-12//99
	Portsmouth-Rochester PMSA, NH-ME	S	8.45 MW	7.41 AW	17570 AAW	NHBLS	10//99-12//99

AAW	Average annual wage	AOH	Average offered, high	ASH	Average starting, high	H	Hourly	M	Monthly	S	Special: hourly and annual
AE	Average entry wage	AOL	Average offered, low	ASL	Average starting, low	HI	Highest wage paid	MTC	Median total compensation	TQ	Third quartile wage
AEX	Average experienced wage	APH	Average pay, high range	AW	Average wage paid	HR	High end range	MW	Median wage paid	W	Weekly
AO	Average offered	APL	Average pay, low range	FQ	First quartile wage	LR	Low end range	SQ	Second quartile wage	Y	Yearly

Occupation/Type/Industry	Location	Per	Low	Mid	High	Source	Date
Counter and Rental Clerk	New Jersey	S	7.57 MW	8.85 AW	18400 AAW	NJBLS	10//99-12//99
	Atlantic-Cape May PMSA, NJ	S	7.46 MW	6.55 AW	15510 AAW	NJBLS	10//99-12//99
	Bergen-Passaic PMSA, NJ	S	10.54 MW	9.27 AW	21920 AAW	NJBLS	10//99-12//99
	Jersey City PMSA, NJ	S	7.99 MW	6.98 AW	16620 AAW	NJBLS	10//99-12//99
	Middlesex-Somerset- Hunterdon PMSA, NJ	S	8.63 MW	7.61 AW	17950 AAW	NJBLS	10//99-12//99
	Monmouth-Ocean PMSA, NJ	S	7.80 MW	6.60 AW	16220 AAW	NJBLS	10//99-12//99
	Newark PMSA, NJ	S	9.01 MW	7.82 AW	18740 AAW	NJBLS	10//99-12//99
	Trenton PMSA, NJ	S	9.00 MW	7.83 AW	18720 AAW	NJBLS	10//99-12//99
	Vineland-Millville-Bridgeton PMSA, NJ	S	9.07 MW	7.87 AW	18860 AAW	NJBLS	10//99-12//99
	New Mexico	S	6.95 MW	7.45 AW	15490 AAW	NMBLS	10//99-12//99
	Albuquerque MSA, NM	S	7.55 MW	6.86 AW	15710 AAW	NMBLS	10//99-12//99
	Las Cruces MSA, NM	S	7.85 MW	7.21 AW	16330 AAW	NMBLS	10//99-12//99
	Santa Fe MSA, NM	S	7.61 MW	7.22 AW	15840 AAW	NMBLS	10//99-12//99
	New York	S	7.43 MW	8.47 AW	17610 AAW	NYBLS	10//99-12//99
	Albany-Schenectady-Troy MSA, NY	S	8.09 MW	7.12 AW	16840 AAW	NYBLS	10//99-12//99
	Binghamton MSA, NY	S	8.89 MW	7.46 AW	18490 AAW	NYBLS	10//99-12//99
	Buffalo-Niagara Falls MSA, NY	S	7.57 MW	7.05 AW	15740 AAW	NYBLS	10//99-12//99
	Dutchess County PMSA, NY	S	8.05 MW	7.46 AW	16740 AAW	NYBLS	10//99-12//99
	Elmira MSA, NY	S	7.91 MW	6.51 AW	16450 AAW	NYBLS	10//99-12//99
	Glens Falls MSA, NY	S	7.42 MW	6.63 AW	15430 AAW	NYBLS	10//99-12//99
	Jamestown MSA, NY	S	8.05 MW	6.82 AW	16740 AAW	NYBLS	10//99-12//99
	Nassau-Suffolk PMSA, NY	S	8.52 MW	7.33 AW	17720 AAW	NYBLS	10//99-12//99
	New York PMSA, NY	S	9.10 MW	7.94 AW	18930 AAW	NYBLS	10//99-12//99
	Newburgh PMSA, NY-PA	S	7.28 MW	6.62 AW	15140 AAW	NYBLS	10//99-12//99
	Rochester MSA, NY	S	7.59 MW	6.71 AW	15790 AAW	NYBLS	10//99-12//99
	Syracuse MSA, NY	S	7.65 MW	6.78 AW	15920 AAW	NYBLS	10//99-12//99
	Utica-Rome MSA, NY	S	7.55 MW	6.84 AW	15710 AAW	NYBLS	10//99-12//99
	North Carolina	S	6.89 MW	7.72 AW	16050 AAW	NCBLS	10//99-12//99
	Asheville MSA, NC	S	8.36 MW	7.33 AW	17380 AAW	NCBLS	10//99-12//99
	Charlotte-Gastonia-Rock Hill MSA, NC-SC	S	8.24 MW	7.24 AW	17150 AAW	NCBLS	10//99-12//99
	Fayetteville MSA, NC	S	6.68 MW	6.16 AW	13890 AAW	NCBLS	10//99-12//99
	Goldsboro MSA, NC	S	7.40 MW	6.76 AW	15400 AAW	NCBLS	10//99-12//99
	Greensboro--Winston-Salem-- High Point MSA, NC	S	7.96 MW	7.44 AW	16560 AAW	NCBLS	10//99-12//99
	Greenville MSA, NC	S	7.55 MW	6.51 AW	15700 AAW	NCBLS	10//99-12//99
	Hickory-Morganton-Lenoir MSA, NC	S	8.05 MW	7.48 AW	16730 AAW	NCBLS	10//99-12//99
	Jacksonville MSA, NC	S	7.01 MW	6.17 AW	14590 AAW	NCBLS	10//99-12//99
	Raleigh-Durham-Chapel Hill MSA, NC	S	7.60 MW	7.04 AW	15800 AAW	NCBLS	10//99-12//99
	Rocky Mount MSA, NC	S	7.43 MW	6.71 AW	15450 AAW	NCBLS	10//99-12//99
	Wilmington MSA, NC	S	7.80 MW	6.84 AW	16220 AAW	NCBLS	10//99-12//99
	North Dakota	S	6.23 MW	6.94 AW	14440 AAW	NDBLS	10//99-12//99
	Bismarck MSA, ND	S	6.76 MW	6.29 AW	14060 AAW	NDBLS	10//99-12//99
	Fargo-Moorhead MSA, ND-MN	S	6.72 MW	6.31 AW	13970 AAW	NDBLS	10//99-12//99
	Grand Forks MSA, ND-MN	S	7.37 MW	6.23 AW	15330 AAW	NDBLS	10//99-12//99
	Ohio	S	6.84 MW	7.68 AW	15970 AAW	OHBLS	10//99-12//99
	Akron PMSA, OH	S	8.01 MW	7.39 AW	16660 AAW	OHBLS	10//99-12//99
	Canton-Massillon MSA, OH	S	7.66 MW	7.26 AW	15940 AAW	OHBLS	10//99-12//99
	Cincinnati PMSA, OH-KY-IN	S	7.62 MW	6.85 AW	15840 AAW	OHBLS	10//99-12//99
	Cleveland-Lorain-Elyria PMSA, OH	S	7.85 MW	7.33 AW	16320 AAW	OHBLS	10//99-12//99
	Columbus MSA, OH	S	8.71 MW	7.60 AW	18120 AAW	OHBLS	10//99-12//99
	Dayton-Springfield MSA, OH	S	7.30 MW	6.20 AW	15190 AAW	OHBLS	10//99-12//99
	Hamilton-Middletown PMSA, OH	S	7.35 MW	6.59 AW	15280 AAW	OHBLS	10//99-12//99
	Lima MSA, OH	S	6.87 MW	6.35 AW	14280 AAW	OHBLS	10//99-12//99
	Mansfield MSA, OH	S	7.77 MW	7.16 AW	16160 AAW	OHBLS	10//99-12//99
	Steubenville-Weirton MSA, OH-WV	S	6.66 MW	6.26 AW	13850 AAW	OHBLS	10//99-12//99
	Toledo MSA, OH	S	7.50 MW	6.68 AW	15600 AAW	OHBLS	10//99-12//99
	Youngstown-Warren MSA, OH	S	7.07 MW	6.52 AW	14710 AAW	OHBLS	10//99-12//99
	Oklahoma	S	7.31 MW	7.74 AW	16100 AAW	OKBLS	10//99-12//99
	Lawton MSA, OK	S	6.78 MW	6.14 AW	14100 AAW	OKBLS	10//99-12//99
	Oklahoma City MSA, OK	S	7.39 MW	6.84 AW	15360 AAW	OKBLS	10//99-12//99
	Tulsa MSA, OK	S	8.39 MW	7.98 AW	17440 AAW	OKBLS	10//99-12//99

AAW Average annual wage	AOH Average offered, high	ASH Average starting, high	H Hourly	M Monthly	S Special: hourly and annual
AE Average entry wage	AOL Average offered, low	ASL Average starting, low	HI Highest wage paid	MTC Median total compensation	TQ Third quartile wage
AEX Average experienced wage	APH Average pay, high range	AW Average wage paid	HR High end range	MW Median wage paid	W Weekly
AO Average offered	APL Average pay, low range	FQ First quartile wage	LR Low end range	SQ Second quartile wage	Y Yearly

Counter and Rental Clerk

Occupation/Type/Industry	Location	Per	Low	Mid	High	Source	Date
	Oregon	S	7.73 MW	8.59 AW	17860 AAW	ORBLS	10//99-12//99
	Corvallis MSA, OR	S	7.97 MW	6.82 AW	16580 AAW	ORBLS	10//99-12//99
	Eugene-Springfield MSA, OR	S	8.57 MW	7.88 AW	17830 AAW	ORBLS	10//99-12//99
	Medford-Ashland MSA, OR	S	8.36 MW	7.96 AW	17400 AAW	ORBLS	10//99-12//99
	Portland-Vancouver PMSA, OR-WA	S	8.82 MW	7.81 AW	18340 AAW	ORBLS	10//99-12//99
	Salem PMSA, OR	S	8.22 MW	7.72 AW	17100 AAW	ORBLS	10//99-12//99
	Pennsylvania	S	6.77 MW	7.72 AW	16060 AAW	PABLS	10//99-12//99
	Allentown-Bethlehem-Easton MSA, PA	S	7.67 MW	6.60 AW	15960 AAW	PABLS	10//99-12//99
	Altoona MSA, PA	S	6.25 MW	6.09 AW	13000 AAW	PABLS	10//99-12//99
	Erie MSA, PA	S	7.11 MW	6.53 AW	14790 AAW	PABLS	10//99-12//99
	Harrisburg-Lebanon-Carlisle MSA, PA	S	7.41 MW	6.83 AW	15420 AAW	PABLS	10//99-12//99
	Johnstown MSA, PA	S	6.87 MW	6.30 AW	14280 AAW	PABLS	10//99-12//99
	Lancaster MSA, PA	S	7.80 MW	7.12 AW	16220 AAW	PABLS	10//99-12//99
	Philadelphia PMSA, PA-NJ	S	8.80 MW	7.88 AW	18310 AAW	PABLS	10//99-12//99
	Pittsburgh MSA, PA	S	7.13 MW	6.56 AW	14820 AAW	PABLS	10//99-12//99
	Reading MSA, PA	S	7.38 MW	6.38 AW	15350 AAW	PABLS	10//99-12//99
	Scranton--Wilkes-Barre--Hazleton MSA, PA	S	7.55 MW	6.97 AW	15700 AAW	PABLS	10//99-12//99
	Sharon MSA, PA	S	6.26 MW	6.05 AW	13030 AAW	PABLS	10//99-12//99
	State College MSA, PA	S	7.91 MW	7.20 AW	16460 AAW	PABLS	10//99-12//99
	Williamsport MSA, PA	S	7.01 MW	6.51 AW	14570 AAW	PABLS	10//99-12//99
	York MSA, PA	S	7.09 MW	6.79 AW	14740 AAW	PABLS	10//99-12//99
	Rhode Island	S	7.24 MW	7.99 AW	16610 AAW	RIBLS	10//99-12//99
	Providence-Fall River-Warwick MSA, RI-MA	S	7.76 MW	6.97 AW	16140 AAW	RIBLS	10//99-12//99
	South Carolina	S	6.81 MW	7.57 AW	15740 AAW	SCBLS	10//99-12//99
	Charleston-North Charleston MSA, SC	S	7.49 MW	6.65 AW	15580 AAW	SCBLS	10//99-12//99
	Columbia MSA, SC	S	7.86 MW	7.33 AW	16340 AAW	SCBLS	10//99-12//99
	Florence MSA, SC	S	8.83 MW	8.41 AW	18370 AAW	SCBLS	10//99-12//99
	Greenville-Spartanburg-Anderson MSA, SC	S	7.51 MW	6.65 AW	15620 AAW	SCBLS	10//99-12//99
	Myrtle Beach MSA, SC	S	8.06 MW	7.44 AW	16770 AAW	SCBLS	10//99-12//99
	Sumter MSA, SC	S	6.74 MW	6.17 AW	14010 AAW	SCBLS	10//99-12//99
	South Dakota	S	6.47 MW	7.02 AW	14600 AAW	SDBLS	10//99-12//99
	Rapid City MSA, SD	S	8.07 MW	7.49 AW	16780 AAW	SDBLS	10//99-12//99
	Sioux Falls MSA, SD	S	7.31 MW	7.00 AW	15200 AAW	SDBLS	10//99-12//99
	Tennessee	S	6.77 MW	7.69 AW	15990 AAW	TNBLS	10//99-12//99
	Chattanooga MSA, TN-GA	S	7.68 MW	6.99 AW	15980 AAW	TNBLS	10//99-12//99
	Clarksville-Hopkinsville MSA, TN-KY	S	9.05 MW	6.56 AW	18820 AAW	TNBLS	10//99-12//99
	Jackson MSA, TN	S	7.20 MW	6.79 AW	14970 AAW	TNBLS	10//99-12//99
	Johnson City-Kingsport-Bristol MSA, TN-VA	S	7.20 MW	6.25 AW	14970 AAW	TNBLS	10//99-12//99
	Knoxville MSA, TN	S	7.78 MW	7.34 AW	16170 AAW	TNBLS	10//99-12//99
	Memphis MSA, TN-AR-MS	S	8.50 MW	7.26 AW	17670 AAW	MSBLS	10//99-12//99
	Nashville MSA, TN	S	7.48 MW	6.96 AW	15550 AAW	TNBLS	10//99-12//99
	Texas	S	6.82 MW	7.86 AW	16340 AAW	TXBLS	10//99-12//99
	Abilene MSA, TX	S	7.11 MW	6.46 AW	14790 AAW	TXBLS	10//99-12//99
	Amarillo MSA, TX	S	7.31 MW	6.50 AW	15190 AAW	TXBLS	10//99-12//99
	Austin-San Marcos MSA, TX	S	7.95 MW	7.50 AW	16530 AAW	TXBLS	10//99-12//99
	Beaumont-Port Arthur MSA, TX	S	7.12 MW	6.19 AW	14800 AAW	TXBLS	10//99-12//99
	Brazoria PMSA, TX	S	7.45 MW	6.25 AW	15490 AAW	TXBLS	10//99-12//99
	Brownsville-Harlingen-San Benito MSA, TX	S	7.00 MW	6.19 AW	14550 AAW	TXBLS	10//99-12//99
	Bryan-College Station MSA, TX	S	6.89 MW	6.27 AW	14320 AAW	TXBLS	10//99-12//99
	Corpus Christi MSA, TX	S	7.41 MW	6.20 AW	15410 AAW	TXBLS	10//99-12//99
	Dallas PMSA, TX	S	8.11 MW	6.92 AW	16860 AAW	TXBLS	10//99-12//99
	El Paso MSA, TX	S	7.33 MW	6.30 AW	15240 AAW	TXBLS	10//99-12//99
	Fort Worth-Arlington PMSA, TX	S	8.43 MW	7.46 AW	17520 AAW	TXBLS	10//99-12//99
	Galveston-Texas City PMSA, TX	S	8.11 MW	7.28 AW	16870 AAW	TXBLS	10//99-12//99
	Houston PMSA, TX	S	8.10 MW	7.20 AW	16850 AAW	TXBLS	10//99-12//99
	Killeen-Temple MSA, TX	S	6.94 MW	6.33 AW	14430 AAW	TXBLS	10//99-12//99
	Laredo MSA, TX	S	7.13 MW	6.22 AW	14830 AAW	TXBLS	10//99-12//99
	Longview-Marshall MSA, TX	S	7.86 MW	7.26 AW	16340 AAW	TXBLS	10//99-12//99

AAW	Average annual wage	AOH	Average offered, high	ASH	Average starting, high	H	Hourly
AE	Average entry wage	AOL	Average offered, low	ASL	Average starting, low	HI	Highest wage paid
AEX	Average experienced wage	APH	Average pay, high range	AW	Average wage paid	HR	High end range
AO	Average offered	APL	Average pay, low range	FQ	First quartile wage	LR	Low end range

M	Monthly	S	Special: hourly and annual
MTC	Median total compensation	TQ	Third quartile wage
MW	Median wage paid	W	Weekly
SQ	Second quartile wage	Y	Yearly

Occupation/Type/Industry	Location	Per	Low	Mid	High	Source	Date
Counter and Rental Clerk	Lubbock MSA, TX	S	7.49 MW	6.67 AW	15580 AAW	TXBLS	10//99-12//99
	McAllen-Edinburg-Mission MSA, TX	S	6.96 MW	6.13 AW	14470 AAW	TXBLS	10//99-12//99
	Odessa-Midland MSA, TX	S	7.90 MW	6.65 AW	16440 AAW	TXBLS	10//99-12//99
	San Angelo MSA, TX	S	7.19 MW	6.39 AW	14960 AAW	TXBLS	10//99-12//99
	San Antonio MSA, TX	S	7.88 MW	6.94 AW	16390 AAW	TXBLS	10//99-12//99
	Sherman-Denison MSA, TX	S	7.49 MW	6.46 AW	15580 AAW	TXBLS	10//99-12//99
	Texarkana MSA, TX-Texarkana, AR	S	7.23 MW	6.21 AW	15030 AAW	TXBLS	10//99-12//99
	Tyler MSA, TX	S	7.54 MW	6.71 AW	15690 AAW	TXBLS	10//99-12//99
	Victoria MSA, TX	S	7.63 MW	6.36 AW	15880 AAW	TXBLS	10//99-12//99
	Waco MSA, TX	S	7.11 MW	6.59 AW	14800 AAW	TXBLS	10//99-12//99
	Wichita Falls MSA, TX	S	8.25 MW	6.58 AW	17160 AAW	TXBLS	10//99-12//99
	Utah	S	7.46 MW	7.94 AW	16520 AAW	UTBLS	10//99-12//99
	Provo-Orem MSA, UT	S	7.34 MW	6.72 AW	15280 AAW	UTBLS	10//99-12//99
	Salt Lake City-Ogden MSA, UT	S	8.14 MW	7.69 AW	16930 AAW	UTBLS	10//99-12//99
	Vermont	S	7 MW	7.80 AW	16220 AAW	VTBLS	10//99-12//99
	Burlington MSA, VT	S	7.57 MW	7.08 AW	15740 AAW	VTBLS	10//99-12//99
	Virginia	S	6.73 MW	7.64 AW	15890 AAW	VABLS	10//99-12//99
	Charlottesville MSA, VA	S	7.72 MW	7.55 AW	16060 AAW	VABLS	10//99-12//99
	Danville MSA, VA	S	7.18 MW	6.89 AW	14930 AAW	VABLS	10//99-12//99
	Lynchburg MSA, VA	S	7.38 MW	6.90 AW	15350 AAW	VABLS	10//99-12//99
	Norfolk-Virginia Beach-Newport News MSA, VA-NC	S	7.51 MW	6.64 AW	15620 AAW	VABLS	10//99-12//99
	Richmond-Petersburg MSA, VA	S	7.64 MW	6.44 AW	15880 AAW	VABLS	10//99-12//99
	Roanoke MSA, VA	S	8.50 MW	7.46 AW	17680 AAW	VABLS	10//99-12//99
	Washington	S	7.57 MW	8.54 AW	17750 AAW	WABLS	10//99-12//99
	Bellingham MSA, WA	S	8.75 MW	8.11 AW	18200 AAW	WABLS	10//99-12//99
	Bremerton PMSA, WA	S	8.23 MW	8.15 AW	17120 AAW	WABLS	10//99-12//99
	Olympia PMSA, WA	S	8.97 MW	7.77 AW	18660 AAW	WABLS	10//99-12//99
	Richland-Kennewick-Pasco MSA, WA	S	8.62 MW	7.51 AW	17930 AAW	WABLS	10//99-12//99
	Seattle-Bellevue-Everett PMSA, WA	S	8.76 MW	7.69 AW	18210 AAW	WABLS	10//99-12//99
	Spokane MSA, WA	S	7.91 MW	6.86 AW	16450 AAW	WABLS	10//99-12//99
	Tacoma PMSA, WA	S	8.22 MW	7.05 AW	17090 AAW	WABLS	10//99-12//99
	Yakima MSA, WA	S	8.44 MW	8.52 AW	17560 AAW	WABLS	10//99-12//99
	West Virginia	S	6.27 MW	7.05 AW	14660 AAW	WVBLS	10//99-12//99
	Charleston MSA, WV	S	7.17 MW	6.23 AW	14910 AAW	WVBLS	10//99-12//99
	Huntington-Ashland MSA, WV-KY-OH	S	6.53 MW	6.19 AW	13570 AAW	WVBLS	10//99-12//99
	Parkersburg-Marietta MSA, WV-OH	S	7.92 MW	6.64 AW	16480 AAW	WVBLS	10//99-12//99
	Wheeling MSA, WV-OH	S	7.40 MW	6.72 AW	15400 AAW	WVBLS	10//99-12//99
	Wisconsin	S	7.08 MW	7.53 AW	15660 AAW	WIBLS	10//99-12//99
	Appleton-Oshkosh-Neenah MSA, WI	S	7.26 MW	6.21 AW	15090 AAW	WIBLS	10//99-12//99
	Eau Claire MSA, WI	S	7.88 MW	7.41 AW	16400 AAW	WIBLS	10//99-12//99
	Green Bay MSA, WI	S	7.37 MW	7.22 AW	15320 AAW	WIBLS	10//99-12//99
	Janesville-Beloit MSA, WI	S	8.69 MW	7.95 AW	18080 AAW	WIBLS	10//99-12//99
	Kenosha PMSA, WI	S	7.17 MW	6.98 AW	14920 AAW	WIBLS	10//99-12//99
	La Crosse MSA, WI-MN	S	7.24 MW	6.37 AW	15060 AAW	WIBLS	10//99-12//99
	Madison MSA, WI	S	7.51 MW	7.01 AW	15630 AAW	WIBLS	10//99-12//99
	Milwaukee-Waukesha PMSA, WI	S	7.81 MW	7.42 AW	16240 AAW	WIBLS	10//99-12//99
	Racine PMSA, WI	S	7.17 MW	6.56 AW	14910 AAW	WIBLS	10//99-12//99
	Sheboygan MSA, WI	S	7.30 MW	7.19 AW	15190 AAW	WIBLS	10//99-12//99
	Wausau MSA, WI	S	7.85 MW	7.54 AW	16330 AAW	WIBLS	10//99-12//99
	Wyoming	S	6.35 MW	7.05 AW	14660 AAW	WYBLS	10//99-12//99
	Casper MSA, WY	S	7.12 MW	6.63 AW	14810 AAW	WYBLS	10//99-12//99
	Cheyenne MSA, WY	S	7.21 MW	6.33 AW	14990 AAW	WYBLS	10//99-12//99
	Puerto Rico	S	6.18 MW	6.71 AW	13960 AAW	PRBLS	10//99-12//99
	Caguas PMSA, PR	S	6.28 MW	6.08 AW	13070 AAW	PRBLS	10//99-12//99
	Mayaguez MSA, PR	S	6.36 MW	6.05 AW	13230 AAW	PRBLS	10//99-12//99
	San Juan-Bayamon PMSA, PR	S	6.82 MW	6.21 AW	14180 AAW	PRBLS	10//99-12//99
	Virgin Islands	S	7.31 MW	7.53 AW	15670 AAW	VIBLS	10//99-12//99
	Guam	S	6.83 MW	7.37 AW	15330 AAW	GUBLS	10//99-12//99

AAW	Average annual wage	AOH	Average offered, high	ASH	Average starting, high	H	Hourly	M	Monthly	S	Special: hourly and annual
AE	Average entry wage	AOL	Average offered, low	ASL	Average starting, low	HI	Highest wage paid	MTC	Median total compensation	TQ	Third quartile wage
AEX	Average experienced wage	APH	Average pay, high range	AW	Average wage paid	HR	High end range	MW	Median wage paid	W	Weekly
AO	Average offered	APL	Average pay, low range	FQ	First quartile wage	LR	Low end range	SQ	Second quartile wage	Y	Yearly

Occupation/Type/Industry	Location	Per	Low	Mid	High	Source	Date
Counter Attendant							
Cafeteria, Food Concession, and Coffee Shop	Alabama	S	6.11 MW	6.09 AW	12660 AAW	ALBLS	10//99-12//99
Cafeteria, Food Concession, and Coffee Shop	Alaska	S	7.15 MW	7.90 AW	16440 AAW	AKBLS	10//99-12//99
Cafeteria, Food Concession, and Coffee Shop	Arizona	S	6.11 MW	6.15 AW	12790 AAW	AZBLS	10//99-12//99
Cafeteria, Food Concession, and Coffee Shop	Arkansas	S	6.4 MW	6.51 AW	13530 AAW	ARBLS	10//99-12//99
Cafeteria, Food Concession, and Coffee Shop	California	S	6.76 MW	7.52 AW	15650 AAW	CABLS	10//99-12//99
Cafeteria, Food Concession, and Coffee Shop	Colorado	S	6.88 MW	6.90 AW	14360 AAW	COBLS	10//99-12//99
Cafeteria, Food Concession, and Coffee Shop	Connecticut	S	7.03 MW	7.46 AW	15520 AAW	CTBLS	10//99-12//99
Cafeteria, Food Concession, and Coffee Shop	Delaware	S	6.55 MW	7.14 AW	14840 AAW	DEBLS	10//99-12//99
Cafeteria, Food Concession, and Coffee Shop	District of Columbia	S	6.96 MW	7.61 AW	15830 AAW	DCBLS	10//99-12//99
Cafeteria, Food Concession, and Coffee Shop	Florida	S	6.19 MW	6.54 AW	13610 AAW	FLBLS	10//99-12//99
Cafeteria, Food Concession, and Coffee Shop	Georgia	S	6.5 MW	6.78 AW	14100 AAW	GABLS	10//99-12//99
Cafeteria, Food Concession, and Coffee Shop	Hawaii	S	7.1 MW	7.57 AW	15750 AAW	HIBLS	10//99-12//99
Cafeteria, Food Concession, and Coffee Shop	Idaho	S	5.95 MW	6.21 AW	12910 AAW	IDBLS	10//99-12//99
Cafeteria, Food Concession, and Coffee Shop	Illinois	S	6.65 MW	6.99 AW	14540 AAW	ILBLS	10//99-12//99
Cafeteria, Food Concession, and Coffee Shop	Indiana	S	6.24 MW	6.49 AW	13500 AAW	INBLS	10//99-12//99
Cafeteria, Food Concession, and Coffee Shop	Iowa	S	6.24 MW	6.32 AW	13140 AAW	IABLS	10//99-12//99
Cafeteria, Food Concession, and Coffee Shop	Kansas	S	6.71 MW	6.99 AW	14530 AAW	KSBLS	10//99-12//99
Cafeteria, Food Concession, and Coffee Shop	Kentucky	S	6.42 MW	6.59 AW	13700 AAW	KYBLS	10//99-12//99
Cafeteria, Food Concession, and Coffee Shop	Louisiana	S	6.22 MW	6.61 AW	13740 AAW	LABLS	10//99-12//99
Cafeteria, Food Concession, and Coffee Shop	Maine	S	6.04 MW	6.34 AW	13180 AAW	MEBLS	10//99-12//99
Cafeteria, Food Concession, and Coffee Shop	Maryland	S	6.9 MW	7.26 AW	15100 AAW	MDBLS	10//99-12//99
Cafeteria, Food Concession, and Coffee Shop	Massachusetts	S	6.47 MW	6.87 AW	14290 AAW	MABLS	10//99-12//99
Cafeteria, Food Concession, and Coffee Shop	Michigan	S	6.71 MW	7.04 AW	14640 AAW	MIBLS	10//99-12//99
Cafeteria, Food Concession, and Coffee Shop	Minnesota	S	7.09 MW	7.41 AW	15420 AAW	MNBLS	10//99-12//99
Cafeteria, Food Concession, and Coffee Shop	Mississippi	S	6.03 MW	6.13 AW	12750 AAW	MSBLS	10//99-12//99
Cafeteria, Food Concession, and Coffee Shop	Missouri	S	6.3 MW	6.56 AW	13650 AAW	MOBLS	10//99-12//99
Cafeteria, Food Concession, and Coffee Shop	Montana	S	6.06 MW	6.33 AW	13170 AAW	MTBLS	10//99-12//99
Cafeteria, Food Concession, and Coffee Shop	Nebraska	S	6.49 MW	6.65 AW	13840 AAW	NEBLS	10//99-12//99
Cafeteria, Food Concession, and Coffee Shop	Nevada	S	8.02 MW	8.29 AW	17250 AAW	NVBLS	10//99-12//99
Cafeteria, Food Concession, and Coffee Shop	New Hampshire	S	6.08 MW	6.56 AW	13640 AAW	NHBLS	10//99-12//99
Cafeteria, Food Concession, and Coffee Shop	New Jersey	S	6.52 MW	6.88 AW	14320 AAW	NJBLS	10//99-12//99
Cafeteria, Food Concession, and Coffee Shop	New Mexico	S	6.13 MW	6.29 AW	13080 AAW	NMBLS	10//99-12//99
Cafeteria, Food Concession, and Coffee Shop	New York	S	6.2 MW	6.63 AW	13800 AAW	NYBLS	10//99-12//99
Cafeteria, Food Concession, and Coffee Shop	North Carolina	S	6.42 MW	6.57 AW	13670 AAW	NCBLS	10//99-12//99
Cafeteria, Food Concession, and Coffee Shop	North Dakota	S	6.25 MW	6.35 AW	13210 AAW	NDBLS	10//99-12//99

AAW Average annual wage	**AOH** Average offered, high	**ASH** Average starting, high	**H** Hourly	**M** Monthly	**S** Special: hourly and annual
AE Average entry wage	**AOL** Average offered, low	**ASL** Average starting, low	**HI** Highest wage paid	**MTC** Median total compensation	**TQ** Third quartile wage
AEX Average experienced wage	**APH** Average pay, high range	**AW** Average wage paid	**HR** High end range	**MW** Median wage paid	**W** Weekly
AO Average offered	**APL** Average pay, low range	**FQ** First quartile wage	**LR** Low end range	**SQ** Second quartile wage	**Y** Yearly

Occupation/Type/Industry	Location	Per	Low	Mid	High	Source	Date
Counter Attendant							
Cafeteria, Food Concession, and Coffee Shop	Ohio	S	6.32 MW	6.83 AW	14200 AAW	OHBLS	10//99-12//99
Cafeteria, Food Concession, and Coffee Shop	Oklahoma	S	6.12 MW	6.23 AW	12950 AAW	OKBLS	10//99-12//99
Cafeteria, Food Concession, and Coffee Shop	Oregon	S	7.27 MW	7.61 AW	15840 AAW	ORBLS	10//99-12//99
Cafeteria, Food Concession, and Coffee Shop	Pennsylvania	S	6.17 MW	6.57 AW	13660 AAW	PABLS	10//99-12//99
Cafeteria, Food Concession, and Coffee Shop	Rhode Island	S	6.49 MW	6.78 AW	14110 AAW	RIBLS	10//99-12//99
Cafeteria, Food Concession, and Coffee Shop	South Carolina	S	6.11 MW	6.38 AW	13280 AAW	SCBLS	10//99-12//99
Cafeteria, Food Concession, and Coffee Shop	South Dakota	S	6.65 MW	7.16 AW	14880 AAW	SDBLS	10//99-12//99
Cafeteria, Food Concession, and Coffee Shop	Tennessee	S	6.42 MW	6.56 AW	13650 AAW	TNBLS	10//99-12//99
Cafeteria, Food Concession, and Coffee Shop	Texas	S	6.34 MW	6.57 AW	13670 AAW	TXBLS	10//99-12//99
Cafeteria, Food Concession, and Coffee Shop	Utah	S	6.65 MW	6.74 AW	14030 AAW	UTBLS	10//99-12//99
Cafeteria, Food Concession, and Coffee Shop	Vermont	S	6.59 MW	6.92 AW	14380 AAW	VTBLS	10//99-12//99
Cafeteria, Food Concession, and Coffee Shop	Virginia	S	6.46 MW	6.72 AW	13970 AAW	VABLS	10//99-12//99
Cafeteria, Food Concession, and Coffee Shop	Washington	S	7.13 MW	7.85 AW	16330 AAW	WABLS	10//99-12//99
Cafeteria, Food Concession, and Coffee Shop	West Virginia	S	6.11 MW	6.04 AW	12560 AAW	WVBLS	10//99-12//99
Cafeteria, Food Concession, and Coffee Shop	Wisconsin	S	6.68 MW	6.87 AW	14290 AAW	WIBLS	10//99-12//99
Cafeteria, Food Concession, and Coffee Shop	Wyoming	S	6.07 MW	6.55 AW	13620 AAW	WYBLS	10//99-12//99
Cafeteria, Food Concession, and Coffee Shop	Puerto Rico	S	5.9 MW	5.79 AW	12040 AAW	PRBLS	10//99-12//99
Cafeteria, Food Concession, and Coffee Shop	Virgin Islands	S	6.4 MW	6.36 AW	13220 AAW	VIBLS	10//99-12//99
Cafeteria, Food Concession, and Coffee Shop	Guam	S	6.11 MW	6.04 AW	12560 AAW	GUBLS	10//99-12//99
County Manager	Midwest	Y		64040 AW		PUBMAN	1998
	Mountain	Y		54679 AW		PUBMAN	1998
	Northeast	Y		70245 AW		PUBMAN	1998
	Southeast	Y		68279 AW		PUBMAN	1998
	West Coast	Y		96371 AW		PUBMAN	1998
Courier and Messenger	Alabama	S	7.36 MW	7.46 AW	15520 AAW	ALBLS	10//99-12//99
	Birmingham MSA, AL	S	7.63 MW	7.52 AW	15870 AAW	ALBLS	10//99-12//99
	Decatur MSA, AL	S	8.81 MW	7.18 AW	18330 AAW	ALBLS	10//99-12//99
	Dothan MSA, AL	S	7.55 MW	7.57 AW	15710 AAW	ALBLS	10//99-12//99
	Gadsden MSA, AL	S	7.27 MW	7.40 AW	15110 AAW	ALBLS	10//99-12//99
	Huntsville MSA, AL	S	7.23 MW	6.93 AW	15030 AAW	ALBLS	10//99-12//99
	Mobile MSA, AL	S	7.01 MW	6.86 AW	14590 AAW	ALBLS	10//99-12//99
	Montgomery MSA, AL	S	7.61 MW	7.53 AW	15820 AAW	ALBLS	10//99-12//99
	Tuscaloosa MSA, AL	S	6.06 MW	5.94 AW	12600 AAW	ALBLS	10//99-12//99
	Alaska	S	9.83 MW	10.62 AW	22080 AAW	AKBLS	10//99-12//99
	Anchorage MSA, AK	S	9.98 MW	9.49 AW	20750 AAW	AKBLS	10//99-12//99
	Arizona	S	8.57 MW	8.96 AW	18640 AAW	AZBLS	10//99-12//99
	Phoenix-Mesa MSA, AZ	S	9.25 MW	8.82 AW	19250 AAW	AZBLS	10//99-12//99
	Tucson MSA, AZ	S	8.34 MW	7.73 AW	17350 AAW	AZBLS	10//99-12//99
	Arkansas	S	7.6 MW	7.90 AW	16430 AAW	ARBLS	10//99-12//99
	Fayetteville-Springdale-Rogers MSA, AR	S	7.66 MW	7.41 AW	15930 AAW	ARBLS	10//99-12//99
	Jonesboro MSA, AR	S	6.96 MW	7.01 AW	14470 AAW	ARBLS	10//99-12//99
	Little Rock-North Little Rock MSA, AR	S	8.45 MW	8.39 AW	17570 AAW	ARBLS	10//99-12//99
	Pine Bluff MSA, AR	S	5.75 MW	5.94 AW	11950 AAW	ARBLS	10//99-12//99
	California	S	8.67 MW	9.98 AW	20760 AAW	CABLS	10//99-12//99
	Bakersfield MSA, CA	S	11.68 MW	10.15 AW	24300 AAW	CABLS	10//99-12//99
	Chico-Paradise MSA, CA	S	8.01 MW	7.81 AW	16670 AAW	CABLS	10//99-12//99
	Fresno MSA, CA	S	7.82 MW	7.08 AW	16270 AAW	CABLS	10//99-12//99
	Los Angeles-Long Beach PMSA, CA	S	9.49 MW	8.27 AW	19750 AAW	CABLS	10//99-12//99

AAW Average annual wage	**AOH** Average offered, high	**ASH** Average starting, high	**H** Hourly	**M** Monthly	**S** Special: hourly and annual
AE Average entry wage	**AOL** Average offered, low	**ASL** Average starting, low	**HI** Highest wage paid	**MTC** Median total compensation	**TQ** Third quartile wage
AEX Average experienced wage	**APH** Average pay, high range	**AW** Average wage paid	**HR** High end range	**MW** Median wage paid	**W** Weekly
AO Average offered	**APL** Average pay, low range	**FQ** First quartile wage	**LR** Low end range	**SQ** Second quartile wage	**Y** Yearly

343

Occupation/Type/Industry	Location	Per	Low	Mid	High	Source	Date
Courier and Messenger	Oakland PMSA, CA	S	13.96 MW	12.45 AW	29030 AAW	CABLS	10//99-12//99
	Orange County PMSA, CA	S	8.52 MW	7.03 AW	17720 AAW	CABLS	10//99-12//99
	Riverside-San Bernardino PMSA, CA	S	8.03 MW	7.64 AW	16700 AAW	CABLS	10//99-12//99
	Sacramento PMSA, CA	S	10.17 MW	8.66 AW	21150 AAW	CABLS	10//99-12//99
	Salinas MSA, CA	S	10.74 MW	9.01 AW	22340 AAW	CABLS	10//99-12//99
	San Diego MSA, CA	S	8.81 MW	8.26 AW	18330 AAW	CABLS	10//99-12//99
	San Francisco PMSA, CA	S	13.20 MW	12.35 AW	27460 AAW	CABLS	10//99-12//99
	San Jose PMSA, CA	S	10.20 MW	8.91 AW	21210 AAW	CABLS	10//99-12//99
	San Luis Obispo-Atascadero-Paso Robles MSA, CA	S	7.73 MW	7.25 AW	16080 AAW	CABLS	10//99-12//99
	Santa Barbara-Santa Maria-Lompoc MSA, CA	S	9.80 MW	9.63 AW	20370 AAW	CABLS	10//99-12//99
	Santa Rosa PMSA, CA	S	8.79 MW	7.86 AW	18290 AAW	CABLS	10//99-12//99
	Stockton-Lodi MSA, CA	S	9.95 MW	8.40 AW	20690 AAW	CABLS	10//99-12//99
	Vallejo-Fairfield-Napa PMSA, CA	S	10.70 MW	10.01 AW	22260 AAW	CABLS	10//99-12//99
	Ventura PMSA, CA	S	8.24 MW	7.60 AW	17150 AAW	CABLS	10//99-12//99
	Colorado	S	8.79 MW	9.20 AW	19140 AAW	COBLS	10//99-12//99
	Boulder-Longmont PMSA, CO	S	8.57 MW	8.29 AW	17830 AAW	COBLS	10//99-12//99
	Colorado Springs MSA, CO	S	8.76 MW	8.50 AW	18220 AAW	COBLS	10//99-12//99
	Denver PMSA, CO	S	9.34 MW	8.95 AW	19420 AAW	COBLS	10//99-12//99
	Fort Collins-Loveland MSA, CO	S	8.91 MW	8.36 AW	18530 AAW	COBLS	10//99-12//99
	Grand Junction MSA, CO	S	8.26 MW	8.65 AW	17190 AAW	COBLS	10//99-12//99
	Pueblo MSA, CO	S	9.49 MW	7.67 AW	19730 AAW	COBLS	10//99-12//99
	Connecticut	S	10.44 MW	10.50 AW	21840 AAW	CTBLS	10//99-12//99
	Bridgeport PMSA, CT	S	10.52 MW	9.87 AW	21880 AAW	CTBLS	10//99-12//99
	Danbury PMSA, CT	S	10.47 MW	9.14 AW	21780 AAW	CTBLS	10//99-12//99
	Hartford MSA, CT	S	10.62 MW	10.97 AW	22090 AAW	CTBLS	10//99-12//99
	Stamford-Norwalk PMSA, CT	S	9.99 MW	9.51 AW	20780 AAW	CTBLS	10//99-12//99
	Waterbury PMSA, CT	S	11.40 MW	11.33 AW	23720 AAW	CTBLS	10//99-12//99
	Delaware	S	8.65 MW	9.04 AW	18810 AAW	DEBLS	10//99-12//99
	Dover MSA, DE	S	8.23 MW	7.83 AW	17120 AAW	DEBLS	10//99-12//99
	Wilmington-Newark PMSA, DE-MD	S	9.66 MW	9.12 AW	20100 AAW	DEBLS	10//99-12//99
	District of Columbia	S	8.88 MW	9.51 AW	19780 AAW	DCBLS	10//99-12//99
	Washington PMSA, DC-MD-VA-WV	S	10.37 MW	10.24 AW	21570 AAW	DCBLS	10//99-12//99
	Florida	S	8.26 MW	8.87 AW	18450 AAW	FLBLS	10//99-12//99
	Fort Lauderdale PMSA, FL	S	9.14 MW	8.37 AW	19020 AAW	FLBLS	10//99-12//99
	Fort Myers-Cape Coral MSA, FL	S	6.46 MW	5.97 AW	13440 AAW	FLBLS	10//99-12//99
	Fort Pierce-Port St. Lucie MSA, FL	S	7.79 MW	7.36 AW	16200 AAW	FLBLS	10//99-12//99
	Fort Walton Beach MSA, FL	S	8.48 MW	8.25 AW	17630 AAW	FLBLS	10//99-12//99
	Gainesville MSA, FL	S	8.25 MW	8.13 AW	17150 AAW	FLBLS	10//99-12//99
	Jacksonville MSA, FL	S	8.75 MW	8.18 AW	18200 AAW	FLBLS	10//99-12//99
	Lakeland-Winter Haven MSA, FL	S	7.80 MW	7.80 AW	16230 AAW	FLBLS	10//99-12//99
	Melbourne-Titusville-Palm Bay MSA, FL	S	8.16 MW	7.87 AW	16980 AAW	FLBLS	10//99-12//99
	Miami PMSA, FL	S	10.44 MW	10.39 AW	21710 AAW	FLBLS	10//99-12//99
	Naples MSA, FL	S	9.44 MW	8.63 AW	19630 AAW	FLBLS	10//99-12//99
	Ocala MSA, FL	S	8.45 MW	8.82 AW	17580 AAW	FLBLS	10//99-12//99
	Orlando MSA, FL	S	8.26 MW	7.75 AW	17190 AAW	FLBLS	10//99-12//99
	Panama City MSA, FL	S	7.35 MW	6.75 AW	15290 AAW	FLBLS	10//99-12//99
	Pensacola MSA, FL	S	7.42 MW	7.24 AW	15430 AAW	FLBLS	10//99-12//99
	Punta Gorda MSA, FL	S	8.09 MW	8.07 AW	16830 AAW	FLBLS	10//99-12//99
	Sarasota-Bradenton MSA, FL	S	8.40 MW	8.15 AW	17470 AAW	FLBLS	10//99-12//99
	Tallahassee MSA, FL	S	8.06 MW	7.59 AW	16770 AAW	FLBLS	10//99-12//99
	Tampa-St. Petersburg-Clearwater MSA, FL	S	8.13 MW	7.94 AW	16910 AAW	FLBLS	10//99-12//99
	West Palm Beach-Boca Raton MSA, FL	S	8.49 MW	8.02 AW	17660 AAW	FLBLS	10//99-12//99
	Georgia	S	8.17 MW	8.51 AW	17710 AAW	GABLS	10//99-12//99
	Atlanta MSA, GA	S	9.13 MW	8.76 AW	19000 AAW	GABLS	10//99-12//99
	Augusta-Aiken MSA, GA-SC	S	7.83 MW	7.37 AW	16280 AAW	GABLS	10//99-12//99
	Columbus MSA, GA-AL	S	7.94 MW	7.88 AW	16520 AAW	GABLS	10//99-12//99
	Macon MSA, GA	S	8.05 MW	7.88 AW	16740 AAW	GABLS	10//99-12//99
	Savannah MSA, GA	S	7.75 MW	7.36 AW	16120 AAW	GABLS	10//99-12//99
	Hawaii	S	8.41 MW	9.08 AW	18880 AAW	HIBLS	10//99-12//99

AAW Average annual wage	**AOH** Average offered, high	**ASH** Average starting, high	**H** Hourly	**M** Monthly	**S** Special: hourly and annual
AE Average entry wage	**AOL** Average offered, low	**ASL** Average starting, low	**HI** Highest wage paid	**MTC** Median total compensation	**TQ** Third quartile wage
AEX Average experienced wage	**APH** Average pay, high range	**AW** Average wage paid	**HR** High end range	**MW** Median wage paid	**W** Weekly
AO Average offered	**APL** Average pay, low range	**FQ** First quartile wage	**LR** Low end range	**SQ** Second quartile wage	**Y** Yearly

Occupation/Type/Industry	Location	Per	Low	Mid	High	Source	Date
Courier and Messenger	Honolulu MSA, HI	S	8.93 MW	8.11 AW	18580 AAW	HIBLS	10//99-12//99
	Idaho	S	7.65 MW	7.79 AW	16200 AAW	IDBLS	10//99-12//99
	Boise City MSA, ID	S	7.98 MW	7.76 AW	16600 AAW	IDBLS	10//99-12//99
	Illinois	S	9.09 MW	9.37 AW	19490 AAW	ILBLS	10//99-12//99
	Bloomington-Normal MSA, IL	S	9.82 MW	9.81 AW	20420 AAW	ILBLS	10//99-12//99
	Champaign-Urbana MSA, IL	S	7.36 MW	6.95 AW	15300 AAW	ILBLS	10//99-12//99
	Chicago PMSA, IL	S	9.54 MW	9.32 AW	19840 AAW	ILBLS	10//99-12//99
	Kankakee PMSA, IL	S	8.37 MW	8.88 AW	17410 AAW	ILBLS	10//99-12//99
	Peoria-Pekin MSA, IL	S	9.27 MW	8.67 AW	19280 AAW	ILBLS	10//99-12//99
	Rockford MSA, IL	S	9.02 MW	8.15 AW	18770 AAW	ILBLS	10//99-12//99
	Springfield MSA, IL	S	7.88 MW	7.92 AW	16390 AAW	ILBLS	10//99-12//99
	Indiana	S	7.33 MW	7.80 AW	16230 AAW	INBLS	10//99-12//99
	Bloomington MSA, IN	S	7.43 MW	7.19 AW	15450 AAW	INBLS	10//99-12//99
	Evansville-Henderson MSA, IN-KY	S	7.72 MW	7.45 AW	16060 AAW	INBLS	10//99-12//99
	Fort Wayne MSA, IN	S	8.52 MW	7.90 AW	17720 AAW	INBLS	10//99-12//99
	Gary PMSA, IN	S	7.08 MW	6.42 AW	14720 AAW	INBLS	10//99-12//99
	Indianapolis MSA, IN	S	8.23 MW	7.78 AW	17120 AAW	INBLS	10//99-12//99
	Muncie MSA, IN	S	6.58 MW	6.56 AW	13690 AAW	INBLS	10//99-12//99
	South Bend MSA, IN	S	7.68 MW	7.36 AW	15970 AAW	INBLS	10//99-12//99
	Terre Haute MSA, IN	S	7.46 MW	7.29 AW	15510 AAW	INBLS	10//99-12//99
	Iowa	S	7.67 MW	8.05 AW	16750 AAW	IABLS	10//99-12//99
	Cedar Rapids MSA, IA	S	7.63 MW	6.86 AW	15860 AAW	IABLS	10//99-12//99
	Davenport-Moline-Rock Island MSA, IA-IL	S	8.76 MW	8.21 AW	18220 AAW	IABLS	10//99-12//99
	Des Moines MSA, IA	S	8.46 MW	8.03 AW	17600 AAW	IABLS	10//99-12//99
	Dubuque MSA, IA	S	7.10 MW	7.09 AW	14770 AAW	IABLS	10//99-12//99
	Iowa City MSA, IA	S	8.63 MW	7.95 AW	17960 AAW	IABLS	10//99-12//99
	Sioux City MSA, IA-NE	S	8.56 MW	7.77 AW	17800 AAW	IABLS	10//99-12//99
	Waterloo-Cedar Falls MSA, IA	S	8.03 MW	8.69 AW	16710 AAW	IABLS	10//99-12//99
	Kansas	S	7.84 MW	8.06 AW	16770 AAW	KSBLS	10//99-12//99
	Lawrence MSA, KS	S	7.92 MW	7.77 AW	16480 AAW	KSBLS	10//99-12//99
	Topeka MSA, KS	S	8.37 MW	8.22 AW	17400 AAW	KSBLS	10//99-12//99
	Wichita MSA, KS	S	7.47 MW	6.97 AW	15540 AAW	KSBLS	10//99-12//99
	Kentucky	S	7.84 MW	8.30 AW	17260 AAW	KYBLS	10//99-12//99
	Lexington MSA, KY	S	8.55 MW	8.09 AW	17780 AAW	KYBLS	10//99-12//99
	Louisville MSA, KY-IN	S	8.00 MW	7.80 AW	16650 AAW	KYBLS	10//99-12//99
	Owensboro MSA, KY	S	8.23 MW	7.92 AW	17130 AAW	KYBLS	10//99-12//99
	Louisiana	S	7.29 MW	8.06 AW	16760 AAW	LABLS	10//99-12//99
	Alexandria MSA, LA	S	7.31 MW	6.80 AW	15190 AAW	LABLS	10//99-12//99
	Baton Rouge MSA, LA	S	7.82 MW	7.27 AW	16270 AAW	LABLS	10//99-12//99
	Lafayette MSA, LA	S	6.78 MW	6.40 AW	14100 AAW	LABLS	10//99-12//99
	Lake Charles MSA, LA	S	6.64 MW	6.56 AW	13820 AAW	LABLS	10//99-12//99
	Monroe MSA, LA	S	7.20 MW	6.47 AW	14970 AAW	LABLS	10//99-12//99
	New Orleans MSA, LA	S	9.36 MW	8.96 AW	19470 AAW	LABLS	10//99-12//99
	Shreveport-Bossier City MSA, LA	S	7.63 MW	6.81 AW	15860 AAW	LABLS	10//99-12//99
	Maine	S	8.05 MW	8.39 AW	17450 AAW	MEBLS	10//99-12//99
	Maryland	S	10.43 MW	10.60 AW	22040 AAW	MDBLS	10//99-12//99
	Baltimore PMSA, MD	S	10.57 MW	9.72 AW	21990 AAW	MDBLS	10//99-12//99
	Hagerstown PMSA, MD	S	8.60 MW	7.96 AW	17880 AAW	MDBLS	10//99-12//99
	Massachusetts	S	9.8 MW	10.08 AW	20980 AAW	MABLS	10//99-12//99
	Boston PMSA, MA-NH	S	10.11 MW	9.79 AW	21020 AAW	MABLS	10//99-12//99
	Brockton PMSA, MA	S	8.94 MW	8.88 AW	18590 AAW	MABLS	10//99-12//99
	Lawrence PMSA, MA-NH	S	9.09 MW	9.31 AW	18910 AAW	MABLS	10//99-12//99
	Springfield MSA, MA	S	10.96 MW	11.18 AW	22800 AAW	MABLS	10//99-12//99
	Worcester PMSA, MA-CT	S	9.72 MW	9.73 AW	20220 AAW	MABLS	10//99-12//99
	Michigan	S	8.35 MW	8.51 AW	17700 AAW	MIBLS	10//99-12//99
	Ann Arbor PMSA, MI	S	8.30 MW	7.96 AW	17270 AAW	MIBLS	10//99-12//99
	Benton Harbor MSA, MI	S	8.20 MW	7.95 AW	17050 AAW	MIBLS	10//99-12//99
	Detroit PMSA, MI	S	8.90 MW	8.84 AW	18500 AAW	MIBLS	10//99-12//99
	Grand Rapids-Muskegon-Holland MSA, MI	S	8.79 MW	8.11 AW	18290 AAW	MIBLS	10//99-12//99
	Jackson MSA, MI	S	7.93 MW	8.00 AW	16500 AAW	MIBLS	10//99-12//99
	Kalamazoo-Battle Creek MSA, MI	S	7.71 MW	7.59 AW	16030 AAW	MIBLS	10//99-12//99
	Lansing-East Lansing MSA, MI	S	9.20 MW	8.21 AW	19130 AAW	MIBLS	10//99-12//99
	Saginaw-Bay City-Midland MSA, MI	S	7.43 MW	7.17 AW	15450 AAW	MIBLS	10//99-12//99
	Minnesota	S	10.01 MW	10.03 AW	20860 AAW	MNBLS	10//99-12//99
	Minneapolis-St. Paul MSA, MN-WI	S	10.28 MW	10.30 AW	21380 AAW	MNBLS	10//99-12//99

AAW Average annual wage	AOH Average offered, high	ASH Average starting, high	H Hourly	M Monthly	S Special: hourly and annual
AE Average entry wage	AOL Average offered, low	ASL Average starting, low	HI Highest wage paid	MTC Median total compensation	TQ Third quartile wage
AEX Average experienced wage	APH Average pay, high range	AW Average wage paid	HR High end range	MW Median wage paid	W Weekly
AO Average offered	APL Average pay, low range	FQ First quartile wage	LR Low end range	SQ Second quartile wage	Y Yearly

Occupation/Type/Industry	Location	Per	Low	Mid	High	Source	Date
Courier and Messenger	Mississippi	S	6.62 MW	6.87 AW	14300 AAW	MSBLS	10//99-12//99
	Biloxi-Gulfport-Pascagoula MSA, MS	S	6.95 MW	6.77 AW	14450 AAW	MSBLS	10//99-12//99
	Hattiesburg MSA, MS	S	7.09 MW	6.96 AW	14750 AAW	MSBLS	10//99-12//99
	Jackson MSA, MS	S	6.69 MW	6.50 AW	13910 AAW	MSBLS	10//99-12//99
	Missouri	S	7.64 MW	8.30 AW	17270 AAW	MOBLS	10//99-12//99
	Kansas City MSA, MO-KS	S	9.01 MW	8.70 AW	18740 AAW	MOBLS	10//99-12//99
	St. Louis MSA, MO-IL	S	8.25 MW	7.48 AW	17170 AAW	MOBLS	10//99-12//99
	Montana	S	7.21 MW	7.63 AW	15870 AAW	MTBLS	10//99-12//99
	Billings MSA, MT	S	6.72 MW	5.97 AW	13970 AAW	MTBLS	10//99-12//99
	Nebraska	S	7.47 MW	7.68 AW	15970 AAW	NEBLS	10//99-12//99
	Lincoln MSA, NE	S	7.54 MW	7.42 AW	15680 AAW	NEBLS	10//99-12//99
	Omaha MSA, NE-IA	S	7.86 MW	7.66 AW	16340 AAW	NEBLS	10//99-12//99
	Nevada	S	8.26 MW	8.63 AW	17940 AAW	NVBLS	10//99-12//99
	Las Vegas MSA, NV-AZ	S	8.46 MW	8.12 AW	17600 AAW	NVBLS	10//99-12//99
	Reno MSA, NV	S	9.23 MW	8.84 AW	19210 AAW	NVBLS	10//99-12//99
	New Hampshire	S	8.35 MW	8.78 AW	18260 AAW	NHBLS	10//99-12//99
	Manchester PMSA, NH	S	8.51 MW	8.14 AW	17710 AAW	NHBLS	10//99-12//99
	Portsmouth-Rochester PMSA, NH-ME	S	9.58 MW	9.42 AW	19920 AAW	NHBLS	10//99-12//99
	New Jersey	S	9.89 MW	10.49 AW	21820 AAW	NJBLS	10//99-12//99
	Atlantic-Cape May PMSA, NJ	S	12.27 MW	11.95 AW	25520 AAW	NJBLS	10//99-12//99
	Bergen-Passaic PMSA, NJ	S	10.48 MW	9.95 AW	21800 AAW	NJBLS	10//99-12//99
	Jersey City PMSA, NJ	S	9.48 MW	8.82 AW	19710 AAW	NJBLS	10//99-12//99
	Middlesex-Somerset-Hunterdon PMSA, NJ	S	10.48 MW	9.83 AW	21800 AAW	NJBLS	10//99-12//99
	Monmouth-Ocean PMSA, NJ	S	10.04 MW	9.41 AW	20890 AAW	NJBLS	10//99-12//99
	Newark PMSA, NJ	S	11.00 MW	10.54 AW	22880 AAW	NJBLS	10//99-12//99
	Trenton PMSA, NJ	S	10.15 MW	9.55 AW	21110 AAW	NJBLS	10//99-12//99
	New Mexico	S	7.2 MW	7.71 AW	16050 AAW	NMBLS	10//99-12//99
	Albuquerque MSA, NM	S	7.50 MW	7.16 AW	15600 AAW	NMBLS	10//99-12//99
	Las Cruces MSA, NM	S	6.69 MW	6.17 AW	13920 AAW	NMBLS	10//99-12//99
	Santa Fe MSA, NM	S	9.97 MW	10.94 AW	20730 AAW	NMBLS	10//99-12//99
	New York	S	8.48 MW	9.19 AW	19110 AAW	NYBLS	10//99-12//99
	Albany-Schenectady-Troy MSA, NY	S	8.43 MW	7.90 AW	17540 AAW	NYBLS	10//99-12//99
	Binghamton MSA, NY	S	9.59 MW	8.53 AW	19940 AAW	NYBLS	10//99-12//99
	Buffalo-Niagara Falls MSA, NY	S	8.02 MW	7.52 AW	16680 AAW	NYBLS	10//99-12//99
	Dutchess County PMSA, NY	S	9.47 MW	8.88 AW	19700 AAW	NYBLS	10//99-12//99
	Glens Falls MSA, NY	S	8.56 MW	8.39 AW	17800 AAW	NYBLS	10//99-12//99
	Nassau-Suffolk PMSA, NY	S	12.28 MW	12.66 AW	25540 AAW	NYBLS	10//99-12//99
	New York PMSA, NY	S	8.64 MW	7.86 AW	17970 AAW	NYBLS	10//99-12//99
	Newburgh PMSA, NY-PA	S	9.43 MW	8.71 AW	19610 AAW	NYBLS	10//99-12//99
	Rochester MSA, NY	S	10.22 MW	8.74 AW	21250 AAW	NYBLS	10//99-12//99
	Syracuse MSA, NY	S	7.81 MW	7.30 AW	16230 AAW	NYBLS	10//99-12//99
	Utica-Rome MSA, NY	S	8.50 MW	8.03 AW	17670 AAW	NYBLS	10//99-12//99
	North Carolina	S	8.74 MW	8.85 AW	18410 AAW	NCBLS	10//99-12//99
	Charlotte-Gastonia-Rock Hill MSA, NC-SC	S	8.33 MW	8.25 AW	17320 AAW	NCBLS	10//99-12//99
	Greensboro--Winston-Salem--High Point MSA, NC	S	9.19 MW	9.40 AW	19120 AAW	NCBLS	10//99-12//99
	Hickory-Morganton-Lenoir MSA, NC	S	8.53 MW	8.00 AW	17730 AAW	NCBLS	10//99-12//99
	Raleigh-Durham-Chapel Hill MSA, NC	S	9.92 MW	9.56 AW	20640 AAW	NCBLS	10//99-12//99
	Rocky Mount MSA, NC	S	9.01 MW	9.10 AW	18750 AAW	NCBLS	10//99-12//99
	North Dakota	S	7.52 MW	7.83 AW	16290 AAW	NDBLS	10//99-12//99
	Fargo-Moorhead MSA, ND-MN	S	8.29 MW	8.09 AW	17240 AAW	NDBLS	10//99-12//99
	Ohio	S	8.24 MW	8.59 AW	17870 AAW	OHBLS	10//99-12//99
	Akron PMSA, OH	S	7.32 MW	7.37 AW	15230 AAW	OHBLS	10//99-12//99
	Canton-Massillon MSA, OH	S	7.58 MW	7.48 AW	15770 AAW	OHBLS	10//99-12//99
	Cincinnati PMSA, OH-KY-IN	S	8.98 MW	8.64 AW	18680 AAW	OHBLS	10//99-12//99
	Cleveland-Lorain-Elyria PMSA, OH	S	9.25 MW	8.97 AW	19230 AAW	OHBLS	10//99-12//99
	Columbus MSA, OH	S	8.63 MW	8.30 AW	17950 AAW	OHBLS	10//99-12//99
	Dayton-Springfield MSA, OH	S	9.04 MW	8.61 AW	18810 AAW	OHBLS	10//99-12//99
	Lima MSA, OH	S	7.94 MW	7.28 AW	16510 AAW	OHBLS	10//99-12//99
	Steubenville-Weirton MSA, OH-WV	S	7.84 MW	7.60 AW	16300 AAW	OHBLS	10//99-12//99
	Toledo MSA, OH	S	8.43 MW	8.09 AW	17520 AAW	OHBLS	10//99-12//99

AAW	Average annual wage	AOH	Average offered, high	ASH	Average starting, high	H	Hourly	M	Monthly	S	Special: hourly and annual
AE	Average entry wage	AOL	Average offered, low	ASL	Average starting, low	HI	Highest wage paid	MTC	Median total compensation	TQ	Third quartile wage
AEX	Average experienced wage	APH	Average pay, high range	AW	Average wage paid	HR	High end range	MW	Median wage paid	W	Weekly
AO	Average offered	APL	Average pay, low range	FQ	First quartile wage	LR	Low end range	SQ	Second quartile wage	Y	Yearly

Occupation/Type/Industry	Location	Per	Low	Mid	High	Source	Date
Courier and Messenger	Youngstown-Warren MSA, OH	S	8.40 MW	8.06 AW	17460 AAW	OHBLS	10//99-12//99
	Oklahoma	S	7.89 MW	8.68 AW	18060 AAW	OKBLS	10//99-12//99
	Oklahoma City MSA, OK	S	8.48 MW	8.05 AW	17630 AAW	OKBLS	10//99-12//99
	Tulsa MSA, OK	S	9.58 MW	8.08 AW	19930 AAW	OKBLS	10//99-12//99
	Oregon	S	8.47 MW	9.22 AW	19180 AAW	ORBLS	10//99-12//99
	Eugene-Springfield MSA, OR	S	8.66 MW	8.10 AW	18010 AAW	ORBLS	10//99-12//99
	Medford-Ashland MSA, OR	S	8.78 MW	8.30 AW	18260 AAW	ORBLS	10//99-12//99
	Portland-Vancouver PMSA, OR-WA	S	9.42 MW	8.70 AW	19600 AAW	ORBLS	10//99-12//99
	Pennsylvania	S	8.53 MW	9.07 AW	18860 AAW	PABLS	10//99-12//99
	Allentown-Bethlehem-Easton MSA, PA	S	9.10 MW	9.29 AW	18940 AAW	PABLS	10//99-12//99
	Erie MSA, PA	S	7.37 MW	7.35 AW	15330 AAW	PABLS	10//99-12//99
	Harrisburg-Lebanon-Carlisle MSA, PA	S	9.42 MW	8.65 AW	19590 AAW	PABLS	10//99-12//99
	Johnstown MSA, PA	S	7.40 MW	7.17 AW	15400 AAW	PABLS	10//99-12//99
	Philadelphia PMSA, PA-NJ	S	9.74 MW	9.52 AW	20250 AAW	PABLS	10//99-12//99
	Pittsburgh MSA, PA	S	8.59 MW	8.12 AW	17870 AAW	PABLS	10//99-12//99
	Reading MSA, PA	S	8.25 MW	7.89 AW	17150 AAW	PABLS	10//99-12//99
	Scranton--Wilkes-Barre--Hazleton MSA, PA	S	8.29 MW	8.11 AW	17250 AAW	PABLS	10//99-12//99
	York MSA, PA	S	8.29 MW	7.83 AW	17240 AAW	PABLS	10//99-12//99
	Rhode Island	S	8.26 MW	9.32 AW	19390 AAW	RIBLS	10//99-12//99
	Providence-Fall River-Warwick MSA, RI-MA	S	8.98 MW	8.11 AW	18670 AAW	RIBLS	10//99-12//99
	South Carolina	S	7.43 MW	7.68 AW	15960 AAW	SCBLS	10//99-12//99
	Charleston-North Charleston MSA, SC	S	7.69 MW	7.34 AW	16000 AAW	SCBLS	10//99-12//99
	Columbia MSA, SC	S	7.61 MW	7.42 AW	15830 AAW	SCBLS	10//99-12//99
	Florence MSA, SC	S	7.27 MW	6.58 AW	15130 AAW	SCBLS	10//99-12//99
	Greenville-Spartanburg-Anderson MSA, SC	S	8.56 MW	8.27 AW	17810 AAW	SCBLS	10//99-12//99
	South Dakota	S	7.05 MW	7.43 AW	15460 AAW	SDBLS	10//99-12//99
	Rapid City MSA, SD	S	6.67 MW	6.17 AW	13870 AAW	SDBLS	10//99-12//99
	Tennessee	S	7.81 MW	8.24 AW	17130 AAW	TNBLS	10//99-12//99
	Chattanooga MSA, TN-GA	S	7.97 MW	7.42 AW	16580 AAW	TNBLS	10//99-12//99
	Johnson City-Kingsport-Bristol MSA, TN-VA	S	7.78 MW	7.43 AW	16190 AAW	TNBLS	10//99-12//99
	Knoxville MSA, TN	S	8.47 MW	7.78 AW	17610 AAW	TNBLS	10//99-12//99
	Memphis MSA, TN-AR-MS	S	8.86 MW	8.37 AW	18430 AAW	MSBLS	10//99-12//99
	Nashville MSA, TN	S	8.15 MW	7.85 AW	16950 AAW	TNBLS	10//99-12//99
	Texas	S	7.64 MW	8.50 AW	17680 AAW	TXBLS	10//99-12//99
	Abilene MSA, TX	S	6.53 MW	6.09 AW	13570 AAW	TXBLS	10//99-12//99
	Amarillo MSA, TX	S	7.48 MW	7.39 AW	15550 AAW	TXBLS	10//99-12//99
	Austin-San Marcos MSA, TX	S	6.91 MW	6.58 AW	14370 AAW	TXBLS	10//99-12//99
	Beaumont-Port Arthur MSA, TX	S	7.38 MW	6.39 AW	15340 AAW	TXBLS	10//99-12//99
	Brownsville-Harlingen-San Benito MSA, TX	S	6.48 MW	6.19 AW	13480 AAW	TXBLS	10//99-12//99
	Bryan-College Station MSA, TX	S	6.52 MW	6.25 AW	13560 AAW	TXBLS	10//99-12//99
	Corpus Christi MSA, TX	S	8.88 MW	8.46 AW	18460 AAW	TXBLS	10//99-12//99
	Dallas PMSA, TX	S	10.40 MW	9.60 AW	21640 AAW	TXBLS	10//99-12//99
	El Paso MSA, TX	S	6.95 MW	6.21 AW	14450 AAW	TXBLS	10//99-12//99
	Fort Worth-Arlington PMSA, TX	S	8.05 MW	7.88 AW	16750 AAW	TXBLS	10//99-12//99
	Galveston-Texas City PMSA, TX	S	8.65 MW	7.94 AW	18000 AAW	TXBLS	10//99-12//99
	Houston PMSA, TX	S	9.71 MW	8.44 AW	20190 AAW	TXBLS	10//99-12//99
	Killeen-Temple MSA, TX	S	6.87 MW	6.98 AW	14280 AAW	TXBLS	10//99-12//99
	Laredo MSA, TX	S	6.70 MW	6.39 AW	13940 AAW	TXBLS	10//99-12//99
	Longview-Marshall MSA, TX	S	8.69 MW	6.24 AW	18080 AAW	TXBLS	10//99-12//99
	Lubbock MSA, TX	S	7.36 MW	7.12 AW	15300 AAW	TXBLS	10//99-12//99
	McAllen-Edinburg-Mission MSA, TX	S	6.87 MW	6.62 AW	14290 AAW	TXBLS	10//99-12//99
	San Angelo MSA, TX	S	6.69 MW	6.39 AW	13920 AAW	TXBLS	10//99-12//99
	San Antonio MSA, TX	S	8.44 MW	7.92 AW	17550 AAW	TXBLS	10//99-12//99
	Sherman-Denison MSA, TX	S	7.40 MW	7.47 AW	15390 AAW	TXBLS	10//99-12//99
	Tyler MSA, TX	S	6.86 MW	6.10 AW	14280 AAW	TXBLS	10//99-12//99
	Waco MSA, TX	S	7.00 MW	6.54 AW	14550 AAW	TXBLS	10//99-12//99
	Wichita Falls MSA, TX	S	6.38 MW	6.19 AW	13280 AAW	TXBLS	10//99-12//99
	Utah	S	7.92 MW	8.18 AW	17020 AAW	UTBLS	10//99-12//99

AAW	Average annual wage	AOH	Average offered, high	ASH	Average starting, high	H	Hourly	M	Monthly	S	Special: hourly and annual
AE	Average entry wage	AOL	Average offered, low	ASL	Average starting, low	HI	Highest wage paid	MTC	Median total compensation	TQ	Third quartile wage
AEX	Average experienced wage	APH	Average pay, high range	AW	Average wage paid	HR	High end range	MW	Median wage paid	W	Weekly
AO	Average offered	APL	Average pay, low range	FQ	First quartile wage	LR	Low end range	SQ	Second quartile wage	Y	Yearly

Occupation/Type/Industry	Location	Per	Low	Mid	High	Source	Date
Courier and Messenger	Provo-Orem MSA, UT	S	7.59 MW	7.48 AW	15780 AAW	UTBLS	10//99-12//99
	Salt Lake City-Ogden MSA, UT	S	8.30 MW	8.00 AW	17260 AAW	UTBLS	10//99-12//99
	Vermont	S	6.09 MW	7.65 AW	15920 AAW	VTBLS	10//99-12//99
	Burlington MSA, VT	S	6.98 MW	6.02 AW	14530 AAW	VTBLS	10//99-12//99
	Virginia	S	8.34 MW	9.11 AW	18950 AAW	VABLS	10//99-12//99
	Lynchburg MSA, VA	S	8.25 MW	7.38 AW	17170 AAW	VABLS	10//99-12//99
	Norfolk-Virginia Beach-Newport News MSA, VA-NC	S	8.39 MW	7.68 AW	17440 AAW	VABLS	10//99-12//99
	Richmond-Petersburg MSA, VA	S	8.98 MW	8.50 AW	18680 AAW	VABLS	10//99-12//99
	Roanoke MSA, VA	S	7.59 MW	7.29 AW	15780 AAW	VABLS	10//99-12//99
	Washington	S	9.35 MW	9.43 AW	19620 AAW	WABLS	10//99-12//99
	Bellingham MSA, WA	S	9.00 MW	8.75 AW	18720 AAW	WABLS	10//99-12//99
	Bremerton PMSA, WA	S	9.65 MW	9.89 AW	20060 AAW	WABLS	10//99-12//99
	Olympia PMSA, WA	S	7.77 MW	7.76 AW	16170 AAW	WABLS	10//99-12//99
	Richland-Kennewick-Pasco MSA, WA	S	9.09 MW	9.44 AW	18910 AAW	WABLS	10//99-12//99
	Seattle-Bellevue-Everett PMSA, WA	S	10.45 MW	10.10 AW	21740 AAW	WABLS	10//99-12//99
	Spokane MSA, WA	S	9.42 MW	9.35 AW	19590 AAW	WABLS	10//99-12//99
	Tacoma PMSA, WA	S	10.13 MW	9.85 AW	21080 AAW	WABLS	10//99-12//99
	West Virginia	S	7.33 MW	7.50 AW	15610 AAW	WVBLS	10//99-12//99
	Charleston MSA, WV	S	7.92 MW	7.67 AW	16480 AAW	WVBLS	10//99-12//99
	Huntington-Ashland MSA, WV-KY-OH	S	7.35 MW	6.21 AW	15290 AAW	WVBLS	10//99-12//99
	Wheeling MSA, WV-OH	S	7.10 MW	6.67 AW	14780 AAW	WVBLS	10//99-12//99
	Wisconsin	S	8.4 MW	8.68 AW	18050 AAW	WIBLS	10//99-12//99
	Appleton-Oshkosh-Neenah MSA, WI	S	9.10 MW	9.22 AW	18930 AAW	WIBLS	10//99-12//99
	Green Bay MSA, WI	S	9.00 MW	8.57 AW	18720 AAW	WIBLS	10//99-12//99
	Janesville-Beloit MSA, WI	S	8.74 MW	8.65 AW	18180 AAW	WIBLS	10//99-12//99
	Kenosha PMSA, WI	S	7.28 MW	6.98 AW	15150 AAW	WIBLS	10//99-12//99
	Madison MSA, WI	S	10.34 MW	9.67 AW	21500 AAW	WIBLS	10//99-12//99
	Milwaukee-Waukesha PMSA, WI	S	8.54 MW	8.22 AW	17770 AAW	WIBLS	10//99-12//99
	Wausau MSA, WI	S	8.77 MW	8.38 AW	18250 AAW	WIBLS	10//99-12//99
	Wyoming	S	6.73 MW	6.66 AW	13850 AAW	WYBLS	10//99-12//99
	Puerto Rico	S	6.15 MW	6.73 AW	14000 AAW	PRBLS	10//99-12//99
	Arecibo PMSA, PR	S	6.11 MW	6.11 AW	12720 AAW	PRBLS	10//99-12//99
	Caguas PMSA, PR	S	6.12 MW	6.19 AW	12730 AAW	PRBLS	10//99-12//99
	Mayaguez MSA, PR	S	6.20 MW	5.97 AW	12900 AAW	PRBLS	10//99-12//99
	Ponce MSA, PR	S	6.47 MW	6.20 AW	13460 AAW	PRBLS	10//99-12//99
	San Juan-Bayamon PMSA, PR	S	6.73 MW	6.15 AW	14010 AAW	PRBLS	10//99-12//99
	Virgin Islands	S	7.44 MW	7.89 AW	16420 AAW	VIBLS	10//99-12//99
	Guam	S	7.8 MW	8.24 AW	17130 AAW	GUBLS	10//99-12//99
Court, Municipal, and License Clerk	Alabama	S	11.59 MW	13.17 AW	27380 AAW	ALBLS	10//99-12//99
	Anniston MSA, AL	S	11.74 MW	10.33 AW	24430 AAW	ALBLS	10//99-12//99
	Birmingham MSA, AL	S	13.37 MW	11.93 AW	27800 AAW	ALBLS	10//99-12//99
	Dothan MSA, AL	S	11.23 MW	10.26 AW	23370 AAW	ALBLS	10//99-12//99
	Florence MSA, AL	S	12.68 MW	10.12 AW	26380 AAW	ALBLS	10//99-12//99
	Huntsville MSA, AL	S	12.33 MW	11.04 AW	25640 AAW	ALBLS	10//99-12//99
	Alaska	S	14.97 MW	15.82 AW	32900 AAW	AKBLS	10//99-12//99
	Arizona	S	10.77 MW	11.36 AW	23630 AAW	AZBLS	10//99-12//99
	Flagstaff MSA, AZ-UT	S	11.90 MW	11.36 AW	24750 AAW	AZBLS	10//99-12//99
	Tucson MSA, AZ	S	10.76 MW	10.30 AW	22380 AAW	AZBLS	10//99-12//99
	Yuma MSA, AZ	S	10.85 MW	10.64 AW	22560 AAW	AZBLS	10//99-12//99
	Arkansas	S	8.91 MW	9.44 AW	19640 AAW	ARBLS	10//99-12//99
	Fayetteville-Springdale-Rogers MSA, AR	S	10.61 MW	9.93 AW	22060 AAW	ARBLS	10//99-12//99
	Fort Smith MSA, AR-OK	S	10.43 MW	10.38 AW	21690 AAW	ARBLS	10//99-12//99
	Little Rock-North Little Rock MSA, AR	S	10.94 MW	10.52 AW	22750 AAW	ARBLS	10//99-12//99
	California	S	15.18 MW	16.02 AW	33320 AAW	CABLS	10//99-12//99
	Fresno MSA, CA	S	15.47 MW	14.55 AW	32170 AAW	CABLS	10//99-12//99
	Oakland PMSA, CA	S	15.54 MW	14.52 AW	32320 AAW	CABLS	10//99-12//99
	Riverside-San Bernardino PMSA, CA	S	16.23 MW	15.49 AW	33770 AAW	CABLS	10//99-12//99
	Sacramento PMSA, CA	S	15.74 MW	14.85 AW	32730 AAW	CABLS	10//99-12//99

AAW	Average annual wage	AOH	Average offered, high	ASH	Average starting, high
AE	Average entry wage	AOL	Average offered, low	ASL	Average starting, low
AEX	Average experienced wage	APH	Average pay, high range	AW	Average wage paid
AO	Average offered	APL	Average pay, low range	FQ	First quartile wage

H	Hourly	M	Monthly
HI	Highest wage paid	MTC	Median total compensation
HR	High end range	MW	Median wage paid
LR	Low end range	SQ	Second quartile wage

S	Special: hourly and annual
TQ	Third quartile wage
W	Weekly
Y	Yearly

Occupation/Type/Industry	Location	Per	Low	Mid	High	Source	Date
Court, Municipal, and License Clerk	San Francisco PMSA, CA	S	23.30 MW	23.92 AW	48470 AAW	CABLS	10//99-12//99
	San José PMSA, CA	S	15.74 MW	14.52 AW	32730 AAW	CABLS	10//99-12//99
	Ventura PMSA, CA	S	15.63 MW	14.60 AW	32500 AAW	CABLS	10//99-12//99
	Colorado	S	13.28 MW	13.43 AW	27940 AAW	COBLS	10//99-12//99
	Boulder-Longmont PMSA, CO	S	13.44 MW	13.41 AW	27960 AAW	COBLS	10//99-12//99
	Colorado Springs MSA, CO	S	14.26 MW	12.96 AW	29660 AAW	COBLS	10//99-12//99
	Denver PMSA, CO	S	14.98 MW	14.62 AW	31150 AAW	COBLS	10//99-12//99
	Fort Collins-Loveland MSA, CO	S	12.90 MW	13.53 AW	26830 AAW	COBLS	10//99-12//99
	Grand Junction MSA, CO	S	13.10 MW	12.36 AW	27240 AAW	COBLS	10//99-12//99
	Greeley PMSA, CO	S	13.01 MW	12.72 AW	27060 AAW	COBLS	10//99-12//99
	Connecticut	S	15.29 MW	15.65 AW	32560 AAW	CTBLS	10//99-12//99
	New Haven-Meriden PMSA, CT	S	15.33 MW	14.81 AW	31890 AAW	CTBLS	10//99-12//99
	Stamford-Norwalk PMSA, CT	S	17.78 MW	17.65 AW	36980 AAW	CTBLS	10//99-12//99
	Washington PMSA, DC-MD-VA-WV	S	15.33 MW	14.86 AW	31900 AAW	DCBLS	10//99-12//99
	Florida	S	10.63 MW	11.31 AW	23520 AAW	FLBLS	10//99-12//99
	Fort Lauderdale PMSA, FL	S	11.98 MW	11.26 AW	24910 AAW	FLBLS	10//99-12//99
	Fort Pierce-Port St. Lucie MSA, FL	S	11.40 MW	10.67 AW	23720 AAW	FLBLS	10//99-12//99
	Jacksonville MSA, FL	S	10.05 MW	9.67 AW	20910 AAW	FLBLS	10//99-12//99
	Lakeland-Winter Haven MSA, FL	S	11.28 MW	10.29 AW	23460 AAW	FLBLS	10//99-12//99
	Melbourne-Titusville-Palm Bay MSA, FL	S	10.91 MW	10.55 AW	22700 AAW	FLBLS	10//99-12//99
	Naples MSA, FL	S	9.90 MW	9.80 AW	20590 AAW	FLBLS	10//99-12//99
	Orlando MSA, FL	S	10.91 MW	10.36 AW	22690 AAW	FLBLS	10//99-12//99
	Pensacola MSA, FL	S	10.74 MW	10.49 AW	22340 AAW	FLBLS	10//99-12//99
	Tampa-St. Petersburg-Clearwater MSA, FL	S	12.31 MW	11.81 AW	25590 AAW	FLBLS	10//99-12//99
	West Palm Beach-Boca Raton MSA, FL	S	12.19 MW	11.30 AW	25350 AAW	FLBLS	10//99-12//99
	Georgia	S	10.57 MW	11.08 AW	23040 AAW	GABLS	10//99-12//99
	Atlanta MSA, GA	S	11.88 MW	11.57 AW	24720 AAW	GABLS	10//99-12//99
	Augusta-Aiken MSA, GA-SC	S	11.04 MW	10.64 AW	22960 AAW	GABLS	10//99-12//99
	Columbus MSA, GA-AL	S	11.37 MW	10.12 AW	23650 AAW	GABLS	10//99-12//99
	Savannah MSA, GA	S	9.31 MW	8.43 AW	19370 AAW	GABLS	10//99-12//99
	Hawaii	S	14.01 MW	14.79 AW	30750 AAW	HIBLS	10//99-12//99
	Idaho	S	10.51 MW	10.84 AW	22550 AAW	IDBLS	10//99-12//99
	Illinois	S	11.81 MW	12.03 AW	25030 AAW	ILBLS	10//99-12//99
	Champaign-Urbana MSA, IL	S	12.54 MW	12.23 AW	26080 AAW	ILBLS	10//99-12//99
	Chicago PMSA, IL	S	12.99 MW	12.74 AW	27020 AAW	ILBLS	10//99-12//99
	Peoria-Pekin MSA, IL	S	12.53 MW	12.51 AW	26060 AAW	ILBLS	10//99-12//99
	Rockford MSA, IL	S	9.54 MW	6.86 AW	19840 AAW	ILBLS	10//99-12//99
	Springfield MSA, IL	S	11.26 MW	11.17 AW	23410 AAW	ILBLS	10//99-12//99
	Indiana	S	10.2 MW	10.35 AW	21520 AAW	INBLS	10//99-12//99
	Elkhart-Goshen MSA, IN	S	10.68 MW	10.48 AW	22220 AAW	INBLS	10//99-12//99
	Evansville-Henderson MSA, IN-KY	S	9.56 MW	9.76 AW	19890 AAW	INBLS	10//99-12//99
	Fort Wayne MSA, IN	S	11.32 MW	11.26 AW	23540 AAW	INBLS	10//99-12//99
	Gary PMSA, IN	S	11.22 MW	10.08 AW	23340 AAW	INBLS	10//99-12//99
	Indianapolis MSA, IN	S	9.05 MW	9.25 AW	18830 AAW	INBLS	10//99-12//99
	Lafayette MSA, IN	S	10.12 MW	10.11 AW	21060 AAW	INBLS	10//99-12//99
	South Bend MSA, IN	S	10.36 MW	10.66 AW	21550 AAW	INBLS	10//99-12//99
	Iowa	S	11.77 MW	12.14 AW	25240 AAW	IABLS	10//99-12//99
	Davenport-Moline-Rock Island MSA, IA-IL	S	12.81 MW	12.64 AW	26640 AAW	IABLS	10//99-12//99
	Des Moines MSA, IA	S	14.61 MW	12.65 AW	30380 AAW	IABLS	10//99-12//99
	Iowa City MSA, IA	S	12.29 MW	11.70 AW	25560 AAW	IABLS	10//99-12//99
	Kansas	S	10.81 MW	10.58 AW	22010 AAW	KSBLS	10//99-12//99
	Lawrence MSA, KS	S	10.45 MW	10.17 AW	21740 AAW	KSBLS	10//99-12//99
	Wichita MSA, KS	S	10.79 MW	10.96 AW	22450 AAW	KSBLS	10//99-12//99
	Kentucky	S	9.16 MW	9.61 AW	20000 AAW	KYBLS	10//99-12//99
	Louisiana	S	10.53 MW	11.25 AW	23400 AAW	LABLS	10//99-12//99
	Baton Rouge MSA, LA	S	10.58 MW	10.86 AW	22000 AAW	LABLS	10//99-12//99
	Lafayette MSA, LA	S	11.27 MW	12.18 AW	23440 AAW	LABLS	10//99-12//99
	Lake Charles MSA, LA	S	12.24 MW	10.91 AW	25450 AAW	LABLS	10//99-12//99
	Monroe MSA, LA	S	10.81 MW	9.89 AW	22470 AAW	LABLS	10//99-12//99
	New Orleans MSA, LA	S	12.00 MW	11.09 AW	24960 AAW	LABLS	10//99-12//99

AAW Average annual wage	AOH Average offered, high	ASH Average starting, high	H Hourly	M Monthly	S Special: hourly and annual
AE Average entry wage	AOL Average offered, low	ASL Average starting, low	HI Highest wage paid	MTC Median total compensation	TQ Third quartile wage
AEX Average experienced wage	APH Average pay, high range	AW Average wage paid	HR High end range	MW Median wage paid	W Weekly
AO Average offered	APL Average pay, low range	FQ First quartile wage	LR Low end range	SQ Second quartile wage	Y Yearly

Court, Municipal, and License Clerk

Occupation/Type/Industry	Location	Per	Low	Mid	High	Source	Date
Court, Municipal, and License Clerk	Shreveport-Bossier City MSA, LA	S	10.32 MW	9.13 AW	21460 AAW	LABLS	10//99-12//99
	Maine	S	11.2 MW	11.33 AW	23560 AAW	MEBLS	10//99-12//99
	Maryland	S	12.05 MW	12.58 AW	26170 AAW	MDBLS	10//99-12//99
	Massachusetts	S	13.46 MW	13.84 AW	28800 AAW	MABLS	10//99-12//99
	Boston PMSA, MA-NH	S	14.06 MW	13.49 AW	29240 AAW	MABLS	10//99-12//99
	Fitchburg-Leominster PMSA, MA	S	11.64 MW	10.58 AW	24210 AAW	MABLS	10//99-12//99
	Lawrence PMSA, MA-NH	S	13.86 MW	14.18 AW	28820 AAW	MABLS	10//99-12//99
	Lowell PMSA, MA-NH	S	13.05 MW	13.06 AW	27130 AAW	MABLS	10//99-12//99
	New Bedford PMSA, MA	S	13.46 MW	13.78 AW	27990 AAW	MABLS	10//99-12//99
	Springfield MSA, MA	S	14.39 MW	14.59 AW	29940 AAW	MABLS	10//99-12//99
	Worcester PMSA, MA-CT	S	16.93 MW	15.54 AW	35210 AAW	MABLS	10//99-12//99
	Michigan	S	14.62 MW	14.52 AW	30200 AAW	MIBLS	10//99-12//99
	Ann Arbor PMSA, MI	S	14.49 MW	14.62 AW	30140 AAW	MIBLS	10//99-12//99
	Detroit PMSA, MI	S	15.09 MW	15.09 AW	31390 AAW	MIBLS	10//99-12//99
	Flint PMSA, MI	S	14.89 MW	14.93 AW	30970 AAW	MIBLS	10//99-12//99
	Grand Rapids-Muskegon-Holland MSA, MI	S	14.11 MW	13.68 AW	29340 AAW	MIBLS	10//99-12//99
	Kalamazoo-Battle Creek MSA, MI	S	12.82 MW	13.51 AW	26660 AAW	MIBLS	10//99-12//99
	Lansing-East Lansing MSA, MI	S	15.84 MW	15.15 AW	32940 AAW	MIBLS	10//99-12//99
	Saginaw-Bay City-Midland MSA, MI	S	14.92 MW	15.09 AW	31020 AAW	MIBLS	10//99-12//99
	Minnesota	S	12.76 MW	13.04 AW	27110 AAW	MNBLS	10//99-12//99
	Duluth-Superior MSA, MN-WI	S	14.68 MW	14.58 AW	30530 AAW	MNBLS	10//99-12//99
	Mississippi	S	9.81 MW	10.20 AW	21220 AAW	MSBLS	10//99-12//99
	Biloxi-Gulfport-Pascagoula MSA, MS	S	10.33 MW	10.11 AW	21500 AAW	MSBLS	10//99-12//99
	Hattiesburg MSA, MS	S	9.44 MW	8.93 AW	19630 AAW	MSBLS	10//99-12//99
	Jackson MSA, MS	S	11.84 MW	11.24 AW	24640 AAW	MSBLS	10//99-12//99
	Missouri	S	9.98 MW	10.77 AW	22410 AAW	MOBLS	10//99-12//99
	St. Louis MSA, MO-IL	S	12.27 MW	11.56 AW	25520 AAW	MOBLS	10//99-12//99
	Montana	S	9.91 MW	10.08 AW	20960 AAW	MTBLS	10//99-12//99
	Great Falls MSA, MT	S	9.96 MW	9.81 AW	20720 AAW	MTBLS	10//99-12//99
	Nebraska	S	11.54 MW	11.78 AW	24510 AAW	NEBLS	10//99-12//99
	Omaha MSA, NE-IA	S	12.94 MW	11.53 AW	26920 AAW	NEBLS	10//99-12//99
	Nevada	S	14.5 MW	15.11 AW	31430 AAW	NVBLS	10//99-12//99
	Las Vegas MSA, NV-AZ	S	15.45 MW	14.49 AW	32130 AAW	NVBLS	10//99-12//99
	New Hampshire	S	10.09 MW	10.11 AW	21020 AAW	NHBLS	10//99-12//99
	Portsmouth-Rochester PMSA, NH-ME	S	11.62 MW	11.30 AW	24170 AAW	NHBLS	10//99-12//99
	New Jersey	S	14.4 MW	15.25 AW	31720 AAW	NJBLS	10//99-12//99
	Atlantic-Cape May PMSA, NJ	S	14.57 MW	14.47 AW	30310 AAW	NJBLS	10//99-12//99
	Bergen-Passaic PMSA, NJ	S	17.29 MW	16.18 AW	35960 AAW	NJBLS	10//99-12//99
	Jersey City PMSA, NJ	S	15.81 MW	14.69 AW	32890 AAW	NJBLS	10//99-12//99
	Middlesex-Somerset-Hunterdon PMSA, NJ	S	12.80 MW	11.65 AW	26630 AAW	NJBLS	10//99-12//99
	Monmouth-Ocean PMSA, NJ	S	16.22 MW	14.71 AW	33740 AAW	NJBLS	10//99-12//99
	Newark PMSA, NJ	S	15.23 MW	15.00 AW	31670 AAW	NJBLS	10//99-12//99
	New Mexico	S	11.53 MW	11.67 AW	24280 AAW	NMBLS	10//99-12//99
	Las Cruces MSA, NM	S	12.42 MW	11.70 AW	25830 AAW	NMBLS	10//99-12//99
	Santa Fe MSA, NM	S	12.29 MW	11.47 AW	25570 AAW	NMBLS	10//99-12//99
	Albany-Schenectady-Troy MSA, NY	S	18.57 MW	16.79 AW	38630 AAW	NYBLS	10//99-12//99
	Binghamton MSA, NY	S	13.24 MW	14.14 AW	27540 AAW	NYBLS	10//99-12//99
	Buffalo-Niagara Falls MSA, NY	S	15.29 MW	13.76 AW	31800 AAW	NYBLS	10//99-12//99
	Dutchess County PMSA, NY	S	12.96 MW	13.37 AW	26960 AAW	NYBLS	10//99-12//99
	Elmira MSA, NY	S	14.50 MW	12.14 AW	30170 AAW	NYBLS	10//99-12//99
	Glens Falls MSA, NY	S	10.10 MW	10.27 AW	21000 AAW	NYBLS	10//99-12//99
	Jamestown MSA, NY	S	9.66 MW	9.32 AW	20100 AAW	NYBLS	10//99-12//99
	Nassau-Suffolk PMSA, NY	S	17.74 MW	15.42 AW	36910 AAW	NYBLS	10//99-12//99
	New York PMSA, NY	S	19.70 MW	18.87 AW	40980 AAW	NYBLS	10//99-12//99
	Newburgh PMSA, NY-PA	S	16.78 MW	15.22 AW	34900 AAW	NYBLS	10//99-12//99
	Rochester MSA, NY	S	12.84 MW	12.24 AW	26700 AAW	NYBLS	10//99-12//99
	Syracuse MSA, NY	S	12.17 MW	12.08 AW	25310 AAW	NYBLS	10//99-12//99
	Utica-Rome MSA, NY	S	9.50 MW	8.45 AW	19770 AAW	NYBLS	10//99-12//99
	North Carolina	S	10.23 MW	10.49 AW	21810 AAW	NCBLS	10//99-12//99
	Charlotte-Gastonia-Rock Hill MSA, NC-SC	S	11.88 MW	11.18 AW	24720 AAW	NCBLS	10//99-12//99

AAW	Average annual wage	AOH	Average offered, high	ASH	Average starting, high
AE	Average entry wage	AOL	Average offered, low	ASL	Average starting, low
AEX	Average experienced wage	APH	Average pay, high range	AW	Average wage paid
AO	Average offered	APL	Average pay, low range	FQ	First quartile wage

H	Hourly	M	Monthly
HI	Highest wage paid	MTC	Median total compensation
HR	High end range	MW	Median wage paid
LR	Low end range	SQ	Second quartile wage

S	Special: hourly and annual
TQ	Third quartile wage
W	Weekly
Y	Yearly

Occupation/Type/Industry	Location	Per	Low	Mid	High	Source	Date
Court, Municipal, and License Clerk							
	Greensboro--Winston-Salem-- High Point MSA, NC	S	11.48 MW	10.48 AW	23870 AAW	NCBLS	10//99-12//99
	North Dakota	S	10.27 MW	10.40 AW	21630 AAW	NDBLS	10//99-12//99
	Grand Forks MSA, ND-MN	S	12.60 MW	10.48 AW	26210 AAW	NDBLS	10//99-12//99
	Ohio	S	12.01 MW	12.92 AW	26870 AAW	OHBLS	10//99-12//99
	Akron PMSA, OH	S	13.24 MW	12.67 AW	27540 AAW	OHBLS	10//99-12//99
	Canton-Massillon MSA, OH	S	12.39 MW	11.75 AW	25780 AAW	OHBLS	10//99-12//99
	Cincinnati PMSA, OH-KY-IN	S	11.33 MW	11.06 AW	23560 AAW	OHBLS	10//99-12//99
	Cleveland-Lorain-Elyria PMSA, OH	S	12.91 MW	12.36 AW	26860 AAW	OHBLS	10//99-12//99
	Dayton-Springfield MSA, OH	S	12.61 MW	12.09 AW	26220 AAW	OHBLS	10//99-12//99
	Mansfield MSA, OH	S	10.12 MW	9.56 AW	21050 AAW	OHBLS	10//99-12//99
	Steubenville-Weirton MSA, OH-WV	S	8.83 MW	7.56 AW	18370 AAW	OHBLS	10//99-12//99
	Toledo MSA, OH	S	11.23 MW	10.60 AW	23370 AAW	OHBLS	10//99-12//99
	Youngstown-Warren MSA, OH	S	10.38 MW	10.42 AW	21590 AAW	OHBLS	10//99-12//99
	Oklahoma	S	9.97 MW	10.44 AW	21710 AAW	OKBLS	10//99-12//99
	Oklahoma City MSA, OK	S	11.30 MW	10.45 AW	23500 AAW	OKBLS	10//99-12//99
	Tulsa MSA, OK	S	12.65 MW	12.01 AW	26310 AAW	OKBLS	10//99-12//99
	Oregon	S	13.4 MW	13.32 AW	27710 AAW	ORBLS	10//99-12//99
	Portland-Vancouver PMSA, OR-WA	S	13.74 MW	13.72 AW	28590 AAW	ORBLS	10//99-12//99
	Pennsylvania	S	12.26 MW	12.64 AW	26300 AAW	PABLS	10//99-12//99
	Allentown-Bethlehem-Easton MSA, PA	S	15.18 MW	14.62 AW	31580 AAW	PABLS	10//99-12//99
	Harrisburg-Lebanon-Carlisle MSA, PA	S	11.30 MW	11.03 AW	23510 AAW	PABLS	10//99-12//99
	Lancaster MSA, PA	S	11.84 MW	11.98 AW	24630 AAW	PABLS	10//99-12//99
	Philadelphia PMSA, PA-NJ	S	14.98 MW	14.65 AW	31150 AAW	PABLS	10//99-12//99
	Scranton--Wilkes-Barre-- Hazleton MSA, PA	S	9.81 MW	9.50 AW	20410 AAW	PABLS	10//99-12//99
	York MSA, PA	S	11.52 MW	11.37 AW	23970 AAW	PABLS	10//99-12//99
	Rhode Island	S	14.73 MW	15.04 AW	31290 AAW	RIBLS	10//99-12//99
	Providence-Fall River- Warwick MSA, RI-MA	S	15.07 MW	14.82 AW	31340 AAW	RIBLS	10//99-12//99
	South Carolina	S	10.13 MW	10.35 AW	21530 AAW	SCBLS	10//99-12//99
	Charleston-North Charleston MSA, SC	S	10.41 MW	10.39 AW	21660 AAW	SCBLS	10//99-12//99
	Columbia MSA, SC	S	11.06 MW	10.71 AW	23010 AAW	SCBLS	10//99-12//99
	Greenville-Spartanburg- Anderson MSA, SC	S	10.82 MW	10.33 AW	22500 AAW	SCBLS	10//99-12//99
	South Dakota	S	8.64 MW	8.91 AW	18530 AAW	SDBLS	10//99-12//99
	Tennessee	S	10.75 MW	11.54 AW	24000 AAW	TNBLS	10//99-12//99
	Chattanooga MSA, TN-GA	S	10.52 MW	9.97 AW	21870 AAW	TNBLS	10//99-12//99
	Knoxville MSA, TN	S	10.43 MW	10.49 AW	21700 AAW	TNBLS	10//99-12//99
	Memphis MSA, TN-AR-MS	S	12.29 MW	11.83 AW	25560 AAW	MSBLS	10//99-12//99
	Nashville MSA, TN	S	12.49 MW	11.16 AW	25970 AAW	TNBLS	10//99-12//99
	Texas	S	9.23 MW	9.79 AW	20370 AAW	TXBLS	10//99-12//99
	Austin-San Marcos MSA, TX	S	10.99 MW	10.46 AW	22860 AAW	TXBLS	10//99-12//99
	Beaumont-Port Arthur MSA, TX	S	12.09 MW	11.99 AW	25140 AAW	TXBLS	10//99-12//99
	Brazoria PMSA, TX	S	10.28 MW	9.88 AW	21380 AAW	TXBLS	10//99-12//99
	Brownsville-Harlingen-San Benito MSA, TX	S	9.62 MW	7.73 AW	20010 AAW	TXBLS	10//99-12//99
	Bryan-College Station MSA, TX	S	9.24 MW	9.12 AW	19220 AAW	TXBLS	10//99-12//99
	Corpus Christi MSA, TX	S	8.14 MW	8.02 AW	16930 AAW	TXBLS	10//99-12//99
	Dallas PMSA, TX	S	12.84 MW	11.96 AW	26710 AAW	TXBLS	10//99-12//99
	Fort Worth-Arlington PMSA, TX	S	10.90 MW	10.22 AW	22670 AAW	TXBLS	10//99-12//99
	Galveston-Texas City PMSA, TX	S	9.95 MW	9.86 AW	20690 AAW	TXBLS	10//99-12//99
	Killeen-Temple MSA, TX	S	8.66 MW	8.35 AW	18020 AAW	TXBLS	10//99-12//99
	Longview-Marshall MSA, TX	S	8.63 MW	8.51 AW	17950 AAW	TXBLS	10//99-12//99
	McAllen-Edinburg-Mission MSA, TX	S	9.42 MW	8.87 AW	19600 AAW	TXBLS	10//99-12//99
	San Antonio MSA, TX	S	10.18 MW	9.93 AW	21170 AAW	TXBLS	10//99-12//99
	Texarkana MSA, TX- Texarkana, AR	S	8.94 MW	8.31 AW	18590 AAW	TXBLS	10//99-12//99
	Waco MSA, TX	S	9.43 MW	9.33 AW	19610 AAW	TXBLS	10//99-12//99
	Utah	S	10.04 MW	10.43 AW	21680 AAW	UTBLS	10//99-12//99

AAW	Average annual wage	AOH	Average offered, high	ASH	Average starting, high
AE	Average entry wage	AOL	Average offered, low	ASL	Average starting, low
AEX	Average experienced wage	APH	Average pay, high range	AW	Average wage paid
AO	Average offered	APL	Average pay, low range	FQ	First quartile wage

H	Hourly	M	Monthly	S	Special: hourly and annual
HI	Highest wage paid	MTC	Median total compensation	TQ	Third quartile wage
HR	High end range	MW	Median wage paid	W	Weekly
LR	Low end range	SQ	Second quartile wage	Y	Yearly

Occupation/Type/Industry	Location	Per	Low	Mid	High	Source	Date
Court, Municipal, and License Clerk	Provo-Orem MSA, UT	S	10.52 MW	10.25 AW	21880 AAW	UTBLS	10//99-12//99
	Salt Lake City-Ogden MSA, UT	S	11.05 MW	10.35 AW	22980 AAW	UTBLS	10//99-12//99
	Vermont	S	11.92 MW	12.68 AW	26380 AAW	VTBLS	10//99-12//99
	Virginia	S	12.73 MW	13.54 AW	28170 AAW	VABLS	10//99-12//99
	Charlottesville MSA, VA	S	14.34 MW	12.98 AW	29840 AAW	VABLS	10//99-12//99
	Danville MSA, VA	S	12.93 MW	12.83 AW	26900 AAW	VABLS	10//99-12//99
	Lynchburg MSA, VA	S	13.24 MW	12.37 AW	27530 AAW	VABLS	10//99-12//99
	Norfolk-Virginia Beach-Newport News MSA, VA-NC	S	13.61 MW	12.60 AW	28310 AAW	VABLS	10//99-12//99
	Richmond-Petersburg MSA, VA	S	13.42 MW	12.65 AW	27920 AAW	VABLS	10//99-12//99
	Roanoke MSA, VA	S	12.09 MW	11.21 AW	25140 AAW	VABLS	10//99-12//99
	Washington	S	15.05 MW	15.16 AW	31520 AAW	WABLS	10//99-12//99
	Bellingham MSA, WA	S	14.68 MW	14.02 AW	30520 AAW	WABLS	10//99-12//99
	Bremerton PMSA, WA	S	13.85 MW	14.12 AW	28800 AAW	WABLS	10//99-12//99
	Richland-Kennewick-Pasco MSA, WA	S	14.46 MW	13.93 AW	30080 AAW	WABLS	10//99-12//99
	Tacoma PMSA, WA	S	15.89 MW	15.61 AW	33050 AAW	WABLS	10//99-12//99
	West Virginia	S	8.39 MW	9.12 AW	18970 AAW	WVBLS	10//99-12//99
	Charleston MSA, WV	S	8.57 MW	8.58 AW	17820 AAW	WVBLS	10//99-12//99
	Huntington-Ashland MSA, WV-KY-OH	S	9.74 MW	9.75 AW	20270 AAW	WVBLS	10//99-12//99
	Parkersburg-Marietta MSA, WV-OH	S	9.33 MW	9.41 AW	19400 AAW	WVBLS	10//99-12//99
	Wheeling MSA, WV-OH	S	9.15 MW	8.54 AW	19020 AAW	WVBLS	10//99-12//99
	Wisconsin	S	11.72 MW	11.21 AW	23320 AAW	WIBLS	10//99-12//99
	Appleton-Oshkosh-Neenah MSA, WI	S	12.09 MW	12.11 AW	25150 AAW	WIBLS	10//99-12//99
	Eau Claire MSA, WI	S	9.89 MW	8.32 AW	20560 AAW	WIBLS	10//99-12//99
	Green Bay MSA, WI	S	12.32 MW	12.24 AW	25620 AAW	WIBLS	10//99-12//99
	Kenosha PMSA, WI	S	11.88 MW	11.50 AW	24710 AAW	WIBLS	10//99-12//99
	La Crosse MSA, WI-MN	S	9.81 MW	10.09 AW	20400 AAW	WIBLS	10//99-12//99
	Milwaukee-Waukesha PMSA, WI	S	13.84 MW	13.86 AW	28780 AAW	WIBLS	10//99-12//99
	Racine PMSA, WI	S	13.66 MW	13.22 AW	28410 AAW	WIBLS	10//99-12//99
	Wausau MSA, WI	S	9.44 MW	8.26 AW	19630 AAW	WIBLS	10//99-12//99
	Wyoming	S	9.69 MW	10.00 AW	20800 AAW	WYBLS	10//99-12//99
	Puerto Rico	S	6.58 MW	7.91 AW	16450 AAW	PRBLS	10//99-12//99
	San Juan-Bayamon PMSA, PR	S	10.80 MW	10.10 AW	22460 AAW	PRBLS	10//99-12//99
Court Reporter	United States	Y		54000 AW		WSJ2	1999
	Alabama	S	9.94 MW	12.58 AW	26170 AAW	ALBLS	10//99-12//99
	Montgomery MSA, AL	S	9.90 MW	6.45 AW	20600 AAW	ALBLS	10//99-12//99
	Arizona	S	17.63 MW	16.97 AW	35290 AAW	AZBLS	10//99-12//99
	Arkansas	S	6.64 MW	8.44 AW	17560 AAW	ARBLS	10//99-12//99
	California	S	20.04 MW	22.82 AW	47460 AAW	CABLS	10//99-12//99
	Bakersfield MSA, CA	S	28.38 MW	29.69 AW	59030 AAW	CABLS	10//99-12//99
	Fresno MSA, CA	S	19.96 MW	18.94 AW	41520 AAW	CABLS	10//99-12//99
	Los Angeles-Long Beach PMSA, CA	S	21.25 MW	19.59 AW	44190 AAW	CABLS	10//99-12//99
	Orange County PMSA, CA	S	16.83 MW	14.61 AW	35000 AAW	CABLS	10//99-12//99
	Riverside-San Bernardino PMSA, CA	S	22.75 MW	20.08 AW	47320 AAW	CABLS	10//99-12//99
	Colorado	S	16.23 MW	18.71 AW	38910 AAW	COBLS	10//99-12//99
	Denver PMSA, CO	S	18.40 MW	15.72 AW	38280 AAW	COBLS	10//99-12//99
	Washington PMSA, DC-MD-VA-WV	S	16.45 MW	13.01 AW	34220 AAW	DCBLS	10//99-12//99
	Florida	S	13.88 MW	16.66 AW	34650 AAW	FLBLS	10//99-12//99
	Georgia	S	20.62 MW	20.57 AW	42790 AAW	GABLS	10//99-12//99
	Idaho	S	18.01 MW	16.68 AW	34700 AAW	IDBLS	10//99-12//99
	Indiana	S	12.13 MW	12.43 AW	25860 AAW	INBLS	10//99-12//99
	Fort Wayne MSA, IN	S	15.59 MW	14.83 AW	32430 AAW	INBLS	10//99-12//99
	Indianapolis MSA, IN	S	12.07 MW	12.16 AW	25100 AAW	INBLS	10//99-12//99
	Iowa	S	22.65 MW	20.87 AW	43410 AAW	IABLS	10//99-12//99
	Kansas	S	18.99 MW	19.67 AW	40920 AAW	KSBLS	10//99-12//99
	Wichita MSA, KS	S	16.39 MW	14.68 AW	34100 AAW	KSBLS	10//99-12//99
	Louisiana	S	11.28 MW	11.53 AW	23980 AAW	LABLS	10//99-12//99
	Shreveport-Bossier City MSA, LA	S	18.27 MW	15.44 AW	37990 AAW	LABLS	10//99-12//99

AAW	Average annual wage	**AOH**	Average offered, high	**ASH**	Average starting, high	**H**	Hourly
AE	Average entry wage	**AOL**	Average offered, low	**ASL**	Average starting, low	**HI**	Highest wage paid
AEX	Average experienced wage	**APH**	Average pay, high range	**AW**	Average wage paid	**HR**	High end range
AO	Average offered	**APL**	Average pay, low range	**FQ**	First quartile wage	**LR**	Low end range

M	Monthly	**S**	Special: hourly and annual
MTC	Median total compensation	**TQ**	Third quartile wage
MW	Median wage paid	**W**	Weekly
SQ	Second quartile wage	**Y**	Yearly

Occupation/Type/Industry	Location	Per	Low	Mid	High	Source	Date
Court Reporter	Maryland	S	17.72 MW	16.83 AW	35010 AAW	MDBLS	10//99-12//99
	Baltimore PMSA, MD	S	17.80 MW	18.54 AW	37030 AAW	MDBLS	10//99-12//99
	Massachusetts	S	19.53 MW	19.35 AW	40250 AAW	MABLS	10//99-12//99
	Michigan	S	19.87 MW	19.69 AW	40960 AAW	MIBLS	10//99-12//99
	Ann Arbor PMSA, MI	S	17.20 MW	15.73 AW	35770 AAW	MIBLS	10//99-12//99
	Detroit PMSA, MI	S	21.66 MW	22.70 AW	45050 AAW	MIBLS	10//99-12//99
	Lansing-East Lansing MSA, MI	S	17.26 MW	16.91 AW	35900 AAW	MIBLS	10//99-12//99
	Mississippi	S	10.06 MW	11.74 AW	24430 AAW	MSBLS	10//99-12//99
	Missouri	S	10.2 MW	10.59 AW	22020 AAW	MOBLS	10//99-12//99
	Montana	S	14.87 MW	14.01 AW	29150 AAW	MTBLS	10//99-12//99
	Billings MSA, MT	S	12.80 MW	14.67 AW	26620 AAW	MTBLS	10//99-12//99
	New Jersey	S	13.31 MW	16.60 AW	34520 AAW	NJBLS	10//99-12//99
	Bergen-Passaic PMSA, NJ	S	18.68 MW	18.07 AW	38860 AAW	NJBLS	10//99-12//99
	Newark PMSA, NJ	S	14.48 MW	12.01 AW	30120 AAW	NJBLS	10//99-12//99
	New Mexico	S	18.24 MW	16.52 AW	34370 AAW	NMBLS	10//99-12//99
	Santa Fe MSA, NM	S	19.19 MW	19.21 AW	39920 AAW	NMBLS	10//99-12//99
	Buffalo-Niagara Falls MSA, NY	S	19.60 MW	16.75 AW	40760 AAW	NYBLS	10//99-12//99
	North Carolina	S	15.54 MW	15.84 AW	32960 AAW	NCBLS	10//99-12//99
	Rocky Mount MSA, NC	S	12.15 MW	10.31 AW	25280 AAW	NCBLS	10//99-12//99
	North Dakota	S	12.13 MW	12.00 AW	24950 AAW	NDBLS	10//99-12//99
	Ohio	S	19.13 MW	20.31 AW	42250 AAW	OHBLS	10//99-12//99
	Cleveland-Lorain-Elyria PMSA, OH	S	22.89 MW	21.70 AW	47610 AAW	OHBLS	10//99-12//99
	Columbus MSA, OH	S	18.97 MW	17.71 AW	39470 AAW	OHBLS	10//99-12//99
	Dayton-Springfield MSA, OH	S	24.14 MW	23.81 AW	50210 AAW	OHBLS	10//99-12//99
	Toledo MSA, OH	S	20.91 MW	20.96 AW	43500 AAW	OHBLS	10//99-12//99
	Youngstown-Warren MSA, OH	S	18.31 MW	17.75 AW	38080 AAW	OHBLS	10//99-12//99
	Oklahoma	S	22.74 MW	19.23 AW	40000 AAW	OKBLS	10//99-12//99
	Oklahoma City MSA, OK	S	22.61 MW	23.87 AW	47030 AAW	OKBLS	10//99-12//99
	Oregon	S	22.31 MW	25.99 AW	54060 AAW	ORBLS	10//99-12//99
	Portland-Vancouver PMSA, OR-WA	S	29.20 MW	25.31 AW	60730 AAW	ORBLS	10//99-12//99
	Salem PMSA, OR	S	11.16 MW	9.88 AW	23210 AAW	ORBLS	10//99-12//99
	Pennsylvania	S	17.15 MW	17.36 AW	36110 AAW	PABLS	10//99-12//99
	Philadelphia PMSA, PA-NJ	S	17.89 MW	17.98 AW	37210 AAW	PABLS	10//99-12//99
	Pittsburgh MSA, PA	S	19.72 MW	18.39 AW	41020 AAW	PABLS	10//99-12//99
	Reading MSA, PA	S	17.67 MW	18.15 AW	36750 AAW	PABLS	10//99-12//99
	South Carolina	S	13.33 MW	15.24 AW	31700 AAW	SCBLS	10//99-12//99
	South Dakota	S	15.91 MW	16.14 AW	33580 AAW	SDBLS	10//99-12//99
	Rapid City MSA, SD	S	16.33 MW	16.13 AW	33960 AAW	SDBLS	10//99-12//99
	Texas	S	16.94 MW	19.60 AW	40770 AAW	TXBLS	10//99-12//99
	Dallas PMSA, TX	S	18.01 MW	15.74 AW	37470 AAW	TXBLS	10//99-12//99
	Fort Worth-Arlington PMSA, TX	S	18.56 MW	16.93 AW	38600 AAW	TXBLS	10//99-12//99
	Houston PMSA, TX	S	20.40 MW	18.86 AW	42420 AAW	TXBLS	10//99-12//99
	Utah	S	10.63 MW	11.33 AW	23560 AAW	UTBLS	10//99-12//99
	Virginia	S	13.12 MW	16.95 AW	35250 AAW	VABLS	10//99-12//99
	Washington	S	23.79 MW	22.36 AW	46510 AAW	WABLS	10//99-12//99
	West Virginia	S	30.92 MW	30.12 AW	62650 AAW	WVBLS	10//99-12//99
	Wisconsin	S	17.19 MW	18.28 AW	38030 AAW	WIBLS	10//99-12//99
	Milwaukee-Waukesha PMSA, WI	S	19.02 MW	18.07 AW	39560 AAW	WIBLS	10//99-12//99
Crane and Tower Operator	Alabama	S	14.31 MW	14.95 AW	31090 AAW	ALBLS	10//99-12//99
	Birmingham MSA, AL	S	14.53 MW	13.87 AW	30230 AAW	ALBLS	10//99-12//99
	Decatur MSA, AL	S	14.28 MW	13.33 AW	29710 AAW	ALBLS	10//99-12//99
	Mobile MSA, AL	S	16.86 MW	15.46 AW	35060 AAW	ALBLS	10//99-12//99
	Montgomery MSA, AL	S	15.73 MW	16.75 AW	32720 AAW	ALBLS	10//99-12//99
	Tuscaloosa MSA, AL	S	16.54 MW	17.51 AW	34410 AAW	ALBLS	10//99-12//99
	Alaska	S	22.72 MW	22.90 AW	47640 AAW	AKBLS	10//99-12//99
	Arizona	S	14.49 MW	14.90 AW	31000 AAW	AZBLS	10//99-12//99
	Phoenix-Mesa MSA, AZ	S	14.88 MW	13.52 AW	30950 AAW	AZBLS	10//99-12//99
	Tucson MSA, AZ	S	15.96 MW	16.93 AW	33210 AAW	AZBLS	10//99-12//99
	Arkansas	S	11.5 MW	12.62 AW	26240 AAW	ARBLS	10//99-12//99
	Fort Smith MSA, AR-OK	S	12.39 MW	10.97 AW	25780 AAW	ARBLS	10//99-12//99
	Little Rock-North Little Rock MSA, AR	S	12.99 MW	12.70 AW	27030 AAW	ARBLS	10//99-12//99
	Pine Bluff MSA, AR	S	14.22 MW	14.55 AW	29570 AAW	ARBLS	10//99-12//99
	California	S	17.07 MW	19.02 AW	39560 AAW	CABLS	10//99-12//99
	Bakersfield MSA, CA	S	18.45 MW	16.97 AW	38380 AAW	CABLS	10//99-12//99
	Los Angeles-Long Beach PMSA, CA	S	19.86 MW	18.40 AW	41300 AAW	CABLS	10//99-12//99

Occupation/Type/Industry	Location	Per	Low	Mid	High	Source	Date
Crane and Tower Operator	Oakland PMSA, CA	S	24.12 MW	24.36 AW	50160 AAW	CABLS	10//99-12//99
	Riverside-San Bernardino PMSA, CA	S	17.05 MW	15.87 AW	35460 AAW	CABLS	10//99-12//99
	Sacramento PMSA, CA	S	22.06 MW	22.05 AW	45880 AAW	CABLS	10//99-12//99
	San Diego MSA, CA	S	20.07 MW	18.83 AW	41740 AAW	CABLS	10//99-12//99
	San Jose PMSA, CA	S	17.93 MW	16.35 AW	37300 AAW	CABLS	10//99-12//99
	Santa Barbara-Santa Maria-Lompoc MSA, CA	S	21.98 MW	23.13 AW	45710 AAW	CABLS	10//99-12//99
	Stockton-Lodi MSA, CA	S	15.49 MW	14.38 AW	32220 AAW	CABLS	10//99-12//99
	Colorado	S	15.95 MW	16.16 AW	33620 AAW	COBLS	10//99-12//99
	Colorado Springs MSA, CO	S	14.44 MW	14.63 AW	30030 AAW	COBLS	10//99-12//99
	Denver PMSA, CO	S	16.80 MW	16.79 AW	34930 AAW	COBLS	10//99-12//99
	Fort Collins-Loveland MSA, CO	S	15.79 MW	15.71 AW	32850 AAW	COBLS	10//99-12//99
	Greeley PMSA, CO	S	16.46 MW	17.59 AW	34250 AAW	COBLS	10//99-12//99
	Connecticut	S	17.19 MW	18.07 AW	37580 AAW	CTBLS	10//99-12//99
	Hartford MSA, CT	S	16.87 MW	16.70 AW	35090 AAW	CTBLS	10//99-12//99
	New Haven-Meriden PMSA, CT	S	17.17 MW	16.35 AW	35710 AAW	CTBLS	10//99-12//99
	New London-Norwich MSA, CT-RI	S	17.32 MW	16.06 AW	36020 AAW	CTBLS	10//99-12//99
	Delaware	S	15.93 MW	16.27 AW	33830 AAW	DEBLS	10//99-12//99
	Wilmington-Newark PMSA, DE-MD	S	15.59 MW	15.51 AW	32430 AAW	DEBLS	10//99-12//99
	Washington PMSA, DC-MD-VA-WV	S	16.84 MW	16.66 AW	35020 AAW	DCBLS	10//99-12//99
	Florida	S	15.32 MW	15.85 AW	32970 AAW	FLBLS	10//99-12//99
	Daytona Beach MSA, FL	S	12.25 MW	10.55 AW	25470 AAW	FLBLS	10//99-12//99
	Fort Lauderdale PMSA, FL	S	20.09 MW	19.04 AW	41780 AAW	FLBLS	10//99-12//99
	Jacksonville MSA, FL	S	12.76 MW	12.39 AW	26530 AAW	FLBLS	10//99-12//99
	Lakeland-Winter Haven MSA, FL	S	13.62 MW	13.82 AW	28330 AAW	FLBLS	10//99-12//99
	Miami PMSA, FL	S	17.27 MW	16.92 AW	35920 AAW	FLBLS	10//99-12//99
	Naples MSA, FL	S	19.12 MW	19.23 AW	39770 AAW	FLBLS	10//99-12//99
	Orlando MSA, FL	S	15.85 MW	16.53 AW	32970 AAW	FLBLS	10//99-12//99
	Panama City MSA, FL	S	14.76 MW	13.91 AW	30710 AAW	FLBLS	10//99-12//99
	Pensacola MSA, FL	S	17.52 MW	17.12 AW	36450 AAW	FLBLS	10//99-12//99
	Sarasota-Bradenton MSA, FL	S	9.54 MW	8.38 AW	19840 AAW	FLBLS	10//99-12//99
	Tampa-St. Petersburg-Clearwater MSA, FL	S	14.17 MW	14.03 AW	29470 AAW	FLBLS	10//99-12//99
	West Palm Beach-Boca Raton MSA, FL	S	15.33 MW	14.94 AW	31900 AAW	FLBLS	10//99-12//99
	Georgia	S	13.29 MW	14.01 AW	29150 AAW	GABLS	10//99-12//99
	Atlanta MSA, GA	S	14.36 MW	13.61 AW	29870 AAW	GABLS	10//99-12//99
	Augusta-Aiken MSA, GA-SC	S	17.57 MW	16.77 AW	36540 AAW	GABLS	10//99-12//99
	Columbus MSA, GA-AL	S	11.40 MW	10.15 AW	23720 AAW	GABLS	10//99-12//99
	Savannah MSA, GA	S	19.54 MW	16.82 AW	40640 AAW	GABLS	10//99-12//99
	Hawaii	S	25.72 MW	24.82 AW	51630 AAW	HIBLS	10//99-12//99
	Honolulu MSA, HI	S	24.72 MW	25.76 AW	51420 AAW	HIBLS	10//99-12//99
	Idaho	S	14.7 MW	15.01 AW	31220 AAW	IDBLS	10//99-12//99
	Boise City MSA, ID	S	14.18 MW	13.98 AW	29500 AAW	IDBLS	10//99-12//99
	Illinois	S	14.82 MW	15.58 AW	32400 AAW	ILBLS	10//99-12//99
	Chicago PMSA, IL	S	15.90 MW	15.14 AW	33070 AAW	ILBLS	10//99-12//99
	Peoria-Pekin MSA, IL	S	17.03 MW	17.29 AW	35430 AAW	ILBLS	10//99-12//99
	Rockford MSA, IL	S	19.08 MW	15.42 AW	39690 AAW	ILBLS	10//99-12//99
	Indiana	S	16.84 MW	16.91 AW	35180 AAW	INBLS	10//99-12//99
	Evansville-Henderson MSA, IN-KY	S	14.40 MW	14.23 AW	29950 AAW	INBLS	10//99-12//99
	Fort Wayne MSA, IN	S	15.69 MW	15.22 AW	32630 AAW	INBLS	10//99-12//99
	Gary PMSA, IN	S	17.97 MW	18.03 AW	37370 AAW	INBLS	10//99-12//99
	Indianapolis MSA, IN	S	17.08 MW	15.68 AW	35540 AAW	INBLS	10//99-12//99
	Lafayette MSA, IN	S	15.51 MW	12.99 AW	32260 AAW	INBLS	10//99-12//99
	South Bend MSA, IN	S	17.91 MW	18.60 AW	37260 AAW	INBLS	10//99-12//99
	Iowa	S	16.79 MW	16.43 AW	34180 AAW	IABLS	10//99-12//99
	Cedar Rapids MSA, IA	S	19.40 MW	18.82 AW	40340 AAW	IABLS	10//99-12//99
	Davenport-Moline-Rock Island MSA, IA-IL	S	14.82 MW	14.68 AW	30820 AAW	IABLS	10//99-12//99
	Des Moines MSA, IA	S	15.19 MW	14.31 AW	31590 AAW	IABLS	10//99-12//99
	Kansas	S	16.93 MW	20.05 AW	41710 AAW	KSBLS	10//99-12//99
	Kentucky	S	15.67 MW	15.51 AW	32270 AAW	KYBLS	10//99-12//99
	Lexington MSA, KY	S	13.33 MW	14.44 AW	27730 AAW	KYBLS	10//99-12//99
	Louisville MSA, KY-IN	S	14.81 MW	12.71 AW	30810 AAW	KYBLS	10//99-12//99

Occupation/Type/Industry	Location	Per	Low	Mid	High	Source	Date
Crane and Tower Operator	Louisiana	S	13.99 MW	14.24 AW	29630 AAW	LABLS	10//99-12//99
	Baton Rouge MSA, LA	S	13.96 MW	14.31 AW	29030 AAW	LABLS	10//99-12//99
	Houma MSA, LA	S	14.28 MW	14.22 AW	29700 AAW	LABLS	10//99-12//99
	Lafayette MSA, LA	S	13.80 MW	13.84 AW	28710 AAW	LABLS	10//99-12//99
	Lake Charles MSA, LA	S	14.76 MW	14.44 AW	30700 AAW	LABLS	10//99-12//99
	Monroe MSA, LA	S	13.14 MW	11.71 AW	27330 AAW	LABLS	10//99-12//99
	New Orleans MSA, LA	S	15.42 MW	14.53 AW	32070 AAW	LABLS	10//99-12//99
	Maine	S	15.8 MW	15.54 AW	32320 AAW	MEBLS	10//99-12//99
	Portland MSA, ME	S	15.45 MW	15.63 AW	32130 AAW	MEBLS	10//99-12//99
	Maryland	S	14.89 MW	15.52 AW	32270 AAW	MDBLS	10//99-12//99
	Baltimore PMSA, MD	S	15.34 MW	14.80 AW	31900 AAW	MDBLS	10//99-12//99
	Massachusetts	S	19.02 MW	20.84 AW	43340 AAW	MABLS	10//99-12//99
	Boston PMSA, MA-NH	S	22.59 MW	20.00 AW	46990 AAW	MABLS	10//99-12//99
	New Bedford PMSA, MA	S	18.97 MW	16.80 AW	39450 AAW	MABLS	10//99-12//99
	Worcester PMSA, MA-CT	S	17.37 MW	15.80 AW	36130 AAW	MABLS	10//99-12//99
	Michigan	S	16.32 MW	17.38 AW	36140 AAW	MIBLS	10//99-12//99
	Ann Arbor PMSA, MI	S	21.21 MW	22.48 AW	44120 AAW	MIBLS	10//99-12//99
	Detroit PMSA, MI	S	17.34 MW	16.22 AW	36060 AAW	MIBLS	10//99-12//99
	Grand Rapids-Muskegon-Holland MSA, MI	S	15.96 MW	13.78 AW	33190 AAW	MIBLS	10//99-12//99
	Kalamazoo-Battle Creek MSA, MI	S	17.96 MW	16.98 AW	37350 AAW	MIBLS	10//99-12//99
	Saginaw-Bay City-Midland MSA, MI	S	17.21 MW	17.44 AW	35800 AAW	MIBLS	10//99-12//99
	Minnesota	S	16.05 MW	17.25 AW	35870 AAW	MNBLS	10//99-12//99
	Minneapolis-St. Paul MSA, MN-WI	S	16.61 MW	15.73 AW	34560 AAW	MNBLS	10//99-12//99
	Mississippi	S	13.67 MW	14.04 AW	29210 AAW	MSBLS	10//99-12//99
	Biloxi-Gulfport-Pascagoula MSA, MS	S	14.57 MW	14.81 AW	30310 AAW	MSBLS	10//99-12//99
	Jackson MSA, MS	S	12.49 MW	12.70 AW	25980 AAW	MSBLS	10//99-12//99
	Missouri	S	16.56 MW	17.09 AW	35550 AAW	MOBLS	10//99-12//99
	Kansas City MSA, MO-KS	S	18.69 MW	20.22 AW	38880 AAW	MOBLS	10//99-12//99
	St. Louis MSA, MO-IL	S	16.21 MW	15.60 AW	33720 AAW	MOBLS	10//99-12//99
	Montana	S	14.88 MW	15.75 AW	32760 AAW	MTBLS	10//99-12//99
	Billings MSA, MT	S	16.22 MW	15.36 AW	33740 AAW	MTBLS	10//99-12//99
	Nebraska	S	14.32 MW	14.01 AW	29150 AAW	NEBLS	10//99-12//99
	Omaha MSA, NE-IA	S	15.21 MW	15.07 AW	31630 AAW	NEBLS	10//99-12//99
	Nevada	S	22.49 MW	22.92 AW	47670 AAW	NVBLS	10//99-12//99
	Las Vegas MSA, NV-AZ	S	23.58 MW	23.71 AW	49050 AAW	NVBLS	10//99-12//99
	New Hampshire	S	15.34 MW	15.50 AW	32230 AAW	NHBLS	10//99-12//99
	Nashua PMSA, NH	S	15.18 MW	13.13 AW	31580 AAW	NHBLS	10//99-12//99
	New Jersey	S	17.54 MW	18.89 AW	39300 AAW	NJBLS	10//99-12//99
	Jersey City PMSA, NJ	S	15.32 MW	16.47 AW	31860 AAW	NJBLS	10//99-12//99
	Middlesex-Somerset-Hunterdon PMSA, NJ	S	16.97 MW	15.94 AW	35300 AAW	NJBLS	10//99-12//99
	Newark PMSA, NJ	S	22.05 MW	19.71 AW	45860 AAW	NJBLS	10//99-12//99
	New Mexico	S	14.76 MW	14.72 AW	30610 AAW	NMBLS	10//99-12//99
	New York	S	16.18 MW	18.63 AW	38750 AAW	NYBLS	10//99-12//99
	Albany-Schenectady-Troy MSA, NY	S	16.74 MW	16.11 AW	34830 AAW	NYBLS	10//99-12//99
	Buffalo-Niagara Falls MSA, NY	S	16.60 MW	16.05 AW	34530 AAW	NYBLS	10//99-12//99
	Nassau-Suffolk PMSA, NY	S	18.69 MW	15.04 AW	38870 AAW	NYBLS	10//99-12//99
	New York PMSA, NY	S	25.26 MW	21.10 AW	52540 AAW	NYBLS	10//99-12//99
	Syracuse MSA, NY	S	16.77 MW	14.94 AW	34890 AAW	NYBLS	10//99-12//99
	Utica-Rome MSA, NY	S	17.89 MW	16.63 AW	37220 AAW	NYBLS	10//99-12//99
	North Carolina	S	11.26 MW	12.75 AW	26530 AAW	NCBLS	10//99-12//99
	Charlotte-Gastonia-Rock Hill MSA, NC-SC	S	14.28 MW	13.90 AW	29700 AAW	NCBLS	10//99-12//99
	Greensboro--Winston-Salem--High Point MSA, NC	S	10.96 MW	10.11 AW	22790 AAW	NCBLS	10//99-12//99
	Raleigh-Durham-Chapel Hill MSA, NC	S	11.90 MW	10.26 AW	24760 AAW	NCBLS	10//99-12//99
	Rocky Mount MSA, NC	S	17.88 MW	16.70 AW	37190 AAW	NCBLS	10//99-12//99
	North Dakota	S	16.55 MW	16.31 AW	33930 AAW	NDBLS	10//99-12//99
	Fargo-Moorhead MSA, ND-MN	S	16.69 MW	16.27 AW	34720 AAW	NDBLS	10//99-12//99
	Grand Forks MSA, ND-MN	S	13.50 MW	10.42 AW	28070 AAW	NDBLS	10//99-12//99
	Ohio	S	15.49 MW	16.46 AW	34240 AAW	OHBLS	10//99-12//99
	Akron PMSA, OH	S	15.15 MW	12.80 AW	31520 AAW	OHBLS	10//99-12//99
	Canton-Massillon MSA, OH	S	17.43 MW	17.76 AW	36250 AAW	OHBLS	10//99-12//99

Occupation/Type/Industry	Location	Per	Low	Mid	High	Source	Date
Crane and Tower Operator	Cincinnati PMSA, OH-KY-IN	S	16.00 MW	15.58 AW	33280 AAW	OHBLS	10//99-12//99
	Cleveland-Lorain-Elyria						
	PMSA, OH	S	17.11 MW	15.57 AW	35580 AAW	OHBLS	10//99-12//99
	Columbus MSA, OH	S	13.58 MW	11.84 AW	28240 AAW	OHBLS	10//99-12//99
	Dayton-Springfield MSA, OH	S	18.90 MW	21.14 AW	39300 AAW	OHBLS	10//99-12//99
	Mansfield MSA, OH	S	20.97 MW	23.31 AW	43620 AAW	OHBLS	10//99-12//99
	Toledo MSA, OH	S	17.79 MW	17.82 AW	37010 AAW	OHBLS	10//99-12//99
	Youngstown-Warren MSA, OH	S	14.03 MW	13.84 AW	29170 AAW	OHBLS	10//99-12//99
	Oklahoma	S	15.01 MW	15.36 AW	31940 AAW	OKBLS	10//99-12//99
	Oklahoma City MSA, OK	S	16.82 MW	17.71 AW	34990 AAW	OKBLS	10//99-12//99
	Tulsa MSA, OK	S	15.42 MW	14.66 AW	32080 AAW	OKBLS	10//99-12//99
	Oregon	S	16.74 MW	17.28 AW	35940 AAW	ORBLS	10//99-12//99
	Eugene-Springfield MSA, OR	S	13.90 MW	13.55 AW	28920 AAW	ORBLS	10//99-12//99
	Portland-Vancouver PMSA,						
	OR-WA	S	17.58 MW	17.32 AW	36560 AAW	ORBLS	10//99-12//99
	Pennsylvania	S	15.3 MW	15.63 AW	32500 AAW	PABLS	10//99-12//99
	Allentown-Bethlehem-Easton						
	MSA, PA	S	13.44 MW	13.23 AW	27960 AAW	PABLS	10//99-12//99
	Erie MSA, PA	S	16.25 MW	17.05 AW	33810 AAW	PABLS	10//99-12//99
	Harrisburg-Lebanon-Carlisle						
	MSA, PA	S	17.16 MW	17.56 AW	35700 AAW	PABLS	10//99-12//99
	Johnstown MSA, PA	S	15.63 MW	15.56 AW	32520 AAW	PABLS	10//99-12//99
	Lancaster MSA, PA	S	15.82 MW	15.05 AW	32910 AAW	PABLS	10//99-12//99
	Philadelphia PMSA, PA-NJ	S	17.43 MW	15.85 AW	36240 AAW	PABLS	10//99-12//99
	Pittsburgh MSA, PA	S	16.37 MW	15.86 AW	34060 AAW	PABLS	10//99-12//99
	Reading MSA, PA	S	16.24 MW	16.08 AW	33790 AAW	PABLS	10//99-12//99
	Scranton--Wilkes-Barre--						
	Hazleton MSA, PA	S	14.89 MW	14.01 AW	30970 AAW	PABLS	10//99-12//99
	Sharon MSA, PA	S	17.47 MW	15.21 AW	36330 AAW	PABLS	10//99-12//99
	State College MSA, PA	S	13.65 MW	8.40 AW	28390 AAW	PABLS	10//99-12//99
	York MSA, PA	S	13.75 MW	13.59 AW	28600 AAW	PABLS	10//99-12//99
	Rhode Island	S	14.94 MW	14.97 AW	31130 AAW	RIBLS	10//99-12//99
	Providence-Fall River-						
	Warwick MSA, RI-MA	S	14.99 MW	14.79 AW	31180 AAW	RIBLS	10//99-12//99
	South Carolina	S	14.36 MW	16.22 AW	33740 AAW	SCBLS	10//99-12//99
	Charleston-North Charleston						
	MSA, SC	S	19.69 MW	16.38 AW	40950 AAW	SCBLS	10//99-12//99
	Columbia MSA, SC	S	13.72 MW	14.00 AW	28530 AAW	SCBLS	10//99-12//99
	Greenville-Spartanburg-						
	Anderson MSA, SC	S	14.40 MW	13.38 AW	29950 AAW	SCBLS	10//99-12//99
	Myrtle Beach MSA, SC	S	14.82 MW	15.18 AW	30830 AAW	SCBLS	10//99-12//99
	South Dakota	S	12.16 MW	13.17 AW	27380 AAW	SDBLS	10//99-12//99
	Sioux Falls MSA, SD	S	14.22 MW	13.13 AW	29580 AAW	SDBLS	10//99-12//99
	Tennessee	S	12.89 MW	13.79 AW	28680 AAW	TNBLS	10//99-12//99
	Chattanooga MSA, TN-GA	S	12.00 MW	11.50 AW	24960 AAW	TNBLS	10//99-12//99
	Johnson City-Kingsport-Bristol						
	MSA, TN-VA	S	11.03 MW	11.10 AW	22940 AAW	TNBLS	10//99-12//99
	Knoxville MSA, TN	S	14.43 MW	12.65 AW	30020 AAW	TNBLS	10//99-12//99
	Memphis MSA, TN-AR-MS	S	14.79 MW	13.42 AW	30760 AAW	MSBLS	10//99-12//99
	Nashville MSA, TN	S	14.60 MW	14.28 AW	30380 AAW	TNBLS	10//99-12//99
	Texas	S	14.26 MW	14.81 AW	30790 AAW	TXBLS	10//99-12//99
	Austin-San Marcos MSA, TX	S	15.05 MW	13.40 AW	31300 AAW	TXBLS	10//99-12//99
	Beaumont-Port Arthur MSA,						
	TX	S	14.17 MW	13.33 AW	29470 AAW	TXBLS	10//99-12//99
	Brazoria PMSA, TX	S	15.82 MW	15.35 AW	32910 AAW	TXBLS	10//99-12//99
	Brownsville-Harlingen-San						
	Benito MSA, TX	S	9.79 MW	8.77 AW	20370 AAW	TXBLS	10//99-12//99
	Corpus Christi MSA, TX	S	12.22 MW	12.10 AW	25410 AAW	TXBLS	10//99-12//99
	Dallas PMSA, TX	S	14.10 MW	13.66 AW	29320 AAW	TXBLS	10//99-12//99
	Fort Worth-Arlington PMSA,						
	TX	S	14.66 MW	14.59 AW	30500 AAW	TXBLS	10//99-12//99
	Houston PMSA, TX	S	15.55 MW	14.85 AW	32340 AAW	TXBLS	10//99-12//99
	Longview-Marshall MSA, TX	S	13.41 MW	12.59 AW	27900 AAW	TXBLS	10//99-12//99
	McAllen-Edinburg-Mission						
	MSA, TX	S	10.09 MW	10.33 AW	20990 AAW	TXBLS	10//99-12//99
	San Antonio MSA, TX	S	11.58 MW	11.26 AW	24090 AAW	TXBLS	10//99-12//99
	Waco MSA, TX	S	12.20 MW	11.80 AW	25370 AAW	TXBLS	10//99-12//99
	Utah	S	17.58 MW	17.20 AW	35770 AAW	UTBLS	10//99-12//99
	Vermont	S	15.66 MW	16.54 AW	34400 AAW	VTBLS	10//99-12//99
	Burlington MSA, VT	S	15.14 MW	15.04 AW	31490 AAW	VTBLS	10//99-12//99
	Virginia	S	15.32 MW	15.54 AW	32320 AAW	VABLS	10//99-12//99

AAW Average annual wage	AOH Average offered, high	ASH Average starting, high	H Hourly	M Monthly	S Special: hourly and annual
AE Average entry wage	AOL Average offered, low	ASL Average starting, low	HI Highest wage paid	MTC Median total compensation	TQ Third quartile wage
AEX Average experienced wage	APH Average pay, high range	AW Average wage paid	HR High end range	MW Median wage paid	W Weekly
AO Average offered	APL Average pay, low range	FQ First quartile wage	LR Low end range	SQ Second quartile wage	Y Yearly

Occupation/Type/Industry	Location	Per	Low	Mid	High	Source	Date
Crane and Tower Operator	Richmond-Petersburg MSA, VA	S	16.46 MW	16.78 AW	34240 AAW	VABLS	10//99-12//99
	Roanoke MSA, VA	S	14.14 MW	13.81 AW	29400 AAW	VABLS	10//99-12//99
	Washington	S	21.88 MW	21.92 AW	45600 AAW	WABLS	10//99-12//99
	Spokane MSA, WA	S	14.58 MW	13.28 AW	30330 AAW	WABLS	10//99-12//99
	Tacoma PMSA, WA	S	22.53 MW	23.51 AW	46850 AAW	WABLS	10//99-12//99
	West Virginia	S	15.24 MW	15.50 AW	32240 AAW	WVBLS	10//99-12//99
	Charleston MSA, WV	S	11.27 MW	10.27 AW	23440 AAW	WVBLS	10//99-12//99
	Huntington-Ashland MSA, WV-KY-OH	S	17.02 MW	17.63 AW	35410 AAW	WVBLS	10//99-12//99
	Parkersburg-Marietta MSA, WV-OH	S	17.28 MW	15.98 AW	35950 AAW	WVBLS	10//99-12//99
	Wisconsin	S	14.61 MW	15.90 AW	33060 AAW	WIBLS	10//99-12//99
	Appleton-Oshkosh-Neenah MSA, WI	S	17.27 MW	15.52 AW	35930 AAW	WIBLS	10//99-12//99
	Green Bay MSA, WI	S	17.09 MW	12.66 AW	35560 AAW	WIBLS	10//99-12//99
	Madison MSA, WI	S	16.01 MW	14.35 AW	33300 AAW	WIBLS	10//99-12//99
	Milwaukee-Waukesha PMSA, WI	S	16.20 MW	14.64 AW	33700 AAW	WIBLS	10//99-12//99
	Racine PMSA, WI	S	14.96 MW	15.16 AW	31110 AAW	WIBLS	10//99-12//99
	Wausau MSA, WI	S	13.94 MW	14.33 AW	28990 AAW	WIBLS	10//99-12//99
	Wyoming	S	16.26 MW	17.44 AW	36280 AAW	WYBLS	10//99-12//99
	Puerto Rico	S	9.25 MW	11.82 AW	24590 AAW	PRBLS	10//99-12//99
	Ponce MSA, PR	S	13.34 MW	11.34 AW	27740 AAW	PRBLS	10//99-12//99
	San Juan-Bayamon PMSA, PR	S	12.15 MW	9.33 AW	25270 AAW	PRBLS	10//99-12//99
	Virgin Islands	S	12.73 MW	13.54 AW	28160 AAW	VIBLS	10//99-12//99
Crane Operator	United States	H		38.83 AW		ENR1	2000
Creative Director							
Advertising	East	Y		163000 AW		ADAGE1	2000
Advertising	Midwest	Y		114000 AW		ADAGE1	2000
Advertising	South	Y		118000 AW		ADAGE1	2000
Advertising	West	Y		114000 AW		ADAGE1	2000
Credit Analyst	Alabama	S	14.85 MW	15.27 AW	31760 AAW	ALBLS	10//99-12//99
	Alaska	S	17.92 MW	18.81 AW	39120 AAW	AKBLS	10//99-12//99
	Arizona	S	11.43 MW	14.59 AW	30340 AAW	AZBLS	10//99-12//99
	Arkansas	S	15.18 MW	15.70 AW	32650 AAW	ARBLS	10//99-12//99
	California	S	21.59 MW	23.71 AW	49320 AAW	CABLS	10//99-12//99
	Colorado	S	19.18 MW	21.17 AW	44040 AAW	COBLS	10//99-12//99
	Connecticut	S	20.65 MW	23.17 AW	48180 AAW	CTBLS	10//99-12//99
	Delaware	S	13.17 MW	14.46 AW	30080 AAW	DEBLS	10//99-12//99
	District of Columbia	S	19.15 MW	19.75 AW	41070 AAW	DCBLS	10//99-12//99
	Florida	S	16.83 MW	18.76 AW	39020 AAW	FLBLS	10//99-12//99
	Georgia	S	18.75 MW	20.98 AW	43630 AAW	GABLS	10//99-12//99
	Hawaii	S	20.22 MW	22.69 AW	47200 AAW	HIBLS	10//99-12//99
	Idaho	S	17.96 MW	19.16 AW	39860 AAW	IDBLS	10//99-12//99
	Illinois	S	18 MW	20.51 AW	42650 AAW	ILBLS	10//99-12//99
	Indiana	S	15.55 MW	16.88 AW	35100 AAW	INBLS	10//99-12//99
	Iowa	S	14.81 MW	16.04 AW	33360 AAW	IABLS	10//99-12//99
	Kansas	S	18.55 MW	20.54 AW	42720 AAW	KSBLS	10//99-12//99
	Kentucky	S	15.78 MW	17.25 AW	35880 AAW	KYBLS	10//99-12//99
	Louisiana	S	16.15 MW	17.36 AW	36110 AAW	LABLS	10//99-12//99
	Maine	S	15.85 MW	17.45 AW	36290 AAW	MEBLS	10//99-12//99
	Maryland	S	15.67 MW	17.24 AW	35850 AAW	MDBLS	10//99-12//99
	Massachusetts	S	18.63 MW	22.18 AW	46130 AAW	MABLS	10//99-12//99
	Michigan	S	17.44 MW	19.79 AW	41160 AAW	MIBLS	10//99-12//99
	Minnesota	S	17.42 MW	18.70 AW	38890 AAW	MNBLS	10//99-12//99
	Mississippi	S	12.79 MW	15.58 AW	32410 AAW	MSBLS	10//99-12//99
	Missouri	S	15.87 MW	18.30 AW	38060 AAW	MOBLS	10//99-12//99
	Montana	S	17.31 MW	18.66 AW	38810 AAW	MTBLS	10//99-12//99
	Nebraska	S	13.71 MW	14.25 AW	29640 AAW	NEBLS	10//99-12//99
	Nevada	S	18.74 MW	22.36 AW	46510 AAW	NVBLS	10//99-12//99
	New Hampshire	S	17.66 MW	18.28 AW	38020 AAW	NHBLS	10//99-12//99
	New Jersey	S	20.67 MW	22.22 AW	46210 AAW	NJBLS	10//99-12//99
	New Mexico	S	18.26 MW	18.61 AW	38700 AAW	NMBLS	10//99-12//99
	New York	S	24.22 MW	25.93 AW	53930 AAW	NYBLS	10//99-12//99
	North Carolina	S	18.15 MW	21.79 AW	45330 AAW	NCBLS	10//99-12//99
	North Dakota	S	17.45 MW	19.72 AW	41010 AAW	NDBLS	10//99-12//99
	Ohio	S	16.82 MW	18.00 AW	37450 AAW	OHBLS	10//99-12//99
	Oklahoma	S	16.29 MW	17.88 AW	37180 AAW	OKBLS	10//99-12//99
	Oregon	S	19.82 MW	20.97 AW	43620 AAW	ORBLS	10//99-12//99

AAW	Average annual wage	AOH	Average offered, high	ASH	Average starting, high	H	Hourly	M	Monthly	S	Special: hourly and annual
AE	Average entry wage	AOL	Average offered, low	ASL	Average starting, low	HI	Highest wage paid	MTC	Median total compensation	TQ	Third quartile wage
AEX	Average experienced wage	APH	Average pay, high range	AW	Average wage paid	HR	High end range	MW	Median wage paid	W	Weekly
AO	Average offered	APL	Average pay, low range	FQ	First quartile wage	LR	Low end range	SQ	Second quartile wage	Y	Yearly

Occupation/Type/Industry	Location	Per	Low	Mid	High	Source	Date
Credit Analyst	Pennsylvania	S	17.92 MW	19.66 AW	40900 AAW	PABLS	10//99-12//99
	Rhode Island	S	18.3 MW	19.27 AW	40080 AAW	RIBLS	10//99-12//99
	South Carolina	S	16.09 MW	18.84 AW	39180 AAW	SCBLS	10//99-12//99
	Tennessee	S	17.39 MW	18.38 AW	38220 AAW	TNBLS	10//99-12//99
	Texas	S	18.71 MW	20.20 AW	42020 AAW	TXBLS	10//99-12//99
	Utah	S	14.68 MW	15.94 AW	33160 AAW	UTBLS	10//99-12//99
	Vermont	S	17.24 MW	18.07 AW	37580 AAW	VTBLS	10//99-12//99
	Virginia	S	21.07 MW	21.88 AW	45510 AAW	VABLS	10//99-12//99
	Washington	S	20.97 MW	24.44 AW	50840 AAW	WABLS	10//99-12//99
	West Virginia	S	13.73 MW	14.55 AW	30270 AAW	WVBLS	10//99-12//99
	Wisconsin	S	13.56 MW	16.01 AW	33290 AAW	WIBLS	10//99-12//99
	Puerto Rico	S	12.88 MW	13.65 AW	28380 AAW	PRBLS	10//99-12//99
Credit & Collections Manager	Los Angeles County, CA	Y		66139 AW		LABJ	1999
Credit Authorizer, Checker, and Clerk	Alabama	S	10.12 MW	11.52 AW	23970 AAW	ALBLS	10//99-12//99
	Alaska	S	11.83 MW	12.27 AW	25530 AAW	AKBLS	10//99-12//99
	Arizona	S	9.3 MW	10.29 AW	21400 AAW	AZBLS	10//99-12//99
	Arkansas	S	9.58 MW	9.88 AW	20560 AAW	ARBLS	10//99-12//99
	California	S	12.83 MW	13.83 AW	28770 AAW	CABLS	10//99-12//99
	Colorado	S	12.23 MW	13.48 AW	28030 AAW	COBLS	10//99-12//99
	Connecticut	S	13.37 MW	13.98 AW	29080 AAW	CTBLS	10//99-12//99
	Delaware	S	12.38 MW	14.58 AW	30320 AAW	DEBLS	10//99-12//99
	District of Columbia	S	13.45 MW	14.54 AW	30240 AAW	DCBLS	10//99-12//99
	Florida	S	10.89 MW	11.87 AW	24680 AAW	FLBLS	10//99-12//99
	Georgia	S	10.58 MW	11.80 AW	24540 AAW	GABLS	10//99-12//99
	Hawaii	S	12.3 MW	13.44 AW	27950 AAW	HIBLS	10//99-12//99
	Idaho	S	8.67 MW	9.92 AW	20630 AAW	IDBLS	10//99-12//99
	Illinois	S	9.93 MW	12.11 AW	25180 AAW	ILBLS	10//99-12//99
	Indiana	S	11.11 MW	11.63 AW	24180 AAW	INBLS	10//99-12//99
	Iowa	S	10.68 MW	11.60 AW	24130 AAW	IABLS	10//99-12//99
	Kansas	S	10.3 MW	11.03 AW	22950 AAW	KSBLS	10//99-12//99
	Kentucky	S	11.14 MW	11.32 AW	23550 AAW	KYBLS	10//99-12//99
	Louisiana	S	9.04 MW	9.37 AW	19490 AAW	LABLS	10//99-12//99
	Maine	S	11.37 MW	11.47 AW	23860 AAW	MEBLS	10//99-12//99
	Maryland	S	10.03 MW	10.17 AW	21150 AAW	MDBLS	10//99-12//99
	Massachusetts	S	13.51 MW	13.46 AW	27990 AAW	MABLS	10//99-12//99
	Michigan	S	12.71 MW	13.76 AW	28620 AAW	MIBLS	10//99-12//99
	Minnesota	S	13.97 MW	14.43 AW	30000 AAW	MNBLS	10//99-12//99
	Mississippi	S	9.73 MW	10.51 AW	21860 AAW	MSBLS	10//99-12//99
	Missouri	S	12.92 MW	14.61 AW	30380 AAW	MOBLS	10//99-12//99
	Montana	S	12.36 MW	12.39 AW	25770 AAW	MTBLS	10//99-12//99
	Nebraska	S	8.12 MW	8.83 AW	18370 AAW	NEBLS	10//99-12//99
	Nevada	S	12.48 MW	12.87 AW	26780 AAW	NVBLS	10//99-12//99
	New Hampshire	S	10.5 MW	11.35 AW	23620 AAW	NHBLS	10//99-12//99
	New Jersey	S	14.43 MW	14.43 AW	30010 AAW	NJBLS	10//99-12//99
	New Mexico	S	9.74 MW	10.83 AW	22520 AAW	NMBLS	10//99-12//99
	New York	S	14.35 MW	14.12 AW	29370 AAW	NYBLS	10//99-12//99
	North Carolina	S	12.08 MW	12.91 AW	26840 AAW	NCBLS	10//99-12//99
	North Dakota	S	14.18 MW	13.23 AW	27510 AAW	NDBLS	10//99-12//99
	Ohio	S	10.57 MW	11.43 AW	23770 AAW	OHBLS	10//99-12//99
	Oklahoma	S	8.06 MW	9.38 AW	19500 AAW	OKBLS	10//99-12//99
	Oregon	S	11.99 MW	14.65 AW	30470 AAW	ORBLS	10//99-12//99
	Pennsylvania	S	10.15 MW	10.41 AW	21650 AAW	PABLS	10//99-12//99
	Rhode Island	S	14.14 MW	14.35 AW	29840 AAW	RIBLS	10//99-12//99
	South Carolina	S	8.48 MW	10.72 AW	22300 AAW	SCBLS	10//99-12//99
	South Dakota	S	9.21 MW	9.27 AW	19270 AAW	SDBLS	10//99-12//99
	Tennessee	S	11.66 MW	12.98 AW	27000 AAW	TNBLS	10//99-12//99
	Texas	S	11.93 MW	12.63 AW	26270 AAW	TXBLS	10//99-12//99
	Vermont	S	9.98 MW	10.58 AW	22010 AAW	VTBLS	10//99-12//99
	Virginia	S	11.51 MW	11.60 AW	24130 AAW	VABLS	10//99-12//99
	Washington	S	13.53 MW	14.10 AW	29320 AAW	WABLS	10//99-12//99
	West Virginia	S	9.11 MW	9.11 AW	18940 AAW	WVBLS	10//99-12//99
	Wisconsin	S	11.97 MW	12.22 AW	25420 AAW	WIBLS	10//99-12//99
	Wyoming	S	8.29 MW	10.81 AW	22480 AAW	WYBLS	10//99-12//99
	Puerto Rico	S	9.85 MW	9.97 AW	20730 AAW	PRBLS	10//99-12//99
	Virgin Islands	S	9.64 MW	9.72 AW	20210 AAW	VIBLS	10//99-12//99
Criminal Justice and Law Enforcement Teacher Postsecondary	Alabama	Y		37620 AAW		ALBLS	10//99-12//99

AAW Average annual wage	**AOH** Average offered, high	**ASH** Average starting, high	**H** Hourly	**M** Monthly	**S** Special: hourly and annual
AE Average entry wage	**AOL** Average offered, low	**ASL** Average starting, low	**HI** Highest wage paid	**MTC** Median total compensation	**TQ** Third quartile wage
AEX Average experienced wage	**APH** Average pay, high range	**AW** Average wage paid	**HR** High end range	**MW** Median wage paid	**W** Weekly
AO Average offered	**APL** Average pay, low range	**FQ** First quartile wage	**LR** Low end range	**SQ** Second quartile wage	**Y** Yearly

Occupation/Type/Industry	Location	Per	Low	Mid	High	Source	Date
Criminal Justice and Law Enforcement Teacher							
Postsecondary	California	Y		45950 AAW		CABLS	10//99-12//99
Postsecondary	Colorado	Y		40830 AAW		COBLS	10//99-12//99
Postsecondary	Florida	Y		42940 AAW		FLBLS	10//99-12//99
Postsecondary	Georgia	Y		44310 AAW		GABLS	10//99-12//99
Postsecondary	Illinois	Y		48420 AAW		ILBLS	10//99-12//99
Postsecondary	Indiana	Y		42850 AAW		INBLS	10//99-12//99
Postsecondary	Iowa	Y		54670 AAW		IABLS	10//99-12//99
Postsecondary	Kansas	Y		35840 AAW		KSBLS	10//99-12//99
Postsecondary	Kentucky	Y		37680 AAW		KYBLS	10//99-12//99
Postsecondary	Louisiana	Y		46360 AAW		LABLS	10//99-12//99
Postsecondary	Maine	Y		39770 AAW		MEBLS	10//99-12//99
Postsecondary	Maryland	Y		49060 AAW		MDBLS	10//99-12//99
Postsecondary	Massachusetts	Y		43060 AAW		MABLS	10//99-12//99
Postsecondary	Michigan	Y		43820 AAW		MIBLS	10//99-12//99
Postsecondary	Mississippi	Y		31400 AAW		MSBLS	10//99-12//99
Postsecondary	Missouri	Y		36590 AAW		MOBLS	10//99-12//99
Postsecondary	New Hampshire	Y		36710 AAW		NHBLS	10//99-12//99
Postsecondary	New Jersey	Y		53260 AAW		NJBLS	10//99-12//99
Postsecondary	New York	Y		52320 AAW		NYBLS	10//99-12//99
Postsecondary	North Carolina	Y		38100 AAW		NCBLS	10//99-12//99
Postsecondary	North Dakota	Y		38450 AAW		NDBLS	10//99-12//99
Postsecondary	Ohio	Y		41770 AAW		OHBLS	10//99-12//99
Postsecondary	Oklahoma	Y		38400 AAW		OKBLS	10//99-12//99
Postsecondary	Pennsylvania	Y		50270 AAW		PABLS	10//99-12//99
Postsecondary	South Carolina	Y		49200 AAW		SCBLS	10//99-12//99
Postsecondary	Tennessee	Y		43880 AAW		TNBLS	10//99-12//99
Postsecondary	Texas	Y		42550 AAW		TXBLS	10//99-12//99
Postsecondary	Vermont	Y		51110 AAW		VTBLS	10//99-12//99
Postsecondary	Virginia	Y		38860 AAW		VABLS	10//99-12//99
Postsecondary	Washington	Y		28680 AAW		WABLS	10//99-12//99
Postsecondary	West Virginia	Y		42120 AAW		WVBLS	10//99-12//99
Postsecondary	Wisconsin	Y		48030 AAW		WIBLS	10//99-12//99
Crop Manager							
Agriculture	United States	Y	25000 APL	30750 AW	40000 APL	FAJO	1998
Crossing Guard	Alabama	S	6.26 MW	6.57 AW	13670 AAW	ALBLS	10//99-12//99
	Birmingham MSA, AL	S	6.98 MW	6.76 AW	14510 AAW	ALBLS	10//99-12//99
	Mobile MSA, AL	S	7.54 MW	6.68 AW	15690 AAW	ALBLS	10//99-12//99
	Arizona	S	7.19 MW	7.35 AW	15280 AAW	AZBLS	10//99-12//99
	Phoenix-Mesa MSA, AZ	S	7.47 MW	7.35 AW	15540 AAW	AZBLS	10//99-12//99
	Tucson MSA, AZ	S	6.35 MW	6.28 AW	13200 AAW	AZBLS	10//99-12//99
	Arkansas	S	6.03 MW	6.62 AW	13760 AAW	ARBLS	10//99-12//99
	California	S	7.77 MW	8.54 AW	17760 AAW	CABLS	10//99-12//99
	Bakersfield MSA, CA	S	7.35 MW	7.47 AW	15290 AAW	CABLS	10//99-12//99
	Los Angeles-Long Beach PMSA, CA	S	8.15 MW	7.67 AW	16960 AAW	CABLS	10//99-12//99
	Modesto MSA, CA	S	8.21 MW	7.69 AW	17070 AAW	CABLS	10//99-12//99
	Oakland PMSA, CA	S	8.54 MW	7.81 AW	17770 AAW	CABLS	10//99-12//99
	Orange County PMSA, CA	S	7.65 MW	7.65 AW	15920 AAW	CABLS	10//99-12//99
	Redding MSA, CA	S	11.87 MW	8.71 AW	24680 AAW	CABLS	10//99-12//99
	Riverside-San Bernardino PMSA, CA	S	8.47 MW	7.75 AW	17620 AAW	CABLS	10//99-12//99
	Sacramento PMSA, CA	S	8.65 MW	8.16 AW	17990 AAW	CABLS	10//99-12//99
	Salinas MSA, CA	S	8.84 MW	7.97 AW	18390 AAW	CABLS	10//99-12//99
	San Diego MSA, CA	S	6.80 MW	6.51 AW	14150 AAW	CABLS	10//99-12//99
	San Francisco PMSA, CA	S	10.87 MW	9.10 AW	22610 AAW	CABLS	10//99-12//99
	San Jose PMSA, CA	S	8.49 MW	7.84 AW	17650 AAW	CABLS	10//99-12//99
	San Luis Obispo-Atascadero-Paso Robles MSA, CA	S	8.43 MW	7.79 AW	17530 AAW	CABLS	10//99-12//99
	Santa Rosa PMSA, CA	S	8.73 MW	8.31 AW	18160 AAW	CABLS	10//99-12//99
	Vallejo-Fairfield-Napa PMSA, CA	S	8.93 MW	8.35 AW	18570 AAW	CABLS	10//99-12//99
	Ventura PMSA, CA	S	7.72 MW	7.50 AW	16060 AAW	CABLS	10//99-12//99
	Visalia-Tulare-Porterville MSA, CA	S	8.22 MW	8.51 AW	17090 AAW	CABLS	10//99-12//99
	Yuba City MSA, CA	S	8.31 MW	7.67 AW	17280 AAW	CABLS	10//99-12//99
	Colorado	S	8.46 MW	9.14 AW	19000 AAW	COBLS	10//99-12//99
	Boulder-Longmont PMSA, CO	S	6.82 MW	6.28 AW	14190 AAW	COBLS	10//99-12//99
	Colorado Springs MSA, CO	S	7.68 MW	7.94 AW	15980 AAW	COBLS	10//99-12//99

AAW Average annual wage	AOH Average offered, high	ASH Average starting, high	H Hourly	M Monthly	S Special: hourly and annual
AE Average entry wage	AOL Average offered, low	ASL Average starting, low	HI Highest wage paid	MTC Median total compensation	TQ Third quartile wage
AEX Average experienced wage	APH Average pay, high range	AW Average wage paid	HR High end range	MW Median wage paid	W Weekly
AO Average offered	APL Average pay, low range	FQ First quartile wage	LR Low end range	SQ Second quartile wage	Y Yearly

Occupation/Type/Industry	Location	Per	Low	Mid	High	Source	Date
Crossing Guard	Denver PMSA, CO	S	9.13 MW	8.18 AW	18990 AAW	COBLS	10//99-12//99
	Connecticut	S	7.99 MW	9.19 AW	19120 AAW	CTBLS	10//99-12//99
	Danbury PMSA, CT	S	8.80 MW	8.04 AW	18310 AAW	CTBLS	10//99-12//99
	Hartford MSA, CT	S	10.81 MW	10.27 AW	22490 AAW	CTBLS	10//99-12//99
	New Haven-Meriden PMSA, CT	S	7.03 MW	6.36 AW	14620 AAW	CTBLS	10//99-12//99
	New London-Norwich MSA, CT-RI	S	8.89 MW	8.87 AW	18490 AAW	CTBLS	10//99-12//99
	Stamford-Norwalk PMSA, CT	S	7.92 MW	7.66 AW	16470 AAW	CTBLS	10//99-12//99
	Delaware	S	6.54 MW	7.69 AW	16000 AAW	DEBLS	10//99-12//99
	Washington PMSA, DC-MD-VA-WV	S	10.29 MW	9.97 AW	21400 AAW	DCBLS	10//99-12//99
	Florida	S	6.86 MW	7.31 AW	15200 AAW	FLBLS	10//99-12//99
	Fort Lauderdale PMSA, FL	S	7.67 MW	6.46 AW	15960 AAW	FLBLS	10//99-12//99
	Fort Pierce-Port St. Lucie MSA, FL	S	9.60 MW	8.99 AW	19970 AAW	FLBLS	10//99-12//99
	Jacksonville MSA, FL	S	6.53 MW	6.25 AW	13580 AAW	FLBLS	10//99-12//99
	Melbourne-Titusville-Palm Bay MSA, FL	S	8.46 MW	8.33 AW	17600 AAW	FLBLS	10//99-12//99
	Miami PMSA, FL	S	7.09 MW	6.91 AW	14750 AAW	FLBLS	10//99-12//99
	Orlando MSA, FL	S	7.48 MW	7.67 AW	15560 AAW	FLBLS	10//99-12//99
	Tampa-St. Petersburg-Clearwater MSA, FL	S	7.80 MW	7.59 AW	16220 AAW	FLBLS	10//99-12//99
	West Palm Beach-Boca Raton MSA, FL	S	9.54 MW	9.16 AW	19850 AAW	FLBLS	10//99-12//99
	Georgia	S	7.14 MW	7.86 AW	16340 AAW	GABLS	10//99-12//99
	Atlanta MSA, GA	S	7.94 MW	7.51 AW	16520 AAW	GABLS	10//99-12//99
	Savannah MSA, GA	S	6.34 MW	6.16 AW	13190 AAW	GABLS	10//99-12//99
	Hawaii	S	6.06 MW	7.45 AW	15500 AAW	HIBLS	10//99-12//99
	Illinois	S	9.49 MW	9.49 AW	19730 AAW	ILBLS	10//99-12//99
	Champaign-Urbana MSA, IL	S	8.48 MW	8.02 AW	17640 AAW	ILBLS	10//99-12//99
	Rockford MSA, IL	S	9.56 MW	8.10 AW	19890 AAW	ILBLS	10//99-12//99
	Indiana	S	6.01 MW	6.74 AW	14030 AAW	INBLS	10//99-12//99
	Elkhart-Goshen MSA, IN	S	6.61 MW	6.66 AW	13740 AAW	INBLS	10//99-12//99
	Fort Wayne MSA, IN	S	6.35 MW	5.91 AW	13220 AAW	INBLS	10//99-12//99
	Gary PMSA, IN	S	6.63 MW	6.12 AW	13790 AAW	INBLS	10//99-12//99
	Indianapolis MSA, IN	S	8.23 MW	6.03 AW	17110 AAW	INBLS	10//99-12//99
	Iowa	S	6.91 MW	7.66 AW	15930 AAW	IABLS	10//99-12//99
	Davenport-Moline-Rock Island MSA, IA-IL	S	7.82 MW	7.83 AW	16260 AAW	IABLS	10//99-12//99
	Kansas	S	7.2 MW	7.46 AW	15510 AAW	KSBLS	10//99-12//99
	Wichita MSA, KS	S	6.58 MW	6.36 AW	13680 AAW	KSBLS	10//99-12//99
	Kentucky	S	7.4 MW	7.89 AW	16410 AAW	KYBLS	10//99-12//99
	Louisville MSA, KY-IN	S	6.58 MW	6.28 AW	13690 AAW	KYBLS	10//99-12//99
	Louisiana	S	6.21 MW	6.69 AW	13910 AAW	LABLS	10//99-12//99
	Baton Rouge MSA, LA	S	6.67 MW	6.40 AW	13880 AAW	LABLS	10//99-12//99
	Lafayette MSA, LA	S	8.68 MW	6.61 AW	18060 AAW	LABLS	10//99-12//99
	New Orleans MSA, LA	S	6.17 MW	6.08 AW	12840 AAW	LABLS	10//99-12//99
	Maine	S	6.44 MW	6.55 AW	13620 AAW	MEBLS	10//99-12//99
	Bangor MSA, ME	S	6.76 MW	6.81 AW	14060 AAW	MEBLS	10//99-12//99
	Lewiston-Auburn MSA, ME	S	6.46 MW	6.29 AW	13430 AAW	MEBLS	10//99-12//99
	Portland MSA, ME	S	6.83 MW	7.08 AW	14200 AAW	MEBLS	10//99-12//99
	Maryland	S	9.49 MW	9.47 AW	19700 AAW	MDBLS	10//99-12//99
	Baltimore PMSA, MD	S	9.28 MW	9.44 AW	19310 AAW	MDBLS	10//99-12//99
	Massachusetts	S	8.18 MW	8.57 AW	17820 AAW	MABLS	10//99-12//99
	Boston PMSA, MA-NH	S	8.17 MW	7.65 AW	17000 AAW	MABLS	10//99-12//99
	Brockton PMSA, MA	S	10.25 MW	10.43 AW	21330 AAW	MABLS	10//99-12//99
	Fitchburg-Leominster PMSA, MA	S	8.94 MW	8.36 AW	18600 AAW	MABLS	10//99-12//99
	Lawrence PMSA, MA-NH	S	7.97 MW	8.67 AW	16580 AAW	MABLS	10//99-12//99
	Lowell PMSA, MA-NH	S	9.37 MW	9.71 AW	19490 AAW	MABLS	10//99-12//99
	Springfield MSA, MA	S	8.80 MW	9.06 AW	18310 AAW	MABLS	10//99-12//99
	Worcester PMSA, MA-CT	S	10.41 MW	10.06 AW	21650 AAW	MABLS	10//99-12//99
	Michigan	S	6.81 MW	7.44 AW	15480 AAW	MIBLS	10//99-12//99
	Ann Arbor PMSA, MI	S	7.41 MW	7.04 AW	15400 AAW	MIBLS	10//99-12//99
	Benton Harbor MSA, MI	S	6.39 MW	5.96 AW	13290 AAW	MIBLS	10//99-12//99
	Detroit PMSA, MI	S	7.21 MW	6.58 AW	14990 AAW	MIBLS	10//99-12//99
	Grand Rapids-Muskegon-Holland MSA, MI	S	9.47 MW	8.88 AW	19690 AAW	MIBLS	10//99-12//99
	Lansing-East Lansing MSA, MI	S	7.96 MW	7.89 AW	16560 AAW	MIBLS	10//99-12//99
	Saginaw-Bay City-Midland MSA, MI	S	6.88 MW	6.40 AW	14320 AAW	MIBLS	10//99-12//99

Occupation/Type/Industry	Location	Per	Low	Mid	High	Source	Date
Crossing Guard	Minnesota	S	6.55 MW	7.65 AW	15910 AAW	MNBLS	10//99-12//99
	Duluth-Superior MSA, MN-WI	S	7.55 MW	7.61 AW	15700 AAW	MNBLS	10//99-12//99
	Minneapolis-St. Paul MSA, MN-WI	S	7.58 MW	6.39 AW	15780 AAW	MNBLS	10//99-12//99
	Mississippi	S	7 MW	7.74 AW	16090 AAW	MSBLS	10//99-12//99
	Biloxi-Gulfport-Pascagoula MSA, MS	S	9.23 MW	7.88 AW	19190 AAW	MSBLS	10//99-12//99
	Missouri	S	8.33 MW	8.48 AW	17650 AAW	MOBLS	10//99-12//99
	Kansas City MSA, MO-KS	S	8.35 MW	7.81 AW	17370 AAW	MOBLS	10//99-12//99
	Montana	S	7.37 MW	8.38 AW	17430 AAW	MTBLS	10//99-12//99
	Nevada	S	8.29 MW	8.91 AW	18540 AAW	NVBLS	10//99-12//99
	Las Vegas MSA, NV-AZ	S	8.39 MW	8.34 AW	17440 AAW	NVBLS	10//99-12//99
	New Hampshire	S	7.44 MW	7.54 AW	15680 AAW	NHBLS	10//99-12//99
	New Jersey	S	8.24 MW	8.69 AW	18070 AAW	NJBLS	10//99-12//99
	Atlantic-Cape May PMSA, NJ	S	7.92 MW	7.79 AW	16480 AAW	NJBLS	10//99-12//99
	Bergen-Passaic PMSA, NJ	S	9.59 MW	10.84 AW	19940 AAW	NJBLS	10//99-12//99
	Jersey City PMSA, NJ	S	7.88 MW	7.83 AW	16380 AAW	NJBLS	10//99-12//99
	Middlesex-Somerset-Hunterdon PMSA, NJ	S	9.71 MW	9.52 AW	20200 AAW	NJBLS	10//99-12//99
	Monmouth-Ocean PMSA, NJ	S	7.26 MW	6.78 AW	15090 AAW	NJBLS	10//99-12//99
	Newark PMSA, NJ	S	8.85 MW	8.86 AW	18410 AAW	NJBLS	10//99-12//99
	Trenton PMSA, NJ	S	12.48 MW	12.21 AW	25960 AAW	NJBLS	10//99-12//99
	Vineland-Millville-Bridgeton PMSA, NJ	S	7.40 MW	6.48 AW	15400 AAW	NJBLS	10//99-12//99
	New Mexico	S	6.26 MW	6.77 AW	14080 AAW	NMBLS	10//99-12//99
	New York	S	11.32 MW	10.81 AW	22480 AAW	NYBLS	10//99-12//99
	Albany-Schenectady-Troy MSA, NY	S	6.73 MW	5.99 AW	13990 AAW	NYBLS	10//99-12//99
	Glens Falls MSA, NY	S	10.05 MW	9.58 AW	20910 AAW	NYBLS	10//99-12//99
	Rochester MSA, NY	S	7.63 MW	6.21 AW	15880 AAW	NYBLS	10//99-12//99
	Syracuse MSA, NY	S	7.08 MW	6.13 AW	14720 AAW	NYBLS	10//99-12//99
	Utica-Rome MSA, NY	S	6.01 MW	5.97 AW	12510 AAW	NYBLS	10//99-12//99
	North Carolina	S	6.62 MW	7.30 AW	15190 AAW	NCBLS	10//99-12//99
	Charlotte-Gastonia-Rock Hill MSA, NC-SC	S	7.77 MW	7.80 AW	16150 AAW	NCBLS	10//99-12//99
	Greensboro--Winston-Salem--High Point MSA, NC	S	8.17 MW	8.44 AW	16990 AAW	NCBLS	10//99-12//99
	North Dakota	S	6.48 MW	7.33 AW	15240 AAW	NDBLS	10//99-12//99
	Ohio	S	7.55 MW	9.12 AW	18970 AAW	OHBLS	10//99-12//99
	Akron PMSA, OH	S	6.96 MW	6.85 AW	14480 AAW	OHBLS	10//99-12//99
	Cincinnati PMSA, OH-KY-IN	S	7.30 MW	6.62 AW	15180 AAW	OHBLS	10//99-12//99
	Columbus MSA, OH	S	8.95 MW	7.60 AW	18620 AAW	OHBLS	10//99-12//99
	Toledo MSA, OH	S	7.58 MW	7.35 AW	15760 AAW	OHBLS	10//99-12//99
	Youngstown-Warren MSA, OH	S	6.40 MW	6.22 AW	13310 AAW	OHBLS	10//99-12//99
	Oklahoma	S	7.51 MW	8.74 AW	18180 AAW	OKBLS	10//99-12//99
	Tulsa MSA, OK	S	10.02 MW	11.41 AW	20830 AAW	OKBLS	10//99-12//99
	Oregon	S	10.72 MW	13.06 AW	27170 AAW	ORBLS	10//99-12//99
	Eugene-Springfield MSA, OR	S	15.48 MW	17.61 AW	32200 AAW	ORBLS	10//99-12//99
	Portland-Vancouver PMSA, OR-WA	S	11.41 MW	9.33 AW	23740 AAW	ORBLS	10//99-12//99
	Pennsylvania	S	6.53 MW	7.21 AW	14990 AAW	PABLS	10//99-12//99
	Allentown-Bethlehem-Easton MSA, PA	S	7.54 MW	7.59 AW	15670 AAW	PABLS	10//99-12//99
	Harrisburg-Lebanon-Carlisle MSA, PA	S	7.03 MW	6.79 AW	14630 AAW	PABLS	10//99-12//99
	Lancaster MSA, PA	S	6.97 MW	6.61 AW	14490 AAW	PABLS	10//99-12//99
	Philadelphia PMSA, PA-NJ	S	7.50 MW	6.71 AW	15600 AAW	PABLS	10//99-12//99
	Pittsburgh MSA, PA	S	7.35 MW	6.81 AW	15290 AAW	PABLS	10//99-12//99
	Reading MSA, PA	S	8.88 MW	9.47 AW	18470 AAW	PABLS	10//99-12//99
	Scranton--Wilkes-Barre--Hazleton MSA, PA	S	6.29 MW	5.97 AW	13080 AAW	PABLS	10//99-12//99
	Williamsport MSA, PA	S	6.69 MW	6.56 AW	13920 AAW	PABLS	10//99-12//99
	York MSA, PA	S	9.09 MW	9.27 AW	18910 AAW	PABLS	10//99-12//99
	Rhode Island	S	6.92 MW	9.87 AW	20540 AAW	RIBLS	10//99-12//99
	Providence-Fall River-Warwick MSA, RI-MA	S	9.88 MW	7.35 AW	20550 AAW	RIBLS	10//99-12//99
	South Carolina	S	6.74 MW	7.79 AW	16210 AAW	SCBLS	10//99-12//99
	Columbia MSA, SC	S	8.67 MW	8.21 AW	18030 AAW	SCBLS	10//99-12//99
	South Dakota	S	7.83 MW	7.84 AW	16300 AAW	SDBLS	10//99-12//99
	Tennessee	S	7 MW	7.64 AW	15900 AAW	TNBLS	10//99-12//99
	Johnson City-Kingsport-Bristol MSA, TN-VA	S	9.60 MW	9.44 AW	19960 AAW	TNBLS	10//99-12//99

AAW	Average annual wage	**AOH**	Average offered, high	**ASH**	Average starting, high	**H**	Hourly	**M**	Monthly	**S**	Special: hourly and annual
AE	Average entry wage	**AOL**	Average offered, low	**ASL**	Average starting, low	**HI**	Highest wage paid	**MTC**	Median total compensation	**TQ**	Third quartile wage
AEX	Average experienced wage	**APH**	Average pay, high range	**AW**	Average wage paid	**HR**	High end range	**MW**	Median wage paid	**W**	Weekly
AO	Average offered	**APL**	Average pay, low range	**FQ**	First quartile wage	**LR**	Low end range	**SQ**	Second quartile wage	**Y**	Yearly

Occupation/Type/Industry	Location	Per	Low	Mid	High	Source	Date
Crossing Guard	Knoxville MSA, TN	S	6.99 MW	5.97 AW	14540 AAW	TNBLS	10//99-12//99
	Memphis MSA, TN-AR-MS	S	8.29 MW	8.24 AW	17240 AAW	MSBLS	10//99-12//99
	Nashville MSA, TN	S	7.29 MW	6.97 AW	15150 AAW	TNBLS	10//99-12//99
	Texas	S	6.43 MW	7.05 AW	14660 AAW	TXBLS	10//99-12//99
	Austin-San Marcos MSA, TX	S	7.14 MW	7.05 AW	14840 AAW	TXBLS	10//99-12//99
	Beaumont-Port Arthur MSA, TX	S	6.83 MW	6.05 AW	14210 AAW	TXBLS	10//99-12//99
	Brazoria PMSA, TX	S	8.95 MW	8.83 AW	18620 AAW	TXBLS	10//99-12//99
	Dallas PMSA, TX	S	6.69 MW	6.29 AW	13910 AAW	TXBLS	10//99-12//99
	El Paso MSA, TX	S	6.37 MW	6.19 AW	13260 AAW	TXBLS	10//99-12//99
	Fort Worth-Arlington PMSA, TX	S	8.38 MW	7.36 AW	17430 AAW	TXBLS	10//99-12//99
	Galveston-Texas City PMSA, TX	S	7.70 MW	6.49 AW	16010 AAW	TXBLS	10//99-12//99
	Houston PMSA, TX	S	7.47 MW	6.73 AW	15530 AAW	TXBLS	10//99-12//99
	McAllen-Edinburg-Mission MSA, TX	S	6.25 MW	6.21 AW	13000 AAW	TXBLS	10//99-12//99
	San Antonio MSA, TX	S	8.74 MW	8.26 AW	18180 AAW	TXBLS	10//99-12//99
	Utah	S	7.48 MW	7.57 AW	15750 AAW	UTBLS	10//99-12//99
	Provo-Orem MSA, UT	S	6.90 MW	7.17 AW	14360 AAW	UTBLS	10//99-12//99
	Salt Lake City-Ogden MSA, UT	S	7.82 MW	7.80 AW	16260 AAW	UTBLS	10//99-12//99
	Vermont	S	8.13 MW	8.30 AW	17270 AAW	VTBLS	10//99-12//99
	Burlington MSA, VT	S	9.75 MW	10.52 AW	20270 AAW	VTBLS	10//99-12//99
	Virginia	S	8.08 MW	8.94 AW	18600 AAW	VABLS	10//99-12//99
	Norfolk-Virginia Beach-Newport News MSA, VA-NC	S	8.77 MW	7.30 AW	18230 AAW	VABLS	10//99-12//99
	Richmond-Petersburg MSA, VA	S	9.25 MW	8.08 AW	19240 AAW	VABLS	10//99-12//99
	Washington	S	11.03 MW	13.08 AW	27210 AAW	WABLS	10//99-12//99
	Seattle-Bellevue-Everett PMSA, WA	S	10.16 MW	8.35 AW	21130 AAW	WABLS	10//99-12//99
	Spokane MSA, WA	S	17.27 MW	17.88 AW	35930 AAW	WABLS	10//99-12//99
	Tacoma PMSA, WA	S	18.79 MW	19.31 AW	39070 AAW	WABLS	10//99-12//99
	West Virginia	S	7.23 MW	7.24 AW	15070 AAW	WVBLS	10//99-12//99
	Wisconsin	S	7.77 MW	7.88 AW	16400 AAW	WIBLS	10//99-12//99
	Appleton-Oshkosh-Neenah MSA, WI	S	6.61 MW	6.59 AW	13760 AAW	WIBLS	10//99-12//99
	Eau Claire MSA, WI	S	6.67 MW	6.35 AW	13870 AAW	WIBLS	10//99-12//99
	Milwaukee-Waukesha PMSA, WI	S	8.48 MW	8.77 AW	17640 AAW	WIBLS	10//99-12//99
	Racine PMSA, WI	S	7.92 MW	7.89 AW	16470 AAW	WIBLS	10//99-12//99
	Wausau MSA, WI	S	7.31 MW	7.15 AW	15200 AAW	WIBLS	10//99-12//99
	Wyoming	S	9.1 MW	8.77 AW	18240 AAW	WYBLS	10//99-12//99
	Casper MSA, WY	S	10.71 MW	9.36 AW	22280 AAW	WYBLS	10//99-12//99
Crushing, Grinding, and Polishing Machine Setter, Operator, and Tender	Alabama	S	10.5 MW	11.45 AW	23810 AAW	ALBLS	10//99-12//99
	Birmingham MSA, AL	S	10.87 MW	11.13 AW	22620 AAW	ALBLS	10//99-12//99
	Florence MSA, AL	S	13.34 MW	13.09 AW	27760 AAW	ALBLS	10//99-12//99
	Huntsville MSA, AL	S	12.17 MW	12.22 AW	25310 AAW	ALBLS	10//99-12//99
	Alaska	S	28.81 MW	26.41 AW	54920 AAW	AKBLS	10//99-12//99
	Arizona	S	9.85 MW	10.84 AW	22550 AAW	AZBLS	10//99-12//99
	Phoenix-Mesa MSA, AZ	S	11.31 MW	10.36 AW	23530 AAW	AZBLS	10//99-12//99
	Arkansas	S	9.6 MW	9.71 AW	20200 AAW	ARBLS	10//99-12//99
	Fort Smith MSA, AR-OK	S	8.61 MW	8.03 AW	17920 AAW	ARBLS	10//99-12//99
	California	S	9.18 MW	10.40 AW	21620 AAW	CABLS	10//99-12//99
	Bakersfield MSA, CA	S	15.15 MW	18.11 AW	31520 AAW	CABLS	10//99-12//99
	Fresno MSA, CA	S	10.03 MW	11.08 AW	20860 AAW	CABLS	10//99-12//99
	Los Angeles-Long Beach PMSA, CA	S	11.19 MW	10.03 AW	23280 AAW	CABLS	10//99-12//99
	Oakland PMSA, CA	S	10.77 MW	8.46 AW	22410 AAW	CABLS	10//99-12//99
	Orange County PMSA, CA	S	9.73 MW	9.52 AW	20240 AAW	CABLS	10//99-12//99
	Riverside-San Bernardino PMSA, CA	S	8.07 MW	7.23 AW	16790 AAW	CABLS	10//99-12//99
	San Diego MSA, CA	S	7.96 MW	7.77 AW	16550 AAW	CABLS	10//99-12//99
	San Jose PMSA, CA	S	9.90 MW	8.18 AW	20590 AAW	CABLS	10//99-12//99
	Santa Rosa PMSA, CA	S	15.00 MW	15.26 AW	31200 AAW	CABLS	10//99-12//99
	Stockton-Lodi MSA, CA	S	9.98 MW	8.22 AW	20760 AAW	CABLS	10//99-12//99
	Colorado	S	14.82 MW	15.14 AW	31500 AAW	COBLS	10//99-12//99

AAW	Average annual wage	AOH	Average offered, high	ASH	Average starting, high	H	Hourly	M	Monthly	S	Special: hourly and annual
AE	Average entry wage	AOL	Average offered, low	ASL	Average starting, low	HI	Highest wage paid	MTC	Median total compensation	TQ	Third quartile wage
AEX	Average experienced wage	APH	Average pay, high range	AW	Average wage paid	HR	High end range	MW	Median wage paid	W	Weekly
AO	Average offered	APL	Average pay, low range	FQ	First quartile wage	LR	Low end range	SQ	Second quartile wage	Y	Yearly

362

Occupation/Type/Industry	Location	Per	Low	Mid	High	Source	Date
Crushing, Grinding, and Polishing Machine Setter, Operator, and Tender							
	Denver PMSA, CO	S	15.86 MW	15.10 AW	32990 AAW	COBLS	10//99-12//99
	Connecticut	S	12.03 MW	12.44 AW	25880 AAW	CTBLS	10//99-12//99
	Danbury PMSA, CT	S	16.48 MW	16.84 AW	34290 AAW	CTBLS	10//99-12//99
	Hartford MSA, CT	S	11.90 MW	11.59 AW	24750 AAW	CTBLS	10//99-12//99
	New Haven-Meriden PMSA, CT	S	14.16 MW	13.66 AW	29460 AAW	CTBLS	10//99-12//99
	Wilmington-Newark PMSA, DE-MD	S	12.93 MW	12.37 AW	26900 AAW	DEBLS	10//99-12//99
	Florida	S	9.88 MW	10.26 AW	21330 AAW	FLBLS	10//99-12//99
	Fort Lauderdale PMSA, FL	S	10.24 MW	9.75 AW	21300 AAW	FLBLS	10//99-12//99
	Jacksonville MSA, FL	S	11.70 MW	11.52 AW	24340 AAW	FLBLS	10//99-12//99
	Lakeland-Winter Haven MSA, FL	S	10.43 MW	10.24 AW	21700 AAW	FLBLS	10//99-12//99
	Miami PMSA, FL	S	8.46 MW	8.78 AW	17600 AAW	FLBLS	10//99-12//99
	Ocala MSA, FL	S	11.60 MW	10.59 AW	24120 AAW	FLBLS	10//99-12//99
	Orlando MSA, FL	S	10.62 MW	10.02 AW	22090 AAW	FLBLS	10//99-12//99
	West Palm Beach-Boca Raton MSA, FL	S	11.61 MW	10.98 AW	24150 AAW	FLBLS	10//99-12//99
	Georgia	S	11.89 MW	11.85 AW	24650 AAW	GABLS	10//99-12//99
	Atlanta MSA, GA	S	12.46 MW	12.16 AW	25910 AAW	GABLS	10//99-12//99
	Idaho	S	9.41 MW	9.73 AW	20240 AAW	IDBLS	10//99-12//99
	Boise City MSA, ID	S	9.17 MW	8.94 AW	19070 AAW	IDBLS	10//99-12//99
	Illinois	S	11.83 MW	13.26 AW	27590 AAW	ILBLS	10//99-12//99
	Chicago PMSA, IL	S	11.84 MW	10.62 AW	24630 AAW	ILBLS	10//99-12//99
	Peoria-Pekin MSA, IL	S	10.54 MW	10.42 AW	21920 AAW	ILBLS	10//99-12//99
	Indiana	S	13.15 MW	14.34 AW	29820 AAW	INBLS	10//99-12//99
	Elkhart-Goshen MSA, IN	S	13.94 MW	12.59 AW	28990 AAW	INBLS	10//99-12//99
	Evansville-Henderson MSA, IN-KY	S	8.07 MW	7.96 AW	16780 AAW	INBLS	10//99-12//99
	Fort Wayne MSA, IN	S	14.13 MW	12.88 AW	29380 AAW	INBLS	10//99-12//99
	Indianapolis MSA, IN	S	12.44 MW	12.51 AW	25870 AAW	INBLS	10//99-12//99
	Iowa	S	13.55 MW	12.66 AW	26330 AAW	IABLS	10//99-12//99
	Cedar Rapids MSA, IA	S	12.26 MW	11.83 AW	25500 AAW	IABLS	10//99-12//99
	Des Moines MSA, IA	S	14.08 MW	14.76 AW	29290 AAW	IABLS	10//99-12//99
	Kansas	S	10.02 MW	10.55 AW	21950 AAW	KSBLS	10//99-12//99
	Kentucky	S	9.99 MW	10.01 AW	20820 AAW	KYBLS	10//99-12//99
	Lexington MSA, KY	S	9.50 MW	9.32 AW	19750 AAW	KYBLS	10//99-12//99
	Louisville MSA, KY-IN	S	11.31 MW	11.70 AW	23530 AAW	KYBLS	10//99-12//99
	Louisiana	S	9.8 MW	10.72 AW	22300 AAW	LABLS	10//99-12//99
	Maine	S	12.82 MW	12.72 AW	26470 AAW	MEBLS	10//99-12//99
	Maryland	S	14.19 MW	13.70 AW	28490 AAW	MDBLS	10//99-12//99
	Massachusetts	S	14.71 MW	14.98 AW	31160 AAW	MABLS	10//99-12//99
	Boston PMSA, MA-NH	S	16.13 MW	15.51 AW	33550 AAW	MABLS	10//99-12//99
	Springfield MSA, MA	S	12.60 MW	12.47 AW	26200 AAW	MABLS	10//99-12//99
	Worcester PMSA, MA-CT	S	14.22 MW	14.80 AW	29580 AAW	MABLS	10//99-12//99
	Michigan	S	13.81 MW	14.01 AW	29140 AAW	MIBLS	10//99-12//99
	Detroit PMSA, MI	S	13.33 MW	13.53 AW	27720 AAW	MIBLS	10//99-12//99
	Minnesota	S	13.32 MW	13.96 AW	29040 AAW	MNBLS	10//99-12//99
	Minneapolis-St. Paul MSA, MN-WI	S	17.08 MW	17.98 AW	35520 AAW	MNBLS	10//99-12//99
	Mississippi	S	10.46 MW	12.42 AW	25840 AAW	MSBLS	10//99-12//99
	Biloxi-Gulfport-Pascagoula MSA, MS	S	15.00 MW	15.16 AW	31200 AAW	MSBLS	10//99-12//99
	Missouri	S	12.75 MW	12.96 AW	26950 AAW	MOBLS	10//99-12//99
	Kansas City MSA, MO-KS	S	13.07 MW	12.15 AW	27180 AAW	MOBLS	10//99-12//99
	St. Louis MSA, MO-IL	S	13.32 MW	13.20 AW	27710 AAW	MOBLS	10//99-12//99
	Montana	S	14.55 MW	13.54 AW	28160 AAW	MTBLS	10//99-12//99
	Nebraska	S	17.29 MW	15.83 AW	32920 AAW	NEBLS	10//99-12//99
	Omaha MSA, NE-IA	S	16.65 MW	17.84 AW	34630 AAW	NEBLS	10//99-12//99
	Nevada	S	13.34 MW	13.65 AW	28390 AAW	NVBLS	10//99-12//99
	Las Vegas MSA, NV-AZ	S	12.05 MW	12.00 AW	25070 AAW	NVBLS	10//99-12//99
	New Hampshire	S	12.3 MW	12.77 AW	26560 AAW	NHBLS	10//99-12//99
	New Jersey	S	11.95 MW	12.01 AW	24980 AAW	NJBLS	10//99-12//99
	Bergen-Passaic PMSA, NJ	S	10.81 MW	10.48 AW	22480 AAW	NJBLS	10//99-12//99
	Middlesex-Somerset-Hunterdon PMSA, NJ	S	11.14 MW	11.47 AW	23170 AAW	NJBLS	10//99-12//99
	Newark PMSA, NJ	S	12.78 MW	12.85 AW	26590 AAW	NJBLS	10//99-12//99
	New Mexico	S	14.41 MW	13.04 AW	27130 AAW	NMBLS	10//99-12//99
	Albuquerque MSA, NM	S	13.53 MW	13.84 AW	28140 AAW	NMBLS	10//99-12//99
	New York	S	14.1 MW	13.53 AW	28140 AAW	NYBLS	10//99-12//99

AAW	Average annual wage	AOH	Average offered, high	ASH	Average starting, high
AE	Average entry wage	AOL	Average offered, low	ASL	Average starting, low
AEX	Average experienced wage	APH	Average pay, high range	AW	Average wage paid
AO	Average offered	APL	Average pay, low range	FQ	First quartile wage

H	Hourly	M	Monthly
HI	Highest wage paid	MTC	Median total compensation
HR	High end range	MW	Median wage paid
LR	Low end range	SQ	Second quartile wage

S	Special: hourly and annual
TQ	Third quartile wage
W	Weekly
Y	Yearly

Occupation/Type/Industry	Location	Per	Low	Mid	High	Source	Date
Crushing, Grinding, and Polishing Machine Setter, Operator, and Tender							
	Albany-Schenectady-Troy MSA, NY	S	10.72 MW	9.97 AW	22310 AAW	NYBLS	10//99-12//99
	Binghamton MSA, NY	S	10.27 MW	10.12 AW	21370 AAW	NYBLS	10//99-12//99
	Buffalo-Niagara Falls MSA, NY	S	16.50 MW	16.59 AW	34310 AAW	NYBLS	10//99-12//99
	New York PMSA, NY	S	9.58 MW	8.13 AW	19920 AAW	NYBLS	10//99-12//99
	Rochester MSA, NY	S	12.26 MW	12.19 AW	25490 AAW	NYBLS	10//99-12//99
	Syracuse MSA, NY	S	10.32 MW	10.22 AW	21470 AAW	NYBLS	10//99-12//99
	Utica-Rome MSA, NY	S	11.93 MW	11.88 AW	24820 AAW	NYBLS	10//99-12//99
	North Carolina	S	11.25 MW	12.04 AW	25050 AAW	NCBLS	10//99-12//99
	Charlotte-Gastonia-Rock Hill MSA, NC-SC	S	11.69 MW	11.99 AW	24320 AAW	NCBLS	10//99-12//99
	Greensboro--Winston-Salem--High Point MSA, NC	S	9.58 MW	9.00 AW	19930 AAW	NCBLS	10//99-12//99
	Hickory-Morganton-Lenoir MSA, NC	S	13.53 MW	14.58 AW	28150 AAW	NCBLS	10//99-12//99
	Ohio	S	11.64 MW	12.16 AW	25280 AAW	OHBLS	10//99-12//99
	Akron PMSA, OH	S	10.38 MW	9.84 AW	21590 AAW	OHBLS	10//99-12//99
	Canton-Massillon MSA, OH	S	10.63 MW	11.43 AW	22110 AAW	OHBLS	10//99-12//99
	Cincinnati PMSA, OH-KY-IN	S	11.39 MW	10.44 AW	23690 AAW	OHBLS	10//99-12//99
	Cleveland-Lorain-Elyria PMSA, OH	S	11.43 MW	11.46 AW	23770 AAW	OHBLS	10//99-12//99
	Columbus MSA, OH	S	12.64 MW	11.27 AW	26290 AAW	OHBLS	10//99-12//99
	Dayton-Springfield MSA, OH	S	11.10 MW	10.50 AW	23100 AAW	OHBLS	10//99-12//99
	Hamilton-Middletown PMSA, OH	S	15.05 MW	15.21 AW	31300 AAW	OHBLS	10//99-12//99
	Toledo MSA, OH	S	13.49 MW	14.31 AW	28050 AAW	OHBLS	10//99-12//99
	Youngstown-Warren MSA, OH	S	12.68 MW	11.89 AW	26370 AAW	OHBLS	10//99-12//99
	Oklahoma	S	10.7 MW	11.35 AW	23600 AAW	OKBLS	10//99-12//99
	Tulsa MSA, OK	S	10.54 MW	9.90 AW	21930 AAW	OKBLS	10//99-12//99
	Oregon	S	13.3 MW	13.39 AW	27850 AAW	ORBLS	10//99-12//99
	Eugene-Springfield MSA, OR	S	11.96 MW	12.04 AW	24880 AAW	ORBLS	10//99-12//99
	Portland-Vancouver PMSA, OR-WA	S	12.93 MW	12.91 AW	26900 AAW	ORBLS	10//99-12//99
	Pennsylvania	S	12.98 MW	13.10 AW	27240 AAW	PABLS	10//99-12//99
	Allentown-Bethlehem-Easton MSA, PA	S	13.02 MW	13.36 AW	27070 AAW	PABLS	10//99-12//99
	Erie MSA, PA	S	10.09 MW	9.34 AW	20990 AAW	PABLS	10//99-12//99
	Lancaster MSA, PA	S	14.49 MW	13.62 AW	30130 AAW	PABLS	10//99-12//99
	Philadelphia PMSA, PA-NJ	S	14.08 MW	13.33 AW	29290 AAW	PABLS	10//99-12//99
	Pittsburgh MSA, PA	S	12.71 MW	13.00 AW	26430 AAW	PABLS	10//99-12//99
	Reading MSA, PA	S	13.34 MW	13.60 AW	27750 AAW	PABLS	10//99-12//99
	Scranton--Wilkes-Barre--Hazleton MSA, PA	S	14.15 MW	14.44 AW	29440 AAW	PABLS	10//99-12//99
	York MSA, PA	S	13.68 MW	13.36 AW	28460 AAW	PABLS	10//99-12//99
	Rhode Island	S	6.71 MW	9.26 AW	19260 AAW	RIBLS	10//99-12//99
	Providence-Fall River-Warwick MSA, RI-MA	S	9.26 MW	6.71 AW	19260 AAW	RIBLS	10//99-12//99
	South Carolina	S	12.98 MW	14.12 AW	29370 AAW	SCBLS	10//99-12//99
	Greenville-Spartanburg-Anderson MSA, SC	S	16.07 MW	17.64 AW	33420 AAW	SCBLS	10//99-12//99
	South Dakota	S	9.88 MW	10.21 AW	21230 AAW	SDBLS	10//99-12//99
	Sioux Falls MSA, SD	S	10.93 MW	11.16 AW	22740 AAW	SDBLS	10//99-12//99
	Tennessee	S	10.31 MW	10.35 AW	21530 AAW	TNBLS	10//99-12//99
	Chattanooga MSA, TN-GA	S	10.92 MW	10.54 AW	22720 AAW	TNBLS	10//99-12//99
	Johnson City-Kingsport-Bristol MSA, TN-VA	S	8.23 MW	7.66 AW	17120 AAW	TNBLS	10//99-12//99
	Knoxville MSA, TN	S	10.07 MW	10.42 AW	20950 AAW	TNBLS	10//99-12//99
	Memphis MSA, TN-AR-MS	S	10.54 MW	10.32 AW	21930 AAW	MSBLS	10//99-12//99
	Nashville MSA, TN	S	10.25 MW	8.64 AW	21330 AAW	TNBLS	10//99-12//99
	Texas	S	9.49 MW	10.32 AW	21470 AAW	TXBLS	10//99-12//99
	Dallas PMSA, TX	S	10.17 MW	9.66 AW	21160 AAW	TXBLS	10//99-12//99
	El Paso MSA, TX	S	6.04 MW	6.00 AW	12550 AAW	TXBLS	10//99-12//99
	Fort Worth-Arlington PMSA, TX	S	14.21 MW	14.09 AW	29560 AAW	TXBLS	10//99-12//99
	Houston PMSA, TX	S	13.07 MW	11.99 AW	27180 AAW	TXBLS	10//99-12//99
	Longview-Marshall MSA, TX	S	9.73 MW	9.96 AW	20240 AAW	TXBLS	10//99-12//99
	San Antonio MSA, TX	S	11.49 MW	9.33 AW	23910 AAW	TXBLS	10//99-12//99
	Waco MSA, TX	S	8.54 MW	8.55 AW	17750 AAW	TXBLS	10//99-12//99
	Utah	S	11.85 MW	12.34 AW	25670 AAW	UTBLS	10//99-12//99

AAW Average annual wage	**AOH** Average offered, high	**ASH** Average starting, high	**H** Hourly	**M** Monthly	**S** Special: hourly and annual
AE Average entry wage	**AOL** Average offered, low	**ASL** Average starting, low	**HI** Highest wage paid	**MTC** Median total compensation	**TQ** Third quartile wage
AEX Average experienced wage	**APH** Average pay, high range	**AW** Average wage paid	**HR** High end range	**MW** Median wage paid	**W** Weekly
AO Average offered	**APL** Average pay, low range	**FQ** First quartile wage	**LR** Low end range	**SQ** Second quartile wage	**Y** Yearly

Occupation/Type/Industry	Location	Per	Low	Mid	High	Source	Date
Crushing, Grinding, and Polishing Machine Setter, Operator, and Tender							
	Vermont	S	14.7 MW	13.90 AW	28920 AAW	VTBLS	10//99-12/99
	Virginia	S	13.15 MW	12.59 AW	26190 AAW	VABLS	10//99-12/99
	Roanoke MSA, VA	S	11.09 MW	10.58 AW	23070 AAW	VABLS	10//99-12/99
	Washington	S	12.01 MW	12.25 AW	25480 AAW	WABLS	10//99-12/99
	Seattle-Bellevue-Everett PMSA, WA	S	13.47 MW	13.95 AW	28010 AAW	WABLS	10//99-12/99
	Spokane MSA, WA	S	9.44 MW	8.83 AW	19640 AAW	WABLS	10//99-12/99
	Tacoma PMSA, WA	S	7.70 MW	7.71 AW	16010 AAW	WABLS	10//99-12/99
	Wisconsin	S	10.38 MW	11.42 AW	23750 AAW	WIBLS	10//99-12/99
	Appleton-Oshkosh-Neenah MSA, WI	S	12.20 MW	12.25 AW	25380 AAW	WIBLS	10//99-12/99
	Green Bay MSA, WI	S	16.21 MW	16.93 AW	33720 AAW	WIBLS	10//99-12/99
	Janesville-Beloit MSA, WI	S	9.38 MW	8.40 AW	19500 AAW	WIBLS	10//99-12/99
	Madison MSA, WI	S	10.13 MW	9.79 AW	21070 AAW	WIBLS	10//99-12/99
	Milwaukee-Waukesha PMSA, WI	S	12.63 MW	11.62 AW	26270 AAW	WIBLS	10//99-12/99
	Wausau MSA, WI	S	11.83 MW	11.58 AW	24610 AAW	WIBLS	10//99-12/99
	Wyoming	S	23.32 MW	20.87 AW	43410 AAW	WYBLS	10//99-12/99
	Puerto Rico	S	9.83 MW	9.52 AW	19800 AAW	PRBLS	10//99-12/99
	San Juan-Bayamon PMSA, PR	S	10.24 MW	10.60 AW	21290 AAW	PRBLS	10//99-12/99
Customer Service Representative	Alabama	S	9.49 MW	10.09 AW	20990 AAW	ALBLS	10//99-12/99
	Alaska	S	12.05 MW	13.24 AW	27540 AAW	AKBLS	10//99-12/99
	Arizona	S	9.8 MW	10.65 AW	22150 AAW	AZBLS	10//99-12/99
	Arkansas	S	10.1 MW	10.88 AW	22630 AAW	ARBLS	10//99-12/99
	California	S	13.03 MW	14.20 AW	29540 AAW	CABLS	10//99-12/99
	Colorado	S	11.4 MW	12.28 AW	25540 AAW	COBLS	10//99-12/99
	Connecticut	S	13.26 MW	13.78 AW	28650 AAW	CTBLS	10//99-12/99
	Delaware	S	11.79 MW	12.51 AW	26020 AAW	DEBLS	10//99-12/99
	District of Columbia	S	13.39 MW	14.07 AW	29250 AAW	DCBLS	10//99-12/99
	Florida	S	10.26 MW	11.06 AW	23000 AAW	FLBLS	10//99-12/99
	Georgia	S	11.59 MW	12.16 AW	25300 AAW	GABLS	10//99-12/99
	Hawaii	S	11.83 MW	12.32 AW	25630 AAW	HIBLS	10//99-12/99
	Idaho	S	10.13 MW	10.66 AW	22170 AAW	IDBLS	10//99-12/99
	Illinois	S	11.46 MW	12.09 AW	25150 AAW	ILBLS	10//99-12/99
	Indiana	S	11.16 MW	11.88 AW	24720 AAW	INBLS	10//99-12/99
	Iowa	S	9.81 MW	10.36 AW	21540 AAW	IABLS	10//99-12/99
	Kansas	S	10.66 MW	10.94 AW	22750 AAW	KSBLS	10//99-12/99
	Kentucky	S	11.82 MW	11.99 AW	24940 AAW	KYBLS	10//99-12/99
	Louisiana	S	8.67 MW	9.45 AW	19650 AAW	LABLS	10//99-12/99
	Maine	S	11.26 MW	11.39 AW	23700 AAW	MEBLS	10//99-12/99
	Maryland	S	10.56 MW	11.10 AW	23090 AAW	MDBLS	10//99-12/99
	Michigan	S	12.47 MW	13.67 AW	28430 AAW	MIBLS	10//99-12/99
	Minnesota	S	11.78 MW	12.28 AW	25550 AAW	MNBLS	10//99-12/99
	Mississippi	S	9.41 MW	10.14 AW	21100 AAW	MSBLS	10//99-12/99
	Missouri	S	11.49 MW	12.32 AW	25630 AAW	MOBLS	10//99-12/99
	Montana	S	8.96 MW	9.53 AW	19820 AAW	MTBLS	10//99-12/99
	Nebraska	S	8.82 MW	9.67 AW	20120 AAW	NEBLS	10//99-12/99
	Nevada	S	10.87 MW	11.71 AW	24370 AAW	NVBLS	10//99-12/99
	New Hampshire	S	11.6 MW	12.22 AW	25410 AAW	NHBLS	10//99-12/99
	New Jersey	S	13.16 MW	13.72 AW	28540 AAW	NJBLS	10//99-12/99
	New Mexico	S	9.69 MW	10.28 AW	21380 AAW	NMBLS	10//99-12/99
	New York	S	12.27 MW	13.92 AW	28950 AAW	NYBLS	10//99-12/99
	North Carolina	S	10.68 MW	11.40 AW	23700 AAW	NCBLS	10//99-12/99
	North Dakota	S	8.31 MW	10.29 AW	21410 AAW	NDBLS	10//99-12/99
	Ohio	S	11.56 MW	12.37 AW	25730 AAW	OHBLS	10//99-12/99
	Oklahoma	S	10.97 MW	11.72 AW	24370 AAW	OKBLS	10//99-12/99
	Oregon	S	10.82 MW	11.72 AW	24370 AAW	ORBLS	10//99-12/99
	Pennsylvania	S	10.56 MW	11.54 AW	24010 AAW	PABLS	10//99-12/99
	Rhode Island	S	11.68 MW	11.42 AW	23750 AAW	RIBLS	10//99-12/99
	South Carolina	S	10.35 MW	11.24 AW	23370 AAW	SCBLS	10//99-12/99
	South Dakota	S	9.08 MW	9.26 AW	19270 AAW	SDBLS	10//99-12/99
	Tennessee	S	9.83 MW	10.42 AW	21680 AAW	TNBLS	10//99-12/99
	Texas	S	10.51 MW	11.40 AW	23700 AAW	TXBLS	10//99-12/99
	Utah	S	9.7 MW	10.34 AW	21500 AAW	UTBLS	10//99-12/99
	Vermont	S	11.85 MW	12.52 AW	26040 AAW	VTBLS	10//99-12/99
	Virginia	S	11.57 MW	12.07 AW	25110 AAW	VABLS	10//99-12/99
	Washington	S	12.83 MW	13.61 AW	28320 AAW	WABLS	10//99-12/99
	West Virginia	S	10.26 MW	10.76 AW	22370 AAW	WVBLS	10//99-12/99
	Wisconsin	S	11.64 MW	12.52 AW	26040 AAW	WIBLS	10//99-12/99

AAW	Average annual wage	AOH	Average offered, high	ASH	Average starting, high	H	Hourly	M	Monthly	S	Special: hourly and annual
AE	Average entry wage	AOL	Average offered, low	ASL	Average starting, low	HI	Highest wage paid	MTC	Median total compensation	TQ	Third quartile wage
AEX	Average experienced wage	APH	Average pay, high range	AW	Average wage paid	HR	High end range	MW	Median wage paid	W	Weekly
AO	Average offered	APL	Average pay, low range	FQ	First quartile wage	LR	Low end range	SQ	Second quartile wage	Y	Yearly

Occupation/Type/Industry	Location	Per	Low	Mid	High	Source	Date
Customer Service Representative	Wyoming	S	9.26 MW	9.90 AW	20580 AAW	WYBLS	10//99-12//99
	Puerto Rico	S	7.89 MW	8.86 AW	18420 AAW	PRBLS	10//99-12//99
	Virgin Islands	S	10.2 MW	11.07 AW	23020 AAW	VIBLS	10//99-12//99
	Guam	S	9.85 MW	10.40 AW	21640 AAW	GUBLS	10//99-12//99
Sales Organization	United States	Y	15000 APL	22656 MW	52932 APH	SMR	1999
Cutter and Trimmer							
Hand	Alabama	S	8.5 MW	8.61 AW	17910 AAW	ALBLS	10//99-12//99
Hand	Arizona	S	8.6 MW	10.04 AW	20890 AAW	AZBLS	10//99-12//99
Hand	Arkansas	S	6.12 MW	6.28 AW	13060 AAW	ARBLS	10//99-12//99
Hand	California	S	7.76 MW	8.39 AW	17450 AAW	CABLS	10//99-12//99
Hand	Connecticut	S	8.48 MW	12.24 AW	25450 AAW	CTBLS	10//99-12//99
Hand	Florida	S	9.15 MW	10.08 AW	20970 AAW	FLBLS	10//99-12//99
Hand	Georgia	S	8.63 MW	10.94 AW	22750 AAW	GABLS	10//99-12//99
Hand	Hawaii	S	6.08 MW	6.27 AW	13030 AAW	HIBLS	10//99-12//99
Hand	Idaho	S	6.32 MW	7.14 AW	14860 AAW	IDBLS	10//99-12//99
Hand	Illinois	S	9.04 MW	11.92 AW	24790 AAW	ILBLS	10//99-12//99
Hand	Indiana	S	11.68 MW	11.42 AW	23760 AAW	INBLS	10//99-12//99
Hand	Iowa	S	11.09 MW	11.42 AW	23760 AAW	IABLS	10//99-12//99
Hand	Kansas	S	8.89 MW	9.20 AW	19130 AAW	KSBLS	10//99-12//99
Hand	Kentucky	S	9.09 MW	9.03 AW	18770 AAW	KYBLS	10//99-12//99
Hand	Louisiana	S	9.49 MW	9.22 AW	19180 AAW	LABLS	10//99-12//99
Hand	Maine	S	9.48 MW	9.19 AW	19110 AAW	MEBLS	10//99-12//99
Hand	Maryland	S	10.01 MW	10.51 AW	21860 AAW	MDBLS	10//99-12//99
Hand	Massachusetts	S	9.51 MW	10.33 AW	21490 AAW	MABLS	10//99-12//99
Hand	Michigan	S	13.16 MW	15.93 AW	33140 AAW	MIBLS	10//99-12//99
Hand	Minnesota	S	22.28 MW	18.34 AW	38140 AAW	MNBLS	10//99-12//99
Hand	Mississippi	S	9.32 MW	9.30 AW	19340 AAW	MSBLS	10//99-12//99
Hand	Missouri	S	21.58 MW	17.53 AW	36460 AAW	MOBLS	10//99-12//99
Hand	Montana	S	11.03 MW	10.93 AW	22740 AAW	MTBLS	10//99-12//99
Hand	Nebraska	S	8.77 MW	8.57 AW	17830 AAW	NEBLS	10//99-12//99
Hand	Nevada	S	14.94 MW	14.15 AW	29430 AAW	NVBLS	10//99-12//99
Hand	New Hampshire	S	9.58 MW	9.59 AW	19960 AAW	NHBLS	10//99-12//99
Hand	New Jersey	S	10.72 MW	12.14 AW	25260 AAW	NJBLS	10//99-12//99
Hand	New Mexico	S	6.15 MW	6.35 AW	13200 AAW	NMBLS	10//99-12//99
Hand	New York	S	9.92 MW	11.33 AW	23560 AAW	NYBLS	10//99-12//99
Hand	North Carolina	S	11.83 MW	12.39 AW	25770 AAW	NCBLS	10//99-12//99
Hand	Ohio	S	8.78 MW	9.62 AW	20000 AAW	OHBLS	10//99-12//99
Hand	Oklahoma	S	7.56 MW	7.82 AW	16260 AAW	OKBLS	10//99-12//99
Hand	Oregon	S	9.32 MW	9.69 AW	20160 AAW	ORBLS	10//99-12//99
Hand	Pennsylvania	S	10.31 MW	10.49 AW	21820 AAW	PABLS	10//99-12//99
Hand	South Carolina	S	8.98 MW	8.99 AW	18710 AAW	SCBLS	10//99-12//99
Hand	South Dakota	S	9.4 MW	9.25 AW	19240 AAW	SDBLS	10//99-12//99
Hand	Tennessee	S	8.1 MW	8.90 AW	18510 AAW	TNBLS	10//99-12//99
Hand	Texas	S	7.53 MW	7.95 AW	16540 AAW	TXBLS	10//99-12//99
Hand	Utah	S	7.91 MW	8.12 AW	16900 AAW	UTBLS	10//99-12//99
Hand	Vermont	S	11.83 MW	12.00 AW	24970 AAW	VTBLS	10//99-12//99
Hand	Virginia	S	13.38 MW	15.77 AW	32800 AAW	VABLS	10//99-12//99
Hand	Washington	S	10.41 MW	12.08 AW	25120 AAW	WABLS	10//99-12//99
Hand	Wisconsin	S	10.03 MW	10.60 AW	22050 AAW	WIBLS	10//99-12//99
Hand	Puerto Rico	S	6.1 MW	6.03 AW	12550 AAW	PRBLS	10//99-12//99
Cutting and Slicing Machine Setter, Operator, and Tender	Alabama	S	8.78 MW	10.71 AW	22270 AAW	ALBLS	10//99-12//99
	Birmingham MSA, AL	S	12.15 MW	11.16 AW	25260 AAW	ALBLS	10//99-12//99
	Decatur MSA, AL	S	11.20 MW	8.79 AW	23300 AAW	ALBLS	10//99-12//99
	Florence MSA, AL	S	9.85 MW	9.66 AW	20480 AAW	ALBLS	10//99-12//99
	Montgomery MSA, AL	S	9.30 MW	8.48 AW	19340 AAW	ALBLS	10//99-12//99
	Arizona	S	10.51 MW	10.63 AW	22110 AAW	AZBLS	10//99-12//99
	Phoenix-Mesa MSA, AZ	S	10.50 MW	10.36 AW	21840 AAW	AZBLS	10//99-12//99
	Tucson MSA, AZ	S	11.19 MW	11.73 AW	23280 AAW	AZBLS	10//99-12//99
	Arkansas	S	9.96 MW	10.06 AW	20930 AAW	ARBLS	10//99-12//99
	Fayetteville-Springdale-Rogers MSA, AR	S	8.90 MW	8.03 AW	18520 AAW	ARBLS	10//99-12//99
	Fort Smith MSA, AR-OK	S	10.12 MW	10.26 AW	21050 AAW	ARBLS	10//99-12//99
	Little Rock-North Little Rock MSA, AR	S	11.35 MW	11.02 AW	23620 AAW	ARBLS	10//99-12//99
	California	S	9.5 MW	10.57 AW	21990 AAW	CABLS	10//99-12//99
	Bakersfield MSA, CA	S	7.51 MW	7.54 AW	15620 AAW	CABLS	10//99-12//99
	Fresno MSA, CA	S	9.17 MW	8.55 AW	19070 AAW	CABLS	10//99-12//99
	Los Angeles-Long Beach PMSA, CA	S	9.96 MW	9.14 AW	20720 AAW	CABLS	10//99-12//99

AAW	Average annual wage	AOH	Average offered, high	ASH	Average starting, high	H	Hourly	M	Monthly
AE	Average entry wage	AOL	Average offered, low	ASL	Average starting, low	HI	Highest wage paid	MTC	Median total compensation
AEX	Average experienced wage	APH	Average pay, high range	AW	Average wage paid	HR	High end range	MW	Median wage paid
AO	Average offered	APL	Average pay, low range	FQ	First quartile wage	LR	Low end range	SQ	Second quartile wage

S   Special: hourly and annual
TQ   Third quartile wage
W   Weekly
Y   Yearly

Occupation/Type/Industry	Location	Per	Low	Mid	High	Source	Date
Cutting and Slicing Machine Setter, Operator, and Tender	Merced MSA, CA	S	9.67 MW	9.56 AW	20120 AAW	CABLS	10//99-12//99
	Oakland PMSA, CA	S	11.58 MW	10.48 AW	24090 AAW	CABLS	10//99-12//99
	Orange County PMSA, CA	S	12.34 MW	11.40 AW	25670 AAW	CABLS	10//99-12//99
	Riverside-San Bernardino PMSA, CA	S	11.46 MW	10.76 AW	23850 AAW	CABLS	10//99-12//99
	Sacramento PMSA, CA	S	10.68 MW	9.96 AW	22220 AAW	CABLS	10//99-12//99
	San Diego MSA, CA	S	10.39 MW	9.01 AW	21610 AAW	CABLS	10//99-12//99
	San Francisco PMSA, CA	S	13.57 MW	12.68 AW	28240 AAW	CABLS	10//99-12//99
	San Jose PMSA, CA	S	11.03 MW	9.69 AW	22950 AAW	CABLS	10//99-12//99
	Santa Cruz-Watsonville PMSA, CA	S	15.15 MW	15.68 AW	31520 AAW	CABLS	10//99-12//99
	Santa Rosa PMSA, CA	S	12.67 MW	11.59 AW	26350 AAW	CABLS	10//99-12//99
	Vallejo-Fairfield-Napa PMSA, CA	S	10.70 MW	10.05 AW	22260 AAW	CABLS	10//99-12//99
	Visalia-Tulare-Porterville MSA, CA	S	8.50 MW	7.76 AW	17670 AAW	CABLS	10//99-12//99
	Colorado	S	11.8 MW	11.89 AW	24740 AAW	COBLS	10//99-12//99
	Boulder-Longmont PMSA, CO	S	11.58 MW	10.32 AW	24080 AAW	COBLS	10//99-12//99
	Colorado Springs MSA, CO	S	11.90 MW	11.70 AW	24740 AAW	COBLS	10//99-12//99
	Denver PMSA, CO	S	12.24 MW	12.21 AW	25450 AAW	COBLS	10//99-12//99
	Fort Collins-Loveland MSA, CO	S	11.05 MW	10.56 AW	22980 AAW	COBLS	10//99-12//99
	Connecticut	S	11.92 MW	12.05 AW	25050 AAW	CTBLS	10//99-12//99
	Bridgeport PMSA, CT	S	11.23 MW	11.43 AW	23360 AAW	CTBLS	10//99-12//99
	Danbury PMSA, CT	S	11.35 MW	10.99 AW	23610 AAW	CTBLS	10//99-12//99
	Hartford MSA, CT	S	12.63 MW	12.76 AW	26260 AAW	CTBLS	10//99-12//99
	New Haven-Meriden PMSA, CT	S	11.74 MW	11.70 AW	24420 AAW	CTBLS	10//99-12//99
	New London-Norwich MSA, CT-RI	S	13.25 MW	14.01 AW	27550 AAW	CTBLS	10//99-12//99
	Stamford-Norwalk PMSA, CT	S	14.76 MW	14.10 AW	30690 AAW	CTBLS	10//99-12//99
	Waterbury PMSA, CT	S	11.06 MW	10.76 AW	23010 AAW	CTBLS	10//99-12//99
	Delaware	S	13.78 MW	13.07 AW	27190 AAW	DEBLS	10//99-12//99
	Wilmington-Newark PMSA, DE-MD	S	12.72 MW	12.75 AW	26460 AAW	DEBLS	10//99-12//99
	Washington PMSA, DC-MD-VA-WV	S	12.42 MW	11.26 AW	25830 AAW	DCBLS	10//99-12//99
	Florida	S	9.54 MW	10.01 AW	20820 AAW	FLBLS	10//99-12//99
	Daytona Beach MSA, FL	S	9.11 MW	8.78 AW	18960 AAW	FLBLS	10//99-12//99
	Fort Lauderdale PMSA, FL	S	10.89 MW	10.78 AW	22640 AAW	FLBLS	10//99-12//99
	Jacksonville MSA, FL	S	9.63 MW	9.09 AW	20030 AAW	FLBLS	10//99-12//99
	Lakeland-Winter Haven MSA, FL	S	10.32 MW	9.67 AW	21470 AAW	FLBLS	10//99-12//99
	Miami PMSA, FL	S	10.59 MW	10.23 AW	22030 AAW	FLBLS	10//99-12//99
	Orlando MSA, FL	S	10.85 MW	10.41 AW	22570 AAW	FLBLS	10//99-12//99
	Sarasota-Bradenton MSA, FL	S	12.25 MW	11.68 AW	25480 AAW	FLBLS	10//99-12//99
	Tallahassee MSA, FL	S	10.63 MW	10.16 AW	22120 AAW	FLBLS	10//99-12//99
	Tampa-St. Petersburg-Clearwater MSA, FL	S	9.37 MW	8.72 AW	19480 AAW	FLBLS	10//99-12//99
	West Palm Beach-Boca Raton MSA, FL	S	10.58 MW	9.98 AW	22000 AAW	FLBLS	10//99-12//99
	Georgia	S	9.94 MW	10.28 AW	21390 AAW	GABLS	10//99-12//99
	Atlanta MSA, GA	S	11.18 MW	10.83 AW	23260 AAW	GABLS	10//99-12//99
	Augusta-Aiken MSA, GA-SC	S	11.22 MW	11.75 AW	23330 AAW	GABLS	10//99-12//99
	Columbus MSA, GA-AL	S	10.27 MW	10.16 AW	21360 AAW	GABLS	10//99-12//99
	Macon MSA, GA	S	10.05 MW	9.72 AW	20910 AAW	GABLS	10//99-12//99
	Hawaii	S	11.82 MW	12.18 AW	25330 AAW	HIBLS	10//99-12//99
	Honolulu MSA, HI	S	12.64 MW	12.84 AW	26290 AAW	HIBLS	10//99-12//99
	Idaho	S	11.29 MW	11.26 AW	23420 AAW	IDBLS	10//99-12//99
	Boise City MSA, ID	S	11.38 MW	11.69 AW	23680 AAW	IDBLS	10//99-12//99
	Illinois	S	10.85 MW	11.92 AW	24800 AAW	ILBLS	10//99-12//99
	Chicago PMSA, IL	S	11.90 MW	10.64 AW	24750 AAW	ILBLS	10//99-12//99
	Decatur MSA, IL	S	14.22 MW	14.65 AW	29570 AAW	ILBLS	10//99-12//99
	Rockford MSA, IL	S	11.90 MW	11.56 AW	24750 AAW	ILBLS	10//99-12//99
	Indiana	S	11.61 MW	11.75 AW	24440 AAW	INBLS	10//99-12//99
	Elkhart-Goshen MSA, IN	S	10.45 MW	10.12 AW	21730 AAW	INBLS	10//99-12//99
	Evansville-Henderson MSA, IN-KY	S	10.23 MW	10.26 AW	21280 AAW	INBLS	10//99-12//99
	Fort Wayne MSA, IN	S	12.51 MW	11.99 AW	26020 AAW	INBLS	10//99-12//99
	Gary PMSA, IN	S	11.91 MW	11.52 AW	24780 AAW	INBLS	10//99-12//99
	Indianapolis MSA, IN	S	12.51 MW	11.96 AW	26030 AAW	INBLS	10//99-12//99

AAW	Average annual wage	AOH	Average offered, high	ASH	Average starting, high	H	Hourly	M	Monthly	S	Special: hourly and annual
AE	Average entry wage	AOL	Average offered, low	ASL	Average starting, low	HI	Highest wage paid	MTC	Median total compensation	TQ	Third quartile wage
AEX	Average experienced wage	APH	Average pay, high range	AW	Average wage paid	HR	High end range	MW	Median wage paid	W	Weekly
AO	Average offered	APL	Average pay, low range	FQ	First quartile wage	LR	Low end range	SQ	Second quartile wage	Y	Yearly

Occupation/Type/Industry	Location	Per	Low	Mid	High	Source	Date
Cutting and Slicing Machine Setter, Operator, and Tender	Muncie MSA, IN	S	11.45 MW	10.86 AW	23820 AAW	INBLS	10//99-12//99
	South Bend MSA, IN	S	10.65 MW	9.66 AW	22160 AAW	INBLS	10//99-12//99
	Terre Haute MSA, IN	S	12.06 MW	12.20 AW	25070 AAW	INBLS	10//99-12//99
	Iowa	S	13.44 MW	13.68 AW	28460 AAW	IABLS	10//99-12//99
	Des Moines MSA, IA	S	11.85 MW	11.55 AW	24650 AAW	IABLS	10//99-12//99
	Kansas	S	9.9 MW	10.28 AW	21380 AAW	KSBLS	10//99-12//99
	Topeka MSA, KS	S	10.54 MW	10.20 AW	21920 AAW	KSBLS	10//99-12//99
	Wichita MSA, KS	S	9.80 MW	9.73 AW	20380 AAW	KSBLS	10//99-12//99
	Kentucky	S	11.12 MW	11.71 AW	24370 AAW	KYBLS	10//99-12//99
	Lexington MSA, KY	S	13.19 MW	14.11 AW	27440 AAW	KYBLS	10//99-12//99
	Louisville MSA, KY-IN	S	12.19 MW	12.23 AW	25360 AAW	KYBLS	10//99-12//99
	Louisiana	S	11.36 MW	11.44 AW	23790 AAW	LABLS	10//99-12//99
	Baton Rouge MSA, LA	S	11.61 MW	12.56 AW	24140 AAW	LABLS	10//99-12//99
	Monroe MSA, LA	S	9.88 MW	9.89 AW	20560 AAW	LABLS	10//99-12//99
	New Orleans MSA, LA	S	9.91 MW	9.75 AW	20620 AAW	LABLS	10//99-12//99
	Shreveport-Bossier City MSA, LA	S	12.17 MW	13.75 AW	25320 AAW	LABLS	10//99-12//99
	Maine	S	9.47 MW	10.36 AW	21560 AAW	MEBLS	10//99-12//99
	Portland MSA, ME	S	11.67 MW	10.50 AW	24270 AAW	MEBLS	10//99-12//99
	Maryland	S	12.58 MW	12.56 AW	26130 AAW	MDBLS	10//99-12//99
	Baltimore PMSA, MD	S	12.76 MW	13.10 AW	26550 AAW	MDBLS	10//99-12//99
	Hagerstown PMSA, MD	S	11.40 MW	10.20 AW	23720 AAW	MDBLS	10//99-12//99
	Massachusetts	S	12.72 MW	12.90 AW	26830 AAW	MABLS	10//99-12//99
	Boston PMSA, MA-NH	S	13.15 MW	13.02 AW	27340 AAW	MABLS	10//99-12//99
	Brockton PMSA, MA	S	13.31 MW	11.85 AW	27670 AAW	MABLS	10//99-12//99
	Fitchburg-Leominster PMSA, MA	S	12.33 MW	12.02 AW	25650 AAW	MABLS	10//99-12//99
	Lawrence PMSA, MA-NH	S	10.98 MW	11.27 AW	22830 AAW	MABLS	10//99-12//99
	Lowell PMSA, MA-NH	S	11.63 MW	10.89 AW	24190 AAW	MABLS	10//99-12//99
	Springfield MSA, MA	S	13.28 MW	13.17 AW	27620 AAW	MABLS	10//99-12//99
	Worcester PMSA, MA-CT	S	12.83 MW	12.48 AW	26680 AAW	MABLS	10//99-12//99
	Michigan	S	11.24 MW	11.68 AW	24290 AAW	MIBLS	10//99-12//99
	Benton Harbor MSA, MI	S	12.11 MW	11.91 AW	25190 AAW	MIBLS	10//99-12//99
	Detroit PMSA, MI	S	12.48 MW	11.27 AW	25950 AAW	MIBLS	10//99-12//99
	Grand Rapids-Muskegon-Holland MSA, MI	S	11.51 MW	11.21 AW	23930 AAW	MIBLS	10//99-12//99
	Kalamazoo-Battle Creek MSA, MI	S	12.26 MW	12.16 AW	25500 AAW	MIBLS	10//99-12//99
	Minnesota	S	14.07 MW	14.07 AW	29260 AAW	MNBLS	10//99-12//99
	Minneapolis-St. Paul MSA, MN-WI	S	14.68 MW	14.54 AW	30540 AAW	MNBLS	10//99-12//99
	Mississippi	S	9.87 MW	10.53 AW	21890 AAW	MSBLS	10//99-12//99
	Biloxi-Gulfport-Pascagoula MSA, MS	S	11.13 MW	9.83 AW	23160 AAW	MSBLS	10//99-12//99
	Jackson MSA, MS	S	11.20 MW	11.36 AW	23290 AAW	MSBLS	10//99-12//99
	Missouri	S	9.46 MW	9.99 AW	20770 AAW	MOBLS	10//99-12//99
	Kansas City MSA, MO-KS	S	11.22 MW	10.84 AW	23340 AAW	MOBLS	10//99-12//99
	St. Louis MSA, MO-IL	S	10.28 MW	10.01 AW	21380 AAW	MOBLS	10//99-12//99
	Nebraska	S	10.69 MW	10.82 AW	22510 AAW	NEBLS	10//99-12//99
	Omaha MSA, NE-IA	S	11.30 MW	11.43 AW	23510 AAW	NEBLS	10//99-12//99
	Nevada	S	16.76 MW	15.71 AW	32680 AAW	NVBLS	10//99-12//99
	New Hampshire	S	11.04 MW	11.38 AW	23660 AAW	NHBLS	10//99-12//99
	Nashua PMSA, NH	S	10.65 MW	9.91 AW	22160 AAW	NHBLS	10//99-12//99
	Portsmouth-Rochester PMSA, NH-ME	S	13.34 MW	13.57 AW	27740 AAW	NHBLS	10//99-12//99
	New Jersey	S	12.88 MW	13.17 AW	27400 AAW	NJBLS	10//99-12//99
	Bergen-Passaic PMSA, NJ	S	12.84 MW	13.29 AW	26710 AAW	NJBLS	10//99-12//99
	Jersey City PMSA, NJ	S	11.35 MW	10.96 AW	23610 AAW	NJBLS	10//99-12//99
	Middlesex-Somerset-Hunterdon PMSA, NJ	S	14.00 MW	13.90 AW	29110 AAW	NJBLS	10//99-12//99
	Monmouth-Ocean PMSA, NJ	S	10.49 MW	10.48 AW	21820 AAW	NJBLS	10//99-12//99
	Newark PMSA, NJ	S	14.16 MW	12.67 AW	29450 AAW	NJBLS	10//99-12//99
	Trenton PMSA, NJ	S	12.64 MW	13.00 AW	26300 AAW	NJBLS	10//99-12//99
	Vineland-Millville-Bridgeton PMSA, NJ	S	11.20 MW	11.50 AW	23290 AAW	NJBLS	10//99-12//99
	New Mexico	S	7.84 MW	8.24 AW	17140 AAW	NMBLS	10//99-12//99
	Albuquerque MSA, NM	S	9.56 MW	8.93 AW	19880 AAW	NMBLS	10//99-12//99
	Las Cruces MSA, NM	S	7.88 MW	7.70 AW	16380 AAW	NMBLS	10//99-12//99
	New York	S	10.49 MW	11.44 AW	23790 AAW	NYBLS	10//99-12//99
	Albany-Schenectady-Troy MSA, NY	S	12.99 MW	14.25 AW	27020 AAW	NYBLS	10//99-12//99

AAW Average annual wage	AOH Average offered, high	ASH Average starting, high	H Hourly	M Monthly	S Special: hourly and annual
AE Average entry wage	AOL Average offered, low	ASL Average starting, low	HI Highest wage paid	MTC Median total compensation	TQ Third quartile wage
AEX Average experienced wage	APH Average pay, high range	AW Average wage paid	HR High end range	MW Median wage paid	W Weekly
AO Average offered	APL Average pay, low range	FQ First quartile wage	LR Low end range	SQ Second quartile wage	Y Yearly

Occupation/Type/Industry	Location	Per	Low	Mid	High	Source	Date
Cutting and Slicing Machine Setter, Operator, and Tender	Binghamton MSA, NY	S	11.30 MW	11.46 AW	23500 AAW	NYBLS	10//99-12//99
	Buffalo-Niagara Falls MSA, NY	S	11.43 MW	10.71 AW	23770 AAW	NYBLS	10//99-12//99
	Dutchess County PMSA, NY	S	11.83 MW	12.04 AW	24600 AAW	NYBLS	10//99-12//99
	Glens Falls MSA, NY	S	11.35 MW	10.15 AW	23610 AAW	NYBLS	10//99-12//99
	Nassau-Suffolk PMSA, NY	S	11.62 MW	11.27 AW	24170 AAW	NYBLS	10//99-12//99
	New York PMSA, NY	S	9.92 MW	8.63 AW	20640 AAW	NYBLS	10//99-12//99
	Newburgh PMSA, NY-PA	S	10.20 MW	9.43 AW	21210 AAW	NYBLS	10//99-12//99
	Rochester MSA, NY	S	15.83 MW	15.86 AW	32920 AAW	NYBLS	10//99-12//99
	Syracuse MSA, NY	S	12.32 MW	12.78 AW	25620 AAW	NYBLS	10//99-12//99
	North Carolina	S	11.79 MW	12.45 AW	25900 AAW	NCBLS	10//99-12//99
	Charlotte-Gastonia-Rock Hill MSA, NC-SC	S	12.39 MW	12.14 AW	25770 AAW	NCBLS	10//99-12//99
	Greensboro--Winston-Salem--High Point MSA, NC	S	13.20 MW	12.37 AW	27450 AAW	NCBLS	10//99-12//99
	Hickory-Morganton-Lenoir MSA, NC	S	10.87 MW	10.79 AW	22600 AAW	NCBLS	10//99-12//99
	Raleigh-Durham-Chapel Hill MSA, NC	S	12.06 MW	11.39 AW	25080 AAW	NCBLS	10//99-12//99
	Wilmington MSA, NC	S	9.25 MW	8.90 AW	19230 AAW	NCBLS	10//99-12//99
	Ohio	S	10.72 MW	11.00 AW	22890 AAW	OHBLS	10//99-12//99
	Akron PMSA, OH	S	10.13 MW	9.76 AW	21080 AAW	OHBLS	10//99-12//99
	Canton-Massillon MSA, OH	S	10.51 MW	10.83 AW	21850 AAW	OHBLS	10//99-12//99
	Cincinnati PMSA, OH-KY-IN	S	12.34 MW	11.61 AW	25660 AAW	OHBLS	10//99-12//99
	Cleveland-Lorain-Elyria PMSA, OH	S	11.62 MW	11.61 AW	24160 AAW	OHBLS	10//99-12//99
	Columbus MSA, OH	S	11.27 MW	11.08 AW	23440 AAW	OHBLS	10//99-12//99
	Dayton-Springfield MSA, OH	S	10.88 MW	10.13 AW	22630 AAW	OHBLS	10//99-12//99
	Hamilton-Middletown PMSA, OH	S	13.02 MW	11.91 AW	27070 AAW	OHBLS	10//99-12//99
	Lima MSA, OH	S	9.01 MW	9.17 AW	18750 AAW	OHBLS	10//99-12//99
	Mansfield MSA, OH	S	9.58 MW	9.54 AW	19930 AAW	OHBLS	10//99-12//99
	Toledo MSA, OH	S	10.59 MW	10.82 AW	22020 AAW	OHBLS	10//99-12//99
	Youngstown-Warren MSA, OH	S	10.57 MW	10.58 AW	21980 AAW	OHBLS	10//99-12//99
	Oklahoma	S	10.56 MW	11.62 AW	24180 AAW	OKBLS	10//99-12//99
	Oklahoma City MSA, OK	S	8.26 MW	7.88 AW	17180 AAW	OKBLS	10//99-12//99
	Tulsa MSA, OK	S	11.49 MW	11.48 AW	23890 AAW	OKBLS	10//99-12//99
	Oregon	S	10.49 MW	11.48 AW	23890 AAW	ORBLS	10//99-12//99
	Portland-Vancouver PMSA, OR-WA	S	11.84 MW	11.27 AW	24630 AAW	ORBLS	10//99-12//99
	Pennsylvania	S	11.44 MW	11.57 AW	24060 AAW	PABLS	10//99-12//99
	Allentown-Bethlehem-Easton MSA, PA	S	12.65 MW	12.60 AW	26310 AAW	PABLS	10//99-12//99
	Altoona MSA, PA	S	12.91 MW	14.29 AW	26850 AAW	PABLS	10//99-12//99
	Harrisburg-Lebanon-Carlisle MSA, PA	S	12.19 MW	12.84 AW	25360 AAW	PABLS	10//99-12//99
	Lancaster MSA, PA	S	13.10 MW	11.57 AW	27240 AAW	PABLS	10//99-12//99
	Philadelphia PMSA, PA-NJ	S	11.62 MW	11.45 AW	24170 AAW	PABLS	10//99-12//99
	Pittsburgh MSA, PA	S	11.63 MW	11.48 AW	24190 AAW	PABLS	10//99-12//99
	Reading MSA, PA	S	8.86 MW	8.67 AW	18430 AAW	PABLS	10//99-12//99
	Scranton--Wilkes-Barre--Hazleton MSA, PA	S	11.67 MW	12.03 AW	24270 AAW	PABLS	10//99-12//99
	York MSA, PA	S	12.62 MW	12.49 AW	26250 AAW	PABLS	10//99-12//99
	Rhode Island	S	11.25 MW	11.53 AW	23980 AAW	RIBLS	10//99-12//99
	Providence-Fall River-Warwick MSA, RI-MA	S	11.71 MW	11.73 AW	24350 AAW	RIBLS	10//99-12//99
	South Carolina	S	10.92 MW	11.92 AW	24790 AAW	SCBLS	10//99-12//99
	Greenville-Spartanburg-Anderson MSA, SC	S	13.50 MW	11.52 AW	28070 AAW	SCBLS	10//99-12//99
	South Dakota	S	10.8 MW	10.50 AW	21850 AAW	SDBLS	10//99-12//99
	Sioux Falls MSA, SD	S	10.90 MW	11.01 AW	22670 AAW	SDBLS	10//99-12//99
	Tennessee	S	10.87 MW	11.30 AW	23510 AAW	TNBLS	10//99-12//99
	Chattanooga MSA, TN-GA	S	10.77 MW	10.63 AW	22390 AAW	TNBLS	10//99-12//99
	Johnson City-Kingsport-Bristol MSA, TN-VA	S	9.63 MW	9.60 AW	20040 AAW	TNBLS	10//99-12//99
	Knoxville MSA, TN	S	9.68 MW	9.64 AW	20140 AAW	TNBLS	10//99-12//99
	Memphis MSA, TN-AR-MS	S	11.99 MW	12.11 AW	24940 AAW	MSBLS	10//99-12//99
	Nashville MSA, TN	S	14.38 MW	14.14 AW	29910 AAW	TNBLS	10//99-12//99
	Texas	S	9.34 MW	9.83 AW	20450 AAW	TXBLS	10//99-12//99
	Austin-San Marcos MSA, TX	S	9.79 MW	8.76 AW	20370 AAW	TXBLS	10//99-12//99
	Dallas PMSA, TX	S	10.67 MW	10.09 AW	22200 AAW	TXBLS	10//99-12//99

AAW	Average annual wage	AOH	Average offered, high	ASH	Average starting, high	H	Hourly	M	Monthly	S	Special: hourly and annual
AE	Average entry wage	AOL	Average offered, low	ASL	Average starting, low	HI	Highest wage paid	MTC	Median total compensation	TQ	Third quartile wage
AEX	Average experienced wage	APH	Average pay, high range	AW	Average wage paid	HR	High end range	MW	Median wage paid	W	Weekly
AO	Average offered	APL	Average pay, low range	FQ	First quartile wage	LR	Low end range	SQ	Second quartile wage	Y	Yearly

Occupation/Type/Industry	Location	Per	Low	Mid	High	Source	Date
Cutting and Slicing Machine Setter, Operator, and Tender	El Paso MSA, TX	S	8.08 MW	7.83 AW	16810 AAW	TXBLS	10//99-12//99
	Fort Worth-Arlington PMSA, TX	S	9.18 MW	8.74 AW	19090 AAW	TXBLS	10//99-12//99
	Houston PMSA, TX	S	10.07 MW	9.93 AW	20930 AAW	TXBLS	10//99-12//99
	Odessa-Midland MSA, TX	S	7.53 MW	7.52 AW	15660 AAW	TXBLS	10//99-12//99
	San Antonio MSA, TX	S	9.18 MW	8.87 AW	19100 AAW	TXBLS	10//99-12//99
	Texarkana MSA, TX-Texarkana, AR	S	9.34 MW	9.19 AW	19420 AAW	TXBLS	10//99-12//99
	Tyler MSA, TX	S	14.33 MW	16.39 AW	29810 AAW	TXBLS	10//99-12//99
	Utah	S	9.73 MW	10.08 AW	20960 AAW	UTBLS	10//99-12//99
	Provo-Orem MSA, UT	S	8.94 MW	8.48 AW	18590 AAW	UTBLS	10//99-12//99
	Vermont	S	11.37 MW	11.40 AW	23700 AAW	VTBLS	10//99-12//99
	Burlington MSA, VT	S	11.94 MW	12.07 AW	24830 AAW	VTBLS	10//99-12//99
	Virginia	S	10.1 MW	10.90 AW	22670 AAW	VABLS	10//99-12//99
	Lynchburg MSA, VA	S	11.99 MW	12.38 AW	24940 AAW	VABLS	10//99-12//99
	Norfolk-Virginia Beach-Newport News MSA, VA-NC	S	8.72 MW	8.37 AW	18140 AAW	VABLS	10//99-12//99
	Richmond-Petersburg MSA, VA	S	11.77 MW	10.30 AW	24480 AAW	VABLS	10//99-12//99
	Roanoke MSA, VA	S	10.72 MW	10.03 AW	22290 AAW	VABLS	10//99-12//99
	Washington	S	10.47 MW	11.59 AW	24100 AAW	WABLS	10//99-12//99
	Olympia PMSA, WA	S	10.61 MW	10.28 AW	22060 AAW	WABLS	10//99-12//99
	Seattle-Bellevue-Everett PMSA, WA	S	11.61 MW	10.73 AW	24150 AAW	WABLS	10//99-12//99
	Tacoma PMSA, WA	S	12.84 MW	12.76 AW	26710 AAW	WABLS	10//99-12//99
	Yakima MSA, WA	S	10.91 MW	10.21 AW	22680 AAW	WABLS	10//99-12//99
	West Virginia	S	12.07 MW	12.06 AW	25090 AAW	WVBLS	10//99-12//99
	Charleston MSA, WV	S	12.24 MW	12.76 AW	25460 AAW	WVBLS	10//99-12//99
	Huntington-Ashland MSA, WV-KY-OH	S	8.77 MW	8.06 AW	18240 AAW	WVBLS	10//99-12//99
	Parkersburg-Marietta MSA, WV-OH	S	9.72 MW	9.60 AW	20210 AAW	WVBLS	10//99-12//99
	Wisconsin	S	12.02 MW	12.13 AW	25230 AAW	WIBLS	10//99-12//99
	Appleton-Oshkosh-Neenah MSA, WI	S	13.54 MW	13.69 AW	28160 AAW	WIBLS	10//99-12//99
	Green Bay MSA, WI	S	13.30 MW	13.43 AW	27660 AAW	WIBLS	10//99-12//99
	Janesville-Beloit MSA, WI	S	11.36 MW	11.77 AW	23630 AAW	WIBLS	10//99-12//99
	La Crosse MSA, WI-MN	S	11.15 MW	10.53 AW	23190 AAW	WIBLS	10//99-12//99
	Milwaukee-Waukesha PMSA, WI	S	12.63 MW	12.36 AW	26280 AAW	WIBLS	10//99-12//99
	Racine PMSA, WI	S	12.15 MW	11.05 AW	25260 AAW	WIBLS	10//99-12//99
	Sheboygan MSA, WI	S	11.24 MW	11.62 AW	23380 AAW	WIBLS	10//99-12//99
	Wausau MSA, WI	S	11.28 MW	11.26 AW	23470 AAW	WIBLS	10//99-12//99
	Wyoming	S	10.11 MW	11.05 AW	22980 AAW	WYBLS	10//99-12//99
	Puerto Rico	S	6.03 MW	6.39 AW	13290 AAW	PRBLS	10//99-12//99
	Caguas PMSA, PR	S	7.05 MW	6.35 AW	14670 AAW	PRBLS	10//99-12//99
	San Juan-Bayamon PMSA, PR	S	6.52 MW	6.22 AW	13570 AAW	PRBLS	10//99-12//99
Cutting, Punching, and Press Machine Setter, Operator, and Tender							
Metals and Plastics	Alabama	S	10.97 MW	11.31 AW	23530 AAW	ALBLS	10//99-12//99
Metals and Plastics	Birmingham MSA, AL	S	10.40 MW	10.09 AW	21630 AAW	ALBLS	10//99-12//99
Metals and Plastics	Decatur MSA, AL	S	15.52 MW	18.07 AW	32280 AAW	ALBLS	10//99-12//99
Metals and Plastics	Dothan MSA, AL	S	8.20 MW	8.08 AW	17050 AAW	ALBLS	10//99-12//99
Metals and Plastics	Gadsden MSA, AL	S	9.46 MW	9.12 AW	19670 AAW	ALBLS	10//99-12//99
Metals and Plastics	Huntsville MSA, AL	S	12.31 MW	12.33 AW	25600 AAW	ALBLS	10//99-12//99
Metals and Plastics	Montgomery MSA, AL	S	8.13 MW	7.69 AW	16920 AAW	ALBLS	10//99-12//99
Metals and Plastics	Tuscaloosa MSA, AL	S	9.41 MW	8.64 AW	19570 AAW	ALBLS	10//99-12//99
Metals and Plastics	Arizona	S	9.2 MW	9.57 AW	19900 AAW	AZBLS	10//99-12//99
Metals and Plastics	Phoenix-Mesa MSA, AZ	S	9.60 MW	9.10 AW	19980 AAW	AZBLS	10//99-12//99
Metals and Plastics	Tucson MSA, AZ	S	9.70 MW	9.57 AW	20170 AAW	AZBLS	10//99-12//99
Metals and Plastics	Arkansas	S	9.94 MW	10.09 AW	21000 AAW	ARBLS	10//99-12//99
Metals and Plastics	Fayetteville-Springdale-Rogers MSA, AR	S	10.78 MW	10.99 AW	22420 AAW	ARBLS	10//99-12//99
Metals and Plastics	Fort Smith MSA, AR-OK	S	12.41 MW	12.57 AW	25820 AAW	ARBLS	10//99-12//99
Metals and Plastics	Little Rock-North Little Rock MSA, AR	S	9.60 MW	9.97 AW	19960 AAW	ARBLS	10//99-12//99
Metals and Plastics	Pine Bluff MSA, AR	S	12.09 MW	12.16 AW	25140 AAW	ARBLS	10//99-12//99

AAW Average annual wage	**AOH** Average offered, high	**ASH** Average starting, high	**H** Hourly	**M** Monthly	**S** Special: hourly and annual
AE Average entry wage	**AOL** Average offered, low	**ASL** Average starting, low	**HI** Highest wage paid	**MTC** Median total compensation	**TQ** Third quartile wage
AEX Average experienced wage	**APH** Average pay, high range	**AW** Average wage paid	**HR** High end range	**MW** Median wage paid	**W** Weekly
AO Average offered	**APL** Average pay, low range	**FQ** First quartile wage	**LR** Low end range	**SQ** Second quartile wage	**Y** Yearly

Occupation/Type/Industry	Location	Per	Low	Mid	High	Source	Date
Cutting, Punching, and Press Machine Setter, Operator, and Tender							
Metals and Plastics	California	S	10.39 MW	11.34 AW	23580 AAW	CABLS	10//99-12//99
Metals and Plastics	Bakersfield MSA, CA	S	11.23 MW	10.20 AW	23360 AAW	CABLS	10//99-12//99
Metals and Plastics	Chico-Paradise MSA, CA	S	15.46 MW	14.77 AW	32160 AAW	CABLS	10//99-12//99
Metals and Plastics	Fresno MSA, CA	S	9.95 MW	9.71 AW	20690 AAW	CABLS	10//99-12//99
Metals and Plastics	Los Angeles-Long Beach PMSA, CA	S	11.81 MW	11.00 AW	24570 AAW	CABLS	10//99-12//99
Metals and Plastics	Merced MSA, CA	S	11.65 MW	12.01 AW	24230 AAW	CABLS	10//99-12//99
Metals and Plastics	Modesto MSA, CA	S	11.71 MW	11.81 AW	24350 AAW	CABLS	10//99-12//99
Metals and Plastics	Oakland PMSA, CA	S	14.31 MW	13.99 AW	29770 AAW	CABLS	10//99-12//99
Metals and Plastics	Orange County PMSA, CA	S	10.12 MW	9.45 AW	21050 AAW	CABLS	10//99-12//99
Metals and Plastics	Riverside-San Bernardino PMSA, CA	S	9.15 MW	8.96 AW	19040 AAW	CABLS	10//99-12//99
Metals and Plastics	Sacramento PMSA, CA	S	11.07 MW	11.06 AW	23030 AAW	CABLS	10//99-12//99
Metals and Plastics	San Diego MSA, CA	S	10.26 MW	9.40 AW	21350 AAW	CABLS	10//99-12//99
Metals and Plastics	San Francisco PMSA, CA	S	12.52 MW	12.16 AW	26050 AAW	CABLS	10//99-12//99
Metals and Plastics	San Jose PMSA, CA	S	15.55 MW	15.87 AW	32350 AAW	CABLS	10//99-12//99
Metals and Plastics	San Luis Obispo-Atascadero-Paso Robles MSA, CA	S	9.28 MW	8.18 AW	19290 AAW	CABLS	10//99-12//99
Metals and Plastics	Santa Barbara-Santa Maria-Lompoc MSA, CA	S	9.86 MW	9.06 AW	20510 AAW	CABLS	10//99-12//99
Metals and Plastics	Santa Cruz-Watsonville PMSA, CA	S	10.21 MW	9.57 AW	21240 AAW	CABLS	10//99-12//99
Metals and Plastics	Santa Rosa PMSA, CA	S	10.19 MW	10.07 AW	21180 AAW	CABLS	10//99-12//99
Metals and Plastics	Stockton-Lodi MSA, CA	S	10.19 MW	9.35 AW	21190 AAW	CABLS	10//99-12//99
Metals and Plastics	Vallejo-Fairfield-Napa PMSA, CA	S	10.44 MW	9.95 AW	21720 AAW	CABLS	10//99-12//99
Metals and Plastics	Ventura PMSA, CA	S	9.11 MW	8.30 AW	18950 AAW	CABLS	10//99-12//99
Metals and Plastics	Visalia-Tulare-Porterville MSA, CA	S	8.95 MW	8.13 AW	18620 AAW	CABLS	10//99-12//99
Metals and Plastics	Colorado	S	10.69 MW	11.23 AW	23370 AAW	COBLS	10//99-12//99
Metals and Plastics	Colorado Springs MSA, CO	S	10.24 MW	9.76 AW	21310 AAW	COBLS	10//99-12//99
Metals and Plastics	Denver PMSA, CO	S	12.76 MW	12.33 AW	26550 AAW	COBLS	10//99-12//99
Metals and Plastics	Fort Collins-Loveland MSA, CO	S	9.24 MW	8.35 AW	19230 AAW	COBLS	10//99-12//99
Metals and Plastics	Connecticut	S	12.85 MW	13.19 AW	27440 AAW	CTBLS	10//99-12//99
Metals and Plastics	Bridgeport PMSA, CT	S	11.09 MW	10.03 AW	23060 AAW	CTBLS	10//99-12//99
Metals and Plastics	Danbury PMSA, CT	S	15.88 MW	15.84 AW	33030 AAW	CTBLS	10//99-12//99
Metals and Plastics	Hartford MSA, CT	S	13.89 MW	13.18 AW	28900 AAW	CTBLS	10//99-12//99
Metals and Plastics	New Haven-Meriden PMSA, CT	S	12.37 MW	12.38 AW	25730 AAW	CTBLS	10//99-12//99
Metals and Plastics	New London-Norwich MSA, CT-RI	S	12.30 MW	12.31 AW	25580 AAW	CTBLS	10//99-12//99
Metals and Plastics	Stamford-Norwalk PMSA, CT	S	12.22 MW	10.65 AW	25410 AAW	CTBLS	10//99-12//99
Metals and Plastics	Waterbury PMSA, CT	S	11.98 MW	11.89 AW	24930 AAW	CTBLS	10//99-12//99
Metals and Plastics	Delaware	S	11.47 MW	11.62 AW	24180 AAW	DEBLS	10//99-12//99
Metals and Plastics	Wilmington-Newark PMSA, DE-MD	S	11.79 MW	11.84 AW	24530 AAW	DEBLS	10//99-12//99
Metals and Plastics	Washington PMSA, DC-MD-VA-WV	S	14.24 MW	14.25 AW	29630 AAW	DCBLS	10//99-12//99
Metals and Plastics	Florida	S	9.29 MW	9.74 AW	20260 AAW	FLBLS	10//99-12//99
Metals and Plastics	Daytona Beach MSA, FL	S	9.06 MW	9.12 AW	18850 AAW	FLBLS	10//99-12//99
Metals and Plastics	Fort Lauderdale PMSA, FL	S	11.12 MW	11.37 AW	23130 AAW	FLBLS	10//99-12//99
Metals and Plastics	Fort Walton Beach MSA, FL	S	8.09 MW	7.99 AW	16830 AAW	FLBLS	10//99-12//99
Metals and Plastics	Jacksonville MSA, FL	S	9.22 MW	9.17 AW	19170 AAW	FLBLS	10//99-12//99
Metals and Plastics	Lakeland-Winter Haven MSA, FL	S	9.02 MW	8.71 AW	18760 AAW	FLBLS	10//99-12//99
Metals and Plastics	Melbourne-Titusville-Palm Bay MSA, FL	S	9.57 MW	9.44 AW	19900 AAW	FLBLS	10//99-12//99
Metals and Plastics	Miami PMSA, FL	S	8.75 MW	8.15 AW	18190 AAW	FLBLS	10//99-12//99
Metals and Plastics	Ocala MSA, FL	S	9.56 MW	9.25 AW	19880 AAW	FLBLS	10//99-12//99
Metals and Plastics	Orlando MSA, FL	S	11.38 MW	11.34 AW	23670 AAW	FLBLS	10//99-12//99
Metals and Plastics	Pensacola MSA, FL	S	8.42 MW	8.20 AW	17520 AAW	FLBLS	10//99-12//99
Metals and Plastics	Sarasota-Bradenton MSA, FL	S	9.61 MW	8.94 AW	19990 AAW	FLBLS	10//99-12//99
Metals and Plastics	Tampa-St. Petersburg-Clearwater MSA, FL	S	9.31 MW	8.50 AW	19360 AAW	FLBLS	10//99-12//99
Metals and Plastics	West Palm Beach-Boca Raton MSA, FL	S	12.78 MW	13.52 AW	26570 AAW	FLBLS	10//99-12//99
Metals and Plastics	Georgia	S	10.32 MW	10.86 AW	22590 AAW	GABLS	10//99-12//99
Metals and Plastics	Albany MSA, GA	S	9.52 MW	9.24 AW	19800 AAW	GABLS	10//99-12//99

AAW	Average annual wage	AOH	Average offered, high	ASH	Average starting, high	H	Hourly	M	Monthly	S	Special: hourly and annual
AE	Average entry wage	AOL	Average offered, low	ASL	Average starting, low	HI	Highest wage paid	MTC	Median total compensation	TQ	Third quartile wage
AEX	Average experienced wage	APH	Average pay, high range	AW	Average wage paid	HR	High end range	MW	Median wage paid	W	Weekly
AO	Average offered	APL	Average pay, low range	FQ	First quartile wage	LR	Low end range	SQ	Second quartile wage	Y	Yearly

Occupation/Type/Industry	Location	Per	Low	Mid	High	Source	Date
Cutting, Punching, and Press Machine Setter, Operator, and Tender							
Metals and Plastics	Athens MSA, GA	S	9.37 MW	7.94 AW	19490 AAW	GABLS	10//99-12//99
Metals and Plastics	Atlanta MSA, GA	S	12.51 MW	11.97 AW	26010 AAW	GABLS	10//99-12//99
Metals and Plastics	Augusta-Aiken MSA, GA-SC	S	9.50 MW	8.46 AW	19750 AAW	GABLS	10//99-12//99
Metals and Plastics	Columbus MSA, GA-AL	S	9.33 MW	9.25 AW	19410 AAW	GABLS	10//99-12//99
Metals and Plastics	Savannah MSA, GA	S	8.34 MW	8.08 AW	17340 AAW	GABLS	10//99-12//99
Metals and Plastics	Hawaii	S	12.89 MW	13.63 AW	28360 AAW	HIBLS	10//99-12//99
Metals and Plastics	Honolulu MSA, HI	S	13.63 MW	12.89 AW	28360 AAW	HIBLS	10//99-12//99
Metals and Plastics	Idaho	S	9.66 MW	10.21 AW	21230 AAW	IDBLS	10//99-12//99
Metals and Plastics	Boise City MSA, ID	S	10.55 MW	10.05 AW	21950 AAW	IDBLS	10//99-12//99
Metals and Plastics	Illinois	S	11.1 MW	11.19 AW	23270 AAW	ILBLS	10//99-12//99
Metals and Plastics	Champaign-Urbana MSA, IL	S	11.46 MW	11.70 AW	23840 AAW	ILBLS	10//99-12//99
Metals and Plastics	Chicago PMSA, IL	S	11.14 MW	11.15 AW	23170 AAW	ILBLS	10//99-12//99
Metals and Plastics	Decatur MSA, IL	S	17.71 MW	17.00 AW	36840 AAW	ILBLS	10//99-12//99
Metals and Plastics	Kankakee PMSA, IL	S	12.28 MW	12.13 AW	25550 AAW	ILBLS	10//99-12//99
Metals and Plastics	Peoria-Pekin MSA, IL	S	11.53 MW	12.00 AW	23980 AAW	ILBLS	10//99-12//99
Metals and Plastics	Rockford MSA, IL	S	11.08 MW	10.30 AW	23050 AAW	ILBLS	10//99-12//99
Metals and Plastics	Springfield MSA, IL	S	15.16 MW	15.20 AW	31530 AAW	ILBLS	10//99-12//99
Metals and Plastics	Indiana	S	10.94 MW	11.37 AW	23650 AAW	INBLS	10//99-12//99
Metals and Plastics	Bloomington MSA, IN	S	10.27 MW	10.66 AW	21370 AAW	INBLS	10//99-12//99
Metals and Plastics	Elkhart-Goshen MSA, IN	S	10.31 MW	10.08 AW	21440 AAW	INBLS	10//99-12//99
Metals and Plastics	Evansville-Henderson MSA, IN-KY	S	10.54 MW	10.19 AW	21930 AAW	INBLS	10//99-12//99
Metals and Plastics	Fort Wayne MSA, IN	S	11.39 MW	11.13 AW	23700 AAW	INBLS	10//99-12//99
Metals and Plastics	Gary PMSA, IN	S	15.53 MW	16.21 AW	32300 AAW	INBLS	10//99-12//99
Metals and Plastics	Indianapolis MSA, IN	S	9.71 MW	9.35 AW	20190 AAW	INBLS	10//99-12//99
Metals and Plastics	Kokomo MSA, IN	S	15.11 MW	13.32 AW	31430 AAW	INBLS	10//99-12//99
Metals and Plastics	Lafayette MSA, IN	S	8.30 MW	7.79 AW	17270 AAW	INBLS	10//99-12//99
Metals and Plastics	Muncie MSA, IN	S	9.50 MW	9.55 AW	19760 AAW	INBLS	10//99-12//99
Metals and Plastics	South Bend MSA, IN	S	10.71 MW	11.03 AW	22270 AAW	INBLS	10//99-12//99
Metals and Plastics	Terre Haute MSA, IN	S	9.46 MW	9.21 AW	19670 AAW	INBLS	10//99-12//99
Metals and Plastics	Iowa	S	12.48 MW	12.32 AW	25630 AAW	IABLS	10//99-12//99
Metals and Plastics	Cedar Rapids MSA, IA	S	17.62 MW	18.45 AW	36660 AAW	IABLS	10//99-12//99
Metals and Plastics	Davenport-Moline-Rock Island MSA, IA-IL	S	10.43 MW	10.35 AW	21680 AAW	IABLS	10//99-12//99
Metals and Plastics	Des Moines MSA, IA	S	13.48 MW	14.56 AW	28030 AAW	IABLS	10//99-12//99
Metals and Plastics	Dubuque MSA, IA	S	12.34 MW	12.76 AW	25670 AAW	IABLS	10//99-12//99
Metals and Plastics	Waterloo-Cedar Falls MSA, IA	S	12.67 MW	12.66 AW	26350 AAW	IABLS	10//99-12//99
Metals and Plastics	Kansas	S	11.21 MW	12.14 AW	25250 AAW	KSBLS	10//99-12//99
Metals and Plastics	Topeka MSA, KS	S	12.72 MW	12.57 AW	26460 AAW	KSBLS	10//99-12//99
Metals and Plastics	Wichita MSA, KS	S	12.97 MW	11.65 AW	26980 AAW	KSBLS	10//99-12//99
Metals and Plastics	Kentucky	S	11.89 MW	12.10 AW	25170 AAW	KYBLS	10//99-12//99
Metals and Plastics	Lexington MSA, KY	S	12.24 MW	12.50 AW	25460 AAW	KYBLS	10//99-12//99
Metals and Plastics	Louisville MSA, KY-IN	S	10.97 MW	10.44 AW	22820 AAW	KYBLS	10//99-12//99
Metals and Plastics	Louisiana	S	9.91 MW	10.09 AW	20980 AAW	LABLS	10//99-12//99
Metals and Plastics	Baton Rouge MSA, LA	S	8.91 MW	8.17 AW	18530 AAW	LABLS	10//99-12//99
Metals and Plastics	Lafayette MSA, LA	S	13.29 MW	9.94 AW	27640 AAW	LABLS	10//99-12//99
Metals and Plastics	New Orleans MSA, LA	S	11.90 MW	11.58 AW	24740 AAW	LABLS	10//99-12//99
Metals and Plastics	Shreveport-Bossier City MSA, LA	S	7.24 MW	6.95 AW	15050 AAW	LABLS	10//99-12//99
Metals and Plastics	Maine	S	10.46 MW	10.76 AW	22390 AAW	MEBLS	10//99-12//99
Metals and Plastics	Portland MSA, ME	S	11.00 MW	10.02 AW	22890 AAW	MEBLS	10//99-12//99
Metals and Plastics	Maryland	S	12.33 MW	12.55 AW	26110 AAW	MDBLS	10//99-12//99
Metals and Plastics	Baltimore PMSA, MD	S	12.67 MW	12.52 AW	26340 AAW	MDBLS	10//99-12//99
Metals and Plastics	Massachusetts	S	11.47 MW	12.18 AW	25330 AAW	MABLS	10//99-12//99
Metals and Plastics	Boston PMSA, MA-NH	S	12.41 MW	11.17 AW	25810 AAW	MABLS	10//99-12//99
Metals and Plastics	Brockton PMSA, MA	S	10.80 MW	10.77 AW	22470 AAW	MABLS	10//99-12//99
Metals and Plastics	Fitchburg-Leominster PMSA, MA	S	9.52 MW	8.47 AW	19810 AAW	MABLS	10//99-12//99
Metals and Plastics	Lawrence PMSA, MA-NH	S	10.96 MW	10.27 AW	22790 AAW	MABLS	10//99-12//99
Metals and Plastics	Lowell PMSA, MA-NH	S	12.24 MW	11.53 AW	25470 AAW	MABLS	10//99-12//99
Metals and Plastics	New Bedford PMSA, MA	S	12.76 MW	12.69 AW	26530 AAW	MABLS	10//99-12//99
Metals and Plastics	Springfield MSA, MA	S	12.81 MW	12.46 AW	26640 AAW	MABLS	10//99-12//99
Metals and Plastics	Worcester PMSA, MA-CT	S	13.03 MW	12.53 AW	27100 AAW	MABLS	10//99-12//99
Metals and Plastics	Michigan	S	10.65 MW	12.54 AW	26080 AAW	MIBLS	10//99-12//99
Metals and Plastics	Ann Arbor PMSA, MI	S	15.55 MW	13.90 AW	32340 AAW	MIBLS	10//99-12//99
Metals and Plastics	Benton Harbor MSA, MI	S	9.86 MW	9.17 AW	20500 AAW	MIBLS	10//99-12//99
Metals and Plastics	Detroit PMSA, MI	S	12.33 MW	10.38 AW	25640 AAW	MIBLS	10//99-12//99
Metals and Plastics	Flint PMSA, MI	S	22.73 MW	23.78 AW	47270 AAW	MIBLS	10//99-12//99

Occupation/Type/Industry	Location	Per	Low	Mid	High	Source	Date
Cutting, Punching, and Press Machine Setter, Operator, and Tender							
Metals and Plastics	Grand Rapids-Muskegon-Holland MSA, MI	S	13.60 MW	12.60 AW	28280 AAW	MIBLS	10//99-12//99
Metals and Plastics	Jackson MSA, MI	S	10.53 MW	9.99 AW	21890 AAW	MIBLS	10//99-12//99
Metals and Plastics	Kalamazoo-Battle Creek MSA, MI	S	11.26 MW	9.18 AW	23410 AAW	MIBLS	10//99-12//99
Metals and Plastics	Lansing-East Lansing MSA, MI	S	10.29 MW	9.89 AW	21390 AAW	MIBLS	10//99-12//99
Metals and Plastics	Saginaw-Bay City-Midland MSA, MI	S	11.89 MW	11.94 AW	24730 AAW	MIBLS	10//99-12//99
Metals and Plastics	Minnesota	S	12.57 MW	12.53 AW	26070 AAW	MNBLS	10//99-12//99
Metals and Plastics	Duluth-Superior MSA, MN-WI	S	8.96 MW	8.36 AW	18630 AAW	MNBLS	10//99-12//99
Metals and Plastics	Minneapolis-St. Paul MSA, MN-WI	S	12.78 MW	12.86 AW	26570 AAW	MNBLS	10//99-12//99
Metals and Plastics	Mississippi	S	10.2 MW	10.44 AW	21710 AAW	MSBLS	10//99-12//99
Metals and Plastics	Jackson MSA, MS	S	8.81 MW	8.29 AW	18330 AAW	MSBLS	10//99-12//99
Metals and Plastics	Missouri	S	10.46 MW	10.74 AW	22330 AAW	MOBLS	10//99-12//99
Metals and Plastics	Joplin MSA, MO	S	9.70 MW	9.69 AW	20180 AAW	MOBLS	10//99-12//99
Metals and Plastics	Kansas City MSA, MO-KS	S	12.84 MW	12.55 AW	26700 AAW	MOBLS	10//99-12//99
Metals and Plastics	St. Louis MSA, MO-IL	S	11.49 MW	11.13 AW	23890 AAW	MOBLS	10//99-12//99
Metals and Plastics	Montana	S	10.65 MW	10.51 AW	21850 AAW	MTBLS	10//99-12//99
Metals and Plastics	Nebraska	S	8.4 MW	9.33 AW	19410 AAW	NEBLS	10//99-12//99
Metals and Plastics	Lincoln MSA, NE	S	11.39 MW	10.29 AW	23690 AAW	NEBLS	10//99-12//99
Metals and Plastics	Omaha MSA, NE-IA	S	8.78 MW	7.81 AW	18260 AAW	NEBLS	10//99-12//99
Metals and Plastics	Nevada	S	11.19 MW	11.79 AW	24530 AAW	NVBLS	10//99-12//99
Metals and Plastics	Las Vegas MSA, NV-AZ	S	11.89 MW	9.80 AW	24740 AAW	NVBLS	10//99-12//99
Metals and Plastics	Reno MSA, NV	S	11.70 MW	11.69 AW	24330 AAW	NVBLS	10//99-12//99
Metals and Plastics	New Hampshire	S	8.39 MW	9.10 AW	18930 AAW	NHBLS	10//99-12//99
Metals and Plastics	Manchester PMSA, NH	S	8.49 MW	7.91 AW	17660 AAW	NHBLS	10//99-12//99
Metals and Plastics	Nashua PMSA, NH	S	9.84 MW	9.57 AW	20460 AAW	NHBLS	10//99-12//99
Metals and Plastics	Portsmouth-Rochester PMSA, NH-ME	S	9.61 MW	9.34 AW	19990 AAW	NHBLS	10//99-12//99
Metals and Plastics	New Jersey	S	10.42 MW	11.08 AW	23040 AAW	NJBLS	10//99-12//99
Metals and Plastics	Bergen-Passaic PMSA, NJ	S	12.70 MW	12.66 AW	26420 AAW	NJBLS	10//99-12//99
Metals and Plastics	Jersey City PMSA, NJ	S	10.19 MW	9.06 AW	21200 AAW	NJBLS	10//99-12//99
Metals and Plastics	Middlesex-Somerset-Hunterdon PMSA, NJ	S	11.78 MW	10.82 AW	24500 AAW	NJBLS	10//99-12//99
Metals and Plastics	Monmouth-Ocean PMSA, NJ	S	11.70 MW	11.59 AW	24340 AAW	NJBLS	10//99-12//99
Metals and Plastics	Newark PMSA, NJ	S	9.78 MW	9.10 AW	20340 AAW	NJBLS	10//99-12//99
Metals and Plastics	Trenton PMSA, NJ	S	9.64 MW	9.38 AW	20040 AAW	NJBLS	10//99-12//99
Metals and Plastics	New Mexico	S	8.58 MW	8.81 AW	18320 AAW	NMBLS	10//99-12//99
Metals and Plastics	Albuquerque MSA, NM	S	8.78 MW	8.60 AW	18260 AAW	NMBLS	10//99-12//99
Metals and Plastics	Las Cruces MSA, NM	S	7.10 MW	7.36 AW	14770 AAW	NMBLS	10//99-12//99
Metals and Plastics	New York	S	9.87 MW	10.50 AW	21850 AAW	NYBLS	10//99-12//99
Metals and Plastics	Albany-Schenectady-Troy MSA, NY	S	11.11 MW	9.99 AW	23110 AAW	NYBLS	10//99-12//99
Metals and Plastics	Binghamton MSA, NY	S	10.15 MW	11.11 AW	21120 AAW	NYBLS	10//99-12//99
Metals and Plastics	Buffalo-Niagara Falls MSA, NY	S	10.78 MW	9.97 AW	22420 AAW	NYBLS	10//99-12//99
Metals and Plastics	Dutchess County PMSA, NY	S	14.39 MW	14.72 AW	29930 AAW	NYBLS	10//99-12//99
Metals and Plastics	Elmira MSA, NY	S	9.86 MW	9.23 AW	20500 AAW	NYBLS	10//99-12//99
Metals and Plastics	Glens Falls MSA, NY	S	13.82 MW	14.04 AW	28740 AAW	NYBLS	10//99-12//99
Metals and Plastics	Jamestown MSA, NY	S	8.30 MW	8.20 AW	17260 AAW	NYBLS	10//99-12//99
Metals and Plastics	Nassau-Suffolk PMSA, NY	S	10.74 MW	9.89 AW	22330 AAW	NYBLS	10//99-12//99
Metals and Plastics	New York PMSA, NY	S	10.06 MW	9.35 AW	20930 AAW	NYBLS	10//99-12//99
Metals and Plastics	Newburgh PMSA, NY-PA	S	11.24 MW	11.66 AW	23380 AAW	NYBLS	10//99-12//99
Metals and Plastics	Rochester MSA, NY	S	10.44 MW	9.74 AW	21710 AAW	NYBLS	10//99-12//99
Metals and Plastics	Syracuse MSA, NY	S	9.65 MW	9.24 AW	20070 AAW	NYBLS	10//99-12//99
Metals and Plastics	Utica-Rome MSA, NY	S	10.90 MW	10.00 AW	22670 AAW	NYBLS	10//99-12//99
Metals and Plastics	North Carolina	S	10.31 MW	10.93 AW	22730 AAW	NCBLS	10//99-12//99
Metals and Plastics	Asheville MSA, NC	S	12.36 MW	12.88 AW	25710 AAW	NCBLS	10//99-12//99
Metals and Plastics	Charlotte-Gastonia-Rock Hill MSA, NC-SC	S	11.60 MW	10.71 AW	24120 AAW	NCBLS	10//99-12//99
Metals and Plastics	Fayetteville MSA, NC	S	8.36 MW	8.09 AW	17380 AAW	NCBLS	10//99-12//99
Metals and Plastics	Goldsboro MSA, NC	S	7.38 MW	7.28 AW	15350 AAW	NCBLS	10//99-12//99
Metals and Plastics	Greensboro--Winston-Salem--High Point MSA, NC	S	10.81 MW	10.63 AW	22480 AAW	NCBLS	10//99-12//99
Metals and Plastics	Hickory-Morganton-Lenoir MSA, NC	S	9.63 MW	9.44 AW	20030 AAW	NCBLS	10//99-12//99
Metals and Plastics	Raleigh-Durham-Chapel Hill MSA, NC	S	11.41 MW	10.74 AW	23730 AAW	NCBLS	10//99-12//99

Occupation/Type/Industry	Location	Per	Low	Mid	High	Source	Date
Cutting, Punching, and Press Machine Setter, Operator, and Tender							
Metals and Plastics	Rocky Mount MSA, NC	S	12.26 MW	11.92 AW	25500 AAW	NCBLS	10//99-12//99
Metals and Plastics	North Dakota	S	9.26 MW	9.44 AW	19640 AAW	NDBLS	10//99-12//99
Metals and Plastics	Bismarck MSA, ND	S	8.48 MW	8.45 AW	17640 AAW	NDBLS	10//99-12//99
Metals and Plastics	Fargo-Moorhead MSA, ND-MN	S	9.77 MW	9.53 AW	20320 AAW	NDBLS	10//99-12//99
Metals and Plastics	Ohio	S	10.83 MW	11.84 AW	24630 AAW	OHBLS	10//99-12//99
Metals and Plastics	Akron PMSA, OH	S	10.10 MW	9.69 AW	21010 AAW	OHBLS	10//99-12//99
Metals and Plastics	Canton-Massillon MSA, OH	S	12.17 MW	11.76 AW	25310 AAW	OHBLS	10//99-12//99
Metals and Plastics	Cincinnati PMSA, OH-KY-IN	S	13.63 MW	13.12 AW	28340 AAW	OHBLS	10//99-12//99
Metals and Plastics	Cleveland-Lorain-Elyria PMSA, OH	S	12.28 MW	11.99 AW	25540 AAW	OHBLS	10//99-12//99
Metals and Plastics	Columbus MSA, OH	S	12.54 MW	10.14 AW	26090 AAW	OHBLS	10//99-12//99
Metals and Plastics	Dayton-Springfield MSA, OH	S	10.66 MW	9.74 AW	22170 AAW	OHBLS	10//99-12//99
Metals and Plastics	Lima MSA, OH	S	11.15 MW	10.54 AW	23190 AAW	OHBLS	10//99-12//99
Metals and Plastics	Mansfield MSA, OH	S	12.81 MW	8.89 AW	26640 AAW	OHBLS	10//99-12//99
Metals and Plastics	Toledo MSA, OH	S	10.80 MW	10.08 AW	22470 AAW	OHBLS	10//99-12//99
Metals and Plastics	Youngstown-Warren MSA, OH	S	13.91 MW	13.09 AW	28930 AAW	OHBLS	10//99-12//99
Metals and Plastics	Oklahoma	S	8.45 MW	9.63 AW	20040 AAW	OKBLS	10//99-12//99
Metals and Plastics	Oklahoma City MSA, OK	S	7.84 MW	7.70 AW	16300 AAW	OKBLS	10//99-12//99
Metals and Plastics	Tulsa MSA, OK	S	10.70 MW	9.98 AW	22260 AAW	OKBLS	10//99-12//99
Metals and Plastics	Oregon	S	12.05 MW	12.71 AW	26430 AAW	ORBLS	10//99-12//99
Metals and Plastics	Eugene-Springfield MSA, OR	S	10.71 MW	10.48 AW	22280 AAW	ORBLS	10//99-12//99
Metals and Plastics	Portland-Vancouver PMSA, OR-WA	S	13.24 MW	12.56 AW	27530 AAW	ORBLS	10//99-12//99
Metals and Plastics	Salem PMSA, OR	S	11.77 MW	12.08 AW	24480 AAW	ORBLS	10//99-12//99
Metals and Plastics	Pennsylvania	S	12.49 MW	12.73 AW	26480 AAW	PABLS	10//99-12//99
Metals and Plastics	Allentown-Bethlehem-Easton MSA, PA	S	12.31 MW	12.36 AW	25600 AAW	PABLS	10//99-12//99
Metals and Plastics	Altoona MSA, PA	S	8.46 MW	6.49 AW	17600 AAW	PABLS	10//99-12//99
Metals and Plastics	Erie MSA, PA	S	10.00 MW	9.89 AW	20800 AAW	PABLS	10//99-12//99
Metals and Plastics	Harrisburg-Lebanon-Carlisle MSA, PA	S	14.67 MW	14.55 AW	30500 AAW	PABLS	10//99-12//99
Metals and Plastics	Johnstown MSA, PA	S	11.70 MW	11.46 AW	24340 AAW	PABLS	10//99-12//99
Metals and Plastics	Lancaster MSA, PA	S	16.91 MW	17.02 AW	35180 AAW	PABLS	10//99-12//99
Metals and Plastics	Philadelphia PMSA, PA-NJ	S	13.54 MW	13.52 AW	28170 AAW	PABLS	10//99-12//99
Metals and Plastics	Pittsburgh MSA, PA	S	12.76 MW	11.78 AW	26540 AAW	PABLS	10//99-12//99
Metals and Plastics	Reading MSA, PA	S	14.37 MW	14.73 AW	29880 AAW	PABLS	10//99-12//99
Metals and Plastics	Scranton--Wilkes-Barre--Hazleton MSA, PA	S	12.12 MW	12.43 AW	25210 AAW	PABLS	10//99-12//99
Metals and Plastics	Sharon MSA, PA	S	12.75 MW	12.30 AW	26520 AAW	PABLS	10//99-12//99
Metals and Plastics	Williamsport MSA, PA	S	9.58 MW	9.52 AW	19920 AAW	PABLS	10//99-12//99
Metals and Plastics	York MSA, PA	S	14.40 MW	13.66 AW	29940 AAW	PABLS	10//99-12//99
Metals and Plastics	Rhode Island	S	9.26 MW	10.07 AW	20940 AAW	RIBLS	10//99-12//99
Metals and Plastics	Providence-Fall River-Warwick MSA, RI-MA	S	10.24 MW	9.54 AW	21310 AAW	RIBLS	10//99-12//99
Metals and Plastics	South Carolina	S	11.15 MW	11.26 AW	23420 AAW	SCBLS	10//99-12//99
Metals and Plastics	Charleston-North Charleston MSA, SC	S	7.61 MW	7.64 AW	15820 AAW	SCBLS	10//99-12//99
Metals and Plastics	Columbia MSA, SC	S	13.82 MW	12.51 AW	28740 AAW	SCBLS	10//99-12//99
Metals and Plastics	Florence MSA, SC	S	15.42 MW	17.18 AW	32070 AAW	SCBLS	10//99-12//99
Metals and Plastics	Greenville-Spartanburg-Anderson MSA, SC	S	10.82 MW	10.41 AW	22510 AAW	SCBLS	10//99-12//99
Metals and Plastics	South Dakota	S	10.37 MW	10.67 AW	22200 AAW	SDBLS	10//99-12//99
Metals and Plastics	Rapid City MSA, SD	S	8.85 MW	9.07 AW	18410 AAW	SDBLS	10//99-12//99
Metals and Plastics	Sioux Falls MSA, SD	S	12.75 MW	12.55 AW	26520 AAW	SDBLS	10//99-12//99
Metals and Plastics	Tennessee	S	10.05 MW	10.39 AW	21600 AAW	TNBLS	10//99-12//99
Metals and Plastics	Chattanooga MSA, TN-GA	S	10.83 MW	10.91 AW	22520 AAW	TNBLS	10//99-12//99
Metals and Plastics	Clarksville-Hopkinsville MSA, TN-KY	S	11.29 MW	11.50 AW	23480 AAW	TNBLS	10//99-12//99
Metals and Plastics	Jackson MSA, TN	S	9.44 MW	8.86 AW	19630 AAW	TNBLS	10//99-12//99
Metals and Plastics	Johnson City-Kingsport-Bristol MSA, TN-VA	S	9.20 MW	8.93 AW	19130 AAW	TNBLS	10//99-12//99
Metals and Plastics	Knoxville MSA, TN	S	11.21 MW	10.84 AW	23310 AAW	TNBLS	10//99-12//99
Metals and Plastics	Memphis MSA, TN-AR-MS	S	10.59 MW	10.74 AW	22020 AAW	MSBLS	10//99-12//99
Metals and Plastics	Nashville MSA, TN	S	11.01 MW	10.00 AW	22910 AAW	TNBLS	10//99-12//99
Metals and Plastics	Texas	S	9.04 MW	9.53 AW	19830 AAW	TXBLS	10//99-12//99
Metals and Plastics	Abilene MSA, TX	S	9.05 MW	10.77 AW	18820 AAW	TXBLS	10//99-12//99
Metals and Plastics	Austin-San Marcos MSA, TX	S	10.13 MW	9.44 AW	21060 AAW	TXBLS	10//99-12//99

Occupation/Type/Industry	Location	Per	Low	Mid	High	Source	Date
Cutting, Punching, and Press Machine Setter, Operator, and Tender							
Metals and Plastics	Beaumont-Port Arthur MSA, TX	S	10.30 MW	10.63 AW	21420 AAW	TXBLS	10//99-12//99
Metals and Plastics	Brownsville-Harlingen-San Benito MSA, TX	S	9.16 MW	9.31 AW	19060 AAW	TXBLS	10//99-12//99
Metals and Plastics	Corpus Christi MSA, TX	S	8.55 MW	8.58 AW	17790 AAW	TXBLS	10//99-12//99
Metals and Plastics	Dallas PMSA, TX	S	9.96 MW	9.44 AW	20730 AAW	TXBLS	10//99-12//99
Metals and Plastics	El Paso MSA, TX	S	8.45 MW	8.57 AW	17570 AAW	TXBLS	10//99-12//99
Metals and Plastics	Fort Worth-Arlington PMSA, TX	S	9.17 MW	8.25 AW	19070 AAW	TXBLS	10//99-12//99
Metals and Plastics	Houston PMSA, TX	S	10.25 MW	9.88 AW	21320 AAW	TXBLS	10//99-12//99
Metals and Plastics	Killeen-Temple MSA, TX	S	8.56 MW	8.97 AW	17800 AAW	TXBLS	10//99-12//99
Metals and Plastics	Longview-Marshall MSA, TX	S	8.75 MW	8.43 AW	18200 AAW	TXBLS	10//99-12//99
Metals and Plastics	Lubbock MSA, TX	S	10.38 MW	10.24 AW	21590 AAW	TXBLS	10//99-12//99
Metals and Plastics	Odessa-Midland MSA, TX	S	8.32 MW	7.82 AW	17310 AAW	TXBLS	10//99-12//99
Metals and Plastics	San Antonio MSA, TX	S	8.31 MW	7.97 AW	17280 AAW	TXBLS	10//99-12//99
Metals and Plastics	Sherman-Denison MSA, TX	S	8.71 MW	8.31 AW	18120 AAW	TXBLS	10//99-12//99
Metals and Plastics	Texarkana MSA, TX-Texarkana, AR	S	11.83 MW	12.08 AW	24600 AAW	TXBLS	10//99-12//99
Metals and Plastics	Tyler MSA, TX	S	10.24 MW	10.28 AW	21300 AAW	TXBLS	10//99-12//99
Metals and Plastics	Utah	S	10.05 MW	10.30 AW	21410 AAW	UTBLS	10//99-12//99
Metals and Plastics	Provo-Orem MSA, UT	S	11.49 MW	11.77 AW	23890 AAW	UTBLS	10//99-12//99
Metals and Plastics	Salt Lake City-Ogden MSA, UT	S	10.07 MW	9.78 AW	20940 AAW	UTBLS	10//99-12//99
Metals and Plastics	Vermont	S	9.76 MW	10.06 AW	20910 AAW	VTBLS	10//99-12//99
Metals and Plastics	Burlington MSA, VT	S	12.22 MW	12.26 AW	25420 AAW	VTBLS	10//99-12//99
Metals and Plastics	Virginia	S	14.14 MW	13.36 AW	27790 AAW	VABLS	10//99-12//99
Metals and Plastics	Lynchburg MSA, VA	S	11.30 MW	11.69 AW	23510 AAW	VABLS	10//99-12//99
Metals and Plastics	Norfolk-Virginia Beach-Newport News MSA, VA-NC	S	13.67 MW	14.30 AW	28430 AAW	VABLS	10//99-12//99
Metals and Plastics	Richmond-Petersburg MSA, VA	S	11.62 MW	11.37 AW	24180 AAW	VABLS	10//99-12//99
Metals and Plastics	Washington	S	11.91 MW	12.73 AW	26480 AAW	WABLS	10//99-12//99
Metals and Plastics	Bellingham MSA, WA	S	13.58 MW	13.90 AW	28240 AAW	WABLS	10//99-12//99
Metals and Plastics	Olympia PMSA, WA	S	19.11 MW	19.22 AW	39750 AAW	WABLS	10//99-12//99
Metals and Plastics	Seattle-Bellevue-Everett PMSA, WA	S	11.81 MW	11.54 AW	24560 AAW	WABLS	10//99-12//99
Metals and Plastics	Spokane MSA, WA	S	10.98 MW	10.99 AW	22840 AAW	WABLS	10//99-12//99
Metals and Plastics	Tacoma PMSA, WA	S	13.46 MW	11.65 AW	27990 AAW	WABLS	10//99-12//99
Metals and Plastics	Yakima MSA, WA	S	9.71 MW	8.49 AW	20190 AAW	WABLS	10//99-12//99
Metals and Plastics	West Virginia	S	8.26 MW	8.51 AW	17690 AAW	WVBLS	10//99-12//99
Metals and Plastics	Huntington-Ashland MSA, WV-KY-OH	S	12.40 MW	10.11 AW	25800 AAW	WVBLS	10//99-12//99
Metals and Plastics	Parkersburg-Marietta MSA, WV-OH	S	8.58 MW	8.46 AW	17850 AAW	WVBLS	10//99-12//99
Metals and Plastics	Wisconsin	S	11.03 MW	11.75 AW	24440 AAW	WIBLS	10//99-12//99
Metals and Plastics	Appleton-Oshkosh-Neenah MSA, WI	S	11.67 MW	11.94 AW	24270 AAW	WIBLS	10//99-12//99
Metals and Plastics	Eau Claire MSA, WI	S	12.18 MW	12.14 AW	25330 AAW	WIBLS	10//99-12//99
Metals and Plastics	Green Bay MSA, WI	S	12.06 MW	11.52 AW	25080 AAW	WIBLS	10//99-12//99
Metals and Plastics	Janesville-Beloit MSA, WI	S	12.03 MW	11.47 AW	25030 AAW	WIBLS	10//99-12//99
Metals and Plastics	Kenosha PMSA, WI	S	11.38 MW	10.83 AW	23670 AAW	WIBLS	10//99-12//99
Metals and Plastics	La Crosse MSA, WI-MN	S	12.12 MW	12.24 AW	25220 AAW	WIBLS	10//99-12//99
Metals and Plastics	Madison MSA, WI	S	12.12 MW	12.29 AW	25210 AAW	WIBLS	10//99-12//99
Metals and Plastics	Milwaukee-Waukesha PMSA, WI	S	12.22 MW	11.17 AW	25430 AAW	WIBLS	10//99-12//99
Metals and Plastics	Racine PMSA, WI	S	11.18 MW	10.59 AW	23260 AAW	WIBLS	10//99-12//99
Metals and Plastics	Sheboygan MSA, WI	S	12.94 MW	13.51 AW	26920 AAW	WIBLS	10//99-12//99
Metals and Plastics	Wausau MSA, WI	S	12.82 MW	12.80 AW	26660 AAW	WIBLS	10//99-12//99
Metals and Plastics	Wyoming	S	10.19 MW	10.11 AW	21030 AAW	WYBLS	10//99-12//99
Metals and Plastics	Puerto Rico	S	6.55 MW	6.94 AW	14430 AAW	PRBLS	10//99-12//99
Metals and Plastics	Caguas PMSA, PR	S	6.49 MW	6.18 AW	13490 AAW	PRBLS	10//99-12//99
Metals and Plastics	Mayaguez MSA, PR	S	5.96 MW	6.06 AW	12390 AAW	PRBLS	10//99-12//99
Metals and Plastics	San Juan-Bayamon PMSA, PR	S	7.26 MW	6.87 AW	15100 AAW	PRBLS	10//99-12//99
Cytotechnologist							
Medical Laboratory	Atlantic	H	15.00 AE	18.70 AW	21.70 APH	LABMED2	1998
Medical Laboratory	East North Central	H	15.70 AE	19.40 AW	21.00 APH	LABMED2	1998
Medical Laboratory	Far West	H	17.70 AE	23.50 AW	24.00 APH	LABMED2	1998

AAW	Average annual wage	AOH	Average offered, high	ASH	Average starting, high
AE	Average entry wage	AOL	Average offered, low	ASL	Average starting, low
AEX	Average experienced wage	APH	Average pay, high range	AW	Average wage paid
AO	Average offered	APL	Average pay, low range	FQ	First quartile wage

H	Hourly	M	Monthly
HI	Highest wage paid	MTC	Median total compensation
HR	High end range	MW	Median wage paid
LR	Low end range	SQ	Second quartile wage

S	Special: hourly and annual
TQ	Third quartile wage
W	Weekly
Y	Yearly

Occupation/Type/Industry	Location	Per	Low	Mid	High	Source	Date
Cytotechnologist							
Medical Laboratory	Northeast	H	14.60 AE	19.00 AW	21.70 APH	LABMED2	1998
Medical Laboratory	West North Central	H	15.20 AE	18.00 AW	21.00 APH	LABMED2	1998
Medical Laboratory	West South Central	H	16.20 AE	21.50 AW	21.80 APH	LABMED2	1998
Dairy Herd Worker							
Beginner	Northeast	Y		19764 AE		DHMAN	11//99
Midlevel	Northeast	Y		23544 AW		DHMAN	11//99
Supervisory Level	Northeast	Y		29579 AW		DHMAN	11//99
Dairy Manager							
Agriculture	United States	Y	25000 APL	25000 AW	40000 APL	FAJO	1998
Dancer	United States	Y		18000 AW		DANCE	2000
	California	S	10.71 MW	12.20 AW	25370 AAW	CABLS	10//99-12//99
	Connecticut	S	15.37 MW	16.93 AW	35210 AAW	CTBLS	10//99-12//99
	Hartford MSA, CT	S	17.27 MW	15.61 AW	35920 AAW	CTBLS	10//99-12//99
	Florida	S	11.7 MW	10.83 AW	22530 AAW	FLBLS	10//99-12//99
	Orlando MSA, FL	S	10.96 MW	11.85 AW	22790 AAW	FLBLS	10//99-12//99
	Tampa-St. Petersburg-Clearwater MSA, FL	S	11.43 MW	11.90 AW	23770 AAW	FLBLS	10//99-12//99
	Georgia	S	12.95 MW	13.13 AW	27300 AAW	GABLS	10//99-12//99
	Atlanta MSA, GA	S	13.26 MW	13.02 AW	27580 AAW	GABLS	10//99-12//99
	Illinois	S	13.01 MW	14.50 AW	30170 AAW	ILBLS	10//99-12//99
	Chicago PMSA, IL	S	16.83 MW	17.88 AW	35000 AAW	ILBLS	10//99-12//99
	Louisiana	S	15.44 MW	15.74 AW	32750 AAW	LABLS	10//99-12//99
	Minnesota	S	11.83 MW	11.47 AW	23850 AAW	MNBLS	10//99-12//99
	Nevada	S	15.64 MW	16.68 AW	34700 AAW	NVBLS	10//99-12//99
	Las Vegas MSA, NV-AZ	S	17.52 MW	15.71 AW	36440 AAW	NVBLS	10//99-12//99
	New Jersey	S	7.73 MW	7.98 AW	16590 AAW	NJBLS	10//99-12//99
	New York	S	25.42 MW	23.38 AW	48640 AAW	NYBLS	10//99-12//99
	New York PMSA, NY	S	23.89 MW	26.49 AW	49690 AAW	NYBLS	10//99-12//99
	North Carolina	S	6.34 MW	9.90 AW	20600 AAW	NCBLS	10//99-12//99
	Pennsylvania	S	12.53 MW	15.12 AW	31450 AAW	PABLS	10//99-12//99
	Philadelphia PMSA, PA-NJ	S	11.17 MW	7.25 AW	23240 AAW	PABLS	10//99-12//99
	South Carolina	S	7.05 MW	8.43 AW	17530 AAW	SCBLS	10//99-12//99
	Tennessee	S	9.72 MW	10.33 AW	21480 AAW	TNBLS	10//99-12//99
	Salt Lake City-Ogden MSA, UT	S	7.14 MW	6.15 AW	14840 AAW	UTBLS	10//99-12//99
	Virginia	S	16.3 MW	16.14 AW	33560 AAW	VABLS	10//99-12//99
	Washington	S	16.85 MW	18.45 AW	38370 AAW	WABLS	10//99-12//99
	Seattle-Bellevue-Everett PMSA, WA	S	19.96 MW	19.71 AW	41510 AAW	WABLS	10//99-12//99
	Puerto Rico	S	6.25 MW	7.04 AW	14640 AAW	PRBLS	10//99-12//99
Major Ballet Company	United States	Y		55000 AW		DANCE	2000
Data Entry Keyer	Alabama	S	9.25 MW	9.61 AW	19990 AAW	ALBLS	10//99-12//99
	Anniston MSA, AL	S	9.26 MW	9.11 AW	19250 AAW	ALBLS	10//99-12//99
	Auburn-Opelika MSA, AL	S	8.10 MW	7.66 AW	16850 AAW	ALBLS	10//99-12//99
	Birmingham MSA, AL	S	10.76 MW	10.88 AW	22380 AAW	ALBLS	10//99-12//99
	Decatur MSA, AL	S	8.37 MW	8.04 AW	17400 AAW	ALBLS	10//99-12//99
	Dothan MSA, AL	S	8.31 MW	8.21 AW	17290 AAW	ALBLS	10//99-12//99
	Florence MSA, AL	S	9.09 MW	9.04 AW	18900 AAW	ALBLS	10//99-12//99
	Gadsden MSA, AL	S	8.55 MW	7.94 AW	17780 AAW	ALBLS	10//99-12//99
	Huntsville MSA, AL	S	9.24 MW	8.76 AW	19220 AAW	ALBLS	10//99-12//99
	Mobile MSA, AL	S	8.74 MW	8.28 AW	18180 AAW	ALBLS	10//99-12//99
	Montgomery MSA, AL	S	8.81 MW	8.69 AW	18330 AAW	ALBLS	10//99-12//99
	Tuscaloosa MSA, AL	S	8.57 MW	8.82 AW	17830 AAW	ALBLS	10//99-12//99
	Alaska	S	10.47 MW	11.36 AW	23620 AAW	AKBLS	10//99-12//99
	Anchorage MSA, AK	S	11.10 MW	10.19 AW	23090 AAW	AKBLS	10//99-12//99
	Arizona	S	9.62 MW	10.08 AW	20970 AAW	AZBLS	10//99-12//99
	Flagstaff MSA, AZ-UT	S	9.48 MW	9.28 AW	19710 AAW	AZBLS	10//99-12//99
	Phoenix-Mesa MSA, AZ	S	10.20 MW	9.72 AW	21220 AAW	AZBLS	10//99-12//99
	Tucson MSA, AZ	S	9.58 MW	9.21 AW	19920 AAW	AZBLS	10//99-12//99
	Yuma MSA, AZ	S	8.58 MW	8.35 AW	17850 AAW	AZBLS	10//99-12//99
	Arkansas	S	9.54 MW	9.67 AW	20110 AAW	ARBLS	10//99-12//99
	Fayetteville-Springdale-Rogers MSA, AR	S	8.44 MW	8.20 AW	17550 AAW	ARBLS	10//99-12//99
	Fort Smith MSA, AR-OK	S	8.32 MW	8.13 AW	17310 AAW	ARBLS	10//99-12//99
	Little Rock-North Little Rock MSA, AR	S	10.41 MW	10.80 AW	21650 AAW	ARBLS	10//99-12//99
	California	S	10.59 MW	11.00 AW	22870 AAW	CABLS	10//99-12//99
	Bakersfield MSA, CA	S	10.32 MW	9.82 AW	21460 AAW	CABLS	10//99-12//99

AAW Average annual wage	AOH Average offered, high	ASH Average starting, high	H Hourly	M Monthly	S Special: hourly and annual
AE Average entry wage	AOL Average offered, low	ASL Average starting, low	HI Highest wage paid	MTC Median total compensation	TQ Third quartile wage
AEX Average experienced wage	APH Average pay, high range	AW Average wage paid	HR High end range	MW Median wage paid	W Weekly
AO Average offered	APL Average pay, low range	FQ First quartile wage	LR Low end range	SQ Second quartile wage	Y Yearly

Occupation/Type/Industry	Location	Per	Low	Mid	High	Source	Date
Data Entry Keyer	Chico-Paradise MSA, CA	S	8.20 MW	7.39 AW	17050 AAW	CABLS	10//99-12//99
	Los Angeles-Long Beach PMSA, CA	S	10.62 MW	10.24 AW	22080 AAW	CABLS	10//99-12//99
	Merced MSA, CA	S	13.15 MW	13.39 AW	27350 AAW	CABLS	10//99-12//99
	Modesto MSA, CA	S	11.05 MW	11.44 AW	22980 AAW	CABLS	10//99-12//99
	Oakland PMSA, CA	S	11.17 MW	10.89 AW	23240 AAW	CABLS	10//99-12//99
	Orange County PMSA, CA	S	10.72 MW	10.26 AW	22290 AAW	CABLS	10//99-12//99
	Redding MSA, CA	S	10.81 MW	10.36 AW	22480 AAW	CABLS	10//99-12//99
	Riverside-San Bernardino PMSA, CA	S	11.29 MW	10.86 AW	23480 AAW	CABLS	10//99-12//99
	Sacramento PMSA, CA	S	11.37 MW	11.32 AW	23650 AAW	CABLS	10//99-12//99
	Salinas MSA, CA	S	11.38 MW	11.06 AW	23670 AAW	CABLS	10//99-12//99
	San Diego MSA, CA	S	10.47 MW	10.15 AW	21780 AAW	CABLS	10//99-12//99
	San Francisco PMSA, CA	S	12.25 MW	11.66 AW	25480 AAW	CABLS	10//99-12//99
	San Jose PMSA, CA	S	12.10 MW	11.83 AW	25170 AAW	CABLS	10//99-12//99
	San Luis Obispo-Atascadero-Paso Robles MSA, CA	S	9.71 MW	9.48 AW	20190 AAW	CABLS	10//99-12//99
	Santa Barbara-Santa Maria-Lompoc MSA, CA	S	10.69 MW	10.56 AW	22230 AAW	CABLS	10//99-12//99
	Santa Cruz-Watsonville PMSA, CA	S	10.11 MW	10.13 AW	21030 AAW	CABLS	10//99-12//99
	Santa Rosa PMSA, CA	S	10.68 MW	10.38 AW	22210 AAW	CABLS	10//99-12//99
	Stockton-Lodi MSA, CA	S	9.48 MW	9.33 AW	19710 AAW	CABLS	10//99-12//99
	Vallejo-Fairfield-Napa PMSA, CA	S	10.46 MW	10.75 AW	21760 AAW	CABLS	10//99-12//99
	Ventura PMSA, CA	S	11.84 MW	10.32 AW	24640 AAW	CABLS	10//99-12//99
	Yolo PMSA, CA	S	10.64 MW	10.44 AW	22120 AAW	CABLS	10//99-12//99
	Colorado	S	9.69 MW	10.18 AW	21170 AAW	COBLS	10//99-12//99
	Boulder-Longmont PMSA, CO	S	9.24 MW	8.98 AW	19220 AAW	COBLS	10//99-12//99
	Colorado Springs MSA, CO	S	10.39 MW	9.96 AW	21620 AAW	COBLS	10//99-12//99
	Denver PMSA, CO	S	10.13 MW	9.88 AW	21080 AAW	COBLS	10//99-12//99
	Fort Collins-Loveland MSA, CO	S	9.35 MW	8.89 AW	19440 AAW	COBLS	10//99-12//99
	Greeley PMSA, CO	S	10.72 MW	9.03 AW	22300 AAW	COBLS	10//99-12//99
	Pueblo MSA, CO	S	8.71 MW	8.39 AW	18130 AAW	COBLS	10//99-12//99
	Connecticut	S	10.48 MW	10.75 AW	22370 AAW	CTBLS	10//99-12//99
	Bridgeport PMSA, CT	S	11.28 MW	10.86 AW	23460 AAW	CTBLS	10//99-12//99
	Danbury PMSA, CT	S	12.14 MW	11.41 AW	25250 AAW	CTBLS	10//99-12//99
	Hartford MSA, CT	S	10.56 MW	10.08 AW	21970 AAW	CTBLS	10//99-12//99
	New Haven-Meriden PMSA, CT	S	10.53 MW	10.41 AW	21890 AAW	CTBLS	10//99-12//99
	New London-Norwich MSA, CT-RI	S	10.78 MW	10.29 AW	22410 AAW	CTBLS	10//99-12//99
	Stamford-Norwalk PMSA, CT	S	10.70 MW	10.98 AW	22260 AAW	CTBLS	10//99-12//99
	Waterbury PMSA, CT	S	10.58 MW	10.45 AW	22000 AAW	CTBLS	10//99-12//99
	Delaware	S	9.61 MW	10.25 AW	21320 AAW	DEBLS	10//99-12//99
	Dover MSA, DE	S	10.27 MW	10.02 AW	21370 AAW	DEBLS	10//99-12//99
	Wilmington-Newark PMSA, DE-MD	S	10.48 MW	9.77 AW	21790 AAW	DEBLS	10//99-12//99
	District of Columbia	S	10.59 MW	11.47 AW	23860 AAW	DCBLS	10//99-12//99
	Washington PMSA, DC-MD-VA-WV	S	10.73 MW	10.43 AW	22320 AAW	DCBLS	10//99-12//99
	Florida	S	8.89 MW	9.33 AW	19410 AAW	FLBLS	10//99-12//99
	Daytona Beach MSA, FL	S	8.25 MW	8.03 AW	17170 AAW	FLBLS	10//99-12//99
	Fort Lauderdale PMSA, FL	S	11.08 MW	10.87 AW	23040 AAW	FLBLS	10//99-12//99
	Fort Myers-Cape Coral MSA, FL	S	8.34 MW	8.11 AW	17340 AAW	FLBLS	10//99-12//99
	Fort Pierce-Port St. Lucie MSA, FL	S	8.14 MW	7.92 AW	16940 AAW	FLBLS	10//99-12//99
	Fort Walton Beach MSA, FL	S	8.91 MW	8.85 AW	18540 AAW	FLBLS	10//99-12//99
	Gainesville MSA, FL	S	8.28 MW	8.11 AW	17220 AAW	FLBLS	10//99-12//99
	Jacksonville MSA, FL	S	9.46 MW	9.14 AW	19680 AAW	FLBLS	10//99-12//99
	Lakeland-Winter Haven MSA, FL	S	8.91 MW	8.24 AW	18530 AAW	FLBLS	10//99-12//99
	Melbourne-Titusville-Palm Bay MSA, FL	S	9.09 MW	9.11 AW	18900 AAW	FLBLS	10//99-12//99
	Miami PMSA, FL	S	9.57 MW	9.43 AW	19900 AAW	FLBLS	10//99-12//99
	Naples MSA, FL	S	10.31 MW	10.00 AW	21450 AAW	FLBLS	10//99-12//99
	Ocala MSA, FL	S	8.48 MW	8.67 AW	17640 AAW	FLBLS	10//99-12//99
	Orlando MSA, FL	S	8.90 MW	8.42 AW	18520 AAW	FLBLS	10//99-12//99
	Panama City MSA, FL	S	9.90 MW	9.58 AW	20590 AAW	FLBLS	10//99-12//99
	Pensacola MSA, FL	S	8.53 MW	8.19 AW	17740 AAW	FLBLS	10//99-12//99

AAW Average annual wage	**AOH** Average offered, high	**ASH** Average starting, high	**H** Hourly	**M** Monthly	**S** Special: hourly and annual
AE Average entry wage	**AOL** Average offered, low	**ASL** Average starting, low	**HI** Highest wage paid	**MTC** Median total compensation	**TQ** Third quartile wage
AEX Average experienced wage	**APH** Average pay, high range	**AW** Average wage paid	**HR** High end range	**MW** Median wage paid	**W** Weekly
AO Average offered	**APL** Average pay, low range	**FQ** First quartile wage	**LR** Low end range	**SQ** Second quartile wage	**Y** Yearly

Occupation/Type/Industry	Location	Per	Low	Mid	High	Source	Date
Data Entry Keyer	Punta Gorda MSA, FL	S	7.80 MW	7.60 AW	16220 AAW	FLBLS	10//99-12//99
	Sarasota-Bradenton MSA, FL	S	8.35 MW	8.10 AW	17360 AAW	FLBLS	10//99-12//99
	Tallahassee MSA, FL	S	9.01 MW	8.73 AW	18730 AAW	FLBLS	10//99-12//99
	Tampa-St. Petersburg-Clearwater MSA, FL	S	9.63 MW	9.27 AW	20030 AAW	FLBLS	10//99-12//99
	West Palm Beach-Boca Raton MSA, FL	S	9.31 MW	8.98 AW	19360 AAW	FLBLS	10//99-12//99
	Georgia	S	9.94 MW	10.16 AW	21120 AAW	GABLS	10//99-12//99
	Albany MSA, GA	S	7.84 MW	7.71 AW	16300 AAW	GABLS	10//99-12//99
	Athens MSA, GA	S	9.10 MW	8.76 AW	18930 AAW	GABLS	10//99-12//99
	Atlanta MSA, GA	S	10.59 MW	10.31 AW	22020 AAW	GABLS	10//99-12//99
	Augusta-Aiken MSA, GA-SC	S	9.53 MW	9.51 AW	19820 AAW	GABLS	10//99-12//99
	Columbus MSA, GA-AL	S	9.98 MW	10.19 AW	20770 AAW	GABLS	10//99-12//99
	Macon MSA, GA	S	8.76 MW	8.85 AW	18220 AAW	GABLS	10//99-12//99
	Savannah MSA, GA	S	8.70 MW	8.65 AW	18100 AAW	GABLS	10//99-12//99
	Hawaii	S	10.42 MW	10.66 AW	22170 AAW	HIBLS	10//99-12//99
	Honolulu MSA, HI	S	10.53 MW	10.34 AW	21900 AAW	HIBLS	10//99-12//99
	Idaho	S	9.54 MW	10.02 AW	20850 AAW	IDBLS	10//99-12//99
	Boise City MSA, ID	S	10.18 MW	8.91 AW	21180 AAW	IDBLS	10//99-12//99
	Illinois	S	9.93 MW	10.14 AW	21090 AAW	ILBLS	10//99-12//99
	Bloomington-Normal MSA, IL	S	9.13 MW	8.47 AW	18980 AAW	ILBLS	10//99-12//99
	Chicago PMSA, IL	S	10.47 MW	10.18 AW	21780 AAW	ILBLS	10//99-12//99
	Decatur MSA, IL	S	7.93 MW	7.51 AW	16490 AAW	ILBLS	10//99-12//99
	Kankakee PMSA, IL	S	8.29 MW	7.83 AW	17250 AAW	ILBLS	10//99-12//99
	Rockford MSA, IL	S	8.70 MW	8.41 AW	18090 AAW	ILBLS	10//99-12//99
	Springfield MSA, IL	S	9.06 MW	8.99 AW	18850 AAW	ILBLS	10//99-12//99
	Indiana	S	9.24 MW	9.52 AW	19810 AAW	INBLS	10//99-12//99
	Bloomington MSA, IN	S	8.47 MW	8.21 AW	17620 AAW	INBLS	10//99-12//99
	Elkhart-Goshen MSA, IN	S	9.56 MW	9.16 AW	19880 AAW	INBLS	10//99-12//99
	Evansville-Henderson MSA, IN-KY	S	8.28 MW	8.14 AW	17210 AAW	INBLS	10//99-12//99
	Fort Wayne MSA, IN	S	10.60 MW	10.88 AW	22040 AAW	INBLS	10//99-12//99
	Gary PMSA, IN	S	10.30 MW	10.84 AW	21420 AAW	INBLS	10//99-12//99
	Indianapolis MSA, IN	S	9.61 MW	9.31 AW	19990 AAW	INBLS	10//99-12//99
	Kokomo MSA, IN	S	8.86 MW	8.10 AW	18430 AAW	INBLS	10//99-12//99
	Lafayette MSA, IN	S	8.44 MW	8.09 AW	17550 AAW	INBLS	10//99-12//99
	Muncie MSA, IN	S	7.81 MW	7.87 AW	16240 AAW	INBLS	10//99-12//99
	South Bend MSA, IN	S	9.37 MW	9.28 AW	19490 AAW	INBLS	10//99-12//99
	Iowa	S	9.21 MW	9.55 AW	19870 AAW	IABLS	10//99-12//99
	Cedar Rapids MSA, IA	S	10.05 MW	10.50 AW	20890 AAW	IABLS	10//99-12//99
	Des Moines MSA, IA	S	9.29 MW	8.88 AW	19320 AAW	IABLS	10//99-12//99
	Iowa City MSA, IA	S	9.50 MW	8.79 AW	19750 AAW	IABLS	10//99-12//99
	Sioux City MSA, IA-NE	S	8.81 MW	8.59 AW	18330 AAW	IABLS	10//99-12//99
	Waterloo-Cedar Falls MSA, IA	S	8.61 MW	8.19 AW	17900 AAW	IABLS	10//99-12//99
	Kansas	S	9.69 MW	10.01 AW	20820 AAW	KSBLS	10//99-12//99
	Lawrence MSA, KS	S	9.68 MW	9.67 AW	20140 AAW	KSBLS	10//99-12//99
	Topeka MSA, KS	S	8.80 MW	8.34 AW	18290 AAW	KSBLS	10//99-12//99
	Wichita MSA, KS	S	11.62 MW	11.52 AW	24180 AAW	KSBLS	10//99-12//99
	Kentucky	S	8.42 MW	8.81 AW	18330 AAW	KYBLS	10//99-12//99
	Lexington MSA, KY	S	8.36 MW	8.07 AW	17400 AAW	KYBLS	10//99-12//99
	Louisville MSA, KY-IN	S	9.53 MW	9.34 AW	19810 AAW	KYBLS	10//99-12//99
	Owensboro MSA, KY	S	8.73 MW	8.83 AW	18150 AAW	KYBLS	10//99-12//99
	Louisiana	S	8.4 MW	8.88 AW	18480 AAW	LABLS	10//99-12//99
	Baton Rouge MSA, LA	S	10.08 MW	10.10 AW	20960 AAW	LABLS	10//99-12//99
	Houma MSA, LA	S	7.45 MW	7.11 AW	15500 AAW	LABLS	10//99-12//99
	Lafayette MSA, LA	S	8.31 MW	7.96 AW	17290 AAW	LABLS	10//99-12//99
	Monroe MSA, LA	S	7.42 MW	7.01 AW	15440 AAW	LABLS	10//99-12//99
	New Orleans MSA, LA	S	8.61 MW	8.31 AW	17910 AAW	LABLS	10//99-12//99
	Shreveport-Bossier City MSA, LA	S	9.77 MW	8.74 AW	20330 AAW	LABLS	10//99-12//99
	Maine	S	8.95 MW	9.23 AW	19210 AAW	MEBLS	10//99-12//99
	Bangor MSA, ME	S	9.13 MW	8.94 AW	18990 AAW	MEBLS	10//99-12//99
	Portland MSA, ME	S	9.90 MW	9.84 AW	20600 AAW	MEBLS	10//99-12//99
	Maryland	S	9.58 MW	9.94 AW	20680 AAW	MDBLS	10//99-12//99
	Baltimore PMSA, MD	S	9.93 MW	9.62 AW	20660 AAW	MDBLS	10//99-12//99
	Cumberland MSA, MD-WV	S	7.90 MW	7.05 AW	16430 AAW	MDBLS	10//99-12//99
	Hagerstown PMSA, MD	S	7.99 MW	7.56 AW	16620 AAW	MDBLS	10//99-12//99
	Massachusetts	S	10.66 MW	11.13 AW	23160 AAW	MABLS	10//99-12//99
	Barnstable-Yarmouth MSA, MA	S	9.98 MW	9.85 AW	20770 AAW	MABLS	10//99-12//99
	Boston PMSA, MA-NH	S	11.42 MW	10.80 AW	23750 AAW	MABLS	10//99-12//99
	Brockton PMSA, MA	S	9.85 MW	9.04 AW	20490 AAW	MABLS	10//99-12//99

AAW Average annual wage	**AOH** Average offered, high	**ASH** Average starting, high	**H** Hourly	**M** Monthly	**S** Special: hourly and annual
AE Average entry wage	**AOL** Average offered, low	**ASL** Average starting, low	**HI** Highest wage paid	**MTC** Median total compensation	**TQ** Third quartile wage
AEX Average experienced wage	**APH** Average pay, high range	**AW** Average wage paid	**HR** High end range	**MW** Median wage paid	**W** Weekly
AO Average offered	**APL** Average pay, low range	**FQ** First quartile wage	**LR** Low end range	**SQ** Second quartile wage	**Y** Yearly

Occupation/Type/Industry	Location	Per	Low	Mid	High	Source	Date
Data Entry Keyer	Fitchburg-Leominster PMSA, MA	S	10.28 MW	10.35 AW	21380 AAW	MABLS	10//99-12//99
	Lawrence PMSA, MA-NH	S	10.87 MW	10.56 AW	22620 AAW	MABLS	10//99-12//99
	Lowell PMSA, MA-NH	S	12.21 MW	11.59 AW	25390 AAW	MABLS	10//99-12//99
	New Bedford PMSA, MA	S	10.60 MW	10.10 AW	22050 AAW	MABLS	10//99-12//99
	Pittsfield MSA, MA	S	10.18 MW	9.76 AW	21180 AAW	MABLS	10//99-12//99
	Springfield MSA, MA	S	10.03 MW	9.76 AW	20850 AAW	MABLS	10//99-12//99
	Worcester PMSA, MA-CT	S	10.39 MW	10.53 AW	21610 AAW	MABLS	10//99-12//99
	Michigan	S	9.58 MW	10.14 AW	21080 AAW	MIBLS	10//99-12//99
	Ann Arbor PMSA, MI	S	9.94 MW	9.76 AW	20670 AAW	MIBLS	10//99-12//99
	Detroit PMSA, MI	S	10.50 MW	9.78 AW	21830 AAW	MIBLS	10//99-12//99
	Flint PMSA, MI	S	9.30 MW	8.28 AW	19350 AAW	MIBLS	10//99-12//99
	Grand Rapids-Muskegon-Holland MSA, MI	S	9.46 MW	9.07 AW	19680 AAW	MIBLS	10//99-12//99
	Jackson MSA, MI	S	9.33 MW	8.93 AW	19400 AAW	MIBLS	10//99-12//99
	Lansing-East Lansing MSA, MI	S	10.85 MW	10.06 AW	22580 AAW	MIBLS	10//99-12//99
	Saginaw-Bay City-Midland MSA, MI	S	8.87 MW	8.06 AW	18460 AAW	MIBLS	10//99-12//99
	Minnesota	S	10.34 MW	10.54 AW	21930 AAW	MNBLS	10//99-12//99
	Minneapolis-St. Paul MSA, MN-WI	S	10.99 MW	10.58 AW	22860 AAW	MNBLS	10//99-12//99
	Rochester MSA, MN	S	9.16 MW	9.22 AW	19050 AAW	MNBLS	10//99-12//99
	St. Cloud MSA, MN	S	9.29 MW	9.03 AW	19320 AAW	MNBLS	10//99-12//99
	Mississippi	S	8.21 MW	8.55 AW	17780 AAW	MSBLS	10//99-12//99
	Biloxi-Gulfport-Pascagoula MSA, MS	S	8.93 MW	8.87 AW	18570 AAW	MSBLS	10//99-12//99
	Hattiesburg MSA, MS	S	8.72 MW	8.60 AW	18130 AAW	MSBLS	10//99-12//99
	Jackson MSA, MS	S	9.00 MW	8.35 AW	18710 AAW	MSBLS	10//99-12//99
	Missouri	S	8.98 MW	9.40 AW	19540 AAW	MOBLS	10//99-12//99
	Columbia MSA, MO	S	9.06 MW	8.54 AW	18830 AAW	MOBLS	10//99-12//99
	Kansas City MSA, MO-KS	S	9.98 MW	9.74 AW	20760 AAW	MOBLS	10//99-12//99
	St. Louis MSA, MO-IL	S	9.38 MW	8.81 AW	19510 AAW	MOBLS	10//99-12//99
	Springfield MSA, MO	S	8.08 MW	7.74 AW	16800 AAW	MOBLS	10//99-12//99
	Montana	S	8.41 MW	8.86 AW	18420 AAW	MTBLS	10//99-12//99
	Billings MSA, MT	S	8.78 MW	8.74 AW	18260 AAW	MTBLS	10//99-12//99
	Great Falls MSA, MT	S	8.25 MW	7.97 AW	17150 AAW	MTBLS	10//99-12//99
	Missoula MSA, MT	S	8.49 MW	8.10 AW	17660 AAW	MTBLS	10//99-12//99
	Nebraska	S	8.89 MW	9.02 AW	18760 AAW	NEBLS	10//99-12//99
	Lincoln MSA, NE	S	9.27 MW	9.02 AW	19290 AAW	NEBLS	10//99-12//99
	Omaha MSA, NE-IA	S	9.14 MW	8.95 AW	19010 AAW	NEBLS	10//99-12//99
	Nevada	S	9.11 MW	9.33 AW	19410 AAW	NVBLS	10//99-12//99
	Las Vegas MSA, NV-AZ	S	9.37 MW	9.22 AW	19480 AAW	NVBLS	10//99-12//99
	Reno MSA, NV	S	9.00 MW	8.48 AW	18730 AAW	NVBLS	10//99-12//99
	New Hampshire	S	9.73 MW	10.04 AW	20890 AAW	NHBLS	10//99-12//99
	Manchester PMSA, NH	S	10.03 MW	9.68 AW	20860 AAW	NHBLS	10//99-12//99
	Nashua PMSA, NH	S	10.15 MW	9.78 AW	21110 AAW	NHBLS	10//99-12//99
	Portsmouth-Rochester PMSA, NH-ME	S	9.69 MW	9.33 AW	20160 AAW	NHBLS	10//99-12//99
	New Jersey	S	10.69 MW	11.08 AW	23050 AAW	NJBLS	10//99-12//99
	Atlantic-Cape May PMSA, NJ	S	10.94 MW	10.23 AW	22760 AAW	NJBLS	10//99-12//99
	Bergen-Passaic PMSA, NJ	S	10.84 MW	10.37 AW	22550 AAW	NJBLS	10//99-12//99
	Jersey City PMSA, NJ	S	11.90 MW	11.61 AW	24750 AAW	NJBLS	10//99-12//99
	Middlesex-Somerset-Hunterdon PMSA, NJ	S	10.84 MW	10.58 AW	22550 AAW	NJBLS	10//99-12//99
	Monmouth-Ocean PMSA, NJ	S	10.74 MW	9.99 AW	22330 AAW	NJBLS	10//99-12//99
	Newark PMSA, NJ	S	10.96 MW	10.38 AW	22800 AAW	NJBLS	10//99-12//99
	Trenton PMSA, NJ	S	12.26 MW	12.18 AW	25510 AAW	NJBLS	10//99-12//99
	Vineland-Millville-Bridgeton PMSA, NJ	S	11.32 MW	11.02 AW	23550 AAW	NJBLS	10//99-12//99
	New Mexico	S	8.49 MW	9.08 AW	18890 AAW	NMBLS	10//99-12//99
	Albuquerque MSA, NM	S	9.29 MW	8.62 AW	19320 AAW	NMBLS	10//99-12//99
	Las Cruces MSA, NM	S	8.77 MW	8.04 AW	18240 AAW	NMBLS	10//99-12//99
	Santa Fe MSA, NM	S	8.31 MW	8.23 AW	17290 AAW	NMBLS	10//99-12//99
	New York	S	11.15 MW	11.48 AW	23890 AAW	NYBLS	10//99-12//99
	Albany-Schenectady-Troy MSA, NY	S	11.04 MW	11.34 AW	22970 AAW	NYBLS	10//99-12//99
	Binghamton MSA, NY	S	8.47 MW	8.38 AW	17620 AAW	NYBLS	10//99-12//99
	Buffalo-Niagara Falls MSA, NY	S	9.79 MW	9.47 AW	20370 AAW	NYBLS	10//99-12//99
	Dutchess County PMSA, NY	S	10.06 MW	9.78 AW	20930 AAW	NYBLS	10//99-12//99
	Elmira MSA, NY	S	11.01 MW	11.13 AW	22890 AAW	NYBLS	10//99-12//99
	Glens Falls MSA, NY	S	9.68 MW	10.27 AW	20130 AAW	NYBLS	10//99-12//99

AAW	Average annual wage	AOH	Average offered, high	ASH	Average starting, high
AE	Average entry wage	AOL	Average offered, low	ASL	Average starting, low
AEX	Average experienced wage	APH	Average pay, high range	AW	Average wage paid
AO	Average offered	APL	Average pay, low range	FQ	First quartile wage

H	Hourly	M	Monthly
HI	Highest wage paid	MTC	Median total compensation
HR	High end range	MW	Median wage paid
LR	Low end range	SQ	Second quartile wage

S	Special: hourly and annual
TQ	Third quartile wage
W	Weekly
Y	Yearly

Occupation/Type/Industry	Location	Per	Low	Mid	High	Source	Date
Data Entry Keyer	Jamestown MSA, NY	S	9.43 MW	9.47 AW	19620 AAW	NYBLS	10//99-12//99
	Nassau-Suffolk PMSA, NY	S	11.30 MW	10.90 AW	23500 AAW	NYBLS	10//99-12//99
	New York PMSA, NY	S	12.51 MW	11.97 AW	26030 AAW	NYBLS	10//99-12//99
	Newburgh PMSA, NY-PA	S	10.73 MW	10.96 AW	22320 AAW	NYBLS	10//99-12//99
	Rochester MSA, NY	S	9.30 MW	8.81 AW	19350 AAW	NYBLS	10//99-12//99
	Syracuse MSA, NY	S	10.88 MW	11.19 AW	22620 AAW	NYBLS	10//99-12//99
	Utica-Rome MSA, NY	S	9.72 MW	9.18 AW	20220 AAW	NYBLS	10//99-12//99
	North Carolina	S	9.72 MW	9.83 AW	20440 AAW	NCBLS	10//99-12//99
	Asheville MSA, NC	S	8.91 MW	8.77 AW	18540 AAW	NCBLS	10//99-12//99
	Charlotte-Gastonia-Rock Hill MSA, NC-SC	S	9.54 MW	9.61 AW	19850 AAW	NCBLS	10//99-12//99
	Greensboro--Winston-Salem-- High Point MSA, NC	S	10.23 MW	10.02 AW	21280 AAW	NCBLS	10//99-12//99
	Greenville MSA, NC	S	8.54 MW	8.47 AW	17770 AAW	NCBLS	10//99-12//99
	Hickory-Morganton-Lenoir MSA, NC	S	9.93 MW	9.76 AW	20650 AAW	NCBLS	10//99-12//99
	Jacksonville MSA, NC	S	8.07 MW	8.39 AW	16780 AAW	NCBLS	10//99-12//99
	Raleigh-Durham-Chapel Hill MSA, NC	S	10.11 MW	10.02 AW	21040 AAW	NCBLS	10//99-12//99
	Rocky Mount MSA, NC	S	9.57 MW	9.01 AW	19910 AAW	NCBLS	10//99-12//99
	Wilmington MSA, NC	S	8.86 MW	8.47 AW	18420 AAW	NCBLS	10//99-12//99
	North Dakota	S	7.91 MW	8.08 AW	16810 AAW	NDBLS	10//99-12//99
	Bismarck MSA, ND	S	8.20 MW	8.10 AW	17060 AAW	NDBLS	10//99-12//99
	Fargo-Moorhead MSA, ND-MN	S	8.90 MW	8.25 AW	18520 AAW	NDBLS	10//99-12//99
	Grand Forks MSA, ND-MN	S	8.85 MW	8.92 AW	18400 AAW	NDBLS	10//99-12//99
	Ohio	S	9.51 MW	9.77 AW	20320 AAW	OHBLS	10//99-12//99
	Akron PMSA, OH	S	10.19 MW	10.07 AW	21190 AAW	OHBLS	10//99-12//99
	Canton-Massillon MSA, OH	S	9.07 MW	9.09 AW	18870 AAW	OHBLS	10//99-12//99
	Cincinnati PMSA, OH-KY-IN	S	9.91 MW	9.57 AW	20600 AAW	OHBLS	10//99-12//99
	Cleveland-Lorain-Elyria PMSA, OH	S	10.16 MW	9.66 AW	21140 AAW	OHBLS	10//99-12//99
	Columbus MSA, OH	S	9.79 MW	9.73 AW	20350 AAW	OHBLS	10//99-12//99
	Dayton-Springfield MSA, OH	S	10.03 MW	9.74 AW	20870 AAW	OHBLS	10//99-12//99
	Hamilton-Middletown PMSA, OH	S	9.39 MW	9.05 AW	19540 AAW	OHBLS	10//99-12//99
	Lima MSA, OH	S	9.66 MW	9.61 AW	20090 AAW	OHBLS	10//99-12//99
	Mansfield MSA, OH	S	8.86 MW	8.58 AW	18440 AAW	OHBLS	10//99-12//99
	Steubenville-Weirton MSA, OH-WV	S	9.26 MW	8.21 AW	19260 AAW	OHBLS	10//99-12//99
	Toledo MSA, OH	S	8.93 MW	8.69 AW	18580 AAW	OHBLS	10//99-12//99
	Youngstown-Warren MSA, OH	S	9.18 MW	8.41 AW	19080 AAW	OHBLS	10//99-12//99
	Oklahoma	S	8.61 MW	9.64 AW	20040 AAW	OKBLS	10//99-12//99
	Lawton MSA, OK	S	6.59 MW	6.34 AW	13720 AAW	OKBLS	10//99-12//99
	Oklahoma City MSA, OK	S	10.39 MW	8.97 AW	21600 AAW	OKBLS	10//99-12//99
	Tulsa MSA, OK	S	9.45 MW	8.69 AW	19660 AAW	OKBLS	10//99-12//99
	Oregon	S	9.96 MW	10.21 AW	21240 AAW	ORBLS	10//99-12//99
	Eugene-Springfield MSA, OR	S	9.47 MW	9.39 AW	19700 AAW	ORBLS	10//99-12//99
	Medford-Ashland MSA, OR	S	9.10 MW	8.99 AW	18920 AAW	ORBLS	10//99-12//99
	Portland-Vancouver PMSA, OR-WA	S	10.47 MW	10.16 AW	21780 AAW	ORBLS	10//99-12//99
	Salem PMSA, OR	S	10.19 MW	9.85 AW	21190 AAW	ORBLS	10//99-12//99
	Pennsylvania	S	9.37 MW	9.68 AW	20140 AAW	PABLS	10//99-12//99
	Allentown-Bethlehem-Easton MSA, PA	S	10.70 MW	10.00 AW	22260 AAW	PABLS	10//99-12//99
	Altoona MSA, PA	S	8.31 MW	7.37 AW	17280 AAW	PABLS	10//99-12//99
	Erie MSA, PA	S	9.22 MW	8.99 AW	19170 AAW	PABLS	10//99-12//99
	Harrisburg-Lebanon-Carlisle MSA, PA	S	9.76 MW	9.59 AW	20290 AAW	PABLS	10//99-12//99
	Johnstown MSA, PA	S	7.31 MW	6.66 AW	15210 AAW	PABLS	10//99-12//99
	Lancaster MSA, PA	S	9.67 MW	9.33 AW	20110 AAW	PABLS	10//99-12//99
	Philadelphia PMSA, PA-NJ	S	10.05 MW	9.85 AW	20910 AAW	PABLS	10//99-12//99
	Pittsburgh MSA, PA	S	9.64 MW	9.01 AW	20050 AAW	PABLS	10//99-12//99
	Reading MSA, PA	S	8.44 MW	8.14 AW	17550 AAW	PABLS	10//99-12//99
	Scranton--Wilkes-Barre-- Hazleton MSA, PA	S	8.59 MW	8.30 AW	17860 AAW	PABLS	10//99-12//99
	Sharon MSA, PA	S	8.88 MW	9.35 AW	18470 AAW	PABLS	10//99-12//99
	State College MSA, PA	S	8.18 MW	7.81 AW	17010 AAW	PABLS	10//99-12//99
	Williamsport MSA, PA	S	8.20 MW	7.96 AW	17050 AAW	PABLS	10//99-12//99
	York MSA, PA	S	10.57 MW	10.93 AW	21990 AAW	PABLS	10//99-12//99
	Rhode Island	S	9.93 MW	10.51 AW	21870 AAW	RIBLS	10//99-12//99

AAW Average annual wage	**AOH** Average offered, high	**ASH** Average starting, high	**H** Hourly	**M** Monthly	**S** Special: hourly and annual
AE Average entry wage	**AOL** Average offered, low	**ASL** Average starting, low	**HI** Highest wage paid	**MTC** Median total compensation	**TQ** Third quartile wage
AEX Average experienced wage	**APH** Average pay, high range	**AW** Average wage paid	**HR** High end range	**MW** Median wage paid	**W** Weekly
AO Average offered	**APL** Average pay, low range	**FQ** First quartile wage	**LR** Low end range	**SQ** Second quartile wage	**Y** Yearly

Occupation/Type/Industry	Location	Per	Low	Mid	High	Source	Date
Data Entry Keyer	Providence-Fall River-Warwick MSA, RI-MA	s	10.54 MW	9.99 AW	21910 AAW	RIBLS	10//99-12//99
	South Carolina	s	8.79 MW	9.24 AW	19210 AAW	SCBLS	10//99-12//99
	Charleston-North Charleston MSA, SC	s	9.80 MW	9.35 AW	20380 AAW	SCBLS	10//99-12//99
	Columbia MSA, SC	s	9.09 MW	8.54 AW	18900 AAW	SCBLS	10//99-12//99
	Florence MSA, SC	s	9.02 MW	8.85 AW	18760 AAW	SCBLS	10//99-12//99
	Greenville-Spartanburg-Anderson MSA, SC	s	9.08 MW	8.81 AW	18900 AAW	SCBLS	10//99-12//99
	Myrtle Beach MSA, SC	s	8.95 MW	8.64 AW	18620 AAW	SCBLS	10//99-12//99
	Sumter MSA, SC	s	9.28 MW	9.36 AW	19290 AAW	SCBLS	10//99-12//99
	South Dakota	s	8.3 MW	9.08 AW	18880 AAW	SDBLS	10//99-12//99
	Rapid City MSA, SD	s	7.60 MW	7.61 AW	15800 AAW	SDBLS	10//99-12//99
	Sioux Falls MSA, SD	s	9.82 MW	8.84 AW	20420 AAW	SDBLS	10//99-12//99
	Tennessee	s	9.12 MW	9.47 AW	19690 AAW	TNBLS	10//99-12//99
	Chattanooga MSA, TN-GA	s	11.06 MW	11.27 AW	23000 AAW	TNBLS	10//99-12//99
	Clarksville-Hopkinsville MSA, TN-KY	s	9.78 MW	9.71 AW	20340 AAW	TNBLS	10//99-12//99
	Jackson MSA, TN	s	10.16 MW	10.82 AW	21130 AAW	TNBLS	10//99-12//99
	Johnson City-Kingsport-Bristol MSA, TN-VA	s	8.84 MW	8.76 AW	18390 AAW	TNBLS	10//99-12//99
	Knoxville MSA, TN	s	8.45 MW	8.13 AW	17570 AAW	TNBLS	10//99-12//99
	Memphis MSA, TN-AR-MS	s	8.64 MW	8.40 AW	17970 AAW	MSBLS	10//99-12//99
	Nashville MSA, TN	s	10.24 MW	10.15 AW	21300 AAW	TNBLS	10//99-12//99
	Texas	s	9.52 MW	9.71 AW	20190 AAW	TXBLS	10//99-12//99
	Amarillo MSA, TX	s	8.06 MW	7.99 AW	16760 AAW	TXBLS	10//99-12//99
	Austin-San Marcos MSA, TX	s	10.15 MW	10.02 AW	21100 AAW	TXBLS	10//99-12//99
	Brazoria PMSA, TX	s	8.85 MW	8.48 AW	18420 AAW	TXBLS	10//99-12//99
	Brownsville-Harlingen-San Benito MSA, TX	s	8.91 MW	7.76 AW	18520 AAW	TXBLS	10//99-12//99
	Bryan-College Station MSA, TX	s	8.57 MW	8.26 AW	17820 AAW	TXBLS	10//99-12//99
	Corpus Christi MSA, TX	s	9.22 MW	9.21 AW	19190 AAW	TXBLS	10//99-12//99
	Dallas PMSA, TX	s	10.20 MW	9.95 AW	21220 AAW	TXBLS	10//99-12//99
	El Paso MSA, TX	s	7.78 MW	7.47 AW	16190 AAW	TXBLS	10//99-12//99
	Fort Worth-Arlington PMSA, TX	s	10.43 MW	9.69 AW	21680 AAW	TXBLS	10//99-12//99
	Galveston-Texas City PMSA, TX	s	9.19 MW	8.97 AW	19120 AAW	TXBLS	10//99-12//99
	Houston PMSA, TX	s	9.49 MW	9.27 AW	19740 AAW	TXBLS	10//99-12//99
	Killeen-Temple MSA, TX	s	7.88 MW	7.82 AW	16380 AAW	TXBLS	10//99-12//99
	Longview-Marshall MSA, TX	s	9.31 MW	8.54 AW	19360 AAW	TXBLS	10//99-12//99
	Lubbock MSA, TX	s	7.92 MW	7.60 AW	16480 AAW	TXBLS	10//99-12//99
	Odessa-Midland MSA, TX	s	8.19 MW	8.00 AW	17030 AAW	TXBLS	10//99-12//99
	San Angelo MSA, TX	s	9.46 MW	8.62 AW	19680 AAW	TXBLS	10//99-12//99
	San Antonio MSA, TX	s	8.84 MW	8.35 AW	18400 AAW	TXBLS	10//99-12//99
	Sherman-Denison MSA, TX	s	8.75 MW	8.16 AW	18200 AAW	TXBLS	10//99-12//99
	Texarkana MSA, TX-Texarkana, AR	s	8.19 MW	7.83 AW	17040 AAW	TXBLS	10//99-12//99
	Tyler MSA, TX	s	8.57 MW	8.65 AW	17820 AAW	TXBLS	10//99-12//99
	Victoria MSA, TX	s	8.09 MW	8.22 AW	16830 AAW	TXBLS	10//99-12//99
	Waco MSA, TX	s	8.62 MW	8.37 AW	17930 AAW	TXBLS	10//99-12//99
	Wichita Falls MSA, TX	s	9.11 MW	8.40 AW	18940 AAW	TXBLS	10//99-12//99
	Utah	s	8.97 MW	9.34 AW	19440 AAW	UTBLS	10//99-12//99
	Provo-Orem MSA, UT	s	8.55 MW	8.32 AW	17780 AAW	UTBLS	10//99-12//99
	Salt Lake City-Ogden MSA, UT	s	9.55 MW	9.22 AW	19850 AAW	UTBLS	10//99-12//99
	Vermont	s	9.68 MW	9.53 AW	19820 AAW	VTBLS	10//99-12//99
	Burlington MSA, VT	s	10.03 MW	10.64 AW	20860 AAW	VTBLS	10//99-12//99
	Virginia	s	9.42 MW	9.66 AW	20100 AAW	VABLS	10//99-12//99
	Charlottesville MSA, VA	s	10.60 MW	10.15 AW	22040 AAW	VABLS	10//99-12//99
	Norfolk-Virginia Beach-Newport News MSA, VA-NC	s	8.69 MW	8.28 AW	18060 AAW	VABLS	10//99-12//99
	Richmond-Petersburg MSA, VA	s	8.74 MW	8.56 AW	18190 AAW	VABLS	10//99-12//99
	Washington	s	10.42 MW	10.80 AW	22470 AAW	WABLS	10//99-12//99
	Bellingham MSA, WA	s	10.58 MW	11.02 AW	22010 AAW	WABLS	10//99-12//99
	Olympia PMSA, WA	s	10.05 MW	9.74 AW	20890 AAW	WABLS	10//99-12//99
	Richland-Kennewick-Pasco MSA, WA	s	10.14 MW	9.46 AW	21090 AAW	WABLS	10//99-12//99

AAW Average annual wage	AOH Average offered, high	ASH Average starting, high	H Hourly	M Monthly	S Special: hourly and annual
AE Average entry wage	AOL Average offered, low	ASL Average starting, low	HI Highest wage paid	MTC Median total compensation	TQ Third quartile wage
AEX Average experienced wage	APH Average pay, high range	AW Average wage paid	HR High end range	MW Median wage paid	W Weekly
AO Average offered	APL Average pay, low range	FQ First quartile wage	LR Low end range	SQ Second quartile wage	Y Yearly

Occupation/Type/Industry	Location	Per	Low	Mid	High	Source	Date
Data Entry Keyer	Seattle-Bellevue-Everett PMSA, WA	S	11.13 MW	10.72 AW	23140 AAW	WABLS	10//99-12//99
	Spokane MSA, WA	S	9.12 MW	8.90 AW	18970 AAW	WABLS	10//99-12//99
	Tacoma PMSA, WA	S	9.76 MW	9.54 AW	20290 AAW	WABLS	10//99-12//99
	Yakima MSA, WA	S	9.99 MW	10.05 AW	20780 AAW	WABLS	10//99-12//99
	West Virginia	S	8.46 MW	9.23 AW	19190 AAW	WVBLS	10//99-12//99
	Charleston MSA, WV	S	10.25 MW	10.81 AW	21310 AAW	WVBLS	10//99-12//99
	Huntington-Ashland MSA, WV-KY-OH	S	7.67 MW	7.14 AW	15950 AAW	WVBLS	10//99-12//99
	Parkersburg-Marietta MSA, WV-OH	S	8.48 MW	7.88 AW	17640 AAW	WVBLS	10//99-12//99
	Wheeling MSA, WV-OH	S	8.02 MW	7.32 AW	16670 AAW	WVBLS	10//99-12//99
	Wisconsin	S	8.76 MW	8.94 AW	18590 AAW	WIBLS	10//99-12//99
	Appleton-Oshkosh-Neenah MSA, WI	S	9.19 MW	8.49 AW	19110 AAW	WIBLS	10//99-12//99
	Eau Claire MSA, WI	S	9.38 MW	9.02 AW	19510 AAW	WIBLS	10//99-12//99
	Green Bay MSA, WI	S	9.16 MW	8.86 AW	19050 AAW	WIBLS	10//99-12//99
	Janesville-Beloit MSA, WI	S	8.41 MW	8.02 AW	17500 AAW	WIBLS	10//99-12//99
	Kenosha PMSA, WI	S	9.51 MW	9.28 AW	19770 AAW	WIBLS	10//99-12//99
	La Crosse MSA, WI-MN	S	8.63 MW	8.38 AW	17950 AAW	WIBLS	10//99-12//99
	Madison MSA, WI	S	10.06 MW	9.95 AW	20920 AAW	WIBLS	10//99-12//99
	Milwaukee-Waukesha PMSA, WI	S	9.28 MW	9.19 AW	19310 AAW	WIBLS	10//99-12//99
	Racine PMSA, WI	S	9.51 MW	9.43 AW	19780 AAW	WIBLS	10//99-12//99
	Sheboygan MSA, WI	S	9.48 MW	9.13 AW	19720 AAW	WIBLS	10//99-12//99
	Wyoming	S	8.08 MW	8.67 AW	18030 AAW	WYBLS	10//99-12//99
	Casper MSA, WY	S	7.85 MW	7.73 AW	16320 AAW	WYBLS	10//99-12//99
	Cheyenne MSA, WY	S	8.09 MW	7.89 AW	16830 AAW	WYBLS	10//99-12//99
	Puerto Rico	S	6.38 MW	6.81 AW	14160 AAW	PRBLS	10//99-12//99
	Aguadilla MSA, PR	S	6.77 MW	6.56 AW	14090 AAW	PRBLS	10//99-12//99
	Arecibo PMSA, PR	S	5.94 MW	6.02 AW	12360 AAW	PRBLS	10//99-12//99
	Caguas PMSA, PR	S	6.18 MW	6.27 AW	12860 AAW	PRBLS	10//99-12//99
	Mayaguez MSA, PR	S	7.13 MW	6.66 AW	14830 AAW	PRBLS	10//99-12//99
	Ponce MSA, PR	S	6.94 MW	6.46 AW	14440 AAW	PRBLS	10//99-12//99
	San Juan-Bayamon PMSA, PR	S	6.91 MW	6.43 AW	14370 AAW	PRBLS	10//99-12//99
	Virgin Islands	S	9.25 MW	9.34 AW	19430 AAW	VIBLS	10//99-12//99
	Guam	S	8 MW	8.10 AW	16850 AAW	GUBLS	10//99-12//99
Data Warehouse Analyst Information Technology	United States	Y	67750 APL		89000 APH	USBANK	2000
Data Warehouse Manager Information Technology	United States	Y	77250 APL		98250 APH	USBANK	2000
Database Administrator	United States	Y		62400 AW		ENT	2000
	Alabama	S	20.35 MW	21.64 AW	45010 AAW	ALBLS	10//99-12//99
	Birmingham MSA, AL	S	19.98 MW	18.46 AW	41550 AAW	ALBLS	10//99-12//99
	Huntsville MSA, AL	S	21.76 MW	21.66 AW	45250 AAW	ALBLS	10//99-12//99
	Mobile MSA, AL	S	20.64 MW	19.44 AW	42930 AAW	ALBLS	10//99-12//99
	Montgomery MSA, AL	S	24.21 MW	24.20 AW	50350 AAW	ALBLS	10//99-12//99
	Alaska	S	25.21 MW	26.25 AW	54590 AAW	AKBLS	10//99-12//99
	Anchorage MSA, AK	S	26.69 MW	25.10 AW	55510 AAW	AKBLS	10//99-12//99
	Arizona	S	24.47 MW	25.77 AW	53610 AAW	AZBLS	10//99-12//99
	Phoenix-Mesa MSA, AZ	S	26.20 MW	24.83 AW	54500 AAW	AZBLS	10//99-12//99
	Tucson MSA, AZ	S	24.03 MW	23.31 AW	49980 AAW	AZBLS	10//99-12//99
	Fayetteville-Springdale-Rogers MSA, AR	S	18.09 MW	14.90 AW	37630 AAW	ARBLS	10//99-12//99
	Fort Smith MSA, AR-OK	S	22.90 MW	22.21 AW	47630 AAW	ARBLS	10//99-12//99
	California	S	25.62 MW	27.08 AW	56330 AAW	CABLS	10//99-12//99
	Bakersfield MSA, CA	S	26.24 MW	23.82 AW	54570 AAW	CABLS	10//99-12//99
	Fresno MSA, CA	S	24.21 MW	22.79 AW	50360 AAW	CABLS	10//99-12//99
	Los Angeles-Long Beach PMSA, CA	S	27.60 MW	27.08 AW	57400 AAW	CABLS	10//99-12//99
	Modesto MSA, CA	S	23.87 MW	23.89 AW	49650 AAW	CABLS	10//99-12//99
	Oakland PMSA, CA	S	30.05 MW	29.11 AW	62510 AAW	CABLS	10//99-12//99
	Orange County PMSA, CA	S	23.53 MW	22.37 AW	48950 AAW	CABLS	10//99-12//99
	Riverside-San Bernardino PMSA, CA	S	23.83 MW	23.60 AW	49570 AAW	CABLS	10//99-12//99
	Sacramento PMSA, CA	S	23.24 MW	20.95 AW	48330 AAW	CABLS	10//99-12//99
	Salinas MSA, CA	S	25.83 MW	24.63 AW	53720 AAW	CABLS	10//99-12//99
	San Diego MSA, CA	S	23.79 MW	22.67 AW	49480 AAW	CABLS	10//99-12//99
	San Francisco PMSA, CA	S	28.44 MW	27.83 AW	59160 AAW	CABLS	10//99-12//99
	San Jose PMSA, CA	S	29.40 MW	29.63 AW	61160 AAW	CABLS	10//99-12//99

AAW Average annual wage	AOH Average offered, high	ASH Average starting, high	H Hourly	M Monthly	S Special: hourly and annual
AE Average entry wage	AOL Average offered, low	ASL Average starting, low	HI Highest wage paid	MTC Median total compensation	TQ Third quartile wage
AEX Average experienced wage	APH Average pay, high range	AW Average wage paid	HR High end range	MW Median wage paid	W Weekly
AO Average offered	APL Average pay, low range	FQ First quartile wage	LR Low end range	SQ Second quartile wage	Y Yearly

Occupation/Type/Industry	Location	Per	Low	Mid	High	Source	Date
Database Administrator	San Luis Obispo-Atascadero-Paso Robles MSA, CA	S	27.86 MW	29.14 AW	57960 AAW	CABLS	10//99-12//99
	Santa Barbara-Santa Maria-Lompoc MSA, CA	S	27.55 MW	29.17 AW	57300 AAW	CABLS	10//99-12//99
	Santa Cruz-Watsonville PMSA, CA	S	22.44 MW	20.04 AW	46680 AAW	CABLS	10//99-12//99
	Santa Rosa PMSA, CA	S	24.88 MW	23.71 AW	51740 AAW	CABLS	10//99-12//99
	Stockton-Lodi MSA, CA	S	28.32 MW	26.64 AW	58910 AAW	CABLS	10//99-12//99
	Vallejo-Fairfield-Napa PMSA, CA	S	27.06 MW	25.63 AW	56280 AAW	CABLS	10//99-12//99
	Ventura PMSA, CA	S	31.73 MW	31.79 AW	66000 AAW	CABLS	10//99-12//99
	Visalia-Tulare-Porterville MSA, CA	S	24.25 MW	23.53 AW	50450 AAW	CABLS	10//99-12//99
	Yolo PMSA, CA	S	26.08 MW	25.02 AW	54250 AAW	CABLS	10//99-12//99
	Colorado	S	24.85 MW	25.52 AW	53080 AAW	COBLS	10//99-12//99
	Boulder-Longmont PMSA, CO	S	23.90 MW	22.77 AW	49700 AAW	COBLS	10//99-12//99
	Colorado Springs MSA, CO	S	25.23 MW	25.39 AW	52470 AAW	COBLS	10//99-12//99
	Denver PMSA, CO	S	26.75 MW	25.91 AW	55650 AAW	COBLS	10//99-12//99
	Fort Collins-Loveland MSA, CO	S	25.35 MW	26.10 AW	52730 AAW	COBLS	10//99-12//99
	Greeley PMSA, CO	S	27.04 MW	28.51 AW	56240 AAW	COBLS	10//99-12//99
	Connecticut	S	25.69 MW	26.91 AW	55970 AAW	CTBLS	10//99-12//99
	Bridgeport PMSA, CT	S	27.07 MW	25.60 AW	56300 AAW	CTBLS	10//99-12//99
	Danbury PMSA, CT	S	22.46 MW	22.31 AW	46720 AAW	CTBLS	10//99-12//99
	Hartford MSA, CT	S	26.69 MW	25.60 AW	55510 AAW	CTBLS	10//99-12//99
	New Haven-Meriden PMSA, CT	S	23.49 MW	21.68 AW	48850 AAW	CTBLS	10//99-12//99
	New London-Norwich MSA, CT-RI	S	22.82 MW	21.31 AW	47470 AAW	CTBLS	10//99-12//99
	Stamford-Norwalk PMSA, CT	S	30.10 MW	29.50 AW	62600 AAW	CTBLS	10//99-12//99
	Waterbury PMSA, CT	S	25.35 MW	23.84 AW	52730 AAW	CTBLS	10//99-12//99
	Delaware	S	25.56 MW	25.54 AW	53120 AAW	DEBLS	10//99-12//99
	Wilmington-Newark PMSA, DE-MD	S	25.90 MW	26.15 AW	53870 AAW	DEBLS	10//99-12//99
	District of Columbia	S	24.38 MW	25.06 AW	52120 AAW	DCBLS	10//99-12//99
	Washington PMSA, DC-MD-VA-WV	S	26.69 MW	24.29 AW	55510 AAW	DCBLS	10//99-12//99
	Florida	S	22.45 MW	24.15 AW	50230 AAW	FLBLS	10//99-12//99
	Daytona Beach MSA, FL	S	22.61 MW	19.87 AW	47040 AAW	FLBLS	10//99-12//99
	Fort Lauderdale PMSA, FL	S	27.21 MW	22.08 AW	56590 AAW	FLBLS	10//99-12//99
	Fort Myers-Cape Coral MSA, FL	S	19.37 MW	16.57 AW	40300 AAW	FLBLS	10//99-12//99
	Fort Pierce-Port St. Lucie MSA, FL	S	21.44 MW	17.66 AW	44600 AAW	FLBLS	10//99-12//99
	Fort Walton Beach MSA, FL	S	29.51 MW	26.17 AW	61380 AAW	FLBLS	10//99-12//99
	Gainesville MSA, FL	S	18.80 MW	18.82 AW	39110 AAW	FLBLS	10//99-12//99
	Lakeland-Winter Haven MSA, FL	S	22.15 MW	19.77 AW	46070 AAW	FLBLS	10//99-12//99
	Melbourne-Titusville-Palm Bay MSA, FL	S	21.36 MW	20.76 AW	44420 AAW	FLBLS	10//99-12//99
	Miami PMSA, FL	S	24.28 MW	23.37 AW	50500 AAW	FLBLS	10//99-12//99
	Orlando MSA, FL	S	21.67 MW	21.07 AW	45080 AAW	FLBLS	10//99-12//99
	Pensacola MSA, FL	S	21.97 MW	21.31 AW	45700 AAW	FLBLS	10//99-12//99
	Sarasota-Bradenton MSA, FL	S	21.03 MW	19.68 AW	43730 AAW	FLBLS	10//99-12//99
	Tallahassee MSA, FL	S	20.01 MW	20.01 AW	41610 AAW	FLBLS	10//99-12//99
	Tampa-St. Petersburg-Clearwater MSA, FL	S	22.53 MW	21.12 AW	46870 AAW	FLBLS	10//99-12//99
	West Palm Beach-Boca Raton MSA, FL	S	22.77 MW	20.69 AW	47360 AAW	FLBLS	10//99-12//99
	Georgia	S	20.78 MW	23.11 AW	48060 AAW	GABLS	10//99-12//99
	Athens MSA, GA	S	21.91 MW	21.38 AW	45580 AAW	GABLS	10//99-12//99
	Atlanta MSA, GA	S	23.18 MW	20.68 AW	48220 AAW	GABLS	10//99-12//99
	Augusta-Aiken MSA, GA-SC	S	19.21 MW	19.22 AW	39970 AAW	GABLS	10//99-12//99
	Columbus MSA, GA-AL	S	23.13 MW	20.65 AW	48110 AAW	GABLS	10//99-12//99
	Macon MSA, GA	S	26.53 MW	23.77 AW	55180 AAW	GABLS	10//99-12//99
	Savannah MSA, GA	S	23.34 MW	22.04 AW	48550 AAW	GABLS	10//99-12//99
	Hawaii	S	25.98 MW	25.66 AW	53370 AAW	HIBLS	10//99-12//99
	Honolulu MSA, HI	S	25.93 MW	26.43 AW	53940 AAW	HIBLS	10//99-12//99
	Idaho	S	22.14 MW	21.44 AW	44600 AAW	IDBLS	10//99-12//99
	Boise City MSA, ID	S	20.59 MW	20.07 AW	42830 AAW	IDBLS	10//99-12//99
	Illinois	S	21.99 MW	24.21 AW	50350 AAW	ILBLS	10//99-12//99
	Bloomington-Normal MSA, IL	S	25.81 MW	28.27 AW	53680 AAW	ILBLS	10//99-12//99

AAW	Average annual wage	AOH	Average offered, high	ASH	Average starting, high
AE	Average entry wage	AOL	Average offered, low	ASL	Average starting, low
AEX	Average experienced wage	APH	Average pay, high range	AW	Average wage paid
AO	Average offered	APL	Average pay, low range	FQ	First quartile wage

H	Hourly	M	Monthly
HI	Highest wage paid	MTC	Median total compensation
HR	High end range	MW	Median wage paid
LR	Low end range	SQ	Second quartile wage

S	Special: hourly and annual
TQ	Third quartile wage
W	Weekly
Y	Yearly

Occupation/Type/Industry	Location	Per	Low	Mid	High	Source	Date
Database Administrator	Champaign-Urbana MSA, IL	S	24.79 MW	22.78 AW	51570 AAW	ILBLS	10//99-12//99
	Chicago PMSA, IL	S	24.52 MW	22.28 AW	51000 AAW	ILBLS	10//99-12//99
	Peoria-Pekin MSA, IL	S	21.44 MW	21.29 AW	44600 AAW	ILBLS	10//99-12//99
	Rockford MSA, IL	S	18.48 MW	15.64 AW	38440 AAW	ILBLS	10//99-12//99
	Indiana	S	20.5 MW	22.10 AW	45970 AAW	INBLS	10//99-12//99
	Evansville-Henderson MSA, IN-KY	S	18.31 MW	16.30 AW	38080 AAW	INBLS	10//99-12//99
	Fort Wayne MSA, IN	S	24.26 MW	23.59 AW	50450 AAW	INBLS	10//99-12//99
	Gary PMSA, IN	S	21.59 MW	19.87 AW	44910 AAW	INBLS	10//99-12//99
	Indianapolis MSA, IN	S	24.40 MW	23.49 AW	50760 AAW	INBLS	10//99-12//99
	Lafayette MSA, IN	S	19.41 MW	17.21 AW	40370 AAW	INBLS	10//99-12//99
	Muncie MSA, IN	S	19.23 MW	18.07 AW	39990 AAW	INBLS	10//99-12//99
	South Bend MSA, IN	S	21.44 MW	20.50 AW	44590 AAW	INBLS	10//99-12//99
	Iowa	S	21.95 MW	22.76 AW	47330 AAW	IABLS	10//99-12//99
	Davenport-Moline-Rock Island MSA, IA-IL	S	21.81 MW	21.91 AW	45360 AAW	IABLS	10//99-12//99
	Des Moines MSA, IA	S	24.04 MW	23.19 AW	50010 AAW	IABLS	10//99-12//99
	Kansas	S	23.41 MW	25.11 AW	52240 AAW	KSBLS	10//99-12//99
	Topeka MSA, KS	S	23.01 MW	22.23 AW	47860 AAW	KSBLS	10//99-12//99
	Wichita MSA, KS	S	30.25 MW	27.73 AW	62910 AAW	KSBLS	10//99-12//99
	Kentucky	S	22.13 MW	22.61 AW	47030 AAW	KYBLS	10//99-12//99
	Lexington MSA, KY	S	23.32 MW	23.41 AW	48500 AAW	KYBLS	10//99-12//99
	Louisville MSA, KY-IN	S	21.52 MW	20.62 AW	44760 AAW	KYBLS	10//99-12//99
	Louisiana	S	19.54 MW	21.38 AW	44470 AAW	LABLS	10//99-12//99
	Baton Rouge MSA, LA	S	21.66 MW	19.38 AW	45050 AAW	LABLS	10//99-12//99
	New Orleans MSA, LA	S	22.82 MW	20.86 AW	47460 AAW	LABLS	10//99-12//99
	Maine	S	20.96 MW	22.32 AW	46430 AAW	MEBLS	10//99-12//99
	Portland MSA, ME	S	24.60 MW	24.59 AW	51170 AAW	MEBLS	10//99-12//99
	Maryland	S	23.3 MW	26.27 AW	54640 AAW	MDBLS	10//99-12//99
	Baltimore PMSA, MD	S	23.30 MW	22.18 AW	48470 AAW	MDBLS	10//99-12//99
	Massachusetts	S	25.12 MW	26.66 AW	55460 AAW	MABLS	10//99-12//99
	Boston PMSA, MA-NH	S	27.09 MW	25.83 AW	56350 AAW	MABLS	10//99-12//99
	Brockton PMSA, MA	S	29.20 MW	31.22 AW	60730 AAW	MABLS	10//99-12//99
	Lawrence PMSA, MA-NH	S	24.53 MW	23.75 AW	51030 AAW	MABLS	10//99-12//99
	Lowell PMSA, MA-NH	S	28.12 MW	27.17 AW	58480 AAW	MABLS	10//99-12//99
	Springfield MSA, MA	S	21.24 MW	18.86 AW	44180 AAW	MABLS	10//99-12//99
	Worcester PMSA, MA-CT	S	25.11 MW	22.97 AW	52220 AAW	MABLS	10//99-12//99
	Michigan	S	21.69 MW	23.35 AW	48570 AAW	MIBLS	10//99-12//99
	Ann Arbor PMSA, MI	S	26.25 MW	27.27 AW	54590 AAW	MIBLS	10//99-12//99
	Detroit PMSA, MI	S	24.48 MW	23.04 AW	50920 AAW	MIBLS	10//99-12//99
	Flint PMSA, MI	S	24.57 MW	21.52 AW	51100 AAW	MIBLS	10//99-12//99
	Grand Rapids-Muskegon-Holland MSA, MI	S	20.33 MW	19.20 AW	42280 AAW	MIBLS	10//99-12//99
	Kalamazoo-Battle Creek MSA, MI	S	23.00 MW	22.49 AW	47850 AAW	MIBLS	10//99-12//99
	Lansing-East Lansing MSA, MI	S	23.84 MW	22.92 AW	49590 AAW	MIBLS	10//99-12//99
	Saginaw-Bay City-Midland MSA, MI	S	20.39 MW	18.88 AW	42400 AAW	MIBLS	10//99-12//99
	Minnesota	S	24.18 MW	26.00 AW	54080 AAW	MNBLS	10//99-12//99
	Duluth-Superior MSA, MN-WI	S	23.40 MW	24.05 AW	48660 AAW	MNBLS	10//99-12//99
	Minneapolis-St. Paul MSA, MN-WI	S	26.65 MW	24.71 AW	55430 AAW	MNBLS	10//99-12//99
	Rochester MSA, MN	S	27.39 MW	28.71 AW	56960 AAW	MNBLS	10//99-12//99
	St. Cloud MSA, MN	S	21.54 MW	22.11 AW	44800 AAW	MNBLS	10//99-12//99
	Mississippi	S	20.16 MW	20.93 AW	43540 AAW	MSBLS	10//99-12//99
	Biloxi-Gulfport-Pascagoula MSA, MS	S	20.58 MW	18.85 AW	42810 AAW	MSBLS	10//99-12//99
	Jackson MSA, MS	S	21.81 MW	21.00 AW	45360 AAW	MSBLS	10//99-12//99
	Missouri	S	24.55 MW	25.63 AW	53300 AAW	MOBLS	10//99-12//99
	Kansas City MSA, MO-KS	S	26.07 MW	24.99 AW	54220 AAW	MOBLS	10//99-12//99
	St. Louis MSA, MO-IL	S	25.57 MW	24.47 AW	53190 AAW	MOBLS	10//99-12//99
	Springfield MSA, MO	S	24.58 MW	24.64 AW	51120 AAW	MOBLS	10//99-12//99
	Montana	S	17.22 MW	19.17 AW	39870 AAW	MTBLS	10//99-12//99
	Nebraska	S	24 MW	24.28 AW	50500 AAW	NEBLS	10//99-12//99
	Lincoln MSA, NE	S	23.76 MW	22.50 AW	49420 AAW	NEBLS	10//99-12//99
	Omaha MSA, NE-IA	S	25.16 MW	24.85 AW	52340 AAW	NEBLS	10//99-12//99
	Nevada	S	22.06 MW	25.33 AW	52690 AAW	NVBLS	10//99-12//99
	Las Vegas MSA, NV-AZ	S	23.45 MW	21.46 AW	48770 AAW	NVBLS	10//99-12//99
	Reno MSA, NV	S	21.79 MW	21.44 AW	45320 AAW	NVBLS	10//99-12//99
	New Hampshire	S	23.79 MW	24.82 AW	51620 AAW	NHBLS	10//99-12//99
	Nashua PMSA, NH	S	29.01 MW	29.70 AW	60330 AAW	NHBLS	10//99-12//99
	New Jersey	S	28.06 MW	28.88 AW	60060 AAW	NJBLS	10//99-12//99

AAW Average annual wage	**AOH** Average offered, high	**ASH** Average starting, high	**H** Hourly	**M** Monthly	**S** Special: hourly and annual
AE Average entry wage	**AOL** Average offered, low	**ASL** Average starting, low	**HI** Highest wage paid	**MTC** Median total compensation	**TQ** Third quartile wage
AEX Average experienced wage	**APH** Average pay, high range	**AW** Average wage paid	**HR** High end range	**MW** Median wage paid	**W** Weekly
AO Average offered	**APL** Average pay, low range	**FQ** First quartile wage	**LR** Low end range	**SQ** Second quartile wage	**Y** Yearly

Occupation/Type/Industry	Location	Per	Low	Mid	High	Source	Date
Database Administrator	Atlantic-Cape May PMSA, NJ	S	30.22 MW	29.18 AW	62850 AAW	NJBLS	10//99-12//99
	Bergen-Passaic PMSA, NJ	S	27.44 MW	27.96 AW	57080 AAW	NJBLS	10//99-12//99
	Jersey City PMSA, NJ	S	31.35 MW	31.65 AW	65200 AAW	NJBLS	10//99-12//99
	Middlesex-Somerset-Hunterdon PMSA, NJ	S	29.12 MW	25.80 AW	60560 AAW	NJBLS	10//99-12//99
	Monmouth-Ocean PMSA, NJ	S	30.44 MW	28.66 AW	63320 AAW	NJBLS	10//99-12//99
	Newark PMSA, NJ	S	29.29 MW	29.57 AW	60930 AAW	NJBLS	10//99-12//99
	Trenton PMSA, NJ	S	28.98 MW	30.10 AW	60270 AAW	NJBLS	10//99-12//99
	New Mexico	S	20.13 MW	20.89 AW	43450 AAW	NMBLS	10//99-12//99
	Albuquerque MSA, NM	S	21.08 MW	19.83 AW	43860 AAW	NMBLS	10//99-12//99
	Santa Fe MSA, NM	S	21.17 MW	21.69 AW	44020 AAW	NMBLS	10//99-12//99
	New York	S	27.92 MW	28.63 AW	59550 AAW	NYBLS	10//99-12//99
	Albany-Schenectady-Troy MSA, NY	S	25.92 MW	25.85 AW	53900 AAW	NYBLS	10//99-12//99
	Binghamton MSA, NY	S	25.16 MW	26.42 AW	52330 AAW	NYBLS	10//99-12//99
	Buffalo-Niagara Falls MSA, NY	S	23.33 MW	22.64 AW	48530 AAW	NYBLS	10//99-12//99
	Dutchess County PMSA, NY	S	29.48 MW	30.32 AW	61330 AAW	NYBLS	10//99-12//99
	Elmira MSA, NY	S	21.04 MW	21.63 AW	43760 AAW	NYBLS	10//99-12//99
	Nassau-Suffolk PMSA, NY	S	26.52 MW	26.67 AW	55150 AAW	NYBLS	10//99-12//99
	New York PMSA, NY	S	30.74 MW	30.01 AW	63930 AAW	NYBLS	10//99-12//99
	Rochester MSA, NY	S	24.71 MW	24.58 AW	51390 AAW	NYBLS	10//99-12//99
	Syracuse MSA, NY	S	23.27 MW	21.68 AW	48400 AAW	NYBLS	10//99-12//99
	Utica-Rome MSA, NY	S	21.78 MW	19.90 AW	45300 AAW	NYBLS	10//99-12//99
	North Carolina	S	22.72 MW	24.25 AW	50450 AAW	NCBLS	10//99-12//99
	Asheville MSA, NC	S	17.37 MW	16.35 AW	36140 AAW	NCBLS	10//99-12//99
	Charlotte-Gastonia-Rock Hill MSA, NC-SC	S	24.18 MW	22.43 AW	50290 AAW	NCBLS	10//99-12//99
	Greensboro--Winston-Salem--High Point MSA, NC	S	27.47 MW	25.70 AW	57140 AAW	NCBLS	10//99-12//99
	Greenville MSA, NC	S	19.46 MW	19.32 AW	40480 AAW	NCBLS	10//99-12//99
	Hickory-Morganton-Lenoir MSA, NC	S	23.26 MW	22.30 AW	48390 AAW	NCBLS	10//99-12//99
	Raleigh-Durham-Chapel Hill MSA, NC	S	25.35 MW	24.17 AW	52720 AAW	NCBLS	10//99-12//99
	Wilmington MSA, NC	S	19.50 MW	18.26 AW	40560 AAW	NCBLS	10//99-12//99
	North Dakota	S	18.85 MW	19.35 AW	40250 AAW	NDBLS	10//99-12//99
	Fargo-Moorhead MSA, ND-MN	S	20.34 MW	19.64 AW	42310 AAW	NDBLS	10//99-12//99
	Ohio	S	23.78 MW	24.67 AW	51310 AAW	OHBLS	10//99-12//99
	Akron PMSA, OH	S	23.66 MW	22.84 AW	49220 AAW	OHBLS	10//99-12//99
	Canton-Massillon MSA, OH	S	20.34 MW	19.16 AW	42300 AAW	OHBLS	10//99-12//99
	Cincinnati PMSA, OH-KY-IN	S	25.18 MW	24.66 AW	52380 AAW	OHBLS	10//99-12//99
	Cleveland-Lorain-Elyria PMSA, OH	S	23.57 MW	22.03 AW	49020 AAW	OHBLS	10//99-12//99
	Columbus MSA, OH	S	24.39 MW	23.40 AW	50720 AAW	OHBLS	10//99-12//99
	Dayton-Springfield MSA, OH	S	28.95 MW	29.09 AW	60220 AAW	OHBLS	10//99-12//99
	Hamilton-Middletown PMSA, OH	S	23.37 MW	21.90 AW	48620 AAW	OHBLS	10//99-12//99
	Toledo MSA, OH	S	21.13 MW	19.65 AW	43960 AAW	OHBLS	10//99-12//99
	Youngstown-Warren MSA, OH	S	22.95 MW	21.40 AW	47730 AAW	OHBLS	10//99-12//99
	Oklahoma	S	19.56 MW	21.18 AW	44060 AAW	OKBLS	10//99-12//99
	Oklahoma City MSA, OK	S	20.06 MW	18.69 AW	41720 AAW	OKBLS	10//99-12//99
	Tulsa MSA, OK	S	24.03 MW	22.32 AW	49980 AAW	OKBLS	10//99-12//99
	Oregon	S	22.4 MW	23.23 AW	48320 AAW	ORBLS	10//99-12//99
	Eugene-Springfield MSA, OR	S	23.44 MW	23.62 AW	48760 AAW	ORBLS	10//99-12//99
	Portland-Vancouver PMSA, OR-WA	S	24.67 MW	23.80 AW	51320 AAW	ORBLS	10//99-12//99
	Salem PMSA, OR	S	22.43 MW	22.87 AW	46660 AAW	ORBLS	10//99-12//99
	Pennsylvania	S	24.84 MW	25.87 AW	53810 AAW	PABLS	10//99-12//99
	Allentown-Bethlehem-Easton MSA, PA	S	29.81 MW	33.26 AW	62010 AAW	PABLS	10//99-12//99
	Altoona MSA, PA	S	17.33 MW	16.72 AW	36040 AAW	PABLS	10//99-12//99
	Erie MSA, PA	S	20.00 MW	19.00 AW	41600 AAW	PABLS	10//99-12//99
	Harrisburg-Lebanon-Carlisle MSA, PA	S	25.53 MW	24.94 AW	53090 AAW	PABLS	10//99-12//99
	Johnstown MSA, PA	S	21.66 MW	20.74 AW	45060 AAW	PABLS	10//99-12//99
	Lancaster MSA, PA	S	22.90 MW	21.23 AW	47630 AAW	PABLS	10//99-12//99
	Philadelphia PMSA, PA-NJ	S	26.75 MW	25.05 AW	55640 AAW	PABLS	10//99-12//99
	Pittsburgh MSA, PA	S	26.20 MW	25.56 AW	54490 AAW	PABLS	10//99-12//99
	Reading MSA, PA	S	21.92 MW	19.86 AW	45590 AAW	PABLS	10//99-12//99

AAW Average annual wage	**AOH** Average offered, high	**ASH** Average starting, high	**H** Hourly	**M** Monthly	**S** Special: hourly and annual
AE Average entry wage	**AOL** Average offered, low	**ASL** Average starting, low	**HI** Highest wage paid	**MTC** Median total compensation	**TQ** Third quartile wage
AEX Average experienced wage	**APH** Average pay, high range	**AW** Average wage paid	**HR** High end range	**MW** Median wage paid	**W** Weekly
AO Average offered	**APL** Average pay, low range	**FQ** First quartile wage	**LR** Low end range	**SQ** Second quartile wage	**Y** Yearly

Occupation/Type/Industry	Location	Per	Low	Mid	High	Source	Date
Database Administrator	Scranton--Wilkes-Barre--						
	Hazleton MSA, PA	S	22.37 MW	21.80 AW	46530 AAW	PABLS	10//99-12//99
	York MSA, PA	S	20.17 MW	18.64 AW	41950 AAW	PABLS	10//99-12//99
	Rhode Island	S	24.3 MW	25.63 AW	53300 AAW	RIBLS	10//99-12//99
	Providence-Fall River-						
	Warwick MSA, RI-MA	S	26.99 MW	25.87 AW	56140 AAW	RIBLS	10//99-12//99
	South Carolina	S	20.08 MW	21.57 AW	44870 AAW	SCBLS	10//99-12//99
	Charleston-North Charleston						
	MSA, SC	S	21.72 MW	20.77 AW	45190 AAW	SCBLS	10//99-12//99
	Columbia MSA, SC	S	22.93 MW	22.37 AW	47690 AAW	SCBLS	10//99-12//99
	Greenville-Spartanburg-						
	Anderson MSA, SC	S	21.00 MW	18.59 AW	43680 AAW	SCBLS	10//99-12//99
	Sumter MSA, SC	S	18.43 MW	20.64 AW	38340 AAW	SCBLS	10//99-12//99
	South Dakota	S	21.41 MW	21.77 AW	45280 AAW	SDBLS	10//99-12//99
	Sioux Falls MSA, SD	S	23.00 MW	23.14 AW	47830 AAW	SDBLS	10//99-12//99
	Tennessee	S	22.86 MW	23.05 AW	47950 AAW	TNBLS	10//99-12//99
	Chattanooga MSA, TN-GA	S	19.23 MW	17.99 AW	40000 AAW	TNBLS	10//99-12//99
	Knoxville MSA, TN	S	20.34 MW	20.31 AW	42310 AAW	TNBLS	10//99-12//99
	Memphis MSA, TN-AR-MS	S	24.36 MW	24.04 AW	50660 AAW	MSBLS	10//99-12//99
	Nashville MSA, TN	S	23.07 MW	22.55 AW	47990 AAW	TNBLS	10//99-12//99
	Texas	S	23.12 MW	24.20 AW	50330 AAW	TXBLS	10//99-12//99
	Abilene MSA, TX	S	19.64 MW	18.83 AW	40860 AAW	TXBLS	10//99-12//99
	Amarillo MSA, TX	S	22.39 MW	22.39 AW	46570 AAW	TXBLS	10//99-12//99
	Austin-San Marcos MSA, TX	S	24.63 MW	23.59 AW	51230 AAW	TXBLS	10//99-12//99
	Beaumont-Port Arthur MSA,						
	TX	S	21.24 MW	20.84 AW	44170 AAW	TXBLS	10//99-12//99
	Brownsville-Harlingen-San						
	Benito MSA, TX	S	20.60 MW	20.25 AW	42850 AAW	TXBLS	10//99-12//99
	Corpus Christi MSA, TX	S	20.89 MW	20.98 AW	43460 AAW	TXBLS	10//99-12//99
	Dallas PMSA, TX	S	27.06 MW	27.74 AW	56280 AAW	TXBLS	10//99-12//99
	El Paso MSA, TX	S	18.02 MW	16.38 AW	37490 AAW	TXBLS	10//99-12//99
	Fort Worth-Arlington PMSA,						
	TX	S	22.70 MW	22.03 AW	47220 AAW	TXBLS	10//99-12//99
	Galveston-Texas City PMSA,						
	TX	S	21.23 MW	19.14 AW	44160 AAW	TXBLS	10//99-12//99
	Houston PMSA, TX	S	23.39 MW	21.34 AW	48650 AAW	TXBLS	10//99-12//99
	Killeen-Temple MSA, TX	S	20.71 MW	18.89 AW	43080 AAW	TXBLS	10//99-12//99
	Lubbock MSA, TX	S	19.45 MW	18.18 AW	40460 AAW	TXBLS	10//99-12//99
	McAllen-Edinburg-Mission						
	MSA, TX	S	19.77 MW	20.34 AW	41120 AAW	TXBLS	10//99-12//99
	Odessa-Midland MSA, TX	S	22.67 MW	22.46 AW	47150 AAW	TXBLS	10//99-12//99
	San Angelo MSA, TX	S	21.94 MW	23.70 AW	45640 AAW	TXBLS	10//99-12//99
	San Antonio MSA, TX	S	22.22 MW	20.76 AW	46230 AAW	TXBLS	10//99-12//99
	Waco MSA, TX	S	18.22 MW	16.81 AW	37890 AAW	TXBLS	10//99-12//99
	Utah	S	23.47 MW	23.83 AW	49560 AAW	UTBLS	10//99-12//99
	Provo-Orem MSA, UT	S	23.04 MW	22.11 AW	47910 AAW	UTBLS	10//99-12//99
	Salt Lake City-Ogden MSA,						
	UT	S	24.39 MW	24.34 AW	50730 AAW	UTBLS	10//99-12//99
	Vermont	S	23.09 MW	23.76 AW	49420 AAW	VTBLS	10//99-12//99
	Burlington MSA, VT	S	26.21 MW	25.86 AW	54520 AAW	VTBLS	10//99-12//99
	Virginia	S	23.34 MW	25.19 AW	52390 AAW	VABLS	10//99-12//99
	Charlottesville MSA, VA	S	24.00 MW	24.20 AW	49920 AAW	VABLS	10//99-12//99
	Lynchburg MSA, VA	S	19.74 MW	19.37 AW	41060 AAW	VABLS	10//99-12//99
	Norfolk-Virginia Beach-						
	Newport News MSA, VA-						
	NC	S	24.06 MW	23.08 AW	50050 AAW	VABLS	10//99-12//99
	Richmond-Petersburg MSA,						
	VA	S	26.63 MW	27.50 AW	55390 AAW	VABLS	10//99-12//99
	Roanoke MSA, VA	S	21.97 MW	19.02 AW	45710 AAW	VABLS	10//99-12//99
	Olympia PMSA, WA	S	19.12 MW	17.83 AW	39770 AAW	WABLS	10//99-12//99
	Spokane MSA, WA	S	23.99 MW	22.34 AW	49900 AAW	WABLS	10//99-12//99
	Tacoma PMSA, WA	S	23.64 MW	21.35 AW	49160 AAW	WABLS	10//99-12//99
	Yakima MSA, WA	S	19.42 MW	18.28 AW	40400 AAW	WABLS	10//99-12//99
	West Virginia	S	18.55 MW	20.38 AW	42400 AAW	WVBLS	10//99-12//99
	Charleston MSA, WV	S	21.77 MW	20.54 AW	45290 AAW	WVBLS	10//99-12//99
	Huntington-Ashland MSA,						
	WV-KY-OH	S	17.35 MW	17.19 AW	36100 AAW	WVBLS	10//99-12//99
	Parkersburg-Marietta MSA,						
	WV-OH	S	20.86 MW	20.20 AW	43390 AAW	WVBLS	10//99-12//99
	Wisconsin	S	21.85 MW	22.64 AW	47100 AAW	WIBLS	10//99-12//99
	Appleton-Oshkosh-Neenah						
	MSA, WI	S	21.26 MW	20.62 AW	44210 AAW	WIBLS	10//99-12//99

AAW	Average annual wage	AOH	Average offered, high	ASH	Average starting, high	H	Hourly			M	Monthly		S	Special: hourly and annual
AE	Average entry wage	AOL	Average offered, low	ASL	Average starting, low	HI	Highest wage paid		MTC	Median total compensation	TQ	Third quartile wage
AEX	Average experienced wage	APH	Average pay, high range	AW	Average wage paid	HR	High end range		MW	Median wage paid	W	Weekly
AO	Average offered	APL	Average pay, low range	FQ	First quartile wage	LR	Low end range		SQ	Second quartile wage	Y	Yearly

Occupation/Type/Industry	Location	Per	Low	Mid	High	Source	Date
Database Administrator	Eau Claire MSA, WI	S	16.62 MW	16.79 AW	34580 AAW	WIBLS	10//99-12//99
	Green Bay MSA, WI	S	22.92 MW	21.66 AW	47670 AAW	WIBLS	10//99-12//99
	Janesville-Beloit MSA, WI	S	20.49 MW	18.50 AW	42630 AAW	WIBLS	10//99-12//99
	La Crosse MSA, WI-MN	S	21.25 MW	19.56 AW	44200 AAW	WIBLS	10//99-12//99
	Madison MSA, WI	S	24.00 MW	23.30 AW	49910 AAW	WIBLS	10//99-12//99
	Milwaukee-Waukesha PMSA, WI	S	23.00 MW	22.37 AW	47830 AAW	WIBLS	10//99-12//99
	Racine PMSA, WI	S	22.12 MW	22.08 AW	46000 AAW	WIBLS	10//99-12//99
	Wyoming	S	20.5 MW	21.94 AW	45630 AAW	WYBLS	10//99-12//99
	Puerto Rico	S	17.01 MW	19.15 AW	39840 AAW	PRBLS	10//99-12//99
	San Juan-Bayamon PMSA, PR	S	19.76 MW	16.88 AW	41100 AAW	PRBLS	10//99-12//99
CRM/SFA Environment	United States	Y		67100 AW		ENT	2000
Data Warehouse	United States	Y		65600 AW		ENT	2000
E-Commerce Environment	United States	Y		64200 AW		ENT	2000
ERP Environment	United States	Y		64500 AW		ENT	2000
SCM System	United States	Y		63500 AW		ENT	2000
Database Manager							
Information Technology	United States	Y	74000 APL		95750 APH	USBANK	2000
Demonstrator and Product Promoter	Alabama	S	7.98 MW	10.06 AW	20920 AAW	ALBLS	10//99-12//99
	Alaska	S	8.16 MW	8.76 AW	18230 AAW	AKBLS	10//99-12//99
	Arizona	S	9.97 MW	11.03 AW	22950 AAW	AZBLS	10//99-12//99
	Arkansas	S	7.74 MW	8.65 AW	18000 AAW	ARBLS	10//99-12//99
	California	S	9.01 MW	10.33 AW	21490 AAW	CABLS	10//99-12//99
	Colorado	S	8.68 MW	10.19 AW	21190 AAW	COBLS	10//99-12//99
	Connecticut	S	10.6 MW	12.76 AW	26530 AAW	CTBLS	10//99-12//99
	Delaware	S	7.88 MW	8.46 AW	17600 AAW	DEBLS	10//99-12//99
	Florida	S	7.82 MW	9.94 AW	20680 AAW	FLBLS	10//99-12//99
	Georgia	S	8.71 MW	9.48 AW	19720 AAW	GABLS	10//99-12//99
	Hawaii	S	8.04 MW	9.41 AW	19580 AAW	HIBLS	10//99-12//99
	Idaho	S	6.89 MW	7.32 AW	15230 AAW	IDBLS	10//99-12//99
	Illinois	S	9.35 MW	10.78 AW	22430 AAW	ILBLS	10//99-12//99
	Indiana	S	7.93 MW	8.92 AW	18540 AAW	INBLS	10//99-12//99
	Iowa	S	9.76 MW	11.37 AW	23660 AAW	IABLS	10//99-12//99
	Kansas	S	8 MW	8.84 AW	18380 AAW	KSBLS	10//99-12//99
	Kentucky	S	8.22 MW	9.18 AW	19080 AAW	KYBLS	10//99-12//99
	Louisiana	S	8.42 MW	9.40 AW	19560 AAW	LABLS	10//99-12//99
	Maine	S	8.54 MW	10.78 AW	22430 AAW	MEBLS	10//99-12//99
	Maryland	S	9.89 MW	11.62 AW	24170 AAW	MDBLS	10//99-12//99
	Massachusetts	S	11.48 MW	13.84 AW	28780 AAW	MABLS	10//99-12//99
	Michigan	S	8.36 MW	10.13 AW	21070 AAW	MIBLS	10//99-12//99
	Minnesota	S	8.46 MW	9.89 AW	20580 AAW	MNBLS	10//99-12//99
	Mississippi	S	6.15 MW	6.55 AW	13630 AAW	MSBLS	10//99-12//99
	Missouri	S	8.71 MW	11.69 AW	24310 AAW	MOBLS	10//99-12//99
	Montana	S	6.75 MW	6.81 AW	14170 AAW	MTBLS	10//99-12//99
	Nebraska	S	7.82 MW	8.37 AW	17420 AAW	NEBLS	10//99-12//99
	Nevada	S	9.82 MW	17.06 AW	35490 AAW	NVBLS	10//99-12//99
	New Hampshire	S	8.63 MW	9.63 AW	20020 AAW	NHBLS	10//99-12//99
	New Jersey	S	9.61 MW	11.37 AW	23640 AAW	NJBLS	10//99-12//99
	New Mexico	S	8.61 MW	9.58 AW	19930 AAW	NMBLS	10//99-12//99
	New York	S	8.03 MW	10.04 AW	20890 AAW	NYBLS	10//99-12//99
	North Dakota	S	7.19 MW	7.44 AW	15480 AAW	NDBLS	10//99-12//99
	Ohio	S	13.85 MW	13.77 AW	28650 AAW	OHBLS	10//99-12//99
	Oklahoma	S	9.75 MW	10.17 AW	21150 AAW	OKBLS	10//99-12//99
	Oregon	S	7.87 MW	8.22 AW	17100 AAW	ORBLS	10//99-12//99
	Pennsylvania	S	9.29 MW	11.45 AW	23810 AAW	PABLS	10//99-12//99
	Rhode Island	S	11.92 MW	13.72 AW	28530 AAW	RIBLS	10//99-12//99
	South Carolina	S	8.2 MW	9.78 AW	20350 AAW	SCBLS	10//99-12//99
	South Dakota	S	7.33 MW	7.58 AW	15760 AAW	SDBLS	10//99-12//99
	Tennessee	S	8.25 MW	9.40 AW	19550 AAW	TNBLS	10//99-12//99
	Texas	S	8.9 MW	9.73 AW	20230 AAW	TXBLS	10//99-12//99
	Utah	S	9.4 MW	11.09 AW	23070 AAW	UTBLS	10//99-12//99
	Vermont	S	16.56 MW	19.31 AW	40170 AAW	VTBLS	10//99-12//99
	Virginia	S	7.44 MW	8.06 AW	16760 AAW	VABLS	10//99-12//99
	Washington	S	8.39 MW	11.32 AW	23540 AAW	WABLS	10//99-12//99
	West Virginia	S	8.57 MW	8.96 AW	18630 AAW	WVBLS	10//99-12//99
	Wisconsin	S	7.44 MW	7.99 AW	16620 AAW	WIBLS	10//99-12//99
	Wyoming	S	7.57 MW	7.67 AW	15940 AAW	WYBLS	10//99-12//99
	Puerto Rico	S	6.3 MW	7.18 AW	14920 AAW	PRBLS	10//99-12//99

AAW Average annual wage	**AOH** Average offered, high	**ASH** Average starting, high	**H** Hourly	**M** Monthly	**S** Special: hourly and annual	
AE Average entry wage	**AOL** Average offered, low	**ASL** Average starting, low	**HI** Highest wage paid	**MTC** Median total compensation	**TQ** Third quartile wage	
AEX Average experienced wage	**APH** Average pay, high range	**AW** Average wage paid	**HR** High end range	**MW** Median wage paid	**W** Weekly	
AO Average offered	**APL** Average pay, low range	**FQ** First quartile wage	**LR** Low end range	**SQ** Second quartile wage	**Y** Yearly	

Occupation/Type/Industry	Location	Per	Low	Mid	High	Source	Date
Dental Assistant	Alabama	S	8.8 MW	8.94 AW	18590 AAW	ALBLS	10//99-12//99
	Alaska	S	15.18 MW	15.13 AW	31470 AAW	AKBLS	10//99-12//99
	Arizona	S	10.68 MW	10.93 AW	22720 AAW	AZBLS	10//99-12//99
	Arkansas	S	9.29 MW	9.25 AW	19240 AAW	ARBLS	10//99-12//99
	California	S	13.03 MW	13.40 AW	27880 AAW	CABLS	10//99-12//99
	Colorado	S	11.45 MW	11.75 AW	24440 AAW	COBLS	10//99-12//99
	Connecticut	S	12.48 MW	13.24 AW	27540 AAW	CTBLS	10//99-12//99
	Delaware	S	12.21 MW	12.22 AW	25430 AAW	DEBLS	10//99-12//99
	District of Columbia	S	13.99 MW	14.57 AW	30310 AAW	DCBLS	10//99-12//99
	Florida	S	11.13 MW	11.49 AW	23900 AAW	FLBLS	10//99-12//99
	Georgia	S	10.44 MW	10.30 AW	21420 AAW	GABLS	10//99-12//99
	Hawaii	S	11.27 MW	11.88 AW	24700 AAW	HIBLS	10//99-12//99
	Idaho	S	10.63 MW	10.53 AW	21910 AAW	IDBLS	10//99-12//99
	Illinois	S	9.86 MW	10.14 AW	21100 AAW	ILBLS	10//99-12//99
	Indiana	S	10.85 MW	10.96 AW	22790 AAW	INBLS	10//99-12//99
	Iowa	S	10.13 MW	10.40 AW	21630 AAW	IABLS	10//99-12//99
	Kansas	S	10.12 MW	9.87 AW	20530 AAW	KSBLS	10//99-12//99
	Kentucky	S	9.73 MW	10.01 AW	20810 AAW	KYBLS	10//99-12//99
	Louisiana	S	8.38 MW	8.59 AW	17860 AAW	LABLS	10//99-12//99
	Maine	S	11.26 MW	11.32 AW	23540 AAW	MEBLS	10//99-12//99
	Maryland	S	11.98 MW	12.47 AW	25930 AAW	MDBLS	10//99-12//99
	Massachusetts	S	13.42 MW	13.31 AW	27680 AAW	MABLS	10//99-12//99
	Michigan	S	11.46 MW	11.60 AW	24120 AAW	MIBLS	10//99-12//99
	Minnesota	S	12.91 MW	13.01 AW	27070 AAW	MNBLS	10//99-12//99
	Mississippi	S	8.76 MW	9.19 AW	19110 AAW	MSBLS	10//99-12//99
	Missouri	S	9.52 MW	10.46 AW	21760 AAW	MOBLS	10//99-12//99
	Montana	S	9.98 MW	10.57 AW	21980 AAW	MTBLS	10//99-12//99
	Nebraska	S	10.05 MW	10.07 AW	20950 AAW	NEBLS	10//99-12//99
	Nevada	S	11.81 MW	12.39 AW	25780 AAW	NVBLS	10//99-12//99
	New Hampshire	S	12.71 MW	12.65 AW	26310 AAW	NHBLS	10//99-12//99
	New Jersey	S	12.58 MW	13.36 AW	27790 AAW	NJBLS	10//99-12//99
	New Mexico	S	10.61 MW	10.73 AW	22320 AAW	NMBLS	10//99-12//99
	New York	S	10.95 MW	11.05 AW	22990 AAW	NYBLS	10//99-12//99
	North Carolina	S	11.84 MW	11.95 AW	24860 AAW	NCBLS	10//99-12//99
	North Dakota	S	10.9 MW	10.79 AW	22450 AAW	NDBLS	10//99-12//99
	Ohio	S	10.96 MW	11.05 AW	22980 AAW	OHBLS	10//99-12//99
	Oklahoma	S	9.8 MW	9.99 AW	20770 AAW	OKBLS	10//99-12//99
	Oregon	S	13.1 MW	13.15 AW	27360 AAW	ORBLS	10//99-12//99
	Pennsylvania	S	10.22 MW	10.54 AW	21910 AAW	PABLS	10//99-12//99
	Rhode Island	S	13.11 MW	13.14 AW	27330 AAW	RIBLS	10//99-12//99
	South Carolina	S	10.42 MW	10.37 AW	21570 AAW	SCBLS	10//99-12//99
	South Dakota	S	9.97 MW	9.85 AW	20490 AAW	SDBLS	10//99-12//99
	Tennessee	S	10.94 MW	11.30 AW	23510 AAW	TNBLS	10//99-12//99
	Texas	S	10.51 MW	11.28 AW	23460 AAW	TXBLS	10//99-12//99
	Utah	S	9.53 MW	9.72 AW	20210 AAW	UTBLS	10//99-12//99
	Vermont	S	11.93 MW	12.40 AW	25790 AAW	VTBLS	10//99-12//99
	Virginia	S	10.9 MW	11.33 AW	23580 AAW	VABLS	10//99-12//99
	Washington	S	13.18 MW	13.45 AW	27970 AAW	WABLS	10//99-12//99
	West Virginia	S	8.65 MW	9.01 AW	18740 AAW	WVBLS	10//99-12//99
	Wisconsin	S	10.73 MW	10.81 AW	22490 AAW	WIBLS	10//99-12//99
	Wyoming	S	9.68 MW	9.74 AW	20250 AAW	WYBLS	10//99-12//99
	Puerto Rico	S	6.23 MW	6.27 AW	13050 AAW	PRBLS	10//99-12//99
	Virgin Islands	S	8.34 MW	8.57 AW	17820 AAW	VIBLS	10//99-12//99
	Guam	S	12.72 MW	13.22 AW	27510 AAW	GUBLS	10//99-12//99
Dental Hygienist	United States	Y	31750 AE			CARWO1	2000
	United States	W		759 AW		TQUES	1999
	United States	H		19.46 AW		NCS98	1998
	Alabama	S	12.72 MW	12.99 AW	27020 AAW	ALBLS	10//99-12//99
	Anniston MSA, AL	S	12.70 MW	12.13 AW	26420 AAW	ALBLS	10//99-12//99
	Auburn-Opelika MSA, AL	S	14.33 MW	14.65 AW	29800 AAW	ALBLS	10//99-12//99
	Birmingham MSA, AL	S	11.99 MW	12.49 AW	24940 AAW	ALBLS	10//99-12//99
	Dothan MSA, AL	S	12.49 MW	12.60 AW	25980 AAW	ALBLS	10//99-12//99
	Mobile MSA, AL	S	12.92 MW	12.80 AW	26880 AAW	ALBLS	10//99-12//99
	Montgomery MSA, AL	S	14.59 MW	14.52 AW	30350 AAW	ALBLS	10//99-12//99
	Alaska	S	36.07 MW	32.77 AW	68160 AAW	AKBLS	10//99-12//99
	Anchorage MSA, AK	S	35.17 MW	38.35 AW	73140 AAW	AKBLS	10//99-12//99
	Arizona	S	31.27 MW	28.53 AW	59340 AAW	AZBLS	10//99-12//99
	Flagstaff MSA, AZ-UT	S	21.59 MW	19.07 AW	44900 AAW	AZBLS	10//99-12//99
	Phoenix-Mesa MSA, AZ	S	29.23 MW	32.34 AW	60790 AAW	AZBLS	10//99-12//99
	Tucson MSA, AZ	S	27.17 MW	28.24 AW	56510 AAW	AZBLS	10//99-12//99
	Arkansas	S	18.38 MW	17.88 AW	37190 AAW	ARBLS	10//99-12//99
	Fort Smith MSA, AR-OK	S	21.66 MW	21.82 AW	45060 AAW	ARBLS	10//99-12//99

AAW Average annual wage	**AOH** Average offered, high	**ASH** Average starting, high	**H** Hourly	**M** Monthly	**S** Special: hourly and annual
AE Average entry wage	**AOL** Average offered, low	**ASL** Average starting, low	**HI** Highest wage paid	**MTC** Median total compensation	**TQ** Third quartile wage
AEX Average experienced wage	**APH** Average pay, high range	**AW** Average wage paid	**HR** High end range	**MW** Median wage paid	**W** Weekly
AO Average offered	**APL** Average pay, low range	**FQ** First quartile wage	**LR** Low end range	**SQ** Second quartile wage	**Y** Yearly

Occupation/Type/Industry	Location	Per	Low	Mid	High	Source	Date
Dental Hygienist	California	S	30.02 MW	26.45 AW	55020 AAW	CABLS	10//99-12//99
	Bakersfield MSA, CA	S	27.61 MW	31.79 AW	57440 AAW	CABLS	10//99-12//99
	Chico-Paradise MSA, CA	S	18.52 MW	12.82 AW	38530 AAW	CABLS	10//99-12//99
	Los Angeles-Long Beach PMSA, CA	S	24.26 MW	28.32 AW	50460 AAW	CABLS	10//99-12//99
	Merced MSA, CA	S	26.27 MW	31.66 AW	54640 AAW	CABLS	10//99-12//99
	Riverside-San Bernardino PMSA, CA	S	23.66 MW	25.43 AW	49210 AAW	CABLS	10//99-12//99
	Sacramento PMSA, CA	S	30.94 MW	34.35 AW	64360 AAW	CABLS	10//99-12//99
	Salinas MSA, CA	S	29.83 MW	34.19 AW	62050 AAW	CABLS	10//99-12//99
	San Diego MSA, CA	S	29.36 MW	32.45 AW	61060 AAW	CABLS	10//99-12//99
	San Francisco PMSA, CA	S	31.56 MW	35.55 AW	65650 AAW	CABLS	10//99-12//99
	San Jose PMSA, CA	S	29.08 MW	31.48 AW	60480 AAW	CABLS	10//99-12//99
	Stockton-Lodi MSA, CA	S	24.20 MW	19.42 AW	50340 AAW	CABLS	10//99-12//99
	Vallejo-Fairfield-Napa PMSA, CA	S	27.36 MW	32.37 AW	56900 AAW	CABLS	10//99-12//99
	Visalia-Tulare-Porterville MSA, CA	S	24.91 MW	27.68 AW	51800 AAW	CABLS	10//99-12//99
	Colorado	S	30.07 MW	27.65 AW	57520 AAW	COBLS	10//99-12//99
	Boulder-Longmont PMSA, CO	S	26.00 MW	24.74 AW	54080 AAW	COBLS	10//99-12//99
	Grand Junction MSA, CO	S	23.59 MW	23.49 AW	49080 AAW	COBLS	10//99-12//99
	Connecticut	S	29.99 MW	28.21 AW	58670 AAW	CTBLS	10//99-12//99
	Bridgeport PMSA, CT	S	28.65 MW	30.72 AW	59590 AAW	CTBLS	10//99-12//99
	Danbury PMSA, CT	S	27.64 MW	28.75 AW	57500 AAW	CTBLS	10//99-12//99
	Hartford MSA, CT	S	30.07 MW	33.53 AW	62550 AAW	CTBLS	10//99-12//99
	New London-Norwich MSA, CT-RI	S	24.01 MW	23.39 AW	49930 AAW	CTBLS	10//99-12//99
	Stamford-Norwalk PMSA, CT	S	27.48 MW	29.51 AW	57160 AAW	CTBLS	10//99-12//99
	Waterbury PMSA, CT	S	26.82 MW	25.89 AW	55780 AAW	CTBLS	10//99-12//99
	Delaware	S	21.28 MW	21.93 AW	45610 AAW	DEBLS	10//99-12//99
	Dover MSA, DE	S	22.81 MW	22.90 AW	47440 AAW	DEBLS	10//99-12//99
	Wilmington-Newark PMSA, DE-MD	S	21.23 MW	20.99 AW	44150 AAW	DEBLS	10//99-12//99
	District of Columbia	S	18.38 MW	20.57 AW	42790 AAW	DCBLS	10//99-12//99
	Washington PMSA, DC-MD-VA-WV	S	28.42 MW	30.27 AW	59110 AAW	DCBLS	10//99-12//99
	Florida	S	21.07 MW	21.15 AW	44000 AAW	FLBLS	10//99-12//99
	Daytona Beach MSA, FL	S	17.97 MW	18.10 AW	37380 AAW	FLBLS	10//99-12//99
	Fort Lauderdale PMSA, FL	S	23.91 MW	23.00 AW	49730 AAW	FLBLS	10//99-12//99
	Fort Myers-Cape Coral MSA, FL	S	23.67 MW	23.12 AW	49230 AAW	FLBLS	10//99-12//99
	Fort Pierce-Port St. Lucie MSA, FL	S	22.72 MW	22.89 AW	47260 AAW	FLBLS	10//99-12//99
	Fort Walton Beach MSA, FL	S	17.34 MW	17.84 AW	36070 AAW	FLBLS	10//99-12//99
	Gainesville MSA, FL	S	17.29 MW	17.54 AW	35960 AAW	FLBLS	10//99-12//99
	Jacksonville MSA, FL	S	20.97 MW	19.32 AW	43630 AAW	FLBLS	10//99-12//99
	Lakeland-Winter Haven MSA, FL	S	22.41 MW	24.00 AW	46610 AAW	FLBLS	10//99-12//99
	Melbourne-Titusville-Palm Bay MSA, FL	S	17.31 MW	13.54 AW	36000 AAW	FLBLS	10//99-12//99
	Miami PMSA, FL	S	25.13 MW	23.86 AW	52260 AAW	FLBLS	10//99-12//99
	Naples MSA, FL	S	26.94 MW	31.19 AW	56030 AAW	FLBLS	10//99-12//99
	Ocala MSA, FL	S	17.23 MW	18.34 AW	35830 AAW	FLBLS	10//99-12//99
	Orlando MSA, FL	S	22.11 MW	22.95 AW	45980 AAW	FLBLS	10//99-12//99
	Panama City MSA, FL	S	17.95 MW	16.27 AW	37340 AAW	FLBLS	10//99-12//99
	Pensacola MSA, FL	S	15.86 MW	15.88 AW	33000 AAW	FLBLS	10//99-12//99
	Punta Gorda MSA, FL	S	24.39 MW	23.11 AW	50720 AAW	FLBLS	10//99-12//99
	Tallahassee MSA, FL	S	18.16 MW	18.28 AW	37770 AAW	FLBLS	10//99-12//99
	Georgia	S	18.82 MW	19.43 AW	40410 AAW	GABLS	10//99-12//99
	Athens MSA, GA	S	19.88 MW	19.55 AW	41350 AAW	GABLS	10//99-12//99
	Atlanta MSA, GA	S	20.44 MW	19.19 AW	42510 AAW	GABLS	10//99-12//99
	Augusta-Aiken MSA, GA-SC	S	16.48 MW	16.55 AW	34280 AAW	GABLS	10//99-12//99
	Columbus MSA, GA-AL	S	15.48 MW	15.35 AW	32200 AAW	GABLS	10//99-12//99
	Savannah MSA, GA	S	19.11 MW	19.77 AW	39740 AAW	GABLS	10//99-12//99
	Hawaii	S	29.14 MW	27.24 AW	56660 AAW	HIBLS	10//99-12//99
	Honolulu MSA, HI	S	24.83 MW	24.03 AW	51650 AAW	HIBLS	10//99-12//99
	Idaho	S	30.58 MW	28.18 AW	58610 AAW	IDBLS	10//99-12//99
	Pocatello MSA, ID	S	22.44 MW	21.33 AW	46680 AAW	IDBLS	10//99-12//99
	Illinois	S	22.64 MW	22.55 AW	46910 AAW	ILBLS	10//99-12//99
	Chicago PMSA, IL	S	25.84 MW	24.76 AW	53740 AAW	ILBLS	10//99-12//99
	Decatur MSA, IL	S	15.89 MW	15.76 AW	33060 AAW	ILBLS	10//99-12//99
	Kankakee PMSA, IL	S	22.76 MW	23.31 AW	47330 AAW	ILBLS	10//99-12//99

AAW Average annual wage	AOH Average offered, high	ASH Average starting, high	H Hourly	M Monthly	S Special: hourly and annual
AE Average entry wage	AOL Average offered, low	ASL Average starting, low	HI Highest wage paid	MTC Median total compensation	TQ Third quartile wage
AEX Average experienced wage	APH Average pay, high range	AW Average wage paid	HR High end range	MW Median wage paid	W Weekly
AO Average offered	APL Average pay, low range	FQ First quartile wage	LR Low end range	SQ Second quartile wage	Y Yearly

Occupation/Type/Industry	Location	Per	Low	Mid	High	Source	Date
Dental Hygienist	Peoria-Pekin MSA, IL	S	22.72 MW	20.09 AW	47260 AAW	ILBLS	10//99-12/99
	Springfield MSA, IL	S	22.18 MW	22.91 AW	46130 AAW	ILBLS	10//99-12/99
	Indiana	S	21.47 MW	21.81 AW	45370 AAW	INBLS	10//99-12/99
	Bloomington MSA, IN	S	13.83 MW	13.05 AW	28770 AAW	INBLS	10//99-12/99
	Elkhart-Goshen MSA, IN	S	21.27 MW	21.98 AW	44240 AAW	INBLS	10//99-12/99
	Fort Wayne MSA, IN	S	20.69 MW	21.73 AW	43030 AAW	INBLS	10//99-12/99
	Gary PMSA, IN	S	22.75 MW	22.98 AW	47320 AAW	INBLS	10//99-12/99
	Indianapolis MSA, IN	S	25.83 MW	23.46 AW	53730 AAW	INBLS	10//99-12/99
	Kokomo MSA, IN	S	20.42 MW	22.35 AW	42470 AAW	INBLS	10//99-12/99
	Lafayette MSA, IN	S	19.12 MW	22.07 AW	39760 AAW	INBLS	10//99-12/99
	South Bend MSA, IN	S	20.00 MW	20.38 AW	41600 AAW	INBLS	10//99-12/99
	Iowa	S	19.61 MW	19.45 AW	40460 AAW	IABLS	10//99-12/99
	Cedar Rapids MSA, IA	S	19.48 MW	19.10 AW	40520 AAW	IABLS	10//99-12/99
	Des Moines MSA, IA	S	23.00 MW	23.29 AW	47850 AAW	IABLS	10//99-12/99
	Iowa City MSA, IA	S	23.31 MW	22.84 AW	48490 AAW	IABLS	10//99-12/99
	Sioux City MSA, IA-NE	S	22.98 MW	23.44 AW	47790 AAW	IABLS	10//99-12/99
	Kansas	S	20.86 MW	20.81 AW	43280 AAW	KSBLS	10//99-12/99
	Lawrence MSA, KS	S	18.94 MW	15.90 AW	39400 AAW	KSBLS	10//99-12/99
	Topeka MSA, KS	S	24.47 MW	24.19 AW	50890 AAW	KSBLS	10//99-12/99
	Kentucky	S	18.3 MW	17.82 AW	37060 AAW	KYBLS	10//99-12/99
	Louisville MSA, KY-IN	S	17.06 MW	17.07 AW	35480 AAW	KYBLS	10//99-12/99
	Louisiana	S	21.74 MW	20.90 AW	43460 AAW	LABLS	10//99-12/99
	Houma MSA, LA	S	13.32 MW	12.83 AW	27710 AAW	LABLS	10//99-12/99
	Monroe MSA, LA	S	18.50 MW	18.52 AW	38470 AAW	LABLS	10//99-12/99
	New Orleans MSA, LA	S	19.49 MW	21.49 AW	40530 AAW	LABLS	10//99-12/99
	Maine	S	19.25 MW	19.53 AW	40630 AAW	MEBLS	10//99-12/99
	Lewiston-Auburn MSA, ME	S	20.00 MW	19.55 AW	41590 AAW	MEBLS	10//99-12/99
	Maryland	S	24.58 MW	23.83 AW	49560 AAW	MDBLS	10//99-12/99
	Baltimore PMSA, MD	S	21.33 MW	21.83 AW	44360 AAW	MDBLS	10//99-12/99
	Cumberland MSA, MD-WV	S	18.28 MW	18.31 AW	38020 AAW	MDBLS	10//99-12/99
	Hagerstown PMSA, MD	S	19.89 MW	19.48 AW	41370 AAW	MDBLS	10//99-12/99
	Massachusetts	S	23.53 MW	23.90 AW	49710 AAW	MABLS	10//99-12/99
	Boston PMSA, MA-NH	S	23.36 MW	23.35 AW	48590 AAW	MABLS	10//99-12/99
	Fitchburg-Leominster PMSA, MA	S	26.82 MW	24.16 AW	55790 AAW	MABLS	10//99-12/99
	Lawrence PMSA, MA-NH	S	23.75 MW	23.43 AW	49400 AAW	MABLS	10//99-12/99
	New Bedford PMSA, MA	S	22.83 MW	20.62 AW	47490 AAW	MABLS	10//99-12/99
	Pittsfield MSA, MA	S	20.36 MW	22.68 AW	42350 AAW	MABLS	10//99-12/99
	Michigan	S	21.44 MW	21.06 AW	43800 AAW	MIBLS	10//99-12/99
	Detroit PMSA, MI	S	22.50 MW	22.96 AW	46800 AAW	MIBLS	10//99-12/99
	Flint PMSA, MI	S	18.06 MW	19.91 AW	37570 AAW	MIBLS	10//99-12/99
	Jackson MSA, MI	S	20.66 MW	21.77 AW	42970 AAW	MIBLS	10//99-12/99
	Saginaw-Bay City-Midland MSA, MI	S	16.73 MW	18.23 AW	34790 AAW	MIBLS	10//99-12/99
	Minnesota	S	23.82 MW	24.79 AW	51560 AAW	MNBLS	10//99-12/99
	Duluth-Superior MSA, MN-WI	S	17.60 MW	17.91 AW	36610 AAW	MNBLS	10//99-12/99
	Minneapolis-St. Paul MSA, MN-WI	S	26.00 MW	24.93 AW	54090 AAW	MNBLS	10//99-12/99
	Rochester MSA, MN	S	21.17 MW	21.56 AW	44030 AAW	MNBLS	10//99-12/99
	Mississippi	S	13.99 MW	15.07 AW	31340 AAW	MSBLS	10//99-12/99
	Biloxi-Gulfport-Pascagoula MSA, MS	S	14.33 MW	11.49 AW	29810 AAW	MSBLS	10//99-12/99
	Hattiesburg MSA, MS	S	16.42 MW	15.99 AW	34140 AAW	MSBLS	10//99-12/99
	Jackson MSA, MS	S	12.48 MW	10.25 AW	25950 AAW	MSBLS	10//99-12/99
	Missouri	S	20.94 MW	19.82 AW	41230 AAW	MOBLS	10//99-12/99
	Columbia MSA, MO	S	22.29 MW	23.06 AW	46370 AAW	MOBLS	10//99-12/99
	Montana	S	25.5 MW	26.64 AW	55410 AAW	MTBLS	10//99-12/99
	Nebraska	S	22 MW	22.18 AW	46130 AAW	NEBLS	10//99-12/99
	Lincoln MSA, NE	S	23.52 MW	22.37 AW	48920 AAW	NEBLS	10//99-12/99
	Omaha MSA, NE-IA	S	23.06 MW	23.93 AW	47970 AAW	NEBLS	10//99-12/99
	Nevada	S	28.69 MW	27.81 AW	57840 AAW	NVBLS	10//99-12/99
	Las Vegas MSA, NV-AZ	S	26.15 MW	24.54 AW	54400 AAW	NVBLS	10//99-12/99
	New Hampshire	S	22.95 MW	23.03 AW	47900 AAW	NHBLS	10//99-12/99
	Manchester PMSA, NH	S	23.64 MW	23.52 AW	49170 AAW	NHBLS	10//99-12/99
	Nashua PMSA, NH	S	22.93 MW	23.02 AW	47700 AAW	NHBLS	10//99-12/99
	Portsmouth-Rochester PMSA, NH-ME	S	18.77 MW	21.45 AW	39040 AAW	NHBLS	10//99-12/99
	New Jersey	S	26.79 MW	26.33 AW	54770 AAW	NJBLS	10//99-12/99
	Bergen-Passaic PMSA, NJ	S	24.81 MW	23.97 AW	51610 AAW	NJBLS	10//99-12/99
	Middlesex-Somerset-Hunterdon PMSA, NJ	S	27.30 MW	28.83 AW	56790 AAW	NJBLS	10//99-12/99
	Newark PMSA, NJ	S	30.01 MW	29.88 AW	62430 AAW	NJBLS	10//99-12/99

AAW	Average annual wage	AOH	Average offered, high	ASH Average starting, high	H Hourly	M Monthly	S Special: hourly and annual
AE	Average entry wage	AOL	Average offered, low	ASL Average starting, low	HI Highest wage paid	MTC Median total compensation	TQ Third quartile wage
AEX	Average experienced wage	APH	Average pay, high range	AW Average wage paid	HR High end range	MW Median wage paid	W Weekly
AO	Average offered	APL	Average pay, low range	FQ First quartile wage	LR Low end range	SQ Second quartile wage	Y Yearly

Occupation/Type/Industry	Location	Per	Low	Mid	High	Source	Date
Dental Hygienist	Trenton PMSA, NJ	S	26.73 MW	29.60 AW	55590 AAW	NJBLS	10//99-12//99
	Vineland-Millville-Bridgeton PMSA, NJ	S	22.25 MW	19.86 AW	46280 AAW	NJBLS	10//99-12//99
	New Mexico	S	26.88 MW	26.50 AW	55130 AAW	NMBLS	10//99-12//99
	Albuquerque MSA, NM	S	26.62 MW	27.12 AW	55370 AAW	NMBLS	10//99-12//99
	Santa Fe MSA, NM	S	27.41 MW	26.24 AW	57010 AAW	NMBLS	10//99-12//99
	New York	S	21.74 MW	22.88 AW	47600 AAW	NYBLS	10//99-12//99
	Albany-Schenectady-Troy MSA, NY	S	20.62 MW	21.08 AW	42890 AAW	NYBLS	10//99-12//99
	Binghamton MSA, NY	S	15.77 MW	16.86 AW	32810 AAW	NYBLS	10//99-12//99
	Buffalo-Niagara Falls MSA, NY	S	17.52 MW	17.88 AW	36430 AAW	NYBLS	10//99-12//99
	Jamestown MSA, NY	S	17.68 MW	17.68 AW	36770 AAW	NYBLS	10//99-12//99
	New York PMSA, NY	S	25.16 MW	26.15 AW	52330 AAW	NYBLS	10//99-12//99
	Newburgh PMSA, NY-PA	S	24.90 MW	24.48 AW	51780 AAW	NYBLS	10//99-12//99
	Syracuse MSA, NY	S	17.74 MW	18.32 AW	36900 AAW	NYBLS	10//99-12//99
	Utica-Rome MSA, NY	S	21.36 MW	22.07 AW	44420 AAW	NYBLS	10//99-12//99
	North Carolina	S	19.84 MW	19.86 AW	41300 AAW	NCBLS	10//99-12//99
	Asheville MSA, NC	S	18.61 MW	18.80 AW	38720 AAW	NCBLS	10//99-12//99
	Charlotte-Gastonia-Rock Hill MSA, NC-SC	S	18.96 MW	17.96 AW	39440 AAW	NCBLS	10//99-12//99
	Fayetteville MSA, NC	S	17.47 MW	17.66 AW	36340 AAW	NCBLS	10//99-12//99
	Goldsboro MSA, NC	S	15.99 MW	18.24 AW	33260 AAW	NCBLS	10//99-12//99
	Greenville MSA, NC	S	22.79 MW	20.58 AW	47410 AAW	NCBLS	10//99-12//99
	Jacksonville MSA, NC	S	15.63 MW	13.75 AW	32510 AAW	NCBLS	10//99-12//99
	Raleigh-Durham-Chapel Hill MSA, NC	S	21.21 MW	21.86 AW	44120 AAW	NCBLS	10//99-12//99
	Wilmington MSA, NC	S	15.58 MW	18.01 AW	32410 AAW	NCBLS	10//99-12//99
	North Dakota	S	19.13 MW	18.98 AW	39480 AAW	NDBLS	10//99-12//99
	Bismarck MSA, ND	S	19.20 MW	18.79 AW	39940 AAW	NDBLS	10//99-12//99
	Fargo-Moorhead MSA, ND-MN	S	20.36 MW	20.15 AW	42350 AAW	NDBLS	10//99-12//99
	Grand Forks MSA, ND-MN	S	23.33 MW	23.33 AW	48520 AAW	NDBLS	10//99-12//99
	Ohio	S	22.03 MW	21.72 AW	45180 AAW	OHBLS	10//99-12//99
	Akron PMSA, OH	S	22.28 MW	22.43 AW	46340 AAW	OHBLS	10//99-12//99
	Cincinnati PMSA, OH-KY-IN	S	20.65 MW	21.80 AW	42950 AAW	OHBLS	10//99-12//99
	Cleveland-Lorain-Elyria PMSA, OH	S	20.29 MW	21.75 AW	42200 AAW	OHBLS	10//99-12//99
	Columbus MSA, OH	S	23.98 MW	23.35 AW	49870 AAW	OHBLS	10//99-12//99
	Hamilton-Middletown PMSA, OH	S	19.55 MW	19.46 AW	40660 AAW	OHBLS	10//99-12//99
	Mansfield MSA, OH	S	17.28 MW	17.25 AW	35940 AAW	OHBLS	10//99-12//99
	Steubenville-Weirton MSA, OH-WV	S	18.05 MW	18.54 AW	37550 AAW	OHBLS	10//99-12//99
	Toledo MSA, OH	S	20.30 MW	20.37 AW	42230 AAW	OHBLS	10//99-12//99
	Oklahoma	S	22.91 MW	22.70 AW	47220 AAW	OKBLS	10//99-12//99
	Lawton MSA, OK	S	21.62 MW	20.03 AW	44960 AAW	OKBLS	10//99-12//99
	Oklahoma City MSA, OK	S	22.46 MW	22.70 AW	46710 AAW	OKBLS	10//99-12//99
	Tulsa MSA, OK	S	25.49 MW	24.79 AW	53010 AAW	OKBLS	10//99-12//99
	Oregon	S	32.57 MW	29.72 AW	61830 AAW	ORBLS	10//99-12//99
	Corvallis MSA, OR	S	24.46 MW	23.93 AW	50870 AAW	ORBLS	10//99-12//99
	Eugene-Springfield MSA, OR	S	28.18 MW	29.98 AW	58610 AAW	ORBLS	10//99-12//99
	Portland-Vancouver PMSA, OR-WA	S	31.07 MW	34.11 AW	64630 AAW	ORBLS	10//99-12//99
	Pennsylvania	S	18.97 MW	19.01 AW	39540 AAW	PABLS	10//99-12//99
	Harrisburg-Lebanon-Carlisle MSA, PA	S	18.36 MW	17.90 AW	38180 AAW	PABLS	10//99-12//99
	Johnstown MSA, PA	S	13.29 MW	12.76 AW	27650 AAW	PABLS	10//99-12//99
	Lancaster MSA, PA	S	17.22 MW	20.51 AW	35820 AAW	PABLS	10//99-12//99
	Philadelphia PMSA, PA-NJ	S	24.81 MW	25.02 AW	51600 AAW	PABLS	10//99-12//99
	Pittsburgh MSA, PA	S	14.80 MW	15.69 AW	30790 AAW	PABLS	10//99-12//99
	State College MSA, PA	S	19.09 MW	18.96 AW	39710 AAW	PABLS	10//99-12//99
	York MSA, PA	S	22.04 MW	22.51 AW	45850 AAW	PABLS	10//99-12//99
	Rhode Island	S	24.61 MW	25.38 AW	52780 AAW	RIBLS	10//99-12//99
	Providence-Fall River-Warwick MSA, RI-MA	S	25.34 MW	24.50 AW	52710 AAW	RIBLS	10//99-12//99
	South Carolina	S	17.65 MW	17.47 AW	36330 AAW	SCBLS	10//99-12//99
	Charleston-North Charleston MSA, SC	S	18.14 MW	17.87 AW	37740 AAW	SCBLS	10//99-12//99
	Greenville-Spartanburg-Anderson MSA, SC	S	17.71 MW	18.15 AW	36830 AAW	SCBLS	10//99-12//99
	South Dakota	S	17.98 MW	18.14 AW	37740 AAW	SDBLS	10//99-12//99

AAW	Average annual wage	AOH	Average offered, high	ASH	Average starting, high	H	Hourly	M	Monthly	S	Special: hourly and annual
AE	Average entry wage	AOL	Average offered, low	ASL	Average starting, low	HI	Highest wage paid	MTC	Median total compensation	TQ	Third quartile wage
AEX	Average experienced wage	APH	Average pay, high range	AW	Average wage paid	HR	High end range	MW	Median wage paid	W	Weekly
AO	Average offered	APL	Average pay, low range	FQ	First quartile wage	LR	Low end range	SQ	Second quartile wage	Y	Yearly

Occupation/Type/Industry	Location	Per	Low	Mid	High	Source	Date
Dental Hygienist	Sioux Falls MSA, SD	S	17.76 MW	18.24 AW	36940 AAW	SDBLS	10//99-12//99
	Tennessee	S	18.58 MW	18.84 AW	39190 AAW	TNBLS	10//99-12//99
	Chattanooga MSA, TN-GA	S	17.20 MW	17.71 AW	35780 AAW	TNBLS	10//99-12//99
	Clarksville-Hopkinsville MSA, TN-KY	S	17.87 MW	18.78 AW	37180 AAW	TNBLS	10//99-12//99
	Jackson MSA, TN	S	20.85 MW	21.22 AW	43370 AAW	TNBLS	10//99-12//99
	Johnson City-Kingsport-Bristol MSA, TN-VA	S	19.33 MW	20.62 AW	40220 AAW	TNBLS	10//99-12//99
	Memphis MSA, TN-AR-MS	S	19.33 MW	19.86 AW	40210 AAW	MSBLS	10//99-12//99
	Texas	S	21.4 MW	22.43 AW	46640 AAW	TXBLS	10//99-12//99
	Abilene MSA, TX	S	12.85 MW	9.99 AW	26730 AAW	TXBLS	10//99-12//99
	Amarillo MSA, TX	S	14.96 MW	15.99 AW	31110 AAW	TXBLS	10//99-12//99
	Bryan-College Station MSA, TX	S	18.87 MW	17.65 AW	39250 AAW	TXBLS	10//99-12//99
	Corpus Christi MSA, TX	S	17.43 MW	17.95 AW	36260 AAW	TXBLS	10//99-12//99
	Dallas PMSA, TX	S	26.42 MW	28.55 AW	54960 AAW	TXBLS	10//99-12//99
	Fort Worth-Arlington PMSA, TX	S	25.76 MW	26.76 AW	53590 AAW	TXBLS	10//99-12//99
	Houston PMSA, TX	S	22.25 MW	21.07 AW	46280 AAW	TXBLS	10//99-12//99
	Killeen-Temple MSA, TX	S	16.82 MW	16.13 AW	34990 AAW	TXBLS	10//99-12//99
	Longview-Marshall MSA, TX	S	18.81 MW	18.51 AW	39120 AAW	TXBLS	10//99-12//99
	McAllen-Edinburg-Mission MSA, TX	S	28.71 MW	30.16 AW	59720 AAW	TXBLS	10//99-12//99
	San Antonio MSA, TX	S	21.85 MW	21.20 AW	45440 AAW	TXBLS	10//99-12//99
	Texarkana MSA, TX-Texarkana, AR	S	19.46 MW	20.10 AW	40490 AAW	TXBLS	10//99-12//99
	Wichita Falls MSA, TX	S	16.24 MW	16.76 AW	33780 AAW	TXBLS	10//99-12//99
	Utah	S	28.68 MW	27.40 AW	57000 AAW	UTBLS	10//99-12//99
	Provo-Orem MSA, UT	S	26.43 MW	27.09 AW	54970 AAW	UTBLS	10//99-12//99
	Vermont	S	20.26 MW	19.67 AW	40910 AAW	VTBLS	10//99-12//99
	Burlington MSA, VT	S	18.18 MW	18.05 AW	37820 AAW	VTBLS	10//99-12//99
	Virginia	S	25.33 MW	26.96 AW	56080 AAW	VABLS	10//99-12//99
	Charlottesville MSA, VA	S	21.06 MW	21.36 AW	43800 AAW	VABLS	10//99-12//99
	Danville MSA, VA	S	22.11 MW	23.19 AW	45980 AAW	VABLS	10//99-12//99
	Lynchburg MSA, VA	S	25.60 MW	24.17 AW	53250 AAW	VABLS	10//99-12//99
	Norfolk-Virginia Beach-Newport News MSA, VA-NC	S	25.74 MW	24.63 AW	53540 AAW	VABLS	10//99-12//99
	Richmond-Petersburg MSA, VA	S	25.76 MW	24.42 AW	53580 AAW	VABLS	10//99-12//99
	Washington	S	35.08 MW	31.67 AW	65870 AAW	WABLS	10//99-12//99
	Bellingham MSA, WA	S	30.81 MW	34.58 AW	64090 AAW	WABLS	10//99-12//99
	Bremerton PMSA, WA	S	28.81 MW	33.59 AW	59920 AAW	WABLS	10//99-12//99
	Olympia PMSA, WA	S	28.20 MW	28.25 AW	58660 AAW	WABLS	10//99-12//99
	Richland-Kennewick-Pasco MSA, WA	S	26.47 MW	32.05 AW	55050 AAW	WABLS	10//99-12//99
	Seattle-Bellevue-Everett PMSA, WA	S	32.59 MW	36.04 AW	67780 AAW	WABLS	10//99-12//99
	Spokane MSA, WA	S	32.41 MW	34.90 AW	67400 AAW	WABLS	10//99-12//99
	Yakima MSA, WA	S	26.81 MW	29.74 AW	55770 AAW	WABLS	10//99-12//99
	West Virginia	S	16.06 MW	15.43 AW	32090 AAW	WVBLS	10//99-12//99
	Huntington-Ashland MSA, WV-KY-OH	S	19.00 MW	17.64 AW	39510 AAW	WVBLS	10//99-12//99
	Parkersburg-Marietta MSA, WV-OH	S	17.45 MW	19.03 AW	36290 AAW	WVBLS	10//99-12//99
	Wheeling MSA, WV-OH	S	12.48 MW	12.33 AW	25950 AAW	WVBLS	10//99-12//99
	Wisconsin	S	20.69 MW	19.52 AW	40600 AAW	WIBLS	10//99-12//99
	Green Bay MSA, WI	S	22.09 MW	22.52 AW	45940 AAW	WIBLS	10//99-12//99
	Kenosha PMSA, WI	S	23.57 MW	23.12 AW	49030 AAW	WIBLS	10//99-12//99
	La Crosse MSA, WI-MN	S	23.02 MW	23.43 AW	47890 AAW	WIBLS	10//99-12//99
	Madison MSA, WI	S	21.70 MW	22.19 AW	45140 AAW	WIBLS	10//99-12//99
	Milwaukee-Waukesha PMSA, WI	S	17.72 MW	17.84 AW	36850 AAW	WIBLS	10//99-12//99
	Sheboygan MSA, WI	S	22.93 MW	23.29 AW	47700 AAW	WIBLS	10//99-12//99
	Wyoming	S	20.62 MW	21.08 AW	43850 AAW	WYBLS	10//99-12//99
	Cheyenne MSA, WY	S	22.62 MW	23.05 AW	47040 AAW	WYBLS	10//99-12//99
	Puerto Rico	S	11.47 MW	13.03 AW	27110 AAW	PRBLS	10//99-12//99
	San Juan-Bayamon PMSA, PR	S	11.76 MW	11.37 AW	24460 AAW	PRBLS	10//99-12//99
	Virgin Islands	S	17.45 MW	18.92 AW	39350 AAW	VIBLS	10//99-12//99
	Guam	S	13.51 MW	15.67 AW	32590 AAW	GUBLS	10//99-12//99
Dental Laboratory Technician	Alabama	S	11.45 MW	11.99 AW	24950 AAW	ALBLS	10//99-12//99
	Arizona	S	12.86 MW	13.90 AW	28900 AAW	AZBLS	10//99-12//99

Occupation/Type/Industry	Location	Per	Low	Mid	High	Source	Date
Dental Laboratory Technician	Arkansas	S	12.34 MW	13.44 AW	27950 AAW	ARBLS	10//99-12//99
	California	S	12.49 MW	14.31 AW	29760 AAW	CABLS	10//99-12//99
	Colorado	S	13.31 MW	13.98 AW	29080 AAW	COBLS	10//99-12//99
	Connecticut	S	13.18 MW	14.23 AW	29600 AAW	CTBLS	10//99-12//99
	Delaware	S	15.11 MW	18.99 AW	39500 AAW	DEBLS	10//99-12//99
	Florida	S	11.48 MW	12.44 AW	25870 AAW	FLBLS	10//99-12//99
	Georgia	S	13.3 MW	14.38 AW	29920 AAW	GABLS	10//99-12//99
	Hawaii	S	11.31 MW	11.49 AW	23900 AAW	HIBLS	10//99-12//99
	Idaho	S	10.73 MW	12.68 AW	26360 AAW	IDBLS	10//99-12//99
	Illinois	S	13.53 MW	13.98 AW	29080 AAW	ILBLS	10//99-12//99
	Indiana	S	12.69 MW	13.60 AW	28300 AAW	INBLS	10//99-12//99
	Iowa	S	12.52 MW	13.22 AW	27490 AAW	IABLS	10//99-12//99
	Kansas	S	10.63 MW	11.86 AW	24670 AAW	KSBLS	10//99-12//99
	Kentucky	S	11.49 MW	13.39 AW	27860 AAW	KYBLS	10//99-12//99
	Louisiana	S	10.29 MW	11.62 AW	24170 AAW	LABLS	10//99-12//99
	Maryland	S	11.15 MW	12.38 AW	25750 AAW	MDBLS	10//99-12//99
	Massachusetts	S	15.22 MW	18.28 AW	38020 AAW	MABLS	10//99-12//99
	Michigan	S	13.36 MW	16.60 AW	34520 AAW	MIBLS	10//99-12//99
	Minnesota	S	11.35 MW	12.58 AW	26170 AAW	MNBLS	10//99-12//99
	Mississippi	S	9.61 MW	11.03 AW	22950 AAW	MSBLS	10//99-12//99
	Missouri	S	10.96 MW	13.87 AW	28840 AAW	MOBLS	10//99-12//99
	Montana	S	30.64 MW	25.97 AW	54010 AAW	MTBLS	10//99-12//99
	Nebraska	S	13.83 MW	14.32 AW	29790 AAW	NEBLS	10//99-12//99
	Nevada	S	13.08 MW	13.88 AW	28860 AAW	NVBLS	10//99-12//99
	New Hampshire	S	11.8 MW	13.31 AW	27680 AAW	NHBLS	10//99-12//99
	New Jersey	S	16.74 MW	18.32 AW	38110 AAW	NJBLS	10//99-12//99
	New Mexico	S	10.44 MW	11.34 AW	23590 AAW	NMBLS	10//99-12//99
	New York	S	13.49 MW	14.98 AW	31150 AAW	NYBLS	10//99-12//99
	North Carolina	S	12.81 MW	13.98 AW	29080 AAW	NCBLS	10//99-12//99
	North Dakota	S	9.86 MW	11.77 AW	24480 AAW	NDBLS	10//99-12//99
	Ohio	S	12.32 MW	13.68 AW	28460 AAW	OHBLS	10//99-12//99
	Oklahoma	S	15.09 MW	14.94 AW	31080 AAW	OKBLS	10//99-12//99
	Oregon	S	16.27 MW	15.82 AW	32910 AAW	ORBLS	10//99-12//99
	Pennsylvania	S	11.64 MW	13.96 AW	29040 AAW	PABLS	10//99-12//99
	Rhode Island	S	14.68 MW	15.05 AW	31300 AAW	RIBLS	10//99-12//99
	South Carolina	S	11.41 MW	12.53 AW	26060 AAW	SCBLS	10//99-12//99
	South Dakota	S	11.56 MW	11.66 AW	24250 AAW	SDBLS	10//99-12//99
	Tennessee	S	11.46 MW	12.52 AW	26050 AAW	TNBLS	10//99-12//99
	Texas	S	10.91 MW	11.63 AW	24190 AAW	TXBLS	10//99-12//99
	Utah	S	11.83 MW	14.87 AW	30920 AAW	UTBLS	10//99-12//99
	Vermont	S	13.97 MW	14.05 AW	29220 AAW	VTBLS	10//99-12//99
	Virginia	S	11.78 MW	13.44 AW	27950 AAW	VABLS	10//99-12//99
	Washington	S	12.89 MW	14.45 AW	30060 AAW	WABLS	10//99-12//99
	Wisconsin	S	12.42 MW	14.35 AW	29840 AAW	WIBLS	10//99-12//99
Dentist	United States	Y		110160 AW		DENE	1999
	United States	H		34.90 AW		NCS98	1998
	Alabama	S	54.78 MW	56.41 AW	117320 AAW	ALBLS	10//99-12//99
	Birmingham MSA, AL	S	49.19 MW	47.31 AW	102320 AAW	ALBLS	10//99-12//99
	Alaska	S	62.71 MW	59.98 AW	124760 AAW	AKBLS	10//99-12//99
	Anchorage MSA, AK	S	59.98 MW	62.71 AW	124760 AAW	AKBLS	10//99-12//99
	Arizona	S	56.2 MW	52.99 AW	110220 AAW	AZBLS	10//99-12//99
	Phoenix-Mesa MSA, AZ	S	56.43 MW	60.04 AW	117380 AAW	AZBLS	10//99-12//99
	Tucson MSA, AZ	S	37.69 MW	38.56 AW	78400 AAW	AZBLS	10//99-12//99
	Little Rock-North Little Rock MSA, AR	S	45.27 MW	46.78 AW	94160 AAW	ARBLS	10//99-12//99
	California	S	54.94 MW	55.90 AW	116270 AAW	CABLS	10//99-12//99
	Bakersfield MSA, CA	S	44.89 MW	43.50 AW	93360 AAW	CABLS	10//99-12//99
	Fresno MSA, CA	S	42.03 MW	41.78 AW	87420 AAW	CABLS	10//99-12//99
	Los Angeles County, CA	Y		128841 AW		LABJ	1999
	Orange County PMSA, CA	S	52.52 MW	44.59 AW	109250 AAW	CABLS	10//99-12//99
	Salinas MSA, CA	S	46.13 MW	47.98 AW	95950 AAW	CABLS	10//99-12//99
	San Diego MSA, CA	S	40.09 MW	39.56 AW	83380 AAW	CABLS	10//99-12//99
	San Francisco PMSA, CA	S	47.85 MW	49.52 AW	99530 AAW	CABLS	10//99-12//99
	Vallejo-Fairfield-Napa PMSA, CA	S	38.81 MW	39.41 AW	80730 AAW	CABLS	10//99-12//99
	Connecticut	S	53.27 MW	48.62 AW	101140 AAW	CTBLS	10//99-12//99
	Danbury PMSA, CT	S	62.25 MW		129480 AAW	CTBLS	10//99-12//99
	New London-Norwich MSA, CT-RI	S	51.62 MW	54.79 AW	107360 AAW	CTBLS	10//99-12//99
	Waterbury PMSA, CT	S	48.94 MW	43.58 AW	101790 AAW	CTBLS	10//99-12//99
	District of Columbia	S	51.1 MW	52.33 AW	108850 AAW	DCBLS	10//99-12//99

AAW	Average annual wage	AOH	Average offered, high	ASH	Average starting, high	H	Hourly
AE	Average entry wage	AOL	Average offered, low	ASL	Average starting, low	HI	Highest wage paid
AEX	Average experienced wage	APH	Average pay, high range	AW	Average wage paid	HR	High end range
AO	Average offered	APL	Average pay, low range	FQ	First quartile wage	LR	Low end range

M	Monthly	S	Special: hourly and annual
MTC	Median total compensation	TQ	Third quartile wage
MW	Median wage paid	W	Weekly
SQ	Second quartile wage	Y	Yearly

Occupation/Type/Industry	Location	Per	Low	Mid	High	Source	Date
Dentist	Washington PMSA, DC-MD-VA-WV	S	56.59 MW		117710 AAW	DCBLS	10//99-12//99
	Florida	S	58.86 MW	54.77 AW	113920 AAW	FLBLS	10//99-12//99
	Fort Myers-Cape Coral MSA, FL	S	59.11 MW	69.24 AW	122940 AAW	FLBLS	10//99-12//99
	Fort Pierce-Port St. Lucie MSA, FL	S	58.86 MW	62.44 AW	122420 AAW	FLBLS	10//99-12//99
	Gainesville MSA, FL	S	61.53 MW	65.56 AW	127980 AAW	FLBLS	10//99-12//99
	Lakeland-Winter Haven MSA, FL	S	55.34 MW	57.40 AW	115110 AAW	FLBLS	10//99-12//99
	Melbourne-Titusville-Palm Bay MSA, FL	S	56.00 MW	53.06 AW	116480 AAW	FLBLS	10//99-12//99
	Miami PMSA, FL	S	47.55 MW	49.28 AW	98900 AAW	FLBLS	10//99-12//99
	Pensacola MSA, FL	S	59.28 MW	62.47 AW	123300 AAW	FLBLS	10//99-12//99
	Tallahassee MSA, FL	S	39.10 MW	39.46 AW	81330 AAW	FLBLS	10//99-12//99
	Tampa-St. Petersburg-Clearwater MSA, FL	S	55.42 MW	58.12 AW	115280 AAW	FLBLS	10//99-12//99
	Georgia	S		58.46 AW	121610 AAW	GABLS	10//99-12//99
	Athens MSA, GA	S	65.30 MW		135820 AAW	GABLS	10//99-12//99
	Idaho	S	40.87 MW	40.17 AW	83550 AAW	IDBLS	10//99-12//99
	Illinois	S	41.63 MW	40.13 AW	83470 AAW	ILBLS	10//99-12//99
	Chicago PMSA, IL	S	34.76 MW	37.21 AW	72310 AAW	ILBLS	10//99-12//99
	Kankakee PMSA, IL	S	69.58 MW		144720 AAW	ILBLS	10//99-12//99
	Indiana	S	34.13 MW	42.52 AW	88430 AAW	INBLS	10//99-12//99
	Indianapolis MSA, IN	S	30.85 MW	30.89 AW	64170 AAW	INBLS	10//99-12//99
	Iowa	S	41.73 MW	44.02 AW	91570 AAW	IABLS	10//99-12//99
	Kansas	S	49.82 MW	49.09 AW	102110 AAW	KSBLS	10//99-12//99
	Topeka MSA, KS	S	52.29 MW	60.94 AW	108760 AAW	KSBLS	10//99-12//99
	Louisville MSA, KY-IN	S	44.45 MW	47.38 AW	92450 AAW	KYBLS	10//99-12//99
	Louisiana	S	25.88 MW	37.36 AW	77700 AAW	LABLS	10//99-12//99
	Maryland	S	63.22 MW	52.24 AW	108660 AAW	MDBLS	10//99-12//99
	Baltimore PMSA, MD	S	58.82 MW	62.47 AW	122340 AAW	MDBLS	10//99-12//99
	Massachusetts	S	63.39 MW	56.48 AW	117480 AAW	MABLS	10//99-12//99
	Boston PMSA, MA-NH	S	48.79 MW	49.75 AW	101490 AAW	MABLS	10//99-12//99
	Lawrence PMSA, MA-NH	S	50.28 MW	50.32 AW	104580 AAW	MABLS	10//99-12//99
	Michigan	S		60.19 AW	125190 AAW	MIBLS	10//99-12//99
	Detroit PMSA, MI	S	47.65 MW	42.75 AW	99110 AAW	MIBLS	10//99-12//99
	Jackson MSA, MI	S	62.40 MW		129780 AAW	MIBLS	10//99-12//99
	Saginaw-Bay City-Midland MSA, MI	S	57.17 MW	68.09 AW	118920 AAW	MIBLS	10//99-12//99
	Minnesota	S		57.19 AW	118950 AAW	MNBLS	10//99-12//99
	Duluth-Superior MSA, MN-WI	S	54.38 MW	52.10 AW	113100 AAW	MNBLS	10//99-12//99
	Minneapolis-St. Paul MSA, MN-WI	S	56.96 MW		118480 AAW	MNBLS	10//99-12//99
	Mississippi	S	65.55 MW	52.34 AW	108870 AAW	MSBLS	10//99-12//99
	Jackson MSA, MS	S	44.77 MW	40.60 AW	93120 AAW	MSBLS	10//99-12//99
	Las Vegas MSA, NV-AZ	S	62.96 MW	67.99 AW	130950 AAW	NVBLS	10//99-12//99
	New Hampshire	S	52.9 MW	50.83 AW	105730 AAW	NHBLS	10//99-12//99
	Nashua PMSA, NH	S	48.86 MW	49.63 AW	101630 AAW	NHBLS	10//99-12//99
	New Jersey	S	58.91 MW	53.20 AW	110660 AAW	NJBLS	10//99-12//99
	Bergen-Passaic PMSA, NJ	S	49.53 MW	53.66 AW	103030 AAW	NJBLS	10//99-12//99
	Middlesex-Somerset-Hunterdon PMSA, NJ	S	54.36 MW	61.38 AW	113060 AAW	NJBLS	10//99-12//99
	Newark PMSA, NJ	S	42.42 MW	42.73 AW	88230 AAW	NJBLS	10//99-12//99
	Trenton PMSA, NJ	S	55.81 MW	61.01 AW	116090 AAW	NJBLS	10//99-12//99
	Vineland-Millville-Bridgeton PMSA, NJ	S	59.57 MW		123900 AAW	NJBLS	10//99-12//99
	New Mexico	S	58.33 MW	53.16 AW	110570 AAW	NMBLS	10//99-12//99
	Albuquerque MSA, NM	S	49.72 MW	49.07 AW	103420 AAW	NMBLS	10//99-12//99
	North Carolina	S		55.80 AW	116070 AAW	NCBLS	10//99-12//99
	Fayetteville MSA, NC	S	56.38 MW	54.72 AW	117280 AAW	NCBLS	10//99-12//99
	Jacksonville MSA, NC	S	52.48 MW	51.23 AW	109150 AAW	NCBLS	10//99-12//99
	Raleigh-Durham-Chapel Hill MSA, NC	S	38.34 MW	39.15 AW	79750 AAW	NCBLS	10//99-12//99
	North Dakota	S	42.17 MW	50.78 AW	105630 AAW	NDBLS	10//99-12//99
	Cincinnati PMSA, OH-KY-IN	S	67.43 MW		140250 AAW	OHBLS	10//99-12//99
	Cleveland-Lorain-Elyria PMSA, OH	S	36.35 MW	33.82 AW	75610 AAW	OHBLS	10//99-12//99
	Hamilton-Middletown PMSA, OH	S	66.38 MW		138070 AAW	OHBLS	10//99-12//99
	Toledo MSA, OH	S	67.27 MW		139930 AAW	OHBLS	10//99-12//99
	Lawton MSA, OK	S	61.76 MW		128470 AAW	OKBLS	10//99-12//99

Occupation/Type/Industry	Location	Per	Low	Mid	High	Source	Date
Dentist	Oklahoma City MSA, OK	S	27.43 MW	29.28 AW	57060 AAW	OKBLS	10//99-12//99
	Oregon	S		60.30 AW	125430 AAW	ORBLS	10//99-12//99
	Portland-Vancouver PMSA, OR-WA	S	61.62 MW		128170 AAW	ORBLS	10//99-12//99
	Pennsylvania	S	50.24 MW	48.51 AW	100890 AAW	PABLS	10//99-12//99
	Harrisburg-Lebanon-Carlisle MSA, PA	S	36.95 MW	39.15 AW	76850 AAW	PABLS	10//99-12//99
	Lancaster MSA, PA	S	56.43 MW	55.35 AW	117380 AAW	PABLS	10//99-12//99
	Philadelphia PMSA, PA-NJ	S	51.67 MW	57.10 AW	107480 AAW	PABLS	10//99-12//99
	Rhode Island	S	60.6 MW	55.87 AW	116210 AAW	RIBLS	10//99-12//99
	Providence-Fall River-Warwick MSA, RI-MA	S	56.88 MW	60.98 AW	118300 AAW	RIBLS	10//99-12//99
	South Carolina	S		66.38 AW	138070 AAW	SCBLS	10//99-12//99
	South Dakota	S		58.11 AW	120870 AAW	SDBLS	10//99-12//99
	Tennessee	S		60.55 AW	125940 AAW	TNBLS	10//99-12//99
	Johnson City-Kingsport-Bristol MSA, TN-VA	S	63.15 MW		131360 AAW	TNBLS	10//99-12//99
	Memphis MSA, TN-AR-MS	S	55.93 MW	62.41 AW	116330 AAW	MSBLS	10//99-12//99
	Texas	S	44.51 MW	41.70 AW	86740 AAW	TXBLS	10//99-12//99
	Dallas PMSA, TX	S	42.50 MW	46.28 AW	88390 AAW	TXBLS	10//99-12//99
	Fort Worth-Arlington PMSA, TX	S	41.43 MW	46.78 AW	86180 AAW	TXBLS	10//99-12//99
	Houston PMSA, TX	S	39.30 MW	34.46 AW	81750 AAW	TXBLS	10//99-12//99
	San Antonio MSA, TX	S	37.23 MW	37.53 AW	77430 AAW	TXBLS	10//99-12//99
	Utah	S	42.7 MW	45.26 AW	94150 AAW	UTBLS	10//99-12//99
	Provo-Orem MSA, UT	S	45.88 MW	41.97 AW	95430 AAW	UTBLS	10//99-12//99
	Salt Lake City-Ogden MSA, UT	S	46.71 MW	56.55 AW	97160 AAW	UTBLS	10//99-12//99
	Virginia	S		64.74 AW	134660 AAW	VABLS	10//99-12//99
	Lynchburg MSA, VA	S	58.31 MW	61.85 AW	121280 AAW	VABLS	10//99-12//99
	Washington	S		63.47 AW	132010 AAW	WABLS	10//99-12//99
	Olympia PMSA, WA	S	39.56 MW	39.72 AW	82280 AAW	WABLS	10//99-12//99
	Seattle-Bellevue-Everett PMSA, WA	S	42.94 MW	45.91 AW	89320 AAW	WABLS	10//99-12//99
	West Virginia	S	46.54 MW	51.69 AW	107510 AAW	WVBLS	10//99-12//99
	Wheeling MSA, WV-OH	S	43.79 MW	39.96 AW	91090 AAW	WVBLS	10//99-12//99
	Wisconsin	S	44.73 MW	43.31 AW	90080 AAW	WIBLS	10//99-12//99
	Appleton-Oshkosh-Neenah MSA, WI	S	59.09 MW	62.42 AW	122900 AAW	WIBLS	10//99-12//99
	La Crosse MSA, WI-MN	S	48.92 MW	49.84 AW	101760 AAW	WIBLS	10//99-12//99
	Madison MSA, WI	S	59.87 MW		124530 AAW	WIBLS	10//99-12//99
	Milwaukee-Waukesha PMSA, WI	S	37.28 MW	41.30 AW	77550 AAW	WIBLS	10//99-12//99
	Wyoming	S	38.97 MW	42.34 AW	88070 AAW	WYBLS	10//99-12//99
	Cheyenne MSA, WY	S	42.41 MW	38.96 AW	88210 AAW	WYBLS	10//99-12//99
	Puerto Rico	S	20.11 MW	22.72 AW	47260 AAW	PRBLS	10//99-12//99
	San Juan-Bayamon PMSA, PR	S	22.40 MW	20.10 AW	46590 AAW	PRBLS	10//99-12//99
	Guam	S	54.16 MW	52.47 AW	109130 AAW	GUBLS	10//99-12//99
Department Head							
Dietary/Food Service, Hospital	United States	Y		58200 AW		HFK2	1998
Facility/Plant Operations, Hospital	United States	Y		68200 AW		HFK2	1998
Housekeeping/Environmental Services, Hospital	United States	Y		48500 AW		HFK2	1998
Plant Engineering, Hospital	United States	Y		61200 AW		HFK2	1998
Purchasing/Materials Management, Hospital	United States	Y		62000 AW		HFK2	1998
Risk Management, Hospital	United States	Y		61600 AW		HFK2	1998
Security, Hospital	United States	Y		48300 AW		HFK2	1998
Derrick Operator							
Oil and Gas	Alaska	S	21.86 MW	20.15 AW	41920 AAW	AKBLS	10//99-12//99
Oil and Gas	Arkansas	S	11.08 MW	11.05 AW	22980 AAW	ARBLS	10//99-12//99
Oil and Gas	California	S	20.81 MW	18.26 AW	37970 AAW	CABLS	10//99-12//99
Oil and Gas	Colorado	S	11.4 MW	12.22 AW	25420 AAW	COBLS	10//99-12//99
Oil and Gas	Kansas	S	9.85 MW	9.95 AW	20700 AAW	KSBLS	10//99-12//99
Oil and Gas	Kentucky	S	9.86 MW	10.61 AW	22060 AAW	KYBLS	10//99-12//99
Oil and Gas	Louisiana	S	19.1 MW	18.21 AW	37880 AAW	LABLS	10//99-12//99
Oil and Gas	Michigan	S	12.51 MW	13.13 AW	27320 AAW	MIBLS	10//99-12//99
Oil and Gas	Mississippi	S	17.33 MW	16.10 AW	33480 AAW	MSBLS	10//99-12//99
Oil and Gas	Montana	S	12.27 MW	12.25 AW	25470 AAW	MTBLS	10//99-12//99
Oil and Gas	New Mexico	S	11.16 MW	11.30 AW	23510 AAW	NMBLS	10//99-12//99
Oil and Gas	Oklahoma	S	9.74 MW	9.72 AW	20220 AAW	OKBLS	10//99-12//99

AAW Average annual wage	**AOH** Average offered, high	**ASH** Average starting, high	**H** Hourly	**M** Monthly	**S** Special: hourly and annual
AE Average entry wage	**AOL** Average offered, low	**ASL** Average starting, low	**HI** Highest wage paid	**MTC** Median total compensation	**TQ** Third quartile wage
AEX Average experienced wage	**APH** Average pay, high range	**AW** Average wage paid	**HR** High end range	**MW** Median wage paid	**W** Weekly
AO Average offered	**APL** Average pay, low range	**FQ** First quartile wage	**LR** Low end range	**SQ** Second quartile wage	**Y** Yearly

Occupation/Type/Industry	Location	Per	Low	Mid	High	Source	Date
Derrick Operator							
Oil and Gas	Pennsylvania	S	11.28 MW	11.44 AW	23790 AAW	PABLS	10//99-12//99
Oil and Gas	Texas	S	12.43 MW	13.23 AW	27510 AAW	TXBLS	10//99-12//99
Oil and Gas	Utah	S	12.92 MW	13.33 AW	27720 AAW	UTBLS	10//99-12//99
Oil and Gas	West Virginia	S	9.79 MW	9.95 AW	20700 AAW	WVBLS	10//99-12//99
Oil and Gas	Wyoming	S	15.37 MW	15.58 AW	32400 AAW	WYBLS	10//99-12//99
Designer	United States	H		22.49 AW		NCS98	1998
Designer/Stylist							
Computer-aided Design, Apparel Industry	United States	Y		43575 AW		BOBBIN	1999
Desktop Publisher	Alabama	S	10.93 MW	11.44 AW	23800 AAW	ALBLS	10//99-12//99
	Arizona	S	19.64 MW	19.93 AW	41450 AAW	AZBLS	10//99-12//99
	Arkansas	S	11.95 MW	11.42 AW	23750 AAW	ARBLS	10//99-12//99
	California	S	14.26 MW	15.48 AW	32200 AAW	CABLS	10//99-12//99
	Colorado	S	14.26 MW	14.34 AW	29820 AAW	COBLS	10//99-12//99
	Connecticut	S	18.49 MW	17.77 AW	36960 AAW	CTBLS	10//99-12//99
	Delaware	S	12.47 MW	13.11 AW	27280 AAW	DEBLS	10//99-12//99
	District of Columbia	S	15.12 MW	17.18 AW	35740 AAW	DCBLS	10//99-12//99
	Florida	S	12.89 MW	13.44 AW	27960 AAW	FLBLS	10//99-12//99
	Georgia	S	12.89 MW	13.37 AW	27820 AAW	GABLS	10//99-12//99
	Hawaii	S	14.74 MW	14.23 AW	29590 AAW	HIBLS	10//99-12//99
	Idaho	S	8.59 MW	9.60 AW	19960 AAW	IDBLS	10//99-12//99
	Illinois	S	18.07 MW	21.09 AW	43880 AAW	ILBLS	10//99-12//99
	Indiana	S	11.19 MW	11.71 AW	24360 AAW	INBLS	10//99-12//99
	Iowa	S	10.49 MW	11.38 AW	23670 AAW	IABLS	10//99-12//99
	Kansas	S	10.97 MW	11.36 AW	23620 AAW	KSBLS	10//99-12//99
	Kentucky	S	11.09 MW	12.15 AW	25280 AAW	KYBLS	10//99-12//99
	Louisiana	S	12.08 MW	12.38 AW	25750 AAW	LABLS	10//99-12//99
	Maine	S	13.43 MW	13.52 AW	28130 AAW	MEBLS	10//99-12//99
	Maryland	S	14.91 MW	16.16 AW	33610 AAW	MDBLS	10//99-12//99
	Massachusetts	S	17.64 MW	17.25 AW	35870 AAW	MABLS	10//99-12//99
	Michigan	S	14.12 MW	13.98 AW	29070 AAW	MIBLS	10//99-12//99
	Minnesota	S	14.93 MW	14.92 AW	31040 AAW	MNBLS	10//99-12//99
	Mississippi	S	9.26 MW	9.55 AW	19860 AAW	MSBLS	10//99-12//99
	Missouri	S	8.82 MW	9.25 AW	19230 AAW	MOBLS	10//99-12//99
	Montana	S	11.66 MW	10.87 AW	22610 AAW	MTBLS	10//99-12//99
	Nebraska	S	10.03 MW	10.43 AW	21690 AAW	NEBLS	10//99-12//99
	Nevada	S	17.96 MW	19.47 AW	40500 AAW	NVBLS	10//99-12//99
	New Hampshire	S	15.32 MW	15.59 AW	32420 AAW	NHBLS	10//99-12//99
	New Jersey	S	16.97 MW	17.23 AW	35830 AAW	NJBLS	10//99-12//99
	New Mexico	S	13.68 MW	12.45 AW	25890 AAW	NMBLS	10//99-12//99
	New York	S	18.2 MW	18.41 AW	38280 AAW	NYBLS	10//99-12//99
	North Carolina	S	14.1 MW	14.06 AW	29250 AAW	NCBLS	10//99-12//99
	North Dakota	S	10.77 MW	11.43 AW	23770 AAW	NDBLS	10//99-12//99
	Ohio	S	12.78 MW	13.22 AW	27490 AAW	OHBLS	10//99-12//99
	Oklahoma	S	11.48 MW	11.37 AW	23660 AAW	OKBLS	10//99-12//99
	Oregon	S	12.31 MW	12.49 AW	25980 AAW	ORBLS	10//99-12//99
	Pennsylvania	S	14.74 MW	15.02 AW	31240 AAW	PABLS	10//99-12//99
	Rhode Island	S	14.67 MW	14.37 AW	29890 AAW	RIBLS	10//99-12//99
	South Carolina	S	13.98 MW	14.30 AW	29750 AAW	SCBLS	10//99-12//99
	South Dakota	S	9.02 MW	9.05 AW	18820 AAW	SDBLS	10//99-12//99
	Tennessee	S	10.14 MW	10.83 AW	22520 AAW	TNBLS	10//99-12//99
	Texas	S	12.24 MW	13.34 AW	27750 AAW	TXBLS	10//99-12//99
	Utah	S	13.63 MW	13.38 AW	27820 AAW	UTBLS	10//99-12//99
	Vermont	S	11.24 MW	11.08 AW	23050 AAW	VTBLS	10//99-12//99
	Virginia	S	16.91 MW	17.10 AW	35570 AAW	VABLS	10//99-12//99
	Washington	S	14.09 MW	14.75 AW	30690 AAW	WABLS	10//99-12//99
	West Virginia	S	9.17 MW	9.09 AW	18910 AAW	WVBLS	10//99-12//99
	Wisconsin	S	13.64 MW	13.79 AW	28690 AAW	WIBLS	10//99-12//99
	Wyoming	S	10.75 MW	10.36 AW	21540 AAW	WYBLS	10//99-12//99
	Puerto Rico	S	13.98 MW	13.19 AW	27430 AAW	PRBLS	10//99-12//99
Detective							
Police	United States	Y		46180 AW		DENE	1999
Detective and Criminal Investigator	Alabama	S	16.33 MW	18.01 AW	37460 AAW	ALBLS	10//99-12//99
	Montgomery MSA, AL	S	18.91 MW	16.01 AW	39340 AAW	ALBLS	10//99-12//99
	Alaska	S	23.68 MW	23.91 AW	49740 AAW	AKBLS	10//99-12//99
	Arizona	S	19.8 MW	21.07 AW	43830 AAW	AZBLS	10//99-12//99
	Flagstaff MSA, AZ-UT	S	21.36 MW	21.65 AW	44430 AAW	AZBLS	10//99-12//99

AAW Average annual wage	**AOH** Average offered, high	**ASH** Average starting, high	**H** Hourly	**M** Monthly	**S** Special: hourly and annual
AE Average entry wage	**AOL** Average offered, low	**ASL** Average starting, low	**HI** Highest wage paid	**MTC** Median total compensation	**TQ** Third quartile wage
AEX Average experienced wage	**APH** Average pay, high range	**AW** Average wage paid	**HR** High end range	**MW** Median wage paid	**W** Weekly
AO Average offered	**APL** Average pay, low range	**FQ** First quartile wage	**LR** Low end range	**SQ** Second quartile wage	**Y** Yearly

Occupation/Type/Industry	Location	Per	Low	Mid	High	Source	Date
Detective and Criminal Investigator	Phoenix-Mesa MSA, AZ	S	20.75 MW	19.52 AW	43170 AAW	AZBLS	10//99-12//99
	Yuma MSA, AZ	S	23.23 MW	21.41 AW	48320 AAW	AZBLS	10//99-12//99
	Arkansas	S	13.37 MW	16.21 AW	33720 AAW	ARBLS	10//99-12//99
	Fayetteville-Springdale-Rogers MSA, AR	S	15.64 MW	13.17 AW	32530 AAW	ARBLS	10//99-12//99
	Fort Smith MSA, AR-OK	S	19.55 MW	16.59 AW	40670 AAW	ARBLS	10//99-12//99
	Little Rock-North Little Rock MSA, AR	S	20.11 MW	19.24 AW	41840 AAW	ARBLS	10//99-12//99
	California	S	27.64 MW	27.48 AW	57150 AAW	CABLS	10//99-12//99
	Los Angeles-Long Beach PMSA, CA	S	27.75 MW	28.43 AW	57720 AAW	CABLS	10//99-12//99
	Merced MSA, CA	S	27.86 MW	27.59 AW	57950 AAW	CABLS	10//99-12//99
	Modesto MSA, CA	S	26.18 MW	25.18 AW	54460 AAW	CABLS	10//99-12//99
	Oakland PMSA, CA	S	29.10 MW	29.25 AW	60530 AAW	CABLS	10//99-12//99
	Redding MSA, CA	S	27.17 MW	27.11 AW	56520 AAW	CABLS	10//99-12//99
	Riverside-San Bernardino PMSA, CA	S	27.00 MW	26.08 AW	56150 AAW	CABLS	10//99-12//99
	Sacramento PMSA, CA	S	23.59 MW	22.86 AW	49070 AAW	CABLS	10//99-12//99
	Salinas MSA, CA	S	25.84 MW	25.13 AW	53760 AAW	CABLS	10//99-12//99
	San Jose PMSA, CA	S	28.14 MW	28.56 AW	58540 AAW	CABLS	10//99-12//99
	San Luis Obispo-Atascadero-Paso Robles MSA, CA	S	21.75 MW	20.62 AW	45250 AAW	CABLS	10//99-12//99
	Santa Barbara-Santa Maria-Lompoc MSA, CA	S	30.73 MW	30.88 AW	63920 AAW	CABLS	10//99-12//99
	Santa Cruz-Watsonville PMSA, CA	S	29.12 MW	29.50 AW	60570 AAW	CABLS	10//99-12//99
	Santa Rosa PMSA, CA	S	29.58 MW	30.42 AW	61520 AAW	CABLS	10//99-12//99
	Ventura PMSA, CA	S	27.39 MW	27.33 AW	56970 AAW	CABLS	10//99-12//99
	Colorado	S	27.92 MW	26.45 AW	55020 AAW	COBLS	10//99-12//99
	Denver PMSA, CO	S	27.75 MW	29.18 AW	57720 AAW	COBLS	10//99-12//99
	Grand Junction MSA, CO	S	24.75 MW	24.33 AW	51490 AAW	COBLS	10//99-12//99
	Connecticut	S	24.42 MW	24.59 AW	51140 AAW	CTBLS	10//99-12//99
	Bridgeport PMSA, CT	S	24.01 MW	24.32 AW	49950 AAW	CTBLS	10//99-12//99
	Danbury PMSA, CT	S	23.56 MW	24.08 AW	49010 AAW	CTBLS	10//99-12//99
	Hartford MSA, CT	S	24.26 MW	24.26 AW	50460 AAW	CTBLS	10//99-12//99
	New Haven-Meriden PMSA, CT	S	23.22 MW	23.62 AW	48310 AAW	CTBLS	10//99-12//99
	New London-Norwich MSA, CT-RI	S	23.40 MW	23.97 AW	48680 AAW	CTBLS	10//99-12//99
	Stamford-Norwalk PMSA, CT	S	23.68 MW	24.18 AW	49250 AAW	CTBLS	10//99-12//99
	Delaware	S	19 MW	19.86 AW	41310 AAW	DEBLS	10//99-12//99
	Washington PMSA, DC-MD-VA-WV	S	28.34 MW	28.90 AW	58940 AAW	DCBLS	10//99-12//99
	Florida	S	19.63 MW	21.26 AW	44230 AAW	FLBLS	10//99-12//99
	Fort Lauderdale PMSA, FL	S	23.80 MW	23.29 AW	49490 AAW	FLBLS	10//99-12//99
	Fort Myers-Cape Coral MSA, FL	S	19.98 MW	18.10 AW	41560 AAW	FLBLS	10//99-12//99
	Fort Pierce-Port St. Lucie MSA, FL	S	19.20 MW	17.45 AW	39930 AAW	FLBLS	10//99-12//99
	Gainesville MSA, FL	S	19.96 MW	18.76 AW	41510 AAW	FLBLS	10//99-12//99
	Melbourne-Titusville-Palm Bay MSA, FL	S	19.61 MW	18.38 AW	40790 AAW	FLBLS	10//99-12//99
	Miami PMSA, FL	S	21.57 MW	19.58 AW	44860 AAW	FLBLS	10//99-12//99
	Orlando MSA, FL	S	21.74 MW	20.19 AW	45220 AAW	FLBLS	10//99-12//99
	Pensacola MSA, FL	S	20.96 MW	19.85 AW	43600 AAW	FLBLS	10//99-12//99
	Sarasota-Bradenton MSA, FL	S	22.12 MW	19.79 AW	46010 AAW	FLBLS	10//99-12//99
	Tampa-St. Petersburg-Clearwater MSA, FL	S	21.36 MW	19.61 AW	44440 AAW	FLBLS	10//99-12//99
	West Palm Beach-Boca Raton MSA, FL	S	21.72 MW	21.11 AW	45180 AAW	FLBLS	10//99-12//99
	Georgia	S	16.65 MW	19.22 AW	39980 AAW	GABLS	10//99-12//99
	Atlanta MSA, GA	S	20.96 MW	19.01 AW	43590 AAW	GABLS	10//99-12//99
	Augusta-Aiken MSA, GA-SC	S	16.98 MW	14.85 AW	35310 AAW	GABLS	10//99-12//99
	Columbus MSA, GA-AL	S	18.54 MW	16.66 AW	38570 AAW	GABLS	10//99-12//99
	Macon MSA, GA	S	20.33 MW	18.67 AW	42290 AAW	GABLS	10//99-12//99
	Hawaii	S	24.34 MW	24.22 AW	50380 AAW	HIBLS	10//99-12//99
	Idaho	S	17.87 MW	19.12 AW	39770 AAW	IDBLS	10//99-12//99
	Boise City MSA, ID	S	20.62 MW	19.02 AW	42900 AAW	IDBLS	10//99-12//99
	Illinois	S	23.14 MW	23.95 AW	49820 AAW	ILBLS	10//99-12//99
	Champaign-Urbana MSA, IL	S	22.45 MW	20.50 AW	46700 AAW	ILBLS	10//99-12//99
	Chicago PMSA, IL	S	25.36 MW	26.36 AW	52740 AAW	ILBLS	10//99-12//99

AAW Average annual wage	AOH Average offered, high	ASH Average starting, high	H Hourly	M Monthly	S Special: hourly and annual
AE Average entry wage	AOL Average offered, low	ASL Average starting, low	HI Highest wage paid	MTC Median total compensation	TQ Third quartile wage
AEX Average experienced wage	APH Average pay, high range	AW Average wage paid	HR High end range	MW Median wage paid	W Weekly
AO Average offered	APL Average pay, low range	FQ First quartile wage	LR Low end range	SQ Second quartile wage	Y Yearly

Occupation/Type/Industry	Location	Per	Low	Mid	High	Source	Date
Detective and Criminal Investigator	Peoria-Pekin MSA, IL	S	20.06 MW	19.47 AW	41730 AAW	ILBLS	10//99-12//99
	Rockford MSA, IL	S	20.43 MW	18.91 AW	42500 AAW	ILBLS	10//99-12//99
	Springfield MSA, IL	S	20.66 MW	19.42 AW	42970 AAW	ILBLS	10//99-12//99
	Indiana	S	16.96 MW	17.60 AW	36600 AAW	INBLS	10//99-12//99
	Elkhart-Goshen MSA, IN	S	19.11 MW	18.01 AW	39750 AAW	INBLS	10//99-12//99
	Evansville-Henderson MSA, IN-KY	S	19.14 MW	16.19 AW	39820 AAW	INBLS	10//99-12//99
	Fort Wayne MSA, IN	S	19.02 MW	18.07 AW	39560 AAW	INBLS	10//99-12//99
	Gary PMSA, IN	S	20.90 MW	19.05 AW	43470 AAW	INBLS	10//99-12//99
	Indianapolis MSA, IN	S	17.39 MW	16.73 AW	36170 AAW	INBLS	10//99-12//99
	Lafayette MSA, IN	S	17.95 MW	18.38 AW	37340 AAW	INBLS	10//99-12//99
	Iowa	S	22.25 MW	21.64 AW	45010 AAW	IABLS	10//99-12//99
	Cedar Rapids MSA, IA	S	24.34 MW	24.56 AW	50630 AAW	IABLS	10//99-12//99
	Davenport-Moline-Rock Island MSA, IA-IL	S	21.84 MW	21.51 AW	45420 AAW	IABLS	10//99-12//99
	Kansas	S	18.29 MW	20.51 AW	42670 AAW	KSBLS	10//99-12//99
	Wichita MSA, KS	S	17.47 MW	16.22 AW	36340 AAW	KSBLS	10//99-12//99
	Kentucky	S	16.94 MW	19.34 AW	40230 AAW	KYBLS	10//99-12//99
	Lexington MSA, KY	S	20.70 MW	19.85 AW	43060 AAW	KYBLS	10//99-12//99
	Louisville MSA, KY-IN	S	21.06 MW	19.17 AW	43800 AAW	KYBLS	10//99-12//99
	Louisiana	S	14.18 MW	16.67 AW	34670 AAW	LABLS	10//99-12//99
	Baton Rouge MSA, LA	S	20.22 MW	17.97 AW	42050 AAW	LABLS	10//99-12//99
	Houma MSA, LA	S	14.48 MW	12.21 AW	30110 AAW	LABLS	10//99-12//99
	Lafayette MSA, LA	S	13.42 MW	12.65 AW	27910 AAW	LABLS	10//99-12//99
	Lake Charles MSA, LA	S	12.71 MW	11.32 AW	26430 AAW	LABLS	10//99-12//99
	New Orleans MSA, LA	S	17.34 MW	13.97 AW	36060 AAW	LABLS	10//99-12//99
	Shreveport-Bossier City MSA, LA	S	20.18 MW	18.64 AW	41970 AAW	LABLS	10//99-12//99
	Maine	S	17.44 MW	18.45 AW	38380 AAW	MEBLS	10//99-12//99
	Bangor MSA, ME	S	16.14 MW	16.00 AW	33570 AAW	MEBLS	10//99-12//99
	Portland MSA, ME	S	17.70 MW	18.04 AW	36820 AAW	MEBLS	10//99-12//99
	Maryland	S	23.51 MW	23.73 AW	49360 AAW	MDBLS	10//99-12//99
	Baltimore PMSA, MD	S	22.47 MW	21.89 AW	46740 AAW	MDBLS	10//99-12//99
	Massachusetts	S	26.41 MW	26.25 AW	54610 AAW	MABLS	10//99-12//99
	Boston PMSA, MA-NH	S	25.31 MW	25.66 AW	52650 AAW	MABLS	10//99-12//99
	Lawrence PMSA, MA-NH	S	23.07 MW	22.83 AW	47980 AAW	MABLS	10//99-12//99
	Springfield MSA, MA	S	23.02 MW	21.34 AW	47880 AAW	MABLS	10//99-12//99
	Worcester PMSA, MA-CT	S	26.27 MW	24.63 AW	54640 AAW	MABLS	10//99-12//99
	Michigan	S	24.4 MW	25.28 AW	52580 AAW	MIBLS	10//99-12//99
	Ann Arbor PMSA, MI	S	24.96 MW	24.50 AW	51910 AAW	MIBLS	10//99-12//99
	Benton Harbor MSA, MI	S	23.11 MW	23.76 AW	48060 AAW	MIBLS	10//99-12//99
	Flint PMSA, MI	S	24.15 MW	23.59 AW	50230 AAW	MIBLS	10//99-12//99
	Grand Rapids-Muskegon-Holland MSA, MI	S	24.25 MW	23.97 AW	50430 AAW	MIBLS	10//99-12//99
	Kalamazoo-Battle Creek MSA, MI	S	24.91 MW	24.07 AW	51800 AAW	MIBLS	10//99-12//99
	Lansing-East Lansing MSA, MI	S	23.16 MW	23.38 AW	48170 AAW	MIBLS	10//99-12//99
	Saginaw-Bay City-Midland MSA, MI	S	20.96 MW	20.21 AW	43600 AAW	MIBLS	10//99-12//99
	Minnesota	S	23.34 MW	23.78 AW	49470 AAW	MNBLS	10//99-12//99
	Duluth-Superior MSA, MN-WI	S	21.40 MW	20.70 AW	44500 AAW	MNBLS	10//99-12//99
	Minneapolis-St. Paul MSA, MN-WI	S	24.69 MW	24.14 AW	51360 AAW	MNBLS	10//99-12//99
	Mississippi	S	14.2 MW	15.74 AW	32730 AAW	MSBLS	10//99-12//99
	Biloxi-Gulfport-Pascagoula MSA, MS	S	18.45 MW	15.83 AW	38380 AAW	MSBLS	10//99-12//99
	Hattiesburg MSA, MS	S	16.04 MW	13.84 AW	33370 AAW	MSBLS	10//99-12//99
	Missouri	S	18.52 MW	20.24 AW	42110 AAW	MOBLS	10//99-12//99
	Kansas City MSA, MO-KS	S	21.77 MW	19.96 AW	45290 AAW	MOBLS	10//99-12//99
	St. Louis MSA, MO-IL	S	21.58 MW	19.67 AW	44880 AAW	MOBLS	10//99-12//99
	Springfield MSA, MO	S	17.31 MW	15.61 AW	36010 AAW	MOBLS	10//99-12//99
	Montana	S	19.38 MW	20.52 AW	42670 AAW	MTBLS	10//99-12//99
	Missoula MSA, MT	S	20.66 MW	19.56 AW	42980 AAW	MTBLS	10//99-12//99
	Nebraska	S	20.12 MW	20.52 AW	42680 AAW	NEBLS	10//99-12//99
	Omaha MSA, NE-IA	S	21.73 MW	21.45 AW	45200 AAW	NEBLS	10//99-12//99
	Nevada	S	23.34 MW	23.73 AW	49370 AAW	NVBLS	10//99-12//99
	Las Vegas MSA, NV-AZ	S	23.88 MW	23.68 AW	49670 AAW	NVBLS	10//99-12//99
	New Hampshire	S	19.91 MW	20.43 AW	42500 AAW	NHBLS	10//99-12//99
	Manchester PMSA, NH	S	20.25 MW	20.13 AW	42110 AAW	NHBLS	10//99-12//99
	New Jersey	S	30.92 MW	29.38 AW	61100 AAW	NJBLS	10//99-12//99
	Atlantic-Cape May PMSA, NJ	S	26.73 MW	28.30 AW	55600 AAW	NJBLS	10//99-12//99

AAW	Average annual wage	**AOH**	Average offered, high	**ASH**	Average starting, high	**H**	Hourly	**M**	Monthly
AE	Average entry wage	**AOL**	Average offered, low	**ASL**	Average starting, low	**HI**	Highest wage paid	**MTC**	Median total compensation
AEX	Average experienced wage	**APH**	Average pay, high range	**AW**	Average wage paid	**HR**	High end range	**MW**	Median wage paid
AO	Average offered	**APL**	Average pay, low range	**FQ**	First quartile wage	**LR**	Low end range	**SQ**	Second quartile wage

S Special: hourly and annual   **TQ** Third quartile wage   **W** Weekly   **Y** Yearly

Occupation/Type/Industry	Location	Per	Low	Mid	High	Source	Date
Detective and Criminal Investigator							
	Bergen-Passaic PMSA, NJ	S	31.35 MW	33.72 AW	65210 AAW	NJBLS	10//99-12//99
	Jersey City PMSA, NJ	S	33.65 MW	36.94 AW	69990 AAW	NJBLS	10//99-12//99
	Middlesex-Somerset- Hunterdon PMSA, NJ	S	30.88 MW	31.65 AW	64230 AAW	NJBLS	10//99-12//99
	Monmouth-Ocean PMSA, NJ	S	29.04 MW	29.70 AW	60390 AAW	NJBLS	10//99-12//99
	Newark PMSA, NJ	S	28.84 MW	30.60 AW	59990 AAW	NJBLS	10//99-12//99
	Trenton PMSA, NJ	S	29.70 MW	30.82 AW	61780 AAW	NJBLS	10//99-12//99
	Vineland-Millville-Bridgeton PMSA, NJ	S	23.67 MW	21.28 AW	49230 AAW	NJBLS	10//99-12//99
	New Mexico	S	16.69 MW	18.76 AW	39010 AAW	NMBLS	10//99-12//99
	Albuquerque MSA, NM	S	21.90 MW	22.73 AW	45560 AAW	NMBLS	10//99-12//99
	New York	S	22.94 MW	24.26 AW	50470 AAW	NYBLS	10//99-12//99
	Albany-Schenectady-Troy MSA, NY	S	23.03 MW	21.96 AW	47890 AAW	NYBLS	10//99-12//99
	Buffalo-Niagara Falls MSA, NY	S	22.87 MW	23.15 AW	47570 AAW	NYBLS	10//99-12//99
	Dutchess County PMSA, NY	S	24.39 MW	24.57 AW	50730 AAW	NYBLS	10//99-12//99
	New York PMSA, NY	S	22.01 MW	19.98 AW	45780 AAW	NYBLS	10//99-12//99
	Newburgh PMSA, NY-PA	S	19.16 MW	19.28 AW	39840 AAW	NYBLS	10//99-12//99
	Rochester MSA, NY	S	24.40 MW	24.25 AW	50750 AAW	NYBLS	10//99-12//99
	Syracuse MSA, NY	S	23.11 MW	22.92 AW	48080 AAW	NYBLS	10//99-12//99
	North Carolina	S	16.28 MW	17.94 AW	37320 AAW	NCBLS	10//99-12//99
	Asheville MSA, NC	S	18.06 MW	16.08 AW	37570 AAW	NCBLS	10//99-12//99
	Charlotte-Gastonia-Rock Hill MSA, NC-SC	S	20.66 MW	18.83 AW	42970 AAW	NCBLS	10//99-12//99
	Goldsboro MSA, NC	S	13.03 MW	13.18 AW	27100 AAW	NCBLS	10//99-12//99
	Greensboro--Winston-Salem-- High Point MSA, NC	S	18.42 MW	16.87 AW	38320 AAW	NCBLS	10//99-12//99
	Greenville MSA, NC	S	20.45 MW	20.51 AW	42540 AAW	NCBLS	10//99-12//99
	Hickory-Morganton-Lenoir MSA, NC	S	17.11 MW	15.32 AW	35590 AAW	NCBLS	10//99-12//99
	Raleigh-Durham-Chapel Hill MSA, NC	S	19.88 MW	19.82 AW	41350 AAW	NCBLS	10//99-12//99
	Rocky Mount MSA, NC	S	13.46 MW	13.03 AW	27990 AAW	NCBLS	10//99-12//99
	Wilmington MSA, NC	S	19.39 MW	16.04 AW	40320 AAW	NCBLS	10//99-12//99
	North Dakota	S	18.63 MW	19.59 AW	40740 AAW	NDBLS	10//99-12//99
	Ohio	S	21.49 MW	21.71 AW	45160 AAW	OHBLS	10//99-12//99
	Akron PMSA, OH	S	23.37 MW	22.21 AW	48610 AAW	OHBLS	10//99-12//99
	Canton-Massillon MSA, OH	S	18.55 MW	18.97 AW	38580 AAW	OHBLS	10//99-12//99
	Cincinnati PMSA, OH-KY-IN	S	21.85 MW	22.47 AW	45440 AAW	OHBLS	10//99-12//99
	Cleveland-Lorain-Elyria PMSA, OH	S	23.22 MW	23.09 AW	48300 AAW	OHBLS	10//99-12//99
	Columbus MSA, OH	S	22.68 MW	23.22 AW	47160 AAW	OHBLS	10//99-12//99
	Dayton-Springfield MSA, OH	S	22.66 MW	21.90 AW	47140 AAW	OHBLS	10//99-12//99
	Lima MSA, OH	S	20.43 MW	20.47 AW	42500 AAW	OHBLS	10//99-12//99
	Toledo MSA, OH	S	20.72 MW	18.77 AW	43110 AAW	OHBLS	10//99-12//99
	Youngstown-Warren MSA, OH	S	20.36 MW	19.37 AW	42350 AAW	OHBLS	10//99-12//99
	Oklahoma	S	19.81 MW	20.15 AW	41910 AAW	OKBLS	10//99-12//99
	Tulsa MSA, OK	S	20.85 MW	20.14 AW	43370 AAW	OKBLS	10//99-12//99
	Oregon	S	22.74 MW	23.36 AW	48590 AAW	ORBLS	10//99-12//99
	Portland-Vancouver PMSA, OR-WA	S	24.40 MW	23.87 AW	50750 AAW	ORBLS	10//99-12//99
	Pennsylvania	S	24.4 MW	24.93 AW	51850 AAW	PABLS	10//99-12//99
	Allentown-Bethlehem-Easton MSA, PA	S	22.88 MW	21.91 AW	47590 AAW	PABLS	10//99-12//99
	Erie MSA, PA	S	24.65 MW	23.97 AW	51260 AAW	PABLS	10//99-12//99
	Harrisburg-Lebanon-Carlisle MSA, PA	S	24.96 MW	24.07 AW	51910 AAW	PABLS	10//99-12//99
	Lancaster MSA, PA	S	22.63 MW	22.76 AW	47060 AAW	PABLS	10//99-12//99
	Philadelphia PMSA, PA-NJ	S	26.59 MW	26.23 AW	55300 AAW	PABLS	10//99-12//99
	Pittsburgh MSA, PA	S	27.60 MW	29.37 AW	57410 AAW	PABLS	10//99-12//99
	Scranton--Wilkes-Barre-- Hazleton MSA, PA	S	22.75 MW	22.55 AW	47320 AAW	PABLS	10//99-12//99
	Rhode Island	S	19.96 MW	21.37 AW	44440 AAW	RIBLS	10//99-12//99
	Providence-Fall River- Warwick MSA, RI-MA	S	20.00 MW	19.30 AW	41600 AAW	RIBLS	10//99-12//99
	South Carolina	S	13.97 MW	15.46 AW	32160 AAW	SCBLS	10//99-12//99
	Charleston-North Charleston MSA, SC	S	20.79 MW	18.28 AW	43250 AAW	SCBLS	10//99-12//99
	Greenville-Spartanburg- Anderson MSA, SC	S	16.79 MW	15.40 AW	34910 AAW	SCBLS	10//99-12//99

AAW	Average annual wage	AOH	Average offered, high	ASH	Average starting, high	H	Hourly	M	Monthly	S	Special: hourly and annual
AE	Average entry wage	AOL	Average offered, low	ASL	Average starting, low	HI	Highest wage paid	MTC	Median total compensation	TQ	Third quartile wage
AEX	Average experienced wage	APH	Average pay, high range	AW	Average wage paid	HR	High end range	MW	Median wage paid	W	Weekly
AO	Average offered	APL	Average pay, low range	FQ	First quartile wage	LR	Low end range	SQ	Second quartile wage	Y	Yearly

Occupation/Type/Industry	Location	Per	Low	Mid	High	Source	Date
Detective and Criminal Investigator	Myrtle Beach MSA, SC	S	17.24 MW	16.21 AW	35870 AAW	SCBLS	10//99-12/99
	South Dakota	S	19.58 MW	20.43 AW	42490 AAW	SDBLS	10//99-12/99
	Rapid City MSA, SD	S	22.40 MW	20.86 AW	46590 AAW	SDBLS	10//99-12/99
	Tennessee	S	16.53 MW	18.04 AW	37530 AAW	TNBLS	10//99-12/99
	Chattanooga MSA, TN-GA	S	17.65 MW	16.37 AW	36720 AAW	TNBLS	10//99-12/99
	Clarksville-Hopkinsville MSA, TN-KY	S	15.05 MW	15.27 AW	31310 AAW	TNBLS	10//99-12/99
	Johnson City-Kingsport-Bristol MSA, TN-VA	S	18.10 MW	16.05 AW	37660 AAW	TNBLS	10//99-12/99
	Knoxville MSA, TN	S	20.71 MW	19.09 AW	43080 AAW	TNBLS	10//99-12/99
	Memphis MSA, TN-AR-MS	S	19.18 MW	17.06 AW	39890 AAW	MSBLS	10//99-12/99
	Nashville MSA, TN	S	19.86 MW	18.62 AW	41300 AAW	TNBLS	10//99-12/99
	Texas	S	20.7	20.91 AW	43500 AAW	TXBLS	10//99-12/99
	Austin-San Marcos MSA, TX	S	20.63 MW	20.60 AW	42910 AAW	TXBLS	10//99-12/99
	Beaumont-Port Arthur MSA, TX	S	18.08 MW	16.70 AW	37610 AAW	TXBLS	10//99-12/99
	Brazoria PMSA, TX	S	17.58 MW	16.10 AW	36580 AAW	TXBLS	10//99-12/99
	Brownsville-Harlingen-San Benito MSA, TX	S	17.17 MW	13.64 AW	35700 AAW	TXBLS	10//99-12/99
	Bryan-College Station MSA, TX	S	19.38 MW	19.26 AW	40310 AAW	TXBLS	10//99-12/99
	Corpus Christi MSA, TX	S	22.21 MW	23.59 AW	46200 AAW	TXBLS	10//99-12/99
	Dallas PMSA, TX	S	22.11 MW	22.31 AW	45980 AAW	TXBLS	10//99-12/99
	El Paso MSA, TX	S	21.77 MW	20.07 AW	45280 AAW	TXBLS	10//99-12/99
	Fort Worth-Arlington PMSA, TX	S	22.47 MW	22.87 AW	46730 AAW	TXBLS	10//99-12/99
	Galveston-Texas City PMSA, TX	S	18.26 MW	18.05 AW	37990 AAW	TXBLS	10//99-12/99
	Houston PMSA, TX	S	23.51 MW	23.31 AW	48890 AAW	TXBLS	10//99-12/99
	Killeen-Temple MSA, TX	S	15.69 MW	14.03 AW	32640 AAW	TXBLS	10//99-12/99
	Laredo MSA, TX	S	20.34 MW	19.63 AW	42300 AAW	TXBLS	10//99-12/99
	Longview-Marshall MSA, TX	S	15.12 MW	14.74 AW	31450 AAW	TXBLS	10//99-12/99
	Lubbock MSA, TX	S	20.42 MW	19.57 AW	42460 AAW	TXBLS	10//99-12/99
	McAllen-Edinburg-Mission MSA, TX	S	19.81 MW	19.18 AW	41200 AAW	TXBLS	10//99-12/99
	San Angelo MSA, TX	S	23.49 MW	24.31 AW	48850 AAW	TXBLS	10//99-12/99
	San Antonio MSA, TX	S	21.93 MW	23.31 AW	45620 AAW	TXBLS	10//99-12/99
	Tyler MSA, TX	S	20.78 MW	19.52 AW	43220 AAW	TXBLS	10//99-12/99
	Waco MSA, TX	S	19.54 MW	18.73 AW	40630 AAW	TXBLS	10//99-12/99
	Wichita Falls MSA, TX	S	15.23 MW	14.44 AW	31670 AAW	TXBLS	10//99-12/99
	Utah	S	17.27 MW	19.07 AW	39670 AAW	UTBLS	10//99-12/99
	Provo-Orem MSA, UT	S	14.70 MW	13.85 AW	30580 AAW	UTBLS	10//99-12/99
	Salt Lake City-Ogden MSA, UT	S	20.86 MW	19.35 AW	43400 AAW	UTBLS	10//99-12/99
	Vermont	S	19.89 MW	20.84 AW	43350 AAW	VTBLS	10//99-12/99
	Burlington MSA, VT	S	19.13 MW	18.59 AW	39800 AAW	VTBLS	10//99-12/99
	Virginia	S	27.06 MW	26.62 AW	55360 AAW	VABLS	10//99-12/99
	Charlottesville MSA, VA	S	24.62 MW	24.65 AW	51220 AAW	VABLS	10//99-12/99
	Lynchburg MSA, VA	S	20.06 MW	18.45 AW	41720 AAW	VABLS	10//99-12/99
	Norfolk-Virginia Beach-Newport News MSA, VA-NC	S	25.18 MW	25.88 AW	52370 AAW	VABLS	10//99-12/99
	Roanoke MSA, VA	S	24.06 MW	24.72 AW	50040 AAW	VABLS	10//99-12/99
	Washington	S	25.71 MW	25.29 AW	52600 AAW	WABLS	10//99-12/99
	Bremerton PMSA, WA	S	24.82 MW	24.16 AW	51630 AAW	WABLS	10//99-12/99
	Seattle-Bellevue-Everett PMSA, WA	S	27.89 MW	29.40 AW	58000 AAW	WABLS	10//99-12/99
	Tacoma PMSA, WA	S	25.33 MW	25.14 AW	52680 AAW	WABLS	10//99-12/99
	Yakima MSA, WA	S	19.22 MW	18.51 AW	39970 AAW	WABLS	10//99-12/99
	West Virginia	S	14.17 MW	17.28 AW	35950 AAW	WVBLS	10//99-12/99
	Huntington-Ashland MSA, WV-KY-OH	S	15.22 MW	13.76 AW	31660 AAW	WVBLS	10//99-12/99
	Wisconsin	S	22.34 MW	22.35 AW	46490 AAW	WIBLS	10//99-12/99
	Appleton-Oshkosh-Neenah MSA, WI	S	20.36 MW	19.62 AW	42350 AAW	WIBLS	10//99-12/99
	Eau Claire MSA, WI	S	21.14 MW	21.07 AW	43970 AAW	WIBLS	10//99-12/99
	Janesville-Beloit MSA, WI	S	24.57 MW	23.65 AW	51100 AAW	WIBLS	10//99-12/99
	Madison MSA, WI	S	21.88 MW	21.59 AW	45510 AAW	WIBLS	10//99-12/99
	Milwaukee-Waukesha PMSA, WI	S	24.08 MW	23.90 AW	50080 AAW	WIBLS	10//99-12/99
	Wyoming	S	18.61 MW	20.38 AW	42390 AAW	WYBLS	10//99-12/99

AAW Average annual wage	AOH Average offered, high	ASH Average starting, high	H Hourly	M Monthly	S Special: hourly and annual
AE Average entry wage	AOL Average offered, low	ASL Average starting, low	HI Highest wage paid	MTC Median total compensation	TQ Third quartile wage
AEX Average experienced wage	APH Average pay, high range	AW Average wage paid	HR High end range	MW Median wage paid	W Weekly
AO Average offered	APL Average pay, low range	FQ First quartile wage	LR Low end range	SQ Second quartile wage	Y Yearly

Occupation/Type/Industry	Location	Per	Low	Mid	High	Source	Date
Detective and Criminal Investigator	Puerto Rico	S	12.2 MW	15.36 AW	31960 AAW	PRBLS	10//99-12//99
Diagnostic Medical Sonographer	Alabama	S	18.59 MW	19.20 AW	39940 AAW	ALBLS	10//99-12//99
	Alaska	S	24.85 MW	26.00 AW	54080 AAW	AKBLS	10//99-12//99
	Arizona	S	20.26 MW	21.28 AW	44260 AAW	AZBLS	10//99-12//99
	Arkansas	S	15.61 MW	16.38 AW	34080 AAW	ARBLS	10//99-12//99
	California	S	25.3 MW	25.32 AW	52660 AAW	CABLS	10//99-12//99
	Colorado	S	23.19 MW	22.27 AW	46320 AAW	COBLS	10//99-12//99
	Connecticut	S	20.96 MW	22.03 AW	45820 AAW	CTBLS	10//99-12//99
	District of Columbia	S	20.93 MW	21.04 AW	43770 AAW	DCBLS	10//99-12//99
	Florida	S	20.19 MW	20.82 AW	43310 AAW	FLBLS	10//99-12//99
	Georgia	S	19.31 MW	19.70 AW	40980 AAW	GABLS	10//99-12//99
	Hawaii	S	24.31 MW	23.94 AW	49790 AAW	HIBLS	10//99-12//99
	Idaho	S	20.1 MW	20.48 AW	42600 AAW	IDBLS	10//99-12//99
	Illinois	S	19.21 MW	19.97 AW	41530 AAW	ILBLS	10//99-12//99
	Indiana	S	19.12 MW	19.15 AW	39820 AAW	INBLS	10//99-12//99
	Iowa	S	19.27 MW	19.27 AW	40080 AAW	IABLS	10//99-12//99
	Kansas	S	18.5 MW	18.74 AW	38990 AAW	KSBLS	10//99-12//99
	Kentucky	S	18.89 MW	18.72 AW	38940 AAW	KYBLS	10//99-12//99
	Louisiana	S	18.68 MW	19.07 AW	39660 AAW	LABLS	10//99-12//99
	Maine	S	19.14 MW	20.02 AW	41640 AAW	MEBLS	10//99-12//99
	Maryland	S	23.31 MW	22.62 AW	47060 AAW	MDBLS	10//99-12//99
	Massachusetts	S	21.61 MW	21.18 AW	44050 AAW	MABLS	10//99-12//99
	Michigan	S	18.98 MW	18.82 AW	39150 AAW	MIBLS	10//99-12//99
	Minnesota	S	20.31 MW	20.51 AW	42650 AAW	MNBLS	10//99-12//99
	Mississippi	S	16.79 MW	21.44 AW	44580 AAW	MSBLS	10//99-12//99
	Missouri	S	19.46 MW	19.58 AW	40720 AAW	MOBLS	10//99-12//99
	Montana	S	19.38 MW	19.52 AW	40600 AAW	MTBLS	10//99-12//99
	Nebraska	S	18.17 MW	18.50 AW	38470 AAW	NEBLS	10//99-12//99
	Nevada	S	22.94 MW	22.10 AW	45960 AAW	NVBLS	10//99-12//99
	New Hampshire	S	20.33 MW	21.11 AW	43900 AAW	NHBLS	10//99-12//99
	New Jersey	S	20.81 MW	21.62 AW	44970 AAW	NJBLS	10//99-12//99
	New Mexico	S	23.29 MW	22.57 AW	46940 AAW	NMBLS	10//99-12//99
	New York	S	20.59 MW	22.25 AW	46280 AAW	NYBLS	10//99-12//99
	North Carolina	S	20 MW	20.06 AW	41720 AAW	NCBLS	10//99-12//99
	North Dakota	S	20.2 MW	20.57 AW	42780 AAW	NDBLS	10//99-12//99
	Ohio	S	18.7 MW	18.70 AW	38890 AAW	OHBLS	10//99-12//99
	Oklahoma	S	19.28 MW	19.07 AW	39670 AAW	OKBLS	10//99-12//99
	Oregon	S	23.94 MW	23.87 AW	49640 AAW	ORBLS	10//99-12//99
	Pennsylvania	S	18.74 MW	20.18 AW	41980 AAW	PABLS	10//99-12//99
	Rhode Island	S	19.6 MW	19.86 AW	41320 AAW	RIBLS	10//99-12//99
	South Carolina	S	20.17 MW	21.35 AW	44400 AAW	SCBLS	10//99-12//99
	South Dakota	S	19.54 MW	19.32 AW	40180 AAW	SDBLS	10//99-12//99
	Tennessee	S	18.94 MW	19.12 AW	39770 AAW	TNBLS	10//99-12//99
	Texas	S	19.76 MW	19.87 AW	41340 AAW	TXBLS	10//99-12//99
	Utah	S	19.29 MW	19.45 AW	40460 AAW	UTBLS	10//99-12//99
	Vermont	S	18.72 MW	19.10 AW	39730 AAW	VTBLS	10//99-12//99
	Virginia	S	19.1 MW	19.21 AW	39960 AAW	VABLS	10//99-12//99
	Washington	S	23.64 MW	24.14 AW	50220 AAW	WABLS	10//99-12//99
	West Virginia	S	17.65 MW	19.67 AW	40910 AAW	WVBLS	10//99-12//99
	Wisconsin	S	20.31 MW	20.83 AW	43330 AAW	WIBLS	10//99-12//99
	Wyoming	S	16.89 MW	17.31 AW	36000 AAW	WYBLS	10//99-12//99
	Puerto Rico	S	8.02 MW	8.35 AW	17380 AAW	PRBLS	10//99-12//99
Dietetic Technician	Alabama	S	8.15 MW	9.01 AW	18740 AAW	ALBLS	10//99-12//99
	Arizona	S	9.26 MW	9.97 AW	20730 AAW	AZBLS	10//99-12//99
	Arkansas	S	8.44 MW	9.22 AW	19180 AAW	ARBLS	10//99-12//99
	California	S	11.51 MW	11.96 AW	24880 AAW	CABLS	10//99-12//99
	Colorado	S	9 MW	9.28 AW	19300 AAW	COBLS	10//99-12//99
	Connecticut	S	12.14 MW	12.40 AW	25780 AAW	CTBLS	10//99-12//99
	Delaware	S	8.17 MW	8.73 AW	18150 AAW	DEBLS	10//99-12//99
	District of Columbia	S	7.1 MW	8.66 AW	18010 AAW	DCBLS	10//99-12//99
	Florida	S	8.29 MW	8.93 AW	18580 AAW	FLBLS	10//99-12//99
	Illinois	S	7.5 MW	8.41 AW	17490 AAW	ILBLS	10//99-12//99
	Indiana	S	8.65 MW	8.68 AW	18060 AAW	INBLS	10//99-12//99
	Iowa	S	7.24 MW	7.48 AW	15560 AAW	IABLS	10//99-12//99
	Kansas	S	7.62 MW	8.09 AW	16830 AAW	KSBLS	10//99-12//99
	Kentucky	S	8.47 MW	8.97 AW	18650 AAW	KYBLS	10//99-12//99
	Louisiana	S	6.57 MW	7.67 AW	15950 AAW	LABLS	10//99-12//99
	Maine	S	11.29 MW	11.36 AW	23630 AAW	MEBLS	10//99-12//99
	Maryland	S	11.02 MW	10.47 AW	21770 AAW	MDBLS	10//99-12//99

Occupation/Type/Industry	Location	Per	Low	Mid	High	Source	Date
Dietetic Technician	Massachusetts	S	8.3 MW	9.12 AW	18970 AAW	MABLS	10//99-12//99
	Michigan	S	10.93 MW	11.08 AW	23050 AAW	MIBLS	10//99-12//99
	Minnesota	S	12.82 MW	13.11 AW	27270 AAW	MNBLS	10//99-12//99
	Mississippi	S	7.87 MW	8.39 AW	17440 AAW	MSBLS	10//99-12//99
	Missouri	S	7.85 MW	8.30 AW	17260 AAW	MOBLS	10//99-12//99
	Montana	S	10.11 MW	9.87 AW	20530 AAW	MTBLS	10//99-12//99
	Nebraska	S	7.56 MW	7.91 AW	16440 AAW	NEBLS	10//99-12//99
	Nevada	S	9.64 MW	10.11 AW	21020 AAW	NVBLS	10//99-12//99
	New Hampshire	S	9.48 MW	9.87 AW	20530 AAW	NHBLS	10//99-12//99
	New Jersey	S	13.28 MW	13.85 AW	28820 AAW	NJBLS	10//99-12//99
	New Mexico	S	8.26 MW	9.54 AW	19850 AAW	NMBLS	10//99-12//99
	New York	S	11.74 MW	12.50 AW	26000 AAW	NYBLS	10//99-12//99
	North Carolina	S	8.12 MW	9.46 AW	19670 AAW	NCBLS	10//99-12//99
	North Dakota	S	10.69 MW	10.32 AW	21470 AAW	NDBLS	10//99-12//99
	Ohio	S	11.57 MW	11.36 AW	23620 AAW	OHBLS	10//99-12//99
	Oklahoma	S	7.2 MW	7.64 AW	15890 AAW	OKBLS	10//99-12//99
	Oregon	S	12.04 MW	11.05 AW	22990 AAW	ORBLS	10//99-12//99
	Pennsylvania	S	10.22 MW	10.71 AW	22270 AAW	PABLS	10//99-12//99
	Rhode Island	S	9.05 MW	9.96 AW	20730 AAW	RIBLS	10//99-12//99
	South Carolina	S	7.88 MW	9.18 AW	19100 AAW	SCBLS	10//99-12//99
	South Dakota	S	9.2 MW	9.29 AW	19310 AAW	SDBLS	10//99-12//99
	Tennessee	S	8.77 MW	10.15 AW	21110 AAW	TNBLS	10//99-12//99
	Texas	S	7.8 MW	8.86 AW	18420 AAW	TXBLS	10//99-12//99
	Utah	S	8.43 MW	9.28 AW	19310 AAW	UTBLS	10//99-12//99
	Virginia	S	9.21 MW	9.03 AW	18780 AAW	VABLS	10//99-12//99
	Washington	S	11.42 MW	11.43 AW	23770 AAW	WABLS	10//99-12//99
	West Virginia	S	9.32 MW	9.86 AW	20520 AAW	WVBLS	10//99-12//99
	Wisconsin	S	8.62 MW	9.10 AW	18930 AAW	WIBLS	10//99-12//99
	Puerto Rico	S	6.48 MW	7.40 AW	15390 AAW	PRBLS	10//99-12//99
Dietitian	United States	H		16.54 AW		NCS98	1998
Hospital	Florida	H			20.17 HI	BJTAMP	2000
Dietitian and Nutritionist	Alabama	S	17.53 MW	17.82 AW	37060 AAW	ALBLS	10//99-12//99
	Alaska	S	21.69 MW	21.27 AW	44240 AAW	AKBLS	10//99-12//99
	Arizona	S	17.03 MW	17.70 AW	36820 AAW	AZBLS	10//99-12//99
	Arkansas	S	15.28 MW	15.61 AW	32480 AAW	ARBLS	10//99-12//99
	California	S	20.73 MW	21.09 AW	43880 AAW	CABLS	10//99-12//99
	Colorado	S	16.66 MW	16.64 AW	34620 AAW	COBLS	10//99-12//99
	Connecticut	S	21.28 MW	22.38 AW	46560 AAW	CTBLS	10//99-12//99
	Delaware	S	16.19 MW	16.97 AW	35300 AAW	DEBLS	10//99-12//99
	District of Columbia	S	20.94 MW	21.44 AW	44600 AAW	DCBLS	10//99-12//99
	Florida	S	17.06 MW	17.75 AW	36910 AAW	FLBLS	10//99-12//99
	Georgia	S	17.74 MW	17.76 AW	36950 AAW	GABLS	10//99-12//99
	Hawaii	S	21.98 MW	22.68 AW	47170 AAW	HIBLS	10//99-12//99
	Idaho	S	16.95 MW	16.30 AW	33900 AAW	IDBLS	10//99-12//99
	Illinois	S	15.6 MW	15.89 AW	33040 AAW	ILBLS	10//99-12//99
	Indiana	S	17.26 MW	17.90 AW	37230 AAW	INBLS	10//99-12//99
	Iowa	S	15.68 MW	15.45 AW	32130 AAW	IABLS	10//99-12//99
	Kansas	S	16.73 MW	17.33 AW	36050 AAW	KSBLS	10//99-12//99
	Kentucky	S	16.98 MW	18.02 AW	37480 AAW	KYBLS	10//99-12//99
	Louisiana	S	15.62 MW	16.50 AW	34320 AAW	LABLS	10//99-12//99
	Maine	S	15.81 MW	15.17 AW	31560 AAW	MEBLS	10//99-12//99
	Maryland	S	17.56 MW	17.45 AW	36290 AAW	MDBLS	10//99-12//99
	Massachusetts	S	18.99 MW	20.37 AW	42360 AAW	MABLS	10//99-12//99
	Michigan	S	17.14 MW	17.85 AW	37120 AAW	MIBLS	10//99-12//99
	Minnesota	S	18.11 MW	18.19 AW	37840 AAW	MNBLS	10//99-12//99
	Mississippi	S	15.82 MW	16.27 AW	33850 AAW	MSBLS	10//99-12//99
	Missouri	S	14.95 MW	15.12 AW	31460 AAW	MOBLS	10//99-12//99
	Montana	S	17.24 MW	17.72 AW	36850 AAW	MTBLS	10//99-12//99
	Nebraska	S	13.32 MW	13.71 AW	28520 AAW	NEBLS	10//99-12//99
	Nevada	S	18.47 MW	18.16 AW	37780 AAW	NVBLS	10//99-12//99
	New Hampshire	S	17.71 MW	17.71 AW	36840 AAW	NHBLS	10//99-12//99
	New Jersey	S	19.99 MW	21.54 AW	44810 AAW	NJBLS	10//99-12//99
	New Mexico	S	15.23 MW	15.67 AW	32590 AAW	NMBLS	10//99-12//99
	New York	S	18.98 MW	19.60 AW	40760 AAW	NYBLS	10//99-12//99
	North Carolina	S	16.12 MW	16.70 AW	34740 AAW	NCBLS	10//99-12//99
	North Dakota	S	14.72 MW	15.08 AW	31360 AAW	NDBLS	10//99-12//99
	Ohio	S	17.58 MW	17.53 AW	36470 AAW	OHBLS	10//99-12//99
	Oklahoma	S	11.73 MW	12.74 AW	26510 AAW	OKBLS	10//99-12//99
	Oregon	S	19.66 MW	19.25 AW	40040 AAW	ORBLS	10//99-12//99
	Pennsylvania	S	17.1 MW	16.90 AW	35150 AAW	PABLS	10//99-12//99
	Rhode Island	S	17.78 MW	19.23 AW	39990 AAW	RIBLS	10//99-12//99

AAW Average annual wage	**AOH** Average offered, high	**ASH** Average starting, high	**H** Hourly	**M** Monthly	**S** Special: hourly and annual
AE Average entry/wage	**AOL** Average offered, low	**ASL** Average starting, low	**HI** Highest wage paid	**MTC** Median total compensation	**TQ** Third quartile wage
AEX Average experienced wage	**APH** Average pay, high range	**AW** Average wage paid	**HR** High end range	**MW** Median wage paid	**W** Weekly
AO Average offered	**APL** Average pay, low range	**FQ** First quartile wage	**LR** Low end range	**SQ** Second quartile wage	**Y** Yearly

Occupation/Type/Industry	Location	Per	Low	Mid	High	Source	Date
Dietitian and Nutritionist	South Carolina	S	14.23 MW	14.22 AW	29580 AAW	SCBLS	10//99-12//99
	South Dakota	S	15.5 MW	16.06 AW	33400 AAW	SDBLS	10//99-12//99
	Tennessee	S	16.21 MW	16.20 AW	33700 AAW	TNBLS	10//99-12//99
	Texas	S	16.45 MW	16.79 AW	34930 AAW	TXBLS	10//99-12//99
	Utah	S	15.08 MW	15.06 AW	31320 AAW	UTBLS	10//99-12//99
	Vermont	S	19.59 MW	20.32 AW	42260 AAW	VTBLS	10//99-12//99
	Virginia	S	17.01 MW	18.11 AW	37670 AAW	VABLS	10//99-12//99
	Washington	S	19.15 MW	19.21 AW	39960 AAW	WABLS	10//99-12//99
	West Virginia	S	15.27 MW	16.87 AW	35080 AAW	WVBLS	10//99-12//99
	Wisconsin	S	17.73 MW	18.35 AW	38180 AAW	WIBLS	10//99-12//99
	Wyoming	S	16.7 MW	16.65 AW	34620 AAW	WYBLS	10//99-12//99
	Puerto Rico	S	10.91 MW	10.96 AW	22790 AAW	PRBLS	10//99-12//99
Dining Room and Cafeteria Attendant and Bartender Helper	Alabama	S	6.07 MW	6.30 AW	13090 AAW	ALBLS	10//99-12//99
	Alaska	S	7.07 MW	7.72 AW	16050 AAW	AKBLS	10//99-12//99
	Arizona	S	6.07 MW	6.26 AW	13020 AAW	AZBLS	10//99-12//99
	Arkansas	S	6.11 MW	6.27 AW	13040 AAW	ARBLS	10//99-12//99
	California	S	6.42 MW	6.91 AW	14370 AAW	CABLS	10//99-12//99
	Colorado	S	6.07 MW	6.37 AW	13250 AAW	COBLS	10//99-12//99
	Connecticut	S	7.69 MW	8.32 AW	17300 AAW	CTBLS	10//99-12//99
	Delaware	S	6.67 MW	7.31 AW	15200 AAW	DEBLS	10//99-12//99
	District of Columbia	S	7.51 MW	8.21 AW	17080 AAW	DCBLS	10//99-12//99
	Florida	S	6.26 MW	6.54 AW	13590 AAW	FLBLS	10//99-12//99
	Georgia	S	6.24 MW	6.65 AW	13820 AAW	GABLS	10//99-12//99
	Hawaii	S	6.86 MW	8.35 AW	17360 AAW	HIBLS	10//99-12//99
	Idaho	S	6.08 MW	5.99 AW	12470 AAW	IDBLS	10//99-12//99
	Illinois	S	6.49 MW	6.83 AW	14200 AAW	ILBLS	10//99-12//99
	Indiana	S	6.26 MW	6.41 AW	13330 AAW	INBLS	10//99-12//99
	Iowa	S	6.17 MW	6.45 AW	13410 AAW	IABLS	10//99-12//99
	Kansas	S	6.35 MW	6.59 AW	13710 AAW	KSBLS	10//99-12//99
	Kentucky	S	6.35 MW	6.58 AW	13680 AAW	KYBLS	10//99-12//99
	Louisiana	S	6.04 MW	6.06 AW	12610 AAW	LABLS	10//99-12//99
	Maine	S	6.35 MW	6.72 AW	13970 AAW	MEBLS	10//99-12//99
	Maryland	S	6.2 MW	6.58 AW	13690 AAW	MDBLS	10//99-12//99
	Massachusetts	S	6.89 MW	7.56 AW	15730 AAW	MABLS	10//99-12//99
	Michigan	S	6.49 MW	6.73 AW	14000 AAW	MIBLS	10//99-12//99
	Minnesota	S	6.4 MW	6.72 AW	13980 AAW	MNBLS	10//99-12//99
	Mississippi	S	6.08 MW	6.28 AW	13070 AAW	MSBLS	10//99-12//99
	Missouri	S	6.17 MW	6.42 AW	13350 AAW	MOBLS	10//99-12//99
	Montana	S	5.93 MW	5.89 AW	12260 AAW	MTBLS	10//99-12//99
	Nebraska	S	6.18 MW	6.39 AW	13280 AAW	NEBLS	10//99-12//99
	Nevada	S	7.37 MW	7.56 AW	15720 AAW	NVBLS	10//99-12//99
	New Hampshire	S	6.21 MW	6.49 AW	13510 AAW	NHBLS	10//99-12//99
	New Jersey	S	6.54 MW	6.98 AW	14510 AAW	NJBLS	10//99-12//99
	New Mexico	S	5.96 MW	6.02 AW	12520 AAW	NMBLS	10//99-12//99
	New York	S	6.3 MW	7.04 AW	14650 AAW	NYBLS	10//99-12//99
	North Carolina	S	6.44 MW	6.63 AW	13780 AAW	NCBLS	10//99-12//99
	North Dakota	S	6.24 MW	6.39 AW	13300 AAW	NDBLS	10//99-12//99
	Ohio	S	6.21 MW	6.51 AW	13550 AAW	OHBLS	10//99-12//99
	Oklahoma	S	5.99 MW	6.04 AW	12570 AAW	OKBLS	10//99-12//99
	Oregon	S	6.8 MW	7.22 AW	15010 AAW	ORBLS	10//99-12//99
	Pennsylvania	S	6.25 MW	6.55 AW	13610 AAW	PABLS	10//99-12//99
	Rhode Island	S	6.57 MW	7.14 AW	14840 AAW	RIBLS	10//99-12//99
	South Carolina	S	6.38 MW	6.57 AW	13660 AAW	SCBLS	10//99-12//99
	South Dakota	S	6.04 MW	6.10 AW	12700 AAW	SDBLS	10//99-12//99
	Tennessee	S	6.37 MW	6.54 AW	13610 AAW	TNBLS	10//99-12//99
	Texas	S	6.01 MW	6.10 AW	12680 AAW	TXBLS	10//99-12//99
	Utah	S	6.27 MW	6.53 AW	13580 AAW	UTBLS	10//99-12//99
	Vermont	S	6.47 MW	6.85 AW	14250 AAW	VTBLS	10//99-12//99
	Virginia	S	6.3 MW	6.54 AW	13610 AAW	VABLS	10//99-12//99
	Washington	S	6.39 MW	7.05 AW	14670 AAW	WABLS	10//99-12//99
	West Virginia	S	6.06 MW	6.12 AW	12730 AAW	WVBLS	10//99-12//99
	Wisconsin	S	6.11 MW	6.37 AW	13250 AAW	WIBLS	10//99-12//99
	Wyoming	S	6.18 MW	6.25 AW	13000 AAW	WYBLS	10//99-12//99
	Puerto Rico	S	6.19 MW	6.50 AW	13520 AAW	PRBLS	10//99-12//99
	Guam	S	6.07 MW	6.32 AW	13150 AAW	GUBLS	10//99-12//99
Director							
Computer-aided Design, Apparel Industry	United States	Y		66200 AW		BOBBIN	1999
Female, Logistics	United States	Y	80000 FQ	110000 SQ	140000 TQ	TRAFWD	2000

AAW	Average annual wage	AOH	Average offered, high	ASH	Average starting, high	H	Hourly
AE	Average entry wage	AOL	Average offered, low	ASL	Average starting, low	HI	Highest wage paid
AEX	Average experienced wage	APH	Average pay, high range	AW	Average wage paid	HR	High end range
AO	Average offered	APL	Average pay, low range	FQ	First quartile wage	LR	Low end range

M	Monthly	S	Special: hourly and annual
MTC	Median total compensation	TQ	Third quartile wage
MW	Median wage paid	W	Weekly
SQ	Second quartile wage	Y	Yearly

Occupation/Type/Industry	Location	Per	Low	Mid	High	Source	Date
Director of Sales On-line Enterprise	United States	Y		110500 AAW		WSJ1	2000
Director, Religious Activities and Education	Alaska	S	13.13 MW	12.98 AW	27010 AAW	AKBLS	10//99-12//99
	Anchorage MSA, AK	S	14.24 MW	13.61 AW	29620 AAW	AKBLS	10//99-12//99
	Arizona	S	15.92 MW	16.81 AW	34970 AAW	AZBLS	10//99-12//99
	Phoenix-Mesa MSA, AZ	S	17.61 MW	16.44 AW	36640 AAW	AZBLS	10//99-12//99
	California	S	12.9 MW	14.41 AW	29970 AAW	CABLS	10//99-12//99
	Bakersfield MSA, CA	S	11.37 MW	12.47 AW	23640 AAW	CABLS	10//99-12//99
	Fresno MSA, CA	S	9.76 MW	10.90 AW	20300 AAW	CABLS	10//99-12//99
	Los Angeles-Long Beach PMSA, CA	S	15.65 MW	13.41 AW	32550 AAW	CABLS	10//99-12//99
	Oakland PMSA, CA	S	16.96 MW	17.05 AW	35280 AAW	CABLS	10//99-12//99
	Orange County PMSA, CA	S	16.78 MW	15.71 AW	34900 AAW	CABLS	10//99-12//99
	Riverside-San Bernardino PMSA, CA	S	11.81 MW	11.56 AW	24560 AAW	CABLS	10//99-12//99
	Sacramento PMSA, CA	S	11.13 MW	9.94 AW	23150 AAW	CABLS	10//99-12//99
	San Diego MSA, CA	S	14.07 MW	14.64 AW	29260 AAW	CABLS	10//99-12//99
	San Francisco PMSA, CA	S	17.03 MW	16.13 AW	35430 AAW	CABLS	10//99-12//99
	San Jose PMSA, CA	S	16.42 MW	14.16 AW	34150 AAW	CABLS	10//99-12//99
	Stockton-Lodi MSA, CA	S	8.30 MW	6.45 AW	17260 AAW	CABLS	10//99-12//99
	Ventura PMSA, CA	S	10.79 MW	8.38 AW	22450 AAW	CABLS	10//99-12//99
	Colorado	S	18.88 MW	18.80 AW	39110 AAW	COBLS	10//99-12//99
	Connecticut	S	13.59 MW	15.30 AW	31830 AAW	CTBLS	10//99-12//99
	Hartford MSA, CT	S	14.09 MW	12.69 AW	29300 AAW	CTBLS	10//99-12//99
	District of Columbia	S	15.29 MW	15.12 AW	31440 AAW	DCBLS	10//99-12//99
	Washington PMSA, DC-MD-VA-WV	S	14.36 MW	13.84 AW	29870 AAW	DCBLS	10//99-12//99
	Florida	S	11.57 MW	11.87 AW	24680 AAW	FLBLS	10//99-12//99
	Fort Lauderdale PMSA, FL	S	11.25 MW	11.71 AW	23390 AAW	FLBLS	10//99-12//99
	Fort Myers-Cape Coral MSA, FL	S	11.72 MW	12.10 AW	24390 AAW	FLBLS	10//99-12//99
	Jacksonville MSA, FL	S	11.31 MW	10.30 AW	23520 AAW	FLBLS	10//99-12//99
	Miami PMSA, FL	S	10.43 MW	9.97 AW	21700 AAW	FLBLS	10//99-12//99
	Orlando MSA, FL	S	15.20 MW	15.47 AW	31610 AAW	FLBLS	10//99-12//99
	Pensacola MSA, FL	S	10.25 MW	10.74 AW	21320 AAW	FLBLS	10//99-12//99
	Sarasota-Bradenton MSA, FL	S	8.57 MW	6.10 AW	17830 AAW	FLBLS	10//99-12//99
	Tampa-St. Petersburg-Clearwater MSA, FL	S	13.69 MW	11.92 AW	28480 AAW	FLBLS	10//99-12//99
	Hawaii	S	13.03 MW	13.16 AW	27380 AAW	HIBLS	10//99-12//99
	Honolulu MSA, HI	S	13.10 MW	12.95 AW	27250 AAW	HIBLS	10//99-12//99
	Illinois	S	14.46 MW	15.89 AW	33060 AAW	ILBLS	10//99-12//99
	Chicago PMSA, IL	S	15.97 MW	14.46 AW	33220 AAW	ILBLS	10//99-12//99
	Indiana	S	11.03 MW	11.08 AW	23040 AAW	INBLS	10//99-12//99
	Iowa	S	10.9 MW	12.24 AW	25460 AAW	IABLS	10//99-12//99
	Kentucky	S	12.36 MW	12.29 AW	25570 AAW	KYBLS	10//99-12//99
	Louisville MSA, KY-IN	S	10.78 MW	10.86 AW	22430 AAW	KYBLS	10//99-12//99
	Maryland	S	10.77 MW	12.13 AW	25230 AAW	MDBLS	10//99-12//99
	Baltimore PMSA, MD	S	13.50 MW	13.01 AW	28080 AAW	MDBLS	10//99-12//99
	Michigan	S	10.16 MW	10.86 AW	22580 AAW	MIBLS	10//99-12//99
	Ann Arbor PMSA, MI	S	12.13 MW	12.57 AW	25230 AAW	MIBLS	10//99-12//99
	Detroit PMSA, MI	S	11.33 MW	11.87 AW	23580 AAW	MIBLS	10//99-12//99
	Grand Rapids-Muskegon-Holland MSA, MI	S	13.52 MW	12.95 AW	28110 AAW	MIBLS	10//99-12//99
	Kalamazoo-Battle Creek MSA, MI	S	11.66 MW	12.06 AW	24240 AAW	MIBLS	10//99-12//99
	Lansing-East Lansing MSA, MI	S	12.43 MW	11.57 AW	25850 AAW	MIBLS	10//99-12//99
	Saginaw-Bay City-Midland MSA, MI	S	8.22 MW	7.88 AW	17100 AAW	MIBLS	10//99-12//99
	Minnesota	S	14.28 MW	13.85 AW	28810 AAW	MNBLS	10//99-12//99
	Minneapolis-St. Paul MSA, MN-WI	S	15.37 MW	15.12 AW	31970 AAW	MNBLS	10//99-12//99
	St. Louis MSA, MO-IL	S	18.90 MW	15.83 AW	39310 AAW	MOBLS	10//99-12//99
	Montana	S	9.54 MW	10.41 AW	21660 AAW	MTBLS	10//99-12//99
	Billings MSA, MT	S	15.32 MW	12.81 AW	31870 AAW	MTBLS	10//99-12//99
	Great Falls MSA, MT	S	11.63 MW	10.62 AW	24190 AAW	MTBLS	10//99-12//99
	New Hampshire	S	13.27 MW	13.77 AW	28640 AAW	NHBLS	10//99-12//99
	New Jersey	S	17.43 MW	18.16 AW	37770 AAW	NJBLS	10//99-12//99
	Middlesex-Somerset-Hunterdon PMSA, NJ	S	15.44 MW	15.70 AW	32110 AAW	NJBLS	10//99-12//99
	New York	S	13.52 MW	14.59 AW	30340 AAW	NYBLS	10//99-12//99

AAW Average annual wage	AOH Average offered, high	ASH Average starting, high	**H** Hourly	**M** Monthly	**S** Special: hourly and annual
AE Average entry wage	AOL Average offered, low	ASL Average starting, low	**HI** Highest wage paid	MTC Median total compensation	**TQ** Third quartile wage
AEX Average experienced wage	APH Average pay, high range	AW Average wage paid	**HR** High end range	MW Median wage paid	**W** Weekly
AO Average offered	APL Average pay, low range	FQ First quartile wage	**LR** Low end range	SQ Second quartile wage	**Y** Yearly

Occupation/Type/Industry	Location	Per	Low	Mid	High	Source	Date
Director, Religious Activities and Education							
	Albany-Schenectady-Troy MSA, NY	S	11.96 MW	10.06 AW	24870 AAW	NYBLS	10//99-12//99
	Binghamton MSA, NY	S	10.96 MW	11.18 AW	22800 AAW	NYBLS	10//99-12//99
	Buffalo-Niagara Falls MSA, NY	S	11.12 MW	10.40 AW	23120 AAW	NYBLS	10//99-12//99
	Jamestown MSA, NY	S	6.90 MW	6.04 AW	14350 AAW	NYBLS	10//99-12//99
	Nassau-Suffolk PMSA, NY	S	17.05 MW	15.15 AW	35470 AAW	NYBLS	10//99-12//99
	New York PMSA, NY	S	16.80 MW	17.23 AW	34950 AAW	NYBLS	10//99-12//99
	Rochester MSA, NY	S	12.91 MW	12.97 AW	26840 AAW	NYBLS	10//99-12//99
	North Carolina	S	13.74 MW	15.54 AW	32330 AAW	NCBLS	10//99-12//99
	Ohio	S	12.92 MW	13.00 AW	27040 AAW	OHBLS	10//99-12//99
	Dayton-Springfield MSA, OH	S	16.36 MW	17.94 AW	34020 AAW	OHBLS	10//99-12//99
	Toledo MSA, OH	S	15.27 MW	15.51 AW	31760 AAW	OHBLS	10//99-12//99
	Oklahoma	S	14.25 MW	15.13 AW	31470 AAW	OKBLS	10//99-12//99
	Oregon	S	13.88 MW	13.10 AW	27240 AAW	ORBLS	10//99-12//99
	Corvallis MSA, OR	S	13.32 MW	14.60 AW	27700 AAW	ORBLS	10//99-12//99
	Eugene-Springfield MSA, OR	S	11.30 MW	9.77 AW	23500 AAW	ORBLS	10//99-12//99
	Medford-Ashland MSA, OR	S	9.76 MW	8.56 AW	20310 AAW	ORBLS	10//99-12//99
	Portland-Vancouver PMSA, OR-WA	S	14.40 MW	14.41 AW	29950 AAW	ORBLS	10//99-12//99
	Salem PMSA, OR	S	13.60 MW	14.50 AW	28300 AAW	ORBLS	10//99-12//99
	Pennsylvania	S	12.55 MW	13.06 AW	27170 AAW	PABLS	10//99-12//99
	Philadelphia PMSA, PA-NJ	S	16.10 MW	16.52 AW	33480 AAW	PABLS	10//99-12//99
	Scranton--Wilkes-Barre--Hazleton MSA, PA	S	12.42 MW	12.49 AW	25820 AAW	PABLS	10//99-12//99
	South Carolina	S	12.38 MW	13.08 AW	27210 AAW	SCBLS	10//99-12//99
	Tennessee	S	13.95 MW	13.94 AW	28990 AAW	TNBLS	10//99-12//99
	Knoxville MSA, TN	S	14.33 MW	14.05 AW	29800 AAW	TNBLS	10//99-12//99
	Memphis MSA, TN-AR-MS	S	14.62 MW	14.50 AW	30420 AAW	MSBLS	10//99-12//99
	Texas	S	11.93 MW	13.99 AW	29090 AAW	TXBLS	10//99-12//99
	Dallas PMSA, TX	S	14.00 MW	12.42 AW	29130 AAW	TXBLS	10//99-12//99
	Utah	S	14.93 MW	17.45 AW	36300 AAW	UTBLS	10//99-12//99
	Virginia	S	12.67 MW	13.04 AW	27130 AAW	VABLS	10//99-12//99
	Norfolk-Virginia Beach-Newport News MSA, VA-NC	S	13.03 MW	12.27 AW	27110 AAW	VABLS	10//99-12//99
	Richmond-Petersburg MSA, VA	S	11.80 MW	12.37 AW	24530 AAW	VABLS	10//99-12//99
	Washington	S	15.42 MW	16.59 AW	34520 AAW	WABLS	10//99-12//99
	Seattle-Bellevue-Everett PMSA, WA	S	14.57 MW	13.94 AW	30300 AAW	WABLS	10//99-12//99
	Wisconsin	S	9.67 MW	10.45 AW	21730 AAW	WIBLS	10//99-12//99
Dishwasher							
	Alabama	S	6.19 MW	6.18 AW	12860 AAW	ALBLS	10//99-12//99
	Anniston MSA, AL	S	6.24 MW	6.26 AW	12980 AAW	ALBLS	10//99-12//99
	Auburn-Opelika MSA, AL	S	5.85 MW	6.00 AW	12160 AAW	ALBLS	10//99-12//99
	Birmingham MSA, AL	S	6.47 MW	6.43 AW	13450 AAW	ALBLS	10//99-12//99
	Decatur MSA, AL	S	6.12 MW	6.16 AW	12720 AAW	ALBLS	10//99-12//99
	Dothan MSA, AL	S	6.07 MW	6.13 AW	12620 AAW	ALBLS	10//99-12//99
	Florence MSA, AL	S	5.90 MW	6.03 AW	12280 AAW	ALBLS	10//99-12//99
	Gadsden MSA, AL	S	6.26 MW	6.28 AW	13030 AAW	ALBLS	10//99-12//99
	Huntsville MSA, AL	S	6.35 MW	6.31 AW	13210 AAW	ALBLS	10//99-12//99
	Mobile MSA, AL	S	5.97 MW	6.07 AW	12420 AAW	ALBLS	10//99-12//99
	Montgomery MSA, AL	S	5.92 MW	6.02 AW	12310 AAW	ALBLS	10//99-12//99
	Tuscaloosa MSA, AL	S	6.02 MW	6.07 AW	12520 AAW	ALBLS	10//99-12//99
	Alaska	S	7.62 MW	7.74 AW	16100 AAW	AKBLS	10//99-12//99
	Anchorage MSA, AK	S	8.03 MW	8.01 AW	16710 AAW	AKBLS	10//99-12//99
	Arizona	S	6.04 MW	5.94 AW	12350 AAW	AZBLS	10//99-12//99
	Flagstaff MSA, AZ-UT	S	6.01 MW	6.08 AW	12500 AAW	AZBLS	10//99-12//99
	Phoenix-Mesa MSA, AZ	S	5.93 MW	6.04 AW	12330 AAW	AZBLS	10//99-12//99
	Tucson MSA, AZ	S	5.98 MW	6.06 AW	12440 AAW	AZBLS	10//99-12//99
	Yuma MSA, AZ	S	5.77 MW	5.96 AW	11990 AAW	AZBLS	10//99-12//99
	Arkansas	S	6.16 MW	6.17 AW	12830 AAW	ARBLS	10//99-12//99
	Fayetteville-Springdale-Rogers MSA, AR	S	5.81 MW	5.98 AW	12090 AAW	ARBLS	10//99-12//99
	Fort Smith MSA, AR-OK	S	6.50 MW	6.33 AW	13520 AAW	ARBLS	10//99-12//99
	Little Rock-North Little Rock MSA, AR	S	6.12 MW	6.12 AW	12730 AAW	ARBLS	10//99-12//99
	California	S	6.6 MW	6.96 AW	14480 AAW	CABLS	10//99-12//99
	Bakersfield MSA, CA	S	6.49 MW	6.37 AW	13500 AAW	CABLS	10//99-12//99
	Chico-Paradise MSA, CA	S	6.30 MW	6.28 AW	13110 AAW	CABLS	10//99-12//99

AAW	Average annual wage	AOH	Average offered, high	ASH	Average starting, high
AE	Average entry wage	AOL	Average offered, low	ASL	Average starting, low
AEX	Average experienced wage	APH	Average pay, high range	AW	Average wage paid
AO	Average offered	APL	Average pay, low range	FQ	First quartile wage

H	Hourly	M	Monthly	S	Special: hourly and annual
HI	Highest wage paid	MTC	Median total compensation	TQ	Third quartile wage
HR	High end range	MW	Median wage paid	W	Weekly
LR	Low end range	SQ	Second quartile wage	Y	Yearly

Occupation/Type/Industry	Location	Per	Low	Mid	High	Source	Date
Dishwasher	Fresno MSA, CA	S	6.40 MW	6.32 AW	13300 AAW	CABLS	10//99-12//99
	Los Angeles-Long Beach PMSA, CA	S	7.22 MW	6.76 AW	15010 AAW	CABLS	10//99-12//99
	Merced MSA, CA	S	6.61 MW	6.38 AW	13760 AAW	CABLS	10//99-12//99
	Modesto MSA, CA	S	6.80 MW	6.62 AW	14140 AAW	CABLS	10//99-12//99
	Oakland PMSA, CA	S	7.32 MW	7.02 AW	15220 AAW	CABLS	10//99-12//99
	Orange County PMSA, CA	S	6.46 MW	6.36 AW	13440 AAW	CABLS	10//99-12//99
	Redding MSA, CA	S	6.41 MW	6.33 AW	13320 AAW	CABLS	10//99-12//99
	Riverside-San Bernardino PMSA, CA	S	6.50 MW	6.37 AW	13510 AAW	CABLS	10//99-12//99
	Sacramento PMSA, CA	S	6.90 MW	6.74 AW	14340 AAW	CABLS	10//99-12//99
	Salinas MSA, CA	S	6.83 MW	6.64 AW	14200 AAW	CABLS	10//99-12//99
	San Diego MSA, CA	S	7.14 MW	7.15 AW	14860 AAW	CABLS	10//99-12//99
	San Francisco PMSA, CA	S	7.85 MW	7.31 AW	16320 AAW	CABLS	10//99-12//99
	San Jose PMSA, CA	S	7.07 MW	7.00 AW	14700 AAW	CABLS	10//99-12//99
	San Luis Obispo-Atascadero-Paso Robles MSA, CA	S	7.15 MW	7.27 AW	14870 AAW	CABLS	10//99-12//99
	Santa Barbara-Santa Maria-Lompoc MSA, CA	S	6.44 MW	6.32 AW	13400 AAW	CABLS	10//99-12//99
	Santa Cruz-Watsonville PMSA, CA	S	7.08 MW	7.03 AW	14720 AAW	CABLS	10//99-12//99
	Santa Rosa PMSA, CA	S	7.38 MW	7.16 AW	15350 AAW	CABLS	10//99-12//99
	Stockton-Lodi MSA, CA	S	6.36 MW	6.31 AW	13240 AAW	CABLS	10//99-12//99
	Vallejo-Fairfield-Napa PMSA, CA	S	6.85 MW	6.60 AW	14240 AAW	CABLS	10//99-12//99
	Ventura PMSA, CA	S	6.92 MW	6.60 AW	14400 AAW	CABLS	10//99-12//99
	Visalia-Tulare-Porterville MSA, CA	S	6.45 MW	6.35 AW	13420 AAW	CABLS	10//99-12//99
	Yolo PMSA, CA	S	6.40 MW	6.33 AW	13320 AAW	CABLS	10//99-12//99
	Yuba City MSA, CA	S	6.54 MW	6.41 AW	13610 AAW	CABLS	10//99-12//99
	Colorado	S	6.93 MW	7.01 AW	14580 AAW	COBLS	10//99-12//99
	Boulder-Longmont PMSA, CO	S	6.05 MW	6.07 AW	12580 AAW	COBLS	10//99-12//99
	Colorado Springs MSA, CO	S	7.09 MW	7.19 AW	14750 AAW	COBLS	10//99-12//99
	Denver PMSA, CO	S	7.34 MW	7.42 AW	15260 AAW	COBLS	10//99-12//99
	Fort Collins-Loveland MSA, CO	S	6.98 MW	7.22 AW	14530 AAW	COBLS	10//99-12//99
	Grand Junction MSA, CO	S	6.32 MW	6.33 AW	13140 AAW	COBLS	10//99-12//99
	Greeley PMSA, CO	S	6.16 MW	6.19 AW	12810 AAW	COBLS	10//99-12//99
	Pueblo MSA, CO	S	5.96 MW	6.03 AW	12400 AAW	COBLS	10//99-12//99
	Connecticut	S	7.53 MW	7.81 AW	16240 AAW	CTBLS	10//99-12//99
	Bridgeport PMSA, CT	S	8.34 MW	8.07 AW	17340 AAW	CTBLS	10//99-12//99
	Danbury PMSA, CT	S	7.57 MW	7.57 AW	15750 AAW	CTBLS	10//99-12//99
	Hartford MSA, CT	S	7.65 MW	7.26 AW	15920 AAW	CTBLS	10//99-12//99
	New Haven-Meriden PMSA, CT	S	8.15 MW	7.75 AW	16940 AAW	CTBLS	10//99-12//99
	New London-Norwich MSA, CT-RI	S	7.31 MW	7.05 AW	15200 AAW	CTBLS	10//99-12//99
	Stamford-Norwalk PMSA, CT	S	7.70 MW	7.32 AW	16010 AAW	CTBLS	10//99-12//99
	Waterbury PMSA, CT	S	8.36 MW	8.07 AW	17380 AAW	CTBLS	10//99-12//99
	Delaware	S	6.45 MW	6.66 AW	13840 AAW	DEBLS	10//99-12//99
	Dover MSA, DE	S	6.80 MW	6.61 AW	14150 AAW	DEBLS	10//99-12//99
	Wilmington-Newark PMSA, DE-MD	S	6.56 MW	6.39 AW	13640 AAW	DEBLS	10//99-12//99
	District of Columbia	S	7 MW	7.77 AW	16150 AAW	DCBLS	10//99-12//99
	Washington PMSA, DC-MD-VA-WV	S	7.64 MW	7.48 AW	15890 AAW	DCBLS	10//99-12//99
	Florida	S	6.53 MW	6.68 AW	13890 AAW	FLBLS	10//99-12//99
	Daytona Beach MSA, FL	S	6.13 MW	6.13 AW	12750 AAW	FLBLS	10//99-12//99
	Fort Lauderdale PMSA, FL	S	6.55 MW	6.45 AW	13620 AAW	FLBLS	10//99-12//99
	Fort Myers-Cape Coral MSA, FL	S	6.57 MW	6.60 AW	13670 AAW	FLBLS	10//99-12//99
	Fort Pierce-Port St. Lucie MSA, FL	S	6.50 MW	6.39 AW	13530 AAW	FLBLS	10//99-12//99
	Fort Walton Beach MSA, FL	S	7.11 MW	7.36 AW	14780 AAW	FLBLS	10//99-12//99
	Gainesville MSA, FL	S	5.89 MW	6.02 AW	12250 AAW	FLBLS	10//99-12//99
	Jacksonville MSA, FL	S	6.17 MW	6.17 AW	12840 AAW	FLBLS	10//99-12//99
	Lakeland-Winter Haven MSA, FL	S	6.50 MW	6.42 AW	13520 AAW	FLBLS	10//99-12//99
	Melbourne-Titusville-Palm Bay MSA, FL	S	6.49 MW	6.51 AW	13490 AAW	FLBLS	10//99-12//99
	Miami PMSA, FL	S	6.64 MW	6.68 AW	13810 AAW	FLBLS	10//99-12//99
	Naples MSA, FL	S	7.57 MW	7.58 AW	15740 AAW	FLBLS	10//99-12//99

AAW Average annual wage	AOH Average offered, high	ASH Average starting, high	H Hourly	M Monthly	S Special: hourly and annual
AE Average entry wage	AOL Average offered, low	ASL Average starting, low	HI Highest wage paid	MTC Median total compensation	TQ Third quartile wage
AEX Average experienced wage	APH Average pay, high range	AW Average wage paid	HR High end range	MW Median wage paid	W Weekly
AO Average offered	APL Average pay, low range	FQ First quartile wage	LR Low end range	SQ Second quartile wage	Y Yearly

Occupation/Type/Industry	Location	Per	Low	Mid	High	Source	Date
Dishwasher	Ocala MSA, FL	S	6.00 MW	6.08 AW	12490 AAW	FLBLS	10//99-12//99
	Orlando MSA, FL	S	6.78 MW	6.54 AW	14090 AAW	FLBLS	10//99-12//99
	Panama City MSA, FL	S	6.31 MW	6.26 AW	13110 AAW	FLBLS	10//99-12//99
	Pensacola MSA, FL	S	7.59 MW	7.64 AW	15790 AAW	FLBLS	10//99-12//99
	Punta Gorda MSA, FL	S	5.97 MW	6.06 AW	12410 AAW	FLBLS	10//99-12//99
	Sarasota-Bradenton MSA, FL	S	7.04 MW	7.16 AW	14640 AAW	FLBLS	10//99-12//99
	Tallahassee MSA, FL	S	6.40 MW	6.33 AW	13300 AAW	FLBLS	10//99-12//99
	Tampa-St. Petersburg-Clearwater MSA, FL	S	6.46 MW	6.38 AW	13430 AAW	FLBLS	10//99-12//99
	West Palm Beach-Boca Raton MSA, FL	S	7.00 MW	6.66 AW	14560 AAW	FLBLS	10//99-12//99
	Georgia	S	6.24 MW	6.30 AW	13100 AAW	GABLS	10//99-12//99
	Albany MSA, GA	S	5.84 MW	5.99 AW	12140 AAW	GABLS	10//99-12//99
	Athens MSA, GA	S	6.83 MW	6.29 AW	14210 AAW	GABLS	10//99-12//99
	Atlanta MSA, GA	S	6.85 MW	6.92 AW	14250 AAW	GABLS	10//99-12//99
	Augusta-Aiken MSA, GA-SC	S	5.87 MW	6.01 AW	12220 AAW	GABLS	10//99-12//99
	Columbus MSA, GA-AL	S	5.83 MW	5.99 AW	12130 AAW	GABLS	10//99-12//99
	Macon MSA, GA	S	5.77 MW	5.96 AW	12010 AAW	GABLS	10//99-12//99
	Savannah MSA, GA	S	5.91 MW	6.03 AW	12300 AAW	GABLS	10//99-12//99
	Hawaii	S	7.49 MW	8.07 AW	16780 AAW	HIBLS	10//99-12//99
	Honolulu MSA, HI	S	8.03 MW	6.82 AW	16700 AAW	HIBLS	10//99-12//99
	Idaho	S	6.38 MW	6.50 AW	13520 AAW	IDBLS	10//99-12//99
	Boise City MSA, ID	S	6.87 MW	6.87 AW	14290 AAW	IDBLS	10//99-12//99
	Pocatello MSA, ID	S	6.04 MW	6.11 AW	12560 AAW	IDBLS	10//99-12//99
	Illinois	S	6.37 MW	6.45 AW	13410 AAW	ILBLS	10//99-12//99
	Bloomington-Normal MSA, IL	S	6.60 MW	6.70 AW	13730 AAW	ILBLS	10//99-12//99
	Chicago PMSA, IL	S	6.73 MW	6.74 AW	13990 AAW	ILBLS	10//99-12//99
	Decatur MSA, IL	S	7.94 MW	8.13 AW	16520 AAW	ILBLS	10//99-12//99
	Kankakee PMSA, IL	S	6.11 MW	6.14 AW	12700 AAW	ILBLS	10//99-12//99
	Peoria-Pekin MSA, IL	S	6.17 MW	6.20 AW	12830 AAW	ILBLS	10//99-12//99
	Rockford MSA, IL	S	6.07 MW	6.13 AW	12630 AAW	ILBLS	10//99-12//99
	Springfield MSA, IL	S	8.14 MW	8.93 AW	16930 AAW	ILBLS	10//99-12//99
	Indiana	S	7.14 MW	7.26 AW	15100 AAW	INBLS	10//99-12//99
	Bloomington MSA, IN	S	7.80 MW	7.96 AW	16220 AAW	INBLS	10//99-12//99
	Elkhart-Goshen MSA, IN	S	6.01 MW	6.07 AW	12500 AAW	INBLS	10//99-12//99
	Evansville-Henderson MSA, IN-KY	S	6.04 MW	6.11 AW	12560 AAW	INBLS	10//99-12//99
	Fort Wayne MSA, IN	S	6.73 MW	6.65 AW	13990 AAW	INBLS	10//99-12//99
	Gary PMSA, IN	S	6.49 MW	6.40 AW	13500 AAW	INBLS	10//99-12//99
	Indianapolis MSA, IN	S	8.65 MW	8.91 AW	18000 AAW	INBLS	10//99-12//99
	Lafayette MSA, IN	S	6.41 MW	6.42 AW	13320 AAW	INBLS	10//99-12//99
	Muncie MSA, IN	S	6.87 MW	6.63 AW	14280 AAW	INBLS	10//99-12//99
	South Bend MSA, IN	S	7.56 MW	7.62 AW	15730 AAW	INBLS	10//99-12//99
	Terre Haute MSA, IN	S	7.28 MW	7.08 AW	15140 AAW	INBLS	10//99-12//99
	Iowa	S	6.63 MW	6.67 AW	13870 AAW	IABLS	10//99-12//99
	Cedar Rapids MSA, IA	S	6.78 MW	6.97 AW	14110 AAW	IABLS	10//99-12//99
	Davenport-Moline-Rock Island MSA, IA-IL	S	5.97 MW	6.05 AW	12420 AAW	IABLS	10//99-12//99
	Des Moines MSA, IA	S	6.99 MW	7.10 AW	14550 AAW	IABLS	10//99-12//99
	Dubuque MSA, IA	S	6.59 MW	6.22 AW	13720 AAW	IABLS	10//99-12//99
	Iowa City MSA, IA	S	7.51 MW	7.60 AW	15630 AAW	IABLS	10//99-12//99
	Sioux City MSA, IA-NE	S	5.99 MW	6.08 AW	12460 AAW	IABLS	10//99-12//99
	Waterloo-Cedar Falls MSA, IA	S	5.75 MW	5.95 AW	11960 AAW	IABLS	10//99-12//99
	Kansas	S	6.4 MW	6.44 AW	13390 AAW	KSBLS	10//99-12//99
	Lawrence MSA, KS	S	6.29 MW	6.29 AW	13080 AAW	KSBLS	10//99-12//99
	Topeka MSA, KS	S	6.94 MW	7.20 AW	14440 AAW	KSBLS	10//99-12//99
	Wichita MSA, KS	S	6.42 MW	6.35 AW	13350 AAW	KSBLS	10//99-12//99
	Kentucky	S	7.1 MW	7.11 AW	14780 AAW	KYBLS	10//99-12//99
	Lexington MSA, KY	S	8.19 MW	8.15 AW	17040 AAW	KYBLS	10//99-12//99
	Louisville MSA, KY-IN	S	7.32 MW	7.37 AW	15220 AAW	KYBLS	10//99-12//99
	Owensboro MSA, KY	S	5.81 MW	5.98 AW	12090 AAW	KYBLS	10//99-12//99
	Louisiana	S	6.09 MW	6.04 AW	12550 AAW	LABLS	10//99-12//99
	Alexandria MSA, LA	S	5.87 MW	6.01 AW	12200 AAW	LABLS	10//99-12//99
	Baton Rouge MSA, LA	S	6.20 MW	6.22 AW	12900 AAW	LABLS	10//99-12//99
	Houma MSA, LA	S	5.85 MW	6.00 AW	12160 AAW	LABLS	10//99-12//99
	Lafayette MSA, LA	S	6.09 MW	6.14 AW	12670 AAW	LABLS	10//99-12//99
	Lake Charles MSA, LA	S	5.83 MW	5.99 AW	12130 AAW	LABLS	10//99-12//99
	Monroe MSA, LA	S	5.75 MW	5.95 AW	11960 AAW	LABLS	10//99-12//99
	New Orleans MSA, LA	S	6.06 MW	6.10 AW	12610 AAW	LABLS	10//99-12//99
	Shreveport-Bossier City MSA, LA	S	5.87 MW	6.01 AW	12210 AAW	LABLS	10//99-12//99
	Maine	S	6.32 MW	6.60 AW	13730 AAW	MEBLS	10//99-12//99

AAW Average annual wage	AOH Average offered, high	ASH Average starting, high	H Hourly	M Monthly	S Special: hourly and annual
AE Average entry wage	AOL Average offered, low	ASL Average starting, low	HI Highest wage paid	MTC Median total compensation	TQ Third quartile wage
AEX Average experienced wage	APH Average pay, high range	AW Average wage paid	HR High end range	MW Median wage paid	W Weekly
AO Average offered	APL Average pay, low range	FQ First quartile wage	LR Low end range	SQ Second quartile wage	Y Yearly

Occupation/Type/Industry	Location	Per	Low	Mid	High	Source	Date
Dishwasher	Bangor MSA, ME	S	6.13 MW	6.07 AW	12740 AAW	MEBLS	10//99-12//99
	Lewiston-Auburn MSA, ME	S	5.81 MW	5.98 AW	12090 AAW	MEBLS	10//99-12//99
	Portland MSA, ME	S	6.78 MW	6.42 AW	14100 AAW	MEBLS	10//99-12//99
	Maryland	S	6.93 MW	6.99 AW	14530 AAW	MDBLS	10//99-12//99
	Baltimore PMSA, MD	S	7.07 MW	7.18 AW	14710 AAW	MDBLS	10//99-12//99
	Cumberland MSA, MD-WV	S	5.97 MW	6.06 AW	12430 AAW	MDBLS	10//99-12//99
	Hagerstown PMSA, MD	S	6.00 MW	6.08 AW	12470 AAW	MDBLS	10//99-12//99
	Massachusetts	S	7.59 MW	7.73 AW	16080 AAW	MABLS	10//99-12//99
	Barnstable-Yarmouth MSA, MA	S	7.27 MW	7.04 AW	15130 AAW	MABLS	10//99-12//99
	Boston PMSA, MA-NH	S	8.08 MW	7.82 AW	16800 AAW	MABLS	10//99-12//99
	Brockton PMSA, MA	S	7.92 MW	7.83 AW	16480 AAW	MABLS	10//99-12//99
	Fitchburg-Leominster PMSA, MA	S	6.95 MW	7.12 AW	14450 AAW	MABLS	10//99-12//99
	Lawrence PMSA, MA-NH	S	7.27 MW	7.17 AW	15120 AAW	MABLS	10//99-12//99
	Lowell PMSA, MA-NH	S	7.86 MW	7.62 AW	16350 AAW	MABLS	10//99-12//99
	New Bedford PMSA, MA	S	6.42 MW	6.12 AW	13350 AAW	MABLS	10//99-12//99
	Pittsfield MSA, MA	S	6.89 MW	7.02 AW	14330 AAW	MABLS	10//99-12//99
	Springfield MSA, MA	S	7.24 MW	7.35 AW	15050 AAW	MABLS	10//99-12//99
	Worcester PMSA, MA-CT	S	7.48 MW	7.52 AW	15550 AAW	MABLS	10//99-12//99
	Michigan	S	7.36 MW	7.24 AW	15060 AAW	MIBLS	10//99-12//99
	Ann Arbor PMSA, MI	S	8.01 MW	7.99 AW	16650 AAW	MIBLS	10//99-12//99
	Benton Harbor MSA, MI	S	6.49 MW	6.36 AW	13490 AAW	MIBLS	10//99-12//99
	Detroit PMSA, MI	S	7.72 MW	7.70 AW	16060 AAW	MIBLS	10//99-12//99
	Flint PMSA, MI	S	6.78 MW	6.61 AW	14100 AAW	MIBLS	10//99-12//99
	Grand Rapids-Muskegon-Holland MSA, MI	S	6.62 MW	6.62 AW	13770 AAW	MIBLS	10//99-12//99
	Jackson MSA, MI	S	6.93 MW	7.09 AW	14400 AAW	MIBLS	10//99-12//99
	Kalamazoo-Battle Creek MSA, MI	S	7.18 MW	7.39 AW	14920 AAW	MIBLS	10//99-12//99
	Lansing-East Lansing MSA, MI	S	6.40 MW	6.29 AW	13320 AAW	MIBLS	10//99-12//99
	Saginaw-Bay City-Midland MSA, MI	S	6.54 MW	6.31 AW	13610 AAW	MIBLS	10//99-12//99
	Minnesota	S	7.08 MW	7.19 AW	14960 AAW	MNBLS	10//99-12//99
	Duluth-Superior MSA, MN-WI	S	5.95 MW	6.04 AW	12370 AAW	MNBLS	10//99-12//99
	Minneapolis-St. Paul MSA, MN-WI	S	7.56 MW	7.56 AW	15710 AAW	MNBLS	10//99-12//99
	Rochester MSA, MN	S	6.67 MW	6.52 AW	13880 AAW	MNBLS	10//99-12//99
	St. Cloud MSA, MN	S	6.20 MW	6.17 AW	12890 AAW	MNBLS	10//99-12//99
	Mississippi	S	6.1 MW	6.06 AW	12600 AAW	MSBLS	10//99-12//99
	Biloxi-Gulfport-Pascagoula MSA, MS	S	6.62 MW	6.53 AW	13760 AAW	MSBLS	10//99-12//99
	Hattiesburg MSA, MS	S	5.75 MW	5.95 AW	11960 AAW	MSBLS	10//99-12//99
	Jackson MSA, MS	S	5.95 MW	6.03 AW	12370 AAW	MSBLS	10//99-12//99
	Missouri	S	6.49 MW	6.54 AW	13600 AAW	MOBLS	10//99-12//99
	Kansas City MSA, MO-KS	S	6.82 MW	6.98 AW	14180 AAW	MOBLS	10//99-12//99
	St. Joseph MSA, MO	S	5.75 MW	5.95 AW	11960 AAW	MOBLS	10//99-12//99
	St. Louis MSA, MO-IL	S	6.52 MW	6.45 AW	13560 AAW	MOBLS	10//99-12//99
	Springfield MSA, MO	S	6.08 MW	6.11 AW	12640 AAW	MOBLS	10//99-12//99
	Montana	S	6.03 MW	5.92 AW	12320 AAW	MTBLS	10//99-12//99
	Billings MSA, MT	S	5.82 MW	5.98 AW	12100 AAW	MTBLS	10//99-12//99
	Great Falls MSA, MT	S	5.75 MW	5.95 AW	11960 AAW	MTBLS	10//99-12//99
	Missoula MSA, MT	S	5.75 MW	5.95 AW	11960 AAW	MTBLS	10//99-12//99
	Nebraska	S	6.37 MW	6.43 AW	13370 AAW	NEBLS	10//99-12//99
	Lincoln MSA, NE	S	7.21 MW	7.37 AW	14990 AAW	NEBLS	10//99-12//99
	Omaha MSA, NE-IA	S	6.86 MW	6.98 AW	14270 AAW	NEBLS	10//99-12//99
	Nevada	S	7.7 MW	7.71 AW	16040 AAW	NVBLS	10//99-12//99
	Las Vegas MSA, NV-AZ	S	8.20 MW	8.41 AW	17050 AAW	NVBLS	10//99-12//99
	Reno MSA, NV	S	6.49 MW	6.38 AW	13500 AAW	NVBLS	10//99-12//99
	New Hampshire	S	6.7 MW	7.06 AW	14680 AAW	NHBLS	10//99-12//99
	Manchester PMSA, NH	S	8.01 MW	8.00 AW	16660 AAW	NHBLS	10//99-12//99
	Nashua PMSA, NH	S	7.43 MW	7.42 AW	15450 AAW	NHBLS	10//99-12//99
	Portsmouth-Rochester PMSA, NH-ME	S	8.54 MW	8.74 AW	17760 AAW	NHBLS	10//99-12//99
	New Jersey	S	7.18 MW	7.42 AW	15430 AAW	NJBLS	10//99-12//99
	Atlantic-Cape May PMSA, NJ	S	9.61 MW	10.81 AW	19990 AAW	NJBLS	10//99-12//99
	Bergen-Passaic PMSA, NJ	S	8.00 MW	7.47 AW	16650 AAW	NJBLS	10//99-12//99
	Jersey City PMSA, NJ	S	7.21 MW	7.21 AW	15000 AAW	NJBLS	10//99-12//99
	Middlesex-Somerset-Hunterdon PMSA, NJ	S	6.98 MW	6.75 AW	14520 AAW	NJBLS	10//99-12//99
	Monmouth-Ocean PMSA, NJ	S	6.65 MW	6.72 AW	13830 AAW	NJBLS	10//99-12//99
	Newark PMSA, NJ	S	6.91 MW	6.76 AW	14380 AAW	NJBLS	10//99-12//99

AAW	Average annual wage	AOH	Average offered, high	ASH	Average starting, high	H	Hourly	M	Monthly	S	Special: hourly and annual
AE	Average entry wage	AOL	Average offered, low	ASL	Average starting, low	HI	Highest wage paid	MTC	Median total compensation	TQ	Third quartile wage
AEX	Average experienced wage	APH	Average pay, high range	AW	Average wage paid	HR	High end range	MW	Median wage paid	W	Weekly
AO	Average offered	APL	Average pay, low range	FQ	First quartile wage	LR	Low end range	SQ	Second quartile wage	Y	Yearly

Occupation/Type/Industry	Location	Per	Low	Mid	High	Source	Date
Dishwasher	Trenton PMSA, NJ	S	7.52 MW	7.59 AW	15650 AAW	NJBLS	10//99-12//99
	New Mexico	S	6.3 MW	6.32 AW	13150 AAW	NMBLS	10//99-12//99
	Albuquerque MSA, NM	S	6.50 MW	6.48 AW	13520 AAW	NMBLS	10//99-12//99
	Las Cruces MSA, NM	S	5.75 MW	5.95 AW	11960 AAW	NMBLS	10//99-12//99
	Santa Fe MSA, NM	S	6.57 MW	6.64 AW	13660 AAW	NMBLS	10//99-12//99
	New York	S	6.5 MW	6.89 AW	14340 AAW	NYBLS	10//99-12//99
	Albany-Schenectady-Troy MSA, NY	S	7.46 MW	7.58 AW	15510 AAW	NYBLS	10//99-12//99
	Binghamton MSA, NY	S	6.01 MW	6.07 AW	12490 AAW	NYBLS	10//99-12//99
	Buffalo-Niagara Falls MSA, NY	S	6.01 MW	6.06 AW	12500 AAW	NYBLS	10//99-12//99
	Dutchess County PMSA, NY	S	6.80 MW	6.61 AW	14150 AAW	NYBLS	10//99-12//99
	Elmira MSA, NY	S	6.53 MW	6.31 AW	13580 AAW	NYBLS	10//99-12//99
	Glens Falls MSA, NY	S	6.10 MW	6.05 AW	12680 AAW	NYBLS	10//99-12//99
	Jamestown MSA, NY	S	5.78 MW	5.97 AW	12030 AAW	NYBLS	10//99-12//99
	Nassau-Suffolk PMSA, NY	S	7.13 MW	6.73 AW	14830 AAW	NYBLS	10//99-12//99
	Newburgh PMSA, NY-PA	S	6.16 MW	6.17 AW	12810 AAW	NYBLS	10//99-12//99
	Rochester MSA, NY	S	6.57 MW	6.29 AW	13660 AAW	NYBLS	10//99-12//99
	Syracuse MSA, NY	S	6.43 MW	6.43 AW	13360 AAW	NYBLS	10//99-12//99
	Utica-Rome MSA, NY	S	6.07 MW	6.09 AW	12630 AAW	NYBLS	10//99-12//99
	North Carolina	S	6.95 MW	6.85 AW	14250 AAW	NCBLS	10//99-12//99
	Asheville MSA, NC	S	6.52 MW	6.53 AW	13560 AAW	NCBLS	10//99-12//99
	Charlotte-Gastonia-Rock Hill MSA, NC-SC	S	7.24 MW	7.45 AW	15050 AAW	NCBLS	10//99-12//99
	Fayetteville MSA, NC	S	6.34 MW	6.29 AW	13200 AAW	NCBLS	10//99-12//99
	Goldsboro MSA, NC	S	5.90 MW	6.02 AW	12270 AAW	NCBLS	10//99-12//99
	Greensboro--Winston-Salem--High Point MSA, NC	S	6.72 MW	6.54 AW	13990 AAW	NCBLS	10//99-12//99
	Greenville MSA, NC	S	6.15 MW	6.19 AW	12800 AAW	NCBLS	10//99-12//99
	Hickory-Morganton-Lenoir MSA, NC	S	6.36 MW	6.26 AW	13230 AAW	NCBLS	10//99-12//99
	Jacksonville MSA, NC	S	6.14 MW	6.18 AW	12770 AAW	NCBLS	10//99-12//99
	Raleigh-Durham-Chapel Hill MSA, NC	S	7.42 MW	7.51 AW	15430 AAW	NCBLS	10//99-12//99
	Rocky Mount MSA, NC	S	6.22 MW	6.15 AW	12940 AAW	NCBLS	10//99-12//99
	Wilmington MSA, NC	S	6.15 MW	6.17 AW	12780 AAW	NCBLS	10//99-12//99
	North Dakota	S	6.23 MW	6.42 AW	13360 AAW	NDBLS	10//99-12//99
	Bismarck MSA, ND	S	6.51 MW	6.27 AW	13550 AAW	NDBLS	10//99-12//99
	Fargo-Moorhead MSA, ND-MN	S	6.24 MW	6.21 AW	12980 AAW	NDBLS	10//99-12//99
	Grand Forks MSA, ND-MN	S	6.99 MW	6.23 AW	14540 AAW	NDBLS	10//99-12//99
	Ohio	S	6.58 MW	6.66 AW	13860 AAW	OHBLS	10//99-12//99
	Akron PMSA, OH	S	6.44 MW	6.41 AW	13400 AAW	OHBLS	10//99-12//99
	Canton-Massillon MSA, OH	S	6.26 MW	6.26 AW	13030 AAW	OHBLS	10//99-12//99
	Cincinnati PMSA, OH-KY-IN	S	6.84 MW	6.84 AW	14230 AAW	OHBLS	10//99-12//99
	Cleveland-Lorain-Elyria PMSA, OH	S	7.16 MW	7.26 AW	14890 AAW	OHBLS	10//99-12//99
	Columbus MSA, OH	S	7.48 MW	7.57 AW	15550 AAW	OHBLS	10//99-12//99
	Dayton-Springfield MSA, OH	S	6.59 MW	6.46 AW	13710 AAW	OHBLS	10//99-12//99
	Hamilton-Middletown PMSA, OH	S	6.30 MW	6.27 AW	13110 AAW	OHBLS	10//99-12//99
	Lima MSA, OH	S	6.10 MW	6.15 AW	12690 AAW	OHBLS	10//99-12//99
	Mansfield MSA, OH	S	6.23 MW	6.25 AW	12960 AAW	OHBLS	10//99-12//99
	Steubenville-Weirton MSA, OH-WV	S	5.75 MW	5.95 AW	11960 AAW	OHBLS	10//99-12//99
	Toledo MSA, OH	S	6.33 MW	6.27 AW	13170 AAW	OHBLS	10//99-12//99
	Youngstown-Warren MSA, OH	S	5.97 MW	6.04 AW	12410 AAW	OHBLS	10//99-12//99
	Oklahoma	S	6.16 MW	6.12 AW	12740 AAW	OKBLS	10//99-12//99
	Enid MSA, OK	S	5.97 MW	6.06 AW	12420 AAW	OKBLS	10//99-12//99
	Lawton MSA, OK	S	5.75 MW	5.95 AW	11960 AAW	OKBLS	10//99-12//99
	Oklahoma City MSA, OK	S	6.39 MW	6.37 AW	13290 AAW	OKBLS	10//99-12//99
	Tulsa MSA, OK	S	5.99 MW	6.07 AW	12450 AAW	OKBLS	10//99-12//99
	Oregon	S	7.16 MW	7.29 AW	15160 AAW	ORBLS	10//99-12//99
	Corvallis MSA, OR	S	7.07 MW	6.75 AW	14700 AAW	ORBLS	10//99-12//99
	Eugene-Springfield MSA, OR	S	7.20 MW	7.14 AW	14970 AAW	ORBLS	10//99-12//99
	Medford-Ashland MSA, OR	S	7.45 MW	7.54 AW	15500 AAW	ORBLS	10//99-12//99
	Portland-Vancouver PMSA, OR-WA	S	7.25 MW	7.04 AW	15090 AAW	ORBLS	10//99-12//99
	Salem PMSA, OR	S	7.38 MW	7.30 AW	15340 AAW	ORBLS	10//99-12//99
	Pennsylvania	S	6.6 MW	6.91 AW	14360 AAW	PABLS	10//99-12//99
	Allentown-Bethlehem-Easton MSA, PA	S	6.01 MW	6.08 AW	12510 AAW	PABLS	10//99-12//99

Dishwasher

Occupation/Type/Industry	Location	Per	Low	Mid	High	Source	Date
Dishwasher	Altoona MSA, PA	S	6.32 MW	6.33 AW	13150 AAW	PABLS	10//99-12//99
	Erie MSA, PA	S	6.87 MW	6.62 AW	14290 AAW	PABLS	10//99-12//99
	Harrisburg-Lebanon-Carlisle MSA, PA	S	6.70 MW	6.47 AW	13930 AAW	PABLS	10//99-12//99
	Johnstown MSA, PA	S	6.18 MW	6.21 AW	12860 AAW	PABLS	10//99-12//99
	Lancaster MSA, PA	S	7.43 MW	7.32 AW	15450 AAW	PABLS	10//99-12//99
	Philadelphia PMSA, PA-NJ	S	7.26 MW	7.29 AW	15100 AAW	PABLS	10//99-12//99
	Pittsburgh MSA, PA	S	7.57 MW	7.11 AW	15740 AAW	PABLS	10//99-12//99
	Reading MSA, PA	S	6.33 MW	6.22 AW	13160 AAW	PABLS	10//99-12//99
	Scranton--Wilkes-Barre--Hazleton MSA, PA	S	6.56 MW	6.49 AW	13650 AAW	PABLS	10//99-12//99
	Sharon MSA, PA	S	6.13 MW	6.06 AW	12750 AAW	PABLS	10//99-12//99
	State College MSA, PA	S	5.94 MW	6.03 AW	12350 AAW	PABLS	10//99-12//99
	Williamsport MSA, PA	S	6.81 MW	6.61 AW	14160 AAW	PABLS	10//99-12//99
	York MSA, PA	S	6.87 MW	6.86 AW	14290 AAW	PABLS	10//99-12//99
	Rhode Island	S	6.57 MW	6.82 AW	14180 AAW	RIBLS	10//99-12//99
	Providence-Fall River-Warwick MSA, RI-MA	S	6.60 MW	6.39 AW	13730 AAW	RIBLS	10//99-12//99
	South Carolina	S	6.28 MW	6.34 AW	13190 AAW	SCBLS	10//99-12//99
	Charleston-North Charleston MSA, SC	S	6.21 MW	6.22 AW	12920 AAW	SCBLS	10//99-12//99
	Columbia MSA, SC	S	6.47 MW	6.40 AW	13450 AAW	SCBLS	10//99-12//99
	Florence MSA, SC	S	6.05 MW	6.11 AW	12580 AAW	SCBLS	10//99-12//99
	Greenville-Spartanburg-Anderson MSA, SC	S	6.14 MW	6.16 AW	12760 AAW	SCBLS	10//99-12//99
	Myrtle Beach MSA, SC	S	6.75 MW	6.67 AW	14040 AAW	SCBLS	10//99-12//99
	Sumter MSA, SC	S	6.34 MW	6.17 AW	13190 AAW	SCBLS	10//99-12//99
	South Dakota	S	6.26 MW	6.31 AW	13120 AAW	SDBLS	10//99-12//99
	Rapid City MSA, SD	S	5.88 MW	6.00 AW	12230 AAW	SDBLS	10//99-12//99
	Sioux Falls MSA, SD	S	6.61 MW	6.45 AW	13740 AAW	SDBLS	10//99-12//99
	Tennessee	S	6.8 MW	6.88 AW	14300 AAW	TNBLS	10//99-12//99
	Chattanooga MSA, TN-GA	S	6.98 MW	7.24 AW	14520 AAW	TNBLS	10//99-12//99
	Clarksville-Hopkinsville MSA, TN-KY	S	6.14 MW	6.11 AW	12770 AAW	TNBLS	10//99-12//99
	Jackson MSA, TN	S	5.99 MW	6.08 AW	12470 AAW	TNBLS	10//99-12//99
	Johnson City-Kingsport-Bristol MSA, TN-VA	S	6.57 MW	6.64 AW	13670 AAW	TNBLS	10//99-12//99
	Knoxville MSA, TN	S	6.86 MW	7.08 AW	14280 AAW	TNBLS	10//99-12//99
	Memphis MSA, TN-AR-MS	S	6.27 MW	6.18 AW	13030 AAW	MSBLS	10//99-12//99
	Nashville MSA, TN	S	7.99 MW	8.13 AW	16610 AAW	TNBLS	10//99-12//99
	Texas	S	6.16 MW	6.15 AW	12790 AAW	TXBLS	10//99-12//99
	Abilene MSA, TX	S	5.78 MW	5.97 AW	12030 AAW	TXBLS	10//99-12//99
	Amarillo MSA, TX	S	6.70 MW	6.87 AW	13930 AAW	TXBLS	10//99-12//99
	Austin-San Marcos MSA, TX	S	6.43 MW	6.40 AW	13380 AAW	TXBLS	10//99-12//99
	Beaumont-Port Arthur MSA, TX	S	6.25 MW	6.26 AW	12990 AAW	TXBLS	10//99-12//99
	Brazoria PMSA, TX	S	6.35 MW	6.36 AW	13210 AAW	TXBLS	10//99-12//99
	Brownsville-Harlingen-San Benito MSA, TX	S	5.75 MW	5.95 AW	11960 AAW	TXBLS	10//99-12//99
	Bryan-College Station MSA, TX	S	6.14 MW	6.17 AW	12760 AAW	TXBLS	10//99-12//99
	Corpus Christi MSA, TX	S	5.75 MW	5.95 AW	11960 AAW	TXBLS	10//99-12//99
	Dallas PMSA, TX	S	6.14 MW	6.17 AW	12760 AAW	TXBLS	10//99-12//99
	El Paso MSA, TX	S	5.78 MW	5.96 AW	12020 AAW	TXBLS	10//99-12//99
	Fort Worth-Arlington PMSA, TX	S	6.29 MW	6.29 AW	13080 AAW	TXBLS	10//99-12//99
	Galveston-Texas City PMSA, TX	S	6.44 MW	6.47 AW	13400 AAW	TXBLS	10//99-12//99
	Houston PMSA, TX	S	5.92 MW	6.03 AW	12320 AAW	TXBLS	10//99-12//99
	Killeen-Temple MSA, TX	S	6.31 MW	6.28 AW	13120 AAW	TXBLS	10//99-12//99
	Laredo MSA, TX	S	5.75 MW	5.95 AW	11960 AAW	TXBLS	10//99-12//99
	Longview-Marshall MSA, TX	S	6.04 MW	6.10 AW	12550 AAW	TXBLS	10//99-12//99
	Lubbock MSA, TX	S	5.91 MW	6.03 AW	12300 AAW	TXBLS	10//99-12//99
	McAllen-Edinburg-Mission MSA, TX	S	5.82 MW	5.98 AW	12110 AAW	TXBLS	10//99-12//99
	Odessa-Midland MSA, TX	S	6.10 MW	6.15 AW	12700 AAW	TXBLS	10//99-12//99
	San Angelo MSA, TX	S	6.47 MW	6.36 AW	13460 AAW	TXBLS	10//99-12//99
	San Antonio MSA, TX	S	6.79 MW	6.61 AW	14120 AAW	TXBLS	10//99-12//99
	Sherman-Denison MSA, TX	S	6.09 MW	6.14 AW	12670 AAW	TXBLS	10//99-12//99
	Texarkana MSA, TX-Texarkana, AR	S	5.89 MW	6.02 AW	12250 AAW	TXBLS	10//99-12//99
	Tyler MSA, TX	S	6.23 MW	6.25 AW	12960 AAW	TXBLS	10//99-12//99

AAW Average annual wage	**AOH** Average offered, high	**ASH** Average starting, high	**H** Hourly	**M** Monthly	**S** Special: hourly and annual
AE Average entry wage	**AOL** Average offered, low	**ASL** Average starting, low	**HI** Highest wage paid	**MTC** Median total compensation	**TQ** Third quartile wage
AEX Average experienced wage	**APH** Average pay, high range	**AW** Average wage paid	**HR** High end range	**MW** Median wage paid	**W** Weekly
AO Average offered	**APL** Average pay, low range	**FQ** First quartile wage	**LR** Low end range	**SQ** Second quartile wage	**Y** Yearly

Occupation/Type/Industry	Location	Per	Low	Mid	High	Source	Date
Dishwasher	Victoria MSA, TX	S	5.75 MW	5.95 AW	11960 AAW	TXBLS	10//99-12//99
	Waco MSA, TX	S	5.92 MW	6.01 AW	12310 AAW	TXBLS	10//99-12//99
	Wichita Falls MSA, TX	S	5.75 MW	5.95 AW	11960 AAW	TXBLS	10//99-12//99
	Utah	S	6.39 MW	6.42 AW	13340 AAW	UTBLS	10//99-12//99
	Provo-Orem MSA, UT	S	6.72 MW	6.65 AW	13990 AAW	UTBLS	10//99-12//99
	Salt Lake City-Ogden MSA, UT	S	6.60 MW	6.63 AW	13730 AAW	UTBLS	10//99-12//99
	Vermont	S	7.1 MW	7.26 AW	15100 AAW	VTBLS	10//99-12//99
	Burlington MSA, VT	S	7.46 MW	7.43 AW	15520 AAW	VTBLS	10//99-12//99
	Virginia	S	6.89 MW	6.99 AW	14540 AAW	VABLS	10//99-12//99
	Charlottesville MSA, VA	S	6.70 MW	6.82 AW	13940 AAW	VABLS	10//99-12//99
	Danville MSA, VA	S	5.88 MW	6.02 AW	12240 AAW	VABLS	10//99-12//99
	Lynchburg MSA, VA	S	6.43 MW	6.29 AW	13370 AAW	VABLS	10//99-12//99
	Norfolk-Virginia Beach-Newport News MSA, VA-NC	S	6.97 MW	6.49 AW	14500 AAW	VABLS	10//99-12//99
	Richmond-Petersburg MSA, VA	S	6.52 MW	6.47 AW	13550 AAW	VABLS	10//99-12//99
	Roanoke MSA, VA	S	6.67 MW	6.57 AW	13860 AAW	VABLS	10//99-12//99
	Washington	S	6.67 MW	7.03 AW	14620 AAW	WABLS	10//99-12//99
	Bellingham MSA, WA	S	6.76 MW	6.43 AW	14060 AAW	WABLS	10//99-12//99
	Bremerton PMSA, WA	S	6.45 MW	6.35 AW	13420 AAW	WABLS	10//99-12//99
	Olympia PMSA, WA	S	6.78 MW	6.39 AW	14100 AAW	WABLS	10//99-12//99
	Richland-Kennewick-Pasco MSA, WA	S	6.87 MW	6.46 AW	14290 AAW	WABLS	10//99-12//99
	Seattle-Bellevue-Everett PMSA, WA	S	7.74 MW	7.66 AW	16100 AAW	WABLS	10//99-12//99
	Spokane MSA, WA	S	6.32 MW	6.28 AW	13140 AAW	WABLS	10//99-12//99
	Tacoma PMSA, WA	S	6.80 MW	6.55 AW	14150 AAW	WABLS	10//99-12//99
	Yakima MSA, WA	S	6.44 MW	6.33 AW	13390 AAW	WABLS	10//99-12//99
	West Virginia	S	6.03 MW	5.92 AW	12310 AAW	WVBLS	10//99-12//99
	Charleston MSA, WV	S	6.01 MW	6.09 AW	12500 AAW	WVBLS	10//99-12//99
	Huntington-Ashland MSA, WV-KY-OH	S	6.16 MW	6.12 AW	12810 AAW	WVBLS	10//99-12//99
	Parkersburg-Marietta MSA, WV-OH	S	5.93 MW	6.04 AW	12340 AAW	WVBLS	10//99-12//99
	Wheeling MSA, WV-OH	S	5.85 MW	6.00 AW	12160 AAW	WVBLS	10//99-12//99
	Wisconsin	S	6.56 MW	6.67 AW	13870 AAW	WIBLS	10//99-12//99
	Appleton-Oshkosh-Neenah MSA, WI	S	7.17 MW	6.80 AW	14920 AAW	WIBLS	10//99-12//99
	Eau Claire MSA, WI	S	7.36 MW	7.52 AW	15300 AAW	WIBLS	10//99-12//99
	Green Bay MSA, WI	S	6.21 MW	6.22 AW	12920 AAW	WIBLS	10//99-12//99
	Janesville-Beloit MSA, WI	S	6.41 MW	6.31 AW	13330 AAW	WIBLS	10//99-12//99
	Kenosha PMSA, WI	S	6.26 MW	6.22 AW	13020 AAW	WIBLS	10//99-12//99
	La Crosse MSA, WI-MN	S	6.09 MW	6.13 AW	12670 AAW	WIBLS	10//99-12//99
	Madison MSA, WI	S	7.17 MW	7.04 AW	14920 AAW	WIBLS	10//99-12//99
	Milwaukee-Waukesha PMSA, WI	S	6.53 MW	6.52 AW	13580 AAW	WIBLS	10//99-12//99
	Racine PMSA, WI	S	6.56 MW	6.54 AW	13650 AAW	WIBLS	10//99-12//99
	Sheboygan MSA, WI	S	6.18 MW	6.20 AW	12850 AAW	WIBLS	10//99-12//99
	Wausau MSA, WI	S	5.86 MW	6.00 AW	12190 AAW	WIBLS	10//99-12//99
	Wyoming	S	5.98 MW	5.85 AW	12160 AAW	WYBLS	10//99-12//99
	Casper MSA, WY	S	5.93 MW	6.04 AW	12340 AAW	WYBLS	10//99-12//99
	Cheyenne MSA, WY	S	5.92 MW	6.01 AW	12320 AAW	WYBLS	10//99-12//99
	Puerto Rico	S	5.98 MW	5.81 AW	12090 AAW	PRBLS	10//99-12//99
	Arecibo PMSA, PR	S	5.75 MW	5.95 AW	11960 AAW	PRBLS	10//99-12//99
	Caguas PMSA, PR	S	5.86 MW	6.00 AW	12180 AAW	PRBLS	10//99-12//99
	Mayaguez MSA, PR	S	5.75 MW	5.95 AW	11960 AAW	PRBLS	10//99-12//99
	San Juan-Bayamon PMSA, PR	S	5.81 MW	5.98 AW	12080 AAW	PRBLS	10//99-12//99
	Virgin Islands	S	6.2 MW	6.22 AW	12940 AAW	VIBLS	10//99-12//99
	Guam	S	6 MW	5.87 AW	12210 AAW	GUBLS	10//99-12//99
Dispatcher							
Except Police, Fire, and Ambulance	Alabama	S	12.71 MW	13.22 AW	27500 AAW	ALBLS	10//99-12//99
Except Police, Fire, and Ambulance	Anniston MSA, AL	S	15.18 MW	15.57 AW	31570 AAW	ALBLS	10//99-12//99
Except Police, Fire, and Ambulance	Auburn-Opelika MSA, AL	S	15.86 MW	13.70 AW	32980 AAW	ALBLS	10//99-12//99
Except Police, Fire, and Ambulance	Birmingham MSA, AL	S	14.08 MW	14.02 AW	29290 AAW	ALBLS	10//99-12//99
Except Police, Fire, and Ambulance	Decatur MSA, AL	S	12.10 MW	11.84 AW	25170 AAW	ALBLS	10//99-12//99
Except Police, Fire, and Ambulance	Dothan MSA, AL	S	12.24 MW	10.32 AW	25470 AAW	ALBLS	10//99-12//99
Except Police, Fire, and Ambulance	Florence MSA, AL	S	13.38 MW	12.58 AW	27820 AAW	ALBLS	10//99-12//99
Except Police, Fire, and Ambulance	Gadsden MSA, AL	S	12.80 MW	12.44 AW	26630 AAW	ALBLS	10//99-12//99
Except Police, Fire, and Ambulance	Huntsville MSA, AL	S	11.35 MW	11.15 AW	23610 AAW	ALBLS	10//99-12//99
Except Police, Fire, and Ambulance	Mobile MSA, AL	S	11.34 MW	9.55 AW	23590 AAW	ALBLS	10//99-12//99

AAW	Average annual wage	AOH	Average offered, high	ASH	Average starting, high
AE	Average entry wage	AOL	Average offered, low	ASL	Average starting, low
AEX	Average experienced wage	APH	Average pay, high range	AW	Average wage paid
AO	Average offered	APL	Average pay, low range	FQ	First quartile wage

H	Hourly	M	Monthly	S	Special: hourly and annual
HI	Highest wage paid	MTC	Median total compensation	TQ	Third quartile wage
HR	High end range	MW	Median wage paid	W	Weekly
LR	Low end range	SQ	Second quartile wage	Y	Yearly

Dispatcher

Occupation/Type/Industry	Location	Per	Low	Mid	High	Source	Date
Dispatcher							
Except Police, Fire, and Ambulance	Montgomery MSA, AL	S	13.97 MW	13.59 AW	29060 AAW	ALBLS	10//99-12//99
Except Police, Fire, and Ambulance	Tuscaloosa MSA, AL	S	11.56 MW	10.13 AW	24050 AAW	ALBLS	10//99-12//99
Except Police, Fire, and Ambulance	Alaska	S	13.35 MW	14.77 AW	30730 AAW	AKBLS	10//99-12//99
Except Police, Fire, and Ambulance	Anchorage MSA, AK	S	14.48 MW	13.01 AW	30120 AAW	AKBLS	10//99-12//99
Except Police, Fire, and Ambulance	Arizona	S	10.76 MW	12.52 AW	26030 AAW	AZBLS	10//99-12//99
Except Police, Fire, and Ambulance	Phoenix-Mesa MSA, AZ	S	12.55 MW	10.95 AW	26110 AAW	AZBLS	10//99-12//99
Except Police, Fire, and Ambulance	Tucson MSA, AZ	S	12.66 MW	9.50 AW	26330 AAW	AZBLS	10//99-12//99
Except Police, Fire, and Ambulance	Yuma MSA, AZ	S	11.29 MW	11.11 AW	23490 AAW	AZBLS	10//99-12//99
Except Police, Fire, and Ambulance	Arkansas	S	13 MW	13.87 AW	28850 AAW	ARBLS	10//99-12//99
Except Police, Fire, and Ambulance	Fayetteville-Springdale-Rogers MSA, AR	S	15.55 MW	15.57 AW	32340 AAW	ARBLS	10//99-12//99
Except Police, Fire, and Ambulance	Fort Smith MSA, AR-OK	S	12.14 MW	12.26 AW	25260 AAW	ARBLS	10//99-12//99
Except Police, Fire, and Ambulance	Jonesboro MSA, AR	S	10.96 MW	11.36 AW	22790 AAW	ARBLS	10//99-12//99
Except Police, Fire, and Ambulance	Little Rock-North Little Rock MSA, AR	S	13.77 MW	12.77 AW	28640 AAW	ARBLS	10//99-12//99
Except Police, Fire, and Ambulance	California	S	13.74 MW	14.72 AW	30610 AAW	CABLS	10//99-12//99
Except Police, Fire, and Ambulance	Bakersfield MSA, CA	S	14.68 MW	13.59 AW	30530 AAW	CABLS	10//99-12//99
Except Police, Fire, and Ambulance	Chico-Paradise MSA, CA	S	11.70 MW	11.19 AW	24330 AAW	CABLS	10//99-12//99
Except Police, Fire, and Ambulance	Fresno MSA, CA	S	14.55 MW	14.26 AW	30260 AAW	CABLS	10//99-12//99
Except Police, Fire, and Ambulance	Los Angeles-Long Beach PMSA, CA	S	15.20 MW	14.40 AW	31610 AAW	CABLS	10//99-12//99
Except Police, Fire, and Ambulance	Merced MSA, CA	S	14.25 MW	13.69 AW	29640 AAW	CABLS	10//99-12//99
Except Police, Fire, and Ambulance	Modesto MSA, CA	S	14.87 MW	15.05 AW	30920 AAW	CABLS	10//99-12//99
Except Police, Fire, and Ambulance	Oakland PMSA, CA	S	16.89 MW	15.55 AW	35130 AAW	CABLS	10//99-12//99
Except Police, Fire, and Ambulance	Orange County PMSA, CA	S	13.96 MW	13.46 AW	29040 AAW	CABLS	10//99-12//99
Except Police, Fire, and Ambulance	Redding MSA, CA	S	15.16 MW	14.94 AW	31520 AAW	CABLS	10//99-12//99
Except Police, Fire, and Ambulance	Riverside-San Bernardino PMSA, CA	S	14.20 MW	12.87 AW	29540 AAW	CABLS	10//99-12//99
Except Police, Fire, and Ambulance	Sacramento PMSA, CA	S	17.22 MW	14.73 AW	35820 AAW	CABLS	10//99-12//99
Except Police, Fire, and Ambulance	Salinas MSA, CA	S	14.64 MW	13.75 AW	30460 AAW	CABLS	10//99-12//99
Except Police, Fire, and Ambulance	San Diego MSA, CA	S	11.82 MW	10.76 AW	24580 AAW	CABLS	10//99-12//99
Except Police, Fire, and Ambulance	San Francisco PMSA, CA	S	15.44 MW	14.37 AW	32120 AAW	CABLS	10//99-12//99
Except Police, Fire, and Ambulance	San Jose PMSA, CA	S	16.76 MW	15.62 AW	34850 AAW	CABLS	10//99-12//99
Except Police, Fire, and Ambulance	San Luis Obispo-Atascadero-Paso Robles MSA, CA	S	15.69 MW	15.45 AW	32640 AAW	CABLS	10//99-12//99
Except Police, Fire, and Ambulance	Santa Barbara-Santa Maria-Lompoc MSA, CA	S	12.55 MW	11.23 AW	26110 AAW	CABLS	10//99-12//99
Except Police, Fire, and Ambulance	Santa Cruz-Watsonville PMSA, CA	S	14.53 MW	14.61 AW	30230 AAW	CABLS	10//99-12//99
Except Police, Fire, and Ambulance	Santa Rosa PMSA, CA	S	15.22 MW	13.95 AW	31660 AAW	CABLS	10//99-12//99
Except Police, Fire, and Ambulance	Stockton-Lodi MSA, CA	S	15.69 MW	15.44 AW	32630 AAW	CABLS	10//99-12//99
Except Police, Fire, and Ambulance	Vallejo-Fairfield-Napa PMSA, CA	S	15.73 MW	15.08 AW	32710 AAW	CABLS	10//99-12//99
Except Police, Fire, and Ambulance	Ventura PMSA, CA	S	15.21 MW	13.11 AW	31640 AAW	CABLS	10//99-12//99
Except Police, Fire, and Ambulance	Visalia-Tulare-Porterville MSA, CA	S	16.37 MW	15.60 AW	34040 AAW	CABLS	10//99-12//99
Except Police, Fire, and Ambulance	Yolo PMSA, CA	S	15.34 MW	16.09 AW	31900 AAW	CABLS	10//99-12//99
Except Police, Fire, and Ambulance	Yuba City MSA, CA	S	12.92 MW	12.47 AW	26880 AAW	CABLS	10//99-12//99
Except Police, Fire, and Ambulance	Colorado	S	12.19 MW	13.21 AW	27470 AAW	COBLS	10//99-12//99
Except Police, Fire, and Ambulance	Colorado Springs MSA, CO	S	11.44 MW	11.27 AW	23800 AAW	COBLS	10//99-12//99
Except Police, Fire, and Ambulance	Denver PMSA, CO	S	13.49 MW	12.52 AW	28060 AAW	COBLS	10//99-12//99
Except Police, Fire, and Ambulance	Fort Collins-Loveland MSA, CO	S	12.03 MW	10.27 AW	25020 AAW	COBLS	10//99-12//99
Except Police, Fire, and Ambulance	Grand Junction MSA, CO	S	12.10 MW	11.01 AW	25170 AAW	COBLS	10//99-12//99
Except Police, Fire, and Ambulance	Greeley PMSA, CO	S	11.03 MW	8.75 AW	22930 AAW	COBLS	10//99-12//99
Except Police, Fire, and Ambulance	Pueblo MSA, CO	S	11.32 MW	10.33 AW	23550 AAW	COBLS	10//99-12//99
Except Police, Fire, and Ambulance	Connecticut	S	13.87 MW	14.56 AW	30290 AAW	CTBLS	10//99-12//99
Except Police, Fire, and Ambulance	Bridgeport PMSA, CT	S	15.11 MW	13.86 AW	31420 AAW	CTBLS	10//99-12//99
Except Police, Fire, and Ambulance	Danbury PMSA, CT	S	13.35 MW	11.84 AW	27770 AAW	CTBLS	10//99-12//99
Except Police, Fire, and Ambulance	Hartford MSA, CT	S	15.23 MW	14.71 AW	31680 AAW	CTBLS	10//99-12//99
Except Police, Fire, and Ambulance	New Haven-Meriden PMSA, CT	S	14.23 MW	13.88 AW	29600 AAW	CTBLS	10//99-12//99
Except Police, Fire, and Ambulance	New London-Norwich MSA, CT-RI	S	12.58 MW	12.13 AW	26160 AAW	CTBLS	10//99-12//99
Except Police, Fire, and Ambulance	Stamford-Norwalk PMSA, CT	S	14.81 MW	14.32 AW	30810 AAW	CTBLS	10//99-12//99
Except Police, Fire, and Ambulance	Waterbury PMSA, CT	S	14.02 MW	12.71 AW	29160 AAW	CTBLS	10//99-12//99
Except Police, Fire, and Ambulance	Delaware	S	14.55 MW	14.98 AW	31160 AAW	DEBLS	10//99-12//99
Except Police, Fire, and Ambulance	Dover MSA, DE	S	11.90 MW	10.54 AW	24750 AAW	DEBLS	10//99-12//99
Except Police, Fire, and Ambulance	Wilmington-Newark PMSA, DE-MD	S	15.51 MW	15.30 AW	32270 AAW	DEBLS	10//99-12//99
Except Police, Fire, and Ambulance	District of Columbia	S	11.37 MW	11.37 AW	23650 AAW	DCBLS	10//99-12//99

Dispatcher

Occupation/Type/Industry	Location	Per	Low	Mid	High	Source	Date
Dispatcher							
Except Police, Fire, and Ambulance	Washington PMSA, DC-MD-VA-WV	S	13.11 MW	12.32 AW	27260 AAW	DCBLS	10//99-12//99
Except Police, Fire, and Ambulance	Florida	S	11.44 MW	12.34 AW	25670 AAW	FLBLS	10//99-12//99
Except Police, Fire, and Ambulance	Daytona Beach MSA, FL	S	10.28 MW	9.48 AW	21380 AAW	FLBLS	10//99-12//99
Except Police, Fire, and Ambulance	Fort Lauderdale PMSA, FL	S	11.38 MW	10.39 AW	23660 AAW	FLBLS	10//99-12//99
Except Police, Fire, and Ambulance	Fort Myers-Cape Coral MSA, FL	S	11.30 MW	10.52 AW	23490 AAW	FLBLS	10//99-12//99
Except Police, Fire, and Ambulance	Fort Pierce-Port St. Lucie MSA, FL	S	11.96 MW	11.34 AW	24880 AAW	FLBLS	10//99-12//99
Except Police, Fire, and Ambulance	Fort Walton Beach MSA, FL	S	10.85 MW	10.75 AW	22580 AAW	FLBLS	10//99-12//99
Except Police, Fire, and Ambulance	Gainesville MSA, FL	S	14.67 MW	10.40 AW	30510 AAW	FLBLS	10//99-12//99
Except Police, Fire, and Ambulance	Jacksonville MSA, FL	S	13.23 MW	12.00 AW	27520 AAW	FLBLS	10//99-12//99
Except Police, Fire, and Ambulance	Lakeland-Winter Haven MSA, FL	S	13.82 MW	12.96 AW	28750 AAW	FLBLS	10//99-12//99
Except Police, Fire, and Ambulance	Melbourne-Titusville-Palm Bay MSA, FL	S	11.30 MW	11.11 AW	23500 AAW	FLBLS	10//99-12//99
Except Police, Fire, and Ambulance	Miami PMSA, FL	S	11.99 MW	11.37 AW	24940 AAW	FLBLS	10//99-12//99
Except Police, Fire, and Ambulance	Ocala MSA, FL	S	13.08 MW	11.27 AW	27210 AAW	FLBLS	10//99-12//99
Except Police, Fire, and Ambulance	Orlando MSA, FL	S	12.67 MW	11.62 AW	26350 AAW	FLBLS	10//99-12//99
Except Police, Fire, and Ambulance	Panama City MSA, FL	S	11.52 MW	11.32 AW	23960 AAW	FLBLS	10//99-12//99
Except Police, Fire, and Ambulance	Pensacola MSA, FL	S	12.04 MW	11.12 AW	25030 AAW	FLBLS	10//99-12//99
Except Police, Fire, and Ambulance	Sarasota-Bradenton MSA, FL	S	11.95 MW	10.82 AW	24860 AAW	FLBLS	10//99-12//99
Except Police, Fire, and Ambulance	Tallahassee MSA, FL	S	10.34 MW	9.69 AW	21510 AAW	FLBLS	10//99-12//99
Except Police, Fire, and Ambulance	Tampa-St. Petersburg-Clearwater MSA, FL	S	12.60 MW	11.97 AW	26210 AAW	FLBLS	10//99-12//99
Except Police, Fire, and Ambulance	West Palm Beach-Boca Raton MSA, FL	S	13.41 MW	12.78 AW	27890 AAW	FLBLS	10//99-12//99
Except Police, Fire, and Ambulance	Georgia	S	12.48 MW	13.09 AW	27220 AAW	GABLS	10//99-12//99
Except Police, Fire, and Ambulance	Albany MSA, GA	S	11.82 MW	11.03 AW	24590 AAW	GABLS	10//99-12//99
Except Police, Fire, and Ambulance	Atlanta MSA, GA	S	13.09 MW	12.51 AW	27240 AAW	GABLS	10//99-12//99
Except Police, Fire, and Ambulance	Augusta-Aiken MSA, GA-SC	S	12.51 MW	11.08 AW	26020 AAW	GABLS	10//99-12//99
Except Police, Fire, and Ambulance	Columbus MSA, GA-AL	S	11.41 MW	10.45 AW	23730 AAW	GABLS	10//99-12//99
Except Police, Fire, and Ambulance	Macon MSA, GA	S	12.59 MW	12.14 AW	26200 AAW	GABLS	10//99-12//99
Except Police, Fire, and Ambulance	Savannah MSA, GA	S	12.53 MW	10.98 AW	26060 AAW	GABLS	10//99-12//99
Except Police, Fire, and Ambulance	Hawaii	S	11.33 MW	12.06 AW	25090 AAW	HIBLS	10//99-12//99
Except Police, Fire, and Ambulance	Honolulu MSA, HI	S	12.21 MW	11.40 AW	25390 AAW	HIBLS	10//99-12//99
Except Police, Fire, and Ambulance	Idaho	S	11.39 MW	11.88 AW	24720 AAW	IDBLS	10//99-12//99
Except Police, Fire, and Ambulance	Boise City MSA, ID	S	11.13 MW	10.01 AW	23160 AAW	IDBLS	10//99-12//99
Except Police, Fire, and Ambulance	Illinois	S	14.04 MW	14.97 AW	31140 AAW	ILBLS	10//99-12//99
Except Police, Fire, and Ambulance	Bloomington-Normal MSA, IL	S	17.27 MW	15.54 AW	35920 AAW	ILBLS	10//99-12//99
Except Police, Fire, and Ambulance	Champaign-Urbana MSA, IL	S	13.48 MW	15.19 AW	28040 AAW	ILBLS	10//99-12//99
Except Police, Fire, and Ambulance	Chicago PMSA, IL	S	15.30 MW	14.48 AW	31830 AAW	ILBLS	10//99-12//99
Except Police, Fire, and Ambulance	Decatur MSA, IL	S	14.64 MW	13.99 AW	30440 AAW	ILBLS	10//99-12//99
Except Police, Fire, and Ambulance	Peoria-Pekin MSA, IL	S	14.44 MW	14.19 AW	30020 AAW	ILBLS	10//99-12//99
Except Police, Fire, and Ambulance	Rockford MSA, IL	S	16.19 MW	16.96 AW	33670 AAW	ILBLS	10//99-12//99
Except Police, Fire, and Ambulance	Springfield MSA, IL	S	14.81 MW	13.57 AW	30810 AAW	ILBLS	10//99-12//99
Except Police, Fire, and Ambulance	Indiana	S	14.08 MW	15.20 AW	31610 AAW	INBLS	10//99-12//99
Except Police, Fire, and Ambulance	Bloomington MSA, IN	S	13.67 MW	11.91 AW	28440 AAW	INBLS	10//99-12//99
Except Police, Fire, and Ambulance	Elkhart-Goshen MSA, IN	S	12.93 MW	11.59 AW	26900 AAW	INBLS	10//99-12//99
Except Police, Fire, and Ambulance	Evansville-Henderson MSA, IN-KY	S	11.16 MW	9.95 AW	23220 AAW	INBLS	10//99-12//99
Except Police, Fire, and Ambulance	Fort Wayne MSA, IN	S	15.60 MW	16.21 AW	32450 AAW	INBLS	10//99-12//99
Except Police, Fire, and Ambulance	Gary PMSA, IN	S	15.59 MW	14.31 AW	32430 AAW	INBLS	10//99-12//99
Except Police, Fire, and Ambulance	Indianapolis MSA, IN	S	17.22 MW	16.42 AW	35810 AAW	INBLS	10//99-12//99
Except Police, Fire, and Ambulance	Lafayette MSA, IN	S	12.52 MW	12.08 AW	26040 AAW	INBLS	10//99-12//99
Except Police, Fire, and Ambulance	South Bend MSA, IN	S	14.62 MW	13.87 AW	30410 AAW	INBLS	10//99-12//99
Except Police, Fire, and Ambulance	Terre Haute MSA, IN	S	12.06 MW	10.71 AW	25090 AAW	INBLS	10//99-12//99
Except Police, Fire, and Ambulance	Iowa	S	13.43 MW	13.70 AW	28490 AAW	IABLS	10//99-12//99
Except Police, Fire, and Ambulance	Cedar Rapids MSA, IA	S	11.98 MW	12.66 AW	24910 AAW	IABLS	10//99-12//99
Except Police, Fire, and Ambulance	Davenport-Moline-Rock Island MSA, IA-IL	S	13.70 MW	13.21 AW	28510 AAW	IABLS	10//99-12//99
Except Police, Fire, and Ambulance	Des Moines MSA, IA	S	14.93 MW	14.73 AW	31050 AAW	IABLS	10//99-12//99
Except Police, Fire, and Ambulance	Dubuque MSA, IA	S	16.87 MW	18.05 AW	35080 AAW	IABLS	10//99-12//99
Except Police, Fire, and Ambulance	Sioux City MSA, IA-NE	S	14.23 MW	14.68 AW	29600 AAW	IABLS	10//99-12//99
Except Police, Fire, and Ambulance	Waterloo-Cedar Falls MSA, IA	S	14.36 MW	13.45 AW	29870 AAW	IABLS	10//99-12//99
Except Police, Fire, and Ambulance	Kansas	S	13.37 MW	14.21 AW	29550 AAW	KSBLS	10//99-12//99
Except Police, Fire, and Ambulance	Topeka MSA, KS	S	12.98 MW	11.62 AW	27010 AAW	KSBLS	10//99-12//99
Except Police, Fire, and Ambulance	Wichita MSA, KS	S	16.67 MW	12.70 AW	34670 AAW	KSBLS	10//99-12//99
Except Police, Fire, and Ambulance	Kentucky	S	11.57 MW	12.41 AW	25810 AAW	KYBLS	10//99-12//99
Except Police, Fire, and Ambulance	Lexington MSA, KY	S	11.18 MW	10.24 AW	23250 AAW	KYBLS	10//99-12//99
Except Police, Fire, and Ambulance	Louisville MSA, KY-IN	S	13.04 MW	12.13 AW	27120 AAW	KYBLS	10//99-12//99

AAW	Average annual wage	AOH	Average offered, high	ASH	Average starting, high
AE	Average entry wage	AOL	Average offered, low	ASL	Average starting, low
AEX	Average experienced wage	APH	Average pay, high range	AW	Average wage paid
AO	Average offered	APL	Average pay, low range	FQ	First quartile wage

H	Hourly	M	Monthly	S	Special: hourly and annual
HI	Highest wage paid	MTC	Median total compensation	TQ	Third quartile wage
HR	High end range	MW	Median wage paid	W	Weekly
LR	Low end range	SQ	Second quartile wage	Y	Yearly

Dispatcher

Occupation/Type/Industry	Location	Per	Low	Mid	High	Source	Date
Except Police, Fire, and Ambulance	Owensboro MSA, KY	s	12.97 mw	12.02 aw	26980 aaw	KYBLS	10//99-12//99
Except Police, Fire, and Ambulance	Louisiana	s	12.69 mw	13.23 aw	27520 aaw	LABLS	10//99-12//99
Except Police, Fire, and Ambulance	Baton Rouge MSA, LA	s	12.47 mw	12.45 aw	25940 aaw	LABLS	10//99-12//99
Except Police, Fire, and Ambulance	Houma MSA, LA	s	12.56 mw	10.63 aw	26130 aaw	LABLS	10//99-12//99
Except Police, Fire, and Ambulance	Lafayette MSA, LA	s	16.25 mw	17.47 aw	33800 aaw	LABLS	10//99-12//99
Except Police, Fire, and Ambulance	Lake Charles MSA, LA	s	12.95 mw	12.06 aw	26930 aaw	LABLS	10//99-12//99
Except Police, Fire, and Ambulance	Monroe MSA, LA	s	11.51 mw	10.73 aw	23930 aaw	LABLS	10//99-12//99
Except Police, Fire, and Ambulance	New Orleans MSA, LA	s	11.86 mw	11.60 aw	24680 aaw	LABLS	10//99-12//99
Except Police, Fire, and Ambulance	Shreveport-Bossier City MSA, LA	s	11.56 mw	10.79 aw	24050 aaw	LABLS	10//99-12//99
Except Police, Fire, and Ambulance	Maine	s	12.44 mw	13.21 aw	27470 aaw	MEBLS	10//99-12//99
Except Police, Fire, and Ambulance	Lewiston-Auburn MSA, ME	s	12.84 mw	12.71 aw	26700 aaw	MEBLS	10//99-12//99
Except Police, Fire, and Ambulance	Portland MSA, ME	s	14.78 mw	14.09 aw	30750 aaw	MEBLS	10//99-12//99
Except Police, Fire, and Ambulance	Maryland	s	13.12 mw	13.86 aw	28820 aaw	MDBLS	10//99-12//99
Except Police, Fire, and Ambulance	Baltimore PMSA, MD	s	13.26 mw	12.94 aw	27590 aaw	MDBLS	10//99-12//99
Except Police, Fire, and Ambulance	Hagerstown PMSA, MD	s	13.91 mw	13.36 aw	28940 aaw	MDBLS	10//99-12//99
Except Police, Fire, and Ambulance	Massachusetts	s	13.1 mw	14.11 aw	29360 aaw	MABLS	10//99-12//99
Except Police, Fire, and Ambulance	Barnstable-Yarmouth MSA, MA	s	12.86 mw	12.47 aw	26760 aaw	MABLS	10//99-12//99
Except Police, Fire, and Ambulance	Boston PMSA, MA-NH	s	14.38 mw	13.13 aw	29900 aaw	MABLS	10//99-12//99
Except Police, Fire, and Ambulance	Brockton PMSA, MA	s	15.01 mw	16.40 aw	31210 aaw	MABLS	10//99-12//99
Except Police, Fire, and Ambulance	Lawrence PMSA, MA-NH	s	12.78 mw	11.64 aw	26580 aaw	MABLS	10//99-12//99
Except Police, Fire, and Ambulance	Lowell PMSA, MA-NH	s	15.63 mw	15.88 aw	32520 aaw	MABLS	10//99-12//99
Except Police, Fire, and Ambulance	New Bedford PMSA, MA	s	10.94 mw	8.73 aw	22760 aaw	MABLS	10//99-12//99
Except Police, Fire, and Ambulance	Pittsfield MSA, MA	s	12.13 mw	10.38 aw	25230 aaw	MABLS	10//99-12//99
Except Police, Fire, and Ambulance	Springfield MSA, MA	s	15.57 mw	13.25 aw	32380 aaw	MABLS	10//99-12//99
Except Police, Fire, and Ambulance	Worcester PMSA, MA-CT	s	13.58 mw	12.77 aw	28250 aaw	MABLS	10//99-12//99
Except Police, Fire, and Ambulance	Michigan	s	13.81 mw	14.76 aw	30710 aaw	MIBLS	10//99-12//99
Except Police, Fire, and Ambulance	Ann Arbor PMSA, MI	s	13.94 mw	11.50 aw	29000 aaw	MIBLS	10//99-12//99
Except Police, Fire, and Ambulance	Benton Harbor MSA, MI	s	13.30 mw	10.55 aw	27670 aaw	MIBLS	10//99-12//99
Except Police, Fire, and Ambulance	Detroit PMSA, MI	s	15.23 mw	15.04 aw	31670 aaw	MIBLS	10//99-12//99
Except Police, Fire, and Ambulance	Flint PMSA, MI	s	14.19 mw	12.74 aw	29520 aaw	MIBLS	10//99-12//99
Except Police, Fire, and Ambulance	Grand Rapids-Muskegon-Holland MSA, MI	s	14.81 mw	13.66 aw	30810 aaw	MIBLS	10//99-12//99
Except Police, Fire, and Ambulance	Jackson MSA, MI	s	21.05 mw	12.63 aw	43790 aaw	MIBLS	10//99-12//99
Except Police, Fire, and Ambulance	Kalamazoo-Battle Creek MSA, MI	s	11.04 mw	10.65 aw	22960 aaw	MIBLS	10//99-12//99
Except Police, Fire, and Ambulance	Lansing-East Lansing MSA, MI	s	13.84 mw	13.27 aw	28790 aaw	MIBLS	10//99-12//99
Except Police, Fire, and Ambulance	Saginaw-Bay City-Midland MSA, MI	s	13.42 mw	13.74 aw	27910 aaw	MIBLS	10//99-12//99
Except Police, Fire, and Ambulance	Minnesota	s	13.97 mw	14.90 aw	30990 aaw	MNBLS	10//99-12//99
Except Police, Fire, and Ambulance	Duluth-Superior MSA, MN-WI	s	14.74 mw	14.79 aw	30660 aaw	MNBLS	10//99-12//99
Except Police, Fire, and Ambulance	Minneapolis-St. Paul MSA, MN-WI	s	15.22 mw	14.12 aw	31660 aaw	MNBLS	10//99-12//99
Except Police, Fire, and Ambulance	Rochester MSA, MN	s	13.65 mw	12.74 aw	28390 aaw	MNBLS	10//99-12//99
Except Police, Fire, and Ambulance	St. Cloud MSA, MN	s	12.18 mw	11.37 aw	25330 aaw	MNBLS	10//99-12//99
Except Police, Fire, and Ambulance	Mississippi	s	10.78 mw	11.72 aw	24370 aaw	MSBLS	10//99-12//99
Except Police, Fire, and Ambulance	Biloxi-Gulfport-Pascagoula MSA, MS	s	11.20 mw	10.52 aw	23300 aaw	MSBLS	10//99-12//99
Except Police, Fire, and Ambulance	Jackson MSA, MS	s	12.14 mw	10.86 aw	25250 aaw	MSBLS	10//99-12//99
Except Police, Fire, and Ambulance	Missouri	s	14.04 mw	14.78 aw	30750 aaw	MOBLS	10//99-12//99
Except Police, Fire, and Ambulance	Kansas City MSA, MO-KS	s	15.30 mw	14.98 aw	31820 aaw	MOBLS	10//99-12//99
Except Police, Fire, and Ambulance	St. Louis MSA, MO-IL	s	14.27 mw	11.96 aw	29680 aaw	MOBLS	10//99-12//99
Except Police, Fire, and Ambulance	Montana	s	10.63 mw	12.56 aw	26120 aaw	MTBLS	10//99-12//99
Except Police, Fire, and Ambulance	Billings MSA, MT	s	12.48 mw	10.21 aw	25960 aaw	MTBLS	10//99-12//99
Except Police, Fire, and Ambulance	Missoula MSA, MT	s	14.30 mw	14.13 aw	29740 aaw	MTBLS	10//99-12//99
Except Police, Fire, and Ambulance	Nebraska	s	15.75 mw	18.68 aw	38850 aaw	NEBLS	10//99-12//99
Except Police, Fire, and Ambulance	Lincoln MSA, NE	s	13.95 mw	14.22 aw	29020 aaw	NEBLS	10//99-12//99
Except Police, Fire, and Ambulance	Omaha MSA, NE-IA	s	20.07 mw	16.26 aw	41750 aaw	NEBLS	10//99-12//99
Except Police, Fire, and Ambulance	Nevada	s	11.4 mw	13.12 aw	27290 aaw	NVBLS	10//99-12//99
Except Police, Fire, and Ambulance	Las Vegas MSA, NV-AZ	s	12.87 mw	11.19 aw	26770 aaw	NVBLS	10//99-12//99
Except Police, Fire, and Ambulance	Reno MSA, NV	s	13.92 mw	12.31 aw	28960 aaw	NVBLS	10//99-12//99
Except Police, Fire, and Ambulance	New Hampshire	s	12.69 mw	13.28 aw	27610 aaw	NHBLS	10//99-12//99
Except Police, Fire, and Ambulance	Manchester PMSA, NH	s	14.36 mw	13.43 aw	29880 aaw	NHBLS	10//99-12//99
Except Police, Fire, and Ambulance	Nashua PMSA, NH	s	11.70 mw	11.13 aw	24340 aaw	NHBLS	10//99-12//99
Except Police, Fire, and Ambulance	Portsmouth-Rochester PMSA, NH-ME	s	14.48 mw	13.98 aw	30110 aaw	NHBLS	10//99-12//99
Except Police, Fire, and Ambulance	New Jersey	s	14.21 mw	15.24 aw	31690 aaw	NJBLS	10//99-12//99
Except Police, Fire, and Ambulance	Atlantic-Cape May PMSA, NJ	s	15.10 mw	13.39 aw	31400 aaw	NJBLS	10//99-12//99
Except Police, Fire, and Ambulance	Bergen-Passaic PMSA, NJ	s	16.17 mw	15.16 aw	33640 aaw	NJBLS	10//99-12//99
Except Police, Fire, and Ambulance	Jersey City PMSA, NJ	s	17.79 mw	15.71 aw	37010 aaw	NJBLS	10//99-12//99

AAW Average annual wage	AOH Average offered, high	ASH Average starting, high	H Hourly	M Monthly	S Special: hourly and annual
AE Average entry wage	AOL Average offered, low	ASL Average starting, low	HI Highest wage paid	MTC Median total compensation	TQ Third quartile wage
AEX Average experienced wage	APH Average pay, high range	AW Average wage paid	HR High end range	MW Median wage paid	W Weekly
AO Average offered	APL Average pay, low range	FQ First quartile wage	LR Low end range	SQ Second quartile wage	Y Yearly

Occupation/Type/Industry	Location	Per	Low	Mid	High	Source	Date
Dispatcher							
Except Police, Fire, and Ambulance	Middlesex-Somerset-Hunterdon PMSA, NJ	S	15.80 MW	15.32 AW	32870 AAW	NJBLS	10//99-12//99
Except Police, Fire, and Ambulance	Monmouth-Ocean PMSA, NJ	S	16.43 MW	16.54 AW	34170 AAW	NJBLS	10//99-12//99
Except Police, Fire, and Ambulance	Newark PMSA, NJ	S	14.64 MW	14.04 AW	30440 AAW	NJBLS	10//99-12//99
Except Police, Fire, and Ambulance	Trenton PMSA, NJ	S	12.76 MW	11.96 AW	26550 AAW	NJBLS	10//99-12//99
Except Police, Fire, and Ambulance	Vineland-Millville-Bridgeton PMSA, NJ	S	12.04 MW	11.97 AW	25040 AAW	NJBLS	10//99-12//99
Except Police, Fire, and Ambulance	New Mexico	S	9.66 MW	10.63 AW	22120 AAW	NMBLS	10//99-12//99
Except Police, Fire, and Ambulance	Albuquerque MSA, NM	S	10.00 MW	8.68 AW	20810 AAW	NMBLS	10//99-12//99
Except Police, Fire, and Ambulance	Las Cruces MSA, NM	S	10.73 MW	10.27 AW	22310 AAW	NMBLS	10//99-12//99
Except Police, Fire, and Ambulance	Santa Fe MSA, NM	S	10.60 MW	10.42 AW	22050 AAW	NMBLS	10//99-12//99
Except Police, Fire, and Ambulance	New York	S	15.5 MW	17.15 AW	35680 AAW	NYBLS	10//99-12//99
Except Police, Fire, and Ambulance	Albany-Schenectady-Troy MSA, NY	S	14.76 MW	13.87 AW	30700 AAW	NYBLS	10//99-12//99
Except Police, Fire, and Ambulance	Binghamton MSA, NY	S	10.19 MW	8.66 AW	21190 AAW	NYBLS	10//99-12//99
Except Police, Fire, and Ambulance	Buffalo-Niagara Falls MSA, NY	S	14.67 MW	14.41 AW	30510 AAW	NYBLS	10//99-12//99
Except Police, Fire, and Ambulance	Dutchess County PMSA, NY	S	12.76 MW	11.68 AW	26540 AAW	NYBLS	10//99-12//99
Except Police, Fire, and Ambulance	Elmira MSA, NY	S	14.02 MW	12.85 AW	29160 AAW	NYBLS	10//99-12//99
Except Police, Fire, and Ambulance	Glens Falls MSA, NY	S	12.95 MW	11.11 AW	26930 AAW	NYBLS	10//99-12//99
Except Police, Fire, and Ambulance	Jamestown MSA, NY	S	14.65 MW	14.02 AW	30470 AAW	NYBLS	10//99-12//99
Except Police, Fire, and Ambulance	Nassau-Suffolk PMSA, NY	S	16.16 MW	15.93 AW	33600 AAW	NYBLS	10//99-12//99
Except Police, Fire, and Ambulance	New York PMSA, NY	S	18.69 MW	17.34 AW	38870 AAW	NYBLS	10//99-12//99
Except Police, Fire, and Ambulance	Rochester MSA, NY	S	17.81 MW	15.10 AW	37040 AAW	NYBLS	10//99-12//99
Except Police, Fire, and Ambulance	Syracuse MSA, NY	S	13.94 MW	12.53 AW	28990 AAW	NYBLS	10//99-12//99
Except Police, Fire, and Ambulance	Utica-Rome MSA, NY	S	14.40 MW	10.61 AW	29950 AAW	NYBLS	10//99-12//99
Except Police, Fire, and Ambulance	North Carolina	S	13.41 MW	14.00 AW	29110 AAW	NCBLS	10//99-12//99
Except Police, Fire, and Ambulance	Asheville MSA, NC	S	11.14 MW	10.70 AW	23160 AAW	NCBLS	10//99-12//99
Except Police, Fire, and Ambulance	Charlotte-Gastonia-Rock Hill MSA, NC-SC	S	14.94 MW	14.07 AW	31070 AAW	NCBLS	10//99-12//99
Except Police, Fire, and Ambulance	Fayetteville MSA, NC	S	12.49 MW	10.85 AW	25980 AAW	NCBLS	10//99-12//99
Except Police, Fire, and Ambulance	Greensboro--Winston-Salem--High Point MSA, NC	S	13.61 MW	13.89 AW	28300 AAW	NCBLS	10//99-12//99
Except Police, Fire, and Ambulance	Greenville MSA, NC	S	12.71 MW	12.67 AW	26430 AAW	NCBLS	10//99-12//99
Except Police, Fire, and Ambulance	Hickory-Morganton-Lenoir MSA, NC	S	15.91 MW	16.37 AW	33100 AAW	NCBLS	10//99-12//99
Except Police, Fire, and Ambulance	Jacksonville MSA, NC	S	10.44 MW	10.07 AW	21710 AAW	NCBLS	10//99-12//99
Except Police, Fire, and Ambulance	Raleigh-Durham-Chapel Hill MSA, NC	S	15.41 MW	14.61 AW	32050 AAW	NCBLS	10//99-12//99
Except Police, Fire, and Ambulance	Wilmington MSA, NC	S	12.85 MW	12.15 AW	26730 AAW	NCBLS	10//99-12//99
Except Police, Fire, and Ambulance	North Dakota	S	13.03 MW	13.52 AW	28130 AAW	NDBLS	10//99-12//99
Except Police, Fire, and Ambulance	Bismarck MSA, ND	S	13.31 MW	12.39 AW	27690 AAW	NDBLS	10//99-12//99
Except Police, Fire, and Ambulance	Fargo-Moorhead MSA, ND-MN	S	14.29 MW	13.34 AW	29720 AAW	NDBLS	10//99-12//99
Except Police, Fire, and Ambulance	Grand Forks MSA, ND-MN	S	14.21 MW	13.63 AW	29560 AAW	NDBLS	10//99-12//99
Except Police, Fire, and Ambulance	Ohio	S	13.12 MW	13.85 AW	28800 AAW	OHBLS	10//99-12//99
Except Police, Fire, and Ambulance	Akron PMSA, OH	S	13.94 MW	13.88 AW	28990 AAW	OHBLS	10//99-12//99
Except Police, Fire, and Ambulance	Canton-Massillon MSA, OH	S	13.95 MW	13.74 AW	29010 AAW	OHBLS	10//99-12//99
Except Police, Fire, and Ambulance	Cincinnati PMSA, OH-KY-IN	S	14.47 MW	13.93 AW	30100 AAW	OHBLS	10//99-12//99
Except Police, Fire, and Ambulance	Cleveland-Lorain-Elyria PMSA, OH	S	14.75 MW	13.56 AW	30670 AAW	OHBLS	10//99-12//99
Except Police, Fire, and Ambulance	Columbus MSA, OH	S	12.65 MW	12.06 AW	26310 AAW	OHBLS	10//99-12//99
Except Police, Fire, and Ambulance	Dayton-Springfield MSA, OH	S	13.95 MW	13.53 AW	29020 AAW	OHBLS	10//99-12//99
Except Police, Fire, and Ambulance	Hamilton-Middletown PMSA, OH	S	15.37 MW	15.48 AW	31960 AAW	OHBLS	10//99-12//99
Except Police, Fire, and Ambulance	Lima MSA, OH	S	12.16 MW	10.90 AW	25300 AAW	OHBLS	10//99-12//99
Except Police, Fire, and Ambulance	Mansfield MSA, OH	S	12.54 MW	11.23 AW	26090 AAW	OHBLS	10//99-12//99
Except Police, Fire, and Ambulance	Toledo MSA, OH	S	13.36 MW	12.03 AW	27790 AAW	OHBLS	10//99-12//99
Except Police, Fire, and Ambulance	Youngstown-Warren MSA, OH	S	14.61 MW	12.98 AW	30380 AAW	OHBLS	10//99-12//99
Except Police, Fire, and Ambulance	Oklahoma	S	11.27 MW	12.66 AW	26340 AAW	OKBLS	10//99-12//99
Except Police, Fire, and Ambulance	Enid MSA, OK	S	11.02 MW	10.28 AW	22920 AAW	OKBLS	10//99-12//99
Except Police, Fire, and Ambulance	Lawton MSA, OK	S	9.85 MW	9.91 AW	20490 AAW	OKBLS	10//99-12//99
Except Police, Fire, and Ambulance	Oklahoma City MSA, OK	S	13.25 MW	12.07 AW	27560 AAW	OKBLS	10//99-12//99
Except Police, Fire, and Ambulance	Tulsa MSA, OK	S	12.90 MW	10.75 AW	26840 AAW	OKBLS	10//99-12//99
Except Police, Fire, and Ambulance	Oregon	S	13.22 MW	15.02 AW	31240 AAW	ORBLS	10//99-12//99
Except Police, Fire, and Ambulance	Eugene-Springfield MSA, OR	S	14.46 MW	14.09 AW	30080 AAW	ORBLS	10//99-12//99
Except Police, Fire, and Ambulance	Medford-Ashland MSA, OR	S	11.57 MW	10.24 AW	24070 AAW	ORBLS	10//99-12//99
Except Police, Fire, and Ambulance	Portland-Vancouver PMSA, OR-WA	S	15.06 MW	13.20 AW	31320 AAW	ORBLS	10//99-12//99
Except Police, Fire, and Ambulance	Salem PMSA, OR	S	13.54 MW	10.94 AW	28150 AAW	ORBLS	10//99-12//99
Except Police, Fire, and Ambulance	Pennsylvania	S	12.86 MW	14.31 AW	29760 AAW	PABLS	10//99-12//99

AAW	Average annual wage	AOH	Average offered, high	ASH	Average starting, high
AE	Average entry wage	AOL	Average offered, low	ASL	Average starting, low
AEX	Average experienced wage	APH	Average pay, high range	AW	Average wage paid
AO	Average offered	APL	Average pay, low range	FQ	First quartile wage

H	Hourly	M	Monthly	S	Special: hourly and annual
HI	Highest wage paid	MTC	Median total compensation	TQ	Third quartile wage
HR	High end range	MW	Median wage paid	W	Weekly
LR	Low end range	SQ	Second quartile wage	Y	Yearly

Occupation/Type/Industry	Location	Per	Low	Mid	High	Source	Date
Dispatcher							
Except Police, Fire, and Ambulance	Allentown-Bethlehem-Easton MSA, PA	S	13.15 MW	12.85 AW	27340 AAW	PABLS	10//99-12//99
Except Police, Fire, and Ambulance	Altoona MSA, PA	S	14.07 MW	12.63 AW	29270 AAW	PABLS	10//99-12//99
Except Police, Fire, and Ambulance	Erie MSA, PA	S	13.02 MW	13.26 AW	27080 AAW	PABLS	10//99-12//99
Except Police, Fire, and Ambulance	Harrisburg-Lebanon-Carlisle MSA, PA	S	14.64 MW	14.24 AW	30450 AAW	PABLS	10//99-12//99
Except Police, Fire, and Ambulance	Johnstown MSA, PA	S	11.16 MW	11.27 AW	23200 AAW	PABLS	10//99-12//99
Except Police, Fire, and Ambulance	Lancaster MSA, PA	S	13.23 MW	11.39 AW	27520 AAW	PABLS	10//99-12//99
Except Police, Fire, and Ambulance	Philadelphia PMSA, PA-NJ	S	13.95 MW	11.99 AW	29020 AAW	PABLS	10//99-12//99
Except Police, Fire, and Ambulance	Pittsburgh MSA, PA	S	16.42 MW	14.64 AW	34150 AAW	PABLS	10//99-12//99
Except Police, Fire, and Ambulance	Reading MSA, PA	S	13.47 MW	12.13 AW	28010 AAW	PABLS	10//99-12//99
Except Police, Fire, and Ambulance	Scranton--Wilkes-Barre--Hazleton MSA, PA	S	12.95 MW	12.37 AW	26940 AAW	PABLS	10//99-12//99
Except Police, Fire, and Ambulance	Sharon MSA, PA	S	11.25 MW	9.12 AW	23410 AAW	PABLS	10//99-12//99
Except Police, Fire, and Ambulance	State College MSA, PA	S	13.09 MW	11.57 AW	27230 AAW	PABLS	10//99-12//99
Except Police, Fire, and Ambulance	Williamsport MSA, PA	S	10.80 MW	10.95 AW	22470 AAW	PABLS	10//99-12//99
Except Police, Fire, and Ambulance	York MSA, PA	S	14.08 MW	13.43 AW	29280 AAW	PABLS	10//99-12//99
Except Police, Fire, and Ambulance	Rhode Island	S	13.07 MW	13.97 AW	29070 AAW	RIBLS	10//99-12//99
Except Police, Fire, and Ambulance	Providence-Fall River-Warwick MSA, RI-MA	S	13.73 MW	13.08 AW	28550 AAW	RIBLS	10//99-12//99
Except Police, Fire, and Ambulance	South Carolina	S	12.66 MW	13.51 AW	28100 AAW	SCBLS	10//99-12//99
Except Police, Fire, and Ambulance	Charleston-North Charleston MSA, SC	S	14.17 MW	12.68 AW	29480 AAW	SCBLS	10//99-12//99
Except Police, Fire, and Ambulance	Columbia MSA, SC	S	13.23 MW	12.86 AW	27520 AAW	SCBLS	10//99-12//99
Except Police, Fire, and Ambulance	Florence MSA, SC	S	11.32 MW	10.08 AW	23540 AAW	SCBLS	10//99-12//99
Except Police, Fire, and Ambulance	Greenville-Spartanburg-Anderson MSA, SC	S	15.03 MW	15.27 AW	31250 AAW	SCBLS	10//99-12//99
Except Police, Fire, and Ambulance	Myrtle Beach MSA, SC	S	13.24 MW	13.47 AW	27530 AAW	SCBLS	10//99-12//99
Except Police, Fire, and Ambulance	Sumter MSA, SC	S	13.91 MW	13.24 AW	28930 AAW	SCBLS	10//99-12//99
Except Police, Fire, and Ambulance	South Dakota	S	10.69 MW	11.07 AW	23020 AAW	SDBLS	10//99-12//99
Except Police, Fire, and Ambulance	Rapid City MSA, SD	S	8.62 MW	7.06 AW	17940 AAW	SDBLS	10//99-12//99
Except Police, Fire, and Ambulance	Sioux Falls MSA, SD	S	13.25 MW	12.24 AW	27560 AAW	SDBLS	10//99-12//99
Except Police, Fire, and Ambulance	Tennessee	S	12.29 MW	13.11 AW	27260 AAW	TNBLS	10//99-12//99
Except Police, Fire, and Ambulance	Chattanooga MSA, TN-GA	S	12.95 MW	12.08 AW	26940 AAW	TNBLS	10//99-12//99
Except Police, Fire, and Ambulance	Clarksville-Hopkinsville MSA, TN-KY	S	10.04 MW	9.08 AW	20870 AAW	TNBLS	10//99-12//99
Except Police, Fire, and Ambulance	Jackson MSA, TN	S	13.63 MW	12.82 AW	28350 AAW	TNBLS	10//99-12//99
Except Police, Fire, and Ambulance	Johnson City-Kingsport-Bristol MSA, TN-VA	S	10.22 MW	9.97 AW	21260 AAW	TNBLS	10//99-12//99
Except Police, Fire, and Ambulance	Knoxville MSA, TN	S	13.72 MW	14.13 AW	28530 AAW	TNBLS	10//99-12//99
Except Police, Fire, and Ambulance	Memphis MSA, TN-AR-MS	S	13.97 MW	12.77 AW	29050 AAW	MSBLS	10//99-12//99
Except Police, Fire, and Ambulance	Nashville MSA, TN	S	13.50 MW	12.05 AW	28080 AAW	TNBLS	10//99-12//99
Except Police, Fire, and Ambulance	Texas	S	11.51 MW	12.66 AW	26340 AAW	TXBLS	10//99-12//99
Except Police, Fire, and Ambulance	Abilene MSA, TX	S	13.07 MW	13.17 AW	27190 AAW	TXBLS	10//99-12//99
Except Police, Fire, and Ambulance	Amarillo MSA, TX	S	12.80 MW	11.44 AW	26630 AAW	TXBLS	10//99-12//99
Except Police, Fire, and Ambulance	Austin-San Marcos MSA, TX	S	12.49 MW	11.47 AW	25980 AAW	TXBLS	10//99-12//99
Except Police, Fire, and Ambulance	Beaumont-Port Arthur MSA, TX	S	11.54 MW	10.78 AW	24010 AAW	TXBLS	10//99-12//99
Except Police, Fire, and Ambulance	Brazoria PMSA, TX	S	12.34 MW	10.18 AW	25660 AAW	TXBLS	10//99-12//99
Except Police, Fire, and Ambulance	Brownsville-Harlingen-San Benito MSA, TX	S	10.05 MW	9.33 AW	20900 AAW	TXBLS	10//99-12//99
Except Police, Fire, and Ambulance	Bryan-College Station MSA, TX	S	13.88 MW	13.56 AW	28880 AAW	TXBLS	10//99-12//99
Except Police, Fire, and Ambulance	Corpus Christi MSA, TX	S	13.07 MW	12.16 AW	27180 AAW	TXBLS	10//99-12//99
Except Police, Fire, and Ambulance	Dallas PMSA, TX	S	13.16 MW	11.80 AW	27380 AAW	TXBLS	10//99-12//99
Except Police, Fire, and Ambulance	El Paso MSA, TX	S	10.57 MW	10.27 AW	21990 AAW	TXBLS	10//99-12//99
Except Police, Fire, and Ambulance	Fort Worth-Arlington PMSA, TX	S	12.49 MW	11.30 AW	25980 AAW	TXBLS	10//99-12//99
Except Police, Fire, and Ambulance	Galveston-Texas City PMSA, TX	S	12.98 MW	11.07 AW	27000 AAW	TXBLS	10//99-12//99
Except Police, Fire, and Ambulance	Houston PMSA, TX	S	12.78 MW	11.93 AW	26580 AAW	TXBLS	10//99-12//99
Except Police, Fire, and Ambulance	Killeen-Temple MSA, TX	S	11.88 MW	10.72 AW	24720 AAW	TXBLS	10//99-12//99
Except Police, Fire, and Ambulance	Laredo MSA, TX	S	9.98 MW	8.47 AW	20760 AAW	TXBLS	10//99-12//99
Except Police, Fire, and Ambulance	Longview-Marshall MSA, TX	S	10.48 MW	9.95 AW	21810 AAW	TXBLS	10//99-12//99
Except Police, Fire, and Ambulance	Lubbock MSA, TX	S	12.53 MW	11.01 AW	26070 AAW	TXBLS	10//99-12//99
Except Police, Fire, and Ambulance	McAllen-Edinburg-Mission MSA, TX	S	9.23 MW	7.96 AW	19210 AAW	TXBLS	10//99-12//99
Except Police, Fire, and Ambulance	Odessa-Midland MSA, TX	S	16.57 MW	15.49 AW	34460 AAW	TXBLS	10//99-12//99
Except Police, Fire, and Ambulance	San Angelo MSA, TX	S	12.52 MW	13.04 AW	26040 AAW	TXBLS	10//99-12//99
Except Police, Fire, and Ambulance	San Antonio MSA, TX	S	12.08 MW	10.78 AW	25130 AAW	TXBLS	10//99-12//99

AAW Average annual wage	**AOH** Average offered, high	**ASH** Average starting, high	**H** Hourly	**M** Monthly	**S** Special: hourly and annual
AE Average entry wage	**AOL** Average offered, low	**ASL** Average starting, low	**HI** Highest wage paid	**MTC** Median total compensation	**TQ** Third quartile wage
AEX Average experienced wage	**APH** Average pay; high range	**AW** Average wage paid	**HR** High end range	**MW** Median wage paid	**W** Weekly
AO Average offered	**APL** Average pay, low range	**FQ** First quartile wage	**LR** Low end range	**SQ** Second quartile wage	**Y** Yearly

Occupation/Type/Industry	Location	Per	Low	Mid	High	Source	Date
Dispatcher							
Except Police, Fire, and Ambulance	Texarkana MSA, TX-Texarkana, AR	s	10.79 MW	10.11 AW	22450 AAW	TXBLS	10//99-12//99
Except Police, Fire, and Ambulance	Tyler MSA, TX	s	12.03 MW	11.41 AW	25020 AAW	TXBLS	10//99-12//99
Except Police, Fire, and Ambulance	Victoria MSA, TX	s	11.43 MW	11.07 AW	23780 AAW	TXBLS	10//99-12//99
Except Police, Fire, and Ambulance	Waco MSA, TX	s	10.46 MW	9.51 AW	21750 AAW	TXBLS	10//99-12//99
Except Police, Fire, and Ambulance	Wichita Falls MSA, TX	s	12.89 MW	12.58 AW	26810 AAW	TXBLS	10//99-12//99
Except Police, Fire, and Ambulance	Utah	s	13.67 MW	14.68 AW	30540 AAW	UTBLS	10//99-12//99
Except Police, Fire, and Ambulance	Salt Lake City-Ogden MSA, UT	s	14.89 MW	14.48 AW	30960 AAW	UTBLS	10//99-12//99
Except Police, Fire, and Ambulance	Vermont	s	12.46 MW	13.07 AW	27200 AAW	VTBLS	10//99-12//99
Except Police, Fire, and Ambulance	Burlington MSA, VT	s	13.34 MW	12.66 AW	27750 AAW	VTBLS	10//99-12//99
Except Police, Fire, and Ambulance	Virginia	s	11.21 MW	12.25 AW	25480 AAW	VABLS	10//99-12//99
Except Police, Fire, and Ambulance	Lynchburg MSA, VA	s	10.93 MW	10.55 AW	22730 AAW	VABLS	10//99-12//99
Except Police, Fire, and Ambulance	Norfolk-Virginia Beach-Newport News MSA, VA-NC	s	10.77 MW	10.01 AW	22390 AAW	VABLS	10//99-12//99
Except Police, Fire, and Ambulance	Richmond-Petersburg MSA, VA	s	13.57 MW	12.40 AW	28230 AAW	VABLS	10//99-12//99
Except Police, Fire, and Ambulance	Roanoke MSA, VA	s	12.95 MW	12.55 AW	26940 AAW	VABLS	10//99-12//99
Except Police, Fire, and Ambulance	Washington	s	14.76 MW	15.53 AW	32310 AAW	WABLS	10//99-12//99
Except Police, Fire, and Ambulance	Bellingham MSA, WA	s	13.90 MW	13.48 AW	28920 AAW	WABLS	10//99-12//99
Except Police, Fire, and Ambulance	Bremerton PMSA, WA	s	13.96 MW	13.04 AW	29050 AAW	WABLS	10//99-12//99
Except Police, Fire, and Ambulance	Olympia PMSA, WA	s	11.83 MW	10.68 AW	24610 AAW	WABLS	10//99-12//99
Except Police, Fire, and Ambulance	Richland-Kennewick-Pasco MSA, WA	s	17.43 MW	16.36 AW	36250 AAW	WABLS	10//99-12//99
Except Police, Fire, and Ambulance	Seattle-Bellevue-Everett PMSA, WA	s	16.55 MW	15.81 AW	34430 AAW	WABLS	10//99-12//99
Except Police, Fire, and Ambulance	Spokane MSA, WA	s	13.01 MW	12.22 AW	27060 AAW	WABLS	10//99-12//99
Except Police, Fire, and Ambulance	Tacoma PMSA, WA	s	16.87 MW	17.47 AW	35090 AAW	WABLS	10//99-12//99
Except Police, Fire, and Ambulance	Yakima MSA, WA	s	13.77 MW	13.96 AW	28640 AAW	WABLS	10//99-12//99
Except Police, Fire, and Ambulance	West Virginia	s	12.28 MW	13.29 AW	27650 AAW	WVBLS	10//99-12//99
Except Police, Fire, and Ambulance	Charleston MSA, WV	s	14.56 MW	14.03 AW	30280 AAW	WVBLS	10//99-12//99
Except Police, Fire, and Ambulance	Huntington-Ashland MSA, WV-KY-OH	s	14.42 MW	15.20 AW	29990 AAW	WVBLS	10//99-12//99
Except Police, Fire, and Ambulance	Parkersburg-Marietta MSA, WV-OH	s	11.39 MW	10.93 AW	23690 AAW	WVBLS	10//99-12//99
Except Police, Fire, and Ambulance	Wheeling MSA, WV-OH	s	13.62 MW	13.79 AW	28340 AAW	WVBLS	10//99-12//99
Except Police, Fire, and Ambulance	Wisconsin	s	13.79 MW	14.74 AW	30660 AAW	WIBLS	10//99-12//99
Except Police, Fire, and Ambulance	Appleton-Oshkosh-Neenah MSA, WI	s	13.73 MW	12.62 AW	28550 AAW	WIBLS	10//99-12//99
Except Police, Fire, and Ambulance	Eau Claire MSA, WI	s	13.74 MW	12.38 AW	28590 AAW	WIBLS	10//99-12//99
Except Police, Fire, and Ambulance	Green Bay MSA, WI	s	15.35 MW	14.59 AW	31930 AAW	WIBLS	10//99-12//99
Except Police, Fire, and Ambulance	Kenosha PMSA, WI	s	13.40 MW	14.26 AW	27870 AAW	WIBLS	10//99-12//99
Except Police, Fire, and Ambulance	La Crosse MSA, WI-MN	s	12.98 MW	12.43 AW	26990 AAW	WIBLS	10//99-12//99
Except Police, Fire, and Ambulance	Madison MSA, WI	s	15.00 MW	13.14 AW	31190 AAW	WIBLS	10//99-12//99
Except Police, Fire, and Ambulance	Milwaukee-Waukesha PMSA, WI	s	15.39 MW	15.14 AW	32020 AAW	WIBLS	10//99-12//99
Except Police, Fire, and Ambulance	Sheboygan MSA, WI	s	14.05 MW	11.66 AW	29210 AAW	WIBLS	10//99-12//99
Except Police, Fire, and Ambulance	Wausau MSA, WI	s	14.60 MW	14.57 AW	30380 AAW	WIBLS	10//99-12//99
Except Police, Fire, and Ambulance	Wyoming	s	10.33 MW	11.31 AW	23520 AAW	WYBLS	10//99-12//99
Except Police, Fire, and Ambulance	Cheyenne MSA, WY	s	10.36 MW	10.80 AW	21550 AAW	WYBLS	10//99-12//99
Except Police, Fire, and Ambulance	Puerto Rico	s	6.94 MW	8.75 AW	18200 AAW	PRBLS	10//99-12//99
Except Police, Fire, and Ambulance	Caguas PMSA, PR	s	7.00 MW	6.33 AW	14550 AAW	PRBLS	10//99-12//99
Except Police, Fire, and Ambulance	Mayaguez MSA, PR	s	7.96 MW	6.58 AW	16570 AAW	PRBLS	10//99-12//99
Except Police, Fire, and Ambulance	San Juan-Bayamon PMSA, PR	s	9.10 MW	7.49 AW	18930 AAW	PRBLS	10//99-12//99
Except Police, Fire, and Ambulance	Virgin Islands	s	10.63 MW	11.00 AW	22880 AAW	VIBLS	10//99-12//99
Except Police, Fire, and Ambulance	Guam	s	11.35 MW	11.75 AW	24440 AAW	GUBLS	10//99-12//99
Door-To-Door Sales Worker, News and Street Vendor, and Related Worker							
	Alabama	s	13.42 MW	15.80 AW	32850 AAW	ALBLS	10//99-12//99
	Arizona	s	6.72 MW	8.04 AW	16710 AAW	AZBLS	10//99-12//99
	Arkansas	s	6.29 MW	7.53 AW	15670 AAW	ARBLS	10//99-12//99
	California	s	8.12 MW	11.25 AW	23390 AAW	CABLS	10//99-12//99
	Connecticut	s	15.47 MW	17.10 AW	35560 AAW	CTBLS	10//99-12//99
	Florida	s	11.55 MW	14.06 AW	29250 AAW	FLBLS	10//99-12//99
	Georgia	s	12.29 MW	14.27 AW	29680 AAW	GABLS	10//99-12//99
	Hawaii	s	6.68 MW	10.87 AW	22620 AAW	HIBLS	10//99-12//99
	Idaho	s	6.71 MW	7.68 AW	15980 AAW	IDBLS	10//99-12//99
	Illinois	s	10.6 MW	11.84 AW	24630 AAW	ILBLS	10//99-12//99
	Indiana	s	13.93 MW	15.18 AW	31570 AAW	INBLS	10//99-12//99

AAW	Average annual wage	AOH	Average offered, high	ASH	Average starting, high	H	Hourly	M	Monthly	S	Special: hourly and annual
AE	Average entry wage	AOL	Average offered, low	ASL	Average starting, low	HI	Highest wage paid	MTC	Median total compensation	TQ	Third quartile wage
AEX	Average experienced wage	APH	Average pay, high range	AW	Average wage paid	HR	High end range	MW	Median wage paid	W	Weekly
AO	Average offered	APL	Average pay, low range	FQ	First quartile wage	LR	Low end range	SQ	Second quartile wage	Y	Yearly

Occupation/Type/Industry	Location	Per	Low	Mid	High	Source	Date
Door-To-Door Sales Worker, News and Street Vendor, and Related Worker	Kentucky	S	16.42 MW	17.95 AW	37330 AAW	KYBLS	10//99-12/99
	Louisiana	S	14.88 MW	17.05 AW	35460 AAW	LABLS	10//99-12/99
	Maine	S	10.52 MW	12.00 AW	24950 AAW	MEBLS	10//99-12/99
	Maryland	S	10.75 MW	13.63 AW	28360 AAW	MDBLS	10//99-12/99
	Michigan	S	12.66 MW	13.31 AW	27690 AAW	MIBLS	10//99-12/99
	Minnesota	S	10.23 MW	12.90 AW	26830 AAW	MNBLS	10//99-12/99
	Mississippi	S	19.58 MW	20.79 AW	43240 AAW	MSBLS	10//99-12/99
	Missouri	S	19.73 MW	24.33 AW	50600 AAW	MOBLS	10//99-12/99
	Nebraska	S	8.08 MW	8.75 AW	18210 AAW	NEBLS	10//99-12/99
	Nevada	S	15.72 MW	17.42 AW	36240 AAW	NVBLS	10//99-12/99
	New Hampshire	S	15.95 MW	19.28 AW	40110 AAW	NHBLS	10//99-12/99
	New Jersey	S	9.51 MW	10.14 AW	21090 AAW	NJBLS	10//99-12/99
	New Mexico	S	10.32 MW	13.17 AW	27390 AAW	NMBLS	10//99-12/99
	New York	S	8.29 MW	10.98 AW	22830 AAW	NYBLS	10//99-12/99
	North Carolina	S	16.13 MW	18.94 AW	39380 AAW	NCBLS	10//99-12/99
	North Dakota	S	14.67 MW	14.69 AW	30560 AAW	NDBLS	10//99-12/99
	Ohio	S	15.58 MW	15.27 AW	31750 AAW	OHBLS	10//99-12/99
	Oklahoma	S	11.68 MW	16.25 AW	33790 AAW	OKBLS	10//99-12/99
	Pennsylvania	S	12.38 MW	12.99 AW	27010 AAW	PABLS	10//99-12/99
	Tennessee	S	21.1 MW	22.80 AW	47430 AAW	TNBLS	10//99-12/99
	Texas	S	12.83 MW	15.97 AW	33220 AAW	TXBLS	10//99-12/99
	Utah	S	15.2 MW	16.46 AW	34240 AAW	UTBLS	10//99-12/99
	Virginia	S	10.13 MW	10.85 AW	22570 AAW	VABLS	10//99-12/99
	Washington	S	16.89 MW	16.39 AW	34090 AAW	WABLS	10//99-12/99
	West Virginia	S	14.48 MW	13.51 AW	28090 AAW	WVBLS	10//99-12/99
	Wisconsin	S	7.7 MW	8.99 AW	18690 AAW	WIBLS	10//99-12/99
	Puerto Rico	S	7.03 MW	9.95 AW	20700 AAW	PRBLS	10//99-12/99
Draft Beer Manager Beer Wholesaling	United States	Y	43250 MW	43368 AW		BEVW	1999
Drafter	United States	H		18.84 AW		NCS98	1998
Dredge Operator	Alabama	S	9.26 MW	10.38 AW	21590 AAW	ALBLS	10//99-12/99
	California	S	15.78 MW	17.65 AW	36700 AAW	CABLS	10//99-12/99
	Connecticut	S	15.23 MW	15.19 AW	31600 AAW	CTBLS	10//99-12/99
	Delaware	S	12.66 MW	12.28 AW	25530 AAW	DEBLS	10//99-12/99
	Florida	S	13.38 MW	13.33 AW	27720 AAW	FLBLS	10//99-12/99
	Illinois	S	13.72 MW	15.25 AW	31730 AAW	ILBLS	10//99-12/99
	Indiana	S	11.28 MW	11.72 AW	24380 AAW	INBLS	10//99-12/99
	Kansas	S	9.24 MW	9.46 AW	19680 AAW	KSBLS	10//99-12/99
	Louisiana	S	10.03 MW	11.17 AW	23230 AAW	LABLS	10//99-12/99
	Minnesota	S	13.07 MW	15.01 AW	31220 AAW	MNBLS	10//99-12/99
	Mississippi	S	9.45 MW	9.81 AW	20410 AAW	MSBLS	10//99-12/99
	Missouri	S	16.96 MW	15.47 AW	32170 AAW	MOBLS	10//99-12/99
	Nebraska	S	8.44 MW	9.89 AW	20570 AAW	NEBLS	10//99-12/99
	New Jersey	S	14.97 MW	17.48 AW	36360 AAW	NJBLS	10//99-12/99
	North Carolina	S	12.13 MW	12.08 AW	25120 AAW	NCBLS	10//99-12/99
	Ohio	S	13.69 MW	13.88 AW	28880 AAW	OHBLS	10//99-12/99
	Oklahoma	S	10.84 MW	11.45 AW	23830 AAW	OKBLS	10//99-12/99
	Pennsylvania	S	16.83 MW	17.80 AW	37010 AAW	PABLS	10//99-12/99
	South Carolina	S	11.78 MW	14.92 AW	31030 AAW	SCBLS	10//99-12/99
	Tennessee	S	10.41 MW	10.43 AW	21700 AAW	TNBLS	10//99-12/99
	Texas	S	11.21 MW	13.00 AW	27040 AAW	TXBLS	10//99-12/99
	Virginia	S	13.37 MW	14.71 AW	30600 AAW	VABLS	10//99-12/99
	Puerto Rico	S	7.42 MW	7.44 AW	15470 AAW	PRBLS	10//99-12/99
Drilling and Boring Machine Tool Setter, Operator, and Tender							
Metals and Plastics	Alabama	S	12 MW	11.73 AW	24390 AAW	ALBLS	10//99-12/99
Metals and Plastics	Birmingham MSA, AL	S	12.80 MW	12.50 AW	26610 AAW	ALBLS	10//99-12/99
Metals and Plastics	Dothan MSA, AL	S	8.10 MW	7.99 AW	16850 AAW	ALBLS	10//99-12/99
Metals and Plastics	Gadsden MSA, AL	S	8.46 MW	8.41 AW	17600 AAW	ALBLS	10//99-12/99
Metals and Plastics	Arizona	S	13.11 MW	14.49 AW	30130 AAW	AZBLS	10//99-12/99
Metals and Plastics	Phoenix-Mesa MSA, AZ	S	15.13 MW	13.68 AW	31460 AAW	AZBLS	10//99-12/99
Metals and Plastics	Tucson MSA, AZ	S	12.89 MW	12.23 AW	26810 AAW	AZBLS	10//99-12/99
Metals and Plastics	Arkansas	S	9.53 MW	9.79 AW	20360 AAW	ARBLS	10//99-12/99
Metals and Plastics	Little Rock-North Little Rock MSA, AR	S	6.75 MW	6.57 AW	14050 AAW	ARBLS	10//99-12/99
Metals and Plastics	California	S	9.8 MW	10.81 AW	22490 AAW	CABLS	10//99-12/99

AAW Average annual wage	**AOH** Average offered, high	**ASH** Average starting, high	**H** Hourly	**M** Monthly	**S** Special: hourly and annual
AE Average entry wage	**AOL** Average offered, low	**ASL** Average starting, low	**HI** Highest wage paid	**MTC** Median total compensation	**TQ** Third quartile wage
AEX Average experienced wage	**APH** Average pay, high range	**AW** Average wage paid	**HR** High end range	**MW** Median wage paid	**W** Weekly
AO Average offered	**APL** Average pay, low range	**FQ** First quartile wage	**LR** Low end range	**SQ** Second quartile wage	**Y** Yearly

Occupation/Type/Industry	Location	Per	Low	Mid	High	Source	Date
Drilling and Boring Machine Tool Setter, Operator, and Tender							
Metals and Plastics	Bakersfield MSA, CA	S	9.78 MW	9.77 AW	20340 AAW	CABLS	10//99-12//99
Metals and Plastics	Fresno MSA, CA	S	12.59 MW	12.87 AW	26180 AAW	CABLS	10//99-12//99
Metals and Plastics	Los Angeles-Long Beach PMSA, CA	S	10.17 MW	9.18 AW	21160 AAW	CABLS	10//99-12//99
Metals and Plastics	Oakland PMSA, CA	S	14.00 MW	14.25 AW	29130 AAW	CABLS	10//99-12//99
Metals and Plastics	Orange County PMSA, CA	S	10.17 MW	9.61 AW	21160 AAW	CABLS	10//99-12//99
Metals and Plastics	Riverside-San Bernardino PMSA, CA	S	12.19 MW	11.58 AW	25360 AAW	CABLS	10//99-12//99
Metals and Plastics	Sacramento PMSA, CA	S	8.83 MW	8.74 AW	18360 AAW	CABLS	10//99-12//99
Metals and Plastics	San Diego MSA, CA	S	9.31 MW	9.11 AW	19370 AAW	CABLS	10//99-12//99
Metals and Plastics	San Francisco PMSA, CA	S	10.55 MW	10.15 AW	21940 AAW	CABLS	10//99-12//99
Metals and Plastics	San Jose PMSA, CA	S	14.18 MW	12.62 AW	29500 AAW	CABLS	10//99-12//99
Metals and Plastics	Ventura PMSA, CA	S	9.94 MW	10.35 AW	20680 AAW	CABLS	10//99-12//99
Metals and Plastics	Visalia-Tulare-Porterville MSA, CA	S	7.09 MW	7.18 AW	14740 AAW	CABLS	10//99-12//99
Metals and Plastics	Colorado	S	12.24 MW	12.85 AW	26730 AAW	COBLS	10//99-12//99
Metals and Plastics	Denver PMSA, CO	S	13.39 MW	12.56 AW	27850 AAW	COBLS	10//99-12//99
Metals and Plastics	Connecticut	S	10.72 MW	12.08 AW	25130 AAW	CTBLS	10//99-12//99
Metals and Plastics	Bridgeport PMSA, CT	S	15.60 MW	15.32 AW	32440 AAW	CTBLS	10//99-12//99
Metals and Plastics	Danbury PMSA, CT	S	13.60 MW	13.26 AW	28280 AAW	CTBLS	10//99-12//99
Metals and Plastics	Hartford MSA, CT	S	12.72 MW	10.57 AW	26450 AAW	CTBLS	10//99-12//99
Metals and Plastics	New Haven-Meriden PMSA, CT	S	12.85 MW	13.18 AW	26740 AAW	CTBLS	10//99-12//99
Metals and Plastics	Stamford-Norwalk PMSA, CT	S	10.94 MW	9.81 AW	22760 AAW	CTBLS	10//99-12//99
Metals and Plastics	Waterbury PMSA, CT	S	8.10 MW	7.87 AW	16850 AAW	CTBLS	10//99-12//99
Metals and Plastics	Washington PMSA, DC-MD-VA-WV	S	12.02 MW	12.25 AW	25010 AAW	DCBLS	10//99-12//99
Metals and Plastics	Florida	S	9.74 MW	10.18 AW	21170 AAW	FLBLS	10//99-12//99
Metals and Plastics	Fort Lauderdale PMSA, FL	S	10.52 MW	11.27 AW	21880 AAW	FLBLS	10//99-12//99
Metals and Plastics	Jacksonville MSA, FL	S	11.60 MW	11.26 AW	24130 AAW	FLBLS	10//99-12//99
Metals and Plastics	Miami PMSA, FL	S	8.16 MW	7.79 AW	16960 AAW	FLBLS	10//99-12//99
Metals and Plastics	Orlando MSA, FL	S	9.69 MW	9.71 AW	20160 AAW	FLBLS	10//99-12//99
Metals and Plastics	Tampa-St. Petersburg-Clearwater MSA, FL	S	12.15 MW	12.26 AW	25270 AAW	FLBLS	10//99-12//99
Metals and Plastics	Georgia	S	12.07 MW	12.35 AW	25700 AAW	GABLS	10//99-12//99
Metals and Plastics	Athens MSA, GA	S	15.39 MW	15.59 AW	32020 AAW	GABLS	10//99-12//99
Metals and Plastics	Atlanta MSA, GA	S	12.26 MW	11.42 AW	25490 AAW	GABLS	10//99-12//99
Metals and Plastics	Augusta-Aiken MSA, GA-SC	S	11.40 MW	11.21 AW	23710 AAW	GABLS	10//99-12//99
Metals and Plastics	Macon MSA, GA	S	15.08 MW	15.20 AW	31370 AAW	GABLS	10//99-12//99
Metals and Plastics	Illinois	S	11.95 MW	12.45 AW	25890 AAW	ILBLS	10//99-12//99
Metals and Plastics	Chicago PMSA, IL	S	10.77 MW	10.47 AW	22410 AAW	ILBLS	10//99-12//99
Metals and Plastics	Peoria-Pekin MSA, IL	S	22.00 MW	22.60 AW	45770 AAW	ILBLS	10//99-12//99
Metals and Plastics	Rockford MSA, IL	S	16.18 MW	15.97 AW	33650 AAW	ILBLS	10//99-12//99
Metals and Plastics	Indiana	S	11.21 MW	11.91 AW	24780 AAW	INBLS	10//99-12//99
Metals and Plastics	Elkhart-Goshen MSA, IN	S	9.53 MW	9.37 AW	19830 AAW	INBLS	10//99-12//99
Metals and Plastics	Fort Wayne MSA, IN	S	10.39 MW	9.84 AW	21600 AAW	INBLS	10//99-12//99
Metals and Plastics	Gary PMSA, IN	S	12.82 MW	13.59 AW	26660 AAW	INBLS	10//99-12//99
Metals and Plastics	Indianapolis MSA, IN	S	14.43 MW	14.23 AW	30020 AAW	INBLS	10//99-12//99
Metals and Plastics	South Bend MSA, IN	S	11.23 MW	10.05 AW	23350 AAW	INBLS	10//99-12//99
Metals and Plastics	Iowa	S	14.46 MW	14.98 AW	31170 AAW	IABLS	10//99-12//99
Metals and Plastics	Davenport-Moline-Rock Island MSA, IA-IL	S	14.89 MW	15.09 AW	30960 AAW	IABLS	10//99-12//99
Metals and Plastics	Waterloo-Cedar Falls MSA, IA	S	19.04 MW	19.16 AW	39600 AAW	IABLS	10//99-12//99
Metals and Plastics	Kansas	S	8.88 MW	8.60 AW	17880 AAW	KSBLS	10//99-12//99
Metals and Plastics	Kentucky	S	12.07 MW	11.89 AW	24740 AAW	KYBLS	10//99-12//99
Metals and Plastics	Lexington MSA, KY	S	12.13 MW	12.17 AW	25240 AAW	KYBLS	10//99-12//99
Metals and Plastics	Louisville MSA, KY-IN	S	11.93 MW	12.10 AW	24820 AAW	KYBLS	10//99-12//99
Metals and Plastics	Louisiana	S	10.92 MW	11.16 AW	23220 AAW	LABLS	10//99-12//99
Metals and Plastics	Baton Rouge MSA, LA	S	8.04 MW	8.76 AW	16730 AAW	LABLS	10//99-12//99
Metals and Plastics	Maine	S	10.44 MW	10.87 AW	22610 AAW	MEBLS	10//99-12//99
Metals and Plastics	Maryland	S	14.68 MW	14.61 AW	30380 AAW	MDBLS	10//99-12//99
Metals and Plastics	Baltimore PMSA, MD	S	16.36 MW	17.73 AW	34030 AAW	MDBLS	10//99-12//99
Metals and Plastics	Massachusetts	S	12.37 MW	12.36 AW	25710 AAW	MABLS	10//99-12//99
Metals and Plastics	Boston PMSA, MA-NH	S	12.75 MW	13.46 AW	26520 AAW	MABLS	10//99-12//99
Metals and Plastics	Lawrence PMSA, MA-NH	S	10.99 MW	11.33 AW	22860 AAW	MABLS	10//99-12//99
Metals and Plastics	Lowell PMSA, MA-NH	S	13.52 MW	13.35 AW	28120 AAW	MABLS	10//99-12//99
Metals and Plastics	Springfield MSA, MA	S	11.45 MW	10.25 AW	23820 AAW	MABLS	10//99-12//99
Metals and Plastics	Worcester PMSA, MA-CT	S	12.14 MW	11.91 AW	25240 AAW	MABLS	10//99-12//99
Metals and Plastics	Michigan	S	11.94 MW	13.83 AW	28770 AAW	MIBLS	10//99-12//99
Metals and Plastics	Ann Arbor PMSA, MI	S	17.49 MW	15.95 AW	36380 AAW	MIBLS	10//99-12//99

AAW	Average annual wage	AOH	Average offered, high	ASH	Average starting, high	H	Hourly	M	Monthly	S	Special: hourly and annual
AE	Average entry wage	AOL	Average offered, low	ASL	Average starting, low	HI	Highest wage paid	MTC	Median total compensation	TQ	Third quartile wage
AEX	Average experienced wage	APH	Average pay, high range	AW	Average wage paid	HR	High end range	MW	Median wage paid	W	Weekly
AO	Average offered	APL	Average pay, low range	FQ	First quartile wage	LR	Low end range	SQ	Second quartile wage	Y	Yearly

Occupation/Type/Industry	Location	Per	Low	Mid	High	Source	Date
Drilling and Boring Machine Tool Setter, Operator, and Tender							
Metals and Plastics	Benton Harbor MSA, MI	S	13.17 MW	14.22 AW	27400 AAW	MIBLS	10//99-12//99
Metals and Plastics	Detroit PMSA, MI	S	15.16 MW	12.64 AW	31530 AAW	MIBLS	10//99-12//99
Metals and Plastics	Flint PMSA, MI	S	15.63 MW	14.77 AW	32510 AAW	MIBLS	10//99-12//99
Metals and Plastics	Grand Rapids-Muskegon-Holland MSA, MI	S	15.75 MW	14.57 AW	32760 AAW	MIBLS	10//99-12//99
Metals and Plastics	Jackson MSA, MI	S	16.65 MW	16.87 AW	34640 AAW	MIBLS	10//99-12//99
Metals and Plastics	Kalamazoo-Battle Creek MSA, MI	S	9.67 MW	8.45 AW	20110 AAW	MIBLS	10//99-12//99
Metals and Plastics	Lansing-East Lansing MSA, MI	S	14.27 MW	14.57 AW	29690 AAW	MIBLS	10//99-12//99
Metals and Plastics	Saginaw-Bay City-Midland MSA, MI	S	12.43 MW	10.12 AW	25850 AAW	MIBLS	10//99-12//99
Metals and Plastics	Minnesota	S	12.98 MW	13.42 AW	27910 AAW	MNBLS	10//99-12//99
Metals and Plastics	Minneapolis-St. Paul MSA, MN-WI	S	14.92 MW	14.54 AW	31030 AAW	MNBLS	10//99-12//99
Metals and Plastics	Mississippi	S	11.71 MW	11.75 AW	24430 AAW	MSBLS	10//99-12//99
Metals and Plastics	Missouri	S	12.08 MW	11.86 AW	24660 AAW	MOBLS	10//99-12//99
Metals and Plastics	Joplin MSA, MO	S	12.79 MW	12.66 AW	26610 AAW	MOBLS	10//99-12//99
Metals and Plastics	Kansas City MSA, MO-KS	S	12.94 MW	13.81 AW	26910 AAW	MOBLS	10//99-12//99
Metals and Plastics	St. Louis MSA, MO-IL	S	11.39 MW	11.36 AW	23690 AAW	MOBLS	10//99-12//99
Metals and Plastics	Nebraska	S	12.69 MW	13.63 AW	28340 AAW	NEBLS	10//99-12//99
Metals and Plastics	Lincoln MSA, NE	S	9.63 MW	9.68 AW	20020 AAW	NEBLS	10//99-12//99
Metals and Plastics	Omaha MSA, NE-IA	S	15.06 MW	16.54 AW	31320 AAW	NEBLS	10//99-12//99
Metals and Plastics	Nevada	S	10.29 MW	10.67 AW	22200 AAW	NVBLS	10//99-12//99
Metals and Plastics	New Hampshire	S	13.27 MW	13.55 AW	28190 AAW	NHBLS	10//99-12//99
Metals and Plastics	Nashua PMSA, NH	S	14.12 MW	14.22 AW	29380 AAW	NHBLS	10//99-12//99
Metals and Plastics	New Jersey	S	10.49 MW	12.09 AW	25150 AAW	NJBLS	10//99-12//99
Metals and Plastics	Bergen-Passaic PMSA, NJ	S	12.16 MW	11.23 AW	25290 AAW	NJBLS	10//99-12//99
Metals and Plastics	Middlesex-Somerset-Hunterdon PMSA, NJ	S	12.25 MW	10.69 AW	25470 AAW	NJBLS	10//99-12//99
Metals and Plastics	Albuquerque MSA, NM	S	11.42 MW	10.92 AW	23750 AAW	NMBLS	10//99-12//99
Metals and Plastics	New York	S	11.14 MW	11.49 AW	23890 AAW	NYBLS	10//99-12//99
Metals and Plastics	Albany-Schenectady-Troy MSA, NY	S	9.90 MW	9.56 AW	20590 AAW	NYBLS	10//99-12//99
Metals and Plastics	Binghamton MSA, NY	S	11.43 MW	11.45 AW	23770 AAW	NYBLS	10//99-12//99
Metals and Plastics	Buffalo-Niagara Falls MSA, NY	S	12.81 MW	12.37 AW	26640 AAW	NYBLS	10//99-12//99
Metals and Plastics	Nassau-Suffolk PMSA, NY	S	11.94 MW	11.30 AW	24840 AAW	NYBLS	10//99-12//99
Metals and Plastics	New York PMSA, NY	S	12.12 MW	10.29 AW	25220 AAW	NYBLS	10//99-12//99
Metals and Plastics	Rochester MSA, NY	S	10.05 MW	8.51 AW	20900 AAW	NYBLS	10//99-12//99
Metals and Plastics	Syracuse MSA, NY	S	11.35 MW	11.64 AW	23600 AAW	NYBLS	10//99-12//99
Metals and Plastics	North Carolina	S	13.44 MW	13.39 AW	27840 AAW	NCBLS	10//99-12//99
Metals and Plastics	Charlotte-Gastonia-Rock Hill MSA, NC-SC	S	13.89 MW	13.23 AW	28890 AAW	NCBLS	10//99-12//99
Metals and Plastics	Greensboro--Winston-Salem--High Point MSA, NC	S	10.49 MW	10.05 AW	21820 AAW	NCBLS	10//99-12//99
Metals and Plastics	Hickory-Morganton-Lenoir MSA, NC	S	11.43 MW	11.12 AW	23780 AAW	NCBLS	10//99-12//99
Metals and Plastics	Ohio	S	14.07 MW	14.01 AW	29140 AAW	OHBLS	10//99-12//99
Metals and Plastics	Akron PMSA, OH	S	14.44 MW	14.50 AW	30040 AAW	OHBLS	10//99-12//99
Metals and Plastics	Canton-Massillon MSA, OH	S	18.15 MW	18.32 AW	37760 AAW	OHBLS	10//99-12//99
Metals and Plastics	Cincinnati PMSA, OH-KY-IN	S	14.22 MW	12.86 AW	29580 AAW	OHBLS	10//99-12//99
Metals and Plastics	Dayton-Springfield MSA, OH	S	16.82 MW	17.04 AW	34980 AAW	OHBLS	10//99-12//99
Metals and Plastics	Hamilton-Middletown PMSA, OH	S	13.01 MW	13.65 AW	27060 AAW	OHBLS	10//99-12//99
Metals and Plastics	Mansfield MSA, OH	S	11.76 MW	11.91 AW	24460 AAW	OHBLS	10//99-12//99
Metals and Plastics	Youngstown-Warren MSA, OH	S	13.04 MW	13.10 AW	27110 AAW	OHBLS	10//99-12//99
Metals and Plastics	Oklahoma	S	10.34 MW	11.00 AW	22870 AAW	OKBLS	10//99-12//99
Metals and Plastics	Tulsa MSA, OK	S	10.43 MW	9.91 AW	21690 AAW	OKBLS	10//99-12//99
Metals and Plastics	Oregon	S	12.18 MW	13.83 AW	28760 AAW	ORBLS	10//99-12//99
Metals and Plastics	Portland-Vancouver PMSA, OR-WA	S	15.55 MW	13.16 AW	32350 AAW	ORBLS	10//99-12//99
Metals and Plastics	Pennsylvania	S	12.95 MW	14.04 AW	29200 AAW	PABLS	10//99-12//99
Metals and Plastics	Allentown-Bethlehem-Easton MSA, PA	S	9.81 MW	9.81 AW	20410 AAW	PABLS	10//99-12//99
Metals and Plastics	Erie MSA, PA	S	12.30 MW	12.15 AW	25590 AAW	PABLS	10//99-12//99
Metals and Plastics	Harrisburg-Lebanon-Carlisle MSA, PA	S	16.06 MW	15.13 AW	33410 AAW	PABLS	10//99-12//99
Metals and Plastics	Philadelphia PMSA, PA-NJ	S	17.82 MW	15.71 AW	37060 AAW	PABLS	10//99-12//99
Metals and Plastics	Pittsburgh MSA, PA	S	13.30 MW	13.12 AW	27660 AAW	PABLS	10//99-12//99
Metals and Plastics	Reading MSA, PA	S	14.74 MW	14.86 AW	30660 AAW	PABLS	10//99-12//99

AAW	Average annual wage	AOH	Average offered, high	ASH	Average starting, high
AE	Average entry wage	AOL	Average offered, low	ASL	Average starting, low
AEX	Average experienced wage	APH	Average pay, high range	AW	Average wage paid
AO	Average offered	APL	Average pay, low range	FQ	First quartile wage

H	Hourly	M	Monthly
HI	Highest wage paid	MTC	Median total compensation
HR	High end range	MW	Median wage paid
LR	Low end range	SQ	Second quartile wage

S	Special: hourly and annual
TQ	Third quartile wage
W	Weekly
Y	Yearly

Occupation/Type/Industry	Location	Per	Low	Mid	High	Source	Date
Drilling and Boring Machine Tool Setter, Operator, and Tender							
Metals and Plastics	Scranton--Wilkes-Barre-- Hazleton MSA, PA	S	12.27 MW	12.81 AW	25520 AAW	PABLS	10//99-12//99
Metals and Plastics	York MSA, PA	S	15.23 MW	15.27 AW	31680 AAW	PABLS	10//99-12//99
Metals and Plastics	Rhode Island	S	10.37 MW	12.25 AW	25480 AAW	RIBLS	10//99-12//99
Metals and Plastics	Providence-Fall River- Warwick MSA, RI-MA	S	12.36 MW	10.64 AW	25700 AAW	RIBLS	10//99-12//99
Metals and Plastics	South Carolina	S	12.03 MW	12.13 AW	25220 AAW	SCBLS	10//99-12//99
Metals and Plastics	Charleston-North Charleston MSA, SC	S	8.36 MW	8.27 AW	17400 AAW	SCBLS	10//99-12//99
Metals and Plastics	Greenville-Spartanburg- Anderson MSA, SC	S	12.31 MW	12.22 AW	25610 AAW	SCBLS	10//99-12//99
Metals and Plastics	South Dakota	S	8.56 MW	8.88 AW	18480 AAW	SDBLS	10//99-12//99
Metals and Plastics	Sioux Falls MSA, SD	S	8.58 MW	8.06 AW	17840 AAW	SDBLS	10//99-12//99
Metals and Plastics	Tennessee	S	11.52 MW	11.30 AW	23510 AAW	TNBLS	10//99-12//99
Metals and Plastics	Chattanooga MSA, TN-GA	S	10.70 MW	10.31 AW	22250 AAW	TNBLS	10//99-12//99
Metals and Plastics	Johnson City-Kingsport-Bristol MSA, TN-VA	S	12.18 MW	12.43 AW	25330 AAW	TNBLS	10//99-12//99
Metals and Plastics	Knoxville MSA, TN	S	10.79 MW	10.27 AW	22440 AAW	TNBLS	10//99-12//99
Metals and Plastics	Memphis MSA, TN-AR-MS	S	10.31 MW	11.48 AW	21450 AAW	MSBLS	10//99-12//99
Metals and Plastics	Nashville MSA, TN	S	12.71 MW	12.12 AW	26440 AAW	TNBLS	10//99-12//99
Metals and Plastics	Texas	S	10.37 MW	11.68 AW	24300 AAW	TXBLS	10//99-12//99
Metals and Plastics	Austin-San Marcos MSA, TX	S	7.73 MW	7.70 AW	16070 AAW	TXBLS	10//99-12//99
Metals and Plastics	Brownsville-Harlingen-San Benito MSA, TX	S	9.10 MW	9.26 AW	18920 AAW	TXBLS	10//99-12//99
Metals and Plastics	Dallas PMSA, TX	S	10.91 MW	10.48 AW	22690 AAW	TXBLS	10//99-12//99
Metals and Plastics	El Paso MSA, TX	S	10.20 MW	10.57 AW	21210 AAW	TXBLS	10//99-12//99
Metals and Plastics	Fort Worth-Arlington PMSA, TX	S	16.62 MW	16.94 AW	34580 AAW	TXBLS	10//99-12//99
Metals and Plastics	Houston PMSA, TX	S	10.54 MW	9.68 AW	21930 AAW	TXBLS	10//99-12//99
Metals and Plastics	Odessa-Midland MSA, TX	S	11.15 MW	11.70 AW	23180 AAW	TXBLS	10//99-12//99
Metals and Plastics	San Antonio MSA, TX	S	11.13 MW	11.49 AW	23150 AAW	TXBLS	10//99-12//99
Metals and Plastics	Vermont	S	14.4 MW	13.79 AW	28670 AAW	VTBLS	10//99-12//99
Metals and Plastics	Burlington MSA, VT	S	13.50 MW	14.10 AW	28070 AAW	VTBLS	10//99-12//99
Metals and Plastics	Virginia	S	11.88 MW	11.71 AW	24360 AAW	VABLS	10//99-12//99
Metals and Plastics	Lynchburg MSA, VA	S	12.35 MW	12.17 AW	25690 AAW	VABLS	10//99-12//99
Metals and Plastics	Norfolk-Virginia Beach- Newport News MSA, VA-NC	S	12.19 MW	12.36 AW	25340 AAW	VABLS	10//99-12//99
Metals and Plastics	Richmond-Petersburg MSA, VA	S	10.28 MW	8.22 AW	21380 AAW	VABLS	10//99-12//99
Metals and Plastics	Washington	S	22.11 MW	19.03 AW	39570 AAW	WABLS	10//99-12//99
Metals and Plastics	Seattle-Bellevue-Everett PMSA, WA	S	20.67 MW	23.04 AW	42990 AAW	WABLS	10//99-12//99
Metals and Plastics	Spokane MSA, WA	S	10.94 MW	9.98 AW	22750 AAW	WABLS	10//99-12//99
Metals and Plastics	West Virginia	S	7.67 MW	8.07 AW	16790 AAW	WVBLS	10//99-12//99
Metals and Plastics	Huntington-Ashland MSA, WV-KY-OH	S	14.42 MW	13.48 AW	30000 AAW	WVBLS	10//99-12//99
Metals and Plastics	Parkersburg-Marietta MSA, WV-OH	S	7.05 MW	7.31 AW	14670 AAW	WVBLS	10//99-12//99
Metals and Plastics	Wisconsin	S	12.65 MW	13.36 AW	27790 AAW	WIBLS	10//99-12//99
Metals and Plastics	Appleton-Oshkosh-Neenah MSA, WI	S	14.08 MW	13.82 AW	29290 AAW	WIBLS	10//99-12//99
Metals and Plastics	Green Bay MSA, WI	S	11.14 MW	10.52 AW	23170 AAW	WIBLS	10//99-12//99
Metals and Plastics	Janesville-Beloit MSA, WI	S	8.78 MW	7.97 AW	18270 AAW	WIBLS	10//99-12//99
Metals and Plastics	Madison MSA, WI	S	12.38 MW	12.31 AW	25740 AAW	WIBLS	10//99-12//99
Metals and Plastics	Milwaukee-Waukesha PMSA, WI	S	14.75 MW	14.87 AW	30670 AAW	WIBLS	10//99-12//99
Metals and Plastics	Racine PMSA, WI	S	10.80 MW	10.11 AW	22460 AAW	WIBLS	10//99-12//99
Metals and Plastics	Wausau MSA, WI	S	13.53 MW	12.79 AW	28150 AAW	WIBLS	10//99-12//99
Metals and Plastics	Puerto Rico	S	6.55 MW	7.16 AW	14900 AAW	PRBLS	10//99-12//99
Metals and Plastics	San Juan-Bayamon PMSA, PR	S	8.17 MW	7.43 AW	17000 AAW	PRBLS	10//99-12//99
Drilling Engineer							
10-15 Years Experience, Petroleum	United States	Y	40000 APL	87700 AW	150000 APH	OILL	5/28/98-9/3/98
Drilling Supervisor							
10-15 Years Experience, Petroleum	United States	Y	30000 APL	40800 AW	50000 APH	OILL	5/28/98-9/3/98
Driver/Sales Worker	Alabama	S	8.09 MW	9.58 AW	19930 AAW	ALBLS	10//99-12//99
	Alaska	S	8.33 MW	10.24 AW	21300 AAW	AKBLS	10//99-12//99

AAW	Average annual wage	AOH	Average offered, high	ASH	Average starting, high	H	Hourly	M	Monthly	S	Special: hourly and annual
AE	Average entry wage	AOL	Average offered, low	ASL	Average starting, low	HI	Highest wage paid	MTC	Median total compensation	TQ	Third quartile wage
AEX	Average experienced wage	APH	Average pay, high range	AW	Average wage paid	HR	High end range	MW	Median wage paid	W	Weekly
AO	Average offered	APL	Average pay, low range	FQ	First quartile wage	LR	Low end range	SQ	Second quartile wage	Y	Yearly

Occupation/Type/Industry	Location	Per	Low	Mid	High	Source	Date
Driver/Sales Worker	Arizona	S	10.19 MW	10.99 AW	22860 AAW	AZBLS	10//99-12//99
	Arkansas	S	10.94 MW	11.23 AW	23360 AAW	ARBLS	10//99-12//99
	California	S	9.33 MW	11.12 AW	23130 AAW	CABLS	10//99-12//99
	Colorado	S	6.66 MW	9.23 AW	19190 AAW	COBLS	10//99-12//99
	Connecticut	S	9.96 MW	11.19 AW	23280 AAW	CTBLS	10//99-12//99
	Delaware	S	11.13 MW	12.17 AW	25320 AAW	DEBLS	10//99-12//99
	District of Columbia	S	11.29 MW	10.91 AW	22690 AAW	DCBLS	10//99-12//99
	Florida	S	10.37 MW	10.59 AW	22020 AAW	FLBLS	10//99-12//99
	Georgia	S	10.66 MW	11.36 AW	23620 AAW	GABLS	10//99-12//99
	Hawaii	S	9.34 MW	11.31 AW	23520 AAW	HIBLS	10//99-12//99
	Idaho	S	9.26 MW	9.99 AW	20780 AAW	IDBLS	10//99-12//99
	Illinois	S	12.37 MW	13.26 AW	27570 AAW	ILBLS	10//99-12//99
	Indiana	S	10.14 MW	11.35 AW	23610 AAW	INBLS	10//99-12//99
	Iowa	S	8.66 MW	10.28 AW	21380 AAW	IABLS	10//99-12//99
	Kansas	S	10.63 MW	11.26 AW	23420 AAW	KSBLS	10//99-12//99
	Kentucky	S	8.86 MW	10.04 AW	20880 AAW	KYBLS	10//99-12//99
	Louisiana	S	10.36 MW	10.39 AW	21610 AAW	LABLS	10//99-12//99
	Maine	S	10.15 MW	10.88 AW	22630 AAW	MEBLS	10//99-12//99
	Maryland	S	10.3 MW	10.94 AW	22760 AAW	MDBLS	10//99-12//99
	Massachusetts	S	11.74 MW	12.14 AW	25250 AAW	MABLS	10//99-12//99
	Michigan	S	8.12 MW	10.62 AW	22090 AAW	MIBLS	10//99-12//99
	Minnesota	S	8.7 MW	10.27 AW	21360 AAW	MNBLS	10//99-12//99
	Mississippi	S	9.53 MW	10.25 AW	21310 AAW	MSBLS	10//99-12//99
	Missouri	S	9.25 MW	10.75 AW	22360 AAW	MOBLS	10//99-12//99
	Montana	S	11.2 MW	11.12 AW	23130 AAW	MTBLS	10//99-12//99
	Nebraska	S	8.68 MW	9.92 AW	20620 AAW	NEBLS	10//99-12//99
	Nevada	S	9.29 MW	10.63 AW	22110 AAW	NVBLS	10//99-12//99
	New Hampshire	S	8.38 MW	10.00 AW	20810 AAW	NHBLS	10//99-12//99
	New Jersey	S	11.63 MW	13.50 AW	28090 AAW	NJBLS	10//99-12//99
	New Mexico	S	7.21 MW	8.67 AW	18020 AAW	NMBLS	10//99-12//99
	New York	S	10.46 MW	11.61 AW	24140 AAW	NYBLS	10//99-12//99
	North Carolina	S	10 MW	10.76 AW	22370 AAW	NCBLS	10//99-12//99
	North Dakota	S	7.52 MW	8.93 AW	18580 AAW	NDBLS	10//99-12//99
	Ohio	S	9 MW	10.76 AW	22380 AAW	OHBLS	10//99-12//99
	Oklahoma	S	9.98 MW	10.68 AW	22220 AAW	OKBLS	10//99-12//99
	Oregon	S	11.43 MW	12.09 AW	25150 AAW	ORBLS	10//99-12//99
	Pennsylvania	S	9.08 MW	10.62 AW	22080 AAW	PABLS	10//99-12//99
	Rhode Island	S	6.95 MW	9.47 AW	19690 AAW	RIBLS	10//99-12//99
	South Carolina	S	9.3 MW	9.70 AW	20170 AAW	SCBLS	10//99-12//99
	South Dakota	S	13.18 MW	12.74 AW	26490 AAW	SDBLS	10//99-12//99
	Tennessee	S	10.44 MW	11.02 AW	22920 AAW	TNBLS	10//99-12//99
	Texas	S	9.13 MW	9.94 AW	20670 AAW	TXBLS	10//99-12//99
	Utah	S	7.38 MW	9.60 AW	19970 AAW	UTBLS	10//99-12//99
	Vermont	S	9.93 MW	10.56 AW	21960 AAW	VTBLS	10//99-12//99
	Virginia	S	9.72 MW	10.35 AW	21540 AAW	VABLS	10//99-12//99
	Washington	S	10.71 MW	11.88 AW	24700 AAW	WABLS	10//99-12//99
	West Virginia	S	7.91 MW	9.26 AW	19250 AAW	WVBLS	10//99-12//99
	Wisconsin	S	9.05 MW	10.50 AW	21830 AAW	WIBLS	10//99-12//99
	Wyoming	S	6.66 MW	8.48 AW	17650 AAW	WYBLS	10//99-12//99
	Puerto Rico	S	6.08 MW	6.52 AW	13570 AAW	PRBLS	10//99-12//99
	Virgin Islands	S	9.52 MW	9.72 AW	20220 AAW	VIBLS	10//99-12//99
	Guam	S	6.57 MW	7.01 AW	14590 AAW	GUBLS	10//99-12//99
Drywall and Ceiling Tile Installer	Alabama	S	9.62 MW	9.48 AW	19710 AAW	ALBLS	10//99-12//99
	Alaska	S	16.38 MW	16.82 AW	34980 AAW	AKBLS	10//99-12//99
	Anchorage MSA, AK	S	17.53 MW	17.46 AW	36450 AAW	AKBLS	10//99-12//99
	Arizona	S	12.02 MW	12.35 AW	25690 AAW	AZBLS	10//99-12//99
	Phoenix-Mesa MSA, AZ	S	12.64 MW	12.28 AW	26290 AAW	AZBLS	10//99-12//99
	Tucson MSA, AZ	S	11.64 MW	11.78 AW	24210 AAW	AZBLS	10//99-12//99
	Arkansas	S	12.05 MW	11.96 AW	24870 AAW	ARBLS	10//99-12//99
	Little Rock-North Little Rock MSA, AR	S	11.57 MW	11.86 AW	24070 AAW	ARBLS	10//99-12//99
	California	S	18.71 MW	18.87 AW	39260 AAW	CABLS	10//99-12//99
	Bakersfield MSA, CA	S	12.43 MW	12.34 AW	25850 AAW	CABLS	10//99-12//99
	Fresno MSA, CA	S	12.74 MW	11.94 AW	26490 AAW	CABLS	10//99-12//99
	Los Angeles-Long Beach PMSA, CA	S	18.36 MW	18.47 AW	38190 AAW	CABLS	10//99-12//99
	Modesto MSA, CA	S	21.82 MW	23.52 AW	45380 AAW	CABLS	10//99-12//99
	Orange County PMSA, CA	S	20.25 MW	20.94 AW	42120 AAW	CABLS	10//99-12//99
	Riverside-San Bernardino PMSA, CA	S	17.23 MW	16.75 AW	35840 AAW	CABLS	10//99-12//99
	Sacramento PMSA, CA	S	16.50 MW	16.01 AW	34320 AAW	CABLS	10//99-12//99
	San Diego MSA, CA	S	18.75 MW	18.89 AW	38990 AAW	CABLS	10//99-12//99

AAW Average annual wage	**AOH** Average offered, high	**ASH** Average starting, high	**H** Hourly	**M** Monthly	**S** Special: hourly and annual
AE Average entry wage	**AOL** Average offered, low	**ASL** Average starting, low	**HI** Highest wage paid	**MTC** Median total compensation	**TQ** Third quartile wage
AEX Average experienced wage	**APH** Average pay, high range	**AW** Average wage paid	**HR** High end range	**MW** Median wage paid	**W** Weekly
AO Average offered	**APL** Average pay, low range	**FQ** First quartile wage	**LR** Low end range	**SQ** Second quartile wage	**Y** Yearly

Occupation/Type/Industry	Location	Per	Low	Mid	High	Source	Date
Drywall and Ceiling Tile Installer	San Francisco PMSA, CA	S	24.73 MW	24.85 AW	51430 AAW	CABLS	10//99-12//99
	San Jose PMSA, CA	S	24.01 MW	24.77 AW	49940 AAW	CABLS	10//99-12//99
	Santa Rosa PMSA, CA	S	22.82 MW	23.64 AW	47460 AAW	CABLS	10//99-12//99
	Stockton-Lodi MSA, CA	S	20.38 MW	19.93 AW	42380 AAW	CABLS	10//99-12//99
	Vallejo-Fairfield-Napa PMSA, CA	S	17.02 MW	16.75 AW	35410 AAW	CABLS	10//99-12//99
	Ventura PMSA, CA	S	20.09 MW	23.22 AW	41780 AAW	CABLS	10//99-12//99
	Yuba City MSA, CA	S	10.39 MW	9.23 AW	21610 AAW	CABLS	10//99-12//99
	Colorado	S	14.76 MW	14.30 AW	29740 AAW	COBLS	10//99-12//99
	Denver PMSA, CO	S	14.45 MW	14.86 AW	30050 AAW	COBLS	10//99-12//99
	Connecticut	S	19.12 MW	19.09 AW	39700 AAW	CTBLS	10//99-12//99
	Delaware	S	14.22 MW	14.69 AW	30560 AAW	DEBLS	10//99-12//99
	Wilmington-Newark PMSA, DE-MD	S	18.21 MW	17.85 AW	37880 AAW	DEBLS	10//99-12//99
	Washington PMSA, DC-MD-VA-WV	S	15.57 MW	15.21 AW	32380 AAW	DCBLS	10//99-12//99
	Florida	S	12.89 MW	13.30 AW	27660 AAW	FLBLS	10//99-12//99
	Fort Myers-Cape Coral MSA, FL	S	14.16 MW	13.41 AW	29460 AAW	FLBLS	10//99-12//99
	Jacksonville MSA, FL	S	11.93 MW	11.69 AW	24810 AAW	FLBLS	10//99-12//99
	Lakeland-Winter Haven MSA, FL	S	11.28 MW	11.38 AW	23460 AAW	FLBLS	10//99-12//99
	Melbourne-Titusville-Palm Bay MSA, FL	S	10.76 MW	9.87 AW	22370 AAW	FLBLS	10//99-12//99
	Miami PMSA, FL	S	16.20 MW	15.06 AW	33690 AAW	FLBLS	10//99-12//99
	Pensacola MSA, FL	S	11.34 MW	11.66 AW	23580 AAW	FLBLS	10//99-12//99
	Tallahassee MSA, FL	S	12.10 MW	10.57 AW	25180 AAW	FLBLS	10//99-12//99
	Tampa-St. Petersburg-Clearwater MSA, FL	S	12.95 MW	12.92 AW	26940 AAW	FLBLS	10//99-12//99
	West Palm Beach-Boca Raton MSA, FL	S	14.61 MW	14.76 AW	30380 AAW	FLBLS	10//99-12//99
	Georgia	S	16.25 MW	16.27 AW	33830 AAW	GABLS	10//99-12//99
	Atlanta MSA, GA	S	16.75 MW	16.71 AW	34840 AAW	GABLS	10//99-12//99
	Augusta-Aiken MSA, GA-SC	S	12.16 MW	12.13 AW	25290 AAW	GABLS	10//99-12//99
	Savannah MSA, GA	S	15.16 MW	15.25 AW	31530 AAW	GABLS	10//99-12//99
	Hawaii	S	28.95 MW	26.48 AW	55070 AAW	HIBLS	10//99-12//99
	Honolulu MSA, HI	S	27.53 MW	29.17 AW	57270 AAW	HIBLS	10//99-12//99
	Idaho	S	15.22 MW	15.11 AW	31430 AAW	IDBLS	10//99-12//99
	Boise City MSA, ID	S	15.16 MW	15.25 AW	31530 AAW	IDBLS	10//99-12//99
	Illinois	S	23.07 MW	22.11 AW	45990 AAW	ILBLS	10//99-12//99
	Chicago PMSA, IL	S	22.27 MW	23.51 AW	46330 AAW	ILBLS	10//99-12//99
	Indiana	S	22.46 MW	20.31 AW	42250 AAW	INBLS	10//99-12//99
	Bloomington MSA, IN	S	11.11 MW	11.66 AW	23110 AAW	INBLS	10//99-12//99
	Indianapolis MSA, IN	S	20.99 MW	22.40 AW	43650 AAW	INBLS	10//99-12//99
	Iowa	S	14.49 MW	14.77 AW	30720 AAW	IABLS	10//99-12//99
	Des Moines MSA, IA	S	15.80 MW	16.50 AW	32870 AAW	IABLS	10//99-12//99
	Iowa City MSA, IA	S	13.53 MW	12.98 AW	28130 AAW	IABLS	10//99-12//99
	Kansas	S	15.02 MW	14.99 AW	31170 AAW	KSBLS	10//99-12//99
	Wichita MSA, KS	S	15.35 MW	15.83 AW	31930 AAW	KSBLS	10//99-12//99
	Kentucky	S	14.54 MW	14.08 AW	29280 AAW	KYBLS	10//99-12//99
	Louisville MSA, KY-IN	S	13.69 MW	14.18 AW	28470 AAW	KYBLS	10//99-12//99
	Louisiana	S	13.72 MW	13.28 AW	27610 AAW	LABLS	10//99-12//99
	Lafayette MSA, LA	S	12.19 MW	12.18 AW	25350 AAW	LABLS	10//99-12//99
	New Orleans MSA, LA	S	13.45 MW	13.99 AW	27980 AAW	LABLS	10//99-12//99
	Maine	S	11.46 MW	12.41 AW	25820 AAW	MEBLS	10//99-12//99
	Lewiston-Auburn MSA, ME	S	11.75 MW	10.50 AW	24450 AAW	MEBLS	10//99-12//99
	Maryland	S	15.78 MW	15.92 AW	33110 AAW	MDBLS	10//99-12//99
	Baltimore PMSA, MD	S	15.96 MW	15.93 AW	33190 AAW	MDBLS	10//99-12//99
	Massachusetts	S	20.3 MW	20.21 AW	42050 AAW	MABLS	10//99-12//99
	Boston PMSA, MA-NH	S	20.63 MW	20.64 AW	42910 AAW	MABLS	10//99-12//99
	Michigan	S	16.58 MW	17.23 AW	35840 AAW	MIBLS	10//99-12//99
	Detroit PMSA, MI	S	18.97 MW	20.37 AW	39460 AAW	MIBLS	10//99-12//99
	Lansing-East Lansing MSA, MI	S	12.36 MW	12.14 AW	25720 AAW	MIBLS	10//99-12//99
	Minnesota	S	21 MW	20.53 AW	42710 AAW	MNBLS	10//99-12//99
	Minneapolis-St. Paul MSA, MN-WI	S	21.95 MW	23.08 AW	45660 AAW	MNBLS	10//99-12//99
	Mississippi	S	11.64 MW	11.31 AW	23530 AAW	MSBLS	10//99-12//99
	Biloxi-Gulfport-Pascagoula MSA, MS	S	15.64 MW	15.49 AW	32540 AAW	MSBLS	10//99-12//99
	Kansas City MSA, MO-KS	S	19.04 MW	19.63 AW	39610 AAW	MOBLS	10//99-12//99
	Montana	S	16.57 MW	16.67 AW	34670 AAW	MTBLS	10//99-12//99
	Nebraska	S	14.1 MW	13.70 AW	28500 AAW	NEBLS	10//99-12//99

AAW	Average annual wage	AOH	Average offered, high	ASH	Average starting, high	H	Hourly	M	Monthly	S	Special: hourly and annual
AE	Average entry wage	AOL	Average offered, low	ASL	Average starting, low	HI	Highest wage paid	MTC	Median total compensation	TQ	Third quartile wage
AEX	Average experienced wage	APH	Average pay, high range	AW	Average wage paid	HR	High end range	MW	Median wage paid	W	Weekly
AO	Average offered	APL	Average pay, low range	FQ	First quartile wage	LR	Low end range	SQ	Second quartile wage	Y	Yearly

Occupation/Type/Industry	Location	Per	Low	Mid	High	Source	Date
Drywall and Ceiling Tile Installer	Lincoln MSA, NE	S	12.71 MW	12.34 AW	26440 AAW	NEBLS	10//99-12//99
	Nevada	S	14.5 MW	15.70 AW	32660 AAW	NVBLS	10//99-12//99
	Las Vegas MSA, NV-AZ	S	15.41 MW	14.59 AW	32060 AAW	NVBLS	10//99-12//99
	New Hampshire	S	14.75 MW	15.12 AW	31450 AAW	NHBLS	10//99-12//99
	New Jersey	S	27.21 MW	23.24 AW	48340 AAW	NJBLS	10//99-12//99
	Monmouth-Ocean PMSA, NJ	S	22.32 MW	20.48 AW	46420 AAW	NJBLS	10//99-12//99
	New Mexico	S	17.02 MW	15.70 AW	32650 AAW	NMBLS	10//99-12//99
	Albuquerque MSA, NM	S	15.86 MW	17.40 AW	32990 AAW	NMBLS	10//99-12//99
	New York	S	29.53 MW	26.61 AW	55340 AAW	NYBLS	10//99-12//99
	Nassau-Suffolk PMSA, NY	S	31.93 MW	32.00 AW	66420 AAW	NYBLS	10//99-12//99
	New York PMSA, NY	S	32.09 MW	31.86 AW	66740 AAW	NYBLS	10//99-12//99
	Rochester MSA, NY	S	17.89 MW	18.53 AW	37200 AAW	NYBLS	10//99-12//99
	Syracuse MSA, NY	S	18.02 MW	18.78 AW	37470 AAW	NYBLS	10//99-12//99
	North Carolina	S	11.41 MW	11.61 AW	24150 AAW	NCBLS	10//99-12//99
	Charlotte-Gastonia-Rock Hill MSA, NC-SC	S	10.23 MW	9.96 AW	21280 AAW	NCBLS	10//99-12//99
	Greensboro--Winston-Salem--High Point MSA, NC	S	13.41 MW	13.01 AW	27890 AAW	NCBLS	10//99-12//99
	Raleigh-Durham-Chapel Hill MSA, NC	S	14.43 MW	14.90 AW	30010 AAW	NCBLS	10//99-12//99
	Wilmington MSA, NC	S	11.54 MW	11.88 AW	23990 AAW	NCBLS	10//99-12//99
	Fargo-Moorhead MSA, ND-MN	S	12.82 MW	13.03 AW	26670 AAW	NDBLS	10//99-12//99
	Ohio	S	14.79 MW	14.79 AW	30760 AAW	OHBLS	10//99-12//99
	Cincinnati PMSA, OH-KY-IN	S	15.83 MW	15.59 AW	32940 AAW	OHBLS	10//99-12//99
	Dayton-Springfield MSA, OH	S	14.13 MW	14.76 AW	29390 AAW	OHBLS	10//99-12//99
	Toledo MSA, OH	S	18.23 MW	18.60 AW	37920 AAW	OHBLS	10//99-12//99
	Youngstown-Warren MSA, OH	S	17.43 MW	18.13 AW	36260 AAW	OHBLS	10//99-12//99
	Oklahoma	S	13.3 MW	13.21 AW	27470 AAW	OKBLS	10//99-12//99
	Oklahoma City MSA, OK	S	12.76 MW	12.67 AW	26540 AAW	OKBLS	10//99-12//99
	Tulsa MSA, OK	S	13.78 MW	14.01 AW	28660 AAW	OKBLS	10//99-12//99
	Oregon	S	18.32 MW	18.14 AW	37730 AAW	ORBLS	10//99-12//99
	Eugene-Springfield MSA, OR	S	19.32 MW	19.32 AW	40190 AAW	ORBLS	10//99-12//99
	Medford-Ashland MSA, OR	S	21.06 MW	19.08 AW	43790 AAW	ORBLS	10//99-12//99
	Portland-Vancouver PMSA, OR-WA	S	16.95 MW	16.49 AW	35260 AAW	ORBLS	10//99-12//99
	Pennsylvania	S	13.91 MW	15.61 AW	32470 AAW	PABLS	10//99-12//99
	Allentown-Bethlehem-Easton MSA, PA	S	15.38 MW	13.02 AW	31980 AAW	PABLS	10//99-12//99
	Erie MSA, PA	S	10.86 MW	11.13 AW	22590 AAW	PABLS	10//99-12//99
	Harrisburg-Lebanon-Carlisle MSA, PA	S	14.43 MW	14.73 AW	30010 AAW	PABLS	10//99-12//99
	Philadelphia PMSA, PA-NJ	S	21.33 MW	23.50 AW	44360 AAW	PABLS	10//99-12//99
	Pittsburgh MSA, PA	S	13.41 MW	12.00 AW	27890 AAW	PABLS	10//99-12//99
	Rhode Island	S	18.03 MW	17.82 AW	37070 AAW	RIBLS	10//99-12//99
	Providence-Fall River-Warwick MSA, RI-MA	S	18.93 MW	18.72 AW	39370 AAW	RIBLS	10//99-12//99
	South Carolina	S	11.49 MW	11.45 AW	23810 AAW	SCBLS	10//99-12//99
	Charleston-North Charleston MSA, SC	S	10.93 MW	10.43 AW	22740 AAW	SCBLS	10//99-12//99
	Columbia MSA, SC	S	13.77 MW	13.59 AW	28640 AAW	SCBLS	10//99-12//99
	Greenville-Spartanburg-Anderson MSA, SC	S	14.34 MW	13.41 AW	29820 AAW	SCBLS	10//99-12//99
	South Dakota	S	12.92 MW	13.06 AW	27170 AAW	SDBLS	10//99-12//99
	Tennessee	S	14.7 MW	14.05 AW	29220 AAW	TNBLS	10//99-12//99
	Chattanooga MSA, TN-GA	S	15.12 MW	15.23 AW	31440 AAW	TNBLS	10//99-12//99
	Knoxville MSA, TN	S	12.71 MW	12.79 AW	26430 AAW	TNBLS	10//99-12//99
	Memphis MSA, TN-AR-MS	S	14.65 MW	14.99 AW	30480 AAW	MSBLS	10//99-12//99
	Nashville MSA, TN	S	14.75 MW	14.99 AW	30680 AAW	TNBLS	10//99-12//99
	Texas	S	12.27 MW	12.75 AW	26520 AAW	TXBLS	10//99-12//99
	Abilene MSA, TX	S	10.79 MW	11.09 AW	22450 AAW	TXBLS	10//99-12//99
	Amarillo MSA, TX	S	12.31 MW	12.50 AW	25610 AAW	TXBLS	10//99-12//99
	Austin-San Marcos MSA, TX	S	13.73 MW	13.60 AW	28550 AAW	TXBLS	10//99-12//99
	Corpus Christi MSA, TX	S	8.70 MW	8.77 AW	18090 AAW	TXBLS	10//99-12//99
	Dallas PMSA, TX	S	14.46 MW	13.33 AW	30070 AAW	TXBLS	10//99-12//99
	El Paso MSA, TX	S	10.06 MW	9.80 AW	20930 AAW	TXBLS	10//99-12//99
	Fort Worth-Arlington PMSA, TX	S	12.86 MW	12.41 AW	26760 AAW	TXBLS	10//99-12//99
	Houston PMSA, TX	S	12.13 MW	11.79 AW	25230 AAW	TXBLS	10//99-12//99
	McAllen-Edinburg-Mission MSA, TX	S	7.60 MW	7.65 AW	15810 AAW	TXBLS	10//99-12//99
	San Angelo MSA, TX	S	10.48 MW	9.84 AW	21800 AAW	TXBLS	10//99-12//99

AAW	Average annual wage	AOH	Average offered, high	ASH	Average starting, high	H	Hourly	M	Monthly	S	Special: hourly and annual
AE	Average entry wage	AOL	Average offered, low	ASL	Average starting, low	HI	Highest wage paid	MTC	Median total compensation	TQ	Third quartile wage
AEX	Average experienced wage	APH	Average pay, high range	AW	Average wage paid	HR	High end range	MW	Median wage paid	W	Weekly
AO	Average offered	APL	Average pay, low range	FQ	First quartile wage	LR	Low end range	SQ	Second quartile wage	Y	Yearly

Occupation/Type/Industry	Location	Per	Low	Mid	High	Source	Date
Drywall and Ceiling Tile Installer	San Antonio MSA, TX	S	11.22 MW	11.57 AW	23340 AAW	TXBLS	10//99-12//99
	Utah	S	12.97 MW	13.36 AW	27790 AAW	UTBLS	10//99-12//99
	Virginia	S	13.26 MW	13.03 AW	27110 AAW	VABLS	10//99-12//99
	Norfolk-Virginia Beach-Newport News MSA, VA-NC	S	11.70 MW	13.07 AW	24330 AAW	VABLS	10//99-12//99
	Richmond-Petersburg MSA, VA	S	13.31 MW	13.47 AW	27690 AAW	VABLS	10//99-12//99
	Roanoke MSA, VA	S	12.32 MW	12.28 AW	25630 AAW	VABLS	10//99-12//99
	Washington	S	21.69 MW	19.86 AW	41300 AAW	WABLS	10//99-12//99
	Bremerton PMSA, WA	S	25.40 MW	28.74 AW	52840 AAW	WABLS	10//99-12//99
	Seattle-Bellevue-Everett PMSA, WA	S	22.76 MW	23.90 AW	47350 AAW	WABLS	10//99-12//99
	Spokane MSA, WA	S	16.76 MW	15.33 AW	34870 AAW	WABLS	10//99-12//99
	Tacoma PMSA, WA	S	23.83 MW	23.52 AW	49560 AAW	WABLS	10//99-12//99
	Yakima MSA, WA	S	18.78 MW	19.14 AW	39070 AAW	WABLS	10//99-12//99
	West Virginia	S	12.39 MW	13.64 AW	28360 AAW	WVBLS	10//99-12//99
	Wisconsin	S	18.83 MW	18.77 AW	39040 AAW	WIBLS	10//99-12//99
	Green Bay MSA, WI	S	16.19 MW	17.79 AW	33670 AAW	WIBLS	10//99-12//99
	Madison MSA, WI	S	19.31 MW	19.21 AW	40170 AAW	WIBLS	10//99-12//99
	Milwaukee-Waukesha PMSA, WI	S	20.31 MW	20.30 AW	42240 AAW	WIBLS	10//99-12//99
	Wyoming	S	11.45 MW	11.22 AW	23330 AAW	WYBLS	10//99-12//99
	Casper MSA, WY	S	9.79 MW	9.55 AW	20350 AAW	WYBLS	10//99-12//99
	Puerto Rico	S	10.96 MW	12.58 AW	26170 AAW	PRBLS	10//99-12//99
Earth Driller							
Except Oil and Gas	Alabama	S	11.11 MW	12.35 AW	25700 AAW	ALBLS	10//99-12//99
Except Oil and Gas	Alaska	S	18.86 MW	20.35 AW	42330 AAW	AKBLS	10//99-12//99
Except Oil and Gas	Arizona	S	13.55 MW	13.61 AW	28310 AAW	AZBLS	10//99-12//99
Except Oil and Gas	Arkansas	S	10.49 MW	12.07 AW	25100 AAW	ARBLS	10//99-12//99
Except Oil and Gas	California	S	17.53 MW	18.40 AW	38280 AAW	CABLS	10//99-12//99
Except Oil and Gas	Colorado	S	16.07 MW	17.17 AW	35710 AAW	COBLS	10//99-12//99
Except Oil and Gas	Connecticut	S	18.83 MW	20.00 AW	41610 AAW	CTBLS	10//99-12//99
Except Oil and Gas	Florida	S	12.04 MW	12.71 AW	26430 AAW	FLBLS	10//99-12//99
Except Oil and Gas	Georgia	S	12.82 MW	13.12 AW	27300 AAW	GABLS	10//99-12//99
Except Oil and Gas	Hawaii	S	21.63 MW	22.15 AW	46070 AAW	HIBLS	10//99-12//99
Except Oil and Gas	Idaho	S	15.97 MW	17.18 AW	35740 AAW	IDBLS	10//99-12//99
Except Oil and Gas	Illinois	S	17.78 MW	17.38 AW	36160 AAW	ILBLS	10//99-12//99
Except Oil and Gas	Indiana	S	14.75 MW	15.33 AW	31890 AAW	INBLS	10//99-12//99
Except Oil and Gas	Iowa	S	12.42 MW	12.76 AW	26550 AAW	IABLS	10//99-12//99
Except Oil and Gas	Kansas	S	12.66 MW	13.02 AW	27070 AAW	KSBLS	10//99-12//99
Except Oil and Gas	Kentucky	S	11.25 MW	11.79 AW	24520 AAW	KYBLS	10//99-12//99
Except Oil and Gas	Louisiana	S	17.61 MW	16.98 AW	35310 AAW	LABLS	10//99-12//99
Except Oil and Gas	Maine	S	12.27 MW	12.40 AW	25800 AAW	MEBLS	10//99-12//99
Except Oil and Gas	Maryland	S	14.71 MW	14.49 AW	30130 AAW	MDBLS	10//99-12//99
Except Oil and Gas	Massachusetts	S	17.92 MW	17.71 AW	36830 AAW	MABLS	10//99-12//99
Except Oil and Gas	Michigan	S	13.35 MW	14.47 AW	30110 AAW	MIBLS	10//99-12//99
Except Oil and Gas	Minnesota	S	14.6 MW	14.65 AW	30470 AAW	MNBLS	10//99-12//99
Except Oil and Gas	Mississippi	S	11.64 MW	11.85 AW	24650 AAW	MSBLS	10//99-12//99
Except Oil and Gas	Missouri	S	15.22 MW	17.25 AW	35880 AAW	MOBLS	10//99-12//99
Except Oil and Gas	Montana	S	14.83 MW	14.62 AW	30400 AAW	MTBLS	10//99-12//99
Except Oil and Gas	Nebraska	S	11.29 MW	11.27 AW	23440 AAW	NEBLS	10//99-12//99
Except Oil and Gas	Nevada	S	17.27 MW	19.46 AW	40470 AAW	NVBLS	10//99-12//99
Except Oil and Gas	New Hampshire	S	14.72 MW	15.54 AW	32320 AAW	NHBLS	10//99-12//99
Except Oil and Gas	New Jersey	S	16.73 MW	18.20 AW	37860 AAW	NJBLS	10//99-12//99
Except Oil and Gas	New Mexico	S	12.36 MW	13.71 AW	28510 AAW	NMBLS	10//99-12//99
Except Oil and Gas	New York	S	15.47 MW	15.79 AW	32840 AAW	NYBLS	10//99-12//99
Except Oil and Gas	North Carolina	S	10.81 MW	11.51 AW	23930 AAW	NCBLS	10//99-12//99
Except Oil and Gas	North Dakota	S	16.3 MW	17.83 AW	37080 AAW	NDBLS	10//99-12//99
Except Oil and Gas	Ohio	S	14.27 MW	14.95 AW	31090 AAW	OHBLS	10//99-12//99
Except Oil and Gas	Oklahoma	S	8.72 MW	10.20 AW	21210 AAW	OKBLS	10//99-12//99
Except Oil and Gas	Oregon	S	16.01 MW	17.10 AW	35560 AAW	ORBLS	10//99-12//99
Except Oil and Gas	Pennsylvania	S	12.78 MW	13.51 AW	28090 AAW	PABLS	10//99-12//99
Except Oil and Gas	Rhode Island	S	18.91 MW	18.31 AW	38090 AAW	RIBLS	10//99-12//99
Except Oil and Gas	South Carolina	S	12.91 MW	13.56 AW	28210 AAW	SCBLS	10//99-12//99
Except Oil and Gas	South Dakota	S	13.92 MW	13.43 AW	27920 AAW	SDBLS	10//99-12//99
Except Oil and Gas	Tennessee	S	12.06 MW	12.61 AW	26230 AAW	TNBLS	10//99-12//99
Except Oil and Gas	Texas	S	12.78 MW	13.39 AW	27850 AAW	TXBLS	10//99-12//99
Except Oil and Gas	Utah	S	15.27 MW	15.20 AW	31610 AAW	UTBLS	10//99-12//99
Except Oil and Gas	Vermont	S	14.12 MW	13.08 AW	27210 AAW	VTBLS	10//99-12//99
Except Oil and Gas	Virginia	S	11.57 MW	12.27 AW	25520 AAW	VABLS	10//99-12//99
Except Oil and Gas	Washington	S	13.07 MW	12.96 AW	26960 AAW	WABLS	10//99-12//99

AAW Average annual wage	AOH Average offered, high	ASH Average starting, high	H Hourly	M Monthly	S Special: hourly and annual
AE Average entry wage	AOL Average offered, low	ASL Average starting, low	HI Highest wage paid	MTC Median total compensation	TQ Third quartile wage
AEX Average experienced wage	APH Average pay, high range	AW Average wage paid	HR High end range	MW Median wage paid	W Weekly
AO Average offered	APL Average pay, low range	FQ First quartile wage	LR Low end range	SQ Second quartile wage	Y Yearly

Occupation/Type/Industry	Location	Per	Low	Mid	High	Source	Date
Earth Driller							
Except Oil and Gas	West Virginia	S	18.47 mw	21.22 aw	44130 aaw	WVBLS	10//99-12//99
Except Oil and Gas	Wisconsin	S	13.88 mw	14.28 aw	29710 aaw	WIBLS	10//99-12//99
Except Oil and Gas	Wyoming	S	16.2 mw	18.23 aw	37930 aaw	WYBLS	10//99-12//99
Except Oil and Gas	Puerto Rico	S	8.74 mw	11.50 aw	23930 aaw	PRBLS	10//99-12//99
Economic Development Officer							
Real Estate	United States	Y		78300 aw		TRAVWK4	2000
Economics Teacher							
Postsecondary	Alabama	Y		52220 aaw		ALBLS	10//99-12//99
Postsecondary	Phoenix-Mesa MSA, AZ	Y		40210 aaw		AZBLS	10//99-12//99
Postsecondary	Arkansas	Y		63070 aaw		ARBLS	10//99-12//99
Postsecondary	California	Y		60440 aaw		CABLS	10//99-12//99
Postsecondary	Los Angeles-Long Beach PMSA, CA	Y		58700 aaw		CABLS	10//99-12//99
Postsecondary	Riverside-San Bernardino PMSA, CA	Y		57850 aaw		CABLS	10//99-12//99
Postsecondary	San Diego MSA, CA	Y		60650 aaw		CABLS	10//99-12//99
Postsecondary	San Francisco PMSA, CA	Y		63750 aaw		CABLS	10//99-12//99
Postsecondary	Colorado	Y		58390 aaw		COBLS	10//99-12//99
Postsecondary	Denver PMSA, CO	Y		58430 aaw		COBLS	10//99-12//99
Postsecondary	Connecticut	Y		64800 aaw		CTBLS	10//99-12//99
Postsecondary	District of Columbia	Y		56060 aaw		DCBLS	10//99-12//99
Postsecondary	Washington PMSA, DC-MD-VA-WV	Y		60810 aaw		DCBLS	10//99-12//99
Postsecondary	Florida	Y		69680 aaw		FLBLS	10//99-12//99
Postsecondary	Miami PMSA, FL	Y		71010 aaw		FLBLS	10//99-12//99
Postsecondary	Orlando MSA, FL	Y		58750 aaw		FLBLS	10//99-12//99
Postsecondary	Tampa-St. Petersburg-Clearwater MSA, FL	Y		64840 aaw		FLBLS	10//99-12//99
Postsecondary	Georgia	Y		52080 aaw		GABLS	10//99-12//99
Postsecondary	Atlanta MSA, GA	Y		52240 aaw		GABLS	10//99-12//99
Postsecondary	Indiana	Y		64100 aaw		INBLS	10//99-12//99
Postsecondary	Iowa	Y		61330 aaw		IABLS	10//99-12//99
Postsecondary	Kansas	Y		45180 aaw		KSBLS	10//99-12//99
Postsecondary	Kentucky	Y		61400 aaw		KYBLS	10//99-12//99
Postsecondary	Louisiana	Y		71300 aaw		LABLS	10//99-12//99
Postsecondary	Maryland	Y		60540 aaw		MDBLS	10//99-12//99
Postsecondary	Baltimore PMSA, MD	Y		54290 aaw		MDBLS	10//99-12//99
Postsecondary	Massachusetts	Y		64810 aaw		MABLS	10//99-12//99
Postsecondary	Boston PMSA, MA-NH	Y		66960 aaw		MABLS	10//99-12//99
Postsecondary	Springfield MSA, MA	Y		70840 aaw		MABLS	10//99-12//99
Postsecondary	Worcester PMSA, MA-CT	Y		58590 aaw		MABLS	10//99-12//99
Postsecondary	Michigan	Y		68180 aaw		MIBLS	10//99-12//99
Postsecondary	Detroit PMSA, MI	Y		52100 aaw		MIBLS	10//99-12//99
Postsecondary	Kalamazoo-Battle Creek MSA, MI	Y		58880 aaw		MIBLS	10//99-12//99
Postsecondary	Minnesota	Y		62690 aaw		MNBLS	10//99-12//99
Postsecondary	Minneapolis-St. Paul MSA, MN-WI	Y		73980 aaw		MNBLS	10//99-12//99
Postsecondary	Mississippi	Y		48140 aaw		MSBLS	10//99-12//99
Postsecondary	Jackson MSA, MS	Y		44190 aaw		MSBLS	10//99-12//99
Postsecondary	Montana	Y		64420 aaw		MTBLS	10//99-12//99
Postsecondary	New Hampshire	Y		70890 aaw		NHBLS	10//99-12//99
Postsecondary	New Jersey	Y		65560 aaw		NJBLS	10//99-12//99
Postsecondary	Newark PMSA, NJ	Y		61130 aaw		NJBLS	10//99-12//99
Postsecondary	New York	Y		57850 aaw		NYBLS	10//99-12//99
Postsecondary	Albany-Schenectady-Troy MSA, NY	Y		58240 aaw		NYBLS	10//99-12//99
Postsecondary	New York PMSA, NY	Y		59510 aaw		NYBLS	10//99-12//99
Postsecondary	North Carolina	Y		53640 aaw		NCBLS	10//99-12//99
Postsecondary	Charlotte-Gastonia-Rock Hill MSA, NC-SC	Y		56150 aaw		NCBLS	10//99-12//99
Postsecondary	Raleigh-Durham-Chapel Hill MSA, NC	Y		53200 aaw		NCBLS	10//99-12//99
Postsecondary	Ohio	Y		52310 aaw		OHBLS	10//99-12//99
Postsecondary	Cincinnati PMSA, OH-KY-IN	Y		50400 aaw		OHBLS	10//99-12//99
Postsecondary	Cleveland-Lorain-Elyria PMSA, OH	Y		52450 aaw		OHBLS	10//99-12//99
Postsecondary	Columbus MSA, OH	Y		53190 aaw		OHBLS	10//99-12//99
Postsecondary	Dayton-Springfield MSA, OH	Y		45210 aaw		OHBLS	10//99-12//99
Postsecondary	Oklahoma	Y		52030 aaw		OKBLS	10//99-12//99

AAW	Average annual wage	AOH	Average offered, high	ASH	Average starting, high	H	Hourly	M	Monthly	S	Special: hourly and annual
AE	Average entry wage	AOL	Average offered, low	ASL	Average starting, low	HI	Highest wage paid	MTC	Median total compensation	TQ	Third quartile wage
AEX	Average experienced wage	APH	Average pay, high range	AW	Average wage paid	HR	High end range	MW	Median wage paid	W	Weekly
AO	Average offered	APL	Average pay, low range	FQ	First quartile wage	LR	Low end range	SQ	Second quartile wage	Y	Yearly

Occupation/Type/Industry	Location	Per	Low	Mid	High	Source	Date
Economics Teacher							
Postsecondary	Oklahoma City MSA, OK	Y		46120 AAW		OKBLS	10//99-12//99
Postsecondary	Oregon	Y		55270 AAW		ORBLS	10//99-12//99
Postsecondary	Portland-Vancouver PMSA, OR-WA	Y		56260 AAW		ORBLS	10//99-12//99
Postsecondary	Pennsylvania	Y		62270 AAW		PABLS	10//99-12//99
Postsecondary	Allentown-Bethlehem-Easton MSA, PA	Y		45670 AAW		PABLS	10//99-12//99
Postsecondary	Harrisburg-Lebanon-Carlisle MSA, PA	Y		63300 AAW		PABLS	10//99-12//99
Postsecondary	Philadelphia PMSA, PA-NJ	Y		65630 AAW		PABLS	10//99-12//99
Postsecondary	Pittsburgh MSA, PA	Y		58660 AAW		PABLS	10//99-12//99
Postsecondary	Reading MSA, PA	Y		60510 AAW		PABLS	10//99-12//99
Postsecondary	Scranton--Wilkes-Barre--Hazleton MSA, PA	Y		53750 AAW		PABLS	10//99-12//99
Postsecondary	Rhode Island	Y		70720 AAW		RIBLS	10//99-12//99
Postsecondary	Providence-Fall River-Warwick MSA, RI-MA	Y		72590 AAW		RIBLS	10//99-12//99
Postsecondary	South Carolina	Y		55630 AAW		SCBLS	10//99-12//99
Postsecondary	South Dakota	Y		50580 AAW		SDBLS	10//99-12//99
Postsecondary	Tennessee	Y		65620 AAW		TNBLS	10//99-12//99
Postsecondary	Nashville MSA, TN	Y		73380 AAW		TNBLS	10//99-12//99
Postsecondary	Texas	Y		54400 AAW		TXBLS	10//99-12//99
Postsecondary	Bryan-College Station MSA, TX	Y		48290 AAW		TXBLS	10//99-12//99
Postsecondary	Dallas PMSA, TX	Y		49090 AAW		TXBLS	10//99-12//99
Postsecondary	El Paso MSA, TX	Y		43300 AAW		TXBLS	10//99-12//99
Postsecondary	Houston PMSA, TX	Y		68210 AAW		TXBLS	10//99-12//99
Postsecondary	San Antonio MSA, TX	Y		62640 AAW		TXBLS	10//99-12//99
Postsecondary	Vermont	Y		51790 AAW		VTBLS	10//99-12//99
Postsecondary	Virginia	Y		58670 AAW		VABLS	10//99-12//99
Postsecondary	Norfolk-Virginia Beach-Newport News MSA, VA-NC	Y		66640 AAW		VABLS	10//99-12//99
Postsecondary	Washington	Y		49510 AAW		WABLS	10//99-12//99
Postsecondary	Seattle-Bellevue-Everett PMSA, WA	Y		55200 AAW		WABLS	10//99-12//99
Postsecondary	Spokane MSA, WA	Y		45940 AAW		WABLS	10//99-12//99
Postsecondary	Tacoma PMSA, WA	Y		50070 AAW		WABLS	10//99-12//99
Postsecondary	West Virginia	Y		54530 AAW		WVBLS	10//99-12//99
Postsecondary	Milwaukee-Waukesha PMSA, WI	Y		56140 AAW		WIBLS	10//99-12//99
Postsecondary	Puerto Rico	Y		34250 AAW		PRBLS	10//99-12//99
Postsecondary	San Juan-Bayamon PMSA, PR	Y		31140 AAW		PRBLS	10//99-12//99
Economist							
	United States	H		25.93 AW		NCS98	1998
	Alabama	S	27.66 MW	25.82 AW	53710 AAW	ALBLS	10//99-12//99
	Alaska	S	28.73 MW	29.24 AW	60820 AAW	AKBLS	10//99-12//99
	Anchorage MSA, AK	S	30.29 MW	30.74 AW	63000 AAW	AKBLS	10//99-12//99
	Arizona	S	29.93 MW	28.80 AW	59900 AAW	AZBLS	10//99-12//99
	Phoenix-Mesa MSA, AZ	S	29.11 MW	30.14 AW	60560 AAW	AZBLS	10//99-12//99
	Arkansas	S	25.47 MW	25.95 AW	53980 AAW	ARBLS	10//99-12//99
	California	S	30.63 MW	30.47 AW	63390 AAW	CABLS	10//99-12//99
	Los Angeles-Long Beach PMSA, CA	S	28.97 MW	27.88 AW	60270 AAW	CABLS	10//99-12//99
	Riverside-San Bernardino PMSA, CA	S	27.98 MW	27.23 AW	58210 AAW	CABLS	10//99-12//99
	San Francisco PMSA, CA	S	31.11 MW	30.92 AW	64720 AAW	CABLS	10//99-12//99
	San Jose PMSA, CA	S	31.08 MW	35.64 AW	64640 AAW	CABLS	10//99-12//99
	Colorado	S	27.52 MW	26.39 AW	54900 AAW	COBLS	10//99-12//99
	Denver PMSA, CO	S	25.87 MW	26.79 AW	53820 AAW	COBLS	10//99-12//99
	Wilmington-Newark PMSA, DE-MD	S	31.19 MW	25.21 AW	64880 AAW	DEBLS	10//99-12//99
	Florida	S	22.9 MW	24.51 AW	50990 AAW	FLBLS	10//99-12//99
	Tampa-St. Petersburg-Clearwater MSA, FL	S	28.26 MW	29.07 AW	58770 AAW	FLBLS	10//99-12//99
	Georgia	S	24.37 MW	25.26 AW	52530 AAW	GABLS	10//99-12//99
	Atlanta MSA, GA	S	26.47 MW	25.62 AW	55060 AAW	GABLS	10//99-12//99
	Hawaii	S	24.71 MW	25.31 AW	52640 AAW	HIBLS	10//99-12//99
	Honolulu MSA, HI	S	26.18 MW	25.39 AW	54450 AAW	HIBLS	10//99-12//99
	Illinois	S	20.14 MW	23.82 AW	49550 AAW	ILBLS	10//99-12//99
	Chicago PMSA, IL	S	24.36 MW	20.29 AW	50670 AAW	ILBLS	10//99-12//99
	Indiana	S	25.79 MW	27.97 AW	58170 AAW	INBLS	10//99-12//99

AAW	Average annual wage	AOH	Average offered, high	ASH	Average starting, high
AE	Average entry wage	AOL	Average offered, low	ASL	Average starting, low
AEX	Average experienced wage	APH	Average pay, high range	AW	Average wage paid
AO	Average offered	APL	Average pay, low range	FQ	First quartile wage

H	Hourly	
HI	Highest wage paid	
HR	High end range	
LR	Low end range	

M	Monthly	S	Special: hourly and annual
MTC	Median total compensation	TQ	Third quartile wage
MW	Median wage paid	W	Weekly
SQ	Second quartile wage	Y	Yearly

Occupation/Type/Industry	Location	Per	Low	Mid	High	Source	Date
Economist	Louisiana	S	22.1 MW	22.62 AW	47040 AAW	LABLS	10//99-12//99
	New Orleans MSA, LA	S	22.05 MW	22.21 AW	45870 AAW	LABLS	10//99-12//99
	Maryland	S	32.42 MW	31.89 AW	66330 AAW	MDBLS	10//99-12//99
	Baltimore PMSA, MD	S	30.34 MW	27.57 AW	63100 AAW	MDBLS	10//99-12//99
	Massachusetts	S	28 MW	30.27 AW	62970 AAW	MABLS	10//99-12//99
	Boston PMSA, MA-NH	S	30.47 MW	27.46 AW	63380 AAW	MABLS	10//99-12//99
	Michigan	S	26.65 MW	27.34 AW	56870 AAW	MIBLS	10//99-12//99
	Detroit PMSA, MI	S	28.06 MW	26.53 AW	58370 AAW	MIBLS	10//99-12//99
	Minnesota	S	26.95 MW	29.99 AW	62370 AAW	MNBLS	10//99-12//99
	Minneapolis-St. Paul MSA, MN-WI	S	30.43 MW	27.33 AW	63280 AAW	MNBLS	10//99-12//99
	Mississippi	S	36.57 MW	32.94 AW	68520 AAW	MSBLS	10//99-12//99
	Jackson MSA, MS	S	24.84 MW	23.56 AW	51660 AAW	MSBLS	10//99-12//99
	Missouri	S	24.37 MW	24.31 AW	50550 AAW	MOBLS	10//99-12//99
	Kansas City MSA, MO-KS	S	23.02 MW	23.64 AW	47880 AAW	MOBLS	10//99-12//99
	Nebraska	S	23.4 MW	22.81 AW	47440 AAW	NEBLS	10//99-12//99
	Lincoln MSA, NE	S	19.70 MW	16.59 AW	40970 AAW	NEBLS	10//99-12//99
	New Hampshire	S	17.28 MW	19.72 AW	41010 AAW	NHBLS	10//99-12//99
	New Jersey	S	28.12 MW	26.44 AW	55000 AAW	NJBLS	10//99-12//99
	Newark PMSA, NJ	S	31.16 MW	31.01 AW	64810 AAW	NJBLS	10//99-12//99
	New York	S	22.14 MW	26.81 AW	55770 AAW	NYBLS	10//99-12//99
	New York PMSA, NY	S	28.83 MW	23.83 AW	59970 AAW	NYBLS	10//99-12//99
	North Carolina	S	25.64 MW	24.71 AW	51400 AAW	NCBLS	10//99-12//99
	Raleigh-Durham-Chapel Hill MSA, NC	S	24.50 MW	25.36 AW	50960 AAW	NCBLS	10//99-12//99
	Ohio	S	22.63 MW	24.28 AW	50500 AAW	OHBLS	10//99-12//99
	Cincinnati PMSA, OH-KY-IN	S	30.16 MW	29.08 AW	62730 AAW	OHBLS	10//99-12//99
	Cleveland-Lorain-Elyria PMSA, OH	S	27.11 MW	24.95 AW	56380 AAW	OHBLS	10//99-12//99
	Columbus MSA, OH	S	23.57 MW	23.01 AW	49040 AAW	OHBLS	10//99-12//99
	Oregon	S	26.75 MW	26.74 AW	55630 AAW	ORBLS	10//99-12//99
	Portland-Vancouver PMSA, OR-WA	S	27.56 MW	27.36 AW	57330 AAW	ORBLS	10//99-12//99
	Pennsylvania	S	26.07 MW	27.89 AW	58010 AAW	PABLS	10//99-12//99
	Philadelphia PMSA, PA-NJ	S	27.79 MW	25.67 AW	57800 AAW	PABLS	10//99-12//99
	Pittsburgh MSA, PA	S	26.44 MW	28.21 AW	55000 AAW	PABLS	10//99-12//99
	Tennessee	S	27.34 MW	30.88 AW	64230 AAW	TNBLS	10//99-12//99
	Texas	S	27.27 MW	33.21 AW	69080 AAW	TXBLS	10//99-12//99
	Dallas PMSA, TX	S	36.22 MW	28.40 AW	75340 AAW	TXBLS	10//99-12//99
	Fort Worth-Arlington PMSA, TX	S	33.72 MW	26.34 AW	70140 AAW	TXBLS	10//99-12//99
	San Antonio MSA, TX	S	28.07 MW	25.77 AW	58380 AAW	TXBLS	10//99-12//99
	Utah	S	22.05 MW	21.64 AW	45000 AAW	UTBLS	10//99-12//99
	Salt Lake City-Ogden MSA, UT	S	21.46 MW	21.65 AW	44640 AAW	UTBLS	10//99-12//99
	Virginia	S	38.4 MW	36.72 AW	76370 AAW	VABLS	10//99-12//99
	Norfolk-Virginia Beach-Newport News MSA, VA-NC	S	17.48 MW	12.76 AW	36360 AAW	VABLS	10//99-12//99
	Richmond-Petersburg MSA, VA	S	32.09 MW	31.16 AW	66760 AAW	VABLS	10//99-12//99
	Washington	S	25.27 MW	27.40 AW	56990 AAW	WABLS	10//99-12//99
	Seattle-Bellevue-Everett PMSA, WA	S	29.86 MW	28.09 AW	62100 AAW	WABLS	10//99-12//99
	West Virginia	S	15.45 MW	24.14 AW	50220 AAW	WVBLS	10//99-12//99
	Wisconsin	S	16.14 MW	18.56 AW	38600 AAW	WIBLS	10//99-12//99
	Milwaukee-Waukesha PMSA, WI	S	17.54 MW	14.76 AW	36480 AAW	WIBLS	10//99-12//99
Editor	Alabama	S	14.8 MW	15.47 AW	32170 AAW	ALBLS	10//99-12//99
	Anniston MSA, AL	S	15.87 MW	15.94 AW	33000 AAW	ALBLS	10//99-12//99
	Birmingham MSA, AL	S	15.81 MW	15.57 AW	32880 AAW	ALBLS	10//99-12//99
	Decatur MSA, AL	S	18.73 MW	16.85 AW	38960 AAW	ALBLS	10//99-12//99
	Mobile MSA, AL	S	10.77 MW	10.05 AW	22400 AAW	ALBLS	10//99-12//99
	Montgomery MSA, AL	S	16.70 MW	15.74 AW	34730 AAW	ALBLS	10//99-12//99
	Alaska	S	19.71 MW	19.65 AW	40870 AAW	AKBLS	10//99-12//99
	Anchorage MSA, AK	S	22.30 MW	22.51 AW	46380 AAW	AKBLS	10//99-12//99
	Arizona	S	17.99 MW	19.15 AW	39830 AAW	AZBLS	10//99-12//99
	Phoenix-Mesa MSA, AZ	S	19.19 MW	17.74 AW	39910 AAW	AZBLS	10//99-12//99
	Tucson MSA, AZ	S	18.98 MW	18.30 AW	39470 AAW	AZBLS	10//99-12//99
	Arkansas	S	13.37 MW	16.88 AW	35110 AAW	ARBLS	10//99-12//99
	Fayetteville-Springdale-Rogers MSA, AR	S	12.54 MW	12.27 AW	26090 AAW	ARBLS	10//99-12//99

AAW	Average annual wage	AOH	Average offered, high	ASH	Average starting, high	H	Hourly	M	Monthly	S	Special: hourly and annual
AE	Average entry wage	AOL	Average offered, low	ASL	Average starting, low	HI	Highest wage paid	MTC	Median total compensation	TQ	Third quartile wage
AEX	Average experienced wage	APH	Average pay, high range	AW	Average wage paid	HR	High end range	MW	Median wage paid	W	Weekly
AO	Average offered	APL	Average pay, low range	FQ	First quartile wage	LR	Low end range	SQ	Second quartile wage	Y	Yearly

Occupation/Type/Industry	Location	Per	Low	Mid	High	Source	Date
Editor	Little Rock-North Little Rock MSA, AR	S	17.91 MW	12.66 AW	37260 AAW	ARBLS	10//99-12//99
	California	S	19.82 MW	21.63 AW	45000 AAW	CABLS	10//99-12//99
	Chico-Paradise MSA, CA	S	14.20 MW	13.06 AW	29530 AAW	CABLS	10//99-12//99
	Fresno MSA, CA	S	22.46 MW	20.95 AW	46720 AAW	CABLS	10//99-12//99
	Los Angeles-Long Beach PMSA, CA	S	23.50 MW	23.33 AW	48890 AAW	CABLS	10//99-12//99
	Modesto MSA, CA	S	15.57 MW	14.72 AW	32390 AAW	CABLS	10//99-12//99
	Oakland PMSA, CA	S	20.95 MW	19.78 AW	43570 AAW	CABLS	10//99-12//99
	Orange County PMSA, CA	S	20.76 MW	19.21 AW	43190 AAW	CABLS	10//99-12//99
	Riverside-San Bernardino PMSA, CA	S	21.18 MW	21.76 AW	44060 AAW	CABLS	10//99-12//99
	Sacramento PMSA, CA	S	19.86 MW	16.32 AW	41310 AAW	CABLS	10//99-12//99
	Salinas MSA, CA	S	16.85 MW	16.12 AW	35040 AAW	CABLS	10//99-12//99
	San Diego MSA, CA	S	19.44 MW	12.48 AW	40430 AAW	CABLS	10//99-12//99
	San Francisco PMSA, CA	S	24.00 MW	22.25 AW	49920 AAW	CABLS	10//99-12//99
	San Jose PMSA, CA	S	21.31 MW	18.78 AW	44320 AAW	CABLS	10//99-12//99
	San Luis Obispo-Atascadero-Paso Robles MSA, CA	S	16.00 MW	14.57 AW	33280 AAW	CABLS	10//99-12//99
	Santa Barbara-Santa Maria-Lompoc MSA, CA	S	15.49 MW	15.40 AW	32220 AAW	CABLS	10//99-12//99
	Santa Cruz-Watsonville PMSA, CA	S	19.73 MW	17.75 AW	41040 AAW	CABLS	10//99-12//99
	Santa Rosa PMSA, CA	S	17.17 MW	15.96 AW	35720 AAW	CABLS	10//99-12//99
	Stockton-Lodi MSA, CA	S	18.42 MW	16.63 AW	38310 AAW	CABLS	10//99-12//99
	Vallejo-Fairfield-Napa PMSA, CA	S	17.18 MW	16.71 AW	35740 AAW	CABLS	10//99-12//99
	Ventura PMSA, CA	S	16.99 MW	12.59 AW	35340 AAW	CABLS	10//99-12//99
	Colorado	S	17.92 MW	19.54 AW	40630 AAW	COBLS	10//99-12//99
	Colorado Springs MSA, CO	S	17.25 MW	16.34 AW	35880 AAW	COBLS	10//99-12//99
	Denver PMSA, CO	S	22.14 MW	21.72 AW	46050 AAW	COBLS	10//99-12//99
	Fort Collins-Loveland MSA, CO	S	24.68 MW	28.62 AW	51330 AAW	COBLS	10//99-12//99
	Connecticut	S	18.39 MW	20.62 AW	42880 AAW	CTBLS	10//99-12//99
	Bridgeport PMSA, CT	S	14.09 MW	12.65 AW	29320 AAW	CTBLS	10//99-12//99
	Danbury PMSA, CT	S	19.02 MW	18.43 AW	39570 AAW	CTBLS	10//99-12//99
	New London-Norwich MSA, CT-RI	S	22.55 MW	22.38 AW	46910 AAW	CTBLS	10//99-12//99
	Stamford-Norwalk PMSA, CT	S	24.86 MW	21.19 AW	51710 AAW	CTBLS	10//99-12//99
	Waterbury PMSA, CT	S	20.29 MW	21.66 AW	42200 AAW	CTBLS	10//99-12//99
	Delaware	S	20.65 MW	21.67 AW	45080 AAW	DEBLS	10//99-12//99
	Wilmington-Newark PMSA, DE-MD	S	22.39 MW	20.47 AW	46570 AAW	DEBLS	10//99-12//99
	District of Columbia	S	23.43 MW	25.00 AW	52010 AAW	DCBLS	10//99-12//99
	Washington PMSA, DC-MD-VA-WV	S	22.38 MW	20.44 AW	46540 AAW	DCBLS	10//99-12//99
	Florida	S	15.85 MW	18.01 AW	37460 AAW	FLBLS	10//99-12//99
	Daytona Beach MSA, FL	S	22.09 MW	19.15 AW	45960 AAW	FLBLS	10//99-12//99
	Fort Lauderdale PMSA, FL	S	17.15 MW	15.49 AW	35670 AAW	FLBLS	10//99-12//99
	Fort Myers-Cape Coral MSA, FL	S	15.46 MW	14.56 AW	32160 AAW	FLBLS	10//99-12//99
	Fort Walton Beach MSA, FL	S	22.67 MW	19.56 AW	47150 AAW	FLBLS	10//99-12//99
	Gainesville MSA, FL	S	15.09 MW	14.50 AW	31390 AAW	FLBLS	10//99-12//99
	Jacksonville MSA, FL	S	18.80 MW	16.43 AW	39110 AAW	FLBLS	10//99-12//99
	Lakeland-Winter Haven MSA, FL	S	11.72 MW	10.28 AW	24370 AAW	FLBLS	10//99-12//99
	Miami PMSA, FL	S	26.12 MW	21.48 AW	54320 AAW	FLBLS	10//99-12//99
	Orlando MSA, FL	S	20.22 MW	19.29 AW	42070 AAW	FLBLS	10//99-12//99
	Pensacola MSA, FL	S	15.13 MW	14.78 AW	31480 AAW	FLBLS	10//99-12//99
	Sarasota-Bradenton MSA, FL	S	21.01 MW	17.87 AW	43710 AAW	FLBLS	10//99-12//99
	Tallahassee MSA, FL	S	14.27 MW	12.00 AW	29680 AAW	FLBLS	10//99-12//99
	Tampa-St. Petersburg-Clearwater MSA, FL	S	11.91 MW	8.25 AW	24760 AAW	FLBLS	10//99-12//99
	West Palm Beach-Boca Raton MSA, FL	S	25.13 MW	22.54 AW	52260 AAW	FLBLS	10//99-12//99
	Georgia	S	16.61 MW	18.27 AW	38010 AAW	GABLS	10//99-12//99
	Athens MSA, GA	S	9.22 MW	6.52 AW	19170 AAW	GABLS	10//99-12//99
	Atlanta MSA, GA	S	20.02 MW	17.73 AW	41640 AAW	GABLS	10//99-12//99
	Augusta-Aiken MSA, GA-SC	S	15.89 MW	15.78 AW	33040 AAW	GABLS	10//99-12//99
	Macon MSA, GA	S	14.16 MW	14.33 AW	29450 AAW	GABLS	10//99-12//99
	Hawaii	S	18.39 MW	18.61 AW	38700 AAW	HIBLS	10//99-12//99
	Honolulu MSA, HI	S	17.75 MW	18.00 AW	36930 AAW	HIBLS	10//99-12//99

Occupation/Type/Industry	Location	Per	Low	Mid	High	Source	Date
Editor	Idaho	S	13.3 MW	14.03 AW	29180 AAW	IDBLS	10//99-12/99
	Boise City MSA, ID	S	12.25 MW	10.84 AW	25480 AAW	IDBLS	10//99-12/99
	Illinois	S	20.18 MW	21.76 AW	45250 AAW	ILBLS	10//99-12/99
	Bloomington-Normal MSA, IL	S	19.90 MW	20.02 AW	41380 AAW	ILBLS	10//99-12/99
	Chicago PMSA, IL	S	22.48 MW	21.07 AW	46760 AAW	ILBLS	10//99-12/99
	Rockford MSA, IL	S	19.31 MW	17.88 AW	40170 AAW	ILBLS	10//99-12/99
	Springfield MSA, IL	S	18.50 MW	18.03 AW	38480 AAW	ILBLS	10//99-12/99
	Indiana	S	15.44 MW	16.10 AW	33480 AAW	INBLS	10//99-12/99
	Bloomington MSA, IN	S	13.00 MW	13.11 AW	27040 AAW	INBLS	10//99-12/99
	Evansville-Henderson MSA, IN-KY	S	16.08 MW	15.80 AW	33460 AAW	INBLS	10//99-12/99
	Fort Wayne MSA, IN	S	16.76 MW	15.60 AW	34870 AAW	INBLS	10//99-12/99
	Gary PMSA, IN	S	18.49 MW	17.75 AW	38460 AAW	INBLS	10//99-12/99
	Indianapolis MSA, IN	S	16.42 MW	15.72 AW	34140 AAW	INBLS	10//99-12/99
	Lafayette MSA, IN	S	16.78 MW	15.89 AW	34890 AAW	INBLS	10//99-12/99
	Iowa	S	12.27 MW	13.44 AW	27960 AAW	IABLS	10//99-12/99
	Cedar Rapids MSA, IA	S	14.28 MW	12.55 AW	29710 AAW	IABLS	10//99-12/99
	Davenport-Moline-Rock Island MSA, IA-IL	S	14.52 MW	12.21 AW	30200 AAW	IABLS	10//99-12/99
	Des Moines MSA, IA	S	18.41 MW	16.45 AW	38280 AAW	IABLS	10//99-12/99
	Dubuque MSA, IA	S	15.41 MW	14.48 AW	32050 AAW	IABLS	10//99-12/99
	Iowa City MSA, IA	S	13.05 MW	13.24 AW	27140 AAW	IABLS	10//99-12/99
	Waterloo-Cedar Falls MSA, IA	S	14.83 MW	12.61 AW	30840 AAW	IABLS	10//99-12/99
	Kansas	S	14.33 MW	15.83 AW	32920 AAW	KSBLS	10//99-12/99
	Lawrence MSA, KS	S	17.61 MW	16.02 AW	36620 AAW	KSBLS	10//99-12/99
	Wichita MSA, KS	S	21.34 MW	23.02 AW	44380 AAW	KSBLS	10//99-12/99
	Kentucky	S	13.05 MW	15.54 AW	32330 AAW	KYBLS	10//99-12/99
	Lexington MSA, KY	S	18.68 MW	16.41 AW	38850 AAW	KYBLS	10//99-12/99
	Louisville MSA, KY-IN	S	18.84 MW	17.15 AW	39190 AAW	KYBLS	10//99-12/99
	Louisiana	S	13.7 MW	15.76 AW	32770 AAW	LABLS	10//99-12/99
	Alexandria MSA, LA	S	15.47 MW	15.69 AW	32170 AAW	LABLS	10//99-12/99
	Baton Rouge MSA, LA	S	16.23 MW	14.64 AW	33760 AAW	LABLS	10//99-12/99
	Lafayette MSA, LA	S	15.33 MW	13.24 AW	31880 AAW	LABLS	10//99-12/99
	New Orleans MSA, LA	S	15.28 MW	12.29 AW	31780 AAW	LABLS	10//99-12/99
	Shreveport-Bossier City MSA, LA	S	19.22 MW	15.63 AW	39980 AAW	LABLS	10//99-12/99
	Maine	S	15.74 MW	16.64 AW	34600 AAW	MEBLS	10//99-12/99
	Portland MSA, ME	S	18.02 MW	16.14 AW	37480 AAW	MEBLS	10//99-12/99
	Maryland	S	17.45 MW	19.37 AW	40300 AAW	MDBLS	10//99-12/99
	Baltimore PMSA, MD	S	21.77 MW	18.99 AW	45290 AAW	MDBLS	10//99-12/99
	Massachusetts	S	22.03 MW	22.74 AW	47310 AAW	MABLS	10//99-12/99
	Boston PMSA, MA-NH	S	23.22 MW	22.48 AW	48290 AAW	MABLS	10//99-12/99
	Springfield MSA, MA	S	18.00 MW	16.47 AW	37450 AAW	MABLS	10//99-12/99
	Worcester PMSA, MA-CT	S	22.37 MW	20.56 AW	46530 AAW	MABLS	10//99-12/99
	Minnesota	S	17.39 MW	19.88 AW	41340 AAW	MNBLS	10//99-12/99
	Minneapolis-St. Paul MSA, MN-WI	S	21.07 MW	18.43 AW	43820 AAW	MNBLS	10//99-12/99
	St. Cloud MSA, MN	S	9.88 MW	10.90 AW	20560 AAW	MNBLS	10//99-12/99
	Mississippi	S	15.16 MW	15.29 AW	31790 AAW	MSBLS	10//99-12/99
	Biloxi-Gulfport-Pascagoula MSA, MS	S	16.60 MW	15.76 AW	34530 AAW	MSBLS	10//99-12/99
	Jackson MSA, MS	S	14.40 MW	14.75 AW	29960 AAW	MSBLS	10//99-12/99
	Missouri	S	12.53 MW	14.36 AW	29860 AAW	MOBLS	10//99-12/99
	Kansas City MSA, MO-KS	S	17.43 MW	15.19 AW	36240 AAW	MOBLS	10//99-12/99
	St. Louis MSA, MO-IL	S	17.98 MW	17.28 AW	37400 AAW	MOBLS	10//99-12/99
	Montana	S	13.47 MW	14.38 AW	29900 AAW	MTBLS	10//99-12/99
	Billings MSA, MT	S	20.58 MW	20.06 AW	42810 AAW	MTBLS	10//99-12/99
	Nebraska	S	17.59 MW	17.12 AW	35620 AAW	NEBLS	10//99-12/99
	Lincoln MSA, NE	S	12.76 MW	8.35 AW	26530 AAW	NEBLS	10//99-12/99
	Omaha MSA, NE-IA	S	17.91 MW	18.22 AW	37250 AAW	NEBLS	10//99-12/99
	Nevada	S	20 MW	21.90 AW	45550 AAW	NVBLS	10//99-12/99
	Las Vegas MSA, NV-AZ	S	22.79 MW	20.71 AW	47410 AAW	NVBLS	10//99-12/99
	Reno MSA, NV	S	20.18 MW	19.38 AW	41980 AAW	NVBLS	10//99-12/99
	New Hampshire	S	17.9 MW	18.15 AW	37760 AAW	NHBLS	10//99-12/99
	Nashua PMSA, NH	S	20.19 MW	19.03 AW	41990 AAW	NHBLS	10//99-12/99
	New Jersey	S	19.76 MW	21.84 AW	45430 AAW	NJBLS	10//99-12/99
	Bergen-Passaic PMSA, NJ	S	19.71 MW	18.35 AW	41010 AAW	NJBLS	10//99-12/99
	Middlesex-Somerset-Hunterdon PMSA, NJ	S	20.73 MW	20.74 AW	43120 AAW	NJBLS	10//99-12/99
	Monmouth-Ocean PMSA, NJ	S	24.27 MW	22.75 AW	50480 AAW	NJBLS	10//99-12/99
	Newark PMSA, NJ	S	24.49 MW	16.69 AW	50940 AAW	NJBLS	10//99-12/99
	Trenton PMSA, NJ	S	20.04 MW	17.37 AW	41690 AAW	NJBLS	10//99-12/99

AAW Average annual wage	**AOH** Average offered, high	**ASH** Average starting, high	**H** Hourly	**M** Monthly	**S** Special: hourly and annual
AE Average entry wage	**AOL** Average offered, low	**ASL** Average starting, low	**HI** Highest wage paid	**MTC** Median total compensation	**TQ** Third quartile wage
AEX Average experienced wage	**APH** Average pay, high range	**AW** Average wage paid	**HR** High end range	**MW** Median wage paid	**W** Weekly
AO Average offered	**APL** Average pay, low range	**FQ** First quartile wage	**LR** Low end range	**SQ** Second quartile wage	**Y** Yearly

Occupation/Type/Industry	Location	Per	Low	Mid	High	Source	Date
Editor	New Mexico	S	17.09 MW	17.83 AW	37090 AAW	NMBLS	10//99-12//99
	Albuquerque MSA, NM	S	17.48 MW	17.05 AW	36360 AAW	NMBLS	10//99-12//99
	Santa Fe MSA, NM	S	20.85 MW	15.62 AW	43360 AAW	NMBLS	10//99-12//99
	New York PMSA, NY	S	28.67 MW	23.75 AW	59630 AAW	NYBLS	10//99-12//99
	North Carolina	S	15.87 MW	17.53 AW	36450 AAW	NCBLS	10//99-12//99
	Asheville MSA, NC	S	17.30 MW	15.91 AW	35990 AAW	NCBLS	10//99-12//99
	Charlotte-Gastonia-Rock Hill MSA, NC-SC	S	19.35 MW	19.22 AW	40250 AAW	NCBLS	10//99-12//99
	Greensboro--Winston-Salem-- High Point MSA, NC	S	15.57 MW	15.14 AW	32380 AAW	NCBLS	10//99-12//99
	Hickory-Morganton-Lenoir MSA, NC	S	14.27 MW	12.59 AW	29680 AAW	NCBLS	10//99-12//99
	Raleigh-Durham-Chapel Hill MSA, NC	S	19.01 MW	16.55 AW	39550 AAW	NCBLS	10//99-12//99
	North Dakota	S	15.52 MW	15.84 AW	32950 AAW	NDBLS	10//99-12//99
	Bismarck MSA, ND	S	16.04 MW	15.93 AW	33360 AAW	NDBLS	10//99-12//99
	Grand Forks MSA, ND-MN	S	15.83 MW	16.11 AW	32920 AAW	NDBLS	10//99-12//99
	Ohio	S	15.77 MW	17.07 AW	35500 AAW	OHBLS	10//99-12//99
	Akron PMSA, OH	S	17.14 MW	15.81 AW	35650 AAW	OHBLS	10//99-12//99
	Canton-Massillon MSA, OH	S	17.71 MW	15.83 AW	36830 AAW	OHBLS	10//99-12//99
	Cincinnati PMSA, OH-KY-IN	S	17.21 MW	15.91 AW	35790 AAW	OHBLS	10//99-12//99
	Cleveland-Lorain-Elyria PMSA, OH	S	18.70 MW	17.25 AW	38890 AAW	OHBLS	10//99-12//99
	Columbus MSA, OH	S	15.91 MW	14.67 AW	33100 AAW	OHBLS	10//99-12//99
	Dayton-Springfield MSA, OH	S	14.86 MW	12.88 AW	30920 AAW	OHBLS	10//99-12//99
	Lima MSA, OH	S	15.77 MW	14.92 AW	32790 AAW	OHBLS	10//99-12//99
	Toledo MSA, OH	S	20.57 MW	21.78 AW	42790 AAW	OHBLS	10//99-12//99
	Youngstown-Warren MSA, OH	S	19.74 MW	20.39 AW	41070 AAW	OHBLS	10//99-12//99
	Oklahoma	S	10.25 MW	12.22 AW	25410 AAW	OKBLS	10//99-12//99
	Oklahoma City MSA, OK	S	13.85 MW	13.14 AW	28800 AAW	OKBLS	10//99-12//99
	Tulsa MSA, OK	S	13.58 MW	10.62 AW	28250 AAW	OKBLS	10//99-12//99
	Oregon	S	13.88 MW	15.77 AW	32800 AAW	ORBLS	10//99-12//99
	Corvallis MSA, OR	S	11.72 MW	9.74 AW	24380 AAW	ORBLS	10//99-12//99
	Eugene-Springfield MSA, OR	S	15.22 MW	12.39 AW	31650 AAW	ORBLS	10//99-12//99
	Portland-Vancouver PMSA, OR-WA	S	18.48 MW	16.98 AW	38440 AAW	ORBLS	10//99-12//99
	Pennsylvania	S	19 MW	20.99 AW	43660 AAW	PABLS	10//99-12//99
	Allentown-Bethlehem-Easton MSA, PA	S	17.78 MW	17.03 AW	36980 AAW	PABLS	10//99-12//99
	Erie MSA, PA	S	18.31 MW	18.92 AW	38090 AAW	PABLS	10//99-12//99
	Harrisburg-Lebanon-Carlisle MSA, PA	S	22.29 MW	22.51 AW	46360 AAW	PABLS	10//99-12//99
	Johnstown MSA, PA	S	17.77 MW	17.99 AW	36950 AAW	PABLS	10//99-12//99
	Lancaster MSA, PA	S	19.05 MW	18.39 AW	39620 AAW	PABLS	10//99-12//99
	Philadelphia PMSA, PA-NJ	S	22.95 MW	20.11 AW	47740 AAW	PABLS	10//99-12//99
	Pittsburgh MSA, PA	S	17.76 MW	17.67 AW	36930 AAW	PABLS	10//99-12//99
	Scranton--Wilkes-Barre-- Hazleton MSA, PA	S	19.07 MW	16.44 AW	39660 AAW	PABLS	10//99-12//99
	Rhode Island	S	18.77 MW	19.52 AW	40590 AAW	RIBLS	10//99-12//99
	Providence-Fall River- Warwick MSA, RI-MA	S	20.30 MW	19.27 AW	42230 AAW	RIBLS	10//99-12//99
	South Carolina	S	16.64 MW	18.48 AW	38450 AAW	SCBLS	10//99-12//99
	Charleston-North Charleston MSA, SC	S	13.23 MW	12.47 AW	27510 AAW	SCBLS	10//99-12//99
	Greenville-Spartanburg- Anderson MSA, SC	S	18.29 MW	16.44 AW	38030 AAW	SCBLS	10//99-12//99
	South Dakota	S	10.95 MW	12.06 AW	25080 AAW	SDBLS	10//99-12//99
	Rapid City MSA, SD	S	13.42 MW	12.64 AW	27900 AAW	SDBLS	10//99-12//99
	Sioux Falls MSA, SD	S	16.46 MW	15.42 AW	34230 AAW	SDBLS	10//99-12//99
	Tennessee	S	18.06 MW	19.22 AW	39980 AAW	TNBLS	10//99-12//99
	Chattanooga MSA, TN-GA	S	15.70 MW	14.54 AW	32660 AAW	TNBLS	10//99-12//99
	Knoxville MSA, TN	S	17.28 MW	17.72 AW	35940 AAW	TNBLS	10//99-12//99
	Memphis MSA, TN-AR-MS	S	21.95 MW	22.95 AW	45660 AAW	MSBLS	10//99-12//99
	Nashville MSA, TN	S	19.52 MW	17.87 AW	40590 AAW	TNBLS	10//99-12//99
	Texas	S	16.08 MW	17.35 AW	36080 AAW	TXBLS	10//99-12//99
	Amarillo MSA, TX	S	15.32 MW	12.99 AW	31870 AAW	TXBLS	10//99-12//99
	Austin-San Marcos MSA, TX	S	15.93 MW	14.09 AW	33140 AAW	TXBLS	10//99-12//99
	Beaumont-Port Arthur MSA, TX	S	15.63 MW	14.34 AW	32500 AAW	TXBLS	10//99-12//99
	Bryan-College Station MSA, TX	S	22.31 MW	23.04 AW	46400 AAW	TXBLS	10//99-12//99
	Corpus Christi MSA, TX	S	11.53 MW	10.18 AW	23970 AAW	TXBLS	10//99-12//99

AAW Average annual wage	**AOH** Average offered, high	**ASH** Average starting, high	**H** Hourly	**M** Monthly	**S** Special: hourly and annual
AE Average entry wage	**AOL** Average offered, low	**ASL** Average starting, low	**HI** Highest wage paid	**MTC** Median total compensation	**TQ** Third quartile wage
AEX Average experienced wage	**APH** Average pay, high range	**AW** Average wage paid	**HR** High end range	**MW** Median wage paid	**W** Weekly
AO Average offered	**APL** Average pay, low range	**FQ** First quartile wage	**LR** Low end range	**SQ** Second quartile wage	**Y** Yearly

Occupation/Type/Industry	Location	Per	Low	Mid	High	Source	Date
Editor	Dallas PMSA, TX	S	17.29 MW	15.78 AW	35950 AAW	TXBLS	10//99-12//99
	Fort Worth-Arlington PMSA, TX	S	19.75 MW	19.06 AW	41080 AAW	TXBLS	10//99-12//99
	Houston PMSA, TX	S	19.78 MW	18.88 AW	41150 AAW	TXBLS	10//99-12//99
	Killeen-Temple MSA, TX	S	17.31 MW	17.37 AW	36000 AAW	TXBLS	10//99-12//99
	Lubbock MSA, TX	S	12.88 MW	12.12 AW	26790 AAW	TXBLS	10//99-12//99
	San Antonio MSA, TX	S	17.06 MW	16.27 AW	35490 AAW	TXBLS	10//99-12//99
	Waco MSA, TX	S	16.91 MW	15.45 AW	35160 AAW	TXBLS	10//99-12//99
	Provo-Orem MSA, UT	S	19.15 MW	19.03 AW	39840 AAW	UTBLS	10//99-12//99
	Salt Lake City-Ogden MSA, UT	S	22.26 MW	23.63 AW	46300 AAW	UTBLS	10//99-12//99
	Vermont	S	14.09 MW	15.00 AW	31200 AAW	VTBLS	10//99-12//99
	Burlington MSA, VT	S	12.76 MW	10.52 AW	26540 AAW	VTBLS	10//99-12//99
	Virginia	S	19.11 MW	20.81 AW	43290 AAW	VABLS	10//99-12//99
	Charlottesville MSA, VA	S	20.79 MW	16.78 AW	43240 AAW	VABLS	10//99-12//99
	Norfolk-Virginia Beach-Newport News MSA, VA-NC	S	22.29 MW	19.26 AW	46370 AAW	VABLS	10//99-12//99
	Richmond-Petersburg MSA, VA	S	22.80 MW	21.25 AW	47420 AAW	VABLS	10//99-12//99
	Roanoke MSA, VA	S	17.74 MW	15.53 AW	36890 AAW	VABLS	10//99-12//99
	Washington	S	22.38 MW	22.64 AW	47080 AAW	WABLS	10//99-12//99
	Bellingham MSA, WA	S	18.04 MW	17.23 AW	37520 AAW	WABLS	10//99-12//99
	Richland-Kennewick-Pasco MSA, WA	S	24.11 MW	23.67 AW	50160 AAW	WABLS	10//99-12//99
	Seattle-Bellevue-Everett PMSA, WA	S	24.48 MW	23.90 AW	50910 AAW	WABLS	10//99-12//99
	Spokane MSA, WA	S	19.77 MW	16.32 AW	41110 AAW	WABLS	10//99-12//99
	Tacoma PMSA, WA	S	19.15 MW	22.05 AW	39820 AAW	WABLS	10//99-12//99
	West Virginia	S	14.85 MW	14.36 AW	29880 AAW	WVBLS	10//99-12//99
	Wisconsin	S	15.09 MW	15.80 AW	32860 AAW	WIBLS	10//99-12//99
	Appleton-Oshkosh-Neenah MSA, WI	S	18.23 MW	17.92 AW	37910 AAW	WIBLS	10//99-12//99
	Eau Claire MSA, WI	S	13.10 MW	10.59 AW	27250 AAW	WIBLS	10//99-12//99
	Janesville-Beloit MSA, WI	S	16.50 MW	17.01 AW	34330 AAW	WIBLS	10//99-12//99
	Kenosha PMSA, WI	S	13.92 MW	12.94 AW	28950 AAW	WIBLS	10//99-12//99
	Madison MSA, WI	S	15.60 MW	15.97 AW	32450 AAW	WIBLS	10//99-12//99
	Milwaukee-Waukesha PMSA, WI	S	15.82 MW	14.46 AW	32900 AAW	WIBLS	10//99-12//99
	Wyoming	S	12.51 MW	12.48 AW	25950 AAW	WYBLS	10//99-12//99
	Puerto Rico	S	18.4 MW	19.58 AW	40730 AAW	PRBLS	10//99-12//99
	San Juan-Bayamon PMSA, PR	S	20.23 MW	19.18 AW	42080 AAW	PRBLS	10//99-12//99
Newspaper, 10 Years Experienc	Utica, NY	Y		36000 AW		CJR	1999
Newspaper, 10 Years Experienc	Gainsville, TX	Y		25000 AW		CJR	1999
Newspaper, 28 Years Experienc	Racine, WI	Y		69000 AW		CJR	1999
Newspaper, 30 Years Experience	Greenville, TX	Y		35000 AW		CJR	1999
Newspaper, 5-10 Years Experience	Defiance, OH	Y		40000 AW		CJR	1999
Publishing, Revenues $10-99.9 million	United States	Y		42833 AW		PUBWK	1999
Publishing, Revenues $100+ million	United States	Y		41320 AW		PUBWK	1999
Publishing, Revenues under $10 million	United States	Y		45000 AW		PUBWK	1999
Editor, Reporter	United States	H		23.35 AW		NCS98	1998
Editorial Assistant							
Publishing, Revenues $10-99.9 million	United States	Y		28933 AW		PUBWK	1999
Publishing, Revenues $100+ million	United States	Y		28150 AW		PUBWK	1999
Publishing, Revenues under $10 million	United States	Y		24283 AW		PUBWK	1999
Education Administrator							
Elementary and Secondary School	Alabama	Y		58050 AAW		ALBLS	10//99-12//99
Elementary and Secondary School	Anniston MSA, AL	Y		47890 AAW		ALBLS	10//99-12//99
Elementary and Secondary School	Auburn-Opelika MSA, AL	Y		52150 AAW		ALBLS	10//99-12//99
Elementary and Secondary School	Birmingham MSA, AL	Y		62770 AAW		ALBLS	10//99-12//99
Elementary and Secondary School	Decatur MSA, AL	Y		59120 AAW		ALBLS	10//99-12//99
Elementary and Secondary School	Dothan MSA, AL	Y		62290 AAW		ALBLS	10//99-12//99
Elementary and Secondary School	Florence MSA, AL	Y		58960 AAW		ALBLS	10//99-12//99
Elementary and Secondary School	Huntsville MSA, AL	Y		64770 AAW		ALBLS	10//99-12//99
Elementary and Secondary School	Montgomery MSA, AL	Y		42430 AAW		ALBLS	10//99-12//99
Elementary and Secondary School	Alaska	Y		69870 AAW		AKBLS	10//99-12//99
Elementary and Secondary School	Arizona	Y		62100 AAW		AZBLS	10//99-12//99
Elementary and Secondary School	Flagstaff MSA, AZ-UT	Y		46820 AAW		AZBLS	10//99-12//99
Elementary and Secondary School	Phoenix-Mesa MSA, AZ	Y		64230 AAW		AZBLS	10//99-12//99
Elementary and Secondary School	Tucson MSA, AZ	Y		61040 AAW		AZBLS	10//99-12//99

AAW	Average annual wage	AOH	Average offered, high	ASH	Average starting, high	H	Hourly	M	Monthly
AE	Average entry wage	AOL	Average offered, low	ASL	Average starting, low	HI	Highest wage paid	MTC	Median total compensation
AEX	Average experienced wage	APH	Average pay, high range	AW	Average wage paid	HR	High end range	MW	Median wage paid
AO	Average offered	APL	Average pay, low range	FQ	First quartile wage	LR	Low end range	SQ	Second quartile wage

S Special: hourly and annual
TQ Third quartile wage
W Weekly
Y Yearly

Occupation/Type/Industry	Location	Per	Low	Mid	High	Source	Date
Education Administrator							
Elementary and Secondary School	Arkansas	Y		54610 AAW		ARBLS	10//99-12//99
Elementary and Secondary School	Fayetteville-Springdale-Rogers MSA, AR	Y		57680 AAW		ARBLS	10//99-12//99
Elementary and Secondary School	Fort Smith MSA, AR-OK	Y		56560 AAW		ARBLS	10//99-12//99
Elementary and Secondary School	Jonesboro MSA, AR	Y		47850 AAW		ARBLS	10//99-12//99
Elementary and Secondary School	Little Rock-North Little Rock MSA, AR	Y		59300 AAW		ARBLS	10//99-12//99
Elementary and Secondary School	California	Y		77940 AAW		CABLS	10//99-12//99
Elementary and Secondary School	Bakersfield MSA, CA	Y		66010 AAW		CABLS	10//99-12//99
Elementary and Secondary School	Fresno MSA, CA	Y		68190 AAW		CABLS	10//99-12//99
Elementary and Secondary School	Los Angeles-Long Beach PMSA, CA	Y		83710 AAW		CABLS	10//99-12//99
Elementary and Secondary School	Merced MSA, CA	Y		76160 AAW		CABLS	10//99-12//99
Elementary and Secondary School	Oakland PMSA, CA	Y		75060 AAW		CABLS	10//99-12//99
Elementary and Secondary School	Orange County PMSA, CA	Y		86990 AAW		CABLS	10//99-12//99
Elementary and Secondary School	Redding MSA, CA	Y		60660 AAW		CABLS	10//99-12//99
Elementary and Secondary School	Riverside-San Bernardino PMSA, CA	Y		73810 AAW		CABLS	10//99-12//99
Elementary and Secondary School	Sacramento PMSA, CA	Y		81530 AAW		CABLS	10//99-12//99
Elementary and Secondary School	Salinas MSA, CA	Y		74710 AAW		CABLS	10//99-12//99
Elementary and Secondary School	San Diego MSA, CA	Y		80420 AAW		CABLS	10//99-12//99
Elementary and Secondary School	San Francisco PMSA, CA	Y		78000 AAW		CABLS	10//99-12//99
Elementary and Secondary School	San Jose PMSA, CA	Y		89870 AAW		CABLS	10//99-12//99
Elementary and Secondary School	San Luis Obispo-Atascadero-Paso Robles MSA, CA	Y		73130 AAW		CABLS	10//99-12//99
Elementary and Secondary School	Santa Barbara-Santa Maria-Lompoc MSA, CA	Y		70740 AAW		CABLS	10//99-12//99
Elementary and Secondary School	Santa Rosa PMSA, CA	Y		70890 AAW		CABLS	10//99-12//99
Elementary and Secondary School	Stockton-Lodi MSA, CA	Y		79320 AAW		CABLS	10//99-12//99
Elementary and Secondary School	Vallejo-Fairfield-Napa PMSA, CA	Y		61970 AAW		CABLS	10//99-12//99
Elementary and Secondary School	Ventura PMSA, CA	Y		73960 AAW		CABLS	10//99-12//99
Elementary and Secondary School	Visalia-Tulare-Porterville MSA, CA	Y		77240 AAW		CABLS	10//99-12//99
Elementary and Secondary School	Yolo PMSA, CA	Y		73720 AAW		CABLS	10//99-12//99
Elementary and Secondary School	Yuba City MSA, CA	Y		62630 AAW		CABLS	10//99-12//99
Elementary and Secondary School	Colorado	Y		62950 AAW		COBLS	10//99-12//99
Elementary and Secondary School	Denver PMSA, CO	Y		64180 AAW		COBLS	10//99-12//99
Elementary and Secondary School	Connecticut	Y		80650 AAW		CTBLS	10//99-12//99
Elementary and Secondary School	Bridgeport PMSA, CT	Y		87130 AAW		CTBLS	10//99-12//99
Elementary and Secondary School	Danbury PMSA, CT	Y		72610 AAW		CTBLS	10//99-12//99
Elementary and Secondary School	Hartford MSA, CT	Y		82440 AAW		CTBLS	10//99-12//99
Elementary and Secondary School	New Haven-Meriden PMSA, CT	Y		82250 AAW		CTBLS	10//99-12//99
Elementary and Secondary School	New London-Norwich MSA, CT-RI	Y		77370 AAW		CTBLS	10//99-12//99
Elementary and Secondary School	Stamford-Norwalk PMSA, CT	Y		77060 AAW		CTBLS	10//99-12//99
Elementary and Secondary School	Waterbury PMSA, CT	Y		78050 AAW		CTBLS	10//99-12//99
Elementary and Secondary School	District of Columbia	Y		110420 AAW		DCBLS	10//99-12//99
Elementary and Secondary School	Washington PMSA, DC-MD-VA-WV	Y		69440 AAW		DCBLS	10//99-12//99
Elementary and Secondary School	Florida	Y		60580 AAW		FLBLS	10//99-12//99
Elementary and Secondary School	Fort Myers-Cape Coral MSA, FL	Y		45940 AAW		FLBLS	10//99-12//99
Elementary and Secondary School	Fort Pierce-Port St. Lucie MSA, FL	Y		66610 AAW		FLBLS	10//99-12//99
Elementary and Secondary School	Jacksonville MSA, FL	Y		62940 AAW		FLBLS	10//99-12//99
Elementary and Secondary School	Miami PMSA, FL	Y		51840 AAW		FLBLS	10//99-12//99
Elementary and Secondary School	Orlando MSA, FL	Y		59310 AAW		FLBLS	10//99-12//99
Elementary and Secondary School	Pensacola MSA, FL	Y		61790 AAW		FLBLS	10//99-12//99
Elementary and Secondary School	Sarasota-Bradenton MSA, FL	Y		72420 AAW		FLBLS	10//99-12//99
Elementary and Secondary School	Tampa-St. Petersburg-Clearwater MSA, FL	Y		62200 AAW		FLBLS	10//99-12//99
Elementary and Secondary School	West Palm Beach-Boca Raton MSA, FL	Y		77230 AAW		FLBLS	10//99-12//99
Elementary and Secondary School	Georgia	Y		64360 AAW		GABLS	10//99-12//99
Elementary and Secondary School	Athens MSA, GA	Y		65110 AAW		GABLS	10//99-12//99
Elementary and Secondary School	Atlanta MSA, GA	Y		67260 AAW		GABLS	10//99-12//99
Elementary and Secondary School	Augusta-Aiken MSA, GA-SC	Y		61380 AAW		GABLS	10//99-12//99
Elementary and Secondary School	Columbus MSA, GA-AL	Y		52690 AAW		GABLS	10//99-12//99
Elementary and Secondary School	Macon MSA, GA	Y		62580 AAW		GABLS	10//99-12//99

AAW Average annual wage	AOH Average offered, high	ASH Average starting, high	H Hourly	M Monthly	S Special: hourly and annual
AE Average entry wage	AOL Average offered, low	ASL Average starting, low	HI Highest wage paid	MTC Median total compensation	TQ Third quartile wage
AEX Average experienced wage	APH Average pay, high range	AW Average wage paid	HR High end range	MW Median wage paid	W Weekly
AO Average offered	APL Average pay, low range	FQ First quartile wage	LR Low end range	SQ Second quartile wage	Y Yearly

Occupation/Type/Industry	Location	Per	Low	Mid	High	Source	Date
Education Administrator							
Elementary and Secondary School	Savannah MSA, GA	Y		51160 AAW		GABLS	10//99-12//99
Elementary and Secondary School	Hawaii	Y		62930 AAW		HIBLS	10//99-12//99
Elementary and Secondary School	Honolulu MSA, HI	Y		72840 AAW		HIBLS	10//99-12//99
Elementary and Secondary School	Idaho	Y		56520 AAW		IDBLS	10//99-12//99
Elementary and Secondary School	Boise City MSA, ID	Y		64090 AAW		IDBLS	10//99-12//99
Elementary and Secondary School	Illinois	Y		71270 AAW		ILBLS	10//99-12//99
Elementary and Secondary School	Bloomington-Normal MSA, IL	Y		84570 AAW		ILBLS	10//99-12//99
Elementary and Secondary School	Champaign-Urbana MSA, IL	Y		66250 AAW		ILBLS	10//99-12//99
Elementary and Secondary School	Chicago PMSA, IL	Y		76540 AAW		ILBLS	10//99-12//99
Elementary and Secondary School	Kankakee PMSA, IL	Y		64890 AAW		ILBLS	10//99-12//99
Elementary and Secondary School	Peoria-Pekin MSA, IL	Y		61740 AAW		ILBLS	10//99-12//99
Elementary and Secondary School	Rockford MSA, IL	Y		64640 AAW		ILBLS	10//99-12//99
Elementary and Secondary School	Springfield MSA, IL	Y		56580 AAW		ILBLS	10//99-12//99
Elementary and Secondary School	Indiana	Y		63140 AAW		INBLS	10//99-12//99
Elementary and Secondary School	Elkhart-Goshen MSA, IN	Y		69930 AAW		INBLS	10//99-12//99
Elementary and Secondary School	Evansville-Henderson MSA, IN-KY	Y		47720 AAW		INBLS	10//99-12//99
Elementary and Secondary School	Fort Wayne MSA, IN	Y		64710 AAW		INBLS	10//99-12//99
Elementary and Secondary School	Gary PMSA, IN	Y		63220 AAW		INBLS	10//99-12//99
Elementary and Secondary School	Indianapolis MSA, IN	Y		63930 AAW		INBLS	10//99-12//99
Elementary and Secondary School	Kokomo MSA, IN	Y		61310 AAW		INBLS	10//99-12//99
Elementary and Secondary School	Lafayette MSA, IN	Y		64150 AAW		INBLS	10//99-12//99
Elementary and Secondary School	Terre Haute MSA, IN	Y		57490 AAW		INBLS	10//99-12//99
Elementary and Secondary School	Iowa	Y		58070 AAW		IABLS	10//99-12//99
Elementary and Secondary School	Cedar Rapids MSA, IA	Y		54190 AAW		IABLS	10//99-12//99
Elementary and Secondary School	Davenport-Moline-Rock Island MSA, IA-IL	Y		68820 AAW		IABLS	10//99-12//99
Elementary and Secondary School	Des Moines MSA, IA	Y		63670 AAW		IABLS	10//99-12//99
Elementary and Secondary School	Dubuque MSA, IA	Y		60250 AAW		IABLS	10//99-12//99
Elementary and Secondary School	Sioux City MSA, IA-NE	Y		79230 AAW		IABLS	10//99-12//99
Elementary and Secondary School	Waterloo-Cedar Falls MSA, IA	Y		59730 AAW		IABLS	10//99-12//99
Elementary and Secondary School	Kansas	Y		56810 AAW		KSBLS	10//99-12//99
Elementary and Secondary School	Wichita MSA, KS	Y		56160 AAW		KSBLS	10//99-12//99
Elementary and Secondary School	Kentucky	Y		56820 AAW		KYBLS	10//99-12//99
Elementary and Secondary School	Lexington MSA, KY	Y		57930 AAW		KYBLS	10//99-12//99
Elementary and Secondary School	Louisville MSA, KY-IN	Y		59540 AAW		KYBLS	10//99-12//99
Elementary and Secondary School	Louisiana	Y		52030 AAW		LABLS	10//99-12//99
Elementary and Secondary School	Baton Rouge MSA, LA	Y		56010 AAW		LABLS	10//99-12//99
Elementary and Secondary School	New Orleans MSA, LA	Y		53490 AAW		LABLS	10//99-12//99
Elementary and Secondary School	Shreveport-Bossier City MSA, LA	Y		50760 AAW		LABLS	10//99-12//99
Elementary and Secondary School	Maine	Y		52510 AAW		MEBLS	10//99-12//99
Elementary and Secondary School	Bangor MSA, ME	Y		49770 AAW		MEBLS	10//99-12//99
Elementary and Secondary School	Lewiston-Auburn MSA, ME	Y		44720 AAW		MEBLS	10//99-12//99
Elementary and Secondary School	Portland MSA, ME	Y		58200 AAW		MEBLS	10//99-12//99
Elementary and Secondary School	Maryland	Y		67220 AAW		MDBLS	10//99-12//99
Elementary and Secondary School	Baltimore PMSA, MD	Y		66110 AAW		MDBLS	10//99-12//99
Elementary and Secondary School	Massachusetts	Y		66020 AAW		MABLS	10//99-12//99
Elementary and Secondary School	Barnstable-Yarmouth MSA, MA	Y		64060 AAW		MABLS	10//99-12//99
Elementary and Secondary School	Boston PMSA, MA-NH	Y		67930 AAW		MABLS	10//99-12//99
Elementary and Secondary School	Brockton PMSA, MA	Y		69460 AAW		MABLS	10//99-12//99
Elementary and Secondary School	Fitchburg-Leominster PMSA, MA	Y		62240 AAW		MABLS	10//99-12//99
Elementary and Secondary School	Lawrence PMSA, MA-NH	Y		73880 AAW		MABLS	10//99-12//99
Elementary and Secondary School	Lowell PMSA, MA-NH	Y		70640 AAW		MABLS	10//99-12//99
Elementary and Secondary School	Pittsfield MSA, MA	Y		65690 AAW		MABLS	10//99-12//99
Elementary and Secondary School	Springfield MSA, MA	Y		56540 AAW		MABLS	10//99-12//99
Elementary and Secondary School	Worcester PMSA, MA-CT	Y		67010 AAW		MABLS	10//99-12//99
Elementary and Secondary School	Ann Arbor PMSA, MI	Y		73510 AAW		MIBLS	10//99-12//99
Elementary and Secondary School	Benton Harbor MSA, MI	Y		61820 AAW		MIBLS	10//99-12//99
Elementary and Secondary School	Detroit PMSA, MI	Y		72640 AAW		MIBLS	10//99-12//99
Elementary and Secondary School	Flint PMSA, MI	Y		71270 AAW		MIBLS	10//99-12//99
Elementary and Secondary School	Grand Rapids-Muskegon-Holland MSA, MI	Y		69790 AAW		MIBLS	10//99-12//99
Elementary and Secondary School	Jackson MSA, MI	Y		61970 AAW		MIBLS	10//99-12//99
Elementary and Secondary School	Kalamazoo-Battle Creek MSA, MI	Y		66490 AAW		MIBLS	10//99-12//99
Elementary and Secondary School	Lansing-East Lansing MSA, MI	Y		65340 AAW		MIBLS	10//99-12//99
Elementary and Secondary School	Saginaw-Bay City-Midland MSA, MI	Y		69860 AAW		MIBLS	10//99-12//99

AAW Average annual wage	**AOH** Average offered, high	**ASH** Average starting, high	**H** Hourly	**M** Monthly	**S** Special: hourly and annual
AE Average entry wage	**AOL** Average offered, low	**ASL** Average starting, low	**HI** Highest wage paid	**MTC** Median total compensation	**TQ** Third quartile wage
AEX Average experienced wage	**APH** Average pay, high range	**AW** Average wage paid	**HR** High end range	**MW** Median wage paid	**W** Weekly
AO Average offered	**APL** Average pay, low range	**FQ** First quartile wage	**LR** Low end range	**SQ** Second quartile wage	**Y** Yearly

Occupation/Type/Industry	Location	Per	Low	Mid	High	Source	Date
Education Administrator							
Elementary and Secondary School	Minnesota	Y		70510 AAW		MNBLS	10//99-12//99
Elementary and Secondary School	Duluth-Superior MSA, MN-WI	Y		60440 AAW		MNBLS	10//99-12//99
Elementary and Secondary School	Minneapolis-St. Paul MSA, MN-WI	Y		75710 AAW		MNBLS	10//99-12//99
Elementary and Secondary School	St. Cloud MSA, MN	Y		72520 AAW		MNBLS	10//99-12//99
Elementary and Secondary School	Mississippi	Y		53200 AAW		MSBLS	10//99-12//99
Elementary and Secondary School	Biloxi-Gulfport-Pascagoula MSA, MS	Y		58710 AAW		MSBLS	10//99-12//99
Elementary and Secondary School	Hattiesburg MSA, MS	Y		51970 AAW		MSBLS	10//99-12//99
Elementary and Secondary School	Jackson MSA, MS	Y		50160 AAW		MSBLS	10//99-12//99
Elementary and Secondary School	Missouri	Y		59570 AAW		MOBLS	10//99-12//99
Elementary and Secondary School	Columbia MSA, MO	Y		45530 AAW		MOBLS	10//99-12//99
Elementary and Secondary School	Joplin MSA, MO	Y		50340 AAW		MOBLS	10//99-12//99
Elementary and Secondary School	Kansas City MSA, MO-KS	Y		62220 AAW		MOBLS	10//99-12//99
Elementary and Secondary School	St. Joseph MSA, MO	Y		63690 AAW		MOBLS	10//99-12//99
Elementary and Secondary School	St. Louis MSA, MO-IL	Y		65510 AAW		MOBLS	10//99-12//99
Elementary and Secondary School	Springfield MSA, MO	Y		56930 AAW		MOBLS	10//99-12//99
Elementary and Secondary School	Montana	Y		51170 AAW		MTBLS	10//99-12//99
Elementary and Secondary School	Great Falls MSA, MT	Y		44850 AAW		MTBLS	10//99-12//99
Elementary and Secondary School	Missoula MSA, MT	Y		55040 AAW		MTBLS	10//99-12//99
Elementary and Secondary School	Nebraska	Y		60320 AAW		NEBLS	10//99-12//99
Elementary and Secondary School	Omaha MSA, NE-IA	Y		57890 AAW		NEBLS	10//99-12//99
Elementary and Secondary School	Nevada	Y		66840 AAW		NVBLS	10//99-12//99
Elementary and Secondary School	Las Vegas MSA, NV-AZ	Y		95720 AAW		NVBLS	10//99-12//99
Elementary and Secondary School	New Hampshire	Y		55650 AAW		NHBLS	10//99-12//99
Elementary and Secondary School	Portsmouth-Rochester PMSA, NH-ME	Y		57060 AAW		NHBLS	10//99-12//99
Elementary and Secondary School	New Jersey	Y		83750 AAW		NJBLS	10//99-12//99
Elementary and Secondary School	Atlantic-Cape May PMSA, NJ	Y		77210 AAW		NJBLS	10//99-12//99
Elementary and Secondary School	Bergen-Passaic PMSA, NJ	Y		96770 AAW		NJBLS	10//99-12//99
Elementary and Secondary School	Jersey City PMSA, NJ	Y		93440 AAW		NJBLS	10//99-12//99
Elementary and Secondary School	Middlesex-Somerset-Hunterdon PMSA, NJ	Y		86380 AAW		NJBLS	10//99-12//99
Elementary and Secondary School	Monmouth-Ocean PMSA, NJ	Y		85940 AAW		NJBLS	10//99-12//99
Elementary and Secondary School	Newark PMSA, NJ	Y		74760 AAW		NJBLS	10//99-12//99
Elementary and Secondary School	Trenton PMSA, NJ	Y		81500 AAW		NJBLS	10//99-12//99
Elementary and Secondary School	Vineland-Millville-Bridgeton PMSA, NJ	Y		77410 AAW		NJBLS	10//99-12//99
Elementary and Secondary School	New Mexico	Y		51430 AAW		NMBLS	10//99-12//99
Elementary and Secondary School	Albuquerque MSA, NM	Y		51070 AAW		NMBLS	10//99-12//99
Elementary and Secondary School	Santa Fe MSA, NM	Y		44330 AAW		NMBLS	10//99-12//99
Elementary and Secondary School	New York	Y		79960 AAW		NYBLS	10//99-12//99
Elementary and Secondary School	Binghamton MSA, NY	Y		72490 AAW		NYBLS	10//99-12//99
Elementary and Secondary School	Buffalo-Niagara Falls MSA, NY	Y		77680 AAW		NYBLS	10//99-12//99
Elementary and Secondary School	Dutchess County PMSA, NY	Y		75520 AAW		NYBLS	10//99-12//99
Elementary and Secondary School	Glens Falls MSA, NY	Y		66990 AAW		NYBLS	10//99-12//99
Elementary and Secondary School	Jamestown MSA, NY	Y		66080 AAW		NYBLS	10//99-12//99
Elementary and Secondary School	Nassau-Suffolk PMSA, NY	Y		89500 AAW		NYBLS	10//99-12//99
Elementary and Secondary School	New York PMSA, NY	Y		97440 AAW		NYBLS	10//99-12//99
Elementary and Secondary School	Newburgh PMSA, NY-PA	Y		67310 AAW		NYBLS	10//99-12//99
Elementary and Secondary School	Rochester MSA, NY	Y		78730 AAW		NYBLS	10//99-12//99
Elementary and Secondary School	Syracuse MSA, NY	Y		64390 AAW		NYBLS	10//99-12//99
Elementary and Secondary School	Utica-Rome MSA, NY	Y		66210 AAW		NYBLS	10//99-12//99
Elementary and Secondary School	North Carolina	Y		57400 AAW		NCBLS	10//99-12//99
Elementary and Secondary School	Asheville MSA, NC	Y		54840 AAW		NCBLS	10//99-12//99
Elementary and Secondary School	Charlotte-Gastonia-Rock Hill MSA, NC-SC	Y		60020 AAW		NCBLS	10//99-12//99
Elementary and Secondary School	Greensboro--Winston-Salem--High Point MSA, NC	Y		63930 AAW		NCBLS	10//99-12//99
Elementary and Secondary School	Hickory-Morganton-Lenoir MSA, NC	Y		51450 AAW		NCBLS	10//99-12//99
Elementary and Secondary School	Raleigh-Durham-Chapel Hill MSA, NC	Y		56560 AAW		NCBLS	10//99-12//99
Elementary and Secondary School	Rocky Mount MSA, NC	Y		51320 AAW		NCBLS	10//99-12//99
Elementary and Secondary School	Wilmington MSA, NC	Y		53860 AAW		NCBLS	10//99-12//99
Elementary and Secondary School	North Dakota	Y		51520 AAW		NDBLS	10//99-12//99
Elementary and Secondary School	Fargo-Moorhead MSA, ND-MN	Y		57510 AAW		NDBLS	10//99-12//99
Elementary and Secondary School	Grand Forks MSA, ND-MN	Y		59220 AAW		NDBLS	10//99-12//99
Elementary and Secondary School	Ohio	Y		62230 AAW		OHBLS	10//99-12//99

AAW Average annual wage	**AOH** Average offered, high	**ASH** Average starting, high	**H** Hourly	**M** Monthly	**S** Special: hourly and annual
AE Average entry wage	**AOL** Average offered, low	**ASL** Average starting, low	**HI** Highest wage paid	**MTC** Median total compensation	**TQ** Third quartile wage
AEX Average experienced wage	**APH** Average pay, high range	**AW** Average wage paid	**HR** High end range	**MW** Median wage paid	**W** Weekly
AO Average offered	**APL** Average pay, low range	**FQ** First quartile wage	**LR** Low end range	**SQ** Second quartile wage	**Y** Yearly

Occupation/Type/Industry	Location	Per	Low	Mid	High	Source	Date
Education Administrator							
Elementary and Secondary School	Akron PMSA, OH	Y		61420 AAW		OHBLS	10//99-12//99
Elementary and Secondary School	Canton-Massillon MSA, OH	Y		63400 AAW		OHBLS	10//99-12//99
Elementary and Secondary School	Cincinnati PMSA, OH-KY-IN	Y		61590 AAW		OHBLS	10//99-12//99
Elementary and Secondary School	Cleveland-Lorain-Elyria PMSA, OH	Y		68540 AAW		OHBLS	10//99-12//99
Elementary and Secondary School	Columbus MSA, OH	Y		70180 AAW		OHBLS	10//99-12//99
Elementary and Secondary School	Dayton-Springfield MSA, OH	Y		62000 AAW		OHBLS	10//99-12//99
Elementary and Secondary School	Hamilton-Middletown PMSA, OH	Y		62830 AAW		OHBLS	10//99-12//99
Elementary and Secondary School	Lima MSA, OH	Y		54420 AAW		OHBLS	10//99-12//99
Elementary and Secondary School	Mansfield MSA, OH	Y		62360 AAW		OHBLS	10//99-12//99
Elementary and Secondary School	Toledo MSA, OH	Y		61200 AAW		OHBLS	10//99-12//99
Elementary and Secondary School	Youngstown-Warren MSA, OH	Y		55660 AAW		OHBLS	10//99-12//99
Elementary and Secondary School	Oklahoma	Y		50780 AAW		OKBLS	10//99-12//99
Elementary and Secondary School	Enid MSA, OK	Y		32300 AAW		OKBLS	10//99-12//99
Elementary and Secondary School	Oklahoma City MSA, OK	Y		49490 AAW		OKBLS	10//99-12//99
Elementary and Secondary School	Tulsa MSA, OK	Y		58400 AAW		OKBLS	10//99-12//99
Elementary and Secondary School	Oregon	Y		68020 AAW		ORBLS	10//99-12//99
Elementary and Secondary School	Corvallis MSA, OR	Y		61460 AAW		ORBLS	10//99-12//99
Elementary and Secondary School	Medford-Ashland MSA, OR	Y		64610 AAW		ORBLS	10//99-12//99
Elementary and Secondary School	Portland-Vancouver PMSA, OR-WA	Y		71030 AAW		ORBLS	10//99-12//99
Elementary and Secondary School	Salem PMSA, OR	Y		67410 AAW		ORBLS	10//99-12//99
Elementary and Secondary School	Pennsylvania	Y		64400 AAW		PABLS	10//99-12//99
Elementary and Secondary School	Allentown-Bethlehem-Easton MSA, PA	Y		67620 AAW		PABLS	10//99-12//99
Elementary and Secondary School	Altoona MSA, PA	Y		61960 AAW		PABLS	10//99-12//99
Elementary and Secondary School	Erie MSA, PA	Y		66100 AAW		PABLS	10//99-12//99
Elementary and Secondary School	Harrisburg-Lebanon-Carlisle MSA, PA	Y		60640 AAW		PABLS	10//99-12//99
Elementary and Secondary School	Johnstown MSA, PA	Y		58850 AAW		PABLS	10//99-12//99
Elementary and Secondary School	Lancaster MSA, PA	Y		68180 AAW		PABLS	10//99-12//99
Elementary and Secondary School	Philadelphia PMSA, PA-NJ	Y		70430 AAW		PABLS	10//99-12//99
Elementary and Secondary School	Pittsburgh MSA, PA	Y		71060 AAW		PABLS	10//99-12//99
Elementary and Secondary School	Reading MSA, PA	Y		70630 AAW		PABLS	10//99-12//99
Elementary and Secondary School	Scranton--Wilkes-Barre--Hazleton MSA, PA	Y		43010 AAW		PABLS	10//99-12//99
Elementary and Secondary School	Sharon MSA, PA	Y		62450 AAW		PABLS	10//99-12//99
Elementary and Secondary School	State College MSA, PA	Y		63450 AAW		PABLS	10//99-12//99
Elementary and Secondary School	Williamsport MSA, PA	Y		44580 AAW		PABLS	10//99-12//99
Elementary and Secondary School	York MSA, PA	Y		64200 AAW		PABLS	10//99-12//99
Elementary and Secondary School	Rhode Island	Y		66010 AAW		RIBLS	10//99-12//99
Elementary and Secondary School	Providence-Fall River-Warwick MSA, RI-MA	Y		66630 AAW		RIBLS	10//99-12//99
Elementary and Secondary School	South Carolina	Y		60430 AAW		SCBLS	10//99-12//99
Elementary and Secondary School	Columbia MSA, SC	Y		63840 AAW		SCBLS	10//99-12//99
Elementary and Secondary School	Florence MSA, SC	Y		45110 AAW		SCBLS	10//99-12//99
Elementary and Secondary School	Greenville-Spartanburg-Anderson MSA, SC	Y		60620 AAW		SCBLS	10//99-12//99
Elementary and Secondary School	Sumter MSA, SC	Y		47070 AAW		SCBLS	10//99-12//99
Elementary and Secondary School	South Dakota	Y		48630 AAW		SDBLS	10//99-12//99
Elementary and Secondary School	Sioux Falls MSA, SD	Y		49050 AAW		SDBLS	10//99-12//99
Elementary and Secondary School	Tennessee	Y		55150 AAW		TNBLS	10//99-12//99
Elementary and Secondary School	Chattanooga MSA, TN-GA	Y		61620 AAW		TNBLS	10//99-12//99
Elementary and Secondary School	Johnson City-Kingsport-Bristol MSA, TN-VA	Y		44210 AAW		TNBLS	10//99-12//99
Elementary and Secondary School	Knoxville MSA, TN	Y		53130 AAW		TNBLS	10//99-12//99
Elementary and Secondary School	Memphis MSA, TN-AR-MS	Y		64670 AAW		MSBLS	10//99-12//99
Elementary and Secondary School	Nashville MSA, TN	Y		58280 AAW		TNBLS	10//99-12//99
Elementary and Secondary School	Texas	Y		57330 AAW		TXBLS	10//99-12//99
Elementary and Secondary School	Austin-San Marcos MSA, TX	Y		67230 AAW		TXBLS	10//99-12//99
Elementary and Secondary School	Beaumont-Port Arthur MSA, TX	Y		51990 AAW		TXBLS	10//99-12//99
Elementary and Secondary School	Bryan-College Station MSA, TX	Y		29620 AAW		TXBLS	10//99-12//99
Elementary and Secondary School	Corpus Christi MSA, TX	Y		66420 AAW		TXBLS	10//99-12//99
Elementary and Secondary School	Dallas PMSA, TX	Y		53190 AAW		TXBLS	10//99-12//99
Elementary and Secondary School	El Paso MSA, TX	Y		57420 AAW		TXBLS	10//99-12//99
Elementary and Secondary School	Fort Worth-Arlington PMSA, TX	Y		68320 AAW		TXBLS	10//99-12//99

Education Administrator

Occupation/Type/Industry	Location	Per	Low	Mid	High	Source	Date
Education Administrator							
Elementary and Secondary School	Galveston-Texas City PMSA, TX	Y		61100 AAW		TXBLS	10//99-12//99
Elementary and Secondary School	Houston PMSA, TX	Y		60680 AAW		TXBLS	10//99-12//99
Elementary and Secondary School	Killeen-Temple MSA, TX	Y		53300 AAW		TXBLS	10//99-12//99
Elementary and Secondary School	Longview-Marshall MSA, TX	Y		53310 AAW		TXBLS	10//99-12//99
Elementary and Secondary School	McAllen-Edinburg-Mission MSA, TX	Y		56790 AAW		TXBLS	10//99-12//99
Elementary and Secondary School	San Angelo MSA, TX	Y		43950 AAW		TXBLS	10//99-12//99
Elementary and Secondary School	San Antonio MSA, TX	Y		57790 AAW		TXBLS	10//99-12//99
Elementary and Secondary School	Sherman-Denison MSA, TX	Y		56880 AAW		TXBLS	10//99-12//99
Elementary and Secondary School	Texarkana MSA, TX-Texarkana, AR	Y		46990 AAW		TXBLS	10//99-12//99
Elementary and Secondary School	Waco MSA, TX	Y		53470 AAW		TXBLS	10//99-12//99
Elementary and Secondary School	Utah	Y		64230 AAW		UTBLS	10//99-12//99
Elementary and Secondary School	Provo-Orem MSA, UT	Y		63740 AAW		UTBLS	10//99-12//99
Elementary and Secondary School	Vermont	Y		56720 AAW		VTBLS	10//99-12//99
Elementary and Secondary School	Burlington MSA, VT	Y		60960 AAW		VTBLS	10//99-12//99
Elementary and Secondary School	Virginia	Y		60030 AAW		VABLS	10//99-12//99
Elementary and Secondary School	Charlottesville MSA, VA	Y		61090 AAW		VABLS	10//99-12//99
Elementary and Secondary School	Danville MSA, VA	Y		56760 AAW		VABLS	10//99-12//99
Elementary and Secondary School	Norfolk-Virginia Beach-Newport News MSA, VA-NC	Y		62520 AAW		VABLS	10//99-12//99
Elementary and Secondary School	Richmond-Petersburg MSA, VA	Y		58520 AAW		VABLS	10//99-12//99
Elementary and Secondary School	Roanoke MSA, VA	Y		57590 AAW		VABLS	10//99-12//99
Elementary and Secondary School	Washington	Y		72750 AAW		WABLS	10//99-12//99
Elementary and Secondary School	Bellingham MSA, WA	Y		73570 AAW		WABLS	10//99-12//99
Elementary and Secondary School	Richland-Kennewick-Pasco MSA, WA	Y		66080 AAW		WABLS	10//99-12//99
Elementary and Secondary School	Seattle-Bellevue-Everett PMSA, WA	Y		79620 AAW		WABLS	10//99-12//99
Elementary and Secondary School	Spokane MSA, WA	Y		71800 AAW		WABLS	10//99-12//99
Elementary and Secondary School	Tacoma PMSA, WA	Y		75810 AAW		WABLS	10//99-12//99
Elementary and Secondary School	Yakima MSA, WA	Y		66820 AAW		WABLS	10//99-12//99
Elementary and Secondary School	West Virginia	Y		49830 AAW		WVBLS	10//99-12//99
Elementary and Secondary School	Huntington-Ashland MSA, WV-KY-OH	Y		52850 AAW		WVBLS	10//99-12//99
Elementary and Secondary School	Wheeling MSA, WV-OH	Y		53930 AAW		WVBLS	10//99-12//99
Elementary and Secondary School	Wisconsin	Y		65800 AAW		WIBLS	10//99-12//99
Elementary and Secondary School	Appleton-Oshkosh-Neenah MSA, WI	Y		65010 AAW		WIBLS	10//99-12//99
Elementary and Secondary School	Eau Claire MSA, WI	Y		56140 AAW		WIBLS	10//99-12//99
Elementary and Secondary School	Green Bay MSA, WI	Y		65140 AAW		WIBLS	10//99-12//99
Elementary and Secondary School	Janesville-Beloit MSA, WI	Y		65610 AAW		WIBLS	10//99-12//99
Elementary and Secondary School	Kenosha PMSA, WI	Y		69380 AAW		WIBLS	10//99-12//99
Elementary and Secondary School	La Crosse MSA, WI-MN	Y		62570 AAW		WIBLS	10//99-12//99
Elementary and Secondary School	Madison MSA, WI	Y		62530 AAW		WIBLS	10//99-12//99
Elementary and Secondary School	Milwaukee-Waukesha PMSA, WI	Y		69630 AAW		WIBLS	10//99-12//99
Elementary and Secondary School	Racine PMSA, WI	Y		65880 AAW		WIBLS	10//99-12//99
Elementary and Secondary School	Sheboygan MSA, WI	Y		62300 AAW		WIBLS	10//99-12//99
Elementary and Secondary School	Wyoming	Y		52820 AAW		WYBLS	10//99-12//99
Elementary and Secondary School	Puerto Rico	Y		25490 AAW		PRBLS	10//99-12//99
Elementary and Secondary School	Caguas PMSA, PR	Y		25540 AAW		PRBLS	10//99-12//99
Elementary and Secondary School	San Juan-Bayamon PMSA, PR	Y		25920 AAW		PRBLS	10//99-12//99
Elementary and Secondary School	Virgin Islands	Y		73390 AAW		VIBLS	10//99-12//99
Postsecondary	Alabama	S	26.06 MW	28.96 AW	60240 AAW	ALBLS	10//99-12//99
Postsecondary	Birmingham MSA, AL	S	24.96 MW	21.35 AW	51920 AAW	ALBLS	10//99-12//99
Postsecondary	Huntsville MSA, AL	S	28.85 MW	24.99 AW	60010 AAW	ALBLS	10//99-12//99
Postsecondary	Mobile MSA, AL	S	33.40 MW	31.46 AW	69470 AAW	ALBLS	10//99-12//99
Postsecondary	Montgomery MSA, AL	S	30.81 MW	29.63 AW	64090 AAW	ALBLS	10//99-12//99
Postsecondary	Arizona	S	30.82 MW	31.36 AW	65230 AAW	AZBLS	10//99-12//99
Postsecondary	Phoenix-Mesa MSA, AZ	S	29.44 MW	31.51 AW	61240 AAW	AZBLS	10//99-12//99
Postsecondary	Arkansas	S	30.99 MW	32.30 AW	67180 AAW	ARBLS	10//99-12//99
Postsecondary	Little Rock-North Little Rock MSA, AR	S	34.85 MW	34.97 AW	72480 AAW	ARBLS	10//99-12//99
Postsecondary	California	S	31.36 MW	31.37 AW	65250 AAW	CABLS	10//99-12//99
Postsecondary	Los Angeles-Long Beach PMSA, CA	S	30.12 MW	28.37 AW	62640 AAW	CABLS	10//99-12//99
Postsecondary	Oakland PMSA, CA	S	30.46 MW	28.90 AW	63360 AAW	CABLS	10//99-12//99

AAW	Average annual wage	AOH	Average offered, high	ASH	Average starting, high	H	Hourly	M	Monthly	S	Special: hourly and annual
AE	Average entry wage	AOL	Average offered, low	ASL	Average starting, low	HI	Highest wage paid	MTC	Median total compensation	TQ	Third quartile wage
AEX	Average experienced wage	APH	Average pay, high range	AW	Average wage paid	HR	High end range	MW	Median wage paid	W	Weekly
AO	Average offered	APL	Average pay, low range	FQ	First quartile wage	LR	Low end range	SQ	Second quartile wage	Y	Yearly

Education Administrator

Occupation/Type/Industry	Location	Per	Low	Mid	High	Source	Date
Postsecondary	Orange County PMSA, CA	S	32.82 MW	33.56 AW	68270 AAW	CABLS	10//99-12//99
Postsecondary	Riverside-San Bernardino PMSA, CA	S	31.72 MW	31.39 AW	65970 AAW	CABLS	10//99-12//99
Postsecondary	Sacramento PMSA, CA	S	35.03 MW	36.36 AW	72850 AAW	CABLS	10//99-12//99
Postsecondary	San Diego MSA, CA	S	31.79 MW	32.17 AW	66130 AAW	CABLS	10//99-12//99
Postsecondary	San Francisco PMSA, CA	S	36.21 MW	38.39 AW	75320 AAW	CABLS	10//99-12//99
Postsecondary	Ventura PMSA, CA	S	25.69 MW	21.36 AW	53430 AAW	CABLS	10//99-12//99
Postsecondary	Colorado	S	20.84 MW	25.39 AW	52820 AAW	COBLS	10//99-12//99
Postsecondary	Denver PMSA, CO	S	26.63 MW	21.15 AW	55400 AAW	COBLS	10//99-12//99
Postsecondary	Connecticut	S	22.98 MW	26.31 AW	54720 AAW	CTBLS	10//99-12//99
Postsecondary	Bridgeport PMSA, CT	S	31.40 MW	34.70 AW	65320 AAW	CTBLS	10//99-12//99
Postsecondary	Hartford MSA, CT	S	30.14 MW	27.22 AW	62680 AAW	CTBLS	10//99-12//99
Postsecondary	Washington PMSA, DC-MD-VA-WV	S	31.81 MW	28.60 AW	66160 AAW	DCBLS	10//99-12//99
Postsecondary	Florida	S	28.26 MW	29.88 AW	62150 AAW	FLBLS	10//99-12//99
Postsecondary	Daytona Beach MSA, FL	S	40.06 MW	39.57 AW	83320 AAW	FLBLS	10//99-12//99
Postsecondary	Fort Lauderdale PMSA, FL	S	26.69 MW	27.90 AW	55520 AAW	FLBLS	10//99-12//99
Postsecondary	Fort Myers-Cape Coral MSA, FL	S	32.10 MW	25.64 AW	66760 AAW	FLBLS	10//99-12//99
Postsecondary	Jacksonville MSA, FL	S	28.48 MW	29.70 AW	59250 AAW	FLBLS	10//99-12//99
Postsecondary	Lakeland-Winter Haven MSA, FL	S	32.45 MW	31.38 AW	67490 AAW	FLBLS	10//99-12//99
Postsecondary	Melbourne-Titusville-Palm Bay MSA, FL	S	32.02 MW	31.43 AW	66600 AAW	FLBLS	10//99-12//99
Postsecondary	Miami PMSA, FL	S	31.65 MW	26.45 AW	65830 AAW	FLBLS	10//99-12//99
Postsecondary	Orlando MSA, FL	S	30.18 MW	29.40 AW	62770 AAW	FLBLS	10//99-12//99
Postsecondary	Pensacola MSA, FL	S	24.78 MW	22.94 AW	51540 AAW	FLBLS	10//99-12//99
Postsecondary	Tallahassee MSA, FL	S	29.98 MW	27.29 AW	62360 AAW	FLBLS	10//99-12//99
Postsecondary	Tampa-St. Petersburg-Clearwater MSA, FL	S	29.67 MW	27.11 AW	61710 AAW	FLBLS	10//99-12//99
Postsecondary	West Palm Beach-Boca Raton MSA, FL	S	25.75 MW	24.87 AW	53550 AAW	FLBLS	10//99-12//99
Postsecondary	Georgia	S	36.77 MW	36.94 AW	76830 AAW	GABLS	10//99-12//99
Postsecondary	Atlanta MSA, GA	S	36.67 MW	34.53 AW	76270 AAW	GABLS	10//99-12//99
Postsecondary	Augusta-Aiken MSA, GA-SC	S	39.76 MW	43.12 AW	82700 AAW	GABLS	10//99-12//99
Postsecondary	Macon MSA, GA	S	32.83 MW	33.38 AW	68280 AAW	GABLS	10//99-12//99
Postsecondary	Savannah MSA, GA	S	35.10 MW	36.21 AW	73010 AAW	GABLS	10//99-12//99
Postsecondary	Idaho	S	25.14 MW	28.79 AW	59890 AAW	IDBLS	10//99-12//99
Postsecondary	Boise City MSA, ID	S	41.53 MW	44.44 AW	86370 AAW	IDBLS	10//99-12//99
Postsecondary	Illinois	S	20.42 MW	22.37 AW	46530 AAW	ILBLS	10//99-12//99
Postsecondary	Chicago PMSA, IL	S	21.66 MW	19.81 AW	45060 AAW	ILBLS	10//99-12//99
Postsecondary	Indiana	S	23.07 MW	24.88 AW	51760 AAW	INBLS	10//99-12//99
Postsecondary	Gary PMSA, IN	S	32.36 MW	29.91 AW	67320 AAW	INBLS	10//99-12//99
Postsecondary	Indianapolis MSA, IN	S	24.82 MW	23.12 AW	51620 AAW	INBLS	10//99-12//99
Postsecondary	Iowa	S	33.02 MW	35.53 AW	73900 AAW	IABLS	10//99-12//99
Postsecondary	Des Moines MSA, IA	S	34.02 MW	35.69 AW	70760 AAW	IABLS	10//99-12//99
Postsecondary	Kansas	S	26.72 MW	28.91 AW	60130 AAW	KSBLS	10//99-12//99
Postsecondary	Wichita MSA, KS	S	22.25 MW	21.96 AW	46280 AAW	KSBLS	10//99-12//99
Postsecondary	Kentucky	S	26.1 MW	27.24 AW	56650 AAW	KYBLS	10//99-12//99
Postsecondary	Louisville MSA, KY-IN	S	26.34 MW	25.62 AW	54790 AAW	KYBLS	10//99-12//99
Postsecondary	Louisiana	S	20.1 MW	21.77 AW	45280 AAW	LABLS	10//99-12//99
Postsecondary	Baton Rouge MSA, LA	S	21.95 MW	20.09 AW	45660 AAW	LABLS	10//99-12//99
Postsecondary	New Orleans MSA, LA	S	22.19 MW	20.46 AW	46160 AAW	LABLS	10//99-12//99
Postsecondary	Shreveport-Bossier City MSA, LA	S	22.06 MW	20.69 AW	45890 AAW	LABLS	10//99-12//99
Postsecondary	Maine	S	23.87 MW	25.70 AW	53460 AAW	MEBLS	10//99-12//99
Postsecondary	Bangor MSA, ME	S	27.80 MW	24.85 AW	57830 AAW	MEBLS	10//99-12//99
Postsecondary	Maryland	S	31.06 MW	34.24 AW	71220 AAW	MDBLS	10//99-12//99
Postsecondary	Baltimore PMSA, MD	S	34.03 MW	31.58 AW	70780 AAW	MDBLS	10//99-12//99
Postsecondary	Massachusetts	S	26.95 MW	32.11 AW	66800 AAW	MABLS	10//99-12//99
Postsecondary	Boston PMSA, MA-NH	S	33.52 MW	28.17 AW	69720 AAW	MABLS	10//99-12//99
Postsecondary	Springfield MSA, MA	S	23.68 MW	20.06 AW	49260 AAW	MABLS	10//99-12//99
Postsecondary	Worcester PMSA, MA-CT	S	26.92 MW	25.54 AW	55990 AAW	MABLS	10//99-12//99
Postsecondary	Minnesota	S	32.12 MW	34.04 AW	70800 AAW	MNBLS	10//99-12//99
Postsecondary	Minneapolis-St. Paul MSA, MN-WI	S	35.62 MW	33.37 AW	74100 AAW	MNBLS	10//99-12//99
Postsecondary	Mississippi	S	31.59 MW	30.95 AW	64380 AAW	MSBLS	10//99-12//99
Postsecondary	Jackson MSA, MS	S	31.69 MW	32.34 AW	65920 AAW	MSBLS	10//99-12//99
Postsecondary	Missouri	S	30.61 MW	31.07 AW	64620 AAW	MOBLS	10//99-12//99
Postsecondary	Kansas City MSA, MO-KS	S	32.68 MW	31.38 AW	67980 AAW	MOBLS	10//99-12//99
Postsecondary	Montana	S	32.23 MW	32.50 AW	67600 AAW	MTBLS	10//99-12//99

AAW	Average annual wage	AOH	Average offered, high	ASH	Average starting, high	H	Hourly	M	Monthly	S	Special: hourly and annual
AE	Average entry wage	AOL	Average offered, low	ASL	Average starting, low	HI	Highest wage paid	MTC	Median total compensation	TQ	Third quartile wage
AEX	Average experienced wage	APH	Average pay, high range	AW	Average wage paid	HR	High end range	MW	Median wage paid	W	Weekly
AO	Average offered	APL	Average pay, low range	FQ	First quartile wage	LR	Low end range	SQ	Second quartile wage	Y	Yearly

Occupation/Type/Industry	Location	Per	Low	Mid	High	Source	Date
Education Administrator							
Postsecondary	Nebraska	S	25.67 MW	27.22 AW	56620 AAW	NEBLS	10//99-12//99
Postsecondary	Lincoln MSA, NE	S	27.08 MW	25.84 AW	56320 AAW	NEBLS	10//99-12//99
Postsecondary	Omaha MSA, NE-IA	S	30.61 MW	28.81 AW	63670 AAW	NEBLS	10//99-12//99
Postsecondary	Las Vegas MSA, NV-AZ	S	36.49 MW	32.94 AW	75910 AAW	NVBLS	10//99-12//99
Postsecondary	New Hampshire	S	19.49 MW	20.69 AW	43030 AAW	NHBLS	10//99-12//99
Postsecondary	Manchester PMSA, NH	S	23.52 MW	22.08 AW	48920 AAW	NHBLS	10//99-12//99
Postsecondary	Nashua PMSA, NH	S	29.73 MW	30.49 AW	61840 AAW	NHBLS	10//99-12//99
Postsecondary	New Jersey	S	32.45 MW	35.30 AW	73430 AAW	NJBLS	10//99-12//99
Postsecondary	Bergen-Passaic PMSA, NJ	S	34.36 MW	33.24 AW	71460 AAW	NJBLS	10//99-12//99
Postsecondary	Monmouth-Ocean PMSA, NJ	S	35.83 MW	34.17 AW	74530 AAW	NJBLS	10//99-12//99
Postsecondary	Newark PMSA, NJ	S	34.06 MW	31.68 AW	70840 AAW	NJBLS	10//99-12//99
Postsecondary	Trenton PMSA, NJ	S	35.80 MW	33.41 AW	74470 AAW	NJBLS	10//99-12//99
Postsecondary	New Mexico	S	22.46 MW	23.79 AW	49480 AAW	NMBLS	10//99-12//99
Postsecondary	New York	S	34.09 MW	34.03 AW	70780 AAW	NYBLS	10//99-12//99
Postsecondary	Albany-Schenectady-Troy MSA, NY	S	30.40 MW	26.72 AW	63230 AAW	NYBLS	10//99-12//99
Postsecondary	Buffalo-Niagara Falls MSA, NY	S	31.78 MW	29.99 AW	66100 AAW	NYBLS	10//99-12//99
Postsecondary	Nassau-Suffolk PMSA, NY	S	35.98 MW	36.76 AW	74840 AAW	NYBLS	10//99-12//99
Postsecondary	New York PMSA, NY	S	39.02 MW	39.18 AW	81160 AAW	NYBLS	10//99-12//99
Postsecondary	Rochester MSA, NY	S	32.65 MW	31.86 AW	67910 AAW	NYBLS	10//99-12//99
Postsecondary	Syracuse MSA, NY	S	25.84 MW	24.87 AW	53740 AAW	NYBLS	10//99-12//99
Postsecondary	Utica-Rome MSA, NY	S	25.54 MW	24.85 AW	53110 AAW	NYBLS	10//99-12//99
Postsecondary	North Carolina	S	21.52 MW	24.60 AW	51180 AAW	NCBLS	10//99-12//99
Postsecondary	Asheville MSA, NC	S	20.50 MW	19.88 AW	42630 AAW	NCBLS	10//99-12//99
Postsecondary	Charlotte-Gastonia-Rock Hill MSA, NC-SC	S	24.33 MW	21.81 AW	50600 AAW	NCBLS	10//99-12//99
Postsecondary	Fayetteville MSA, NC	S	24.71 MW	21.35 AW	51400 AAW	NCBLS	10//99-12//99
Postsecondary	Greensboro--Winston-Salem--High Point MSA, NC	S	28.23 MW	22.25 AW	58720 AAW	NCBLS	10//99-12//99
Postsecondary	Raleigh-Durham-Chapel Hill MSA, NC	S	21.99 MW	20.31 AW	45730 AAW	NCBLS	10//99-12//99
Postsecondary	North Dakota	S	14.59 MW	15.32 AW	31860 AAW	NDBLS	10//99-12//99
Postsecondary	Ohio	S	27.6 MW	29.08 AW	60490 AAW	OHBLS	10//99-12//99
Postsecondary	Akron PMSA, OH	S	29.74 MW	25.85 AW	61850 AAW	OHBLS	10//99-12//99
Postsecondary	Cincinnati PMSA, OH-KY-IN	S	26.83 MW	25.03 AW	55800 AAW	OHBLS	10//99-12//99
Postsecondary	Cleveland-Lorain-Elyria PMSA, OH	S	40.34 MW	41.47 AW	83910 AAW	OHBLS	10//99-12//99
Postsecondary	Toledo MSA, OH	S	26.11 MW	27.41 AW	54300 AAW	OHBLS	10//99-12//99
Postsecondary	Oklahoma	S	31.83 MW	31.33 AW	65160 AAW	OKBLS	10//99-12//99
Postsecondary	Oklahoma City MSA, OK	S	32.67 MW	33.40 AW	67960 AAW	OKBLS	10//99-12//99
Postsecondary	Oregon	S	28 MW	28.59 AW	59460 AAW	ORBLS	10//99-12//99
Postsecondary	Portland-Vancouver PMSA, OR-WA	S	30.03 MW	29.64 AW	62460 AAW	ORBLS	10//99-12//99
Postsecondary	Pennsylvania	S	23.91 MW	27.56 AW	57320 AAW	PABLS	10//99-12//99
Postsecondary	Allentown-Bethlehem-Easton MSA, PA	S	25.28 MW	23.37 AW	52580 AAW	PABLS	10//99-12//99
Postsecondary	Harrisburg-Lebanon-Carlisle MSA, PA	S	32.97 MW	22.52 AW	68570 AAW	PABLS	10//99-12//99
Postsecondary	Lancaster MSA, PA	S	37.20 MW	37.80 AW	77380 AAW	PABLS	10//99-12//99
Postsecondary	Philadelphia PMSA, PA-NJ	S	24.97 MW	21.64 AW	51930 AAW	PABLS	10//99-12//99
Postsecondary	Pittsburgh MSA, PA	S	33.79 MW	31.79 AW	70280 AAW	PABLS	10//99-12//99
Postsecondary	Sharon MSA, PA	S	27.27 MW	23.07 AW	56710 AAW	PABLS	10//99-12//99
Postsecondary	Rhode Island	S	32.4 MW	34.99 AW	72780 AAW	RIBLS	10//99-12//99
Postsecondary	Providence-Fall River-Warwick MSA, RI-MA	S	34.94 MW	32.33 AW	72670 AAW	RIBLS	10//99-12//99
Postsecondary	South Carolina	S	19.66 MW	22.92 AW	47680 AAW	SCBLS	10//99-12//99
Postsecondary	Greenville-Spartanburg-Anderson MSA, SC	S	19.10 MW	18.32 AW	39740 AAW	SCBLS	10//99-12//99
Postsecondary	South Dakota	S	33.41 MW	33.55 AW	69780 AAW	SDBLS	10//99-12//99
Postsecondary	Tennessee	S	24.96 MW	29.14 AW	60620 AAW	TNBLS	10//99-12//99
Postsecondary	Chattanooga MSA, TN-GA	S	28.33 MW	29.07 AW	58930 AAW	TNBLS	10//99-12//99
Postsecondary	Johnson City-Kingsport-Bristol MSA, TN-VA	S	25.13 MW	21.02 AW	52270 AAW	TNBLS	10//99-12//99
Postsecondary	Memphis MSA, TN-AR-MS	S	27.81 MW	25.85 AW	57840 AAW	MSBLS	10//99-12//99
Postsecondary	Nashville MSA, TN	S	56.93 MW		118400 AAW	TNBLS	10//99-12//99
Postsecondary	Texas	S	23.72 MW	29.40 AW	61160 AAW	TXBLS	10//99-12//99
Postsecondary	Fort Worth-Arlington PMSA, TX	S	36.24 MW	32.58 AW	75370 AAW	TXBLS	10//99-12//99
Postsecondary	San Antonio MSA, TX	S	27.28 MW	25.83 AW	56750 AAW	TXBLS	10//99-12//99
Postsecondary	Utah	S	22.82 MW	23.83 AW	49560 AAW	UTBLS	10//99-12//99

AAW	Average annual wage	AOH	Average offered, high	ASH	Average starting, high
AE	Average entry wage	AOL	Average offered, low	ASL	Average starting, low
AEX	Average experienced wage	APH	Average pay, high range	AW	Average wage paid
AO	Average offered	APL	Average pay, low range	FQ	First quartile wage

H	Hourly	M	Monthly
HI	Highest wage paid	MTC	Median total compensation
HR	High end range	MW	Median wage paid
LR	Low end range	SQ	Second quartile wage

S	Special: hourly and annual
TQ	Third quartile wage
W	Weekly
Y	Yearly

Education Administrator

Occupation/Type/Industry	Location	Per	Low	Mid	High	Source	Date
Postsecondary	Vermont	S	22.12 MW	23.10 AW	48040 AAW	VTBLS	10//99-12//99
Postsecondary	Virginia	S	26.54 MW	29.42 AW	61200 AAW	VABLS	10//99-12//99
Postsecondary	Norfolk-Virginia Beach-Newport News MSA, VA-NC	S	31.26 MW	28.72 AW	65030 AAW	VABLS	10//99-12//99
Postsecondary	Roanoke MSA, VA	S	18.59 MW	17.59 AW	38660 AAW	VABLS	10//99-12//99
Postsecondary	Washington	S	26.67 MW	27.53 AW	57270 AAW	WABLS	10//99-12//99
Postsecondary	Richland-Kennewick-Pasco MSA, WA	S	30.74 MW	31.09 AW	63940 AAW	WABLS	10//99-12//99
Postsecondary	Seattle-Bellevue-Everett PMSA, WA	S	27.11 MW	26.51 AW	56390 AAW	WABLS	10//99-12//99
Postsecondary	Tacoma PMSA, WA	S	29.70 MW	29.67 AW	61770 AAW	WABLS	10//99-12//99
Postsecondary	West Virginia	S	19.85 MW	24.81 AW	51600 AAW	WVBLS	10//99-12//99
Postsecondary	Huntington-Ashland MSA, WV-KY-OH	S	29.01 MW	25.39 AW	60340 AAW	WVBLS	10//99-12//99
Postsecondary	Wisconsin	S	24.55 MW	26.27 AW	54640 AAW	WIBLS	10//99-12//99
Postsecondary	Madison MSA, WI	S	22.88 MW	22.13 AW	47600 AAW	WIBLS	10//99-12//99
Postsecondary	Milwaukee-Waukesha PMSA, WI	S	28.23 MW	26.07 AW	58720 AAW	WIBLS	10//99-12//99
Postsecondary	Wyoming	S	30.52 MW	33.17 AW	68980 AAW	WYBLS	10//99-12//99
Postsecondary	Puerto Rico	S	21.33 MW	22.96 AW	47760 AAW	PRBLS	10//99-12//99
Postsecondary	Mayaguez MSA, PR	S	24.22 MW	27.77 AW	50380 AAW	PRBLS	10//99-12//99
Postsecondary	San Juan-Bayamon PMSA, PR	S	23.47 MW	21.76 AW	48820 AAW	PRBLS	10//99-12//99
Preschool and Child Care Center/Program	Alabama	S	13.22 MW	14.57 AW	30310 AAW	ALBLS	10//99-12//99
Preschool and Child Care Center/Program	Birmingham MSA, AL	S	19.34 MW	18.90 AW	40220 AAW	ALBLS	10//99-12//99
Preschool and Child Care Center/Program	Alaska	S	18.06 MW	18.00 AW	37440 AAW	AKBLS	10//99-12//99
Preschool and Child Care Center/Program	Arizona	S	11.97 MW	15.83 AW	32930 AAW	AZBLS	10//99-12//99
Preschool and Child Care Center/Program	Tucson MSA, AZ	S	18.23 MW	16.46 AW	37920 AAW	AZBLS	10//99-12//99
Preschool and Child Care Center/Program	Arkansas	S	8.54 MW	10.78 AW	22420 AAW	ARBLS	10//99-12//99
Preschool and Child Care Center/Program	Fayetteville-Springdale-Rogers MSA, AR	S	14.14 MW	14.27 AW	29410 AAW	ARBLS	10//99-12//99
Preschool and Child Care Center/Program	Little Rock-North Little Rock MSA, AR	S	16.03 MW	16.45 AW	33350 AAW	ARBLS	10//99-12//99
Preschool and Child Care Center/Program	California	S	17.77 MW	19.10 AW	39730 AAW	CABLS	10//99-12//99
Preschool and Child Care Center/Program	Bakersfield MSA, CA	S	18.39 MW	17.85 AW	38260 AAW	CABLS	10//99-12//99
Preschool and Child Care Center/Program	Los Angeles-Long Beach PMSA, CA	S	20.24 MW	19.29 AW	42090 AAW	CABLS	10//99-12//99
Preschool and Child Care Center/Program	Modesto MSA, CA	S	23.71 MW	23.20 AW	49310 AAW	CABLS	10//99-12//99
Preschool and Child Care Center/Program	Oakland PMSA, CA	S	26.77 MW	25.66 AW	55670 AAW	CABLS	10//99-12//99
Preschool and Child Care Center/Program	Orange County PMSA, CA	S	15.11 MW	14.60 AW	31430 AAW	CABLS	10//99-12//99
Preschool and Child Care Center/Program	Riverside-San Bernardino PMSA, CA	S	16.25 MW	14.50 AW	33800 AAW	CABLS	10//99-12//99
Preschool and Child Care Center/Program	Sacramento PMSA, CA	S	22.27 MW	20.26 AW	46310 AAW	CABLS	10//99-12//99
Preschool and Child Care Center/Program	San Jose PMSA, CA	S	24.36 MW	17.92 AW	50660 AAW	CABLS	10//99-12//99
Preschool and Child Care Center/Program	San Luis Obispo-Atascadero-Paso Robles MSA, CA	S	16.58 MW	13.46 AW	34490 AAW	CABLS	10//99-12//99
Preschool and Child Care Center/Program	Stockton-Lodi MSA, CA	S	20.57 MW	20.12 AW	42780 AAW	CABLS	10//99-12//99
Preschool and Child Care Center/Program	Colorado	S	12.84 MW	14.29 AW	29730 AAW	COBLS	10//99-12//99
Preschool and Child Care Center/Program	Boulder-Longmont PMSA, CO	S	14.97 MW	13.36 AW	31130 AAW	COBLS	10//99-12//99
Preschool and Child Care Center/Program	Denver PMSA, CO	S	14.51 MW	12.70 AW	30170 AAW	COBLS	10//99-12//99
Preschool and Child Care Center/Program	Pueblo MSA, CO	S	16.54 MW	13.77 AW	34400 AAW	COBLS	10//99-12//99
Preschool and Child Care Center/Program	Connecticut	S	16.63 MW	21.16 AW	44020 AAW	CTBLS	10//99-12//99
Preschool and Child Care Center/Program	Bridgeport PMSA, CT	S	28.54 MW	25.65 AW	59350 AAW	CTBLS	10//99-12//99
Preschool and Child Care Center/Program	Hartford MSA, CT	S	17.03 MW	14.69 AW	35430 AAW	CTBLS	10//99-12//99
Preschool and Child Care Center/Program	New Haven-Meriden PMSA, CT	S	20.66 MW	20.39 AW	42960 AAW	CTBLS	10//99-12//99
Preschool and Child Care Center/Program	New London-Norwich MSA, CT-RI	S	35.27 MW	37.81 AW	73360 AAW	CTBLS	10//99-12//99
Preschool and Child Care Center/Program	Stamford-Norwalk PMSA, CT	S	29.79 MW	23.85 AW	61960 AAW	CTBLS	10//99-12//99
Preschool and Child Care Center/Program	District of Columbia	S	15.03 MW	14.51 AW	30180 AAW	DCBLS	10//99-12//99
Preschool and Child Care Center/Program	Washington PMSA, DC-MD-VA-WV	S	15.29 MW	14.89 AW	31800 AAW	DCBLS	10//99-12//99
Preschool and Child Care Center/Program	Florida	S	13.45 MW	16.00 AW	33270 AAW	FLBLS	10//99-12//99
Preschool and Child Care Center/Program	Fort Pierce-Port St. Lucie MSA, FL	S	13.35 MW	13.15 AW	27760 AAW	FLBLS	10//99-12//99
Preschool and Child Care Center/Program	Gainesville MSA, FL	S	29.07 MW	30.41 AW	60460 AAW	FLBLS	10//99-12//99
Preschool and Child Care Center/Program	Jacksonville MSA, FL	S	13.17 MW	11.83 AW	27390 AAW	FLBLS	10//99-12//99
Preschool and Child Care Center/Program	Lakeland-Winter Haven MSA, FL	S	13.68 MW	13.83 AW	28450 AAW	FLBLS	10//99-12//99
Preschool and Child Care Center/Program	Melbourne-Titusville-Palm Bay MSA, FL	S	26.44 MW	30.16 AW	55000 AAW	FLBLS	10//99-12//99

AAW	Average annual wage	AOH	Average offered, high	ASH	Average starting, high	H	Hourly
AE	Average entry wage	AOL	Average offered, low	ASL	Average starting, low	HI	Highest wage paid
AEX	Average experienced wage	APH	Average pay, high range	AW	Average wage paid	HR	High end range
AO	Average offered	APL	Average pay, low range	FQ	First quartile wage	LR	Low end range

M   Monthly   S   Special: hourly and annual
MTC Median total compensation   TQ   Third quartile wage
MW Median wage paid   W   Weekly
SQ Second quartile wage   Y   Yearly

Education Administrator

Occupation/Type/Industry	Location	Per	Low	Mid	High	Source	Date
Education Administrator							
Preschool and Child Care Center/Program	Miami PMSA, FL	S	13.22 MW	11.72 AW	27490 AAW	FLBLS	10//99-12//99
Preschool and Child Care Center/Program	Orlando MSA, FL	S	14.31 MW	12.48 AW	29760 AAW	FLBLS	10//99-12//99
Preschool and Child Care Center/Program	Pensacola MSA, FL	S	20.71 MW	21.59 AW	43080 AAW	FLBLS	10//99-12//99
Preschool and Child Care Center/Program	Sarasota-Bradenton MSA, FL	S	14.62 MW	12.73 AW	30410 AAW	FLBLS	10//99-12//99
Preschool and Child Care Center/Program	Tampa-St. Petersburg-Clearwater MSA, FL	S	18.50 MW	17.36 AW	38470 AAW	FLBLS	10//99-12//99
Preschool and Child Care Center/Program	West Palm Beach-Boca Raton MSA, FL	S	14.19 MW	13.68 AW	29500 AAW	FLBLS	10//99-12//99
Preschool and Child Care Center/Program	Georgia	S	17.3 MW	18.01 AW	37450 AAW	GABLS	10//99-12//99
Preschool and Child Care Center/Program	Atlanta MSA, GA	S	18.77 MW	17.97 AW	39040 AAW	GABLS	10//99-12//99
Preschool and Child Care Center/Program	Columbus MSA, GA-AL	S	10.78 MW	9.87 AW	22430 AAW	GABLS	10//99-12//99
Preschool and Child Care Center/Program	Macon MSA, GA	S	11.26 MW	11.08 AW	23430 AAW	GABLS	10//99-12//99
Preschool and Child Care Center/Program	Hawaii	S	15.56 MW	17.27 AW	35920 AAW	HIBLS	10//99-12//99
Preschool and Child Care Center/Program	Honolulu MSA, HI	S	18.31 MW	15.79 AW	38090 AAW	HIBLS	10//99-12//99
Preschool and Child Care Center/Program	Idaho	S	36.69 MW	34.82 AW	72430 AAW	IDBLS	10//99-12//99
Preschool and Child Care Center/Program	Illinois	S	18.11 MW	21.56 AW	44840 AAW	ILBLS	10//99-12//99
Preschool and Child Care Center/Program	Bloomington-Normal MSA, IL	S	18.95 MW	18.22 AW	39410 AAW	ILBLS	10//99-12//99
Preschool and Child Care Center/Program	Chicago PMSA, IL	S	23.32 MW	20.20 AW	48500 AAW	ILBLS	10//99-12//99
Preschool and Child Care Center/Program	Peoria-Pekin MSA, IL	S	16.88 MW	12.88 AW	35110 AAW	ILBLS	10//99-12//99
Preschool and Child Care Center/Program	Indiana	S	10.7 MW	15.86 AW	32980 AAW	INBLS	10//99-12//99
Preschool and Child Care Center/Program	Fort Wayne MSA, IN	S	17.61 MW	15.87 AW	36640 AAW	INBLS	10//99-12//99
Preschool and Child Care Center/Program	Gary PMSA, IN	S	17.37 MW	16.76 AW	36130 AAW	INBLS	10//99-12//99
Preschool and Child Care Center/Program	Lafayette MSA, IN	S	12.70 MW	12.30 AW	26430 AAW	INBLS	10//99-12//99
Preschool and Child Care Center/Program	Muncie MSA, IN	S	13.47 MW	12.21 AW	28010 AAW	INBLS	10//99-12//99
Preschool and Child Care Center/Program	Iowa	S	12.6 MW	16.66 AW	34660 AAW	IABLS	10//99-12//99
Preschool and Child Care Center/Program	Cedar Rapids MSA, IA	S	18.95 MW	11.96 AW	39420 AAW	IABLS	10//99-12//99
Preschool and Child Care Center/Program	Davenport-Moline-Rock Island MSA, IA-IL	S	16.16 MW	12.09 AW	33610 AAW	IABLS	10//99-12//99
Preschool and Child Care Center/Program	Des Moines MSA, IA	S	14.30 MW	14.35 AW	29740 AAW	IABLS	10//99-12//99
Preschool and Child Care Center/Program	Iowa City MSA, IA	S	20.25 MW	22.64 AW	42110 AAW	IABLS	10//99-12//99
Preschool and Child Care Center/Program	Waterloo-Cedar Falls MSA, IA	S	22.27 MW	23.97 AW	46330 AAW	IABLS	10//99-12//99
Preschool and Child Care Center/Program	Kansas	S	27.2 MW	23.05 AW	47950 AAW	KSBLS	10//99-12//99
Preschool and Child Care Center/Program	Wichita MSA, KS	S	28.83 MW	30.49 AW	59970 AAW	KSBLS	10//99-12//99
Preschool and Child Care Center/Program	Kentucky	S	11.05 MW	13.77 AW	28650 AAW	KYBLS	10//99-12//99
Preschool and Child Care Center/Program	Louisville MSA, KY-IN	S	17.94 MW	13.12 AW	37320 AAW	KYBLS	10//99-12//99
Preschool and Child Care Center/Program	Louisiana	S	8.48 MW	13.00 AW	27040 AAW	LABLS	10//99-12//99
Preschool and Child Care Center/Program	Maine	S	13.48 MW	14.19 AW	29500 AAW	MEBLS	10//99-12//99
Preschool and Child Care Center/Program	Maryland	S	10.97 MW	12.73 AW	26470 AAW	MDBLS	10//99-12//99
Preschool and Child Care Center/Program	Baltimore PMSA, MD	S	11.66 MW	10.39 AW	24250 AAW	MDBLS	10//99-12//99
Preschool and Child Care Center/Program	Brockton PMSA, MA	S	13.52 MW	12.81 AW	28120 AAW	MABLS	10//99-12//99
Preschool and Child Care Center/Program	Lawrence PMSA, MA-NH	S	14.85 MW	15.13 AW	30890 AAW	MABLS	10//99-12//99
Preschool and Child Care Center/Program	Lowell PMSA, MA-NH	S	13.25 MW	12.30 AW	27560 AAW	MABLS	10//99-12//99
Preschool and Child Care Center/Program	New Bedford PMSA, MA	S	17.87 MW	14.35 AW	37180 AAW	MABLS	10//99-12//99
Preschool and Child Care Center/Program	Springfield MSA, MA	S	16.86 MW	16.24 AW	35070 AAW	MABLS	10//99-12//99
Preschool and Child Care Center/Program	Worcester PMSA, MA-CT	S	15.43 MW	14.89 AW	32080 AAW	MABLS	10//99-12//99
Preschool and Child Care Center/Program	Michigan	S	16.66 MW	22.89 AW	47610 AAW	MIBLS	10//99-12//99
Preschool and Child Care Center/Program	Ann Arbor PMSA, MI	S	21.76 MW	16.90 AW	45260 AAW	MIBLS	10//99-12//99
Preschool and Child Care Center/Program	Detroit PMSA, MI	S	31.80 MW	37.04 AW	66150 AAW	MIBLS	10//99-12//99
Preschool and Child Care Center/Program	Flint PMSA, MI	S	19.58 MW	16.37 AW	40720 AAW	MIBLS	10//99-12//99
Preschool and Child Care Center/Program	Grand Rapids-Muskegon-Holland MSA, MI	S	18.66 MW	15.38 AW	38820 AAW	MIBLS	10//99-12//99
Preschool and Child Care Center/Program	Lansing-East Lansing MSA, MI	S	13.82 MW	12.43 AW	28750 AAW	MIBLS	10//99-12//99
Preschool and Child Care Center/Program	Saginaw-Bay City-Midland MSA, MI	S	28.70 MW	30.48 AW	59700 AAW	MIBLS	10//99-12//99
Preschool and Child Care Center/Program	Minnesota	S	12.34 MW	13.77 AW	28630 AAW	MNBLS	10//99-12//99
Preschool and Child Care Center/Program	Duluth-Superior MSA, MN-WI	S	13.01 MW	12.10 AW	27060 AAW	MNBLS	10//99-12//99
Preschool and Child Care Center/Program	Minneapolis-St. Paul MSA, MN-WI	S	14.23 MW	12.37 AW	29590 AAW	MNBLS	10//99-12//99
Preschool and Child Care Center/Program	Mississippi	S	18.95 MW	21.45 AW	44620 AAW	MSBLS	10//99-12//99
Preschool and Child Care Center/Program	Jackson MSA, MS	S	21.18 MW	17.62 AW	44060 AAW	MSBLS	10//99-12//99
Preschool and Child Care Center/Program	Missouri	S	12.03 MW	14.02 AW	29160 AAW	MOBLS	10//99-12//99
Preschool and Child Care Center/Program	Kansas City MSA, MO-KS	S	15.00 MW	11.19 AW	31200 AAW	MOBLS	10//99-12//99
Preschool and Child Care Center/Program	St. Louis MSA, MO-IL	S	15.26 MW	13.05 AW	31750 AAW	MOBLS	10//99-12//99
Preschool and Child Care Center/Program	Montana	S	30.27 MW	27.70 AW	57620 AAW	MTBLS	10//99-12//99
Preschool and Child Care Center/Program	Nebraska	S	13.82 MW	21.08 AW	43850 AAW	NEBLS	10//99-12//99
Preschool and Child Care Center/Program	Lincoln MSA, NE	S	14.47 MW	14.38 AW	30100 AAW	NEBLS	10//99-12//99
Preschool and Child Care Center/Program	Nevada	S	12.73 MW	13.23 AW	27520 AAW	NVBLS	10//99-12//99
Preschool and Child Care Center/Program	Las Vegas MSA, NV-AZ	S	13.55 MW	13.24 AW	28190 AAW	NVBLS	10//99-12//99
Preschool and Child Care Center/Program	New Hampshire	S	17 MW	18.10 AW	37640 AAW	NHBLS	10//99-12//99
Preschool and Child Care Center/Program	New Jersey	S	21.44 MW	29.52 AW	61400 AAW	NJBLS	10//99-12//99
Preschool and Child Care Center/Program	Atlantic-Cape May PMSA, NJ	S	30.06 MW	16.23 AW	62520 AAW	NJBLS	10//99-12//99

AAW	Average annual wage	AOH	Average offered, high	ASH	Average starting, high	H	Hourly	M	Monthly	S	Special: hourly and annual
AE	Average entry wage	AOL	Average offered, low	ASL	Average starting, low	HI	Highest wage paid	MTC	Median total compensation	TQ	Third quartile wage
AEX	Average experienced wage	APH	Average pay, high range	AW	Average wage paid	HR	High end range	MW	Median wage paid	W	Weekly
AO	Average offered	APL	Average pay, low range	FQ	First quartile wage	LR	Low end range	SQ	Second quartile wage	Y	Yearly

Occupation/Type/Industry	Location	Per	Low	Mid	High	Source	Date
Education Administrator							
Preschool and Child Care Center/Program	Bergen-Passaic PMSA, NJ	S	28.67 MW	21.07 AW	59630 AAW	NJBLS	10//99-12//99
Preschool and Child Care Center/Program	Jersey City PMSA, NJ	S	24.68 MW	16.84 AW	51340 AAW	NJBLS	10//99-12//99
Preschool and Child Care Center/Program	Newark PMSA, NJ	S	22.19 MW	21.63 AW	46150 AAW	NJBLS	10//99-12//99
Preschool and Child Care Center/Program	Trenton PMSA, NJ	S	18.59 MW	16.78 AW	38670 AAW	NJBLS	10//99-12//99
Preschool and Child Care Center/Program	Vineland-Millville-Bridgeton PMSA, NJ	S	36.23 MW	42.34 AW	75360 AAW	NJBLS	10//99-12//99
Preschool and Child Care Center/Program	New Mexico	S	22.91 MW	21.91 AW	45570 AAW	NMBLS	10//99-12//99
Preschool and Child Care Center/Program	Albuquerque MSA, NM	S	14.78 MW	14.83 AW	30750 AAW	NMBLS	10//99-12//99
Preschool and Child Care Center/Program	Las Cruces MSA, NM	S	23.91 MW	24.29 AW	49730 AAW	NMBLS	10//99-12//99
Preschool and Child Care Center/Program	Santa Fe MSA, NM	S	18.33 MW	16.79 AW	38140 AAW	NMBLS	10//99-12//99
Preschool and Child Care Center/Program	New York	S	18.16 MW	19.11 AW	39750 AAW	NYBLS	10//99-12//99
Preschool and Child Care Center/Program	Albany-Schenectady-Troy MSA, NY	S	17.53 MW	16.97 AW	36470 AAW	NYBLS	10//99-12//99
Preschool and Child Care Center/Program	Binghamton MSA, NY	S	14.36 MW	12.77 AW	29880 AAW	NYBLS	10//99-12//99
Preschool and Child Care Center/Program	Buffalo-Niagara Falls MSA, NY	S	18.33 MW	10.84 AW	38130 AAW	NYBLS	10//99-12//99
Preschool and Child Care Center/Program	Dutchess County PMSA, NY	S	22.46 MW	22.94 AW	46720 AAW	NYBLS	10//99-12//99
Preschool and Child Care Center/Program	Nassau-Suffolk PMSA, NY	S	18.34 MW	17.41 AW	38150 AAW	NYBLS	10//99-12//99
Preschool and Child Care Center/Program	New York PMSA, NY	S	21.82 MW	19.84 AW	45380 AAW	NYBLS	10//99-12//99
Preschool and Child Care Center/Program	Rochester MSA, NY	S	23.08 MW	23.49 AW	48000 AAW	NYBLS	10//99-12//99
Preschool and Child Care Center/Program	Syracuse MSA, NY	S	16.85 MW	16.08 AW	35060 AAW	NYBLS	10//99-12//99
Preschool and Child Care Center/Program	Utica-Rome MSA, NY	S	12.49 MW	12.27 AW	25980 AAW	NYBLS	10//99-12//99
Preschool and Child Care Center/Program	North Carolina	S	15.96 MW	17.44 AW	36280 AAW	NCBLS	10//99-12//99
Preschool and Child Care Center/Program	Asheville MSA, NC	S	19.23 MW	22.00 AW	40000 AAW	NCBLS	10//99-12//99
Preschool and Child Care Center/Program	Charlotte-Gastonia-Rock Hill MSA, NC-SC	S	23.01 MW	17.93 AW	47850 AAW	NCBLS	10//99-12//99
Preschool and Child Care Center/Program	Greensboro--Winston-Salem--High Point MSA, NC	S	21.62 MW	20.90 AW	44980 AAW	NCBLS	10//99-12//99
Preschool and Child Care Center/Program	Raleigh-Durham-Chapel Hill MSA, NC	S	17.00 MW	15.73 AW	35350 AAW	NCBLS	10//99-12//99
Preschool and Child Care Center/Program	North Dakota	S	10.59 MW	14.14 AW	29410 AAW	NDBLS	10//99-12//99
Preschool and Child Care Center/Program	Ohio	S	14.47 MW	16.15 AW	33600 AAW	OHBLS	10//99-12//99
Preschool and Child Care Center/Program	Akron PMSA, OH	S	14.54 MW	13.78 AW	30240 AAW	OHBLS	10//99-12//99
Preschool and Child Care Center/Program	Canton-Massillon MSA, OH	S	14.47 MW	11.21 AW	30090 AAW	OHBLS	10//99-12//99
Preschool and Child Care Center/Program	Cincinnati PMSA, OH-KY-IN	S	14.33 MW	13.46 AW	29800 AAW	OHBLS	10//99-12//99
Preschool and Child Care Center/Program	Cleveland-Lorain-Elyria PMSA, OH	S	20.53 MW	18.13 AW	42690 AAW	OHBLS	10//99-12//99
Preschool and Child Care Center/Program	Columbus MSA, OH	S	17.62 MW	15.72 AW	36650 AAW	OHBLS	10//99-12//99
Preschool and Child Care Center/Program	Dayton-Springfield MSA, OH	S	12.43 MW	11.14 AW	25850 AAW	OHBLS	10//99-12//99
Preschool and Child Care Center/Program	Toledo MSA, OH	S	12.59 MW	11.55 AW	26190 AAW	OHBLS	10//99-12//99
Preschool and Child Care Center/Program	Youngstown-Warren MSA, OH	S	22.44 MW	19.24 AW	46680 AAW	OHBLS	10//99-12//99
Preschool and Child Care Center/Program	Oklahoma	S	11.15 MW	12.31 AW	25600 AAW	OKBLS	10//99-12//99
Preschool and Child Care Center/Program	Oklahoma City MSA, OK	S	11.47 MW	8.45 AW	23860 AAW	OKBLS	10//99-12//99
Preschool and Child Care Center/Program	Tulsa MSA, OK	S	11.77 MW	11.72 AW	24480 AAW	OKBLS	10//99-12//99
Preschool and Child Care Center/Program	Oregon	S	19.34 MW	20.70 AW	43050 AAW	ORBLS	10//99-12//99
Preschool and Child Care Center/Program	Portland-Vancouver PMSA, OR-WA	S	21.21 MW	19.93 AW	44120 AAW	ORBLS	10//99-12//99
Preschool and Child Care Center/Program	Pennsylvania	S	14.36 MW	16.31 AW	33920 AAW	PABLS	10//99-12//99
Preschool and Child Care Center/Program	Allentown-Bethlehem-Easton MSA, PA	S	16.00 MW	14.36 AW	33280 AAW	PABLS	10//99-12//99
Preschool and Child Care Center/Program	Harrisburg-Lebanon-Carlisle MSA, PA	S	23.79 MW	21.14 AW	49480 AAW	PABLS	10//99-12//99
Preschool and Child Care Center/Program	Pittsburgh MSA, PA	S	18.43 MW	18.90 AW	38340 AAW	PABLS	10//99-12//99
Preschool and Child Care Center/Program	Rhode Island	S	24.55 MW	24.89 AW	51770 AAW	RIBLS	10//99-12//99
Preschool and Child Care Center/Program	Providence-Fall River-Warwick MSA, RI-MA	S	24.51 MW	23.94 AW	50970 AAW	RIBLS	10//99-12//99
Preschool and Child Care Center/Program	Columbia MSA, SC	S	34.30 MW	36.43 AW	71350 AAW	SCBLS	10//99-12//99
Preschool and Child Care Center/Program	Greenville-Spartanburg-Anderson MSA, SC	S	17.53 MW	12.70 AW	36460 AAW	SCBLS	10//99-12//99
Preschool and Child Care Center/Program	Sumter MSA, SC	S	6.35 MW	6.11 AW	13200 AAW	SCBLS	10//99-12//99
Preschool and Child Care Center/Program	South Dakota	S	13.38 MW	15.29 AW	31800 AAW	SDBLS	10//99-12//99
Preschool and Child Care Center/Program	Sioux Falls MSA, SD	S	12.99 MW	12.53 AW	27010 AAW	SDBLS	10//99-12//99
Preschool and Child Care Center/Program	Tennessee	S	14.6 MW	16.25 AW	33800 AAW	TNBLS	10//99-12//99
Preschool and Child Care Center/Program	Clarksville-Hopkinsville MSA, TN-KY	S	15.79 MW	15.43 AW	32840 AAW	TNBLS	10//99-12//99
Preschool and Child Care Center/Program	Johnson City-Kingsport-Bristol MSA, TN-VA	S	14.25 MW	14.27 AW	29650 AAW	TNBLS	10//99-12//99
Preschool and Child Care Center/Program	Knoxville MSA, TN	S	18.02 MW	15.50 AW	37490 AAW	TNBLS	10//99-12//99
Preschool and Child Care Center/Program	Memphis MSA, TN-AR-MS	S	16.39 MW	12.63 AW	34090 AAW	MSBLS	10//99-12//99
Preschool and Child Care Center/Program	Nashville MSA, TN	S	17.20 MW	17.31 AW	35770 AAW	TNBLS	10//99-12//99
Preschool and Child Care Center/Program	Texas	S	19.38 MW	20.29 AW	42210 AAW	TXBLS	10//99-12//99

AAW	Average annual wage	AOH	Average offered, high	ASH	Average starting, high
AE	Average entry wage	AOL	Average offered, low	ASL	Average starting, low
AEX	Average experienced wage	APH	Average pay, high range	AW	Average wage paid
AO	Average offered	APL	Average pay, low range	FQ	First quartile wage

H	Hourly	M	Monthly
HI	Highest wage paid	MTC	Median total compensation
HR	High end range	MW	Median wage paid
LR	Low end range	SQ	Second quartile wage

S	Special: hourly and annual
TQ	Third quartile wage
W	Weekly
Y	Yearly

Occupation/Type/Industry	Location	Per	Low	Mid	High	Source	Date
Education Administrator							
Preschool and Child Care Center/Program	Amarillo MSA, TX	S	19.23 mw	18.97 aw	40000 aaw	TXBLS	10//99-12/99
Preschool and Child Care Center/Program	Austin-San Marcos MSA, TX	S	14.83 mw	12.51 aw	30840 aaw	TXBLS	10//99-12/99
Preschool and Child Care Center/Program	Dallas PMSA, TX	S	24.48 mw	21.04 aw	50910 aaw	TXBLS	10//99-12/99
Preschool and Child Care Center/Program	Fort Worth-Arlington PMSA, TX	S	26.20 mw	26.18 aw	54490 aaw	TXBLS	10//99-12/99
Preschool and Child Care Center/Program	Houston PMSA, TX	S	23.72 mw	20.56 aw	49330 aaw	TXBLS	10//99-12/99
Preschool and Child Care Center/Program	Longview-Marshall MSA, TX	S	24.80 mw	28.80 aw	51580 aaw	TXBLS	10//99-12/99
Preschool and Child Care Center/Program	San Antonio MSA, TX	S	14.10 mw	12.12 aw	29320 aaw	TXBLS	10//99-12/99
Preschool and Child Care Center/Program	Salt Lake City-Ogden MSA, UT	S	16.06 mw	15.63 aw	33410 aaw	UTBLS	10//99-12/99
Preschool and Child Care Center/Program	Vermont	S	20.71 mw	23.75 aw	49400 aaw	VTBLS	10//99-12/99
Preschool and Child Care Center/Program	Virginia	S	11.56 mw	13.78 aw	28660 aaw	VABLS	10//99-12/99
Preschool and Child Care Center/Program	Charlottesville MSA, VA	S	17.47 mw	18.21 aw	36350 aaw	VABLS	10//99-12/99
Preschool and Child Care Center/Program	Lynchburg MSA, VA	S	11.51 mw	10.14 aw	23930 aaw	VABLS	10//99-12/99
Preschool and Child Care Center/Program	Norfolk-Virginia Beach-Newport News MSA, VA-NC	S	13.58 mw	11.26 aw	28250 aaw	VABLS	10//99-12/99
Preschool and Child Care Center/Program	Richmond-Petersburg MSA, VA	S	10.32 mw	9.80 aw	21470 aaw	VABLS	10//99-12/99
Preschool and Child Care Center/Program	Roanoke MSA, VA	S	10.16 mw	8.45 aw	21140 aaw	VABLS	10//99-12/99
Preschool and Child Care Center/Program	Washington	S	17.08 mw	21.48 aw	44690 aaw	WABLS	10//99-12/99
Preschool and Child Care Center/Program	Richland-Kennewick-Pasco MSA, WA	S	16.36 mw	15.51 aw	34030 aaw	WABLS	10//99-12/99
Preschool and Child Care Center/Program	Seattle-Bellevue-Everett PMSA, WA	S	22.35 mw	20.32 aw	46490 aaw	WABLS	10//99-12/99
Preschool and Child Care Center/Program	Spokane MSA, WA	S	14.83 mw	14.12 aw	30850 aaw	WABLS	10//99-12/99
Preschool and Child Care Center/Program	Tacoma PMSA, WA	S	32.30 mw	37.01 aw	67190 aaw	WABLS	10//99-12/99
Preschool and Child Care Center/Program	Madison MSA, WI	S	27.33 mw	28.20 aw	56850 aaw	WIBLS	10//99-12/99
Preschool and Child Care Center/Program	Wyoming	S	26.61 mw	24.98 aw	51960 aaw	WYBLS	10//99-12/99
Preschool and Child Care Center/Program	Puerto Rico	S	14.63 mw	14.44 aw	30040 aaw	PRBLS	10//99-12/99
Preschool and Child Care Center/Program	San Juan-Bayamon PMSA, PR	S	15.39 mw	15.28 aw	32010 aaw	PRBLS	10//99-12/99
Education Teacher							
Postsecondary	Alabama	Y		44910 aaw		ALBLS	10//99-12/99
Postsecondary	Birmingham MSA, AL	Y		46780 aaw		ALBLS	10//99-12/99
Postsecondary	Tuscaloosa MSA, AL	Y		41380 aaw		ALBLS	10//99-12/99
Postsecondary	Arizona	Y		35900 aaw		AZBLS	10//99-12/99
Postsecondary	Phoenix-Mesa MSA, AZ	Y		33440 aaw		AZBLS	10//99-12/99
Postsecondary	Arkansas	Y		47450 aaw		ARBLS	10//99-12/99
Postsecondary	California	Y		46140 aaw		CABLS	10//99-12/99
Postsecondary	Los Angeles-Long Beach PMSA, CA	Y		43410 aaw		CABLS	10//99-12/99
Postsecondary	Riverside-San Bernardino PMSA, CA	Y		52310 aaw		CABLS	10//99-12/99
Postsecondary	San Francisco PMSA, CA	Y		47410 aaw		CABLS	10//99-12/99
Postsecondary	Colorado	Y		42010 aaw		COBLS	10//99-12/99
Postsecondary	Denver PMSA, CO	Y		41970 aaw		COBLS	10//99-12/99
Postsecondary	Connecticut	Y		50540 aaw		CTBLS	10//99-12/99
Postsecondary	Hartford MSA, CT	Y		57520 aaw		CTBLS	10//99-12/99
Postsecondary	District of Columbia	Y		39200 aaw		DCBLS	10//99-12/99
Postsecondary	Washington PMSA, DC-MD-VA-WV	Y		46600 aaw		DCBLS	10//99-12/99
Postsecondary	Florida	Y		61980 aaw		FLBLS	10//99-12/99
Postsecondary	Jacksonville MSA, FL	Y		65380 aaw		FLBLS	10//99-12/99
Postsecondary	Miami PMSA, FL	Y		60690 aaw		FLBLS	10//99-12/99
Postsecondary	Tampa-St. Petersburg-Clearwater MSA, FL	Y		64960 aaw		FLBLS	10//99-12/99
Postsecondary	West Palm Beach-Boca Raton MSA, FL	Y		53620 aaw		FLBLS	10//99-12/99
Postsecondary	Georgia	Y		44380 aaw		GABLS	10//99-12/99
Postsecondary	Atlanta MSA, GA	Y		44970 aaw		GABLS	10//99-12/99
Postsecondary	Savannah MSA, GA	Y		51230 aaw		GABLS	10//99-12/99
Postsecondary	Idaho	Y		48170 aaw		IDBLS	10//99-12/99
Postsecondary	Illinois	Y		45260 aaw		ILBLS	10//99-12/99
Postsecondary	Chicago PMSA, IL	Y		46300 aaw		ILBLS	10//99-12/99
Postsecondary	Indiana	Y		39840 aaw		INBLS	10//99-12/99
Postsecondary	Fort Wayne MSA, IN	Y		36820 aaw		INBLS	10//99-12/99
Postsecondary	Gary PMSA, IN	Y		41630 aaw		INBLS	10//99-12/99
Postsecondary	Indianapolis MSA, IN	Y		37320 aaw		INBLS	10//99-12/99
Postsecondary	Iowa	Y		44480 aaw		IABLS	10//99-12/99
Postsecondary	Kansas	Y		36700 aaw		KSBLS	10//99-12/99
Postsecondary	Kentucky	Y		46370 aaw		KYBLS	10//99-12/99

AAW	Average annual wage	AOH	Average offered, high	ASH	Average starting, high	H	Hourly	M	Monthly	S	Special: hourly and annual
AE	Average entry wage	AOL	Average offered, low	ASL	Average starting, low	HI	Highest wage paid	MTC	Median total compensation	TQ	Third quartile wage
AEX	Average experienced wage	APH	Average pay, high range	AW	Average wage paid	HR	High end range	MW	Median wage paid	W	Weekly
AO	Average offered	APL	Average pay, low range	FQ	First quartile wage	LR	Low end range	SQ	Second quartile wage	Y	Yearly

Education Teacher

Occupation/Type/Industry	Location	Per	Low	Mid	High	Source	Date
Education Teacher							
Postsecondary	Louisiana	Y		41930 AAW		LABLS	10//99-12//99
Postsecondary	Maine	Y		45930 AAW		MEBLS	10//99-12//99
Postsecondary	Maryland	Y		52640 AAW		MDBLS	10//99-12//99
Postsecondary	Baltimore PMSA, MD	Y		46670 AAW		MDBLS	10//99-12//99
Postsecondary	Massachusetts	Y		45710 AAW		MABLS	10//99-12//99
Postsecondary	Boston PMSA, MA-NH	Y		43950 AAW		MABLS	10//99-12//99
Postsecondary	Springfield MSA, MA	Y		47090 AAW		MABLS	10//99-12//99
Postsecondary	Worcester PMSA, MA-CT	Y		50780 AAW		MABLS	10//99-12//99
Postsecondary	Michigan	Y		54030 AAW		MIBLS	10//99-12//99
Postsecondary	Detroit PMSA, MI	Y		42370 AAW		MIBLS	10//99-12//99
Postsecondary	Grand Rapids-Muskegon-Holland MSA, MI	Y		42630 AAW		MIBLS	10//99-12//99
Postsecondary	Minnesota	Y		48960 AAW		MNBLS	10//99-12//99
Postsecondary	Minneapolis-St. Paul MSA, MN-WI	Y		49120 AAW		MNBLS	10//99-12//99
Postsecondary	Mississippi	Y		41390 AAW		MSBLS	10//99-12//99
Postsecondary	Jackson MSA, MS	Y		36400 AAW		MSBLS	10//99-12//99
Postsecondary	Missouri	Y		38880 AAW		MOBLS	10//99-12//99
Postsecondary	St. Louis MSA, MO-IL	Y		32940 AAW		MOBLS	10//99-12//99
Postsecondary	Montana	Y		51200 AAW		MTBLS	10//99-12//99
Postsecondary	Nevada	Y		41400 AAW		NVBLS	10//99-12//99
Postsecondary	New Hampshire	Y		49270 AAW		NHBLS	10//99-12//99
Postsecondary	New Jersey	Y		52090 AAW		NJBLS	10//99-12//99
Postsecondary	Bergen-Passaic PMSA, NJ	Y		52530 AAW		NJBLS	10//99-12//99
Postsecondary	Jersey City PMSA, NJ	Y		46780 AAW		NJBLS	10//99-12//99
Postsecondary	Newark PMSA, NJ	Y		51500 AAW		NJBLS	10//99-12//99
Postsecondary	Albany-Schenectady-Troy MSA, NY	Y		37110 AAW		NYBLS	10//99-12//99
Postsecondary	Buffalo-Niagara Falls MSA, NY	Y		38660 AAW		NYBLS	10//99-12//99
Postsecondary	New York PMSA, NY	Y		40910 AAW		NYBLS	10//99-12//99
Postsecondary	North Carolina	Y		44600 AAW		NCBLS	10//99-12//99
Postsecondary	Charlotte-Gastonia-Rock Hill MSA, NC-SC	Y		42190 AAW		NCBLS	10//99-12//99
Postsecondary	Greensboro--Winston-Salem--High Point MSA, NC	Y		49660 AAW		NCBLS	10//99-12//99
Postsecondary	Hickory-Morganton-Lenoir MSA, NC	Y		34520 AAW		NCBLS	10//99-12//99
Postsecondary	Raleigh-Durham-Chapel Hill MSA, NC	Y		48220 AAW		NCBLS	10//99-12//99
Postsecondary	North Dakota	Y		40480 AAW		NDBLS	10//99-12//99
Postsecondary	Ohio	Y		41390 AAW		OHBLS	10//99-12//99
Postsecondary	Cincinnati PMSA, OH-KY-IN	Y		43510 AAW		OHBLS	10//99-12//99
Postsecondary	Cleveland-Lorain-Elyria PMSA, OH	Y		46980 AAW		OHBLS	10//99-12//99
Postsecondary	Columbus MSA, OH	Y		33470 AAW		OHBLS	10//99-12//99
Postsecondary	Dayton-Springfield MSA, OH	Y		41930 AAW		OHBLS	10//99-12//99
Postsecondary	Oklahoma	Y		45530 AAW		OKBLS	10//99-12//99
Postsecondary	Oklahoma City MSA, OK	Y		42960 AAW		OKBLS	10//99-12//99
Postsecondary	Tulsa MSA, OK	Y		47910 AAW		OKBLS	10//99-12//99
Postsecondary	Oregon	Y		44140 AAW		ORBLS	10//99-12//99
Postsecondary	Portland-Vancouver PMSA, OR-WA	Y		46620 AAW		ORBLS	10//99-12//99
Postsecondary	Pennsylvania	Y		49000 AAW		PABLS	10//99-12//99
Postsecondary	Allentown-Bethlehem-Easton MSA, PA	Y		44260 AAW		PABLS	10//99-12//99
Postsecondary	Erie MSA, PA	Y		51620 AAW		PABLS	10//99-12//99
Postsecondary	Harrisburg-Lebanon-Carlisle MSA, PA	Y		47230 AAW		PABLS	10//99-12//99
Postsecondary	Philadelphia PMSA, PA-NJ	Y		49450 AAW		PABLS	10//99-12//99
Postsecondary	Pittsburgh MSA, PA	Y		47300 AAW		PABLS	10//99-12//99
Postsecondary	Reading MSA, PA	Y		46050 AAW		PABLS	10//99-12//99
Postsecondary	Scranton--Wilkes-Barre--Hazleton MSA, PA	Y		42650 AAW		PABLS	10//99-12//99
Postsecondary	Rhode Island	Y		53220 AAW		RIBLS	10//99-12//99
Postsecondary	Providence-Fall River-Warwick MSA, RI-MA	Y		53050 AAW		RIBLS	10//99-12//99
Postsecondary	South Carolina	Y		48980 AAW		SCBLS	10//99-12//99
Postsecondary	Charleston-North Charleston MSA, SC	Y		44440 AAW		SCBLS	10//99-12//99

AAW	Average annual wage	AOH	Average offered, high	ASH	Average starting, high	H	Hourly	M	Monthly	S	Special: hourly and annual
AE	Average entry wage	AOL	Average offered, low	ASL	Average starting, low	HI	Highest wage paid	MTC	Median total compensation	TQ	Third quartile wage
AEX	Average experienced wage	APH	Average pay, high range	AW	Average wage paid	HR	High end range	MW	Median wage paid	W	Weekly
AO	Average offered	APL	Average pay, low range	FQ	First quartile wage	LR	Low end range	SQ	Second quartile wage	Y	Yearly

Occupation/Type/Industry	Location	Per	Low	Mid	High	Source	Date
Education Teacher							
Postsecondary	Greenville-Spartanburg-Anderson MSA, SC	Y		51040 AAW		SCBLS	10//99-12//99
Postsecondary	South Dakota	Y		40210 AAW		SDBLS	10//99-12//99
Postsecondary	Tennessee	Y		42320 AAW		TNBLS	10//99-12//99
Postsecondary	Johnson City-Kingsport-Bristol MSA, TN-VA	Y		33120 AAW		TNBLS	10//99-12//99
Postsecondary	Nashville MSA, TN	Y		45300 AAW		TNBLS	10//99-12//99
Postsecondary	Texas	Y		41150 AAW		TXBLS	10//99-12//99
Postsecondary	Austin-San Marcos MSA, TX	Y		40440 AAW		TXBLS	10//99-12//99
Postsecondary	Dallas PMSA, TX	Y		55750 AAW		TXBLS	10//99-12//99
Postsecondary	El Paso MSA, TX	Y		33360 AAW		TXBLS	10//99-12//99
Postsecondary	Fort Worth-Arlington PMSA, TX	Y		40870 AAW		TXBLS	10//99-12//99
Postsecondary	Houston PMSA, TX	Y		41720 AAW		TXBLS	10//99-12//99
Postsecondary	McAllen-Edinburg-Mission MSA, TX	Y		47460 AAW		TXBLS	10//99-12//99
Postsecondary	Odessa-Midland MSA, TX	Y		42400 AAW		TXBLS	10//99-12//99
Postsecondary	San Antonio MSA, TX	Y		55530 AAW		TXBLS	10//99-12//99
Postsecondary	Vermont	Y		45340 AAW		VTBLS	10//99-12//99
Postsecondary	Virginia	Y		51370 AAW		VABLS	10//99-12//99
Postsecondary	Norfolk-Virginia Beach-Newport News MSA, VA-NC	Y		52920 AAW		VABLS	10//99-12//99
Postsecondary	Washington	Y		46660 AAW		WABLS	10//99-12//99
Postsecondary	Seattle-Bellevue-Everett PMSA, WA	Y		47860 AAW		WABLS	10//99-12//99
Postsecondary	Tacoma PMSA, WA	Y		52870 AAW		WABLS	10//99-12//99
Postsecondary	West Virginia	Y		51370 AAW		WVBLS	10//99-12//99
Postsecondary	Charleston MSA, WV	Y		44990 AAW		WVBLS	10//99-12//99
Postsecondary	Wisconsin	Y		44390 AAW		WIBLS	10//99-12//99
Postsecondary	Milwaukee-Waukesha PMSA, WI	Y		41470 AAW		WIBLS	10//99-12//99
Postsecondary	Puerto Rico	Y		30660 AAW		PRBLS	10//99-12//99
Postsecondary	Arecibo PMSA, PR	Y		33850 AAW		PRBLS	10//99-12//99
Postsecondary	Mayaguez MSA, PR	Y		29690 AAW		PRBLS	10//99-12//99
Postsecondary	San Juan-Bayamon PMSA, PR	Y		30000 AAW		PRBLS	10//99-12//99
Educational, Vocational, and School Counselor							
	Alabama	S	19.01 MW	19.33 AW	40210 AAW	ALBLS	10//99-12//99
	Anniston MSA, AL	S	17.17 MW	17.38 AW	35720 AAW	ALBLS	10//99-12//99
	Auburn-Opelika MSA, AL	S	18.97 MW	19.15 AW	39450 AAW	ALBLS	10//99-12//99
	Birmingham MSA, AL	S	20.53 MW	21.83 AW	42690 AAW	ALBLS	10//99-12//99
	Decatur MSA, AL	S	20.78 MW	20.63 AW	43220 AAW	ALBLS	10//99-12//99
	Dothan MSA, AL	S	20.76 MW	20.80 AW	43180 AAW	ALBLS	10//99-12//99
	Florence MSA, AL	S	18.93 MW	19.05 AW	39370 AAW	ALBLS	10//99-12//99
	Gadsden MSA, AL	S	17.54 MW	18.37 AW	36480 AAW	ALBLS	10//99-12//99
	Huntsville MSA, AL	S	19.72 MW	20.47 AW	41010 AAW	ALBLS	10//99-12//99
	Mobile MSA, AL	S	19.43 MW	17.86 AW	40420 AAW	ALBLS	10//99-12//99
	Montgomery MSA, AL	S	18.10 MW	18.32 AW	37660 AAW	ALBLS	10//99-12//99
	Tuscaloosa MSA, AL	S	21.42 MW	20.72 AW	44550 AAW	ALBLS	10//99-12//99
	Alaska	S	22.91 MW	23.29 AW	48450 AAW	AKBLS	10//99-12//99
	Arizona	S	15.64 MW	16.94 AW	35230 AAW	AZBLS	10//99-12//99
	Flagstaff MSA, AZ-UT	S	17.33 MW	15.58 AW	36050 AAW	AZBLS	10//99-12//99
	Phoenix-Mesa MSA, AZ	S	17.20 MW	15.12 AW	35780 AAW	AZBLS	10//99-12//99
	Tucson MSA, AZ	S	16.58 MW	16.53 AW	34490 AAW	AZBLS	10//99-12//99
	Yuma MSA, AZ	S	14.07 MW	14.98 AW	29270 AAW	AZBLS	10//99-12//99
	Arkansas	S	18.42 MW	18.24 AW	37940 AAW	ARBLS	10//99-12//99
	Fayetteville-Springdale-Rogers MSA, AR	S	19.19 MW	18.83 AW	39920 AAW	ARBLS	10//99-12//99
	Fort Smith MSA, AR-OK	S	19.02 MW	19.26 AW	39560 AAW	ARBLS	10//99-12//99
	Jonesboro MSA, AR	S	17.31 MW	18.30 AW	36010 AAW	ARBLS	10//99-12//99
	Little Rock-North Little Rock MSA, AR	S	18.47 MW	18.65 AW	38410 AAW	ARBLS	10//99-12//99
	California	S	22.08 MW	21.84 AW	45440 AAW	CABLS	10//99-12//99
	Bakersfield MSA, CA	S	24.65 MW	25.89 AW	51270 AAW	CABLS	10//99-12//99
	Chico-Paradise MSA, CA	S	20.56 MW	21.16 AW	42770 AAW	CABLS	10//99-12//99
	Fresno MSA, CA	S	24.12 MW	26.00 AW	50170 AAW	CABLS	10//99-12//99
	Los Angeles-Long Beach PMSA, CA	S	24.94 MW	27.07 AW	51880 AAW	CABLS	10//99-12//99
	Merced MSA, CA	S	29.58 MW	26.96 AW	61530 AAW	CABLS	10//99-12//99
	Modesto MSA, CA	S	22.21 MW	22.99 AW	46200 AAW	CABLS	10//99-12//99

AAW	Average annual wage	AOH	Average offered, high	ASH	Average starting, high	H	Hourly	M	Monthly	S	Special: hourly and annual
AE	Average entry wage	AOL	Average offered, low	ASL	Average starting, low	HI	Highest wage paid	MTC	Median total compensation	TQ	Third quartile wage
AEX	Average experienced wage	APH	Average pay, high range	AW	Average wage paid	HR	High end range	MW	Median wage paid	W	Weekly
AO	Average offered	APL	Average pay, low range	FQ	First quartile wage	LR	Low end range	SQ	Second quartile wage	Y	Yearly

Occupation/Type/Industry	Location	Per	Low	Mid	High	Source	Date
Educational, Vocational, and School Counselor							
	Oakland PMSA, CA	S	16.67 MW	15.64 AW	34680 AAW	CABLS	10//99-12//99
	Orange County PMSA, CA	S	18.69 MW	16.49 AW	38880 AAW	CABLS	10//99-12//99
	Redding MSA, CA	S	19.67 MW	18.87 AW	40920 AAW	CABLS	10//99-12//99
	Riverside-San Bernardino PMSA, CA	S	21.62 MW	22.49 AW	44970 AAW	CABLS	10//99-12//99
	Sacramento PMSA, CA	S	19.26 MW	18.36 AW	40060 AAW	CABLS	10//99-12//99
	Salinas MSA, CA	S	23.56 MW	27.25 AW	49000 AAW	CABLS	10//99-12//99
	San Diego MSA, CA	S	22.30 MW	23.72 AW	46390 AAW	CABLS	10//99-12//99
	San Francisco PMSA, CA	S	19.63 MW	17.81 AW	40820 AAW	CABLS	10//99-12//99
	San Jose PMSA, CA	S	22.83 MW	22.29 AW	47480 AAW	CABLS	10//99-12//99
	San Luis Obispo-Atascadero-Paso Robles MSA, CA	S	25.84 MW	28.27 AW	53740 AAW	CABLS	10//99-12//99
	Santa Barbara-Santa Maria-Lompoc MSA, CA	S	17.82 MW	17.21 AW	37060 AAW	CABLS	10//99-12//99
	Santa Cruz-Watsonville PMSA, CA	S	27.64 MW	21.95 AW	57480 AAW	CABLS	10//99-12//99
	Santa Rosa PMSA, CA	S	20.86 MW	20.19 AW	43400 AAW	CABLS	10//99-12//99
	Stockton-Lodi MSA, CA	S	20.32 MW	20.58 AW	42270 AAW	CABLS	10//99-12//99
	Vallejo-Fairfield-Napa PMSA, CA	S	19.11 MW	19.13 AW	39740 AAW	CABLS	10//99-12//99
	Ventura PMSA, CA	S	24.32 MW	24.86 AW	50580 AAW	CABLS	10//99-12//99
	Visalia-Tulare-Porterville MSA, CA	S	15.78 MW	12.12 AW	32820 AAW	CABLS	10//99-12//99
	Yolo PMSA, CA	S	18.12 MW	16.80 AW	37680 AAW	CABLS	10//99-12//99
	Yuba City MSA, CA	S	19.74 MW	16.24 AW	41060 AAW	CABLS	10//99-12//99
	Colorado	S	17.66 MW	19.22 AW	39970 AAW	COBLS	10//99-12//99
	Boulder-Longmont PMSA, CO	S	21.07 MW	19.62 AW	43830 AAW	COBLS	10//99-12//99
	Colorado Springs MSA, CO	S	23.15 MW	21.04 AW	48150 AAW	COBLS	10//99-12//99
	Denver PMSA, CO	S	20.08 MW	18.41 AW	41770 AAW	COBLS	10//99-12//99
	Greeley PMSA, CO	S	17.54 MW	17.88 AW	36490 AAW	COBLS	10//99-12//99
	Connecticut	S	19.67 MW	20.73 AW	43120 AAW	CTBLS	10//99-12//99
	Bridgeport PMSA, CT	S	20.59 MW	19.26 AW	42830 AAW	CTBLS	10//99-12//99
	Danbury PMSA, CT	S	16.74 MW	12.90 AW	34830 AAW	CTBLS	10//99-12//99
	Hartford MSA, CT	S	21.64 MW	21.28 AW	45010 AAW	CTBLS	10//99-12//99
	New Haven-Meriden PMSA, CT	S	22.96 MW	22.80 AW	47750 AAW	CTBLS	10//99-12//99
	New London-Norwich MSA, CT-RI	S	19.41 MW	17.06 AW	40380 AAW	CTBLS	10//99-12//99
	Stamford-Norwalk PMSA, CT	S	17.41 MW	14.76 AW	36200 AAW	CTBLS	10//99-12//99
	Waterbury PMSA, CT	S	22.28 MW	23.07 AW	46350 AAW	CTBLS	10//99-12//99
	District of Columbia	S	18.06 MW	18.90 AW	39310 AAW	DCBLS	10//99-12//99
	Washington PMSA, DC-MD-VA-WV	S	19.86 MW	18.85 AW	41310 AAW	DCBLS	10//99-12//99
	Florida	S	17.92 MW	18.37 AW	38220 AAW	FLBLS	10//99-12//99
	Fort Myers-Cape Coral MSA, FL	S	18.48 MW	17.42 AW	38450 AAW	FLBLS	10//99-12//99
	Fort Pierce-Port St. Lucie MSA, FL	S	19.32 MW	19.92 AW	40180 AAW	FLBLS	10//99-12//99
	Gainesville MSA, FL	S	19.36 MW	18.41 AW	40270 AAW	FLBLS	10//99-12//99
	Jacksonville MSA, FL	S	19.01 MW	18.59 AW	39540 AAW	FLBLS	10//99-12//99
	Melbourne-Titusville-Palm Bay MSA, FL	S	15.58 MW	15.51 AW	32400 AAW	FLBLS	10//99-12//99
	Miami PMSA, FL	S	11.95 MW	11.14 AW	24860 AAW	FLBLS	10//99-12//99
	Ocala MSA, FL	S	13.06 MW	12.05 AW	27160 AAW	FLBLS	10//99-12//99
	Orlando MSA, FL	S	19.66 MW	19.65 AW	40890 AAW	FLBLS	10//99-12//99
	Pensacola MSA, FL	S	19.35 MW	18.92 AW	40250 AAW	FLBLS	10//99-12//99
	Sarasota-Bradenton MSA, FL	S	19.33 MW	19.69 AW	40200 AAW	FLBLS	10//99-12//99
	Tallahassee MSA, FL	S	18.72 MW	16.70 AW	38950 AAW	FLBLS	10//99-12//99
	Tampa-St. Petersburg-Clearwater MSA, FL	S	19.33 MW	18.16 AW	40200 AAW	FLBLS	10//99-12//99
	West Palm Beach-Boca Raton MSA, FL	S	20.96 MW	19.41 AW	43590 AAW	FLBLS	10//99-12//99
	Georgia	S	21.95 MW	21.54 AW	44790 AAW	GABLS	10//99-12//99
	Albany MSA, GA	S	19.66 MW	21.94 AW	40890 AAW	GABLS	10//99-12//99
	Atlanta MSA, GA	S	22.51 MW	22.87 AW	46830 AAW	GABLS	10//99-12//99
	Augusta-Aiken MSA, GA-SC	S	19.31 MW	19.25 AW	40170 AAW	GABLS	10//99-12//99
	Columbus MSA, GA-AL	S	21.37 MW	20.70 AW	44460 AAW	GABLS	10//99-12//99
	Macon MSA, GA	S	22.51 MW	22.68 AW	46820 AAW	GABLS	10//99-12//99
	Savannah MSA, GA	S	19.61 MW	19.74 AW	40790 AAW	GABLS	10//99-12//99
	Hawaii	S	20.41 MW	22.02 AW	45800 AAW	HIBLS	10//99-12//99
	Honolulu MSA, HI	S	22.28 MW	20.32 AW	46330 AAW	HIBLS	10//99-12//99

AAW	Average annual wage	AOH	Average offered, high	ASH	Average starting, high	H	Hourly
AE	Average entry wage	AOL	Average offered, low	ASL	Average starting, low	HI	Highest wage paid
AEX	Average experienced wage	APH	Average pay, high range	AW	Average wage paid	HR	High end range
AO	Average offered	APL	Average pay, low range	FQ	First quartile wage	LR	Low end range

M	Monthly	S	Special: hourly and annual
MTC	Median total compensation	TQ	Third quartile wage
MW	Median wage paid	W	Weekly
SQ	Second quartile wage	Y	Yearly

Occupation/Type/Industry	Location	Per	Low	Mid	High	Source	Date
Educational, Vocational, and School Counselor							
	Idaho	S	19.04 MW	19.70 AW	40980 AAW	IDBLS	10//99-12//99
	Boise City MSA, ID	S	21.45 MW	20.77 AW	44610 AAW	IDBLS	10//99-12//99
	Pocatello MSA, ID	S	18.77 MW	17.17 AW	39040 AAW	IDBLS	10//99-12//99
	Illinois	S	18.89 MW	20.52 AW	42680 AAW	ILBLS	10//99-12//99
	Champaign-Urbana MSA, IL	S	17.24 MW	14.96 AW	35850 AAW	ILBLS	10//99-12//99
	Chicago PMSA, IL	S	21.66 MW	20.34 AW	45040 AAW	ILBLS	10//99-12//99
	Decatur MSA, IL	S	17.79 MW	20.33 AW	37000 AAW	ILBLS	10//99-12//99
	Peoria-Pekin MSA, IL	S	18.57 MW	16.95 AW	38630 AAW	ILBLS	10//99-12//99
	Rockford MSA, IL	S	23.85 MW	22.36 AW	49600 AAW	ILBLS	10//99-12//99
	Springfield MSA, IL	S	16.79 MW	15.50 AW	34910 AAW	ILBLS	10//99-12//99
	Indiana	S	18.52 MW	19.55 AW	40660 AAW	INBLS	10//99-12//99
	Elkhart-Goshen MSA, IN	S	28.94 MW	27.06 AW	60200 AAW	INBLS	10//99-12//99
	Evansville-Henderson MSA, IN-KY	S	17.26 MW	16.08 AW	35910 AAW	INBLS	10//99-12//99
	Fort Wayne MSA, IN	S	21.33 MW	22.13 AW	44370 AAW	INBLS	10//99-12//99
	Gary PMSA, IN	S	20.78 MW	21.29 AW	43210 AAW	INBLS	10//99-12//99
	Indianapolis MSA, IN	S	22.32 MW	22.12 AW	46420 AAW	INBLS	10//99-12//99
	Kokomo MSA, IN	S	20.87 MW	21.57 AW	43410 AAW	INBLS	10//99-12//99
	Lafayette MSA, IN	S	20.29 MW	20.80 AW	42210 AAW	INBLS	10//99-12//99
	Muncie MSA, IN	S	15.87 MW	15.04 AW	33000 AAW	INBLS	10//99-12//99
	South Bend MSA, IN	S	14.80 MW	14.73 AW	30780 AAW	INBLS	10//99-12//99
	Terre Haute MSA, IN	S	18.70 MW	19.89 AW	38900 AAW	INBLS	10//99-12//99
	Iowa	S	17.09 MW	16.92 AW	35200 AAW	IABLS	10//99-12//99
	Cedar Rapids MSA, IA	S	14.86 MW	14.23 AW	30920 AAW	IABLS	10//99-12//99
	Davenport-Moline-Rock Island MSA, IA-IL	S	19.19 MW	17.83 AW	39900 AAW	IABLS	10//99-12//99
	Des Moines MSA, IA	S	18.24 MW	18.11 AW	37930 AAW	IABLS	10//99-12//99
	Dubuque MSA, IA	S	18.01 MW	19.19 AW	37460 AAW	IABLS	10//99-12//99
	Sioux City MSA, IA-NE	S	14.51 MW	12.79 AW	30190 AAW	IABLS	10//99-12//99
	Waterloo-Cedar Falls MSA, IA	S	16.58 MW	16.20 AW	34480 AAW	IABLS	10//99-12//99
	Kansas	S	18.83 MW	18.46 AW	38410 AAW	KSBLS	10//99-12//99
	Topeka MSA, KS	S	20.12 MW	20.33 AW	41850 AAW	KSBLS	10//99-12//99
	Wichita MSA, KS	S	18.93 MW	19.38 AW	39380 AAW	KSBLS	10//99-12//99
	Kentucky	S	20.79 MW	20.61 AW	42870 AAW	KYBLS	10//99-12//99
	Lexington MSA, KY	S	20.34 MW	20.06 AW	42300 AAW	KYBLS	10//99-12//99
	Louisville MSA, KY-IN	S	22.45 MW	22.45 AW	46700 AAW	KYBLS	10//99-12//99
	Louisiana	S	18.43 MW	18.82 AW	39140 AAW	LABLS	10//99-12//99
	Baton Rouge MSA, LA	S	17.17 MW	17.61 AW	35720 AAW	LABLS	10//99-12//99
	Monroe MSA, LA	S	17.07 MW	17.25 AW	35500 AAW	LABLS	10//99-12//99
	New Orleans MSA, LA	S	19.08 MW	19.15 AW	39680 AAW	LABLS	10//99-12//99
	Maine	S	15.85 MW	16.21 AW	33720 AAW	MEBLS	10//99-12//99
	Bangor MSA, ME	S	17.23 MW	16.33 AW	35840 AAW	MEBLS	10//99-12//99
	Lewiston-Auburn MSA, ME	S	17.10 MW	16.70 AW	35560 AAW	MEBLS	10//99-12//99
	Portland MSA, ME	S	14.94 MW	13.90 AW	31080 AAW	MEBLS	10//99-12//99
	Maryland	S	14.46 MW	16.47 AW	34250 AAW	MDBLS	10//99-12//99
	Baltimore PMSA, MD	S	15.16 MW	13.40 AW	31530 AAW	MDBLS	10//99-12//99
	Massachusetts	S	20.9 MW	19.90 AW	41390 AAW	MABLS	10//99-12//99
	Barnstable-Yarmouth MSA, MA	S	14.15 MW	11.53 AW	29440 AAW	MABLS	10//99-12//99
	Boston PMSA, MA-NH	S	20.76 MW	21.79 AW	43170 AAW	MABLS	10//99-12//99
	Brockton PMSA, MA	S	21.92 MW	21.73 AW	45580 AAW	MABLS	10//99-12//99
	Fitchburg-Leominster PMSA, MA	S	20.13 MW	21.67 AW	41860 AAW	MABLS	10//99-12//99
	Lawrence PMSA, MA-NH	S	16.81 MW	15.71 AW	34960 AAW	MABLS	10//99-12//99
	Lowell PMSA, MA-NH	S	22.00 MW	22.33 AW	45750 AAW	MABLS	10//99-12//99
	New Bedford PMSA, MA	S	15.95 MW	11.30 AW	33180 AAW	MABLS	10//99-12//99
	Pittsfield MSA, MA	S	18.93 MW	18.25 AW	39370 AAW	MABLS	10//99-12//99
	Springfield MSA, MA	S	16.98 MW	17.38 AW	35320 AAW	MABLS	10//99-12//99
	Worcester PMSA, MA-CT	S	19.52 MW	21.54 AW	40600 AAW	MABLS	10//99-12//99
	Michigan	S	22.44 MW	22.68 AW	47180 AAW	MIBLS	10//99-12//99
	Ann Arbor PMSA, MI	S	22.89 MW	22.46 AW	47620 AAW	MIBLS	10//99-12//99
	Benton Harbor MSA, MI	S	23.16 MW	22.67 AW	48170 AAW	MIBLS	10//99-12//99
	Detroit PMSA, MI	S	24.38 MW	24.83 AW	50710 AAW	MIBLS	10//99-12//99
	Flint PMSA, MI	S	24.61 MW	27.63 AW	51180 AAW	MIBLS	10//99-12//99
	Grand Rapids-Muskegon-Holland MSA, MI	S	23.11 MW	22.74 AW	48080 AAW	MIBLS	10//99-12//99
	Jackson MSA, MI	S	24.83 MW	24.84 AW	51640 AAW	MIBLS	10//99-12//99
	Kalamazoo-Battle Creek MSA, MI	S	19.97 MW	21.34 AW	41540 AAW	MIBLS	10//99-12//99
	Lansing-East Lansing MSA, MI	S	21.26 MW	21.35 AW	44230 AAW	MIBLS	10//99-12//99

AAW	Average annual wage	AOH	Average offered, high	ASH	Average starting, high
AE	Average entry wage	AOL	Average offered, low	ASL	Average starting, low
AEX	Average experienced wage	APH	Average pay, high range	AW	Average wage paid
AO	Average offered	APL	Average pay, low range	FQ	First quartile wage

H	Hourly	M	Monthly
HI	Highest wage paid	MTC	Median total compensation
HR	High end range	MW	Median wage paid
LR	Low end range	SQ	Second quartile wage

S	Special: hourly and annual
TQ	Third quartile wage
W	Weekly
Y	Yearly

Occupation/Type/Industry	Location	Per	Low	Mid	High	Source	Date
Educational, Vocational, and School Counselor	Saginaw-Bay City-Midland MSA, MI	S	20.65 MW	19.51 AW	42960 AAW	MIBLS	10//99-12//99
	Minnesota	S	16.91 MW	18.34 AW	38150 AAW	MNBLS	10//99-12//99
	Duluth-Superior MSA, MN-WI	S	19.44 MW	18.16 AW	40430 AAW	MNBLS	10//99-12//99
	Minneapolis-St. Paul MSA, MN-WI	S	18.57 MW	16.67 AW	38630 AAW	MNBLS	10//99-12//99
	St. Cloud MSA, MN	S	20.95 MW	19.45 AW	43570 AAW	MNBLS	10//99-12//99
	Mississippi	S	16.75 MW	16.92 AW	35200 AAW	MSBLS	10//99-12//99
	Biloxi-Gulfport-Pascagoula MSA, MS	S	19.23 MW	18.80 AW	40000 AAW	MSBLS	10//99-12//99
	Jackson MSA, MS	S	15.57 MW	15.05 AW	32390 AAW	MSBLS	10//99-12//99
	Missouri	S	17.68 MW	18.08 AW	37600 AAW	MOBLS	10//99-12//99
	Columbia MSA, MO	S	17.66 MW	17.39 AW	36740 AAW	MOBLS	10//99-12//99
	Joplin MSA, MO	S	14.16 MW	14.18 AW	29460 AAW	MOBLS	10//99-12//99
	Kansas City MSA, MO-KS	S	19.69 MW	19.78 AW	40950 AAW	MOBLS	10//99-12//99
	Springfield MSA, MO	S	16.04 MW	17.03 AW	33360 AAW	MOBLS	10//99-12//99
	Montana	S	14.61 MW	14.64 AW	30460 AAW	MTBLS	10//99-12//99
	Billings MSA, MT	S	18.64 MW	18.88 AW	38780 AAW	MTBLS	10//99-12//99
	Great Falls MSA, MT	S	18.80 MW	19.45 AW	39100 AAW	MTBLS	10//99-12//99
	Missoula MSA, MT	S	12.80 MW	13.18 AW	26620 AAW	MTBLS	10//99-12//99
	Nebraska	S	17.86 MW	17.78 AW	36990 AAW	NEBLS	10//99-12//99
	Omaha MSA, NE-IA	S	18.28 MW	17.47 AW	38020 AAW	NEBLS	10//99-12//99
	Nevada	S	21.23 MW	21.74 AW	45210 AAW	NVBLS	10//99-12//99
	New Hampshire	S	17.3 MW	17.57 AW	36550 AAW	NHBLS	10//99-12//99
	Manchester PMSA, NH	S	19.48 MW	19.23 AW	40520 AAW	NHBLS	10//99-12//99
	Nashua PMSA, NH	S	19.53 MW	18.91 AW	40620 AAW	NHBLS	10//99-12//99
	Portsmouth-Rochester PMSA, NH-ME	S	19.83 MW	18.72 AW	41240 AAW	NHBLS	10//99-12//99
	New Jersey	S	26.41 MW	25.75 AW	53560 AAW	NJBLS	10//99-12//99
	Atlantic-Cape May PMSA, NJ	S	24.07 MW	24.22 AW	50080 AAW	NJBLS	10//99-12//99
	Bergen-Passaic PMSA, NJ	S	28.47 MW	31.30 AW	59220 AAW	NJBLS	10//99-12//99
	Middlesex-Somerset-Hunterdon PMSA, NJ	S	25.52 MW	26.03 AW	53070 AAW	NJBLS	10//99-12//99
	Monmouth-Ocean PMSA, NJ	S	25.28 MW	26.10 AW	52590 AAW	NJBLS	10//99-12//99
	Newark PMSA, NJ	S	25.10 MW	25.44 AW	52210 AAW	NJBLS	10//99-12//99
	Trenton PMSA, NJ	S	26.29 MW	27.86 AW	54670 AAW	NJBLS	10//99-12//99
	Vineland-Millville-Bridgeton PMSA, NJ	S	21.54 MW	22.11 AW	44810 AAW	NJBLS	10//99-12//99
	New Mexico	S	16.41 MW	16.57 AW	34470 AAW	NMBLS	10//99-12//99
	Albuquerque MSA, NM	S	15.50 MW	15.38 AW	32230 AAW	NMBLS	10//99-12//99
	Las Cruces MSA, NM	S	15.80 MW	15.41 AW	32870 AAW	NMBLS	10//99-12//99
	Santa Fe MSA, NM	S	19.42 MW	17.56 AW	40400 AAW	NMBLS	10//99-12//99
	New York	S	20.32 MW	22.31 AW	46400 AAW	NYBLS	10//99-12//99
	Binghamton MSA, NY	S	18.59 MW	18.24 AW	38660 AAW	NYBLS	10//99-12//99
	Buffalo-Niagara Falls MSA, NY	S	20.90 MW	21.20 AW	43460 AAW	NYBLS	10//99-12//99
	Dutchess County PMSA, NY	S	17.92 MW	17.38 AW	37270 AAW	NYBLS	10//99-12//99
	Elmira MSA, NY	S	17.05 MW	16.26 AW	35470 AAW	NYBLS	10//99-12//99
	Glens Falls MSA, NY	S	22.56 MW	21.59 AW	46920 AAW	NYBLS	10//99-12//99
	Jamestown MSA, NY	S	19.65 MW	18.82 AW	40870 AAW	NYBLS	10//99-12//99
	Nassau-Suffolk PMSA, NY	S	29.64 MW	29.37 AW	61660 AAW	NYBLS	10//99-12//99
	New York PMSA, NY	S	23.03 MW	20.35 AW	47900 AAW	NYBLS	10//99-12//99
	Newburgh PMSA, NY-PA	S	23.26 MW	23.81 AW	48390 AAW	NYBLS	10//99-12//99
	Rochester MSA, NY	S	21.99 MW	19.92 AW	45730 AAW	NYBLS	10//99-12//99
	Syracuse MSA, NY	S	17.49 MW	17.80 AW	36380 AAW	NYBLS	10//99-12//99
	Utica-Rome MSA, NY	S	20.90 MW	20.77 AW	43470 AAW	NYBLS	10//99-12//99
	North Carolina	S	16.55 MW	16.82 AW	34990 AAW	NCBLS	10//99-12//99
	Asheville MSA, NC	S	15.46 MW	16.28 AW	32150 AAW	NCBLS	10//99-12//99
	Charlotte-Gastonia-Rock Hill MSA, NC-SC	S	17.69 MW	17.88 AW	36800 AAW	NCBLS	10//99-12//99
	Fayetteville MSA, NC	S	17.34 MW	17.15 AW	36060 AAW	NCBLS	10//99-12//99
	Goldsboro MSA, NC	S	16.98 MW	17.60 AW	35310 AAW	NCBLS	10//99-12//99
	Greensboro--Winston-Salem--High Point MSA, NC	S	19.12 MW	18.95 AW	39760 AAW	NCBLS	10//99-12//99
	Hickory-Morganton-Lenoir MSA, NC	S	17.20 MW	16.38 AW	35780 AAW	NCBLS	10//99-12//99
	Raleigh-Durham-Chapel Hill MSA, NC	S	14.63 MW	12.51 AW	30440 AAW	NCBLS	10//99-12//99
	Rocky Mount MSA, NC	S	16.99 MW	15.93 AW	35340 AAW	NCBLS	10//99-12//99
	Wilmington MSA, NC	S	16.46 MW	16.77 AW	34240 AAW	NCBLS	10//99-12//99
	North Dakota	S	15.23 MW	15.39 AW	32010 AAW	NDBLS	10//99-12//99

Occupation/Type/Industry	Location	Per	Low	Mid	High	Source	Date
Educational, Vocational, and School Counselor	Bismarck MSA, ND	S	13.44 MW	14.86 AW	27950 AAW	NDBLS	10//99-12/99
	Fargo-Moorhead MSA, ND-MN	S	15.95 MW	15.32 AW	33170 AAW	NDBLS	10//99-12/99
	Grand Forks MSA, ND-MN	S	19.37 MW	18.68 AW	40280 AAW	NDBLS	10//99-12/99
	Ohio	S	22.55 MW	21.77 AW	45280 AAW	OHBLS	10//99-12/99
	Akron PMSA, OH	S	21.49 MW	22.27 AW	44700 AAW	OHBLS	10//99-12/99
	Canton-Massillon MSA, OH	S	22.63 MW	22.93 AW	47070 AAW	OHBLS	10//99-12/99
	Cincinnati PMSA, OH-KY-IN	S	22.66 MW	23.12 AW	47140 AAW	OHBLS	10//99-12/99
	Cleveland-Lorain-Elyria PMSA, OH	S	24.38 MW	24.70 AW	50710 AAW	OHBLS	10//99-12/99
	Columbus MSA, OH	S	23.67 MW	24.22 AW	49230 AAW	OHBLS	10//99-12/99
	Dayton-Springfield MSA, OH	S	21.31 MW	22.91 AW	44320 AAW	OHBLS	10//99-12/99
	Hamilton-Middletown PMSA, OH	S	23.33 MW	24.81 AW	48520 AAW	OHBLS	10//99-12/99
	Lima MSA, OH	S	21.27 MW	20.86 AW	44240 AAW	OHBLS	10//99-12/99
	Steubenville-Weirton MSA, OH-WV	S	20.81 MW	21.44 AW	43280 AAW	OHBLS	10//99-12/99
	Toledo MSA, OH	S	23.28 MW	23.42 AW	48420 AAW	OHBLS	10//99-12/99
	Youngstown-Warren MSA, OH	S	16.95 MW	17.37 AW	35260 AAW	OHBLS	10//99-12/99
	Oklahoma	S	15.14 MW	15.45 AW	32150 AAW	OKBLS	10//99-12/99
	Enid MSA, OK	S	15.44 MW	15.34 AW	32110 AAW	OKBLS	10//99-12/99
	Oklahoma City MSA, OK	S	15.08 MW	14.44 AW	31360 AAW	OKBLS	10//99-12/99
	Tulsa MSA, OK	S	16.83 MW	16.54 AW	35000 AAW	OKBLS	10//99-12/99
	Oregon	S	21.61 MW	21.28 AW	44260 AAW	ORBLS	10//99-12/99
	Eugene-Springfield MSA, OR	S	21.05 MW	21.41 AW	43780 AAW	ORBLS	10//99-12/99
	Medford-Ashland MSA, OR	S	23.15 MW	22.84 AW	48140 AAW	ORBLS	10//99-12/99
	Portland-Vancouver PMSA, OR-WA	S	21.58 MW	21.38 AW	44890 AAW	ORBLS	10//99-12/99
	Salem PMSA, OR	S	19.49 MW	21.16 AW	40550 AAW	ORBLS	10//99-12/99
	Pennsylvania	S	19.04 MW	19.79 AW	41170 AAW	PABLS	10//99-12/99
	Allentown-Bethlehem-Easton MSA, PA	S	18.92 MW	17.19 AW	39360 AAW	PABLS	10//99-12/99
	Altoona MSA, PA	S	20.47 MW	21.58 AW	42590 AAW	PABLS	10//99-12/99
	Erie MSA, PA	S	17.40 MW	13.02 AW	36200 AAW	PABLS	10//99-12/99
	Harrisburg-Lebanon-Carlisle MSA, PA	S	18.65 MW	19.22 AW	38800 AAW	PABLS	10//99-12/99
	Johnstown MSA, PA	S	20.85 MW	19.83 AW	43360 AAW	PABLS	10//99-12/99
	Lancaster MSA, PA	S	19.26 MW	20.56 AW	40060 AAW	PABLS	10//99-12/99
	Philadelphia PMSA, PA-NJ	S	20.80 MW	19.65 AW	43260 AAW	PABLS	10//99-12/99
	Pittsburgh MSA, PA	S	21.36 MW	21.45 AW	44430 AAW	PABLS	10//99-12/99
	Reading MSA, PA	S	22.88 MW	23.04 AW	47590 AAW	PABLS	10//99-12/99
	Scranton--Wilkes-Barre--Hazleton MSA, PA	S	21.02 MW	20.04 AW	43720 AAW	PABLS	10//99-12/99
	Sharon MSA, PA	S	21.27 MW	21.90 AW	44230 AAW	PABLS	10//99-12/99
	Williamsport MSA, PA	S	17.54 MW	16.79 AW	36480 AAW	PABLS	10//99-12/99
	York MSA, PA	S	23.00 MW	23.35 AW	47850 AAW	PABLS	10//99-12/99
	Rhode Island	S	22.12 MW	21.95 AW	45650 AAW	RIBLS	10//99-12/99
	Providence-Fall River-Warwick MSA, RI-MA	S	21.60 MW	22.06 AW	44930 AAW	RIBLS	10//99-12/99
	South Carolina	S	18.03 MW	18.07 AW	37590 AAW	SCBLS	10//99-12/99
	Charleston-North Charleston MSA, SC	S	18.77 MW	18.55 AW	39050 AAW	SCBLS	10//99-12/99
	Columbia MSA, SC	S	20.08 MW	19.44 AW	41760 AAW	SCBLS	10//99-12/99
	Florence MSA, SC	S	17.85 MW	18.09 AW	37140 AAW	SCBLS	10//99-12/99
	Greenville-Spartanburg-Anderson MSA, SC	S	15.98 MW	15.73 AW	33240 AAW	SCBLS	10//99-12/99
	Sumter MSA, SC	S	11.61 MW	10.44 AW	24150 AAW	SCBLS	10//99-12/99
	South Dakota	S	14.69 MW	15.07 AW	31350 AAW	SDBLS	10//99-12/99
	Sioux Falls MSA, SD	S	16.67 MW	16.26 AW	34660 AAW	SDBLS	10//99-12/99
	Tennessee	S	15.99 MW	15.98 AW	33240 AAW	TNBLS	10//99-12/99
	Chattanooga MSA, TN-GA	S	11.51 MW	11.04 AW	23940 AAW	TNBLS	10//99-12/99
	Clarksville-Hopkinsville MSA, TN-KY	S	18.66 MW	18.58 AW	38820 AAW	TNBLS	10//99-12/99
	Jackson MSA, TN	S	15.98 MW	16.52 AW	33240 AAW	TNBLS	10//99-12/99
	Johnson City-Kingsport-Bristol MSA, TN-VA	S	14.71 MW	14.50 AW	30590 AAW	TNBLS	10//99-12/99
	Knoxville MSA, TN	S	18.34 MW	17.21 AW	38150 AAW	TNBLS	10//99-12/99
	Memphis MSA, TN-AR-MS	S	18.46 MW	19.30 AW	38390 AAW	MSBLS	10//99-12/99
	Nashville MSA, TN	S	16.42 MW	16.49 AW	34160 AAW	TNBLS	10//99-12/99
	Texas	S	20.93 MW	20.46 AW	42550 AAW	TXBLS	10//99-12/99
	Abilene MSA, TX	S	15.49 MW	14.36 AW	32220 AAW	TXBLS	10//99-12/99

AAW Average annual wage	AOH Average offered, high	ASH Average starting, high	H Hourly	M Monthly	S Special: hourly and annual
AE Average entry wage	AOL Average offered, low	ASL Average starting, low	HI Highest wage paid	MTC Median total compensation	TQ Third quartile wage
AEX Average experienced wage	APH Average pay, high range	AW Average wage paid	HR High end range	MW Median wage paid	W Weekly
AO Average offered	APL Average pay, low range	FQ First quartile wage	LR Low end range	SQ Second quartile wage	Y Yearly

Occupation/Type/Industry	Location	Per	Low	Mid	High	Source	Date
Educational, Vocational, and School Counselor	Austin-San Marcos MSA, TX	S	19.88 MW	20.83 AW	41350 AAW	TXBLS	10//99-12//99
	Beaumont-Port Arthur MSA, TX	S	21.46 MW	22.06 AW	44630 AAW	TXBLS	10//99-12//99
	Brazoria PMSA, TX	S	21.77 MW	22.55 AW	45280 AAW	TXBLS	10//99-12//99
	Brownsville-Harlingen-San Benito MSA, TX	S	20.20 MW	20.81 AW	42010 AAW	TXBLS	10//99-12//99
	Bryan-College Station MSA, TX	S	15.49 MW	15.18 AW	32220 AAW	TXBLS	10//99-12//99
	Corpus Christi MSA, TX	S	23.57 MW	25.16 AW	49020 AAW	TXBLS	10//99-12//99
	Dallas PMSA, TX	S	21.31 MW	20.36 AW	44320 AAW	TXBLS	10//99-12//99
	El Paso MSA, TX	S	17.67 MW	17.64 AW	36750 AAW	TXBLS	10//99-12//99
	Fort Worth-Arlington PMSA, TX	S	22.65 MW	22.83 AW	47110 AAW	TXBLS	10//99-12//99
	Galveston-Texas City PMSA, TX	S	22.13 MW	22.34 AW	46040 AAW	TXBLS	10//99-12//99
	Houston PMSA, TX	S	20.83 MW	22.03 AW	43320 AAW	TXBLS	10//99-12//99
	Killeen-Temple MSA, TX	S	20.35 MW	20.91 AW	42330 AAW	TXBLS	10//99-12//99
	Longview-Marshall MSA, TX	S	15.10 MW	15.17 AW	31400 AAW	TXBLS	10//99-12//99
	Lubbock MSA, TX	S	18.21 MW	17.71 AW	37880 AAW	TXBLS	10//99-12//99
	McAllen-Edinburg-Mission MSA, TX	S	21.77 MW	22.20 AW	45290 AAW	TXBLS	10//99-12//99
	San Angelo MSA, TX	S	19.62 MW	19.63 AW	40820 AAW	TXBLS	10//99-12//99
	San Antonio MSA, TX	S	20.63 MW	21.72 AW	42920 AAW	TXBLS	10//99-12//99
	Sherman-Denison MSA, TX	S	21.84 MW	20.57 AW	45420 AAW	TXBLS	10//99-12//99
	Texarkana MSA, TX-Texarkana, AR	S	19.70 MW	19.60 AW	40980 AAW	TXBLS	10//99-12//99
	Tyler MSA, TX	S	19.14 MW	19.33 AW	39800 AAW	TXBLS	10//99-12//99
	Victoria MSA, TX	S	22.23 MW	22.58 AW	46230 AAW	TXBLS	10//99-12//99
	Waco MSA, TX	S	18.77 MW	19.00 AW	39030 AAW	TXBLS	10//99-12//99
	Wichita Falls MSA, TX	S	16.76 MW	18.51 AW	34850 AAW	TXBLS	10//99-12//99
	Utah	S	14.07 MW	15.27 AW	31750 AAW	UTBLS	10//99-12//99
	Salt Lake City-Ogden MSA, UT	S	15.54 MW	14.28 AW	32320 AAW	UTBLS	10//99-12//99
	Vermont	S	18.18 MW	18.01 AW	37450 AAW	VTBLS	10//99-12//99
	Burlington MSA, VT	S	16.47 MW	15.60 AW	34260 AAW	VTBLS	10//99-12//99
	Virginia	S	19.37 MW	20.21 AW	42040 AAW	VABLS	10//99-12//99
	Charlottesville MSA, VA	S	17.02 MW	15.87 AW	35400 AAW	VABLS	10//99-12//99
	Danville MSA, VA	S	18.74 MW	18.32 AW	38980 AAW	VABLS	10//99-12//99
	Lynchburg MSA, VA	S	18.56 MW	17.64 AW	38610 AAW	VABLS	10//99-12//99
	Norfolk-Virginia Beach-Newport News MSA, VA-NC	S	19.12 MW	18.71 AW	39760 AAW	VABLS	10//99-12//99
	Richmond-Petersburg MSA, VA	S	21.83 MW	21.35 AW	45410 AAW	VABLS	10//99-12//99
	Roanoke MSA, VA	S	18.22 MW	18.92 AW	37890 AAW	VABLS	10//99-12//99
	Washington	S	19.35 MW	19.33 AW	40200 AAW	WABLS	10//99-12//99
	Bellingham MSA, WA	S	20.99 MW	20.82 AW	43670 AAW	WABLS	10//99-12//99
	Bremerton PMSA, WA	S	17.52 MW	18.19 AW	36450 AAW	WABLS	10//99-12//99
	Olympia PMSA, WA	S	17.88 MW	16.57 AW	37190 AAW	WABLS	10//99-12//99
	Richland-Kennewick-Pasco MSA, WA	S	20.20 MW	20.04 AW	42020 AAW	WABLS	10//99-12//99
	Seattle-Bellevue-Everett PMSA, WA	S	19.09 MW	18.80 AW	39720 AAW	WABLS	10//99-12//99
	Spokane MSA, WA	S	17.98 MW	19.28 AW	37390 AAW	WABLS	10//99-12//99
	Tacoma PMSA, WA	S	21.90 MW	22.49 AW	45560 AAW	WABLS	10//99-12//99
	Yakima MSA, WA	S	18.96 MW	18.94 AW	39430 AAW	WABLS	10//99-12//99
	West Virginia	S	17.88 MW	17.14 AW	35640 AAW	WVBLS	10//99-12//99
	Huntington-Ashland MSA, WV-KY-OH	S	18.70 MW	18.68 AW	38900 AAW	WVBLS	10//99-12//99
	Wheeling MSA, WV-OH	S	19.43 MW	20.00 AW	40420 AAW	WVBLS	10//99-12//99
	Wisconsin	S	19.35 MW	19.89 AW	41380 AAW	WIBLS	10//99-12//99
	Appleton-Oshkosh-Neenah MSA, WI	S	20.60 MW	20.54 AW	42850 AAW	WIBLS	10//99-12//99
	Eau Claire MSA, WI	S	21.14 MW	21.68 AW	43980 AAW	WIBLS	10//99-12//99
	Green Bay MSA, WI	S	21.29 MW	20.79 AW	44280 AAW	WIBLS	10//99-12//99
	Kenosha PMSA, WI	S	21.48 MW	20.84 AW	44680 AAW	WIBLS	10//99-12//99
	La Crosse MSA, WI-MN	S	18.85 MW	18.52 AW	39200 AAW	WIBLS	10//99-12//99
	Madison MSA, WI	S	17.18 MW	16.58 AW	35740 AAW	WIBLS	10//99-12//99
	Milwaukee-Waukesha PMSA, WI	S	20.92 MW	19.56 AW	43520 AAW	WIBLS	10//99-12//99
	Racine PMSA, WI	S	19.69 MW	20.72 AW	40960 AAW	WIBLS	10//99-12//99

AAW Average annual wage	AOH Average offered, high	ASH Average starting, high	H Hourly	M Monthly	S Special: hourly and annual
AE Average entry wage	AOL Average offered, low	ASL Average starting, low	HI Highest wage paid	MTC Median total compensation	TQ Third quartile wage
AEX Average experienced wage	APH Average pay, high range	AW Average wage paid	HR High end range	MW Median wage paid	W Weekly
AO Average offered	APL Average pay, low range	FQ First quartile wage	LR Low end range	SQ Second quartile wage	Y Yearly

Occupation/Type/Industry	Location	Per	Low	Mid	High	Source	Date
Educational, Vocational, and School Counselor	Sheboygan MSA, WI	S	20.03 MW	20.52 AW	41660 AAW	WIBLS	10//99-12//99
	Wausau MSA, WI	S	19.56 MW	19.67 AW	40690 AAW	WIBLS	10//99-12//99
	Wyoming	S	15.85 MW	16.72 AW	34770 AAW	WYBLS	10//99-12//99
	Mayaguez MSA, PR	S	10.46 MW	10.10 AW	21760 AAW	PRBLS	10//99-12//99
	Guam	S	15.34 MW	14.40 AW	29960 AAW	GUBLS	10//99-12//99
Electric Motor, Power Tool, and Related Repairer	Alabama	S	13.88 MW	13.95 AW	29020 AAW	ALBLS	10//99-12//99
	Birmingham MSA, AL	S	14.69 MW	14.60 AW	30550 AAW	ALBLS	10//99-12//99
	Arizona	S	17.6 MW	16.99 AW	35340 AAW	AZBLS	10//99-12//99
	Phoenix-Mesa MSA, AZ	S	18.39 MW	18.64 AW	38240 AAW	AZBLS	10//99-12//99
	Tucson MSA, AZ	S	10.06 MW	9.79 AW	20930 AAW	AZBLS	10//99-12//99
	Arkansas	S	11.59 MW	11.63 AW	24190 AAW	ARBLS	10//99-12//99
	Little Rock-North Little Rock MSA, AR	S	11.85 MW	11.74 AW	24640 AAW	ARBLS	10//99-12//99
	California	S	14.2 MW	15.05 AW	31300 AAW	CABLS	10//99-12//99
	Chico-Paradise MSA, CA	S	10.31 MW	7.63 AW	21430 AAW	CABLS	10//99-12//99
	Fresno MSA, CA	S	16.95 MW	15.54 AW	35260 AAW	CABLS	10//99-12//99
	Los Angeles-Long Beach PMSA, CA	S	14.46 MW	13.02 AW	30070 AAW	CABLS	10//99-12//99
	Modesto MSA, CA	S	14.44 MW	14.25 AW	30040 AAW	CABLS	10//99-12//99
	Oakland PMSA, CA	S	19.19 MW	19.08 AW	39920 AAW	CABLS	10//99-12//99
	Riverside-San Bernardino PMSA, CA	S	12.29 MW	12.87 AW	25570 AAW	CABLS	10//99-12//99
	Sacramento PMSA, CA	S	14.52 MW	13.37 AW	30200 AAW	CABLS	10//99-12//99
	San Diego MSA, CA	S	14.59 MW	15.06 AW	30340 AAW	CABLS	10//99-12//99
	Santa Cruz-Watsonville PMSA, CA	S	15.84 MW	17.19 AW	32950 AAW	CABLS	10//99-12//99
	Stockton-Lodi MSA, CA	S	17.49 MW	17.37 AW	36370 AAW	CABLS	10//99-12//99
	Colorado	S	11.9 MW	12.76 AW	26540 AAW	COBLS	10//99-12//99
	Denver PMSA, CO	S	15.29 MW	13.48 AW	31800 AAW	COBLS	10//99-12//99
	Connecticut	S	12.92 MW	14.09 AW	29320 AAW	CTBLS	10//99-12//99
	Hartford MSA, CT	S	17.13 MW	16.84 AW	35630 AAW	CTBLS	10//99-12//99
	Florida	S	14.14 MW	14.11 AW	29340 AAW	FLBLS	10//99-12//99
	Fort Lauderdale PMSA, FL	S	13.56 MW	13.78 AW	28200 AAW	FLBLS	10//99-12//99
	Jacksonville MSA, FL	S	14.33 MW	14.73 AW	29810 AAW	FLBLS	10//99-12//99
	Lakeland-Winter Haven MSA, FL	S	13.32 MW	13.04 AW	27700 AAW	FLBLS	10//99-12//99
	Melbourne-Titusville-Palm Bay MSA, FL	S	16.23 MW	13.51 AW	33760 AAW	FLBLS	10//99-12//99
	Miami PMSA, FL	S	12.70 MW	12.61 AW	26420 AAW	FLBLS	10//99-12//99
	Orlando MSA, FL	S	12.69 MW	12.44 AW	26400 AAW	FLBLS	10//99-12//99
	Pensacola MSA, FL	S	12.99 MW	12.69 AW	27020 AAW	FLBLS	10//99-12//99
	Tampa-St. Petersburg-Clearwater MSA, FL	S	17.95 MW	16.39 AW	37340 AAW	FLBLS	10//99-12//99
	Georgia	S	15.23 MW	15.79 AW	32840 AAW	GABLS	10//99-12//99
	Atlanta MSA, GA	S	16.26 MW	16.05 AW	33820 AAW	GABLS	10//99-12//99
	Columbus MSA, GA-AL	S	12.90 MW	12.77 AW	26840 AAW	GABLS	10//99-12//99
	Hawaii	S	11.22 MW	11.70 AW	24340 AAW	HIBLS	10//99-12//99
	Honolulu MSA, HI	S	11.74 MW	11.27 AW	24410 AAW	HIBLS	10//99-12//99
	Idaho	S	10.41 MW	10.64 AW	22120 AAW	IDBLS	10//99-12//99
	Boise City MSA, ID	S	12.75 MW	12.28 AW	26520 AAW	IDBLS	10//99-12//99
	Illinois	S	18.67 MW	18.22 AW	37900 AAW	ILBLS	10//99-12//99
	Chicago PMSA, IL	S	20.31 MW	20.02 AW	42250 AAW	ILBLS	10//99-12//99
	Peoria-Pekin MSA, IL	S	15.61 MW	15.70 AW	32470 AAW	ILBLS	10//99-12//99
	Indiana	S	15.63 MW	17.17 AW	35710 AAW	INBLS	10//99-12//99
	Evansville-Henderson MSA, IN-KY	S	15.86 MW	15.87 AW	32980 AAW	INBLS	10//99-12//99
	Gary PMSA, IN	S	17.00 MW	17.10 AW	35350 AAW	INBLS	10//99-12//99
	Indianapolis MSA, IN	S	19.25 MW	15.49 AW	40050 AAW	INBLS	10//99-12//99
	South Bend MSA, IN	S	15.95 MW	15.50 AW	33190 AAW	INBLS	10//99-12//99
	Terre Haute MSA, IN	S	17.69 MW	18.56 AW	36800 AAW	INBLS	10//99-12//99
	Iowa	S	11.35 MW	11.61 AW	24140 AAW	IABLS	10//99-12//99
	Davenport-Moline-Rock Island MSA, IA-IL	S	11.15 MW	10.68 AW	23190 AAW	IABLS	10//99-12//99
	Des Moines MSA, IA	S	12.88 MW	12.67 AW	26800 AAW	IABLS	10//99-12//99
	Kansas	S	14.35 MW	14.41 AW	29980 AAW	KSBLS	10//99-12//99
	Kentucky	S	16.25 MW	15.75 AW	32750 AAW	KYBLS	10//99-12//99
	Louisville MSA, KY-IN	S	18.20 MW	18.59 AW	37850 AAW	KYBLS	10//99-12//99
	Louisiana	S	14.91 MW	14.42 AW	29990 AAW	LABLS	10//99-12//99
	Baton Rouge MSA, LA	S	15.05 MW	15.17 AW	31300 AAW	LABLS	10//99-12//99

AAW Average annual wage	**AOH** Average offered, high	**ASH** Average starting, high	**H** Hourly	**M** Monthly	**S** Special: hourly and annual
AE Average entry wage	**AOL** Average offered, low	**ASL** Average starting, low	**HI** Highest wage paid	**MTC** Median total compensation	**TQ** Third quartile wage
AEX Average experienced wage	**APH** Average pay, high range	**AW** Average wage paid	**HR** High end range	**MW** Median wage paid	**W** Weekly
AO Average offered	**APL** Average pay, low range	**FQ** First quartile wage	**LR** Low end range	**SQ** Second quartile wage	**Y** Yearly

Electric Motor, Power Tool, and Related Repairer

Occupation/Type/Industry	Location	Per	Low	Mid	High	Source	Date
Electric Motor, Power Tool, and Related Repairer	New Orleans MSA, LA	S	13.35 MW	12.82 AW	27770 AAW	LABLS	10//99-12//99
	Maine	S	13.36 MW	15.44 AW	32110 AAW	MEBLS	10//99-12//99
	Portland MSA, ME	S	14.13 MW	13.86 AW	29380 AAW	MEBLS	10//99-12//99
	Maryland	S	20.44 MW	20.08 AW	41760 AAW	MDBLS	10//99-12//99
	Baltimore PMSA, MD	S	18.76 MW	19.06 AW	39030 AAW	MDBLS	10//99-12//99
	Massachusetts	S	17.94 MW	17.33 AW	36040 AAW	MABLS	10//99-12//99
	Boston PMSA, MA-NH	S	17.31 MW	17.89 AW	35990 AAW	MABLS	10//99-12//99
	Springfield MSA, MA	S	19.70 MW	19.49 AW	40970 AAW	MABLS	10//99-12//99
	Michigan	S	15.43 MW	15.67 AW	32600 AAW	MIBLS	10//99-12//99
	Detroit PMSA, MI	S	16.13 MW	16.51 AW	33540 AAW	MIBLS	10//99-12//99
	Grand Rapids-Muskegon- Holland MSA, MI	S	15.53 MW	15.82 AW	32300 AAW	MIBLS	10//99-12//99
	Minnesota	S	17.95 MW	19.97 AW	41540 AAW	MNBLS	10//99-12//99
	St. Cloud MSA, MN	S	14.37 MW	13.80 AW	29880 AAW	MNBLS	10//99-12//99
	Mississippi	S	11.8 MW	12.40 AW	25780 AAW	MSBLS	10//99-12//99
	Missouri	S	12.78 MW	12.91 AW	26850 AAW	MOBLS	10//99-12//99
	Kansas City MSA, MO-KS	S	16.85 MW	16.80 AW	35040 AAW	MOBLS	10//99-12//99
	Montana	S	16.53 MW	17.51 AW	36410 AAW	MTBLS	10//99-12//99
	Billings MSA, MT	S	17.36 MW	15.39 AW	36100 AAW	MTBLS	10//99-12//99
	Nebraska	S	14.73 MW	14.92 AW	31040 AAW	NEBLS	10//99-12//99
	Lincoln MSA, NE	S	14.38 MW	14.34 AW	29910 AAW	NEBLS	10//99-12//99
	Nevada	S	13.46 MW	13.45 AW	27990 AAW	NVBLS	10//99-12//99
	Las Vegas MSA, NV-AZ	S	13.45 MW	13.46 AW	27990 AAW	NVBLS	10//99-12//99
	New Hampshire	S	18.19 MW	16.61 AW	34560 AAW	NHBLS	10//99-12//99
	New Jersey	S	11.56 MW	12.14 AW	25260 AAW	NJBLS	10//99-12//99
	Bergen-Passaic PMSA, NJ	S	10.75 MW	10.12 AW	22360 AAW	NJBLS	10//99-12//99
	Newark PMSA, NJ	S	13.20 MW	12.79 AW	27460 AAW	NJBLS	10//99-12//99
	New York	S	7.16 MW	10.50 AW	21850 AAW	NYBLS	10//99-12//99
	Buffalo-Niagara Falls MSA, NY	S	16.87 MW	17.80 AW	35090 AAW	NYBLS	10//99-12//99
	Nassau-Suffolk PMSA, NY	S	15.96 MW	18.50 AW	33190 AAW	NYBLS	10//99-12//99
	North Carolina	S	13.94 MW	14.50 AW	30150 AAW	NCBLS	10//99-12//99
	Asheville MSA, NC	S	17.36 MW	17.30 AW	36100 AAW	NCBLS	10//99-12//99
	Charlotte-Gastonia-Rock Hill MSA, NC-SC	S	14.36 MW	13.67 AW	29870 AAW	NCBLS	10//99-12//99
	Fayetteville MSA, NC	S	13.47 MW	13.03 AW	28020 AAW	NCBLS	10//99-12//99
	Greensboro--Winston-Salem-- High Point MSA, NC	S	15.52 MW	15.35 AW	32270 AAW	NCBLS	10//99-12//99
	Hickory-Morganton-Lenoir MSA, NC	S	13.46 MW	12.72 AW	28000 AAW	NCBLS	10//99-12//99
	Raleigh-Durham-Chapel Hill MSA, NC	S	14.68 MW	14.70 AW	30530 AAW	NCBLS	10//99-12//99
	North Dakota	S	10.25 MW	10.40 AW	21630 AAW	NDBLS	10//99-12//99
	Ohio	S	15.32 MW	16.07 AW	33420 AAW	OHBLS	10//99-12//99
	Cincinnati PMSA, OH-KY-IN	S	16.69 MW	18.69 AW	34710 AAW	OHBLS	10//99-12//99
	Cleveland-Lorain-Elyria PMSA, OH	S	15.94 MW	14.65 AW	33150 AAW	OHBLS	10//99-12//99
	Columbus MSA, OH	S	15.07 MW	13.80 AW	31340 AAW	OHBLS	10//99-12//99
	Toledo MSA, OH	S	16.05 MW	15.48 AW	33370 AAW	OHBLS	10//99-12//99
	Oklahoma	S	11.96 MW	13.31 AW	27690 AAW	OKBLS	10//99-12//99
	Tulsa MSA, OK	S	10.50 MW	8.14 AW	21830 AAW	OKBLS	10//99-12//99
	Oregon	S	10.48 MW	11.84 AW	24630 AAW	ORBLS	10//99-12//99
	Eugene-Springfield MSA, OR	S	12.29 MW	11.94 AW	25570 AAW	ORBLS	10//99-12//99
	Portland-Vancouver PMSA, OR-WA	S	14.56 MW	13.68 AW	30290 AAW	ORBLS	10//99-12//99
	Pennsylvania	S	12.73 MW	13.28 AW	27620 AAW	PABLS	10//99-12//99
	Allentown-Bethlehem-Easton MSA, PA	S	17.92 MW	18.44 AW	37270 AAW	PABLS	10//99-12//99
	Harrisburg-Lebanon-Carlisle MSA, PA	S	14.65 MW	15.03 AW	30470 AAW	PABLS	10//99-12//99
	Lancaster MSA, PA	S	14.49 MW	14.30 AW	30130 AAW	PABLS	10//99-12//99
	Philadelphia PMSA, PA-NJ	S	12.69 MW	11.95 AW	26380 AAW	PABLS	10//99-12//99
	Pittsburgh MSA, PA	S	11.49 MW	10.38 AW	23890 AAW	PABLS	10//99-12//99
	Scranton--Wilkes-Barre-- Hazleton MSA, PA	S	6.72 MW	6.91 AW	13990 AAW	PABLS	10//99-12//99
	South Carolina	S	8.75 MW	10.10 AW	21000 AAW	SCBLS	10//99-12//99
	Greenville-Spartanburg- Anderson MSA, SC	S	9.73 MW	8.33 AW	20230 AAW	SCBLS	10//99-12//99
	Tennessee	S	14.13 MW	14.04 AW	29200 AAW	TNBLS	10//99-12//99
	Chattanooga MSA, TN-GA	S	12.82 MW	13.00 AW	26670 AAW	TNBLS	10//99-12//99
	Knoxville MSA, TN	S	13.93 MW	12.75 AW	28980 AAW	TNBLS	10//99-12//99

Occupation/Type/Industry	Location	Per	Low	Mid	High	Source	Date
Electric Motor, Power Tool, and Related Repairer	Memphis MSA, TN-AR-MS	S	14.46 MW	14.74 AW	30080 AAW	MSBLS	10//99-12//99
	Texas	S	12.8 MW	14.69 AW	30540 AAW	TXBLS	10//99-12//99
	Amarillo MSA, TX	S	10.22 MW	9.36 AW	21250 AAW	TXBLS	10//99-12//99
	Austin-San Marcos MSA, TX	S	11.29 MW	11.50 AW	23480 AAW	TXBLS	10//99-12//99
	Dallas PMSA, TX	S	15.91 MW	14.33 AW	33100 AAW	TXBLS	10//99-12//99
	Fort Worth-Arlington PMSA, TX	S	11.13 MW	11.25 AW	23150 AAW	TXBLS	10//99-12//99
	Houston PMSA, TX	S	19.18 MW	15.89 AW	39890 AAW	TXBLS	10//99-12//99
	Lubbock MSA, TX	S	9.83 MW	9.26 AW	20450 AAW	TXBLS	10//99-12//99
	Utah	S	15.56 MW	18.14 AW	37720 AAW	UTBLS	
	Salt Lake City-Ogden MSA, UT	S	19.08 MW	16.47 AW	39700 AAW	UTBLS	10//99-12//99
	Virginia	S	15.26 MW	15.87 AW	33000 AAW	VABLS	10//99-12//99
	Lynchburg MSA, VA	S	13.54 MW	10.74 AW	28160 AAW	VABLS	10//99-12//99
	Norfolk-Virginia Beach-Newport News MSA, VA-NC	S	15.79 MW	15.20 AW	32830 AAW	VABLS	10//99-12//99
	Richmond-Petersburg MSA, VA	S	21.41 MW	20.59 AW	44520 AAW	VABLS	10//99-12//99
	Washington	S	18.38 MW	18.35 AW	38160 AAW	WABLS	10//99-12//99
	Seattle-Bellevue-Everett PMSA, WA	S	19.58 MW	19.72 AW	40740 AAW	WABLS	10//99-12//99
	Spokane MSA, WA	S	15.44 MW	14.75 AW	32120 AAW	WABLS	10//99-12//99
	Tacoma PMSA, WA	S	18.09 MW	18.08 AW	37630 AAW	WABLS	10//99-12//99
	West Virginia	S	11.78 MW	11.60 AW	24130 AAW	WVBLS	10//99-12//99
	Wisconsin	S	12.95 MW	14.43 AW	30020 AAW	WIBLS	10//99-12//99
	Milwaukee-Waukesha PMSA, WI	S	22.59 MW	23.55 AW	46980 AAW	WIBLS	10//99-12//99
	Puerto Rico	S	8.54 MW	10.03 AW	20850 AAW	PRBLS	10//99-12//99
	San Juan-Bayamon PMSA, PR	S	10.06 MW	8.41 AW	20920 AAW	PRBLS	10//99-12//99
Electrical and Electronic Engineering Technician	Alabama	S	16.86 MW	17.86 AW	37150 AAW	ALBLS	10//99-12//99
	Anniston MSA, AL	S	14.96 MW	16.02 AW	31120 AAW	ALBLS	10//99-12//99
	Auburn-Opelika MSA, AL	S	18.84 MW	19.10 AW	39190 AAW	ALBLS	10//99-12//99
	Birmingham MSA, AL	S	17.39 MW	16.28 AW	36160 AAW	ALBLS	10//99-12//99
	Decatur MSA, AL	S	21.18 MW	20.80 AW	44050 AAW	ALBLS	10//99-12//99
	Dothan MSA, AL	S	22.18 MW	22.35 AW	46130 AAW	ALBLS	10//99-12//99
	Florence MSA, AL	S	17.38 MW	18.60 AW	36150 AAW	ALBLS	10//99-12//99
	Huntsville MSA, AL	S	17.84 MW	15.71 AW	37110 AAW	ALBLS	10//99-12//99
	Mobile MSA, AL	S	20.17 MW	19.80 AW	41950 AAW	ALBLS	10//99-12//99
	Montgomery MSA, AL	S	17.14 MW	17.14 AW	35650 AAW	ALBLS	10//99-12//99
	Alaska	S	25.76 MW	27.19 AW	56550 AAW	AKBLS	10//99-12//99
	Anchorage MSA, AK	S	25.85 MW	24.88 AW	53780 AAW	AKBLS	10//99-12//99
	Arizona	S	18.71 MW	18.75 AW	38990 AAW	AZBLS	10//99-12//99
	Phoenix-Mesa MSA, AZ	S	18.89 MW	18.90 AW	39280 AAW	AZBLS	10//99-12//99
	Tucson MSA, AZ	S	17.37 MW	17.78 AW	36130 AAW	AZBLS	10//99-12//99
	Arkansas	S	16.07 MW	17.22 AW	35830 AAW	ARBLS	10//99-12//99
	Fayetteville-Springdale-Rogers MSA, AR	S	18.22 MW	18.83 AW	37900 AAW	ARBLS	10//99-12//99
	Little Rock-North Little Rock MSA, AR	S	16.71 MW	17.21 AW	34750 AAW	ARBLS	10//99-12//99
	California	S	19.7 MW	20.28 AW	42180 AAW	CABLS	10//99-12//99
	Fresno MSA, CA	S	23.52 MW	21.62 AW	48920 AAW	CABLS	10//99-12//99
	Los Angeles-Long Beach PMSA, CA	S	20.00 MW	19.01 AW	41590 AAW	CABLS	10//99-12//99
	Modesto MSA, CA	S	16.18 MW	15.78 AW	33650 AAW	CABLS	10//99-12//99
	Oakland PMSA, CA	S	21.89 MW	21.58 AW	45540 AAW	CABLS	10//99-12//99
	Orange County PMSA, CA	S	18.86 MW	17.68 AW	39220 AAW	CABLS	10//99-12//99
	Redding MSA, CA	S	17.96 MW	18.90 AW	37370 AAW	CABLS	10//99-12//99
	Riverside-San Bernardino PMSA, CA	S	18.92 MW	18.87 AW	39360 AAW	CABLS	10//99-12//99
	Sacramento PMSA, CA	S	20.34 MW	18.00 AW	42310 AAW	CABLS	10//99-12//99
	San Diego MSA, CA	S	20.36 MW	19.93 AW	42340 AAW	CABLS	10//99-12//99
	San Francisco PMSA, CA	S	20.16 MW	19.41 AW	41930 AAW	CABLS	10//99-12//99
	San Jose PMSA, CA	S	20.51 MW	20.66 AW	42670 AAW	CABLS	10//99-12//99
	San Luis Obispo-Atascadero-Paso Robles MSA, CA	S	26.30 MW	29.07 AW	54700 AAW	CABLS	10//99-12//99
	Santa Barbara-Santa Maria-Lompoc MSA, CA	S	19.44 MW	16.87 AW	40430 AAW	CABLS	10//99-12//99

AAW Average annual wage	AOH Average offered, high	ASH Average starting, high	H Hourly	M Monthly	S Special: hourly and annual
AE Average entry wage	AOL Average offered, low	ASL Average starting, low	HI Highest wage paid	MTC Median total compensation	TQ Third quartile wage
AEX Average experienced wage	APH Average pay, high range	AW Average wage paid	HR High end range	MW Median wage paid	W Weekly
AO Average offered	APL Average pay, low range	FQ First quartile wage	LR Low end range	SQ Second quartile wage	Y Yearly

Occupation/Type/Industry	Location	Per	Low	Mid	High	Source	Date
Electrical and Electronic Engineering Technician	Santa Cruz-Watsonville PMSA, CA	S	18.29 MW	16.47 AW	38040 AAW	CABLS	10//99-12//99
	Santa Rosa PMSA, CA	S	18.12 MW	17.29 AW	37690 AAW	CABLS	10//99-12//99
	Vallejo-Fairfield-Napa PMSA, CA	S	18.79 MW	16.85 AW	39080 AAW	CABLS	10//99-12//99
	Ventura PMSA, CA	S	24.26 MW	24.55 AW	50460 AAW	CABLS	10//99-12//99
	Visalia-Tulare-Porterville MSA, CA	S	15.65 MW	15.49 AW	32550 AAW	CABLS	10//99-12//99
	Colorado	S	21.42 MW	24.92 AW	51830 AAW	COBLS	10//99-12//99
	Boulder-Longmont PMSA, CO	S	26.72 MW	24.85 AW	55570 AAW	COBLS	10//99-12//99
	Colorado Springs MSA, CO	S	18.44 MW	18.07 AW	38360 AAW	COBLS	10//99-12//99
	Fort Collins-Loveland MSA, CO	S	19.22 MW	17.96 AW	39980 AAW	COBLS	10//99-12//99
	Grand Junction MSA, CO	S	16.91 MW	17.71 AW	35170 AAW	COBLS	10//99-12//99
	Greeley PMSA, CO	S	15.76 MW	15.13 AW	32770 AAW	COBLS	10//99-12//99
	Pueblo MSA, CO	S	17.08 MW	18.17 AW	35530 AAW	COBLS	10//99-12//99
	Connecticut	S	19.77 MW	20.25 AW	42120 AAW	CTBLS	10//99-12//99
	Bridgeport PMSA, CT	S	19.11 MW	17.29 AW	39750 AAW	CTBLS	10//99-12//99
	Danbury PMSA, CT	S	20.79 MW	21.43 AW	43250 AAW	CTBLS	10//99-12//99
	Hartford MSA, CT	S	20.66 MW	20.11 AW	42970 AAW	CTBLS	10//99-12//99
	New Haven-Meriden PMSA, CT	S	19.01 MW	19.26 AW	39540 AAW	CTBLS	10//99-12//99
	New London-Norwich MSA, CT-RI	S	19.14 MW	19.17 AW	39820 AAW	CTBLS	10//99-12//99
	Stamford-Norwalk PMSA, CT	S	22.98 MW	23.33 AW	47800 AAW	CTBLS	10//99-12//99
	Waterbury PMSA, CT	S	18.91 MW	17.16 AW	39320 AAW	CTBLS	10//99-12//99
	Delaware	S	23.16 MW	22.19 AW	46150 AAW	DEBLS	10//99-12//99
	Wilmington-Newark PMSA, DE-MD	S	22.49 MW	23.45 AW	46790 AAW	DEBLS	10//99-12//99
	District of Columbia	S	21.73 MW	21.88 AW	45500 AAW	DCBLS	10//99-12//99
	Washington PMSA, DC-MD-VA-WV	S	20.22 MW	19.72 AW	42050 AAW	DCBLS	10//99-12//99
	Florida	S	15.82 MW	16.98 AW	35330 AAW	FLBLS	10//99-12//99
	Daytona Beach MSA, FL	S	16.85 MW	17.03 AW	35060 AAW	FLBLS	10//99-12//99
	Fort Lauderdale PMSA, FL	S	17.18 MW	16.46 AW	35730 AAW	FLBLS	10//99-12//99
	Fort Myers-Cape Coral MSA, FL	S	16.23 MW	16.78 AW	33760 AAW	FLBLS	10//99-12//99
	Fort Pierce-Port St. Lucie MSA, FL	S	17.39 MW	18.46 AW	36170 AAW	FLBLS	10//99-12//99
	Fort Walton Beach MSA, FL	S	19.45 MW	19.24 AW	40450 AAW	FLBLS	10//99-12//99
	Gainesville MSA, FL	S	19.78 MW	19.36 AW	41130 AAW	FLBLS	10//99-12//99
	Jacksonville MSA, FL	S	16.81 MW	15.98 AW	34970 AAW	FLBLS	10//99-12//99
	Lakeland-Winter Haven MSA, FL	S	17.57 MW	18.14 AW	36550 AAW	FLBLS	10//99-12//99
	Melbourne-Titusville-Palm Bay MSA, FL	S	14.09 MW	13.93 AW	29300 AAW	FLBLS	10//99-12//99
	Miami PMSA, FL	S	20.59 MW	20.49 AW	42820 AAW	FLBLS	10//99-12//99
	Naples MSA, FL	S	12.18 MW	10.09 AW	25340 AAW	FLBLS	10//99-12//99
	Orlando MSA, FL	S	15.92 MW	15.19 AW	33110 AAW	FLBLS	10//99-12//99
	Pensacola MSA, FL	S	16.05 MW	16.86 AW	33380 AAW	FLBLS	10//99-12//99
	Sarasota-Bradenton MSA, FL	S	15.55 MW	13.71 AW	32350 AAW	FLBLS	10//99-12//99
	Tallahassee MSA, FL	S	15.91 MW	14.33 AW	33100 AAW	FLBLS	10//99-12//99
	Tampa-St. Petersburg-Clearwater MSA, FL	S	18.34 MW	17.85 AW	38150 AAW	FLBLS	10//99-12//99
	West Palm Beach-Boca Raton MSA, FL	S	17.44 MW	17.30 AW	36280 AAW	FLBLS	10//99-12//99
	Georgia	S	18.4 MW	19.36 AW	40270 AAW	GABLS	10//99-12//99
	Athens MSA, GA	S	16.25 MW	15.20 AW	33800 AAW	GABLS	10//99-12//99
	Atlanta MSA, GA	S	19.80 MW	18.21 AW	41180 AAW	GABLS	10//99-12//99
	Augusta-Aiken MSA, GA-SC	S	20.67 MW	19.57 AW	42990 AAW	GABLS	10//99-12//99
	Columbus MSA, GA-AL	S	16.19 MW	17.33 AW	33670 AAW	GABLS	10//99-12//99
	Macon MSA, GA	S	20.78 MW	20.72 AW	43210 AAW	GABLS	10//99-12//99
	Savannah MSA, GA	S	17.39 MW	18.42 AW	36160 AAW	GABLS	10//99-12//99
	Hawaii	S	19.24 MW	20.20 AW	42010 AAW	HIBLS	10//99-12//99
	Honolulu MSA, HI	S	20.59 MW	19.52 AW	42830 AAW	HIBLS	10//99-12//99
	Idaho	S	19.44 MW	19.01 AW	39540 AAW	IDBLS	10//99-12//99
	Boise City MSA, ID	S	18.19 MW	18.82 AW	37840 AAW	IDBLS	10//99-12//99
	Illinois	S	16.49 MW	17.09 AW	35540 AAW	ILBLS	10//99-12//99
	Bloomington-Normal MSA, IL	S	25.33 MW	25.65 AW	52680 AAW	ILBLS	10//99-12//99
	Champaign-Urbana MSA, IL	S	18.72 MW	18.84 AW	38940 AAW	ILBLS	10//99-12//99
	Chicago PMSA, IL	S	16.96 MW	16.37 AW	35270 AAW	ILBLS	10//99-12//99

Occupation/Type/Industry	Location	Per	Low	Mid	High	Source	Date
Electrical and Electronic Engineering Technician	Peoria-Pekin MSA, IL	S	19.17 MW	19.17 AW	39870 AAW	ILBLS	10//99-12//99
	Rockford MSA, IL	S	16.65 MW	18.24 AW	34630 AAW	ILBLS	10//99-12//99
	Springfield MSA, IL	S	18.24 MW	18.34 AW	37940 AAW	ILBLS	10//99-12//99
	Indiana	S	16.49 MW	17.12 AW	35620 AAW	INBLS	10//99-12//99
	Elkhart-Goshen MSA, IN	S	15.95 MW	15.59 AW	33170 AAW	INBLS	10//99-12//99
	Evansville-Henderson MSA, IN-KY	S	15.53 MW	15.93 AW	32300 AAW	INBLS	10//99-12//99
	Fort Wayne MSA, IN	S	17.99 MW	17.59 AW	37410 AAW	INBLS	10//99-12//99
	Gary PMSA, IN	S	17.91 MW	17.72 AW	37260 AAW	INBLS	10//99-12//99
	Indianapolis MSA, IN	S	15.37 MW	14.89 AW	31980 AAW	INBLS	10//99-12//99
	Kokomo MSA, IN	S	12.86 MW	12.37 AW	26740 AAW	INBLS	10//99-12//99
	Lafayette MSA, IN	S	16.26 MW	16.97 AW	33820 AAW	INBLS	10//99-12//99
	South Bend MSA, IN	S	16.82 MW	17.54 AW	34980 AAW	INBLS	10//99-12//99
	Terre Haute MSA, IN	S	15.47 MW	14.80 AW	32180 AAW	INBLS	10//99-12//99
	Iowa	S	17.24 MW	17.56 AW	36530 AAW	IABLS	10//99-12//99
	Davenport-Moline-Rock Island MSA, IA-IL	S	18.98 MW	18.88 AW	39480 AAW	IABLS	10//99-12//99
	Des Moines MSA, IA	S	22.44 MW	20.89 AW	46670 AAW	IABLS	10//99-12//99
	Sioux City MSA, IA-NE	S	22.09 MW	20.57 AW	45950 AAW	IABLS	10//99-12//99
	Waterloo-Cedar Falls MSA, IA	S	18.95 MW	19.06 AW	39410 AAW	IABLS	10//99-12//99
	Kansas	S	18.16 MW	17.86 AW	37150 AAW	KSBLS	10//99-12//99
	Topeka MSA, KS	S	17.30 MW	17.57 AW	35980 AAW	KSBLS	10//99-12//99
	Wichita MSA, KS	S	18.70 MW	18.99 AW	38900 AAW	KSBLS	10//99-12//99
	Kentucky	S	18.97 MW	18.87 AW	39240 AAW	KYBLS	10//99-12//99
	Lexington MSA, KY	S	15.96 MW	15.82 AW	33190 AAW	KYBLS	10//99-12//99
	Louisville MSA, KY-IN	S	19.85 MW	19.91 AW	41290 AAW	KYBLS	10//99-12//99
	Owensboro MSA, KY	S	19.49 MW	19.36 AW	40540 AAW	KYBLS	10//99-12//99
	Louisiana	S	18.81 MW	18.58 AW	38640 AAW	LABLS	10//99-12//99
	Alexandria MSA, LA	S	19.03 MW	19.18 AW	39570 AAW	LABLS	10//99-12//99
	Baton Rouge MSA, LA	S	16.83 MW	16.97 AW	35000 AAW	LABLS	10//99-12//99
	Lafayette MSA, LA	S	19.01 MW	19.30 AW	39550 AAW	LABLS	10//99-12//99
	Lake Charles MSA, LA	S	22.79 MW	23.21 AW	47400 AAW	LABLS	10//99-12//99
	Monroe MSA, LA	S	16.62 MW	17.74 AW	34570 AAW	LABLS	10//99-12//99
	New Orleans MSA, LA	S	18.66 MW	18.70 AW	38810 AAW	LABLS	10//99-12//99
	Shreveport-Bossier City MSA, LA	S	19.28 MW	19.37 AW	40110 AAW	LABLS	10//99-12//99
	Maine	S	20.51 MW	21.34 AW	44380 AAW	MEBLS	10//99-12//99
	Lewiston-Auburn MSA, ME	S	20.52 MW	20.04 AW	42690 AAW	MEBLS	10//99-12//99
	Portland MSA, ME	S	17.37 MW	16.86 AW	36140 AAW	MEBLS	10//99-12//99
	Maryland	S	18.74 MW	18.92 AW	39360 AAW	MDBLS	10//99-12//99
	Baltimore PMSA, MD	S	17.49 MW	18.06 AW	36370 AAW	MDBLS	10//99-12//99
	Hagerstown PMSA, MD	S	14.92 MW	15.60 AW	31040 AAW	MDBLS	10//99-12//99
	Massachusetts	S	19.79 MW	20.44 AW	42510 AAW	MABLS	10//99-12//99
	Boston PMSA, MA-NH	S	20.80 MW	20.12 AW	43260 AAW	MABLS	10//99-12//99
	Lawrence PMSA, MA-NH	S	20.15 MW	18.28 AW	41920 AAW	MABLS	10//99-12//99
	Lowell PMSA, MA-NH	S	20.31 MW	19.86 AW	42230 AAW	MABLS	10//99-12//99
	New Bedford PMSA, MA	S	17.18 MW	17.03 AW	35730 AAW	MABLS	10//99-12//99
	Springfield MSA, MA	S	17.34 MW	16.89 AW	36060 AAW	MABLS	10//99-12//99
	Worcester PMSA, MA-CT	S	19.20 MW	19.18 AW	39930 AAW	MABLS	10//99-12//99
	Michigan	S	19.09 MW	19.81 AW	41210 AAW	MIBLS	10//99-12//99
	Ann Arbor PMSA, MI	S	19.43 MW	18.79 AW	40410 AAW	MIBLS	10//99-12//99
	Detroit PMSA, MI	S	21.28 MW	20.13 AW	44270 AAW	MIBLS	10//99-12//99
	Flint PMSA, MI	S	18.33 MW	18.43 AW	38120 AAW	MIBLS	10//99-12//99
	Grand Rapids-Muskegon-Holland MSA, MI	S	17.26 MW	15.77 AW	35910 AAW	MIBLS	10//99-12//99
	Jackson MSA, MI	S	17.00 MW	17.66 AW	35360 AAW	MIBLS	10//99-12//99
	Kalamazoo-Battle Creek MSA, MI	S	18.59 MW	17.96 AW	38680 AAW	MIBLS	10//99-12//99
	Lansing-East Lansing MSA, MI	S	20.30 MW	21.36 AW	42230 AAW	MIBLS	10//99-12//99
	Saginaw-Bay City-Midland MSA, MI	S	23.01 MW	23.07 AW	47860 AAW	MIBLS	10//99-12//99
	Minnesota	S	18.68 MW	18.81 AW	39110 AAW	MNBLS	10//99-12//99
	Duluth-Superior MSA, MN-WI	S	14.87 MW	13.60 AW	30930 AAW	MNBLS	10//99-12//99
	Minneapolis-St. Paul MSA, MN-WI	S	19.74 MW	19.26 AW	41060 AAW	MNBLS	10//99-12//99
	Rochester MSA, MN	S	18.92 MW	19.17 AW	39360 AAW	MNBLS	10//99-12//99
	St. Cloud MSA, MN	S	12.74 MW	11.77 AW	26500 AAW	MNBLS	10//99-12//99
	Mississippi	S	17.66 MW	18.54 AW	38560 AAW	MSBLS	10//99-12//99
	Biloxi-Gulfport-Pascagoula MSA, MS	S	20.11 MW	19.47 AW	41820 AAW	MSBLS	10//99-12//99
	Jackson MSA, MS	S	17.64 MW	17.00 AW	36690 AAW	MSBLS	10//99-12//99

AAW	Average annual wage	AOH	Average offered, high	ASH	Average starting, high	H	Hourly	M	Monthly	S	Special: hourly and annual
AE	Average entry wage	AOL	Average offered, low	ASL	Average starting, low	HI	Highest wage paid	MTC	Median total compensation	TQ	Third quartile wage
AEX	Average experienced wage	APH	Average pay, high range	AW	Average wage paid	HR	High end range	MW	Median wage paid	W	Weekly
AO	Average offered	APL	Average pay, low range	FQ	First quartile wage	LR	Low end range	SQ	Second quartile wage	Y	Yearly

Occupation/Type/Industry	Location	Per	Low	Mid	High	Source	Date
Electrical and Electronic Engineering Technician	Missouri	S	17.27 MW	17.20 AW	35780 AAW	MOBLS	10//99-12//99
	Columbia MSA, MO	S	14.96 MW	13.39 AW	31120 AAW	MOBLS	10//99-12//99
	Kansas City MSA, MO-KS	S	20.51 MW	19.87 AW	42660 AAW	MOBLS	10//99-12//99
	St. Louis MSA, MO-IL	S	17.56 MW	17.41 AW	36520 AAW	MOBLS	10//99-12//99
	Springfield MSA, MO	S	17.27 MW	16.86 AW	35920 AAW	MOBLS	10//99-12//99
	Montana	S	18.84 MW	18.79 AW	39080 AAW	MTBLS	10//99-12//99
	Billings MSA, MT	S	20.39 MW	19.76 AW	42410 AAW	MTBLS	10//99-12//99
	Missoula MSA, MT	S	18.72 MW	18.73 AW	38940 AAW	MTBLS	10//99-12//99
	Nebraska	S	17.16 MW	16.82 AW	34980 AAW	NEBLS	10//99-12//99
	Lincoln MSA, NE	S	16.75 MW	16.73 AW	34850 AAW	NEBLS	10//99-12//99
	Omaha MSA, NE-IA	S	16.21 MW	16.67 AW	33720 AAW	NEBLS	10//99-12//99
	Nevada	S	18.68 MW	18.72 AW	38940 AAW	NVBLS	10//99-12//99
	Las Vegas MSA, NV-AZ	S	21.82 MW	20.95 AW	45390 AAW	NVBLS	10//99-12//99
	Reno MSA, NV	S	15.90 MW	15.98 AW	33080 AAW	NVBLS	10//99-12//99
	New Hampshire	S	17.89 MW	18.76 AW	39020 AAW	NHBLS	10//99-12//99
	Manchester PMSA, NH	S	20.58 MW	20.40 AW	42810 AAW	NHBLS	10//99-12//99
	Nashua PMSA, NH	S	16.47 MW	16.07 AW	34260 AAW	NHBLS	10//99-12//99
	Portsmouth-Rochester PMSA, NH-ME	S	16.85 MW	16.18 AW	35040 AAW	NHBLS	10//99-12//99
	New Jersey	S	19.36 MW	20.26 AW	42140 AAW	NJBLS	10//99-12//99
	Atlantic-Cape May PMSA, NJ	S	24.08 MW	24.03 AW	50090 AAW	NJBLS	10//99-12//99
	Bergen-Passaic PMSA, NJ	S	20.50 MW	19.78 AW	42640 AAW	NJBLS	10//99-12//99
	Jersey City PMSA, NJ	S	22.42 MW	20.52 AW	46640 AAW	NJBLS	10//99-12//99
	Middlesex-Somerset-Hunterdon PMSA, NJ	S	23.07 MW	20.66 AW	47990 AAW	NJBLS	10//99-12//99
	Monmouth-Ocean PMSA, NJ	S	18.45 MW	18.61 AW	38380 AAW	NJBLS	10//99-12//99
	Newark PMSA, NJ	S	18.84 MW	18.09 AW	39180 AAW	NJBLS	10//99-12//99
	New Mexico	S	18.52 MW	18.90 AW	39320 AAW	NMBLS	10//99-12//99
	Albuquerque MSA, NM	S	18.29 MW	17.51 AW	38040 AAW	NMBLS	10//99-12//99
	New York	S	18.97 MW	19.07 AW	39670 AAW	NYBLS	10//99-12//99
	Albany-Schenectady-Troy MSA, NY	S	20.47 MW	20.72 AW	42570 AAW	NYBLS	10//99-12//99
	Binghamton MSA, NY	S	16.22 MW	13.37 AW	33740 AAW	NYBLS	10//99-12//99
	Buffalo-Niagara Falls MSA, NY	S	16.54 MW	15.78 AW	34410 AAW	NYBLS	10//99-12//99
	Dutchess County PMSA, NY	S	20.19 MW	20.95 AW	41990 AAW	NYBLS	10//99-12//99
	Elmira MSA, NY	S	15.67 MW	13.19 AW	32590 AAW	NYBLS	10//99-12//99
	Glens Falls MSA, NY	S	21.34 MW	22.52 AW	44380 AAW	NYBLS	10//99-12//99
	Nassau-Suffolk PMSA, NY	S	18.72 MW	18.64 AW	38950 AAW	NYBLS	10//99-12//99
	New York PMSA, NY	S	19.21 MW	18.96 AW	39950 AAW	NYBLS	10//99-12//99
	Newburgh PMSA, NY-PA	S	20.07 MW	19.72 AW	41740 AAW	NYBLS	10//99-12//99
	Rochester MSA, NY	S	18.30 MW	18.60 AW	38060 AAW	NYBLS	10//99-12//99
	Syracuse MSA, NY	S	23.67 MW	24.05 AW	49230 AAW	NYBLS	10//99-12//99
	Utica-Rome MSA, NY	S	14.93 MW	10.29 AW	31050 AAW	NYBLS	10//99-12//99
	North Carolina	S	16.97 MW	18.67 AW	38840 AAW	NCBLS	10//99-12//99
	Asheville MSA, NC	S	16.03 MW	15.88 AW	33350 AAW	NCBLS	10//99-12//99
	Charlotte-Gastonia-Rock Hill MSA, NC-SC	S	19.75 MW	18.60 AW	41070 AAW	NCBLS	10//99-12//99
	Fayetteville MSA, NC	S	18.73 MW	18.87 AW	38950 AAW	NCBLS	10//99-12//99
	Goldsboro MSA, NC	S	15.61 MW	12.91 AW	32480 AAW	NCBLS	10//99-12//99
	Greensboro--Winston-Salem--High Point MSA, NC	S	20.72 MW	18.23 AW	43090 AAW	NCBLS	10//99-12//99
	Greenville MSA, NC	S	19.88 MW	19.59 AW	41340 AAW	NCBLS	10//99-12//99
	Hickory-Morganton-Lenoir MSA, NC	S	18.85 MW	18.49 AW	39210 AAW	NCBLS	10//99-12//99
	Raleigh-Durham-Chapel Hill MSA, NC	S	18.73 MW	17.03 AW	38970 AAW	NCBLS	10//99-12//99
	Rocky Mount MSA, NC	S	17.17 MW	17.09 AW	35710 AAW	NCBLS	10//99-12//99
	Wilmington MSA, NC	S	18.55 MW	18.64 AW	38580 AAW	NCBLS	10//99-12//99
	North Dakota	S	13.94 MW	14.58 AW	30330 AAW	NDBLS	10//99-12//99
	Bismarck MSA, ND	S	15.10 MW	15.07 AW	31420 AAW	NDBLS	10//99-12//99
	Fargo-Moorhead MSA, ND-MN	S	14.71 MW	14.34 AW	30600 AAW	NDBLS	10//99-12//99
	Ohio	S	17.74 MW	18.58 AW	38640 AAW	OHBLS	10//99-12//99
	Canton-Massillon MSA, OH	S	18.19 MW	18.91 AW	37850 AAW	OHBLS	10//99-12//99
	Cincinnati PMSA, OH-KY-IN	S	19.10 MW	19.37 AW	39720 AAW	OHBLS	10//99-12//99
	Cleveland-Lorain-Elyria PMSA, OH	S	19.19 MW	18.30 AW	39900 AAW	OHBLS	10//99-12//99
	Columbus MSA, OH	S	17.59 MW	17.62 AW	36580 AAW	OHBLS	10//99-12//99
	Dayton-Springfield MSA, OH	S	21.03 MW	20.38 AW	43750 AAW	OHBLS	10//99-12//99
	Lima MSA, OH	S	18.69 MW	17.99 AW	38880 AAW	OHBLS	10//99-12//99

Occupation/Type/Industry	Location	Per	Low	Mid	High	Source	Date
Electrical and Electronic Engineering Technician	Mansfield MSA, OH	S	18.11 MW	18.36 AW	37670 AAW	OHBLS	10//99-12//99
	Steubenville-Weirton MSA, OH-WV	S	21.40 MW	20.72 AW	44520 AAW	OHBLS	10//99-12//99
	Toledo MSA, OH	S	20.49 MW	17.30 AW	42620 AAW	OHBLS	10//99-12//99
	Oklahoma	S	18.88 MW	19.19 AW	39920 AAW	OKBLS	10//99-12//99
	Lawton MSA, OK	S	16.60 MW	14.17 AW	34540 AAW	OKBLS	10//99-12//99
	Oklahoma City MSA, OK	S	19.78 MW	19.58 AW	41150 AAW	OKBLS	10//99-12//99
	Tulsa MSA, OK	S	20.37 MW	18.04 AW	42380 AAW	OKBLS	10//99-12//99
	Oregon	S	16.83 MW	17.06 AW	35490 AAW	ORBLS	10//99-12//99
	Eugene-Springfield MSA, OR	S	23.05 MW	23.07 AW	47950 AAW	ORBLS	10//99-12//99
	Medford-Ashland MSA, OR	S	15.44 MW	15.99 AW	32120 AAW	ORBLS	10//99-12//99
	Portland-Vancouver PMSA, OR-WA	S	17.22 MW	17.76 AW	35820 AAW	ORBLS	10//99-12//99
	Salem PMSA, OR	S	22.16 MW	23.20 AW	46100 AAW	ORBLS	10//99-12//99
	Pennsylvania	S	17.78 MW	18.70 AW	38890 AAW	PABLS	10//99-12//99
	Allentown-Bethlehem-Easton MSA, PA	S	17.37 MW	16.81 AW	36130 AAW	PABLS	10//99-12//99
	Erie MSA, PA	S	17.62 MW	15.91 AW	36640 AAW	PABLS	10//99-12//99
	Harrisburg-Lebanon-Carlisle MSA, PA	S	19.63 MW	18.20 AW	40820 AAW	PABLS	10//99-12//99
	Johnstown MSA, PA	S	18.29 MW	18.46 AW	38040 AAW	PABLS	10//99-12//99
	Lancaster MSA, PA	S	17.99 MW	18.21 AW	37410 AAW	PABLS	10//99-12//99
	Philadelphia PMSA, PA-NJ	S	19.86 MW	18.80 AW	41310 AAW	PABLS	10//99-12//99
	Pittsburgh MSA, PA	S	18.67 MW	17.89 AW	38840 AAW	PABLS	10//99-12//99
	Reading MSA, PA	S	15.11 MW	13.47 AW	31420 AAW	PABLS	10//99-12//99
	Scranton--Wilkes-Barre--Hazleton MSA, PA	S	16.74 MW	17.37 AW	34820 AAW	PABLS	10//99-12//99
	State College MSA, PA	S	14.86 MW	14.73 AW	30900 AAW	PABLS	10//99-12//99
	Williamsport MSA, PA	S	14.97 MW	14.49 AW	31130 AAW	PABLS	10//99-12//99
	York MSA, PA	S	16.53 MW	15.84 AW	34380 AAW	PABLS	10//99-12//99
	Rhode Island	S	18.15 MW	18.64 AW	38780 AAW	RIBLS	10//99-12//99
	Providence-Fall River-Warwick MSA, RI-MA	S	17.41 MW	15.95 AW	36220 AAW	RIBLS	10//99-12//99
	South Carolina	S	19.73 MW	20.04 AW	41680 AAW	SCBLS	10//99-12//99
	Charleston-North Charleston MSA, SC	S	21.01 MW	20.34 AW	43700 AAW	SCBLS	10//99-12//99
	Columbia MSA, SC	S	19.73 MW	19.56 AW	41030 AAW	SCBLS	10//99-12//99
	Florence MSA, SC	S	18.92 MW	19.08 AW	39360 AAW	SCBLS	10//99-12//99
	Greenville-Spartanburg-Anderson MSA, SC	S	18.92 MW	18.71 AW	39360 AAW	SCBLS	10//99-12//99
	Myrtle Beach MSA, SC	S	21.14 MW	20.47 AW	43980 AAW	SCBLS	10//99-12//99
	Sumter MSA, SC	S	25.98 MW	21.29 AW	54030 AAW	SCBLS	10//99-12//99
	South Dakota	S	14.32 MW	14.60 AW	30370 AAW	SDBLS	10//99-12//99
	Tennessee	S	18.88 MW	18.49 AW	38470 AAW	TNBLS	10//99-12//99
	Chattanooga MSA, TN-GA	S	17.99 MW	18.37 AW	37420 AAW	TNBLS	10//99-12//99
	Jackson MSA, TN	S	19.11 MW	19.17 AW	39750 AAW	TNBLS	10//99-12//99
	Johnson City-Kingsport-Bristol MSA, TN-VA	S	19.06 MW	18.89 AW	39640 AAW	TNBLS	10//99-12//99
	Knoxville MSA, TN	S	16.26 MW	16.12 AW	33830 AAW	TNBLS	10//99-12//99
	Memphis MSA, TN-AR-MS	S	14.57 MW	14.53 AW	30320 AAW	MSBLS	10//99-12//99
	Nashville MSA, TN	S	21.43 MW	22.68 AW	44570 AAW	TNBLS	10//99-12//99
	Texas	S	19.14 MW	19.74 AW	41050 AAW	TXBLS	10//99-12//99
	Abilene MSA, TX	S	19.15 MW	18.70 AW	39840 AAW	TXBLS	10//99-12//99
	Amarillo MSA, TX	S	22.86 MW	23.83 AW	47560 AAW	TXBLS	10//99-12//99
	Austin-San Marcos MSA, TX	S	20.55 MW	19.77 AW	42740 AAW	TXBLS	10//99-12//99
	Beaumont-Port Arthur MSA, TX	S	25.06 MW	24.61 AW	52130 AAW	TXBLS	10//99-12//99
	Brazoria PMSA, TX	S	11.99 MW	14.08 AW	24950 AAW	TXBLS	10//99-12//99
	Brownsville-Harlingen-San Benito MSA, TX	S	17.43 MW	16.37 AW	36260 AAW	TXBLS	10//99-12//99
	Bryan-College Station MSA, TX	S	18.80 MW	18.96 AW	39100 AAW	TXBLS	10//99-12//99
	Corpus Christi MSA, TX	S	18.83 MW	17.84 AW	39170 AAW	TXBLS	10//99-12//99
	Dallas PMSA, TX	S	20.60 MW	20.12 AW	42840 AAW	TXBLS	10//99-12//99
	El Paso MSA, TX	S	20.20 MW	19.71 AW	42010 AAW	TXBLS	10//99-12//99
	Fort Worth-Arlington PMSA, TX	S	22.11 MW	19.55 AW	45990 AAW	TXBLS	10//99-12//99
	Houston PMSA, TX	S	18.41 MW	17.97 AW	38280 AAW	TXBLS	10//99-12//99
	Killeen-Temple MSA, TX	S	19.55 MW	16.75 AW	40660 AAW	TXBLS	10//99-12//99
	Lubbock MSA, TX	S	16.66 MW	15.91 AW	34650 AAW	TXBLS	10//99-12//99
	Odessa-Midland MSA, TX	S	19.74 MW	19.54 AW	41060 AAW	TXBLS	10//99-12//99

AAW Average annual wage	**AOH** Average offered, high	**ASH** Average starting, high	**H** Hourly	**M** Monthly	**S** Special: hourly and annual
AE Average entry wage	**AOL** Average offered, low	**ASL** Average starting, low	**HI** Highest wage paid	**MTC** Median total compensation	**TQ** Third quartile wage
AEX Average experienced wage	**APH** Average pay, high range	**AW** Average wage paid	**HR** High end range	**MW** Median wage paid	**W** Weekly
AO Average offered	**APL** Average pay, low range	**FQ** First quartile wage	**LR** Low end range	**SQ** Second quartile wage	**Y** Yearly

Occupation/Type/Industry	Location	Per	Low	Mid	High	Source	Date
Electrical and Electronic Engineering Technician	San Antonio MSA, TX	S	15.60 MW	14.79 AW	32440 AAW	TXBLS	10//99-12//99
	Sherman-Denison MSA, TX	S	22.21 MW	21.58 AW	46190 AAW	TXBLS	10//99-12//99
	Tyler MSA, TX	S	16.47 MW	16.28 AW	34250 AAW	TXBLS	10//99-12//99
	Waco MSA, TX	S	20.73 MW	22.27 AW	43120 AAW	TXBLS	10//99-12//99
	Utah	S	11.71 MW	13.09 AW	27220 AAW	UTBLS	10//99-12//99
	Salt Lake City-Ogden MSA, UT	S	18.42 MW	18.62 AW	38320 AAW	UTBLS	10//99-12//99
	Vermont	S	14.87 MW	14.87 AW	30930 AAW	VTBLS	10//99-12//99
	Burlington MSA, VT	S	13.44 MW	13.15 AW	27950 AAW	VTBLS	10//99-12//99
	Virginia	S	18.72 MW	18.99 AW	39500 AAW	VABLS	10//99-12//99
	Charlottesville MSA, VA	S	15.28 MW	13.95 AW	31780 AAW	VABLS	10//99-12//99
	Lynchburg MSA, VA	S	20.49 MW	19.17 AW	42620 AAW	VABLS	10//99-12//99
	Norfolk-Virginia Beach-Newport News MSA, VA-NC	S	18.67 MW	18.43 AW	38840 AAW	VABLS	10//99-12//99
	Richmond-Petersburg MSA, VA	S	19.41 MW	19.18 AW	40370 AAW	VABLS	10//99-12//99
	Roanoke MSA, VA	S	17.99 MW	18.83 AW	37430 AAW	VABLS	10//99-12//99
	Washington	S	21.17 MW	19.96 AW	41520 AAW	WABLS	10//99-12//99
	Richland-Kennewick-Pasco MSA, WA	S	19.58 MW	20.06 AW	40720 AAW	WABLS	10//99-12//99
	Seattle-Bellevue-Everett PMSA, WA	S	21.74 MW	22.39 AW	45220 AAW	WABLS	10//99-12//99
	Spokane MSA, WA	S	17.36 MW	18.05 AW	36100 AAW	WABLS	10//99-12//99
	Tacoma PMSA, WA	S	20.81 MW	20.02 AW	43280 AAW	WABLS	10//99-12//99
	Yakima MSA, WA	S	15.27 MW	15.45 AW	31770 AAW	WABLS	10//99-12//99
	West Virginia	S	19.4 MW	18.77 AW	39050 AAW	WVBLS	10//99-12//99
	Charleston MSA, WV	S	14.97 MW	13.14 AW	31130 AAW	WVBLS	10//99-12//99
	Huntington-Ashland MSA, WV-KY-OH	S	22.45 MW	22.87 AW	46700 AAW	WVBLS	10//99-12//99
	Parkersburg-Marietta MSA, WV-OH	S	16.65 MW	14.34 AW	34640 AAW	WVBLS	10//99-12//99
	Wheeling MSA, WV-OH	S	18.67 MW	18.67 AW	38840 AAW	WVBLS	10//99-12//99
	Wisconsin	S	16.59 MW	17.54 AW	36490 AAW	WIBLS	10//99-12//99
	Appleton-Oshkosh-Neenah MSA, WI	S	15.39 MW	14.95 AW	32020 AAW	WIBLS	10//99-12//99
	Eau Claire MSA, WI	S	19.96 MW	19.36 AW	41520 AAW	WIBLS	10//99-12//99
	Green Bay MSA, WI	S	17.57 MW	16.80 AW	36540 AAW	WIBLS	10//99-12//99
	Janesville-Beloit MSA, WI	S	17.68 MW	17.83 AW	36780 AAW	WIBLS	10//99-12//99
	Kenosha PMSA, WI	S	11.37 MW	10.17 AW	23640 AAW	WIBLS	10//99-12//99
	La Crosse MSA, WI-MN	S	21.91 MW	20.98 AW	45570 AAW	WIBLS	10//99-12//99
	Madison MSA, WI	S	18.31 MW	17.00 AW	38080 AAW	WIBLS	10//99-12//99
	Milwaukee-Waukesha PMSA, WI	S	19.20 MW	18.77 AW	39940 AAW	WIBLS	10//99-12//99
	Racine PMSA, WI	S	18.09 MW	16.48 AW	37640 AAW	WIBLS	10//99-12//99
	Sheboygan MSA, WI	S	18.38 MW	18.52 AW	38230 AAW	WIBLS	10//99-12//99
	Wausau MSA, WI	S	23.78 MW	20.59 AW	49450 AAW	WIBLS	10//99-12//99
	Wyoming	S	19.47 MW	20.25 AW	42110 AAW	WYBLS	10//99-12//99
	Casper MSA, WY	S	14.41 MW	14.95 AW	29970 AAW	WYBLS	10//99-12//99
	Cheyenne MSA, WY	S	18.08 MW	18.23 AW	37620 AAW	WYBLS	10//99-12//99
	Puerto Rico	S	12.94 MW	13.17 AW	27380 AAW	PRBLS	10//99-12//99
	Caguas PMSA, PR	S	13.88 MW	14.13 AW	28870 AAW	PRBLS	10//99-12//99
	Mayaguez MSA, PR	S	13.68 MW	14.41 AW	28460 AAW	PRBLS	10//99-12//99
	San Juan-Bayamon PMSA, PR	S	12.81 MW	12.48 AW	26640 AAW	PRBLS	10//99-12//99
	Virgin Islands	S	18.43 MW	18.69 AW	38880 AAW	VIBLS	10//99-12//99
	Guam	S	13.64 MW	14.62 AW	30400 AAW	GUBLS	10//99-12//99
Electrical and Electronic Equipment Assembler	Alabama	S	9.89 MW	10.88 AW	22620 AAW	ALBLS	10//99-12//99
	Arizona	S	9.03 MW	9.47 AW	19710 AAW	AZBLS	10//99-12//99
	Arkansas	S	13.78 MW	12.11 AW	25200 AAW	ARBLS	10//99-12//99
	California	S	10.21 MW	10.87 AW	22610 AAW	CABLS	10//99-12//99
	Colorado	S	9.72 MW	9.78 AW	20340 AAW	COBLS	10//99-12//99
	Delaware	S	12.55 MW	12.43 AW	25860 AAW	DEBLS	10//99-12//99
	Florida	S	7.54 MW	7.83 AW	16290 AAW	FLBLS	10//99-12//99
	Georgia	S	8.89 MW	9.08 AW	18890 AAW	GABLS	10//99-12//99
	Idaho	S	8.81 MW	11.92 AW	24800 AAW	IDBLS	10//99-12//99
	Illinois	S	10.22 MW	10.23 AW	21270 AAW	ILBLS	10//99-12//99
	Indiana	S	8.62 MW	8.88 AW	18480 AAW	INBLS	10//99-12//99
	Iowa	S	9.61 MW	10.29 AW	21390 AAW	IABLS	10//99-12//99
	Kansas	S	10.89 MW	11.94 AW	24830 AAW	KSBLS	10//99-12//99

AAW	Average annual wage	AOH	Average offered, high	ASH	Average starting, high	H	Hourly	M	Monthly	S	Special: hourly and annual
AE	Average entry wage	AOL	Average offered, low	ASL	Average starting, low	HI	Highest wage paid	MTC	Median total compensation	TQ	Third quartile wage
AEX	Average experienced wage	APH	Average pay, high range	AW	Average wage paid	HR	High end range	MW	Median wage paid	W	Weekly
AO	Average offered	APL	Average pay, low range	FQ	First quartile wage	LR	Low end range	SQ	Second quartile wage	Y	Yearly

Occupation/Type/Industry	Location	Per	Low	Mid	High	Source	Date
Electrical and Electronic Equipment Assembler	Kentucky	S	9.53 MW	10.19 AW	21190 AAW	KYBLS	10//99-12//99
	Louisiana	S	7.52 MW	8.59 AW	17880 AAW	LABLS	10//99-12//99
	Maine	S	11.9 MW	11.66 AW	24240 AAW	MEBLS	10//99-12//99
	Maryland	S	10.21 MW	10.83 AW	22520 AAW	MDBLS	10//99-12//99
	Massachusetts	S	11.5 MW	11.72 AW	24380 AAW	MABLS	10//99-12//99
	Michigan	S	10.58 MW	11.61 AW	24150 AAW	MIBLS	10//99-12//99
	Minnesota	S	11.01 MW	11.70 AW	24340 AAW	MNBLS	10//99-12//99
	Mississippi	S	6.95 MW	7.92 AW	16470 AAW	MSBLS	10//99-12//99
	Missouri	S	9.63 MW	10.09 AW	20980 AAW	MOBLS	10//99-12//99
	Montana	S	9.59 MW	10.10 AW	21000 AAW	MTBLS	10//99-12//99
	Nebraska	S	8.22 MW	9.92 AW	20630 AAW	NEBLS	10//99-12//99
	Nevada	S	8.66 MW	9.45 AW	19660 AAW	NVBLS	10//99-12//99
	New Hampshire	S	11.6 MW	11.58 AW	24080 AAW	NHBLS	10//99-12//99
	New Jersey	S	10.91 MW	11.41 AW	23720 AAW	NJBLS	10//99-12//99
	New Mexico	S	9.31 MW	9.41 AW	19560 AAW	NMBLS	10//99-12//99
	New York	S	10.46 MW	11.25 AW	23410 AAW	NYBLS	10//99-12//99
	North Carolina	S	10.3 MW	11.20 AW	23300 AAW	NCBLS	10//99-12//99
	North Dakota	S	8.07 MW	8.82 AW	18350 AAW	NDBLS	10//99-12//99
	Ohio	S	9.94 MW	10.50 AW	21850 AAW	OHBLS	10//99-12//99
	Oklahoma	S	11.15 MW	10.52 AW	21880 AAW	OKBLS	10//99-12//99
	Oregon	S	10.04 MW	10.58 AW	22000 AAW	ORBLS	10//99-12//99
	Pennsylvania	S	11.59 MW	11.83 AW	24610 AAW	PABLS	10//99-12//99
	Rhode Island	S	9.89 MW	10.97 AW	22820 AAW	RIBLS	10//99-12//99
	South Carolina	S	11.46 MW	11.78 AW	24510 AAW	SCBLS	10//99-12//99
	South Dakota	S	7.96 MW	8.03 AW	16690 AAW	SDBLS	10//99-12//99
	Tennessee	S	10 MW	10.70 AW	22250 AAW	TNBLS	10//99-12//99
	Texas	S	8.98 MW	10.64 AW	22130 AAW	TXBLS	10//99-12//99
	Vermont	S	8.53 MW	9.19 AW	19110 AAW	VTBLS	10//99-12//99
	Virginia	S	9.43 MW	9.85 AW	20490 AAW	VABLS	10//99-12//99
	Washington	S	8.74 MW	9.82 AW	20420 AAW	WABLS	10//99-12//99
	Wisconsin	S	9.65 MW	10.80 AW	22470 AAW	WIBLS	10//99-12//99
	Wyoming	S	15.17 MW	15.64 AW	32540 AAW	WYBLS	10//99-12//99
	Puerto Rico	S	6.29 MW	6.34 AW	13180 AAW	PRBLS	10//99-12//99
Electrical and Electronics Drafter	Alabama	S	18.92 MW	19.45 AW	40460 AAW	ALBLS	10//99-12//99
	Birmingham MSA, AL	S	19.28 MW	17.49 AW	40100 AAW	ALBLS	10//99-12//99
	Huntsville MSA, AL	S	19.75 MW	19.36 AW	41090 AAW	ALBLS	10//99-12//99
	Alaska	S	20.53 MW	22.58 AW	46960 AAW	AKBLS	10//99-12//99
	Anchorage MSA, AK	S	21.25 MW	19.62 AW	44200 AAW	AKBLS	10//99-12//99
	Arizona	S	20.4 MW	20.20 AW	42020 AAW	AZBLS	10//99-12//99
	Phoenix-Mesa MSA, AZ	S	20.13 MW	20.32 AW	41870 AAW	AZBLS	10//99-12//99
	Tucson MSA, AZ	S	20.83 MW	20.91 AW	43320 AAW	AZBLS	10//99-12//99
	Arkansas	S	15.93 MW	16.63 AW	34590 AAW	ARBLS	10//99-12//99
	Little Rock-North Little Rock MSA, AR	S	15.72 MW	15.53 AW	32690 AAW	ARBLS	10//99-12//99
	California	S	19.77 MW	21.26 AW	44220 AAW	CABLS	10//99-12//99
	Los Angeles-Long Beach PMSA, CA	S	23.52 MW	23.77 AW	48930 AAW	CABLS	10//99-12//99
	Oakland PMSA, CA	S	23.42 MW	21.59 AW	48720 AAW	CABLS	10//99-12//99
	Orange County PMSA, CA	S	16.98 MW	14.78 AW	35320 AAW	CABLS	10//99-12//99
	Riverside-San Bernardino PMSA, CA	S	17.28 MW	15.66 AW	35950 AAW	CABLS	10//99-12//99
	Sacramento PMSA, CA	S	16.02 MW	15.54 AW	33320 AAW	CABLS	10//99-12//99
	San Diego MSA, CA	S	21.23 MW	21.85 AW	44150 AAW	CABLS	10//99-12//99
	San Francisco PMSA, CA	S	22.20 MW	21.06 AW	46170 AAW	CABLS	10//99-12//99
	San Jose PMSA, CA	S	22.94 MW	20.26 AW	47720 AAW	CABLS	10//99-12//99
	Santa Rosa PMSA, CA	S	16.64 MW	15.42 AW	34610 AAW	CABLS	10//99-12//99
	Vallejo-Fairfield-Napa PMSA, CA	S	18.62 MW	18.40 AW	38720 AAW	CABLS	10//99-12//99
	Ventura PMSA, CA	S	20.47 MW	19.13 AW	42570 AAW	CABLS	10//99-12//99
	Colorado	S	16.9 MW	18.33 AW	38130 AAW	COBLS	10//99-12//99
	Boulder-Longmont PMSA, CO	S	18.02 MW	18.08 AW	37490 AAW	COBLS	10//99-12//99
	Denver PMSA, CO	S	20.76 MW	22.60 AW	43190 AAW	COBLS	10//99-12//99
	Fort Collins-Loveland MSA, CO	S	18.87 MW	19.01 AW	39250 AAW	COBLS	10//99-12//99
	Connecticut	S	16.36 MW	18.02 AW	37490 AAW	CTBLS	10//99-12//99
	Bridgeport PMSA, CT	S	17.71 MW	16.24 AW	36840 AAW	CTBLS	10//99-12//99
	Danbury PMSA, CT	S	18.60 MW	16.58 AW	38680 AAW	CTBLS	10//99-12//99
	Hartford MSA, CT	S	18.05 MW	15.61 AW	37540 AAW	CTBLS	10//99-12//99
	New Haven-Meriden PMSA, CT	S	18.38 MW	17.91 AW	38230 AAW	CTBLS	10//99-12//99

AAW	Average annual wage	AOH	Average offered, high	ASH	Average starting, high	H	Hourly
AE	Average entry wage	AOL	Average offered, low	ASL	Average starting, low	HI	Highest wage paid
AEX	Average experienced wage	APH	Average pay, high range	AW	Average wage paid	HR	High end range
AO	Average offered	APL	Average pay, low range	FQ	First quartile wage	LR	Low end range

M	Monthly	S	Special: hourly and annual
MTC	Median total compensation	TQ	Third quartile wage
MW	Median wage paid	W	Weekly
SQ	Second quartile wage	Y	Yearly

Occupation/Type/Industry	Location	Per	Low	Mid	High	Source	Date
Electrical and Electronics Drafter	Stamford-Norwalk PMSA, CT	S	14.71 MW	13.50 AW	30590 AAW	CTBLS	10//99-12//99
	Delaware	S	17.31 MW	18.39 AW	38240 AAW	DEBLS	10//99-12//99
	Wilmington-Newark PMSA, DE-MD	S	18.48 MW	17.49 AW	38440 AAW	DEBLS	10//99-12//99
	Washington PMSA, DC-MD-VA-WV	S	18.18 MW	17.58 AW	37810 AAW	DCBLS	10//99-12//99
	Florida	S	15.99 MW	16.79 AW	34920 AAW	FLBLS	10//99-12//99
	Fort Lauderdale PMSA, FL	S	18.00 MW	18.02 AW	37440 AAW	FLBLS	10//99-12//99
	Fort Myers-Cape Coral MSA, FL	S	14.78 MW	14.91 AW	30750 AAW	FLBLS	10//99-12//99
	Jacksonville MSA, FL	S	13.67 MW	14.11 AW	28430 AAW	FLBLS	10//99-12//99
	Lakeland-Winter Haven MSA, FL	S	15.02 MW	15.10 AW	31240 AAW	FLBLS	10//99-12//99
	Melbourne-Titusville-Palm Bay MSA, FL	S	16.56 MW	17.74 AW	34450 AAW	FLBLS	10//99-12//99
	Miami PMSA, FL	S	18.26 MW	17.27 AW	37980 AAW	FLBLS	10//99-12//99
	Orlando MSA, FL	S	15.66 MW	15.33 AW	32570 AAW	FLBLS	10//99-12//99
	Tampa-St. Petersburg-Clearwater MSA, FL	S	16.82 MW	17.13 AW	34990 AAW	FLBLS	10//99-12//99
	West Palm Beach-Boca Raton MSA, FL	S	20.48 MW	21.51 AW	42600 AAW	FLBLS	10//99-12//99
	Georgia	S	17.3 MW	18.15 AW	37750 AAW	GABLS	10//99-12//99
	Atlanta MSA, GA	S	17.34 MW	16.01 AW	36060 AAW	GABLS	10//99-12//99
	Macon MSA, GA	S	18.55 MW	16.52 AW	38590 AAW	GABLS	10//99-12//99
	Hawaii	S	12.13 MW	13.91 AW	28930 AAW	HIBLS	10//99-12//99
	Honolulu MSA, HI	S	13.31 MW	11.19 AW	27680 AAW	HIBLS	10//99-12//99
	Idaho	S	16.17 MW	15.11 AW	31440 AAW	IDBLS	10//99-12//99
	Illinois	S	15.91 MW	16.95 AW	35250 AAW	ILBLS	10//99-12//99
	Chicago PMSA, IL	S	18.10 MW	16.34 AW	37640 AAW	ILBLS	10//99-12//99
	Peoria-Pekin MSA, IL	S	15.74 MW	15.64 AW	32750 AAW	ILBLS	10//99-12//99
	Rockford MSA, IL	S	16.44 MW	15.67 AW	34200 AAW	ILBLS	10//99-12//99
	Springfield MSA, IL	S	12.12 MW	12.13 AW	25200 AAW	ILBLS	10//99-12//99
	Indiana	S	15.53 MW	15.50 AW	32230 AAW	INBLS	10//99-12//99
	Elkhart-Goshen MSA, IN	S	20.04 MW	19.26 AW	41690 AAW	INBLS	10//99-12//99
	Fort Wayne MSA, IN	S	14.34 MW	13.72 AW	29830 AAW	INBLS	10//99-12//99
	Gary PMSA, IN	S	15.69 MW	13.44 AW	32630 AAW	INBLS	10//99-12//99
	South Bend MSA, IN	S	14.17 MW	14.84 AW	29480 AAW	INBLS	10//99-12//99
	Iowa	S	14.87 MW	15.21 AW	31630 AAW	IABLS	10//99-12//99
	Davenport-Moline-Rock Island MSA, IA-IL	S	12.34 MW	11.48 AW	25670 AAW	IABLS	10//99-12//99
	Kansas	S	15.07 MW	16.13 AW	33550 AAW	KSBLS	10//99-12//99
	Wichita MSA, KS	S	15.06 MW	13.03 AW	31320 AAW	KSBLS	10//99-12//99
	Kentucky	S	14.68 MW	15.61 AW	32470 AAW	KYBLS	10//99-12//99
	Lexington MSA, KY	S	14.23 MW	13.77 AW	29610 AAW	KYBLS	10//99-12//99
	Louisville MSA, KY-IN	S	20.11 MW	20.89 AW	41840 AAW	KYBLS	10//99-12//99
	Louisiana	S	16.35 MW	17.74 AW	36910 AAW	LABLS	10//99-12//99
	New Orleans MSA, LA	S	15.22 MW	15.11 AW	31650 AAW	LABLS	10//99-12//99
	Maine	S	19.83 MW	19.62 AW	40810 AAW	MEBLS	10//99-12//99
	Maryland	S	23.02 MW	21.80 AW	45340 AAW	MDBLS	10//99-12//99
	Baltimore PMSA, MD	S	23.19 MW	23.91 AW	48240 AAW	MDBLS	10//99-12//99
	Massachusetts	S	19.06 MW	19.61 AW	40780 AAW	MABLS	10//99-12//99
	Boston PMSA, MA-NH	S	19.09 MW	18.32 AW	39710 AAW	MABLS	10//99-12//99
	Lawrence PMSA, MA-NH	S	23.38 MW	24.07 AW	48620 AAW	MABLS	10//99-12//99
	Lowell PMSA, MA-NH	S	22.60 MW	23.16 AW	47000 AAW	MABLS	10//99-12//99
	Worcester PMSA, MA-CT	S	19.58 MW	19.00 AW	40730 AAW	MABLS	10//99-12//99
	Michigan	S	17.21 MW	17.41 AW	36210 AAW	MIBLS	10//99-12//99
	Ann Arbor PMSA, MI	S	18.64 MW	18.44 AW	38770 AAW	MIBLS	10//99-12//99
	Detroit PMSA, MI	S	17.76 MW	17.63 AW	36930 AAW	MIBLS	10//99-12//99
	Grand Rapids-Muskegon-Holland MSA, MI	S	16.06 MW	16.55 AW	33410 AAW	MIBLS	10//99-12//99
	Minnesota	S	17.87 MW	18.59 AW	38670 AAW	MNBLS	10//99-12//99
	Minneapolis-St. Paul MSA, MN-WI	S	20.59 MW	20.23 AW	42830 AAW	MNBLS	10//99-12//99
	Mississippi	S	15.79 MW	16.62 AW	34560 AAW	MSBLS	10//99-12//99
	Biloxi-Gulfport-Pascagoula MSA, MS	S	20.89 MW	20.91 AW	43450 AAW	MSBLS	10//99-12//99
	Jackson MSA, MS	S	15.89 MW	15.02 AW	33060 AAW	MSBLS	10//99-12//99
	Missouri	S	13.44 MW	15.48 AW	32210 AAW	MOBLS	10//99-12//99
	Kansas City MSA, MO-KS	S	14.99 MW	13.15 AW	31180 AAW	MOBLS	10//99-12//99
	St. Louis MSA, MO-IL	S	16.28 MW	15.54 AW	33860 AAW	MOBLS	10//99-12//99
	Montana	S	18.21 MW	18.56 AW	38610 AAW	MTBLS	10//99-12//99
	Lincoln MSA, NE	S	17.69 MW	15.03 AW	36800 AAW	NEBLS	10//99-12//99

Occupation/Type/Industry	Location	Per	Low	Mid	High	Source	Date
Electrical and Electronics Drafter	Nevada	s	18.84 mw	19.26 aw	40050 aaw	NVBLS	10//99-12//99
	Las Vegas MSA, NV-AZ	s	19.50 mw	18.96 aw	40550 aaw	NVBLS	10//99-12//99
	Reno MSA, NV	s	19.28 mw	19.22 aw	40110 aaw	NVBLS	10//99-12//99
	New Hampshire	s	22.37 mw	21.71 aw	45150 aaw	NHBLS	10//99-12//99
	Manchester PMSA, NH	s	23.23 mw	24.04 aw	48320 aaw	NHBLS	10//99-12//99
	Nashua PMSA, NH	s	19.84 mw	19.71 aw	41260 aaw	NHBLS	10//99-12//99
	New Jersey	s	20.35 mw	21.78 aw	45290 aaw	NJBLS	10//99-12//99
	Bergen-Passaic PMSA, NJ	s	17.56 mw	15.84 aw	36520 aaw	NJBLS	10//99-12//99
	Monmouth-Ocean PMSA, NJ	s	21.22 mw	19.80 aw	44150 aaw	NJBLS	10//99-12//99
	Newark PMSA, NJ	s	22.83 mw	21.41 aw	47490 aaw	NJBLS	10//99-12//99
	Trenton PMSA, NJ	s	22.23 mw	20.61 aw	46230 aaw	NJBLS	10//99-12//99
	New Mexico	s	17.67 mw	17.64 aw	36690 aaw	NMBLS	10//99-12//99
	New York	s	20.71 mw	21.15 aw	44000 aaw	NYBLS	10//99-12//99
	Albany-Schenectady-Troy MSA, NY	s	17.14 mw	17.59 aw	35650 aaw	NYBLS	10//99-12//99
	Buffalo-Niagara Falls MSA, NY	s	20.61 mw	22.74 aw	42860 aaw	NYBLS	10//99-12//99
	Dutchess County PMSA, NY	s	23.20 mw	23.91 aw	48250 aaw	NYBLS	10//99-12//99
	Nassau-Suffolk PMSA, NY	s	21.90 mw	22.10 aw	45550 aaw	NYBLS	10//99-12//99
	New York PMSA, NY	s	21.79 mw	20.50 aw	45320 aaw	NYBLS	10//99-12//99
	Rochester MSA, NY	s	17.94 mw	16.50 aw	37310 aaw	NYBLS	10//99-12//99
	Syracuse MSA, NY	s	24.79 mw	27.21 aw	51560 aaw	NYBLS	10//99-12//99
	North Carolina	s	17.79 mw	18.36 aw	38190 aaw	NCBLS	10//99-12//99
	Asheville MSA, NC	s	17.81 mw	18.30 aw	37040 aaw	NCBLS	10//99-12//99
	Charlotte-Gastonia-Rock Hill MSA, NC-SC	s	19.02 mw	18.54 aw	39560 aaw	NCBLS	10//99-12//99
	Greensboro--Winston-Salem--High Point MSA, NC	s	18.69 mw	17.97 aw	38880 aaw	NCBLS	10//99-12//99
	Raleigh-Durham-Chapel Hill MSA, NC	s	19.92 mw	21.98 aw	41430 aaw	NCBLS	10//99-12//99
	North Dakota	s	18.47 mw	17.56 aw	36530 aaw	NDBLS	10//99-12//99
	Ohio	s	15.88 mw	17.61 aw	36630 aaw	OHBLS	10//99-12//99
	Canton-Massillon MSA, OH	s	17.83 mw	18.57 aw	37090 aaw	OHBLS	10//99-12//99
	Cleveland-Lorain-Elyria PMSA, OH	s	21.62 mw	20.94 aw	44980 aaw	OHBLS	10//99-12//99
	Hamilton-Middletown PMSA, OH	s	19.55 mw	19.57 aw	40660 aaw	OHBLS	10//99-12//99
	Oklahoma	s	16.94 mw	19.09 aw	39700 aaw	OKBLS	10//99-12//99
	Oklahoma City MSA, OK	s	14.73 mw	14.42 aw	30640 aaw	OKBLS	10//99-12//99
	Tulsa MSA, OK	s	22.52 mw	21.04 aw	46840 aaw	OKBLS	10//99-12//99
	Oregon	s	13.41 mw	14.33 aw	29810 aaw	ORBLS	10//99-12//99
	Portland-Vancouver PMSA, OR-WA	s	13.86 mw	12.91 aw	28820 aaw	ORBLS	10//99-12//99
	Pennsylvania	s	17.25 mw	17.46 aw	36330 aaw	PABLS	10//99-12//99
	Allentown-Bethlehem-Easton MSA, PA	s	15.59 mw	15.12 aw	32420 aaw	PABLS	10//99-12//99
	Harrisburg-Lebanon-Carlisle MSA, PA	s	14.54 mw	17.10 aw	30230 aaw	PABLS	10//99-12//99
	Philadelphia PMSA, PA-NJ	s	18.77 mw	17.72 aw	39040 aaw	PABLS	10//99-12//99
	Pittsburgh MSA, PA	s	18.50 mw	18.90 aw	38470 aaw	PABLS	10//99-12//99
	Reading MSA, PA	s	17.12 mw	17.35 aw	35620 aaw	PABLS	10//99-12//99
	State College MSA, PA	s	19.67 mw	16.59 aw	40920 aaw	PABLS	10//99-12//99
	York MSA, PA	s	13.93 mw	13.21 aw	28970 aaw	PABLS	10//99-12//99
	Rhode Island	s	18.27 mw	18.72 aw	38940 aaw	RIBLS	10//99-12//99
	Providence-Fall River-Warwick MSA, RI-MA	s	17.49 mw	17.19 aw	36380 aaw	RIBLS	10//99-12//99
	South Carolina	s	22.18 mw	22.81 aw	47450 aaw	SCBLS	10//99-12//99
	Charleston-North Charleston MSA, SC	s	17.50 mw	17.50 aw	36400 aaw	SCBLS	10//99-12//99
	Columbia MSA, SC	s	15.33 mw	15.51 aw	31890 aaw	SCBLS	10//99-12//99
	Florence MSA, SC	s	13.21 mw	12.39 aw	27470 aaw	SCBLS	10//99-12//99
	Greenville-Spartanburg-Anderson MSA, SC	s	22.84 mw	22.31 aw	47520 aaw	SCBLS	10//99-12//99
	South Dakota	s	16.33 mw	17.06 aw	35490 aaw	SDBLS	10//99-12//99
	Tennessee	s	12.91 mw	14.47 aw	30100 aaw	TNBLS	10//99-12//99
	Johnson City-Kingsport-Bristol MSA, TN-VA	s	12.13 mw	12.15 aw	25230 aaw	TNBLS	10//99-12//99
	Knoxville MSA, TN	s	17.13 mw	12.99 aw	35630 aaw	TNBLS	10//99-12//99
	Nashville MSA, TN	s	16.51 mw	15.43 aw	34350 aaw	TNBLS	10//99-12//99
	Texas	s	18.53 mw	20.08 aw	41760 aaw	TXBLS	10//99-12//99
	Austin-San Marcos MSA, TX	s	17.92 mw	16.46 aw	37280 aaw	TXBLS	10//99-12//99
	Corpus Christi MSA, TX	s	15.08 mw	15.13 aw	31370 aaw	TXBLS	10//99-12//99

AAW	Average annual wage	**AOH**	Average offered, high	**ASH**	Average starting, high	**H**	Hourly	**M**	Monthly	**S**	Special: hourly and annual
AE	Average entry wage	**AOL**	Average offered, low	**ASL**	Average starting, low	**HI**	Highest wage paid	**MTC**	Median total compensation	**TQ**	Third quartile wage
AEX	Average experienced wage	**APH**	Average pay, high range	**AW**	Average wage paid	**HR**	High end range	**MW**	Median wage paid	**W**	Weekly
AO	Average offered	**APL**	Average pay, low range	**FQ**	First quartile wage	**LR**	Low end range	**SQ**	Second quartile wage	**Y**	Yearly

Occupation/Type/Industry	Location	Per	Low	Mid	High	Source	Date
Electrical and Electronics Drafter	Dallas PMSA, TX	S	14.54 MW	13.22 AW	30240 AAW	TXBLS	10//99-12//99
	El Paso MSA, TX	S	18.47 MW	19.06 AW	38420 AAW	TXBLS	10//99-12//99
	Fort Worth-Arlington PMSA, TX	S	13.33 MW	13.36 AW	27720 AAW	TXBLS	10//99-12//99
	Houston PMSA, TX	S	24.78 MW	23.94 AW	51540 AAW	TXBLS	10//99-12//99
	Longview-Marshall MSA, TX	S	17.33 MW	16.90 AW	36040 AAW	TXBLS	10//99-12//99
	San Antonio MSA, TX	S	20.86 MW	21.46 AW	43380 AAW	TXBLS	10//99-12//99
	Waco MSA, TX	S	18.08 MW	15.14 AW	37610 AAW	TXBLS	10//99-12//99
	Utah	S	15.59 MW	15.79 AW	32840 AAW	UTBLS	10//99-12//99
	Salt Lake City-Ogden MSA, UT	S	15.74 MW	15.85 AW	32740 AAW	UTBLS	10//99-12//99
	Vermont	S	17.77 MW	17.57 AW	36550 AAW	VTBLS	10//99-12//99
	Burlington MSA, VT	S	18.28 MW	18.60 AW	38020 AAW	VTBLS	10//99-12//99
	Virginia	S	16.4 MW	17.24 AW	35860 AAW	VABLS	10//99-12//99
	Norfolk-Virginia Beach-Newport News MSA, VA-NC	S	14.26 MW	14.03 AW	29660 AAW	VABLS	10//99-12//99
	Richmond-Petersburg MSA, VA	S	21.31 MW	20.19 AW	44320 AAW	VABLS	10//99-12//99
	Washington	S	16.99 MW	17.51 AW	36420 AAW	WABLS	10//99-12//99
	Seattle-Bellevue-Everett PMSA, WA	S	20.56 MW	19.75 AW	42760 AAW	WABLS	10//99-12//99
	Spokane MSA, WA	S	13.34 MW	14.19 AW	27750 AAW	WABLS	10//99-12//99
	Tacoma PMSA, WA	S	18.59 MW	20.08 AW	38680 AAW	WABLS	10//99-12//99
	West Virginia	S	16.42 MW	16.36 AW	34030 AAW	WVBLS	10//99-12//99
	Wisconsin	S	16.95 MW	18.91 AW	39330 AAW	WIBLS	10//99-12//99
	Eau Claire MSA, WI	S	15.62 MW	15.47 AW	32500 AAW	WIBLS	10//99-12//99
	Green Bay MSA, WI	S	21.82 MW	21.95 AW	45390 AAW	WIBLS	10//99-12//99
	Madison MSA, WI	S	14.62 MW	13.28 AW	30410 AAW	WIBLS	10//99-12//99
	Milwaukee-Waukesha PMSA, WI	S	20.00 MW	18.55 AW	41600 AAW	WIBLS	10//99-12//99
Electrical and Electronics Installer and Repairer							
Transportation Equipment	Alabama	S	22.57 MW	19.68 AW	40940 AAW	ALBLS	10//99-12//99
Transportation Equipment	Alaska	S	20 MW	20.43 AW	42500 AAW	AKBLS	10//99-12//99
Transportation Equipment	Arizona	S	21.24 MW	21.37 AW	44450 AAW	AZBLS	10//99-12//99
Transportation Equipment	Phoenix-Mesa MSA, AZ	S	21.22 MW	20.97 AW	44130 AAW	AZBLS	10//99-12//99
Transportation Equipment	California	S	16.33 MW	15.88 AW	33030 AAW	CABLS	10//99-12//99
Transportation Equipment	Los Angeles-Long Beach PMSA, CA	S	15.41 MW	14.48 AW	32040 AAW	CABLS	10//99-12//99
Transportation Equipment	Oakland PMSA, CA	S	15.96 MW	15.88 AW	33210 AAW	CABLS	10//99-12//99
Transportation Equipment	Orange County PMSA, CA	S	18.79 MW	19.33 AW	39090 AAW	CABLS	10//99-12//99
Transportation Equipment	Riverside-San Bernardino PMSA, CA	S	21.22 MW	20.78 AW	44140 AAW	CABLS	10//99-12//99
Transportation Equipment	San Diego MSA, CA	S	14.09 MW	14.50 AW	29300 AAW	CABLS	10//99-12//99
Transportation Equipment	Ventura PMSA, CA	S	15.63 MW	18.23 AW	32510 AAW	CABLS	10//99-12//99
Transportation Equipment	Colorado	S	19 MW	18.32 AW	38100 AAW	COBLS	10//99-12//99
Transportation Equipment	Denver PMSA, CO	S	17.81 MW	18.85 AW	37050 AAW	COBLS	10//99-12//99
Transportation Equipment	Connecticut	S	22.03 MW	19.79 AW	41150 AAW	CTBLS	10//99-12//99
Transportation Equipment	New London-Norwich MSA, CT-RI	S	20.71 MW	21.98 AW	43070 AAW	CTBLS	10//99-12//99
Transportation Equipment	Delaware	S	10.54 MW	12.47 AW	25950 AAW	DEBLS	10//99-12//99
Transportation Equipment	Washington PMSA, DC-MD-VA-WV	S	16.08 MW	17.91 AW	33450 AAW	DCBLS	10//99-12//99
Transportation Equipment	Florida	S	13.32 MW	14.06 AW	29240 AAW	FLBLS	10//99-12//99
Transportation Equipment	Fort Lauderdale PMSA, FL	S	15.55 MW	15.08 AW	32340 AAW	FLBLS	10//99-12//99
Transportation Equipment	Jacksonville MSA, FL	S	15.01 MW	14.97 AW	31220 AAW	FLBLS	10//99-12//99
Transportation Equipment	Miami PMSA, FL	S	14.45 MW	14.19 AW	30050 AAW	FLBLS	10//99-12//99
Transportation Equipment	Orlando MSA, FL	S	11.45 MW	10.95 AW	23810 AAW	FLBLS	10//99-12//99
Transportation Equipment	Tampa-St. Petersburg-Clearwater MSA, FL	S	17.53 MW	15.24 AW	36460 AAW	FLBLS	10//99-12//99
Transportation Equipment	Georgia	S	15.14 MW	14.46 AW	30080 AAW	GABLS	10//99-12//99
Transportation Equipment	Atlanta MSA, GA	S	14.34 MW	15.40 AW	29840 AAW	GABLS	10//99-12//99
Transportation Equipment	Idaho	S	18.41 MW	17.88 AW	37180 AAW	IDBLS	10//99-12//99
Transportation Equipment	Illinois	S	17.79 MW	17.51 AW	36420 AAW	ILBLS	10//99-12//99
Transportation Equipment	Chicago PMSA, IL	S	18.42 MW	16.73 AW	38320 AAW	ILBLS	10//99-12//99
Transportation Equipment	Indiana	S	16.19 MW	16.11 AW	33510 AAW	INBLS	10//99-12//99
Transportation Equipment	Kansas	S	16.72 MW	16.15 AW	33590 AAW	KSBLS	10//99-12//99
Transportation Equipment	Kentucky	S	9.54 MW	10.59 AW	22030 AAW	KYBLS	10//99-12//99
Transportation Equipment	Louisiana	S	10.23 MW	12.26 AW	25490 AAW	LABLS	10//99-12//99
Transportation Equipment	Maryland	S	22.91 MW	20.42 AW	42470 AAW	MDBLS	10//99-12//99

AAW Average annual wage	**AOH** Average offered, high	**ASH** Average starting, high	**H** Hourly	**M** Monthly	**S** Special: hourly and annual
AE Average entry wage	**AOL** Average offered, low	**ASL** Average starting, low	**HI** Highest wage paid	**MTC** Median total compensation	**TQ** Third quartile wage
AEX Average experienced wage	**APH** Average pay, high range	**AW** Average wage paid	**HR** High end range	**MW** Median wage paid	**W** Weekly
AO Average offered	**APL** Average pay, low range	**FQ** First quartile wage	**LR** Low end range	**SQ** Second quartile wage	**Y** Yearly

Occupation/Type/Industry	Location	Per	Low	Mid	High	Source	Date

Electrical and Electronics
Installer and Repairer

Occupation/Type/Industry	Location	Per	Low	Mid	High	Source	Date
Transportation Equipment	Massachusetts	S	10.79 MW	12.58 AW	26170 AAW	MABLS	10//99-12//99
Transportation Equipment	Boston PMSA, MA-NH	S	9.66 MW	9.69 AW	20100 AAW	MABLS	10//99-12//99
Transportation Equipment	Michigan	S	20.93 MW	20.58 AW	42800 AAW	MIBLS	10//99-12//99
Transportation Equipment	Minnesota	S	19.85 MW	19.96 AW	41520 AAW	MNBLS	10//99-12//99
Transportation Equipment	Nebraska	S	16.73 MW	17.36 AW	36110 AAW	NEBLS	10//99-12//99
Transportation Equipment	Nevada	S	16.07 MW	15.77 AW	32790 AAW	NVBLS	10//99-12//99
Transportation Equipment	Las Vegas MSA, NV-AZ	S	15.13 MW	15.10 AW	31460 AAW	NVBLS	10//99-12//99
Transportation Equipment	New Jersey	S	19.01 MW	18.64 AW	38770 AAW	NJBLS	10//99-12//99
Transportation Equipment	New Mexico	S	18 MW	17.37 AW	36140 AAW	NMBLS	10//99-12//99
Transportation Equipment	New York	S	15.8 MW	15.97 AW	33220 AAW	NYBLS	10//99-12//99
Transportation Equipment	New York PMSA, NY	S	17.73 MW	17.75 AW	36890 AAW	NYBLS	10//99-12//99
Transportation Equipment	North Carolina	S	14.23 MW	14.75 AW	30680 AAW	NCBLS	10//99-12//99
Transportation Equipment	Ohio	S	16.22 MW	16.63 AW	34580 AAW	OHBLS	10//99-12//99
Transportation Equipment	Oklahoma	S	14.35 MW	13.54 AW	28160 AAW	OKBLS	10//99-12//99
Transportation Equipment	Pennsylvania	S	17.91 MW	19.34 AW	40230 AAW	PABLS	10//99-12//99
Transportation Equipment	Rhode Island	S	7.23 MW	8.24 AW	17140 AAW	RIBLS	10//99-12//99
Transportation Equipment	South Carolina	S	17.3 MW	17.75 AW	36930 AAW	SCBLS	10//99-12//99
Transportation Equipment	Tennessee	S	14.99 MW	14.78 AW	30750 AAW	TNBLS	10//99-12//99
Transportation Equipment	Texas	S	10.28 MW	12.02 AW	25010 AAW	TXBLS	10//99-12//99
Transportation Equipment	Dallas PMSA, TX	S	12.76 MW	10.42 AW	26550 AAW	TXBLS	10//99-12//99
Transportation Equipment	Houston PMSA, TX	S	11.09 MW	9.78 AW	23060 AAW	TXBLS	10//99-12//99
Transportation Equipment	Virginia	S	14.42 MW	14.61 AW	30380 AAW	VABLS	10//99-12//99
Transportation Equipment	Norfolk-Virginia Beach-Newport News MSA, VA-NC	S	14.07 MW	13.60 AW	29270 AAW	VABLS	10//99-12//99
Transportation Equipment	Washington	S	19.02 MW	18.94 AW	39390 AAW	WABLS	10//99-12//99
Transportation Equipment	Seattle-Bellevue-Everett PMSA, WA	S	19.04 MW	19.14 AW	39600 AAW	WABLS	10//99-12//99
Transportation Equipment	Wisconsin	S	15.31 MW	15.48 AW	32200 AAW	WIBLS	10//99-12//99
Transportation Equipment	Milwaukee-Waukesha PMSA, WI	S	20.22 MW	19.74 AW	42050 AAW	WIBLS	10//99-12//99
Transportation Equipment	Wyoming	S	11.81 MW	13.07 AW	27180 AAW	WYBLS	10//99-12//99
Transportation Equipment	Puerto Rico	S	6.12 MW	6.40 AW	13300 AAW	PRBLS	10//99-12//99.

Electrical and Electronics
Repairer

Occupation/Type/Industry	Location	Per	Low	Mid	High	Source	Date
Commercial and Industrial Equipment	Alabama	S	16.38 MW	16.79 AW	34930 AAW	ALBLS	10//99-12//99
Commercial and Industrial Equipment	Birmingham MSA, AL	S	15.79 MW	15.51 AW	32830 AAW	ALBLS	10//99-12//99
Commercial and Industrial Equipment	Decatur MSA, AL	S	14.51 MW	14.47 AW	30180 AAW	ALBLS	10//99-12//99
Commercial and Industrial Equipment	Huntsville MSA, AL	S	22.17 MW	20.65 AW	46120 AAW	ALBLS	10//99-12//99
Commercial and Industrial Equipment	Mobile MSA, AL	S	17.35 MW	17.81 AW	36080 AAW	ALBLS	10//99-12//99
Commercial and Industrial Equipment	Alaska	S	29.53 MW	28.79 AW	59890 AAW	AKBLS	10//99-12//99
Commercial and Industrial Equipment	Arizona	S	18.04 MW	18.06 AW	37560 AAW	AZBLS	10//99-12//99
Commercial and Industrial Equipment	Phoenix-Mesa MSA, AZ	S	16.86 MW	16.56 AW	35070 AAW	AZBLS	10//99-12//99
Commercial and Industrial Equipment	Tucson MSA, AZ	S	19.68 MW	19.84 AW	40940 AAW	AZBLS	10//99-12//99
Commercial and Industrial Equipment	Arkansas	S	16.25 MW	17.38 AW	36150 AAW	ARBLS	10//99-12//99
Commercial and Industrial Equipment	California	S	18.32 MW	18.57 AW	38620 AAW	CABLS	10//99-12//99
Commercial and Industrial Equipment	Fresno MSA, CA	S	17.64 MW	17.34 AW	36680 AAW	CABLS	10//99-12//99
Commercial and Industrial Equipment	Los Angeles-Long Beach PMSA, CA	S	18.66 MW	17.53 AW	38810 AAW	CABLS	10//99-12//99
Commercial and Industrial Equipment	Modesto MSA, CA	S	14.33 MW	17.14 AW	29810 AAW	CABLS	10//99-12//99
Commercial and Industrial Equipment	Oakland PMSA, CA	S	19.25 MW	19.27 AW	40040 AAW	CABLS	10//99-12//99
Commercial and Industrial Equipment	Orange County PMSA, CA	S	16.36 MW	15.98 AW	34020 AAW	CABLS	10//99-12//99
Commercial and Industrial Equipment	Riverside-San Bernardino PMSA, CA	S	17.82 MW	18.40 AW	37070 AAW	CABLS	10//99-12//99
Commercial and Industrial Equipment	Sacramento PMSA, CA	S	19.36 MW	19.95 AW	40260 AAW	CABLS	10//99-12//99
Commercial and Industrial Equipment	San Diego MSA, CA	S	19.52 MW	19.66 AW	40610 AAW	CABLS	10//99-12//99
Commercial and Industrial Equipment	San Francisco PMSA, CA	S	22.70 MW	23.23 AW	47220 AAW	CABLS	10//99-12//99
Commercial and Industrial Equipment	San Jose PMSA, CA	S	21.19 MW	20.28 AW	44080 AAW	CABLS	10//99-12//99
Commercial and Industrial Equipment	Santa Barbara-Santa Maria-Lompoc MSA, CA	S	20.65 MW	20.19 AW	42950 AAW	CABLS	10//99-12//99
Commercial and Industrial Equipment	Ventura PMSA, CA	S	21.82 MW	23.13 AW	45390 AAW	CABLS	10//99-12//99
Commercial and Industrial Equipment	Colorado	S	16.8 MW	18.17 AW	37790 AAW	COBLS	10//99-12//99
Commercial and Industrial Equipment	Colorado Springs MSA, CO	S	22.67 MW	20.61 AW	47150 AAW	COBLS	10//99-12//99
Commercial and Industrial Equipment	Denver PMSA, CO	S	18.62 MW	18.10 AW	38720 AAW	COBLS	10//99-12//99
Commercial and Industrial Equipment	Fort Collins-Loveland MSA, CO	S	21.53 MW	19.62 AW	44790 AAW	COBLS	10//99-12//99
Commercial and Industrial Equipment	Connecticut	S	15.63 MW	16.14 AW	33570 AAW	CTBLS	10//99-12//99
Commercial and Industrial Equipment	Bridgeport PMSA, CT	S	17.44 MW	17.88 AW	36280 AAW	CTBLS	10//99-12//99
Commercial and Industrial Equipment	Hartford MSA, CT	S	17.26 MW	16.33 AW	35910 AAW	CTBLS	10//99-12//99

AAW Average annual wage	**AOH** Average offered, high	**ASH** Average starting, high	**H** Hourly	**M** Monthly	**S** Special: hourly and annual
AE Average entry wage	**AOL** Average offered, low	**ASL** Average starting, low	**HI** Highest wage paid	**MTC** Median total compensation	**TQ** Third quartile wage
AEX Average experienced wage	**APH** Average pay, high range	**AW** Average wage paid	**HR** High end range	**MW** Median wage paid	**W** Weekly
AO Average offered	**APL** Average pay, low range	**FQ** First quartile wage	**LR** Low end range	**SQ** Second quartile wage	**Y** Yearly

Occupation/Type/Industry	Location	Per	Low	Mid	High	Source	Date
Electrical and Electronics							
Repairer							
Commercial and Industrial Equipment	New Haven-Meriden PMSA, CT	S	14.43 MW	13.68 AW	30010 AAW	CTBLS	10//99-12//99
Commercial and Industrial Equipment	Delaware	S	20.93 MW	21.50 AW	44720 AAW	DEBLS	10//99-12//99
Commercial and Industrial Equipment	Dover MSA, DE	S	18.22 MW	18.49 AW	37900 AAW	DEBLS	10//99-12//99
Commercial and Industrial Equipment	Wilmington-Newark PMSA, DE-MD	S	22.62 MW	22.18 AW	47040 AAW	DEBLS	10//99-12//99
Commercial and Industrial Equipment	Washington PMSA, DC-MD-VA-WV	S	17.67 MW	16.64 AW	36750 AAW	DCBLS	10//99-12//99
Commercial and Industrial Equipment	Florida	S	16.77 MW	15.95 AW	33180 AAW	FLBLS	10//99-12//99
Commercial and Industrial Equipment	Fort Lauderdale PMSA, FL	S	17.81 MW	18.53 AW	37040 AAW	FLBLS	10//99-12//99
Commercial and Industrial Equipment	Fort Myers-Cape Coral MSA, FL	S	16.87 MW	16.49 AW	35100 AAW	FLBLS	10//99-12//99
Commercial and Industrial Equipment	Jacksonville MSA, FL	S	17.47 MW	17.87 AW	36330 AAW	FLBLS	10//99-12//99
Commercial and Industrial Equipment	Lakeland-Winter Haven MSA, FL	S	15.83 MW	16.63 AW	32930 AAW	FLBLS	10//99-12//99
Commercial and Industrial Equipment	Melbourne-Titusville-Palm Bay MSA, FL	S	19.69 MW	19.71 AW	40950 AAW	FLBLS	10//99-12//99
Commercial and Industrial Equipment	Miami PMSA, FL	S	15.98 MW	17.46 AW	33250 AAW	FLBLS	10//99-12//99
Commercial and Industrial Equipment	Orlando MSA, FL	S	12.54 MW	11.79 AW	26090 AAW	FLBLS	10//99-12//99
Commercial and Industrial Equipment	Panama City MSA, FL	S	17.92 MW	18.69 AW	37280 AAW	FLBLS	10//99-12//99
Commercial and Industrial Equipment	Pensacola MSA, FL	S	14.65 MW	12.68 AW	30470 AAW	FLBLS	10//99-12//99
Commercial and Industrial Equipment	Sarasota-Bradenton MSA, FL	S	12.20 MW	12.42 AW	25370 AAW	FLBLS	10//99-12//99
Commercial and Industrial Equipment	Tampa-St. Petersburg-Clearwater MSA, FL	S	17.41 MW	16.52 AW	36210 AAW	FLBLS	10//99-12//99
Commercial and Industrial Equipment	West Palm Beach-Boca Raton MSA, FL	S	14.48 MW	13.42 AW	30120 AAW	FLBLS	10//99-12//99
Commercial and Industrial Equipment	Georgia	S	16.79 MW	16.72 AW	34770 AAW	GABLS	10//99-12//99
Commercial and Industrial Equipment	Albany MSA, GA	S	15.62 MW	14.78 AW	32490 AAW	GABLS	10//99-12//99
Commercial and Industrial Equipment	Atlanta MSA, GA	S	16.55 MW	15.77 AW	34430 AAW	GABLS	10//99-12//99
Commercial and Industrial Equipment	Columbus MSA, GA-AL	S	15.58 MW	15.61 AW	32410 AAW	GABLS	10//99-12//99
Commercial and Industrial Equipment	Savannah MSA, GA	S	17.82 MW	17.60 AW	37060 AAW	GABLS	10//99-12//99
Commercial and Industrial Equipment	Hawaii	S	23.95 MW	23.48 AW	48830 AAW	HIBLS	10//99-12//99
Commercial and Industrial Equipment	Honolulu MSA, HI	S	24.21 MW	24.35 AW	50350 AAW	HIBLS	10//99-12//99
Commercial and Industrial Equipment	Idaho	S	16.33 MW	15.87 AW	33000 AAW	IDBLS	10//99-12//99
Commercial and Industrial Equipment	Illinois	S	16.89 MW	17.90 AW	37230 AAW	ILBLS	10//99-12//99
Commercial and Industrial Equipment	Chicago PMSA, IL	S	18.32 MW	17.45 AW	38100 AAW	ILBLS	10//99-12//99
Commercial and Industrial Equipment	Peoria-Pekin MSA, IL	S	18.36 MW	19.13 AW	38190 AAW	ILBLS	10//99-12//99
Commercial and Industrial Equipment	Rockford MSA, IL	S	17.52 MW	15.44 AW	36440 AAW	ILBLS	10//99-12//99
Commercial and Industrial Equipment	Indiana	S	17.46 MW	18.05 AW	37550 AAW	INBLS	10//99-12//99
Commercial and Industrial Equipment	Evansville-Henderson MSA, IN-KY	S	13.82 MW	13.18 AW	28750 AAW	INBLS	10//99-12//99
Commercial and Industrial Equipment	Fort Wayne MSA, IN	S	14.97 MW	15.71 AW	31140 AAW	INBLS	10//99-12//99
Commercial and Industrial Equipment	Gary PMSA, IN	S	16.61 MW	16.28 AW	34540 AAW	INBLS	10//99-12//99
Commercial and Industrial Equipment	Indianapolis MSA, IN	S	21.27 MW	23.06 AW	44250 AAW	INBLS	10//99-12//99
Commercial and Industrial Equipment	Lafayette MSA, IN	S	17.45 MW	17.56 AW	36290 AAW	INBLS	10//99-12//99
Commercial and Industrial Equipment	South Bend MSA, IN	S	15.35 MW	15.20 AW	31920 AAW	INBLS	10//99-12//99
Commercial and Industrial Equipment	Iowa	S	16.29 MW	16.89 AW	35140 AAW	IABLS	10//99-12//99
Commercial and Industrial Equipment	Cedar Rapids MSA, IA	S	18.95 MW	21.49 AW	39410 AAW	IABLS	10//99-12//99
Commercial and Industrial Equipment	Des Moines MSA, IA	S	15.20 MW	15.08 AW	31610 AAW	IABLS	10//99-12//99
Commercial and Industrial Equipment	Sioux City MSA, IA-NE	S	16.76 MW	16.64 AW	34870 AAW	IABLS	10//99-12//99
Commercial and Industrial Equipment	Waterloo-Cedar Falls MSA, IA	S	11.66 MW	10.31 AW	24260 AAW	IABLS	10//99-12//99
Commercial and Industrial Equipment	Kansas	S	17.62 MW	18.10 AW	37640 AAW	KSBLS	10//99-12//99
Commercial and Industrial Equipment	Topeka MSA, KS	S	16.07 MW	15.92 AW	33420 AAW	KSBLS	10//99-12//99
Commercial and Industrial Equipment	Wichita MSA, KS	S	19.21 MW	19.58 AW	39960 AAW	KSBLS	10//99-12//99
Commercial and Industrial Equipment	Kentucky	S	16.17 MW	17.87 AW	37170 AAW	KYBLS	10//99-12//99
Commercial and Industrial Equipment	Lexington MSA, KY	S	15.77 MW	15.31 AW	32800 AAW	KYBLS	10//99-12//99
Commercial and Industrial Equipment	Louisville MSA, KY-IN	S	18.33 MW	16.19 AW	38130 AAW	KYBLS	10//99-12//99
Commercial and Industrial Equipment	Louisiana	S	18.33 MW	17.65 AW	36720 AAW	LABLS	10//99-12//99
Commercial and Industrial Equipment	Baton Rouge MSA, LA	S	21.55 MW	22.01 AW	44830 AAW	LABLS	10//99-12//99
Commercial and Industrial Equipment	Houma MSA, LA	S	20.97 MW	22.47 AW	43630 AAW	LABLS	10//99-12//99
Commercial and Industrial Equipment	Lafayette MSA, LA	S	16.50 MW	15.22 AW	34320 AAW	LABLS	10//99-12//99
Commercial and Industrial Equipment	New Orleans MSA, LA	S	14.23 MW	13.00 AW	29590 AAW	LABLS	10//99-12//99
Commercial and Industrial Equipment	Shreveport-Bossier City MSA, LA	S	19.70 MW	19.49 AW	40980 AAW	LABLS	10//99-12//99
Commercial and Industrial Equipment	Maine	S	16.76 MW	16.72 AW	34770 AAW	MEBLS	10//99-12//99
Commercial and Industrial Equipment	Portland MSA, ME	S	19.57 MW	19.07 AW	40710 AAW	MEBLS	10//99-12//99
Commercial and Industrial Equipment	Maryland	S	19.98 MW	20.75 AW	43170 AAW	MDBLS	10//99-12//99
Commercial and Industrial Equipment	Baltimore PMSA, MD	S	20.91 MW	19.91 AW	43480 AAW	MDBLS	10//99-12//99
Commercial and Industrial Equipment	Massachusetts	S	18.54 MW	19.57 AW	40710 AAW	MABLS	10//99-12//99
Commercial and Industrial Equipment	Boston PMSA, MA-NH	S	20.48 MW	19.51 AW	42610 AAW	MABLS	10//99-12//99

AAW Average annual wage	**AOH** Average offered, high	**ASH** Average starting, high	**H** Hourly	**M** Monthly	**S** Special: hourly and annual
AE Average entry wage	**AOL** Average offered, low	**ASL** Average starting, low	**HI** Highest wage paid	**MTC** Median total compensation	**TQ** Third quartile wage
AEX Average experienced wage	**APH** Average pay, high range	**AW** Average wage paid	**HR** High end range	**MW** Median wage paid	**W** Weekly
AO Average offered	**APL** Average pay, low range	**FQ** First quartile wage	**LR** Low end range	**SQ** Second quartile wage	**Y** Yearly

Occupation/Type/Industry	Location	Per	Low	Mid	High	Source	Date
Electrical and Electronics							
Repairer							
Commercial and Industrial Equipment	Brockton PMSA, MA	S	16.45 MW	15.66 AW	34210 AAW	MABLS	10//99-12//99
Commercial and Industrial Equipment	Lawrence PMSA, MA-NH	S	18.71 MW	15.64 AW	38910 AAW	MABLS	10//99-12//99
Commercial and Industrial Equipment	Springfield MSA, MA	S	16.11 MW	15.45 AW	33510 AAW	MABLS	10//99-12//99
Commercial and Industrial Equipment	Worcester PMSA, MA-CT	S	17.44 MW	16.82 AW	36270 AAW	MABLS	10//99-12//99
Commercial and Industrial Equipment	Michigan	S	17.18 MW	17.33 AW	36050 AAW	MIBLS	10//99-12//99
Commercial and Industrial Equipment	Ann Arbor PMSA, MI	S	23.13 MW	18.97 AW	48110 AAW	MIBLS	10//99-12//99
Commercial and Industrial Equipment	Detroit PMSA, MI	S	16.94 MW	16.92 AW	35230 AAW	MIBLS	10//99-12//99
Commercial and Industrial Equipment	Grand Rapids-Muskegon-Holland MSA, MI	S	16.36 MW	16.93 AW	34040 AAW	MIBLS	10//99-12//99
Commercial and Industrial Equipment	Kalamazoo-Battle Creek MSA, MI	S	21.64 MW	23.42 AW	45020 AAW	MIBLS	10//99-12//99
Commercial and Industrial Equipment	Minnesota	S	18.84 MW	18.94 AW	39390 AAW	MNBLS	10//99-12//99
Commercial and Industrial Equipment	Minneapolis-St. Paul MSA, MN-WI	S	20.77 MW	20.49 AW	43200 AAW	MNBLS	10//99-12//99
Commercial and Industrial Equipment	St. Cloud MSA, MN	S	11.61 MW	11.63 AW	24140 AAW	MNBLS	10//99-12//99
Commercial and Industrial Equipment	Mississippi	S	13.9 MW	13.53 AW	28150 AAW	MSBLS	10//99-12//99
Commercial and Industrial Equipment	Hattiesburg MSA, MS	S	11.94 MW	10.51 AW	24830 AAW	MSBLS	10//99-12//99
Commercial and Industrial Equipment	Jackson MSA, MS	S	12.32 MW	11.45 AW	25620 AAW	MSBLS	10//99-12//99
Commercial and Industrial Equipment	Missouri	S	16.74 MW	16.89 AW	35130 AAW	MOBLS	10//99-12//99
Commercial and Industrial Equipment	Kansas City MSA, MO-KS	S	16.21 MW	16.00 AW	33720 AAW	MOBLS	10//99-12//99
Commercial and Industrial Equipment	St. Joseph MSA, MO	S	13.80 MW	14.06 AW	28710 AAW	MOBLS	10//99-12//99
Commercial and Industrial Equipment	St. Louis MSA, MO-IL	S	19.67 MW	19.56 AW	40900 AAW	MOBLS	10//99-12//99
Commercial and Industrial Equipment	Montana	S	17.34 MW	18.71 AW	38920 AAW	MTBLS	10//99-12//99
Commercial and Industrial Equipment	Missoula MSA, MT	S	16.34 MW	15.55 AW	33990 AAW	MTBLS	10//99-12//99
Commercial and Industrial Equipment	Nebraska	S	15.32 MW	15.51 AW	32260 AAW	NEBLS	10//99-12//99
Commercial and Industrial Equipment	Lincoln MSA, NE	S	15.59 MW	15.37 AW	32430 AAW	NEBLS	10//99-12//99
Commercial and Industrial Equipment	Omaha MSA, NE-IA	S	15.56 MW	15.46 AW	32370 AAW	NEBLS	10//99-12//99
Commercial and Industrial Equipment	Nevada	S	17.54 MW	17.64 AW	36690 AAW	NVBLS	10//99-12//99
Commercial and Industrial Equipment	Las Vegas MSA, NV-AZ	S	17.63 MW	17.35 AW	36670 AAW	NVBLS	10//99-12//99
Commercial and Industrial Equipment	New Hampshire	S	16.26 MW	16.13 AW	33560 AAW	NHBLS	10//99-12//99
Commercial and Industrial Equipment	Nashua PMSA, NH	S	13.14 MW	13.03 AW	27330 AAW	NHBLS	10//99-12//99
Commercial and Industrial Equipment	Portsmouth-Rochester PMSA, NH-ME	S	16.91 MW	16.64 AW	35180 AAW	NHBLS	10//99-12//99
Commercial and Industrial Equipment	New Jersey	S	18.39 MW	18.48 AW	38440 AAW	NJBLS	10//99-12//99
Commercial and Industrial Equipment	Bergen-Passaic PMSA, NJ	S	19.42 MW	19.03 AW	40400 AAW	NJBLS	10//99-12//99
Commercial and Industrial Equipment	Jersey City PMSA, NJ	S	17.11 MW	17.26 AW	35600 AAW	NJBLS	10//99-12//99
Commercial and Industrial Equipment	Middlesex-Somerset-Hunterdon PMSA, NJ	S	16.68 MW	14.98 AW	34690 AAW	NJBLS	10//99-12//99
Commercial and Industrial Equipment	Monmouth-Ocean PMSA, NJ	S	16.66 MW	15.77 AW	34650 AAW	NJBLS	10//99-12//99
Commercial and Industrial Equipment	Newark PMSA, NJ	S	19.29 MW	19.51 AW	40130 AAW	NJBLS	10//99-12//99
Commercial and Industrial Equipment	Trenton PMSA, NJ	S	15.46 MW	15.58 AW	32160 AAW	NJBLS	10//99-12//99
Commercial and Industrial Equipment	New Mexico	S	19.39 MW	18.84 AW	39180 AAW	NMBLS	10//99-12//99
Commercial and Industrial Equipment	Albuquerque MSA, NM	S	17.32 MW	17.97 AW	36030 AAW	NMBLS	10//99-12//99
Commercial and Industrial Equipment	New York	S	15.25 MW	15.39 AW	32000 AAW	NYBLS	10//99-12//99
Commercial and Industrial Equipment	Albany-Schenectady-Troy MSA, NY	S	17.08 MW	17.12 AW	35520 AAW	NYBLS	10//99-12//99
Commercial and Industrial Equipment	Buffalo-Niagara Falls MSA, NY	S	14.00 MW	12.85 AW	29130 AAW	NYBLS	10//99-12//99
Commercial and Industrial Equipment	Jamestown MSA, NY	S	15.42 MW	15.26 AW	32070 AAW	NYBLS	10//99-12//99
Commercial and Industrial Equipment	Nassau-Suffolk PMSA, NY	S	15.46 MW	15.48 AW	32150 AAW	NYBLS	10//99-12//99
Commercial and Industrial Equipment	New York PMSA, NY	S	15.00 MW	15.05 AW	31200 AAW	NYBLS	10//99-12//99
Commercial and Industrial Equipment	Rochester MSA, NY	S	16.32 MW	15.49 AW	33940 AAW	NYBLS	10//99-12//99
Commercial and Industrial Equipment	Syracuse MSA, NY	S	13.65 MW	12.77 AW	28380 AAW	NYBLS	10//99-12//99
Commercial and Industrial Equipment	North Carolina	S	14.93 MW	14.82 AW	30830 AAW	NCBLS	10//99-12//99
Commercial and Industrial Equipment	Asheville MSA, NC	S	17.15 MW	16.42 AW	35670 AAW	NCBLS	10//99-12//99
Commercial and Industrial Equipment	Charlotte-Gastonia-Rock Hill MSA, NC-SC	S	14.75 MW	14.81 AW	30680 AAW	NCBLS	10//99-12//99
Commercial and Industrial Equipment	Fayetteville MSA, NC	S	16.10 MW	15.56 AW	33480 AAW	NCBLS	10//99-12//99
Commercial and Industrial Equipment	Greensboro--Winston-Salem--High Point MSA, NC	S	17.13 MW	17.15 AW	35640 AAW	NCBLS	10//99-12//99
Commercial and Industrial Equipment	Hickory-Morganton-Lenoir MSA, NC	S	13.85 MW	14.76 AW	28800 AAW	NCBLS	10//99-12//99
Commercial and Industrial Equipment	Raleigh-Durham-Chapel Hill MSA, NC	S	15.86 MW	15.49 AW	32980 AAW	NCBLS	10//99-12//99
Commercial and Industrial Equipment	Wilmington MSA, NC	S	8.69 MW	7.90 AW	18080 AAW	NCBLS	10//99-12//99
Commercial and Industrial Equipment	North Dakota	S	15.96 MW	15.95 AW	33170 AAW	NDBLS	10//99-12//99
Commercial and Industrial Equipment	Bismarck MSA, ND	S	14.76 MW	14.60 AW	30700 AAW	NDBLS	10//99-12//99
Commercial and Industrial Equipment	Ohio	S	17.92 MW	17.27 AW	35920 AAW	OHBLS	10//99-12//99
Commercial and Industrial Equipment	Akron PMSA, OH	S	12.38 MW	11.92 AW	25740 AAW	OHBLS	10//99-12//99
Commercial and Industrial Equipment	Canton-Massillon MSA, OH	S	14.18 MW	14.87 AW	29500 AAW	OHBLS	10//99-12//99

AAW	Average annual wage	AOH	Average offered, high	ASH	Average starting, high	H	Hourly	M	Monthly	S	Special: hourly and annual
AE	Average entry wage	AOL	Average offered, low	ASL	Average starting, low	HI	Highest wage paid	MTC	Median total compensation	TQ	Third quartile wage
AEX	Average experienced wage	APH	Average pay, high range	AW	Average wage paid	HR	High end range	MW	Median wage paid	W	Weekly
AO	Average offered	APL	Average pay, low range	FQ	First quartile wage	LR	Low end range	SQ	Second quartile wage	Y	Yearly

465

Occupation/Type/Industry	Location	Per	Low	Mid	High	Source	Date
Electrical and Electronics Repairer							
Commercial and Industrial Equipment	Cincinnati PMSA, OH-KY-IN	S	20.96 MW	22.62 AW	43590 AAW	OHBLS	10//99-12/99
Commercial and Industrial Equipment	Cleveland-Lorain-Elyria PMSA, OH	S	18.24 MW	18.78 AW	37940 AAW	OHBLS	10//99-12/99
Commercial and Industrial Equipment	Columbus MSA, OH	S	18.00 MW	18.00 AW	37440 AAW	OHBLS	10//99-12/99
Commercial and Industrial Equipment	Toledo MSA, OH	S	19.03 MW	18.38 AW	39580 AAW	OHBLS	10//99-12/99
Commercial and Industrial Equipment	Youngstown-Warren MSA, OH	S	20.08 MW	20.83 AW	41770 AAW	OHBLS	10//99-12/99
Commercial and Industrial Equipment	Oklahoma	S	16.45 MW	15.87 AW	33000 AAW	OKBLS	10//99-12/99
Commercial and Industrial Equipment	Tulsa MSA, OK	S	13.27 MW	12.12 AW	27600 AAW	OKBLS	10//99-12/99
Commercial and Industrial Equipment	Oregon	S	18.87 MW	18.54 AW	38570 AAW	ORBLS	10//99-12/99
Commercial and Industrial Equipment	Portland-Vancouver PMSA, OR-WA	S	19.24 MW	19.27 AW	40030 AAW	ORBLS	10//99-12/99
Commercial and Industrial Equipment	Pennsylvania	S	18.49 MW	18.81 AW	39120 AAW	PABLS	10//99-12/99
Commercial and Industrial Equipment	Allentown-Bethlehem-Easton MSA, PA	S	16.34 MW	18.15 AW	33980 AAW	PABLS	10//99-12/99
Commercial and Industrial Equipment	Harrisburg-Lebanon-Carlisle MSA, PA	S	20.53 MW	20.23 AW	42690 AAW	PABLS	10//99-12/99
Commercial and Industrial Equipment	Philadelphia PMSA, PA-NJ	S	19.13 MW	18.70 AW	39800 AAW	PABLS	10//99-12/99
Commercial and Industrial Equipment	Pittsburgh MSA, PA	S	20.64 MW	19.84 AW	42940 AAW	PABLS	10//99-12/99
Commercial and Industrial Equipment	Reading MSA, PA	S	15.23 MW	14.48 AW	31680 AAW	PABLS	10//99-12/99
Commercial and Industrial Equipment	Scranton--Wilkes-Barre--Hazleton MSA, PA	S	26.96 MW	28.40 AW	56080 AAW	PABLS	10//99-12/99
Commercial and Industrial Equipment	York MSA, PA	S	19.46 MW	19.29 AW	40480 AAW	PABLS	10//99-12/99
Commercial and Industrial Equipment	Rhode Island	S	16.32 MW	20.29 AW	42200 AAW	RIBLS	10//99-12/99
Commercial and Industrial Equipment	Providence-Fall River-Warwick MSA, RI-MA	S	21.45 MW	16.88 AW	44620 AAW	RIBLS	10//99-12/99
Commercial and Industrial Equipment	South Carolina	S	18.72 MW	18.87 AW	39250 AAW	SCBLS	10//99-12/99
Commercial and Industrial Equipment	Charleston-North Charleston MSA, SC	S	16.10 MW	16.54 AW	33480 AAW	SCBLS	10//99-12/99
Commercial and Industrial Equipment	Columbia MSA, SC	S	15.61 MW	16.19 AW	32470 AAW	SCBLS	10//99-12/99
Commercial and Industrial Equipment	Greenville-Spartanburg-Anderson MSA, SC	S	19.88 MW	20.06 AW	41340 AAW	SCBLS	10//99-12/99
Commercial and Industrial Equipment	South Dakota	S	15.06 MW	16.42 AW	34150 AAW	SDBLS	10//99-12/99
Commercial and Industrial Equipment	Sioux Falls MSA, SD	S	14.57 MW	13.64 AW	30300 AAW	SDBLS	10//99-12/99
Commercial and Industrial Equipment	Tennessee	S	18.1 MW	17.50 AW	36400 AAW	TNBLS	10//99-12/99
Commercial and Industrial Equipment	Chattanooga MSA, TN-GA	S	15.62 MW	16.21 AW	32500 AAW	TNBLS	10//99-12/99
Commercial and Industrial Equipment	Clarksville-Hopkinsville MSA, TN-KY	S	22.07 MW	20.02 AW	45910 AAW	TNBLS	10//99-12/99
Commercial and Industrial Equipment	Johnson City-Kingsport-Bristol MSA, TN-VA	S	18.94 MW	19.06 AW	39400 AAW	TNBLS	10//99-12/99
Commercial and Industrial Equipment	Knoxville MSA, TN	S	13.83 MW	12.96 AW	28770 AAW	TNBLS	10//99-12/99
Commercial and Industrial Equipment	Memphis MSA, TN-AR-MS	S	15.99 MW	16.10 AW	33260 AAW	MSBLS	10//99-12/99
Commercial and Industrial Equipment	Nashville MSA, TN	S	15.19 MW	13.52 AW	31590 AAW	TNBLS	10//99-12/99
Commercial and Industrial Equipment	Texas	S	14.46 MW	14.83 AW	30850 AAW	TXBLS	10//99-12/99
Commercial and Industrial Equipment	Austin-San Marcos MSA, TX	S	16.17 MW	15.59 AW	33630 AAW	TXBLS	10//99-12/99
Commercial and Industrial Equipment	Beaumont-Port Arthur MSA, TX	S	15.84 MW	15.98 AW	32950 AAW	TXBLS	10//99-12/99
Commercial and Industrial Equipment	Bryan-College Station MSA, TX	S	13.82 MW	12.61 AW	28740 AAW	TXBLS	10//99-12/99
Commercial and Industrial Equipment	Dallas PMSA, TX	S	13.85 MW	13.06 AW	28810 AAW	TXBLS	10//99-12/99
Commercial and Industrial Equipment	El Paso MSA, TX	S	16.01 MW	14.64 AW	33310 AAW	TXBLS	10//99-12/99
Commercial and Industrial Equipment	Fort Worth-Arlington PMSA, TX	S	17.53 MW	15.99 AW	36460 AAW	TXBLS	10//99-12/99
Commercial and Industrial Equipment	Houston PMSA, TX	S	12.82 MW	10.11 AW	26660 AAW	TXBLS	10//99-12/99
Commercial and Industrial Equipment	Longview-Marshall MSA, TX	S	14.07 MW	12.67 AW	29260 AAW	TXBLS	10//99-12/99
Commercial and Industrial Equipment	Odessa-Midland MSA, TX	S	15.59 MW	15.59 AW	32430 AAW	TXBLS	10//99-12/99
Commercial and Industrial Equipment	Waco MSA, TX	S	13.06 MW	13.96 AW	27170 AAW	TXBLS	10//99-12/99
Commercial and Industrial Equipment	Utah	S	17.03 MW	16.58 AW	34480 AAW	UTBLS	10//99-12/99
Commercial and Industrial Equipment	Salt Lake City-Ogden MSA, UT	S	17.17 MW	17.85 AW	35720 AAW	UTBLS	10//99-12/99
Commercial and Industrial Equipment	Vermont	S	20.84 MW	21.88 AW	45520 AAW	VTBLS	10//99-12/99
Commercial and Industrial Equipment	Burlington MSA, VT	S	27.03 MW	28.09 AW	56220 AAW	VTBLS	10//99-12/99
Commercial and Industrial Equipment	Virginia	S	15.99 MW	16.12 AW	33530 AAW	VABLS	10//99-12/99
Commercial and Industrial Equipment	Norfolk-Virginia Beach-Newport News MSA, VA-NC	S	16.59 MW	16.31 AW	34510 AAW	VABLS	10//99-12/99
Commercial and Industrial Equipment	Richmond-Petersburg MSA, VA	S	17.07 MW	17.74 AW	35510 AAW	VABLS	10//99-12/99
Commercial and Industrial Equipment	Washington	S	19.32 MW	20.51 AW	42670 AAW	WABLS	10//99-12/99
Commercial and Industrial Equipment	Seattle-Bellevue-Everett PMSA, WA	S	22.59 MW	20.59 AW	46980 AAW	WABLS	10//99-12/99

AAW	Average annual wage	AOH	Average offered, high	ASH	Average starting, high	H	Hourly	M	Monthly	S	Special: hourly and annual
AE	Average entry wage	AOL	Average offered, low	ASL	Average starting, low	HI	Highest wage paid	MTC	Median total compensation	TQ	Third quartile wage
AEX	Average experienced wage	APH	Average pay, high range	AW	Average wage paid	HR	High end range	MW	Median wage paid	W	Weekly
AO	Average offered	APL	Average pay, low range	FQ	First quartile wage	LR	Low end range	SQ	Second quartile wage	Y	Yearly

Electrical and Electronics Repairer

Occupation/Type/Industry	Location	Per	Low	Mid	High	Source	Date
Commercial and Industrial Equipment	Spokane MSA, WA	S	15.45 MW	15.25 AW	32130 AAW	WABLS	10//99-12//99
Commercial and Industrial Equipment	Yakima MSA, WA	S	18.64 MW	19.53 AW	38780 AAW	WABLS	10//99-12//99
Commercial and Industrial Equipment	West Virginia	S	19.88 MW	19.66 AW	40890 AAW	WVBLS	10//99-12//99
Commercial and Industrial Equipment	Parkersburg-Marietta MSA, WV-OH	S	20.98 MW	20.61 AW	43630 AAW	WVBLS	10//99-12//99
Commercial and Industrial Equipment	Wisconsin	S	15.92 MW	16.24 AW	33770 AAW	WIBLS	10//99-12//99
Commercial and Industrial Equipment	Green Bay MSA, WI	S	16.56 MW	17.54 AW	34440 AAW	WIBLS	10//99-12//99
Commercial and Industrial Equipment	Madison MSA, WI	S	15.08 MW	15.27 AW	31360 AAW	WIBLS	10//99-12//99
Commercial and Industrial Equipment	Milwaukee-Waukesha PMSA, WI	S	15.90 MW	15.54 AW	33070 AAW	WIBLS	10//99-12//99
Commercial and Industrial Equipment	Sheboygan MSA, WI	S	17.17 MW	16.97 AW	35710 AAW	WIBLS	10//99-12//99
Commercial and Industrial Equipment	Wyoming	S	19.09 MW	19.16 AW	39850 AAW	WYBLS	10//99-12//99
Commercial and Industrial Equipment	Puerto Rico	S	9.11 MW	9.52 AW	19800 AAW	PRBLS	10//99-12//99
Commercial and Industrial Equipment	Caguas PMSA, PR	S	9.60 MW	9.57 AW	19980 AAW	PRBLS	10//99-12//99
Commercial and Industrial Equipment	San Juan-Bayamon PMSA, PR	S	9.28 MW	8.44 AW	19310 AAW	PRBLS	10//99-12//99
Commercial and Industrial Equipment	Guam	S	12.78 MW	13.72 AW	28540 AAW	GUBLS	10//99-12//99
Powerhouse, Substation, and Relay	Alabama	S	19.28 MW	19.33 AW	40210 AAW	ALBLS	10//99-12//99
Powerhouse, Substation, and Relay	Alaska	S	31.3 MW	31.34 AW	65180 AAW	AKBLS	10//99-12//99
Powerhouse, Substation, and Relay	Arizona	S	24.4 MW	24.32 AW	50590 AAW	AZBLS	10//99-12//99
Powerhouse, Substation, and Relay	Phoenix-Mesa MSA, AZ	S	26.23 MW	26.14 AW	54550 AAW	AZBLS	10//99-12//99
Powerhouse, Substation, and Relay	Arkansas	S	21.29 MW	20.75 AW	43160 AAW	ARBLS	10//99-12//99
Powerhouse, Substation, and Relay	California	S	24.36 MW	23.30 AW	48450 AAW	CABLS	10//99-12//99
Powerhouse, Substation, and Relay	Oakland PMSA, CA	S	24.10 MW	24.53 AW	50130 AAW	CABLS	10//99-12//99
Powerhouse, Substation, and Relay	Ventura PMSA, CA	S	17.66 MW	16.02 AW	36730 AAW	CABLS	10//99-12//99
Powerhouse, Substation, and Relay	Connecticut	S	24.05 MW	23.85 AW	49610 AAW	CTBLS	10//99-12//99
Powerhouse, Substation, and Relay	Washington PMSA, DC-MD-VA-WV	S	23.72 MW	24.14 AW	49340 AAW	DCBLS	10//99-12//99
Powerhouse, Substation, and Relay	Florida	S	17.92 MW	16.41 AW	34130 AAW	FLBLS	10//99-12//99
Powerhouse, Substation, and Relay	Orlando MSA, FL	S	19.75 MW	19.42 AW	41070 AAW	FLBLS	10//99-12//99
Powerhouse, Substation, and Relay	Tampa-St. Petersburg-Clearwater MSA, FL	S	18.50 MW	18.84 AW	38490 AAW	FLBLS	10//99-12//99
Powerhouse, Substation, and Relay	Georgia	S	16.39 MW	16.46 AW	34240 AAW	GABLS	10//99-12//99
Powerhouse, Substation, and Relay	Atlanta MSA, GA	S	14.87 MW	13.79 AW	30920 AAW	GABLS	10//99-12//99
Powerhouse, Substation, and Relay	Illinois	S	20.85 MW	20.69 AW	43040 AAW	ILBLS	10//99-12//99
Powerhouse, Substation, and Relay	Indiana	S	23.74 MW	22.58 AW	46960 AAW	INBLS	10//99-12//99
Powerhouse, Substation, and Relay	Gary PMSA, IN	S	26.07 MW	29.11 AW	54230 AAW	INBLS	10//99-12//99
Powerhouse, Substation, and Relay	Indianapolis MSA, IN	S	18.71 MW	19.60 AW	38920 AAW	INBLS	10//99-12//99
Powerhouse, Substation, and Relay	Iowa	S	23.38 MW	22.85 AW	47520 AAW	IABLS	10//99-12//99
Powerhouse, Substation, and Relay	Kansas	S	23.07 MW	19.76 AW	41110 AAW	KSBLS	10//99-12//99
Powerhouse, Substation, and Relay	Kentucky	S	22.11 MW	21.88 AW	45500 AAW	KYBLS	10//99-12//99
Powerhouse, Substation, and Relay	Louisiana	S	23.11 MW	20.60 AW	42850 AAW	LABLS	10//99-12//99
Powerhouse, Substation, and Relay	Maine	S	19.89 MW	20.99 AW	43650 AAW	MEBLS	10//99-12//99
Powerhouse, Substation, and Relay	Massachusetts	S	22.78 MW	21.93 AW	45610 AAW	MABLS	10//99-12//99
Powerhouse, Substation, and Relay	Michigan	S	22.81 MW	22.36 AW	46510 AAW	MIBLS	10//99-12//99
Powerhouse, Substation, and Relay	Minnesota	S	22.15 MW	20.40 AW	42430 AAW	MNBLS	10//99-12//99
Powerhouse, Substation, and Relay	Mississippi	S	19.89 MW	20.06 AW	41720 AAW	MSBLS	10//99-12//99
Powerhouse, Substation, and Relay	St. Louis MSA, MO-IL	S	23.76 MW	24.24 AW	49410 AAW	MOBLS	10//99-12//99
Powerhouse, Substation, and Relay	Montana	S	24.62 MW	24.55 AW	51070 AAW	MTBLS	10//99-12//99
Powerhouse, Substation, and Relay	Nebraska	S	23.4 MW	22.53 AW	46860 AAW	NEBLS	10//99-12//99
Powerhouse, Substation, and Relay	New Hampshire	S	21.59 MW	21.69 AW	45120 AAW	NHBLS	10//99-12//99
Powerhouse, Substation, and Relay	New Jersey	S	23.97 MW	23.54 AW	48960 AAW	NJBLS	10//99-12//99
Powerhouse, Substation, and Relay	Middlesex-Somerset-Hunterdon PMSA, NJ	S	19.94 MW	19.35 AW	41480 AAW	NJBLS	10//99-12//99
Powerhouse, Substation, and Relay	New York	S	24.3 MW	22.79 AW	47400 AAW	NYBLS	10//99-12//99
Powerhouse, Substation, and Relay	Albany-Schenectady-Troy MSA, NY	S	28.96 MW	30.11 AW	60240 AAW	NYBLS	10//99-12//99
Powerhouse, Substation, and Relay	Nassau-Suffolk PMSA, NY	S	19.62 MW	22.40 AW	40820 AAW	NYBLS	10//99-12//99
Powerhouse, Substation, and Relay	North Carolina	S	15.55 MW	16.32 AW	33950 AAW	NCBLS	10//99-12//99
Powerhouse, Substation, and Relay	Charlotte-Gastonia-Rock Hill MSA, NC-SC	S	22.55 MW	23.30 AW	46910 AAW	NCBLS	10//99-12//99
Powerhouse, Substation, and Relay	North Dakota	S	24.24 MW	23.77 AW	49440 AAW	NDBLS	10//99-12//99
Powerhouse, Substation, and Relay	Ohio	S	16.71 MW	18.37 AW	38200 AAW	OHBLS	10//99-12//99
Powerhouse, Substation, and Relay	Cincinnati PMSA, OH-KY-IN	S	19.40 MW	18.63 AW	40350 AAW	OHBLS	10//99-12//99
Powerhouse, Substation, and Relay	Cleveland-Lorain-Elyria PMSA, OH	S	18.81 MW	19.90 AW	39130 AAW	OHBLS	10//99-12//99
Powerhouse, Substation, and Relay	Columbus MSA, OH	S	21.81 MW	22.37 AW	45370 AAW	OHBLS	10//99-12//99
Powerhouse, Substation, and Relay	Oklahoma	S	13.66 MW	16.77 AW	34870 AAW	OKBLS	10//99-12//99
Powerhouse, Substation, and Relay	Oregon	S	27.97 MW	27.14 AW	56460 AAW	ORBLS	10//99-12//99
Powerhouse, Substation, and Relay	Pennsylvania	S	24.62 MW	24.16 AW	50240 AAW	PABLS	10//99-12//99
Powerhouse, Substation, and Relay	Philadelphia PMSA, PA-NJ	S	25.30 MW	25.08 AW	52620 AAW	PABLS	10//99-12//99

AAW	Average annual wage	AOH	Average offered, high	ASH	Average starting, high	H	Hourly	M	Monthly	S	Special: hourly and annual
AE	Average entry wage	AOL	Average offered, low	ASL	Average starting, low	HI	Highest wage paid	MTC	Median total compensation	TQ	Third quartile wage
AEX	Average experienced wage	APH	Average pay, high range	AW	Average wage paid	HR	High end range	MW	Median wage paid	W	Weekly
AO	Average offered	APL	Average pay, low range	FQ	First quartile wage	LR	Low end range	SQ	Second quartile wage	Y	Yearly

Occupation/Type/Industry	Location	Per	Low	Mid	High	Source	Date
Electrical and Electronics Repairer							
Powerhouse, Substation, and Relay	South Carolina	S	21.92 MW	21.88 AW	45500 AAW	SCBLS	10//99-12//99
Powerhouse, Substation, and Relay	South Dakota	S	24.34 MW	24.12 AW	50170 AAW	SDBLS	10//99-12//99
Powerhouse, Substation, and Relay	Tennessee	S	15.9 MW	16.76 AW	34860 AAW	TNBLS	10//99-12//99
Powerhouse, Substation, and Relay	Texas	S	18.8 MW	18.45 AW	38380 AAW	TXBLS	10//99-12//99
Powerhouse, Substation, and Relay	Dallas PMSA, TX	S	15.15 MW	15.40 AW	31510 AAW	TXBLS	10//99-12//99
Powerhouse, Substation, and Relay	Houston PMSA, TX	S	18.27 MW	18.56 AW	38000 AAW	TXBLS	10//99-12//99
Powerhouse, Substation, and Relay	Utah	S	21.44 MW	22.00 AW	45770 AAW	UTBLS	10//99-12//99
Powerhouse, Substation, and Relay	Vermont	S	20.37 MW	20.54 AW	42730 AAW	VTBLS	10//99-12//99
Powerhouse, Substation, and Relay	Virginia	S	24.03 MW	23.49 AW	48850 AAW	VABLS	10//99-12//99
Powerhouse, Substation, and Relay	Washington	S	28.62 MW	27.72 AW	57660 AAW	WABLS	10//99-12//99
Powerhouse, Substation, and Relay	West Virginia	S	24.05 MW	23.56 AW	49010 AAW	WVBLS	10//99-12//99
Powerhouse, Substation, and Relay	Wisconsin	S	29.04 MW	28.15 AW	58560 AAW	WIBLS	10//99-12//99
Powerhouse, Substation, and Relay	Wyoming	S	23.2 MW	21.58 AW	44880 AAW	WYBLS	10//99-12//99
Electrical/Electronic Technician	United States	H		18.33 AW		NCS98	1998
Electrical Engineer	Alabama	S	27.12 MW	26.66 AW	55460 AAW	ALBLS	10//99-12//99
	Anniston MSA, AL	S	23.19 MW	21.37 AW	48230 AAW	ALBLS	10//99-12//99
	Birmingham MSA, AL	S	29.08 MW	29.81 AW	60480 AAW	ALBLS	10//99-12//99
	Decatur MSA, AL	S	29.42 MW	29.36 AW	61190 AAW	ALBLS	10//99-12//99
	Dothan MSA, AL	S	23.30 MW	26.38 AW	48470 AAW	ALBLS	10//99-12//99
	Florence MSA, AL	S	28.38 MW	27.76 AW	59030 AAW	ALBLS	10//99-12//99
	Huntsville MSA, AL	S	26.47 MW	26.54 AW	55050 AAW	ALBLS	10//99-12//99
	Mobile MSA, AL	S	32.23 MW	31.64 AW	67040 AAW	ALBLS	10//99-12//99
	Montgomery MSA, AL	S	19.17 MW	18.78 AW	39870 AAW	ALBLS	10//99-12//99
	Alaska	S	28.03 MW	28.49 AW	59260 AAW	AKBLS	10//99-12//99
	Anchorage MSA, AK	S	27.51 MW	26.52 AW	57230 AAW	AKBLS	10//99-12//99
	Arizona	S	33.89 MW	34.20 AW	71130 AAW	AZBLS	10//99-12//99
	Phoenix-Mesa MSA, AZ	S	34.50 MW	34.34 AW	71760 AAW	AZBLS	10//99-12//99
	Tucson MSA, AZ	S	30.68 MW	28.66 AW	63820 AAW	AZBLS	10//99-12//99
	Arkansas	S	28.08 MW	27.29 AW	56770 AAW	ARBLS	10//99-12//99
	Fayetteville-Springdale-Rogers MSA, AR	S	28.28 MW	28.34 AW	58830 AAW	ARBLS	10//99-12//99
	Little Rock-North Little Rock MSA, AR	S	22.58 MW	23.83 AW	46970 AAW	ARBLS	10//99-12//99
	California	S	30.34 MW	29.94 AW	62280 AAW	CABLS	10//99-12//99
	Bakersfield MSA, CA	S	27.18 MW	30.15 AW	56540 AAW	CABLS	10//99-12//99
	Fresno MSA, CA	S	27.36 MW	27.90 AW	56900 AAW	CABLS	10//99-12//99
	Los Angeles-Long Beach PMSA, CA	S	31.22 MW	30.24 AW	64930 AAW	CABLS	10//99-12//99
	Modesto MSA, CA	S	27.49 MW	26.67 AW	57190 AAW	CABLS	10//99-12//99
	Oakland PMSA, CA	S	22.24 MW	18.24 AW	46250 AAW	CABLS	10//99-12//99
	Orange County PMSA, CA	S	29.52 MW	29.94 AW	61400 AAW	CABLS	10//99-12//99
	Redding MSA, CA	S	31.87 MW	31.86 AW	66300 AAW	CABLS	10//99-12//99
	Riverside-San Bernardino PMSA, CA	S	28.17 MW	27.89 AW	58590 AAW	CABLS	10//99-12//99
	Sacramento PMSA, CA	S	29.45 MW	28.95 AW	61260 AAW	CABLS	10//99-12//99
	San Diego MSA, CA	S	20.39 MW	16.73 AW	42420 AAW	CABLS	10//99-12//99
	San Francisco PMSA, CA	S	32.24 MW	31.58 AW	67050 AAW	CABLS	10//99-12//99
	San Jose PMSA, CA	S	35.73 MW	34.83 AW	74320 AAW	CABLS	10//99-12//99
	Santa Barbara-Santa Maria-Lompoc MSA, CA	S	34.37 MW	33.96 AW	71490 AAW	CABLS	10//99-12//99
	Santa Rosa PMSA, CA	S	34.44 MW	34.19 AW	71630 AAW	CABLS	10//99-12//99
	Vallejo-Fairfield-Napa PMSA, CA	S	32.36 MW	32.06 AW	67320 AAW	CABLS	10//99-12//99
	Ventura PMSA, CA	S	36.08 MW	34.70 AW	75040 AAW	CABLS	10//99-12//99
	Colorado	S	28.17 MW	28.21 AW	58670 AAW	COBLS	10//99-12//99
	Boulder-Longmont PMSA, CO	S	29.80 MW	27.85 AW	61990 AAW	COBLS	10//99-12//99
	Colorado Springs MSA, CO	S	27.49 MW	27.12 AW	57190 AAW	COBLS	10//99-12//99
	Denver PMSA, CO	S	28.92 MW	28.69 AW	60160 AAW	COBLS	10//99-12//99
	Fort Collins-Loveland MSA, CO	S	27.19 MW	28.36 AW	56550 AAW	COBLS	10//99-12//99
	Connecticut	S	27.14 MW	27.99 AW	58230 AAW	CTBLS	10//99-12//99
	Bridgeport PMSA, CT	S	29.69 MW	29.82 AW	61750 AAW	CTBLS	10//99-12//99
	Danbury PMSA, CT	S	30.69 MW	33.27 AW	63840 AAW	CTBLS	10//99-12//99
	Hartford MSA, CT	S	27.52 MW	26.61 AW	57240 AAW	CTBLS	10//99-12//99
	New Haven-Meriden PMSA, CT	S	31.02 MW	31.08 AW	64520 AAW	CTBLS	10//99-12//99
	New London-Norwich MSA, CT-RI	S	29.40 MW	29.83 AW	61160 AAW	CTBLS	10//99-12//99

AAW	Average annual wage	AOH	Average offered, high	ASH	Average starting, high
AE	Average entry wage	AOL	Average offered, low	ASL	Average starting, low
AEX	Average experienced wage	APH	Average pay, high range	AW	Average wage paid
AO	Average offered	APL	Average pay, low range	FQ	First quartile wage

H	Hourly	M	Monthly	S	Special: hourly and annual
HI	Highest wage paid	MTC	Median total compensation	TQ	Third quartile wage
HR	High end range	MW	Median wage paid	W	Weekly
LR	Low end range	SQ	Second quartile wage	Y	Yearly

Occupation/Type/Industry	Location	Per	Low	Mid	High	Source	Date
Electrical Engineer	Stamford-Norwalk PMSA, CT	S	31.10 MW	30.51 AW	64690 AAW	CTBLS	10//99-12//99
	Waterbury PMSA, CT	S	22.90 MW	20.54 AW	47630 AAW	CTBLS	10//99-12//99
	Delaware	S	23.51 MW	25.21 AW	52440 AAW	DEBLS	10//99-12//99
	Wilmington-Newark PMSA, DE-MD	S	25.07 MW	22.50 AW	52140 AAW	DEBLS	10//99-12//99
	Washington PMSA, DC-MD-VA-WV	S	30.89 MW	30.29 AW	64240 AAW	DCBLS	10//99-12//99
	Florida	S	25.79 MW	26.81 AW	55770 AAW	FLBLS	10//99-12//99
	Fort Lauderdale PMSA, FL	S	24.66 MW	24.00 AW	51300 AAW	FLBLS	10//99-12//99
	Fort Walton Beach MSA, FL	S	35.83 MW	34.60 AW	74520 AAW	FLBLS	10//99-12//99
	Gainesville MSA, FL	S	25.34 MW	24.78 AW	52710 AAW	FLBLS	10//99-12//99
	Jacksonville MSA, FL	S	27.05 MW	26.96 AW	56270 AAW	FLBLS	10//99-12//99
	Lakeland-Winter Haven MSA, FL	S	21.89 MW	23.50 AW	45530 AAW	FLBLS	10//99-12//99
	Melbourne-Titusville-Palm Bay MSA, FL	S	24.46 MW	24.67 AW	50880 AAW	FLBLS	10//99-12//99
	Miami PMSA, FL	S	29.30 MW	28.13 AW	60940 AAW	FLBLS	10//99-12//99
	Orlando MSA, FL	S	26.43 MW	25.47 AW	54980 AAW	FLBLS	10//99-12//99
	Pensacola MSA, FL	S	35.09 MW	31.83 AW	72990 AAW	FLBLS	10//99-12//99
	Sarasota-Bradenton MSA, FL	S	32.38 MW	26.84 AW	67340 AAW	FLBLS	10//99-12//99
	Tallahassee MSA, FL	S	23.67 MW	23.98 AW	49220 AAW	FLBLS	10//99-12//99
	Tampa-St. Petersburg-Clearwater MSA, FL	S	28.96 MW	29.25 AW	60230 AAW	FLBLS	10//99-12//99
	West Palm Beach-Boca Raton MSA, FL	S	25.36 MW	24.14 AW	52740 AAW	FLBLS	10//99-12//99
	Georgia	S	28.88 MW	29.56 AW	61490 AAW	GABLS	10//99-12//99
	Albany MSA, GA	S	33.56 MW	35.22 AW	69810 AAW	GABLS	10//99-12//99
	Athens MSA, GA	S	29.79 MW	30.15 AW	61960 AAW	GABLS	10//99-12//99
	Atlanta MSA, GA	S	29.51 MW	28.51 AW	61380 AAW	GABLS	10//99-12//99
	Macon MSA, GA	S	26.92 MW	26.40 AW	56000 AAW	GABLS	10//99-12//99
	Hawaii	S	28.83 MW	28.28 AW	58820 AAW	HIBLS	10//99-12//99
	Honolulu MSA, HI	S	28.18 MW	28.76 AW	58620 AAW	HIBLS	10//99-12//99
	Idaho	S	28.61 MW	29.07 AW	60470 AAW	IDBLS	10//99-12//99
	Illinois	S	27.07 MW	27.87 AW	57960 AAW	ILBLS	10//99-12//99
	Bloomington-Normal MSA, IL	S	25.49 MW	27.76 AW	53020 AAW	ILBLS	10//99-12//99
	Champaign-Urbana MSA, IL	S	27.64 MW	28.35 AW	57500 AAW	ILBLS	10//99-12//99
	Chicago PMSA, IL	S	28.16 MW	27.67 AW	58580 AAW	ILBLS	10//99-12//99
	Peoria-Pekin MSA, IL	S	26.93 MW	24.94 AW	56010 AAW	ILBLS	10//99-12//99
	Rockford MSA, IL	S	29.13 MW	27.69 AW	60580 AAW	ILBLS	10//99-12//99
	Indiana	S	24.83 MW	25.34 AW	52710 AAW	INBLS	10//99-12//99
	Elkhart-Goshen MSA, IN	S	21.53 MW	21.82 AW	44780 AAW	INBLS	10//99-12//99
	Evansville-Henderson MSA, IN-KY	S	27.91 MW	25.84 AW	58050 AAW	INBLS	10//99-12//99
	Fort Wayne MSA, IN	S	23.41 MW	23.46 AW	48680 AAW	INBLS	10//99-12//99
	Gary PMSA, IN	S	26.48 MW	26.59 AW	55080 AAW	INBLS	10//99-12//99
	Indianapolis MSA, IN	S	23.72 MW	22.92 AW	49340 AAW	INBLS	10//99-12//99
	Lafayette MSA, IN	S	26.37 MW	26.26 AW	54850 AAW	INBLS	10//99-12//99
	South Bend MSA, IN	S	26.83 MW	25.86 AW	55810 AAW	INBLS	10//99-12//99
	Terre Haute MSA, IN	S	36.85 MW	36.73 AW	76640 AAW	INBLS	10//99-12//99
	Iowa	S	27.66 MW	27.46 AW	57130 AAW	IABLS	10//99-12//99
	Davenport-Moline-Rock Island MSA, IA-IL	S	28.68 MW	26.11 AW	59660 AAW	IABLS	10//99-12//99
	Des Moines MSA, IA	S	25.33 MW	24.79 AW	52680 AAW	IABLS	10//99-12//99
	Kansas	S	23.71 MW	25.27 AW	52550 AAW	KSBLS	10//99-12//99
	Wichita MSA, KS	S	27.14 MW	24.66 AW	56460 AAW	KSBLS	10//99-12//99
	Kentucky	S	29.09 MW	28.82 AW	59940 AAW	KYBLS	10//99-12//99
	Lexington MSA, KY	S	29.04 MW	28.49 AW	60400 AAW	KYBLS	10//99-12//99
	Louisville MSA, KY-IN	S	30.21 MW	30.44 AW	62850 AAW	KYBLS	10//99-12//99
	Louisiana	S	27.44 MW	28.34 AW	58950 AAW	LABLS	10//99-12//99
	Baton Rouge MSA, LA	S	31.33 MW	31.47 AW	65170 AAW	LABLS	10//99-12//99
	New Orleans MSA, LA	S	28.41 MW	26.50 AW	59090 AAW	LABLS	10//99-12//99
	Maine	S	25.81 MW	26.34 AW	54790 AAW	MEBLS	10//99-12//99
	Portland MSA, ME	S	23.64 MW	23.64 AW	49170 AAW	MEBLS	10//99-12//99
	Maryland	S	27.79 MW	28.91 AW	60140 AAW	MDBLS	10//99-12//99
	Baltimore PMSA, MD	S	26.12 MW	25.12 AW	54330 AAW	MDBLS	10//99-12//99
	Massachusetts	S	29.82 MW	30.31 AW	63040 AAW	MABLS	10//99-12//99
	Boston PMSA, MA-NH	S	29.89 MW	29.11 AW	62170 AAW	MABLS	10//99-12//99
	Lawrence PMSA, MA-NH	S	33.12 MW	32.60 AW	68880 AAW	MABLS	10//99-12//99
	Lowell PMSA, MA-NH	S	31.37 MW	31.96 AW	65250 AAW	MABLS	10//99-12//99
	Pittsfield MSA, MA	S	34.08 MW	33.24 AW	70880 AAW	MABLS	10//99-12//99
	Springfield MSA, MA	S	30.39 MW	30.62 AW	63220 AAW	MABLS	10//99-12//99
	Worcester PMSA, MA-CT	S	33.44 MW	32.43 AW	69560 AAW	MABLS	10//99-12//99

AAW Average annual wage	**AOH** Average offered, high	**ASH** Average starting, high	**H** Hourly	**M** Monthly	**S** Special: hourly and annual
AE Average entry wage	**AOL** Average offered, low	**ASL** Average starting, low	**HI** Highest wage paid	**MTC** Median total compensation	**TQ** Third quartile wage
AEX Average experienced wage	**APH** Average pay, high range	**AW** Average wage paid	**HR** High end range	**MW** Median wage paid	**W** Weekly
AO Average offered	**APL** Average pay, low range	**FQ** First quartile wage	**LR** Low end range	**SQ** Second quartile wage	**Y** Yearly

Occupation/Type/Industry	Location	Per	Low	Mid	High	Source	Date
Electrical Engineer	Michigan	S	29.8 MW	30.29 AW	63000 AAW	MIBLS	10//99-12//99
	Ann Arbor PMSA, MI	S	33.17 MW	32.66 AW	68990 AAW	MIBLS	10//99-12//99
	Detroit PMSA, MI	S	31.05 MW	30.66 AW	64590 AAW	MIBLS	10//99-12//99
	Grand Rapids-Muskegon-Holland MSA, MI	S	26.96 MW	25.55 AW	56070 AAW	MIBLS	
	Kalamazoo-Battle Creek MSA, MI	S	32.12 MW	34.77 AW	66810 AAW	MIBLS	10//99-12//99
	Lansing-East Lansing MSA, MI	S	24.13 MW	23.09 AW	50200 AAW	MIBLS	10//99-12//99
	Saginaw-Bay City-Midland MSA, MI	S	32.29 MW	33.80 AW	67160 AAW	MIBLS	10//99-12//99
	Minnesota	S	28.03 MW	28.33 AW	58930 AAW	MNBLS	10//99-12//99
	Minneapolis-St. Paul MSA, MN-WI	S	29.29 MW	28.94 AW	60930 AAW	MNBLS	10//99-12//99
	Mississippi	S	23.87 MW	24.76 AW	51500 AAW	MSBLS	10//99-12//99
	Jackson MSA, MS	S	21.85 MW	20.48 AW	45440 AAW	MSBLS	10//99-12//99
	Missouri	S	28.92 MW	28.88 AW	60060 AAW	MOBLS	10//99-12//99
	Columbia MSA, MO	S	22.94 MW	22.69 AW	47710 AAW	MOBLS	10//99-12//99
	Kansas City MSA, MO-KS	S	29.80 MW	29.42 AW	61990 AAW	MOBLS	10//99-12//99
	St. Louis MSA, MO-IL	S	27.56 MW	27.49 AW	57320 AAW	MOBLS	10//99-12//99
	Montana	S	25.94 MW	26.77 AW	55670 AAW	MTBLS	10//99-12//99
	Billings MSA, MT	S	30.98 MW	30.45 AW	64440 AAW	MTBLS	10//99-12//99
	Nebraska	S	26.36 MW	27.32 AW	56820 AAW	NEBLS	10//99-12//99
	Lincoln MSA, NE	S	24.57 MW	24.67 AW	51110 AAW	NEBLS	10//99-12//99
	Omaha MSA, NE-IA	S	20.87 MW	19.94 AW	43400 AAW	NEBLS	10//99-12//99
	Nevada	S	27.08 MW	28.62 AW	59520 AAW	NVBLS	10//99-12//99
	Las Vegas MSA, NV-AZ	S	30.05 MW	30.25 AW	62510 AAW	NVBLS	10//99-12//99
	Reno MSA, NV	S	28.81 MW	26.93 AW	59920 AAW	NVBLS	10//99-12//99
	New Hampshire	S	30.91 MW	31.63 AW	65790 AAW	NHBLS	10//99-12//99
	Manchester PMSA, NH	S	32.11 MW	32.57 AW	66780 AAW	NHBLS	10//99-12//99
	Nashua PMSA, NH	S	34.53 MW	36.80 AW	71830 AAW	NHBLS	10//99-12//99
	Portsmouth-Rochester PMSA, NH-ME	S	29.84 MW	28.35 AW	62070 AAW	NHBLS	10//99-12//99
	New Jersey	S	31.9 MW	31.98 AW	66520 AAW	NJBLS	10//99-12//99
	Bergen-Passaic PMSA, NJ	S	31.84 MW	32.46 AW	66220 AAW	NJBLS	10//99-12//99
	Jersey City PMSA, NJ	S	31.26 MW	31.48 AW	65010 AAW	NJBLS	10//99-12//99
	Middlesex-Somerset-Hunterdon PMSA, NJ	S	36.96 MW	35.94 AW	76880 AAW	NJBLS	10//99-12//99
	Monmouth-Ocean PMSA, NJ	S	34.76 MW	32.33 AW	72300 AAW	NJBLS	10//99-12//99
	Newark PMSA, NJ	S	29.70 MW	30.83 AW	61780 AAW	NJBLS	10//99-12//99
	Trenton PMSA, NJ	S	27.98 MW	26.20 AW	58200 AAW	NJBLS	10//99-12//99
	New Mexico	S	29.97 MW	31.62 AW	65770 AAW	NMBLS	10//99-12//99
	Albuquerque MSA, NM	S	33.10 MW	30.85 AW	68840 AAW	NMBLS	10//99-12//99
	New York	S	32.16 MW	32.45 AW	67500 AAW	NYBLS	10//99-12//99
	Albany-Schenectady-Troy MSA, NY	S	22.38 MW	20.17 AW	46540 AAW	NYBLS	10//99-12//99
	Binghamton MSA, NY	S	30.88 MW	30.69 AW	64220 AAW	NYBLS	10//99-12//99
	Buffalo-Niagara Falls MSA, NY	S	27.68 MW	26.63 AW	57570 AAW	NYBLS	10//99-12//99
	Dutchess County PMSA, NY	S	27.95 MW	25.47 AW	58140 AAW	NYBLS	10//99-12//99
	Glens Falls MSA, NY	S	21.96 MW	20.54 AW	45680 AAW	NYBLS	10//99-12//99
	Nassau-Suffolk PMSA, NY	S	36.41 MW	37.20 AW	75730 AAW	NYBLS	10//99-12//99
	New York PMSA, NY	S	32.06 MW	30.79 AW	66690 AAW	NYBLS	10//99-12//99
	Rochester MSA, NY	S	27.45 MW	26.97 AW	57090 AAW	NYBLS	10//99-12//99
	Syracuse MSA, NY	S	30.98 MW	29.78 AW	64430 AAW	NYBLS	10//99-12//99
	Utica-Rome MSA, NY	S	27.55 MW	28.72 AW	57300 AAW	NYBLS	10//99-12//99
	North Carolina	S	30.38 MW	30.96 AW	64390 AAW	NCBLS	10//99-12//99
	Asheville MSA, NC	S	22.77 MW	24.03 AW	47370 AAW	NCBLS	10//99-12//99
	Charlotte-Gastonia-Rock Hill MSA, NC-SC	S	30.16 MW	29.83 AW	62730 AAW	NCBLS	10//99-12//99
	Greensboro--Winston-Salem--High Point MSA, NC	S	27.85 MW	27.55 AW	57940 AAW	NCBLS	10//99-12//99
	Raleigh-Durham-Chapel Hill MSA, NC	S	33.52 MW	33.68 AW	69720 AAW	NCBLS	10//99-12//99
	Rocky Mount MSA, NC	S	28.85 MW	29.20 AW	60010 AAW	NCBLS	10//99-12//99
	Wilmington MSA, NC	S	30.96 MW	31.04 AW	64400 AAW	NCBLS	10//99-12//99
	North Dakota	S	28.32 MW	28.80 AW	59890 AAW	NDBLS	10//99-12//99
	Ohio	S	28.62 MW	28.94 AW	60190 AAW	OHBLS	10//99-12//99
	Akron PMSA, OH	S	32.08 MW	25.70 AW	66720 AAW	OHBLS	10//99-12//99
	Canton-Massillon MSA, OH	S	23.99 MW	25.40 AW	49900 AAW	OHBLS	10//99-12//99
	Cincinnati PMSA, OH-KY-IN	S	26.18 MW	25.38 AW	54460 AAW	OHBLS	10//99-12//99
	Cleveland-Lorain-Elyria PMSA, OH	S	30.26 MW	29.91 AW	62940 AAW	OHBLS	10//99-12//99

AAW	Average annual wage	AOH	Average offered, high	ASH	Average starting, high	H	Hourly	M	Monthly	S	Special: hourly and annual
AE	Average entry wage	AOL	Average offered, low	ASL	Average starting, low	HI	Highest wage paid	MTC	Median total compensation	TQ	Third quartile wage
AEX	Average experienced wage	APH	Average pay, high range	AW	Average wage paid	HR	High end range	MW	Median wage paid	W	Weekly
AO	Average offered	APL	Average pay, low range	FQ	First quartile wage	LR	Low end range	SQ	Second quartile wage	Y	Yearly

Electrical Engineer

Occupation/Type/Industry	Location	Per	Low	Mid	High	Source	Date
Electrical Engineer	Columbus MSA, OH	S	30.82 MW	30.06 AW	64110 AAW	OHBLS	10//99-12//99
	Dayton-Springfield MSA, OH	S	28.95 MW	29.51 AW	60210 AAW	OHBLS	10//99-12//99
	Hamilton-Middletown PMSA, OH	S	30.37 MW	28.45 AW	63170 AAW	OHBLS	10//99-12//99
	Lima MSA, OH	S	22.76 MW	20.95 AW	47340 AAW	OHBLS	10//99-12//99
	Mansfield MSA, OH	S	22.08 MW	21.28 AW	45920 AAW	OHBLS	10//99-12//99
	Steubenville-Weirton MSA, OH-WV	S	24.24 MW	25.54 AW	50410 AAW	OHBLS	10//99-12//99
	Toledo MSA, OH	S	25.11 MW	24.25 AW	52240 AAW	OHBLS	10//99-12//99
	Youngstown-Warren MSA, OH	S	21.18 MW	17.80 AW	44050 AAW	OHBLS	10//99-12//99
	Oklahoma	S	22.61 MW	22.73 AW	47280 AAW	OKBLS	10//99-12//99
	Oklahoma City MSA, OK	S	26.44 MW	25.73 AW	55000 AAW	OKBLS	10//99-12//99
	Tulsa MSA, OK	S	26.36 MW	26.21 AW	54830 AAW	OKBLS	10//99-12//99
	Oregon	S	31.32 MW	31.24 AW	64970 AAW	ORBLS	10//99-12//99
	Eugene-Springfield MSA, OR	S	33.69 MW	34.49 AW	70080 AAW	ORBLS	10//99-12//99
	Portland-Vancouver PMSA, OR-WA	S	31.09 MW	31.27 AW	64660 AAW	ORBLS	10//99-12//99
	Salem PMSA, OR	S	30.71 MW	30.97 AW	63880 AAW	ORBLS	10//99-12//99
	Pennsylvania	S	28.02 MW	28.43 AW	59120 AAW	PABLS	10//99-12//99
	Allentown-Bethlehem-Easton MSA, PA	S	32.42 MW	32.21 AW	67430 AAW	PABLS	10//99-12//99
	Harrisburg-Lebanon-Carlisle MSA, PA	S	26.81 MW	26.80 AW	55760 AAW	PABLS	10//99-12//99
	Lancaster MSA, PA	S	27.71 MW	27.09 AW	57640 AAW	PABLS	10//99-12//99
	Philadelphia PMSA, PA-NJ	S	28.24 MW	27.56 AW	58730 AAW	PABLS	10//99-12//99
	Pittsburgh MSA, PA	S	31.56 MW	31.50 AW	65650 AAW	PABLS	10//99-12//99
	Reading MSA, PA	S	22.14 MW	21.49 AW	46050 AAW	PABLS	10//99-12//99
	Scranton--Wilkes-Barre--Hazleton MSA, PA	S	30.10 MW	30.35 AW	62610 AAW	PABLS	10//99-12//99
	York MSA, PA	S	25.81 MW	24.85 AW	53670 AAW	PABLS	10//99-12//99
	Rhode Island	S	26.54 MW	27.24 AW	56670 AAW	RIBLS	10//99-12//99
	Providence-Fall River-Warwick MSA, RI-MA	S	27.67 MW	27.16 AW	57550 AAW	RIBLS	10//99-12//99
	South Carolina	S	33.49 MW	33.09 AW	68830 AAW	SCBLS	10//99-12//99
	Charleston-North Charleston MSA, SC	S	28.83 MW	29.55 AW	59960 AAW	SCBLS	10//99-12//99
	Columbia MSA, SC	S	26.53 MW	26.38 AW	55190 AAW	SCBLS	10//99-12//99
	Greenville-Spartanburg-Anderson MSA, SC	S	30.52 MW	30.56 AW	63480 AAW	SCBLS	10//99-12//99
	Myrtle Beach MSA, SC	S	29.06 MW	27.97 AW	60450 AAW	SCBLS	10//99-12//99
	Sumter MSA, SC	S	22.76 MW	20.04 AW	47340 AAW	SCBLS	10//99-12//99
	South Dakota	S	25.63 MW	26.88 AW	55910 AAW	SDBLS	10//99-12//99
	Sioux Falls MSA, SD	S	24.45 MW	24.07 AW	50850 AAW	SDBLS	10//99-12//99
	Tennessee	S	25.91 MW	27.14 AW	56460 AAW	TNBLS	10//99-12//99
	Jackson MSA, TN	S	27.56 MW	27.20 AW	57330 AAW	TNBLS	10//99-12//99
	Johnson City-Kingsport-Bristol MSA, TN-VA	S	29.30 MW	28.09 AW	60940 AAW	TNBLS	10//99-12//99
	Knoxville MSA, TN	S	28.42 MW	28.21 AW	59110 AAW	TNBLS	10//99-12//99
	Memphis MSA, TN-AR-MS	S	27.78 MW	25.58 AW	57780 AAW	MSBLS	10//99-12//99
	Nashville MSA, TN	S	27.81 MW	28.29 AW	57850 AAW	TNBLS	10//99-12//99
	Texas	S	32.13 MW	32.81 AW	68250 AAW	TXBLS	10//99-12//99
	Austin-San Marcos MSA, TX	S	29.68 MW	29.01 AW	61730 AAW	TXBLS	10//99-12//99
	Beaumont-Port Arthur MSA, TX	S	31.78 MW	31.10 AW	66110 AAW	TXBLS	10//99-12//99
	Dallas PMSA, TX	S	32.49 MW	31.96 AW	67580 AAW	TXBLS	10//99-12//99
	El Paso MSA, TX	S	30.21 MW	29.81 AW	62840 AAW	TXBLS	10//99-12//99
	Fort Worth-Arlington PMSA, TX	S	29.35 MW	29.74 AW	61050 AAW	TXBLS	10//99-12//99
	Galveston-Texas City PMSA, TX	S	34.68 MW	34.23 AW	72140 AAW	TXBLS	10//99-12//99
	Houston PMSA, TX	S	37.55 MW	37.40 AW	78110 AAW	TXBLS	10//99-12//99
	Longview-Marshall MSA, TX	S	32.89 MW	32.10 AW	68410 AAW	TXBLS	10//99-12//99
	Lubbock MSA, TX	S	28.28 MW	27.64 AW	58810 AAW	TXBLS	10//99-12//99
	San Antonio MSA, TX	S	27.78 MW	28.50 AW	57780 AAW	TXBLS	10//99-12//99
	Tyler MSA, TX	S	32.51 MW	32.00 AW	67610 AAW	TXBLS	10//99-12//99
	Utah	S	28.53 MW	28.59 AW	59470 AAW	UTBLS	10//99-12//99
	Salt Lake City-Ogden MSA, UT	S	28.65 MW	28.22 AW	59590 AAW	UTBLS	10//99-12//99
	Vermont	S	32.47 MW	31.68 AW	65890 AAW	VTBLS	10//99-12//99
	Burlington MSA, VT	S	32.31 MW	33.64 AW	67200 AAW	VTBLS	10//99-12//99
	Virginia	S	27.73 MW	27.78 AW	57780 AAW	VABLS	10//99-12//99
	Lynchburg MSA, VA	S	27.20 MW	26.58 AW	56580 AAW	VABLS	10//99-12//99

AAW Average annual wage	AOH Average offered, high	ASH Average starting, high	H Hourly	M Monthly	S Special: hourly and annual
AE Average entry wage	AOL Average offered, low	ASL Average starting, low	HI Highest wage paid	MTC Median total compensation	TQ Third quartile wage
AEX Average experienced wage	APH Average pay, high range	AW Average wage paid	HR High end range	MW Median wage paid	W Weekly
AO Average offered	APL Average pay, low range	FQ First quartile wage	LR Low end range	SQ Second quartile wage	Y Yearly

Occupation/Type/Industry	Location	Per	Low	Mid	High	Source	Date
Electrical Engineer	Norfolk-Virginia Beach-Newport News MSA, VA-NC	S	24.55 MW	25.37 AW	51050 AAW	VABLS	10//99-12//99
	Richmond-Petersburg MSA, VA	S	27.04 MW	27.14 AW	56240 AAW	VABLS	10//99-12//99
	Roanoke MSA, VA	S	27.89 MW	28.49 AW	58010 AAW	VABLS	10//99-12//99
	Washington	S	27.76 MW	27.75 AW	57720 AAW	WABLS	10//99-12//99
	Richland-Kennewick-Pasco MSA, WA	S	29.80 MW	30.28 AW	61980 AAW	WABLS	10//99-12//99
	Seattle-Bellevue-Everett PMSA, WA	S	28.56 MW	28.53 AW	59410 AAW	WABLS	10//99-12//99
	Spokane MSA, WA	S	22.43 MW	22.08 AW	46660 AAW	WABLS	10//99-12//99
	Tacoma PMSA, WA	S	23.80 MW	23.96 AW	49500 AAW	WABLS	10//99-12//99
	West Virginia	S	27.81 MW	25.60 AW	53250 AAW	WVBLS	10//99-12//99
	Huntington-Ashland MSA, WV-KY-OH	S	30.61 MW	30.97 AW	63660 AAW	WVBLS	10//99-12//99
	Wisconsin	S	27.01 MW	28.00 AW	58230 AAW	WIBLS	10//99-12//99
	Appleton-Oshkosh-Neenah MSA, WI	S	22.85 MW	22.51 AW	47520 AAW	WIBLS	10//99-12//99
	Eau Claire MSA, WI	S	27.61 MW	26.68 AW	57420 AAW	WIBLS	10//99-12//99
	Green Bay MSA, WI	S	27.70 MW	27.08 AW	57620 AAW	WIBLS	10//99-12//99
	Madison MSA, WI	S	25.44 MW	24.96 AW	52910 AAW	WIBLS	10//99-12//99
	Milwaukee-Waukesha PMSA, WI	S	31.24 MW	31.60 AW	64980 AAW	WIBLS	10//99-12//99
	Racine PMSA, WI	S	28.36 MW	29.39 AW	58990 AAW	WIBLS	10//99-12//99
	Wyoming	S	28.17 MW	29.73 AW	61850 AAW	WYBLS	10//99-12//99
	Puerto Rico	S	17.91 MW	18.71 AW	38910 AAW	PRBLS	10//99-12//99
	San Juan-Bayamon PMSA, PR	S	18.75 MW	18.15 AW	39000 AAW	PRBLS	10//99-12//99
	Guam	S	18.86 MW	20.12 AW	41840 AAW	GUBLS	10//99-12//99
Electrical Power-Line Installer and Repairer	Alabama	S	20.14 MW	19.82 AW	41230 AAW	ALBLS	10//99-12//99
	Birmingham MSA, AL	S	21.39 MW	21.37 AW	44490 AAW	ALBLS	10//99-12//99
	Mobile MSA, AL	S	18.62 MW	18.76 AW	38740 AAW	ALBLS	10//99-12//99
	Alaska	S	31.91 MW	29.71 AW	61800 AAW	AKBLS	10//99-12//99
	Anchorage MSA, AK	S	27.90 MW	29.72 AW	58040 AAW	AKBLS	10//99-12//99
	Arizona	S	21.97 MW	22.44 AW	46670 AAW	AZBLS	10//99-12//99
	Tucson MSA, AZ	S	21.88 MW	21.54 AW	45500 AAW	AZBLS	10//99-12//99
	Yuma MSA, AZ	S	18.22 MW	17.73 AW	37890 AAW	AZBLS	10//99-12//99
	Arkansas	S	18.63 MW	18.23 AW	37930 AAW	ARBLS	10//99-12//99
	Fayetteville-Springdale-Rogers MSA, AR	S	21.57 MW	21.30 AW	44870 AAW	ARBLS	10//99-12//99
	Little Rock-North Little Rock MSA, AR	S	17.42 MW	17.89 AW	36230 AAW	ARBLS	10//99-12//99
	California	S	24.62 MW	25.44 AW	52910 AAW	CABLS	10//99-12//99
	Los Angeles-Long Beach PMSA, CA	S	21.49 MW	22.19 AW	44690 AAW	CABLS	10//99-12//99
	Oakland PMSA, CA	S	26.30 MW	26.74 AW	54700 AAW	CABLS	10//99-12//99
	Riverside-San Bernardino PMSA, CA	S	27.31 MW	24.28 AW	56810 AAW	CABLS	10//99-12//99
	Sacramento PMSA, CA	S	23.56 MW	23.18 AW	49010 AAW	CABLS	10//99-12//99
	San Diego MSA, CA	S	24.59 MW	25.01 AW	51150 AAW	CABLS	10//99-12//99
	Visalia-Tulare-Porterville MSA, CA	S	25.42 MW	26.66 AW	52870 AAW	CABLS	10//99-12//99
	Connecticut	S	24.29 MW	24.22 AW	50380 AAW	CTBLS	10//99-12//99
	Hartford MSA, CT	S	23.15 MW	23.02 AW	48160 AAW	CTBLS	10//99-12//99
	New London-Norwich MSA, CT-RI	S	24.43 MW	24.39 AW	50800 AAW	CTBLS	10//99-12//99
	Delaware	S	20.55 MW	19.13 AW	39780 AAW	DEBLS	10//99-12//99
	Wilmington-Newark PMSA, DE-MD	S	21.40 MW	21.99 AW	44520 AAW	DEBLS	10//99-12//99
	Washington PMSA, DC-MD-VA-WV	S	19.05 MW	20.26 AW	39610 AAW	DCBLS	10//99-12//99
	Florida	S	18.08 MW	17.09 AW	35550 AAW	FLBLS	10//99-12//99
	Fort Lauderdale PMSA, FL	S	15.53 MW	17.15 AW	32310 AAW	FLBLS	10//99-12//99
	Lakeland-Winter Haven MSA, FL	S	17.87 MW	18.07 AW	37170 AAW	FLBLS	10//99-12//99
	Orlando MSA, FL	S	18.23 MW	18.51 AW	37920 AAW	FLBLS	10//99-12//99
	Sarasota-Bradenton MSA, FL	S	16.15 MW	17.78 AW	33580 AAW	FLBLS	10//99-12//99
	Tampa-St. Petersburg-Clearwater MSA, FL	S	17.46 MW	18.32 AW	36320 AAW	FLBLS	10//99-12//99

AAW Average annual wage	**AOH** Average offered, high	**ASH** Average starting, high	**H** Hourly	**M** Monthly	**S** Special: hourly and annual
AE Average entry wage	**AOL** Average offered, low	**ASL** Average starting, low	**HI** Highest wage paid	**MTC** Median total compensation	**TQ** Third quartile wage
AEX Average experienced wage	**APH** Average pay, high range	**AW** Average wage paid	**HR** High end range	**MW** Median wage paid	**W** Weekly
AO Average offered	**APL** Average pay, low range	**FQ** First quartile wage	**LR** Low end range	**SQ** Second quartile wage	**Y** Yearly

Occupation/Type/Industry	Location	Per	Low	Mid	High	Source	Date
Electrical Power-Line Installer and Repairer							
	West Palm Beach-Boca Raton MSA, FL	S	18.56 MW	18.71 AW	38610 AAW	FLBLS	10//99-12//99
	Georgia	S	16.57 MW	16.77 AW	34880 AAW	GABLS	10//99-12//99
	Albany MSA, GA	S	15.11 MW	15.14 AW	31440 AAW	GABLS	10//99-12//99
	Athens MSA, GA	S	18.22 MW	18.01 AW	37910 AAW	GABLS	10//99-12//99
	Atlanta MSA, GA	S	16.70 MW	16.51 AW	34740 AAW	GABLS	10//99-12//99
	Augusta-Aiken MSA, GA-SC	S	16.42 MW	14.96 AW	34160 AAW	GABLS	10//99-12//99
	Columbus MSA, GA-AL	S	14.77 MW	13.45 AW	30720 AAW	GABLS	10//99-12//99
	Macon MSA, GA	S	17.21 MW	17.31 AW	35790 AAW	GABLS	10//99-12//99
	Idaho	S	22.9 MW	23.23 AW	48310 AAW	IDBLS	10//99-12//99
	Boise City MSA, ID	S	20.14 MW	18.51 AW	41890 AAW	IDBLS	10//99-12//99
	Illinois	S	24.14 MW	24.73 AW	51440 AAW	ILBLS	10//99-12//99
	Bloomington-Normal MSA, IL	S	21.77 MW	22.56 AW	45290 AAW	ILBLS	10//99-12//99
	Chicago PMSA, IL	S	25.41 MW	24.82 AW	52860 AAW	ILBLS	10//99-12//99
	Decatur MSA, IL	S	26.43 MW	25.31 AW	54970 AAW	ILBLS	10//99-12//99
	Peoria-Pekin MSA, IL	S	25.77 MW	25.97 AW	53610 AAW	ILBLS	10//99-12//99
	Rockford MSA, IL	S	25.19 MW	26.19 AW	52390 AAW	ILBLS	10//99-12//99
	Indiana	S	19.74 MW	19.57 AW	40700 AAW	INBLS	10//99-12//99
	Fort Wayne MSA, IN	S	19.81 MW	20.09 AW	41200 AAW	INBLS	10//99-12//99
	Gary PMSA, IN	S	23.04 MW	23.44 AW	47920 AAW	INBLS	10//99-12//99
	Indianapolis MSA, IN	S	17.90 MW	16.81 AW	37220 AAW	INBLS	10//99-12//99
	Lafayette MSA, IN	S	19.37 MW	19.28 AW	40290 AAW	INBLS	10//99-12//99
	Terre Haute MSA, IN	S	21.90 MW	21.38 AW	45540 AAW	INBLS	10//99-12//99
	Iowa	S	21.88 MW	21.02 AW	43710 AAW	IABLS	10//99-12//99
	Cedar Rapids MSA, IA	S	22.21 MW	22.90 AW	46200 AAW	IABLS	10//99-12//99
	Davenport-Moline-Rock Island MSA, IA-IL	S	22.13 MW	22.57 AW	46040 AAW	IABLS	10//99-12//99
	Des Moines MSA, IA	S	22.39 MW	22.68 AW	46570 AAW	IABLS	10//99-12//99
	Kansas	S	21.53 MW	20.55 AW	42750 AAW	KSBLS	10//99-12//99
	Topeka MSA, KS	S	21.76 MW	22.43 AW	45250 AAW	KSBLS	10//99-12//99
	Wichita MSA, KS	S	18.62 MW	18.49 AW	38740 AAW	KSBLS	10//99-12//99
	Kentucky	S	19.84 MW	19.73 AW	41030 AAW	KYBLS	10//99-12//99
	Louisville MSA, KY-IN	S	20.41 MW	19.99 AW	42460 AAW	KYBLS	10//99-12//99
	Louisiana	S	14.87 MW	15.65 AW	32540 AAW	LABLS	10//99-12//99
	Alexandria MSA, LA	S	13.66 MW	14.21 AW	28410 AAW	LABLS	10//99-12//99
	Baton Rouge MSA, LA	S	18.65 MW	18.85 AW	38780 AAW	LABLS	10//99-12//99
	Shreveport-Bossier City MSA, LA	S	14.91 MW	13.54 AW	31010 AAW	LABLS	10//99-12//99
	Maine	S	18.31 MW	18.01 AW	37460 AAW	MEBLS	10//99-12//99
	Maryland	S	20.34 MW	19.37 AW	40280 AAW	MDBLS	10//99-12//99
	Baltimore PMSA, MD	S	19.00 MW	17.71 AW	39520 AAW	MDBLS	10//99-12//99
	Massachusetts	S	23.48 MW	23.43 AW	48730 AAW	MABLS	10//99-12//99
	Boston PMSA, MA-NH	S	24.13 MW	23.80 AW	50190 AAW	MABLS	10//99-12//99
	Lawrence PMSA, MA-NH	S	20.48 MW	21.74 AW	42590 AAW	MABLS	10//99-12//99
	Worcester PMSA, MA-CT	S	22.58 MW	21.90 AW	46970 AAW	MABLS	10//99-12//99
	Michigan	S	22.71 MW	22.63 AW	47070 AAW	MIBLS	10//99-12//99
	Detroit PMSA, MI	S	22.81 MW	22.83 AW	47440 AAW	MIBLS	10//99-12//99
	Grand Rapids-Muskegon-Holland MSA, MI	S	24.37 MW	23.45 AW	50690 AAW	MIBLS	10//99-12//99
	Saginaw-Bay City-Midland MSA, MI	S	17.54 MW	16.24 AW	36480 AAW	MIBLS	10//99-12//99
	Minnesota	S	22.31 MW	21.91 AW	45570 AAW	MNBLS	10//99-12//99
	Minneapolis-St. Paul MSA, MN-WI	S	23.12 MW	23.42 AW	48090 AAW	MNBLS	10//99-12//99
	Mississippi	S	16.37 MW	16.14 AW	33570 AAW	MSBLS	10//99-12//99
	Missouri	S	20.47 MW	19.61 AW	40790 AAW	MOBLS	10//99-12//99
	Kansas City MSA, MO-KS	S	20.99 MW	22.27 AW	43670 AAW	MOBLS	10//99-12//99
	St. Louis MSA, MO-IL	S	21.83 MW	21.75 AW	45410 AAW	MOBLS	10//99-12//99
	Montana	S	22.76 MW	22.09 AW	45940 AAW	MTBLS	10//99-12//99
	Nebraska	S	17.9 MW	18.47 AW	38420 AAW	NEBLS	10//99-12//99
	Nevada	S	24.6 MW	23.92 AW	49760 AAW	NVBLS	10//99-12//99
	Las Vegas MSA, NV-AZ	S	23.38 MW	25.80 AW	48630 AAW	NVBLS	10//99-12//99
	Reno MSA, NV	S	26.70 MW	25.75 AW	55540 AAW	NVBLS	10//99-12//99
	New Hampshire	S	18.94 MW	17.62 AW	36650 AAW	NHBLS	10//99-12//99
	Nashua PMSA, NH	S	16.00 MW	14.42 AW	33280 AAW	NHBLS	10//99-12//99
	Portsmouth-Rochester PMSA, NH-ME	S	20.85 MW	21.06 AW	43370 AAW	NHBLS	10//99-12//99
	New Jersey	S	24.9 MW	25.54 AW	53120 AAW	NJBLS	10//99-12//99
	Middlesex-Somerset-Hunterdon PMSA, NJ	S	23.11 MW	22.87 AW	48060 AAW	NJBLS	10//99-12//99
	Monmouth-Ocean PMSA, NJ	S	25.91 MW	26.02 AW	53900 AAW	NJBLS	10//99-12//99

AAW Average annual wage	**AOH** Average offered, high	**ASH** Average starting, high	**H** Hourly	**M** Monthly	**S** Special: hourly and annual
AE Average entry wage	**AOL** Average offered, low	**ASL** Average starting, low	**HI** Highest wage paid	**MTC** Median total compensation	**TQ** Third quartile wage
AEX Average experienced wage	**APH** Average pay, high range	**AW** Average wage paid	**HR** High end range	**MW** Median wage paid	**W** Weekly
AO Average offered	**APL** Average pay, low range	**FQ** First quartile wage	**LR** Low end range	**SQ** Second quartile wage	**Y** Yearly

Occupation/Type/Industry	Location	Per	Low	Mid	High	Source	Date
Electrical Power-Line Installer and Repairer							
	Newark PMSA, NJ	S	26.95 MW	26.90 AW	56050 AAW	NJBLS	10//99-12//99
	New Mexico	S	19.68 MW	19.36 AW	40270 AAW	NMBLS	10//99-12//99
	Las Cruces MSA, NM	S	19.77 MW	19.89 AW	41120 AAW	NMBLS	10//99-12//99
	New York	S	29.53 MW	28.29 AW	58840 AAW	NYBLS	10//99-12//99
	Nassau-Suffolk PMSA, NY	S	27.42 MW	27.09 AW	57030 AAW	NYBLS	10//99-12//99
	New York PMSA, NY	S	28.39 MW	28.95 AW	59060 AAW	NYBLS	10//99-12//99
	Newburgh PMSA, NY-PA	S	26.94 MW	25.88 AW	56040 AAW	NYBLS	10//99-12//99
	Rochester MSA, NY	S	28.20 MW	30.30 AW	58660 AAW	NYBLS	10//99-12//99
	North Carolina	S	17.73 MW	17.72 AW	36860 AAW	NCBLS	10//99-12//99
	Charlotte-Gastonia-Rock Hill MSA, NC-SC	S	19.14 MW	20.12 AW	39820 AAW	NCBLS	10//99-12//99
	Goldsboro MSA, NC	S	15.21 MW	15.04 AW	31630 AAW	NCBLS	10//99-12//99
	Greensboro--Winston-Salem-- High Point MSA, NC	S	15.90 MW	14.06 AW	33070 AAW	NCBLS	10//99-12//99
	Hickory-Morganton-Lenoir MSA, NC	S	21.32 MW	22.13 AW	44350 AAW	NCBLS	10//99-12//99
	Raleigh-Durham-Chapel Hill MSA, NC	S	20.30 MW	20.65 AW	42230 AAW	NCBLS	10//99-12//99
	Wilmington MSA, NC	S	17.21 MW	16.87 AW	35800 AAW	NCBLS	10//99-12//99
	North Dakota	S	20.43 MW	20.09 AW	41780 AAW	NDBLS	10//99-12//99
	Bismarck MSA, ND	S	21.07 MW	20.12 AW	43820 AAW	NDBLS	10//99-12//99
	Ohio	S	20.6 MW	19.57 AW	40700 AAW	OHBLS	10//99-12//99
	Canton-Massillon MSA, OH	S	22.91 MW	23.51 AW	47650 AAW	OHBLS	10//99-12//99
	Cincinnati PMSA, OH-KY-IN	S	22.34 MW	22.46 AW	46470 AAW	OHBLS	10//99-12//99
	Cleveland-Lorain-Elyria PMSA, OH	S	18.08 MW	17.97 AW	37600 AAW	OHBLS	10//99-12//99
	Columbus MSA, OH	S	20.94 MW	21.66 AW	43550 AAW	OHBLS	10//99-12//99
	Toledo MSA, OH	S	19.99 MW	21.71 AW	41570 AAW	OHBLS	10//99-12//99
	Oklahoma	S	18.01 MW	17.62 AW	36640 AAW	OKBLS	10//99-12//99
	Tulsa MSA, OK	S	19.28 MW	19.23 AW	40110 AAW	OKBLS	10//99-12//99
	Oregon	S	26.1 MW	26.77 AW	55680 AAW	ORBLS	10//99-12//99
	Eugene-Springfield MSA, OR	S	26.04 MW	25.55 AW	54160 AAW	ORBLS	10//99-12//99
	Portland-Vancouver PMSA, OR-WA	S	27.20 MW	27.28 AW	56580 AAW	ORBLS	10//99-12//99
	Pennsylvania	S	21.39 MW	21.27 AW	44250 AAW	PABLS	10//99-12//99
	Allentown-Bethlehem-Easton MSA, PA	S	24.85 MW	23.69 AW	51690 AAW	PABLS	10//99-12//99
	Harrisburg-Lebanon-Carlisle MSA, PA	S	25.36 MW	24.96 AW	52740 AAW	PABLS	10//99-12//99
	Johnstown MSA, PA	S	24.07 MW	23.48 AW	50060 AAW	PABLS	10//99-12//99
	Philadelphia PMSA, PA-NJ	S	18.13 MW	16.93 AW	37700 AAW	PABLS	10//99-12//99
	Pittsburgh MSA, PA	S	18.86 MW	20.19 AW	39230 AAW	PABLS	10//99-12//99
	Reading MSA, PA	S	25.36 MW	24.22 AW	52740 AAW	PABLS	10//99-12//99
	Scranton--Wilkes-Barre-- Hazleton MSA, PA	S	27.43 MW	27.56 AW	57060 AAW	PABLS	10//99-12//99
	York MSA, PA	S	24.84 MW	23.58 AW	51660 AAW	PABLS	10//99-12//99
	Rhode Island	S	20.04 MW	20.60 AW	42840 AAW	RIBLS	10//99-12//99
	Providence-Fall River- Warwick MSA, RI-MA	S	21.03 MW	20.86 AW	43740 AAW	RIBLS	10//99-12//99
	South Carolina	S	17.15 MW	17.69 AW	36790 AAW	SCBLS	10//99-12//99
	Charleston-North Charleston MSA, SC	S	16.25 MW	16.53 AW	33790 AAW	SCBLS	10//99-12//99
	Columbia MSA, SC	S	23.05 MW	22.35 AW	47940 AAW	SCBLS	10//99-12//99
	Greenville-Spartanburg- Anderson MSA, SC	S	15.97 MW	15.47 AW	33220 AAW	SCBLS	10//99-12//99
	Myrtle Beach MSA, SC	S	15.09 MW	15.91 AW	31380 AAW	SCBLS	10//99-12//99
	South Dakota	S	18.36 MW	18.42 AW	38310 AAW	SDBLS	10//99-12//99
	Rapid City MSA, SD	S	18.55 MW	18.28 AW	38590 AAW	SDBLS	10//99-12//99
	Sioux Falls MSA, SD	S	19.72 MW	18.98 AW	41020 AAW	SDBLS	10//99-12//99
	Tennessee	S	18.81 MW	18.26 AW	37980 AAW	TNBLS	10//99-12//99
	Jackson MSA, TN	S	21.02 MW	20.65 AW	43730 AAW	TNBLS	10//99-12//99
	Johnson City-Kingsport-Bristol MSA, TN-VA	S	18.91 MW	20.24 AW	39330 AAW	TNBLS	10//99-12//99
	Nashville MSA, TN	S	16.96 MW	17.28 AW	35270 AAW	TNBLS	10//99-12//99
	Texas	S	17.31 MW	16.75 AW	34850 AAW	TXBLS	10//99-12//99
	Austin-San Marcos MSA, TX	S	12.61 MW	12.25 AW	26240 AAW	TXBLS	10//99-12//99
	Beaumont-Port Arthur MSA, TX	S	20.00 MW	19.94 AW	41610 AAW	TXBLS	10//99-12//99
	Brownsville-Harlingen-San Benito MSA, TX	S	15.37 MW	15.75 AW	31970 AAW	TXBLS	10//99-12//99
	Dallas PMSA, TX	S	15.65 MW	16.23 AW	32560 AAW	TXBLS	10//99-12//99

AAW	Average annual wage	AOH	Average offered, high	ASH	Average starting, high
AE	Average entry wage	AOL	Average offered, low	ASL	Average starting, low
AEX	Average experienced wage	APH	Average pay, high range	AW	Average wage paid
AO	Average offered	APL	Average pay, low range	FQ	First quartile wage

H	Hourly
HI	Highest wage paid
HR	High end range
LR	Low end range

M	Monthly
MTC	Median total compensation
MW	Median wage paid
SQ	Second quartile wage

S	Special: hourly and annual
TQ	Third quartile wage
W	Weekly
Y	Yearly

Occupation/Type/Industry	Location	Per	Low	Mid	High	Source	Date
Electrical Power-Line Installer and Repairer							
	Fort Worth-Arlington PMSA, TX	S	15.38 MW	15.12 AW	31980 AAW	TXBLS	10//99-12//99
	Galveston-Texas City PMSA, TX	S	20.30 MW	20.45 AW	42210 AAW	TXBLS	10//99-12//99
	Houston PMSA, TX	S	17.57 MW	17.88 AW	36540 AAW	TXBLS	10//99-12//99
	Longview-Marshall MSA, TX	S	18.10 MW	18.18 AW	37660 AAW	TXBLS	10//99-12//99
	San Antonio MSA, TX	S	14.46 MW	13.72 AW	30080 AAW	TXBLS	10//99-12//99
	Texarkana MSA, TX-Texarkana, AR	S	19.96 MW	20.79 AW	41510 AAW	TXBLS	10//99-12//99
	Utah	S	21.74 MW	21.34 AW	44390 AAW	UTBLS	10//99-12//99
	Provo-Orem MSA, UT	S	18.80 MW	19.74 AW	39100 AAW	UTBLS	10//99-12//99
	Salt Lake City-Ogden MSA, UT	S	22.70 MW	22.78 AW	47220 AAW	UTBLS	10//99-12//99
	Vermont	S	21.63 MW	19.70 AW	40980 AAW	VTBLS	10//99-12//99
	Burlington MSA, VT	S	20.64 MW	21.01 AW	42930 AAW	VTBLS	10//99-12//99
	Virginia	S	20.51 MW	19.42 AW	40390 AAW	VABLS	10//99-12//99
	Lynchburg MSA, VA	S	17.98 MW	19.96 AW	37400 AAW	VABLS	10//99-12//99
	Richmond-Petersburg MSA, VA	S	19.00 MW	20.50 AW	39530 AAW	VABLS	10//99-12//99
	Washington	S	25.15 MW	24.35 AW	50640 AAW	WABLS	10//99-12//99
	Richland-Kennewick-Pasco MSA, WA	S	26.69 MW	26.50 AW	55510 AAW	WABLS	10//99-12//99
	Seattle-Bellevue-Everett PMSA, WA	S	27.69 MW	29.06 AW	57590 AAW	WABLS	10//99-12//99
	Tacoma PMSA, WA	S	29.01 MW	30.24 AW	60340 AAW	WABLS	10//99-12//99
	West Virginia	S	21.5 MW	19.21 AW	39950 AAW	WVBLS	10//99-12//99
	Huntington-Ashland MSA, WV-KY-OH	S	12.01 MW	8.33 AW	24980 AAW	WVBLS	10//99-12//99
	Wheeling MSA, WV-OH	S	21.47 MW	22.63 AW	44660 AAW	WVBLS	10//99-12//99
	Wisconsin	S	22.07 MW	21.74 AW	45230 AAW	WIBLS	10//99-12//99
	La Crosse MSA, WI-MN	S	21.19 MW	22.09 AW	44070 AAW	WIBLS	10//99-12//99
	Sheboygan MSA, WI	S	22.02 MW	22.44 AW	45810 AAW	WIBLS	10//99-12//99
	Wyoming	S	22.76 MW	22.56 AW	46920 AAW	WYBLS	10//99-12//99
	Cheyenne MSA, WY	S	21.20 MW	21.57 AW	44100 AAW	WYBLS	10//99-12//99
Electrician							
	United States	H		35.58 AW		ENR1	2000
	Alabama	S	14.92 MW	15.88 AW	33040 AAW	ALBLS	10//99-12//99
	Anniston MSA, AL	S	13.82 MW	12.75 AW	28750 AAW	ALBLS	10//99-12//99
	Auburn-Opelika MSA, AL	S	11.55 MW	11.40 AW	24020 AAW	ALBLS	10//99-12//99
	Birmingham MSA, AL	S	14.29 MW	13.91 AW	29720 AAW	ALBLS	10//99-12//99
	Decatur MSA, AL	S	19.16 MW	16.96 AW	39840 AAW	ALBLS	10//99-12//99
	Dothan MSA, AL	S	12.08 MW	11.34 AW	25120 AAW	ALBLS	10//99-12//99
	Florence MSA, AL	S	20.21 MW	21.90 AW	42040 AAW	ALBLS	10//99-12//99
	Gadsden MSA, AL	S	11.70 MW	11.74 AW	24340 AAW	ALBLS	10//99-12//99
	Huntsville MSA, AL	S	17.60 MW	15.85 AW	36600 AAW	ALBLS	10//99-12//99
	Mobile MSA, AL	S	14.46 MW	14.51 AW	30070 AAW	ALBLS	10//99-12//99
	Montgomery MSA, AL	S	13.56 MW	13.71 AW	28200 AAW	ALBLS	10//99-12//99
	Tuscaloosa MSA, AL	S	16.12 MW	16.61 AW	33520 AAW	ALBLS	10//99-12//99
	Alaska	S	25.87 MW	24.55 AW	51060 AAW	AKBLS	10//99-12//99
	Anchorage MSA, AK	S	26.04 MW	28.33 AW	54160 AAW	AKBLS	10//99-12//99
	Arizona	S	15.57 MW	16.14 AW	33570 AAW	AZBLS	10//99-12//99
	Flagstaff MSA, AZ-UT	S	12.52 MW	12.02 AW	26030 AAW	AZBLS	10//99-12//99
	Phoenix-Mesa MSA, AZ	S	16.16 MW	15.62 AW	33620 AAW	AZBLS	10//99-12//99
	Tucson MSA, AZ	S	16.01 MW	15.68 AW	33290 AAW	AZBLS	10//99-12//99
	Yuma MSA, AZ	S	14.64 MW	14.50 AW	30440 AAW	AZBLS	10//99-12//99
	Arkansas	S	14.41 MW	14.90 AW	30990 AAW	ARBLS	10//99-12//99
	Fayetteville-Springdale-Rogers MSA, AR	S	13.34 MW	13.17 AW	27750 AAW	ARBLS	10//99-12//99
	Fort Smith MSA, AR-OK	S	13.18 MW	13.13 AW	27410 AAW	ARBLS	10//99-12//99
	Jonesboro MSA, AR	S	15.62 MW	15.64 AW	32490 AAW	ARBLS	10//99-12//99
	Little Rock-North Little Rock MSA, AR	S	13.40 MW	13.76 AW	27870 AAW	ARBLS	10//99-12//99
	Pine Bluff MSA, AR	S	16.04 MW	16.29 AW	33370 AAW	ARBLS	10//99-12//99
	California	S	21.08 MW	22.66 AW	47140 AAW	CABLS	10//99-12//99
	Bakersfield MSA, CA	S	18.42 MW	18.03 AW	38320 AAW	CABLS	10//99-12//99
	Chico-Paradise MSA, CA	S	22.35 MW	22.67 AW	46480 AAW	CABLS	10//99-12//99
	Fresno MSA, CA	S	21.56 MW	23.24 AW	44850 AAW	CABLS	10//99-12//99
	Los Angeles-Long Beach PMSA, CA	S	21.27 MW	20.31 AW	44230 AAW	CABLS	10//99-12//99
	Merced MSA, CA	S	19.76 MW	19.72 AW	41090 AAW	CABLS	10//99-12//99
	Modesto MSA, CA	S	17.56 MW	16.73 AW	36520 AAW	CABLS	10//99-12//99

AAW	Average annual wage	AOH	Average offered, high	ASH	Average starting, high	H	Hourly	M	Monthly	S	Special: hourly and annual
AE	Average entry wage	AOL	Average offered, low	ASL	Average starting, low	HI	Highest wage paid	MTC	Median total compensation	TQ	Third quartile wage
AEX	Average experienced wage	APH	Average pay, high range	AW	Average wage paid	HR	High end range	MW	Median wage paid	W	Weekly
AO	Average offered	APL	Average pay, low range	FQ	First quartile wage	LR	Low end range	SQ	Second quartile wage	Y	Yearly

Occupation/Type/Industry	Location	Per	Low	Mid	High	Source	Date
Electrician	Oakland PMSA, CA	S	32.52 MW	36.49 AW	67650 AAW	CABLS	10//99-12//99
	Orange County PMSA, CA	S	22.29 MW	22.58 AW	46370 AAW	CABLS	10//99-12//99
	Redding MSA, CA	S	13.31 MW	12.14 AW	27690 AAW	CABLS	10//99-12//99
	Riverside-San Bernardino PMSA, CA	S	19.64 MW	18.85 AW	40860 AAW	CABLS	10//99-12//99
	Sacramento PMSA, CA	S	21.17 MW	20.80 AW	44020 AAW	CABLS	10//99-12//99
	Salinas MSA, CA	S	23.53 MW	20.88 AW	48950 AAW	CABLS	10//99-12//99
	San Diego MSA, CA	S	18.39 MW	18.14 AW	38240 AAW	CABLS	10//99-12//99
	San Francisco PMSA, CA	S	26.80 MW	25.67 AW	55740 AAW	CABLS	10//99-12//99
	San Jose PMSA, CA	S	21.28 MW	19.81 AW	44260 AAW	CABLS	10//99-12//99
	San Luis Obispo-Atascadero-Paso Robles MSA, CA	S	24.10 MW	24.36 AW	50120 AAW	CABLS	10//99-12//99
	Santa Barbara-Santa Maria-Lompoc MSA, CA	S	21.31 MW	20.63 AW	44320 AAW	CABLS	10//99-12//99
	Santa Cruz-Watsonville PMSA, CA	S	30.13 MW	33.29 AW	62660 AAW	CABLS	10//99-12//99
	Santa Rosa PMSA, CA	S	15.64 MW	14.86 AW	32530 AAW	CABLS	10//99-12//99
	Stockton-Lodi MSA, CA	S	20.02 MW	18.58 AW	41640 AAW	CABLS	10//99-12//99
	Vallejo-Fairfield-Napa PMSA, CA	S	23.60 MW	22.86 AW	49090 AAW	CABLS	10//99-12//99
	Ventura PMSA, CA	S	18.34 MW	17.59 AW	38160 AAW	CABLS	10//99-12//99
	Visalia-Tulare-Porterville MSA, CA	S	18.83 MW	16.74 AW	39170 AAW	CABLS	10//99-12//99
	Colorado	S	21.22 MW	20.08 AW	41770 AAW	COBLS	10//99-12//99
	Boulder-Longmont PMSA, CO	S	18.43 MW	18.59 AW	38340 AAW	COBLS	10//99-12//99
	Colorado Springs MSA, CO	S	19.57 MW	20.09 AW	40710 AAW	COBLS	10//99-12//99
	Denver PMSA, CO	S	20.66 MW	22.32 AW	42970 AAW	COBLS	10//99-12//99
	Connecticut	S	20.87 MW	21.53 AW	44790 AAW	CTBLS	10//99-12//99
	Bridgeport PMSA, CT	S	19.41 MW	19.43 AW	40360 AAW	CTBLS	10//99-12//99
	Danbury PMSA, CT	S	18.20 MW	18.08 AW	37860 AAW	CTBLS	10//99-12//99
	Hartford MSA, CT	S	19.67 MW	19.27 AW	40910 AAW	CTBLS	10//99-12//99
	New Haven-Meriden PMSA, CT	S	21.45 MW	22.63 AW	44610 AAW	CTBLS	10//99-12//99
	New London-Norwich MSA, CT-RI	S	19.38 MW	19.52 AW	40320 AAW	CTBLS	10//99-12//99
	Stamford-Norwalk PMSA, CT	S	24.02 MW	20.56 AW	49970 AAW	CTBLS	10//99-12//99
	Waterbury PMSA, CT	S	20.58 MW	20.62 AW	42800 AAW	CTBLS	10//99-12//99
	Delaware	S	19.4 MW	19.71 AW	41000 AAW	DEBLS	10//99-12//99
	Dover MSA, DE	S	12.35 MW	11.97 AW	25690 AAW	DEBLS	10//99-12//99
	Wilmington-Newark PMSA, DE-MD	S	20.85 MW	20.92 AW	43370 AAW	DEBLS	10//99-12//99
	District of Columbia	S	24.03 MW	23.71 AW	49310 AAW	DCBLS	10//99-12//99
	Washington PMSA, DC-MD-VA-WV	S	18.05 MW	17.50 AW	37540 AAW	DCBLS	10//99-12//99
	Florida	S	13.71 MW	14.51 AW	30180 AAW	FLBLS	10//99-12//99
	Daytona Beach MSA, FL	S	13.68 MW	14.02 AW	28450 AAW	FLBLS	10//99-12//99
	Fort Lauderdale PMSA, FL	S	16.56 MW	16.90 AW	34450 AAW	FLBLS	10//99-12//99
	Fort Myers-Cape Coral MSA, FL	S	13.71 MW	13.61 AW	28530 AAW	FLBLS	10//99-12//99
	Fort Pierce-Port St. Lucie MSA, FL	S	13.85 MW	13.69 AW	28810 AAW	FLBLS	10//99-12//99
	Fort Walton Beach MSA, FL	S	15.35 MW	14.97 AW	31930 AAW	FLBLS	10//99-12//99
	Gainesville MSA, FL	S	11.58 MW	10.96 AW	24090 AAW	FLBLS	10//99-12//99
	Jacksonville MSA, FL	S	16.07 MW	15.78 AW	33420 AAW	FLBLS	10//99-12//99
	Lakeland-Winter Haven MSA, FL	S	15.77 MW	15.61 AW	32790 AAW	FLBLS	10//99-12//99
	Melbourne-Titusville-Palm Bay MSA, FL	S	13.66 MW	13.21 AW	28410 AAW	FLBLS	10//99-12//99
	Miami PMSA, FL	S	15.51 MW	14.94 AW	32260 AAW	FLBLS	10//99-12//99
	Naples MSA, FL	S	14.60 MW	14.57 AW	30360 AAW	FLBLS	10//99-12//99
	Ocala MSA, FL	S	13.43 MW	12.36 AW	27940 AAW	FLBLS	10//99-12//99
	Orlando MSA, FL	S	12.78 MW	12.11 AW	26590 AAW	FLBLS	10//99-12//99
	Panama City MSA, FL	S	13.18 MW	11.53 AW	27420 AAW	FLBLS	10//99-12//99
	Pensacola MSA, FL	S	13.01 MW	12.40 AW	27070 AAW	FLBLS	10//99-12//99
	Sarasota-Bradenton MSA, FL	S	12.90 MW	12.60 AW	26830 AAW	FLBLS	10//99-12//99
	Tallahassee MSA, FL	S	12.76 MW	12.62 AW	26550 AAW	FLBLS	10//99-12//99
	Tampa-St. Petersburg-Clearwater MSA, FL	S	13.52 MW	12.79 AW	28120 AAW	FLBLS	10//99-12//99
	West Palm Beach-Boca Raton MSA, FL	S	16.17 MW	15.13 AW	33620 AAW	FLBLS	10//99-12//99
	Georgia	S	17.62 MW	18.32 AW	38120 AAW	GABLS	10//99-12//99
	Albany MSA, GA	S	17.43 MW	16.53 AW	36240 AAW	GABLS	10//99-12//99

AAW Average annual wage	**AOH** Average offered, high	**ASH** Average starting, high	**H** Hourly	**M** Monthly	**S** Special: hourly and annual
AE Average entry wage	**AOL** Average offered, low	**ASL** Average starting, low	**HI** Highest wage paid	**MTC** Median total compensation	**TQ** Third quartile wage
AEX Average experienced wage	**APH** Average pay, high range	**AW** Average wage paid	**HR** High end range	**MW** Median wage paid	**W** Weekly
AO Average offered	**APL** Average pay, low range	**FQ** First quartile wage	**LR** Low end range	**SQ** Second quartile wage	**Y** Yearly

Electrician

Occupation/Type/Industry	Location	Per	Low	Mid	High	Source	Date
Electrician	Athens MSA, GA	S	16.38 MW	15.86 AW	34060 AAW	GABLS	10//99-12//99
	Atlanta MSA, GA	S	19.38 MW	20.78 AW	40310 AAW	GABLS	10//99-12//99
	Augusta-Aiken MSA, GA-SC	S	17.71 MW	16.75 AW	36830 AAW	GABLS	10//99-12//99
	Columbus MSA, GA-AL	S	15.33 MW	15.05 AW	31890 AAW	GABLS	10//99-12//99
	Macon MSA, GA	S	17.93 MW	18.12 AW	37300 AAW	GABLS	10//99-12//99
	Hawaii	S	21.46 MW	21.95 AW	45650 AAW	HIBLS	10//99-12//99
	Honolulu MSA, HI	S	24.84 MW	26.13 AW	51670 AAW	HIBLS	10//99-12//99
	Idaho	S	18.2 MW	17.96 AW	37360 AAW	IDBLS	10//99-12//99
	Boise City MSA, ID	S	18.26 MW	18.91 AW	37990 AAW	IDBLS	10//99-12//99
	Illinois	S	24.59 MW	24.89 AW	51760 AAW	ILBLS	10//99-12//99
	Bloomington-Normal MSA, IL	S	21.90 MW	22.89 AW	45550 AAW	ILBLS	10//99-12//99
	Champaign-Urbana MSA, IL	S	24.06 MW	23.29 AW	50040 AAW	ILBLS	10//99-12//99
	Chicago PMSA, IL	S	25.73 MW	25.64 AW	53530 AAW	ILBLS	10//99-12//99
	Kankakee PMSA, IL	S	23.01 MW	23.63 AW	47860 AAW	ILBLS	10//99-12//99
	Peoria-Pekin MSA, IL	S	22.43 MW	23.78 AW	46650 AAW	ILBLS	10//99-12//99
	Rockford MSA, IL	S	21.35 MW	20.76 AW	44400 AAW	ILBLS	10//99-12//99
	Springfield MSA, IL	S	25.32 MW	27.53 AW	52660 AAW	ILBLS	10//99-12//99
	Indiana	S	19.98 MW	19.30 AW	40150 AAW	INBLS	10//99-12//99
	Bloomington MSA, IN	S	17.85 MW	16.18 AW	37130 AAW	INBLS	10//99-12//99
	Elkhart-Goshen MSA, IN	S	20.71 MW	22.89 AW	43080 AAW	INBLS	10//99-12//99
	Evansville-Henderson MSA, IN-KY	S	20.50 MW	22.41 AW	42640 AAW	INBLS	10//99-12//99
	Fort Wayne MSA, IN	S	16.79 MW	16.30 AW	34910 AAW	INBLS	10//99-12//99
	Gary PMSA, IN	S	21.93 MW	23.00 AW	45620 AAW	INBLS	10//99-12//99
	Indianapolis MSA, IN	S	18.83 MW	18.87 AW	39180 AAW	INBLS	10//99-12//99
	Kokomo MSA, IN	S	22.77 MW	23.94 AW	47350 AAW	INBLS	10//99-12//99
	Lafayette MSA, IN	S	20.32 MW	22.41 AW	42260 AAW	INBLS	10//99-12//99
	Muncie MSA, IN	S	16.16 MW	13.14 AW	33610 AAW	INBLS	10//99-12//99
	South Bend MSA, IN	S	18.77 MW	19.06 AW	39040 AAW	INBLS	10//99-12//99
	Terre Haute MSA, IN	S	20.45 MW	23.11 AW	42530 AAW	INBLS	10//99-12//99
	Iowa	S	16.86 MW	17.61 AW	36620 AAW	IABLS	10//99-12//99
	Cedar Rapids MSA, IA	S	22.26 MW	23.67 AW	46290 AAW	IABLS	10//99-12//99
	Davenport-Moline-Rock Island MSA, IA-IL	S	18.68 MW	18.87 AW	38860 AAW	IABLS	10//99-12//99
	Des Moines MSA, IA	S	15.60 MW	15.21 AW	32450 AAW	IABLS	10//99-12//99
	Dubuque MSA, IA	S	17.67 MW	18.15 AW	36750 AAW	IABLS	10//99-12//99
	Iowa City MSA, IA	S	15.58 MW	15.45 AW	32400 AAW	IABLS	10//99-12//99
	Sioux City MSA, IA-NE	S	18.56 MW	18.51 AW	38610 AAW	IABLS	10//99-12//99
	Waterloo-Cedar Falls MSA, IA	S	15.15 MW	15.26 AW	31510 AAW	IABLS	10//99-12//99
	Kansas	S	14.44 MW	14.76 AW	30690 AAW	KSBLS	10//99-12//99
	Lawrence MSA, KS	S	17.15 MW	16.90 AW	35680 AAW	KSBLS	10//99-12//99
	Topeka MSA, KS	S	17.77 MW	17.75 AW	36950 AAW	KSBLS	10//99-12//99
	Wichita MSA, KS	S	16.59 MW	16.00 AW	34500 AAW	KSBLS	10//99-12//99
	Kentucky	S	17.05 MW	17.74 AW	36900 AAW	KYBLS	10//99-12//99
	Lexington MSA, KY	S	16.48 MW	15.70 AW	34290 AAW	KYBLS	10//99-12//99
	Louisville MSA, KY-IN	S	18.58 MW	18.12 AW	38650 AAW	KYBLS	10//99-12//99
	Owensboro MSA, KY	S	15.92 MW	15.52 AW	33110 AAW	KYBLS	10//99-12//99
	Louisiana	S	15.26 MW	15.18 AW	31560 AAW	LABLS	10//99-12//99
	Alexandria MSA, LA	S	14.34 MW	14.87 AW	29830 AAW	LABLS	10//99-12//99
	Baton Rouge MSA, LA	S	14.51 MW	14.78 AW	30180 AAW	LABLS	10//99-12//99
	Houma MSA, LA	S	13.28 MW	12.73 AW	27620 AAW	LABLS	10//99-12//99
	Lafayette MSA, LA	S	16.87 MW	17.24 AW	35100 AAW	LABLS	10//99-12//99
	Lake Charles MSA, LA	S	14.34 MW	14.34 AW	29840 AAW	LABLS	10//99-12//99
	Monroe MSA, LA	S	14.93 MW	15.06 AW	31050 AAW	LABLS	10//99-12//99
	New Orleans MSA, LA	S	15.71 MW	15.90 AW	32680 AAW	LABLS	10//99-12//99
	Shreveport-Bossier City MSA, LA	S	15.26 MW	17.13 AW	31750 AAW	LABLS	10//99-12//99
	Maine	S	15.72 MW	16.07 AW	33430 AAW	MEBLS	10//99-12//99
	Bangor MSA, ME	S	13.96 MW	14.31 AW	29040 AAW	MEBLS	10//99-12//99
	Lewiston-Auburn MSA, ME	S	18.98 MW	16.92 AW	39470 AAW	MEBLS	10//99-12//99
	Portland MSA, ME	S	16.01 MW	15.70 AW	33300 AAW	MEBLS	10//99-12//99
	Maryland	S	17.5 MW	18.47 AW	38430 AAW	MDBLS	10//99-12//99
	Baltimore PMSA, MD	S	18.07 MW	16.48 AW	37590 AAW	MDBLS	10//99-12//99
	Hagerstown PMSA, MD	S	15.06 MW	14.33 AW	31320 AAW	MDBLS	10//99-12//99
	Massachusetts	S	21.99 MW	22.76 AW	47330 AAW	MABLS	10//99-12//99
	Barnstable-Yarmouth MSA, MA	S	17.56 MW	17.99 AW	36530 AAW	MABLS	10//99-12//99
	Boston PMSA, MA-NH	S	24.29 MW	25.34 AW	50510 AAW	MABLS	10//99-12//99
	Brockton PMSA, MA	S	16.80 MW	13.43 AW	34950 AAW	MABLS	10//99-12//99
	Fitchburg-Leominster PMSA, MA	S	14.36 MW	14.33 AW	29870 AAW	MABLS	10//99-12//99
	Lawrence PMSA, MA-NH	S	18.27 MW	18.47 AW	38000 AAW	MABLS	10//99-12//99

Occupation/Type/Industry	Location	Per	Low	Mid	High	Source	Date
Electrician	Lowell PMSA, MA-NH	S	19.25 MW	19.07 AW	40050 AAW	MABLS	10//99-12//99
	New Bedford PMSA, MA	S	21.02 MW	22.33 AW	43720 AAW	MABLS	10//99-12//99
	Springfield MSA, MA	S	18.70 MW	18.98 AW	38890 AAW	MABLS	10//99-12//99
	Worcester PMSA, MA-CT	S	27.09 MW	26.49 AW	56340 AAW	MABLS	10//99-12//99
	Michigan	S	27.46 MW	25.21 AW	52440 AAW	MIBLS	10//99-12//99
	Ann Arbor PMSA, MI	S	21.28 MW	22.09 AW	44260 AAW	MIBLS	10//99-12//99
	Benton Harbor MSA, MI	S	20.63 MW	20.63 AW	42910 AAW	MIBLS	10//99-12//99
	Detroit PMSA, MI	S	27.97 MW	29.59 AW	58170 AAW	MIBLS	10//99-12//99
	Flint PMSA, MI	S	26.31 MW	27.42 AW	54730 AAW	MIBLS	10//99-12//99
	Grand Rapids-Muskegon- Holland MSA, MI	S	18.61 MW	18.15 AW	38700 AAW	MIBLS	10//99-12//99
	Jackson MSA, MI	S	26.41 MW	27.75 AW	54940 AAW	MIBLS	10//99-12//99
	Kalamazoo-Battle Creek MSA, MI	S	25.79 MW	27.49 AW	53640 AAW	MIBLS	10//99-12//99
	Lansing-East Lansing MSA, MI	S	23.30 MW	23.32 AW	48460 AAW	MIBLS	10//99-12//99
	Saginaw-Bay City-Midland MSA, MI	S	24.89 MW	25.70 AW	51770 AAW	MIBLS	10//99-12//99
	Minnesota	S	22.14 MW	21.59 AW	44920 AAW	MNBLS	10//99-12//99
	Duluth-Superior MSA, MN-WI	S	21.45 MW	22.66 AW	44610 AAW	MNBLS	10//99-12//99
	Minneapolis-St. Paul MSA, MN-WI	S	22.75 MW	23.04 AW	47310 AAW	MNBLS	10//99-12//99
	Rochester MSA, MN	S	22.22 MW	23.79 AW	46210 AAW	MNBLS	10//99-12//99
	St. Cloud MSA, MN	S	18.09 MW	18.96 AW	37620 AAW	MNBLS	10//99-12//99
	Mississippi	S	15.34 MW	15.75 AW	32760 AAW	MSBLS	10//99-12//99
	Biloxi-Gulfport-Pascagoula MSA, MS	S	15.04 MW	15.15 AW	31280 AAW	MSBLS	10//99-12//99
	Hattiesburg MSA, MS	S	13.13 MW	13.28 AW	27310 AAW	MSBLS	10//99-12//99
	Jackson MSA, MS	S	17.39 MW	18.15 AW	36170 AAW	MSBLS	10//99-12//99
	Missouri	S	21.63 MW	20.21 AW	42040 AAW	MOBLS	10//99-12//99
	Columbia MSA, MO	S	16.18 MW	15.59 AW	33660 AAW	MOBLS	10//99-12//99
	Joplin MSA, MO	S	15.01 MW	14.86 AW	31220 AAW	MOBLS	10//99-12//99
	Kansas City MSA, MO-KS	S	17.18 MW	15.87 AW	35730 AAW	MOBLS	10//99-12//99
	St. Louis MSA, MO-IL	S	21.83 MW	22.91 AW	45400 AAW	MOBLS	10//99-12//99
	Springfield MSA, MO	S	14.93 MW	14.39 AW	31050 AAW	MOBLS	10//99-12//99
	Montana	S	18.91 MW	18.33 AW	38130 AAW	MTBLS	10//99-12//99
	Billings MSA, MT	S	18.64 MW	19.53 AW	38770 AAW	MTBLS	10//99-12//99
	Missoula MSA, MT	S	17.12 MW	16.90 AW	35610 AAW	MTBLS	10//99-12//99
	Nebraska	S	16.59 MW	17.28 AW	35950 AAW	NEBLS	10//99-12//99
	Lincoln MSA, NE	S	17.15 MW	18.13 AW	35660 AAW	NEBLS	10//99-12//99
	Omaha MSA, NE-IA	S	18.89 MW	21.56 AW	39300 AAW	NEBLS	10//99-12//99
	Nevada	S	21.15 MW	20.72 AW	43100 AAW	NVBLS	10//99-12//99
	Las Vegas MSA, NV-AZ	S	21.04 MW	21.78 AW	43760 AAW	NVBLS	10//99-12//99
	Reno MSA, NV	S	20.04 MW	19.33 AW	41690 AAW	NVBLS	10//99-12//99
	New Hampshire	S	16.28 MW	16.61 AW	34550 AAW	NHBLS	10//99-12//99
	Manchester PMSA, NH	S	17.06 MW	17.78 AW	35490 AAW	NHBLS	10//99-12//99
	Nashua PMSA, NH	S	18.54 MW	16.53 AW	38560 AAW	NHBLS	10//99-12//99
	Portsmouth-Rochester PMSA, NH-ME	S	16.23 MW	16.62 AW	33760 AAW	NHBLS	10//99-12//99
	New Jersey	S	22.98 MW	23.32 AW	48510 AAW	NJBLS	10//99-12//99
	Bergen-Passaic PMSA, NJ	S	26.12 MW	28.91 AW	54320 AAW	NJBLS	10//99-12//99
	Jersey City PMSA, NJ	S	25.90 MW	24.11 AW	53860 AAW	NJBLS	10//99-12//99
	Monmouth-Ocean PMSA, NJ	S	23.68 MW	20.25 AW	49250 AAW	NJBLS	10//99-12//99
	Newark PMSA, NJ	S	23.63 MW	23.88 AW	49140 AAW	NJBLS	10//99-12//99
	Trenton PMSA, NJ	S	23.64 MW	24.10 AW	49170 AAW	NJBLS	10//99-12//99
	Vineland-Millville-Bridgeton PMSA, NJ	S	24.29 MW	27.97 AW	50520 AAW	NJBLS	10//99-12//99
	New Mexico	S	17.27 MW	16.98 AW	35320 AAW	NMBLS	10//99-12//99
	Albuquerque MSA, NM	S	17.59 MW	18.05 AW	36590 AAW	NMBLS	10//99-12//99
	Las Cruces MSA, NM	S	16.75 MW	15.55 AW	34850 AAW	NMBLS	10//99-12//99
	Santa Fe MSA, NM	S	17.53 MW	18.40 AW	36470 AAW	NMBLS	10//99-12//99
	New York	S	30.04 MW	28.51 AW	59290 AAW	NYBLS	10//99-12//99
	Albany-Schenectady-Troy MSA, NY	S	17.95 MW	17.69 AW	37330 AAW	NYBLS	10//99-12//99
	Binghamton MSA, NY	S	13.31 MW	13.63 AW	27680 AAW	NYBLS	10//99-12//99
	Buffalo-Niagara Falls MSA, NY	S	21.12 MW	22.97 AW	43930 AAW	NYBLS	10//99-12//99
	Dutchess County PMSA, NY	S	21.29 MW	23.18 AW	44290 AAW	NYBLS	10//99-12//99
	Elmira MSA, NY	S	22.90 MW	24.03 AW	47640 AAW	NYBLS	10//99-12//99
	Glens Falls MSA, NY	S	17.59 MW	16.31 AW	36580 AAW	NYBLS	10//99-12//99
	Jamestown MSA, NY	S	19.19 MW	20.95 AW	39900 AAW	NYBLS	10//99-12//99
	New York PMSA, NY	S	29.79 MW	31.24 AW	61960 AAW	NYBLS	10//99-12//99
	Newburgh PMSA, NY-PA	S	18.34 MW	17.34 AW	38150 AAW	NYBLS	10//99-12//99

AAW Average annual wage	**AOH** Average offered, high	**ASH** Average starting, high	**H** Hourly	**M** Monthly	**S** Special: hourly and annual
AE Average entry wage	**AOL** Average offered, low	**ASL** Average starting, low	**HI** Highest wage paid	**MTC** Median total compensation	**TQ** Third quartile wage
AEX Average experienced wage	**APH** Average pay, high range	**AW** Average wage paid	**HR** High end range	**MW** Median wage paid	**W** Weekly
AO Average offered	**APL** Average pay, low range	**FQ** First quartile wage	**LR** Low end range	**SQ** Second quartile wage	**Y** Yearly

Occupation/Type/Industry	Location	Per	Low	Mid	High	Source	Date
Electrician	Rochester MSA, NY	S	22.82 MW	23.06 AW	47460 AAW	NYBLS	10//99-12//99
	Syracuse MSA, NY	S	15.58 MW	15.69 AW	32400 AAW	NYBLS	10//99-12//99
	Utica-Rome MSA, NY	S	17.07 MW	17.47 AW	35500 AAW	NYBLS	10//99-12//99
	North Carolina	S	14.49 MW	14.66 AW	30500 AAW	NCBLS	10//99-12//99
	Asheville MSA, NC	S	12.17 MW	11.81 AW	25310 AAW	NCBLS	10//99-12//99
	Charlotte-Gastonia-Rock Hill MSA, NC-SC	S	15.68 MW	15.19 AW	32620 AAW	NCBLS	10//99-12//99
	Fayetteville MSA, NC	S	13.41 MW	13.14 AW	27890 AAW	NCBLS	10//99-12//99
	Goldsboro MSA, NC	S	14.22 MW	13.81 AW	29570 AAW	NCBLS	10//99-12//99
	Greensboro--Winston-Salem--High Point MSA, NC	S	16.16 MW	15.54 AW	33610 AAW	NCBLS	10//99-12//99
	Greenville MSA, NC	S	11.53 MW	11.63 AW	23970 AAW	NCBLS	10//99-12//99
	Hickory-Morganton-Lenoir MSA, NC	S	12.87 MW	12.55 AW	26770 AAW	NCBLS	10//99-12//99
	Jacksonville MSA, NC	S	13.52 MW	13.07 AW	28120 AAW	NCBLS	10//99-12//99
	Raleigh-Durham-Chapel Hill MSA, NC	S	14.27 MW	14.45 AW	29680 AAW	NCBLS	10//99-12//99
	Rocky Mount MSA, NC	S	12.45 MW	12.33 AW	25900 AAW	NCBLS	10//99-12//99
	Wilmington MSA, NC	S	13.46 MW	12.79 AW	28010 AAW	NCBLS	10//99-12//99
	North Dakota	S	18.4 MW	17.96 AW	37350 AAW	NDBLS	10//99-12//99
	Fargo-Moorhead MSA, ND-MN	S	21.86 MW	22.40 AW	45460 AAW	NDBLS	10//99-12//99
	Grand Forks MSA, ND-MN	S	15.65 MW	15.24 AW	32560 AAW	NDBLS	10//99-12//99
	Ohio	S	20.97 MW	20.71 AW	43080 AAW	OHBLS	10//99-12//99
	Akron PMSA, OH	S	18.27 MW	19.11 AW	37990 AAW	OHBLS	10//99-12//99
	Canton-Massillon MSA, OH	S	16.10 MW	15.27 AW	33490 AAW	OHBLS	10//99-12//99
	Cincinnati PMSA, OH-KY-IN	S	18.04 MW	18.11 AW	37520 AAW	OHBLS	10//99-12//99
	Cleveland-Lorain-Elyria PMSA, OH	S	23.68 MW	25.40 AW	49250 AAW	OHBLS	10//99-12//99
	Columbus MSA, OH	S	18.23 MW	17.91 AW	37920 AAW	OHBLS	10//99-12//99
	Dayton-Springfield MSA, OH	S	22.55 MW	23.57 AW	46900 AAW	OHBLS	10//99-12//99
	Hamilton-Middletown PMSA, OH	S	20.99 MW	18.78 AW	43670 AAW	OHBLS	10//99-12//99
	Lima MSA, OH	S	17.27 MW	15.73 AW	35920 AAW	OHBLS	10//99-12//99
	Steubenville-Weirton MSA, OH-WV	S	18.71 MW	19.01 AW	38920 AAW	OHBLS	10//99-12//99
	Toledo MSA, OH	S	20.96 MW	22.81 AW	43610 AAW	OHBLS	10//99-12//99
	Youngstown-Warren MSA, OH	S	23.19 MW	24.05 AW	48230 AAW	OHBLS	10//99-12//99
	Oklahoma	S	16.18 MW	16.68 AW	34690 AAW	OKBLS	10//99-12//99
	Enid MSA, OK	S	15.24 MW	15.42 AW	31690 AAW	OKBLS	10//99-12//99
	Lawton MSA, OK	S	15.46 MW	15.29 AW	32150 AAW	OKBLS	10//99-12//99
	Oklahoma City MSA, OK	S	16.40 MW	15.89 AW	34100 AAW	OKBLS	10//99-12//99
	Tulsa MSA, OK	S	17.20 MW	17.55 AW	35770 AAW	OKBLS	10//99-12//99
	Oregon	S	24.47 MW	23.85 AW	49600 AAW	ORBLS	10//99-12//99
	Corvallis MSA, OR	S	21.88 MW	22.98 AW	45500 AAW	ORBLS	10//99-12//99
	Eugene-Springfield MSA, OR	S	23.66 MW	24.16 AW	49200 AAW	ORBLS	10//99-12//99
	Medford-Ashland MSA, OR	S	22.45 MW	23.60 AW	46700 AAW	ORBLS	10//99-12//99
	Portland-Vancouver PMSA, OR-WA	S	25.58 MW	27.30 AW	53210 AAW	ORBLS	10//99-12//99
	Salem PMSA, OR	S	22.42 MW	23.37 AW	46640 AAW	ORBLS	10//99-12//99
	Pennsylvania	S	18.56 MW	19.69 AW	40960 AAW	PABLS	10//99-12//99
	Allentown-Bethlehem-Easton MSA, PA	S	21.66 MW	22.13 AW	45050 AAW	PABLS	10//99-12//99
	Altoona MSA, PA	S	16.48 MW	15.40 AW	34280 AAW	PABLS	10//99-12//99
	Erie MSA, PA	S	21.42 MW	22.36 AW	44550 AAW	PABLS	10//99-12//99
	Harrisburg-Lebanon-Carlisle MSA, PA	S	16.77 MW	17.49 AW	34880 AAW	PABLS	10//99-12//99
	Johnstown MSA, PA	S	17.47 MW	17.39 AW	36350 AAW	PABLS	10//99-12//99
	Lancaster MSA, PA	S	20.49 MW	19.56 AW	42610 AAW	PABLS	10//99-12//99
	Philadelphia PMSA, PA-NJ	S	23.35 MW	24.66 AW	48560 AAW	PABLS	10//99-12//99
	Pittsburgh MSA, PA	S	18.79 MW	18.18 AW	39080 AAW	PABLS	10//99-12//99
	Reading MSA, PA	S	19.63 MW	20.54 AW	40840 AAW	PABLS	10//99-12//99
	Scranton--Wilkes-Barre--Hazleton MSA, PA	S	19.60 MW	17.61 AW	40760 AAW	PABLS	10//99-12//99
	Sharon MSA, PA	S	14.46 MW	14.30 AW	30070 AAW	PABLS	10//99-12//99
	Williamsport MSA, PA	S	12.56 MW	12.53 AW	26120 AAW	PABLS	10//99-12//99
	York MSA, PA	S	15.67 MW	15.35 AW	32600 AAW	PABLS	10//99-12//99
	Rhode Island	S	18.17 MW	18.01 AW	37470 AAW	RIBLS	10//99-12//99
	Providence-Fall River-Warwick MSA, RI-MA	S	18.25 MW	18.34 AW	37970 AAW	RIBLS	10//99-12//99
	South Carolina	S	15.22 MW	15.75 AW	32770 AAW	SCBLS	10//99-12//99

Occupation/Type/Industry	Location	Per	Low	Mid	High	Source	Date
Electrician	Charleston-North Charleston MSA, SC	S	18.12 MW	17.23 AW	37690 AAW	SCBLS	10//99-12//99
	Columbia MSA, SC	S	16.96 MW	16.26 AW	35270 AAW	SCBLS	10//99-12//99
	Florence MSA, SC	S	13.83 MW	13.89 AW	28760 AAW	SCBLS	10//99-12//99
	Greenville-Spartanburg-Anderson MSA, SC	S	13.61 MW	12.61 AW	28310 AAW	SCBLS	10//99-12//99
	Myrtle Beach MSA, SC	S	12.85 MW	12.93 AW	26720 AAW	SCBLS	10//99-12//99
	Sumter MSA, SC	S	15.38 MW	15.31 AW	31980 AAW	SCBLS	10//99-12//99
	South Dakota	S	15.28 MW	15.26 AW	31740 AAW	SDBLS	10//99-12//99
	Rapid City MSA, SD	S	14.02 MW	14.13 AW	29160 AAW	SDBLS	10//99-12//99
	Sioux Falls MSA, SD	S	16.16 MW	16.68 AW	33600 AAW	SDBLS	10//99-12//99
	Tennessee	S	17.29 MW	17.07 AW	35510 AAW	TNBLS	10//99-12//99
	Chattanooga MSA, TN-GA	S	19.48 MW	21.91 AW	40510 AAW	TNBLS	10//99-12//99
	Clarksville-Hopkinsville MSA, TN-KY	S	17.38 MW	17.80 AW	36150 AAW	TNBLS	10//99-12//99
	Jackson MSA, TN	S	15.33 MW	14.56 AW	31880 AAW	TNBLS	10//99-12//99
	Johnson City-Kingsport-Bristol MSA, TN-VA	S	15.01 MW	14.35 AW	31220 AAW	TNBLS	10//99-12//99
	Knoxville MSA, TN	S	18.78 MW	19.21 AW	39050 AAW	TNBLS	10//99-12//99
	Memphis MSA, TN-AR-MS	S	17.13 MW	17.61 AW	35630 AAW	MSBLS	10//99-12//99
	Nashville MSA, TN	S	16.34 MW	16.59 AW	33990 AAW	TNBLS	10//99-12//99
	Texas	S	17	16.97 AW	35300 AAW	TXBLS	10//99-12//99
	Abilene MSA, TX	S	14.73 MW	15.07 AW	30630 AAW	TXBLS	10//99-12//99
	Amarillo MSA, TX	S	19.61 MW	19.75 AW	40780 AAW	TXBLS	10//99-12//99
	Austin-San Marcos MSA, TX	S	17.94 MW	18.39 AW	37320 AAW	TXBLS	10//99-12//99
	Beaumont-Port Arthur MSA, TX	S	18.62 MW	18.74 AW	38740 AAW	TXBLS	10//99-12//99
	Brazoria PMSA, TX	S	20.66 MW	21.76 AW	42970 AAW	TXBLS	10//99-12//99
	Brownsville-Harlingen-San Benito MSA, TX	S	10.44 MW	10.06 AW	21710 AAW	TXBLS	10//99-12//99
	Bryan-College Station MSA, TX	S	12.99 MW	13.59 AW	27020 AAW	TXBLS	10//99-12//99
	Corpus Christi MSA, TX	S	15.99 MW	15.69 AW	33260 AAW	TXBLS	10//99-12//99
	Dallas PMSA, TX	S	16.67 MW	16.38 AW	34670 AAW	TXBLS	10//99-12//99
	El Paso MSA, TX	S	13.57 MW	13.84 AW	28230 AAW	TXBLS	10//99-12//99
	Fort Worth-Arlington PMSA, TX	S	19.13 MW	17.87 AW	39800 AAW	TXBLS	10//99-12//99
	Galveston-Texas City PMSA, TX	S	16.61 MW	17.73 AW	34560 AAW	TXBLS	10//99-12//99
	Houston PMSA, TX	S	17.12 MW	17.17 AW	35600 AAW	TXBLS	10//99-12//99
	Killeen-Temple MSA, TX	S	13.80 MW	13.29 AW	28710 AAW	TXBLS	10//99-12//99
	Laredo MSA, TX	S	14.74 MW	14.99 AW	30660 AAW	TXBLS	10//99-12//99
	Longview-Marshall MSA, TX	S	12.95 MW	11.97 AW	26940 AAW	TXBLS	10//99-12//99
	Lubbock MSA, TX	S	14.76 MW	15.45 AW	30710 AAW	TXBLS	10//99-12//99
	McAllen-Edinburg-Mission MSA, TX	S	12.38 MW	10.51 AW	25750 AAW	TXBLS	10//99-12//99
	Odessa-Midland MSA, TX	S	14.04 MW	13.67 AW	29210 AAW	TXBLS	10//99-12//99
	San Angelo MSA, TX	S	14.72 MW	15.22 AW	30620 AAW	TXBLS	10//99-12//99
	San Antonio MSA, TX	S	17.61 MW	18.55 AW	36640 AAW	TXBLS	10//99-12//99
	Sherman-Denison MSA, TX	S	18.02 MW	18.38 AW	37470 AAW	TXBLS	10//99-12//99
	Texarkana MSA, TX-Texarkana, AR	S	17.18 MW	18.22 AW	35730 AAW	TXBLS	10//99-12//99
	Tyler MSA, TX	S	14.14 MW	13.86 AW	29410 AAW	TXBLS	10//99-12//99
	Victoria MSA, TX	S	16.55 MW	16.50 AW	34410 AAW	TXBLS	10//99-12//99
	Waco MSA, TX	S	14.77 MW	15.16 AW	30720 AAW	TXBLS	10//99-12//99
	Wichita Falls MSA, TX	S	13.49 MW	13.10 AW	28060 AAW	TXBLS	10//99-12//99
	Utah	S	18.54 MW	18.26 AW	37970 AAW	UTBLS	10//99-12//99
	Provo-Orem MSA, UT	S	15.93 MW	15.80 AW	33140 AAW	UTBLS	10//99-12//99
	Salt Lake City-Ogden MSA, UT	S	19.30 MW	20.04 AW	40150 AAW	UTBLS	10//99-12//99
	Vermont	S	17.11 MW	17.09 AW	35550 AAW	VTBLS	10//99-12//99
	Burlington MSA, VT	S	17.14 MW	17.44 AW	35660 AAW	VTBLS	10//99-12//99
	Virginia	S	15.45 MW	15.85 AW	32960 AAW	VABLS	10//99-12//99
	Charlottesville MSA, VA	S	14.33 MW	12.81 AW	29810 AAW	VABLS	10//99-12//99
	Danville MSA, VA	S	13.75 MW	14.35 AW	28600 AAW	VABLS	10//99-12//99
	Lynchburg MSA, VA	S	13.95 MW	12.85 AW	29020 AAW	VABLS	10//99-12//99
	Norfolk-Virginia Beach-Newport News MSA, VA-NC	S	15.22 MW	14.95 AW	31660 AAW	VABLS	10//99-12//99
	Richmond-Petersburg MSA, VA	S	18.30 MW	18.81 AW	38060 AAW	VABLS	10//99-12//99
	Roanoke MSA, VA	S	13.67 MW	13.15 AW	28440 AAW	VABLS	10//99-12//99

AAW Average annual wage	**AOH** Average offered, high	**ASH** Average starting, high	**H** Hourly	**M** Monthly	**S** Special: hourly and annual
AE Average entry wage	**AOL** Average offered, low	**ASL** Average starting, low	**HI** Highest wage paid	**MTC** Median total compensation	**TQ** Third quartile wage
AEX Average experienced wage	**APH** Average pay, high range	**AW** Average wage paid	**HR** High end range	**MW** Median wage paid	**W** Weekly
AO Average offered	**APL** Average pay, low range	**FQ** First quartile wage	**LR** Low end range	**SQ** Second quartile wage	**Y** Yearly

Occupation/Type/Industry	Location	Per	Low	Mid	High	Source	Date
Electrician	Washington	S	22.51 MW	22.18 AW	46130 AAW	WABLS	10//99-12//99
	Bellingham MSA, WA	S	21.36 MW	22.12 AW	44430 AAW	WABLS	10//99-12//99
	Olympia PMSA, WA	S	21.94 MW	23.47 AW	45630 AAW	WABLS	10//99-12//99
	Richland-Kennewick-Pasco MSA, WA	S	23.24 MW	24.17 AW	48340 AAW	WABLS	10//99-12//99
	Seattle-Bellevue-Everett PMSA, WA	S	22.77 MW	23.68 AW	47370 AAW	WABLS	10//99-12//99
	Spokane MSA, WA	S	19.91 MW	19.91 AW	41420 AAW	WABLS	10//99-12//99
	Tacoma PMSA, WA	S	20.23 MW	20.69 AW	42080 AAW	WABLS	10//99-12//99
	Yakima MSA, WA	S	16.41 MW	12.89 AW	34140 AAW	WABLS	10//99-12//99
	West Virginia	S	18.26 MW	17.42 AW	36240 AAW	WVBLS	10//99-12//99
	Charleston MSA, WV	S	18.00 MW	19.26 AW	37440 AAW	WVBLS	10//99-12//99
	Huntington-Ashland MSA, WV-KY-OH	S	20.83 MW	22.57 AW	43320 AAW	WVBLS	10//99-12//99
	Parkersburg-Marietta MSA, WV-OH	S	20.36 MW	21.77 AW	42350 AAW	WVBLS	10//99-12//99
	Wheeling MSA, WV-OH	S	15.14 MW	13.30 AW	31500 AAW	WVBLS	10//99-12//99
	Wisconsin	S	22.89 MW	22.31 AW	46400 AAW	WIBLS	10//99-12//99
	Appleton-Oshkosh-Neenah MSA, WI	S	22.20 MW	22.04 AW	46180 AAW	WIBLS	10//99-12//99
	Eau Claire MSA, WI	S	17.75 MW	15.72 AW	36930 AAW	WIBLS	10//99-12//99
	Green Bay MSA, WI	S	20.53 MW	22.14 AW	42710 AAW	WIBLS	10//99-12//99
	Janesville-Beloit MSA, WI	S	21.12 MW	22.30 AW	43930 AAW	WIBLS	10//99-12//99
	Kenosha PMSA, WI	S	22.99 MW	24.09 AW	47830 AAW	WIBLS	10//99-12//99
	La Crosse MSA, WI-MN	S	16.30 MW	16.09 AW	33910 AAW	WIBLS	10//99-12//99
	Madison MSA, WI	S	20.13 MW	21.64 AW	41860 AAW	WIBLS	10//99-12//99
	Milwaukee-Waukesha PMSA, WI	S	26.53 MW	26.70 AW	55180 AAW	WIBLS	10//99-12//99
	Racine PMSA, WI	S	20.64 MW	22.68 AW	42930 AAW	WIBLS	10//99-12//99
	Sheboygan MSA, WI	S	20.75 MW	19.98 AW	43150 AAW	WIBLS	10//99-12//99
	Wausau MSA, WI	S	21.26 MW	22.90 AW	44220 AAW	WIBLS	10//99-12//99
	Wyoming	S	18.42 MW	17.57 AW	36540 AAW	WYBLS	10//99-12//99
	Casper MSA, WY	S	16.08 MW	17.65 AW	33440 AAW	WYBLS	10//99-12//99
	Cheyenne MSA, WY	S	16.43 MW	17.76 AW	34170 AAW	WYBLS	10//99-12//99
	Puerto Rico	S	8.45 MW	9.12 AW	18970 AAW	PRBLS	10//99-12//99
	Aguadilla MSA, PR	S	7.38 MW	6.88 AW	15350 AAW	PRBLS	10//99-12//99
	Arecibo PMSA, PR	S	6.72 MW	6.23 AW	13970 AAW	PRBLS	10//99-12//99
	Caguas PMSA, PR	S	8.31 MW	8.57 AW	17280 AAW	PRBLS	10//99-12//99
	Mayaguez MSA, PR	S	8.21 MW	7.73 AW	17070 AAW	PRBLS	10//99-12//99
	Ponce MSA, PR	S	8.26 MW	7.89 AW	17190 AAW	PRBLS	10//99-12//99
	San Juan-Bayamon PMSA, PR	S	9.48 MW	9.17 AW	19730 AAW	PRBLS	10//99-12//99
	Virgin Islands	S	11.54 MW	12.28 AW	25550 AAW	VIBLS	10//99-12//99
	Guam	S	12.84 MW	13.97 AW	29060 AAW	GUBLS	10//99-12//99
Nonunion, Construction	Central	H		17.80 AW		ENR3	2000
Nonunion, Construction	Middle Atlantic	H		16.64 AW		ENR3	2000
Nonunion, Construction	New England	H		18.06 AW		ENR3	2000
Nonunion, Construction	Southeast	H		17.11 AW		ENR3	2000
Nonunion, Construction	West	H		19.64 AW		ENR3	2000
Electro-Mechanical Technician	Alabama	S	10.61 MW	11.69 AW	24320 AAW	ALBLS	10//99-12//99
	Arizona	S	18.02 MW	17.70 AW	36820 AAW	AZBLS	10//99-12//99
	Arkansas	S	15.95 MW	17.70 AW	36820 AAW	ARBLS	10//99-12//99
	California	S	17 MW	18.17 AW	37790 AAW	CABLS	10//99-12//99
	Colorado	S	17.69 MW	16.88 AW	35110 AAW	COBLS	10//99-12//99
	Connecticut	S	15.35 MW	15.63 AW	32510 AAW	CTBLS	10//99-12//99
	Florida	S	16.77 MW	17.76 AW	36950 AAW	FLBLS	10//99-12//99
	Georgia	S	10.23 MW	11.72 AW	24380 AAW	GABLS	10//99-12//99
	Hawaii	S	15.81 MW	16.46 AW	34230 AAW	HIBLS	10//99-12//99
	Idaho	S	23.86 MW	23.20 AW	48250 AAW	IDBLS	10//99-12//99
	Illinois	S	23.09 MW	25.32 AW	52660 AAW	ILBLS	10//99-12//99
	Indiana	S	16.47 MW	16.45 AW	34220 AAW	INBLS	10//99-12//99
	Iowa	S	12.28 MW	13.30 AW	27660 AAW	IABLS	10//99-12//99
	Kansas	S	14.82 MW	14.51 AW	30180 AAW	KSBLS	10//99-12//99
	Kentucky	S	14 MW	14.96 AW	31110 AAW	KYBLS	10//99-12//99
	Louisiana	S	22.9 MW	21.36 AW	44430 AAW	LABLS	10//99-12//99
	Maine	S	15.55 MW	16.79 AW	34930 AAW	MEBLS	10//99-12//99
	Maryland	S	16.7 MW	17.93 AW	37290 AAW	MDBLS	10//99-12//99
	Massachusetts	S	18.77 MW	19.35 AW	40240 AAW	MABLS	10//99-12//99
	Michigan	S	16.18 MW	17.31 AW	36000 AAW	MIBLS	10//99-12//99
	Minnesota	S	18.64 MW	18.73 AW	38970 AAW	MNBLS	10//99-12//99
	Mississippi	S	13.41 MW	15.63 AW	32500 AAW	MSBLS	10//99-12//99
	Missouri	S	18.54 MW	19.28 AW	40090 AAW	MOBLS	10//99-12//99
	Montana	S	14.39 MW	14.86 AW	30910 AAW	MTBLS	10//99-12//99

AAW Average annual wage	AOH Average offered, high	ASH Average starting, high	H Hourly	M Monthly	S Special: hourly and annual
AE Average entry wage	AOL Average offered, low	ASL Average starting, low	HI Highest wage paid	MTC Median total compensation	TQ Third quartile wage
AEX Average experienced wage	APH Average pay, high range	AW Average wage paid	HR High end range	MW Median wage paid	W Weekly
AO Average offered	APL Average pay, low range	FQ First quartile wage	LR Low end range	SQ Second quartile wage	Y Yearly

Occupation/Type/Industry	Location	Per	Low	Mid	High	Source	Date
Electro-Mechanical Technician	Nebraska	S	17.93 MW	19.26 AW	40060 AAW	NEBLS	10//99-12//99
	Nevada	S	16.11 MW	16.35 AW	34010 AAW	NVBLS	10//99-12//99
	New Hampshire	S	13.21 MW	14.07 AW	29270 AAW	NHBLS	10//99-12//99
	New Jersey	S	14.49 MW	15.92 AW	33110 AAW	NJBLS	10//99-12//99
	New Mexico	S	12.85 MW	12.85 AW	26730 AAW	NMBLS	10//99-12//99
	New York	S	15.84 MW	16.63 AW	34590 AAW	NYBLS	10//99-12//99
	North Carolina	S	17.39 MW	17.62 AW	36650 AAW	NCBLS	10//99-12//99
	Ohio	S	16.14 MW	16.57 AW	34470 AAW	OHBLS	10//99-12//99
	Oregon	S	17.95 MW	16.83 AW	35020 AAW	ORBLS	10//99-12//99
	Pennsylvania	S	17.7 MW	18.18 AW	37810 AAW	PABLS	10//99-12//99
	Rhode Island	S	23.66 MW	26.41 AW	54930 AAW	RIBLS	10//99-12//99
	South Carolina	S	22.66 MW	22.93 AW	47700 AAW	SCBLS	10//99-12//99
	Tennessee	S	14.9 MW	14.94 AW	31070 AAW	TNBLS	10//99-12//99
	Texas	S	15.15 MW	16.25 AW	33790 AAW	TXBLS	10//99-12//99
	Utah	S	16.66 MW	16.60 AW	34530 AAW	UTBLS	10//99-12//99
	Virginia	S	13.5 MW	15.64 AW	32530 AAW	VABLS	10//99-12//99
	Washington	S	22.69 MW	21.74 AW	45210 AAW	WABLS	10//99-12//99
	West Virginia	S	18.14 MW	17.83 AW	37090 AAW	WVBLS	10//99-12//99
	Wisconsin	S	18.9 MW	19.22 AW	39990 AAW	WIBLS	10//99-12//99
	Puerto Rico	S	8.04 MW	8.77 AW	18230 AAW	PRBLS	10//99-12//99
Electromechanical Equipment Assembler	Alabama	S	8.44 MW	9.53 AW	19830 AAW	ALBLS	10//99-12//99
	Arizona	S	9.12 MW	9.37 AW	19500 AAW	AZBLS	10//99-12//99
	California	S	9.56 MW	10.09 AW	20980 AAW	CABLS	10//99-12//99
	Colorado	S	9.15 MW	9.30 AW	19340 AAW	COBLS	10//99-12//99
	Connecticut	S	13.87 MW	14.65 AW	30470 AAW	CTBLS	10//99-12//99
	Florida	S	10.61 MW	11.42 AW	23750 AAW	FLBLS	10//99-12//99
	Georgia	S	12.55 MW	13.09 AW	27220 AAW	GABLS	10//99-12//99
	Illinois	S	10.78 MW	11.47 AW	23860 AAW	ILBLS	10//99-12//99
	Indiana	S	10.2 MW	11.35 AW	23600 AAW	INBLS	10//99-12//99
	Iowa	S	10.72 MW	11.38 AW	23670 AAW	IABLS	10//99-12//99
	Kansas	S	7.62 MW	7.87 AW	16380 AAW	KSBLS	10//99-12//99
	Kentucky	S	10.98 MW	9.98 AW	20750 AAW	KYBLS	10//99-12//99
	Maine	S	10.39 MW	10.69 AW	22240 AAW	MEBLS	10//99-12//99
	Maryland	S	11.68 MW	12.15 AW	25270 AAW	MDBLS	10//99-12//99
	Massachusetts	S	12.5 MW	12.92 AW	26870 AAW	MABLS	10//99-12//99
	Michigan	S	12.76 MW	13.22 AW	27490 AAW	MIBLS	10//99-12//99
	Minnesota	S	14.22 MW	13.62 AW	28330 AAW	MNBLS	10//99-12//99
	Mississippi	S	7.72 MW	7.94 AW	16520 AAW	MSBLS	10//99-12//99
	Missouri	S	11.82 MW	13.97 AW	29060 AAW	MOBLS	10//99-12//99
	Nebraska	S	14.41 MW	13.63 AW	28360 AAW	NEBLS	10//99-12//99
	Nevada	S	9.7 MW	9.96 AW	20710 AAW	NVBLS	10//99-12//99
	New Hampshire	S	11.09 MW	11.21 AW	23330 AAW	NHBLS	10//99-12//99
	New Jersey	S	12.48 MW	13.97 AW	29060 AAW	NJBLS	10//99-12//99
	New York	S	10.17 MW	11.53 AW	23970 AAW	NYBLS	10//99-12//99
	North Carolina	S	9.43 MW	9.86 AW	20500 AAW	NCBLS	10//99-12//99
	Ohio	S	11.08 MW	11.13 AW	23150 AAW	OHBLS	10//99-12//99
	Oklahoma	S	9.78 MW	10.03 AW	20860 AAW	OKBLS	10//99-12//99
	Oregon	S	10.4 MW	10.88 AW	22620 AAW	ORBLS	10//99-12//99
	Pennsylvania	S	14.21 MW	14.55 AW	30260 AAW	PABLS	10//99-12//99
	Rhode Island	S	8.63 MW	9.32 AW	19390 AAW	RIBLS	10//99-12//99
	South Carolina	S	12.24 MW	12.87 AW	26770 AAW	SCBLS	10//99-12//99
	Tennessee	S	10.51 MW	11.14 AW	23180 AAW	TNBLS	10//99-12//99
	Texas	S	10.01 MW	10.73 AW	22320 AAW	TXBLS	10//99-12//99
	Utah	S	11.33 MW	11.60 AW	24120 AAW	UTBLS	10//99-12//99
	Virginia	S	10.29 MW	11.66 AW	24260 AAW	VABLS	10//99-12//99
	Washington	S	12.46 MW	12.55 AW	26100 AAW	WABLS	10//99-12//99
	Puerto Rico	S	6.02 MW	6.05 AW	12580 AAW	PRBLS	10//99-12//99
Electronic Equipment Installer and Repairer							
Motor Vehicle	Alabama	S	14.83 MW	14.13 AW	29390 AAW	ALBLS	10//99-12//99
Motor Vehicle	Arkansas	S	9.85 MW	10.69 AW	22240 AAW	ARBLS	10//99-12//99
Motor Vehicle	California	S	10.89 MW	11.51 AW	23950 AAW	CABLS	10//99-12//99
Motor Vehicle	Los Angeles-Long Beach PMSA, CA	S	10.98 MW	10.44 AW	22840 AAW	CABLS	10//99-12//99
Motor Vehicle	Colorado	S	8.3 MW	10.35 AW	21520 AAW	COBLS	10//99-12//99
Motor Vehicle	Denver PMSA, CO	S	15.96 MW	17.66 AW	33200 AAW	COBLS	10//99-12//99
Motor Vehicle	Washington PMSA, DC-MD-VA-WV	S	11.62 MW	11.90 AW	24160 AAW	DCBLS	10//99-12//99
Motor Vehicle	Florida	S	10.94 MW	12.02 AW	25000 AAW	FLBLS	10//99-12//99

AAW Average annual wage	**AOH** Average offered, high	**ASH** Average starting, high	**H** Hourly	**M** Monthly	**S** Special: hourly and annual
AE Average entry wage	**AOL** Average offered, low	**ASL** Average starting, low	**HI** Highest wage paid	**MTC** Median total compensation	**TQ** Third quartile wage
AEX Average experienced wage	**APH** Average pay, high range	**AW** Average wage paid	**HR** High end range	**MW** Median wage paid	**W** Weekly
AO Average offered	**APL** Average pay, low range	**FQ** First quartile wage	**LR** Low end range	**SQ** Second quartile wage	**Y** Yearly

Occupation/Type/Industry	Location	Per	Low	Mid	High	Source	Date
Electronic Equipment Installer and Repairer							
Motor Vehicle	Orlando MSA, FL	S	12.36 MW	12.20 AW	25700 AAW	FLBLS	10//99-12//99
Motor Vehicle	Georgia	S	11.05 MW	11.01 AW	22890 AAW	GABLS	10//99-12//99
Motor Vehicle	Atlanta MSA, GA	S	11.01 MW	11.06 AW	22900 AAW	GABLS	10//99-12//99
Motor Vehicle	Idaho	S	11.11 MW	14.09 AW	29300 AAW	IDBLS	10//99-12//99
Motor Vehicle	Illinois	S	13.25 MW	13.14 AW	27330 AAW	ILBLS	10//99-12//99
Motor Vehicle	Chicago PMSA, IL	S	12.93 MW	13.28 AW	26880 AAW	ILBLS	10//99-12//99
Motor Vehicle	Indiana	S	13.47 MW	14.12 AW	29370 AAW	INBLS	10//99-12//99
Motor Vehicle	Iowa	S	10.21 MW	11.70 AW	24340 AAW	IABLS	10//99-12//99
Motor Vehicle	Kentucky	S	8.8 MW	9.93 AW	20650 AAW	KYBLS	10//99-12//99
Motor Vehicle	Louisville MSA, KY-IN	S	10.06 MW	8.86 AW	20920 AAW	KYBLS	10//99-12//99
Motor Vehicle	Louisiana	S	12.01 MW	12.13 AW	25220 AAW	LABLS	10//99-12//99
Motor Vehicle	Maryland	S	12.01 MW	11.94 AW	24840 AAW	MDBLS	10//99-12//99
Motor Vehicle	Massachusetts	S	14.45 MW	14.83 AW	30840 AAW	MABLS	10//99-12//99
Motor Vehicle	Boston PMSA, MA-NH	S	14.48 MW	13.35 AW	30130 AAW	MABLS	10//99-12//99
Motor Vehicle	Michigan	S	13.02 MW	14.45 AW	30070 AAW	MIBLS	10//99-12//99
Motor Vehicle	Detroit PMSA, MI	S	17.03 MW	18.33 AW	35420 AAW	MIBLS	10//99-12//99
Motor Vehicle	Mississippi	S	7.73 MW	7.87 AW	16370 AAW	MSBLS	10//99-12//99
Motor Vehicle	Missouri	S	11.78 MW	12.70 AW	26410 AAW	MOBLS	10//99-12//99
Motor Vehicle	Nevada	S	8.37 MW	11.05 AW	22970 AAW	NVBLS	10//99-12//99
Motor Vehicle	New Jersey	S	13.35 MW	13.98 AW	29080 AAW	NJBLS	10//99-12//99
Motor Vehicle	New York	S	13.59 MW	13.49 AW	28060 AAW	NYBLS	10//99-12//99
Motor Vehicle	Albany-Schenectady-Troy MSA, NY	S	15.26 MW	15.08 AW	31740 AAW	NYBLS	10//99-12//99
Motor Vehicle	New York PMSA, NY	S	18.27 MW	19.19 AW	38000 AAW	NYBLS	10//99-12//99
Motor Vehicle	North Carolina	S	14.74 MW	14.78 AW	30750 AAW	NCBLS	10//99-12//99
Motor Vehicle	Ohio	S	10.7 MW	11.50 AW	23910 AAW	OHBLS	10//99-12//99
Motor Vehicle	Oklahoma	S	11.49 MW	12.78 AW	26580 AAW	OKBLS	10//99-12//99
Motor Vehicle	Oregon	S	11.78 MW	12.81 AW	26650 AAW	ORBLS	10//99-12//99
Motor Vehicle	Portland-Vancouver PMSA, OR-WA	S	15.60 MW	15.60 AW	32460 AAW	ORBLS	10//99-12//99
Motor Vehicle	Pennsylvania	S	10.05 MW	11.03 AW	22950 AAW	PABLS	10//99-12//99
Motor Vehicle	Rhode Island	S	11.93 MW	11.71 AW	24350 AAW	RIBLS	10//99-12//99
Motor Vehicle	South Carolina	S	8.27 MW	8.55 AW	17780 AAW	SCBLS	10//99-12//99
Motor Vehicle	Tennessee	S	10.58 MW	10.87 AW	22620 AAW	TNBLS	10//99-12//99
Motor Vehicle	Texas	S	12.23 MW	15.21 AW	31630 AAW	TXBLS	10//99-12//99
Motor Vehicle	Dallas PMSA, TX	S	14.12 MW	12.98 AW	29360 AAW	TXBLS	10//99-12//99
Motor Vehicle	Texarkana MSA, TX-Texarkana, AR	S	8.95 MW	9.23 AW	18620 AAW	TXBLS	10//99-12//99
Motor Vehicle	Utah	S	12.18 MW	12.41 AW	25800 AAW	UTBLS	10//99-12//99
Motor Vehicle	Salt Lake City-Ogden MSA, UT	S	12.77 MW	12.73 AW	26570 AAW	UTBLS	10//99-12//99
Motor Vehicle	Virginia	S	8.76 MW	10.08 AW	20960 AAW	VABLS	10//99-12//99
Motor Vehicle	Washington	S	17.07 MW	17.02 AW	35400 AAW	WABLS	10//99-12//99
Motor Vehicle	Seattle-Bellevue-Everett PMSA, WA	S	16.73 MW	16.99 AW	34800 AAW	WABLS	10//99-12//99
Motor Vehicle	Wisconsin	S	10.96 MW	11.39 AW	23700 AAW	WIBLS	10//99-12//99
Motor Vehicle	Milwaukee-Waukesha PMSA, WI	S	11.37 MW	10.98 AW	23640 AAW	WIBLS	10//99-12//99
Motor Vehicle	Puerto Rico	S	6.46 MW	7.47 AW	15550 AAW	PRBLS	10//99-12//99
Electronic Home Entertainment Equipment Installer and Repairer							
	Alabama	S	10.82 MW	11.48 AW	23880 AAW	ALBLS	10//99-12//99
	Arizona	S	10.65 MW	12.86 AW	26750 AAW	AZBLS	10//99-12//99
	Arkansas	S	9.96 MW	10.53 AW	21900 AAW	ARBLS	10//99-12//99
	California	S	11.16 MW	14.02 AW	29160 AAW	CABLS	10//99-12//99
	Colorado	S	12.99 MW	13.99 AW	29100 AAW	COBLS	10//99-12//99
	Connecticut	S	13.85 MW	14.46 AW	30080 AAW	CTBLS	10//99-12//99
	Delaware	S	17.74 MW	16.19 AW	33670 AAW	DEBLS	10//99-12//99
	Florida	S	13.18 MW	13.81 AW	28730 AAW	FLBLS	10//99-12//99
	Georgia	S	10.61 MW	11.91 AW	24770 AAW	GABLS	10//99-12//99
	Hawaii	S	17.22 MW	16.03 AW	33340 AAW	HIBLS	10//99-12//99
	Idaho	S	12.44 MW	13.33 AW	27730 AAW	IDBLS	10//99-12//99
	Illinois	S	13.65 MW	13.25 AW	27560 AAW	ILBLS	10//99-12//99
	Indiana	S	13.6 MW	13.51 AW	28100 AAW	INBLS	10//99-12//99
	Iowa	S	12.17 MW	11.87 AW	24690 AAW	IABLS	10//99-12//99
	Kansas	S	11.69 MW	11.73 AW	24390 AAW	KSBLS	10//99-12//99
	Kentucky	S	11.72 MW	15.36 AW	31950 AAW	KYBLS	10//99-12//99
	Louisiana	S	11.79 MW	11.89 AW	24730 AAW	LABLS	10//99-12//99

Occupation/Type/Industry	Location	Per	Low	Mid	High	Source	Date
Electronic Home Entertainment Equipment Installer and Repairer							
	Maine	S	10.32 MW	11.54 AW	24010 AAW	MEBLS	10//99-12//99
	Maryland	S	17.98 MW	16.48 AW	34280 AAW	MDBLS	10//99-12//99
	Massachusetts	S	14.9 MW	14.59 AW	30350 AAW	MABLS	10//99-12//99
	Michigan	S	10.5 MW	11.63 AW	24180 AAW	MIBLS	10//99-12//99
	Minnesota	S	8.33 MW	12.81 AW	26650 AAW	MNBLS	10//99-12//99
	Mississippi	S	8.64 MW	9.32 AW	19390 AAW	MSBLS	10//99-12//99
	Missouri	S	11.6 MW	12.47 AW	25950 AAW	MOBLS	10//99-12//99
	Montana	S	12.05 MW	12.17 AW	25310 AAW	MTBLS	10//99-12//99
	Nebraska	S	11.63 MW	12.30 AW	25570 AAW	NEBLS	10//99-12//99
	Nevada	S	16.65 MW	14.99 AW	31190 AAW	NVBLS	10//99-12//99
	New Hampshire	S	12.59 MW	13.63 AW	28360 AAW	NHBLS	10//99-12//99
	New Jersey	S	13.16 MW	14.14 AW	29410 AAW	NJBLS	10//99-12//99
	New Mexico	S	8.98 MW	10.66 AW	22180 AAW	NMBLS	10//99-12//99
	New York	S	12.9 MW	14.25 AW	29630 AAW	NYBLS	10//99-12//99
	North Carolina	S	12.99 MW	13.13 AW	27320 AAW	NCBLS	10//99-12//99
	North Dakota	S	11.06 MW	11.09 AW	23070 AAW	NDBLS	10//99-12//99
	Ohio	S	12.1 MW	13.31 AW	27680 AAW	OHBLS	10//99-12//99
	Oklahoma	S	11.84 MW	11.53 AW	23970 AAW	OKBLS	10//99-12//99
	Oregon	S	10.35 MW	11.64 AW	24210 AAW	ORBLS	10//99-12//99
	Pennsylvania	S	10.14 MW	11.40 AW	23710 AAW	PABLS	10//99-12//99
	South Carolina	S	6.19 MW	6.39 AW	13290 AAW	SCBLS	10//99-12//99
	South Dakota	S	10.16 MW	11.00 AW	22870 AAW	SDBLS	10//99-12//99
	Tennessee	S	10.63 MW	14.09 AW	29300 AAW	TNBLS	10//99-12//99
	Texas	S	10.88 MW	11.72 AW	24380 AAW	TXBLS	10//99-12//99
	Utah	S	10.63 MW	11.28 AW	23470 AAW	UTBLS	10//99-12//99
	Vermont	S	10.32 MW	10.71 AW	22270 AAW	VTBLS	10//99-12//99
	Virginia	S	10.52 MW	12.94 AW	26920 AAW	VABLS	10//99-12//99
	Washington	S	14.64 MW	14.52 AW	30200 AAW	WABLS	10//99-12//99
	West Virginia	S	8.42 MW	8.80 AW	18310 AAW	WVBLS	10//99-12//99
	Wisconsin	S	11.91 MW	12.18 AW	25340 AAW	WIBLS	10//99-12//99
	Puerto Rico	S	11.63 MW	11.09 AW	23060 AAW	PRBLS	10//99-12//99
	Guam	S	8.23 MW	9.94 AW	20670 AAW	GUBLS	10//99-12//99
Electronics Engineer							
Except Computer	Alabama	S	32.45 MW	32.70 AW	68020 AAW	ALBLS	10//99-12//99
Except Computer	Birmingham MSA, AL	S	35.36 MW	37.72 AW	73550 AAW	ALBLS	10//99-12//99
Except Computer	Mobile MSA, AL	S	32.55 MW	32.18 AW	67700 AAW	ALBLS	10//99-12//99
Except Computer	Alaska	S	30.99 MW	30.85 AW	64160 AAW	AKBLS	10//99-12//99
Except Computer	Arizona	S	35.1 MW	34.95 AW	72700 AAW	AZBLS	10//99-12//99
Except Computer	Phoenix-Mesa MSA, AZ	S	35.68 MW	36.28 AW	74210 AAW	AZBLS	10//99-12//99
Except Computer	Tucson MSA, AZ	S	30.60 MW	31.15 AW	63650 AAW	AZBLS	10//99-12//99
Except Computer	Arkansas	S	27.84 MW	28.57 AW	59430 AAW	ARBLS	10//99-12//99
Except Computer	California	S	30.7 MW	30.62 AW	63690 AAW	CABLS	10//99-12//99
Except Computer	Los Angeles-Long Beach PMSA, CA	S	28.35 MW	28.28 AW	58970 AAW	CABLS	10//99-12//99
Except Computer	Oakland PMSA, CA	S	33.71 MW	34.77 AW	70110 AAW	CABLS	10//99-12//99
Except Computer	Orange County PMSA, CA	S	27.92 MW	27.80 AW	58080 AAW	CABLS	10//99-12//99
Except Computer	Sacramento PMSA, CA	S	28.71 MW	29.45 AW	59710 AAW	CABLS	10//99-12//99
Except Computer	San Diego MSA, CA	S	30.28 MW	30.56 AW	62990 AAW	CABLS	10//99-12//99
Except Computer	San Francisco PMSA, CA	S	31.16 MW	30.64 AW	64820 AAW	CABLS	10//99-12//99
Except Computer	San Jose PMSA, CA	S	30.95 MW	30.54 AW	64370 AAW	CABLS	10//99-12//99
Except Computer	Santa Barbara-Santa Maria-Lompoc MSA, CA	S	32.66 MW	32.68 AW	67930 AAW	CABLS	10//99-12//99
Except Computer	Santa Cruz-Watsonville PMSA, CA	S	35.86 MW	37.01 AW	74580 AAW	CABLS	10//99-12//99
Except Computer	Santa Rosa PMSA, CA	S	28.14 MW	28.90 AW	58540 AAW	CABLS	10//99-12//99
Except Computer	Colorado	S	31.55 MW	31.76 AW	66060 AAW	COBLS	10//99-12//99
Except Computer	Colorado Springs MSA, CO	S	33.80 MW	32.98 AW	70310 AAW	COBLS	10//99-12//99
Except Computer	Denver PMSA, CO	S	30.39 MW	29.89 AW	63210 AAW	COBLS	10//99-12//99
Except Computer	Fort Collins-Loveland MSA, CO	S	31.23 MW	31.05 AW	64950 AAW	COBLS	10//99-12//99
Except Computer	Greeley PMSA, CO	S	30.89 MW	30.45 AW	64250 AAW	COBLS	10//99-12//99
Except Computer	Connecticut	S	27.46 MW	29.44 AW	61240 AAW	CTBLS	10//99-12//99
Except Computer	Bridgeport PMSA, CT	S	26.11 MW	23.43 AW	54300 AAW	CTBLS	10//99-12//99
Except Computer	Hartford MSA, CT	S	29.64 MW	29.04 AW	61650 AAW	CTBLS	10//99-12//99
Except Computer	New Haven-Meriden PMSA, CT	S	31.77 MW	31.41 AW	66090 AAW	CTBLS	10//99-12//99
Except Computer	Washington PMSA, DC-MD-VA-WV	S	36.59 MW	35.45 AW	76110 AAW	DCBLS	10//99-12//99
Except Computer	Florida	S	26.79 MW	26.57 AW	55270 AAW	FLBLS	10//99-12//99

AAW Average annual wage	**AOH** Average offered, high	**ASH** Average starting, high	**H** Hourly	**M** Monthly	**S** Special: hourly and annual
AE Average entry wage	**AOL** Average offered, low	**ASL** Average starting, low	**HI** Highest wage paid	**MTC** Median total compensation	**TQ** Third quartile wage
AEX Average experienced wage	**APH** Average pay, high range	**AW** Average wage paid	**HR** High end range	**MW** Median wage paid	**W** Weekly
AO Average offered	**APL** Average pay, low range	**FQ** First quartile wage	**LR** Low end range	**SQ** Second quartile wage	**Y** Yearly

Electronics Engineer

Occupation/Type/Industry	Location	Per	Low	Mid	High	Source	Date
Electronics Engineer							
Except Computer	Fort Lauderdale PMSA, FL	S	24.75 MW	24.37 AW	51470 AAW	FLBLS	10//99-12//99
Except Computer	Melbourne-Titusville-Palm Bay MSA, FL	S	28.89 MW	29.10 AW	60080 AAW	FLBLS	10//99-12//99
Except Computer	Miami PMSA, FL	S	22.52 MW	21.05 AW	46850 AAW	FLBLS	10//99-12//99
Except Computer	Pensacola MSA, FL	S	29.77 MW	29.69 AW	61920 AAW	FLBLS	10//99-12//99
Except Computer	Tampa-St. Petersburg-Clearwater MSA, FL	S	26.07 MW	27.37 AW	54220 AAW	FLBLS	
Except Computer	West Palm Beach-Boca Raton MSA, FL	S	24.85 MW	25.06 AW	51690 AAW	FLBLS	10//99-12//99
Except Computer	Georgia	S	29.38 MW	29.75 AW	61880 AAW	GABLS	10//99-12//99
Except Computer	Atlanta MSA, GA	S	30.25 MW	29.68 AW	62910 AAW	GABLS	10//99-12//99
Except Computer	Idaho	S	24.52 MW	23.42 AW	48700 AAW	IDBLS	10//99-12//99
Except Computer	Boise City MSA, ID	S	22.64 MW	23.47 AW	47090 AAW	IDBLS	10//99-12//99
Except Computer	Illinois	S	28.46 MW	28.58 AW	59450 AAW	ILBLS	10//99-12//99
Except Computer	Chicago PMSA, IL	S	28.71 MW	28.74 AW	59730 AAW	ILBLS	10//99-12//99
Except Computer	Rockford MSA, IL	S	35.06 MW	33.66 AW	72930 AAW	ILBLS	10//99-12//99
Except Computer	Indiana	S	27.66 MW	26.29 AW	54680 AAW	INBLS	10//99-12//99
Except Computer	Elkhart-Goshen MSA, IN	S	19.35 MW	15.88 AW	40250 AAW	INBLS	10//99-12//99
Except Computer	Fort Wayne MSA, IN	S	26.41 MW	26.35 AW	54930 AAW	INBLS	10//99-12//99
Except Computer	Indianapolis MSA, IN	S	26.28 MW	26.86 AW	54650 AAW	INBLS	10//99-12//99
Except Computer	Kansas	S	21.98 MW	25.89 AW	53850 AAW	KSBLS	10//99-12//99
Except Computer	Wichita MSA, KS	S	27.45 MW	22.66 AW	57090 AAW	KSBLS	10//99-12//99
Except Computer	Kentucky	S	29.96 MW	28.65 AW	59590 AAW	KYBLS	10//99-12//99
Except Computer	Lexington MSA, KY	S	28.84 MW	29.86 AW	59990 AAW	KYBLS	10//99-12//99
Except Computer	Louisville MSA, KY-IN	S	29.61 MW	30.38 AW	61590 AAW	KYBLS	10//99-12//99
Except Computer	Louisiana	S	33.34 MW	31.12 AW	64740 AAW	LABLS	10//99-12//99
Except Computer	New Orleans MSA, LA	S	30.95 MW	32.01 AW	64380 AAW	LABLS	10//99-12//99
Except Computer	Maryland	S	33.33 MW	34.09 AW	70900 AAW	MDBLS	10//99-12//99
Except Computer	Baltimore PMSA, MD	S	33.07 MW	32.94 AW	68780 AAW	MDBLS	10//99-12//99
Except Computer	Massachusetts	S	32.43 MW	33.18 AW	69010 AAW	MABLS	10//99-12//99
Except Computer	Boston PMSA, MA-NH	S	33.01 MW	32.08 AW	68670 AAW	MABLS	10//99-12//99
Except Computer	Lawrence PMSA, MA-NH	S	32.34 MW	32.60 AW	67260 AAW	MABLS	10//99-12//99
Except Computer	Lowell PMSA, MA-NH	S	35.30 MW	35.36 AW	73420 AAW	MABLS	10//99-12//99
Except Computer	Springfield MSA, MA	S	32.13 MW	32.94 AW	66830 AAW	MABLS	10//99-12//99
Except Computer	Worcester PMSA, MA-CT	S	31.20 MW	31.57 AW	64900 AAW	MABLS	10//99-12//99
Except Computer	Michigan	S	25.73 MW	27.84 AW	57910 AAW	MIBLS	10//99-12//99
Except Computer	Ann Arbor PMSA, MI	S	32.25 MW	35.24 AW	67080 AAW	MIBLS	10//99-12//99
Except Computer	Detroit PMSA, MI	S	26.48 MW	25.11 AW	55070 AAW	MIBLS	10//99-12//99
Except Computer	Grand Rapids-Muskegon-Holland MSA, MI	S	29.46 MW	25.17 AW	61270 AAW	MIBLS	
Except Computer	Minnesota	S	32.36 MW	32.84 AW	68300 AAW	MNBLS	
Except Computer	Minneapolis-St. Paul MSA, MN-WI	S	33.75 MW	33.71 AW	70210 AAW	MNBLS	10//99-12//99
Except Computer	Mississippi	S	25.68 MW	26.14 AW	54370 AAW	MSBLS	10//99-12//99
Except Computer	Biloxi-Gulfport-Pascagoula MSA, MS	S	25.21 MW	23.88 AW	52440 AAW	MSBLS	
Except Computer	Missouri	S	23 MW	24.31 AW	50550 AAW	MOBLS	10//99-12//99
Except Computer	Kansas City MSA, MO-KS	S	26.22 MW	25.13 AW	54530 AAW	MOBLS	10//99-12//99
Except Computer	St. Louis MSA, MO-IL	S	24.60 MW	21.75 AW	51170 AAW	MOBLS	10//99-12//99
Except Computer	Montana	S	19.3 MW	20.25 AW	42110 AAW	MTBLS	10//99-12//99
Except Computer	Nebraska	S	26.38 MW	26.09 AW	54270 AAW	NEBLS	10//99-12//99
Except Computer	Omaha MSA, NE-IA	S	27.54 MW	27.82 AW	57290 AAW	NEBLS	10//99-12//99
Except Computer	Nevada	S	28.74 MW	28.17 AW	58600 AAW	NVBLS	10//99-12//99
Except Computer	Las Vegas MSA, NV-AZ	S	27.85 MW	28.35 AW	57920 AAW	NVBLS	10//99-12//99
Except Computer	New Hampshire	S	29.72 MW	31.23 AW	64960 AAW	NHBLS	10//99-12//99
Except Computer	Nashua PMSA, NH	S	35.38 MW	37.59 AW	73590 AAW	NHBLS	10//99-12//99
Except Computer	New Jersey	S	34.17 MW	34.28 AW	71300 AAW	NJBLS	10//99-12//99
Except Computer	Bergen-Passaic PMSA, NJ	S	38.17 MW	39.01 AW	79400 AAW	NJBLS	10//99-12//99
Except Computer	Middlesex-Somerset-Hunterdon PMSA, NJ	S	29.26 MW	27.41 AW	60850 AAW	NJBLS	10//99-12//99
Except Computer	Newark PMSA, NJ	S	34.37 MW	33.12 AW	71500 AAW	NJBLS	10//99-12//99
Except Computer	New Mexico	S	31.92 MW	32.41 AW	67410 AAW	NMBLS	10//99-12//99
Except Computer	Albuquerque MSA, NM	S	32.66 MW	32.17 AW	67930 AAW	NMBLS	10//99-12//99
Except Computer	New York	S	28.63 MW	28.98 AW	60280 AAW	NYBLS	10//99-12//99
Except Computer	Albany-Schenectady-Troy MSA, NY	S	33.50 MW	34.29 AW	69680 AAW	NYBLS	10//99-12//99
Except Computer	Binghamton MSA, NY	S	29.12 MW	29.73 AW	60570 AAW	NYBLS	10//99-12//99
Except Computer	Buffalo-Niagara Falls MSA, NY	S	32.14 MW	31.63 AW	66860 AAW	NYBLS	10//99-12//99
Except Computer	Nassau-Suffolk PMSA, NY	S	28.12 MW	27.66 AW	58480 AAW	NYBLS	10//99-12//99
Except Computer	New York PMSA, NY	S	31.04 MW	29.78 AW	64560 AAW	NYBLS	10//99-12//99

AAW	Average annual wage	AOH	Average offered, high	ASH	Average starting, high
AE	Average entry wage	AOL	Average offered, low	ASL	Average starting, low
AEX	Average experienced wage	APH	Average pay, high range	AW	Average wage paid
AO	Average offered	APL	Average pay, low range	FQ	First quartile wage

H	Hourly	M	Monthly	S	Special: hourly and annual
HI	Highest wage paid	MTC	Median total compensation	TQ	Third quartile wage
HR	High end range	MW	Median wage paid	W	Weekly
LR	Low end range	SQ	Second quartile wage	Y	Yearly

Electronics Engineer

Occupation/Type/Industry	Location	Per	Low	Mid	High	Source	Date
Except Computer	Rochester MSA, NY	S	29.85 MW	29.49 AW	62080 AAW	NYBLS	10//99-12/99
Except Computer	Syracuse MSA, NY	S	28.41 MW	28.15 AW	59100 AAW	NYBLS	10//99-12/99
Except Computer	North Carolina	S	28.69 MW	28.90 AW	60110 AAW	NCBLS	10//99-12/99
Except Computer	Asheville MSA, NC	S	23.36 MW	24.31 AW	48580 AAW	NCBLS	10//99-12/99
Except Computer	Charlotte-Gastonia-Rock Hill MSA, NC-SC	S	25.98 MW	25.02 AW	54030 AAW	NCBLS	10//99-12/99
Except Computer	Greensboro--Winston-Salem--High Point MSA, NC	S	30.58 MW	31.13 AW	63610 AAW	NCBLS	10//99-12/99
Except Computer	Raleigh-Durham-Chapel Hill MSA, NC	S	27.38 MW	28.46 AW	56940 AAW	NCBLS	10//99-12/99
Except Computer	North Dakota	S	25.2 MW	25.49 AW	53030 AAW	NDBLS	10//99-12/99
Except Computer	Ohio	S	28.45 MW	28.40 AW	59060 AAW	OHBLS	10//99-12/99
Except Computer	Akron PMSA, OH	S	25.72 MW	25.40 AW	53500 AAW	OHBLS	10//99-12/99
Except Computer	Cincinnati PMSA, OH-KY-IN	S	25.68 MW	25.79 AW	53420 AAW	OHBLS	10//99-12/99
Except Computer	Cleveland-Lorain-Elyria PMSA, OH	S	28.37 MW	27.71 AW	59010 AAW	OHBLS	10//99-12/99
Except Computer	Columbus MSA, OH	S	26.31 MW	27.00 AW	54720 AAW	OHBLS	10//99-12/99
Except Computer	Mansfield MSA, OH	S	21.59 MW	20.10 AW	44910 AAW	OHBLS	10//99-12/99
Except Computer	Toledo MSA, OH	S	24.64 MW	26.87 AW	51260 AAW	OHBLS	10//99-12/99
Except Computer	Tulsa MSA, OK	S	26.18 MW	26.85 AW	54450 AAW	OKBLS	10//99-12/99
Except Computer	Oregon	S	25.24 MW	25.34 AW	52710 AAW	ORBLS	10//99-12/99
Except Computer	Eugene-Springfield MSA, OR	S	19.79 MW	19.36 AW	41150 AAW	ORBLS	10//99-12/99
Except Computer	Portland-Vancouver PMSA, OR-WA	S	26.45 MW	25.94 AW	55010 AAW	ORBLS	10//99-12/99
Except Computer	Salem PMSA, OR	S	23.95 MW	23.55 AW	49810 AAW	ORBLS	10//99-12/99
Except Computer	Pennsylvania	S	25.15 MW	25.67 AW	53390 AAW	PABLS	10//99-12/99
Except Computer	Philadelphia PMSA, PA-NJ	S	27.37 MW	26.62 AW	56920 AAW	PABLS	10//99-12/99
Except Computer	Pittsburgh MSA, PA	S	23.40 MW	22.50 AW	48670 AAW	PABLS	10//99-12/99
Except Computer	State College MSA, PA	S	26.86 MW	26.35 AW	55870 AAW	PABLS	10//99-12/99
Except Computer	York MSA, PA	S	23.07 MW	23.14 AW	47980 AAW	PABLS	10//99-12/99
Except Computer	Providence-Fall River-Warwick MSA, RI-MA	S	34.95 MW	31.94 AW	72690 AAW	RIBLS	10//99-12/99
Except Computer	South Carolina	S	34.05 MW	33.50 AW	69680 AAW	SCBLS	10//99-12/99
Except Computer	Greenville-Spartanburg-Anderson MSA, SC	S	27.14 MW	29.36 AW	56450 AAW	SCBLS	10//99-12/99
Except Computer	South Dakota	S	24.12 MW	25.59 AW	53230 AAW	SDBLS	10//99-12/99
Except Computer	Tennessee	S	25.95 MW	25.23 AW	52480 AAW	TNBLS	10//99-12/99
Except Computer	Chattanooga MSA, TN-GA	S	23.47 MW	23.71 AW	48820 AAW	TNBLS	10//99-12/99
Except Computer	Knoxville MSA, TN	S	23.78 MW	23.73 AW	49460 AAW	TNBLS	10//99-12/99
Except Computer	Memphis MSA, TN-AR-MS	S	23.94 MW	20.60 AW	49800 AAW	MSBLS	10//99-12/99
Except Computer	Nashville MSA, TN	S	33.95 MW	32.37 AW	70610 AAW	TNBLS	10//99-12/99
Except Computer	Texas	S	31.47 MW	31.97 AW	66490 AAW	TXBLS	10//99-12/99
Except Computer	Austin-San Marcos MSA, TX	S	33.90 MW	33.91 AW	70510 AAW	TXBLS	10//99-12/99
Except Computer	Dallas PMSA, TX	S	31.79 MW	31.21 AW	66130 AAW	TXBLS	10//99-12/99
Except Computer	El Paso MSA, TX	S	35.35 MW	35.23 AW	73520 AAW	TXBLS	10//99-12/99
Except Computer	Fort Worth-Arlington PMSA, TX	S	33.39 MW	32.53 AW	69450 AAW	TXBLS	10//99-12/99
Except Computer	Houston PMSA, TX	S	31.68 MW	29.84 AW	65900 AAW	TXBLS	10//99-12/99
Except Computer	Waco MSA, TX	S	34.36 MW	34.79 AW	71480 AAW	TXBLS	10//99-12/99
Except Computer	Utah	S	27.46 MW	27.45 AW	57100 AAW	UTBLS	10//99-12/99
Except Computer	Salt Lake City-Ogden MSA, UT	S	27.82 MW	27.81 AW	57870 AAW	UTBLS	10//99-12/99
Except Computer	Virginia	S	34.17 MW	37.18 AW	77330 AAW	VABLS	10//99-12/99
Except Computer	Norfolk-Virginia Beach-Newport News MSA, VA-NC	S	30.40 MW	30.54 AW	63230 AAW	VABLS	10//99-12/99
Except Computer	Richmond-Petersburg MSA, VA	S	34.23 MW	31.64 AW	71200 AAW	VABLS	10//99-12/99
Except Computer	Washington	S	25.84 MW	26.95 AW	56060 AAW	WABLS	10//99-12/99
Except Computer	Seattle-Bellevue-Everett PMSA, WA	S	26.49 MW	25.56 AW	55110 AAW	WABLS	10//99-12/99
Except Computer	Spokane MSA, WA	S	23.00 MW	23.04 AW	47850 AAW	WABLS	10//99-12/99
Except Computer	West Virginia	S	25.57 MW	26.07 AW	54230 AAW	WVBLS	10//99-12/99
Except Computer	Wisconsin	S	22.77 MW	23.15 AW	48150 AAW	WIBLS	10//99-12/99
Except Computer	Green Bay MSA, WI	S	25.84 MW	25.71 AW	53740 AAW	WIBLS	10//99-12/99
Except Computer	Janesville-Beloit MSA, WI	S	19.26 MW	19.25 AW	40060 AAW	WIBLS	10//99-12/99
Except Computer	Madison MSA, WI	S	24.62 MW	25.53 AW	51210 AAW	WIBLS	10//99-12/99
Except Computer	Milwaukee-Waukesha PMSA, WI	S	23.46 MW	23.54 AW	48790 AAW	WIBLS	10//99-12/99
Except Computer	Puerto Rico	S	23.61 MW	24.14 AW	50210 AAW	PRBLS	10//99-12/99
Except Computer	San Juan-Bayamon PMSA, PR	S	23.23 MW	22.29 AW	48310 AAW	PRBLS	10//99-12/99

AAW Average annual wage	AOH Average offered, high	ASH Average starting, high	H Hourly	M Monthly	S Special: hourly and annual
AE Average entry wage	AOL Average offered, low	ASL Average starting, low	HI Highest wage paid	MTC Median total compensation	TQ Third quartile wage
AEX Average experienced wage	APH Average pay, high range	AW Average wage paid	HR High end range	MW Median wage paid	W Weekly
AO Average offered	APL Average pay, low range	FQ First quartile wage	LR Low end range	SQ Second quartile wage	Y Yearly

Occupation/Type/Industry	Location	Per	Low	Mid	High	Source	Date
Elementary School Teacher							
Except Special Education	Alabama	Y		34750 AAW		ALBLS	10//99-12//99
Except Special Education	Anniston MSA, AL	Y		36020 AAW		ALBLS	10//99-12//99
Except Special Education	Birmingham MSA, AL	Y		33670 AAW		ALBLS	10//99-12//99
Except Special Education	Decatur MSA, AL	Y		36520 AAW		ALBLS	10//99-12//99
Except Special Education	Dothan MSA, AL	Y		36450 AAW		ALBLS	10//99-12//99
Except Special Education	Florence MSA, AL	Y		35980 AAW		ALBLS	10//99-12//99
Except Special Education	Huntsville MSA, AL	Y		36890 AAW		ALBLS	10//99-12//99
Except Special Education	Mobile MSA, AL	Y		30070 AAW		ALBLS	10//99-12//99
Except Special Education	Montgomery MSA, AL	Y		33430 AAW		ALBLS	10//99-12//99
Except Special Education	Tuscaloosa MSA, AL	Y		47100 AAW		ALBLS	10//99-12//99
Except Special Education	Alaska	Y		48320 AAW		AKBLS	10//99-12//99
Except Special Education	Arizona	Y		34870 AAW		AZBLS	10//99-12//99
Except Special Education	Flagstaff MSA, AZ-UT	Y		29750 AAW		AZBLS	10//99-12//99
Except Special Education	Phoenix-Mesa MSA, AZ	Y		35890 AAW		AZBLS	10//99-12//99
Except Special Education	Tucson MSA, AZ	Y		36610 AAW		AZBLS	10//99-12//99
Except Special Education	Yuma MSA, AZ	Y		33130 AAW		AZBLS	10//99-12//99
Except Special Education	Arkansas	Y		32050 AAW		ARBLS	10//99-12//99
Except Special Education	Fayetteville-Springdale-Rogers MSA, AR	Y		39580 AAW		ARBLS	10//99-12//99
Except Special Education	Fort Smith MSA, AR-OK	Y		32820 AAW		ARBLS	10//99-12//99
Except Special Education	Jonesboro MSA, AR	Y		31640 AAW		ARBLS	10//99-12//99
Except Special Education	Little Rock-North Little Rock MSA, AR	Y		31780 AAW		ARBLS	10//99-12//99
Except Special Education	California	Y		45270 AAW		CABLS	10//99-12//99
Except Special Education	Bakersfield MSA, CA	Y		44120 AAW		CABLS	10//99-12//99
Except Special Education	Chico-Paradise MSA, CA	Y		41990 AAW		CABLS	10//99-12//99
Except Special Education	Fresno MSA, CA	Y		43220 AAW		CABLS	10//99-12//99
Except Special Education	Los Angeles-Long Beach PMSA, CA	Y		48270 AAW		CABLS	10//99-12//99
Except Special Education	Merced MSA, CA	Y		40430 AAW		CABLS	10//99-12//99
Except Special Education	Modesto MSA, CA	Y		44040 AAW		CABLS	10//99-12//99
Except Special Education	Oakland PMSA, CA	Y		43910 AAW		CABLS	10//99-12//99
Except Special Education	Orange County PMSA, CA	Y		43290 AAW		CABLS	10//99-12//99
Except Special Education	Redding MSA, CA	Y		37890 AAW		CABLS	10//99-12//99
Except Special Education	Riverside-San Bernardino PMSA, CA	Y		46340 AAW		CABLS	10//99-12//99
Except Special Education	Sacramento PMSA, CA	Y		44200 AAW		CABLS	10//99-12//99
Except Special Education	Salinas MSA, CA	Y		43970 AAW		CABLS	10//99-12//99
Except Special Education	San Diego MSA, CA	Y		43940 AAW		CABLS	10//99-12//99
Except Special Education	San Francisco PMSA, CA	Y		41400 AAW		CABLS	10//99-12//99
Except Special Education	San Jose PMSA, CA	Y		46530 AAW		CABLS	10//99-12//99
Except Special Education	San Luis Obispo-Atascadero-Paso Robles MSA, CA	Y		43640 AAW		CABLS	10//99-12//99
Except Special Education	Santa Barbara-Santa Maria-Lompoc MSA, CA	Y		43260 AAW		CABLS	10//99-12//99
Except Special Education	Santa Cruz-Watsonville PMSA, CA	Y		41390 AAW		CABLS	10//99-12//99
Except Special Education	Santa Rosa PMSA, CA	Y		42330 AAW		CABLS	10//99-12//99
Except Special Education	Stockton-Lodi MSA, CA	Y		44060 AAW		CABLS	10//99-12//99
Except Special Education	Vallejo-Fairfield-Napa PMSA, CA	Y		38850 AAW		CABLS	10//99-12//99
Except Special Education	Ventura PMSA, CA	Y		49780 AAW		CABLS	10//99-12//99
Except Special Education	Visalia-Tulare-Porterville MSA, CA	Y		43660 AAW		CABLS	10//99-12//99
Except Special Education	Yolo PMSA, CA	Y		39070 AAW		CABLS	10//99-12//99
Except Special Education	Yuba City MSA, CA	Y		51850 AAW		CABLS	10//99-12//99
Except Special Education	Colorado	Y		38560 AAW		COBLS	10//99-12//99
Except Special Education	Boulder-Longmont PMSA, CO	Y		39500 AAW		COBLS	10//99-12//99
Except Special Education	Denver PMSA, CO	Y		37620 AAW		COBLS	10//99-12//99
Except Special Education	Fort Collins-Loveland MSA, CO	Y		39730 AAW		COBLS	10//99-12//99
Except Special Education	Grand Junction MSA, CO	Y		35660 AAW		COBLS	10//99-12//99
Except Special Education	Greeley PMSA, CO	Y		33170 AAW		COBLS	10//99-12//99
Except Special Education	Connecticut	Y		48010 AAW		CTBLS	10//99-12//99
Except Special Education	Bridgeport PMSA, CT	Y		50850 AAW		CTBLS	10//99-12//99
Except Special Education	Danbury PMSA, CT	Y		46770 AAW		CTBLS	10//99-12//99
Except Special Education	Hartford MSA, CT	Y		49160 AAW		CTBLS	10//99-12//99
Except Special Education	New Haven-Meriden PMSA, CT	Y		48870 AAW		CTBLS	10//99-12//99
Except Special Education	New London-Norwich MSA, CT-RI	Y		49030 AAW		CTBLS	10//99-12//99

AAW	Average annual wage	AOH	Average offered, high	ASH	Average starting, high	H	Hourly
AE	Average entry wage	AOL	Average offered, low	ASL	Average starting, low	HI	Highest wage paid
AEX	Average experienced wage	APH	Average pay, high range	AW	Average wage paid	HR	High end range
AO	Average offered	APL	Average pay, low range	FQ	First quartile wage	LR	Low end range

M	Monthly	S	Special: hourly and annual
MTC	Median total compensation	TQ	Third quartile wage
MW	Median wage paid	W	Weekly
SQ	Second quartile wage	Y	Yearly

Elementary School Teacher

Occupation/Type/Industry	Location	Per	Low	Mid	High	Source	Date
Except Special Education	Stamford-Norwalk PMSA, CT	Y		38960 AAW		CTBLS	10//99-12//99
Except Special Education	Waterbury PMSA, CT	Y		47030 AAW		CTBLS	10//99-12//99
Except Special Education	District of Columbia	Y		41580 AAW		DCBLS	10//99-12//99
Except Special Education	Washington PMSA, DC-MD-VA-WV	Y		37090 AAW		DCBLS	10//99-12//99
Except Special Education	Florida	Y		35470 AAW		FLBLS	10//99-12//99
Except Special Education	Fort Myers-Cape Coral MSA, FL	Y		31200 AAW		FLBLS	10//99-12//99
Except Special Education	Fort Pierce-Port St. Lucie MSA, FL	Y		40560 AAW		FLBLS	10//99-12//99
Except Special Education	Jacksonville MSA, FL	Y		42330 AAW		FLBLS	10//99-12//99
Except Special Education	Melbourne-Titusville-Palm Bay MSA, FL	Y		22570 AAW		FLBLS	10//99-12//99
Except Special Education	Miami PMSA, FL	Y		27750 AAW		FLBLS	10//99-12//99
Except Special Education	Pensacola MSA, FL	Y		33140 AAW		FLBLS	10//99-12//99
Except Special Education	Sarasota-Bradenton MSA, FL	Y		37920 AAW		FLBLS	10//99-12//99
Except Special Education	Tampa-St. Petersburg-Clearwater MSA, FL	Y		38940 AAW		FLBLS	10//99-12//99
Except Special Education	West Palm Beach-Boca Raton MSA, FL	Y		37990 AAW		FLBLS	10//99-12//99
Except Special Education	Georgia	Y		40090 AAW		GABLS	10//99-12//99
Except Special Education	Albany MSA, GA	Y		40020 AAW		GABLS	10//99-12//99
Except Special Education	Athens MSA, GA	Y		43700 AAW		GABLS	10//99-12//99
Except Special Education	Atlanta MSA, GA	Y		41180 AAW		GABLS	10//99-12//99
Except Special Education	Augusta-Aiken MSA, GA-SC	Y		41290 AAW		GABLS	10//99-12//99
Except Special Education	Columbus MSA, GA-AL	Y		37950 AAW		GABLS	10//99-12//99
Except Special Education	Macon MSA, GA	Y		40460 AAW		GABLS	10//99-12//99
Except Special Education	Savannah MSA, GA	Y		40050 AAW		GABLS	10//99-12//99
Except Special Education	Idaho	Y		37190 AAW		IDBLS	10//99-12//99
Except Special Education	Boise City MSA, ID	Y		34670 AAW		IDBLS	10//99-12//99
Except Special Education	Illinois	Y		38320 AAW		ILBLS	10//99-12//99
Except Special Education	Bloomington-Normal MSA, IL	Y		38120 AAW		ILBLS	10//99-12//99
Except Special Education	Champaign-Urbana MSA, IL	Y		38040 AAW		ILBLS	10//99-12//99
Except Special Education	Chicago PMSA, IL	Y		40660 AAW		ILBLS	10//99-12//99
Except Special Education	Kankakee PMSA, IL	Y		39910 AAW		ILBLS	10//99-12//99
Except Special Education	Peoria-Pekin MSA, IL	Y		33260 AAW		ILBLS	10//99-12//99
Except Special Education	Rockford MSA, IL	Y		42280 AAW		ILBLS	10//99-12//99
Except Special Education	Springfield MSA, IL	Y		34860 AAW		ILBLS	10//99-12//99
Except Special Education	Indiana	Y		41660 AAW		INBLS	10//99-12//99
Except Special Education	Bloomington MSA, IN	Y		37280 AAW		INBLS	10//99-12//99
Except Special Education	Elkhart-Goshen MSA, IN	Y		41190 AAW		INBLS	10//99-12//99
Except Special Education	Evansville-Henderson MSA, IN-KY	Y		40570 AAW		INBLS	10//99-12//99
Except Special Education	Fort Wayne MSA, IN	Y		40380 AAW		INBLS	10//99-12//99
Except Special Education	Gary PMSA, IN	Y		39160 AAW		INBLS	10//99-12//99
Except Special Education	Indianapolis MSA, IN	Y		46400 AAW		INBLS	10//99-12//99
Except Special Education	Kokomo MSA, IN	Y		41660 AAW		INBLS	10//99-12//99
Except Special Education	Lafayette MSA, IN	Y		42070 AAW		INBLS	10//99-12//99
Except Special Education	Muncie MSA, IN	Y		36730 AAW		INBLS	10//99-12//99
Except Special Education	South Bend MSA, IN	Y		38830 AAW		INBLS	10//99-12//99
Except Special Education	Terre Haute MSA, IN	Y		39040 AAW		INBLS	10//99-12//99
Except Special Education	Iowa	Y		33070 AAW		IABLS	10//99-12//99
Except Special Education	Cedar Rapids MSA, IA	Y		34110 AAW		IABLS	10//99-12//99
Except Special Education	Davenport-Moline-Rock Island MSA, IA-IL	Y		38920 AAW		IABLS	10//99-12//99
Except Special Education	Des Moines MSA, IA	Y		33170 AAW		IABLS	10//99-12//99
Except Special Education	Dubuque MSA, IA	Y		32390 AAW		IABLS	10//99-12//99
Except Special Education	Iowa City MSA, IA	Y		32960 AAW		IABLS	10//99-12//99
Except Special Education	Sioux City MSA, IA-NE	Y		27550 AAW		IABLS	10//99-12//99
Except Special Education	Waterloo-Cedar Falls MSA, IA	Y		29580 AAW		IABLS	10//99-12//99
Except Special Education	Kansas	Y		32210 AAW		KSBLS	10//99-12//99
Except Special Education	Lawrence MSA, KS	Y		28340 AAW		KSBLS	10//99-12//99
Except Special Education	Topeka MSA, KS	Y		32130 AAW		KSBLS	10//99-12//99
Except Special Education	Wichita MSA, KS	Y		32220 AAW		KSBLS	10//99-12//99
Except Special Education	Kentucky	Y		35720 AAW		KYBLS	10//99-12//99
Except Special Education	Lexington MSA, KY	Y		36240 AAW		KYBLS	10//99-12//99
Except Special Education	Louisiana	Y		35560 AAW		LABLS	10//99-12//99
Except Special Education	Baton Rouge MSA, LA	Y		32660 AAW		LABLS	10//99-12//99
Except Special Education	Lafayette MSA, LA	Y		34150 AAW		LABLS	10//99-12//99
Except Special Education	New Orleans MSA, LA	Y		35470 AAW		LABLS	10//99-12//99
Except Special Education	Maine	Y		34360 AAW		MEBLS	10//99-12//99

AAW	Average annual wage	AOH	Average offered, high	ASH	Average starting, high	H	Hourly	M	Monthly	S	Special: hourly and annual
AE	Average entry wage	AOL	Average offered, low	ASL	Average starting, low	HI	Highest wage paid	MTC	Median total compensation	TQ	Third quartile wage
AEX	Average experienced wage	APH	Average pay, high range	AW	Average wage paid	HR	High end range	MW	Median wage paid	W	Weekly
AO	Average offered	APL	Average pay, low range	FQ	First quartile wage	LR	Low end range	SQ	Second quartile wage	Y	Yearly

Occupation/Type/Industry	Location	Per	Low	Mid	High	Source	Date
Elementary School Teacher							
Except Special Education	Bangor MSA, ME	Y		32500 AAW		MEBLS	10//99-12//99
Except Special Education	Lewiston-Auburn MSA, ME	Y		40010 AAW		MEBLS	10//99-12//99
Except Special Education	Portland MSA, ME	Y		36650 AAW		MEBLS	10//99-12//99
Except Special Education	Maryland	Y		37240 AAW		MDBLS	10//99-12//99
Except Special Education	Baltimore PMSA, MD	Y		39350 AAW		MDBLS	10//99-12//99
Except Special Education	Hagerstown PMSA, MD	Y		38060 AAW		MDBLS	10//99-12//99
Except Special Education	Massachusetts	Y		43520 AAW		MABLS	10//99-12//99
Except Special Education	Barnstable-Yarmouth MSA, MA	Y		40720 AAW		MABLS	10//99-12//99
Except Special Education	Boston PMSA, MA-NH	Y		45160 AAW		MABLS	10//99-12//99
Except Special Education	Brockton PMSA, MA	Y		43430 AAW		MABLS	10//99-12//99
Except Special Education	Fitchburg-Leominster PMSA, MA	Y		41630 AAW		MABLS	10//99-12//99
Except Special Education	Lawrence PMSA, MA-NH	Y		41770 AAW		MABLS	10//99-12//99
Except Special Education	Lowell PMSA, MA-NH	Y		41080 AAW		MABLS	10//99-12//99
Except Special Education	New Bedford PMSA, MA	Y		43330 AAW		MABLS	10//99-12//99
Except Special Education	Pittsfield MSA, MA	Y		36460 AAW		MABLS	10//99-12//99
Except Special Education	Springfield MSA, MA	Y		39950 AAW		MABLS	10//99-12//99
Except Special Education	Worcester PMSA, MA-CT	Y		45800 AAW		MABLS	10//99-12//99
Except Special Education	Michigan	Y		42980 AAW		MIBLS	10//99-12//99
Except Special Education	Ann Arbor PMSA, MI	Y		47460 AAW		MIBLS	10//99-12//99
Except Special Education	Benton Harbor MSA, MI	Y		40930 AAW		MIBLS	10//99-12//99
Except Special Education	Detroit PMSA, MI	Y		43630 AAW		MIBLS	10//99-12//99
Except Special Education	Flint PMSA, MI	Y		41760 AAW		MIBLS	10//99-12//99
Except Special Education	Grand Rapids-Muskegon-Holland MSA, MI	Y		43020 AAW		MIBLS	10//99-12//99
Except Special Education	Kalamazoo-Battle Creek MSA, MI	Y		44970 AAW		MIBLS	10//99-12//99
Except Special Education	Lansing-East Lansing MSA, MI	Y		43220 AAW		MIBLS	10//99-12//99
Except Special Education	Saginaw-Bay City-Midland MSA, MI	Y		45060 AAW		MIBLS	10//99-12//99
Except Special Education	Minnesota	Y		40160 AAW		MNBLS	10//99-12//99
Except Special Education	Duluth-Superior MSA, MN-WI	Y		37870 AAW		MNBLS	10//99-12//99
Except Special Education	Minneapolis-St. Paul MSA, MN-WI	Y		42220 AAW		MNBLS	10//99-12//99
Except Special Education	Rochester MSA, MN	Y		37480 AAW		MNBLS	10//99-12//99
Except Special Education	St. Cloud MSA, MN	Y		40070 AAW		MNBLS	10//99-12//99
Except Special Education	Mississippi	Y		28700 AAW		MSBLS	10//99-12//99
Except Special Education	Biloxi-Gulfport-Pascagoula MSA, MS	Y		32300 AAW		MSBLS	10//99-12//99
Except Special Education	Hattiesburg MSA, MS	Y		28810 AAW		MSBLS	10//99-12//99
Except Special Education	Jackson MSA, MS	Y		27450 AAW		MSBLS	10//99-12//99
Except Special Education	Missouri	Y		32770 AAW		MOBLS	10//99-12//99
Except Special Education	Joplin MSA, MO	Y		27320 AAW		MOBLS	10//99-12//99
Except Special Education	Kansas City MSA, MO-KS	Y		34100 AAW		MOBLS	10//99-12//99
Except Special Education	St. Louis MSA, MO-IL	Y		36560 AAW		MOBLS	10//99-12//99
Except Special Education	Springfield MSA, MO	Y		29820 AAW		MOBLS	10//99-12//99
Except Special Education	Montana	Y		32590 AAW		MTBLS	10//99-12//99
Except Special Education	Billings MSA, MT	Y		33330 AAW		MTBLS	10//99-12//99
Except Special Education	Great Falls MSA, MT	Y		33040 AAW		MTBLS	10//99-12//99
Except Special Education	Missoula MSA, MT	Y		36860 AAW		MTBLS	10//99-12//99
Except Special Education	Nebraska	Y		31900 AAW		NEBLS	10//99-12//99
Except Special Education	Omaha MSA, NE-IA	Y		33900 AAW		NEBLS	10//99-12//99
Except Special Education	Nevada	Y		37410 AAW		NVBLS	10//99-12//99
Except Special Education	New Hampshire	Y		36800 AAW		NHBLS	10//99-12//99
Except Special Education	Manchester PMSA, NH	Y		37260 AAW		NHBLS	10//99-12//99
Except Special Education	Nashua PMSA, NH	Y		40690 AAW		NHBLS	10//99-12//99
Except Special Education	Portsmouth-Rochester PMSA, NH-ME	Y		38980 AAW		NHBLS	10//99-12//99
Except Special Education	New Jersey	Y		49780 AAW		NJBLS	10//99-12//99
Except Special Education	Atlantic-Cape May PMSA, NJ	Y		44970 AAW		NJBLS	10//99-12//99
Except Special Education	Bergen-Passaic PMSA, NJ	Y		51840 AAW		NJBLS	10//99-12//99
Except Special Education	Jersey City PMSA, NJ	Y		53450 AAW		NJBLS	10//99-12//99
Except Special Education	Middlesex-Somerset-Hunterdon PMSA, NJ	Y		52730 AAW		NJBLS	10//99-12//99
Except Special Education	Monmouth-Ocean PMSA, NJ	Y		49160 AAW		NJBLS	10//99-12//99
Except Special Education	Newark PMSA, NJ	Y		48380 AAW		NJBLS	10//99-12//99
Except Special Education	Trenton PMSA, NJ	Y		52060 AAW		NJBLS	10//99-12//99
Except Special Education	Vineland-Millville-Bridgeton PMSA, NJ	Y		43530 AAW		NJBLS	10//99-12//99
Except Special Education	New Mexico	Y		34150 AAW		NMBLS	10//99-12//99

AAW	Average annual wage	AOH	Average offered, high	ASH	Average starting, high	H	Hourly	M	Monthly	S	Special: hourly and annual
AE	Average entry wage	AOL	Average offered, low	ASL	Average starting, low	HI	Highest wage paid	MTC	Median total compensation	TQ	Third quartile wage
AEX	Average experienced wage	APH	Average pay, high range	AW	Average wage paid	HR	High end range	MW	Median wage paid	W	Weekly
AO	Average offered	APL	Average pay, low range	FQ	First quartile wage	LR	Low end range	SQ	Second quartile wage	Y	Yearly

489

Occupation/Type/Industry	Location	Per	Low	Mid	High	Source	Date
Elementary School Teacher							
Except Special Education	Las Cruces MSA, NM	Y		31420 AAW		NMBLS	10//99-12//99
Except Special Education	New York	Y		46430 AAW		NYBLS	10//99-12//99
Except Special Education	Albany-Schenectady-Troy MSA, NY	Y		44930 AAW		NYBLS	10//99-12//99
Except Special Education	Binghamton MSA, NY	Y		41290 AAW		NYBLS	10//99-12//99
Except Special Education	Buffalo-Niagara Falls MSA, NY	Y		44640 AAW		NYBLS	10//99-12//99
Except Special Education	Dutchess County PMSA, NY	Y		41100 AAW		NYBLS	10//99-12//99
Except Special Education	Glens Falls MSA, NY	Y		46460 AAW		NYBLS	10//99-12//99
Except Special Education	Jamestown MSA, NY	Y		44150 AAW		NYBLS	10//99-12//99
Except Special Education	Nassau-Suffolk PMSA, NY	Y		57910 AAW		NYBLS	10//99-12//99
Except Special Education	New York PMSA, NY	Y		45220 AAW		NYBLS	10//99-12//99
Except Special Education	Newburgh PMSA, NY-PA	Y		38890 AAW		NYBLS	10//99-12//99
Except Special Education	Rochester MSA, NY	Y		49880 AAW		NYBLS	10//99-12//99
Except Special Education	Syracuse MSA, NY	Y		43430 AAW		NYBLS	10//99-12//99
Except Special Education	Utica-Rome MSA, NY	Y		40870 AAW		NYBLS	10//99-12//99
Except Special Education	North Carolina	Y		33430 AAW		NCBLS	10//99-12//99
Except Special Education	Asheville MSA, NC	Y		33340 AAW		NCBLS	10//99-12//99
Except Special Education	Charlotte-Gastonia-Rock Hill MSA, NC-SC	Y		34570 AAW		NCBLS	10//99-12//99
Except Special Education	Fayetteville MSA, NC	Y		33040 AAW		NCBLS	10//99-12//99
Except Special Education	Greensboro--Winston-Salem--High Point MSA, NC	Y		34540 AAW		NCBLS	10//99-12//99
Except Special Education	Hickory-Morganton-Lenoir MSA, NC	Y		32420 AAW		NCBLS	10//99-12//99
Except Special Education	Raleigh-Durham-Chapel Hill MSA, NC	Y		34510 AAW		NCBLS	10//99-12//99
Except Special Education	Rocky Mount MSA, NC	Y		34630 AAW		NCBLS	10//99-12//99
Except Special Education	Wilmington MSA, NC	Y		34000 AAW		NCBLS	10//99-12//99
Except Special Education	North Dakota	Y		30020 AAW		NDBLS	10//99-12//99
Except Special Education	Fargo-Moorhead MSA, ND-MN	Y		34510 AAW		NDBLS	10//99-12//99
Except Special Education	Grand Forks MSA, ND-MN	Y		33600 AAW		NDBLS	10//99-12//99
Except Special Education	Ohio	Y		38830 AAW		OHBLS	10//99-12//99
Except Special Education	Akron PMSA, OH	Y		39440 AAW		OHBLS	10//99-12//99
Except Special Education	Canton-Massillon MSA, OH	Y		35520 AAW		OHBLS	10//99-12//99
Except Special Education	Cincinnati PMSA, OH-KY-IN	Y		37970 AAW		OHBLS	10//99-12//99
Except Special Education	Cleveland-Lorain-Elyria PMSA, OH	Y		44170 AAW		OHBLS	10//99-12//99
Except Special Education	Columbus MSA, OH	Y		42700 AAW		OHBLS	10//99-12//99
Except Special Education	Dayton-Springfield MSA, OH	Y		38020 AAW		OHBLS	10//99-12//99
Except Special Education	Hamilton-Middletown PMSA, OH	Y		40300 AAW		OHBLS	10//99-12//99
Except Special Education	Lima MSA, OH	Y		35290 AAW		OHBLS	10//99-12//99
Except Special Education	Mansfield MSA, OH	Y		38590 AAW		OHBLS	10//99-12//99
Except Special Education	Steubenville-Weirton MSA, OH-WV	Y		34300 AAW		OHBLS	10//99-12//99
Except Special Education	Toledo MSA, OH	Y		36250 AAW		OHBLS	10//99-12//99
Except Special Education	Youngstown-Warren MSA, OH	Y		35070 AAW		OHBLS	10//99-12//99
Except Special Education	Oklahoma	Y		29990 AAW		OKBLS	10//99-12//99
Except Special Education	Enid MSA, OK	Y		31150 AAW		OKBLS	10//99-12//99
Except Special Education	Oklahoma City MSA, OK	Y		28340 AAW		OKBLS	10//99-12//99
Except Special Education	Tulsa MSA, OK	Y		30140 AAW		OKBLS	10//99-12//99
Except Special Education	Oregon	Y		40760 AAW		ORBLS	10//99-12//99
Except Special Education	Corvallis MSA, OR	Y		30410 AAW		ORBLS	10//99-12//99
Except Special Education	Eugene-Springfield MSA, OR	Y		40810 AAW		ORBLS	10//99-12//99
Except Special Education	Medford-Ashland MSA, OR	Y		37440 AAW		ORBLS	10//99-12//99
Except Special Education	Portland-Vancouver PMSA, OR-WA	Y		41880 AAW		ORBLS	10//99-12//99
Except Special Education	Salem PMSA, OR	Y		38140 AAW		ORBLS	10//99-12//99
Except Special Education	Pennsylvania	Y		45780 AAW		PABLS	10//99-12//99
Except Special Education	Allentown-Bethlehem-Easton MSA, PA	Y		44650 AAW		PABLS	10//99-12//99
Except Special Education	Altoona MSA, PA	Y		42760 AAW		PABLS	10//99-12//99
Except Special Education	Erie MSA, PA	Y		43010 AAW		PABLS	10//99-12//99
Except Special Education	Harrisburg-Lebanon-Carlisle MSA, PA	Y		40020 AAW		PABLS	10//99-12//99
Except Special Education	Johnstown MSA, PA	Y		38600 AAW		PABLS	10//99-12//99
Except Special Education	Lancaster MSA, PA	Y		48840 AAW		PABLS	10//99-12//99
Except Special Education	Philadelphia PMSA, PA-NJ	Y		49470 AAW		PABLS	10//99-12//99
Except Special Education	Pittsburgh MSA, PA	Y		42530 AAW		PABLS	10//99-12//99

AAW Average annual wage	**AOH** Average offered, high	**ASH** Average starting, high	**H** Hourly	**M** Monthly	**S** Special: hourly and annual
AE Average entry wage	**AOL** Average offered, low	**ASL** Average starting, low	**HI** Highest wage paid	**MTC** Median total compensation	**TQ** Third quartile wage
AEX Average experienced wage	**APH** Average pay, high range	**AW** Average wage paid	**HR** High end range	**MW** Median wage paid	**W** Weekly
AO Average offered	**APL** Average pay, low range	**FQ** First quartile wage	**LR** Low end range	**SQ** Second quartile wage	**Y** Yearly

Occupation/Type/Industry	Location	Per	Low	Mid	High	Source	Date
Elementary School Teacher							
Except Special Education	Reading MSA, PA	Y		47220 AAW		PABLS	10//99-12//99
Except Special Education	Scranton--Wilkes-Barre-- Hazleton MSA, PA	Y		46420 AAW		PABLS	10//99-12//99
Except Special Education	Sharon MSA, PA	Y		42630 AAW		PABLS	10//99-12//99
Except Special Education	State College MSA, PA	Y		42280 AAW		PABLS	10//99-12//99
Except Special Education	Williamsport MSA, PA	Y		42190 AAW		PABLS	10//99-12//99
Except Special Education	York MSA, PA	Y		47930 AAW		PABLS	10//99-12//99
Except Special Education	Rhode Island	Y		47620 AAW		RIBLS	10//99-12//99
Except Special Education	Providence-Fall River- Warwick MSA, RI-MA	Y		46650 AAW		RIBLS	10//99-12//99
Except Special Education	South Carolina	Y		35570 AAW		SCBLS	10//99-12//99
Except Special Education	Charleston-North Charleston MSA, SC	Y		33260 AAW		SCBLS	10//99-12//99
Except Special Education	Columbia MSA, SC	Y		35740 AAW		SCBLS	10//99-12//99
Except Special Education	Florence MSA, SC	Y		32520 AAW		SCBLS	10//99-12//99
Except Special Education	Greenville-Spartanburg- Anderson MSA, SC	Y		35420 AAW		SCBLS	10//99-12//99
Except Special Education	Sumter MSA, SC	Y		32170 AAW		SCBLS	10//99-12//99
Except Special Education	South Dakota	Y		29840 AAW		SDBLS	10//99-12//99
Except Special Education	Tennessee	Y		33540 AAW		TNBLS	10//99-12//99
Except Special Education	Chattanooga MSA, TN-GA	Y		35160 AAW		TNBLS	10//99-12//99
Except Special Education	Jackson MSA, TN	Y		33760 AAW		TNBLS	10//99-12//99
Except Special Education	Johnson City-Kingsport-Bristol MSA, TN-VA	Y		33410 AAW		TNBLS	10//99-12//99
Except Special Education	Knoxville MSA, TN	Y		34590 AAW		TNBLS	10//99-12//99
Except Special Education	Memphis MSA, TN-AR-MS	Y		37630 AAW		MSBLS	10//99-12//99
Except Special Education	Nashville MSA, TN	Y		30670 AAW		TNBLS	10//99-12//99
Except Special Education	Texas	Y		35280 AAW		TXBLS	10//99-12//99
Except Special Education	Abilene MSA, TX	Y		34710 AAW		TXBLS	10//99-12//99
Except Special Education	Austin-San Marcos MSA, TX	Y		34710 AAW		TXBLS	10//99-12//99
Except Special Education	Beaumont-Port Arthur MSA, TX	Y		36280 AAW		TXBLS	10//99-12//99
Except Special Education	Brazoria PMSA, TX	Y		36440 AAW		TXBLS	10//99-12//99
Except Special Education	Brownsville-Harlingen-San Benito MSA, TX	Y		35020 AAW		TXBLS	10//99-12//99
Except Special Education	Bryan-College Station MSA, TX	Y		28520 AAW		TXBLS	10//99-12//99
Except Special Education	Corpus Christi MSA, TX	Y		36930 AAW		TXBLS	10//99-12//99
Except Special Education	Dallas PMSA, TX	Y		34070 AAW		TXBLS	10//99-12//99
Except Special Education	El Paso MSA, TX	Y		35550 AAW		TXBLS	10//99-12//99
Except Special Education	Fort Worth-Arlington PMSA, TX	Y		36720 AAW		TXBLS	10//99-12//99
Except Special Education	Galveston-Texas City PMSA, TX	Y		38370 AAW		TXBLS	10//99-12//99
Except Special Education	Houston PMSA, TX	Y		36750 AAW		TXBLS	10//99-12//99
Except Special Education	Killeen-Temple MSA, TX	Y		33700 AAW		TXBLS	10//99-12//99
Except Special Education	Longview-Marshall MSA, TX	Y		33530 AAW		TXBLS	10//99-12//99
Except Special Education	McAllen-Edinburg-Mission MSA, TX	Y		35710 AAW		TXBLS	10//99-12//99
Except Special Education	San Angelo MSA, TX	Y		33490 AAW		TXBLS	10//99-12//99
Except Special Education	San Antonio MSA, TX	Y		38010 AAW		TXBLS	10//99-12//99
Except Special Education	Sherman-Denison MSA, TX	Y		34000 AAW		TXBLS	10//99-12//99
Except Special Education	Texarkana MSA, TX- Texarkana, AR	Y		31330 AAW		TXBLS	10//99-12//99
Except Special Education	Victoria MSA, TX	Y		35200 AAW		TXBLS	10//99-12//99
Except Special Education	Waco MSA, TX	Y		32590 AAW		TXBLS	10//99-12//99
Except Special Education	Utah	Y		33340 AAW		UTBLS	10//99-12//99
Except Special Education	Salt Lake City-Ogden MSA, UT	Y		34400 AAW		UTBLS	10//99-12//99
Except Special Education	Vermont	Y		37750 AAW		VTBLS	10//99-12//99
Except Special Education	Burlington MSA, VT	Y		40660 AAW		VTBLS	10//99-12//99
Except Special Education	Virginia	Y		36560 AAW		VABLS	10//99-12//99
Except Special Education	Charlottesville MSA, VA	Y		44230 AAW		VABLS	10//99-12//99
Except Special Education	Lynchburg MSA, VA	Y		27380 AAW		VABLS	10//99-12//99
Except Special Education	Norfolk-Virginia Beach- Newport News MSA, VA-NC	Y		35060 AAW		VABLS	10//99-12//99
Except Special Education	Richmond-Petersburg MSA, VA	Y		41880 AAW		VABLS	10//99-12//99
Except Special Education	Roanoke MSA, VA	Y		38020 AAW		VABLS	10//99-12//99
Except Special Education	Washington	Y		39670 AAW		WABLS	10//99-12//99

AAW	Average annual wage	AOH	Average offered, high	ASH	Average starting, high	H	Hourly	M	Monthly	S	Special: hourly and annual
AE	Average entry wage	AOL	Average offered, low	ASL	Average starting, low	HI	Highest wage paid	MTC	Median total compensation	TQ	Third quartile wage
AEX	Average experienced wage	APH	Average pay, high range	AW	Average wage paid	HR	High end range	MW	Median wage paid	W	Weekly
AO	Average offered	APL	Average pay, low range	FQ	First quartile wage	LR	Low end range	SQ	Second quartile wage	Y	Yearly

Occupation/Type/Industry	Location	Per	Low	Mid	High	Source	Date
Elementary School Teacher							
Except Special Education	Bellingham MSA, WA	Y		37900 AAW		WABLS	10//99-12//99
Except Special Education	Bremerton PMSA, WA	Y		38810 AAW		WABLS	10//99-12//99
Except Special Education	Olympia PMSA, WA	Y		39780 AAW		WABLS	10//99-12//99
Except Special Education	Richland-Kennewick-Pasco MSA, WA	Y		45470 AAW		WABLS	10//99-12//99
Except Special Education	Seattle-Bellevue-Everett PMSA, WA	Y		40350 AAW		WABLS	10//99-12//99
Except Special Education	Spokane MSA, WA	Y		36910 AAW		WABLS	10//99-12//99
Except Special Education	Tacoma PMSA, WA	Y		40220 AAW		WABLS	10//99-12//99
Except Special Education	Yakima MSA, WA	Y		39580 AAW		WABLS	10//99-12//99
Except Special Education	West Virginia	Y		35180 AAW		WVBLS	10//99-12//99
Except Special Education	Huntington-Ashland MSA, WV-KY-OH	Y		37080 AAW		WVBLS	10//99-12//99
Except Special Education	Parkersburg-Marietta MSA, WV-OH	Y		33950 AAW		WVBLS	10//99-12//99
Except Special Education	Wheeling MSA, WV-OH	Y		36510 AAW		WVBLS	10//99-12//99
Except Special Education	Wisconsin	Y		38850 AAW		WIBLS	10//99-12//99
Except Special Education	Appleton-Oshkosh-Neenah MSA, WI	Y		40900 AAW		WIBLS	10//99-12//99
Except Special Education	Eau Claire MSA, WI	Y		37790 AAW		WIBLS	10//99-12//99
Except Special Education	Green Bay MSA, WI	Y		39800 AAW		WIBLS	10//99-12//99
Except Special Education	Janesville-Beloit MSA, WI	Y		37940 AAW		WIBLS	10//99-12//99
Except Special Education	Kenosha PMSA, WI	Y		37060 AAW		WIBLS	10//99-12//99
Except Special Education	La Crosse MSA, WI-MN	Y		35170 AAW		WIBLS	10//99-12//99
Except Special Education	Madison MSA, WI	Y		38250 AAW		WIBLS	10//99-12//99
Except Special Education	Milwaukee-Waukesha PMSA, WI	Y		41000 AAW		WIBLS	10//99-12//99
Except Special Education	Racine PMSA, WI	Y		37910 AAW		WIBLS	10//99-12//99
Except Special Education	Sheboygan MSA, WI	Y		40480 AAW		WIBLS	10//99-12//99
Except Special Education	Wausau MSA, WI	Y		38980 AAW		WIBLS	10//99-12//99
Except Special Education	Wyoming	Y		36610 AAW		WYBLS	10//99-12//99
Elevator Installer and Repairer	Arizona	S	19.02 MW	17.82 AW	37070 AAW	AZBLS	10//99-12//99
	California	S	33.35 MW	29.19 AW	60710 AAW	CABLS	10//99-12//99
	Connecticut	S	30.21 MW	28.40 AW	59080 AAW	CTBLS	10//99-12//99
	District of Columbia	S	21.62 MW	18.78 AW	39060 AAW	DCBLS	10//99-12//99
	Florida	S	18.65 MW	17.99 AW	37420 AAW	FLBLS	10//99-12//99
	Georgia	S	13.19 MW	16.25 AW	33790 AAW	GABLS	10//99-12//99
	Illinois	S	27.25 MW	26.51 AW	55140 AAW	ILBLS	10//99-12//99
	Indiana	S	29.94 MW	28.20 AW	58660 AAW	INBLS	10//99-12//99
	Iowa	S	22.22 MW	22.49 AW	46770 AAW	IABLS	10//99-12//99
	Kentucky	S	20.77 MW	19.84 AW	41260 AAW	KYBLS	10//99-12//99
	Maine	S	22.67 MW	22.44 AW	46670 AAW	MEBLS	10//99-12//99
	Maryland	S	22.92 MW	22.93 AW	47690 AAW	MDBLS	10//99-12//99
	Massachusetts	S	29.54 MW	27.24 AW	56660 AAW	MABLS	10//99-12//99
	Michigan	S	25.32 MW	26.18 AW	54450 AAW	MIBLS	10//99-12//99
	Minnesota	S	25.75 MW	25.69 AW	53420 AAW	MNBLS	10//99-12//99
	Mississippi	S	17.07 MW	18.03 AW	37500 AAW	MSBLS	10//99-12//99
	Nebraska	S	22.54 MW	22.23 AW	46230 AAW	NEBLS	10//99-12//99
	Nevada	S	33.71 MW	33.02 AW	68680 AAW	NVBLS	10//99-12//99
	New Jersey	S	26.37 MW	26.14 AW	54370 AAW	NJBLS	10//99-12//99
	New Mexico	S	23.42 MW	22.49 AW	46780 AAW	NMBLS	10//99-12//99
	New York	S	26.92 MW	29.22 AW	60790 AAW	NYBLS	10//99-12//99
	North Carolina	S	21.59 MW	20.97 AW	43620 AAW	NCBLS	10//99-12//99
	Oklahoma	S	19.81 MW	20.34 AW	42310 AAW	OKBLS	10//99-12//99
	Pennsylvania	S	29.07 MW	28.07 AW	58380 AAW	PABLS	10//99-12//99
	South Carolina	S	12.8 MW	13.57 AW	28230 AAW	SCBLS	10//99-12//99
	Tennessee	S	17.97 MW	17.55 AW	36500 AAW	TNBLS	10//99-12//99
	Texas	S	15.55 MW	16.07 AW	33420 AAW	TXBLS	10//99-12//99
	Virginia	S	18 MW	19.36 AW	40270 AAW	VABLS	10//99-12//99
	West Virginia	S	21.42 MW	20.10 AW	41800 AAW	WVBLS	10//99-12//99
	Wisconsin	S	22.25 MW	23.33 AW	48530 AAW	WIBLS	10//99-12//99
	Puerto Rico	S	14.35 MW	13.52 AW	28120 AAW	PRBLS	10//99-12//99
Eligibility Interviewer							
Government Program	Alabama	S	14.48 MW	14.48 AW	30130 AAW	ALBLS	10//99-12//99
Government Program	Alaska	S	18.07 MW	18.42 AW	38320 AAW	AKBLS	10//99-12//99
Government Program	Arkansas	S	9.29 MW	9.85 AW	20490 AAW	ARBLS	10//99-12//99
Government Program	California	S	12.79 MW	13.12 AW	27290 AAW	CABLS	10//99-12//99
Government Program	Colorado	S	12.69 MW	12.83 AW	26680 AAW	COBLS	10//99-12//99
Government Program	Florida	S	11.88 MW	11.76 AW	24450 AAW	FLBLS	10//99-12//99
Government Program	Georgia	S	12.73 MW	13.71 AW	28520 AAW	GABLS	10//99-12//99

AAW Average annual wage	AOH Average offered, high	ASH Average starting, high	H Hourly	M Monthly	S Special: hourly and annual
AE Average entry wage	AOL Average offered, low	ASL Average starting, low	HI Highest wage paid	MTC Median total compensation	TQ Third quartile wage
AEX Average experienced wage	APH Average pay, high range	AW Average wage paid	HR High end range	MW Median wage paid	W Weekly
AO Average offered	APL Average pay, low range	FQ First quartile wage	LR Low end range	SQ Second quartile wage	Y Yearly

Occupation/Type/Industry	Location	Per	Low	Mid	High	Source	Date
Eligibility Interviewer							
Government Program	Idaho	S	10.65 MW	11.40 AW	23710 AAW	IDBLS	10//99-12//99
Government Program	Illinois	S	12.31 MW	14.39 AW	29920 AAW	ILBLS	10//99-12//99
Government Program	Indiana	S	11.25 MW	11.59 AW	24120 AAW	INBLS	10//99-12//99
Government Program	Iowa	S	14.88 MW	14.64 AW	30450 AAW	IABLS	10//99-12//99
Government Program	Michigan	S	18.11 MW	17.54 AW	36490 AAW	MIBLS	10//99-12//99
Government Program	Minnesota	S	16.05 MW	16.26 AW	33820 AAW	MNBLS	10//99-12//99
Government Program	Mississippi	S	10.65 MW	11.18 AW	23240 AAW	MSBLS	10//99-12//99
Government Program	Missouri	S	12.34 MW	12.74 AW	26500 AAW	MOBLS	10//99-12//99
Government Program	New Jersey	S	17.18 MW	17.72 AW	36850 AAW	NJBLS	10//99-12//99
Government Program	New York	S	14.84 MW	15.27 AW	31760 AAW	NYBLS	10//99-12//99
Government Program	North Carolina	S	11.77 MW	11.87 AW	24700 AAW	NCBLS	10//99-12//99
Government Program	North Dakota	S	12.12 MW	12.17 AW	25310 AAW	NDBLS	10//99-12//99
Government Program	Ohio	S	13.88 MW	14.47 AW	30110 AAW	OHBLS	10//99-12//99
Government Program	Oregon	S	13.73 MW	13.69 AW	28470 AAW	ORBLS	10//99-12//99
Government Program	Pennsylvania	S	17.03 MW	17.40 AW	36200 AAW	PABLS	10//99-12//99
Government Program	South Carolina	S	12.19 MW	13.09 AW	27230 AAW	SCBLS	10//99-12//99
Government Program	Texas	S	13 MW	13.11 AW	27260 AAW	TXBLS	10//99-12//99
Government Program	Utah	S	12.14 MW	12.14 AW	25240 AAW	UTBLS	10//99-12//99
Government Program	Virginia	S	12.74 MW	13.28 AW	27620 AAW	VABLS	10//99-12//99
Government Program	Washington	S	17.45 MW	16.78 AW	34910 AAW	WABLS	10//99-12//99
Government Program	West Virginia	S	10.03 MW	10.20 AW	21220 AAW	WVBLS	10//99-12//99
Government Program	Wisconsin	S	15.09 MW	15.40 AW	32030 AAW	WIBLS	10//99-12//99
Government Program	Puerto Rico	S	7.52 MW	8.50 AW	17690 AAW	PRBLS	10//99-12//99
Embalmer	Alabama	S	12.36 MW	12.80 AW	26620 AAW	ALBLS	10//99-12//99
	Arizona	S	12.6 MW	12.48 AW	25950 AAW	AZBLS	10//99-12//99
	Phoenix-Mesa MSA, AZ	S	12.45 MW	12.29 AW	25900 AAW	AZBLS	10//99-12//99
	Arkansas	S	14.33 MW	14.57 AW	30310 AAW	ARBLS	10//99-12//99
	California	S	15.62 MW	16.12 AW	33530 AAW	CABLS	10//99-12//99
	Bakersfield MSA, CA	S	18.77 MW	18.01 AW	39050 AAW	CABLS	10//99-12//99
	Fresno MSA, CA	S	12.67 MW	11.41 AW	26350 AAW	CABLS	10//99-12//99
	San Diego MSA, CA	S	11.56 MW	11.08 AW	24050 AAW	CABLS	10//99-12//99
	Colorado	S	11.39 MW	12.22 AW	25410 AAW	COBLS	10//99-12//99
	Connecticut	S	24.68 MW	24.70 AW	51380 AAW	CTBLS	10//99-12//99
	Bridgeport PMSA, CT	S	20.74 MW	19.78 AW	43150 AAW	CTBLS	10//99-12//99
	Hartford MSA, CT	S	29.28 MW	33.33 AW	60900 AAW	CTBLS	10//99-12//99
	Florida	S	12.18 MW	12.23 AW	25450 AAW	FLBLS	10//99-12//99
	Miami PMSA, FL	S	12.07 MW	10.39 AW	25110 AAW	FLBLS	10//99-12//99
	Tampa-St. Petersburg-Clearwater MSA, FL	S	12.07 MW	11.53 AW	25100 AAW	FLBLS	10//99-12//99
	Georgia	S	11.89 MW	11.97 AW	24900 AAW	GABLS	10//99-12//99
	Augusta-Aiken MSA, GA-SC	S	12.70 MW	13.12 AW	26420 AAW	GABLS	10//99-12//99
	Macon MSA, GA	S	12.30 MW	12.66 AW	25580 AAW	GABLS	10//99-12//99
	Idaho	S	14.57 MW	13.13 AW	27310 AAW	IDBLS	10//99-12//99
	Illinois	S	14 MW	15.51 AW	32260 AAW	ILBLS	10//99-12//99
	Chicago PMSA, IL	S	17.51 MW	14.39 AW	36410 AAW	ILBLS	10//99-12//99
	Indiana	S	12.93 MW	14.26 AW	29660 AAW	INBLS	10//99-12//99
	Iowa	S	15.46 MW	15.57 AW	32380 AAW	IABLS	10//99-12//99
	Des Moines MSA, IA	S	14.27 MW	14.98 AW	29690 AAW	IABLS	10//99-12//99
	Kansas	S	14.66 MW	14.07 AW	29270 AAW	KSBLS	10//99-12//99
	Kentucky	S	14.93 MW	14.35 AW	29840 AAW	KYBLS	10//99-12//99
	Lexington MSA, KY	S	13.73 MW	12.97 AW	28560 AAW	KYBLS	10//99-12//99
	Louisville MSA, KY-IN	S	16.57 MW	16.69 AW	34460 AAW	KYBLS	10//99-12//99
	Louisiana	S	15.26 MW	14.64 AW	30450 AAW	LABLS	10//99-12//99
	New Orleans MSA, LA	S	14.01 MW	14.01 AW	29130 AAW	LABLS	10//99-12//99
	Maine	S	15.05 MW	14.94 AW	31080 AAW	MEBLS	10//99-12//99
	Maryland	S	17.67 MW	18.86 AW	39220 AAW	MDBLS	10//99-12//99
	Massachusetts	S	14.59 MW	14.43 AW	30010 AAW	MABLS	10//99-12//99
	Boston PMSA, MA-NH	S	15.16 MW	16.68 AW	31540 AAW	MABLS	10//99-12//99
	Michigan	S	14.47 MW	13.94 AW	28990 AAW	MIBLS	10//99-12//99
	Detroit PMSA, MI	S	14.29 MW	14.87 AW	29720 AAW	MIBLS	10//99-12//99
	Grand Rapids-Muskegon-Holland MSA, MI	S	13.47 MW	14.09 AW	28020 AAW	MIBLS	10//99-12//99
	Mississippi	S	14.32 MW	14.15 AW	29430 AAW	MSBLS	10//99-12//99
	Jackson MSA, MS	S	14.24 MW	14.40 AW	29620 AAW	MSBLS	10//99-12//99
	Missouri	S	14.01 MW	16.17 AW	33640 AAW	MOBLS	10//99-12//99
	St. Louis MSA, MO-IL	S	18.16 MW	15.81 AW	37770 AAW	MOBLS	10//99-12//99
	Omaha MSA, NE-IA	S	17.34 MW	16.06 AW	36060 AAW	NEBLS	10//99-12//99
	Nevada	S	13.44 MW	12.83 AW	26680 AAW	NVBLS	10//99-12//99
	Las Vegas MSA, NV-AZ	S	11.29 MW	9.13 AW	23480 AAW	NVBLS	10//99-12//99
	New Jersey	S	15.27 MW	15.35 AW	31920 AAW	NJBLS	10//99-12//99
	New York	S	13.05 MW	14.07 AW	29270 AAW	NYBLS	10//99-12//99

AAW Average annual wage	**AOH** Average offered, high	**ASH** Average starting, high	**H** Hourly	**M** Monthly	**S** Special: hourly and annual
AE Average entry wage	**AOL** Average offered, low	**ASL** Average starting, low	**HI** Highest wage paid	**MTC** Median total compensation	**TQ** Third quartile wage
AEX Average experienced wage	**APH** Average pay, high range	**AW** Average wage paid	**HR** High end range	**MW** Median wage paid	**W** Weekly
AO Average offered	**APL** Average pay, low range	**FQ** First quartile wage	**LR** Low end range	**SQ** Second quartile wage	**Y** Yearly

Occupation/Type/Industry	Location	Per	Low	Mid	High	Source	Date
Embalmer	North Carolina	s	13.66 MW	15.57 AW	32400 AAW	NCBLS	10//99-12//99
	Greensboro--Winston-Salem-- High Point MSA, NC	s	19.16 MW	17.81 AW	39860 AAW	NCBLS	10//99-12//99
	North Dakota	s	12.13 MW	12.00 AW	24950 AAW	NDBLS	10//99-12//99
	Ohio	s	20.35 MW	18.38 AW	38220 AAW	OHBLS	10//99-12//99
	Cincinnati PMSA, OH-KY-IN	s	18.50 MW	17.53 AW	38490 AAW	OHBLS	10//99-12//99
	Columbus MSA, OH	s	15.71 MW	15.90 AW	32670 AAW	OHBLS	10//99-12//99
	Oklahoma	s	14.43 MW	16.53 AW	34370 AAW	OKBLS	10//99-12//99
	Pennsylvania	s	11.62 MW	14.09 AW	29300 AAW	PABLS	10//99-12//99
	Rhode Island	s	17.67 MW	18.01 AW	37460 AAW	RIBLS	10//99-12//99
	Providence-Fall River- Warwick MSA, RI-MA	s	17.59 MW	17.88 AW	36590 AAW	RIBLS	10//99-12//99
	South Carolina	s	15.29 MW	16.00 AW	33290 AAW	SCBLS	10//99-12//99
	Charleston-North Charleston MSA, SC	s	10.70 MW	10.42 AW	22260 AAW	SCBLS	10//99-12//99
	Greenville-Spartanburg- Anderson MSA, SC	s	19.30 MW	20.74 AW	40130 AAW	SCBLS	10//99-12//99
	Myrtle Beach MSA, SC	s	16.65 MW	17.82 AW	34640 AAW	SCBLS	10//99-12//99
	Tennessee	s	10.66 MW	12.46 AW	25910 AAW	TNBLS	10//99-12//99
	Memphis MSA, TN-AR-MS	s	13.16 MW	12.77 AW	27370 AAW	MSBLS	10//99-12//99
	Texas	s	11.59 MW	12.14 AW	25250 AAW	TXBLS	10//99-12//99
	Houston PMSA, TX	s	11.44 MW	10.50 AW	23790 AAW	TXBLS	10//99-12//99
	Virginia	s	11.6 MW	12.04 AW	25040 AAW	VABLS	10//99-12//99
	Richmond-Petersburg MSA, VA	s	14.58 MW	14.71 AW	30330 AAW	VABLS	10//99-12//99
	Washington	s	19.2 MW	19.49 AW	40530 AAW	WABLS	10//99-12//99
	Seattle-Bellevue-Everett PMSA, WA	s	19.34 MW	19.12 AW	40230 AAW	WABLS	10//99-12//99
	West Virginia	s	14.52 MW	13.07 AW	27190 AAW	WVBLS	10//99-12//99
	Wisconsin	s	12.91 MW	15.74 AW	32730 AAW	WIBLS	10//99-12//99
	Puerto Rico	s	7.43 MW	7.48 AW	15560 AAW	PRBLS	10//99-12//99
	San Juan-Bayamon PMSA, PR	s	8.31 MW	8.23 AW	17270 AAW	PRBLS	10//99-12//99
Emergency Management Specialist	Alabama	s	14.99 MW	14.91 AW	31010 AAW	ALBLS	10//99-12//99
	Arizona	s	20.04 MW	20.25 AW	42130 AAW	AZBLS	10//99-12//99
	Arkansas	s	11.33 MW	12.52 AW	26040 AAW	ARBLS	10//99-12//99
	California	s	23.96 MW	25.43 AW	52890 AAW	CABLS	10//99-12//99
	Connecticut	s	17.84 MW	19.94 AW	41470 AAW	CTBLS	10//99-12//99
	District of Columbia	s	15.71 MW	17.13 AW	35620 AAW	DCBLS	10//99-12//99
	Florida	s	17.95 MW	21.24 AW	44190 AAW	FLBLS	10//99-12//99
	Georgia	s	16.31 MW	16.05 AW	33390 AAW	GABLS	10//99-12//99
	Hawaii	s	22.22 MW	23.45 AW	48790 AAW	HIBLS	10//99-12//99
	Idaho	s	11.61 MW	15.88 AW	33040 AAW	IDBLS	10//99-12//99
	Illinois	s	15.02 MW	16.56 AW	34440 AAW	ILBLS	10//99-12//99
	Indiana	s	12.34 MW	13.27 AW	27590 AAW	INBLS	10//99-12//99
	Iowa	s	12.49 MW	14.97 AW	31140 AAW	IABLS	10//99-12//99
	Kansas	s	13.93 MW	13.54 AW	28160 AAW	KSBLS	10//99-12//99
	Kentucky	s	14.37 MW	15.50 AW	32230 AAW	KYBLS	10//99-12//99
	Louisiana	s	17.21 MW	21.05 AW	43780 AAW	LABLS	10//99-12//99
	Maine	s	14.58 MW	15.51 AW	32260 AAW	MEBLS	10//99-12//99
	Maryland	s	20.52 MW	21.73 AW	45190 AAW	MDBLS	10//99-12//99
	Massachusetts	s	23.49 MW	23.25 AW	48370 AAW	MABLS	10//99-12//99
	Michigan	s	16.54 MW	18.45 AW	38380 AAW	MIBLS	10//99-12//99
	Minnesota	s	17.07 MW	18.80 AW	39110 AAW	MNBLS	10//99-12//99
	Mississippi	s	10.84 MW	12.03 AW	25030 AAW	MSBLS	10//99-12//99
	Missouri	s	15.74 MW	16.92 AW	35200 AAW	MOBLS	10//99-12//99
	Montana	s	13.86 MW	14.66 AW	30500 AAW	MTBLS	10//99-12//99
	Nebraska	s	17.99 MW	19.21 AW	39970 AAW	NEBLS	10//99-12//99
	Nevada	s	19.74 MW	20.65 AW	42940 AAW	NVBLS	10//99-12//99
	New Hampshire	s	17.2 MW	16.30 AW	33910 AAW	NHBLS	10//99-12//99
	New Jersey	s	19.61 MW	22.50 AW	46810 AAW	NJBLS	10//99-12//99
	New Mexico	s	16.26 MW	18.82 AW	39140 AAW	NMBLS	10//99-12//99
	New York	s	31.46 MW	32.08 AW	66720 AAW	NYBLS	10//99-12//99
	North Carolina	s	17.38 MW	18.20 AW	37850 AAW	NCBLS	10//99-12//99
	North Dakota	s	14.29 MW	13.84 AW	28800 AAW	NDBLS	10//99-12//99
	Ohio	s	15.85 MW	17.30 AW	35980 AAW	OHBLS	10//99-12//99
	Oklahoma	s	18.84 MW	20.66 AW	42980 AAW	OKBLS	10//99-12//99
	Oregon	s	15.49 MW	16.82 AW	34990 AAW	ORBLS	10//99-12//99
	Pennsylvania	s	20.72 MW	21.52 AW	44760 AAW	PABLS	10//99-12//99
	South Carolina	s	16.98 MW	18.57 AW	38630 AAW	SCBLS	10//99-12//99
	South Dakota	s	11.44 MW	11.99 AW	24930 AAW	SDBLS	10//99-12//99

Occupation/Type/Industry	Location	Per	Low	Mid	High	Source	Date
Emergency Management Specialist	Tennessee	S	15.61 MW	17.12 AW	35600 AAW	TNBLS	10//99-12//99
	Texas	S	21.75 MW	23.15 AW	48150 AAW	TXBLS	10//99-12//99
	Utah	S	22.7 MW	22.19 AW	46160 AAW	UTBLS	10//99-12//99
	Virginia	S	20.84 MW	21.48 AW	44670 AAW	VABLS	10//99-12//99
	Washington	S	16.35 MW	17.97 AW	37380 AAW	WABLS	10//99-12//99
	West Virginia	S	12.04 MW	13.85 AW	28800 AAW	WVBLS	10//99-12//99
	Wisconsin	S	16.17 MW	18.44 AW	38360 AAW	WIBLS	10//99-12//99
	Wyoming	S	10.57 MW	14.13 AW	29390 AAW	WYBLS	10//99-12//99
	Puerto Rico	S	7.8 MW	9.37 AW	19490 AAW	PRBLS	10//99-12//99
Emergency Medical Technician and Paramedic	Alabama	S	10.06 MW	10.78 AW	22420 AAW	ALBLS	10//99-12//99
	Birmingham MSA, AL	S	12.53 MW	11.35 AW	26070 AAW	ALBLS	10//99-12//99
	Dothan MSA, AL	S	10.86 MW	10.65 AW	22590 AAW	ALBLS	10//99-12//99
	Mobile MSA, AL	S	9.92 MW	9.70 AW	20630 AAW	ALBLS	10//99-12//99
	Montgomery MSA, AL	S	11.06 MW	10.32 AW	22990 AAW	ALBLS	10//99-12//99
	Alaska	S	14.79 MW	16.61 AW	34540 AAW	AKBLS	10//99-12//99
	Arizona	S	8.3 MW	9.61 AW	19990 AAW	AZBLS	10//99-12//99
	Tucson MSA, AZ	S	13.02 MW	12.64 AW	27080 AAW	AZBLS	10//99-12//99
	Arkansas	S	9.65 MW	10.07 AW	20950 AAW	ARBLS	10//99-12//99
	Fayetteville-Springdale-Rogers MSA, AR	S	10.63 MW	10.61 AW	22120 AAW	ARBLS	10//99-12//99
	Fort Smith MSA, AR-OK	S	9.57 MW	8.89 AW	19900 AAW	ARBLS	10//99-12//99
	Little Rock-North Little Rock MSA, AR	S	11.22 MW	10.86 AW	23330 AAW	ARBLS	10//99-12//99
	California	S	11.45 MW	12.99 AW	27020 AAW	CABLS	10//99-12//99
	Fresno MSA, CA	S	12.18 MW	11.20 AW	25340 AAW	CABLS	10//99-12//99
	Los Angeles-Long Beach PMSA, CA	S	10.72 MW	8.70 AW	22290 AAW	CABLS	10//99-12//99
	Modesto MSA, CA	S	10.82 MW	9.49 AW	22510 AAW	CABLS	10//99-12//99
	Oakland PMSA, CA	S	12.39 MW	13.08 AW	25770 AAW	CABLS	10//99-12//99
	Orange County PMSA, CA	S	11.58 MW	9.24 AW	24080 AAW	CABLS	10//99-12//99
	Redding MSA, CA	S	10.52 MW	9.51 AW	21880 AAW	CABLS	10//99-12//99
	Riverside-San Bernardino PMSA, CA	S	12.67 MW	10.48 AW	26350 AAW	CABLS	10//99-12//99
	Sacramento PMSA, CA	S	16.93 MW	14.10 AW	35220 AAW	CABLS	10//99-12//99
	San Diego MSA, CA	S	14.70 MW	12.36 AW	30570 AAW	CABLS	10//99-12//99
	San Francisco PMSA, CA	S	13.54 MW	13.91 AW	28170 AAW	CABLS	10//99-12//99
	San Luis Obispo-Atascadero-Paso Robles MSA, CA	S	14.09 MW	14.00 AW	29310 AAW	CABLS	10//99-12//99
	Santa Rosa PMSA, CA	S	10.18 MW	9.26 AW	21180 AAW	CABLS	10//99-12//99
	Vallejo-Fairfield-Napa PMSA, CA	S	13.27 MW	11.73 AW	27590 AAW	CABLS	10//99-12//99
	Visalia-Tulare-Porterville MSA, CA	S	9.20 MW	7.33 AW	19130 AAW	CABLS	10//99-12//99
	Colorado	S	11 MW	11.89 AW	24720 AAW	COBLS	10//99-12//99
	Denver PMSA, CO	S	14.30 MW	12.60 AW	29750 AAW	COBLS	10//99-12//99
	Fort Collins-Loveland MSA, CO	S	13.46 MW	11.90 AW	27990 AAW	COBLS	10//99-12//99
	Pueblo MSA, CO	S	11.14 MW	11.17 AW	23170 AAW	COBLS	10//99-12//99
	Connecticut	S	11.97 MW	12.82 AW	26670 AAW	CTBLS	10//99-12//99
	Bridgeport PMSA, CT	S	12.75 MW	12.32 AW	26530 AAW	CTBLS	10//99-12//99
	Danbury PMSA, CT	S	12.75 MW	12.67 AW	26530 AAW	CTBLS	10//99-12//99
	Hartford MSA, CT	S	13.06 MW	11.91 AW	27170 AAW	CTBLS	10//99-12//99
	New Haven-Meriden PMSA, CT	S	12.38 MW	11.62 AW	25740 AAW	CTBLS	10//99-12//99
	Stamford-Norwalk PMSA, CT	S	15.61 MW	15.56 AW	32480 AAW	CTBLS	10//99-12//99
	District of Columbia	S	10.55 MW	11.91 AW	24780 AAW	DCBLS	10//99-12//99
	Washington PMSA, DC-MD-VA-WV	S	11.55 MW	10.29 AW	24020 AAW	DCBLS	10//99-12//99
	Florida	S	10.67 MW	11.76 AW	24460 AAW	FLBLS	10//99-12//99
	Daytona Beach MSA, FL	S	10.28 MW	9.97 AW	21390 AAW	FLBLS	10//99-12//99
	Fort Lauderdale PMSA, FL	S	13.37 MW	12.31 AW	27820 AAW	FLBLS	10//99-12//99
	Jacksonville MSA, FL	S	11.29 MW	10.39 AW	23480 AAW	FLBLS	10//99-12//99
	Melbourne-Titusville-Palm Bay MSA, FL	S	10.90 MW	10.28 AW	22660 AAW	FLBLS	10//99-12//99
	Miami PMSA, FL	S	11.10 MW	9.85 AW	23080 AAW	FLBLS	10//99-12//99
	Orlando MSA, FL	S	12.29 MW	11.23 AW	25570 AAW	FLBLS	10//99-12//99
	Pensacola MSA, FL	S	12.30 MW	12.35 AW	25590 AAW	FLBLS	10//99-12//99
	Sarasota-Bradenton MSA, FL	S	12.73 MW	11.30 AW	26480 AAW	FLBLS	10//99-12//99
	Tallahassee MSA, FL	S	8.86 MW	8.31 AW	18420 AAW	FLBLS	10//99-12//99

AAW Average annual wage	AOH Average offered, high	ASH Average starting, high	H Hourly	M Monthly	S Special: hourly and annual
AE Average entry wage	AOL Average offered, low	ASL Average starting, low	HI Highest wage paid	MTC Median total compensation	TQ Third quartile wage
AEX Average experienced wage	APH Average pay, high range	AW Average wage paid	HR High end range	MW Median wage paid	W Weekly
AO Average offered	APL Average pay, low range	FQ First quartile wage	LR Low end range	SQ Second quartile wage	Y Yearly

Occupation/Type/Industry	Location	Per	Low	Mid	High	Source	Date
Emergency Medical Technician and Paramedic	Tampa-St. Petersburg-Clearwater MSA, FL	S	12.12 MW	10.57 AW	25220 AAW	FLBLS	10//99-12//99
	West Palm Beach-Boca Raton MSA, FL	S	14.45 MW	12.95 AW	30060 AAW	FLBLS	10//99-12//99
	Georgia	S	9.62 MW	10.21 AW	21240 AAW	GABLS	10//99-12//99
	Atlanta MSA, GA	S	10.58 MW	9.89 AW	22000 AAW	GABLS	10//99-12//99
	Augusta-Aiken MSA, GA-SC	S	12.22 MW	9.23 AW	25410 AAW	GABLS	10//99-12//99
	Columbus MSA, GA-AL	S	8.99 MW	8.91 AW	18690 AAW	GABLS	10//99-12//99
	Macon MSA, GA	S	10.78 MW	9.75 AW	22410 AAW	GABLS	10//99-12//99
	Hawaii	S	14.84 MW	14.77 AW	30720 AAW	HIBLS	10//99-12//99
	Honolulu MSA, HI	S	14.35 MW	14.30 AW	29850 AAW	HIBLS	10//99-12//99
	Idaho	S	11.47 MW	12.44 AW	25880 AAW	IDBLS	10//99-12//99
	Boise City MSA, ID	S	13.66 MW	12.74 AW	28420 AAW	IDBLS	10//99-12//99
	Illinois	S	10.02 MW	11.51 AW	23930 AAW	ILBLS	10//99-12//99
	Chicago PMSA, IL	S	12.91 MW	11.28 AW	26860 AAW	ILBLS	10//99-12//99
	Peoria-Pekin MSA, IL	S	9.63 MW	8.56 AW	20030 AAW	ILBLS	10//99-12//99
	Springfield MSA, IL	S	9.18 MW	7.82 AW	19090 AAW	ILBLS	10//99-12//99
	Indiana	S	9.89 MW	10.33 AW	21480 AAW	INBLS	10//99-12//99
	Elkhart-Goshen MSA, IN	S	10.49 MW	10.45 AW	21810 AAW	INBLS	10//99-12//99
	Evansville-Henderson MSA, IN-KY	S	11.68 MW	11.11 AW	24290 AAW	INBLS	10//99-12//99
	Fort Wayne MSA, IN	S	10.10 MW	9.26 AW	21000 AAW	INBLS	10//99-12//99
	Gary PMSA, IN	S	10.46 MW	9.44 AW	21750 AAW	INBLS	10//99-12//99
	Indianapolis MSA, IN	S	11.61 MW	11.38 AW	24140 AAW	INBLS	10//99-12//99
	South Bend MSA, IN	S	9.58 MW	9.07 AW	19920 AAW	INBLS	10//99-12//99
	Iowa	S	9.08 MW	9.50 AW	19760 AAW	IABLS	10//99-12//99
	Davenport-Moline-Rock Island MSA, IA-IL	S	10.68 MW	10.64 AW	22220 AAW	IABLS	10//99-12//99
	Des Moines MSA, IA	S	11.55 MW	10.55 AW	24030 AAW	IABLS	10//99-12//99
	Waterloo-Cedar Falls MSA, IA	S	9.73 MW	9.23 AW	20250 AAW	IABLS	10//99-12//99
	Kansas	S	8.15 MW	8.82 AW	18350 AAW	KSBLS	10//99-12//99
	Wichita MSA, KS	S	7.88 MW	7.45 AW	16400 AAW	KSBLS	10//99-12//99
	Kentucky	S	8.34 MW	8.63 AW	17950 AAW	KYBLS	10//99-12//99
	Lexington MSA, KY	S	11.73 MW	10.86 AW	24390 AAW	KYBLS	10//99-12//99
	Louisville MSA, KY-IN	S	9.26 MW	8.47 AW	19270 AAW	KYBLS	10//99-12//99
	Louisiana	S	9.99 MW	10.67 AW	22190 AAW	LABLS	10//99-12//99
	Baton Rouge MSA, LA	S	11.08 MW	9.97 AW	23040 AAW	LABLS	10//99-12//99
	Houma MSA, LA	S	10.92 MW	10.94 AW	22700 AAW	LABLS	10//99-12//99
	New Orleans MSA, LA	S	10.64 MW	10.11 AW	22130 AAW	LABLS	10//99-12//99
	Maine	S	9.72 MW	9.85 AW	20490 AAW	MEBLS	10//99-12//99
	Portland MSA, ME	S	11.69 MW	11.37 AW	24320 AAW	MEBLS	10//99-12//99
	Maryland	S	10.71 MW	12.22 AW	25420 AAW	MDBLS	10//99-12//99
	Baltimore PMSA, MD	S	14.35 MW	14.17 AW	29840 AAW	MDBLS	10//99-12//99
	Massachusetts	S	10.78 MW	12.23 AW	25430 AAW	MABLS	10//99-12//99
	Boston PMSA, MA-NH	S	12.60 MW	11.07 AW	26210 AAW	MABLS	10//99-12//99
	Lawrence PMSA, MA-NH	S	10.60 MW	9.90 AW	22040 AAW	MABLS	10//99-12//99
	Lowell PMSA, MA-NH	S	12.81 MW	11.82 AW	26640 AAW	MABLS	10//99-12//99
	New Bedford PMSA, MA	S	11.57 MW	10.45 AW	24060 AAW	MABLS	10//99-12//99
	Springfield MSA, MA	S	11.39 MW	10.37 AW	23690 AAW	MABLS	10//99-12//99
	Worcester PMSA, MA-CT	S	11.09 MW	10.48 AW	23060 AAW	MABLS	10//99-12//99
	Michigan	S	11.01 MW	11.13 AW	23140 AAW	MIBLS	10//99-12//99
	Ann Arbor PMSA, MI	S	10.99 MW	10.06 AW	22850 AAW	MIBLS	10//99-12//99
	Benton Harbor MSA, MI	S	10.83 MW	8.81 AW	22530 AAW	MIBLS	10//99-12//99
	Detroit PMSA, MI	S	12.27 MW	12.22 AW	25520 AAW	MIBLS	10//99-12//99
	Flint PMSA, MI	S	9.52 MW	8.37 AW	19800 AAW	MIBLS	10//99-12//99
	Grand Rapids-Muskegon-Holland MSA, MI	S	10.42 MW	10.79 AW	21680 AAW	MIBLS	10//99-12//99
	Kalamazoo-Battle Creek MSA, MI	S	8.92 MW	8.73 AW	18560 AAW	MIBLS	10//99-12//99
	Lansing-East Lansing MSA, MI	S	10.61 MW	9.04 AW	22080 AAW	MIBLS	10//99-12//99
	Minnesota	S	10.32 MW	11.15 AW	23190 AAW	MNBLS	10//99-12//99
	Duluth-Superior MSA, MN-WI	S	9.53 MW	9.72 AW	19830 AAW	MNBLS	10//99-12//99
	Minneapolis-St. Paul MSA, MN-WI	S	13.04 MW	12.62 AW	27120 AAW	MNBLS	10//99-12//99
	Mississippi	S	9.76 MW	9.94 AW	20680 AAW	MSBLS	10//99-12//99
	Missouri	S	10.09 MW	11.97 AW	24900 AAW	MOBLS	10//99-12//99
	Kansas City MSA, MO-KS	S	11.53 MW	11.24 AW	23990 AAW	MOBLS	10//99-12//99
	St. Louis MSA, MO-IL	S	14.47 MW	11.39 AW	30100 AAW	MOBLS	10//99-12//99
	Montana	S	8.81 MW	9.52 AW	19810 AAW	MTBLS	10//99-12//99
	Nebraska	S	8.73 MW	10.16 AW	21120 AAW	NEBLS	10//99-12//99
	Omaha MSA, NE-IA	S	13.36 MW	10.65 AW	27780 AAW	NEBLS	10//99-12//99

AAW Average annual wage	**AOH** Average offered, high	**ASH** Average starting, high	**H** Hourly	**M** Monthly	**S** Special: hourly and annual
AE Average entry wage	**AOL** Average offered, low	**ASL** Average starting, low	**HI** Highest wage paid	**MTC** Median total compensation	**TQ** Third quartile wage
AEX Average experienced wage	**APH** Average pay, high range	**AW** Average wage paid	**HR** High end range	**MW** Median wage paid	**W** Weekly
AO Average offered	**APL** Average pay, low range	**FQ** First quartile wage	**LR** Low end range	**SQ** Second quartile wage	**Y** Yearly

Occupation/Type/Industry	Location	Per	Low	Mid	High	Source	Date
Emergency Medical Technician and Paramedic							
	Nevada	S	12.56 MW	13.47 AW	28010 AAW	NVBLS	10//99-12//99
	Reno MSA, NV	S	11.69 MW	11.43 AW	24320 AAW	NVBLS	10//99-12//99
	New Hampshire	S	10.41 MW	10.90 AW	22670 AAW	NHBLS	10//99-12//99
	Portsmouth-Rochester PMSA, NH-ME	S	11.96 MW	12.13 AW	24880 AAW	NHBLS	10//99-12//99
	New Jersey	S	10.74 MW	12.09 AW	25140 AAW	NJBLS	10//99-12//99
	Atlantic-Cape May PMSA, NJ	S	8.98 MW	8.49 AW	18670 AAW	NJBLS	10//99-12//99
	Bergen-Passaic PMSA, NJ	S	11.65 MW	10.67 AW	24230 AAW	NJBLS	10//99-12//99
	Jersey City PMSA, NJ	S	13.43 MW	12.72 AW	27940 AAW	NJBLS	10//99-12//99
	Middlesex-Somerset-Hunterdon PMSA, NJ	S	12.14 MW	10.47 AW	25240 AAW	NJBLS	10//99-12//99
	Monmouth-Ocean PMSA, NJ	S	12.51 MW	10.87 AW	26030 AAW	NJBLS	10//99-12//99
	Newark PMSA, NJ	S	12.72 MW	11.48 AW	26450 AAW	NJBLS	10//99-12//99
	Trenton PMSA, NJ	S	14.93 MW	16.34 AW	31050 AAW	NJBLS	10//99-12//99
	Vineland-Millville-Bridgeton PMSA, NJ	S	10.94 MW	10.38 AW	22750 AAW	NJBLS	10//99-12//99
	New Mexico	S	11.17 MW	11.51 AW	23940 AAW	NMBLS	10//99-12//99
	Albuquerque MSA, NM	S	12.33 MW	11.89 AW	25640 AAW	NMBLS	10//99-12//99
	New York	S	12.16 MW	12.99 AW	27020 AAW	NYBLS	10//99-12//99
	Albany-Schenectady-Troy MSA, NY	S	11.38 MW	10.78 AW	23670 AAW	NYBLS	10//99-12//99
	Buffalo-Niagara Falls MSA, NY	S	10.68 MW	10.92 AW	22210 AAW	NYBLS	10//99-12//99
	Nassau-Suffolk PMSA, NY	S	20.58 MW	21.86 AW	42810 AAW	NYBLS	10//99-12//99
	New York PMSA, NY	S	14.10 MW	13.75 AW	29330 AAW	NYBLS	10//99-12//99
	Rochester MSA, NY	S	10.95 MW	11.25 AW	22770 AAW	NYBLS	10//99-12//99
	North Carolina	S	10.5 MW	10.91 AW	22690 AAW	NCBLS	10//99-12//99
	Charlotte-Gastonia-Rock Hill MSA, NC-SC	S	11.12 MW	10.90 AW	23120 AAW	NCBLS	10//99-12//99
	Goldsboro MSA, NC	S	11.52 MW	10.29 AW	23970 AAW	NCBLS	10//99-12//99
	Greensboro--Winston-Salem--High Point MSA, NC	S	11.27 MW	10.40 AW	23440 AAW	NCBLS	10//99-12//99
	Greenville MSA, NC	S	11.22 MW	11.31 AW	23340 AAW	NCBLS	10//99-12//99
	Raleigh-Durham-Chapel Hill MSA, NC	S	11.13 MW	10.23 AW	23150 AAW	NCBLS	10//99-12//99
	North Dakota	S	10.05 MW	10.35 AW	21530 AAW	NDBLS	10//99-12//99
	Fargo-Moorhead MSA, ND-MN	S	10.90 MW	10.02 AW	22670 AAW	NDBLS	10//99-12//99
	Grand Forks MSA, ND-MN	S	10.40 MW	10.01 AW	21630 AAW	NDBLS	10//99-12//99
	Ohio	S	10.37 MW	11.12 AW	23120 AAW	OHBLS	10//99-12//99
	Akron PMSA, OH	S	12.14 MW	11.40 AW	25250 AAW	OHBLS	10//99-12//99
	Canton-Massillon MSA, OH	S	10.78 MW	10.77 AW	22430 AAW	OHBLS	10//99-12//99
	Cincinnati PMSA, OH-KY-IN	S	11.55 MW	10.37 AW	24030 AAW	OHBLS	10//99-12//99
	Cleveland-Lorain-Elyria PMSA, OH	S	11.81 MW	11.18 AW	24570 AAW	OHBLS	10//99-12//99
	Columbus MSA, OH	S	12.13 MW	11.43 AW	25240 AAW	OHBLS	10//99-12//99
	Dayton-Springfield MSA, OH	S	9.70 MW	9.09 AW	20180 AAW	OHBLS	10//99-12//99
	Hamilton-Middletown PMSA, OH	S	10.64 MW	10.17 AW	22140 AAW	OHBLS	10//99-12//99
	Mansfield MSA, OH	S	7.78 MW	7.59 AW	16170 AAW	OHBLS	10//99-12//99
	Steubenville-Weirton MSA, OH-WV	S	8.05 MW	7.81 AW	16750 AAW	OHBLS	10//99-12//99
	Toledo MSA, OH	S	11.15 MW	11.57 AW	23190 AAW	OHBLS	10//99-12//99
	Youngstown-Warren MSA, OH	S	9.68 MW	9.37 AW	20130 AAW	OHBLS	10//99-12//99
	Oklahoma	S	8.64 MW	9.09 AW	18900 AAW	OKBLS	10//99-12//99
	Oklahoma City MSA, OK	S	10.86 MW	10.52 AW	22590 AAW	OKBLS	10//99-12//99
	Tulsa MSA, OK	S	9.28 MW	9.05 AW	19310 AAW	OKBLS	10//99-12//99
	Oregon	S	10.95 MW	12.68 AW	26380 AAW	ORBLS	10//99-12//99
	Eugene-Springfield MSA, OR	S	15.16 MW	17.31 AW	31530 AAW	ORBLS	10//99-12//99
	Portland-Vancouver PMSA, OR-WA	S	13.19 MW	11.27 AW	27440 AAW	ORBLS	10//99-12//99
	Salem PMSA, OR	S	11.68 MW	10.15 AW	24300 AAW	ORBLS	10//99-12//99
	Pennsylvania	S	9.58 MW	9.79 AW	20370 AAW	PABLS	10//99-12//99
	Allentown-Bethlehem-Easton MSA, PA	S	10.90 MW	11.05 AW	22680 AAW	PABLS	10//99-12//99
	Altoona MSA, PA	S	6.91 MW	7.04 AW	14370 AAW	PABLS	10//99-12//99
	Harrisburg-Lebanon-Carlisle MSA, PA	S	9.93 MW	9.62 AW	20640 AAW	PABLS	10//99-12//99
	Johnstown MSA, PA	S	7.39 MW	6.82 AW	15380 AAW	PABLS	10//99-12//99
	Lancaster MSA, PA	S	8.65 MW	8.23 AW	18000 AAW	PABLS	10//99-12//99
	Philadelphia PMSA, PA-NJ	S	10.71 MW	10.30 AW	22280 AAW	PABLS	10//99-12//99

Occupation/Type/Industry	Location	Per	Low	Mid	High	Source	Date
Emergency Medical Technician and Paramedic	Pittsburgh MSA, PA	S	10.06 MW	9.86 AW	20930 AAW	PABLS	10//99-12//99
	Reading MSA, PA	S	9.15 MW	9.49 AW	19030 AAW	PABLS	10//99-12//99
	Scranton--Wilkes-Barre--Hazleton MSA, PA	S	8.93 MW	8.48 AW	18570 AAW	PABLS	10//99-12//99
	Sharon MSA, PA	S	9.59 MW	9.52 AW	19950 AAW	PABLS	10//99-12//99
	York MSA, PA	S	8.28 MW	7.96 AW	17230 AAW	PABLS	10//99-12//99
	Rhode Island	S	9.92 MW	10.65 AW	22140 AAW	RIBLS	10//99-12//99
	Providence-Fall River-Warwick MSA, RI-MA	S	10.86 MW	10.09 AW	22580 AAW	RIBLS	10//99-12//99
	South Carolina	S	9.99 MW	10.58 AW	22000 AAW	SCBLS	10//99-12//99
	Charleston-North Charleston MSA, SC	S	9.20 MW	8.94 AW	19140 AAW	SCBLS	10//99-12//99
	Columbia MSA, SC	S	10.00 MW	9.47 AW	20810 AAW	SCBLS	10//99-12//99
	Greenville-Spartanburg-Anderson MSA, SC	S	11.04 MW	10.82 AW	22970 AAW	SCBLS	10//99-12//99
	South Dakota	S	8.69 MW	9.58 AW	19930 AAW	SDBLS	10//99-12//99
	Tennessee	S	10.13 MW	11.33 AW	23560 AAW	TNBLS	10//99-12//99
	Chattanooga MSA, TN-GA	S	11.05 MW	10.08 AW	22980 AAW	TNBLS	10//99-12//99
	Clarksville-Hopkinsville MSA, TN-KY	S	9.42 MW	9.56 AW	19590 AAW	TNBLS	10//99-12//99
	Johnson City-Kingsport-Bristol MSA, TN-VA	S	9.40 MW	8.95 AW	19560 AAW	TNBLS	10//99-12//99
	Knoxville MSA, TN	S	10.57 MW	10.01 AW	21980 AAW	TNBLS	10//99-12//99
	Memphis MSA, TN-AR-MS	S	14.31 MW	13.24 AW	29770 AAW	MSBLS	10//99-12//99
	Nashville MSA, TN	S	12.44 MW	10.94 AW	25870 AAW	TNBLS	10//99-12//99
	Texas	S	9.61 MW	10.19 AW	21190 AAW	TXBLS	10//99-12//99
	Austin-San Marcos MSA, TX	S	12.17 MW	10.68 AW	25310 AAW	TXBLS	10//99-12//99
	Beaumont-Port Arthur MSA, TX	S	10.56 MW	9.99 AW	21960 AAW	TXBLS	10//99-12//99
	Brazoria PMSA, TX	S	11.23 MW	10.08 AW	23360 AAW	TXBLS	10//99-12//99
	Brownsville-Harlingen-San Benito MSA, TX	S	10.27 MW	8.93 AW	21360 AAW	TXBLS	10//99-12//99
	Corpus Christi MSA, TX	S	12.43 MW	9.85 AW	25850 AAW	TXBLS	10//99-12//99
	Dallas PMSA, TX	S	10.26 MW	9.58 AW	21330 AAW	TXBLS	10//99-12//99
	El Paso MSA, TX	S	11.30 MW	11.40 AW	23500 AAW	TXBLS	10//99-12//99
	Fort Worth-Arlington PMSA, TX	S	10.32 MW	9.60 AW	21460 AAW	TXBLS	10//99-12//99
	Houston PMSA, TX	S	10.52 MW	10.01 AW	21880 AAW	TXBLS	10//99-12//99
	Killeen-Temple MSA, TX	S	10.33 MW	11.16 AW	21480 AAW	TXBLS	10//99-12//99
	Laredo MSA, TX	S	11.39 MW	11.69 AW	23700 AAW	TXBLS	10//99-12//99
	Lubbock MSA, TX	S	9.90 MW	9.52 AW	20590 AAW	TXBLS	10//99-12//99
	McAllen-Edinburg-Mission MSA, TX	S	8.81 MW	8.05 AW	18320 AAW	TXBLS	10//99-12//99
	Odessa-Midland MSA, TX	S	10.39 MW	9.76 AW	21600 AAW	TXBLS	10//99-12//99
	San Antonio MSA, TX	S	10.25 MW	10.05 AW	21320 AAW	TXBLS	10//99-12//99
	Sherman-Denison MSA, TX	S	8.90 MW	8.87 AW	18510 AAW	TXBLS	10//99-12//99
	Utah	S	9.43 MW	9.47 AW	19690 AAW	UTBLS	10//99-12//99
	Provo-Orem MSA, UT	S	7.30 MW	6.45 AW	15180 AAW	UTBLS	10//99-12//99
	Salt Lake City-Ogden MSA, UT	S	10.91 MW	10.35 AW	22690 AAW	UTBLS	10//99-12//99
	Vermont	S	9.29 MW	9.63 AW	20040 AAW	VTBLS	10//99-12//99
	Burlington MSA, VT	S	8.74 MW	8.71 AW	18180 AAW	VTBLS	10//99-12//99
	Virginia	S	11.26 MW	12.17 AW	25310 AAW	VABLS	10//99-12//99
	Charlottesville MSA, VA	S	11.37 MW	10.07 AW	23640 AAW	VABLS	10//99-12//99
	Norfolk-Virginia Beach-Newport News MSA, VA-NC	S	12.67 MW	11.65 AW	26350 AAW	VABLS	10//99-12//99
	Richmond-Petersburg MSA, VA	S	14.83 MW	13.63 AW	30850 AAW	VABLS	10//99-12//99
	Roanoke MSA, VA	S	11.64 MW	11.52 AW	24220 AAW	VABLS	10//99-12//99
	Washington	S	11.55 MW	14.63 AW	30420 AAW	WABLS	10//99-12//99
	Bremerton PMSA, WA	S	22.91 MW	27.90 AW	47640 AAW	WABLS	10//99-12//99
	Richland-Kennewick-Pasco MSA, WA	S	22.18 MW	22.57 AW	46120 AAW	WABLS	10//99-12//99
	Seattle-Bellevue-Everett PMSA, WA	S	12.67 MW	8.06 AW	26360 AAW	WABLS	10//99-12//99
	Spokane MSA, WA	S	15.17 MW	11.80 AW	31560 AAW	WABLS	10//99-12//99
	Tacoma PMSA, WA	S	24.15 MW	28.65 AW	50240 AAW	WABLS	10//99-12//99
	West Virginia	S	8.65 MW	9.07 AW	18860 AAW	WVBLS	10//99-12//99
	Charleston MSA, WV	S	10.00 MW	9.39 AW	20810 AAW	WVBLS	10//99-12//99

AAW Average annual wage	**AOH** Average offered, high	**ASH** Average starting, high	**H** Hourly	**M** Monthly	**S** Special: hourly and annual
AE Average entry wage	**AOL** Average offered, low	**ASL** Average starting, low	**HI** Highest wage paid	**MTC** Median total compensation	**TQ** Third quartile wage
AEX Average experienced wage	**APH** Average pay, high range	**AW** Average wage paid	**HR** High end range	**MW** Median wage paid	**W** Weekly
AO Average offered	**APL** Average pay, low range	**FQ** First quartile wage	**LR** Low end range	**SQ** Second quartile wage	**Y** Yearly

Occupation/Type/Industry	Location	Per	Low	Mid	High	Source	Date
Emergency Medical Technician and Paramedic	Huntington-Ashland MSA, WV-KY-OH	S	10.23 MW	9.91 AW	21270 AAW	WVBLS	10//99-12//99
	Parkersburg-Marietta MSA, WV-OH	S	9.71 MW	9.64 AW	20190 AAW	WVBLS	10//99-12//99
	Wheeling MSA, WV-OH	S	7.71 MW	7.00 AW	16040 AAW	WVBLS	10//99-12//99
	Wisconsin	S	9.52 MW	10.41 AW	21660 AAW	WIBLS	10//99-12//99
	Appleton-Oshkosh-Neenah MSA, WI	S	9.59 MW	9.44 AW	19950 AAW	WIBLS	10//99-12//99
	Green Bay MSA, WI	S	10.97 MW	8.86 AW	22810 AAW	WIBLS	10//99-12//99
	Janesville-Beloit MSA, WI	S	11.06 MW	11.20 AW	22990 AAW	WIBLS	10//99-12//99
	Kenosha PMSA, WI	S	9.49 MW	9.04 AW	19740 AAW	WIBLS	10//99-12//99
	La Crosse MSA, WI-MN	S	10.19 MW	9.74 AW	21200 AAW	WIBLS	10//99-12//99
	Madison MSA, WI	S	11.50 MW	9.66 AW	23920 AAW	WIBLS	10//99-12//99
	Milwaukee-Waukesha PMSA, WI	S	11.38 MW	9.81 AW	23680 AAW	WIBLS	10//99-12//99
	Racine PMSA, WI	S	9.32 MW	9.17 AW	19380 AAW	WIBLS	10//99-12//99
	Sheboygan MSA, WI	S	7.51 MW	6.06 AW	15630 AAW	WIBLS	10//99-12//99
	Wyoming	S	8.33 MW	8.82 AW	18350 AAW	WYBLS	10//99-12//99
	Puerto Rico	S	6.39 MW	7.28 AW	15130 AAW	PRBLS	10//99-12//99
	Caguas PMSA, PR	S	7.58 MW	6.91 AW	15760 AAW	PRBLS	10//99-12//99
	Ponce MSA, PR	S	7.69 MW	6.76 AW	15990 AAW	PRBLS	10//99-12//99
	San Juan-Bayamon PMSA, PR	S	7.80 MW	6.76 AW	16230 AAW	PRBLS	10//99-12//99
Employee Relations Specialist Human Resources	United States	Y		50800 AW		HRMAG	1999
Employment and Recruiting Manager	United States	Y		73000 AW		TRAVWK2	1999
Employment, Recruitment, and Placement Specialist	Alabama	S	17.83 MW	17.43 AW	36260 AAW	ALBLS	10//99-12//99
	Birmingham MSA, AL	S	18.10 MW	18.24 AW	37640 AAW	ALBLS	10//99-12//99
	Mobile MSA, AL	S	17.86 MW	18.46 AW	37150 AAW	ALBLS	10//99-12//99
	Montgomery MSA, AL	S	16.38 MW	16.08 AW	34060 AAW	ALBLS	10//99-12//99
	Alaska	S	19.07 MW	20.12 AW	41850 AAW	AKBLS	10//99-12//99
	Anchorage MSA, AK	S	21.91 MW	21.99 AW	45570 AAW	AKBLS	10//99-12//99
	Arizona	S	14.5 MW	16.68 AW	34700 AAW	AZBLS	10//99-12//99
	Flagstaff MSA, AZ-UT	S	13.70 MW	13.97 AW	28500 AAW	AZBLS	10//99-12//99
	Phoenix-Mesa MSA, AZ	S	17.63 MW	15.06 AW	36660 AAW	AZBLS	10//99-12//99
	Tucson MSA, AZ	S	13.19 MW	12.56 AW	27440 AAW	AZBLS	10//99-12//99
	Arkansas	S	12.43 MW	13.56 AW	28200 AAW	ARBLS	10//99-12//99
	Fayetteville-Springdale-Rogers MSA, AR	S	13.01 MW	12.26 AW	27070 AAW	ARBLS	10//99-12//99
	Fort Smith MSA, AR-OK	S	11.10 MW	9.53 AW	23090 AAW	ARBLS	10//99-12//99
	Jonesboro MSA, AR	S	12.81 MW	13.86 AW	26650 AAW	ARBLS	10//99-12//99
	Little Rock-North Little Rock MSA, AR	S	14.70 MW	13.50 AW	30570 AAW	ARBLS	10//99-12//99
	California	S	19.92 MW	23.53 AW	48950 AAW	CABLS	10//99-12//99
	Bakersfield MSA, CA	S	19.28 MW	18.75 AW	40100 AAW	CABLS	10//99-12//99
	Chico-Paradise MSA, CA	S	16.29 MW	15.90 AW	33880 AAW	CABLS	10//99-12//99
	Fresno MSA, CA	S	14.47 MW	13.58 AW	30110 AAW	CABLS	10//99-12//99
	Los Angeles-Long Beach PMSA, CA	S	21.81 MW	19.65 AW	45360 AAW	CABLS	10//99-12//99
	Modesto MSA, CA	S	15.82 MW	15.63 AW	32920 AAW	CABLS	10//99-12//99
	Oakland PMSA, CA	S	21.35 MW	20.76 AW	44400 AAW	CABLS	10//99-12//99
	Orange County PMSA, CA	S	22.93 MW	20.67 AW	47700 AAW	CABLS	10//99-12//99
	Redding MSA, CA	S	22.74 MW	22.11 AW	47290 AAW	CABLS	10//99-12//99
	Riverside-San Bernardino PMSA, CA	S	17.41 MW	15.71 AW	36220 AAW	CABLS	10//99-12//99
	Salinas MSA, CA	S	20.63 MW	19.91 AW	42900 AAW	CABLS	10//99-12//99
	San Diego MSA, CA	S	17.79 MW	16.58 AW	37000 AAW	CABLS	10//99-12//99
	San Francisco PMSA, CA	S	36.12 MW	32.24 AW	75130 AAW	CABLS	10//99-12//99
	San Jose PMSA, CA	S	23.61 MW	21.16 AW	49110 AAW	CABLS	10//99-12//99
	San Luis Obispo-Atascadero-Paso Robles MSA, CA	S	20.76 MW	19.80 AW	43180 AAW	CABLS	10//99-12//99
	Santa Barbara-Santa Maria-Lompoc MSA, CA	S	23.92 MW	17.49 AW	49750 AAW	CABLS	10//99-12//99
	Santa Cruz-Watsonville PMSA, CA	S	20.04 MW	16.90 AW	41690 AAW	CABLS	10//99-12//99
	Santa Rosa PMSA, CA	S	23.54 MW	20.62 AW	48970 AAW	CABLS	10//99-12//99
	Stockton-Lodi MSA, CA	S	16.20 MW	15.80 AW	33700 AAW	CABLS	10//99-12//99

AAW Average annual wage	**AOH** Average offered, high	**ASH** Average starting, high	**H** Hourly	**M** Monthly	**S** Special: hourly and annual
AE Average entry wage	**AOL** Average offered, low	**ASL** Average starting, low	**HI** Highest wage paid	**MTC** Median total compensation	**TQ** Third quartile wage
AEX Average experienced wage	**APH** Average pay, high range	**AW** Average wage paid	**HR** High end range	**MW** Median wage paid	**W** Weekly
AO Average offered	**APL** Average pay, low range	**FQ** First quartile wage	**LR** Low end range	**SQ** Second quartile wage	**Y** Yearly

Occupation/Type/Industry	Location	Per	Low	Mid	High	Source	Date
Employment, Recruitment, and Placement Specialist	Vallejo-Fairfield-Napa PMSA, CA	S	18.51 MW	18.50 AW	38510 AAW	CABLS	10//99-12//99
	Visalia-Tulare-Porterville MSA, CA	S	13.86 MW	12.89 AW	28820 AAW	CABLS	10//99-12//99
	Yolo PMSA, CA	S	18.63 MW	18.14 AW	38750 AAW	CABLS	10//99-12//99
	Colorado	S	16.5 MW	19.30 AW	40140 AAW	COBLS	10//99-12//99
	Boulder-Longmont PMSA, CO	S	21.12 MW	18.74 AW	43920 AAW	COBLS	10//99-12//99
	Colorado Springs MSA, CO	S	18.18 MW	16.70 AW	37820 AAW	COBLS	10//99-12//99
	Denver PMSA, CO	S	19.60 MW	16.40 AW	40770 AAW	COBLS	10//99-12//99
	Fort Collins-Loveland MSA, CO	S	18.14 MW	15.88 AW	37730 AAW	COBLS	10//99-12//99
	Greeley PMSA, CO	S	19.25 MW	16.34 AW	40030 AAW	COBLS	10//99-12//99
	Connecticut	S	18.68 MW	23.38 AW	48630 AAW	CTBLS	10//99-12//99
	Bridgeport PMSA, CT	S	23.43 MW	22.70 AW	48730 AAW	CTBLS	10//99-12//99
	Danbury PMSA, CT	S	20.28 MW	15.75 AW	42190 AAW	CTBLS	10//99-12//99
	Hartford MSA, CT	S	19.45 MW	16.62 AW	40460 AAW	CTBLS	10//99-12//99
	New Haven-Meriden PMSA, CT	S	18.22 MW	16.76 AW	37900 AAW	CTBLS	10//99-12//99
	New London-Norwich MSA, CT-RI	S	15.05 MW	14.40 AW	31300 AAW	CTBLS	10//99-12//99
	Stamford-Norwalk PMSA, CT	S	36.73 MW	26.87 AW	76400 AAW	CTBLS	10//99-12//99
	Delaware	S	15.01 MW	15.79 AW	32840 AAW	DEBLS	10//99-12//99
	Dover MSA, DE	S	14.39 MW	14.69 AW	29940 AAW	DEBLS	10//99-12//99
	Wilmington-Newark PMSA, DE-MD	S	15.94 MW	15.03 AW	33160 AAW	DEBLS	10//99-12//99
	District of Columbia	S	16.65 MW	18.99 AW	39490 AAW	DCBLS	10//99-12//99
	Washington PMSA, DC-MD-VA-WV	S	20.67 MW	19.76 AW	42990 AAW	DCBLS	10//99-12//99
	Florida	S	13.22 MW	15.46 AW	32160 AAW	FLBLS	10//99-12//99
	Daytona Beach MSA, FL	S	21.00 MW	22.14 AW	43680 AAW	FLBLS	10//99-12//99
	Fort Lauderdale PMSA, FL	S	14.07 MW	12.63 AW	29270 AAW	FLBLS	10//99-12//99
	Fort Myers-Cape Coral MSA, FL	S	17.94 MW	17.66 AW	37320 AAW	FLBLS	10//99-12//99
	Fort Pierce-Port St. Lucie MSA, FL	S	8.76 MW	7.96 AW	18210 AAW	FLBLS	10//99-12//99
	Fort Walton Beach MSA, FL	S	14.40 MW	11.63 AW	29960 AAW	FLBLS	10//99-12//99
	Gainesville MSA, FL	S	13.52 MW	11.74 AW	28120 AAW	FLBLS	10//99-12//99
	Jacksonville MSA, FL	S	18.27 MW	18.61 AW	38000 AAW	FLBLS	10//99-12//99
	Lakeland-Winter Haven MSA, FL	S	14.88 MW	13.55 AW	30950 AAW	FLBLS	10//99-12//99
	Melbourne-Titusville-Palm Bay MSA, FL	S	15.39 MW	14.40 AW	32000 AAW	FLBLS	10//99-12//99
	Miami PMSA, FL	S	13.28 MW	11.75 AW	27630 AAW	FLBLS	10//99-12//99
	Naples MSA, FL	S	14.90 MW	12.99 AW	30980 AAW	FLBLS	10//99-12//99
	Ocala MSA, FL	S	13.39 MW	12.64 AW	27850 AAW	FLBLS	10//99-12//99
	Orlando MSA, FL	S	16.98 MW	16.41 AW	35320 AAW	FLBLS	10//99-12//99
	Panama City MSA, FL	S	26.68 MW	35.89 AW	55500 AAW	FLBLS	10//99-12//99
	Pensacola MSA, FL	S	18.99 MW	17.24 AW	39500 AAW	FLBLS	10//99-12//99
	Sarasota-Bradenton MSA, FL	S	15.88 MW	13.77 AW	33030 AAW	FLBLS	10//99-12//99
	Tallahassee MSA, FL	S	14.41 MW	13.35 AW	29980 AAW	FLBLS	10//99-12//99
	Tampa-St. Petersburg-Clearwater MSA, FL	S	16.67 MW	14.12 AW	34670 AAW	FLBLS	10//99-12//99
	West Palm Beach-Boca Raton MSA, FL	S	17.78 MW	16.57 AW	36980 AAW	FLBLS	10//99-12//99
	Georgia	S	16.75 MW	17.57 AW	36550 AAW	GABLS	10//99-12//99
	Albany MSA, GA	S	13.80 MW	13.86 AW	28700 AAW	GABLS	10//99-12//99
	Athens MSA, GA	S	16.29 MW	16.39 AW	33880 AAW	GABLS	10//99-12//99
	Atlanta MSA, GA	S	18.45 MW	17.69 AW	38380 AAW	GABLS	10//99-12//99
	Augusta-Aiken MSA, GA-SC	S	22.18 MW	16.87 AW	46130 AAW	GABLS	10//99-12//99
	Columbus MSA, GA-AL	S	16.63 MW	15.68 AW	34590 AAW	GABLS	10//99-12//99
	Macon MSA, GA	S	15.63 MW	13.30 AW	32510 AAW	GABLS	10//99-12//99
	Savannah MSA, GA	S	13.85 MW	12.86 AW	28800 AAW	GABLS	10//99-12//99
	Idaho	S	16.72 MW	17.06 AW	35480 AAW	IDBLS	10//99-12//99
	Boise City MSA, ID	S	16.33 MW	14.92 AW	33960 AAW	IDBLS	10//99-12//99
	Illinois	S	15.14 MW	16.38 AW	34080 AAW	ILBLS	10//99-12//99
	Bloomington-Normal MSA, IL	S	18.65 MW	18.54 AW	38780 AAW	ILBLS	10//99-12//99
	Champaign-Urbana MSA, IL	S	14.63 MW	14.61 AW	30440 AAW	ILBLS	10//99-12//99
	Chicago PMSA, IL	S	16.33 MW	15.23 AW	33980 AAW	ILBLS	10//99-12//99
	Kankakee PMSA, IL	S	13.70 MW	13.58 AW	28500 AAW	ILBLS	10//99-12//99
	Peoria-Pekin MSA, IL	S	17.21 MW	15.53 AW	35800 AAW	ILBLS	10//99-12//99
	Rockford MSA, IL	S	15.40 MW	12.78 AW	32030 AAW	ILBLS	10//99-12//99

AAW Average annual wage	**AOH** Average offered, high	**ASH** Average starting, high	**H** Hourly	**M** Monthly	**S** Special: hourly and annual
AE Average entry wage	**AOL** Average offered, low	**ASL** Average starting, low	**HI** Highest wage paid	**MTC** Median total compensation	**TQ** Third quartile wage
AEX Average experienced wage	**APH** Average pay, high range	**AW** Average wage paid	**HR** High end range	**MW** Median wage paid	**W** Weekly
AO Average offered	**APL** Average pay, low range	**FQ** First quartile wage	**LR** Low end range	**SQ** Second quartile wage	**Y** Yearly

Occupation/Type/Industry	Location	Per	Low	Mid	High	Source	Date
Employment, Recruitment, and Placement Specialist	Springfield MSA, IL	S	17.22 MW	17.51 AW	35820 AAW	ILBLS	10//99-12//99
	Indiana	S	15.14 MW	18.13 AW	37710 AAW	INBLS	10//99-12//99
	Bloomington MSA, IN	S	18.68 MW	15.71 AW	38840 AAW	INBLS	10//99-12//99
	Elkhart-Goshen MSA, IN	S	14.50 MW	13.68 AW	30150 AAW	INBLS	10//99-12//99
	Evansville-Henderson MSA, IN-KY	S	17.89 MW	15.85 AW	37200 AAW	INBLS	10//99-12//99
	Fort Wayne MSA, IN	S	15.77 MW	13.37 AW	32800 AAW	INBLS	10//99-12//99
	Gary PMSA, IN	S	21.16 MW	16.80 AW	44010 AAW	INBLS	10//99-12//99
	Indianapolis MSA, IN	S	21.05 MW	16.58 AW	43790 AAW	INBLS	10//99-12//99
	Kokomo MSA, IN	S	13.23 MW	13.81 AW	27530 AAW	INBLS	10//99-12//99
	Lafayette MSA, IN	S	10.91 MW	9.88 AW	22680 AAW	INBLS	10//99-12//99
	Muncie MSA, IN	S	12.10 MW	10.89 AW	25160 AAW	INBLS	10//99-12//99
	South Bend MSA, IN	S	12.39 MW	11.80 AW	25770 AAW	INBLS	10//99-12//99
	Terre Haute MSA, IN	S	13.33 MW	13.94 AW	27730 AAW	INBLS	10//99-12//99
	Iowa	S	16.56 MW	18.81 AW	39120 AAW	IABLS	10//99-12//99
	Davenport-Moline-Rock Island MSA, IA-IL	S	23.69 MW	19.03 AW	49270 AAW	IABLS	10//99-12//99
	Des Moines MSA, IA	S	18.48 MW	17.49 AW	38450 AAW	IABLS	10//99-12//99
	Dubuque MSA, IA	S	14.24 MW	14.06 AW	29620 AAW	IABLS	10//99-12//99
	Iowa City MSA, IA	S	17.75 MW	19.05 AW	36920 AAW	IABLS	10//99-12//99
	Sioux City MSA, IA-NE	S	15.19 MW	14.64 AW	31600 AAW	IABLS	10//99-12//99
	Waterloo-Cedar Falls MSA, IA	S	17.26 MW	16.75 AW	35900 AAW	IABLS	10//99-12//99
	Kansas	S	18.57 MW	21.16 AW	44010 AAW	KSBLS	10//99-12//99
	Lawrence MSA, KS	S	14.80 MW	13.58 AW	30780 AAW	KSBLS	10//99-12//99
	Topeka MSA, KS	S	18.09 MW	13.43 AW	37620 AAW	KSBLS	10//99-12//99
	Wichita MSA, KS	S	20.41 MW	17.32 AW	42450 AAW	KSBLS	10//99-12//99
	Kentucky	S	15.67 MW	16.01 AW	33300 AAW	KYBLS	10//99-12//99
	Lexington MSA, KY	S	16.04 MW	15.53 AW	33360 AAW	KYBLS	10//99-12//99
	Louisville MSA, KY-IN	S	16.34 MW	16.16 AW	34000 AAW	KYBLS	10//99-12//99
	Louisiana	S	14.28 MW	14.92 AW	31040 AAW	LABLS	10//99-12//99
	Baton Rouge MSA, LA	S	17.17 MW	17.52 AW	35710 AAW	LABLS	10//99-12//99
	Lafayette MSA, LA	S	14.84 MW	13.94 AW	30860 AAW	LABLS	10//99-12//99
	Monroe MSA, LA	S	19.28 MW	19.79 AW	40110 AAW	LABLS	10//99-12//99
	New Orleans MSA, LA	S	14.67 MW	14.41 AW	30510 AAW	LABLS	10//99-12//99
	Shreveport-Bossier City MSA, LA	S	15.61 MW	14.64 AW	32480 AAW	LABLS	10//99-12//99
	Maine	S	13.89 MW	17.69 AW	36800 AAW	MEBLS	10//99-12//99
	Bangor MSA, ME	S	12.59 MW	12.20 AW	26190 AAW	MEBLS	10//99-12//99
	Portland MSA, ME	S	18.75 MW	18.01 AW	39000 AAW	MEBLS	10//99-12//99
	Maryland	S	17.44 MW	19.12 AW	39760 AAW	MDBLS	10//99-12//99
	Baltimore PMSA, MD	S	17.70 MW	16.74 AW	36820 AAW	MDBLS	10//99-12//99
	Massachusetts	S	18.6 MW	22.28 AW	46340 AAW	MABLS	10//99-12//99
	Barnstable-Yarmouth MSA, MA	S	19.65 MW	16.35 AW	40870 AAW	MABLS	10//99-12//99
	Boston PMSA, MA-NH	S	23.78 MW	19.57 AW	49460 AAW	MABLS	10//99-12//99
	Brockton PMSA, MA	S	14.21 MW	12.60 AW	29560 AAW	MABLS	10//99-12//99
	Lowell PMSA, MA-NH	S	23.99 MW	23.57 AW	49900 AAW	MABLS	10//99-12//99
	New Bedford PMSA, MA	S	15.85 MW	15.48 AW	32960 AAW	MABLS	10//99-12//99
	Springfield MSA, MA	S	16.54 MW	16.00 AW	34400 AAW	MABLS	10//99-12//99
	Worcester PMSA, MA-CT	S	16.96 MW	14.91 AW	35270 AAW	MABLS	10//99-12//99
	Michigan	S	17.54 MW	19.75 AW	41080 AAW	MIBLS	10//99-12//99
	Ann Arbor PMSA, MI	S	20.23 MW	19.00 AW	42080 AAW	MIBLS	10//99-12//99
	Benton Harbor MSA, MI	S	19.20 MW	16.61 AW	39940 AAW	MIBLS	10//99-12//99
	Detroit PMSA, MI	S	20.23 MW	18.60 AW	42080 AAW	MIBLS	10//99-12//99
	Flint PMSA, MI	S	17.37 MW	17.44 AW	36130 AAW	MIBLS	10//99-12//99
	Grand Rapids-Muskegon-Holland MSA, MI	S	19.08 MW	18.05 AW	39690 AAW	MIBLS	10//99-12//99
	Jackson MSA, MI	S	24.36 MW	16.01 AW	50660 AAW	MIBLS	10//99-12//99
	Kalamazoo-Battle Creek MSA, MI	S	18.46 MW	16.76 AW	38390 AAW	MIBLS	10//99-12//99
	Lansing-East Lansing MSA, MI	S	25.12 MW	19.81 AW	52260 AAW	MIBLS	10//99-12//99
	Saginaw-Bay City-Midland MSA, MI	S	13.84 MW	12.51 AW	28790 AAW	MIBLS	10//99-12//99
	Minnesota	S	21.66 MW	23.92 AW	49760 AAW	MNBLS	10//99-12//99
	Duluth-Superior MSA, MN-WI	S	17.16 MW	16.58 AW	35680 AAW	MNBLS	10//99-12//99
	Minneapolis-St. Paul MSA, MN-WI	S	24.50 MW	22.03 AW	50970 AAW	MNBLS	10//99-12//99
	St. Cloud MSA, MN	S	18.65 MW	17.79 AW	38800 AAW	MNBLS	10//99-12//99
	Mississippi	S	14.27 MW	15.20 AW	31620 AAW	MSBLS	10//99-12//99
	Biloxi-Gulfport-Pascagoula MSA, MS	S	14.23 MW	13.09 AW	29600 AAW	MSBLS	10//99-12//99

AAW	Average annual wage	AOH	Average offered, high	ASH	Average starting, high
AE	Average entry wage	AOL	Average offered, low	ASL	Average starting, low
AEX	Average experienced wage	APH	Average pay, high range	AW	Average wage paid
AO	Average offered	APL	Average pay, low range	FQ	First quartile wage

H	Hourly		
HI	Highest wage paid	M	Monthly
HR	High end range	MTC	Median total compensation
LR	Low end range	MW	Median wage paid
		SQ	Second quartile wage

S	Special: hourly and annual
TQ	Third quartile wage
W	Weekly
Y	Yearly

Occupation/Type/Industry	Location	Per	Low	Mid	High	Source	Date
Employment, Recruitment, and Placement Specialist	Hattiesburg MSA, MS	S	11.05 MW	9.64 AW	22990 AAW	MSBLS	10//99-12//99
	Jackson MSA, MS	S	15.89 MW	14.15 AW	33060 AAW	MSBLS	10//99-12//99
	Missouri	S	14.16 MW	16.44 AW	34200 AAW	MOBLS	10//99-12//99
	Columbia MSA, MO	S	14.00 MW	13.37 AW	29110 AAW	MOBLS	10//99-12//99
	Joplin MSA, MO	S	19.14 MW	15.29 AW	39810 AAW	MOBLS	10//99-12//99
	Kansas City MSA, MO-KS	S	21.57 MW	18.55 AW	44860 AAW	MOBLS	10//99-12//99
	St. Louis MSA, MO-IL	S	17.83 MW	15.18 AW	37080 AAW	MOBLS	10//99-12//99
	Billings MSA, MT	S	16.94 MW	17.59 AW	35240 AAW	MTBLS	10//99-12//99
	Missoula MSA, MT	S	11.50 MW	10.97 AW	23910 AAW	MTBLS	10//99-12//99
	Nebraska	S	16.57 MW	19.61 AW	40780 AAW	NEBLS	10//99-12//99
	Lincoln MSA, NE	S	15.63 MW	14.82 AW	32520 AAW	NEBLS	10//99-12//99
	Omaha MSA, NE-IA	S	21.85 MW	18.64 AW	45450 AAW	NEBLS	10//99-12//99
	Nevada	S	13.42 MW	15.82 AW	32900 AAW	NVBLS	10//99-12//99
	Las Vegas MSA, NV-AZ	S	15.52 MW	13.44 AW	32280 AAW	NVBLS	10//99-12//99
	Reno MSA, NV	S	17.02 MW	13.45 AW	35400 AAW	NVBLS	10//99-12//99
	New Hampshire	S	18.47 MW	25.80 AW	53660 AAW	NHBLS	10//99-12//99
	Manchester PMSA, NH	S	23.89 MW	20.84 AW	49700 AAW	NHBLS	10//99-12//99
	Nashua PMSA, NH	S	18.47 MW	17.69 AW	38410 AAW	NHBLS	10//99-12//99
	New Jersey	S	20.92 MW	23.37 AW	48620 AAW	NJBLS	10//99-12//99
	Atlantic-Cape May PMSA, NJ	S	16.90 MW	17.28 AW	35150 AAW	NJBLS	10//99-12//99
	Bergen-Passaic PMSA, NJ	S	22.69 MW	20.15 AW	47190 AAW	NJBLS	10//99-12//99
	Jersey City PMSA, NJ	S	17.86 MW	16.12 AW	37150 AAW	NJBLS	10//99-12//99
	Middlesex-Somerset-Hunterdon PMSA, NJ	S	23.36 MW	20.58 AW	48590 AAW	NJBLS	10//99-12//99
	Newark PMSA, NJ	S	23.96 MW	23.47 AW	49830 AAW	NJBLS	10//99-12//99
	New Mexico	S	14.65 MW	16.42 AW	34160 AAW	NMBLS	10//99-12//99
	Albuquerque MSA, NM	S	18.99 MW	16.90 AW	39510 AAW	NMBLS	10//99-12//99
	Las Cruces MSA, NM	S	13.68 MW	13.41 AW	28450 AAW	NMBLS	10//99-12//99
	Santa Fe MSA, NM	S	14.76 MW	14.44 AW	30700 AAW	NMBLS	10//99-12//99
	New York	S	18.21 MW	20.04 AW	41680 AAW	NYBLS	10//99-12//99
	Albany-Schenectady-Troy MSA, NY	S	19.45 MW	16.94 AW	40460 AAW	NYBLS	10//99-12//99
	Binghamton MSA, NY	S	17.92 MW	16.64 AW	37260 AAW	NYBLS	10//99-12//99
	Buffalo-Niagara Falls MSA, NY	S	18.80 MW	17.45 AW	39100 AAW	NYBLS	10//99-12//99
	Dutchess County PMSA, NY	S	20.86 MW	16.61 AW	43390 AAW	NYBLS	10//99-12//99
	Jamestown MSA, NY	S	12.61 MW	11.57 AW	26230 AAW	NYBLS	10//99-12//99
	Nassau-Suffolk PMSA, NY	S	21.87 MW	20.71 AW	45490 AAW	NYBLS	10//99-12//99
	New York PMSA, NY	S	21.34 MW	19.42 AW	44380 AAW	NYBLS	10//99-12//99
	Newburgh PMSA, NY-PA	S	20.50 MW	16.24 AW	42640 AAW	NYBLS	10//99-12//99
	Rochester MSA, NY	S	16.82 MW	13.35 AW	34990 AAW	NYBLS	10//99-12//99
	Syracuse MSA, NY	S	18.32 MW	17.13 AW	38100 AAW	NYBLS	10//99-12//99
	Utica-Rome MSA, NY	S	12.16 MW	11.53 AW	25280 AAW	NYBLS	10//99-12//99
	North Carolina	S	15.53 MW	17.54 AW	36480 AAW	NCBLS	10//99-12//99
	Asheville MSA, NC	S	17.47 MW	14.72 AW	36340 AAW	NCBLS	10//99-12//99
	Charlotte-Gastonia-Rock Hill MSA, NC-SC	S	15.64 MW	14.60 AW	32540 AAW	NCBLS	10//99-12//99
	Fayetteville MSA, NC	S	16.64 MW	16.83 AW	34620 AAW	NCBLS	10//99-12//99
	Greensboro--Winston-Salem--High Point MSA, NC	S	17.68 MW	16.21 AW	36780 AAW	NCBLS	10//99-12//99
	Greenville MSA, NC	S	16.88 MW	15.55 AW	35110 AAW	NCBLS	10//99-12//99
	Hickory-Morganton-Lenoir MSA, NC	S	13.94 MW	12.99 AW	29000 AAW	NCBLS	10//99-12//99
	Raleigh-Durham-Chapel Hill MSA, NC	S	20.61 MW	18.66 AW	42870 AAW	NCBLS	10//99-12//99
	Rocky Mount MSA, NC	S	13.02 MW	12.03 AW	27070 AAW	NCBLS	10//99-12//99
	Wilmington MSA, NC	S	15.05 MW	12.86 AW	31310 AAW	NCBLS	10//99-12//99
	Fargo-Moorhead MSA, ND-MN	S	15.53 MW	15.27 AW	32290 AAW	NDBLS	10//99-12//99
	Ohio	S	15.79 MW	17.12 AW	35610 AAW	OHBLS	10//99-12//99
	Akron PMSA, OH	S	16.80 MW	15.70 AW	34940 AAW	OHBLS	10//99-12//99
	Canton-Massillon MSA, OH	S	15.34 MW	14.62 AW	31900 AAW	OHBLS	10//99-12//99
	Cincinnati PMSA, OH-KY-IN	S	16.28 MW	15.21 AW	33860 AAW	OHBLS	10//99-12//99
	Cleveland-Lorain-Elyria PMSA, OH	S	19.08 MW	17.95 AW	39690 AAW	OHBLS	10//99-12//99
	Columbus MSA, OH	S	17.70 MW	16.49 AW	36820 AAW	OHBLS	10//99-12//99
	Dayton-Springfield MSA, OH	S	16.84 MW	14.64 AW	35030 AAW	OHBLS	10//99-12//99
	Hamilton-Middletown PMSA, OH	S	14.70 MW	14.48 AW	30570 AAW	OHBLS	10//99-12//99
	Lima MSA, OH	S	14.67 MW	13.29 AW	30510 AAW	OHBLS	10//99-12//99
	Mansfield MSA, OH	S	18.35 MW	16.63 AW	38160 AAW	OHBLS	10//99-12//99

Occupation/Type/Industry	Location	Per	Low	Mid	High	Source	Date
Employment, Recruitment, and Placement Specialist							
	Toledo MSA, OH	S	14.91 MW	13.98 AW	31020 AAW	OHBLS	10//99-12//99
	Youngstown-Warren MSA, OH	S	21.36 MW	18.84 AW	44420 AAW	OHBLS	10//99-12//99
	Oklahoma	S	14.04 MW	15.10 AW	31400 AAW	OKBLS	10//99-12//99
	Oklahoma City MSA, OK	S	15.76 MW	14.63 AW	32780 AAW	OKBLS	10//99-12//99
	Tulsa MSA, OK	S	16.04 MW	15.10 AW	33350 AAW	OKBLS	10//99-12//99
	Oregon	S	15.79 MW	16.84 AW	35040 AAW	ORBLS	10//99-12//99
	Corvallis MSA, OR	S	22.95 MW	21.18 AW	47730 AAW	ORBLS	10//99-12//99
	Eugene-Springfield MSA, OR	S	13.77 MW	12.41 AW	28650 AAW	ORBLS	10//99-12//99
	Medford-Ashland MSA, OR	S	14.84 MW	15.10 AW	30870 AAW	ORBLS	10//99-12//99
	Portland-Vancouver PMSA, OR-WA	S	17.73 MW	16.62 AW	36880 AAW	ORBLS	10//99-12//99
	Pennsylvania	S	18.51 MW	19.44 AW	40440 AAW	PABLS	10//99-12//99
	Allentown-Bethlehem-Easton MSA, PA	S	19.04 MW	18.01 AW	39610 AAW	PABLS	10//99-12//99
	Altoona MSA, PA	S	18.78 MW	19.21 AW	39050 AAW	PABLS	10//99-12//99
	Erie MSA, PA	S	16.89 MW	15.55 AW	35130 AAW	PABLS	10//99-12//99
	Johnstown MSA, PA	S	19.14 MW	19.49 AW	39810 AAW	PABLS	10//99-12//99
	Lancaster MSA, PA	S	19.29 MW	18.72 AW	40130 AAW	PABLS	10//99-12//99
	Philadelphia PMSA, PA-NJ	S	20.41 MW	19.02 AW	42460 AAW	PABLS	10//99-12//99
	Pittsburgh MSA, PA	S	20.31 MW	19.38 AW	42240 AAW	PABLS	10//99-12//99
	Reading MSA, PA	S	16.36 MW	14.06 AW	34030 AAW	PABLS	10//99-12//99
	Scranton--Wilkes-Barre--Hazleton MSA, PA	S	15.99 MW	14.70 AW	33260 AAW	PABLS	10//99-12//99
	Sharon MSA, PA	S	13.03 MW	9.82 AW	27090 AAW	PABLS	10//99-12//99
	State College MSA, PA	S	14.09 MW	12.93 AW	29320 AAW	PABLS	10//99-12//99
	York MSA, PA	S	18.37 MW	18.28 AW	38210 AAW	PABLS	10//99-12//99
	Rhode Island	S	18.78 MW	19.24 AW	40020 AAW	RIBLS	10//99-12//99
	Providence-Fall River-Warwick MSA, RI-MA	S	18.74 MW	18.47 AW	38990 AAW	RIBLS	10//99-12//99
	South Carolina	S	15.25 MW	17.13 AW	35640 AAW	SCBLS	10//99-12//99
	Charleston-North Charleston MSA, SC	S	14.37 MW	12.53 AW	29890 AAW	SCBLS	10//99-12//99
	Columbia MSA, SC	S	17.23 MW	16.70 AW	35830 AAW	SCBLS	10//99-12//99
	Florence MSA, SC	S	13.84 MW	13.93 AW	28780 AAW	SCBLS	10//99-12//99
	Greenville-Spartanburg-Anderson MSA, SC	S	17.93 MW	16.06 AW	37290 AAW	SCBLS	10//99-12//99
	Myrtle Beach MSA, SC	S	14.84 MW	13.95 AW	30870 AAW	SCBLS	10//99-12//99
	South Dakota	S	14.29 MW	15.23 AW	31680 AAW	SDBLS	10//99-12//99
	Sioux Falls MSA, SD	S	15.69 MW	15.15 AW	32640 AAW	SDBLS	10//99-12//99
	Tennessee	S	13.08 MW	16.12 AW	33520 AAW	TNBLS	10//99-12//99
	Chattanooga MSA, TN-GA	S	23.06 MW	18.83 AW	47970 AAW	TNBLS	10//99-12//99
	Clarksville-Hopkinsville MSA, TN-KY	S	11.35 MW	11.40 AW	23610 AAW	TNBLS	10//99-12//99
	Johnson City-Kingsport-Bristol MSA, TN-VA	S	17.40 MW	16.13 AW	36200 AAW	TNBLS	10//99-12//99
	Knoxville MSA, TN	S	14.02 MW	12.97 AW	29160 AAW	TNBLS	10//99-12//99
	Memphis MSA, TN-AR-MS	S	14.67 MW	11.96 AW	30510 AAW	MSBLS	10//99-12//99
	Nashville MSA, TN	S	18.04 MW	14.05 AW	37520 AAW	TNBLS	10//99-12//99
	Texas	S	14.96 MW	16.69 AW	34710 AAW	TXBLS	10//99-12//99
	Amarillo MSA, TX	S	13.42 MW	11.78 AW	27910 AAW	TXBLS	10//99-12//99
	Austin-San Marcos MSA, TX	S	15.96 MW	15.06 AW	33200 AAW	TXBLS	10//99-12//99
	Beaumont-Port Arthur MSA, TX	S	16.60 MW	15.59 AW	34530 AAW	TXBLS	10//99-12//99
	Brazoria PMSA, TX	S	18.84 MW	16.22 AW	39180 AAW	TXBLS	10//99-12//99
	Bryan-College Station MSA, TX	S	17.20 MW	17.11 AW	35770 AAW	TXBLS	10//99-12//99
	Corpus Christi MSA, TX	S	14.45 MW	14.29 AW	30050 AAW	TXBLS	10//99-12//99
	Dallas PMSA, TX	S	17.81 MW	16.31 AW	37050 AAW	TXBLS	10//99-12//99
	El Paso MSA, TX	S	16.76 MW	14.45 AW	34870 AAW	TXBLS	10//99-12//99
	Fort Worth-Arlington PMSA, TX	S	20.97 MW	18.09 AW	43620 AAW	TXBLS	10//99-12//99
	Galveston-Texas City PMSA, TX	S	19.08 MW	17.26 AW	39690 AAW	TXBLS	10//99-12//99
	Houston PMSA, TX	S	16.50 MW	15.48 AW	34320 AAW	TXBLS	10//99-12//99
	Killeen-Temple MSA, TX	S	16.18 MW	13.79 AW	33660 AAW	TXBLS	10//99-12//99
	Laredo MSA, TX	S	13.99 MW	13.00 AW	29100 AAW	TXBLS	10//99-12//99
	Longview-Marshall MSA, TX	S	14.69 MW	14.81 AW	30560 AAW	TXBLS	10//99-12//99
	Lubbock MSA, TX	S	15.72 MW	15.44 AW	32700 AAW	TXBLS	10//99-12//99
	Odessa-Midland MSA, TX	S	17.47 MW	17.80 AW	36330 AAW	TXBLS	10//99-12//99
	San Angelo MSA, TX	S	12.18 MW	10.98 AW	25340 AAW	TXBLS	10//99-12//99
	San Antonio MSA, TX	S	17.38 MW	16.21 AW	36150 AAW	TXBLS	10//99-12//99

AAW	Average annual wage	AOH	Average offered, high	ASH	Average starting, high
AE	Average entry wage	AOL	Average offered, low	ASL	Average starting, low
AEX	Average experienced wage	APH	Average pay, high range	AW	Average wage paid
AO	Average offered	APL	Average pay, low range	FQ	First quartile wage

H	Hourly	M	Monthly
HI	Highest wage paid	MTC	Median total compensation
HR	High end range	MW	Median wage paid
LR	Low end range	SQ	Second quartile wage

S	Special: hourly and annual
TQ	Third quartile wage
W	Weekly
Y	Yearly

Occupation/Type/Industry	Location	Per	Low	Mid	High	Source	Date
Employment, Recruitment, and Placement Specialist	Texarkana MSA, TX-Texarkana, AR	S	12.67 MW	12.50 AW	26350 AAW	TXBLS	10//99-12//99
	Tyler MSA, TX	S	16.28 MW	15.04 AW	33870 AAW	TXBLS	10//99-12//99
	Victoria MSA, TX	S	13.88 MW	13.80 AW	28860 AAW	TXBLS	10//99-12//99
	Waco MSA, TX	S	14.66 MW	14.59 AW	30490 AAW	TXBLS	10//99-12//99
	Wichita Falls MSA, TX	S	14.71 MW	14.98 AW	30590 AAW	TXBLS	10//99-12//99
	Utah	S	15.83 MW	16.67 AW	34680 AAW	UTBLS	10//99-12//99
	Provo-Orem MSA, UT	S	18.32 MW	16.77 AW	38100 AAW	UTBLS	10//99-12//99
	Vermont	S	20.29 MW	20.23 AW	42070 AAW	VTBLS	10//99-12//99
	Burlington MSA, VT	S	15.52 MW	10.63 AW	32280 AAW	VTBLS	10//99-12//99
	Virginia	S	19.04 MW	19.71 AW	41000 AAW	VABLS	10//99-12//99
	Charlottesville MSA, VA	S	17.18 MW	14.46 AW	35740 AAW	VABLS	10//99-12//99
	Lynchburg MSA, VA	S	18.82 MW	18.34 AW	39160 AAW	VABLS	10//99-12//99
	Norfolk-Virginia Beach-Newport News MSA, VA-NC	S	17.91 MW	16.80 AW	37260 AAW	VABLS	10//99-12//99
	Richmond-Petersburg MSA, VA	S	18.69 MW	17.96 AW	38870 AAW	VABLS	10//99-12//99
	Roanoke MSA, VA	S	17.31 MW	17.19 AW	36010 AAW	VABLS	10//99-12//99
	Washington	S	19.05 MW	21.78 AW	45310 AAW	WABLS	10//99-12//99
	Bellingham MSA, WA	S	18.75 MW	19.07 AW	38990 AAW	WABLS	10//99-12//99
	Bremerton PMSA, WA	S	17.22 MW	16.61 AW	35810 AAW	WABLS	10//99-12//99
	Richland-Kennewick-Pasco MSA, WA	S	17.89 MW	16.45 AW	37220 AAW	WABLS	10//99-12//99
	Seattle-Bellevue-Everett PMSA, WA	S	24.31 MW	20.78 AW	50560 AAW	WABLS	10//99-12//99
	Spokane MSA, WA	S	16.91 MW	16.96 AW	35170 AAW	WABLS	10//99-12//99
	Tacoma PMSA, WA	S	16.08 MW	15.53 AW	33440 AAW	WABLS	10//99-12//99
	West Virginia	S	12.81 MW	14.33 AW	29810 AAW	WVBLS	10//99-12//99
	Charleston MSA, WV	S	16.31 MW	14.83 AW	33920 AAW	WVBLS	10//99-12//99
	Huntington-Ashland MSA, WV-KY-OH	S	13.93 MW	12.48 AW	28980 AAW	WVBLS	10//99-12//99
	Wisconsin	S	15.9 MW	16.80 AW	34950 AAW	WIBLS	10//99-12//99
	Appleton-Oshkosh-Neenah MSA, WI	S	17.03 MW	15.05 AW	35430 AAW	WIBLS	10//99-12//99
	Eau Claire MSA, WI	S	15.23 MW	13.19 AW	31680 AAW	WIBLS	10//99-12//99
	Green Bay MSA, WI	S	16.36 MW	15.43 AW	34040 AAW	WIBLS	10//99-12//99
	Janesville-Beloit MSA, WI	S	21.87 MW	23.22 AW	45480 AAW	WIBLS	10//99-12//99
	La Crosse MSA, WI-MN	S	19.47 MW	16.67 AW	40500 AAW	WIBLS	10//99-12//99
	Madison MSA, WI	S	16.54 MW	15.39 AW	34400 AAW	WIBLS	10//99-12//99
	Milwaukee-Waukesha PMSA, WI	S	17.66 MW	17.49 AW	36730 AAW	WIBLS	10//99-12//99
	Racine PMSA, WI	S	15.40 MW	14.40 AW	32030 AAW	WIBLS	10//99-12//99
	Sheboygan MSA, WI	S	14.94 MW	13.74 AW	31070 AAW	WIBLS	10//99-12//99
	Wausau MSA, WI	S	16.10 MW	15.95 AW	33490 AAW	WIBLS	10//99-12//99
	Puerto Rico	S	8.81 MW	10.50 AW	21830 AAW	PRBLS	10//99-12//99
	Caguas PMSA, PR	S	12.57 MW	10.29 AW	26140 AAW	PRBLS	10//99-12//99
	Ponce MSA, PR	S	9.13 MW	8.09 AW	18990 AAW	PRBLS	10//99-12//99
	San Juan-Bayamon PMSA, PR	S	10.27 MW	8.72 AW	21370 AAW	PRBLS	10//99-12//99
EMT-Basic							
Emergency Medical Services	United States	Y	19009 AE	23322 AW	26087 HI	JEMS	1998
Emergency Medical Services	North Central	Y		24993 AW		JEMS	1998
Emergency Medical Services	Northeast	Y		20024 AW		JEMS	1998
Emergency Medical Services	Northwest	Y		28575 AW		JEMS	1998
Emergency Medical Services	South Central	Y		18241 AW		JEMS	1998
Emergency Medical Services	Southeast	Y		22728 AW		JEMS	1998
Emergency Medical Services	Southwest	Y		33134 AW		JEMS	1998
EMT-Intermediate							
Emergency Medical Services	United States	Y	19729 AE	21833 AW	29575 HI	JEMS	1998
Emergency Medical Services	North Central	Y		20256 AW		JEMS	1998
Emergency Medical Services	Northeast	Y		21561 AW		JEMS	1998
Emergency Medical Services	Northwest	Y		22442 AW		JEMS	1998
Emergency Medical Services	South Central	Y		21531 AW		JEMS	1998
Emergency Medical Services	Southeast	Y		25233 AW		JEMS	1998
Emergency Medical Services	Southwest	Y		27000 AW		JEMS	1998
EMT-Paramedic							
Emergency Medical Services	United States	Y	24585 AE	29303 AW	34877 HI	JEMS	1998
Emergency Medical Services	North Central	Y		30179 AW		JEMS	1998

Occupation/Type/Industry	Location	Per	Low	Mid	High	Source	Date
EMT-Paramedic							
Emergency Medical Services	Northeast	Y		29451 AW		JEMS	1998
Emergency Medical Services	Northwest	Y		33790 AW		JEMS	1998
Emergency Medical Services	South Central	Y		22174 AW		JEMS	1998
Emergency Medical Services	Southeast	Y		26871 AW		JEMS	1998
Emergency Medical Services	Southwest	Y		37842 AW		JEMS	1998
Engine and Other Machine Assembler							
	Alabama	S	9.02 MW	10.12 AW	21050 AAW	ALBLS	10//99-12//99
	Arizona	S	7.93 MW	9.13 AW	19000 AAW	AZBLS	10//99-12//99
	Arkansas	S	14.8 MW	14.24 AW	29620 AAW	ARBLS	10//99-12//99
	California	S	11.81 MW	11.78 AW	24510 AAW	CABLS	10//99-12//99
	Colorado	S	8.44 MW	9.00 AW	18710 AAW	COBLS	10//99-12//99
	Connecticut	S	15.66 MW	16.13 AW	33540 AAAW	CTBLS	10//99-12//99
	Florida	S	9.03 MW	10.42 AW	21670 AAW	FLBLS	10//99-12//99
	Georgia	S	9.97 MW	10.36 AW	21550 AAW	GABLS	10//99-12//99
	Illinois	S	8.2 MW	9.50 AW	19750 AAW	ILBLS	10//99-12//99
	Indiana	S	16.26 MW	16.58 AW	34480 AAW	INBLS	10//99-12//99
	Iowa	S	18.67 MW	17.39 AW	36170 AAW	IABLS	10//99-12//99
	Kansas	S	12.05 MW	11.78 AW	24490 AAW	KSBLS	10//99-12//99
	Kentucky	S	8.74 MW	9.19 AW	19110 AAW	KYBLS	10//99-12//99
	Louisiana	S	15.08 MW	14.69 AW	30540 AAW	LABLS	10//99-12//99
	Maryland	S	14.89 MW	15.04 AW	31280 AAW	MDBLS	10//99-12//99
	Massachusetts	S	15.6 MW	15.56 AW	32370 AAW	MABLS	10//99-12//99
	Michigan	S	19.03 MW	18.48 AW	38450 AAW	MIBLS	10//99-12//99
	Minnesota	S	14.06 MW	13.87 AW	28850 AAW	MNBLS	10//99-12//99
	Mississippi	S	8.45 MW	8.67 AW	18040 AAW	MSBLS	10//99-12//99
	Nebraska	S	9.77 MW	9.85 AW	20490 AAW	NEBLS	10//99-12//99
	Nevada	S	13.53 MW	13.37 AW	27800 AAW	NVBLS	10//99-12//99
	New Jersey	S	15.17 MW	15.15 AW	31510 AAW	NJBLS	10//99-12//99
	New Mexico	S	8.88 MW	8.64 AW	17970 AAW	NMBLS	10//99-12//99
	New York	S	9.84 MW	10.70 AW	22250 AAW	NYBLS	10//99-12//99
	North Carolina	S	13.12 MW	14.48 AW	30130 AAW	NCBLS	10//99-12//99
	Ohio	S	15.81 MW	16.25 AW	33790 AAW	OHBLS	10//99-12//99
	Oregon	S	19.03 MW	18.41 AW	38290 AAW	ORBLS	10//99-12//99
	Pennsylvania	S	12.41 MW	12.40 AW	25800 AAW	PABLS	10//99-12//99
	South Carolina	S	10.91 MW	12.96 AW	26950 AAW	SCBLS	10//99-12//99
	South Dakota	S	9.93 MW	9.93 AW	20660 AAW	SDBLS	10//99-12//99
	Tennessee	S	14.34 MW	14.15 AW	29420 AAW	TNBLS	10//99-12//99
	Texas	S	8.59 MW	9.42 AW	19600 AAW	TXBLS	10//99-12//99
	Virginia	S	11.55 MW	11.92 AW	24800 AAW	VABLS	10//99-12//99
	Washington	S	12.88 MW	12.85 AW	26720 AAW	WABLS	10//99-12//99
	Wisconsin	S	14.66 MW	15.34 AW	31910 AAW	WIBLS	10//99-12//99
Engineer	San Francisco, CA	Y		100948 MW		INTECH	2000
	San Francisco, CA	Y		54000 AEX		JOM	1999
	San Jose, CA	Y		100500 MW		INTECH	2000
	Stamford-Norwalk-Bridgeport, CT	Y		80500 MW		INTECH	2000
	Washingon Area, DC	Y		85036 MW		INTECH	2000
	Washington, DC	Y		64242 AEX		JOM	1999
	Chicago, IL	Y		56527 AEX		JOM	1999
	Manchester-Nashua, NH	Y		85000 MW		INTECH	2000
	Newark-Jersey City, NJ	Y		89440 MW		INTECH	2000
	Albany-Schenectady-Troy, NY	Y		83450 MW		INTECH	2000
	Nassau-Suffolk Counties, NY	Y		94920 MW		INTECH	2000
	New York City, NY	Y		86625 MW		INTECH	2000
	Tulsa, OK	Y		80500 MW		INTECH	2000
	Houston, TX	Y		87000 MW		INTECH	2000
Academic Environment	United States	Y		66900 AW		JOM2	1998
Aeronautical, Entry Level	United States	Y	41179 AE			AVWEEK2	1998
Aeronautical, Senior, 5 Years Experience	United States	Y		63751 AW		AVWEEK2	1998
Aeronautical, Senior Specialist	United States	Y	41179 AE	93527 AW		AVWEEK2	1998
Aerospace	United States	H		30.96 AW		NCS98	1998
Chemical	United States	Y	44033 AE			CIVENG	1999
Chemical	United States	H		33.37 AW		NCS98	1998
Civil	United States	Y	37543 AE			CIVENG	1999
Civil	United States	H		27.69 AW		NCS98	1998
Corrosion	United States	Y		73770 AW		MATPER	1999
Design/Consgruction, Wood Processing Industry	United States	Y		77667 AW		WOODT	6//98
Electrical	United States	Y	45691 AE			CIVENG	1999

Occupation/Type/Industry	Location	Per	Low	Mid	High	Source	Date
Engineer							
Electrical and Electronic	United States	H		30.37 AW		NCS98	1998
Electrical, Automobile Industry	Fort Wayne, IN	Y		57074 AW		SITSEL	2000
Electrical, Automobile Industry	Grand Rapids, MI	Y		60141 AW		SITSEL	2000
Electrical, Automobile Industry	St. Louis, MO	Y		58613 AW		SITSEL	2000
Electrical, Automobile Industry	Greenville, SC	Y		54340 AW		SITSEL	2000
Industrial	United States	H		25.26 AW		NCS98	1998
Industrial	United States	Y	39750 AE			CIVENG	1999
Industrial Environment	United States	Y		63300 AW		JOM2	1998
Industrial, Fabricated Metal Products Industry	United States	Y		48275 MW		IIES	1998
Industrial, Financial Institutions	United States	Y		88900 MW		IIES	1998
Industrial, Food/Beverage/Tobacco Industries	United States	Y		107375 MW		IIES	1998
Industrial, Furniture Manufacturer	United States	Y		44000 MW		IIES	1998
Industrial, Machinery Industry	United States	Y		49300 MW		IIES	1998
Industrial, Non-Engineering Consulting	United States	Y		82000 MW		IIES	1998
Industrial, Printing/Publishing	United States	Y		42250 MW		IIES	1998
Industrial, Textile Mill	United States	Y		45000 MW		IIES	1998
Manufacturing, Assembly	East North Central	Y		64291 AW		ASSEMB	2000
Manufacturing, Assembly	East South Central	Y		64293 AW		ASSEMB	2000
Manufacturing, Assembly	Middle Atlantic	Y		63837 AW		ASSEMB	2000
Manufacturing, Assembly	Mountain	Y		63576 AW		ASSEMB	2000
Manufacturing, Assembly	New England	Y		65138 AW		ASSEMB	2000
Manufacturing, Assembly	Pacific	Y		65713 AW		ASSEMB	2000
Manufacturing, Assembly	South Atlantic	Y		64573 AW		ASSEMB	2000
Manufacturing, Assembly	West North Central	Y		63825 AW		ASSEMB	2000
Manufacturing, Assembly	West South Central	Y		63351 AW		ASSEMB	2000
Mechanical	United States	Y	44166 AE			CIVENG	1999
Mechanical	United States	H		26.28 AW		NCS98	1998
Merallurgical and Materials	United States	H		27.28 AW		NCS98	1998
Mining	United States	H		30.49 AW		NCS98	1998
Nuclear	United States	H		34.60 AW		NCS98	1998
Petroleum	United States	H		43.02 AW		NCS98	1998
Quality Control, Chemicals	United States	Y		65127 AW		QPRO	4//99-5//99
Quality Control, Computers and Electronics	United States	Y		57899 AW		QPRO	4//99-5//99
Quality Control, Electrical Products	United States	Y		48634 AW		QPRO	4//99-5//99
Quality Control, Fabricated Metal Products	United States	Y		45240 AW		QPRO	4//99-5//99
Quality Control, Food and Related	United States	Y		59417 AW		QPRO	4//99-5//99
Quality Control, Machinery Industry	United States	Y		50639 AW		QPRO	4//99-5//99
Quality Control, Medical Devices	United States	Y		51165 AW		QPRO	4//99-5//99
Quality Control, Paper Industry	United States	Y		59650 AW		QPRO	4//99-5//99
Quality Control, Primary Metals	United States	Y		52083 AW		QPRO	4//99-5//99
Quality Control, Rubber and Plastics	United States	Y		48418 AW		QPRO	4//99-5//99
Quality Control, Transportation/Aerospace	United States	Y		52338 AW		QPRO	4//99-5//99
Quality Control, Utilities	United States	Y		65000 AW		QPRO	4//99-5//99
Engineering Manager	Alabama	S	36.94 MW	35.99 AW	74850 AAW	ALBLS	10//99-12//99
	Anniston MSA, AL	S	29.65 MW	30.32 AW	61680 AAW	ALBLS	10//99-12//99
	Auburn-Opelika MSA, AL	S	32.76 MW	30.85 AW	68140 AAW	ALBLS	10//99-12//99
	Birmingham MSA, AL	S	34.70 MW	35.16 AW	72180 AAW	ALBLS	10//99-12//99
	Decatur MSA, AL	S	36.05 MW	37.88 AW	74990 AAW	ALBLS	10//99-12//99
	Dothan MSA, AL	S	32.60 MW	34.60 AW	67810 AAW	ALBLS	10//99-12//99
	Florence MSA, AL	S	32.41 MW	31.03 AW	67420 AAW	ALBLS	10//99-12//99
	Huntsville MSA, AL	S	39.08 MW	39.44 AW	81280 AAW	ALBLS	10//99-12//99
	Mobile MSA, AL	S	35.79 MW	36.63 AW	74430 AAW	ALBLS	10//99-12//99
	Montgomery MSA, AL	S	29.65 MW	29.48 AW	61670 AAW	ALBLS	10//99-12//99
	Tuscaloosa MSA, AL	S	30.45 MW	33.43 AW	63330 AAW	ALBLS	10//99-12//99
	Alaska	S	33.88 MW	36.66 AW	76240 AAW	AKBLS	10//99-12//99
	Anchorage MSA, AK	S	37.93 MW	34.32 AW	78900 AAW	AKBLS	10//99-12//99
	Arizona	S	39.82 MW	40.87 AW	85010 AAW	AZBLS	10//99-12//99
	Flagstaff MSA, AZ-UT	S	33.78 MW	32.83 AW	70260 AAW	AZBLS	10//99-12//99
	Phoenix-Mesa MSA, AZ	S	42.07 MW	41.05 AW	87510 AAW	AZBLS	10//99-12//99
	Tucson MSA, AZ	S	39.54 MW	37.90 AW	82230 AAW	AZBLS	10//99-12//99
	Yuma MSA, AZ	S	35.57 MW	37.05 AW	73980 AAW	AZBLS	10//99-12//99
	Arkansas	S	31.75 MW	32.39 AW	67370 AAW	ARBLS	10//99-12//99
	Fayetteville-Springdale-Rogers MSA, AR	S	29.65 MW	29.43 AW	61680 AAW	ARBLS	10//99-12//99
	Fort Smith MSA, AR-OK	S	30.95 MW	31.75 AW	64380 AAW	ARBLS	10//99-12//99
	Little Rock-North Little Rock MSA, AR	S	32.08 MW	32.10 AW	66730 AAW	ARBLS	10//99-12//99
	California	S	42.98 MW	43.22 AW	89900 AAW	CABLS	10//99-12//99
	Bakersfield MSA, CA	S	43.77 MW	43.83 AW	91040 AAW	CABLS	10//99-12//99

AAW Average annual wage	**AOH** Average offered, high	**ASH** Average starting, high	**H** Hourly	**M** Monthly	**S** Special: hourly and annual
AE Average entry wage	**AOL** Average offered, low	**ASL** Average starting, low	**HI** Highest wage paid	**MTC** Median total compensation	**TQ** Third quartile wage
AEX Average experienced wage	**APH** Average pay, high range	**AW** Average wage paid	**HR** High end range	**MW** Median wage paid	**W** Weekly
AO Average offered	**APL** Average pay, low range	**FQ** First quartile wage	**LR** Low end range	**SQ** Second quartile wage	**Y** Yearly

Occupation/Type/Industry	Location	Per	Low	Mid	High	Source	Date
Engineering Manager	Chico-Paradise MSA, CA	S	28.41 MW	29.44 AW	59090 AAW	CABLS	10//99-12//99
	Fresno MSA, CA	S	28.91 MW	25.94 AW	60130 AAW	CABLS	10//99-12//99
	Los Angeles-Long Beach PMSA, CA	S	38.31 MW	37.27 AW	79680 AAW	CABLS	10//99-12//99
	Merced MSA, CA	S	24.42 MW	20.61 AW	50790 AAW	CABLS	10//99-12//99
	Modesto MSA, CA	S	36.76 MW	36.43 AW	76450 AAW	CABLS	10//99-12//99
	Oakland PMSA, CA	S	44.99 MW	46.04 AW	93590 AAW	CABLS	10//99-12//99
	Orange County PMSA, CA	S	43.82 MW	44.32 AW	91150 AAW	CABLS	10//99-12//99
	Redding MSA, CA	S	32.18 MW	29.33 AW	66940 AAW	CABLS	10//99-12//99
	Riverside-San Bernardino PMSA, CA	S	39.88 MW	39.90 AW	82950 AAW	CABLS	10//99-12//99
	Sacramento PMSA, CA	S	41.17 MW	39.74 AW	85630 AAW	CABLS	10//99-12//99
	Salinas MSA, CA	S	33.15 MW	32.49 AW	68950 AAW	CABLS	10//99-12//99
	San Diego MSA, CA	S	39.55 MW	39.68 AW	82260 AAW	CABLS	10//99-12//99
	San Francisco PMSA, CA	S	45.26 MW	42.54 AW	94140 AAW	CABLS	10//99-12//99
	San Jose PMSA, CA	S	51.28 MW	52.78 AW	106670 AAW	CABLS	10//99-12//99
	San Luis Obispo-Atascadero-Paso Robles MSA, CA	S	34.31 MW	35.64 AW	71370 AAW	CABLS	10//99-12//99
	Santa Barbara-Santa Maria-Lompoc MSA, CA	S	39.58 MW	39.91 AW	82330 AAW	CABLS	10//99-12//99
	Santa Cruz-Watsonville PMSA, CA	S	47.19 MW	49.68 AW	98160 AAW	CABLS	10//99-12//99
	Santa Rosa PMSA, CA	S	42.38 MW	40.73 AW	88150 AAW	CABLS	10//99-12//99
	Stockton-Lodi MSA, CA	S	33.71 MW	32.38 AW	70120 AAW	CABLS	10//99-12//99
	Vallejo-Fairfield-Napa PMSA, CA	S	36.99 MW	37.10 AW	76930 AAW	CABLS	10//99-12//99
	Ventura PMSA, CA	S	42.73 MW	41.60 AW	88880 AAW	CABLS	10//99-12//99
	Visalia-Tulare-Porterville MSA, CA	S	32.70 MW	33.88 AW	68010 AAW	CABLS	10//99-12//99
	Yolo PMSA, CA	S	42.48 MW	42.40 AW	88370 AAW	CABLS	10//99-12//99
	Colorado	S	37.96 MW	38.57 AW	80230 AAW	COBLS	10//99-12//99
	Boulder-Longmont PMSA, CO	S	43.31 MW	43.13 AW	90090 AAW	COBLS	10//99-12//99
	Colorado Springs MSA, CO	S	42.43 MW	42.33 AW	88250 AAW	COBLS	10//99-12//99
	Denver PMSA, CO	S	37.44 MW	36.73 AW	77880 AAW	COBLS	10//99-12//99
	Fort Collins-Loveland MSA, CO	S	42.32 MW	42.58 AW	88030 AAW	COBLS	10//99-12//99
	Grand Junction MSA, CO	S	33.48 MW	31.85 AW	69640 AAW	COBLS	10//99-12//99
	Greeley PMSA, CO	S	34.78 MW	32.37 AW	72350 AAW	COBLS	10//99-12//99
	Pueblo MSA, CO	S	33.88 MW	34.19 AW	70470 AAW	COBLS	10//99-12//99
	Connecticut	S	40.25 MW	41.20 AW	85690 AAW	CTBLS	10//99-12//99
	Bridgeport PMSA, CT	S	42.89 MW	41.78 AW	89220 AAW	CTBLS	10//99-12//99
	Danbury PMSA, CT	S	36.31 MW	34.24 AW	75530 AAW	CTBLS	10//99-12//99
	Hartford MSA, CT	S	41.19 MW	40.43 AW	85670 AAW	CTBLS	10//99-12//99
	New Haven-Meriden PMSA, CT	S	39.74 MW	38.11 AW	82660 AAW	CTBLS	10//99-12//99
	New London-Norwich MSA, CT-RI	S	37.87 MW	38.06 AW	78770 AAW	CTBLS	10//99-12//99
	Stamford-Norwalk PMSA, CT	S	46.99 MW	47.93 AW	97750 AAW	CTBLS	10//99-12//99
	Waterbury PMSA, CT	S	40.80 MW	41.04 AW	84860 AAW	CTBLS	10//99-12//99
	Delaware	S	36.48 MW	36.73 AW	76410 AAW	DEBLS	10//99-12//99
	Wilmington-Newark PMSA, DE-MD	S	37.35 MW	37.16 AW	77680 AAW	DEBLS	10//99-12//99
	Washington PMSA, DC-MD-VA-WV	S	42.20 MW	42.16 AW	87780 AAW	DCBLS	10//99-12//99
	Florida	S	36.21 MW	37.18 AW	77340 AAW	FLBLS	10//99-12//99
	Daytona Beach MSA, FL	S	32.81 MW	31.29 AW	68240 AAW	FLBLS	10//99-12//99
	Fort Lauderdale PMSA, FL	S	41.66 MW	38.25 AW	86640 AAW	FLBLS	10//99-12//99
	Fort Myers-Cape Coral MSA, FL	S	30.94 MW	28.32 AW	64360 AAW	FLBLS	10//99-12//99
	Fort Pierce-Port St. Lucie MSA, FL	S	31.56 MW	30.42 AW	65650 AAW	FLBLS	10//99-12//99
	Gainesville MSA, FL	S	40.78 MW	38.10 AW	84830 AAW	FLBLS	10//99-12//99
	Jacksonville MSA, FL	S	36.61 MW	37.06 AW	76160 AAW	FLBLS	10//99-12//99
	Lakeland-Winter Haven MSA, FL	S	31.56 MW	30.17 AW	65640 AAW	FLBLS	10//99-12//99
	Melbourne-Titusville-Palm Bay MSA, FL	S	39.56 MW	37.94 AW	82290 AAW	FLBLS	10//99-12//99
	Miami PMSA, FL	S	35.16 MW	31.88 AW	73140 AAW	FLBLS	10//99-12//99
	Naples MSA, FL	S	40.14 MW	43.24 AW	83480 AAW	FLBLS	10//99-12//99
	Ocala MSA, FL	S	25.95 MW	26.37 AW	53980 AAW	FLBLS	10//99-12//99
	Orlando MSA, FL	S	40.07 MW	39.06 AW	83350 AAW	FLBLS	10//99-12//99
	Panama City MSA, FL	S	34.99 MW	35.99 AW	72780 AAW	FLBLS	10//99-12//99

AAW	Average annual wage	AOH	Average offered, high	ASH	Average starting, high
AE	Average entry wage	AOL	Average offered, low	ASL	Average starting, low
AEX	Average experienced wage	APH	Average pay, high range	AW	Average wage paid
AO	Average offered	APL	Average pay, low range	FQ	First quartile wage

H	Hourly	M	Monthly
HI	Highest wage paid	MTC	Median total compensation
HR	High end range	MW	Median wage paid
LR	Low end range	SQ	Second quartile wage

S	Special: hourly and annual		
TQ	Third quartile wage		
W	Weekly		
Y	Yearly		

Occupation/Type/Industry	Location	Per	Low	Mid	High	Source	Date
Engineering Manager	Pensacola MSA, FL	S	37.98 MW	38.50 AW	79010 AAW	FLBLS	10//99-12//99
	Sarasota-Bradenton MSA, FL	S	34.18 MW	33.94 AW	71090 AAW	FLBLS	10//99-12//99
	Tallahassee MSA, FL	S	35.01 MW	35.58 AW	72830 AAW	FLBLS	10//99-12//99
	Tampa-St. Petersburg-Clearwater MSA, FL	S	34.93 MW	34.87 AW	72650 AAW	FLBLS	10//99-12//99
	West Palm Beach-Boca Raton MSA, FL	S	39.20 MW	38.24 AW	81540 AAW	FLBLS	10//99-12//99
	Georgia	S	41.15 MW	42.28 AW	87930 AAW	GABLS	10//99-12//99
	Albany MSA, GA	S	29.36 MW	29.47 AW	61060 AAW	GABLS	10//99-12//99
	Athens MSA, GA	S	35.50 MW	36.79 AW	73830 AAW	GABLS	10//99-12//99
	Atlanta MSA, GA	S	44.75 MW	45.12 AW	93070 AAW	GABLS	10//99-12//99
	Columbus MSA, GA-AL	S	35.11 MW	31.99 AW	73030 AAW	GABLS	10//99-12//99
	Savannah MSA, GA	S	34.07 MW	33.33 AW	70860 AAW	GABLS	10//99-12//99
	Hawaii	S	34.35 MW	35.04 AW	72880 AAW	HIBLS	10//99-12//99
	Idaho	S	41.01 MW	40.47 AW	84180 AAW	IDBLS	10//99-12//99
	Boise City MSA, ID	S	43.91 MW	45.70 AW	91330 AAW	IDBLS	10//99-12//99
	Illinois	S	37.89 MW	39.20 AW	81540 AAW	ILBLS	10//99-12//99
	Champaign-Urbana MSA, IL	S	32.52 MW	32.41 AW	67640 AAW	ILBLS	10//99-12//99
	Chicago PMSA, IL	S	40.49 MW	39.12 AW	84230 AAW	ILBLS	10//99-12//99
	Kankakee PMSA, IL	S	30.75 MW	31.45 AW	63960 AAW	ILBLS	10//99-12//99
	Peoria-Pekin MSA, IL	S	40.77 MW	40.14 AW	84810 AAW	ILBLS	10//99-12//99
	Rockford MSA, IL	S	33.05 MW	34.12 AW	68750 AAW	ILBLS	10//99-12//99
	Springfield MSA, IL	S	29.18 MW	29.66 AW	60700 AAW	ILBLS	10//99-12//99
	Indiana	S	32.66 MW	34.19 AW	71100 AAW	INBLS	10//99-12//99
	Bloomington MSA, IN	S	26.04 MW	21.40 AW	54170 AAW	INBLS	10//99-12//99
	Elkhart-Goshen MSA, IN	S	25.51 MW	24.92 AW	53060 AAW	INBLS	10//99-12//99
	Evansville-Henderson MSA, IN-KY	S	31.48 MW	31.89 AW	65470 AAW	INBLS	10//99-12//99
	Fort Wayne MSA, IN	S	31.61 MW	30.81 AW	65760 AAW	INBLS	10//99-12//99
	Gary PMSA, IN	S	32.03 MW	32.00 AW	66610 AAW	INBLS	10//99-12//99
	Indianapolis MSA, IN	S	34.26 MW	33.05 AW	71250 AAW	INBLS	10//99-12//99
	Kokomo MSA, IN	S	50.46 MW	52.07 AW	104950 AAW	INBLS	10//99-12//99
	Lafayette MSA, IN	S	45.69 MW	44.80 AW	95030 AAW	INBLS	10//99-12//99
	Muncie MSA, IN	S	33.57 MW	36.29 AW	69830 AAW	INBLS	10//99-12//99
	South Bend MSA, IN	S	37.29 MW	35.94 AW	77560 AAW	INBLS	10//99-12//99
	Terre Haute MSA, IN	S	40.13 MW	39.80 AW	83470 AAW	INBLS	10//99-12//99
	Iowa	S	29 MW	30.69 AW	63830 AAW	IABLS	10//99-12//99
	Davenport-Moline-Rock Island MSA, IA-IL	S	31.33 MW	32.18 AW	65170 AAW	IABLS	10//99-12//99
	Des Moines MSA, IA	S	29.10 MW	29.29 AW	60520 AAW	IABLS	10//99-12//99
	Sioux City MSA, IA-NE	S	28.69 MW	30.27 AW	59680 AAW	IABLS	10//99-12//99
	Kansas	S	32.16 MW	33.30 AW	69260 AAW	KSBLS	10//99-12//99
	Topeka MSA, KS	S	32.46 MW	32.50 AW	67520 AAW	KSBLS	10//99-12//99
	Wichita MSA, KS	S	31.58 MW	31.35 AW	65690 AAW	KSBLS	10//99-12//99
	Kentucky	S	32.05 MW	32.88 AW	68390 AAW	KYBLS	10//99-12//99
	Lexington MSA, KY	S	32.32 MW	31.12 AW	67230 AAW	KYBLS	10//99-12//99
	Louisville MSA, KY-IN	S	34.86 MW	34.24 AW	72510 AAW	KYBLS	10//99-12//99
	Owensboro MSA, KY	S	28.69 MW	28.56 AW	59680 AAW	KYBLS	10//99-12//99
	Louisiana	S	35.27 MW	36.26 AW	75430 AAW	LABLS	10//99-12//99
	Alexandria MSA, LA	S	33.12 MW	33.92 AW	68900 AAW	LABLS	10//99-12//99
	Baton Rouge MSA, LA	S	38.04 MW	36.48 AW	79120 AAW	LABLS	10//99-12//99
	Houma MSA, LA	S	29.14 MW	29.94 AW	60620 AAW	LABLS	10//99-12//99
	Lafayette MSA, LA	S	29.02 MW	27.16 AW	60350 AAW	LABLS	10//99-12//99
	Lake Charles MSA, LA	S	37.92 MW	39.30 AW	78870 AAW	LABLS	10//99-12//99
	Monroe MSA, LA	S	41.58 MW	37.57 AW	86490 AAW	LABLS	10//99-12//99
	New Orleans MSA, LA	S	37.89 MW	36.95 AW	78810 AAW	LABLS	10//99-12//99
	Shreveport-Bossier City MSA, LA	S	28.06 MW	25.58 AW	58360 AAW	LABLS	10//99-12//99
	Maine	S	30.4 MW	31.19 AW	64880 AAW	MEBLS	10//99-12//99
	Bangor MSA, ME	S	36.67 MW	33.67 AW	76260 AAW	MEBLS	10//99-12//99
	Lewiston-Auburn MSA, ME	S	32.39 MW	35.43 AW	67370 AAW	MEBLS	10//99-12//99
	Portland MSA, ME	S	27.68 MW	25.18 AW	57570 AAW	MEBLS	10//99-12//99
	Maryland	S	39.22 MW	39.31 AW	81770 AAW	MDBLS	10//99-12//99
	Baltimore PMSA, MD	S	36.41 MW	36.02 AW	75720 AAW	MDBLS	10//99-12//99
	Hagerstown PMSA, MD	S	38.10 MW	36.43 AW	79250 AAW	MDBLS	10//99-12//99
	Massachusetts	S	42.31 MW	43.39 AW	90250 AAW	MABLS	10//99-12//99
	Boston PMSA, MA-NH	S	45.09 MW	44.09 AW	93780 AAW	MABLS	10//99-12//99
	Brockton PMSA, MA	S	37.05 MW	37.68 AW	77060 AAW	MABLS	10//99-12//99
	Fitchburg-Leominster PMSA, MA	S	37.70 MW	39.67 AW	78410 AAW	MABLS	10//99-12//99
	Lawrence PMSA, MA-NH	S	38.21 MW	39.24 AW	79470 AAW	MABLS	10//99-12//99
	Lowell PMSA, MA-NH	S	43.27 MW	41.44 AW	90000 AAW	MABLS	10//99-12//99

AAW	Average annual wage	AOH	Average offered, high	ASH	Average starting, high	H	Hourly	M	Monthly	S	Special: hourly and annual
AE	Average entry wage	AOL	Average offered, low	ASL	Average starting, low	HI	Highest wage paid	MTC	Median total compensation	TQ	Third quartile wage
AEX	Average experienced wage	APH	Average pay, high range	AW	Average wage paid	HR	High end range	MW	Median wage paid	W	Weekly
AO	Average offered	APL	Average pay, low range	FQ	First quartile wage	LR	Low end range	SQ	Second quartile wage	Y	Yearly

Occupation/Type/Industry	Location	Per	Low	Mid	High	Source	Date
Engineering Manager	New Bedford PMSA, MA	S	37.21 MW	37.58 AW	77390 AAW	MABLS	10//99-12//99
	Pittsfield MSA, MA	S	27.73 MW	25.68 AW	57690 AAW	MABLS	10//99-12//99
	Springfield MSA, MA	S	33.68 MW	31.93 AW	70050 AAW	MABLS	10//99-12//99
	Worcester PMSA, MA-CT	S	37.76 MW	37.99 AW	78540 AAW	MABLS	10//99-12//99
	Michigan	S	39.8 MW	40.56 AW	84360 AAW	MIBLS	10//99-12//99
	Ann Arbor PMSA, MI	S	37.15 MW	36.94 AW	77280 AAW	MIBLS	10//99-12//99
	Benton Harbor MSA, MI	S	29.84 MW	30.43 AW	62070 AAW	MIBLS	10//99-12//99
	Detroit PMSA, MI	S	41.90 MW	41.18 AW	87150 AAW	MIBLS	10//99-12//99
	Flint PMSA, MI	S	53.39 MW	55.43 AW	111060 AAW	MIBLS	10//99-12//99
	Grand Rapids-Muskegon-Holland MSA, MI	S	37.46 MW	37.65 AW	77920 AAW	MIBLS	10//99-12//99
	Jackson MSA, MI	S	37.12 MW	33.91 AW	77220 AAW	MIBLS	10//99-12//99
	Kalamazoo-Battle Creek MSA, MI	S	40.76 MW	40.34 AW	84780 AAW	MIBLS	10//99-12//99
	Lansing-East Lansing MSA, MI	S	37.48 MW	37.81 AW	77960 AAW	MIBLS	10//99-12//99
	Saginaw-Bay City-Midland MSA, MI	S	39.68 MW	38.77 AW	82540 AAW	MIBLS	10//99-12//99
	Minnesota	S	40.54 MW	41.28 AW	85870 AAW	MNBLS	10//99-12//99
	Duluth-Superior MSA, MN-WI	S	36.19 MW	36.39 AW	75270 AAW	MNBLS	10//99-12//99
	Minneapolis-St. Paul MSA, MN-WI	S	41.81 MW	41.00 AW	86970 AAW	MNBLS	10//99-12//99
	Mississippi	S	32.55 MW	32.21 AW	67000 AAW	MSBLS	10//99-12//99
	Biloxi-Gulfport-Pascagoula MSA, MS	S	36.97 MW	37.70 AW	76900 AAW	MSBLS	10//99-12//99
	Jackson MSA, MS	S	32.53 MW	32.16 AW	67660 AAW	MSBLS	10//99-12//99
	Missouri	S	35.24 MW	35.79 AW	74450 AAW	MOBLS	10//99-12//99
	Joplin MSA, MO	S	26.11 MW	24.61 AW	54300 AAW	MOBLS	10//99-12//99
	Kansas City MSA, MO-KS	S	37.58 MW	36.27 AW	78170 AAW	MOBLS	10//99-12//99
	St. Louis MSA, MO-IL	S	35.73 MW	35.65 AW	74330 AAW	MOBLS	10//99-12//99
	Springfield MSA, MO	S	37.50 MW	33.33 AW	77990 AAW	MOBLS	10//99-12//99
	Montana	S	28.13 MW	28.87 AW	60050 AAW	MTBLS	10//99-12//99
	Billings MSA, MT	S	27.26 MW	29.21 AW	56700 AAW	MTBLS	10//99-12//99
	Nebraska	S	34.62 MW	33.75 AW	70210 AAW	NEBLS	10//99-12//99
	Lincoln MSA, NE	S	35.03 MW	30.22 AW	72860 AAW	NEBLS	10//99-12//99
	Omaha MSA, NE-IA	S	34.51 MW	36.28 AW	71780 AAW	NEBLS	10//99-12//99
	Nevada	S	36.09 MW	36.99 AW	76930 AAW	NVBLS	10//99-12//99
	Las Vegas MSA, NV-AZ	S	37.38 MW	37.63 AW	77740 AAW	NVBLS	10//99-12//99
	Reno MSA, NV	S	38.93 MW	35.53 AW	80970 AAW	NVBLS	10//99-12//99
	New Hampshire	S	34.79 MW	36.41 AW	75730 AAW	NHBLS	10//99-12//99
	Manchester PMSA, NH	S	33.70 MW	31.84 AW	70090 AAW	NHBLS	10//99-12//99
	Nashua PMSA, NH	S	43.83 MW	42.17 AW	91170 AAW	NHBLS	10//99-12//99
	Portsmouth-Rochester PMSA, NH-ME	S	35.18 MW	33.45 AW	73160 AAW	NHBLS	10//99-12//99
	New Jersey	S	45.24 MW	45.11 AW	93830 AAW	NJBLS	10//99-12//99
	Atlantic-Cape May PMSA, NJ	S	44.36 MW	46.13 AW	92260 AAW	NJBLS	10//99-12//99
	Bergen-Passaic PMSA, NJ	S	48.84 MW	49.60 AW	101600 AAW	NJBLS	10//99-12//99
	Jersey City PMSA, NJ	S	44.37 MW	41.84 AW	92300 AAW	NJBLS	10//99-12//99
	Middlesex-Somerset-Hunterdon PMSA, NJ	S	44.28 MW	43.64 AW	92090 AAW	NJBLS	10//99-12//99
	Monmouth-Ocean PMSA, NJ	S	42.06 MW	42.62 AW	87490 AAW	NJBLS	10//99-12//99
	Newark PMSA, NJ	S	44.87 MW	45.85 AW	93330 AAW	NJBLS	10//99-12//99
	Trenton PMSA, NJ	S	46.46 MW	46.88 AW	96640 AAW	NJBLS	10//99-12//99
	New Mexico	S	39.8 MW	39.10 AW	81330 AAW	NMBLS	10//99-12//99
	Albuquerque MSA, NM	S	41.55 MW	41.52 AW	86420 AAW	NMBLS	10//99-12//99
	Santa Fe MSA, NM	S	34.05 MW	33.10 AW	70820 AAW	NMBLS	10//99-12//99
	New York	S	40.91 MW	41.70 AW	86740 AAW	NYBLS	10//99-12//99
	Albany-Schenectady-Troy MSA, NY	S	36.62 MW	34.16 AW	76160 AAW	NYBLS	10//99-12//99
	Binghamton MSA, NY	S	44.90 MW	46.77 AW	93400 AAW	NYBLS	10//99-12//99
	Buffalo-Niagara Falls MSA, NY	S	35.98 MW	35.86 AW	74830 AAW	NYBLS	10//99-12//99
	Dutchess County PMSA, NY	S	49.39 MW	52.07 AW	102730 AAW	NYBLS	10//99-12//99
	Elmira MSA, NY	S	31.02 MW	31.34 AW	64520 AAW	NYBLS	10//99-12//99
	Glens Falls MSA, NY	S	38.64 MW	34.19 AW	80360 AAW	NYBLS	10//99-12//99
	Jamestown MSA, NY	S	29.58 MW	21.26 AW	61520 AAW	NYBLS	10//99-12//99
	Nassau-Suffolk PMSA, NY	S	44.09 MW	44.99 AW	91710 AAW	NYBLS	10//99-12//99
	New York PMSA, NY	S	42.99 MW	41.07 AW	89410 AAW	NYBLS	10//99-12//99
	Newburgh PMSA, NY-PA	S	37.95 MW	35.68 AW	78940 AAW	NYBLS	10//99-12//99
	Rochester MSA, NY	S	39.08 MW	39.01 AW	81290 AAW	NYBLS	10//99-12//99
	Syracuse MSA, NY	S	39.57 MW	40.20 AW	82320 AAW	NYBLS	10//99-12//99
	Utica-Rome MSA, NY	S	36.46 MW	33.61 AW	75830 AAW	NYBLS	10//99-12//99
	North Carolina	S	35.57 MW	35.63 AW	74110 AAW	NCBLS	10//99-12//99

AAW	Average annual wage	AOH	Average offered, high	ASH	Average starting, high	H	Hourly	M	Monthly	S	Special: hourly and annual
AE	Average entry wage	AOL	Average offered, low	ASL	Average starting, low	HI	Highest wage paid	MTC	Median total compensation	TQ	Third quartile wage
AEX	Average experienced wage	APH	Average pay, high range	AW	Average wage paid	HR	High end range	MW	Median wage paid	W	Weekly
AO	Average offered	APL	Average pay, low range	FQ	First quartile wage	LR	Low end range	SQ	Second quartile wage	Y	Yearly

Occupation/Type/Industry	Location	Per	Low	Mid	High	Source	Date
Engineering Manager	Asheville MSA, NC	S	31.19 MW	30.00 AW	64870 AAW	NCBLS	10//99-12//99
	Charlotte-Gastonia-Rock Hill MSA, NC-SC	S	33.87 MW	33.04 AW	70450 AAW	NCBLS	10//99-12//99
	Fayetteville MSA, NC	S	31.23 MW	31.31 AW	64960 AAW	NCBLS	10//99-12//99
	Greensboro--Winston-Salem--High Point MSA, NC	S	38.05 MW	38.73 AW	79150 AAW	NCBLS	10//99-12//99
	Greenville MSA, NC	S	36.33 MW	36.51 AW	75560 AAW	NCBLS	10//99-12//99
	Hickory-Morganton-Lenoir MSA, NC	S	32.99 MW	32.15 AW	68620 AAW	NCBLS	10//99-12//99
	Raleigh-Durham-Chapel Hill MSA, NC	S	37.99 MW	38.21 AW	79010 AAW	NCBLS	10//99-12//99
	Rocky Mount MSA, NC	S	33.33 MW	35.51 AW	69340 AAW	NCBLS	10//99-12//99
	Wilmington MSA, NC	S	34.59 MW	36.01 AW	71940 AAW	NCBLS	10//99-12//99
	North Dakota	S	24.74 MW	26.55 AW	55220 AAW	NDBLS	10//99-12//99
	Ohio	S	35.83 MW	35.63 AW	74100 AAW	OHBLS	10//99-12//99
	Akron PMSA, OH	S	34.07 MW	33.04 AW	70870 AAW	OHBLS	10//99-12//99
	Canton-Massillon MSA, OH	S	34.93 MW	33.50 AW	72650 AAW	OHBLS	10//99-12//99
	Cincinnati PMSA, OH-KY-IN	S	36.88 MW	35.66 AW	76700 AAW	OHBLS	10//99-12//99
	Cleveland-Lorain-Elyria PMSA, OH	S	36.13 MW	37.41 AW	75150 AAW	OHBLS	10//99-12//99
	Columbus MSA, OH	S	35.26 MW	33.91 AW	73340 AAW	OHBLS	10//99-12//99
	Dayton-Springfield MSA, OH	S	38.37 MW	38.67 AW	79810 AAW	OHBLS	10//99-12//99
	Hamilton-Middletown PMSA, OH	S	35.54 MW	34.00 AW	73910 AAW	OHBLS	10//99-12//99
	Lima MSA, OH	S	28.92 MW	29.75 AW	60150 AAW	OHBLS	10//99-12//99
	Mansfield MSA, OH	S	35.21 MW	34.29 AW	73240 AAW	OHBLS	10//99-12//99
	Steubenville-Weirton MSA, OH-WV	S	29.12 MW	29.40 AW	60570 AAW	OHBLS	10//99-12//99
	Toledo MSA, OH	S	33.07 MW	32.61 AW	68780 AAW	OHBLS	10//99-12//99
	Youngstown-Warren MSA, OH	S	30.39 MW	27.00 AW	63210 AAW	OHBLS	10//99-12//99
	Oklahoma	S	34.11 MW	33.77 AW	70240 AAW	OKBLS	10//99-12//99
	Oklahoma City MSA, OK	S	35.94 MW	34.51 AW	74750 AAW	OKBLS	10//99-12//99
	Tulsa MSA, OK	S	33.15 MW	35.46 AW	68950 AAW	OKBLS	10//99-12//99
	Oregon	S	39.31 MW	40.98 AW	85240 AAW	ORBLS	10//99-12//99
	Eugene-Springfield MSA, OR	S	35.98 MW	37.97 AW	74830 AAW	ORBLS	10//99-12//99
	Medford-Ashland MSA, OR	S	40.12 MW	37.59 AW	83450 AAW	ORBLS	10//99-12//99
	Portland-Vancouver PMSA, OR-WA	S	41.66 MW	39.99 AW	86650 AAW	ORBLS	10//99-12//99
	Salem PMSA, OR	S	36.78 MW	37.52 AW	76500 AAW	ORBLS	10//99-12//99
	Pennsylvania	S	36.01 MW	35.91 AW	74690 AAW	PABLS	10//99-12//99
	Allentown-Bethlehem-Easton MSA, PA	S	36.17 MW	34.08 AW	75240 AAW	PABLS	10//99-12//99
	Altoona MSA, PA	S	31.90 MW	32.85 AW	66360 AAW	PABLS	10//99-12//99
	Erie MSA, PA	S	29.98 MW	29.13 AW	62360 AAW	PABLS	10//99-12//99
	Harrisburg-Lebanon-Carlisle MSA, PA	S	37.21 MW	36.50 AW	77390 AAW	PABLS	10//99-12//99
	Johnstown MSA, PA	S	20.36 MW	17.25 AW	42340 AAW	PABLS	10//99-12//99
	Lancaster MSA, PA	S	37.08 MW	33.15 AW	77130 AAW	PABLS	10//99-12//99
	Philadelphia PMSA, PA-NJ	S	38.38 MW	37.54 AW	79820 AAW	PABLS	10//99-12//99
	Pittsburgh MSA, PA	S	37.38 MW	38.43 AW	77750 AAW	PABLS	10//99-12//99
	Reading MSA, PA	S	34.49 MW	34.02 AW	71730 AAW	PABLS	10//99-12//99
	Scranton--Wilkes-Barre--Hazleton MSA, PA	S	33.21 MW	33.13 AW	69080 AAW	PABLS	10//99-12//99
	State College MSA, PA	S	32.17 MW	31.26 AW	66910 AAW	PABLS	10//99-12//99
	York MSA, PA	S	32.00 MW	31.63 AW	66560 AAW	PABLS	10//99-12//99
	Rhode Island	S	39.29 MW	39.12 AW	81370 AAW	RIBLS	10//99-12//99
	Providence-Fall River-Warwick MSA, RI-MA	S	37.57 MW	38.03 AW	78140 AAW	RIBLS	10//99-12//99
	South Carolina	S	36.72 MW	36.03 AW	74940 AAW	SCBLS	10//99-12//99
	Columbia MSA, SC	S	34.98 MW	31.47 AW	72750 AAW	SCBLS	10//99-12//99
	Florence MSA, SC	S	33.40 MW	37.08 AW	69470 AAW	SCBLS	10//99-12//99
	Greenville-Spartanburg-Anderson MSA, SC	S	37.33 MW	37.82 AW	77640 AAW	SCBLS	10//99-12//99
	Myrtle Beach MSA, SC	S	37.16 MW	35.82 AW	77290 AAW	SCBLS	10//99-12//99
	Sumter MSA, SC	S	34.51 MW	34.42 AW	71790 AAW	SCBLS	10//99-12//99
	South Dakota	S	32.72 MW	33.53 AW	69750 AAW	SDBLS	10//99-12//99
	Rapid City MSA, SD	S	39.30 MW	38.64 AW	81740 AAW	SDBLS	10//99-12//99
	Sioux Falls MSA, SD	S	33.80 MW	33.17 AW	70300 AAW	SDBLS	10//99-12//99
	Tennessee	S	33.95 MW	34.03 AW	70770 AAW	TNBLS	10//99-12//99
	Chattanooga MSA, TN-GA	S	33.95 MW	35.10 AW	70620 AAW	TNBLS	10//99-12//99
	Clarksville-Hopkinsville MSA, TN-KY	S	33.43 MW	32.05 AW	69520 AAW	TNBLS	10//99-12//99

AAW Average annual wage	**AOH** Average offered, high	**ASH** Average starting, high	**H** Hourly	**M** Monthly	**S** Special: hourly and annual
AE Average entry wage	**AOL** Average offered, low	**ASL** Average starting, low	**HI** Highest wage paid	**MTC** Median total compensation	**TQ** Third quartile wage
AEX Average experienced wage	**APH** Average pay, high range	**AW** Average wage paid	**HR** High end range	**MW** Median wage paid	**W** Weekly
AO Average offered	**APL** Average pay, low range	**FQ** First quartile wage	**LR** Low end range	**SQ** Second quartile wage	**Y** Yearly

Occupation/Type/Industry	Location	Per	Low	Mid	High	Source	Date
Engineering Manager	Johnson City-Kingsport-Bristol MSA, TN-VA	S	32.96 MW	35.88 AW	68560 AAW	TNBLS	10//99-12//99
	Knoxville MSA, TN	S	36.40 MW	37.34 AW	75710 AAW	TNBLS	10//99-12//99
	Memphis MSA, TN-AR-MS	S	35.42 MW	34.30 AW	73680 AAW	MSBLS	10//99-12//99
	Nashville MSA, TN	S	34.42 MW	34.16 AW	71590 AAW	TNBLS	10//99-12//99
	Texas	S	39.8 MW	40.23 AW	83680 AAW	TXBLS	10//99-12//99
	Austin-San Marcos MSA, TX	S	41.11 MW	40.43 AW	85520 AAW	TXBLS	10//99-12//99
	Beaumont-Port Arthur MSA, TX	S	43.27 MW	42.59 AW	90000 AAW	TXBLS	10//99-12//99
	Brazoria PMSA, TX	S	30.99 MW	29.64 AW	64450 AAW	TXBLS	10//99-12//99
	Brownsville-Harlingen-San Benito MSA, TX	S	35.42 MW	33.06 AW	73670 AAW	TXBLS	10//99-12//99
	Bryan-College Station MSA, TX	S	49.71 MW	53.21 AW	103390 AAW	TXBLS	10//99-12//99
	Corpus Christi MSA, TX	S	46.37 MW	46.41 AW	96440 AAW	TXBLS	10//99-12//99
	Dallas PMSA, TX	S	39.45 MW	38.73 AW	82050 AAW	TXBLS	10//99-12//99
	El Paso MSA, TX	S	38.70 MW	38.33 AW	80500 AAW	TXBLS	10//99-12//99
	Fort Worth-Arlington PMSA, TX	S	39.80 MW	40.02 AW	82780 AAW	TXBLS	10//99-12//99
	Galveston-Texas City PMSA, TX	S	38.90 MW	39.22 AW	80920 AAW	TXBLS	10//99-12//99
	Houston PMSA, TX	S	42.68 MW	42.18 AW	88780 AAW	TXBLS	10//99-12//99
	Killeen-Temple MSA, TX	S	36.18 MW	34.47 AW	75260 AAW	TXBLS	10//99-12//99
	Laredo MSA, TX	S	32.53 MW	35.53 AW	67660 AAW	TXBLS	10//99-12//99
	Longview-Marshall MSA, TX	S	30.25 MW	29.37 AW	62910 AAW	TXBLS	10//99-12//99
	Lubbock MSA, TX	S	28.14 MW	27.46 AW	58520 AAW	TXBLS	10//99-12//99
	Odessa-Midland MSA, TX	S	44.14 MW	45.50 AW	91800 AAW	TXBLS	10//99-12//99
	San Antonio MSA, TX	S	35.65 MW	34.65 AW	74140 AAW	TXBLS	10//99-12//99
	Sherman-Denison MSA, TX	S	43.85 MW	46.67 AW	91210 AAW	TXBLS	10//99-12//99
	Texarkana MSA, TX-Texarkana, AR	S	30.98 MW	32.16 AW	64430 AAW	TXBLS	10//99-12//99
	Tyler MSA, TX	S	35.25 MW	37.12 AW	73330 AAW	TXBLS	10//99-12//99
	Victoria MSA, TX	S	29.31 MW	28.10 AW	60970 AAW	TXBLS	10//99-12//99
	Wichita Falls MSA, TX	S	40.71 MW	39.05 AW	84680 AAW	TXBLS	10//99-12//99
	Provo-Orem MSA, UT	S	30.77 MW	28.42 AW	64000 AAW	UTBLS	10//99-12//99
	Salt Lake City-Ogden MSA, UT	S	35.46 MW	34.07 AW	73760 AAW	UTBLS	10//99-12//99
	Vermont	S	37.19 MW	40.95 AW	85170 AAW	VTBLS	10//99-12//99
	Burlington MSA, VT	S	47.79 MW	40.37 AW	99410 AAW	VTBLS	10//99-12//99
	Virginia	S	39.2 MW	39.21 AW	81560 AAW	VABLS	10//99-12//99
	Charlottesville MSA, VA	S	34.39 MW	31.58 AW	71540 AAW	VABLS	10//99-12//99
	Lynchburg MSA, VA	S	37.12 MW	37.89 AW	77210 AAW	VABLS	10//99-12//99
	Norfolk-Virginia Beach-Newport News MSA, VA-NC	S	37.25 MW	37.47 AW	77470 AAW	VABLS	10//99-12//99
	Richmond-Petersburg MSA, VA	S	31.62 MW	30.30 AW	65770 AAW	VABLS	10//99-12//99
	Roanoke MSA, VA	S	33.96 MW	34.93 AW	70640 AAW	VABLS	10//99-12//99
	Washington	S	39.19 MW	39.03 AW	81170 AAW	WABLS	10//99-12//99
	Olympia PMSA, WA	S	32.74 MW	31.98 AW	68110 AAW	WABLS	10//99-12//99
	Richland-Kennewick-Pasco MSA, WA	S	37.21 MW	38.13 AW	77400 AAW	WABLS	10//99-12//99
	Seattle-Bellevue-Everett PMSA, WA	S	40.22 MW	40.81 AW	83650 AAW	WABLS	10//99-12//99
	Spokane MSA, WA	S	34.05 MW	34.65 AW	70830 AAW	WABLS	10//99-12//99
	Tacoma PMSA, WA	S	36.17 MW	34.92 AW	75240 AAW	WABLS	10//99-12//99
	West Virginia	S	30.08 MW	30.48 AW	63390 AAW	WVBLS	10//99-12//99
	Charleston MSA, WV	S	31.04 MW	31.10 AW	64550 AAW	WVBLS	10//99-12//99
	Huntington-Ashland MSA, WV-KY-OH	S	34.87 MW	35.07 AW	72540 AAW	WVBLS	10//99-12//99
	Parkersburg-Marietta MSA, WV-OH	S	35.10 MW	35.73 AW	73000 AAW	WVBLS	10//99-12//99
	Wheeling MSA, WV-OH	S	32.81 MW	35.22 AW	68240 AAW	WVBLS	10//99-12//99
	Wisconsin	S	33 MW	33.71 AW	70120 AAW	WIBLS	10//99-12//99
	Appleton-Oshkosh-Neenah MSA, WI	S	33.81 MW	31.75 AW	70330 AAW	WIBLS	10//99-12//99
	Eau Claire MSA, WI	S	31.72 MW	30.44 AW	65980 AAW	WIBLS	10//99-12//99
	Green Bay MSA, WI	S	33.06 MW	32.45 AW	68770 AAW	WIBLS	10//99-12//99
	Janesville-Beloit MSA, WI	S	32.04 MW	32.21 AW	66630 AAW	WIBLS	10//99-12//99
	Kenosha PMSA, WI	S	27.32 MW	27.02 AW	56820 AAW	WIBLS	10//99-12//99
	La Crosse MSA, WI-MN	S	31.44 MW	30.76 AW	65400 AAW	WIBLS	10//99-12//99
	Madison MSA, WI	S	32.33 MW	31.34 AW	67250 AAW	WIBLS	10//99-12//99

AAW	Average annual wage	AOH	Average offered, high	ASH	Average starting, high	H	Hourly	M	Monthly	S	Special: hourly and annual
AE	Average entry wage	AOL	Average offered, low	ASL	Average starting, low	HI	Highest wage paid	MTC	Median total compensation	TQ	Third quartile wage
AEX	Average experienced wage	APH	Average pay, high range	AW	Average wage paid	HR	High end range	MW	Median wage paid	W	Weekly
AO	Average offered	APL	Average pay, low range	FQ	First quartile wage	LR	Low end range	SQ	Second quartile wage	Y	Yearly

Occupation/Type/Industry	Location	Per	Low	Mid	High	Source	Date
Engineering Manager	Milwaukee-Waukesha PMSA, WI	S	36.02 MW	35.73 AW	74920 AAW	WIBLS	10//99-12//99
	Racine PMSA, WI	S	35.39 MW	37.62 AW	73620 AAW	WIBLS	10//99-12//99
	Sheboygan MSA, WI	S	31.47 MW	32.10 AW	65460 AAW	WIBLS	10//99-12//99
	Wausau MSA, WI	S	26.06 MW	24.51 AW	54200 AAW	WIBLS	10//99-12//99
	Wyoming	S	34.18 MW	37.21 AW	77390 AAW	WYBLS	10//99-12//99
	Casper MSA, WY	S	39.63 MW	37.83 AW	82440 AAW	WYBLS	10//99-12//99
	Puerto Rico	S	33.01 MW	32.77 AW	68170 AAW	PRBLS	10//99-12//99
	Caguas PMSA, PR	S	36.68 MW	37.45 AW	76290 AAW	PRBLS	10//99-12//99
	Mayaguez MSA, PR	S	31.81 MW	29.58 AW	66160 AAW	PRBLS	10//99-12//99
	San Juan-Bayamon PMSA, PR	S	33.10 MW	34.20 AW	68840 AAW	PRBLS	10//99-12//99
	Guam	S	25.63 MW	28.07 AW	58390 AAW	GUBLS	10//99-12//99
Mechanical Contracting Firm	United States	Y		56000 AW		CONTR	1998
Engineering Teacher							
Postsecondary	Alabama	Y		69000 AAW		ALBLS	10//99-12//99
Postsecondary	Arizona	Y		50730 AAW		AZBLS	10//99-12//99
Postsecondary	California	Y		60560 AAW		CABLS	10//99-12//99
Postsecondary	San Francisco PMSA, CA	Y		41570 AAW		CABLS	10//99-12//99
Postsecondary	Colorado	Y		69500 AAW		COBLS	10//99-12//99
Postsecondary	Washington PMSA, DC-MD-VA-WV	Y		69960 AAW		DCBLS	10//99-12//99
Postsecondary	Florida	Y		68340 AAW		FLBLS	10//99-12//99
Postsecondary	Fort Lauderdale PMSA, FL	Y		47990 AAW		FLBLS	10//99-12//99
Postsecondary	Melbourne-Titusville-Palm Bay MSA, FL	Y		52880 AAW		FLBLS	10//99-12//99
Postsecondary	Tampa-St. Petersburg-Clearwater MSA, FL	Y		67480 AAW		FLBLS	10//99-12//99
Postsecondary	Georgia	Y		60110 AAW		GABLS	10//99-12//99
Postsecondary	Atlanta MSA, GA	Y		60300 AAW		GABLS	10//99-12//99
Postsecondary	Idaho	Y		63550 AAW		IDBLS	10//99-12//99
Postsecondary	Indiana	Y		62200 AAW		INBLS	10//99-12//99
Postsecondary	Kansas	Y		59790 AAW		KSBLS	10//99-12//99
Postsecondary	Louisiana	Y		63150 AAW		LABLS	10//99-12//99
Postsecondary	Maryland	Y		67810 AAW		MDBLS	10//99-12//99
Postsecondary	Massachusetts	Y		62480 AAW		MABLS	10//99-12//99
Postsecondary	Boston PMSA, MA-NH	Y		63300 AAW		MABLS	10//99-12//99
Postsecondary	Michigan	Y		72750 AAW		MIBLS	10//99-12//99
Postsecondary	Detroit PMSA, MI	Y		68640 AAW		MIBLS	10//99-12//99
Postsecondary	Montana	Y		51940 AAW		MTBLS	10//99-12//99
Postsecondary	New Jersey	Y		73590 AAW		NJBLS	10//99-12//99
Postsecondary	Newark PMSA, NJ	Y		79180 AAW		NJBLS	10//99-12//99
Postsecondary	New York	Y		60200 AAW		NYBLS	10//99-12//99
Postsecondary	Nassau-Suffolk PMSA, NY	Y		68750 AAW		NYBLS	10//99-12//99
Postsecondary	New York PMSA, NY	Y		60280 AAW		NYBLS	10//99-12//99
Postsecondary	North Carolina	Y		56380 AAW		NCBLS	10//99-12//99
Postsecondary	Charlotte-Gastonia-Rock Hill MSA, NC-SC	Y		49260 AAW		NCBLS	10//99-12//99
Postsecondary	Greensboro--Winston-Salem--High Point MSA, NC	Y		55940 AAW		NCBLS	10//99-12//99
Postsecondary	Ohio	Y		49650 AAW		OHBLS	10//99-12//99
Postsecondary	Cleveland-Lorain-Elyria PMSA, OH	Y		52420 AAW		OHBLS	10//99-12//99
Postsecondary	Dayton-Springfield MSA, OH	Y		39900 AAW		OHBLS	10//99-12//99
Postsecondary	Toledo MSA, OH	Y		50500 AAW		OHBLS	10//99-12//99
Postsecondary	Oklahoma	Y		68350 AAW		OKBLS	10//99-12//99
Postsecondary	Oregon	Y		62860 AAW		ORBLS	10//99-12//99
Postsecondary	Portland-Vancouver PMSA, OR-WA	Y		62410 AAW		ORBLS	10//99-12//99
Postsecondary	Pennsylvania	Y		72050 AAW		PABLS	10//99-12//99
Postsecondary	Erie MSA, PA	Y		65380 AAW		PABLS	10//99-12//99
Postsecondary	Harrisburg-Lebanon-Carlisle MSA, PA	Y		60750 AAW		PABLS	10//99-12//99
Postsecondary	Philadelphia PMSA, PA-NJ	Y		69740 AAW		PABLS	10//99-12//99
Postsecondary	Rhode Island	Y		74450 AAW		RIBLS	10//99-12//99
Postsecondary	Providence-Fall River-Warwick MSA, RI-MA	Y		73340 AAW		RIBLS	10//99-12//99
Postsecondary	South Carolina	Y		54800 AAW		SCBLS	10//99-12//99
Postsecondary	Tennessee	Y		61240 AAW		TNBLS	10//99-12//99
Postsecondary	Memphis MSA, TN-AR-MS	Y		55170 AAW		MSBLS	10//99-12//99
Postsecondary	Texas	Y		61440 AAW		TXBLS	10//99-12//99
Postsecondary	Dallas PMSA, TX	Y		61500 AAW		TXBLS	10//99-12//99
Postsecondary	Houston PMSA, TX	Y		68060 AAW		TXBLS	10//99-12//99

AAW	Average annual wage	**AOH**	Average offered, high	**ASH**	Average starting, high	**H**	Hourly	**M**	Monthly	**S**	Special: hourly and annual
AE	Average entry wage	**AOL**	Average offered, low	**ASL**	Average starting, low	**HI**	Highest wage paid	**MTC**	Median total compensation	**TQ**	Third quartile wage
AEX	Average experienced wage	**APH**	Average pay, high range	**AW**	Average wage paid	**HR**	High end range	**MW**	Median wage paid	**W**	Weekly
AO	Average offered	**APL**	Average pay, low range	**FQ**	First quartile wage	**LR**	Low end range	**SQ**	Second quartile wage	**Y**	Yearly

Occupation/Type/Industry	Location	Per	Low	Mid	High	Source	Date
Engineering Teacher							
Postsecondary	San Antonio MSA, TX	Y		59240 AAW		TXBLS	10//99-12//99
Postsecondary	Virginia	Y		66960 AAW		VABLS	10//99-12//99
Postsecondary	Washington	Y		69860 AAW		WABLS	10//99-12//99
Postsecondary	Puerto Rico	Y		40240 AAW		PRBLS	10//99-12//99
Postsecondary	San Juan-Bayamon PMSA, PR	Y		39720 AAW		PRBLS	10//99-12//99
English Language and Literature Teacher							
Postsecondary	Alabama	Y		35580 AAW		ALBLS	10//99-12//99
Postsecondary	Mobile MSA, AL	Y		32850 AAW		ALBLS	10//99-12//99
Postsecondary	Montgomery MSA, AL	Y		34160 AAW		ALBLS	10//99-12//99
Postsecondary	Arizona	Y		33680 AAW		AZBLS	10//99-12//99
Postsecondary	Phoenix-Mesa MSA, AZ	Y		33290 AAW		AZBLS	10//99-12//99
Postsecondary	Arkansas	Y		41060 AAW		ARBLS	10//99-12//99
Postsecondary	California	Y		54160 AAW		CABLS	10//99-12//99
Postsecondary	Fresno MSA, CA	Y		46340 AAW		CABLS	10//99-12//99
Postsecondary	Los Angeles-Long Beach PMSA, CA	Y		48510 AAW		CABLS	10//99-12//99
Postsecondary	Orange County PMSA, CA	Y		54270 AAW		CABLS	10//99-12//99
Postsecondary	Riverside-San Bernardino PMSA, CA	Y		53020 AAW		CABLS	10//99-12//99
Postsecondary	Sacramento PMSA, CA	Y		44310 AAW		CABLS	10//99-12//99
Postsecondary	San Diego MSA, CA	Y		54240 AAW		CABLS	10//99-12//99
Postsecondary	San Francisco PMSA, CA	Y		66150 AAW		CABLS	10//99-12//99
Postsecondary	Colorado	Y		43310 AAW		COBLS	10//99-12//99
Postsecondary	Colorado Springs MSA, CO	Y		47290 AAW		COBLS	10//99-12//99
Postsecondary	Denver PMSA, CO	Y		42570 AAW		COBLS	10//99-12//99
Postsecondary	Connecticut	Y		50560 AAW		CTBLS	10//99-12//99
Postsecondary	Hartford MSA, CT	Y		59970 AAW		CTBLS	10//99-12//99
Postsecondary	New Haven-Meriden PMSA, CT	Y		45340 AAW		CTBLS	10//99-12//99
Postsecondary	District of Columbia	Y		45270 AAW		DCBLS	10//99-12//99
Postsecondary	Washington PMSA, DC-MD-VA-WV	Y		45270 AAW		DCBLS	10//99-12//99
Postsecondary	Florida	Y		51270 AAW		FLBLS	10//99-12//99
Postsecondary	Melbourne-Titusville-Palm Bay MSA, FL	Y		35720 AAW		FLBLS	10//99-12//99
Postsecondary	Miami PMSA, FL	Y		57710 AAW		FLBLS	10//99-12//99
Postsecondary	Orlando MSA, FL	Y		41540 AAW		FLBLS	10//99-12//99
Postsecondary	Tampa-St. Petersburg-Clearwater MSA, FL	Y		60260 AAW		FLBLS	10//99-12//99
Postsecondary	West Palm Beach-Boca Raton MSA, FL	Y		52030 AAW		FLBLS	10//99-12//99
Postsecondary	Georgia	Y		40880 AAW		GABLS	10//99-12//99
Postsecondary	Atlanta MSA, GA	Y		41680 AAW		GABLS	10//99-12//99
Postsecondary	Savannah MSA, GA	Y		45310 AAW		GABLS	10//99-12//99
Postsecondary	Idaho	Y		47300 AAW		IDBLS	10//99-12//99
Postsecondary	Illinois	Y		41650 AAW		ILBLS	10//99-12//99
Postsecondary	Chicago PMSA, IL	Y		41850 AAW		ILBLS	10//99-12//99
Postsecondary	Indiana	Y		38680 AAW		INBLS	10//99-12//99
Postsecondary	Fort Wayne MSA, IN	Y		41150 AAW		INBLS	10//99-12//99
Postsecondary	Gary PMSA, IN	Y		38270 AAW		INBLS	10//99-12//99
Postsecondary	Indianapolis MSA, IN	Y		35710 AAW		INBLS	10//99-12//99
Postsecondary	South Bend MSA, IN	Y		35810 AAW		INBLS	10//99-12//99
Postsecondary	Iowa	Y		43330 AAW		IABLS	10//99-12//99
Postsecondary	Des Moines MSA, IA	Y		47520 AAW		IABLS	10//99-12//99
Postsecondary	Kansas	Y		32040 AAW		KSBLS	10//99-12//99
Postsecondary	Kentucky	Y		40130 AAW		KYBLS	10//99-12//99
Postsecondary	Louisiana	Y		38760 AAW		LABLS	10//99-12//99
Postsecondary	Maine	Y		43560 AAW		MEBLS	10//99-12//99
Postsecondary	Portland MSA, ME	Y		45830 AAW		MEBLS	10//99-12//99
Postsecondary	Maryland	Y		45900 AAW		MDBLS	10//99-12//99
Postsecondary	Baltimore PMSA, MD	Y		46570 AAW		MDBLS	10//99-12//99
Postsecondary	Massachusetts	Y		46510 AAW		MABLS	10//99-12//99
Postsecondary	Boston PMSA, MA-NH	Y		43260 AAW		MABLS	10//99-12//99
Postsecondary	Brockton PMSA, MA	Y		42330 AAW		MABLS	10//99-12//99
Postsecondary	Springfield MSA, MA	Y		59000 AAW		MABLS	10//99-12//99
Postsecondary	Worcester PMSA, MA-CT	Y		52710 AAW		MABLS	10//99-12//99
Postsecondary	Michigan	Y		49780 AAW		MIBLS	10//99-12//99
Postsecondary	Ann Arbor PMSA, MI	Y		54640 AAW		MIBLS	10//99-12//99
Postsecondary	Detroit PMSA, MI	Y		52380 AAW		MIBLS	10//99-12//99

AAW Average annual wage	**AOH** Average offered, high	**ASH** Average starting, high	**H** Hourly	**M** Monthly	**S** Special: hourly and annual
AE Average entry wage	**AOL** Average offered, low	**ASL** Average starting, low	**HI** Highest wage paid	**MTC** Median total compensation	**TQ** Third quartile wage
AEX Average experienced wage	**APH** Average pay, high range	**AW** Average wage paid	**HR** High end range	**MW** Median wage paid	**W** Weekly
AO Average offered	**APL** Average pay, low range	**FQ** First quartile wage	**LR** Low end range	**SQ** Second quartile wage	**Y** Yearly

Occupation/Type/Industry	Location	Per	Low	Mid	High	Source	Date
English Language and Literature Teacher							
Postsecondary	Kalamazoo-Battle Creek MSA, MI	Y		52800 AAW		MIBLS	10//99-12//99
Postsecondary	Minnesota	Y		49450 AAW		MNBLS	10//99-12//99
Postsecondary	Duluth-Superior MSA, MN-WI	Y		44210 AAW		MNBLS	10//99-12//99
Postsecondary	Minneapolis-St. Paul MSA, MN-WI	Y		48820 AAW		MNBLS	10//99-12//99
Postsecondary	St. Cloud MSA, MN	Y		53800 AAW		MNBLS	10//99-12//99
Postsecondary	Mississippi	Y		39780 AAW		MSBLS	10//99-12//99
Postsecondary	Jackson MSA, MS	Y		32720 AAW		MSBLS	10//99-12//99
Postsecondary	Missouri	Y		37670 AAW		MOBLS	10//99-12//99
Postsecondary	Montana	Y		41560 AAW		MTBLS	10//99-12//99
Postsecondary	Omaha MSA, NE-IA	Y		40000 AAW		NEBLS	10//99-12//99
Postsecondary	Nevada	Y		39890 AAW		NVBLS	10//99-12//99
Postsecondary	Las Vegas MSA, NV-AZ	Y		43970 AAW		NVBLS	10//99-12//99
Postsecondary	New Hampshire	Y		50910 AAW		NHBLS	10//99-12//99
Postsecondary	Manchester PMSA, NH	Y		40490 AAW		NHBLS	10//99-12//99
Postsecondary	Nashua PMSA, NH	Y		49010 AAW		NHBLS	10//99-12//99
Postsecondary	New Jersey	Y		53500 AAW		NJBLS	10//99-12//99
Postsecondary	Bergen-Passaic PMSA, NJ	Y		54870 AAW		NJBLS	10//99-12//99
Postsecondary	Jersey City PMSA, NJ	Y		57220 AAW		NJBLS	10//99-12//99
Postsecondary	Monmouth-Ocean PMSA, NJ	Y		49280 AAW		NJBLS	10//99-12//99
Postsecondary	Newark PMSA, NJ	Y		54700 AAW		NJBLS	10//99-12//99
Postsecondary	New Mexico	Y		44660 AAW		NMBLS	10//99-12//99
Postsecondary	New York	Y		50660 AAW		NYBLS	10//99-12//99
Postsecondary	Albany-Schenectady-Troy MSA, NY	Y		45260 AAW		NYBLS	10//99-12//99
Postsecondary	Buffalo-Niagara Falls MSA, NY	Y		52620 AAW		NYBLS	10//99-12//99
Postsecondary	Nassau-Suffolk PMSA, NY	Y		61370 AAW		NYBLS	10//99-12//99
Postsecondary	New York PMSA, NY	Y		52150 AAW		NYBLS	10//99-12//99
Postsecondary	Utica-Rome MSA, NY	Y		49460 AAW		NYBLS	10//99-12//99
Postsecondary	North Carolina	Y		42410 AAW		NCBLS	10//99-12//99
Postsecondary	Asheville MSA, NC	Y		41480 AAW		NCBLS	10//99-12//99
Postsecondary	Charlotte-Gastonia-Rock Hill MSA, NC-SC	Y		38710 AAW		NCBLS	10//99-12//99
Postsecondary	Fayetteville MSA, NC	Y		36590 AAW		NCBLS	10//99-12//99
Postsecondary	Greensboro--Winston-Salem--High Point MSA, NC	Y		42570 AAW		NCBLS	10//99-12//99
Postsecondary	Hickory-Morganton-Lenoir MSA, NC	Y		36810 AAW		NCBLS	10//99-12//99
Postsecondary	Raleigh-Durham-Chapel Hill MSA, NC	Y		46420 AAW		NCBLS	10//99-12//99
Postsecondary	Rocky Mount MSA, NC	Y		37870 AAW		NCBLS	10//99-12//99
Postsecondary	Wilmington MSA, NC	Y		48170 AAW		NCBLS	10//99-12//99
Postsecondary	North Dakota	Y		42080 AAW		NDBLS	10//99-12//99
Postsecondary	Ohio	Y		39870 AAW		OHBLS	10//99-12//99
Postsecondary	Canton-Massillon MSA, OH	Y		37160 AAW		OHBLS	10//99-12//99
Postsecondary	Cincinnati PMSA, OH-KY-IN	Y		36280 AAW		OHBLS	10//99-12//99
Postsecondary	Cleveland-Lorain-Elyria PMSA, OH	Y		41120 AAW		OHBLS	10//99-12//99
Postsecondary	Columbus MSA, OH	Y		40480 AAW		OHBLS	10//99-12//99
Postsecondary	Dayton-Springfield MSA, OH	Y		31200 AAW		OHBLS	10//99-12//99
Postsecondary	Oklahoma	Y		39750 AAW		OKBLS	10//99-12//99
Postsecondary	Oklahoma City MSA, OK	Y		41890 AAW		OKBLS	10//99-12//99
Postsecondary	Oregon	Y		46740 AAW		ORBLS	10//99-12//99
Postsecondary	Portland-Vancouver PMSA, OR-WA	Y		45600 AAW		ORBLS	10//99-12//99
Postsecondary	Pennsylvania	Y		54500 AAW		PABLS	10//99-12//99
Postsecondary	Allentown-Bethlehem-Easton MSA, PA	Y		47400 AAW		PABLS	10//99-12//99
Postsecondary	Philadelphia PMSA, PA-NJ	Y		56700 AAW		PABLS	10//99-12//99
Postsecondary	Pittsburgh MSA, PA	Y		54380 AAW		PABLS	10//99-12//99
Postsecondary	Reading MSA, PA	Y		47880 AAW		PABLS	10//99-12//99
Postsecondary	Scranton--Wilkes-Barre--Hazleton MSA, PA	Y		44580 AAW		PABLS	10//99-12//99
Postsecondary	Rhode Island	Y		65880 AAW		RIBLS	10//99-12//99
Postsecondary	Providence-Fall River-Warwick MSA, RI-MA	Y		65520 AAW		RIBLS	10//99-12//99
Postsecondary	South Carolina	Y		42260 AAW		SCBLS	10//99-12//99

AAW Average annual wage	**AOH** Average offered, high	**ASH** Average starting, high	**H** Hourly	**M** Monthly	**S** Special: hourly and annual
AE Average entry wage	**AOL** Average offered, low	**ASL** Average starting, low	**HI** Highest wage paid	**MTC** Median total compensation	**TQ** Third quartile wage
AEX Average experienced wage	**APH** Average pay, high range	**AW** Average wage paid	**HR** High end range	**MW** Median wage paid	**W** Weekly
AO Average offered	**APL** Average pay, low range	**FQ** First quartile wage	**LR** Low end range	**SQ** Second quartile wage	**Y** Yearly

Occupation/Type/Industry	Location	Per	Low	Mid	High	Source	Date
English Language and Literature Teacher							
Postsecondary	Greenville-Spartanburg-Anderson MSA, SC	Y		40830 AAW		SCBLS	10//99-12//99
Postsecondary	Sumter MSA, SC	Y		36010 AAW		SCBLS	10//99-12//99
Postsecondary	South Dakota	Y		37700 AAW		SDBLS	10//99-12//99
Postsecondary	Rapid City MSA, SD	Y		42960 AAW		SDBLS	10//99-12//99
Postsecondary	Tennessee	Y		39860 AAW		TNBLS	10//99-12//99
Postsecondary	Johnson City-Kingsport-Bristol MSA, TN-VA	Y		38060 AAW		TNBLS	10//99-12//99
Postsecondary	Memphis MSA, TN-AR-MS	Y		42040 AAW		MSBLS	10//99-12//99
Postsecondary	Nashville MSA, TN	Y		44950 AAW		TNBLS	10//99-12//99
Postsecondary	Texas	Y		41710 AAW		TXBLS	10//99-12//99
Postsecondary	Dallas PMSA, TX	Y		47720 AAW		TXBLS	10//99-12//99
Postsecondary	El Paso MSA, TX	Y		37080 AAW		TXBLS	10//99-12//99
Postsecondary	Fort Worth-Arlington PMSA, TX	Y		36370 AAW		TXBLS	10//99-12//99
Postsecondary	Houston PMSA, TX	Y		45580 AAW		TXBLS	10//99-12//99
Postsecondary	Killeen-Temple MSA, TX	Y		32540 AAW		TXBLS	10//99-12//99
Postsecondary	Longview-Marshall MSA, TX	Y		35900 AAW		TXBLS	10//99-12//99
Postsecondary	Odessa-Midland MSA, TX	Y		41000 AAW		TXBLS	10//99-12//99
Postsecondary	San Antonio MSA, TX	Y		50400 AAW		TXBLS	10//99-12//99
Postsecondary	Vermont	Y		48900 AAW		VTBLS	10//99-12//99
Postsecondary	Burlington MSA, VT	Y		47670 AAW		VTBLS	10//99-12//99
Postsecondary	Virginia	Y		45940 AAW		VABLS	10//99-12//99
Postsecondary	Norfolk-Virginia Beach-Newport News MSA, VA-NC	Y		43690 AAW		VABLS	10//99-12//99
Postsecondary	Richmond-Petersburg MSA, VA	Y		45780 AAW		VABLS	10//99-12//99
Postsecondary	Washington	Y		39220 AAW		WABLS	10//99-12//99
Postsecondary	Seattle-Bellevue-Everett PMSA, WA	Y		42720 AAW		WABLS	10//99-12//99
Postsecondary	Spokane MSA, WA	Y		36050 AAW		WABLS	10//99-12//99
Postsecondary	Tacoma PMSA, WA	Y		39660 AAW		WABLS	10//99-12//99
Postsecondary	West Virginia	Y		51380 AAW		WVBLS	10//99-12//99
Postsecondary	Wisconsin	Y		40540 AAW		WIBLS	10//99-12//99
Postsecondary	Milwaukee-Waukesha PMSA, WI	Y		31910 AAW		WIBLS	10//99-12//99
Postsecondary	Wyoming	Y		40920 AAW		WYBLS	10//99-12//99
Postsecondary	Puerto Rico	Y		33510 AAW		PRBLS	10//99-12//99
Postsecondary	San Juan-Bayamon PMSA, PR	Y		37690 AAW		PRBLS	10//99-12//99
Enologist							
Winery/Vineyard, Over 150K Cases/Year	United States	Y	38950 MW	43513 AW		PWV	1999
Environmental Engineer	Alabama	S	24.81 MW	24.94 AW	51870 AAW	ALBLS	10//99-12//99
	Birmingham MSA, AL	S	26.51 MW	25.82 AW	55140 AAW	ALBLS	10//99-12//99
	Decatur MSA, AL	S	28.01 MW	28.85 AW	58250 AAW	ALBLS	10//99-12//99
	Huntsville MSA, AL	S	21.82 MW	19.96 AW	45380 AAW	ALBLS	10//99-12//99
	Mobile MSA, AL	S	25.53 MW	25.46 AW	53100 AAW	ALBLS	10//99-12//99
	Alaska	S	31.42 MW	34.29 AW	71320 AAW	AKBLS	10//99-12//99
	Anchorage MSA, AK	S	33.96 MW	30.90 AW	70630 AAW	AKBLS	10//99-12//99
	Arizona	S	25.88 MW	28.55 AW	59390 AAW	AZBLS	10//99-12//99
	Phoenix-Mesa MSA, AZ	S	28.89 MW	25.99 AW	60090 AAW	AZBLS	10//99-12//99
	Arkansas	S	24.21 MW	26.53 AW	55190 AAW	ARBLS	10//99-12//99
	Fayetteville-Springdale-Rogers MSA, AR	S	31.70 MW	29.90 AW	65930 AAW	ARBLS	10//99-12//99
	Little Rock-North Little Rock MSA, AR	S	27.53 MW	23.89 AW	57260 AAW	ARBLS	10//99-12//99
	California	S	28.63 MW	29.91 AW	62210 AAW	CABLS	10//99-12//99
	Bakersfield MSA, CA	S	30.30 MW	31.06 AW	63030 AAW	CABLS	10//99-12//99
	Fresno MSA, CA	S	24.27 MW	21.47 AW	50480 AAW	CABLS	10//99-12//99
	Los Angeles-Long Beach PMSA, CA	S	30.12 MW	29.42 AW	62650 AAW	CABLS	10//99-12//99
	Oakland PMSA, CA	S	24.42 MW	21.45 AW	50800 AAW	CABLS	10//99-12//99
	Orange County PMSA, CA	S	29.72 MW	28.80 AW	61810 AAW	CABLS	10//99-12//99
	Riverside-San Bernardino PMSA, CA	S	25.15 MW	25.15 AW	52300 AAW	CABLS	10//99-12//99
	San Diego MSA, CA	S	28.76 MW	29.01 AW	59820 AAW	CABLS	10//99-12//99
	San Francisco PMSA, CA	S	28.20 MW	28.11 AW	58660 AAW	CABLS	10//99-12//99

AAW Average annual wage	**AOH** Average offered, high	**ASH** Average starting, high	**H** Hourly	**M** Monthly	**S** Special: hourly and annual
AE Average entry wage	**AOL** Average offered, low	**ASL** Average starting, low	**HI** Highest wage paid	**MTC** Median total compensation	**TQ** Third quartile wage
AEX Average experienced wage	**APH** Average pay, high range	**AW** Average wage paid	**HR** High end range	**MW** Median wage paid	**W** Weekly
AO Average offered	**APL** Average pay, low range	**FQ** First quartile wage	**LR** Low end range	**SQ** Second quartile wage	**Y** Yearly

Environmental Engineer

Occupation/Type/Industry	Location	Per	Low	Mid	High	Source	Date
Environmental Engineer	Santa Barbara-Santa Maria-Lompoc MSA, CA	S	29.71 MW	30.47 AW	61800 AAW	CABLS	10//99-12//99
	Santa Rosa PMSA, CA	S	24.16 MW	23.59 AW	50240 AAW	CABLS	10//99-12//99
	Vallejo-Fairfield-Napa PMSA, CA	S	29.15 MW	28.79 AW	60640 AAW	CABLS	10//99-12//99
	Colorado	S	29.15 MW	28.94 AW	60190 AAW	COBLS	10//99-12//99
	Denver PMSA, CO	S	30.43 MW	30.63 AW	63290 AAW	COBLS	10//99-12//99
	Connecticut	S	28.43 MW	28.48 AW	59240 AAW	CTBLS	10//99-12//99
	New Haven-Meriden PMSA, CT	S	23.62 MW	22.66 AW	49130 AAW	CTBLS	10//99-12//99
	Stamford-Norwalk PMSA, CT	S	27.50 MW	23.04 AW	57200 AAW	CTBLS	10//99-12//99
	Delaware	S	20.19 MW	22.47 AW	46740 AAW	DEBLS	10//99-12//99
	Wilmington-Newark PMSA, DE-MD	S	22.12 MW	19.92 AW	46000 AAW	DEBLS	10//99-12//99
	Washington PMSA, DC-MD-VA-WV	S	27.80 MW	27.42 AW	57820 AAW	DCBLS	10//99-12//99
	Florida	S	23.05 MW	27.16 AW	56500 AAW	FLBLS	10//99-12//99
	Fort Lauderdale PMSA, FL	S	24.11 MW	24.14 AW	50160 AAW	FLBLS	10//99-12//99
	Fort Myers-Cape Coral MSA, FL	S	25.54 MW	21.86 AW	53120 AAW	FLBLS	10//99-12//99
	Gainesville MSA, FL	S	24.83 MW	24.01 AW	51640 AAW	FLBLS	10//99-12//99
	Jacksonville MSA, FL	S	23.83 MW	23.76 AW	49580 AAW	FLBLS	10//99-12//99
	Lakeland-Winter Haven MSA, FL	S	25.35 MW	26.29 AW	52730 AAW	FLBLS	10//99-12//99
	Melbourne-Titusville-Palm Bay MSA, FL	S	35.24 MW	26.93 AW	73290 AAW	FLBLS	10//99-12//99
	Miami PMSA, FL	S	28.71 MW	29.43 AW	59720 AAW	FLBLS	10//99-12//99
	Orlando MSA, FL	S	20.87 MW	21.32 AW	43410 AAW	FLBLS	10//99-12//99
	Pensacola MSA, FL	S	20.64 MW	19.64 AW	42940 AAW	FLBLS	10//99-12//99
	Tampa-St. Petersburg-Clearwater MSA, FL	S	32.58 MW	24.61 AW	67760 AAW	FLBLS	10//99-12//99
	West Palm Beach-Boca Raton MSA, FL	S	26.70 MW	19.49 AW	55540 AAW	FLBLS	10//99-12//99
	Georgia	S	24.84 MW	25.44 AW	52920 AAW	GABLS	10//99-12//99
	Atlanta MSA, GA	S	25.14 MW	24.60 AW	52300 AAW	GABLS	10//99-12//99
	Augusta-Aiken MSA, GA-SC	S	31.04 MW	31.68 AW	64560 AAW	GABLS	10//99-12//99
	Macon MSA, GA	S	28.58 MW	28.59 AW	59440 AAW	GABLS	10//99-12//99
	Savannah MSA, GA	S	28.93 MW	30.24 AW	60180 AAW	GABLS	10//99-12//99
	Idaho	S	27.48 MW	28.00 AW	58240 AAW	IDBLS	10//99-12//99
	Illinois	S	28.3 MW	28.25 AW	58760 AAW	ILBLS	10//99-12//99
	Chicago PMSA, IL	S	30.28 MW	30.26 AW	62980 AAW	ILBLS	10//99-12//99
	Indiana	S	22.23 MW	23.18 AW	48220 AAW	INBLS	10//99-12//99
	Bloomington MSA, IN	S	23.17 MW	20.04 AW	48190 AAW	INBLS	10//99-12//99
	Indianapolis MSA, IN	S	24.18 MW	23.18 AW	50280 AAW	INBLS	10//99-12//99
	Iowa	S	20.01 MW	20.68 AW	43020 AAW	IABLS	10//99-12//99
	Kansas	S	25.84 MW	25.88 AW	53830 AAW	KSBLS	10//99-12//99
	Kentucky	S	26.72 MW	26.68 AW	55490 AAW	KYBLS	10//99-12//99
	Lexington MSA, KY	S	27.08 MW	26.99 AW	56320 AAW	KYBLS	10//99-12//99
	Louisville MSA, KY-IN	S	25.09 MW	24.16 AW	52190 AAW	KYBLS	10//99-12//99
	Louisiana	S	25.89 MW	27.71 AW	57640 AAW	LABLS	10//99-12//99
	Baton Rouge MSA, LA	S	25.58 MW	24.61 AW	53210 AAW	LABLS	10//99-12//99
	New Orleans MSA, LA	S	33.69 MW	32.43 AW	70070 AAW	LABLS	10//99-12//99
	Maine	S	23.98 MW	23.94 AW	49800 AAW	MEBLS	10//99-12//99
	Maryland	S	31.03 MW	30.97 AW	64420 AAW	MDBLS	10//99-12//99
	Massachusetts	S	27.3 MW	26.77 AW	55690 AAW	MABLS	10//99-12//99
	Boston PMSA, MA-NH	S	26.91 MW	27.41 AW	55980 AAW	MABLS	10//99-12//99
	Lawrence PMSA, MA-NH	S	27.17 MW	26.90 AW	56510 AAW	MABLS	10//99-12//99
	Lowell PMSA, MA-NH	S	29.84 MW	30.15 AW	62070 AAW	MABLS	10//99-12//99
	New Bedford PMSA, MA	S	26.33 MW	25.32 AW	54770 AAW	MABLS	10//99-12//99
	Michigan	S	22.98 MW	24.87 AW	51730 AAW	MIBLS	10//99-12//99
	Ann Arbor PMSA, MI	S	22.61 MW	20.18 AW	47030 AAW	MIBLS	10//99-12//99
	Detroit PMSA, MI	S	24.41 MW	20.72 AW	50770 AAW	MIBLS	10//99-12//99
	Grand Rapids-Muskegon-Holland MSA, MI	S	24.36 MW	24.67 AW	50670 AAW	MIBLS	10//99-12//99
	Saginaw-Bay City-Midland MSA, MI	S	26.80 MW	25.58 AW	55740 AAW	MIBLS	10//99-12//99
	Minnesota	S	26.04 MW	26.45 AW	55010 AAW	MNBLS	10//99-12//99
	Duluth-Superior MSA, MN-WI	S	25.08 MW	23.47 AW	52160 AAW	MNBLS	10//99-12//99
	Minneapolis-St. Paul MSA, MN-WI	S	26.73 MW	25.68 AW	55600 AAW	MNBLS	10//99-12//99
	Mississippi	S	24.63 MW	24.31 AW	50560 AAW	MSBLS	10//99-12//99

AAW Average annual wage	**AOH** Average offered, high	**ASH** Average starting, high	**H** Hourly	**M** Monthly	**S** Special: hourly and annual
AE Average entry wage	**AOL** Average offered, low	**ASL** Average starting, low	**HI** Highest wage paid	**MTC** Median total compensation	**TQ** Third quartile wage
AEX Average experienced wage	**APH** Average pay, high range	**AW** Average wage paid	**HR** High end range	**MW** Median wage paid	**W** Weekly
AO Average offered	**APL** Average pay, low range	**FQ** First quartile wage	**LR** Low end range	**SQ** Second quartile wage	**Y** Yearly

Occupation/Type/Industry	Location	Per	Low	Mid	High	Source	Date
Environmental Engineer	Biloxi-Gulfport-Pascagoula						
	MSA, MS	S	20.27 MW	21.82 AW	42160 AAW	MSBLS	10//99-12//99
	Missouri	S	21.4 MW	24.02 AW	49960 AAW	MOBLS	10//99-12//99
	Kansas City MSA, MO-KS	S	26.39 MW	26.79 AW	54890 AAW	MOBLS	10//99-12//99
	Springfield MSA, MO	S	21.23 MW	22.04 AW	44160 AAW	MOBLS	10//99-12//99
	Montana	S	22.38 MW	23.43 AW	48730 AAW	MTBLS	10//99-12//99
	Billings MSA, MT	S	24.55 MW	22.70 AW	51070 AAW	MTBLS	10//99-12//99
	Nebraska	S	25.79 MW	25.91 AW	53890 AAW	NEBLS	10//99-12//99
	Omaha MSA, NE-IA	S	26.60 MW	27.03 AW	55330 AAW	NEBLS	10//99-12//99
	Nevada	S	26.59 MW	28.42 AW	59110 AAW	NVBLS	10//99-12//99
	Las Vegas MSA, NV-AZ	S	25.77 MW	25.84 AW	53600 AAW	NVBLS	10//99-12//99
	Reno MSA, NV	S	32.82 MW	36.95 AW	68270 AAW	NVBLS	10//99-12//99
	New Hampshire	S	20.73 MW	24.11 AW	50140 AAW	NHBLS	10//99-12//99
	Portsmouth-Rochester PMSA,						
	NH-ME	S	21.07 MW	18.96 AW	43820 AAW	NHBLS	10//99-12//99
	New Jersey	S	24.63 MW	26.20 AW	54500 AAW	NJBLS	10//99-12//99
	Bergen-Passaic PMSA, NJ	S	24.79 MW	23.83 AW	51570 AAW	NJBLS	10//99-12//99
	Jersey City PMSA, NJ	S	24.67 MW	24.31 AW	51310 AAW	NJBLS	10//99-12//99
	Middlesex-Somerset-						
	Hunterdon PMSA, NJ	S	24.86 MW	23.39 AW	51710 AAW	NJBLS	10//99-12//99
	Monmouth-Ocean PMSA, NJ	S	26.52 MW	28.01 AW	55160 AAW	NJBLS	10//99-12//99
	Newark PMSA, NJ	S	27.80 MW	26.05 AW	57820 AAW	NJBLS	10//99-12//99
	New Mexico	S	21.99 MW	23.74 AW	49370 AAW	NMBLS	10//99-12//99
	Albuquerque MSA, NM	S	29.05 MW	26.23 AW	60420 AAW	NMBLS	10//99-12//99
	New York	S	29.28 MW	29.88 AW	62160 AAW	NYBLS	10//99-12//99
	Binghamton MSA, NY	S	31.64 MW	30.96 AW	65810 AAW	NYBLS	10//99-12//99
	Buffalo-Niagara Falls MSA,						
	NY	S	26.67 MW	24.85 AW	55470 AAW	NYBLS	10//99-12//99
	Nassau-Suffolk PMSA, NY	S	29.98 MW	28.46 AW	62350 AAW	NYBLS	10//99-12//99
	New York PMSA, NY	S	28.39 MW	28.10 AW	59060 AAW	NYBLS	10//99-12//99
	Newburgh PMSA, NY-PA	S	27.12 MW	26.81 AW	56420 AAW	NYBLS	10//99-12//99
	Rochester MSA, NY	S	31.73 MW	31.01 AW	65990 AAW	NYBLS	10//99-12//99
	Syracuse MSA, NY	S	22.96 MW	21.80 AW	47750 AAW	NYBLS	10//99-12//99
	North Carolina	S	24.3 MW	25.78 AW	53610 AAW	NCBLS	10//99-12//99
	Asheville MSA, NC	S	22.20 MW	20.41 AW	46170 AAW	NCBLS	10//99-12//99
	Charlotte-Gastonia-Rock Hill						
	MSA, NC-SC	S	24.88 MW	22.88 AW	51760 AAW	NCBLS	10//99-12//99
	Raleigh-Durham-Chapel Hill						
	MSA, NC	S	27.18 MW	25.94 AW	56530 AAW	NCBLS	10//99-12//99
	Wilmington MSA, NC	S	24.47 MW	22.78 AW	50900 AAW	NCBLS	10//99-12//99
	North Dakota	S	18.16 MW	19.25 AW	40050 AAW	NDBLS	10//99-12//99
	Ohio	S	24.19 MW	24.60 AW	51160 AAW	OHBLS	10//99-12//99
	Akron PMSA, OH	S	26.25 MW	25.51 AW	54610 AAW	OHBLS	10//99-12//99
	Canton-Massillon MSA, OH	S	20.20 MW	18.55 AW	42010 AAW	OHBLS	10//99-12//99
	Cincinnati PMSA, OH-KY-IN	S	26.46 MW	26.90 AW	55050 AAW	OHBLS	10//99-12//99
	Cleveland-Lorain-Elyria						
	PMSA, OH	S	26.57 MW	24.79 AW	55280 AAW	OHBLS	10//99-12//99
	Columbus MSA, OH	S	24.12 MW	23.83 AW	50170 AAW	OHBLS	10//99-12//99
	Dayton-Springfield MSA, OH	S	23.89 MW	24.31 AW	49680 AAW	OHBLS	10//99-12//99
	Youngstown-Warren MSA, OH	S	26.43 MW	27.90 AW	54970 AAW	OHBLS	10//99-12//99
	Oklahoma	S	24.8 MW	23.39 AW	48640 AAW	OKBLS	10//99-12//99
	Oklahoma City MSA, OK	S	25.13 MW	26.71 AW	52270 AAW	OKBLS	10//99-12//99
	Tulsa MSA, OK	S	22.71 MW	24.54 AW	47240 AAW	OKBLS	10//99-12//99
	Oregon	S	27.38 MW	28.31 AW	58890 AAW	ORBLS	10//99-12//99
	Portland-Vancouver PMSA,						
	OR-WA	S	28.48 MW	27.19 AW	59240 AAW	ORBLS	10//99-12//99
	Pennsylvania	S	28.24 MW	28.53 AW	59340 AAW	PABLS	10//99-12//99
	Allentown-Bethlehem-Easton						
	MSA, PA	S	34.72 MW	31.69 AW	72230 AAW	PABLS	10//99-12//99
	Harrisburg-Lebanon-Carlisle						
	MSA, PA	S	27.11 MW	26.62 AW	56380 AAW	PABLS	10//99-12//99
	Lancaster MSA, PA	S	22.19 MW	22.86 AW	46150 AAW	PABLS	10//99-12//99
	Philadelphia PMSA, PA-NJ	S	27.73 MW	26.47 AW	57680 AAW	PABLS	10//99-12//99
	Pittsburgh MSA, PA	S	29.89 MW	29.74 AW	62160 AAW	PABLS	10//99-12//99
	Reading MSA, PA	S	26.96 MW	25.34 AW	56080 AAW	PABLS	10//99-12//99
	Rhode Island	S	27.33 MW	28.40 AW	59080 AAW	RIBLS	10//99-12//99
	Providence-Fall River-						
	Warwick MSA, RI-MA	S	28.24 MW	27.19 AW	58740 AAW	RIBLS	10//99-12//99
	South Carolina	S	28.31 MW	26.98 AW	56110 AAW	SCBLS	10//99-12//99
	Charleston-North Charleston						
	MSA, SC	S	24.06 MW	26.82 AW	50040 AAW	SCBLS	10//99-12//99
	Columbia MSA, SC	S	26.91 MW	25.90 AW	55970 AAW	SCBLS	10//99-12//99

517

Occupation/Type/Industry	Location	Per	Low	Mid	High	Source	Date
Environmental Engineer	Greenville-Spartanburg-Anderson MSA, SC	S	25.00 MW	23.72 AW	52010 AAW	SCBLS	10//99-12//99
	South Dakota	S	23.04 MW	24.67 AW	51310 AAW	SDBLS	10//99-12//99
	Tennessee	S	22.67 MW	23.48 AW	48830 AAW	TNBLS	10//99-12//99
	Chattanooga MSA, TN-GA	S	24.21 MW	22.37 AW	50360 AAW	TNBLS	10//99-12//99
	Johnson City-Kingsport-Bristol MSA, TN-VA	S	22.53 MW	23.27 AW	46860 AAW	TNBLS	10//99-12//99
	Knoxville MSA, TN	S	27.05 MW	26.44 AW	56270 AAW	TNBLS	10//99-12//99
	Memphis MSA, TN-AR-MS	S	25.29 MW	24.85 AW	52600 AAW	MSBLS	10//99-12//99
	Nashville MSA, TN	S	21.10 MW	20.37 AW	43890 AAW	TNBLS	10//99-12//99
	Texas	S	27.99 MW	28.38 AW	59030 AAW	TXBLS	10//99-12//99
	Austin-San Marcos MSA, TX	S	25.28 MW	25.26 AW	52590 AAW	TXBLS	10//99-12//99
	Beaumont-Port Arthur MSA, TX	S	28.68 MW	29.05 AW	59650 AAW	TXBLS	10//99-12//99
	Corpus Christi MSA, TX	S	29.51 MW	28.73 AW	61380 AAW	TXBLS	10//99-12//99
	Dallas PMSA, TX	S	29.95 MW	30.33 AW	62290 AAW	TXBLS	10//99-12//99
	El Paso MSA, TX	S	22.86 MW	22.41 AW	47550 AAW	TXBLS	10//99-12//99
	Fort Worth-Arlington PMSA, TX	S	25.37 MW	24.76 AW	52770 AAW	TXBLS	10//99-12//99
	Galveston-Texas City PMSA, TX	S	20.48 MW	19.84 AW	42600 AAW	TXBLS	10//99-12//99
	Houston PMSA, TX	S	30.32 MW	29.59 AW	63070 AAW	TXBLS	10//99-12//99
	Longview-Marshall MSA, TX	S	23.59 MW	28.18 AW	49060 AAW	TXBLS	10//99-12//99
	Odessa-Midland MSA, TX	S	23.70 MW	21.23 AW	49290 AAW	TXBLS	10//99-12//99
	San Antonio MSA, TX	S	27.79 MW	26.69 AW	57810 AAW	TXBLS	10//99-12//99
	Waco MSA, TX	S	28.54 MW	28.50 AW	59370 AAW	TXBLS	10//99-12//99
	Utah	S	25.26 MW	26.17 AW	54430 AAW	UTBLS	10//99-12//99
	Salt Lake City-Ogden MSA, UT	S	26.08 MW	24.99 AW	54250 AAW	UTBLS	10//99-12//99
	Vermont	S	29.12 MW	28.42 AW	59110 AAW	VTBLS	10//99-12//99
	Virginia	S	26.25 MW	27.73 AW	57670 AAW	VABLS	10//99-12//99
	Charlottesville MSA, VA	S	24.98 MW	24.07 AW	51970 AAW	VABLS	10//99-12//99
	Lynchburg MSA, VA	S	37.49 MW	38.84 AW	77980 AAW	VABLS	10//99-12//99
	Norfolk-Virginia Beach-Newport News MSA, VA-NC	S	25.50 MW	25.66 AW	53030 AAW	VABLS	10//99-12//99
	Washington	S	28.6 MW	28.32 AW	58910 AAW	WABLS	10//99-12//99
	Seattle-Bellevue-Everett PMSA, WA	S	28.06 MW	28.36 AW	58370 AAW	WABLS	10//99-12//99
	Spokane MSA, WA	S	28.59 MW	29.25 AW	59460 AAW	WABLS	10//99-12//99
	Tacoma PMSA, WA	S	36.90 MW	32.99 AW	76760 AAW	WABLS	10//99-12//99
	West Virginia	S	20.58 MW	24.08 AW	50080 AAW	WVBLS	10//99-12//99
	Charleston MSA, WV	S	25.21 MW	20.40 AW	52430 AAW	WVBLS	10//99-12//99
	Parkersburg-Marietta MSA, WV-OH	S	25.37 MW	29.40 AW	52780 AAW	WVBLS	10//99-12//99
	Wisconsin	S	26.85 MW	27.15 AW	56470 AAW	WIBLS	10//99-12//99
	Appleton-Oshkosh-Neenah MSA, WI	S	28.12 MW	28.69 AW	58490 AAW	WIBLS	10//99-12//99
	Eau Claire MSA, WI	S	26.81 MW	27.09 AW	55770 AAW	WIBLS	10//99-12//99
	Madison MSA, WI	S	28.96 MW	28.86 AW	60250 AAW	WIBLS	10//99-12//99
	Milwaukee-Waukesha PMSA, WI	S	25.17 MW	24.76 AW	52360 AAW	WIBLS	10//99-12//99
	Wyoming	S	25 MW	25.76 AW	53580 AAW	WYBLS	10//99-12//99
	Puerto Rico	S	21.56 MW	21.39 AW	44490 AAW	PRBLS	10//99-12//99
	San Juan-Bayamon PMSA, PR	S	21.09 MW	20.10 AW	43860 AAW	PRBLS	10//99-12//99
Senior	United States	Y		72411 AW		ENR1	2000
Environmental Engineering Technician	Alabama	S	12.58 MW	13.10 AW	27250 AAW	ALBLS	10//99-12//99
	Alaska	S	19.19 MW	19.25 AW	40030 AAW	AKBLS	10//99-12//99
	Arizona	S	14.23 MW	15.13 AW	31470 AAW	AZBLS	10//99-12//99
	Phoenix-Mesa MSA, AZ	S	14.60 MW	13.38 AW	30360 AAW	AZBLS	10//99-12//99
	Arkansas	S	14.56 MW	15.55 AW	32350 AAW	ARBLS	10//99-12//99
	Fayetteville-Springdale-Rogers MSA, AR	S	15.74 MW	15.06 AW	32740 AAW	ARBLS	10//99-12//99
	California	S	17.85 MW	19.36 AW	40270 AAW	CABLS	10//99-12//99
	Los Angeles-Long Beach PMSA, CA	S	20.99 MW	19.97 AW	43650 AAW	CABLS	10//99-12//99
	Oakland PMSA, CA	S	17.07 MW	17.15 AW	35510 AAW	CABLS	10//99-12//99
	Orange County PMSA, CA	S	18.29 MW	16.58 AW	38050 AAW	CABLS	10//99-12//99
	Riverside-San Bernardino PMSA, CA	S	24.44 MW	28.62 AW	50830 AAW	CABLS	10//99-12//99

AAW Average annual wage	**AOH** Average offered, high	**ASH** Average starting, high	**H** Hourly	**M** Monthly	**S** Special: hourly and annual
AE Average entry wage	**AOL** Average offered, low	**ASL** Average starting, low	**HI** Highest wage paid	**MTC** Median total compensation	**TQ** Third quartile wage
AEX Average experienced wage	**APH** Average pay, high range	**AW** Average wage paid	**HR** High end range	**MW** Median wage paid	**W** Weekly
AO Average offered	**APL** Average pay, low range	**FQ** First quartile wage	**LR** Low end range	**SQ** Second quartile wage	**Y** Yearly

Occupation/Type/Industry	Location	Per	Low	Mid	High	Source	Date
Environmental Engineering Technician	Sacramento PMSA, CA	S	17.60 MW	16.87 AW	36610 AAW	CABLS	10//99-12//99
	San Diego MSA, CA	S	19.31 MW	20.74 AW	40170 AAW	CABLS	10//99-12//99
	Santa Rosa PMSA, CA	S	18.87 MW	18.46 AW	39250 AAW	CABLS	10//99-12//99
	Colorado	S	16.09 MW	16.82 AW	34990 AAW	COBLS	10//99-12//99
	Denver PMSA, CO	S	16.93 MW	16.09 AW	35220 AAW	COBLS	10//99-12//99
	Connecticut	S	16.19 MW	16.85 AW	35050 AAW	CTBLS	10//99-12//99
	Hartford MSA, CT	S	16.22 MW	15.80 AW	33750 AAW	CTBLS	10//99-12//99
	Delaware	S	12.58 MW	13.73 AW	28570 AAW	DEBLS	10//99-12//99
	Washington PMSA, DC-MD-VA-WV	S	14.86 MW	14.90 AW	30920 AAW	DCBLS	10//99-12//99
	Florida	S	14.13 MW	14.73 AW	30640 AAW	FLBLS	10//99-12//99
	Fort Lauderdale PMSA, FL	S	13.83 MW	13.11 AW	28770 AAW	FLBLS	10//99-12//99
	Fort Myers-Cape Coral MSA, FL	S	14.46 MW	13.68 AW	30080 AAW	FLBLS	10//99-12//99
	Jacksonville MSA, FL	S	17.40 MW	15.91 AW	36180 AAW	FLBLS	10//99-12//99
	Orlando MSA, FL	S	13.73 MW	12.87 AW	28560 AAW	FLBLS	10//99-12//99
	Tampa-St. Petersburg-Clearwater MSA, FL	S	14.34 MW	13.40 AW	29830 AAW	FLBLS	10//99-12//99
	West Palm Beach-Boca Raton MSA, FL	S	16.10 MW	17.06 AW	33480 AAW	FLBLS	10//99-12//99
	Augusta-Aiken MSA, GA-SC	S	29.73 MW	29.99 AW	61830 AAW	GABLS	10//99-12//99
	Hawaii	S	15.99 MW	17.36 AW	36110 AAW	HIBLS	10//99-12//99
	Honolulu MSA, HI	S	17.36 MW	15.99 AW	36110 AAW	HIBLS	10//99-12//99
	Idaho	S	15.92 MW	16.18 AW	33650 AAW	IDBLS	10//99-12//99
	Illinois	S	14.41 MW	14.45 AW	30060 AAW	ILBLS	10//99-12//99
	Chicago PMSA, IL	S	16.68 MW	15.62 AW	34700 AAW	ILBLS	10//99-12//99
	Indiana	S	17.86 MW	17.56 AW	36530 AAW	INBLS	10//99-12//99
	Evansville-Henderson MSA, IN-KY	S	18.64 MW	18.76 AW	38760 AAW	INBLS	10//99-12//99
	Indianapolis MSA, IN	S	17.21 MW	17.61 AW	35790 AAW	INBLS	10//99-12//99
	Iowa	S	17.88 MW	18.59 AW	38660 AAW	IABLS	10//99-12//99
	Des Moines MSA, IA	S	17.86 MW	18.56 AW	37150 AAW	IABLS	10//99-12//99
	Kansas	S	19.97 MW	21.25 AW	44200 AAW	KSBLS	10//99-12//99
	Kentucky	S	15.95 MW	15.69 AW	32630 AAW	KYBLS	10//99-12//99
	Lexington MSA, KY	S	16.39 MW	17.90 AW	34100 AAW	KYBLS	10//99-12//99
	Louisiana	S	12.76 MW	14.70 AW	30570 AAW	LABLS	10//99-12//99
	Baton Rouge MSA, LA	S	12.71 MW	12.22 AW	26430 AAW	LABLS	10//99-12//99
	New Orleans MSA, LA	S	28.99 MW	30.32 AW	60310 AAW	LABLS	10//99-12//99
	Maine	S	14.22 MW	15.18 AW	31580 AAW	MEBLS	10//99-12//99
	Maryland	S	17.27 MW	17.60 AW	36610 AAW	MDBLS	10//99-12//99
	Massachusetts	S	16.11 MW	16.23 AW	33760 AAW	MABLS	10//99-12//99
	Boston PMSA, MA-NH	S	19.06 MW	18.66 AW	39640 AAW	MABLS	10//99-12//99
	Michigan	S	17.08 MW	19.50 AW	40560 AAW	MIBLS	10//99-12//99
	Detroit PMSA, MI	S	20.68 MW	19.04 AW	43000 AAW	MIBLS	10//99-12//99
	Grand Rapids-Muskegon-Holland MSA, MI	S	18.51 MW	15.50 AW	38500 AAW	MIBLS	10//99-12//99
	Lansing-East Lansing MSA, MI	S	15.80 MW	14.51 AW	32870 AAW	MIBLS	10//99-12//99
	Minnesota	S	19.28 MW	19.34 AW	40220 AAW	MNBLS	10//99-12//99
	Minneapolis-St. Paul MSA, MN-WI	S	19.63 MW	21.20 AW	40830 AAW	MNBLS	10//99-12//99
	Mississippi	S	13.3 MW	15.44 AW	32110 AAW	MSBLS	10//99-12//99
	Biloxi-Gulfport-Pascagoula MSA, MS	S	17.84 MW	18.65 AW	37100 AAW	MSBLS	10//99-12//99
	Missouri	S	16.77 MW	19.44 AW	40440 AAW	MOBLS	10//99-12//99
	Montana	S	14.2 MW	14.20 AW	29550 AAW	MTBLS	10//99-12//99
	Nebraska	S	16.28 MW	16.75 AW	34830 AAW	NEBLS	10//99-12//99
	Omaha MSA, NE-IA	S	19.18 MW	19.23 AW	39890 AAW	NEBLS	10//99-12//99
	Nevada	S	15.96 MW	16.73 AW	34800 AAW	NVBLS	10//99-12//99
	Las Vegas MSA, NV-AZ	S	16.19 MW	15.45 AW	33680 AAW	NVBLS	10//99-12//99
	New Hampshire	S	15.43 MW	15.93 AW	33140 AAW	NHBLS	10//99-12//99
	New Jersey	S	22.78 MW	22.23 AW	46230 AAW	NJBLS	10//99-12//99
	Bergen-Passaic PMSA, NJ	S	18.33 MW	16.90 AW	38130 AAW	NJBLS	10//99-12//99
	Middlesex-Somerset-Hunterdon PMSA, NJ	S	24.82 MW	24.80 AW	51620 AAW	NJBLS	10//99-12//99
	Monmouth-Ocean PMSA, NJ	S	16.18 MW	15.91 AW	33640 AAW	NJBLS	10//99-12//99
	New Mexico	S	16.08 MW	16.60 AW	34530 AAW	NMBLS	10//99-12//99
	New York	S	18.23 MW	18.16 AW	37770 AAW	NYBLS	10//99-12//99
	Albany-Schenectady-Troy MSA, NY	S	19.04 MW	19.10 AW	39600 AAW	NYBLS	10//99-12//99
	Buffalo-Niagara Falls MSA, NY	S	17.49 MW	16.79 AW	36380 AAW	NYBLS	10//99-12//99

AAW	Average annual wage	AOH	Average offered, high	ASH	Average starting, high	H	Hourly	M	Monthly	S	Special: hourly and annual
AE	Average entry wage	AOL	Average offered, low	ASL	Average starting, low	HI	Highest wage paid	MTC	Median total compensation	TQ	Third quartile wage
AEX	Average experienced wage	APH	Average pay, high range	AW	Average wage paid	HR	High end range	MW	Median wage paid	W	Weekly
AO	Average offered	APL	Average pay, low range	FQ	First quartile wage	LR	Low end range	SQ	Second quartile wage	Y	Yearly

Occupation/Type/Industry	Location	Per	Low	Mid	High	Source	Date
Environmental Engineering Technician	Nassau-Suffolk PMSA, NY	S	17.18 MW	17.70 AW	35730 AAW	NYBLS	10//99-12//99
	Newburgh PMSA, NY-PA	S	22.36 MW	23.66 AW	46500 AAW	NYBLS	10//99-12//99
	Rochester MSA, NY	S	18.96 MW	18.95 AW	39440 AAW	NYBLS	10//99-12//99
	Syracuse MSA, NY	S	16.08 MW	15.06 AW	33450 AAW	NYBLS	10//99-12//99
	North Carolina	S	15.4 MW	17.38 AW	36140 AAW	NCBLS	10//99-12//99
	Asheville MSA, NC	S	14.77 MW	15.01 AW	30720 AAW	NCBLS	10//99-12//99
	Charlotte-Gastonia-Rock Hill MSA, NC-SC	S	18.95 MW	15.67 AW	39410 AAW	NCBLS	10//99-12//99
	Raleigh-Durham-Chapel Hill MSA, NC	S	17.25 MW	17.24 AW	35870 AAW	NCBLS	10//99-12//99
	Ohio	S	14.18 MW	14.63 AW	30440 AAW	OHBLS	10//99-12//99
	Cincinnati PMSA, OH-KY-IN	S	14.91 MW	14.07 AW	31020 AAW	OHBLS	10//99-12//99
	Cleveland-Lorain-Elyria PMSA, OH	S	17.21 MW	17.64 AW	35800 AAW	OHBLS	10//99-12//99
	Columbus MSA, OH	S	17.38 MW	17.24 AW	36150 AAW	OHBLS	10//99-12//99
	Dayton-Springfield MSA, OH	S	15.29 MW	15.36 AW	31810 AAW	OHBLS	10//99-12//99
	Oklahoma	S	10.54 MW	12.13 AW	25240 AAW	OKBLS	10//99-12//99
	Oklahoma City MSA, OK	S	12.36 MW	10.76 AW	25720 AAW	OKBLS	10//99-12//99
	Pennsylvania	S	13.16 MW	16.63 AW	34580 AAW	PABLS	10//99-12//99
	Philadelphia PMSA, PA-NJ	S	17.33 MW	13.30 AW	36050 AAW	PABLS	10//99-12//99
	Pittsburgh MSA, PA	S	16.49 MW	14.46 AW	34310 AAW	PABLS	10//99-12//99
	Reading MSA, PA	S	15.84 MW	15.24 AW	32940 AAW	PABLS	10//99-12//99
	Rhode Island	S	15.85 MW	15.41 AW	32050 AAW	RIBLS	10//99-12//99
	Providence-Fall River-Warwick MSA, RI-MA	S	15.49 MW	15.95 AW	32230 AAW	RIBLS	10//99-12//99
	South Carolina	S	15.96 MW	20.03 AW	41660 AAW	SCBLS	10//99-12//99
	Greenville-Spartanburg-Anderson MSA, SC	S	14.58 MW	14.92 AW	30330 AAW	SCBLS	10//99-12//99
	Tennessee	S	12.91 MW	13.65 AW	28400 AAW	TNBLS	10//99-12//99
	Johnson City-Kingsport-Bristol MSA, TN-VA	S	10.88 MW	10.29 AW	22630 AAW	TNBLS	10//99-12//99
	Knoxville MSA, TN	S	13.36 MW	13.47 AW	27790 AAW	TNBLS	10//99-12//99
	Nashville MSA, TN	S	16.72 MW	13.97 AW	34790 AAW	TNBLS	10//99-12//99
	Texas	S	14.07 MW	15.19 AW	31580 AAW	TXBLS	10//99-12//99
	Beaumont-Port Arthur MSA, TX	S	20.36 MW	17.42 AW	42340 AAW	TXBLS	10//99-12//99
	Dallas PMSA, TX	S	19.22 MW	17.70 AW	39990 AAW	TXBLS	10//99-12//99
	El Paso MSA, TX	S	15.68 MW	15.03 AW	32610 AAW	TXBLS	10//99-12//99
	Fort Worth-Arlington PMSA, TX	S	12.09 MW	11.08 AW	25140 AAW	TXBLS	10//99-12//99
	Houston PMSA, TX	S	14.86 MW	14.24 AW	30910 AAW	TXBLS	10//99-12//99
	San Antonio MSA, TX	S	13.68 MW	10.70 AW	28450 AAW	TXBLS	10//99-12//99
	Utah	S	14.61 MW	15.57 AW	32390 AAW	UTBLS	10//99-12//99
	Salt Lake City-Ogden MSA, UT	S	15.78 MW	14.43 AW	32820 AAW	UTBLS	10//99-12//99
	Vermont	S	14.21 MW	15.93 AW	33130 AAW	VTBLS	10//99-12//99
	Virginia	S	13.83 MW	15.46 AW	32150 AAW	VABLS	10//99-12//99
	Richmond-Petersburg MSA, VA	S	20.74 MW	22.56 AW	43150 AAW	VABLS	10//99-12//99
	Washington	S	16.74 MW	17.64 AW	36690 AAW	WABLS	10//99-12//99
	Bremerton PMSA, WA	S	20.02 MW	20.38 AW	41640 AAW	WABLS	10//99-12//99
	Seattle-Bellevue-Everett PMSA, WA	S	17.51 MW	16.54 AW	36430 AAW	WABLS	10//99-12//99
	West Virginia	S	13.78 MW	13.69 AW	28470 AAW	WVBLS	10//99-12//99
	Huntington-Ashland MSA, WV-KY-OH	S	10.39 MW	10.21 AW	21610 AAW	WVBLS	10//99-12//99
	Wisconsin	S	18.72 MW	18.96 AW	39450 AAW	WIBLS	10//99-12//99
	Milwaukee-Waukesha PMSA, WI	S	22.15 MW	21.06 AW	46070 AAW	WIBLS	10//99-12//99
	Puerto Rico	S	13.93 MW	14.18 AW	29490 AAW	PRBLS	10//99-12//99
	San Juan-Bayamon PMSA, PR	S	14.22 MW	14.00 AW	29580 AAW	PRBLS	10//99-12//99
Environmental Science and Protection Technician, Including Health	Alabama	S	16.42 MW	18.30 AW	38070 AAW	ALBLS	10//99-12//99
	Alaska	S	16.99 MW	18.00 AW	37450 AAW	AKBLS	10//99-12//99
	Anchorage MSA, AK	S	18.94 MW	18.05 AW	39400 AAW	AKBLS	10//99-12//99
	Arizona	S	21.76 MW	21.40 AW	44510 AAW	AZBLS	10//99-12//99
	Phoenix-Mesa MSA, AZ	S	22.96 MW	23.19 AW	47750 AAW	AZBLS	10//99-12//99
	Arkansas	S	10.13 MW	10.98 AW	22840 AAW	ARBLS	10//99-12//99

AAW	Average annual wage	AOH	Average offered, high	ASH	Average starting, high	H	Hourly	S	Special: hourly and annual
AE	Average entry wage	AOL	Average offered, low	ASL	Average starting, low	HI	Highest wage paid	TQ	Third quartile wage
AEX	Average experienced wage	APH	Average pay, high range	AW	Average wage paid	HR	High end range	W	Weekly
AO	Average offered	APL	Average pay, low range	FQ	First quartile wage	LR	Low end range	Y	Yearly

Additional legend: M Monthly, MTC Median total compensation, MW Median wage paid, SQ Second quartile wage

Occupation/Type/Industry	Location	Per	Low	Mid	High	Source	Date
Environmental Science and Protection Technician, Including Health							
	Little Rock-North Little Rock MSA, AR	S	9.72 MW	9.43 AW	20210 AAW	ARBLS	10//99-12//99
	California	S	18.85 MW	20.44 AW	42520 AAW	CABLS	10//99-12//99
	Los Angeles-Long Beach PMSA, CA	S	21.34 MW	19.54 AW	44380 AAW	CABLS	10//99-12//99
	Oakland PMSA, CA	S	20.95 MW	19.92 AW	43570 AAW	CABLS	10//99-12//99
	Orange County PMSA, CA	S	17.88 MW	16.35 AW	37180 AAW	CABLS	10//99-12//99
	Riverside-San Bernardino PMSA, CA	S	13.35 MW	11.83 AW	27760 AAW	CABLS	10//99-12//99
	Sacramento PMSA, CA	S	14.73 MW	14.21 AW	30650 AAW	CABLS	10//99-12//99
	San Diego MSA, CA	S	19.29 MW	19.09 AW	40120 AAW	CABLS	10//99-12//99
	San Francisco PMSA, CA	S	21.18 MW	18.14 AW	44050 AAW	CABLS	10//99-12//99
	San Jose PMSA, CA	S	26.30 MW	24.08 AW	54690 AAW	CABLS	10//99-12//99
	Vallejo-Fairfield-Napa PMSA, CA	S	13.11 MW	12.55 AW	27270 AAW	CABLS	10//99-12//99
	Colorado	S	17.85 MW	18.19 AW	37830 AAW	COBLS	10//99-12//99
	Denver PMSA, CO	S	18.06 MW	16.72 AW	37550 AAW	COBLS	10//99-12//99
	Connecticut	S	15.49 MW	16.59 AW	34510 AAW	CTBLS	10//99-12//99
	Bridgeport PMSA, CT	S	14.87 MW	13.83 AW	30930 AAW	CTBLS	10//99-12//99
	Hartford MSA, CT	S	16.51 MW	15.11 AW	34350 AAW	CTBLS	10//99-12//99
	Delaware	S	18.99 MW	18.94 AW	39400 AAW	DEBLS	10//99-12//99
	Washington PMSA, DC-MD-VA-WV	S	17.41 MW	16.03 AW	36220 AAW	DCBLS	10//99-12//99
	Florida	S	14.43 MW	14.64 AW	30450 AAW	FLBLS	10//99-12//99
	Daytona Beach MSA, FL	S	11.62 MW	10.69 AW	24160 AAW	FLBLS	10//99-12//99
	Fort Pierce-Port St. Lucie MSA, FL	S	14.47 MW	14.66 AW	30110 AAW	FLBLS	10//99-12//99
	Fort Walton Beach MSA, FL	S	9.19 MW	7.92 AW	19110 AAW	FLBLS	10//99-12//99
	Lakeland-Winter Haven MSA, FL	S	15.71 MW	15.19 AW	32690 AAW	FLBLS	10//99-12//99
	Melbourne-Titusville-Palm Bay MSA, FL	S	12.66 MW	8.44 AW	26320 AAW	FLBLS	10//99-12//99
	Tampa-St. Petersburg-Clearwater MSA, FL	S	14.34 MW	13.23 AW	29820 AAW	FLBLS	10//99-12//99
	Georgia	S	15.73 MW	16.88 AW	35100 AAW	GABLS	10//99-12//99
	Atlanta MSA, GA	S	18.46 MW	16.09 AW	38400 AAW	GABLS	10//99-12//99
	Augusta-Aiken MSA, GA-SC	S	18.43 MW	18.49 AW	38330 AAW	GABLS	10//99-12//99
	Idaho	S	23.09 MW	21.67 AW	45080 AAW	IDBLS	10//99-12//99
	Boise City MSA, ID	S	20.25 MW	20.31 AW	42120 AAW	IDBLS	10//99-12//99
	Illinois	S	13.77 MW	14.83 AW	30840 AAW	ILBLS	10//99-12//99
	Chicago PMSA, IL	S	14.65 MW	13.57 AW	30460 AAW	ILBLS	10//99-12//99
	Indiana	S	16.67 MW	17.41 AW	36210 AAW	INBLS	10//99-12//99
	Gary PMSA, IN	S	13.92 MW	11.68 AW	28960 AAW	INBLS	10//99-12//99
	Iowa	S	16.82 MW	16.61 AW	34540 AAW	IABLS	10//99-12//99
	Cedar Rapids MSA, IA	S	17.92 MW	17.68 AW	37280 AAW	IABLS	10//99-12//99
	Davenport-Moline-Rock Island MSA, IA-IL	S	14.52 MW	12.97 AW	30200 AAW	IABLS	10//99-12//99
	Kansas	S	14.97 MW	15.93 AW	33140 AAW	KSBLS	10//99-12//99
	Kentucky	S	14.45 MW	16.10 AW	33500 AAW	KYBLS	10//99-12//99
	Lexington MSA, KY	S	12.76 MW	11.89 AW	26540 AAW	KYBLS	10//99-12//99
	Louisville MSA, KY-IN	S	14.85 MW	12.21 AW	30880 AAW	KYBLS	10//99-12//99
	Louisiana	S	16.02 MW	16.51 AW	34340 AAW	LABLS	10//99-12//99
	Baton Rouge MSA, LA	S	14.51 MW	10.44 AW	30180 AAW	LABLS	10//99-12//99
	Lafayette MSA, LA	S	18.77 MW	19.90 AW	39050 AAW	LABLS	10//99-12//99
	New Orleans MSA, LA	S	16.80 MW	16.73 AW	34940 AAW	LABLS	10//99-12//99
	Maine	S	12.73 MW	13.00 AW	27050 AAW	MEBLS	10//99-12//99
	Maryland	S	17.45 MW	17.77 AW	36950 AAW	MDBLS	10//99-12//99
	Massachusetts	S	14.92 MW	15.59 AW	32430 AAW	MABLS	10//99-12//99
	Boston PMSA, MA-NH	S	14.94 MW	14.76 AW	31080 AAW	MABLS	10//99-12//99
	Fitchburg-Leominster PMSA, MA	S	18.03 MW	16.08 AW	37490 AAW	MABLS	10//99-12//99
	Lawrence PMSA, MA-NH	S	16.54 MW	15.73 AW	34410 AAW	MABLS	10//99-12//99
	Michigan	S	17.73 MW	17.72 AW	36850 AAW	MIBLS	10//99-12//99
	Detroit PMSA, MI	S	18.78 MW	18.52 AW	39050 AAW	MIBLS	10//99-12//99
	Grand Rapids-Muskegon-Holland MSA, MI	S	18.21 MW	18.26 AW	37870 AAW	MIBLS	10//99-12//99
	Minnesota	S	16.44 MW	17.76 AW	36930 AAW	MNBLS	10//99-12//99
	Duluth-Superior MSA, MN-WI	S	16.95 MW	15.94 AW	35260 AAW	MNBLS	10//99-12//99
	Minneapolis-St. Paul MSA, MN-WI	S	17.12 MW	16.22 AW	35610 AAW	MNBLS	10//99-12//99

AAW Average annual wage	**AOH** Average offered, high	**ASH** Average starting, high	**H** Hourly	**M** Monthly	**S** Special: hourly and annual
AE Average entry wage	**AOL** Average offered, low	**ASL** Average starting, low	**HI** Highest wage paid	**MTC** Median total compensation	**TQ** Third quartile wage
AEX Average experienced wage	**APH** Average pay, high range	**AW** Average wage paid	**HR** High end range	**MW** Median wage paid	**W** Weekly
AO Average offered	**APL** Average pay, low range	**FQ** First quartile wage	**LR** Low end range	**SQ** Second quartile wage	**Y** Yearly

Occupation/Type/Industry	Location	Per	Low	Mid	High	Source	Date
Environmental Science and Protection Technician, Including Health							
	Mississippi	S	16.53 MW	16.54 AW	34400 AAW	MSBLS	10//99-12//99
	Biloxi-Gulfport-Pascagoula MSA, MS	S	22.32 MW	26.84 AW	46430 AAW	MSBLS	10//99-12//99
	Jackson MSA, MS	S	17.08 MW	18.41 AW	35530 AAW	MSBLS	10//99-12//99
	Missouri	S	17.27 MW	17.76 AW	36940 AAW	MOBLS	10//99-12//99
	Kansas City MSA, MO-KS	S	17.47 MW	15.44 AW	36330 AAW	MOBLS	10//99-12//99
	St. Louis MSA, MO-IL	S	17.39 MW	16.33 AW	36170 AAW	MOBLS	10//99-12//99
	Montana	S	10.09 MW	11.31 AW	23520 AAW	MTBLS	10//99-12//99
	Nebraska	S	11.84 MW	11.97 AW	24900 AAW	NEBLS	10//99-12//99
	Omaha MSA, NE-IA	S	14.61 MW	13.05 AW	30390 AAW	NEBLS	10//99-12//99
	Nevada	S	21.62 MW	20.79 AW	43240 AAW	NVBLS	10//99-12//99
	New Hampshire	S	14.96 MW	14.63 AW	30420 AAW	NHBLS	10//99-12//99
	New Jersey	S	17.14 MW	18.03 AW	37500 AAW	NJBLS	10//99-12//99
	Middlesex-Somerset-Hunterdon PMSA, NJ	S	19.06 MW	18.22 AW	39650 AAW	NJBLS	10//99-12//99
	Newark PMSA, NJ	S	18.43 MW	17.40 AW	38340 AAW	NJBLS	10//99-12//99
	Trenton PMSA, NJ	S	17.36 MW	16.70 AW	36110 AAW	NJBLS	10//99-12//99
	New Mexico	S	11.39 MW	11.69 AW	24320 AAW	NMBLS	10//99-12//99
	New York	S	11.3 MW	12.89 AW	26820 AAW	NYBLS	10//99-12//99
	Albany-Schenectady-Troy MSA, NY	S	10.16 MW	9.75 AW	21130 AAW	NYBLS	10//99-12//99
	Binghamton MSA, NY	S	14.49 MW	13.56 AW	30140 AAW	NYBLS	10//99-12//99
	Buffalo-Niagara Falls MSA, NY	S	17.48 MW	17.86 AW	36350 AAW	NYBLS	10//99-12//99
	Nassau-Suffolk PMSA, NY	S	15.25 MW	14.63 AW	31720 AAW	NYBLS	10//99-12//99
	New York PMSA, NY	S	14.27 MW	13.14 AW	29680 AAW	NYBLS	10//99-12//99
	Syracuse MSA, NY	S	12.61 MW	10.61 AW	26240 AAW	NYBLS	10//99-12//99
	North Carolina	S	15.1 MW	15.73 AW	32720 AAW	NCBLS	10//99-12//99
	Charlotte-Gastonia-Rock Hill MSA, NC-SC	S	17.75 MW	16.96 AW	36920 AAW	NCBLS	10//99-12//99
	Fayetteville MSA, NC	S	15.65 MW	15.34 AW	32550 AAW	NCBLS	10//99-12//99
	Greensboro--Winston-Salem--High Point MSA, NC	S	15.91 MW	13.69 AW	33080 AAW	NCBLS	10//99-12//99
	Hickory-Morganton-Lenoir MSA, NC	S	14.44 MW	13.41 AW	30040 AAW	NCBLS	10//99-12//99
	North Dakota	S	21.68 MW	21.81 AW	45360 AAW	NDBLS	10//99-12//99
	Ohio	S	16.53 MW	16.68 AW	34690 AAW	OHBLS	10//99-12//99
	Akron PMSA, OH	S	18.96 MW	19.17 AW	39450 AAW	OHBLS	10//99-12//99
	Canton-Massillon MSA, OH	S	21.71 MW	18.67 AW	45160 AAW	OHBLS	10//99-12//99
	Cincinnati PMSA, OH-KY-IN	S	17.01 MW	16.69 AW	35390 AAW	OHBLS	10//99-12//99
	Cleveland-Lorain-Elyria PMSA, OH	S	17.90 MW	17.19 AW	37220 AAW	OHBLS	10//99-12//99
	Youngstown-Warren MSA, OH	S	16.00 MW	15.84 AW	33280 AAW	OHBLS	10//99-12//99
	Oklahoma	S	11.27 MW	12.63 AW	26280 AAW	OKBLS	10//99-12//99
	Oklahoma City MSA, OK	S	20.82 MW	20.01 AW	43310 AAW	OKBLS	10//99-12//99
	Tulsa MSA, OK	S	10.23 MW	9.90 AW	21270 AAW	OKBLS	10//99-12//99
	Oregon	S	18.18 MW	17.31 AW	36010 AAW	ORBLS	10//99-12//99
	Pennsylvania	S	17.91 MW	17.59 AW	36590 AAW	PABLS	10//99-12//99
	Harrisburg-Lebanon-Carlisle MSA, PA	S	20.19 MW	22.30 AW	42000 AAW	PABLS	10//99-12//99
	Philadelphia PMSA, PA-NJ	S	16.96 MW	16.66 AW	35280 AAW	PABLS	10//99-12//99
	Pittsburgh MSA, PA	S	18.42 MW	19.67 AW	38310 AAW	PABLS	10//99-12//99
	Reading MSA, PA	S	12.45 MW	12.61 AW	25890 AAW	PABLS	10//99-12//99
	Rhode Island	S	18.24 MW	17.91 AW	37250 AAW	RIBLS	10//99-12//99
	Providence-Fall River-Warwick MSA, RI-MA	S	17.91 MW	18.27 AW	37250 AAW	RIBLS	10//99-12//99
	South Carolina	S	19.33 MW	19.70 AW	40970 AAW	SCBLS	10//99-12//99
	Charleston-North Charleston MSA, SC	S	20.59 MW	16.85 AW	42820 AAW	SCBLS	10//99-12//99
	Columbia MSA, SC	S	19.26 MW	15.57 AW	40070 AAW	SCBLS	10//99-12//99
	Greenville-Spartanburg-Anderson MSA, SC	S	21.51 MW	22.10 AW	44750 AAW	SCBLS	10//99-12//99
	South Dakota	S	12.22 MW	12.33 AW	25650 AAW	SDBLS	10//99-12//99
	Tennessee	S	12.42 MW	13.37 AW	27800 AAW	TNBLS	10//99-12//99
	Memphis MSA, TN-AR-MS	S	13.90 MW	11.86 AW	28920 AAW	MSBLS	10//99-12//99
	Nashville MSA, TN	S	11.66 MW	11.10 AW	24250 AAW	TNBLS	10//99-12//99
	Texas	S	18.58 MW	18.89 AW	39300 AAW	TXBLS	10//99-12//99
	Austin-San Marcos MSA, TX	S	17.19 MW	15.46 AW	35750 AAW	TXBLS	10//99-12//99
	Beaumont-Port Arthur MSA, TX	S	16.42 MW	14.67 AW	34150 AAW	TXBLS	10//99-12//99

AAW Average annual wage	**AOH** Average offered, high	**ASH** Average starting, high	**H** Hourly	**M** Monthly	**S** Special: hourly and annual
AE Average entry wage	**AOL** Average offered, low	**ASL** Average starting, low	**HI** Highest wage paid	**MTC** Median total compensation	**TQ** Third quartile wage
AEX Average experienced wage	**APH** Average pay, high range	**AW** Average wage paid	**HR** High end range	**MW** Median wage paid	**W** Weekly
AO Average offered	**APL** Average pay, low range	**FQ** First quartile wage	**LR** Low end range	**SQ** Second quartile wage	**Y** Yearly

Occupation/Type/Industry	Location	Per	Low	Mid	High	Source	Date
Environmental Science and Protection Technician, Including Health							
	Corpus Christi MSA, TX	S	17.04 MW	13.87 AW	35440 AAW	TXBLS	10//99-12//99
	Dallas PMSA, TX	S	15.78 MW	15.33 AW	32820 AAW	TXBLS	10//99-12//99
	El Paso MSA, TX	S	16.50 MW	13.29 AW	34320 AAW	TXBLS	10//99-12//99
	Fort Worth-Arlington PMSA, TX	S	19.92 MW	21.30 AW	41430 AAW	TXBLS	10//99-12//99
	Houston PMSA, TX	S	22.38 MW	24.40 AW	46540 AAW	TXBLS	10//99-12//99
	Odessa-Midland MSA, TX	S	16.20 MW	17.45 AW	33700 AAW	TXBLS	10//99-12//99
	San Antonio MSA, TX	S	14.27 MW	13.18 AW	29670 AAW	TXBLS	10//99-12//99
	Utah	S	18.3 MW	18.93 AW	39360 AAW	UTBLS	10//99-12//99
	Salt Lake City-Ogden MSA, UT	S	19.77 MW	19.19 AW	41130 AAW	UTBLS	10//99-12//99
	Vermont	S	11.79 MW	13.15 AW	27350 AAW	VTBLS	10//99-12//99
	Virginia	S	17.03 MW	17.15 AW	35680 AAW	VABLS	10//99-12//99
	Norfolk-Virginia Beach-Newport News MSA, VA-NC	S	16.92 MW	16.66 AW	35200 AAW	VABLS	10//99-12//99
	Richmond-Petersburg MSA, VA	S	15.13 MW	15.27 AW	31480 AAW	VABLS	10//99-12//99
	Roanoke MSA, VA	S	12.05 MW	10.07 AW	25050 AAW	VABLS	10//99-12//99
	Washington	S	17.49 MW	17.52 AW	36440 AAW	WABLS	10//99-12//99
	Seattle-Bellevue-Everett PMSA, WA	S	17.83 MW	17.53 AW	37090 AAW	WABLS	10//99-12//99
	Tacoma PMSA, WA	S	18.19 MW	18.90 AW	37840 AAW	WABLS	10//99-12//99
	West Virginia	S	10.31 MW	11.79 AW	24530 AAW	WVBLS	10//99-12//99
	Charleston MSA, WV	S	11.46 MW	10.65 AW	23840 AAW	WVBLS	10//99-12//99
	Wisconsin	S	14.45 MW	14.46 AW	30080 AAW	WIBLS	10//99-12//99
	Milwaukee-Waukesha PMSA, WI	S	13.65 MW	13.88 AW	28390 AAW	WIBLS	10//99-12//99
	Wyoming	S	9.01 MW	10.19 AW	21180 AAW	WYBLS	10//99-12//99
	Puerto Rico	S	11.72 MW	11.01 AW	22890 AAW	PRBLS	10//99-12//99
	San Juan-Bayamon PMSA, PR	S	11.01 MW	11.74 AW	22890 AAW	PRBLS	10//99-12//99
Environmental Science Teacher							
Postsecondary	California	Y		60010 AAW		CABLS	10//99-12//99
Postsecondary	Florida	Y		74580 AAW		FLBLS	10//99-12//99
Postsecondary	Illinois	Y		41980 AAW		ILBLS	10//99-12//99
Postsecondary	Iowa	Y		58370 AAW		IABLS	10//99-12//99
Postsecondary	Michigan	Y		47780 AAW		MIBLS	10//99-12//99
Postsecondary	Minnesota	Y		71330 AAW		MNBLS	10//99-12//99
Postsecondary	Nevada	Y		41840 AAW		NVBLS	10//99-12//99
Postsecondary	New York	Y		54170 AAW		NYBLS	10//99-12//99
Postsecondary	North Carolina	Y		48510 AAW		NCBLS	10//99-12//99
Postsecondary	Ohio	Y		54820 AAW		OHBLS	10//99-12//99
Postsecondary	Pennsylvania	Y		59370 AAW		PABLS	10//99-12//99
Postsecondary	Tennessee	Y		56200 AAW		TNBLS	10//99-12//99
Postsecondary	Texas	Y		53410 AAW		TXBLS	10//99-12//99
Postsecondary	Washington	Y		36830 AAW		WABLS	10//99-12//99
Postsecondary	Wisconsin	Y		56210 AAW		WIBLS	10//99-12//99
Postsecondary	Wyoming	Y		56250 AAW		WYBLS	10//99-12//99
Environmental Scientist and Specialist, Including Health							
	Alabama	S	17.72 MW	18.06 AW	37560 AAW	ALBLS	10//99-12//99
	Birmingham MSA, AL	S	19.37 MW	19.26 AW	40290 AAW	ALBLS	10//99-12//99
	Huntsville MSA, AL	S	20.23 MW	19.63 AW	42070 AAW	ALBLS	10//99-12//99
	Mobile MSA, AL	S	17.88 MW	16.77 AW	37180 AAW	ALBLS	10//99-12//99
	Alaska	S	24.53 MW	24.73 AW	51430 AAW	AKBLS	10//99-12//99
	Anchorage MSA, AK	S	24.48 MW	24.22 AW	50930 AAW	AKBLS	10//99-12//99
	Arizona	S	20.25 MW	22.16 AW	46090 AAW	AZBLS	10//99-12//99
	Phoenix-Mesa MSA, AZ	S	22.48 MW	20.46 AW	46760 AAW	AZBLS	10//99-12//99
	Arkansas	S	19.14 MW	19.49 AW	40530 AAW	ARBLS	10//99-12//99
	Little Rock-North Little Rock MSA, AR	S	19.17 MW	19.05 AW	39870 AAW	ARBLS	10//99-12//99
	California	S	26.62 MW	28.36 AW	58990 AAW	CABLS	10//99-12//99
	Bakersfield MSA, CA	S	32.08 MW	31.64 AW	66730 AAW	CABLS	10//99-12//99
	Fresno MSA, CA	S	23.92 MW	23.74 AW	49760 AAW	CABLS	10//99-12//99
	Los Angeles-Long Beach PMSA, CA	S	28.43 MW	24.26 AW	59140 AAW	CABLS	10//99-12//99
	Oakland PMSA, CA	S	28.49 MW	27.26 AW	59260 AAW	CABLS	10//99-12//99
	Orange County PMSA, CA	S	27.25 MW	26.66 AW	56670 AAW	CABLS	10//99-12//99

AAW	Average annual wage	AOH	Average offered, high	ASH	Average starting, high	H	Hourly		M	Monthly	S	Special: hourly and annual
AE	Average entry wage	AOL	Average offered, low	ASL	Average starting, low	HI	Highest wage paid		MTC	Median total compensation	TQ	Third quartile wage
AEX	Average experienced wage	APH	Average pay, high range	AW	Average wage paid	HR	High end range		MW	Median wage paid	W	Weekly
AO	Average offered	APL	Average pay, low range	FQ	First quartile wage	LR	Low end range		SQ	Second quartile wage	Y	Yearly

523

Occupation/Type/Industry	Location	Per	Low	Mid	High	Source	Date
Environmental Scientist and Specialist, Including Health	Riverside-San Bernardino PMSA, CA	S	25.12 MW	23.64 AW	52240 AAW	CABLS	10//99-12//99
	San Diego MSA, CA	S	25.32 MW	24.57 AW	52670 AAW	CABLS	10//99-12//99
	San Francisco PMSA, CA	S	28.91 MW	28.18 AW	60130 AAW	CABLS	10//99-12//99
	San Jose PMSA, CA	S	34.50 MW	37.51 AW	71770 AAW	CABLS	10//99-12//99
	Santa Barbara-Santa Maria-Lompoc MSA, CA	S	27.57 MW	25.36 AW	57360 AAW	CABLS	10//99-12//99
	Santa Cruz-Watsonville PMSA, CA	S	15.61 MW	13.56 AW	32470 AAW	CABLS	10//99-12//99
	Ventura PMSA, CA	S	30.10 MW	30.47 AW	62610 AAW	CABLS	10//99-12//99
	Yolo PMSA, CA	S	26.02 MW	21.30 AW	54110 AAW	CABLS	10//99-12//99
	Colorado	S	24.26 MW	24.87 AW	51720 AAW	COBLS	10//99-12//99
	Boulder-Longmont PMSA, CO	S	20.94 MW	22.05 AW	43550 AAW	COBLS	10//99-12//99
	Denver PMSA, CO	S	26.15 MW	25.65 AW	54390 AAW	COBLS	10//99-12//99
	Connecticut	S	23.07 MW	23.98 AW	49870 AAW	CTBLS	10//99-12//99
	Bridgeport PMSA, CT	S	25.19 MW	23.65 AW	52400 AAW	CTBLS	10//99-12//99
	Danbury PMSA, CT	S	29.91 MW	25.34 AW	62220 AAW	CTBLS	10//99-12//99
	Hartford MSA, CT	S	23.45 MW	22.53 AW	48770 AAW	CTBLS	10//99-12//99
	Delaware	S	18.26 MW	18.60 AW	38690 AAW	DEBLS	10//99-12//99
	Wilmington-Newark PMSA, DE-MD	S	18.43 MW	17.92 AW	38330 AAW	DEBLS	10//99-12//99
	Washington PMSA, DC-MD-VA-WV	S	28.52 MW	28.17 AW	59320 AAW	DCBLS	10//99-12//99
	Florida	S	19.76 MW	20.60 AW	42840 AAW	FLBLS	10//99-12//99
	Fort Lauderdale PMSA, FL	S	19.61 MW	17.35 AW	40780 AAW	FLBLS	10//99-12//99
	Fort Myers-Cape Coral MSA, FL	S	18.35 MW	16.64 AW	38160 AAW	FLBLS	10//99-12//99
	Fort Pierce-Port St. Lucie MSA, FL	S	30.42 MW	30.82 AW	63280 AAW	FLBLS	10//99-12//99
	Gainesville MSA, FL	S	19.06 MW	18.80 AW	39640 AAW	FLBLS	10//99-12//99
	Jacksonville MSA, FL	S	22.67 MW	22.18 AW	47140 AAW	FLBLS	10//99-12//99
	Lakeland-Winter Haven MSA, FL	S	20.11 MW	19.30 AW	41820 AAW	FLBLS	10//99-12//99
	Melbourne-Titusville-Palm Bay MSA, FL	S	19.83 MW	19.43 AW	41240 AAW	FLBLS	10//99-12//99
	Miami PMSA, FL	S	21.99 MW	21.12 AW	45750 AAW	FLBLS	10//99-12//99
	Orlando MSA, FL	S	22.44 MW	21.95 AW	46670 AAW	FLBLS	10//99-12//99
	Panama City MSA, FL	S	13.63 MW	10.54 AW	28360 AAW	FLBLS	10//99-12//99
	Sarasota-Bradenton MSA, FL	S	19.45 MW	19.26 AW	40460 AAW	FLBLS	10//99-12//99
	Tampa-St. Petersburg-Clearwater MSA, FL	S	19.68 MW	18.70 AW	40940 AAW	FLBLS	10//99-12//99
	West Palm Beach-Boca Raton MSA, FL	S	21.63 MW	20.42 AW	44990 AAW	FLBLS	10//99-12//99
	Georgia	S	20.1 MW	21.51 AW	44740 AAW	GABLS	10//99-12//99
	Atlanta MSA, GA	S	22.20 MW	20.35 AW	46170 AAW	GABLS	10//99-12//99
	Augusta-Aiken MSA, GA-SC	S	22.55 MW	21.43 AW	46910 AAW	GABLS	10//99-12//99
	Savannah MSA, GA	S	18.10 MW	17.11 AW	37640 AAW	GABLS	10//99-12//99
	Idaho	S	21.8 MW	24.57 AW	51110 AAW	IDBLS	10//99-12//99
	Illinois	S	28.48 MW	27.86 AW	57950 AAW	ILBLS	10//99-12//99
	Chicago PMSA, IL	S	28.76 MW	29.20 AW	59810 AAW	ILBLS	10//99-12//99
	Indiana	S	18.38 MW	19.04 AW	39610 AAW	INBLS	10//99-12//99
	Bloomington MSA, IN	S	18.38 MW	17.39 AW	38220 AAW	INBLS	10//99-12//99
	Fort Wayne MSA, IN	S	16.85 MW	17.03 AW	35050 AAW	INBLS	10//99-12//99
	Gary PMSA, IN	S	16.54 MW	17.19 AW	34400 AAW	INBLS	10//99-12//99
	Indianapolis MSA, IN	S	20.31 MW	20.99 AW	42240 AAW	INBLS	10//99-12//99
	South Bend MSA, IN	S	15.51 MW	14.76 AW	32260 AAW	INBLS	10//99-12//99
	Iowa	S	16.28 MW	22.04 AW	45850 AAW	IABLS	10//99-12//99
	Des Moines MSA, IA	S	20.49 MW	16.23 AW	42630 AAW	IABLS	10//99-12//99
	Kansas	S	20.87 MW	21.92 AW	45600 AAW	KSBLS	10//99-12//99
	Lawrence MSA, KS	S	23.60 MW	22.31 AW	49090 AAW	KSBLS	10//99-12//99
	Wichita MSA, KS	S	19.27 MW	18.27 AW	40070 AAW	KSBLS	10//99-12//99
	Kentucky	S	17.34 MW	18.02 AW	37470 AAW	KYBLS	10//99-12//99
	Lexington MSA, KY	S	16.19 MW	15.88 AW	33680 AAW	KYBLS	10//99-12//99
	Louisville MSA, KY-IN	S	17.46 MW	16.26 AW	36320 AAW	KYBLS	10//99-12//99
	Louisiana	S	16.58 MW	17.46 AW	36320 AAW	LABLS	10//99-12//99
	Baton Rouge MSA, LA	S	15.26 MW	15.10 AW	31750 AAW	LABLS	10//99-12//99
	Lake Charles MSA, LA	S	21.85 MW	22.40 AW	45440 AAW	LABLS	10//99-12//99
	New Orleans MSA, LA	S	20.64 MW	19.87 AW	42920 AAW	LABLS	10//99-12//99
	Maryland	S	22.92 MW	23.77 AW	49440 AAW	MDBLS	10//99-12//99
	Baltimore PMSA, MD	S	21.55 MW	21.03 AW	44830 AAW	MDBLS	10//99-12//99
	Massachusetts	S	23.59 MW	24.21 AW	50350 AAW	MABLS	10//99-12//99

AAW Average annual wage	AOH Average offered, high	ASH Average starting, high	H Hourly	M Monthly	S Special: hourly and annual
AE Average entry wage	AOL Average offered, low	ASL Average starting, low	HI Highest wage paid	MTC Median total compensation	TQ Third quartile wage
AEX Average experienced wage	APH Average pay, high range	AW Average wage paid	HR High end range	MW Median wage paid	W Weekly
AO Average offered	APL Average pay, low range	FQ First quartile wage	LR Low end range	SQ Second quartile wage	Y Yearly

Occupation/Type/Industry	Location	Per	Low	Mid	High	Source	Date
Environmental Scientist and Specialist, Including Health							
	Barnstable-Yarmouth MSA, MA	S	21.73 MW	20.56 AW	45190 AAW	MABLS	10//99-12//99
	Boston PMSA, MA-NH	S	25.31 MW	25.01 AW	52650 AAW	MABLS	10//99-12//99
	Lowell PMSA, MA-NH	S	23.85 MW	21.52 AW	49610 AAW	MABLS	10//99-12//99
	Michigan	S	21.42 MW	21.31 AW	44330 AAW	MIBLS	10//99-12//99
	Ann Arbor PMSA, MI	S	21.24 MW	21.29 AW	44180 AAW	MIBLS	10//99-12//99
	Detroit PMSA, MI	S	20.88 MW	20.22 AW	43440 AAW	MIBLS	10//99-12//99
	Grand Rapids-Muskegon-Holland MSA, MI	S	19.49 MW	19.13 AW	40530 AAW	MIBLS	10//99-12//99
	Saginaw-Bay City-Midland MSA, MI	S	19.16 MW	18.44 AW	39850 AAW	MIBLS	10//99-12//99
	Minnesota	S	21.89 MW	21.26 AW	44220 AAW	MNBLS	10//99-12//99
	Duluth-Superior MSA, MN-WI	S	23.14 MW	23.84 AW	48120 AAW	MNBLS	10//99-12//99
	Minneapolis-St. Paul MSA, MN-WI	S	19.40 MW	18.05 AW	40340 AAW	MNBLS	10//99-12//99
	Missouri	S	16.39 MW	17.38 AW	36140 AAW	MOBLS	10//99-12//99
	Kansas City MSA, MO-KS	S	20.34 MW	18.57 AW	42300 AAW	MOBLS	10//99-12//99
	St. Louis MSA, MO-IL	S	19.12 MW	17.18 AW	39770 AAW	MOBLS	10//99-12//99
	Montana	S	18.61 MW	24.37 AW	50700 AAW	MTBLS	10//99-12//99
	Omaha MSA, NE-IA	S	20.19 MW	19.90 AW	41990 AAW	NEBLS	10//99-12//99
	Nevada	S	23.52 MW	23.76 AW	49420 AAW	NVBLS	10//99-12//99
	Las Vegas MSA, NV-AZ	S	24.37 MW	24.12 AW	50700 AAW	NVBLS	10//99-12//99
	Reno MSA, NV	S	24.89 MW	25.04 AW	51780 AAW	NVBLS	10//99-12//99
	New Hampshire	S	21.54 MW	22.24 AW	46250 AAW	NHBLS	10//99-12//99
	New Jersey	S	25.84 MW	26.06 AW	54210 AAW	NJBLS	10//99-12//99
	Atlantic-Cape May PMSA, NJ	S	25.34 MW	25.76 AW	52700 AAW	NJBLS	10//99-12//99
	Bergen-Passaic PMSA, NJ	S	23.03 MW	21.80 AW	47900 AAW	NJBLS	10//99-12//99
	Middlesex-Somerset-Hunterdon PMSA, NJ	S	26.99 MW	27.70 AW	56130 AAW	NJBLS	10//99-12//99
	Monmouth-Ocean PMSA, NJ	S	23.19 MW	24.34 AW	48240 AAW	NJBLS	10//99-12//99
	Newark PMSA, NJ	S	28.57 MW	26.19 AW	59420 AAW	NJBLS	10//99-12//99
	New Mexico	S	17.99 MW	18.64 AW	38770 AAW	NMBLS	10//99-12//99
	Albuquerque MSA, NM	S	22.20 MW	20.81 AW	46180 AAW	NMBLS	10//99-12//99
	Las Cruces MSA, NM	S	17.54 MW	16.64 AW	36480 AAW	NMBLS	10//99-12//99
	Santa Fe MSA, NM	S	17.10 MW	16.96 AW	35570 AAW	NMBLS	10//99-12//99
	New York	S	22.92 MW	22.98 AW	47800 AAW	NYBLS	10//99-12//99
	Albany-Schenectady-Troy MSA, NY	S	25.58 MW	24.75 AW	53200 AAW	NYBLS	10//99-12//99
	Binghamton MSA, NY	S	20.50 MW	15.07 AW	42640 AAW	NYBLS	10//99-12//99
	Buffalo-Niagara Falls MSA, NY	S	20.68 MW	18.97 AW	43010 AAW	NYBLS	10//99-12//99
	Dutchess County PMSA, NY	S	21.38 MW	21.84 AW	44470 AAW	NYBLS	10//99-12//99
	Glens Falls MSA, NY	S	15.79 MW	13.66 AW	32840 AAW	NYBLS	10//99-12//99
	Nassau-Suffolk PMSA, NY	S	22.04 MW	20.12 AW	45840 AAW	NYBLS	10//99-12//99
	New York PMSA, NY	S	24.74 MW	24.34 AW	51460 AAW	NYBLS	10//99-12//99
	Rochester MSA, NY	S	18.88 MW	16.49 AW	39260 AAW	NYBLS	10//99-12//99
	Syracuse MSA, NY	S	14.23 MW	13.15 AW	29600 AAW	NYBLS	10//99-12//99
	North Carolina	S	20.11 MW	23.32 AW	48520 AAW	NCBLS	10//99-12//99
	Asheville MSA, NC	S	16.82 MW	15.87 AW	34980 AAW	NCBLS	10//99-12//99
	Charlotte-Gastonia-Rock Hill MSA, NC-SC	S	24.90 MW	24.21 AW	51790 AAW	NCBLS	10//99-12//99
	Greensboro--Winston-Salem--High Point MSA, NC	S	18.21 MW	16.68 AW	37880 AAW	NCBLS	10//99-12//99
	Raleigh-Durham-Chapel Hill MSA, NC	S	26.40 MW	22.97 AW	54900 AAW	NCBLS	10//99-12//99
	Wilmington MSA, NC	S	17.15 MW	16.34 AW	35670 AAW	NCBLS	10//99-12//99
	Ohio	S	20.22 MW	20.84 AW	43350 AAW	OHBLS	10//99-12//99
	Akron PMSA, OH	S	16.82 MW	17.24 AW	34980 AAW	OHBLS	10//99-12//99
	Cincinnati PMSA, OH-KY-IN	S	20.21 MW	18.74 AW	42040 AAW	OHBLS	10//99-12//99
	Cleveland-Lorain-Elyria PMSA, OH	S	18.31 MW	17.92 AW	38090 AAW	OHBLS	10//99-12//99
	Columbus MSA, OH	S	21.70 MW	20.00 AW	45130 AAW	OHBLS	10//99-12//99
	Dayton-Springfield MSA, OH	S	23.41 MW	22.76 AW	48700 AAW	OHBLS	10//99-12//99
	Toledo MSA, OH	S	19.68 MW	16.41 AW	40930 AAW	OHBLS	10//99-12//99
	Youngstown-Warren MSA, OH	S	17.30 MW	16.99 AW	35990 AAW	OHBLS	10//99-12//99
	Tulsa MSA, OK	S	17.93 MW	15.86 AW	37300 AAW	OKBLS	10//99-12//99
	Oregon	S	26.59 MW	26.15 AW	54390 AAW	ORBLS	10//99-12//99
	Eugene-Springfield MSA, OR	S	29.30 MW	30.29 AW	60950 AAW	ORBLS	10//99-12//99
	Pennsylvania	S	21.33 MW	22.70 AW	47210 AAW	PABLS	10//99-12//99
	Harrisburg-Lebanon-Carlisle MSA, PA	S	21.56 MW	20.30 AW	44840 AAW	PABLS	10//99-12//99

AAW Average annual wage	AOH Average offered, high	ASH Average starting, high	H Hourly	M Monthly	S Special: hourly and annual
AE Average entry wage	AOL Average offered, low	ASL Average starting, low	HI Highest wage paid	MTC Median total compensation	TQ Third quartile wage
AEX Average experienced wage	APH Average pay, high range	AW Average wage paid	HR High end range	MW Median wage paid	W Weekly
AO Average offered	APL Average pay, low range	FQ First quartile wage	LR Low end range	SQ Second quartile wage	Y Yearly

Occupation/Type/Industry	Location	Per	Low	Mid	High	Source	Date
Environmental Scientist and Specialist, Including Health	Lancaster MSA, PA	S	20.52 MW	15.29 AW	42680 AAW	PABLS	10//99-12//99
	Philadelphia PMSA, PA-NJ	S	24.36 MW	24.46 AW	50670 AAW	PABLS	10//99-12//99
	Pittsburgh MSA, PA	S	18.77 MW	16.65 AW	39030 AAW	PABLS	10//99-12//99
	Providence-Fall River-Warwick MSA, RI-MA	S	24.58 MW	24.35 AW	51130 AAW	RIBLS	10//99-12//99
	South Carolina	S	18.75 MW	19.58 AW	40720 AAW	SCBLS	10//99-12//99
	Charleston-North Charleston MSA, SC	S	22.20 MW	21.75 AW	46180 AAW	SCBLS	10//99-12//99
	Greenville-Spartanburg-Anderson MSA, SC	S	20.20 MW	20.23 AW	42010 AAW	SCBLS	10//99-12//99
	Knoxville MSA, TN	S	15.78 MW	14.33 AW	32820 AAW	TNBLS	10//99-12//99
	Memphis MSA, TN-AR-MS	S	20.87 MW	18.88 AW	43410 AAW	MSBLS	10//99-12//99
	Nashville MSA, TN	S	17.04 MW	16.67 AW	35440 AAW	TNBLS	10//99-12//99
	Texas	S	20.25 MW	22.38 AW	46560 AAW	TXBLS	10//99-12//99
	Austin-San Marcos MSA, TX	S	19.60 MW	18.91 AW	40780 AAW	TXBLS	10//99-12//99
	Beaumont-Port Arthur MSA, TX	S	22.25 MW	23.46 AW	46270 AAW	TXBLS	10//99-12//99
	Corpus Christi MSA, TX	S	23.33 MW	19.74 AW	48520 AAW	TXBLS	10//99-12//99
	El Paso MSA, TX	S	15.37 MW	14.75 AW	31980 AAW	TXBLS	10//99-12//99
	Fort Worth-Arlington PMSA, TX	S	17.18 MW	15.31 AW	35720 AAW	TXBLS	10//99-12//99
	Houston PMSA, TX	S	25.86 MW	23.64 AW	53800 AAW	TXBLS	10//99-12//99
	San Antonio MSA, TX	S	17.02 MW	16.37 AW	35400 AAW	TXBLS	10//99-12//99
	Utah	S	19.94 MW	20.57 AW	42790 AAW	UTBLS	10//99-12//99
	Salt Lake City-Ogden MSA, UT	S	20.60 MW	19.98 AW	42840 AAW	UTBLS	10//99-12//99
	Virginia	S	20.82 MW	23.52 AW	48910 AAW	VABLS	10//99-12//99
	Norfolk-Virginia Beach-Newport News MSA, VA-NC	S	19.63 MW	19.09 AW	40820 AAW	VABLS	10//99-12//99
	Washington	S	20.65 MW	21.90 AW	45560 AAW	WABLS	10//99-12//99
	Bellingham MSA, WA	S	28.83 MW	30.04 AW	59960 AAW	WABLS	10//99-12//99
	Richland-Kennewick-Pasco MSA, WA	S	29.96 MW	26.97 AW	62310 AAW	WABLS	10//99-12//99
	Seattle-Bellevue-Everett PMSA, WA	S	20.53 MW	18.54 AW	42710 AAW	WABLS	10//99-12//99
	Tacoma PMSA, WA	S	26.83 MW	28.92 AW	55800 AAW	WABLS	10//99-12//99
	West Virginia	S	16.32 MW	16.91 AW	35170 AAW	WVBLS	10//99-12//99
	Huntington-Ashland MSA, WV-KY-OH	S	24.34 MW	20.88 AW	50630 AAW	WVBLS	10//99-12//99
	Wisconsin	S	19.9 MW	20.23 AW	42080 AAW	WIBLS	10//99-12//99
	Appleton-Oshkosh-Neenah MSA, WI	S	22.40 MW	21.97 AW	46590 AAW	WIBLS	10//99-12//99
	Green Bay MSA, WI	S	21.59 MW	20.35 AW	44900 AAW	WIBLS	10//99-12//99
	Milwaukee-Waukesha PMSA, WI	S	20.32 MW	19.63 AW	42270 AAW	WIBLS	10//99-12//99
	Wausau MSA, WI	S	18.38 MW	21.62 AW	38240 AAW	WIBLS	10//99-12//99
	Wyoming	S	15.32 MW	16.29 AW	33880 AAW	WYBLS	10//99-12//99
	Puerto Rico	S	17.89 MW	19.23 AW	39990 AAW	PRBLS	10//99-12//99
	San Juan-Bayamon PMSA, PR	S	18.85 MW	17.75 AW	39210 AAW	PRBLS	10//99-12//99
	Guam	S	17.59 MW	19.89 AW	41360 AAW	GUBLS	10//99-12//99
Epidemiologist	California	S	21.67 MW	21.97 AW	45700 AAW	CABLS	10//99-12//99
	Florida	S	23.75 MW	24.37 AW	50680 AAW	FLBLS	10//99-12//99
	Georgia	S	24.04 MW	26.65 AW	55430 AAW	GABLS	10//99-12//99
	Illinois	S	21.27 MW	22.10 AW	45960 AAW	ILBLS	10//99-12//99
	Maryland	S	26.04 MW	30.35 AW	63130 AAW	MDBLS	10//99-12//99
	Baltimore PMSA, MD	S	31.33 MW	27.07 AW	65170 AAW	MDBLS	10//99-12//99
	Boston PMSA, MA-NH	S	24.95 MW	25.12 AW	51890 AAW	MABLS	10//99-12//99
	Michigan	S	22.62 MW	21.91 AW	45580 AAW	MIBLS	10//99-12//99
	Minnesota	S	32.67 MW	33.19 AW	69040 AAW	MNBLS	10//99-12//99
	Minneapolis-St. Paul MSA, MN-WI	S	33.88 MW	33.50 AW	70470 AAW	MNBLS	10//99-12//99
	Mississippi	S	12.92 MW	13.35 AW	27760 AAW	MSBLS	10//99-12//99
	Missouri	S	21.89 MW	22.91 AW	47640 AAW	MOBLS	10//99-12//99
	North Carolina	S	19.98 MW	20.25 AW	42120 AAW	NCBLS	10//99-12//99
	Pennsylvania	S	24 MW	24.33 AW	50600 AAW	PABLS	10//99-12//99
	Texas	S	22.05 MW	23.48 AW	48850 AAW	TXBLS	10//99-12//99
	Salt Lake City-Ogden MSA, UT	S	19.36 MW	18.96 AW	40280 AAW	UTBLS	10//99-12//99
	Washington	S	25.98 MW	26.19 AW	54470 AAW	WABLS	10//99-12//99

AAW Average annual wage	**AOH** Average offered, high	**ASH** Average starting, high	**H** Hourly	**M** Monthly	**S** Special: hourly and annual
AE Average entry wage	**AOL** Average offered, low	**ASL** Average starting, low	**HI** Highest wage paid	**MTC** Median total compensation	**TQ** Third quartile wage
AEX Average experienced wage	**APH** Average pay, high range	**AW** Average wage paid	**HR** High end range	**MW** Median wage paid	**W** Weekly
AO Average offered	**APL** Average pay, low range	**FQ** First quartile wage	**LR** Low end range	**SQ** Second quartile wage	**Y** Yearly

Occupation/Type/Industry	Location	Per	Low	Mid	High	Source	Date
Epidemiologist	Seattle-Bellevue-Everett PMSA, WA	S	25.90 MW	25.56 AW	53880 AAW	WABLS	10//99-12//99
	Wisconsin	S	23.48 MW	23.28 AW	48410 AAW	WIBLS	10//99-12//99
Etcher and Engraver	Alabama	S	8.74 MW	9.57 AW	19900 AAW	ALBLS	10//99-12//99
	Alaska	S	9.67 MW	10.03 AW	20860 AAW	AKBLS	10//99-12//99
	Arizona	S	10 MW	9.97 AW	20740 AAW	AZBLS	10//99-12//99
	Arkansas	S	9.17 MW	9.93 AW	20660 AAW	ARBLS	10//99-12//99
	California	S	9.55 MW	10.52 AW	21880 AAW	CABLS	10//99-12//99
	Colorado	S	9.6 MW	9.87 AW	20530 AAW	COBLS	10//99-12//99
	Connecticut	S	11.02 MW	11.25 AW	23390 AAW	CTBLS	10//99-12//99
	Florida	S	8.93 MW	10.12 AW	21050 AAW	FLBLS	10//99-12//99
	Georgia	S	10.21 MW	10.34 AW	21500 AAW	GABLS	10//99-12//99
	Hawaii	S	7.86 MW	9.39 AW	19520 AAW	HIBLS	10//99-12//99
	Illinois	S	12.22 MW	14.28 AW	29700 AAW	ILBLS	10//99-12//99
	Indiana	S	9.16 MW	10.14 AW	21090 AAW	INBLS	10//99-12//99
	Iowa	S	10.64 MW	10.18 AW	21170 AAW	IABLS	10//99-12//99
	Kansas	S	8.5 MW	8.47 AW	17620 AAW	KSBLS	10//99-12//99
	Kentucky	S	10.36 MW	12.02 AW	25000 AAW	KYBLS	10//99-12//99
	Maryland	S	10.43 MW	11.05 AW	22990 AAW	MDBLS	10//99-12//99
	Massachusetts	S	10.53 MW	11.54 AW	24000 AAW	MABLS	10//99-12//99
	Michigan	S	9.88 MW	10.60 AW	22040 AAW	MIBLS	10//99-12//99
	Minnesota	S	11.79 MW	12.69 AW	26390 AAW	MNBLS	10//99-12//99
	Missouri	S	9.73 MW	10.17 AW	21150 AAW	MOBLS	10//99-12//99
	New Jersey	S	13.61 MW	13.82 AW	28750 AAW	NJBLS	10//99-12//99
	New York	S	10.41 MW	11.02 AW	22920 AAW	NYBLS	10//99-12//99
	North Carolina	S	8.54 MW	9.72 AW	20210 AAW	NCBLS	10//99-12//99
	Ohio	S	10.29 MW	10.82 AW	22510 AAW	OHBLS	10//99-12//99
	Oklahoma	S	7.67 MW	7.76 AW	16140 AAW	OKBLS	10//99-12//99
	Pennsylvania	S	10.56 MW	10.70 AW	22250 AAW	PABLS	10//99-12//99
	Rhode Island	S	18.11 MW	19.62 AW	40810 AAW	RIBLS	10//99-12//99
	South Carolina	S	8.08 MW	8.65 AW	17990 AAW	SCBLS	10//99-12//99
	South Dakota	S	8.24 MW	8.15 AW	16960 AAW	SDBLS	10//99-12//99
	Tennessee	S	12.2 MW	11.57 AW	24070 AAW	TNBLS	10//99-12//99
	Texas	S	7.86 MW	8.59 AW	17870 AAW	TXBLS	10//99-12//99
	Utah	S	9.04 MW	9.63 AW	20040 AAW	UTBLS	10//99-12//99
	Virginia	S	7.96 MW	8.87 AW	18450 AAW	VABLS	10//99-12//99
	Washington	S	7.81 MW	8.58 AW	17850 AAW	WABLS	10//99-12//99
	Wisconsin	S	10.06 MW	11.30 AW	23510 AAW	WIBLS	10//99-12//99
	Puerto Rico	S	6.39 MW	6.94 AW	14440 AAW	PRBLS	10//99-12//99
Excavating and Loading Machine and Dragline Operator	Alabama	S	12.41 MW	14.46 AW	30070 AAW	ALBLS	10//99-12//99
	Birmingham MSA, AL	S	16.09 MW	13.05 AW	33470 AAW	ALBLS	10//99-12//99
	Florence MSA, AL	S	11.23 MW	11.84 AW	23370 AAW	ALBLS	10//99-12//99
	Mobile MSA, AL	S	10.76 MW	10.89 AW	22390 AAW	ALBLS	10//99-12//99
	Montgomery MSA, AL	S	10.85 MW	10.61 AW	22580 AAW	ALBLS	10//99-12//99
	Alaska	S	24.82 MW	23.67 AW	49230 AAW	AKBLS	10//99-12//99
	Anchorage MSA, AK	S	19.34 MW	17.80 AW	40220 AAW	AKBLS	10//99-12//99
	Arizona	S	14.85 MW	15.50 AW	32240 AAW	AZBLS	10//99-12//99
	Flagstaff MSA, AZ-UT	S	15.25 MW	15.97 AW	31730 AAW	AZBLS	10//99-12//99
	Phoenix-Mesa MSA, AZ	S	16.83 MW	15.76 AW	35000 AAW	AZBLS	10//99-12//99
	Arkansas	S	10.75 MW	10.57 AW	21990 AAW	ARBLS	10//99-12//99
	Fayetteville-Springdale-Rogers MSA, AR	S	12.19 MW	11.60 AW	25350 AAW	ARBLS	10//99-12//99
	Fort Smith MSA, AR-OK	S	11.33 MW	11.46 AW	23560 AAW	ARBLS	10//99-12//99
	Little Rock-North Little Rock MSA, AR	S	11.14 MW	11.04 AW	23170 AAW	ARBLS	10//99-12//99
	California	S	17.98 MW	19.51 AW	40580 AAW	CABLS	10//99-12//99
	Bakersfield MSA, CA	S	14.96 MW	14.02 AW	31120 AAW	CABLS	10//99-12//99
	Los Angeles-Long Beach PMSA, CA	S	19.76 MW	19.52 AW	41090 AAW	CABLS	10//99-12//99
	Modesto MSA, CA	S	19.07 MW	14.00 AW	39670 AAW	CABLS	10//99-12//99
	Oakland PMSA, CA	S	25.17 MW	24.48 AW	52350 AAW	CABLS	10//99-12//99
	Orange County PMSA, CA	S	19.59 MW	19.79 AW	40750 AAW	CABLS	10//99-12//99
	Riverside-San Bernardino PMSA, CA	S	18.00 MW	17.64 AW	37440 AAW	CABLS	10//99-12//99
	Sacramento PMSA, CA	S	17.69 MW	16.07 AW	36790 AAW	CABLS	10//99-12//99
	San Diego MSA, CA	S	23.81 MW	25.15 AW	49520 AAW	CABLS	10//99-12//99
	San Francisco PMSA, CA	S	26.90 MW	28.57 AW	55960 AAW	CABLS	10//99-12//99
	San Jose PMSA, CA	S	24.16 MW	25.41 AW	50260 AAW	CABLS	10//99-12//99

AAW Average annual wage	AOH Average offered, high	ASH Average starting, high	H Hourly	M Monthly	S Special: hourly and annual
AE Average entry wage	AOL Average offered, low	ASL Average starting, low	HI Highest wage paid	MTC Median total compensation	TQ Third quartile wage
AEX Average experienced wage	APH Average pay, high range	AW Average wage paid	HR High end range	MW Median wage paid	W Weekly
AO Average offered	APL Average pay, low range	FQ First quartile wage	LR Low end range	SQ Second quartile wage	Y Yearly

Occupation/Type/Industry	Location	Per	Low	Mid	High	Source	Date
Excavating and Loading Machine and Dragline Operator	Santa Barbara-Santa Maria-Lompoc MSA, CA	S	15.21 MW	14.92 AW	31640 AAW	CABLS	10//99-12//99
	Santa Rosa PMSA, CA	S	18.71 MW	18.55 AW	38910 AAW	CABLS	10//99-12//99
	Ventura PMSA, CA	S	23.12 MW	22.66 AW	48100 AAW	CABLS	10//99-12//99
	Yolo PMSA, CA	S	20.81 MW	19.67 AW	43270 AAW	CABLS	10//99-12//99
	Colorado	S	14.57 MW	14.91 AW	31020 AAW	COBLS	10//99-12//99
	Colorado Springs MSA, CO	S	15.08 MW	15.24 AW	31360 AAW	COBLS	10//99-12//99
	Denver PMSA, CO	S	16.06 MW	15.60 AW	33400 AAW	COBLS	10//99-12//99
	Fort Collins-Loveland MSA, CO	S	13.92 MW	13.52 AW	28950 AAW	COBLS	10//99-12//99
	Grand Junction MSA, CO	S	15.31 MW	14.66 AW	31850 AAW	COBLS	10//99-12//99
	Greeley PMSA, CO	S	14.62 MW	14.28 AW	30400 AAW	COBLS	10//99-12//99
	Connecticut	S	16.74 MW	17.58 AW	36560 AAW	CTBLS	10//99-12//99
	Bridgeport PMSA, CT	S	20.91 MW	19.67 AW	43500 AAW	CTBLS	10//99-12//99
	Hartford MSA, CT	S	16.56 MW	16.21 AW	34450 AAW	CTBLS	10//99-12//99
	Stamford-Norwalk PMSA, CT	S	18.60 MW	18.71 AW	38690 AAW	CTBLS	10//99-12//99
	Delaware	S	11.77 MW	12.77 AW	26570 AAW	DEBLS	10//99-12//99
	Wilmington-Newark PMSA, DE-MD	S	14.64 MW	15.82 AW	30460 AAW	DEBLS	10//99-12//99
	Washington PMSA, DC-MD-VA-WV	S	13.87 MW	13.92 AW	28850 AAW	DCBLS	10//99-12//99
	Florida	S	11.73 MW	12.25 AW	25490 AAW	FLBLS	10//99-12//99
	Fort Lauderdale PMSA, FL	S	15.48 MW	15.00 AW	32190 AAW	FLBLS	10//99-12//99
	Fort Myers-Cape Coral MSA, FL	S	11.98 MW	12.20 AW	24910 AAW	FLBLS	10//99-12//99
	Lakeland-Winter Haven MSA, FL	S	12.67 MW	12.12 AW	26350 AAW	FLBLS	10//99-12//99
	Miami PMSA, FL	S	12.64 MW	11.87 AW	26280 AAW	FLBLS	10//99-12//99
	Ocala MSA, FL	S	13.48 MW	12.08 AW	28050 AAW	FLBLS	10//99-12//99
	Orlando MSA, FL	S	11.02 MW	11.23 AW	22930 AAW	FLBLS	10//99-12//99
	Sarasota-Bradenton MSA, FL	S	11.68 MW	11.47 AW	24300 AAW	FLBLS	10//99-12//99
	Tallahassee MSA, FL	S	11.83 MW	11.66 AW	24600 AAW	FLBLS	10//99-12//99
	Tampa-St. Petersburg-Clearwater MSA, FL	S	11.62 MW	11.25 AW	24160 AAW	FLBLS	10//99-12//99
	West Palm Beach-Boca Raton MSA, FL	S	12.15 MW	11.79 AW	25270 AAW	FLBLS	10//99-12//99
	Georgia	S	12.73 MW	12.89 AW	26810 AAW	GABLS	10//99-12//99
	Albany MSA, GA	S	11.39 MW	11.05 AW	23690 AAW	GABLS	10//99-12//99
	Athens MSA, GA	S	12.83 MW	12.75 AW	26700 AAW	GABLS	10//99-12//99
	Atlanta MSA, GA	S	13.69 MW	13.21 AW	28470 AAW	GABLS	10//99-12//99
	Augusta-Aiken MSA, GA-SC	S	12.27 MW	11.38 AW	25520 AAW	GABLS	10//99-12//99
	Columbus MSA, GA-AL	S	12.54 MW	12.33 AW	26090 AAW	GABLS	10//99-12//99
	Macon MSA, GA	S	13.09 MW	12.64 AW	27220 AAW	WABLS	10//99-12//99
	Savannah MSA, GA	S	12.56 MW	12.26 AW	26130 AAW	GABLS	10//99-12//99
	Hawaii	S	28.93 MW	26.98 AW	56120 AAW	HIBLS	10//99-12//99
	Idaho	S	13.97 MW	14.04 AW	29200 AAW	IDBLS	10//99-12//99
	Boise City MSA, ID	S	13.69 MW	13.61 AW	28480 AAW	IDBLS	10//99-12//99
	Illinois	S	17.13 MW	18.13 AW	37700 AAW	ILBLS	10//99-12//99
	Chicago PMSA, IL	S	20.79 MW	19.21 AW	43250 AAW	ILBLS	10//99-12//99
	Kankakee PMSA, IL	S	19.94 MW	18.99 AW	41480 AAW	ILBLS	10//99-12//99
	Peoria-Pekin MSA, IL	S	20.07 MW	21.08 AW	41750 AAW	ILBLS	10//99-12//99
	Rockford MSA, IL	S	20.67 MW	18.72 AW	43000 AAW	ILBLS	10//99-12//99
	Indiana	S	15.7 MW	16.87 AW	35080 AAW	INBLS	10//99-12//99
	Evansville-Henderson MSA, IN-KY	S	18.13 MW	17.74 AW	37710 AAW	INBLS	10//99-12//99
	Fort Wayne MSA, IN	S	16.61 MW	15.73 AW	34540 AAW	INBLS	10//99-12//99
	Gary PMSA, IN	S	20.75 MW	21.87 AW	43160 AAW	INBLS	10//99-12//99
	Indianapolis MSA, IN	S	15.34 MW	14.31 AW	31900 AAW	INBLS	10//99-12//99
	Lafayette MSA, IN	S	17.60 MW	15.90 AW	36610 AAW	INBLS	10//99-12//99
	Terre Haute MSA, IN	S	15.74 MW	12.88 AW	32730 AAW	INBLS	10//99-12//99
	Iowa	S	13.05 MW	13.69 AW	28480 AAW	IABLS	10//99-12//99
	Cedar Rapids MSA, IA	S	16.03 MW	15.88 AW	33350 AAW	IABLS	10//99-12//99
	Des Moines MSA, IA	S	15.71 MW	16.54 AW	32680 AAW	IABLS	10//99-12//99
	Iowa City MSA, IA	S	17.04 MW	15.33 AW	35440 AAW	IABLS	10//99-12//99
	Kansas	S	13.53 MW	14.46 AW	30080 AAW	KSBLS	10//99-12//99
	Lawrence MSA, KS	S	13.91 MW	13.75 AW	28930 AAW	KSBLS	10//99-12//99
	Topeka MSA, KS	S	12.74 MW	12.10 AW	26500 AAW	KSBLS	10//99-12//99
	Wichita MSA, KS	S	13.86 MW	13.36 AW	28820 AAW	KSBLS	10//99-12//99
	Kentucky	S	12.94 MW	14.15 AW	29440 AAW	KYBLS	10//99-12//99
	Lexington MSA, KY	S	17.75 MW	16.25 AW	36920 AAW	KYBLS	10//99-12//99
	Louisville MSA, KY-IN	S	15.62 MW	15.36 AW	32490 AAW	KYBLS	10//99-12//99

AAW Average annual wage	AOH Average offered, high	ASH Average starting, high	H Hourly	M Monthly	S Special: hourly and annual
AE Average entry wage	AOL Average offered, low	ASL Average starting, low	HI Highest wage paid	MTC Median total compensation	TQ Third quartile wage
AEX Average experienced wage	APH Average pay, high range	AW Average wage paid	HR High end range	MW Median wage paid	W Weekly
AO Average offered	APL Average pay, low range	FQ First quartile wage	LR Low end range	SQ Second quartile wage	Y Yearly

Occupation/Type/Industry	Location	Per	Low	Mid	High	Source	Date
Excavating and Loading Machine and Dragline Operator	Louisiana	S	11.42 MW	11.56 AW	24040 AAW	LABLS	10//99-12//99
	Alexandria MSA, LA	S	11.40 MW	11.57 AW	23720 AAW	LABLS	10//99-12//99
	Baton Rouge MSA, LA	S	11.43 MW	11.72 AW	23770 AAW	LABLS	10//99-12//99
	Lafayette MSA, LA	S	11.39 MW	11.27 AW	23690 AAW	LABLS	10//99-12//99
	Lake Charles MSA, LA	S	11.60 MW	11.04 AW	24140 AAW	LABLS	10//99-12//99
	New Orleans MSA, LA	S	11.63 MW	11.62 AW	24190 AAW	LABLS	10//99-12//99
	Shreveport-Bossier City MSA, LA	S	11.73 MW	11.92 AW	24390 AAW	LABLS	10//99-12//99
	Maine	S	11.9 MW	12.43 AW	25850 AAW	MEBLS	10//99-12//99
	Bangor MSA, ME	S	16.68 MW	16.07 AW	34700 AAW	MEBLS	10//99-12//99
	Portland MSA, ME	S	13.02 MW	12.67 AW	27090 AAW	MEBLS	10//99-12//99
	Maryland	S	13.87 MW	13.79 AW	28680 AAW	MDBLS	10//99-12//99
	Baltimore PMSA, MD	S	13.26 MW	13.31 AW	27580 AAW	MDBLS	10//99-12//99
	Massachusetts	S	17.35 MW	19.10 AW	39730 AAW	MABLS	10//99-12//99
	Barnstable-Yarmouth MSA, MA	S	16.72 MW	17.38 AW	34790 AAW	MABLS	10//99-12//99
	Boston PMSA, MA-NH	S	20.14 MW	17.46 AW	41890 AAW	MABLS	10//99-12//99
	Brockton PMSA, MA	S	21.14 MW	19.90 AW	43970 AAW	MABLS	10//99-12//99
	Fitchburg-Leominster PMSA, MA	S	16.60 MW	16.91 AW	34530 AAW	MABLS	10//99-12//99
	Lawrence PMSA, MA-NH	S	16.92 MW	15.02 AW	35200 AAW	MABLS	10//99-12//99
	Lowell PMSA, MA-NH	S	20.05 MW	18.73 AW	41700 AAW	MABLS	10//99-12//99
	Springfield MSA, MA	S	17.21 MW	16.49 AW	35800 AAW	MABLS	10//99-12//99
	Worcester PMSA, MA-CT	S	16.92 MW	17.14 AW	35190 AAW	MABLS	10//99-12//99
	Michigan	S	15.28 MW	15.64 AW	32530 AAW	MIBLS	10//99-12//99
	Ann Arbor PMSA, MI	S	16.10 MW	15.84 AW	33500 AAW	MIBLS	10//99-12//99
	Benton Harbor MSA, MI	S	14.54 MW	13.55 AW	30240 AAW	MIBLS	10//99-12//99
	Detroit PMSA, MI	S	19.64 MW	19.70 AW	40850 AAW	MIBLS	10//99-12//99
	Grand Rapids-Muskegon-Holland MSA, MI	S	14.83 MW	16.00 AW	30850 AAW	MIBLS	10//99-12//99
	Jackson MSA, MI	S	13.70 MW	11.83 AW	28500 AAW	MIBLS	10//99-12//99
	Kalamazoo-Battle Creek MSA, MI	S	14.97 MW	14.98 AW	31130 AAW	MIBLS	10//99-12//99
	Lansing-East Lansing MSA, MI	S	16.72 MW	17.40 AW	34770 AAW	MIBLS	10//99-12//99
	Minnesota	S	18.36 MW	18.29 AW	38050 AAW	MNBLS	10//99-12//99
	Duluth-Superior MSA, MN-WI	S	17.66 MW	17.98 AW	36730 AAW	MNBLS	10//99-12//99
	Minneapolis-St. Paul MSA, MN-WI	S	20.86 MW	21.42 AW	43380 AAW	MNBLS	10//99-12//99
	St. Cloud MSA, MN	S	14.20 MW	14.31 AW	29530 AAW	MNBLS	10//99-12//99
	Mississippi	S	11.48 MW	12.24 AW	25450 AAW	MSBLS	10//99-12//99
	Jackson MSA, MS	S	13.61 MW	12.54 AW	28310 AAW	MSBLS	10//99-12//99
	Missouri	S	16.74 MW	17.00 AW	35370 AAW	MOBLS	10//99-12//99
	Kansas City MSA, MO-KS	S	19.39 MW	18.76 AW	40330 AAW	MOBLS	10//99-12//99
	St. Louis MSA, MO-IL	S	18.96 MW	21.08 AW	39430 AAW	MOBLS	10//99-12//99
	Montana	S	15.08 MW	15.64 AW	32540 AAW	MTBLS	10//99-12//99
	Nebraska	S	13.13 MW	13.81 AW	28730 AAW	NEBLS	10//99-12//99
	Omaha MSA, NE-IA	S	14.84 MW	15.03 AW	30860 AAW	NEBLS	10//99-12//99
	Nevada	S	16.27 MW	18.48 AW	38440 AAW	NVBLS	10//99-12//99
	Las Vegas MSA, NV-AZ	S	18.72 MW	15.91 AW	38930 AAW	NVBLS	10//99-12//99
	New Hampshire	S	14.7 MW	14.83 AW	30850 AAW	NHBLS	10//99-12//99
	Nashua PMSA, NH	S	14.49 MW	14.44 AW	30130 AAW	NHBLS	10//99-12//99
	Portsmouth-Rochester PMSA, NH-ME	S	14.82 MW	14.01 AW	30830 AAW	NHBLS	10//99-12//99
	New Jersey	S	18.82 MW	20.32 AW	42270 AAW	NJBLS	10//99-12//99
	Bergen-Passaic PMSA, NJ	S	21.50 MW	20.14 AW	44720 AAW	NJBLS	10//99-12//99
	Jersey City PMSA, NJ	S	25.75 MW	28.55 AW	53570 AAW	NJBLS	10//99-12//99
	Middlesex-Somerset-Hunterdon PMSA, NJ	S	19.96 MW	18.63 AW	41510 AAW	NJBLS	10//99-12//99
	Monmouth-Ocean PMSA, NJ	S	18.32 MW	18.13 AW	38100 AAW	NJBLS	10//99-12//99
	Newark PMSA, NJ	S	19.98 MW	18.92 AW	41570 AAW	NJBLS	10//99-12//99
	New Mexico	S	12.41 MW	13.21 AW	27490 AAW	NMBLS	10//99-12//99
	Albuquerque MSA, NM	S	12.81 MW	12.39 AW	26640 AAW	NMBLS	10//99-12//99
	Las Cruces MSA, NM	S	8.65 MW	8.90 AW	17990 AAW	NMBLS	10//99-12//99
	New York	S	19.54 MW	20.30 AW	42230 AAW	NYBLS	10//99-12//99
	Albany-Schenectady-Troy MSA, NY	S	16.13 MW	13.76 AW	33560 AAW	NYBLS	10//99-12//99
	Binghamton MSA, NY	S	14.61 MW	13.44 AW	30390 AAW	NYBLS	10//99-12//99
	Buffalo-Niagara Falls MSA, NY	S	19.34 MW	18.84 AW	40220 AAW	NYBLS	10//99-12//99
	Dutchess County PMSA, NY	S	19.35 MW	18.27 AW	40250 AAW	NYBLS	10//99-12//99
	New York PMSA, NY	S	29.62 MW	32.15 AW	61600 AAW	NYBLS	10//99-12//99

Occupation/Type/Industry	Location	Per	Low	Mid	High	Source	Date
Excavating and Loading Machine and Dragline Operator							
	Rochester MSA, NY	S	12.68 MW	12.71 AW	26370 AAW	NYBLS	10//99-12//99
	North Carolina	S	11.45 MW	11.85 AW	24660 AAW	NCBLS	10//99-12//99
	Charlotte-Gastonia-Rock Hill MSA, NC-SC	S	12.33 MW	11.50 AW	25660 AAW	NCBLS	10//99-12//99
	Fayetteville MSA, NC	S	14.16 MW	13.67 AW	29450 AAW	NCBLS	10//99-12//99
	Greensboro--Winston-Salem--High Point MSA, NC	S	11.94 MW	12.23 AW	24840 AAW	NCBLS	10//99-12//99
	Hickory-Morganton-Lenoir MSA, NC	S	12.99 MW	12.77 AW	27010 AAW	NCBLS	10//99-12//99
	Raleigh-Durham-Chapel Hill MSA, NC	S	13.68 MW	12.71 AW	28450 AAW	NCBLS	10//99-12//99
	Wilmington MSA, NC	S	12.43 MW	12.22 AW	25850 AAW	NCBLS	10//99-12//99
	North Dakota	S	15.87 MW	16.53 AW	34380 AAW	NDBLS	10//99-12//99
	Ohio	S	15.87 MW	16.63 AW	34600 AAW	OHBLS	10//99-12//99
	Canton-Massillon MSA, OH	S	16.70 MW	16.29 AW	34740 AAW	OHBLS	10//99-12//99
	Cincinnati PMSA, OH-KY-IN	S	16.56 MW	15.93 AW	34450 AAW	OHBLS	10//99-12//99
	Cleveland-Lorain-Elyria PMSA, OH	S	19.26 MW	19.68 AW	40060 AAW	OHBLS	10//99-12//99
	Columbus MSA, OH	S	17.05 MW	16.57 AW	35450 AAW	OHBLS	10//99-12//99
	Steubenville-Weirton MSA, OH-WV	S	17.26 MW	17.78 AW	35890 AAW	OHBLS	10//99-12//99
	Toledo MSA, OH	S	16.97 MW	15.90 AW	35300 AAW	OHBLS	10//99-12//99
	Youngstown-Warren MSA, OH	S	15.74 MW	16.83 AW	32730 AAW	OHBLS	10//99-12//99
	Oklahoma	S	11.2 MW	11.52 AW	23970 AAW	OKBLS	10//99-12//99
	Enid MSA, OK	S	13.04 MW	12.75 AW	27120 AAW	OKBLS	10//99-12//99
	Oklahoma City MSA, OK	S	11.05 MW	10.94 AW	22990 AAW	OKBLS	10//99-12//99
	Tulsa MSA, OK	S	12.96 MW	12.33 AW	26950 AAW	OKBLS	10//99-12//99
	Oregon	S	16.4 MW	17.51 AW	36420 AAW	ORBLS	10//99-12//99
	Corvallis MSA, OR	S	15.05 MW	14.81 AW	31310 AAW	ORBLS	10//99-12//99
	Eugene-Springfield MSA, OR	S	16.38 MW	14.55 AW	34070 AAW	ORBLS	10//99-12//99
	Portland-Vancouver PMSA, OR-WA	S	18.85 MW	18.43 AW	39200 AAW	ORBLS	10//99-12//99
	Salem PMSA, OR	S	18.87 MW	18.25 AW	39250 AAW	ORBLS	10//99-12//99
	Pennsylvania	S	13.84 MW	14.51 AW	30190 AAW	PABLS	10//99-12//99
	Allentown-Bethlehem-Easton MSA, PA	S	16.13 MW	16.10 AW	33540 AAW	PABLS	10//99-12//99
	Altoona MSA, PA	S	11.96 MW	10.79 AW	24880 AAW	PABLS	10//99-12//99
	Harrisburg-Lebanon-Carlisle MSA, PA	S	14.53 MW	13.18 AW	30220 AAW	PABLS	10//99-12//99
	Johnstown MSA, PA	S	13.20 MW	13.50 AW	27460 AAW	PABLS	10//99-12//99
	Philadelphia PMSA, PA-NJ	S	17.96 MW	17.32 AW	37350 AAW	PABLS	10//99-12//99
	Pittsburgh MSA, PA	S	14.46 MW	13.33 AW	30080 AAW	PABLS	10//99-12//99
	Reading MSA, PA	S	14.94 MW	14.72 AW	31060 AAW	PABLS	10//99-12//99
	Scranton--Wilkes-Barre--Hazleton MSA, PA	S	13.80 MW	13.16 AW	28710 AAW	PABLS	10//99-12//99
	York MSA, PA	S	15.22 MW	15.05 AW	31650 AAW	PABLS	10//99-12//99
	Rhode Island	S	17.94 MW	17.70 AW	36820 AAW	RIBLS	10//99-12//99
	Providence-Fall River-Warwick MSA, RI-MA	S	17.96 MW	17.92 AW	37350 AAW	RIBLS	10//99-12//99
	South Carolina	S	11.84 MW	12.24 AW	25450 AAW	SCBLS	10//99-12//99
	Charleston-North Charleston MSA, SC	S	12.62 MW	12.40 AW	26250 AAW	SCBLS	10//99-12//99
	Columbia MSA, SC	S	12.01 MW	11.57 AW	24970 AAW	SCBLS	10//99-12//99
	Greenville-Spartanburg-Anderson MSA, SC	S	12.18 MW	11.70 AW	25340 AAW	SCBLS	10//99-12//99
	Myrtle Beach MSA, SC	S	10.56 MW	10.19 AW	21960 AAW	SCBLS	10//99-12//99
	South Dakota	S	12.04 MW	12.19 AW	25360 AAW	SDBLS	10//99-12//99
	Rapid City MSA, SD	S	12.24 MW	12.06 AW	25450 AAW	SDBLS	10//99-12//99
	Sioux Falls MSA, SD	S	12.38 MW	11.91 AW	25740 AAW	SDBLS	10//99-12//99
	Tennessee	S	12.05 MW	12.13 AW	25220 AAW	TNBLS	10//99-12//99
	Chattanooga MSA, TN-GA	S	12.67 MW	12.60 AW	26350 AAW	TNBLS	10//99-12//99
	Johnson City-Kingsport-Bristol MSA, TN-VA	S	10.50 MW	10.71 AW	21840 AAW	TNBLS	10//99-12//99
	Knoxville MSA, TN	S	11.00 MW	10.90 AW	22870 AAW	TNBLS	10//99-12//99
	Memphis MSA, TN-AR-MS	S	12.27 MW	11.60 AW	25510 AAW	MSBLS	10//99-12//99
	Nashville MSA, TN	S	12.88 MW	12.88 AW	26780 AAW	TNBLS	10//99-12//99
	Texas	S	10.93 MW	11.28 AW	23470 AAW	TXBLS	10//99-12//99
	Austin-San Marcos MSA, TX	S	11.34 MW	11.19 AW	23580 AAW	TXBLS	10//99-12//99
	Beaumont-Port Arthur MSA, TX	S	11.41 MW	11.24 AW	23730 AAW	TXBLS	10//99-12//99
	Brazoria PMSA, TX	S	11.58 MW	10.37 AW	24080 AAW	TXBLS	10//99-12//99

AAW Average annual wage	**AOH** Average offered, high	**ASH** Average starting, high	**H** Hourly	**M** Monthly	**S** Special: hourly and annual
AE Average entry wage	**AOL** Average offered, low	**ASL** Average starting, low	**HI** Highest wage paid	**MTC** Median total compensation	**TQ** Third quartile wage
AEX Average experienced wage	**APH** Average pay, high range	**AW** Average wage paid	**HR** High end range	**MW** Median wage paid	**W** Weekly
AO Average offered	**APL** Average pay, low range	**FQ** First quartile wage	**LR** Low end range	**SQ** Second quartile wage	**Y** Yearly

Occupation/Type/Industry	Location	Per	Low	Mid	High	Source	Date
Excavating and Loading Machine and Dragline Operator	Corpus Christi MSA, TX	S	10.53 MW	10.24 AW	21900 AAW	TXBLS	10//99-12//99
	Dallas PMSA, TX	S	11.51 MW	11.27 AW	23940 AAW	TXBLS	10//99-12//99
	Fort Worth-Arlington PMSA, TX	S	13.90 MW	12.88 AW	28910 AAW	TXBLS	10//99-12//99
	Houston PMSA, TX	S	11.43 MW	11.01 AW	23780 AAW	TXBLS	10//99-12//99
	Longview-Marshall MSA, TX	S	14.52 MW	14.26 AW	30190 AAW	TXBLS	10//99-12//99
	McAllen-Edinburg-Mission MSA, TX	S	8.86 MW	8.90 AW	18430 AAW	TXBLS	10//99-12//99
	Odessa-Midland MSA, TX	S	11.82 MW	10.91 AW	24590 AAW	TXBLS	10//99-12//99
	San Antonio MSA, TX	S	10.48 MW	10.04 AW	21790 AAW	TXBLS	10//99-12//99
	Waco MSA, TX	S	10.83 MW	10.87 AW	22530 AAW	TXBLS	10//99-12//99
	Utah	S	15.36 MW	16.09 AW	33460 AAW	UTBLS	10//99-12//99
	Vermont	S	11.23 MW	11.50 AW	23920 AAW	VTBLS	10//99-12//99
	Burlington MSA, VT	S	11.68 MW	11.47 AW	24290 AAW	VTBLS	10//99-12//99
	Virginia	S	12.15 MW	12.44 AW	25870 AAW	VABLS	10//99-12//99
	Lynchburg MSA, VA	S	11.02 MW	11.03 AW	22910 AAW	VABLS	10//99-12//99
	Norfolk-Virginia Beach-Newport News MSA, VA-NC	S	13.03 MW	12.53 AW	27100 AAW	VABLS	10//99-12//99
	Richmond-Petersburg MSA, VA	S	11.77 MW	11.39 AW	24480 AAW	VABLS	10//99-12//99
	Roanoke MSA, VA	S	11.45 MW	11.24 AW	23810 AAW	VABLS	10//99-12//99
	Washington	S	18.75 MW	19.35 AW	40250 AAW	WABLS	10//99-12//99
	Bellingham MSA, WA	S	17.19 MW	16.66 AW	35750 AAW	WABLS	10//99-12//99
	Seattle-Bellevue-Everett PMSA, WA	S	19.38 MW	18.71 AW	40300 AAW	WABLS	10//99-12//99
	Tacoma PMSA, WA	S	21.79 MW	21.50 AW	45310 AAW	WABLS	10//99-12//99
	West Virginia	S	14.72 MW	15.18 AW	31580 AAW	WVBLS	10//99-12//99
	Charleston MSA, WV	S	15.19 MW	13.46 AW	31600 AAW	WVBLS	10//99-12//99
	Huntington-Ashland MSA, WV-KY-OH	S	14.10 MW	12.67 AW	29320 AAW	WVBLS	10//99-12//99
	Parkersburg-Marietta MSA, WV-OH	S	13.28 MW	14.33 AW	27620 AAW	WVBLS	10//99-12//99
	Wheeling MSA, WV-OH	S	13.63 MW	12.70 AW	28350 AAW	WVBLS	10//99-12//99
	Wisconsin	S	15.6 MW	17.20 AW	35770 AAW	WIBLS	10//99-12//99
	Appleton-Oshkosh-Neenah MSA, WI	S	17.47 MW	16.27 AW	36340 AAW	WIBLS	10//99-12//99
	Eau Claire MSA, WI	S	18.95 MW	21.21 AW	39420 AAW	WIBLS	10//99-12//99
	Green Bay MSA, WI	S	19.17 MW	16.05 AW	39880 AAW	WIBLS	10//99-12//99
	Madison MSA, WI	S	18.88 MW	18.68 AW	39270 AAW	WIBLS	10//99-12//99
	Milwaukee-Waukesha PMSA, WI	S	16.43 MW	15.38 AW	34180 AAW	WIBLS	10//99-12//99
	Wyoming	S	20.52 MW	18.99 AW	39490 AAW	WYBLS	10//99-12//99
	Cheyenne MSA, WY	S	10.66 MW	11.27 AW	22180 AAW	WYBLS	10//99-12//99
	Puerto Rico	S	8.39 MW	8.39 AW	17450 AAW	PRBLS	10//99-12//99
	Aguadilla MSA, PR	S	6.48 MW	6.38 AW	13480 AAW	PRBLS	10//99-12//99
	Arecibo PMSA, PR	S	6.59 MW	6.55 AW	13700 AAW	PRBLS	10//99-12//99
	Caguas PMSA, PR	S	8.20 MW	8.22 AW	17050 AAW	PRBLS	10//99-12//99
	Mayaguez MSA, PR	S	9.55 MW	8.68 AW	19860 AAW	PRBLS	10//99-12//99
	Ponce MSA, PR	S	7.48 MW	7.35 AW	15550 AAW	PRBLS	10//99-12//99
	San Juan-Bayamon PMSA, PR	S	8.84 MW	8.81 AW	18390 AAW	PRBLS	10//99-12//99
	Guam	S	11.52 MW	11.52 AW	23960 AAW	GUBLS	10//99-12//99
Executive							
International Facility	United States	Y		69407 AW		BOM	1998
Executive Secretary and Administrative Assistant	Alabama	S	12.01 MW	12.58 AW	26160 AAW	ALBLS	10//99-12//99
	Anniston MSA, AL	S	10.89 MW	10.10 AW	22650 AAW	ALBLS	10//99-12//99
	Auburn-Opelika MSA, AL	S	10.82 MW	10.43 AW	22490 AAW	ALBLS	10//99-12//99
	Birmingham MSA, AL	S	13.73 MW	13.29 AW	28560 AAW	ALBLS	10//99-12//99
	Decatur MSA, AL	S	12.38 MW	11.82 AW	25750 AAW	ALBLS	10//99-12//99
	Dothan MSA, AL	S	11.17 MW	10.81 AW	23230 AAW	ALBLS	10//99-12//99
	Florence MSA, AL	S	11.11 MW	10.48 AW	23100 AAW	ALBLS	10//99-12//99
	Gadsden MSA, AL	S	10.27 MW	9.99 AW	21370 AAW	ALBLS	10//99-12//99
	Huntsville MSA, AL	S	12.75 MW	12.11 AW	26510 AAW	ALBLS	10//99-12//99
	Mobile MSA, AL	S	11.85 MW	11.59 AW	24650 AAW	ALBLS	10//99-12//99
	Montgomery MSA, AL	S	12.93 MW	11.63 AW	26890 AAW	ALBLS	10//99-12//99
	Tuscaloosa MSA, AL	S	11.10 MW	10.44 AW	23090 AAW	ALBLS	10//99-12//99
	Alaska	S	16 MW	16.70 AW	34740 AAW	AKBLS	10//99-12//99
	Anchorage MSA, AK	S	15.79 MW	14.90 AW	32840 AAW	AKBLS	10//99-12//99

AAW Average annual wage	AOH Average offered, high	ASH Average starting, high	H Hourly	M Monthly	S Special: hourly and annual
AE Average entry salary	AOL Average offered, low	ASL Average starting, low	HI Highest wage paid	MTC Median total compensation	TQ Third quartile wage
AEX Average experienced wage	APH Average pay, high range	AW Average wage paid	HR High end range	MW Median wage paid	W Weekly
AO Average offered	APL Average pay, low range	FQ First quartile wage	LR Low end range	SQ Second quartile wage	Y Yearly

Occupation/Type/Industry	Location	Per	Low	Mid	High	Source	Date
Executive Secretary and Administrative Assistant	Arizona	S	13.45 MW	14.16 AW	29460 AAW	AZBLS	10//99-12//99
	Flagstaff MSA, AZ-UT	S	13.42 MW	12.60 AW	27900 AAW	AZBLS	10//99-12//99
	Phoenix-Mesa MSA, AZ	S	14.69 MW	14.06 AW	30560 AAW	AZBLS	10//99-12//99
	Tucson MSA, AZ	S	12.65 MW	12.38 AW	26320 AAW	AZBLS	10//99-12//99
	Yuma MSA, AZ	S	12.33 MW	11.43 AW	25640 AAW	AZBLS	10//99-12//99
	Arkansas	S	11.94 MW	12.44 AW	25880 AAW	ARBLS	10//99-12//99
	Fayetteville-Springdale-Rogers MSA, AR	S	11.58 MW	11.10 AW	24080 AAW	ARBLS	10//99-12//99
	Fort Smith MSA, AR-OK	S	12.51 MW	11.59 AW	26030 AAW	ARBLS	10//99-12//99
	Jonesboro MSA, AR	S	13.81 MW	12.25 AW	28730 AAW	ARBLS	10//99-12//99
	Little Rock-North Little Rock MSA, AR	S	13.20 MW	12.57 AW	27460 AAW	ARBLS	10//99-12//99
	Pine Bluff MSA, AR	S	11.75 MW	11.53 AW	24440 AAW	ARBLS	10//99-12//99
	California	S	15.93 MW	16.65 AW	34630 AAW	CABLS	10//99-12//99
	Bakersfield MSA, CA	S	14.40 MW	13.99 AW	29950 AAW	CABLS	10//99-12//99
	Chico-Paradise MSA, CA	S	12.02 MW	10.66 AW	25000 AAW	CABLS	10//99-12//99
	Fresno MSA, CA	S	16.09 MW	15.19 AW	33470 AAW	CABLS	10//99-12//99
	Los Angeles-Long Beach PMSA, CA	S	16.75 MW	16.23 AW	34840 AAW	CABLS	10//99-12//99
	Merced MSA, CA	S	12.55 MW	10.59 AW	26100 AAW	CABLS	10//99-12//99
	Modesto MSA, CA	S	14.15 MW	13.90 AW	29420 AAW	CABLS	10//99-12//99
	Oakland PMSA, CA	S	17.74 MW	16.72 AW	36910 AAW	CABLS	10//99-12//99
	Orange County PMSA, CA	S	17.02 MW	16.51 AW	35390 AAW	CABLS	10//99-12//99
	Redding MSA, CA	S	13.78 MW	12.34 AW	28660 AAW	CABLS	10//99-12//99
	Riverside-San Bernardino PMSA, CA	S	14.93 MW	14.69 AW	31060 AAW	CABLS	10//99-12//99
	Sacramento PMSA, CA	S	14.11 MW	13.82 AW	29360 AAW	CABLS	10//99-12//99
	Salinas MSA, CA	S	15.05 MW	14.71 AW	31300 AAW	CABLS	10//99-12//99
	San Diego MSA, CA	S	15.27 MW	14.66 AW	31750 AAW	CABLS	10//99-12//99
	San Francisco PMSA, CA	S	17.64 MW	16.39 AW	36680 AAW	CABLS	10//99-12//99
	San Jose PMSA, CA	S	20.45 MW	20.19 AW	42540 AAW	CABLS	10//99-12//99
	San Luis Obispo-Atascadero-Paso Robles MSA, CA	S	13.14 MW	12.19 AW	27330 AAW	CABLS	10//99-12//99
	Santa Barbara-Santa Maria-Lompoc MSA, CA	S	15.13 MW	14.83 AW	31480 AAW	CABLS	10//99-12//99
	Santa Cruz-Watsonville PMSA, CA	S	15.58 MW	15.32 AW	32400 AAW	CABLS	10//99-12//99
	Santa Rosa PMSA, CA	S	15.68 MW	14.91 AW	32620 AAW	CABLS	10//99-12//99
	Stockton-Lodi MSA, CA	S	15.41 MW	14.49 AW	32060 AAW	CABLS	10//99-12//99
	Vallejo-Fairfield-Napa PMSA, CA	S	13.35 MW	13.24 AW	27770 AAW	CABLS	10//99-12//99
	Ventura PMSA, CA	S	16.88 MW	15.69 AW	35110 AAW	CABLS	10//99-12//99
	Visalia-Tulare-Porterville MSA, CA	S	14.43 MW	13.59 AW	30010 AAW	CABLS	10//99-12//99
	Yolo PMSA, CA	S	13.55 MW	12.94 AW	28170 AAW	CABLS	10//99-12//99
	Yuba City MSA, CA	S	14.93 MW	14.25 AW	31060 AAW	CABLS	10//99-12//99
	Colorado	S	15.31 MW	15.70 AW	32660 AAW	COBLS	10//99-12//99
	Boulder-Longmont PMSA, CO	S	16.50 MW	15.73 AW	34320 AAW	COBLS	10//99-12//99
	Colorado Springs MSA, CO	S	14.81 MW	14.39 AW	30810 AAW	COBLS	10//99-12//99
	Denver PMSA, CO	S	16.15 MW	15.66 AW	33600 AAW	COBLS	10//99-12//99
	Fort Collins-Loveland MSA, CO	S	13.07 MW	12.72 AW	27190 AAW	COBLS	10//99-12//99
	Grand Junction MSA, CO	S	12.49 MW	11.32 AW	25980 AAW	COBLS	10//99-12//99
	Greeley PMSA, CO	S	14.40 MW	14.40 AW	29950 AAW	COBLS	10//99-12//99
	Pueblo MSA, CO	S	14.87 MW	15.36 AW	30940 AAW	COBLS	10//99-12//99
	Connecticut	S	16.64 MW	17.42 AW	36240 AAW	CTBLS	10//99-12//99
	Bridgeport PMSA, CT	S	16.05 MW	15.60 AW	33390 AAW	CTBLS	10//99-12//99
	Danbury PMSA, CT	S	15.76 MW	15.41 AW	32780 AAW	CTBLS	10//99-12//99
	Hartford MSA, CT	S	17.77 MW	17.15 AW	36960 AAW	CTBLS	10//99-12//99
	New Haven-Meriden PMSA, CT	S	15.98 MW	15.64 AW	33230 AAW	CTBLS	10//99-12//99
	New London-Norwich MSA, CT-RI	S	14.34 MW	14.06 AW	29820 AAW	CTBLS	10//99-12//99
	Stamford-Norwalk PMSA, CT	S	19.91 MW	19.11 AW	41400 AAW	CTBLS	10//99-12//99
	Waterbury PMSA, CT	S	16.37 MW	15.81 AW	34040 AAW	CTBLS	10//99-12//99
	Delaware	S	14.87 MW	15.30 AW	31830 AAW	DEBLS	10//99-12//99
	Dover MSA, DE	S	12.29 MW	12.13 AW	25560 AAW	DEBLS	10//99-12//99
	Wilmington-Newark PMSA, DE-MD	S	15.90 MW	15.30 AW	33060 AAW	DEBLS	10//99-12//99
	District of Columbia	S	15.08 MW	16.50 AW	34320 AAW	DCBLS	10//99-12//99

Occupation/Type/Industry	Location	Per	Low	Mid	High	Source	Date
Executive Secretary and Administrative Assistant	Washington PMSA, DC-MD-VA-WV	S	16.24 MW	15.39 AW	33780 AAW	DCBLS	10//99-12//99
	Florida	S	12.93 MW	13.55 AW	28180 AAW	FLBLS	10//99-12//99
	Daytona Beach MSA, FL	S	12.54 MW	12.23 AW	26090 AAW	FLBLS	10//99-12//99
	Fort Lauderdale PMSA, FL	S	14.52 MW	13.94 AW	30210 AAW	FLBLS	10//99-12//99
	Fort Myers-Cape Coral MSA, FL	S	13.78 MW	13.57 AW	28660 AAW	FLBLS	10//99-12//99
	Fort Pierce-Port St. Lucie MSA, FL	S	13.35 MW	12.77 AW	27760 AAW	FLBLS	10//99-12//99
	Fort Walton Beach MSA, FL	S	12.61 MW	11.25 AW	26220 AAW	FLBLS	10//99-12//99
	Gainesville MSA, FL	S	12.86 MW	12.41 AW	26750 AAW	FLBLS	10//99-12//99
	Jacksonville MSA, FL	S	13.26 MW	12.74 AW	27580 AAW	FLBLS	10//99-12//99
	Lakeland-Winter Haven MSA, FL	S	11.91 MW	11.64 AW	24780 AAW	FLBLS	10//99-12//99
	Melbourne-Titusville-Palm Bay MSA, FL	S	11.92 MW	11.61 AW	24790 AAW	FLBLS	10//99-12//99
	Miami PMSA, FL	S	14.64 MW	13.77 AW	30440 AAW	FLBLS	10//99-12//99
	Naples MSA, FL	S	14.08 MW	13.91 AW	29290 AAW	FLBLS	10//99-12//99
	Ocala MSA, FL	S	12.15 MW	11.57 AW	25270 AAW	FLBLS	10//99-12//99
	Orlando MSA, FL	S	13.70 MW	12.91 AW	28500 AAW	FLBLS	10//99-12//99
	Panama City MSA, FL	S	11.95 MW	11.82 AW	24860 AAW	FLBLS	10//99-12//99
	Pensacola MSA, FL	S	11.12 MW	10.36 AW	23130 AAW	FLBLS	10//99-12//99
	Punta Gorda MSA, FL	S	11.14 MW	10.39 AW	23160 AAW	FLBLS	10//99-12//99
	Sarasota-Bradenton MSA, FL	S	12.10 MW	11.80 AW	25170 AAW	FLBLS	10//99-12//99
	Tallahassee MSA, FL	S	13.06 MW	12.84 AW	27170 AAW	FLBLS	10//99-12//99
	Tampa-St. Petersburg-Clearwater MSA, FL	S	13.19 MW	12.80 AW	27440 AAW	FLBLS	10//99-12//99
	West Palm Beach-Boca Raton MSA, FL	S	15.05 MW	14.66 AW	31300 AAW	FLBLS	10//99-12//99
	Georgia	S	13.39 MW	14.19 AW	29510 AAW	GABLS	10//99-12//99
	Albany MSA, GA	S	13.35 MW	12.46 AW	27760 AAW	GABLS	10//99-12//99
	Atlanta MSA, GA	S	14.99 MW	14.28 AW	31170 AAW	GABLS	10//99-12//99
	Augusta-Aiken MSA, GA-SC	S	13.38 MW	11.67 AW	27820 AAW	GABLS	10//99-12//99
	Columbus MSA, GA-AL	S	11.79 MW	11.87 AW	24510 AAW	GABLS	10//99-12//99
	Macon MSA, GA	S	12.25 MW	11.52 AW	25480 AAW	GABLS	10//99-12//99
	Savannah MSA, GA	S	12.50 MW	12.15 AW	25990 AAW	GABLS	10//99-12//99
	Hawaii	S	15.34 MW	15.87 AW	33020 AAW	HIBLS	10//99-12//99
	Honolulu MSA, HI	S	15.99 MW	15.42 AW	33260 AAW	HIBLS	10//99-12//99
	Idaho	S	12.12 MW	12.29 AW	25560 AAW	IDBLS	10//99-12//99
	Boise City MSA, ID	S	12.88 MW	12.72 AW	26780 AAW	IDBLS	10//99-12//99
	Pocatello MSA, ID	S	12.23 MW	12.11 AW	25430 AAW	IDBLS	10//99-12//99
	Illinois	S	14.06 MW	14.49 AW	30130 AAW	ILBLS	10//99-12//99
	Bloomington-Normal MSA, IL	S	14.32 MW	14.59 AW	29790 AAW	ILBLS	10//99-12//99
	Champaign-Urbana MSA, IL	S	12.56 MW	11.44 AW	26130 AAW	ILBLS	10//99-12//99
	Chicago PMSA, IL	S	15.24 MW	14.71 AW	31700 AAW	ILBLS	10//99-12//99
	Decatur MSA, IL	S	9.47 MW	9.11 AW	19700 AAW	ILBLS	10//99-12//99
	Kankakee PMSA, IL	S	11.31 MW	10.70 AW	23530 AAW	ILBLS	10//99-12//99
	Peoria-Pekin MSA, IL	S	12.73 MW	12.57 AW	26480 AAW	ILBLS	10//99-12//99
	Rockford MSA, IL	S	12.71 MW	12.51 AW	26440 AAW	ILBLS	10//99-12//99
	Indiana	S	13.15 MW	13.50 AW	28090 AAW	INBLS	10//99-12//99
	Bloomington MSA, IN	S	11.82 MW	11.66 AW	24590 AAW	INBLS	10//99-12//99
	Elkhart-Goshen MSA, IN	S	13.21 MW	12.79 AW	27470 AAW	INBLS	10//99-12//99
	Evansville-Henderson MSA, IN-KY	S	12.84 MW	12.91 AW	26710 AAW	INBLS	10//99-12//99
	Fort Wayne MSA, IN	S	13.96 MW	13.89 AW	29040 AAW	INBLS	10//99-12//99
	Gary PMSA, IN	S	14.42 MW	14.07 AW	29990 AAW	INBLS	10//99-12//99
	Indianapolis MSA, IN	S	14.76 MW	14.45 AW	30710 AAW	INBLS	10//99-12//99
	Kokomo MSA, IN	S	15.04 MW	13.44 AW	31290 AAW	INBLS	10//99-12//99
	Lafayette MSA, IN	S	16.49 MW	17.37 AW	34300 AAW	INBLS	10//99-12//99
	Muncie MSA, IN	S	12.37 MW	11.70 AW	25720 AAW	INBLS	10//99-12//99
	South Bend MSA, IN	S	12.72 MW	12.39 AW	26450 AAW	INBLS	10//99-12//99
	Terre Haute MSA, IN	S	12.33 MW	11.44 AW	25640 AAW	INBLS	10//99-12//99
	Iowa	S	12.62 MW	12.94 AW	26920 AAW	IABLS	10//99-12//99
	Cedar Rapids MSA, IA	S	12.04 MW	11.75 AW	25030 AAW	IABLS	10//99-12//99
	Davenport-Moline-Rock Island MSA, IA-IL	S	11.75 MW	11.34 AW	24440 AAW	IABLS	10//99-12//99
	Des Moines MSA, IA	S	14.63 MW	14.42 AW	30430 AAW	IABLS	10//99-12//99
	Dubuque MSA, IA	S	10.70 MW	10.73 AW	22260 AAW	IABLS	10//99-12//99
	Iowa City MSA, IA	S	11.48 MW	10.71 AW	23880 AAW	IABLS	10//99-12//99
	Sioux City MSA, IA-NE	S	11.83 MW	10.91 AW	24610 AAW	IABLS	10//99-12//99
	Waterloo-Cedar Falls MSA, IA	S	12.87 MW	12.44 AW	26760 AAW	IABLS	10//99-12//99

AAW Average annual wage	**AOH** Average offered, high	**ASH** Average starting, high	**H** Hourly	**M** Monthly	**S** Special: hourly and annual
AE Average entry wage	**AOL** Average offered, low	**ASL** Average starting, low	**HI** Highest wage paid	**MTC** Median total compensation	**TQ** Third quartile wage
AEX Average experienced wage	**APH** Average pay, high range	**AW** Average wage paid	**HR** High end range	**MW** Median wage paid	**W** Weekly
AO Average offered	**APL** Average pay, low range	**FQ** First quartile wage	**LR** Low end range	**SQ** Second quartile wage	**Y** Yearly

Occupation/Type/Industry	Location	Per	Low	Mid	High	Source	Date
Executive Secretary and Administrative Assistant	Kansas	S	14.46 MW	14.64 AW	30460 AAW	KSBLS	10//99-12//99
	Lawrence MSA, KS	S	14.48 MW	14.49 AW	30120 AAW	KSBLS	10//99-12//99
	Topeka MSA, KS	S	13.39 MW	12.86 AW	27850 AAW	KSBLS	10//99-12//99
	Wichita MSA, KS	S	15.33 MW	14.98 AW	31880 AAW	KSBLS	10//99-12//99
	Kentucky	S	12.55 MW	13.04 AW	27110 AAW	KYBLS	10//99-12//99
	Lexington MSA, KY	S	13.25 MW	13.18 AW	27560 AAW	KYBLS	10//99-12//99
	Louisville MSA, KY-IN	S	13.14 MW	12.48 AW	27330 AAW	KYBLS	10//99-12//99
	Owensboro MSA, KY	S	11.53 MW	11.04 AW	23980 AAW	KYBLS	10//99-12//99
	Louisiana	S	12.47 MW	12.90 AW	26840 AAW	LABLS	10//99-12//99
	Alexandria MSA, LA	S	11.74 MW	11.81 AW	24420 AAW	LABLS	10//99-12//99
	Baton Rouge MSA, LA	S	13.62 MW	13.24 AW	28330 AAW	LABLS	10//99-12//99
	Houma MSA, LA	S	12.03 MW	11.29 AW	25030 AAW	LABLS	10//99-12//99
	Lafayette MSA, LA	S	11.32 MW	11.18 AW	23550 AAW	LABLS	10//99-12//99
	Lake Charles MSA, LA	S	13.36 MW	13.01 AW	27790 AAW	LABLS	10//99-12//99
	Monroe MSA, LA	S	10.76 MW	9.79 AW	22380 AAW	LABLS	10//99-12//99
	New Orleans MSA, LA	S	13.09 MW	12.65 AW	27230 AAW	LABLS	10//99-12//99
	Shreveport-Bossier City MSA, LA	S	13.00 MW	12.42 AW	27040 AAW	LABLS	10//99-12//99
	Maine	S	12.38 MW	12.95 AW	26930 AAW	MEBLS	10//99-12//99
	Bangor MSA, ME	S	11.58 MW	11.36 AW	24090 AAW	MEBLS	10//99-12//99
	Lewiston-Auburn MSA, ME	S	12.39 MW	11.59 AW	25780 AAW	MEBLS	10//99-12//99
	Portland MSA, ME	S	13.39 MW	12.82 AW	27860 AAW	MEBLS	10//99-12//99
	Baltimore PMSA, MD	S	16.01 MW	15.49 AW	33290 AAW	MDBLS	10//99-12//99
	Hagerstown PMSA, MD	S	14.65 MW	14.91 AW	30480 AAW	MDBLS	10//99-12//99
	Massachusetts	S	15.63 MW	16.24 AW	33790 AAW	MABLS	10//99-12//99
	Barnstable-Yarmouth MSA, MA	S	13.16 MW	12.74 AW	27380 AAW	MABLS	10//99-12//99
	Boston PMSA, MA-NH	S	16.89 MW	16.09 AW	35130 AAW	MABLS	10//99-12//99
	Brockton PMSA, MA	S	15.47 MW	15.18 AW	32170 AAW	MABLS	10//99-12//99
	Fitchburg-Leominster PMSA, MA	S	16.13 MW	17.18 AW	33540 AAW	MABLS	10//99-12//99
	Lawrence PMSA, MA-NH	S	15.21 MW	14.93 AW	31640 AAW	MABLS	10//99-12//99
	Lowell PMSA, MA-NH	S	15.53 MW	14.99 AW	32300 AAW	MABLS	10//99-12//99
	New Bedford PMSA, MA	S	12.94 MW	12.77 AW	26920 AAW	MABLS	10//99-12//99
	Pittsfield MSA, MA	S	12.66 MW	12.61 AW	26320 AAW	MABLS	10//99-12//99
	Springfield MSA, MA	S	13.60 MW	13.28 AW	28290 AAW	MABLS	10//99-12//99
	Worcester PMSA, MA-CT	S	15.80 MW	15.24 AW	32860 AAW	MABLS	10//99-12//99
	Michigan	S	14.61 MW	15.41 AW	32040 AAW	MIBLS	10//99-12//99
	Ann Arbor PMSA, MI	S	15.22 MW	14.82 AW	31660 AAW	MIBLS	10//99-12//99
	Benton Harbor MSA, MI	S	14.79 MW	13.87 AW	30760 AAW	MIBLS	10//99-12//99
	Detroit PMSA, MI	S	16.14 MW	15.34 AW	33570 AAW	MIBLS	10//99-12//99
	Flint PMSA, MI	S	14.29 MW	12.81 AW	29720 AAW	MIBLS	10//99-12//99
	Grand Rapids-Muskegon-Holland MSA, MI	S	14.19 MW	13.35 AW	29520 AAW	MIBLS	10//99-12//99
	Jackson MSA, MI	S	14.14 MW	13.81 AW	29400 AAW	MIBLS	10//99-12//99
	Kalamazoo-Battle Creek MSA, MI	S	15.28 MW	14.79 AW	31790 AAW	MIBLS	10//99-12//99
	Lansing-East Lansing MSA, MI	S	16.13 MW	16.54 AW	33550 AAW	MIBLS	10//99-12//99
	Saginaw-Bay City-Midland MSA, MI	S	14.41 MW	13.68 AW	29980 AAW	MIBLS	10//99-12//99
	Minnesota	S	14.76 MW	15.20 AW	31610 AAW	MNBLS	10//99-12//99
	Duluth-Superior MSA, MN-WI	S	13.98 MW	13.25 AW	29080 AAW	MNBLS	10//99-12//99
	Minneapolis-St. Paul MSA, MN-WI	S	15.71 MW	15.27 AW	32670 AAW	MNBLS	10//99-12//99
	Rochester MSA, MN	S	13.14 MW	12.67 AW	27340 AAW	MNBLS	10//99-12//99
	St. Cloud MSA, MN	S	12.15 MW	10.74 AW	25270 AAW	MNBLS	10//99-12//99
	Mississippi	S	11.75 MW	12.41 AW	25810 AAW	MSBLS	10//99-12//99
	Biloxi-Gulfport-Pascagoula MSA, MS	S	11.47 MW	10.64 AW	23860 AAW	MSBLS	10//99-12//99
	Hattiesburg MSA, MS	S	10.66 MW	10.14 AW	22160 AAW	MSBLS	10//99-12//99
	Jackson MSA, MS	S	13.09 MW	12.65 AW	27220 AAW	MSBLS	10//99-12//99
	Missouri	S	13.24 MW	14.11 AW	29340 AAW	MOBLS	10//99-12//99
	Joplin MSA, MO	S	11.94 MW	11.59 AW	24830 AAW	MOBLS	10//99-12//99
	Kansas City MSA, MO-KS	S	14.47 MW	14.33 AW	30100 AAW	MOBLS	10//99-12//99
	St. Joseph MSA, MO	S	12.29 MW	12.18 AW	25560 AAW	MOBLS	10//99-12//99
	St. Louis MSA, MO-IL	S	15.23 MW	14.24 AW	31690 AAW	MOBLS	10//99-12//99
	Springfield MSA, MO	S	12.09 MW	11.60 AW	25150 AAW	MOBLS	10//99-12//99
	Montana	S	10.47 MW	11.19 AW	23260 AAW	MTBLS	10//99-12//99
	Billings MSA, MT	S	10.89 MW	10.06 AW	22640 AAW	MTBLS	10//99-12//99
	Great Falls MSA, MT	S	10.36 MW	10.00 AW	21550 AAW	MTBLS	10//99-12//99
	Missoula MSA, MT	S	10.55 MW	9.94 AW	21940 AAW	MTBLS	10//99-12//99

AAW Average annual wage	**AOH** Average offered, high	**ASH** Average starting, high	**H** Hourly	**M** Monthly	**S** Special: hourly and annual
AE Average entry wage	**AOL** Average offered, low	**ASL** Average starting, low	**HI** Highest wage paid	**MTC** Median total compensation	**TQ** Third quartile wage
AEX Average experienced wage	**APH** Average pay, high range	**AW** Average wage paid	**HR** High end range	**MW** Median wage paid	**W** Weekly
AO Average offered	**APL** Average pay, low range	**FQ** First quartile wage	**LR** Low end range	**SQ** Second quartile wage	**Y** Yearly

Left Page

Industry	Location	Per	Low	Mid			
	Milwaukee-Waukesha PMSA, WI	S	14.28 MW				
	Racine PMSA, WI	S	12.33 MW				
	Sheboygan MSA, WI	S	11.70 MW				
	Wausau MSA, WI	S	11.18 MW				
	Wyoming	S	11.4 MW				
	Casper MSA, WY	S	12.68 MW				
	Cheyenne MSA, WY	S	11.41 MW	11.36			
	Puerto Rico	S	9.52 MW	10.19 AW			
	Aguadilla MSA, PR	S	8.43 MW	8.24 AW	17260		
	Arecibo PMSA, PR	S	8.30 MW	7.62 AW	17520		
	Caguas PMSA, PR	S	8.42 MW	7.68 AW	19210 AAW	PRBL	
	Mayaguez MSA, PR	S	9.24 MW	9.35 AW	18350	PRBLS	
	Ponce MSA, PR	S	8.82 MW	8.76 AW	22140 AAW	PRBLS	
	San Juan-Bayamon PMSA, PR	S	10.64 MW	9.91 AW	28660 AAW	VIBLS	10//9
	Virgin Islands	S	13.06 MW	13.78 AW	24870 AAW	GUBLS	10//99-12/9
	Guam	S	11.7 MW	11.96 AW			

rker, Ordnance xpert, and Blaster

	Location	Per	Low	Mid		Source	Date
	Alabama	S	15.62 MW	15.58 AW	32400 AAW	ALBLS	10//99-12//99
	Alaska	S	22.35 MW	21.77 AW	45280 AAW	AKBLS	10//99-12//99
	Arizona	S	16.49 MW	17.35 AW	36090 AAW	AZBLS	10//99-12//99
	California	S	15.94 MW	17.18 AW	35740 AAW	CABLS	10//99-12//99
	Colorado	S	20.51 MW	20.92 AW	43520 AAW	COBLS	10//99-12//99
	Florida	S	13.28 MW	13.40 AW	27880 AAW	FLBLS	10//99-12//99
	Georgia	S	13.89 MW	14.23 AW	29600 AAW	GABLS	10//99-12//99
	Illinois	S	18.28 MW	18.44 AW	38360 AAW	ILBLS	10//99-12//99
	Iowa	S	16.34 MW	17.26 AW	35900 AAW	IABLS	10//99-12//99
	Kansas	S	11.32 MW	11.49 AW	23910 AAW	KSBLS	10//99-12//99
	Kentucky	S	14.22 MW	14.72 AW	30620 AAW	KYBLS	10//99-12//99
	Massachusetts	S	22.52 MW	22.11 AW	46000 AAW	MABLS	10//99-12//99
	Missouri	S	13.2 MW	14.17 AW	29470 AAW	MOBLS	10//99-12//99
	Nevada	S	17.92 MW	17.35 AW	36080 AAW	NVBLS	10//99-12//99
	New Jersey	S	18.43 MW	19.04 AW	39590 AAW	NJBLS	10//99-12//99
	New York	S	14.99 MW	16.15 AW	31720 AAW	NYBLS	10//99-12//99
	North Carolina	S	14.36 MW	15.25 AW	33600 AAW	NCBLS	10//99-12//99
	Ohio	S	13.5 MW	15.60 AW	32460 AAW	OHBLS	10//99-12//99
	Oregon	S	16.91 MW	16.80 AW	34950 AAW	ORBLS	10//99-12//99
	Pennsylvania	S	15.82 MW	15.61 AW	32480 AAW	PABLS	10//99-12//99
	South Dakota	S	15.64 MW	15.76 AW	32780 AAW	SDBLS	10//99-12//99
	Tennessee	S	14.4 MW	15.11 AW	31420 AAW	TNBLS	10//99-12//99
	Texas	S	10.51 MW	11.92 AW	24790 AAW	TXBLS	10//99-12//99
	Vermont	S	14 MW	13.33 AW	27720 AAW	VTBLS	10//99-12//99
	Virginia	S	14.51 MW	15.05 AW	31300 AAW	VABLS	10//99-12//99
	Washington	S	18.84 MW	18.92 AW	39360 AAW	WABLS	10//99-12//99
	West Virginia	S	15.66 MW	17.34 AW	36060 AAW	WVBLS	10//99-12//99

xtruding and Drawing Machine Setter, Operator, and Tender

Industry	Location	Per	Low	Mid		Source	Date
Metals and Plastics	Alabama	S	11.82 MW	11.55 AW	24030 AAW	ALBLS	10//99-12//99
Metals and Plastics	Arizona	S	10.05 MW	9.80 AW	20390 AAW	AZBLS	10//99-12//99
Metals and Plastics	Phoenix-Mesa MSA, AZ	S	10.05 MW	10.50 AW	20890 AAW	AZBLS	10//99-12//99
Metals and Plastics	Arkansas	S	12.99 MW	12.61 AW	26240 AAW	ARBLS	10//99-12//99
Metals and Plastics	Fort Smith MSA, AR-OK	S	10.02 MW	9.74 AW	20840 AAW	ARBLS	10//99-12//99
Metals and Plastics	Little Rock-North Little Rock MSA, AR	S	11.43 MW	11.79 AW	23770 AAW	ARBLS	10//99-12//99
Metals and Plastics	California	S	9.33 MW	10.20 AW	21220 AAW	CABLS	10//99-12//99
Metals and Plastics	Fresno MSA, CA	S	8.88 MW	6.47 AW	18470 AAW	CABLS	10//99-12//99
Metals and Plastics	Los Angeles-Long Beach PMSA, CA	S	9.93 MW	9.24 AW	20650 AAW	CABLS	10//99-12//99
Metals and Plastics	Modesto MSA, CA	S	9.88 MW	9.82 AW	20560 AAW	CABLS	10//99-12//99
Metals and Plastics	Oakland PMSA, CA	S	10.52 MW	9.75 AW	21890 AAW	CABLS	10//99-12//99
Metals and Plastics	Orange County PMSA, CA	S	9.51 MW	8.74 AW	19780 AAW	CABLS	10//99-12//99
Metals and Plastics	Riverside-San Bernardino PMSA, CA	S	11.96 MW	10.56 AW	24870 AAW	CABLS	10//99-12//99
Metals and Plastics	Sacramento PMSA, CA	S	11.58 MW	11.29 AW	24080 AAW	CABLS	10//99-12//99
Metals and Plastics	San Diego MSA, CA	S	8.54 MW	7.96 AW	17760 AAW	CABLS	10//99-12//99
Metals and Plastics	San Jose PMSA, CA	S	11.75 MW	11.39 AW	24430 AAW	CABLS	10//99-12//99
Metals and Plastics	Ventura PMSA, CA	S	9.04 MW	8.01 AW	18800 AAW	CABLS	10//99-12//99
Metals and Plastics	Visalia-Tulare-Porterville MSA, CA	S	13.34 MW	14.52 AW	27750 AAW	CABLS	10//99-12//99

Right Page

Occupation/Type/Industry	Location	Per	Low	Mid	High	Source	Date
Executive Secretary and Administrative Assistant	Nebraska	S	11.98 MW	12.47 AW	25940 AAW	NEBLS	10//99-12//99
	Lincoln MSA, NE	S	12.59 MW	12.07 AW	26180 AAW	NEBLS	10//99-12//99
	Omaha MSA, NE-IA	S	12.94 MW	12.43 AW	26920 AAW	NEBLS	10//99-12//99
	Nevada	S	13.23 MW	14.06 AW	29240 AAW	NVBLS	10//99-12//99
	Las Vegas MSA, NV-AZ	S	14.27 MW	13.59 AW	29680 AAW	NVBLS	10//99-12//99
	Reno MSA, NV	S	13.56 MW	12.90 AW	28200 AAW	NVBLS	10//99-12//99
	New Hampshire	S	13.28 MW	14.21 AW	29560 AAW	NHBLS	10//99-12//99
	Manchester PMSA, NH	S	15.16 MW	14.47 AW	31540 AAW	NHBLS	10//99-12//99
	Nashua PMSA, NH	S	14.59 MW	14.09 AW	30350 AAW	NHBLS	10//99-12//99
	Portsmouth-Rochester PMSA, NH-ME	S	13.34 MW	13.17 AW	27750 AAW	NHBLS	10//99-12//99
	New Jersey	S	17.5 MW	18.02 AW	37470 AAW	NJBLS	10//99-12//99
	Atlantic-Cape May PMSA, NJ	S	15.90 MW	15.05 AW	33070 AAW	NJBLS	10//99-12//99
	Bergen-Passaic PMSA, NJ	S	17.48 MW	16.44 AW	36360 AAW	NJBLS	10//99-12//99
	Jersey City PMSA, NJ	S	18.21 MW	18.21 AW	37870 AAW	NJBLS	10//99-12//99
	Middlesex-Somerset-Hunterdon PMSA, NJ	S	18.75 MW	18.38 AW	39000 AAW	NJBLS	10//99-12//99
	Monmouth-Ocean PMSA, NJ	S	17.57 MW	17.59 AW	36550 AAW	NJBLS	10//99-12//99
	Newark PMSA, NJ	S	18.86 MW	18.39 AW	39230 AAW	NJBLS	10//99-12//99
	Trenton PMSA, NJ	S	18.15 MW	18.12 AW	37750 AAW	NJBLS	10//99-12//99
	Vineland-Millville-Bridgeton PMSA, NJ	S	14.89 MW	14.82 AW	30960 AAW	NJBLS	10//99-12//99
	New Mexico	S	12.31 MW	12.72 AW	26460 AAW	NMBLS	10//99-12//99
	Albuquerque MSA, NM	S	13.07 MW	13.08 AW	27190 AAW	NMBLS	10//99-12//99
	Las Cruces MSA, NM	S	11.21 MW	11.07 AW	23310 AAW	NMBLS	10//99-12//99
	Santa Fe MSA, NM	S	14.67 MW	13.01 AW	30520 AAW	NMBLS	10//99-12//99
	New York	S	15.97 MW	16.74 AW	34820 AAW	NYBLS	10//99-12//99
	Albany-Schenectady-Troy MSA, NY	S	15.64 MW	15.00 AW	32540 AAW	NYBLS	10//99-12//99
	Binghamton MSA, NY	S	12.69 MW	11.64 AW	26400 AAW	NYBLS	10//99-12//99
	Buffalo-Niagara Falls MSA, NY	S	13.32 MW	12.27 AW	27700 AAW	NYBLS	10//99-12//99
	Dutchess County PMSA, NY	S	14.95 MW	14.76 AW	31100 AAW	NYBLS	10//99-12//99
	Elmira MSA, NY	S	13.56 MW	12.39 AW	28200 AAW	NYBLS	10//99-12//99
	Glens Falls MSA, NY	S	12.89 MW	12.04 AW	26800 AAW	NYBLS	10//99-12//99
	Jamestown MSA, NY	S	12.42 MW	11.18 AW	25840 AAW	NYBLS	10//99-12//99
	Nassau-Suffolk PMSA, NY	S	17.10 MW	16.51 AW	35560 AAW	NYBLS	10//99-12//99
	New York PMSA, NY	S	17.95 MW	17.28 AW	37330 AAW	NYBLS	10//99-12//99
	Newburgh PMSA, NY-PA	S	14.80 MW	13.84 AW	30780 AAW	NYBLS	10//99-12//99
	Rochester MSA, NY	S	13.26 MW	12.94 AW	27580 AAW	NYBLS	10//99-12//99
	Syracuse MSA, NY	S	14.20 MW	13.22 AW	29530 AAW	NYBLS	10//99-12//99
	Utica-Rome MSA, NY	S	12.64 MW	11.69 AW	26290 AAW	NYBLS	10//99-12//99
	North Carolina	S	13.04 MW	13.43 AW	27930 AAW	NCBLS	10//99-12//99
	Asheville MSA, NC	S	12.40 MW	12.10 AW	25790 AAW	NCBLS	10//99-12//99
	Charlotte-Gastonia-Rock Hill MSA, NC-SC	S	13.97 MW	13.43 AW	29050 AAW	NCBLS	10//99-12//99
	Fayetteville MSA, NC	S	13.17 MW	12.33 AW	27400 AAW	NCBLS	10//99-12//99
	Goldsboro MSA, NC	S	11.16 MW	10.48 AW	23200 AAW	NCBLS	10//99-12//99
	Greensboro--Winston-Salem--High Point MSA, NC	S	13.63 MW	13.18 AW	28350 AAW	NCBLS	10//99-12//99
	Greenville MSA, NC	S	10.97 MW	10.22 AW	22810 AAW	NCBLS	10//99-12//99
	Hickory-Morganton-Lenoir MSA, NC	S	13.26 MW	12.81 AW	27580 AAW	NCBLS	10//99-12//99
	Jacksonville MSA, NC	S	11.39 MW	10.69 AW	23690 AAW	NCBLS	10//99-12//99
	Raleigh-Durham-Chapel Hill MSA, NC	S	14.40 MW	14.18 AW	29960 AAW	NCBLS	10//99-12//99
	Rocky Mount MSA, NC	S	13.41 MW	13.11 AW	27900 AAW	NCBLS	10//99-12//99
	Wilmington MSA, NC	S	13.04 MW	12.83 AW	27130 AAW	NCBLS	10//99-12//99
	North Dakota	S	10.42 MW	11.35 AW	23610 AAW	NDBLS	10//99-12//99
	Bismarck MSA, ND	S	12.67 MW	11.88 AW	26360 AAW	NDBLS	10//99-12//99
	Fargo-Moorhead MSA, ND-MN	S	11.91 MW	10.71 AW	24770 AAW	NDBLS	10//99-12//99
	Grand Forks MSA, ND-MN	S	12.59 MW	10.66 AW	26200 AAW	NDBLS	10//99-12//99
	Ohio	S	13.62 MW	14.32 AW	29790 AAW	OHBLS	10//99-12//99
	Akron PMSA, OH	S	13.99 MW	13.78 AW	29090 AAW	OHBLS	10//99-12//99
	Canton-Massillon MSA, OH	S	13.56 MW	12.28 AW	28200 AAW	OHBLS	10//99-12//99
	Cincinnati PMSA, OH-KY-IN	S	14.62 MW	13.68 AW	30410 AAW	OHBLS	10//99-12//99
	Cleveland-Lorain-Elyria PMSA, OH	S	14.40 MW	14.03 AW	29950 AAW	OHBLS	10//99-12//99
	Columbus MSA, OH	S	15.61 MW	14.48 AW	32460 AAW	OHBLS	10//99-12//99
	Dayton-Springfield MSA, OH	S	13.80 MW	13.32 AW	28700 AAW	OHBLS	10//99-12//99

Executive Secretary and Administrative Assistant

Occupation/Type/Industry	Location	Per	Low	Mid	High	Source	Date
	Hamilton-Middletown PMSA, OH	s	13.21 MW	12.63 AW	27470 AAW	OHBLS	10//99-12/99
	Lima MSA, OH	s	12.43 MW	11.11 AW	25840 AAW	OHBLS	10//99-12/99
	Mansfield MSA, OH	s	12.47 MW	11.88 AW	25940 AAW	OHBLS	10//99-12/99
	Steubenville-Weirton MSA, OH-WV	s	12.57 MW	11.70 AW	26150 AAW	OHBLS	10//99-12/99
	Toledo MSA, OH	s	13.50 MW	13.13 AW	28080 AAW	OHBLS	10//99-12/99
	Youngstown-Warren MSA, OH	s	13.31 MW	12.55 AW	27690 AAW	OHBLS	10//99-12/99
	Oklahoma	s	11.75 MW	12.33 AW	25650 AAW	OKBLS	10//99-12/99
	Enid MSA, OK	s	11.96 MW	11.82 AW	24870 AAW	OKBLS	10//99-12/99
	Lawton MSA, OK	s	15.61 MW	12.09 AW	32460 AAW	OKBLS	10//99-12/99
	Oklahoma City MSA, OK	s	11.91 MW	11.72 AW	24760 AAW	OKBLS	10//99-12/99
	Tulsa MSA, OK	s	13.62 MW	12.80 AW	28320 AAW	OKBLS	10//99-12/99
	Oregon	s	14.11 MW	14.63 AW	30430 AAW	ORBLS	10//99-12/99
	Corvallis MSA, OR	s	13.04 MW	12.54 AW	27120 AAW	ORBLS	10//99-12/99
	Eugene-Springfield MSA, OR	s	14.02 MW	13.35 AW	29160 AAW	ORBLS	10//99-12/99
	Medford-Ashland MSA, OR	s	13.56 MW	13.54 AW	28210 AAW	ORBLS	10//99-12/99
	Portland-Vancouver PMSA, OR-WA	s	15.12 MW	14.64 AW	31450 AAW	ORBLS	10//99-12/99
	Salem PMSA, OR	s	13.91 MW	13.28 AW	28930 AAW	ORBLS	10//99-12/99
	Pennsylvania	s	13.41 MW	14.09 AW	29310 AAW	PABLS	10//99-12/99
	Allentown-Bethlehem-Easton MSA, PA	s	12.22 MW	11.89 AW	25410 AAW	PABLS	10//99-12/99
	Altoona MSA, PA	s	11.24 MW	10.81 AW	23370 AAW	PABLS	10//99-12/99
	Erie MSA, PA	s	12.90 MW	12.32 AW	26820 AAW	PABLS	10//99-12/99
	Harrisburg-Lebanon-Carlisle MSA, PA	s	13.49 MW	12.99 AW	28070 AAW	PABLS	10//99-12/99
	Johnstown MSA, PA	s	11.75 MW	11.75 AW	24440 AAW	PABLS	10//99-12/99
	Lancaster MSA, PA	s	12.07 MW	11.90 AW	25110 AAW	PABLS	10//99-12/99
	Philadelphia PMSA, PA-NJ	s	15.58 MW	15.06 AW	32420 AAW	PABLS	10//99-12/99
	Pittsburgh MSA, PA	s	14.25 MW	13.27 AW	29630 AAW	PABLS	10//99-12/99
	Reading MSA, PA	s	14.04 MW	13.44 AW	29200 AAW	PABLS	10//99-12/99
	Scranton--Wilkes-Barre--Hazleton MSA, PA	s	12.16 MW	11.71 AW	25290 AAW	PABLS	10//99-12/99
	Sharon MSA, PA	s	13.39 MW	13.09 AW	27860 AAW	PABLS	10//99-12/99
	State College MSA, PA	s	12.28 MW	11.99 AW	25530 AAW	PABLS	10//99-12/99
	Williamsport MSA, PA	s	10.02 MW	8.22 AW	20840 AAW	PABLS	10//99-12/99
	York MSA, PA	s	13.04 MW	12.31 AW	27120 AAW	PABLS	10//99-12/99
	Rhode Island	s	14.78 MW	15.91 AW	33090 AAW	RIBLS	10//99-12/99
	Providence-Fall River-Warwick MSA, RI-MA	s	16.69 MW	15.35 AW	34710 AAW	RIBLS	10//99-12/99
	South Carolina	s	12.32 MW	13.54 AW	28160 AAW	SCBLS	10//99-12/99
	Charleston-North Charleston MSA, SC	s	12.94 MW	12.00 AW	26920 AAW	SCBLS	10//99-12/99
	Columbia MSA, SC	s	14.66 MW	12.16 AW	30500 AAW	SCBLS	10//99-12/99
	Florence MSA, SC	s	13.52 MW	12.11 AW	28120 AAW	SCBLS	10//99-12/99
	Greenville-Spartanburg-Anderson MSA, SC	s	13.06 MW	12.75 AW	27170 AAW	SCBLS	10//99-12/99
	Myrtle Beach MSA, SC	s	12.24 MW	10.50 AW	25470 AAW	SCBLS	10//99-12/99
	Sumter MSA, SC	s	13.51 MW	11.12 AW	28100 AAW	SCBLS	10//99-12/99
	South Dakota	s	11.6 MW	11.78 AW	24500 AAW	SDBLS	10//99-12/99
	Rapid City MSA, SD	s	11.47 MW	11.33 AW	23850 AAW	SDBLS	10//99-12/99
	Sioux Falls MSA, SD	s	12.34 MW	12.18 AW	25670 AAW	SDBLS	10//99-12/99
	Tennessee	s	12.58 MW	13.08 AW	27210 AAW	TNBLS	10//99-12/99
	Chattanooga MSA, TN-GA	s	13.15 MW	12.38 AW	27350 AAW	TNBLS	10//99-12/99
	Clarksville-Hopkinsville MSA, TN-KY	s	10.56 MW	10.23 AW	21960 AAW	TNBLS	10//99-12/99
	Jackson MSA, TN	s	13.03 MW	12.51 AW	27100 AAW	TNBLS	10//99-12/99
	Johnson City-Kingsport-Bristol MSA, TN-VA	s	11.68 MW	10.91 AW	24290 AAW	TNBLS	10//99-12/99
	Knoxville MSA, TN	s	12.19 MW	11.83 AW	25350 AAW	TNBLS	10//99-12/99
	Memphis MSA, TN-AR-MS	s	13.29 MW	12.65 AW	27650 AAW	MSBLS	10//99-12/99
	Nashville MSA, TN	s	13.96 MW	13.52 AW	29030 AAW	TNBLS	10//99-12/99
	Texas	s	13.85 MW	14.33 AW	29800 AAW	TXBLS	10//99-12/99
	Abilene MSA, TX	s	11.67 MW	11.66 AW	24280 AAW	TXBLS	10//99-12/99
	Amarillo MSA, TX	s	11.56 MW	10.96 AW	24050 AAW	TXBLS	10//99-12/99
	Austin-San Marcos MSA, TX	s	13.54 MW	12.87 AW	28160 AAW	TXBLS	10//99-12/99
	Beaumont-Port Arthur MSA, TX	s	13.03 MW	12.39 AW	27100 AAW	TXBLS	10//99-12/99
	Brazoria PMSA, TX	s	15.97 MW	15.66 AW	33220 AAW	TXBLS	10//99-12/99

AAW　Average annual wage
AE　Average entry wage
AEX　Average experienced wage
AO　Average offered
AOH　Average offered, high
AOL　Average offered, low
APH　Average pay, high range
APL　Average pay, low range
ASH　Average starting, high
ASL　Average starting, low
AW　Average wage paid
FQ　First quartile wage
H　Hourly
HI　Highest wage paid
HR　High end range
LR　Low end range
M　Monthly
MTC　Median total compensation
MW　Median wage paid
SQ　Second quartile wage
S　Special: hourly and annual
TQ　Third quartile wage
W　Weekly
Y　Yearly

Executive Secretary and Administrative Assistant (continued)

.../Industry	Location	Per	Low	Mid	High	Source	Date
	Brownsville-Harlingen-San Benito MSA, TX						
	Bryan-College Station MSA, TX	s	11...				
	Corpus Christi MSA, TX	s	14.1...				
	Dallas PMSA, TX	s	11.78...				
	El Paso MSA, TX	s	15.41 M...				
	Fort Worth-Arlington PMSA, TX	s	11.92 M...				
	Galveston-Texas City PMSA, TX	s	14.28 MW				
	Houston PMSA, TX	s	13.65 MW				
	Killeen-Temple MSA, TX	s	15.56 MW				
	Laredo MSA, TX	s	12.09 MW				
	Longview-Marshall MSA, TX	s	12.34 MW	11....			
	Lubbock MSA, TX	s	11.90 MW	11.4...			
	McAllen-Edinburg-Mission MSA, TX	s	11.47 MW	11.4...			
	Odessa-Midland MSA, TX	s	12.44 MW	12.45 AW			
	San Angelo MSA, TX	s	12.93 MW	12.29 AW			
	San Antonio MSA, TX	s	11.84 MW	11.33 AW			
	Sherman-Denison MSA, TX	s	13.61 MW	12.81 AW			
	Texarkana MSA, TX-Texarkana, AR	s	11.84 MW	11.05 AW			
	Tyler MSA, TX	s	11.40 MW	10.85 AW	2...		
	Victoria MSA, TX	s	13.51 MW	12.69 AW	28...		
	Waco MSA, TX	s	11.83 MW	11.90 AW	246...		
	Wichita Falls MSA, TX	s	11.08 MW	10.56 AW	2305...		
	Utah	s	12.97 MW	11.97 AW	26980		
	Provo-Orem MSA, UT	s	12.64 MW	13.63 AW	28350...		
	Salt Lake City-Ogden MSA, UT	s	12.38 MW	12.09 AW	25750...		
	Vermont	s	13.18 MW	12.76 AW	27410...		
	Burlington MSA, VT	s	14.47 MW	15.76 AW	32780...		
	Virginia	s	17.31 MW	14.29 AW	36000...		
	Charlottesville MSA, VA	s	13.96 MW	14.64 AW	30450...	VA...	
	Danville MSA, VA	s	12.92 MW	11.97 AW	26870...	VABL...	
	Lynchburg MSA, VA	s	11.55 MW	10.80 AW	24010...	VABL...	
	Norfolk-Virginia Beach-Newport News MSA, VA-NC	s	11.83 MW	11.52 AW	24610 AAW	VABL...	
	Richmond-Petersburg MSA, VA	s	13.23 MW	12.53 AW	27510	VABLS	
	Roanoke MSA, VA	s	14.39 MW	14.04 AW	29930 AAW	VABLS	
	Washington	s	12.52 MW	12.22 AW	26050 AAW	VABLS	
	Bellingham MSA, WA	s	15.48 MW	15.86 AW	32990 AAW	WABLS	
	Bremerton PMSA, WA	s	14.14 MW	13.90 AW	29420 AAW	WABLS	
	Richland-Kennewick-Pasco MSA, WA	s	14.38 MW	13.94 AW	29910 AAW	WABLS	
	Seattle-Bellevue-Everett PMSA, WA	s	13.86 MW	14.24 AW	28830 AAW	WABLS	
	Spokane MSA, WA	s	16.41 MW	15.92 AW	34140 AAW	WABLS	10/99-1...
	Tacoma PMSA, WA	s	14.62 MW	14.38 AW	30410 AAW	WABLS	10//99-12/...
	Yakima MSA, WA	s	14.50 MW	14.37 AW	30150 AAW	WABLS	10//99-12/5...
	West Virginia	s	13.59 MW	12.83 AW	28260 AAW	WABLS	10//99-12/99
	Charleston MSA, WV	s	11.17 MW	12.12 AW	25220 AAW	WVBLS	10//99-12/99
	Huntington-Ashland MSA, WV-KY-OH	s	13.92 MW	13.58 AW	28960 AAW	WVBLS	10//99-12/99
	Parkersburg-Marietta MSA, WV-OH	s	12.05 MW	11.76 AW	25070 AAW	WVBLS	10//99-12/99
	Wheeling MSA, WV-OH	s	10.76 MW	9.97 AW	22380 AAW	WVBLS	
	Wisconsin	s	10.43 MW	8.82 AW	21690 AAW	WVBLS	10//99-12/99
	Appleton-Oshkosh-Neenah MSA, WI	s	12.44 MW	12.92 AW	26870 AAW	WIBLS	10//99-12/99
	Eau Claire MSA, WI	s	11.51 MW	11.24 AW	23950 AAW	WIBLS	10//99-12/99
	Green Bay MSA, WI	s	10.68 MW	10.30 AW	22220 AAW	WIBLS	10//99-12/99
	Janesville-Beloit MSA, WI	s	12.23 MW	11.69 AW	25440 AAW	WIBLS	10//99-12/99
	Kenosha PMSA, WI	s	11.69 MW	10.89 AW	24320 AAW	WIBLS	10//99-12/99
	La Crosse MSA, WI-MN	s	12.74 MW	11.85 AW	26510 AAW	WIBLS	10//99-12/99
	Madison MSA, WI	s	10.85 MW	10.15 AW	22570 AAW	WIBLS	10//99-12/99
		s	14.36 MW	13.64 AW	29860 AAW	WIBLS	

AAW　Average annual wage
AE　Average entry wage
AEX　Average experienced wage
AO　Average offered
AOH　Average offered, high
AOL　Average offered, low
APH　Average pay, high range
APL　Average pay, low range
ASH　Average starting, high
ASL　Average starting, low
AW　Average wage paid
FQ　First quartile wage
H　Hourly
HI　Highest wage paid
HR　High end range
LR　Low end range
M　Monthly
MTC　Median total compensation
MW　Median wage paid
SQ　Second quartile wage
S　Special: hourly and annual
TQ　Third quartile wage
W　Weekly
Y　Yearly

Occupation/Type/Industry	Location	Per	Low	Mid	High	Source	Date
Extruding and Drawing Machine Setter, Operator, and Tender							
Metals and Plastics	Colorado	S	11.33 MW	12.59 AW	26190 AAW	COBLS	10//99-12/99
Metals and Plastics	Denver PMSA, CO	S	14.04 MW	12.80 AW	29210 AAW	COBLS	10//99-12/99
Metals and Plastics	Connecticut	S	11.88 MW	12.38 AW	25750 AAW	CTBLS	10//99-12/99
Metals and Plastics	Bridgeport PMSA, CT	S	12.13 MW	12.03 AW	25240 AAW	CTBLS	10//99-12/99
Metals and Plastics	Hartford MSA, CT	S	13.79 MW	13.03 AW	28690 AAW	CTBLS	10//99-12/99
Metals and Plastics	New Haven-Meriden PMSA, CT	S	11.26 MW	10.57 AW	23420 AAW	CTBLS	10//99-12/99
Metals and Plastics	New London-Norwich MSA, CT-RI	S	11.31 MW	10.29 AW	23530 AAW	CTBLS	10//99-12/99
Metals and Plastics	Stamford-Norwalk PMSA, CT	S	10.53 MW	10.53 AW	21890 AAW	CTBLS	10//99-12/99
Metals and Plastics	Waterbury PMSA, CT	S	11.49 MW	11.48 AW	23890 AAW	CTBLS	10//99-12/99
Metals and Plastics	Delaware	S	9.69 MW	10.51 AW	21860 AAW	DEBLS	10//99-12/99
Metals and Plastics	Washington PMSA, DC-MD-VA-WV	S	11.71 MW	11.59 AW	24350 AAW	DCBLS	10//99-12/99
Metals and Plastics	Florida	S	9.6 MW	10.17 AW	21160 AAW	FLBLS	10//99-12/99
Metals and Plastics	Fort Lauderdale PMSA, FL	S	9.30 MW	8.48 AW	19350 AAW	FLBLS	10//99-12/99
Metals and Plastics	Jacksonville MSA, FL	S	10.33 MW	10.05 AW	21490 AAW	FLBLS	10//99-12/99
Metals and Plastics	Lakeland-Winter Haven MSA, FL	S	9.10 MW	8.86 AW	18940 AAW	FLBLS	10//99-12/99
Metals and Plastics	Miami PMSA, FL	S	8.49 MW	7.72 AW	17670 AAW	FLBLS	10//99-12/99
Metals and Plastics	Orlando MSA, FL	S	10.41 MW	9.89 AW	21650 AAW	FLBLS	10//99-12/99
Metals and Plastics	Tampa-St. Petersburg-Clearwater MSA, FL	S	10.22 MW	9.51 AW	21260 AAW	FLBLS	10//99-12/99
Metals and Plastics	Georgia	S	12.29 MW	12.63 AW	26260 AAW	GABLS	10//99-12/99
Metals and Plastics	Atlanta MSA, GA	S	14.49 MW	14.42 AW	30130 AAW	GABLS	10//99-12/99
Metals and Plastics	Columbus MSA, GA-AL	S	9.65 MW	9.69 AW	20080 AAW	GABLS	10//99-12/99
Metals and Plastics	Macon MSA, GA	S	11.62 MW	11.86 AW	24170 AAW	GABLS	10//99-12/99
Metals and Plastics	Idaho	S	9.9 MW	9.53 AW	19820 AAW	IDBLS	10//99-12/99
Metals and Plastics	Illinois	S	11.37 MW	12.44 AW	25870 AAW	ILBLS	10//99-12/99
Metals and Plastics	Chicago PMSA, IL	S	12.65 MW	11.30 AW	26310 AAW	ILBLS	10//99-12/99
Metals and Plastics	Indiana	S	12.12 MW	12.25 AW	25490 AAW	INBLS	10//99-12/99
Metals and Plastics	Elkhart-Goshen MSA, IN	S	10.03 MW	11.00 AW	20870 AAW	INBLS	10//99-12/99
Metals and Plastics	Evansville-Henderson MSA, IN-KY	S	10.78 MW	10.06 AW	22430 AAW	INBLS	10//99-12/99
Metals and Plastics	Fort Wayne MSA, IN	S	11.52 MW	11.67 AW	23950 AAW	INBLS	10//99-12/99
Metals and Plastics	Indianapolis MSA, IN	S	12.99 MW	12.41 AW	27020 AAW	INBLS	10//99-12/99
Metals and Plastics	South Bend MSA, IN	S	12.18 MW	12.14 AW	25340 AAW	INBLS	10//99-12/99
Metals and Plastics	Iowa	S	12.69 MW	12.60 AW	26210 AAW	IABLS	10//99-12/99
Metals and Plastics	Cedar Rapids MSA, IA	S	15.78 MW	15.53 AW	32820 AAW	IABLS	10//99-12/99
Metals and Plastics	Kansas	S	10.27 MW	10.49 AW	21820 AAW	KSBLS	10//99-12/99
Metals and Plastics	Kentucky	S	10.7 MW	11.55 AW	24030 AAW	KYBLS	10//99-12/99
Metals and Plastics	Lexington MSA, KY	S	9.48 MW	9.06 AW	19720 AAW	KYBLS	10//99-12/99
Metals and Plastics	Louisville MSA, KY-IN	S	9.99 MW	9.63 AW	20780 AAW	KYBLS	10//99-12/99
Metals and Plastics	Louisiana	S	12.87 MW	12.72 AW	26460 AAW	LABLS	10//99-12/99
Metals and Plastics	Baton Rouge MSA, LA	S	12.58 MW	12.84 AW	26160 AAW	LABLS	10//99-12/99
Metals and Plastics	Maine	S	11.55 MW	11.67 AW	24270 AAW	MEBLS	10//99-12/99
Metals and Plastics	Maryland	S	10.51 MW	10.91 AW	22700 AAW	MDBLS	10//99-12/99
Metals and Plastics	Baltimore PMSA, MD	S	10.91 MW	10.49 AW	22690 AAW	MDBLS	10//99-12/99
Metals and Plastics	Massachusetts	S	12.46 MW	12.49 AW	25980 AAW	MABLS	10//99-12/99
Metals and Plastics	Boston PMSA, MA-NH	S	12.77 MW	12.34 AW	26570 AAW	MABLS	10//99-12/99
Metals and Plastics	Brockton PMSA, MA	S	10.24 MW	10.13 AW	21300 AAW	MABLS	10//99-12/99
Metals and Plastics	Fitchburg-Leominster PMSA, MA	S	14.54 MW	14.89 AW	30250 AAW	MABLS	10//99-12/99
Metals and Plastics	Lowell PMSA, MA-NH	S	11.10 MW	11.39 AW	23080 AAW	MABLS	10//99-12/99
Metals and Plastics	New Bedford PMSA, MA	S	13.39 MW	13.40 AW	27840 AAW	MABLS	10//99-12/99
Metals and Plastics	Springfield MSA, MA	S	11.90 MW	11.54 AW	24750 AAW	MABLS	10//99-12/99
Metals and Plastics	Worcester PMSA, MA-CT	S	12.06 MW	11.87 AW	25090 AAW	MABLS	10//99-12/99
Metals and Plastics	Michigan	S	10.46 MW	11.09 AW	23070 AAW	MIBLS	10//99-12/99
Metals and Plastics	Ann Arbor PMSA, MI	S	12.36 MW	11.42 AW	25700 AAW	MIBLS	10//99-12/99
Metals and Plastics	Detroit PMSA, MI	S	10.52 MW	9.93 AW	21890 AAW	MIBLS	10//99-12/99
Metals and Plastics	Grand Rapids-Muskegon-Holland MSA, MI	S	11.88 MW	11.60 AW	24700 AAW	MIBLS	10//99-12/99
Metals and Plastics	Jackson MSA, MI	S	11.94 MW	11.68 AW	24830 AAW	MIBLS	10//99-12/99
Metals and Plastics	Kalamazoo-Battle Creek MSA, MI	S	9.85 MW	9.54 AW	20490 AAW	MIBLS	10//99-12/99
Metals and Plastics	Minnesota	S	12.14 MW	12.12 AW	25210 AAW	MNBLS	10//99-12/99
Metals and Plastics	Minneapolis-St. Paul MSA, MN-WI	S	12.07 MW	12.01 AW	25110 AAW	MNBLS	10//99-12/99
Metals and Plastics	Mississippi	S	9.74 MW	9.79 AW	20370 AAW	MSBLS	10//99-12/99
Metals and Plastics	Missouri	S	11.74 MW	11.37 AW	23640 AAW	MOBLS	10//99-12/99

Occupation/Type/Industry	Location	Per	Low	Mid	High	Source	Date
Extruding and Drawing Machine Setter, Operator, and Tender							
Metals and Plastics	Kansas City MSA, MO-KS	S	11.41 MW	10.82 AW	23740 AAW	MOBLS	10//99-12//99
Metals and Plastics	St. Louis MSA, MO-IL	S	10.32 MW	9.90 AW	21470 AAW	MOBLS	10//99-12//99
Metals and Plastics	Nebraska	S	9.81 MW	9.91 AW	20610 AAW	NEBLS	10//99-12//99
Metals and Plastics	Nevada	S	12.98 MW	12.91 AW	26850 AAW	NVBLS	10//99-12//99
Metals and Plastics	Las Vegas MSA, NV-AZ	S	11.60 MW	11.84 AW	24130 AAW	NVBLS	10//99-12//99
Metals and Plastics	New Hampshire	S	11.05 MW	11.49 AW	23890 AAW	NHBLS	10//99-12//99
Metals and Plastics	Manchester PMSA, NH	S	10.03 MW	9.93 AW	20870 AAW	NHBLS	10//99-12//99
Metals and Plastics	New Jersey	S	12.1 MW	12.70 AW	26420 AAW	NJBLS	10//99-12//99
Metals and Plastics	Bergen-Passaic PMSA, NJ	S	12.36 MW	11.87 AW	25700 AAW	NJBLS	10//99-12//99
Metals and Plastics	Middlesex-Somerset-Hunterdon PMSA, NJ	S	13.64 MW	12.20 AW	28380 AAW	NJBLS	10//99-12//99
Metals and Plastics	Monmouth-Ocean PMSA, NJ	S	11.82 MW	11.97 AW	24580 AAW	NJBLS	10//99-12//99
Metals and Plastics	Newark PMSA, NJ	S	12.12 MW	11.88 AW	25210 AAW	NJBLS	10//99-12//99
Metals and Plastics	New Mexico	S	10.64 MW	15.96 AW	33200 AAW	NMBLS	10//99-12//99
Metals and Plastics	New York	S	10.04 MW	10.83 AW	22530 AAW	NYBLS	10//99-12//99
Metals and Plastics	Albany-Schenectady-Troy MSA, NY	S	12.26 MW	11.90 AW	25500 AAW	NYBLS	10//99-12//99
Metals and Plastics	Glens Falls MSA, NY	S	14.77 MW	15.01 AW	30720 AAW	NYBLS	10//99-12//99
Metals and Plastics	Nassau-Suffolk PMSA, NY	S	9.77 MW	9.37 AW	20320 AAW	NYBLS	10//99-12//99
Metals and Plastics	New York PMSA, NY	S	13.43 MW	13.93 AW	27930 AAW	NYBLS	10//99-12//99
Metals and Plastics	Newburgh PMSA, NY-PA	S	11.69 MW	11.77 AW	24310 AAW	NYBLS	10//99-12//99
Metals and Plastics	Syracuse MSA, NY	S	10.76 MW	10.77 AW	22380 AAW	NYBLS	10//99-12//99
Metals and Plastics	Utica-Rome MSA, NY	S	10.94 MW	10.57 AW	22750 AAW	NYBLS	10//99-12//99
Metals and Plastics	North Carolina	S	9.96 MW	10.91 AW	22690 AAW	NCBLS	10//99-12//99
Metals and Plastics	Charlotte-Gastonia-Rock Hill MSA, NC-SC	S	16.88 MW	15.68 AW	35110 AAW	NCBLS	10//99-12//99
Metals and Plastics	Greensboro--Winston-Salem--High Point MSA, NC	S	11.68 MW	11.67 AW	24290 AAW	NCBLS	10//99-12//99
Metals and Plastics	Hickory-Morganton-Lenoir MSA, NC	S	13.18 MW	13.74 AW	27420 AAW	NCBLS	10//99-12//99
Metals and Plastics	Raleigh-Durham-Chapel Hill MSA, NC	S	10.79 MW	10.31 AW	22440 AAW	NCBLS	10//99-12//99
Metals and Plastics	Ohio	S	12.53 MW	12.68 AW	26380 AAW	OHBLS	10//99-12//99
Metals and Plastics	Akron PMSA, OH	S	11.24 MW	11.00 AW	23370 AAW	OHBLS	10//99-12//99
Metals and Plastics	Cincinnati PMSA, OH-KY-IN	S	11.35 MW	11.05 AW	23600 AAW	OHBLS	10//99-12//99
Metals and Plastics	Cleveland-Lorain-Elyria PMSA, OH	S	14.20 MW	12.62 AW	29540 AAW	OHBLS	10//99-12//99
Metals and Plastics	Columbus MSA, OH	S	14.07 MW	14.54 AW	29270 AAW	OHBLS	10//99-12//99
Metals and Plastics	Dayton-Springfield MSA, OH	S	14.35 MW	14.91 AW	29860 AAW	OHBLS	10//99-12//99
Metals and Plastics	Hamilton-Middletown PMSA, OH	S	13.42 MW	12.69 AW	27910 AAW	OHBLS	10//99-12//99
Metals and Plastics	Toledo MSA, OH	S	11.85 MW	10.65 AW	24640 AAW	OHBLS	10//99-12//99
Metals and Plastics	Oklahoma	S	8.58 MW	10.64 AW	22130 AAW	OKBLS	10//99-12//99
Metals and Plastics	Oklahoma City MSA, OK	S	8.56 MW	7.90 AW	17810 AAW	OKBLS	10//99-12//99
Metals and Plastics	Tulsa MSA, OK	S	13.20 MW	11.95 AW	27450 AAW	OKBLS	10//99-12//99
Metals and Plastics	Oregon	S	10.95 MW	10.87 AW	22600 AAW	ORBLS	10//99-12//99
Metals and Plastics	Portland-Vancouver PMSA, OR-WA	S	9.84 MW	8.66 AW	20460 AAW	ORBLS	10//99-12//99
Metals and Plastics	Pennsylvania	S	13.37 MW	13.02 AW	27080 AAW	PABLS	10//99-12//99
Metals and Plastics	Allentown-Bethlehem-Easton MSA, PA	S	10.11 MW	9.95 AW	21030 AAW	PABLS	10//99-12//99
Metals and Plastics	Erie MSA, PA	S	11.78 MW	12.26 AW	24500 AAW	PABLS	10//99-12//99
Metals and Plastics	Philadelphia PMSA, PA-NJ	S	13.80 MW	13.70 AW	28700 AAW	PABLS	10//99-12//99
Metals and Plastics	Pittsburgh MSA, PA	S	14.32 MW	14.82 AW	29790 AAW	PABLS	10//99-12//99
Metals and Plastics	Reading MSA, PA	S	14.72 MW	14.81 AW	30620 AAW	PABLS	10//99-12//99
Metals and Plastics	Scranton--Wilkes-Barre--Hazleton MSA, PA	S	13.48 MW	13.68 AW	28050 AAW	PABLS	10//99-12//99
Metals and Plastics	Williamsport MSA, PA	S	9.82 MW	9.49 AW	20430 AAW	PABLS	10//99-12//99
Metals and Plastics	York MSA, PA	S	13.28 MW	13.19 AW	27620 AAW	PABLS	10//99-12//99
Metals and Plastics	Rhode Island	S	8.02 MW	9.14 AW	19010 AAW	RIBLS	10//99-12//99
Metals and Plastics	Providence-Fall River-Warwick MSA, RI-MA	S	9.29 MW	8.11 AW	19330 AAW	RIBLS	10//99-12//99
Metals and Plastics	South Carolina	S	13 MW	14.22 AW	29570 AAW	SCBLS	10//99-12//99
Metals and Plastics	Charleston-North Charleston MSA, SC	S	11.96 MW	12.02 AW	24880 AAW	SCBLS	10//99-12//99
Metals and Plastics	Greenville-Spartanburg-Anderson MSA, SC	S	13.07 MW	12.49 AW	27200 AAW	SCBLS	10//99-12//99
Metals and Plastics	South Dakota	S	9.63 MW	9.75 AW	20280 AAW	SDBLS	10//99-12//99
Metals and Plastics	Sioux Falls MSA, SD	S	9.36 MW	8.97 AW	19470 AAW	SDBLS	10//99-12//99
Metals and Plastics	Tennessee	S	11.41 MW	11.29 AW	23490 AAW	TNBLS	10//99-12//99

AAW Average annual wage	**AOH** Average offered, high	**ASH** Average starting, high	**H** Hourly	**M** Monthly	**S** Special: hourly and annual
AE Average entry wage	**AOL** Average offered, low	**ASL** Average starting, low	**HI** Highest wage paid	**MTC** Median total compensation	**TQ** Third quartile wage
AEX Average experienced wage	**APH** Average pay, high range	**AW** Average wage paid	**HR** High end range	**MW** Median wage paid	**W** Weekly
AO Average offered	**APL** Average pay, low range	**FQ** First quartile wage	**LR** Low end range	**SQ** Second quartile wage	**Y** Yearly

Occupation/Type/Industry	Location	Per	Low	Mid	High	Source	Date
Extruding and Drawing Machine Setter, Operator, and Tender							
Metals and Plastics	Chattanooga MSA, TN-GA	S	12.33 MW	12.32 AW	25650 AAW	TNBLS	10//99-12//99
Metals and Plastics	Memphis MSA, TN-AR-MS	S	10.07 MW	9.92 AW	20950 AAW	MSBLS	10//99-12//99
Metals and Plastics	Nashville MSA, TN	S	12.50 MW	12.21 AW	26010 AAW	TNBLS	10//99-12//99
Metals and Plastics	Texas	S	10.34 MW	10.77 AW	22400 AAW	TXBLS	10//99-12//99
Metals and Plastics	Dallas PMSA, TX	S	9.92 MW	9.95 AW	20630 AAW	TXBLS	10//99-12//99
Metals and Plastics	El Paso MSA, TX	S	13.19 MW	14.18 AW	27420 AAW	TXBLS	10//99-12//99
Metals and Plastics	Fort Worth-Arlington PMSA, TX	S	10.45 MW	10.50 AW	21740 AAW	TXBLS	10//99-12//99
Metals and Plastics	Houston PMSA, TX	S	11.45 MW	10.33 AW	23810 AAW	TXBLS	10//99-12//99
Metals and Plastics	San Antonio MSA, TX	S	10.75 MW	10.22 AW	22360 AAW	TXBLS	10//99-12//99
Metals and Plastics	Waco MSA, TX	S	13.30 MW	12.43 AW	27670 AAW	TXBLS	10//99-12//99
Metals and Plastics	Utah	S	11.86 MW	11.86 AW	24670 AAW	UTBLS	10//99-12//99
Metals and Plastics	Salt Lake City-Ogden MSA, UT	S	11.90 MW	11.86 AW	24750 AAW	UTBLS	10//99-12//99
Metals and Plastics	Vermont	S	9.54 MW	10.46 AW	21760 AAW	VTBLS	10//99-12//99
Metals and Plastics	Virginia	S	12.65 MW	12.37 AW	25720 AAW	VABLS	10//99-12//99
Metals and Plastics	Norfolk-Virginia Beach-Newport News MSA, VA-NC	S	11.38 MW	11.61 AW	23660 AAW	VABLS	10//99-12//99
Metals and Plastics	Washington	S	10.53 MW	12.19 AW	25350 AAW	WABLS	10//99-12//99
Metals and Plastics	Seattle-Bellevue-Everett PMSA, WA	S	8.95 MW	8.12 AW	18610 AAW	WABLS	10//99-12//99
Metals and Plastics	Huntington-Ashland MSA, WV-KY-OH	S	13.37 MW	10.76 AW	27810 AAW	WVBLS	10//99-12//99
Metals and Plastics	Wisconsin	S	12.2 MW	12.18 AW	25330 AAW	WIBLS	10//99-12//99
Metals and Plastics	Green Bay MSA, WI	S	9.15 MW	6.72 AW	19030 AAW	WIBLS	10//99-12//99
Metals and Plastics	Janesville-Beloit MSA, WI	S	10.03 MW	9.79 AW	20860 AAW	WIBLS	10//99-12//99
Metals and Plastics	Milwaukee-Waukesha PMSA, WI	S	12.76 MW	12.15 AW	26550 AAW	WIBLS	10//99-12//99
Metals and Plastics	Racine PMSA, WI	S	11.18 MW	10.37 AW	23260 AAW	WIBLS	10//99-12//99
Metals and Plastics	Sheboygan MSA, WI	S	12.94 MW	12.94 AW	26910 AAW	WIBLS	10//99-12//99
Metals and Plastics	Puerto Rico	S	6.8 MW	7.99 AW	16620 AAW	PRBLS	10//99-12//99
Metals and Plastics	San Juan-Bayamon PMSA, PR	S	6.28 MW	6.25 AW	13050 AAW	PRBLS	10//99-12//99
Extruding and Forming Machine Setter, Operator, and Tender							
Synthetic and Glass Fiber	Alabama	S	12.1 MW	11.98 AW	24910 AAW	ALBLS	10//99-12//99
Synthetic and Glass Fiber	Arizona	S	8.25 MW	9.11 AW	18950 AAW	AZBLS	10//99-12//99
Synthetic and Glass Fiber	Arkansas	S	12.19 MW	12.45 AW	25900 AAW	ARBLS	10//99-12//99
Synthetic and Glass Fiber	California	S	9.22 MW	9.74 AW	20250 AAW	CABLS	10//99-12//99
Synthetic and Glass Fiber	Los Angeles-Long Beach PMSA, CA	S	9.34 MW	9.11 AW	19420 AAW	CABLS	10//99-12//99
Synthetic and Glass Fiber	Oakland PMSA, CA	S	14.28 MW	12.13 AW	29700 AAW	CABLS	10//99-12//99
Synthetic and Glass Fiber	Riverside-San Bernardino PMSA, CA	S	10.70 MW	9.80 AW	22250 AAW	CABLS	10//99-12//99
Synthetic and Glass Fiber	Connecticut	S	8.37 MW	9.13 AW	18990 AAW	CTBLS	10//99-12//99
Synthetic and Glass Fiber	New London-Norwich MSA, CT-RI	S	9.13 MW	8.37 AW	18990 AAW	CTBLS	10//99-12//99
Synthetic and Glass Fiber	Delaware	S	14.63 MW	14.04 AW	29200 AAW	DEBLS	10//99-12//99
Synthetic and Glass Fiber	Florida	S	10.15 MW	10.53 AW	21890 AAW	FLBLS	10//99-12//99
Synthetic and Glass Fiber	Georgia	S	9.59 MW	9.84 AW	20460 AAW	GABLS	10//99-12//99
Synthetic and Glass Fiber	Atlanta MSA, GA	S	7.24 MW	6.71 AW	15070 AAW	GABLS	10//99-12//99
Synthetic and Glass Fiber	Illinois	S	11.6 MW	11.40 AW	23720 AAW	ILBLS	10//99-12//99
Synthetic and Glass Fiber	Iowa	S	18.95 MW	18.27 AW	38000 AAW	IABLS	10//99-12//99
Synthetic and Glass Fiber	Kentucky	S	10.16 MW	10.68 AW	22220 AAW	KYBLS	10//99-12//99
Synthetic and Glass Fiber	Massachusetts	S	11.78 MW	11.82 AW	24590 AAW	MABLS	10//99-12//99
Synthetic and Glass Fiber	Boston PMSA, MA-NH	S	11.81 MW	11.75 AW	24560 AAW	MABLS	10//99-12//99
Synthetic and Glass Fiber	Worcester PMSA, MA-CT	S	11.88 MW	11.90 AW	24710 AAW	MABLS	10//99-12//99
Synthetic and Glass Fiber	Mississippi	S	10.54 MW	11.68 AW	24290 AAW	MSBLS	10//99-12//99
Synthetic and Glass Fiber	Missouri	S	8.41 MW	8.46 AW	17600 AAW	MOBLS	10//99-12//99
Synthetic and Glass Fiber	New Jersey	S	11.28 MW	11.05 AW	22980 AAW	NJBLS	10//99-12//99
Synthetic and Glass Fiber	New York	S	13.78 MW	12.62 AW	26250 AAW	NYBLS	10//99-12//99
Synthetic and Glass Fiber	New York PMSA, NY	S	11.98 MW	12.66 AW	24920 AAW	NYBLS	10//99-12//99
Synthetic and Glass Fiber	North Carolina	S	13.26 MW	12.31 AW	25600 AAW	NCBLS	10//99-12//99
Synthetic and Glass Fiber	Charlotte-Gastonia-Rock Hill MSA, NC-SC	S	11.51 MW	11.14 AW	23930 AAW	NCBLS	10//99-12//99
Synthetic and Glass Fiber	Greensboro--Winston-Salem--High Point MSA, NC	S	12.52 MW	12.54 AW	26040 AAW	NCBLS	10//99-12//99
Synthetic and Glass Fiber	Ohio	S	12.31 MW	12.36 AW	25700 AAW	OHBLS	10//99-12//99
Synthetic and Glass Fiber	Akron PMSA, OH	S	10.50 MW	9.91 AW	21830 AAW	OHBLS	10//99-12//99

AAW	Average annual wage	AOH	Average offered, high	ASH	Average starting, high	H	Hourly	M	Monthly	S	Special: hourly and annual
AE	Average entry wage	AOL	Average offered, low	ASL	Average starting, low	HI	Highest wage paid	MTC	Median total compensation	TQ	Third quartile wage
AEX	Average experienced wage	APH	Average pay, high range	AW	Average wage paid	HR	High end range	MW	Median wage paid	W	Weekly
AO	Average offered	APL	Average pay, low range	FQ	First quartile wage	LR	Low end range	SQ	Second quartile wage	Y	Yearly

Occupation/Type/Industry	Location	Per	Low	Mid	High	Source	Date
Extruding and Forming Machine Setter, Operator, and Tender							
Synthetic and Glass Fiber	Cincinnati PMSA, OH-KY-IN	S	13.87 MW	14.21 AW	28850 AAW	OHBLS	10//99-12//99
Synthetic and Glass Fiber	Cleveland-Lorain-Elyria PMSA, OH	S	12.65 MW	12.49 AW	26320 AAW	OHBLS	10//99-12//99
Synthetic and Glass Fiber	Oklahoma	S	10.82 MW	10.62 AW	22090 AAW	OKBLS	10//99-12//99
Synthetic and Glass Fiber	Tulsa MSA, OK	S	11.12 MW	11.11 AW	23130 AAW	OKBLS	10//99-12//99
Synthetic and Glass Fiber	Pennsylvania	S	15.26 MW	15.13 AW	31470 AAW	PABLS	10//99-12//99
Synthetic and Glass Fiber	Philadelphia PMSA, PA-NJ	S	13.62 MW	13.34 AW	28330 AAW	PABLS	10//99-12//99
Synthetic and Glass Fiber	Scranton--Wilkes-Barre--Hazleton MSA, PA	S	15.02 MW	14.98 AW	31250 AAW	PABLS	10//99-12//99
Synthetic and Glass Fiber	Rhode Island	S	10.95 MW	10.85 AW	22570 AAW	RIBLS	10//99-12//99
Synthetic and Glass Fiber	Providence-Fall River-Warwick MSA, RI-MA	S	10.93 MW	11.09 AW	22730 AAW	RIBLS	10//99-12//99
Synthetic and Glass Fiber	South Carolina	S	10.71 MW	11.37 AW	23640 AAW	SCBLS	10//99-12//99
Synthetic and Glass Fiber	Greenville-Spartanburg-Anderson MSA, SC	S	12.09 MW	11.50 AW	25160 AAW	SCBLS	10//99-12//99
Synthetic and Glass Fiber	Tennessee	S	14.89 MW	14.21 AW	29550 AAW	TNBLS	10//99-12//99
Synthetic and Glass Fiber	Johnson City-Kingsport-Bristol MSA, TN-VA	S	13.92 MW	14.75 AW	28960 AAW	TNBLS	10//99-12//99
Synthetic and Glass Fiber	Memphis MSA, TN-AR-MS	S	11.59 MW	10.58 AW	24110 AAW	MSBLS	10//99-12//99
Synthetic and Glass Fiber	Nashville MSA, TN	S	15.04 MW	15.20 AW	31280 AAW	TNBLS	10//99-12//99
Synthetic and Glass Fiber	Utah	S	8.07 MW	8.38 AW	17430 AAW	UTBLS	10//99-12//99
Synthetic and Glass Fiber	Salt Lake City-Ogden MSA, UT	S	8.38 MW	8.07 AW	17430 AAW	UTBLS	10//99-12//99
Synthetic and Glass Fiber	Vermont	S	12.4 MW	12.56 AW	26120 AAW	VTBLS	10//99-12//99
Synthetic and Glass Fiber	Virginia	S	11.04 MW	12.05 AW	25070 AAW	VABLS	10//99-12//99
Synthetic and Glass Fiber	Washington	S	8.91 MW	9.63 AW	20030 AAW	WABLS	10//99-12//99
Synthetic and Glass Fiber	Wisconsin	S	13.13 MW	12.72 AW	26460 AAW	WIBLS	10//99-12//99
Synthetic and Glass Fiber	Appleton-Oshkosh-Neenah MSA, WI	S	13.63 MW	13.66 AW	28340 AAW	WIBLS	10//99-12//99
Extruding, Forming, Pressing, and Compacting Machine Setter, Operator, and Tender	Alabama	S	16.5 MW	14.75 AW	30680 AAW	ALBLS	10//99-12//99
	Birmingham MSA, AL	S	12.35 MW	11.29 AW	25680 AAW	ALBLS	10//99-12//99
	Montgomery MSA, AL	S	11.29 MW	11.18 AW	23480 AAW	ALBLS	10//99-12//99
	Arizona	S	10.16 MW	11.07 AW	23030 AAW	AZBLS	10//99-12//99
	Phoenix-Mesa MSA, AZ	S	10.34 MW	10.09 AW	21510 AAW	AZBLS	10//99-12//99
	Tucson MSA, AZ	S	8.61 MW	8.49 AW	17900 AAW	AZBLS	10//99-12//99
	Arkansas	S	11.33 MW	11.71 AW	24360 AAW	ARBLS	10//99-12//99
	Fort Smith MSA, AR-OK	S	10.86 MW	10.25 AW	22590 AAW	ARBLS	10//99-12//99
	Jonesboro MSA, AR	S	9.94 MW	10.08 AW	20680 AAW	ARBLS	10//99-12//99
	Little Rock-North Little Rock MSA, AR	S	10.14 MW	10.68 AW	21090 AAW	ARBLS	10//99-12//99
	California	S	9.29 MW	10.28 AW	21390 AAW	CABLS	10//99-12//99
	Fresno MSA, CA	S	12.45 MW	10.69 AW	25910 AAW	CABLS	10//99-12//99
	Los Angeles-Long Beach PMSA, CA	S	10.26 MW	9.02 AW	21340 AAW	CABLS	10//99-12//99
	Modesto MSA, CA	S	12.17 MW	12.28 AW	25310 AAW	CABLS	10//99-12//99
	Oakland PMSA, CA	S	11.38 MW	10.68 AW	23660 AAW	CABLS	10//99-12//99
	Orange County PMSA, CA	S	9.07 MW	9.17 AW	18860 AAW	CABLS	10//99-12//99
	Riverside-San Bernardino PMSA, CA	S	9.01 MW	8.47 AW	18740 AAW	CABLS	10//99-12//99
	Sacramento PMSA, CA	S	10.94 MW	9.93 AW	22750 AAW	CABLS	10//99-12//99
	San Diego MSA, CA	S	9.07 MW	7.97 AW	18860 AAW	CABLS	10//99-12//99
	San Francisco PMSA, CA	S	9.70 MW	6.84 AW	20170 AAW	CABLS	10//99-12//99
	San Jose PMSA, CA	S	11.84 MW	11.88 AW	24630 AAW	CABLS	10//99-12//99
	Santa Barbara-Santa Maria-Lompoc MSA, CA	S	9.95 MW	9.26 AW	20690 AAW	CABLS	10//99-12//99
	Stockton-Lodi MSA, CA	S	10.86 MW	10.19 AW	22590 AAW	CABLS	10//99-12//99
	Vallejo-Fairfield-Napa PMSA, CA	S	10.29 MW	9.23 AW	21400 AAW	CABLS	10//99-12//99
	Ventura PMSA, CA	S	10.52 MW	9.11 AW	21870 AAW	CABLS	10//99-12//99
	Fort Collins-Loveland MSA, CO	S	11.28 MW	10.12 AW	23470 AAW	COBLS	10//99-12//99
	Greeley PMSA, CO	S	10.27 MW	9.58 AW	21350 AAW	COBLS	10//99-12//99
	Connecticut	S	10.44 MW	11.36 AW	23630 AAW	CTBLS	10//99-12//99
	Bridgeport PMSA, CT	S	12.23 MW	12.02 AW	25450 AAW	CTBLS	10//99-12//99
	Danbury PMSA, CT	S	12.12 MW	12.05 AW	25210 AAW	CTBLS	10//99-12//99

AAW	Average annual wage	AOH	Average offered, high	ASH	Average starting, high	H	Hourly	M	Monthly	S	Special: hourly and annual
AE	Average entry wage	AOL	Average offered, low	ASL	Average starting, low	HI	Highest wage paid	MTC	Median total compensation	TQ	Third quartile wage
AEX	Average experienced wage	APH	Average pay, high range	AW	Average wage paid	HR	High end range	MW	Median wage paid	W	Weekly
AO	Average offered	APL	Average pay, low range	FQ	First quartile wage	LR	Low end range	SQ	Second quartile wage	Y	Yearly

Occupation/Type/Industry	Location	Per	Low	Mid	High	Source	Date
Extruding, Forming, Pressing, and Compacting Machine Setter, Operator, and Tender	New London-Norwich MSA, CT-RI	S	10.87 MW	9.99 AW	22610 AAW	CTBLS	10//99-12//99
	Stamford-Norwalk PMSA, CT	S	12.57 MW	14.09 AW	26140 AAW	CTBLS	10//99-12//99
	Waterbury PMSA, CT	S	11.79 MW	11.13 AW	24530 AAW	CTBLS	10//99-12//99
	Delaware	S	15.27 MW	14.98 AW	31150 AAW	DEBLS	10//99-12//99
	Wilmington-Newark PMSA, DE-MD	S	15.98 MW	17.43 AW	33250 AAW	DEBLS	10//99-12//99
	Washington PMSA, DC-MD-VA-WV	S	11.34 MW	11.01 AW	23590 AAW	DCBLS	10//99-12//99
	Florida	S	9.48 MW	10.01 AW	20820 AAW	FLBLS	10//99-12//99
	Lakeland-Winter Haven MSA, FL	S	9.92 MW	9.72 AW	20640 AAW	FLBLS	10//99-12//99
	Miami PMSA, FL	S	9.11 MW	8.33 AW	18960 AAW	FLBLS	10//99-12//99
	Orlando MSA, FL	S	10.58 MW	9.06 AW	22010 AAW	FLBLS	10//99-12//99
	Georgia	S	11.06 MW	11.21 AW	23320 AAW	GABLS	10//99-12//99
	Albany MSA, GA	S	10.77 MW	11.26 AW	22410 AAW	GABLS	10//99-12//99
	Atlanta MSA, GA	S	11.82 MW	11.56 AW	24580 AAW	GABLS	10//99-12//99
	Augusta-Aiken MSA, GA-SC	S	12.01 MW	12.35 AW	24990 AAW	GABLS	10//99-12//99
	Macon MSA, GA	S	12.08 MW	12.25 AW	25130 AAW	GABLS	10//99-12//99
	Idaho	S	10.52 MW	10.81 AW	22490 AAW	IDBLS	10//99-12//99
	Illinois	S	12.55 MW	13.28 AW	27620 AAW	ILBLS	10//99-12//99
	Chicago PMSA, IL	S	13.14 MW	12.42 AW	27330 AAW	ILBLS	10//99-12//99
	Indiana	S	11.61 MW	12.10 AW	25170 AAW	INBLS	10//99-12//99
	Elkhart-Goshen MSA, IN	S	10.56 MW	10.07 AW	21960 AAW	INBLS	10//99-12//99
	Evansville-Henderson MSA, IN-KY	S	12.27 MW	11.93 AW	25530 AAW	INBLS	10//99-12//99
	Fort Wayne MSA, IN	S	12.00 MW	10.50 AW	24960 AAW	INBLS	10//99-12//99
	Gary PMSA, IN	S	14.78 MW	14.94 AW	30740 AAW	INBLS	10//99-12//99
	Indianapolis MSA, IN	S	11.10 MW	10.44 AW	23090 AAW	INBLS	10//99-12//99
	Iowa	S	12.84 MW	13.04 AW	27120 AAW	IABLS	10//99-12//99
	Des Moines MSA, IA	S	11.47 MW	11.65 AW	23850 AAW	IABLS	10//99-12//99
	Dubuque MSA, IA	S	11.57 MW	10.97 AW	24070 AAW	IABLS	10//99-12//99
	Kansas	S	10.59 MW	10.86 AW	22590 AAW	KSBLS	10//99-12//99
	Topeka MSA, KS	S	11.62 MW	10.48 AW	24170 AAW	KSBLS	10//99-12//99
	Kentucky	S	10.73 MW	11.20 AW	23290 AAW	KYBLS	10//99-12//99
	Lexington MSA, KY	S	11.12 MW	10.82 AW	23120 AAW	KYBLS	10//99-12//99
	Louisville MSA, KY-IN	S	12.98 MW	11.57 AW	27000 AAW	KYBLS	10//99-12//99
	Louisiana	S	12.52 MW	13.45 AW	27970 AAW	LABLS	10//99-12//99
	Lafayette MSA, LA	S	10.73 MW	10.88 AW	22320 AAW	LABLS	10//99-12//99
	Monroe MSA, LA	S	9.10 MW	9.34 AW	18920 AAW	LABLS	10//99-12//99
	New Orleans MSA, LA	S	10.41 MW	10.12 AW	21640 AAW	LABLS	10//99-12//99
	Maine	S	10.2 MW	10.31 AW	21450 AAW	MEBLS	10//99-12//99
	Maryland	S	14.4 MW	13.61 AW	28310 AAW	MDBLS	10//99-12//99
	Baltimore PMSA, MD	S	13.32 MW	13.65 AW	27700 AAW	MDBLS	10//99-12//99
	Massachusetts	S	11.92 MW	12.47 AW	25940 AAW	MABLS	10//99-12//99
	Boston PMSA, MA-NH	S	12.32 MW	11.82 AW	25620 AAW	MABLS	10//99-12//99
	Lawrence PMSA, MA-NH	S	12.60 MW	11.73 AW	26220 AAW	MABLS	10//99-12//99
	Michigan	S	11.17 MW	11.52 AW	23960 AAW	MIBLS	10//99-12//99
	Ann Arbor PMSA, MI	S	13.02 MW	12.57 AW	27080 AAW	MIBLS	10//99-12//99
	Detroit PMSA, MI	S	10.87 MW	10.69 AW	22620 AAW	MIBLS	10//99-12//99
	Grand Rapids-Muskegon-Holland MSA, MI	S	11.32 MW	12.01 AW	23540 AAW	MIBLS	10//99-12//99
	Kalamazoo-Battle Creek MSA, MI	S	11.80 MW	12.23 AW	24550 AAW	MIBLS	10//99-12//99
	Saginaw-Bay City-Midland MSA, MI	S	13.43 MW	14.22 AW	27940 AAW	MIBLS	10//99-12//99
	Minnesota	S	13.17 MW	13.33 AW	27730 AAW	MNBLS	10//99-12//99
	Minneapolis-St. Paul MSA, MN-WI	S	13.40 MW	13.03 AW	27870 AAW	MNBLS	10//99-12//99
	Mississippi	S	10.37 MW	11.27 AW	23440 AAW	MSBLS	10//99-12//99
	Jackson MSA, MS	S	13.85 MW	9.09 AW	28800 AAW	MSBLS	10//99-12//99
	Missouri	S	10.92 MW	10.94 AW	22750 AAW	MOBLS	10//99-12//99
	Joplin MSA, MO	S	11.49 MW	11.35 AW	23900 AAW	MOBLS	10//99-12//99
	Kansas City MSA, MO-KS	S	11.54 MW	11.53 AW	24010 AAW	MOBLS	10//99-12//99
	St. Louis MSA, MO-IL	S	11.46 MW	11.41 AW	23850 AAW	MOBLS	10//99-12//99
	Nebraska	S	11.06 MW	10.91 AW	22700 AAW	NEBLS	10//99-12//99
	Omaha MSA, NE-IA	S	9.89 MW	9.71 AW	20560 AAW	NEBLS	10//99-12//99
	Nevada	S	11.54 MW	11.80 AW	24540 AAW	NVBLS	10//99-12//99
	Reno MSA, NV	S	11.38 MW	11.22 AW	23670 AAW	NVBLS	10//99-12//99
	Nashua PMSA, NH	S	10.56 MW	10.61 AW	21970 AAW	NHBLS	10//99-12//99

AAW Average annual wage	**AOH** Average offered, high	**ASH** Average starting, high	**H** Hourly	**M** Monthly	**S** Special: hourly and annual
AE Average entry wage	**AOL** Average offered, low	**ASL** Average starting, low	**HI** Highest wage paid	**MTC** Median total compensation	**TQ** Third quartile wage
AEX Average experienced wage	**APH** Average pay, high range	**AW** Average wage paid	**HR** High end range	**MW** Median wage paid	**W** Weekly
AO Average offered	**APL** Average pay, low range	**FQ** First quartile wage	**LR** Low end range	**SQ** Second quartile wage	**Y** Yearly

Occupation/Type/Industry	Location	Per	Low	Mid	High	Source	Date
Extruding, Forming, Pressing, and Compacting Machine Setter, Operator, and Tender	New Jersey	S	11.43 MW	11.98 AW	24910 AAW	NJBLS	10//99-12//99
	Bergen-Passaic PMSA, NJ	S	10.25 MW	9.63 AW	21320 AAW	NJBLS	10//99-12//99
	Middlesex-Somerset-Hunterdon PMSA, NJ	S	13.11 MW	12.01 AW	27260 AAW	NJBLS	10//99-12//99
	Monmouth-Ocean PMSA, NJ	S	9.60 MW	9.06 AW	19970 AAW	NJBLS	10//99-12//99
	Newark PMSA, NJ	S	10.64 MW	10.95 AW	22140 AAW	NJBLS	10//99-12//99
	Trenton PMSA, NJ	S	12.53 MW	12.50 AW	26060 AAW	NJBLS	10//99-12//99
	Vineland-Millville-Bridgeton PMSA, NJ	S	10.81 MW	9.69 AW	22480 AAW	NJBLS	10//99-12//99
	New Mexico	S	7.91 MW	8.30 AW	17270 AAW	NMBLS	10//99-12//99
	Albuquerque MSA, NM	S	9.83 MW	9.57 AW	20450 AAW	NMBLS	10//99-12//99
	New York	S	11.71 MW	12.28 AW	25550 AAW	NYBLS	10//99-12//99
	Albany-Schenectady-Troy MSA, NY	S	12.12 MW	12.61 AW	25220 AAW	NYBLS	10//99-12//99
	Buffalo-Niagara Falls MSA, NY	S	9.73 MW	9.21 AW	20240 AAW	NYBLS	10//99-12//99
	Nassau-Suffolk PMSA, NY	S	10.77 MW	9.52 AW	22410 AAW	NYBLS	10//99-12//99
	New York PMSA, NY	S	10.24 MW	9.23 AW	21300 AAW	NYBLS	10//99-12//99
	Newburgh PMSA, NY-PA	S	13.12 MW	12.14 AW	27290 AAW	NYBLS	10//99-12//99
	Rochester MSA, NY	S	15.13 MW	16.51 AW	31470 AAW	NYBLS	10//99-12//99
	Syracuse MSA, NY	S	14.66 MW	15.48 AW	30480 AAW	NYBLS	10//99-12//99
	North Carolina	S	12.49 MW	13.13 AW	27320 AAW	NCBLS	10//99-12//99
	Charlotte-Gastonia-Rock Hill MSA, NC-SC	S	14.34 MW	14.61 AW	29820 AAW	NCBLS	10//99-12//99
	Greensboro--Winston-Salem--High Point MSA, NC	S	14.27 MW	12.31 AW	29690 AAW	NCBLS	10//99-12//99
	Hickory-Morganton-Lenoir MSA, NC	S	11.69 MW	12.15 AW	24310 AAW	NCBLS	10//99-12//99
	Raleigh-Durham-Chapel Hill MSA, NC	S	11.82 MW	11.62 AW	24580 AAW	NCBLS	10//99-12//99
	Ohio	S	11.65 MW	12.12 AW	25210 AAW	OHBLS	10//99-12//99
	Akron PMSA, OH	S	12.19 MW	11.97 AW	25350 AAW	OHBLS	10//99-12//99
	Cincinnati PMSA, OH-KY-IN	S	12.28 MW	12.35 AW	25540 AAW	OHBLS	10//99-12//99
	Cleveland-Lorain-Elyria PMSA, OH	S	11.38 MW	11.18 AW	23670 AAW	OHBLS	10//99-12//99
	Columbus MSA, OH	S	13.72 MW	14.30 AW	28540 AAW	OHBLS	10//99-12//99
	Dayton-Springfield MSA, OH	S	14.43 MW	12.13 AW	30020 AAW	OHBLS	10//99-12//99
	Toledo MSA, OH	S	12.71 MW	13.18 AW	26440 AAW	OHBLS	10//99-12//99
	Youngstown-Warren MSA, OH	S	13.70 MW	12.67 AW	28490 AAW	OHBLS	10//99-12//99
	Oklahoma	S	10.75 MW	11.29 AW	23470 AAW	OKBLS	10//99-12//99
	Oklahoma City MSA, OK	S	11.60 MW	11.50 AW	24130 AAW	OKBLS	10//99-12//99
	Tulsa MSA, OK	S	10.95 MW	10.02 AW	22780 AAW	OKBLS	10//99-12//99
	Oregon	S	12.03 MW	12.40 AW	25800 AAW	ORBLS	10//99-12//99
	Eugene-Springfield MSA, OR	S	12.26 MW	12.29 AW	25500 AAW	ORBLS	10//99-12//99
	Portland-Vancouver PMSA, OR-WA	S	11.58 MW	10.40 AW	24090 AAW	ORBLS	10//99-12//99
	Salem PMSA, OR	S	11.54 MW	11.09 AW	24000 AAW	ORBLS	10//99-12//99
	Pennsylvania	S	13.24 MW	13.39 AW	27850 AAW	PABLS	10//99-12//99
	Allentown-Bethlehem-Easton MSA, PA	S	11.62 MW	11.33 AW	24160 AAW	PABLS	10//99-12//99
	Erie MSA, PA	S	15.45 MW	16.92 AW	32130 AAW	PABLS	10//99-12//99
	Harrisburg-Lebanon-Carlisle MSA, PA	S	12.45 MW	13.34 AW	25890 AAW	PABLS	10//99-12//99
	Lancaster MSA, PA	S	13.13 MW	12.06 AW	27310 AAW	PABLS	10//99-12//99
	Philadelphia PMSA, PA-NJ	S	14.29 MW	14.50 AW	29730 AAW	PABLS	10//99-12//99
	Pittsburgh MSA, PA	S	12.91 MW	12.66 AW	26860 AAW	PABLS	10//99-12//99
	Reading MSA, PA	S	14.55 MW	14.96 AW	30250 AAW	PABLS	10//99-12//99
	Scranton--Wilkes-Barre--Hazleton MSA, PA	S	14.02 MW	13.37 AW	29160 AAW	PABLS	10//99-12//99
	Sharon MSA, PA	S	9.20 MW	8.27 AW	19140 AAW	PABLS	10//99-12//99
	York MSA, PA	S	11.56 MW	11.83 AW	24040 AAW	PABLS	10//99-12//99
	Rhode Island	S	8.4 MW	9.18 AW	19100 AAW	RIBLS	10//99-12//99
	Providence-Fall River-Warwick MSA, RI-MA	S	9.80 MW	8.66 AW	20380 AAW	RIBLS	10//99-12//99
	South Carolina	S	12.18 MW	13.19 AW	27440 AAW	SCBLS	10//99-12//99
	Charleston-North Charleston MSA, SC	S	10.73 MW	10.96 AW	22320 AAW	SCBLS	10//99-12//99
	Greenville-Spartanburg-Anderson MSA, SC	S	14.99 MW	14.52 AW	31180 AAW	SCBLS	10//99-12//99
	South Dakota	S	11.45 MW	11.36 AW	23630 AAW	SDBLS	10//99-12//99

Occupation/Type/Industry	Location	Per	Low	Mid	High	Source	Date
Extruding, Forming, Pressing, and Compacting Machine Setter, Operator, and Tender	Sioux Falls MSA, SD	S	11.78 MW	11.34 AW	24510 AAW	SDBLS	10//99-12//99
	Tennessee	S	11.32 MW	11.53 AW	23990 AAW	TNBLS	10//99-12//99
	Chattanooga MSA, TN-GA	S	10.08 MW	9.98 AW	20960 AAW	TNBLS	10//99-12//99
	Clarksville-Hopkinsville MSA, TN-KY	S	10.16 MW	9.93 AW	21140 AAW	TNBLS	10//99-12//99
	Jackson MSA, TN	S	12.16 MW	12.48 AW	25300 AAW	TNBLS	10//99-12//99
	Knoxville MSA, TN	S	11.37 MW	10.67 AW	23640 AAW	TNBLS	10//99-12//99
	Memphis MSA, TN-AR-MS	S	10.65 MW	10.25 AW	22160 AAW	MSBLS	10//99-12//99
	Nashville MSA, TN	S	13.63 MW	14.17 AW	28360 AAW	TNBLS	10//99-12//99
	Texas	S	10.37 MW	10.83 AW	22530 AAW	TXBLS	10//99-12//99
	Dallas PMSA, TX	S	9.72 MW	9.56 AW	20220 AAW	TXBLS	10//99-12//99
	Fort Worth-Arlington PMSA, TX	S	10.57 MW	10.90 AW	21990 AAW	TXBLS	10//99-12//99
	Houston PMSA, TX	S	10.75 MW	9.36 AW	22360 AAW	TXBLS	10//99-12//99
	Longview-Marshall MSA, TX	S	10.21 MW	11.20 AW	21240 AAW	TXBLS	10//99-12//99
	San Antonio MSA, TX	S	9.23 MW	8.50 AW	19200 AAW	TXBLS	10//99-12//99
	Waco MSA, TX	S	10.00 MW	9.96 AW	20800 AAW	TXBLS	10//99-12//99
	Provo-Orem MSA, UT	S	11.35 MW	10.72 AW	23610 AAW	UTBLS	10//99-12//99
	Vermont	S	11.64 MW	12.23 AW	25450 AAW	VTBLS	10//99-12//99
	Virginia	S	10.68 MW	12.27 AW	25520 AAW	VABLS	10//99-12//99
	Richmond-Petersburg MSA, VA	S	16.45 MW	17.46 AW	34220 AAW	VABLS	10//99-12//99
	Washington	S	12.57 MW	13.41 AW	27880 AAW	WABLS	10//99-12//99
	Seattle-Bellevue-Everett PMSA, WA	S	12.57 MW	11.56 AW	26140 AAW	WABLS	10//99-12//99
	West Virginia	S	13.91 MW	12.57 AW	26150 AAW	WVBLS	10//99-12//99
	Parkersburg-Marietta MSA, WV-OH	S	15.12 MW	15.21 AW	31450 AAW	WVBLS	10//99-12//99
	Wheeling MSA, WV-OH	S	10.47 MW	10.32 AW	21770 AAW	WVBLS	10//99-12//99
	Wisconsin	S	11.29 MW	11.64 AW	24220 AAW	WIBLS	10//99-12//99
	Appleton-Oshkosh-Neenah MSA, WI	S	13.82 MW	14.46 AW	28750 AAW	WIBLS	10//99-12//99
	Green Bay MSA, WI	S	11.39 MW	10.94 AW	23700 AAW	WIBLS	10//99-12//99
	Madison MSA, WI	S	12.01 MW	11.16 AW	24970 AAW	WIBLS	10//99-12//99
	Milwaukee-Waukesha PMSA, WI	S	10.80 MW	9.77 AW	22450 AAW	WIBLS	10//99-12//99
	Racine PMSA, WI	S	10.40 MW	10.32 AW	21630 AAW	WIBLS	10//99-12//99
	Sheboygan MSA, WI	S	12.10 MW	11.94 AW	25160 AAW	WIBLS	10//99-12//99
	Puerto Rico	S	7.87 MW	8.26 AW	17170 AAW	PRBLS	10//99-12//99
	San Juan-Bayamon PMSA, PR	S	8.61 MW	9.11 AW	17920 AAW	PRBLS	10//99-12//99
Fabric and Apparel Patternmaker	Alabama	S	8.11 MW	8.94 AW	18590 AAW	ALBLS	10//99-12//99
	Arizona	S	9.89 MW	9.95 AW	20700 AAW	AZBLS	10//99-12//99
	Arkansas	S	7.78 MW	8.08 AW	16800 AAW	ARBLS	10//99-12//99
	California	S	14.12 MW	16.07 AW	33420 AAW	CABLS	10//99-12//99
	Florida	S	7.74 MW	9.45 AW	19660 AAW	FLBLS	10//99-12//99
	Georgia	S	10.04 MW	10.19 AW	21190 AAW	GABLS	10//99-12//99
	Hawaii	S	10.22 MW	11.43 AW	23780 AAW	HIBLS	10//99-12//99
	Illinois	S	10.52 MW	11.47 AW	23860 AAW	ILBLS	10//99-12//99
	Indiana	S	9.1 MW	9.86 AW	20500 AAW	INBLS	10//99-12//99
	Iowa	S	8.9 MW	9.45 AW	19670 AAW	IABLS	10//99-12//99
	Kansas	S	8.5 MW	8.56 AW	17810 AAW	KSBLS	10//99-12//99
	Kentucky	S	8.82 MW	10.58 AW	22000 AAW	KYBLS	10//99-12//99
	Maine	S	10.7 MW	11.42 AW	23750 AAW	MEBLS	10//99-12//99
	Massachusetts	S	10.58 MW	12.13 AW	25240 AAW	MABLS	10//99-12//99
	Michigan	S	15.16 MW	15.11 AW	31430 AAW	MIBLS	10//99-12//99
	Minnesota	S	10.12 MW	10.38 AW	21590 AAW	MNBLS	10//99-12//99
	Mississippi	S	8.61 MW	9.44 AW	19640 AAW	MSBLS	10//99-12//99
	New Hampshire	S	11.53 MW	13.28 AW	27610 AAW	NHBLS	10//99-12//99
	New Jersey	S	11.9 MW	15.54 AW	32320 AAW	NJBLS	10//99-12//99
	New York	S	14.87 MW	18.47 AW	38420 AAW	NYBLS	10//99-12//99
	North Carolina	S	11.1 MW	12.12 AW	25210 AAW	NCBLS	10//99-12//99
	Ohio	S	8.07 MW	8.79 AW	18290 AAW	OHBLS	10//99-12//99
	Oregon	S	11.27 MW	13.64 AW	28370 AAW	ORBLS	10//99-12//99
	Pennsylvania	S	10.58 MW	12.12 AW	25210 AAW	PABLS	10//99-12//99
	South Carolina	S	11.65 MW	12.25 AW	25480 AAW	SCBLS	10//99-12//99
	Tennessee	S	10.85 MW	11.48 AW	23870 AAW	TNBLS	10//99-12//99
	Texas	S	8.1 MW	8.94 AW	18600 AAW	TXBLS	10//99-12//99
	Virginia	S	11.21 MW	11.10 AW	23100 AAW	VABLS	10//99-12//99
	Washington	S	8.35 MW	8.87 AW	18450 AAW	WABLS	10//99-12//99

AAW	Average annual wage	AOH	Average offered, high	ASH	Average starting, high
AE	Average entry wage	AOL	Average offered, low	ASL	Average starting, low
AEX	Average experienced wage	APH	Average pay, high range	AW	Average wage paid
AO	Average offered	APL	Average pay, low range	FQ	First quartile wage

H	Hourly	M	Monthly	S	Special: hourly and annual
HI	Highest wage paid	MTC	Median total compensation	TQ	Third quartile wage
HR	High end range	MW	Median wage paid	W	Weekly
LR	Low end range	SQ	Second quartile wage	Y	Yearly

Occupation/Type/Industry	Location	Per	Low	Mid	High	Source	Date
Fabric and Apparel Patternmaker	Wisconsin	S	9.92 MW	10.77 AW	22410 AAW	WIBLS	10//99-12//99
	Puerto Rico	S	6.04 MW	6.37 AW	13260 AAW	PRBLS	10//99-12//99
Fabric Mender							
Except Garment	California	S	14.56 MW	13.32 AW	27700 AAW	CABLS	10//99-12//99
Except Garment	Connecticut	S	19.03 MW	18.90 AW	39310 AAW	CTBLS	10//99-12//99
Except Garment	Florida	S	17.56 MW	14.81 AW	30800 AAW	FLBLS	10//99-12//99
Except Garment	Georgia	S	7.71 MW	8.38 AW	17430 AAW	GABLS	10//99-12//99
Except Garment	Atlanta MSA, GA	S	7.54 MW	7.50 AW	15680 AAW	GABLS	10//99-12//99
Except Garment	Illinois	S	18.72 MW	17.52 AW	36450 AAW	ILBLS	10//99-12//99
Except Garment	Kansas	S	10.14 MW	12.43 AW	25850 AAW	KSBLS	10//99-12//99
Except Garment	Louisiana	S	7.57 MW	9.77 AW	20320 AAW	LABLS	10//99-12//99
Except Garment	Maine	S	13.9 MW	13.35 AW	27760 AAW	MEBLS	10//99-12//99
Except Garment	Massachusetts	S	12.52 MW	13.32 AW	27710 AAW	MABLS	10//99-12//99
Except Garment	Mississippi	S	7.21 MW	10.30 AW	21420 AAW	MSBLS	10//99-12//99
Except Garment	New Hampshire	S	9.74 MW	10.11 AW	21030 AAW	NHBLS	10//99-12//99
Except Garment	New York	S	7.76 MW	9.65 AW	20080 AAW	NYBLS	10//99-12//99
Except Garment	New York PMSA, NY	S	7.23 MW	6.77 AW	15030 AAW	NYBLS	10//99-12//99
Except Garment	North Carolina	S	10.07 MW	10.44 AW	21720 AAW	NCBLS	10//99-12//99
Except Garment	Ohio	S	18.88 MW	17.83 AW	37090 AAW	OHBLS	10//99-12//99
Except Garment	Cleveland-Lorain-Elyria PMSA, OH	S	19.06 MW	19.20 AW	39650 AAW	OHBLS	10//99-12//99
Except Garment	Dayton-Springfield MSA, OH	S	12.21 MW	9.90 AW	25390 AAW	OHBLS	10//99-12//99
Except Garment	Oklahoma	S	14.21 MW	13.92 AW	28960 AAW	OKBLS	10//99-12//99
Except Garment	Pennsylvania	S	8.03 MW	9.32 AW	19380 AAW	PABLS	10//99-12//99
Except Garment	Harrisburg-Lebanon-Carlisle MSA, PA	S	9.15 MW	8.64 AW	19040 AAW	PABLS	10//99-12//99
Except Garment	Philadelphia PMSA, PA-NJ	S	9.83 MW	6.72 AW	20440 AAW	PABLS	10//99-12//99
Except Garment	Scranton--Wilkes-Barre--Hazleton MSA, PA	S	8.11 MW	7.68 AW	16870 AAW	PABLS	10//99-12//99
Except Garment	South Carolina	S	9.41 MW	9.59 AW	19960 AAW	SCBLS	10//99-12//99
Except Garment	Tennessee	S	6.68 MW	9.60 AW	19970 AAW	TNBLS	10//99-12//99
Except Garment	Texas	S	10.42 MW	11.99 AW	24940 AAW	TXBLS	10//99-12//99
Except Garment	West Virginia	S	7.73 MW	7.84 AW	16310 AAW	WVBLS	10//99-12//99
Faculty							
Top, Accounting	United States	Y		67276 AW		PRISM	2000
Top, Business Management	United States	Y		71282 AW		PRISM	2000
Top, Chemical Engineering	United States	Y		73863 AW		PRISM	2000
Top, Dentistry	United States	Y		70196 AW		PRISM	2000
Top, Electrical and Communications Engineering	United States	Y		71259 AW		PRISM	2000
Top, Financial Management and Services	United States	Y		71259 AW		PRISM	2000
Top, Human Resources Management	United States	Y		67253 AW		PRISM	2000
Top, Law	United States	Y		95655 AW		PRISM	2000
Top, Mechanical Engineering	United States	Y		68340 AW		PRISM	2000
Faller	Alabama	S	10.83 MW	10.45 AW	21730 AAW	ALBLS	10//99-12//99
	Arizona	S	6.29 MW	6.71 AW	13960 AAW	AZBLS	10//99-12//99
	Arkansas	S	7.93 MW	8.87 AW	18460 AAW	ARBLS	10//99-12//99
	California	S	21.57 MW	21.37 AW	44440 AAW	CABLS	10//99-12//99
	Connecticut	S	15.35 MW	15.37 AW	31970 AAW	CTBLS	10//99-12//99
	Florida	S	9.84 MW	9.88 AW	20560 AAW	FLBLS	10//99-12//99
	Georgia	S	11.72 MW	11.04 AW	22960 AAW	GABLS	10//99-12//99
	Idaho	S	28.9 MW	27.13 AW	56430 AAW	IDBLS	10//99-12//99
	Indiana	S	11.59 MW	11.51 AW	23940 AAW	INBLS	10//99-12//99
	Kentucky	S	9.15 MW	9.47 AW	19700 AAW	KYBLS	10//99-12//99
	Louisiana	S	9.12 MW	9.14 AW	19010 AAW	LABLS	10//99-12//99
	Maine	S	14.28 MW	12.66 AW	26340 AAW	MEBLS	10//99-12//99
	Michigan	S	9.77 MW	10.25 AW	21310 AAW	MIBLS	10//99-12//99
	Mississippi	S	8.92 MW	9.12 AW	18970 AAW	MSBLS	10//99-12//99
	Missouri	S	9.48 MW	9.04 AW	18810 AAW	MOBLS	10//99-12//99
	New Hampshire	S	15.25 MW	15.16 AW	31530 AAW	NHBLS	10//99-12//99
	New York	S	7.33 MW	8.17 AW	16990 AAW	NYBLS	10//99-12//99
	North Carolina	S	10.44 MW	10.65 AW	22150 AAW	NCBLS	10//99-12//99
	Ohio	S	10.14 MW	10.29 AW	21400 AAW	OHBLS	10//99-12//99
	Oklahoma	S	14.46 MW	14.43 AW	30020 AAW	OKBLS	10//99-12//99
	Oregon	S	18.52 MW	19.22 AW	39970 AAW	ORBLS	10//99-12//99
	Pennsylvania	S	14.21 MW	12.86 AW	26740 AAW	PABLS	10//99-12//99
	South Carolina	S	8.98 MW	9.83 AW	20440 AAW	SCBLS	10//99-12//99
	Tennessee	S	12.09 MW	11.93 AW	24810 AAW	TNBLS	10//99-12//99
	Virginia	S	10.24 MW	10.93 AW	22730 AAW	VABLS	10//99-12//99
	Washington	S	21.69 MW	20.86 AW	43380 AAW	WABLS	10//99-12//99

AAW	Average annual wage	AOH	Average offered, high	ASH	Average starting, high	H	Hourly			M	Monthly			S	Special: hourly and annual
AE	Average entry wage	AOL	Average offered, low	ASL	Average starting, low	HI	Highest wage paid	MTC	Median total compensation	TQ	Third quartile wage
AEX	Average experienced wage	APH	Average pay, high range	AW	Average wage paid	HR	High end range	MW	Median wage paid	W	Weekly
AO	Average offered	APL	Average pay, low range	FQ	First quartile wage	LR	Low end range	SQ	Second quartile wage	Y	Yearly

Occupation/Type/Industry	Location	Per	Low	Mid	High	Source	Date
Faller	Wisconsin	S	10.11 MW	13.97 AW	29050 AAW	WIBLS	10//99-12//99
Family and General Practitioner	Alabama	S	62.33 MW	58.40 AW	121470 AAW	ALBLS	10//99-12//99
	Birmingham MSA, AL	S	59.32 MW	63.12 AW	123380 AAW	ALBLS	10//99-12//99
	Alaska	S	51.71 MW	50.64 AW	105340 AAW	AKBLS	10//99-12//99
	Anchorage MSA, AK	S	50.62 MW	50.28 AW	105300 AAW	AKBLS	10//99-12//99
	Arizona	S	59.59 MW	50.45 AW	104930 AAW	AZBLS	10//99-12//99
	Phoenix-Mesa MSA, AZ	S	49.91 MW	60.72 AW	103820 AAW	AZBLS	10//99-12//99
	Tucson MSA, AZ	S	58.34 MW		121350 AAW	AZBLS	10//99-12//99
	Arkansas	S	53.94 MW	52.44 AW	109060 AAW	ARBLS	10//99-12//99
	Fayetteville-Springdale-Rogers MSA, AR	S	59.44 MW	63.35 AW	123640 AAW	ARBLS	10//99-12//99
	California	S	40.55 MW	37.97 AW	78990 AAW	CABLS	10//99-12//99
	Chico-Paradise MSA, CA	S	49.01 MW	49.94 AW	101940 AAW	CABLS	10//99-12//99
	Fresno MSA, CA	S	48.11 MW	49.55 AW	100070 AAW	CABLS	10//99-12//99
	Los Angeles-Long Beach PMSA, CA	S	31.17 MW	23.78 AW	64820 AAW	CABLS	
	Oakland PMSA, CA	S	51.34 MW	52.53 AW	106790 AAW	CABLS	10//99-12//99
	Orange County PMSA, CA	S	46.30 MW	45.92 AW	96300 AAW	CABLS	10//99-12//99
	Sacramento PMSA, CA	S	39.70 MW	45.69 AW	82580 AAW	CABLS	10//99-12//99
	Salinas MSA, CA	S	63.80 MW		132690 AAW	CABLS	10//99-12//99
	San Diego MSA, CA	S	38.58 MW	38.90 AW	80250 AAW	CABLS	10//99-12//99
	San Francisco PMSA, CA	S	55.24 MW	56.64 AW	114890 AAW	CABLS	10//99-12//99
	Santa Barbara-Santa Maria-Lompoc MSA, CA	S	54.78 MW	59.71 AW	113940 AAW	CABLS	10//99-12//99
	Santa Rosa PMSA, CA	S	39.06 MW	39.31 AW	81240 AAW	CABLS	10//99-12//99
	Vallejo-Fairfield-Napa PMSA, CA	S	29.99 MW	20.93 AW	62380 AAW	CABLS	10//99-12//99
	Connecticut	S	47.22 MW	45.35 AW	94330 AAW	CTBLS	10//99-12//99
	Bridgeport PMSA, CT	S	49.32 MW	50.22 AW	102600 AAW	CTBLS	10//99-12//99
	Danbury PMSA, CT	S	63.89 MW		132900 AAW	CTBLS	10//99-12//99
	Hartford MSA, CT	S	47.97 MW	43.86 AW	99780 AAW	CTBLS	10//99-12//99
	New London-Norwich MSA, CT-RI	S	45.73 MW	52.35 AW	95120 AAW	CTBLS	
	Washington PMSA, DC-MD-VA-WV	S	42.85 MW	43.84 AW	89130 AAW	DCBLS	10//99-12//99
	Florida	S	62.37 MW	54.25 AW	112840 AAW	FLBLS	10//99-12//99
	Daytona Beach MSA, FL	S	55.79 MW	64.51 AW	116050 AAW	FLBLS	10//99-12//99
	Fort Lauderdale PMSA, FL	S	63.15 MW	68.78 AW	131360 AAW	FLBLS	10//99-12//99
	Fort Myers-Cape Coral MSA, FL	S	59.24 MW	66.26 AW	123230 AAW	FLBLS	10//99-12//99
	Fort Pierce-Port St. Lucie MSA, FL	S	49.36 MW	53.44 AW	102670 AAW	FLBLS	10//99-12//99
	Gainesville MSA, FL	S	49.75 MW	50.04 AW	103470 AAW	FLBLS	10//99-12//99
	Jacksonville MSA, FL	S	51.85 MW	56.81 AW	107850 AAW	FLBLS	10//99-12//99
	Lakeland-Winter Haven MSA, FL	S	62.76 MW		130550 AAW	FLBLS	10//99-12//99
	Melbourne-Titusville-Palm Bay MSA, FL	S	60.45 MW	66.29 AW	125730 AAW	FLBLS	10//99-12//99
	Orlando MSA, FL	S	57.04 MW	63.28 AW	118650 AAW	FLBLS	10//99-12//99
	Sarasota-Bradenton MSA, FL	S	60.45 MW	63.68 AW	125730 AAW	FLBLS	10//99-12//99
	Tampa-St. Petersburg-Clearwater MSA, FL	S	54.95 MW	59.35 AW	114290 AAW	FLBLS	10//99-12//99
	West Palm Beach-Boca Raton MSA, FL	S	47.95 MW	50.21 AW	99730 AAW	FLBLS	10//99-12//99
	Georgia	S		56.84 AW	118230 AAW	GABLS	10//99-12//99
	Columbus MSA, GA-AL	S	58.93 MW	67.90 AW	122570 AAW	GABLS	10//99-12//99
	Hawaii	S	41.01 MW	39.07 AW	81270 AAW	HIBLS	10//99-12//99
	Illinois	S	46.51 MW	44.09 AW	91700 AAW	ILBLS	10//99-12//99
	Bloomington-Normal MSA, IL	S	51.78 MW		107710 AAW	ILBLS	10//99-12//99
	Chicago PMSA, IL	S	39.59 MW	43.75 AW	82340 AAW	ILBLS	10//99-12//99
	Peoria-Pekin MSA, IL	S	59.66 MW	63.25 AW	124100 AAW	ILBLS	10//99-12//99
	Rockford MSA, IL	S	51.54 MW	53.40 AW	107190 AAW	ILBLS	10//99-12//99
	Springfield MSA, IL	S	41.77 MW	43.68 AW	86890 AAW	ILBLS	10//99-12//99
	Indiana	S	64.18 MW	58.82 AW	122350 AAW	INBLS	10//99-12//99
	Evansville-Henderson MSA, IN-KY	S	60.06 MW	62.85 AW	124930 AAW	INBLS	10//99-12//99
	Gary PMSA, IN	S	61.66 MW		128250 AAW	INBLS	10//99-12//99
	Indianapolis MSA, IN	S	56.15 MW	60.55 AW	116790 AAW	INBLS	10//99-12//99
	Terre Haute MSA, IN	S	59.10 MW		122920 AAW	INBLS	10//99-12//99
	Iowa	S	52.58 MW	46.56 AW	96840 AAW	IABLS	10//99-12//99
	Waterloo-Cedar Falls MSA, IA	S	61.92 MW		128800 AAW	IABLS	10//99-12//99
	Kansas	S		61.15 AW	127200 AAW	KSBLS	

AAW	Average annual wage	AOH	Average offered, high	ASH	Average starting, high
AE	Average entry salaries	AOL	Average offered, low	ASL	Average starting, low
AEX	Average experienced wage	APH	Average pay, high range	AW	Average wage paid
AO	Average offered	APL	Average pay, low range	FQ	First quartile wage

H	Hourly	M	Monthly	S	Special: hourly and annual
HI	Highest wage paid	MTC	Median total compensation	TQ	Third quartile wage
HR	High end range	MW	Median wage paid	W	Weekly
LR	Low end range	SQ	Second quartile wage	Y	Yearly

Occupation/Type/Industry	Location	Per	Low	Mid	High	Source	Date
Family and General Practitioner	Wichita MSA, KS	S	63.60 MW		132300 AAW	KSBLS	10//99-12//99
	Kentucky	S		62.24 AW	129450 AAW	KYBLS	10//99-12//99
	Louisville MSA, KY-IN	S	60.20 MW	68.62 AW	125230 AAW	KYBLS	10//99-12//99
	Louisiana	S	54.73 MW	50.07 AW	104140 AAW	LABLS	10//99-12//99
	Baton Rouge MSA, LA	S	38.93 MW	38.25 AW	80980 AAW	LABLS	10//99-12//99
	Monroe MSA, LA	S	52.56 MW	51.07 AW	109330 AAW	LABLS	10//99-12//99
	New Orleans MSA, LA	S	46.81 MW	53.12 AW	97370 AAW	LABLS	10//99-12//99
	Maine	S	53.26 MW	53.47 AW	111220 AAW	MEBLS	10//99-12//99
	Lewiston-Auburn MSA, ME	S	53.93 MW	63.63 AW	112180 AAW	MEBLS	10//99-12//99
	Maryland	S	39.78 MW	39.77 AW	82710 AAW	MDBLS	10//99-12//99
	Hagerstown PMSA, MD	S	55.24 MW	63.52 AW	114900 AAW	MDBLS	10//99-12//99
	Massachusetts	S	43.77 MW	40.32 AW	83870 AAW	MABLS	10//99-12//99
	Boston PMSA, MA-NH	S	34.85 MW	25.73 AW	72490 AAW	MABLS	10//99-12//99
	Worcester PMSA, MA-CT	S	33.16 MW	20.98 AW	68980 AAW	MABLS	10//99-12//99
	Michigan	S		62.59 AW	130200 AAW	MIBLS	10//99-12//99
	Ann Arbor PMSA, MI	S	58.01 MW	66.63 AW	120650 AAW	MIBLS	10//99-12//99
	Detroit PMSA, MI	S	65.34 MW		135910 AAW	MIBLS	10//99-12//99
	Lansing-East Lansing MSA, MI	S	58.97 MW	62.41 AW	122660 AAW	MIBLS	10//99-12//99
	Minnesota	S	61.09 MW	57.37 AW	119330 AAW	MNBLS	10//99-12//99
	Minneapolis-St. Paul MSA, MN-WI	S	58.41 MW	63.89 AW	121490 AAW	MNBLS	10//99-12//99
	Mississippi	S	48.83 MW	46.56 AW	96850 AAW	MSBLS	10//99-12//99
	Hattiesburg MSA, MS	S	48.40 MW	50.19 AW	100670 AAW	MSBLS	10//99-12//99
	Missouri	S	57.7 MW	51.55 AW	107230 AAW	MOBLS	10//99-12//99
	Springfield MSA, MO	S	55.45 MW	61.05 AW	115330 AAW	MOBLS	10//99-12//99
	Montana	S	52.79 MW	52.03 AW	108220 AAW	MTBLS	10//99-12//99
	Nebraska	S	64.34 MW	57.21 AW	119000 AAW	NEBLS	10//99-12//99
	Lincoln MSA, NE	S	61.37 MW	67.07 AW	127640 AAW	NEBLS	10//99-12//99
	Omaha MSA, NE-IA	S	53.78 MW	57.57 AW	111850 AAW	NEBLS	10//99-12//99
	Nevada	S	62.69 MW	59.15 AW	123020 AAW	NVBLS	10//99-12//99
	Las Vegas MSA, NV-AZ	S	62.12 MW		129210 AAW	NVBLS	10//99-12//99
	Reno MSA, NV	S	51.03 MW	51.09 AW	106140 AAW	NVBLS	10//99-12//99
	New Hampshire	S	53.51 MW	48.33 AW	100520 AAW	NHBLS	10//99-12//99
	Manchester PMSA, NH	S	32.80 MW	23.84 AW	68230 AAW	NHBLS	10//99-12//99
	New Jersey	S		64.28 AW	133690 AAW	NJBLS	10//99-12//99
	Bergen-Passaic PMSA, NJ	S	52.54 MW	54.41 AW	109290 AAW	NJBLS	10//99-12//99
	Middlesex-Somerset-Hunterdon PMSA, NJ	S	47.40 MW	48.58 AW	98590 AAW	NJBLS	10//99-12//99
	Monmouth-Ocean PMSA, NJ	S	55.29 MW	56.06 AW	115000 AAW	NJBLS	10//99-12//99
	Newark PMSA, NJ	S	66.15 MW		137600 AAW	NJBLS	10//99-12//99
	New Mexico	S	57.34 MW	53.61 AW	111510 AAW	NMBLS	10//99-12//99
	Albuquerque MSA, NM	S	48.69 MW	52.66 AW	101270 AAW	NMBLS	10//99-12//99
	Las Cruces MSA, NM	S	38.35 MW	30.85 AW	79770 AAW	NMBLS	10//99-12//99
	Santa Fe MSA, NM	S	57.32 MW	59.13 AW	119220 AAW	NMBLS	10//99-12//99
	New York	S	49.93 MW	45.87 AW	95420 AAW	NYBLS	10//99-12//99
	Binghamton MSA, NY	S	65.40 MW		136030 AAW	NYBLS	10//99-12//99
	Nassau-Suffolk PMSA, NY	S	49.66 MW	51.33 AW	103290 AAW	NYBLS	10//99-12//99
	New York PMSA, NY	S	41.84 MW	47.27 AW	87020 AAW	NYBLS	10//99-12//99
	Newburgh PMSA, NY-PA	S	45.02 MW	49.74 AW	93640 AAW	NYBLS	10//99-12//99
	Rochester MSA, NY	S	50.28 MW	50.95 AW	104590 AAW	NYBLS	10//99-12//99
	Syracuse MSA, NY	S	45.01 MW	48.80 AW	93630 AAW	NYBLS	10//99-12//99
	North Carolina	S	57.5 MW	53.89 AW	112090 AAW	NCBLS	10//99-12//99
	Asheville MSA, NC	S	54.10 MW	53.27 AW	112530 AAW	NCBLS	10//99-12//99
	Greensboro--Winston-Salem--High Point MSA, NC	S	52.53 MW	44.76 AW	109260 AAW	NCBLS	10//99-12//99
	Hickory-Morganton-Lenoir MSA, NC	S	59.53 MW	65.84 AW	123810 AAW	NCBLS	10//99-12//99
	Raleigh-Durham-Chapel Hill MSA, NC	S	50.21 MW	51.89 AW	104430 AAW	NCBLS	10//99-12//99
	Wilmington MSA, NC	S	63.96 MW		133040 AAW	NCBLS	10//99-12//99
	North Dakota	S	58.3 MW	54.92 AW	114240 AAW	NDBLS	10//99-12//99
	Fargo-Moorhead MSA, ND-MN	S	58.66 MW	66.90 AW	122010 AAW	NDBLS	10//99-12//99
	Ohio	S	55.93 MW	49.78 AW	103550 AAW	OHBLS	10//99-12//99
	Akron PMSA, OH	S	47.87 MW	49.36 AW	99570 AAW	OHBLS	10//99-12//99
	Canton-Massillon MSA, OH	S	52.77 MW	56.55 AW	109770 AAW	OHBLS	10//99-12//99
	Cincinnati PMSA, OH-KY-IN	S	48.91 MW	59.83 AW	101730 AAW	OHBLS	10//99-12//99
	Columbus MSA, OH	S	59.20 MW	63.16 AW	123140 AAW	OHBLS	10//99-12//99
	Dayton-Springfield MSA, OH	S	50.49 MW	54.15 AW	105020 AAW	OHBLS	10//99-12//99
	Youngstown-Warren MSA, OH	S	58.55 MW	64.80 AW	121770 AAW	OHBLS	10//99-12//99
	Oklahoma	S	65.57 MW	57.25 AW	119080 AAW	OKBLS	10//99-12//99
	Oklahoma City MSA, OK	S	50.74 MW	54.99 AW	105550 AAW	OKBLS	10//99-12//99

AAW Average annual wage	**AOH** Average offered, high	**ASH** Average starting, high	**H** Hourly	**M** Monthly	**S** Special: hourly and annual
AE Average entry wage	**AOL** Average offered, low	**ASL** Average starting, low	**HI** Highest wage paid	**MTC** Median total compensation	**TQ** Third quartile wage
AEX Average experienced wage	**APH** Average pay, high range	**AW** Average wage paid	**HR** High end range	**MW** Median wage paid	**W** Weekly
AO Average offered	**APL** Average pay, low range	**FQ** First quartile wage	**LR** Low end range	**SQ** Second quartile wage	**Y** Yearly

Occupation/Type/Industry	Location	Per	Low	Mid	High	Source	Date
Family and General Practitioner	Tulsa MSA, OK	S	60.52 MW		125880 AAW	OKBLS	10//99-12//99
	Oregon	S	50.74 MW	50.77 AW	105610 AAW	ORBLS	10//99-12//99
	Portland-Vancouver PMSA, OR-WA	S	49.81 MW	50.03 AW	103590 AAW	ORBLS	10//99-12//99
	Pennsylvania	S	54.69 MW	48.73 AW	101350 AAW	PABLS	10//99-12//99
	Allentown-Bethlehem-Easton MSA, PA	S	61.88 MW		128710 AAW	PABLS	10//99-12//99
	Erie MSA, PA	S	59.64 MW	67.41 AW	124060 AAW	PABLS	10//99-12//99
	Harrisburg-Lebanon-Carlisle MSA, PA	S	43.02 MW	46.62 AW	89480 AAW	PABLS	10//99-12//99
	Lancaster MSA, PA	S	48.72 MW	49.79 AW	101330 AAW	PABLS	10//99-12//99
	Philadelphia PMSA, PA-NJ	S	54.28 MW	62.81 AW	112900 AAW	PABLS	10//99-12//99
	Pittsburgh MSA, PA	S	52.62 MW	56.17 AW	109460 AAW	PABLS	10//99-12//99
	Reading MSA, PA	S	16.10 MW	6.23 AW	33490 AAW	PABLS	10//99-12//99
	York MSA, PA	S	39.07 MW	39.45 AW	81270 AAW	PABLS	10//99-12//99
	Rhode Island	S	45.4 MW	47.47 AW	98740 AAW	RIBLS	10//99-12//99
	Providence-Fall River-Warwick MSA, RI-MA	S	48.10 MW	43.99 AW	100040 AAW	RIBLS	10//99-12//99
	South Carolina	S	65.68 MW	57.55 AW	119700 AAW	SCBLS	10//99-12//99
	Columbia MSA, SC	S	50.27 MW	50.50 AW	104550 AAW	SCBLS	10//99-12//99
	Florence MSA, SC	S	53.43 MW	59.16 AW	111130 AAW	SCBLS	10//99-12//99
	Greenville-Spartanburg-Anderson MSA, SC	S	56.45 MW	62.85 AW	117420 AAW	SCBLS	10//99-12//99
	Myrtle Beach MSA, SC	S	66.88 MW		139120 AAW	SCBLS	10//99-12//99
	Tennessee	S	67.39 MW	57.87 AW	120370 AAW	TNBLS	10//99-12//99
	Clarksville-Hopkinsville MSA, TN-KY	S	45.80 MW	47.64 AW	95260 AAW	TNBLS	10//99-12//99
	Knoxville MSA, TN	S	54.91 MW	58.90 AW	114220 AAW	TNBLS	10//99-12//99
	Memphis MSA, TN-AR-MS	S	52.46 MW	52.83 AW	109110 AAW	MSBLS	10//99-12//99
	Texas	S	56.68 MW	49.53 AW	103030 AAW	TXBLS	10//99-12//99
	Beaumont-Port Arthur MSA, TX	S	56.10 MW	59.93 AW	116680 AAW	TXBLS	10//99-12//99
	Corpus Christi MSA, TX	S	60.73 MW		126320 AAW	TXBLS	10//99-12//99
	Dallas PMSA, TX	S	51.14 MW	51.98 AW	106370 AAW	TXBLS	10//99-12//99
	Fort Worth-Arlington PMSA, TX	S	62.50 MW	66.78 AW	130000 AAW	TXBLS	10//99-12//99
	Houston PMSA, TX	S	56.19 MW	54.95 AW	116880 AAW	TXBLS	10//99-12//99
	Lubbock MSA, TX	S	61.66 MW	69.56 AW	128260 AAW	TXBLS	10//99-12//99
	San Antonio MSA, TX	S	57.11 MW	64.04 AW	118790 AAW	TXBLS	10//99-12//99
	Utah	S	50.87 MW	49.04 AW	102010 AAW	UTBLS	10//99-12//99
	Salt Lake City-Ogden MSA, UT	S	48.58 MW	48.55 AW	101040 AAW	UTBLS	10//99-12//99
	Vermont	S	53.38 MW	51.92 AW	107990 AAW	VTBLS	10//99-12//99
	Virginia	S	51.73 MW	49.17 AW	102270 AAW	VABLS	10//99-12//99
	Norfolk-Virginia Beach-Newport News MSA, VA-NC	S	49.98 MW	50.59 AW	103970 AAW	VABLS	10//99-12//99
	Richmond-Petersburg MSA, VA	S	55.48 MW	53.65 AW	115390 AAW	VABLS	10//99-12//99
	Roanoke MSA, VA	S	48.67 MW	49.79 AW	101240 AAW	VABLS	10//99-12//99
	Washington	S	55.38 MW	52.35 AW	108900 AAW	WABLS	10//99-12//99
	Bremerton PMSA, WA	S	47.86 MW	47.10 AW	99550 AAW	WABLS	10//99-12//99
	Richland-Kennewick-Pasco MSA, WA	S	59.43 MW	63.36 AW	123610 AAW	WABLS	10//99-12//99
	Seattle-Bellevue-Everett PMSA, WA	S	52.09 MW	53.39 AW	108360 AAW	WABLS	10//99-12//99
	Spokane MSA, WA	S	56.83 MW	60.77 AW	118200 AAW	WABLS	10//99-12//99
	Yakima MSA, WA	S	25.39 MW	19.18 AW	52810 AAW	WABLS	10//99-12//99
	West Virginia	S	65.44 MW	58.72 AW	122130 AAW	WVBLS	10//99-12//99
	Charleston MSA, WV	S	48.65 MW	49.70 AW	101190 AAW	WVBLS	10//99-12//99
	Huntington-Ashland MSA, WV-KY-OH	S	49.03 MW	50.86 AW	101990 AAW	WVBLS	10//99-12//99
	Wheeling MSA, WV-OH	S	62.94 MW		130920 AAW	WVBLS	10//99-12//99
	Wisconsin	S		63.02 AW	131070 AAW	WIBLS	10//99-12//99
	Madison MSA, WI	S	56.87 MW	64.89 AW	118300 AAW	WIBLS	10//99-12//99
	Milwaukee-Waukesha PMSA, WI	S	62.34 MW		129660 AAW	WIBLS	10//99-12//99
	Wyoming	S	51.25 MW	50.65 AW	105350 AAW	WYBLS	10//99-12//99
	Cheyenne MSA, WY	S	50.89 MW	50.65 AW	105840 AAW	WYBLS	10//99-12//99
	Puerto Rico	S	21.85 MW	25.86 AW	53790 AAW	PRBLS	10//99-12//99
	Arecibo PMSA, PR	S	16.96 MW	17.46 AW	35280 AAW	PRBLS	10//99-12//99

AAW	Average annual wage	**AOH**	Average offered, high	**ASH**	Average starting, high	**H**	Hourly	**M**	Monthly	**S**	Special: hourly and annual
AE	Average entry wage	**AOL**	Average offered, low	**ASL**	Average starting, low	**HI**	Highest wage paid	**MTC**	Median total compensation **TQ** Third quartile wage
AEX	Average experienced wage	**APH**	Average pay, high range	**AW**	Average wage paid	**HR**	High end range	**MW**	Median wage paid **W** Weekly
AO	Average offered	**APL**	Average pay, low range	**FQ**	First quartile wage	**LR**	Low end range	**SQ**	Second quartile wage **Y** Yearly

Occupation/Type/Industry	Location	Per	Low	Mid	High	Source	Date
Farm and Home Management Advisor	Arkansas	S	14.32 MW	14.76 AW	30690 AAW	ARBLS	10//99-12//99
	California	S	19.01 MW	21.44 AW	44600 AAW	CABLS	10//99-12//99
	Colorado	S	16.32 MW	17.53 AW	36460 AAW	COBLS	10//99-12//99
	Connecticut	S	21.03 MW	21.69 AW	45120 AAW	CTBLS	10//99-12//99
	Georgia	S	15.64 MW	15.99 AW	33260 AAW	GABLS	10//99-12//99
	Hawaii	S	29.54 MW	30.22 AW	62870 AAW	HIBLS	10//99-12//99
	Illinois	S	16.39 MW	15.73 AW	32710 AAW	ILBLS	10//99-12//99
	Indiana	S	10.14 MW	10.39 AW	21610 AAW	INBLS	10//99-12//99
	Kansas	S	14.01 MW	14.68 AW	30530 AAW	KSBLS	10//99-12//99
	Louisiana	S	20.73 MW	21.86 AW	45470 AAW	LABLS	10//99-12//99
	Maryland	S	13.03 MW	15.40 AW	32040 AAW	MDBLS	10//99-12//99
	Minnesota	S	18.63 MW	19.12 AW	39780 AAW	MNBLS	10//99-12//99
	Mississippi	S	7.75 MW	12.26 AW	25510 AAW	MSBLS	10//99-12//99
	Montana	S	15.7 MW	16.96 AW	35270 AAW	MTBLS	10//99-12//99
	New Jersey	S	15.3 MW	15.98 AW	33240 AAW	NJBLS	10//99-12//99
	New York	S	17.45 MW	18.16 AW	37780 AAW	NYBLS	10//99-12//99
	North Dakota	S	17.42 MW	17.11 AW	35580 AAW	NDBLS	10//99-12//99
	Oklahoma	S	9.84 MW	10.54 AW	21930 AAW	OKBLS	10//99-12//99
	Oregon	S	16.11 MW	17.87 AW	37170 AAW	ORBLS	10//99-12//99
	Pennsylvania	S	14.56 MW	16.69 AW	34710 AAW	PABLS	10//99-12//99
	South Carolina	S	15.12 MW	15.98 AW	33230 AAW	SCBLS	10//99-12//99
	Texas	S	14.64 MW	16.47 AW	34260 AAW	TXBLS	10//99-12//99
	Virginia	S	20.82 MW	21.82 AW	45380 AAW	VABLS	10//99-12//99
	Washington	S	20.79 MW	20.68 AW	43020 AAW	WABLS	10//99-12//99
	West Virginia	S	7.81 MW	9.72 AW	20220 AAW	WVBLS	10//99-12//99
	Wisconsin	S	18.2 MW	18.27 AW	38010 AAW	WIBLS	10//99-12//99
	Wyoming	S	16.58 MW	17.39 AW	36180 AAW	WYBLS	10//99-12//99
	Puerto Rico	S	9.18 MW	12.02 AW	25010 AAW	PRBLS	10//99-12//99
Farm Equipment Mechanic	Alabama	S	10.84 MW	11.42 AW	23750 AAW	ALBLS	10//99-12//99
	Arizona	S	12.53 MW	13.38 AW	27830 AAW	AZBLS	10//99-12//99
	Arkansas	S	12 MW	12.03 AW	25020 AAW	ARBLS	10//99-12//99
	California	S	13 MW	13.37 AW	27800 AAW	CABLS	10//99-12//99
	Colorado	S	11.69 MW	11.91 AW	24770 AAW	COBLS	10//99-12//99
	Connecticut	S	16.53 MW	16.50 AW	34320 AAW	CTBLS	10//99-12//99
	Delaware	S	13.56 MW	14.39 AW	29920 AAW	DEBLS	10//99-12//99
	Florida	S	11.92 MW	12.37 AW	25720 AAW	FLBLS	10//99-12//99
	Georgia	S	10.58 MW	10.23 AW	21280 AAW	GABLS	10//99-12//99
	Hawaii	S	15.52 MW	15.54 AW	32330 AAW	HIBLS	10//99-12//99
	Idaho	S	13.11 MW	13.39 AW	27860 AAW	IDBLS	10//99-12//99
	Illinois	S	11.56 MW	11.98 AW	24910 AAW	ILBLS	10//99-12//99
	Indiana	S	11.65 MW	11.89 AW	24720 AAW	INBLS	10//99-12//99
	Iowa	S	11.26 MW	12.23 AW	25430 AAW	IABLS	10//99-12//99
	Kansas	S	11.3 MW	11.73 AW	24390 AAW	KSBLS	10//99-12//99
	Kentucky	S	9.35 MW	9.72 AW	20210 AAW	KYBLS	10//99-12//99
	Louisiana	S	10.67 MW	11.06 AW	23010 AAW	LABLS	10//99-12//99
	Maine	S	9.49 MW	9.07 AW	18850 AAW	MEBLS	10//99-12//99
	Maryland	S	13 MW	13.61 AW	28320 AAW	MDBLS	10//99-12//99
	Michigan	S	11.94 MW	12.33 AW	25650 AAW	MIBLS	10//99-12//99
	Minnesota	S	12.14 MW	12.55 AW	26110 AAW	MNBLS	10//99-12//99
	Mississippi	S	10.97 MW	11.31 AW	23520 AAW	MSBLS	10//99-12//99
	Missouri	S	11.06 MW	11.19 AW	23270 AAW	MOBLS	10//99-12//99
	Montana	S	11.1 MW	11.28 AW	23450 AAW	MTBLS	10//99-12//99
	Nebraska	S	10.22 MW	10.55 AW	21940 AAW	NEBLS	10//99-12//99
	Nevada	S	13.28 MW	14.36 AW	29870 AAW	NVBLS	10//99-12//99
	New Hampshire	S	11.72 MW	12.09 AW	25150 AAW	NHBLS	10//99-12//99
	New Jersey	S	13.26 MW	13.52 AW	28110 AAW	NJBLS	10//99-12//99
	New Mexico	S	10.58 MW	11.06 AW	23000 AAW	NMBLS	10//99-12//99
	New York	S	10.37 MW	11.22 AW	23330 AAW	NYBLS	10//99-12//99
	North Carolina	S	12.35 MW	12.48 AW	25960 AAW	NCBLS	10//99-12//99
	North Dakota	S	11.75 MW	11.83 AW	24600 AAW	NDBLS	10//99-12//99
	Ohio	S	10.83 MW	11.07 AW	23030 AAW	OHBLS	10//99-12//99
	Oklahoma	S	8.42 MW	9.76 AW	20310 AAW	OKBLS	10//99-12//99
	Oregon	S	13.41 MW	13.28 AW	27620 AAW	ORBLS	10//99-12//99
	Pennsylvania	S	11.7 MW	12.30 AW	25590 AAW	PABLS	10//99-12//99
	South Carolina	S	10.32 MW	10.51 AW	21850 AAW	SCBLS	10//99-12//99
	South Dakota	S	10.71 MW	11.06 AW	23010 AAW	SDBLS	10//99-12//99
	Tennessee	S	10.25 MW	10.49 AW	21810 AAW	TNBLS	10//99-12//99
	Texas	S	10.42 MW	12.24 AW	25450 AAW	TXBLS	10//99-12//99
	Vermont	S	11.75 MW	12.08 AW	25120 AAW	VTBLS	10//99-12//99
	Virginia	S	11.8 MW	11.86 AW	24670 AAW	VABLS	10//99-12//99

AAW Average annual wage	**AOH** Average offered, high	**ASH** Average starting, high	**H** Hourly	**M** Monthly	**S** Special: hourly and annual
AE Average entry wage	**AOL** Average offered, low	**ASL** Average starting, low	**HI** Highest wage paid	**MTC** Median total compensation	**TQ** Third quartile wage
AEX Average experienced wage	**APH** Average pay, high range	**AW** Average wage paid	**HR** High end range	**MW** Median wage paid	**W** Weekly
AO Average offered	**APL** Average pay, low range	**FQ** First quartile wage	**LR** Low end range	**SQ** Second quartile wage	**Y** Yearly

Occupation/Type/Industry	Location	Per	Low	Mid	High	Source	Date
Farm Equipment Mechanic	Washington	S	12.77 MW	12.95 AW	26940 AAW	WABLS	10//99-12//99
	West Virginia	S	9.28 MW	9.27 AW	19290 AAW	WVBLS	10//99-12//99
	Wisconsin	S	10.66 MW	11.12 AW	23120 AAW	WIBLS	10//99-12//99
	Wyoming	S	12.44 MW	12.91 AW	26840 AAW	WYBLS	10//99-12//99
	Puerto Rico	S	10.8 MW	11.70 AW	24350 AAW	PRBLS	10//99-12//99
Farm Labor Contractor	California	S	6.57 MW	9.08 AW	18880 AAW	CABLS	10//99-12//99
	Florida	S	6.44 MW	8.12 AW	16890 AAW	FLBLS	10//99-12//99
	Illinois	S	5.95 MW	5.75 AW	11960 AAW	ILBLS	10//99-12//99
	Iowa	S	8.79 MW	7.90 AW	16440 AAW	IABLS	10//99-12//99
	Texas	S	7.88 MW	8.03 AW	16690 AAW	TXBLS	10//99-12//99
Farm, Ranch, and Other Agricultural Manager	Alabama	S	18.53 MW	21.01 AW	43690 AAW	ALBLS	10//99-12//99
	Arizona	S	21.17 MW	23.56 AW	49010 AAW	AZBLS	10//99-12//99
	California	S	28.2 MW	27.32 AW	56830 AAW	CABLS	10//99-12//99
	Colorado	S	17.84 MW	17.80 AW	37020 AAW	COBLS	10//99-12//99
	Florida	S	17.81 MW	19.14 AW	39820 AAW	FLBLS	10//99-12//99
	Georgia	S	20.08 MW	21.73 AW	45200 AAW	GABLS	10//99-12//99
	Idaho	S	19.74 MW	22.54 AW	46890 AAW	IDBLS	10//99-12//99
	Illinois	S	19.89 MW	21.03 AW	43740 AAW	ILBLS	10//99-12//99
	Indiana	S	15.96 MW	19.49 AW	40540 AAW	INBLS	10//99-12//99
	Iowa	S	19.26 MW	21.65 AW	45040 AAW	IABLS	10//99-12//99
	Kansas	S	10.72 MW	20.77 AW	43200 AAW	KSBLS	10//99-12//99
	Kentucky	S	22.59 MW	23.47 AW	48830 AAW	KYBLS	10//99-12//99
	Mississippi	S	10.33 MW	11.69 AW	24310 AAW	MSBLS	10//99-12//99
	Missouri	S	17.45 MW	16.48 AW	34280 AAW	MOBLS	10//99-12//99
	Nebraska	S	19.31 MW	22.64 AW	47100 AAW	NEBLS	10//99-12//99
	Nevada	S	19.69 MW	23.46 AW	48800 AAW	NVBLS	10//99-12//99
	New Mexico	S	15.91 MW	16.09 AW	33470 AAW	NMBLS	10//99-12//99
	New York	S	15.58 MW	17.26 AW	35900 AAW	NYBLS	10//99-12//99
	Oklahoma	S	23.27 MW	21.33 AW	44360 AAW	OKBLS	10//99-12//99
	Pennsylvania	S	19.86 MW	21.55 AW	44830 AAW	PABLS	10//99-12//99
	South Carolina	S	32.97 MW	35.86 AW	74580 AAW	SCBLS	10//99-12//99
	Tennessee	S	14.38 MW	16.03 AW	33340 AAW	TNBLS	10//99-12//99
	Texas	S	15.46 MW	17.87 AW	37160 AAW	TXBLS	10//99-12//99
	Utah	S	19.52 MW	20.68 AW	43010 AAW	UTBLS	10//99-12//99
	Virginia	S	18.32 MW	20.15 AW	41910 AAW	VABLS	10//99-12//99
	Washington	S	22.37 MW	25.63 AW	53300 AAW	WABLS	10//99-12//99
	Wisconsin	S	10.67 MW	16.48 AW	34280 AAW	WIBLS	10//99-12//99
Farmworker and Laborer, Crop, Nursery, and Greenhouse	Alabama	S	6.61 MW	6.93 AW	14420 AAW	ALBLS	10//99-12//99
	Arizona	S	6.04 MW	6.09 AW	12660 AAW	AZBLS	10//99-12//99
	Arkansas	S	6.05 MW	6.13 AW	12740 AAW	ARBLS	10//99-12//99
	California	S	6.39 MW	6.63 AW	13780 AAW	CABLS	10//99-12//99
	Colorado	S	7.43 MW	7.82 AW	16270 AAW	COBLS	10//99-12//99
	Connecticut	S	9.28 MW	9.28 AW	19310 AAW	CTBLS	10//99-12//99
	Delaware	S	8.57 MW	9.29 AW	19310 AAW	DEBLS	10//99-12//99
	Florida	S	6.55 MW	7.02 AW	14600 AAW	FLBLS	10//99-12//99
	Georgia	S	6.16 MW	6.51 AW	13550 AAW	GABLS	10//99-12//99
	Hawaii	S	9.22 MW	8.95 AW	18620 AAW	HIBLS	10//99-12//99
	Idaho	S	6.27 MW	6.59 AW	13710 AAW	IDBLS	10//99-12//99
	Illinois	S	7.77 MW	8.90 AW	18510 AAW	ILBLS	10//99-12//99
	Indiana	S	6.87 MW	7.31 AW	15200 AAW	INBLS	10//99-12//99
	Iowa	S	9.08 MW	8.85 AW	18410 AAW	IABLS	10//99-12//99
	Kansas	S	6.88 MW	7.51 AW	15620 AAW	KSBLS	10//99-12//99
	Kentucky	S	7.85 MW	8.00 AW	16640 AAW	KYBLS	10//99-12//99
	Louisiana	S	6.53 MW	6.76 AW	14060 AAW	LABLS	10//99-12//99
	Maryland	S	9.95 MW	10.16 AW	21130 AAW	MDBLS	10//99-12//99
	Massachusetts	S	9.45 MW	9.24 AW	19210 AAW	MABLS	10//99-12//99
	Michigan	S	7.98 MW	8.15 AW	16950 AAW	MIBLS	10//99-12//99
	Minnesota	S	7.36 MW	7.80 AW	16220 AAW	MNBLS	10//99-12//99
	Missouri	S	7.59 MW	7.86 AW	16340 AAW	MOBLS	10//99-12//99
	Montana	S	7.9 MW	8.83 AW	18380 AAW	MTBLS	10//99-12//99
	Nebraska	S	7.06 MW	7.54 AW	15680 AAW	NEBLS	10//99-12//99
	Nevada	S	7.87 MW	8.08 AW	16810 AAW	NVBLS	10//99-12//99
	New Hampshire	S	8.68 MW	8.85 AW	18410 AAW	NHBLS	10//99-12//99
	New Jersey	S	8.33 MW	8.40 AW	17470 AAW	NJBLS	10//99-12//99
	New Mexico	S	5.96 MW	5.84 AW	12150 AAW	NMBLS	10//99-12//99
	New York	S	7.73 MW	8.11 AW	16870 AAW	NYBLS	10//99-12//99
	North Carolina	S	6.12 MW	6.34 AW	13190 AAW	NCBLS	10//99-12//99

AAW	Average annual wage	**AOH**	Average offered, high	**ASH**	Average starting, high	**H**	Hourly	**M** Monthly
AE	Average entry wage	**AOL**	Average offered, low	**ASL**	Average starting, low	**HI**	Highest wage paid	**MTC** Median total compensation
AEX	Average experienced wage	**APH**	Average pay, high range	**AW**	Average wage paid	**HR**	High end range	**MW** Median wage paid
AO	Average offered	**APL**	Average pay, low range	**FQ**	First quartile wage	**LR**	Low end range	**SQ** Second quartile wage

S	Special: hourly and annual	
TQ	Third quartile wage	
W	Weekly	
Y	Yearly	

Occupation/Type/Industry	Location	Per	Low	Mid	High	Source	Date
Farmworker and Laborer, Crop, Nursery, and Greenhouse	North Dakota	S	7.36 MW	8.19 AW	17040 AAW	NDBLS	10//99-12//99
	Ohio	S	8.42 MW	8.96 AW	18640 AAW	OHBLS	10//99-12//99
	Oklahoma	S	6.74 MW	6.86 AW	14270 AAW	OKBLS	10//99-12//99
	Pennsylvania	S	7.41 MW	7.58 AW	15760 AAW	PABLS	10//99-12//99
	Rhode Island	S	17.29 MW	14.08 AW	29280 AAW	RIBLS	10//99-12//99
	South Carolina	S	6.34 MW	6.62 AW	13770 AAW	SCBLS	10//99-12//99
	South Dakota	S	7.55 MW	7.46 AW	15520 AAW	SDBLS	10//99-12//99
	Tennessee	S	7.57 MW	7.85 AW	16330 AAW	TNBLS	10//99-12//99
	Texas	S	6.16 MW	6.42 AW	13350 AAW	TXBLS	10//99-12//99
	Vermont	S	8.77 MW	9.11 AW	18950 AAW	VTBLS	10//99-12//99
	Virginia	S	7.95 MW	8.53 AW	17750 AAW	VABLS	10//99-12//99
	Washington	S	7.7 MW	7.90 AW	16420 AAW	WABLS	10//99-12//99
	Wisconsin	S	7.95 MW	8.22 AW	17100 AAW	WIBLS	10//99-12//99
	Wyoming	S	7.63 MW	8.86 AW	18430 AAW	WYBLS	10//99-12//99
	Puerto Rico	S	6.47 MW	7.30 AW	15180 AAW	PRBLS	10//99-12//99
Farmworker, Farm and Ranch Animal	Alabama	S	7.42 MW	7.87 AW	16370 AAW	ALBLS	10//99-12//99
	Arizona	S	6.71 MW	7.29 AW	15170 AAW	AZBLS	10//99-12//99
	Arkansas	S	7.75 MW	7.96 AW	16550 AAW	ARBLS	10//99-12//99
	California	S	6.62 MW	7.48 AW	15570 AAW	CABLS	10//99-12//99
	Colorado	S	7.24 MW	8.01 AW	16650 AAW	COBLS	10//99-12//99
	Connecticut	S	7.27 MW	7.99 AW	16620 AAW	CTBLS	10//99-12//99
	Delaware	S	8.12 MW	8.57 AW	17820 AAW	DEBLS	10//99-12//99
	Florida	S	6.72 MW	7.34 AW	15260 AAW	FLBLS	10//99-12//99
	Georgia	S	6.96 MW	7.38 AW	15340 AAW	GABLS	10//99-12//99
	Idaho	S	6.79 MW	7.47 AW	15540 AAW	IDBLS	10//99-12//99
	Illinois	S	7.88 MW	8.10 AW	16850 AAW	ILBLS	10//99-12//99
	Indiana	S	7.25 MW	7.56 AW	15720 AAW	INBLS	10//99-12//99
	Iowa	S	8.22 MW	8.90 AW	18510 AAW	IABLS	10//99-12//99
	Kansas	S	7.18 MW	7.43 AW	15460 AAW	KSBLS	10//99-12//99
	Kentucky	S	8.63 MW	8.64 AW	17970 AAW	KYBLS	10//99-12//99
	Louisiana	S	6.89 MW	7.22 AW	15020 AAW	LABLS	10//99-12//99
	Maryland	S	8.28 MW	8.55 AW	17770 AAW	MDBLS	10//99-12//99
	Massachusetts	S	7.75 MW	7.86 AW	16350 AAW	MABLS	10//99-12//99
	Michigan	S	6.58 MW	7.10 AW	14770 AAW	MIBLS	10//99-12//99
	Minnesota	S	7.79 MW	8.18 AW	17020 AAW	MNBLS	10//99-12//99
	Mississippi	S	6.56 MW	7.10 AW	14760 AAW	MSBLS	10//99-12//99
	Missouri	S	8.27 MW	8.74 AW	18180 AAW	MOBLS	10//99-12//99
	Montana	S	7.35 MW	8.22 AW	17100 AAW	MTBLS	10//99-12//99
	Nebraska	S	6.62 MW	8.07 AW	16780 AAW	NEBLS	10//99-12//99
	New Hampshire	S	7.3 MW	7.81 AW	16240 AAW	NHBLS	10//99-12//99
	New Jersey	S	8.1 MW	8.31 AW	17290 AAW	NJBLS	10//99-12//99
	New Mexico	S	6.72 MW	7.44 AW	15480 AAW	NMBLS	10//99-12//99
	New York	S	7.33 MW	8.45 AW	17570 AAW	NYBLS	10//99-12//99
	North Carolina	S	7.76 MW	8.27 AW	17200 AAW	NCBLS	10//99-12//99
	Ohio	S	7.58 MW	7.73 AW	16090 AAW	OHBLS	10//99-12//99
	Oklahoma	S	6.72 MW	7.20 AW	14980 AAW	OKBLS	10//99-12//99
	Oregon	S	8.17 MW	8.77 AW	18250 AAW	ORBLS	10//99-12//99
	Pennsylvania	S	9.06 MW	9.65 AW	20070 AAW	PABLS	10//99-12//99
	South Carolina	S	7.74 MW	8.14 AW	16920 AAW	SCBLS	10//99-12//99
	South Dakota	S	8.28 MW	8.59 AW	17870 AAW	SDBLS	10//99-12//99
	Tennessee	S	6.58 MW	8.03 AW	16700 AAW	TNBLS	10//99-12//99
	Texas	S	7.36 MW	8.02 AW	16690 AAW	TXBLS	10//99-12//99
	Utah	S	6.64 MW	7.59 AW	15790 AAW	UTBLS	10//99-12//99
	Virginia	S	8.34 MW	8.93 AW	18570 AAW	VABLS	10//99-12//99
	Washington	S	7.9 MW	8.31 AW	17290 AAW	WABLS	10//99-12//99
	Wisconsin	S	7.58 MW	7.82 AW	16260 AAW	WIBLS	10//99-12//99
	Wyoming	S	7.91 MW	8.46 AW	17590 AAW	WYBLS	10//99-12//99
Fashion Designer	Arizona	S	18.97 MW	20.30 AW	42220 AAW	AZBLS	10//99-12//99
	Phoenix-Mesa MSA, AZ	S	20.53 MW	17.45 AW	42700 AAW	AZBLS	10//99-12//99
	Arkansas	S	12.29 MW	15.12 AW	31450 AAW	ARBLS	10//99-12//99
	California	S	23.36 MW	28.58 AW	59450 AAW	CABLS	10//99-12//99
	Los Angeles-Long Beach PMSA, CA	S	29.78 MW	25.94 AW	61930 AAW	CABLS	10//99-12//99
	Oakland PMSA, CA	S	39.50 MW	27.33 AW	82170 AAW	CABLS	10//99-12//99
	Orange County PMSA, CA	S	19.33 MW	17.69 AW	40210 AAW	CABLS	10//99-12//99
	San Diego MSA, CA	S	19.80 MW	18.99 AW	41190 AAW	CABLS	10//99-12//99
	San Francisco PMSA, CA	S	23.86 MW	19.82 AW	49630 AAW	CABLS	10//99-12//99
	Colorado	S	15.02 MW	15.13 AW	31470 AAW	COBLS	10//99-12//99

AAW	Average annual wage	AOH	Average offered, high	ASH Average starting, high	H Hourly	M Monthly	S Special: hourly and annual
AE	Average entry wage	AOL	Average offered, low	ASL Average starting, low	HI Highest wage paid	MTC Median total compensation	TQ Third quartile wage
AEX	Average experienced wage	APH	Average pay, high range	AW Average wage paid	HR High end range	MW Median wage paid	W Weekly
AO	Average offered	APL	Average pay, low range	FQ First quartile wage	LR Low end range	SQ Second quartile wage	Y Yearly

Occupation/Type/Industry	Location	Per	Low	Mid	High	Source	Date
Fashion Designer	Connecticut	S	21.03 MW	27.87 AW	57960 AAW	CTBLS	10//99-12//99
	Danbury PMSA, CT	S	29.71 MW	32.69 AW	61800 AAW	CTBLS	10//99-12//99
	Washington PMSA, DC-MD-VA-WV	S	20.34 MW	15.36 AW	42300 AAW	DCBLS	10//99-12//99
	Florida	S	15.98 MW	19.39 AW	40330 AAW	FLBLS	10//99-12//99
	Fort Lauderdale PMSA, FL	S	15.82 MW	17.69 AW	32910 AAW	FLBLS	10//99-12//99
	Miami PMSA, FL	S	19.22 MW	19.90 AW	39970 AAW	FLBLS	10//99-12//99
	Orlando MSA, FL	S	10.41 MW	8.69 AW	21660 AAW	FLBLS	10//99-12//99
	Georgia	S	20.53 MW	25.88 AW	53820 AAW	GABLS	10//99-12//99
	Atlanta MSA, GA	S	26.68 MW	20.76 AW	55500 AAW	GABLS	10//99-12//99
	Illinois	S	13.32 MW	15.18 AW	31580 AAW	ILBLS	10//99-12//99
	Chicago PMSA, IL	S	15.18 MW	13.33 AW	31580 AAW	ILBLS	10//99-12//99
	Indiana	S	11.72 MW	18.32 AW	38100 AAW	INBLS	10//99-12//99
	Iowa	S	13.26 MW	11.93 AW	24820 AAW	IABLS	10//99-12//99
	Louisiana	S	11.76 MW	11.22 AW	23330 AAW	LABLS	10//99-12//99
	Massachusetts	S	21.45 MW	23.96 AW	49840 AAW	MABLS	10//99-12//99
	Minnesota	S	12.46 MW	13.16 AW	27380 AAW	MNBLS	10//99-12//99
	New Jersey	S	25.92 MW	30.41 AW	63260 AAW	NJBLS	10//99-12//99
	Newark PMSA, NJ	S	30.38 MW	20.73 AW	63180 AAW	NJBLS	10//99-12//99
	New York	S	25.07 MW	28.65 AW	59600 AAW	NYBLS	10//99-12//99
	New York PMSA, NY	S	28.68 MW	25.04 AW	59660 AAW	NYBLS	10//99-12//99
	North Carolina	S	19.46 MW	23.24 AW	48340 AAW	NCBLS	10//99-12//99
	Greensboro--Winston-Salem--High Point MSA, NC	S	22.27 MW	18.31 AW	46330 AAW	NCBLS	10//99-12//99
	Columbus MSA, OH	S	36.68 MW	35.23 AW	76290 AAW	OHBLS	10//99-12//99
	Oklahoma	S	13.86 MW	12.59 AW	26190 AAW	OKBLS	10//99-12//99
	Oregon	S	17.55 MW	22.12 AW	46010 AAW	ORBLS	10//99-12//99
	Portland-Vancouver PMSA, OR-WA	S	22.12 MW	17.55 AW	46010 AAW	ORBLS	10//99-12//99
	Pennsylvania	S	21.12 MW	20.63 AW	42920 AAW	PABLS	10//99-12//99
	Philadelphia PMSA, PA-NJ	S	14.62 MW	11.94 AW	30420 AAW	PABLS	10//99-12//99
	South Carolina	S	11.54 MW	13.87 AW	28840 AAW	SCBLS	10//99-12//99
	Tennessee	S	19.09 MW	19.11 AW	39750 AAW	TNBLS	10//99-12//99
	Austin-San Marcos MSA, TX	S	7.75 MW	7.64 AW	16110 AAW	TXBLS	10//99-12//99
	Vermont	S	15.16 MW	15.23 AW	31680 AAW	VTBLS	10//99-12//99
	Virginia	S	15.88 MW	22.18 AW	46140 AAW	VABLS	10//99-12//99
	Washington	S	15.69 MW	18.12 AW	37690 AAW	WABLS	10//99-12//99
	Seattle-Bellevue-Everett PMSA, WA	S	18.10 MW	15.29 AW	37640 AAW	WABLS	10//99-12//99
	Puerto Rico	S	6.44 MW	6.76 AW	14070 AAW	PRBLS	10//99-12//99
	San Juan-Bayamon PMSA, PR	S	7.03 MW	6.66 AW	14630 AAW	PRBLS	10//99-12//99
Fence Erector	Alabama	S	8.73 MW	9.67 AW	20110 AAW	ALBLS	10//99-12//99
	Alaska	S	15.3 MW	14.83 AW	30850 AAW	AKBLS	10//99-12//99
	Arizona	S	9.88 MW	10.06 AW	20920 AAW	AZBLS	10//99-12//99
	Arkansas	S	7.65 MW	7.67 AW	15960 AAW	ARBLS	10//99-12//99
	California	S	11.09 MW	13.12 AW	27290 AAW	CABLS	10//99-12//99
	Colorado	S	11.42 MW	11.88 AW	24710 AAW	COBLS	10//99-12//99
	Florida	S	8.86 MW	9.61 AW	19980 AAW	FLBLS	10//99-12//99
	Georgia	S	10.45 MW	9.95 AW	20690 AAW	GABLS	10//99-12//99
	Idaho	S	9.39 MW	9.93 AW	20650 AAW	IDBLS	10//99-12//99
	Indiana	S	7.38 MW	8.24 AW	17140 AAW	INBLS	10//99-12//99
	Kentucky	S	7.5 MW	7.53 AW	15650 AAW	KYBLS	10//99-12//99
	Louisiana	S	7.44 MW	8.15 AW	16950 AAW	LABLS	10//99-12//99
	Maine	S	9.45 MW	9.90 AW	20600 AAW	MEBLS	10//99-12//99
	Maryland	S	12.52 MW	12.83 AW	26680 AAW	MDBLS	10//99-12//99
	Massachusetts	S	12.2 MW	12.85 AW	26720 AAW	MABLS	10//99-12//99
	Michigan	S	12.36 MW	13.56 AW	28210 AAW	MIBLS	10//99-12//99
	Mississippi	S	7.02 MW	7.38 AW	15350 AAW	MSBLS	10//99-12//99
	Missouri	S	9.69 MW	10.55 AW	21950 AAW	MOBLS	10//99-12//99
	Nevada	S	12.02 MW	12.61 AW	26230 AAW	NVBLS	10//99-12//99
	New Hampshire	S	8.39 MW	8.61 AW	17900 AAW	NHBLS	10//99-12//99
	New Jersey	S	13.47 MW	13.97 AW	29070 AAW	NJBLS	10//99-12//99
	New Mexico	S	6.57 MW	7.27 AW	15120 AAW	NMBLS	10//99-12//99
	New York	S	9.74 MW	10.32 AW	21470 AAW	NYBLS	10//99-12//99
	North Carolina	S	10.07 MW	10.88 AW	22620 AAW	NCBLS	10//99-12//99
	Ohio	S	10.73 MW	10.68 AW	22220 AAW	OHBLS	10//99-12//99
	Oklahoma	S	9.17 MW	10.15 AW	21120 AAW	OKBLS	10//99-12//99
	Pennsylvania	S	9.72 MW	10.18 AW	21160 AAW	PABLS	10//99-12//99
	South Carolina	S	8.42 MW	8.83 AW	18370 AAW	SCBLS	10//99-12//99
	Tennessee	S	8.66 MW	9.02 AW	18770 AAW	TNBLS	10//99-12//99
	Texas	S	6.81 MW	8.08 AW	16800 AAW	TXBLS	10//99-12//99
	Vermont	S	9.7 MW	10.01 AW	20820 AAW	VTBLS	10//99-12//99

AAW	Average annual wage	AOH	Average offered, high	ASH	Average starting, high	H	Hourly	M	Monthly	S	Special: hourly and annual
AE	Average entry wage	AOL	Average offered, low	ASL	Average starting, low	HI	Highest wage paid	MTC	Median total compensation	TQ	Third quartile wage
AEX	Average experienced wage	APH	Average pay, high range	AW	Average wage paid	HR	High end range	MW	Median wage paid	W	Weekly
AO	Average offered	APL	Average pay, low range	FQ	First quartile wage	LR	Low end range	SQ	Second quartile wage	Y	Yearly

Occupation/Type/Industry	Location	Per	Low	Mid	High	Source	Date
Fence Erector	Virginia	S	9.89 MW	10.00 AW	20790 AAW	VABLS	10//99-12//99
	Washington	S	11.9 MW	12.28 AW	25530 AAW	WABLS	10//99-12//99
	West Virginia	S	8.96 MW	9.82 AW	20420 AAW	WVBLS	10//99-12//99
	Wisconsin	S	11.9 MW	11.91 AW	24770 AAW	WIBLS	10//99-12//99
	Wyoming	S	10.32 MW	10.70 AW	22250 AAW	WYBLS	10//99-12//99
Fiberglass Laminator and Fabricator	Alabama	S	7.8 MW	9.46 AW	19670 AAW	ALBLS	10//99-12//99
	Arizona	S	10.58 MW	11.51 AW	23950 AAW	AZBLS	10//99-12//99
	Phoenix-Mesa MSA, AZ	S	10.98 MW	9.61 AW	22830 AAW	AZBLS	10//99-12//99
	Arkansas	S	7.85 MW	7.94 AW	16510 AAW	ARBLS	10//99-12//99
	California	S	9.71 MW	11.50 AW	23920 AAW	CABLS	10//99-12//99
	Los Angeles-Long Beach PMSA, CA	S	9.73 MW	9.56 AW	20240 AAW	CABLS	10//99-12//99
	Oakland PMSA, CA	S	17.41 MW	18.61 AW	36220 AAW	CABLS	10//99-12//99
	Orange County PMSA, CA	S	8.96 MW	8.36 AW	18630 AAW	CABLS	10//99-12//99
	Riverside-San Bernardino PMSA, CA	S	13.07 MW	7.93 AW	27180 AAW	CABLS	10//99-12//99
	Washington PMSA, DC-MD-VA-WV	S	7.89 MW	6.53 AW	16400 AAW	DCBLS	10//99-12//99
	Florida	S	9.37 MW	9.97 AW	20730 AAW	FLBLS	10//99-12//99
	Fort Lauderdale PMSA, FL	S	12.42 MW	12.23 AW	25830 AAW	FLBLS	10//99-12//99
	Fort Myers-Cape Coral MSA, FL	S	13.39 MW	13.88 AW	27850 AAW	FLBLS	10//99-12//99
	Fort Pierce-Port St. Lucie MSA, FL	S	12.98 MW	13.22 AW	27010 AAW	FLBLS	10//99-12//99
	Jacksonville MSA, FL	S	10.09 MW	9.58 AW	20980 AAW	FLBLS	10//99-12//99
	Melbourne-Titusville-Palm Bay MSA, FL	S	10.03 MW	9.76 AW	20860 AAW	FLBLS	10//99-12//99
	Miami PMSA, FL	S	8.67 MW	8.15 AW	18040 AAW	FLBLS	10//99-12//99
	Orlando MSA, FL	S	9.91 MW	9.84 AW	20620 AAW	FLBLS	10//99-12//99
	Sarasota-Bradenton MSA, FL	S	9.74 MW	9.72 AW	20260 AAW	FLBLS	10//99-12//99
	Tampa-St. Petersburg-Clearwater MSA, FL	S	9.66 MW	9.42 AW	20090 AAW	FLBLS	10//99-12//99
	West Palm Beach-Boca Raton MSA, FL	S	13.26 MW	13.04 AW	27570 AAW	FLBLS	10//99-12//99
	Georgia	S	8.12 MW	8.83 AW	18360 AAW	GABLS	10//99-12//99
	Atlanta MSA, GA	S	8.30 MW	7.84 AW	17260 AAW	GABLS	10//99-12//99
	Augusta-Aiken MSA, GA-SC	S	12.77 MW	12.06 AW	26570 AAW	GABLS	10//99-12//99
	Illinois	S	8.26 MW	8.75 AW	18190 AAW	ILBLS	10//99-12//99
	Chicago PMSA, IL	S	8.17 MW	8.05 AW	16990 AAW	ILBLS	10//99-12//99
	Peoria-Pekin MSA, IL	S	15.27 MW	15.14 AW	31770 AAW	ILBLS	10//99-12//99
	Indiana	S	8.29 MW	9.95 AW	20690 AAW	INBLS	10//99-12//99
	Elkhart-Goshen MSA, IN	S	14.86 MW	13.61 AW	30900 AAW	INBLS	10//99-12//99
	Indianapolis MSA, IN	S	11.70 MW	10.66 AW	24330 AAW	INBLS	10//99-12//99
	Davenport-Moline-Rock Island MSA, IA-IL	S	16.15 MW	17.84 AW	33590 AAW	IABLS	10//99-12//99
	Kansas	S	9.95 MW	10.10 AW	21010 AAW	KSBLS	10//99-12//99
	Kentucky	S	10.43 MW	10.84 AW	22550 AAW	KYBLS	10//99-12//99
	Louisiana	S	10.17 MW	10.08 AW	20960 AAW	LABLS	10//99-12//99
	Maryland	S	7.88 MW	8.24 AW	17150 AAW	MDBLS	10//99-12//99
	Boston PMSA, MA-NH	S	10.58 MW	9.80 AW	22000 AAW	MABLS	10//99-12//99
	Michigan	S	12.77 MW	14.56 AW	30290 AAW	MIBLS	10//99-12//99
	Detroit PMSA, MI	S	18.61 MW	20.36 AW	38710 AAW	MIBLS	10//99-12//99
	Grand Rapids-Muskegon-Holland MSA, MI	S	12.84 MW	12.77 AW	26700 AAW	MIBLS	10//99-12//99
	Minnesota	S	9.64 MW	9.57 AW	19910 AAW	MNBLS	10//99-12//99
	Minneapolis-St. Paul MSA, MN-WI	S	11.67 MW	10.61 AW	24270 AAW	MNBLS	10//99-12//99
	Mississippi	S	13.18 MW	13.10 AW	27260 AAW	MSBLS	10//99-12//99
	Missouri	S	14.19 MW	12.81 AW	26640 AAW	MOBLS	10//99-12//99
	Nevada	S	14.44 MW	15.12 AW	31450 AAW	NVBLS	10//99-12//99
	Las Vegas MSA, NV-AZ	S	13.68 MW	12.39 AW	28450 AAW	NVBLS	10//99-12//99
	New Jersey	S	12.19 MW	12.49 AW	25990 AAW	NJBLS	10//99-12//99
	Bergen-Passaic PMSA, NJ	S	16.62 MW	17.59 AW	34580 AAW	NJBLS	10//99-12//99
	New York	S	11.63 MW	11.42 AW	23760 AAW	NYBLS	10//99-12//99
	North Carolina	S	8.28 MW	9.37 AW	19490 AAW	NCBLS	10//99-12//99
	Charlotte-Gastonia-Rock Hill MSA, NC-SC	S	10.54 MW	8.84 AW	21910 AAW	NCBLS	10//99-12//99
	North Dakota	S	8.04 MW	10.44 AW	21710 AAW	NDBLS	10//99-12//99
	Ohio	S	10.04 MW	10.53 AW	21900 AAW	OHBLS	10//99-12//99

AAW Average annual wage	**AOH** Average offered, high	**ASH** Average starting, high	**H** Hourly	**M** Monthly	**S** Special: hourly and annual
AE Average entry wage	**AOL** Average offered, low	**ASL** Average starting, low	**HI** Highest wage paid	**MTC** Median total compensation	**TQ** Third quartile wage
AEX Average experienced wage	**APH** Average pay, high range	**AW** Average wage paid	**HR** High end range	**MW** Median wage paid	**W** Weekly
AO Average offered	**APL** Average pay, low range	**FQ** First quartile wage	**LR** Low end range	**SQ** Second quartile wage	**Y** Yearly

Occupation/Type/Industry	Location	Per	Low	Mid	High	Source	Date
Fiberglass Laminator and Fabricator	Cleveland-Lorain-Elyria PMSA, OH	S	11.59 MW	11.36 AW	24120 AAW	OHBLS	10//99-12//99
	Oklahoma City MSA, OK	S	9.22 MW	9.37 AW	19190 AAW	OKBLS	10//99-12//99
	Oregon	S	11.14 MW	10.89 AW	22650 AAW	ORBLS	10//99-12//99
	Portland-Vancouver PMSA, OR-WA	S	13.60 MW	14.11 AW	28290 AAW	ORBLS	10//99-12//99
	Pennsylvania	S	10.03 MW	10.33 AW	21490 AAW	PABLS	10//99-12//99
	Pittsburgh MSA, PA	S	9.42 MW	8.42 AW	19590 AAW	PABLS	10//99-12//99
	Rhode Island	S	15.58 MW	16.67 AW	34670 AAW	RIBLS	10//99-12//99
	Providence-Fall River-Warwick MSA, RI-MA	S	16.82 MW	15.76 AW	34980 AAW	RIBLS	10//99-12//99
	South Carolina	S	10.28 MW	12.48 AW	25960 AAW	SCBLS	10//99-12//99
	Charleston-North Charleston MSA, SC	S	12.37 MW	13.51 AW	25720 AAW	SCBLS	10//99-12//99
	Greenville-Spartanburg-Anderson MSA, SC	S	16.55 MW	18.01 AW	34430 AAW	SCBLS	10//99-12//99
	Tennessee	S	10.04 MW	10.06 AW	20930 AAW	TNBLS	10//99-12//99
	Chattanooga MSA, TN-GA	S	11.30 MW	11.72 AW	23500 AAW	TNBLS	10//99-12//99
	Knoxville MSA, TN	S	8.71 MW	9.21 AW	18110 AAW	TNBLS	10//99-12//99
	Memphis MSA, TN-AR-MS	S	10.43 MW	9.87 AW	21690 AAW	MSBLS	10//99-12//99
	Nashville MSA, TN	S	11.01 MW	11.45 AW	22890 AAW	TNBLS	10//99-12//99
	Texas	S	12.05 MW	13.05 AW	27150 AAW	TXBLS	10//99-12//99
	Dallas PMSA, TX	S	9.63 MW	8.82 AW	20030 AAW	TXBLS	10//99-12//99
	San Antonio MSA, TX	S	8.83 MW	8.71 AW	18380 AAW	TXBLS	10//99-12//99
	Utah	S	12.46 MW	13.72 AW	28550 AAW	UTBLS	10//99-12//99
	Salt Lake City-Ogden MSA, UT	S	13.38 MW	12.07 AW	27840 AAW	UTBLS	10//99-12//99
	Vermont	S	11.45 MW	13.43 AW	27940 AAW	VTBLS	10//99-12//99
	Burlington MSA, VT	S	14.77 MW	17.33 AW	30720 AAW	VTBLS	10//99-12//99
	Virginia	S	9.42 MW	10.01 AW	20820 AAW	VABLS	10//99-12//99
	Washington	S	14.49 MW	14.22 AW	29570 AAW	WABLS	10//99-12//99
	Seattle-Bellevue-Everett PMSA, WA	S	14.51 MW	13.66 AW	30180 AAW	WABLS	10//99-12//99
	Wisconsin	S	14.03 MW	12.68 AW	26370 AAW	WIBLS	10//99-12//99
	Milwaukee-Waukesha PMSA, WI	S	13.34 MW	14.65 AW	27740 AAW	WIBLS	10//99-12//99
File Clerk	Alabama	S	7.5 MW	7.82 AW	16260 AAW	ALBLS	10//99-12//99
	Anniston MSA, AL	S	8.00 MW	7.55 AW	16640 AAW	ALBLS	10//99-12//99
	Auburn-Opelika MSA, AL	S	6.46 MW	6.38 AW	13430 AAW	ALBLS	10//99-12//99
	Birmingham MSA, AL	S	8.37 MW	8.13 AW	17410 AAW	ALBLS	10//99-12//99
	Decatur MSA, AL	S	6.84 MW	6.24 AW	14230 AAW	ALBLS	10//99-12//99
	Dothan MSA, AL	S	7.24 MW	6.99 AW	15070 AAW	ALBLS	10//99-12//99
	Florence MSA, AL	S	6.41 MW	6.03 AW	13330 AAW	ALBLS	10//99-12//99
	Huntsville MSA, AL	S	7.65 MW	7.30 AW	15900 AAW	ALBLS	10//99-12//99
	Mobile MSA, AL	S	8.41 MW	7.95 AW	17480 AAW	ALBLS	10//99-12//99
	Montgomery MSA, AL	S	7.74 MW	7.48 AW	16110 AAW	ALBLS	10//99-12//99
	Tuscaloosa MSA, AL	S	7.78 MW	7.13 AW	16180 AAW	ALBLS	10//99-12//99
	Alaska	S	8.3 MW	9.63 AW	20020 AAW	AKBLS	10//99-12//99
	Anchorage MSA, AK	S	9.84 MW	8.41 AW	20470 AAW	AKBLS	10//99-12//99
	Arizona	S	7.65 MW	7.83 AW	16280 AAW	AZBLS	10//99-12//99
	Flagstaff MSA, AZ-UT	S	7.69 MW	7.46 AW	15990 AAW	AZBLS	10//99-12//99
	Phoenix-Mesa MSA, AZ	S	8.02 MW	7.84 AW	16690 AAW	AZBLS	10//99-12//99
	Tucson MSA, AZ	S	7.43 MW	7.01 AW	15450 AAW	AZBLS	10//99-12//99
	Yuma MSA, AZ	S	7.30 MW	6.80 AW	15190 AAW	AZBLS	10//99-12//99
	Arkansas	S	7.45 MW	7.70 AW	16010 AAW	ARBLS	10//99-12//99
	Fayetteville-Springdale-Rogers MSA, AR	S	7.02 MW	6.97 AW	14600 AAW	ARBLS	10//99-12//99
	Fort Smith MSA, AR-OK	S	7.58 MW	7.23 AW	15780 AAW	ARBLS	10//99-12//99
	Jonesboro MSA, AR	S	7.46 MW	7.18 AW	15510 AAW	ARBLS	10//99-12//99
	Little Rock-North Little Rock MSA, AR	S	8.22 MW	7.82 AW	17090 AAW	ARBLS	10//99-12//99
	California	S	9.33 MW	9.88 AW	20550 AAW	CABLS	10//99-12//99
	Bakersfield MSA, CA	S	8.25 MW	7.53 AW	17160 AAW	CABLS	10//99-12//99
	Chico-Paradise MSA, CA	S	7.43 MW	6.90 AW	15440 AAW	CABLS	10//99-12//99
	Fresno MSA, CA	S	8.21 MW	7.50 AW	17080 AAW	CABLS	10//99-12//99
	Los Angeles-Long Beach PMSA, CA	S	10.07 MW	9.79 AW	20950 AAW	CABLS	10//99-12//99
	Merced MSA, CA	S	11.86 MW	8.12 AW	24660 AAW	CABLS	10//99-12//99
	Modesto MSA, CA	S	7.20 MW	6.59 AW	14970 AAW	CABLS	10//99-12//99
	Oakland PMSA, CA	S	11.05 MW	10.54 AW	22980 AAW	CABLS	10//99-12//99

AAW	Average annual wage	AOH	Average offered, high	ASH Average starting, high
AE	Average entry wage	AOL	Average offered, low	ASL Average starting, low
AEX	Average experienced wage	APH	Average pay, high range	AW Average wage paid
AO	Average offered	APL	Average pay, low range	FQ First quartile wage

H	Hourly	M	Monthly
HI	Highest wage paid	MTC	Median total compensation
HR	High end range	MW	Median wage paid
LR	Low end range	SQ	Second quartile wage

S	Special: hourly and annual
TQ	Third quartile wage
W	Weekly
Y	Yearly

Occupation/Type/Industry	Location	Per	Low	Mid	High	Source	Date
File Clerk	Orange County PMSA, CA	S	10.01 MW	9.02 AW	20820 AAW	CABLS	10//99-12//99
	Redding MSA, CA	S	7.47 MW	6.92 AW	15530 AAW	CABLS	10//99-12//99
	Riverside-San Bernardino PMSA, CA	S	9.43 MW	8.86 AW	19610 AAW	CABLS	10//99-12//99
	Sacramento PMSA, CA	S	10.05 MW	8.94 AW	20900 AAW	CABLS	10//99-12//99
	Salinas MSA, CA	S	8.03 MW	7.82 AW	16700 AAW	CABLS	10//99-12//99
	San Diego MSA, CA	S	9.21 MW	8.43 AW	19150 AAW	CABLS	10//99-12//99
	San Francisco PMSA, CA	S	11.19 MW	11.01 AW	23270 AAW	CABLS	10//99-12//99
	San Jose PMSA, CA	S	10.42 MW	10.79 AW	21680 AAW	CABLS	10//99-12//99
	San Luis Obispo-Atascadero-Paso Robles MSA, CA	S	7.21 MW	6.31 AW	15010 AAW	CABLS	10//99-12//99
	Santa Barbara-Santa Maria-Lompoc MSA, CA	S	8.92 MW	8.53 AW	18560 AAW	CABLS	10//99-12//99
	Santa Cruz-Watsonville PMSA, CA	S	8.88 MW	7.72 AW	18470 AAW	CABLS	10//99-12//99
	Santa Rosa PMSA, CA	S	7.90 MW	7.48 AW	16420 AAW	CABLS	10//99-12//99
	Stockton-Lodi MSA, CA	S	7.97 MW	7.69 AW	16580 AAW	CABLS	10//99-12//99
	Vallejo-Fairfield-Napa PMSA, CA	S	9.26 MW	8.56 AW	19260 AAW	CABLS	10//99-12//99
	Ventura PMSA, CA	S	8.96 MW	8.95 AW	18640 AAW	CABLS	10//99-12//99
	Visalia-Tulare-Porterville MSA, CA	S	7.54 MW	7.18 AW	15680 AAW	CABLS	10//99-12//99
	Yolo PMSA, CA	S	9.98 MW	9.71 AW	20760 AAW	CABLS	10//99-12//99
	Yuba City MSA, CA	S	8.03 MW	7.75 AW	16710 AAW	CABLS	10//99-12//99
	Colorado	S	8.48 MW	8.72 AW	18130 AAW	COBLS	10//99-12//99
	Boulder-Longmont PMSA, CO	S	8.65 MW	8.38 AW	17990 AAW	COBLS	10//99-12//99
	Colorado Springs MSA, CO	S	8.25 MW	7.88 AW	17150 AAW	COBLS	10//99-12//99
	Denver PMSA, CO	S	9.19 MW	8.90 AW	19110 AAW	COBLS	10//99-12//99
	Fort Collins-Loveland MSA, CO	S	7.65 MW	7.35 AW	15910 AAW	COBLS	10//99-12//99
	Grand Junction MSA, CO	S	7.29 MW	6.70 AW	15160 AAW	COBLS	10//99-12//99
	Greeley PMSA, CO	S	8.58 MW	8.04 AW	17840 AAW	COBLS	10//99-12//99
	Pueblo MSA, CO	S	7.46 MW	7.48 AW	15510 AAW	COBLS	10//99-12//99
	Connecticut	S	9.41 MW	9.73 AW	20250 AAW	CTBLS	10//99-12//99
	Bridgeport PMSA, CT	S	9.34 MW	8.88 AW	19420 AAW	CTBLS	10//99-12//99
	Danbury PMSA, CT	S	9.00 MW	8.60 AW	18720 AAW	CTBLS	10//99-12//99
	Hartford MSA, CT	S	9.84 MW	9.81 AW	20460 AAW	CTBLS	10//99-12//99
	New Haven-Meriden PMSA, CT	S	10.25 MW	10.07 AW	21320 AAW	CTBLS	10//99-12//99
	New London-Norwich MSA, CT-RI	S	9.06 MW	8.41 AW	18850 AAW	CTBLS	10//99-12//99
	Stamford-Norwalk PMSA, CT	S	11.03 MW	10.31 AW	22950 AAW	CTBLS	10//99-12//99
	Waterbury PMSA, CT	S	8.84 MW	8.04 AW	18400 AAW	CTBLS	10//99-12//99
	Delaware	S	9.38 MW	10.06 AW	20930 AAW	DEBLS	10//99-12//99
	Dover MSA, DE	S	8.47 MW	7.49 AW	17620 AAW	DEBLS	10//99-12//99
	Wilmington-Newark PMSA, DE-MD	S	10.34 MW	9.57 AW	21520 AAW	DEBLS	10//99-12//99
	District of Columbia	S	10.07 MW	10.51 AW	21850 AAW	DCBLS	10//99-12//99
	Washington PMSA, DC-MD-VA-WV	S	10.23 MW	9.84 AW	21270 AAW	DCBLS	10//99-12//99
	Florida	S	8.18 MW	8.67 AW	18040 AAW	FLBLS	10//99-12//99
	Daytona Beach MSA, FL	S	7.43 MW	7.03 AW	15460 AAW	FLBLS	10//99-12//99
	Fort Lauderdale PMSA, FL	S	9.32 MW	8.89 AW	19390 AAW	FLBLS	10//99-12//99
	Fort Myers-Cape Coral MSA, FL	S	7.84 MW	7.64 AW	16300 AAW	FLBLS	10//99-12//99
	Fort Pierce-Port St. Lucie MSA, FL	S	7.91 MW	7.55 AW	16440 AAW	FLBLS	10//99-12//99
	Fort Walton Beach MSA, FL	S	7.28 MW	7.16 AW	15130 AAW	FLBLS	10//99-12//99
	Gainesville MSA, FL	S	8.23 MW	8.02 AW	17120 AAW	FLBLS	10//99-12//99
	Jacksonville MSA, FL	S	8.81 MW	8.18 AW	18310 AAW	FLBLS	10//99-12//99
	Lakeland-Winter Haven MSA, FL	S	7.85 MW	7.49 AW	16330 AAW	FLBLS	10//99-12//99
	Melbourne-Titusville-Palm Bay MSA, FL	S	9.64 MW	8.93 AW	20060 AAW	FLBLS	10//99-12//99
	Miami PMSA, FL	S	9.00 MW	8.52 AW	18720 AAW	FLBLS	10//99-12//99
	Naples MSA, FL	S	9.33 MW	9.58 AW	19400 AAW	FLBLS	10//99-12//99
	Ocala MSA, FL	S	8.03 MW	7.75 AW	16690 AAW	FLBLS	10//99-12//99
	Orlando MSA, FL	S	9.21 MW	8.09 AW	19150 AAW	FLBLS	10//99-12//99
	Panama City MSA, FL	S	8.39 MW	7.82 AW	17450 AAW	FLBLS	10//99-12//99
	Pensacola MSA, FL	S	6.92 MW	6.47 AW	14390 AAW	FLBLS	10//99-12//99
	Punta Gorda MSA, FL	S	7.48 MW	7.50 AW	15570 AAW	FLBLS	10//99-12//99
	Sarasota-Bradenton MSA, FL	S	8.28 MW	8.24 AW	17220 AAW	FLBLS	10//99-12//99

AAW Average annual wage	**AOH** Average offered, high	**ASH** Average starting, high	**H** Hourly	**M** Monthly	**S** Special: hourly and annual
AE Average entry wage	**AOL** Average offered, low	**ASL** Average starting, low	**HI** Highest wage paid	**MTC** Median total compensation	**TQ** Third quartile wage
AEX Average experienced wage	**APH** Average pay, high range	**AW** Average wage paid	**HR** High end range	**MW** Median wage paid	**W** Weekly
AO Average offered	**APL** Average pay, low range	**FQ** First quartile wage	**LR** Low end range	**SQ** Second quartile wage	**Y** Yearly

Occupation/Type/Industry	Location	Per	Low	Mid	High	Source	Date
File Clerk	Tampa-St. Petersburg-Clearwater MSA, FL	s	8.72 MW	8.21 AW	18150 AAW	FLBLS	10//99-12//99
	West Palm Beach-Boca Raton MSA, FL	s	8.95 MW	8.40 AW	18610 AAW	FLBLS	10//99-12//99
	Georgia	s	8.37 MW	9.07 AW	18870 AAW	GABLS	10//99-12//99
	Albany MSA, GA	s	8.29 MW	8.22 AW	17240 AAW	GABLS	10//99-12//99
	Athens MSA, GA	s	7.95 MW	7.88 AW	16530 AAW	GABLS	10//99-12//99
	Atlanta MSA, GA	s	9.77 MW	8.72 AW	20320 AAW	GABLS	10//99-12//99
	Augusta-Aiken MSA, GA-SC	s	8.53 MW	8.53 AW	17740 AAW	GABLS	10//99-12//99
	Columbus MSA, GA-AL	s	7.71 MW	7.42 AW	16040 AAW	GABLS	10//99-12//99
	Macon MSA, GA	s	7.79 MW	7.23 AW	16190 AAW	GABLS	10//99-12//99
	Savannah MSA, GA	s	7.36 MW	7.14 AW	15310 AAW	GABLS	10//99-12//99
	Hawaii	s	8.59 MW	9.10 AW	18940 AAW	HIBLS	10//99-12//99
	Honolulu MSA, HI	s	9.12 MW	8.57 AW	18970 AAW	HIBLS	10//99-12//99
	Idaho	s	8.61 MW	8.64 AW	17980 AAW	IDBLS	10//99-12//99
	Boise City MSA, ID	s	9.12 MW	9.02 AW	18980 AAW	IDBLS	10//99-12//99
	Pocatello MSA, ID	s	8.84 MW	8.44 AW	18400 AAW	IDBLS	10//99-12//99
	Illinois	s	8.78 MW	9.07 AW	18870 AAW	ILBLS	10//99-12//99
	Bloomington-Normal MSA, IL	s	7.17 MW	7.16 AW	14920 AAW	ILBLS	10//99-12//99
	Champaign-Urbana MSA, IL	s	8.80 MW	9.16 AW	18300 AAW	ILBLS	10//99-12//99
	Chicago PMSA, IL	s	9.47 MW	9.21 AW	19700 AAW	ILBLS	10//99-12//99
	Decatur MSA, IL	s	6.66 MW	6.45 AW	13850 AAW	ILBLS	10//99-12//99
	Kankakee PMSA, IL	s	6.75 MW	6.46 AW	14040 AAW	ILBLS	10//99-12//99
	Peoria-Pekin MSA, IL	s	8.17 MW	7.98 AW	17000 AAW	ILBLS	10//99-12//99
	Rockford MSA, IL	s	8.20 MW	7.94 AW	17050 AAW	ILBLS	10//99-12//99
	Springfield MSA, IL	s	8.52 MW	8.02 AW	17730 AAW	ILBLS	10//99-12//99
	Indiana	s	7.89 MW	8.05 AW	16740 AAW	INBLS	10//99-12//99
	Bloomington MSA, IN	s	8.81 MW	8.75 AW	18320 AAW	INBLS	10//99-12//99
	Elkhart-Goshen MSA, IN	s	8.27 MW	8.24 AW	17190 AAW	INBLS	10//99-12//99
	Evansville-Henderson MSA, IN-KY	s	7.66 MW	7.44 AW	15940 AAW	INBLS	10//99-12//99
	Fort Wayne MSA, IN	s	8.68 MW	8.59 AW	18050 AAW	INBLS	10//99-12//99
	Gary PMSA, IN	s	7.17 MW	6.71 AW	14920 AAW	INBLS	10//99-12//99
	Indianapolis MSA, IN	s	8.50 MW	8.35 AW	17680 AAW	INBLS	10//99-12//99
	Kokomo MSA, IN	s	7.36 MW	7.05 AW	15310 AAW	INBLS	10//99-12//99
	Lafayette MSA, IN	s	7.73 MW	7.62 AW	16070 AAW	INBLS	10//99-12//99
	Muncie MSA, IN	s	7.88 MW	8.24 AW	16400 AAW	INBLS	10//99-12//99
	South Bend MSA, IN	s	8.13 MW	7.83 AW	16910 AAW	INBLS	10//99-12//99
	Terre Haute MSA, IN	s	7.92 MW	7.48 AW	16480 AAW	INBLS	10//99-12//99
	Iowa	s	8.16 MW	8.33 AW	17330 AAW	IABLS	10//99-12//99
	Cedar Rapids MSA, IA	s	8.24 MW	8.09 AW	17140 AAW	IABLS	10//99-12//99
	Davenport-Moline-Rock Island MSA, IA-IL	s	7.71 MW	7.50 AW	16030 AAW	IABLS	10//99-12//99
	Des Moines MSA, IA	s	8.83 MW	8.67 AW	18360 AAW	IABLS	10//99-12//99
	Iowa City MSA, IA	s	7.23 MW	6.50 AW	15030 AAW	IABLS	10//99-12//99
	Sioux City MSA, IA-NE	s	8.51 MW	7.82 AW	17700 AAW	IABLS	10//99-12//99
	Waterloo-Cedar Falls MSA, IA	s	8.29 MW	8.30 AW	17240 AAW	IABLS	10//99-12//99
	Kansas	s	7.89 MW	8.33 AW	17320 AAW	KSBLS	10//99-12//99
	Topeka MSA, KS	s	7.40 MW	7.43 AW	15380 AAW	KSBLS	10//99-12//99
	Wichita MSA, KS	s	7.48 MW	7.08 AW	15560 AAW	KSBLS	10//99-12//99
	Kentucky	s	7.66 MW	7.82 AW	16270 AAW	KYBLS	10//99-12//99
	Lexington MSA, KY	s	7.98 MW	7.88 AW	16590 AAW	KYBLS	10//99-12//99
	Louisville MSA, KY-IN	s	7.99 MW	7.83 AW	16620 AAW	KYBLS	10//99-12//99
	Owensboro MSA, KY	s	8.30 MW	7.83 AW	17270 AAW	KYBLS	10//99-12//99
	Louisiana	s	6.86 MW	7.29 AW	15160 AAW	LABLS	10//99-12//99
	Alexandria MSA, LA	s	7.54 MW	7.21 AW	15680 AAW	LABLS	10//99-12//99
	Baton Rouge MSA, LA	s	7.14 MW	6.62 AW	14860 AAW	LABLS	10//99-12//99
	Houma MSA, LA	s	7.05 MW	6.98 AW	14670 AAW	LABLS	10//99-12//99
	Lafayette MSA, LA	s	6.94 MW	6.66 AW	14430 AAW	LABLS	10//99-12//99
	Lake Charles MSA, LA	s	7.09 MW	6.57 AW	14750 AAW	LABLS	10//99-12//99
	Monroe MSA, LA	s	6.73 MW	6.67 AW	14000 AAW	LABLS	10//99-12//99
	New Orleans MSA, LA	s	7.94 MW	7.61 AW	16520 AAW	LABLS	10//99-12//99
	Shreveport-Bossier City MSA, LA	s	7.03 MW	6.61 AW	14630 AAW	LABLS	10//99-12//99
	Maine	s	7.51 MW	7.71 AW	16040 AAW	MEBLS	10//99-12//99
	Bangor MSA, ME	s	7.83 MW	7.70 AW	16280 AAW	MEBLS	10//99-12//99
	Lewiston-Auburn MSA, ME	s	7.96 MW	7.86 AW	16550 AAW	MEBLS	10//99-12//99
	Portland MSA, ME	s	8.44 MW	8.24 AW	17560 AAW	MEBLS	10//99-12//99
	Maryland	s	9.39 MW	9.66 AW	20090 AAW	MDBLS	10//99-12//99
	Baltimore PMSA, MD	s	9.21 MW	9.13 AW	19150 AAW	MDBLS	10//99-12//99
	Cumberland MSA, MD-WV	s	7.39 MW	6.15 AW	15370 AAW	MDBLS	10//99-12//99
	Hagerstown PMSA, MD	s	9.22 MW	8.34 AW	19190 AAW	MDBLS	10//99-12//99

AAW	Average annual wage	AOH	Average offered, high	ASH	Average starting, high	H	Hourly	M	Monthly	S	Special: hourly and annual
AE	Average entry wage	AOL	Average offered, low	ASL	Average starting, low	HI	Highest wage paid	MTC	Median total compensation	TQ	Third quartile wage
AEX	Average experienced wage	APH	Average pay, high range	AW	Average wage paid	HR	High end range	MW	Median wage paid	W	Weekly
AO	Average offered	APL	Average pay, low range	FQ	First quartile wage	LR	Low end range	SQ	Second quartile wage	Y	Yearly

Occupation/Type/Industry	Location	Per	Low	Mid	High	Source	Date
File Clerk	Massachusetts	S	9.11 MW	9.64 AW	20040 AAW	MABLS	10//99-12//99
	Barnstable-Yarmouth MSA, MA	S	10.14 MW	9.94 AW	21090 AAW	MABLS	10//99-12//99
	Boston PMSA, MA-NH	S	9.81 MW	9.27 AW	20400 AAW	MABLS	10//99-12//99
	Brockton PMSA, MA	S	9.46 MW	9.10 AW	19680 AAW	MABLS	10//99-12//99
	Lawrence PMSA, MA-NH	S	9.96 MW	10.10 AW	20720 AAW	MABLS	10//99-12//99
	Lowell PMSA, MA-NH	S	9.62 MW	9.15 AW	20010 AAW	MABLS	10//99-12//99
	New Bedford PMSA, MA	S	8.23 MW	8.16 AW	17130 AAW	MABLS	10//99-12//99
	Pittsfield MSA, MA	S	10.61 MW	9.77 AW	22080 AAW	MABLS	10//99-12//99
	Springfield MSA, MA	S	9.82 MW	9.24 AW	20420 AAW	MABLS	10//99-12//99
	Worcester PMSA, MA-CT	S	8.92 MW	8.72 AW	18560 AAW	MABLS	10//99-12//99
	Michigan	S	8.34 MW	8.45 AW	17580 AAW	MIBLS	10//99-12//99
	Ann Arbor PMSA, MI	S	8.90 MW	8.87 AW	18520 AAW	MIBLS	10//99-12//99
	Benton Harbor MSA, MI	S	8.17 MW	7.87 AW	16990 AAW	MIBLS	10//99-12//99
	Detroit PMSA, MI	S	8.55 MW	8.60 AW	17790 AAW	MIBLS	10//99-12//99
	Flint PMSA, MI	S	7.67 MW	7.49 AW	15960 AAW	MIBLS	10//99-12//99
	Grand Rapids-Muskegon-Holland MSA, MI	S	9.51 MW	9.22 AW	19770 AAW	MIBLS	10//99-12//99
	Jackson MSA, MI	S	7.25 MW	7.01 AW	15080 AAW	MIBLS	10//99-12//99
	Kalamazoo-Battle Creek MSA, MI	S	8.31 MW	7.86 AW	17290 AAW	MIBLS	10//99-12//99
	Lansing-East Lansing MSA, MI	S	8.47 MW	8.56 AW	17620 AAW	MIBLS	10//99-12//99
	Saginaw-Bay City-Midland MSA, MI	S	6.92 MW	6.43 AW	14380 AAW	MIBLS	10//99-12//99
	Minnesota	S	9.01 MW	9.15 AW	19040 AAW	MNBLS	10//99-12//99
	Duluth-Superior MSA, MN-WI	S	8.03 MW	7.56 AW	16690 AAW	MNBLS	10//99-12//99
	Minneapolis-St. Paul MSA, MN-WI	S	9.41 MW	9.29 AW	19570 AAW	MNBLS	10//99-12//99
	St. Cloud MSA, MN	S	8.65 MW	8.51 AW	17990 AAW	MNBLS	10//99-12//99
	Mississippi	S	6.92 MW	7.36 AW	15310 AAW	MSBLS	10//99-12//99
	Biloxi-Gulfport-Pascagoula MSA, MS	S	7.10 MW	6.64 AW	14760 AAW	MSBLS	10//99-12//99
	Hattiesburg MSA, MS	S	6.93 MW	6.64 AW	14420 AAW	MSBLS	10//99-12//99
	Jackson MSA, MS	S	7.83 MW	7.67 AW	16290 AAW	MSBLS	10//99-12//99
	Missouri	S	7.99 MW	8.32 AW	17300 AAW	MOBLS	10//99-12//99
	Joplin MSA, MO	S	6.70 MW	6.08 AW	13940 AAW	MOBLS	10//99-12//99
	Kansas City MSA, MO-KS	S	9.52 MW	9.37 AW	19810 AAW	MOBLS	10//99-12//99
	St. Joseph MSA, MO	S	7.38 MW	6.92 AW	15360 AAW	MOBLS	10//99-12//99
	St. Louis MSA, MO-IL	S	8.08 MW	7.75 AW	16800 AAW	MOBLS	10//99-12//99
	Springfield MSA, MO	S	7.15 MW	6.75 AW	14860 AAW	MOBLS	10//99-12//99
	Montana	S	7.22 MW	7.74 AW	16100 AAW	MTBLS	10//99-12//99
	Billings MSA, MT	S	7.89 MW	7.42 AW	16400 AAW	MTBLS	10//99-12//99
	Great Falls MSA, MT	S	8.40 MW	7.79 AW	17480 AAW	MTBLS	10//99-12//99
	Missoula MSA, MT	S	7.29 MW	7.27 AW	15170 AAW	MTBLS	10//99-12//99
	Nebraska	S	7.16 MW	7.48 AW	15550 AAW	NEBLS	10//99-12//99
	Omaha MSA, NE-IA	S	8.81 MW	8.35 AW	18320 AAW	NEBLS	10//99-12//99
	Nevada	S	8.15 MW	8.47 AW	17620 AAW	NVBLS	10//99-12//99
	Las Vegas MSA, NV-AZ	S	8.34 MW	8.16 AW	17350 AAW	NVBLS	10//99-12//99
	Reno MSA, NV	S	8.82 MW	8.52 AW	18340 AAW	NVBLS	10//99-12//99
	New Hampshire	S	8.16 MW	8.36 AW	17380 AAW	NHBLS	10//99-12//99
	Manchester PMSA, NH	S	8.81 MW	8.61 AW	18330 AAW	NHBLS	10//99-12//99
	Nashua PMSA, NH	S	9.05 MW	8.89 AW	18820 AAW	NHBLS	10//99-12//99
	Portsmouth-Rochester PMSA, NH-ME	S	7.99 MW	7.83 AW	16610 AAW	NHBLS	10//99-12//99
	New Jersey	S	9.42 MW	10.41 AW	21650 AAW	NJBLS	10//99-12//99
	Atlantic-Cape May PMSA, NJ	S	8.92 MW	8.31 AW	18550 AAW	NJBLS	10//99-12//99
	Bergen-Passaic PMSA, NJ	S	8.94 MW	8.32 AW	18600 AAW	NJBLS	10//99-12//99
	Jersey City PMSA, NJ	S	9.35 MW	8.78 AW	19440 AAW	NJBLS	10//99-12//99
	Middlesex-Somerset-Hunterdon PMSA, NJ	S	13.19 MW	12.69 AW	27430 AAW	NJBLS	10//99-12//99
	Monmouth-Ocean PMSA, NJ	S	10.69 MW	9.49 AW	22240 AAW	NJBLS	10//99-12//99
	Newark PMSA, NJ	S	9.91 MW	9.24 AW	20610 AAW	NJBLS	10//99-12//99
	Trenton PMSA, NJ	S	10.98 MW	9.85 AW	22830 AAW	NJBLS	10//99-12//99
	Vineland-Millville-Bridgeton PMSA, NJ	S	9.44 MW	8.49 AW	19640 AAW	NJBLS	10//99-12//99
	New Mexico	S	7.41 MW	7.57 AW	15740 AAW	NMBLS	10//99-12//99
	Albuquerque MSA, NM	S	7.94 MW	7.83 AW	16510 AAW	NMBLS	10//99-12//99
	Santa Fe MSA, NM	S	7.79 MW	7.58 AW	16210 AAW	NMBLS	10//99-12//99
	New York	S	9.06 MW	9.69 AW	20160 AAW	NYBLS	10//99-12//99
	Albany-Schenectady-Troy MSA, NY	S	9.28 MW	8.94 AW	19310 AAW	NYBLS	10//99-12//99
	Binghamton MSA, NY	S	7.40 MW	7.16 AW	15400 AAW	NYBLS	10//99-12//99

AAW Average annual wage	**AOH** Average offered, high	**ASH** Average starting, high	**H** Hourly	**M** Monthly	**S** Special: hourly and annual
AE Average entry wage	**AOL** Average offered, low	**ASL** Average starting, low	**HI** Highest wage paid	**MTC** Median total compensation	**TQ** Third quartile wage
AEX Average experienced wage	**APH** Average pay, high range	**AW** Average wage paid	**HR** High end range	**MW** Median wage paid	**W** Weekly
AO Average offered	**APL** Average pay, low range	**FQ** First quartile wage	**LR** Low end range	**SQ** Second quartile wage	**Y** Yearly

Occupation/Type/Industry	Location	Per	Low	Mid	High	Source	Date
File Clerk	Buffalo-Niagara Falls MSA, NY	S	8.08 MW	7.38 AW	16810 AAW	NYBLS	10//99-12//99
	Dutchess County PMSA, NY	S	8.58 MW	8.08 AW	17840 AAW	NYBLS	10//99-12//99
	Elmira MSA, NY	S	7.22 MW	6.69 AW	15030 AAW	NYBLS	10//99-12//99
	Glens Falls MSA, NY	S	8.07 MW	7.69 AW	16790 AAW	NYBLS	10//99-12//99
	Nassau-Suffolk PMSA, NY	S	9.47 MW	9.29 AW	19700 AAW	NYBLS	10//99-12//99
	New York PMSA, NY	S	10.35 MW	9.77 AW	21520 AAW	NYBLS	10//99-12//99
	Newburgh PMSA, NY-PA	S	7.99 MW	7.36 AW	16610 AAW	NYBLS	10//99-12//99
	Rochester MSA, NY	S	8.73 MW	8.11 AW	18150 AAW	NYBLS	10//99-12//99
	Syracuse MSA, NY	S	8.35 MW	8.03 AW	17370 AAW	NYBLS	10//99-12//99
	Utica-Rome MSA, NY	S	7.91 MW	7.27 AW	16450 AAW	NYBLS	10//99-12//99
	North Carolina	S	8.16 MW	8.56 AW	17800 AAW	NCBLS	10//99-12//99
	Asheville MSA, NC	S	8.25 MW	8.21 AW	17160 AAW	NCBLS	10//99-12//99
	Charlotte-Gastonia-Rock Hill MSA, NC-SC	S	8.88 MW	8.60 AW	18470 AAW	NCBLS	10//99-12//99
	Fayetteville MSA, NC	S	7.06 MW	6.67 AW	14690 AAW	NCBLS	10//99-12//99
	Goldsboro MSA, NC	S	7.06 MW	7.28 AW	14680 AAW	NCBLS	10//99-12//99
	Greensboro--Winston-Salem-- High Point MSA, NC	S	8.81 MW	8.27 AW	18320 AAW	NCBLS	10//99-12//99
	Greenville MSA, NC	S	8.61 MW	7.80 AW	17920 AAW	NCBLS	10//99-12//99
	Hickory-Morganton-Lenoir MSA, NC	S	8.31 MW	8.15 AW	17280 AAW	NCBLS	10//99-12//99
	Raleigh-Durham-Chapel Hill MSA, NC	S	9.14 MW	8.60 AW	19010 AAW	NCBLS	10//99-12//99
	Rocky Mount MSA, NC	S	7.28 MW	7.23 AW	15150 AAW	NCBLS	10//99-12//99
	Wilmington MSA, NC	S	8.82 MW	8.91 AW	18340 AAW	NCBLS	10//99-12//99
	North Dakota	S	6.75 MW	7.03 AW	14610 AAW	NDBLS	10//99-12//99
	Bismarck MSA, ND	S	6.89 MW	6.59 AW	14330 AAW	NDBLS	10//99-12//99
	Fargo-Moorhead MSA, ND-MN	S	7.59 MW	7.45 AW	15780 AAW	NDBLS	10//99-12//99
	Ohio	S	8.13 MW	8.62 AW	17920 AAW	OHBLS	10//99-12//99
	Akron PMSA, OH	S	8.36 MW	8.02 AW	17400 AAW	OHBLS	10//99-12//99
	Canton-Massillon MSA, OH	S	8.39 MW	8.15 AW	17450 AAW	OHBLS	10//99-12//99
	Cincinnati PMSA, OH-KY-IN	S	8.98 MW	8.60 AW	18670 AAW	OHBLS	10//99-12//99
	Cleveland-Lorain-Elyria PMSA, OH	S	8.83 MW	8.38 AW	18370 AAW	OHBLS	10//99-12//99
	Columbus MSA, OH	S	9.47 MW	8.65 AW	19690 AAW	OHBLS	10//99-12//99
	Dayton-Springfield MSA, OH	S	8.34 MW	7.95 AW	17340 AAW	OHBLS	10//99-12//99
	Hamilton-Middletown PMSA, OH	S	7.60 MW	7.13 AW	15800 AAW	OHBLS	10//99-12//99
	Lima MSA, OH	S	7.24 MW	6.95 AW	15050 AAW	OHBLS	10//99-12//99
	Mansfield MSA, OH	S	8.68 MW	8.39 AW	18050 AAW	OHBLS	10//99-12//99
	Steubenville-Weirton MSA, OH-WV	S	7.85 MW	6.98 AW	16340 AAW	OHBLS	10//99-12//99
	Toledo MSA, OH	S	8.24 MW	7.83 AW	17130 AAW	OHBLS	10//99-12//99
	Youngstown-Warren MSA, OH	S	7.07 MW	6.48 AW	14710 AAW	OHBLS	10//99-12//99
	Oklahoma	S	7.45 MW	7.93 AW	16490 AAW	OKBLS	10//99-12//99
	Enid MSA, OK	S	7.55 MW	7.14 AW	15700 AAW	OKBLS	10//99-12//99
	Lawton MSA, OK	S	6.52 MW	6.13 AW	13570 AAW	OKBLS	10//99-12//99
	Oklahoma City MSA, OK	S	8.10 MW	7.63 AW	16860 AAW	OKBLS	10//99-12//99
	Tulsa MSA, OK	S	8.63 MW	8.18 AW	17960 AAW	OKBLS	10//99-12//99
	Oregon	S	8.68 MW	9.06 AW	18840 AAW	ORBLS	10//99-12//99
	Corvallis MSA, OR	S	7.33 MW	6.50 AW	15250 AAW	ORBLS	10//99-12//99
	Eugene-Springfield MSA, OR	S	8.26 MW	7.96 AW	17180 AAW	ORBLS	10//99-12//99
	Medford-Ashland MSA, OR	S	8.54 MW	7.63 AW	17760 AAW	ORBLS	10//99-12//99
	Portland-Vancouver PMSA, OR-WA	S	9.40 MW	9.29 AW	19560 AAW	ORBLS	10//99-12//99
	Salem PMSA, OR	S	8.62 MW	8.25 AW	17930 AAW	ORBLS	10//99-12//99
	Pennsylvania	S	8.27 MW	8.82 AW	18350 AAW	PABLS	10//99-12//99
	Allentown-Bethlehem-Easton MSA, PA	S	8.48 MW	8.29 AW	17630 AAW	PABLS	10//99-12//99
	Altoona MSA, PA	S	8.57 MW	7.97 AW	17830 AAW	PABLS	10//99-12//99
	Erie MSA, PA	S	7.98 MW	6.95 AW	16600 AAW	PABLS	10//99-12//99
	Harrisburg-Lebanon-Carlisle MSA, PA	S	9.92 MW	9.02 AW	20640 AAW	PABLS	10//99-12//99
	Johnstown MSA, PA	S	8.54 MW	8.33 AW	17760 AAW	PABLS	10//99-12//99
	Lancaster MSA, PA	S	9.35 MW	8.06 AW	19440 AAW	PABLS	10//99-12//99
	Philadelphia PMSA, PA-NJ	S	9.09 MW	8.61 AW	18900 AAW	PABLS	10//99-12//99
	Pittsburgh MSA, PA	S	8.62 MW	8.19 AW	17940 AAW	PABLS	10//99-12//99
	Reading MSA, PA	S	9.54 MW	9.15 AW	19840 AAW	PABLS	10//99-12//99
	Scranton--Wilkes-Barre-- Hazleton MSA, PA	S	7.60 MW	7.21 AW	15810 AAW	PABLS	10//99-12//99

AAW Average annual wage	AOH Average offered, high	ASH Average starting, high	H Hourly	M Monthly	S Special: hourly and annual
AE Average entry wage	AOL Average offered, low	ASL Average starting, low	HI Highest wage paid	MTC Median total compensation	TQ Third quartile wage
AEX Average experienced wage	APH Average pay, high range	AW Average wage paid	HR High end range	MW Median wage paid	W Weekly
AO Average offered	APL Average pay, low range	FQ First quartile wage	LR Low end range	SQ Second quartile wage	Y Yearly

Occupation/Type/Industry	Location	Per	Low	Mid	High	Source	Date
File Clerk	Sharon MSA, PA	S	8.18 MW	7.54 AW	17020 AAW	PABLS	10//99-12//99
	State College MSA, PA	S	9.06 MW	8.57 AW	18840 AAW	PABLS	10//99-12//99
	Williamsport MSA, PA	S	8.67 MW	7.95 AW	18020 AAW	PABLS	10//99-12//99
	York MSA, PA	S	9.29 MW	8.94 AW	19320 AAW	PABLS	10//99-12//99
	Rhode Island	S	8.95 MW	9.83 AW	20440 AAW	RIBLS	10//99-12//99
	Providence-Fall River- Warwick MSA, RI-MA	S	9.62 MW	8.78 AW	20020 AAW	RIBLS	10//99-12//99
	South Carolina	S	7.78 MW	8.07 AW	16790 AAW	SCBLS	10//99-12//99
	Charleston-North Charleston MSA, SC	S	7.35 MW	7.15 AW	15290 AAW	SCBLS	10//99-12//99
	Columbia MSA, SC	S	8.75 MW	8.43 AW	18200 AAW	SCBLS	10//99-12//99
	Florence MSA, SC	S	8.01 MW	7.90 AW	16670 AAW	SCBLS	10//99-12//99
	Greenville-Spartanburg- Anderson MSA, SC	S	8.12 MW	7.82 AW	16900 AAW	SCBLS	10//99-12//99
	Myrtle Beach MSA, SC	S	8.62 MW	8.32 AW	17920 AAW	SCBLS	10//99-12//99
	Sumter MSA, SC	S	9.95 MW	8.17 AW	20690 AAW	SCBLS	10//99-12//99
	South Dakota	S	8.22 MW	8.85 AW	18410 AAW	SDBLS	10//99-12//99
	Rapid City MSA, SD	S	8.25 MW	8.14 AW	17150 AAW	SDBLS	10//99-12//99
	Sioux Falls MSA, SD	S	10.05 MW	9.01 AW	20910 AAW	SDBLS	10//99-12//99
	Tennessee	S	7.95 MW	8.10 AW	16840 AAW	TNBLS	10//99-12//99
	Chattanooga MSA, TN-GA	S	8.26 MW	7.94 AW	17170 AAW	TNBLS	10//99-12//99
	Clarksville-Hopkinsville MSA, TN-KY	S	7.02 MW	6.72 AW	14600 AAW	TNBLS	10//99-12//99
	Jackson MSA, TN	S	7.77 MW	7.50 AW	16160 AAW	TNBLS	10//99-12//99
	Johnson City-Kingsport-Bristol MSA, TN-VA	S	7.86 MW	7.68 AW	16350 AAW	TNBLS	10//99-12//99
	Knoxville MSA, TN	S	7.61 MW	7.57 AW	15830 AAW	TNBLS	10//99-12//99
	Memphis MSA, TN-AR-MS	S	8.05 MW	7.89 AW	16750 AAW	MSBLS	10//99-12//99
	Nashville MSA, TN	S	8.64 MW	8.42 AW	17970 AAW	TNBLS	10//99-12//99
	Texas	S	8.03 MW	8.56 AW	17810 AAW	TXBLS	10//99-12//99
	Abilene MSA, TX	S	6.65 MW	6.32 AW	13830 AAW	TXBLS	10//99-12//99
	Amarillo MSA, TX	S	8.16 MW	7.80 AW	16980 AAW	TXBLS	10//99-12//99
	Austin-San Marcos MSA, TX	S	8.43 MW	8.11 AW	17530 AAW	TXBLS	10//99-12//99
	Beaumont-Port Arthur MSA, TX	S	7.15 MW	6.56 AW	14860 AAW	TXBLS	10//99-12//99
	Brazoria PMSA, TX	S	7.36 MW	6.63 AW	15310 AAW	TXBLS	10//99-12//99
	Brownsville-Harlingen-San Benito MSA, TX	S	6.35 MW	6.20 AW	13210 AAW	TXBLS	10//99-12//99
	Bryan-College Station MSA, TX	S	7.10 MW	6.62 AW	14780 AAW	TXBLS	10//99-12//99
	Corpus Christi MSA, TX	S	7.43 MW	7.25 AW	15440 AAW	TXBLS	10//99-12//99
	Dallas PMSA, TX	S	10.15 MW	9.51 AW	21120 AAW	TXBLS	10//99-12//99
	El Paso MSA, TX	S	7.39 MW	6.94 AW	15370 AAW	TXBLS	10//99-12//99
	Fort Worth-Arlington PMSA, TX	S	8.16 MW	7.53 AW	16970 AAW	TXBLS	10//99-12//99
	Galveston-Texas City PMSA, TX	S	7.94 MW	7.49 AW	16520 AAW	TXBLS	10//99-12//99
	Houston PMSA, TX	S	8.77 MW	8.27 AW	18250 AAW	TXBLS	10//99-12//99
	Killeen-Temple MSA, TX	S	8.43 MW	7.97 AW	17530 AAW	TXBLS	10//99-12//99
	Laredo MSA, TX	S	6.73 MW	6.27 AW	13990 AAW	TXBLS	10//99-12//99
	Longview-Marshall MSA, TX	S	7.88 MW	7.23 AW	16400 AAW	TXBLS	10//99-12//99
	Lubbock MSA, TX	S	6.60 MW	6.39 AW	13730 AAW	TXBLS	10//99-12//99
	McAllen-Edinburg-Mission MSA, TX	S	7.69 MW	7.58 AW	16000 AAW	TXBLS	10//99-12//99
	Odessa-Midland MSA, TX	S	7.16 MW	6.45 AW	14890 AAW	TXBLS	10//99-12//99
	San Angelo MSA, TX	S	7.28 MW	7.25 AW	15150 AAW	TXBLS	10//99-12//99
	San Antonio MSA, TX	S	7.79 MW	7.60 AW	16210 AAW	TXBLS	10//99-12//99
	Texarkana MSA, TX- Texarkana, AR	S	7.11 MW	6.90 AW	14790 AAW	TXBLS	10//99-12//99
	Tyler MSA, TX	S	7.28 MW	7.09 AW	15130 AAW	TXBLS	10//99-12//99
	Victoria MSA, TX	S	7.44 MW	6.54 AW	15470 AAW	TXBLS	10//99-12//99
	Waco MSA, TX	S	7.56 MW	6.81 AW	15720 AAW	TXBLS	10//99-12//99
	Wichita Falls MSA, TX	S	7.14 MW	6.75 AW	14850 AAW	TXBLS	10//99-12//99
	Utah	S	8.16 MW	8.49 AW	17650 AAW	UTBLS	10//99-12//99
	Provo-Orem MSA, UT	S	7.88 MW	7.77 AW	16390 AAW	UTBLS	10//99-12//99
	Salt Lake City-Ogden MSA, UT	S	8.74 MW	8.41 AW	18170 AAW	UTBLS	10//99-12//99
	Vermont	S	8.49 MW	9.00 AW	18710 AAW	VTBLS	10//99-12//99
	Burlington MSA, VT	S	9.52 MW	9.53 AW	19800 AAW	VTBLS	10//99-12//99
	Virginia	S	8.15 MW	8.71 AW	18110 AAW	VABLS	10//99-12//99
	Charlottesville MSA, VA	S	8.43 MW	8.31 AW	17530 AAW	VABLS	10//99-12//99
	Danville MSA, VA	S	7.62 MW	7.18 AW	15850 AAW	VABLS	10//99-12//99

AAW	Average annual wage	**AOH**	Average offered, high	**ASH**	Average starting, high	**H**	Hourly	**M**	Monthly	**S**	Special: hourly and annual
AE	Average entry wage	**AOL**	Average offered, low	**ASL**	Average starting, low	**HI**	Highest wage paid	**MTC**	Median total compensation	**TQ**	Third quartile wage
AEX	Average experienced wage	**APH**	Average pay, high range	**AW**	Average wage paid	**HR**	High end range	**MW**	Median wage paid	**W**	Weekly
AO	Average offered	**APL**	Average pay, low range	**FQ**	First quartile wage	**LR**	Low end range	**SQ**	Second quartile wage	**Y**	Yearly

Occupation/Type/Industry	Location	Per	Low	Mid	High	Source	Date
File Clerk	Lynchburg MSA, VA	S	8.25 MW	7.99 AW	17160 AAW	VABLS	10//99-12//99
	Norfolk-Virginia Beach-Newport News MSA, VA-NC	S	7.69 MW	7.30 AW	16000 AAW	VABLS	10//99-12//99
	Richmond-Petersburg MSA, VA	S	8.25 MW	7.79 AW	17170 AAW	VABLS	10//99-12//99
	Roanoke MSA, VA	S	8.32 MW	8.00 AW	17300 AAW	VABLS	10//99-12//99
	Washington	S	8.81 MW	9.27 AW	19270 AAW	WABLS	10//99-12//99
	Bellingham MSA, WA	S	8.56 MW	7.85 AW	17800 AAW	WABLS	10//99-12//99
	Bremerton PMSA, WA	S	8.10 MW	7.91 AW	16840 AAW	WABLS	10//99-12//99
	Olympia PMSA, WA	S	8.88 MW	8.79 AW	18470 AAW	WABLS	10//99-12//99
	Richland-Kennewick-Pasco MSA, WA	S	8.10 MW	7.47 AW	16850 AAW	WABLS	10//99-12//99
	Seattle-Bellevue-Everett PMSA, WA	S	9.81 MW	9.32 AW	20400 AAW	WABLS	10//99-12//99
	Spokane MSA, WA	S	7.95 MW	7.57 AW	16540 AAW	WABLS	10//99-12//99
	Tacoma PMSA, WA	S	8.63 MW	8.22 AW	17950 AAW	WABLS	10//99-12//99
	Yakima MSA, WA	S	7.81 MW	7.37 AW	16240 AAW	WABLS	10//99-12//99
	West Virginia	S	7.19 MW	8.02 AW	16680 AAW	WVBLS	10//99-12//99
	Charleston MSA, WV	S	8.21 MW	6.87 AW	17080 AAW	WVBLS	10//99-12//99
	Huntington-Ashland MSA, WV-KY-OH	S	7.86 MW	7.00 AW	16350 AAW	WVBLS	10//99-12//99
	Parkersburg-Marietta MSA, WV-OH	S	7.80 MW	7.12 AW	16220 AAW	WVBLS	10//99-12//99
	Wheeling MSA, WV-OH	S	7.69 MW	7.16 AW	15990 AAW	WVBLS	10//99-12//99
	Wisconsin	S	8.24 MW	8.58 AW	17850 AAW	WIBLS	10//99-12//99
	Appleton-Oshkosh-Neenah MSA, WI	S	8.83 MW	8.38 AW	18360 AAW	WIBLS	10//99-12//99
	Eau Claire MSA, WI	S	8.25 MW	8.12 AW	17160 AAW	WIBLS	10//99-12//99
	Green Bay MSA, WI	S	9.10 MW	8.18 AW	18920 AAW	WIBLS	10//99-12//99
	Janesville-Beloit MSA, WI	S	8.88 MW	8.51 AW	18480 AAW	WIBLS	10//99-12//99
	La Crosse MSA, WI-MN	S	7.55 MW	7.38 AW	15690 AAW	WIBLS	10//99-12//99
	Madison MSA, WI	S	8.72 MW	8.53 AW	18140 AAW	WIBLS	10//99-12//99
	Milwaukee-Waukesha PMSA, WI	S	8.70 MW	8.43 AW	18090 AAW	WIBLS	10//99-12//99
	Racine PMSA, WI	S	8.79 MW	8.37 AW	18280 AAW	WIBLS	10//99-12//99
	Wausau MSA, WI	S	8.41 MW	8.05 AW	17500 AAW	WIBLS	10//99-12//99
	Wyoming	S	6.94 MW	7.11 AW	14790 AAW	WYBLS	10//99-12//99
	Casper MSA, WY	S	8.24 MW	7.69 AW	17130 AAW	WYBLS	10//99-12//99
	Cheyenne MSA, WY	S	6.82 MW	6.58 AW	14180 AAW	WYBLS	10//99-12//99
	Puerto Rico	S	6.16 MW	6.73 AW	14000 AAW	PRBLS	10//99-12//99
	Arecibo PMSA, PR	S	6.40 MW	6.23 AW	13310 AAW	PRBLS	10//99-12//99
	Caguas PMSA, PR	S	6.67 MW	6.20 AW	13880 AAW	PRBLS	10//99-12//99
	Ponce MSA, PR	S	6.02 MW	6.03 AW	12520 AAW	PRBLS	10//99-12//99
	San Juan-Bayamon PMSA, PR	S	6.78 MW	6.19 AW	14110 AAW	PRBLS	10//99-12//99
	Virgin Islands	S	7.66 MW	7.61 AW	15820 AAW	VIBLS	10//99-12//99
Film and Video Editor	Alabama	S	11.66 MW	13.64 AW	28380 AAW	ALBLS	10//99-12//99
	Arizona	S	12.18 MW	14.55 AW	30260 AAW	AZBLS	10//99-12//99
	Arkansas	S	13.36 MW	13.46 AW	28000 AAW	ARBLS	10//99-12//99
	California	S	26.82 MW	25.34 AW	52700 AAW	CABLS	10//99-12//99
	Colorado	S	16.37 MW	17.25 AW	35870 AAW	COBLS	10//99-12//99
	Connecticut	S	16.42 MW	20.38 AW	42380 AAW	CTBLS	10//99-12//99
	District of Columbia	S	15.51 MW	18.03 AW	37510 AAW	DCBLS	10//99-12//99
	Florida	S	13.63 MW	14.59 AW	30360 AAW	FLBLS	10//99-12//99
	Georgia	S	14.55 MW	17.54 AW	36490 AAW	GABLS	10//99-12//99
	Hawaii	S	15.55 MW	17.60 AW	36600 AAW	HIBLS	10//99-12//99
	Illinois	S	14 MW	19.56 AW	40680 AAW	ILBLS	10//99-12//99
	Indiana	S	13.4 MW	15.78 AW	32830 AAW	INBLS	10//99-12//99
	Iowa	S	10.59 MW	12.36 AW	25710 AAW	IABLS	10//99-12//99
	Kentucky	S	9.89 MW	10.26 AW	21330 AAW	KYBLS	10//99-12//99
	Louisiana	S	15.46 MW	17.34 AW	36060 AAW	LABLS	10//99-12//99
	Maine	S	15.24 MW	14.66 AW	30490 AAW	MEBLS	10//99-12//99
	Maryland	S	21.39 MW	21.11 AW	43900 AAW	MDBLS	10//99-12//99
	Massachusetts	S	22.28 MW	22.86 AW	47540 AAW	MABLS	10//99-12//99
	Michigan	S	21.33 MW	23.49 AW	48850 AAW	MIBLS	10//99-12//99
	Minnesota	S	19.75 MW	22.88 AW	47600 AAW	MNBLS	10//99-12//99
	Mississippi	S	20.21 MW	17.00 AW	35360 AAW	MSBLS	10//99-12//99
	Montana	S	17.61 MW	20.02 AW	41630 AAW	MTBLS	10//99-12//99
	Nebraska	S	8.73 MW	11.86 AW	24660 AAW	NEBLS	10//99-12//99
	Nevada	S	12.44 MW	14.26 AW	29670 AAW	NVBLS	10//99-12//99
	New Jersey	S	22.23 MW	22.89 AW	47610 AAW	NJBLS	10//99-12//99
	New Mexico	S	16.15 MW	19.64 AW	40850 AAW	NMBLS	10//99-12//99

AAW	Average annual wage	AOH	Average offered, high	ASH	Average starting, high	H	Hourly	M	Monthly	S	Special: hourly and annual
AE	Average entry wage	AOL	Average offered, low	ASL	Average starting, low	HI	Highest wage paid	MTC	Median total compensation	TQ	Third quartile wage
AEX	Average experienced wage	APH	Average pay, high range	AW	Average wage paid	HR	High end range	MW	Median wage paid	W	Weekly
AO	Average offered	APL	Average pay, low range	FQ	First quartile wage	LR	Low end range	SQ	Second quartile wage	Y	Yearly

Occupation/Type/Industry	Location	Per	Low	Mid	High	Source	Date
Film and Video Editor	New York	S	23.41 MW	26.60 AW	55330 AAW	NYBLS	10//99-12//99
	North Carolina	S	13.37 MW	15.63 AW	32500 AAW	NCBLS	10//99-12//99
	Ohio	S	14.57 MW	16.64 AW	34610 AAW	OHBLS	10//99-12//99
	Oregon	S	12.58 MW	15.15 AW	31520 AAW	ORBLS	10//99-12//99
	Pennsylvania	S	20.18 MW	21.71 AW	45160 AAW	PABLS	10//99-12//99
	Rhode Island	S	13.79 MW	14.86 AW	30920 AAW	RIBLS	10//99-12//99
	South Carolina	S	15.69 MW	18.15 AW	37760 AAW	SCBLS	10//99-12//99
	Tennessee	S	13.45 MW	17.70 AW	36820 AAW	TNBLS	10//99-12//99
	Texas	S	12.58 MW	13.97 AW	29060 AAW	TXBLS	10//99-12//99
	Utah	S	16.42 MW	18.38 AW	38230 AAW	UTBLS	10//99-12//99
	Vermont	S	17.81 MW	20.36 AW	42350 AAW	VTBLS	10//99-12//99
	Virginia	S	14.64 MW	17.03 AW	35420 AAW	VABLS	10//99-12//99
	Washington	S	16.32 MW	18.09 AW	37640 AAW	WABLS	10//99-12//99
	West Virginia	S	9.84 MW	10.91 AW	22680 AAW	WVBLS	10//99-12//99
	Wisconsin	S	9.14 MW	14.82 AW	30820 AAW	WIBLS	10//99-12//99
	Puerto Rico	S	10.08 MW	11.21 AW	23320 AAW	PRBLS	10//99-12//99
Financial Analyst	Alabama	S	18.98 MW	20.66 AW	42980 AAW	ALBLS	10//99-12//99
	Birmingham MSA, AL	S	20.15 MW	18.94 AW	41900 AAW	ALBLS	10//99-12//99
	Huntsville MSA, AL	S	17.63 MW	16.53 AW	36670 AAW	ALBLS	10//99-12//99
	Montgomery MSA, AL	S	20.90 MW	22.95 AW	43480 AAW	ALBLS	10//99-12//99
	Alaska	S	24.05 MW	24.72 AW	51410 AAW	AKBLS	10//99-12//99
	Anchorage MSA, AK	S	24.42 MW	24.11 AW	50800 AAW	AKBLS	10//99-12//99
	Arizona	S	26.79 MW	26.50 AW	55120 AAW	AZBLS	10//99-12//99
	Phoenix-Mesa MSA, AZ	S	26.75 MW	26.96 AW	55640 AAW	AZBLS	10//99-12//99
	Tucson MSA, AZ	S.	25.21 MW	25.37 AW	52440 AAW	AZBLS	10//99-12//99
	Arkansas	S	17.91 MW	19.04 AW	39610 AAW	ARBLS	10//99-12//99
	Little Rock-North Little Rock MSA, AR	S	19.51 MW	18.65 AW	40580 AAW	ARBLS	10//99-12//99
	California	S	27.17 MW	30.45 AW	63340 AAW	CABLS	10//99-12//99
	Bakersfield MSA, CA	S	24.48 MW	22.79 AW	50920 AAW	CABLS	10//99-12//99
	Fresno MSA, CA	S	23.66 MW	24.93 AW	49210 AAW	CABLS	10//99-12//99
	Los Angeles-Long Beach PMSA, CA	S	32.15 MW	26.95 AW	66870 AAW	CABLS	10//99-12//99
	Oakland PMSA, CA	S	27.21 MW	26.64 AW	56590 AAW	CABLS	10//99-12//99
	Orange County PMSA, CA	S	34.71 MW	28.83 AW	72190 AAW	CABLS	10//99-12//99
	Riverside-San Bernardino PMSA, CA	S	26.00 MW	24.12 AW	54080 AAW	CABLS	10//99-12//99
	Sacramento PMSA, CA	S	26.44 MW	25.13 AW	54990 AAW	CABLS	10//99-12//99
	Salinas MSA, CA	S	24.41 MW	24.50 AW	50770 AAW	CABLS	10//99-12//99
	San Diego MSA, CA	S	24.04 MW	21.41 AW	50000 AAW	CABLS	10//99-12//99
	San Francisco PMSA, CA	S	30.37 MW	29.33 AW	63160 AAW	CABLS	10//99-12//99
	San Jose PMSA, CA	S	30.46 MW	30.37 AW	63360 AAW	CABLS	10//99-12//99
	Santa Barbara-Santa Maria-Lompoc MSA, CA	S	30.60 MW	30.04 AW	63650 AAW	CABLS	10//99-12//99
	Santa Rosa PMSA, CA	S	28.08 MW	25.39 AW	58410 AAW	CABLS	10//99-12//99
	Ventura PMSA, CA	S	31.15 MW	31.57 AW	64790 AAW	CABLS	10//99-12//99
	Colorado	S	23.91 MW	29.95 AW	62290 AAW	COBLS	10//99-12//99
	Denver PMSA, CO	S	30.46 MW	23.86 AW	63360 AAW	COBLS	10//99-12//99
	Connecticut	S	21.43 MW	25.67 AW	53390 AAW	CTBLS	10//99-12//99
	Bridgeport PMSA, CT	S	32.86 MW	28.02 AW	68350 AAW	CTBLS	10//99-12//99
	New Haven-Meriden PMSA, CT	S	21.78 MW	21.17 AW	45310 AAW	CTBLS	10//99-12//99
	Stamford-Norwalk PMSA, CT	S	25.10 MW	21.20 AW	52220 AAW	CTBLS	10//99-12//99
	Waterbury PMSA, CT	S	28.79 MW	28.83 AW	59870 AAW	CTBLS	10//99-12//99
	Delaware	S	23.05 MW	25.56 AW	53170 AAW	DEBLS	10//99-12//99
	Wilmington-Newark PMSA, DE-MD	S	25.66 MW	23.02 AW	53360 AAW	DEBLS	10//99-12//99
	District of Columbia	S	27.76 MW	29.52 AW	61410 AAW	DCBLS	10//99-12//99
	Washington PMSA, DC-MD-VA-WV	S	26.26 MW	24.70 AW	54630 AAW	DCBLS	10//99-12//99
	Florida	S	18.79 MW	21.65 AW	45030 AAW	FLBLS	10//99-12//99
	Fort Lauderdale PMSA, FL	S	30.82 MW	29.76 AW	64120 AAW	FLBLS	10//99-12//99
	Jacksonville MSA, FL	S	17.76 MW	16.54 AW	36940 AAW	FLBLS	10//99-12//99
	Melbourne-Titusville-Palm Bay MSA, FL	S	21.64 MW	21.51 AW	45000 AAW	FLBLS	10//99-12//99
	Miami PMSA, FL	S	23.95 MW	20.45 AW	49810 AAW	FLBLS	10//99-12//99
	Orlando MSA, FL	S	21.97 MW	18.95 AW	45690 AAW	FLBLS	10//99-12//99
	Pensacola MSA, FL	S	21.73 MW	21.42 AW	45190 AAW	FLBLS	10//99-12//99
	Sarasota-Bradenton MSA, FL	S	23.57 MW	23.76 AW	49030 AAW	FLBLS	10//99-12//99
	Tampa-St. Petersburg-Clearwater MSA, FL	S	19.84 MW	16.60 AW	41260 AAW	FLBLS	10//99-12//99

AAW Average annual wage	AOH Average offered, high	ASH Average starting, high	H Hourly	M Monthly	S Special; hourly and annual
AE Average entry wage	AOL Average offered, low	ASL Average starting, low	HI Highest wage paid	MTC Median total compensation	TQ Third quartile wage
AEX Average experienced wage	APH Average pay, high range	AW Average wage paid	HR High end range	MW Median wage paid	W Weekly
AO Average offered	APL Average pay, low range	FQ First quartile wage	LR Low end range	SQ Second quartile wage	Y Yearly

Financial Analyst

Occupation/Type/Industry	Location	Per	Low	Mid	High	Source	Date
Financial Analyst	West Palm Beach-Boca Raton MSA, FL	S	18.49 MW	16.57 AW	38470 AAW	FLBLS	10//99-12//99
	Georgia	S	19.06 MW	21.74 AW	45230 AAW	GABLS	10//99-12//99
	Atlanta MSA, GA	S	22.92 MW	20.53 AW	47680 AAW	GABLS	10//99-12//99
	Augusta-Aiken MSA, GA-SC	S	22.03 MW	20.29 AW	45820 AAW	GABLS	10//99-12//99
	Columbus MSA, GA-AL	S	21.56 MW	19.71 AW	44840 AAW	GABLS	10//99-12//99
	Macon MSA, GA	S	22.34 MW	20.13 AW	46470 AAW	GABLS	10//99-12//99
	Hawaii	S	20.55 MW	22.37 AW	46530 AAW	HIBLS	10//99-12//99
	Honolulu MSA, HI	S	22.21 MW	20.44 AW	46190 AAW	HIBLS	10//99-12//99
	Idaho	S	15.8 MW	19.49 AW	40540 AAW	IDBLS	10//99-12//99
	Boise City MSA, ID	S	17.30 MW	15.35 AW	35980 AAW	IDBLS	10//99-12//99
	Illinois	S	22.32 MW	25.76 AW	53580 AAW	ILBLS	10//99-12//99
	Bloomington-Normal MSA, IL	S	26.28 MW	23.73 AW	54670 AAW	ILBLS	10//99-12//99
	Champaign-Urbana MSA, IL	S	22.48 MW	22.72 AW	46750 AAW	ILBLS	10//99-12//99
	Chicago PMSA, IL	S	26.14 MW	22.50 AW	54370 AAW	ILBLS	10//99-12//99
	Peoria-Pekin MSA, IL	S	23.50 MW	22.00 AW	48880 AAW	ILBLS	10//99-12//99
	Indiana	S	22.64 MW	23.22 AW	48290 AAW	INBLS	10//99-12//99
	Fort Wayne MSA, IN	S	25.57 MW	24.03 AW	53190 AAW	INBLS	10//99-12//99
	Gary PMSA, IN	S	21.47 MW	22.65 AW	44650 AAW	INBLS	10//99-12//99
	Indianapolis MSA, IN	S	25.78 MW	23.50 AW	53620 AAW	INBLS	10//99-12//99
	Kokomo MSA, IN	S	18.02 MW	13.13 AW	37480 AAW	INBLS	10//99-12//99
	South Bend MSA, IN	S	14.41 MW	12.41 AW	29970 AAW	INBLS	10//99-12//99
	Iowa	S	19.62 MW	21.42 AW	44550 AAW	IABLS	10//99-12//99
	Des Moines MSA, IA	S	21.08 MW	18.99 AW	43840 AAW	IABLS	10//99-12//99
	Waterloo-Cedar Falls MSA, IA	S	22.50 MW	18.51 AW	46800 AAW	IABLS	10//99-12//99
	Kansas	S	20.75 MW	23.76 AW	49430 AAW	KSBLS	10//99-12//99
	Topeka MSA, KS	S	22.69 MW	21.27 AW	47190 AAW	KSBLS	10//99-12//99
	Wichita MSA, KS	S	22.58 MW	20.75 AW	46960 AAW	KSBLS	10//99-12//99
	Kentucky	S	19.73 MW	22.87 AW	47570 AAW	KYBLS	10//99-12//99
	Lexington MSA, KY	S	18.32 MW	16.65 AW	38110 AAW	KYBLS	10//99-12//99
	Louisville MSA, KY-IN	S	24.91 MW	22.21 AW	51820 AAW	KYBLS	10//99-12//99
	Louisiana	S	19.68 MW	20.71 AW	43080 AAW	LABLS	10//99-12//99
	Baton Rouge MSA, LA	S	21.05 MW	21.00 AW	43790 AAW	LABLS	10//99-12//99
	New Orleans MSA, LA	S	25.31 MW	23.40 AW	52640 AAW	LABLS	10//99-12//99
	Maine	S	18.17 MW	18.55 AW	38570 AAW	MEBLS	10//99-12//99
	Portland MSA, ME	S	18.36 MW	17.79 AW	38180 AAW	MEBLS	10//99-12//99
	Maryland	S	21.62 MW	22.78 AW	47390 AAW	MDBLS	10//99-12//99
	Baltimore PMSA, MD	S	22.18 MW	21.25 AW	46140 AAW	MDBLS	10//99-12//99
	Massachusetts	S	23.31 MW	26.62 AW	55370 AAW	MABLS	10//99-12//99
	Barnstable-Yarmouth MSA, MA	S	26.73 MW	29.74 AW	55590 AAW	MABLS	10//99-12//99
	Boston PMSA, MA-NH	S	26.72 MW	23.15 AW	55580 AAW	MABLS	10//99-12//99
	Lawrence PMSA, MA-NH	S	28.99 MW	24.32 AW	60290 AAW	MABLS	10//99-12//99
	Lowell PMSA, MA-NH	S	25.85 MW	25.37 AW	53770 AAW	MABLS	10//99-12//99
	Worcester PMSA, MA-CT	S	23.83 MW	21.39 AW	49560 AAW	MABLS	10//99-12//99
	Michigan	S	26.79 MW	31.47 AW	65470 AAW	MIBLS	10//99-12//99
	Ann Arbor PMSA, MI	S	29.64 MW	27.17 AW	61650 AAW	MIBLS	10//99-12//99
	Detroit PMSA, MI	S	32.67 MW	26.93 AW	67950 AAW	MIBLS	10//99-12//99
	Flint PMSA, MI	S	25.46 MW	22.82 AW	52950 AAW	MIBLS	10//99-12//99
	Grand Rapids-Muskegon-Holland MSA, MI	S	33.38 MW	34.34 AW	69430 AAW	MIBLS	10//99-12//99
	Kalamazoo-Battle Creek MSA, MI	S	21.64 MW	20.39 AW	45010 AAW	MIBLS	10//99-12//99
	Saginaw-Bay City-Midland MSA, MI	S	24.18 MW	24.11 AW	50290 AAW	MIBLS	10//99-12//99
	Minnesota	S	28.99 MW	32.35 AW	67280 AAW	MNBLS	10//99-12//99
	Minneapolis-St. Paul MSA, MN-WI	S	32.77 MW	29.32 AW	68170 AAW	MNBLS	10//99-12//99
	Rochester MSA, MN	S	27.31 MW	25.77 AW	56810 AAW	MNBLS	10//99-12//99
	Mississippi	S	15.9 MW	16.86 AW	35070 AAW	MSBLS	10//99-12//99
	Biloxi-Gulfport-Pascagoula MSA, MS	S	20.31 MW	18.85 AW	42250 AAW	MSBLS	10//99-12//99
	Jackson MSA, MS	S	16.20 MW	15.58 AW	33690 AAW	MSBLS	10//99-12//99
	Missouri	S	21.96 MW	24.79 AW	51570 AAW	MOBLS	10//99-12//99
	Kansas City MSA, MO-KS	S	26.44 MW	22.17 AW	55000 AAW	MOBLS	10//99-12//99
	St. Louis MSA, MO-IL	S	21.44 MW	19.27 AW	44590 AAW	MOBLS	10//99-12//99
	Montana	S	18.53 MW	19.75 AW	41070 AAW	MTBLS	10//99-12//99
	Nebraska	S	15.66 MW	16.12 AW	33540 AAW	NEBLS	10//99-12//99
	Omaha MSA, NE-IA	S	19.05 MW	18.18 AW	39610 AAW	NEBLS	10//99-12//99
	Nevada	S	17.17 MW	18.63 AW	38740 AAW	NVBLS	10//99-12//99
	Las Vegas MSA, NV-AZ	S	17.86 MW	15.22 AW	37150 AAW	NVBLS	10//99-12//99
	Reno MSA, NV	S	21.26 MW	20.45 AW	44220 AAW	NVBLS	10//99-12//99

AAW	Average annual wage	AOH	Average offered, high	ASH	Average starting, high	H	Hourly	M	Monthly	S	Special: hourly and annual
AE	Average entry wage	AOL	Average offered, low	ASL	Average starting, low	HI	Highest wage paid	MTC	Median total compensation	TQ	Third quartile wage
AEX	Average experienced wage	APH	Average pay, high range	AW	Average wage paid	HR	High end range	MW	Median wage paid	W	Weekly
AO	Average offered	APL	Average pay, low range	FQ	First quartile wage	LR	Low end range	SQ	Second quartile wage	Y	Yearly

Occupation/Type/Industry	Location	Per	Low	Mid	High	Source	Date
Financial Analyst	New Hampshire	S	20.71 mw	25.95 aw	53970 aaw	NHBLS	10//99-12//99
	Manchester PMSA, NH	S	24.08 mw	18.53 aw	50090 aaw	NHBLS	10//99-12//99
	Nashua PMSA, NH	S	27.06 mw	22.61 aw	56290 aaw	NHBLS	10//99-12//99
	New Jersey	S	26.2 mw	29.54 aw	61450 aaw	NJBLS	10//99-12//99
	Atlantic-Cape May PMSA, NJ	S	20.49 mw	19.11 aw	42630 aaw	NJBLS	10//99-12//99
	Bergen-Passaic PMSA, NJ	S	28.61 mw	28.28 aw	59500 aaw	NJBLS	10//99-12//99
	Jersey City PMSA, NJ	S	29.96 mw	24.83 aw	62320 aaw	NJBLS	10//99-12//99
	Middlesex-Somerset-Hunterdon PMSA, NJ	S	29.20 mw	26.79 aw	60740 aaw	NJBLS	10//99-12//99
	Monmouth-Ocean PMSA, NJ	S	35.61 mw	29.62 aw	74070 aaw	NJBLS	10//99-12//99
	Newark PMSA, NJ	S	28.90 mw	25.02 aw	60100 aaw	NJBLS	10//99-12//99
	Trenton PMSA, NJ	S	32.63 mw	28.66 aw	67860 aaw	NJBLS	10//99-12//99
	New Mexico	S	20.88 mw	21.93 aw	45620 aaw	NMBLS	10//99-12//99
	Albuquerque MSA, NM	S	23.61 mw	22.24 aw	49120 aaw	NMBLS	10//99-12//99
	Santa Fe MSA, NM	S	17.19 mw	15.69 aw	35760 aaw	NMBLS	10//99-12//99
	New York	S	26.51 mw	32.23 aw	67030 aaw	NYBLS	10//99-12//99
	Albany-Schenectady-Troy MSA, NY	S	23.27 mw	22.03 aw	48400 aaw	NYBLS	10//99-12//99
	Binghamton MSA, NY	S	26.27 mw	25.28 aw	54650 aaw	NYBLS	10//99-12//99
	Buffalo-Niagara Falls MSA, NY	S	20.60 mw	19.34 aw	42840 aaw	NYBLS	10//99-12//99
	Nassau-Suffolk PMSA, NY	S	24.81 mw	22.83 aw	51610 aaw	NYBLS	10//99-12//99
	New York PMSA, NY	S	34.36 mw	28.22 aw	71470 aaw	NYBLS	10//99-12//99
	Newburgh PMSA, NY-PA	S	27.18 mw	23.10 aw	56530 aaw	NYBLS	10//99-12//99
	Rochester MSA, NY	S	20.09 mw	19.31 aw	41800 aaw	NYBLS	10//99-12//99
	Syracuse MSA, NY	S	21.14 mw	21.82 aw	43980 aaw	NYBLS	10//99-12//99
	North Carolina	S	18.22 mw	19.81 aw	41200 aaw	NCBLS	10//99-12//99
	Charlotte-Gastonia-Rock Hill MSA, NC-SC	S	19.04 mw	17.75 aw	39610 aaw	NCBLS	10//99-12//99
	Greensboro--Winston-Salem--High Point MSA, NC	S	17.16 mw	15.75 aw	35690 aaw	NCBLS	10//99-12//99
	Raleigh-Durham-Chapel Hill MSA, NC	S	24.23 mw	23.70 aw	50390 aaw	NCBLS	10//99-12//99
	Wilmington MSA, NC	S	21.21 mw	20.29 aw	44110 aaw	NCBLS	10//99-12//99
	North Dakota	S	19.65 mw	20.41 aw	42440 aaw	NDBLS	10//99-12//99
	Ohio	S	21.09 mw	24.78 aw	51550 aaw	OHBLS	10//99-12//99
	Akron PMSA, OH	S	25.29 mw	22.51 aw	52600 aaw	OHBLS	10//99-12//99
	Cincinnati PMSA, OH-KY-IN	S	21.85 mw	19.04 aw	45460 aaw	OHBLS	10//99-12//99
	Cleveland-Lorain-Elyria PMSA, OH	S	29.76 mw	25.41 aw	61890 aaw	OHBLS	10//99-12//99
	Columbus MSA, OH	S	21.58 mw	20.61 aw	44880 aaw	OHBLS	10//99-12//99
	Dayton-Springfield MSA, OH	S	21.88 mw	19.89 aw	45510 aaw	OHBLS	10//99-12//99
	Toledo MSA, OH	S	29.88 mw	20.28 aw	62150 aaw	OHBLS	10//99-12//99
	Oklahoma	S	15.79 mw	17.69 aw	36790 aaw	OKBLS	10//99-12//99
	Oklahoma City MSA, OK	S	17.69 mw	15.72 aw	36800 aaw	OKBLS	10//99-12//99
	Tulsa MSA, OK	S	18.47 mw	16.18 aw	38420 aaw	OKBLS	10//99-12//99
	Oregon	S	24 mw	28.06 aw	58360 aaw	ORBLS	10//99-12//99
	Corvallis MSA, OR	S	28.65 mw	30.28 aw	59600 aaw	ORBLS	10//99-12//99
	Eugene-Springfield MSA, OR	S	26.38 mw	27.05 aw	54870 aaw	ORBLS	10//99-12//99
	Portland-Vancouver PMSA, OR-WA	S	28.01 mw	23.41 aw	58260 aaw	ORBLS	10//99-12//99
	Pennsylvania	S	20.28 mw	24.75 aw	51480 aaw	PABLS	10//99-12//99
	Allentown-Bethlehem-Easton MSA, PA	S	18.13 mw	17.61 aw	37710 aaw	PABLS	10//99-12//99
	Altoona MSA, PA	S	18.63 mw	16.99 aw	38760 aaw	PABLS	10//99-12//99
	Erie MSA, PA	S	23.22 mw	21.50 aw	48290 aaw	PABLS	10//99-12//99
	Lancaster MSA, PA	S	21.78 mw	20.35 aw	45310 aaw	PABLS	10//99-12//99
	Philadelphia PMSA, PA-NJ	S	26.36 mw	23.07 aw	54840 aaw	PABLS	10//99-12//99
	Pittsburgh MSA, PA	S	23.83 mw	17.53 aw	49560 aaw	PABLS	10//99-12//99
	Scranton--Wilkes-Barre--Hazleton MSA, PA	S	17.10 mw	16.56 aw	35560 aaw	PABLS	10//99-12//99
	State College MSA, PA	S	39.95 mw	38.21 aw	83100 aaw	PABLS	10//99-12//99
	Rhode Island	S	22.29 mw	26.80 aw	55740 aaw	RIBLS	10//99-12//99
	Providence-Fall River-Warwick MSA, RI-MA	S	26.81 mw	22.44 aw	55770 aaw	RIBLS	10//99-12//99
	South Carolina	S	17.24 mw	21.86 aw	45470 aaw	SCBLS	10//99-12//99
	Charleston-North Charleston MSA, SC	S	18.36 mw	16.59 aw	38180 aaw	SCBLS	10//99-12//99
	Columbia MSA, SC	S	20.45 mw	16.06 aw	42530 aaw	SCBLS	10//99-12//99
	Greenville-Spartanburg-Anderson MSA, SC	S	19.62 mw	18.49 aw	40820 aaw	SCBLS	10//99-12//99
	South Dakota	S	13.79 mw	16.92 aw	35200 aaw	SDBLS	10//99-12//99

AAW Average annual wage · AE Average entry wage · AEX Average experienced wage · AO Average offered
AOH Average offered, high · AOL Average offered, low · APH Average pay, high range · APL Average pay, low range
ASH Average starting, high · ASL Average starting, low · AW Average wage paid · FQ First quartile wage
H Hourly · HI Highest wage paid · HR High end range · LR Low end range
M Monthly · MTC Median total compensation · MW Median wage paid · SQ Second quartile wage
S Special: hourly and annual · TQ Third quartile wage · W Weekly · Y Yearly

Occupation/Type/Industry	Location	Per	Low	Mid	High	Source	Date
Financial Analyst	Sioux Falls MSA, SD	S	16.02 MW	15.14 AW	33320 AAW	SDBLS	10//99-12//99
	Tennessee	S	21.46 MW	23.45 AW	48780 AAW	TNBLS	10//99-12//99
	Chattanooga MSA, TN-GA	S	21.87 MW	21.30 AW	45490 AAW	TNBLS	10//99-12//99
	Knoxville MSA, TN	S	26.02 MW	23.75 AW	54120 AAW	TNBLS	10//99-12//99
	Memphis MSA, TN-AR-MS	S	25.20 MW	22.45 AW	52410 AAW	MSBLS	10//99-12//99
	Nashville MSA, TN	S	21.19 MW	19.78 AW	44070 AAW	TNBLS	10//99-12//99
	Texas	S	26.91 MW	28.11 AW	58470 AAW	TXBLS	10//99-12//99
	Austin-San Marcos MSA, TX	S	28.17 MW	28.93 AW	58580 AAW	TXBLS	10//99-12//99
	Beaumont-Port Arthur MSA, TX	S	26.99 MW	28.04 AW	56140 AAW	TXBLS	10//99-12//99
	Corpus Christi MSA, TX	S	25.45 MW	25.30 AW	52930 AAW	TXBLS	10//99-12//99
	Dallas PMSA, TX	S	27.98 MW	25.97 AW	58190 AAW	TXBLS	10//99-12//99
	Fort Worth-Arlington PMSA, TX	S	21.96 MW	20.86 AW	45670 AAW	TXBLS	10//99-12//99
	Houston PMSA, TX	S	32.09 MW	33.04 AW	66740 AAW	TXBLS	10//99-12//99
	Lubbock MSA, TX	S	28.93 MW	30.23 AW	60170 AAW	TXBLS	10//99-12//99
	San Antonio MSA, TX	S	24.92 MW	24.15 AW	51830 AAW	TXBLS	10//99-12//99
	Tyler MSA, TX	S	17.00 MW	17.40 AW	35350 AAW	TXBLS	10//99-12//99
	Utah	S	23.1 MW	32.84 AW	68310 AAW	UTBLS	10//99-12//99
	Provo-Orem MSA, UT	S	22.50 MW	20.84 AW	46800 AAW	UTBLS	10//99-12//99
	Vermont	S	26.34 MW	27.44 AW	57080 AAW	VTBLS	10//99-12//99
	Burlington MSA, VT	S	25.23 MW	24.59 AW	52480 AAW	VTBLS	10//99-12//99
	Virginia	S	23.73 MW	24.84 AW	51680 AAW	VABLS	10//99-12//99
	Norfolk-Virginia Beach-Newport News MSA, VA-NC	S	21.83 MW	20.74 AW	45410 AAW	VABLS	10//99-12//99
	Richmond-Petersburg MSA, VA	S	27.15 MW	26.16 AW	56460 AAW	VABLS	10//99-12//99
	Roanoke MSA, VA	S	21.95 MW	21.50 AW	45650 AAW	VABLS	10//99-12//99
	Washington	S	28.46 MW	33.77 AW	70230 AAW	WABLS	10//99-12//99
	Seattle-Bellevue-Everett PMSA, WA	S	34.41 MW	28.99 AW	71570 AAW	WABLS	10//99-12//99
	Tacoma PMSA, WA	S	21.16 MW	20.25 AW	44020 AAW	WABLS	10//99-12//99
	West Virginia	S	15.99 MW	17.12 AW	35610 AAW	WVBLS	10//99-12//99
	Charleston MSA, WV	S	15.90 MW	15.50 AW	33080 AAW	WVBLS	10//99-12//99
	Wisconsin	S	22.86 MW	24.49 AW	50940 AAW	WIBLS	10//99-12//99
	Appleton-Oshkosh-Neenah MSA, WI	S	23.78 MW	15.05 AW	49470 AAW	WIBLS	10//99-12//99
	Eau Claire MSA, WI	S	22.96 MW	22.13 AW	47770 AAW	WIBLS	10//99-12//99
	Green Bay MSA, WI	S	23.13 MW	22.91 AW	48110 AAW	WIBLS	10//99-12//99
	Madison MSA, WI	S	24.46 MW	21.90 AW	50880 AAW	WIBLS	10//99-12//99
	Milwaukee-Waukesha PMSA, WI	S	24.89 MW	23.48 AW	51780 AAW	WIBLS	10//99-12//99
	Wyoming	S	23.84 MW	23.66 AW	49210 AAW	WYBLS	10//99-12//99
	Puerto Rico	S	17.94 MW	18.31 AW	38090 AAW	PRBLS	10//99-12//99
	Caguas PMSA, PR	S	20.91 MW	20.21 AW	43490 AAW	PRBLS	10//99-12//99
	San Juan-Bayamon PMSA, PR	S	18.00 MW	17.37 AW	37430 AAW	PRBLS	10//99-12//99
Financial Examiner	Alabama	S	26.16 MW	26.24 AW	54570 AAW	ALBLS	10//99-12//99
	Arizona	S	18.65 MW	19.97 AW	41540 AAW	AZBLS	10//99-12//99
	California	S	25.16 MW	27.26 AW	56710 AAW	CABLS	10//99-12//99
	Colorado	S	23.59 MW	24.86 AW	51710 AAW	COBLS	10//99-12//99
	Connecticut	S	26.82 MW	27.69 AW	57600 AAW	CTBLS	10//99-12//99
	Georgia	S	21.53 MW	25.56 AW	53170 AAW	GABLS	10//99-12//99
	Idaho	S	22.84 MW	23.79 AW	49490 AAW	IDBLS	10//99-12//99
	Illinois	S	23.77 MW	25.94 AW	53960 AAW	ILBLS	10//99-12//99
	Indiana	S	23.97 MW	24.56 AW	51080 AAW	INBLS	10//99-12//99
	Iowa	S	19.65 MW	21.18 AW	44060 AAW	IABLS	10//99-12//99
	Kansas	S	24.85 MW	25.36 AW	52760 AAW	KSBLS	10//99-12//99
	Louisiana	S	22.63 MW	22.99 AW	47810 AAW	LABLS	10//99-12//99
	Maine	S	18.72 MW	19.08 AW	39690 AAW	MEBLS	10//99-12//99
	Maryland	S	20.85 MW	23.66 AW	49220 AAW	MDBLS	10//99-12//99
	Michigan	S	29.92 MW	34.21 AW	71150 AAW	MIBLS	10//99-12//99
	Minnesota	S	27.11 MW	27.22 AW	56620 AAW	MNBLS	10//99-12//99
	Mississippi	S	19.88 MW	21.81 AW	45360 AAW	MSBLS	10//99-12//99
	Missouri	S	26.47 MW	28.13 AW	58520 AAW	MOBLS	10//99-12//99
	Nebraska	S	24 MW	29.47 AW	61300 AAW	NEBLS	10//99-12//99
	New Hampshire	S	27.69 MW	25.81 AW	53680 AAW	NHBLS	10//99-12//99
	New Jersey	S	32.57 MW	37.53 AW	78070 AAW	NJBLS	10//99-12//99
	New Mexico	S	19.17 MW	22.28 AW	46340 AAW	NMBLS	10//99-12//99
	New York	S	34.81 MW	38.39 AW	79840 AAW	NYBLS	10//99-12//99
	North Carolina	S	24.13 MW	25.50 AW	53030 AAW	NCBLS	10//99-12//99
	North Dakota	S	20.47 MW	22.58 AW	46960 AAW	NDBLS	10//99-12//99

AAW Average annual wage	**AOH** Average offered, high	**ASH** Average starting, high	**H** Hourly	**M** Monthly	**S** Special: hourly and annual
AE Average entry wage	**AOL** Average offered, low	**ASL** Average starting, low	**HI** Highest wage paid	**MTC** Median total compensation	**TQ** Third quartile wage
AEX Average experienced wage	**APH** Average pay, high range	**AW** Average wage paid	**HR** High end range	**MW** Median wage paid	**W** Weekly
AO Average offered	**APL** Average pay, low range	**FQ** First quartile wage	**LR** Low end range	**SQ** Second quartile wage	**Y** Yearly

Occupation/Type/Industry	Location	Per	Low	Mid	High	Source	Date
Financial Examiner	Ohio	S	23.67 MW	24.72 AW	51420 AAW	OHBLS	10//99-12//99
	Oklahoma	S	15.11 MW	18.68 AW	38860 AAW	OKBLS	10//99-12//99
	Oregon	S	24.33 MW	25.43 AW	52900 AAW	ORBLS	10//99-12//99
	Pennsylvania	S	23.28 MW	24.54 AW	51040 AAW	PABLS	10//99-12//99
	Rhode Island	S	16.72 MW	22.18 AW	46140 AAW	RIBLS	10//99-12//99
	South Carolina	S	16.2 MW	18.35 AW	38170 AAW	SCBLS	10//99-12//99
	Tennessee	S	22.75 MW	25.75 AW	53550 AAW	TNBLS	10//99-12//99
	Texas	S	23.48 MW	24.09 AW	50110 AAW	TXBLS	10//99-12//99
	Utah	S	17.79 MW	19.10 AW	39730 AAW	UTBLS	10//99-12//99
	Virginia	S	21.43 MW	23.28 AW	48430 AAW	VABLS	10//99-12//99
	Washington	S	22.48 MW	25.98 AW	54040 AAW	WABLS	10//99-12//99
	West Virginia	S	21.06 MW	22.90 AW	47620 AAW	WVBLS	10//99-12//99
	Wisconsin	S	18.14 MW	20.17 AW	41960 AAW	WIBLS	10//99-12//99
	Puerto Rico	S	12.05 MW	13.51 AW	28110 AAW	PRBLS	10//99-12//99
Financial Manager	Alabama	S	23.18 MW	24.81 AW	51600 AAW	ALBLS	10//99-12//99
	Anniston MSA, AL	S	21.85 MW	20.04 AW	45450 AAW	ALBLS	10//99-12//99
	Auburn-Opelika MSA, AL	S	25.05 MW	23.87 AW	52100 AAW	ALBLS	10//99-12//99
	Birmingham MSA, AL	S	26.08 MW	23.52 AW	54250 AAW	ALBLS	10//99-12//99
	Decatur MSA, AL	S	23.15 MW	23.01 AW	48150 AAW	ALBLS	10//99-12//99
	Dothan MSA, AL	S	24.03 MW	24.32 AW	49990 AAW	ALBLS	10//99-12//99
	Florence MSA, AL	S	25.20 MW	22.70 AW	52420 AAW	ALBLS	10//99-12//99
	Gadsden MSA, AL	S	22.01 MW	23.63 AW	45790 AAW	ALBLS	10//99-12//99
	Huntsville MSA, AL	S	26.05 MW	23.86 AW	54180 AAW	ALBLS	10//99-12//99
	Mobile MSA, AL	S	23.62 MW	24.24 AW	49120 AAW	ALBLS	10//99-12//99
	Montgomery MSA, AL	S	26.18 MW	23.79 AW	54450 AAW	ALBLS	10//99-12//99
	Tuscaloosa MSA, AL	S	22.76 MW	21.71 AW	47350 AAW	ALBLS	10//99-12//99
	Alaska	S	25.18 MW	27.23 AW	56640 AAW	AKBLS	10//99-12//99
	Anchorage MSA, AK	S	28.37 MW	25.07 AW	59020 AAW	AKBLS	10//99-12//99
	Arizona	S	27.11 MW	29.84 AW	62070 AAW	AZBLS	10//99-12//99
	Flagstaff MSA, AZ-UT	S	25.74 MW	24.36 AW	53540 AAW	AZBLS	10//99-12//99
	Phoenix-Mesa MSA, AZ	S	30.97 MW	28.47 AW	64420 AAW	AZBLS	10//99-12//99
	Tucson MSA, AZ	S	25.86 MW	22.08 AW	53790 AAW	AZBLS	10//99-12//99
	Yuma MSA, AZ	S	30.31 MW	25.46 AW	63050 AAW	AZBLS	10//99-12//99
	Arkansas	S	25.32 MW	26.88 AW	55900 AAW	ARBLS	10//99-12//99
	Fayetteville-Springdale-Rogers MSA, AR	S	22.39 MW	21.39 AW	46580 AAW	ARBLS	10//99-12//99
	Fort Smith MSA, AR-OK	S	32.63 MW	28.98 AW	67860 AAW	ARBLS	10//99-12//99
	Jonesboro MSA, AR	S	21.95 MW	17.64 AW	45660 AAW	ARBLS	10//99-12//99
	Little Rock-North Little Rock MSA, AR	S	30.46 MW	29.71 AW	63350 AAW	ARBLS	10//99-12//99
	Pine Bluff MSA, AR	S	23.16 MW	23.70 AW	48170 AAW	ARBLS	10//99-12//99
	California	S	32.3 MW	34.77 AW	72310 AAW	CABLS	10//99-12//99
	Bakersfield MSA, CA	S	25.92 MW	23.62 AW	53920 AAW	CABLS	10//99-12//99
	Chico-Paradise MSA, CA	S	23.46 MW	21.06 AW	48790 AAW	CABLS	10//99-12//99
	Fresno MSA, CA	S	28.66 MW	25.52 AW	59610 AAW	CABLS	10//99-12//99
	Los Angeles-Long Beach PMSA, CA	S	36.25 MW	33.08 AW	75400 AAW	CABLS	10//99-12//99
	Merced MSA, CA	S	28.55 MW	27.93 AW	59370 AAW	CABLS	10//99-12//99
	Modesto MSA, CA	S	27.07 MW	25.91 AW	56310 AAW	CABLS	10//99-12//99
	Oakland PMSA, CA	S	36.73 MW	34.30 AW	76400 AAW	CABLS	10//99-12//99
	Orange County PMSA, CA	S	36.05 MW	34.85 AW	74990 AAW	CABLS	10//99-12//99
	Redding MSA, CA	S	25.05 MW	23.93 AW	52100 AAW	CABLS	10//99-12//99
	Riverside-San Bernardino PMSA, CA	S	28.23 MW	25.74 AW	58730 AAW	CABLS	10//99-12//99
	Sacramento PMSA, CA	S	30.45 MW	29.27 AW	63340 AAW	CABLS	10//99-12//99
	Salinas MSA, CA	S	36.16 MW	35.12 AW	75210 AAW	CABLS	10//99-12//99
	San Diego MSA, CA	S	31.80 MW	30.48 AW	66140 AAW	CABLS	10//99-12//99
	San Francisco PMSA, CA	S	37.35 MW	34.67 AW	77690 AAW	CABLS	10//99-12//99
	San Jose PMSA, CA	S	39.45 MW	36.68 AW	82050 AAW	CABLS	10//99-12//99
	San Luis Obispo-Atascadero-Paso Robles MSA, CA	S	27.60 MW	22.24 AW	57410 AAW	CABLS	10//99-12//99
	Santa Barbara-Santa Maria-Lompoc MSA, CA	S	29.77 MW	25.87 AW	61930 AAW	CABLS	10//99-12//99
	Santa Cruz-Watsonville PMSA, CA	S	28.43 MW	21.72 AW	59130 AAW	CABLS	10//99-12//99
	Santa Rosa PMSA, CA	S	29.00 MW	25.24 AW	60330 AAW	CABLS	10//99-12//99
	Stockton-Lodi MSA, CA	S	32.01 MW	29.10 AW	66580 AAW	CABLS	10//99-12//99
	Vallejo-Fairfield-Napa PMSA, CA	S	31.40 MW	28.63 AW	65320 AAW	CABLS	10//99-12//99
	Ventura PMSA, CA	S	35.19 MW	29.82 AW	73190 AAW	CABLS	10//99-12//99
	Visalia-Tulare-Porterville MSA, CA	S	26.34 MW	24.40 AW	54780 AAW	CABLS	10//99-12//99

Occupation/Type/Industry	Location	Per	Low	Mid	High	Source	Date
Financial Manager	Yolo PMSA, CA	S	27.44 MW	28.37 AW	57070 AAW	CABLS	10//99-12//99
	Yuba City MSA, CA	S	28.28 MW	24.96 AW	58820 AAW	CABLS	10//99-12//99
	Colorado	S	30.65 MW	32.98 AW	68590 AAW	COBLS	10//99-12//99
	Boulder-Longmont PMSA, CO	S	32.71 MW	29.38 AW	68030 AAW	COBLS	10//99-12//99
	Colorado Springs MSA, CO	S	29.65 MW	26.30 AW	61660 AAW	COBLS	10//99-12//99
	Denver PMSA, CO	S	35.13 MW	32.61 AW	73070 AAW	COBLS	10//99-12//99
	Fort Collins-Loveland MSA, CO	S	31.48 MW	26.96 AW	65480 AAW	COBLS	10//99-12//99
	Greeley PMSA, CO	S	26.79 MW	26.37 AW	55710 AAW	COBLS	10//99-12//99
	Pueblo MSA, CO	S	29.22 MW	29.55 AW	60780 AAW	COBLS	10//99-12//99
	Connecticut	S	34.85 MW	36.28 AW	75460 AAW	CTBLS	10//99-12//99
	Bridgeport PMSA, CT	S	34.54 MW	33.46 AW	71840 AAW	CTBLS	10//99-12//99
	Danbury PMSA, CT	S	27.77 MW	25.54 AW	57760 AAW	CTBLS	10//99-12//99
	Hartford MSA, CT	S	38.44 MW	37.80 AW	79960 AAW	CTBLS	10//99-12//99
	New Haven-Meriden PMSA, CT	S	31.60 MW	30.34 AW	65740 AAW	CTBLS	10//99-12//99
	New London-Norwich MSA, CT-RI	S	33.92 MW	32.35 AW	70560 AAW	CTBLS	10//99-12//99
	Stamford-Norwalk PMSA, CT	S	38.83 MW	36.11 AW	80770 AAW	CTBLS	10//99-12//99
	Waterbury PMSA, CT	S	33.36 MW	31.69 AW	69400 AAW	CTBLS	10//99-12//99
	Delaware	S	25.67 MW	28.39 AW	59060 AAW	DEBLS	10//99-12//99
	Dover MSA, DE	S	24.83 MW	23.10 AW	51650 AAW	DEBLS	10//99-12//99
	Wilmington-Newark PMSA, DE-MD	S	29.49 MW	26.44 AW	61340 AAW	DEBLS	10//99-12//99
	District of Columbia	S	36.12 MW	36.01 AW	74900 AAW	DCBLS	10//99-12//99
	Washington PMSA, DC-MD-VA-WV	S	35.59 MW	34.21 AW	74020 AAW	DCBLS	10//99-12//99
	Florida	S	28.17 MW	30.41 AW	63250 AAW	FLBLS	10//99-12//99
	Daytona Beach MSA, FL	S	22.76 MW	20.75 AW	47350 AAW	FLBLS	10//99-12//99
	Fort Lauderdale PMSA, FL	S	28.83 MW	25.32 AW	59970 AAW	FLBLS	10//99-12//99
	Fort Myers-Cape Coral MSA, FL	S	25.44 MW	24.64 AW	52920 AAW	FLBLS	10//99-12//99
	Fort Pierce-Port St. Lucie MSA, FL	S	26.59 MW	24.63 AW	55300 AAW	FLBLS	10//99-12//99
	Jacksonville MSA, FL	S	31.49 MW	30.58 AW	65490 AAW	FLBLS	10//99-12//99
	Lakeland-Winter Haven MSA, FL	S	29.84 MW	27.29 AW	62070 AAW	FLBLS	10//99-12//99
	Melbourne-Titusville-Palm Bay MSA, FL	S	27.94 MW	28.02 AW	58110 AAW	FLBLS	10//99-12//99
	Miami PMSA, FL	S	32.44 MW	30.96 AW	67470 AAW	FLBLS	10//99-12//99
	Naples MSA, FL	S	26.36 MW	24.00 AW	54830 AAW	FLBLS	10//99-12//99
	Ocala MSA, FL	S	22.30 MW	18.04 AW	46390 AAW	FLBLS	10//99-12//99
	Panama City MSA, FL	S	20.00 MW	16.51 AW	41610 AAW	FLBLS	10//99-12//99
	Punta Gorda MSA, FL	S	23.03 MW	23.91 AW	47910 AAW	FLBLS	10//99-12//99
	Sarasota-Bradenton MSA, FL	S	29.76 MW	28.01 AW	61890 AAW	FLBLS	10//99-12//99
	Tallahassee MSA, FL	S	27.25 MW	26.76 AW	56670 AAW	FLBLS	10//99-12//99
	Tampa-St. Petersburg-Clearwater MSA, FL	S	31.17 MW	29.02 AW	64830 AAW	FLBLS	10//99-12//99
	West Palm Beach-Boca Raton MSA, FL	S	29.67 MW	27.26 AW	61720 AAW	FLBLS	10//99-12//99
	Georgia	S	28.79 MW	31.82 AW	66180 AAW	GABLS	10//99-12//99
	Albany MSA, GA	S	22.66 MW	20.69 AW	47140 AAW	GABLS	10//99-12//99
	Athens MSA, GA	S	26.50 MW	25.40 AW	55120 AAW	GABLS	10//99-12//99
	Atlanta MSA, GA	S	33.77 MW	31.10 AW	70250 AAW	GABLS	10//99-12//99
	Augusta-Aiken MSA, GA-SC	S	29.02 MW	27.53 AW	60360 AAW	GABLS	10//99-12//99
	Columbus MSA, GA-AL	S	23.25 MW	20.17 AW	48350 AAW	GABLS	10//99-12//99
	Macon MSA, GA	S	26.15 MW	25.47 AW	54390 AAW	GABLS	10//99-12//99
	Savannah MSA, GA	S	30.79 MW	26.26 AW	64050 AAW	GABLS	10//99-12//99
	Hawaii	S	26.79 MW	29.24 AW	60830 AAW	HIBLS	10//99-12//99
	Honolulu MSA, HI	S	29.27 MW	27.35 AW	60880 AAW	HIBLS	10//99-12//99
	Idaho	S	24.89 MW	28.12 AW	58500 AAW	IDBLS	10//99-12//99
	Boise City MSA, ID	S	30.60 MW	27.73 AW	63650 AAW	IDBLS	10//99-12//99
	Pocatello MSA, ID	S	23.99 MW	23.46 AW	49890 AAW	IDBLS	10//99-12//99
	Illinois	S	32.37 MW	33.78 AW	70270 AAW	ILBLS	10//99-12//99
	Bloomington-Normal MSA, IL	S	34.19 MW	33.07 AW	71110 AAW	ILBLS	10//99-12//99
	Champaign-Urbana MSA, IL	S	27.52 MW	26.88 AW	57250 AAW	ILBLS	10//99-12//99
	Chicago PMSA, IL	S	35.42 MW	33.81 AW	73660 AAW	ILBLS	10//99-12//99
	Decatur MSA, IL	S	27.56 MW	25.03 AW	57330 AAW	ILBLS	10//99-12//99
	Kankakee PMSA, IL	S	26.55 MW	29.25 AW	55210 AAW	ILBLS	10//99-12//99
	Peoria-Pekin MSA, IL	S	25.14 MW	23.68 AW	52300 AAW	ILBLS	10//99-12//99
	Rockford MSA, IL	S	27.29 MW	27.16 AW	56770 AAW	ILBLS	10//99-12//99
	Springfield MSA, IL	S	30.23 MW	30.56 AW	62880 AAW	ILBLS	10//99-12//99

Occupation/Type/Industry	Location	Per	Low	Mid	High	Source	Date
Financial Manager	Indiana	S	26.73 MW	29.46 AW	61270 AAW	INBLS	10//99-12//99
	Bloomington MSA, IN	S	26.51 MW	24.99 AW	55150 AAW	INBLS	10//99-12//99
	Elkhart-Goshen MSA, IN	S	26.89 MW	24.71 AW	55930 AAW	INBLS	10//99-12//99
	Evansville-Henderson MSA, IN-KY	S	27.83 MW	24.99 AW	57880 AAW	INBLS	10//99-12//99
	Fort Wayne MSA, IN	S	26.44 MW	22.60 AW	55000 AAW	INBLS	10//99-12//99
	Gary PMSA, IN	S	30.37 MW	27.24 AW	63170 AAW	INBLS	10//99-12//99
	Indianapolis MSA, IN	S	32.68 MW	30.46 AW	67980 AAW	INBLS	10//99-12//99
	Kokomo MSA, IN	S	30.71 MW	28.57 AW	63880 AAW	INBLS	10//99-12//99
	Lafayette MSA, IN	S	30.79 MW	28.64 AW	64040 AAW	INBLS	10//99-12//99
	Muncie MSA, IN	S	28.38 MW	26.42 AW	59020 AAW	INBLS	10//99-12//99
	South Bend MSA, IN	S	28.24 MW	25.12 AW	58730 AAW	INBLS	10//99-12//99
	Terre Haute MSA, IN	S	24.54 MW	22.42 AW	51040 AAW	INBLS	10//99-12//99
	Iowa	S	25.16 MW	27.25 AW	56670 AAW	IABLS	10//99-12//99
	Cedar Rapids MSA, IA	S	28.93 MW	25.26 AW	60170 AAW	IABLS	10//99-12//99
	Davenport-Moline-Rock Island MSA, IA-IL	S	26.30 MW	25.31 AW	54710 AAW	IABLS	10//99-12//99
	Des Moines MSA, IA	S	28.97 MW	26.72 AW	60260 AAW	IABLS	10//99-12//99
	Dubuque MSA, IA	S	26.03 MW	23.78 AW	54150 AAW	IABLS	10//99-12//99
	Iowa City MSA, IA	S	24.43 MW	20.79 AW	50820 AAW	IABLS	10//99-12//99
	Sioux City MSA, IA-NE	S	25.96 MW	24.70 AW	54000 AAW	IABLS	10//99-12//99
	Waterloo-Cedar Falls MSA, IA	S	26.83 MW	25.62 AW	55810 AAW	IABLS	10//99-12//99
	Kansas	S	24.98 MW	27.29 AW	56760 AAW	KSBLS	10//99-12//99
	Lawrence MSA, KS	S	19.42 MW	14.49 AW	40390 AAW	KSBLS	10//99-12//99
	Topeka MSA, KS	S	24.70 MW	22.42 AW	51370 AAW	KSBLS	10//99-12//99
	Wichita MSA, KS	S	26.62 MW	24.54 AW	55370 AAW	KSBLS	10//99-12//99
	Kentucky	S	22.57 MW	24.50 AW	50960 AAW	KYBLS	10//99-12//99
	Lexington MSA, KY	S	26.93 MW	26.98 AW	56010 AAW	KYBLS	10//99-12//99
	Louisville MSA, KY-IN	S	25.39 MW	22.39 AW	52810 AAW	KYBLS	10//99-12//99
	Owensboro MSA, KY	S	22.90 MW	22.93 AW	47630 AAW	KYBLS	10//99-12//99
	Louisiana	S	25.5 MW	27.59 AW	57380 AAW	LABLS	10//99-12//99
	Alexandria MSA, LA	S	24.45 MW	24.04 AW	50860 AAW	LABLS	10//99-12//99
	Baton Rouge MSA, LA	S	26.26 MW	25.18 AW	54620 AAW	LABLS	10//99-12//99
	Houma MSA, LA	S	26.13 MW	20.91 AW	54340 AAW	LABLS	10//99-12//99
	Lafayette MSA, LA	S	27.61 MW	27.37 AW	57420 AAW	LABLS	10//99-12//99
	Lake Charles MSA, LA	S	32.61 MW	25.96 AW	67830 AAW	LABLS	10//99-12//99
	Monroe MSA, LA	S	21.13 MW	17.92 AW	43960 AAW	LABLS	10//99-12//99
	New Orleans MSA, LA	S	28.21 MW	25.58 AW	58680 AAW	LABLS	10//99-12//99
	Shreveport-Bossier City MSA, LA	S	27.55 MW	27.43 AW	57310 AAW	LABLS	10//99-12//99
	Maine	S	25.13 MW	27.84 AW	57910 AAW	MEBLS	10//99-12//99
	Bangor MSA, ME	S	26.75 MW	25.83 AW	55640 AAW	MEBLS	10//99-12//99
	Lewiston-Auburn MSA, ME	S	24.25 MW	22.99 AW	50440 AAW	MEBLS	10//99-12//99
	Portland MSA, ME	S	28.68 MW	25.82 AW	59660 AAW	MEBLS	10//99-12//99
	Maryland	S	28.66 MW	30.27 AW	62970 AAW	MDBLS	10//99-12//99
	Baltimore PMSA, MD	S	29.69 MW	27.87 AW	61760 AAW	MDBLS	10//99-12//99
	Cumberland MSA, MD-WV	S	18.39 MW	18.61 AW	38260 AAW	MDBLS	10//99-12//99
	Hagerstown PMSA, MD	S	22.74 MW	21.59 AW	47300 AAW	MDBLS	10//99-12//99
	Massachusetts	S	36.3 MW	39.80 AW	82780 AAW	MABLS	10//99-12//99
	Barnstable-Yarmouth MSA, MA	S	26.00 MW	25.06 AW	54080 AAW	MABLS	10//99-12//99
	Boston PMSA, MA-NH	S	43.46 MW	40.23 AW	90400 AAW	MABLS	10//99-12//99
	Brockton PMSA, MA	S	29.81 MW	28.87 AW	62000 AAW	MABLS	10//99-12//99
	Fitchburg-Leominster PMSA, MA	S	25.85 MW	22.10 AW	53770 AAW	MABLS	10//99-12//99
	Lawrence PMSA, MA-NH	S	31.13 MW	28.90 AW	64740 AAW	MABLS	10//99-12//99
	Lowell PMSA, MA-NH	S	34.54 MW	33.36 AW	71840 AAW	MABLS	10//99-12//99
	New Bedford PMSA, MA	S	30.64 MW	28.26 AW	63740 AAW	MABLS	10//99-12//99
	Pittsfield MSA, MA	S	26.46 MW	23.31 AW	55030 AAW	MABLS	10//99-12//99
	Springfield MSA, MA	S	31.11 MW	29.72 AW	64700 AAW	MABLS	10//99-12//99
	Worcester PMSA, MA-CT	S	25.90 MW	23.95 AW	53870 AAW	MABLS	10//99-12//99
	Michigan	S	31.62 MW	34.48 AW	71730 AAW	MIBLS	10//99-12//99
	Ann Arbor PMSA, MI	S	30.44 MW	27.73 AW	63320 AAW	MIBLS	10//99-12//99
	Benton Harbor MSA, MI	S	25.30 MW	23.40 AW	52620 AAW	MIBLS	10//99-12//99
	Detroit PMSA, MI	S	37.15 MW	34.72 AW	77280 AAW	MIBLS	10//99-12//99
	Flint PMSA, MI	S	29.98 MW	25.25 AW	62360 AAW	MIBLS	10//99-12//99
	Grand Rapids-Muskegon-Holland MSA, MI	S	30.56 MW	26.75 AW	63570 AAW	MIBLS	10//99-12//99
	Jackson MSA, MI	S	32.86 MW	31.58 AW	68340 AAW	MIBLS	10//99-12//99
	Kalamazoo-Battle Creek MSA, MI	S	33.24 MW	29.93 AW	69140 AAW	MIBLS	10//99-12//99
	Lansing-East Lansing MSA, MI	S	31.71 MW	29.95 AW	65950 AAW	MIBLS	10//99-12//99

AAW Average annual wage	**AOH** Average offered, high	**ASH** Average starting, high	**H** Hourly	**M** Monthly	**S** Special: hourly and annual
AE Average entry wage	**AOL** Average offered, low	**ASL** Average starting, low	**HI** Highest wage paid	**MTC** Median total compensation	**TQ** Third quartile wage
AEX Average experienced wage	**APH** Average pay, high range	**AW** Average wage paid	**HR** High end range	**MW** Median wage paid	**W** Weekly
AO Average offered	**APL** Average pay, low range	**FQ** First quartile wage	**LR** Low end range	**SQ** Second quartile wage	**Y** Yearly

Occupation/Type/Industry	Location	Per	Low	Mid	High	Source	Date
Financial Manager	Saginaw-Bay City-Midland						
	MSA, MI	S	30.91 MW	26.27 AW	64300 AAW	MIBLS	10//99-12//99
	Minnesota	S	33.35 MW	36.04 AW	74960 AAW	MNBLS	10//99-12//99
	Duluth-Superior MSA, MN-WI	S	31.08 MW	28.29 AW	64650 AAW	MNBLS	10//99-12//99
	Minneapolis-St. Paul MSA,						
	MN-WI	S	37.33 MW	34.44 AW	77650 AAW	MNBLS	10//99-12//99
	Rochester MSA, MN	S	34.91 MW	31.98 AW	72610 AAW	MNBLS	10//99-12//99
	St. Cloud MSA, MN	S	36.25 MW	33.00 AW	75390 AAW	MNBLS	10//99-12//99
	Mississippi	S	24.59 MW	26.19 AW	54470 AAW	MSBLS	10//99-12//99
	Biloxi-Gulfport-Pascagoula						
	MSA, MS	S	26.00 MW	23.49 AW	54080 AAW	MSBLS	10//99-12//99
	Hattiesburg MSA, MS	S	19.59 MW	19.29 AW	40740 AAW	MSBLS	10//99-12//99
	Jackson MSA, MS	S	29.32 MW	26.69 AW	60980 AAW	MSBLS	10//99-12//99
	Missouri	S	26.19 MW	28.39 AW	59040 AAW	MOBLS	10//99-12//99
	Columbia MSA, MO	S	24.43 MW	22.42 AW	50820 AAW	MOBLS	10//99-12//99
	Joplin MSA, MO	S	22.67 MW	19.85 AW	47150 AAW	MOBLS	10//99-12//99
	Kansas City MSA, MO-KS	S	30.91 MW	28.80 AW	64280 AAW	MOBLS	10//99-12//99
	St. Joseph MSA, MO	S	26.80 MW	27.43 AW	55740 AAW	MOBLS	10//99-12//99
	St. Louis MSA, MO-IL	S	31.10 MW	29.39 AW	64700 AAW	MOBLS	10//99-12//99
	Springfield MSA, MO	S	21.63 MW	19.91 AW	44990 AAW	MOBLS	10//99-12//99
	Montana	S	19.78 MW	22.26 AW	46310 AAW	MTBLS	10//99-12//99
	Billings MSA, MT	S	23.72 MW	20.90 AW	49340 AAW	MTBLS	10//99-12//99
	Great Falls MSA, MT	S	24.18 MW	21.72 AW	50290 AAW	MTBLS	10//99-12//99
	Missoula MSA, MT	S	22.78 MW	21.02 AW	47380 AAW	MTBLS	10//99-12//99
	Nebraska	S	25.47 MW	27.38 AW	56940 AAW	NEBLS	10//99-12//99
	Lincoln MSA, NE	S	27.66 MW	25.38 AW	57530 AAW	NEBLS	10//99-12//99
	Omaha MSA, NE-IA	S	29.22 MW	26.88 AW	60770 AAW	NEBLS	10//99-12//99
	Nevada	S	28.59 MW	30.93 AW	64330 AAW	NVBLS	10//99-12//99
	Las Vegas MSA, NV-AZ	S	31.53 MW	29.76 AW	65580 AAW	NVBLS	10//99-12//99
	Reno MSA, NV	S	31.53 MW	26.85 AW	65580 AAW	NVBLS	10//99-12//99
	New Hampshire	S	26.98 MW	29.14 AW	60610 AAW	NHBLS	10//99-12//99
	Manchester PMSA, NH	S	31.59 MW	28.23 AW	65710 AAW	NHBLS	10//99-12//99
	Nashua PMSA, NH	S	29.38 MW	27.33 AW	61100 AAW	NHBLS	10//99-12//99
	New Jersey	S	39.77 MW	41.43 AW	86170 AAW	NJBLS	10//99-12//99
	Atlantic-Cape May PMSA, NJ	S	35.08 MW	32.48 AW	72960 AAW	NJBLS	10//99-12//99
	Bergen-Passaic PMSA, NJ	S	41.87 MW	43.54 AW	87100 AAW	NJBLS	10//99-12//99
	Jersey City PMSA, NJ	S	46.67 MW	43.51 AW	97070 AAW	NJBLS	10//99-12//99
	Middlesex-Somerset-						
	Hunterdon PMSA, NJ	S	40.80 MW	39.14 AW	84870 AAW	NJBLS	10//99-12//99
	Monmouth-Ocean PMSA, NJ	S	39.90 MW	36.42 AW	82980 AAW	NJBLS	10//99-12//99
	Newark PMSA, NJ	S	43.14 MW	40.79 AW	89730 AAW	NJBLS	10//99-12//99
	Trenton PMSA, NJ	S	36.26 MW	35.27 AW	75420 AAW	NJBLS	10//99-12//99
	Vineland-Millville-Bridgeton						
	PMSA, NJ	S	30.07 MW	26.53 AW	62550 AAW	NJBLS	10//99-12//99
	New Mexico	S	23.81 MW	26.31 AW	54720 AAW	NMBLS	10//99-12//99
	Albuquerque MSA, NM	S	27.71 MW	24.67 AW	57640 AAW	NMBLS	10//99-12//99
	Las Cruces MSA, NM	S	26.87 MW	24.66 AW	55880 AAW	NMBLS	10//99-12//99
	Santa Fe MSA, NM	S	25.08 MW	23.39 AW	52160 AAW	NMBLS	10//99-12//99
	Albany-Schenectady-Troy						
	MSA, NY	S	35.02 MW	34.57 AW	72850 AAW	NYBLS	10//99-12//99
	Binghamton MSA, NY	S	29.41 MW	26.39 AW	61170 AAW	NYBLS	10//99-12//99
	Buffalo-Niagara Falls MSA,						
	NY	S	30.15 MW	27.79 AW	62710 AAW	NYBLS	10//99-12//99
	Dutchess County PMSA, NY	S	33.42 MW	28.77 AW	69510 AAW	NYBLS	10//99-12//99
	Elmira MSA, NY	S	27.73 MW	27.44 AW	57680 AAW	NYBLS	10//99-12//99
	Glens Falls MSA, NY	S	38.53 MW	33.98 AW	80140 AAW	NYBLS	10//99-12//99
	Jamestown MSA, NY	S	25.17 MW	22.54 AW	52350 AAW	NYBLS	10//99-12//99
	Nassau-Suffolk PMSA, NY	S	40.65 MW	39.01 AW	84540 AAW	NYBLS	10//99-12//99
	New York PMSA, NY	S	47.60 MW	49.49 AW	99010 AAW	NYBLS	10//99-12//99
	Newburgh PMSA, NY-PA	S	31.04 MW	26.92 AW	64560 AAW	NYBLS	10//99-12//99
	Rochester MSA, NY	S	33.13 MW	32.32 AW	68900 AAW	NYBLS	10//99-12//99
	Syracuse MSA, NY	S	35.08 MW	33.29 AW	72970 AAW	NYBLS	10//99-12//99
	Utica-Rome MSA, NY	S	30.40 MW	27.65 AW	63240 AAW	NYBLS	10//99-12//99
	North Carolina	S	29.32 MW	31.35 AW	65220 AAW	NCBLS	10//99-12//99
	Asheville MSA, NC	S	24.82 MW	21.14 AW	51620 AAW	NCBLS	10//99-12//99
	Charlotte-Gastonia-Rock Hill						
	MSA, NC-SC	S	34.49 MW	31.89 AW	71740 AAW	NCBLS	10//99-12//99
	Fayetteville MSA, NC	S	28.07 MW	26.73 AW	58380 AAW	NCBLS	10//99-12//99
	Goldsboro MSA, NC	S	21.85 MW	19.59 AW	45450 AAW	NCBLS	10//99-12//99
	Greensboro--Winston-Salem--						
	High Point MSA, NC	S	29.33 MW	26.88 AW	61010 AAW	NCBLS	10//99-12//99

AAW Average annual wage	**AOH** Average offered, high	**ASH** Average starting, high	**H** Hourly	**M** Monthly	**S** Special: hourly and annual
AE Average entry wage	**AOL** Average offered, low	**ASL** Average starting, low	**HI** Highest wage paid	**MTC** Median total compensation	**TQ** Third quartile wage
AEX Average experienced wage	**APH** Average pay, high range	**AW** Average wage paid	**HR** High end range	**MW** Median wage paid	**W** Weekly
AO Average offered	**APL** Average pay, low range	**FQ** First quartile wage	**LR** Low end range	**SQ** Second quartile wage	**Y** Yearly

Occupation/Type/Industry	Location	Per	Low	Mid	High	Source	Date
Financial Manager	Hickory-Morganton-Lenoir MSA, NC	S	28.72 MW	25.53 AW	59730 AAW	NCBLS	10//99-12/99
	Jacksonville MSA, NC	S	23.16 MW	23.88 AW	48180 AAW	NCBLS	10//99-12/99
	Raleigh-Durham-Chapel Hill MSA, NC	S	32.49 MW	30.34 AW	67570 AAW	NCBLS	10//99-12/99
	Rocky Mount MSA, NC	S	31.27 MW	27.18 AW	65040 AAW	NCBLS	10//99-12/99
	Wilmington MSA, NC	S	26.48 MW	24.71 AW	55070 AAW	NCBLS	10//99-12/99
	North Dakota	S	21.68 MW	22.78 AW	47380 AAW	NDBLS	10//99-12/99
	Bismarck MSA, ND	S	21.80 MW	20.23 AW	45350 AAW	NDBLS	10//99-12/99
	Fargo-Moorhead MSA, ND-MN	S	26.48 MW	23.21 AW	55080 AAW	NDBLS	10//99-12/99
	Grand Forks MSA, ND-MN	S	29.93 MW	26.61 AW	62260 AAW	NDBLS	10//99-12/99
	Ohio	S	27.98 MW	30.60 AW	63640 AAW	OHBLS	10//99-12/99
	Akron PMSA, OH	S	27.93 MW	26.13 AW	58100 AAW	OHBLS	10//99-12/99
	Canton-Massillon MSA, OH	S	27.61 MW	27.04 AW	57420 AAW	OHBLS	10//99-12/99
	Cincinnati PMSA, OH-KY-IN	S	30.11 MW	27.31 AW	62630 AAW	OHBLS	10//99-12/99
	Columbus MSA, OH	S	30.85 MW	27.18 AW	64170 AAW	OHBLS	10//99-12/99
	Dayton-Springfield MSA, OH	S	31.44 MW	29.85 AW	65390 AAW	OHBLS	10//99-12/99
	Hamilton-Middletown PMSA, OH	S	26.75 MW	25.44 AW	55640 AAW	OHBLS	10//99-12/99
	Lima MSA, OH	S	25.27 MW	22.32 AW	52550 AAW	OHBLS	10//99-12/99
	Mansfield MSA, OH	S	28.80 MW	26.67 AW	59900 AAW	OHBLS	10//99-12/99
	Steubenville-Weirton MSA, OH-WV	S	29.23 MW	25.89 AW	60790 AAW	OHBLS	10//99-12/99
	Toledo MSA, OH	S	31.15 MW	27.59 AW	64790 AAW	OHBLS	10//99-12/99
	Youngstown-Warren MSA, OH	S	26.77 MW	25.15 AW	55680 AAW	OHBLS	10//99-12/99
	Oklahoma	S	23.5 MW	26.45 AW	55010 AAW	OKBLS	10//99-12/99
	Enid MSA, OK	S	25.69 MW	23.18 AW	53420 AAW	OKBLS	10//99-12/99
	Lawton MSA, OK	S	20.05 MW	19.42 AW	41700 AAW	OKBLS	10//99-12/99
	Oklahoma City MSA, OK	S	27.29 MW	24.01 AW	56770 AAW	OKBLS	10//99-12/99
	Oregon	S	27.86 MW	30.03 AW	62460 AAW	ORBLS	10//99-12/99
	Corvallis MSA, OR	S	24.37 MW	24.30 AW	50690 AAW	ORBLS	10//99-12/99
	Eugene-Springfield MSA, OR	S	26.80 MW	23.75 AW	55750 AAW	ORBLS	10//99-12/99
	Medford-Ashland MSA, OR	S	28.18 MW	26.75 AW	58620 AAW	ORBLS	10//99-12/99
	Portland-Vancouver PMSA, OR-WA	S	32.00 MW	30.05 AW	66550 AAW	ORBLS	10//99-12/99
	Salem PMSA, OR	S	28.20 MW	24.76 AW	58660 AAW	ORBLS	10//99-12/99
	Pennsylvania	S	26.09 MW	29.56 AW	61480 AAW	PABLS	10//99-12/99
	Allentown-Bethlehem-Easton MSA, PA	S	30.04 MW	29.21 AW	62480 AAW	PABLS	10//99-12/99
	Altoona MSA, PA	S	29.80 MW	27.06 AW	61980 AAW	PABLS	10//99-12/99
	Erie MSA, PA	S	25.63 MW	23.15 AW	53310 AAW	PABLS	10//99-12/99
	Harrisburg-Lebanon-Carlisle MSA, PA	S	31.40 MW	28.71 AW	65320 AAW	PABLS	10//99-12/99
	Johnstown MSA, PA	S	23.14 MW	21.94 AW	48130 AAW	PABLS	10//99-12/99
	Lancaster MSA, PA	S	26.28 MW	23.33 AW	54660 AAW	PABLS	10//99-12/99
	Philadelphia PMSA, PA-NJ	S	33.99 MW	30.79 AW	70700 AAW	PABLS	10//99-12/99
	Reading MSA, PA	S	18.23 MW	13.08 AW	37910 AAW	PABLS	10//99-12/99
	Scranton--Wilkes-Barre--Hazleton MSA, PA	S	25.58 MW	24.00 AW	53210 AAW	PABLS	10//99-12/99
	Sharon MSA, PA	S	29.86 MW	24.49 AW	62100 AAW	PABLS	10//99-12/99
	State College MSA, PA	S	24.17 MW	22.74 AW	50260 AAW	PABLS	10//99-12/99
	Williamsport MSA, PA	S	26.98 MW	27.25 AW	56120 AAW	PABLS	10//99-12/99
	York MSA, PA	S	26.57 MW	24.90 AW	55260 AAW	PABLS	10//99-12/99
	Rhode Island	S	38.68 MW	41.80 AW	86940 AAW	RIBLS	10//99-12/99
	Providence-Fall River-Warwick MSA, RI-MA	S	39.45 MW	36.45 AW	82050 AAW	RIBLS	10//99-12/99
	South Carolina	S	23.63 MW	25.15 AW	52310 AAW	SCBLS	10//99-12/99
	Charleston-North Charleston MSA, SC	S	24.70 MW	23.63 AW	51380 AAW	SCBLS	10//99-12/99
	Columbia MSA, SC	S	24.86 MW	23.50 AW	51710 AAW	SCBLS	10//99-12/99
	Florence MSA, SC	S	24.20 MW	21.27 AW	50340 AAW	SCBLS	10//99-12/99
	Greenville-Spartanburg-Anderson MSA, SC	S	27.24 MW	26.38 AW	56660 AAW	SCBLS	10//99-12/99
	Myrtle Beach MSA, SC	S	22.46 MW	17.88 AW	46720 AAW	SCBLS	10//99-12/99
	Sumter MSA, SC	S	30.14 MW	28.12 AW	62690 AAW	SCBLS	10//99-12/99
	South Dakota	S	30.12 MW	31.10 AW	64700 AAW	SDBLS	10//99-12/99
	Rapid City MSA, SD	S	32.64 MW	31.83 AW	67890 AAW	SDBLS	10//99-12/99
	Sioux Falls MSA, SD	S	30.78 MW	30.09 AW	64030 AAW	SDBLS	10//99-12/99
	Tennessee	S	25.09 MW	28.24 AW	58740 AAW	TNBLS	10//99-12/99
	Chattanooga MSA, TN-GA	S	23.90 MW	21.82 AW	49720 AAW	TNBLS	10//99-12/99

Occupation/Type/Industry	Location	Per	Low	Mid	High	Source	Date
Financial Manager	Clarksville-Hopkinsville MSA, TN-KY	S	22.25 MW	22.42 AW	46270 AAW	TNBLS	10//99-12//99
	Jackson MSA, TN	S	21.90 MW	19.37 AW	45550 AAW	TNBLS	10//99-12//99
	Johnson City-Kingsport-Bristol MSA, TN-VA	S	22.51 MW	21.07 AW	46820 AAW	TNBLS	10//99-12//99
	Knoxville MSA, TN	S	25.88 MW	22.85 AW	53840 AAW	TNBLS	10//99-12//99
	Memphis MSA, TN-AR-MS	S	32.89 MW	30.76 AW	68410 AAW	MSBLS	10//99-12//99
	Nashville MSA, TN	S	28.64 MW	25.38 AW	59580 AAW	TNBLS	10//99-12//99
	Texas	S	29.6 MW	31.40 AW	65310 AAW	TXBLS	10//99-12//99
	Abilene MSA, TX	S	23.67 MW	24.34 AW	49220 AAW	TXBLS	10//99-12//99
	Amarillo MSA, TX	S	24.52 MW	21.07 AW	51010 AAW	TXBLS	10//99-12//99
	Austin-San Marcos MSA, TX	S	32.90 MW	30.76 AW	68420 AAW	TXBLS	10//99-12//99
	Beaumont-Port Arthur MSA, TX	S	29.03 MW	27.96 AW	60390 AAW	TXBLS	10//99-12//99
	Brazoria PMSA, TX	S	23.46 MW	19.85 AW	48790 AAW	TXBLS	10//99-12//99
	Brownsville-Harlingen-San Benito MSA, TX	S	23.27 MW	19.26 AW	48410 AAW	TXBLS	10//99-12//99
	Bryan-College Station MSA, TX	S	25.33 MW	21.16 AW	52680 AAW	TXBLS	10//99-12//99
	Corpus Christi MSA, TX	S	21.18 MW	17.95 AW	44050 AAW	TXBLS	10//99-12//99
	Dallas PMSA, TX	S	36.08 MW	34.73 AW	75050 AAW	TXBLS	10//99-12//99
	El Paso MSA, TX	S	28.85 MW	25.11 AW	60000 AAW	TXBLS	10//99-12//99
	Fort Worth-Arlington PMSA, TX	S	32.18 MW	31.37 AW	66940 AAW	TXBLS	10//99-12//99
	Houston PMSA, TX	S	32.70 MW	30.06 AW	68020 AAW	TXBLS	10//99-12//99
	Killeen-Temple MSA, TX	S	25.48 MW	24.44 AW	53000 AAW	TXBLS	10//99-12//99
	Laredo MSA, TX	S	37.46 MW	31.85 AW	77910 AAW	TXBLS	10//99-12//99
	Longview-Marshall MSA, TX	S	28.04 MW	27.27 AW	58320 AAW	TXBLS	10//99-12//99
	Lubbock MSA, TX	S	22.89 MW	18.99 AW	47610 AAW	TXBLS	10//99-12//99
	McAllen-Edinburg-Mission MSA, TX	S	27.96 MW	25.74 AW	58160 AAW	TXBLS	10//99-12//99
	Odessa-Midland MSA, TX	S	24.36 MW	23.10 AW	50680 AAW	TXBLS	10//99-12//99
	San Antonio MSA, TX	S	29.83 MW	28.67 AW	62040 AAW	TXBLS	10//99-12//99
	Sherman-Denison MSA, TX	S	24.63 MW	23.78 AW	51220 AAW	TXBLS	10//99-12//99
	Texarkana MSA, TX-Texarkana, AR	S	21.09 MW	19.05 AW	43870 AAW	TXBLS	10//99-12//99
	Tyler MSA, TX	S	28.83 MW	26.99 AW	59960 AAW	TXBLS	10//99-12//99
	Victoria MSA, TX	S	27.78 MW	24.39 AW	57790 AAW	TXBLS	10//99-12//99
	Wichita Falls MSA, TX	S	23.63 MW	19.39 AW	49150 AAW	TXBLS	10//99-12//99
	Utah	S	26.16 MW	28.11 AW	58460 AAW	UTBLS	10//99-12//99
	Provo-Orem MSA, UT	S	26.96 MW	25.10 AW	56070 AAW	UTBLS	10//99-12//99
	Salt Lake City-Ogden MSA, UT	S	28.67 MW	26.80 AW	59630 AAW	UTBLS	10//99-12//99
	Vermont	S	31.08 MW	33.27 AW	69200 AAW	VTBLS	10//99-12//99
	Burlington MSA, VT	S	31.10 MW	30.37 AW	64690 AAW	VTBLS	10//99-12//99
	Virginia	S	32.73 MW	33.69 AW	70080 AAW	VABLS	10//99-12//99
	Charlottesville MSA, VA	S	21.26 MW	16.61 AW	44220 AAW	VABLS	10//99-12//99
	Danville MSA, VA	S	23.47 MW	21.88 AW	48810 AAW	VABLS	10//99-12//99
	Lynchburg MSA, VA	S	30.40 MW	27.85 AW	63240 AAW	VABLS	10//99-12//99
	Norfolk-Virginia Beach-Newport News MSA, VA-NC	S	30.30 MW	30.65 AW	63020 AAW	VABLS	10//99-12//99
	Richmond-Petersburg MSA, VA	S	33.08 MW	31.69 AW	68800 AAW	VABLS	10//99-12//99
	Roanoke MSA, VA	S	26.17 MW	22.80 AW	54420 AAW	VABLS	10//99-12//99
	Washington	S	31.92 MW	33.29 AW	69250 AAW	WABLS	10//99-12//99
	Bellingham MSA, WA	S	26.88 MW	23.98 AW	55900 AAW	WABLS	10//99-12//99
	Bremerton PMSA, WA	S	40.22 MW	33.90 AW	83660 AAW	WABLS	10//99-12//99
	Olympia PMSA, WA	S	28.43 MW	28.56 AW	59140 AAW	WABLS	10//99-12//99
	Richland-Kennewick-Pasco MSA, WA	S	30.45 MW	26.24 AW	63330 AAW	WABLS	10//99-12//99
	Seattle-Bellevue-Everett PMSA, WA	S	34.90 MW	33.55 AW	72600 AAW	WABLS	10//99-12//99
	Spokane MSA, WA	S	28.89 MW	25.51 AW	60100 AAW	WABLS	10//99-12//99
	Tacoma PMSA, WA	S	30.22 MW	28.89 AW	62860 AAW	WABLS	10//99-12//99
	Yakima MSA, WA	S	28.39 MW	28.80 AW	59050 AAW	WABLS	10//99-12//99
	West Virginia	S	20.97 MW	24.25 AW	50440 AAW	WVBLS	10//99-12//99
	Charleston MSA, WV	S	28.49 MW	23.93 AW	59250 AAW	WVBLS	10//99-12//99
	Huntington-Ashland MSA, WV-KY-OH	S	24.16 MW	20.71 AW	50260 AAW	WVBLS	10//99-12//99
	Parkersburg-Marietta MSA, WV-OH	S	22.05 MW	19.29 AW	45850 AAW	WVBLS	10//99-12//99

AAW Average annual wage	**AOH** Average offered, high	**ASH** Average starting, high	**H** Hourly	**M** Monthly	**S** Special: hourly and annual
AE Average entry wage	**AOL** Average offered, low	**ASL** Average starting, low	**HI** Highest wage paid	**MTC** Median total compensation	**TQ** Third quartile wage
AEX Average experienced wage	**APH** Average pay, high range	**AW** Average wage paid	**HR** High end range	**MW** Median wage paid	**W** Weekly
AO Average offered	**APL** Average pay, low range	**FQ** First quartile wage	**LR** Low end range	**SQ** Second quartile wage	**Y** Yearly

Occupation/Type/Industry	Location	Per	Low	Mid	High	Source	Date
Financial Manager	Wheeling MSA, WV-OH	S	20.19 MW	18.86 AW	42000 AAW	WVBLS	10//99-12//99
	Wisconsin	S	25.05 MW	27.27 AW	56720 AAW	WIBLS	10//99-12//99
	Appleton-Oshkosh-Neenah MSA, WI	S	25.04 MW	24.14 AW	52090 AAW	WIBLS	10//99-12//99
	Eau Claire MSA, WI	S	25.29 MW	22.77 AW	52600 AAW	WIBLS	10//99-12//99
	Green Bay MSA, WI	S	29.73 MW	26.76 AW	61840 AAW	WIBLS	10//99-12//99
	Janesville-Beloit MSA, WI	S	22.96 MW	18.68 AW	47760 AAW	WIBLS	10//99-12//99
	Kenosha PMSA, WI	S	22.67 MW	22.57 AW	47140 AAW	WIBLS	10//99-12//99
	La Crosse MSA, WI-MN	S	21.11 MW	20.55 AW	43910 AAW	WIBLS	10//99-12//99
	Madison MSA, WI	S	25.57 MW	23.71 AW	53180 AAW	WIBLS	10//99-12//99
	Milwaukee-Waukesha PMSA, WI	S	31.00 MW	29.27 AW	64490 AAW	WIBLS	10//99-12//99
	Racine PMSA, WI	S	26.66 MW	23.55 AW	55440 AAW	WIBLS	10//99-12//99
	Sheboygan MSA, WI	S	28.67 MW	29.63 AW	59620 AAW	WIBLS	10//99-12//99
	Wausau MSA, WI	S	21.87 MW	21.24 AW	45500 AAW	WIBLS	10//99-12//99
	Wyoming	S	20.65 MW	22.50 AW	46790 AAW	WYBLS	10//99-12//99
	Casper MSA, WY	S	23.08 MW	20.29 AW	48010 AAW	WYBLS	10//99-12//99
	Cheyenne MSA, WY	S	22.83 MW	21.32 AW	47480 AAW	WYBLS	10//99-12//99
	Puerto Rico	S	20.93 MW	23.71 AW	49310 AAW	PRBLS	10//99-12//99
	Aguadilla MSA, PR	S	20.41 MW	20.78 AW	42450 AAW	PRBLS	10//99-12//99
	Arecibo PMSA, PR	S	20.83 MW	16.61 AW	43320 AAW	PRBLS	10//99-12//99
	Caguas PMSA, PR	S	22.45 MW	19.47 AW	46690 AAW	PRBLS	10//99-12//99
	Mayaguez MSA, PR	S	21.83 MW	19.53 AW	45410 AAW	PRBLS	10//99-12//99
	Ponce MSA, PR	S	21.80 MW	19.37 AW	45350 AAW	PRBLS	10//99-12//99
	San Juan-Bayamon PMSA, PR	S	24.47 MW	21.89 AW	50900 AAW	PRBLS	10//99-12//99
	Virgin Islands	S	25.87 MW	27.16 AW	56490 AAW	VIBLS	10//99-12//99
	Guam	S	19.86 MW	21.39 AW	44490 AAW	GUBLS	10//99-12//99
Financial Planner	United States	Y		73180 AW		INVNEWS	2000
Sole Proprietor	United States	Y		87559 AW		INVNEWS	2000
Sole Proprietor	United States	Y		87559 AW		INVNEWS	2000
Fine Artist, Including Painter, Sculptor, and Illustrator	Alabama	S	14.17 MW	14.13 AW	29380 AAW	ALBLS	10//99-12//99
	Arizona	S	10.05 MW	15.13 AW	31460 AAW	AZBLS	10//99-12//99
	Phoenix-Mesa MSA, AZ	S	10.74 MW	9.86 AW	22340 AAW	AZBLS	10//99-12//99
	Arkansas	S	9.68 MW	10.19 AW	21190 AAW	ARBLS	10//99-12//99
	Little Rock-North Little Rock MSA, AR	S	11.21 MW	9.96 AW	23310 AAW	ARBLS	10//99-12//99
	California	S	18.41 MW	19.32 AW	40190 AAW	CABLS	10//99-12//99
	Los Angeles-Long Beach PMSA, CA	S	20.72 MW	21.74 AW	43100 AAW	CABLS	10//99-12//99
	San Diego MSA, CA	S	16.65 MW	16.05 AW	34620 AAW	CABLS	10//99-12//99
	San Francisco PMSA, CA	S	19.11 MW	17.69 AW	39740 AAW	CABLS	10//99-12//99
	San Jose PMSA, CA	S	24.07 MW	21.16 AW	50060 AAW	CABLS	10//99-12//99
	Connecticut	S	16.7 MW	18.19 AW	37840 AAW	CTBLS	10//99-12//99
	District of Columbia	S	21.98 MW	21.62 AW	44970 AAW	DCBLS	10//99-12//99
	Washington PMSA, DC-MD-VA-WV	S	20.27 MW	20.71 AW	42160 AAW	DCBLS	10//99-12//99
	Florida	S	15.27 MW	22.95 AW	47740 AAW	FLBLS	10//99-12//99
	Fort Lauderdale PMSA, FL	S	9.92 MW	11.44 AW	20620 AAW	FLBLS	10//99-12//99
	Jacksonville MSA, FL	S	11.89 MW	11.64 AW	24740 AAW	FLBLS	10//99-12//99
	Orlando MSA, FL	S	15.95 MW	14.45 AW	33180 AAW	FLBLS	10//99-12//99
	Tallahassee MSA, FL	S	14.33 MW	13.40 AW	29800 AAW	FLBLS	10//99-12//99
	West Palm Beach-Boca Raton MSA, FL	S	14.76 MW	15.10 AW	30700 AAW	FLBLS	10//99-12//99
	Macon MSA, GA	S	10.58 MW	9.79 AW	22000 AAW	GABLS	10//99-12//99
	Hawaii	S	14.41 MW	18.99 AW	39500 AAW	HIBLS	10//99-12//99
	Honolulu MSA, HI	S	18.99 MW	14.41 AW	39500 AAW	HIBLS	10//99-12//99
	Idaho	S	12.65 MW	13.79 AW	28690 AAW	IDBLS	10//99-12//99
	Illinois	S	12.46 MW	12.64 AW	26290 AAW	ILBLS	10//99-12//99
	Chicago PMSA, IL	S	12.60 MW	12.42 AW	26210 AAW	ILBLS	10//99-12//99
	Indiana	S	13.09 MW	14.32 AW	29790 AAW	INBLS	10//99-12//99
	Indianapolis MSA, IN	S	12.99 MW	12.78 AW	27020 AAW	INBLS	10//99-12//99
	Iowa	S	12.26 MW	12.98 AW	26990 AAW	IABLS	10//99-12//99
	Kansas	S	12.54 MW	14.98 AW	31150 AAW	KSBLS	10//99-12//99
	Kentucky	S	14.71 MW	14.41 AW	29970 AAW	KYBLS	10//99-12//99
	Lexington MSA, KY	S	14.26 MW	14.26 AW	29660 AAW	KYBLS	10//99-12//99
	Louisiana	S	8.25 MW	8.87 AW	18440 AAW	LABLS	10//99-12//99
	New Orleans MSA, LA	S	8.42 MW	8.14 AW	17500 AAW	LABLS	10//99-12//99
	Maryland	S	15.56 MW	17.11 AW	35580 AAW	MDBLS	10//99-12//99
	Baltimore PMSA, MD	S	16.94 MW	15.18 AW	35220 AAW	MDBLS	10//99-12//99

AAW	Average annual wage	**AOH**	Average offered, high	**ASH**	Average starting, high	**H**	Hourly	**M**	Monthly	**S**	Special: hourly and annual
AE	Average entry wage	**AOL**	Average offered, low	**ASL**	Average starting, low	**HI**	Highest wage paid	**MTC**	Median total compensation	**TQ**	Third quartile wage
AEX	Average experienced wage	**APH**	Average pay, high range	**AW**	Average wage paid	**HR**	High end range	**MW**	Median wage paid	**W**	Weekly
AO	Average offered	**APL**	Average pay, low range	**FQ**	First quartile wage	**LR**	Low end range	**SQ**	Second quartile wage	**Y**	Yearly

Occupation/Type/Industry	Location	Per	Low	Mid	High	Source	Date
Fine Artist, Including Painter, Sculptor, and Illustrator	Massachusetts	S	18.53 MW	19.17 AW	39870 AAW	MABLS	10//99-12//99
	Boston PMSA, MA-NH	S	17.87 MW	18.54 AW	37180 AAW	MABLS	10//99-12//99
	Minnesota	S	19.61 MW	20.25 AW	42110 AAW	MNBLS	10//99-12//99
	Minneapolis-St. Paul MSA, MN-WI	S	20.24 MW	19.64 AW	42110 AAW	MNBLS	10//99-12//99
	Missouri	S	9.82 MW	12.81 AW	26640 AAW	MOBLS	10//99-12//99
	St. Louis MSA, MO-IL	S	15.63 MW	15.25 AW	32510 AAW	MOBLS	10//99-12//99
	Nebraska	S	12.17 MW	13.89 AW	28890 AAW	NEBLS	10//99-12//99
	Omaha MSA, NE-IA	S	14.05 MW	13.65 AW	29220 AAW	NEBLS	10//99-12//99
	Nevada	S	17.22 MW	16.65 AW	34640 AAW	NVBLS	10//99-12//99
	Las Vegas MSA, NV-AZ	S	15.70 MW	10.47 AW	32650 AAW	NVBLS	10//99-12//99
	New Hampshire	S	13.87 MW	15.24 AW	31690 AAW	NHBLS	10//99-12//99
	New Jersey	S	11.07 MW	12.95 AW	26950 AAW	NJBLS	10//99-12//99
	Bergen-Passaic PMSA, NJ	S	9.40 MW	10.85 AW	19540 AAW	NJBLS	10//99-12//99
	Newark PMSA, NJ	S	11.19 MW	9.88 AW	23280 AAW	NJBLS	10//99-12//99
	New Mexico	S	18.29 MW	18.78 AW	39050 AAW	NMBLS	10//99-12//99
	Santa Fe MSA, NM	S	25.18 MW	27.61 AW	52380 AAW	NMBLS	10//99-12//99
	New York	S	14.24 MW	15.75 AW	32760 AAW	NYBLS	10//99-12//99
	New York PMSA, NY	S	14.93 MW	14.42 AW	31050 AAW	NYBLS	10//99-12//99
	North Carolina	S	14.69 MW	14.20 AW	29540 AAW	NCBLS	10//99-12//99
	Charlotte-Gastonia-Rock Hill MSA, NC-SC	S	12.86 MW	13.66 AW	26750 AAW	NCBLS	10//99-12//99
	Ohio	S	15.65 MW	16.43 AW	34180 AAW	OHBLS	10//99-12//99
	Akron PMSA, OH	S	21.64 MW	22.26 AW	45010 AAW	OHBLS	10//99-12//99
	Cincinnati PMSA, OH-KY-IN	S	16.96 MW	15.49 AW	35280 AAW	OHBLS	10//99-12//99
	Cleveland-Lorain-Elyria PMSA, OH	S	14.80 MW	15.06 AW	30780 AAW	OHBLS	10//99-12//99
	Columbus MSA, OH	S	13.57 MW	12.96 AW	28220 AAW	OHBLS	10//99-12//99
	Dayton-Springfield MSA, OH	S	16.27 MW	15.97 AW	33850 AAW	OHBLS	10//99-12//99
	Oregon	S	11.21 MW	15.01 AW	31220 AAW	ORBLS	10//99-12//99
	Portland-Vancouver PMSA, OR-WA	S	13.42 MW	10.51 AW	27910 AAW	ORBLS	10//99-12//99
	Pennsylvania	S	15.01 MW	15.73 AW	32720 AAW	PABLS	10//99-12//99
	Philadelphia PMSA, PA-NJ	S	17.24 MW	16.64 AW	35860 AAW	PABLS	10//99-12//99
	Rhode Island	S	14.97 MW	21.78 AW	45300 AAW	RIBLS	10//99-12//99
	South Carolina	S	13.28 MW	20.19 AW	42000 AAW	SCBLS	10//99-12//99
	South Dakota	S	10.53 MW	13.69 AW	28480 AAW	SDBLS	10//99-12//99
	Tennessee	S	12.83 MW	14.59 AW	30340 AAW	TNBLS	10//99-12//99
	Nashville MSA, TN	S	16.85 MW	17.87 AW	35050 AAW	TNBLS	10//99-12//99
	Texas	S	15.08 MW	15.38 AW	31990 AAW	TXBLS	10//99-12//99
	Houston PMSA, TX	S	15.32 MW	15.23 AW	31870 AAW	TXBLS	10//99-12//99
	Vermont	S	8.26 MW	9.34 AW	19420 AAW	VTBLS	10//99-12//99
	Virginia	S	13.56 MW	13.65 AW	28390 AAW	VABLS	10//99-12//99
	Norfolk-Virginia Beach-Newport News MSA, VA-NC	S	16.39 MW	17.63 AW	34090 AAW	VABLS	10//99-12//99
	Richmond-Petersburg MSA, VA	S	12.99 MW	10.67 AW	27010 AAW	VABLS	10//99-12//99
	Washington	S	15.92 MW	16.41 AW	34120 AAW	WABLS	10//99-12//99
	Seattle-Bellevue-Everett PMSA, WA	S	17.52 MW	16.13 AW	36450 AAW	WABLS	10//99-12//99
	West Virginia	S	7.63 MW	9.64 AW	20040 AAW	WVBLS	10//99-12//99
	Wisconsin	S	11.32 MW	12.34 AW	25660 AAW	WIBLS	10//99-12//99
	Milwaukee-Waukesha PMSA, WI	S	15.82 MW	17.01 AW	32900 AAW	WIBLS	10//99-12//99
Finisher							
Garment Company, $10-25 Million in Sales	Los Angeles, CA	H		7.50 AW		CAAPN	1998
Fire Fighter	United States	W	513 LR		832 HR	TQUES	1999
	Alabama	S	13.15 MW	13.58 AW	28250 AAW	ALBLS	10//99-12//99
	Birmingham MSA, AL	S	16.18 MW	15.89 AW	33660 AAW	ALBLS	10//99-12//99
	Arizona	S	15.33 MW	15.49 AW	32220 AAW	AZBLS	10//99-12//99
	Flagstaff MSA, AZ-UT	S	11.86 MW	12.33 AW	24660 AAW	AZBLS	10//99-12//99
	Phoenix-Mesa MSA, AZ	S	19.46 MW	20.24 AW	40490 AAW	AZBLS	10//99-12//99
	Tucson MSA, AZ	S	12.51 MW	12.91 AW	26030 AAW	AZBLS	10//99-12//99
	Yuma MSA, AZ	S	13.18 MW	12.64 AW	27420 AAW	AZBLS	10//99-12//99
	Arkansas	S	12.7 MW	12.93 AW	26900 AAW	ARBLS	10//99-12//99
	Fayetteville-Springdale-Rogers MSA, AR	S	11.27 MW	10.99 AW	23430 AAW	ARBLS	10//99-12//99
	California	S	21.43 MW	21.75 AW	45240 AAW	CABLS	10//99-12//99

AAW	Average annual wage	AOH	Average offered, high	ASH	Average starting, high	H	Hourly	M	Monthly	S	Special: hourly and annual
AE	Average entry wage	AOL	Average offered, low	ASL	Average starting, low	HI	Highest wage paid	MTC	Median total compensation	TQ	Third quartile wage
AEX	Average experienced wage	APH	Average pay, high range	AW	Average wage paid	HR	High end range	MW	Median wage paid	W	Weekly
AO	Average offered	APL	Average pay, low range	FQ	First quartile wage	LR	Low end range	SQ	Second quartile wage	Y	Yearly

Occupation/Type/Industry	Location	Per	Low	Mid	High	Source	Date
Fire Fighter	Bakersfield MSA, CA	s	14.19 MW	13.57 AW	29500 AAW	CABLS	10//99-12//99
	Fresno MSA, CA	s	21.01 MW	20.63 AW	43710 AAW	CABLS	10//99-12//99
	Los Angeles-Long Beach PMSA, CA	s	25.80 MW	25.72 AW	53670 AAW	CABLS	10//99-12//99
	Merced MSA, CA	s	18.40 MW	18.66 AW	38260 AAW	CABLS	10//99-12//99
	Oakland PMSA, CA	s	29.43 MW	30.76 AW	61220 AAW	CABLS	10//99-12//99
	Riverside-San Bernardino PMSA, CA	s	17.84 MW	16.66 AW	37100 AAW	CABLS	10//99-12//99
	Sacramento PMSA, CA	s	18.71 MW	16.50 AW	38910 AAW	CABLS	10//99-12//99
	Salinas MSA, CA	s	15.58 MW	14.45 AW	32400 AAW	CABLS	10//99-12//99
	San Diego MSA, CA	s	19.45 MW	20.30 AW	40460 AAW	CABLS	10//99-12//99
	San Francisco PMSA, CA	s	25.59 MW	25.30 AW	53220 AAW	CABLS	10//99-12//99
	San Jose PMSA, CA	s	23.60 MW	23.57 AW	49090 AAW	CABLS	10//99-12//99
	San Luis Obispo-Atascadero-Paso Robles MSA, CA	s	16.29 MW	15.79 AW	33880 AAW	CABLS	10//99-12//99
	Santa Barbara-Santa Maria-Lompoc MSA, CA	s	22.02 MW	22.42 AW	45800 AAW	CABLS	10//99-12//99
	Santa Cruz-Watsonville PMSA, CA	s	24.14 MW	24.82 AW	50200 AAW	CABLS	10//99-12//99
	Stockton-Lodi MSA, CA	s	16.93 MW	15.56 AW	35210 AAW	CABLS	10//99-12//99
	Vallejo-Fairfield-Napa PMSA, CA	s	21.76 MW	21.60 AW	45250 AAW	CABLS	10//99-12//99
	Ventura PMSA, CA	s	20.22 MW	18.69 AW	42060 AAW	CABLS	10//99-12//99
	Visalia-Tulare-Porterville MSA, CA	s	16.77 MW	17.22 AW	34890 AAW	CABLS	10//99-12//99
	Yolo PMSA, CA	s	17.68 MW	16.52 AW	36770 AAW	CABLS	10//99-12//99
	Yuba City MSA, CA	s	20.92 MW	20.78 AW	43510 AAW	CABLS	10//99-12//99
	Colorado	s	18.22 MW	18.01 AW	37450 AAW	COBLS	10//99-12//99
	Denver PMSA, CO	s	18.62 MW	18.63 AW	38740 AAW	COBLS	10//99-12//99
	Fort Collins-Loveland MSA, CO	s	19.62 MW	21.69 AW	40810 AAW	COBLS	10//99-12//99
	Connecticut	s	22.07 MW	21.25 AW	44190 AAW	CTBLS	10//99-12//99
	Hartford MSA, CT	s	21.05 MW	21.74 AW	43780 AAW	CTBLS	10//99-12//99
	New Haven-Meriden PMSA, CT	s	22.79 MW	23.27 AW	47400 AAW	CTBLS	10//99-12//99
	New London-Norwich MSA, CT-RI	s	15.87 MW	17.76 AW	33010 AAW	CTBLS	10//99-12//99
	Stamford-Norwalk PMSA, CT	s	23.28 MW	23.85 AW	48430 AAW	CTBLS	10//99-12//99
	Delaware	s	18.48 MW	17.67 AW	36760 AAW	DEBLS	10//99-12//99
	Wilmington-Newark PMSA, DE-MD	s	17.89 MW	18.59 AW	37210 AAW	DEBLS	10//99-12//99
	Washington PMSA, DC-MD-VA-WV	s	17.33 MW	17.21 AW	36040 AAW	DCBLS	10//99-12//99
	Florida	s	14.64 MW	14.97 AW	31140 AAW	FLBLS	10//99-12//99
	Daytona Beach MSA, FL	s	12.52 MW	11.03 AW	26040 AAW	FLBLS	10//99-12//99
	Fort Lauderdale PMSA, FL	s	17.44 MW	17.41 AW	36270 AAW	FLBLS	10//99-12//99
	Fort Myers-Cape Coral MSA, FL	s	15.10 MW	14.61 AW	31400 AAW	FLBLS	10//99-12//99
	Fort Walton Beach MSA, FL	s	12.34 MW	11.75 AW	25670 AAW	FLBLS	10//99-12//99
	Gainesville MSA, FL	s	9.44 MW	8.85 AW	19630 AAW	FLBLS	10//99-12//99
	Jacksonville MSA, FL	s	12.05 MW	11.33 AW	25060 AAW	FLBLS	10//99-12//99
	Lakeland-Winter Haven MSA, FL	s	11.76 MW	11.37 AW	24470 AAW	FLBLS	10//99-12//99
	Melbourne-Titusville-Palm Bay MSA, FL	s	13.12 MW	12.56 AW	27280 AAW	FLBLS	10//99-12//99
	Miami PMSA, FL	s	20.53 MW	20.84 AW	42700 AAW	FLBLS	10//99-12//99
	Naples MSA, FL	s	14.89 MW	14.99 AW	30980 AAW	FLBLS	10//99-12//99
	Orlando MSA, FL	s	11.65 MW	11.06 AW	24230 AAW	FLBLS	10//99-12//99
	Pensacola MSA, FL	s	11.46 MW	11.41 AW	23830 AAW	FLBLS	10//99-12//99
	Sarasota-Bradenton MSA, FL	s	15.15 MW	14.51 AW	31510 AAW	FLBLS	10//99-12//99
	Tampa-St. Petersburg-Clearwater MSA, FL	s	14.76 MW	15.07 AW	30690 AAW	FLBLS	10//99-12//99
	Georgia	s	13.28 MW	13.93 AW	28970 AAW	GABLS	10//99-12//99
	Atlanta MSA, GA	s	15.49 MW	15.60 AW	32210 AAW	GABLS	10//99-12//99
	Macon MSA, GA	s	11.71 MW	11.40 AW	24370 AAW	GABLS	10//99-12//99
	Savannah MSA, GA	s	15.17 MW	15.01 AW	31560 AAW	GABLS	10//99-12//99
	Hawaii	s	15.78 MW	16.24 AW	33770 AAW	HIBLS	10//99-12//99
	Idaho	s	8.94 MW	9.76 AW	20290 AAW	IDBLS	10//99-12//99
	Boise City MSA, ID	s	15.43 MW	13.83 AW	32090 AAW	IDBLS	10//99-12//99
	Illinois	s	16.36 MW	16.65 AW	34630 AAW	ILBLS	10//99-12//99
	Bloomington-Normal MSA, IL	s	17.18 MW	19.62 AW	35730 AAW	ILBLS	10//99-12//99
	Chicago PMSA, IL	s	19.59 MW	20.39 AW	40750 AAW	ILBLS	10//99-12//99

AAW	Average annual wage	AOH	Average offered, high	ASH	Average starting, high	H	Hourly	M	Monthly	S	Special: hourly and annual
AE	Average entry wage	AOL	Average offered, low	ASL	Average starting, low	HI	Highest wage paid	MTC	Median total compensation	TQ	Third quartile wage
AEX	Average experienced wage	APH	Average pay, high range	AW	Average wage paid	HR	High end range	MW	Median wage paid	W	Weekly
AO	Average offered	APL	Average pay, low range	FQ	First quartile wage	LR	Low end range	SQ	Second quartile wage	Y	Yearly

Fire Fighter

Occupation/Type/Industry	Location	Per	Low	Mid	High	Source	Date
Fire Fighter	Rockford MSA, IL	S	18.53 MW	19.01 AW	38550 AAW	ILBLS	10//99-12//99
	Springfield MSA, IL	S	18.32 MW	18.48 AW	38110 AAW	ILBLS	10//99-12//99
	Indiana	S	14.61 MW	14.44 AW	30020 AAW	INBLS	10//99-12//99
	Evansville-Henderson MSA, IN-KY	S	13.14 MW	13.26 AW	27330 AAW	INBLS	10//99-12//99
	Gary PMSA, IN	S	14.16 MW	14.48 AW	29450 AAW	INBLS	10//99-12//99
	Indianapolis MSA, IN	S	15.53 MW	15.56 AW	32310 AAW	INBLS	10//99-12//99
	Iowa	S	12.19 MW	11.85 AW	24650 AAW	IABLS	10//99-12//99
	Davenport-Moline-Rock Island MSA, IA-IL	S	11.83 MW	11.05 AW	24610 AAW	IABLS	10//99-12//99
	Des Moines MSA, IA	S	10.87 MW	11.93 AW	22610 AAW	IABLS	10//99-12//99
	Kansas	S	10.49 MW	11.44 AW	23790 AAW	KSBLS	10//99-12//99
	Wichita MSA, KS	S	13.33 MW	14.35 AW	27720 AAW	KSBLS	10//99-12//99
	Kentucky	S	9.63 MW	10.01 AW	20830 AAW	KYBLS	10//99-12//99
	Louisville MSA, KY-IN	S	10.40 MW	9.39 AW	21620 AAW	KYBLS	10//99-12//99
	Louisiana	S	11.65 MW	12.81 AW	26650 AAW	LABLS	10//99-12//99
	Baton Rouge MSA, LA	S	13.13 MW	11.96 AW	27320 AAW	LABLS	10//99-12//99
	Lafayette MSA, LA	S	6.33 MW	6.27 AW	13160 AAW	LABLS	10//99-12//99
	Lake Charles MSA, LA	S	11.39 MW	10.02 AW	23700 AAW	LABLS	10//99-12//99
	New Orleans MSA, LA	S	12.61 MW	11.42 AW	26230 AAW	LABLS	10//99-12//99
	Maine	S	10.5 MW	10.82 AW	22510 AAW	MEBLS	10//99-12//99
	Bangor MSA, ME	S	11.74 MW	10.89 AW	24420 AAW	MEBLS	10//99-12//99
	Portland MSA, ME	S	10.86 MW	9.49 AW	22580 AAW	MEBLS	10//99-12//99
	Maryland	S	17.79 MW	17.94 AW	37320 AAW	MDBLS	10//99-12//99
	Baltimore PMSA, MD	S	17.36 MW	17.46 AW	36110 AAW	MDBLS	10//99-12//99
	Massachusetts	S	17.13 MW	16.86 AW	35060 AAW	MABLS	10//99-12//99
	Barnstable-Yarmouth MSA, MA	S	20.96 MW	21.45 AW	43590 AAW	MABLS	10//99-12//99
	Boston PMSA, MA-NH	S	17.80 MW	18.12 AW	37010 AAW	MABLS	10//99-12//99
	Brockton PMSA, MA	S	17.08 MW	17.61 AW	35530 AAW	MABLS	10//99-12//99
	Lawrence PMSA, MA-NH	S	14.07 MW	13.27 AW	29270 AAW	MABLS	10//99-12//99
	Springfield MSA, MA	S	16.09 MW	15.59 AW	33460 AAW	MABLS	10//99-12//99
	Michigan	S	15.74 MW	15.71 AW	32680 AAW	MIBLS	10//99-12//99
	Ann Arbor PMSA, MI	S	12.80 MW	8.67 AW	26630 AAW	MIBLS	10//99-12//99
	Benton Harbor MSA, MI	S	12.88 MW	11.02 AW	26790 AAW	MIBLS	10//99-12//99
	Detroit PMSA, MI	S	18.39 MW	18.48 AW	38240 AAW	MIBLS	10//99-12//99
	Flint PMSA, MI	S	13.23 MW	12.41 AW	27530 AAW	MIBLS	10//99-12//99
	Grand Rapids-Muskegon-Holland MSA, MI	S	15.12 MW	14.46 AW	31460 AAW	MIBLS	10//99-12//99
	Kalamazoo-Battle Creek MSA, MI	S	14.55 MW	14.54 AW	30270 AAW	MIBLS	10//99-12//99
	Saginaw-Bay City-Midland MSA, MI	S	13.41 MW	14.36 AW	27890 AAW	MIBLS	10//99-12//99
	Minnesota	S	8.35 MW	8.91 AW	18520 AAW	MNBLS	10//99-12//99
	Duluth-Superior MSA, MN-WI	S	9.68 MW	7.86 AW	20140 AAW	MNBLS	10//99-12//99
	Minneapolis-St. Paul MSA, MN-WI	S	9.37 MW	8.73 AW	19490 AAW	MNBLS	10//99-12//99
	St. Cloud MSA, MN	S	7.12 MW	7.42 AW	14810 AAW	MNBLS	10//99-12//99
	Mississippi	S	11.79 MW	11.71 AW	24350 AAW	MSBLS	10//99-12//99
	Biloxi-Gulfport-Pascagoula MSA, MS	S	12.17 MW	12.56 AW	25320 AAW	MSBLS	10//99-12//99
	Jackson MSA, MS	S	13.40 MW	13.77 AW	27870 AAW	MSBLS	10//99-12//99
	Missouri	S	14.49 MW	15.52 AW	32270 AAW	MOBLS	10//99-12//99
	St. Louis MSA, MO-IL	S	16.70 MW	16.89 AW	34730 AAW	MOBLS	10//99-12//99
	Montana	S	15.5 MW	15.34 AW	31910 AAW	MTBLS	10//99-12//99
	Nebraska	S	15.87 MW	16.02 AW	33310 AAW	NEBLS	10//99-12//99
	Nevada	S	17.81 MW	18.65 AW	38790 AAW	NVBLS	10//99-12//99
	Las Vegas MSA, NV-AZ	S	18.05 MW	18.07 AW	37540 AAW	NVBLS	10//99-12//99
	Reno MSA, NV	S	17.46 MW	16.06 AW	36310 AAW	NVBLS	10//99-12//99
	New Hampshire	S	14.65 MW	14.03 AW	29180 AAW	NHBLS	10//99-12//99
	Manchester PMSA, NH	S	15.46 MW	17.13 AW	32150 AAW	NHBLS	10//99-12//99
	Nashua PMSA, NH	S	15.38 MW	17.28 AW	31990 AAW	NHBLS	10//99-12//99
	Portsmouth-Rochester PMSA, NH-ME	S	15.58 MW	15.70 AW	32410 AAW	NHBLS	10//99-12//99
	New Jersey	S	24.58 MW	24.53 AW	51030 AAW	NJBLS	10//99-12//99
	Atlantic-Cape May PMSA, NJ	S	24.72 MW	25.95 AW	51430 AAW	NJBLS	10//99-12//99
	Bergen-Passaic PMSA, NJ	S	27.55 MW	29.91 AW	57300 AAW	NJBLS	10//99-12//99
	Jersey City PMSA, NJ	S	26.84 MW	28.46 AW	55830 AAW	NJBLS	10//99-12//99
	Middlesex-Somerset-Hunterdon PMSA, NJ	S	28.43 MW	31.06 AW	59130 AAW	NJBLS	10//99-12//99
	Monmouth-Ocean PMSA, NJ	S	19.88 MW	21.27 AW	41350 AAW	NJBLS	10//99-12//99
	Newark PMSA, NJ	S	24.14 MW	23.65 AW	50210 AAW	NJBLS	10//99-12//99

AAW Average annual wage	**AOH** Average offered, high	**ASH** Average starting, high	**H** Hourly	**M** Monthly	**S** Special: hourly and annual
AE Average entry wage	**AOL** Average offered, low	**ASL** Average starting, low	**HI** Highest wage paid	**MTC** Median total compensation	**TQ** Third quartile wage
AEX Average experienced wage	**APH** Average pay, high range	**AW** Average wage paid	**HR** High end range	**MW** Median wage paid	**W** Weekly
AO Average offered	**APL** Average pay, low range	**FQ** First quartile wage	**LR** Low end range	**SQ** Second quartile wage	**Y** Yearly

Occupation/Type/Industry	Location	Per	Low	Mid	High	Source	Date
Fire Fighter	Vineland-Millville-Bridgeton PMSA, NJ	S	25.64 MW	27.30 AW	53330 AAW	NJBLS	10//99-12//99
	New Mexico	S	12.02 MW	11.91 AW	24780 AAW	NMBLS	10//99-12//99
	Santa Fe MSA, NM	S	10.98 MW	11.02 AW	22840 AAW	NMBLS	10//99-12//99
	New York	S	22.95 MW	22.19 AW	46160 AAW	NYBLS	10//99-12//99
	Nassau-Suffolk PMSA, NY	S	23.93 MW	24.26 AW	49780 AAW	NYBLS	10//99-12//99
	Rochester MSA, NY	S	16.08 MW	16.34 AW	33450 AAW	NYBLS	10//99-12//99
	North Carolina	S	12.16 MW	12.59 AW	26180 AAW	NCBLS	10//99-12//99
	Greensboro--Winston-Salem-- High Point MSA, NC	S	12.04 MW	11.56 AW	25050 AAW	NCBLS	10//99-12//99
	Raleigh-Durham-Chapel Hill MSA, NC	S	13.22 MW	12.10 AW	27500 AAW	NCBLS	10//99-12//99
	North Dakota	S	14.43 MW	13.11 AW	27270 AAW	NDBLS	10//99-12//99
	Grand Forks MSA, ND-MN	S	12.61 MW	12.02 AW	26230 AAW	NDBLS	10//99-12//99
	Ohio	S	14.47 MW	14.23 AW	29590 AAW	OHBLS	10//99-12//99
	Akron PMSA, OH	S	16.19 MW	16.94 AW	33670 AAW	OHBLS	10//99-12//99
	Canton-Massillon MSA, OH	S	13.39 MW	14.81 AW	27840 AAW	OHBLS	10//99-12//99
	Cincinnati PMSA, OH-KY-IN	S	12.38 MW	11.30 AW	25740 AAW	OHBLS	10//99-12//99
	Cleveland-Lorain-Elyria PMSA, OH	S	15.05 MW	16.34 AW	31300 AAW	OHBLS	10//99-12//99
	Columbus MSA, OH	S	15.73 MW	17.03 AW	32720 AAW	OHBLS	10//99-12//99
	Dayton-Springfield MSA, OH	S	14.39 MW	14.55 AW	29920 AAW	OHBLS	10//99-12//99
	Hamilton-Middletown PMSA, OH	S	11.60 MW	10.54 AW	24120 AAW	OHBLS	10//99-12//99
	Mansfield MSA, OH	S	14.51 MW	14.72 AW	30190 AAW	OHBLS	10//99-12//99
	Steubenville-Weirton MSA, OH-WV	S	14.19 MW	14.44 AW	29520 AAW	OHBLS	10//99-12//99
	Toledo MSA, OH	S	12.79 MW	11.80 AW	26610 AAW	OHBLS	10//99-12//99
	Youngstown-Warren MSA, OH	S	11.81 MW	10.99 AW	24560 AAW	OHBLS	10//99-12//99
	Oklahoma	S	14.76 MW	14.93 AW	31040 AAW	OKBLS	10//99-12//99
	Tulsa MSA, OK	S	14.75 MW	15.04 AW	30670 AAW	OKBLS	10//99-12//99
	Oregon	S	18.49 MW	18.05 AW	37550 AAW	ORBLS	10//99-12//99
	Portland-Vancouver PMSA, OR-WA	S	20.03 MW	19.49 AW	41660 AAW	ORBLS	10//99-12//99
	Salem PMSA, OR	S	16.86 MW	18.03 AW	35070 AAW	ORBLS	10//99-12//99
	Pennsylvania	S	16.08 MW	16.46 AW	34240 AAW	PABLS	10//99-12//99
	Harrisburg-Lebanon-Carlisle MSA, PA	S	16.16 MW	16.60 AW	33610 AAW	PABLS	10//99-12//99
	Philadelphia PMSA, PA-NJ	S	15.34 MW	15.11 AW	31910 AAW	PABLS	10//99-12//99
	Scranton--Wilkes-Barre-- Hazleton MSA, PA	S	16.75 MW	17.96 AW	34830 AAW	PABLS	10//99-12//99
	Sharon MSA, PA	S	13.78 MW	15.50 AW	28650 AAW	PABLS	10//99-12//99
	York MSA, PA	S	16.05 MW	15.85 AW	33380 AAW	PABLS	10//99-12//99
	Rhode Island	S	18.28 MW	18.05 AW	37550 AAW	RIBLS	10//99-12//99
	Providence-Fall River- Warwick MSA, RI-MA	S	17.23 MW	17.84 AW	35830 AAW	RIBLS	10//99-12//99
	South Carolina	S	12.02 MW	12.50 AW	25990 AAW	SCBLS	10//99-12//99
	Charleston-North Charleston MSA, SC	S	12.32 MW	11.49 AW	25620 AAW	SCBLS	10//99-12//99
	Greenville-Spartanburg- Anderson MSA, SC	S	13.49 MW	13.30 AW	28050 AAW	SCBLS	10//99-12//99
	Myrtle Beach MSA, SC	S	10.13 MW	10.07 AW	21070 AAW	SCBLS	10//99-12//99
	South Dakota	S	12.59 MW	13.06 AW	27160 AAW	SDBLS	10//99-12//99
	Tennessee	S	15.11 MW	14.55 AW	30260 AAW	TNBLS	10//99-12//99
	Knoxville MSA, TN	S	14.17 MW	14.43 AW	29470 AAW	TNBLS	10//99-12//99
	Memphis MSA, TN-AR-MS	S	16.89 MW	18.17 AW	35140 AAW	MSBLS	10//99-12//99
	Nashville MSA, TN	S	15.42 MW	15.79 AW	32070 AAW	TNBLS	10//99-12//99
	Texas	S	16.63 MW	16.58 AW	34480 AAW	TXBLS	10//99-12//99
	Austin-San Marcos MSA, TX	S	13.51 MW	12.67 AW	28100 AAW	TXBLS	10//99-12//99
	Beaumont-Port Arthur MSA, TX	S	15.75 MW	15.82 AW	32750 AAW	TXBLS	10//99-12//99
	Brownsville-Harlingen-San Benito MSA, TX	S	10.28 MW	9.84 AW	21390 AAW	TXBLS	10//99-12//99
	Corpus Christi MSA, TX	S	17.55 MW	17.97 AW	36510 AAW	TXBLS	10//99-12//99
	Dallas PMSA, TX	S	19.59 MW	19.96 AW	40760 AAW	TXBLS	10//99-12//99
	El Paso MSA, TX	S	17.05 MW	17.48 AW	35460 AAW	TXBLS	10//99-12//99
	Fort Worth-Arlington PMSA, TX	S	18.24 MW	18.45 AW	37930 AAW	TXBLS	10//99-12//99
	Galveston-Texas City PMSA, TX	S	11.22 MW	10.10 AW	23330 AAW	TXBLS	10//99-12//99
	Houston PMSA, TX	S	17.58 MW	18.28 AW	36570 AAW	TXBLS	10//99-12//99
	Killeen-Temple MSA, TX	S	12.49 MW	12.53 AW	25980 AAW	TXBLS	10//99-12//99

AAW Average annual wage	**AOH** Average offered, high	**ASH** Average starting, high	**H** Hourly	**M** Monthly	**S** Special: hourly and annual
AE Average entry wage	**AOL** Average offered, low	**ASL** Average starting, low	**HI** Highest wage paid	**MTC** Median total compensation	**TQ** Third quartile wage
AEX Average experienced wage	**APH** Average pay, high range	**AW** Average wage paid	**HR** High end range	**MW** Median wage paid	**W** Weekly
AO Average offered	**APL** Average pay, low range	**FQ** First quartile wage	**LR** Low end range	**SQ** Second quartile wage	**Y** Yearly

Occupation/Type/Industry	Location	Per	Low	Mid	High	Source	Date
Fire Fighter	McAllen-Edinburg-Mission MSA, TX	S	10.95 ᴍᴡ	10.35 ᴀᴡ	22790 ᴀᴀᴡ	TXBLS	10//99-12//99
	Utah	S	10.25 ᴍᴡ	11.63 ᴀᴡ	24190 ᴀᴀᴡ	UTBLS	10//99-12//99
	Provo-Orem MSA, UT	S	8.19 ᴍᴡ	7.23 ᴀᴡ	17040 ᴀᴀᴡ	UTBLS	10//99-12//99
	Salt Lake City-Ogden MSA, UT	S	13.99 ᴍᴡ	13.04 ᴀᴡ	29110 ᴀᴀᴡ	UTBLS	10//99-12//99
	Vermont	S	10.64 ᴍᴡ	11.03 ᴀᴡ	22940 ᴀᴀᴡ	VTBLS	10//99-12//99
	Burlington MSA, VT	S	11.01 ᴍᴡ	10.72 ᴀᴡ	22900 ᴀᴀᴡ	VTBLS	10//99-12//99
	Virginia	S	15.04 ᴍᴡ	15.71 ᴀᴡ	32670 ᴀᴀᴡ	VABLS	10//99-12//99
	Charlottesville MSA, VA	S	15.77 ᴍᴡ	15.52 ᴀᴡ	32800 ᴀᴀᴡ	VABLS	10//99-12//99
	Norfolk-Virginia Beach-Newport News MSA, VA-NC	S	14.28 ᴍᴡ	14.18 ᴀᴡ	29710 ᴀᴀᴡ	VABLS	10//99-12//99
	Richmond-Petersburg MSA, VA	S	15.17 ᴍᴡ	14.74 ᴀᴡ	31550 ᴀᴀᴡ	VABLS	10//99-12//99
	Roanoke MSA, VA	S	14.29 ᴍᴡ	14.27 ᴀᴡ	29730 ᴀᴀᴡ	VABLS	10//99-12//99
	Washington	S	17.37 ᴍᴡ	17.93 ᴀᴡ	37290 ᴀᴀᴡ	WABLS	10//99-12//99
	Bellingham MSA, WA	S	20.82 ᴍᴡ	20.85 ᴀᴡ	43300 ᴀᴀᴡ	WABLS	10//99-12//99
	Bremerton PMSA, WA	S	17.90 ᴍᴡ	15.62 ᴀᴡ	37240 ᴀᴀᴡ	WABLS	10//99-12//99
	Olympia PMSA, WA	S	20.63 ᴍᴡ	19.37 ᴀᴡ	42900 ᴀᴀᴡ	WABLS	10//99-12//99
	Richland-Kennewick-Pasco MSA, WA	S	21.10 ᴍᴡ	21.95 ᴀᴡ	43890 ᴀᴀᴡ	WABLS	10//99-12//99
	Seattle-Bellevue-Everett PMSA, WA	S	19.27 ᴍᴡ	19.80 ᴀᴡ	40080 ᴀᴀᴡ	WABLS	10//99-12//99
	Spokane MSA, WA	S	18.78 ᴍᴡ	20.09 ᴀᴡ	39050 ᴀᴀᴡ	WABLS	10//99-12//99
	Tacoma PMSA, WA	S	22.00 ᴍᴡ	21.51 ᴀᴡ	45750 ᴀᴀᴡ	WABLS	10//99-12//99
	Yakima MSA, WA	S	15.35 ᴍᴡ	16.89 ᴀᴡ	31930 ᴀᴀᴡ	WABLS	10//99-12//99
	West Virginia	S	13.32 ᴍᴡ	13.23 ᴀᴡ	27520 ᴀᴀᴡ	WVBLS	10//99-12//99
	Huntington-Ashland MSA, WV-KY-OH	S	12.26 ᴍᴡ	12.13 ᴀᴡ	25490 ᴀᴀᴡ	WVBLS	10//99-12//99
	Parkersburg-Marietta MSA, WV-OH	S	12.60 ᴍᴡ	12.66 ᴀᴡ	26200 ᴀᴀᴡ	WVBLS	10//99-12//99
	Wisconsin	S	14.13 ᴍᴡ	14.88 ᴀᴡ	30950 ᴀᴀᴡ	WIBLS	10//99-12//99
	Appleton-Oshkosh-Neenah MSA, WI	S	12.02 ᴍᴡ	11.79 ᴀᴡ	25000 ᴀᴀᴡ	WIBLS	10//99-12//99
	Janesville-Beloit MSA, WI	S	13.00 ᴍᴡ	11.00 ᴀᴡ	27040 ᴀᴀᴡ	WIBLS	10//99-12//99
	Kenosha PMSA, WI	S	15.25 ᴍᴡ	14.53 ᴀᴡ	31710 ᴀᴀᴡ	WIBLS	10//99-12//99
	La Crosse MSA, WI-MN	S	9.82 ᴍᴡ	9.96 ᴀᴡ	20430 ᴀᴀᴡ	WIBLS	10//99-12//99
	Milwaukee-Waukesha PMSA, WI	S	17.26 ᴍᴡ	16.13 ᴀᴡ	35900 ᴀᴀᴡ	WIBLS	10//99-12//99
	Racine PMSA, WI	S	15.64 ᴍᴡ	12.90 ᴀᴡ	32540 ᴀᴀᴡ	WIBLS	10//99-12//99
	Wausau MSA, WI	S	12.23 ᴍᴡ	12.73 ᴀᴡ	25440 ᴀᴀᴡ	WIBLS	10//99-12//99
	Wyoming	S	14.57 ᴍᴡ	14.73 ᴀᴡ	30640 ᴀᴀᴡ	WYBLS	10//99-12//99
	Cheyenne MSA, WY	S	11.95 ᴍᴡ	11.64 ᴀᴡ	24860 ᴀᴀᴡ	WYBLS	10//99-12//99
Fire Inspector	United States	H		18.48 ᴀᴡ		NCS98	1998
Fire Inspector and Investigator	Alabama	S	15.89 ᴍᴡ	16.31 ᴀᴡ	33920 ᴀᴀᴡ	ALBLS	10//99-12//99
	Alaska	S	30.71 ᴍᴡ	30.45 ᴀᴡ	63350 ᴀᴀᴡ	AKBLS	10//99-12//99
	Arizona	S	19.37 ᴍᴡ	20.17 ᴀᴡ	41950 ᴀᴀᴡ	AZBLS	10//99-12//99
	Phoenix-Mesa MSA, AZ	S	20.92 ᴍᴡ	20.10 ᴀᴡ	43510 ᴀᴀᴡ	AZBLS	10//99-12//99
	Tucson MSA, AZ	S	18.54 ᴍᴡ	17.83 ᴀᴡ	38560 ᴀᴀᴡ	AZBLS	10//99-12//99
	California	S	28.58 ᴍᴡ	28.14 ᴀᴡ	58520 ᴀᴀᴡ	CABLS	10//99-12//99
	Los Angeles-Long Beach PMSA, CA	S	27.29 ᴍᴡ	27.24 ᴀᴡ	56750 ᴀᴀᴡ	CABLS	10//99-12//99
	Oakland PMSA, CA	S	30.71 ᴍᴡ	31.27 ᴀᴡ	63880 ᴀᴀᴡ	CABLS	10//99-12//99
	Riverside-San Bernardino PMSA, CA	S	26.00 ᴍᴡ	26.65 ᴀᴡ	54080 ᴀᴀᴡ	CABLS	10//99-12//99
	San Francisco PMSA, CA	S	33.36 ᴍᴡ	33.81 ᴀᴡ	69390 ᴀᴀᴡ	CABLS	10//99-12//99
	San Jose PMSA, CA	S	35.01 ᴍᴡ	37.10 ᴀᴡ	72820 ᴀᴀᴡ	CABLS	10//99-12//99
	Connecticut	S	21.79 ᴍᴡ	21.30 ᴀᴡ	44290 ᴀᴀᴡ	CTBLS	10//99-12//99
	Bridgeport PMSA, CT	S	19.47 ᴍᴡ	22.45 ᴀᴡ	40510 ᴀᴀᴡ	CTBLS	10//99-12//99
	Hartford MSA, CT	S	22.23 ᴍᴡ	21.40 ᴀᴡ	46240 ᴀᴀᴡ	CTBLS	10//99-12//99
	New Haven-Meriden PMSA, CT	S	19.17 ᴍᴡ	21.63 ᴀᴡ	39880 ᴀᴀᴡ	CTBLS	10//99-12//99
	New London-Norwich MSA, CT-RI	S	17.19 ᴍᴡ	18.08 ᴀᴡ	35750 ᴀᴀᴡ	CTBLS	10//99-12//99
	Stamford-Norwalk PMSA, CT	S	26.52 ᴍᴡ	28.32 ᴀᴡ	55160 ᴀᴀᴡ	CTBLS	10//99-12//99
	Florida	S	18.12 ᴍᴡ	19.26 ᴀᴡ	40060 ᴀᴀᴡ	FLBLS	10//99-12//99
	Daytona Beach MSA, FL	S	14.93 ᴍᴡ	14.74 ᴀᴡ	31060 ᴀᴀᴡ	FLBLS	10//99-12//99
	Fort Lauderdale PMSA, FL	S	24.65 ᴍᴡ	23.52 ᴀᴡ	51280 ᴀᴀᴡ	FLBLS	10//99-12//99
	Lakeland-Winter Haven MSA, FL	S	16.05 ᴍᴡ	16.59 ᴀᴡ	33380 ᴀᴀᴡ	FLBLS	10//99-12//99

AAW Average annual wage	**AOH** Average offered, high	**ASH** Average starting, high	**H** Hourly	**M** Monthly	**S** Special: hourly and annual
AE Average entry wage	**AOL** Average offered, low	**ASL** Average starting, low	**HI** Highest wage paid	**MTC** Median total compensation	**TQ** Third quartile wage
AEX Average experienced wage	**APH** Average pay, high range	**AW** Average wage paid	**HR** High end range	**MW** Median wage paid	**W** Weekly
AO Average offered	**APL** Average pay, low range	**FQ** First quartile wage	**LR** Low end range	**SQ** Second quartile wage	**Y** Yearly

Occupation/Type/Industry	Location	Per	Low	Mid	High	Source	Date
Fire Inspector and Investigator	Melbourne-Titusville-Palm Bay MSA, FL	S	20.30 MW	18.89 AW	42220 AAW	FLBLS	10//99-12//99
	Orlando MSA, FL	S	17.69 MW	18.07 AW	36790 AAW	FLBLS	10//99-12//99
	Tampa-St. Petersburg-Clearwater MSA, FL	S	17.42 MW	16.75 AW	36230 AAW	FLBLS	10//99-12//99
	Georgia	S	15.88 MW	16.48 AW	34280 AAW	GABLS	10//99-12//99
	Atlanta MSA, GA	S	18.26 MW	18.05 AW	37970 AAW	GABLS	10//99-12//99
	Illinois	S	20.56 MW	21.82 AW	45380 AAW	ILBLS	10//99-12//99
	Indiana	S	15.57 MW	16.01 AW	33300 AAW	INBLS	10//99-12//99
	Indianapolis MSA, IN	S	15.49 MW	15.08 AW	32210 AAW	INBLS	10//99-12//99
	Iowa	S	19.26 MW	19.91 AW	41410 AAW	IABLS	10//99-12//99
	Kansas	S	18.24 MW	18.75 AW	39000 AAW	KSBLS	10//99-12//99
	Kentucky	S	15.64 MW	16.19 AW	33680 AAW	KYBLS	10//99-12//99
	Louisiana	S	12.5 MW	13.20 AW	27460 AAW	LABLS	10//99-12//99
	Lafayette MSA, LA	S	12.21 MW	12.18 AW	25410 AAW	LABLS	10//99-12//99
	Maryland	S	26.15 MW	25.70 AW	53450 AAW	MDBLS	10//99-12//99
	Massachusetts	S	17.04 MW	16.90 AW	35150 AAW	MABLS	10//99-12//99
	Boston PMSA, MA-NH	S	18.07 MW	17.72 AW	37580 AAW	MABLS	10//99-12//99
	Michigan	S	20.99 MW	21.22 AW	44140 AAW	MIBLS	10//99-12//99
	Detroit PMSA, MI	S	22.71 MW	22.59 AW	47240 AAW	MIBLS	10//99-12//99
	Saginaw-Bay City-Midland MSA, MI	S	19.00 MW	20.99 AW	39520 AAW	MIBLS	10//99-12//99
	Minnesota	S	20.73 MW	20.47 AW	42580 AAW	MNBLS	10//99-12//99
	Minneapolis-St. Paul MSA, MN-WI	S	20.23 MW	20.93 AW	42080 AAW	MNBLS	10//99-12//99
	Mississippi	S	19.71 MW	18.24 AW	37940 AAW	MSBLS	10//99-12//99
	Missouri	S	20.47 MW	19.94 AW	41480 AAW	MOBLS	10//99-12//99
	St. Louis MSA, MO-IL	S	21.92 MW	21.75 AW	45600 AAW	MOBLS	10//99-12//99
	Montana	S	15.36 MW	15.51 AW	32270 AAW	MTBLS	10//99-12//99
	Nevada	S	24.61 MW	24.85 AW	51690 AAW	NVBLS	10//99-12//99
	New Hampshire	S	19.41 MW	19.58 AW	40720 AAW	NHBLS	10//99-12//99
	New Jersey	S	16.6 MW	19.57 AW	40700 AAW	NJBLS	10//99-12//99
	Bergen-Passaic PMSA, NJ	S	19.61 MW	20.25 AW	40790 AAW	NJBLS	10//99-12//99
	Middlesex-Somerset-Hunterdon PMSA, NJ	S	17.81 MW	15.90 AW	37050 AAW	NJBLS	10//99-12//99
	Monmouth-Ocean PMSA, NJ	S	15.80 MW	17.08 AW	32860 AAW	NJBLS	10//99-12//99
	Newark PMSA, NJ	S	21.81 MW	16.22 AW	45370 AAW	NJBLS	10//99-12//99
	Trenton PMSA, NJ	S	18.77 MW	16.28 AW	39050 AAW	NJBLS	10//99-12//99
	New Mexico	S	17.46 MW	16.75 AW	34840 AAW	NMBLS	10//99-12//99
	New York	S	17.53 MW	18.30 AW	38060 AAW	NYBLS	10//99-12//99
	Nassau-Suffolk PMSA, NY	S	18.75 MW	16.46 AW	39000 AAW	NYBLS	10//99-12//99
	New York PMSA, NY	S	19.31 MW	20.19 AW	40160 AAW	NYBLS	10//99-12//99
	Rochester MSA, NY	S	15.62 MW	15.17 AW	32490 AAW	NYBLS	10//99-12//99
	Syracuse MSA, NY	S	19.45 MW	18.16 AW	40450 AAW	NYBLS	10//99-12//99
	North Carolina	S	15.87 MW	16.22 AW	33740 AAW	NCBLS	10//99-12//99
	Charlotte-Gastonia-Rock Hill MSA, NC-SC	S	18.92 MW	18.64 AW	39360 AAW	NCBLS	10//99-12//99
	Greensboro--Winston-Salem--High Point MSA, NC	S	15.20 MW	15.32 AW	31620 AAW	NCBLS	10//99-12//99
	Raleigh-Durham-Chapel Hill MSA, NC	S	17.10 MW	16.81 AW	35570 AAW	NCBLS	10//99-12//99
	Ohio	S	20.35 MW	19.65 AW	40880 AAW	OHBLS	10//99-12//99
	Cincinnati PMSA, OH-KY-IN	S	19.80 MW	21.53 AW	41180 AAW	OHBLS	10//99-12//99
	Cleveland-Lorain-Elyria PMSA, OH	S	20.68 MW	21.03 AW	43010 AAW	OHBLS	10//99-12//99
	Oklahoma	S	10.3 MW	12.80 AW	26620 AAW	OKBLS	10//99-12//99
	Oregon	S	28.25 MW	27.67 AW	57550 AAW	ORBLS	10//99-12//99
	Pennsylvania	S	20.16 MW	19.42 AW	40400 AAW	PABLS	10//99-12//99
	Philadelphia PMSA, PA-NJ	S	20.59 MW	20.03 AW	42830 AAW	PABLS	10//99-12//99
	Pittsburgh MSA, PA	S	17.25 MW	18.51 AW	35870 AAW	PABLS	10//99-12//99
	Rhode Island	S	19.24 MW	19.54 AW	40640 AAW	RIBLS	10//99-12//99
	Providence-Fall River-Warwick MSA, RI-MA	S	19.44 MW	19.13 AW	40440 AAW	RIBLS	10//99-12//99
	South Carolina	S	16.12 MW	15.73 AW	32720 AAW	SCBLS	10//99-12//99
	Charleston-North Charleston MSA, SC	S	14.43 MW	12.69 AW	30010 AAW	SCBLS	10//99-12//99
	Greenville-Spartanburg-Anderson MSA, SC	S	14.31 MW	13.50 AW	29760 AAW	SCBLS	10//99-12//99
	Tennessee	S	16.95 MW	17.80 AW	37020 AAW	TNBLS	10//99-12//99
	Nashville MSA, TN	S	18.06 MW	18.44 AW	37550 AAW	TNBLS	10//99-12//99
	Texas	S	19.71 MW	19.90 AW	41400 AAW	TXBLS	10//99-12//99
	Dallas PMSA, TX	S	23.46 MW	23.77 AW	48800 AAW	TXBLS	10//99-12//99

AAW	Average annual wage	AOH	Average offered, high	ASH	Average starting, high
AE	Average entry wage	AOL	Average offered, low	ASL	Average starting, low
AEX	Average experienced wage	APH	Average pay, high range	AW	Average wage paid
AO	Average offered	APL	Average pay, low range	FQ	First quartile wage

H	Hourly
HI	Highest wage paid
HR	High end range
LR	Low end range

M	Monthly
MTC	Median total compensation
MW	Median wage paid
SQ	Second quartile wage

S	Special: hourly and annual
TQ	Third quartile wage
W	Weekly
Y	Yearly

Occupation/Type/Industry	Location	Per	Low	Mid	High	Source	Date
Fire Inspector and Investigator	Fort Worth-Arlington PMSA, TX	S	22.58 MW	22.83 AW	46980 AAW	TXBLS	10//99-12//99
	Houston PMSA, TX	S	19.19 MW	19.26 AW	39920 AAW	TXBLS	10//99-12//99
	Utah	S	19.7 MW	19.29 AW	40120 AAW	UTBLS	10//99-12//99
	Salt Lake City-Ogden MSA, UT	S	20.60 MW	20.28 AW	42850 AAW	UTBLS	10//99-12//99
	Virginia	S	18.93 MW	19.64 AW	40860 AAW	VABLS	10//99-12//99
	Norfolk-Virginia Beach-Newport News MSA, VA-NC	S	20.17 MW	19.45 AW	41960 AAW	VABLS	10//99-12//99
	Washington	S	26.3 MW	26.51 AW	55150 AAW	WABLS	10//99-12//99
	Seattle-Bellevue-Everett PMSA, WA	S	26.86 MW	26.48 AW	55860 AAW	WABLS	10//99-12//99
	West Virginia	S	13.18 MW	13.41 AW	27890 AAW	WVBLS	10//99-12//99
	Wisconsin	S	8.76 MW	11.84 AW	24640 AAW	WIBLS	10//99-12//99
	Appleton-Oshkosh-Neenah MSA, WI	S	11.02 MW	6.44 AW	22930 AAW	WIBLS	10//99-12//99
	Wyoming	S	16.62 MW	17.95 AW	37330 AAW	WYBLS	10//99-12//99
Firefighter	United States	H		15.54 AW		NCS98	1998
Supervisory	United States	H		20.00 AW		NCS98	1998
First-Line Supervisor/Manager							
Construction Trade and Extraction Workers	Alabama	S	18.76 MW	19.51 AW	40590 AAW	ALBLS	10//99-12//99
Construction Trade and Extraction Workers	Anniston MSA, AL	S	16.87 MW	16.18 AW	35090 AAW	ALBLS	10//99-12//99
Construction Trade and Extraction Workers	Auburn-Opelika MSA, AL	S	14.11 MW	13.20 AW	29340 AAW	ALBLS	10//99-12//99
Construction Trade and Extraction Workers	Birmingham MSA, AL	S	23.09 MW	21.28 AW	48020 AAW	ALBLS	10//99-12//99
Construction Trade and Extraction Workers	Decatur MSA, AL	S	17.90 MW	17.70 AW	37230 AAW	ALBLS	10//99-12//99
Construction Trade and Extraction Workers	Dothan MSA, AL	S	12.81 MW	12.01 AW	26640 AAW	ALBLS	10//99-12//99
Construction Trade and Extraction Workers	Florence MSA, AL	S	17.01 MW	17.35 AW	35380 AAW	ALBLS	10//99-12//99
Construction Trade and Extraction Workers	Gadsden MSA, AL	S	14.47 MW	13.85 AW	30100 AAW	ALBLS	10//99-12//99
Construction Trade and Extraction Workers	Huntsville MSA, AL	S	18.73 MW	18.26 AW	38950 AAW	ALBLS	10//99-12//99
Construction Trade and Extraction Workers	Mobile MSA, AL	S	19.19 MW	18.63 AW	39910 AAW	ALBLS	10//99-12//99
Construction Trade and Extraction Workers	Montgomery MSA, AL	S	19.46 MW	19.77 AW	40490 AAW	ALBLS	10//99-12//99
Construction Trade and Extraction Workers	Tuscaloosa MSA, AL	S	19.21 MW	19.18 AW	39960 AAW	ALBLS	10//99-12//99
Construction Trade and Extraction Workers	Alaska	S	27.87 MW	28.57 AW	59430 AAW	AKBLS	10//99-12//99
Construction Trade and Extraction Workers	Anchorage MSA, AK	S	30.49 MW	30.45 AW	63410 AAW	AKBLS	10//99-12//99
Construction Trade and Extraction Workers	Arizona	S	20.38 MW	21.46 AW	44640 AAW	AZBLS	10//99-12//99
Construction Trade and Extraction Workers	Flagstaff MSA, AZ-UT	S	18.35 MW	16.98 AW	38160 AAW	AZBLS	10//99-12//99
Construction Trade and Extraction Workers	Phoenix-Mesa MSA, AZ	S	21.84 MW	20.75 AW	45430 AAW	AZBLS	10//99-12//99
Construction Trade and Extraction Workers	Tucson MSA, AZ	S	21.00 MW	20.04 AW	43680 AAW	AZBLS	10//99-12//99
Construction Trade and Extraction Workers	Yuma MSA, AZ	S	17.07 MW	16.46 AW	35520 AAW	AZBLS	10//99-12//99
Construction Trade and Extraction Workers	Arkansas	S	15.17 MW	15.96 AW	33210 AAW	ARBLS	10//99-12//99
Construction Trade and Extraction Workers	Fayetteville-Springdale-Rogers MSA, AR	S	17.37 MW	16.69 AW	36130 AAW	ARBLS	10//99-12//99
Construction Trade and Extraction Workers	Fort Smith MSA, AR-OK	S	16.22 MW	14.98 AW	33740 AAW	ARBLS	10//99-12//99
Construction Trade and Extraction Workers	Jonesboro MSA, AR	S	16.33 MW	13.11 AW	33970 AAW	ARBLS	10//99-12//99
Construction Trade and Extraction Workers	Little Rock-North Little Rock MSA, AR	S	17.18 MW	16.28 AW	35740 AAW	ARBLS	10//99-12//99
Construction Trade and Extraction Workers	Pine Bluff MSA, AR	S	17.22 MW	16.66 AW	35810 AAW	ARBLS	10//99-12//99
Construction Trade and Extraction Workers	California	S	25.36 MW	25.85 AW	53770 AAW	CABLS	10//99-12//99
Construction Trade and Extraction Workers	Bakersfield MSA, CA	S	21.45 MW	21.30 AW	44620 AAW	CABLS	10//99-12//99
Construction Trade and Extraction Workers	Chico-Paradise MSA, CA	S	24.01 MW	24.76 AW	49940 AAW	CABLS	10//99-12//99
Construction Trade and Extraction Workers	Fresno MSA, CA	S	22.99 MW	23.21 AW	47820 AAW	CABLS	10//99-12//99
Construction Trade and Extraction Workers	Los Angeles-Long Beach PMSA, CA	S	24.80 MW	24.41 AW	51580 AAW	CABLS	10//99-12//99
Construction Trade and Extraction Workers	Merced MSA, CA	S	22.78 MW	21.27 AW	47380 AAW	CABLS	10//99-12//99
Construction Trade and Extraction Workers	Modesto MSA, CA	S	22.91 MW	22.11 AW	47650 AAW	CABLS	10//99-12//99
Construction Trade and Extraction Workers	Oakland PMSA, CA	S	28.43 MW	27.57 AW	59130 AAW	CABLS	10//99-12//99
Construction Trade and Extraction Workers	Orange County PMSA, CA	S	26.28 MW	26.36 AW	54660 AAW	CABLS	10//99-12//99
Construction Trade and Extraction Workers	Redding MSA, CA	S	21.90 MW	22.11 AW	45560 AAW	CABLS	10//99-12//99
Construction Trade and Extraction Workers	Riverside-San Bernardino PMSA, CA	S	23.66 MW	23.72 AW	49220 AAW	CABLS	10//99-12//99
Construction Trade and Extraction Workers	Sacramento PMSA, CA	S	26.57 MW	25.66 AW	55270 AAW	CABLS	10//99-12//99
Construction Trade and Extraction Workers	Salinas MSA, CA	S	25.40 MW	25.75 AW	52840 AAW	CABLS	10//99-12//99
Construction Trade and Extraction Workers	San Diego MSA, CA	S	27.02 MW	27.13 AW	56190 AAW	CABLS	10//99-12//99
Construction Trade and Extraction Workers	San Francisco PMSA, CA	S	31.55 MW	31.32 AW	65620 AAW	CABLS	10//99-12//99
Construction Trade and Extraction Workers	San Jose PMSA, CA	S	28.11 MW	27.35 AW	58470 AAW	CABLS	10//99-12//99
Construction Trade and Extraction Workers	San Luis Obispo-Atascadero-Paso Robles MSA, CA	S	24.54 MW	24.82 AW	51050 AAW	CABLS	10//99-12//99
Construction Trade and Extraction Workers	Santa Barbara-Santa Maria-Lompoc MSA, CA	S	25.05 MW	24.28 AW	52110 AAW	CABLS	10//99-12//99

AAW Average annual wage	AOH Average offered, high	ASH Average starting, high	H Hourly	M Monthly	S Special: hourly and annual
AE Average entry wage	AOL Average offered, low	ASL Average starting, low	HI Highest wage paid	MTC Median total compensation	TQ Third quartile wage
AEX Average experienced wage	APH Average pay, high range	AW Average wage paid	HR High end range	MW Median wage paid	W Weekly
AO Average offered	APL Average pay, low range	FQ First quartile wage	LR Low end range	SQ Second quartile wage	Y Yearly

Occupation/Type/Industry	Location	Per	Low	Mid	High	Source	Date
First-Line Supervisor/Manager							
Construction Trade and Extraction Workers	Santa Cruz-Watsonville PMSA, CA	S	21.28 MW	20.87 AW	44250 AAW	CABLS	10//99-12//99
Construction Trade and Extraction Workers	Santa Rosa PMSA, CA	S	24.51 MW	23.09 AW	50980 AAW	CABLS	10//99-12//99
Construction Trade and Extraction Workers	Stockton-Lodi MSA, CA	S	22.79 MW	21.27 AW	47410 AAW	CABLS	10//99-12//99
Construction Trade and Extraction Workers	Vallejo-Fairfield-Napa PMSA, CA	S	26.17 MW	25.92 AW	54420 AAW	CABLS	10//99-12//99
Construction Trade and Extraction Workers	Ventura PMSA, CA	S	26.26 MW	26.31 AW	54630 AAW	CABLS	10//99-12//99
Construction Trade and Extraction Workers	Visalia-Tulare-Porterville MSA, CA	S	18.42 MW	18.75 AW	38320 AAW	CABLS	10//99-12//99
Construction Trade and Extraction Workers	Yolo PMSA, CA	S	20.52 MW	18.56 AW	42680 AAW	CABLS	10//99-12//99
Construction Trade and Extraction Workers	Yuba City MSA, CA	S	20.88 MW	19.59 AW	43420 AAW	CABLS	10//99-12//99
Construction Trade and Extraction Workers	Colorado	S	20.03 MW	20.82 AW	43310 AAW	COBLS	10//99-12//99
Construction Trade and Extraction Workers	Boulder-Longmont PMSA, CO	S	21.27 MW	19.77 AW	44230 AAW	COBLS	10//99-12//99
Construction Trade and Extraction Workers	Colorado Springs MSA, CO	S	18.63 MW	18.61 AW	38740 AAW	COBLS	10//99-12//99
Construction Trade and Extraction Workers	Denver PMSA, CO	S	21.15 MW	20.68 AW	43990 AAW	COBLS	10//99-12//99
Construction Trade and Extraction Workers	Fort Collins-Loveland MSA, CO	S	20.96 MW	19.80 AW	43590 AAW	COBLS	10//99-12//99
Construction Trade and Extraction Workers	Grand Junction MSA, CO	S	18.22 MW	17.66 AW	37890 AAW	COBLS	10//99-12//99
Construction Trade and Extraction Workers	Greeley PMSA, CO	S	21.84 MW	20.48 AW	45430 AAW	COBLS	10//99-12//99
Construction Trade and Extraction Workers	Pueblo MSA, CO	S	18.88 MW	18.63 AW	39260 AAW	COBLS	10//99-12//99
Construction Trade and Extraction Workers	Connecticut	S	23 MW	23.81 AW	49530 AAW	CTBLS	10//99-12//99
Construction Trade and Extraction Workers	Bridgeport PMSA, CT	S	25.77 MW	24.70 AW	53590 AAW	CTBLS	10//99-12//99
Construction Trade and Extraction Workers	Danbury PMSA, CT	S	23.09 MW	19.83 AW	48030 AAW	CTBLS	10//99-12//99
Construction Trade and Extraction Workers	Hartford MSA, CT	S	22.31 MW	22.21 AW	46400 AAW	CTBLS	10//99-12//99
Construction Trade and Extraction Workers	New Haven-Meriden PMSA, CT	S	25.01 MW	24.20 AW	52020 AAW	CTBLS	10//99-12//99
Construction Trade and Extraction Workers	New London-Norwich MSA, CT-RI	S	22.56 MW	22.26 AW	46920 AAW	CTBLS	10//99-12//99
Construction Trade and Extraction Workers	Stamford-Norwalk PMSA, CT	S	28.27 MW	25.25 AW	58790 AAW	CTBLS	10//99-12//99
Construction Trade and Extraction Workers	Waterbury PMSA, CT	S	20.97 MW	19.97 AW	43610 AAW	CTBLS	10//99-12//99
Construction Trade and Extraction Workers	Delaware	S	18.44 MW	19.50 AW	40570 AAW	DEBLS	10//99-12//99
Construction Trade and Extraction Workers	Dover MSA, DE	S	18.43 MW	17.53 AW	38330 AAW	DEBLS	10//99-12//99
Construction Trade and Extraction Workers	Wilmington-Newark PMSA, DE-MD	S	19.71 MW	19.07 AW	40990 AAW	DEBLS	10//99-12//99
Construction Trade and Extraction Workers	District of Columbia	S	25.61 MW	25.52 AW	53080 AAW	DCBLS	10//99-12//99
Construction Trade and Extraction Workers	Washington PMSA, DC-MD-VA-WV	S	21.97 MW	20.84 AW	45700 AAW	DCBLS	10//99-12//99
Construction Trade and Extraction Workers	Florida	S	17.75 MW	18.58 AW	38650 AAW	FLBLS	10//99-12//99
Construction Trade and Extraction Workers	Daytona Beach MSA, FL	S	16.67 MW	16.64 AW	34680 AAW	FLBLS	10//99-12//99
Construction Trade and Extraction Workers	Fort Lauderdale PMSA, FL	S	20.36 MW	20.05 AW	42360 AAW	FLBLS	10//99-12//99
Construction Trade and Extraction Workers	Fort Myers-Cape Coral MSA, FL	S	19.48 MW	19.03 AW	40510 AAW	FLBLS	10//99-12//99
Construction Trade and Extraction Workers	Fort Pierce-Port St. Lucie MSA, FL	S	15.72 MW	15.40 AW	32700 AAW	FLBLS	10//99-12//99
Construction Trade and Extraction Workers	Fort Walton Beach MSA, FL	S	16.56 MW	16.56 AW	34440 AAW	FLBLS	10//99-12//99
Construction Trade and Extraction Workers	Gainesville MSA, FL	S	14.31 MW	14.07 AW	29770 AAW	FLBLS	10//99-12//99
Construction Trade and Extraction Workers	Jacksonville MSA, FL	S	18.26 MW	18.13 AW	37970 AAW	FLBLS	10//99-12//99
Construction Trade and Extraction Workers	Lakeland-Winter Haven MSA, FL	S	17.89 MW	18.21 AW	37200 AAW	FLBLS	10//99-12//99
Construction Trade and Extraction Workers	Melbourne-Titusville-Palm Bay MSA, FL	S	18.36 MW	18.20 AW	38180 AAW	FLBLS	10//99-12//99
Construction Trade and Extraction Workers	Miami PMSA, FL	S	21.65 MW	20.01 AW	45040 AAW	FLBLS	10//99-12//99
Construction Trade and Extraction Workers	Naples MSA, FL	S	17.20 MW	17.62 AW	35770 AAW	FLBLS	10//99-12//99
Construction Trade and Extraction Workers	Ocala MSA, FL	S	13.20 MW	13.42 AW	27460 AAW	FLBLS	10//99-12//99
Construction Trade and Extraction Workers	Orlando MSA, FL	S	17.70 MW	16.96 AW	36820 AAW	FLBLS	10//99-12//99
Construction Trade and Extraction Workers	Panama City MSA, FL	S	16.05 MW	15.55 AW	33390 AAW	FLBLS	10//99-12//99
Construction Trade and Extraction Workers	Pensacola MSA, FL	S	16.48 MW	16.16 AW	34290 AAW	FLBLS	10//99-12//99
Construction Trade and Extraction Workers	Punta Gorda MSA, FL	S	16.67 MW	15.92 AW	34670 AAW	FLBLS	10//99-12//99
Construction Trade and Extraction Workers	Sarasota-Bradenton MSA, FL	S	20.00 MW	19.58 AW	41600 AAW	FLBLS	10//99-12//99
Construction Trade and Extraction Workers	Tallahassee MSA, FL	S	16.27 MW	15.67 AW	33840 AAW	FLBLS	10//99-12//99
Construction Trade and Extraction Workers	Tampa-St. Petersburg-Clearwater MSA, FL	S	18.52 MW	17.70 AW	38520 AAW	FLBLS	10//99-12//99
Construction Trade and Extraction Workers	West Palm Beach-Boca Raton MSA, FL	S	18.50 MW	18.24 AW	38480 AAW	FLBLS	10//99-12//99
Construction Trade and Extraction Workers	Georgia	S	19.19 MW	20.15 AW	41920 AAW	GABLS	10//99-12//99
Construction Trade and Extraction Workers	Albany MSA, GA	S	18.72 MW	18.51 AW	38940 AAW	GABLS	10//99-12//99
Construction Trade and Extraction Workers	Athens MSA, GA	S	18.39 MW	16.15 AW	38260 AAW	GABLS	10//99-12//99
Construction Trade and Extraction Workers	Atlanta MSA, GA	S	21.68 MW	20.46 AW	45090 AAW	GABLS	10//99-12//99
Construction Trade and Extraction Workers	Columbus MSA, GA-AL	S	17.64 MW	16.50 AW	36700 AAW	GABLS	10//99-12//99
Construction Trade and Extraction Workers	Macon MSA, GA	S	19.37 MW	18.66 AW	40280 AAW	GABLS	10//99-12//99
Construction Trade and Extraction Workers	Savannah MSA, GA	S	22.03 MW	22.49 AW	45830 AAW	GABLS	10//99-12//99

Occupation/Type/Industry	Location	Per	Low	Mid	High	Source	Date
First-Line Supervisor/Manager							
Construction Trade and Extraction Workers	Hawaii	S	23.97 MW	25.43 AW	52890 AAW	HIBLS	10//99-12//99
Construction Trade and Extraction Workers	Honolulu MSA, HI	S	25.54 MW	24.00 AW	53110 AAW	HIBLS	10//99-12//99
Construction Trade and Extraction Workers	Idaho	S	19.5 MW	20.45 AW	42530 AAW	IDBLS	10//99-12//99
Construction Trade and Extraction Workers	Boise City MSA, ID	S	19.96 MW	19.77 AW	41520 AAW	IDBLS	10//99-12//99
Construction Trade and Extraction Workers	Pocatello MSA, ID	S	15.76 MW	15.16 AW	32790 AAW	IDBLS	10//99-12//99
Construction Trade and Extraction Workers	Illinois	S	26.68 MW	26.47 AW	55050 AAW	ILBLS	10//99-12//99
Construction Trade and Extraction Workers	Bloomington-Normal MSA, IL	S	20.40 MW	20.97 AW	42440 AAW	ILBLS	10//99-12//99
Construction Trade and Extraction Workers	Champaign-Urbana MSA, IL	S	23.06 MW	24.34 AW	47950 AAW	ILBLS	10//99-12//99
Construction Trade and Extraction Workers	Chicago PMSA, IL	S	28.79 MW	29.23 AW	59880 AAW	ILBLS	10//99-12//99
Construction Trade and Extraction Workers	Decatur MSA, IL	S	22.55 MW	23.86 AW	46910 AAW	ILBLS	10//99-12//99
Construction Trade and Extraction Workers	Kankakee PMSA, IL	S	24.24 MW	22.89 AW	50430 AAW	ILBLS	10//99-12//99
Construction Trade and Extraction Workers	Peoria-Pekin MSA, IL	S	24.22 MW	24.34 AW	50380 AAW	ILBLS	10//99-12//99
Construction Trade and Extraction Workers	Rockford MSA, IL	S	24.86 MW	24.63 AW	51700 AAW	ILBLS	10//99-12//99
Construction Trade and Extraction Workers	Springfield MSA, IL	S	19.67 MW	21.62 AW	40920 AAW	ILBLS	10//99-12//99
Construction Trade and Extraction Workers	Indiana	S	20.17 MW	21.65 AW	45030 AAW	INBLS	10//99-12//99
Construction Trade and Extraction Workers	Bloomington MSA, IN	S	18.87 MW	18.21 AW	39260 AAW	INBLS	10//99-12//99
Construction Trade and Extraction Workers	Elkhart-Goshen MSA, IN	S	17.17 MW	15.88 AW	35720 AAW	INBLS	10//99-12//99
Construction Trade and Extraction Workers	Evansville-Henderson MSA, IN-KY	S	20.01 MW	17.10 AW	41620 AAW	INBLS	10//99-12//99
Construction Trade and Extraction Workers	Fort Wayne MSA, IN	S	21.56 MW	19.23 AW	44840 AAW	INBLS	10//99-12//99
Construction Trade and Extraction Workers	Gary PMSA, IN	S	26.63 MW	24.78 AW	55390 AAW	INBLS	10//99-12//99
Construction Trade and Extraction Workers	Indianapolis MSA, IN	S	21.88 MW	21.62 AW	45510 AAW	INBLS	10//99-12//99
Construction Trade and Extraction Workers	Kokomo MSA, IN	S	18.12 MW	16.20 AW	37680 AAW	INBLS	10//99-12//99
Construction Trade and Extraction Workers	Lafayette MSA, IN	S	17.08 MW	13.03 AW	35530 AAW	INBLS	10//99-12//99
Construction Trade and Extraction Workers	Muncie MSA, IN	S	19.23 MW	16.73 AW	40000 AAW	INBLS	10//99-12//99
Construction Trade and Extraction Workers	South Bend MSA, IN	S	38.79 MW	45.19 AW	80680 AAW	INBLS	10//99-12//99
Construction Trade and Extraction Workers	Terre Haute MSA, IN	S	14.90 MW	14.17 AW	30990 AAW	INBLS	10//99-12//99
Construction Trade and Extraction Workers	Iowa	S	18.55 MW	19.55 AW	40660 AAW	IABLS	10//99-12//99
Construction Trade and Extraction Workers	Cedar Rapids MSA, IA	S	24.45 MW	25.22 AW	50850 AAW	IABLS	10//99-12//99
Construction Trade and Extraction Workers	Davenport-Moline-Rock Island MSA, IA-IL	S	22.15 MW	20.40 AW	46070 AAW	IABLS	10//99-12//99
Construction Trade and Extraction Workers	Des Moines MSA, IA	S	22.42 MW	22.01 AW	46630 AAW	IABLS	10//99-12//99
Construction Trade and Extraction Workers	Dubuque MSA, IA	S	14.70 MW	10.50 AW	30570 AAW	IABLS	10//99-12//99
Construction Trade and Extraction Workers	Iowa City MSA, IA	S	17.09 MW	17.22 AW	35540 AAW	IABLS	10//99-12//99
Construction Trade and Extraction Workers	Sioux City MSA, IA-NE	S	18.94 MW	18.55 AW	39390 AAW	IABLS	10//99-12//99
Construction Trade and Extraction Workers	Waterloo-Cedar Falls MSA, IA	S	16.15 MW	15.82 AW	33600 AAW	IABLS	10//99-12//99
Construction Trade and Extraction Workers	Kansas	S	18.42 MW	19.13 AW	39800 AAW	KSBLS	10//99-12//99
Construction Trade and Extraction Workers	Lawrence MSA, KS	S	17.97 MW	17.39 AW	37380 AAW	KSBLS	10//99-12//99
Construction Trade and Extraction Workers	Topeka MSA, KS	S	18.46 MW	17.79 AW	38400 AAW	KSBLS	10//99-12//99
Construction Trade and Extraction Workers	Wichita MSA, KS	S	19.60 MW	19.37 AW	40770 AAW	KSBLS	10//99-12//99
Construction Trade and Extraction Workers	Kentucky	S	18.14 MW	18.65 AW	38800 AAW	KYBLS	10//99-12//99
Construction Trade and Extraction Workers	Lexington MSA, KY	S	20.16 MW	18.72 AW	41940 AAW	KYBLS	10//99-12//99
Construction Trade and Extraction Workers	Louisville MSA, KY-IN	S	20.44 MW	20.21 AW	42510 AAW	KYBLS	10//99-12//99
Construction Trade and Extraction Workers	Owensboro MSA, KY	S	15.95 MW	15.48 AW	33180 AAW	KYBLS	10//99-12//99
Construction Trade and Extraction Workers	Louisiana	S	17 MW	17.72 AW	36850 AAW	LABLS	10//99-12//99
Construction Trade and Extraction Workers	Alexandria MSA, LA	S	15.37 MW	13.35 AW	31960 AAW	LABLS	10//99-12//99
Construction Trade and Extraction Workers	Baton Rouge MSA, LA	S	19.29 MW	18.64 AW	40110 AAW	LABLS	10//99-12//99
Construction Trade and Extraction Workers	Houma MSA, LA	S	16.80 MW	17.47 AW	34950 AAW	LABLS	10//99-12//99
Construction Trade and Extraction Workers	Lafayette MSA, LA	S	18.05 MW	17.10 AW	37550 AAW	LABLS	10//99-12//99
Construction Trade and Extraction Workers	Lake Charles MSA, LA	S	18.61 MW	16.31 AW	38710 AAW	LABLS	10//99-12//99
Construction Trade and Extraction Workers	Monroe MSA, LA	S	14.34 MW	12.76 AW	29820 AAW	LABLS	10//99-12//99
Construction Trade and Extraction Workers	New Orleans MSA, LA	S	18.91 MW	18.00 AW	39330 AAW	LABLS	10//99-12//99
Construction Trade and Extraction Workers	Shreveport-Bossier City MSA, LA	S	14.07 MW	12.49 AW	29260 AAW	LABLS	10//99-12//99
Construction Trade and Extraction Workers	Maine	S	18.1 MW	18.19 AW	37830 AAW	MEBLS	10//99-12//99
Construction Trade and Extraction Workers	Bangor MSA, ME	S	18.61 MW	17.57 AW	38710 AAW	MEBLS	10//99-12//99
Construction Trade and Extraction Workers	Lewiston-Auburn MSA, ME	S	18.10 MW	18.90 AW	37650 AAW	MEBLS	10//99-12//99
Construction Trade and Extraction Workers	Portland MSA, ME	S	18.67 MW	17.99 AW	38840 AAW	MEBLS	10//99-12//99
Construction Trade and Extraction Workers	Maryland	S	20 MW	20.57 AW	42790 AAW	MDBLS	10//99-12//99
Construction Trade and Extraction Workers	Baltimore PMSA, MD	S	20.35 MW	19.90 AW	42330 AAW	MDBLS	10//99-12//99
Construction Trade and Extraction Workers	Cumberland MSA, MD-WV	S	17.62 MW	17.99 AW	36650 AAW	MDBLS	10//99-12//99
Construction Trade and Extraction Workers	Hagerstown PMSA, MD	S	16.16 MW	15.81 AW	33610 AAW	MDBLS	10//99-12//99
Construction Trade and Extraction Workers	Massachusetts	S	25.68 MW	26.30 AW	54700 AAW	MABLS	10//99-12//99
Construction Trade and Extraction Workers	Barnstable-Yarmouth MSA, MA	S	23.55 MW	23.27 AW	48980 AAW	MABLS	10//99-12//99
Construction Trade and Extraction Workers	Boston PMSA, MA-NH	S	27.68 MW	27.01 AW	57570 AAW	MABLS	10//99-12//99
Construction Trade and Extraction Workers	Brockton PMSA, MA	S	26.84 MW	25.75 AW	55830 AAW	MABLS	10//99-12//99
Construction Trade and Extraction Workers	Fitchburg-Leominster PMSA, MA	S	23.75 MW	23.26 AW	49400 AAW	MABLS	10//99-12//99
Construction Trade and Extraction Workers	Lawrence PMSA, MA-NH	S	25.29 MW	25.42 AW	52610 AAW	MABLS	10//99-12//99
Construction Trade and Extraction Workers	Lowell PMSA, MA-NH	S	21.52 MW	21.06 AW	44770 AAW	MABLS	10//99-12//99

581

Occupation/Type/Industry	Location	Per	Low	Mid	High	Source	Date
First-Line Supervisor/Manager							
Construction Trade and Extraction Workers	New Bedford PMSA, MA	S	27.10 MW	28.88 AW	56370 AAW	MABLS	10//99-12//99
Construction Trade and Extraction Workers	Pittsfield MSA, MA	S	22.79 MW	22.78 AW	47410 AAW	MABLS	10//99-12//99
Construction Trade and Extraction Workers	Springfield MSA, MA	S	23.91 MW	23.65 AW	49740 AAW	MABLS	10//99-12//99
Construction Trade and Extraction Workers	Worcester PMSA, MA-CT	S	24.65 MW	24.77 AW	51280 AAW	MABLS	10//99-12//99
Construction Trade and Extraction Workers	Michigan	S	23.01 MW	25.15 AW	52310 AAW	MIBLS	10//99-12//99
Construction Trade and Extraction Workers	Ann Arbor PMSA, MI	S	29.60 MW	28.34 AW	61580 AAW	MIBLS	10//99-12//99
Construction Trade and Extraction Workers	Benton Harbor MSA, MI	S	23.34 MW	19.96 AW	48540 AAW	MIBLS	10//99-12//99
Construction Trade and Extraction Workers	Detroit PMSA, MI	S	25.46 MW	23.60 AW	52950 AAW	MIBLS	10//99-12//99
Construction Trade and Extraction Workers	Flint PMSA, MI	S	23.94 MW	22.84 AW	49800 AAW	MIBLS	10//99-12//99
Construction Trade and Extraction Workers	Grand Rapids-Muskegon-Holland MSA, MI	S	26.41 MW	23.79 AW	54930 AAW	MIBLS	10//99-12//99
Construction Trade and Extraction Workers	Jackson MSA, MI	S	29.91 MW	24.55 AW	62210 AAW	MIBLS	10//99-12//99
Construction Trade and Extraction Workers	Kalamazoo-Battle Creek MSA, MI	S	24.91 MW	23.29 AW	51820 AAW	MIBLS	10//99-12//99
Construction Trade and Extraction Workers	Lansing-East Lansing MSA, MI	S	23.48 MW	23.22 AW	48850 AAW	MIBLS	10//99-12//99
Construction Trade and Extraction Workers	Saginaw-Bay City-Midland MSA, MI	S	25.34 MW	23.82 AW	52700 AAW	MIBLS	10//99-12//99
Construction Trade and Extraction Workers	Minnesota	S	24.73 MW	24.76 AW	51500 AAW	MNBLS	10//99-12//99
Construction Trade and Extraction Workers	Duluth-Superior MSA, MN-WI	S	22.39 MW	23.25 AW	46560 AAW	MNBLS	10//99-12//99
Construction Trade and Extraction Workers	Minneapolis-St. Paul MSA, MN-WI	S	27.13 MW	27.17 AW	56430 AAW	MNBLS	10//99-12//99
Construction Trade and Extraction Workers	Rochester MSA, MN	S	22.22 MW	21.68 AW	46210 AAW	MNBLS	10//99-12//99
Construction Trade and Extraction Workers	St. Cloud MSA, MN	S	22.33 MW	21.92 AW	46440 AAW	MNBLS	10//99-12//99
Construction Trade and Extraction Workers	Mississippi	S	17.86 MW	20.00 AW	41600 AAW	MSBLS	10//99-12//99
Construction Trade and Extraction Workers	Biloxi-Gulfport-Pascagoula MSA, MS	S	18.95 MW	18.77 AW	39420 AAW	MSBLS	10//99-12//99
Construction Trade and Extraction Workers	Hattiesburg MSA, MS	S	16.00 MW	15.42 AW	33280 AAW	MSBLS	10//99-12//99
Construction Trade and Extraction Workers	Jackson MSA, MS	S	26.84 MW	23.15 AW	55830 AAW	MSBLS	10//99-12//99
Construction Trade and Extraction Workers	Missouri	S	20.74 MW	21.81 AW	45370 AAW	MOBLS	10//99-12//99
Construction Trade and Extraction Workers	Columbia MSA, MO	S	19.82 MW	19.66 AW	41220 AAW	MOBLS	10//99-12//99
Construction Trade and Extraction Workers	Joplin MSA, MO	S	20.78 MW	19.24 AW	43220 AAW	MOBLS	10//99-12//99
Construction Trade and Extraction Workers	Kansas City MSA, MO-KS	S	23.04 MW	22.19 AW	47930 AAW	MOBLS	10//99-12//99
Construction Trade and Extraction Workers	St. Joseph MSA, MO	S	21.79 MW	22.13 AW	45320 AAW	MOBLS	10//99-12//99
Construction Trade and Extraction Workers	St. Louis MSA, MO-IL	S	23.79 MW	23.51 AW	49480 AAW	MOBLS	10//99-12//99
Construction Trade and Extraction Workers	Springfield MSA, MO	S	19.14 MW	19.11 AW	39810 AAW	MOBLS	10//99-12//99
Construction Trade and Extraction Workers	Montana	S	19.89 MW	20.29 AW	42210 AAW	MTBLS	10//99-12//99
Construction Trade and Extraction Workers	Billings MSA, MT	S	21.91 MW	22.88 AW	45570 AAW	MTBLS	10//99-12//99
Construction Trade and Extraction Workers	Great Falls MSA, MT	S	20.05 MW	19.69 AW	41700 AAW	MTBLS	10//99-12//99
Construction Trade and Extraction Workers	Missoula MSA, MT	S	18.24 MW	18.49 AW	37940 AAW	MTBLS	10//99-12//99
Construction Trade and Extraction Workers	Nebraska	S	18.16 MW	19.06 AW	39650 AAW	NEBLS	10//99-12//99
Construction Trade and Extraction Workers	Lincoln MSA, NE	S	20.12 MW	18.90 AW	41860 AAW	NEBLS	10//99-12//99
Construction Trade and Extraction Workers	Omaha MSA, NE-IA	S	20.58 MW	19.32 AW	42810 AAW	NEBLS	10//99-12//99
Construction Trade and Extraction Workers	Nevada	S	22.68 MW	23.07 AW	47990 AAW	NVBLS	10//99-12//99
Construction Trade and Extraction Workers	Las Vegas MSA, NV-AZ	S	22.82 MW	22.38 AW	47470 AAW	NVBLS	10//99-12//99
Construction Trade and Extraction Workers	Reno MSA, NV	S	22.30 MW	22.04 AW	46380 AAW	NVBLS	10//99-12//99
Construction Trade and Extraction Workers	New Hampshire	S	17.62 MW	18.49 AW	38450 AAW	NHBLS	10//99-12//99
Construction Trade and Extraction Workers	Manchester PMSA, NH	S	20.75 MW	20.45 AW	43150 AAW	NHBLS	10//99-12//99
Construction Trade and Extraction Workers	Nashua PMSA, NH	S	18.97 MW	18.42 AW	39450 AAW	NHBLS	10//99-12//99
Construction Trade and Extraction Workers	Portsmouth-Rochester PMSA, NH-ME	S	17.83 MW	17.56 AW	37080 AAW	NHBLS	10//99-12//99
Construction Trade and Extraction Workers	New Jersey	S	27.38 MW	28.47 AW	59210 AAW	NJBLS	10//99-12//99
Construction Trade and Extraction Workers	Atlantic-Cape May PMSA, NJ	S	28.65 MW	29.78 AW	59600 AAW	NJBLS	10//99-12//99
Construction Trade and Extraction Workers	Bergen-Passaic PMSA, NJ	S	32.81 MW	34.81 AW	68230 AAW	NJBLS	10//99-12//99
Construction Trade and Extraction Workers	Jersey City PMSA, NJ	S	28.84 MW	25.41 AW	59980 AAW	NJBLS	10//99-12//99
Construction Trade and Extraction Workers	Middlesex-Somerset-Hunterdon PMSA, NJ	S	26.93 MW	24.84 AW	56020 AAW	NJBLS	10//99-12//99
Construction Trade and Extraction Workers	Monmouth-Ocean PMSA, NJ	S	26.75 MW	25.84 AW	55630 AAW	NJBLS	10//99-12//99
Construction Trade and Extraction Workers	Newark PMSA, NJ	S	29.87 MW	28.61 AW	62130 AAW	NJBLS	10//99-12//99
Construction Trade and Extraction Workers	Trenton PMSA, NJ	S	26.60 MW	23.89 AW	55320 AAW	NJBLS	10//99-12//99
Construction Trade and Extraction Workers	New Mexico	S	19.53 MW	19.73 AW	41040 AAW	NMBLS	10//99-12//99
Construction Trade and Extraction Workers	Albuquerque MSA, NM	S	18.97 MW	18.60 AW	39460 AAW	NMBLS	10//99-12//99
Construction Trade and Extraction Workers	Las Cruces MSA, NM	S	16.97 MW	16.25 AW	35310 AAW	NMBLS	10//99-12//99
Construction Trade and Extraction Workers	Santa Fe MSA, NM	S	18.58 MW	16.94 AW	38640 AAW	NMBLS	10//99-12//99
Construction Trade and Extraction Workers	New York	S	25.52 MW	27.67 AW	57550 AAW	NYBLS	10//99-12//99
Construction Trade and Extraction Workers	Albany-Schenectady-Troy MSA, NY	S	23.12 MW	21.03 AW	48080 AAW	NYBLS	10//99-12//99
Construction Trade and Extraction Workers	Binghamton MSA, NY	S	20.15 MW	19.12 AW	41920 AAW	NYBLS	10//99-12//99
Construction Trade and Extraction Workers	Buffalo-Niagara Falls MSA, NY	S	23.16 MW	22.98 AW	48160 AAW	NYBLS	10//99-12//99
Construction Trade and Extraction Workers	Dutchess County PMSA, NY	S	17.39 MW	15.35 AW	36170 AAW	NYBLS	10//99-12//99
Construction Trade and Extraction Workers	Elmira MSA, NY	S	31.91 MW	24.69 AW	66360 AAW	NYBLS	10//99-12//99

AAW Average annual wage	**AOH** Average offered, high	**ASH** Average starting, high	**H** Hourly	**M** Monthly	**S** Special: hourly and annual
AE Average entry wage	**AOL** Average offered, low	**ASL** Average starting, low	**HI** Highest wage paid	**MTC** Median total compensation	**TQ** Third quartile wage
AEX Average experienced wage	**APH** Average pay, high range	**AW** Average wage paid	**HR** High end range	**MW** Median wage paid	**W** Weekly
AO Average offered	**APL** Average pay, low range	**FQ** First quartile wage	**LR** Low end range	**SQ** Second quartile wage	**Y** Yearly

Occupation/Type/Industry	Location	Per	Low	Mid	High	Source	Date

First-Line Supervisor/Manager

Occupation/Type/Industry	Location	Per	Low	Mid	High	Source	Date
Construction Trade and Extraction Workers	Glens Falls MSA, NY	S	18.21 MW	18.00 AW	37880 AAW	NYBLS	10//99-12//99
Construction Trade and Extraction Workers	Jamestown MSA, NY	S	23.08 MW	21.46 AW	48010 AAW	NYBLS	10//99-12//99
Construction Trade and Extraction Workers	Nassau-Suffolk PMSA, NY	S	29.42 MW	26.01 AW	61200 AAW	NYBLS	10//99-12//99
Construction Trade and Extraction Workers	New York PMSA, NY	S	32.60 MW	33.76 AW	67810 AAW	NYBLS	10//99-12//99
Construction Trade and Extraction Workers	Newburgh PMSA, NY-PA	S	26.19 MW	26.90 AW	54470 AAW	NYBLS	10//99-12//99
Construction Trade and Extraction Workers	Rochester MSA, NY	S	25.05 MW	22.97 AW	52100 AAW	NYBLS	10//99-12//99
Construction Trade and Extraction Workers	Syracuse MSA, NY	S	23.43 MW	22.97 AW	48740 AAW	NYBLS	10//99-12//99
Construction Trade and Extraction Workers	Utica-Rome MSA, NY	S	18.15 MW	15.58 AW	37760 AAW	NYBLS	10//99-12//99
Construction Trade and Extraction Workers	North Carolina	S	18 MW	19.40 AW	40350 AAW	NCBLS	10//99-12//99
Construction Trade and Extraction Workers	Asheville MSA, NC	S	19.60 MW	19.83 AW	40760 AAW	NCBLS	10//99-12//99
Construction Trade and Extraction Workers	Charlotte-Gastonia-Rock Hill MSA, NC-SC	S	23.56 MW	22.27 AW	49010 AAW	NCBLS	10//99-12//99
Construction Trade and Extraction Workers	Fayetteville MSA, NC	S	14.38 MW	14.08 AW	29900 AAW	NCBLS	10//99-12//99
Construction Trade and Extraction Workers	Goldsboro MSA, NC	S	17.41 MW	16.25 AW	36210 AAW	NCBLS	10//99-12//99
Construction Trade and Extraction Workers	Greensboro--Winston-Salem--High Point MSA, NC	S	18.78 MW	17.79 AW	39070 AAW	NCBLS	10//99-12//99
Construction Trade and Extraction Workers	Greenville MSA, NC	S	16.77 MW	16.14 AW	34880 AAW	NCBLS	10//99-12//99
Construction Trade and Extraction Workers	Hickory-Morganton-Lenoir MSA, NC	S	19.25 MW	17.22 AW	40030 AAW	NCBLS	10//99-12//99
Construction Trade and Extraction Workers	Jacksonville MSA, NC	S	16.15 MW	14.34 AW	33590 AAW	NCBLS	10//99-12//99
Construction Trade and Extraction Workers	Raleigh-Durham-Chapel Hill MSA, NC	S	18.39 MW	18.01 AW	38260 AAW	NCBLS	10//99-12//99
Construction Trade and Extraction Workers	Rocky Mount MSA, NC	S	18.79 MW	18.58 AW	39090 AAW	NCBLS	10//99-12//99
Construction Trade and Extraction Workers	Wilmington MSA, NC	S	15.66 MW	15.16 AW	32560 AAW	NCBLS	10//99-12//99
Construction Trade and Extraction Workers	North Dakota	S	16.96 MW	17.78 AW	36990 AAW	NDBLS	10//99-12//99
Construction Trade and Extraction Workers	Bismarck MSA, ND	S	19.11 MW	16.22 AW	39750 AAW	NDBLS	10//99-12//99
Construction Trade and Extraction Workers	Fargo-Moorhead MSA, ND-MN	S	17.03 MW	16.29 AW	35430 AAW	NDBLS	10//99-12//99
Construction Trade and Extraction Workers	Grand Forks MSA, ND-MN	S	18.42 MW	16.95 AW	38320 AAW	NDBLS	10//99-12//99
Construction Trade and Extraction Workers	Ohio	S	21.37 MW	21.54 AW	44810 AAW	OHBLS	10//99-12//99
Construction Trade and Extraction Workers	Akron PMSA, OH	S	19.94 MW	19.21 AW	41480 AAW	OHBLS	10//99-12//99
Construction Trade and Extraction Workers	Canton-Massillon MSA, OH	S	21.29 MW	22.66 AW	44280 AAW	OHBLS	10//99-12//99
Construction Trade and Extraction Workers	Cincinnati PMSA, OH-KY-IN	S	21.02 MW	20.40 AW	43710 AAW	OHBLS	10//99-12//99
Construction Trade and Extraction Workers	Cleveland-Lorain-Elyria PMSA, OH	S	22.96 MW	22.85 AW	47760 AAW	OHBLS	10//99-12//99
Construction Trade and Extraction Workers	Columbus MSA, OH	S	20.59 MW	20.24 AW	42830 AAW	OHBLS	10//99-12//99
Construction Trade and Extraction Workers	Dayton-Springfield MSA, OH	S	21.19 MW	20.50 AW	44080 AAW	OHBLS	10//99-12//99
Construction Trade and Extraction Workers	Hamilton-Middletown PMSA, OH	S	21.80 MW	21.56 AW	45330 AAW	OHBLS	10//99-12//99
Construction Trade and Extraction Workers	Lima MSA, OH	S	18.34 MW	16.78 AW	38150 AAW	OHBLS	10//99-12//99
Construction Trade and Extraction Workers	Mansfield MSA, OH	S	21.70 MW	20.29 AW	45130 AAW	OHBLS	10//99-12//99
Construction Trade and Extraction Workers	Steubenville-Weirton MSA, OH-WV	S	20.63 MW	20.19 AW	42910 AAW	OHBLS	10//99-12//99
Construction Trade and Extraction Workers	Toledo MSA, OH	S	22.32 MW	22.61 AW	46420 AAW	OHBLS	10//99-12//99
Construction Trade and Extraction Workers	Youngstown-Warren MSA, OH	S	21.15 MW	20.23 AW	44000 AAW	OHBLS	10//99-12//99
Construction Trade and Extraction Workers	Oklahoma	S	18.65 MW	18.74 AW	38990 AAW	OKBLS	10//99-12//99
Construction Trade and Extraction Workers	Enid MSA, OK	S	20.19 MW	20.49 AW	41990 AAW	OKBLS	10//99-12//99
Construction Trade and Extraction Workers	Lawton MSA, OK	S	17.61 MW	17.43 AW	36620 AAW	OKBLS	10//99-12//99
Construction Trade and Extraction Workers	Oklahoma City MSA, OK	S	19.24 MW	19.03 AW	40010 AAW	OKBLS	10//99-12//99
Construction Trade and Extraction Workers	Tulsa MSA, OK	S	18.95 MW	18.96 AW	39420 AAW	OKBLS	10//99-12//99
Construction Trade and Extraction Workers	Oregon	S	23.83 MW	24.57 AW	51110 AAW	ORBLS	10//99-12//99
Construction Trade and Extraction Workers	Corvallis MSA, OR	S	22.42 MW	21.64 AW	46640 AAW	ORBLS	10//99-12//99
Construction Trade and Extraction Workers	Eugene-Springfield MSA, OR	S	21.97 MW	22.64 AW	45710 AAW	ORBLS	10//99-12//99
Construction Trade and Extraction Workers	Medford-Ashland MSA, OR	S	31.22 MW	33.31 AW	64940 AAW	ORBLS	10//99-12//99
Construction Trade and Extraction Workers	Portland-Vancouver PMSA, OR-WA	S	26.79 MW	25.22 AW	55730 AAW	ORBLS	10//99-12//99
Construction Trade and Extraction Workers	Salem PMSA, OR	S	23.86 MW	23.34 AW	49620 AAW	ORBLS	10//99-12//99
Construction Trade and Extraction Workers	Pennsylvania	S	20.47 MW	21.62 AW	44980 AAW	PABLS	10//99-12//99
Construction Trade and Extraction Workers	Allentown-Bethlehem-Easton MSA, PA	S	18.96 MW	17.83 AW	39440 AAW	PABLS	10//99-12//99
Construction Trade and Extraction Workers	Altoona MSA, PA	S	13.27 MW	10.72 AW	27590 AAW	PABLS	10//99-12//99
Construction Trade and Extraction Workers	Erie MSA, PA	S	23.01 MW	23.72 AW	47850 AAW	PABLS	10//99-12//99
Construction Trade and Extraction Workers	Harrisburg-Lebanon-Carlisle MSA, PA	S	24.54 MW	23.47 AW	51050 AAW	PABLS	10//99-12//99
Construction Trade and Extraction Workers	Johnstown MSA, PA	S	19.98 MW	19.42 AW	41550 AAW	PABLS	10//99-12//99
Construction Trade and Extraction Workers	Lancaster MSA, PA	S	20.95 MW	22.07 AW	43580 AAW	PABLS	10//99-12//99
Construction Trade and Extraction Workers	Philadelphia PMSA, PA-NJ	S	22.52 MW	20.55 AW	46830 AAW	PABLS	10//99-12//99
Construction Trade and Extraction Workers	Pittsburgh MSA, PA	S	23.80 MW	22.42 AW	49500 AAW	PABLS	10//99-12//99
Construction Trade and Extraction Workers	Reading MSA, PA	S	20.68 MW	19.79 AW	43020 AAW	PABLS	10//99-12//99
Construction Trade and Extraction Workers	Scranton--Wilkes-Barre--Hazleton MSA, PA	S	18.39 MW	17.64 AW	38240 AAW	PABLS	10//99-12//99

AAW Average annual wage	**AOH** Average offered, high	**ASH** Average starting, high	**H** Hourly	**M** Monthly	**S** Special: hourly and annual
AE Average entry wage	**AOL** Average offered, low	**ASL** Average starting, low	**HI** Highest wage paid	**MTC** Median total compensation	**TQ** Third quartile wage
AEX Average experienced wage	**APH** Average pay, high range	**AW** Average wage paid	**HR** High end range	**MW** Median wage paid	**W** Weekly
AO Average offered	**APL** Average pay, low range	**FQ** First quartile wage	**LR** Low end range	**SQ** Second quartile wage	**Y** Yearly

Occupation/Type/Industry	Location	Per	Low	Mid	High	Source	Date

First-Line Supervisor/Manager

Occupation/Type/Industry	Location	Per	Low	Mid	High	Source	Date
Construction Trade and Extraction Workers	Sharon MSA, PA	S	20.80 MW	19.29 AW	43270 AAW	PABLS	10//99-12//99
Construction Trade and Extraction Workers	State College MSA, PA	S	18.04 MW	17.31 AW	37520 AAW	PABLS	10//99-12//99
Construction Trade and Extraction Workers	Williamsport MSA, PA	S	18.19 MW	16.71 AW	37840 AAW	PABLS	10//99-12//99
Construction Trade and Extraction Workers	York MSA, PA	S	23.06 MW	21.52 AW	47960 AAW	PABLS	10//99-12//99
Construction Trade and Extraction Workers	Rhode Island	S	24.42 MW	25.51 AW	53070 AAW	RIBLS	10//99-12//99
Construction Trade and Extraction Workers	Providence-Fall River-Warwick MSA, RI-MA	S	25.55 MW	24.38 AW	53130 AAW	RIBLS	10//99-12//99
Construction Trade and Extraction Workers	South Carolina	S	17.76 MW	19.15 AW	39830 AAW	SCBLS	10//99-12//99
Construction Trade and Extraction Workers	Charleston-North Charleston MSA, SC	S	17.97 MW	16.95 AW	37370 AAW	SCBLS	10//99-12//99
Construction Trade and Extraction Workers	Columbia MSA, SC	S	16.74 MW	16.94 AW	34820 AAW	SCBLS	10//99-12//99
Construction Trade and Extraction Workers	Florence MSA, SC	S	17.89 MW	16.55 AW	37220 AAW	SCBLS	10//99-12//99
Construction Trade and Extraction Workers	Greenville-Spartanburg-Anderson MSA, SC	S	17.71 MW	16.48 AW	36830 AAW	SCBLS	10//99-12//99
Construction Trade and Extraction Workers	Myrtle Beach MSA, SC	S	15.76 MW	15.58 AW	32780 AAW	SCBLS	10//99-12//99
Construction Trade and Extraction Workers	Sumter MSA, SC	S	16.17 MW	14.79 AW	33640 AAW	SCBLS	10//99-12//99
Construction Trade and Extraction Workers	South Dakota	S	18.01 MW	18.65 AW	38790 AAW	SDBLS	10//99-12//99
Construction Trade and Extraction Workers	Rapid City MSA, SD	S	19.55 MW	19.26 AW	40670 AAW	SDBLS	10//99-12//99
Construction Trade and Extraction Workers	Sioux Falls MSA, SD	S	19.44 MW	19.02 AW	40440 AAW	SDBLS	10//99-12//99
Construction Trade and Extraction Workers	Tennessee	S	18.29 MW	19.23 AW	40000 AAW	TNBLS	10//99-12//99
Construction Trade and Extraction Workers	Chattanooga MSA, TN-GA	S	17.46 MW	16.53 AW	36320 AAW	TNBLS	10//99-12//99
Construction Trade and Extraction Workers	Clarksville-Hopkinsville MSA, TN-KY	S	16.28 MW	15.51 AW	33860 AAW	TNBLS	10//99-12//99
Construction Trade and Extraction Workers	Jackson MSA, TN	S	20.00 MW	20.10 AW	41590 AAW	TNBLS	10//99-12//99
Construction Trade and Extraction Workers	Johnson City-Kingsport-Bristol MSA, TN-VA	S	17.98 MW	17.74 AW	37400 AAW	TNBLS	10//99-12//99
Construction Trade and Extraction Workers	Knoxville MSA, TN	S	19.68 MW	19.17 AW	40940 AAW	TNBLS	10//99-12//99
Construction Trade and Extraction Workers	Memphis MSA, TN-AR-MS	S	19.81 MW	19.35 AW	41210 AAW	MSBLS	10//99-12//99
Construction Trade and Extraction Workers	Nashville MSA, TN	S	20.98 MW	19.20 AW	43640 AAW	TNBLS	10//99-12//99
Construction Trade and Extraction Workers	Texas	S	18.94 MW	19.92 AW	41430 AAW	TXBLS	10//99-12//99
Construction Trade and Extraction Workers	Abilene MSA, TX	S	21.90 MW	22.70 AW	45540 AAW	TXBLS	10//99-12//99
Construction Trade and Extraction Workers	Amarillo MSA, TX	S	18.13 MW	16.21 AW	37720 AAW	TXBLS	10//99-12//99
Construction Trade and Extraction Workers	Austin-San Marcos MSA, TX	S	19.60 MW	19.51 AW	40760 AAW	TXBLS	10//99-12//99
Construction Trade and Extraction Workers	Beaumont-Port Arthur MSA, TX	S	18.74 MW	18.25 AW	38980 AAW	TXBLS	10//99-12//99
Construction Trade and Extraction Workers	Brazoria PMSA, TX	S	17.23 MW	17.85 AW	35830 AAW	TXBLS	10//99-12//99
Construction Trade and Extraction Workers	Brownsville-Harlingen-San Benito MSA, TX	S	11.20 MW	10.12 AW	23300 AAW	TXBLS	10//99-12//99
Construction Trade and Extraction Workers	Bryan-College Station MSA, TX	S	20.91 MW	21.04 AW	43500 AAW	TXBLS	10//99-12//99
Construction Trade and Extraction Workers	Corpus Christi MSA, TX	S	16.80 MW	15.36 AW	34940 AAW	TXBLS	10//99-12//99
Construction Trade and Extraction Workers	Dallas PMSA, TX	S	19.62 MW	19.17 AW	40820 AAW	TXBLS	10//99-12//99
Construction Trade and Extraction Workers	El Paso MSA, TX	S	18.89 MW	17.61 AW	39290 AAW	TXBLS	10//99-12//99
Construction Trade and Extraction Workers	Fort Worth-Arlington PMSA, TX	S	21.98 MW	20.62 AW	45710 AAW	TXBLS	10//99-12//99
Construction Trade and Extraction Workers	Galveston-Texas City PMSA, TX	S	19.32 MW	19.09 AW	40180 AAW	TXBLS	10//99-12//99
Construction Trade and Extraction Workers	Houston PMSA, TX	S	21.20 MW	19.46 AW	44100 AAW	TXBLS	10//99-12//99
Construction Trade and Extraction Workers	Killeen-Temple MSA, TX	S	17.04 MW	15.88 AW	35440 AAW	TXBLS	10//99-12//99
Construction Trade and Extraction Workers	Laredo MSA, TX	S	15.80 MW	12.74 AW	32870 AAW	TXBLS	10//99-12//99
Construction Trade and Extraction Workers	Longview-Marshall MSA, TX	S	20.07 MW	19.06 AW	41750 AAW	TXBLS	10//99-12//99
Construction Trade and Extraction Workers	Lubbock MSA, TX	S	18.44 MW	16.51 AW	38360 AAW	TXBLS	10//99-12//99
Construction Trade and Extraction Workers	McAllen-Edinburg-Mission MSA, TX	S	16.62 MW	17.44 AW	34560 AAW	TXBLS	10//99-12//99
Construction Trade and Extraction Workers	Odessa-Midland MSA, TX	S	20.30 MW	20.44 AW	42230 AAW	TXBLS	10//99-12//99
Construction Trade and Extraction Workers	San Angelo MSA, TX	S	16.29 MW	15.13 AW	33890 AAW	TXBLS	10//99-12//99
Construction Trade and Extraction Workers	San Antonio MSA, TX	S	16.71 MW	15.53 AW	34760 AAW	TXBLS	10//99-12//99
Construction Trade and Extraction Workers	Sherman-Denison MSA, TX	S	15.46 MW	15.47 AW	32150 AAW	TXBLS	10//99-12//99
Construction Trade and Extraction Workers	Texarkana MSA, TX-Texarkana, AR	S	14.97 MW	13.98 AW	31140 AAW	TXBLS	10//99-12//99
Construction Trade and Extraction Workers	Tyler MSA, TX	S	17.69 MW	18.11 AW	36780 AAW	TXBLS	10//99-12//99
Construction Trade and Extraction Workers	Victoria MSA, TX	S	15.66 MW	13.86 AW	32560 AAW	TXBLS	10//99-12//99
Construction Trade and Extraction Workers	Waco MSA, TX	S	17.79 MW	16.68 AW	37010 AAW	TXBLS	10//99-12//99
Construction Trade and Extraction Workers	Wichita Falls MSA, TX	S	18.18 MW	16.72 AW	37810 AAW	TXBLS	10//99-12//99
Construction Trade and Extraction Workers	Utah	S	18.4 MW	19.35 AW	40250 AAW	UTBLS	10//99-12//99
Construction Trade and Extraction Workers	Provo-Orem MSA, UT	S	19.50 MW	19.61 AW	40570 AAW	UTBLS	10//99-12//99
Construction Trade and Extraction Workers	Salt Lake City-Ogden MSA, UT	S	19.80 MW	18.94 AW	41190 AAW	UTBLS	10//99-12//99
Construction Trade and Extraction Workers	Vermont	S	19.84 MW	21.31 AW	44320 AAW	VTBLS	10//99-12//99
Construction Trade and Extraction Workers	Burlington MSA, VT	S	21.83 MW	19.56 AW	45410 AAW	VTBLS	10//99-12//99
Construction Trade and Extraction Workers	Virginia	S	19.4 MW	20.29 AW	42210 AAW	VABLS	10//99-12//99

Occupation/Type/Industry	Location	Per	Low	Mid	High	Source	Date
First-Line Supervisor/Manager							
Construction Trade and Extraction Workers	Charlottesville MSA, VA	S	15.07 MW	14.76 AW	31350 AAW	VABLS	10//99-12//99
Construction Trade and Extraction Workers	Danville MSA, VA	S	16.30 MW	15.42 AW	33900 AAW	VABLS	10//99-12//99
Construction Trade and Extraction Workers	Lynchburg MSA, VA	S	16.43 MW	15.63 AW	34170 AAW	VABLS	10//99-12//99
Construction Trade and Extraction Workers	Norfolk-Virginia Beach-Newport News MSA, VA-NC	S	20.47 MW	19.84 AW	42570 AAW	VABLS	10//99-12//99
Construction Trade and Extraction Workers	Richmond-Petersburg MSA, VA	S	20.81 MW	20.02 AW	43290 AAW	VABLS	10//99-12//99
Construction Trade and Extraction Workers	Roanoke MSA, VA	S	17.21 MW	16.64 AW	35800 AAW	VABLS	10//99-12//99
Construction Trade and Extraction Workers	Washington	S	23.71 MW	25.20 AW	52420 AAW	WABLS	10//99-12//99
Construction Trade and Extraction Workers	Bellingham MSA, WA	S	24.80 MW	23.34 AW	51580 AAW	WABLS	10//99-12//99
Construction Trade and Extraction Workers	Olympia PMSA, WA	S	25.00 MW	22.65 AW	52000 AAW	WABLS	10//99-12//99
Construction Trade and Extraction Workers	Richland-Kennewick-Pasco MSA, WA	S	21.32 MW	20.67 AW	44350 AAW	WABLS	10//99-12//99
Construction Trade and Extraction Workers	Seattle-Bellevue-Everett PMSA, WA	S	25.95 MW	24.76 AW	53980 AAW	WABLS	10//99-12//99
Construction Trade and Extraction Workers	Spokane MSA, WA	S	22.81 MW	22.74 AW	47430 AAW	WABLS	10//99-12//99
Construction Trade and Extraction Workers	Tacoma PMSA, WA	S	27.29 MW	25.38 AW	56770 AAW	WABLS	10//99-12//99
Construction Trade and Extraction Workers	Yakima MSA, WA	S	20.51 MW	19.78 AW	42650 AAW	WABLS	10//99-12//99
Construction Trade and Extraction Workers	West Virginia	S	22.25 MW	21.12 AW	43940 AAW	WVBLS	10//99-12//99
Construction Trade and Extraction Workers	Charleston MSA, WV	S	20.91 MW	20.78 AW	43500 AAW	WVBLS	10//99-12//99
Construction Trade and Extraction Workers	Huntington-Ashland MSA, WV-KY-OH	S	18.83 MW	18.08 AW	39170 AAW	WVBLS	10//99-12//99
Construction Trade and Extraction Workers	Parkersburg-Marietta MSA, WV-OH	S	19.09 MW	19.70 AW	39700 AAW	WVBLS	10//99-12//99
Construction Trade and Extraction Workers	Wheeling MSA, WV-OH	S	19.40 MW	16.28 AW	40360 AAW	WVBLS	10//99-12//99
Construction Trade and Extraction Workers	Wisconsin	S	22.83 MW	22.83 AW	47490 AAW	WIBLS	10//99-12//99
Construction Trade and Extraction Workers	Appleton-Oshkosh-Neenah MSA, WI	S	21.82 MW	21.46 AW	45380 AAW	WIBLS	10//99-12//99
Construction Trade and Extraction Workers	Eau Claire MSA, WI	S	22.26 MW	22.77 AW	46310 AAW	WIBLS	10//99-12//99
Construction Trade and Extraction Workers	Green Bay MSA, WI	S	19.30 MW	19.35 AW	40140 AAW	WIBLS	10//99-12//99
Construction Trade and Extraction Workers	Janesville-Beloit MSA, WI	S	21.04 MW	20.60 AW	43760 AAW	WIBLS	10//99-12//99
Construction Trade and Extraction Workers	Kenosha PMSA, WI	S	21.57 MW	20.64 AW	44860 AAW	WIBLS	.10//99-12//99
Construction Trade and Extraction Workers	La Crosse MSA, WI-MN	S	18.06 MW	14.72 AW	37560 AAW	WIBLS	10//99-12//99
Construction Trade and Extraction Workers	Madison MSA, WI	S	22.99 MW	23.50 AW	47810 AAW	WIBLS	10//99-12//99
Construction Trade and Extraction Workers	Milwaukee-Waukesha PMSA, WI	S	25.37 MW	24.69 AW	52770 AAW	WIBLS	10//99-12//99
Construction Trade and Extraction Workers	Racine PMSA, WI	S	20.50 MW	20.99 AW	42640 AAW	WIBLS	10//99-12//99
Construction Trade and Extraction Workers	Sheboygan MSA, WI	S	16.94 MW	15.91 AW	35230 AAW	WIBLS	10//99-12//99
Construction Trade and Extraction Workers	Wausau MSA, WI	S	19.68 MW	20.73 AW	40930 AAW	WIBLS	10//99-12//99
Construction Trade and Extraction Workers	Wyoming	S	18.63 MW	19.89 AW	41370 AAW	WYBLS	10//99-12//99
Construction Trade and Extraction Workers	Casper MSA, WY	S	19.53 MW	19.08 AW	40620 AAW	WYBLS	10//99-12//99
Construction Trade and Extraction Workers	Cheyenne MSA, WY	S	17.63 MW	17.43 AW	36660 AAW	WYBLS	10//99-12//99
Construction Trade and Extraction Workers	Puerto Rico	S	10.14 MW	10.41 AW	21650 AAW	PRBLS	10//99-12//99
Construction Trade and Extraction Workers	Aguadilla MSA, PR	S	8.12 MW	8.55 AW	16900 AAW	PRBLS	10//99-12//99
Construction Trade and Extraction Workers	Arecibo PMSA, PR	S	7.65 MW	7.72 AW	15910 AAW	PRBLS	10//99-12//99
Construction Trade and Extraction Workers	Caguas PMSA, PR	S	10.34 MW	10.10 AW	21500 AAW	PRBLS	10//99-12//99
Construction Trade and Extraction Workers	Mayaguez MSA, PR	S	9.08 MW	9.12 AW	18880 AAW	PRBLS	10//99-12//99
Construction Trade and Extraction Workers	Ponce MSA, PR	S	8.28 MW	7.97 AW	17220 AAW	PRBLS	10//99-12//99
Construction Trade and Extraction Workers	San Juan-Bayamon PMSA, PR	S	10.95 MW	10.79 AW	22770 AAW	PRBLS	10//99-12//99
Construction Trade and Extraction Workers	Virgin Islands	S	17.51 MW	17.87 AW	37170 AAW	VIBLS	10//99-12//99
Construction Trade and Extraction Workers	Guam	S	13.3 MW	14.77 AW	30720 AAW	GUBLS	10//99-12//99
Correctional Officers	Alabama	S	15.36 MW	15.82 AW	32910 AAW	ALBLS	10//99-12//99
Correctional Officers	Alaska	S	30.42 MW	30.69 AW	63840 AAW	AKBLS	10//99-12//99
Correctional Officers	Arkansas	S	20 MW	19.61 AW	40800 AAW	ARBLS	10//99-12//99
Correctional Officers	California	S	30.12 MW	29.44 AW	61220 AAW	CABLS	10//99-12//99
Correctional Officers	Florida	S	18.22 MW	18.99 AW	39500 AAW	FLBLS	10//99-12//99
Correctional Officers	Jacksonville MSA, FL	S	20.30 MW	19.93 AW	42220 AAW	FLBLS	10//99-12//99
Correctional Officers	Sarasota-Bradenton MSA, FL	S	20.32 MW	20.34 AW	42260 AAW	FLBLS	10//99-12//99
Correctional Officers	Tampa-St. Petersburg-Clearwater MSA, FL	S	16.84 MW	16.61 AW	35020 AAW	FLBLS	10//99-12//99
Correctional Officers	West Palm Beach-Boca Raton MSA, FL	S	27.60 MW	29.74 AW	57410 AAW	FLBLS	10//99-12//99
Correctional Officers	Georgia	S	14.7 MW	15.48 AW	32190 AAW	GABLS	10//99-12//99
Correctional Officers	Atlanta MSA, GA	S	18.01 MW	17.91 AW	37460 AAW	GABLS	10//99-12//99
Correctional Officers	Illinois	S	24.23 MW	24.31 AW	50560 AAW	ILBLS	10//99-12//99
Correctional Officers	Chicago PMSA, IL	S	24.67 MW	24.75 AW	51310 AAW	ILBLS	10//99-12//99
Correctional Officers	Iowa	S	19.64 MW	20.10 AW	41800 AAW	IABLS	10//99-12//99
Correctional Officers	Lexington MSA, KY	S	18.41 MW	17.68 AW	38290 AAW	KYBLS	10//99-12//99
Correctional Officers	Louisville MSA, KY-IN	S	15.66 MW	15.52 AW	32570 AAW	KYBLS	10//99-12//99
Correctional Officers	Maryland	S	28.03 MW	27.45 AW	57090 AAW	MDBLS	10//99-12//99

AAW Average annual wage	**AOH** Average offered, high	**ASH** Average starting, high	**H** Hourly	**M** Monthly	**S** Special: hourly and annual
AE Average entry wage	**AOL** Average offered, low	**ASL** Average starting, low	**HI** Highest wage paid	**MTC** Median total compensation	**TQ** Third quartile wage
AEX Average experienced wage	**APH** Average pay, high range	**AW** Average wage paid	**HR** High end range	**MW** Median wage paid	**W** Weekly
AO Average offered	**APL** Average pay, low range	**FQ** First quartile wage	**LR** Low end range	**SQ** Second quartile wage	**Y** Yearly

Occupation/Type/Industry	Location	Per	Low	Mid	High	Source	Date
First-Line Supervisor/Manager							
Correctional Officers	Baltimore PMSA, MD	S	27.69 MW	28.07 AW	57600 AAW	MDBLS	10//99-12//99
Correctional Officers	Massachusetts	S	23.7 MW	23.69 AW	49280 AAW	MABLS	10//99-12//99
Correctional Officers	Michigan	S	21.98 MW	22.19 AW	46160 AAW	MIBLS	10//99-12//99
Correctional Officers	Detroit PMSA, MI	S	22.40 MW	22.32 AW	46590 AAW	MIBLS	10//99-12//99
Correctional Officers	Minnesota	S	28.37 MW	26.06 AW	54210 AAW	MNBLS	10//99-12//99
Correctional Officers	Mississippi	S	12.99 MW	13.96 AW	29030 AAW	MSBLS	10//99-12//99
Correctional Officers	Kansas City MSA, MO-KS	S	20.04 MW	19.50 AW	41690 AAW	MOBLS	10//99-12//99
Correctional Officers	Omaha MSA, NE-IA	S	17.26 MW	18.01 AW	35910 AAW	NEBLS	10//99-12//99
Correctional Officers	New Jersey	S	22.74 MW	24.61 AW	51190 AAW	NJBLS	10//99-12//99
Correctional Officers	Newark PMSA, NJ	S	18.90 MW	17.86 AW	39300 AAW	NJBLS	10//99-12//99
Correctional Officers	New Mexico	S	12.59 MW	13.31 AW	27690 AAW	NMBLS	10//99-12//99
Correctional Officers	Albany-Schenectady-Troy MSA, NY	S	26.73 MW	26.08 AW	55600 AAW	NYBLS	10//99-12//99
Correctional Officers	North Carolina	S	16.26 MW	17.87 AW	37160 AAW	NCBLS	10//99-12//99
Correctional Officers	Ohio	S	19.55 MW	20.58 AW	42810 AAW	OHBLS	10//99-12//99
Correctional Officers	Oregon	S	20.47 MW	21.13 AW	43950 AAW	ORBLS	10//99-12//99
Correctional Officers	Portland-Vancouver PMSA, OR-WA	S	20.91 MW	20.80 AW	43490 AAW	ORBLS	10//99-12//99
Correctional Officers	Pennsylvania	S	19.14 MW	18.96 AW	39440 AAW	PABLS	10//99-12//99
Correctional Officers	Philadelphia PMSA, PA-NJ	S	20.52 MW	20.14 AW	42690 AAW	PABLS	10//99-12//99
Correctional Officers	Pittsburgh MSA, PA	S	16.57 MW	15.40 AW	34470 AAW	PABLS	10//99-12//99
Correctional Officers	South Carolina	S	16.83 MW	18.80 AW	39100 AAW	SCBLS	10//99-12//99
Correctional Officers	Tennessee	S	15.25 MW	15.52 AW	32280 AAW	TNBLS	10//99-12//99
Correctional Officers	Austin-San Marcos MSA, TX	S	13.98 MW	13.02 AW	29090 AAW	TXBLS	10//99-12//99
Correctional Officers	Dallas PMSA, TX	S	20.31 MW	19.34 AW	42240 AAW	TXBLS	10//99-12//99
Correctional Officers	Virginia	S	16.94 MW	17.95 AW	37330 AAW	VABLS	10//99-12//99
Correctional Officers	Charlottesville MSA, VA	S	17.64 MW	16.74 AW	36700 AAW	VABLS	10//99-12//99
Correctional Officers	Washington	S	19.4 MW	19.63 AW	40840 AAW	WABLS	10//99-12//99
Correctional Officers	West Virginia	S	15.13 MW	16.55 AW	34430 AAW	WVBLS	10//99-12//99
Correctional Officers	Wisconsin	S	17.83 MW	17.39 AW	36180 AAW	WIBLS	10//99-12//99
Correctional Officers	Puerto Rico	S	11.22 MW	13.38 AW	27820 AAW	PRBLS	10//99-12//99
Correctional Officers	San Juan-Bayamon PMSA, PR	S	11.62 MW	10.37 AW	24160 AAW	PRBLS	10//99-12//99
Farming, Fishing, and Forestry Workers	Alaska	S	24.76 MW	23.73 AW	49350 AAW	AKBLS	10//99-12//99
Farming, Fishing, and Forestry Workers	Arizona	S	11.81 MW	12.36 AW	25710 AAW	AZBLS	10//99-12//99
Farming, Fishing, and Forestry Workers	Arkansas	S	14.71 MW	15.72 AW	32690 AAW	ARBLS	10//99-12//99
Farming, Fishing, and Forestry Workers	California	S	12.13 MW	14.61 AW	30390 AAW	CABLS	10//99-12//99
Farming, Fishing, and Forestry Workers	Colorado	S	15.39 MW	17.20 AW	35770 AAW	COBLS	10//99-12//99
Farming, Fishing, and Forestry Workers	Connecticut	S	21.35 MW	22.64 AW	47100 AAW	CTBLS	10//99-12//99
Farming, Fishing, and Forestry Workers	Delaware	S	18.51 MW	17.58 AW	36570 AAW	DEBLS	10//99-12//99
Farming, Fishing, and Forestry Workers	District of Columbia	S	19.85 MW	25.90 AW	53880 AAW	DCBLS	10//99-12//99
Farming, Fishing, and Forestry Workers	Florida	S	14.09 MW	14.82 AW	30830 AAW	FLBLS	10//99-12//99
Farming, Fishing, and Forestry Workers	Georgia	S	15.17 MW	15.52 AW	32280 AAW	GABLS	10//99-12//99
Farming, Fishing, and Forestry Workers	Hawaii	S	15.04 MW	16.47 AW	34260 AAW	HIBLS	10//99-12//99
Farming, Fishing, and Forestry Workers	Idaho	S	18.66 MW	18.44 AW	38360 AAW	IDBLS	10//99-12//99
Farming, Fishing, and Forestry Workers	Illinois	S	18.28 MW	19.15 AW	39830 AAW	ILBLS	10//99-12//99
Farming, Fishing, and Forestry Workers	Indiana	S	16.41 MW	16.15 AW	33600 AAW	INBLS	10//99-12//99
Farming, Fishing, and Forestry Workers	Iowa	S	21.69 MW	21.23 AW	44160 AAW	IABLS	10//99-12//99
Farming, Fishing, and Forestry Workers	Kansas	S	15.06 MW	15.46 AW	32150 AAW	KSBLS	10//99-12//99
Farming, Fishing, and Forestry Workers	Kentucky	S	12.58 MW	13.83 AW	28760 AAW	KYBLS	10//99-12//99
Farming, Fishing, and Forestry Workers	Louisiana	S	15.03 MW	15.56 AW	32360 AAW	LABLS	10//99-12//99
Farming, Fishing, and Forestry Workers	Maine	S	10.01 MW	11.51 AW	23950 AAW	MEBLS	10//99-12//99
Farming, Fishing, and Forestry Workers	Massachusetts	S	13.1 MW	16.46 AW	34230 AAW	MABLS	10//99-12//99
Farming, Fishing, and Forestry Workers	Michigan	S	20.04 MW	21.73 AW	45190 AAW	MIBLS	10//99-12//99
Farming, Fishing, and Forestry Workers	Minnesota	S	17.57 MW	18.16 AW	37770 AAW	MNBLS	10//99-12//99
Farming, Fishing, and Forestry Workers	Mississippi	S	9.98 MW	10.85 AW	22570 AAW	MSBLS	10//99-12//99
Farming, Fishing, and Forestry Workers	Missouri	S	11.28 MW	13.99 AW	29100 AAW	MOBLS	10//99-12//99
Farming, Fishing, and Forestry Workers	Montana	S	18.55 MW	17.24 AW	35850 AAW	MTBLS	10//99-12//99
Farming, Fishing, and Forestry Workers	Nebraska	S	14.6 MW	14.56 AW	30290 AAW	NEBLS	10//99-12//99
Farming, Fishing, and Forestry Workers	New Hampshire	S	13.45 MW	15.65 AW	32550 AAW	NHBLS	10//99-12//99
Farming, Fishing, and Forestry Workers	New Jersey	S	17.5 MW	20.20 AW	42010 AAW	NJBLS	10//99-12//99
Farming, Fishing, and Forestry Workers	New Mexico	S	9.98 MW	10.57 AW	21980 AAW	NMBLS	10//99-12//99
Farming, Fishing, and Forestry Workers	New York	S	12.8 MW	14.44 AW	30020 AAW	NYBLS	10//99-12//99
Farming, Fishing, and Forestry Workers	North Carolina	S	16.62 MW	16.93 AW	35210 AAW	NCBLS	10//99-12//99
Farming, Fishing, and Forestry Workers	Ohio	S	14.15 MW	15.43 AW	32100 AAW	OHBLS	10//99-12//99
Farming, Fishing, and Forestry Workers	Oklahoma	S	13.95 MW	14.04 AW	29210 AAW	OKBLS	10//99-12//99
Farming, Fishing, and Forestry Workers	Oregon	S	15.79 MW	17.04 AW	35440 AAW	ORBLS	10//99-12//99
Farming, Fishing, and Forestry Workers	Pennsylvania	S	12.75 MW	14.79 AW	30770 AAW	PABLS	10//99-12//99
Farming, Fishing, and Forestry Workers	Rhode Island	S	18.32 MW	16.96 AW	35270 AAW	RIBLS	10//99-12//99
Farming, Fishing, and Forestry Workers	South Carolina	S	16.45 MW	18.94 AW	39390 AAW	SCBLS	10//99-12//99
Farming, Fishing, and Forestry Workers	South Dakota	S	15.58 MW	15.34 AW	31910 AAW	SDBLS	10//99-12//99
Farming, Fishing, and Forestry Workers	Tennessee	S	17.89 MW	16.88 AW	35110 AAW	TNBLS	10//99-12//99

AAW	Average annual wage	AOH	Average offered, high	ASH	Average starting, high	H	Hourly	M	Monthly	S	Special: hourly and annual
AE	Average entry wage	AOL	Average offered, low	ASL	Average starting, low	HI	Highest wage paid	MTC	Median total compensation	TQ	Third quartile wage
AEX	Average experienced wage	APH	Average pay, high range	AW	Average wage paid	HR	High end range	MW	Median wage paid	W	Weekly
AO	Average offered	APL	Average pay, low range	FQ	First quartile wage	LR	Low end range	SQ	Second quartile wage	Y	Yearly

First-Line Supervisor/Manager

Occupation/Type/Industry	Location	Per	Low	Mid	High	Source	Date
Farming, Fishing, and Forestry Workers	Texas	S	12.9 MW	13.67 AW	28440 AAW	TXBLS	10//99-12//99
Farming, Fishing, and Forestry Workers	Utah	S	17.92 MW	17.14 AW	35640 AAW	UTBLS	10//99-12//99
Farming, Fishing, and Forestry Workers	Virginia	S	15.49 MW	17.30 AW	35990 AAW	VABLS	10//99-12//99
Farming, Fishing, and Forestry Workers	Washington	S	18.26 MW	19.67 AW	40910 AAW	WABLS	10//99-12//99
Farming, Fishing, and Forestry Workers	Wisconsin	S	17.4 MW	16.71 AW	34750 AAW	WIBLS	10//99-12//99
Farming, Fishing, and Forestry Workers	Wyoming	S	17.13 MW	15.71 AW	32680 AAW	WYBLS	10//99-12//99
Farming, Fishing, and Forestry Workers	Puerto Rico	S	12.49 MW	11.34 AW	23590 AAW	PRBLS	10//99-12//99
Fire Fighting and Prevention Workers	Alabama	S	17.57 MW	18.24 AW	37940 AAW	ALBLS	10//99-12//99
Fire Fighting and Prevention Workers	Birmingham MSA, AL	S	19.69 MW	20.11 AW	40960 AAW	ALBLS	10//99-12//99
Fire Fighting and Prevention Workers	Alaska	S	25.8 MW	25.74 AW	53530 AAW	AKBLS	10//99-12//99
Fire Fighting and Prevention Workers	Arizona	S	24.94 MW	25.22 AW	52470 AAW	AZBLS	10//99-12//99
Fire Fighting and Prevention Workers	Phoenix-Mesa MSA, AZ	S	26.98 MW	27.93 AW	56110 AAW	AZBLS	10//99-12//99
Fire Fighting and Prevention Workers	Tucson MSA, AZ	S	23.94 MW	23.75 AW	49800 AAW	AZBLS	10//99-12//99
Fire Fighting and Prevention Workers	Yuma MSA, AZ	S	22.84 MW	22.97 AW	47500 AAW	AZBLS	10//99-12//99
Fire Fighting and Prevention Workers	Arkansas	S	16.66 MW	17.54 AW	36480 AAW	ARBLS	10//99-12//99
Fire Fighting and Prevention Workers	Little Rock-North Little Rock MSA, AR	S	19.97 MW	19.01 AW	41540 AAW	ARBLS	10//99-12//99
Fire Fighting and Prevention Workers	California	S	28.61 MW	29.72 AW	61810 AAW	CABLS	10//99-12//99
Fire Fighting and Prevention Workers	Los Angeles-Long Beach PMSA, CA	S	34.75 MW	37.00 AW	72280 AAW	CABLS	10//99-12//99
Fire Fighting and Prevention Workers	Merced MSA, CA	S	25.13 MW	24.94 AW	52280 AAW	CABLS	10//99-12//99
Fire Fighting and Prevention Workers	Oakland PMSA, CA	S	36.34 MW	38.64 AW	75590 AAW	CABLS	10//99-12//99
Fire Fighting and Prevention Workers	Riverside-San Bernardino PMSA, CA	S	27.80 MW	27.10 AW	57820 AAW	CABLS	10//99-12//99
Fire Fighting and Prevention Workers	Sacramento PMSA, CA	S	25.25 MW	24.55 AW	52520 AAW	CABLS	10//99-12//99
Fire Fighting and Prevention Workers	San Diego MSA, CA	S	30.50 MW	34.91 AW	63450 AAW	CABLS	10//99-12//99
Fire Fighting and Prevention Workers	San Francisco PMSA, CA	S	29.19 MW	26.16 AW	60710 AAW	CABLS	10//99-12//99
Fire Fighting and Prevention Workers	San Jose PMSA, CA	S	31.84 MW	34.65 AW	66240 AAW	CABLS	10//99-12//99
Fire Fighting and Prevention Workers	San Luis Obispo-Atascadero-Paso Robles MSA, CA	S	25.87 MW	25.18 AW	53820 AAW	CABLS	10//99-12//99
Fire Fighting and Prevention Workers	Santa Barbara-Santa Maria-Lompoc MSA, CA	S	34.43 MW	36.97 AW	71620 AAW	CABLS	10//99-12//99
Fire Fighting and Prevention Workers	Santa Cruz-Watsonville PMSA, CA	S	29.67 MW	29.54 AW	61720 AAW	CABLS	10//99-12//99
Fire Fighting and Prevention Workers	Santa Rosa PMSA, CA	S	28.46 MW	30.21 AW	59200 AAW	CABLS	10//99-12//99
Fire Fighting and Prevention Workers	Vallejo-Fairfield-Napa PMSA, CA	S	25.80 MW	24.79 AW	53670 AAW	CABLS	10//99-12//99
Fire Fighting and Prevention Workers	Ventura PMSA, CA	S	28.83 MW	26.50 AW	59970 AAW	CABLS	10//99-12//99
Fire Fighting and Prevention Workers	Visalia-Tulare-Porterville MSA, CA	S	20.87 MW	20.57 AW	43410 AAW	CABLS	10//99-12//99
Fire Fighting and Prevention Workers	Yolo PMSA, CA	S	33.62 MW	34.16 AW	69940 AAW	CABLS	10//99-12//99
Fire Fighting and Prevention Workers	Yuba City MSA, CA	S	29.76 MW	34.43 AW	61890 AAW	CABLS	10//99-12//99
Fire Fighting and Prevention Workers	Colorado	S	29.14 MW	27.98 AW	58200 AAW	COBLS	10//99-12//99
Fire Fighting and Prevention Workers	Denver PMSA, CO	S	29.98 MW	30.97 AW	62360 AAW	COBLS	10//99-12//99
Fire Fighting and Prevention Workers	Fort Collins-Loveland MSA, CO	S	30.05 MW	31.33 AW	62500 AAW	COBLS	10//99-12//99
Fire Fighting and Prevention Workers	Connecticut	S	27.63 MW	28.75 AW	59800 AAW	CTBLS	10//99-12//99
Fire Fighting and Prevention Workers	Bridgeport PMSA, CT	S	28.10 MW	29.72 AW	58460 AAW	CTBLS	10//99-12//99
Fire Fighting and Prevention Workers	Hartford MSA, CT	S	28.11 MW	26.90 AW	58460 AAW	CTBLS	10//99-12//99
Fire Fighting and Prevention Workers	New Haven-Meriden PMSA, CT	S	24.97 MW	24.83 AW	51940 AAW	CTBLS	10//99-12//99
Fire Fighting and Prevention Workers	Stamford-Norwalk PMSA, CT	S	29.88 MW	29.53 AW	62140 AAW	CTBLS	10//99-12//99
Fire Fighting and Prevention Workers	Delaware	S	24.56 MW	24.61 AW	51200 AAW	DEBLS	10//99-12//99
Fire Fighting and Prevention Workers	Wilmington-Newark PMSA, DE-MD	S	25.46 MW	25.06 AW	52950 AAW	DEBLS	10//99-12//99
Fire Fighting and Prevention Workers	Washington PMSA, DC-MD-VA-WV	S	27.30 MW	26.61 AW	56780 AAW	DCBLS	10//99-12//99
Fire Fighting and Prevention Workers	Florida	S	21.66 MW	21.80 AW	45350 AAW	FLBLS	10//99-12//99
Fire Fighting and Prevention Workers	Daytona Beach MSA, FL	S	18.85 MW	17.77 AW	39210 AAW	FLBLS	10//99-12//99
Fire Fighting and Prevention Workers	Fort Lauderdale PMSA, FL	S	25.32 MW	24.85 AW	52670 AAW	FLBLS	10//99-12//99
Fire Fighting and Prevention Workers	Fort Myers-Cape Coral MSA, FL	S	23.01 MW	22.68 AW	47870 AAW	FLBLS	10//99-12//99
Fire Fighting and Prevention Workers	Jacksonville MSA, FL	S	20.30 MW	21.09 AW	42230 AAW	FLBLS	10//99-12//99
Fire Fighting and Prevention Workers	Melbourne-Titusville-Palm Bay MSA, FL	S	19.14 MW	18.54 AW	39810 AAW	FLBLS	10//99-12//99
Fire Fighting and Prevention Workers	Miami PMSA, FL	S	26.36 MW	26.85 AW	54830 AAW	FLBLS	10//99-12//99
Fire Fighting and Prevention Workers	Naples MSA, FL	S	22.05 MW	21.74 AW	45860 AAW	FLBLS	10//99-12//99
Fire Fighting and Prevention Workers	Orlando MSA, FL	S	22.54 MW	21.34 AW	46890 AAW	FLBLS	10//99-12//99
Fire Fighting and Prevention Workers	Panama City MSA, FL	S	18.54 MW	16.06 AW	38560 AAW	FLBLS	10//99-12//99
Fire Fighting and Prevention Workers	Pensacola MSA, FL	S	15.90 MW	14.96 AW	33080 AAW	FLBLS	10//99-12//99
Fire Fighting and Prevention Workers	Sarasota-Bradenton MSA, FL	S	20.52 MW	19.90 AW	42690 AAW	FLBLS	10//99-12//99

AAW	Average annual wage	AOH	Average offered, high	ASH	Average starting, high
AE	Average entry wage	AOL	Average offered, low	ASL	Average starting, low
AEX	Average experienced wage	APH	Average pay, high range	AW	Average wage paid
AO	Average offered	APL	Average pay, low range	FQ	First quartile wage

H	Hourly	M	Monthly
HI	Highest wage paid	MTC	Median total compensation
HR	High end range	MW	Median wage paid
LR	Low end range	SQ	Second quartile wage

S	Special: hourly and annual
TQ	Third quartile wage
W	Weekly
Y	Yearly

Occupation/Type/Industry	Location	Per	Low	Mid	High	Source	Date
First-Line Supervisor/Manager							
Fire Fighting and Prevention Workers	Tampa-St. Petersburg-Clearwater MSA, FL	S	20.50 MW	21.14 AW	42640 AAW	FLBLS	10//99-12//99
Fire Fighting and Prevention Workers	West Palm Beach-Boca Raton MSA, FL	S	24.74 MW	23.50 AW	51460 AAW	FLBLS	10//99-12//99
Fire Fighting and Prevention Workers	Georgia	S	19.5 MW	19.43 AW	40410 AAW	GABLS	10//99-12//99
Fire Fighting and Prevention Workers	Atlanta MSA, GA	S	21.21 MW	22.21 AW	44110 AAW	GABLS	10//99-12//99
Fire Fighting and Prevention Workers	Augusta-Aiken MSA, GA-SC	S	24.52 MW	23.43 AW	51010 AAW	GABLS	10//99-12//99
Fire Fighting and Prevention Workers	Macon MSA, GA	S	18.32 MW	17.76 AW	38100 AAW	GABLS	10//99-12//99
Fire Fighting and Prevention Workers	Savannah MSA, GA	S	21.64 MW	21.24 AW	45000 AAW	GABLS	10//99-12//99
Fire Fighting and Prevention Workers	Hawaii	S	23.75 MW	23.03 AW	47910 AAW	HIBLS	10//99-12//99
Fire Fighting and Prevention Workers	Idaho	S	19.4 MW	26.17 AW	54440 AAW	IDBLS	10//99-12//99
Fire Fighting and Prevention Workers	Boise City MSA, ID	S	29.84 MW	25.35 AW	62070 AAW	IDBLS	10//99-12//99
Fire Fighting and Prevention Workers	Illinois	S	24.07 MW	23.20 AW	48260 AAW	ILBLS	10//99-12//99
Fire Fighting and Prevention Workers	Chicago PMSA, IL	S	26.74 MW	27.49 AW	55610 AAW	ILBLS	10//99-12//99
Fire Fighting and Prevention Workers	Springfield MSA, IL	S	22.71 MW	23.07 AW	47240 AAW	ILBLS	10//99-12//99
Fire Fighting and Prevention Workers	Indiana	S	18.41 MW	18.43 AW	38330 AAW	INBLS	10//99-12//99
Fire Fighting and Prevention Workers	Gary PMSA, IN	S	18.63 MW	18.66 AW	38750 AAW	INBLS	10//99-12//99
Fire Fighting and Prevention Workers	Indianapolis MSA, IN	S	20.39 MW	21.60 AW	42420 AAW	INBLS	10//99-12//99
Fire Fighting and Prevention Workers	Iowa	S	15.72 MW	15.38 AW	31980 AAW	IABLS	10//99-12//99
Fire Fighting and Prevention Workers	Davenport-Moline-Rock Island MSA, IA-IL	S	19.95 MW	20.63 AW	41500 AAW	IABLS	10//99-12//99
Fire Fighting and Prevention Workers	Sioux City MSA, IA-NE	S	20.99 MW	18.42 AW	43670 AAW	IABLS	10//99-12//99
Fire Fighting and Prevention Workers	Kansas	S	16.65 MW	19.67 AW	40920 AAW	KSBLS	10//99-12//99
Fire Fighting and Prevention Workers	Kentucky	S	16.9 MW	18.40 AW	38260 AAW	KYBLS	10//99-12//99
Fire Fighting and Prevention Workers	Louisville MSA, KY-IN	S	23.41 MW	23.95 AW	48690 AAW	KYBLS	10//99-12//99
Fire Fighting and Prevention Workers	Louisiana	S	15.94 MW	17.13 AW	35630 AAW	LABLS	10//99-12//99
Fire Fighting and Prevention Workers	Baton Rouge MSA, LA	S	16.51 MW	15.59 AW	34330 AAW	LABLS	10//99-12//99
Fire Fighting and Prevention Workers	Lafayette MSA, LA	S	14.86 MW	14.95 AW	30910 AAW	LABLS	10//99-12//99
Fire Fighting and Prevention Workers	Lake Charles MSA, LA	S	15.42 MW	15.44 AW	32080 AAW	LABLS	10//99-12//99
Fire Fighting and Prevention Workers	New Orleans MSA, LA	S	16.97 MW	15.93 AW	35310 AAW	LABLS	10//99-12//99
Fire Fighting and Prevention Workers	Shreveport-Bossier City MSA, LA	S	24.69 MW	24.69 AW	51350 AAW	LABLS	10//99-12//99
Fire Fighting and Prevention Workers	Maine	S	18.36 MW	17.52 AW	36430 AAW	MEBLS	10//99-12//99
Fire Fighting and Prevention Workers	Bangor MSA, ME	S	16.16 MW	17.10 AW	33610 AAW	MEBLS	10//99-12//99
Fire Fighting and Prevention Workers	Maryland	S	23.98 MW	25.09 AW	52180 AAW	MDBLS	10//99-12//99
Fire Fighting and Prevention Workers	Baltimore PMSA, MD	S	24.45 MW	23.31 AW	50860 AAW	MDBLS	10//99-12//99
Fire Fighting and Prevention Workers	Massachusetts	S	23.07 MW	23.41 AW	48690 AAW	MABLS	10//99-12//99
Fire Fighting and Prevention Workers	Barnstable-Yarmouth MSA, MA	S	25.24 MW	25.10 AW	52500 AAW	MABLS	10//99-12//99
Fire Fighting and Prevention Workers	Boston PMSA, MA-NH	S	23.48 MW	21.72 AW	48830 AAW	MABLS	10//99-12//99
Fire Fighting and Prevention Workers	Brockton PMSA, MA	S	24.91 MW	23.98 AW	51810 AAW	MABLS	10//99-12//99
Fire Fighting and Prevention Workers	Lowell PMSA, MA-NH	S	24.73 MW	22.78 AW	51430 AAW	MABLS	10//99-12//99
Fire Fighting and Prevention Workers	Springfield MSA, MA	S	24.36 MW	24.03 AW	50670 AAW	MABLS	10//99-12//99
Fire Fighting and Prevention Workers	Michigan	S	23.25 MW	22.46 AW	46720 AAW	MIBLS	10//99-12//99
Fire Fighting and Prevention Workers	Ann Arbor PMSA, MI	S	24.66 MW	24.63 AW	51300 AAW	MIBLS	10//99-12//99
Fire Fighting and Prevention Workers	Benton Harbor MSA, MI	S	19.22 MW	19.15 AW	39970 AAW	MIBLS	10//99-12//99
Fire Fighting and Prevention Workers	Detroit PMSA, MI	S	25.50 MW	25.67 AW	53040 AAW	MIBLS	10//99-12//99
Fire Fighting and Prevention Workers	Grand Rapids-Muskegon-Holland MSA, MI	S	23.92 MW	23.15 AW	49760 AAW	MIBLS	10//99-12//99
Fire Fighting and Prevention Workers	Kalamazoo-Battle Creek MSA, MI	S	17.45 MW	16.06 AW	36300 AAW	MIBLS	10//99-12//99
Fire Fighting and Prevention Workers	Saginaw-Bay City-Midland MSA, MI	S	25.56 MW	26.98 AW	53170 AAW	MIBLS	10//99-12//99
Fire Fighting and Prevention Workers	Minnesota	S	9.62 MW	13.63 AW	28360 AAW	MNBLS	10//99-12//99
Fire Fighting and Prevention Workers	Minneapolis-St. Paul MSA, MN-WI	S	16.97 MW	12.68 AW	35290 AAW	MNBLS	10//99-12//99
Fire Fighting and Prevention Workers	Mississippi	S	15.97 MW	18.38 AW	38220 AAW	MSBLS	10//99-12//99
Fire Fighting and Prevention Workers	Biloxi-Gulfport-Pascagoula MSA, MS	S	16.98 MW	17.18 AW	35320 AAW	MSBLS	10//99-12//99
Fire Fighting and Prevention Workers	Jackson MSA, MS	S	25.09 MW	28.03 AW	52200 AAW	MSBLS	10//99-12//99
Fire Fighting and Prevention Workers	Missouri	S	22.48 MW	22.28 AW	46350 AAW	MOBLS	10//99-12//99
Fire Fighting and Prevention Workers	Kansas City MSA, MO-KS	S	25.78 MW	26.00 AW	53620 AAW	MOBLS	10//99-12//99
Fire Fighting and Prevention Workers	St. Louis MSA, MO-IL	S	23.73 MW	24.51 AW	49350 AAW	MOBLS	10//99-12//99
Fire Fighting and Prevention Workers	Montana	S	15.49 MW	15.49 AW	32210 AAW	MTBLS	10//99-12//99
Fire Fighting and Prevention Workers	Nevada	S	25.81 MW	26.79 AW	55720 AAW	NVBLS	10//99-12//99
Fire Fighting and Prevention Workers	Las Vegas MSA, NV-AZ	S	28.28 MW	26.75 AW	58820 AAW	NVBLS	10//99-12//99
Fire Fighting and Prevention Workers	Reno MSA, NV	S	22.79 MW	20.19 AW	47410 AAW	NVBLS	10//99-12//99
Fire Fighting and Prevention Workers	New Hampshire	S	19.37 MW	18.26 AW	37970 AAW	NHBLS	10//99-12//99
Fire Fighting and Prevention Workers	Manchester PMSA, NH	S	16.98 MW	18.19 AW	35320 AAW	NHBLS	10//99-12//99
Fire Fighting and Prevention Workers	Portsmouth-Rochester PMSA, NH-ME	S	21.49 MW	21.31 AW	44710 AAW	NHBLS	10//99-12//99

AAW	Average annual wage	AOH	Average offered, high	ASH	Average starting, high
AE	Average entry wage	AOL	Average offered, low	ASL	Average starting, low
AEX	Average experienced wage	APH	Average pay, high range	AW	Average wage paid
AO	Average offered	APL	Average pay, low range	FQ	First quartile wage

H	Hourly	M	Monthly	S	Special: hourly and annual
HI	Highest wage paid	MTC	Median total compensation	TQ	Third quartile wage
HR	High end range	MW	Median wage paid	W	Weekly
LR	Low end range	SQ	Second quartile wage	Y	Yearly

Occupation/Type/Industry	Location	Per	Low	Mid	High	Source	Date

First-Line Supervisor/Manager

Occupation/Type/Industry	Location	Per	Low	Mid	High	Source	Date
Fire Fighting and Prevention Workers	New Jersey	S	34.56 MW	31.60 AW	65720 AAW	NJBLS	10//99-12//99
Fire Fighting and Prevention Workers	Atlantic-Cape May PMSA, NJ	S	24.66 MW	25.82 AW	51300 AAW	NJBLS	10//99-12//99
Fire Fighting and Prevention Workers	Bergen-Passaic PMSA, NJ	S	30.73 MW	33.57 AW	63910 AAW	NJBLS	10//99-12//99
Fire Fighting and Prevention Workers	Jersey City PMSA, NJ	S	38.84 MW	39.61 AW	80780 AAW	NJBLS	10//99-12//99
Fire Fighting and Prevention Workers	Middlesex-Somerset- Hunterdon PMSA, NJ	S	38.68 MW	42.21 AW	80450 AAW	NJBLS	10//99-12//99
Fire Fighting and Prevention Workers	Monmouth-Ocean PMSA, NJ	S	27.09 MW	28.44 AW	56360 AAW	NJBLS	10//99-12//99
Fire Fighting and Prevention Workers	Newark PMSA, NJ	S	31.85 MW	34.54 AW	66250 AAW	NJBLS	10//99-12//99
Fire Fighting and Prevention Workers	New Mexico	S	16.52 MW	17.22 AW	35820 AAW	NMBLS	10//99-12//99
Fire Fighting and Prevention Workers	New York	S	30.24 MW	29.94 AW	62280 AAW	NYBLS	10//99-12//99
Fire Fighting and Prevention Workers	Nassau-Suffolk PMSA, NY	S	27.05 MW	29.44 AW	56270 AAW	NYBLS	10//99-12//99
Fire Fighting and Prevention Workers	North Carolina	S	19.64 MW	19.38 AW	40310 AAW	NCBLS	10//99-12//99
Fire Fighting and Prevention Workers	Greensboro--Winston-Salem-- High Point MSA, NC	S	17.90 MW	16.83 AW	37230 AAW	NCBLS	10//99-12//99
Fire Fighting and Prevention Workers	Raleigh-Durham-Chapel Hill MSA, NC	S	21.37 MW	21.46 AW	44450 AAW	NCBLS	10//99-12//99
Fire Fighting and Prevention Workers	North Dakota	S	22.33 MW	22.05 AW	45870 AAW	NDBLS	10//99-12//99
Fire Fighting and Prevention Workers	Ohio	S	22.77 MW	21.74 AW	45220 AAW	OHBLS	10//99-12//99
Fire Fighting and Prevention Workers	Akron PMSA, OH	S	22.85 MW	23.59 AW	47530 AAW	OHBLS	10//99-12//99
Fire Fighting and Prevention Workers	Canton-Massillon MSA, OH	S	19.25 MW	22.54 AW	40050 AAW	OHBLS	10//99-12//99
Fire Fighting and Prevention Workers	Cincinnati PMSA, OH-KY-IN	S	20.78 MW	21.55 AW	43220 AAW	OHBLS	10//99-12//99
Fire Fighting and Prevention Workers	Cleveland-Lorain-Elyria PMSA, OH	S	24.50 MW	24.72 AW	50970 AAW	OHBLS	10//99-12//99
Fire Fighting and Prevention Workers	Dayton-Springfield MSA, OH	S	21.25 MW	20.13 AW	44210 AAW	OHBLS	10//99-12//99
Fire Fighting and Prevention Workers	Hamilton-Middletown PMSA, OH	S	19.31 MW	19.44 AW	40160 AAW	OHBLS	10//99-12//99
Fire Fighting and Prevention Workers	Mansfield MSA, OH	S	13.89 MW	16.56 AW	28890 AAW	OHBLS	10//99-12//99
Fire Fighting and Prevention Workers	Steubenville-Weirton MSA, OH-WV	S	18.76 MW	18.91 AW	39020 AAW	OHBLS	10//99-12//99
Fire Fighting and Prevention Workers	Toledo MSA, OH	S	20.57 MW	20.84 AW	42780 AAW	OHBLS	10//99-12//99
Fire Fighting and Prevention Workers	Youngstown-Warren MSA, OH	S	15.22 MW	15.72 AW	31660 AAW	OHBLS	10//99-12//99
Fire Fighting and Prevention Workers	Oklahoma	S	16.53 MW	17.85 AW	37130 AAW	OKBLS	10//99-12//99
Fire Fighting and Prevention Workers	Oklahoma City MSA, OK	S	20.87 MW	21.11 AW	43410 AAW	OKBLS	10//99-12//99
Fire Fighting and Prevention Workers	Tulsa MSA, OK	S	16.81 MW	16.01 AW	34970 AAW	OKBLS	10//99-12//99
Fire Fighting and Prevention Workers	Oregon	S	25.19 MW	25.78 AW	53630 AAW	ORBLS	10//99-12//99
Fire Fighting and Prevention Workers	Portland-Vancouver PMSA, OR-WA	S	26.81 MW	26.68 AW	55760 AAW	ORBLS	10//99-12//99
Fire Fighting and Prevention Workers	Pennsylvania	S	24.03 MW	23.11 AW	48060 AAW	PABLS	10//99-12//99
Fire Fighting and Prevention Workers	Philadelphia PMSA, PA-NJ	S	20.13 MW	19.89 AW	41870 AAW	PABLS	10//99-12//99
Fire Fighting and Prevention Workers	Scranton--Wilkes-Barre-- Hazleton MSA, PA	S	21.06 MW	22.52 AW	43800 AAW	PABLS	10//99-12//99
Fire Fighting and Prevention Workers	Rhode Island	S	20.64 MW	21.60 AW	44920 AAW	RIBLS	10//99-12//99
Fire Fighting and Prevention Workers	Providence-Fall River- Warwick MSA, RI-MA	S	21.43 MW	20.35 AW	44570 AAW	RIBLS	10//99-12//99
Fire Fighting and Prevention Workers	South Carolina	S	16.24 MW	17.47 AW	36350 AAW	SCBLS	10//99-12//99
Fire Fighting and Prevention Workers	Greenville-Spartanburg- Anderson MSA, SC	S	13.92 MW	12.51 AW	28960 AAW	SCBLS	10//99-12//99
Fire Fighting and Prevention Workers	South Dakota	S	19.17 MW	19.69 AW	40960 AAW	SDBLS	10//99-12//99
Fire Fighting and Prevention Workers	Tennessee	S	21.56 MW	20.84 AW	43350 AAW	TNBLS	10//99-12//99
Fire Fighting and Prevention Workers	Johnson City-Kingsport-Bristol MSA, TN-VA	S	19.38 MW	18.90 AW	40310 AAW	TNBLS	10//99-12//99
Fire Fighting and Prevention Workers	Knoxville MSA, TN	S	18.77 MW	18.78 AW	39030 AAW	TNBLS	10//99-12//99
Fire Fighting and Prevention Workers	Memphis MSA, TN-AR-MS	S	23.26 MW	23.68 AW	48390 AAW	MSBLS	10//99-12//99
Fire Fighting and Prevention Workers	Texas	S	21.92 MW	22.53 AW	46860 AAW	TXBLS	10//99-12//99
Fire Fighting and Prevention Workers	Austin-San Marcos MSA, TX	S	22.82 MW	18.41 AW	47460 AAW	TXBLS	10//99-12//99
Fire Fighting and Prevention Workers	Beaumont-Port Arthur MSA, TX	S	20.75 MW	19.63 AW	43160 AAW	TXBLS	10//99-12//99
Fire Fighting and Prevention Workers	Brownsville-Harlingen-San Benito MSA, TX	S	13.96 MW	13.32 AW	29030 AAW	TXBLS	10//99-12//99
Fire Fighting and Prevention Workers	Corpus Christi MSA, TX	S	27.65 MW	29.79 AW	57510 AAW	TXBLS	10//99-12//99
Fire Fighting and Prevention Workers	Dallas PMSA, TX	S	25.66 MW	25.85 AW	53380 AAW	TXBLS	10//99-12//99
Fire Fighting and Prevention Workers	Fort Worth-Arlington PMSA, TX	S	24.16 MW	24.58 AW	50240 AAW	TXBLS	10//99-12//99
Fire Fighting and Prevention Workers	Galveston-Texas City PMSA, TX	S	20.03 MW	19.94 AW	41650 AAW	TXBLS	10//99-12//99
Fire Fighting and Prevention Workers	Houston PMSA, TX	S	24.32 MW	24.39 AW	50580 AAW	TXBLS	10//99-12//99
Fire Fighting and Prevention Workers	Killeen-Temple MSA, TX	S	16.61 MW	15.60 AW	34540 AAW	TXBLS	10//99-12//99
Fire Fighting and Prevention Workers	McAllen-Edinburg-Mission MSA, TX	S	19.66 MW	19.25 AW	40890 AAW	TXBLS	10//99-12//99
Fire Fighting and Prevention Workers	Tyler MSA, TX	S	19.85 MW	19.50 AW	41290 AAW	TXBLS	10//99-12//99
Fire Fighting and Prevention Workers	Utah	S	22.32 MW	23.15 AW	48160 AAW	UTBLS	10//99-12//99

AAW Average annual wage	AOH Average offered, high	ASH Average starting, high	H Hourly	M Monthly	S Special: hourly and annual
AE Average entry wage	AOL Average offered, low	ASL Average starting, low	HI Highest wage paid	MTC Median total compensation	TQ Third quartile wage
AEX Average experienced wage	APH Average pay, high range	AW Average wage paid	HR High end range	MW Median wage paid	W Weekly
AO Average offered	APL Average pay, low range	FQ First quartile wage	LR Low end range	SQ Second quartile wage	Y Yearly

Occupation/Type/Industry	Location	Per	Low	Mid	High	Source	Date
First-Line Supervisor/Manager							
Fire Fighting and Prevention Workers	Provo-Orem MSA, UT	S	19.37 MW	19.48 AW	40300 AAW	UTBLS	10//99-12//99
Fire Fighting and Prevention Workers	Salt Lake City-Ogden MSA, UT	S	24.35 MW	24.29 AW	50660 AAW	UTBLS	10//99-12//99
Fire Fighting and Prevention Workers	Virginia	S	21.28 MW	23.25 AW	48370 AAW	VABLS	10//99-12//99
Fire Fighting and Prevention Workers	Norfolk-Virginia Beach-Newport News MSA, VA-NC	S	20.52 MW	19.53 AW	42680 AAW	VABLS	10//99-12//99
Fire Fighting and Prevention Workers	Richmond-Petersburg MSA, VA	S	21.84 MW	21.42 AW	45430 AAW	VABLS	10//99-12//99
Fire Fighting and Prevention Workers	Washington	S	29.3 MW	28.16 AW	58570 AAW	WABLS	10//99-12//99
Fire Fighting and Prevention Workers	Bremerton PMSA, WA	S	25.06 MW	25.10 AW	52120 AAW	WABLS	10//99-12//99
Fire Fighting and Prevention Workers	Seattle-Bellevue-Everett PMSA, WA	S	30.53 MW	31.31 AW	63500 AAW	WABLS	10//99-12//99
Fire Fighting and Prevention Workers	Tacoma PMSA, WA	S	27.53 MW	28.64 AW	57260 AAW	WABLS	10//99-12//99
Fire Fighting and Prevention Workers	Yakima MSA, WA	S	22.66 MW	22.78 AW	47140 AAW	WABLS	10//99-12//99
Fire Fighting and Prevention Workers	West Virginia	S	15.9 MW	16.56 AW	34450 AAW	WVBLS	10//99-12//99
Fire Fighting and Prevention Workers	Charleston MSA, WV	S	18.28 MW	16.34 AW	38020 AAW	WVBLS	10//99-12//99
Fire Fighting and Prevention Workers	Wisconsin	S	22.13 MW	19.77 AW	41120 AAW	WIBLS	10//99-12//99
Fire Fighting and Prevention Workers	Appleton-Oshkosh-Neenah MSA, WI	S	17.95 MW	22.05 AW	37340 AAW	WIBLS	10//99-12//99
Fire Fighting and Prevention Workers	Kenosha PMSA, WI	S	26.01 MW	25.49 AW	54100 AAW	WIBLS	10//99-12//99
Fire Fighting and Prevention Workers	Wyoming	S	22.11 MW	23.20 AW	48260 AAW	WYBLS	10//99-12//99
Food Preparation and Serving Workers	Alabama	S	9.51 MW	10.20 AW	21220 AAW	ALBLS	10//99-12//99
Food Preparation and Serving Workers	Anniston MSA, AL	S	8.94 MW	7.97 AW	18600 AAW	ALBLS	10//99-12//99
Food Preparation and Serving Workers	Auburn-Opelika MSA, AL	S	9.38 MW	8.23 AW	19500 AAW	ALBLS	10//99-12//99
Food Preparation and Serving Workers	Birmingham MSA, AL	S	10.29 MW	9.21 AW	21410 AAW	ALBLS	10//99-12//99
Food Preparation and Serving Workers	Decatur MSA, AL	S	9.79 MW	9.15 AW	20360 AAW	ALBLS	10//99-12//99
Food Preparation and Serving Workers	Dothan MSA, AL	S	8.25 MW	7.84 AW	17160 AAW	ALBLS	10//99-12//99
Food Preparation and Serving Workers	Florence MSA, AL	S	8.06 MW	8.19 AW	16760 AAW	ALBLS	10//99-12//99
Food Preparation and Serving Workers	Gadsden MSA, AL	S	6.53 MW	6.38 AW	13570 AAW	ALBLS	10//99-12//99
Food Preparation and Serving Workers	Huntsville MSA, AL	S	10.40 MW	9.38 AW	21630 AAW	ALBLS	10//99-12//99
Food Preparation and Serving Workers	Mobile MSA, AL	S	9.85 MW	9.36 AW	20490 AAW	ALBLS	10//99-12//99
Food Preparation and Serving Workers	Montgomery MSA, AL	S	9.78 MW	9.20 AW	20340 AAW	ALBLS	10//99-12//99
Food Preparation and Serving Workers	Tuscaloosa MSA, AL	S	8.58 MW	7.99 AW	17840 AAW	ALBLS	10//99-12//99
Food Preparation and Serving Workers	Alaska	S	12.77 MW	13.45 AW	27980 AAW	AKBLS	10//99-12//99
Food Preparation and Serving Workers	Anchorage MSA, AK	S	12.48 MW	11.86 AW	25950 AAW	AKBLS	10//99-12//99
Food Preparation and Serving Workers	Arizona	S	9.78 MW	10.18 AW	21180 AAW	AZBLS	10//99-12//99
Food Preparation and Serving Workers	Flagstaff MSA, AZ-UT	S	10.07 MW	9.71 AW	20950 AAW	AZBLS	10//99-12//99
Food Preparation and Serving Workers	Phoenix-Mesa MSA, AZ	S	10.19 MW	9.70 AW	21180 AAW	AZBLS	10//99-12//99
Food Preparation and Serving Workers	Tucson MSA, AZ	S	10.61 MW	10.40 AW	22070 AAW	AZBLS	10//99-12//99
Food Preparation and Serving Workers	Yuma MSA, AZ	S	7.59 MW	6.73 AW	15790 AAW	AZBLS	10//99-12//99
Food Preparation and Serving Workers	Arkansas	S	9.37 MW	10.06 AW	20920 AAW	ARBLS	10//99-12//99
Food Preparation and Serving Workers	Fayetteville-Springdale-Rogers MSA, AR	S	10.10 MW	9.50 AW	21020 AAW	ARBLS	10//99-12//99
Food Preparation and Serving Workers	Fort Smith MSA, AR-OK	S	9.55 MW	9.13 AW	19860 AAW	ARBLS	10//99-12//99
Food Preparation and Serving Workers	Jonesboro MSA, AR	S	7.98 MW	7.58 AW	16600 AAW	ARBLS	10//99-12//99
Food Preparation and Serving Workers	Little Rock-North Little Rock MSA, AR	S	12.84 MW	12.51 AW	26710 AAW	ARBLS	10//99-12//99
Food Preparation and Serving Workers	Pine Bluff MSA, AR	S	9.14 MW	8.31 AW	19020 AAW	ARBLS	10//99-12//99
Food Preparation and Serving Workers	California	S	11.73 MW	12.28 AW	25540 AAW	CABLS	10//99-12//99
Food Preparation and Serving Workers	Bakersfield MSA, CA	S	11.93 MW	11.57 AW	24810 AAW	CABLS	10//99-12//99
Food Preparation and Serving Workers	Chico-Paradise MSA, CA	S	10.24 MW	8.62 AW	21290 AAW	CABLS	10//99-12//99
Food Preparation and Serving Workers	Fresno MSA, CA	S	13.48 MW	13.58 AW	28030 AAW	CABLS	10//99-12//99
Food Preparation and Serving Workers	Los Angeles-Long Beach PMSA, CA	S	14.41 MW	14.59 AW	29980 AAW	CABLS	10//99-12//99
Food Preparation and Serving Workers	Merced MSA, CA	S	10.15 MW	9.81 AW	21120 AAW	CABLS	10//99-12//99
Food Preparation and Serving Workers	Modesto MSA, CA	S	11.33 MW	11.84 AW	23560 AAW	CABLS	10//99-12//99
Food Preparation and Serving Workers	Oakland PMSA, CA	S	12.70 MW	12.01 AW	26420 AAW	CABLS	10//99-12//99
Food Preparation and Serving Workers	Orange County PMSA, CA	S	11.97 MW	10.31 AW	24890 AAW	CABLS	10//99-12//99
Food Preparation and Serving Workers	Redding MSA, CA	S	9.74 MW	9.56 AW	20260 AAW	CABLS	10//99-12//99
Food Preparation and Serving Workers	Riverside-San Bernardino PMSA, CA	S	10.52 MW	9.99 AW	21890 AAW	CABLS	10//99-12//99
Food Preparation and Serving Workers	Sacramento PMSA, CA	S	13.34 MW	13.59 AW	27750 AAW	CABLS	10//99-12//99
Food Preparation and Serving Workers	Salinas MSA, CA	S	11.42 MW	10.23 AW	23740 AAW	CABLS	10//99-12//99
Food Preparation and Serving Workers	San Diego MSA, CA	S	10.90 MW	9.93 AW	22660 AAW	CABLS	10//99-12//99
Food Preparation and Serving Workers	San Francisco PMSA, CA	S	14.89 MW	14.85 AW	30960 AAW	CABLS	10//99-12//99
Food Preparation and Serving Workers	San Jose PMSA, CA	S	12.41 MW	12.20 AW	25820 AAW	CABLS	10//99-12//99
Food Preparation and Serving Workers	San Luis Obispo-Atascadero-Paso Robles MSA, CA	S	13.31 MW	12.36 AW	27680 AAW	CABLS	10//99-12//99
Food Preparation and Serving Workers	Santa Barbara-Santa Maria-Lompoc MSA, CA	S	11.21 MW	10.77 AW	23330 AAW	CABLS	10//99-12//99

AAW Average annual wage	AOH Average offered, high	ASH Average starting, high	H Hourly	M Monthly	S Special: hourly and annual
AE Average entry wage	AOL Average offered, low	ASL Average starting, low	HI Highest wage paid	MTC Median total compensation	TQ Third quartile wage
AEX Average experienced wage	APH Average pay, high range	AW Average wage paid	HR High end range	MW Median wage paid	W Weekly
AO Average offered	APL Average pay, low range	FQ First quartile wage	LR Low end range	SQ Second quartile wage	Y Yearly

Occupation/Type/Industry	Location	Per	Low	Mid	High	Source	Date

First-Line Supervisor/Manager

Occupation/Type/Industry	Location	Per	Low	Mid	High	Source	Date
Food Preparation and Serving Workers	Santa Cruz-Watsonville PMSA, CA	S	9.33 MW	8.39 AW	19400 AAW	CABLS	10//99-12//99
Food Preparation and Serving Workers	Santa Rosa PMSA, CA	S	11.79 MW	11.36 AW	24510 AAW	CABLS	10//99-12//99
Food Preparation and Serving Workers	Stockton-Lodi MSA, CA	S	12.68 MW	12.27 AW	26370 AAW	CABLS	10//99-12//99
Food Preparation and Serving Workers	Vallejo-Fairfield-Napa PMSA, CA	S	10.37 MW	7.72 AW	21570 AAW	CABLS	10//99-12//99
Food Preparation and Serving Workers	Ventura PMSA, CA	S	11.15 MW	9.18 AW	23200 AAW	CABLS	10//99-12//99
Food Preparation and Serving Workers	Visalia-Tulare-Porterville MSA, CA	S	10.23 MW	11.39 AW	21270 AAW	CABLS	10//99-12//99
Food Preparation and Serving Workers	Yolo PMSA, CA	S	12.20 MW	12.01 AW	25370 AAW	CABLS	10//99-12//99
Food Preparation and Serving Workers	Yuba City MSA, CA	S	9.52 MW	8.50 AW	19800 AAW	CABLS	10//99-12//99
Food Preparation and Serving Workers	Colorado	S	10.66 MW	11.74 AW	24420 AAW	COBLS	10//99-12//99
Food Preparation and Serving Workers	Boulder-Longmont PMSA, CO	S	11.15 MW	11.50 AW	23190 AAW	COBLS	10//99-12//99
Food Preparation and Serving Workers	Colorado Springs MSA, CO	S	12.66 MW	12.59 AW	26340 AAW	COBLS	10//99-12//99
Food Preparation and Serving Workers	Denver PMSA, CO	S	12.98 MW	11.43 AW	26990 AAW	COBLS	10//99-12//99
Food Preparation and Serving Workers	Fort Collins-Loveland MSA, CO	S	8.24 MW	7.77 AW	17150 AAW	COBLS	10//99-12//99
Food Preparation and Serving Workers	Grand Junction MSA, CO	S	9.62 MW	8.96 AW	20010 AAW	COBLS	10//99-12//99
Food Preparation and Serving Workers	Greeley PMSA, CO	S	11.75 MW	10.39 AW	24440 AAW	COBLS	10//99-12//99
Food Preparation and Serving Workers	Pueblo MSA, CO	S	9.66 MW	9.79 AW	20100 AAW	COBLS	10//99-12//99
Food Preparation and Serving Workers	Connecticut	S	13.32 MW	13.90 AW	28910 AAW	CTBLS	10//99-12//99
Food Preparation and Serving Workers	Bridgeport PMSA, CT	S	15.90 MW	16.16 AW	33080 AAW	CTBLS	10//99-12//99
Food Preparation and Serving Workers	Danbury PMSA, CT	S	12.50 MW	12.25 AW	26000 AAW	CTBLS	10//99-12//99
Food Preparation and Serving Workers	Hartford MSA, CT	S	13.77 MW	13.67 AW	28640 AAW	CTBLS	10//99-12//99
Food Preparation and Serving Workers	New Haven-Meriden PMSA, CT	S	15.79 MW	15.74 AW	32850 AAW	CTBLS	10//99-12//99
Food Preparation and Serving Workers	New London-Norwich MSA, CT-RI	S	12.28 MW	11.52 AW	25550 AAW	CTBLS	10//99-12//99
Food Preparation and Serving Workers	Stamford-Norwalk PMSA, CT	S	14.16 MW	13.43 AW	29450 AAW	CTBLS	10//99-12//99
Food Preparation and Serving Workers	Waterbury PMSA, CT	S	15.16 MW	12.99 AW	31530 AAW	CTBLS	10//99-12//99
Food Preparation and Serving Workers	Delaware	S	11.36 MW	12.21 AW	25390 AAW	DEBLS	10//99-12//99
Food Preparation and Serving Workers	Dover MSA, DE	S	13.04 MW	12.61 AW	27120 AAW	DEBLS	10//99-12//99
Food Preparation and Serving Workers	Wilmington-Newark PMSA, DE-MD	S	12.21 MW	10.82 AW	25390 AAW	DEBLS	10//99-12//99
Food Preparation and Serving Workers	District of Columbia	S	12.04 MW	13.32 AW	27710 AAW	DCBLS	10//99-12//99
Food Preparation and Serving Workers	Washington PMSA, DC-MD-VA-WV	S	12.79 MW	11.96 AW	26600 AAW	DCBLS	10//99-12//99
Food Preparation and Serving Workers	Florida	S	11.16 MW	11.87 AW	24680 AAW	FLBLS	10//99-12//99
Food Preparation and Serving Workers	Daytona Beach MSA, FL	S	10.26 MW	9.21 AW	21340 AAW	FLBLS	10//99-12//99
Food Preparation and Serving Workers	Fort Lauderdale PMSA, FL	S	14.28 MW	14.44 AW	29710 AAW	FLBLS	10//99-12//99
Food Preparation and Serving Workers	Fort Myers-Cape Coral MSA, FL	S	12.38 MW	11.09 AW	25750 AAW	FLBLS	10//99-12//99
Food Preparation and Serving Workers	Fort Pierce-Port St. Lucie MSA, FL	S	9.86 MW	8.03 AW	20510 AAW	FLBLS	10//99-12//99
Food Preparation and Serving Workers	Fort Walton Beach MSA, FL	S	12.93 MW	13.50 AW	26900 AAW	FLBLS	10//99-12//99
Food Preparation and Serving Workers	Gainesville MSA, FL	S	9.44 MW	8.38 AW	19640 AAW	FLBLS	10//99-12//99
Food Preparation and Serving Workers	Jacksonville MSA, FL	S	11.80 MW	11.69 AW	24540 AAW	FLBLS	10//99-12//99
Food Preparation and Serving Workers	Lakeland-Winter Haven MSA, FL	S	13.00 MW	14.19 AW	27050 AAW	FLBLS	10//99-12//99
Food Preparation and Serving Workers	Melbourne-Titusville-Palm Bay MSA, FL	S	11.39 MW	11.40 AW	23680 AAW	FLBLS	10//99-12//99
Food Preparation and Serving Workers	Miami PMSA, FL	S	14.96 MW	14.71 AW	31120 AAW	FLBLS	10//99-12//99
Food Preparation and Serving Workers	Naples MSA, FL	S	13.34 MW	12.81 AW	27740 AAW	FLBLS	10//99-12//99
Food Preparation and Serving Workers	Ocala MSA, FL	S	8.40 MW	8.06 AW	17480 AAW	FLBLS	10//99-12//99
Food Preparation and Serving Workers	Orlando MSA, FL	S	11.52 MW	11.13 AW	23960 AAW	FLBLS	10//99-12//99
Food Preparation and Serving Workers	Panama City MSA, FL	S	10.89 MW	10.16 AW	22660 AAW	FLBLS	10//99-12//99
Food Preparation and Serving Workers	Pensacola MSA, FL	S	9.45 MW	9.14 AW	19650 AAW	FLBLS	10//99-12//99
Food Preparation and Serving Workers	Punta Gorda MSA, FL	S	10.14 MW	9.54 AW	21090 AAW	FLBLS	10//99-12//99
Food Preparation and Serving Workers	Sarasota-Bradenton MSA, FL	S	11.35 MW	10.42 AW	23600 AAW	FLBLS	10//99-12//99
Food Preparation and Serving Workers	Tallahassee MSA, FL	S	10.89 MW	10.90 AW	22640 AAW	FLBLS	10//99-12//99
Food Preparation and Serving Workers	Tampa-St. Petersburg-Clearwater MSA, FL	S	11.21 MW	9.86 AW	23310 AAW	FLBLS	10//99-12//99
Food Preparation and Serving Workers	West Palm Beach-Boca Raton MSA, FL	S	11.17 MW	8.72 AW	23220 AAW	FLBLS	10//99-12//99
Food Preparation and Serving Workers	Georgia	S	10.69 MW	10.81 AW	22480 AAW	GABLS	10//99-12//99
Food Preparation and Serving Workers	Albany MSA, GA	S	11.20 MW	10.85 AW	23290 AAW	GABLS	10//99-12//99
Food Preparation and Serving Workers	Athens MSA, GA	S	11.51 MW	11.58 AW	23940 AAW	GABLS	10//99-12//99
Food Preparation and Serving Workers	Atlanta MSA, GA	S	10.72 MW	10.12 AW	22300 AAW	GABLS	10//99-12//99
Food Preparation and Serving Workers	Augusta-Aiken MSA, GA-SC	S	10.74 MW	11.15 AW	22350 AAW	GABLS	10//99-12//99
Food Preparation and Serving Workers	Columbus MSA, GA-AL	S	11.08 MW	11.42 AW	23050 AAW	GABLS	10//99-12//99
Food Preparation and Serving Workers	Macon MSA, GA	S	11.20 MW	11.43 AW	23300 AAW	GABLS	10//99-12//99

AAW	Average annual wage	AOH	Average offered, high	ASH	Average starting, high	H	Hourly	M	Monthly	S	Special: hourly and annual
AE	Average entry wage	AOL	Average offered, low	ASL	Average starting, low	HI	Highest wage paid	MTC	Median total compensation	TQ	Third quartile wage
AEX	Average experienced wage	APH	Average pay, high range	AW	Average wage paid	HR	High end range	MW	Median wage paid	W	Weekly
AO	Average offered	APL	Average pay, low range	FQ	First quartile wage	LR	Low end range	SQ	Second quartile wage	Y	Yearly

Occupation/Type/Industry	Location	Per	Low	Mid	High	Source	Date
First-Line Supervisor/Manager							
Food Preparation and Serving Workers	Savannah MSA, GA	S	10.37 MW	10.30 AW	21580 AAW	GABLS	10//99-12//99
Food Preparation and Serving Workers	Hawaii	S	12.49 MW	12.48 AW	25950 AAW	HIBLS	10//99-12//99
Food Preparation and Serving Workers	Honolulu MSA, HI	S	12.02 MW	11.78 AW	25010 AAW	HIBLS	10//99-12//99
Food Preparation and Serving Workers	Idaho	S	8.18 MW	9.03 AW	18770 AAW	IDBLS	10//99-12//99
Food Preparation and Serving Workers	Boise City MSA, ID	S	10.14 MW	9.08 AW	21090 AAW	IDBLS	10//99-12//99
Food Preparation and Serving Workers	Pocatello MSA, ID	S	9.34 MW	9.33 AW	19420 AAW	IDBLS	10//99-12//99
Food Preparation and Serving Workers	Illinois	S	12.71 MW	13.74 AW	28580 AAW	ILBLS	10//99-12//99
Food Preparation and Serving Workers	Bloomington-Normal MSA, IL	S	10.07 MW	10.27 AW	20940 AAW	ILBLS	10//99-12//99
Food Preparation and Serving Workers	Champaign-Urbana MSA, IL	S	8.57 MW	7.96 AW	17820 AAW	ILBLS	10//99-12//99
Food Preparation and Serving Workers	Chicago PMSA, IL	S	15.27 MW	14.72 AW	31760 AAW	ILBLS	10//99-12//99
Food Preparation and Serving Workers	Decatur MSA, IL	S	8.31 MW	8.10 AW	17290 AAW	ILBLS	10//99-12//99
Food Preparation and Serving Workers	Kankakee PMSA, IL	S	8.64 MW	8.18 AW	17970 AAW	ILBLS	10//99-12//99
Food Preparation and Serving Workers	Peoria-Pekin MSA, IL	S	10.02 MW	8.05 AW	20830 AAW	ILBLS	10//99-12//99
Food Preparation and Serving Workers	Rockford MSA, IL	S	7.94 MW	7.71 AW	16520 AAW	ILBLS	10//99-12//99
Food Preparation and Serving Workers	Springfield MSA, IL	S	16.19 MW	17.50 AW	33680 AAW	ILBLS	10//99-12//99
Food Preparation and Serving Workers	Indiana	S	10 MW	10.74 AW	22330 AAW	INBLS	10//99-12//99
Food Preparation and Serving Workers	Bloomington MSA, IN	S	9.60 MW	8.28 AW	19970 AAW	INBLS	10//99-12//99
Food Preparation and Serving Workers	Elkhart-Goshen MSA, IN	S	10.62 MW	10.08 AW	22100 AAW	INBLS	10//99-12//99
Food Preparation and Serving Workers	Evansville-Henderson MSA, IN-KY	S	9.54 MW	9.12 AW	19850 AAW	INBLS	10//99-12//99
Food Preparation and Serving Workers	Fort Wayne MSA, IN	S	13.05 MW	12.11 AW	27150 AAW	INBLS	10//99-12//99
Food Preparation and Serving Workers	Gary PMSA, IN	S	11.22 MW	10.45 AW	23350 AAW	INBLS	10//99-12//99
Food Preparation and Serving Workers	Indianapolis MSA, IN	S	12.52 MW	12.17 AW	26040 AAW	INBLS	10//99-12//99
Food Preparation and Serving Workers	Kokomo MSA, IN	S	11.07 MW	10.36 AW	23030 AAW	INBLS	10//99-12//99
Food Preparation and Serving Workers	Lafayette MSA, IN	S	9.47 MW	8.34 AW	19710 AAW	INBLS	10//99-12//99
Food Preparation and Serving Workers	Muncie MSA, IN	S	13.10 MW	13.34 AW	27240 AAW	INBLS	10//99-12//99
Food Preparation and Serving Workers	South Bend MSA, IN	S	11.96 MW	11.62 AW	24870 AAW	INBLS	10//99-12//99
Food Preparation and Serving Workers	Terre Haute MSA, IN	S	8.89 MW	8.39 AW	18500 AAW	INBLS	10//99-12//99
Food Preparation and Serving Workers	Iowa	S	8.87 MW	9.98 AW	20750 AAW	IABLS	10//99-12//99
Food Preparation and Serving Workers	Cedar Rapids MSA, IA	S	10.13 MW	9.45 AW	21060 AAW	IABLS	10//99-12//99
Food Preparation and Serving Workers	Davenport-Moline-Rock Island MSA, IA-IL	S	8.73 MW	8.13 AW	18150 AAW	IABLS	10//99-12//99
Food Preparation and Serving Workers	Des Moines MSA, IA	S	10.95 MW	10.40 AW	22780 AAW	IABLS	10//99-12//99
Food Preparation and Serving Workers	Dubuque MSA, IA	S	10.55 MW	8.98 AW	21950 AAW	IABLS	10//99-12//99
Food Preparation and Serving Workers	Sioux City MSA, IA-NE	S	8.80 MW	8.30 AW	18300 AAW	IABLS	10//99-12//99
Food Preparation and Serving Workers	Waterloo-Cedar Falls MSA, IA	S	8.73 MW	8.01 AW	18160 AAW	IABLS	10//99-12//99
Food Preparation and Serving Workers	Kansas	S	9.39 MW	10.08 AW	20960 AAW	KSBLS	10//99-12//99
Food Preparation and Serving Workers	Lawrence MSA, KS	S	9.23 MW	8.76 AW	19200 AAW	KSBLS	10//99-12//99
Food Preparation and Serving Workers	Topeka MSA, KS	S	9.69 MW	9.22 AW	20160 AAW	KSBLS	10//99-12//99
Food Preparation and Serving Workers	Wichita MSA, KS	S	12.18 MW	11.75 AW	25340 AAW	KSBLS	10//99-12//99
Food Preparation and Serving Workers	Kentucky	S	9.62 MW	10.45 AW	21740 AAW	KYBLS	10//99-12//99
Food Preparation and Serving Workers	Lexington MSA, KY	S	10.92 MW	10.75 AW	22710 AAW	KYBLS	10//99-12//99
Food Preparation and Serving Workers	Louisville MSA, KY-IN	S	10.07 MW	9.12 AW	20940 AAW	KYBLS	10//99-12//99
Food Preparation and Serving Workers	Owensboro MSA, KY	S	12.66 MW	12.60 AW	26340 AAW	KYBLS	10//99-12//99
Food Preparation and Serving Workers	Louisiana	S	9.58 MW	10.06 AW	20920 AAW	LABLS	10//99-12//99
Food Preparation and Serving Workers	Alexandria MSA, LA	S	8.70 MW	7.43 AW	18100 AAW	LABLS	10//99-12//99
Food Preparation and Serving Workers	Baton Rouge MSA, LA	S	10.99 MW	10.72 AW	22850 AAW	LABLS	10//99-12//99
Food Preparation and Serving Workers	Houma MSA, LA	S	11.42 MW	10.76 AW	23740 AAW	LABLS	10//99-12//99
Food Preparation and Serving Workers	Lafayette MSA, LA	S	10.21 MW	9.20 AW	21240 AAW	LABLS	10//99-12//99
Food Preparation and Serving Workers	Lake Charles MSA, LA	S	9.78 MW	9.04 AW	20330 AAW	LABLS	10//99-12//99
Food Preparation and Serving Workers	Monroe MSA, LA	S	8.16 MW	7.89 AW	16970 AAW	LABLS	10//99-12//99
Food Preparation and Serving Workers	New Orleans MSA, LA	S	10.21 MW	10.21 AW	21230 AAW	LABLS	10//99-12//99
Food Preparation and Serving Workers	Shreveport-Bossier City MSA, LA	S	9.88 MW	9.74 AW	20540 AAW	LABLS	10//99-12//99
Food Preparation and Serving Workers	Maine	S	9.06 MW	10.08 AW	20970 AAW	MEBLS	10//99-12//99
Food Preparation and Serving Workers	Bangor MSA, ME	S	9.89 MW	9.78 AW	20570 AAW	MEBLS	10//99-12//99
Food Preparation and Serving Workers	Lewiston-Auburn MSA, ME	S	8.88 MW	8.33 AW	18460 AAW	MEBLS	10//99-12//99
Food Preparation and Serving Workers	Portland MSA, ME	S	8.43 MW	8.03 AW	17540 AAW	MEBLS	10//99-12//99
Food Preparation and Serving Workers	Maryland	S	13.67 MW	15.16 AW	31540 AAW	MDBLS	10//99-12//99
Food Preparation and Serving Workers	Baltimore PMSA, MD	S	17.29 MW	14.79 AW	35950 AAW	MDBLS	10//99-12//99
Food Preparation and Serving Workers	Cumberland MSA, MD-WV	S	9.51 MW	9.33 AW	19780 AAW	MDBLS	10//99-12//99
Food Preparation and Serving Workers	Hagerstown PMSA, MD	S	13.87 MW	14.38 AW	28840 AAW	MDBLS	10//99-12//99
Food Preparation and Serving Workers	Massachusetts	S	12.73 MW	13.46 AW	27990 AAW	MABLS	10//99-12//99
Food Preparation and Serving Workers	Barnstable-Yarmouth MSA, MA	S	14.24 MW	12.76 AW	29620 AAW	MABLS	10//99-12//99
Food Preparation and Serving Workers	Boston PMSA, MA-NH	S	13.90 MW	13.07 AW	28910 AAW	MABLS	10//99-12//99
Food Preparation and Serving Workers	Brockton PMSA, MA	S	11.72 MW	11.39 AW	24370 AAW	MABLS	10//99-12//99
Food Preparation and Serving Workers	Fitchburg-Leominster PMSA, MA	S	13.76 MW	14.15 AW	28610 AAW	MABLS	10//99-12//99
Food Preparation and Serving Workers	Lawrence PMSA, MA-NH	S	15.34 MW	14.44 AW	31900 AAW	MABLS	10//99-12//99
Food Preparation and Serving Workers	Lowell PMSA, MA-NH	S	14.13 MW	12.55 AW	29380 AAW	MABLS	10//99-12//99

AAW Average annual wage	AOH Average offered, high	ASH Average starting, high	H Hourly	M Monthly	S Special: hourly and annual
AE Average entry wage	AOL Average offered, low	ASL Average starting, low	HI Highest wage paid	MTC Median total compensation	TQ Third quartile wage
AEX Average experienced wage	APH Average pay, high range	AW Average wage paid	HR High end range	MW Median wage paid	W Weekly
AO Average offered	APL Average pay, low range	FQ First quartile wage	LR Low end range	SQ Second quartile wage	Y Yearly

Occupation/Type/Industry	Location	Per	Low	Mid	High	Source	Date
First-Line Supervisor/Manager							
Food Preparation and Serving Workers	New Bedford PMSA, MA	S	11.31 MW	10.88 AW	23520 AAW	MABLS	10//99-12//99
Food Preparation and Serving Workers	Pittsfield MSA, MA	S	12.65 MW	12.56 AW	26310 AAW	MABLS	10//99-12//99
Food Preparation and Serving Workers	Springfield MSA, MA	S	12.58 MW	12.76 AW	26170 AAW	MABLS	10//99-12//99
Food Preparation and Serving Workers	Worcester PMSA, MA-CT	S	12.96 MW	12.46 AW	26960 AAW	MABLS	10//99-12//99
Food Preparation and Serving Workers	Michigan	S	12.18 MW	12.57 AW	26150 AAW	MIBLS	10//99-12//99
Food Preparation and Serving Workers	Ann Arbor PMSA, MI	S	12.43 MW	11.90 AW	25850 AAW	MIBLS	10//99-12//99
Food Preparation and Serving Workers	Benton Harbor MSA, MI	S	9.29 MW	9.08 AW	19320 AAW	MIBLS	10//99-12//99
Food Preparation and Serving Workers	Detroit PMSA, MI	S	12.54 MW	12.61 AW	26070 AAW	MIBLS	10//99-12//99
Food Preparation and Serving Workers	Flint PMSA, MI	S	13.87 MW	13.94 AW	28860 AAW	MIBLS	10//99-12//99
Food Preparation and Serving Workers	Grand Rapids-Muskegon-Holland MSA, MI	S	13.24 MW	12.34 AW	27530 AAW	MIBLS	10//99-12//99
Food Preparation and Serving Workers	Jackson MSA, MI	S	14.75 MW	15.08 AW	30670 AAW	MIBLS	10//99-12//99
Food Preparation and Serving Workers	Kalamazoo-Battle Creek MSA, MI	S	12.42 MW	11.88 AW	25840 AAW	MIBLS	10//99-12//99
Food Preparation and Serving Workers	Lansing-East Lansing MSA, MI	S	11.80 MW	10.86 AW	24540 AAW	MIBLS	10//99-12//99
Food Preparation and Serving Workers	Saginaw-Bay City-Midland MSA, MI	S	12.93 MW	12.81 AW	26900 AAW	MIBLS	10//99-12//99
Food Preparation and Serving Workers	Minnesota	S	10.44 MW	11.02 AW	22920 AAW	MNBLS	10//99-12//99
Food Preparation and Serving Workers	Duluth-Superior MSA, MN-WI	S	10.13 MW	9.84 AW	21080 AAW	MNBLS	10//99-12//99
Food Preparation and Serving Workers	Minneapolis-St. Paul MSA, MN-WI	S	11.52 MW	10.94 AW	23960 AAW	MNBLS	10//99-12//99
Food Preparation and Serving Workers	Rochester MSA, MN	S	10.16 MW	9.45 AW	21140 AAW	MNBLS	10//99-12//99
Food Preparation and Serving Workers	St. Cloud MSA, MN	S	8.92 MW	8.03 AW	18550 AAW	MNBLS	10//99-12//99
Food Preparation and Serving Workers	Mississippi	S	8.06 MW	8.72 AW	18130 AAW	MSBLS	10//99-12//99
Food Preparation and Serving Workers	Biloxi-Gulfport-Pascagoula MSA, MS	S	8.85 MW	7.88 AW	18410 AAW	MSBLS	10//99-12//99
Food Preparation and Serving Workers	Hattiesburg MSA, MS	S	8.99 MW	8.12 AW	18700 AAW	MSBLS	10//99-12//99
Food Preparation and Serving Workers	Jackson MSA, MS	S	9.05 MW	8.57 AW	18820 AAW	MSBLS	10//99-12//99
Food Preparation and Serving Workers	Missouri	S	8.91 MW	9.88 AW	20560 AAW	MOBLS	10//99-12//99
Food Preparation and Serving Workers	Columbia MSA, MO	S	9.52 MW	8.21 AW	19800 AAW	MOBLS	10//99-12//99
Food Preparation and Serving Workers	Kansas City MSA, MO-KS	S	8.70 MW	6.73 AW	18100 AAW	MOBLS	10//99-12//99
Food Preparation and Serving Workers	St. Joseph MSA, MO	S	9.08 MW	8.75 AW	18890 AAW	MOBLS	10//99-12//99
Food Preparation and Serving Workers	St. Louis MSA, MO-IL	S	12.61 MW	10.73 AW	26220 AAW	MOBLS	10//99-12//99
Food Preparation and Serving Workers	Springfield MSA, MO	S	10.18 MW	8.61 AW	21180 AAW	MOBLS	10//99-12//99
Food Preparation and Serving Workers	Montana	S	9.05 MW	9.12 AW	18970 AAW	MTBLS	10//99-12//99
Food Preparation and Serving Workers	Billings MSA, MT	S	8.82 MW	8.91 AW	18350 AAW	MTBLS	10//99-12//99
Food Preparation and Serving Workers	Great Falls MSA, MT	S	8.30 MW	8.31 AW	17260 AAW	MTBLS	10//99-12//99
Food Preparation and Serving Workers	Missoula MSA, MT	S	10.10 MW	8.33 AW	21010 AAW	MTBLS	10//99-12//99
Food Preparation and Serving Workers	Nebraska	S	9.73 MW	10.43 AW	21690 AAW	NEBLS	10//99-12//99
Food Preparation and Serving Workers	Lincoln MSA, NE	S	12.03 MW	11.93 AW	25010 AAW	NEBLS	10//99-12//99
Food Preparation and Serving Workers	Omaha MSA, NE-IA	S	10.58 MW	9.42 AW	22000 AAW	NEBLS	10//99-12//99
Food Preparation and Serving Workers	Nevada	S	10.72 MW	11.77 AW	24490 AAW	NVBLS	10//99-12//99
Food Preparation and Serving Workers	Las Vegas MSA, NV-AZ	S	11.49 MW	10.46 AW	23900 AAW	NVBLS	10//99-12//99
Food Preparation and Serving Workers	Reno MSA, NV	S	11.52 MW	10.47 AW	23960 AAW	NVBLS	10//99-12//99
Food Preparation and Serving Workers	New Hampshire	S	10.29 MW	10.75 AW	22350 AAW	NHBLS	10//99-12//99
Food Preparation and Serving Workers	Manchester PMSA, NH	S	9.01 MW	6.73 AW	18740 AAW	NHBLS	10//99-12//99
Food Preparation and Serving Workers	Nashua PMSA, NH	S	10.17 MW	9.93 AW	21160 AAW	NHBLS	10//99-12//99
Food Preparation and Serving Workers	Portsmouth-Rochester PMSA, NH-ME	S	13.07 MW	12.61 AW	27190 AAW	NHBLS	10//99-12//99
Food Preparation and Serving Workers	New Jersey	S	12.4 MW	13.35 AW	27780 AAW	NJBLS	10//99-12//99
Food Preparation and Serving Workers	Atlantic-Cape May PMSA, NJ	S	16.37 MW	16.97 AW	34050 AAW	NJBLS	10//99-12//99
Food Preparation and Serving Workers	Bergen-Passaic PMSA, NJ	S	11.27 MW	9.82 AW	23450 AAW	NJBLS	10//99-12//99
Food Preparation and Serving Workers	Jersey City PMSA, NJ	S	13.34 MW	12.54 AW	27760 AAW	NJBLS	10//99-12//99
Food Preparation and Serving Workers	Middlesex-Somerset-Hunterdon PMSA, NJ	S	13.75 MW	13.28 AW	28590 AAW	NJBLS	10//99-12//99
Food Preparation and Serving Workers	Monmouth-Ocean PMSA, NJ	S	14.84 MW	14.74 AW	30870 AAW	NJBLS	10//99-12//99
Food Preparation and Serving Workers	Newark PMSA, NJ	S	12.41 MW	10.46 AW	25820 AAW	NJBLS	10//99-12//99
Food Preparation and Serving Workers	Vineland-Millville-Bridgeton PMSA, NJ	S	13.62 MW	12.39 AW	28330 AAW	NJBLS	10//99-12//99
Food Preparation and Serving Workers	New Mexico	S	8.12 MW	8.75 AW	18200 AAW	NMBLS	10//99-12//99
Food Preparation and Serving Workers	Albuquerque MSA, NM	S	9.38 MW	8.65 AW	19520 AAW	NMBLS	10//99-12//99
Food Preparation and Serving Workers	Las Cruces MSA, NM	S	7.52 MW	6.64 AW	15630 AAW	NMBLS	10//99-12//99
Food Preparation and Serving Workers	Santa Fe MSA, NM	S	8.24 MW	7.79 AW	17140 AAW	NMBLS	10//99-12//99
Food Preparation and Serving Workers	New York	S	9.83 MW	11.49 AW	23900 AAW	NYBLS	10//99-12//99
Food Preparation and Serving Workers	Albany-Schenectady-Troy MSA, NY	S	13.44 MW	12.25 AW	27950 AAW	NYBLS	10//99-12//99
Food Preparation and Serving Workers	Binghamton MSA, NY	S	9.78 MW	8.93 AW	20340 AAW	NYBLS	10//99-12//99
Food Preparation and Serving Workers	Buffalo-Niagara Falls MSA, NY	S	9.42 MW	8.50 AW	19600 AAW	NYBLS	10//99-12//99
Food Preparation and Serving Workers	Elmira MSA, NY	S	9.36 MW	8.17 AW	19460 AAW	NYBLS	10//99-12//99
Food Preparation and Serving Workers	Glens Falls MSA, NY	S	10.49 MW	9.33 AW	21810 AAW	NYBLS	10//99-12//99

AAW	Average annual wage	AOH	Average offered, high	ASH	Average starting, high
AE	Average entry wage	AOL	Average offered, low	ASL	Average starting, low
AEX	Average experienced wage	APH	Average pay, high range	AW	Average wage paid
AO	Average offered	APL	Average pay, low range	FQ	First quartile wage

H	Hourly	M	Monthly	S	Special: hourly and annual
HI	Highest wage paid	MTC	Median total compensation	TQ	Third quartile wage
HR	High end range	MW	Median wage paid	W	Weekly
LR	Low end range	SQ	Second quartile wage	Y	Yearly

Occupation/Type/Industry	Location	Per	Low	Mid	High	Source	Date
First-Line Supervisor/Manager							
Food Preparation and Serving Workers	Jamestown MSA, NY	S	10.26 MW	9.65 AW	21340 AAW	NYBLS	10//99-12//99
Food Preparation and Serving Workers	Nassau-Suffolk PMSA, NY	S	9.75 MW	6.98 AW	20280 AAW	NYBLS	10//99-12//99
Food Preparation and Serving Workers	New York PMSA, NY	S	17.79 MW	17.38 AW	37000 AAW	NYBLS	10//99-12//99
Food Preparation and Serving Workers	Newburgh PMSA, NY-PA	S	11.40 MW	10.38 AW	23720 AAW	NYBLS	10//99-12//99
Food Preparation and Serving Workers	Rochester MSA, NY	S	13.21 MW	12.93 AW	27470 AAW	NYBLS	10//99-12//99
Food Preparation and Serving Workers	Syracuse MSA, NY	S	11.47 MW	10.55 AW	23860 AAW	NYBLS	10//99-12//99
Food Preparation and Serving Workers	Utica-Rome MSA, NY	S	7.42 MW	6.30 AW	15430 AAW	NYBLS	10//99-12//99
Food Preparation and Serving Workers	North Carolina	S	9.99 MW	10.92 AW	22720 AAW	NCBLS	10//99-12//99
Food Preparation and Serving Workers	Asheville MSA, NC	S	10.72 MW	8.40 AW	22300 AAW	NCBLS	10//99-12//99
Food Preparation and Serving Workers	Charlotte-Gastonia-Rock Hill MSA, NC-SC	S	11.33 MW	10.58 AW	23570 AAW	NCBLS	10//99-12//99
Food Preparation and Serving Workers	Fayetteville MSA, NC	S	10.02 MW	9.77 AW	20840 AAW	NCBLS	10//99-12//99
Food Preparation and Serving Workers	Goldsboro MSA, NC	S	8.96 MW	8.58 AW	18630 AAW	NCBLS	10//99-12//99
Food Preparation and Serving Workers	Greensboro--Winston-Salem-- High Point MSA, NC	S	11.65 MW	10.68 AW	24230 AAW	NCBLS	10//99-12//99
Food Preparation and Serving Workers	Greenville MSA, NC	S	9.58 MW	9.62 AW	19920 AAW	NCBLS	10//99-12//99
Food Preparation and Serving Workers	Hickory-Morganton-Lenoir MSA, NC	S	10.60 MW	10.05 AW	22040 AAW	NCBLS	10//99-12//99
Food Preparation and Serving Workers	Jacksonville MSA, NC	S	7.02 MW	6.15 AW	14600 AAW	NCBLS	10//99-12//99
Food Preparation and Serving Workers	Raleigh-Durham-Chapel Hill MSA, NC	S	11.55 MW	11.07 AW	24030 AAW	NCBLS	10//99-12//99
Food Preparation and Serving Workers	Rocky Mount MSA, NC	S	9.32 MW	9.51 AW	19380 AAW	NCBLS	10//99-12//99
Food Preparation and Serving Workers	Wilmington MSA, NC	S	10.67 MW	10.43 AW	22190 AAW	NCBLS	10//99-12//99
Food Preparation and Serving Workers	North Dakota	S	8.01 MW	8.68 AW	18050 AAW	NDBLS	10//99-12//99
Food Preparation and Serving Workers	Bismarck MSA, ND	S	7.61 MW	7.61 AW	15820 AAW	NDBLS	10//99-12//99
Food Preparation and Serving Workers	Fargo-Moorhead MSA, ND-MN	S	8.76 MW	7.95 AW	18220 AAW	NDBLS	10//99-12//99
Food Preparation and Serving Workers	Grand Forks MSA, ND-MN	S	8.82 MW	8.36 AW	18350 AAW	NDBLS	10//99-12//99
Food Preparation and Serving Workers	Ohio	S	10.24 MW	10.75 AW	22350 AAW	OHBLS	10//99-12//99
Food Preparation and Serving Workers	Akron PMSA, OH	S	9.71 MW	9.14 AW	20200 AAW	OHBLS	10//99-12//99
Food Preparation and Serving Workers	Canton-Massillon MSA, OH	S	11.64 MW	11.83 AW	24210 AAW	OHBLS	10//99-12//99
Food Preparation and Serving Workers	Cincinnati PMSA, OH-KY-IN	S	10.82 MW	9.92 AW	22500 AAW	OHBLS	10//99-12//99
Food Preparation and Serving Workers	Cleveland-Lorain-Elyria PMSA, OH	S	11.87 MW	11.54 AW	24680 AAW	OHBLS	10//99-12//99
Food Preparation and Serving Workers	Columbus MSA, OH	S	11.50 MW	10.83 AW	23920 AAW	OHBLS	10//99-12//99
Food Preparation and Serving Workers	Dayton-Springfield MSA, OH	S	11.86 MW	11.25 AW	24670 AAW	OHBLS	10//99-12//99
Food Preparation and Serving Workers	Hamilton-Middletown PMSA, OH	S	11.09 MW	10.67 AW	23070 AAW	OHBLS	10//99-12//99
Food Preparation and Serving Workers	Lima MSA, OH	S	8.01 MW	7.77 AW	16650 AAW	OHBLS	10//99-12//99
Food Preparation and Serving Workers	Mansfield MSA, OH	S	8.75 MW	8.02 AW	18200 AAW	OHBLS	10//99-12//99
Food Preparation and Serving Workers	Steubenville-Weirton MSA, OH-WV	S	7.95 MW	7.29 AW	16530 AAW	OHBLS	10//99-12//99
Food Preparation and Serving Workers	Toledo MSA, OH	S	10.62 MW	10.16 AW	22080 AAW	OHBLS	10//99-12//99
Food Preparation and Serving Workers	Youngstown-Warren MSA, OH	S	9.49 MW	8.01 AW	19740 AAW	OHBLS	10//99-12//99
Food Preparation and Serving Workers	Oklahoma	S	8.27 MW	9.35 AW	19450 AAW	OKBLS	10//99-12//99
Food Preparation and Serving Workers	Lawton MSA, OK	S	9.89 MW	9.61 AW	20570 AAW	OKBLS	10//99-12//99
Food Preparation and Serving Workers	Oklahoma City MSA, OK	S	8.36 MW	7.98 AW	17390 AAW	OKBLS	10//99-12//99
Food Preparation and Serving Workers	Tulsa MSA, OK	S	9.46 MW	8.24 AW	19670 AAW	OKBLS	10//99-12//99
Food Preparation and Serving Workers	Oregon	S	10.86 MW	11.55 AW	24030 AAW	ORBLS	10//99-12//99
Food Preparation and Serving Workers	Corvallis MSA, OR	S	12.38 MW	11.55 AW	25750 AAW	ORBLS	10//99-12//99
Food Preparation and Serving Workers	Eugene-Springfield MSA, OR	S	9.97 MW	9.68 AW	20750 AAW	ORBLS	10//99-12//99
Food Preparation and Serving Workers	Medford-Ashland MSA, OR	S	10.97 MW	10.38 AW	22820 AAW	ORBLS	10//99-12//99
Food Preparation and Serving Workers	Portland-Vancouver PMSA, OR-WA	S	12.58 MW	12.37 AW	26170 AAW	ORBLS	10//99-12//99
Food Preparation and Serving Workers	Salem PMSA, OR	S	10.29 MW	9.68 AW	21410 AAW	ORBLS	10//99-12//99
Food Preparation and Serving Workers	Pennsylvania	S	10.83 MW	13.20 AW	27460 AAW	PABLS	10//99-12//99
Food Preparation and Serving Workers	Allentown-Bethlehem-Easton MSA, PA	S	12.04 MW	12.09 AW	25040 AAW	PABLS	10//99-12//99
Food Preparation and Serving Workers	Altoona MSA, PA	S	9.92 MW	8.59 AW	20630 AAW	PABLS	10//99-12//99
Food Preparation and Serving Workers	Erie MSA, PA	S	11.51 MW	10.93 AW	23930 AAW	PABLS	10//99-12//99
Food Preparation and Serving Workers	Harrisburg-Lebanon-Carlisle MSA, PA	S	12.49 MW	12.10 AW	25980 AAW	PABLS	10//99-12//99
Food Preparation and Serving Workers	Johnstown MSA, PA	S	10.24 MW	8.91 AW	21290 AAW	PABLS	10//99-12//99
Food Preparation and Serving Workers	Philadelphia PMSA, PA-NJ	S	13.37 MW	13.34 AW	27810 AAW	PABLS	10//99-12//99
Food Preparation and Serving Workers	Pittsburgh MSA, PA	S	11.41 MW	10.45 AW	23720 AAW	PABLS	10//99-12//99
Food Preparation and Serving Workers	Reading MSA, PA	S	12.48 MW	11.79 AW	25960 AAW	PABLS	10//99-12//99
Food Preparation and Serving Workers	Scranton--Wilkes-Barre-- Hazleton MSA, PA	S	10.01 MW	9.79 AW	20820 AAW	PABLS	10//99-12//99
Food Preparation and Serving Workers	Sharon MSA, PA	S	9.54 MW	9.45 AW	19840 AAW	PABLS	10//99-12//99
Food Preparation and Serving Workers	State College MSA, PA	S	11.49 MW	11.10 AW	23890 AAW	PABLS	10//99-12//99
Food Preparation and Serving Workers	Williamsport MSA, PA	S	11.47 MW	9.55 AW	23850 AAW	PABLS	10//99-12//99

AAW Average annual wage	**AOH** Average offered, high	**ASH** Average starting, high	**H** Hourly	**M** Monthly	**S** Special: hourly and annual
AE Average entry wage	**AOL** Average offered, low	**ASL** Average starting, low	**HI** Highest wage paid	**MTC** Median total compensation	**TQ** Third quartile wage
AEX Average experienced wage	**APH** Average pay, high range	**AW** Average wage paid	**HR** High end range	**MW** Median wage paid	**W** Weekly
AO Average offered	**APL** Average pay, low range	**FQ** First quartile wage	**LR** Low end range	**SQ** Second quartile wage	**Y** Yearly

Occupation/Type/Industry	Location	Per	Low	Mid	High	Source	Date
First-Line Supervisor/Manager							
Food Preparation and Serving Workers	York MSA, PA	S	12.04 MW	10.49 AW	25030 AAW	PABLS	10//99-12//99
Food Preparation and Serving Workers	Rhode Island	S	12.89 MW	14.20 AW	29540 AAW	RIBLS	10//99-12//99
Food Preparation and Serving Workers	Providence-Fall River-Warwick MSA, RI-MA	S	14.12 MW	12.95 AW	29370 AAW	RIBLS	10//99-12//99
Food Preparation and Serving Workers	South Carolina	S	8.16 MW	9.23 AW	19200 AAW	SCBLS	10//99-12//99
Food Preparation and Serving Workers	Charleston-North Charleston MSA, SC	S	12.95 MW	10.58 AW	26940 AAW	SCBLS	10//99-12//99
Food Preparation and Serving Workers	Columbia MSA, SC	S	9.71 MW	9.55 AW	20190 AAW	SCBLS	10//99-12//99
Food Preparation and Serving Workers	Florence MSA, SC	S	8.91 MW	9.12 AW	18530 AAW	SCBLS	10//99-12//99
Food Preparation and Serving Workers	Greenville-Spartanburg-Anderson MSA, SC	S	11.19 MW	10.48 AW	23270 AAW	SCBLS	10//99-12//99
Food Preparation and Serving Workers	Myrtle Beach MSA, SC	S	11.90 MW	11.26 AW	24750 AAW	SCBLS	10//99-12//99
Food Preparation and Serving Workers	Sumter MSA, SC	S	9.38 MW	8.42 AW	19500 AAW	SCBLS	10//99-12//99
Food Preparation and Serving Workers	South Dakota	S	10.61 MW	10.78 AW	22420 AAW	SDBLS	10//99-12//99
Food Preparation and Serving Workers	Rapid City MSA, SD	S	10.56 MW	10.39 AW	21960 AAW	SDBLS	10//99-12//99
Food Preparation and Serving Workers	Sioux Falls MSA, SD	S	10.99 MW	10.68 AW	22850 AAW	SDBLS	10//99-12//99
Food Preparation and Serving Workers	Tennessee	S	10.98 MW	11.46 AW	23830 AAW	TNBLS	10//99-12//99
Food Preparation and Serving Workers	Chattanooga MSA, TN-GA	S	10.91 MW	11.00 AW	22690 AAW	TNBLS	10//99-12//99
Food Preparation and Serving Workers	Clarksville-Hopkinsville MSA, TN-KY	S	8.84 MW	7.98 AW	18380 AAW	TNBLS	10//99-12//99
Food Preparation and Serving Workers	Jackson MSA, TN	S	8.84 MW	9.02 AW	18390 AAW	TNBLS	10//99-12//99
Food Preparation and Serving Workers	Johnson City-Kingsport-Bristol MSA, TN-VA	S	11.23 MW	10.46 AW	23370 AAW	TNBLS	10//99-12//99
Food Preparation and Serving Workers	Knoxville MSA, TN	S	13.93 MW	13.05 AW	28970 AAW	TNBLS	10//99-12//99
Food Preparation and Serving Workers	Memphis MSA, TN-AR-MS	S	10.89 MW	10.42 AW	22660 AAW	MSBLS	10//99-12//99
Food Preparation and Serving Workers	Nashville MSA, TN	S	11.59 MW	11.33 AW	24120 AAW	TNBLS	10//99-12//99
Food Preparation and Serving Workers	Texas	S	10.51 MW	11.12 AW	23130 AAW	TXBLS	10//99-12//99
Food Preparation and Serving Workers	Abilene MSA, TX	S	8.51 MW	6.74 AW	17700 AAW	TXBLS	10//99-12//99
Food Preparation and Serving Workers	Amarillo MSA, TX	S	8.35 MW	7.80 AW	17370 AAW	TXBLS	10//99-12//99
Food Preparation and Serving Workers	Austin-San Marcos MSA, TX	S	11.93 MW	11.96 AW	24810 AAW	TXBLS	10//99-12//99
Food Preparation and Serving Workers	Beaumont-Port Arthur MSA, TX	S	9.40 MW	9.11 AW	19560 AAW	TXBLS	10//99-12//99
Food Preparation and Serving Workers	Brazoria PMSA, TX	S	9.66 MW	8.80 AW	20090 AAW	TXBLS	10//99-12//99
Food Preparation and Serving Workers	Brownsville-Harlingen-San Benito MSA, TX	S	7.52 MW	7.47 AW	15650 AAW	TXBLS	10//99-12//99
Food Preparation and Serving Workers	Bryan-College Station MSA, TX	S	9.52 MW	8.72 AW	19810 AAW	TXBLS	10//99-12//99
Food Preparation and Serving Workers	Corpus Christi MSA, TX	S	8.73 MW	8.29 AW	18170 AAW	TXBLS	10//99-12//99
Food Preparation and Serving Workers	Dallas PMSA, TX	S	12.55 MW	12.05 AW	26100 AAW	TXBLS	10//99-12//99
Food Preparation and Serving Workers	El Paso MSA, TX	S	11.94 MW	12.82 AW	24830 AAW	TXBLS	10//99-12//99
Food Preparation and Serving Workers	Fort Worth-Arlington PMSA, TX	S	14.42 MW	13.28 AW	30000 AAW	TXBLS	10//99-12//99
Food Preparation and Serving Workers	Galveston-Texas City PMSA, TX	S	10.23 MW	9.60 AW	21280 AAW	TXBLS	10//99-12//99
Food Preparation and Serving Workers	Houston PMSA, TX	S	9.88 MW	9.59 AW	20540 AAW	TXBLS	10//99-12//99
Food Preparation and Serving Workers	Killeen-Temple MSA, TX	S	8.84 MW	7.79 AW	18380 AAW	TXBLS	10//99-12//99
Food Preparation and Serving Workers	Laredo MSA, TX	S	9.41 MW	8.50 AW	19580 AAW	TXBLS	10//99-12//99
Food Preparation and Serving Workers	Longview-Marshall MSA, TX	S	10.68 MW	10.25 AW	22220 AAW	TXBLS	10//99-12//99
Food Preparation and Serving Workers	Lubbock MSA, TX	S	10.42 MW	9.67 AW	21680 AAW	TXBLS	10//99-12//99
Food Preparation and Serving Workers	McAllen-Edinburg-Mission MSA, TX	S	8.50 MW	7.96 AW	17680 AAW	TXBLS	10//99-12//99
Food Preparation and Serving Workers	Odessa-Midland MSA, TX	S	9.05 MW	8.00 AW	18820 AAW	TXBLS	10//99-12//99
Food Preparation and Serving Workers	San Angelo MSA, TX	S	8.00 MW	7.23 AW	16650 AAW	TXBLS	10//99-12//99
Food Preparation and Serving Workers	San Antonio MSA, TX	S	13.11 MW	12.62 AW	27260 AAW	TXBLS	10//99-12//99
Food Preparation and Serving Workers	Sherman-Denison MSA, TX	S	9.67 MW	8.80 AW	20110 AAW	TXBLS	10//99-12//99
Food Preparation and Serving Workers	Texarkana MSA, TX-Texarkana, AR	S	8.51 MW	7.76 AW	17690 AAW	TXBLS	10//99-12//99
Food Preparation and Serving Workers	Tyler MSA, TX	S	8.41 MW	7.11 AW	17490 AAW	TXBLS	10//99-12//99
Food Preparation and Serving Workers	Victoria MSA, TX	S	9.83 MW	9.92 AW	20460 AAW	TXBLS	10//99-12//99
Food Preparation and Serving Workers	Waco MSA, TX	S	8.91 MW	8.17 AW	18530 AAW	TXBLS	10//99-12//99
Food Preparation and Serving Workers	Wichita Falls MSA, TX	S	10.45 MW	11.08 AW	21750 AAW	TXBLS	10//99-12//99
Food Preparation and Serving Workers	Utah	S	9.85 MW	10.35 AW	21520 AAW	UTBLS	10//99-12//99
Food Preparation and Serving Workers	Provo-Orem MSA, UT	S	10.83 MW	9.79 AW	22520 AAW	UTBLS	10//99-12//99
Food Preparation and Serving Workers	Salt Lake City-Ogden MSA, UT	S	10.24 MW	9.82 AW	21290 AAW	UTBLS	10//99-12//99
Food Preparation and Serving Workers	Vermont	S	13.33 MW	13.56 AW	28210 AAW	VTBLS	10//99-12//99
Food Preparation and Serving Workers	Burlington MSA, VT	S	13.52 MW	13.93 AW	28120 AAW	VTBLS	10//99-12//99
Food Preparation and Serving Workers	Virginia	S	10.21 MW	11.00 AW	22870 AAW	VABLS	10//99-12//99
Food Preparation and Serving Workers	Charlottesville MSA, VA	S	11.94 MW	11.28 AW	24840 AAW	VABLS	10//99-12//99
Food Preparation and Serving Workers	Danville MSA, VA	S	10.24 MW	9.39 AW	21300 AAW	VABLS	10//99-12//99
Food Preparation and Serving Workers	Lynchburg MSA, VA	S	9.59 MW	8.59 AW	19950 AAW	VABLS	10//99-12//99

AAW Average annual wage	AOH Average offered, high	ASH Average starting, high	H Hourly	M Monthly	S Special: hourly and annual
AE Average entry wage	AOL Average offered, low	ASL Average starting, low	HI Highest wage paid	MTC Median total compensation	TQ Third quartile wage
AEX Average experienced wage	APH Average pay, high range	AW Average wage paid	HR High end range	MW Median wage paid	W Weekly
AO Average offered	APL Average pay, low range	FQ First quartile wage	LR Low end range	SQ Second quartile wage	Y Yearly

Occupation/Type/Industry	Location	Per	Low	Mid	High	Source	Date
First-Line Supervisor/Manager							
Food Preparation and Serving Workers	Norfolk-Virginia Beach-Newport News MSA, VA-NC	S	9.18 MW	8.34 AW	19080 AAW	VABLS	10//99-12//99
Food Preparation and Serving Workers	Richmond-Petersburg MSA, VA	S	12.58 MW	13.10 AW	26170 AAW	VABLS	10//99-12//99
Food Preparation and Serving Workers	Roanoke MSA, VA	S	11.63 MW	11.14 AW	24180 AAW	VABLS	10//99-12//99
Food Preparation and Serving Workers	Washington	S	12.21 MW	12.47 AW	25940 AAW	WABLS	10//99-12//99
Food Preparation and Serving Workers	Bellingham MSA, WA	S	15.69 MW	15.69 AW	32630 AAW	WABLS	10//99-12//99
Food Preparation and Serving Workers	Bremerton PMSA, WA	S	12.99 MW	12.53 AW	27020 AAW	WABLS	10//99-12//99
Food Preparation and Serving Workers	Olympia PMSA, WA	S	15.50 MW	13.86 AW	32230 AAW	WABLS	10//99-12//99
Food Preparation and Serving Workers	Richland-Kennewick-Pasco MSA, WA	S	10.49 MW	8.00 AW	21820 AAW	WABLS	10//99-12//99
Food Preparation and Serving Workers	Seattle-Bellevue-Everett PMSA, WA	S	12.03 MW	11.99 AW	25020 AAW	WABLS	10//99-12//99
Food Preparation and Serving Workers	Spokane MSA, WA	S	13.18 MW	12.74 AW	27420 AAW	WABLS	10//99-12//99
Food Preparation and Serving Workers	Tacoma PMSA, WA	S	12.58 MW	12.19 AW	26170 AAW	WABLS	10//99-12//99
Food Preparation and Serving Workers	Yakima MSA, WA	S	11.24 MW	10.58 AW	23390 AAW	WABLS	10//99-12//99
Food Preparation and Serving Workers	West Virginia	S	8.14 MW	8.64 AW	17970 AAW	WVBLS	10//99-12//99
Food Preparation and Serving Workers	Charleston MSA, WV	S	10.75 MW	9.98 AW	22350 AAW	WVBLS	10//99-12//99
Food Preparation and Serving Workers	Huntington-Ashland MSA, WV-KY-OH	S	8.52 MW	7.92 AW	17710 AAW	WVBLS	10//99-12//99
Food Preparation and Serving Workers	Parkersburg-Marietta MSA, WV-OH	S	8.32 MW	7.98 AW	17310 AAW	WVBLS	10//99-12//99
Food Preparation and Serving Workers	Wheeling MSA, WV-OH	S	9.57 MW	9.26 AW	19900 AAW	WVBLS	10//99-12//99
Food Preparation and Serving Workers	Wisconsin	S	10.76 MW	11.53 AW	23980 AAW	WIBLS	10//99-12//99
Food Preparation and Serving Workers	Appleton-Oshkosh-Neenah MSA, WI	S	10.11 MW	9.58 AW	21030 AAW	WIBLS	10//99-12//99
Food Preparation and Serving Workers	Eau Claire MSA, WI	S	10.47 MW	10.16 AW	21780 AAW	WIBLS	10//99-12//99
Food Preparation and Serving Workers	Green Bay MSA, WI	S	15.22 MW	15.42 AW	31660 AAW	WIBLS	10//99-12//99
Food Preparation and Serving Workers	Janesville-Beloit MSA, WI	S	10.96 MW	10.42 AW	22800 AAW	WIBLS	10//99-12//99
Food Preparation and Serving Workers	Kenosha PMSA, WI	S	10.12 MW	10.20 AW	21050 AAW	WIBLS	10//99-12//99
Food Preparation and Serving Workers	La Crosse MSA, WI-MN	S	8.81 MW	8.11 AW	18320 AAW	WIBLS	10//99-12//99
Food Preparation and Serving Workers	Madison MSA, WI	S	10.97 MW	10.72 AW	22810 AAW	WIBLS	10//99-12//99
Food Preparation and Serving Workers	Milwaukee-Waukesha PMSA, WI	S	11.76 MW	11.28 AW	24460 AAW	WIBLS	10//99-12//99
Food Preparation and Serving Workers	Racine PMSA, WI	S	10.83 MW	10.40 AW	22530 AAW	WIBLS	10//99-12//99
Food Preparation and Serving Workers	Sheboygan MSA, WI	S	14.03 MW	11.93 AW	29180 AAW	WIBLS	10//99-12//99
Food Preparation and Serving Workers	Wausau MSA, WI	S	10.25 MW	10.00 AW	21320 AAW	WIBLS	10//99-12//99
Food Preparation and Serving Workers	Wyoming	S	9.3 MW	9.92 AW	20640 AAW	WYBLS	10//99-12//99
Food Preparation and Serving Workers	Casper MSA, WY	S	11.65 MW	13.54 AW	24230 AAW	WYBLS	10//99-12//99
Food Preparation and Serving Workers	Cheyenne MSA, WY	S	8.66 MW	8.31 AW	18000 AAW	WYBLS	10//99-12//99
Food Preparation and Serving Workers	Puerto Rico	S	8.33 MW	8.71 AW	18120 AAW	PRBLS	10//99-12//99
Food Preparation and Serving Workers	Aguadilla MSA, PR	S	6.70 MW	6.35 AW	13940 AAW	PRBLS	10//99-12//99
Food Preparation and Serving Workers	Arecibo PMSA, PR	S	6.16 MW	6.12 AW	12820 AAW	PRBLS	10//99-12//99
Food Preparation and Serving Workers	Caguas PMSA, PR	S	7.44 MW	6.71 AW	15480 AAW	PRBLS	10//99-12//99
Food Preparation and Serving Workers	Mayaguez MSA, PR	S	6.85 MW	6.45 AW	14250 AAW	PRBLS	10//99-12//99
Food Preparation and Serving Workers	Ponce MSA, PR	S	7.50 MW	7.17 AW	15590 AAW	PRBLS	10//99-12//99
Food Preparation and Serving Workers	San Juan-Bayamon PMSA, PR	S	9.54 MW	9.04 AW	19840 AAW	PRBLS	10//99-12//99
Food Preparation and Serving Workers	Virgin Islands	S	11.3 MW	12.01 AW	24970 AAW	VIBLS	10//99-12//99
Food Preparation and Serving Workers	Guam	S	7.98 MW	8.68 AW	18060 AAW	GUBLS	10//99-12//99
Helpers, Laborers, and Material Movers, Hand	Alabama	S	14.68 MW	15.99 AW	33250 AAW	ALBLS	10//99-12//99
Helpers, Laborers, and Material Movers, Hand	Anniston MSA, AL	S	20.79 MW	20.15 AW	43240 AAW	ALBLS	10//99-12//99
Helpers, Laborers, and Material Movers, Hand	Birmingham MSA, AL	S	15.67 MW	15.59 AW	32600 AAW	ALBLS	10//99-12//99
Helpers, Laborers, and Material Movers, Hand	Dothan MSA, AL	S	15.08 MW	14.65 AW	31360 AAW	ALBLS	10//99-12//99
Helpers, Laborers, and Material Movers, Hand	Florence MSA, AL	S	15.41 MW	12.92 AW	32050 AAW	ALBLS	10//99-12//99
Helpers, Laborers, and Material Movers, Hand	Gadsden MSA, AL	S	13.25 MW	10.38 AW	27560 AAW	ALBLS	10//99-12//99
Helpers, Laborers, and Material Movers, Hand	Huntsville MSA, AL	S	22.87 MW	21.30 AW	47570 AAW	ALBLS	10//99-12//99
Helpers, Laborers, and Material Movers, Hand	Mobile MSA, AL	S	16.01 MW	14.23 AW	33290 AAW	ALBLS	10//99-12//99
Helpers, Laborers, and Material Movers, Hand	Montgomery MSA, AL	S	14.74 MW	13.09 AW	30660 AAW	ALBLS	10//99-12//99
Helpers, Laborers, and Material Movers, Hand	Tuscaloosa MSA, AL	S	21.34 MW	21.79 AW	44390 AAW	ALBLS	10//99-12//99

AAW	Average annual wage	AOH	Average offered, high	ASH	Average starting, high	H	Hourly	M	Monthly	S	Special: hourly and annual
AE	Average entry wage	AOL	Average offered, low	ASL	Average starting, low	HI	Highest wage paid	MTC	Median total compensation	TQ	Third quartile wage
AEX	Average experienced wage	APH	Average pay, high range	AW	Average wage paid	HR	High end range	MW	Median wage paid	W	Weekly
AO	Average offered	APL	Average pay, low range	FQ	First quartile wage	LR	Low end range	SQ	Second quartile wage	Y	Yearly

First-Line Supervisor/Manager

Occupation/Type/Industry	Location	Per	Low	Mid	High	Source	Date
Helpers, Laborers, and Material Movers, Hand	Alaska	S	16.76 MW	19.23 AW	40000 AAW	AKBLS	10//99-12//99
Helpers, Laborers, and Material Movers, Hand	Anchorage MSA, AK	S	19.16 MW	16.30 AW	39850 AAW	AKBLS	10//99-12//99
Helpers, Laborers, and Material Movers, Hand	Arizona	S	15.62 MW	17.45 AW	36290 AAW	AZBLS	10//99-12//99
Helpers, Laborers, and Material Movers, Hand	Flagstaff MSA, AZ-UT	S	16.25 MW	17.85 AW	33800 AAW	AZBLS	10//99-12//99
Helpers, Laborers, and Material Movers, Hand	Phoenix-Mesa MSA, AZ	S	18.07 MW	15.86 AW	37590 AAW	AZBLS	10//99-12//99
Helpers, Laborers, and Material Movers, Hand	Tucson MSA, AZ	S	13.86 MW	13.74 AW	28820 AAW	AZBLS	10//99-12//99
Helpers, Laborers, and Material Movers, Hand	Yuma MSA, AZ	S	12.01 MW	12.86 AW	24980 AAW	AZBLS	10//99-12//99
Helpers, Laborers, and Material Movers, Hand	Arkansas	S	12.98 MW	14.11 AW	29350 AAW	ARBLS	10//99-12//99
Helpers, Laborers, and Material Movers, Hand	Fayetteville-Springdale-Rogers MSA, AR	S	12.65 MW	11.72 AW	26300 AAW	ARBLS	10//99-12//99
Helpers, Laborers, and Material Movers, Hand	Fort Smith MSA, AR-OK	S	12.86 MW	12.12 AW	26750 AAW	ARBLS	10//99-12//99
Helpers, Laborers, and Material Movers, Hand	Little Rock-North Little Rock MSA, AR	S	15.21 MW	14.72 AW	31640 AAW	ARBLS	10//99-12//99
Helpers, Laborers, and Material Movers, Hand	Pine Bluff MSA, AR	S	14.73 MW	14.25 AW	30640 AAW	ARBLS	10//99-12//99
Helpers, Laborers, and Material Movers, Hand	California	S	17.9 MW	18.46 AW	38400 AAW	CABLS	10//99-12//99
Helpers, Laborers, and Material Movers, Hand	Bakersfield MSA, CA	S	20.08 MW	19.34 AW	41760 AAW	CABLS	10//99-12//99
Helpers, Laborers, and Material Movers, Hand	Fresno MSA, CA	S	18.74 MW	18.19 AW	38980 AAW	CABLS	10//99-12//99
Helpers, Laborers, and Material Movers, Hand	Los Angeles-Long Beach PMSA, CA	S	17.93 MW	16.83 AW	37300 AAW	CABLS	10//99-12//99
Helpers, Laborers, and Material Movers, Hand	Merced MSA, CA	S	15.80 MW	14.95 AW	32870 AAW	CABLS	10//99-12//99
Helpers, Laborers, and Material Movers, Hand	Modesto MSA, CA	S	17.83 MW	17.18 AW	37080 AAW	CABLS	10//99-12//99
Helpers, Laborers, and Material Movers, Hand	Oakland PMSA, CA	S	21.53 MW	19.96 AW	44770 AAW	CABLS	10//99-12//99
Helpers, Laborers, and Material Movers, Hand	Orange County PMSA, CA	S	17.50 MW	16.68 AW	36400 AAW	CABLS	10//99-12//99
Helpers, Laborers, and Material Movers, Hand	Riverside-San Bernardino PMSA, CA	S	19.82 MW	19.02 AW	41230 AAW	CABLS	10//99-12//99
Helpers, Laborers, and Material Movers, Hand	Sacramento PMSA, CA	S	19.90 MW	19.24 AW	41390 AAW	CABLS	10//99-12//99
Helpers, Laborers, and Material Movers, Hand	Salinas MSA, CA	S	18.68 MW	18.27 AW	38860 AAW	CABLS	10//99-12//99
Helpers, Laborers, and Material Movers, Hand	San Diego MSA, CA	S	15.74 MW	14.70 AW	32730 AAW	CABLS	10//99-12//99
Helpers, Laborers, and Material Movers, Hand	San Francisco PMSA, CA	S	18.77 MW	18.44 AW	39030 AAW	CABLS	10//99-12//99
Helpers, Laborers, and Material Movers, Hand	San Jose PMSA, CA	S	20.74 MW	20.71 AW	43150 AAW	CABLS	10//99-12//99
Helpers, Laborers, and Material Movers, Hand	San Luis Obispo-Atascadero-Paso Robles MSA, CA	S	19.48 MW	19.05 AW	40510 AAW	CABLS	10//99-12//99
Helpers, Laborers, and Material Movers, Hand	Santa Barbara-Santa Maria-Lompoc MSA, CA	S	13.63 MW	12.60 AW	28350 AAW	CABLS	10//99-12//99
Helpers, Laborers, and Material Movers, Hand	Santa Cruz-Watsonville PMSA, CA	S	14.25 MW	12.43 AW	29630 AAW	CABLS	10//99-12//99
Helpers, Laborers, and Material Movers, Hand	Santa Rosa PMSA, CA	S	15.20 MW	12.70 AW	31620 AAW	CABLS	10//99-12//99
Helpers, Laborers, and Material Movers, Hand	Stockton-Lodi MSA, CA	S	19.49 MW	19.43 AW	40550 AAW	CABLS	10//99-12//99

AAW Average annual wage	AOH Average offered, high	ASH Average starting, high	H Hourly	M Monthly	S Special: hourly and annual
AE Average entry wage	AOL Average offered, low	ASL Average starting, low	HI Highest wage paid	MTC Median total compensation	TQ Third quartile wage
AEX Average experienced wage	APH Average pay, high range	AW Average wage paid	HR High end range	MW Median wage paid	W Weekly
AO Average offered	APL Average pay, low range	FQ First quartile wage	LR Low end range	SQ Second quartile wage	Y Yearly

597

Occupation/Type/Industry	Location	Per	Low	Mid	High	Source	Date
First-Line Supervisor/Manager							
Helpers, Laborers, and Material Movers, Hand	Vallejo-Fairfield-Napa PMSA, CA	S	19.47 MW	19.24 AW	40500 AAW	CABLS	10//99-12//99
Helpers, Laborers, and Material Movers, Hand	Ventura PMSA, CA	S	16.23 MW	16.01 AW	33760 AAW	CABLS	10//99-12//99
Helpers, Laborers, and Material Movers, Hand	Visalia-Tulare-Porterville MSA, CA	S	18.38 MW	16.89 AW	38240 AAW	CABLS	10//99-12//99
Helpers, Laborers, and Material Movers, Hand	Yolo PMSA, CA	S	19.75 MW	19.69 AW	41080 AAW	CABLS	10//99-12//99
Helpers, Laborers, and Material Movers, Hand	Yuba City MSA, CA	S	14.98 MW	13.09 AW	31160 AAW	CABLS	10//99-12//99
Helpers, Laborers, and Material Movers, Hand	Colorado	S	16.55 MW	17.26 AW	35890 AAW	COBLS	10//99-12//99
Helpers, Laborers, and Material Movers, Hand	Boulder-Longmont PMSA, CO	S	14.98 MW	14.95 AW	31160 AAW	COBLS	10//99-12//99
Helpers, Laborers, and Material Movers, Hand	Colorado Springs MSA, CO	S	15.24 MW	14.30 AW	31710 AAW	COBLS	10//99-12//99
Helpers, Laborers, and Material Movers, Hand	Denver PMSA, CO	S	17.64 MW	16.78 AW	36690 AAW	COBLS	10//99-12//99
Helpers, Laborers, and Material Movers, Hand	Fort Collins-Loveland MSA, CO	S	20.01 MW	20.21 AW	41610 AAW	COBLS	10//99-12//99
Helpers, Laborers, and Material Movers, Hand	Grand Junction MSA, CO	S	20.36 MW	19.40 AW	42340 AAW	COBLS	10//99-12//99
Helpers, Laborers, and Material Movers, Hand	Greeley PMSA, CO	S	17.39 MW	16.49 AW	36180 AAW	COBLS	10//99-12//99
Helpers, Laborers, and Material Movers, Hand	Pueblo MSA, CO	S	13.20 MW	10.20 AW	27450 AAW	COBLS	10//99-12//99
Helpers, Laborers, and Material Movers, Hand	Connecticut	S	16.98 MW	18.11 AW	37670 AAW	CTBLS	10//99-12//99
Helpers, Laborers, and Material Movers, Hand	Bridgeport PMSA, CT	S	15.26 MW	14.62 AW	31750 AAW	CTBLS	10//99-12//99
Helpers, Laborers, and Material Movers, Hand	Danbury PMSA, CT	S	16.41 MW	15.62 AW	34130 AAW	CTBLS	10//99-12//99
Helpers, Laborers, and Material Movers, Hand	Hartford MSA, CT	S	18.28 MW	17.46 AW	38030 AAW	CTBLS	10//99-12//99
Helpers, Laborers, and Material Movers, Hand	New Haven-Meriden PMSA, CT	S	22.72 MW	20.05 AW	47250 AAW	CTBLS	10//99-12//99
Helpers, Laborers, and Material Movers, Hand	New London-Norwich MSA, CT-RI	S	16.97 MW	16.40 AW	35290 AAW	CTBLS	10//99-12//99
Helpers, Laborers, and Material Movers, Hand	Stamford-Norwalk PMSA, CT	S	17.16 MW	16.23 AW	35700 AAW	CTBLS	10//99-12//99
Helpers, Laborers, and Material Movers, Hand	Waterbury PMSA, CT	S	21.59 MW	18.53 AW	44900 AAW	CTBLS	10//99-12//99
Helpers, Laborers, and Material Movers, Hand	Delaware	S	17.69 MW	18.48 AW	38450 AAW	DEBLS	10//99-12//99
Helpers, Laborers, and Material Movers, Hand	Wilmington-Newark PMSA, DE-MD	S	19.03 MW	18.49 AW	39580 AAW	DEBLS	10//99-12//99
Helpers, Laborers, and Material Movers, Hand	District of Columbia	S	15 MW	15.36 AW	31940 AAW	DCBLS	10//99-12//99
Helpers, Laborers, and Material Movers, Hand	Washington PMSA, DC-MD-VA-WV	S	17.06 MW	16.12 AW	35480 AAW	DCBLS	10//99-12//99
Helpers, Laborers, and Material Movers, Hand	Florida	S	14.33 MW	15.75 AW	32750 AAW	FLBLS	10//99-12//99
Helpers, Laborers, and Material Movers, Hand	Daytona Beach MSA, FL	S	15.18 MW	14.12 AW	31570 AAW	FLBLS	10//99-12//99
Helpers, Laborers, and Material Movers, Hand	Fort Lauderdale PMSA, FL	S	16.12 MW	16.03 AW	33530 AAW	FLBLS	10//99-12//99
Helpers, Laborers, and Material Movers, Hand	Fort Myers-Cape Coral MSA, FL	S	12.43 MW	11.96 AW	25850 AAW	FLBLS	10//99-12//99
Helpers, Laborers, and Material Movers, Hand	Fort Pierce-Port St. Lucie MSA, FL	S	14.89 MW	14.81 AW	30970 AAW	FLBLS	10//99-12//99

AAW Average annual wage	**AOH** Average offered, high	**ASH** Average starting, high	**H** Hourly	**M** Monthly	**S** Special: hourly and annual
AE Average entry wage	**AOL** Average offered, low	**ASL** Average starting, low	**HI** Highest wage paid	**MTC** Median total compensation	**TQ** Third quartile wage
AEX Average experienced wage	**APH** Average pay, high range	**AW** Average wage paid	**HR** High end range	**MW** Median wage paid	**W** Weekly
AO Average offered	**APL** Average pay, low range	**FQ** First quartile wage	**LR** Low end range	**SQ** Second quartile wage	**Y** Yearly

First-Line Supervisor/Manager

Occupation/Type/Industry	Location	Per	Low	Mid	High	Source	Date
First-Line Supervisor/Manager							
Helpers, Laborers, and Material Movers, Hand	Fort Walton Beach MSA, FL	S	12.33 MW	11.23 AW	25650 AAW	FLBLS	10//99-12//99
Helpers, Laborers, and Material Movers, Hand	Gainesville MSA, FL	S	16.04 MW	14.67 AW	33370 AAW	FLBLS	10//99-12//99
Helpers, Laborers, and Material Movers, Hand	Jacksonville MSA, FL	S	18.22 MW	15.83 AW	37910 AAW	FLBLS	10//99-12//99
Helpers, Laborers, and Material Movers, Hand	Lakeland-Winter Haven MSA, FL	S	17.70 MW	16.58 AW	36820 AAW	FLBLS	10//99-12//99
Helpers, Laborers, and Material Movers, Hand	Melbourne-Titusville-Palm Bay MSA, FL	S	13.06 MW	12.17 AW	27160 AAW	FLBLS	10//99-12//99
Helpers, Laborers, and Material Movers, Hand	Miami PMSA, FL	S	15.75 MW	14.87 AW	32760 AAW	FLBLS	10//99-12//99
Helpers, Laborers, and Material Movers, Hand	Naples MSA, FL	S	12.37 MW	12.32 AW	25730 AAW	FLBLS	10//99-12//99
Helpers, Laborers, and Material Movers, Hand	Ocala MSA, FL	S	18.77 MW	18.22 AW	39040 AAW	FLBLS	10//99-12//99
Helpers, Laborers, and Material Movers, Hand	Orlando MSA, FL	S	17.89 MW	15.79 AW	37210 AAW	FLBLS	10//99-12//99
Helpers, Laborers, and Material Movers, Hand	Pensacola MSA, FL	S	13.60 MW	12.46 AW	28300 AAW	FLBLS	10//99-12//99
Helpers, Laborers, and Material Movers, Hand	Sarasota-Bradenton MSA, FL	S	17.78 MW	14.48 AW	36970 AAW	FLBLS	10//99-12//99
Helpers, Laborers, and Material Movers, Hand	Tallahassee MSA, FL	S	12.73 MW	12.40 AW	26480 AAW	FLBLS	10//99-12//99
Helpers, Laborers, and Material Movers, Hand	Tampa-St. Petersburg-Clearwater MSA, FL	S	14.71 MW	13.21 AW	30610 AAW	FLBLS	10//99-12//99
Helpers, Laborers, and Material Movers, Hand	West Palm Beach-Boca Raton MSA, FL	S	13.13 MW	12.55 AW	27310 AAW	FLBLS	10//99-12//99
Helpers, Laborers, and Material Movers, Hand	Georgia	S	16.97 MW	17.66 AW	36740 AAW	GABLS	10//99-12//99
Helpers, Laborers, and Material Movers, Hand	Athens MSA, GA	S	16.32 MW	16.01 AW	33940 AAW	GABLS	10//99-12//99
Helpers, Laborers, and Material Movers, Hand	Atlanta MSA, GA	S	18.80 MW	18.66 AW	39100 AAW	GABLS	10//99-12//99
Helpers, Laborers, and Material Movers, Hand	Augusta-Aiken MSA, GA-SC	S	15.47 MW	15.29 AW	32170 AAW	GABLS	10//99-12//99
Helpers, Laborers, and Material Movers, Hand	Columbus MSA, GA-AL	S	16.04 MW	15.57 AW	33360 AAW	GABLS	10//99-12//99
Helpers, Laborers, and Material Movers, Hand	Macon MSA, GA	S	17.24 MW	16.87 AW	35860 AAW	GABLS	10//99-12//99
Helpers, Laborers, and Material Movers, Hand	Savannah MSA, GA	S	15.64 MW	15.06 AW	32530 AAW	GABLS	10//99-12//99
Helpers, Laborers, and Material Movers, Hand	Hawaii	S	15.81 MW	17.00 AW	35350 AAW	HIBLS	10//99-12//99
Helpers, Laborers, and Material Movers, Hand	Honolulu MSA, HI	S	17.58 MW	15.65 AW	36570 AAW	HIBLS	10//99-12//99
Helpers, Laborers, and Material Movers, Hand	Idaho	S	14.83 MW	16.55 AW	34430 AAW	IDBLS	10//99-12//99
Helpers, Laborers, and Material Movers, Hand	Boise City MSA, ID	S	16.22 MW	16.58 AW	33750 AAW	IDBLS	10//99-12//99
Helpers, Laborers, and Material Movers, Hand	Illinois	S	15.37 MW	16.92 AW	35190 AAW	ILBLS	10//99-12//99
Helpers, Laborers, and Material Movers, Hand	Bloomington-Normal MSA, IL	S	14.41 MW	12.75 AW	29980 AAW	ILBLS	10//99-12//99
Helpers, Laborers, and Material Movers, Hand	Champaign-Urbana MSA, IL	S	19.08 MW	15.93 AW	39690 AAW	ILBLS	10//99-12//99
Helpers, Laborers, and Material Movers, Hand	Chicago PMSA, IL	S	17.33 MW	15.67 AW	36040 AAW	ILBLS	10//99-12//99
Helpers, Laborers, and Material Movers, Hand	Peoria-Pekin MSA, IL	S	16.00 MW	15.50 AW	33290 AAW	ILBLS	10//99-12//99
Helpers, Laborers, and Material Movers, Hand	Rockford MSA, IL	S	14.87 MW	14.45 AW	30940 AAW	ILBLS	10//99-12//99
Helpers, Laborers, and Material Movers, Hand	Springfield MSA, IL	S	14.99 MW	15.19 AW	31170 AAW	ILBLS	10//99-12//99
Helpers, Laborers, and Material Movers, Hand	Indiana	S	14.77 MW	15.78 AW	32820 AAW	INBLS	10//99-12//99

AAW Average annual wage	**AOH** Average offered, high	**ASH** Average starting, high	**H** Hourly	**M** Monthly	**S** Special: hourly and annual
AE Average entry wage	**AOL** Average offered, low	**ASL** Average starting, low	**HI** Highest wage paid	**MTC** Median total compensation	**TQ** Third quartile wage
AEX Average experienced wage	**APH** Average pay, high range	**AW** Average wage paid	**HR** High end range	**MW** Median wage paid	**W** Weekly
AO Average offered	**APL** Average pay, low range	**FQ** First quartile wage	**LR** Low end range	**SQ** Second quartile wage	**Y** Yearly

Occupation/Type/Industry	Location	Per	Low	Mid	High	Source	Date
First-Line Supervisor/Manager							
Helpers, Laborers, and Material Movers, Hand	Elkhart-Goshen MSA, IN	S	16.40 MW	16.92 AW	34100 AAW	INBLS	10//99-12//99
Helpers, Laborers, and Material Movers, Hand	Evansville-Henderson MSA, IN-KY	S	14.47 MW	14.01 AW	30100 AAW	INBLS	10//99-12//99
Helpers, Laborers, and Material Movers, Hand	Fort Wayne MSA, IN	S	14.69 MW	12.85 AW	30550 AAW	INBLS	10//99-12//99
Helpers, Laborers, and Material Movers, Hand	Gary PMSA, IN	S	17.34 MW	16.08 AW	36070 AAW	INBLS	10//99-12//99
Helpers, Laborers, and Material Movers, Hand	Indianapolis MSA, IN	S	15.66 MW	14.57 AW	32580 AAW	INBLS	10//99-12//99
Helpers, Laborers, and Material Movers, Hand	Kokomo MSA, IN	S	15.81 MW	15.21 AW	32880 AAW	INBLS	10//99-12//99
Helpers, Laborers, and Material Movers, Hand	Lafayette MSA, IN	S	15.25 MW	13.01 AW	31720 AAW	INBLS	10//99-12//99
Helpers, Laborers, and Material Movers, Hand	South Bend MSA, IN	S	16.67 MW	15.21 AW	34680 AAW	INBLS	10//99-12//99
Helpers, Laborers, and Material Movers, Hand	Terre Haute MSA, IN	S	15.52 MW	13.08 AW	32280 AAW	INBLS	10//99-12//99
Helpers, Laborers, and Material Movers, Hand	Iowa	S	16.4 MW	16.07 AW	33430 AAW	IABLS	10//99-12//99
Helpers, Laborers, and Material Movers, Hand	Cedar Rapids MSA, IA	S	15.53 MW	15.21 AW	32300 AAW	IABLS	10//99-12//99
Helpers, Laborers, and Material Movers, Hand	Davenport-Moline-Rock Island MSA, IA-IL	S	17.95 MW	18.28 AW	37330 AAW	IABLS	10//99-12//99
Helpers, Laborers, and Material Movers, Hand	Des Moines MSA, IA	S	17.32 MW	17.50 AW	36030 AAW	IABLS	10//99-12//99
Helpers, Laborers, and Material Movers, Hand	Dubuque MSA, IA	S	18.04 MW	18.65 AW	37520 AAW	IABLS	10//99-12//99
Helpers, Laborers, and Material Movers, Hand	Iowa City MSA, IA	S	14.12 MW	14.61 AW	29370 AAW	IABLS	10//99-12//99
Helpers, Laborers, and Material Movers, Hand	Sioux City MSA, IA-NE	S	15.06 MW	14.74 AW	31330 AAW	IABLS	10//99-12//99
Helpers, Laborers, and Material Movers, Hand	Waterloo-Cedar Falls MSA, IA	S	12.26 MW	11.22 AW	25500 AAW	IABLS	10//99-12//99
Helpers, Laborers, and Material Movers, Hand	Kansas	S	13.93 MW	14.75 AW	30680 AAW	KSBLS	10//99-12//99
Helpers, Laborers, and Material Movers, Hand	Topeka MSA, KS	S	15.62 MW	15.11 AW	32490 AAW	KSBLS	10//99-12//99
Helpers, Laborers, and Material Movers, Hand	Wichita MSA, KS	S	16.38 MW	15.47 AW	34070 AAW	KSBLS	10//99-12//99
Helpers, Laborers, and Material Movers, Hand	Kentucky	S	14.7 MW	15.99 AW	33260 AAW	KYBLS	10//99-12//99
Helpers, Laborers, and Material Movers, Hand	Lexington MSA, KY	S	13.61 MW	13.81 AW	28300 AAW	KYBLS	10//99-12//99
Helpers, Laborers, and Material Movers, Hand	Louisville MSA, KY-IN	S	15.23 MW	15.12 AW	31690 AAW	KYBLS	10//99-12//99
Helpers, Laborers, and Material Movers, Hand	Louisiana	S	16.94 MW	18.25 AW	37960 AAW	LABLS	10//99-12//99
Helpers, Laborers, and Material Movers, Hand	Baton Rouge MSA, LA	S	14.75 MW	14.13 AW	30680 AAW	LABLS	10//99-12//99
Helpers, Laborers, and Material Movers, Hand	Houma MSA, LA	S	12.84 MW	11.79 AW	26720 AAW	LABLS	10//99-12//99
Helpers, Laborers, and Material Movers, Hand	Lafayette MSA, LA	S	18.14 MW	15.47 AW	37730 AAW	LABLS	10//99-12//99
Helpers, Laborers, and Material Movers, Hand	Lake Charles MSA, LA	S	19.68 MW	22.67 AW	40930 AAW	LABLS	10//99-12//99
Helpers, Laborers, and Material Movers, Hand	Monroe MSA, LA	S	16.57 MW	13.07 AW	34470 AAW	LABLS	10//99-12//99
Helpers, Laborers, and Material Movers, Hand	New Orleans MSA, LA	S	16.68 MW	17.47 AW	34690 AAW	LABLS	10//99-12//99
Helpers, Laborers, and Material Movers, Hand	Shreveport-Bossier City MSA, LA	S	17.76 MW	15.81 AW	36940 AAW	LABLS	10//99-12//99
Helpers, Laborers, and Material Movers, Hand	Maine	S	14.91 MW	15.72 AW	32700 AAW	MEBLS	10//99-12//99
Helpers, Laborers, and Material Movers, Hand	Bangor MSA, ME	S	13.55 MW	13.97 AW	28170 AAW	MEBLS	10//99-12//99

AAW Average annual wage	**AOH** Average offered, high	**ASH** Average starting, high	**H** Hourly	**M** Monthly	**S** Special: hourly and annual
AE Average entry wage	**AOL** Average offered, low	**ASL** Average starting, low	**HI** Highest wage paid	**MTC** Median total compensation	**TQ** Third quartile wage
AEX Average experienced wage	**APH** Average pay, high range	**AW** Average wage paid	**HR** High end range	**MW** Median wage paid	**W** Weekly
AO Average offered	**APL** Average pay, low range	**FQ** First quartile wage	**LR** Low end range	**SQ** Second quartile wage	**Y** Yearly

First-Line Supervisor/Manager

Occupation/Type/Industry	Location	Per	Low	Mid	High	Source	Date
Helpers, Laborers, and Material Movers, Hand	Portland MSA, ME	S	16.92 MW	15.32 AW	35190 AAW	MEBLS	10//99-12//99
Helpers, Laborers, and Material Movers, Hand	Maryland	S	15.23 MW	15.99 AW	33260 AAW	MDBLS	10//99-12//99
Helpers, Laborers, and Material Movers, Hand	Baltimore PMSA, MD	S	15.40 MW	15.12 AW	32030 AAW	MDBLS	10//99-12//99
Helpers, Laborers, and Material Movers, Hand	Hagerstown PMSA, MD	S	14.21 MW	14.89 AW	29550 AAW	MDBLS	10//99-12//99
Helpers, Laborers, and Material Movers, Hand	Massachusetts	S	17.14 MW	17.54 AW	36490 AAW	MABLS	10//99-12//99
Helpers, Laborers, and Material Movers, Hand	Boston PMSA, MA-NH	S	17.11 MW	16.82 AW	35600 AAW	MABLS	10//99-12//99
Helpers, Laborers, and Material Movers, Hand	Brockton PMSA, MA	S	17.20 MW	16.92 AW	35780 AAW	MABLS	10//99-12//99
Helpers, Laborers, and Material Movers, Hand	Fitchburg-Leominster PMSA, MA	S	18.56 MW	16.92 AW	38610 AAW	MABLS	10//99-12//99
Helpers, Laborers, and Material Movers, Hand	Lawrence PMSA, MA-NH	S	17.62 MW	16.86 AW	36640 AAW	MABLS	10//99-12//99
Helpers, Laborers, and Material Movers, Hand	Lowell PMSA, MA-NH	S	16.53 MW	15.97 AW	34390 AAW	MABLS	10//99-12//99
Helpers, Laborers, and Material Movers, Hand	New Bedford PMSA, MA	S	18.74 MW	17.97 AW	38970 AAW	MABLS	10//99-12//99
Helpers, Laborers, and Material Movers, Hand	Springfield MSA, MA	S	18.42 MW	17.87 AW	38320 AAW	MABLS	10//99-12//99
Helpers, Laborers, and Material Movers, Hand	Worcester PMSA, MA-CT	S	18.41 MW	16.93 AW	38290 AAW	MABLS	10//99-12//99
Helpers, Laborers, and Material Movers, Hand	Michigan	S	16.52 MW	18.59 AW	38680 AAW	MIBLS	10//99-12//99
Helpers, Laborers, and Material Movers, Hand	Ann Arbor PMSA, MI	S	18.41 MW	17.75 AW	38300 AAW	MIBLS	10//99-12//99
Helpers, Laborers, and Material Movers, Hand	Benton Harbor MSA, MI	S	23.65 MW	19.74 AW	49190 AAW	MIBLS	10//99-12//99
Helpers, Laborers, and Material Movers, Hand	Detroit PMSA, MI	S	18.83 MW	16.43 AW	39170 AAW	MIBLS	10//99-12//99
Helpers, Laborers, and Material Movers, Hand	Flint PMSA, MI	S	17.77 MW	15.63 AW	36970 AAW	MIBLS	10//99-12//99
Helpers, Laborers, and Material Movers, Hand	Grand Rapids-Muskegon-Holland MSA, MI	S	18.61 MW	16.27 AW	38710 AAW	MIBLS	10//99-12//99
Helpers, Laborers, and Material Movers, Hand	Jackson MSA, MI	S	16.04 MW	16.14 AW	33350 AAW	MIBLS	10//99-12//99
Helpers, Laborers, and Material Movers, Hand	Kalamazoo-Battle Creek MSA, MI	S	17.53 MW	16.06 AW	36470 AAW	MIBLS	10//99-12//99
Helpers, Laborers, and Material Movers, Hand	Lansing-East Lansing MSA, MI	S	16.32 MW	16.04 AW	33940 AAW	MIBLS	10//99-12//99
Helpers, Laborers, and Material Movers, Hand	Saginaw-Bay City-Midland MSA, MI	S	17.00 MW	16.22 AW	35360 AAW	MIBLS	10//99-12//99
Helpers, Laborers, and Material Movers, Hand	Minnesota	S	17.8 MW	18.71 AW	38920 AAW	MNBLS	10//99-12//99
Helpers, Laborers, and Material Movers, Hand	Duluth-Superior MSA, MN-WI	S	20.22 MW	17.89 AW	42050 AAW	MNBLS	10//99-12//99
Helpers, Laborers, and Material Movers, Hand	Minneapolis-St. Paul MSA, MN-WI	S	19.49 MW	18.31 AW	40540 AAW	MNBLS	10//99-12//99
Helpers, Laborers, and Material Movers, Hand	Rochester MSA, MN	S	14.76 MW	13.62 AW	30690 AAW	MNBLS	10//99-12//99
Helpers, Laborers, and Material Movers, Hand	St. Cloud MSA, MN	S	15.32 MW	14.15 AW	31860 AAW	MNBLS	10//99-12//99
Helpers, Laborers, and Material Movers, Hand	Mississippi	S	14.28 MW	14.85 AW	30890 AAW	MSBLS	10//99-12//99
Helpers, Laborers, and Material Movers, Hand	Biloxi-Gulfport-Pascagoula MSA, MS	S	18.88 MW	18.35 AW	39270 AAW	MSBLS	10//99-12//99
Helpers, Laborers, and Material Movers, Hand	Hattiesburg MSA, MS	S	15.77 MW	14.29 AW	32800 AAW	MSBLS	10//99-12//99
Helpers, Laborers, and Material Movers, Hand	Jackson MSA, MS	S	13.65 MW	13.46 AW	28380 AAW	MSBLS	10//99-12//99

AAW Average annual wage	AOH Average offered, high	ASH Average starting, high	H Hourly	M Monthly	S Special: hourly and annual
AE Average entry wage	AOL Average offered, low	ASL Average starting, low	HI Highest wage paid	MTC Median total compensation	TQ Third quartile wage
AEX Average experienced wage	APH Average pay, high range	AW Average wage paid	HR High end range	MW Median wage paid	W Weekly
AO Average offered	APL Average pay, low range	FQ First quartile wage	LR Low end range	SQ Second quartile wage	Y Yearly

Occupation/Type/Industry	Location	Per	Low	Mid	High	Source	Date
First-Line Supervisor/Manager							
Helpers, Laborers, and Material Movers, Hand	Missouri	S	16.27 MW	16.24 AW	33780 AAW	MOBLS	10//99-12//99
Helpers, Laborers, and Material Movers, Hand	Columbia MSA, MO	S	13.19 MW	10.37 AW	27440 AAW	MOBLS	10//99-12//99
Helpers, Laborers, and Material Movers, Hand	Joplin MSA, MO	S	14.09 MW	11.88 AW	29310 AAW	MOBLS	10//99-12//99
Helpers, Laborers, and Material Movers, Hand	Kansas City MSA, MO-KS	S	16.08 MW	15.66 AW	33440 AAW	MOBLS	10//99-12//99
Helpers, Laborers, and Material Movers, Hand	St. Joseph MSA, MO	S	13.98 MW	11.77 AW	29070 AAW	MOBLS	10//99-12//99
Helpers, Laborers, and Material Movers, Hand	St. Louis MSA, MO-IL	S	17.69 MW	17.99 AW	36790 AAW	MOBLS	10//99-12//99
Helpers, Laborers, and Material Movers, Hand	Springfield MSA, MO	S	15.41 MW	15.16 AW	32050 AAW	MOBLS	10//99-12//99
Helpers, Laborers, and Material Movers, Hand	Montana	S	10.15 MW	11.62 AW	24170 AAW	MTBLS	10//99-12//99
Helpers, Laborers, and Material Movers, Hand	Billings MSA, MT	S	11.69 MW	10.70 AW	24320 AAW	MTBLS	10//99-12//99
Helpers, Laborers, and Material Movers, Hand	Nebraska	S	11.29 MW	12.69 AW	26390 AAW	NEBLS	10//99-12//99
Helpers, Laborers, and Material Movers, Hand	Lincoln MSA, NE	S	13.21 MW	13.68 AW	27480 AAW	NEBLS	10//99-12//99
Helpers, Laborers, and Material Movers, Hand	Omaha MSA, NE-IA	S	17.22 MW	16.50 AW	35820 AAW	NEBLS	10//99-12//99
Helpers, Laborers, and Material Movers, Hand	Nevada	S	13.2 MW	14.55 AW	30260 AAW	NVBLS	10//99-12//99
Helpers, Laborers, and Material Movers, Hand	Las Vegas MSA, NV-AZ	S	14.57 MW	13.00 AW	30310 AAW	NVBLS	10//99-12//99
Helpers, Laborers, and Material Movers, Hand	Reno MSA, NV	S	14.89 MW	15.19 AW	30980 AAW	NVBLS	10//99-12//99
Helpers, Laborers, and Material Movers, Hand	New Hampshire	S	13.89 MW	14.66 AW	30500 AAW	NHBLS	10//99-12//99
Helpers, Laborers, and Material Movers, Hand	Manchester PMSA, NH	S	13.36 MW	11.45 AW	27780 AAW	NHBLS	10//99-12//99
Helpers, Laborers, and Material Movers, Hand	Nashua PMSA, NH	S	15.62 MW	13.47 AW	32490 AAW	NHBLS	10//99-12//99
Helpers, Laborers, and Material Movers, Hand	Portsmouth-Rochester PMSA, NH-ME	S	15.28 MW	15.62 AW	31780 AAW	NHBLS	10//99-12//99
Helpers, Laborers, and Material Movers, Hand	New Jersey	S	18.47 MW	19.09 AW	39720 AAW	NJBLS	10//99-12//99
Helpers, Laborers, and Material Movers, Hand	Atlantic-Cape May PMSA, NJ	S	18.04 MW	18.72 AW	37530 AAW	NJBLS	10//99-12//99
Helpers, Laborers, and Material Movers, Hand	Bergen-Passaic PMSA, NJ	S	17.04 MW	15.62 AW	35450 AAW	NJBLS	10//99-12//99
Helpers, Laborers, and Material Movers, Hand	Jersey City PMSA, NJ	S	17.88 MW	16.38 AW	37190 AAW	NJBLS	10//99-12//99
Helpers, Laborers, and Material Movers, Hand	Middlesex-Somerset-Hunterdon PMSA, NJ	S	21.83 MW	21.58 AW	45400 AAW	NJBLS	10//99-12//99
Helpers, Laborers, and Material Movers, Hand	Monmouth-Ocean PMSA, NJ	S	16.35 MW	14.44 AW	34010 AAW	NJBLS	10//99-12//99
Helpers, Laborers, and Material Movers, Hand	Newark PMSA, NJ	S	19.18 MW	19.54 AW	39890 AAW	NJBLS	10//99-12//99
Helpers, Laborers, and Material Movers, Hand	Trenton PMSA, NJ	S	16.82 MW	16.24 AW	34990 AAW	NJBLS	10//99-12//99
Helpers, Laborers, and Material Movers, Hand	Vineland-Millville-Bridgeton PMSA, NJ	S	14.67 MW	14.51 AW	30520 AAW	NJBLS	10//99-12//99
Helpers, Laborers, and Material Movers, Hand	New Mexico	S	12.75 MW	13.99 AW	29100 AAW	NMBLS	10//99-12//99
Helpers, Laborers, and Material Movers, Hand	Albuquerque MSA, NM	S	17.94 MW	18.26 AW	37310 AAW	NMBLS	10//99-12//99
Helpers, Laborers, and Material Movers, Hand	Santa Fe MSA, NM	S	14.74 MW	13.27 AW	30660 AAW	NMBLS	10//99-12//99
Helpers, Laborers, and Material Movers, Hand	New York	S	17.59 MW	18.83 AW	39160 AAW	NYBLS	10//99-12//99
Helpers, Laborers, and Material Movers, Hand	Albany-Schenectady-Troy MSA, NY	S	16.36 MW	15.60 AW	34030 AAW	NYBLS	10//99-12//99

AAW	Average annual wage	AOH	Average offered, high	ASH	Average starting, high	H	Hourly	M	Monthly	S	Special: hourly and annual
AE	Average entry wage	AOL	Average offered, low	ASL	Average starting, low	HI	Highest wage paid	MTC	Median total compensation	TQ	Third quartile wage
AEX	Average experienced wage	APH	Average pay, high range	AW	Average wage paid	HR	High end range	MW	Median wage paid	W	Weekly
AO	Average offered	APL	Average pay, low range	FQ	First quartile wage	LR	Low end range	SQ	Second quartile wage	Y	Yearly

First-Line Supervisor/Manager

Occupation/Type/Industry	Location	Per	Low	Mid	High	Source	Date
Helpers, Laborers, and Material Movers, Hand	Binghamton MSA, NY	S	18.31 MW	18.07 AW	38090 AAW	NYBLS	10//99-12//99
Helpers, Laborers, and Material Movers, Hand	Buffalo-Niagara Falls MSA, NY	S	14.17 MW	13.04 AW	29460 AAW	NYBLS	10//99-12//99
Helpers, Laborers, and Material Movers, Hand	Dutchess County PMSA, NY	S	18.81 MW	18.60 AW	39130 AAW	NYBLS	10//99-12//99
Helpers, Laborers, and Material Movers, Hand	Elmira MSA, NY	S	26.21 MW	22.43 AW	54510 AAW	NYBLS	10//99-12//99
Helpers, Laborers, and Material Movers, Hand	Glens Falls MSA, NY	S	17.42 MW	15.33 AW	36230 AAW	NYBLS	10//99-12//99
Helpers, Laborers, and Material Movers, Hand	Jamestown MSA, NY	S	19.91 MW	18.34 AW	41410 AAW	NYBLS	10//99-12//99
Helpers, Laborers, and Material Movers, Hand	Nassau-Suffolk PMSA, NY	S	17.14 MW	15.17 AW	35650 AAW	NYBLS	10//99-12//99
Helpers, Laborers, and Material Movers, Hand	New York PMSA, NY	S	21.40 MW	20.27 AW	44510 AAW	NYBLS	10//99-12//99
Helpers, Laborers, and Material Movers, Hand	Newburgh PMSA, NY-PA	S	15.84 MW	13.16 AW	32950 AAW	NYBLS	10//99-12//99
Helpers, Laborers, and Material Movers, Hand	Rochester MSA, NY	S	15.71 MW	15.04 AW	32670 AAW	NYBLS	10//99-12//99
Helpers, Laborers, and Material Movers, Hand	Syracuse MSA, NY	S	18.06 MW	17.70 AW	37560 AAW	NYBLS	10//99-12//99
Helpers, Laborers, and Material Movers, Hand	Utica-Rome MSA, NY	S	17.38 MW	16.29 AW	36150 AAW	NYBLS	10//99-12//99
Helpers, Laborers, and Material Movers, Hand	North Carolina	S	14.45 MW	14.93 AW	31040 AAW	NCBLS	10//99-12//99
Helpers, Laborers, and Material Movers, Hand	Asheville MSA, NC	S	16.72 MW	17.88 AW	34770 AAW	NCBLS	10//99-12//99
Helpers, Laborers, and Material Movers, Hand	Charlotte-Gastonia-Rock Hill MSA, NC-SC	S	15.44 MW	14.80 AW	32120 AAW	NCBLS	10//99-12//99
Helpers, Laborers, and Material Movers, Hand	Fayetteville MSA, NC	S	13.12 MW	12.67 AW	27280 AAW	NCBLS	10//99-12//99
Helpers, Laborers, and Material Movers, Hand	Goldsboro MSA, NC	S	13.99 MW	12.47 AW	29100 AAW	NCBLS	10//99-12//99
Helpers, Laborers, and Material Movers, Hand	Greensboro--Winston-Salem--High Point MSA, NC	S	15.53 MW	16.21 AW	32300 AAW	NCBLS	10//99-12//99
Helpers, Laborers, and Material Movers, Hand	Greenville MSA, NC	S	11.44 MW	11.12 AW	23790 AAW	NCBLS	10//99-12//99
Helpers, Laborers, and Material Movers, Hand	Hickory-Morganton-Lenoir MSA, NC	S	13.43 MW	12.63 AW	27930 AAW	NCBLS	10//99-12//99
Helpers, Laborers, and Material Movers, Hand	Raleigh-Durham-Chapel Hill MSA, NC	S	14.27 MW	13.22 AW	29670 AAW	NCBLS	10//99-12//99
Helpers, Laborers, and Material Movers, Hand	Wilmington MSA, NC	S	12.95 MW	9.99 AW	26930 AAW	NCBLS	10//99-12//99
Helpers, Laborers, and Material Movers, Hand	North Dakota	S	14.39 MW	14.65 AW	30470 AAW	NDBLS	10//99-12//99
Helpers, Laborers, and Material Movers, Hand	Fargo-Moorhead MSA, ND-MN	S	14.11 MW	14.01 AW	29340 AAW	NDBLS	10//99-12//99
Helpers, Laborers, and Material Movers, Hand	Ohio	S	14.86 MW	15.78 AW	32830 AAW	OHBLS	10//99-12//99
Helpers, Laborers, and Material Movers, Hand	Akron PMSA, OH	S	16.60 MW	17.39 AW	34530 AAW	OHBLS	10//99-12//99
Helpers, Laborers, and Material Movers, Hand	Canton-Massillon MSA, OH	S	15.37 MW	14.85 AW	31970 AAW	OHBLS	10//99-12//99
Helpers, Laborers, and Material Movers, Hand	Cincinnati PMSA, OH-KY-IN	S	16.70 MW	15.52 AW	34740 AAW	OHBLS	10//99-12//99
Helpers, Laborers, and Material Movers, Hand	Cleveland-Lorain-Elyria PMSA, OH	S	16.60 MW	15.90 AW	34530 AAW	OHBLS	10//99-12//99
Helpers, Laborers, and Material Movers, Hand	Columbus MSA, OH	S	14.82 MW	14.15 AW	30820 AAW	OHBLS	10//99-12//99
Helpers, Laborers, and Material Movers, Hand	Dayton-Springfield MSA, OH	S	15.36 MW	13.90 AW	31950 AAW	OHBLS	10//99-12//99

AAW	Average annual wage	AOH	Average offered, high	ASH	Average starting, high
AE	Average entry wage	AOL	Average offered, low	ASL	Average starting, low
AEX	Average experienced wage	APH	Average pay, high range	AW	Average wage paid
AO	Average offered	APL	Average pay, low range	FQ	First quartile wage

H	Hourly	M	Monthly	S	Special: hourly and annual
HI	Highest wage paid	MTC	Median total compensation	TQ	Third quartile wage
HR	High end range	MW	Median wage paid	W	Weekly
LR	Low end range	SQ	Second quartile wage	Y	Yearly

Occupation/Type/Industry	Location	Per	Low	Mid	High	Source	Date
First-Line Supervisor/Manager							
Helpers, Laborers, and Material Movers, Hand	Hamilton-Middletown PMSA, OH	S	19.99 MW	18.94 AW	41580 AAW	OHBLS	10//99-12//99
Helpers, Laborers, and Material Movers, Hand	Lima MSA, OH	S	14.48 MW	15.00 AW	30120 AAW	OHBLS	10//99-12//99
Helpers, Laborers, and Material Movers, Hand	Steubenville-Weirton MSA, OH-WV	S	19.42 MW	20.19 AW	40390 AAW	OHBLS	10//99-12//99
Helpers, Laborers, and Material Movers, Hand	Toledo MSA, OH	S	16.36 MW	15.03 AW	34040 AAW	OHBLS	10//99-12//99
Helpers, Laborers, and Material Movers, Hand	Youngstown-Warren MSA, OH	S	17.56 MW	15.24 AW	36530 AAW	OHBLS	10//99-12//99
Helpers, Laborers, and Material Movers, Hand	Oklahoma	S	13.85 MW	15.14 AW	31490 AAW	OKBLS	10//99-12//99
Helpers, Laborers, and Material Movers, Hand	Oklahoma City MSA, OK	S	16.31 MW	15.64 AW	33920 AAW	OKBLS	10//99-12//99
Helpers, Laborers, and Material Movers, Hand	Tulsa MSA, OK	S	14.16 MW	12.83 AW	29440 AAW	OKBLS	10//99-12//99
Helpers, Laborers, and Material Movers, Hand	Oregon	S	16.31 MW	17.31 AW	36000 AAW	ORBLS	10//99-12//99
Helpers, Laborers, and Material Movers, Hand	Portland-Vancouver PMSA, OR-WA	S	17.38 MW	16.48 AW	36160 AAW	ORBLS	10//99-12//99
Helpers, Laborers, and Material Movers, Hand	Salem PMSA, OR	S	18.26 MW	18.52 AW	37970 AAW	ORBLS	10//99-12//99
Helpers, Laborers, and Material Movers, Hand	Pennsylvania	S	15.42 MW	15.94 AW	33150 AAW	PABLS	10//99-12//99
Helpers, Laborers, and Material Movers, Hand	Allentown-Bethlehem-Easton MSA, PA	S	16.23 MW	14.75 AW	33760 AAW	PABLS	10//99-12//99
Helpers, Laborers, and Material Movers, Hand	Altoona MSA, PA	S	11.42 MW	10.22 AW	23760 AAW	PABLS	10//99-12//99
Helpers, Laborers, and Material Movers, Hand	Erie MSA, PA	S	15.96 MW	15.39 AW	33200 AAW	PABLS	10//99-12//99
Helpers, Laborers, and Material Movers, Hand	Harrisburg-Lebanon-Carlisle MSA, PA	S	16.13 MW	15.85 AW	33550 AAW	PABLS	10//99-12//99
Helpers, Laborers, and Material Movers, Hand	Johnstown MSA, PA	S	13.08 MW	11.20 AW	27200 AAW	PABLS	10//99-12//99
Helpers, Laborers, and Material Movers, Hand	Lancaster MSA, PA	S	16.10 MW	16.29 AW	33480 AAW	PABLS	10//99-12//99
Helpers, Laborers, and Material Movers, Hand	Philadelphia PMSA, PA-NJ	S	18.08 MW	17.24 AW	37600 AAW	PABLS	10//99-12//99
Helpers, Laborers, and Material Movers, Hand	Pittsburgh MSA, PA	S	16.28 MW	15.63 AW	33850 AAW	PABLS	10//99-12//99
Helpers, Laborers, and Material Movers, Hand	Reading MSA, PA	S	13.85 MW	10.73 AW	28800 AAW	PABLS	10//99-12//99
Helpers, Laborers, and Material Movers, Hand	Scranton--Wilkes-Barre--Hazleton MSA, PA	S	15.09 MW	14.66 AW	31380 AAW	PABLS	10//99-12//99
Helpers, Laborers, and Material Movers, Hand	Sharon MSA, PA	S	12.97 MW	12.35 AW	26970 AAW	PABLS	10//99-12//99
Helpers, Laborers, and Material Movers, Hand	State College MSA, PA	S	14.90 MW	13.20 AW	31000 AAW	PABLS	10//99-12//99
Helpers, Laborers, and Material Movers, Hand	York MSA, PA	S	14.93 MW	14.79 AW	31060 AAW	PABLS	10//99-12//99
Helpers, Laborers, and Material Movers, Hand	Rhode Island	S	16.65 MW	17.93 AW	37290 AAW	RIBLS	10//99-12//99
Helpers, Laborers, and Material Movers, Hand	Providence-Fall River-Warwick MSA, RI-MA	S	18.15 MW	17.85 AW	37740 AAW	RIBLS	10//99-12//99
Helpers, Laborers, and Material Movers, Hand	South Carolina	S	14.11 MW	14.91 AW	31020 AAW	SCBLS	10//99-12//99
Helpers, Laborers, and Material Movers, Hand	Charleston-North Charleston MSA, SC	S	14.20 MW	12.61 AW	29540 AAW	SCBLS	10//99-12//99
Helpers, Laborers, and Material Movers, Hand	Columbia MSA, SC	S	17.31 MW	16.73 AW	36010 AAW	SCBLS	10//99-12//99
Helpers, Laborers, and Material Movers, Hand	Florence MSA, SC	S	17.27 MW	17.85 AW	35930 AAW	SCBLS	10//99-12//99

AAW Average annual wage	**AOH** Average offered, high	**ASH** Average starting, high	**H** Hourly	**M** Monthly	**S** Special: hourly and annual
AE Average entry wage	**AOL** Average offered, low	**ASL** Average starting, low	**HI** Highest wage paid	**MTC** Median total compensation	**TQ** Third quartile wage
AEX Average experienced wage	**APH** Average pay, high range	**AW** Average wage paid	**HR** High end range	**MW** Median wage paid	**W** Weekly
AO Average offered	**APL** Average pay, low range	**FQ** First quartile wage	**LR** Low end range	**SQ** Second quartile wage	**Y** Yearly

First-Line Supervisor/Manager

Occupation/Type/Industry	Location	Per	Low	Mid	High	Source	Date
First-Line Supervisor/Manager							
Helpers, Laborers, and Material Movers, Hand	Greenville-Spartanburg-Anderson MSA, SC	S	16.91 MW	16.11 AW	35180 AAW	SCBLS	10//99-12//99
Helpers, Laborers, and Material Movers, Hand	Myrtle Beach MSA, SC	S	13.33 MW	12.72 AW	27720 AAW	SCBLS	10//99-12//99
Helpers, Laborers, and Material Movers, Hand	Sumter MSA, SC	S	13.85 MW	13.16 AW	28810 AAW	SCBLS	10//99-12//99
Helpers, Laborers, and Material Movers, Hand	South Dakota	S	14.02 MW	13.98 AW	29070 AAW	SDBLS	10//99-12//99
Helpers, Laborers, and Material Movers, Hand	Sioux Falls MSA, SD	S	14.49 MW	14.68 AW	30140 AAW	SDBLS	10//99-12//99
Helpers, Laborers, and Material Movers, Hand	Tennessee	S	16.35 MW	17.31 AW	36000 AAW	TNBLS	10//99-12//99
Helpers, Laborers, and Material Movers, Hand	Chattanooga MSA, TN-GA	S	12.36 MW	10.92 AW	25710 AAW	TNBLS	10//99-12//99
Helpers, Laborers, and Material Movers, Hand	Clarksville-Hopkinsville MSA, TN-KY	S	14.29 MW	14.49 AW	29730 AAW	TNBLS	10//99-12//99
Helpers, Laborers, and Material Movers, Hand	Jackson MSA, TN	S	11.81 MW	10.09 AW	24570 AAW	TNBLS	10//99-12//99
Helpers, Laborers, and Material Movers, Hand	Johnson City-Kingsport-Bristol MSA, TN-VA	S	16.54 MW	16.47 AW	34410 AAW	TNBLS	10//99-12//99
Helpers, Laborers, and Material Movers, Hand	Knoxville MSA, TN	S	16.94 MW	16.03 AW	35230 AAW	TNBLS	10//99-12//99
Helpers, Laborers, and Material Movers, Hand	Memphis MSA, TN-AR-MS	S	17.27 MW	16.46 AW	35910 AAW	MSBLS	10//99-12//99
Helpers, Laborers, and Material Movers, Hand	Nashville MSA, TN	S	17.96 MW	16.63 AW	37360 AAW	TNBLS	10//99-12//99
Helpers, Laborers, and Material Movers, Hand	Texas	S	15.23 MW	15.91 AW	33090 AAW	TXBLS	10//99-12//99
Helpers, Laborers, and Material Movers, Hand	Abilene MSA, TX	S	13.35 MW	13.28 AW	27770 AAW	TXBLS	10//99-12//99
Helpers, Laborers, and Material Movers, Hand	Amarillo MSA, TX	S	14.40 MW	12.18 AW	29950 AAW	TXBLS	10//99-12//99
Helpers, Laborers, and Material Movers, Hand	Austin-San Marcos MSA, TX	S	13.78 MW	14.20 AW	28660 AAW	TXBLS	10//99-12//99
Helpers, Laborers, and Material Movers, Hand	Beaumont-Port Arthur MSA, TX	S	14.53 MW	13.18 AW	30230 AAW	TXBLS	10//99-12//99
Helpers, Laborers, and Material Movers, Hand	Brazoria PMSA, TX	S	14.71 MW	12.38 AW	30590 AAW	TXBLS	10//99-12//99
Helpers, Laborers, and Material Movers, Hand	Brownsville-Harlingen-San Benito MSA, TX	S	11.99 MW	11.79 AW	24940 AAW	TXBLS	10//99-12//99
Helpers, Laborers, and Material Movers, Hand	Corpus Christi MSA, TX	S	16.04 MW	14.26 AW	33360 AAW	TXBLS	10//99-12//99
Helpers, Laborers, and Material Movers, Hand	Dallas PMSA, TX	S	16.77 MW	16.57 AW	34880 AAW	TXBLS	10//99-12//99
Helpers, Laborers, and Material Movers, Hand	El Paso MSA, TX	S	15.12 MW	14.42 AW	31450 AAW	TXBLS	10//99-12//99
Helpers, Laborers, and Material Movers, Hand	Fort Worth-Arlington PMSA, TX	S	16.43 MW	15.43 AW	34180 AAW	TXBLS	10//99-12//99
Helpers, Laborers, and Material Movers, Hand	Galveston-Texas City PMSA, TX	S	17.66 MW	17.29 AW	36740 AAW	TXBLS	10//99-12//99
Helpers, Laborers, and Material Movers, Hand	Houston PMSA, TX	S	16.75 MW	16.17 AW	34850 AAW	TXBLS	10//99-12//99
Helpers, Laborers, and Material Movers, Hand	Killeen-Temple MSA, TX	S	13.46 MW	13.77 AW	27990 AAW	TXBLS	10//99-12//99
Helpers, Laborers, and Material Movers, Hand	Laredo MSA, TX	S	17.35 MW	16.13 AW	36080 AAW	TXBLS	10//99-12//99
Helpers, Laborers, and Material Movers, Hand	Longview-Marshall MSA, TX	S	11.96 MW	12.10 AW	24870 AAW	TXBLS	10//99-12//99
Helpers, Laborers, and Material Movers, Hand	Lubbock MSA, TX	S	14.60 MW	14.64 AW	30370 AAW	TXBLS	10//99-12//99
Helpers, Laborers, and Material Movers, Hand	McAllen-Edinburg-Mission MSA, TX	S	13.22 MW	11.97 AW	27490 AAW	TXBLS	10//99-12//99

AAW Average annual wage	AOH Average offered, high	ASH Average starting, high	H Hourly	M Monthly	S Special: hourly and annual
AE Average entry wage	AOL Average offered, low	ASL Average starting, low	HI Highest wage paid	MTC Median total compensation	TQ Third quartile wage
AEX Average experienced wage	APH Average pay, high range	AW Average wage paid	HR High end range	MW Median wage paid	W Weekly
AO Average offered	APL Average pay, low range	FQ First quartile wage	LR Low end range	SQ Second quartile wage	Y Yearly

Occupation/Type/Industry	Location	Per	Low	Mid	High	Source	Date
First-Line Supervisor/Manager							
Helpers, Laborers, and Material Movers, Hand	Odessa-Midland MSA, TX	S	15.80 MW	14.20 AW	32860 AAW	TXBLS	10//99-12//99
Helpers, Laborers, and Material Movers, Hand	San Antonio MSA, TX	S	15.64 MW	15.28 AW	32520 AAW	TXBLS	10//99-12//99
Helpers, Laborers, and Material Movers, Hand	Sherman-Denison MSA, TX	S	11.96 MW	10.64 AW	24890 AAW	TXBLS	10//99-12//99
Helpers, Laborers, and Material Movers, Hand	Texarkana MSA, TX-Texarkana, AR	S	15.97 MW	16.23 AW	33230 AAW	TXBLS	10//99-12//99
Helpers, Laborers, and Material Movers, Hand	Tyler MSA, TX	S	14.38 MW	14.78 AW	29900 AAW	TXBLS	10//99-12//99
Helpers, Laborers, and Material Movers, Hand	Victoria MSA, TX	S	12.45 MW	13.01 AW	25900 AAW	TXBLS	10//99-12//99
Helpers, Laborers, and Material Movers, Hand	Waco MSA, TX	S	17.26 MW	15.04 AW	35890 AAW	TXBLS	10//99-12//99
Helpers, Laborers, and Material Movers, Hand	Wichita Falls MSA, TX	S	11.83 MW	10.29 AW	24610 AAW	TXBLS	10//99-12//99
Helpers, Laborers, and Material Movers, Hand	Utah	S	14.19 MW	15.72 AW	32700 AAW	UTBLS	10//99-12//99
Helpers, Laborers, and Material Movers, Hand	Provo-Orem MSA, UT	S	14.37 MW	14.68 AW	29900 AAW	UTBLS	10//99-12//99
Helpers, Laborers, and Material Movers, Hand	Salt Lake City-Ogden MSA, UT	S	15.72 MW	14.35 AW	32690 AAW	UTBLS	10//99-12//99
Helpers, Laborers, and Material Movers, Hand	Vermont	S	17.82 MW	20.54 AW	42730 AAW	VTBLS	10//99-12//99
Helpers, Laborers, and Material Movers, Hand	Virginia	S	14.61 MW	15.72 AW	32700 AAW	VABLS	10//99-12//99
Helpers, Laborers, and Material Movers, Hand	Danville MSA, VA	S	12.28 MW	11.28 AW	25550 AAW	VABLS	10//99-12//99
Helpers, Laborers, and Material Movers, Hand	Lynchburg MSA, VA	S	18.02 MW	17.37 AW	37480 AAW	VABLS	10//99-12//99
Helpers, Laborers, and Material Movers, Hand	Norfolk-Virginia Beach-Newport News MSA, VA-NC	S	16.46 MW	14.29 AW	34240 AAW	VABLS	10//99-12//99
Helpers, Laborers, and Material Movers, Hand	Richmond-Petersburg MSA, VA	S	13.88 MW	13.37 AW	28870 AAW	VABLS	10//99-12//99
Helpers, Laborers, and Material Movers, Hand	Roanoke MSA, VA	S	14.15 MW	12.25 AW	29440 AAW	VABLS	10//99-12//99
Helpers, Laborers, and Material Movers, Hand	Washington	S	16.77 MW	18.52 AW	38520 AAW	WABLS	10//99-12//99
Helpers, Laborers, and Material Movers, Hand	Bellingham MSA, WA	S	21.35 MW	21.89 AW	44400 AAW	WABLS	10//99-12//99
Helpers, Laborers, and Material Movers, Hand	Olympia PMSA, WA	S	17.27 MW	15.17 AW	35920 AAW	WABLS	10//99-12//99
Helpers, Laborers, and Material Movers, Hand	Richland-Kennewick-Pasco MSA, WA	S	15.36 MW	15.46 AW	31940 AAW	WABLS	10//99-12//99
Helpers, Laborers, and Material Movers, Hand	Seattle-Bellevue-Everett PMSA, WA	S	17.74 MW	16.57 AW	36900 AAW	WABLS	10//99-12//99
Helpers, Laborers, and Material Movers, Hand	Spokane MSA, WA	S	17.87 MW	17.09 AW	37170 AAW	WABLS	10//99-12//99
Helpers, Laborers, and Material Movers, Hand	Tacoma PMSA, WA	S	20.91 MW	18.76 AW	43490 AAW	WABLS	10//99-12//99
Helpers, Laborers, and Material Movers, Hand	Yakima MSA, WA	S	17.13 MW	17.85 AW	35630 AAW	WABLS	10//99-12//99
Helpers, Laborers, and Material Movers, Hand	West Virginia	S	14.3 MW	16.52 AW	34350 AAW	WVBLS	10//99-12//99
Helpers, Laborers, and Material Movers, Hand	Charleston MSA, WV	S	15.75 MW	16.19 AW	32750 AAW	WVBLS	10//99-12//99
Helpers, Laborers, and Material Movers, Hand	Huntington-Ashland MSA, WV-KY-OH	S	12.27 MW	10.13 AW	25520 AAW	WVBLS	10//99-12//99
Helpers, Laborers, and Material Movers, Hand	Parkersburg-Marietta MSA, WV-OH	S	16.16 MW	17.22 AW	33610 AAW	WVBLS	10//99-12//99

Occupation/Type/Industry	Location	Per	Low	Mid	High	Source	Date
First-Line Supervisor/Manager							
Helpers, Laborers, and Material Movers, Hand	Wheeling MSA, WV-OH	S	14.34 MW	13.45 AW	29830 AAW	WVBLS	10//99-12//99
Helpers, Laborers, and Material Movers, Hand	Wisconsin	S	16.04 MW	16.93 AW	35210 AAW	WIBLS	10//99-12//99
Helpers, Laborers, and Material Movers, Hand	Appleton-Oshkosh-Neenah MSA, WI	S	20.77 MW	19.50 AW	43210 AAW	WIBLS	10//99-12//99
Helpers, Laborers, and Material Movers, Hand	Eau Claire MSA, WI	S	17.40 MW	15.44 AW	36190 AAW	WIBLS	10//99-12//99
Helpers, Laborers, and Material Movers, Hand	Green Bay MSA, WI	S	16.62 MW	15.86 AW	34560 AAW	WIBLS	10//99-12//99
Helpers, Laborers, and Material Movers, Hand	La Crosse MSA, WI-MN	S	17.83 MW	18.08 AW	37080 AAW	WIBLS	10//99-12//99
Helpers, Laborers, and Material Movers, Hand	Madison MSA, WI	S	17.93 MW	18.36 AW	37290 AAW	WIBLS	10//99-12//99
Helpers, Laborers, and Material Movers, Hand	Milwaukee-Waukesha PMSA, WI	S	16.70 MW	16.03 AW	34730 AAW	WIBLS	10//99-12//99
Helpers, Laborers, and Material Movers, Hand	Racine PMSA, WI	S	16.72 MW	14.95 AW	34770 AAW	WIBLS	10//99-12//99
Helpers, Laborers, and Material Movers, Hand	Wausau MSA, WI	S	14.55 MW	14.35 AW	30260 AAW	WIBLS	10//99-12//99
Helpers, Laborers, and Material Movers, Hand	Wyoming	S	17.03 MW	16.73 AW	34810 AAW	WYBLS	10//99-12//99
Helpers, Laborers, and Material Movers, Hand	Cheyenne MSA, WY	S	17.19 MW	17.43 AW	35750 AAW	WYBLS	10//99-12//99
Helpers, Laborers, and Material Movers, Hand	Puerto Rico	S	9.55 MW	11.05 AW	22990 AAW	PRBLS	10//99-12//99
Helpers, Laborers, and Material Movers, Hand	Mayaguez MSA, PR	S	10.78 MW	8.91 AW	22430 AAW	PRBLS	10//99-12//99
Helpers, Laborers, and Material Movers, Hand	Ponce MSA, PR	S	10.91 MW	11.34 AW	22700 AAW	PRBLS	10//99-12//99
Helpers, Laborers, and Material Movers, Hand	San Juan-Bayamon PMSA, PR	S	11.50 MW	9.93 AW	23920 AAW	PRBLS	10//99-12//99
Helpers, Laborers, and Material Movers, Hand	Guam	S	11.13 MW	12.74 AW	26500 AAW	GUBLS	10//99-12//99
Housekeeping and Janitorial Workers	Alabama	S	8.77 MW	9.60 AW	19980 AAW	ALBLS	10//99-12//99
Housekeeping and Janitorial Workers	Alaska	S	12.45 MW	14.80 AW	30790 AAW	AKBLS	10//99-12//99
Housekeeping and Janitorial Workers	Arizona	S	10.12 MW	10.48 AW	21790 AAW	AZBLS	10//99-12//99
Housekeeping and Janitorial Workers	Arkansas	S	8.44 MW	9.20 AW	19130 AAW	ARBLS	10//99-12//99
Housekeeping and Janitorial Workers	California	S	11.04 MW	12.24 AW	25460 AAW	CABLS	10//99-12//99
Housekeeping and Janitorial Workers	Colorado	S	10.95 MW	11.78 AW	24500 AAW	COBLS	10//99-12//99
Housekeeping and Janitorial Workers	Connecticut	S	13.2 MW	14.42 AW	29990 AAW	CTBLS	10//99-12//99
Housekeeping and Janitorial Workers	Delaware	S	12.33 MW	12.69 AW	26400 AAW	DEBLS	10//99-12//99
Housekeeping and Janitorial Workers	District of Columbia	S	7.74 MW	9.03 AW	18790 AAW	DCBLS	10//99-12//99
Housekeeping and Janitorial Workers	Florida	S	10.57 MW	11.12 AW	23140 AAW	FLBLS	10//99-12//99
Housekeeping and Janitorial Workers	Georgia	S	10.31 MW	10.88 AW	22630 AAW	GABLS	10//99-12//99
Housekeeping and Janitorial Workers	Hawaii	S	13.41 MW	13.94 AW	28990 AAW	HIBLS	10//99-12//99
Housekeeping and Janitorial Workers	Idaho	S	8.7 MW	9.48 AW	19730 AAW	IDBLS	10//99-12//99
Housekeeping and Janitorial Workers	Illinois	S	10.78 MW	11.94 AW	24840 AAW	ILBLS	10//99-12//99
Housekeeping and Janitorial Workers	Indiana	S	10.58 MW	11.36 AW	23630 AAW	INBLS	10//99-12//99
Housekeeping and Janitorial Workers	Iowa	S	9.42 MW	10.44 AW	21720 AAW	IABLS	10//99-12//99
Housekeeping and Janitorial Workers	Kansas	S	9.38 MW	10.14 AW	21090 AAW	KSBLS	10//99-12//99
Housekeeping and Janitorial Workers	Kentucky	S	9.42 MW	10.12 AW	21060 AAW	KYBLS	10//99-12//99
Housekeeping and Janitorial Workers	Louisiana	S	9.25 MW	10.17 AW	21150 AAW	LABLS	10//99-12//99
Housekeeping and Janitorial Workers	Maine	S	11.1 MW	11.46 AW	23830 AAW	MEBLS	10//99-12//99
Housekeeping and Janitorial Workers	Maryland	S	11.23 MW	12.24 AW	25460 AAW	MDBLS	10//99-12//99
Housekeeping and Janitorial Workers	Massachusetts	S	13.85 MW	14.20 AW	29540 AAW	MABLS	10//99-12//99
Housekeeping and Janitorial Workers	Michigan	S	10.77 MW	12.31 AW	25610 AAW	MIBLS	10//99-12//99
Housekeeping and Janitorial Workers	Minnesota	S	11.92 MW	12.58 AW	26160 AAW	MNBLS	10//99-12//99
Housekeeping and Janitorial Workers	Mississippi	S	9.22 MW	10.07 AW	20950 AAW	MSBLS	10//99-12//99
Housekeeping and Janitorial Workers	Missouri	S	9.98 MW	10.98 AW	22830 AAW	MOBLS	10//99-12//99
Housekeeping and Janitorial Workers	Montana	S	8.97 MW	9.97 AW	20740 AAW	MTBLS	10//99-12//99
Housekeeping and Janitorial Workers	Nebraska	S	9.93 MW	10.72 AW	22310 AAW	NEBLS	10//99-12//99
Housekeeping and Janitorial Workers	Nevada	S	12.04 MW	12.07 AW	25110 AAW	NVBLS	10//99-12//99
Housekeeping and Janitorial Workers	New Hampshire	S	11.61 MW	11.94 AW	24840 AAW	NHBLS	10//99-12//99
Housekeeping and Janitorial Workers	New Jersey	S	14.17 MW	15.28 AW	31770 AAW	NJBLS	10//99-12//99
Housekeeping and Janitorial Workers	New Mexico	S	9.47 MW	9.99 AW	20790 AAW	NMBLS	10//99-12//99
Housekeeping and Janitorial Workers	New York	S	14.84 MW	15.46 AW	32150 AAW	NYBLS	10//99-12//99
Housekeeping and Janitorial Workers	North Carolina	S	9.2 MW	9.99 AW	20790 AAW	NCBLS	10//99-12//99
Housekeeping and Janitorial Workers	North Dakota	S	9.16 MW	9.70 AW	20170 AAW	NDBLS	10//99-12//99

AAW	Average annual wage	AOH	Average offered, high	ASH	Average starting, high	H	Hourly	M	Monthly	S	Special: hourly and annual
AE	Average entry wage	AOL	Average offered, low	ASL	Average starting, low	HI	Highest wage paid	MTC	Median total compensation	TQ	Third quartile wage
AEX	Average experienced wage	APH	Average pay, high range	AW	Average wage paid	HR	High end range	MW	Median wage paid	W	Weekly
AO	Average offered	APL	Average pay, low range	FQ	First quartile wage	LR	Low end range	SQ	Second quartile wage	Y	Yearly

Occupation/Type/Industry	Location	Per	Low	Mid	High	Source	Date
First-Line Supervisor/Manager							
Housekeeping and Janitorial Workers	Ohio	S	10.94 MW	11.82 AW	24600 AAW	OHBLS	10//99-12//99
Housekeeping and Janitorial Workers	Oklahoma	S	9.26 MW	10.17 AW	21160 AAW	OKBLS	10//99-12//99
Housekeeping and Janitorial Workers	Oregon	S	9.95 MW	11.19 AW	23280 AAW	ORBLS	10//99-12//99
Housekeeping and Janitorial Workers	Pennsylvania	S	11.87 MW	12.76 AW	26540 AAW	PABLS	10//99-12//99
Housekeeping and Janitorial Workers	Rhode Island	S	13.78 MW	13.02 AW	27090 AAW	RIBLS	10//99-12//99
Housekeeping and Janitorial Workers	South Carolina	S	9.37 MW	10.35 AW	21530 AAW	SCBLS	10//99-12//99
Housekeeping and Janitorial Workers	South Dakota	S	9.92 MW	10.28 AW	21390 AAW	SDBLS	10//99-12//99
Housekeeping and Janitorial Workers	Tennessee	S	9.08 MW	9.70 AW	20170 AAW	TNBLS	10//99-12//99
Housekeeping and Janitorial Workers	Texas	S	9.52 MW	10.57 AW	21970 AAW	TXBLS	10//99-12//99
Housekeeping and Janitorial Workers	Utah	S	10.02 MW	11.08 AW	23050 AAW	UTBLS	10//99-12//99
Housekeeping and Janitorial Workers	Vermont	S	11.18 MW	12.49 AW	25980 AAW	VTBLS	10//99-12//99
Housekeeping and Janitorial Workers	Virginia	S	11.04 MW	11.52 AW	23950 AAW	VABLS	10//99-12//99
Housekeeping and Janitorial Workers	Washington	S	11.73 MW	12.24 AW	25450 AAW	WABLS	10//99-12//99
Housekeeping and Janitorial Workers	West Virginia	S	9.32 MW	9.96 AW	20710 AAW	WVBLS	10//99-12//99
Housekeeping and Janitorial Workers	Wisconsin	S	10.17 MW	10.98 AW	22840 AAW	WIBLS	10//99-12//99
Housekeeping and Janitorial Workers	Wyoming	S	8.83 MW	9.28 AW	19290 AAW	WYBLS	10//99-12//99
Housekeeping and Janitorial Workers	Puerto Rico	S	8.15 MW	8.61 AW	17910 AAW	PRBLS	10//99-12//99
Housekeeping and Janitorial Workers	Virgin Islands	S	10.72 MW	11.21 AW	23320 AAW	VIBLS	10//99-12//99
Housekeeping and Janitorial Workers	Guam	S	9.11 MW	10.63 AW	22110 AAW	GUBLS	10//99-12//99
Landscaping, Lawn Service, and Groundskeeping Workers	Alabama	S	11.22 MW	12.63 AW	26260 AAW	ALBLS	10//99-12//99
Landscaping, Lawn Service, and Groundskeeping Workers	Alaska	S	19.1 MW	19.44 AW	40440 AAW	AKBLS	10//99-12//99
Landscaping, Lawn Service, and Groundskeeping Workers	Arizona	S	11.26 MW	13.04 AW	27120 AAW	AZBLS	10//99-12//99
Landscaping, Lawn Service, and Groundskeeping Workers	Arkansas	S	11.81 MW	12.48 AW	25970 AAW	ARBLS	10//99-12//99
Landscaping, Lawn Service, and Groundskeeping Workers	California	S	16.11 MW	17.18 AW	35740 AAW	CABLS	10//99-12//99
Landscaping, Lawn Service, and Groundskeeping Workers	Colorado	S	15.9 MW	16.47 AW	34260 AAW	COBLS	10//99-12//99
Landscaping, Lawn Service, and Groundskeeping Workers	Connecticut	S	20.26 MW	21.10 AW	43890 AAW	CTBLS	10//99-12//99
Landscaping, Lawn Service, and Groundskeeping Workers	Delaware	S	17.14 MW	17.71 AW	36830 AAW	DEBLS	10//99-12//99
Landscaping, Lawn Service, and Groundskeeping Workers	District of Columbia	S	12.6 MW	14.22 AW	29580 AAW	DCBLS	10//99-12//99
Landscaping, Lawn Service, and Groundskeeping Workers	Florida	S	12.22 MW	13.30 AW	27670 AAW	FLBLS	10//99-12//99
Landscaping, Lawn Service, and Groundskeeping Workers	Georgia	S	14.53 MW	15.62 AW	32500 AAW	GABLS	10//99-12//99
Landscaping, Lawn Service, and Groundskeeping Workers	Hawaii	S	15.61 MW	16.05 AW	33380 AAW	HIBLS	10//99-12//99
Landscaping, Lawn Service, and Groundskeeping Workers	Idaho	S	13.14 MW	14.63 AW	30430 AAW	IDBLS	10//99-12//99
Landscaping, Lawn Service, and Groundskeeping Workers	Illinois	S	14.77 MW	15.03 AW	31260 AAW	ILBLS	10//99-12//99
Landscaping, Lawn Service, and Groundskeeping Workers	Indiana	S	14.21 MW	15.07 AW	31350 AAW	INBLS	10//99-12//99
Landscaping, Lawn Service, and Groundskeeping Workers	Iowa	S	12.25 MW	12.74 AW	26510 AAW	IABLS	10//99-12//99
Landscaping, Lawn Service, and Groundskeeping Workers	Kansas	S	13.29 MW	15.08 AW	31370 AAW	KSBLS	10//99-12//99
Landscaping, Lawn Service, and Groundskeeping Workers	Kentucky	S	12.44 MW	13.58 AW	28240 AAW	KYBLS	10//99-12//99
Landscaping, Lawn Service, and Groundskeeping Workers	Louisiana	S	12.46 MW	13.95 AW	29030 AAW	LABLS	10//99-12//99
Landscaping, Lawn Service, and Groundskeeping Workers	Maine	S	12.56 MW	12.90 AW	26840 AAW	MEBLS	10//99-12//99
Landscaping, Lawn Service, and Groundskeeping Workers	Maryland	S	14.28 MW	15.39 AW	32020 AAW	MDBLS	10//99-12//99
Landscaping, Lawn Service, and Groundskeeping Workers	Massachusetts	S	18.26 MW	25.69 AW	53440 AAW	MABLS	10//99-12//99
Landscaping, Lawn Service, and Groundskeeping Workers	Michigan	S	14.55 MW	15.69 AW	32630 AAW	MIBLS	10//99-12//99
Landscaping, Lawn Service, and Groundskeeping Workers	Minnesota	S	15.73 MW	18.22 AW	37910 AAW	MNBLS	10//99-12//99
Landscaping, Lawn Service, and Groundskeeping Workers	Mississippi	S	14.3 MW	14.92 AW	31030 AAW	MSBLS	10//99-12//99

AAW Average annual wage	AOH Average offered, high	ASH Average starting, high	H Hourly	M Monthly	S Special: hourly and annual
AE Average entry wage	AOL Average offered, low	ASL Average starting, low	HI Highest wage paid	MTC Median total compensation	TQ Third quartile wage
AEX Average experienced wage	APH Average pay, high range	AW Average wage paid	HR High end range	MW Median wage paid	W Weekly
AO Average offered	APL Average pay, low range	FQ First quartile wage	LR Low end range	SQ Second quartile wage	Y Yearly

Occupation/Type/Industry	Location	Per	Low	Mid	High	Source	Date
First-Line Supervisor/Manager							
Landscaping, Lawn Service, and Groundskeeping Workers	Missouri	S	13.94 MW	15.28 AW	31790 AAW	MOBLS	10//99-12//99
Landscaping, Lawn Service, and Groundskeeping Workers	Montana	S	12.73 MW	13.76 AW	28620 AAW	MTBLS	10//99-12//99
Landscaping, Lawn Service, and Groundskeeping Workers	Nebraska	S	12.61 MW	13.80 AW	28700 AAW	NEBLS	10//99-12//99
Landscaping, Lawn Service, and Groundskeeping Workers	Nevada	S	12.62 MW	13.21 AW	27470 AAW	NVBLS	10//99-12//99
Landscaping, Lawn Service, and Groundskeeping Workers	New Hampshire	S	13.16 MW	14.45 AW	30060 AAW	NHBLS	10//99-12//99
Landscaping, Lawn Service, and Groundskeeping Workers	New Jersey	S	17.49 MW	19.11 AW	39740 AAW	NJBLS	10//99-12//99
Landscaping, Lawn Service, and Groundskeeping Workers	New Mexico	S	11.18 MW	11.58 AW	24080 AAW	NMBLS	10//99-12//99
Landscaping, Lawn Service, and Groundskeeping Workers	New York	S	19.41 MW	21.38 AW	44470 AAW	NYBLS	10//99-12//99
Landscaping, Lawn Service, and Groundskeeping Workers	North Carolina	S	14.47 MW	15.40 AW	32020 AAW	NCBLS	10//99-12//99
Landscaping, Lawn Service, and Groundskeeping Workers	North Dakota	S	11.07 MW	11.92 AW	24800 AAW	NDBLS	10//99-12//99
Landscaping, Lawn Service, and Groundskeeping Workers	Ohio	S	13.45 MW	15.02 AW	31250 AAW	OHBLS	10//99-12//99
Landscaping, Lawn Service, and Groundskeeping Workers	Oklahoma	S	10.54 MW	10.88 AW	22620 AAW	OKBLS	10//99-12//99
Landscaping, Lawn Service, and Groundskeeping Workers	Oregon	S	17.24 MW	17.99 AW	37410 AAW	ORBLS	10//99-12//99
Landscaping, Lawn Service, and Groundskeeping Workers	Pennsylvania	S	14.19 MW	15.58 AW	32400 AAW	PABLS	10//99-12//99
Landscaping, Lawn Service, and Groundskeeping Workers	Rhode Island	S	15.85 MW	18.54 AW	38560 AAW	RIBLS	10//99-12//99
Landscaping, Lawn Service, and Groundskeeping Workers	South Carolina	S	12.67 MW	13.51 AW	28090 AAW	SCBLS	10//99-12//99
Landscaping, Lawn Service, and Groundskeeping Workers	South Dakota	S	13.77 MW	13.48 AW	28050 AAW	SDBLS	10//99-12//99
Landscaping, Lawn Service, and Groundskeeping Workers	Tennessee	S	11.29 MW	12.24 AW	25450 AAW	TNBLS	10//99-12//99
Landscaping, Lawn Service, and Groundskeeping Workers	Texas	S	11.28 MW	12.33 AW	25640 AAW	TXBLS	10//99-12//99
Landscaping, Lawn Service, and Groundskeeping Workers	Utah	S	13.08 MW	13.83 AW	28770 AAW	UTBLS	10//99-12//99
Landscaping, Lawn Service, and Groundskeeping Workers	Vermont	S	16.29 MW	16.89 AW	35120 AAW	VTBLS	10//99-12//99
Landscaping, Lawn Service, and Groundskeeping Workers	Virginia	S	13.53 MW	15.12 AW	31460 AAW	VABLS	10//99-12//99
Landscaping, Lawn Service, and Groundskeeping Workers	Washington	S	16.21 MW	18.01 AW	37460 AAW	WABLS	10//99-12//99
Landscaping, Lawn Service, and Groundskeeping Workers	West Virginia	S	9.07 MW	10.67 AW	22190 AAW	WVBLS	10//99-12//99
Landscaping, Lawn Service, and Groundskeeping Workers	Wisconsin	S	15.13 MW	16.63 AW	34590 AAW	WIBLS	10//99-12//99
Landscaping, Lawn Service, and Groundskeeping Workers	Wyoming	S	10.3 MW	12.57 AW	26140 AAW	WYBLS	10//99-12//99
Landscaping, Lawn Service, and Groundskeeping Workers	Puerto Rico	S	7.34 MW	8.55 AW	17770 AAW	PRBLS	10//99-12//99
Landscaping, Lawn Service, and Groundskeeping Workers	Virgin Islands	S	13.02 MW	13.67 AW	28440 AAW	VIBLS	10//99-12//99
Landscaping, Lawn Service, and Groundskeeping Workers	Guam	S	10.39 MW	10.87 AW	22620 AAW	GUBLS	10//99-12//99
Mechanics, Installers, and Repairers	Alabama	S	18.53 MW	19.78 AW	41140 AAW	ALBLS	10//99-12//99
Mechanics, Installers, and Repairers	Anniston MSA, AL	S	21.23 MW	20.28 AW	44150 AAW	ALBLS	10//99-12//99
Mechanics, Installers, and Repairers	Auburn-Opelika MSA, AL	S	17.21 MW	16.25 AW	35790 AAW	ALBLS	10//99-12//99
Mechanics, Installers, and Repairers	Birmingham MSA, AL	S	20.31 MW	20.49 AW	42250 AAW	ALBLS	10//99-12//99
Mechanics, Installers, and Repairers	Decatur MSA, AL	S	20.17 MW	18.83 AW	41940 AAW	ALBLS	10//99-12//99
Mechanics, Installers, and Repairers	Dothan MSA, AL	S	17.95 MW	16.47 AW	37340 AAW	ALBLS	10//99-12//99
Mechanics, Installers, and Repairers	Florence MSA, AL	S	16.52 MW	15.19 AW	34370 AAW	ALBLS	10//99-12//99
Mechanics, Installers, and Repairers	Gadsden MSA, AL	S	19.87 MW	17.00 AW	41340 AAW	ALBLS	10//99-12//99
Mechanics, Installers, and Repairers	Huntsville MSA, AL	S	22.64 MW	18.92 AW	47090 AAW	ALBLS	10//99-12//99
Mechanics, Installers, and Repairers	Mobile MSA, AL	S	20.26 MW	18.47 AW	42140 AAW	ALBLS	10//99-12//99
Mechanics, Installers, and Repairers	Montgomery MSA, AL	S	17.61 MW	16.24 AW	36620 AAW	ALBLS	10//99-12//99
Mechanics, Installers, and Repairers	Tuscaloosa MSA, AL	S	18.43 MW	16.77 AW	38330 AAW	ALBLS	10//99-12//99
Mechanics, Installers, and Repairers	Alaska	S	28.51 MW	27.84 AW	57920 AAW	AKBLS	10//99-12//99

AAW	Average annual wage	AOH	Average offered, high	ASH	Average starting, high
AE	Average entry wage	AOL	Average offered, low	ASL	Average starting, low
AEX	Average experienced wage	APH	Average pay, high range	AW	Average wage paid
AO	Average offered	APL	Average pay, low range	FQ	First quartile wage

H	Hourly	M	Monthly	S	Special: hourly and annual
HI	Highest wage paid	MTC	Median total compensation	TQ	Third quartile wage
HR	High end range	MW	Median wage paid	W	Weekly
LR	Low end range	SQ	Second quartile wage	Y	Yearly

Occupation/Type/Industry	Location	Per	Low	Mid	High	Source	Date
First-Line Supervisor/Manager							
Mechanics, Installers, and Repairers	Anchorage MSA, AK	S	26.57 MW	27.39 AW	55270 AAW	AKBLS	10//99-12//99
Mechanics, Installers, and Repairers	Arizona	S	21.49 MW	21.84 AW	45420 AAW	AZBLS	10//99-12//99
Mechanics, Installers, and Repairers	Flagstaff MSA, AZ-UT	S	19.20 MW	17.45 AW	39940 AAW	AZBLS	10//99-12//99
Mechanics, Installers, and Repairers	Phoenix-Mesa MSA, AZ	S	22.46 MW	22.26 AW	46710 AAW	AZBLS	10//99-12//99
Mechanics, Installers, and Repairers	Tucson MSA, AZ	S	20.17 MW	20.21 AW	41950 AAW	AZBLS	10//99-12//99
Mechanics, Installers, and Repairers	Yuma MSA, AZ	S	20.60 MW	20.48 AW	42850 AAW	AZBLS	10//99-12//99
Mechanics, Installers, and Repairers	Arkansas	S	17.01 MW	18.14 AW	37740 AAW	ARBLS	10//99-12//99
Mechanics, Installers, and Repairers	Fayetteville-Springdale-Rogers MSA, AR	S	16.30 MW	15.43 AW	33910 AAW	ARBLS	10//99-12//99
Mechanics, Installers, and Repairers	Fort Smith MSA, AR-OK	S	16.91 MW	15.33 AW	35180 AAW	ARBLS	10//99-12//99
Mechanics, Installers, and Repairers	Jonesboro MSA, AR	S	18.55 MW	16.40 AW	38590 AAW	ARBLS	10//99-12//99
Mechanics, Installers, and Repairers	Little Rock-North Little Rock MSA, AR	S	19.96 MW	18.84 AW	41510 AAW	ARBLS	10//99-12//99
Mechanics, Installers, and Repairers	Pine Bluff MSA, AR	S	16.57 MW	17.36 AW	34460 AAW	ARBLS	10//99-12//99
Mechanics, Installers, and Repairers	California	S	23.44 MW	24.11 AW	50140 AAW	CABLS	10//99-12//99
Mechanics, Installers, and Repairers	Bakersfield MSA, CA	S	24.42 MW	23.18 AW	50790 AAW	CABLS	10//99-12//99
Mechanics, Installers, and Repairers	Chico-Paradise MSA, CA	S	23.53 MW	24.36 AW	48930 AAW	CABLS	10//99-12//99
Mechanics, Installers, and Repairers	Fresno MSA, CA	S	22.56 MW	20.57 AW	46930 AAW	CABLS	10//99-12//99
Mechanics, Installers, and Repairers	Los Angeles-Long Beach PMSA, CA	S	24.38 MW	24.16 AW	50700 AAW	CABLS	10//99-12//99
Mechanics, Installers, and Repairers	Merced MSA, CA	S	21.35 MW	19.73 AW	44410 AAW	CABLS	10//99-12//99
Mechanics, Installers, and Repairers	Modesto MSA, CA	S	19.26 MW	18.15 AW	40060 AAW	CABLS	10//99-12//99
Mechanics, Installers, and Repairers	Oakland PMSA, CA	S	30.38 MW	28.00 AW	63180 AAW	CABLS	10//99-12//99
Mechanics, Installers, and Repairers	Orange County PMSA, CA	S	25.35 MW	23.58 AW	52720 AAW	CABLS	10//99-12//99
Mechanics, Installers, and Repairers	Redding MSA, CA	S	22.85 MW	22.46 AW	47530 AAW	CABLS	10//99-12//99
Mechanics, Installers, and Repairers	Riverside-San Bernardino PMSA, CA	S	22.93 MW	23.05 AW	47700 AAW	CABLS	10//99-12//99
Mechanics, Installers, and Repairers	Sacramento PMSA, CA	S	24.96 MW	25.19 AW	51930 AAW	CABLS	10//99-12//99
Mechanics, Installers, and Repairers	Salinas MSA, CA	S	22.86 MW	21.01 AW	47550 AAW	CABLS	10//99-12//99
Mechanics, Installers, and Repairers	San Diego MSA, CA	S	22.16 MW	21.37 AW	46100 AAW	CABLS	10//99-12//99
Mechanics, Installers, and Repairers	San Francisco PMSA, CA	S	25.93 MW	25.22 AW	53930 AAW	CABLS	10//99-12//99
Mechanics, Installers, and Repairers	San Jose PMSA, CA	S	25.03 MW	24.17 AW	52050 AAW	CABLS	10//99-12//99
Mechanics, Installers, and Repairers	Santa Barbara-Santa Maria-Lompoc MSA, CA	S	24.02 MW	24.79 AW	49970 AAW	CABLS	10//99-12//99
Mechanics, Installers, and Repairers	Santa Cruz-Watsonville PMSA, CA	S	19.69 MW	18.83 AW	40960 AAW	CABLS	10//99-12//99
Mechanics, Installers, and Repairers	Santa Rosa PMSA, CA	S	21.73 MW	21.84 AW	45200 AAW	CABLS	10//99-12//99
Mechanics, Installers, and Repairers	Stockton-Lodi MSA, CA	S	22.08 MW	22.43 AW	45930 AAW	CABLS	10//99-12//99
Mechanics, Installers, and Repairers	Vallejo-Fairfield-Napa PMSA, CA	S	22.34 MW	21.99 AW	46460 AAW	CABLS	10//99-12//99
Mechanics, Installers, and Repairers	Ventura PMSA, CA	S	20.74 MW	19.71 AW	43150 AAW	CABLS	10//99-12//99
Mechanics, Installers, and Repairers	Visalia-Tulare-Porterville MSA, CA	S	20.05 MW	20.68 AW	41710 AAW	CABLS	10//99-12//99
Mechanics, Installers, and Repairers	Yolo PMSA, CA	S	23.09 MW	22.84 AW	48030 AAW	CABLS	10//99-12//99
Mechanics, Installers, and Repairers	Yuba City MSA, CA	S	22.61 MW	22.80 AW	47020 AAW	CABLS	10//99-12//99
Mechanics, Installers, and Repairers	Colorado	S	21.98 MW	22.31 AW	46410 AAW	COBLS	10//99-12//99
Mechanics, Installers, and Repairers	Boulder-Longmont PMSA, CO	S	23.44 MW	22.40 AW	48750 AAW	COBLS	10//99-12//99
Mechanics, Installers, and Repairers	Colorado Springs MSA, CO	S	21.50 MW	19.82 AW	44710 AAW	COBLS	10//99-12//99
Mechanics, Installers, and Repairers	Denver PMSA, CO	S	23.75 MW	23.69 AW	49410 AAW	COBLS	10//99-12//99
Mechanics, Installers, and Repairers	Fort Collins-Loveland MSA, CO	S	20.46 MW	20.64 AW	42560 AAW	COBLS	10//99-12//99
Mechanics, Installers, and Repairers	Greeley PMSA, CO	S	21.23 MW	20.28 AW	44160 AAW	COBLS	10//99-12//99
Mechanics, Installers, and Repairers	Connecticut	S	23.88 MW	24.84 AW	51670 AAW	CTBLS	10//99-12//99
Mechanics, Installers, and Repairers	Bridgeport PMSA, CT	S	23.80 MW	22.96 AW	49500 AAW	CTBLS	10//99-12//99
Mechanics, Installers, and Repairers	Danbury PMSA, CT	S	29.00 MW	26.31 AW	60310 AAW	CTBLS	10//99-12//99
Mechanics, Installers, and Repairers	Hartford MSA, CT	S	24.31 MW	23.86 AW	50570 AAW	CTBLS	10//99-12//99
Mechanics, Installers, and Repairers	New Haven-Meriden PMSA, CT	S	21.96 MW	21.96 AW	45670 AAW	CTBLS	10//99-12//99
Mechanics, Installers, and Repairers	New London-Norwich MSA, CT-RI	S	26.77 MW	23.44 AW	55670 AAW	CTBLS	10//99-12//99
Mechanics, Installers, and Repairers	Stamford-Norwalk PMSA, CT	S	30.21 MW	27.18 AW	62840 AAW	CTBLS	10//99-12//99
Mechanics, Installers, and Repairers	Waterbury PMSA, CT	S	22.26 MW	22.14 AW	46300 AAW	CTBLS	10//99-12//99
Mechanics, Installers, and Repairers	Delaware	S	21.32 MW	22.32 AW	46430 AAW	DEBLS	10//99-12//99
Mechanics, Installers, and Repairers	Dover MSA, DE	S	20.46 MW	21.18 AW	42560 AAW	DEBLS	10//99-12//99
Mechanics, Installers, and Repairers	Wilmington-Newark PMSA, DE-MD	S	22.43 MW	21.42 AW	46650 AAW	DEBLS	10//99-12//99
Mechanics, Installers, and Repairers	District of Columbia	S	24.94 MW	24.82 AW	51620 AAW	DCBLS	10//99-12//99
Mechanics, Installers, and Repairers	Washington PMSA, DC-MD-VA-WV	S	23.42 MW	21.90 AW	48710 AAW	DCBLS	10//99-12//99
Mechanics, Installers, and Repairers	Florida	S	19.02 MW	20.00 AW	41600 AAW	FLBLS	10//99-12//99
Mechanics, Installers, and Repairers	Daytona Beach MSA, FL	S	14.55 MW	13.18 AW	30260 AAW	FLBLS	10//99-12//99

AAW Average annual wage	**AOH** Average offered, high	**ASH** Average starting, high	**H** Hourly	**M** Monthly	**S** Special: hourly and annual
AE Average entry wage	**AOL** Average offered, low	**ASL** Average starting, low	**HI** Highest wage paid	**MTC** Median total compensation	**TQ** Third quartile wage
AEX Average experienced wage	**APH** Average pay, high range	**AW** Average wage paid	**HR** High end range	**MW** Median wage paid	**W** Weekly
AO Average offered	**APL** Average pay, low range	**FQ** First quartile wage	**LR** Low end range	**SQ** Second quartile wage	**Y** Yearly

Occupation/Type/Industry	Location	Per	Low	Mid	High	Source	Date
First-Line Supervisor/Manager							
Mechanics, Installers, and Repairers	Fort Lauderdale PMSA, FL	S	23.58 MW	21.66 AW	49040 AAW	FLBLS	10//99-12//99
Mechanics, Installers, and Repairers	Fort Myers-Cape Coral MSA, FL	S	16.37 MW	15.01 AW	34050 AAW	FLBLS	10//99-12//99
Mechanics, Installers, and Repairers	Fort Pierce-Port St. Lucie MSA, FL	S	18.26 MW	18.01 AW	37980 AAW	FLBLS	10//99-12//99
Mechanics, Installers, and Repairers	Fort Walton Beach MSA, FL	S	20.23 MW	20.70 AW	42080 AAW	FLBLS	10//99-12//99
Mechanics, Installers, and Repairers	Gainesville MSA, FL	S	15.41 MW	13.22 AW	32040 AAW	FLBLS	10//99-12//99
Mechanics, Installers, and Repairers	Jacksonville MSA, FL	S	19.70 MW	19.66 AW	40980 AAW	FLBLS	10//99-12//99
Mechanics, Installers, and Repairers	Lakeland-Winter Haven MSA, FL	S	19.59 MW	18.50 AW	40750 AAW	FLBLS	10//99-12//99
Mechanics, Installers, and Repairers	Melbourne-Titusville-Palm Bay MSA, FL	S	20.41 MW	19.26 AW	42440 AAW	FLBLS	10//99-12//99
Mechanics, Installers, and Repairers	Miami PMSA, FL	S	18.57 MW	18.63 AW	38620 AAW	FLBLS	10//99-12//99
Mechanics, Installers, and Repairers	Naples MSA, FL	S	18.60 MW	19.09 AW	38680 AAW	FLBLS	10//99-12//99
Mechanics, Installers, and Repairers	Ocala MSA, FL	S	20.25 MW	18.75 AW	42130 AAW	FLBLS	10//99-12//99
Mechanics, Installers, and Repairers	Orlando MSA, FL	S	19.67 MW	18.21 AW	40910 AAW	FLBLS	10//99-12//99
Mechanics, Installers, and Repairers	Panama City MSA, FL	S	20.84 MW	21.17 AW	43350 AAW	FLBLS	10//99-12//99
Mechanics, Installers, and Repairers	Pensacola MSA, FL	S	19.17 MW	16.94 AW	39860 AAW	FLBLS	10//99-12//99
Mechanics, Installers, and Repairers	Punta Gorda MSA, FL	S	16.51 MW	17.56 AW	34340 AAW	FLBLS	10//99-12//99
Mechanics, Installers, and Repairers	Sarasota-Bradenton MSA, FL	S	20.61 MW	18.10 AW	42870 AAW	FLBLS	10//99-12//99
Mechanics, Installers, and Repairers	Tallahassee MSA, FL	S	18.30 MW	18.40 AW	38070 AAW	FLBLS	10//99-12//99
Mechanics, Installers, and Repairers	Tampa-St. Petersburg-Clearwater MSA, FL	S	22.56 MW	20.85 AW	46910 AAW	FLBLS	10//99-12//99
Mechanics, Installers, and Repairers	West Palm Beach-Boca Raton MSA, FL	S	20.81 MW	19.10 AW	43290 AAW	FLBLS	10//99-12//99
Mechanics, Installers, and Repairers	Georgia	S	20.19 MW	21.51 AW	44730 AAW	GABLS	10//99-12//99
Mechanics, Installers, and Repairers	Albany MSA, GA	S	20.77 MW	20.47 AW	43200 AAW	GABLS	10//99-12//99
Mechanics, Installers, and Repairers	Athens MSA, GA	S	23.76 MW	22.02 AW	49430 AAW	GABLS	10//99-12//99
Mechanics, Installers, and Repairers	Atlanta MSA, GA	S	22.78 MW	20.80 AW	47380 AAW	GABLS	10//99-12//99
Mechanics, Installers, and Repairers	Augusta-Aiken MSA, GA-SC	S	20.40 MW	18.64 AW	42420 AAW	GABLS	10//99-12//99
Mechanics, Installers, and Repairers	Columbus MSA, GA-AL	S	18.83 MW	17.45 AW	39170 AAW	GABLS	10//99-12//99
Mechanics, Installers, and Repairers	Savannah MSA, GA	S	22.19 MW	22.25 AW	46160 AAW	GABLS	10//99-12//99
Mechanics, Installers, and Repairers	Hawaii	S	24.11 MW	24.24 AW	50420 AAW	HIBLS	10//99-12//99
Mechanics, Installers, and Repairers	Honolulu MSA, HI	S	24.94 MW	25.12 AW	51870 AAW	HIBLS	10//99-12//99
Mechanics, Installers, and Repairers	Idaho	S	17.56 MW	19.62 AW	40800 AAW	IDBLS	10//99-12//99
Mechanics, Installers, and Repairers	Boise City MSA, ID	S	19.27 MW	16.75 AW	40070 AAW	IDBLS	10//99-12//99
Mechanics, Installers, and Repairers	Pocatello MSA, ID	S	18.61 MW	18.54 AW	38710 AAW	IDBLS	10//99-12//99
Mechanics, Installers, and Repairers	Illinois	S	21.54 MW	22.50 AW	46810 AAW	ILBLS	10//99-12//99
Mechanics, Installers, and Repairers	Bloomington-Normal MSA, IL	S	24.66 MW	23.54 AW	51280 AAW	ILBLS	10//99-12//99
Mechanics, Installers, and Repairers	Champaign-Urbana MSA, IL	S	20.55 MW	19.82 AW	42740 AAW	ILBLS	10//99-12//99
Mechanics, Installers, and Repairers	Chicago PMSA, IL	S	24.12 MW	23.00 AW	50170 AAW	ILBLS	10//99-12//99
Mechanics, Installers, and Repairers	Decatur MSA, IL	S	22.48 MW	23.67 AW	46750 AAW	ILBLS	10//99-12//99
Mechanics, Installers, and Repairers	Kankakee PMSA, IL	S	21.71 MW	21.46 AW	45170 AAW	ILBLS	10//99-12//99
Mechanics, Installers, and Repairers	Peoria-Pekin MSA, IL	S	20.99 MW	20.10 AW	43650 AAW	ILBLS	10//99-12//99
Mechanics, Installers, and Repairers	Rockford MSA, IL	S	24.27 MW	23.67 AW	50490 AAW	ILBLS	10//99-12//99
Mechanics, Installers, and Repairers	Springfield MSA, IL	S	18.65 MW	16.36 AW	38800 AAW	ILBLS	10//99-12//99
Mechanics, Installers, and Repairers	Indiana	S	19.31 MW	20.42 AW	42470 AAW	INBLS	10//99-12//99
Mechanics, Installers, and Repairers	Bloomington MSA, IN	S	21.39 MW	19.39 AW	44480 AAW	INBLS	10//99-12//99
Mechanics, Installers, and Repairers	Elkhart-Goshen MSA, IN	S	20.34 MW	20.62 AW	42300 AAW	INBLS	10//99-12//99
Mechanics, Installers, and Repairers	Evansville-Henderson MSA, IN-KY	S	21.07 MW	20.43 AW	43830 AAW	INBLS	10//99-12//99
Mechanics, Installers, and Repairers	Fort Wayne MSA, IN	S	20.35 MW	19.88 AW	42330 AAW	INBLS	10//99-12//99
Mechanics, Installers, and Repairers	Gary PMSA, IN	S	24.25 MW	22.38 AW	50450 AAW	INBLS	10//99-12//99
Mechanics, Installers, and Repairers	Indianapolis MSA, IN	S	19.97 MW	18.87 AW	41540 AAW	INBLS	10//99-12//99
Mechanics, Installers, and Repairers	Kokomo MSA, IN	S	24.21 MW	27.02 AW	50360 AAW	INBLS	10//99-12//99
Mechanics, Installers, and Repairers	Lafayette MSA, IN	S	19.32 MW	18.84 AW	40180 AAW	INBLS	10//99-12//99
Mechanics, Installers, and Repairers	Muncie MSA, IN	S	21.42 MW	16.93 AW	44560 AAW	INBLS	10//99-12//99
Mechanics, Installers, and Repairers	South Bend MSA, IN	S	20.03 MW	17.67 AW	41670 AAW	INBLS	10//99-12//99
Mechanics, Installers, and Repairers	Terre Haute MSA, IN	S	17.49 MW	16.41 AW	36380 AAW	INBLS	10//99-12//99
Mechanics, Installers, and Repairers	Iowa	S	16.76 MW	18.14 AW	37720 AAW	IABLS	10//99-12//99
Mechanics, Installers, and Repairers	Cedar Rapids MSA, IA	S	22.65 MW	22.76 AW	47100 AAW	IABLS	10//99-12//99
Mechanics, Installers, and Repairers	Davenport-Moline-Rock Island MSA, IA-IL	S	19.26 MW	18.00 AW	40060 AAW	IABLS	10//99-12//99
Mechanics, Installers, and Repairers	Des Moines MSA, IA	S	20.81 MW	20.29 AW	43290 AAW	IABLS	10//99-12//99
Mechanics, Installers, and Repairers	Dubuque MSA, IA	S	19.26 MW	19.38 AW	40070 AAW	IABLS	10//99-12//99
Mechanics, Installers, and Repairers	Iowa City MSA, IA	S	17.18 MW	16.78 AW	35740 AAW	IABLS	10//99-12//99
Mechanics, Installers, and Repairers	Sioux City MSA, IA-NE	S	19.26 MW	18.78 AW	40060 AAW	IABLS	10//99-12//99
Mechanics, Installers, and Repairers	Waterloo-Cedar Falls MSA, IA	S	19.07 MW	16.96 AW	39660 AAW	IABLS	10//99-12//99
Mechanics, Installers, and Repairers	Kansas	S	18.78 MW	19.80 AW	41190 AAW	KSBLS	10//99-12//99
Mechanics, Installers, and Repairers	Lawrence MSA, KS	S	20.80 MW	19.41 AW	43260 AAW	KSBLS	10//99-12//99
Mechanics, Installers, and Repairers	Topeka MSA, KS	S	19.80 MW	19.87 AW	41180 AAW	KSBLS	10//99-12//99

AAW	Average annual wage	AOH	Average offered, high	ASH	Average starting, high	H	Hourly	M	Monthly	S	Special: hourly and annual
AE	Average entry wage	AOL	Average offered, low	ASL	Average starting, low	HI	Highest wage paid	MTC	Median total compensation	TQ	Third quartile wage
AEX	Average experienced wage	APH	Average pay, high range	AW	Average wage paid	HR	High end range	MW	Median wage paid	W	Weekly
AO	Average offered	APL	Average pay, low range	FQ	First quartile wage	LR	Low end range	SQ	Second quartile wage	Y	Yearly

Occupation/Type/Industry	Location	Per	Low	Mid	High	Source	Date
First-Line Supervisor/Manager							
Mechanics, Installers, and Repairers	Wichita MSA, KS	S	20.68 MW	20.24 AW	43010 AAW	KSBLS	10//99-12//99
Mechanics, Installers, and Repairers	Kentucky	S	17.72 MW	19.22 AW	39970 AAW	KYBLS	10//99-12//99
Mechanics, Installers, and Repairers	Lexington MSA, KY	S	17.39 MW	15.98 AW	36180 AAW	KYBLS	10//99-12//99
Mechanics, Installers, and Repairers	Louisville MSA, KY-IN	S	20.16 MW	18.84 AW	41930 AAW	KYBLS	10//99-12//99
Mechanics, Installers, and Repairers	Owensboro MSA, KY	S	18.13 MW	20.64 AW	37710 AAW	KYBLS	10//99-12//99
Mechanics, Installers, and Repairers	Louisiana	S	18.58 MW	19.53 AW	40630 AAW	LABLS	10//99-12//99
Mechanics, Installers, and Repairers	Alexandria MSA, LA	S	17.59 MW	16.14 AW	36590 AAW	LABLS	10//99-12//99
Mechanics, Installers, and Repairers	Baton Rouge MSA, LA	S	19.93 MW	18.28 AW	41450 AAW	LABLS	10//99-12//99
Mechanics, Installers, and Repairers	Houma MSA, LA	S	17.77 MW	17.96 AW	36960 AAW	LABLS	10//99-12//99
Mechanics, Installers, and Repairers	Lafayette MSA, LA	S	21.57 MW	21.94 AW	44870 AAW	LABLS	10//99-12//99
Mechanics, Installers, and Repairers	Lake Charles MSA, LA	S	21.73 MW	23.46 AW	45190 AAW	LABLS	10//99-12//99
Mechanics, Installers, and Repairers	Monroe MSA, LA	S	21.89 MW	19.94 AW	45530 AAW	LABLS	10//99-12//99
Mechanics, Installers, and Repairers	New Orleans MSA, LA	S	19.04 MW	18.22 AW	39600 AAW	LABLS	10//99-12//99
Mechanics, Installers, and Repairers	Shreveport-Bossier City MSA, LA	S	18.70 MW	18.08 AW	38890 AAW	LABLS	10//99-12//99
Mechanics, Installers, and Repairers	Maine	S	18.91 MW	19.77 AW	41130 AAW	MEBLS	10//99-12//99
Mechanics, Installers, and Repairers	Bangor MSA, ME	S	16.98 MW	16.55 AW	35320 AAW	MEBLS	10//99-12//99
Mechanics, Installers, and Repairers	Lewiston-Auburn MSA, ME	S	19.58 MW	18.58 AW	40720 AAW	MEBLS	10//99-12//99
Mechanics, Installers, and Repairers	Portland MSA, ME	S	21.34 MW	19.66 AW	44390 AAW	MEBLS	10//99-12//99
Mechanics, Installers, and Repairers	Maryland	S	20.03 MW	22.25 AW	46290 AAW	MDBLS	10//99-12//99
Mechanics, Installers, and Repairers	Baltimore PMSA, MD	S	21.32 MW	20.49 AW	44350 AAW	MDBLS	10//99-12//99
Mechanics, Installers, and Repairers	Cumberland MSA, MD-WV	S	15.57 MW	14.76 AW	32380 AAW	MDBLS	10//99-12//99
Mechanics, Installers, and Repairers	Hagerstown PMSA, MD	S	31.90 MW	19.91 AW	66360 AAW	MDBLS	10//99-12//99
Mechanics, Installers, and Repairers	Massachusetts	S	21.54 MW	22.44 AW	46680 AAW	MABLS	10//99-12//99
Mechanics, Installers, and Repairers	Barnstable-Yarmouth MSA, MA	S	22.78 MW	22.63 AW	47370 AAW	MABLS	10//99-12//99
Mechanics, Installers, and Repairers	Boston PMSA, MA-NH	S	23.11 MW	22.03 AW	48070 AAW	MABLS	10//99-12//99
Mechanics, Installers, and Repairers	Brockton PMSA, MA	S	24.05 MW	23.97 AW	50030 AAW	MABLS	10//99-12//99
Mechanics, Installers, and Repairers	Fitchburg-Leominster PMSA, MA	S	22.27 MW	23.25 AW	46310 AAW	MABLS	10//99-12//99
Mechanics, Installers, and Repairers	Lawrence PMSA, MA-NH	S	23.82 MW	22.32 AW	49550 AAW	MABLS	10//99-12//99
Mechanics, Installers, and Repairers	Lowell PMSA, MA-NH	S	23.40 MW	23.83 AW	48660 AAW	MABLS	10//99-12//99
Mechanics, Installers, and Repairers	New Bedford PMSA, MA	S	21.69 MW	21.12 AW	45120 AAW	MABLS	10//99-12//99
Mechanics, Installers, and Repairers	Pittsfield MSA, MA	S	21.59 MW	22.55 AW	44900 AAW	MABLS	10//99-12//99
Mechanics, Installers, and Repairers	Springfield MSA, MA	S	21.88 MW	20.74 AW	45510 AAW	MABLS	10//99-12//99
Mechanics, Installers, and Repairers	Worcester PMSA, MA-CT	S	19.73 MW	19.35 AW	41040 AAW	MABLS	10//99-12//99
Mechanics, Installers, and Repairers	Michigan	S	24.5 MW	25.96 AW	54010 AAW	MIBLS	10//99-12//99
Mechanics, Installers, and Repairers	Ann Arbor PMSA, MI	S	23.41 MW	23.40 AW	48700 AAW	MIBLS	10//99-12//99
Mechanics, Installers, and Repairers	Benton Harbor MSA, MI	S	17.70 MW	16.34 AW	36820 AAW	MIBLS	10//99-12//99
Mechanics, Installers, and Repairers	Detroit PMSA, MI	S	26.78 MW	27.36 AW	55700 AAW	MIBLS	10//99-12//99
Mechanics, Installers, and Repairers	Flint PMSA, MI	S	20.10 MW	18.87 AW	41820 AAW	MIBLS	10//99-12//99
Mechanics, Installers, and Repairers	Grand Rapids-Muskegon-Holland MSA, MI	S	33.98 MW	25.68 AW	70670 AAW	MIBLS	10//99-12//99
Mechanics, Installers, and Repairers	Jackson MSA, MI	S	27.95 MW	22.42 AW	58140 AAW	MIBLS	10//99-12//99
Mechanics, Installers, and Repairers	Kalamazoo-Battle Creek MSA, MI	S	22.94 MW	22.81 AW	47710 AAW	MIBLS	10//99-12//99
Mechanics, Installers, and Repairers	Lansing-East Lansing MSA, MI	S	20.08 MW	20.49 AW	41760 AAW	MIBLS	10//99-12//99
Mechanics, Installers, and Repairers	Saginaw-Bay City-Midland MSA, MI	S	24.29 MW	21.83 AW	50510 AAW	MIBLS	10//99-12//99
Mechanics, Installers, and Repairers	Minnesota	S	20.08 MW	22.49 AW	46770 AAW	MNBLS	10//99-12//99
Mechanics, Installers, and Repairers	Duluth-Superior MSA, MN-WI	S	21.43 MW	21.38 AW	44580 AAW	MNBLS	10//99-12//99
Mechanics, Installers, and Repairers	Minneapolis-St. Paul MSA, MN-WI	S	21.00 MW	20.29 AW	43680 AAW	MNBLS	10//99-12//99
Mechanics, Installers, and Repairers	Rochester MSA, MN	S	23.03 MW	21.76 AW	47900 AAW	MNBLS	10//99-12//99
Mechanics, Installers, and Repairers	St. Cloud MSA, MN	S	20.44 MW	18.92 AW	42520 AAW	MNBLS	10//99-12//99
Mechanics, Installers, and Repairers	Mississippi	S	17.11 MW	17.92 AW	37270 AAW	MSBLS	10//99-12//99
Mechanics, Installers, and Repairers	Biloxi-Gulfport-Pascagoula MSA, MS	S	19.49 MW	19.45 AW	40540 AAW	MSBLS	10//99-12//99
Mechanics, Installers, and Repairers	Hattiesburg MSA, MS	S	16.32 MW	15.11 AW	33960 AAW	MSBLS	10//99-12//99
Mechanics, Installers, and Repairers	Jackson MSA, MS	S	17.80 MW	16.97 AW	37020 AAW	MSBLS	10//99-12//99
Mechanics, Installers, and Repairers	Missouri	S	18.3 MW	19.37 AW	40300 AAW	MOBLS	10//99-12//99
Mechanics, Installers, and Repairers	Columbia MSA, MO	S	17.55 MW	17.44 AW	36500 AAW	MOBLS	10//99-12//99
Mechanics, Installers, and Repairers	Joplin MSA, MO	S	19.33 MW	21.30 AW	40210 AAW	MOBLS	10//99-12//99
Mechanics, Installers, and Repairers	Kansas City MSA, MO-KS	S	21.25 MW	20.29 AW	44190 AAW	MOBLS	10//99-12//99
Mechanics, Installers, and Repairers	St. Joseph MSA, MO	S	19.64 MW	18.29 AW	40860 AAW	MOBLS	10//99-12//99
Mechanics, Installers, and Repairers	St. Louis MSA, MO-IL	S	20.78 MW	19.96 AW	43220 AAW	MOBLS	10//99-12//99
Mechanics, Installers, and Repairers	Springfield MSA, MO	S	18.33 MW	16.82 AW	38120 AAW	MOBLS	10//99-12//99
Mechanics, Installers, and Repairers	Montana	S	18.22 MW	19.22 AW	39970 AAW	MTBLS	10//99-12//99
Mechanics, Installers, and Repairers	Billings MSA, MT	S	19.06 MW	16.53 AW	39650 AAW	MTBLS	10//99-12//99
Mechanics, Installers, and Repairers	Great Falls MSA, MT	S	20.75 MW	21.20 AW	43160 AAW	MTBLS	10//99-12//99
Mechanics, Installers, and Repairers	Missoula MSA, MT	S	18.00 MW	17.64 AW	37450 AAW	MTBLS	10//99-12//99

AAW Average annual wage	**AOH** Average offered, high	**ASH** Average starting, high	**H** Hourly	**M** Monthly	**S** Special: hourly and annual
AE Average entry wage	**AOL** Average offered, low	**ASL** Average starting, low	**HI** Highest wage paid	**MTC** Median total compensation	**TQ** Third quartile wage
AEX Average experienced wage	**APH** Average pay, high range	**AW** Average wage paid	**HR** High end range	**MW** Median wage paid	**W** Weekly
AO Average offered	**APL** Average pay, low range	**FQ** First quartile wage	**LR** Low end range	**SQ** Second quartile wage	**Y** Yearly

Occupation/Type/Industry	Location	Per	Low	Mid	High	Source	Date
First-Line Supervisor/Manager							
Mechanics, Installers, and Repairers	Nebraska	S	16.42 MW	16.82 AW	34990 AAW	NEBLS	10//99-12//99
Mechanics, Installers, and Repairers	Lincoln MSA, NE	S	17.24 MW	17.37 AW	35850 AAW	NEBLS	10//99-12//99
Mechanics, Installers, and Repairers	Omaha MSA, NE-IA	S	18.95 MW	18.45 AW	39410 AAW	NEBLS	10//99-12//99
Mechanics, Installers, and Repairers	Nevada	S	20.88 MW	21.88 AW	45510 AAW	NVBLS	10//99-12//99
Mechanics, Installers, and Repairers	Las Vegas MSA, NV-AZ	S	20.99 MW	19.97 AW	43650 AAW	NVBLS	10//99-12//99
Mechanics, Installers, and Repairers	Reno MSA, NV	S	23.84 MW	22.74 AW	49600 AAW	NVBLS	10//99-12//99
Mechanics, Installers, and Repairers	New Hampshire	S	19.94 MW	20.17 AW	41950 AAW	NHBLS	10//99-12//99
Mechanics, Installers, and Repairers	Manchester PMSA, NH	S	21.19 MW	22.03 AW	44080 AAW	NHBLS	10//99-12//99
Mechanics, Installers, and Repairers	Nashua PMSA, NH	S	20.98 MW	19.01 AW	43630 AAW	NHBLS	10//99-12//99
Mechanics, Installers, and Repairers	Portsmouth-Rochester PMSA, NH-ME	S	18.94 MW	18.64 AW	39400 AAW	NHBLS	10//99-12//99
Mechanics, Installers, and Repairers	New Jersey	S	24.78 MW	25.39 AW	52800 AAW	NJBLS	10//99-12//99
Mechanics, Installers, and Repairers	Atlantic-Cape May PMSA, NJ	S	25.66 MW	24.28 AW	53380 AAW	NJBLS	10//99-12//99
Mechanics, Installers, and Repairers	Bergen-Passaic PMSA, NJ	S	25.95 MW	25.74 AW	53970 AAW	NJBLS	10//99-12//99
Mechanics, Installers, and Repairers	Jersey City PMSA, NJ	S	23.90 MW	23.62 AW	49710 AAW	NJBLS	10//99-12//99
Mechanics, Installers, and Repairers	Middlesex-Somerset-Hunterdon PMSA, NJ	S	26.60 MW	25.79 AW	55320 AAW	NJBLS	10//99-12//99
Mechanics, Installers, and Repairers	Monmouth-Ocean PMSA, NJ	S	27.10 MW	25.83 AW	56370 AAW	NJBLS	10//99-12//99
Mechanics, Installers, and Repairers	Newark PMSA, NJ	S	25.65 MW	24.93 AW	53340 AAW	NJBLS	10//99-12//99
Mechanics, Installers, and Repairers	Trenton PMSA, NJ	S	22.90 MW	23.00 AW	47630 AAW	NJBLS	10//99-12//99
Mechanics, Installers, and Repairers	Vineland-Millville-Bridgeton PMSA, NJ	S	20.83 MW	20.79 AW	43320 AAW	NJBLS	10//99-12//99
Mechanics, Installers, and Repairers	New Mexico	S	17.61 MW	18.03 AW	37500 AAW	NMBLS	10//99-12//99
Mechanics, Installers, and Repairers	Albuquerque MSA, NM	S	18.47 MW	17.78 AW	38420 AAW	NMBLS	10//99-12//99
Mechanics, Installers, and Repairers	Las Cruces MSA, NM	S	18.62 MW	18.90 AW	38740 AAW	NMBLS	10//99-12//99
Mechanics, Installers, and Repairers	Santa Fe MSA, NM	S	16.94 MW	15.76 AW	35230 AAW	NMBLS	10//99-12//99
Mechanics, Installers, and Repairers	New York	S	23.06 MW	24.99 AW	51980 AAW	NYBLS	10//99-12//99
Mechanics, Installers, and Repairers	Albany-Schenectady-Troy MSA, NY	S	21.70 MW	19.97 AW	45140 AAW	NYBLS	10//99-12//99
Mechanics, Installers, and Repairers	Binghamton MSA, NY	S	22.00 MW	20.89 AW	45770 AAW	NYBLS	10//99-12//99
Mechanics, Installers, and Repairers	Buffalo-Niagara Falls MSA, NY	S	21.23 MW	20.60 AW	44160 AAW	NYBLS	10//99-12//99
Mechanics, Installers, and Repairers	Dutchess County PMSA, NY	S	24.11 MW	23.57 AW	50150 AAW	NYBLS	10//99-12//99
Mechanics, Installers, and Repairers	Elmira MSA, NY	S	15.68 MW	13.34 AW	32620 AAW	NYBLS	10//99-12//99
Mechanics, Installers, and Repairers	Glens Falls MSA, NY	S	19.88 MW	19.00 AW	41350 AAW	NYBLS	10//99-12//99
Mechanics, Installers, and Repairers	Jamestown MSA, NY	S	18.73 MW	17.94 AW	38970 AAW	NYBLS	10//99-12//99
Mechanics, Installers, and Repairers	Nassau-Suffolk PMSA, NY	S	27.93 MW	26.50 AW	58100 AAW	NYBLS	10//99-12//99
Mechanics, Installers, and Repairers	New York PMSA, NY	S	28.83 MW	25.72 AW	59970 AAW	NYBLS	10//99-12//99
Mechanics, Installers, and Repairers	Newburgh PMSA, NY-PA	S	21.55 MW	22.11 AW	44820 AAW	NYBLS	10//99-12//99
Mechanics, Installers, and Repairers	Rochester MSA, NY	S	21.30 MW	20.38 AW	44310 AAW	NYBLS	10//99-12//99
Mechanics, Installers, and Repairers	Syracuse MSA, NY	S	23.65 MW	21.03 AW	49200 AAW	NYBLS	10//99-12//99
Mechanics, Installers, and Repairers	Utica-Rome MSA, NY	S	19.85 MW	16.18 AW	41290 AAW	NYBLS	10//99-12//99
Mechanics, Installers, and Repairers	North Carolina	S	19.46 MW	20.85 AW	43370 AAW	NCBLS	10//99-12//99
Mechanics, Installers, and Repairers	Asheville MSA, NC	S	19.66 MW	17.39 AW	40900 AAW	NCBLS	10//99-12//99
Mechanics, Installers, and Repairers	Charlotte-Gastonia-Rock Hill MSA, NC-SC	S	22.89 MW	20.47 AW	47600 AAW	NCBLS	10//99-12//99
Mechanics, Installers, and Repairers	Fayetteville MSA, NC	S	18.69 MW	18.60 AW	38870 AAW	NCBLS	10//99-12//99
Mechanics, Installers, and Repairers	Goldsboro MSA, NC	S	17.15 MW	17.72 AW	35670 AAW	NCBLS	10//99-12//99
Mechanics, Installers, and Repairers	Greensboro--Winston-Salem--High Point MSA, NC	S	19.88 MW	19.36 AW	41360 AAW	NCBLS	10//99-12//99
Mechanics, Installers, and Repairers	Hickory-Morganton-Lenoir MSA, NC	S	19.24 MW	17.83 AW	40030 AAW	NCBLS	10//99-12//99
Mechanics, Installers, and Repairers	Jacksonville MSA, NC	S	16.48 MW	15.41 AW	34280 AAW	NCBLS	10//99-12//99
Mechanics, Installers, and Repairers	Raleigh-Durham-Chapel Hill MSA, NC	S	24.24 MW	21.82 AW	50420 AAW	NCBLS	10//99-12//99
Mechanics, Installers, and Repairers	Rocky Mount MSA, NC	S	16.48 MW	15.69 AW	34280 AAW	NCBLS	10//99-12//99
Mechanics, Installers, and Repairers	Wilmington MSA, NC	S	22.36 MW	20.25 AW	46500 AAW	NCBLS	10//99-12//99
Mechanics, Installers, and Repairers	North Dakota	S	18.17 MW	18.13 AW	37720 AAW	NDBLS	10//99-12//99
Mechanics, Installers, and Repairers	Bismarck MSA, ND	S	15.25 MW	14.95 AW	31730 AAW	NDBLS	10//99-12//99
Mechanics, Installers, and Repairers	Fargo-Moorhead MSA, ND-MN	S	16.81 MW	17.68 AW	34960 AAW	NDBLS	10//99-12//99
Mechanics, Installers, and Repairers	Grand Forks MSA, ND-MN	S	18.12 MW	17.85 AW	37700 AAW	NDBLS	10//99-12//99
Mechanics, Installers, and Repairers	Ohio	S	19.36 MW	20.51 AW	42670 AAW	OHBLS	10//99-12//99
Mechanics, Installers, and Repairers	Akron PMSA, OH	S	19.45 MW	19.11 AW	40460 AAW	OHBLS	10//99-12//99
Mechanics, Installers, and Repairers	Canton-Massillon MSA, OH	S	19.59 MW	19.24 AW	40750 AAW	OHBLS	10//99-12//99
Mechanics, Installers, and Repairers	Cincinnati PMSA, OH-KY-IN	S	23.45 MW	20.60 AW	48770 AAW	OHBLS	10//99-12//99
Mechanics, Installers, and Repairers	Cleveland-Lorain-Elyria PMSA, OH	S	20.82 MW	19.65 AW	43310 AAW	OHBLS	10//99-12//99
Mechanics, Installers, and Repairers	Columbus MSA, OH	S	19.54 MW	18.29 AW	40640 AAW	OHBLS	10//99-12//99
Mechanics, Installers, and Repairers	Dayton-Springfield MSA, OH	S	22.80 MW	22.46 AW	47410 AAW	OHBLS	10//99-12//99

AAW	Average annual wage	AOH	Average offered, high	ASH	Average starting, high
AE	Average entry wage	AOL	Average offered, low	ASL	Average starting, low
AEX	Average experienced wage	APH	Average pay, high range	AW	Average wage paid
AO	Average offered	APL	Average pay, low range	FQ	First quartile wage

H	Hourly	M	Monthly
HI	Highest wage paid	MTC	Median total compensation
HR	High end range	MW	Median wage paid
LR	Low end range	SQ	Second quartile wage

S	Special: hourly and annual
TQ	Third quartile wage
W	Weekly
Y	Yearly

Occupation/Type/Industry	Location	Per	Low	Mid	High	Source	Date
First-Line Supervisor/Manager							
Mechanics, Installers, and Repairers	Hamilton-Middletown PMSA, OH	S	19.01 MW	19.28 AW	39550 AAW	OHBLS	10//99-12//99
Mechanics, Installers, and Repairers	Lima MSA, OH	S	16.33 MW	15.77 AW	33960 AAW	OHBLS	10//99-12//99
Mechanics, Installers, and Repairers	Mansfield MSA, OH	S	19.55 MW	18.94 AW	40670 AAW	OHBLS	10//99-12//99
Mechanics, Installers, and Repairers	Steubenville-Weirton MSA, OH-WV	S	21.57 MW	22.51 AW	44870 AAW	OHBLS	10//99-12//99
Mechanics, Installers, and Repairers	Toledo MSA, OH	S	21.60 MW	20.48 AW	44930 AAW	OHBLS	10//99-12//99
Mechanics, Installers, and Repairers	Youngstown-Warren MSA, OH	S	20.73 MW	18.64 AW	43120 AAW	OHBLS	10//99-12//99
Mechanics, Installers, and Repairers	Oklahoma	S	19.49 MW	20.35 AW	42330 AAW	OKBLS	10//99-12//99
Mechanics, Installers, and Repairers	Enid MSA, OK	S	16.92 MW	16.93 AW	35190 AAW	OKBLS	10//99-12//99
Mechanics, Installers, and Repairers	Lawton MSA, OK	S	15.50 MW	15.24 AW	32230 AAW	OKBLS	10//99-12//99
Mechanics, Installers, and Repairers	Oklahoma City MSA, OK	S	20.47 MW	20.44 AW	42590 AAW	OKBLS	10//99-12//99
Mechanics, Installers, and Repairers	Tulsa MSA, OK	S	22.75 MW	23.31 AW	47320 AAW	OKBLS	10//99-12//99
Mechanics, Installers, and Repairers	Oregon	S	23.46 MW	23.84 AW	49580 AAW	ORBLS	10//99-12//99
Mechanics, Installers, and Repairers	Corvallis MSA, OR	S	18.96 MW	16.19 AW	39440 AAW	ORBLS	10//99-12//99
Mechanics, Installers, and Repairers	Eugene-Springfield MSA, OR	S	26.01 MW	27.26 AW	54100 AAW	ORBLS	10//99-12//99
Mechanics, Installers, and Repairers	Medford-Ashland MSA, OR	S	24.53 MW	23.89 AW	51030 AAW	ORBLS	10//99-12//99
Mechanics, Installers, and Repairers	Portland-Vancouver PMSA, OR-WA	S	24.08 MW	23.94 AW	50090 AAW	ORBLS	10//99-12//99
Mechanics, Installers, and Repairers	Salem PMSA, OR	S	20.34 MW	19.90 AW	42310 AAW	ORBLS	10//99-12//99
Mechanics, Installers, and Repairers	Pennsylvania	S	20.91 MW	21.75 AW	45250 AAW	PABLS	10//99-12//99
Mechanics, Installers, and Repairers	Allentown-Bethlehem-Easton MSA, PA	S	23.11 MW	21.35 AW	48080 AAW	PABLS	10//99-12//99
Mechanics, Installers, and Repairers	Altoona MSA, PA	S	18.89 MW	16.93 AW	39300 AAW	PABLS	10//99-12//99
Mechanics, Installers, and Repairers	Erie MSA, PA	S	18.66 MW	17.96 AW	38800 AAW	PABLS	10//99-12//99
Mechanics, Installers, and Repairers	Harrisburg-Lebanon-Carlisle MSA, PA	S	20.39 MW	19.77 AW	42410 AAW	PABLS	10//99-12//99
Mechanics, Installers, and Repairers	Johnstown MSA, PA	S	16.98 MW	17.11 AW	35310 AAW	PABLS	10//99-12//99
Mechanics, Installers, and Repairers	Lancaster MSA, PA	S	22.25 MW	21.39 AW	46280 AAW	PABLS	10//99-12//99
Mechanics, Installers, and Repairers	Philadelphia PMSA, PA-NJ	S	23.42 MW	22.96 AW	48720 AAW	PABLS	10//99-12//99
Mechanics, Installers, and Repairers	Pittsburgh MSA, PA	S	21.74 MW	20.94 AW	45230 AAW	PABLS	10//99-12//99
Mechanics, Installers, and Repairers	Reading MSA, PA	S	20.84 MW	19.88 AW	43340 AAW	PABLS	10//99-12//99
Mechanics, Installers, and Repairers	Scranton--Wilkes-Barre--Hazleton MSA, PA	S	22.68 MW	21.29 AW	47170 AAW	PABLS	10//99-12//99
Mechanics, Installers, and Repairers	Sharon MSA, PA	S	17.61 MW	17.68 AW	36620 AAW	PABLS	10//99-12//99
Mechanics, Installers, and Repairers	State College MSA, PA	S	17.84 MW	15.72 AW	37120 AAW	PABLS	10//99-12//99
Mechanics, Installers, and Repairers	Williamsport MSA, PA	S	17.35 MW	15.72 AW	36090 AAW	PABLS	10//99-12//99
Mechanics, Installers, and Repairers	York MSA, PA	S	22.08 MW	21.29 AW	45940 AAW	PABLS	10//99-12//99
Mechanics, Installers, and Repairers	Rhode Island	S	20.22 MW	20.74 AW	43140 AAW	RIBLS	10//99-12//99
Mechanics, Installers, and Repairers	Providence-Fall River-Warwick MSA, RI-MA	S	20.76 MW	20.28 AW	43180 AAW	RIBLS	10//99-12//99
Mechanics, Installers, and Repairers	South Carolina	S	20.71 MW	21.53 AW	44780 AAW	SCBLS	10//99-12//99
Mechanics, Installers, and Repairers	Charleston-North Charleston MSA, SC	S	22.01 MW	21.54 AW	45790 AAW	SCBLS	10//99-12//99
Mechanics, Installers, and Repairers	Columbia MSA, SC	S	23.22 MW	21.17 AW	48300 AAW	SCBLS	10//99-12//99
Mechanics, Installers, and Repairers	Florence MSA, SC	S	17.87 MW	16.41 AW	37170 AAW	SCBLS	10//99-12//99
Mechanics, Installers, and Repairers	Greenville-Spartanburg-Anderson MSA, SC	S	20.96 MW	21.67 AW	43600 AAW	SCBLS	10//99-12//99
Mechanics, Installers, and Repairers	Myrtle Beach MSA, SC	S	20.29 MW	18.17 AW	42210 AAW	SCBLS	10//99-12//99
Mechanics, Installers, and Repairers	Sumter MSA, SC	S	18.70 MW	19.39 AW	38900 AAW	SCBLS	10//99-12//99
Mechanics, Installers, and Repairers	South Dakota	S	19.54 MW	19.77 AW	41120 AAW	SDBLS	10//99-12//99
Mechanics, Installers, and Repairers	Rapid City MSA, SD	S	20.40 MW	19.85 AW	42420 AAW	SDBLS	10//99-12//99
Mechanics, Installers, and Repairers	Sioux Falls MSA, SD	S	18.88 MW	18.60 AW	39260 AAW	SDBLS	10//99-12//99
Mechanics, Installers, and Repairers	Tennessee	S	17.56 MW	18.75 AW	39000 AAW	TNBLS	10//99-12//99
Mechanics, Installers, and Repairers	Chattanooga MSA, TN-GA	S	20.03 MW	19.93 AW	41660 AAW	TNBLS	10//99-12//99
Mechanics, Installers, and Repairers	Clarksville-Hopkinsville MSA, TN-KY	S	21.27 MW	22.33 AW	44240 AAW	TNBLS	10//99-12//99
Mechanics, Installers, and Repairers	Jackson MSA, TN	S	18.56 MW	17.51 AW	38600 AAW	TNBLS	10//99-12//99
Mechanics, Installers, and Repairers	Johnson City-Kingsport-Bristol MSA, TN-VA	S	19.30 MW	16.80 AW	40140 AAW	TNBLS	10//99-12//99
Mechanics, Installers, and Repairers	Knoxville MSA, TN	S	17.72 MW	17.03 AW	36850 AAW	TNBLS	10//99-12//99
Mechanics, Installers, and Repairers	Memphis MSA, TN-AR-MS	S	17.31 MW	16.26 AW	36010 AAW	MSBLS	10//99-12//99
Mechanics, Installers, and Repairers	Nashville MSA, TN	S	20.38 MW	19.33 AW	42390 AAW	TNBLS	10//99-12//99
Mechanics, Installers, and Repairers	Texas	S	18.68 MW	19.94 AW	41480 AAW	TXBLS	10//99-12//99
Mechanics, Installers, and Repairers	Abilene MSA, TX	S	22.09 MW	22.69 AW	45950 AAW	TXBLS	10//99-12//99
Mechanics, Installers, and Repairers	Amarillo MSA, TX	S	17.86 MW	15.02 AW	37140 AAW	TXBLS	10//99-12//99
Mechanics, Installers, and Repairers	Austin-San Marcos MSA, TX	S	21.47 MW	20.63 AW	44670 AAW	TXBLS	10//99-12//99
Mechanics, Installers, and Repairers	Beaumont-Port Arthur MSA, TX	S	23.02 MW	22.53 AW	47890 AAW	TXBLS	10//99-12//99
Mechanics, Installers, and Repairers	Brazoria PMSA, TX	S	17.81 MW	15.82 AW	37050 AAW	TXBLS	10//99-12//99

AAW	Average annual wage	AOH	Average offered, high	ASH	Average starting, high	H	Hourly	M	Monthly	S	Special: hourly and annual
AE	Average entry wage	AOL	Average offered, low	ASL	Average starting, low	HI	Highest wage paid	MTC	Median total compensation	TQ	Third quartile wage
AEX	Average experienced wage	APH	Average pay, high range	AW	Average wage paid	HR	High end range	MW	Median wage paid	W	Weekly
AO	Average offered	APL	Average pay, low range	FQ	First quartile wage	LR	Low end range	SQ	Second quartile wage	Y	Yearly

Occupation/Type/Industry	Location	Per	Low	Mid	High	Source	Date
First-Line Supervisor/Manager							
Mechanics, Installers, and Repairers	Brownsville-Harlingen-San Benito MSA, TX	S	16.55 MW	15.36 AW	34430 AAW	TXBLS	10//99-12//99
Mechanics, Installers, and Repairers	Bryan-College Station MSA, TX	S	16.06 MW	14.87 AW	33400 AAW	TXBLS	10//99-12//99
Mechanics, Installers, and Repairers	Corpus Christi MSA, TX	S	17.77 MW	16.72 AW	36970 AAW	TXBLS	10//99-12//99
Mechanics, Installers, and Repairers	Dallas PMSA, TX	S	21.55 MW	20.77 AW	44820 AAW	TXBLS	10//99-12//99
Mechanics, Installers, and Repairers	El Paso MSA, TX	S	15.40 MW	14.45 AW	32030 AAW	TXBLS	10//99-12//99
Mechanics, Installers, and Repairers	Fort Worth-Arlington PMSA, TX	S	19.31 MW	18.76 AW	40170 AAW	TXBLS	10//99-12//99
Mechanics, Installers, and Repairers	Galveston-Texas City PMSA, TX	S	20.17 MW	22.52 AW	41950 AAW	TXBLS	10//99-12//99
Mechanics, Installers, and Repairers	Houston PMSA, TX	S	20.33 MW	18.66 AW	42280 AAW	TXBLS	10//99-12//99
Mechanics, Installers, and Repairers	Killeen-Temple MSA, TX	S	16.69 MW	15.92 AW	34720 AAW	TXBLS	10//99-12//99
Mechanics, Installers, and Repairers	Laredo MSA, TX	S	16.36 MW	13.43 AW	34030 AAW	TXBLS	10//99-12//99
Mechanics, Installers, and Repairers	Longview-Marshall MSA, TX	S	17.07 MW	15.50 AW	35510 AAW	TXBLS	10//99-12//99
Mechanics, Installers, and Repairers	Lubbock MSA, TX	S	18.48 MW	16.84 AW	38450 AAW	TXBLS	
Mechanics, Installers, and Repairers	McAllen-Edinburg-Mission MSA, TX	S	16.65 MW	15.87 AW	34620 AAW	TXBLS	10//99-12//99
Mechanics, Installers, and Repairers	Odessa-Midland MSA, TX	S	18.93 MW	16.25 AW	39380 AAW	TXBLS	10//99-12//99
Mechanics, Installers, and Repairers	San Angelo MSA, TX	S	19.05 MW	16.28 AW	39610 AAW	TXBLS	10//99-12//99
Mechanics, Installers, and Repairers	San Antonio MSA, TX	S	19.13 MW	17.45 AW	39780 AAW	TXBLS	10//99-12//99
Mechanics, Installers, and Repairers	Sherman-Denison MSA, TX	S	18.67 MW	18.84 AW	38830 AAW	TXBLS	10//99-12//99
Mechanics, Installers, and Repairers	Texarkana MSA, TX-Texarkana, AR		18.30 MW	17.90 AW	38060 AAW	TXBLS	10//99-12//99
Mechanics, Installers, and Repairers	Tyler MSA, TX	S	19.07 MW	18.05 AW	39670 AAW	TXBLS	10//99-12//99
Mechanics, Installers, and Repairers	Victoria MSA, TX	S	18.70 MW	17.56 AW	38890 AAW	TXBLS	10//99-12//99
Mechanics, Installers, and Repairers	Waco MSA, TX	S	16.65 MW	14.91 AW	34630 AAW	TXBLS	10//99-12//99
Mechanics, Installers, and Repairers	Wichita Falls MSA, TX	S	17.00 MW	16.04 AW	35360 AAW	TXBLS	10//99-12//99
Mechanics, Installers, and Repairers	Utah	S	18.92 MW	19.35 AW	40260 AAW	UTBLS	10//99-12//99
Mechanics, Installers, and Repairers	Provo-Orem MSA, UT	S	17.17 MW	17.43 AW	35700 AAW	UTBLS	10//99-12//99
Mechanics, Installers, and Repairers	Salt Lake City-Ogden MSA, UT	S	20.71 MW	20.27 AW	43080 AAW	UTBLS	10//99-12//99
Mechanics, Installers, and Repairers	Vermont	S	19.69 MW	20.32 AW	42260 AAW	VTBLS	10//99-12//99
Mechanics, Installers, and Repairers	Burlington MSA, VT	S	20.12 MW	19.75 AW	41860 AAW	VTBLS	10//99-12//99
Mechanics, Installers, and Repairers	Virginia	S	20.2 MW	21.13 AW	43940 AAW	VABLS	10//99-12//99
Mechanics, Installers, and Repairers	Charlottesville MSA, VA	S	20.84 MW	18.67 AW	43340 AAW	VABLS	10//99-12//99
Mechanics, Installers, and Repairers	Danville MSA, VA	S	15.66 MW	14.69 AW	32570 AAW	VABLS	10//99-12//99
Mechanics, Installers, and Repairers	Lynchburg MSA, VA	S	21.71 MW	20.97 AW	45170 AAW	VABLS	10//99-12//99
Mechanics, Installers, and Repairers	Norfolk-Virginia Beach-Newport News MSA, VA-NC	S	20.87 MW	20.01 AW	43400 AAW	VABLS	10//99-12//99
Mechanics, Installers, and Repairers	Richmond-Petersburg MSA, VA	S	22.09 MW	21.36 AW	45940 AAW	VABLS	10//99-12//99
Mechanics, Installers, and Repairers	Roanoke MSA, VA	S	21.63 MW	21.07 AW	45000 AAW	VABLS	10//99-12//99
Mechanics, Installers, and Repairers	Washington	S	22.62 MW	23.80 AW	49500 AAW	WABLS	10//99-12//99
Mechanics, Installers, and Repairers	Bellingham MSA, WA	S	25.39 MW	22.32 AW	52800 AAW	WABLS	10//99-12//99
Mechanics, Installers, and Repairers	Bremerton PMSA, WA	S	25.90 MW	25.08 AW	53880 AAW	WABLS	10//99-12//99
Mechanics, Installers, and Repairers	Olympia PMSA, WA	S	26.39 MW	24.09 AW	54880 AAW	WABLS	10//99-12//99
Mechanics, Installers, and Repairers	Richland-Kennewick-Pasco MSA, WA	S	24.68 MW	24.97 AW	51340 AAW	WABLS	10//99-12//99
Mechanics, Installers, and Repairers	Seattle-Bellevue-Everett PMSA, WA	S	24.07 MW	22.98 AW	50070 AAW	WABLS	10//99-12//99
Mechanics, Installers, and Repairers	Spokane MSA, WA	S	23.67 MW	20.77 AW	49230 AAW	WABLS	10//99-12//99
Mechanics, Installers, and Repairers	Tacoma PMSA, WA	S	24.70 MW	22.83 AW	51390 AAW	WABLS	10//99-12//99
Mechanics, Installers, and Repairers	Yakima MSA, WA	S	17.55 MW	16.08 AW	36510 AAW	WABLS	10//99-12//99
Mechanics, Installers, and Repairers	West Virginia	S	16.9 MW	18.77 AW	39040 AAW	WVBLS	10//99-12//99
Mechanics, Installers, and Repairers	Charleston MSA, WV	S	20.55 MW	20.64 AW	42730 AAW	WVBLS	10//99-12//99
Mechanics, Installers, and Repairers	Huntington-Ashland MSA, WV-KY-OH	S	18.75 MW	16.71 AW	39000 AAW	WVBLS	10//99-12//99
Mechanics, Installers, and Repairers	Parkersburg-Marietta MSA, WV-OH	S	18.15 MW	16.10 AW	37740 AAW	WVBLS	10//99-12//99
Mechanics, Installers, and Repairers	Wheeling MSA, WV-OH	S	19.85 MW	18.75 AW	41280 AAW	WVBLS	10//99-12//99
Mechanics, Installers, and Repairers	Wisconsin	S	22.91 MW	23.73 AW	49350 AAW	WIBLS	10//99-12//99
Mechanics, Installers, and Repairers	Appleton-Oshkosh-Neenah MSA, WI	S	25.21 MW	27.48 AW	52430 AAW	WIBLS	10//99-12//99
Mechanics, Installers, and Repairers	Eau Claire MSA, WI	S	21.13 MW	20.49 AW	43940 AAW	WIBLS	10//99-12//99
Mechanics, Installers, and Repairers	Green Bay MSA, WI	S	25.53 MW	25.93 AW	53090 AAW	WIBLS	10//99-12//99
Mechanics, Installers, and Repairers	Janesville-Beloit MSA, WI	S	20.30 MW	18.58 AW	42230 AAW	WIBLS	10//99-12//99
Mechanics, Installers, and Repairers	Kenosha PMSA, WI	S	15.89 MW	15.29 AW	33040 AAW	WIBLS	10//99-12//99
Mechanics, Installers, and Repairers	La Crosse MSA, WI-MN	S	20.56 MW	18.68 AW	42770 AAW	WIBLS	10//99-12//99
Mechanics, Installers, and Repairers	Madison MSA, WI	S	22.72 MW	23.05 AW	47250 AAW	WIBLS	10//99-12//99

AAW	Average annual wage	AOH	Average offered, high	ASH	Average starting, high	H	Hourly	M	Monthly	S	Special: hourly and annual
AE	Average entry wage	AOL	Average offered, low	ASL	Average starting, low	HI	Highest wage paid	MTC	Median total compensation	TQ	Third quartile wage
AEX	Average experienced wage	APH	Average pay, high range	AW	Average wage paid	HR	High end range	MW	Median wage paid	W	Weekly
AO	Average offered	APL	Average pay, low range	FQ	First quartile wage	LR	Low end range	SQ	Second quartile wage	Y	Yearly

Occupation/Type/Industry	Location	Per	Low	Mid	High	Source	Date
First-Line Supervisor/Manager							
Mechanics, Installers, and Repairers	Milwaukee-Waukesha PMSA, WI	S	26.45 MW	25.90 AW	55010 AAW	WIBLS	10//99-12//99
Mechanics, Installers, and Repairers	Racine PMSA, WI	S	24.43 MW	24.77 AW	50820 AAW	WIBLS	10//99-12//99
Mechanics, Installers, and Repairers	Sheboygan MSA, WI	S	24.57 MW	23.92 AW	51110 AAW	WIBLS	10//99-12//99
Mechanics, Installers, and Repairers	Wausau MSA, WI	S	21.03 MW	19.53 AW	43750 AAW	WIBLS	10//99-12//99
Mechanics, Installers, and Repairers	Wyoming	S	20.72 MW	21.14 AW	43970 AAW	WYBLS	10//99-12//99
Mechanics, Installers, and Repairers	Casper MSA, WY	S	18.17 MW	17.79 AW	37780 AAW	WYBLS	10//99-12//99
Mechanics, Installers, and Repairers	Cheyenne MSA, WY	S	19.20 MW	19.21 AW	39940 AAW	WYBLS	10//99-12//99
Mechanics, Installers, and Repairers	Puerto Rico	S	15.62 MW	16.00 AW	33290 AAW	PRBLS	10//99-12//99
Mechanics, Installers, and Repairers	Aguadilla MSA, PR	S	13.06 MW	13.65 AW	27170 AAW	PRBLS	10//99-12//99
Mechanics, Installers, and Repairers	Arecibo PMSA, PR	S	16.70 MW	16.49 AW	34740 AAW	PRBLS	10//99-12//99
Mechanics, Installers, and Repairers	Caguas PMSA, PR	S	15.05 MW	13.74 AW	31300 AAW	PRBLS	10//99-12//99
Mechanics, Installers, and Repairers	Mayaguez MSA, PR	S	13.28 MW	12.25 AW	27630 AAW	PRBLS	10//99-12//99
Mechanics, Installers, and Repairers	Ponce MSA, PR	S	13.85 MW	12.35 AW	28800 AAW	PRBLS	10//99-12//99
Mechanics, Installers, and Repairers	San Juan-Bayamon PMSA, PR	S	16.53 MW	16.24 AW	34380 AAW	PRBLS	10//99-12//99
Mechanics, Installers, and Repairers	Virgin Islands	S	15.72 MW	16.44 AW	34190 AAW	VIBLS	10//99-12//99
Mechanics, Installers, and Repairers	Guam	S	18.77 MW	18.51 AW	38490 AAW	GUBLS	10//99-12//99
Non-Retail Sales Workers	Alabama	S	20.88 MW	21.82 AW	45390 AAW	ALBLS	10//99-12//99
Non-Retail Sales Workers	Birmingham MSA, AL	S	22.26 MW	23.78 AW	46310 AAW	ALBLS	10//99-12//99
Non-Retail Sales Workers	Dothan MSA, AL	S	18.81 MW	17.94 AW	39120 AAW	ALBLS	10//99-12//99
Non-Retail Sales Workers	Huntsville MSA, AL	S	22.30 MW	13.83 AW	46380 AAW	ALBLS	10//99-12//99
Non-Retail Sales Workers	Mobile MSA, AL	S	18.52 MW	15.78 AW	38520 AAW	ALBLS	10//99-12//99
Non-Retail Sales Workers	Montgomery MSA, AL	S	28.03 MW	29.80 AW	58300 AAW	ALBLS	10//99-12//99
Non-Retail Sales Workers	Tuscaloosa MSA, AL	S	23.42 MW	23.79 AW	48700 AAW	ALBLS	10//99-12//99
Non-Retail Sales Workers	Alaska	S	17.79 MW	20.70 AW	43060 AAW	AKBLS	10//99-12//99
Non-Retail Sales Workers	Anchorage MSA, AK	S	24.15 MW	21.11 AW	50230 AAW	AKBLS	10//99-12//99
Non-Retail Sales Workers	Arizona	S	23.7 MW	24.32 AW	50580 AAW	AZBLS	10//99-12//99
Non-Retail Sales Workers	Flagstaff MSA, AZ-UT	S	16.83 MW	13.39 AW	35000 AAW	AZBLS	10//99-12//99
Non-Retail Sales Workers	Phoenix-Mesa MSA, AZ	S	24.90 MW	24.15 AW	51800 AAW	AZBLS	10//99-12//99
Non-Retail Sales Workers	Tucson MSA, AZ	S	16.22 MW	13.67 AW	33730 AAW	AZBLS	10//99-12//99
Non-Retail Sales Workers	Arkansas	S	13.62 MW	15.95 AW	33190 AAW	ARBLS	10//99-12//99
Non-Retail Sales Workers	Fort Smith MSA, AR-OK	S	19.26 MW	15.99 AW	40060 AAW	ARBLS	10//99-12//99
Non-Retail Sales Workers	Jonesboro MSA, AR	S	20.96 MW	20.95 AW	43600 AAW	ARBLS	10//99-12//99
Non-Retail Sales Workers	Little Rock-North Little Rock MSA, AR	S	17.68 MW	16.64 AW	36770 AAW	ARBLS	10//99-12//99
Non-Retail Sales Workers	California	S	26.21 MW	28.20 AW	58660 AAW	CABLS	10//99-12//99
Non-Retail Sales Workers	Bakersfield MSA, CA	S	25.80 MW	24.34 AW	53650 AAW	CABLS	10//99-12//99
Non-Retail Sales Workers	Chico-Paradise MSA, CA	S	23.82 MW	25.06 AW	49550 AAW	CABLS	10//99-12//99
Non-Retail Sales Workers	Fresno MSA, CA	S	27.13 MW	26.63 AW	56420 AAW	CABLS	10//99-12//99
Non-Retail Sales Workers	Los Angeles-Long Beach PMSA, CA	S	28.26 MW	26.29 AW	58790 AAW	CABLS	10//99-12//99
Non-Retail Sales Workers	Merced MSA, CA	S	17.90 MW	15.02 AW	37240 AAW	CABLS	10//99-12//99
Non-Retail Sales Workers	Modesto MSA, CA	S	22.77 MW	19.71 AW	47360 AAW	CABLS	10//99-12//99
Non-Retail Sales Workers	Oakland PMSA, CA	S	33.29 MW	31.60 AW	69240 AAW	CABLS	10//99-12//99
Non-Retail Sales Workers	Orange County PMSA, CA	S	29.02 MW	28.23 AW	60360 AAW	CABLS	10//99-12//99
Non-Retail Sales Workers	Redding MSA, CA	S	22.37 MW	20.18 AW	46530 AAW	CABLS	10//99-12//99
Non-Retail Sales Workers	Riverside-San Bernardino PMSA, CA	S	32.33 MW	29.48 AW	67240 AAW	CABLS	10//99-12//99
Non-Retail Sales Workers	Sacramento PMSA, CA	S	23.56 MW	22.48 AW	49000 AAW	CABLS	10//99-12//99
Non-Retail Sales Workers	Salinas MSA, CA	S	28.31 MW	27.92 AW	58890 AAW	CABLS	10//99-12//99
Non-Retail Sales Workers	San Diego MSA, CA	S	23.42 MW	19.13 AW	48720 AAW	CABLS	10//99-12//99
Non-Retail Sales Workers	San Francisco PMSA, CA	S	28.73 MW	26.38 AW	59760 AAW	CABLS	10//99-12//99
Non-Retail Sales Workers	San Jose PMSA, CA	S	32.43 MW	32.79 AW	67440 AAW	CABLS	10//99-12//99
Non-Retail Sales Workers	San Luis Obispo-Atascadero-Paso Robles MSA, CA	S	24.11 MW	25.41 AW	50150 AAW	CABLS	10//99-12//99
Non-Retail Sales Workers	Santa Barbara-Santa Maria-Lompoc MSA, CA	S	35.83 MW	28.20 AW	74520 AAW	CABLS	10//99-12//99
Non-Retail Sales Workers	Santa Cruz-Watsonville PMSA, CA	S	26.33 MW	24.27 AW	54770 AAW	CABLS	10//99-12//99
Non-Retail Sales Workers	Santa Rosa PMSA, CA	S	25.26 MW	24.37 AW	52530 AAW	CABLS	10//99-12//99
Non-Retail Sales Workers	Stockton-Lodi MSA, CA	S	26.16 MW	23.65 AW	54420 AAW	CABLS	10//99-12//99
Non-Retail Sales Workers	Vallejo-Fairfield-Napa PMSA, CA	S	26.37 MW	26.07 AW	54840 AAW	CABLS	10//99-12//99
Non-Retail Sales Workers	Ventura PMSA, CA	S	29.95 MW	28.31 AW	62290 AAW	CABLS	10//99-12//99
Non-Retail Sales Workers	Visalia-Tulare-Porterville MSA, CA	S	20.42 MW	18.30 AW	42480 AAW	CABLS	10//99-12//99
Non-Retail Sales Workers	Yolo PMSA, CA	S	26.11 MW	23.42 AW	54320 AAW	CABLS	10//99-12//99
Non-Retail Sales Workers	Colorado	S	21.44 MW	23.92 AW	49760 AAW	COBLS	10//99-12//99
Non-Retail Sales Workers	Boulder-Longmont PMSA, CO	S	26.69 MW	21.49 AW	55520 AAW	COBLS	10//99-12//99
Non-Retail Sales Workers	Colorado Springs MSA, CO	S	18.30 MW	16.29 AW	38070 AAW	COBLS	10//99-12//99
Non-Retail Sales Workers	Denver PMSA, CO	S	25.47 MW	23.56 AW	52980 AAW	COBLS	10//99-12//99

AAW Average annual wage	**AOH** Average offered, high	**ASH** Average starting, high	**H** Hourly	**M** Monthly	**S** Special: hourly and annual
AE Average entry wage	**AOL** Average offered, low	**ASL** Average starting, low	**HI** Highest wage paid	**MTC** Median total compensation	**TQ** Third quartile wage
AEX Average experienced wage	**APH** Average pay, high range	**AW** Average wage paid	**HR** High end range	**MW** Median wage paid	**W** Weekly
AO Average offered	**APL** Average pay, low range	**FQ** First quartile wage	**LR** Low end range	**SQ** Second quartile wage	**Y** Yearly

Occupation/Type/Industry	Location	Per	Low	Mid	High	Source	Date
First-Line Supervisor/Manager							
Non-Retail Sales Workers	Fort Collins-Loveland MSA, CO	S	23.41 MW	20.31 AW	48690 AAW	COBLS	10//99-12//99
Non-Retail Sales Workers	Grand Junction MSA, CO	S	20.83 MW	18.29 AW	43330 AAW	COBLS	10//99-12//99
Non-Retail Sales Workers	Pueblo MSA, CO	S	16.25 MW	12.83 AW	33800 AAW	COBLS	10//99-12//99
Non-Retail Sales Workers	Connecticut	S	25.68 MW	27.83 AW	57890 AAW	CTBLS	10//99-12//99
Non-Retail Sales Workers	Bridgeport PMSA, CT	S	28.12 MW	25.35 AW	58490 AAW	CTBLS	10//99-12//99
Non-Retail Sales Workers	Danbury PMSA, CT	S	22.05 MW	18.45 AW	45870 AAW	CTBLS	10//99-12//99
Non-Retail Sales Workers	Hartford MSA, CT	S	29.38 MW	27.41 AW	61100 AAW	CTBLS	10//99-12//99
Non-Retail Sales Workers	New Haven-Meriden PMSA, CT	S	28.93 MW	25.06 AW	60180 AAW	CTBLS	10//99-12//99
Non-Retail Sales Workers	New London-Norwich MSA, CT-RI	S	22.81 MW	20.64 AW	47450 AAW	CTBLS	10//99-12//99
Non-Retail Sales Workers	Stamford-Norwalk PMSA, CT	S	31.85 MW	31.47 AW	66250 AAW	CTBLS	10//99-12//99
Non-Retail Sales Workers	Waterbury PMSA, CT	S	24.90 MW	24.24 AW	51790 AAW	CTBLS	10//99-12//99
Non-Retail Sales Workers	Delaware	S	21.33 MW	22.56 AW	46930 AAW	DEBLS	10//99-12//99
Non-Retail Sales Workers	Dover MSA, DE	S	24.90 MW	19.71 AW	51790 AAW	DEBLS	10//99-12//99
Non-Retail Sales Workers	Wilmington-Newark PMSA, DE-MD	S	21.49 MW	20.71 AW	44700 AAW	DEBLS	10//99-12//99
Non-Retail Sales Workers	District of Columbia	S	16.37 MW	17.62 AW	36640 AAW	DCBLS	10//99-12//99
Non-Retail Sales Workers	Washington PMSA, DC-MD-VA-WV	S	23.52 MW	19.01 AW	48930 AAW	DCBLS	10//99-12//99
Non-Retail Sales Workers	Florida	S	18.02 MW	21.30 AW	44300 AAW	FLBLS	10//99-12//99
Non-Retail Sales Workers	Daytona Beach MSA, FL	S	17.82 MW	14.27 AW	37080 AAW	FLBLS	10//99-12//99
Non-Retail Sales Workers	Fort Lauderdale PMSA, FL	S	23.46 MW	18.85 AW	48800 AAW	FLBLS	10//99-12//99
Non-Retail Sales Workers	Fort Myers-Cape Coral MSA, FL	S	18.41 MW	16.02 AW	38280 AAW	FLBLS	10//99-12//99
Non-Retail Sales Workers	Fort Pierce-Port St. Lucie MSA, FL	S	20.27 MW	20.10 AW	42170 AAW	FLBLS	10//99-12//99
Non-Retail Sales Workers	Fort Walton Beach MSA, FL	S	13.93 MW	10.89 AW	28980 AAW	FLBLS	10//99-12//99
Non-Retail Sales Workers	Gainesville MSA, FL	S	17.11 MW	15.04 AW	35600 AAW	FLBLS	10//99-12//99
Non-Retail Sales Workers	Jacksonville MSA, FL	S	22.49 MW	19.01 AW	46780 AAW	FLBLS	10//99-12//99
Non-Retail Sales Workers	Lakeland-Winter Haven MSA, FL	S	19.31 MW	16.01 AW	40160 AAW	FLBLS	10//99-12//99
Non-Retail Sales Workers	Melbourne-Titusville-Palm Bay MSA, FL	S	21.88 MW	16.76 AW	45500 AAW	FLBLS	10//99-12//99
Non-Retail Sales Workers	Miami PMSA, FL	S	21.16 MW	19.85 AW	44020 AAW	FLBLS	10//99-12//99
Non-Retail Sales Workers	Naples MSA, FL	S	25.25 MW	17.43 AW	52510 AAW	FLBLS	10//99-12//99
Non-Retail Sales Workers	Ocala MSA, FL	S	21.31 MW	18.82 AW	44320 AAW	FLBLS	10//99-12//99
Non-Retail Sales Workers	Orlando MSA, FL	S	23.52 MW	18.43 AW	48930 AAW	FLBLS	10//99-12//99
Non-Retail Sales Workers	Panama City MSA, FL	S	18.11 MW	16.07 AW	37670 AAW	FLBLS	10//99-12//99
Non-Retail Sales Workers	Pensacola MSA, FL	S	14.45 MW	9.09 AW	30050 AAW	FLBLS	10//99-12//99
Non-Retail Sales Workers	Punta Gorda MSA, FL	S	13.74 MW	14.39 AW	28580 AAW	FLBLS	10//99-12//99
Non-Retail Sales Workers	Sarasota-Bradenton MSA, FL	S	18.04 MW	15.93 AW	37530 AAW	FLBLS	10//99-12//99
Non-Retail Sales Workers	Tallahassee MSA, FL	S	18.96 MW	15.17 AW	39450 AAW	FLBLS	10//99-12//99
Non-Retail Sales Workers	Tampa-St. Petersburg-Clearwater MSA, FL	S	21.82 MW	18.99 AW	45380 AAW	FLBLS	10//99-12//99
Non-Retail Sales Workers	West Palm Beach-Boca Raton MSA, FL	S	21.71 MW	18.15 AW	45150 AAW	FLBLS	10//99-12//99
Non-Retail Sales Workers	Georgia	S	14.19 MW	17.55 AW	36510 AAW	GABLS	10//99-12//99
Non-Retail Sales Workers	Albany MSA, GA	S	18.84 MW	16.30 AW	39190 AAW	GABLS	10//99-12//99
Non-Retail Sales Workers	Atlanta MSA, GA	S	16.96 MW	13.58 AW	35280 AAW	GABLS	10//99-12//99
Non-Retail Sales Workers	Augusta-Aiken MSA, GA-SC	S	14.14 MW	12.81 AW	29420 AAW	GABLS	10//99-12//99
Non-Retail Sales Workers	Columbus MSA, GA-AL	S	26.39 MW	21.31 AW	54890 AAW	GABLS	10//99-12//99
Non-Retail Sales Workers	Macon MSA, GA	S	16.81 MW	16.72 AW	34970 AAW	GABLS	10//99-12//99
Non-Retail Sales Workers	Savannah MSA, GA	S	21.68 MW	14.72 AW	45100 AAW	GABLS	10//99-12//99
Non-Retail Sales Workers	Hawaii	S	16.95 MW	19.25 AW	40030 AAW	HIBLS	10//99-12//99
Non-Retail Sales Workers	Honolulu MSA, HI	S	20.93 MW	17.89 AW	43530 AAW	HIBLS	10//99-12//99
Non-Retail Sales Workers	Idaho	S	20.08 MW	20.32 AW	42260 AAW	IDBLS	10//99-12//99
Non-Retail Sales Workers	Boise City MSA, ID	S	24.32 MW	24.41 AW	50580 AAW	IDBLS	10//99-12//99
Non-Retail Sales Workers	Illinois	S	20.33 MW	23.13 AW	48100 AAW	ILBLS	10//99-12//99
Non-Retail Sales Workers	Bloomington-Normal MSA, IL	S	27.97 MW	28.02 AW	58180 AAW	ILBLS	10//99-12//99
Non-Retail Sales Workers	Champaign-Urbana MSA, IL	S	22.72 MW	19.24 AW	47250 AAW	ILBLS	10//99-12//99
Non-Retail Sales Workers	Chicago PMSA, IL	S	23.63 MW	21.31 AW	49150 AAW	ILBLS	10//99-12//99
Non-Retail Sales Workers	Peoria-Pekin MSA, IL	S	22.20 MW	19.12 AW	46170 AAW	ILBLS	10//99-12//99
Non-Retail Sales Workers	Rockford MSA, IL	S	19.58 MW	16.30 AW	40720 AAW	ILBLS	10//99-12//99
Non-Retail Sales Workers	Springfield MSA, IL	S	14.89 MW	10.53 AW	30960 AAW	ILBLS	10//99-12//99
Non-Retail Sales Workers	Indiana	S	21.62 MW	27.17 AW	56510 AAW	INBLS	10//99-12//99
Non-Retail Sales Workers	Bloomington MSA, IN	S	22.48 MW	19.07 AW	46770 AAW	INBLS	10//99-12//99
Non-Retail Sales Workers	Elkhart-Goshen MSA, IN	S	20.96 MW	18.88 AW	43610 AAW	INBLS	10//99-12//99
Non-Retail Sales Workers	Evansville-Henderson MSA, IN-KY	S	21.11 MW	18.78 AW	43910 AAW	INBLS	10//99-12//99

AAW	Average annual wage	AOH	Average offered, high	ASH	Average starting, high	H	Hourly
AE	Average entry wage	AOL	Average offered, low	ASL	Average starting, low	HI	Highest wage paid
AEX	Average experienced wage	APH	Average pay, high range	AW	Average wage paid	HR	High end range
AO	Average offered	APL	Average pay, low range	FQ	First quartile wage	LR	Low end range

M	Monthly	S	Special: hourly and annual
MTC	Median total compensation	TQ	Third quartile wage
MW	Median wage paid	W	Weekly
SQ	Second quartile wage	Y	Yearly

Occupation/Type/Industry	Location	Per	Low	Mid	High	Source	Date
First-Line Supervisor/Manager							
Non-Retail Sales Workers	Fort Wayne MSA, IN	S	27.26 MW	23.87 AW	56690 AAW	INBLS	10//99-12//99
Non-Retail Sales Workers	Gary PMSA, IN	S	18.70 MW	17.30 AW	38890 AAW	INBLS	10//99-12//99
Non-Retail Sales Workers	Indianapolis MSA, IN	S	29.87 MW	24.44 AW	62130 AAW	INBLS	10//99-12//99
Non-Retail Sales Workers	Kokomo MSA, IN	S	40.65 MW	38.36 AW	84560 AAW	INBLS	10//99-12//99
Non-Retail Sales Workers	Lafayette MSA, IN	S	26.28 MW	19.71 AW	54660 AAW	INBLS	10//99-12//99
Non-Retail Sales Workers	Muncie MSA, IN	S	25.99 MW	12.05 AW	54050 AAW	INBLS	10//99-12//99
Non-Retail Sales Workers	South Bend MSA, IN	S	20.02 MW	18.45 AW	41650 AAW	INBLS	10//99-12//99
Non-Retail Sales Workers	Terre Haute MSA, IN	S	17.91 MW	17.12 AW	37250 AAW	INBLS	10//99-12//99
Non-Retail Sales Workers	Iowa	S	16.29 MW	19.08 AW	39700 AAW	IABLS	10//99-12//99
Non-Retail Sales Workers	Cedar Rapids MSA, IA	S	25.68 MW	22.69 AW	53410 AAW	IABLS	10//99-12//99
Non-Retail Sales Workers	Davenport-Moline-Rock Island MSA, IA-IL	S	16.36 MW	15.87 AW	34040 AAW	IABLS	10//99-12//99
Non-Retail Sales Workers	Des Moines MSA, IA	S	21.57 MW	16.39 AW	44860 AAW	IABLS	10//99-12//99
Non-Retail Sales Workers	Dubuque MSA, IA	S	18.86 MW	18.33 AW	39230 AAW	IABLS	10//99-12//99
Non-Retail Sales Workers	Waterloo-Cedar Falls MSA, IA	S	15.23 MW	13.20 AW	31690 AAW	IABLS	10//99-12//99
Non-Retail Sales Workers	Kansas	S	19.39 MW	21.25 AW	44190 AAW	KSBLS	10//99-12//99
Non-Retail Sales Workers	Lawrence MSA, KS	S	20.50 MW	19.77 AW	42630 AAW	KSBLS	10//99-12//99
Non-Retail Sales Workers	Topeka MSA, KS	S	14.45 MW	10.37 AW	30060 AAW	KSBLS	10//99-12//99
Non-Retail Sales Workers	Wichita MSA, KS	S	22.22 MW	20.30 AW	46220 AAW	KSBLS	10//99-12//99
Non-Retail Sales Workers	Kentucky	S	16.83 MW	21.35 AW	44410 AAW	KYBLS	10//99-12//99
Non-Retail Sales Workers	Lexington MSA, KY	S	26.51 MW	19.83 AW	55130 AAW	KYBLS	10//99-12//99
Non-Retail Sales Workers	Louisville MSA, KY-IN	S	20.47 MW	18.38 AW	42570 AAW	KYBLS	10//99-12//99
Non-Retail Sales Workers	Owensboro MSA, KY	S	16.63 MW	14.45 AW	34580 AAW	KYBLS	10//99-12//99
Non-Retail Sales Workers	Louisiana	S	15.62 MW	18.57 AW	38630 AAW	LABLS	10//99-12//99
Non-Retail Sales Workers	Alexandria MSA, LA	S	13.75 MW	11.42 AW	28610 AAW	LABLS	10//99-12//99
Non-Retail Sales Workers	Baton Rouge MSA, LA	S	23.44 MW	22.47 AW	48760 AAW	LABLS	10//99-12//99
Non-Retail Sales Workers	Houma MSA, LA	S	15.19 MW	12.70 AW	31590 AAW	LABLS	10//99-12//99
Non-Retail Sales Workers	Lafayette MSA, LA	S	14.90 MW	10.20 AW	30990 AAW	LABLS	10//99-12//99
Non-Retail Sales Workers	Lake Charles MSA, LA	S	11.14 MW	11.02 AW	23170 AAW	LABLS	10//99-12//99
Non-Retail Sales Workers	New Orleans MSA, LA	S	19.66 MW	17.97 AW	40900 AAW	LABLS	10//99-12//99
Non-Retail Sales Workers	Shreveport-Bossier City MSA, LA	S	18.96 MW	16.23 AW	39430 AAW	LABLS	10//99-12//99
Non-Retail Sales Workers	Maine	S	18.51 MW	18.95 AW	39410 AAW	MEBLS	10//99-12//99
Non-Retail Sales Workers	Bangor MSA, ME	S	17.77 MW	16.46 AW	36960 AAW	MEBLS	10//99-12//99
Non-Retail Sales Workers	Lewiston-Auburn MSA, ME	S	18.72 MW	18.52 AW	38930 AAW	MEBLS	10//99-12//99
Non-Retail Sales Workers	Portland MSA, ME	S	17.98 MW	16.75 AW	37390 AAW	MEBLS	10//99-12//99
Non-Retail Sales Workers	Maryland	S	17.68 MW	23.27 AW	48400 AAW	MDBLS	10//99-12//99
Non-Retail Sales Workers	Baltimore PMSA, MD	S	24.00 MW	20.39 AW	49920 AAW	MDBLS	10//99-12//99
Non-Retail Sales Workers	Hagerstown PMSA, MD	S	18.45 MW	17.31 AW	38370 AAW	MDBLS	10//99-12//99
Non-Retail Sales Workers	Massachusetts	S	26.03 MW	26.90 AW	55960 AAW	MABLS	10//99-12//99
Non-Retail Sales Workers	Barnstable-Yarmouth MSA, MA	S	16.92 MW	14.22 AW	35180 AAW	MABLS	10//99-12//99
Non-Retail Sales Workers	Boston PMSA, MA-NH	S	31.30 MW	30.39 AW	65100 AAW	MABLS	10//99-12//99
Non-Retail Sales Workers	Brockton PMSA, MA	S	25.05 MW	23.89 AW	52110 AAW	MABLS	10//99-12//99
Non-Retail Sales Workers	Fitchburg-Leominster PMSA, MA	S	20.48 MW	22.36 AW	42590 AAW	MABLS	10//99-12//99
Non-Retail Sales Workers	Lawrence PMSA, MA-NH	S	26.12 MW	25.44 AW	54330 AAW	MABLS	10//99-12//99
Non-Retail Sales Workers	Lowell PMSA, MA-NH	S	25.12 MW	24.41 AW	52250 AAW	MABLS	10//99-12//99
Non-Retail Sales Workers	Pittsfield MSA, MA	S	18.27 MW	16.45 AW	38000 AAW	MABLS	10//99-12//99
Non-Retail Sales Workers	Springfield MSA, MA	S	21.11 MW	16.87 AW	43900 AAW	MABLS	10//99-12//99
Non-Retail Sales Workers	Worcester PMSA, MA-CT	S	29.38 MW	28.04 AW	61100 AAW	MABLS	10//99-12//99
Non-Retail Sales Workers	Michigan	S	27.14 MW	31.84 AW	66230 AAW	MIBLS	10//99-12//99
Non-Retail Sales Workers	Ann Arbor PMSA, MI	S	36.37 MW	33.63 AW	75640 AAW	MIBLS	10//99-12//99
Non-Retail Sales Workers	Benton Harbor MSA, MI	S	32.32 MW	23.22 AW	67220 AAW	MIBLS	10//99-12//99
Non-Retail Sales Workers	Detroit PMSA, MI	S	35.55 MW	32.69 AW	73950 AAW	MIBLS	10//99-12//99
Non-Retail Sales Workers	Flint PMSA, MI	S	30.78 MW	22.93 AW	64020 AAW	MIBLS	10//99-12//99
Non-Retail Sales Workers	Grand Rapids-Muskegon-Holland MSA, MI	S	33.66 MW	27.46 AW	70020 AAW	MIBLS	10//99-12//99
Non-Retail Sales Workers	Jackson MSA, MI	S	36.32 MW	29.14 AW	75550 AAW	MIBLS	10//99-12//99
Non-Retail Sales Workers	Kalamazoo-Battle Creek MSA, MI	S	20.96 MW	18.45 AW	43600 AAW	MIBLS	10//99-12//99
Non-Retail Sales Workers	Lansing-East Lansing MSA, MI	S	23.62 MW	21.52 AW	49130 AAW	MIBLS	10//99-12//99
Non-Retail Sales Workers	Saginaw-Bay City-Midland MSA, MI	S	27.17 MW	26.13 AW	56510 AAW	MIBLS	10//99-12//99
Non-Retail Sales Workers	Minnesota	S	26.37 MW	29.37 AW	61080 AAW	MNBLS	10//99-12//99
Non-Retail Sales Workers	Duluth-Superior MSA, MN-WI	S	20.25 MW	18.90 AW	42120 AAW	MNBLS	10//99-12//99
Non-Retail Sales Workers	Minneapolis-St. Paul MSA, MN-WI	S	30.64 MW	27.89 AW	63730 AAW	MNBLS	10//99-12//99
Non-Retail Sales Workers	Rochester MSA, MN	S	24.71 MW	18.64 AW	51400 AAW	MNBLS	10//99-12//99
Non-Retail Sales Workers	St. Cloud MSA, MN	S	24.32 MW	22.88 AW	50590 AAW	MNBLS	10//99-12//99
Non-Retail Sales Workers	Mississippi	S	17.75 MW	20.21 AW	42030 AAW	MSBLS	10//99-12//99

AAW Average annual wage	**AOH** Average offered, high	**ASH** Average starting, high	**H** Hourly	**M** Monthly	**S** Special: hourly and annual
AE Average entry wage	**AOL** Average offered, low	**ASL** Average starting, low	**HI** Highest wage paid	**MTC** Median total compensation	**TQ** Third quartile wage
AEX Average experienced wage	**APH** Average pay, high range	**AW** Average wage paid	**HR** High end range	**MW** Median wage paid	**W** Weekly
AO Average offered	**APL** Average pay, low range	**FQ** First quartile wage	**LR** Low end range	**SQ** Second quartile wage	**Y** Yearly

First-Line Supervisor/Manager

Occupation/Type/Industry	Location	Per	Low	Mid	High	Source	Date
Non-Retail Sales Workers	Biloxi-Gulfport-Pascagoula MSA, MS	S	17.46 MW	16.90 AW	36310 AAW	MSBLS	10//99-12//99
Non-Retail Sales Workers	Hattiesburg MSA, MS	S	17.45 MW	17.36 AW	36300 AAW	MSBLS	10//99-12//99
Non-Retail Sales Workers	Jackson MSA, MS	S	24.19 MW	19.37 AW	50310 AAW	MSBLS	10//99-12//99
Non-Retail Sales Workers	Missouri	S	16.01 MW	18.89 AW	39280 AAW	MOBLS	10//99-12//99
Non-Retail Sales Workers	Columbia MSA, MO	S	17.11 MW	17.49 AW	35580 AAW	MOBLS	10//99-12//99
Non-Retail Sales Workers	Joplin MSA, MO	S	17.20 MW	16.48 AW	35770 AAW	MOBLS	10//99-12//99
Non-Retail Sales Workers	St. Joseph MSA, MO	S	19.70 MW	18.51 AW	40980 AAW	MOBLS	10//99-12//99
Non-Retail Sales Workers	St. Louis MSA, MO-IL	S	20.00 MW	15.63 AW	41610 AAW	MOBLS	10//99-12//99
Non-Retail Sales Workers	Springfield MSA, MO	S	21.71 MW	19.31 AW	45150 AAW	MOBLS	10//99-12//99
Non-Retail Sales Workers	Montana	S	19.05 MW	21.59 AW	44910 AAW	MTBLS	10//99-12//99
Non-Retail Sales Workers	Billings MSA, MT	S	19.85 MW	16.40 AW	41280 AAW	MTBLS	10//99-12//99
Non-Retail Sales Workers	Missoula MSA, MT	S	25.60 MW	20.89 AW	53240 AAW	MTBLS	10//99-12//99
Non-Retail Sales Workers	Nebraska	S	20.58 MW	21.34 AW	44390 AAW	NEBLS	10//99-12//99
Non-Retail Sales Workers	Lincoln MSA, NE	S	16.19 MW	17.49 AW	33670 AAW	NEBLS	10//99-12//99
Non-Retail Sales Workers	Omaha MSA, NE-IA	S	22.84 MW	22.29 AW	47500 AAW	NEBLS	10//99-12//99
Non-Retail Sales Workers	Nevada	S	13.48 MW	19.65 AW	40880 AAW	NVBLS	10//99-12//99
Non-Retail Sales Workers	Las Vegas MSA, NV-AZ	S	17.91 MW	12.37 AW	37260 AAW	NVBLS	10//99-12//99
Non-Retail Sales Workers	Reno MSA, NV	S	24.01 MW	23.31 AW	49950 AAW	NVBLS	10//99-12//99
Non-Retail Sales Workers	New Hampshire	S	22.21 MW	24.44 AW	50840 AAW	NHBLS	10//99-12//99
Non-Retail Sales Workers	Manchester PMSA, NH	S	23.71 MW	21.00 AW	49310 AAW	NHBLS	10//99-12//99
Non-Retail Sales Workers	Nashua PMSA, NH	S	26.95 MW	27.21 AW	56070 AAW	NHBLS	10//99-12//99
Non-Retail Sales Workers	Portsmouth-Rochester PMSA, NH-ME	S	22.00 MW	20.67 AW	45750 AAW	NHBLS	10//99-12//99
Non-Retail Sales Workers	New Jersey	S	35.1 MW	35.82 AW	74510 AAW	NJBLS	10//99-12//99
Non-Retail Sales Workers	Bergen-Passaic PMSA, NJ	S	40.26 MW	39.81 AW	83740 AAW	NJBLS	10//99-12//99
Non-Retail Sales Workers	Jersey City PMSA, NJ	S	35.66 MW	35.79 AW	74170 AAW	NJBLS	10//99-12//99
Non-Retail Sales Workers	Middlesex-Somerset-Hunterdon PMSA, NJ	S	36.39 MW	36.57 AW	75680 AAW	NJBLS	10//99-12//99
Non-Retail Sales Workers	Monmouth-Ocean PMSA, NJ	S	31.27 MW	26.72 AW	65040 AAW	NJBLS	10//99-12//99
Non-Retail Sales Workers	Newark PMSA, NJ	S	38.57 MW	36.53 AW	80220 AAW	NJBLS	10//99-12//99
Non-Retail Sales Workers	Trenton PMSA, NJ	S	30.88 MW	29.29 AW	64240 AAW	NJBLS	10//99-12//99
Non-Retail Sales Workers	Vineland-Millville-Bridgeton PMSA, NJ	S	34.81 MW	38.15 AW	72400 AAW	NJBLS	10//99-12//99
Non-Retail Sales Workers	New Mexico	S	18.46 MW	20.47 AW	42590 AAW	NMBLS	10//99-12//99
Non-Retail Sales Workers	Albuquerque MSA, NM	S	21.49 MW	19.25 AW	44700 AAW	NMBLS	10//99-12//99
Non-Retail Sales Workers	Santa Fe MSA, NM	S	18.92 MW	17.00 AW	39350 AAW	NMBLS	10//99-12//99
Non-Retail Sales Workers	New York	S	35.37 MW	39.38 AW	81920 AAW	NYBLS	10//99-12//99
Non-Retail Sales Workers	Albany-Schenectady-Troy MSA, NY	S	29.15 MW	25.73 AW	60620 AAW	NYBLS	10//99-12//99
Non-Retail Sales Workers	Binghamton MSA, NY	S	31.90 MW	26.36 AW	66360 AAW	NYBLS	10//99-12//99
Non-Retail Sales Workers	Buffalo-Niagara Falls MSA, NY	S	30.38 MW	22.43 AW	63190 AAW	NYBLS	10//99-12//99
Non-Retail Sales Workers	Dutchess County PMSA, NY	S	30.39 MW	25.82 AW	63210 AAW	NYBLS	10//99-12//99
Non-Retail Sales Workers	Elmira MSA, NY	S	28.88 MW	25.18 AW	60070 AAW	NYBLS	10//99-12//99
Non-Retail Sales Workers	Glens Falls MSA, NY	S	28.45 MW	18.24 AW	59180 AAW	NYBLS	10//99-12//99
Non-Retail Sales Workers	Jamestown MSA, NY	S	20.05 MW	16.91 AW	41710 AAW	NYBLS	10//99-12//99
Non-Retail Sales Workers	Nassau-Suffolk PMSA, NY	S	43.07 MW	39.57 AW	89590 AAW	NYBLS	10//99-12//99
Non-Retail Sales Workers	New York PMSA, NY	S	44.02 MW	42.41 AW	91570 AAW	NYBLS	10//99-12//99
Non-Retail Sales Workers	Newburgh PMSA, NY-PA	S	32.09 MW	23.65 AW	66750 AAW	NYBLS	10//99-12//99
Non-Retail Sales Workers	Rochester MSA, NY	S	30.56 MW	26.60 AW	63560 AAW	NYBLS	10//99-12//99
Non-Retail Sales Workers	Syracuse MSA, NY	S	30.90 MW	25.07 AW	64260 AAW	NYBLS	10//99-12//99
Non-Retail Sales Workers	Utica-Rome MSA, NY	S	31.33 MW	23.29 AW	65170 AAW	NYBLS	10//99-12//99
Non-Retail Sales Workers	North Carolina	S	14.85 MW	17.25 AW	35880 AAW	NCBLS	10//99-12//99
Non-Retail Sales Workers	Asheville MSA, NC	S	15.08 MW	15.26 AW	31370 AAW	NCBLS	10//99-12//99
Non-Retail Sales Workers	Charlotte-Gastonia-Rock Hill MSA, NC-SC	S	18.45 MW	15.86 AW	38380 AAW	NCBLS	10//99-12//99
Non-Retail Sales Workers	Fayetteville MSA, NC	S	14.30 MW	13.06 AW	29750 AAW	NCBLS	10//99-12//99
Non-Retail Sales Workers	Goldsboro MSA, NC	S	11.44 MW	8.41 AW	23790 AAW	NCBLS	10//99-12//99
Non-Retail Sales Workers	Greensboro--Winston-Salem--High Point MSA, NC	S	19.26 MW	15.25 AW	40050 AAW	NCBLS	10//99-12//99
Non-Retail Sales Workers	Greenville MSA, NC	S	14.67 MW	12.86 AW	30520 AAW	NCBLS	10//99-12//99
Non-Retail Sales Workers	Hickory-Morganton-Lenoir MSA, NC	S	16.00 MW	12.75 AW	33270 AAW	NCBLS	10//99-12//99
Non-Retail Sales Workers	Jacksonville MSA, NC	S	12.24 MW	12.42 AW	25450 AAW	NCBLS	10//99-12//99
Non-Retail Sales Workers	Raleigh-Durham-Chapel Hill MSA, NC	S	20.86 MW	18.01 AW	43390 AAW	NCBLS	10//99-12//99
Non-Retail Sales Workers	Rocky Mount MSA, NC	S	19.64 MW	16.12 AW	40860 AAW	NCBLS	10//99-12//99
Non-Retail Sales Workers	Wilmington MSA, NC	S	23.61 MW	16.98 AW	49100 AAW	NCBLS	10//99-12//99
Non-Retail Sales Workers	North Dakota	S	14.97 MW	16.82 AW	34980 AAW	NDBLS	10//99-12//99
Non-Retail Sales Workers	Bismarck MSA, ND	S	14.72 MW	13.32 AW	30610 AAW	NDBLS	10//99-12//99

AAW	Average annual wage	AOH	Average offered, high	ASH	Average starting, high
AE	Average entry wage	AOL	Average offered, low	ASL	Average starting, low
AEX	Average experienced wage	APH	Average pay, high range	AW	Average wage paid
AO	Average offered	APL	Average pay, low range	FQ	First quartile wage

H	Hourly
HI	Highest wage paid
HR	High end range
LR	Low end range

M	Monthly
MTC	Median total compensation
MW	Median wage paid
SQ	Second quartile wage

S	Special: hourly and annual
TQ	Third quartile wage
W	Weekly
Y	Yearly

Occupation/Type/Industry	Location	Per	Low	Mid	High	Source	Date

First-Line Supervisor/Manager

Occupation/Type/Industry	Location	Per	Low	Mid	High	Source	Date
Non-Retail Sales Workers	Fargo-Moorhead MSA, ND-MN	S	17.32 MW	15.30 AW	36030 AAW	NDBLS	10//99-12/99
Non-Retail Sales Workers	Grand Forks MSA, ND-MN	S	19.42 MW	16.24 AW	40400 AAW	NDBLS	10//99-12/99
Non-Retail Sales Workers	Ohio	S	22.4 MW	26.44 AW	55000 AAW	OHBLS	10//99-12/99
Non-Retail Sales Workers	Akron PMSA, OH	S	31.66 MW	27.05 AW	65840 AAW	OHBLS	10//99-12/99
Non-Retail Sales Workers	Canton-Massillon MSA, OH	S	23.61 MW	21.68 AW	49100 AAW	OHBLS	10//99-12/99
Non-Retail Sales Workers	Cincinnati PMSA, OH-KY-IN	S	26.74 MW	22.57 AW	55620 AAW	OHBLS	10//99-12/99
Non-Retail Sales Workers	Cleveland-Lorain-Elyria PMSA, OH	S	23.87 MW	21.47 AW	49660 AAW	OHBLS	10//99-12/99
Non-Retail Sales Workers	Columbus MSA, OH	S	27.95 MW	24.47 AW	58130 AAW	OHBLS	10//99-12/99
Non-Retail Sales Workers	Dayton-Springfield MSA, OH	S	32.73 MW	28.27 AW	68080 AAW	OHBLS	10//99-12/99
Non-Retail Sales Workers	Hamilton-Middletown PMSA, OH	S	25.15 MW	21.41 AW	52320 AAW	OHBLS	10//99-12/99
Non-Retail Sales Workers	Lima MSA, OH	S	16.05 MW	14.46 AW	33390 AAW	OHBLS	10//99-12/99
Non-Retail Sales Workers	Mansfield MSA, OH	S	19.59 MW	17.75 AW	40740 AAW	OHBLS	10//99-12/99
Non-Retail Sales Workers	Youngstown-Warren MSA, OH	S	18.73 MW	17.62 AW	38960 AAW	OHBLS	10//99-12/99
Non-Retail Sales Workers	Oklahoma	S	17.09 MW	19.50 AW	40570 AAW	OKBLS	10//99-12/99
Non-Retail Sales Workers	Enid MSA, OK	S	22.43 MW	18.75 AW	46660 AAW	OKBLS	10//99-12/99
Non-Retail Sales Workers	Oklahoma City MSA, OK	S	18.14 MW	16.04 AW	37730 AAW	OKBLS	10//99-12/99
Non-Retail Sales Workers	Tulsa MSA, OK	S	21.62 MW	19.21 AW	44970 AAW	OKBLS	10//99-12/99
Non-Retail Sales Workers	Oregon	S	22.74 MW	25.70 AW	53460 AAW	ORBLS	10//99-12/99
Non-Retail Sales Workers	Corvallis MSA, OR	S	23.08 MW	19.50 AW	48000 AAW	ORBLS	10//99-12/99
Non-Retail Sales Workers	Eugene-Springfield MSA, OR	S	26.58 MW	21.37 AW	55290 AAW	ORBLS	10//99-12/99
Non-Retail Sales Workers	Medford-Ashland MSA, OR	S	21.23 MW	20.44 AW	44160 AAW	ORBLS	10//99-12/99
Non-Retail Sales Workers	Portland-Vancouver PMSA, OR-WA	S	26.26 MW	22.81 AW	54610 AAW	ORBLS	10//99-12/99
Non-Retail Sales Workers	Salem PMSA, OR	S	21.43 MW	21.62 AW	44570 AAW	ORBLS	10//99-12/99
Non-Retail Sales Workers	Pennsylvania	S	21.31 MW	23.96 AW	49840 AAW	PABLS	10//99-12/99
Non-Retail Sales Workers	Allentown-Bethlehem-Easton MSA, PA	S	27.51 MW	27.85 AW	57220 AAW	PABLS	10//99-12/99
Non-Retail Sales Workers	Altoona MSA, PA	S	21.82 MW	20.89 AW	45380 AAW	PABLS	10//99-12/99
Non-Retail Sales Workers	Erie MSA, PA	S	20.35 MW	19.78 AW	42340 AAW	PABLS	10//99-12/99
Non-Retail Sales Workers	Harrisburg-Lebanon-Carlisle MSA, PA	S	23.19 MW	21.18 AW	48230 AAW	PABLS	10//99-12/99
Non-Retail Sales Workers	Lancaster MSA, PA	S	21.44 MW	22.23 AW	44590 AAW	PABLS	10//99-12/99
Non-Retail Sales Workers	Philadelphia PMSA, PA-NJ	S	25.64 MW	21.63 AW	53330 AAW	PABLS	10//99-12/99
Non-Retail Sales Workers	Pittsburgh MSA, PA	S	24.72 MW	23.24 AW	51420 AAW	PABLS	10//99-12/99
Non-Retail Sales Workers	Reading MSA, PA	S	23.87 MW	20.70 AW	49650 AAW	PABLS	10//99-12/99
Non-Retail Sales Workers	Scranton--Wilkes-Barre--Hazleton MSA, PA	S	23.05 MW	19.63 AW	47940 AAW	PABLS	10//99-12/99
Non-Retail Sales Workers	Sharon MSA, PA	S	21.43 MW	16.33 AW	44580 AAW	PABLS	10//99-12/99
Non-Retail Sales Workers	Williamsport MSA, PA	S	20.58 MW	20.03 AW	42800 AAW	PABLS	10//99-12/99
Non-Retail Sales Workers	York MSA, PA	S	19.64 MW	17.32 AW	40850 AAW	PABLS	10//99-12/99
Non-Retail Sales Workers	Rhode Island	S	25.21 MW	30.83 AW	64130 AAW	RIBLS	10//99-12/99
Non-Retail Sales Workers	Providence-Fall River-Warwick MSA, RI-MA	S	28.03 MW	22.66 AW	58300 AAW	RIBLS	10//99-12/99
Non-Retail Sales Workers	South Carolina	S	16.07 MW	18.48 AW	38450 AAW	SCBLS	10//99-12/99
Non-Retail Sales Workers	Charleston-North Charleston MSA, SC	S	15.53 MW	11.48 AW	32300 AAW	SCBLS	10//99-12/99
Non-Retail Sales Workers	Columbia MSA, SC	S	20.95 MW	17.88 AW	43570 AAW	SCBLS	10//99-12/99
Non-Retail Sales Workers	Florence MSA, SC	S	14.96 MW	14.30 AW	31110 AAW	SCBLS	10//99-12/99
Non-Retail Sales Workers	Greenville-Spartanburg-Anderson MSA, SC	S	19.34 MW	15.70 AW	40230 AAW	SCBLS	10//99-12/99
Non-Retail Sales Workers	Myrtle Beach MSA, SC	S	16.92 MW	17.23 AW	35200 AAW	SCBLS	10//99-12/99
Non-Retail Sales Workers	South Dakota	S	19.76 MW	22.67 AW	47160 AAW	SDBLS	10//99-12/99
Non-Retail Sales Workers	Rapid City MSA, SD	S	18.10 MW	16.77 AW	37650 AAW	SDBLS	10//99-12/99
Non-Retail Sales Workers	Sioux Falls MSA, SD	S	25.05 MW	21.92 AW	52110 AAW	SDBLS	10//99-12/99
Non-Retail Sales Workers	Tennessee	S	14.87 MW	18.26 AW	37990 AAW	TNBLS	10//99-12/99
Non-Retail Sales Workers	Chattanooga MSA, TN-GA	S	16.44 MW	14.48 AW	34190 AAW	TNBLS	10//99-12/99
Non-Retail Sales Workers	Clarksville-Hopkinsville MSA, TN-KY	S	13.69 MW	13.40 AW	28480 AAW	TNBLS	10//99-12/99
Non-Retail Sales Workers	Jackson MSA, TN	S	14.71 MW	13.02 AW	30590 AAW	TNBLS	10//99-12/99
Non-Retail Sales Workers	Johnson City-Kingsport-Bristol MSA, TN-VA	S	18.33 MW	18.17 AW	38120 AAW	TNBLS	10//99-12/99
Non-Retail Sales Workers	Knoxville MSA, TN	S	15.38 MW	12.16 AW	31980 AAW	TNBLS	10//99-12/99
Non-Retail Sales Workers	Memphis MSA, TN-AR-MS	S	17.54 MW	15.58 AW	36490 AAW	MSBLS	10//99-12/99
Non-Retail Sales Workers	Nashville MSA, TN	S	22.00 MW	19.17 AW	45750 AAW	TNBLS	10//99-12/99
Non-Retail Sales Workers	Texas	S	16.77 MW	21.09 AW	43860 AAW	TXBLS	10//99-12/99
Non-Retail Sales Workers	Abilene MSA, TX	S	13.17 MW	11.55 AW	27400 AAW	TXBLS	10//99-12/99
Non-Retail Sales Workers	Amarillo MSA, TX	S	21.50 MW	19.62 AW	44720 AAW	TXBLS	10//99-12/99
Non-Retail Sales Workers	Austin-San Marcos MSA, TX	S	21.23 MW	19.00 AW	44150 AAW	TXBLS	10//99-12/99

AAW Average annual wage	**AOH** Average offered, high	**ASH** Average starting, high	**H** Hourly	**M** Monthly	**S** Special: hourly and annual
AE Average entry wage	**AOL** Average offered, low	**ASL** Average starting, low	**HI** Highest wage paid	**MTC** Median total compensation	**TQ** Third quartile wage
AEX Average experienced wage	**APH** Average pay, high range	**AW** Average wage paid	**HR** High end range	**MW** Median wage paid	**W** Weekly
AO Average offered	**APL** Average pay, low range	**FQ** First quartile wage	**LR** Low end range	**SQ** Second quartile wage	**Y** Yearly

First-Line Supervisor/Manager

Occupation/Type/Industry	Location	Per	Low	Mid	High	Source	Date
Non-Retail Sales Workers	Brazoria PMSA, TX	S	16.13 MW	10.68 AW	33540 AAW	TXBLS	10//99-12//99
Non-Retail Sales Workers	Brownsville-Harlingen-San Benito MSA, TX	S	25.25 MW	21.55 AW	52530 AAW	TXBLS	10//99-12//99
Non-Retail Sales Workers	Bryan-College Station MSA, TX	S	14.36 MW	11.80 AW	29870 AAW	TXBLS	10//99-12//99
Non-Retail Sales Workers	Corpus Christi MSA, TX	S	22.98 MW	22.95 AW	47800 AAW	TXBLS	10//99-12//99
Non-Retail Sales Workers	Dallas PMSA, TX	S	22.90 MW	17.58 AW	47640 AAW	TXBLS	10//99-12//99
Non-Retail Sales Workers	El Paso MSA, TX	S	13.06 MW	12.67 AW	27160 AAW	TXBLS	10//99-12//99
Non-Retail Sales Workers	Fort Worth-Arlington PMSA, TX	S	20.74 MW	14.59 AW	43150 AAW	TXBLS	10//99-12//99
Non-Retail Sales Workers	Galveston-Texas City PMSA, TX	S	21.26 MW	20.20 AW	44220 AAW	TXBLS	10//99-12//99
Non-Retail Sales Workers	Houston PMSA, TX	S	22.88 MW	20.65 AW	47600 AAW	TXBLS	10//99-12//99
Non-Retail Sales Workers	Killeen-Temple MSA, TX	S	15.07 MW	12.17 AW	31350 AAW	TXBLS	10//99-12//99
Non-Retail Sales Workers	Laredo MSA, TX	S	21.56 MW	19.73 AW	44840 AAW	TXBLS	10//99-12//99
Non-Retail Sales Workers	Longview-Marshall MSA, TX	S	18.22 MW	14.42 AW	37890 AAW	TXBLS	10//99-12//99
Non-Retail Sales Workers	Lubbock MSA, TX	S	16.59 MW	13.99 AW	34510 AAW	TXBLS	10//99-12//99
Non-Retail Sales Workers	McAllen-Edinburg-Mission MSA, TX	S	24.77 MW	20.48 AW	51530 AAW	TXBLS	10//99-12//99
Non-Retail Sales Workers	Odessa-Midland MSA, TX	S	17.39 MW	13.49 AW	36170 AAW	TXBLS	10//99-12//99
Non-Retail Sales Workers	San Antonio MSA, TX	S	21.27 MW	17.41 AW	44240 AAW	TXBLS	10//99-12//99
Non-Retail Sales Workers	Sherman-Denison MSA, TX	S	14.71 MW	12.49 AW	30600 AAW	TXBLS	10//99-12//99
Non-Retail Sales Workers	Texarkana MSA, TX-Texarkana, AR	S	24.74 MW	15.73 AW	51460 AAW	TXBLS	10//99-12//99
Non-Retail Sales Workers	Tyler MSA, TX	S	18.22 MW	17.86 AW	37900 AAW	TXBLS	10//99-12//99
Non-Retail Sales Workers	Waco MSA, TX	S	23.97 MW	18.99 AW	49870 AAW	TXBLS	10//99-12//99
Non-Retail Sales Workers	Wichita Falls MSA, TX	S	19.08 MW	19.66 AW	39690 AAW	TXBLS	10//99-12//99
Non-Retail Sales Workers	Utah	S	18.84 MW	22.46 AW	46710 AAW	UTBLS	10//99-12//99
Non-Retail Sales Workers	Salt Lake City-Ogden MSA, UT	S	24.60 MW	21.61 AW	51170 AAW	UTBLS	10//99-12//99
Non-Retail Sales Workers	Vermont	S	28.05 MW	29.65 AW	61670 AAW	VTBLS	10//99-12//99
Non-Retail Sales Workers	Burlington MSA, VT	S	31.62 MW	25.14 AW	65770 AAW	VTBLS	10//99-12//99
Non-Retail Sales Workers	Virginia	S	21.46 MW	25.13 AW	52280 AAW	VABLS	10//99-12//99
Non-Retail Sales Workers	Charlottesville MSA, VA	S	24.12 MW	21.15 AW	50170 AAW	VABLS	10//99-12//99
Non-Retail Sales Workers	Danville MSA, VA	S	23.98 MW	22.05 AW	49870 AAW	VABLS	10//99-12//99
Non-Retail Sales Workers	Lynchburg MSA, VA	S	24.32 MW	19.35 AW	50590 AAW	VABLS	10//99-12//99
Non-Retail Sales Workers	Norfolk-Virginia Beach-Newport News MSA, VA-NC	S	20.30 MW	17.99 AW	42220 AAW	VABLS	10//99-12//99
Non-Retail Sales Workers	Richmond-Petersburg MSA, VA	S	23.51 MW	21.92 AW	48900 AAW	VABLS	10//99-12//99
Non-Retail Sales Workers	Roanoke MSA, VA	S	33.25 MW	29.25 AW	69170 AAW	VABLS	10//99-12//99
Non-Retail Sales Workers	Washington	S	23.79 MW	27.24 AW	56660 AAW	WABLS	10//99-12//99
Non-Retail Sales Workers	Bellingham MSA, WA	S	25.84 MW	22.32 AW	53750 AAW	WABLS	10//99-12//99
Non-Retail Sales Workers	Bremerton PMSA, WA	S	23.76 MW	17.83 AW	49420 AAW	WABLS	10//99-12//99
Non-Retail Sales Workers	Olympia PMSA, WA	S	23.12 MW	20.58 AW	48100 AAW	WABLS	10//99-12//99
Non-Retail Sales Workers	Richland-Kennewick-Pasco MSA, WA	S	23.59 MW	20.82 AW	49070 AAW	WABLS	10//99-12//99
Non-Retail Sales Workers	Seattle-Bellevue-Everett PMSA, WA	S	27.35 MW	24.55 AW	56890 AAW	WABLS	10//99-12//99
Non-Retail Sales Workers	Spokane MSA, WA	S	39.44 MW	30.98 AW	82040 AAW	WABLS	10//99-12//99
Non-Retail Sales Workers	Tacoma PMSA, WA	S	24.39 MW	21.05 AW	50730 AAW	WABLS	10//99-12//99
Non-Retail Sales Workers	Yakima MSA, WA	S	28.46 MW	28.18 AW	59210 AAW	WABLS	10//99-12//99
Non-Retail Sales Workers	West Virginia	S	17.22 MW	19.17 AW	39880 AAW	WVBLS	10//99-12//99
Non-Retail Sales Workers	Charleston MSA, WV	S	19.00 MW	16.97 AW	39510 AAW	WVBLS	10//99-12//99
Non-Retail Sales Workers	Huntington-Ashland MSA, WV-KY-OH	S	16.82 MW	16.62 AW	34980 AAW	WVBLS	10//99-12//99
Non-Retail Sales Workers	Parkersburg-Marietta MSA, WV-OH	S	17.87 MW	17.66 AW	37180 AAW	WVBLS	10//99-12//99
Non-Retail Sales Workers	Wheeling MSA, WV-OH	S	27.25 MW	19.72 AW	56680 AAW	WVBLS	10//99-12//99
Non-Retail Sales Workers	Wisconsin	S	22.25 MW	24.59 AW	51140 AAW	WIBLS	10//99-12//99
Non-Retail Sales Workers	Appleton-Oshkosh-Neenah MSA, WI	S	22.88 MW	22.53 AW	47590 AAW	WIBLS	10//99-12//99
Non-Retail Sales Workers	Eau Claire MSA, WI	S	24.38 MW	27.14 AW	50710 AAW	WIBLS	10//99-12//99
Non-Retail Sales Workers	Green Bay MSA, WI	S	19.01 MW	19.25 AW	39540 AAW	WIBLS	10//99-12//99
Non-Retail Sales Workers	Janesville-Beloit MSA, WI	S	19.51 MW	18.92 AW	40580 AAW	WIBLS	10//99-12//99
Non-Retail Sales Workers	Kenosha PMSA, WI	S	21.45 MW	22.25 AW	44610 AAW	WIBLS	10//99-12//99
Non-Retail Sales Workers	La Crosse MSA, WI-MN	S	21.57 MW	22.18 AW	44870 AAW	WIBLS	10//99-12//99
Non-Retail Sales Workers	Madison MSA, WI	S	29.42 MW	22.67 AW	61190 AAW	WIBLS	10//99-12//99
Non-Retail Sales Workers	Milwaukee-Waukesha PMSA, WI	S	26.71 MW	24.36 AW	55550 AAW	WIBLS	10//99-12//99

AAW	Average annual wage	AOH	Average offered, high	ASH	Average starting, high
AE	Average entry wage	AOL	Average offered, low	ASL	Average starting, low
AEX	Average experienced wage	APH	Average pay, high range	AW	Average wage paid
AO	Average offered	APL	Average pay, low range	FQ	First quartile wage

H	Hourly
HI	Highest wage paid
HR	High end range
LR	Low end range

M	Monthly
MTC	Median total compensation
MW	Median wage paid
SQ	Second quartile wage

S	Special: hourly and annual
TQ	Third quartile wage
W	Weekly
Y	Yearly

First-Line Supervisor/Manager

Occupation/Type/Industry	Location	Per	Low	Mid	High	Source	Date
Non-Retail Sales Workers	Racine PMSA, WI	S	26.72 MW	27.16 AW	55570 AAW	WIBLS	10//99-12//99
Non-Retail Sales Workers	Sheboygan MSA, WI	S	28.67 MW	20.39 AW	59640 AAW	WIBLS	10//99-12//99
Non-Retail Sales Workers	Wausau MSA, WI	S	21.60 MW	16.89 AW	44940 AAW	WIBLS	10//99-12//99
Non-Retail Sales Workers	Wyoming	S	13.21 MW	14.98 AW	31150 AAW	WYBLS	10//99-12//99
Non-Retail Sales Workers	Casper MSA, WY	S	13.77 MW	8.45 AW	28630 AAW	WYBLS	10//99-12//99
Non-Retail Sales Workers	Puerto Rico	S	14.81 MW	16.90 AW	35150 AAW	PRBLS	10//99-12//99
Non-Retail Sales Workers	Caguas PMSA, PR	S	14.80 MW	12.94 AW	30780 AAW	PRBLS	10//99-12//99
Non-Retail Sales Workers	Mayaguez MSA, PR	S	12.92 MW	11.44 AW	26880 AAW	PRBLS	10//99-12//99
Non-Retail Sales Workers	Ponce MSA, PR	S	17.56 MW	16.32 AW	36530 AAW	PRBLS	10//99-12//99
Non-Retail Sales Workers	San Juan-Bayamon PMSA, PR	S	17.24 MW	14.99 AW	35860 AAW	PRBLS	10//99-12//99
Non-Retail Sales Workers	Virgin Islands	S	14.16 MW	14.80 AW	30780 AAW	VIBLS	10//99-12//99
Non-Retail Sales Workers	Guam	S	13.37 MW	15.10 AW	31400 AAW	GUBLS	10//99-12//99
Office and Administrative Support Workers	Alabama	S	14.12 MW	16.13 AW	33560 AAW	ALBLS	10//99-12//99
Office and Administrative Support Workers	Alaska	S	18.74 MW	19.99 AW	41580 AAW	AKBLS	10//99-12//99
Office and Administrative Support Workers	Arizona	S	15.28 MW	16.61 AW	34560 AAW	AZBLS	10//99-12//99
Office and Administrative Support Workers	Arkansas	S	12.71 MW	13.82 AW	28750 AAW	ARBLS	10//99-12//99
Office and Administrative Support Workers	California	S	17.66 MW	18.55 AW	38590 AAW	CABLS	10//99-12//99
Office and Administrative Support Workers	Colorado	S	16.13 MW	17.25 AW	35880 AAW	COBLS	10//99-12//99
Office and Administrative Support Workers	Connecticut	S	18.01 MW	18.96 AW	39440 AAW	CTBLS	10//99-12//99
Office and Administrative Support Workers	Delaware	S	16.34 MW	17.52 AW	36440 AAW	DEBLS	10//99-12//99
Office and Administrative Support Workers	District of Columbia	S	21.43 MW	25.67 AW	53390 AAW	DCBLS	10//99-12//99
Office and Administrative Support Workers	Florida	S	14.74 MW	16.13 AW	33540 AAW	FLBLS	10//99-12//99
Office and Administrative Support Workers	Georgia	S	14.82 MW	16.22 AW	33740 AAW	GABLS	10//99-12//99
Office and Administrative Support Workers	Hawaii	S	17.27 MW	18.23 AW	37920 AAW	HIBLS	10//99-12//99
Office and Administrative Support Workers	Idaho	S	13.3 MW	14.35 AW	29840 AAW	IDBLS	10//99-12//99
Office and Administrative Support Workers	Illinois	S	15.5 MW	16.86 AW	35080 AAW	ILBLS	10//99-12//99
Office and Administrative Support Workers	Indiana	S	14.36 MW	15.82 AW	32910 AAW	INBLS	10//99-12//99
Office and Administrative Support Workers	Iowa	S	14.14 MW	15.79 AW	32830 AAW	IABLS	10//99-12//99
Office and Administrative Support Workers	Kansas	S	13.89 MW	15.27 AW	31760 AAW	KSBLS	10//99-12//99
Office and Administrative Support Workers	Kentucky	S	14.19 MW	15.55 AW	32350 AAW	KYBLS	10//99-12//99
Office and Administrative Support Workers	Louisiana	S	13.2 MW	14.94 AW	31080 AAW	LABLS	10//99-12//99
Office and Administrative Support Workers	Maine	S	13.32 MW	14.36 AW	29870 AAW	MEBLS	10//99-12//99
Office and Administrative Support Workers	Maryland	S	16.36 MW	17.72 AW	36860 AAW	MDBLS	10//99-12//99
Office and Administrative Support Workers	Massachusetts	S	17.8 MW	19.07 AW	39670 AAW	MABLS	10//99-12//99
Office and Administrative Support Workers	Michigan	S	16.56 MW	17.78 AW	36980 AAW	MIBLS	10//99-12//99
Office and Administrative Support Workers	Minnesota	S	16.68 MW	17.73 AW	36870 AAW	MNBLS	10//99-12//99
Office and Administrative Support Workers	Mississippi	S	12.65 MW	14.00 AW	29110 AAW	MSBLS	10//99-12//99
Office and Administrative Support Workers	Missouri	S	14.82 MW	16.21 AW	33710 AAW	MOBLS	10//99-12//99
Office and Administrative Support Workers	Montana	S	12.89 MW	13.98 AW	29080 AAW	MTBLS	10//99-12//99
Office and Administrative Support Workers	Nebraska	S	13.29 MW	14.65 AW	30470 AAW	NEBLS	10//99-12//99
Office and Administrative Support Workers	Nevada	S	15.21 MW	16.35 AW	34010 AAW	NVBLS	10//99-12//99
Office and Administrative Support Workers	New Hampshire	S	15.02 MW	16.26 AW	33830 AAW	NHBLS	10//99-12//99
Office and Administrative Support Workers	New Jersey	S	19.55 MW	21.02 AW	43720 AAW	NJBLS	10//99-12//99
Office and Administrative Support Workers	New Mexico	S	13.01 MW	14.36 AW	29870 AAW	NMBLS	10//99-12//99
Office and Administrative Support Workers	New York	S	18.46 MW	20.20 AW	42020 AAW	NYBLS	10//99-12//99
Office and Administrative Support Workers	North Carolina	S	14.99 MW	16.15 AW	33590 AAW	NCBLS	10//99-12//99
Office and Administrative Support Workers	North Dakota	S	12.96 MW	14.85 AW	30880 AAW	NDBLS	10//99-12//99
Office and Administrative Support Workers	Ohio	S	14.92 MW	16.07 AW	33430 AAW	OHBLS	10//99-12//99
Office and Administrative Support Workers	Oklahoma	S	13.33 MW	14.92 AW	31040 AAW	OKBLS	10//99-12//99
Office and Administrative Support Workers	Oregon	S	15.93 MW	17.04 AW	35440 AAW	ORBLS	10//99-12//99
Office and Administrative Support Workers	Pennsylvania	S	15.56 MW	16.85 AW	35060 AAW	PABLS	10//99-12//99
Office and Administrative Support Workers	Rhode Island	S	16.79 MW	17.37 AW	36130 AAW	RIBLS	10//99-12//99
Office and Administrative Support Workers	South Carolina	S	13.82 MW	15.39 AW	32010 AAW	SCBLS	10//99-12//99
Office and Administrative Support Workers	South Dakota	S	14.33 MW	15.13 AW	31460 AAW	SDBLS	10//99-12//99
Office and Administrative Support Workers	Tennessee	S	14.08 MW	15.96 AW	33190 AAW	TNBLS	10//99-12//99
Office and Administrative Support Workers	Texas	S	15.63 MW	16.98 AW	35310 AAW	TXBLS	10//99-12//99
Office and Administrative Support Workers	Utah	S	14.71 MW	16.22 AW	33730 AAW	UTBLS	10//99-12//99
Office and Administrative Support Workers	Vermont	S	15.91 MW	16.89 AW	35130 AAW	VTBLS	10//99-12//99
Office and Administrative Support Workers	Virginia	S	15.58 MW	17.11 AW	35600 AAW	VABLS	10//99-12//99
Office and Administrative Support Workers	Washington	S	17.06 MW	18.23 AW	37910 AAW	WABLS	10//99-12//99
Office and Administrative Support Workers	West Virginia	S	13.06 MW	14.72 AW	30610 AAW	WVBLS	10//99-12//99
Office and Administrative Support Workers	Wisconsin	S	15.07 MW	16.17 AW	33630 AAW	WIBLS	10//99-12//99
Office and Administrative Support Workers	Wyoming	S	13.19 MW	14.39 AW	29930 AAW	WYBLS	10//99-12//99
Office and Administrative Support Workers	Puerto Rico	S	11.32 MW	12.63 AW	26270 AAW	PRBLS	10//99-12//99
Office and Administrative Support Workers	Virgin Islands	S	13.15 MW	14.14 AW	29410 AAW	VIBLS	10//99-12//99
Office and Administrative Support Workers	Guam	S	12.28 MW	13.49 AW	28050 AAW	GUBLS	10//99-12//99
Personal Service Workers	Alabama	S	13.86 MW	12.97 AW	26980 AAW	ALBLS	10//99-12//99
Personal Service Workers	Alaska	S	16.16 MW	15.86 AW	32980 AAW	AKBLS	10//99-12//99
Personal Service Workers	Arizona	S	11.94 MW	13.33 AW	27730 AAW	AZBLS	10//99-12//99
Personal Service Workers	Arkansas	S	11.59 MW	11.88 AW	24700 AAW	ARBLS	10//99-12//99
Personal Service Workers	California	S	14.24 MW	15.44 AW	32120 AAW	CABLS	10//99-12//99

Occupation/Type/Industry	Location	Per	Low	Mid	High	Source	Date
First-Line Supervisor/Manager							
Personal Service Workers	Colorado	S	11.44 MW	12.77 AW	26570 AAW	COBLS	10//99-12//99
Personal Service Workers	Connecticut	S	16.78 MW	19.02 AW	39570 AAW	CTBLS	10//99-12//99
Personal Service Workers	Delaware	S	17.58 MW	17.68 AW	36770 AAW	DEBLS	10//99-12//99
Personal Service Workers	District of Columbia	S	13.5 MW	14.69 AW	30550 AAW	DCBLS	10//99-12//99
Personal Service Workers	Florida	S	10.94 MW	12.56 AW	26110 AAW	FLBLS	10//99-12//99
Personal Service Workers	Georgia	S	12.41 MW	13.14 AW	27330 AAW	GABLS	10//99-12//99
Personal Service Workers	Hawaii	S	11.6 MW	12.08 AW	25130 AAW	HIBLS	10//99-12//99
Personal Service Workers	Idaho	S	9.2 MW	9.49 AW	19740 AAW	IDBLS	10//99-12//99
Personal Service Workers	Illinois	S	13.27 MW	15.41 AW	32060 AAW	ILBLS	10//99-12//99
Personal Service Workers	Indiana	S	12.41 MW	16.10 AW	33490 AAW	INBLS	10//99-12//99
Personal Service Workers	Iowa	S	13.91 MW	13.89 AW	28880 AAW	IABLS	10//99-12//99
Personal Service Workers	Kansas	S	11.23 MW	11.98 AW	24910 AAW	KSBLS	10//99-12//99
Personal Service Workers	Kentucky	S	10.16 MW	11.00 AW	22890 AAW	KYBLS	10//99-12//99
Personal Service Workers	Louisiana	S	9.54 MW	10.53 AW	21910 AAW	LABLS	10//99-12//99
Personal Service Workers	Maine	S	11.39 MW	12.39 AW	25770 AAW	MEBLS	10//99-12//99
Personal Service Workers	Maryland	S	14.54 MW	14.93 AW	31050 AAW	MDBLS	10//99-12//99
Personal Service Workers	Massachusetts	S	11.92 MW	13.06 AW	27170 AAW	MABLS	10//99-12//99
Personal Service Workers	Michigan	S	14.37 MW	15.48 AW	32200 AAW	MIBLS	10//99-12//99
Personal Service Workers	Minnesota	S	12.52 MW	13.62 AW	28340 AAW	MNBLS	10//99-12//99
Personal Service Workers	Mississippi	S	10.25 MW	10.95 AW	22770 AAW	MSBLS	10//99-12//99
Personal Service Workers	Missouri	S	10.6 MW	11.37 AW	23640 AAW	MOBLS	10//99-12//99
Personal Service Workers	Montana	S	6.57 MW	9.80 AW	20390 AAW	MTBLS	10//99-12//99
Personal Service Workers	Nebraska	S	12.41 MW	13.95 AW	29020 AAW	NEBLS	10//99-12//99
Personal Service Workers	Nevada	S	11.58 MW	12.84 AW	26710 AAW	NVBLS	10//99-12//99
Personal Service Workers	New Hampshire	S	11.8 MW	12.02 AW	24990 AAW	NHBLS	10//99-12//99
Personal Service Workers	New Jersey	S	13.97 MW	16.16 AW	33600 AAW	NJBLS	10//99-12//99
Personal Service Workers	New Mexico	S	10.26 MW	11.52 AW	23970 AAW	NMBLS	10//99-12//99
Personal Service Workers	New York	S	12.65 MW	14.97 AW	31130 AAW	NYBLS	10//99-12//99
Personal Service Workers	North Carolina	S	11.77 MW	12.57 AW	26150 AAW	NCBLS	10//99-12//99
Personal Service Workers	North Dakota	S	12.77 MW	12.82 AW	26670 AAW	NDBLS	10//99-12//99
Personal Service Workers	Ohio	S	9.95 MW	11.10 AW	23080 AAW	OHBLS	10//99-12//99
Personal Service Workers	Oklahoma	S	12.3 MW	13.12 AW	27290 AAW	OKBLS	10//99-12//99
Personal Service Workers	Oregon	S	14.09 MW	14.87 AW	30930 AAW	ORBLS	10//99-12//99
Personal Service Workers	Pennsylvania	S	13.74 MW	13.71 AW	28510 AAW	PABLS	10//99-12//99
Personal Service Workers	Rhode Island	S	14.31 MW	14.64 AW	30450 AAW	RIBLS	10//99-12//99
Personal Service Workers	South Carolina	S	12.92 MW	16.15 AW	33600 AAW	SCBLS	10//99-12//99
Personal Service Workers	South Dakota	S	12.59 MW	13.25 AW	27570 AAW	SDBLS	10//99-12//99
Personal Service Workers	Tennessee	S	9.79 MW	11.11 AW	23100 AAW	TNBLS	10//99-12//99
Personal Service Workers	Texas	S	12.39 MW	13.77 AW	28630 AAW	TXBLS	10//99-12//99
Personal Service Workers	Utah	S	8.42 MW	10.75 AW	22360 AAW	UTBLS	10//99-12//99
Personal Service Workers	Vermont	S	13.23 MW	14.98 AW	31160 AAW	VTBLS	10//99-12//99
Personal Service Workers	Virginia	S	15.4 MW	15.98 AW	33240 AAW	VABLS	10//99-12//99
Personal Service Workers	Washington	S	13.72 MW	15.35 AW	31940 AAW	WABLS	10//99-12//99
Personal Service Workers	West Virginia	S	9.73 MW	9.69 AW	20150 AAW	WVBLS	10//99-12//99
Personal Service Workers	Wisconsin	S	13.43 MW	13.79 AW	28690 AAW	WIBLS	10//99-12//99
Personal Service Workers	Wyoming	S	10.21 MW	11.60 AW	24120 AAW	WYBLS	10//99-12//99
Personal Service Workers	Puerto Rico	S	10.11 MW	10.35 AW	21530 AAW	PRBLS	10//99-12//99
Personal Service Workers	Virgin Islands	S	11.52 MW	12.81 AW	26650 AAW	VIBLS	10//99-12//99
Personal Service Workers	Guam	S	11.34 MW	12.46 AW	25910 AAW	GUBLS	10//99-12//99
Police and Detectives	Alabama	S	18.95 MW	19.70 AW	40970 AAW	ALBLS	10//99-12//99
Police and Detectives	Birmingham MSA, AL	S	22.91 MW	21.33 AW	47650 AAW	ALBLS	10//99-12//99
Police and Detectives	Decatur MSA, AL	S	19.53 MW	19.18 AW	40630 AAW	ALBLS	10//99-12//99
Police and Detectives	Dothan MSA, AL	S	16.80 MW	16.44 AW	34940 AAW	ALBLS	10//99-12//99
Police and Detectives	Huntsville MSA, AL	S	21.49 MW	19.79 AW	44690 AAW	ALBLS	10//99-12//99
Police and Detectives	Mobile MSA, AL	S	23.20 MW	21.75 AW	48260 AAW	ALBLS	10//99-12//99
Police and Detectives	Tuscaloosa MSA, AL	S	15.79 MW	15.40 AW	32840 AAW	ALBLS	10//99-12//99
Police and Detectives	Alaska	S	33.35 MW	31.53 AW	65580 AAW	AKBLS	10//99-12//99
Police and Detectives	Arizona	S	27.46 MW	27.03 AW	56220 AAW	AZBLS	10//99-12//99
Police and Detectives	Flagstaff MSA, AZ-UT	S	23.23 MW	23.20 AW	48330 AAW	AZBLS	10//99-12//99
Police and Detectives	Phoenix-Mesa MSA, AZ	S	28.12 MW	28.98 AW	58500 AAW	AZBLS	10//99-12//99
Police and Detectives	Tucson MSA, AZ	S	27.79 MW	28.24 AW	57810 AAW	AZBLS	10//99-12//99
Police and Detectives	Arkansas	S	15.56 MW	17.22 AW	35830 AAW	ARBLS	10//99-12//99
Police and Detectives	Fayetteville-Springdale-Rogers MSA, AR	S	17.95 MW	17.13 AW	37340 AAW	ARBLS	10//99-12//99
Police and Detectives	Little Rock-North Little Rock MSA, AR	S	23.20 MW	22.99 AW	48250 AAW	ARBLS	10//99-12//99
Police and Detectives	California	S	35.04 MW	34.30 AW	71350 AAW	CABLS	10//99-12//99
Police and Detectives	Bakersfield MSA, CA	S	30.29 MW	29.88 AW	63000 AAW	CABLS	10//99-12//99
Police and Detectives	Los Angeles-Long Beach PMSA, CA	S	34.74 MW	34.45 AW	72260 AAW	CABLS	10//99-12//99
Police and Detectives	Merced MSA, CA	S	26.80 MW	25.91 AW	55750 AAW	CABLS	10//99-12//99

AAW	Average annual wage	AOH	Average offered, high	ASH	Average starting, high
AE	Average entry wage	AOL	Average offered, low	ASL	Average starting, low
AEX	Average experienced wage	APH	Average pay, high range	AW	Average wage paid
AO	Average offered	APL	Average pay, low range	FQ	First quartile wage

H	Hourly	M	Monthly	S	Special: hourly and annual
HI	Highest wage paid	MTC	Median total compensation	TQ	Third quartile wage
HR	High end range	MW	Median wage paid	W	Weekly
LR	Low end range	SQ	Second quartile wage	Y	Yearly

First-Line Supervisor/Manager

Occupation/Type/Industry	Location	Per	Low	Mid	High	Source	Date
Police and Detectives	Oakland PMSA, CA	S	38.58 MW	39.53 AW	80250 AAW	CABLS	10//99-12//99
Police and Detectives	Orange County PMSA, CA	S	38.88 MW	39.69 AW	80870 AAW	CABLS	10//99-12//99
Police and Detectives	Redding MSA, CA	S	34.34 MW	34.36 AW	71420 AAW	CABLS	10//99-12//99
Police and Detectives	Riverside-San Bernardino PMSA, CA	S	32.74 MW	32.89 AW	68090 AAW	CABLS	10//99-12//99
Police and Detectives	Sacramento PMSA, CA	S	35.80 MW	37.44 AW	74470 AAW	CABLS	10//99-12//99
Police and Detectives	Salinas MSA, CA	S	27.18 MW	24.95 AW	56540 AAW	CABLS	10//99-12//99
Police and Detectives	San Diego MSA, CA	S	34.31 MW	36.10 AW	71360 AAW	CABLS	10//99-12//99
Police and Detectives	San Francisco PMSA, CA	S	39.20 MW	40.41 AW	81530 AAW	CABLS	10//99-12//99
Police and Detectives	San Jose PMSA, CA	S	33.83 MW	34.59 AW	70370 AAW	CABLS	10//99-12//99
Police and Detectives	San Luis Obispo-Atascadero-Paso Robles MSA, CA	S	28.11 MW	26.15 AW	58460 AAW	CABLS	10//99-12//99
Police and Detectives	Santa Barbara-Santa Maria-Lompoc MSA, CA	S	34.48 MW	35.17 AW	71720 AAW	CABLS	10//99-12//99
Police and Detectives	Santa Cruz-Watsonville PMSA, CA	S	33.91 MW	34.70 AW	70540 AAW	CABLS	10//99-12//99
Police and Detectives	Santa Rosa PMSA, CA	S	33.36 MW	34.38 AW	69390 AAW	CABLS	10//99-12//99
Police and Detectives	Stockton-Lodi MSA, CA	S	27.58 MW	26.82 AW	57370 AAW	CABLS	10//99-12//99
Police and Detectives	Vallejo-Fairfield-Napa PMSA, CA	S	34.63 MW	34.50 AW	72030 AAW	CABLS	10//99-12//99
Police and Detectives	Ventura PMSA, CA	S	32.29 MW	33.77 AW	67170 AAW	CABLS	10//99-12//99
Police and Detectives	Visalia-Tulare-Porterville MSA, CA	S	31.58 MW	31.27 AW	65690 AAW	CABLS	10//99-12//99
Police and Detectives	Yolo PMSA, CA	S	29.59 MW	33.07 AW	61550 AAW	CABLS	10//99-12//99
Police and Detectives	Yuba City MSA, CA	S	32.80 MW	33.24 AW	68220 AAW	CABLS	10//99-12//99
Police and Detectives	Colorado	S	28.66 MW	28.29 AW	58840 AAW	COBLS	10//99-12//99
Police and Detectives	Boulder-Longmont PMSA, CO	S	30.11 MW	31.63 AW	62630 AAW	COBLS	10//99-12//99
Police and Detectives	Colorado Springs MSA, CO	S	26.79 MW	26.26 AW	55730 AAW	COBLS	10//99-12//99
Police and Detectives	Denver PMSA, CO	S	30.45 MW	30.90 AW	63330 AAW	COBLS	10//99-12//99
Police and Detectives	Fort Collins-Loveland MSA, CO	S	31.06 MW	32.17 AW	64610 AAW	COBLS	10//99-12//99
Police and Detectives	Grand Junction MSA, CO	S	26.61 MW	25.60 AW	55340 AAW	COBLS	10//99-12//99
Police and Detectives	Pueblo MSA, CO	S	26.69 MW	25.17 AW	55510 AAW	COBLS	10//99-12//99
Police and Detectives	Connecticut	S	27.52 MW	27.34 AW	56860 AAW	CTBLS	10//99-12//99
Police and Detectives	Bridgeport PMSA, CT	S	28.24 MW	28.93 AW	58730 AAW	CTBLS	10//99-12//99
Police and Detectives	Danbury PMSA, CT	S	26.41 MW	26.26 AW	54940 AAW	CTBLS	10//99-12//99
Police and Detectives	Hartford MSA, CT	S	28.34 MW	28.05 AW	58940 AAW	CTBLS	10//99-12//99
Police and Detectives	New Haven-Meriden PMSA, CT	S	26.79 MW	26.02 AW	55720 AAW	CTBLS	10//99-12//99
Police and Detectives	New London-Norwich MSA, CT-RI	S	25.32 MW	24.89 AW	52660 AAW	CTBLS	10//99-12//99
Police and Detectives	Stamford-Norwalk PMSA, CT	S	26.28 MW	29.38 AW	54660 AAW	CTBLS	10//99-12//99
Police and Detectives	Delaware	S	27.62 MW	28.15 AW	58560 AAW	DEBLS	10//99-12//99
Police and Detectives	Wilmington-Newark PMSA, DE-MD	S	28.15 MW	27.19 AW	58560 AAW	DEBLS	10//99-12//99
Police and Detectives	Washington PMSA, DC-MD-VA-WV	S	32.24 MW	33.96 AW	67070 AAW	DCBLS	10//99-12//99
Police and Detectives	Florida	S	25.63 MW	26.55 AW	55220 AAW	FLBLS	10//99-12//99
Police and Detectives	Daytona Beach MSA, FL	S	21.19 MW	19.45 AW	44070 AAW	FLBLS	10//99-12//99
Police and Detectives	Fort Lauderdale PMSA, FL	S	28.60 MW	29.08 AW	59490 AAW	FLBLS	10//99-12//99
Police and Detectives	Fort Pierce-Port St. Lucie MSA, FL	S	24.71 MW	23.79 AW	51410 AAW	FLBLS	10//99-12//99
Police and Detectives	Fort Walton Beach MSA, FL	S	21.13 MW	21.57 AW	43960 AAW	FLBLS	10//99-12//99
Police and Detectives	Gainesville MSA, FL	S	23.44 MW	22.54 AW	48750 AAW	FLBLS	10//99-12//99
Police and Detectives	Jacksonville MSA, FL	S	24.76 MW	23.41 AW	51500 AAW	FLBLS	10//99-12//99
Police and Detectives	Lakeland-Winter Haven MSA, FL	S	20.84 MW	19.48 AW	43340 AAW	FLBLS	10//99-12//99
Police and Detectives	Melbourne-Titusville-Palm Bay MSA, FL	S	24.99 MW	24.27 AW	51980 AAW	FLBLS	10//99-12//99
Police and Detectives	Miami PMSA, FL	S	31.22 MW	33.09 AW	64940 AAW	FLBLS	10//99-12//99
Police and Detectives	Orlando MSA, FL	S	24.47 MW	23.24 AW	50910 AAW	FLBLS	10//99-12//99
Police and Detectives	Panama City MSA, FL	S	21.10 MW	19.20 AW	43880 AAW	FLBLS	10//99-12//99
Police and Detectives	Pensacola MSA, FL	S	23.16 MW	21.81 AW	48160 AAW	FLBLS	10//99-12//99
Police and Detectives	Sarasota-Bradenton MSA, FL	S	25.47 MW	24.90 AW	52980 AAW	FLBLS	10//99-12//99
Police and Detectives	Tampa-St. Petersburg-Clearwater MSA, FL	S	27.51 MW	27.81 AW	57230 AAW	FLBLS	10//99-12//99
Police and Detectives	West Palm Beach-Boca Raton MSA, FL	S	27.46 MW	27.61 AW	57120 AAW	FLBLS	10//99-12//99
Police and Detectives	Georgia	S	19.5 MW	20.58 AW	42800 AAW	GABLS	10//99-12//99
Police and Detectives	Atlanta MSA, GA	S	22.50 MW	22.22 AW	46810 AAW	GABLS	10//99-12//99
Police and Detectives	Augusta-Aiken MSA, GA-SC	S	18.76 MW	18.64 AW	39010 AAW	GABLS	10//99-12//99

Occupation/Type/Industry	Location	Per	Low	Mid	High	Source	Date
First-Line Supervisor/Manager							
Police and Detectives	Columbus MSA, GA-AL	S	20.39 MW	18.14 AW	42410 AAW	GABLS	10//99-12//99
Police and Detectives	Macon MSA, GA	S	18.29 MW	17.23 AW	38040 AAW	GABLS	10//99-12//99
Police and Detectives	Savannah MSA, GA	S	21.22 MW	21.50 AW	44130 AAW	GABLS	10//99-12//99
Police and Detectives	Idaho	S	18.37 MW	19.45 AW	40450 AAW	IDBLS	10//99-12//99
Police and Detectives	Illinois	S	21.04 MW	23.85 AW	49610 AAW	ILBLS	10//99-12//99
Police and Detectives	Bloomington-Normal MSA, IL	S	19.61 MW	17.81 AW	40780 AAW	ILBLS	10//99-12//99
Police and Detectives	Chicago PMSA, IL	S	26.18 MW	25.68 AW	54450 AAW	ILBLS	10//99-12//99
Police and Detectives	Rockford MSA, IL	S	19.76 MW	18.94 AW	41110 AAW	ILBLS	10//99-12//99
Police and Detectives	Springfield MSA, IL	S	18.83 MW	18.05 AW	39160 AAW	ILBLS	10//99-12//99
Police and Detectives	Indiana	S	20.6 MW	20.53 AW	42700 AAW	INBLS	10//99-12//99
Police and Detectives	Elkhart-Goshen MSA, IN	S	19.17 MW	18.89 AW	39880 AAW	INBLS	10//99-12//99
Police and Detectives	Evansville-Henderson MSA, IN-KY	S	20.50 MW	20.45 AW	42640 AAW	INBLS	10//99-12//99
Police and Detectives	Fort Wayne MSA, IN	S	20.54 MW	19.96 AW	42730 AAW	INBLS	10//99-12//99
Police and Detectives	Gary PMSA, IN	S	20.96 MW	20.30 AW	43600 AAW	INBLS	10//99-12//99
Police and Detectives	Indianapolis MSA, IN	S	22.14 MW	22.89 AW	46050 AAW	INBLS	10//99-12//99
Police and Detectives	Lafayette MSA, IN	S	18.35 MW	19.33 AW	38160 AAW	INBLS	10//99-12//99
Police and Detectives	South Bend MSA, IN	S	24.76 MW	23.24 AW	51500 AAW	INBLS	10//99-12//99
Police and Detectives	Iowa	S	20.49 MW	21.28 AW	44270 AAW	IABLS	10//99-12//99
Police and Detectives	Davenport-Moline-Rock Island MSA, IA-IL	S	21.97 MW	20.87 AW	45690 AAW	IABLS	10//99-12//99
Police and Detectives	Des Moines MSA, IA	S	25.78 MW	24.35 AW	53630 AAW	IABLS	10//99-12//99
Police and Detectives	Iowa City MSA, IA	S	25.58 MW	24.72 AW	53210 AAW	IABLS	10//99-12//99
Police and Detectives	Waterloo-Cedar Falls MSA, IA	S	19.92 MW	19.19 AW	41440 AAW	IABLS	10//99-12//99
Police and Detectives	Kansas	S	19.31 MW	20.24 AW	42100 AAW	KSBLS	10//99-12//99
Police and Detectives	Wichita MSA, KS	S	19.96 MW	19.67 AW	41520 AAW	KSBLS	10//99-12//99
Police and Detectives	Kentucky	S	18.28 MW	19.51 AW	40580 AAW	KYBLS	10//99-12//99
Police and Detectives	Lexington MSA, KY	S	21.19 MW	20.69 AW	44080 AAW	KYBLS	10//99-12//99
Police and Detectives	Louisville MSA, KY-IN	S	19.89 MW	18.39 AW	41360 AAW	KYBLS	10//99-12//99
Police and Detectives	Louisiana	S	16.68 MW	17.72 AW	36850 AAW	LABLS	10//99-12//99
Police and Detectives	Alexandria MSA, LA	S	20.54 MW	18.11 AW	42720 AAW	LABLS	10//99-12//99
Police and Detectives	Baton Rouge MSA, LA	S	19.30 MW	18.65 AW	40140 AAW	LABLS	10//99-12//99
Police and Detectives	Houma MSA, LA	S	16.29 MW	15.18 AW	33890 AAW	LABLS	10//99-12//99
Police and Detectives	Lafayette MSA, LA	S	16.11 MW	14.66 AW	33520 AAW	LABLS	10//99-12//99
Police and Detectives	Lake Charles MSA, LA	S	14.04 MW	13.17 AW	29210 AAW	LABLS	10//99-12//99
Police and Detectives	New Orleans MSA, LA	S	19.65 MW	16.69 AW	40870 AAW	LABLS	10//99-12//99
Police and Detectives	Shreveport-Bossier City MSA, LA	S	18.14 MW	15.59 AW	37720 AAW	LABLS	10//99-12//99
Police and Detectives	Maine	S	17.82 MW	18.78 AW	39060 AAW	MEBLS	10//99-12//99
Police and Detectives	Bangor MSA, ME	S	17.50 MW	16.38 AW	36410 AAW	MEBLS	10//99-12//99
Police and Detectives	Portland MSA, ME	S	20.03 MW	19.10 AW	41670 AAW	MEBLS	10//99-12//99
Police and Detectives	Maryland	S	21.13 MW	24.65 AW	51280 AAW	MDBLS	10//99-12//99
Police and Detectives	Baltimore PMSA, MD	S	23.55 MW	20.63 AW	48980 AAW	MDBLS	10//99-12//99
Police and Detectives	Massachusetts	S	25.8 MW	27.22 AW	56620 AAW	MABLS	10//99-12//99
Police and Detectives	Barnstable-Yarmouth MSA, MA	S	26.43 MW	26.93 AW	54970 AAW	MABLS	10//99-12//99
Police and Detectives	Boston PMSA, MA-NH	S	25.38 MW	24.31 AW	52780 AAW	MABLS	10//99-12//99
Police and Detectives	Brockton PMSA, MA	S	29.47 MW	28.73 AW	61300 AAW	MABLS	10//99-12//99
Police and Detectives	Lawrence PMSA, MA-NH	S	29.17 MW	29.74 AW	60670 AAW	MABLS	10//99-12//99
Police and Detectives	Lowell PMSA, MA-NH	S	29.03 MW	26.93 AW	60380 AAW	MABLS	10//99-12//99
Police and Detectives	New Bedford PMSA, MA	S	31.01 MW	31.65 AW	64510 AAW	MABLS	10//99-12//99
Police and Detectives	Pittsfield MSA, MA	S	29.84 MW	29.97 AW	62070 AAW	MABLS	10//99-12//99
Police and Detectives	Springfield MSA, MA	S	28.15 MW	27.39 AW	58550 AAW	MABLS	10//99-12//99
Police and Detectives	Worcester PMSA, MA-CT	S	28.24 MW	26.31 AW	58740 AAW	MABLS	10//99-12//99
Police and Detectives	Michigan	S	26.1 MW	26.34 AW	54780 AAW	MIBLS	10//99-12//99
Police and Detectives	Ann Arbor PMSA, MI	S	28.95 MW	29.91 AW	60220 AAW	MIBLS	10//99-12//99
Police and Detectives	Benton Harbor MSA, MI	S	23.63 MW	21.22 AW	49160 AAW	MIBLS	10//99-12//99
Police and Detectives	Detroit PMSA, MI	S	28.77 MW	29.29 AW	59850 AAW	MIBLS	10//99-12//99
Police and Detectives	Flint PMSA, MI	S	23.64 MW	22.27 AW	49180 AAW	MIBLS	10//99-12//99
Police and Detectives	Grand Rapids-Muskegon-Holland MSA, MI	S	25.64 MW	24.63 AW	53330 AAW	MIBLS	10//99-12//99
Police and Detectives	Kalamazoo-Battle Creek MSA, MI	S	21.60 MW	20.28 AW	44930 AAW	MIBLS	10//99-12//99
Police and Detectives	Lansing-East Lansing MSA, MI	S	25.95 MW	25.49 AW	53980 AAW	MIBLS	10//99-12//99
Police and Detectives	Saginaw-Bay City-Midland MSA, MI	S	24.39 MW	23.80 AW	50740 AAW	MIBLS	10//99-12//99
Police and Detectives	Minnesota	S	25.73 MW	25.79 AW	53650 AAW	MNBLS	10//99-12//99
Police and Detectives	Duluth-Superior MSA, MN-WI	S	25.25 MW	24.93 AW	52510 AAW	MNBLS	10//99-12//99
Police and Detectives	Minneapolis-St. Paul MSA, MN-WI	S	28.59 MW	29.27 AW	59470 AAW	MNBLS	10//99-12//99
Police and Detectives	Mississippi	S	15.62 MW	17.54 AW	36490 AAW	MSBLS	10//99-12//99

Occupation/Type/Industry	Location	Per	Low	Mid	High	Source	Date
First-Line Supervisor/Manager							
Police and Detectives	Biloxi-Gulfport-Pascagoula MSA, MS	S	18.94 mw	16.65 aw	39390 aaw	MSBLS	10//99-12//99
Police and Detectives	Hattiesburg MSA, MS	S	14.21 mw	14.02 aw	29560 aaw	MSBLS	10//99-12//99
Police and Detectives	Jackson MSA, MS	S	23.06 mw	22.57 aw	47970 aaw	MSBLS	10//99-12//99
Police and Detectives	Missouri	S	19.58 mw	20.40 aw	42420 aaw	MOBLS	10//99-12//99
Police and Detectives	Kansas City MSA, MO-KS	S	23.57 mw	23.90 aw	49020 aaw	MOBLS	10//99-12//99
Police and Detectives	St. Louis MSA, MO-IL	S	19.72 mw	19.10 aw	41020 aaw	MOBLS	10//99-12//99
Police and Detectives	Montana	S	18.73 mw	20.06 aw	41730 aaw	MTBLS	10//99-12//99
Police and Detectives	Nebraska	S	18.88 mw	19.77 aw	41130 aaw	NEBLS	10//99-12//99
Police and Detectives	Omaha MSA, NE-IA	S	21.88 mw	20.37 aw	45510 aaw	NEBLS	10//99-12//99
Police and Detectives	Nevada	S	30.29 mw	30.11 aw	62630 aaw	NVBLS	10//99-12//99
Police and Detectives	New Hampshire	S	20.9 mw	20.60 aw	42840 aaw	NHBLS	10//99-12//99
Police and Detectives	Manchester PMSA, NH	S	24.31 mw	23.99 aw	50570 aaw	NHBLS	10//99-12//99
Police and Detectives	Portsmouth-Rochester PMSA, NH-ME	S	23.60 mw	23.04 aw	49090 aaw	NHBLS	10//99-12//99
Police and Detectives	New Jersey	S	35.24 mw	33.89 aw	70490 aaw	NJBLS	10//99-12//99
Police and Detectives	Atlantic-Cape May PMSA, NJ	S	30.93 mw	31.59 aw	64340 aaw	NJBLS	10//99-12//99
Police and Detectives	Bergen-Passaic PMSA, NJ	S	37.10 mw	39.27 aw	77170 aaw	NJBLS	10//99-12//99
Police and Detectives	Jersey City PMSA, NJ	S	38.12 mw	39.17 aw	79290 aaw	NJBLS	10//99-12//99
Police and Detectives	Middlesex-Somerset-Hunterdon PMSA, NJ	S	32.90 mw	35.19 aw	68440 aaw	NJBLS	10//99-12//99
Police and Detectives	Monmouth-Ocean PMSA, NJ	S	36.68 mw	35.90 aw	76290 aaw	NJBLS	10//99-12//99
Police and Detectives	Newark PMSA, NJ	S	31.88 mw	35.03 aw	66320 aaw	NJBLS	10//99-12//99
Police and Detectives	Trenton PMSA, NJ	S	36.23 mw	37.59 aw	75350 aaw	NJBLS	10//99-12//99
Police and Detectives	Vineland-Millville-Bridgeton PMSA, NJ	S	34.70 mw	35.78 aw	72170 aaw	NJBLS	10//99-12//99
Police and Detectives	New Mexico	S	19.6 mw	20.35 aw	42320 aaw	NMBLS	10//99-12//99
Police and Detectives	Albuquerque MSA, NM	S	20.37 mw	18.94 aw	42360 aaw	NMBLS	10//99-12//99
Police and Detectives	Las Cruces MSA, NM	S	22.38 mw	21.15 aw	46550 aaw	NMBLS	10//99-12//99
Police and Detectives	New York	S	31.21 mw	30.85 aw	64160 aaw	NYBLS	10//99-12//99
Police and Detectives	Binghamton MSA, NY	S	22.64 mw	22.83 aw	47080 aaw	NYBLS	10//99-12//99
Police and Detectives	Buffalo-Niagara Falls MSA, NY	S	27.34 mw	26.36 aw	56870 aaw	NYBLS	10//99-12//99
Police and Detectives	Dutchess County PMSA, NY	S	28.00 mw	29.80 aw	58250 aaw	NYBLS	10//99-12//99
Police and Detectives	Glens Falls MSA, NY	S	20.89 mw	19.81 aw	43460 aaw	NYBLS	10//99-12//99
Police and Detectives	Jamestown MSA, NY	S	24.15 mw	24.14 aw	50230 aaw	NYBLS	10//99-12//99
Police and Detectives	Newburgh PMSA, NY-PA	S	25.44 mw	25.98 aw	52920 aaw	NYBLS	10//99-12//99
Police and Detectives	Rochester MSA, NY	S	26.48 mw	26.43 aw	55070 aaw	NYBLS	10//99-12//99
Police and Detectives	Syracuse MSA, NY	S	21.93 mw	21.94 aw	45610 aaw	NYBLS	10//99-12//99
Police and Detectives	Utica-Rome MSA, NY	S	21.15 mw	19.56 aw	43990 aaw	NYBLS	10//99-12//99
Police and Detectives	North Carolina	S	19.58 mw	20.43 aw	42500 aaw	NCBLS	10//99-12//99
Police and Detectives	Charlotte-Gastonia-Rock Hill MSA, NC-SC	S	23.32 mw	22.73 aw	48510 aaw	NCBLS	10//99-12//99
Police and Detectives	Goldsboro MSA, NC	S	17.07 mw	16.87 aw	35500 aaw	NCBLS	10//99-12//99
Police and Detectives	Greensboro--Winston-Salem--High Point MSA, NC	S	22.51 mw	22.19 aw	46810 aaw	NCBLS	10//99-12//99
Police and Detectives	Hickory-Morganton-Lenoir MSA, NC	S	18.29 mw	17.28 aw	38040 aaw	NCBLS	10//99-12//99
Police and Detectives	Jacksonville MSA, NC	S	21.94 mw	21.14 aw	45640 aaw	NCBLS	10//99-12//99
Police and Detectives	Raleigh-Durham-Chapel Hill MSA, NC	S	22.61 mw	22.47 aw	47020 aaw	NCBLS	10//99-12//99
Police and Detectives	Rocky Mount MSA, NC	S	19.11 mw	17.98 aw	39760 aaw	NCBLS	10//99-12//99
Police and Detectives	Wilmington MSA, NC	S	21.39 mw	19.62 aw	44490 aaw	NCBLS	10//99-12//99
Police and Detectives	North Dakota	S	18.89 mw	19.83 aw	41250 aaw	NDBLS	10//99-12//99
Police and Detectives	Fargo-Moorhead MSA, ND-MN	S	21.50 mw	19.70 aw	44710 aaw	NDBLS	10//99-12//99
Police and Detectives	Grand Forks MSA, ND-MN	S	21.65 mw	19.55 aw	45030 aaw	NDBLS	10//99-12//99
Police and Detectives	Ohio	S	23.72 mw	23.93 aw	49780 aaw	OHBLS	10//99-12//99
Police and Detectives	Akron PMSA, OH	S	29.46 mw	30.55 aw	61270 aaw	OHBLS	10//99-12//99
Police and Detectives	Canton-Massillon MSA, OH	S	22.49 mw	23.20 aw	46770 aaw	OHBLS	10//99-12//99
Police and Detectives	Cincinnati PMSA, OH-KY-IN	S	23.50 mw	23.03 aw	48870 aaw	OHBLS	10//99-12//99
Police and Detectives	Cleveland-Lorain-Elyria PMSA, OH	S	25.97 mw	25.33 aw	54030 aaw	OHBLS	10//99-12//99
Police and Detectives	Dayton-Springfield MSA, OH	S	25.77 mw	25.87 aw	53590 aaw	OHBLS	10//99-12//99
Police and Detectives	Hamilton-Middletown PMSA, OH	S	25.92 mw	25.83 aw	53920 aaw	OHBLS	10//99-12//99
Police and Detectives	Lima MSA, OH	S	19.62 mw	20.05 aw	40800 aaw	OHBLS	10//99-12//99
Police and Detectives	Mansfield MSA, OH	S	21.02 mw	20.62 aw	43720 aaw	OHBLS	10//99-12//99
Police and Detectives	Toledo MSA, OH	S	23.35 mw	22.55 aw	48560 aaw	OHBLS	10//99-12//99
Police and Detectives	Youngstown-Warren MSA, OH	S	21.64 mw	21.04 aw	45020 aaw	OHBLS	10//99-12//99
Police and Detectives	Oklahoma	S	17.31 mw	17.69 aw	36800 aaw	OKBLS	10//99-12//99

AAW Average annual wage	**AOH** Average offered, high	**ASH** Average starting, high	**H** Hourly	**M** Monthly	**S** Special: hourly and annual
AE Average entry wage	**AOL** Average offered, low	**ASL** Average starting, low	**HI** Highest wage paid	**MTC** Median total compensation	**TQ** Third quartile wage
AEX Average experienced wage	**APH** Average pay, high range	**AW** Average wage paid	**HR** High end range	**MW** Median wage paid	**W** Weekly
AO Average offered	**APL** Average pay, low range	**FQ** First quartile wage	**LR** Low end range	**SQ** Second quartile wage	**Y** Yearly

Occupation/Type/Industry	Location	Per	Low	Mid	High	Source	Date
First-Line Supervisor/Manager							
Police and Detectives	Oklahoma City MSA, OK	S	22.58 MW	22.12 AW	46970 AAW	OKBLS	10//99-12//99
Police and Detectives	Tulsa MSA, OK	S	17.24 MW	18.13 AW	35870 AAW	OKBLS	10//99-12//99
Police and Detectives	Oregon	S	29.17 MW	28.52 AW	59330 AAW	ORBLS	10//99-12//99
Police and Detectives	Medford-Ashland MSA, OR	S	25.91 MW	25.24 AW	53890 AAW	ORBLS	10//99-12//99
Police and Detectives	Portland-Vancouver PMSA, OR-WA	S	31.84 MW	34.11 AW	66220 AAW	ORBLS	10//99-12//99
Police and Detectives	Salem PMSA, OR	S	25.95 MW	24.53 AW	53980 AAW	ORBLS	10//99-12//99
Police and Detectives	Pennsylvania	S	25.71 MW	26.49 AW	55110 AAW	PABLS	10//99-12//99
Police and Detectives	Allentown-Bethlehem-Easton MSA, PA	S	22.85 MW	22.75 AW	47530 AAW	PABLS	10//99-12//99
Police and Detectives	Altoona MSA, PA	S	20.29 MW	18.76 AW	42210 AAW	PABLS	10//99-12//99
Police and Detectives	Harrisburg-Lebanon-Carlisle MSA, PA	S	28.35 MW	27.44 AW	58960 AAW	PABLS	10//99-12//99
Police and Detectives	Johnstown MSA, PA	S	15.36 MW	14.50 AW	31940 AAW	PABLS	10//99-12//99
Police and Detectives	Lancaster MSA, PA	S	25.60 MW	24.23 AW	53240 AAW	PABLS	10//99-12//99
Police and Detectives	Philadelphia PMSA, PA-NJ	S	30.80 MW	31.90 AW	64060 AAW	PABLS	10//99-12//99
Police and Detectives	Pittsburgh MSA, PA	S	25.08 MW	24.31 AW	52160 AAW	PABLS	10//99-12//99
Police and Detectives	Reading MSA, PA	S	22.67 MW	22.28 AW	47150 AAW	PABLS	10//99-12//99
Police and Detectives	Scranton--Wilkes-Barre--Hazleton MSA, PA	S	20.14 MW	18.78 AW	41900 AAW	PABLS	10//99-12//99
Police and Detectives	Rhode Island	S	24.29 MW	25.23 AW	52470 AAW	RIBLS	10//99-12//99
Police and Detectives	Providence-Fall River-Warwick MSA, RI-MA	S	25.25 MW	24.27 AW	52510 AAW	RIBLS	10//99-12//99
Police and Detectives	South Carolina	S	16.75 MW	18.07 AW	37570 AAW	SCBLS	10//99-12//99
Police and Detectives	Charleston-North Charleston MSA, SC	S	21.73 MW	21.52 AW	45200 AAW	SCBLS	10//99-12//99
Police and Detectives	Columbia MSA, SC	S	18.62 MW	17.03 AW	38730 AAW	SCBLS	10//99-12//99
Police and Detectives	Greenville-Spartanburg-Anderson MSA, SC	S	16.63 MW	14.99 AW	34580 AAW	SCBLS	10//99-12//99
Police and Detectives	Myrtle Beach MSA, SC	S	18.93 MW	18.70 AW	39380 AAW	SCBLS	10//99-12//99
Police and Detectives	South Dakota	S	18.91 MW	19.71 AW	41000 AAW	SDBLS	10//99-12//99
Police and Detectives	Sioux Falls MSA, SD	S	23.22 MW	22.32 AW	48290 AAW	SDBLS	10//99-12//99
Police and Detectives	Tennessee	S	19.98 MW	20.10 AW	41810 AAW	TNBLS	10//99-12//99
Police and Detectives	Chattanooga MSA, TN-GA	S	20.60 MW	19.28 AW	42840 AAW	TNBLS	10//99-12//99
Police and Detectives	Clarksville-Hopkinsville MSA, TN-KY	S	16.20 MW	15.25 AW	33700 AAW	TNBLS	10//99-12//99
Police and Detectives	Johnson City-Kingsport-Bristol MSA, TN-VA	S	19.62 MW	19.19 AW	40820 AAW	TNBLS	10//99-12//99
Police and Detectives	Knoxville MSA, TN	S	20.21 MW	19.27 AW	42040 AAW	TNBLS	10//99-12//99
Police and Detectives	Memphis MSA, TN-AR-MS	S	22.72 MW	23.36 AW	47250 AAW	MSBLS	10//99-12//99
Police and Detectives	Texas	S	24.14 MW	24.51 AW	50970 AAW	TXBLS	10//99-12//99
Police and Detectives	Amarillo MSA, TX	S	24.59 MW	24.39 AW	51140 AAW	TXBLS	10//99-12//99
Police and Detectives	Austin-San Marcos MSA, TX	S	27.16 MW	28.74 AW	56490 AAW	TXBLS	10//99-12//99
Police and Detectives	Beaumont-Port Arthur MSA, TX	S	19.27 MW	18.83 AW	40070 AAW	TXBLS	10//99-12//99
Police and Detectives	Brazoria PMSA, TX	S	19.14 MW	18.99 AW	39800 AAW	TXBLS	10//99-12//99
Police and Detectives	Bryan-College Station MSA, TX	S	23.55 MW	23.13 AW	48990 AAW	TXBLS	10//99-12//99
Police and Detectives	Corpus Christi MSA, TX	S	26.22 MW	27.70 AW	54530 AAW	TXBLS	10//99-12//99
Police and Detectives	Dallas PMSA, TX	S	27.19 MW	28.19 AW	56550 AAW	TXBLS	10//99-12//99
Police and Detectives	El Paso MSA, TX	S	24.68 MW	21.13 AW	51340 AAW	TXBLS	10//99-12//99
Police and Detectives	Fort Worth-Arlington PMSA, TX	S	24.66 MW	24.37 AW	51300 AAW	TXBLS	10//99-12//99
Police and Detectives	Galveston-Texas City PMSA, TX	S	20.48 MW	16.67 AW	42590 AAW	TXBLS	10//99-12//99
Police and Detectives	Houston PMSA, TX	S	28.67 MW	28.07 AW	59640 AAW	TXBLS	10//99-12//99
Police and Detectives	Killeen-Temple MSA, TX	S	16.51 MW	14.90 AW	34340 AAW	TXBLS	10//99-12//99
Police and Detectives	Longview-Marshall MSA, TX	S	18.39 MW	18.31 AW	38240 AAW	TXBLS	10//99-12//99
Police and Detectives	Lubbock MSA, TX	S	23.43 MW	24.12 AW	48720 AAW	TXBLS	10//99-12//99
Police and Detectives	McAllen-Edinburg-Mission MSA, TX	S	22.71 MW	21.17 AW	47230 AAW	TXBLS	10//99-12//99
Police and Detectives	Odessa-Midland MSA, TX	S	22.66 MW	20.92 AW	47140 AAW	TXBLS	10//99-12//99
Police and Detectives	San Antonio MSA, TX	S	26.79 MW	26.69 AW	55710 AAW	TXBLS	10//99-12//99
Police and Detectives	Texarkana MSA, TX-Texarkana, AR	S	19.28 MW	18.95 AW	40090 AAW	TXBLS	10//99-12//99
Police and Detectives	Tyler MSA, TX	S	19.25 MW	19.22 AW	40030 AAW	TXBLS	10//99-12//99
Police and Detectives	Waco MSA, TX	S	19.92 MW	19.14 AW	41430 AAW	TXBLS	10//99-12//99
Police and Detectives	Wichita Falls MSA, TX	S	17.00 MW	16.11 AW	35360 AAW	TXBLS	10//99-12//99
Police and Detectives	Utah	S	23.66 MW	23.74 AW	49380 AAW	UTBLS	10//99-12//99
Police and Detectives	Provo-Orem MSA, UT	S	22.78 MW	23.08 AW	47390 AAW	UTBLS	10//99-12//99

AAW	Average annual wage	AOH	Average offered, high	ASH	Average starting, high	H	Hourly
AE	Average entry wage	AOL	Average offered, low	ASL	Average starting, low	HI	Highest wage paid
AEX	Average experienced wage	APH	Average pay, high range	AW	Average wage paid	HR	High end range
AO	Average offered	APL	Average pay, low range	FQ	First quartile wage	LR	Low end range

M	Monthly	S	Special: hourly and annual
MTC	Median total compensation	TQ	Third quartile wage
MW	Median wage paid	W	Weekly
SQ	Second quartile wage	Y	Yearly

Occupation/Type/Industry	Location	Per	Low	Mid	High	Source	Date
First-Line Supervisor/Manager							
Police and Detectives	Salt Lake City-Ogden MSA, UT	S	24.57 MW	24.29 AW	51100 AAW	UTBLS	10//99-12//99
Police and Detectives	Vermont	S	23.69 MW	25.02 AW	52040 AAW	VTBLS	10//99-12//99
Police and Detectives	Burlington MSA, VT	S	20.87 MW	21.27 AW	43410 AAW	VTBLS	10//99-12//99
Police and Detectives	Virginia	S	24.71 MW	26.37 AW	54850 AAW	VABLS	10//99-12//99
Police and Detectives	Danville MSA, VA	S	28.68 MW	30.34 AW	59650 AAW	VABLS	10//99-12//99
Police and Detectives	Lynchburg MSA, VA	S	19.99 MW	17.84 AW	41580 AAW	VABLS	10//99-12//99
Police and Detectives	Norfolk-Virginia Beach-Newport News MSA, VA-NC	S	23.59 MW	22.83 AW	49070 AAW	VABLS	10//99-12//99
Police and Detectives	Richmond-Petersburg MSA, VA	S	27.41 MW	27.02 AW	57020 AAW	VABLS	10//99-12//99
Police and Detectives	Roanoke MSA, VA	S	23.32 MW	22.58 AW	48510 AAW	VABLS	10//99-12//99
Police and Detectives	Washington	S	31.02 MW	29.54 AW	61440 AAW	WABLS	10//99-12//99
Police and Detectives	Bellingham MSA, WA	S	29.81 MW	31.56 AW	62010 AAW	WABLS	10//99-12//99
Police and Detectives	Bremerton PMSA, WA	S	25.19 MW	24.89 AW	52380 AAW	WABLS	10//99-12//99
Police and Detectives	Olympia PMSA, WA	S	30.10 MW	32.09 AW	62600 AAW	WABLS	10//99-12//99
Police and Detectives	Seattle-Bellevue-Everett PMSA, WA	S	31.57 MW	32.15 AW	65660 AAW	WABLS	10//99-12//99
Police and Detectives	Tacoma PMSA, WA	S	27.79 MW	31.09 AW	57800 AAW	WABLS	10//99-12//99
Police and Detectives	Yakima MSA, WA	S	27.97 MW	29.18 AW	58180 AAW	WABLS	10//99-12//99
Police and Detectives	West Virginia	S	13.67 MW	15.70 AW	32650 AAW	WVBLS	10//99-12//99
Police and Detectives	Charleston MSA, WV	S	23.50 MW	18.27 AW	48880 AAW	WVBLS	10//99-12//99
Police and Detectives	Huntington-Ashland MSA, WV-KY-OH	S	16.33 MW	15.35 AW	33960 AAW	WVBLS	10//99-12//99
Police and Detectives	Parkersburg-Marietta MSA, WV-OH	S	16.51 MW	15.79 AW	34350 AAW	WVBLS	10//99-12//99
Police and Detectives	Wheeling MSA, WV-OH	S	18.06 MW	16.01 AW	37560 AAW	WVBLS	10//99-12//99
Police and Detectives	Wisconsin	S	22.9 MW	23.03 AW	47900 AAW	WIBLS	10//99-12//99
Police and Detectives	Appleton-Oshkosh-Neenah MSA, WI	S	23.35 MW	23.15 AW	48560 AAW	WIBLS	10//99-12//99
Police and Detectives	Eau Claire MSA, WI	S	20.87 MW	20.60 AW	43400 AAW	WIBLS	10//99-12//99
Police and Detectives	Green Bay MSA, WI	S	21.18 MW	20.52 AW	44060 AAW	WIBLS	10//99-12//99
Police and Detectives	Kenosha PMSA, WI	S	23.62 MW	23.87 AW	49120 AAW	WIBLS	10//99-12//99
Police and Detectives	La Crosse MSA, WI-MN	S	24.04 MW	24.08 AW	50010 AAW	WIBLS	10//99-12//99
Police and Detectives	Madison MSA, WI	S	26.24 MW	24.73 AW	54590 AAW	WIBLS	10//99-12//99
Police and Detectives	Milwaukee-Waukesha PMSA, WI	S	27.28 MW	26.72 AW	56750 AAW	WIBLS	10//99-12//99
Police and Detectives	Racine PMSA, WI	S	23.60 MW	22.99 AW	49090 AAW	WIBLS	10//99-12//99
Police and Detectives	Wausau MSA, WI	S	21.08 MW	20.71 AW	43850 AAW	WIBLS	10//99-12//99
Police and Detectives	Wyoming	S	18.78 MW	19.20 AW	39930 AAW	WYBLS	10//99-12//99
Police and Detectives	Cheyenne MSA, WY	S	19.25 MW	18.44 AW	40040 AAW	WYBLS	10//99-12//99
Police and Detectives	San Juan-Bayamon PMSA, PR	S	10.29 MW	10.04 AW	21410 AAW	PRBLS	10//99-12//99
Production and Operating Workers	Alabama	S	17.41 MW	18.86 AW	39220 AAW	ALBLS	10//99-12//99
Production and Operating Workers	Anniston MSA, AL	S	17.95 MW	18.08 AW	37340 AAW	ALBLS	10//99-12//99
Production and Operating Workers	Auburn-Opelika MSA, AL	S	14.37 MW	13.15 AW	29890 AAW	ALBLS	10//99-12//99
Production and Operating Workers	Birmingham MSA, AL	S	20.19 MW	19.55 AW	42000 AAW	ALBLS	10//99-12//99
Production and Operating Workers	Decatur MSA, AL	S	19.92 MW	21.20 AW	41430 AAW	ALBLS	10//99-12//99
Production and Operating Workers	Dothan MSA, AL	S	14.22 MW	12.65 AW	29570 AAW	ALBLS	10//99-12//99
Production and Operating Workers	Florence MSA, AL	S	15.03 MW	14.02 AW	31260 AAW	ALBLS	10//99-12//99
Production and Operating Workers	Gadsden MSA, AL	S	15.67 MW	14.79 AW	32600 AAW	ALBLS	10//99-12//99
Production and Operating Workers	Huntsville MSA, AL	S	21.31 MW	20.91 AW	44330 AAW	ALBLS	10//99-12//99
Production and Operating Workers	Mobile MSA, AL	S	21.28 MW	20.34 AW	44270 AAW	ALBLS	10//99-12//99
Production and Operating Workers	Montgomery MSA, AL	S	15.19 MW	13.62 AW	31590 AAW	ALBLS	10//99-12//99
Production and Operating Workers	Tuscaloosa MSA, AL	S	18.58 MW	17.77 AW	38650 AAW	ALBLS	10//99-12//99
Production and Operating Workers	Alaska	S	32.63 MW	31.75 AW	66040 AAW	AKBLS	10//99-12//99
Production and Operating Workers	Anchorage MSA, AK	S	26.36 MW	25.99 AW	54820 AAW	AKBLS	10//99-12//99
Production and Operating Workers	Arizona	S	17.14 MW	18.63 AW	38740 AAW	AZBLS	10//99-12//99
Production and Operating Workers	Flagstaff MSA, AZ-UT	S	14.12 MW	10.80 AW	29380 AAW	AZBLS	10//99-12//99
Production and Operating Workers	Phoenix-Mesa MSA, AZ	S	18.89 MW	17.52 AW	39290 AAW	AZBLS	10//99-12//99
Production and Operating Workers	Tucson MSA, AZ	S	16.96 MW	15.54 AW	35280 AAW	AZBLS	10//99-12//99
Production and Operating Workers	Yuma MSA, AZ	S	20.12 MW	16.76 AW	41850 AAW	AZBLS	10//99-12//99
Production and Operating Workers	Arkansas	S	14.46 MW	15.92 AW	33120 AAW	ARBLS	10//99-12//99
Production and Operating Workers	Fayetteville-Springdale-Rogers MSA, AR	S	13.42 MW	12.06 AW	27910 AAW	ARBLS	10//99-12//99
Production and Operating Workers	Fort Smith MSA, AR-OK	S	14.77 MW	12.98 AW	30720 AAW	ARBLS	10//99-12//99
Production and Operating Workers	Jonesboro MSA, AR	S	18.07 MW	17.54 AW	37580 AAW	ARBLS	10//99-12//99
Production and Operating Workers	Little Rock-North Little Rock MSA, AR	S	17.64 MW	16.78 AW	36690 AAW	ARBLS	10//99-12//99
Production and Operating Workers	Pine Bluff MSA, AR	S	17.19 MW	15.60 AW	35750 AAW	ARBLS	10//99-12//99
Production and Operating Workers	California	S	19.25 MW	20.70 AW	43050 AAW	CABLS	10//99-12//99

AAW Average annual wage	**AOH** Average offered, high	**ASH** Average starting, high	**H** Hourly	**M** Monthly	**S** Special: hourly and annual
AE Average entry wage	**AOL** Average offered, low	**ASL** Average starting, low	**HI** Highest wage paid	**MTC** Median total compensation	**TQ** Third quartile wage
AEX Average experienced wage	**APH** Average pay, high range	**AW** Average wage paid	**HR** High end range	**MW** Median wage paid	**W** Weekly
AO Average offered	**APL** Average pay, low range	**FQ** First quartile wage	**LR** Low end range	**SQ** Second quartile wage	**Y** Yearly

Occupation/Type/Industry	Location	Per	Low	Mid	High	Source	Date
First-Line Supervisor/Manager							
Production and Operating Workers	Bakersfield MSA, CA	S	23.37 MW	22.11 AW	48610 AAW	CABLS	10//99-12//99
Production and Operating Workers	Chico-Paradise MSA, CA	S	17.68 MW	15.90 AW	36770 AAW	CABLS	10//99-12//99
Production and Operating Workers	Fresno MSA, CA	S	18.16 MW	16.89 AW	37780 AAW	CABLS	10//99-12//99
Production and Operating Workers	Los Angeles-Long Beach PMSA, CA	S	19.87 MW	18.52 AW	41330 AAW	CABLS	10//99-12//99
Production and Operating Workers	Merced MSA, CA	S	18.85 MW	18.19 AW	39210 AAW	CABLS	10//99-12//99
Production and Operating Workers	Modesto MSA, CA	S	19.76 MW	16.94 AW	41110 AAW	CABLS	10//99-12//99
Production and Operating Workers	Oakland PMSA, CA	S	22.72 MW	22.48 AW	47250 AAW	CABLS	10//99-12//99
Production and Operating Workers	Orange County PMSA, CA	S	20.44 MW	18.98 AW	42510 AAW	CABLS	10//99-12//99
Production and Operating Workers	Redding MSA, CA	S	16.07 MW	15.83 AW	33430 AAW	CABLS	10//99-12//99
Production and Operating Workers	Riverside-San Bernardino PMSA, CA	S	18.89 MW	16.89 AW	39300 AAW	CABLS	10//99-12//99
Production and Operating Workers	Sacramento PMSA, CA	S	19.69 MW	18.36 AW	40950 AAW	CABLS	10//99-12//99
Production and Operating Workers	Salinas MSA, CA	S	16.69 MW	13.46 AW	34720 AAW	CABLS	10//99-12//99
Production and Operating Workers	San Diego MSA, CA	S	21.33 MW	19.41 AW	44370 AAW	CABLS	10//99-12//99
Production and Operating Workers	San Francisco PMSA, CA	S	23.05 MW	20.09 AW	47950 AAW	CABLS	10//99-12//99
Production and Operating Workers	San Jose PMSA, CA	S	25.69 MW	24.31 AW	53440 AAW	CABLS	10//99-12//99
Production and Operating Workers	San Luis Obispo-Atascadero-Paso Robles MSA, CA	S	20.62 MW	18.15 AW	42890 AAW	CABLS	10//99-12//99
Production and Operating Workers	Santa Barbara-Santa Maria-Lompoc MSA, CA	S	19.77 MW	18.81 AW	41120 AAW	CABLS	10//99-12//99
Production and Operating Workers	Santa Cruz-Watsonville PMSA, CA	S	17.16 MW	14.63 AW	35690 AAW	CABLS	10//99-12//99
Production and Operating Workers	Santa Rosa PMSA, CA	S	19.83 MW	18.74 AW	41240 AAW	CABLS	10//99-12//99
Production and Operating Workers	Stockton-Lodi MSA, CA	S	20.60 MW	19.44 AW	42850 AAW	CABLS	10//99-12//99
Production and Operating Workers	Vallejo-Fairfield-Napa PMSA, CA	S	18.67 MW	17.67 AW	38840 AAW	CABLS	10//99-12//99
Production and Operating Workers	Ventura PMSA, CA	S	19.09 MW	18.53 AW	39710 AAW	CABLS	10//99-12//99
Production and Operating Workers	Visalia-Tulare-Porterville MSA, CA	S	17.59 MW	17.56 AW	36590 AAW	CABLS	10//99-12//99
Production and Operating Workers	Yolo PMSA, CA	S	20.68 MW	19.69 AW	43020 AAW	CABLS	10//99-12//99
Production and Operating Workers	Yuba City MSA, CA	S	14.36 MW	12.94 AW	29880 AAW	CABLS	10//99-12//99
Production and Operating Workers	Colorado	S	18.71 MW	19.36 AW	40270 AAW	COBLS	10//99-12//99
Production and Operating Workers	Boulder-Longmont PMSA, CO	S	21.33 MW	20.05 AW	44370 AAW	COBLS	10//99-12//99
Production and Operating Workers	Colorado Springs MSA, CO	S	19.26 MW	18.23 AW	40070 AAW	COBLS	10//99-12//99
Production and Operating Workers	Denver PMSA, CO	S	19.07 MW	18.51 AW	39660 AAW	COBLS	10//99-12//99
Production and Operating Workers	Fort Collins-Loveland MSA, CO	S	18.39 MW	18.49 AW	38260 AAW	COBLS	10//99-12//99
Production and Operating Workers	Grand Junction MSA, CO	S	20.48 MW	20.00 AW	42610 AAW	COBLS	10//99-12//99
Production and Operating Workers	Greeley PMSA, CO	S	19.92 MW	19.26 AW	41440 AAW	COBLS	10//99-12//99
Production and Operating Workers	Pueblo MSA, CO	S	18.41 MW	17.69 AW	38300 AAW	COBLS	10//99-12//99
Production and Operating Workers	Connecticut	S	21.41 MW	23.05 AW	47950 AAW	CTBLS	10//99-12//99
Production and Operating Workers	Bridgeport PMSA, CT	S	22.92 MW	21.82 AW	47670 AAW	CTBLS	10//99-12//99
Production and Operating Workers	Danbury PMSA, CT	HR	23.24 MW	21.34 AW	48350 AAW	CTBLS	10//99-12//99
Production and Operating Workers	Hartford MSA, CT	S	23.88 MW	22.83 AW	49670 AAW	CTBLS	10//99-12//99
Production and Operating Workers	New Haven-Meriden PMSA, CT	S	23.04 MW	21.48 AW	47920 AAW	CTBLS	10//99-12//99
Production and Operating Workers	New London-Norwich MSA, CT-RI	S	20.84 MW	19.96 AW	43350 AAW	CTBLS	10//99-12//99
Production and Operating Workers	Stamford-Norwalk PMSA, CT	S	24.38 MW	22.50 AW	50720 AAW	CTBLS	10//99-12//99
Production and Operating Workers	Waterbury PMSA, CT	S	21.59 MW	19.54 AW	44910 AAW	CTBLS	10//99-12//99
Production and Operating Workers	Delaware	S	21.15 MW	23.23 AW	48310 AAW	DEBLS	10//99-12//99
Production and Operating Workers	Dover MSA, DE	S	15.77 MW	15.19 AW	32800 AAW	DEBLS	10//99-12//99
Production and Operating Workers	Wilmington-Newark PMSA, DE-MD	S	26.71 MW	25.85 AW	55570 AAW	DEBLS	10//99-12//99
Production and Operating Workers	District of Columbia	S	22.65 MW	24.11 AW	50150 AAW	DCBLS	10//99-12//99
Production and Operating Workers	Washington PMSA, DC-MD-VA-WV	S	20.73 MW	19.47 AW	43110 AAW	DCBLS	10//99-12//99
Production and Operating Workers	Florida	S	16.83 MW	18.38 AW	38220 AAW	FLBLS	10//99-12//99
Production and Operating Workers	Daytona Beach MSA, FL	S	15.38 MW	14.01 AW	32000 AAW	FLBLS	10//99-12//99
Production and Operating Workers	Fort Lauderdale PMSA, FL	S	17.68 MW	16.19 AW	36780 AAW	FLBLS	10//99-12//99
Production and Operating Workers	Fort Myers-Cape Coral MSA, FL	S	18.27 MW	16.86 AW	37990 AAW	FLBLS	10//99-12//99
Production and Operating Workers	Fort Pierce-Port St. Lucie MSA, FL	S	25.47 MW	24.28 AW	52980 AAW	FLBLS	10//99-12//99
Production and Operating Workers	Fort Walton Beach MSA, FL	S	19.77 MW	17.64 AW	41110 AAW	FLBLS	10//99-12//99
Production and Operating Workers	Gainesville MSA, FL	S	18.13 MW	16.47 AW	37700 AAW	FLBLS	10//99-12//99
Production and Operating Workers	Jacksonville MSA, FL	S	18.29 MW	17.04 AW	38040 AAW	FLBLS	10//99-12//99
Production and Operating Workers	Lakeland-Winter Haven MSA, FL	S	17.45 MW	16.41 AW	36300 AAW	FLBLS	10//99-12//99

AAW	Average annual wage	AOH	Average offered, high	ASH	Average starting, high	H	Hourly	M	Monthly	S	Special: hourly and annual
AE	Average entry wage	AOL	Average offered, low	ASL	Average starting, low	HI	Highest wage paid	MTC	Median total compensation	TQ	Third quartile wage
AEX	Average experienced wage	APH	Average pay, high range	AW	Average wage paid	HR	High end range	MW	Median wage paid	W	Weekly
AO	Average offered	APL	Average pay, low range	FQ	First quartile wage	LR	Low end range	SQ	Second quartile wage	Y	Yearly

Occupation/Type/Industry	Location	Per	Low	Mid	High	Source	Date
First-Line Supervisor/Manager							
Production and Operating Workers	Melbourne-Titusville-Palm Bay MSA, FL	S	15.75 MW	14.44 AW	32770 AAW	FLBLS	10//99-12//99
Production and Operating Workers	Miami PMSA, FL	S	18.79 MW	16.84 AW	39090 AAW	FLBLS	10//99-12//99
Production and Operating Workers	Naples MSA, FL	S	19.46 MW	17.59 AW	40480 AAW	FLBLS	10//99-12//99
Production and Operating Workers	Ocala MSA, FL	S	16.07 MW	14.12 AW	33420 AAW	FLBLS	10//99-12//99
Production and Operating Workers	Orlando MSA, FL	S	18.87 MW	17.17 AW	39250 AAW	FLBLS	10//99-12//99
Production and Operating Workers	Panama City MSA, FL	S	17.53 MW	15.06 AW	36470 AAW	FLBLS	10//99-12//99
Production and Operating Workers	Pensacola MSA, FL	S	21.46 MW	19.99 AW	44630 AAW	FLBLS	10//99-12//99
Production and Operating Workers	Punta Gorda MSA, FL	S	18.56 MW	19.43 AW	38600 AAW	FLBLS	10//99-12//99
Production and Operating Workers	Sarasota-Bradenton MSA, FL	S	17.25 MW	16.67 AW	35880 AAW	FLBLS	10//99-12//99
Production and Operating Workers	Tallahassee MSA, FL	S	14.62 MW	14.42 AW	30400 AAW	FLBLS	10//99-12//99
Production and Operating Workers	Tampa-St. Petersburg-Clearwater MSA, FL	S	18.32 MW	16.69 AW	38100 AAW	FLBLS	10//99-12//99
Production and Operating Workers	West Palm Beach-Boca Raton MSA, FL	S	20.73 MW	20.53 AW	43120 AAW	FLBLS	10//99-12//99
Production and Operating Workers	Georgia	S	17.71 MW	18.62 AW	38730 AAW	GABLS	10//99-12//99
Production and Operating Workers	Albany MSA, GA	S	16.68 MW	12.78 AW	34690 AAW	GABLS	10//99-12//99
Production and Operating Workers	Athens MSA, GA	S	16.98 MW	15.97 AW	35320 AAW	GABLS	10//99-12//99
Production and Operating Workers	Atlanta MSA, GA	S	19.41 MW	18.48 AW	40360 AAW	GABLS	10//99-12//99
Production and Operating Workers	Augusta-Aiken MSA, GA-SC	S	23.28 MW	23.51 AW	48410 AAW	GABLS	10//99-12//99
Production and Operating Workers	Columbus MSA, GA-AL	S	18.90 MW	18.90 AW	39300 AAW	GABLS	10//99-12//99
Production and Operating Workers	Macon MSA, GA	S	19.35 MW	19.35 AW	40240 AAW	GABLS	10//99-12//99
Production and Operating Workers	Savannah MSA, GA	S	19.01 MW	18.75 AW	39540 AAW	GABLS	10//99-12//99
Production and Operating Workers	Hawaii	S	15.65 MW	17.73 AW	36880 AAW	HIBLS	10//99-12//99
Production and Operating Workers	Honolulu MSA, HI	S	17.64 MW	15.57 AW	36700 AAW	HIBLS	10//99-12//99
Production and Operating Workers	Idaho	S	17.92 MW	18.36 AW	38180 AAW	IDBLS	10//99-12//99
Production and Operating Workers	Boise City MSA, ID	S	18.54 MW	18.47 AW	38550 AAW	IDBLS	10//99-12//99
Production and Operating Workers	Pocatello MSA, ID	S	13.82 MW	14.12 AW	28740 AAW	IDBLS	10//99-12//99
Production and Operating Workers	Illinois	S	18.58 MW	19.22 AW	39980 AAW	ILBLS	10//99-12//99
Production and Operating Workers	Bloomington-Normal MSA, IL	S	18.19 MW	17.16 AW	37830 AAW	ILBLS	10//99-12//99
Production and Operating Workers	Champaign-Urbana MSA, IL	S	17.58 MW	16.07 AW	36570 AAW	ILBLS	10//99-12//99
Production and Operating Workers	Chicago PMSA, IL	S	19.77 MW	19.09 AW	41120 AAW	ILBLS	10//99-12//99
Production and Operating Workers	Decatur MSA, IL	S	18.09 MW	16.93 AW	37620 AAW	ILBLS	10//99-12//99
Production and Operating Workers	Kankakee PMSA, IL	S	16.69 MW	16.06 AW	34720 AAW	ILBLS	10//99-12//99
Production and Operating Workers	Peoria-Pekin MSA, IL	S	19.48 MW	18.91 AW	40510 AAW	ILBLS	10//99-12//99
Production and Operating Workers	Rockford MSA, IL	S	19.52 MW	18.80 AW	40590 AAW	ILBLS	10//99-12//99
Production and Operating Workers	Springfield MSA, IL	S	18.70 MW	18.60 AW	38890 AAW	ILBLS	10//99-12//99
Production and Operating Workers	Indiana	S	17.54 MW	18.65 AW	38790 AAW	INBLS	10//99-12//99
Production and Operating Workers	Bloomington MSA, IN	S	16.87 MW	13.99 AW	35080 AAW	INBLS	10//99-12//99
Production and Operating Workers	Elkhart-Goshen MSA, IN	S	16.72 MW	15.69 AW	34790 AAW	INBLS	10//99-12//99
Production and Operating Workers	Evansville-Henderson MSA, IN-KY	S	18.51 MW	17.52 AW	38490 AAW	INBLS	10//99-12//99
Production and Operating Workers	Fort Wayne MSA, IN	S	19.26 MW	18.20 AW	40070 AAW	INBLS	10//99-12//99
Production and Operating Workers	Gary PMSA, IN	S	20.76 MW	20.36 AW	43180 AAW	INBLS	10//99-12//99
Production and Operating Workers	Indianapolis MSA, IN	S	19.05 MW	18.21 AW	39620 AAW	INBLS	10//99-12//99
Production and Operating Workers	Kokomo MSA, IN	S	24.10 MW	23.65 AW	50120 AAW	INBLS	10//99-12//99
Production and Operating Workers	Lafayette MSA, IN	S	23.91 MW	20.22 AW	49730 AAW	INBLS	10//99-12//99
Production and Operating Workers	Muncie MSA, IN	S	16.92 MW	15.85 AW	35190 AAW	INBLS	10//99-12//99
Production and Operating Workers	South Bend MSA, IN	S	16.29 MW	15.40 AW	33880 AAW	INBLS	10//99-12//99
Production and Operating Workers	Terre Haute MSA, IN	S	19.69 MW	22.41 AW	40940 AAW	INBLS	10//99-12//99
Production and Operating Workers	Iowa	S	17.48 MW	18.30 AW	38060 AAW	IABLS	10//99-12//99
Production and Operating Workers	Cedar Rapids MSA, IA	S	23.00 MW	20.35 AW	47840 AAW	IABLS	10//99-12//99
Production and Operating Workers	Davenport-Moline-Rock Island MSA, IA-IL	S	17.22 MW	16.05 AW	35830 AAW	IABLS	10//99-12//99
Production and Operating Workers	Des Moines MSA, IA	S	16.75 MW	16.65 AW	34830 AAW	IABLS	10//99-12//99
Production and Operating Workers	Dubuque MSA, IA	S	17.47 MW	17.66 AW	36330 AAW	IABLS	10//99-12//99
Production and Operating Workers	Iowa City MSA, IA	S	16.53 MW	17.23 AW	34370 AAW	IABLS	10//99-12//99
Production and Operating Workers	Sioux City MSA, IA-NE	S	18.00 MW	18.08 AW	37450 AAW	IABLS	10//99-12//99
Production and Operating Workers	Waterloo-Cedar Falls MSA, IA	S	18.39 MW	17.02 AW	38260 AAW	IABLS	10//99-12//99
Production and Operating Workers	Kansas	S	18.91 MW	19.02 AW	39570 AAW	KSBLS	10//99-12//99
Production and Operating Workers	Topeka MSA, KS	S	18.19 MW	18.16 AW	37840 AAW	KSBLS	10//99-12//99
Production and Operating Workers	Wichita MSA, KS	S	20.33 MW	20.92 AW	42290 AAW	KSBLS	10//99-12//99
Production and Operating Workers	Kentucky	S	17.38 MW	18.66 AW	38800 AAW	KYBLS	10//99-12//99
Production and Operating Workers	Lexington MSA, KY	S	18.16 MW	18.25 AW	37760 AAW	KYBLS	10//99-12//99
Production and Operating Workers	Louisville MSA, KY-IN	S	18.99 MW	17.15 AW	39490 AAW	KYBLS	10//99-12//99
Production and Operating Workers	Owensboro MSA, KY	S	17.41 MW	17.30 AW	36210 AAW	KYBLS	10//99-12//99
Production and Operating Workers	Louisiana	S	19.34 MW	21.73 AW	45200 AAW	LABLS	10//99-12//99
Production and Operating Workers	Alexandria MSA, LA	S	16.55 MW	16.08 AW	34430 AAW	LABLS	10//99-12//99
Production and Operating Workers	Baton Rouge MSA, LA	S	21.83 MW	21.14 AW	45410 AAW	LABLS	10//99-12//99
Production and Operating Workers	Houma MSA, LA	S	21.97 MW	20.19 AW	45690 AAW	LABLS	10//99-12//99
Production and Operating Workers	Lafayette MSA, LA	S	17.99 MW	15.69 AW	37430 AAW	LABLS	10//99-12//99

AAW Average annual wage	**AOH** Average offered, high	**ASH** Average starting, high	**H** Hourly	**M** Monthly	**S** Special: hourly and annual
AE Average entry wage	**AOL** Average offered, low	**ASL** Average starting, low	**HI** Highest wage paid	**MTC** Median total compensation	**TQ** Third quartile wage
AEX Average experienced wage	**APH** Average pay, high range	**AW** Average wage paid	**HR** High end range	**MW** Median wage paid	**W** Weekly
AO Average offered	**APL** Average pay, low range	**FQ** First quartile wage	**LR** Low end range	**SQ** Second quartile wage	**Y** Yearly

Occupation/Type/Industry	Location	Per	Low	Mid	High	Source	Date
First-Line Supervisor/Manager							
Production and Operating Workers	Lake Charles MSA, LA	S	20.96 MW	19.37 AW	43600 AAW	LABLS	10//99-12//99
Production and Operating Workers	Monroe MSA, LA	S	21.73 MW	22.54 AW	45200 AAW	LABLS	10//99-12//99
Production and Operating Workers	New Orleans MSA, LA	S	22.62 MW	19.66 AW	47050 AAW	LABLS	10//99-12//99
Production and Operating Workers	Shreveport-Bossier City MSA, LA	S	16.26 MW	14.14 AW	33820 AAW	LABLS	10//99-12//99
Production and Operating Workers	Maine	S	18.34 MW	19.59 AW	40740 AAW	MEBLS	10//99-12//99
Production and Operating Workers	Bangor MSA, ME	S	15.27 MW	13.57 AW	31750 AAW	MEBLS	10//99-12//99
Production and Operating Workers	Lewiston-Auburn MSA, ME	S	17.18 MW	16.02 AW	35740 AAW	MEBLS	10//99-12//99
Production and Operating Workers	Portland MSA, ME	S	17.86 MW	16.74 AW	37160 AAW	MEBLS	10//99-12//99
Production and Operating Workers	Maryland	S	18.09 MW	19.36 AW	40280 AAW	MDBLS	10//99-12//99
Production and Operating Workers	Baltimore PMSA, MD	S	19.09 MW	18.32 AW	39720 AAW	MDBLS	10//99-12//99
Production and Operating Workers	Cumberland MSA, MD-WV	S	19.86 MW	18.27 AW	41320 AAW	MDBLS	10//99-12//99
Production and Operating Workers	Hagerstown PMSA, MD	S	19.11 MW	16.63 AW	39750 AAW	MDBLS	10//99-12//99
Production and Operating Workers	Massachusetts	S	19.76 MW	20.44 AW	42510 AAW	MABLS	10//99-12//99
Production and Operating Workers	Barnstable-Yarmouth MSA, MA	S	16.54 MW	12.82 AW	34390 AAW	MABLS	10//99-12//99
Production and Operating Workers	Boston PMSA, MA-NH	S	20.37 MW	19.91 AW	42360 AAW	MABLS	10//99-12//99
Production and Operating Workers	Brockton PMSA, MA	S	20.77 MW	20.51 AW	43200 AAW	MABLS	10//99-12//99
Production and Operating Workers	Fitchburg-Leominster PMSA, MA	S	22.34 MW	22.70 AW	46460 AAW	MABLS	10//99-12//99
Production and Operating Workers	Lawrence PMSA, MA-NH	S	20.05 MW	19.02 AW	41700 AAW	MABLS	10//99-12//99
Production and Operating Workers	Lowell PMSA, MA-NH	S	20.06 MW	19.46 AW	41720 AAW	MABLS	10//99-12//99
Production and Operating Workers	New Bedford PMSA, MA	S	19.87 MW	19.82 AW	41330 AAW	MABLS	10//99-12//99
Production and Operating Workers	Pittsfield MSA, MA	S	19.21 MW	17.53 AW	39950 AAW	MABLS	10//99-12//99
Production and Operating Workers	Springfield MSA, MA	S	21.05 MW	20.26 AW	43790 AAW	MABLS	10//99-12//99
Production and Operating Workers	Worcester PMSA, MA-CT	S	20.22 MW	19.75 AW	42060 AAW	MABLS	10//99-12//99
Production and Operating Workers	Michigan	S	21.87 MW	23.59 AW	49060 AAW	MIBLS	10//99-12//99
Production and Operating Workers	Ann Arbor PMSA, MI	S	24.72 MW	21.64 AW	51420 AAW	MIBLS	10//99-12//99
Production and Operating Workers	Benton Harbor MSA, MI	S	20.77 MW	19.03 AW	43190 AAW	MIBLS	10//99-12//99
Production and Operating Workers	Detroit PMSA, MI	S	25.89 MW	25.10 AW	53850 AAW	MIBLS	10//99-12//99
Production and Operating Workers	Flint PMSA, MI	S	27.78 MW	29.25 AW	57790 AAW	MIBLS	10//99-12//99
Production and Operating Workers	Grand Rapids-Muskegon-Holland MSA, MI	S	21.04 MW	19.29 AW	43770 AAW	MIBLS	10//99-12//99
Production and Operating Workers	Jackson MSA, MI	S	19.79 MW	18.57 AW	41170 AAW	MIBLS	10//99-12//99
Production and Operating Workers	Kalamazoo-Battle Creek MSA, MI	S	22.76 MW	20.75 AW	47330 AAW	MIBLS	10//99-12//99
Production and Operating Workers	Lansing-East Lansing MSA, MI	S	21.23 MW	19.82 AW	44160 AAW	MIBLS	10//99-12//99
Production and Operating Workers	Saginaw-Bay City-Midland MSA, MI	S	21.24 MW	20.17 AW	44180 AAW	MIBLS	10//99-12//99
Production and Operating Workers	Minnesota	S	19.32 MW	20.08 AW	41760 AAW	MNBLS	10//99-12//99
Production and Operating Workers	Duluth-Superior MSA, MN-WI	S	19.87 MW	19.98 AW	41320 AAW	MNBLS	10//99-12//99
Production and Operating Workers	Minneapolis-St. Paul MSA, MN-WI	S	21.31 MW	20.30 AW	44330 AAW	MNBLS	10//99-12//99
Production and Operating Workers	Rochester MSA, MN	S	20.22 MW	19.72 AW	42050 AAW	MNBLS	10//99-12//99
Production and Operating Workers	St. Cloud MSA, MN	S	17.22 MW	16.73 AW	35820 AAW	MNBLS	10//99-12//99
Production and Operating Workers	Mississippi	S	15.5 MW	16.14 AW	33570 AAW	MSBLS	10//99-12//99
Production and Operating Workers	Biloxi-Gulfport-Pascagoula MSA, MS	S	20.42 MW	19.51 AW	42470 AAW	MSBLS	10//99-12//99
Production and Operating Workers	Hattiesburg MSA, MS	S	15.71 MW	16.68 AW	32670 AAW	MSBLS	10//99-12//99
Production and Operating Workers	Jackson MSA, MS	S	16.83 MW	16.97 AW	35000 AAW	MSBLS	10//99-12//99
Production and Operating Workers	Missouri	S	16.87 MW	18.43 AW	38330 AAW	MOBLS	10//99-12//99
Production and Operating Workers	Columbia MSA, MO	S	12.66 MW	12.09 AW	26330 AAW	MOBLS	10//99-12//99
Production and Operating Workers	Joplin MSA, MO	S	15.49 MW	14.85 AW	32210 AAW	MOBLS	10//99-12//99
Production and Operating Workers	Kansas City MSA, MO-KS	S	19.57 MW	18.82 AW	40710 AAW	MOBLS	10//99-12//99
Production and Operating Workers	St. Joseph MSA, MO	S	19.70 MW	20.14 AW	40970 AAW	MOBLS	10//99-12//99
Production and Operating Workers	St. Louis MSA, MO-IL	S	20.74 MW	19.10 AW	43140 AAW	MOBLS	10//99-12//99
Production and Operating Workers	Springfield MSA, MO	S	15.83 MW	14.75 AW	32930 AAW	MOBLS	10//99-12//99
Production and Operating Workers	Montana	S	14.82 MW	16.35 AW	34010 AAW	MTBLS	10//99-12//99
Production and Operating Workers	Billings MSA, MT	S	20.85 MW	18.43 AW	43370 AAW	MTBLS	10//99-12//99
Production and Operating Workers	Great Falls MSA, MT	S	16.06 MW	15.48 AW	33400 AAW	MTBLS	10//99-12//99
Production and Operating Workers	Missoula MSA, MT	S	14.29 MW	13.05 AW	29730 AAW	MTBLS	10//99-12//99
Production and Operating Workers	Nebraska	S	15.72 MW	16.73 AW	34790 AAW	NEBLS	10//99-12//99
Production and Operating Workers	Lincoln MSA, NE	S	16.61 MW	15.71 AW	34550 AAW	NEBLS	10//99-12//99
Production and Operating Workers	Omaha MSA, NE-IA	S	17.93 MW	16.63 AW	37290 AAW	NEBLS	10//99-12//99
Production and Operating Workers	Nevada	S	16.25 MW	17.37 AW	36120 AAW	NVBLS	10//99-12//99
Production and Operating Workers	Las Vegas MSA, NV-AZ	S	17.83 MW	16.79 AW	37090 AAW	NVBLS	10//99-12//99
Production and Operating Workers	Reno MSA, NV	S	16.52 MW	15.32 AW	34360 AAW	NVBLS	10//99-12//99
Production and Operating Workers	New Hampshire	S	17.52 MW	18.39 AW	38240 AAW	NHBLS	10//99-12//99
Production and Operating Workers	Manchester PMSA, NH	S	16.91 MW	15.60 AW	35180 AAW	NHBLS	10//99-12//99
Production and Operating Workers	Nashua PMSA, NH	S	20.18 MW	18.85 AW	41970 AAW	NHBLS	10//99-12//99

AAW	Average annual wage	AOH	Average offered, high	ASH	Average starting, high
AE	Average entry wage	AOL	Average offered, low	ASL	Average starting, low
AEX	Average experienced wage	APH	Average pay, high range	AW	Average wage paid
AO	Average offered	APL	Average pay, low range	FQ	First quartile wage

H	Hourly	M	Monthly	S	Special: hourly and annual
HI	Highest wage paid	MTC	Median total compensation	TQ	Third quartile wage
HR	High end range	MW	Median wage paid	W	Weekly
LR	Low end range	SQ	Second quartile wage	Y	Yearly

Occupation/Type/Industry	Location	Per	Low	Mid	High	Source	Date
First-Line Supervisor/Manager							
Production and Operating Workers	Portsmouth-Rochester PMSA, NH-ME	S	16.62 MW	16.14 AW	34570 AAW	NHBLS	10//99-12//99
Production and Operating Workers	New Jersey	S	22.57 MW	23.22 AW	48300 AAW	NJBLS	10//99-12//99
Production and Operating Workers	Atlantic-Cape May PMSA, NJ	S	18.34 MW	17.11 AW	38150 AAW	NJBLS	10//99-12//99
Production and Operating Workers	Bergen-Passaic PMSA, NJ	S	24.48 MW	23.58 AW	50920 AAW	NJBLS	10//99-12//99
Production and Operating Workers	Jersey City PMSA, NJ	S	21.72 MW	20.81 AW	45180 AAW	NJBLS	10//99-12//99
Production and Operating Workers	Middlesex-Somerset-Hunterdon PMSA, NJ	S	23.91 MW	22.81 AW	49740 AAW	NJBLS	10//99-12//99
Production and Operating Workers	Monmouth-Ocean PMSA, NJ	S	22.44 MW	20.52 AW	46670 AAW	NJBLS	10//99-12//99
Production and Operating Workers	Newark PMSA, NJ	S	22.94 MW	23.06 AW	47720 AAW	NJBLS	10//99-12//99
Production and Operating Workers	Trenton PMSA, NJ	S	20.40 MW	19.43 AW	42430 AAW	NJBLS	10//99-12//99
Production and Operating Workers	Vineland-Millville-Bridgeton PMSA, NJ	S	20.88 MW	19.83 AW	43440 AAW	NJBLS	10//99-12//99
Production and Operating Workers	New Mexico	S	14.84 MW	15.87 AW	33010 AAW	NMBLS	10//99-12//99
Production and Operating Workers	Albuquerque MSA, NM	S	14.35 MW	14.36 AW	29850 AAW	NMBLS	10//99-12//99
Production and Operating Workers	Las Cruces MSA, NM	S	17.48 MW	15.45 AW	36350 AAW	NMBLS	10//99-12//99
Production and Operating Workers	Santa Fe MSA, NM	S	14.29 MW	14.45 AW	29730 AAW	NMBLS	10//99-12//99
Production and Operating Workers	New York	S	21.2 MW	22.31 AW	46400 AAW	NYBLS	10//99-12//99
Production and Operating Workers	Albany-Schenectady-Troy MSA, NY	S	18.70 MW	17.26 AW	38890 AAW	NYBLS	10//99-12//99
Production and Operating Workers	Binghamton MSA, NY	S	20.00 MW	19.17 AW	41590 AAW	NYBLS	10//99-12//99
Production and Operating Workers	Buffalo-Niagara Falls MSA, NY	S	20.89 MW	19.66 AW	43450 AAW	NYBLS	10//99-12//99
Production and Operating Workers	Dutchess County PMSA, NY	S	23.71 MW	23.12 AW	49310 AAW	NYBLS	10//99-12//99
Production and Operating Workers	Elmira MSA, NY	S	18.66 MW	18.93 AW	38800 AAW	NYBLS	10//99-12//99
Production and Operating Workers	Glens Falls MSA, NY	S	20.50 MW	19.95 AW	42640 AAW	NYBLS	10//99-12//99
Production and Operating Workers	Jamestown MSA, NY	S	18.16 MW	16.36 AW	37770 AAW	NYBLS	10//99-12//99
Production and Operating Workers	Nassau-Suffolk PMSA, NY	S	23.23 MW	22.06 AW	48310 AAW	NYBLS	10//99-12//99
Production and Operating Workers	New York PMSA, NY	S	24.95 MW	24.21 AW	51900 AAW	NYBLS	10//99-12//99
Production and Operating Workers	Newburgh PMSA, NY-PA	S	20.90 MW	19.67 AW	43480 AAW	NYBLS	10//99-12//99
Production and Operating Workers	Rochester MSA, NY	S	23.23 MW	21.84 AW	48320 AAW	NYBLS	10//99-12//99
Production and Operating Workers	Syracuse MSA, NY	S	20.51 MW	19.06 AW	42670 AAW	NYBLS	10//99-12//99
Production and Operating Workers	Utica-Rome MSA, NY	S	15.19 MW	14.01 AW	31600 AAW	NYBLS	10//99-12//99
Production and Operating Workers	North Carolina	S	17.6 MW	18.81 AW	39120 AAW	NCBLS	10//99-12//99
Production and Operating Workers	Asheville MSA, NC	S	16.35 MW	14.75 AW	34010 AAW	NCBLS	10//99-12//99
Production and Operating Workers	Charlotte-Gastonia-Rock Hill MSA, NC-SC	S	19.65 MW	18.72 AW	40880 AAW	NCBLS	10//99-12//99
Production and Operating Workers	Fayetteville MSA, NC	S	18.77 MW	17.67 AW	39050 AAW	NCBLS	10//99-12//99
Production and Operating Workers	Goldsboro MSA, NC	S	16.51 MW	12.96 AW	34350 AAW	NCBLS	10//99-12//99
Production and Operating Workers	Greensboro--Winston-Salem--High Point MSA, NC	S	17.65 MW	16.57 AW	36720 AAW	NCBLS	10//99-12//99
Production and Operating Workers	Greenville MSA, NC	S	20.78 MW	21.07 AW	43220 AAW	NCBLS	10//99-12//99
Production and Operating Workers	Hickory-Morganton-Lenoir MSA, NC	S	17.10 MW	16.51 AW	35560 AAW	NCBLS	10//99-12//99
Production and Operating Workers	Jacksonville MSA, NC	S	15.60 MW	15.12 AW	32440 AAW	NCBLS	10//99-12//99
Production and Operating Workers	Raleigh-Durham-Chapel Hill MSA, NC	S	23.26 MW	21.72 AW	48380 AAW	NCBLS	10//99-12//99
Production and Operating Workers	Rocky Mount MSA, NC	S	15.24 MW	15.27 AW	31710 AAW	NCBLS	10//99-12//99
Production and Operating Workers	Wilmington MSA, NC	S	22.16 MW	23.50 AW	46090 AAW	NCBLS	10//99-12//99
Production and Operating Workers	North Dakota	S	13.62 MW	14.85 AW	30890 AAW	NDBLS	10//99-12//99
Production and Operating Workers	Bismarck MSA, ND	S	15.29 MW	14.36 AW	31800 AAW	NDBLS	10//99-12//99
Production and Operating Workers	Fargo-Moorhead MSA, ND-MN	S	14.75 MW	13.33 AW	30670 AAW	NDBLS	10//99-12//99
Production and Operating Workers	Grand Forks MSA, ND-MN	S	15.53 MW	14.56 AW	32290 AAW	NDBLS	10//99-12//99
Production and Operating Workers	Ohio	S	18.99 MW	19.90 AW	41390 AAW	OHBLS	10//99-12//99
Production and Operating Workers	Akron PMSA, OH	S	17.77 MW	17.03 AW	36960 AAW	OHBLS	10//99-12//99
Production and Operating Workers	Canton-Massillon MSA, OH	S	19.45 MW	19.27 AW	40450 AAW	OHBLS	10//99-12//99
Production and Operating Workers	Cincinnati PMSA, OH-KY-IN	S	20.19 MW	19.95 AW	42000 AAW	OHBLS	10//99-12//99
Production and Operating Workers	Cleveland-Lorain-Elyria PMSA, OH	S	21.66 MW	20.15 AW	45040 AAW	OHBLS	10//99-12//99
Production and Operating Workers	Columbus MSA, OH	S	18.45 MW	17.78 AW	38370 AAW	OHBLS	10//99-12//99
Production and Operating Workers	Dayton-Springfield MSA, OH	S	21.42 MW	21.79 AW	44550 AAW	OHBLS	10//99-12//99
Production and Operating Workers	Hamilton-Middletown PMSA, OH	S	20.03 MW	21.36 AW	41660 AAW	OHBLS	10//99-12//99
Production and Operating Workers	Mansfield MSA, OH	S	17.99 MW	16.92 AW	37420 AAW	OHBLS	10//99-12//99
Production and Operating Workers	Steubenville-Weirton MSA, OH-WV	S	21.33 MW	20.35 AW	44360 AAW	OHBLS	10//99-12//99
Production and Operating Workers	Toledo MSA, OH	S	22.72 MW	22.90 AW	47260 AAW	OHBLS	10//99-12//99
Production and Operating Workers	Youngstown-Warren MSA, OH	S	19.92 MW	19.10 AW	41440 AAW	OHBLS	10//99-12//99
Production and Operating Workers	Oklahoma	S	17.12 MW	17.87 AW	37170 AAW	OKBLS	10//99-12//99
Production and Operating Workers	Enid MSA, OK	S	21.94 MW	22.44 AW	45630 AAW	OKBLS	10//99-12//99

AAW Average annual wage	**AOH** Average offered, high	**ASH** Average starting, high	**H** Hourly	**M** Monthly	**S** Special: hourly and annual
AE Average entry wage	**AOL** Average offered, low	**ASL** Average starting, low	**HI** Highest wage paid	**MTC** Median total compensation	**TQ** Third quartile wage
AEX Average experienced wage	**APH** Average pay, high range	**AW** Average wage paid	**HR** High end range	**MW** Median wage paid	**W** Weekly
AO Average offered	**APL** Average pay, low range	**FQ** First quartile wage	**LR** Low end range	**SQ** Second quartile wage	**Y** Yearly

Occupation/Type/Industry	Location	Per	Low	Mid	High	Source	Date
First-Line Supervisor/Manager							
Production and Operating Workers	Lawton MSA, OK	S	14.44 MW	13.21 AW	30030 AAW	OKBLS	10//99-12//99
Production and Operating Workers	Oklahoma City MSA, OK	S	18.36 MW	17.01 AW	38180 AAW	OKBLS	10//99-12//99
Production and Operating Workers	Tulsa MSA, OK	S	19.15 MW	18.43 AW	39840 AAW	OKBLS	10//99-12//99
Production and Operating Workers	Oregon	S	19.58 MW	20.45 AW	42540 AAW	ORBLS	10//99-12//99
Production and Operating Workers	Eugene-Springfield MSA, OR	S	17.77 MW	15.60 AW	36960 AAW	ORBLS	10//99-12//99
Production and Operating Workers	Medford-Ashland MSA, OR	S	18.45 MW	18.28 AW	38380 AAW	ORBLS	10//99-12//99
Production and Operating Workers	Portland-Vancouver PMSA, OR-WA	S	21.38 MW	20.06 AW	44470 AAW	ORBLS	10//99-12//99
Production and Operating Workers	Salem PMSA, OR	S	19.34 MW	18.19 AW	40220 AAW	ORBLS	10//99-12//99
Production and Operating Workers	Pennsylvania	S	19.25 MW	20.21 AW	42030 AAW	PABLS	10//99-12//99
Production and Operating Workers	Allentown-Bethlehem-Easton MSA, PA	S	19.98 MW	19.12 AW	41560 AAW	PABLS	10//99-12//99
Production and Operating Workers	Altoona MSA, PA	S	18.91 MW	16.22 AW	39320 AAW	PABLS	10//99-12//99
Production and Operating Workers	Erie MSA, PA	S	17.61 MW	16.56 AW	36630 AAW	PABLS	10//99-12//99
Production and Operating Workers	Harrisburg-Lebanon-Carlisle MSA, PA	S	22.33 MW	20.20 AW	46450 AAW	PABLS	10//99-12//99
Production and Operating Workers	Johnstown MSA, PA	S	18.07 MW	17.37 AW	37590 AAW	PABLS	10//99-12//99
Production and Operating Workers	Lancaster MSA, PA	S	18.26 MW	17.69 AW	37980 AAW	PABLS	10//99-12//99
Production and Operating Workers	Philadelphia PMSA, PA-NJ	S	22.31 MW	21.29 AW	46410 AAW	PABLS	10//99-12//99
Production and Operating Workers	Pittsburgh MSA, PA	S	19.69 MW	18.63 AW	40950 AAW	PABLS	10//99-12//99
Production and Operating Workers	Reading MSA, PA	S	20.12 MW	19.77 AW	41860 AAW	PABLS	10//99-12//99
Production and Operating Workers	Scranton--Wilkes-Barre--Hazleton MSA, PA	S	19.57 MW	19.06 AW	40700 AAW	PABLS	10//99-12//99
Production and Operating Workers	Sharon MSA, PA	S	19.60 MW	19.55 AW	40760 AAW	PABLS	10//99-12//99
Production and Operating Workers	State College MSA, PA	S	19.65 MW	18.66 AW	40860 AAW	PABLS	10//99-12//99
Production and Operating Workers	Williamsport MSA, PA	S	18.60 MW	17.86 AW	38700 AAW	PABLS	10//99-12//99
Production and Operating Workers	York MSA, PA	S	18.22 MW	16.99 AW	37890 AAW	PABLS	10//99-12//99
Production and Operating Workers	Rhode Island	S	19.15 MW	20.53 AW	42690 AAW	RIBLS	10//99-12//99
Production and Operating Workers	Providence-Fall River-Warwick MSA, RI-MA	S	20.48 MW	18.90 AW	42590 AAW	RIBLS	10//99-12//99
Production and Operating Workers	South Carolina	S	19.76 MW	20.14 AW	41890 AAW	SCBLS	10//99-12//99
Production and Operating Workers	Charleston-North Charleston MSA, SC	S	19.64 MW	19.65 AW	40850 AAW	SCBLS	10//99-12//99
Production and Operating Workers	Columbia MSA, SC	S	20.46 MW	19.21 AW	42560 AAW	SCBLS	10//99-12//99
Production and Operating Workers	Florence MSA, SC	S	19.30 MW	19.99 AW	40130 AAW	SCBLS	10//99-12//99
Production and Operating Workers	Greenville-Spartanburg-Anderson MSA, SC	S	21.14 MW	21.84 AW	43980 AAW	SCBLS	10//99-12//99
Production and Operating Workers	Myrtle Beach MSA, SC	S	14.04 MW	12.24 AW	29210 AAW	SCBLS	10//99-12//99
Production and Operating Workers	Sumter MSA, SC	S	17.24 MW	16.74 AW	35870 AAW	SCBLS	10//99-12//99
Production and Operating Workers	South Dakota	S	15.97 MW	16.54 AW	34400 AAW	SDBLS	10//99-12//99
Production and Operating Workers	Rapid City MSA, SD	S	16.59 MW	15.81 AW	34510 AAW	SDBLS	10//99-12//99
Production and Operating Workers	Sioux Falls MSA, SD	S	16.40 MW	15.87 AW	34120 AAW	SDBLS	10//99-12//99
Production and Operating Workers	Tennessee	S	16.24 MW	17.56 AW	36530 AAW	TNBLS	10//99-12//99
Production and Operating Workers	Chattanooga MSA, TN-GA	S	17.55 MW	17.46 AW	36490 AAW	TNBLS	10//99-12//99
Production and Operating Workers	Clarksville-Hopkinsville MSA, TN-KY	S	18.51 MW	18.19 AW	38510 AAW	TNBLS	10//99-12//99
Production and Operating Workers	Jackson MSA, TN	S	16.20 MW	15.29 AW	33700 AAW	TNBLS	10//99-12//99
Production and Operating Workers	Johnson City-Kingsport-Bristol MSA, TN-VA	S	20.69 MW	19.74 AW	43040 AAW	TNBLS	10//99-12//99
Production and Operating Workers	Knoxville MSA, TN	S	18.87 MW	17.46 AW	39260 AAW	TNBLS	10//99-12//99
Production and Operating Workers	Memphis MSA, TN-AR-MS	S	16.40 MW	15.32 AW	34110 AAW	MSBLS	10//99-12//99
Production and Operating Workers	Nashville MSA, TN	S	18.08 MW	16.94 AW	37600 AAW	TNBLS	10//99-12//99
Production and Operating Workers	Texas	S	17.93 MW	19.51 AW	40590 AAW	TXBLS	10//99-12//99
Production and Operating Workers	Abilene MSA, TX	S	17.38 MW	16.50 AW	36150 AAW	TXBLS	10//99-12//99
Production and Operating Workers	Amarillo MSA, TX	S	17.54 MW	15.50 AW	36480 AAW	TXBLS	10//99-12//99
Production and Operating Workers	Austin-San Marcos MSA, TX	S	18.37 MW	17.76 AW	38200 AAW	TXBLS	10//99-12//99
Production and Operating Workers	Beaumont-Port Arthur MSA, TX	S	23.43 MW	23.87 AW	48730 AAW	TXBLS	10//99-12//99
Production and Operating Workers	Brazoria PMSA, TX	S	24.44 MW	24.96 AW	50840 AAW	TXBLS	10//99-12//99
Production and Operating Workers	Brownsville-Harlingen-San Benito MSA, TX	S	13.16 MW	12.06 AW	27360 AAW	TXBLS	10//99-12//99
Production and Operating Workers	Bryan-College Station MSA, TX	S	17.39 MW	15.31 AW	36160 AAW	TXBLS	10//99-12//99
Production and Operating Workers	Corpus Christi MSA, TX	S	19.58 MW	18.30 AW	40730 AAW	TXBLS	10//99-12//99
Production and Operating Workers	Dallas PMSA, TX	S	20.69 MW	18.64 AW	43030 AAW	TXBLS	10//99-12//99
Production and Operating Workers	El Paso MSA, TX	S	15.52 MW	13.64 AW	32280 AAW	TXBLS	10//99-12//99
Production and Operating Workers	Fort Worth-Arlington PMSA, TX	S	18.89 MW	18.00 AW	39290 AAW	TXBLS	10//99-12//99
Production and Operating Workers	Galveston-Texas City PMSA, TX	S	19.02 MW	16.47 AW	39570 AAW	TXBLS	10//99-12//99
Production and Operating Workers	Houston PMSA, TX	S	21.63 MW	20.10 AW	44980 AAW	TXBLS	10//99-12//99

AAW	Average annual wage	AOH	Average offered, high	ASH	Average starting, high	H	Hourly	M	Monthly	S	Special: hourly and annual
AE	Average entry wage	AOL	Average offered, low	ASL	Average starting, low	HI	Highest wage paid	MTC	Median total compensation	TQ	Third quartile wage
AEX	Average experienced wage	APH	Average pay, high range	AW	Average wage paid	HR	High end range	MW	Median wage paid	W	Weekly
AO	Average offered	APL	Average pay, low range	FQ	First quartile wage	LR	Low end range	SQ	Second quartile wage	Y	Yearly

Occupation/Type/Industry	Location	Per	Low	Mid	High	Source	Date
First-Line Supervisor/Manager							
Production and Operating Workers	Killeen-Temple MSA, TX	S	13.18 MW	11.92 AW	27410 AAW	TXBLS	10//99-12//99
Production and Operating Workers	Laredo MSA, TX	S	13.74 MW	11.96 AW	28570 AAW	TXBLS	10//99-12//99
Production and Operating Workers	Longview-Marshall MSA, TX	S	15.15 MW	14.41 AW	31520 AAW	TXBLS	10//99-12//99
Production and Operating Workers	Lubbock MSA, TX	S	14.91 MW	14.24 AW	31020 AAW	TXBLS	10//99-12//99
Production and Operating Workers	McAllen-Edinburg-Mission MSA, TX	S	12.70 MW	10.53 AW	26420 AAW	TXBLS	10//99-12//99
Production and Operating Workers	Odessa-Midland MSA, TX	S	21.86 MW	20.32 AW	45480 AAW	TXBLS	10//99-12//99
Production and Operating Workers	San Angelo MSA, TX	S	14.87 MW	11.30 AW	30940 AAW	TXBLS	10//99-12//99
Production and Operating Workers	San Antonio MSA, TX	S	15.54 MW	14.59 AW	32330 AAW	TXBLS	10//99-12//99
Production and Operating Workers	Sherman-Denison MSA, TX	S	27.76 MW	26.11 AW	57750 AAW	TXBLS	10//99-12//99
Production and Operating Workers	Texarkana MSA, TX- Texarkana, AR	S	16.34 MW	15.34 AW	33980 AAW	TXBLS	10//99-12//99
Production and Operating Workers	Tyler MSA, TX	S	18.86 MW	18.90 AW	39230 AAW	TXBLS	10//99-12//99
Production and Operating Workers	Victoria MSA, TX	S	14.02 MW	14.60 AW	29160 AAW	TXBLS	10//99-12//99
Production and Operating Workers	Waco MSA, TX	S	14.14 MW	12.77 AW	29400 AAW	TXBLS	10//99-12//99
Production and Operating Workers	Wichita Falls MSA, TX	S	14.85 MW	14.78 AW	30880 AAW	TXBLS	10//99-12//99
Production and Operating Workers	Utah	S	15.9 MW	16.97 AW	35300 AAW	UTBLS	10//99-12//99
Production and Operating Workers	Provo-Orem MSA, UT	S	15.85 MW	14.93 AW	32970 AAW	UTBLS	10//99-12//99
Production and Operating Workers	Salt Lake City-Ogden MSA, UT	S	17.85 MW	16.42 AW	37130 AAW	UTBLS	10//99-12//99
Production and Operating Workers	Vermont	S	17.98 MW	19.42 AW	40400 AAW	VTBLS	10//99-12//99
Production and Operating Workers	Burlington MSA, VT	S	18.76 MW	18.00 AW	39010 AAW	VTBLS	10//99-12//99
Production and Operating Workers	Virginia	S	18.66 MW	19.56 AW	40690 AAW	VABLS	10//99-12//99
Production and Operating Workers	Charlottesville MSA, VA	S	18.36 MW	16.01 AW	38190 AAW	VABLS	10//99-12//99
Production and Operating Workers	Danville MSA, VA	S	16.63 MW	17.03 AW	34600 AAW	VABLS	10//99-12//99
Production and Operating Workers	Lynchburg MSA, VA	S	17.44 MW	17.22 AW	36270 AAW	VABLS	10//99-12//99
Production and Operating Workers	Norfolk-Virginia Beach-Newport News MSA, VA-NC	S	22.50 MW	21.49 AW	46800 AAW	VABLS	10//99-12//99
Production and Operating Workers	Richmond-Petersburg MSA, VA	S	21.38 MW	20.14 AW	44480 AAW	VABLS	10//99-12//99
Production and Operating Workers	Roanoke MSA, VA	S	19.13 MW	19.37 AW	39780 AAW	VABLS	10//99-12//99
Production and Operating Workers	Washington	S	19.36 MW	20.52 AW	42680 AAW	WABLS	10//99-12//99
Production and Operating Workers	Bellingham MSA, WA	S	22.03 MW	19.31 AW	45810 AAW	WABLS	10//99-12//99
Production and Operating Workers	Olympia PMSA, WA	S	21.31 MW	21.06 AW	44320 AAW	WABLS	10//99-12//99
Production and Operating Workers	Richland-Kennewick-Pasco MSA, WA	S	19.94 MW	19.33 AW	41480 AAW	WABLS	10//99-12//99
Production and Operating Workers	Seattle-Bellevue-Everett PMSA, WA	S	21.25 MW	20.23 AW	44190 AAW	WABLS	10//99-12//99
Production and Operating Workers	Spokane MSA, WA	S	16.14 MW	15.22 AW	33570 AAW	WABLS	10//99-12//99
Production and Operating Workers	Tacoma PMSA, WA	S	21.09 MW	19.97 AW	43870 AAW	WABLS	10//99-12//99
Production and Operating Workers	Yakima MSA, WA	S	19.70 MW	18.91 AW	40970 AAW	WABLS	10//99-12//99
Production and Operating Workers	West Virginia	S	16.16 MW	18.70 AW	38890 AAW	WVBLS	10//99-12//99
Production and Operating Workers	Charleston MSA, WV	S	16.57 MW	14.16 AW	34460 AAW	WVBLS	10//99-12//99
Production and Operating Workers	Huntington-Ashland MSA, WV-KY-OH	S	26.19 MW	28.31 AW	54480 AAW	WVBLS	10//99-12//99
Production and Operating Workers	Parkersburg-Marietta MSA, WV-OH	S	17.02 MW	16.08 AW	35390 AAW	WVBLS	10//99-12//99
Production and Operating Workers	Wheeling MSA, WV-OH	S	18.28 MW	13.09 AW	38030 AAW	WVBLS	10//99-12//99
Production and Operating Workers	Wisconsin	S	18.01 MW	19.11 AW	39750 AAW	WIBLS	10//99-12//99
Production and Operating Workers	Appleton-Oshkosh-Neenah MSA, WI	S	20.00 MW	19.19 AW	41600 AAW	WIBLS	10//99-12//99
Production and Operating Workers	Eau Claire MSA, WI	S	18.56 MW	17.12 AW	38610 AAW	WIBLS	10//99-12//99
Production and Operating Workers	Green Bay MSA, WI	S	19.46 MW	17.97 AW	40470 AAW	WIBLS	10//99-12//99
Production and Operating Workers	Janesville-Beloit MSA, WI	S	17.67 MW	18.53 AW	36750 AAW	WIBLS	10//99-12//99
Production and Operating Workers	Kenosha PMSA, WI	S	23.68 MW	24.44 AW	49240 AAW	WIBLS	10//99-12//99
Production and Operating Workers	La Crosse MSA, WI-MN	S	16.16 MW	15.58 AW	33610 AAW	WIBLS	10//99-12//99
Production and Operating Workers	Madison MSA, WI	S	18.72 MW	18.08 AW	38940 AAW	WIBLS	10//99-12//99
Production and Operating Workers	Milwaukee-Waukesha PMSA, WI	S	21.45 MW	20.83 AW	44610 AAW	WIBLS	10//99-12//99
Production and Operating Workers	Racine PMSA, WI	S	17.30 MW	17.03 AW	35990 AAW	WIBLS	10//99-12//99
Production and Operating Workers	Sheboygan MSA, WI	S	17.88 MW	17.52 AW	37190 AAW	WIBLS	10//99-12//99
Production and Operating Workers	Wausau MSA, WI	S	16.21 MW	15.71 AW	33730 AAW	WIBLS	10//99-12//99
Production and Operating Workers	Wyoming	S	19.34 MW	20.78 AW	43220 AAW	WYBLS	10//99-12//99
Production and Operating Workers	Casper MSA, WY	S	22.53 MW	19.01 AW	46850 AAW	WYBLS	10//99-12//99
Production and Operating Workers	Cheyenne MSA, WY	S	11.71 MW	10.01 AW	24360 AAW	WYBLS	10//99-12//99
Production and Operating Workers	Puerto Rico	S	12.8 MW	14.31 AW	29770 AAW	PRBLS	10//99-12//99
Production and Operating Workers	Aguadilla MSA, PR	S	14.30 MW	11.52 AW	29740 AAW	PRBLS	10//99-12//99
Production and Operating Workers	Arecibo PMSA, PR	S	13.43 MW	10.65 AW	27930 AAW	PRBLS	10//99-12//99
Production and Operating Workers	Caguas PMSA, PR	S	16.97 MW	15.75 AW	35310 AAW	PRBLS	10//99-12//99
Production and Operating Workers	Mayaguez MSA, PR	S	14.28 MW	13.62 AW	29710 AAW	PRBLS	10//99-12//99

AAW Average annual wage	**AOH** Average offered, high	**ASH** Average starting, high	**H** Hourly	**M** Monthly	**S** Special: hourly and annual
AE Average entry wage	**AOL** Average offered, low	**ASL** Average starting, low	**HI** Highest wage paid	**MTC** Median total compensation	**TQ** Third quartile wage
AEX Average experienced wage	**APH** Average pay, high range	**AW** Average wage paid	**HR** High end range	**MW** Median wage paid	**W** Weekly
AO Average offered	**APL** Average pay, low range	**FQ** First quartile wage	**LR** Low end range	**SQ** Second quartile wage	**Y** Yearly

First-Line Supervisor/Manager

Occupation/Type/Industry	Location	Per	Low	Mid	High	Source	Date
First-Line Supervisor/Manager							
Production and Operating Workers	Ponce MSA, PR	S	12.22 MW	11.57 AW	25420 AAW	PRBLS	10//99-12//99
Production and Operating Workers	San Juan-Bayamon PMSA, PR	S	14.52 MW	13.06 AW	30210 AAW	PRBLS	10//99-12//99
Production and Operating Workers	Virgin Islands	S	17.9 MW	17.53 AW	36450 AAW	VIBLS	10//99-12//99
Production and Operating Workers	Guam	S	16.61 MW	16.35 AW	34010 AAW	GUBLS	10//99-12//99
Retail Sales Workers	Alabama	S	11.19 MW	12.79 AW	26610 AAW	ALBLS	10//99-12//99
Retail Sales Workers	Anniston MSA, AL	S	10.52 MW	10.21 AW	21890 AAW	ALBLS	10//99-12//99
Retail Sales Workers	Auburn-Opelika MSA, AL	S	13.62 MW	11.33 AW	28320 AAW	ALBLS	10//99-12//99
Retail Sales Workers	Birmingham MSA, AL	S	14.37 MW	12.67 AW	29890 AAW	ALBLS	10//99-12//99
Retail Sales Workers	Decatur MSA, AL	S	10.49 MW	9.95 AW	21820 AAW	ALBLS	10//99-12//99
Retail Sales Workers	Dothan MSA, AL	S	13.73 MW	11.74 AW	28560 AAW	ALBLS	10//99-12//99
Retail Sales Workers	Florence MSA, AL	S	11.27 MW	10.08 AW	23450 AAW	ALBLS	10//99-12//99
Retail Sales Workers	Gadsden MSA, AL	S	11.93 MW	10.12 AW	24810 AAW	ALBLS	10//99-12//99
Retail Sales Workers	Huntsville MSA, AL	S	13.93 MW	11.02 AW	28970 AAW	ALBLS	10//99-12//99
Retail Sales Workers	Mobile MSA, AL	S	12.44 MW	10.38 AW	25870 AAW	ALBLS	10//99-12//99
Retail Sales Workers	Montgomery MSA, AL	S	12.25 MW	10.49 AW	25490 AAW	ALBLS	10//99-12//99
Retail Sales Workers	Tuscaloosa MSA, AL	S	12.91 MW	12.00 AW	26840 AAW	ALBLS	10//99-12//99
Retail Sales Workers	Alaska	S	14.38 MW	15.88 AW	33040 AAW	AKBLS	10//99-12//99
Retail Sales Workers	Anchorage MSA, AK	S	17.14 MW	14.45 AW	35650 AAW	AKBLS	10//99-12//99
Retail Sales Workers	Arizona	S	13.24 MW	15.31 AW	31840 AAW	AZBLS	10//99-12//99
Retail Sales Workers	Flagstaff MSA, AZ-UT	S	12.70 MW	10.38 AW	26420 AAW	AZBLS	10//99-12//99
Retail Sales Workers	Phoenix-Mesa MSA, AZ	S	15.86 MW	14.05 AW	32980 AAW	AZBLS	10//99-12//99
Retail Sales Workers	Tucson MSA, AZ	S	15.15 MW	12.07 AW	31520 AAW	AZBLS	10//99-12//99
Retail Sales Workers	Yuma MSA, AZ	S	12.77 MW	10.62 AW	26560 AAW	AZBLS	10//99-12//99
Retail Sales Workers	Arkansas	S	10.28 MW	11.76 AW	24470 AAW	ARBLS	10//99-12//99
Retail Sales Workers	Fayetteville-Springdale-Rogers MSA, AR	S	11.86 MW	10.37 AW	24670 AAW	ARBLS	10//99-12//99
Retail Sales Workers	Fort Smith MSA, AR-OK	S	11.88 MW	10.25 AW	24710 AAW	ARBLS	10//99-12//99
Retail Sales Workers	Jonesboro MSA, AR	S	11.51 MW	9.62 AW	23950 AAW	ARBLS	10//99-12//99
Retail Sales Workers	Little Rock-North Little Rock MSA, AR	S	13.23 MW	11.67 AW	27520 AAW	ARBLS	10//99-12//99
Retail Sales Workers	Pine Bluff MSA, AR	S	11.88 MW	9.81 AW	24700 AAW	ARBLS	10//99-12//99
Retail Sales Workers	California	S	14.6 MW	16.99 AW	35330 AAW	CABLS	10//99-12//99
Retail Sales Workers	Bakersfield MSA, CA	S	13.87 MW	11.83 AW	28850 AAW	CABLS	10//99-12//99
Retail Sales Workers	Chico-Paradise MSA, CA	S	13.44 MW	11.45 AW	27950 AAW	CABLS	10//99-12//99
Retail Sales Workers	Fresno MSA, CA	S	15.09 MW	13.16 AW	31380 AAW	CABLS	10//99-12//99
Retail Sales Workers	Los Angeles-Long Beach PMSA, CA	S	17.48 MW	15.27 AW	36360 AAW	CABLS	10//99-12//99
Retail Sales Workers	Merced MSA, CA	S	14.94 MW	14.30 AW	31080 AAW	CABLS	10//99-12//99
Retail Sales Workers	Modesto MSA, CA	S	15.45 MW	13.98 AW	32130 AAW	CABLS	10//99-12//99
Retail Sales Workers	Oakland PMSA, CA	S	16.58 MW	14.29 AW	34490 AAW	CABLS	10//99-12//99
Retail Sales Workers	Orange County PMSA, CA	S	18.29 MW	15.47 AW	38050 AAW	CABLS	10//99-12//99
Retail Sales Workers	Redding MSA, CA	S	14.22 MW	13.23 AW	29580 AAW	CABLS	10//99-12//99
Retail Sales Workers	Riverside-San Bernardino PMSA, CA	S	16.80 MW	13.58 AW	34950 AAW	CABLS	10//99-12//99
Retail Sales Workers	Sacramento PMSA, CA	S	17.72 MW	14.91 AW	36850 AAW	CABLS	10//99-12//99
Retail Sales Workers	Salinas MSA, CA	S	17.72 MW	15.12 AW	36850 AAW	CABLS	10//99-12//99
Retail Sales Workers	San Diego MSA, CA	S	16.81 MW	14.67 AW	34970 AAW	CABLS	10//99-12//99
Retail Sales Workers	San Francisco PMSA, CA	S	17.80 MW	15.42 AW	37030 AAW	CABLS	10//99-12//99
Retail Sales Workers	San Jose PMSA, CA	S	18.54 MW	14.93 AW	38570 AAW	CABLS	10//99-12//99
Retail Sales Workers	San Luis Obispo-Atascadero-Paso Robles MSA, CA	S	14.21 MW	13.45 AW	29550 AAW	CABLS	10//99-12//99
Retail Sales Workers	Santa Barbara-Santa Maria-Lompoc MSA, CA	S	14.83 MW	12.18 AW	30850 AAW	CABLS	10//99-12//99
Retail Sales Workers	Santa Cruz-Watsonville PMSA, CA	S	15.95 MW	14.33 AW	33170 AAW	CABLS	10//99-12//99
Retail Sales Workers	Santa Rosa PMSA, CA	S	18.04 MW	15.67 AW	37510 AAW	CABLS	10//99-12//99
Retail Sales Workers	Stockton-Lodi MSA, CA	S	15.49 MW	13.17 AW	32230 AAW	CABLS	10//99-12//99
Retail Sales Workers	Vallejo-Fairfield-Napa PMSA, CA	S	15.72 MW	13.62 AW	32690 AAW	CABLS	10//99-12//99
Retail Sales Workers	Ventura PMSA, CA	S	16.01 MW	13.90 AW	33290 AAW	CABLS	10//99-12//99
Retail Sales Workers	Visalia-Tulare-Porterville MSA, CA	S	14.74 MW	12.60 AW	30660 AAW	CABLS	10//99-12//99
Retail Sales Workers	Yolo PMSA, CA	S	15.95 MW	15.37 AW	33180 AAW	CABLS	10//99-12//99
Retail Sales Workers	Yuba City MSA, CA	S	16.02 MW	13.22 AW	33320 AAW	CABLS	10//99-12//99
Retail Sales Workers	Colorado	S	13.83 MW	16.19 AW	33670 AAW	COBLS	10//99-12//99
Retail Sales Workers	Boulder-Longmont PMSA, CO	S	16.13 MW	13.84 AW	33560 AAW	COBLS	10//99-12//99
Retail Sales Workers	Colorado Springs MSA, CO	S	15.22 MW	12.79 AW	31660 AAW	COBLS	10//99-12//99
Retail Sales Workers	Denver PMSA, CO	S	17.38 MW	14.67 AW	36160 AAW	COBLS	10//99-12//99
Retail Sales Workers	Fort Collins-Loveland MSA, CO	S	16.68 MW	14.15 AW	34690 AAW	COBLS	10//99-12//99
Retail Sales Workers	Grand Junction MSA, CO	S	14.54 MW	11.97 AW	30240 AAW	COBLS	10//99-12//99

AAW	Average annual wage	AOH	Average offered, high	ASH	Average starting, high	H	Hourly	M	Monthly	S	Special: hourly and annual
AE	Average entry wage	AOL	Average offered, low	ASL	Average starting, low	HI	Highest wage paid	MTC	Median total compensation	TQ	Third quartile wage
AEX	Average experienced wage	APH	Average pay, high range	AW	Average wage paid	HR	High end range	MW	Median wage paid	W	Weekly
AO	Average offered	APL	Average pay, low range	FQ	First quartile wage	LR	Low end range	SQ	Second quartile wage	Y	Yearly

Occupation/Type/Industry	Location	Per	Low	Mid	High	Source	Date
First-Line Supervisor/Manager							
Retail Sales Workers	Connecticut	S	15.19 MW	16.80 AW	34940 AAW	CTBLS	10//99-12//99
Retail Sales Workers	Bridgeport PMSA, CT	S	17.10 MW	15.20 AW	35570 AAW	CTBLS	10//99-12//99
Retail Sales Workers	Danbury PMSA, CT	S	16.80 MW	15.53 AW	34950 AAW	CTBLS	10//99-12//99
Retail Sales Workers	Hartford MSA, CT	S	16.60 MW	14.93 AW	34530 AAW	CTBLS	10//99-12//99
Retail Sales Workers	New Haven-Meriden PMSA, CT	S	16.97 MW	14.85 AW	35300 AAW	CTBLS	10//99-12//99
Retail Sales Workers	New London-Norwich MSA, CT-RI	S	15.51 MW	12.46 AW	32270 AAW	CTBLS	10//99-12//99
Retail Sales Workers	Stamford-Norwalk PMSA, CT	S	18.06 MW	16.94 AW	37570 AAW	CTBLS	10//99-12//99
Retail Sales Workers	Waterbury PMSA, CT	S	16.90 MW	14.85 AW	35150 AAW	CTBLS	10//99-12//99
Retail Sales Workers	Delaware	S	12.18 MW	14.62 AW	30420 AAW	DEBLS	10//99-12//99
Retail Sales Workers	Dover MSA, DE	S	16.47 MW	14.92 AW	34250 AAW	DEBLS	10//99-12//99
Retail Sales Workers	Wilmington-Newark PMSA, DE-MD	S	14.54 MW	11.79 AW	30240 AAW	DEBLS	10//99-12//99
Retail Sales Workers	District of Columbia	S	14.73 MW	17.28 AW	35940 AAW	DCBLS	10//99-12//99
Retail Sales Workers	Washington PMSA, DC-MD-VA-WV	S	15.13 MW	13.46 AW	31460 AAW	DCBLS	10//99-12//99
Retail Sales Workers	Florida	S	13.04 MW	15.71 AW	32670 AAW	FLBLS	10//99-12//99
Retail Sales Workers	Daytona Beach MSA, FL	S	15.73 MW	12.80 AW	32720 AAW	FLBLS	10//99-12//99
Retail Sales Workers	Fort Lauderdale PMSA, FL	S	15.37 MW	12.71 AW	31980 AAW	FLBLS	10//99-12//99
Retail Sales Workers	Fort Myers-Cape Coral MSA, FL	S	14.22 MW	12.40 AW	29590 AAW	FLBLS	10//99-12//99
Retail Sales Workers	Fort Pierce-Port St. Lucie MSA, FL	S	16.25 MW	14.21 AW	33790 AAW	FLBLS	10//99-12//99
Retail Sales Workers	Fort Walton Beach MSA, FL	S	12.62 MW	11.79 AW	26250 AAW	FLBLS	10//99-12//99
Retail Sales Workers	Gainesville MSA, FL	S	15.11 MW	12.74 AW	31430 AAW	FLBLS	10//99-12//99
Retail Sales Workers	Jacksonville MSA, FL	S	16.09 MW	13.97 AW	33460 AAW	FLBLS	10//99-12//99
Retail Sales Workers	Lakeland-Winter Haven MSA, FL	S	14.60 MW	12.42 AW	30370 AAW	FLBLS	10//99-12//99
Retail Sales Workers	Melbourne-Titusville-Palm Bay MSA, FL	S	14.60 MW	12.55 AW	30370 AAW	FLBLS	10//99-12//99
Retail Sales Workers	Miami PMSA, FL	S	16.53 MW	13.25 AW	34380 AAW	FLBLS	10//99-12//99
Retail Sales Workers	Naples MSA, FL	S	15.77 MW	13.38 AW	32810 AAW	FLBLS	10//99-12//99
Retail Sales Workers	Ocala MSA, FL	S	15.24 MW	13.47 AW	31690 AAW	FLBLS	10//99-12//99
Retail Sales Workers	Orlando MSA, FL	S	15.69 MW	12.78 AW	32640 AAW	FLBLS	10//99-12//99
Retail Sales Workers	Panama City MSA, FL	S	14.75 MW	13.11 AW	30680 AAW	FLBLS	10//99-12//99
Retail Sales Workers	Pensacola MSA, FL	S	13.44 MW	11.56 AW	27960 AAW	FLBLS	10//99-12//99
Retail Sales Workers	Punta Gorda MSA, FL	S	13.53 MW	12.56 AW	28140 AAW	FLBLS	10//99-12//99
Retail Sales Workers	Sarasota-Bradenton MSA, FL	S	15.59 MW	12.83 AW	32420 AAW	FLBLS	10//99-12//99
Retail Sales Workers	Tallahassee MSA, FL	S	12.51 MW	10.73 AW	26030 AAW	FLBLS	10//99-12//99
Retail Sales Workers	Tampa-St. Petersburg-Clearwater MSA, FL	S	16.56 MW	13.48 AW	34450 AAW	FLBLS	10//99-12//99
Retail Sales Workers	West Palm Beach-Boca Raton MSA, FL	S	17.83 MW	14.28 AW	37090 AAW	FLBLS	10//99-12//99
Retail Sales Workers	Georgia	S	12.58 MW	14.29 AW	29720 AAW	GABLS	10//99-12//99
Retail Sales Workers	Albany MSA, GA	S	13.98 MW	12.78 AW	29080 AAW	GABLS	10//99-12//99
Retail Sales Workers	Athens MSA, GA	S	13.33 MW	12.24 AW	27720 AAW	GABLS	10//99-12//99
Retail Sales Workers	Atlanta MSA, GA	S	15.63 MW	13.41 AW	32510 AAW	GABLS	10//99-12//99
Retail Sales Workers	Augusta-Aiken MSA, GA-SC	S	13.03 MW	12.13 AW	27110 AAW	GABLS	10//99-12//99
Retail Sales Workers	Columbus MSA, GA-AL	S	12.20 MW	11.33 AW	25380 AAW	GABLS	10//99-12//99
Retail Sales Workers	Macon MSA, GA	S	12.37 MW	11.40 AW	25730 AAW	GABLS	10//99-12//99
Retail Sales Workers	Savannah MSA, GA	S	12.84 MW	11.15 AW	26710 AAW	GABLS	10//99-12//99
Retail Sales Workers	Hawaii	S	13.47 MW	15.60 AW	32450 AAW	HIBLS	10//99-12//99
Retail Sales Workers	Honolulu MSA, HI	S	15.84 MW	13.58 AW	32940 AAW	HIBLS	10//99-12//99
Retail Sales Workers	Idaho	S	11.6 MW	13.51 AW	28090 AAW	IDBLS	10//99-12//99
Retail Sales Workers	Boise City MSA, ID	S	14.80 MW	12.90 AW	30790 AAW	IDBLS	10//99-12//99
Retail Sales Workers	Pocatello MSA, ID	S	13.45 MW	10.48 AW	27990 AAW	IDBLS	10//99-12//99
Retail Sales Workers	Illinois	S	14.13 MW	16.10 AW	33490 AAW	ILBLS	10//99-12//99
Retail Sales Workers	Bloomington-Normal MSA, IL	S	16.27 MW	13.17 AW	33830 AAW	ILBLS	10//99-12//99
Retail Sales Workers	Champaign-Urbana MSA, IL	S	15.14 MW	13.29 AW	31490 AAW	ILBLS	10//99-12//99
Retail Sales Workers	Chicago PMSA, IL	S	17.78 MW	15.42 AW	36990 AAW	ILBLS	10//99-12//99
Retail Sales Workers	Decatur MSA, IL	S	15.92 MW	14.18 AW	33110 AAW	ILBLS	10//99-12//99
Retail Sales Workers	Kankakee PMSA, IL	S	15.18 MW	17.02 AW	31580 AAW	ILBLS	10//99-12//99
Retail Sales Workers	Peoria-Pekin MSA, IL	S	17.14 MW	13.54 AW	35650 AAW	ILBLS	10//99-12//99
Retail Sales Workers	Rockford MSA, IL	S	14.43 MW	13.50 AW	30010 AAW	ILBLS	10//99-12//99
Retail Sales Workers	Springfield MSA, IL	S	15.44 MW	14.19 AW	32120 AAW	ILBLS	10//99-12//99
Retail Sales Workers	Indiana	S	11.92 MW	13.67 AW	28440 AAW	INBLS	10//99-12//99
Retail Sales Workers	Bloomington MSA, IN	S	13.66 MW	11.99 AW	28410 AAW	INBLS	10//99-12//99
Retail Sales Workers	Elkhart-Goshen MSA, IN	S	15.38 MW	13.97 AW	32000 AAW	INBLS	10//99-12//99
Retail Sales Workers	Evansville-Henderson MSA, IN-KY	S	12.31 MW	10.40 AW	25610 AAW	INBLS	10//99-12//99

AAW	Average annual wage	AOH	Average offered, high	ASH	Average starting, high	H	Hourly	M	Monthly	S	Special: hourly and annual
AE	Average entry wage	AOL	Average offered, low	ASL	Average starting, low	HI	Highest wage paid	MTC	Median total compensation	TQ	Third quartile wage
AEX	Average experienced wage	APH	Average pay, high range	AW	Average wage paid	HR	High end range	MW	Median wage paid	W	Weekly
AO	Average offered	APL	Average pay, low range	FQ	First quartile wage	LR	Low end range	SQ	Second quartile wage	Y	Yearly

First-Line Supervisor/Manager

Occupation/Type/Industry	Location	Per	Low	Mid	High	Source	Date
First-Line Supervisor/Manager							
Retail Sales Workers	Fort Wayne MSA, IN	S	13.41 MW	11.69 AW	27880 AAW	INBLS	10//99-12//99
Retail Sales Workers	Gary PMSA, IN	S	15.69 MW	12.91 AW	32640 AAW	INBLS	10//99-12//99
Retail Sales Workers	Indianapolis MSA, IN	S	14.33 MW	12.73 AW	29800 AAW	INBLS	10//99-12//99
Retail Sales Workers	Kokomo MSA, IN	S	14.69 MW	11.91 AW	30560 AAW	INBLS	10//99-12//99
Retail Sales Workers	Lafayette MSA, IN	S	12.44 MW	11.48 AW	25880 AAW	INBLS	10//99-12//99
Retail Sales Workers	Muncie MSA, IN	S	12.18 MW	11.24 AW	25330 AAW	INBLS	10//99-12//99
Retail Sales Workers	South Bend MSA, IN	S	15.76 MW	12.73 AW	32780 AAW	INBLS	10//99-12//99
Retail Sales Workers	Terre Haute MSA, IN	S	14.62 MW	11.96 AW	30410 AAW	INBLS	10//99-12//99
Retail Sales Workers	Iowa	S	11.7	13.24 AW	27550 AAW	IABLS	10//99-12//99
Retail Sales Workers	Cedar Rapids MSA, IA	S	14.38 MW	12.73 AW	29910 AAW	IABLS	10//99-12//99
Retail Sales Workers	Davenport-Moline-Rock Island MSA, IA-IL	S	15.33 MW	12.25 AW	31880 AAW	IABLS	10//99-12//99
Retail Sales Workers	Des Moines MSA, IA	S	14.29 MW	12.33 AW	29730 AAW	IABLS	10//99-12//99
Retail Sales Workers	Dubuque MSA, IA	S	11.85 MW	10.20 AW	24640 AAW	IABLS	10//99-12//99
Retail Sales Workers	Iowa City MSA, IA	S	13.14 MW	12.07 AW	27320 AAW	IABLS	10//99-12//99
Retail Sales Workers	Sioux City MSA, IA-NE	S	16.96 MW	12.42 AW	35270 AAW	IABLS	10//99-12//99
Retail Sales Workers	Waterloo-Cedar Falls MSA, IA	S	13.37 MW	11.48 AW	27820 AAW	IABLS	10//99-12//99
Retail Sales Workers	Kansas	S	11.06 MW	13.11 AW	27260 AAW	KSBLS	10//99-12//99
Retail Sales Workers	Lawrence MSA, KS	S	11.80 MW	10.52 AW	24530 AAW	KSBLS	10//99-12//99
Retail Sales Workers	Topeka MSA, KS	S	13.44 MW	12.22 AW	27950 AAW	KSBLS	10//99-12//99
Retail Sales Workers	Wichita MSA, KS	S	12.68 MW	11.00 AW	26370 AAW	KSBLS	10//99-12//99
Retail Sales Workers	Kentucky	S	10.57 MW	12.63 AW	26260 AAW	KYBLS	10//99-12//99
Retail Sales Workers	Lexington MSA, KY	S	13.30 MW	11.13 AW	27670 AAW	KYBLS	10//99-12//99
Retail Sales Workers	Louisville MSA, KY-IN	S	14.07 MW	11.59 AW	29270 AAW	KYBLS	10//99-12//99
Retail Sales Workers	Owensboro MSA, KY	S	12.72 MW	10.22 AW	26450 AAW	KYBLS	10//99-12//99
Retail Sales Workers	Louisiana	S	12.33 MW	13.77 AW	28650 AAW	LABLS	10//99-12//99
Retail Sales Workers	Alexandria MSA, LA	S	12.66 MW	10.40 AW	26330 AAW	LABLS	10//99-12//99
Retail Sales Workers	Baton Rouge MSA, LA	S	14.42 MW	12.86 AW	29990 AAW	LABLS	10//99-12//99
Retail Sales Workers	Houma MSA, LA	S	13.72 MW	12.27 AW	28540 AAW	LABLS	10//99-12//99
Retail Sales Workers	Lafayette MSA, LA	S	14.57 MW	12.19 AW	30300 AAW	LABLS	10//99-12//99
Retail Sales Workers	Lake Charles MSA, LA	S	13.21 MW	12.27 AW	27480 AAW	LABLS	10//99-12//99
Retail Sales Workers	Monroe MSA, LA	S	13.73 MW	12.43 AW	28560 AAW	LABLS	10//99-12//99
Retail Sales Workers	New Orleans MSA, LA	S	14.58 MW	12.81 AW	30340 AAW	LABLS	10//99-12//99
Retail Sales Workers	Shreveport-Bossier City MSA, LA	S	13.02 MW	11.96 AW	27090 AAW	LABLS	10//99-12//99
Retail Sales Workers	Maine	S	12.65 MW	13.97 AW	29050 AAW	MEBLS	10//99-12//99
Retail Sales Workers	Bangor MSA, ME	S	14.25 MW	13.35 AW	29640 AAW	MEBLS	10//99-12//99
Retail Sales Workers	Lewiston-Auburn MSA, ME	S	14.50 MW	12.60 AW	30160 AAW	MEBLS	10//99-12//99
Retail Sales Workers	Portland MSA, ME	S	15.12 MW	13.70 AW	31450 AAW	MEBLS	10//99-12//99
Retail Sales Workers	Maryland	S	13.3 MW	15.01 AW	31220 AAW	MDBLS	10//99-12//99
Retail Sales Workers	Baltimore PMSA, MD	S	15.82 MW	13.90 AW	32910 AAW	MDBLS	10//99-12//99
Retail Sales Workers	Cumberland MSA, MD-WV	S	10.33 MW	9.11 AW	21490 AAW	MDBLS	10//99-12//99
Retail Sales Workers	Hagerstown PMSA, MD	S	11.39 MW	9.99 AW	23700 AAW	MDBLS	10//99-12//99
Retail Sales Workers	Massachusetts	S	13.4 MW	15.25 AW	31720 AAW	MABLS	10//99-12//99
Retail Sales Workers	Barnstable-Yarmouth MSA, MA	S	14.98 MW	12.62 AW	31150 AAW	MABLS	10//99-12//99
Retail Sales Workers	Boston PMSA, MA-NH	S	15.93 MW	14.01 AW	33130 AAW	MABLS	10//99-12//99
Retail Sales Workers	Brockton PMSA, MA	S	15.60 MW	14.40 AW	32460 AAW	MABLS	10//99-12//99
Retail Sales Workers	Fitchburg-Leominster PMSA, MA	S	14.51 MW	12.79 AW	30190 AAW	MABLS	10//99-12//99
Retail Sales Workers	Lawrence PMSA, MA-NH	S	13.69 MW	12.54 AW	28460 AAW	MABLS	10//99-12//99
Retail Sales Workers	Lowell PMSA, MA-NH	S	14.70 MW	13.16 AW	30580 AAW	MABLS	10//99-12//99
Retail Sales Workers	New Bedford PMSA, MA	S	13.95 MW	11.59 AW	29020 AAW	MABLS	10//99-12//99
Retail Sales Workers	Pittsfield MSA, MA	S	12.38 MW	11.05 AW	25760 AAW	MABLS	10//99-12//99
Retail Sales Workers	Springfield MSA, MA	S	13.71 MW	12.43 AW	28520 AAW	MABLS	10//99-12//99
Retail Sales Workers	Worcester PMSA, MA-CT	S	14.59 MW	13.75 AW	30350 AAW	MABLS	10//99-12//99
Retail Sales Workers	Michigan	S	13.54 MW	16.30 AW	33900 AAW	MIBLS	10//99-12//99
Retail Sales Workers	Ann Arbor PMSA, MI	S	16.16 MW	13.73 AW	33620 AAW	MIBLS	10//99-12//99
Retail Sales Workers	Benton Harbor MSA, MI	S	13.42 MW	11.94 AW	27920 AAW	MIBLS	10//99-12//99
Retail Sales Workers	Detroit PMSA, MI	S	17.29 MW	13.88 AW	35950 AAW	MIBLS	10//99-12//99
Retail Sales Workers	Flint PMSA, MI	S	15.98 MW	13.13 AW	33240 AAW	MIBLS	10//99-12//99
Retail Sales Workers	Grand Rapids-Muskegon-Holland MSA, MI	S	16.18 MW	14.47 AW	33660 AAW	MIBLS	10//99-12//99
Retail Sales Workers	Jackson MSA, MI	S	15.84 MW	13.48 AW	32950 AAW	MIBLS	10//99-12//99
Retail Sales Workers	Kalamazoo-Battle Creek MSA, MI	S	14.78 MW	13.52 AW	30740 AAW	MIBLS	10//99-12//99
Retail Sales Workers	Lansing-East Lansing MSA, MI	S	17.76 MW	13.47 AW	36940 AAW	MIBLS	10//99-12//99
Retail Sales Workers	Saginaw-Bay City-Midland MSA, MI	S	15.24 MW	13.32 AW	31700 AAW	MIBLS	10//99-12//99
Retail Sales Workers	Minnesota	S	13.28 MW	15.10 AW	31410 AAW	MNBLS	10//99-12//99
Retail Sales Workers	Duluth-Superior MSA, MN-WI	S	12.92 MW	11.74 AW	26870 AAW	MNBLS	10//99-12//99

Occupation/Type/Industry	Location	Per	Low	Mid	High	Source	Date
First-Line Supervisor/Manager							
Retail Sales Workers	Minneapolis-St. Paul MSA, MN-WI	S	16.25 MW	14.25 AW	33800 AAW	MNBLS	10//99-12//99
Retail Sales Workers	Rochester MSA, MN	S	13.29 MW	12.62 AW	27640 AAW	MNBLS	10//99-12//99
Retail Sales Workers	St. Cloud MSA, MN	S	14.77 MW	13.15 AW	30710 AAW	MNBLS	10//99-12//99
Retail Sales Workers	Mississippi	S	12.07 MW	13.57 AW	28220 AAW	MSBLS	10//99-12//99
Retail Sales Workers	Biloxi-Gulfport-Pascagoula MSA, MS	S	12.94 MW	11.67 AW	26920 AAW	MSBLS	10//99-12//99
Retail Sales Workers	Hattiesburg MSA, MS	S	13.75 MW	12.53 AW	28600 AAW	MSBLS	10//99-12//99
Retail Sales Workers	Jackson MSA, MS	S	14.46 MW	12.68 AW	30080 AAW	MSBLS	10//99-12//99
Retail Sales Workers	Missouri	S	11.99 MW	13.71 AW	28530 AAW	MOBLS	10//99-12//99
Retail Sales Workers	Columbia MSA, MO	S	12.97 MW	11.72 AW	26970 AAW	MOBLS	10//99-12//99
Retail Sales Workers	Joplin MSA, MO	S	12.35 MW	10.90 AW	25680 AAW	MOBLS	10//99-12//99
Retail Sales Workers	Kansas City MSA, MO-KS	S	14.87 MW	12.80 AW	30930 AAW	MOBLS	10//99-12//99
Retail Sales Workers	St. Joseph MSA, MO	S	13.06 MW	11.61 AW	27170 AAW	MOBLS	10//99-12//99
Retail Sales Workers	St. Louis MSA, MO-IL	S	14.59 MW	12.97 AW	30350 AAW	MOBLS	10//99-12//99
Retail Sales Workers	Springfield MSA, MO	S	13.50 MW	11.44 AW	28090 AAW	MOBLS	10//99-12//99
Retail Sales Workers	Montana	S	10.56 MW	13.27 AW	27590 AAW	MTBLS	10//99-12//99
Retail Sales Workers	Billings MSA, MT	S	17.07 MW	11.90 AW	35510 AAW	MTBLS	10//99-12//99
Retail Sales Workers	Great Falls MSA, MT	S	15.07 MW	12.12 AW	31340 AAW	MTBLS	10//99-12//99
Retail Sales Workers	Missoula MSA, MT	S	13.16 MW	11.02 AW	27380 AAW	MTBLS	10//99-12//99
Retail Sales Workers	Nebraska	S	12.81 MW	14.32 AW	29790 AAW	NEBLS	10//99-12//99
Retail Sales Workers	Lincoln MSA, NE	S	14.39 MW	12.55 AW	29930 AAW	NEBLS	10//99-12//99
Retail Sales Workers	Omaha MSA, NE-IA	S	15.39 MW	13.06 AW	32020 AAW	NEBLS	10//99-12//99
Retail Sales Workers	Nevada	S	12.54 MW	14.77 AW	30720 AAW	NVBLS	10//99-12//99
Retail Sales Workers	Las Vegas MSA, NV-AZ	S	14.32 MW	12.21 AW	29780 AAW	NVBLS	10//99-12//99
Retail Sales Workers	Reno MSA, NV	S	16.83 MW	14.01 AW	35000 AAW	NVBLS	10//99-12//99
Retail Sales Workers	New Hampshire	S	12.69 MW	14.25 AW	29640 AAW	NHBLS	10//99-12//99
Retail Sales Workers	Manchester PMSA, NH	S	14.89 MW	12.27 AW	30970 AAW	NHBLS	10//99-12//99
Retail Sales Workers	Nashua PMSA, NH	S	15.24 MW	14.13 AW	31700 AAW	NHBLS	10//99-12//99
Retail Sales Workers	Portsmouth-Rochester PMSA, NH-ME	S	14.62 MW	13.04 AW	30410 AAW	NHBLS	10//99-12//99
Retail Sales Workers	New Jersey	S	15.53 MW	18.19 AW	37830 AAW	NJBLS	10//99-12//99
Retail Sales Workers	Atlantic-Cape May PMSA, NJ	S	16.11 MW	14.26 AW	33520 AAW	NJBLS	10//99-12//99
Retail Sales Workers	Bergen-Passaic PMSA, NJ	S	18.58 MW	16.20 AW	38650 AAW	NJBLS	10//99-12//99
Retail Sales Workers	Jersey City PMSA, NJ	S	17.97 MW	15.11 AW	37390 AAW	NJBLS	10//99-12//99
Retail Sales Workers	Middlesex-Somerset-Hunterdon PMSA, NJ	S	17.15 MW	14.78 AW	35660 AAW	NJBLS	10//99-12//99
Retail Sales Workers	Monmouth-Ocean PMSA, NJ	S	18.31 MW	15.66 AW	38090 AAW	NJBLS	10//99-12//99
Retail Sales Workers	Newark PMSA, NJ	S	18.75 MW	16.00 AW	39000 AAW	NJBLS	10//99-12//99
Retail Sales Workers	Vineland-Millville-Bridgeton PMSA, NJ	S	18.25 MW	13.92 AW	37960 AAW	NJBLS	10//99-12//99
Retail Sales Workers	New Mexico	S	11.38 MW	13.06 AW	27170 AAW	NMBLS	10//99-12//99
Retail Sales Workers	Albuquerque MSA, NM	S	14.65 MW	12.30 AW	30470 AAW	NMBLS	10//99-12//99
Retail Sales Workers	Las Cruces MSA, NM	S	11.02 MW	9.81 AW	22920 AAW	NMBLS	10//99-12//99
Retail Sales Workers	Santa Fe MSA, NM	S	13.86 MW	12.16 AW	28830 AAW	NMBLS	10//99-12//99
Retail Sales Workers	New York	S	13.71 MW	17.53 AW	36470 AAW	NYBLS	10//99-12//99
Retail Sales Workers	Albany-Schenectady-Troy MSA, NY	S	15.11 MW	12.84 AW	31420 AAW	NYBLS	10//99-12//99
Retail Sales Workers	Binghamton MSA, NY	S	14.08 MW	13.18 AW	29290 AAW	NYBLS	10//99-12//99
Retail Sales Workers	Buffalo-Niagara Falls MSA, NY	S	14.06 MW	12.42 AW	29250 AAW	NYBLS	10//99-12//99
Retail Sales Workers	Dutchess County PMSA, NY	S	13.72 MW	11.52 AW	28540 AAW	NYBLS	10//99-12//99
Retail Sales Workers	Elmira MSA, NY	S	15.33 MW	12.59 AW	31880 AAW	NYBLS	10//99-12//99
Retail Sales Workers	Glens Falls MSA, NY	S	13.77 MW	11.10 AW	28640 AAW	NYBLS	10//99-12//99
Retail Sales Workers	Jamestown MSA, NY	S	13.13 MW	11.44 AW	27300 AAW	NYBLS	10//99-12//99
Retail Sales Workers	Nassau-Suffolk PMSA, NY	S	18.81 MW	14.34 AW	39130 AAW	NYBLS	10//99-12//99
Retail Sales Workers	New York PMSA, NY	S	19.76 MW	15.34 AW	41090 AAW	NYBLS	10//99-12//99
Retail Sales Workers	Newburgh PMSA, NY-PA	S	15.20 MW	13.09 AW	31610 AAW	NYBLS	10//99-12//99
Retail Sales Workers	Rochester MSA, NY	S	16.79 MW	12.19 AW	34910 AAW	NYBLS	10//99-12//99
Retail Sales Workers	Syracuse MSA, NY	S	15.17 MW	14.04 AW	31560 AAW	NYBLS	10//99-12//99
Retail Sales Workers	Utica-Rome MSA, NY	S	13.48 MW	11.08 AW	28030 AAW	NYBLS	10//99-12//99
Retail Sales Workers	North Carolina	S	11.78 MW	13.93 AW	28980 AAW	NCBLS	10//99-12//99
Retail Sales Workers	Asheville MSA, NC	S	12.62 MW	10.60 AW	26250 AAW	NCBLS	10//99-12//99
Retail Sales Workers	Charlotte-Gastonia-Rock Hill MSA, NC-SC	S	14.57 MW	12.36 AW	30300 AAW	NCBLS	10//99-12//99
Retail Sales Workers	Fayetteville MSA, NC	S	12.00 MW	10.93 AW	24960 AAW	NCBLS	10//99-12//99
Retail Sales Workers	Goldsboro MSA, NC	S	11.16 MW	10.46 AW	23210 AAW	NCBLS	10//99-12//99
Retail Sales Workers	Greensboro--Winston-Salem--High Point MSA, NC	S	14.17 MW	12.49 AW	29470 AAW	NCBLS	10//99-12//99
Retail Sales Workers	Greenville MSA, NC	S	11.97 MW	11.14 AW	24900 AAW	NCBLS	10//99-12//99

AAW	Average annual wage	AOH	Average offered, high	ASH	Average starting, high	H	Hourly	M	Monthly	S	Special: hourly and annual
AE	Average entry wage	AOL	Average offered, low	ASL	Average starting, low	HI	Highest wage paid	MTC	Median total compensation	TQ	Third quartile wage
AEX	Average experienced wage	APH	Average pay, high range	AW	Average wage paid	HR	High end range	MW	Median wage paid	W	Weekly
AO	Average offered	APL	Average pay, low range	FQ	First quartile wage	LR	Low end range	SQ	Second quartile wage	Y	Yearly

Occupation/Type/Industry	Location	Per	Low	Mid	High	Source	Date
First-Line Supervisor/Manager							
Retail Sales Workers	Hickory-Morganton-Lenoir MSA, NC	S	14.17 MW	11.88 AW	29460 AAW	NCBLS	10//99-12//99
Retail Sales Workers	Jacksonville MSA, NC	S	14.04 MW	12.42 AW	29190 AAW	NCBLS	10//99-12//99
Retail Sales Workers	Raleigh-Durham-Chapel Hill MSA, NC	S	14.27 MW	12.45 AW	29690 AAW	NCBLS	10//99-12//99
Retail Sales Workers	Rocky Mount MSA, NC	S	12.80 MW	11.77 AW	26630 AAW	NCBLS	10//99-12//99
Retail Sales Workers	Wilmington MSA, NC	S	13.08 MW	12.19 AW	27220 AAW	NCBLS	10//99-12//99
Retail Sales Workers	North Dakota	S	11.24 MW	12.83 AW	26690 AAW	NDBLS	10//99-12//99
Retail Sales Workers	Bismarck MSA, ND	S	11.69 MW	10.21 AW	24320 AAW	NDBLS	10//99-12//99
Retail Sales Workers	Fargo-Moorhead MSA, ND-MN	S	13.99 MW	12.35 AW	29110 AAW	NDBLS	10//99-12//99
Retail Sales Workers	Grand Forks MSA, ND-MN	S	12.61 MW	11.72 AW	26230 AAW	NDBLS	10//99-12//99
Retail Sales Workers	Ohio	S	12.14 MW	13.83 AW	28770 AAW	OHBLS	10//99-12//99
Retail Sales Workers	Akron PMSA, OH	S	13.40 MW	12.04 AW	27870 AAW	OHBLS	10//99-12//99
Retail Sales Workers	Canton-Massillon MSA, OH	S	11.36 MW	9.77 AW	23620 AAW	OHBLS	10//99-12//99
Retail Sales Workers	Cincinnati PMSA, OH-KY-IN	S	13.98 MW	11.70 AW	29080 AAW	OHBLS	10//99-12//99
Retail Sales Workers	Cleveland-Lorain-Elyria PMSA, OH	S	14.08 MW	12.82 AW	29290 AAW	OHBLS	10//99-12//99
Retail Sales Workers	Columbus MSA, OH	S	15.77 MW	13.69 AW	32810 AAW	OHBLS	10//99-12//99
Retail Sales Workers	Dayton-Springfield MSA, OH	S	14.01 MW	12.45 AW	29140 AAW	OHBLS	10//99-12//99
Retail Sales Workers	Hamilton-Middletown PMSA, OH	S	14.21 MW	12.22 AW	29550 AAW	OHBLS	10//99-12//99
Retail Sales Workers	Lima MSA, OH	S	12.19 MW	10.19 AW	25370 AAW	OHBLS	10//99-12//99
Retail Sales Workers	Mansfield MSA, OH	S	13.00 MW	11.75 AW	27030 AAW	OHBLS	10//99-12//99
Retail Sales Workers	Steubenville-Weirton MSA, OH-WV	S	11.88 MW	10.14 AW	24710 AAW	OHBLS	10//99-12//99
Retail Sales Workers	Toledo MSA, OH	S	14.74 MW	12.36 AW	30660 AAW	OHBLS	10//99-12//99
Retail Sales Workers	Youngstown-Warren MSA, OH	S	13.89 MW	12.04 AW	28890 AAW	OHBLS	10//99-12//99
Retail Sales Workers	Oklahoma	S	10.46 MW	12.35 AW	25680 AAW	OKBLS	10//99-12//99
Retail Sales Workers	Enid MSA, OK	S	10.65 MW	8.46 AW	22140 AAW	OKBLS	10//99-12//99
Retail Sales Workers	Lawton MSA, OK	S	11.67 MW	10.75 AW	24280 AAW	OKBLS	10//99-12//99
Retail Sales Workers	Oklahoma City MSA, OK	S	12.65 MW	10.61 AW	26310 AAW	OKBLS	10//99-12//99
Retail Sales Workers	Tulsa MSA, OK	S	14.53 MW	12.01 AW	30230 AAW	OKBLS	10//99-12//99
Retail Sales Workers	Oregon	S	14.84 MW	17.59 AW	36600 AAW	ORBLS	10//99-12//99
Retail Sales Workers	Corvallis MSA, OR	S	15.67 MW	13.30 AW	32600 AAW	ORBLS	10//99-12//99
Retail Sales Workers	Eugene-Springfield MSA, OR	S	18.94 MW	17.11 AW	39390 AAW	ORBLS	10//99-12//99
Retail Sales Workers	Medford-Ashland MSA, OR	S	15.62 MW	13.52 AW	32490 AAW	ORBLS	10//99-12//99
Retail Sales Workers	Portland-Vancouver PMSA, OR-WA	S	19.19 MW	16.00 AW	39910 AAW	ORBLS	10//99-12//99
Retail Sales Workers	Salem PMSA, OR	S	17.42 MW	14.53 AW	36230 AAW	ORBLS	10//99-12//99
Retail Sales Workers	Pennsylvania	S	12.94 MW	14.27 AW	29690 AAW	PABLS	10//99-12//99
Retail Sales Workers	Allentown-Bethlehem-Easton MSA, PA	S	15.77 MW	14.81 AW	32800 AAW	PABLS	10//99-12//99
Retail Sales Workers	Altoona MSA, PA	S	13.71 MW	12.20 AW	28520 AAW	PABLS	10//99-12//99
Retail Sales Workers	Erie MSA, PA	S	13.58 MW	12.58 AW	28260 AAW	PABLS	10//99-12//99
Retail Sales Workers	Harrisburg-Lebanon-Carlisle MSA, PA	S	15.03 MW	13.84 AW	31270 AAW	PABLS	10//99-12//99
Retail Sales Workers	Johnstown MSA, PA	S	12.70 MW	11.51 AW	26430 AAW	PABLS	10//99-12//99
Retail Sales Workers	Lancaster MSA, PA	S	14.72 MW	13.29 AW	30610 AAW	PABLS	10//99-12//99
Retail Sales Workers	Philadelphia PMSA, PA-NJ	S	16.03 MW	14.48 AW	33330 AAW	PABLS	10//99-12//99
Retail Sales Workers	Pittsburgh MSA, PA	S	13.05 MW	11.71 AW	27140 AAW	PABLS	10//99-12//99
Retail Sales Workers	Reading MSA, PA	S	15.32 MW	13.34 AW	31870 AAW	PABLS	10//99-12//99
Retail Sales Workers	Scranton--Wilkes-Barre--Hazleton MSA, PA	S	13.33 MW	11.97 AW	27730 AAW	PABLS	10//99-12//99
Retail Sales Workers	Sharon MSA, PA	S	12.75 MW	11.68 AW	26520 AAW	PABLS	10//99-12//99
Retail Sales Workers	State College MSA, PA	S	12.04 MW	11.28 AW	25040 AAW	PABLS	10//99-12//99
Retail Sales Workers	Williamsport MSA, PA	S	12.56 MW	11.62 AW	26130 AAW	PABLS	10//99-12//99
Retail Sales Workers	York MSA, PA	S	14.97 MW	13.26 AW	31140 AAW	PABLS	10//99-12//99
Retail Sales Workers	Rhode Island	S	13.9 MW	16.54 AW	34410 AAW	RIBLS	10//99-12//99
Retail Sales Workers	Providence-Fall River-Warwick MSA, RI-MA	S	15.83 MW	13.45 AW	32920 AAW	RIBLS	10//99-12//99
Retail Sales Workers	South Carolina	S	12.01 MW	13.60 AW	28300 AAW	SCBLS	10//99-12//99
Retail Sales Workers	Charleston-North Charleston MSA, SC	S	14.83 MW	12.85 AW	30840 AAW	SCBLS	10//99-12//99
Retail Sales Workers	Columbia MSA, SC	S	14.30 MW	12.62 AW	29750 AAW	SCBLS	10//99-12//99
Retail Sales Workers	Florence MSA, SC	S	15.06 MW	14.49 AW	31320 AAW	SCBLS	10//99-12//99
Retail Sales Workers	Greenville-Spartanburg-Anderson MSA, SC	S	13.92 MW	12.17 AW	28950 AAW	SCBLS	10//99-12//99
Retail Sales Workers	Myrtle Beach MSA, SC	S	14.82 MW	12.72 AW	30820 AAW	SCBLS	10//99-12//99
Retail Sales Workers	Sumter MSA, SC	S	12.28 MW	10.36 AW	25550 AAW	SCBLS	10//99-12//99
Retail Sales Workers	South Dakota	S	13.5 MW	15.49 AW	32210 AAW	SDBLS	10//99-12//99

AAW	Average annual wage	AOH	Average offered, high	ASH	Average starting, high
AE	Average entry wage	AOL	Average offered, low	ASL	Average starting, low
AEX	Average experienced wage	APH	Average pay, high range	AW	Average wage paid
AO	Average offered	APL	Average pay, low range	FQ	First quartile wage

H	Hourly	M	Monthly	S	Special: hourly and annual
HI	Highest wage paid	MTC	Median total compensation	TQ	Third quartile wage
HR	High end range	MW	Median wage paid	W	Weekly
LR	Low end range	SQ	Second quartile wage	Y	Yearly

Occupation/Type/Industry	Location	Per	Low	Mid	High	Source	Date
First-Line Supervisor/Manager							
Retail Sales Workers	Rapid City MSA, SD	S	16.02 MW	13.40 AW	33320 AAW	SDBLS	10//99-12//99
Retail Sales Workers	Sioux Falls MSA, SD	S	15.49 MW	13.51 AW	32210 AAW	SDBLS	10//99-12//99
Retail Sales Workers	Tennessee	S	11.28 MW	13.28 AW	27620 AAW	TNBLS	10//99-12//99
Retail Sales Workers	Chattanooga MSA, TN-GA	S	13.01 MW	10.56 AW	27070 AAW	TNBLS	10//99-12//99
Retail Sales Workers	Clarksville-Hopkinsville MSA, TN-KY	S	11.64 MW	10.25 AW	24210 AAW	TNBLS	10//99-12//99
Retail Sales Workers	Jackson MSA, TN	S	17.57 MW	14.02 AW	36540 AAW	TNBLS	10//99-12//99
Retail Sales Workers	Johnson City-Kingsport-Bristol MSA, TN-VA	S	13.34 MW	10.86 AW	27760 AAW	TNBLS	10//99-12//99
Retail Sales Workers	Knoxville MSA, TN	S	11.64 MW	10.43 AW	24210 AAW	TNBLS	10//99-12//99
Retail Sales Workers	Memphis MSA, TN-AR-MS	S	12.97 MW	11.72 AW	26970 AAW	MSBLS	10//99-12//99
Retail Sales Workers	Nashville MSA, TN	S	15.62 MW	12.63 AW	32500 AAW	TNBLS	10//99-12//99
Retail Sales Workers	Texas	S	12.03 MW	13.64 AW	28380 AAW	TXBLS	10//99-12//99
Retail Sales Workers	Abilene MSA, TX	S	12.19 MW	9.98 AW	25350 AAW	TXBLS	10//99-12//99
Retail Sales Workers	Amarillo MSA, TX	S	12.67 MW	11.63 AW	26360 AAW	TXBLS	10//99-12//99
Retail Sales Workers	Austin-San Marcos MSA, TX	S	13.65 MW	12.32 AW	28380 AAW	TXBLS	10//99-12//99
Retail Sales Workers	Beaumont-Port Arthur MSA, TX	S	12.85 MW	10.72 AW	26720 AAW	TXBLS	10//99-12//99
Retail Sales Workers	Brazoria PMSA, TX	S	12.62 MW	11.55 AW	26250 AAW	TXBLS	10//99-12//99
Retail Sales Workers	Brownsville-Harlingen-San Benito MSA, TX	S	11.98 MW	11.05 AW	24930 AAW	TXBLS	10//99-12//99
Retail Sales Workers	Bryan-College Station MSA, TX	S	14.02 MW	12.32 AW	29160 AAW	TXBLS	10//99-12//99
Retail Sales Workers	Corpus Christi MSA, TX	S	13.15 MW	11.46 AW	27340 AAW	TXBLS	10//99-12//99
Retail Sales Workers	Dallas PMSA, TX	S	15.50 MW	13.69 AW	32250 AAW	TXBLS	10//99-12//99
Retail Sales Workers	El Paso MSA, TX	S	12.25 MW	10.67 AW	25480 AAW	TXBLS	10//99-12//99
Retail Sales Workers	Fort Worth-Arlington PMSA, TX	S	13.50 MW	12.37 AW	28070 AAW	TXBLS	10//99-12//99
Retail Sales Workers	Galveston-Texas City PMSA, TX	S	13.05 MW	12.32 AW	27130 AAW	TXBLS	10//99-12//99
Retail Sales Workers	Houston PMSA, TX	S	14.01 MW	12.47 AW	29140 AAW	TXBLS	10//99-12//99
Retail Sales Workers	Killeen-Temple MSA, TX	S	12.64 MW	11.50 AW	26280 AAW	TXBLS	10//99-12//99
Retail Sales Workers	Laredo MSA, TX	S	11.36 MW	10.87 AW	23620 AAW	TXBLS	10//99-12//99
Retail Sales Workers	Longview-Marshall MSA, TX	S	12.02 MW	9.96 AW	25010 AAW	TXBLS	10//99-12//99
Retail Sales Workers	Lubbock MSA, TX	S	13.61 MW	11.16 AW	28300 AAW	TXBLS	10//99-12//99
Retail Sales Workers	McAllen-Edinburg-Mission MSA, TX	S	12.22 MW	10.20 AW	25420 AAW	TXBLS	10//99-12//99
Retail Sales Workers	Odessa-Midland MSA, TX	S	12.22 MW	10.73 AW	25420 AAW	TXBLS	10//99-12//99
Retail Sales Workers	San Angelo MSA, TX	S	15.99 MW	14.58 AW	33260 AAW	TXBLS	10//99-12//99
Retail Sales Workers	San Antonio MSA, TX	S	14.27 MW	12.81 AW	29670 AAW	TXBLS	10//99-12//99
Retail Sales Workers	Sherman-Denison MSA, TX	S	10.98 MW	8.48 AW	22840 AAW	TXBLS	10//99-12//99
Retail Sales Workers	Texarkana MSA, TX-Texarkana, AR	S	10.68 MW	9.75 AW	22220 AAW	TXBLS	10//99-12//99
Retail Sales Workers	Tyler MSA, TX	S	13.08 MW	11.90 AW	27210 AAW	TXBLS	10//99-12//99
Retail Sales Workers	Victoria MSA, TX	S	13.12 MW	12.33 AW	27300 AAW	TXBLS	10//99-12//99
Retail Sales Workers	Waco MSA, TX	S	12.86 MW	12.19 AW	26750 AAW	TXBLS	10//99-12//99
Retail Sales Workers	Wichita Falls MSA, TX	S	12.60 MW	10.93 AW	26200 AAW	TXBLS	10//99-12//99
Retail Sales Workers	Utah	S	12.17 MW	13.96 AW	29030 AAW	UTBLS	10//99-12//99
Retail Sales Workers	Provo-Orem MSA, UT	S	13.16 MW	10.70 AW	27380 AAW	UTBLS	10//99-12//99
Retail Sales Workers	Salt Lake City-Ogden MSA, UT	S	14.80 MW	12.88 AW	30780 AAW	UTBLS	10//99-12//99
Retail Sales Workers	Vermont	S	14.08 MW	17.16 AW	35680 AAW	VTBLS	10//99-12//99
Retail Sales Workers	Burlington MSA, VT	S	21.40 MW	16.88 AW	44510 AAW	VTBLS	10//99-12//99
Retail Sales Workers	Virginia	S	11.81 MW	13.63 AW	28350 AAW	VABLS	10//99-12//99
Retail Sales Workers	Charlottesville MSA, VA	S	14.12 MW	13.49 AW	29360 AAW	VABLS	10//99-12//99
Retail Sales Workers	Danville MSA, VA	S	11.22 MW	10.35 AW	23330 AAW	VABLS	10//99-12//99
Retail Sales Workers	Lynchburg MSA, VA	S	10.96 MW	9.69 AW	22790 AAW	VABLS	10//99-12//99
Retail Sales Workers	Norfolk-Virginia Beach-Newport News MSA, VA-NC	S	12.20 MW	10.38 AW	25380 AAW	VABLS	10//99-12//99
Retail Sales Workers	Richmond-Petersburg MSA, VA	S	15.27 MW	12.91 AW	31760 AAW	VABLS	10//99-12//99
Retail Sales Workers	Roanoke MSA, VA	S	14.14 MW	11.36 AW	29410 AAW	VABLS	10//99-12//99
Retail Sales Workers	Washington	S	15.16 MW	17.51 AW	36430 AAW	WABLS	10//99-12//99
Retail Sales Workers	Bellingham MSA, WA	S	16.77 MW	15.49 AW	34880 AAW	WABLS	10//99-12//99
Retail Sales Workers	Bremerton PMSA, WA	S	15.45 MW	12.85 AW	32130 AAW	WABLS	10//99-12//99
Retail Sales Workers	Olympia PMSA, WA	S	16.74 MW	15.43 AW	34830 AAW	WABLS	10//99-12//99
Retail Sales Workers	Richland-Kennewick-Pasco MSA, WA	S	17.22 MW	15.95 AW	35820 AAW	WABLS	10//99-12//99
Retail Sales Workers	Seattle-Bellevue-Everett PMSA, WA	S	18.06 MW	15.53 AW	37570 AAW	WABLS	10//99-12//99

AAW Average annual wage	**AOH** Average offered, high	**ASH** Average starting, high	**H** Hourly	**M** Monthly	**S** Special: hourly and annual
AE Average entry wage	**AOL** Average offered, low	**ASL** Average starting, low	**HI** Highest wage paid	**MTC** Median total compensation	**TQ** Third quartile wage
AEX Average experienced wage	**APH** Average pay, high range	**AW** Average wage paid	**HR** High end range	**MW** Median wage paid	**W** Weekly
AO Average offered	**APL** Average pay, low range	**FQ** First quartile wage	**LR** Low end range	**SQ** Second quartile wage	**Y** Yearly

Occupation/Type/Industry	Location	Per	Low	Mid	High	Source	Date
First-Line Supervisor/Manager							
Retail Sales Workers	Spokane MSA, WA	S	16.32 MW	13.40 AW	33950 AAW	WABLS	10//99-12//99
Retail Sales Workers	Tacoma PMSA, WA	S	18.14 MW	15.18 AW	37740 AAW	WABLS	10//99-12//99
Retail Sales Workers	Yakima MSA, WA	S	16.47 MW	15.22 AW	34270 AAW	WABLS	10//99-12//99
Retail Sales Workers	West Virginia	S	10.24 MW	11.70 AW	24340 AAW	WVBLS	10//99-12//99
Retail Sales Workers	Charleston MSA, WV	S	14.07 MW	12.50 AW	29270 AAW	WVBLS	10//99-12//99
Retail Sales Workers	Huntington-Ashland MSA, WV-KY-OH	S	11.57 MW	10.00 AW	24060 AAW	WVBLS	10//99-12//99
Retail Sales Workers	Parkersburg-Marietta MSA, WV-OH	S	12.85 MW	11.15 AW	26720 AAW	WVBLS	10//99-12//99
Retail Sales Workers	Wheeling MSA, WV-OH	S	11.86 MW	11.17 AW	24670 AAW	WVBLS	10//99-12//99
Retail Sales Workers	Wisconsin	S	12.66 MW	15.02 AW	31240 AAW	WIBLS	10//99-12//99
Retail Sales Workers	Appleton-Oshkosh-Neenah MSA, WI	S	15.47 MW	13.13 AW	32180 AAW	WIBLS	10//99-12//99
Retail Sales Workers	Eau Claire MSA, WI	S	12.67 MW	10.38 AW	26360 AAW	WIBLS	10//99-12//99
Retail Sales Workers	Green Bay MSA, WI	S	16.28 MW	13.73 AW	33870 AAW	WIBLS	10//99-12//99
Retail Sales Workers	Janesville-Beloit MSA, WI	S	13.78 MW	12.39 AW	28650 AAW	WIBLS	10//99-12//99
Retail Sales Workers	Kenosha PMSA, WI	S	13.86 MW	12.40 AW	28820 AAW	WIBLS	10//99-12//99
Retail Sales Workers	La Crosse MSA, WI-MN	S	13.76 MW	12.03 AW	28610 AAW	WIBLS	10//99-12//99
Retail Sales Workers	Madison MSA, WI	S	13.72 MW	12.33 AW	28540 AAW	WIBLS	10//99-12//99
Retail Sales Workers	Milwaukee-Waukesha PMSA, WI	S	16.92 MW	13.58 AW	35180 AAW	WIBLS	10//99-12//99
Retail Sales Workers	Racine PMSA, WI	S	14.08 MW	12.77 AW	29280 AAW	WIBLS	10//99-12//99
Retail Sales Workers	Sheboygan MSA, WI	S	15.03 MW	14.29 AW	31260 AAW	WIBLS	10//99-12//99
Retail Sales Workers	Wausau MSA, WI	S	16.27 MW	16.06 AW	33840 AAW	WIBLS	10//99-12//99
Retail Sales Workers	Wyoming	S	10.92 MW	12.46 AW	25920 AAW	WYBLS	10//99-12//99
Retail Sales Workers	Casper MSA, WY	S	12.61 MW	10.74 AW	26220 AAW	WYBLS	10//99-12//99
Retail Sales Workers	Cheyenne MSA, WY	S	15.26 MW	13.13 AW	31740 AAW	WYBLS	10//99-12//99
Retail Sales Workers	Puerto Rico	S	8.85 MW	10.55 AW	21940 AAW	PRBLS	10//99-12//99
Retail Sales Workers	Aguadilla MSA, PR	S	10.06 MW	8.47 AW	20920 AAW	PRBLS	10//99-12//99
Retail Sales Workers	Arecibo PMSA, PR	S	9.72 MW	8.31 AW	20220 AAW	PRBLS	10//99-12//99
Retail Sales Workers	Caguas PMSA, PR	S	10.73 MW	8.36 AW	22310 AAW	PRBLS	10//99-12//99
Retail Sales Workers	Mayaguez MSA, PR	S	10.11 MW	7.85 AW	21020 AAW	PRBLS	10//99-12//99
Retail Sales Workers	Ponce MSA, PR	S	9.97 MW	8.42 AW	20730 AAW	PRBLS	10//99-12//99
Retail Sales Workers	San Juan-Bayamon PMSA, PR	S	10.74 MW	9.18 AW	22350 AAW	PRBLS	10//99-12//99
Retail Sales Workers	Virgin Islands	S	12.73 MW	13.48 AW	28030 AAW	VIBLS	10//99-12//99
Retail Sales Workers	Guam	S	10.58 MW	12.15 AW	25270 AAW	GUBLS	10//99-12//99
Transportation and Material-Moving Machine and Vehicle Operators	Alabama	S	16.6 MW	18.09 AW	37630 AAW	ALBLS	10//99-12//99
Transportation and Material-Moving Machine and Vehicle Operators	Auburn-Opelika MSA, AL	S	16.72 MW	17.70 AW	34770 AAW	ALBLS	10//99-12//99
Transportation and Material-Moving Machine and Vehicle Operators	Birmingham MSA, AL	S	18.88 MW	17.92 AW	39260 AAW	ALBLS	10//99-12//99
Transportation and Material-Moving Machine and Vehicle Operators	Dothan MSA, AL	S	17.88 MW	15.71 AW	37180 AAW	ALBLS	10//99-12//99
Transportation and Material-Moving Machine and Vehicle Operators	Gadsden MSA, AL	S	16.40 MW	16.01 AW	34120 AAW	ALBLS	10//99-12//99
Transportation and Material-Moving Machine and Vehicle Operators	Huntsville MSA, AL	S	16.73 MW	14.17 AW	34790 AAW	ALBLS	10//99-12//99
Transportation and Material-Moving Machine and Vehicle Operators	Mobile MSA, AL	S	15.88 MW	15.02 AW	33020 AAW	ALBLS	10//99-12//99
Transportation and Material-Moving Machine and Vehicle Operators	Montgomery MSA, AL	S	23.56 MW	23.69 AW	49010 AAW	ALBLS	10//99-12//99
Transportation and Material-Moving Machine and Vehicle Operators	Tuscaloosa MSA, AL	S	14.57 MW	13.93 AW	30300 AAW	ALBLS	10//99-12//99
Transportation and Material-Moving Machine and Vehicle Operators	Alaska	S	25.69 MW	26.57 AW	55270 AAW	AKBLS	10//99-12//99
Transportation and Material-Moving Machine and Vehicle Operators	Arizona	S	16.26 MW	17.56 AW	36520 AAW	AZBLS	10//99-12//99
Transportation and Material-Moving Machine and Vehicle Operators	Flagstaff MSA, AZ-UT	S	16.35 MW	13.40 AW	34000 AAW	AZBLS	10//99-12//99
Transportation and Material-Moving Machine and Vehicle Operators	Phoenix-Mesa MSA, AZ	S	17.73 MW	16.42 AW	36870 AAW	AZBLS	10//99-12//99
Transportation and Material-Moving Machine and Vehicle Operators	Tucson MSA, AZ	S	17.01 MW	15.67 AW	35380 AAW	AZBLS	10//99-12//99
Transportation and Material-Moving Machine and Vehicle Operators	Yuma MSA, AZ	S	15.33 MW	15.08 AW	31890 AAW	AZBLS	10//99-12//99
Transportation and Material-Moving Machine and Vehicle Operators	Arkansas	S	18.2 MW	18.94 AW	39390 AAW	ARBLS	10//99-12//99

AAW	Average annual wage	AOH	Average offered, high	ASH	Average starting, high	H	Hourly	M	Monthly	S	Special: hourly and annual
AE	Average entry wage	AOL	Average offered, low	ASL	Average starting, low	HI	Highest wage paid	MTC	Median total compensation	TQ	Third quartile wage
AEX	Average experienced wage	APH	Average pay, high range	AW	Average wage paid	HR	High end range	MW	Median wage paid	W	Weekly
AO	Average offered	APL	Average pay, low range	FQ	First quartile wage	LR	Low end range	SQ	Second quartile wage	Y	Yearly

First-Line Supervisor/Manager

Occupation/Type/Industry	Location	Per	Low	Mid	High	Source	Date
Transportation and Material-Moving Machine and Vehicle Operators	Fayetteville-Springdale-Rogers MSA, AR	S	17.35 MW	17.23 AW	36090 AAW	ARBLS	10//99-12//99
Transportation and Material-Moving Machine and Vehicle Operators	Fort Smith MSA, AR-OK	S	22.72 MW	23.25 AW	47270 AAW	ARBLS	10//99-12//99
Transportation and Material-Moving Machine and Vehicle Operators	Jonesboro MSA, AR	S	19.25 MW	18.80 AW	40040 AAW	ARBLS	10//99-12//99
Transportation and Material-Moving Machine and Vehicle Operators	Little Rock-North Little Rock MSA, AR	S	20.42 MW	19.39 AW	42470 AAW	ARBLS	10//99-12//99
Transportation and Material-Moving Machine and Vehicle Operators	Pine Bluff MSA, AR	S	21.06 MW	19.70 AW	43810 AAW	ARBLS	10//99-12//99
Transportation and Material-Moving Machine and Vehicle Operators	California	S	19.82 MW	20.66 AW	42960 AAW	CABLS	10//99-12//99
Transportation and Material-Moving Machine and Vehicle Operators	Bakersfield MSA, CA	S	20.69 MW	19.70 AW	43030 AAW	CABLS	10//99-12//99
Transportation and Material-Moving Machine and Vehicle Operators	Chico-Paradise MSA, CA	S	17.26 MW	16.49 AW	35900 AAW	CABLS	10//99-12//99
Transportation and Material-Moving Machine and Vehicle Operators	Fresno MSA, CA	S	20.06 MW	19.81 AW	41720 AAW	CABLS	10//99-12//99
Transportation and Material-Moving Machine and Vehicle Operators	Los Angeles-Long Beach PMSA, CA	S	20.02 MW	19.25 AW	41650 AAW	CABLS	10//99-12//99
Transportation and Material-Moving Machine and Vehicle Operators	Merced MSA, CA	S	21.62 MW	19.18 AW	44960 AAW	CABLS	10//99-12//99
Transportation and Material-Moving Machine and Vehicle Operators	Modesto MSA, CA	S	23.83 MW	20.75 AW	49570 AAW	CABLS	10//99-12//99
Transportation and Material-Moving Machine and Vehicle Operators	Oakland PMSA, CA	S	23.57 MW	23.20 AW	49040 AAW	CABLS	10//99-12//99
Transportation and Material-Moving Machine and Vehicle Operators	Orange County PMSA, CA	S	17.96 MW	17.52 AW	37370 AAW	CABLS	10//99-12//99
Transportation and Material-Moving Machine and Vehicle Operators	Redding MSA, CA	S	27.01 MW	25.91 AW	56170 AAW	CABLS	10//99-12//99
Transportation and Material-Moving Machine and Vehicle Operators	Riverside-San Bernardino PMSA, CA	S	21.93 MW	21.58 AW	45620 AAW	CABLS	10//99-12//99
Transportation and Material-Moving Machine and Vehicle Operators	Sacramento PMSA, CA	S	22.10 MW	19.67 AW	45970 AAW	CABLS	10//99-12//99
Transportation and Material-Moving Machine and Vehicle Operators	Salinas MSA, CA	S	17.40 MW	16.53 AW	36190 AAW	CABLS	10//99-12//99
Transportation and Material-Moving Machine and Vehicle Operators	San Diego MSA, CA	S	16.15 MW	12.90 AW	33590 AAW	CABLS	10//99-12//99
Transportation and Material-Moving Machine and Vehicle Operators	San Francisco PMSA, CA	S	23.71 MW	21.58 AW	49310 AAW	CABLS	10//99-12//99
Transportation and Material-Moving Machine and Vehicle Operators	San Jose PMSA, CA	S	23.48 MW	21.18 AW	48840 AAW	CABLS	10//99-12//99
Transportation and Material-Moving Machine and Vehicle Operators	San Luis Obispo-Atascadero-Paso Robles MSA, CA	S	22.33 MW	19.49 AW	46450 AAW	CABLS	10//99-12//99
Transportation and Material-Moving Machine and Vehicle Operators	Santa Barbara-Santa Maria-Lompoc MSA, CA	S	20.11 MW	18.78 AW	41820 AAW	CABLS	10//99-12//99
Transportation and Material-Moving Machine and Vehicle Operators	Santa Cruz-Watsonville PMSA, CA	S	18.17 MW	18.79 AW	37790 AAW	CABLS	10//99-12//99
Transportation and Material-Moving Machine and Vehicle Operators	Santa Rosa PMSA, CA	S	19.77 MW	18.29 AW	41120 AAW	CABLS	10//99-12//99
Transportation and Material-Moving Machine and Vehicle Operators	Stockton-Lodi MSA, CA	S	19.33 MW	18.91 AW	40200 AAW	CABLS	10//99-12//99
Transportation and Material-Moving Machine and Vehicle Operators	Vallejo-Fairfield-Napa PMSA, CA	S	28.33 MW	29.62 AW	58920 AAW	CABLS	10//99-12//99
Transportation and Material-Moving Machine and Vehicle Operators	Ventura PMSA, CA	S	17.41 MW	15.48 AW	36220 AAW	CABLS	10//99-12//99
Transportation and Material-Moving Machine and Vehicle Operators	Visalia-Tulare-Porterville MSA, CA	S	18.27 MW	17.61 AW	37990 AAW	CABLS	10//99-12//99
Transportation and Material-Moving Machine and Vehicle Operators	Yolo PMSA, CA	S	21.70 MW	21.05 AW	45130 AAW	CABLS	10//99-12//99

AAW	Average annual wage	AOH	Average offered, high	ASH	Average starting, high	H	Hourly	M	Monthly	S	Special: hourly and annual
AE	Average entry wage	AOL	Average offered, low	ASL	Average starting, low	HI	Highest wage paid	MTC	Median total compensation	TQ	Third quartile wage
AEX	Average experienced wage	APH	Average pay, high range	AW	Average wage paid	HR	High end range	MW	Median wage paid	W	Weekly
AO	Average offered	APL	Average pay, low range	FQ	First quartile wage	LR	Low end range	SQ	Second quartile wage	Y	Yearly

Occupation/Type/Industry	Location	Per	Low	Mid	High	Source	Date
First-Line Supervisor/Manager							
Transportation and Material-Moving Machine and Vehicle Operators	Yuba City MSA, CA	S	25.03 MW	24.77 AW	52050 AAW	CABLS	10//99-12//99
Transportation and Material-Moving Machine and Vehicle Operators	Colorado	S	18.37 MW	20.05 AW	41700 AAW	COBLS	10//99-12//99
Transportation and Material-Moving Machine and Vehicle Operators	Colorado Springs MSA, CO	S	19.36 MW	17.45 AW	40260 AAW	COBLS	10//99-12//99
Transportation and Material-Moving Machine and Vehicle Operators	Denver PMSA, CO	S	19.67 MW	18.45 AW	40920 AAW	COBLS	10//99-12//99
Transportation and Material-Moving Machine and Vehicle Operators	Fort Collins-Loveland MSA, CO	S	17.44 MW	16.17 AW	36280 AAW	COBLS	10//99-12//99
Transportation and Material-Moving Machine and Vehicle Operators	Grand Junction MSA, CO	S	19.15 MW	18.39 AW	39830 AAW	COBLS	10//99-12//99
Transportation and Material-Moving Machine and Vehicle Operators	Greeley PMSA, CO	S	20.50 MW	22.07 AW	42630 AAW	COBLS	10//99-12//99
Transportation and Material-Moving Machine and Vehicle Operators	Pueblo MSA, CO	S	19.15 MW	16.87 AW	39820 AAW	COBLS	10//99-12//99
Transportation and Material-Moving Machine and Vehicle Operators	Connecticut	S	20.29 MW	21.70 AW	45130 AAW	CTBLS	10//99-12//99
Transportation and Material-Moving Machine and Vehicle Operators	Bridgeport PMSA, CT	S	20.39 MW	18.36 AW	42400 AAW	CTBLS	10//99-12//99
Transportation and Material-Moving Machine and Vehicle Operators	Danbury PMSA, CT	S	20.79 MW	19.24 AW	43240 AAW	CTBLS	10//99-12//99
Transportation and Material-Moving Machine and Vehicle Operators	Hartford MSA, CT	S	21.17 MW	19.86 AW	44040 AAW	CTBLS	10//99-12//99
Transportation and Material-Moving Machine and Vehicle Operators	New Haven-Meriden PMSA, CT	S	20.71 MW	19.14 AW	43070 AAW	CTBLS	10//99-12//99
Transportation and Material-Moving Machine and Vehicle Operators	New London-Norwich MSA, CT-RI	S	18.21 MW	18.44 AW	37880 AAW	CTBLS	10//99-12//99
Transportation and Material-Moving Machine and Vehicle Operators	Stamford-Norwalk PMSA, CT	S	26.46 MW	22.88 AW	55040 AAW	CTBLS	10//99-12//99
Transportation and Material-Moving Machine and Vehicle Operators	Waterbury PMSA, CT	S	22.74 MW	23.40 AW	47290 AAW	CTBLS	10//99-12//99
Transportation and Material-Moving Machine and Vehicle Operators	Delaware	S	19.03 MW	19.42 AW	40380 AAW	DEBLS	10//99-12//99
Transportation and Material-Moving Machine and Vehicle Operators	Dover MSA, DE	S	20.65 MW	18.74 AW	42950 AAW	DEBLS	10//99-12//99
Transportation and Material-Moving Machine and Vehicle Operators	Wilmington-Newark PMSA, DE-MD	S	20.44 MW	20.42 AW	42510 AAW	DEBLS	10//99-12//99
Transportation and Material-Moving Machine and Vehicle Operators	District of Columbia	S	20.46 MW	25.33 AW	52680 AAW	DCBLS	10//99-12//99
Transportation and Material-Moving Machine and Vehicle Operators	Washington PMSA, DC-MD-VA-WV	S	19.20 MW	17.66 AW	39930 AAW	DCBLS	10//99-12//99
Transportation and Material-Moving Machine and Vehicle Operators	Florida	S	17.72 MW	19.15 AW	39820 AAW	FLBLS	10//99-12//99
Transportation and Material-Moving Machine and Vehicle Operators	Daytona Beach MSA, FL	S	20.50 MW	16.88 AW	42640 AAW	FLBLS	10//99-12//99
Transportation and Material-Moving Machine and Vehicle Operators	Fort Lauderdale PMSA, FL	S	18.83 MW	18.56 AW	39170 AAW	FLBLS	10//99-12//99
Transportation and Material-Moving Machine and Vehicle Operators	Fort Myers-Cape Coral MSA, FL	S	17.16 MW	13.15 AW	35700 AAW	FLBLS	10//99-12//99
Transportation and Material-Moving Machine and Vehicle Operators	Fort Pierce-Port St. Lucie MSA, FL	S	15.50 MW	15.03 AW	32230 AAW	FLBLS	10//99-12//99
Transportation and Material-Moving Machine and Vehicle Operators	Fort Walton Beach MSA, FL	S	17.78 MW	12.86 AW	36990 AAW	FLBLS	10//99-12//99
Transportation and Material-Moving Machine and Vehicle Operators	Jacksonville MSA, FL	S	24.22 MW	20.25 AW	50380 AAW	FLBLS	10//99-12//99
Transportation and Material-Moving Machine and Vehicle Operators	Lakeland-Winter Haven MSA, FL	S	17.79 MW	17.73 AW	36990 AAW	FLBLS	10//99-12//99
Transportation and Material-Moving Machine and Vehicle Operators	Melbourne-Titusville-Palm Bay MSA, FL	S	18.74 MW	17.45 AW	38970 AAW	FLBLS	10//99-12//99

AAW Average annual wage	AOH Average offered, high	ASH Average starting, high	H Hourly	M Monthly	S Special: hourly and annual
AE Average entry wage	AOL Average offered, low	ASL Average starting, low	HI Highest wage paid	MTC Median total compensation	TQ Third quartile wage
AEX Average experienced wage	APH Average pay, high range	AW Average wage paid	HR High end range	MW Median wage paid	W Weekly
AO Average offered	APL Average pay, low range	FQ First quartile wage	LR Low end range	SQ Second quartile wage	Y Yearly

Occupation/Type/Industry	Location	Per	Low	Mid	High	Source	Date
First-Line Supervisor/Manager							
Transportation and Material-Moving Machine and Vehicle Operators	Miami PMSA, FL	S	19.76 MW	16.77 AW	41110 AAW	FLBLS	10//99-12//99
Transportation and Material-Moving Machine and Vehicle Operators	Ocala MSA, FL	S	16.02 MW	14.33 AW	33330 AAW	FLBLS	10//99-12//99
Transportation and Material-Moving Machine and Vehicle Operators	Orlando MSA, FL	S	19.96 MW	18.33 AW	41510 AAW	FLBLS	10//99-12//99
Transportation and Material-Moving Machine and Vehicle Operators	Pensacola MSA, FL	S	19.29 MW	16.17 AW	40110 AAW	FLBLS	10//99-12//99
Transportation and Material-Moving Machine and Vehicle Operators	Sarasota-Bradenton MSA, FL	S	14.74 MW	10.57 AW	30650 AAW	FLBLS	10//99-12//99
Transportation and Material-Moving Machine and Vehicle Operators	Tallahassee MSA, FL	S	19.70 MW	17.43 AW	40980 AAW	FLBLS	10//99-12//99
Transportation and Material-Moving Machine and Vehicle Operators	Tampa-St. Petersburg-Clearwater MSA, FL	S	17.75 MW	17.62 AW	36920 AAW	FLBLS	10//99-12//99
Transportation and Material-Moving Machine and Vehicle Operators	West Palm Beach-Boca Raton MSA, FL	S	17.48 MW	15.98 AW	36370 AAW	FLBLS	10//99-12//99
Transportation and Material-Moving Machine and Vehicle Operators	Georgia	S	20.34 MW	22.09 AW	45940 AAW	GABLS	10//99-12//99
Transportation and Material-Moving Machine and Vehicle Operators	Albany MSA, GA	S	17.32 MW	17.78 AW	36020 AAW	GABLS	10//99-12//99
Transportation and Material-Moving Machine and Vehicle Operators	Atlanta MSA, GA	S	24.29 MW	21.56 AW	50530 AAW	GABLS	10//99-12//99
Transportation and Material-Moving Machine and Vehicle Operators	Augusta-Aiken MSA, GA-SC	S	20.32 MW	19.75 AW	42260 AAW	GABLS	10//99-12//99
Transportation and Material-Moving Machine and Vehicle Operators	Columbus MSA, GA-AL	S	18.85 MW	18.47 AW	39220 AAW	GABLS	10//99-12//99
Transportation and Material-Moving Machine and Vehicle Operators	Macon MSA, GA	S	22.28 MW	21.17 AW	46330 AAW	GABLS	10//99-12//99
Transportation and Material-Moving Machine and Vehicle Operators	Savannah MSA, GA	S	21.31 MW	21.14 AW	44320 AAW	GABLS	10//99-12//99
Transportation and Material-Moving Machine and Vehicle Operators	Hawaii	S	20.5 MW	21.70 AW	45130 AAW	HIBLS	10//99-12//99
Transportation and Material-Moving Machine and Vehicle Operators	Honolulu MSA, HI	S	21.66 MW	20.40 AW	45040 AAW	HIBLS	10//99-12//99
Transportation and Material-Moving Machine and Vehicle Operators	Idaho	S	12.73 MW	15.91 AW	33100 AAW	IDBLS	10//99-12//99
Transportation and Material-Moving Machine and Vehicle Operators	Boise City MSA, ID	S	14.94 MW	13.55 AW	31070 AAW	IDBLS	10//99-12//99
Transportation and Material-Moving Machine and Vehicle Operators	Illinois	S	19.65 MW	21.18 AW	44050 AAW	ILBLS	10//99-12//99
Transportation and Material-Moving Machine and Vehicle Operators	Bloomington-Normal MSA, IL	S	25.92 MW	24.32 AW	53920 AAW	ILBLS	10//99-12//99
Transportation and Material-Moving Machine and Vehicle Operators	Chicago PMSA, IL	S	21.51 MW	19.52 AW	44750 AAW	ILBLS	10//99-12//99
Transportation and Material-Moving Machine and Vehicle Operators	Kankakee PMSA, IL	S	19.38 MW	19.00 AW	40300 AAW	ILBLS	10//99-12//99
Transportation and Material-Moving Machine and Vehicle Operators	Peoria-Pekin MSA, IL	S	20.28 MW	19.61 AW	42180 AAW	ILBLS	10//99-12//99
Transportation and Material-Moving Machine and Vehicle Operators	Rockford MSA, IL	S	19.40 MW	18.25 AW	40360 AAW	ILBLS	10//99-12//99
Transportation and Material-Moving Machine and Vehicle Operators	Indiana	S	18.44 MW	19.39 AW	40320 AAW	INBLS	10//99-12//99
Transportation and Material-Moving Machine and Vehicle Operators	Bloomington MSA, IN	S	18.99 MW	14.56 AW	39490 AAW	INBLS	10//99-12//99
Transportation and Material-Moving Machine and Vehicle Operators	Elkhart-Goshen MSA, IN	S	20.53 MW	20.96 AW	42710 AAW	INBLS	10//99-12//99
Transportation and Material-Moving Machine and Vehicle Operators	Evansville-Henderson MSA, IN-KY	S	17.33 MW	16.16 AW	36050 AAW	INBLS	10//99-12//99
Transportation and Material-Moving Machine and Vehicle Operators	Fort Wayne MSA, IN	S	17.60 MW	16.13 AW	36610 AAW	INBLS	10//99-12//99
Transportation and Material-Moving Machine and Vehicle Operators	Gary PMSA, IN	S	21.12 MW	22.26 AW	43920 AAW	INBLS	10//99-12//99
Transportation and Material-Moving Machine and Vehicle Operators	Indianapolis MSA, IN	S	20.77 MW	19.11 AW	43200 AAW	INBLS	10//99-12//99
Transportation and Material-Moving Machine and Vehicle Operators	Kokomo MSA, IN	S	15.71 MW	15.59 AW	32680 AAW	INBLS	10//99-12//99

AAW	Average annual wage	AOH	Average offered, high	ASH	Average starting, high
AE	Average entry wage	AOL	Average offered, low	ASL	Average starting, low
AEX	Average experienced wage	APH	Average pay, high range	AW	Average wage paid
AO	Average offered	APL	Average pay, low range	FQ	First quartile wage

H	Hourly	M	Monthly	S	Special: hourly and annual
HI	Highest wage paid	MTC	Median total compensation	TQ	Third quartile wage
HR	High end range	MW	Median wage paid	W	Weekly
LR	Low end range	SQ	Second quartile wage	Y	Yearly

Occupation/Type/Industry	Location	Per	Low	Mid	High	Source	Date
First-Line Supervisor/Manager							
Transportation and Material-Moving Machine and Vehicle Operators	Lafayette MSA, IN	S	25.79 MW	19.78 AW	53640 AAW	INBLS	10//99-12//99
Transportation and Material-Moving Machine and Vehicle Operators	Muncie MSA, IN	S	20.85 MW	19.55 AW	43380 AAW	INBLS	10//99-12//99
Transportation and Material-Moving Machine and Vehicle Operators	South Bend MSA, IN	S	19.36 MW	18.65 AW	40280 AAW	INBLS	10//99-12//99
Transportation and Material-Moving Machine and Vehicle Operators	Terre Haute MSA, IN	S	15.86 MW	10.55 AW	33000 AAW	INBLS	10//99-12//99
Transportation and Material-Moving Machine and Vehicle Operators	Iowa	S	16.92 MW	17.82 AW	37050 AAW	IABLS	10//99-12//99
Transportation and Material-Moving Machine and Vehicle Operators	Cedar Rapids MSA, IA	S	19.93 MW	19.20 AW	41450 AAW	IABLS	10//99-12//99
Transportation and Material-Moving Machine and Vehicle Operators	Davenport-Moline-Rock Island MSA, IA-IL	S	20.65 MW	19.14 AW	42950 AAW	IABLS	10//99-12//99
Transportation and Material-Moving Machine and Vehicle Operators	Des Moines MSA, IA	S	17.52 MW	15.35 AW	36430 AAW	IABLS	10//99-12//99
Transportation and Material-Moving Machine and Vehicle Operators	Iowa City MSA, IA	S	15.53 MW	15.53 AW	32310 AAW	IABLS	10//99-12//99
Transportation and Material-Moving Machine and Vehicle Operators	Sioux City MSA, IA-NE	S	17.22 MW	15.85 AW	35820 AAW	IABLS	10//99-12//99
Transportation and Material-Moving Machine and Vehicle Operators	Waterloo-Cedar Falls MSA, IA	S	19.46 MW	14.78 AW	40480 AAW	IABLS	10//99-12//99
Transportation and Material-Moving Machine and Vehicle Operators	Kansas	S	16.71 MW	19.72 AW	41030 AAW	KSBLS	10//99-12//99
Transportation and Material-Moving Machine and Vehicle Operators	Topeka MSA, KS	S	18.89 MW	18.33 AW	39290 AAW	KSBLS	10//99-12//99
Transportation and Material-Moving Machine and Vehicle Operators	Wichita MSA, KS	S	17.86 MW	16.01 AW	37150 AAW	KSBLS	10//99-12//99
Transportation and Material-Moving Machine and Vehicle Operators	Kentucky	S	17.5 MW	18.50 AW	38490 AAW	KYBLS	10//99-12//99
Transportation and Material-Moving Machine and Vehicle Operators	Lexington MSA, KY	S	16.83 MW	15.96 AW	35000 AAW	KYBLS	10//99-12//99
Transportation and Material-Moving Machine and Vehicle Operators	Louisville MSA, KY-IN	S	19.91 MW	19.32 AW	41420 AAW	KYBLS	10//99-12//99
Transportation and Material-Moving Machine and Vehicle Operators	Louisiana	S	18.04 MW	18.88 AW	39280 AAW	LABLS	10//99-12//99
Transportation and Material-Moving Machine and Vehicle Operators	Alexandria MSA, LA	S	19.15 MW	18.84 AW	39830 AAW	LABLS	10//99-12//99
Transportation and Material-Moving Machine and Vehicle Operators	Baton Rouge MSA, LA	S	16.92 MW	17.31 AW	35180 AAW	LABLS	10//99-12//99
Transportation and Material-Moving Machine and Vehicle Operators	Houma MSA, LA	S	17.76 MW	17.81 AW	36950 AAW	LABLS	10//99-12//99
Transportation and Material-Moving Machine and Vehicle Operators	Lafayette MSA, LA	S	18.67 MW	18.83 AW	38830 AAW	LABLS	10//99-12//99
Transportation and Material-Moving Machine and Vehicle Operators	Lake Charles MSA, LA	S	16.92 MW	16.99 AW	35200 AAW	LABLS	10//99-12//99
Transportation and Material-Moving Machine and Vehicle Operators	Monroe MSA, LA	S	15.01 MW	12.79 AW	31230 AAW	LABLS	10//99-12//99
Transportation and Material-Moving Machine and Vehicle Operators	New Orleans MSA, LA	S	18.85 MW	16.84 AW	39210 AAW	LABLS	10//99-12//99
Transportation and Material-Moving Machine and Vehicle Operators	Shreveport-Bossier City MSA, LA	S	22.13 MW	20.59 AW	46030 AAW	LABLS	10//99-12//99
Transportation and Material-Moving Machine and Vehicle Operators	Maine	S	17.41 MW	18.49 AW	38460 AAW	MEBLS	10//99-12//99
Transportation and Material-Moving Machine and Vehicle Operators	Bangor MSA, ME	S	14.98 MW	14.68 AW	31160 AAW	MEBLS	10//99-12//99
Transportation and Material-Moving Machine and Vehicle Operators	Lewiston-Auburn MSA, ME	S	16.21 MW	15.19 AW	33710 AAW	MEBLS	10//99-12//99
Transportation and Material-Moving Machine and Vehicle Operators	Portland MSA, ME	S	18.04 MW	17.38 AW	37520 AAW	MEBLS	10//99-12//99
Transportation and Material-Moving Machine and Vehicle Operators	Maryland	S	17.47 MW	17.33 AW	36050 AAW	MDBLS	10//99-12//99
Transportation and Material-Moving Machine and Vehicle Operators	Baltimore PMSA, MD	S	18.41 MW	18.12 AW	38290 AAW	MDBLS	10//99-12//99
Transportation and Material-Moving Machine and Vehicle Operators	Hagerstown PMSA, MD	S	14.86 MW	13.22 AW	30900 AAW	MDBLS	10//99-12//99
Transportation and Material-Moving Machine and Vehicle Operators	Massachusetts	S	19.41 MW	20.42 AW	42470 AAW	MABLS	10//99-12//99

AAW	Average annual wage	AOH	Average offered, high	ASH	Average starting, high	H	Hourly	M	Monthly	S	Special: hourly and annual
AE	Average entry wage	AOL	Average offered, low	ASL	Average starting, low	HI	Highest wage paid	MTC	Median total compensation	TQ	Third quartile wage
AEX	Average experienced wage	APH	Average pay, high range	AW	Average wage paid	HR	High end range	MW	Median wage paid	W	Weekly
AO	Average offered	APL	Average pay, low range	FQ	First quartile wage	LR	Low end range	SQ	Second quartile wage	Y	Yearly

First-Line Supervisor/Manager

Occupation/Type/Industry	Location	Per	Low	Mid	High	Source	Date
Transportation and Material-Moving Machine and Vehicle Operators	Barnstable-Yarmouth MSA, MA	S	21.08 MW	19.32 AW	43850 AAW	MABLS	10//99-12//99
Transportation and Material-Moving Machine and Vehicle Operators	Boston PMSA, MA-NH	S	20.85 MW	19.79 AW	43360 AAW	MABLS	10//99-12//99
Transportation and Material-Moving Machine and Vehicle Operators	Brockton PMSA, MA	S	18.61 MW	18.64 AW	38710 AAW	MABLS	10//99-12//99
Transportation and Material-Moving Machine and Vehicle Operators	Fitchburg-Leominster PMSA, MA	S	23.90 MW	21.50 AW	49720 AAW	MABLS	10//99-12//99
Transportation and Material-Moving Machine and Vehicle Operators	Lawrence PMSA, MA-NH	S	17.47 MW	17.02 AW	36350 AAW	MABLS	10//99-12//99
Transportation and Material-Moving Machine and Vehicle Operators	Lowell PMSA, MA-NH	S	17.82 MW	18.36 AW	37070 AAW	MABLS	10//99-12//99
Transportation and Material-Moving Machine and Vehicle Operators	New Bedford PMSA, MA	S	16.43 MW	14.78 AW	34170 AAW	MABLS	10//99-12//99
Transportation and Material-Moving Machine and Vehicle Operators	Pittsfield MSA, MA	S	16.56 MW	15.64 AW	34430 AAW	MABLS	10//99-12//99
Transportation and Material-Moving Machine and Vehicle Operators	Springfield MSA, MA	S	15.74 MW	15.17 AW	32750 AAW	MABLS	10//99-12//99
Transportation and Material-Moving Machine and Vehicle Operators	Worcester PMSA, MA-CT	S	16.76 MW	15.95 AW	34850 AAW	MABLS	10//99-12//99
Transportation and Material-Moving Machine and Vehicle Operators	Michigan	S	20.49 MW	21.54 AW	44800 AAW	MIBLS	10//99-12//99
Transportation and Material-Moving Machine and Vehicle Operators	Ann Arbor PMSA, MI	S	26.10 MW	25.04 AW	54290 AAW	MIBLS	10//99-12//99
Transportation and Material-Moving Machine and Vehicle Operators	Benton Harbor MSA, MI	S	20.04 MW	15.53 AW	41680 AAW	MIBLS	10//99-12//99
Transportation and Material-Moving Machine and Vehicle Operators	Detroit PMSA, MI	S	21.84 MW	20.94 AW	45420 AAW	MIBLS	10//99-12//99
Transportation and Material-Moving Machine and Vehicle Operators	Flint PMSA, MI	S	20.35 MW	20.65 AW	42320 AAW	MIBLS	10//99-12//99
Transportation and Material-Moving Machine and Vehicle Operators	Grand Rapids-Muskegon-Holland MSA, MI	S	21.25 MW	19.63 AW	44210 AAW	MIBLS	10//99-12//99
Transportation and Material-Moving Machine and Vehicle Operators	Jackson MSA, MI	S	19.16 MW	19.73 AW	39850 AAW	MIBLS	10//99-12//99
Transportation and Material-Moving Machine and Vehicle Operators	Kalamazoo-Battle Creek MSA, MI	S	19.98 MW	19.43 AW	41570 AAW	MIBLS	10//99-12//99
Transportation and Material-Moving Machine and Vehicle Operators	Lansing-East Lansing MSA, MI	S	19.35 MW	19.43 AW	40240 AAW	MIBLS	10//99-12//99
Transportation and Material-Moving Machine and Vehicle Operators	Saginaw-Bay City-Midland MSA, MI	S	23.63 MW	22.47 AW	49160 AAW	MIBLS	10//99-12//99
Transportation and Material-Moving Machine and Vehicle Operators	Minnesota	S	18.3 MW	20.20 AW	42010 AAW	MNBLS	10//99-12//99
Transportation and Material-Moving Machine and Vehicle Operators	Duluth-Superior MSA, MN-WI	S	18.62 MW	17.05 AW	38730 AAW	MNBLS	10//99-12//99
Transportation and Material-Moving Machine and Vehicle Operators	Minneapolis-St. Paul MSA, MN-WI	S	21.25 MW	19.09 AW	44190 AAW	MNBLS	10//99-12//99
Transportation and Material-Moving Machine and Vehicle Operators	Rochester MSA, MN	S	19.69 MW	16.59 AW	40960 AAW	MNBLS	10//99-12//99
Transportation and Material-Moving Machine and Vehicle Operators	St. Cloud MSA, MN	S	19.98 MW	19.40 AW	41550 AAW	MNBLS	10//99-12//99
Transportation and Material-Moving Machine and Vehicle Operators	Mississippi	S	16.41 MW	18.45 AW	38380 AAW	MSBLS	10//99-12//99
Transportation and Material-Moving Machine and Vehicle Operators	Biloxi-Gulfport-Pascagoula MSA, MS	S	18.64 MW	17.30 AW	38770 AAW	MSBLS	10//99-12//99
Transportation and Material-Moving Machine and Vehicle Operators	Hattiesburg MSA, MS	S	14.99 MW	15.09 AW	31170 AAW	MSBLS	10//99-12//99
Transportation and Material-Moving Machine and Vehicle Operators	Jackson MSA, MS	S	20.57 MW	19.49 AW	42790 AAW	MSBLS	10//99-12//99
Transportation and Material-Moving Machine and Vehicle Operators	Missouri	S	17.88 MW	19.09 AW	39710 AAW	MOBLS	10//99-12//99
Transportation and Material-Moving Machine and Vehicle Operators	Columbia MSA, MO	S	16.14 MW	15.95 AW	33570 AAW	MOBLS	10//99-12//99

AAW Average annual wage	AOH Average offered, high	ASH Average starting, high	H Hourly	M Monthly	S Special: hourly and annual
AE Average entry wage	AOL Average offered, low	ASL Average starting, low	HI Highest wage paid	MTC Median total compensation	TQ Third quartile wage
AEX Average experienced wage	APH Average pay, high range	AW Average wage paid	HR High end range	MW Median wage paid	W Weekly
AO Average offered	APL Average pay, low range	FQ First quartile wage	LR Low end range	SQ Second quartile wage	Y Yearly

Occupation/Type/Industry	Location	Per	Low	Mid	High	Source	Date
First-Line Supervisor/Manager							
Transportation and Material-Moving Machine and Vehicle Operators	Joplin MSA, MO	S	11.41 MW	11.78 AW	23720 AAW	MOBLS	10//99-12//99
Transportation and Material-Moving Machine and Vehicle Operators	Kansas City MSA, MO-KS	S	23.42 MW	20.48 AW	48720 AAW	MOBLS	10//99-12//99
Transportation and Material-Moving Machine and Vehicle Operators	St. Louis MSA, MO-IL	S	19.36 MW	18.87 AW	40280 AAW	MOBLS	10//99-12//99
Transportation and Material-Moving Machine and Vehicle Operators	Springfield MSA, MO	S	18.57 MW	16.36 AW	38630 AAW	MOBLS	10//99-12//99
Transportation and Material-Moving Machine and Vehicle Operators	Montana	S	17.33 MW	19.82 AW	41230 AAW	MTBLS	10//99-12//99
Transportation and Material-Moving Machine and Vehicle Operators	Billings MSA, MT	S	20.38 MW	16.32 AW	42390 AAW	MTBLS	10//99-12//99
Transportation and Material-Moving Machine and Vehicle Operators	Missoula MSA, MT	S	16.72 MW	12.91 AW	34770 AAW	MTBLS	10//99-12//99
Transportation and Material-Moving Machine and Vehicle Operators	Nebraska	S	15.89 MW	17.28 AW	35950 AAW	NEBLS	10//99-12//99
Transportation and Material-Moving Machine and Vehicle Operators	Lincoln MSA, NE	S	18.60 MW	16.29 AW	38690 AAW	NEBLS	10//99-12//99
Transportation and Material-Moving Machine and Vehicle Operators	Omaha MSA, NE-IA	S	19.06 MW	17.57 AW	39640 AAW	NEBLS	10//99-12//99
Transportation and Material-Moving Machine and Vehicle Operators	Nevada	S	12.94 MW	16.35 AW	34000 AAW	NVBLS	10//99-12//99
Transportation and Material-Moving Machine and Vehicle Operators	Las Vegas MSA, NV-AZ	S	16.24 MW	12.87 AW	33770 AAW	NVBLS	10//99-12//99
Transportation and Material-Moving Machine and Vehicle Operators	Reno MSA, NV	S	16.40 MW	12.94 AW	34100 AAW	NVBLS	10//99-12//99
Transportation and Material-Moving Machine and Vehicle Operators	New Hampshire	S	17.66 MW	21.84 AW	45420 AAW	NHBLS	10//99-12//99
Transportation and Material-Moving Machine and Vehicle Operators	Manchester PMSA, NH	S	21.21 MW	20.47 AW	44110 AAW	NHBLS	10//99-12//99
Transportation and Material-Moving Machine and Vehicle Operators	Nashua PMSA, NH	S	19.09 MW	18.05 AW	39710 AAW	NHBLS	10//99-12//99
Transportation and Material-Moving Machine and Vehicle Operators	Portsmouth-Rochester PMSA, NH-ME	S	16.23 MW	15.48 AW	33760 AAW	NHBLS	10//99-12//99
Transportation and Material-Moving Machine and Vehicle Operators	New Jersey	S	21.4 MW	21.77 AW	45280 AAW	NJBLS	10//99-12//99
Transportation and Material-Moving Machine and Vehicle Operators	Atlantic-Cape May PMSA, NJ	S	16.43 MW	13.77 AW	34180 AAW	NJBLS	10//99-12//99
Transportation and Material-Moving Machine and Vehicle Operators	Bergen-Passaic PMSA, NJ	S	19.92 MW	18.31 AW	41440 AAW	NJBLS	10//99-12//99
Transportation and Material-Moving Machine and Vehicle Operators	Jersey City PMSA, NJ	S	22.77 MW	22.39 AW	47370 AAW	NJBLS	10//99-12//99
Transportation and Material-Moving Machine and Vehicle Operators	Middlesex-Somerset-Hunterdon PMSA, NJ	S	21.91 MW	21.98 AW	45580 AAW	NJBLS	10//99-12//99
Transportation and Material-Moving Machine and Vehicle Operators	Monmouth-Ocean PMSA, NJ	S	19.19 MW	19.40 AW	39910 AAW	NJBLS	10//99-12//99
Transportation and Material-Moving Machine and Vehicle Operators	Newark PMSA, NJ	S	24.02 MW	23.05 AW	49970 AAW	NJBLS	10//99-12//99
Transportation and Material-Moving Machine and Vehicle Operators	Trenton PMSA, NJ	S	19.43 MW	17.91 AW	40410 AAW	NJBLS	10//99-12//99
Transportation and Material-Moving Machine and Vehicle Operators	Vineland-Millville-Bridgeton PMSA, NJ	S	19.24 MW	18.79 AW	40020 AAW	NJBLS	10//99-12//99
Transportation and Material-Moving Machine and Vehicle Operators	New Mexico	S	16.21 MW	19.30 AW	40130 AAW	NMBLS	10//99-12//99
Transportation and Material-Moving Machine and Vehicle Operators	Albuquerque MSA, NM	S	21.57 MW	16.87 AW	44870 AAW	NMBLS	10//99-12//99
Transportation and Material-Moving Machine and Vehicle Operators	Las Cruces MSA, NM	S	12.73 MW	12.46 AW	26470 AAW	NMBLS	10//99-12//99
Transportation and Material-Moving Machine and Vehicle Operators	New York	S	17.13 MW	19.78 AW	41150 AAW	NYBLS	10//99-12//99
Transportation and Material-Moving Machine and Vehicle Operators	Albany-Schenectady-Troy MSA, NY	S	20.59 MW	19.25 AW	42830 AAW	NYBLS	10//99-12//99
Transportation and Material-Moving Machine and Vehicle Operators	Binghamton MSA, NY	S	19.64 MW	17.19 AW	40850 AAW	NYBLS	10//99-12//99

AAW	Average annual wage	AOH	Average offered, high	ASH	Average starting, high	H
AE	Average entry wage	AOL	Average offered, low	ASL	Average starting, low	HI
AEX	Average experienced wage	APH	Average pay, high range	AW	Average wage paid	HR
AO	Average offered	APL	Average pay, low range	FQ	First quartile wage	LR

- **AAW** Average annual wage
- **AE** Average entry wage
- **AEX** Average experienced wage
- **AO** Average offered
- **AOH** Average offered, high
- **AOL** Average offered, low
- **APH** Average pay, high range
- **APL** Average pay, low range
- **ASH** Average starting, high
- **ASL** Average starting, low
- **AW** Average wage paid
- **FQ** First quartile wage
- **H** Hourly
- **HI** Highest wage paid
- **HR** High end range
- **LR** Low end range
- **M** Monthly
- **MTC** Median total compensation
- **MW** Median wage paid
- **SQ** Second quartile wage
- **S** Special: hourly and annual
- **TQ** Third quartile wage
- **W** Weekly
- **Y** Yearly

First-Line Supervisor/Manager

Occupation/Type/Industry	Location	Per	Low	Mid	High	Source	Date
Transportation and Material-Moving Machine and Vehicle Operators	Buffalo-Niagara Falls MSA, NY	S	21.51 MW	21.13 AW	44750 AAW	NYBLS	10//99-12//99
Transportation and Material-Moving Machine and Vehicle Operators	Dutchess County PMSA, NY	S	21.15 MW	20.99 AW	43990 AAW	NYBLS	10//99-12//99
Transportation and Material-Moving Machine and Vehicle Operators	Elmira MSA, NY	S	15.92 MW	11.69 AW	33110 AAW	NYBLS	10//99-12//99
Transportation and Material-Moving Machine and Vehicle Operators	Glens Falls MSA, NY	S	27.20 MW	23.18 AW	56580 AAW	NYBLS	10//99-12//99
Transportation and Material-Moving Machine and Vehicle Operators	Jamestown MSA, NY	S	16.30 MW	15.24 AW	33900 AAW	NYBLS	10//99-12//99
Transportation and Material-Moving Machine and Vehicle Operators	Nassau-Suffolk PMSA, NY	S	24.76 MW	21.87 AW	51500 AAW	NYBLS	10//99-12//99
Transportation and Material-Moving Machine and Vehicle Operators	New York PMSA, NY	S	18.97 MW	13.34 AW	39460 AAW	NYBLS	10//99-12//99
Transportation and Material-Moving Machine and Vehicle Operators	Newburgh PMSA, NY-PA	S	20.20 MW	19.03 AW	42020 AAW	NYBLS	10//99-12//99
Transportation and Material-Moving Machine and Vehicle Operators	Rochester MSA, NY	S	19.58 MW	19.25 AW	40730 AAW	NYBLS	10//99-12//99
Transportation and Material-Moving Machine and Vehicle Operators	Syracuse MSA, NY	S	16.31 MW	15.08 AW	33930 AAW	NYBLS	10//99-12//99
Transportation and Material-Moving Machine and Vehicle Operators	Utica-Rome MSA, NY	S	24.39 MW	17.58 AW	50730 AAW	NYBLS	10//99-12//99
Transportation and Material-Moving Machine and Vehicle Operators	North Carolina	S	17.56 MW	18.76 AW	39030 AAW	NCBLS	10//99-12//99
Transportation and Material-Moving Machine and Vehicle Operators	Asheville MSA, NC	S	18.29 MW	18.48 AW	38030 AAW	NCBLS	10//99-12//99
Transportation and Material-Moving Machine and Vehicle Operators	Charlotte-Gastonia-Rock Hill MSA, NC-SC	S	19.91 MW	19.53 AW	41400 AAW	NCBLS	10//99-12//99
Transportation and Material-Moving Machine and Vehicle Operators	Fayetteville MSA, NC	S	19.66 MW	16.95 AW	40890 AAW	NCBLS	10//99-12//99
Transportation and Material-Moving Machine and Vehicle Operators	Goldsboro MSA, NC	S	20.46 MW	17.74 AW	42560 AAW	NCBLS	10//99-12//99
Transportation and Material-Moving Machine and Vehicle Operators	Greensboro--Winston-Salem--High Point MSA, NC	S	20.08 MW	19.79 AW	41760 AAW	NCBLS	10//99-12//99
Transportation and Material-Moving Machine and Vehicle Operators	Greenville MSA, NC	S	18.42 MW	17.26 AW	38310 AAW	NCBLS	10//99-12//99
Transportation and Material-Moving Machine and Vehicle Operators	Hickory-Morganton-Lenoir MSA, NC	S	15.11 MW	14.67 AW	31430 AAW	NCBLS	10//99-12//99
Transportation and Material-Moving Machine and Vehicle Operators	Jacksonville MSA, NC	S	14.85 MW	14.43 AW	30890 AAW	NCBLS	10//99-12//99
Transportation and Material-Moving Machine and Vehicle Operators	Raleigh-Durham-Chapel Hill MSA, NC	S	21.15 MW	19.00 AW	43990 AAW	NCBLS	10//99-12//99
Transportation and Material-Moving Machine and Vehicle Operators	Rocky Mount MSA, NC	S	18.19 MW	17.82 AW	37840 AAW	NCBLS	10//99-12//99
Transportation and Material-Moving Machine and Vehicle Operators	Wilmington MSA, NC	S	19.21 MW	18.34 AW	39950 AAW	NCBLS	10//99-12//99
Transportation and Material-Moving Machine and Vehicle Operators	North Dakota	S	13.44 MW	17.55 AW	36510 AAW	NDBLS	10//99-12//99
Transportation and Material-Moving Machine and Vehicle Operators	Bismarck MSA, ND	S	19.26 MW	16.59 AW	40070 AAW	NDBLS	10//99-12//99
Transportation and Material-Moving Machine and Vehicle Operators	Fargo-Moorhead MSA, ND-MN	S	17.52 MW	15.25 AW	36440 AAW	NDBLS	10//99-12//99
Transportation and Material-Moving Machine and Vehicle Operators	Grand Forks MSA, ND-MN	S	22.50 MW	21.29 AW	46810 AAW	NDBLS	10//99-12//99
Transportation and Material-Moving Machine and Vehicle Operators	Ohio	S	18.6 MW	19.64 AW	40840 AAW	OHBLS	10//99-12//99
Transportation and Material-Moving Machine and Vehicle Operators	Akron PMSA, OH	S	21.50 MW	20.75 AW	44720 AAW	OHBLS	10//99-12//99
Transportation and Material-Moving Machine and Vehicle Operators	Canton-Massillon MSA, OH	S	19.44 MW	19.58 AW	40430 AAW	OHBLS	10//99-12//99
Transportation and Material-Moving Machine and Vehicle Operators	Cincinnati PMSA, OH-KY-IN	S	20.55 MW	18.89 AW	42740 AAW	OHBLS	10//99-12//99

AAW	Average annual wage	AOH	Average offered, high	ASH	Average starting, high	H	Hourly
AE	Average entry wage	AOL	Average offered, low	ASL	Average starting, low	HI	Highest wage paid
AEX	Average experienced wage	APH	Average pay, high range	AW	Average wage paid	HR	High end range
AO	Average offered	APL	Average pay, low range	FQ	First quartile wage	LR	Low end range

M Monthly   MTC Median total compensation   MW Median wage paid   SQ Second quartile wage   S Special: hourly and annual   TQ Third quartile wage   W Weekly   Y Yearly

First-Line Supervisor/Manager

Occupation/Type/Industry	Location	Per	Low	Mid	High	Source	Date
Transportation and Material-Moving Machine and Vehicle Operators	Cleveland-Lorain-Elyria PMSA, OH	S	20.85 MW	18.30 AW	43370 AAW	OHBLS	10//99-12//99
Transportation and Material-Moving Machine and Vehicle Operators	Columbus MSA, OH	S	19.54 MW	19.08 AW	40650 AAW	OHBLS	10//99-12//99
Transportation and Material-Moving Machine and Vehicle Operators	Dayton-Springfield MSA, OH	S	18.00 MW	14.21 AW	37430 AAW	OHBLS	10//99-12//99
Transportation and Material-Moving Machine and Vehicle Operators	Hamilton-Middletown PMSA, OH	S	18.60 MW	18.22 AW	38680 AAW	OHBLS	10//99-12//99
Transportation and Material-Moving Machine and Vehicle Operators	Lima MSA, OH	S	14.25 MW	13.55 AW	29640 AAW	OHBLS	10//99-12//99
Transportation and Material-Moving Machine and Vehicle Operators	Mansfield MSA, OH	S	17.43 MW	17.37 AW	36250 AAW	OHBLS	10//99-12//99
Transportation and Material-Moving Machine and Vehicle Operators	Steubenville-Weirton MSA, OH-WV	S	18.74 MW	18.50 AW	38980 AAW	OHBLS	10//99-12//99
Transportation and Material-Moving Machine and Vehicle Operators	Toledo MSA, OH	S	20.83 MW	19.71 AW	43330 AAW	OHBLS	10//99-12//99
Transportation and Material-Moving Machine and Vehicle Operators	Youngstown-Warren MSA, OH	S	20.66 MW	18.37 AW	42970 AAW	OHBLS	10//99-12//99
Transportation and Material-Moving Machine and Vehicle Operators	Oklahoma	S	19.11 MW	18.95 AW	39420 AAW	OKBLS	10//99-12//99
Transportation and Material-Moving Machine and Vehicle Operators	Enid MSA, OK	S	19.33 MW	22.22 AW	40200 AAW	OKBLS	10//99-12//99
Transportation and Material-Moving Machine and Vehicle Operators	Lawton MSA, OK	S	15.15 MW	14.27 AW	31520 AAW	OKBLS	10//99-12//99
Transportation and Material-Moving Machine and Vehicle Operators	Oklahoma City MSA, OK	S	21.76 MW	21.91 AW	45260 AAW	OKBLS	10//99-12//99
Transportation and Material-Moving Machine and Vehicle Operators	Tulsa MSA, OK	S	18.19 MW	18.21 AW	37840 AAW	OKBLS	10//99-12//99
Transportation and Material-Moving Machine and Vehicle Operators	Oregon	S	22.03 MW	24.04 AW	50010 AAW	ORBLS	10//99-12//99
Transportation and Material-Moving Machine and Vehicle Operators	Eugene-Springfield MSA, OR	S	18.02 MW	17.30 AW	37480 AAW	ORBLS	10//99-12//99
Transportation and Material-Moving Machine and Vehicle Operators	Medford-Ashland MSA, OR	S	18.54 MW	18.29 AW	38560 AAW	ORBLS	10//99-12//99
Transportation and Material-Moving Machine and Vehicle Operators	Portland-Vancouver PMSA, OR-WA	S	25.85 MW	25.10 AW	53770 AAW	ORBLS	10//99-12//99
Transportation and Material-Moving Machine and Vehicle Operators	Salem PMSA, OR	S	16.81 MW	15.73 AW	34970 AAW	ORBLS	10//99-12//99
Transportation and Material-Moving Machine and Vehicle Operators	Pennsylvania	S	19.9 MW	20.12 AW	41860 AAW	PABLS	10//99-12//99
Transportation and Material-Moving Machine and Vehicle Operators	Allentown-Bethlehem-Easton MSA, PA	S	20.37 MW	19.41 AW	42370 AAW	PABLS	10//99-12//99
Transportation and Material-Moving Machine and Vehicle Operators	Altoona MSA, PA	S	22.08 MW	21.61 AW	45930 AAW	PABLS	10//99-12//99
Transportation and Material-Moving Machine and Vehicle Operators	Erie MSA, PA	S	18.22 MW	18.62 AW	37900 AAW	PABLS	10//99-12//99
Transportation and Material-Moving Machine and Vehicle Operators	Harrisburg-Lebanon-Carlisle MSA, PA	S	21.52 MW	19.97 AW	44760 AAW	PABLS	10//99-12//99
Transportation and Material-Moving Machine and Vehicle Operators	Johnstown MSA, PA	S	17.74 MW	16.84 AW	36910 AAW	PABLS	10//99-12//99
Transportation and Material-Moving Machine and Vehicle Operators	Lancaster MSA, PA	S	18.27 MW	18.79 AW	37990 AAW	PABLS	10//99-12//99
Transportation and Material-Moving Machine and Vehicle Operators	Philadelphia PMSA, PA-NJ	S	21.22 MW	20.73 AW	44150 AAW	PABLS	10//99-12//99
Transportation and Material-Moving Machine and Vehicle Operators	Pittsburgh MSA, PA	S	20.99 MW	21.67 AW	43660 AAW	PABLS	10//99-12//99
Transportation and Material-Moving Machine and Vehicle Operators	Reading MSA, PA	S	16.51 MW	16.06 AW	34340 AAW	PABLS	10//99-12//99
Transportation and Material-Moving Machine and Vehicle Operators	Scranton--Wilkes-Barre--Hazleton MSA, PA	S	15.53 MW	13.46 AW	32310 AAW	PABLS	10//99-12//99
Transportation and Material-Moving Machine and Vehicle Operators	Sharon MSA, PA	S	13.14 MW	10.29 AW	27330 AAW	PABLS	10//99-12//99

AAW	Average annual wage	AOH	Average offered, high	ASH	Average starting, high	H	Hourly	M	Monthly	S	Special: hourly and annual
AE	Average entry wage	AOL	Average offered, low	ASL	Average starting, low	HI	Highest wage paid	MTC	Median total compensation	TQ	Third quartile wage
AEX	Average experienced wage	APH	Average pay, high range	AW	Average wage paid	HR	High end range	MW	Median wage paid	W	Weekly
AO	Average offered	APL	Average pay, low range	FQ	First quartile wage	LR	Low end range	SQ	Second quartile wage	Y	Yearly

First-Line Supervisor/Manager

Occupation/Type/Industry	Location	Per	Low	Mid	High	Source	Date
Transportation and Material-Moving Machine and Vehicle Operators	Williamsport MSA, PA	S	22.50 MW	23.66 AW	46810 AAW	PABLS	10//99-12//99
Transportation and Material-Moving Machine and Vehicle Operators	York MSA, PA	S	17.61 MW	17.17 AW	36620 AAW	PABLS	10//99-12//99
Transportation and Material-Moving Machine and Vehicle Operators	Rhode Island	S	18.67 MW	19.40 AW	40360 AAW	RIBLS	10//99-12//99
Transportation and Material-Moving Machine and Vehicle Operators	Providence-Fall River-Warwick MSA, RI-MA	S	19.05 MW	18.94 AW	39610 AAW	RIBLS	10//99-12//99
Transportation and Material-Moving Machine and Vehicle Operators	South Carolina	S	21.13 MW	22.53 AW	46860 AAW	SCBLS	10//99-12//99
Transportation and Material-Moving Machine and Vehicle Operators	Charleston-North Charleston MSA, SC	S	21.96 MW	20.15 AW	45670 AAW	SCBLS	10//99-12//99
Transportation and Material-Moving Machine and Vehicle Operators	Columbia MSA, SC	S	24.20 MW	26.28 AW	50340 AAW	SCBLS	10//99-12//99
Transportation and Material-Moving Machine and Vehicle Operators	Florence MSA, SC	S	20.08 MW	19.20 AW	41760 AAW	SCBLS	10//99-12//99
Transportation and Material-Moving Machine and Vehicle Operators	Greenville-Spartanburg-Anderson MSA, SC	S	24.85 MW	28.08 AW	51680 AAW	SCBLS	10//99-12//99
Transportation and Material-Moving Machine and Vehicle Operators	Myrtle Beach MSA, SC	S	20.79 MW	19.80 AW	43240 AAW	SCBLS	10//99-12//99
Transportation and Material-Moving Machine and Vehicle Operators	South Dakota	S	19.07 MW	19.36 AW	40260 AAW	SDBLS	10//99-12//99
Transportation and Material-Moving Machine and Vehicle Operators	Rapid City MSA, SD	S	21.31 MW	21.57 AW	44330 AAW	SDBLS	10//99-12//99
Transportation and Material-Moving Machine and Vehicle Operators	Sioux Falls MSA, SD	S	19.80 MW	19.54 AW	41180 AAW	SDBLS	10//99-12//99
Transportation and Material-Moving Machine and Vehicle Operators	Tennessee	S	17.98 MW	18.66 AW	38820 AAW	TNBLS	10//99-12//99
Transportation and Material-Moving Machine and Vehicle Operators	Chattanooga MSA, TN-GA	S	18.52 MW	18.51 AW	38520 AAW	TNBLS	10//99-12//99
Transportation and Material-Moving Machine and Vehicle Operators	Clarksville-Hopkinsville MSA, TN-KY	S	17.96 MW	17.40 AW	37370 AAW	TNBLS	10//99-12//99
Transportation and Material-Moving Machine and Vehicle Operators	Jackson MSA, TN	S	22.39 MW	22.17 AW	46570 AAW	TNBLS	10//99-12//99
Transportation and Material-Moving Machine and Vehicle Operators	Johnson City-Kingsport-Bristol MSA, TN-VA	S	19.48 MW	18.75 AW	40520 AAW	TNBLS	10//99-12//99
Transportation and Material-Moving Machine and Vehicle Operators	Knoxville MSA, TN	S	19.54 MW	19.36 AW	40640 AAW	TNBLS	10//99-12//99
Transportation and Material-Moving Machine and Vehicle Operators	Memphis MSA, TN-AR-MS	S	19.61 MW	18.00 AW	40790 AAW	MSBLS	10//99-12//99
Transportation and Material-Moving Machine and Vehicle Operators	Nashville MSA, TN	S	17.77 MW	17.23 AW	36960 AAW	TNBLS	10//99-12//99
Transportation and Material-Moving Machine and Vehicle Operators	Texas	S	18.87 MW	19.70 AW	40970 AAW	TXBLS	10//99-12//99
Transportation and Material-Moving Machine and Vehicle Operators	Abilene MSA, TX	S	18.51 MW	18.26 AW	38490 AAW	TXBLS	10//99-12//99
Transportation and Material-Moving Machine and Vehicle Operators	Amarillo MSA, TX	S	18.44 MW	17.85 AW	38350 AAW	TXBLS	10//99-12//99
Transportation and Material-Moving Machine and Vehicle Operators	Austin-San Marcos MSA, TX	S	18.73 MW	15.51 AW	38950 AAW	TXBLS	10//99-12//99
Transportation and Material-Moving Machine and Vehicle Operators	Beaumont-Port Arthur MSA, TX	S	20.34 MW	18.44 AW	42300 AAW	TXBLS	10//99-12//99
Transportation and Material-Moving Machine and Vehicle Operators	Brownsville-Harlingen-San Benito MSA, TX	S	17.03 MW	17.56 AW	35430 AAW	TXBLS	10//99-12//99
Transportation and Material-Moving Machine and Vehicle Operators	Bryan-College Station MSA, TX	S	13.72 MW	11.84 AW	28530 AAW	TXBLS	10//99-12//99
Transportation and Material-Moving Machine and Vehicle Operators	Corpus Christi MSA, TX	S	23.23 MW	20.28 AW	48330 AAW	TXBLS	10//99-12//99
Transportation and Material-Moving Machine and Vehicle Operators	Dallas PMSA, TX	S	18.84 MW	18.71 AW	39180 AAW	TXBLS	10//99-12//99
Transportation and Material-Moving Machine and Vehicle Operators	El Paso MSA, TX	S	17.27 MW	17.96 AW	35920 AAW	TXBLS	10//99-12//99

AAW	Average annual wage	AOH	Average offered, high	ASH	Average starting, high
AE	Average entry wage	AOL	Average offered, low	ASL	Average starting, low
AEX	Average experienced wage	APH	Average pay, high range	AW	Average wage paid
AO	Average offered	APL	Average pay, low range	FQ	First quartile wage

H	Hourly	M	Monthly
HI	Highest wage paid	MTC	Median total compensation
HR	High end range	MW	Median wage paid
LR	Low end range	SQ	Second quartile wage

S	Special: hourly and annual
TQ	Third quartile wage
W	Weekly
Y	Yearly

First-Line Supervisor/Manager

Occupation/Type/Industry	Location	Per	Low	Mid	High	Source	Date
Transportation and Material-Moving Machine and Vehicle Operators	Fort Worth-Arlington PMSA, TX	S	22.97 MW	19.64 AW	47780 AAW	TXBLS	10//99-12//99
Transportation and Material-Moving Machine and Vehicle Operators	Galveston-Texas City PMSA, TX	S	17.70 MW	18.74 AW	36820 AAW	TXBLS	10//99-12//99
Transportation and Material-Moving Machine and Vehicle Operators	Houston PMSA, TX	S	20.74 MW	19.93 AW	43150 AAW	TXBLS	10//99-12//99
Transportation and Material-Moving Machine and Vehicle Operators	Killeen-Temple MSA, TX	S	18.04 MW	15.67 AW	37530 AAW	TXBLS	10//99-12//99
Transportation and Material-Moving Machine and Vehicle Operators	Longview-Marshall MSA, TX	S	17.61 MW	13.21 AW	36630 AAW	TXBLS	10//99-12//99
Transportation and Material-Moving Machine and Vehicle Operators	Lubbock MSA, TX	S	15.77 MW	13.48 AW	32790 AAW	TXBLS	10//99-12//99
Transportation and Material-Moving Machine and Vehicle Operators	McAllen-Edinburg-Mission MSA, TX	S	20.65 MW	18.18 AW	42960 AAW	TXBLS	10//99-12//99
Transportation and Material-Moving Machine and Vehicle Operators	Odessa-Midland MSA, TX	S	12.48 MW	9.74 AW	25950 AAW	TXBLS	10//99-12//99
Transportation and Material-Moving Machine and Vehicle Operators	San Antonio MSA, TX	S	19.86 MW	18.94 AW	41310 AAW	TXBLS	10//99-12//99
Transportation and Material-Moving Machine and Vehicle Operators	Sherman-Denison MSA, TX	S	15.75 MW	15.04 AW	32760 AAW	TXBLS	10//99-12//99
Transportation and Material-Moving Machine and Vehicle Operators	Texarkana MSA, TX-Texarkana, AR	S	13.52 MW	12.46 AW	28120 AAW	TXBLS	10//99-12//99
Transportation and Material-Moving Machine and Vehicle Operators	Tyler MSA, TX	S	16.38 MW	16.65 AW	34070 AAW	TXBLS	10//99-12//99
Transportation and Material-Moving Machine and Vehicle Operators	Waco MSA, TX	S	19.49 MW	18.99 AW	40540 AAW	TXBLS	10//99-12//99
Transportation and Material-Moving Machine and Vehicle Operators	Utah	S	13.27 MW	16.02 AW	33320 AAW	UTBLS	10//99-12//99
Transportation and Material-Moving Machine and Vehicle Operators	Provo-Orem MSA, UT	S	17.77 MW	17.81 AW	36970 AAW	UTBLS	10//99-12//99
Transportation and Material-Moving Machine and Vehicle Operators	Salt Lake City-Ogden MSA, UT	S	15.72 MW	12.64 AW	32700 AAW	UTBLS	10//99-12//99
Transportation and Material-Moving Machine and Vehicle Operators	Vermont	S	18.13 MW	19.70 AW	40970 AAW	VTBLS	10//99-12//99
Transportation and Material-Moving Machine and Vehicle Operators	Burlington MSA, VT	S	21.16 MW	19.35 AW	44010 AAW	VTBLS	10//99-12//99
Transportation and Material-Moving Machine and Vehicle Operators	Virginia	S	17.64 MW	19.18 AW	39890 AAW	VABLS	10//99-12//99
Transportation and Material-Moving Machine and Vehicle Operators	Charlottesville MSA, VA	S	16.80 MW	15.96 AW	34940 AAW	VABLS	10//99-12//99
Transportation and Material-Moving Machine and Vehicle Operators	Danville MSA, VA	S	13.92 MW	14.42 AW	28950 AAW	VABLS	10//99-12//99
Transportation and Material-Moving Machine and Vehicle Operators	Lynchburg MSA, VA	S	18.35 MW	15.44 AW	38160 AAW	VABLS	10//99-12//99
Transportation and Material-Moving Machine and Vehicle Operators	Norfolk-Virginia Beach-Newport News MSA, VA-NC	S	20.33 MW	19.27 AW	42290 AAW	VABLS	10//99-12//99
Transportation and Material-Moving Machine and Vehicle Operators	Richmond-Petersburg MSA, VA	S	16.89 MW	16.55 AW	35130 AAW	VABLS	10//99-12//99
Transportation and Material-Moving Machine and Vehicle Operators	Roanoke MSA, VA	S	18.35 MW	17.67 AW	38180 AAW	VABLS	10//99-12//99
Transportation and Material-Moving Machine and Vehicle Operators	Washington	S	23.68 MW	24.10 AW	50130 AAW	WABLS	10//99-12//99
Transportation and Material-Moving Machine and Vehicle Operators	Bellingham MSA, WA	S	20.37 MW	16.22 AW	42360 AAW	WABLS	10//99-12//99
Transportation and Material-Moving Machine and Vehicle Operators	Bremerton PMSA, WA	S	20.81 MW	21.60 AW	43280 AAW	WABLS	10//99-12//99
Transportation and Material-Moving Machine and Vehicle Operators	Olympia PMSA, WA	S	21.31 MW	20.92 AW	44320 AAW	WABLS	10//99-12//99
Transportation and Material-Moving Machine and Vehicle Operators	Richland-Kennewick-Pasco MSA, WA	S	19.85 MW	20.09 AW	41280 AAW	WABLS	10//99-12//99

AAW	Average annual wage	AOH	Average offered, high	ASH	Average starting, high	H	Hourly	M	Monthly	S	Special: hourly and annual
AE	Average entry wage	AOL	Average offered, low	ASL	Average starting, low	HI	Highest wage paid	MTC	Median total compensation	TQ	Third quartile wage
AEX	Average experienced wage	APH	Average pay, high range	AW	Average wage paid	HR	High end range	MW	Median wage paid	W	Weekly
AO	Average offered	APL	Average pay, low range	FQ	First quartile wage	LR	Low end range	SQ	Second quartile wage	Y	Yearly

First-Line Supervisor/Manager

Occupation/Type/Industry	Location	Per	Low	Mid	High	Source	Date
Transportation and Material-Moving Machine and Vehicle Operators	Seattle-Bellevue-Everett PMSA, WA	S	24.96 MW	24.58 AW	51920 AAW	WABLS	10//99-12//99
Transportation and Material-Moving Machine and Vehicle Operators	Spokane MSA, WA	S	21.81 MW	20.87 AW	45360 AAW	WABLS	10//99-12//99
Transportation and Material-Moving Machine and Vehicle Operators	Tacoma PMSA, WA	S	26.91 MW	25.94 AW	55980 AAW	WABLS	10//99-12//99
Transportation and Material-Moving Machine and Vehicle Operators	Yakima MSA, WA	S	19.38 MW	20.29 AW	40310 AAW	WABLS	10//99-12//99
Transportation and Material-Moving Machine and Vehicle Operators	West Virginia	S	15.03 MW	17.51 AW	36420 AAW	WVBLS	10//99-12//99
Transportation and Material-Moving Machine and Vehicle Operators	Charleston MSA, WV	S	17.66 MW	14.33 AW	36730 AAW	WVBLS	10//99-12//99
Transportation and Material-Moving Machine and Vehicle Operators	Huntington-Ashland MSA, WV-KY-OH	S	15.62 MW	13.19 AW	32490 AAW	WVBLS	10//99-12//99
Transportation and Material-Moving Machine and Vehicle Operators	Parkersburg-Marietta MSA, WV-OH	S	18.08 MW	17.69 AW	37600 AAW	WVBLS	10//99-12//99
Transportation and Material-Moving Machine and Vehicle Operators	Wheeling MSA, WV-OH	S	18.17 MW	14.60 AW	37780 AAW	WVBLS	10//99-12//99
Transportation and Material-Moving Machine and Vehicle Operators	Wisconsin	S	19.77 MW	20.57 AW	42790 AAW	WIBLS	10//99-12//99
Transportation and Material-Moving Machine and Vehicle Operators	Appleton-Oshkosh-Neenah MSA, WI	S	19.83 MW	17.07 AW	41250 AAW	WIBLS	10//99-12//99
Transportation and Material-Moving Machine and Vehicle Operators	Eau Claire MSA, WI	S	18.30 MW	16.11 AW	38060 AAW	WIBLS	10//99-12//99
Transportation and Material-Moving Machine and Vehicle Operators	Green Bay MSA, WI	S	20.08 MW	19.50 AW	41770 AAW	WIBLS	10//99-12//99
Transportation and Material-Moving Machine and Vehicle Operators	Janesville-Beloit MSA, WI	S	19.51 MW	19.78 AW	40590 AAW	WIBLS	10//99-12//99
Transportation and Material-Moving Machine and Vehicle Operators	La Crosse MSA, WI-MN	S	15.73 MW	15.52 AW	32730 AAW	WIBLS	10//99-12//99
Transportation and Material-Moving Machine and Vehicle Operators	Madison MSA, WI	S	20.48 MW	20.25 AW	42610 AAW	WIBLS	10//99-12//99
Transportation and Material-Moving Machine and Vehicle Operators	Milwaukee-Waukesha PMSA, WI	S	22.03 MW	20.72 AW	45830 AAW	WIBLS	10//99-12//99
Transportation and Material-Moving Machine and Vehicle Operators	Racine PMSA, WI	S	16.31 MW	15.13 AW	33920 AAW	WIBLS	10//99-12//99
Transportation and Material-Moving Machine and Vehicle Operators	Sheboygan MSA, WI	S	19.22 MW	20.24 AW	39980 AAW	WIBLS	10//99-12//99
Transportation and Material-Moving Machine and Vehicle Operators	Wyoming	S	19.18 MW	21.05 AW	43790 AAW	WYBLS	10//99-12//99
Transportation and Material-Moving Machine and Vehicle Operators	Casper MSA, WY	S	23.34 MW	20.68 AW	48540 AAW	WYBLS	10//99-12//99
Transportation and Material-Moving Machine and Vehicle Operators	Cheyenne MSA, WY	S	12.52 MW	12.44 AW	26050 AAW	WYBLS	10//99-12//99
Transportation and Material-Moving Machine and Vehicle Operators	Puerto Rico	S	10.48 MW	12.35 AW	25680 AAW	PRBLS	10//99-12//99
Transportation and Material-Moving Machine and Vehicle Operators	Mayaguez MSA, PR	S	10.20 MW	8.40 AW	21220 AAW	PRBLS	10//99-12//99
Transportation and Material-Moving Machine and Vehicle Operators	Ponce MSA, PR	S	10.69 MW	8.95 AW	22230 AAW	PRBLS	10//99-12//99
Transportation and Material-Moving Machine and Vehicle Operators	San Juan-Bayamon PMSA, PR	S	12.84 MW	11.34 AW	26700 AAW	PRBLS	10//99-12//99
Transportation and Material-Moving Machine and Vehicle Operators	Virgin Islands	S	14.89 MW	17.34 AW	36080 AAW	VIBLS	10//99-12//99
Transportation and Material-Moving Machine and Vehicle Operators	Guam	S	13.06 MW	15.35 AW	31930 AAW	GUBLS	10//99-12//99
Fish and Game Warden	Arizona	S	15.85 MW	16.23 AW	33760 AAW	AZBLS	10//99-12//99
	California	S	19.58 MW	20.50 AW	42640 AAW	CABLS	10//99-12//99
	Colorado	S	23.17 MW	21.77 AW	45290 AAW	COBLS	10//99-12//99
	Connecticut	S	17.47 MW	16.78 AW	34910 AAW	CTBLS	10//99-12//99
	Georgia	S	12.67 MW	13.11 AW	27260 AAW	GABLS	10//99-12//99
	Idaho	S	18.81 MW	19.48 AW	40520 AAW	IDBLS	10//99-12//99
	Illinois	S	17.55 MW	17.07 AW	35500 AAW	ILBLS	10//99-12//99
	Massachusetts	S	17.67 MW	19.20 AW	39940 AAW	MABLS	10//99-12//99
	Michigan	S	19.81 MW	20.45 AW	42530 AAW	MIBLS	10//99-12//99
	Mississippi	S	17.6 MW	17.72 AW	36860 AAW	MSBLS	10//99-12//99

AAW	Average annual wage	AOH	Average offered, high	ASH	Average starting, high	H	Hourly	M	Monthly	S	Special: hourly and annual
AE	Average entry wage	AOL	Average offered, low	ASL	Average starting, low	HI	Highest wage paid	MTC	Median total compensation	TQ	Third quartile wage
AEX	Average experienced wage	APH	Average pay, high range	AW	Average wage paid	HR	High end range	MW	Median wage paid	W	Weekly
AO	Average offered	APL	Average pay, low range	FQ	First quartile wage	LR	Low end range	SQ	Second quartile wage	Y	Yearly

Occupation/Type/Industry	Location	Per	Low	Mid	High	Source	Date
Fish and Game Warden	New Hampshire	S	17.85 MW	17.87 AW	37170 AAW	NHBLS	10//99-12//99
	New York	S	22.58 MW	20.94 AW	43560 AAW	NYBLS	10//99-12//99
	Oklahoma	S	11.63 MW	11.55 AW	24030 AAW	OKBLS	10//99-12//99
	Pennsylvania	S	44.94 MW	35.12 AW	73050 AAW	PABLS	10//99-12//99
	South Carolina	S	18.9 MW	18.97 AW	39460 AAW	SCBLS	10//99-12//99
	Texas	S	18.99 MW	19.33 AW	40210 AAW	TXBLS	10//99-12//99
	Virginia	S	15.7 MW	15.53 AW	32310 AAW	VABLS	10//99-12//99
	Washington	S	24.32 MW	23.92 AW	49760 AAW	WABLS	10//99-12//99
	West Virginia	S	15.4 MW	15.62 AW	32480 AAW	WVBLS	10//99-12//99
Fish-head Trimmer							
Cannery	United States	H		7.77 AW		MENHEL	1999
Fitness Trainer and Aerobics Instructor							
	Alabama	S	13.3 MW	13.13 AW	27310 AAW	ALBLS	10//99-12//99
	Alaska	S	13.27 MW	12.89 AW	26810 AAW	AKBLS	10//99-12//99
	Arizona	S	10.02 MW	12.02 AW	25010 AAW	AZBLS	10//99-12//99
	Arkansas	S	7.69 MW	7.81 AW	16250 AAW	ARBLS	10//99-12//99
	California	S	15.94 MW	17.73 AW	36890 AAW	CABLS	10//99-12//99
	Colorado	S	14.58 MW	15.65 AW	32550 AAW	COBLS	10//99-12//99
	Connecticut	S	10.97 MW	14.36 AW	29880 AAW	CTBLS	10//99-12//99
	Delaware	S	8.73 MW	9.24 AW	19220 AAW	DEBLS	10//99-12//99
	District of Columbia	S	36.59 MW	28.32 AW	58900 AAW	DCBLS	10//99-12//99
	Florida	S	10.26 MW	12.66 AW	26340 AAW	FLBLS	10//99-12//99
	Georgia	S	13.31 MW	14.40 AW	29940 AAW	GABLS	10//99-12//99
	Hawaii	S	15.32 MW	16.13 AW	33560 AAW	HIBLS	10//99-12//99
	Idaho	S	14.62 MW	14.32 AW	29790 AAW	IDBLS	10//99-12//99
	Illinois	S	10.75 MW	14.55 AW	30270 AAW	ILBLS	10//99-12//99
	Indiana	S	12.24 MW	14.11 AW	29340 AAW	INBLS	10//99-12//99
	Iowa	S	7.37 MW	8.10 AW	16850 AAW	IABLS	10//99-12//99
	Kansas	S	7.51 MW	10.14 AW	21090 AAW	KSBLS	10//99-12//99
	Kentucky	S	9.55 MW	10.58 AW	22000 AAW	KYBLS	10//99-12//99
	Louisiana	S	9.92 MW	9.84 AW	20460 AAW	LABLS	10//99-12//99
	Maine	S	12.33 MW	12.99 AW	27020 AAW	MEBLS	10//99-12//99
	Maryland	S	14.08 MW	13.78 AW	28650 AAW	MDBLS	10//99-12//99
	Massachusetts	S	10.42 MW	12.22 AW	25420 AAW	MABLS	10//99-12//99
	Michigan	S	12.88 MW	13.45 AW	27980 AAW	MIBLS	10//99-12//99
	Minnesota	S	8.12 MW	9.85 AW	20490 AAW	MNBLS	10//99-12//99
	Mississippi	S	8.88 MW	9.68 AW	20130 AAW	MSBLS	10//99-12//99
	Missouri	S	8.15 MW	10.06 AW	20920 AAW	MOBLS	10//99-12//99
	Montana	S	8.9 MW	8.43 AW	17530 AAW	MTBLS	10//99-12//99
	Nebraska	S	8.49 MW	10.36 AW	21540 AAW	NEBLS	10//99-12//99
	Nevada	S	14.64 MW	14.34 AW	29820 AAW	NVBLS	10//99-12//99
	New Hampshire	S	12.57 MW	12.61 AW	26230 AAW	NHBLS	10//99-12//99
	New Jersey	S	10.71 MW	12.10 AW	25170 AAW	NJBLS	10//99-12//99
	New Mexico	S	9.66 MW	10.49 AW	21820 AAW	NMBLS	10//99-12//99
	New York	S	10.98 MW	15.00 AW	31210 AAW	NYBLS	10//99-12//99
	North Carolina	S	10.14 MW	11.37 AW	23650 AAW	NCBLS	10//99-12//99
	North Dakota	S	9.6 MW	10.25 AW	21310 AAW	NDBLS	10//99-12//99
	Ohio	S	8.19 MW	9.95 AW	20700 AAW	OHBLS	10//99-12//99
	Oklahoma	S	9.06 MW	9.66 AW	20100 AAW	OKBLS	10//99-12//99
	Oregon	S	11.04 MW	13.81 AW	28720 AAW	ORBLS	10//99-12//99
	Pennsylvania	S	8.86 MW	10.80 AW	22460 AAW	PABLS	10//99-12//99
	Rhode Island	S	8.17 MW	9.72 AW	20220 AAW	RIBLS	10//99-12//99
	South Carolina	S	9.26 MW	11.42 AW	23760 AAW	SCBLS	10//99-12//99
	South Dakota	S	11.48 MW	11.42 AW	23750 AAW	SDBLS	10//99-12//99
	Tennessee	S	7.6 MW	8.58 AW	17840 AAW	TNBLS	10//99-12//99
	Texas	S	10.57 MW	13.29 AW	27640 AAW	TXBLS	10//99-12//99
	Vermont	S	11.89 MW	11.53 AW	23980 AAW	VTBLS	10//99-12//99
	Virginia	S	11.09 MW	11.64 AW	24210 AAW	VABLS	10//99-12//99
	Washington	S	12.51 MW	14.69 AW	30560 AAW	WABLS	10//99-12//99
	West Virginia	S	7.4 MW	8.18 AW	17020 AAW	WVBLS	10//99-12//99
	Wisconsin	S	9.9 MW	10.74 AW	22340 AAW	WIBLS	10//99-12//99
	Wyoming	S	6.45 MW	7.66 AW	15930 AAW	WYBLS	10//99-12//99
	Puerto Rico	S	6.49 MW	6.90 AW	14360 AAW	PRBLS	10//99-12//99
Fleet Manager							
Supply Chain Management	United States	Y		57100 AW		AMSHIP	2000
Flight Attendant							
	Alaska	Y		27820 AAW		AKBLS	10//99-12//99
	California	Y		45080 AAW		CABLS	10//99-12//99
	Washington PMSA, DC-MD-VA-WV	Y		58420 AAW		DCBLS	10//99-12//99

AAW Average annual wage	**AOH** Average offered, high	**ASH** Average starting, high	**H** Hourly	**M** Monthly	**S** Special: hourly and annual
AE Average entry wage	**AOL** Average offered, low	**ASL** Average starting, low	**HI** Highest wage paid	**MTC** Median total compensation	**TQ** Third quartile wage
AEX Average experienced wage	**APH** Average pay, high range	**AW** Average wage paid	**HR** High end range	**MW** Median wage paid	**W** Weekly
AO Average offered	**APL** Average pay, low range	**FQ** First quartile wage	**LR** Low end range	**SQ** Second quartile wage	**Y** Yearly

Occupation/Type/Industry	Location	Per	Low	Mid	High	Source	Date
Flight Attendant	Florida	Y		42460 AAW		FLBLS	10//99-12//99
	Tampa-St. Petersburg-Clearwater MSA, FL	Y		44530 AAW		FLBLS	10//99-12//99
	Georgia	Y		41060 AAW		GABLS	10//99-12//99
	Atlanta MSA, GA	Y		41060 AAW		GABLS	10//99-12//99
	Hawaii	Y		53320 AAW		HIBLS	10//99-12//99
	Honolulu MSA, HI	Y		53550 AAW		HIBLS	10//99-12//99
	Illinois	Y		50820 AAW		ILBLS	10//99-12//99
	Chicago PMSA, IL	Y		50870 AAW		ILBLS	10//99-12//99
	Massachusetts	Y		58780 AAW		MABLS	10//99-12//99
	Boston PMSA, MA-NH	Y		58780 AAW		MABLS	10//99-12//99
	Minnesota	Y		37300 AAW		MNBLS	10//99-12//99
	Minneapolis-St. Paul MSA, MN-WI	Y		37480 AAW		MNBLS	10//99-12//99
	New York PMSA, NY	Y		51910 AAW		NYBLS	10//99-12//99
	Raleigh-Durham-Chapel Hill MSA, NC	Y		56830 AAW		NCBLS	10//99-12//99
	Oklahoma	Y		40220 AAW		OKBLS	10//99-12//99
	Tulsa MSA, OK	Y		38540 AAW		OKBLS	10//99-12//99
	Tennessee	Y		38530 AAW		TNBLS	10//99-12//99
	Texas	Y		70990 AAW		TXBLS	10//99-12//99
	Virginia	Y		57840 AAW		VABLS	10//99-12//99
	Washington	Y		59860 AAW		WABLS	10//99-12//99
	Seattle-Bellevue-Everett PMSA, WA	Y		59920 AAW		WABLS	10//99-12//99
	Wisconsin	Y		56410 AAW		WIBLS	10//99-12//99
Floor Layer							
Except Carpet, Wood, and Hard Tile	Arizona	S	12.58 MW	12.52 AW	26040 AAW	AZBLS	10//99-12//99
Except Carpet, Wood, and Hard Tile	California	S	19.9 MW	19.73 AW	41030 AAW	CABLS	10//99-12//99
Except Carpet, Wood, and Hard Tile	Colorado	S	10.19 MW	13.49 AW	28050 AAW	COBLS	10//99-12//99
Except Carpet, Wood, and Hard Tile	Delaware	S	11.37 MW	11.91 AW	24770 AAW	DEBLS	10//99-12//99
Except Carpet, Wood, and Hard Tile	Florida	S	7.11 MW	7.97 AW	16580 AAW	FLBLS	10//99-12//99
Except Carpet, Wood, and Hard Tile	Hawaii	S	15.04 MW	16.07 AW	33420 AAW	HIBLS	10//99-12//99
Except Carpet, Wood, and Hard Tile	Idaho	S	11.54 MW	12.11 AW	25190 AAW	IDBLS	10//99-12//99
Except Carpet, Wood, and Hard Tile	Illinois	S	17.34 MW	16.60 AW	34530 AAW	ILBLS	10//99-12//99
Except Carpet, Wood, and Hard Tile	Indiana	S	10.41 MW	11.45 AW	23810 AAW	INBLS	10//99-12//99
Except Carpet, Wood, and Hard Tile	Iowa	S	8.15 MW	9.25 AW	19240 AAW	IABLS	10//99-12//99
Except Carpet, Wood, and Hard Tile	Kansas	S	22.49 MW	20.15 AW	41900 AAW	KSBLS	10//99-12//99
Except Carpet, Wood, and Hard Tile	Louisiana	S	11.06 MW	10.81 AW	22490 AAW	LABLS	10//99-12//99
Except Carpet, Wood, and Hard Tile	Maryland	S	15.26 MW	15.23 AW	31690 AAW	MDBLS	10//99-12//99
Except Carpet, Wood, and Hard Tile	Massachusetts	S	16.34 MW	18.43 AW	38340 AAW	MABLS	10//99-12//99
Except Carpet, Wood, and Hard Tile	Michigan	S	10.47 MW	12.94 AW	26910 AAW	MIBLS	10//99-12//99
Except Carpet, Wood, and Hard Tile	Minnesota	S	21.14 MW	21.05 AW	43790 AAW	MNBLS	10//99-12//99
Except Carpet, Wood, and Hard Tile	Mississippi	S	9.32 MW	8.96 AW	18630 AAW	MSBLS	10//99-12//99
Except Carpet, Wood, and Hard Tile	New Hampshire	S	18.56 MW	17.86 AW	37150 AAW	NHBLS	10//99-12//99
Except Carpet, Wood, and Hard Tile	New Jersey	S	24.1 MW	23.25 AW	48360 AAW	NJBLS	10//99-12//99
Except Carpet, Wood, and Hard Tile	New York	S	11.88 MW	11.94 AW	24840 AAW	NYBLS	10//99-12//99
Except Carpet, Wood, and Hard Tile	North Carolina	S	11.56 MW	13.58 AW	28240 AAW	NCBLS	10//99-12//99
Except Carpet, Wood, and Hard Tile	Ohio	S	17.09 MW	16.22 AW	33740 AAW	OHBLS	10//99-12//99
Except Carpet, Wood, and Hard Tile	Oklahoma	S	11.91 MW	13.79 AW	28680 AAW	OKBLS	10//99-12//99
Except Carpet, Wood, and Hard Tile	Oregon	S	15.14 MW	15.23 AW	31680 AAW	ORBLS	10//99-12//99
Except Carpet, Wood, and Hard Tile	Pennsylvania	S	10.83 MW	12.23 AW	25430 AAW	PABLS	10//99-12//99
Except Carpet, Wood, and Hard Tile	Tennessee	S	10.81 MW	11.55 AW	24020 AAW	TNBLS	10//99-12//99
Except Carpet, Wood, and Hard Tile	Texas	S	12.53 MW	13.11 AW	27270 AAW	TXBLS	10//99-12//99
Except Carpet, Wood, and Hard Tile	Vermont	S	12.05 MW	12.33 AW	25650 AAW	VTBLS	10//99-12//99
Except Carpet, Wood, and Hard Tile	Virginia	S	11.57 MW	12.40 AW	25780 AAW	VABLS	10//99-12//99
Except Carpet, Wood, and Hard Tile	Washington	S	20.24 MW	20.05 AW	41700 AAW	WABLS	10//99-12//99
Except Carpet, Wood, and Hard Tile	Wisconsin	S	15.33 MW	15.72 AW	32700 AAW	WIBLS	10//99-12//99
Except Carpet, Wood, and Hard Tile	Puerto Rico	S	12.33 MW	12.67 AW	26350 AAW	PRBLS	10//99-12//99
Floor Sander and Finisher	California	S	13.82 MW	14.26 AW	29660 AAW	CABLS	10//99-12//99
	Los Angeles-Long Beach PMSA, CA	S	14.81 MW	14.87 AW	30810 AAW	CABLS	10//99-12//99
	Colorado	S	11.32 MW	12.40 AW	25800 AAW	COBLS	10//99-12//99
	Denver PMSA, CO	S	12.18 MW	10.53 AW	25340 AAW	COBLS	10//99-12//99
	Connecticut	S	13.38 MW	14.57 AW	30310 AAW	CTBLS	10//99-12//99
	Danbury PMSA, CT	S	18.59 MW	18.98 AW	38660 AAW	CTBLS	10//99-12//99
	Washington PMSA, DC-MD-VA-WV	S	14.04 MW	13.32 AW	29200 AAW	DCBLS	10//99-12//99
	Florida	S	10.37 MW	10.65 AW	22150 AAW	FLBLS	10//99-12//99
	Georgia	S	12.55 MW	12.78 AW	26580 AAW	GABLS	10//99-12//99
	Columbus MSA, GA-AL	S	9.26 MW	9.54 AW	19260 AAW	GABLS	10//99-12//99

AAW Average annual wage	**AOH** Average offered, high	**ASH** Average starting, high	**H** Hourly	**M** Monthly	**S** Special: hourly and annual
AE Average entry wage	**AOL** Average offered, low	**ASL** Average starting, low	**HI** Highest wage paid	**MTC** Median total compensation	**TQ** Third quartile wage
AEX Average experienced wage	**APH** Average pay, high range	**AW** Average wage paid	**HR** High end range	**MW** Median wage paid	**W** Weekly
AO Average offered	**APL** Average pay, low range	**FQ** First quartile wage	**LR** Low end range	**SQ** Second quartile wage	**Y** Yearly

Occupation/Type/Industry	Location	Per	Low	Mid	High	Source	Date
Floor Sander and Finisher	Illinois	S	21.23 MW	20.94 AW	43560 AAW	ILBLS	10//99-12//99
	Chicago PMSA, IL	S	21.05 MW	21.49 AW	43780 AAW	ILBLS	10//99-12//99
	Iowa	S	9.54 MW	10.65 AW	22150 AAW	IABLS	10//99-12//99
	Louisiana	S	11.58 MW	11.93 AW	24820 AAW	LABLS	10//99-12//99
	Maryland	S	13.38 MW	15.17 AW	31560 AAW	MDBLS	10//99-12//99
	Baltimore PMSA, MD	S	18.06 MW	19.08 AW	37560 AAW	MDBLS	10//99-12//99
	Massachusetts	S	14.16 MW	15.51 AW	32260 AAW	MABLS	10//99-12//99
	Michigan	S	10.97 MW	13.16 AW	27370 AAW	MIBLS	10//99-12//99
	Mississippi	S	10.13 MW	9.98 AW	20760 AAW	MSBLS	10//99-12//99
	Nebraska	S	11.16 MW	12.11 AW	25190 AAW	NEBLS	10//99-12//99
	New York	S	10.86 MW	11.43 AW	23780 AAW	NYBLS	10//99-12//99
	North Carolina	S	11.28 MW	11.51 AW	23930 AAW	NCBLS	10//99-12//99
	Charlotte-Gastonia-Rock Hill MSA, NC-SC	S	13.35 MW	11.74 AW	27760 AAW	NCBLS	10//99-12//99
	Cincinnati PMSA, OH-KY-IN	S	14.64 MW	12.90 AW	30450 AAW	OHBLS	10//99-12//99
	Oklahoma	S	11.8 MW	11.62 AW	24160 AAW	OKBLS	10//99-12//99
	Oregon	S	12.32 MW	12.94 AW	26910 AAW	ORBLS	10//99-12//99
	Pennsylvania	S	11.66 MW	12.16 AW	25300 AAW	PABLS	10//99-12//99
	South Carolina	S	10.89 MW	11.20 AW	23290 AAW	SCBLS	10//99-12//99
	Tennessee	S	11.31 MW	11.95 AW	24850 AAW	TNBLS	10//99-12//99
	Texas	S	10.87 MW	10.92 AW	22710 AAW	TXBLS	10//99-12//99
	Fort Worth-Arlington PMSA, TX	S	13.52 MW	13.58 AW	28130 AAW	TXBLS	10//99-12//99
	Houston PMSA, TX	S	10.83 MW	10.18 AW	22520 AAW	TXBLS	10//99-12//99
	Vermont	S	12.32 MW	12.66 AW	26340 AAW	VTBLS	10//99-12//99
	Virginia	S	10.01 MW	10.99 AW	22850 AAW	VABLS	10//99-12//99
	Richmond-Petersburg MSA, VA	S	12.29 MW	12.28 AW	25570 AAW	VABLS	10//99-12//99
	Washington	S	11.52 MW	12.43 AW	25850 AAW	WABLS	10//99-12//99
	Wisconsin	S	14.27 MW	14.41 AW	29980 AAW	WIBLS	10//99-12//99
Floral Designer	Alabama	S	6.89 MW	6.94 AW	14430 AAW	ALBLS	10//99-12//99
	Alaska	S	9.65 MW	9.74 AW	20260 AAW	AKBLS	10//99-12//99
	Arizona	S	8.85 MW	9.26 AW	19260 AAW	AZBLS	10//99-12//99
	Arkansas	S	8.24 MW	8.23 AW	17120 AAW	ARBLS	10//99-12//99
	California	S	10.16 MW	10.63 AW	22110 AAW	CABLS	10//99-12//99
	Colorado	S	9.46 MW	9.49 AW	19740 AAW	COBLS	10//99-12//99
	Connecticut	S	11.75 MW	11.85 AW	24640 AAW	CTBLS	10//99-12//99
	Delaware	S	8.53 MW	8.47 AW	17620 AAW	DEBLS	10//99-12//99
	District of Columbia	S	13.79 MW	14.27 AW	29680 AAW	DCBLS	10//99-12//99
	Florida	S	8.24 MW	8.52 AW	17720 AAW	FLBLS	10//99-12//99
	Georgia	S	8.05 MW	8.19 AW	17030 AAW	GABLS	10//99-12//99
	Hawaii	S	9.11 MW	9.21 AW	19160 AAW	HIBLS	10//99-12//99
	Idaho	S	9.67 MW	9.78 AW	20340 AAW	IDBLS	10//99-12//99
	Illinois	S	8.04 MW	8.81 AW	18320 AAW	ILBLS	10//99-12//99
	Indiana	S	7.86 MW	8.25 AW	17160 AAW	INBLS	10//99-12//99
	Iowa	S	7.39 MW	7.39 AW	15370 AAW	IABLS	10//99-12//99
	Kansas	S	8.36 MW	8.20 AW	17060 AAW	KSBLS	10//99-12//99
	Kentucky	S	8.08 MW	8.26 AW	17180 AAW	KYBLS	10//99-12//99
	Louisiana	S	6.29 MW	6.62 AW	13770 AAW	LABLS	10//99-12//99
	Maine	S	9.51 MW	9.12 AW	18970 AAW	MEBLS	10//99-12//99
	Maryland	S	9 MW	8.68 AW	18050 AAW	MDBLS	10//99-12//99
	Michigan	S	9.14 MW	8.84 AW	18390 AAW	MIBLS	10//99-12//99
	Minnesota	S	7.28 MW	8.62 AW	17930 AAW	MNBLS	10//99-12//99
	Mississippi	S	8.02 MW	8.00 AW	16640 AAW	MSBLS	10//99-12//99
	Missouri	S	8.22 MW	8.68 AW	18060 AAW	MOBLS	10//99-12//99
	Montana	S	7.41 MW	7.48 AW	15570 AAW	MTBLS	10//99-12//99
	Nebraska	S	9.2 MW	9.23 AW	19200 AAW	NEBLS	10//99-12//99
	Nevada	S	9.86 MW	9.91 AW	20610 AAW	NVBLS	10//99-12//99
	New Hampshire	S	9.99 MW	10.34 AW	21510 AAW	NHBLS	10//99-12//99
	New Jersey	S	10.72 MW	11.16 AW	23210 AAW	NJBLS	10//99-12//99
	New Mexico	S	7.82 MW	7.94 AW	16510 AAW	NMBLS	10//99-12//99
	New York	S	10.12 MW	11.51 AW	23950 AAW	NYBLS	10//99-12//99
	North Carolina	S	7.61 MW	8.16 AW	16970 AAW	NCBLS	10//99-12//99
	North Dakota	S	7.61 MW	7.61 AW	15830 AAW	NDBLS	10//99-12//99
	Ohio	S	8.06 MW	8.37 AW	17410 AAW	OHBLS	10//99-12//99
	Oklahoma	S	8.83 MW	9.62 AW	20010 AAW	OKBLS	10//99-12//99
	Oregon	S	8.21 MW	8.94 AW	18600 AAW	ORBLS	10//99-12//99
	Pennsylvania	S	8.24 MW	8.79 AW	18280 AAW	PABLS	10//99-12//99
	South Carolina	S	9.57 MW	9.94 AW	20680 AAW	SCBLS	10//99-12//99
	South Dakota	S	7.22 MW	7.35 AW	15290 AAW	SDBLS	10//99-12//99
	Tennessee	S	7.45 MW	7.95 AW	16540 AAW	TNBLS	10//99-12//99
	Texas	S	8.14 MW	8.49 AW	17670 AAW	TXBLS	10//99-12//99

AAW	Average annual wage	AOH	Average offered, high	ASH	Average starting, high	H	Hourly	M	Monthly	S	Special: hourly and annual
AE	Average entry wage	AOL	Average offered, low	ASL	Average starting, low	HI	Highest wage paid	MTC	Median total compensation	TQ	Third quartile wage
AEX	Average experienced wage	APH	Average pay, high range	AW	Average wage paid	HR	High end range	MW	Median wage paid	W	Weekly
AO	Average offered	APL	Average pay, low range	FQ	First quartile wage	LR	Low end range	SQ	Second quartile wage	Y	Yearly

Occupation/Type/Industry	Location	Per	Low	Mid	High	Source	Date
Floral Designer	Utah	S	8.09 MW	8.47 AW	17610 AAW	UTBLS	10//99-12//99
	Vermont	S	9.33 MW	9.66 AW	20100 AAW	VTBLS	10//99-12//99
	Virginia	S	8.25 MW	9.12 AW	18960 AAW	VABLS	10//99-12//99
	Washington	S	11.05 MW	10.84 AW	22540 AAW	WABLS	10//99-12//99
	West Virginia	S	7.26 MW	7.80 AW	16220 AAW	WVBLS	10//99-12//99
	Wisconsin	S	8.88 MW	8.98 AW	18680 AAW	WIBLS	10//99-12//99
	Wyoming	S	7.49 MW	7.75 AW	16130 AAW	WYBLS	10//99-12//99
	Puerto Rico	S	5.99 MW	5.95 AW	12370 AAW	PRBLS	10//99-12//99
	Guam	S	6.63 MW	6.97 AW	14500 AAW	GUBLS	10//99-12//99
Food and Tobacco Roasting, Baking, and Drying Machine Operator and Tender	Alabama	S	6.06 MW	6.60 AW	13730 AAW	ALBLS	10//99-12//99
	Arkansas	S	9.7 MW	9.85 AW	20490 AAW	ARBLS	10//99-12//99
	California	S	8.79 MW	10.18 AW	21170 AAW	CABLS	10//99-12//99
	Fresno MSA, CA	S	8.52 MW	7.90 AW	17730 AAW	CABLS	10//99-12//99
	Los Angeles-Long Beach PMSA, CA	S	8.24 MW	6.74 AW	17140 AAW	CABLS	10//99-12//99
	Oakland PMSA, CA	S	16.39 MW	17.82 AW	34090 AAW	CABLS	10//99-12//99
	Orange County PMSA, CA	S	9.43 MW	11.02 AW	19620 AAW	CABLS	10//99-12//99
	Colorado	S	14.02 MW	12.10 AW	25180 AAW	COBLS	10//99-12//99
	Denver PMSA, CO	S	12.85 MW	14.44 AW	26720 AAW	COBLS	10//99-12//99
	Connecticut	S	14.56 MW	13.54 AW	28160 AAW	CTBLS	10//99-12//99
	Washington PMSA, DC-MD-VA-WV	S	9.68 MW	9.01 AW	20130 AAW	DCBLS	10//99-12//99
	Florida	S	11.94 MW	11.53 AW	23980 AAW	FLBLS	10//99-12//99
	Idaho	S	10.89 MW	9.66 AW	20100 AAW	IDBLS	10//99-12//99
	Illinois	S	14.54 MW	12.97 AW	26970 AAW	ILBLS	10//99-12//99
	Chicago PMSA, IL	S	12.65 MW	14.39 AW	26320 AAW	ILBLS	10//99-12//99
	Indiana	S	11.27 MW	11.02 AW	22920 AAW	INBLS	10//99-12//99
	Louisiana	S	11.36 MW	10.37 AW	21570 AAW	LABLS	10//99-12//99
	New Orleans MSA, LA	S	11.74 MW	11.97 AW	24420 AAW	LABLS	10//99-12//99
	Maryland	S	12.26 MW	12.20 AW	25370 AAW	MDBLS	10//99-12//99
	Baltimore PMSA, MD	S	12.60 MW	12.50 AW	26210 AAW	MDBLS	10//99-12//99
	Massachusetts	S	13.91 MW	12.94 AW	26920 AAW	MABLS	10//99-12//99
	Boston PMSA, MA-NH	S	12.92 MW	13.89 AW	26870 AAW	MABLS	10//99-12//99
	Minnesota	S	11.95 MW	12.06 AW	25090 AAW	MNBLS	10//99-12//99
	Minneapolis-St. Paul MSA, MN-WI	S	9.83 MW	8.35 AW	20450 AAW	MNBLS	10//99-12//99
	Mississippi	S	8.07 MW	8.19 AW	17040 AAW	MSBLS	10//99-12//99
	Missouri	S	12.28 MW	12.47 AW	25930 AAW	MOBLS	10//99-12//99
	Nebraska	S	11.9 MW	11.36 AW	23630 AAW	NEBLS	10//99-12//99
	New Jersey	S	11.89 MW	12.66 AW	26340 AAW	NJBLS	10//99-12//99
	New York	S	8.04 MW	9.61 AW	19990 AAW	NYBLS	10//99-12//99
	New York PMSA, NY	S	9.80 MW	8.13 AW	20390 AAW	NYBLS	10//99-12//99
	North Carolina	S	8.43 MW	13.27 AW	27600 AAW	NCBLS	10//99-12//99
	Greensboro--Winston-Salem--High Point MSA, NC	S	22.81 MW	23.71 AW	47450 AAW	NCBLS	10//99-12//99
	North Dakota	S	11.18 MW	10.93 AW	22730 AAW	NDBLS	10//99-12//99
	Ohio	S	12.17 MW	12.17 AW	25320 AAW	OHBLS	10//99-12//99
	Cincinnati PMSA, OH-KY-IN	S	12.08 MW	12.13 AW	25130 AAW	OHBLS	10//99-12//99
	Oklahoma	S	8.3 MW	10.27 AW	21360 AAW	OKBLS	10//99-12//99
	Oregon	S	11.91 MW	11.80 AW	24550 AAW	ORBLS	10//99-12//99
	Portland-Vancouver PMSA, OR-WA	S	13.70 MW	14.20 AW	28500 AAW	ORBLS	10//99-12//99
	Pennsylvania	S	8.21 MW	9.50 AW	19760 AAW	PABLS	10//99-12//99
	Lancaster MSA, PA	S	7.73 MW	7.73 AW	16090 AAW	PABLS	10//99-12//99
	Philadelphia PMSA, PA-NJ	S	15.11 MW	12.77 AW	31430 AAW	PABLS	10//99-12//99
	York MSA, PA	S	10.39 MW	11.42 AW	21620 AAW	PABLS	10//99-12//99
	South Carolina	S	8.71 MW	9.48 AW	19720 AAW	SCBLS	10//99-12//99
	Tennessee	S	12.35 MW	12.85 AW	26730 AAW	TNBLS	10//99-12//99
	Texas	S	8.27 MW	9.20 AW	19140 AAW	TXBLS	10//99-12//99
	Houston PMSA, TX	S	11.31 MW	11.86 AW	23530 AAW	TXBLS	10//99-12//99
	Virginia	S	6.88 MW	9.51 AW	19780 AAW	VABLS	10//99-12//99
	Washington	S	7.97 MW	9.14 AW	19000 AAW	WABLS	10//99-12//99
	Wisconsin	S	10.62 MW	10.68 AW	22210 AAW	WIBLS	10//99-12//99
	Puerto Rico	S	7.09 MW	6.85 AW	14240 AAW	PRBLS	10//99-12//99
Food Batchmaker	Alabama	S	8.61 MW	8.56 AW	17800 AAW	ALBLS	10//99-12//99
	Mobile MSA, AL	S	6.92 MW	6.61 AW	14390 AAW	ALBLS	10//99-12//99
	Montgomery MSA, AL	S	7.58 MW	7.65 AW	15760 AAW	ALBLS	10//99-12//99
	Alaska	S	11.16 MW	11.31 AW	23520 AAW	AKBLS	10//99-12//99

AAW Average annual wage	AOH Average offered, high	ASH Average starting, high	H Hourly	M Monthly	S Special: hourly and annual
AE Average entry wage	AOL Average offered, low	ASL Average starting, low	HI Highest wage paid	MTC Median total compensation	TQ Third quartile wage
AEX Average experienced wage	APH Average pay, high range	AW Average wage paid	HR High end range	MW Median wage paid	W Weekly
AO Average offered	APL Average pay, low range	FQ First quartile wage	LR Low end range	SQ Second quartile wage	Y Yearly

Occupation/Type/Industry	Location	Per	Low	Mid	High	Source	Date
Food Batchmaker	Arizona	S	7.44 MW	7.51 AW	15620 AAW	AZBLS	10//99-12//99
	Phoenix-Mesa MSA, AZ	S	7.63 MW	7.62 AW	15870 AAW	AZBLS	10//99-12//99
	Tucson MSA, AZ	S	7.74 MW	8.08 AW	16110 AAW	AZBLS	10//99-12//99
	Arkansas	S	10.62 MW	10.85 AW	22560 AAW	ARBLS	10//99-12//99
	Fort Smith MSA, AR-OK	S	12.97 MW	13.69 AW	26980 AAW	ARBLS	10//99-12//99
	California	S	9.31 MW	10.91 AW	22700 AAW	CABLS	10//99-12//99
	Fresno MSA, CA	S	14.03 MW	15.24 AW	29190 AAW	CABLS	10//99-12//99
	Los Angeles-Long Beach PMSA, CA	S	9.82 MW	8.00 AW	20430 AAW	CABLS	10//99-12//99
	Modesto MSA, CA	S	10.64 MW	9.95 AW	22140 AAW	CABLS	10//99-12//99
	Oakland PMSA, CA	S	17.43 MW	16.02 AW	36240 AAW	CABLS	10//99-12//99
	Orange County PMSA, CA	S	9.33 MW	8.57 AW	19410 AAW	CABLS	10//99-12//99
	Riverside-San Bernardino PMSA, CA	S	12.03 MW	12.41 AW	25020 AAW	CABLS	10//99-12//99
	San Diego MSA, CA	S	8.32 MW	7.96 AW	17300 AAW	CABLS	10//99-12//99
	San Francisco PMSA, CA	S	10.96 MW	8.40 AW	22800 AAW	CABLS	10//99-12//99
	Santa Cruz-Watsonville PMSA, CA	S	11.75 MW	10.17 AW	24450 AAW	CABLS	10//99-12//99
	Santa Rosa PMSA, CA	S	15.38 MW	17.35 AW	32000 AAW	CABLS	10//99-12//99
	Stockton-Lodi MSA, CA	S	14.65 MW	14.39 AW	30470 AAW	CABLS	10//99-12//99
	Colorado	S	8.07 MW	8.46 AW	17590 AAW	COBLS	10//99-12//99
	Denver PMSA, CO	S	7.64 MW	7.68 AW	15880 AAW	COBLS	10//99-12//99
	Connecticut	S	9.78 MW	10.80 AW	22460 AAW	CTBLS	10//99-12//99
	Hartford MSA, CT	S	13.10 MW	13.83 AW	27240 AAW	CTBLS	10//99-12//99
	New Haven-Meriden PMSA, CT	S	9.26 MW	8.38 AW	19250 AAW	CTBLS	10//99-12//99
	Delaware	S	9.61 MW	9.73 AW	20240 AAW	DEBLS	10//99-12//99
	Washington PMSA, DC-MD-VA-WV	S	9.07 MW	8.97 AW	18870 AAW	DCBLS	10//99-12//99
	Florida	S	7.64 MW	8.46 AW	17600 AAW	FLBLS	10//99-12//99
	Fort Lauderdale PMSA, FL	S	8.95 MW	9.15 AW	18610 AAW	FLBLS	10//99-12//99
	Lakeland-Winter Haven MSA, FL	S	11.37 MW	11.69 AW	23650 AAW	FLBLS	10//99-12//99
	Tampa-St. Petersburg-Clearwater MSA, FL	S	10.99 MW	10.49 AW	22870 AAW	FLBLS	10//99-12//99
	Georgia	S	9.89 MW	10.05 AW	20910 AAW	GABLS	10//99-12//99
	Atlanta MSA, GA	S	9.47 MW	9.54 AW	19690 AAW	GABLS	10//99-12//99
	Hawaii	S	6.43 MW	7.06 AW	14690 AAW	HIBLS	10//99-12//99
	Honolulu MSA, HI	S	7.17 MW	6.54 AW	14900 AAW	HIBLS	10//99-12//99
	Idaho	S	11.52 MW	10.40 AW	21630 AAW	IDBLS	10//99-12//99
	Boise City MSA, ID	S	9.68 MW	11.18 AW	20130 AAW	IDBLS	10//99-12//99
	Illinois	S	9.43 MW	10.76 AW	22380 AAW	ILBLS	10//99-12//99
	Bloomington-Normal MSA, IL	S	8.62 MW	8.04 AW	17930 AAW	ILBLS	10//99-12//99
	Chicago PMSA, IL	S	10.78 MW	9.44 AW	22430 AAW	ILBLS	10//99-12//99
	Indiana	S	8.95 MW	9.15 AW	19030 AAW	INBLS	10//99-12//99
	Elkhart-Goshen MSA, IN	S	10.21 MW	9.89 AW	21250 AAW	INBLS	10//99-12//99
	Evansville-Henderson MSA, IN-KY	S	9.50 MW	9.58 AW	19750 AAW	INBLS	10//99-12//99
	Fort Wayne MSA, IN	S	8.36 MW	8.70 AW	17380 AAW	INBLS	10//99-12//99
	Gary PMSA, IN	S	6.79 MW	6.29 AW	14130 AAW	INBLS	10//99-12//99
	Iowa	S	14.24 MW	13.23 AW	27510 AAW	IABLS	10//99-12//99
	Waterloo-Cedar Falls MSA, IA	S	8.43 MW	7.93 AW	17530 AAW	IABLS	10//99-12//99
	Kansas	S	7.96 MW	9.44 AW	19650 AAW	KSBLS	10//99-12//99
	Kentucky	S	10.62 MW	11.43 AW	23770 AAW	KYBLS	10//99-12//99
	Louisville MSA, KY-IN	S	9.96 MW	9.87 AW	20710 AAW	KYBLS	10//99-12//99
	Louisiana	S	8 MW	8.36 AW	17380 AAW	LABLS	10//99-12//99
	New Orleans MSA, LA	S	10.83 MW	11.08 AW	22530 AAW	LABLS	10//99-12//99
	Maine	S	9.8 MW	10.12 AW	21050 AAW	MEBLS	10//99-12//99
	Portland MSA, ME	S	8.53 MW	9.03 AW	17730 AAW	MEBLS	10//99-12//99
	Maryland	S	9.64 MW	10.41 AW	21640 AAW	MDBLS	10//99-12//99
	Baltimore PMSA, MD	S	12.54 MW	12.38 AW	26080 AAW	MDBLS	10//99-12//99
	Massachusetts	S	10.19 MW	11.06 AW	23010 AAW	MABLS	10//99-12//99
	Boston PMSA, MA-NH	S	12.25 MW	11.35 AW	25470 AAW	MABLS	10//99-12//99
	Michigan	S	10.21 MW	10.51 AW	21860 AAW	MIBLS	10//99-12//99
	Ann Arbor PMSA, MI	S	11.87 MW	11.77 AW	24690 AAW	MIBLS	10//99-12//99
	Detroit PMSA, MI	S	8.15 MW	7.64 AW	16950 AAW	MIBLS	10//99-12//99
	Grand Rapids-Muskegon-Holland MSA, MI	S	10.86 MW	10.57 AW	22590 AAW	MIBLS	10//99-12//99
	Minnesota	S	12.74 MW	12.98 AW	27000 AAW	MNBLS	10//99-12//99
	Minneapolis-St. Paul MSA, MN-WI	S	13.39 MW	13.24 AW	27840 AAW	MNBLS	10//99-12//99
	St. Cloud MSA, MN	S	14.27 MW	14.79 AW	29680 AAW	MNBLS	10//99-12//99

AAW	Average annual wage	AOH	Average offered, high	ASH	Average starting, high	H	Hourly	M	Monthly	S	Special: hourly and annual
AE	Average entry wage	AOL	Average offered, low	ASL	Average starting, low	HI	Highest wage paid	MTC	Median total compensation	TQ	Third quartile wage
AEX	Average experienced wage	APH	Average pay, high range	AW	Average wage paid	HR	High end range	MW	Median wage paid	W	Weekly
AO	Average offered	APL	Average pay, low range	FQ	First quartile wage	LR	Low end range	SQ	Second quartile wage	Y	Yearly

Occupation/Type/Industry	Location	Per	Low	Mid	High	Source	Date
Food Batchmaker	Mississippi	S	6.79 MW	7.52 AW	15650 AAW	MSBLS	10//99-12//99
	Missouri	S	11.29 MW	10.85 AW	22560 AAW	MOBLS	10//99-12//99
	Joplin MSA, MO	S	7.56 MW	7.63 AW	15730 AAW	MOBLS	10//99-12//99
	Kansas City MSA, MO-KS	S	8.93 MW	8.00 AW	18570 AAW	MOBLS	10//99-12//99
	St. Louis MSA, MO-IL	S	11.37 MW	11.73 AW	23650 AAW	MOBLS	10//99-12//99
	Montana	S	6.42 MW	7.30 AW	15170 AAW	MTBLS	10//99-12//99
	Nebraska	S	13.02 MW	13.17 AW	27400 AAW	NEBLS	10//99-12//99
	Omaha MSA, NE-IA	S	13.50 MW	13.40 AW	28070 AAW	NEBLS	10//99-12//99
	Nevada	S	6.2 MW	6.35 AW	13210 AAW	NVBLS	10//99-12//99
	Las Vegas MSA, NV-AZ	S	6.50 MW	6.29 AW	13530 AAW	NVBLS	10//99-12//99
	New Jersey	S	6.71 MW	7.98 AW	16600 AAW	NJBLS	10//99-12//99
	Bergen-Passaic PMSA, NJ	S	6.66 MW	6.21 AW	13850 AAW	NJBLS	10//99-12//99
	Newark PMSA, NJ	S	7.60 MW	6.62 AW	15800 AAW	NJBLS	10//99-12//99
	Vineland-Millville-Bridgeton PMSA, NJ	S	12.16 MW	12.13 AW	25290 AAW	NJBLS	10//99-12//99
	New Mexico	S	11.04 MW	12.34 AW	25660 AAW	NMBLS	10//99-12//99
	Las Cruces MSA, NM	S	6.21 MW	6.23 AW	12910 AAW	NMBLS	10//99-12//99
	New York	S	8.53 MW	8.94 AW	18600 AAW	NYBLS	10//99-12//99
	Albany-Schenectady-Troy MSA, NY	S	10.42 MW	10.06 AW	21670 AAW	NYBLS	10//99-12//99
	Binghamton MSA, NY	S	7.38 MW	6.52 AW	15350 AAW	NYBLS	10//99-12//99
	Buffalo-Niagara Falls MSA, NY	S	9.76 MW	10.76 AW	20300 AAW	NYBLS	10//99-12//99
	Nassau-Suffolk PMSA, NY	S	7.29 MW	7.02 AW	15170 AAW	NYBLS	10//99-12//99
	New York PMSA, NY	S	9.58 MW	9.70 AW	19940 AAW	NYBLS	10//99-12//99
	Newburgh PMSA, NY-PA	S	7.72 MW	7.64 AW	16060 AAW	NYBLS	10//99-12//99
	Rochester MSA, NY	S	9.62 MW	8.64 AW	20010 AAW	NYBLS	10//99-12//99
	Syracuse MSA, NY	S	9.25 MW	8.68 AW	19250 AAW	NYBLS	10//99-12//99
	Utica-Rome MSA, NY	S	7.43 MW	6.62 AW	15450 AAW	NYBLS	10//99-12//99
	North Carolina	S	9.09 MW	9.42 AW	19590 AAW	NCBLS	10//99-12//99
	Charlotte-Gastonia-Rock Hill MSA, NC-SC	S	8.71 MW	8.20 AW	18120 AAW	NCBLS	10//99-12//99
	Greensboro--Winston-Salem--High Point MSA, NC	S	10.51 MW	10.29 AW	21860 AAW	NCBLS	10//99-12//99
	Raleigh-Durham-Chapel Hill MSA, NC	S	7.98 MW	8.02 AW	16590 AAW	NCBLS	10//99-12//99
	Grand Forks MSA, ND-MN	S	6.71 MW	6.27 AW	13950 AAW	NDBLS	10//99-12//99
	Ohio	S	9.45 MW	10.19 AW	21200 AAW	OHBLS	10//99-12//99
	Akron PMSA, OH	S	7.12 MW	6.83 AW	14800 AAW	OHBLS	10//99-12//99
	Canton-Massillon MSA, OH	S	11.96 MW	12.11 AW	24880 AAW	OHBLS	10//99-12//99
	Cincinnati PMSA, OH-KY-IN	S	14.32 MW	14.90 AW	29780 AAW	OHBLS	10//99-12//99
	Cleveland-Lorain-Elyria PMSA, OH	S	9.21 MW	9.00 AW	19150 AAW	OHBLS	10//99-12//99
	Columbus MSA, OH	S	8.35 MW	7.89 AW	17370 AAW	OHBLS	10//99-12//99
	Dayton-Springfield MSA, OH	S	8.59 MW	8.47 AW	17870 AAW	OHBLS	10//99-12//99
	Toledo MSA, OH	S	7.80 MW	6.14 AW	16220 AAW	OHBLS	10//99-12//99
	Youngstown-Warren MSA, OH	S	6.58 MW	6.25 AW	13690 AAW	OHBLS	10//99-12//99
	Oklahoma	S	9.59 MW	9.56 AW	19890 AAW	OKBLS	10//99-12//99
	Oklahoma City MSA, OK	S	8.80 MW	9.01 AW	18310 AAW	OKBLS	10//99-12//99
	Oregon	S	8.33 MW	9.44 AW	19630 AAW	ORBLS	10//99-12//99
	Portland-Vancouver PMSA, OR-WA	S	9.50 MW	8.74 AW	19770 AAW	ORBLS	10//99-12//99
	Pennsylvania	S	11.67 MW	11.78 AW	24500 AAW	PABLS	10//99-12//99
	Allentown-Bethlehem-Easton MSA, PA	S	12.90 MW	14.27 AW	26840 AAW	PABLS	10//99-12//99
	Erie MSA, PA	S	11.82 MW	12.19 AW	24590 AAW	PABLS	10//99-12//99
	Harrisburg-Lebanon-Carlisle MSA, PA	S	13.60 MW	13.97 AW	28300 AAW	PABLS	10//99-12//99
	Lancaster MSA, PA	S	14.38 MW	15.01 AW	29920 AAW	PABLS	10//99-12//99
	Philadelphia PMSA, PA-NJ	S	10.82 MW	11.26 AW	22510 AAW	PABLS	10//99-12//99
	Pittsburgh MSA, PA	S	8.52 MW	8.43 AW	17730 AAW	PABLS	10//99-12//99
	Reading MSA, PA	S	11.21 MW	11.52 AW	23320 AAW	PABLS	10//99-12//99
	Scranton--Wilkes-Barre--Hazleton MSA, PA	S	7.34 MW	6.39 AW	15270 AAW	PABLS	10//99-12//99
	Sharon MSA, PA	S	8.54 MW	7.30 AW	17760 AAW	PABLS	10//99-12//99
	York MSA, PA	S	11.17 MW	11.76 AW	23230 AAW	PABLS	10//99-12//99
	Rhode Island	S	9.93 MW	9.91 AW	20610 AAW	RIBLS	10//99-12//99
	Providence-Fall River-Warwick MSA, RI-MA	S	9.91 MW	9.93 AW	20610 AAW	RIBLS	10//99-12//99
	South Carolina	S	8.03 MW	8.59 AW	17880 AAW	SCBLS	10//99-12//99
	Tennessee	S	12.63 MW	12.94 AW	26910 AAW	TNBLS	10//99-12//99
	Chattanooga MSA, TN-GA	S	13.99 MW	13.62 AW	29090 AAW	TNBLS	10//99-12//99

AAW Average annual wage	**AOH** Average offered, high	**ASH** Average starting, high	**H** Hourly	**M** Monthly	**S** Special: hourly and annual
AE Average entry wage	**AOL** Average offered, low	**ASL** Average starting, low	**HI** Highest wage paid	**MTC** Median total compensation	**TQ** Third quartile wage
AEX Average experienced wage	**APH** Average pay, high range	**AW** Average wage paid	**HR** High end range	**MW** Median wage paid	**W** Weekly
AO Average offered	**APL** Average pay, low range	**FQ** First quartile wage	**LR** Low end range	**SQ** Second quartile wage	**Y** Yearly

Occupation/Type/Industry	Location	Per	Low	Mid	High	Source	Date
Food Batchmaker	Knoxville MSA, TN	S	16.27 MW	16.75 AW	33840 AAW	TNBLS	10//99-12//99
	Memphis MSA, TN-AR-MS	S	11.78 MW	12.11 AW	24490 AAW	MSBLS	10//99-12//99
	Nashville MSA, TN	S	13.83 MW	14.73 AW	28770 AAW	TNBLS	10//99-12//99
	Texas	S	7.93 MW	8.40 AW	17460 AAW	TXBLS	10//99-12//99
	Austin-San Marcos MSA, TX	S	6.98 MW	7.19 AW	14520 AAW	TXBLS	10//99-12//99
	Corpus Christi MSA, TX	S	7.54 MW	6.63 AW	15680 AAW	TXBLS	10//99-12//99
	Dallas PMSA, TX	S	8.95 MW	9.18 AW	18610 AAW	TXBLS	10//99-12//99
	El Paso MSA, TX	S	5.92 MW	6.01 AW	12310 AAW	TXBLS	10//99-12//99
	Fort Worth-Arlington PMSA, TX	S	7.40 MW	6.53 AW	15390 AAW	TXBLS	10//99-12//99
	Houston PMSA, TX	S	8.76 MW	7.40 AW	18220 AAW	TXBLS	10//99-12//99
	Lubbock MSA, TX	S	7.33 MW	7.36 AW	15240 AAW	TXBLS	10//99-12//99
	McAllen-Edinburg-Mission MSA, TX	S	7.92 MW	6.50 AW	16470 AAW	TXBLS	10//99-12//99
	San Antonio MSA, TX	S	9.03 MW	9.40 AW	18790 AAW	TXBLS	10//99-12//99
	Utah	S	11.82 MW	11.98 AW	24910 AAW	UTBLS	10//99-12//99
	Salt Lake City-Ogden MSA, UT	S	12.09 MW	12.09 AW	25160 AAW	UTBLS	10//99-12//99
	Vermont	S	11.26 MW	11.70 AW	24340 AAW	VTBLS	10//99-12//99
	Virginia	S	7.93 MW	8.39 AW	17450 AAW	VABLS	10//99-12//99
	Norfolk-Virginia Beach-Newport News MSA, VA-NC	S	8.55 MW	8.01 AW	17780 AAW	VABLS	10//99-12//99
	Washington	S	9.78 MW	10.72 AW	22310 AAW	WABLS	10//99-12//99
	Bellingham MSA, WA	S	9.41 MW	9.56 AW	19570 AAW	WABLS	10//99-12//99
	Seattle-Bellevue-Everett PMSA, WA	S	11.22 MW	10.42 AW	23340 AAW	WABLS	10//99-12//99
	Spokane MSA, WA	S	10.43 MW	10.90 AW	21680 AAW	WABLS	10//99-12//99
	Wisconsin	S	10.38 MW	10.44 AW	21720 AAW	WIBLS	10//99-12//99
	Appleton-Oshkosh-Neenah MSA, WI	S	15.78 MW	12.10 AW	32810 AAW	WIBLS	10//99-12//99
	La Crosse MSA, WI-MN	S	9.10 MW	9.22 AW	18930 AAW	WIBLS	10//99-12//99
	Madison MSA, WI	S	12.51 MW	12.65 AW	26010 AAW	WIBLS	10//99-12//99
	Milwaukee-Waukesha PMSA, WI	S	10.54 MW	10.35 AW	21920 AAW	WIBLS	10//99-12//99
	Wausau MSA, WI	S	9.98 MW	10.85 AW	20750 AAW	WIBLS	10//99-12//99
	Puerto Rico	S	6.32 MW	6.93 AW	14410 AAW	PRBLS	10//99-12//99
	San Juan-Bayamon PMSA, PR	S	5.78 MW	5.96 AW	12010 AAW	PRBLS	10//99-12//99
Food Cooking Machine Operator and Tender	Alabama	S	9.95 MW	9.95 AW	20710 AAW	ALBLS	10//99-12//99
	Arizona	S	6.17 MW	6.40 AW	13310 AAW	AZBLS	10//99-12//99
	Arkansas	S	9.43 MW	9.27 AW	19280 AAW	ARBLS	10//99-12//99
	California	S	9.69 MW	10.96 AW	22790 AAW	CABLS	10//99-12//99
	Colorado	S	8.68 MW	8.64 AW	17970 AAW	COBLS	10//99-12//99
	Connecticut	S	13.96 MW	11.67 AW	24270 AAW	CTBLS	10//99-12//99
	Florida	S	7.58 MW	8.35 AW	17380 AAW	FLBLS	10//99-12//99
	Georgia	S	7.97 MW	8.08 AW	16810 AAW	GABLS	10//99-12//99
	Hawaii	S	12.49 MW	11.31 AW	23510 AAW	HIBLS	10//99-12//99
	Idaho	S	9.98 MW	10.04 AW	20890 AAW	IDBLS	10//99-12//99
	Illinois	S	11.64 MW	11.96 AW	24880 AAW	ILBLS	10//99-12//99
	Indiana	S	7.8 MW	8.03 AW	16700 AAW	INBLS	10//99-12//99
	Kansas	S	9.25 MW	9.21 AW	19150 AAW	KSBLS	10//99-12//99
	Kentucky	S	11.43 MW	11.29 AW	23480 AAW	KYBLS	10//99-12//99
	Louisiana	S	8.27 MW	8.47 AW	17610 AAW	LABLS	10//99-12//99
	Maine	S	11.75 MW	11.59 AW	24100 AAW	MEBLS	10//99-12//99
	Maryland	S	9.58 MW	9.66 AW	20090 AAW	MDBLS	10//99-12//99
	Massachusetts	S	11.48 MW	11.71 AW	24350 AAW	MABLS	10//99-12//99
	Michigan	S	13.79 MW	12.92 AW	26860 AAW	MIBLS	10//99-12//99
	Minnesota	S	14.9 MW	14.83 AW	30850 AAW	MNBLS	10//99-12//99
	Nebraska	S	10.51 MW	10.74 AW	22340 AAW	NEBLS	10//99-12//99
	New Hampshire	S	6.65 MW	6.61 AW	13750 AAW	NHBLS	10//99-12//99
	New Jersey	S	12.73 MW	12.42 AW	25830 AAW	NJBLS	10//99-12//99
	New York	S	6.41 MW	7.62 AW	15840 AAW	NYBLS	10//99-12//99
	North Carolina	S	8.2 MW	8.26 AW	17170 AAW	NCBLS	10//99-12//99
	Ohio	S	9.86 MW	10.19 AW	21200 AAW	OHBLS	10//99-12//99
	Pennsylvania	S	10.56 MW	10.54 AW	21920 AAW	PABLS	10//99-12//99
	Tennessee	S	11.74 MW	11.61 AW	24150 AAW	TNBLS	10//99-12//99
	Texas	S	9.57 MW	9.78 AW	20330 AAW	TXBLS	10//99-12//99
	Virginia	S	8.69 MW	8.52 AW	17720 AAW	VABLS	10//99-12//99
	Washington	S	12.29 MW	11.97 AW	24910 AAW	WABLS	10//99-12//99
	Wisconsin	S	14.16 MW	14.79 AW	30770 AAW	WIBLS	10//99-12//99

AAW	Average annual wage	AOH	Average offered, high	ASH	Average starting, high	H	Hourly	M	Monthly	S	Special: hourly and annual
AE	Average entry wage	AOL	Average offered, low	ASL	Average starting, low	HI	Highest wage paid	MTC	Median total compensation	TQ	Third quartile wage
AEX	Average experienced wage	APH	Average pay, high range	AW	Average wage paid	HR	High end range	MW	Median wage paid	W	Weekly
AO	Average offered	APL	Average pay, low range	FQ	First quartile wage	LR	Low end range	SQ	Second quartile wage	Y	Yearly

Occupation/Type/Industry	Location	Per	Low	Mid	High	Source	Date
Food Preparation Worker	Alabama	S	6.4 MW	6.75 AW	14040 AAW	ALBLS	10//99-12//99
	Alaska	S	9.47 MW	9.56 AW	19890 AAW	AKBLS	10//99-12//99
	Arizona	S	6.53 MW	6.64 AW	13800 AAW	AZBLS	10//99-12//99
	Arkansas	S	6.46 MW	6.93 AW	14410 AAW	ARBLS	10//99-12//99
	California	S	7.54 MW	7.90 AW	16430 AAW	CABLS	10//99-12//99
	Colorado	S	7.89 MW	8.31 AW	17280 AAW	COBLS	10//99-12//99
	Connecticut	S	8.79 MW	9.20 AW	19140 AAW	CTBLS	10//99-12//99
	Delaware	S	7.67 MW	7.99 AW	16620 AAW	DEBLS	10//99-12//99
	District of Columbia	S	9.68 MW	9.58 AW	19930 AAW	DCBLS	10//99-12//99
	Florida	S	7.23 MW	7.28 AW	15140 AAW	FLBLS	10//99-12//99
	Georgia	S	6.72 MW	7.09 AW	14750 AAW	GABLS	10//99-12//99
	Hawaii	S	9.74 MW	9.79 AW	20360 AAW	HIBLS	10//99-12//99
	Idaho	S	6.5 MW	6.79 AW	14120 AAW	IDBLS	10//99-12//99
	Illinois	S	6.36 MW	6.55 AW	13620 AAW	ILBLS	10//99-12//99
	Indiana	S	7.48 MW	7.34 AW	15270 AAW	INBLS	10//99-12//99
	Iowa	S	6.55 MW	6.80 AW	14150 AAW	IABLS	10//99-12//99
	Kansas	S	6.71 MW	6.79 AW	14130 AAW	KSBLS	10//99-12//99
	Kentucky	S	7.51 MW	7.68 AW	15970 AAW	KYBLS	10//99-12//99
	Louisiana	S	6.38 MW	6.58 AW	13690 AAW	LABLS	10//99-12//99
	Maine	S	7.74 MW	7.82 AW	16270 AAW	MEBLS	10//99-12//99
	Maryland	S	7.65 MW	8.11 AW	16870 AAW	MDBLS	10//99-12//99
	Massachusetts	S	8.03 MW	8.57 AW	17820 AAW	MABLS	10//99-12//99
	Michigan	S	8.18 MW	8.44 AW	17560 AAW	MIBLS	10//99-12//99
	Minnesota	S	8.27 MW	8.71 AW	18130 AAW	MNBLS	10//99-12//99
	Mississippi	S	6.33 MW	6.53 AW	13580 AAW	MSBLS	10//99-12//99
	Missouri	S	7.02 MW	7.20 AW	14970 AAW	MOBLS	10//99-12//99
	Montana	S	6.46 MW	6.61 AW	13740 AAW	MTBLS	10//99-12//99
	Nebraska	S	6.77 MW	6.98 AW	14510 AAW	NEBLS	10//99-12//99
	Nevada	S	8.46 MW	8.86 AW	18420 AAW	NVBLS	10//99-12//99
	New Hampshire	S	7.94 MW	8.05 AW	16750 AAW	NHBLS	10//99-12//99
	New Jersey	S	7.88 MW	8.48 AW	17650 AAW	NJBLS	10//99-12//99
	New Mexico	S	6.5 MW	6.82 AW	14190 AAW	NMBLS	10//99-12//99
	New York	S	6.88 MW	7.91 AW	16450 AAW	NYBLS	10//99-12//99
	North Carolina	S	7.15 MW	7.24 AW	15060 AAW	NCBLS	10//99-12//99
	North Dakota	S	7.38 MW	8.30 AW	17260 AAW	NDBLS	10//99-12//99
	Ohio	S	7.48 MW	7.64 AW	15890 AAW	OHBLS	10//99-12//99
	Oklahoma	S	6.82 MW	7.08 AW	14720 AAW	OKBLS	10//99-12//99
	Oregon	S	7.98 MW	8.27 AW	17190 AAW	ORBLS	10//99-12//99
	Pennsylvania	S	7.39 MW	7.69 AW	16000 AAW	PABLS	10//99-12//99
	Rhode Island	S	7.11 MW	7.80 AW	16230 AAW	RIBLS	10//99-12//99
	South Carolina	S	6.51 MW	6.85 AW	14240 AAW	SCBLS	10//99-12//99
	South Dakota	S	6.91 MW	6.93 AW	14410 AAW	SDBLS	10//99-12//99
	Tennessee	S	6.63 MW	7.06 AW	14680 AAW	TNBLS	10//99-12//99
	Texas	S	6.63 MW	6.94 AW	14440 AAW	TXBLS	10//99-12//99
	Utah	S	7.64 MW	7.87 AW	16370 AAW	UTBLS	10//99-12//99
	Vermont	S	6.95 MW	7.35 AW	15290 AAW	VTBLS	10//99-12//99
	Virginia	S	6.65 MW	7.33 AW	15250 AAW	VABLS	10//99-12//99
	Washington	S	7.42 MW	7.77 AW	16170 AAW	WABLS	10//99-12//99
	West Virginia	S	6.37 MW	6.74 AW	14020 AAW	WVBLS	10//99-12//99
	Wisconsin	S	6.92 MW	7.25 AW	15080 AAW	WIBLS	10//99-12//99
	Wyoming	S	6.75 MW	7.12 AW	14810 AAW	WYBLS	10//99-12//99
	Virgin Islands	S	7.42 MW	7.48 AW	15570 AAW	VIBLS	10//99-12//99
	Guam	S	6.2 MW	6.29 AW	13080 AAW	GUBLS	10//99-12//99
Food Server							
Nonrestaurant	Alabama	S	6.48 MW	6.55 AW	13630 AAW	ALBLS	10//99-12//99
Nonrestaurant	Arizona	S	7.18 MW	7.00 AW	14550 AAW	AZBLS	10//99-12//99
Nonrestaurant	Arkansas	S	7.19 MW	7.71 AW	16040 AAW	ARBLS	10//99-12//99
Nonrestaurant	California	S	7.58 MW	8.75 AW	18190 AAW	CABLS	10//99-12//99
Nonrestaurant	Colorado	S	7.08 MW	7.37 AW	15320 AAW	COBLS	10//99-12//99
Nonrestaurant	Connecticut	S	9.45 MW	10.21 AW	21240 AAW	CTBLS	10//99-12//99
Nonrestaurant	Delaware	S	7.3 MW	7.79 AW	16200 AAW	DEBLS	10//99-12//99
Nonrestaurant	District of Columbia	S	7.94 MW	9.39 AW	19530 AAW	DCBLS	10//99-12//99
Nonrestaurant	Florida	S	6.51 MW	6.82 AW	14190 AAW	FLBLS	10//99-12//99
Nonrestaurant	Georgia	S	7.58 MW	7.84 AW	16300 AAW	GABLS	10//99-12//99
Nonrestaurant	Hawaii	S	6.72 MW	7.97 AW	16590 AAW	HIBLS	10//99-12//99
Nonrestaurant	Idaho	S	7.17 MW	8.07 AW	16780 AAW	IDBLS	10//99-12//99
Nonrestaurant	Illinois	S	7.06 MW	7.66 AW	15940 AAW	ILBLS	10//99-12//99
Nonrestaurant	Indiana	S	6.87 MW	7.49 AW	15580 AAW	INBLS	10//99-12//99
Nonrestaurant	Iowa	S	6.49 MW	6.82 AW	14180 AAW	IABLS	10//99-12//99
Nonrestaurant	Kansas	S	6.31 MW	6.58 AW	13680 AAW	KSBLS	10//99-12//99
Nonrestaurant	Kentucky	S	6.94 MW	7.05 AW	14660 AAW	KYBLS	10//99-12//99
Nonrestaurant	Louisiana	S	6.19 MW	6.45 AW	13420 AAW	LABLS	10//99-12//99

AAW Average annual wage · AE Average entry wage · AEX Average experienced wage · AO Average offered · AOH Average offered, high · AOL Average offered, low · APH Average pay, high range · APL Average pay, low range · ASH Average starting, high · ASL Average starting, low · AW Average wage paid · FQ First quartile wage · H Hourly · HI Highest wage paid · HR High end range · LR Low end range · M Monthly · MTC Median total compensation · MW Median wage paid · SQ Second quartile wage · S Special: hourly and annual · TQ Third quartile wage · W Weekly · Y Yearly

Occupation/Type/Industry	Location	Per	Low	Mid	High	Source	Date
Food Server							
Nonrestaurant	Maine	s	6.89 MW	6.89 AW	14330 AAW	MEBLS	10//99-12//99
Nonrestaurant	Maryland	s	7.19 MW	7.47 AW	15530 AAW	MDBLS	10//99-12//99
Nonrestaurant	Massachusetts	s	8.68 MW	9.74 AW	20260 AAW	MABLS	10//99-12//99
Nonrestaurant	Michigan	s	6.94 MW	7.50 AW	15600 AAW	MIBLS	10//99-12//99
Nonrestaurant	Minnesota	s	7.53 MW	7.60 AW	15810 AAW	MNBLS	10//99-12//99
Nonrestaurant	Mississippi	s	5.94 MW	6.10 AW	12690 AAW	MSBLS	10//99-12//99
Nonrestaurant	Missouri	s	6.68 MW	7.20 AW	14970 AAW	MOBLS	10//99-12//99
Nonrestaurant	Montana	s	6.13 MW	6.27 AW	13030 AAW	MTBLS	10//99-12//99
Nonrestaurant	Nebraska	s	7.57 MW	7.78 AW	16190 AAW	NEBLS	10//99-12//99
Nonrestaurant	Nevada	s	7.55 MW	7.73 AW	16080 AAW	NVBLS	10//99-12//99
Nonrestaurant	New Hampshire	s	7.05 MW	7.22 AW	15020 AAW	NHBLS	10//99-12//99
Nonrestaurant	New Jersey	s	8.16 MW	8.72 AW	18130 AAW	NJBLS	10//99-12//99
Nonrestaurant	New Mexico	s	6.06 MW	6.44 AW	13400 AAW	NMBLS	10//99-12//99
Nonrestaurant	New York	s	9.95 MW	10.14 AW	21090 AAW	NYBLS	10//99-12//99
Nonrestaurant	North Carolina	s	6.92 MW	7.12 AW	14800 AAW	NCBLS	10//99-12//99
Nonrestaurant	North Dakota	s	6.9 MW	7.34 AW	15260 AAW	NDBLS	10//99-12//99
Nonrestaurant	Ohio	s	7.45 MW	7.72 AW	16060 AAW	OHBLS	10//99-12//99
Nonrestaurant	Oklahoma	s	6.17 MW	6.27 AW	13040 AAW	OKBLS	10//99-12//99
Nonrestaurant	Oregon	s	7.27 MW	7.71 AW	16040 AAW	ORBLS	10//99-12//99
Nonrestaurant	Pennsylvania	s	7.71 MW	7.91 AW	16460 AAW	PABLS	10//99-12//99
Nonrestaurant	Rhode Island	s	10.22 MW	9.54 AW	19830 AAW	RIBLS	10//99-12//99
Nonrestaurant	South Carolina	s	6.6 MW	7.08 AW	14730 AAW	SCBLS	10//99-12//99
Nonrestaurant	South Dakota	s	7.26 MW	7.11 AW	14790 AAW	SDBLS	10//99-12//99
Nonrestaurant	Tennessee	s	6.2 MW	6.66 AW	13860 AAW	TNBLS	10//99-12//99
Nonrestaurant	Texas	s	6.22 MW	6.49 AW	13510 AAW	TXBLS	10//99-12//99
Nonrestaurant	Utah	s	6.76 MW	6.92 AW	14390 AAW	UTBLS	10//99-12//99
Nonrestaurant	Vermont	s	7.27 MW	7.46 AW	15510 AAW	VTBLS	10//99-12//99
Nonrestaurant	Virginia	s	6.73 MW	7.24 AW	15060 AAW	VABLS	10//99-12//99
Nonrestaurant	Washington	s	7.28 MW	7.93 AW	16490 AAW	WABLS	10//99-12//99
Nonrestaurant	West Virginia	s	6.43 MW	6.79 AW	14130 AAW	WVBLS	10//99-12//99
Nonrestaurant	Wisconsin	s	7.61 MW	7.82 AW	16270 AAW	WIBLS	10//99-12//99
Nonrestaurant	Wyoming	s	6.35 MW	6.63 AW	13800 AAW	WYBLS	10//99-12//99
Nonrestaurant	Puerto Rico	s	6.16 MW	6.56 AW	13630 AAW	PRBLS	10//99-12//99
Nonrestaurant	Virgin Islands	s	6.09 MW	6.34 AW	13190 AAW	VIBLS	10//99-12//99
Food Service Manager	Alabama	s	12.84 MW	14.45 AW	30060 AAW	ALBLS	10//99-12//99
	Anniston MSA, AL	s	12.96 MW	11.36 AW	26960 AAW	ALBLS	10//99-12//99
	Auburn-Opelika MSA, AL	s	13.05 MW	12.42 AW	27150 AAW	ALBLS	10//99-12//99
	Birmingham MSA, AL	s	17.37 MW	15.93 AW	36130 AAW	ALBLS	10//99-12//99
	Decatur MSA, AL	s	11.65 MW	10.18 AW	24220 AAW	ALBLS	10//99-12//99
	Dothan MSA, AL	s	12.71 MW	11.28 AW	26440 AAW	ALBLS	10//99-12//99
	Florence MSA, AL	s	10.80 MW	8.47 AW	22470 AAW	ALBLS	10//99-12//99
	Gadsden MSA, AL	s	13.50 MW	13.87 AW	28080 AAW	ALBLS	10//99-12//99
	Huntsville MSA, AL	s	15.74 MW	13.40 AW	32750 AAW	ALBLS	10//99-12//99
	Mobile MSA, AL	s	17.83 MW	16.70 AW	37080 AAW	ALBLS	10//99-12//99
	Montgomery MSA, AL	s	14.13 MW	12.06 AW	29390 AAW	ALBLS	10//99-12//99
	Tuscaloosa MSA, AL	s	11.14 MW	10.04 AW	23160 AAW	ALBLS	10//99-12//99
	Alaska	s	15.43 MW	16.88 AW	35120 AAW	AKBLS	10//99-12//99
	Anchorage MSA, AK	s	19.44 MW	18.69 AW	40430 AAW	AKBLS	10//99-12//99
	Arizona	s	14.8 MW	15.16 AW	31530 AAW	AZBLS	10//99-12//99
	Flagstaff MSA, AZ-UT	s	13.73 MW	12.90 AW	28560 AAW	AZBLS	10//99-12//99
	Phoenix-Mesa MSA, AZ	s	15.05 MW	14.77 AW	31310 AAW	AZBLS	10//99-12//99
	Tucson MSA, AZ	s	15.89 MW	14.96 AW	33050 AAW	AZBLS	10//99-12//99
	Yuma MSA, AZ	s	14.64 MW	12.72 AW	30450 AAW	AZBLS	10//99-12//99
	Arkansas	s	17.81 MW	18.04 AW	37520 AAW	ARBLS	10//99-12//99
	Fayetteville-Springdale-Rogers MSA, AR	s	18.24 MW	19.00 AW	37950 AAW	ARBLS	10//99-12//99
	Fort Smith MSA, AR-OK	s	16.08 MW	14.55 AW	33440 AAW	ARBLS	10//99-12//99
	Jonesboro MSA, AR	s	19.26 MW	19.25 AW	40060 AAW	ARBLS	10//99-12//99
	Little Rock-North Little Rock MSA, AR	s	21.39 MW	22.93 AW	44480 AAW	ARBLS	10//99-12//99
	Pine Bluff MSA, AR	s	17.70 MW	16.75 AW	36810 AAW	ARBLS	10//99-12//99
	California	s	16.84 MW	18.35 AW	38170 AAW	CABLS	10//99-12//99
	Bakersfield MSA, CA	s	12.14 MW	10.55 AW	25250 AAW	CABLS	10//99-12//99
	Chico-Paradise MSA, CA	s	17.40 MW	17.56 AW	36200 AAW	CABLS	10//99-12//99
	Fresno MSA, CA	s	15.70 MW	15.30 AW	32660 AAW	CABLS	10//99-12//99
	Los Angeles-Long Beach PMSA, CA	s	19.91 MW	18.30 AW	41410 AAW	CABLS	10//99-12//99
	Merced MSA, CA	s	14.66 MW	14.36 AW	30490 AAW	CABLS	10//99-12//99
	Modesto MSA, CA	s	16.94 MW	15.58 AW	35230 AAW	CABLS	10//99-12//99
	Oakland PMSA, CA	s	19.02 MW	18.77 AW	39560 AAW	CABLS	10//99-12//99
	Orange County PMSA, CA	s	16.78 MW	15.80 AW	34890 AAW	CABLS	10//99-12//99

AAW	Average annual wage	AOH	Average offered, high	ASH	Average starting, high	H	Hourly	M	Monthly	S	Special: hourly and annual
AE	Average entry wage	AOL	Average offered, low	ASL	Average starting, low	HI	Highest wage paid	MTC	Median total compensation	TQ	Third quartile wage
AEX	Average experienced wage	APH	Average pay, high range	AW	Average wage paid	HR	High end range	MW	Median wage paid	W	Weekly
AO	Average offered	APL	Average pay, low range	FQ	First quartile wage	LR	Low end range	SQ	Second quartile wage	Y	Yearly

Occupation/Type/Industry	Location	Per	Low	Mid	High	Source	Date
Food Service Manager	Redding MSA, CA	S	14.73 MW	15.10 AW	30640 AAW	CABLS	10//99-12//99
	Riverside-San Bernardino PMSA, CA	S	21.93 MW	23.42 AW	45610 AAW	CABLS	10//99-12//99
	Sacramento PMSA, CA	S	21.83 MW	20.23 AW	45400 AAW	CABLS	10//99-12//99
	Salinas MSA, CA	S	16.36 MW	15.71 AW	34040 AAW	CABLS	10//99-12//99
	San Diego MSA, CA	S	18.16 MW	15.53 AW	37760 AAW	CABLS	10//99-12//99
	San Francisco PMSA, CA	S	18.01 MW	17.35 AW	37460 AAW	CABLS	10//99-12//99
	San Jose PMSA, CA	S	22.84 MW	20.32 AW	47510 AAW	CABLS	10//99-12//99
	San Luis Obispo-Atascadero-Paso Robles MSA, CA	S	15.58 MW	13.32 AW	32400 AAW	CABLS	10//99-12//99
	Santa Barbara-Santa Maria-Lompoc MSA, CA	S	18.71 MW	17.92 AW	38920 AAW	CABLS	10//99-12//99
	Santa Cruz-Watsonville PMSA, CA	S	16.46 MW	15.06 AW	34230 AAW	CABLS	10//99-12//99
	Santa Rosa PMSA, CA	S	18.20 MW	16.62 AW	37850 AAW	CABLS	10//99-12//99
	Stockton-Lodi MSA, CA	S	18.14 MW	16.62 AW	37730 AAW	CABLS	10//99-12//99
	Vallejo-Fairfield-Napa PMSA, CA	S	19.99 MW	19.32 AW	41590 AAW	CABLS	10//99-12//99
	Ventura PMSA, CA	S	16.86 MW	15.84 AW	35060 AAW	CABLS	10//99-12//99
	Visalia-Tulare-Porterville MSA, CA	S	13.82 MW	13.21 AW	28740 AAW	CABLS	10//99-12//99
	Yolo PMSA, CA	S	14.99 MW	13.12 AW	31180 AAW	CABLS	10//99-12//99
	Yuba City MSA, CA	S	21.71 MW	16.24 AW	45150 AAW	CABLS	10//99-12//99
	Colorado	S	13.12 MW	14.91 AW	31020 AAW	COBLS	10//99-12//99
	Denver PMSA, CO	S	18.38 MW	17.17 AW	38230 AAW	COBLS	10//99-12//99
	Fort Collins-Loveland MSA, CO	S	12.59 MW	12.26 AW	26200 AAW	COBLS	10//99-12//99
	Grand Junction MSA, CO	S	12.55 MW	12.34 AW	26110 AAW	COBLS	10//99-12//99
	Pueblo MSA, CO	S	11.67 MW	10.35 AW	24280 AAW	COBLS	10//99-12//99
	Connecticut	S	19.76 MW	20.60 AW	42840 AAW	CTBLS	10//99-12//99
	Bridgeport PMSA, CT	S	15.53 MW	14.93 AW	32310 AAW	CTBLS	10//99-12//99
	Danbury PMSA, CT	S	19.33 MW	17.43 AW	40210 AAW	CTBLS	10//99-12//99
	Hartford MSA, CT	S	22.28 MW	22.42 AW	46330 AAW	CTBLS	10//99-12//99
	New Haven-Meriden PMSA, CT	S	14.93 MW	12.69 AW	31050 AAW	CTBLS	10//99-12//99
	New London-Norwich MSA, CT-RI	S	20.92 MW	22.44 AW	43520 AAW	CTBLS	10//99-12//99
	Stamford-Norwalk PMSA, CT	S	28.28 MW	24.49 AW	58820 AAW	CTBLS	10//99-12//99
	Waterbury PMSA, CT	S	21.52 MW	19.98 AW	44760 AAW	CTBLS	10//99-12//99
	Delaware	S	17.3 MW	18.06 AW	37560 AAW	DEBLS	10//99-12//99
	Dover MSA, DE	S	15.46 MW	14.64 AW	32150 AAW	DEBLS	10//99-12//99
	Wilmington-Newark PMSA, DE-MD	S	18.21 MW	16.91 AW	37880 AAW	DEBLS	10//99-12//99
	District of Columbia	S	18.86 MW	19.08 AW	39680 AAW	DCBLS	10//99-12//99
	Washington PMSA, DC-MD-VA-WV	S	16.99 MW	15.84 AW	35340 AAW	DCBLS	10//99-12//99
	Florida	S	15.56 MW	16.67 AW	34680 AAW	FLBLS	10//99-12//99
	Daytona Beach MSA, FL	S	15.85 MW	13.37 AW	32960 AAW	FLBLS	10//99-12//99
	Fort Lauderdale PMSA, FL	S	17.95 MW	16.15 AW	37330 AAW	FLBLS	10//99-12//99
	Fort Myers-Cape Coral MSA, FL	S	15.41 MW	14.78 AW	32050 AAW	FLBLS	10//99-12//99
	Fort Pierce-Port St. Lucie MSA, FL	S	16.66 MW	15.67 AW	34650 AAW	FLBLS	10//99-12//99
	Fort Walton Beach MSA, FL	S	18.26 MW	18.88 AW	37990 AAW	FLBLS	10//99-12//99
	Gainesville MSA, FL	S	16.72 MW	15.41 AW	34770 AAW	FLBLS	10//99-12//99
	Jacksonville MSA, FL	S	16.89 MW	16.06 AW	35130 AAW	FLBLS	10//99-12//99
	Lakeland-Winter Haven MSA, FL	S	19.39 MW	21.55 AW	40330 AAW	FLBLS	10//99-12//99
	Melbourne-Titusville-Palm Bay MSA, FL	S	18.23 MW	17.55 AW	37920 AAW	FLBLS	10//99-12//99
	Miami PMSA, FL	S	18.00 MW	17.65 AW	37450 AAW	FLBLS	10//99-12//99
	Naples MSA, FL	S	18.96 MW	16.84 AW	39440 AAW	FLBLS	10//99-12//99
	Ocala MSA, FL	S	13.15 MW	13.78 AW	27350 AAW	FLBLS	10//99-12//99
	Orlando MSA, FL	S	16.27 MW	15.07 AW	33850 AAW	FLBLS	10//99-12//99
	Panama City MSA, FL	S	15.08 MW	14.94 AW	31370 AAW	FLBLS	10//99-12//99
	Pensacola MSA, FL	S	13.51 MW	13.50 AW	28090 AAW	FLBLS	10//99-12//99
	Punta Gorda MSA, FL	S	16.63 MW	14.35 AW	34590 AAW	FLBLS	10//99-12//99
	Sarasota-Bradenton MSA, FL	S	14.43 MW	13.22 AW	30010 AAW	FLBLS	10//99-12//99
	Tallahassee MSA, FL	S	15.74 MW	14.86 AW	32740 AAW	FLBLS	10//99-12//99
	Tampa-St. Petersburg-Clearwater MSA, FL	S	17.05 MW	16.54 AW	35470 AAW	FLBLS	10//99-12//99

AAW	Average annual wage	AOH	Average offered, high	ASH	Average starting, high
AE	Average entry wage	AOL	Average offered, low	ASL	Average starting, low
AEX	Average experienced wage	APH	Average pay, high range	AW	Average wage paid
AO	Average offered	APL	Average pay, low range	FQ	First quartile wage

H	Hourly	M	Monthly	S	Special: hourly and annual
HI	Highest wage paid	MTC	Median total compensation	TQ	Third quartile wage
HR	High end range	MW	Median wage paid	W	Weekly
LR	Low end range	SQ	Second quartile wage	Y	Yearly

Occupation/Type/Industry	Location	Per	Low	Mid	High	Source	Date
Food Service Manager	West Palm Beach-Boca Raton MSA, FL	S	15.41 MW	15.05 AW	32050 AAW	FLBLS	10//99-12//99
	Georgia	S	14.19 MW	14.89 AW	30980 AAW	GABLS	10//99-12//99
	Albany MSA, GA	S	18.41 MW	18.16 AW	38280 AAW	GABLS	10//99-12//99
	Athens MSA, GA	S	22.31 MW	23.61 AW	46400 AAW	GABLS	10//99-12//99
	Atlanta MSA, GA	S	16.16 MW	15.29 AW	33620 AAW	GABLS	10//99-12//99
	Augusta-Aiken MSA, GA-SC	S	13.33 MW	13.73 AW	27720 AAW	GABLS	10//99-12//99
	Columbus MSA, GA-AL	S	15.03 MW	14.86 AW	31270 AAW	GABLS	10//99-12//99
	Macon MSA, GA	S	14.37 MW	14.57 AW	29900 AAW	GABLS	10//99-12//99
	Savannah MSA, GA	S	13.62 MW	12.50 AW	28340 AAW	GABLS	10//99-12//99
	Hawaii	S	19.57 MW	20.82 AW	43300 AAW	HIBLS	10//99-12//99
	Honolulu MSA, HI	S	19.75 MW	19.10 AW	41080 AAW	HIBLS	10//99-12//99
	Idaho	S	12.18 MW	12.61 AW	26230 AAW	IDBLS	10//99-12//99
	Boise City MSA, ID	S	12.61 MW	11.73 AW	26230 AAW	IDBLS	10//99-12//99
	Pocatello MSA, ID	S	12.62 MW	14.30 AW	26250 AAW	IDBLS	10//99-12//99
	Illinois	S	12.48 MW	12.96 AW	26950 AAW	ILBLS	10//99-12//99
	Bloomington-Normal MSA, IL	S	13.23 MW	12.73 AW	27510 AAW	ILBLS	10//99-12//99
	Champaign-Urbana MSA, IL	S	12.99 MW	12.80 AW	27020 AAW	ILBLS	10//99-12//99
	Chicago PMSA, IL	S	14.25 MW	12.96 AW	29630 AAW	ILBLS	10//99-12//99
	Decatur MSA, IL	S	10.62 MW	10.15 AW	22090 AAW	ILBLS	10//99-12//99
	Kankakee PMSA, IL	S	16.96 MW	16.17 AW	35280 AAW	ILBLS	10//99-12//99
	Rockford MSA, IL	S	15.45 MW	14.81 AW	32140 AAW	ILBLS	10//99-12//99
	Springfield MSA, IL	S	12.97 MW	12.46 AW	26970 AAW	ILBLS	10//99-12//99
	Indiana	S	14.02 MW	14.96 AW	31110 AAW	INBLS	10//99-12//99
	Bloomington MSA, IN	S	15.31 MW	15.02 AW	31850 AAW	INBLS	10//99-12//99
	Elkhart-Goshen MSA, IN	S	10.04 MW	8.00 AW	20870 AAW	INBLS	10//99-12//99
	Evansville-Henderson MSA, IN-KY	S	12.68 MW	11.53 AW	26370 AAW	INBLS	10//99-12//99
	Fort Wayne MSA, IN	S	19.47 MW	18.34 AW	40500 AAW	INBLS	10//99-12//99
	Gary PMSA, IN	S	17.55 MW	16.78 AW	36510 AAW	INBLS	10//99-12//99
	Indianapolis MSA, IN	S	18.43 MW	17.60 AW	38330 AAW	INBLS	10//99-12//99
	Kokomo MSA, IN	S	12.62 MW	10.87 AW	26240 AAW	INBLS	10//99-12//99
	Lafayette MSA, IN	S	14.05 MW	12.47 AW	29230 AAW	INBLS	10//99-12//99
	Muncie MSA, IN	S	15.03 MW	14.97 AW	31260 AAW	INBLS	10//99-12//99
	South Bend MSA, IN	S	13.36 MW	11.14 AW	27800 AAW	INBLS	10//99-12//99
	Terre Haute MSA, IN	S	10.19 MW	9.89 AW	21190 AAW	INBLS	10//99-12//99
	Iowa	S	12.67 MW	13.28 AW	27610 AAW	IABLS	10//99-12//99
	Davenport-Moline-Rock Island MSA, IA-IL	S	11.54 MW	11.51 AW	24000 AAW	IABLS	10//99-12//99
	Des Moines MSA, IA	S	15.55 MW	14.95 AW	32350 AAW	IABLS	10//99-12//99
	Dubuque MSA, IA	S	10.93 MW	11.16 AW	22730 AAW	IABLS	10//99-12//99
	Iowa City MSA, IA	S	15.70 MW	15.12 AW	32650 AAW	IABLS	10//99-12//99
	Sioux City MSA, IA-NE	S	10.27 MW	9.50 AW	21360 AAW	IABLS	10//99-12//99
	Waterloo-Cedar Falls MSA, IA	S	13.57 MW	12.45 AW	28210 AAW	IABLS	10//99-12//99
	Kansas	S	13.16 MW	14.21 AW	29560 AAW	KSBLS	10//99-12//99
	Lawrence MSA, KS	S	14.58 MW	13.05 AW	30320 AAW	KSBLS	10//99-12//99
	Topeka MSA, KS	S	14.81 MW	15.14 AW	30810 AAW	KSBLS	10//99-12//99
	Wichita MSA, KS	S	14.69 MW	14.25 AW	30560 AAW	KSBLS	10//99-12//99
	Kentucky	S	15.27 MW	15.59 AW	32430 AAW	KYBLS	10//99-12//99
	Lexington MSA, KY	S	14.48 MW	14.99 AW	30130 AAW	KYBLS	10//99-12//99
	Louisville MSA, KY-IN	S	17.93 MW	16.97 AW	37290 AAW	KYBLS	10//99-12//99
	Owensboro MSA, KY	S	12.62 MW	12.08 AW	26250 AAW	KYBLS	10//99-12//99
	Louisiana	S	15.64 MW	16.59 AW	34510 AAW	LABLS	10//99-12//99
	Alexandria MSA, LA	S	14.85 MW	14.31 AW	30880 AAW	LABLS	10//99-12//99
	Baton Rouge MSA, LA	S	20.17 MW	18.16 AW	41950 AAW	LABLS	10//99-12//99
	Houma MSA, LA	S	11.81 MW	10.04 AW	24560 AAW	LABLS	10//99-12//99
	Lafayette MSA, LA	S	15.00 MW	11.77 AW	31210 AAW	LABLS	10//99-12//99
	Lake Charles MSA, LA	S	12.60 MW	12.08 AW	26200 AAW	LABLS	10//99-12//99
	Monroe MSA, LA	S	12.20 MW	10.19 AW	25370 AAW	LABLS	10//99-12//99
	New Orleans MSA, LA	S	16.17 MW	15.88 AW	33640 AAW	LABLS	10//99-12//99
	Shreveport-Bossier City MSA, LA	S	18.14 MW	16.11 AW	37730 AAW	LABLS	10//99-12//99
	Maine	S	13.47 MW	13.90 AW	28900 AAW	MEBLS	10//99-12//99
	Bangor MSA, ME	S	14.15 MW	14.10 AW	29430 AAW	MEBLS	10//99-12//99
	Lewiston-Auburn MSA, ME	S	12.89 MW	13.44 AW	26820 AAW	MEBLS	10//99-12//99
	Portland MSA, ME	S	11.28 MW	10.18 AW	23460 AAW	MEBLS	10//99-12//99
	Maryland	S	17.03 MW	21.23 AW	44160 AAW	MDBLS	10//99-12//99
	Baltimore PMSA, MD	S	25.40 MW	20.09 AW	52830 AAW	MDBLS	10//99-12//99
	Cumberland MSA, MD-WV	S	16.89 MW	12.41 AW	35140 AAW	MDBLS	10//99-12//99
	Hagerstown PMSA, MD	S	13.99 MW	13.33 AW	29090 AAW	MDBLS	10//99-12//99
	Massachusetts	S	16.86 MW	17.28 AW	35950 AAW	MABLS	10//99-12//99

AAW	Average annual wage	AOH	Average offered, high	ASH	Average starting, high	H	Hourly	M	Monthly	S	Special: hourly and annual
AE	Average entry wage	AOL	Average offered, low	ASL	Average starting, low	HI	Highest wage paid	MTC	Median total compensation	TQ	Third quartile wage
AEX	Average experienced wage	APH	Average pay, high range	AW	Average wage paid	HR	High end range	MW	Median wage paid	W	Weekly
AO	Average offered	APL	Average pay, low range	FQ	First quartile wage	LR	Low end range	SQ	Second quartile wage	Y	Yearly

Occupation/Type/Industry	Location	Per	Low	Mid	High	Source	Date
Food Service Manager	Barnstable-Yarmouth MSA, MA	S	12.52 MW	10.60 AW	26050 AAW	MABLS	10//99-12/99
	Boston PMSA, MA-NH	S	18.84 MW	18.44 AW	39190 AAW	MABLS	10//99-12/99
	Brockton PMSA, MA	S	18.20 MW	18.30 AW	37860 AAW	MABLS	10//99-12/99
	Fitchburg-Leominster PMSA, MA	S	15.09 MW	14.67 AW	31390 AAW	MABLS	10//99-12/99
	Lawrence PMSA, MA-NH	S	14.20 MW	14.52 AW	29530 AAW	MABLS	10//99-12/99
	Lowell PMSA, MA-NH	S	16.03 MW	15.28 AW	33340 AAW	MABLS	10//99-12/99
	New Bedford PMSA, MA	S	15.26 MW	15.26 AW	31740 AAW	MABLS	10//99-12/99
	Pittsfield MSA, MA	S	14.58 MW	14.69 AW	30320 AAW	MABLS	10//99-12/99
	Springfield MSA, MA	S	17.85 MW	16.58 AW	37140 AAW	MABLS	10//99-12/99
	Worcester PMSA, MA-CT	S	16.51 MW	15.70 AW	34350 AAW	MABLS	10//99-12/99
	Michigan	S	17.75 MW	18.72 AW	38930 AAW	MIBLS	10//99-12/99
	Ann Arbor PMSA, MI	S	17.37 MW	16.58 AW	36130 AAW	MIBLS	10//99-12/99
	Detroit PMSA, MI	S	20.14 MW	19.12 AW	41880 AAW	MIBLS	10//99-12/99
	Flint PMSA, MI	S	20.52 MW	20.28 AW	42670 AAW	MIBLS	10//99-12/99
	Grand Rapids-Muskegon-Holland MSA, MI	S	21.16 MW	20.06 AW	44010 AAW	MIBLS	10//99-12/99
	Kalamazoo-Battle Creek MSA, MI	S	17.73 MW	15.93 AW	36890 AAW	MIBLS	10//99-12/99
	Lansing-East Lansing MSA, MI	S	16.33 MW	16.32 AW	33970 AAW	MIBLS	10//99-12/99
	Saginaw-Bay City-Midland MSA, MI	S	20.64 MW	18.77 AW	42930 AAW	MIBLS	10//99-12/99
	Minnesota	S	14.97 MW	17.53 AW	36450 AAW	MNBLS	10//99-12/99
	Duluth-Superior MSA, MN-WI	S	14.57 MW	14.91 AW	30310 AAW	MNBLS	10//99-12/99
	Minneapolis-St. Paul MSA, MN-WI	S	18.76 MW	15.46 AW	39030 AAW	MNBLS	10//99-12/99
	Rochester MSA, MN	S	13.75 MW	13.68 AW	28600 AAW	MNBLS	10//99-12/99
	St. Cloud MSA, MN	S	14.77 MW	13.02 AW	30710 AAW	MNBLS	10//99-12/99
	Mississippi	S	13.01 MW	14.10 AW	29330 AAW	MSBLS	10//99-12/99
	Biloxi-Gulfport-Pascagoula MSA, MS	S	15.00 MW	14.66 AW	31210 AAW	MSBLS	10//99-12/99
	Hattiesburg MSA, MS	S	13.74 MW	13.20 AW	28580 AAW	MSBLS	10//99-12/99
	Jackson MSA, MS	S	15.14 MW	13.16 AW	31500 AAW	MSBLS	10//99-12/99
	Missouri	S	13.26 MW	14.87 AW	30920 AAW	MOBLS	10//99-12/99
	Columbia MSA, MO	S	14.21 MW	13.38 AW	29560 AAW	MOBLS	10//99-12/99
	Joplin MSA, MO	S	12.95 MW	12.79 AW	26930 AAW	MOBLS	10//99-12/99
	Kansas City MSA, MO-KS	S	13.56 MW	12.30 AW	28200 AAW	MOBLS	10//99-12/99
	St. Joseph MSA, MO	S	12.25 MW	11.48 AW	25480 AAW	MOBLS	10//99-12/99
	St. Louis MSA, MO-IL	S	13.54 MW	12.47 AW	28170 AAW	MOBLS	10//99-12/99
	Springfield MSA, MO	S	13.46 MW	10.65 AW	28000 AAW	MOBLS	10//99-12/99
	Montana	S	10.56 MW	11.52 AW	23970 AAW	MTBLS	10//99-12/99
	Billings MSA, MT	S	9.29 MW	8.16 AW	19320 AAW	MTBLS	10//99-12/99
	Great Falls MSA, MT	S	11.22 MW	9.88 AW	23340 AAW	MTBLS	10//99-12/99
	Missoula MSA, MT	S	12.25 MW	11.76 AW	25470 AAW	MTBLS	10//99-12/99
	Nebraska	S	11.9 MW	13 00 AW	27050 AAW	NEBLS	10//99-12/99
	Lincoln MSA, NE	S	15.11 MW	13.88 AW	31440 AAW	NEBLS	10//99-12/99
	Omaha MSA, NE-IA	S	13.11 MW	12.80 AW	27270 AAW	NEBLS	10//99-12/99
	Nevada	S	15.41 MW	18.00 AW	37440 AAW	NVBLS	10//99-12/99
	Las Vegas MSA, NV-AZ	S	18.61 MW	15.72 AW	38720 AAW	NVBLS	10//99-12/99
	Reno MSA, NV	S	15.87 MW	14.77 AW	33010 AAW	NVBLS	10//99-12/99
	New Hampshire	S	13.29 MW	14.06 AW	29250 AAW	NHBLS	10//99-12/99
	Manchester PMSA, NH	S	15.65 MW	15.33 AW	32550 AAW	NHBLS	10//99-12/99
	Nashua PMSA, NH	S	12.71 MW	11.81 AW	26430 AAW	NHBLS	10//99-12/99
	Portsmouth-Rochester PMSA, NH-ME	S	16.95 MW	17.60 AW	35250 AAW	NHBLS	10//99-12/99
	New Jersey	S	22.77 MW	22.35 AW	46490 AAW	NJBLS	10//99-12/99
	Atlantic-Cape May PMSA, NJ	S	22.98 MW	22.00 AW	47800 AAW	NJBLS	10//99-12/99
	Bergen-Passaic PMSA, NJ	S	21.54 MW	22.36 AW	44810 AAW	NJBLS	
	Middlesex-Somerset-Hunterdon PMSA, NJ	S	21.40 MW	20.34 AW	44510 AAW	NJBLS	10//99-12/99
	Monmouth-Ocean PMSA, NJ	S	18.73 MW	16.51 AW	38960 AAW	NJBLS	10//99-12/99
	Newark PMSA, NJ	S	24.54 MW	24.35 AW	51040 AAW	NJBLS	10//99-12/99
	Trenton PMSA, NJ	S	19.21 MW	18.95 AW	39960 AAW	NJBLS	10//99-12/99
	Vineland-Millville-Bridgeton PMSA, NJ	S	19.70 MW	16.91 AW	40970 AAW	NJBLS	10//99-12/99
	New Mexico	S	12.1 MW	12.86 AW	26750 AAW	NMBLS	10//99-12/99
	Albuquerque MSA, NM	S	13.14 MW	12.09 AW	27320 AAW	NMBLS	10//99-12/99
	Las Cruces MSA, NM	S	15.56 MW	10.24 AW	32360 AAW	NMBLS	10//99-12/99
	Santa Fe MSA, NM	S	13.85 MW	13.54 AW	28820 AAW	NMBLS	10//99-12/99
	New York	S	16.58 MW	18.28 AW	38030 AAW	NYBLS	10//99-12/99

AAW Average annual wage	**AOH** Average offered, high	**ASH** Average starting, high	**H** Hourly	**M** Monthly	**S** Special: hourly and annual
AE Average entry wage	**AOL** Average offered, low	**ASL** Average starting, low	**HI** Highest wage paid	**MTC** Median total compensation	**TQ** Third quartile wage
AEX Average experienced wage	**APH** Average pay, high range	**AW** Average wage paid	**HR** High end range	**MW** Median wage paid	**W** Weekly
AO Average offered	**APL** Average pay, low range	**FQ** First quartile wage	**LR** Low end range	**SQ** Second quartile wage	**Y** Yearly

Occupation/Type/Industry	Location	Per	Low	Mid	High	Source	Date
Food Service Manager	Albany-Schenectady-Troy MSA, NY	S	14.26 MW	12.70 AW	29660 AAW	NYBLS	10//99-12//99
	Binghamton MSA, NY	S	13.17 MW	12.39 AW	27390 AAW	NYBLS	10//99-12//99
	Buffalo-Niagara Falls MSA, NY	S	14.58 MW	13.35 AW	30330 AAW	NYBLS	10//99-12//99
	Dutchess County PMSA, NY	S	17.49 MW	17.11 AW	36380 AAW	NYBLS	10//99-12//99
	Elmira MSA, NY	S	18.32 MW	14.08 AW	38100 AAW	NYBLS	10//99-12//99
	Glens Falls MSA, NY	S	13.74 MW	12.27 AW	28570 AAW	NYBLS	10//99-12//99
	Jamestown MSA, NY	S	17.95 MW	18.97 AW	37350 AAW	NYBLS	10//99-12//99
	Nassau-Suffolk PMSA, NY	S	18.27 MW	17.56 AW	37990 AAW	NYBLS	10//99-12//99
	New York PMSA, NY	S	22.62 MW	21.98 AW	47040 AAW	NYBLS	10//99-12//99
	Newburgh PMSA, NY-PA	S	17.02 MW	16.58 AW	35410 AAW	NYBLS	10//99-12//99
	Syracuse MSA, NY	S	20.42 MW	21.74 AW	42470 AAW	NYBLS	10//99-12//99
	Utica-Rome MSA, NY	S	14.02 MW	13.89 AW	29160 AAW	NYBLS	10//99-12//99
	North Carolina	S	14.62 MW	15.08 AW	31370 AAW	NCBLS	10//99-12//99
	Asheville MSA, NC	S	13.90 MW	13.50 AW	28900 AAW	NCBLS	10//99-12//99
	Charlotte-Gastonia-Rock Hill MSA, NC-SC	S	14.54 MW	14.36 AW	30250 AAW	NCBLS	10//99-12//99
	Goldsboro MSA, NC	S	9.10 MW	8.78 AW	18920 AAW	NCBLS	10//99-12//99
	Greensboro--Winston-Salem--High Point MSA, NC	S	15.14 MW	14.94 AW	31490 AAW	NCBLS	10//99-12//99
	Jacksonville MSA, NC	S	9.30 MW	8.16 AW	19340 AAW	NCBLS	10//99-12//99
	Raleigh-Durham-Chapel Hill MSA, NC	S	15.89 MW	14.65 AW	33050 AAW	NCBLS	10//99-12//99
	Wilmington MSA, NC	S	14.40 MW	13.78 AW	29960 AAW	NCBLS	10//99-12//99
	North Dakota	S	10.83 MW	11.90 AW	24750 AAW	NDBLS	10//99-12//99
	Bismarck MSA, ND	S	12.30 MW	10.81 AW	25590 AAW	NDBLS	10//99-12//99
	Fargo-Moorhead MSA, ND-MN	S	11.90 MW	11.16 AW	24750 AAW	NDBLS	10//99-12//99
	Grand Forks MSA, ND-MN	S	11.21 MW	10.68 AW	23320 AAW	NDBLS	10//99-12//99
	Ohio	S	12.65 MW	13.90 AW	28900 AAW	OHBLS	10//99-12//99
	Akron PMSA, OH	S	12.00 MW	10.21 AW	24950 AAW	OHBLS	10//99-12//99
	Canton-Massillon MSA, OH	S	11.47 MW	8.22 AW	23850 AAW	OHBLS	10//99-12//99
	Cincinnati PMSA, OH-KY-IN	S	15.96 MW	15.09 AW	33190 AAW	OHBLS	10//99-12//99
	Cleveland-Lorain-Elyria PMSA, OH	S	14.99 MW	12.84 AW	31170 AAW	OHBLS	10//99-12//99
	Columbus MSA, OH	S	13.54 MW	12.96 AW	28160 AAW	OHBLS	10//99-12//99
	Dayton-Springfield MSA, OH	S	16.10 MW	14.28 AW	33480 AAW	OHBLS	10//99-12//99
	Hamilton-Middletown PMSA, OH	S	13.80 MW	12.39 AW	28710 AAW	OHBLS	10//99-12//99
	Lima MSA, OH	S	12.88 MW	13.54 AW	26790 AAW	OHBLS	10//99-12//99
	Mansfield MSA, OH	S	12.13 MW	10.66 AW	25230 AAW	OHBLS	10//99-12//99
	Steubenville-Weirton MSA, OH-WV	S	11.09 MW	8.39 AW	23080 AAW	OHBLS	10//99-12//99
	Toledo MSA, OH	S	14.86 MW	14.08 AW	30900 AAW	OHBLS	10//99-12//99
	Youngstown-Warren MSA, OH	S	12.26 MW	11.68 AW	25500 AAW	OHBLS	10//99-12//99
	Oklahoma	S	13.16 MW	13.43 AW	27940 AAW	OKBLS	10//99-12//99
	Enid MSA, OK	S	12.51 MW	10.44 AW	26020 AAW	OKBLS	10//99-12//99
	Lawton MSA, OK	S	11.44 MW	11.60 AW	23790 AAW	OKBLS	10//99-12//99
	Oklahoma City MSA, OK	S	14.22 MW	14.25 AW	29570 AAW	OKBLS	10//99-12//99
	Tulsa MSA, OK	S	15.59 MW	14.56 AW	32420 AAW	OKBLS	10//99-12//99
	Oregon	S	16.36 MW	17.83 AW	37090 AAW	ORBLS	10//99-12//99
	Corvallis MSA, OR	S	17.39 MW	16.83 AW	36170 AAW	ORBLS	10//99-12//99
	Eugene-Springfield MSA, OR	S	18.16 MW	17.31 AW	37780 AAW	ORBLS	10//99-12//99
	Medford-Ashland MSA, OR	S	14.20 MW	14.71 AW	29530 AAW	ORBLS	10//99-12//99
	Salem PMSA, OR	S	18.66 MW	19.04 AW	38810 AAW	ORBLS	10//99-12//99
	Pennsylvania	S	13.64 MW	15.25 AW	31720 AAW	PABLS	10//99-12//99
	Altoona MSA, PA	S	19.90 MW	16.63 AW	41380 AAW	PABLS	10//99-12//99
	Erie MSA, PA	S	13.42 MW	12.78 AW	27920 AAW	PABLS	10//99-12//99
	Harrisburg-Lebanon-Carlisle MSA, PA	S	15.81 MW	14.57 AW	32870 AAW	PABLS	10//99-12//99
	Johnstown MSA, PA	S	12.44 MW	11.89 AW	25870 AAW	PABLS	10//99-12//99
	Lancaster MSA, PA	S	15.91 MW	15.49 AW	33090 AAW	PABLS	10//99-12//99
	Philadelphia PMSA, PA-NJ	S	19.87 MW	20.41 AW	41330 AAW	PABLS	10//99-12//99
	Pittsburgh MSA, PA	S	14.38 MW	13.23 AW	29920 AAW	PABLS	10//99-12//99
	Reading MSA, PA	S	16.16 MW	15.48 AW	33600 AAW	PABLS	10//99-12//99
	Scranton--Wilkes-Barre--Hazleton MSA, PA	S	13.77 MW	13.52 AW	28650 AAW	PABLS	10//99-12//99
	Sharon MSA, PA	S	10.32 MW	9.29 AW	21460 AAW	PABLS	10//99-12//99
	State College MSA, PA	S	15.51 MW	15.52 AW	32270 AAW	PABLS	10//99-12//99
	Williamsport MSA, PA	S	13.53 MW	12.31 AW	28140 AAW	PABLS	10//99-12//99
	York MSA, PA	S	15.50 MW	14.68 AW	32250 AAW	PABLS	10//99-12//99

AAW	Average annual wage	AOH	Average offered, high	ASH	Average starting, high
AE	Average entry wage	AOL	Average offered, low	ASL	Average starting, low
AEX	Average experienced wage	APH	Average pay, high range	AW	Average wage paid
AO	Average offered	APL	Average pay, low range	FQ	First quartile wage

H	Hourly	M	Monthly	S	Special: hourly and annual
HI	Highest wage paid	MTC	Median total compensation	TQ	Third quartile wage
HR	High end range	MW	Median wage paid	W	Weekly
LR	Low end range	SQ	Second quartile wage	Y	Yearly

Occupation/Type/Industry	Location	Per	Low	Mid	High	Source	Date
Food Service Manager	Rhode Island	S	26.95 MW	24.13 AW	50180 AAW	RIBLS	10//99-12//99
	Providence-Fall River- Warwick MSA, RI-MA	S	22.56 MW	23.26 AW	46920 AAW	RIBLS	10//99-12//99
	South Carolina	S	14.4 MW	14.65 AW	30480 AAW	SCBLS	10//99-12//99
	Charleston-North Charleston MSA, SC	S	15.18 MW	14.33 AW	31570 AAW	SCBLS	10//99-12//99
	Columbia MSA, SC	S	12.40 MW	11.35 AW	25790 AAW	SCBLS	10//99-12//99
	Florence MSA, SC	S	12.95 MW	12.33 AW	26940 AAW	SCBLS	10//99-12//99
	Greenville-Spartanburg- Anderson MSA, SC	S	16.00 MW	15.60 AW	33280 AAW	SCBLS	10//99-12//99
	Myrtle Beach MSA, SC	S	15.10 MW	14.41 AW	31420 AAW	SCBLS	10//99-12//99
	Sumter MSA, SC	S	12.23 MW	10.48 AW	25450 AAW	SCBLS	10//99-12//99
	South Dakota	S	16.41 MW	17.42 AW	36240 AAW	SDBLS	10//99-12//99
	Rapid City MSA, SD	S	18.64 MW	17.85 AW	38770 AAW	SDBLS	10//99-12//99
	Sioux Falls MSA, SD	S	16.73 MW	15.97 AW	34800 AAW	SDBLS	10//99-12//99
	Tennessee	S	14 MW	14.73 AW	30640 AAW	TNBLS	10//99-12//99
	Chattanooga MSA, TN-GA	S	14.78 MW	15.39 AW	30740 AAW	TNBLS	10//99-12//99
	Clarksville-Hopkinsville MSA, TN-KY	S	13.63 MW	14.12 AW	28350 AAW	TNBLS	10//99-12//99
	Jackson MSA, TN	S	12.41 MW	12.47 AW	25820 AAW	TNBLS	10//99-12//99
	Johnson City-Kingsport-Bristol MSA, TN-VA	S	14.64 MW	14.64 AW	30460 AAW	TNBLS	10//99-12//99
	Knoxville MSA, TN	S	16.88 MW	15.13 AW	35110 AAW	TNBLS	10//99-12//99
	Memphis MSA, TN-AR-MS	S	14.95 MW	14.24 AW	31090 AAW	MSBLS	10//99-12//99
	Nashville MSA, TN	S	14.01 MW	12.41 AW	29140 AAW	TNBLS	10//99-12//99
	Texas	S	17.83 MW	18.02 AW	37490 AAW	TXBLS	10//99-12//99
	Abilene MSA, TX	S	16.32 MW	18.27 AW	33940 AAW	TXBLS	10//99-12//99
	Amarillo MSA, TX	S	14.98 MW	13.97 AW	31160 AAW	TXBLS	10//99-12//99
	Austin-San Marcos MSA, TX	S	20.26 MW	19.51 AW	42140 AAW	TXBLS	10//99-12//99
	Beaumont-Port Arthur MSA, TX	S	21.35 MW	16.63 AW	44410 AAW	TXBLS	10//99-12//99
	Brownsville-Harlingen-San Benito MSA, TX	S	12.19 MW	13.65 AW	25350 AAW	TXBLS	10//99-12//99
	Bryan-College Station MSA, TX	S	14.47 MW	13.17 AW	30100 AAW	TXBLS	10//99-12//99
	Corpus Christi MSA, TX	S	15.07 MW	14.40 AW	31340 AAW	TXBLS	10//99-12//99
	Dallas PMSA, TX	S	21.31 MW	21.05 AW	44320 AAW	TXBLS	10//99-12//99
	El Paso MSA, TX	S	16.67 MW	17.29 AW	34680 AAW	TXBLS	10//99-12//99
	Fort Worth-Arlington PMSA, TX	S	16.76 MW	16.41 AW	34870 AAW	TXBLS	10//99-12//99
	Galveston-Texas City PMSA, TX	S	16.56 MW	18.23 AW	34450 AAW	TXBLS	10//99-12//99
	Houston PMSA, TX	S	14.20 MW	12.76 AW	29540 AAW	TXBLS	10//99-12//99
	Killeen-Temple MSA, TX	S	14.76 MW	15.01 AW	30700 AAW	TXBLS	10//99-12//99
	Laredo MSA, TX	S	11.80 MW	9.81 AW	24540 AAW	TXBLS	10//99-12//99
	Longview-Marshall MSA, TX	S	14.82 MW	12.81 AW	30830 AAW	TXBLS	10//99-12//99
	Lubbock MSA, TX	S	12.22 MW	11.03 AW	25410 AAW	TXBLS	10//99-12//99
	McAllen-Edinburg-Mission MSA, TX	S	10.98 MW	9.76 AW	22830 AAW	TXBLS	10//99-12//99
	Odessa-Midland MSA, TX	S	14.74 MW	13.71 AW	30650 AAW	TXBLS	10//99-12//99
	San Angelo MSA, TX	S	15.44 MW	15.76 AW	32110 AAW	TXBLS	10//99-12//99
	San Antonio MSA, TX	S	24.32 MW	20.03 AW	50580 AAW	TXBLS	10//99-12//99
	Sherman-Denison MSA, TX	S	14.40 MW	14.94 AW	29950 AAW	TXBLS	10//99-12//99
	Texarkana MSA, TX- Texarkana, AR	S	14.95 MW	14.28 AW	31110 AAW	TXBLS	10//99-12//99
	Tyler MSA, TX	S	12.77 MW	12.64 AW	26550 AAW	TXBLS	10//99-12//99
	Victoria MSA, TX	S	11.85 MW	10.19 AW	24640 AAW	TXBLS	10//99-12//99
	Waco MSA, TX	S	10.51 MW	9.44 AW	21860 AAW	TXBLS	10//99-12//99
	Wichita Falls MSA, TX	S	16.59 MW	16.85 AW	34500 AAW	TXBLS	10//99-12//99
	Utah	S	13.42 MW	14.97 AW	31140 AAW	UTBLS	10//99-12//99
	Provo-Orem MSA, UT	S	15.02 MW	12.86 AW	31240 AAW	UTBLS	10//99-12//99
	Salt Lake City-Ogden MSA, UT	S	17.05 MW	15.83 AW	35470 AAW	UTBLS	10//99-12//99
	Vermont	S	16.28 MW	18.50 AW	38470 AAW	VTBLS	10//99-12//99
	Burlington MSA, VT	S	11.98 MW	10.03 AW	24920 AAW	VTBLS	10//99-12//99
	Virginia	S	14.8 MW	15.57 AW	32380 AAW	VABLS	10//99-12//99
	Charlottesville MSA, VA	S	15.57 MW	14.58 AW	32380 AAW	VABLS	10//99-12//99
	Danville MSA, VA	S	17.60 MW	14.94 AW	36610 AAW	VABLS	10//99-12//99
	Lynchburg MSA, VA	S	21.90 MW	19.57 AW	45550 AAW	VABLS	10//99-12//99
	Norfolk-Virginia Beach- Newport News MSA, VA- NC	S	15.18 MW	14.48 AW	31570 AAW	VABLS	10//99-12//99

AAW	Average annual wage	AOH	Average offered, high	ASH	Average starting, high	H	Hourly	M	Monthly	S	Special: hourly and annual
AE	Average entry wage	AOL	Average offered, low	ASL	Average starting, low	HI	Highest wage paid	MTC	Median total compensation	TQ	Third quartile wage
AEX	Average experienced wage	APH	Average pay, high range	AW	Average wage paid	HR	High end range	MW	Median wage paid	W	Weekly
AO	Average offered	APL	Average pay, low range	FQ	First quartile wage	LR	Low end range	SQ	Second quartile wage	Y	Yearly

Occupation/Type/Industry	Location	Per	Low	Mid	High	Source	Date
Food Service Manager	Richmond-Petersburg MSA, VA	S	15.49 MW	15.23 AW	32230 AAW	VABLS	10//99-12//99
	Roanoke MSA, VA	S	10.69 MW	9.33 AW	22220 AAW	VABLS	10//99-12//99
	Washington	S	16.84 MW	19.97 AW	41550 AAW	WABLS	10//99-12//99
	Bellingham MSA, WA	S	16.77 MW	15.54 AW	34880 AAW	WABLS	10//99-12//99
	Bremerton PMSA, WA	S	18.70 MW	18.28 AW	38890 AAW	WABLS	10//99-12//99
	Seattle-Bellevue-Everett PMSA, WA	S	17.79 MW	15.73 AW	37000 AAW	WABLS	10//99-12//99
	Spokane MSA, WA	S	19.71 MW	17.04 AW	41000 AAW	WABLS	10//99-12//99
	Tacoma PMSA, WA	S	21.11 MW	19.49 AW	43910 AAW	WABLS	10//99-12//99
	Yakima MSA, WA	S	15.77 MW	15.56 AW	32800 AAW	WABLS	10//99-12//99
	West Virginia	S	11.77 MW	13.33 AW	27740 AAW	WVBLS	10//99-12//99
	Charleston MSA, WV	S	12.69 MW	11.60 AW	26400 AAW	WVBLS	10//99-12//99
	Huntington-Ashland MSA, WV-KY-OH	S	11.84 MW	11.61 AW	24630 AAW	WVBLS	10//99-12//99
	Parkersburg-Marietta MSA, WV-OH	S	11.68 MW	10.16 AW	24290 AAW	WVBLS	10//99-12//99
	Wheeling MSA, WV-OH	S	14.42 MW	12.77 AW	30000 AAW	WVBLS	10//99-12//99
	Wisconsin	S	12.74 MW	13.77 AW	28640 AAW	WIBLS	10//99-12//99
	Appleton-Oshkosh-Neenah MSA, WI	S	14.85 MW	14.85 AW	30890 AAW	WIBLS	10//99-12//99
	Eau Claire MSA, WI	S	13.23 MW	12.45 AW	27520 AAW	WIBLS	10//99-12//99
	Green Bay MSA, WI	S	14.44 MW	14.03 AW	30030 AAW	WIBLS	10//99-12//99
	Janesville-Beloit MSA, WI	S	13.75 MW	12.12 AW	28600 AAW	WIBLS	10//99-12//99
	Kenosha PMSA, WI	S	11.40 MW	10.36 AW	23710 AAW	WIBLS	10//99-12//99
	La Crosse MSA, WI-MN	S	11.43 MW	10.50 AW	23780 AAW	WIBLS	10//99-12//99
	Madison MSA, WI	S	13.51 MW	12.51 AW	28090 AAW	WIBLS	10//99-12//99
	Milwaukee-Waukesha PMSA, WI	S	14.33 MW	12.61 AW	29810 AAW	WIBLS	10//99-12//99
	Racine PMSA, WI	S	14.40 MW	13.17 AW	29940 AAW	WIBLS	10//99-12//99
	Sheboygan MSA, WI	S	13.44 MW	12.47 AW	27960 AAW	WIBLS	10//99-12//99
	Wausau MSA, WI	S	14.80 MW	14.26 AW	30780 AAW	WIBLS	10//99-12//99
	Wyoming	S	10.69 MW	11.85 AW	24640 AAW	WYBLS	10//99-12//99
	Casper MSA, WY	S	11.31 MW	10.49 AW	23520 AAW	WYBLS	10//99-12//99
	Cheyenne MSA, WY	S	13.72 MW	13.36 AW	28540 AAW	WYBLS	10//99-12//99
	Puerto Rico	S	15.46 MW	15.48 AW	32200 AAW	PRBLS	10//99-12//99
	Guam	S	13.97 MW	14.67 AW	30520 AAW	GUBLS	10//99-12//99
Food Technologist							
Female, BS Degree	United States	Y		50000 AW		FOODT	11//99
Female, MBA	United States	Y		65000 AW		FOODT	11//99
Female, MS Degree	United States	Y		55000 AW		FOODT	11//99
Female, PhD	United States	Y		65000 AW		FOODT	11//99
Male, BS Degree	United States	Y		65000 AW		FOODT	11//99
Male, MBA	United States	Y		85300 AW		FOODT	11//99
Male, MS Degree	United States	Y		72000 AW		FOODT	11//99
Male, PhD	United States	Y		82450 AW		FOODT	11//99
Football Player							
Professional	United States	Y	175000 APL	1071000 AW	5874200 APH	SPORTS	1999
Foreign Language and Literature Teacher							
Postsecondary	Alabama	Y		40960 AAW		ALBLS	10//99-12//99
Postsecondary	Arizona	Y		37330 AAW		AZBLS	10//99-12//99
Postsecondary	Phoenix-Mesa MSA, AZ	Y		33950 AAW		AZBLS	10//99-12//99
Postsecondary	Arkansas	Y		47260 AAW		ARBLS	10//99-12//99
Postsecondary	California	Y		49560 AAW		CABLS	10//99-12//99
Postsecondary	Los Angeles-Long Beach PMSA, CA	Y		44590 AAW		CABLS	10//99-12//99
Postsecondary	Orange County PMSA, CA	Y		48090 AAW		CABLS	10//99-12//99
Postsecondary	Riverside-San Bernardino PMSA, CA	Y		50020 AAW		CABLS	10//99-12//99
Postsecondary	San Diego MSA, CA	Y		52600 AAW		CABLS	10//99-12//99
Postsecondary	San Francisco PMSA, CA	Y		57760 AAW		CABLS	10//99-12//99
Postsecondary	Colorado	Y		42640 AAW		COBLS	10//99-12//99
Postsecondary	Denver PMSA, CO	Y		40410 AAW		COBLS	10//99-12//99
Postsecondary	Connecticut	Y		51430 AAW		CTBLS	10//99-12//99
Postsecondary	District of Columbia	Y		39320 AAW		DCBLS	10//99-12//99
Postsecondary	Washington PMSA, DC-MD-VA-WV	Y		40230 AAW		DCBLS	10//99-12//99
Postsecondary	Florida	Y		51410 AAW		FLBLS	10//99-12//99

AAW	Average annual wage	AOH	Average offered, high	ASH	Average starting, high	H	Hourly	M	Monthly	S	Special: hourly and annual
AE	Average entry wage	AOL	Average offered, low	ASL	Average starting, low	HI	Highest wage paid	MTC	Median total compensation	TQ	Third quartile wage
AEX	Average experienced wage	APH	Average pay, high range	AW	Average wage paid	HR	High end range	MW	Median wage paid	W	Weekly
AO	Average offered	APL	Average pay, low range	FQ	First quartile wage	LR	Low end range	SQ	Second quartile wage	Y	Yearly

Occupation/Type/Industry	Location	Per	Low	Mid	High	Source	Date
Foreign Language and Literature Teacher							
Postsecondary	Fort Lauderdale PMSA, FL	Y		26950 AAW		FLBLS	10//99-12//99
Postsecondary	Miami PMSA, FL	Y		56770 AAW		FLBLS	10//99-12//99
Postsecondary	Orlando MSA, FL	Y		44480 AAW		FLBLS	10//99-12//99
Postsecondary	Tampa-St. Petersburg-Clearwater MSA, FL	Y		46710 AAW		FLBLS	10//99-12//99
Postsecondary	West Palm Beach-Boca Raton MSA, FL	Y		51500 AAW		FLBLS	10//99-12//99
Postsecondary	Georgia	Y		46040 AAW		GABLS	10//99-12//99
Postsecondary	Atlanta MSA, GA	Y		48030 AAW		GABLS	10//99-12//99
Postsecondary	Savannah MSA, GA	Y		43130 AAW		GABLS	10//99-12//99
Postsecondary	Idaho	Y		45450 AAW		IDBLS	10//99-12//99
Postsecondary	Illinois	Y		49520 AAW		ILBLS	10//99-12//99
Postsecondary	Chicago PMSA, IL	Y		49050 AAW		ILBLS	10//99-12//99
Postsecondary	Indiana	Y		41140 AAW		INBLS	10//99-12//99
Postsecondary	Fort Wayne MSA, IN	Y		42910 AAW		INBLS	10//99-12//99
Postsecondary	Gary PMSA, IN	Y		40110 AAW		INBLS	10//99-12//99
Postsecondary	Indianapolis MSA, IN	Y		40150 AAW		INBLS	10//99-12//99
Postsecondary	Iowa	Y		48650 AAW		IABLS	10//99-12//99
Postsecondary	Kansas	Y		30630 AAW		KSBLS	10//99-12//99
Postsecondary	Kentucky	Y		45470 AAW		KYBLS	10//99-12//99
Postsecondary	Louisiana	Y		43280 AAW		LABLS	10//99-12//99
Postsecondary	Maryland	Y		47120 AAW		MDBLS	10//99-12//99
Postsecondary	Baltimore PMSA, MD	Y		47500 AAW		MDBLS	10//99-12//99
Postsecondary	Massachusetts	Y		49160 AAW		MABLS	10//99-12//99
Postsecondary	Boston PMSA, MA-NH	Y		47670 AAW		MABLS	10//99-12//99
Postsecondary	Brockton PMSA, MA	Y		40420 AAW		MABLS	10//99-12//99
Postsecondary	Springfield MSA, MA	Y		58320 AAW		MABLS	10//99-12//99
Postsecondary	Worcester PMSA, MA-CT	Y		51870 AAW		MABLS	10//99-12//99
Postsecondary	Michigan	Y		46550 AAW		MIBLS	10//99-12//99
Postsecondary	Ann Arbor PMSA, MI	Y		51210 AAW		MIBLS	10//99-12//99
Postsecondary	Kalamazoo-Battle Creek MSA, MI	Y		48250 AAW		MIBLS	10//99-12//99
Postsecondary	Minnesota	Y		45750 AAW		MNBLS	10//99-12//99
Postsecondary	Minneapolis-St. Paul MSA, MN-WI	Y		42460 AAW		MNBLS	10//99-12//99
Postsecondary	St. Cloud MSA, MN	Y		48710 AAW		MNBLS	10//99-12//99
Postsecondary	Mississippi	Y		41750 AAW		MSBLS	10//99-12//99
Postsecondary	Jackson MSA, MS	Y		34930 AAW		MSBLS	10//99-12//99
Postsecondary	Missouri	Y		39740 AAW		MOBLS	10//99-12//99
Postsecondary	St. Louis MSA, MO-IL	Y		40820 AAW		MOBLS	10//99-12//99
Postsecondary	Montana	Y		55550 AAW		MTBLS	10//99-12//99
Postsecondary	Nebraska	Y		36070 AAW		NEBLS	10//99-12//99
Postsecondary	Nevada	Y		37770 AAW		NVBLS	10//99-12//99
Postsecondary	New Hampshire	Y		51660 AAW		NHBLS	10//99-12//99
Postsecondary	New Jersey	Y		53030 AAW		NJBLS	10//99-12//99
Postsecondary	Bergen-Passaic PMSA, NJ	Y		47710 AAW		NJBLS	10//99-12//99
Postsecondary	Jersey City PMSA, NJ	Y		61430 AAW		NJBLS	10//99-12//99
Postsecondary	Newark PMSA, NJ	Y		56700 AAW		NJBLS	10//99-12//99
Postsecondary	New Mexico	Y		44810 AAW		NMBLS	10//99-12//99
Postsecondary	New York	Y		47840 AAW		NYBLS	10//99-12//99
Postsecondary	Albany-Schenectady-Troy MSA, NY	Y		45380 AAW		NYBLS	10//99-12//99
Postsecondary	New York PMSA, NY	Y		49130 AAW		NYBLS	10//99-12//99
Postsecondary	North Carolina	Y		42740 AAW		NCBLS	10//99-12//99
Postsecondary	Asheville MSA, NC	Y		41700 AAW		NCBLS	10//99-12//99
Postsecondary	Charlotte-Gastonia-Rock Hill MSA, NC-SC	Y		43790 AAW		NCBLS	10//99-12//99
Postsecondary	Greensboro--Winston-Salem--High Point MSA, NC	Y		42950 AAW		NCBLS	10//99-12//99
Postsecondary	Hickory-Morganton-Lenoir MSA, NC	Y		38700 AAW		NCBLS	10//99-12//99
Postsecondary	Raleigh-Durham-Chapel Hill MSA, NC	Y		43510 AAW		NCBLS	10//99-12//99
Postsecondary	North Dakota	Y		36810 AAW		NDBLS	10//99-12//99
Postsecondary	Ohio	Y		42090 AAW		OHBLS	10//99-12//99
Postsecondary	Cincinnati PMSA, OH-KY-IN	Y		41790 AAW		OHBLS	10//99-12//99
Postsecondary	Cleveland-Lorain-Elyria PMSA, OH	Y		46060 AAW		OHBLS	10//99-12//99
Postsecondary	Columbus MSA, OH	Y		38550 AAW		OHBLS	10//99-12//99
Postsecondary	Dayton-Springfield MSA, OH	Y		40770 AAW		OHBLS	10//99-12//99

AAW	Average annual wage	**AOH**	Average offered, high	**ASH**	Average starting, high	**H**	Hourly	**M**	Monthly	**S**	Special; hourly and annual
AE	Average entry wage	**AOL**	Average offered, low	**ASL**	Average starting, low	**HI**	Highest wage paid	**MTC**	Median total compensation	**TQ**	Third quartile wage
AEX	Average experienced wage	**APH**	Average pay, high range	**AW**	Average wage paid	**HR**	High end range	**MW**	Median wage paid	**W**	Weekly
AO	Average offered	**APL**	Average pay, low range	**FQ**	First quartile wage	**LR**	Low end range	**SQ**	Second quartile wage	**Y**	Yearly

Occupation/Type/Industry	Location	Per	Low	Mid	High	Source	Date
Foreign Language and Literature Teacher							
Postsecondary	Oklahoma	Y		35770 AAW		OKBLS	10//99-12//99
Postsecondary	Oklahoma City MSA, OK	Y		36750 AAW		OKBLS	10//99-12//99
Postsecondary	Oregon	Y		47060 AAW		ORBLS	10//99-12//99
Postsecondary	Portland-Vancouver PMSA, OR-WA	Y		46880 AAW		ORBLS	10//99-12//99
Postsecondary	Pennsylvania	Y		58660 AAW		PABLS	10//99-12//99
Postsecondary	Allentown-Bethlehem-Easton MSA, PA	Y		45590 AAW		PABLS	10//99-12//99
Postsecondary	Philadelphia PMSA, PA-NJ	Y		61820 AAW		PABLS	10//99-12//99
Postsecondary	Pittsburgh MSA, PA	Y		61200 AAW		PABLS	10//99-12//99
Postsecondary	Reading MSA, PA	Y		47820 AAW		PABLS	10//99-12//99
Postsecondary	Scranton--Wilkes-Barre--Hazleton MSA, PA	Y		46560 AAW		PABLS	10//99-12//99
Postsecondary	Rhode Island	Y		68340 AAW		RIBLS	10//99-12//99
Postsecondary	Providence-Fall River-Warwick MSA, RI-MA	Y		68500 AAW		RIBLS	10//99-12//99
Postsecondary	South Carolina	Y		45260 AAW		SCBLS	10//99-12//99
Postsecondary	Greenville-Spartanburg-Anderson MSA, SC	Y		47190 AAW		SCBLS	10//99-12//99
Postsecondary	South Dakota	Y		36260 AAW		SDBLS	10//99-12//99
Postsecondary	Tennessee	Y		44140 AAW		TNBLS	10//99-12//99
Postsecondary	Johnson City-Kingsport-Bristol MSA, TN-VA	Y		43830 AAW		TNBLS	10//99-12//99
Postsecondary	Memphis MSA, TN-AR-MS	Y		46310 AAW		MSBLS	10//99-12//99
Postsecondary	Nashville MSA, TN	Y		46280 AAW		TNBLS	10//99-12//99
Postsecondary	Texas	Y		39940 AAW		TXBLS	10//99-12//99
Postsecondary	Houston PMSA, TX	Y		42720 AAW		TXBLS	10//99-12//99
Postsecondary	Odessa-Midland MSA, TX	Y		37090 AAW		TXBLS	10//99-12//99
Postsecondary	San Antonio MSA, TX	Y		42140 AAW		TXBLS	10//99-12//99
Postsecondary	Vermont	Y		51100 AAW		VTBLS	10//99-12//99
Postsecondary	Virginia	Y		44780 AAW		VABLS	10//99-12//99
Postsecondary	Richmond-Petersburg MSA, VA	Y		50170 AAW		VABLS	10//99-12//99
Postsecondary	Washington	Y		40170 AAW		WABLS	10//99-12//99
Postsecondary	Seattle-Bellevue-Everett PMSA, WA	Y		45000 AAW		WABLS	10//99-12//99
Postsecondary	Tacoma PMSA, WA	Y		41570 AAW		WABLS	10//99-12//99
Postsecondary	West Virginia	Y		47160 AAW		WVBLS	10//99-12//99
Postsecondary	Wyoming	Y		47950 AAW		WYBLS	10//99-12//99
Postsecondary	Puerto Rico	Y		35330 AAW		PRBLS	10//99-12//99
Postsecondary	San Juan-Bayamon PMSA, PR	Y		38620 AAW		PRBLS	10//99-12//99
Forensic Autopsy Assistant	Louisville, KY	Y		20545 AW		LOUMAG	1999-2000
Forensic Science Technician	California	S	18.45 MW	20.02 AW	41640 AAW	CABLS	10//99-12//99
	Oakland PMSA, CA	S	23.81 MW	23.00 AW	49520 AAW	CABLS	10//99-12//99
	Colorado	S	18.49 MW	18.49 AW	38450 AAW	COBLS	10//99-12//99
	Denver PMSA, CO	S	17.85 MW	17.98 AW	37140 AAW	COBLS	10//99-12//99
	Hartford MSA, CT	S	23.71 MW	20.28 AW	49310 AAW	CTBLS	10//99-12//99
	Washington PMSA, DC-MD-VA-WV	S	23.12 MW	22.92 AW	48090 AAW	DCBLS	10//99-12//99
	Florida	S	16.74 MW	17.11 AW	35580 AAW	FLBLS	10//99-12//99
	Fort Lauderdale PMSA, FL	S	15.24 MW	15.19 AW	31690 AAW	FLBLS	10//99-12//99
	Miami PMSA, FL	S	15.26 MW	15.04 AW	31730 AAW	FLBLS	10//99-12//99
	Tampa-St. Petersburg-Clearwater MSA, FL	S	18.41 MW	18.66 AW	38290 AAW	FLBLS	10//99-12//99
	Georgia	S	12.5 MW	14.51 AW	30170 AAW	GABLS	10//99-12//99
	Atlanta MSA, GA	S	19.42 MW	18.23 AW	40390 AAW	GABLS	10//99-12//99
	Illinois	S	18.02 MW	18.71 AW	38920 AAW	ILBLS	10//99-12//99
	Chicago PMSA, IL	S	19.24 MW	18.42 AW	40010 AAW	ILBLS	10//99-12//99
	Indiana	S	15.63 MW	16.70 AW	34740 AAW	INBLS	10//99-12//99
	Kentucky	S	13.22 MW	14.13 AW	29390 AAW	KYBLS	10//99-12//99
	Maryland	S	16.63 MW	17.50 AW	36410 AAW	MDBLS	10//99-12//99
	Baltimore PMSA, MD	S	15.28 MW	13.83 AW	31790 AAW	MDBLS	10//99-12//99
	Nevada	S	20.82 MW	21.52 AW	44770 AAW	NVBLS	10//99-12//99
	New Mexico	S	17.04 MW	16.80 AW	34950 AAW	NMBLS	10//99-12//99
	New York	S	24.6 MW	24.26 AW	50460 AAW	NYBLS	10//99-12//99
	North Carolina	S	13.69 MW	15.42 AW	32060 AAW	NCBLS	10//99-12//99
	Raleigh-Durham-Chapel Hill MSA, NC	S	15.35 MW	13.20 AW	31920 AAW	NCBLS	10//99-12//99

AAW Average annual wage	**AOH** Average offered, high	**ASH** Average starting, high	**H** Hourly	**M** Monthly	**S** Special: hourly and annual
AE Average entry wage	**AOL** Average offered, low	**ASL** Average starting, low	**HI** Highest wage paid	**MTC** Median total compensation	**TQ** Third quartile wage
AEX Average experienced wage	**APH** Average pay, high range	**AW** Average wage paid	**HR** High end range	**MW** Median wage paid	**W** Weekly
AO Average offered	**APL** Average pay, low range	**FQ** First quartile wage	**LR** Low end range	**SQ** Second quartile wage	**Y** Yearly

Occupation/Type/Industry	Location	Per	Low	Mid	High	Source	Date
Forensic Science Technician	Oklahoma	S	13.57 MW	13.63 AW	28350 AAW	OKBLS	10//99-12//99
	Oregon	S	22.58 MW	22.00 AW	45770 AAW	ORBLS	10//99-12//99
	Pennsylvania	S	15.31 MW	17.17 AW	35710 AAW	PABLS	10//99-12//99
	Texas	S	19.36 MW	19.56 AW	40690 AAW	TXBLS	10//99-12//99
	Dallas PMSA, TX	S	20.77 MW	20.60 AW	43210 AAW	TXBLS	10//99-12//99
	Utah	S	15.64 MW	16.38 AW	34080 AAW	UTBLS	10//99-12//99
	Salt Lake City-Ogden MSA, UT	S	16.35 MW	15.63 AW	34000 AAW	UTBLS	10//99-12//99
	Virginia	S	16.56 MW	17.22 AW	35820 AAW	VABLS	10//99-12//99
	Washington	S	22 MW	21.24 AW	44170 AAW	WABLS	10//99-12//99
	Seattle-Bellevue-Everett PMSA, WA	S	21.55 MW	22.52 AW	44830 AAW	WABLS	10//99-12//99
Forest and Conservation Technician	Alaska	S	13.38 MW	14.23 AW	29590 AAW	AKBLS	10//99-12//99
	Arizona	S	11.66 MW	12.06 AW	25090 AAW	AZBLS	10//99-12//99
	Arkansas	S	13.37 MW	13.54 AW	28150 AAW	ARBLS	10//99-12//99
	California	S	14.18 MW	14.59 AW	30340 AAW	CABLS	10//99-12//99
	Colorado	S	13.68 MW	14.03 AW	29180 AAW	COBLS	10//99-12//99
	Florida	S	13.78 MW	13.71 AW	28510 AAW	FLBLS	10//99-12//99
	Georgia	S	12.71 MW	13.14 AW	27330 AAW	GABLS	10//99-12//99
	Idaho	S	13.86 MW	14.37 AW	29880 AAW	IDBLS	10//99-12//99
	Illinois	S	13.13 MW	12.52 AW	26040 AAW	ILBLS	10//99-12//99
	Indiana	S	14.27 MW	13.55 AW	28180 AAW	INBLS	10//99-12//99
	Iowa	S	9.61 MW	10.56 AW	21960 AAW	IABLS	10//99-12//99
	Kansas	S	13.7 MW	12.34 AW	25670 AAW	KSBLS	10//99-12//99
	Kentucky	S	12.16 MW	12.23 AW	25450 AAW	KYBLS	10//99-12//99
	Louisiana	S	15.29 MW	17.39 AW	36170 AAW	LABLS	10//99-12//99
	Maine	S	14.04 MW	14.24 AW	29610 AAW	MEBLS	10//99-12//99
	Michigan	S	17.1 MW	16.88 AW	35110 AAW	MIBLS	10//99-12//99
	Minnesota	S	10.61 MW	12.49 AW	25990 AAW	MNBLS	10//99-12//99
	Mississippi	S	13.93 MW	14.00 AW	29130 AAW	MSBLS	10//99-12//99
	Missouri	S	13.97 MW	13.17 AW	27380 AAW	MOBLS	10//99-12//99
	Nebraska	S	13.39 MW	12.54 AW	26090 AAW	NEBLS	10//99-12//99
	Nevada	S	13.01 MW	13.60 AW	28290 AAW	NVBLS	10//99-12//99
	New Hampshire	S	12.65 MW	13.22 AW	27500 AAW	NHBLS	10//99-12//99
	New Mexico	S	12.43 MW	12.77 AW	26570 AAW	NMBLS	10//99-12//99
	North Carolina	S	15.12 MW	15.02 AW	31240 AAW	NCBLS	10//99-12//99
	North Dakota	S	11.13 MW	11.48 AW	23870 AAW	NDBLS	10//99-12//99
	Ohio	S	12.56 MW	13.16 AW	27370 AAW	OHBLS	10//99-12//99
	Oklahoma	S	14.31 MW	13.92 AW	28960 AAW	OKBLS	10//99-12//99
	Oregon	S	15.63 MW	15.97 AW	33220 AAW	ORBLS	10//99-12//99
	Pennsylvania	S	14.1 MW	24.97 AW	51930 AAW	PABLS	10//99-12//99
	South Carolina	S	12.29 MW	12.51 AW	26020 AAW	SCBLS	10//99-12//99
	South Dakota	S	9.67 MW	10.54 AW	21930 AAW	SDBLS	10//99-12//99
	Texas	S	12.08 MW	12.30 AW	25580 AAW	TXBLS	10//99-12//99
	Utah	S	10.91 MW	11.88 AW	24710 AAW	UTBLS	10//99-12//99
	Virginia	S	13.21 MW	13.57 AW	28220 AAW	VABLS	10//99-12//99
	Washington	S	15.59 MW	15.82 AW	32910 AAW	WABLS	10//99-12//99
	West Virginia	S	13.19 MW	12.41 AW	25820 AAW	WVBLS	10//99-12//99
	Wisconsin	S	12.82 MW	12.86 AW	26750 AAW	WIBLS	10//99-12//99
	Wyoming	S	13.04 MW	13.22 AW	27500 AAW	WYBLS	10//99-12//99
Forest and Conservation Worker	Arkansas	S	9.65 MW	9.84 AW	20470 AAW	ARBLS	10//99-12//99
	Colorado	S	12.76 MW	12.89 AW	26810 AAW	COBLS	10//99-12//99
	Florida	S	14.07 MW	13.35 AW	27760 AAW	FLBLS	10//99-12//99
	Illinois	S	5.95 MW	5.75 AW	11960 AAW	ILBLS	10//99-12//99
	Iowa	S	11.35 MW	10.98 AW	22840 AAW	IABLS	10//99-12//99
	Louisiana	S	10.93 MW	10.65 AW	22150 AAW	LABLS	10//99-12//99
	Maine	S	9.58 MW	9.43 AW	19620 AAW	MEBLS	10//99-12//99
	Michigan	S	6.51 MW	10.17 AW	21160 AAW	MIBLS	10//99-12//99
	Minnesota	S	14.86 MW	14.49 AW	30140 AAW	MNBLS	10//99-12//99
	Mississippi	S	8.79 MW	8.93 AW	18580 AAW	MSBLS	10//99-12//99
	Missouri	S	12.11 MW	12.55 AW	26100 AAW	MOBLS	10//99-12//99
	Nevada	S	12.16 MW	12.15 AW	25270 AAW	NVBLS	10//99-12//99
	New Hampshire	S	8.62 MW	9.57 AW	19910 AAW	NHBLS	10//99-12//99
	New Jersey	S	12.74 MW	12.97 AW	26990 AAW	NJBLS	10//99-12//99
	New Mexico	S	10.83 MW	10.54 AW	21920 AAW	NMBLS	10//99-12//99
	North Carolina	S	9.17 MW	10.15 AW	21110 AAW	NCBLS	10//99-12//99
	South Dakota	S	7.95 MW	9.32 AW	19380 AAW	SDBLS	10//99-12//99
	Tennessee	S	7.23 MW	8.92 AW	18540 AAW	TNBLS	10//99-12//99
	Texas	S	7.54 MW	8.23 AW	17120 AAW	TXBLS	10//99-12//99

AAW Average annual wage	**AOH** Average offered, high	**ASH** Average starting, high	**H** Hourly	**M** Monthly	**S** Special: hourly and annual
AE Average entry wage	**AOL** Average offered, low	**ASL** Average starting, low	**HI** Highest wage paid	**MTC** Median total compensation	**TQ** Third quartile wage
AEX Average experienced wage	**APH** Average pay, high range	**AW** Average wage paid	**HR** High end range	**MW** Median wage paid	**W** Weekly
AO Average offered	**APL** Average pay, low range	**FQ** First quartile wage	**LR** Low end range	**SQ** Second quartile wage	**Y** Yearly

Occupation/Type/Industry	Location	Per	Low	Mid	High	Source	Date
Forest and Conservation Worker	Virginia	S	8.85 MW	9.79 AW	20370 AAW	VABLS	10//99-12//99
	Wisconsin	S	15.29 MW	15.32 AW	31860 AAW	WIBLS	10//99-12//99
Forest Fire Inspector and Prevention Specialist	Arizona	S	12.39 MW	12.81 AW	26650 AAW	AZBLS	10//99-12//99
	California	S	21.51 MW	21.07 AW	43830 AAW	CABLS	10//99-12//99
	Florida	S	11.39 MW	11.87 AW	24690 AAW	FLBLS	10//99-12//99
	Georgia	S	11.01 MW	13.03 AW	27110 AAW	GABLS	10//99-12//99
	New Jersey	S	16.74 MW	18.73 AW	38960 AAW	NJBLS	10//99-12//99
	Pennsylvania	S	17.04 MW	16.43 AW	34170 AAW	PABLS	10//99-12//99
	South Carolina	S	11.86 MW	11.89 AW	24720 AAW	SCBLS	10//99-12//99
	Virginia	S	7.98 MW	11.24 AW	23390 AAW	VABLS	10//99-12//99
Forester	Alabama	S	21.02 MW	22.43 AW	46660 AAW	ALBLS	10//99-12//99
	Alaska	S	23.54 MW	23.84 AW	49580 AAW	AKBLS	10//99-12//99
	Arizona	S	18.39 MW	18.43 AW	38340 AAW	AZBLS	10//99-12//99
	Arkansas	S	21.02 MW	20.76 AW	43180 AAW	ARBLS	10//99-12//99
	California	S	22.53 MW	23.39 AW	48660 AAW	CABLS	10//99-12//99
	Colorado	S	21.4 MW	22.73 AW	47280 AAW	COBLS	10//99-12//99
	Florida	S	21.69 MW	20.24 AW	42110 AAW	FLBLS	10//99-12//99
	Georgia	S	16.24 MW	18.90 AW	39300 AAW	GABLS	10//99-12//99
	Idaho	S	20.99 MW	22.01 AW	45790 AAW	IDBLS	10//99-12//99
	Illinois	S	25 MW	25.54 AW	53120 AAW	ILBLS	10//99-12//99
	Indiana	S	18.65 MW	19.05 AW	39630 AAW	INBLS	10//99-12//99
	Iowa	S	19.91 MW	19.34 AW	40230 AAW	IABLS	10//99-12//99
	Louisiana	S	20.9 MW	24.14 AW	50210 AAW	LABLS	10//99-12//99
	Maine	S	18.96 MW	18.78 AW	39060 AAW	MEBLS	10//99-12//99
	Michigan	S	21.5 MW	22.26 AW	46300 AAW	MIBLS	10//99-12//99
	Minnesota	S	21.47 MW	21.39 AW	44500 AAW	MNBLS	10//99-12//99
	Mississippi	S	18.13 MW	18.61 AW	38710 AAW	MSBLS	10//99-12//99
	Montana	S	20.04 MW	21.30 AW	44300 AAW	MTBLS	10//99-12//99
	Nevada	S	19.79 MW	20.39 AW	42420 AAW	NVBLS	10//99-12//99
	New Hampshire	S	23.16 MW	23.64 AW	49170 AAW	NHBLS	10//99-12//99
	New Jersey	S	16.01 MW	18.88 AW	39270 AAW	NJBLS	10//99-12//99
	New Mexico	S	19.42 MW	20.23 AW	42080 AAW	NMBLS	10//99-12//99
	New York	S	19.87 MW	20.50 AW	42630 AAW	NYBLS	10//99-12//99
	North Carolina	S	20.79 MW	21.71 AW	45170 AAW	NCBLS	10//99-12//99
	Oregon	S	22.77 MW	23.68 AW	49260 AAW	ORBLS	10//99-12//99
	Pennsylvania	S	19.35 MW	20.55 AW	42740 AAW	PABLS	10//99-12//99
	South Carolina	S	20.72 MW	20.55 AW	42740 AAW	SCBLS	10//99-12//99
	Tennessee	S	16.46 MW	17.31 AW	36000 AAW	TNBLS	10//99-12//99
	Texas	S	16.86 MW	18.02 AW	37490 AAW	TXBLS	10//99-12//99
	Utah	S	19.99 MW	20.80 AW	43270 AAW	UTBLS	10//99-12//99
	Vermont	S	20.53 MW	20.79 AW	43250 AAW	VTBLS	10//99-12//99
	Virginia	S	19.75 MW	20.12 AW	41860 AAW	VABLS	10//99-12//99
	Washington	S	20.31 MW	21.57 AW	44860 AAW	WABLS	10//99-12//99
	West Virginia	S	17.76 MW	17.79 AW	36990 AAW	WVBLS	10//99-12//99
	Wisconsin	S	19 MW	19.58 AW	40720 AAW	WIBLS	10//99-12//99
	Wyoming	S	20.14 MW	20.56 AW	42760 AAW	WYBLS	10//99-12//99
Forestry and Conservation Science Teacher							
Postsecondary	California	Y		56150 AAW		CABLS	10//99-12//99
Postsecondary	Minnesota	Y		62100 AAW		MNBLS	10//99-12//99
Postsecondary	North Carolina	Y		40570 AAW		NCBLS	10//99-12//99
Postsecondary	Ohio	Y		59800 AAW		OHBLS	10//99-12//99
Postsecondary	Pennsylvania	Y		52930 AAW		PABLS	10//99-12//99
Postsecondary	South Carolina	Y		52750 AAW		SCBLS	10//99-12//99
Postsecondary	West Virginia	Y		55760 AAW		WVBLS	10//99-12//99
Forging Machine Setter, Operator, and Tender							
Metals and Plastics	Alabama	S	16.05 MW	16.09 AW	33470 AAW	ALBLS	10//99-12//99
Metals and Plastics	Birmingham MSA, AL	S	18.26 MW	19.62 AW	37990 AAW	ALBLS	10//99-12//99
Metals and Plastics	Arizona	S	9.17 MW	9.62 AW	20000 AAW	AZBLS	10//99-12//99
Metals and Plastics	Arkansas	S	11.56 MW	11.53 AW	23980 AAW	ARBLS	10//99-12//99
Metals and Plastics	Little Rock-North Little Rock MSA, AR	S	11.86 MW	11.88 AW	24660 AAW	ARBLS	10//99-12//99
Metals and Plastics	California	S	9.05 MW	10.56 AW	21960 AAW	CABLS	10//99-12//99
Metals and Plastics	Los Angeles-Long Beach PMSA, CA	S	11.05 MW	8.73 AW	22980 AAW	CABLS	10//99-12//99
Metals and Plastics	Oakland PMSA, CA	S	9.06 MW	8.32 AW	18840 AAW	CABLS	10//99-12//99

AAW	Average annual wage	AOH	Average offered, high	ASH	Average starting, high	H	Hourly	M	Monthly	S	Special: hourly and annual
AE	Average entry wage	AOL	Average offered, low	ASL	Average starting, low	HI	Highest wage paid	MTC	Median total compensation	TQ	Third quartile wage
AEX	Average experienced wage	APH	Average pay, high range	AW	Average wage paid	HR	High end range	MW	Median wage paid	W	Weekly
AO	Average offered	APL	Average pay, low range	FQ	First quartile wage	LR	Low end range	SQ	Second quartile wage	Y	Yearly

Occupation/Type/Industry	Location	Per	Low	Mid	High	Source	Date
Forging Machine Setter, Operator, and Tender							
Metals and Plastics	Orange County PMSA, CA	S	11.85 MW	10.40 AW	24640 AAW	CABLS	10//99-12//99
Metals and Plastics	Riverside-San Bernardino PMSA, CA	S	12.24 MW	11.98 AW	25450 AAW	CABLS	10//99-12//99
Metals and Plastics	Colorado	S	11.26 MW	10.24 AW	21290 AAW	COBLS	10//99-12//99
Metals and Plastics	Connecticut	S	14.11 MW	12.54 AW	26070 AAW	CTBLS	10//99-12//99
Metals and Plastics	Hartford MSA, CT	S	12.47 MW	14.14 AW	25940 AAW	CTBLS	10//99-12//99
Metals and Plastics	Florida	S	8.85 MW	9.58 AW	19930 AAW	FLBLS	10//99-12//99
Metals and Plastics	Jacksonville MSA, FL	S	11.55 MW	11.92 AW	24030 AAW	FLBLS	10//99-12//99
Metals and Plastics	Lakeland-Winter Haven MSA, FL	S	8.43 MW	8.75 AW	17530 AAW	FLBLS	10//99-12//99
Metals and Plastics	Orlando MSA, FL	S	11.98 MW	10.43 AW	24910 AAW	FLBLS	10//99-12//99
Metals and Plastics	Pensacola MSA, FL	S	10.20 MW	10.06 AW	21220 AAW	FLBLS	10//99-12//99
Metals and Plastics	Georgia	S	9.04 MW	8.82 AW	18350 AAW	GABLS	10//99-12//99
Metals and Plastics	Illinois	S	12.02 MW	11.94 AW	24840 AAW	ILBLS	10//99-12//99
Metals and Plastics	Chicago PMSA, IL	S	12.19 MW	12.14 AW	25360 AAW	ILBLS	10//99-12//99
Metals and Plastics	Indiana	S	9.83 MW	10.74 AW	22340 AAW	INBLS	10//99-12//99
Metals and Plastics	Elkhart-Goshen MSA, IN	S	10.35 MW	10.22 AW	21530 AAW	INBLS	10//99-12//99.
Metals and Plastics	Indianapolis MSA, IN	S	12.98 MW	14.46 AW	27000 AAW	INBLS	10//99-12//99
Metals and Plastics	South Bend MSA, IN	S	9.25 MW	8.17 AW	19240 AAW	INBLS	10//99-12//99
Metals and Plastics	Iowa	S	12.79 MW	12.74 AW	26490 AAW	IABLS	10//99-12//99
Metals and Plastics	Kentucky	S	9.99 MW	9.93 AW	20650 AAW	KYBLS	10//99-12//99
Metals and Plastics	Louisville MSA, KY-IN	S	11.63 MW	11.44 AW	24200 AAW	KYBLS	10//99-12//99
Metals and Plastics	Massachusetts	S	14.44 MW	14.94 AW	31070 AAW	MABLS	10//99-12//99
Metals and Plastics	Boston PMSA, MA-NH	S	15.12 MW	15.33 AW	31440 AAW	MABLS	10//99-12//99
Metals and Plastics	Springfield MSA, MA	S	14.72 MW	12.96 AW	30620 AAW	MABLS	10//99-12//99
Metals and Plastics	Worcester PMSA, MA-CT	S	15.72 MW	15.89 AW	32700 AAW	MABLS	10//99-12//99
Metals and Plastics	Michigan	S	18.36 MW	17.19 AW	35760 AAW	MIBLS	10//99-12//99
Metals and Plastics	Ann Arbor PMSA, MI	S	14.22 MW	10.01 AW	29580 AAW	MIBLS	10//99-12//99
Metals and Plastics	Detroit PMSA, MI	S	19.02 MW	21.53 AW	39570 AAW	MIBLS	10//99-12//99
Metals and Plastics	Flint PMSA, MI	S	24.05 MW	24.38 AW	50030 AAW	MIBLS	10//99-12//99
Metals and Plastics	Grand Rapids-Muskegon-Holland MSA, MI	S	14.39 MW	12.05 AW	29920 AAW	MIBLS	10//99-12//99
Metals and Plastics	Jackson MSA, MI	S	13.12 MW	12.48 AW	27280 AAW	MIBLS	10//99-12//99
Metals and Plastics	Kalamazoo-Battle Creek MSA, MI	S	14.57 MW	10.29 AW	30300 AAW	MIBLS	10//99-12//99
Metals and Plastics	Minnesota	S	9.69 MW	9.85 AW	20490 AAW	MNBLS	10//99-12//99
Metals and Plastics	Minneapolis-St. Paul MSA, MN-WI	S	9.70 MW	9.80 AW	20170 AAW	MNBLS	10//99-12//99
Metals and Plastics	Mississippi	S	8.7 MW	9.15 AW	19020 AAW	MSBLS	10//99-12//99
Metals and Plastics	Jackson MSA, MS	S	7.69 MW	6.34 AW	16000 AAW	MSBLS	10//99-12//99
Metals and Plastics	Missouri	S	11.31 MW	11.44 AW	23790 AAW	MOBLS	10//99-12//99
Metals and Plastics	St. Louis MSA, MO-IL	S	13.93 MW	14.62 AW	28980 AAW	MOBLS	10//99-12//99
Metals and Plastics	Montana	S	8.31 MW	9.21 AW	19160 AAW	MTBLS	10//99-12//99
Metals and Plastics	Nebraska	S	11.17 MW	10.63 AW	22120 AAW	NEBLS	10//99-12//99
Metals and Plastics	New Jersey	S	7.71 MW	9.00 AW	18710 AAW	NJBLS	10//99-12//99
Metals and Plastics	Bergen-Passaic PMSA, NJ	S	7.36 MW	6.65 AW	15310 AAW	NJBLS	10//99-12//99
Metals and Plastics	New York	S	16.4 MW	16.70 AW	34730 AAW	NYBLS	10//99-12//99
Metals and Plastics	New York PMSA, NY	S	8.10 MW	7.58 AW	16840 AAW	NYBLS	10//99-12//99
Metals and Plastics	Rochester MSA, NY	S	11.78 MW	11.08 AW	24500 AAW	NYBLS	10//99-12//99
Metals and Plastics	North Carolina	S	7.82 MW	9.33 AW	19400 AAW	NCBLS	10//99-12//99
Metals and Plastics	Charlotte-Gastonia-Rock Hill MSA, NC-SC	S	12.27 MW	13.50 AW	25520 AAW	NCBLS	10//99-12//99
Metals and Plastics	Greensboro--Winston-Salem--High Point MSA, NC	S	7.52 MW	6.26 AW	15650 AAW	NCBLS	10//99-12//99
Metals and Plastics	Hickory-Morganton-Lenoir MSA, NC	S	8.24 MW	8.05 AW	17140 AAW	NCBLS	10//99-12//99
Metals and Plastics	Ohio	S	12.39 MW	13.27 AW	27610 AAW	OHBLS	10//99-12//99
Metals and Plastics	Canton-Massillon MSA, OH	S	12.28 MW	12.26 AW	25550 AAW	OHBLS	10//99-12//99
Metals and Plastics	Cincinnati PMSA, OH-KY-IN	S	11.92 MW	11.01 AW	24800 AAW	OHBLS	10//99-12//99
Metals and Plastics	Cleveland-Lorain-Elyria PMSA, OH	S	14.86 MW	14.93 AW	30910 AAW	OHBLS	10//99-12//99
Metals and Plastics	Columbus MSA, OH	S	12.53 MW	10.75 AW	26050 AAW	OHBLS	10//99-12//99
Metals and Plastics	Dayton-Springfield MSA, OH	S	11.95 MW	12.11 AW	24850 AAW	OHBLS	10//99-12//99
Metals and Plastics	Toledo MSA, OH	S	17.31 MW	19.53 AW	36000 AAW	OHBLS	10//99-12//99
Metals and Plastics	Youngstown-Warren MSA, OH	S	12.61 MW	10.50 AW	26240 AAW	OHBLS	10//99-12//99
Metals and Plastics	Oklahoma	S	7.55 MW	7.70 AW	16010 AAW	OKBLS	10//99-12//99
Metals and Plastics	Oklahoma City MSA, OK	S	7.94 MW	7.82 AW	16520 AAW	OKBLS	10//99-12//99
Metals and Plastics	Tulsa MSA, OK	S	9.91 MW	8.48 AW	20620 AAW	OKBLS	10//99-12//99
Metals and Plastics	Oregon	S	15.3 MW	14.84 AW	30870 AAW	ORBLS	10//99-12//99

AAW	Average annual wage	AOH	Average offered, high	ASH	Average starting, high	H	Hourly	M	Monthly	S	Special: hourly and annual
AE	Average entry wage	AOL	Average offered, low	ASL	Average starting, low	HI	Highest wage paid	MTC	Median total compensation	TQ	Third quartile wage
AEX	Average experienced wage	APH	Average pay, high range	AW	Average wage paid	HR	High end range	MW	Median wage paid	W	Weekly
AO	Average offered	APL	Average pay, low range	FQ	First quartile wage	LR	Low end range	SQ	Second quartile wage	Y	Yearly

Occupation/Type/Industry	Location	Per	Low	Mid	High	Source	Date
Forging Machine Setter, Operator, and Tender							
Metals and Plastics	Portland-Vancouver PMSA, OR-WA	S	14.39 MW	15.06 AW	29930 AAW	ORBLS	10//99-12//99
Metals and Plastics	Pennsylvania	S	13.76 MW	13.27 AW	27610 AAW	PABLS	10//99-12//99
Metals and Plastics	Allentown-Bethlehem-Easton MSA, PA	S	10.42 MW	10.09 AW	21680 AAW	PABLS	10//99-12//99
Metals and Plastics	Erie MSA, PA	S	11.59 MW	10.82 AW	24120 AAW	PABLS	10//99-12//99
Metals and Plastics	Philadelphia PMSA, PA-NJ	S	9.97 MW	9.36 AW	20740 AAW	PABLS	10//99-12//99
Metals and Plastics	Pittsburgh MSA, PA	S	14.02 MW	14.58 AW	29170 AAW	PABLS	10//99-12//99
Metals and Plastics	Rhode Island	S	10.33 MW	10.85 AW	22560 AAW	RIBLS	10//99-12//99
Metals and Plastics	South Carolina	S	11.97 MW	14.47 AW	30100 AAW	SCBLS	10//99-12//99
Metals and Plastics	Columbia MSA, SC	S	9.15 MW	9.04 AW	19030 AAW	SCBLS	10//99-12//99
Metals and Plastics	Greenville-Spartanburg-Anderson MSA, SC	S	18.41 MW	21.69 AW	38290 AAW	SCBLS	10//99-12//99
Metals and Plastics	South Dakota	S	10.13 MW	10.40 AW	21630 AAW	SDBLS	10//99-12//99
Metals and Plastics	Tennessee	S	10.48 MW	11.76 AW	24460 AAW	TNBLS	10//99-12//99
Metals and Plastics	Knoxville MSA, TN	S	14.36 MW	14.66 AW	29860 AAW	TNBLS	10//99-12//99
Metals and Plastics	Memphis MSA, TN-AR-MS	S	9.61 MW	9.57 AW	19990 AAW	MSBLS	10//99-12//99
Metals and Plastics	Nashville MSA, TN	S	17.43 MW	17.86 AW	36260 AAW	TNBLS	10//99-12//99
Metals and Plastics	Texas	S	10.08 MW	10.59 AW	22020 AAW	TXBLS	10//99-12//99
Metals and Plastics	Dallas PMSA, TX	S	8.74 MW	7.94 AW	18180 AAW	TXBLS	10//99-12//99
Metals and Plastics	Fort Worth-Arlington PMSA, TX	S	12.35 MW	10.49 AW	25690 AAW	TXBLS	10//99-12//99
Metals and Plastics	Houston PMSA, TX	S	13.16 MW	12.44 AW	27380 AAW	TXBLS	10//99-12//99
Metals and Plastics	Utah	S	11.71 MW	11.12 AW	23130 AAW	UTBLS	10//99-12//99
Metals and Plastics	Salt Lake City-Ogden MSA, UT	S	8.09 MW	8.66 AW	16820 AAW	UTBLS	10//99-12//99
Metals and Plastics	Vermont	S	10.22 MW	11.28 AW	23470 AAW	VTBLS	10//99-12//99
Metals and Plastics	Virginia	S	10.77 MW	10.57 AW	21990 AAW	VABLS	10//99-12//99
Metals and Plastics	Norfolk-Virginia Beach-Newport News MSA, VA-NC	S	9.64 MW	10.66 AW	20060 AAW	VABLS	10//99-12//99
Metals and Plastics	Washington	S	11.02 MW	12.32 AW	25630 AAW	WABLS	10//99-12//99
Metals and Plastics	West Virginia	S	9.63 MW	9.51 AW	19780 AAW	WVBLS	10//99-12//99
Metals and Plastics	Wisconsin	S	12.47 MW	14.02 AW	29160 AAW	WIBLS	10//99-12//99
Metals and Plastics	Milwaukee-Waukesha PMSA, WI	S	16.95 MW	19.23 AW	35260 AAW	WIBLS	10//99-12//99
Metals and Plastics	Racine PMSA, WI	S	10.44 MW	9.33 AW	21720 AAW	WIBLS	10//99-12//99
Fork Lift Operator							
Manufacturing	United States	Y		23067 AW		WARD3	1998
Foundry Mold and Coremaker	Alabama	S	9.66 MW	9.91 AW	20610 AAW	ALBLS	10//99-12//99
	Auburn-Opelika MSA, AL	S	12.23 MW	12.18 AW	25440 AAW	ALBLS	10//99-12//99
	Birmingham MSA, AL	S	9.71 MW	9.20 AW	20190 AAW	ALBLS	10//99-12//99
	Arizona	S	9.76 MW	9.69 AW	20160 AAW	AZBLS	10//99-12//99
	Phoenix-Mesa MSA, AZ	S	10.20 MW	10.24 AW	21210 AAW	AZBLS	10//99-12//99
	Arkansas	S	11.85 MW	13.86 AW	28820 AAW	ARBLS	10//99-12//99
	California	S	9.66 MW	10.40 AW	21640 AAW	CABLS	10//99-12//99
	Los Angeles-Long Beach PMSA, CA	S	9.50 MW	9.29 AW	19760 AAW	CABLS	10//99-12//99
	Oakland PMSA, CA	S	15.79 MW	15.57 AW	32840 AAW	CABLS	10//99-12//99
	Riverside-San Bernardino PMSA, CA	S	10.04 MW	8.29 AW	20890 AAW	CABLS	10//99-12//99
	San Diego MSA, CA	S	10.59 MW	10.97 AW	22020 AAW	CABLS	10//99-12//99
	Ventura PMSA, CA	S	9.82 MW	9.79 AW	20430 AAW	CABLS	10//99-12//99
	Colorado	S	12.56 MW	13.04 AW	27130 AAW	COBLS	10//99-12//99
	Denver PMSA, CO	S	12.50 MW	12.39 AW	26000 AAW	COBLS	10//99-12//99
	Connecticut	S	12.91 MW	13.62 AW	28330 AAW	CTBLS	10//99-12//99
	Hartford MSA, CT	S	17.15 MW	16.57 AW	35670 AAW	CTBLS	10//99-12//99
	Florida	S	9.45 MW	9.50 AW	19750 AAW	FLBLS	10//99-12//99
	Tampa-St. Petersburg-Clearwater MSA, FL	S	9.54 MW	8.84 AW	19850 AAW	FLBLS	10//99-12//99
	Georgia	S	13.65 MW	13.95 AW	29010 AAW	GABLS	10//99-12//99
	Atlanta MSA, GA	S	10.31 MW	10.53 AW	21450 AAW	GABLS	10//99-12//99
	Idaho	S	9.71 MW	9.70 AW	20170 AAW	IDBLS	10//99-12//99
	Illinois	S	10.26 MW	10.95 AW	22770 AAW	ILBLS	10//99-12//99
	Chicago PMSA, IL	S	10.19 MW	9.98 AW	21200 AAW	ILBLS	10//99-12//99
	Peoria-Pekin MSA, IL	S	16.81 MW	17.56 AW	34960 AAW	ILBLS	10//99-12//99
	Rockford MSA, IL	S	10.58 MW	10.10 AW	22010 AAW	ILBLS	10//99-12//99
	Indiana	S	12.27 MW	13.10 AW	27250 AAW	INBLS	10//99-12//99

AAW	Average annual wage	AOH	Average offered, high	ASH	Average starting, high
AE	Average entry wage	AOL	Average offered, low	ASL	Average starting, low
AEX	Average experienced wage	APH	Average pay, high range	AW	Average wage paid
AO	Average offered	APL	Average pay, low range	FQ	First quartile wage

H	Hourly	M	Monthly
HI	Highest wage paid	MTC	Median total compensation
HR	High end range	MW	Median wage paid
LR	Low end range	SQ	Second quartile wage

S	Special: hourly and annual
TQ	Third quartile wage
W	Weekly
Y	Yearly

Occupation/Type/Industry	Location	Per	Low	Mid	High	Source	Date
Foundry Mold and Coremaker	Fort Wayne MSA, IN	S	13.05 MW	14.00 AW	27150 AAW	INBLS	10//99-12//99
	Iowa	S	11.77 MW	11.69 AW	24320 AAW	IABLS	10//99-12//99
	Kansas	S	9.99 MW	9.98 AW	20750 AAW	KSBLS	10//99-12//99
	Kentucky	S	8.02 MW	8.48 AW	17650 AAW	KYBLS	10//99-12//99
	Louisville MSA, KY-IN	S	8.60 MW	8.16 AW	17880 AAW	KYBLS	10//99-12//99
	Louisiana	S	14.14 MW	12.40 AW	25800 AAW	LABLS	10//99-12//99
	Massachusetts	S	14.44 MW	15.61 AW	32460 AAW	MABLS	10//99-12//99
	Boston PMSA, MA-NH	S	14.68 MW	14.06 AW	30530 AAW	MABLS	10//99-12//99
	Springfield MSA, MA	S	18.50 MW	22.24 AW	38470 AAW	MABLS	10//99-12//99
	Michigan	S	11.45 MW	11.72 AW	24390 AAW	MIBLS	10//99-12//99
	Benton Harbor MSA, MI	S	9.40 MW	9.44 AW	19550 AAW	MIBLS	10//99-12//99
	Detroit PMSA, MI	S	13.53 MW	13.90 AW	28130 AAW	MIBLS	10//99-12//99
	Grand Rapids-Muskegon-Holland MSA, MI	S	11.44 MW	11.56 AW	23790 AAW	MIBLS	10//99-12//99
	Kalamazoo-Battle Creek MSA, MI	S	10.63 MW	10.21 AW	22110 AAW	MIBLS	10//99-12//99
	Minnesota	S	13.95 MW	14.43 AW	30020 AAW	MNBLS	10//99-12//99
	Minneapolis-St. Paul MSA, MN-WI	S	15.35 MW	14.70 AW	31920 AAW	MNBLS	10//99-12//99
	Mississippi	S	10.9 MW	10.53 AW	21900 AAW	MSBLS	10//99-12//99
	Missouri	S	10.31 MW	10.01 AW	20830 AAW	MOBLS	10//99-12//99
	St. Louis MSA, MO-IL	S	11.05 MW	10.53 AW	22980 AAW	MOBLS	10//99-12//99
	Nebraska	S	17.23 MW	15.78 AW	32820 AAW	NEBLS	10//99-12//99
	New Jersey	S	11.54 MW	11.92 AW	24780 AAW	NJBLS	10//99-12//99
	Newark PMSA, NJ	S	11.85 MW	11.17 AW	24640 AAW	NJBLS	10//99-12//99
	New York	S	9.21 MW	12.16 AW	25290 AAW	NYBLS	10//99-12//99
	Buffalo-Niagara Falls MSA, NY	S	11.51 MW	11.01 AW	23940 AAW	NYBLS	10//99-12//99
	North Carolina	S	12.68 MW	13.22 AW	27490 AAW	NCBLS	10//99-12//99
	Charlotte-Gastonia-Rock Hill MSA, NC-SC	S	15.37 MW	15.25 AW	31970 AAW	NCBLS	10//99-12//99
	Greensboro--Winston-Salem--High Point MSA, NC	S	17.91 MW	18.14 AW	37240 AAW	NCBLS	10//99-12//99
	Hickory-Morganton-Lenoir MSA, NC	S	8.66 MW	8.34 AW	18010 AAW	NCBLS	10//99-12//99
	Akron PMSA, OH	S	11.72 MW	11.68 AW	24380 AAW	OHBLS	10//99-12//99
	Cleveland-Lorain-Elyria PMSA, OH	S	11.03 MW	11.48 AW	22940 AAW	OHBLS	10//99-12//99
	Dayton-Springfield MSA, OH	S	14.03 MW	14.39 AW	29190 AAW	OHBLS	10//99-12//99
	Youngstown-Warren MSA, OH	S	10.72 MW	11.00 AW	22290 AAW	OHBLS	10//99-12//99
	Oklahoma	S	10.16 MW	10.26 AW	21340 AAW	OKBLS	10//99-12//99
	Tulsa MSA, OK	S	10.82 MW	11.09 AW	22510 AAW	OKBLS	10//99-12//99
	Oregon	S	15.35 MW	15.55 AW	32350 AAW	ORBLS	10//99-12//99
	Portland-Vancouver PMSA, OR-WA	S	15.62 MW	15.39 AW	32490 AAW	ORBLS	10//99-12//99
	Pennsylvania	S	11.76 MW	12.08 AW	25130 AAW	PABLS	10//99-12//99
	Erie MSA, PA	S	11.88 MW	12.06 AW	24710 AAW	PABLS	10//99-12//99
	Harrisburg-Lebanon-Carlisle MSA, PA	S	14.94 MW	13.29 AW	31070 AAW	PABLS	10//99-12//99
	Pittsburgh MSA, PA	S	10.88 MW	10.48 AW	22620 AAW	PABLS	10//99-12//99
	Reading MSA, PA	S	11.27 MW	11.58 AW	23440 AAW	PABLS	10//99-12//99
	Providence-Fall River-Warwick MSA, RI-MA	S	12.43 MW	11.64 AW	25840 AAW	RIBLS	10//99-12//99
	South Carolina	S	12.19 MW	12.60 AW	26200 AAW	SCBLS	10//99-12//99
	Tennessee	S	12.11 MW	12.09 AW	25160 AAW	TNBLS	10//99-12//99
	Knoxville MSA, TN	S	10.07 MW	9.95 AW	20940 AAW	TNBLS	10//99-12//99
	Texas	S	8.92 MW	9.40 AW	19540 AAW	TXBLS	10//99-12//99
	Dallas PMSA, TX	S	18.02 MW	19.68 AW	37480 AAW	TXBLS	10//99-12//99
	Fort Worth-Arlington PMSA, TX	S	9.96 MW	7.85 AW	20720 AAW	TXBLS	10//99-12//99
	Houston PMSA, TX	S	10.54 MW	11.18 AW	21920 AAW	TXBLS	10//99-12//99
	Longview-Marshall MSA, TX	S	6.03 MW	6.04 AW	12540 AAW	TXBLS	10//99-12//99
	San Antonio MSA, TX	S	8.86 MW	8.83 AW	18430 AAW	TXBLS	10//99-12//99
	Utah	S	11.96 MW	11.74 AW	24410 AAW	UTBLS	10//99-12//99
	Vermont	S	10.03 MW	11.21 AW	23310 AAW	VTBLS	10//99-12//99
	Washington	S	13.65 MW	13.14 AW	27340 AAW	WABLS	10//99-12//99
	Seattle-Bellevue-Everett PMSA, WA	S	13.62 MW	14.00 AW	28320 AAW	WABLS	10//99-12//99
	Wisconsin	S	11.28 MW	11.13 AW	23150 AAW	WIBLS	10//99-12//99
	Milwaukee-Waukesha PMSA, WI	S	11.15 MW	11.61 AW	23200 AAW	WIBLS	10//99-12//99
	Racine PMSA, WI	S	14.61 MW	12.90 AW	30400 AAW	WIBLS	10//99-12//99

AAW Average annual wage	AOH Average offered, high	ASH Average starting, high	H Hourly	M Monthly	S Special: hourly and annual
AE Average entry wage	AOL Average offered, low	ASL Average starting, low	HI Highest wage paid	MTC Median total compensation	TQ Third quartile wage
AEX Average experienced wage	APH Average pay, high range	AW Average wage paid	HR High end range	MW Median wage paid	W Weekly
AO Average offered	APL Average pay, low range	FQ First quartile wage	LR Low end range	SQ Second quartile wage	Y Yearly

Occupation/Type/Industry	Location	Per	Low	Mid	High	Source	Date
Freight Rate Specialist							
Supply Chain Management	United States	Y		38600 AW		AMSHIP	2000
Funeral Attendant	Alabama	S	6.28 MW	7.42 AW	15440 AAW	ALBLS	10//99-12//99
	Arizona	S	8.11 MW	8.71 AW	18110 AAW	AZBLS	10//99-12//99
	Arkansas	S	6.09 MW	6.47 AW	13450 AAW	ARBLS	10//99-12//99
	California	S	9.32 MW	9.42 AW	19590 AAW	CABLS	10//99-12//99
	Colorado	S	8.27 MW	8.50 AW	17680 AAW	COBLS	10//99-12//99
	Connecticut	S	6.76 MW	8.17 AW	16990 AAW	CTBLS	10//99-12//99
	Delaware	S	6.39 MW	7.47 AW	15540 AAW	DEBLS	10//99-12//99
	Florida	S	8.02 MW	9.22 AW	19190 AAW	FLBLS	10//99-12//99
	Georgia	S	7.61 MW	7.72 AW	16060 AAW	GABLS	10//99-12//99
	Idaho	S	11.52 MW	10.98 AW	22830 AAW	IDBLS	10//99-12//99
	Illinois	S	8.19 MW	8.46 AW	17600 AAW	ILBLS	10//99-12//99
	Indiana	S	7.8 MW	8.22 AW	17100 AAW	INBLS	10//99-12//99
	Iowa	S	7.18 MW	7.61 AW	15830 AAW	IABLS	10//99-12//99
	Kansas	S	6.27 MW	7.04 AW	14640 AAW	KSBLS	10//99-12//99
	Kentucky	S	6.3 MW	7.00 AW	14560 AAW	KYBLS	10//99-12//99
	Louisiana	S	6.13 MW	7.12 AW	14800 AAW	LABLS	10//99-12//99
	Maine	S	8.59 MW	8.65 AW	17990 AAW	MEBLS	10//99-12//99
	Maryland	S	9.56 MW	9.85 AW	20490 AAW	MDBLS	10//99-12//99
	Massachusetts	S	7.62 MW	8.03 AW	16700 AAW	MABLS	10//99-12//99
	Michigan	S	8.1 MW	8.29 AW	17240 AAW	MIBLS	10//99-12//99
	Minnesota	S	7.8 MW	8.68 AW	18050 AAW	MNBLS	10//99-12//99
	Mississippi	S	7.8 MW	7.90 AW	16430 AAW	MSBLS	10//99-12//99
	Missouri	S	7.24 MW	7.31 AW	15210 AAW	MOBLS	10//99-12//99
	Montana	S	7.93 MW	8.44 AW	17550 AAW	MTBLS	10//99-12//99
	Nebraska	S	7.15 MW	8.23 AW	17110 AAW	NEBLS	10//99-12//99
	Nevada	S	9.23 MW	9.76 AW	20310 AAW	NVBLS	10//99-12//99
	New Hampshire	S	9.53 MW	9.51 AW	19790 AAW	NHBLS	10//99-12//99
	New Jersey	S	8.58 MW	9.25 AW	19230 AAW	NJBLS	10//99-12//99
	New Mexico	S	7.37 MW	7.14 AW	14840 AAW	NMBLS	10//99-12//99
	New York	S	6.85 MW	8.36 AW	17380 AAW	NYBLS	10//99-12//99
	North Carolina	S	6.96 MW	7.56 AW	15720 AAW	NCBLS	10//99-12//99
	North Dakota	S	9.52 MW	9.61 AW	19980 AAW	NDBLS	10//99-12//99
	Ohio	S	8.08 MW	8.92 AW	18560 AAW	OHBLS	10//99-12//99
	Oklahoma	S	6.69 MW	7.88 AW	16390 AAW	OKBLS	10//99-12//99
	Pennsylvania	S	7.55 MW	8.20 AW	17050 AAW	PABLS	10//99-12//99
	Rhode Island	S	12.58 MW	11.74 AW	24410 AAW	RIBLS	10//99-12//99
	South Carolina	S	7.53 MW	8.18 AW	17020 AAW	SCBLS	10//99-12//99
	South Dakota	S	7.18 MW	7.07 AW	14710 AAW	SDBLS	10//99-12//99
	Tennessee	S	7.75 MW	7.98 AW	16600 AAW	TNBLS	10//99-12//99
	Texas	S	6.58 MW	7.98 AW	16600 AAW	TXBLS	10//99-12//99
	Vermont	S	7.81 MW	10.05 AW	20910 AAW	VTBLS	10//99-12//99
	Virginia	S	8.45 MW	8.76 AW	18210 AAW	VABLS	10//99-12//99
	Washington	S	12.4 MW	13.17 AW	27400 AAW	WABLS	10//99-12//99
	West Virginia	S	6.39 MW	7.26 AW	15100 AAW	WVBLS	10//99-12//99
	Wisconsin	S	6.94 MW	7.61 AW	15820 AAW	WIBLS	10//99-12//99
	Puerto Rico	S	6.16 MW	6.09 AW	12660 AAW	PRBLS	10//99-12//99
Funeral Director	United States	Y		37000 AW		NYT1	1999
	Alabama	S	11.11 MW	11.66 AW	24240 AAW	ALBLS	10//99-12//99
	Arizona	S	16.61 MW	17.01 AW	35370 AAW	AZBLS	10//99-12//99
	Phoenix-Mesa MSA, AZ	S	18.21 MW	17.38 AW	37880 AAW	AZBLS	10//99-12//99
	Arkansas	S	11.28 MW	13.17 AW	27400 AAW	ARBLS	10//99-12//99
	California	S	17.93 MW	20.45 AW	42530 AAW	CABLS	10//99-12//99
	Fresno MSA, CA	S	19.82 MW	16.31 AW	41230 AAW	CABLS	10//99-12//99
	Los Angeles-Long Beach PMSA, CA	S	20.53 MW	16.84 AW	42710 AAW	CABLS	10//99-12//99
	Merced MSA, CA	S	16.65 MW	15.13 AW	34630 AAW	CABLS	10//99-12//99
	Oakland PMSA, CA	S	21.47 MW	19.57 AW	44660 AAW	CABLS	10//99-12//99
	Riverside-San Bernardino PMSA, CA	S	18.58 MW	18.51 AW	38640 AAW	CABLS	10//99-12//99
	Sacramento PMSA, CA	S	19.17 MW	15.56 AW	39880 AAW	CABLS	10//99-12//99
	San Diego MSA, CA	S	24.76 MW	26.51 AW	51510 AAW	CABLS	10//99-12//99
	San Francisco PMSA, CA	S	19.97 MW	19.14 AW	41530 AAW	CABLS	10//99-12//99
	Santa Barbara-Santa Maria-Lompoc MSA, CA	S	34.60 MW	31.03 AW	71960 AAW	CABLS	10//99-12//99
	Santa Cruz-Watsonville PMSA, CA	S	20.47 MW	22.45 AW	42580 AAW	CABLS	10//99-12//99
	Santa Rosa PMSA, CA	S	19.46 MW	19.31 AW	40480 AAW	CABLS	10//99-12//99
	Vallejo-Fairfield-Napa PMSA, CA	S	17.09 MW	16.05 AW	35540 AAW	CABLS	10//99-12//99

AAW	Average annual wage	AOH	Average offered, high	ASH	Average starting, high	H	Hourly			M	Monthly			S	Special: hourly and annual
AE	Average entry wage	AOL	Average offered, low	ASL	Average starting, low	HI	Highest wage paid			MTC	Median total compensation	TQ	Third quartile wage
AEX	Average experienced wage	APH	Average pay, high range	AW	Average wage paid	HR	High end range			MW	Median wage paid	W	Weekly
AO	Average offered	APL	Average pay, low range	FQ	First quartile wage	LR	Low end range			SQ	Second quartile wage	Y	Yearly

Occupation/Type/Industry	Location	Per	Low	Mid	High	Source	Date
Funeral Director	Visalia-Tulare-Porterville MSA, CA	S	28.59 MW	18.94 AW	59470 AAW	CABLS	10//99-12//99
	Colorado	S	13.42 MW	15.27 AW	31770 AAW	COBLS	10//99-12//99
	Fort Collins-Loveland MSA, CO	S	17.64 MW	13.72 AW	36690 AAW	COBLS	10//99-12//99
	Greeley PMSA, CO	S	16.15 MW	13.33 AW	33590 AAW	COBLS	10//99-12//99
	Connecticut	S	19.48 MW	29.09 AW	60510 AAW	CTBLS	10//99-12//99
	Hartford MSA, CT	S	24.32 MW	18.45 AW	50580 AAW	CTBLS	10//99-12//99
	Delaware	S	23.89 MW	24.76 AW	51500 AAW	DEBLS	10//99-12//99
	Wilmington-Newark PMSA, DE-MD	S	24.63 MW	21.33 AW	51240 AAW	DEBLS	10//99-12//99
	Washington PMSA, DC-MD-VA-WV	S	19.06 MW	17.20 AW	39650 AAW	DCBLS	10//99-12//99
	Florida	S	15.31 MW	15.71 AW	32670 AAW	FLBLS	10//99-12//99
	Daytona Beach MSA, FL	S	21.89 MW	17.93 AW	45540 AAW	FLBLS	10//99-12//99
	Jacksonville MSA, FL	S	15.66 MW	14.69 AW	32570 AAW	FLBLS	10//99-12//99
	Miami PMSA, FL	S	16.60 MW	15.61 AW	34530 AAW	FLBLS	10//99-12//99
	Orlando MSA, FL	S	20.12 MW	17.40 AW	41840 AAW	FLBLS	10//99-12//99
	Pensacola MSA, FL	S	17.22 MW	17.36 AW	35820 AAW	FLBLS	10//99-12//99
	Sarasota-Bradenton MSA, FL	S	17.67 MW	16.71 AW	36750 AAW	FLBLS	10//99-12//99
	Tampa-St. Petersburg-Clearwater MSA, FL	S	14.42 MW	12.34 AW	29990 AAW	FLBLS	10//99-12//99
	Georgia	S	16.86 MW	18.33 AW	38130 AAW	GABLS	10//99-12//99
	Augusta-Aiken MSA, GA-SC	S	15.74 MW	14.48 AW	32730 AAW	GABLS	10//99-12//99
	Macon MSA, GA	S	21.95 MW	21.07 AW	45660 AAW	GABLS	10//99-12//99
	Illinois	S	22.08 MW	27.61 AW	57420 AAW	ILBLS	10//99-12//99
	Chicago PMSA, IL	S	26.86 MW	24.10 AW	55860 AAW	ILBLS	10//99-12//99
	Decatur MSA, IL	S	25.87 MW	19.70 AW	53810 AAW	ILBLS	10//99-12//99
	Rockford MSA, IL	S	40.14 MW	37.47 AW	83480 AAW	ILBLS	10//99-12//99
	Indiana	S	15.57 MW	18.68 AW	38860 AAW	INBLS	10//99-12//99
	Evansville-Henderson MSA, IN-KY	S	17.99 MW	14.41 AW	37410 AAW	INBLS	10//99-12//99
	Gary PMSA, IN	S	16.56 MW	15.24 AW	34450 AAW	INBLS	10//99-12//99
	Indianapolis MSA, IN	S	16.15 MW	17.28 AW	33590 AAW	INBLS	10//99-12//99
	South Bend MSA, IN	S	22.54 MW	23.17 AW	46870 AAW	INBLS	10//99-12//99
	Iowa	S	19.75 MW	27.01 AW	56170 AAW	IABLS	10//99-12//99
	Cedar Rapids MSA, IA	S	18.16 MW	15.99 AW	37780 AAW	IABLS	10//99-12//99
	Davenport-Moline-Rock Island MSA, IA-IL	S	23.10 MW	19.89 AW	48060 AAW	IABLS	10//99-12//99
	Des Moines MSA, IA	S	17.40 MW	15.53 AW	36190 AAW	IABLS	10//99-12//99
	Kansas	S	14.65 MW	13.08 AW	27210 AAW	KSBLS	10//99-12//99
	Kentucky	S	16.51 MW	17.22 AW	35810 AAW	KYBLS	10//99-12//99
	Lexington MSA, KY	S	17.62 MW	14.19 AW	36650 AAW	KYBLS	10//99-12//99
	Louisville MSA, KY-IN	S	15.43 MW	9.80 AW	32100 AAW	KYBLS	10//99-12//99
	Louisiana	S	15.14 MW	15.64 AW	32520 AAW	LABLS	10//99-12//99
	Baton Rouge MSA, LA	S	16.26 MW	14.89 AW	33830 AAW	LABLS	10//99-12//99
	Houma MSA, LA	S	13.32 MW	13.33 AW	27710 AAW	LABLS	10//99-12//99
	New Orleans MSA, LA	S	15.90 MW	15.95 AW	33080 AAW	LABLS	10//99-12//99
	Shreveport-Bossier City MSA, LA	S	14.25 MW	13.63 AW	29640 AAW	LABLS	10//99-12//99
	Maine	S	19.06 MW	20.12 AW	41850 AAW	MEBLS	10//99-12//99
	Maryland	S	18.89 MW	21.17 AW	44030 AAW	MDBLS	10//99-12//99
	Baltimore PMSA, MD	S	23.13 MW	20.22 AW	48110 AAW	MDBLS	10//99-12//99
	Massachusetts	S	25.99 MW	26.79 AW	55730 AAW	MABLS	10//99-12//99
	Boston PMSA, MA-NH	S	24.90 MW	21.79 AW	51800 AAW	MABLS	10//99-12//99
	Brockton PMSA, MA	S	34.98 MW	32.38 AW	72760 AAW	MABLS	10//99-12//99
	Lawrence PMSA, MA-NH	S	24.53 MW	21.94 AW	51020 AAW	MABLS	10//99-12//99
	Lowell PMSA, MA-NH	S	18.34 MW	13.11 AW	38140 AAW	MABLS	10//99-12//99
	New Bedford PMSA, MA	S	37.71 MW	39.54 AW	78440 AAW	MABLS	10//99-12//99
	Springfield MSA, MA	S	29.74 MW	26.65 AW	61860 AAW	MABLS	10//99-12//99
	Worcester PMSA, MA-CT	S	29.91 MW	32.79 AW	62200 AAW	MABLS	10//99-12//99
	Michigan	S	19.71 MW	22.95 AW	47740 AAW	MIBLS	10//99-12//99
	Detroit PMSA, MI	S	22.71 MW	17.83 AW	47240 AAW	MIBLS	10//99-12//99
	Flint PMSA, MI	S	29.16 MW	25.41 AW	60660 AAW	MIBLS	10//99-12//99
	Grand Rapids-Muskegon-Holland MSA, MI	S	25.51 MW	21.72 AW	53060 AAW	MIBLS	10//99-12//99
	Kalamazoo-Battle Creek MSA, MI	S	21.73 MW	21.55 AW	45190 AAW	MIBLS	10//99-12//99
	Lansing-East Lansing MSA, MI	S	20.76 MW	19.79 AW	43190 AAW	MIBLS	10//99-12//99
	Saginaw-Bay City-Midland MSA, MI	S	27.10 MW	23.80 AW	56370 AAW	MIBLS	10//99-12//99
	Minnesota	S	17.45 MW	20.03 AW	41660 AAW	MNBLS	10//99-12//99

Funeral Director

Occupation/Type/Industry	Location	Per	Low	Mid	High	Source	Date
Funeral Director	Duluth-Superior MSA, MN-WI	S	18.45 MW	17.54 AW	38370 AAW	MNBLS	10//99-12//99
	Minneapolis-St. Paul MSA, MN-WI	S	22.34 MW	19.51 AW	46470 AAW	MNBLS	10//99-12//99
	St. Cloud MSA, MN	S	26.35 MW	25.84 AW	54810 AAW	MNBLS	10//99-12//99
	Mississippi	S	13.83 MW	14.73 AW	30630 AAW	MSBLS	10//99-12//99
	Hattiesburg MSA, MS	S	16.38 MW	15.31 AW	34060 AAW	MSBLS	10//99-12//99
	Jackson MSA, MS	S	15.24 MW	14.37 AW	31690 AAW	MSBLS	10//99-12//99
	Missouri	S	11.85 MW	14.71 AW	30600 AAW	MOBLS	10//99-12//99
	Kansas City MSA, MO-KS	S	18.81 MW	14.64 AW	39120 AAW	MOBLS	10//99-12//99
	St. Louis MSA, MO-IL	S	16.11 MW	14.15 AW	33510 AAW	MOBLS	10//99-12//99
	Nebraska	S	20.04 MW	22.84 AW	47500 AAW	NEBLS	10//99-12//99
	Omaha MSA, NE-IA	S	23.56 MW	20.29 AW	49000 AAW	NEBLS	10//99-12//99
	Nevada	S	17.62 MW	16.94 AW	35240 AAW	NVBLS	10//99-12//99
	Las Vegas MSA, NV-AZ	S	13.15 MW	11.71 AW	27360 AAW	NVBLS	10//99-12//99
	New Hampshire	S	21.31 MW	24.46 AW	50880 AAW	NHBLS	10//99-12//99
	New Jersey	S	25.11 MW	31.01 AW	64490 AAW	NJBLS	10//99-12//99
	Atlantic-Cape May PMSA, NJ	S	26.56 MW	25.50 AW	55240 AAW	NJBLS	10//99-12//99
	Bergen-Passaic PMSA, NJ	S	32.82 MW	24.29 AW	68270 AAW	NJBLS	10//99-12//99
	Jersey City PMSA, NJ	S	34.23 MW	35.12 AW	71200 AAW	NJBLS	10//99-12//99
	Monmouth-Ocean PMSA, NJ	S	29.31 MW	30.78 AW	60970 AAW	NJBLS	10//99-12//99
	Newark PMSA, NJ	S	31.23 MW	20.18 AW	64950 AAW	NJBLS	10//99-12//99
	New Mexico	S	17.59 MW	17.72 AW	36850 AAW	NMBLS	10//99-12//99
	New York	S	21.72 MW	24.50 AW	50960 AAW	NYBLS	10//99-12//99
	Binghamton MSA, NY	S	19.66 MW	21.80 AW	40890 AAW	NYBLS	10//99-12//99
	Buffalo-Niagara Falls MSA, NY	S	19.61 MW	16.08 AW	40780 AAW	NYBLS	10//99-12//99
	Dutchess County PMSA, NY	S	31.92 MW	25.33 AW	66380 AAW	NYBLS	10//99-12//99
	Jamestown MSA, NY	S	19.49 MW	20.59 AW	40550 AAW	NYBLS	10//99-12//99
	New York PMSA, NY	S	26.35 MW	23.17 AW	54810 AAW	NYBLS	10//99-12//99
	Newburgh PMSA, NY-PA	S	22.15 MW	23.09 AW	46070 AAW	NYBLS	10//99-12//99
	Rochester MSA, NY	S	25.54 MW	21.04 AW	53130 AAW	NYBLS	10//99-12//99
	Syracuse MSA, NY	S	22.99 MW	16.31 AW	47810 AAW	NYBLS	10//99-12//99
	Utica-Rome MSA, NY	S	20.95 MW	19.50 AW	43570 AAW	NYBLS	10//99-12//99
	North Carolina	S	16.21 MW	17.76 AW	36940 AAW	NCBLS	10//99-12//99
	Charlotte-Gastonia-Rock Hill MSA, NC-SC	S	15.49 MW	15.12 AW	32210 AAW	NCBLS	10//99-12//99
	Fayetteville MSA, NC	S	13.45 MW	13.22 AW	27980 AAW	NCBLS	10//99-12//99
	Jacksonville MSA, NC	S	13.62 MW	11.45 AW	28330 AAW	NCBLS	10//99-12//99
	Raleigh-Durham-Chapel Hill MSA, NC	S	18.80 MW	17.04 AW	39110 AAW	NCBLS	10//99-12//99
	Rocky Mount MSA, NC	S	14.67 MW	14.01 AW	30510 AAW	NCBLS	10//99-12//99
	North Dakota	S	23.28 MW	23.19 AW	48230 AAW	NDBLS	10//99-12//99
	Ohio	S	19.64 MW	24.19 AW	50320 AAW	OHBLS	10//99-12//99
	Akron PMSA, OH	S	24.17 MW	20.96 AW	50270 AAW	OHBLS	10//99-12//99
	Columbus MSA, OH	S	15.79 MW	15.97 AW	32840 AAW	OHBLS	10//99-12//99
	Dayton-Springfield MSA, OH	S	28.29 MW	26.36 AW	58850 AAW	OHBLS	10//99-12//99
	Hamilton-Middletown PMSA, OH	S	19.64 MW	13.84 AW	40850 AAW	OHBLS	10//99-12//99
	Lima MSA, OH	S	18.55 MW	13.93 AW	38580 AAW	OHBLS	10//99-12//99
	Oklahoma	S	12.33 MW	14.15 AW	29420 AAW	OKBLS	10//99-12//99
	Lawton MSA, OK	S	18.29 MW	18.25 AW	38040 AAW	OKBLS	10//99-12//99
	Oklahoma City MSA, OK	S	12.85 MW	10.53 AW	26720 AAW	OKBLS	10//99-12//99
	Tulsa MSA, OK	S	14.86 MW	13.30 AW	30900 AAW	OKBLS	10//99-12//99
	Oregon	S	18.9 MW	19.96 AW	41510 AAW	ORBLS	10//99-12//99
	Salem PMSA, OR	S	21.12 MW	17.02 AW	43930 AAW	ORBLS	10//99-12//99
	Pennsylvania	S	23.16 MW	24.17 AW	50270 AAW	PABLS	10//99-12//99
	Allentown-Bethlehem-Easton MSA, PA	S	25.72 MW	24.19 AW	53500 AAW	PABLS	10//99-12//99
	Erie MSA, PA	S	22.37 MW	18.94 AW	46530 AAW	PABLS	10//99-12//99
	Harrisburg-Lebanon-Carlisle MSA, PA	S	23.92 MW	23.68 AW	49750 AAW	PABLS	10//99-12//99
	Lancaster MSA, PA	S	17.88 MW	17.70 AW	37190 AAW	PABLS	10//99-12//99
	Philadelphia PMSA, PA-NJ	S	27.77 MW	23.43 AW	57760 AAW	PABLS	10//99-12//99
	Pittsburgh MSA, PA	S	28.08 MW	31.95 AW	58410 AAW	PABLS	10//99-12//99
	Reading MSA, PA	S	25.82 MW	25.88 AW	53700 AAW	PABLS	10//99-12//99
	Scranton--Wilkes-Barre--Hazleton MSA, PA	S	15.29 MW	13.83 AW	31810 AAW	PABLS	10//99-12//99
	Sharon MSA, PA	S	13.79 MW	12.70 AW	28690 AAW	PABLS	10//99-12//99
	York MSA, PA	S	21.71 MW	19.48 AW	45160 AAW	PABLS	10//99-12//99
	Rhode Island	S	21.5 MW	21.51 AW	44750 AAW	RIBLS	10//99-12//99
	Providence-Fall River-Warwick MSA, RI-MA	S	22.60 MW	21.98 AW	47000 AAW	RIBLS	10//99-12//99

AAW Average annual wage	AOH Average offered, high	ASH Average starting, high	H Hourly	M Monthly	S Special: hourly and annual
AE Average entry wage	AOL Average offered, low	ASL Average starting, low	HI Highest wage paid	MTC Median total compensation	TQ Third quartile wage
AEX Average experienced wage	APH Average pay, high range	AW Average wage paid	HR High end range	MW Median wage paid	W Weekly
AO Average offered	APL Average pay, low range	FQ First quartile wage	LR Low end range	SQ Second quartile wage	Y Yearly

677

Occupation/Type/Industry	Location	Per	Low	Mid	High	Source	Date
Funeral Director	South Carolina	S	17.88 MW	18.59 AW	38660 AAW	SCBLS	10//99-12//99
	Charleston-North Charleston MSA, SC	S	12.63 MW	11.04 AW	26270 AAW	SCBLS	10//99-12//99
	Columbia MSA, SC	S	16.25 MW	13.05 AW	33810 AAW	SCBLS	10//99-12//99
	Florence MSA, SC	S	15.62 MW	17.85 AW	32500 AAW	SCBLS	10//99-12//99
	Greenville-Spartanburg-Anderson MSA, SC	S	21.53 MW	20.23 AW	44790 AAW	SCBLS	10//99-12//99
	Myrtle Beach MSA, SC	S	29.95 MW	23.55 AW	62300 AAW	SCBLS	10//99-12//99
	Sumter MSA, SC	S	17.50 MW	12.81 AW	36400 AAW	SCBLS	10//99-12//99
	South Dakota	S	18.55 MW	19.02 AW	39550 AAW	SDBLS	10//99-12//99
	Tennessee	S	10.67 MW	12.80 AW	26620 AAW	TNBLS	10//99-12//99
	Chattanooga MSA, TN-GA	S	14.90 MW	14.12 AW	30980 AAW	TNBLS	10//99-12//99
	Clarksville-Hopkinsville MSA, TN-KY	S	15.40 MW	14.81 AW	32030 AAW	TNBLS	10//99-12//99
	Johnson City-Kingsport-Bristol MSA, TN-VA	S	14.89 MW	13.51 AW	30970 AAW	TNBLS	10//99-12//99
	Knoxville MSA, TN	S	15.96 MW	14.15 AW	33190 AAW	TNBLS	10//99-12//99
	Memphis MSA, TN-AR-MS	S	14.89 MW	14.20 AW	30960 AAW	MSBLS	10//99-12//99
	Nashville MSA, TN	S	13.28 MW	12.60 AW	27630 AAW	TNBLS	10//99-12//99
	Texas	S	15.78 MW	17.34 AW	36060 AAW	TXBLS	10//99-12//99
	Austin-San Marcos MSA, TX	S	20.94 MW	18.62 AW	43550 AAW	TXBLS	10//99-12//99
	Beaumont-Port Arthur MSA, TX	S	23.75 MW	20.76 AW	49400 AAW	TXBLS	10//99-12//99
	Brownsville-Harlingen-San Benito MSA, TX	S	15.98 MW	15.90 AW	33250 AAW	TXBLS	10//99-12//99
	Corpus Christi MSA, TX	S	16.95 MW	17.31 AW	35250 AAW	TXBLS	10//99-12//99
	Dallas PMSA, TX	S	22.90 MW	21.86 AW	47620 AAW	TXBLS	10//99-12//99
	Fort Worth-Arlington PMSA, TX	S	17.03 MW	15.95 AW	35410 AAW	TXBLS	10//99-12//99
	Galveston-Texas City PMSA, TX	S	16.18 MW	15.18 AW	33660 AAW	TXBLS	10//99-12//99
	Houston PMSA, TX	S	16.46 MW	15.85 AW	34230 AAW	TXBLS	10//99-12//99
	Killeen-Temple MSA, TX	S	15.80 MW	15.96 AW	32860 AAW	TXBLS	10//99-12//99
	Lubbock MSA, TX	S	13.71 MW	12.93 AW	28520 AAW	TXBLS	10//99-12//99
	McAllen-Edinburg-Mission MSA, TX	S	12.46 MW	10.91 AW	25920 AAW	TXBLS	10//99-12//99
	San Antonio MSA, TX	S	16.85 MW	15.37 AW	35040 AAW	TXBLS	10//99-12//99
	Sherman-Denison MSA, TX	S	16.85 MW	16.88 AW	35040 AAW	TXBLS	10//99-12//99
	Wichita Falls MSA, TX	S	17.80 MW	18.00 AW	37010 AAW	TXBLS	10//99-12//99
	Vermont	S	19.13 MW	19.57 AW	40710 AAW	VTBLS	10//99-12//99
	Virginia	S	15.15 MW	17.74 AW	36910 AAW	VABLS	10//99-12//99
	Charlottesville MSA, VA	S	14.31 MW	12.20 AW	29770 AAW	VABLS	10//99-12//99
	Lynchburg MSA, VA	S	17.70 MW	13.13 AW	36810 AAW	VABLS	10//99-12//99
	Richmond-Petersburg MSA, VA	S	25.27 MW	22.89 AW	52560 AAW	VABLS	10//99-12//99
	Washington	S	17.29 MW	17.81 AW	37040 AAW	WABLS	10//99-12//99
	Tacoma PMSA, WA	S	22.36 MW	21.14 AW	46510 AAW	WABLS	10//99-12//99
	West Virginia	S	17.23 MW	18.69 AW	38870 AAW	WVBLS	10//99-12//99
	Huntington-Ashland MSA, WV-KY-OH	S	14.56 MW	14.64 AW	30280 AAW	WVBLS	10//99-12//99
	Wheeling MSA, WV-OH	S	19.18 MW	18.79 AW	39890 AAW	WVBLS	10//99-12//99
	Wisconsin	S	23.76 MW	23.75 AW	49410 AAW	WIBLS	10//99-12//99
	Janesville-Beloit MSA, WI	S	22.90 MW	22.42 AW	47640 AAW	WIBLS	10//99-12//99
	Milwaukee-Waukesha PMSA, WI	S	23.68 MW	27.42 AW	49250 AAW	WIBLS	10//99-12//99
	Racine PMSA, WI	S	35.53 MW	36.44 AW	73890 AAW	WIBLS	10//99-12//99
	Puerto Rico	S	8.01 MW	8.78 AW	18260 AAW	PRBLS	10//99-12//99
	San Juan-Bayamon PMSA, PR	S	9.09 MW	8.40 AW	18910 AAW	PRBLS	10//99-12//99
Funeral Parlor Attendant	Louisville, KY	Y		32000 AW		LOUMAG	1999-2000
Furnace, Kiln, Oven, Drier, and Kettle Operator and Tender	Alabama	S	12.55 MW	12.95 AW	26940 AAW	ALBLS	10//99-12//99
	Birmingham MSA, AL	S	13.41 MW	12.50 AW	27890 AAW	ALBLS	10//99-12//99
	Florence MSA, AL	S	9.84 MW	9.86 AW	20460 AAW	ALBLS	10//99-12//99
	Montgomery MSA, AL	S	8.99 MW	9.31 AW	18710 AAW	ALBLS	10//99-12//99
	Arizona	S	11.5 MW	12.14 AW	25240 AAW	AZBLS	10//99-12//99
	Phoenix-Mesa MSA, AZ	S	12.62 MW	12.32 AW	26240 AAW	AZBLS	10//99-12//99
	Arkansas	S	11.19 MW	11.43 AW	23780 AAW	ARBLS	10//99-12//99
	California	S	13.47 MW	14.39 AW	29940 AAW	CABLS	10//99-12//99
	Oakland PMSA, CA	S	14.78 MW	14.83 AW	30750 AAW	CABLS	10//99-12//99
	Orange County PMSA, CA	S	10.87 MW	10.75 AW	22620 AAW	CABLS	10//99-12//99

AAW	Average annual wage	AOH	Average offered, high	ASH	Average starting, high	H	Hourly	M	Monthly	S	Special: hourly and annual
AE	Average entry wage	AOL	Average offered, low	ASL	Average starting, low	HI	Highest wage paid	MTC	Median total compensation	TQ	Third quartile wage
AEX	Average experienced wage	APH	Average pay, high range	AW	Average wage paid	HR	High end range	MW	Median wage paid	W	Weekly
AO	Average offered	APL	Average pay, low range	FQ	First quartile wage	LR	Low end range	SQ	Second quartile wage	Y	Yearly

Occupation/Type/Industry	Location	Per	Low	Mid	High	Source	Date
Furnace, Kiln, Oven, Drier, and Kettle Operator and Tender	Riverside-San Bernardino PMSA, CA	s	13.83 mw	14.14 aw	28770 aaw	CABLS	10//99-12//99
	San Francisco PMSA, CA	s	15.51 mw	15.15 aw	32260 aaw	CABLS	10//99-12//99
	Ventura PMSA, CA	s	8.00 mw	6.95 aw	16650 aaw	CABLS	10//99-12//99
	Colorado	s	10.22 mw	11.66 aw	24260 aaw	COBLS	10//99-12//99
	Denver PMSA, CO	s	11.65 mw	10.67 aw	24230 aaw	COBLS	10//99-12//99
	Connecticut	s	12.86 mw	14.03 aw	29190 aaw	CTBLS	10//99-12//99
	Hartford MSA, CT	s	13.75 mw	12.34 aw	28590 aaw	CTBLS	10//99-12//99
	Washington PMSA, DC-MD-VA-WV	s	12.58 mw	12.16 aw	26160 aaw	DCBLS	10//99-12//99
	Florida	s	10.19 mw	10.84 aw	22540 aaw	FLBLS	10//99-12//99
	Lakeland-Winter Haven MSA, FL	s	12.12 mw	10.39 aw	25200 aaw	FLBLS	10//99-12//99
	Miami PMSA, FL	s	10.89 mw	10.82 aw	22650 aaw	FLBLS	10//99-12//99
	Tampa-St. Petersburg-Clearwater MSA, FL	s	11.62 mw	10.89 aw	24180 aaw	FLBLS	10//99-12//99
	Georgia	s	10.04 mw	11.10 aw	23080 aaw	GABLS	10//99-12//99
	Albany MSA, GA	s	10.48 mw	9.93 aw	21800 aaw	GABLS	10//99-12//99
	Atlanta MSA, GA	s	11.86 mw	11.01 aw	24660 aaw	GABLS	10//99-12//99
	Augusta-Aiken MSA, GA-SC	s	15.84 mw	15.68 aw	32940 aaw	GABLS	10//99-12//99
	Idaho	s	14.89 mw	14.91 aw	31020 aaw	IDBLS	10//99-12//99
	Illinois	s	13.8 mw	13.97 aw	29050 aaw	ILBLS	10//99-12//99
	Chicago PMSA, IL	s	13.48 mw	12.75 aw	28030 aaw	ILBLS	10//99-12//99
	Indiana	s	12.54 mw	13.58 aw	28240 aaw	INBLS	10//99-12//99
	Fort Wayne MSA, IN	s	15.34 mw	16.98 aw	31900 aaw	INBLS	10//99-12//99
	Gary PMSA, IN	s	13.13 mw	12.82 aw	27310 aaw	INBLS	10//99-12//99
	Indianapolis MSA, IN	s	13.82 mw	11.79 aw	28750 aaw	INBLS	10//99-12//99
	Terre Haute MSA, IN	s	11.85 mw	11.46 aw	24640 aaw	INBLS	10//99-12//99
	Iowa	s	12.09 mw	11.64 aw	24210 aaw	IABLS	10//99-12//99
	Kansas	s	13.89 mw	14.00 aw	29110 aaw	KSBLS	10//99-12//99
	Kentucky	s	13.57 mw	14.49 aw	30140 aaw	KYBLS	10//99-12//99
	Lexington MSA, KY	s	16.94 mw	18.18 aw	35230 aaw	KYBLS	10//99-12//99
	Louisville MSA, KY-IN	s	11.00 mw	11.17 aw	22880 aaw	KYBLS	10//99-12//99
	Louisiana	s	13.02 mw	16.89 aw	35120 aaw	LABLS	10//99-12//99
	Maine	s	10.99 mw	12.20 aw	25370 aaw	MEBLS	10//99-12//99
	Maryland	s	14.22 mw	14.33 aw	29810 aaw	MDBLS	10//99-12//99
	Baltimore PMSA, MD	s	14.07 mw	13.57 aw	29260 aaw	MDBLS	10//99-12//99
	Massachusetts	s	12.95 mw	13.42 aw	27920 aaw	MABLS	10//99-12//99
	Boston PMSA, MA-NH	s	15.31 mw	15.49 aw	31850 aaw	MABLS	10//99-12//99
	Worcester PMSA, MA-CT	s	12.11 mw	11.42 aw	25180 aaw	MABLS	10//99-12//99
	Michigan	s	13.42 mw	14.50 aw	30150 aaw	MIBLS	10//99-12//99
	Detroit PMSA, MI	s	17.37 mw	16.67 aw	36120 aaw	MIBLS	10//99-12//99
	Grand Rapids-Muskegon-Holland MSA, MI	s	16.29 mw	15.64 aw	33880 aaw	MIBLS	10//99-12//99
	Jackson MSA, MI	s	13.29 mw	13.47 aw	27640 aaw	MIBLS	10//99-12//99
	Minnesota	s	18.25 mw	17.88 aw	37190 aaw	MNBLS	10//99-12//99
	Duluth-Superior MSA, MN-WI	s	18.48 mw	18.82 aw	38440 aaw	MNBLS	10//99-12//99
	Minneapolis-St. Paul MSA, MN-WI	s	19.25 mw	20.67 aw	40050 aaw	MNBLS	10//99-12//99
	Mississippi	s	10.41 mw	10.96 aw	22800 aaw	MSBLS	10//99-12//99
	Jackson MSA, MS	s	9.16 mw	9.19 aw	19040 aaw	MSBLS	10//99-12//99
	Missouri	s	12.35 mw	12.58 aw	26160 aaw	MOBLS	10//99-12//99
	St. Louis MSA, MO-IL	s	14.12 mw	13.63 aw	29370 aaw	MOBLS	10//99-12//99
	Montana	s	11.23 mw	11.89 aw	24730 aaw	MTBLS	10//99-12//99
	Nebraska	s	12.96 mw	13.35 aw	27760 aaw	NEBLS	10//99-12//99
	Nevada	s	18.14 mw	17.62 aw	36650 aaw	NVBLS	10//99-12//99
	Las Vegas MSA, NV-AZ	s	16.67 mw	17.46 aw	34670 aaw	NVBLS	10//99-12//99
	New Hampshire	s	11.4 mw	12.01 aw	24980 aaw	NHBLS	10//99-12//99
	New Jersey	s	15.25 mw	16.21 aw	33720 aaw	NJBLS	10//99-12//99
	Bergen-Passaic PMSA, NJ	s	14.81 mw	14.92 aw	30800 aaw	NJBLS	10//99-12//99
	Middlesex-Somerset-Hunterdon PMSA, NJ	s	17.71 mw	16.08 aw	36830 aaw	NJBLS	10//99-12//99
	Newark PMSA, NJ	s	13.63 mw	13.71 aw	28360 aaw	NJBLS	10//99-12//99
	Trenton PMSA, NJ	s	14.97 mw	14.95 aw	31140 aaw	NJBLS	10//99-12//99
	Vineland-Millville-Bridgeton PMSA, NJ	s	13.01 mw	13.89 aw	27060 aaw	NJBLS	10//99-12//99
	New Mexico	s	12.57 mw	12.08 aw	25130 aaw	NMBLS	10//99-12//99
	New York	s	12.57 mw	13.23 aw	27520 aaw	NYBLS	10//99-12//99
	Albany-Schenectady-Troy MSA, NY	s	13.27 mw	12.16 aw	27590 aaw	NYBLS	10//99-12//99

AAW Average annual wage	**AOH** Average offered, high	**ASH** Average starting, high	**H** Hourly	**M** Monthly	**S** Special; hourly and annual
AE Average entry wage	**AOL** Average offered, low	**ASL** Average starting, low	**HI** Highest wage paid	**MTC** Median total compensation	**TQ** Third quartile wage
AEX Average experienced wage	**APH** Average pay, high range	**AW** Average wage paid	**HR** High end range	**MW** Median wage paid	**W** Weekly
AO Average offered	**APL** Average pay, low range	**FQ** First quartile wage	**LR** Low end range	**SQ** Second quartile wage	**Y** Yearly

Occupation/Type/Industry	Location	Per	Low	Mid	High	Source	Date
Furnace, Kiln, Oven, Drier, and Kettle Operator and Tender	Buffalo-Niagara Falls MSA, NY	S	10.91 MW	11.10 AW	22690 AAW	NYBLS	10//99-12//99
	Nassau-Suffolk PMSA, NY	S	15.05 MW	14.87 AW	31310 AAW	NYBLS	10//99-12//99
	New York PMSA, NY	S	12.16 MW	12.36 AW	25300 AAW	NYBLS	10//99-12//99
	Syracuse MSA, NY	S	12.26 MW	12.43 AW	25510 AAW	NYBLS	10//99-12//99
	North Carolina	S	10.02 MW	10.56 AW	21970 AAW	NCBLS	10//99-12//99
	Charlotte-Gastonia-Rock Hill MSA, NC-SC	S	13.80 MW	12.66 AW	28710 AAW	NCBLS	10//99-12//99
	Greensboro--Winston-Salem--High Point MSA, NC	S	11.70 MW	10.61 AW	24330 AAW	NCBLS	10//99-12//99
	Hickory-Morganton-Lenoir MSA, NC	S	10.78 MW	10.71 AW	22410 AAW	NCBLS	10//99-12//99
	Raleigh-Durham-Chapel Hill MSA, NC	S	10.41 MW	10.92 AW	21650 AAW	NCBLS	10//99-12//99
	Ohio	S	11.97 MW	12.69 AW	26390 AAW	OHBLS	10//99-12//99
	Cincinnati PMSA, OH-KY-IN	S	13.35 MW	12.82 AW	27760 AAW	OHBLS	10//99-12//99
	Cleveland-Lorain-Elyria PMSA, OH	S	13.95 MW	12.87 AW	29010 AAW	OHBLS	10//99-12//99
	Columbus MSA, OH	S	13.01 MW	13.19 AW	27060 AAW	OHBLS	10//99-12//99
	Dayton-Springfield MSA, OH	S	11.04 MW	11.19 AW	22970 AAW	OHBLS	10//99-12//99
	Hamilton-Middletown PMSA, OH	S	11.82 MW	11.27 AW	24590 AAW	OHBLS	10//99-12//99
	Toledo MSA, OH	S	13.93 MW	13.64 AW	28970 AAW	OHBLS	10//99-12//99
	Youngstown-Warren MSA, OH	S	10.79 MW	9.60 AW	22440 AAW	OHBLS	10//99-12//99
	Oklahoma	S	12.52 MW	12.94 AW	26910 AAW	OKBLS	10//99-12//99
	Oklahoma City MSA, OK	S	8.99 MW	8.22 AW	18700 AAW	OKBLS	10//99-12//99
	Tulsa MSA, OK	S	11.72 MW	11.37 AW	24380 AAW	OKBLS	10//99-12//99
	Oregon	S	13.82 MW	14.30 AW	29740 AAW	ORBLS	10//99-12//99
	Eugene-Springfield MSA, OR	S	15.52 MW	15.37 AW	32270 AAW	ORBLS	10//99-12//99
	Medford-Ashland MSA, OR	S	12.57 MW	12.32 AW	26140 AAW	ORBLS	10//99-12//99
	Portland-Vancouver PMSA, OR-WA	S	14.45 MW	13.91 AW	30050 AAW	ORBLS	10//99-12//99
	Pennsylvania	S	13.88 MW	14.18 AW	29500 AAW	PABLS	10//99-12//99
	Allentown-Bethlehem-Easton MSA, PA	S	16.66 MW	16.82 AW	34650 AAW	PABLS	10//99-12//99
	Philadelphia PMSA, PA-NJ	S	16.06 MW	14.93 AW	33400 AAW	PABLS	10//99-12//99
	Pittsburgh MSA, PA	S	14.02 MW	13.56 AW	29170 AAW	PABLS	10//99-12//99
	Scranton--Wilkes-Barre--Hazleton MSA, PA	S	14.09 MW	14.53 AW	29300 AAW	PABLS	10//99-12//99
	York MSA, PA	S	13.67 MW	12.77 AW	28430 AAW	PABLS	10//99-12//99
	Rhode Island	S	15.02 MW	13.99 AW	29110 AAW	RIBLS	10//99-12//99
	Providence-Fall River-Warwick MSA, RI-MA	S	14.08 MW	15.02 AW	29290 AAW	RIBLS	10//99-12//99
	South Carolina	S	12.93 MW	14.34 AW	29820 AAW	SCBLS	10//99-12//99
	Columbia MSA, SC	S	15.43 MW	16.65 AW	32090 AAW	SCBLS	10//99-12//99
	Greenville-Spartanburg-Anderson MSA, SC	S	16.45 MW	16.45 AW	34220 AAW	SCBLS	10//99-12//99
	South Dakota	S	14.1 MW	14.18 AW	29490 AAW	SDBLS	10//99-12//99
	Tennessee	S	11.22 MW	11.75 AW	24440 AAW	TNBLS	10//99-12//99
	Chattanooga MSA, TN-GA	S	10.34 MW	10.11 AW	21500 AAW	TNBLS	10//99-12//99
	Johnson City-Kingsport-Bristol MSA, TN-VA	S	12.18 MW	12.07 AW	25320 AAW	TNBLS	10//99-12//99
	Memphis MSA, TN-AR-MS	S	13.99 MW	12.01 AW	29100 AAW	MSBLS	10//99-12//99
	Texas	S	12.24 MW	13.44 AW	27950 AAW	TXBLS	10//99-12//99
	Austin-San Marcos MSA, TX	S	9.99 MW	9.24 AW	20790 AAW	TXBLS	10//99-12//99
	Dallas PMSA, TX	S	11.16 MW	11.42 AW	23210 AAW	TXBLS	10//99-12//99
	Houston PMSA, TX	S	16.64 MW	19.04 AW	34610 AAW	TXBLS	10//99-12//99
	Longview-Marshall MSA, TX	S	7.84 MW	7.37 AW	16300 AAW	TXBLS	10//99-12//99
	San Antonio MSA, TX	S	11.26 MW	11.10 AW	23430 AAW	TXBLS	10//99-12//99
	Utah	S	13.97 MW	13.74 AW	28570 AAW	UTBLS	10//99-12//99
	Salt Lake City-Ogden MSA, UT	S	15.48 MW	16.95 AW	32210 AAW	UTBLS	10//99-12//99
	Vermont	S	10.78 MW	11.33 AW	23570 AAW	VTBLS	10//99-12//99
	Virginia	S	11.56 MW	12.02 AW	25010 AAW	VABLS	10//99-12//99
	Lynchburg MSA, VA	S	11.20 MW	12.31 AW	23300 AAW	VABLS	10//99-12//99
	Norfolk-Virginia Beach-Newport News MSA, VA-NC	S	16.13 MW	17.88 AW	33560 AAW	VABLS	10//99-12//99
	Washington	S	16.33 MW	15.78 AW	32830 AAW	WABLS	10//99-12//99
	Seattle-Bellevue-Everett PMSA, WA	S	13.62 MW	12.41 AW	28340 AAW	WABLS	10//99-12//99

AAW	Average annual wage	AOH	Average offered, high	ASH	Average starting, high
AE	Average entry wage	AOL	Average offered, low	ASL	Average starting, low
AEX	Average experienced wage	APH	Average pay, high range	AW	Average wage paid
AO	Average offered	APL	Average pay, low range	FQ	First quartile wage

H Hourly   M Monthly   S Special: hourly and annual
HI Highest wage paid   MTC Median total compensation   TQ Third quartile wage
HR High end range   MW Median wage paid   W Weekly
LR Low end range   SQ Second quartile wage   Y Yearly

Occupation/Type/Industry	Location	Per	Low	Mid	High	Source	Date
Furnace, Kiln, Oven, Drier, and Kettle Operator and Tender	Tacoma PMSA, WA	S	15.30 MW	14.74 AW	31820 AAW	WABLS	10//99-12//99
	West Virginia	S	11.89 MW	12.65 AW	26320 AAW	WVBLS	10//99-12//99
	Huntington-Ashland MSA, WV-KY-OH	S	9.76 MW	9.60 AW	20290 AAW	WVBLS	10//99-12//99
	Parkersburg-Marietta MSA, WV-OH	S	12.92 MW	12.72 AW	26870 AAW	WVBLS	10//99-12//99
	Wisconsin	S	11.91 MW	12.56 AW	26110 AAW	WIBLS	10//99-12//99
	Appleton-Oshkosh-Neenah MSA, WI	S	14.07 MW	12.71 AW	29270 AAW	WIBLS	10//99-12//99
	Madison MSA, WI	S	12.79 MW	12.47 AW	26590 AAW	WIBLS	10//99-12//99
	Milwaukee-Waukesha PMSA, WI	S	11.97 MW	11.33 AW	24890 AAW	WIBLS	10//99-12//99
	Sheboygan MSA, WI	S	14.60 MW	15.20 AW	30380 AAW	WIBLS	10//99-12//99
	Wyoming	S	14.34 MW	16.40 AW	34110 AAW	WYBLS	10//99-12//99
	Puerto Rico	S	11.62 MW	11.46 AW	23840 AAW	PRBLS	10//99-12//99
	San Juan-Bayamon PMSA, PR	S	11.41 MW	11.71 AW	23740 AAW	PRBLS	10//99-12//99
Furniture Finisher	Alabama	S	9.05 MW	9.03 AW	18790 AAW	ALBLS	10//99-12//99
	Arizona	S	7.36 MW	8.30 AW	17270 AAW	AZBLS	10//99-12//99
	Arkansas	S	8.51 MW	8.81 AW	18320 AAW	ARBLS	10//99-12//99
	California	S	8.55 MW	9.63 AW	20020 AAW	CABLS	10//99-12//99
	Colorado	S	12.04 MW	12.17 AW	25310 AAW	COBLS	10//99-12//99
	Connecticut	S	11.77 MW	12.19 AW	25360 AAW	CTBLS	10//99-12//99
	Delaware	S	12.73 MW	13.09 AW	27230 AAW	DEBLS	10//99-12//99
	Florida	S	10.5 MW	10.81 AW	22490 AAW	FLBLS	10//99-12//99
	Georgia	S	9.56 MW	10.69 AW	22240 AAW	GABLS	10//99-12//99
	Hawaii	S	7.76 MW	8.36 AW	17380 AAW	HIBLS	10//99-12//99
	Idaho	S	8.78 MW	9.55 AW	19860 AAW	IDBLS	10//99-12//99
	Illinois	S	10.17 MW	11.07 AW	23020 AAW	ILBLS	10//99-12//99
	Indiana	S	10.1 MW	10.69 AW	22240 AAW	INBLS	10//99-12//99
	Iowa	S	9.22 MW	8.93 AW	18570 AAW	IABLS	10//99-12//99
	Kansas	S	11.11 MW	11.24 AW	23380 AAW	KSBLS	10//99-12//99
	Kentucky	S	8.87 MW	9.55 AW	19860 AAW	KYBLS	10//99-12//99
	Louisiana	S	9.34 MW	9.96 AW	20720 AAW	LABLS	10//99-12//99
	Maine	S	10.86 MW	11.11 AW	23110 AAW	MEBLS	10//99-12//99
	Maryland	S	11.63 MW	11.51 AW	23950 AAW	MDBLS	10//99-12//99
	Massachusetts	S	10.33 MW	11.39 AW	23690 AAW	MABLS	10//99-12//99
	Michigan	S	12.41 MW	12.66 AW	26330 AAW	MIBLS	10//99-12//99
	Minnesota	S	10.96 MW	10.99 AW	22860 AAW	MNBLS	10//99-12//99
	Mississippi	S	7.58 MW	7.75 AW	16110 AAW	MSBLS	10//99-12//99
	Missouri	S	9.23 MW	9.70 AW	20170 AAW	MOBLS	10//99-12//99
	Montana	S	6.64 MW	7.55 AW	15710 AAW	MTBLS	10//99-12//99
	Nebraska	S	10.92 MW	11.04 AW	22970 AAW	NEBLS	10//99-12//99
	Nevada	S	8.87 MW	9.94 AW	20680 AAW	NVBLS	10//99-12//99
	New Hampshire	S	13.35 MW	13.16 AW	27380 AAW	NHBLS	10//99-12//99
	New Jersey	S	12.4 MW	12.80 AW	26620 AAW	NJBLS	10//99-12//99
	New Mexico	S	9.44 MW	10.24 AW	21290 AAW	NMBLS	10//99-12//99
	New York	S	10.38 MW	11.53 AW	23980 AAW	NYBLS	10//99-12//99
	North Carolina	S	9.86 MW	9.94 AW	20670 AAW	NCBLS	10//99-12//99
	North Dakota	S	9.67 MW	10.84 AW	22550 AAW	NDBLS	10//99-12//99
	Ohio	S	10.51 MW	10.52 AW	21890 AAW	OHBLS	10//99-12//99
	Oklahoma	S	8.45 MW	9.00 AW	18720 AAW	OKBLS	10//99-12//99
	Oregon	S	9.74 MW	10.48 AW	21810 AAW	ORBLS	10//99-12//99
	Pennsylvania	S	10.6 MW	11.04 AW	22970 AAW	PABLS	10//99-12//99
	Rhode Island	S	9.62 MW	10.92 AW	22710 AAW	RIBLS	10//99-12//99
	South Carolina	S	9.87 MW	10.25 AW	21320 AAW	SCBLS	10//99-12//99
	Tennessee	S	9.31 MW	9.36 AW	19460 AAW	TNBLS	10//99-12//99
	Texas	S	8.41 MW	9.02 AW	18750 AAW	TXBLS	10//99-12//99
	Utah	S	11.2 MW	11.79 AW	24530 AAW	UTBLS	10//99-12//99
	Vermont	S	9.86 MW	9.97 AW	20730 AAW	VTBLS	10//99-12//99
	Virginia	S	10.31 MW	11.46 AW	23840 AAW	VABLS	10//99-12//99
	Washington	S	12.44 MW	12.43 AW	25850 AAW	WABLS	10//99-12//99
	West Virginia	S	9.12 MW	9.03 AW	18790 AAW	WVBLS	10//99-12//99
	Wisconsin	S	9.47 MW	9.61 AW	20000 AAW	WIBLS	10//99-12//99
	Wyoming	S	9.93 MW	11.54 AW	24000 AAW	WYBLS	10//99-12//99
	Puerto Rico	S	6.14 MW	6.63 AW	13790 AAW	PRBLS	10//99-12//99
Gaming and Sports Book Writer and Runner	Arizona	S	8.92 MW	8.95 AW	18610 AAW	AZBLS	10//99-12//99
	California	S	6.71 MW	6.98 AW	14520 AAW	CABLS	10//99-12//99
	Iowa	S	9.51 MW	9.15 AW	19030 AAW	IABLS	10//99-12//99

AAW	Average annual wage	AOH	Average offered, high	ASH	Average starting, high	H	Hourly	M	Monthly	S	Special: hourly and annual
AE	Average entry wage	AOL	Average offered, low	ASL	Average starting, low	HI	Highest wage paid	MTC	Median total compensation	TQ	Third quartile wage
AEX	Average experienced wage	APH	Average pay, high range	AW	Average wage paid	HR	High end range	MW	Median wage paid	W	Weekly
AO	Average offered	APL	Average pay, low range	FQ	First quartile wage	LR	Low end range	SQ	Second quartile wage	Y	Yearly

Occupation/Type/Industry	Location	Per	Low	Mid	High	Source	Date
Gaming and Sports Book Writer and Runner	Louisiana	S	7.57 MW	7.66 AW	15920 AAW	LABLS	10//99-12//99
	Minnesota	S	6.32 MW	6.77 AW	14080 AAW	MNBLS	10//99-12//99
	Mississippi	S	6.5 MW	7.67 AW	15950 AAW	MSBLS	10//99-12//99
	Nebraska	S	7.16 MW	7.20 AW	14970 AAW	NEBLS	10//99-12//99
	Nevada	S	8.02 MW	8.17 AW	17000 AAW	NVBLS	10//99-12//99
	New Jersey	S	9.07 MW	8.85 AW	18420 AAW	NJBLS	10//99-12//99
	North Dakota	S	8.12 MW	8.24 AW	17140 AAW	NDBLS	10//99-12//99
	Oklahoma	S	6.09 MW	6.13 AW	12750 AAW	OKBLS	10//99-12//99
	Pennsylvania	S	6.87 MW	6.75 AW	14040 AAW	PABLS	10//99-12//99
	Washington	S	6.38 MW	6.57 AW	13660 AAW	WABLS	10//99-12//99
Gaming Cage Worker	Arizona	S	9.36 MW	9.35 AW	19440 AAW	AZBLS	10//99-12//99
	California	S	10.11 MW	10.10 AW	21020 AAW	CABLS	10//99-12//99
	Illinois	S	9.68 MW	10.17 AW	21150 AAW	ILBLS	10//99-12//99
	Iowa	S	8.79 MW	9.02 AW	18750 AAW	IABLS	10//99-12//99
	Louisiana	S	9.52 MW	9.50 AW	19770 AAW	LABLS	10//99-12//99
	Minnesota	S	11.17 MW	10.78 AW	22410 AAW	MNBLS	10//99-12//99
	Mississippi	S	9.31 MW	10.26 AW	21350 AAW	MSBLS	10//99-12//99
	Missouri	S	9.96 MW	10.04 AW	20880 AAW	MOBLS	10//99-12//99
	Nevada	S	10.52 MW	10.34 AW	21500 AAW	NVBLS	10//99-12//99
	New Mexico	S	8.07 MW	8.19 AW	17030 AAW	NMBLS	10//99-12//99
	New York	S	10.6 MW	10.62 AW	22090 AAW	NYBLS	10//99-12//99
	Oklahoma	S	6.15 MW	6.11 AW	12710 AAW	OKBLS	10//99-12//99
	South Dakota	S	8.17 MW	8.39 AW	17440 AAW	SDBLS	10//99-12//99
	Washington	S	7.95 MW	8.67 AW	18040 AAW	WABLS	10//99-12//99
	Wisconsin	S	8.15 MW	9.61 AW	19990 AAW	WIBLS	10//99-12//99
	Puerto Rico	S	6.13 MW	6.34 AW	13180 AAW	PRBLS	10//99-12//99
Gaming Change Person and Booth Cashier	Arizona	S	9.84 MW	9.87 AW	20530 AAW	AZBLS	10//99-12//99
	California	S	6.54 MW	6.95 AW	14460 AAW	CABLS	10//99-12//99
	Illinois	S	9.42 MW	10.32 AW	21460 AAW	ILBLS	10//99-12//99
	Iowa	S	7.93 MW	8.16 AW	16970 AAW	IABLS	10//99-12//99
	Louisiana	S	8.48 MW	8.60 AW	17890 AAW	LABLS	10//99-12//99
	Maine	S	6.82 MW	7.36 AW	15310 AAW	MEBLS	10//99-12//99
	Maryland	S	7.82 MW	8.40 AW	17460 AAW	MDBLS	10//99-12//99
	Minnesota	S	8.67 MW	8.05 AW	16740 AAW	MNBLS	10//99-12//99
	Mississippi	S	9.2 MW	9.29 AW	19330 AAW	MSBLS	10//99-12//99
	Missouri	S	9.42 MW	9.21 AW	19150 AAW	MOBLS	10//99-12//99
	Montana	S	6.15 MW	6.11 AW	12710 AAW	MTBLS	10//99-12//99
	Nevada	S	8.38 MW	8.58 AW	17840 AAW	NVBLS	10//99-12//99
	New Jersey	S	9.46 MW	9.45 AW	19660 AAW	NJBLS	10//99-12//99
	New Mexico	S	7.77 MW	7.80 AW	16230 AAW	NMBLS	10//99-12//99
	New York	S	8.96 MW	8.97 AW	18660 AAW	NYBLS	10//99-12//99
	Oklahoma	S	6.51 MW	6.61 AW	13740 AAW	OKBLS	10//99-12//99
	South Carolina	S	6.63 MW	8.39 AW	17460 AAW	SCBLS	10//99-12//99
	South Dakota	S	7.65 MW	7.58 AW	15760 AAW	SDBLS	10//99-12//99
	Washington	S	7.98 MW	8.47 AW	17610 AAW	WABLS	10//99-12//99
	Puerto Rico	S	6.55 MW	6.81 AW	14160 AAW	PRBLS	10//99-12//99
Gaming Dealer	Arizona	S	6.24 MW	7.98 AW	16610 AAW	AZBLS	10//99-12//99
	California	S	6.31 MW	6.97 AW	14490 AAW	CABLS	10//99-12//99
	Florida	S	6.12 MW	6.21 AW	12920 AAW	FLBLS	10//99-12//99
	Illinois	S	6.15 MW	6.75 AW	14030 AAW	ILBLS	10//99-12//99
	Iowa	S	6.29 MW	6.71 AW	13970 AAW	IABLS	10//99-12//99
	Louisiana	S	6.09 MW	6.58 AW	13690 AAW	LABLS	10//99-12//99
	Minnesota	S	11.69 MW	11.02 AW	22910 AAW	MNBLS	10//99-12//99
	Mississippi	S	6.25 MW	7.56 AW	15720 AAW	MSBLS	10//99-12//99
	Missouri	S	5.97 MW	5.78 AW	12030 AAW	MOBLS	10//99-12//99
	Nevada	S	5.98 MW	5.93 AW	12320 AAW	NVBLS	10//99-12//99
	New Mexico	S	6.33 MW	6.32 AW	13140 AAW	NMBLS	10//99-12//99
	North Dakota	S	7.79 MW	9.09 AW	18910 AAW	NDBLS	10//99-12//99
	Oklahoma	S	6.16 MW	6.12 AW	12730 AAW	OKBLS	10//99-12//99
	Pennsylvania	S	6.3 MW	6.39 AW	13280 AAW	PABLS	10//99-12//99
	South Dakota	S	7.7 MW	7.66 AW	15940 AAW	SDBLS	10//99-12//99
	Washington	S	6.45 MW	7.60 AW	15800 AAW	WABLS	10//99-12//99
	Wisconsin	S	6.26 MW	7.35 AW	15290 AAW	WIBLS	10//99-12//99
	Puerto Rico	S	6.42 MW	7.14 AW	14840 AAW	PRBLS	10//99-12//99
Gaming Manager	Arizona	S	23.5 MW	26.80 AW	55740 AAW	AZBLS	10//99-12//99
	California	S	25.63 MW	38.52 AW	80110 AAW	CABLS	10//99-12//99

AAW Average annual wage	AOH Average offered, high	ASH Average starting, high	H Hourly	M Monthly	S Special: hourly and annual
AE Average entry wage	AOL Average offered, low	ASL Average starting, low	HI Highest wage paid	MTC Median total compensation	TQ Third quartile wage
AEX Average experienced wage	APH Average pay, high range	AW Average wage paid	HR High end range	MW Median wage paid	W Weekly
AO Average offered	APL Average pay, low range	FQ First quartile wage	LR Low end range	SQ Second quartile wage	Y Yearly

Occupation/Type/Industry	Location	Per	Low	Mid	High	Source	Date
Gaming Manager	Florida	S	22.02 MW	25.90 AW	53870 AAW	FLBLS	10//99-12//99
	Illinois	S	28.07 MW	29.69 AW	61750 AAW	ILBLS	10//99-12//99
	Iowa	S	19.16 MW	22.36 AW	46510 AAW	IABLS	10//99-12//99
	Louisiana	S	27.38 MW	29.56 AW	61480 AAW	LABLS	10//99-12//99
	Michigan	S	16.37 MW	18.16 AW	37760 AAW	MIBLS	10//99-12//99
	Minnesota	S	17.41 MW	19.28 AW	40110 AAW	MNBLS	10//99-12//99
	Mississippi	S	23.87 MW	26.58 AW	55280 AAW	MSBLS	10//99-12//99
	Nevada	S	22.53 MW	27.92 AW	58070 AAW	NVBLS	10//99-12//99
	New Jersey	S	31.52 MW	32.45 AW	67500 AAW	NJBLS	10//99-12//99
	North Dakota	S	15.84 MW	16.74 AW	34820 AAW	NDBLS	10//99-12//99
	Oklahoma	S	12.39 MW	13.30 AW	27670 AAW	OKBLS	10//99-12//99
	South Carolina	S	10.51 MW	14.04 AW	29200 AAW	SCBLS	10//99-12//99
	South Dakota	S	16.83 MW	18.46 AW	38390 AAW	SDBLS	10//99-12//99
	Texas	S	19.2 MW	20.82 AW	43300 AAW	TXBLS	10//99-12//99
	Washington	S	20.97 MW	20.10 AW	41810 AAW	WABLS	10//99-12//99
	West Virginia	S	30.75 MW	29.91 AW	62210 AAW	WVBLS	10//99-12//99
	Wisconsin	S	19.17 MW	19.80 AW	41170 AAW	WIBLS	10//99-12//99
	Puerto Rico	S	21.79 MW	25.71 AW	53480 AAW	PRBLS	10//99-12//99
Gaming Supervisor	Arizona	S	16.7 MW	17.59 AW	36590 AAW	AZBLS	10//99-12//99
	California	S	14.51 MW	15.61 AW	32460 AAW	CABLS	10//99-12//99
	Florida	S	18.46 MW	18.29 AW	38040 AAW	FLBLS	10//99-12//99
	Georgia	S	15.26 MW	16.13 AW	33550 AAW	GABLS	10//99-12//99
	Illinois	S	16.2 MW	17.10 AW	35560 AAW	ILBLS	10//99-12//99
	Indiana	S	17.15 MW	18.35 AW	38180 AAW	INBLS	10//99-12//99
	Iowa	S	14.26 MW	14.92 AW	31040 AAW	IABLS	10//99-12//99
	Louisiana	S	14.57 MW	14.72 AW	30620 AAW	LABLS	10//99-12//99
	Massachusetts	S	18.63 MW	17.72 AW	36860 AAW	MABLS	10//99-12//99
	Minnesota	S	14.11 MW	13.35 AW	27770 AAW	MNBLS	10//99-12//99
	Mississippi	S	18.69 MW	19.32 AW	40190 AAW	MSBLS	10//99-12//99
	Missouri	S	16.45 MW	17.43 AW	36260 AAW	MOBLS	10//99-12//99
	Nevada	S	15.96 MW	16.47 AW	34260 AAW	NVBLS	10//99-12//99
	New Mexico	S	12.23 MW	12.23 AW	25440 AAW	NMBLS	10//99-12//99
	New York	S	17.56 MW	17.76 AW	36950 AAW	NYBLS	10//99-12//99
	North Dakota	S	11.17 MW	12.53 AW	26060 AAW	NDBLS	10//99-12//99
	Oklahoma	S	6.57 MW	7.37 AW	15340 AAW	OKBLS	10//99-12//99
	Oregon	S	14.69 MW	13.45 AW	27980 AAW	ORBLS	10//99-12//99
	South Carolina	S	7.01 MW	6.86 AW	14260 AAW	SCBLS	10//99-12//99
	South Dakota	S	12.81 MW	13.43 AW	27930 AAW	SDBLS	10//99-12//99
	Washington	S	15.18 MW	15.08 AW	31360 AAW	WABLS	10//99-12//99
	West Virginia	S	18.6 MW	18.71 AW	38920 AAW	WVBLS	10//99-12//99
	Wisconsin	S	15.05 MW	15.75 AW	32750 AAW	WIBLS	10//99-12//99
	Puerto Rico	S	11.66 MW	12.08 AW	25120 AAW	PRBLS	10//99-12//99
Gaming Surveillance Officer and Gaming Investigator	Arizona	S	10.53 MW	10.72 AW	22310 AAW	AZBLS	10//99-12//99
	California	S	10.31 MW	10.51 AW	21860 AAW	CABLS	10//99-12//99
	Colorado	S	9.95 MW	10.33 AW	21480 AAW	COBLS	10//99-12//99
	Florida	S	11.08 MW	11.84 AW	24640 AAW	FLBLS	10//99-12//99
	Illinois	S	9.41 MW	9.25 AW	19250 AAW	ILBLS	10//99-12//99
	Iowa	S	9.55 MW	10.55 AW	21940 AAW	IABLS	10//99-12//99
	Louisiana	S	9.3 MW	10.10 AW	21000 AAW	LABLS	10//99-12//99
	Minnesota	S	9.79 MW	10.47 AW	21790 AAW	MNBLS	10//99-12//99
	Mississippi	S	10.11 MW	11.53 AW	23980 AAW	MSBLS	10//99-12//99
	Nevada	S	13.19 MW	13.26 AW	27590 AAW	NVBLS	10//99-12//99
	New Jersey	S	12.79 MW	14.03 AW	29180 AAW	NJBLS	10//99-12//99
	New York	S	11.62 MW	12.19 AW	25350 AAW	NYBLS	10//99-12//99
	South Dakota	S	8.3 MW	9.09 AW	18910 AAW	SDBLS	10//99-12//99
	Washington	S	11.12 MW	11.38 AW	23660 AAW	WABLS	10//99-12//99
	Wisconsin	S	9.13 MW	9.28 AW	19300 AAW	WIBLS	10//99-12//99
	Puerto Rico	S	7.75 MW	7.93 AW	16500 AAW	PRBLS	10//99-12//99
Garment Sewer	Los Angeles County, CA	Y		20304 AW		LABJ	1999
Gas Compressor and Gas Pumping Station Operator	Alabama	S	20.18 MW	18.87 AW	39250 AAW	ALBLS	10//99-12//99
	Arkansas	S	22.07 MW	21.66 AW	45050 AAW	ARBLS	10//99-12//99
	California	S	17.83 MW	17.47 AW	36330 AAW	CABLS	10//99-12//99
	Colorado	S	19.51 MW	19.80 AW	41190 AAW	COBLS	10//99-12//99
	Connecticut	S	20.87 MW	18.55 AW	38590 AAW	CTBLS	10//99-12//99
	Washington PMSA, DC-MD-VA-WV	S	18.21 MW	18.81 AW	37880 AAW	DCBLS	10//99-12//99

AAW Average annual wage	AOH Average offered, high	ASH Average starting, high	H Hourly	M Monthly	S Special: hourly and annual
AE Average entry wage	AOL Average offered, low	ASL Average starting, low	HI Highest wage paid	MTC Median total compensation	TQ Third quartile wage
AEX Average experienced wage	APH Average pay, high range	AW Average wage paid	HR High end range	MW Median wage paid	W Weekly
AO Average offered	APL Average pay, low range	FQ First quartile wage	LR Low end range	SQ Second quartile wage	Y Yearly

Occupation/Type/Industry	Location	Per	Low	Mid	High	Source	Date
Gas Compressor and Gas Pumping Station Operator	Illinois	S	18.2 MW	17.58 AW	36570 AAW	ILBLS	10//99-12//99
	Iowa	S	19.98 MW	18.00 AW	37450 AAW	IABLS	10//99-12//99
	Kansas	S	20.67 MW	19.03 AW	39580 AAW	KSBLS	10//99-12//99
	Louisiana	S	20.41 MW	20.13 AW	41860 AAW	LABLS	10//99-12//99
	Lafayette MSA, LA	S	22.32 MW	22.56 AW	46420 AAW	LABLS	10//99-12//99
	Maryland	S	20.12 MW	20.13 AW	41880 AAW	MDBLS	10//99-12//99
	Massachusetts	S	14.38 MW	14.73 AW	30640 AAW	MABLS	10//99-12//99
	Minnesota	S	19.05 MW	18.87 AW	39250 AAW	MNBLS	10//99-12//99
	Mississippi	S	19.44 MW	18.09 AW	37620 AAW	MSBLS	10//99-12//99
	Missouri	S	17.53 MW	15.69 AW	32630 AAW	MOBLS	10//99-12//99
	St. Louis MSA, MO-IL	S	11.55 MW	8.90 AW	24030 AAW	MOBLS	10//99-12//99
	Montana	S	18.68 MW	18.40 AW	38260 AAW	MTBLS	10//99-12//99
	New Jersey	S	20.09 MW	19.36 AW	40270 AAW	NJBLS	10//99-12//99
	Newark PMSA, NJ	S	21.81 MW	22.35 AW	45370 AAW	NJBLS	10//99-12//99
	New York	S	10.66 MW	12.96 AW	26960 AAW	NYBLS	10//99-12//99
	New York PMSA, NY	S	14.12 MW	13.20 AW	29370 AAW	NYBLS	10//99-12//99
	Pennsylvania	S	18.75 MW	17.96 AW	37350 AAW	PABLS	10//99-12//99
	Pittsburgh MSA, PA	S	19.61 MW	18.91 AW	40790 AAW	PABLS	10//99-12//99
	South Carolina	S	11.13 MW	11.61 AW	24150 AAW	SCBLS	10//99-12//99
	Tennessee	S	18.34 MW	17.98 AW	37400 AAW	TNBLS	10//99-12//99
	Texas	S	18.46 MW	18.30 AW	38070 AAW	TXBLS	10//99-12//99
	El Paso MSA, TX	S	17.34 MW	15.75 AW	36060 AAW	TXBLS	10//99-12//99
	Houston PMSA, TX	S	18.93 MW	18.74 AW	39380 AAW	TXBLS	10//99-12//99
	Longview-Marshall MSA, TX	S	13.91 MW	12.56 AW	28940 AAW	TXBLS	10//99-12//99
	Virginia	S	19.91 MW	19.94 AW	41470 AAW	VABLS	10//99-12//99
	West Virginia	S	20.53 MW	20.24 AW	42100 AAW	WVBLS	10//99-12//99
	Wyoming	S	20.49 MW	20.57 AW	42780 AAW	WYBLS	10//99-12//99
Gas Plant Operator	Alabama	S	18.87 MW	19.10 AW	39730 AAW	ALBLS	10//99-12//99
	Alaska	S	32.4 MW	29.22 AW	60780 AAW	AKBLS	10//99-12//99
	Arkansas	S	19.09 MW	18.78 AW	39070 AAW	ARBLS	10//99-12//99
	Colorado	S	19.32 MW	19.76 AW	41100 AAW	COBLS	10//99-12//99
	Florida	S	18.68 MW	19.34 AW	40230 AAW	FLBLS	10//99-12//99
	Georgia	S	14.93 MW	15.33 AW	31890 AAW	GABLS	10//99-12//99
	Illinois	S	24.48 MW	24.10 AW	50120 AAW	ILBLS	10//99-12//99
	Indiana	S	21.58 MW	21.01 AW	43710 AAW	INBLS	10//99-12//99
	Iowa	S	19.96 MW	19.23 AW	40000 AAW	IABLS	10//99-12//99
	Kansas	S	21.23 MW	20.55 AW	42730 AAW	KSBLS	10//99-12//99
	Kentucky	S	21.81 MW	20.76 AW	43190 AAW	KYBLS	10//99-12//99
	Louisiana	S	20.73 MW	19.98 AW	41550 AAW	LABLS	10//99-12//99
	Massachusetts	S	22.51 MW	22.89 AW	47620 AAW	MABLS	10//99-12//99
	Michigan	S	21.07 MW	20.48 AW	42590 AAW	MIBLS	10//99-12//99
	Minnesota	S	19.55 MW	19.97 AW	41530 AAW	MNBLS	10//99-12//99
	Mississippi	S	20.57 MW	20.34 AW	42310 AAW	MSBLS	10//99-12//99
	Missouri	S	21.35 MW	21.81 AW	45360 AAW	MOBLS	10//99-12//99
	Nebraska	S	18.37 MW	17.94 AW	37310 AAW	NEBLS	10//99-12//99
	New Jersey	S	19.91 MW	19.62 AW	40820 AAW	NJBLS	10//99-12//99
	New Mexico	S	17.77 MW	17.44 AW	36260 AAW	NMBLS	10//99-12//99
	New York	S	24.73 MW	24.77 AW	51520 AAW	NYBLS	10//99-12//99
	North Carolina	S	16.7 MW	17.49 AW	36380 AAW	NCBLS	10//99-12//99
	Ohio	S	21.35 MW	20.83 AW	43330 AAW	OHBLS	10//99-12//99
	Oklahoma	S	16.87 MW	17.01 AW	35370 AAW	OKBLS	10//99-12//99
	Pennsylvania	S	19.91 MW	19.95 AW	41490 AAW	PABLS	10//99-12//99
	Tennessee	S	23.5 MW	23.03 AW	47910 AAW	TNBLS	10//99-12//99
	Texas	S	19.74 MW	19.14 AW	39810 AAW	TXBLS	10//99-12//99
	Virginia	S	18.69 MW	19.12 AW	39780 AAW	VABLS	10//99-12//99
	Washington	S	21.07 MW	21.19 AW	44070 AAW	WABLS	10//99-12//99
	West Virginia	S	21.26 MW	20.04 AW	41690 AAW	WVBLS	10//99-12//99
	Wisconsin	S	23.53 MW	23.39 AW	48640 AAW	WIBLS	10//99-12//99
	Wyoming	S	21.44 MW	20.71 AW	43080 AAW	WYBLS	10//99-12//99
Gas Station Clerk	Louisville, KY	H		6.50 AW		LOUMAG	1999-2000
General and Operations Manager	Alabama	S	21.47 MW	26.46 AW	55040 AAW	ALBLS	10//99-12//99
	Anniston MSA, AL	S	20.80 MW	16.94 AW	43260 AAW	ALBLS	10//99-12//99
	Auburn-Opelika MSA, AL	S	21.33 MW	18.00 AW	44370 AAW	ALBLS	10//99-12//99
	Birmingham MSA, AL	S	30.43 MW	25.08 AW	63300 AAW	ALBLS	10//99-12//99
	Decatur MSA, AL	S	24.55 MW	20.02 AW	51060 AAW	ALBLS	10//99-12//99
	Dothan MSA, AL	S	21.41 MW	16.18 AW	44540 AAW	ALBLS	10//99-12//99
	Florence MSA, AL	S	22.29 MW	19.81 AW	46360 AAW	ALBLS	10//99-12//99
	Gadsden MSA, AL	S	21.49 MW	19.65 AW	44710 AAW	ALBLS	10//99-12//99

Occupation/Type/Industry	Location	Per	Low	Mid	High	Source	Date
General and Operations Manager	Huntsville MSA, AL	S	26.77 MW	22.61 AW	55680 AAW	ALBLS	10//99-12//99
	Mobile MSA, AL	S	28.78 MW	22.88 AW	59860 AAW	ALBLS	10//99-12//99
	Montgomery MSA, AL	S	24.84 MW	19.84 AW	51670 AAW	ALBLS	10//99-12//99
	Tuscaloosa MSA, AL	S	20.56 MW	17.83 AW	42770 AAW	ALBLS	10//99-12//99
	Alaska	S	27.97 MW	30.94 AW	64360 AAW	AKBLS	10//99-12//99
	Anchorage MSA, AK	S	34.93 MW	29.75 AW	72650 AAW	AKBLS	10//99-12//99
	Arizona	S	30.23 MW	33.41 AW	69490 AAW	AZBLS	10//99-12//99
	Flagstaff MSA, AZ-UT	S	28.69 MW	22.80 AW	59680 AAW	AZBLS	10//99-12//99
	Phoenix-Mesa MSA, AZ	S	35.12 MW	32.73 AW	73040 AAW	AZBLS	10//99-12//99
	Tucson MSA, AZ	S	30.89 MW	25.73 AW	64250 AAW	AZBLS	10//99-12//99
	Yuma MSA, AZ	S	28.21 MW	25.75 AW	58680 AAW	AZBLS	10//99-12//99
	Arkansas	S	24.58 MW	28.51 AW	59300 AAW	ARBLS	10//99-12//99
	Fayetteville-Springdale-Rogers MSA, AR	S	25.49 MW	19.97 AW	53020 AAW	ARBLS	10//99-12//99
	Fort Smith MSA, AR-OK	S	26.97 MW	23.68 AW	56100 AAW	ARBLS	10//99-12//99
	Jonesboro MSA, AR	S	26.28 MW	21.09 AW	54650 AAW	ARBLS	10//99-12//99
	Little Rock-North Little Rock MSA, AR	S	32.72 MW	29.23 AW	68050 AAW	ARBLS	10//99-12//99
	Pine Bluff MSA, AR	S	29.85 MW	25.66 AW	62100 AAW	ARBLS	10//99-12//99
	California	S	32.8 MW	36.87 AW	76690 AAW	CABLS	10//99-12//99
	Bakersfield MSA, CA	S	29.95 MW	26.09 AW	62290 AAW	CABLS	10//99-12//99
	Chico-Paradise MSA, CA	S	28.45 MW	23.94 AW	59180 AAW	CABLS	10//99-12//99
	Fresno MSA, CA	S	30.09 MW	25.75 AW	62600 AAW	CABLS	10//99-12//99
	Los Angeles-Long Beach PMSA, CA	S	37.80 MW	33.94 AW	78610 AAW	CABLS	10//99-12//99
	Merced MSA, CA	S	28.88 MW	26.10 AW	60080 AAW	CABLS	10//99-12//99
	Modesto MSA, CA	S	31.22 MW	28.24 AW	64940 AAW	CABLS	10//99-12//99
	Oakland PMSA, CA	S	38.83 MW	34.36 AW	80770 AAW	CABLS	10//99-12//99
	Orange County PMSA, CA	S	40.10 MW	37.15 AW	83400 AAW	CABLS	10//99-12//99
	Redding MSA, CA	S	27.01 MW	24.15 AW	56170 AAW	CABLS	10//99-12//99
	Riverside-San Bernardino PMSA, CA	S	33.42 MW	29.40 AW	69510 AAW	CABLS	10//99-12//99
	Sacramento PMSA, CA	S	32.39 MW	29.32 AW	67360 AAW	CABLS	10//99-12//99
	Salinas MSA, CA	S	33.16 MW	28.87 AW	68970 AAW	CABLS	10//99-12//99
	San Diego MSA, CA	S	35.06 MW	31.11 AW	72920 AAW	CABLS	10//99-12//99
	San Francisco PMSA, CA	S	40.90 MW	37.17 AW	85070 AAW	CABLS	10//99-12//99
	San Jose PMSA, CA	S	43.15 MW	40.74 AW	89750 AAW	CABLS	10//99-12//99
	San Luis Obispo-Atascadero-Paso Robles MSA, CA	S	27.83 MW	24.40 AW	57890 AAW	CABLS	10//99-12//99
	Santa Barbara-Santa Maria-Lompoc MSA, CA	S	34.58 MW	29.83 AW	71930 AAW	CABLS	10//99-12//99
	Santa Cruz-Watsonville PMSA, CA	S	32.50 MW	25.76 AW	67600 AAW	CABLS	10//99-12//99
	Santa Rosa PMSA, CA	S	31.68 MW	26.84 AW	65890 AAW	CABLS	10//99-12//99
	Stockton-Lodi MSA, CA	S	31.82 MW	28.85 AW	66180 AAW	CABLS	10//99-12//99
	Vallejo-Fairfield-Napa PMSA, CA	S	32.75 MW	27.49 AW	68120 AAW	CABLS	10//99-12//99
	Ventura PMSA, CA	S	38.17 MW	34.85 AW	79390 AAW	CABLS	10//99-12//99
	Visalia-Tulare-Porterville MSA, CA	S	29.41 MW	27.41 AW	61170 AAW	CABLS	10//99-12//99
	Yolo PMSA, CA	S	28.24 MW	24.39 AW	58750 AAW	CABLS	10//99-12//99
	Yuba City MSA, CA	S	30.55 MW	26.33 AW	63550 AAW	CABLS	10//99-12//99
	Colorado	S	28.55 MW	32.98 AW	68590 AAW	COBLS	10//99-12//99
	Boulder-Longmont PMSA, CO	S	38.47 MW	37.57 AW	80030 AAW	COBLS	10//99-12//99
	Colorado Springs MSA, CO	S	32.49 MW	26.48 AW	67590 AAW	COBLS	10//99-12//99
	Denver PMSA, CO	S	36.04 MW	31.95 AW	74970 AAW	COBLS	10//99-12//99
	Fort Collins-Loveland MSA, CO	S	34.50 MW	30.02 AW	71760 AAW	COBLS	10//99-12//99
	Grand Junction MSA, CO	S	22.66 MW	19.21 AW	47130 AAW	COBLS	10//99-12//99
	Greeley PMSA, CO	S	27.61 MW	24.54 AW	57430 AAW	COBLS	10//99-12//99
	Connecticut	S	38.54 MW	41.50 AW	86320 AAW	CTBLS	10//99-12//99
	Bridgeport PMSA, CT	S	38.85 MW	34.52 AW	80810 AAW	CTBLS	10//99-12//99
	Danbury PMSA, CT	S	37.92 MW	32.29 AW	78870 AAW	CTBLS	10//99-12//99
	Hartford MSA, CT	S	41.11 MW	39.43 AW	85520 AAW	CTBLS	10//99-12//99
	New Haven-Meriden PMSA, CT	S	41.12 MW	36.99 AW	85530 AAW	CTBLS	10//99-12//99
	New London-Norwich MSA, CT-RI	S	35.42 MW	28.96 AW	73680 AAW	CTBLS	10//99-12//99
	Stamford-Norwalk PMSA, CT	S	46.89 MW	48.65 AW	97540 AAW	CTBLS	10//99-12//99
	Waterbury PMSA, CT	S	35.40 MW	31.82 AW	73640 AAW	CTBLS	10//99-12//99
	Delaware	S	24.62 MW	28.36 AW	58980 AAW	DEBLS	10//99-12//99
	Dover MSA, DE	S	24.23 MW	22.31 AW	50390 AAW	DEBLS	10//99-12//99

AAW	Average annual wage	AOH	Average offered, high	ASH	Average starting, high	H	Hourly	M	Monthly	S	Special: hourly and annual
AE	Average entry wage	AOL	Average offered, low	ASL	Average starting, low	HI	Highest wage paid	MTC	Median total compensation	TQ	Third quartile wage
AEX	Average experienced wage	APH	Average pay, high range	AW	Average wage paid	HR	High end range	MW	Median wage paid	W	Weekly
AO	Average offered	APL	Average pay, low range	FQ	First quartile wage	LR	Low end range	SQ	Second quartile wage	Y	Yearly

Occupation/Type/Industry	Location	Per	Low	Mid	High	Source	Date
General and Operations Manager	Wilmington-Newark PMSA, DE-MD	S	29.63 MW	26.20 AW	61640 AAW	DEBLS	10//99-12//99
	District of Columbia	S	30.17 MW	33.55 AW	69770 AAW	DCBLS	10//99-12//99
	Washington PMSA, DC-MD-VA-WV	S	35.14 MW	33.08 AW	73080 AAW	DCBLS	10//99-12//99
	Florida	S	24.39 MW	28.81 AW	59930 AAW	FLBLS	10//99-12//99
	Daytona Beach MSA, FL	S	22.83 MW	19.08 AW	47490 AAW	FLBLS	10//99-12//99
	Fort Lauderdale PMSA, FL	S	30.36 MW	24.73 AW	63150 AAW	FLBLS	10//99-12//99
	Fort Myers-Cape Coral MSA, FL	S	27.66 MW	23.67 AW	57540 AAW	FLBLS	10//99-12//99
	Fort Pierce-Port St. Lucie MSA, FL	S	27.83 MW	25.27 AW	57880 AAW	FLBLS	10//99-12//99
	Fort Walton Beach MSA, FL	S	24.77 MW	22.00 AW	51530 AAW	FLBLS	10//99-12//99
	Gainesville MSA, FL	S	24.24 MW	20.16 AW	50430 AAW	FLBLS	10//99-12//99
	Jacksonville MSA, FL	S	29.70 MW	25.76 AW	61780 AAW	FLBLS	10//99-12//99
	Lakeland-Winter Haven MSA, FL	S	27.09 MW	23.29 AW	56350 AAW	FLBLS	10//99-12//99
	Melbourne-Titusville-Palm Bay MSA, FL	S	27.51 MW	24.16 AW	57220 AAW	FLBLS	10//99-12//99
	Miami PMSA, FL	S	31.35 MW	27.20 AW	65200 AAW	FLBLS	10//99-12//99
	Naples MSA, FL	S	28.85 MW	27.66 AW	60010 AAW	FLBLS	10//99-12//99
	Ocala MSA, FL	S	22.34 MW	18.59 AW	46460 AAW	FLBLS	10//99-12//99
	Orlando MSA, FL	S	29.41 MW	24.66 AW	61170 AAW	FLBLS	10//99-12//99
	Panama City MSA, FL	S	22.15 MW	17.91 AW	46080 AAW	FLBLS	10//99-12//99
	Pensacola MSA, FL	S	26.15 MW	23.02 AW	54380 AAW	FLBLS	10//99-12//99
	Punta Gorda MSA, FL	S	24.47 MW	18.85 AW	50900 AAW	FLBLS	10//99-12//99
	Sarasota-Bradenton MSA, FL	S	29.90 MW	24.41 AW	62180 AAW	FLBLS	10//99-12//99
	Tallahassee MSA, FL	S	25.85 MW	20.92 AW	53780 AAW	FLBLS	10//99-12//99
	Tampa-St. Petersburg-Clearwater MSA, FL	S	28.88 MW	24.23 AW	60060 AAW	FLBLS	10//99-12//99
	West Palm Beach-Boca Raton MSA, FL	S	30.57 MW	25.67 AW	63590 AAW	FLBLS	10//99-12//99
	Georgia	S	26.91 MW	31.19 AW	64880 AAW	GABLS	10//99-12//99
	Albany MSA, GA	S	24.91 MW	20.56 AW	51820 AAW	GABLS	10//99-12//99
	Athens MSA, GA	S	25.00 MW	20.77 AW	52000 AAW	GABLS	10//99-12//99
	Atlanta MSA, GA	S	34.85 MW	31.38 AW	72490 AAW	GABLS	10//99-12//99
	Augusta-Aiken MSA, GA-SC	S	26.51 MW	23.21 AW	55130 AAW	GABLS	10//99-12//99
	Columbus MSA, GA-AL	S	26.92 MW	24.88 AW	56000 AAW	GABLS	10//99-12//99
	Macon MSA, GA	S	27.65 MW	23.91 AW	57520 AAW	GABLS	10//99-12//99
	Savannah MSA, GA	S	26.55 MW	22.97 AW	55210 AAW	GABLS	10//99-12//99
	Hawaii	S	27.03 MW	31.37 AW	65250 AAW	HIBLS	10//99-12//99
	Honolulu MSA, HI	S	32.15 MW	28.10 AW	66880 AAW	HIBLS	10//99-12//99
	Idaho	S	21.32 MW	25.46 AW	52950 AAW	IDBLS	10//99-12//99
	Boise City MSA, ID	S	27.71 MW	23.81 AW	57630 AAW	IDBLS	10//99-12//99
	Pocatello MSA, ID	S	19.99 MW	15.69 AW	41580 AAW	IDBLS	10//99-12//99
	Illinois	S	26.47 MW	30.28 AW	62970 AAW	ILBLS	10//99-12//99
	Champaign-Urbana MSA, IL	S	26.83 MW	26.26 AW	55800 AAW	ILBLS	10//99-12//99
	Chicago PMSA, IL	S	34.28 MW	30.93 AW	71310 AAW	ILBLS	10//99-12//99
	Decatur MSA, IL	S	25.40 MW	23.57 AW	52830 AAW	ILBLS	10//99-12//99
	Kankakee PMSA, IL	S	24.38 MW	19.41 AW	50700 AAW	ILBLS	10//99-12//99
	Peoria-Pekin MSA, IL	S	28.88 MW	23.99 AW	60060 AAW	ILBLS	10//99-12//99
	Rockford MSA, IL	S	21.63 MW	16.14 AW	44980 AAW	ILBLS	10//99-12//99
	Springfield MSA, IL	S	25.92 MW	23.99 AW	53910 AAW	ILBLS	10//99-12//99
	Indiana	S	28.1 MW	31.71 AW	65960 AAW	INBLS	10//99-12//99
	Bloomington MSA, IN	S	31.48 MW	29.24 AW	65480 AAW	INBLS	10//99-12//99
	Elkhart-Goshen MSA, IN	S	28.73 MW	24.12 AW	59760 AAW	INBLS	10//99-12//99
	Evansville-Henderson MSA, IN-KY	S	27.20 MW	22.94 AW	56570 AAW	INBLS	10//99-12//99
	Fort Wayne MSA, IN	S	33.53 MW	30.25 AW	69730 AAW	INBLS	10//99-12//99
	Gary PMSA, IN	S	34.47 MW	30.08 AW	71700 AAW	INBLS	10//99-12//99
	Indianapolis MSA, IN	S	36.75 MW	35.33 AW	76440 AAW	INBLS	10//99-12//99
	Kokomo MSA, IN	S	30.77 MW	26.86 AW	64000 AAW	INBLS	10//99-12//99
	Lafayette MSA, IN	S	29.62 MW	24.75 AW	61610 AAW	INBLS	10//99-12//99
	Muncie MSA, IN	S	29.91 MW	26.81 AW	62220 AAW	INBLS	10//99-12//99
	South Bend MSA, IN	S	31.46 MW	27.41 AW	65440 AAW	INBLS	10//99-12//99
	Terre Haute MSA, IN	S	30.17 MW	25.41 AW	62760 AAW	INBLS	10//99-12//99
	Iowa	S	21.04 MW	25.05 AW	52110 AAW	IABLS	10//99-12//99
	Cedar Rapids MSA, IA	S	27.59 MW	23.78 AW	57380 AAW	IABLS	10//99-12//99
	Davenport-Moline-Rock Island MSA, IA-IL	S	26.78 MW	23.89 AW	55700 AAW	IABLS	10//99-12//99
	Des Moines MSA, IA	S	31.07 MW	26.60 AW	64620 AAW	IABLS	10//99-12//99
	Dubuque MSA, IA	S	20.26 MW	16.96 AW	42140 AAW	IABLS	10//99-12//99

AAW	Average annual wage	AOH	Average offered, high	ASH	Average starting, high	H	Hourly	M	Monthly	S	Special: hourly and annual
AE	Average entry wage	AOL	Average offered, low	ASL	Average starting, low	HI	Highest wage paid	MTC	Median total compensation	TQ	Third quartile wage
AEX	Average experienced wage	APH	Average pay, high range	AW	Average wage paid	HR	High end range	MW	Median wage paid	W	Weekly
AO	Average offered	APL	Average pay, low range	FQ	First quartile wage	LR	Low end range	SQ	Second quartile wage	Y	Yearly

Occupation/Type/Industry	Location	Per	Low	Mid	High	Source	Date
General and Operations Manager	Iowa City MSA, IA	s	20.87 MW	18.01 AW	43420 AAW	IABLS	10//99-12//99
	Sioux City MSA, IA-NE	s	23.39 MW	19.96 AW	48660 AAW	IABLS	10//99-12//99
	Waterloo-Cedar Falls MSA, IA	s	26.92 MW	21.18 AW	55990 AAW	IABLS	10//99-12//99
	Kansas	s	24.91 MW	28.43 AW	59140 AAW	KSBLS	10//99-12//99
	Lawrence MSA, KS	s	27.85 MW	25.07 AW	57940 AAW	KSBLS	10//99-12//99
	Topeka MSA, KS	s	25.95 MW	22.93 AW	53980 AAW	KSBLS	10//99-12//99
	Wichita MSA, KS	s	27.57 MW	24.80 AW	57350 AAW	KSBLS	10//99-12//99
	Kentucky	s	22.95 MW	26.65 AW	55440 AAW	KYBLS	10//99-12//99
	Lexington MSA, KY	s	29.05 MW	24.52 AW	60410 AAW	KYBLS	10//99-12//99
	Louisville MSA, KY-IN	s	30.47 MW	26.43 AW	63380 AAW	KYBLS	10//99-12//99
	Owensboro MSA, KY	s	27.13 MW	23.44 AW	56440 AAW	KYBLS	10//99-12//99
	Louisiana	s	23.63 MW	27.65 AW	57520 AAW	LABLS	10//99-12//99
	Alexandria MSA, LA	s	27.65 MW	24.25 AW	57510 AAW	LABLS	10//99-12//99
	Baton Rouge MSA, LA	s	29.29 MW	24.54 AW	60930 AAW	LABLS	10//99-12//99
	Houma MSA, LA	s	25.08 MW	21.21 AW	52160 AAW	LABLS	10//99-12//99
	Lafayette MSA, LA	s	25.45 MW	22.37 AW	52940 AAW	LABLS	10//99-12//99
	Lake Charles MSA, LA	s	23.41 MW	22.46 AW	48690 AAW	LABLS	10//99-12//99
	Monroe MSA, LA	s	24.91 MW	22.49 AW	51810 AAW	LABLS	10//99-12//99
	New Orleans MSA, LA	s	29.39 MW	24.77 AW	61130 AAW	LABLS	10//99-12//99
	Shreveport-Bossier City MSA, LA	s	29.20 MW	25.23 AW	60730 AAW	LABLS	10//99-12//99
	Maine	s	21.77 MW	25.29 AW	52610 AAW	MEBLS	10//99-12//99
	Bangor MSA, ME	s	27.40 MW	26.30 AW	57000 AAW	MEBLS	10//99-12//99
	Lewiston-Auburn MSA, ME	s	23.00 MW	21.17 AW	47850 AAW	MEBLS	10//99-12//99
	Portland MSA, ME	s	26.75 MW	23.44 AW	55630 AAW	MEBLS	10//99-12//99
	Maryland	s	28.22 MW	31.99 AW	66550 AAW	MDBLS	10//99-12//99
	Baltimore PMSA, MD	s	31.60 MW	27.31 AW	65720 AAW	MDBLS	10//99-12//99
	Cumberland MSA, MD-WV	s	21.41 MW	18.17 AW	44540 AAW	MDBLS	10//99-12//99
	Hagerstown PMSA, MD	s	27.28 MW	23.64 AW	56740 AAW	MDBLS	10//99-12//99
	Massachusetts	s	34.5 MW	37.35 AW	77690 AAW	MABLS	10//99-12//99
	Barnstable-Yarmouth MSA, MA	s	28.41 MW	25.35 AW	59080 AAW	MABLS	10//99-12//99
	Boston PMSA, MA-NH	s	40.47 MW	38.91 AW	84180 AAW	MABLS	10//99-12//99
	Brockton PMSA, MA	s	34.27 MW	29.96 AW	71290 AAW	MABLS	10//99-12//99
	Fitchburg-Leominster PMSA, MA	s	29.78 MW	27.76 AW	61950 AAW	MABLS	10//99-12//99
	Lawrence PMSA, MA-NH	s	34.12 MW	30.02 AW	70960 AAW	MABLS	10//99-12//99
	Lowell PMSA, MA-NH	s	36.51 MW	34.12 AW	75930 AAW	MABLS	10//99-12//99
	New Bedford PMSA, MA	s	26.53 MW	24.23 AW	55180 AAW	MABLS	10//99-12//99
	Pittsfield MSA, MA	s	28.37 MW	25.08 AW	59010 AAW	MABLS	10//99-12//99
	Springfield MSA, MA	s	32.31 MW	27.70 AW	67200 AAW	MABLS	10//99-12//99
	Worcester PMSA, MA-CT	s	33.81 MW	30.25 AW	70330 AAW	MABLS	10//99-12//99
	Michigan	s	36.28 MW	39.19 AW	81520 AAW	MIBLS	10//99-12//99
	Ann Arbor PMSA, MI	s	36.72 MW	34.54 AW	76390 AAW	MIBLS	10//99-12//99
	Benton Harbor MSA, MI	s	32.96 MW	29.73 AW	68560 AAW	MIBLS	10//99-12//99
	Detroit PMSA, MI	s	42.98 MW	40.54 AW	89390 AAW	MIBLS	10//99-12//99
	Flint PMSA, MI	s	34.87 MW	28.77 AW	72530 AAW	MIBLS	10//99-12//99
	Grand Rapids-Muskegon-Holland MSA, MI	s	38.48 MW	35.45 AW	80040 AAW	MIBLS	10//99-12//99
	Jackson MSA, MI	s	41.06 MW	41.51 AW	85410 AAW	MIBLS	10//99-12//99
	Kalamazoo-Battle Creek MSA, MI	s	36.25 MW	32.62 AW	75400 AAW	MIBLS	10//99-12//99
	Lansing-East Lansing MSA, MI	s	37.18 MW	35.94 AW	77330 AAW	MIBLS	10//99-12//99
	Saginaw-Bay City-Midland MSA, MI	s	36.67 MW	32.00 AW	76280 AAW	MIBLS	10//99-12//99
	Minnesota	s	27.02 MW	31.29 AW	65080 AAW	MNBLS	10//99-12//99
	Duluth-Superior MSA, MN-WI	s	24.39 MW	21.80 AW	50720 AAW	MNBLS	10//99-12//99
	Minneapolis-St. Paul MSA, MN-WI	s	34.42 MW	30.52 AW	71600 AAW	MNBLS	10//99-12//99
	Rochester MSA, MN	s	29.12 MW	26.82 AW	60570 AAW	MNBLS	10//99-12//99
	St. Cloud MSA, MN	s	22.54 MW	20.90 AW	46880 AAW	MNBLS	10//99-12//99
	Mississippi	s	22.96 MW	26.75 AW	55630 AAW	MSBLS	10//99-12//99
	Biloxi-Gulfport-Pascagoula MSA, MS	s	26.64 MW	22.35 AW	55420 AAW	MSBLS	10//99-12//99
	Hattiesburg MSA, MS	s	22.68 MW	20.41 AW	47180 AAW	MSBLS	10//99-12//99
	Jackson MSA, MS	s	29.78 MW	25.97 AW	61940 AAW	MSBLS	10//99-12//99
	Missouri	s	24.94 MW	29.40 AW	61150 AAW	MOBLS	10//99-12//99
	Columbia MSA, MO	s	24.81 MW	21.69 AW	51610 AAW	MOBLS	10//99-12//99
	Joplin MSA, MO	s	28.20 MW	24.56 AW	58650 AAW	MOBLS	10//99-12//99
	Kansas City MSA, MO-KS	s	32.07 MW	28.46 AW	66700 AAW	MOBLS	10//99-12//99
	St. Joseph MSA, MO	s	24.61 MW	19.72 AW	51190 AAW	MOBLS	10//99-12//99
	St. Louis MSA, MO-IL	s	30.99 MW	25.67 AW	64450 AAW	MOBLS	10//99-12//99

AAW	Average annual wage	AOH	Average offered, high	ASH	Average starting, high	H	Hourly	M	Monthly	S	Special: hourly and annual
AE	Average entry wage	AOL	Average offered, low	ASL	Average starting, low	HI	Highest wage paid	MTC	Median total compensation	TQ	Third quartile wage
AEX	Average experienced wage	APH	Average pay, high range	AW	Average wage paid	HR	High end range	MW	Median wage paid	W	Weekly
AO	Average offered	APL	Average pay, low range	FQ	First quartile wage	LR	Low end range	SQ	Second quartile wage	Y	Yearly

Occupation/Type/Industry	Location	Per	Low	Mid	High	Source	Date
General and Operations Manager	Springfield MSA, MO	s	26.17 mw	22.75 aw	54440 aaw	MOBLS	10//99-12//99
	Montana	s	19.74 mw	23.10 aw	48050 aaw	MTBLS	10//99-12//99
	Billings MSA, MT	s	23.86 mw	19.60 aw	49620 aaw	MTBLS	10//99-12//99
	Great Falls MSA, MT	s	18.40 mw	14.13 aw	38280 aaw	MTBLS	10//99-12//99
	Missoula MSA, MT	s	28.41 mw	23.46 aw	59090 aaw	MTBLS	10//99-12//99
	Nebraska	s	20.31 mw	24.85 aw	51680 aaw	NEBLS	10//99-12//99
	Lincoln MSA, NE	s	24.79 mw	20.77 aw	51570 aaw	NEBLS	10//99-12//99
	Omaha MSA, NE-IA	s	29.43 mw	25.20 aw	61210 aaw	NEBLS	10//99-12//99
	Nevada	s	29.86 mw	33.90 aw	70510 aaw	NVBLS	10//99-12//99
	Las Vegas MSA, NV-AZ	s	33.73 mw	30.39 aw	70150 aaw	NVBLS	10//99-12//99
	Reno MSA, NV	s	35.18 mw	29.92 aw	73180 aaw	NVBLS	10//99-12//99
	New Hampshire	s	25.51 mw	29.84 aw	62070 aaw	NHBLS	10//99-12//99
	Manchester PMSA, NH	s	30.99 mw	27.86 aw	64450 aaw	NHBLS	10//99-12//99
	Nashua PMSA, NH	s	34.52 mw	29.13 aw	71800 aaw	NHBLS	10//99-12//99
	Portsmouth-Rochester PMSA, NH-ME	s	31.24 mw	26.84 aw	64990 aaw	NHBLS	10//99-12//99
	New Jersey	s	45.9 mw	46.33 aw	96370 aaw	NJBLS	10//99-12//99
	Bergen-Passaic PMSA, NJ	s	49.66 mw	51.75 aw	103290 aaw	NJBLS	10//99-12//99
	Jersey City PMSA, NJ	s	42.31 mw	40.62 aw	88000 aaw	NJBLS	10//99-12//99
	Middlesex-Somerset-Hunterdon PMSA, NJ	s	47.70 mw	48.02 aw	99230 aaw	NJBLS	10//99-12//99
	Monmouth-Ocean PMSA, NJ	s	44.30 mw	45.60 aw	92140 aaw	NJBLS	10//99-12//99
	Newark PMSA, NJ	s	47.42 mw	46.94 aw	98640 aaw	NJBLS	10//99-12//99
	Trenton PMSA, NJ	s	47.21 mw	47.70 aw	98200 aaw	NJBLS	10//99-12//99
	Vineland-Millville-Bridgeton PMSA, NJ	s	36.71 mw	35.57 aw	76350 aaw	NJBLS	10//99-12//99
	New Mexico	s	22.52 mw	26.19 aw	54470 aaw	NMBLS	10//99-12//99
	Albuquerque MSA, NM	s	29.92 mw	25.84 aw	62230 aaw	NMBLS	10//99-12//99
	Las Cruces MSA, NM	s	22.21 mw	19.03 aw	46200 aaw	NMBLS	10//99-12//99
	Santa Fe MSA, NM	s	25.36 mw	22.57 aw	52750 aaw	NMBLS	10//99-12//99
	New York	s	40.97 mw	43.33 aw	90120 aaw	NYBLS	10//99-12//99
	Albany-Schenectady-Troy MSA, NY	s	33.41 mw	30.71 aw	69500 aaw	NYBLS	10//99-12//99
	Binghamton MSA, NY	s	30.76 mw	27.37 aw	63980 aaw	NYBLS	10//99-12//99
	Buffalo-Niagara Falls MSA, NY	s	39.90 mw	36.98 aw	82990 aaw	NYBLS	10//99-12//99
	Dutchess County PMSA, NY	s	35.70 mw	31.47 aw	74250 aaw	NYBLS	10//99-12//99
	Elmira MSA, NY	s	30.42 mw	30.41 aw	63270 aaw	NYBLS	10//99-12//99
	Glens Falls MSA, NY	s	34.08 mw	31.37 aw	70890 aaw	NYBLS	10//99-12//99
	Jamestown MSA, NY	s	32.19 mw	29.36 aw	66950 aaw	NYBLS	10//99-12//99
	Nassau-Suffolk PMSA, NY	s	42.78 mw	41.06 aw	88980 aaw	NYBLS	10//99-12//99
	New York PMSA, NY	s	48.71 mw	53.03 aw	101320 aaw	NYBLS	10//99-12//99
	Newburgh PMSA, NY-PA	s	34.40 mw	31.36 aw	71560 aaw	NYBLS	10//99-12//99
	Rochester MSA, NY	s	38.38 mw	34.18 aw	79830 aaw	NYBLS	10//99-12//99
	Syracuse MSA, NY	s	36.30 mw	32.57 aw	75500 aaw	NYBLS	10//99-12//99
	Utica-Rome MSA, NY	s	34.54 mw	29.92 aw	71840 aaw	NYBLS	10//99-12//99
	North Carolina	s	24.71 mw	28.95 aw	60210 aaw	NCBLS	10//99-12//99
	Asheville MSA, NC	s	27.14 mw	22.02 aw	56450 aaw	NCBLS	10//99-12//99
	Charlotte-Gastonia-Rock Hill MSA, NC-SC	s	31.70 mw	27.14 aw	65930 aaw	NCBLS	10//99-12//99
	Fayetteville MSA, NC	s	25.99 mw	21.63 aw	54060 aaw	NCBLS	10//99-12//99
	Goldsboro MSA, NC	s	23.13 mw	16.82 aw	48120 aaw	NCBLS	10//99-12//99
	Greensboro--Winston-Salem--High Point MSA, NC	s	31.44 mw	27.37 aw	65400 aaw	NCBLS	10//99-12//99
	Greenville MSA, NC	s	29.26 mw	24.59 aw	60850 aaw	NCBLS	10//99-12//99
	Hickory-Morganton-Lenoir MSA, NC	s	29.47 mw	24.62 aw	61290 aaw	NCBLS	10//99-12//99
	Jacksonville MSA, NC	s	21.77 mw	18.64 aw	45290 aaw	NCBLS	10//99-12//99
	Raleigh-Durham-Chapel Hill MSA, NC	s	29.88 mw	26.12 aw	62150 aaw	NCBLS	10//99-12//99
	Rocky Mount MSA, NC	s	27.37 mw	21.08 aw	56920 aaw	NCBLS	10//99-12//99
	Wilmington MSA, NC	s	25.37 mw	21.44 aw	52770 aaw	NCBLS	10//99-12//99
	North Dakota	s	20.87 mw	24.55 aw	51060 aaw	NDBLS	10//99-12//99
	Bismarck MSA, ND	s	24.24 mw	20.86 aw	50420 aaw	NDBLS	10//99-12//99
	Fargo-Moorhead MSA, ND-MN	s	27.79 mw	24.09 aw	57800 aaw	NDBLS	10//99-12//99
	Grand Forks MSA, ND-MN	s	24.02 mw	21.02 aw	49960 aaw	NDBLS	10//99-12//99
	Ohio	s	26.1 mw	30.47 aw	63380 aaw	OHBLS	10//99-12//99
	Akron PMSA, OH	s	29.05 mw	22.12 aw	60430 aaw	OHBLS	10//99-12//99
	Canton-Massillon MSA, OH	s	25.37 mw	20.77 aw	52760 aaw	OHBLS	10//99-12//99
	Cincinnati PMSA, OH-KY-IN	s	30.91 mw	26.28 aw	64290 aaw	OHBLS	10//99-12//99

AAW Average annual wage	**AOH** Average offered, high	**ASH** Average starting, high	**H** Hourly	**M** Monthly	**S** Special: hourly and annual
AE Average entry wage	**AOL** Average offered, low	**ASL** Average starting, low	**HI** Highest wage paid	**MTC** Median total compensation	**TQ** Third quartile wage
AEX Average experienced wage	**APH** Average pay, high range	**AW** Average wage paid	**HR** High end range	**MW** Median wage paid	**W** Weekly
AO Average offered	**APL** Average pay, low range	**FQ** First quartile wage	**LR** Low end range	**SQ** Second quartile wage	**Y** Yearly

Occupation/Type/Industry	Location	Per	Low	Mid	High	Source	Date
General and Operations Manager	Cleveland-Lorain-Elyria PMSA, OH	S	32.53 MW	28.64 AW	67660 AAW	OHBLS	10//99-12//99
	Columbus MSA, OH	S	31.42 MW	27.09 AW	65360 AAW	OHBLS	10//99-12//99
	Dayton-Springfield MSA, OH	S	32.59 MW	29.59 AW	67790 AAW	OHBLS	10//99-12//99
	Hamilton-Middletown PMSA, OH	S	29.49 MW	25.81 AW	61330 AAW	OHBLS	10//99-12//99
	Lima MSA, OH	S	26.27 MW	23.30 AW	54630 AAW	OHBLS	10//99-12//99
	Mansfield MSA, OH	S	25.79 MW	20.70 AW	53630 AAW	OHBLS	10//99-12//99
	Steubenville-Weirton MSA, OH-WV	S	21.96 MW	18.59 AW	45670 AAW	OHBLS	10//99-12//99
	Toledo MSA, OH	S	33.72 MW	29.62 AW	70130 AAW	OHBLS	10//99-12//99
	Youngstown-Warren MSA, OH	S	26.89 MW	23.75 AW	55930 AAW	OHBLS	10//99-12//99
	Oklahoma	S	20.95 MW	24.54 AW	51030 AAW	OKBLS	10//99-12//99
	Enid MSA, OK	S	20.90 MW	18.27 AW	43470 AAW	OKBLS	10//99-12//99
	Lawton MSA, OK	S	16.69 MW	14.83 AW	34710 AAW	OKBLS	10//99-12//99
	Oklahoma City MSA, OK	S	25.26 MW	22.46 AW	52540 AAW	OKBLS	10//99-12//99
	Tulsa MSA, OK	S	29.02 MW	24.90 AW	60360 AAW	OKBLS	10//99-12//99
	Oregon	S	32.19 MW	35.38 AW	73600 AAW	ORBLS	10//99-12//99
	Corvallis MSA, OR	S	32.58 MW	25.43 AW	67760 AAW	ORBLS	10//99-12//99
	Eugene-Springfield MSA, OR	S	32.21 MW	26.59 AW	66990 AAW	ORBLS	10//99-12//99
	Medford-Ashland MSA, OR	S	26.55 MW	22.18 AW	55220 AAW	ORBLS	10//99-12//99
	Portland-Vancouver PMSA, OR-WA	S	37.92 MW	34.36 AW	78870 AAW	ORBLS	10//99-12//99
	Salem PMSA, OR	S	30.47 MW	26.29 AW	63370 AAW	ORBLS	10//99-12//99
	Pennsylvania	S	27.14 MW	31.50 AW	65520 AAW	PABLS	10//99-12//99
	Allentown-Bethlehem-Easton MSA, PA	S	29.31 MW	25.09 AW	60960 AAW	PABLS	10//99-12//99
	Altoona MSA, PA	S	25.32 MW	19.98 AW	52680 AAW	PABLS	10//99-12//99
	Harrisburg-Lebanon-Carlisle MSA, PA	S	29.60 MW	26.34 AW	61570 AAW	PABLS	10//99-12//99
	Johnstown MSA, PA	S	28.01 MW	25.86 AW	58260 AAW	PABLS	10//99-12//99
	Lancaster MSA, PA	S	30.20 MW	26.44 AW	62820 AAW	PABLS	10//99-12//99
	Philadelphia PMSA, PA-NJ	S	36.94 MW	34.37 AW	76830 AAW	PABLS	10//99-12//99
	Pittsburgh MSA, PA	S	31.29 MW	26.99 AW	65090 AAW	PABLS	10//99-12//99
	Reading MSA, PA	S	27.69 MW	22.57 AW	57590 AAW	PABLS	10//99-12//99
	Scranton--Wilkes-Barre--Hazleton MSA, PA	S	26.50 MW	21.60 AW	55110 AAW	PABLS	10//99-12//99
	Sharon MSA, PA	S	22.35 MW	18.64 AW	46490 AAW	PABLS	10//99-12//99
	State College MSA, PA	S	24.63 MW	20.12 AW	51230 AAW	PABLS	10//99-12//99
	Williamsport MSA, PA	S	23.52 MW	22.20 AW	48910 AAW	PABLS	10//99-12//99
	York MSA, PA	S	27.63 MW	24.32 AW	57480 AAW	PABLS	10//99-12//99
	Rhode Island	S	37.12 MW	40.38 AW	83980 AAW	RIBLS	10//99-12//99
	Providence-Fall River-Warwick MSA, RI-MA	S	36.85 MW	33.89 AW	76650 AAW	RIBLS	10//99-12//99
	South Carolina	S	21.32 MW	25.48 AW	53000 AAW	SCBLS	10//99-12//99
	Charleston-North Charleston MSA, SC	S	25.05 MW	20.71 AW	52110 AAW	SCBLS	10//99-12//99
	Columbia MSA, SC	S	24.97 MW	20.71 AW	51950 AAW	SCBLS	10//99-12//99
	Florence MSA, SC	S	26.77 MW	22.91 AW	55690 AAW	SCBLS	10//99-12//99
	Greenville-Spartanburg-Anderson MSA, SC	S	28.75 MW	25.21 AW	59790 AAW	SCBLS	10//99-12//99
	Myrtle Beach MSA, SC	S	21.21 MW	17.25 AW	44120 AAW	SCBLS	10//99-12//99
	Sumter MSA, SC	S	21.19 MW	19.36 AW	44080 AAW	SCBLS	10//99-12//99
	Rapid City MSA, SD	S	34.09 MW	30.96 AW	70910 AAW	SDBLS	10//99-12//99
	Sioux Falls MSA, SD	S	39.45 MW	34.81 AW	82050 AAW	SDBLS	10//99-12//99
	Tennessee	S	23.59 MW	28.07 AW	58380 AAW	TNBLS	10//99-12//99
	Chattanooga MSA, TN-GA	S	27.23 MW	23.78 AW	56640 AAW	TNBLS	10//99-12//99
	Clarksville-Hopkinsville MSA, TN-KY	S	20.82 MW	16.16 AW	43300 AAW	TNBLS	10//99-12//99
	Jackson MSA, TN	S	24.18 MW	21.18 AW	50300 AAW	TNBLS	10//99-12//99
	Johnson City-Kingsport-Bristol MSA, TN-VA	S	24.57 MW	20.11 AW	51110 AAW	TNBLS	10//99-12//99
	Knoxville MSA, TN	S	26.91 MW	21.84 AW	55960 AAW	TNBLS	10//99-12//99
	Memphis MSA, TN-AR-MS	S	30.14 MW	25.15 AW	62690 AAW	MSBLS	10//99-12//99
	Nashville MSA, TN	S	31.73 MW	26.58 AW	66000 AAW	TNBLS	10//99-12//99
	Texas	S	25.07 MW	29.29 AW	60920 AAW	TXBLS	10//99-12//99
	Abilene MSA, TX	S	20.48 MW	18.06 AW	42590 AAW	TXBLS	10//99-12//99
	Amarillo MSA, TX	S	22.82 MW	18.80 AW	47470 AAW	TXBLS	10//99-12//99
	Austin-San Marcos MSA, TX	S	28.35 MW	24.67 AW	58970 AAW	TXBLS	10//99-12//99
	Beaumont-Port Arthur MSA, TX	S	25.57 MW	22.34 AW	53180 AAW	TXBLS	10//99-12//99
	Brazoria PMSA, TX	S	25.46 MW	21.44 AW	52950 AAW	TXBLS	10//99-12//99

AAW Average annual wage	AOH Average offered, high	ASH Average starting, high	H Hourly	M Monthly	S Special: hourly and annual
AE Average entry wage	AOL Average offered, low	ASL Average starting, low	HI Highest wage paid	MTC Median total compensation	TQ Third quartile wage
AEX Average experienced wage	APH Average pay, high range	AW Average wage paid	HR High end range	MW Median wage paid	W Weekly
AO Average offered	APL Average pay, low range	FQ First quartile wage	LR Low end range	SQ Second quartile wage	Y Yearly

Occupation/Type/Industry	Location	Per	Low	Mid	High	Source	Date
General and Operations Manager	Brownsville-Harlingen-San Benito MSA, TX	S	26.38 MW	20.27 AW	54880 AAW	TXBLS	10//99-12//99
	Bryan-College Station MSA, TX	S	31.11 MW	23.98 AW	64710 AAW	TXBLS	10//99-12//99
	Corpus Christi MSA, TX	S	24.56 MW	21.33 AW	51090 AAW	TXBLS	10//99-12//99
	Dallas PMSA, TX	S	35.15 MW	32.16 AW	73120 AAW	TXBLS	10//99-12//99
	El Paso MSA, TX	S	23.64 MW	20.29 AW	49180 AAW	TXBLS	10//99-12//99
	Fort Worth-Arlington PMSA, TX	S	28.93 MW	25.18 AW	60170 AAW	TXBLS	10//99-12//99
	Galveston-Texas City PMSA, TX	S	24.46 MW	20.43 AW	50880 AAW	TXBLS	10//99-12//99
	Killeen-Temple MSA, TX	S	22.55 MW	20.18 AW	46890 AAW	TXBLS	10//99-12//99
	Laredo MSA, TX	S	24.74 MW	23.03 AW	51470 AAW	TXBLS	10//99-12//99
	Longview-Marshall MSA, TX	S	24.32 MW	20.90 AW	50600 AAW	TXBLS	10//99-12//99
	Lubbock MSA, TX	S	22.98 MW	20.42 AW	47810 AAW	TXBLS	10//99-12//99
	McAllen-Edinburg-Mission MSA, TX	S	22.02 MW	19.14 AW	45800 AAW	TXBLS	10//99-12//99
	Odessa-Midland MSA, TX	S	24.17 MW	20.54 AW	50270 AAW	TXBLS	10//99-12//99
	San Angelo MSA, TX	S	22.73 MW	19.03 AW	47290 AAW	TXBLS	10//99-12//99
	San Antonio MSA, TX	S	31.08 MW	27.27 AW	64660 AAW	TXBLS	10//99-12//99
	Sherman-Denison MSA, TX	S	23.99 MW	21.10 AW	49890 AAW	TXBLS	10//99-12//99
	Texarkana MSA, TX-Texarkana, AR	S	22.04 MW	19.86 AW	45850 AAW	TXBLS	10//99-12//99
	Tyler MSA, TX	S	27.06 MW	24.03 AW	56290 AAW	TXBLS	10//99-12//99
	Victoria MSA, TX	S	23.34 MW	17.67 AW	48550 AAW	TXBLS	10//99-12//99
	Waco MSA, TX	S	26.61 MW	22.39 AW	55360 AAW	TXBLS	10//99-12//99
	Wichita Falls MSA, TX	S	24.32 MW	20.28 AW	50580 AAW	TXBLS	10//99-12//99
	Utah	S	24.66 MW	27.82 AW	57860 AAW	UTBLS	10//99-12//99
	Provo-Orem MSA, UT	S	23.54 MW	20.05 AW	48960 AAW	UTBLS	10//99-12//99
	Salt Lake City-Ogden MSA, UT	S	29.78 MW	26.91 AW	61940 AAW	UTBLS	10//99-12//99
	Vermont	S	37.16 MW	40.93 AW	85130 AAW	VTBLS	10//99-12//99
	Burlington MSA, VT	S	47.95 MW	52.26 AW	99740 AAW	VTBLS	10//99-12//99
	Virginia	S	30.45 MW	33.10 AW	68850 AAW	VABLS	10//99-12//99
	Charlottesville MSA, VA	S	28.85 MW	24.37 AW	60000 AAW	VABLS	10//99-12//99
	Lynchburg MSA, VA	S	25.25 MW	21.09 AW	52510 AAW	VABLS	10//99-12//99
	Norfolk-Virginia Beach-Newport News MSA, VA-NC	S	27.08 MW	22.87 AW	56330 AAW	VABLS	10//99-12//99
	Richmond-Petersburg MSA, VA	S	35.60 MW	33.77 AW	74060 AAW	VABLS	10//99-12//99
	Roanoke MSA, VA	S	26.85 MW	22.70 AW	55840 AAW	VABLS	10//99-12//99
	Washington	S	33 MW	36.98 AW	76920 AAW	WABLS	10//99-12//99
	Bellingham MSA, WA	S	30.94 MW	30.79 AW	64360 AAW	WABLS	10//99-12//99
	Bremerton PMSA, WA	S	27.62 MW	25.30 AW	57440 AAW	WABLS	10//99-12//99
	Richland-Kennewick-Pasco MSA, WA	S	34.04 MW	33.78 AW	70810 AAW	WABLS	10//99-12//99
	Seattle-Bellevue-Everett PMSA, WA	S	41.82 MW	39.60 AW	86990 AAW	WABLS	10//99-12//99
	Spokane MSA, WA	S	35.51 MW	31.34 AW	73860 AAW	WABLS	10//99-12//99
	Tacoma PMSA, WA	S	34.49 MW	30.69 AW	71730 AAW	WABLS	10//99-12//99
	Yakima MSA, WA	S	32.26 MW	29.54 AW	67100 AAW	WABLS	10//99-12//99
	West Virginia	S	19.31 MW	22.89 AW	47610 AAW	WVBLS	10//99-12//99
	Charleston MSA, WV	S	26.13 MW	23.21 AW	54350 AAW	WVBLS	10//99-12//99
	Huntington-Ashland MSA, WV-KY-OH	S	23.35 MW	18.94 AW	48570 AAW	WVBLS	10//99-12//99
	Parkersburg-Marietta MSA, WV-OH	S	20.97 MW	16.84 AW	43610 AAW	WVBLS	10//99-12//99
	Wheeling MSA, WV-OH	S	23.01 MW	19.87 AW	47850 AAW	WVBLS	10//99-12//99
	Wisconsin	S	25.39 MW	29.20 AW	60730 AAW	WIBLS	10//99-12//99
	Appleton-Oshkosh-Neenah MSA, WI	S	28.37 MW	24.73 AW	59010 AAW	WIBLS	10//99-12//99
	Eau Claire MSA, WI	S	25.66 MW	20.18 AW	53370 AAW	WIBLS	10//99-12//99
	Green Bay MSA, WI	S	27.57 MW	25.04 AW	57340 AAW	WIBLS	10//99-12//99
	Janesville-Beloit MSA, WI	S	25.35 MW	21.17 AW	52740 AAW	WIBLS	10//99-12//99
	Kenosha PMSA, WI	S	25.13 MW	18.59 AW	52270 AAW	WIBLS	10//99-12//99
	La Crosse MSA, WI-MN	S	22.79 MW	21.38 AW	47410 AAW	WIBLS	10//99-12//99
	Madison MSA, WI	S	30.26 MW	25.87 AW	62950 AAW	WIBLS	10//99-12//99
	Milwaukee-Waukesha PMSA, WI	S	34.99 MW	31.30 AW	72780 AAW	WIBLS	10//99-12//99
	Racine PMSA, WI	S	28.67 MW	24.33 AW	59640 AAW	WIBLS	10//99-12//99
	Sheboygan MSA, WI	S	33.23 MW	28.41 AW	69130 AAW	WIBLS	10//99-12//99

Occupation/Type/Industry	Location	Per	Low	Mid	High	Source	Date
General and Operations Manager	Wausau MSA, WI	S	28.30 MW	23.75 AW	58870 AAW	WIBLS	10//99-12//99
	Wyoming	S	21.28 MW	25.16 AW	52320 AAW	WYBLS	10//99-12//99
	Casper MSA, WY	S	23.51 MW	19.72 AW	48910 AAW	WYBLS	10//99-12//99
	Cheyenne MSA, WY	S	23.46 MW	20.27 AW	48810 AAW	WYBLS	10//99-12//99
	Puerto Rico	S	26.43 MW	31.42 AW	65360 AAW	PRBLS	10//99-12//99
	Aguadilla MSA, PR	S	27.62 MW	22.25 AW	57450 AAW	PRBLS	10//99-12//99
	Arecibo PMSA, PR	S	26.33 MW	24.24 AW	54780 AAW	PRBLS	10//99-12//99
	Caguas PMSA, PR	S	30.05 MW	25.65 AW	62500 AAW	PRBLS	10//99-12//99
	Mayaguez MSA, PR	S	25.87 MW	19.42 AW	53810 AAW	PRBLS	10//99-12//99
	Ponce MSA, PR	S	24.94 MW	21.22 AW	51880 AAW	PRBLS	10//99-12//99
	San Juan-Bayamon PMSA, PR	S	32.90 MW	27.99 AW	68430 AAW	PRBLS	10//99-12//99
	Virgin Islands	S	28.65 MW	30.96 AW	64400 AAW	VIBLS	10//99-12//99
	Guam	S	19.54 MW	22.47 AW	46730 AAW	GUBLS	10//99-12//99
General Manager							
Auto Dealership	United States	Y		100000 MW		WARD2	1999
Auto Dealership	United States	Y		100480 AW		WARD1	1999
Hotel	United States	Y		77950 AW		HOTEL	1998
Gentleman's Gentleman	United States	Y	50000 LR		100000 HR	COLBIZ	2000
Geographer	California	S	19.06 MW	19.75 AW	41090 AAW	CABLS	10//99-12//99
	Washington PMSA, DC-MD-VA-WV	S	25.47 MW	24.74 AW	52980 AAW	DCBLS	10//99-12//99
	Oregon	S	15.64 MW	17.36 AW	36110 AAW	ORBLS	10//99-12//99
	Utah	S	19.16 MW	19.27 AW	40090 AAW	UTBLS	10//99-12//99
	Virginia	S	24.68 MW	26.22 AW	54530 AAW	VABLS	10//99-12//99
Geography Teacher							
Postsecondary	Alabama	Y		38570 AAW		ALBLS	10//99-12//99
Postsecondary	California	Y		56590 AAW		CABLS	10//99-12//99
Postsecondary	San Francisco PMSA, CA	Y		60870 AAW		CABLS	10//99-12//99
Postsecondary	Colorado	Y		47940 AAW		COBLS	10//99-12//99
Postsecondary	Washington PMSA, DC-MD-VA-WV	Y		54320 AAW		DCBLS	10//99-12//99
Postsecondary	Florida	Y		65370 AAW		FLBLS	10//99-12//99
Postsecondary	Georgia	Y		52380 AAW		GABLS	10//99-12//99
Postsecondary	Illinois	Y		51500 AAW		ILBLS	10//99-12//99
Postsecondary	Chicago PMSA, IL	Y		48980 AAW		ILBLS	10//99-12//99
Postsecondary	Indiana	Y		53720 AAW		INBLS	10//99-12//99
Postsecondary	Iowa	Y		54790 AAW		IABLS	10//99-12//99
Postsecondary	Kentucky	Y		52620 AAW		KYBLS	10//99-12//99
Postsecondary	Maryland	Y		55530 AAW		MDBLS	10//99-12//99
Postsecondary	Baltimore PMSA, MD	Y		54510 AAW		MDBLS	10//99-12//99
Postsecondary	Massachusetts	Y		54370 AAW		MABLS	10//99-12//99
Postsecondary	Michigan	Y		59940 AAW		MIBLS	10//99-12//99
Postsecondary	Minnesota	Y		59210 AAW		MNBLS	10//99-12//99
Postsecondary	Minneapolis-St. Paul MSA, MN-WI	Y		63650 AAW		MNBLS	10//99-12//99
Postsecondary	Missouri	Y		49340 AAW		MOBLS	10//99-12//99
Postsecondary	St. Louis MSA, MO-IL	Y		50750 AAW		MOBLS	10//99-12//99
Postsecondary	Nevada	Y		48750 AAW		NVBLS	10//99-12//99
Postsecondary	New Jersey	Y		62050 AAW		NJBLS	10//99-12//99
Postsecondary	New York	Y		49520 AAW		NYBLS	10//99-12//99
Postsecondary	North Carolina	Y		38610 AAW		NCBLS	10//99-12//99
Postsecondary	Ohio	Y		50760 AAW		OHBLS	10//99-12//99
Postsecondary	Pennsylvania	Y		57230 AAW		PABLS	10//99-12//99
Postsecondary	Allentown-Bethlehem-Easton MSA, PA	Y		56680 AAW		PABLS	10//99-12//99
Postsecondary	Philadelphia PMSA, PA-NJ	Y		58220 AAW		PABLS	10//99-12//99
Postsecondary	Pittsburgh MSA, PA	Y		49610 AAW		PABLS	10//99-12//99
Postsecondary	Scranton--Wilkes-Barre--Hazleton MSA, PA	Y		52860 AAW		PABLS	10//99-12//99
Postsecondary	South Carolina	Y		35200 AAW		SCBLS	10//99-12//99
Postsecondary	Tennessee	Y		46880 AAW		TNBLS	10//99-12//99
Postsecondary	Nashville MSA, TN	Y		49990 AAW		TNBLS	10//99-12//99
Postsecondary	Texas	Y		51810 AAW		TXBLS	10//99-12//99
Postsecondary	Virginia	Y		49780 AAW		VABLS	10//99-12//99
Postsecondary	West Virginia	Y		54630 AAW		WVBLS	10//99-12//99
Geological and Petroleum Technician	Alabama	S	15.42 MW	16.89 AW	35130 AAW	ALBLS	10//99-12//99
	Alaska	S	17.67 MW	18.63 AW	38740 AAW	AKBLS	10//99-12//99

AAW Average annual wage	**AOH** Average offered, high	**ASH** Average starting, high	**H** Hourly	**M** Monthly	**S** Special: hourly and annual
AE Average entry wage	**AOL** Average offered, low	**ASL** Average starting, low	**HI** Highest wage paid	**MTC** Median total compensation	**TQ** Third quartile wage
AEX Average experienced wage	**APH** Average pay, high range	**AW** Average wage paid	**HR** High end range	**MW** Median wage paid	**W** Weekly
AO Average offered	**APL** Average pay, low range	**FQ** First quartile wage	**LR** Low end range	**SQ** Second quartile wage	**Y** Yearly

Occupation/Type/Industry	Location	Per	Low	Mid	High	Source	Date
Geological and Petroleum							
Technician	Arizona	S	16.16 MW	17.72 AW	36870 AAW	AZBLS	10//99-12//99
	California	S	22.42 MW	21.70 AW	45130 AAW	CABLS	10//99-12//99
	Colorado	S	20.38 MW	22.08 AW	45930 AAW	COBLS	10//99-12//99
	Florida	S	10.69 MW	12.05 AW	25070 AAW	FLBLS	10//99-12//99
	Georgia	S	14.22 MW	13.39 AW	27840 AAW	GABLS	10//99-12//99
	Illinois	S	18.18 MW	18.10 AW	37640 AAW	ILBLS	10//99-12//99
	Kansas	S	23.63 MW	21.58 AW	44890 AAW	KSBLS	10//99-12//99
	Louisiana	S	17.53 MW	19.14 AW	39820 AAW	LABLS	10//99-12//99
	Maryland	S	11.77 MW	11.93 AW	24800 AAW	MDBLS	10//99-12//99
	Massachusetts	S	17.1 MW	17.95 AW	37350 AAW	MABLS	10//99-12//99
	Montana	S	17.3 MW	18.47 AW	38430 AAW	MTBLS	10//99-12//99
	Nevada	S	14.45 MW	14.11 AW	29350 AAW	NVBLS	10//99-12//99
	New Mexico	S	19.07 MW	18.40 AW	38270 AAW	NMBLS	10//99-12//99
	North Dakota	S	17.76 MW	14.74 AW	30660 AAW	NDBLS	10//99-12//99
	Oklahoma	S	15.6 MW	15.60 AW	32450 AAW	OKBLS	10//99-12//99
	Pennsylvania	S	18.1 MW	19.29 AW	40120 AAW	PABLS	10//99-12//99
	South Carolina	S	19.08 MW	19.45 AW	40450 AAW	SCBLS	10//99-12//99
	Texas	S	16.87 MW	20.74 AW	43130 AAW	TXBLS	10//99-12//99
	Utah	S	25.52 MW	25.79 AW	53630 AAW	UTBLS	10//99-12//99
	Virginia	S	16.86 MW	18.87 AW	39240 AAW	VABLS	10//99-12//99
	West Virginia	S	15.01 MW	17.42 AW	36240 AAW	WVBLS	10//99-12//99
	Wyoming	S	20.63 MW	22.62 AW	47060 AAW	WYBLS	10//99-12//99
Geoscientist							
Except Hydrologist and Geographer	Alabama	S	21.4 MW	22.06 AW	45880 AAW	ALBLS	10//99-12//99
Except Hydrologist and Geographer	Alaska	S	28.12 MW	27.96 AW	58150 AAW	AKBLS	10//99-12//99
Except Hydrologist and Geographer	Arizona	S	24.36 MW	25.90 AW	53880 AAW	AZBLS	10//99-12//99
Except Hydrologist and Geographer	California	S	25.84 MW	28.56 AW	59400 AAW	CABLS	10//99-12//99
Except Hydrologist and Geographer	Colorado	S	32.81 MW	33.18 AW	69020 AAW	COBLS	10//99-12//99
Except Hydrologist and Geographer	Connecticut	S	20.19 MW	22.96 AW	47770 AAW	CTBLS	10//99-12//99
Except Hydrologist and Geographer	Florida	S	23.43 MW	26.29 AW	54690 AAW	FLBLS	10//99-12//99
Except Hydrologist and Geographer	Georgia	S	20.47 MW	21.10 AW	43880 AAW	GABLS	10//99-12//99
Except Hydrologist and Geographer	Hawaii	S	25.23 MW	26.46 AW	55030 AAW	HIBLS	10//99-12//99
Except Hydrologist and Geographer	Idaho	S	24.13 MW	24.21 AW	50350 AAW	IDBLS	10//99-12//99
Except Hydrologist and Geographer	Illinois	S	27.42 MW	24.38 AW	50700 AAW	ILBLS	10//99-12//99
Except Hydrologist and Geographer	Indiana	S	19.39 MW	20.34 AW	42320 AAW	INBLS	10//99-12//99
Except Hydrologist and Geographer	Iowa	S	21.88 MW	22.68 AW	47170 AAW	IABLS	10//99-12//99
Except Hydrologist and Geographer	Kentucky	S	18.68 MW	19.72 AW	41020 AAW	KYBLS	10//99-12//99
Except Hydrologist and Geographer	Louisiana	S	32.28 MW	33.91 AW	70520 AAW	LABLS	10//99-12//99
Except Hydrologist and Geographer	Maine	S	19.33 MW	19.93 AW	41460 AAW	MEBLS	10//99-12//99
Except Hydrologist and Geographer	Maryland	S	31.76 MW	31.41 AW	65340 AAW	MDBLS	10//99-12//99
Except Hydrologist and Geographer	Massachusetts	S	18.26 MW	19.90 AW	41390 AAW	MABLS	10//99-12//99
Except Hydrologist and Geographer	Michigan	S	20.16 MW	21.42 AW	44550 AAW	MIBLS	10//99-12//99
Except Hydrologist and Geographer	Minnesota	S	16.34 MW	19.77 AW	41120 AAW	MNBLS	10//99-12//99
Except Hydrologist and Geographer	Missouri	S	20.89 MW	21.83 AW	45400 AAW	MOBLS	10//99-12//99
Except Hydrologist and Geographer	Montana	S	25.42 MW	26.22 AW	54540 AAW	MTBLS	10//99-12//99
Except Hydrologist and Geographer	Nebraska	S	21.3 MW	21.43 AW	44570 AAW	NEBLS	10//99-12//99
Except Hydrologist and Geographer	Nevada	S	25.52 MW	26.98 AW	56110 AAW	NVBLS	10//99-12//99
Except Hydrologist and Geographer	New Hampshire	S	23.53 MW	27.22 AW	56620 AAW	NHBLS	10//99-12//99
Except Hydrologist and Geographer	New Jersey	S	24.08 MW	26.05 AW	54190 AAW	NJBLS	10//99-12//99
Except Hydrologist and Geographer	New Mexico	S	23.45 MW	25.07 AW	52150 AAW	NMBLS	10//99-12//99
Except Hydrologist and Geographer	New York	S	23.48 MW	23.76 AW	49420 AAW	NYBLS	10//99-12//99
Except Hydrologist and Geographer	North Carolina	S	18.6 MW	19.99 AW	41570 AAW	NCBLS	10//99-12//99
Except Hydrologist and Geographer	Ohio	S	25.05 MW	24.97 AW	51930 AAW	OHBLS	10//99-12//99
Except Hydrologist and Geographer	Oklahoma	S	36.75 MW	37.33 AW	77640 AAW	OKBLS	10//99-12//99
Except Hydrologist and Geographer	Oregon	S	23.73 MW	24.03 AW	49970 AAW	ORBLS	10//99-12//99
Except Hydrologist and Geographer	Pennsylvania	S	20.65 MW	24.00 AW	49920 AAW	PABLS	10//99-12//99
Except Hydrologist and Geographer	South Carolina	S	30.05 MW	30.29 AW	62990 AAW	SCBLS	10//99-12//99
Except Hydrologist and Geographer	Tennessee	S	22.32 MW	21.69 AW	45120 AAW	TNBLS	10//99-12//99
Except Hydrologist and Geographer	Utah	S	23.61 MW	23.77 AW	49450 AAW	UTBLS	10//99-12//99
Except Hydrologist and Geographer	Vermont	S	22.35 MW	25.22 AW	52450 AAW	VTBLS	10//99-12//99
Except Hydrologist and Geographer	Virginia	S	32.87 MW	33.42 AW	69510 AAW	VABLS	10//99-12//99
Except Hydrologist and Geographer	Washington	S	31.46 MW	33.14 AW	68940 AAW	WABLS	10//99-12//99
Except Hydrologist and Geographer	West Virginia	S	19.65 MW	24.13 AW	50180 AAW	WVBLS	10//99-12//99
Except Hydrologist and Geographer	Wisconsin	S	21.48 MW	22.66 AW	47130 AAW	WIBLS	10//99-12//99
Except Hydrologist and Geographer	Wyoming	S	29.84 MW	28.90 AW	60120 AAW	WYBLS	10//99-12//99
Glazier	United States	W	353 LR		886 HR	TQUES	1999
	Alabama	S	10.66 MW	10.94 AW	22760 AAW	ALBLS	10//99-12//99
	Montgomery MSA, AL	S	12.29 MW	12.23 AW	25550 AAW	ALBLS	10//99-12//99
	Alaska	S	21.87 MW	20.94 AW	43550 AAW	AKBLS	10//99-12//99

AAW	Average annual wage	**AOH**	Average offered, high	**ASH**	Average starting, high	**H**	Hourly	**M**	Monthly	**S**	Special: hourly and annual
AE	Average entry wage	**AOL**	Average offered, low	**ASL**	Average starting, low	**HI**	Highest wage paid	**MTC**	Median total compensation	**TQ**	Third quartile wage
AEX	Average experienced wage	**APH**	Average pay, high range	**AW**	Average wage paid	**HR**	High end range	**MW**	Median wage paid	**W**	Weekly
AO	Average offered	**APL**	Average pay, low range	**FQ**	First quartile wage	**LR**	Low end range	**SQ**	Second quartile wage	**Y**	Yearly

Occupation/Type/Industry	Location	Per	Low	Mid	High	Source	Date
Glazier	Arizona	S	10.29 MW	10.70 AW	22250 AAW	AZBLS	10//99-12//99
	Phoenix-Mesa MSA, AZ	S	12.42 MW	12.02 AW	25840 AAW	AZBLS	10//99-12//99
	Tucson MSA, AZ	S	10.79 MW	10.34 AW	22450 AAW	AZBLS	10//99-12//99
	Arkansas	S	10.99 MW	11.11 AW	23100 AAW	ARBLS	10//99-12//99
	Fayetteville-Springdale-Rogers MSA, AR	S	11.52 MW	11.44 AW	23960 AAW	ARBLS	10//99-12//99
	California	S	15.38 MW	16.83 AW	35010 AAW	CABLS	10//99-12//99
	Chico-Paradise MSA, CA	S	12.33 MW	11.95 AW	25640 AAW	CABLS	10//99-12//99
	Fresno MSA, CA	S	17.31 MW	19.38 AW	36000 AAW	CABLS	10//99-12//99
	Los Angeles-Long Beach PMSA, CA	S	11.33 MW	10.57 AW	23560 AAW	CABLS	10//99-12//99
	Oakland PMSA, CA	S	17.64 MW	15.49 AW	36690 AAW	CABLS	10//99-12//99
	Orange County PMSA, CA	S	14.94 MW	14.05 AW	31070 AAW	CABLS	10//99-12//99
	Riverside-San Bernardino PMSA, CA	S	12.30 MW	13.55 AW	25590 AAW	CABLS	10//99-12//99
	Sacramento PMSA, CA	S	13.29 MW	11.06 AW	27630 AAW	CABLS	10//99-12//99
	San Diego MSA, CA	S	19.84 MW	21.80 AW	41260 AAW	CABLS	10//99-12//99
	San Francisco PMSA, CA	S	26.27 MW	28.92 AW	54630 AAW	CABLS	10//99-12//99
	San Jose PMSA, CA	S	16.14 MW	13.90 AW	33570 AAW	CABLS	10//99-12//99
	Stockton-Lodi MSA, CA	S	15.69 MW	15.84 AW	32630 AAW	CABLS	10//99-12//99
	Vallejo-Fairfield-Napa PMSA, CA	S	14.55 MW	15.51 AW	30260 AAW	CABLS	10//99-12//99
	Visalia-Tulare-Porterville MSA, CA	S	12.59 MW	10.99 AW	26180 AAW	CABLS	10//99-12//99
	Colorado	S	15.33 MW	15.35 AW	31920 AAW	COBLS	10//99-12//99
	Denver PMSA, CO	S	17.55 MW	17.47 AW	36500 AAW	COBLS	10//99-12//99
	Connecticut	S	18.47 MW	19.05 AW	39620 AAW	CTBLS	10//99-12//99
	Bridgeport PMSA, CT	S	18.45 MW	18.59 AW	38380 AAW	CTBLS	10//99-12//99
	Danbury PMSA, CT	S	14.01 MW	14.52 AW	29130 AAW	CTBLS	10//99-12//99
	Hartford MSA, CT	S	20.70 MW	16.14 AW	43060 AAW	CTBLS	10//99-12//99
	Delaware	S	11.58 MW	11.61 AW	24140 AAW	DEBLS	10//99-12//99
	Wilmington-Newark PMSA, DE-MD	S	12.38 MW	11.81 AW	25750 AAW	DEBLS	10//99-12//99
	Washington PMSA, DC-MD-VA-WV	S	16.34 MW	16.78 AW	33980 AAW	DCBLS	10//99-12//99
	Florida	S	12.14 MW	12.20 AW	25370 AAW	FLBLS	10//99-12//99
	Fort Lauderdale PMSA, FL	S	12.17 MW	12.00 AW	25310 AAW	FLBLS	10//99-12//99
	Miami PMSA, FL	S	10.85 MW	11.21 AW	22580 AAW	FLBLS	10//99-12//99
	Orlando MSA, FL	S	12.21 MW	12.32 AW	25390 AAW	FLBLS	10//99-12//99
	Pensacola MSA, FL	S	10.28 MW	10.14 AW	21370 AAW	FLBLS	10//99-12//99
	Tampa-St. Petersburg-Clearwater MSA, FL	S	13.98 MW	14.64 AW	29090 AAW	FLBLS	10//99-12//99
	Georgia	S	12.42 MW	13.15 AW	27350 AAW	GABLS	10//99-12//99
	Atlanta MSA, GA	S	14.87 MW	14.21 AW	30930 AAW	GABLS	10//99-12//99
	Idaho	S	12.35 MW	12.57 AW	26140 AAW	IDBLS	10//99-12//99
	Boise City MSA, ID	S	13.48 MW	14.33 AW	28050 AAW	IDBLS	10//99-12//99
	Pocatello MSA, ID	S	10.31 MW	10.82 AW	21450 AAW	IDBLS	10//99-12//99
	Illinois	S	23.31 MW	21.01 AW	43700 AAW	ILBLS	10//99-12//99
	Chicago PMSA, IL	S	25.68 MW	25.68 AW	53410 AAW	ILBLS	10//99-12//99
	Peoria-Pekin MSA, IL	S	12.58 MW	10.78 AW	26160 AAW	ILBLS	10//99-12//99
	Indiana	S	17.78 MW	16.63 AW	34600 AAW	INBLS	10//99-12//99
	Evansville-Henderson MSA, IN-KY	S	17.43 MW	18.77 AW	36250 AAW	INBLS	10//99-12//99
	Indianapolis MSA, IN	S	19.82 MW	22.37 AW	41220 AAW	INBLS	10//99-12//99
	Iowa	S	16.09 MW	14.45 AW	30050 AAW	IABLS	10//99-12//99
	Davenport-Moline-Rock Island MSA, IA-IL	S	16.03 MW	16.32 AW	33350 AAW	IABLS	10//99-12//99
	Kansas	S	9.16 MW	10.20 AW	21210 AAW	KSBLS	10//99-12//99
	Kentucky	S	12.49 MW	12.48 AW	25960 AAW	KYBLS	10//99-12//99
	Louisville MSA, KY-IN	S	13.08 MW	13.48 AW	27200 AAW	KYBLS	10//99-12//99
	Louisiana	S	11.92 MW	11.67 AW	24270 AAW	LABLS	10//99-12//99
	Houma MSA, LA	S	8.41 MW	8.74 AW	17480 AAW	LABLS	10//99-12//99
	New Orleans MSA, LA	S	13.57 MW	14.25 AW	28230 AAW	LABLS	10//99-12//99
	Maryland	S	14.22 MW	14.21 AW	29550 AAW	MDBLS	10//99-12//99
	Baltimore PMSA, MD	S	14.09 MW	14.19 AW	29320 AAW	MDBLS	10//99-12//99
	Massachusetts	S	18.13 MW	18.75 AW	38990 AAW	MABLS	10//99-12//99
	Lawrence PMSA, MA-NH	S	14.24 MW	14.41 AW	29610 AAW	MABLS	10//99-12//99
	Michigan	S	14.78 MW	14.84 AW	30870 AAW	MIBLS	10//99-12//99
	Detroit PMSA, MI	S	15.44 MW	15.32 AW	32110 AAW	MIBLS	10//99-12//99
	Grand Rapids-Muskegon-Holland MSA, MI	S	13.75 MW	13.14 AW	28600 AAW	MIBLS	10//99-12//99

AAW Average annual wage	AOH Average offered, high	ASH Average starting, high	H Hourly	M Monthly	S Special: hourly and annual
AE Average entry wage	AOL Average offered, low	ASL Average starting, low	HI Highest wage paid	MTC Median total compensation	TQ Third quartile wage
AEX Average experienced wage	APH Average pay, high range	AW Average wage paid	HR High end range	MW Median wage paid	W Weekly
AO Average offered	APL Average pay, low range	FQ First quartile wage	LR Low end range	SQ Second quartile wage	Y Yearly

Occupation/Type/Industry	Location	Per	Low	Mid	High	Source	Date
Glazier	Kalamazoo-Battle Creek MSA, MI	S	15.77 MW	16.47 AW	32810 AAW	MIBLS	10//99-12//99
	Minnesota	S	16.59 MW	18.74 AW	38970 AAW	MNBLS	10//99-12//99
	Minneapolis-St. Paul MSA, MN-WI	S	20.18 MW	18.79 AW	41980 AAW	MNBLS	10//99-12//99
	Mississippi	S	10.15 MW	10.33 AW	21490 AAW	MSBLS	10//99-12//99
	Jackson MSA, MS	S	12.30 MW	12.63 AW	25590 AAW	MSBLS	10//99-12//99
	Missouri	S	14.81 MW	16.58 AW	34480 AAW	MOBLS	10//99-12//99
	Kansas City MSA, MO-KS	S	16.18 MW	13.52 AW	33650 AAW	MOBLS	10//99-12//99
	Montana	S	11.92 MW	11.65 AW	24220 AAW	MTBLS	10//99-12//99
	Nebraska	S	14.32 MW	14.29 AW	29720 AAW	NEBLS	10//99-12//99
	Omaha MSA, NE-IA	S	14.93 MW	14.89 AW	31060 AAW	NEBLS	10//99-12//99
	Nevada	S	13.47 MW	13.91 AW	28940 AAW	NVBLS	10//99-12//99
	Las Vegas MSA, NV-AZ	S	14.49 MW	13.22 AW	30140 AAW	NVBLS	10//99-12//99
	Reno MSA, NV	S	13.14 MW	12.97 AW	27320 AAW	NVBLS	10//99-12//99
	New Hampshire	S	14.32 MW	14.32 AW	29790 AAW	NHBLS	10//99-12//99
	New Jersey	S	18.4 MW	18.44 AW	38340 AAW	NJBLS	10//99-12//99
	Atlantic-Cape May PMSA, NJ	S	18.76 MW	22.65 AW	39030 AAW	NJBLS	10//99-12//99
	Jersey City PMSA, NJ	S	19.87 MW	22.45 AW	41320 AAW	NJBLS	10//99-12//99
	New Mexico	S	9.57 MW	10.13 AW	21070 AAW	NMBLS	10//99-12//99
	Albuquerque MSA, NM	S	12.76 MW	12.27 AW	26550 AAW	NMBLS	10//99-12//99
	New York	S	16.4 MW	18.34 AW	38150 AAW	NYBLS	10//99-12//99
	Albany-Schenectady-Troy MSA, NY	S	13.91 MW	14.81 AW	28940 AAW	NYBLS	10//99-12//99
	Buffalo-Niagara Falls MSA, NY	S	12.99 MW	13.86 AW	27010 AAW	NYBLS	10//99-12//99
	New York PMSA, NY	S	27.97 MW	28.82 AW	58180 AAW	NYBLS	10//99-12//99
	Newburgh PMSA, NY-PA	S	13.58 MW	10.72 AW	28260 AAW	NYBLS	10//99-12//99
	Rochester MSA, NY	S	14.98 MW	15.32 AW	31160 AAW	NYBLS	10//99-12//99
	Utica-Rome MSA, NY	S	11.50 MW	10.84 AW	23910 AAW	NYBLS	10//99-12//99
	North Carolina	S	10.23 MW	11.02 AW	22930 AAW	NCBLS	10//99-12//99
	Charlotte-Gastonia-Rock Hill MSA, NC-SC	S	11.97 MW	12.16 AW	24890 AAW	NCBLS	10//99-12//99
	Hickory-Morganton-Lenoir MSA, NC	S	10.30 MW	9.76 AW	21430 AAW	NCBLS	10//99-12//99
	North Dakota	S	12.72 MW	13.45 AW	27980 AAW	NDBLS	10//99-12//99
	Ohio	S	13.23 MW	14.09 AW	29300 AAW	OHBLS	10//99-12//99
	Canton-Massillon MSA, OH	S	13.70 MW	14.13 AW	28490 AAW	OHBLS	10//99-12//99
	Cincinnati PMSA, OH-KY-IN	S	16.82 MW	18.16 AW	34980 AAW	OHBLS	10//99-12//99
	Cleveland-Lorain-Elyria PMSA, OH	S	15.03 MW	13.30 AW	31270 AAW	OHBLS	10//99-12//99
	Dayton-Springfield MSA, OH	S	12.92 MW	12.58 AW	26870 AAW	OHBLS	10//99-12//99
	Oklahoma	S	10.63 MW	10.78 AW	22410 AAW	OKBLS	10//99-12//99
	Oklahoma City MSA, OK	S	12.28 MW	12.55 AW	25540 AAW	OKBLS	10//99-12//99
	Tulsa MSA, OK	S	9.56 MW	8.86 AW	19880 AAW	OKBLS	10//99-12//99
	Oregon	S	17.74 MW	18.45 AW	38380 AAW	ORBLS	10//99-12//99
	Medford-Ashland MSA, OR	S	11.51 MW	11.67 AW	23950 AAW	ORBLS	10//99-12//99
	Portland-Vancouver PMSA, OR-WA	S	22.04 MW	23.47 AW	45840 AAW	ORBLS	10//99-12//99
	Salem PMSA, OR	S	12.64 MW	12.36 AW	26280 AAW	ORBLS	10//99-12//99
	Pennsylvania	S	21.95 MW	18.88 AW	39260 AAW	PABLS	10//99-12//99
	Harrisburg-Lebanon-Carlisle MSA, PA	S	12.04 MW	12.02 AW	25050 AAW	PABLS	10//99-12//99
	Philadelphia PMSA, PA-NJ	S	21.14 MW	22.83 AW	43960 AAW	PABLS	10//99-12//99
	Pittsburgh MSA, PA	S	22.45 MW	23.93 AW	46690 AAW	PABLS	10//99-12//99
	York MSA, PA	S	10.38 MW	10.01 AW	21600 AAW	PABLS	10//99-12//99
	Rhode Island	S	13.23 MW	14.77 AW	30730 AAW	RIBLS	10//99-12//99
	Providence-Fall River-Warwick MSA, RI-MA	S	14.98 MW	13.97 AW	31150 AAW	RIBLS	10//99-12//99
	South Carolina	S	11.94 MW	11.79 AW	24530 AAW	SCBLS	10//99-12//99
	Charleston-North Charleston MSA, SC	S	11.53 MW	11.24 AW	23980 AAW	SCBLS	10//99-12//99
	South Dakota	S	13.77 MW	13.58 AW	28250 AAW	SDBLS	10//99-12//99
	Tennessee	S	11.82 MW	11.70 AW	24340 AAW	TNBLS	10//99-12//99
	Johnson City-Kingsport-Bristol MSA, TN-VA	S	8.65 MW	8.44 AW	17990 AAW	TNBLS	10//99-12//99
	Knoxville MSA, TN	S	11.30 MW	10.61 AW	23500 AAW	TNBLS	10//99-12//99
	Memphis MSA, TN-AR-MS	S	12.80 MW	12.58 AW	26630 AAW	MSBLS	10//99-12//99
	Texas	S	10.73 MW	11.18 AW	23260 AAW	TXBLS	10//99-12//99
	Austin-San Marcos MSA, TX	S	10.47 MW	9.60 AW	21780 AAW	TXBLS	10//99-12//99
	Corpus Christi MSA, TX	S	10.48 MW	10.98 AW	21810 AAW	TXBLS	10//99-12//99
	Dallas PMSA, TX	S	13.50 MW	13.50 AW	28070 AAW	TXBLS	10//99-12//99

AAW Average annual wage	**AOH** Average offered, high	**ASH** Average starting, high	**H** Hourly	**M** Monthly	**S** Special: hourly and annual
AE Average entry wage	**AOL** Average offered, low	**ASL** Average starting, low	**HI** Highest wage paid	**MTC** Median total compensation	**TQ** Third quartile wage
AEX Average experienced wage	**APH** Average pay, high range	**AW** Average wage paid	**HR** High end range	**MW** Median wage paid	**W** Weekly
AO Average offered	**APL** Average pay, low range	**FQ** First quartile wage	**LR** Low end range	**SQ** Second quartile wage	**Y** Yearly

Occupation/Type/Industry	Location	Per	Low	Mid	High	Source	Date
Glazier	Houston PMSA, TX	S	14.23 MW	14.53 AW	29590 AAW	TXBLS	10//99-12//99
	Lubbock MSA, TX	S	7.86 MW	7.70 AW	16350 AAW	TXBLS	10//99-12//99
	San Antonio MSA, TX	S	12.26 MW	12.19 AW	25500 AAW	TXBLS	10//99-12//99
	Sherman-Denison MSA, TX	S	10.95 MW	11.41 AW	22770 AAW	TXBLS	10//99-12//99
	Tyler MSA, TX	S	11.54 MW	11.35 AW	24000 AAW	TXBLS	10//99-12//99
	Utah	S	11.04 MW	11.84 AW	24630 AAW	UTBLS	10//99-12//99
	Salt Lake City-Ogden MSA, UT	S	11.48 MW	10.66 AW	23880 AAW	UTBLS	10//99-12//99
	Vermont	S	11.93 MW	11.54 AW	24010 AAW	VTBLS	10//99-12//99
	Virginia	S	15.46 MW	15.23 AW	31670 AAW	VABLS	10//99-12//99
	Norfolk-Virginia Beach-Newport News MSA, VA-NC	S	12.80 MW	13.97 AW	26610 AAW	VABLS	10//99-12//99
	Washington	S	19 MW	18.63 AW	38750 AAW	WABLS	10//99-12//99
	Seattle-Bellevue-Everett PMSA, WA	S	22.01 MW	23.18 AW	45780 AAW	WABLS	10//99-12//99
	Tacoma PMSA, WA	S	12.95 MW	12.28 AW	26940 AAW	WABLS	10//99-12//99
	Yakima MSA, WA	S	12.76 MW	13.22 AW	26530 AAW	WABLS	10//99-12//99
	West Virginia	S	7 MW	9.60 AW	19960 AAW	WVBLS	10//99-12//99
	Parkersburg-Marietta MSA, WV-OH	S	18.53 MW	20.07 AW	38550 AAW	WVBLS	10//99-12//99
	Wisconsin	S	11.77 MW	14.52 AW	30190 AAW	WIBLS	10//99-12//99
	Wyoming	S	10.13 MW	10.88 AW	22630 AAW	WYBLS	10//99-12//99
	Puerto Rico	S	6.12 MW	6.09 AW	12660 AAW	PRBLS	10//99-12//99
	San Juan-Bayamon PMSA, PR	S	6.12 MW	6.14 AW	12720 AAW	PRBLS	10//99-12//99
Gospel Music Artist	United States	Y		85000 AW		PETENG	1999
Grader and Sorter							
Agricultural Product	Alabama	S	7.77 MW	8.57 AW	17830 AAW	ALBLS	10//99-12//99
Agricultural Product	Arizona	S	6.34 MW	7.93 AW	16500 AAW	AZBLS	10//99-12//99
Agricultural Product	Arkansas	S	7.95 MW	8.56 AW	17800 AAW	ARBLS	10//99-12//99
Agricultural Product	California	S	6.63 MW	7.09 AW	14750 AAW	CABLS	10//99-12//99
Agricultural Product	Colorado	S	6.07 MW	6.64 AW	13810 AAW	COBLS	10//99-12//99
Agricultural Product	Delaware	S	8.55 MW	9.40 AW	19560 AAW	DEBLS	10//99-12//99
Agricultural Product	Florida	S	6.19 MW	6.46 AW	13440 AAW	FLBLS	10//99-12//99
Agricultural Product	Georgia	S	6.65 MW	7.18 AW	14940 AAW	GABLS	10//99-12//99
Agricultural Product	Hawaii	S	6.53 MW	6.92 AW	14390 AAW	HIBLS	10//99-12//99
Agricultural Product	Idaho	S	6.04 MW	6.15 AW	12790 AAW	IDBLS	10//99-12//99
Agricultural Product	Illinois	S	7.77 MW	8.64 AW	17970 AAW	ILBLS	10//99-12//99
Agricultural Product	Indiana	S	9.63 MW	10.12 AW	21040 AAW	INBLS	10//99-12//99
Agricultural Product	Kansas	S	9.95 MW	9.85 AW	20490 AAW	KSBLS	10//99-12//99
Agricultural Product	Kentucky	S	7.65 MW	8.16 AW	16980 AAW	KYBLS	10//99-12//99
Agricultural Product	Louisiana	S	6.21 MW	7.11 AW	14790 AAW	LABLS	10//99-12//99
Agricultural Product	Maine	S	7.33 MW	7.52 AW	15640 AAW	MEBLS	10//99-12//99
Agricultural Product	Maryland	S	6.89 MW	7.35 AW	15300 AAW	MDBLS	10//99-12//99
Agricultural Product	Massachusetts	S	8.19 MW	9.87 AW	20520 AAW	MABLS	10//99-12//99
Agricultural Product	Michigan	S	6.54 MW	7.73 AW	16070 AAW	MIBLS	10//99-12//99
Agricultural Product	Minnesota	S	10 MW	10.53 AW	21910 AAW	MNBLS	10//99-12//99
Agricultural Product	Mississippi	S	7.02 MW	7.33 AW	15240 AAW	MSBLS	10//99-12//99
Agricultural Product	Missouri	S	6.18 MW	6.70 AW	13930 AAW	MOBLS	10//99-12//99
Agricultural Product	Montana	S	9.2 MW	9.12 AW	18980 AAW	MTBLS	10//99-12//99
Agricultural Product	Nebraska	S	7.94 MW	8.04 AW	16730 AAW	NEBLS	10//99-12//99
Agricultural Product	Nevada	S	7.01 MW	7.27 AW	15110 AAW	NVBLS	10//99-12//99
Agricultural Product	New Hampshire	S	10.08 MW	11.48 AW	23880 AAW	NHBLS	10//99-12//99
Agricultural Product	New Jersey	S	6.13 MW	7.21 AW	14990 AAW	NJBLS	10//99-12//99
Agricultural Product	New Mexico	S	5.96 MW	6.34 AW	13200 AAW	NMBLS	10//99-12//99
Agricultural Product	New York	S	6.45 MW	8.33 AW	17340 AAW	NYBLS	10//99-12//99
Agricultural Product	North Carolina	S	6.28 MW	7.24 AW	15060 AAW	NCBLS	10//99-12//99
Agricultural Product	North Dakota	S	8.35 MW	9.18 AW	19100 AAW	NDBLS	10//99-12//99
Agricultural Product	Ohio	S	7.92 MW	8.71 AW	18110 AAW	OHBLS	10//99-12//99
Agricultural Product	Oklahoma	S	7.48 MW	7.56 AW	15720 AAW	OKBLS	10//99-12//99
Agricultural Product	Oregon	S	7.67 MW	7.94 AW	16510 AAW	ORBLS	10//99-12//99
Agricultural Product	Pennsylvania	S	7.76 MW	8.09 AW	16820 AAW	PABLS	10//99-12//99
Agricultural Product	South Carolina	S	8.69 MW	9.77 AW	20310 AAW	SCBLS	10//99-12//99
Agricultural Product	South Dakota	S	8.3 MW	8.51 AW	17700 AAW	SDBLS	10//99-12//99
Agricultural Product	Tennessee	S	7.24 MW	7.55 AW	15690 AAW	TNBLS	10//99-12//99
Agricultural Product	Texas	S	6.25 MW	7.14 AW	14850 AAW	TXBLS	10//99-12//99
Agricultural Product	Utah	S	7.69 MW	8.16 AW	16970 AAW	UTBLS	10//99-12//99
Agricultural Product	Virginia	S	6.52 MW	7.36 AW	15320 AAW	VABLS	10//99-12//99
Agricultural Product	Washington	S	7.38 MW	7.68 AW	15970 AAW	WABLS	10//99-12//99
Agricultural Product	West Virginia	S	6.69 MW	7.36 AW	15310 AAW	WVBLS	10//99-12//99
Agricultural Product	Wisconsin	S	8.49 MW	8.93 AW	18570 AAW	WIBLS	10//99-12//99

AAW	Average annual wage	AOH	Average offered, high	ASH	Average starting, high	H	Hourly	M	Monthly	S	Special: hourly and annual
AE	Average entry wage	AOL	Average offered, low	ASL	Average starting, low	HI	Highest wage paid	MTC	Median total compensation	TQ	Third quartile wage
AEX	Average experienced wage	APH	Average pay, high range	AW	Average wage paid	HR	High end range	MW	Median wage paid	W	Weekly
AO	Average offered	APL	Average pay, low range	FQ	First quartile wage	LR	Low end range	SQ	Second quartile wage	Y	Yearly

Occupation/Type/Industry	Location	Per	Low	Mid	High	Source	Date
Grader and Sorter							
Agricultural Product	Puerto Rico	S	6.01 MW	6.14 AW	12770 AAW	PRBLS	10//99-12//99
Graduate Teaching Assistant	Alabama	Y		23140 AAW		ALBLS	10//99-12//99
	California	Y		27800 AAW		CABLS	10//99-12//99
	Florida	Y		12460 AAW		FLBLS	10//99-12//99
	Georgia	Y		17680 AAW		GABLS	10//99-12//99
	Louisiana	Y		18400 AAW		LABLS	10//99-12//99
	Maryland	Y		24390 AAW		MDBLS	10//99-12//99
	Minnesota	Y		29330 AAW		MNBLS	10//99-12//99
	Nebraska	Y		15020 AAW		NEBLS	10//99-12//99
	New Jersey	Y		17200 AAW		NJBLS	10//99-12//99
	New York	Y		24900 AAW		NYBLS	10//99-12//99
	North Carolina	Y		19340 AAW		NCBLS	10//99-12//99
	Pennsylvania	Y		15530 AAW		PABLS	10//99-12//99
	South Carolina	Y		20300 AAW		SCBLS	10//99-12//99
	South Dakota	Y		21600 AAW		SDBLS	10//99-12//99
	Tennessee	Y		23810 AAW		TNBLS	10//99-12//99
	Texas	Y		23470 AAW		TXBLS	10//99-12//99
	Vermont	Y		19610 AAW		VTBLS	10//99-12//99
	Virginia	Y		16140 AAW		VABLS	10//99-12//99
	Washington	Y		30380 AAW		WABLS	10//99-12//99
	Puerto Rico	Y		17570 AAW		PRBLS	10//99-12//99
Graphic Designer	Alabama	S	13.84 MW	15.00 AW	31200 AAW	ALBLS	10//99-12//99
	Alaska	S	15.24 MW	15.26 AW	31740 AAW	AKBLS	10//99-12//99
	Arizona	S	15.13 MW	16.47 AW	34260 AAW	AZBLS	10//99-12//99
	Arkansas	S	11.2 MW	11.59 AW	24120 AAW	ARBLS	10//99-12//99
	California	S	18.36 MW	19.66 AW	40900 AAW	CABLS	10//99-12//99
	Colorado	S	16.05 MW	16.83 AW	35010 AAW	COBLS	10//99-12//99
	Connecticut	S	18.15 MW	19.56 AW	40670 AAW	CTBLS	10//99-12//99
	Delaware	S	13.12 MW	13.84 AW	28780 AAW	DEBLS	10//99-12//99
	District of Columbia	S	18.91 MW	19.00 AW	39520 AAW	DCBLS	10//99-12//99
	Florida	S	13.85 MW	15.03 AW	31270 AAW	FLBLS	10//99-12//99
	Georgia	S	16.98 MW	17.84 AW	37100 AAW	GABLS	10//99-12//99
	Hawaii	S	13 MW	14.62 AW	30400 AAW	HIBLS	10//99-12//99
	Idaho	S	14.9 MW	14.70 AW	30570 AAW	IDBLS	10//99-12//99
	Illinois	S	16.88 MW	18.36 AW	38180 AAW	ILBLS	10//99-12//99
	Indiana	S	13.25 MW	15.25 AW	31720 AAW	INBLS	10//99-12//99
	Iowa	S	11.68 MW	12.98 AW	26990 AAW	IABLS	10//99-12//99
	Kansas	S	12.3 MW	12.60 AW	26210 AAW	KSBLS	10//99-12//99
	Kentucky	S	12.67 MW	12.88 AW	26800 AAW	KYBLS	10//99-12//99
	Louisiana	S	10.86 MW	12.00 AW	24960 AAW	LABLS	10//99-12//99
	Maine	S	14.04 MW	15.83 AW	32920 AAW	MEBLS	10//99-12//99
	Maryland	S	16.24 MW	17.93 AW	37290 AAW	MDBLS	10//99-12//99
	Massachusetts	S	18.68 MW	20.27 AW	42160 AAW	MABLS	10//99-12//99
	Michigan	S	16.92 MW	20.19 AW	41990 AAW	MIBLS	10//99-12//99
	Minnesota	S	15.7 MW	16.69 AW	34710 AAW	MNBLS	10//99-12//99
	Mississippi	S	13.54 MW	13.92 AW	28960 AAW	MSBLS	10//99-12//99
	Missouri	S	13.16 MW	14.81 AW	30800 AAW	MOBLS	10//99-12//99
	Montana	S	12.72 MW	13.56 AW	28190 AAW	MTBLS	10//99-12//99
	Nebraska	S	14.72 MW	14.94 AW	31080 AAW	NEBLS	10//99-12//99
	Nevada	S	14.11 MW	14.65 AW	30470 AAW	NVBLS	10//99-12//99
	New Hampshire	S	13.14 MW	14.71 AW	30590 AAW	NHBLS	10//99-12//99
	New Jersey	S	15.67 MW	17.38 AW	36150 AAW	NJBLS	10//99-12//99
	New Mexico	S	15.69 MW	16.78 AW	34900 AAW	NMBLS	10//99-12//99
	New York	S	20.16 MW	21.83 AW	45410 AAW	NYBLS	10//99-12//99
	North Carolina	S	14.86 MW	15.72 AW	32690 AAW	NCBLS	10//99-12//99
	North Dakota	S	11.03 MW	11.82 AW	24570 AAW	NDBLS	10//99-12//99
	Oklahoma	S	10.86 MW	12.77 AW	26550 AAW	OKBLS	10//99-12//99
	Oregon	S	15.96 MW	17.71 AW	36830 AAW	ORBLS	10//99-12//99
	Pennsylvania	S	15.12 MW	16.18 AW	33660 AAW	PABLS	10//99-12//99
	Rhode Island	S	17.52 MW	18.44 AW	38360 AAW	RIBLS	10//99-12//99
	South Carolina	S	16.05 MW	16.62 AW	34560 AAW	SCBLS	10//99-12//99
	South Dakota	S	12.2 MW	13.20 AW	27450 AAW	SDBLS	10//99-12//99
	Tennessee	S	14.42 MW	16.04 AW	33370 AAW	TNBLS	10//99-12//99
	Texas	S	15.84 MW	16.36 AW	34030 AAW	TXBLS	10//99-12//99
	Utah	S	14.91 MW	15.90 AW	33080 AAW	UTBLS	10//99-12//99
	Vermont	S	14.36 MW	15.10 AW	31400 AAW	VTBLS	10//99-12//99
	Virginia	S	15.32 MW	16.36 AW	34030 AAW	VABLS	10//99-12//99
	Washington	S	18.36 MW	18.62 AW	38740 AAW	WABLS	10//99-12//99
	West Virginia	S	9.95 MW	10.36 AW	21550 AAW	WVBLS	10//99-12//99
	Wisconsin	S	15.63 MW	16.40 AW	34100 AAW	WIBLS	10//99-12//99

AAW	Average annual wage	AOH	Average offered, high	ASH	Average starting, high	H	Hourly	M	Monthly	S	Special: hourly and annual
AE	Average entry wage	AOL	Average offered, low	ASL	Average starting, low	HI	Highest wage paid	MTC	Median total compensation	TQ	Third quartile wage
AEX	Average experienced wage	APH	Average pay, high range	AW	Average wage paid	HR	High end range	MW	Median wage paid	W	Weekly
AO	Average offered	APL	Average pay, low range	FQ	First quartile wage	LR	Low end range	SQ	Second quartile wage	Y	Yearly

Occupation/Type/Industry	Location	Per	Low	Mid	High	Source	Date
Graphic Designer	Wyoming	S	9.48 MW	10.58 AW	22010 AAW	WYBLS	10//99-12//99
	Puerto Rico	S	6.7 MW	8.47 AW	17620 AAW	PRBLS	10//99-12//99
	Guam	S	12.68 MW	13.02 AW	27090 AAW	GUBLS	10//99-12//99
Grinding and Polishing Worker							
Hand	Alabama	S	9.17 MW	9.73 AW	20240 AAW	ALBLS	10//99-12//99
Hand	Arizona	S	9.59 MW	9.88 AW	20550 AAW	AZBLS	10//99-12//99
Hand	Arkansas	S	9.83 MW	10.19 AW	21190 AAW	ARBLS	10//99-12//99
Hand	California	S	8.48 MW	9.45 AW	19650 AAW	CABLS	10//99-12//99
Hand	Colorado	S	10.39 MW	11.11 AW	23110 AAW	COBLS	10//99-12//99
Hand	Connecticut	S	12.54 MW	12.86 AW	26760 AAW	CTBLS	10//99-12//99
Hand	Florida	S	9.21 MW	9.56 AW	19890 AAW	FLBLS	10//99-12//99
Hand	Georgia	S	10.11 MW	10.77 AW	22400 AAW	GABLS	10//99-12//99
Hand	Hawaii	S	7.96 MW	8.60 AW	17900 AAW	HIBLS	10//99-12//99
Hand	Idaho	S	9.01 MW	9.59 AW	19950 AAW	IDBLS	10//99-12//99
Hand	Illinois	S	11.25 MW	12.90 AW	26830 AAW	ILBLS	10//99-12//99
Hand	Indiana	S	11.36 MW	13.06 AW	27160 AAW	INBLS	10//99-12//99
Hand	Iowa	S	10.24 MW	11.48 AW	23880 AAW	IABLS	10//99-12//99
Hand	Kansas	S	12.1 MW	20.09 AW	41780 AAW	KSBLS	10//99-12//99
Hand	Kentucky	S	9.71 MW	9.63 AW	20020 AAW	KYBLS	10//99-12//99
Hand	Louisiana	S	8.39 MW	8.86 AW	18430 AAW	LABLS	10//99-12//99
Hand	Maine	S	10.22 MW	10.20 AW	21220 AAW	MEBLS	10//99-12//99
Hand	Maryland	S	11.29 MW	11.51 AW	23950 AAW	MDBLS	10//99-12//99
Hand	Massachusetts	S	12.22 MW	12.84 AW	26710 AAW	MABLS	10//99-12//99
Hand	Michigan	S	11.13 MW	12.86 AW	26750 AAW	MIBLS	10//99-12//99
Hand	Minnesota	S	11.57 MW	11.74 AW	24420 AAW	MNBLS	10//99-12//99
Hand	Mississippi	S	8.81 MW	9.20 AW	19130 AAW	MSBLS	10//99-12//99
Hand	Missouri	S	11.18 MW	12.20 AW	25380 AAW	MOBLS	10//99-12//99
Hand	Montana	S	8 MW	8.46 AW	17600 AAW	MTBLS	10//99-12//99
Hand	Nebraska	S	12.3 MW	12.69 AW	26400 AAW	NEBLS	10//99-12//99
Hand	Nevada	S	8.43 MW	9.36 AW	19470 AAW	NVBLS	10//99-12//99
Hand	New Hampshire	S	10.51 MW	10.86 AW	22580 AAW	NHBLS	10//99-12//99
Hand	New Jersey	S	12.13 MW	13.29 AW	27630 AAW	NJBLS	10//99-12//99
Hand	New Mexico	S	7.44 MW	7.62 AW	15840 AAW	NMBLS	10//99-12//99
Hand	New York	S	9.27 MW	10.18 AW	21170 AAW	NYBLS	10//99-12//99
Hand	North Carolina	S	9.59 MW	10.25 AW	21330 AAW	NCBLS	10//99-12//99
Hand	North Dakota	S	9.64 MW	9.53 AW	19830 AAW	NDBLS	10//99-12//99
Hand	Ohio	S	11.99 MW	13.24 AW	27530 AAW	OHBLS	10//99-12//99
Hand	Oklahoma	S	9.71 MW	10.36 AW	21550 AAW	OKBLS	10//99-12//99
Hand	Oregon	S	8.88 MW	9.57 AW	19910 AAW	ORBLS	10//99-12//99
Hand	Pennsylvania	S	10.96 MW	11.42 AW	23750 AAW	PABLS	10//99-12//99
Hand	Rhode Island	S	10.23 MW	10.38 AW	21580 AAW	RIBLS	10//99-12//99
Hand	South Carolina	S	10.36 MW	11.34 AW	23580 AAW	SCBLS	10//99-12//99
Hand	South Dakota	S	8.38 MW	8.44 AW	17550 AAW	SDBLS	10//99-12//99
Hand	Tennessee	S	9.7 MW	9.85 AW	20480 AAW	TNBLS	10//99-12//99
Hand	Texas	S	8.35 MW	8.80 AW	18310 AAW	TXBLS	10//99-12//99
Hand	Utah	S	9.87 MW	10.59 AW	22020 AAW	UTBLS	10//99-12//99
Hand	Vermont	S	9.8 MW	10.75 AW	22350 AAW	VTBLS	10//99-12//99
Hand	Virginia	S	11.13 MW	11.07 AW	23020 AAW	VABLS	10//99-12//99
Hand	Washington	S	10.16 MW	11.87 AW	24700 AAW	WABLS	10//99-12//99
Hand	West Virginia	S	9.79 MW	9.76 AW	20300 AAW	WVBLS	10//99-12//99
Hand	Wisconsin	S	10.88 MW	11.55 AW	24020 AAW	WIBLS	10//99-12//99
Hand	Puerto Rico	S	7.08 MW	8.17 AW	16980 AAW	PRBLS	10//99-12//99
Grinding, Lapping, Polishing, and Buffing Machine Tool Setter, Operator, and Tender							
Metals and Plastics	Alabama	S	10.56 MW	12.85 AW	26730 AAW	ALBLS	10//99-12//99
Metals and Plastics	Anniston MSA, AL	S	9.56 MW	9.65 AW	19890 AAW	ALBLS	10//99-12//99
Metals and Plastics	Birmingham MSA, AL	S	12.12 MW	8.45 AW	25220 AAW	ALBLS	10//99-12//99
Metals and Plastics	Decatur MSA, AL	S	8.87 MW	8.61 AW	18460 AAW	ALBLS	10//99-12//99
Metals and Plastics	Dothan MSA, AL	S	5.96 MW	6.03 AW	12400 AAW	ALBLS	10//99-12//99
Metals and Plastics	Mobile MSA, AL	S	10.82 MW	10.88 AW	22500 AAW	ALBLS	10//99-12//99
Metals and Plastics	Arizona	S	11.7 MW	12.30 AW	25590 AAW	AZBLS	10//99-12//99
Metals and Plastics	Phoenix-Mesa MSA, AZ	S	13.31 MW	12.37 AW	27690 AAW	AZBLS	10//99-12//99
Metals and Plastics	Tucson MSA, AZ	S	10.43 MW	10.75 AW	21680 AAW	AZBLS	10//99-12//99
Metals and Plastics	Arkansas	S	12.56 MW	12.42 AW	25830 AAW	ARBLS	10//99-12//99
Metals and Plastics	Fayetteville-Springdale-Rogers MSA, AR	S	11.18 MW	11.47 AW	23250 AAW	ARBLS	10//99-12//99
Metals and Plastics	Little Rock-North Little Rock MSA, AR	S	10.28 MW	9.81 AW	21380 AAW	ARBLS	10//99-12//99
Metals and Plastics	California	S	9.39 MW	10.39 AW	21620 AAW	CABLS	10//99-12//99

AAW	Average annual wage	AOH	Average offered, high	ASH	Average starting, high
AE	Average entry wage	AOL	Average offered, low	ASL	Average starting, low
AEX	Average experienced wage	APH	Average pay, high range	AW	Average wage paid
AO	Average offered	APL	Average pay, low range	FQ	First quartile wage

H	Hourly	M	Monthly
HI	Highest wage paid	MTC	Median total compensation
HR	High end range	MW	Median wage paid
LR	Low end range	SQ	Second quartile wage

S	Special: hourly and annual
TQ	Third quartile wage
W	Weekly
Y	Yearly

Occupation/Type/Industry	Location	Per	Low	Mid	High	Source	Date
Grinding, Lapping, Polishing, and Buffing Machine Tool Setter, Operator, and Tender							
Metals and Plastics	Bakersfield MSA, CA	S	8.42 MW	8.02 AW	17510 AAW	CABLS	10//99-12//99
Metals and Plastics	Fresno MSA, CA	S	9.29 MW	8.41 AW	19320 AAW	CABLS	10//99-12//99
Metals and Plastics	Los Angeles-Long Beach PMSA, CA	S	9.86 MW	8.75 AW	20500 AAW	CABLS	10//99-12//99
Metals and Plastics	Modesto MSA, CA	S	9.26 MW	8.50 AW	19260 AAW	CABLS	10//99-12//99
Metals and Plastics	Oakland PMSA, CA	S	15.67 MW	15.55 AW	32590 AAW	CABLS	10//99-12//99
Metals and Plastics	Orange County PMSA, CA	S	9.93 MW	9.57 AW	20660 AAW	CABLS	10//99-12//99
Metals and Plastics	Riverside-San Bernardino PMSA, CA	S	10.53 MW	8.62 AW	21910 AAW	CABLS	10//99-12//99
Metals and Plastics	San Diego MSA, CA	S	9.88 MW	9.16 AW	20560 AAW	CABLS	10//99-12//99
Metals and Plastics	San Francisco PMSA, CA	S	13.66 MW	13.18 AW	28410 AAW	CABLS	10//99-12//99
Metals and Plastics	San Jose PMSA, CA	S	11.46 MW	9.58 AW	23830 AAW	CABLS	10//99-12//99
Metals and Plastics	Santa Barbara-Santa Maria-Lompoc MSA, CA	S	9.33 MW	8.45 AW	19410 AAW	CABLS	10//99-12//99
Metals and Plastics	Santa Rosa PMSA, CA	S	9.08 MW	8.40 AW	18890 AAW	CABLS	10//99-12//99
Metals and Plastics	Stockton-Lodi MSA, CA	S	9.93 MW	9.61 AW	20660 AAW	CABLS	10//99-12//99
Metals and Plastics	Ventura PMSA, CA	S	9.43 MW	9.41 AW	19620 AAW	CABLS	10//99-12//99
Metals and Plastics	Colorado	S	10.91 MW	10.98 AW	22840 AAW	COBLS	10//99-12//99
Metals and Plastics	Denver PMSA, CO	S	11.95 MW	11.76 AW	24860 AAW	COBLS	10//99-12//99
Metals and Plastics	Connecticut	S	13.61 MW	13.96 AW	29040 AAW	CTBLS	10//99-12//99
Metals and Plastics	Bridgeport PMSA, CT	S	15.18 MW	14.78 AW	31570 AAW	CTBLS	10//99-12//99
Metals and Plastics	Hartford MSA, CT	S	14.22 MW	14.08 AW	29590 AAW	CTBLS	10//99-12//99
Metals and Plastics	New Haven-Meriden PMSA, CT	S	13.12 MW	12.54 AW	27280 AAW	CTBLS	10//99-12//99
Metals and Plastics	New London-Norwich MSA, CT-RI	S	12.24 MW	12.13 AW	25460 AAW	CTBLS	10//99-12//99
Metals and Plastics	Waterbury PMSA, CT	S	12.97 MW	12.87 AW	26970 AAW	CTBLS	10//99-12//99
Metals and Plastics	Washington PMSA, DC-MD-VA-WV	S	10.40 MW	9.72 AW	21630 AAW	DCBLS	10//99-12//99
Metals and Plastics	Florida	S	10.1 MW	10.50 AW	21830 AAW	FLBLS	10//99-12//99
Metals and Plastics	Fort Lauderdale PMSA, FL	S	11.01 MW	11.47 AW	22900 AAW	FLBLS	10//99-12//99
Metals and Plastics	Jacksonville MSA, FL	S	8.83 MW	8.47 AW	18370 AAW	FLBLS	10//99-12//99
Metals and Plastics	Lakeland-Winter Haven MSA, FL	S	7.05 MW	6.44 AW	14660 AAW	FLBLS	10//99-12//99
Metals and Plastics	Melbourne-Titusville-Palm Bay MSA, FL	S	8.14 MW	7.32 AW	16930 AAW	FLBLS	10//99-12//99
Metals and Plastics	Miami PMSA, FL	S	9.06 MW	8.72 AW	18840 AAW	FLBLS	10//99-12//99
Metals and Plastics	Orlando MSA, FL	S	11.43 MW	10.47 AW	23770 AAW	FLBLS	10//99-12//99
Metals and Plastics	Sarasota-Bradenton MSA, FL	S	10.17 MW	10.03 AW	21150 AAW	FLBLS	10//99-12//99
Metals and Plastics	Tampa-St. Petersburg-Clearwater MSA, FL	S	12.34 MW	11.00 AW	25660 AAW	FLBLS	10//99-12//99
Metals and Plastics	West Palm Beach-Boca Raton MSA, FL	S	14.49 MW	15.01 AW	30140 AAW	FLBLS	10//99-12//99
Metals and Plastics	Georgia	S	11.64 MW	11.30 AW	23500 AAW	GABLS	10//99-12//99
Metals and Plastics	Atlanta MSA, GA	S	9.12 MW	8.19 AW	18970 AAW	GABLS	10//99-12//99
Metals and Plastics	Augusta-Aiken MSA, GA-SC	S	8.94 MW	9.38 AW	18590 AAW	GABLS	10//99-12//99
Metals and Plastics	Columbus MSA, GA-AL	S	11.46 MW	11.48 AW	23840 AAW	GABLS	10//99-12//99
Metals and Plastics	Idaho	S	10.15 MW	11.98 AW	24930 AAW	IDBLS	10//99-12//99
Metals and Plastics	Illinois	S	12.94 MW	13.21 AW	27480 AAW	ILBLS	10//99-12//99
Metals and Plastics	Chicago PMSA, IL	S	12.76 MW	12.90 AW	26550 AAW	ILBLS	10//99-12//99
Metals and Plastics	Peoria-Pekin MSA, IL	S	19.31 MW	19.57 AW	40160 AAW	ILBLS	10//99-12//99
Metals and Plastics	Rockford MSA, IL	S	13.67 MW	12.55 AW	28430 AAW	ILBLS	10//99-12//99
Metals and Plastics	Indiana	S	12.65 MW	12.65 AW	26310 AAW	INBLS	10//99-12//99
Metals and Plastics	Elkhart-Goshen MSA, IN	S	12.52 MW	12.35 AW	26040 AAW	INBLS	10//99-12//99
Metals and Plastics	Evansville-Henderson MSA, IN-KY	S	11.61 MW	11.94 AW	24150 AAW	INBLS	10//99-12//99
Metals and Plastics	Fort Wayne MSA, IN	S	12.44 MW	12.07 AW	25880 AAW	INBLS	10//99-12//99
Metals and Plastics	Gary PMSA, IN	S	12.38 MW	12.74 AW	25740 AAW	INBLS	10//99-12//99
Metals and Plastics	Indianapolis MSA, IN	S	11.25 MW	11.06 AW	23410 AAW	INBLS	10//99-12//99
Metals and Plastics	Muncie MSA, IN	S	8.46 MW	8.06 AW	17590 AAW	INBLS	10//99-12//99
Metals and Plastics	South Bend MSA, IN	S	11.37 MW	10.54 AW	23650 AAW	INBLS	10//99-12//99
Metals and Plastics	Iowa	S	11.68 MW	11.39 AW	23690 AAW	IABLS	10//99-12//99
Metals and Plastics	Davenport-Moline-Rock Island MSA, IA-IL	S	11.43 MW	10.92 AW	23770 AAW	IABLS	10//99-12//99
Metals and Plastics	Kansas	S	11.75 MW	12.02 AW	25000 AAW	KSBLS	10//99-12//99
Metals and Plastics	Wichita MSA, KS	S	13.55 MW	12.68 AW	28190 AAW	KSBLS	10//99-12//99
Metals and Plastics	Kentucky	S	10.83 MW	11.04 AW	22960 AAW	KYBLS	10//99-12//99
Metals and Plastics	Lexington MSA, KY	S	10.87 MW	10.38 AW	22600 AAW	KYBLS	10//99-12//99
Metals and Plastics	Louisville MSA, KY-IN	S	9.69 MW	8.37 AW	20160 AAW	KYBLS	10//99-12//99

AAW Average annual wage	**AOH** Average offered, high	**ASH** Average starting, high	**H** Hourly	**M** Monthly	**S** Special: hourly and annual
AE Average entry wage	**AOL** Average offered, low	**ASL** Average starting, low	**HI** Highest wage paid	**MTC** Median total compensation	**TQ** Third quartile wage
AEX Average experienced wage	**APH** Average pay, high range	**AW** Average wage paid	**HR** High end range	**MW** Median wage paid	**W** Weekly
AO Average offered	**APL** Average pay, low range	**FQ** First quartile wage	**LR** Low end range	**SQ** Second quartile wage	**Y** Yearly

Occupation/Type/Industry	Location	Per	Low	Mid	High	Source	Date
Grinding, Lapping, Polishing, and Buffing Machine Tool Setter, Operator, and Tender							
Metals and Plastics	Louisiana	S	8.53 MW	8.66 AW	18010 AAW	LABLS	10//99-12//99
Metals and Plastics	Baton Rouge MSA, LA	S	8.05 MW	8.06 AW	16740 AAW	LABLS	10//99-12//99
Metals and Plastics	Houma MSA, LA	S	12.19 MW	12.18 AW	25360 AAW	LABLS	10//99-12//99
Metals and Plastics	New Orleans MSA, LA	S	8.98 MW	9.36 AW	18690 AAW	LABLS	10//99-12//99
Metals and Plastics	Shreveport-Bossier City MSA, LA	S	6.67 MW	6.36 AW	13870 AAW	LABLS	10//99-12//99
Metals and Plastics	Maine	S	9.69 MW	10.44 AW	21710 AAW	MEBLS	10//99-12//99
Metals and Plastics	Portland MSA, ME	S	11.04 MW	9.35 AW	22970 AAW	MEBLS	10//99-12//99
Metals and Plastics	Maryland	S	10.72 MW	13.05 AW	27140 AAW	MDBLS	10//99-12//99
Metals and Plastics	Baltimore PMSA, MD	S	15.78 MW	17.05 AW	32820 AAW	MDBLS	10//99-12//99
Metals and Plastics	Massachusetts	S	13.17 MW	13.39 AW	27850 AAW	MABLS	10//99-12//99
Metals and Plastics	Boston PMSA, MA-NH	S	13.80 MW	13.27 AW	28710 AAW	MABLS	10//99-12//99
Metals and Plastics	Brockton PMSA, MA	S	11.09 MW	11.11 AW	23070 AAW	MABLS	10//99-12//99
Metals and Plastics	Fitchburg-Leominster PMSA, MA	S	16.05 MW	16.82 AW	33380 AAW	MABLS	10//99-12//99
Metals and Plastics	Lawrence PMSA, MA-NH	S	9.67 MW	9.63 AW	20110 AAW	MABLS	10//99-12//99
Metals and Plastics	Lowell PMSA, MA-NH	S	12.87 MW	12.28 AW	26780 AAW	MABLS	10//99-12//99
Metals and Plastics	New Bedford PMSA, MA	S	13.20 MW	14.07 AW	27460 AAW	MABLS	10//99-12//99
Metals and Plastics	Springfield MSA, MA	S	10.59 MW	10.22 AW	22030 AAW	MABLS	10//99-12//99
Metals and Plastics	Worcester PMSA, MA-CT	S	13.99 MW	13.83 AW	29100 AAW	MABLS	10//99-12//99
Metals and Plastics	Michigan	S	14.37 MW	15.21 AW	31630 AAW	MIBLS	10//99-12//99
Metals and Plastics	Ann Arbor PMSA, MI	S	19.12 MW	19.53 AW	39770 AAW	MIBLS	10//99-12//99
Metals and Plastics	Benton Harbor MSA, MI	S	10.93 MW	9.71 AW	22730 AAW	MIBLS	10//99-12//99
Metals and Plastics	Detroit PMSA, MI	S	15.94 MW	15.79 AW	33150 AAW	MIBLS	10//99-12//99
Metals and Plastics	Flint PMSA, MI	S	22.08 MW	24.07 AW	45920 AAW	MIBLS	10//99-12//99
Metals and Plastics	Grand Rapids-Muskegon-Holland MSA, MI	S	13.23 MW	11.55 AW	27530 AAW	MIBLS	10//99-12//99
Metals and Plastics	Jackson MSA, MI	S	15.17 MW	17.29 AW	31550 AAW	MIBLS	10//99-12//99
Metals and Plastics	Kalamazoo-Battle Creek MSA, MI	S	12.29 MW	11.33 AW	25560 AAW	MIBLS	10//99-12//99
Metals and Plastics	Lansing-East Lansing MSA, MI	S	15.51 MW	14.77 AW	32260 AAW	MIBLS	10//99-12//99
Metals and Plastics	Saginaw-Bay City-Midland MSA, MI	S	16.23 MW	15.10 AW	33770 AAW	MIBLS	10//99-12//99
Metals and Plastics	Minnesota	S	14.14 MW	14.39 AW	29940 AAW	MNBLS	10//99-12//99
Metals and Plastics	Minneapolis-St. Paul MSA, MN-WI	S	15.01 MW	14.90 AW	31210 AAW	MNBLS	10//99-12//99
Metals and Plastics	Mississippi	S	9.46 MW	9.82 AW	20420 AAW	MSBLS	10//99-12//99
Metals and Plastics	Missouri	S	9.78 MW	10.41 AW	21660 AAW	MOBLS	10//99-12//99
Metals and Plastics	Kansas City MSA, MO-KS	S	11.44 MW	11.10 AW	23790 AAW	MOBLS	10//99-12//99
Metals and Plastics	St. Louis MSA, MO-IL	S	11.17 MW	10.27 AW	23220 AAW	MOBLS	10//99-12//99
Metals and Plastics	Springfield MSA, MO	S	11.82 MW	11.77 AW	24580 AAW	MOBLS	10//99-12//99
Metals and Plastics	Montana	S	6.49 MW	8.17 AW	17000 AAW	MTBLS	10//99-12//99
Metals and Plastics	Nebraska	S	10.69 MW	10.57 AW	21990 AAW	NEBLS	10//99-12//99
Metals and Plastics	Lincoln MSA, NE	S	10.93 MW	10.30 AW	22730 AAW	NEBLS	10//99-12//99
Metals and Plastics	Omaha MSA, NE-IA	S	11.23 MW	10.59 AW	23360 AAW	NEBLS	10//99-12//99
Metals and Plastics	Nevada	S	10.66 MW	10.82 AW	22500 AAW	NVBLS	10//99-12//99
Metals and Plastics	Las Vegas MSA, NV-AZ	S	10.57 MW	10.33 AW	21990 AAW	NVBLS	10//99-12//99
Metals and Plastics	Reno MSA, NV	S	10.54 MW	10.40 AW	21920 AAW	NVBLS	10//99-12//99
Metals and Plastics	New Hampshire	S	11.65 MW	11.50 AW	23930 AAW	NHBLS	10//99-12//99
Metals and Plastics	Manchester PMSA, NH	S	9.97 MW	9.77 AW	20750 AAW	NHBLS	10//99-12//99
Metals and Plastics	Nashua PMSA, NH	S	11.70 MW	12.04 AW	24340 AAW	NHBLS	10//99-12//99
Metals and Plastics	Portsmouth-Rochester PMSA, NH-ME	S	12.56 MW	12.59 AW	26130 AAW	NHBLS	10//99-12//99
Metals and Plastics	New Jersey	S	12.75 MW	12.57 AW	26140 AAW	NJBLS	10//99-12//99
Metals and Plastics	Bergen-Passaic PMSA, NJ	S	13.90 MW	14.21 AW	28900 AAW	NJBLS	10//99-12//99
Metals and Plastics	Middlesex-Somerset-Hunterdon PMSA, NJ	S	11.96 MW	10.11 AW	24880 AAW	NJBLS	10//99-12//99
Metals and Plastics	Newark PMSA, NJ	S	12.52 MW	12.95 AW	26040 AAW	NJBLS	10//99-12//99
Metals and Plastics	New Mexico	S	8.75 MW	9.42 AW	19600 AAW	NMBLS	10//99-12//99
Metals and Plastics	Albuquerque MSA, NM	S	9.62 MW	8.52 AW	20010 AAW	NMBLS	10//99-12//99
Metals and Plastics	New York	S	10.94 MW	11.35 AW	23610 AAW	NYBLS	10//99-12//99
Metals and Plastics	Albany-Schenectady-Troy MSA, NY	S	12.53 MW	10.36 AW	26060 AAW	NYBLS	10//99-12//99
Metals and Plastics	Buffalo-Niagara Falls MSA, NY	S	13.22 MW	12.36 AW	27490 AAW	NYBLS	10//99-12//99
Metals and Plastics	Elmira MSA, NY	S	10.41 MW	10.77 AW	21660 AAW	NYBLS	10//99-12//99
Metals and Plastics	Jamestown MSA, NY	S	10.40 MW	10.44 AW	21630 AAW	NYBLS	10//99-12//99
Metals and Plastics	Nassau-Suffolk PMSA, NY	S	10.93 MW	10.48 AW	22740 AAW	NYBLS	10//99-12//99
Metals and Plastics	New York PMSA, NY	S	12.20 MW	12.16 AW	25380 AAW	NYBLS	10//99-12//99

AAW	Average annual wage	AOH	Average offered, high	ASH	Average starting, high	H	Hourly	M	Monthly	S	Special: hourly and annual
AE	Average entry wage	AOL	Average offered, low	ASL	Average starting, low	HI	Highest wage paid	MTC	Median total compensation	TQ	Third quartile wage
AEX	Average experienced wage	APH	Average pay, high range	AW	Average wage paid	HR	High end range	MW	Median wage paid	W	Weekly
AO	Average offered	APL	Average pay, low range	FQ	First quartile wage	LR	Low end range	SQ	Second quartile wage	Y	Yearly

Occupation/Type/Industry	Location	Per	Low	Mid	High	Source	Date
Grinding, Lapping, Polishing, and Buffing Machine Tool Setter, Operator, and Tender							
Metals and Plastics	Rochester MSA, NY	S	10.59 MW	9.98 AW	22020 AAW	NYBLS	10//99-12//99
Metals and Plastics	Syracuse MSA, NY	S	9.44 MW	8.79 AW	19630 AAW	NYBLS	10//99-12//99
Metals and Plastics	Utica-Rome MSA, NY	S	9.54 MW	8.78 AW	19840 AAW	NYBLS	10//99-12//99
Metals and Plastics	North Carolina	S	11.81 MW	12.26 AW	25500 AAW	NCBLS	10//99-12//99
Metals and Plastics	Asheville MSA, NC	S	9.63 MW	7.79 AW	20020 AAW	NCBLS	10//99-12//99
Metals and Plastics	Charlotte-Gastonia-Rock Hill MSA, NC-SC	S	13.88 MW	13.36 AW	28870 AAW	NCBLS	10//99-12//99
Metals and Plastics	Greensboro--Winston-Salem--High Point MSA, NC	S	11.03 MW	11.18 AW	22950 AAW	NCBLS	10//99-12//99
Metals and Plastics	Hickory-Morganton-Lenoir MSA, NC	S	12.73 MW	12.01 AW	26470 AAW	NCBLS	10//99-12//99
Metals and Plastics	Raleigh-Durham-Chapel Hill MSA, NC	S	10.19 MW	9.57 AW	21190 AAW	NCBLS	10//99-12//99
Metals and Plastics	Ohio	S	12.92 MW	13.09 AW	27230 AAW	OHBLS	10//99-12//99
Metals and Plastics	Akron PMSA, OH	S	12.35 MW	12.35 AW	25680 AAW	OHBLS	10//99-12//99
Metals and Plastics	Canton-Massillon MSA, OH	S	13.32 MW	13.09 AW	27710 AAW	OHBLS	10//99-12//99
Metals and Plastics	Cincinnati PMSA, OH-KY-IN	S	11.59 MW	11.14 AW	24100 AAW	OHBLS	10//99-12//99
Metals and Plastics	Cleveland-Lorain-Elyria PMSA, OH	S	13.82 MW	14.09 AW	28740 AAW	OHBLS	10//99-12//99
Metals and Plastics	Columbus MSA, OH	S	10.12 MW	10.02 AW	21040 AAW	OHBLS	10//99-12//99
Metals and Plastics	Dayton-Springfield MSA, OH	S	13.70 MW	13.27 AW	28500 AAW	OHBLS	10//99-12//99
Metals and Plastics	Hamilton-Middletown PMSA, OH	S	13.57 MW	13.61 AW	28220 AAW	OHBLS	10//99-12//99
Metals and Plastics	Lima MSA, OH	S	11.49 MW	11.49 AW	23890 AAW	OHBLS	10//99-12//99
Metals and Plastics	Mansfield MSA, OH	S	10.15 MW	9.79 AW	21120 AAW	OHBLS	10//99-12//99
Metals and Plastics	Toledo MSA, OH	S	16.88 MW	14.87 AW	35120 AAW	OHBLS	10//99-12//99
Metals and Plastics	Youngstown-Warren MSA, OH	S	9.71 MW	9.55 AW	20200 AAW	OHBLS	10//99-12//99
Metals and Plastics	Oklahoma	S	10.77 MW	11.35 AW	23610 AAW	OKBLS	10//99-12//99
Metals and Plastics	Oklahoma City MSA, OK	S	9.21 MW	8.33 AW	19160 AAW	OKBLS	10//99-12//99
Metals and Plastics	Tulsa MSA, OK	S	12.79 MW	14.21 AW	26600 AAW	OKBLS	10//99-12//99
Metals and Plastics	Oregon	S	10.62 MW	12.09 AW	25140 AAW	ORBLS	10//99-12//99
Metals and Plastics	Eugene-Springfield MSA, OR	S	9.51 MW	9.63 AW	19780 AAW	ORBLS	10//99-12//99
Metals and Plastics	Portland-Vancouver PMSA, OR-WA	S	11.56 MW	10.66 AW	24050 AAW	ORBLS	10//99-12//99
Metals and Plastics	Salem PMSA, OR	S	9.79 MW	9.77 AW	20370 AAW	ORBLS	10//99-12//99
Metals and Plastics	Pennsylvania	S	11.88 MW	12.24 AW	25460 AAW	PABLS	10//99-12//99
Metals and Plastics	Allentown-Bethlehem-Easton MSA, PA	S	10.74 MW	9.91 AW	22330 AAW	PABLS	10//99-12//99
Metals and Plastics	Erie MSA, PA	S	11.45 MW	11.89 AW	23820 AAW	PABLS	10//99-12//99
Metals and Plastics	Harrisburg-Lebanon-Carlisle MSA, PA	S	13.42 MW	13.27 AW	27920 AAW	PABLS	10//99-12//99
Metals and Plastics	Lancaster MSA, PA	S	12.82 MW	12.94 AW	26660 AAW	PABLS	10//99-12//99
Metals and Plastics	Philadelphia PMSA, PA-NJ	S	13.90 MW	12.96 AW	28900 AAW	PABLS	10//99-12//99
Metals and Plastics	Pittsburgh MSA, PA	S	11.98 MW	11.23 AW	24930 AAW	PABLS	10//99-12//99
Metals and Plastics	Reading MSA, PA	S	11.29 MW	10.44 AW	23470 AAW	PABLS	10//99-12//99
Metals and Plastics	Scranton--Wilkes-Barre--Hazleton MSA, PA	S	11.96 MW	12.49 AW	24890 AAW	PABLS	10//99-12//99
Metals and Plastics	York MSA, PA	S	12.61 MW	14.05 AW	26220 AAW	PABLS	10//99-12//99
Metals and Plastics	Rhode Island	S	9.98 MW	10.58 AW	22010 AAW	RIBLS	10//99-12//99
Metals and Plastics	Providence-Fall River-Warwick MSA, RI-MA	S	10.73 MW	10.20 AW	22310 AAW	RIBLS	10//99-12//99
Metals and Plastics	South Carolina	S	13.43 MW	12.78 AW	26580 AAW	SCBLS	10//99-12//99
Metals and Plastics	Columbia MSA, SC	S	11.23 MW	11.33 AW	23360 AAW	SCBLS	10//99-12//99
Metals and Plastics	Greenville-Spartanburg-Anderson MSA, SC	S	14.77 MW	15.01 AW	30710 AAW	SCBLS	10//99-12//99
Metals and Plastics	South Dakota	S	9.56 MW	9.67 AW	20120 AAW	SDBLS	10//99-12//99
Metals and Plastics	Sioux Falls MSA, SD	S	11.02 MW	10.20 AW	22930 AAW	SDBLS	10//99-12//99
Metals and Plastics	Tennessee	S	10.13 MW	10.81 AW	22490 AAW	TNBLS	10//99-12//99
Metals and Plastics	Chattanooga MSA, TN-GA	S	10.68 MW	10.69 AW	22210 AAW	TNBLS	10//99-12//99
Metals and Plastics	Johnson City-Kingsport-Bristol MSA, TN-VA	S	11.94 MW	11.97 AW	24830 AAW	TNBLS	10//99-12//99
Metals and Plastics	Knoxville MSA, TN	S	12.11 MW	10.98 AW	25190 AAW	TNBLS	10//99-12//99
Metals and Plastics	Memphis MSA, TN-AR-MS	S	10.56 MW	10.19 AW	21970 AAW	MSBLS	10//99-12//99
Metals and Plastics	Nashville MSA, TN	S	12.99 MW	12.35 AW	27020 AAW	TNBLS	10//99-12//99
Metals and Plastics	Texas	S	9.14 MW	10.23 AW	21280 AAW	TXBLS	10//99-12//99
Metals and Plastics	Austin-San Marcos MSA, TX	S	9.80 MW	9.54 AW	20380 AAW	TXBLS	10//99-12//99
Metals and Plastics	Dallas PMSA, TX	S	8.66 MW	8.05 AW	18010 AAW	TXBLS	10//99-12//99
Metals and Plastics	Fort Worth-Arlington PMSA, TX	S	17.41 MW	21.43 AW	36210 AAW	TXBLS	10//99-12//99

AAW Average annual wage	**AOH** Average offered, high	**ASH** Average starting, high	**H** Hourly	**M** Monthly	**S** Special: hourly and annual
AE Average entry wage	**AOL** Average offered, low	**ASL** Average starting, low	**HI** Highest wage paid	**MTC** Median total compensation	**TQ** Third quartile wage
AEX Average experienced wage	**APH** Average pay, high range	**AW** Average wage paid	**HR** High end range	**MW** Median wage paid	**W** Weekly
AO Average offered	**APL** Average pay, low range	**FQ** First quartile wage	**LR** Low end range	**SQ** Second quartile wage	**Y** Yearly

Occupation/Type/Industry	Location	Per	Low	Mid	High	Source	Date
Grinding, Lapping, Polishing, and Buffing Machine Tool Setter, Operator, and Tender							
Metals and Plastics	Houston PMSA, TX	S	10.35 MW	9.57 AW	21520 AAW	TXBLS	10//99-12//99
Metals and Plastics	Longview-Marshall MSA, TX	S	7.22 MW	6.26 AW	15020 AAW	TXBLS	10//99-12//99
Metals and Plastics	Lubbock MSA, TX	S	8.53 MW	9.16 AW	17750 AAW	TXBLS	10//99-12//99
Metals and Plastics	Odessa-Midland MSA, TX	S	11.29 MW	10.27 AW	23470 AAW	TXBLS	10//99-12//99
Metals and Plastics	San Antonio MSA, TX	S	10.21 MW	10.09 AW	21240 AAW	TXBLS	10//99-12//99
Metals and Plastics	Vermont	S	8.89 MW	9.20 AW	19130 AAW	VTBLS	10//99-12//99
Metals and Plastics	Burlington MSA, VT	S	10.69 MW	10.40 AW	22230 AAW	VTBLS	10//99-12//99
Metals and Plastics	Virginia	S	11.62 MW	11.58 AW	24090 AAW	VABLS	10//99-12//99
Metals and Plastics	Norfolk-Virginia Beach-Newport News MSA, VA-NC	S	9.90 MW	9.22 AW	20590 AAW	VABLS	10//99-12//99
Metals and Plastics	Richmond-Petersburg MSA, VA	S	11.86 MW	11.75 AW	24660 AAW	VABLS	10//99-12//99
Metals and Plastics	Washington	S	11.3 MW	12.73 AW	26490 AAW	WABLS	10//99-12//99
Metals and Plastics	Seattle-Bellevue-Everett PMSA, WA	S	14.30 MW	12.47 AW	29740 AAW	WABLS	10//99-12//99
Metals and Plastics	Spokane MSA, WA	S	9.12 MW	9.31 AW	18960 AAW	WABLS	10//99-12//99
Metals and Plastics	Tacoma PMSA, WA	S	12.65 MW	12.44 AW	26320 AAW	WABLS	10//99-12//99
Metals and Plastics	West Virginia	S	11.01 MW	10.32 AW	21470 AAW	WVBLS	10//99-12//99
Metals and Plastics	Wisconsin	S	11.19 MW	12.15 AW	25270 AAW	WIBLS	10//99-12//99
Metals and Plastics	Appleton-Oshkosh-Neenah MSA, WI	S	16.19 MW	15.79 AW	33670 AAW	WIBLS	10//99-12//99
Metals and Plastics	Green Bay MSA, WI	S	13.17 MW	12.55 AW	27400 AAW	WIBLS	10//99-12//99
Metals and Plastics	Kenosha PMSA, WI	S	15.78 MW	16.99 AW	32830 AAW	WIBLS	10//99-12//99
Metals and Plastics	Milwaukee-Waukesha PMSA, WI	S	11.43 MW	10.44 AW	23780 AAW	WIBLS	10//99-12//99
Metals and Plastics	Racine PMSA, WI	S	10.41 MW	10.16 AW	21650 AAW	WIBLS	10//99-12//99
Metals and Plastics	Sheboygan MSA, WI	S	11.80 MW	11.65 AW	24550 AAW	WIBLS	10//99-12//99
Metals and Plastics	Wausau MSA, WI	S	11.03 MW	10.71 AW	22940 AAW	WIBLS	10//99-12//99
Metals and Plastics	Puerto Rico	S	6.76 MW	6.64 AW	13800 AAW	PRBLS	10//99-12//99
Metals and Plastics	San Juan-Bayamon PMSA, PR	S	6.75 MW	6.95 AW	14040 AAW	PRBLS	10//99-12//99
Guard, Police							
Private Service	United States	H		8.78 AW		NCS98	1998
Hairdresser, Hairstylist, and Cosmetologist							
	Alabama	S	6.51 MW	8.80 AW	18310 AAW	ALBLS	10//99-12//99
	Anniston MSA, AL	S	7.22 MW	6.03 AW	15010 AAW	ALBLS	10//99-12//99
	Auburn-Opelika MSA, AL	S	8.70 MW	7.08 AW	18110 AAW	ALBLS	10//99-12//99
	Birmingham MSA, AL	S	10.01 MW	7.08 AW	20830 AAW	ALBLS	10//99-12//99
	Dothan MSA, AL	S	6.94 MW	6.64 AW	14430 AAW	ALBLS	10//99-12//99
	Florence MSA, AL	S	6.61 MW	6.17 AW	13740 AAW	ALBLS	10//99-12//99
	Gadsden MSA, AL	S	6.81 MW	6.38 AW	14170 AAW	ALBLS	10//99-12//99
	Huntsville MSA, AL	S	9.20 MW	6.33 AW	19130 AAW	ALBLS	10//99-12//99
	Mobile MSA, AL	S	5.86 MW	6.00 AW	12180 AAW	ALBLS	10//99-12//99
	Montgomery MSA, AL	S	10.85 MW	8.77 AW	22560 AAW	ALBLS	10//99-12//99
	Tuscaloosa MSA, AL	S	7.72 MW	6.53 AW	16050 AAW	ALBLS	10//99-12//99
	Alaska	S	11.54 MW	11.90 AW	24750 AAW	AKBLS	10//99-12//99
	Anchorage MSA, AK	S	15.01 MW	15.13 AW	31220 AAW	AKBLS	10//99-12//99
	Arizona	S	7.35 MW	8.09 AW	16830 AAW	AZBLS	10//99-12//99
	Flagstaff MSA, AZ-UT	S	8.31 MW	8.29 AW	17290 AAW	AZBLS	10//99-12//99
	Phoenix-Mesa MSA, AZ	S	8.10 MW	7.50 AW	16850 AAW	AZBLS	10//99-12//99
	Tucson MSA, AZ	S	8.45 MW	6.68 AW	17580 AAW	AZBLS	10//99-12//99
	Arkansas	S	6.7 MW	7.02 AW	14600 AAW	ARBLS	10//99-12//99
	Fort Smith MSA, AR-OK	S	7.39 MW	6.75 AW	15360 AAW	ARBLS	10//99-12//99
	Jonesboro MSA, AR	S	7.18 MW	6.66 AW	14940 AAW	ARBLS	10//99-12//99
	Little Rock-North Little Rock MSA, AR	S	6.94 MW	6.83 AW	14430 AAW	ARBLS	10//99-12//99
	Pine Bluff MSA, AR	S	6.23 MW	6.25 AW	12970 AAW	ARBLS	10//99-12//99
	California	S	8 MW	9.57 AW	19900 AAW	CABLS	10//99-12//99
	Bakersfield MSA, CA	S	9.29 MW	8.55 AW	19310 AAW	CABLS	10//99-12//99
	Chico-Paradise MSA, CA	S	7.12 MW	7.20 AW	14820 AAW	CABLS	10//99-12//99
	Fresno MSA, CA	S	9.60 MW	8.15 AW	19960 AAW	CABLS	10//99-12//99
	Los Angeles-Long Beach PMSA, CA	S	9.06 MW	7.66 AW	18840 AAW	CABLS	10//99-12//99
	Merced MSA, CA	S	6.97 MW	6.55 AW	14500 AAW	CABLS	10//99-12//99
	Modesto MSA, CA	S	7.39 MW	7.30 AW	15370 AAW	CABLS	10//99-12//99
	Oakland PMSA, CA	S	8.16 MW	7.58 AW	16980 AAW	CABLS	10//99-12//99
	Orange County PMSA, CA	S	8.21 MW	7.65 AW	17070 AAW	CABLS	10//99-12//99

Occupation/Type/Industry	Location	Per	Low	Mid	High	Source	Date
Hairdresser, Hairstylist, and Cosmetologist	Redding MSA, CA	S	9.04 MW	8.17 AW	18800 AAW	CABLS	10//99-12//99
	Riverside-San Bernardino PMSA, CA	S	9.42 MW	9.12 AW	19590 AAW	CABLS	10//99-12//99
	Sacramento PMSA, CA	S	8.32 MW	8.09 AW	17310 AAW	CABLS	10//99-12//99
	Salinas MSA, CA	S	10.66 MW	9.94 AW	22180 AAW	CABLS	10//99-12//99
	San Diego MSA, CA	S	13.26 MW	14.24 AW	27590 AAW	CABLS	10//99-12//99
	San Francisco PMSA, CA	S	13.70 MW	7.93 AW	28500 AAW	CABLS	10//99-12//99
	San Jose PMSA, CA	S	11.33 MW	9.43 AW	23570 AAW	CABLS	10//99-12//99
	San Luis Obispo-Atascadero-Paso Robles MSA, CA	S	10.34 MW	10.41 AW	21520 AAW	CABLS	10//99-12//99
	Santa Barbara-Santa Maria-Lompoc MSA, CA	S	9.40 MW	8.75 AW	19550 AAW	CABLS	10//99-12//99
	Santa Rosa PMSA, CA	S	9.06 MW	9.23 AW	18840 AAW	CABLS	10//99-12//99
	Stockton-Lodi MSA, CA	S	8.69 MW	9.14 AW	18080 AAW	CABLS	10//99-12//99
	Ventura PMSA, CA	S	7.69 MW	7.31 AW	15990 AAW	CABLS	10//99-12//99
	Visalia-Tulare-Porterville MSA, CA	S	7.51 MW	7.24 AW	15630 AAW	CABLS	10//99-12//99
	Yuba City MSA, CA	S	8.37 MW	8.11 AW	17410 AAW	CABLS	10//99-12//99
	Colorado	S	8.62 MW	8.93 AW	18580 AAW	COBLS	10//99-12//99
	Colorado Springs MSA, CO	S	8.84 MW	9.04 AW	18380 AAW	COBLS	10//99-12//99
	Denver PMSA, CO	S	9.06 MW	8.79 AW	18840 AAW	COBLS	10//99-12//99
	Greeley PMSA, CO	S	6.83 MW	6.47 AW	14210 AAW	COBLS	10//99-12//99
	Pueblo MSA, CO	S	8.94 MW	8.00 AW	18590 AAW	COBLS	10//99-12//99
	Connecticut	S	8.79 MW	10.58 AW	22010 AAW	CTBLS	10//99-12//99
	Bridgeport PMSA, CT	S	8.20 MW	8.01 AW	17060 AAW	CTBLS	10//99-12//99
	Danbury PMSA, CT	S	8.61 MW	8.89 AW	17910 AAW	CTBLS	10//99-12//99
	Hartford MSA, CT	S	12.34 MW	10.69 AW	25660 AAW	CTBLS	10//99-12//99
	New Haven-Meriden PMSA, CT	S	10.05 MW	9.09 AW	20900 AAW	CTBLS	10//99-12//99
	New London-Norwich MSA, CT-RI	S	8.49 MW	7.70 AW	17660 AAW	CTBLS	10//99-12//99
	Stamford-Norwalk PMSA, CT	S	17.43 MW	14.46 AW	36250 AAW	CTBLS	10//99-12//99
	Waterbury PMSA, CT	S	7.88 MW	6.48 AW	16390 AAW	CTBLS	10//99-12//99
	Delaware	S	7.66 MW	10.01 AW	20810 AAW	DEBLS	10//99-12//99
	Dover MSA, DE	S	8.10 MW	6.65 AW	16840 AAW	DEBLS	10//99-12//99
	Wilmington-Newark PMSA, DE-MD	S	10.20 MW	8.48 AW	21210 AAW	DEBLS	10//99-12//99
	District of Columbia	S	11.8 MW	13.41 AW	27890 AAW	DCBLS	10//99-12//99
	Washington PMSA, DC-MD-VA-WV	S	14.82 MW	12.71 AW	30820 AAW	DCBLS	10//99-12//99
	Florida	S	8.54 MW	10.03 AW	20870 AAW	FLBLS	10//99-12//99
	Daytona Beach MSA, FL	S	6.07 MW	6.05 AW	12630 AAW	FLBLS	10//99-12//99
	Fort Lauderdale PMSA, FL	S	7.06 MW	6.54 AW	14680 AAW	FLBLS	10//99-12//99
	Fort Myers-Cape Coral MSA, FL	S	7.92 MW	6.88 AW	16460 AAW	FLBLS	10//99-12//99
	Fort Pierce-Port St. Lucie MSA, FL	S	8.63 MW	9.17 AW	17940 AAW	FLBLS	10//99-12//99
	Fort Walton Beach MSA, FL	S	7.63 MW	7.30 AW	15870 AAW	FLBLS	10//99-12//99
	Gainesville MSA, FL	S	7.94 MW	7.72 AW	16510 AAW	FLBLS	10//99-12//99
	Jacksonville MSA, FL	S	10.09 MW	9.61 AW	21000 AAW	FLBLS	10//99-12//99
	Lakeland-Winter Haven MSA, FL	S	6.96 MW	6.72 AW	14480 AAW	FLBLS	10//99-12//99
	Melbourne-Titusville-Palm Bay MSA, FL	S	7.97 MW	7.75 AW	16580 AAW	FLBLS	10//99-12//99
	Miami PMSA, FL	S	11.57 MW	8.46 AW	24060 AAW	FLBLS	10//99-12//99
	Naples MSA, FL	S	13.89 MW	13.20 AW	28900 AAW	FLBLS	10//99-12//99
	Ocala MSA, FL	S	9.98 MW	8.29 AW	20760 AAW	FLBLS	10//99-12//99
	Orlando MSA, FL	S	10.59 MW	8.23 AW	22020 AAW	FLBLS	10//99-12//99
	Panama City MSA, FL	S	9.05 MW	8.31 AW	18830 AAW	FLBLS	10//99-12//99
	Pensacola MSA, FL	S	6.73 MW	6.40 AW	14000 AAW	FLBLS	10//99-12//99
	Punta Gorda MSA, FL	S	8.93 MW	8.28 AW	18570 AAW	FLBLS	10//99-12//99
	Sarasota-Bradenton MSA, FL	S	10.58 MW	9.51 AW	22000 AAW	FLBLS	10//99-12//99
	Tallahassee MSA, FL	S	12.15 MW	10.17 AW	25270 AAW	FLBLS	10//99-12//99
	Tampa-St. Petersburg-Clearwater MSA, FL	S	11.41 MW	11.01 AW	23730 AAW	FLBLS	10//99-12//99
	Georgia	S	8.3 MW	9.14 AW	19000 AAW	GABLS	10//99-12//99
	Athens MSA, GA	S	9.08 MW	8.65 AW	18890 AAW	GABLS	10//99-12//99
	Atlanta MSA, GA	S	9.01 MW	8.07 AW	18740 AAW	GABLS	10//99-12//99
	Augusta-Aiken MSA, GA-SC	S	8.88 MW	8.50 AW	18460 AAW	GABLS	10//99-12//99
	Columbus MSA, GA-AL	S	9.18 MW	8.93 AW	19100 AAW	GABLS	10//99-12//99
	Macon MSA, GA	S	8.14 MW	7.91 AW	16930 AAW	GABLS	10//99-12//99

AAW Average annual wage	**AOH** Average offered, high	**ASH** Average starting, high	**H** Hourly	**M** Monthly	**S** Special: hourly and annual
AE Average entry wage	**AOL** Average offered, low	**ASL** Average starting, low	**HI** Highest wage paid	**MTC** Median total compensation	**TQ** Third quartile wage
AEX Average experienced wage	**APH** Average pay, high range	**AW** Average wage paid	**HR** High end range	**MW** Median wage paid	**W** Weekly
AO Average offered	**APL** Average pay, low range	**FQ** First quartile wage	**LR** Low end range	**SQ** Second quartile wage	**Y** Yearly

Occupation/Type/Industry	Location	Per	Low	Mid	High	Source	Date
Hairdresser, Hairstylist, and Cosmetologist	Savannah MSA, GA	S	7.31 MW	6.54 AW	15210 AAW	GABLS	10//99-12//99
	Hawaii	S	9.81 MW	9.99 AW	20770 AAW	HIBLS	10//99-12//99
	Honolulu MSA, HI	S	9.97 MW	9.88 AW	20740 AAW	HIBLS	10//99-12//99
	Idaho	S	7.35 MW	7.76 AW	16140 AAW	IDBLS	10//99-12//99
	Boise City MSA, ID	S	6.81 MW	7.02 AW	14150 AAW	IDBLS	10//99-12//99
	Pocatello MSA, ID	S	6.97 MW	6.87 AW	14490 AAW	IDBLS	10//99-12//99
	Illinois	S	9.1 MW	9.53 AW	19830 AAW	ILBLS	10//99-12//99
	Bloomington-Normal MSA, IL	S	11.58 MW	11.15 AW	24090 AAW	ILBLS	10//99-12//99
	Champaign-Urbana MSA, IL	S	10.28 MW	9.47 AW	21380 AAW	ILBLS	10//99-12//99
	Chicago PMSA, IL	S	9.95 MW	11.03 AW	20710 AAW	ILBLS	10//99-12//99
	Decatur MSA, IL	S	8.65 MW	8.04 AW	18000 AAW	ILBLS	10//99-12//99
	Kankakee PMSA, IL	S	8.97 MW	8.29 AW	18660 AAW	ILBLS	10//99-12//99
	Peoria-Pekin MSA, IL	S	9.16 MW	7.92 AW	19060 AAW	ILBLS	10//99-12//99
	Rockford MSA, IL	S	9.36 MW	8.54 AW	19460 AAW	ILBLS	10//99-12//99
	Indiana	S	7.99 MW	8.73 AW	18170 AAW	INBLS	10//99-12//99
	Bloomington MSA, IN	S	8.80 MW	7.68 AW	18310 AAW	INBLS	10//99-12//99
	Elkhart-Goshen MSA, IN	S	6.89 MW	6.72 AW	14330 AAW	INBLS	10//99-12//99
	Evansville-Henderson MSA, IN-KY	S	6.78 MW	6.28 AW	14100 AAW	INBLS	10//99-12//99
	Fort Wayne MSA, IN	S	10.51 MW	11.21 AW	21850 AAW	INBLS	10//99-12//99
	Gary PMSA, IN	S	8.27 MW	8.35 AW	17190 AAW	INBLS	10//99-12//99
	Indianapolis MSA, IN	S	9.72 MW	8.07 AW	20220 AAW	INBLS	10//99-12//99
	Kokomo MSA, IN	S	7.70 MW	7.35 AW	16010 AAW	INBLS	10//99-12//99
	Lafayette MSA, IN	S	11.21 MW	10.39 AW	23310 AAW	INBLS	10//99-12//99
	Muncie MSA, IN	S	6.92 MW	6.49 AW	14400 AAW	INBLS	10//99-12//99
	South Bend MSA, IN	S	9.57 MW	9.29 AW	19910 AAW	INBLS	10//99-12//99
	Terre Haute MSA, IN	S	8.62 MW	7.90 AW	17920 AAW	INBLS	10//99-12//99
	Iowa	S	7.98 MW	9.05 AW	18820 AAW	IABLS	10//99-12//99
	Cedar Rapids MSA, IA	S	9.52 MW	7.97 AW	19790 AAW	IABLS	10//99-12//99
	Davenport-Moline-Rock Island MSA, IA-IL	S	8.96 MW	7.88 AW	18630 AAW	IABLS	10//99-12//99
	Des Moines MSA, IA	S	11.87 MW	10.33 AW	24690 AAW	IABLS	10//99-12//99
	Dubuque MSA, IA	S	9.51 MW	8.34 AW	19790 AAW	IABLS	10//99-12//99
	Iowa City MSA, IA	S	7.87 MW	7.75 AW	16380 AAW	IABLS	10//99-12//99
	Sioux City MSA, IA-NE	S	8.67 MW	8.81 AW	18030 AAW	IABLS	10//99-12//99
	Waterloo-Cedar Falls MSA, IA	S	8.95 MW	8.48 AW	18610 AAW	IABLS	10//99-12//99
	Kansas	S	8.39 MW	9.43 AW	19620 AAW	KSBLS	10//99-12//99
	Lawrence MSA, KS	S	11.80 MW	12.28 AW	24530 AAW	KSBLS	10//99-12//99
	Topeka MSA, KS	S	7.83 MW	7.83 AW	16290 AAW	KSBLS	10//99-12//99
	Wichita MSA, KS	S	9.48 MW	7.71 AW	19710 AAW	KSBLS	10//99-12//99
	Kentucky	S	9.49 MW	10.04 AW	20880 AAW	KYBLS	10//99-12//99
	Lexington MSA, KY	S	9.11 MW	7.45 AW	18950 AAW	KYBLS	10//99-12//99
	Louisville MSA, KY-IN	S	12.27 MW	12.58 AW	25530 AAW	KYBLS	10//99-12//99
	Louisiana	S	8.09 MW	9.08 AW	18880 AAW	LABLS	10//99-12//99
	Alexandria MSA, LA	S	8.29 MW	7.62 AW	17240 AAW	LABLS	10//99-12//99
	Baton Rouge MSA, LA	S	8.27 MW	6.43 AW	17200 AAW	LABLS	10//99-12//99
	Houma MSA, LA	S	7.57 MW	7.63 AW	15740 AAW	LABLS	10//99-12//99
	Lafayette MSA, LA	S	6.06 MW	6.00 AW	12600 AAW	LABLS	10//99-12//99
	Lake Charles MSA, LA	S	6.26 MW	6.12 AW	13020 AAW	LABLS	10//99-12//99
	Monroe MSA, LA	S	7.29 MW	7.32 AW	15160 AAW	LABLS	10//99-12//99
	New Orleans MSA, LA	S	10.98 MW	10.67 AW	22840 AAW	LABLS	10//99-12//99
	Shreveport-Bossier City MSA, LA	S	8.35 MW	7.19 AW	17380 AAW	LABLS	10//99-12//99
	Maine	S	6.86 MW	7.79 AW	16200 AAW	MEBLS	10//99-12//99
	Bangor MSA, ME	S	6.83 MW	6.47 AW	14200 AAW	MEBLS	10//99-12//99
	Lewiston-Auburn MSA, ME	S	9.72 MW	9.91 AW	20220 AAW	MEBLS	10//99-12//99
	Portland MSA, ME	S	7.53 MW	6.83 AW	15670 AAW	MEBLS	10//99-12//99
	Maryland	S	7.98 MW	10.05 AW	20900 AAW	MDBLS	10//99-12//99
	Baltimore PMSA, MD	S	9.46 MW	7.61 AW	19670 AAW	MDBLS	10//99-12//99
	Cumberland MSA, MD-WV	S	6.31 MW	6.18 AW	13130 AAW	MDBLS	10//99-12//99
	Massachusetts	S	8.96 MW	10.29 AW	21400 AAW	MABLS	10//99-12//99
	Barnstable-Yarmouth MSA, MA	S	10.77 MW	10.79 AW	22410 AAW	MABLS	10//99-12//99
	Boston PMSA, MA-NH	S	10.44 MW	8.61 AW	21720 AAW	MABLS	10//99-12//99
	Brockton PMSA, MA	S	9.49 MW	8.88 AW	19730 AAW	MABLS	10//99-12//99
	Lawrence PMSA, MA-NH	S	10.17 MW	9.84 AW	21160 AAW	MABLS	10//99-12//99
	Lowell PMSA, MA-NH	S	9.50 MW	9.63 AW	19750 AAW	MABLS	10//99-12//99
	New Bedford PMSA, MA	S	13.75 MW	10.22 AW	28610 AAW	MABLS	10//99-12//99
	Pittsfield MSA, MA	S	9.67 MW	11.26 AW	20110 AAW	MABLS	10//99-12//99
	Springfield MSA, MA	S	10.62 MW	9.27 AW	22090 AAW	MABLS	10//99-12//99
	Worcester PMSA, MA-CT	S	10.24 MW	8.45 AW	21300 AAW	MABLS	10//99-12//99

AAW Average annual wage	AOH Average offered, high	ASH Average starting, high	H Hourly	M Monthly	S Special: hourly and annual
AE Average entry wage	AOL Average offered, low	ASL Average starting, low	HI Highest wage paid	MTC Median total compensation	TQ Third quartile wage
AEX Average experienced wage	APH Average pay, high range	AW Average wage paid	HR High end range	MW Median wage paid	W Weekly
AO Average offered	APL Average pay, low range	FQ First quartile wage	LR Low end range	SQ Second quartile wage	Y Yearly

Occupation/Type/Industry	Location	Per	Low	Mid	High	Source	Date
Hairdresser, Hairstylist, and Cosmetologist	Michigan	S	9.4 MW	9.83 AW	20440 AAW	MIBLS	10//99-12//99
	Ann Arbor PMSA, MI	S	9.10 MW	8.08 AW	18930 AAW	MIBLS	10//99-12//99
	Benton Harbor MSA, MI	S	8.29 MW	8.04 AW	17250 AAW	MIBLS	10//99-12//99
	Detroit PMSA, MI	S	10.46 MW	9.71 AW	21750 AAW	MIBLS	10//99-12//99
	Flint PMSA, MI	S	7.35 MW	6.81 AW	15280 AAW	MIBLS	10//99-12//99
	Grand Rapids-Muskegon-Holland MSA, MI	S	10.05 MW	10.07 AW	20910 AAW	MIBLS	10//99-12//99
	Jackson MSA, MI	S	8.94 MW	8.49 AW	18590 AAW	MIBLS	10//99-12//99
	Kalamazoo-Battle Creek MSA, MI	S	9.01 MW	8.76 AW	18740 AAW	MIBLS	10//99-12//99
	Lansing-East Lansing MSA, MI	S	9.29 MW	7.91 AW	19310 AAW	MIBLS	10//99-12//99
	Saginaw-Bay City-Midland MSA, MI	S	9.10 MW	9.36 AW	18920 AAW	MIBLS	10//99-12//99
	Minnesota	S	9.95 MW	10.96 AW	22790 AAW	MNBLS	10//99-12//99
	Duluth-Superior MSA, MN-WI	S	8.34 MW	7.93 AW	17340 AAW	MNBLS	10//99-12//99
	Minneapolis-St. Paul MSA, MN-WI	S	11.30 MW	10.04 AW	23510 AAW	MNBLS	10//99-12//99
	Rochester MSA, MN	S	11.47 MW	11.05 AW	23860 AAW	MNBLS	10//99-12//99
	St. Cloud MSA, MN	S	9.67 MW	8.97 AW	20110 AAW	MNBLS	10//99-12//99
	Mississippi	S	8.88 MW	9.79 AW	20370 AAW	MSBLS	10//99-12//99
	Biloxi-Gulfport-Pascagoula MSA, MS	S	11.50 MW	9.31 AW	23920 AAW	MSBLS	10//99-12//99
	Jackson MSA, MS	S	10.48 MW	9.91 AW	21800 AAW	MSBLS	10//99-12//99
	Missouri	S	8.48 MW	9.89 AW	20560 AAW	MOBLS	10//99-12//99
	Columbia MSA, MO	S	7.65 MW	6.68 AW	15900 AAW	MOBLS	10//99-12//99
	Joplin MSA, MO	S	6.59 MW	6.37 AW	13700 AAW	MOBLS	10//99-12//99
	Kansas City MSA, MO-KS	S	11.21 MW	11.03 AW	23310 AAW	MOBLS	10//99-12//99
	St. Joseph MSA, MO	S	8.39 MW	6.74 AW	17440 AAW	MOBLS	10//99-12//99
	St. Louis MSA, MO-IL	S	10.68 MW	8.67 AW	22210 AAW	MOBLS	10//99-12//99
	Springfield MSA, MO	S	8.74 MW	7.54 AW	18180 AAW	MOBLS	10//99-12//99
	Montana	S	7.48 MW	8.45 AW	17570 AAW	MTBLS	10//99-12//99
	Billings MSA, MT	S	10.49 MW	11.70 AW	21810 AAW	MTBLS	10//99-12//99
	Nebraska	S	9.05 MW	9.85 AW	20490 AAW	NEBLS	10//99-12//99
	Lincoln MSA, NE	S	9.99 MW	9.28 AW	20770 AAW	NEBLS	10//99-12//99
	Omaha MSA, NE-IA	S	11.30 MW	10.32 AW	23500 AAW	NEBLS	10//99-12//99
	Nevada	S	7.63 MW	8.28 AW	17230 AAW	NVBLS	10//99-12//99
	Las Vegas MSA, NV-AZ	S	8.42 MW	7.57 AW	17510 AAW	NVBLS	10//99-12//99
	Reno MSA, NV	S	7.27 MW	7.36 AW	15130 AAW	NVBLS	10//99-12//99
	New Hampshire	S	8.12 MW	9.93 AW	20650 AAW	NHBLS	10//99-12//99
	Manchester PMSA, NH	S	12.65 MW	12.92 AW	26320 AAW	NHBLS	10//99-12//99
	Nashua PMSA, NH	S	9.76 MW	8.29 AW	20300 AAW	NHBLS	10//99-12//99
	New Jersey	S	6.85 MW	9.00 AW	18730 AAW	NJBLS	10//99-12//99
	Atlantic-Cape May PMSA, NJ	S	8.69 MW	8.94 AW	18080 AAW	NJBLS	10//99-12//99
	Bergen-Passaic PMSA, NJ	S	6.32 MW	6.07 AW	13150 AAW	NJBLS	10//99-12//99
	Jersey City PMSA, NJ	S	8.98 MW	7.50 AW	18670 AAW	NJBLS	10//99-12//99
	Middlesex-Somerset-Hunterdon PMSA, NJ	S	9.01 MW	6.64 AW	18740 AAW	NJBLS	10//99-12//99
	Monmouth-Ocean PMSA, NJ	S	7.86 MW	7.02 AW	16350 AAW	NJBLS	10//99-12//99
	Vineland-Millville-Bridgeton PMSA, NJ	S	6.99 MW	6.14 AW	14540 AAW	NJBLS	10//99-12//99
	New Mexico	S	6.92 MW	7.31 AW	15200 AAW	NMBLS	10//99-12//99
	Albuquerque MSA, NM	S	7.55 MW	7.13 AW	15700 AAW	NMBLS	10//99-12//99
	Las Cruces MSA, NM	S	7.07 MW	6.19 AW	14710 AAW	NMBLS	10//99-12//99
	Santa Fe MSA, NM	S	6.95 MW	6.30 AW	14460 AAW	NMBLS	10//99-12//99
	New York	S	8.19 MW	14.55 AW	30270 AAW	NYBLS	10//99-12//99
	Albany-Schenectady-Troy MSA, NY	S	8.15 MW	7.85 AW	16960 AAW	NYBLS	10//99-12//99
	Binghamton MSA, NY	S	6.97 MW	6.19 AW	14510 AAW	NYBLS	10//99-12//99
	Buffalo-Niagara Falls MSA, NY	S	5.97 MW	6.05 AW	12420 AAW	NYBLS	10//99-12//99
	Dutchess County PMSA, NY	S	7.62 MW	6.35 AW	15860 AAW	NYBLS	10//99-12//99
	Elmira MSA, NY	S	7.54 MW	7.54 AW	15690 AAW	NYBLS	10//99-12//99
	Glens Falls MSA, NY	S	7.44 MW	7.10 AW	15480 AAW	NYBLS	10//99-12//99
	Jamestown MSA, NY	S	6.81 MW	6.26 AW	14160 AAW	NYBLS	10//99-12//99
	Nassau-Suffolk PMSA, NY	S	9.60 MW	8.36 AW	19960 AAW	NYBLS	10//99-12//99
	Newburgh PMSA, NY-PA	S	7.86 MW	6.70 AW	16350 AAW	NYBLS	10//99-12//99
	Rochester MSA, NY	S	9.62 MW	7.59 AW	20000 AAW	NYBLS	10//99-12//99
	Syracuse MSA, NY	S	7.21 MW	6.96 AW	15000 AAW	NYBLS	10//99-12//99
	Utica-Rome MSA, NY	S	7.59 MW	6.59 AW	15780 AAW	NYBLS	10//99-12//99
	North Carolina	S	7.9 MW	9.06 AW	18850 AAW	NCBLS	10//99-12//99
	Asheville MSA, NC	S	10.54 MW	7.86 AW	21930 AAW	NCBLS	10//99-12//99

AAW Average annual wage	**AOH** Average offered, high	**ASH** Average starting, high	**H** Hourly	**M** Monthly	**S** Special: hourly and annual
AE Average entry wage	**AOL** Average offered, low	**ASL** Average starting, low	**HI** Highest wage paid	**MTC** Median total compensation	**TQ** Third quartile wage
AEX Average experienced wage	**APH** Average pay, high range	**AW** Average wage paid	**HR** High end range	**MW** Median wage paid	**W** Weekly
AO Average offered	**APL** Average pay, low range	**FQ** First quartile wage	**LR** Low end range	**SQ** Second quartile wage	**Y** Yearly

Occupation/Type/Industry	Location	Per	Low	Mid	High	Source	Date
Hairdresser, Hairstylist, and Cosmetologist							
	Charlotte-Gastonia-Rock Hill MSA, NC-SC	S	8.93 MW	8.06 AW	18580 AAW	NCBLS	10//99-12//99
	Fayetteville MSA, NC	S	6.32 MW	6.33 AW	13150 AAW	NCBLS	10//99-12//99
	Goldsboro MSA, NC	S	7.15 MW	7.39 AW	14870 AAW	NCBLS	10//99-12//99
	Greensboro--Winston-Salem-- High Point MSA, NC	S	13.27 MW	13.66 AW	27590 AAW	NCBLS	10//99-12//99
	Greenville MSA, NC	S	8.87 MW	8.15 AW	18440 AAW	NCBLS	10//99-12//99
	Hickory-Morganton-Lenoir MSA, NC	S	7.52 MW	6.65 AW	15640 AAW	NCBLS	10//99-12//99
	Jacksonville MSA, NC	S	7.73 MW	7.71 AW	16070 AAW	NCBLS	10//99-12//99
	Raleigh-Durham-Chapel Hill MSA, NC	S	8.20 MW	7.72 AW	17070 AAW	NCBLS	10//99-12//99
	Rocky Mount MSA, NC	S	7.64 MW	7.69 AW	15900 AAW	NCBLS	10//99-12//99
	Wilmington MSA, NC	S	8.44 MW	7.91 AW	17560 AAW	NCBLS	10//99-12//99
	North Dakota	S	7.59 MW	8.46 AW	17600 AAW	NDBLS	10//99-12//99
	Bismarck MSA, ND	S	8.99 MW	8.31 AW	18700 AAW	NDBLS	10//99-12//99
	Fargo-Moorhead MSA, ND-MN	S	9.02 MW	8.94 AW	18770 AAW	NDBLS	10//99-12//99
	Grand Forks MSA, ND-MN	S	9.05 MW	8.54 AW	18830 AAW	NDBLS	10//99-12//99
	Ohio	S	7.98 MW	9.14 AW	19020 AAW	OHBLS	10//99-12//99
	Akron PMSA, OH	S	8.38 MW	7.30 AW	17420 AAW	OHBLS	10//99-12//99
	Canton-Massillon MSA, OH	S	8.80 MW	8.09 AW	18310 AAW	OHBLS	10//99-12//99
	Cincinnati PMSA, OH-KY-IN	S	10.32 MW	10.74 AW	21470 AAW	OHBLS	10//99-12//99
	Cleveland-Lorain-Elyria PMSA, OH	S	7.85 MW	7.69 AW	16340 AAW	OHBLS	10//99-12//99
	Columbus MSA, OH	S	12.81 MW	10.06 AW	26640 AAW	OHBLS	10//99-12//99
	Dayton-Springfield MSA, OH	S	8.64 MW	8.05 AW	17980 AAW	OHBLS	10//99-12//99
	Hamilton-Middletown PMSA, OH	S	12.26 MW	11.00 AW	25500 AAW	OHBLS	10//99-12//99
	Lima MSA, OH	S	7.35 MW	6.56 AW	15300 AAW	OHBLS	10//99-12//99
	Steubenville-Weirton MSA, OH-WV	S	7.74 MW	7.22 AW	16090 AAW	OHBLS	10//99-12//99
	Toledo MSA, OH	S	12.80 MW	13.18 AW	26620 AAW	OHBLS	10//99-12//99
	Youngstown-Warren MSA, OH	S	8.98 MW	8.97 AW	18680 AAW	OHBLS	10//99-12//99
	Oklahoma	S	7.15 MW	7.54 AW	15690 AAW	OKBLS	10//99-12//99
	Oklahoma City MSA, OK	S	7.38 MW	7.16 AW	15350 AAW	OKBLS	10//99-12//99
	Tulsa MSA, OK	S	7.94 MW	7.39 AW	16510 AAW	OKBLS	10//99-12//99
	Oregon	S	10.13 MW	11.31 AW	23520 AAW	ORBLS	10//99-12//99
	Corvallis MSA, OR	S	9.28 MW	9.20 AW	19300 AAW	ORBLS	10//99-12//99
	Portland-Vancouver PMSA, OR-WA	S	11.31 MW	9.71 AW	23530 AAW	ORBLS	10//99-12//99
	Salem PMSA, OR	S	11.26 MW	9.72 AW	23420 AAW	ORBLS	10//99-12//99
	Pennsylvania	S	7.33 MW	8.74 AW	18170 AAW	PABLS	10//99-12//99
	Allentown-Bethlehem-Easton MSA, PA	S	8.72 MW	8.11 AW	18140 AAW	PABLS	10//99-12//99
	Altoona MSA, PA	S	6.52 MW	6.12 AW	13560 AAW	PABLS	10//99-12//99
	Erie MSA, PA	S	6.84 MW	6.66 AW	14230 AAW	PABLS	10//99-12//99
	Harrisburg-Lebanon-Carlisle MSA, PA	S	8.97 MW	7.23 AW	18660 AAW	PABLS	10//99-12//99
	Johnstown MSA, PA	S	11.61 MW	11.21 AW	24140 AAW	PABLS	10//99-12//99
	Lancaster MSA, PA	S	10.59 MW	10.61 AW	22030 AAW	PABLS	10//99-12//99
	Philadelphia PMSA, PA-NJ	S	8.16 MW	6.53 AW	16970 AAW	PABLS	10//99-12//99
	Pittsburgh MSA, PA	S	9.08 MW	7.88 AW	18880 AAW	PABLS	10//99-12//99
	Scranton--Wilkes-Barre-- Hazleton MSA, PA	S	6.09 MW	6.08 AW	12660 AAW	PABLS	10//99-12//99
	State College MSA, PA	S	7.58 MW	7.32 AW	15780 AAW	PABLS	10//99-12//99
	Williamsport MSA, PA	S	9.10 MW	7.76 AW	18920 AAW	PABLS	10//99-12//99
	York MSA, PA	S	9.35 MW	7.14 AW	19440 AAW	PABLS	10//99-12//99
	Rhode Island	S	8.39 MW	9.56 AW	19890 AAW	RIBLS	10//99-12//99
	Providence-Fall River- Warwick MSA, RI-MA	S	9.09 MW	8.09 AW	18900 AAW	RIBLS	10//99-12//99
	South Carolina	S	9.64 MW	10.89 AW	22650 AAW	SCBLS	10//99-12//99
	Charleston-North Charleston MSA, SC	S	12.68 MW	14.12 AW	26380 AAW	SCBLS	10//99-12//99
	Columbia MSA, SC	S	9.64 MW	8.65 AW	20060 AAW	SCBLS	10//99-12//99
	Greenville-Spartanburg- Anderson MSA, SC	S	13.60 MW	14.62 AW	28290 AAW	SCBLS	10//99-12//99
	Myrtle Beach MSA, SC	S	8.18 MW	7.31 AW	17020 AAW	SCBLS	10//99-12//99
	Sumter MSA, SC	S	7.89 MW	7.75 AW	16410 AAW	SCBLS	10//99-12//99
	South Dakota	S	10.14 MW	10.49 AW	21810 AAW	SDBLS	10//99-12//99
	Rapid City MSA, SD	S	9.69 MW	9.50 AW	20150 AAW	SDBLS	10//99-12//99

AAW Average annual wage	AOH Average offered, high	ASH Average starting, high	H Hourly	M Monthly	S Special: hourly and annual
AE Average entry wage	AOL Average offered, low	ASL Average starting, low	HI Highest wage paid	MTC Median total compensation	TQ Third quartile wage
AEX Average experienced wage	APH Average pay, high range	AW Average wage paid	HR High end range	MW Median wage paid	W Weekly
AO Average offered	APL Average pay, low range	FQ First quartile wage	LR Low end range	SQ Second quartile wage	Y Yearly

Occupation/Type/Industry	Location	Per	Low	Mid	High	Source	Date
Hairdresser, Hairstylist, and Cosmetologist							
	Sioux Falls MSA, SD	S	11.66 MW	11.50 AW	24260 AAW	SDBLS	10//99-12//99
	Tennessee	S	8.12 MW	9.46 AW	19680 AAW	TNBLS	10//99-12//99
	Chattanooga MSA, TN-GA	S	10.45 MW	8.27 AW	21740 AAW	TNBLS	10//99-12//99
	Clarksville-Hopkinsville MSA, TN-KY	S	8.91 MW	9.06 AW	18540 AAW	TNBLS	10//99-12//99
	Johnson City-Kingsport-Bristol MSA, TN-VA	S	7.13 MW	6.63 AW	14830 AAW	TNBLS	10//99-12//99
	Knoxville MSA, TN	S	10.97 MW	9.73 AW	22810 AAW	TNBLS	10//99-12//99
	Memphis MSA, TN-AR-MS	S	9.13 MW	7.84 AW	18980 AAW	MSBLS	10//99-12//99
	Nashville MSA, TN	S	10.46 MW	9.07 AW	21750 AAW	TNBLS	10//99-12//99
	Texas	S	8.1 MW	9.30 AW	19350 AAW	TXBLS	10//99-12//99
	Abilene MSA, TX	S	6.83 MW	6.54 AW	14200 AAW	TXBLS	10//99-12//99
	Amarillo MSA, TX	S	6.45 MW	6.13 AW	13420 AAW	TXBLS	10//99-12//99
	Austin-San Marcos MSA, TX	S	10.78 MW	9.94 AW	22430 AAW	TXBLS	10//99-12//99
	Beaumont-Port Arthur MSA, TX	S	6.15 MW	6.05 AW	12800 AAW	TXBLS	10//99-12//99
	Brazoria PMSA, TX	S	11.93 MW	13.32 AW	24820 AAW	TXBLS	10//99-12//99
	Brownsville-Harlingen-San Benito MSA, TX	S	6.68 MW	6.31 AW	13900 AAW	TXBLS	10//99-12//99
	Bryan-College Station MSA, TX	S	8.56 MW	7.77 AW	17810 AAW	TXBLS	10//99-12//99
	Corpus Christi MSA, TX	S	6.40 MW	6.14 AW	13310 AAW	TXBLS	10//99-12//99
	Dallas PMSA, TX	S	10.17 MW	9.30 AW	21150 AAW	TXBLS	10//99-12//99
	El Paso MSA, TX	S	11.49 MW	13.98 AW	23890 AAW	TXBLS	10//99-12//99
	Fort Worth-Arlington PMSA, TX	S	7.81 MW	7.33 AW	16250 AAW	TXBLS	10//99-12//99
	Galveston-Texas City PMSA, TX	S	7.77 MW	6.38 AW	16170 AAW	TXBLS	10//99-12//99
	Houston PMSA, TX	S	10.83 MW	9.81 AW	22530 AAW	TXBLS	10//99-12//99
	Killeen-Temple MSA, TX	S	12.56 MW	11.06 AW	26120 AAW	TXBLS	10//99-12//99
	Laredo MSA, TX	S	6.51 MW	6.12 AW	13540 AAW	TXBLS	10//99-12//99
	Longview-Marshall MSA, TX	S	6.73 MW	6.30 AW	14000 AAW	TXBLS	10//99-12//99
	Lubbock MSA, TX	S	8.44 MW	8.79 AW	17550 AAW	TXBLS	10//99-12//99
	McAllen-Edinburg-Mission MSA, TX	S	7.51 MW	7.14 AW	15630 AAW	TXBLS	10//99-12//99
	San Angelo MSA, TX	S	7.33 MW	7.08 AW	15240 AAW	TXBLS	10//99-12//99
	San Antonio MSA, TX	S	7.35 MW	7.45 AW	15290 AAW	TXBLS	10//99-12//99
	Sherman-Denison MSA, TX	S	6.32 MW	6.21 AW	13140 AAW	TXBLS	10//99-12//99
	Texarkana MSA, TX-Texarkana, AR	S	7.14 MW	7.29 AW	14860 AAW	TXBLS	10//99-12//99
	Tyler MSA, TX	S	8.09 MW	6.66 AW	16830 AAW	TXBLS	10//99-12//99
	Victoria MSA, TX	S	7.67 MW	7.71 AW	15950 AAW	TXBLS	10//99-12//99
	Waco MSA, TX	S	8.60 MW	8.53 AW	17890 AAW	TXBLS	10//99-12//99
	Wichita Falls MSA, TX	S	7.37 MW	7.07 AW	15320 AAW	TXBLS	10//99-12//99
	Utah	S	8.71 MW	8.71 AW	18130 AAW	UTBLS	10//99-12//99
	Provo-Orem MSA, UT	S	8.66 MW	8.34 AW	18010 AAW	UTBLS	10//99-12//99
	Salt Lake City-Ogden MSA, UT	S	8.78 MW	8.83 AW	18270 AAW	UTBLS	10//99-12//99
	Vermont	S	9.55 MW	9.69 AW	20160 AAW	VTBLS	10//99-12//99
	Burlington MSA, VT	S	10.29 MW	9.57 AW	21410 AAW	VTBLS	10//99-12//99
	Virginia	S	10.71 MW	13.78 AW	28660 AAW	VABLS	10//99-12//99
	Danville MSA, VA	S	8.96 MW	8.45 AW	18630 AAW	VABLS	10//99-12//99
	Lynchburg MSA, VA	S	9.03 MW	9.07 AW	18790 AAW	VABLS	10//99-12//99
	Norfolk-Virginia Beach-Newport News MSA, VA-NC	S	12.88 MW	10.80 AW	26800 AAW	VABLS	10//99-12//99
	Richmond-Petersburg MSA, VA	S	10.76 MW	9.14 AW	22390 AAW	VABLS	10//99-12//99
	Roanoke MSA, VA	S	9.01 MW	8.37 AW	18740 AAW	VABLS	10//99-12//99
	Washington	S	11.37 MW	13.24 AW	27540 AAW	WABLS	10//99-12//99
	Bellingham MSA, WA	S	8.90 MW	9.02 AW	18510 AAW	WABLS	10//99-12//99
	Bremerton PMSA, WA	S	9.64 MW	9.64 AW	20060 AAW	WABLS	10//99-12//99
	Richland-Kennewick-Pasco MSA, WA	S	13.79 MW	13.79 AW	28680 AAW	WABLS	10//99-12//99
	Spokane MSA, WA	S	9.07 MW	8.32 AW	18860 AAW	WABLS	10//99-12//99
	Tacoma PMSA, WA	S	9.35 MW	8.77 AW	19450 AAW	WABLS	10//99-12//99
	Yakima MSA, WA	S	7.77 MW	7.32 AW	16150 AAW	WABLS	10//99-12//99
	West Virginia	S	6.66 MW	7.69 AW	15990 AAW	WVBLS	10//99-12//99
	Charleston MSA, WV	S	9.08 MW	8.31 AW	18880 AAW	WVBLS	10//99-12//99
	Huntington-Ashland MSA, WV-KY-OH	S	7.74 MW	7.20 AW	16100 AAW	WVBLS	10//99-12//99

AAW	Average annual wage	AOH	Average offered, high	ASH	Average starting, high	H	Hourly	M	Monthly	S	Special: hourly and annual
AE	Average entry wage	AOL	Average offered, low	ASL	Average starting, low	HI	Highest wage paid	MTC	Median total compensation	TQ	Third quartile wage
AEX	Average experienced wage	APH	Average pay, high range	AW	Average wage paid	HR	High end range	MW	Median wage paid	W	Weekly
AO	Average offered	APL	Average pay, low range	FQ	First quartile wage	LR	Low end range	SQ	Second quartile wage	Y	Yearly

Occupation/Type/Industry	Location	Per	Low	Mid	High	Source	Date
Hairdresser, Hairstylist, and Cosmetologist							
	Parkersburg-Marietta MSA, WV-OH	S	8.31 MW	7.66 AW	17290 AAW	WVBLS	10//99-12//99
	Wheeling MSA, WV-OH	S	7.10 MW	6.23 AW	14780 AAW	WVBLS	10//99-12//99
	Wisconsin	S	8.66 MW	10.02 AW	20840 AAW	WIBLS	10//99-12//99
	Appleton-Oshkosh-Neenah MSA, WI	S	8.70 MW	8.36 AW	18090 AAW	WIBLS	10//99-12//99
	Eau Claire MSA, WI	S	10.69 MW	10.09 AW	22230 AAW	WIBLS	10//99-12//99
	Green Bay MSA, WI	S	10.29 MW	9.74 AW	21400 AAW	WIBLS	10//99-12//99
	Kenosha PMSA, WI	S	8.86 MW	9.37 AW	18430 AAW	WIBLS	10//99-12//99
	La Crosse MSA, WI-MN	S	8.78 MW	8.22 AW	18260 AAW	WIBLS	10//99-12//99
	Madison MSA, WI	S	15.03 MW	13.84 AW	31260 AAW	WIBLS	10//99-12//99
	Milwaukee-Waukesha PMSA, WI	S	10.88 MW	9.90 AW	22630 AAW	WIBLS	10//99-12//99
	Racine PMSA, WI	S	10.72 MW	10.00 AW	22300 AAW	WIBLS	10//99-12//99
	Sheboygan MSA, WI	S	8.27 MW	7.66 AW	17210 AAW	WIBLS	10//99-12//99
	Wyoming	S	6.61 MW	7.63 AW	15860 AAW	WYBLS	10//99-12//99
	Casper MSA, WY	S	7.76 MW	7.68 AW	16140 AAW	WYBLS	10//99-12//99
	Puerto Rico	S	6.64 MW	8.13 AW	16900 AAW	PRBLS	10//99-12//99
	San Juan-Bayamon PMSA, PR	S	8.19 MW	6.63 AW	17030 AAW	PRBLS	10//99-12//99
	Guam	S	6.72 MW	9.21 AW	19150 AAW	GUBLS	10//99-12//99
Hazardous Materials Removal Worker							
	Alabama	S	12.34 MW	13.91 AW	28930 AAW	ALBLS	10//99-12//99
	Alaska	S	17.11 MW	19.67 AW	40910 AAW	AKBLS	10//99-12//99
	Anchorage MSA, AK	S	18.96 MW	16.54 AW	39430 AAW	AKBLS	10//99-12//99
	Arizona	S	17.19 MW	16.82 AW	34990 AAW	AZBLS	10//99-12//99
	Phoenix-Mesa MSA, AZ	S	16.94 MW	17.38 AW	35240 AAW	AZBLS	10//99-12//99
	Arkansas	S	12 MW	12.90 AW	26840 AAW	ARBLS	10//99-12//99
	Little Rock-North Little Rock MSA, AR	S	12.69 MW	11.54 AW	26400 AAW	ARBLS	10//99-12//99
	California	S	13.57 MW	14.48 AW	30110 AAW	CABLS	10//99-12//99
	Fresno MSA, CA	S	14.55 MW	14.07 AW	30260 AAW	CABLS	10//99-12//99
	Los Angeles-Long Beach PMSA, CA	S	16.18 MW	14.67 AW	33660 AAW	CABLS	10//99-12//99
	Oakland PMSA, CA	S	13.68 MW	12.67 AW	28450 AAW	CABLS	10//99-12//99
	Orange County PMSA, CA	S	12.89 MW	12.52 AW	26810 AAW	CABLS	10//99-12//99
	Riverside-San Bernardino PMSA, CA	S	14.26 MW	12.61 AW	29660 AAW	CABLS	10//99-12//99
	Sacramento PMSA, CA	S	15.66 MW	15.45 AW	32580 AAW	CABLS	10//99-12//99
	San Diego MSA, CA	S	15.19 MW	14.80 AW	31600 AAW	CABLS	10//99-12//99
	San Francisco PMSA, CA	S	17.37 MW	17.71 AW	36130 AAW	CABLS	10//99-12//99
	Colorado	S	14.43 MW	14.20 AW	29530 AAW	COBLS	10//99-12//99
	Colorado Springs MSA, CO	S	14.95 MW	15.00 AW	31090 AAW	COBLS	10//99-12//99
	Connecticut	S	14.4 MW	13.84 AW	28790 AAW	CTBLS	10//99-12//99
	Bridgeport PMSA, CT	S	14.51 MW	15.21 AW	30180 AAW	CTBLS	10//99-12//99
	New Haven-Meriden PMSA, CT	S	14.08 MW	15.65 AW	29290 AAW	CTBLS	10//99-12//99
	Stamford-Norwalk PMSA, CT	S	11.26 MW	10.15 AW	23410 AAW	CTBLS	10//99-12//99
	Delaware	S	12.69 MW	13.02 AW	27080 AAW	DEBLS	10//99-12//99
	Wilmington-Newark PMSA, DE-MD	S	13.05 MW	12.74 AW	27140 AAW	DEBLS	10//99-12//99
	Washington PMSA, DC-MD-VA-WV	S	16.33 MW	15.32 AW	33960 AAW	DCBLS	10//99-12//99
	Florida	S	11.8 MW	13.89 AW	28890 AAW	FLBLS	10//99-12//99
	Jacksonville MSA, FL	S	9.21 MW	8.86 AW	19150 AAW	FLBLS	10//99-12//99
	Melbourne-Titusville-Palm Bay MSA, FL	S	17.14 MW	17.82 AW	35650 AAW	FLBLS	10//99-12//99
	Miami PMSA, FL	S	22.36 MW	21.90 AW	46500 AAW	FLBLS	10//99-12//99
	Tampa-St. Petersburg-Clearwater MSA, FL	S	10.88 MW	10.21 AW	22620 AAW	FLBLS	10//99-12//99
	Georgia	S	15.17 MW	14.76 AW	30690 AAW	GABLS	10//99-12//99
	Atlanta MSA, GA	S	15.72 MW	17.18 AW	32690 AAW	GABLS	10//99-12//99
	Augusta-Aiken MSA, GA-SC	S	17.62 MW	18.02 AW	36650 AAW	GABLS	10//99-12//99
	Hawaii	S	18.45 MW	20.35 AW	42320 AAW	HIBLS	10//99-12//99
	Honolulu MSA, HI	S	20.87 MW	19.50 AW	43400 AAW	HIBLS	10//99-12//99
	Idaho	S	17.7 MW	17.04 AW	35450 AAW	IDBLS	10//99-12//99
	Boise City MSA, ID	S	15.95 MW	16.02 AW	33180 AAW	IDBLS	10//99-12//99
	Illinois	S	21.6 MW	20.13 AW	41870 AAW	ILBLS	10//99-12//99
	Chicago PMSA, IL	S	20.55 MW	22.60 AW	42730 AAW	ILBLS	10//99-12//99
	Indiana	S	11.48 MW	13.80 AW	28700 AAW	INBLS	10//99-12//99
	Iowa	S	12.88 MW	11.88 AW	24700 AAW	IABLS	10//99-12//99

AAW	Average annual wage	AOH	Average offered, high
AE	Average entry wage	AOL	Average offered, low
AEX	Average experienced wage	APH	Average pay, high range
AO	Average offered	APL	Average pay, low range

ASH	Average starting, high	H	Hourly
ASL	Average starting, low	HI	Highest wage paid
AW	Average wage paid	HR	High end range
FQ	First quartile wage	LR	Low end range

M	Monthly	S	Special: hourly and annual
MTC	Median total compensation	TQ	Third quartile wage
MW	Median wage paid	W	Weekly
SQ	Second quartile wage	Y	Yearly

Occupation/Type/Industry	Location	Per	Low	Mid	High	Source	Date
Hazardous Materials Removal Worker	Des Moines MSA, IA	S	14.11 MW	14.55 AW	29340 AAW	IABLS	10//99-12//99
	Kansas	S	13.62 MW	14.06 AW	29240 AAW	KSBLS	10//99-12//99
	Kentucky	S	10.54 MW	11.59 AW	24120 AAW	KYBLS	10//99-12//99
	Louisiana	S	11.41 MW	12.52 AW	26030 AAW	LABLS	10//99-12//99
	New Orleans MSA, LA	S	12.64 MW	12.53 AW	26290 AAW	LABLS	10//99-12//99
	Maine	S	9.66 MW	9.64 AW	20060 AAW	MEBLS	10//99-12//99
	Maryland	S	12.14 MW	13.64 AW	28370 AAW	MDBLS	10//99-12//99
	Baltimore PMSA, MD	S	12.09 MW	11.59 AW	25160 AAW	MDBLS	10//99-12//99
	Massachusetts	S	16.2 MW	17.37 AW	36140 AAW	MABLS	10//99-12//99
	Boston PMSA, MA-NH	S	16.96 MW	15.33 AW	35270 AAW	MABLS	10//99-12//99
	Lawrence PMSA, MA-NH	S	17.43 MW	16.01 AW	36250 AAW	MABLS	10//99-12//99
	Springfield MSA, MA	S	16.29 MW	15.99 AW	33890 AAW	MABLS	10//99-12//99
	Michigan	S	11.16 MW	14.06 AW	29240 AAW	MIBLS	10//99-12//99
	Detroit PMSA, MI	S	17.04 MW	15.19 AW	35430 AAW	MIBLS	10//99-12//99
	Grand Rapids-Muskegon-Holland MSA, MI	S	16.84 MW	13.63 AW	35040 AAW	MIBLS	10//99-12//99
	Lansing-East Lansing MSA, MI	S	10.83 MW	10.32 AW	22530 AAW	MIBLS	10//99-12//99
	Minnesota	S	18.45 MW	18.09 AW	37620 AAW	MNBLS	10//99-12//99
	Duluth-Superior MSA, MN-WI	S	16.33 MW	17.91 AW	33960 AAW	MNBLS	10//99-12//99
	Minneapolis-St. Paul MSA, MN-WI	S	18.60 MW	18.67 AW	38690 AAW	MNBLS	10//99-12//99
	Mississippi	S	11.5 MW	13.02 AW	27080 AAW	MSBLS	10//99-12//99
	Hattiesburg MSA, MS	S	10.62 MW	10.86 AW	22090 AAW	MSBLS	10//99-12//99
	Missouri	S	18.51 MW	18.84 AW	39180 AAW	MOBLS	10//99-12//99
	Kansas City MSA, MO-KS	S	19.31 MW	17.01 AW	40160 AAW	MOBLS	10//99-12//99
	St. Louis MSA, MO-IL	S	16.98 MW	16.11 AW	35320 AAW	MOBLS	10//99-12//99
	Montana	S	14.95 MW	14.88 AW	30960 AAW	MTBLS	10//99-12//99
	Nebraska	S	11.81 MW	12.02 AW	25010 AAW	NEBLS	10//99-12//99
	Nevada	S	15.94 MW	15.80 AW	32860 AAW	NVBLS	10//99-12//99
	New Jersey	S	17.73 MW	17.95 AW	37340 AAW	NJBLS	10//99-12//99
	Bergen-Passaic PMSA, NJ	S	16.21 MW	17.06 AW	33720 AAW	NJBLS	10//99-12//99
	Middlesex-Somerset-Hunterdon PMSA, NJ	S	18.11 MW	18.34 AW	37660 AAW	NJBLS	10//99-12//99
	Monmouth-Ocean PMSA, NJ	S	17.82 MW	16.70 AW	37060 AAW	NJBLS	10//99-12//99
	Newark PMSA, NJ	S	18.60 MW	19.20 AW	38690 AAW	NJBLS	10//99-12//99
	Las Cruces MSA, NM	S	17.73 MW	18.44 AW	36870 AAW	NMBLS	10//99-12//99
	New York	S	20.18 MW	19.48 AW	40520 AAW	NYBLS	10//99-12//99
	Albany-Schenectady-Troy MSA, NY	S	18.41 MW	18.85 AW	38300 AAW	NYBLS	10//99-12//99
	Buffalo-Niagara Falls MSA, NY	S	19.72 MW	19.17 AW	41020 AAW	NYBLS	10//99-12//99
	Nassau-Suffolk PMSA, NY	S	21.09 MW	21.64 AW	43870 AAW	NYBLS	10//99-12//99
	New York PMSA, NY	S	20.40 MW	20.88 AW	42440 AAW	NYBLS	10//99-12//99
	Syracuse MSA, NY	S	11.14 MW	11.51 AW	23160 AAW	NYBLS	10//99-12//99
	North Carolina	S	10.19 MW	10.80 AW	22460 AAW	NCBLS	10//99-12//99
	Charlotte-Gastonia-Rock Hill MSA, NC-SC	S	16.51 MW	15.64 AW	34340 AAW	NCBLS	10//99-12//99
	Greensboro--Winston-Salem--High Point MSA, NC	S	10.30 MW	10.24 AW	21430 AAW	NCBLS	10//99-12//99
	Raleigh-Durham-Chapel Hill MSA, NC	S	11.71 MW	11.34 AW	24350 AAW	NCBLS	10//99-12//99
	Wilmington MSA, NC	S	12.07 MW	12.18 AW	25100 AAW	NCBLS	10//99-12//99
	North Dakota	S	17.23 MW	18.23 AW	37920 AAW	NDBLS	10//99-12//99
	Ohio	S	13.08 MW	14.12 AW	29360 AAW	OHBLS	10//99-12//99
	Cincinnati PMSA, OH-KY-IN	S	13.06 MW	12.44 AW	27150 AAW	OHBLS	10//99-12//99
	Cleveland-Lorain-Elyria PMSA, OH	S	13.95 MW	13.02 AW	29010 AAW	OHBLS	10//99-12//99
	Youngstown-Warren MSA, OH	S	15.74 MW	14.01 AW	32730 AAW	OHBLS	10//99-12//99
	Oklahoma	S	11.64 MW	12.24 AW	25460 AAW	OKBLS	10//99-12//99
	Oklahoma City MSA, OK	S	12.54 MW	11.84 AW	26070 AAW	OKBLS	10//99-12//99
	Oregon	S	15.29 MW	16.28 AW	33870 AAW	ORBLS	10//99-12//99
	Pennsylvania	S	17.22 MW	16.81 AW	34970 AAW	PABLS	10//99-12//99
	Philadelphia PMSA, PA-NJ	S	17.17 MW	17.87 AW	35720 AAW	PABLS	10//99-12//99
	Pittsburgh MSA, PA	S	15.93 MW	15.91 AW	33140 AAW	PABLS	10//99-12//99
	South Carolina	S	14.97 MW	15.23 AW	31670 AAW	SCBLS	10//99-12//99
	Charleston-North Charleston MSA, SC	S	10.29 MW	10.27 AW	21410 AAW	SCBLS	10//99-12//99
	Tennessee	S	10.62 MW	11.53 AW	23980 AAW	TNBLS	10//99-12//99
	Memphis MSA, TN-AR-MS	S	11.75 MW	10.97 AW	24450 AAW	MSBLS	10//99-12//99
	Texas	S	11.27 MW	11.81 AW	24570 AAW	TXBLS	10//99-12//99
	Corpus Christi MSA, TX	S	12.78 MW	11.62 AW	26580 AAW	TXBLS	10//99-12//99

AAW Average annual wage	AOH Average offered, high	ASH Average starting, high	H Hourly
AE Average entry wage	AOL Average offered, low	ASL Average starting, low	HI Highest wage paid
AEX Average experienced wage	APH Average pay, high range	AW Average wage paid	HR High end range
AO Average offered	APL Average pay, low range	FQ First quartile wage	LR Low end range

M Monthly	S Special: hourly and annual	
MTC Median total compensation	TQ Third quartile wage	
MW Median wage paid	W Weekly	
SQ Second quartile wage	Y Yearly	

Occupation/Type/Industry	Location	Per	Low	Mid	High	Source	Date
Hazardous Materials Removal Worker	Houston PMSA, TX	S	12.11 MW	12.14 AW	25180 AAW	TXBLS	10//99-12//99
	Vermont	S	11.92 MW	12.22 AW	25420 AAW	VTBLS	10//99-12//99
	Virginia	S	12.88 MW	14.62 AW	30420 AAW	VABLS	10//99-12//99
	Norfolk-Virginia Beach-Newport News MSA, VA-NC	S	12.32 MW	11.89 AW	25630 AAW	VABLS	10//99-12//99
	Richmond-Petersburg MSA, VA	S	10.85 MW	10.75 AW	22570 AAW	VABLS	10//99-12//99
	Washington	S	17.17 MW	17.79 AW	37000 AAW	WABLS	10//99-12//99
	Richland-Kennewick-Pasco MSA, WA	S	24.50 MW	23.39 AW	50960 AAW	WABLS	10//99-12//99
	Seattle-Bellevue-Everett PMSA, WA	S	18.08 MW	17.51 AW	37610 AAW	WABLS	10//99-12//99
	Tacoma PMSA, WA	S	16.36 MW	15.44 AW	34030 AAW	WABLS	10//99-12//99
	West Virginia	S	14.45 MW	14.38 AW	29910 AAW	WVBLS	10//99-12//99
	Wisconsin	S	13.28 MW	13.84 AW	28790 AAW	WIBLS	10//99-12//99
	Milwaukee-Waukesha PMSA, WI	S	14.11 MW	14.04 AW	29360 AAW	WIBLS	10//99-12//99
	Puerto Rico	S	6.94 MW	9.92 AW	20640 AAW	PRBLS	10//99-12//99
	Ponce MSA, PR	S	8.31 MW	6.71 AW	17280 AAW	PRBLS	10//99-12//99
Health and Safety Engineer							
Except Mining Safety Engineer and Inspector	Alabama	S	24.87 MW	25.34 AW	52710 AAW	ALBLS	10//99-12//99
Except Mining Safety Engineer and Inspector	Arizona	S	25.25 MW	23.34 AW	48550 AAW	AZBLS	10//99-12//99
Except Mining Safety Engineer and Inspector	Arkansas	S	19.4 MW	19.98 AW	41560 AAW	ARBLS	10//99-12//99
Except Mining Safety Engineer and Inspector	California	S	27.77 MW	26.96 AW	56090 AAW	CABLS	10//99-12//99
Except Mining Safety Engineer and Inspector	Colorado	S	25.32 MW	26.44 AW	55000 AAW	COBLS	10//99-12//99
Except Mining Safety Engineer and Inspector	Connecticut	S	24.56 MW	24.82 AW	51630 AAW	CTBLS	10//99-12//99
Except Mining Safety Engineer and Inspector	Delaware	S	28.47 MW	27.22 AW	56610 AAW	DEBLS	10//99-12//99
Except Mining Safety Engineer and Inspector	Florida	S	23.07 MW	22.89 AW	47620 AAW	FLBLS	10//99-12//99
Except Mining Safety Engineer and Inspector	Georgia	S	25.57 MW	26.37 AW	54850 AAW	GABLS	10//99-12//99
Except Mining Safety Engineer and Inspector	Hawaii	S	22.2 MW	22.20 AW	46170 AAW	HIBLS	10//99-12//99
Except Mining Safety Engineer and Inspector	Idaho	S	26.77 MW	27.28 AW	56740 AAW	IDBLS	10//99-12//99
Except Mining Safety Engineer and Inspector	Illinois	S	24.02 MW	23.42 AW	48710 AAW	ILBLS	10//99-12//99
Except Mining Safety Engineer and Inspector	Indiana	S	24.43 MW	25.07 AW	52140 AAW	INBLS	10//99-12//99
Except Mining Safety Engineer and Inspector	Iowa	S	17.27 MW	18.80 AW	39110 AAW	IABLS	10//99-12//99
Except Mining Safety Engineer and Inspector	Kansas	S	25.17 MW	25.79 AW	53640 AAW	KSBLS	10//99-12//99
Except Mining Safety Engineer and Inspector	Kentucky	S	21.64 MW	22.20 AW	46180 AAW	KYBLS	10//99-12//99
Except Mining Safety Engineer and Inspector	Louisiana	S	24.52 MW	25.33 AW	52690 AAW	LABLS	10//99-12//99
Except Mining Safety Engineer and Inspector	Maine	S	21.88 MW	23.29 AW	48440 AAW	MEBLS	10//99-12//99
Except Mining Safety Engineer and Inspector	Maryland	S	29.43 MW	29.31 AW	60970 AAW	MDBLS	10//99-12//99
Except Mining Safety Engineer and Inspector	Massachusetts	S	23.22 MW	24.80 AW	51590 AAW	MABLS	10//99-12//99
Except Mining Safety Engineer and Inspector	Michigan	S	28.34 MW	28.81 AW	59930 AAW	MIBLS	10//99-12//99
Except Mining Safety Engineer and Inspector	Minnesota	S	23.7 MW	23.75 AW	49390 AAW	MNBLS	10//99-12//99
Except Mining Safety Engineer and Inspector	Mississippi	S	26.36 MW	25.21 AW	52430 AAW	MSBLS	10//99-12//99
Except Mining Safety Engineer and Inspector	Missouri	S	25.94 MW	27.39 AW	56970 AAW	MOBLS	10//99-12//99

AAW Average annual wage	**AOH** Average offered, high	**ASH** Average starting, high	**H** Hourly	**M** Monthly	**S** Special: hourly and annual
AE Average entry wage	**AOL** Average offered, low	**ASL** Average starting, low	**HI** Highest wage paid	**MTC** Median total compensation	**TQ** Third quartile wage
AEX Average experienced wage	**APH** Average pay, high range	**AW** Average wage paid	**HR** High end range	**MW** Median wage paid	**W** Weekly
AO Average offered	**APL** Average pay, low range	**FQ** First quartile wage	**LR** Low end range	**SQ** Second quartile wage	**Y** Yearly

Occupation/Type/Industry	Location	Per	Low	Mid	High	Source	Date
Health and Safety Engineer							
Except Mining Safety Engineer and Inspector	Montana	S	24.46 MW	23.86 AW	49620 AAW	MTBLS	10//99-12//99
Except Mining Safety Engineer and Inspector	Nebraska	S	25.62 MW	26.65 AW	55430 AAW	NEBLS	10//99-12//99
Except Mining Safety Engineer and Inspector	Nevada	S	21.75 MW	22.46 AW	46710 AAW	NVBLS	10//99-12//99
Except Mining Safety Engineer and Inspector	New Hampshire	S	24.6 MW	27.06 AW	56280 AAW	NHBLS	10//99-12//99
Except Mining Safety Engineer and Inspector	New Jersey	S	24.99 MW	26.05 AW	54190 AAW	NJBLS	10//99-12//99
Except Mining Safety Engineer and Inspector	New Mexico	S	22.62 MW	22.91 AW	47660 AAW	NMBLS	10//99-12//99
Except Mining Safety Engineer and Inspector	New York	S	28.09 MW	30.09 AW	62580 AAW	NYBLS	10//99-12//99
Except Mining Safety Engineer and Inspector	North Carolina	S	23.74 MW	24.44 AW	50830 AAW	NCBLS	10//99-12//99
Except Mining Safety Engineer and Inspector	North Dakota	S	26.15 MW	27.71 AW	57630 AAW	NDBLS	10//99-12//99
Except Mining Safety Engineer and Inspector	Ohio	S	24.11 MW	24.68 AW	51330 AAW	OHBLS	10//99-12//99
Except Mining Safety Engineer and Inspector	Oklahoma	S	24.28 MW	25.47 AW	52980 AAW	OKBLS	10//99-12//99
Except Mining Safety Engineer and Inspector	Oregon	S	21.28 MW	21.81 AW	45370 AAW	ORBLS	10//99-12//99
Except Mining Safety Engineer and Inspector	Pennsylvania	S	22.44 MW	23.13 AW	48100 AAW	PABLS	10//99-12//99
Except Mining Safety Engineer and Inspector	Rhode Island	S	23.72 MW	23.30 AW	48470 AAW	RIBLS	10//99-12//99
Except Mining Safety Engineer and Inspector	South Carolina	S	32.34 MW	31.94 AW	66430 AAW	SCBLS	10//99-12//99
Except Mining Safety Engineer and Inspector	South Dakota	S	20.64 MW	21.14 AW	43980 AAW	SDBLS	10//99-12//99
Except Mining Safety Engineer and Inspector	Tennessee	S	23.91 MW	24.63 AW	51220 AAW	TNBLS	10//99-12//99
Except Mining Safety Engineer and Inspector	Texas	S	23.77 MW	23.74 AW	49370 AAW	TXBLS	10//99-12//99
Except Mining Safety Engineer and Inspector	Utah	S	22.41 MW	22.39 AW	46580 AAW	UTBLS	10//99-12//99
Except Mining Safety Engineer and Inspector	Vermont	S	20.51 MW	24.25 AW	50440 AAW	VTBLS	10//99-12//99
Except Mining Safety Engineer and Inspector	Virginia	S	22.55 MW	25.46 AW	52950 AAW	VABLS	10//99-12//99
Except Mining Safety Engineer and Inspector	Washington	S	28.39 MW	28.20 AW	58650 AAW	WABLS	10//99-12//99
Except Mining Safety Engineer and Inspector	West Virginia	S	24.93 MW	25.53 AW	53100 AAW	WVBLS	10//99-12//99
Except Mining Safety Engineer and Inspector	Wisconsin	S	21.82 MW	23.34 AW	48550 AAW	WIBLS	10//99-12//99
Except Mining Safety Engineer and Inspector	Wyoming	S	26.15 MW	26.15 AW	54390 AAW	WYBLS	10//99-12//99
Except Mining Safety Engineer and Inspector	Puerto Rico	S	22.64 MW	24.11 AW	50140 AAW	PRBLS	10//99-12//99
Health Educator	Alabama	S	16.32 MW	16.26 AW	33830 AAW	ALBLS	10//99-12//99
	Alaska	S	15.5 MW	16.20 AW	33690 AAW	AKBLS	10//99-12//99
	Arizona	S	28.64 MW	24.93 AW	51860 AAW	AZBLS	10//99-12//99
	Arkansas	S	15.85 MW	17.49 AW	36370 AAW	ARBLS	10//99-12//99
	California	S	14 MW	17.30 AW	35980 AAW	CABLS	10//99-12//99
	Colorado	S	21.37 MW	20.25 AW	42130 AAW	COBLS	10//99-12//99
	Connecticut	S	16.57 MW	18.59 AW	38660 AAW	CTBLS	10//99-12//99
	District of Columbia	S	23.09 MW	23.57 AW	49030 AAW	DCBLS	10//99-12//99
	Florida	S	12.74 MW	13.62 AW	28330 AAW	FLBLS	10//99-12//99
	Georgia	S	11.03 MW	14.96 AW	31110 AAW	GABLS	10//99-12//99
	Hawaii	S	14.64 MW	17.92 AW	37280 AAW	HIBLS	10//99-12//99
	Idaho	S	17.93 MW	15.78 AW	32820 AAW	IDBLS	10//99-12//99
	Illinois	S	16.57 MW	16.63 AW	34590 AAW	ILBLS	10//99-12//99
	Indiana	S	12.93 MW	14.33 AW	29810 AAW	INBLS	10//99-12//99
	Iowa	S	14.66 MW	15.72 AW	32700 AAW	IABLS	10//99-12//99
	Kansas	S	12.67 MW	15.68 AW	32610 AAW	KSBLS	10//99-12//99
	Kentucky	S	14.44 MW	15.19 AW	31600 AAW	KYBLS	10//99-12//99
	Louisiana	S	8.28 MW	9.97 AW	20730 AAW	LABLS	10//99-12//99
	Maine	S	14.96 MW	14.67 AW	30520 AAW	MEBLS	10//99-12//99

Occupation/Type/Industry	Location	Per	Low	Mid	High	Source	Date
Health Educator	Massachusetts	S	14.02 MW	16.94 AW	35230 AAW	MABLS	10//99-12//99
	Michigan	S	18.28 MW	18.57 AW	38630 AAW	MIBLS	10//99-12//99
	Minnesota	S	16.02 MW	16.68 AW	34700 AAW	MNBLS	10//99-12//99
	Mississippi	S	14.06 MW	16.67 AW	34660 AAW	MSBLS	10//99-12//99
	Missouri	S	12.75 MW	14.35 AW	29840 AAW	MOBLS	10//99-12//99
	Montana	S	12.73 MW	13.22 AW	27490 AAW	MTBLS	10//99-12//99
	Nebraska	S	14.81 MW	15.28 AW	31780 AAW	NEBLS	10//99-12//99
	Nevada	S	22.03 MW	21.85 AW	45450 AAW	NVBLS	10//99-12//99
	New Hampshire	S	14.59 MW	15.10 AW	31400 AAW	NHBLS	10//99-12//99
	New Jersey	S	23.6 MW	22.97 AW	47770 AAW	NJBLS	10//99-12//99
	New Mexico	S	11.15 MW	13.25 AW	27570 AAW	NMBLS	10//99-12//99
	New York	S	17.33 MW	17.70 AW	36820 AAW	NYBLS	10//99-12//99
	North Carolina	S	15.21 MW	15.89 AW	33040 AAW	NCBLS	10//99-12//99
	Ohio	S	15.9 MW	15.98 AW	33250 AAW	OHBLS	10//99-12//99
	Oklahoma	S	11.45 MW	13.18 AW	27410 AAW	OKBLS	10//99-12//99
	Oregon	S	9.39 MW	11.94 AW	24830 AAW	ORBLS	10//99-12//99
	Pennsylvania	S	15.37 MW	16.02 AW	33330 AAW	PABLS	10//99-12//99
	Rhode Island	S	22.05 MW	21.67 AW	45070 AAW	RIBLS	10//99-12//99
	South Carolina	S	17.26 MW	18.64 AW	38770 AAW	SCBLS	10//99-12//99
	South Dakota	S	15.76 MW	16.28 AW	33850 AAW	SDBLS	10//99-12//99
	Tennessee	S	21.68 MW	18.87 AW	39250 AAW	TNBLS	10//99-12//99
	Texas	S	16.3 MW	16.65 AW	34630 AAW	TXBLS	10//99-12//99
	Utah	S	15.6 MW	16.23 AW	33750 AAW	UTBLS	10//99-12//99
	Vermont	S	16.3 MW	21.05 AW	43780 AAW	VTBLS	10//99-12//99
	Virginia	S	12.46 MW	13.77 AW	28650 AAW	VABLS	10//99-12//99
	Washington	S	18.41 MW	18.46 AW	38400 AAW	WABLS	10//99-12//99
	West Virginia	S	12.14 MW	13.96 AW	29040 AAW	WVBLS	10//99-12//99
	Wisconsin	S	13.02 MW	14.89 AW	30960 AAW	WIBLS	10//99-12//99
	Wyoming	S	12.69 MW	13.35 AW	27760 AAW	WYBLS	10//99-12//99
	Puerto Rico	S	9.09 MW	9.50 AW	19760 AAW	PRBLS	10//99-12//99
Health Record Technician	United States	H		12.02 AW		NCS98	1998
Health Specialties Teacher							
Postsecondary	Arkansas	Y		43500 AAW		ARBLS	10//99-12//99
Postsecondary	California	Y		64580 AAW		CABLS	10//99-12//99
Postsecondary	Colorado	Y		53300 AAW		COBLS	10//99-12//99
Postsecondary	Connecticut	Y		66730 AAW		CTBLS	10//99-12//99
Postsecondary	District of Columbia	Y		70880 AAW		DCBLS	10//99-12//99
Postsecondary	Florida	Y		76650 AAW		FLBLS	10//99-12//99
Postsecondary	Georgia	Y		67640 AAW		GABLS	10//99-12//99
Postsecondary	Idaho	Y		36690 AAW		IDBLS	10//99-12//99
Postsecondary	Illinois	Y		45420 AAW		ILBLS	10//99-12//99
Postsecondary	Indiana	Y		63860 AAW		INBLS	10//99-12//99
Postsecondary	Iowa	Y		83880 AAW		IABLS	10//99-12//99
Postsecondary	Kansas	Y		54010 AAW		KSBLS	10//99-12//99
Postsecondary	Kentucky	Y		68690 AAW		KYBLS	10//99-12//99
Postsecondary	Louisiana	Y		56790 AAW		LABLS	10//99-12//99
Postsecondary	Maine	Y		52760 AAW		MEBLS	10//99-12//99
Postsecondary	Massachusetts	Y		83280 AAW		MABLS	10//99-12//99
Postsecondary	Michigan	Y		80630 AAW		MIBLS	10//99-12//99
Postsecondary	Missouri	Y		52610 AAW		MOBLS	10//99-12//99
Postsecondary	Montana	Y		63050 AAW		MTBLS	10//99-12//99
Postsecondary	New Jersey	Y		69240 AAW		NJBLS	10//99-12//99
Postsecondary	New Mexico	Y		83860 AAW		NMBLS	10//99-12//99
Postsecondary	New York	Y		70340 AAW		NYBLS	10//99-12//99
Postsecondary	North Carolina	Y		62420 AAW		NCBLS	10//99-12//99
Postsecondary	Ohio	Y		55180 AAW		OHBLS	10//99-12//99
Postsecondary	Oklahoma	Y		63660 AAW		OKBLS	10//99-12//99
Postsecondary	Oregon	Y		58090 AAW		ORBLS	10//99-12//99
Postsecondary	Pennsylvania	Y		50040 AAW		PABLS	10//99-12//99
Postsecondary	South Carolina	Y		53850 AAW		SCBLS	10//99-12//99
Postsecondary	Texas	Y		65710 AAW		TXBLS	10//99-12//99
Postsecondary	Utah	Y		48080 AAW		UTBLS	10//99-12//99
Postsecondary	Virginia	Y		73320 AAW		VABLS	10//99-12//99
Postsecondary	West Virginia	Y		55110 AAW		WVBLS	10//99-12//99
Postsecondary	Wyoming	Y		54280 AAW		WYBLS	10//99-12//99
Postsecondary	Puerto Rico	Y		59420 AAW		PRBLS	10//99-12//99
Heat Treating Equipment Setter, Operator, and Tender							
Metals and Plastics	Alabama	S	12.67 MW	13.33 AW	27720 AAW	ALBLS	10//99-12//99

AAW	Average annual wage	AOH	Average offered, high	ASH	Average starting, high	H	Hourly	M	Monthly	S	Special: hourly and annual
AE	Average entry wage	AOL	Average offered, low	ASL	Average starting, low	HI	Highest wage paid	MTC	Median total compensation	TQ	Third quartile wage
AEX	Average experienced wage	APH	Average pay, high range	AW	Average wage paid	HR	High end range	MW	Median wage paid	W	Weekly
AO	Average offered	APL	Average pay, low range	FQ	First quartile wage	LR	Low end range	SQ	Second quartile wage	Y	Yearly

Occupation/Type/Industry	Location	Per	Low	Mid	High	Source	Date
Heat Treating Equipment Setter, Operator, and Tender							
Metals and Plastics	Birmingham MSA, AL	S	13.69 MW	13.03 AW	28470 AAW	ALBLS	10//99-12//99
Metals and Plastics	Arizona	S	13.02 MW	13.83 AW	28760 AAW	AZBLS	10//99-12//99
Metals and Plastics	Phoenix-Mesa MSA, AZ	S	13.03 MW	11.84 AW	27110 AAW	AZBLS	10//99-12//99
Metals and Plastics	Tucson MSA, AZ	S	14.10 MW	14.34 AW	29340 AAW	AZBLS	10//99-12//99
Metals and Plastics	Arkansas	S	10.1 MW	10.02 AW	20840 AAW	ARBLS	10//99-12//99
Metals and Plastics	California	S	10.59 MW	11.67 AW	24270 AAW	CABLS	10//99-12//99
Metals and Plastics	Los Angeles-Long Beach PMSA, CA	S	11.83 MW	10.99 AW	24610 AAW	CABLS	10//99-12//99
Metals and Plastics	Oakland PMSA, CA	S	14.00 MW	13.43 AW	29110 AAW	CABLS	10//99-12//99
Metals and Plastics	Orange County PMSA, CA	S	10.47 MW	9.30 AW	21780 AAW	CABLS	10//99-12//99
Metals and Plastics	Riverside-San Bernardino PMSA, CA	S	13.31 MW	12.57 AW	27670 AAW	CABLS	10//99-12//99
Metals and Plastics	San Diego MSA, CA	S	12.34 MW	11.98 AW	25660 AAW	CABLS	10//99-12//99
Metals and Plastics	San Francisco PMSA, CA	S	12.22 MW	10.58 AW	25420 AAW	CABLS	10//99-12//99
Metals and Plastics	Vallejo-Fairfield-Napa PMSA, CA	S	16.34 MW	14.56 AW	33990 AAW	CABLS	10//99-12//99
Metals and Plastics	Colorado	S	13.63 MW	13.79 AW	28690 AAW	COBLS	10//99-12//99
Metals and Plastics	Denver PMSA, CO	S	15.20 MW	15.68 AW	31610 AAW	COBLS	10//99-12//99
Metals and Plastics	Connecticut	S	14.12 MW	13.84 AW	28790 AAW	CTBLS	10//99-12//99
Metals and Plastics	Bridgeport PMSA, CT	S	13.51 MW	13.60 AW	28110 AAW	CTBLS	10//99-12//99
Metals and Plastics	Hartford MSA, CT	S	14.03 MW	14.48 AW	29180 AAW	CTBLS	10//99-12//99
Metals and Plastics	New Haven-Meriden PMSA, CT	S	12.92 MW	12.41 AW	26860 AAW	CTBLS	10//99-12//99
Metals and Plastics	Waterbury PMSA, CT	S	14.95 MW	14.75 AW	31100 AAW	CTBLS	10//99-12//99
Metals and Plastics	Delaware	S	14.16 MW	13.00 AW	27040 AAW	DEBLS	10//99-12//99
Metals and Plastics	Wilmington-Newark PMSA, DE-MD	S	12.20 MW	11.60 AW	25370 AAW	DEBLS	10//99-12//99
Metals and Plastics	Florida	S	11.5 MW	11.81 AW	24560 AAW	FLBLS	10//99-12//99
Metals and Plastics	Orlando MSA, FL	S	11.86 MW	13.84 AW	24660 AAW	FLBLS	10//99-12//99
Metals and Plastics	Pensacola MSA, FL	S	12.70 MW	13.80 AW	26410 AAW	FLBLS	10//99-12//99
Metals and Plastics	Tampa-St. Petersburg-Clearwater MSA, FL	S	10.35 MW	9.50 AW	21540 AAW	FLBLS	10//99-12//99
Metals and Plastics	West Palm Beach-Boca Raton MSA, FL	S	13.58 MW	13.22 AW	28250 AAW	FLBLS	10//99-12//99
Metals and Plastics	Georgia	S	12.27 MW	12.31 AW	25610 AAW	GABLS	10//99-12//99
Metals and Plastics	Atlanta MSA, GA	S	12.39 MW	12.39 AW	25780 AAW	GABLS	10//99-12//99
Metals and Plastics	Idaho	S	11.11 MW	10.80 AW	22470 AAW	IDBLS	10//99-12//99
Metals and Plastics	Illinois	S	10.31 MW	11.74 AW	24410 AAW	ILBLS	10//99-12//99
Metals and Plastics	Chicago PMSA, IL	S	11.01 MW	9.90 AW	22910 AAW	ILBLS	10//99-12//99
Metals and Plastics	Rockford MSA, IL	S	11.48 MW	10.72 AW	23870 AAW	ILBLS	10//99-12//99
Metals and Plastics	Indiana	S	13.87 MW	15.02 AW	31240 AAW	INBLS	10//99-12//99
Metals and Plastics	Elkhart-Goshen MSA, IN	S	15.36 MW	14.81 AW	31950 AAW	INBLS	10//99-12//99
Metals and Plastics	Evansville-Henderson MSA, IN-KY	S	11.84 MW	12.18 AW	24630 AAW	INBLS	10//99-12//99
Metals and Plastics	Fort Wayne MSA, IN	S	11.53 MW	10.26 AW	23970 AAW	INBLS	10//99-12//99
Metals and Plastics	Indianapolis MSA, IN	S	16.44 MW	15.70 AW	34190 AAW	INBLS	10//99-12//99
Metals and Plastics	South Bend MSA, IN	S	14.62 MW	14.57 AW	30410 AAW	INBLS	10//99-12//99
Metals and Plastics	Iowa	S	14.8 MW	14.53 AW	30220 AAW	IABLS	10//99-12//99
Metals and Plastics	Davenport-Moline-Rock Island MSA, IA-IL	S	14.23 MW	14.32 AW	29600 AAW	IABLS	10//99-12//99
Metals and Plastics	Kansas	S	13.74 MW	16.02 AW	33320 AAW	KSBLS	10//99-12//99
Metals and Plastics	Wichita MSA, KS	S	17.88 MW	14.44 AW	37190 AAW	KSBLS	10//99-12//99
Metals and Plastics	Kentucky	S	12.81 MW	13.12 AW	27280 AAW	KYBLS	10//99-12//99
Metals and Plastics	Louisville MSA, KY-IN	S	12.83 MW	12.72 AW	26680 AAW	KYBLS	10//99-12//99
Metals and Plastics	Louisiana	S	12.04 MW	12.40 AW	25790 AAW	LABLS	10//99-12//99
Metals and Plastics	Maryland	S	14.79 MW	15.27 AW	31770 AAW	MDBLS	10//99-12//99
Metals and Plastics	Baltimore PMSA, MD	S	14.07 MW	13.49 AW	29250 AAW	MDBLS	10//99-12//99
Metals and Plastics	Massachusetts	S	13.43 MW	13.92 AW	28950 AAW	MABLS	10//99-12//99
Metals and Plastics	Boston PMSA, MA-NH	S	13.51 MW	13.16 AW	28100 AAW	MABLS	10//99-12//99
Metals and Plastics	Fitchburg-Leominster PMSA, MA	S	12.27 MW	11.52 AW	25510 AAW	MABLS	10//99-12//99
Metals and Plastics	Springfield MSA, MA	S	14.19 MW	13.76 AW	29510 AAW	MABLS	10//99-12//99
Metals and Plastics	Worcester PMSA, MA-CT	S	13.40 MW	13.20 AW	27870 AAW	MABLS	10//99-12//99
Metals and Plastics	Michigan	S	11.71 MW	13.38 AW	27820 AAW	MIBLS	10//99-12//99
Metals and Plastics	Ann Arbor PMSA, MI	S	17.41 MW	18.29 AW	36210 AAW	MIBLS	10//99-12//99
Metals and Plastics	Detroit PMSA, MI	S	12.92 MW	11.28 AW	26870 AAW	MIBLS	10//99-12//99
Metals and Plastics	Flint PMSA, MI	S	19.66 MW	21.70 AW	40890 AAW	MIBLS	10//99-12//99
Metals and Plastics	Grand Rapids-Muskegon-Holland MSA, MI	S	14.05 MW	11.47 AW	29230 AAW	MIBLS	10//99-12//99

AAW	Average annual wage	AOH	Average offered, high	ASH	Average starting, high	H	Hourly	M	Monthly	S	Special: hourly and annual
AE	Average entry wage	AOL	Average offered, low	ASL	Average starting, low	HI	Highest wage paid	MTC	Median total compensation	TQ	Third quartile wage
AEX	Average experienced wage	APH	Average pay, high range	AW	Average wage paid	HR	High end range	MW	Median wage paid	W	Weekly
AO	Average offered	APL	Average pay, low range	FQ	First quartile wage	LR	Low end range	SQ	Second quartile wage	Y	Yearly

Occupation/Type/Industry	Location	Per	Low	Mid	High	Source	Date
Heat Treating Equipment Setter, Operator, and Tender							
Metals and Plastics	Kalamazoo-Battle Creek MSA, MI	s	11.65 mw	10.12 aw	24230 aaw	MIBLS	10//99-12//99
Metals and Plastics	Minnesota	s	13.45 mw	14.00 aw	29110 aaw	MNBLS	10//99-12//99
Metals and Plastics	Minneapolis-St. Paul MSA, MN-WI	s	14.10 mw	13.59 aw	29330 aaw	MNBLS	10//99-12//99
Metals and Plastics	Mississippi	s	10.68 mw	10.40 aw	21620 aaw	MSBLS	10//99-12//99
Metals and Plastics	Missouri	s	12.33 mw	12.54 aw	26080 aaw	MOBLS	10//99-12//99
Metals and Plastics	St. Louis MSA, MO-IL	s	13.37 mw	14.02 aw	27810 aaw	MOBLS	10//99-12//99
Metals and Plastics	Nebraska	s	11.98 mw	13.48 aw	28030 aaw	NEBLS	10//99-12//99
Metals and Plastics	New Hampshire	s	13.02 mw	13.33 aw	27720 aaw	NHBLS	10//99-12//99
Metals and Plastics	Portsmouth-Rochester PMSA, NH-ME	s	16.83 mw	17.09 aw	35010 aaw	NHBLS	10//99-12//99
Metals and Plastics	New Jersey	s	11.58 mw	11.43 aw	23780 aaw	NJBLS	10//99-12//99
Metals and Plastics	Bergen-Passaic PMSA, NJ	s	10.36 mw	9.84 aw	21550 aaw	NJBLS	10//99-12//99
Metals and Plastics	Middlesex-Somerset-Hunterdon PMSA, NJ	s	12.72 mw	11.85 aw	26450 aaw	NJBLS	10//99-12//99
Metals and Plastics	Newark PMSA, NJ	s	11.25 mw	11.72 aw	23390 aaw	NJBLS	10//99-12//99
Metals and Plastics	New York	s	13.63 mw	14.48 aw	30130 aaw	NYBLS	10//99-12//99
Metals and Plastics	Buffalo-Niagara Falls MSA, NY	s	16.90 mw	15.12 aw	35140 aaw	NYBLS	10//99-12//99
Metals and Plastics	New York PMSA, NY	s	12.44 mw	11.39 aw	25880 aaw	NYBLS	10//99-12//99
Metals and Plastics	Rochester MSA, NY	s	12.58 mw	11.45 aw	26160 aaw	NYBLS	10//99-12//99
Metals and Plastics	Utica-Rome MSA, NY	s	14.47 mw	14.86 aw	30090 aaw	NYBLS	10//99-12//99
Metals and Plastics	North Carolina	s	12 mw	12.22 aw	25430 aaw	NCBLS	10//99-12//99
Metals and Plastics	Charlotte-Gastonia-Rock Hill MSA, NC-SC	s	13.24 mw	12.84 aw	27540 aaw	NCBLS	10//99-12//99
Metals and Plastics	Greensboro--Winston-Salem--High Point MSA, NC	s	12.13 mw	11.94 aw	25220 aaw	NCBLS	10//99-12//99
Metals and Plastics	Hickory-Morganton-Lenoir MSA, NC	s	12.43 mw	12.51 aw	25850 aaw	NCBLS	10//99-12//99
Metals and Plastics	Ohio	s	12.77 mw	13.65 aw	28380 aaw	OHBLS	10//99-12//99
Metals and Plastics	Akron PMSA, OH	s	12.75 mw	13.27 aw	26520 aaw	OHBLS	10//99-12//99
Metals and Plastics	Canton-Massillon MSA, OH	s	11.47 mw	11.49 aw	23860 aaw	OHBLS	10//99-12//99
Metals and Plastics	Cincinnati PMSA, OH-KY-IN	s	14.21 mw	14.22 aw	29550 aaw	OHBLS	10//99-12//99
Metals and Plastics	Cleveland-Lorain-Elyria PMSA, OH	s	11.93 mw	11.55 aw	24810 aaw	OHBLS	10//99-12//99
Metals and Plastics	Columbus MSA, OH	s	11.71 mw	10.85 aw	24350 aaw	OHBLS	10//99-12//99
Metals and Plastics	Dayton-Springfield MSA, OH	s	17.30 mw	17.48 aw	35990 aaw	OHBLS	10//99-12//99
Metals and Plastics	Hamilton-Middletown PMSA, OH	s	14.64 mw	14.43 aw	30450 aaw	OHBLS	10//99-12//99
Metals and Plastics	Mansfield MSA, OH	s	18.55 mw	19.89 aw	38590 aaw	OHBLS	10//99-12//99
Metals and Plastics	Toledo MSA, OH	s	10.74 mw	10.77 aw	22340 aaw	OHBLS	10//99-12//99
Metals and Plastics	Youngstown-Warren MSA, OH	s	15.27 mw	15.55 aw	31770 aaw	OHBLS	10//99-12//99
Metals and Plastics	Oklahoma	s	12.57 mw	13.41 aw	27900 aaw	OKBLS	10//99-12//99
Metals and Plastics	Tulsa MSA, OK	s	13.05 mw	12.28 aw	27130 aaw	OKBLS	10//99-12//99
Metals and Plastics	Oregon	s	13.12 mw	14.36 aw	29870 aaw	ORBLS	10//99-12//99
Metals and Plastics	Portland-Vancouver PMSA, OR-WA	s	13.35 mw	12.33 aw	27760 aaw	ORBLS	10//99-12//99
Metals and Plastics	Pennsylvania	s	13.91 mw	14.21 aw	29550 aaw	PABLS	10//99-12//99
Metals and Plastics	Allentown-Bethlehem-Easton MSA, PA	s	11.72 mw	11.30 aw	24370 aaw	PABLS	10//99-12//99
Metals and Plastics	Harrisburg-Lebanon-Carlisle MSA, PA	s	17.01 mw	16.64 aw	35370 aaw	PABLS	10//99-12//99
Metals and Plastics	Lancaster MSA, PA	s	14.28 mw	14.04 aw	29690 aaw	PABLS	10//99-12//99
Metals and Plastics	Philadelphia PMSA, PA-NJ	s	14.34 mw	13.48 aw	29830 aaw	PABLS	10//99-12//99
Metals and Plastics	Pittsburgh MSA, PA	s	13.74 mw	12.89 aw	28570 aaw	PABLS	10//99-12//99
Metals and Plastics	Reading MSA, PA	s	13.90 mw	13.61 aw	28910 aaw	PABLS	10//99-12//99
Metals and Plastics	York MSA, PA	s	14.47 mw	13.53 aw	30090 aaw	PABLS	10//99-12//99
Metals and Plastics	Rhode Island	s	10.57 mw	11.14 aw	23170 aaw	RIBLS	10//99-12//99
Metals and Plastics	Providence-Fall River-Warwick MSA, RI-MA	s	11.87 mw	11.20 aw	24680 aaw	RIBLS	10//99-12//99
Metals and Plastics	South Carolina	s	11.57 mw	11.94 aw	24840 aaw	SCBLS	10//99-12//99
Metals and Plastics	Columbia MSA, SC	s	14.13 mw	13.26 aw	29400 aaw	SCBLS	10//99-12//99
Metals and Plastics	South Dakota	s	11.65 mw	11.34 aw	23600 aaw	SDBLS	10//99-12//99
Metals and Plastics	Tennessee	s	11 mw	11.74 aw	24420 aaw	TNBLS	10//99-12//99
Metals and Plastics	Johnson City-Kingsport-Bristol MSA, TN-VA	s	11.83 mw	11.79 aw	24610 aaw	TNBLS	10//99-12//99
Metals and Plastics	Knoxville MSA, TN	s	11.99 mw	11.35 aw	24950 aaw	TNBLS	10//99-12//99
Metals and Plastics	Memphis MSA, TN-AR-MS	s	10.56 mw	10.56 aw	21970 aaw	MSBLS	10//99-12//99
Metals and Plastics	Nashville MSA, TN	s	12.56 mw	10.70 aw	26130 aaw	TNBLS	10//99-12//99

AAW	Average annual wage	AOH	Average offered, high	ASH	Average starting, high
AE	Average entry wage	AOL	Average offered, low	ASL	Average starting, low
AEX	Average experienced wage	APH	Average pay, high range	AW	Average wage paid
AO	Average offered	APL	Average pay, low range	FQ	First quartile wage

H	Hourly	M	Monthly
HI	Highest wage paid	MTC	Median total compensation
HR	High end range	MW	Median wage paid
LR	Low end range	SQ	Second quartile wage

S	Special: hourly and annual
TQ	Third quartile wage
W	Weekly
Y	Yearly

Occupation/Type/Industry	Location	Per	Low	Mid	High	Source	Date
Heat Treating Equipment Setter, Operator, and Tender							
Metals and Plastics	Texas	S	11.34 MW	11.62 AW	24170 AAW	TXBLS	10//99-12//99
Metals and Plastics	Austin-San Marcos MSA, TX	S	11.51 MW	10.91 AW	23940 AAW	TXBLS	10//99-12//99
Metals and Plastics	Dallas PMSA, TX	S	11.19 MW	11.40 AW	23270 AAW	TXBLS	10//99-12//99
Metals and Plastics	El Paso MSA, TX	S	10.26 MW	10.90 AW	21340 AAW	TXBLS	10//99-12//99
Metals and Plastics	Fort Worth-Arlington PMSA, TX	S	13.29 MW	11.97 AW	27640 AAW	TXBLS	10//99-12//99
Metals and Plastics	Houston PMSA, TX	S	11.50 MW	11.11 AW	23930 AAW	TXBLS	10//99-12//99
Metals and Plastics	San Antonio MSA, TX	S	12.28 MW	11.41 AW	25550 AAW	TXBLS	10//99-12//99
Metals and Plastics	Utah	S	10.74 MW	10.77 AW	22410 AAW	UTBLS	10//99-12//99
Metals and Plastics	Vermont	S	13.85 MW	14.24 AW	29620 AAW	VTBLS	10//99-12//99
Metals and Plastics	Virginia	S	11.58 MW	11.87 AW	24690 AAW	VABLS	10//99-12//99
Metals and Plastics	Richmond-Petersburg MSA, VA	S	16.24 MW	15.64 AW	33780 AAW	VABLS	10//99-12//99
Metals and Plastics	Washington	S	15.91 MW	16.83 AW	35010 AAW	WABLS	10//99-12//99
Metals and Plastics	Seattle-Bellevue-Everett PMSA, WA	S	19.09 MW	17.75 AW	39710 AAW	WABLS	10//99-12//99
Metals and Plastics	West Virginia	S	15.95 MW	16.36 AW	34030 AAW	WVBLS	10//99-12//99
Metals and Plastics	Huntington-Ashland MSA, WV-KY-OH	S	13.97 MW	13.86 AW	29060 AAW	WVBLS	10//99-12//99
Metals and Plastics	Wisconsin	S	12.49 MW	12.86 AW	26750 AAW	WIBLS	10//99-12//99
Metals and Plastics	Appleton-Oshkosh-Neenah MSA, WI	S	11.89 MW	11.47 AW	24730 AAW	WIBLS	10//99-12//99
Metals and Plastics	Milwaukee-Waukesha PMSA, WI	S	12.93 MW	12.12 AW	26900 AAW	WIBLS	10//99-12//99
Metals and Plastics	Racine PMSA, WI	S	13.60 MW	13.93 AW	28300 AAW	WIBLS	10//99-12//99
Metals and Plastics	Puerto Rico	S	9.94 MW	11.06 AW	23010 AAW	PRBLS	10//99-12//99
Metals and Plastics	San Juan-Bayamon PMSA, PR	S	11.75 MW	10.36 AW	24450 AAW	PRBLS	10//99-12//99
Heating, Air Conditioning, and Refrigeration Mechanic and Installer							
	Alabama	S	11.7 MW	12.35 AW	25690 AAW	ALBLS	10//99-12//99
	Anniston MSA, AL	S	11.97 MW	10.78 AW	24890 AAW	ALBLS	10//99-12//99
	Auburn-Opelika MSA, AL	S	12.68 MW	11.66 AW	26380 AAW	ALBLS	10//99-12//99
	Birmingham MSA, AL	S	12.87 MW	11.83 AW	26780 AAW	ALBLS	10//99-12//99
	Gadsden MSA, AL	S	11.22 MW	11.35 AW	23340 AAW	ALBLS	10//99-12//99
	Huntsville MSA, AL	S	12.88 MW	12.19 AW	26790 AAW	ALBLS	10//99-12//99
	Mobile MSA, AL	S	12.88 MW	12.11 AW	26800 AAW	ALBLS	10//99-12//99
	Montgomery MSA, AL	S	14.51 MW	14.91 AW	30170 AAW	ALBLS	10//99-12//99
	Tuscaloosa MSA, AL	S	13.23 MW	14.09 AW	27520 AAW	ALBLS	10//99-12//99
	Alaska	S	21.41 MW	21.71 AW	45150 AAW	AKBLS	10//99-12//99
	Anchorage MSA, AK	S	20.21 MW	20.10 AW	42040 AAW	AKBLS	10//99-12//99
	Arizona	S	13.78 MW	14.60 AW	30360 AAW	AZBLS	10//99-12//99
	Flagstaff MSA, AZ-UT	S	14.56 MW	14.51 AW	30290 AAW	AZBLS	10//99-12//99
	Phoenix-Mesa MSA, AZ	S	15.28 MW	14.69 AW	31770 AAW	AZBLS	10//99-12//99
	Tucson MSA, AZ	S	13.35 MW	12.41 AW	27770 AAW	AZBLS	10//99-12//99
	Yuma MSA, AZ	S	13.37 MW	12.04 AW	27810 AAW	AZBLS	10//99-12//99
	Arkansas	S	11.67 MW	12.85 AW	26720 AAW	ARBLS	10//99-12//99
	Fayetteville-Springdale-Rogers MSA, AR	S	15.13 MW	12.07 AW	31460 AAW	ARBLS	10//99-12//99
	Fort Smith MSA, AR-OK	S	12.16 MW	11.78 AW	25300 AAW	ARBLS	10//99-12//99
	Little Rock-North Little Rock MSA, AR	S	12.56 MW	11.80 AW	26120 AAW	ARBLS	10//99-12//99
	Pine Bluff MSA, AR	S	13.27 MW	12.63 AW	27610 AAW	ARBLS	10//99-12//99
	California	S	17.77 MW	18.63 AW	38750 AAW	CABLS	10//99-12//99
	Bakersfield MSA, CA	S	16.61 MW	16.54 AW	34560 AAW	CABLS	10//99-12//99
	Chico-Paradise MSA, CA	S	12.94 MW	12.69 AW	26910 AAW	CABLS	10//99-12//99
	Fresno MSA, CA	S	16.75 MW	16.64 AW	34840 AAW	CABLS	10//99-12//99
	Los Angeles-Long Beach PMSA, CA	S	19.77 MW	18.55 AW	41120 AAW	CABLS	10//99-12//99
	Merced MSA, CA	S	13.95 MW	14.22 AW	29020 AAW	CABLS	10//99-12//99
	Modesto MSA, CA	S	17.43 MW	16.10 AW	36250 AAW	CABLS	10//99-12//99
	Oakland PMSA, CA	S	22.23 MW	20.87 AW	46230 AAW	CABLS	10//99-12//99
	Orange County PMSA, CA	S	17.38 MW	16.44 AW	36150 AAW	CABLS	10//99-12//99
	Redding MSA, CA	S	15.27 MW	15.54 AW	31750 AAW	CABLS	10//99-12//99
	Riverside-San Bernardino PMSA, CA	S	16.99 MW	15.37 AW	35340 AAW	CABLS	10//99-12//99
	Sacramento PMSA, CA	S	17.70 MW	17.33 AW	36820 AAW	CABLS	10//99-12//99
	Salinas MSA, CA	S	24.11 MW	24.36 AW	50140 AAW	CABLS	10//99-12//99
	San Diego MSA, CA	S	17.12 MW	17.22 AW	35610 AAW	CABLS	10//99-12//99

AAW Average annual wage	AOH Average offered, high	ASH Average starting, high	H Hourly	M Monthly	S Special: hourly and annual
AE Average entry wage	AOL Average offered, low	ASL Average starting, low	HI Highest wage paid	MTC Median total compensation	TQ Third quartile wage
AEX Average experienced wage	APH Average pay, high range	AW Average wage paid	HR High end range	MW Median wage paid	W Weekly
AO Average offered	APL Average pay, low range	FQ First quartile wage	LR Low end range	SQ Second quartile wage	Y Yearly

Occupation/Type/Industry	Location	Per	Low	Mid	High	Source	Date
Heating, Air Conditioning, and Refrigeration Mechanic and Installer							
	San Francisco PMSA, CA	S	20.42 MW	20.27 AW	42480 AAW	CABLS	10//99-12//99
	San Jose PMSA, CA	S	20.58 MW	19.41 AW	42810 AAW	CABLS	10//99-12//99
	San Luis Obispo-Atascadero-Paso Robles MSA, CA	S	15.94 MW	11.85 AW	33150 AAW	CABLS	10//99-12//99
	Santa Barbara-Santa Maria-Lompoc MSA, CA	S	19.43 MW	19.20 AW	40420 AAW	CABLS	10//99-12//99
	Santa Rosa PMSA, CA	S	19.24 MW	18.36 AW	40030 AAW	CABLS	10//99-12//99
	Stockton-Lodi MSA, CA	S	16.31 MW	15.32 AW	33910 AAW	CABLS	10//99-12//99
	Vallejo-Fairfield-Napa PMSA, CA	S	17.57 MW	17.96 AW	36550 AAW	CABLS	10//99-12//99
	Ventura PMSA, CA	S	17.53 MW	17.10 AW	36460 AAW	CABLS	10//99-12//99
	Visalia-Tulare-Porterville MSA, CA	S	16.63 MW	16.39 AW	34580 AAW	CABLS	10//99-12//99
	Colorado	S	15.83 MW	16.72 AW	34780 AAW	COBLS	10//99-12//99
	Boulder-Longmont PMSA, CO	S	16.31 MW	15.72 AW	33920 AAW	COBLS	10//99-12//99
	Colorado Springs MSA, CO	S	16.54 MW	15.13 AW	34400 AAW	COBLS	10//99-12//99
	Denver PMSA, CO	S	17.34 MW	16.29 AW	36070 AAW	COBLS	10//99-12//99
	Fort Collins-Loveland MSA, CO	S	17.68 MW	17.19 AW	36780 AAW	COBLS	10//99-12//99
	Pueblo MSA, CO	S	14.21 MW	14.56 AW	29560 AAW	COBLS	10//99-12//99
	Connecticut	S	17.93 MW	18.22 AW	37910 AAW	CTBLS	10//99-12//99
	Bridgeport PMSA, CT	S	17.33 MW	17.58 AW	36050 AAW	CTBLS	10//99-12//99
	Danbury PMSA, CT	S	16.84 MW	17.31 AW	35020 AAW	CTBLS	10//99-12//99
	Hartford MSA, CT	S	17.86 MW	17.93 AW	37150 AAW	CTBLS	10//99-12//99
	New Haven-Meriden PMSA, CT	S	19.74 MW	18.97 AW	41050 AAW	CTBLS	10//99-12//99
	New London-Norwich MSA, CT-RI	S	16.14 MW	15.65 AW	33570 AAW	CTBLS	10//99-12//99
	Stamford-Norwalk PMSA, CT	S	20.05 MW	19.26 AW	41690 AAW	CTBLS	10//99-12//99
	Waterbury PMSA, CT	S	19.01 MW	18.16 AW	39540 AAW	CTBLS	10//99-12//99
	Delaware	S	14.58 MW	16.59 AW	34500 AAW	DEBLS	10//99-12//99
	Dover MSA, DE	S	13.87 MW	13.00 AW	28840 AAW	DEBLS	10//99-12//99
	Wilmington-Newark PMSA, DE-MD	S	18.24 MW	16.65 AW	37930 AAW	DEBLS	10//99-12//99
	District of Columbia	S	18.65 MW	18.58 AW	38650 AAW	DCBLS	10//99-12//99
	Washington PMSA, DC-MD-VA-WV	S	17.11 MW	16.90 AW	35580 AAW	DCBLS	10//99-12//99
	Florida	S	12.49 MW	12.80 AW	26610 AAW	FLBLS	10//99-12//99
	Daytona Beach MSA, FL	S	12.56 MW	12.00 AW	26120 AAW	FLBLS	10//99-12//99
	Fort Lauderdale PMSA, FL	S	13.66 MW	13.32 AW	28410 AAW	FLBLS	10//99-12//99
	Fort Myers-Cape Coral MSA, FL	S	12.27 MW	11.85 AW	25530 AAW	FLBLS	10//99-12//99
	Fort Pierce-Port St. Lucie MSA, FL	S	12.70 MW	12.54 AW	26410 AAW	FLBLS	10//99-12//99
	Fort Walton Beach MSA, FL	S	15.00 MW	13.32 AW	31200 AAW	FLBLS	10//99-12//99
	Gainesville MSA, FL	S	11.38 MW	10.99 AW	23670 AAW	FLBLS	10//99-12//99
	Jacksonville MSA, FL	S	12.54 MW	11.93 AW	26090 AAW	FLBLS	10//99-12//99
	Lakeland-Winter Haven MSA, FL	S	13.44 MW	12.69 AW	27950 AAW	FLBLS	10//99-12//99
	Melbourne-Titusville-Palm Bay MSA, FL	S	14.26 MW	13.65 AW	29660 AAW	FLBLS	10//99-12//99
	Miami PMSA, FL	S	11.67 MW	10.79 AW	24280 AAW	FLBLS	10//99-12//99
	Naples MSA, FL	S	14.60 MW	14.40 AW	30360 AAW	FLBLS	10//99-12//99
	Ocala MSA, FL	S	10.05 MW	10.08 AW	20900 AAW	FLBLS	10//99-12//99
	Orlando MSA, FL	S	13.09 MW	12.81 AW	27230 AAW	FLBLS	10//99-12//99
	Panama City MSA, FL	S	12.37 MW	12.20 AW	25720 AAW	FLBLS	10//99-12//99
	Pensacola MSA, FL	S	11.88 MW	11.69 AW	24710 AAW	FLBLS	10//99-12//99
	Punta Gorda MSA, FL	S	12.33 MW	12.86 AW	25650 AAW	FLBLS	10//99-12//99
	Sarasota-Bradenton MSA, FL	S	13.34 MW	12.85 AW	27760 AAW	FLBLS	10//99-12//99
	Tallahassee MSA, FL	S	11.62 MW	10.86 AW	24160 AAW	FLBLS	10//99-12//99
	Tampa-St. Petersburg-Clearwater MSA, FL	S	12.42 MW	12.44 AW	25830 AAW	FLBLS	10//99-12//99
	West Palm Beach-Boca Raton MSA, FL	S	14.81 MW	14.66 AW	30810 AAW	FLBLS	10//99-12//99
	Georgia	S	13.68 MW	14.01 AW	29130 AAW	GABLS	10//99-12//99
	Albany MSA, GA	S	13.71 MW	13.29 AW	28510 AAW	GABLS	10//99-12//99
	Athens MSA, GA	S	12.90 MW	12.66 AW	26820 AAW	GABLS	10//99-12//99
	Atlanta MSA, GA	S	15.46 MW	14.92 AW	32170 AAW	GABLS	10//99-12//99
	Augusta-Aiken MSA, GA-SC	S	12.66 MW	11.52 AW	26330 AAW	GABLS	10//99-12//99
	Columbus MSA, GA-AL	S	13.21 MW	13.10 AW	27480 AAW	GABLS	10//99-12//99

AAW Average annual wage	**AOH** Average offered, high	**ASH** Average starting, high	**H** Hourly	**M** Monthly
AE Average entry wage	**AOL** Average offered, low	**ASL** Average starting, low	**HI** Highest wage paid	**MTC** Median total compensation
AEX Average experienced wage	**APH** Average pay, high range	**AW** Average wage paid	**HR** High end range	**MW** Median wage paid
AO Average offered	**APL** Average pay, low range	**FQ** First quartile wage	**LR** Low end range	**SQ** Second quartile wage

S Special: hourly and annual		
TQ Third quartile wage		
W Weekly		
Y Yearly		

Occupation/Type/Industry	Location	Per	Low	Mid	High	Source	Date
Heating, Air Conditioning, and Refrigeration Mechanic and Installer							
	Macon MSA, GA	S	12.92 MW	12.37 AW	26880 AAW	GABLS	10//99-12//99
	Savannah MSA, GA	S	13.28 MW	12.99 AW	27620 AAW	GABLS	10//99-12//99
	Hawaii	S	19.32 MW	20.28 AW	42180 AAW	HIBLS	10//99-12//99
	Honolulu MSA, HI	S	20.72 MW	20.64 AW	43110 AAW	HIBLS	10//99-12//99
	Idaho	S	15.04 MW	14.93 AW	31060 AAW	IDBLS	10//99-12//99
	Boise City MSA, ID	S	15.31 MW	15.93 AW	31850 AAW	IDBLS	10//99-12//99
	Illinois	S	15.42 MW	16.80 AW	34930 AAW	ILBLS	10//99-12//99
	Bloomington-Normal MSA, IL	S	19.27 MW	17.40 AW	40080 AAW	ILBLS	10//99-12//99
	Chicago PMSA, IL	S	17.43 MW	16.62 AW	36260 AAW	ILBLS	10//99-12//99
	Decatur MSA, IL	S	20.29 MW	16.95 AW	42210 AAW	ILBLS	10//99-12//99
	Kankakee PMSA, IL	S	22.42 MW	20.14 AW	46640 AAW	ILBLS	10//99-12//99
	Peoria-Pekin MSA, IL	S	18.68 MW	21.67 AW	38860 AAW	ILBLS	10//99-12//99
	Rockford MSA, IL	S	18.81 MW	15.93 AW	39120 AAW	ILBLS	10//99-12//99
	Springfield MSA, IL	S	16.65 MW	14.56 AW	34630 AAW	ILBLS	10//99-12//99
	Indiana	S	14.55 MW	15.04 AW	31290 AAW	INBLS	10//99-12//99
	Elkhart-Goshen MSA, IN	S	13.80 MW	12.63 AW	28700 AAW	INBLS	10//99-12//99
	Evansville-Henderson MSA, IN-KY	S	14.86 MW	13.49 AW	30900 AAW	INBLS	10//99-12//99
	Fort Wayne MSA, IN	S	18.07 MW	17.76 AW	37590 AAW	INBLS	10//99-12//99
	Gary PMSA, IN	S	12.30 MW	11.69 AW	25580 AAW	INBLS	10//99-12//99
	Indianapolis MSA, IN	S	15.08 MW	14.23 AW	31360 AAW	INBLS	10//99-12//99
	Kokomo MSA, IN	S	17.31 MW	15.53 AW	36010 AAW	INBLS	10//99-12//99
	Lafayette MSA, IN	S	12.53 MW	11.79 AW	26050 AAW	INBLS	10//99-12//99
	South Bend MSA, IN	S	15.39 MW	15.27 AW	32010 AAW	INBLS	10//99-12//99
	Terre Haute MSA, IN	S	14.07 MW	14.51 AW	29270 AAW	INBLS	10//99-12//99
	Iowa	S	13.48 MW	14.70 AW	30570 AAW	IABLS	10//99-12//99
	Cedar Rapids MSA, IA	S	16.30 MW	13.10 AW	33900 AAW	IABLS	10//99-12//99
	Davenport-Moline-Rock Island MSA, IA-IL	S	15.58 MW	15.04 AW	32400 AAW	IABLS	10//99-12//99
	Des Moines MSA, IA	S	14.94 MW	13.91 AW	31070 AAW	IABLS	10//99-12//99
	Dubuque MSA, IA	S	13.88 MW	13.26 AW	28880 AAW	IABLS	10//99-12//99
	Iowa City MSA, IA	S	16.21 MW	15.34 AW	33710 AAW	IABLS	10//99-12//99
	Sioux City MSA, IA-NE	S	16.26 MW	14.85 AW	33820 AAW	IABLS	10//99-12//99
	Waterloo-Cedar Falls MSA, IA	S	11.65 MW	10.94 AW	24240 AAW	IABLS	10//99-12//99
	Kansas	S	14.51 MW	15.05 AW	31300 AAW	KSBLS	10//99-12//99
	Lawrence MSA, KS	S	14.78 MW	13.77 AW	30750 AAW	KSBLS	10//99-12//99
	Topeka MSA, KS	S	15.63 MW	15.38 AW	32510 AAW	KSBLS	10//99-12//99
	Wichita MSA, KS	S	15.71 MW	14.53 AW	32670 AAW	KSBLS	10//99-12//99
	Kentucky	S	12.17 MW	12.87 AW	26760 AAW	KYBLS	10//99-12//99
	Lexington MSA, KY	S	14.11 MW	14.08 AW	29340 AAW	KYBLS	10//99-12//99
	Louisville MSA, KY-IN	S	13.95 MW	13.39 AW	29010 AAW	KYBLS	10//99-12//99
	Louisiana	S	12.38 MW	12.84 AW	26710 AAW	LABLS	10//99-12//99
	Alexandria MSA, LA	S	12.93 MW	12.34 AW	26900 AAW	LABLS	10//99-12//99
	Baton Rouge MSA, LA	S	12.54 MW	12.55 AW	26090 AAW	LABLS	10//99-12//99
	Houma MSA, LA	S	12.40 MW	12.18 AW	25800 AAW	LABLS	10//99-12//99
	Lafayette MSA, LA	S	14.17 MW	14.32 AW	29480 AAW	LABLS	10//99-12//99
	Lake Charles MSA, LA	S	14.24 MW	13.56 AW	29620 AAW	LABLS	10//99-12//99
	Monroe MSA, LA	S	13.28 MW	12.98 AW	27630 AAW	LABLS	10//99-12//99
	New Orleans MSA, LA	S	12.75 MW	12.10 AW	26510 AAW	LABLS	10//99-12//99
	Shreveport-Bossier City MSA, LA	S	13.51 MW	12.67 AW	28100 AAW	LABLS	10//99-12//99
	Maine	S	13.02 MW	13.24 AW	27530 AAW	MEBLS	10//99-12//99
	Bangor MSA, ME	S	12.10 MW	11.85 AW	25170 AAW	MEBLS	10//99-12//99
	Lewiston-Auburn MSA, ME	S	12.79 MW	13.05 AW	26600 AAW	MEBLS	10//99-12//99
	Portland MSA, ME	S	16.09 MW	16.08 AW	33460 AAW	MEBLS	10//99-12//99
	Maryland	S	15.89 MW	16.43 AW	34170 AAW	MDBLS	10//99-12//99
	Baltimore PMSA, MD	S	15.24 MW	14.51 AW	31710 AAW	MDBLS	10//99-12//99
	Hagerstown PMSA, MD	S	14.25 MW	13.66 AW	29640 AAW	MDBLS	10//99-12//99
	Massachusetts	S	18.67 MW	18.83 AW	39170 AAW	MABLS	10//99-12//99
	Boston PMSA, MA-NH	S	19.75 MW	19.52 AW	41070 AAW	MABLS	10//99-12//99
	Brockton PMSA, MA	S	15.96 MW	15.88 AW	33200 AAW	MABLS	10//99-12//99
	Lowell PMSA, MA-NH	S	16.38 MW	16.17 AW	34060 AAW	MABLS	10//99-12//99
	New Bedford PMSA, MA	S	18.23 MW	17.56 AW	37910 AAW	MABLS	10//99-12//99
	Springfield MSA, MA	S	16.10 MW	15.85 AW	33490 AAW	MABLS	10//99-12//99
	Worcester PMSA, MA-CT	S	18.14 MW	16.69 AW	37720 AAW	MABLS	10//99-12//99
	Michigan	S	16.08 MW	16.97 AW	35290 AAW	MIBLS	10//99-12//99
	Ann Arbor PMSA, MI	S	21.31 MW	20.73 AW	44320 AAW	MIBLS	10//99-12//99
	Benton Harbor MSA, MI	S	15.84 MW	14.16 AW	32950 AAW	MIBLS	10//99-12//99
	Detroit PMSA, MI	S	17.67 MW	16.98 AW	36750 AAW	MIBLS	10//99-12//99
	Flint PMSA, MI	S	16.26 MW	16.56 AW	33820 AAW	MIBLS	10//99-12//99

AAW Average annual wage	**AOH** Average offered, high	**ASH** Average starting, high	**H** Hourly	**M** Monthly	**S** Special: hourly and annual
AE Average entry wage	**AOL** Average offered, low	**ASL** Average starting, low	**HI** Highest wage paid	**MTC** Median total compensation	**TQ** Third quartile wage
AEX Average experienced wage	**APH** Average pay, high range	**AW** Average wage paid	**HR** High end range	**MW** Median wage paid	**W** Weekly
AO Average offered	**APL** Average pay, low range	**FQ** First quartile wage	**LR** Low end range	**SQ** Second quartile wage	**Y** Yearly

Occupation/Type/Industry	Location	Per	Low	Mid	High	Source	Date
Heating, Air Conditioning, and Refrigeration Mechanic and Installer							
	Grand Rapids-Muskegon-Holland MSA, MI	S	16.69 MW	15.72 AW	34720 AAW	MIBLS	10//99-12//99
	Kalamazoo-Battle Creek MSA, MI	S	14.45 MW	13.38 AW	30060 AAW	MIBLS	10//99-12//99
	Lansing-East Lansing MSA, MI	S	16.73 MW	15.21 AW	34810 AAW	MIBLS	10//99-12//99
	Saginaw-Bay City-Midland MSA, MI	S	14.85 MW	14.77 AW	30890 AAW	MIBLS	10//99-12//99
	Minnesota	S	15.87 MW	16.47 AW	34260 AAW	MNBLS	10//99-12//99
	Duluth-Superior MSA, MN-WI	S	15.90 MW	15.40 AW	33070 AAW	MNBLS	10//99-12//99
	Minneapolis-St. Paul MSA, MN-WI	S	17.83 MW	17.83 AW	37090 AAW	MNBLS	10//99-12//99
	Rochester MSA, MN	S	17.77 MW	15.65 AW	36970 AAW	MNBLS	10//99-12//99
	St. Cloud MSA, MN	S	15.64 MW	13.53 AW	32540 AAW	MNBLS	10//99-12//99
	Mississippi	S	11.51 MW	12.50 AW	25990 AAW	MSBLS	10//99-12//99
	Biloxi-Gulfport-Pascagoula MSA, MS	S	11.79 MW	12.17 AW	24530 AAW	MSBLS	10//99-12//99
	Jackson MSA, MS	S	16.54 MW	16.27 AW	34410 AAW	MSBLS	10//99-12//99
	Missouri	S	13.77 MW	15.09 AW	31390 AAW	MOBLS	10//99-12//99
	Joplin MSA, MO	S	12.42 MW	11.77 AW	25830 AAW	MOBLS	10//99-12//99
	Kansas City MSA, MO-KS	S	16.10 MW	14.98 AW	33480 AAW	MOBLS	10//99-12//99
	St. Louis MSA, MO-IL	S	15.69 MW	14.55 AW	32630 AAW	MOBLS	10//99-12//99
	Springfield MSA, MO	S	15.09 MW	14.17 AW	31390 AAW	MOBLS	10//99-12//99
	Montana	S	13.73 MW	14.38 AW	29920 AAW	MTBLS	10//99-12//99
	Great Falls MSA, MT	S	16.95 MW	17.49 AW	35250 AAW	MTBLS	10//99-12//99
	Nebraska	S	14.46 MW	15.33 AW	31890 AAW	NEBLS	10//99-12//99
	Lincoln MSA, NE	S	14.51 MW	13.83 AW	30190 AAW	NEBLS	10//99-12//99
	Omaha MSA, NE-IA	S	16.86 MW	16.21 AW	35060 AAW	NEBLS	10//99-12//99
	Nevada	S	15.15 MW	15.60 AW	32440 AAW	NVBLS	10//99-12//99
	Las Vegas MSA, NV-AZ	S	15.57 MW	15.02 AW	32380 AAW	NVBLS	10//99-12//99
	Reno MSA, NV	S	15.12 MW	15.12 AW	31440 AAW	NVBLS	10//99-12//99
	New Hampshire	S	14.43 MW	14.54 AW	30250 AAW	NHBLS	10//99-12//99
	Manchester PMSA, NH	S	16.76 MW	16.51 AW	34850 AAW	NHBLS	10//99-12//99
	Nashua PMSA, NH	S	16.50 MW	16.31 AW	34310 AAW	NHBLS	10//99-12//99
	Portsmouth-Rochester PMSA, NH-ME	S	15.30 MW	14.26 AW	31820 AAW	NHBLS	10//99-12//99
	New Jersey	S	18.32 MW	18.61 AW	38710 AAW	NJBLS	10//99-12//99
	Atlantic-Cape May PMSA, NJ	S	16.09 MW	15.78 AW	33460 AAW	NJBLS	10//99-12//99
	Bergen-Passaic PMSA, NJ	S	19.46 MW	19.03 AW	40480 AAW	NJBLS	10//99-12//99
	Jersey City PMSA, NJ	S	18.91 MW	18.23 AW	39330 AAW	NJBLS	10//99-12//99
	Middlesex-Somerset-Hunterdon PMSA, NJ	S	17.25 MW	17.40 AW	35880 AAW	NJBLS	10//99-12//99
	Monmouth-Ocean PMSA, NJ	S	17.12 MW	16.71 AW	35610 AAW	NJBLS	10//99-12//99
	Newark PMSA, NJ	S	19.30 MW	19.06 AW	40140 AAW	NJBLS	10//99-12//99
	Trenton PMSA, NJ	S	18.71 MW	18.59 AW	38910 AAW	NJBLS	10//99-12//99
	Vineland-Millville-Bridgeton PMSA, NJ	S	17.43 MW	17.37 AW	36250 AAW	NJBLS	10//99-12//99
	New Mexico	S	12.55 MW	13.49 AW	28060 AAW	NMBLS	10//99-12//99
	Albuquerque MSA, NM	S	15.91 MW	15.47 AW	33100 AAW	NMBLS	10//99-12//99
	Las Cruces MSA, NM	S	12.01 MW	11.43 AW	24980 AAW	NMBLS	10//99-12//99
	New York	S	16.47 MW	17.41 AW	36220 AAW	NYBLS	10//99-12//99
	Albany-Schenectady-Troy MSA, NY	S	15.38 MW	15.39 AW	31980 AAW	NYBLS	10//99-12//99
	Binghamton MSA, NY	S	17.01 MW	16.02 AW	35390 AAW	NYBLS	10//99-12//99
	Buffalo-Niagara Falls MSA, NY	S	14.93 MW	14.93 AW	31050 AAW	NYBLS	10//99-12//99
	Dutchess County PMSA, NY	S	15.81 MW	15.83 AW	32880 AAW	NYBLS	10//99-12//99
	Elmira MSA, NY	S	13.91 MW	14.86 AW	28940 AAW	NYBLS	10//99-12//99
	Glens Falls MSA, NY	S	13.95 MW	13.78 AW	29020 AAW	NYBLS	10//99-12//99
	Nassau-Suffolk PMSA, NY	S	18.52 MW	17.95 AW	38530 AAW	NYBLS	10//99-12//99
	New York PMSA, NY	S	19.23 MW	18.71 AW	39990 AAW	NYBLS	10//99-12//99
	Newburgh PMSA, NY-PA	S	17.26 MW	17.87 AW	35910 AAW	NYBLS	10//99-12//99
	Rochester MSA, NY	S	15.10 MW	14.57 AW	31400 AAW	NYBLS	10//99-12//99
	Syracuse MSA, NY	S	16.26 MW	15.83 AW	33830 AAW	NYBLS	10//99-12//99
	Utica-Rome MSA, NY	S	11.97 MW	10.66 AW	24900 AAW	NYBLS	10//99-12//99
	North Carolina	S	12.44 MW	12.77 AW	26570 AAW	NCBLS	10//99-12//99
	Asheville MSA, NC	S	11.72 MW	11.48 AW	24370 AAW	NCBLS	10//99-12//99
	Charlotte-Gastonia-Rock Hill MSA, NC-SC	S	13.18 MW	12.50 AW	27410 AAW	NCBLS	10//99-12//99
	Fayetteville MSA, NC	S	10.52 MW	9.90 AW	21890 AAW	NCBLS	10//99-12//99
	Goldsboro MSA, NC	S	12.89 MW	12.47 AW	26800 AAW	NCBLS	10//99-12//99

AAW Average annual wage	**AOH** Average offered, high	**ASH** Average starting, high	**H** Hourly	**M** Monthly	**S** Special: hourly and annual
AE Average entry wage	**AOL** Average offered, low	**ASL** Average starting, low	**HI** Highest wage paid	**MTC** Median total compensation	**TQ** Third quartile wage
AEX Average experienced wage	**APH** Average pay, high range	**AW** Average wage paid	**HR** High end range	**MW** Median wage paid	**W** Weekly
AO Average offered	**APL** Average pay, low range	**FQ** First quartile wage	**LR** Low end range	**SQ** Second quartile wage	**Y** Yearly

Occupation/Type/Industry	Location	Per	Low	Mid	High	Source	Date
Heating, Air Conditioning, and Refrigeration Mechanic and Installer	Greensboro--Winston-Salem-- High Point MSA, NC	S	13.67 MW	13.47 AW	28430 AAW	NCBLS	10//99-12//99
	Hickory-Morganton-Lenoir MSA, NC	S	13.63 MW	13.81 AW	28350 AAW	NCBLS	10//99-12//99
	Jacksonville MSA, NC	S	13.84 MW	13.42 AW	28790 AAW	NCBLS	10//99-12//99
	Raleigh-Durham-Chapel Hill MSA, NC	S	12.97 MW	13.27 AW	26980 AAW	NCBLS	10//99-12//99
	Rocky Mount MSA, NC	S	11.95 MW	12.35 AW	24850 AAW	NCBLS	10//99-12//99
	Wilmington MSA, NC	S	12.07 MW	11.88 AW	25110 AAW	NCBLS	10//99-12//99
	North Dakota	S	13.64 MW	14.50 AW	30160 AAW	NDBLS	10//99-12//99
	Bismarck MSA, ND	S	15.23 MW	13.24 AW	31680 AAW	NDBLS	10//99-12//99
	Fargo-Moorhead MSA, ND-MN	S	14.29 MW	14.13 AW	29710 AAW	NDBLS	10//99-12//99
	Grand Forks MSA, ND-MN	S	14.38 MW	13.21 AW	29920 AAW	NDBLS	10//99-12//99
	Ohio	S	14.59 MW	15.45 AW	32130 AAW	OHBLS	10//99-12//99
	Akron PMSA, OH	S	14.35 MW	14.18 AW	29850 AAW	OHBLS	10//99-12//99
	Canton-Massillon MSA, OH	S	14.36 MW	13.65 AW	29870 AAW	OHBLS	10//99-12//99
	Cincinnati PMSA, OH-KY-IN	S	15.35 MW	14.66 AW	31920 AAW	OHBLS	10//99-12//99
	Cleveland-Lorain-Elyria PMSA, OH	S	18.25 MW	16.75 AW	37960 AAW	OHBLS	10//99-12//99
	Columbus MSA, OH	S	15.33 MW	15.25 AW	31890 AAW	OHBLS	10//99-12//99
	Dayton-Springfield MSA, OH	S	16.88 MW	15.68 AW	35110 AAW	OHBLS	10//99-12//99
	Hamilton-Middletown PMSA, OH	S	14.69 MW	14.15 AW	30550 AAW	OHBLS	10//99-12//99
	Lima MSA, OH	S	13.74 MW	13.53 AW	28580 AAW	OHBLS	10//99-12//99
	Mansfield MSA, OH	S	15.16 MW	16.31 AW	31530 AAW	OHBLS	10//99-12//99
	Steubenville-Weirton MSA, OH-WV	S	11.65 MW	11.34 AW	24230 AAW	OHBLS	10//99-12//99
	Toledo MSA, OH	S	17.09 MW	15.81 AW	35550 AAW	OHBLS	10//99-12//99
	Youngstown-Warren MSA, OH	S	17.64 MW	18.68 AW	36700 AAW	OHBLS	10//99-12//99
	Oklahoma	S	11.81 MW	12.95 AW	26930 AAW	OKBLS	10//99-12//99
	Enid MSA, OK	S	12.75 MW	11.90 AW	26520 AAW	OKBLS	10//99-12//99
	Lawton MSA, OK	S	14.07 MW	13.66 AW	29270 AAW	OKBLS	10//99-12//99
	Oklahoma City MSA, OK	S	12.44 MW	10.47 AW	25880 AAW	OKBLS	10//99-12//99
	Tulsa MSA, OK	S	13.65 MW	12.76 AW	28390 AAW	OKBLS	10//99-12//99
	Oregon	S	16.12 MW	17.31 AW	36000 AAW	ORBLS	10//99-12//99
	Medford-Ashland MSA, OR	S	13.79 MW	13.92 AW	28690 AAW	ORBLS	10//99-12//99
	Portland-Vancouver PMSA, OR-WA	S	19.87 MW	18.61 AW	41320 AAW	ORBLS	10//99-12//99
	Salem PMSA, OR	S	12.69 MW	11.31 AW	26390 AAW	ORBLS	10//99-12//99
	Pennsylvania	S	15.28 MW	16.01 AW	33310 AAW	PABLS	10//99-12//99
	Allentown-Bethlehem-Easton MSA, PA	S	15.76 MW	15.43 AW	32780 AAW	PABLS	10//99-12//99
	Altoona MSA, PA	S	11.39 MW	11.26 AW	23700 AAW	PABLS	10//99-12//99
	Erie MSA, PA	S	14.62 MW	13.88 AW	30410 AAW	PABLS	10//99-12//99
	Harrisburg-Lebanon-Carlisle MSA, PA	S	14.51 MW	14.29 AW	30190 AAW	PABLS	10//99-12//99
	Johnstown MSA, PA	S	12.14 MW	12.07 AW	25250 AAW	PABLS	10//99-12//99
	Lancaster MSA, PA	S	14.58 MW	13.94 AW	30320 AAW	PABLS	10//99-12//99
	Philadelphia PMSA, PA-NJ	S	19.38 MW	18.78 AW	40320 AAW	PABLS	10//99-12//99
	Pittsburgh MSA, PA	S	14.60 MW	14.43 AW	30370 AAW	PABLS	10//99-12//99
	Reading MSA, PA	S	16.09 MW	15.11 AW	33470 AAW	PABLS	10//99-12//99
	Sharon MSA, PA	S	15.13 MW	14.86 AW	31470 AAW	PABLS	10//99-12//99
	State College MSA, PA	S	12.92 MW	12.43 AW	26880 AAW	PABLS	10//99-12//99
	Williamsport MSA, PA	S	13.21 MW	13.18 AW	27470 AAW	PABLS	10//99-12//99
	York MSA, PA	S	15.03 MW	14.85 AW	31250 AAW	PABLS	10//99-12//99
	Rhode Island	S	15.9 MW	16.42 AW	34160 AAW	RIBLS	10//99-12//99
	Providence-Fall River-Warwick MSA, RI-MA	S	17.16 MW	16.62 AW	35690 AAW	RIBLS	10//99-12//99
	South Carolina	S	11.6 MW	12.28 AW	25550 AAW	SCBLS	10//99-12//99
	Charleston-North Charleston MSA, SC	S	11.83 MW	10.91 AW	24610 AAW	SCBLS	10//99-12//99
	Columbia MSA, SC	S	12.86 MW	12.82 AW	26760 AAW	SCBLS	10//99-12//99
	Florence MSA, SC	S	12.61 MW	12.50 AW	26220 AAW	SCBLS	10//99-12//99
	Greenville-Spartanburg-Anderson MSA, SC	S	11.95 MW	11.60 AW	24850 AAW	SCBLS	10//99-12//99
	Myrtle Beach MSA, SC	S	11.18 MW	10.91 AW	23250 AAW	SCBLS	10//99-12//99
	Sumter MSA, SC	S	11.63 MW	10.67 AW	24190 AAW	SCBLS	10//99-12//99
	South Dakota	S	13.01 MW	13.29 AW	27650 AAW	SDBLS	10//99-12//99
	Rapid City MSA, SD	S	14.68 MW	14.03 AW	30530 AAW	SDBLS	10//99-12//99

Occupation/Type/Industry	Location	Per	Low	Mid	High	Source	Date
Heating, Air Conditioning, and Refrigeration Mechanic and Installer							
	Sioux Falls MSA, SD	s	14.19 mw	13.99 aw	29510 aaw	SDBLS	10//99-12//99
	Tennessee	s	13.99 mw	14.71 aw	30600 aaw	TNBLS	10//99-12//99
	Chattanooga MSA, TN-GA	s	12.72 mw	11.60 aw	26450 aaw	TNBLS	10//99-12//99
	Clarksville-Hopkinsville MSA, TN-KY	s	12.73 mw	13.46 aw	26480 aaw	TNBLS	10//99-12//99
	Jackson MSA, TN	s	13.16 mw	10.58 aw	27380 aaw	TNBLS	10//99-12//99
	Johnson City-Kingsport-Bristol MSA, TN-VA	s	11.25 mw	10.95 aw	23390 aaw	TNBLS	10//99-12//99
	Knoxville MSA, TN	s	13.61 mw	13.57 aw	28300 aaw	TNBLS	10//99-12//99
	Memphis MSA, TN-AR-MS	s	16.61 mw	16.60 aw	34550 aaw	MSBLS	10//99-12//99
	Nashville MSA, TN	s	15.72 mw	14.93 aw	32700 aaw	TNBLS	10//99-12//99
	Texas	s	13.36 mw	13.94 aw	29000 aaw	TXBLS	10//99-12//99
	Abilene MSA, TX	s	12.52 mw	11.97 aw	26040 aaw	TXBLS	10//99-12//99
	Amarillo MSA, TX	s	12.58 mw	12.28 aw	26170 aaw	TXBLS	10//99-12//99
	Austin-San Marcos MSA, TX	s	13.63 mw	13.18 aw	28350 aaw	TXBLS	10//99-12//99
	Beaumont-Port Arthur MSA, TX	s	14.29 mw	13.72 aw	29730 aaw	TXBLS	10//99-12//99
	Brazoria PMSA, TX	s	14.13 mw	13.31 aw	29390 aaw	TXBLS	10//99-12//99
	Brownsville-Harlingen-San Benito MSA, TX	s	10.91 mw	9.62 aw	22700 aaw	TXBLS	10//99-12//99
	Bryan-College Station MSA, TX	s	12.08 mw	11.51 aw	25130 aaw	TXBLS	10//99-12//99
	Corpus Christi MSA, TX	s	12.75 mw	12.43 aw	26520 aaw	TXBLS	10//99-12//99
	Dallas PMSA, TX	s	14.59 mw	14.28 aw	30340 aaw	TXBLS	10//99-12//99
	El Paso MSA, TX	s	12.30 mw	11.55 aw	25570 aaw	TXBLS	10//99-12//99
	Fort Worth-Arlington PMSA, TX	s	14.46 mw	14.08 aw	30070 aaw	TXBLS	10//99-12//99
	Galveston-Texas City PMSA, TX	s	14.42 mw	14.86 aw	30000 aaw	TXBLS	10//99-12//99
	Houston PMSA, TX	s	15.02 mw	14.00 aw	31230 aaw	TXBLS	10//99-12//99
	Killeen-Temple MSA, TX	s	13.24 mw	12.93 aw	27540 aaw	TXBLS	10//99-12//99
	Longview-Marshall MSA, TX	s	14.35 mw	14.82 aw	29850 aaw	TXBLS	10//99-12//99
	Lubbock MSA, TX	s	14.70 mw	13.62 aw	30580 aaw	TXBLS	10//99-12//99
	McAllen-Edinburg-Mission MSA, TX	s	9.25 mw	8.49 aw	19230 aaw	TXBLS	10//99-12//99
	Odessa-Midland MSA, TX	s	13.69 mw	13.61 aw	28480 aaw	TXBLS	10//99-12//99
	San Angelo MSA, TX	s	14.78 mw	14.89 aw	30740 aaw	TXBLS	10//99-12//99
	San Antonio MSA, TX	s	13.10 mw	12.25 aw	27260 aaw	TXBLS	10//99-12//99
	Sherman-Denison MSA, TX	s	12.95 mw	12.57 aw	26950 aaw	TXBLS	10//99-12//99
	Tyler MSA, TX	s	13.17 mw	13.51 aw	27400 aaw	TXBLS	10//99-12//99
	Waco MSA, TX	s	12.92 mw	12.83 aw	26880 aaw	TXBLS	10//99-12//99
	Wichita Falls MSA, TX	s	15.65 mw	17.12 aw	32550 aaw	TXBLS	10//99-12//99
	Utah	s	14.6 mw	15.43 aw	32090 aaw	UTBLS	10//99-12//99
	Provo-Orem MSA, UT	s	15.65 mw	14.86 aw	32560 aaw	UTBLS	10//99-12//99
	Salt Lake City-Ogden MSA, UT	s	15.60 mw	14.47 aw	32440 aaw	UTBLS	10//99-12//99
	Vermont	s	13.25 mw	13.62 aw	28340 aaw	VTBLS	10//99-12//99
	Burlington MSA, VT	s	15.48 mw	15.36 aw	32190 aaw	VTBLS	10//99-12//99
	Virginia	s	14.02 mw	14.38 aw	29920 aaw	VABLS	10//99-12//99
	Charlottesville MSA, VA	s	13.96 mw	13.73 aw	29040 aaw	VABLS	10//99-12//99
	Danville MSA, VA	s	12.24 mw	12.10 aw	25470 aaw	VABLS	10//99-12//99
	Lynchburg MSA, VA	s	12.23 mw	12.16 aw	25450 aaw	VABLS	10//99-12//99
	Norfolk-Virginia Beach-Newport News MSA, VA-NC	s	14.53 mw	14.54 aw	30220 aaw	VABLS	10//99-12//99
	Richmond-Petersburg MSA, VA	s	14.31 mw	13.79 aw	29760 aaw	VABLS	10//99-12//99
	Roanoke MSA, VA	s	13.18 mw	12.78 aw	27410 aaw	VABLS	10//99-12//99
	Washington	s	17.67 mw	18.03 aw	37500 aaw	WABLS	10//99-12//99
	Bellingham MSA, WA	s	16.27 mw	15.82 aw	33840 aaw	WABLS	10//99-12//99
	Bremerton PMSA, WA	s	17.98 mw	18.52 aw	37400 aaw	WABLS	10//99-12//99
	Olympia PMSA, WA	s	18.65 mw	18.69 aw	38780 aaw	WABLS	10//99-12//99
	Richland-Kennewick-Pasco MSA, WA	s	13.09 mw	12.95 aw	27220 aaw	WABLS	10//99-12//99
	Seattle-Bellevue-Everett PMSA, WA	s	20.19 mw	19.06 aw	42000 aaw	WABLS	10//99-12//99
	Spokane MSA, WA	s	14.94 mw	14.86 aw	31070 aaw	WABLS	10//99-12//99
	Tacoma PMSA, WA	s	17.54 mw	17.73 aw	36480 aaw	WABLS	10//99-12//99
	Yakima MSA, WA	s	14.29 mw	14.38 aw	29730 aaw	WABLS	10//99-12//99
	West Virginia	s	13.41 mw	14.22 aw	29590 aaw	WVBLS	10//99-12//99

AAW	Average annual wage	AOH	Average offered, high	ASH	Average starting, high
AE	Average entry wage	AOL	Average offered, low	ASL	Average starting, low
AEX	Average experienced wage	APH	Average pay, high range	AW	Average pay wage
AO	Average offered	APL	Average pay, low range	FQ	First quartile wage

H	Hourly	M	Monthly
HI	Highest wage paid	MTC	Median total compensation
HR	High end range	MW	Median wage paid
LR	Low end range	SQ	Second quartile wage

S	Special: hourly and annual
TQ	Third quartile wage
W	Weekly
Y	Yearly

Occupation/Type/Industry	Location	Per	Low	Mid	High	Source	Date
Heating, Air Conditioning, and Refrigeration Mechanic and Installer	Charleston MSA, WV	S	15.44 MW	14.92 AW	32120 AAW	WVBLS	10//99-12//99
	Huntington-Ashland MSA, WV-KY-OH	S	12.78 MW	12.27 AW	26580 AAW	WVBLS	10//99-12//99
	Parkersburg-Marietta MSA, WV-OH	S	13.33 MW	12.82 AW	27720 AAW	WVBLS	10//99-12//99
	Wheeling MSA, WV-OH	S	12.71 MW	11.07 AW	26430 AAW	WVBLS	10//99-12//99
	Wisconsin	S	15.18 MW	16.34 AW	33990 AAW	WIBLS	10//99-12//99
	Appleton-Oshkosh-Neenah MSA, WI	S	14.37 MW	14.56 AW	29880 AAW	WIBLS	10//99-12//99
	Eau Claire MSA, WI	S	15.27 MW	15.35 AW	31750 AAW	WIBLS	10//99-12//99
	Green Bay MSA, WI	S	15.26 MW	15.25 AW	31750 AAW	WIBLS	10//99-12//99
	Janesville-Beloit MSA, WI	S	15.22 MW	13.91 AW	31660 AAW	WIBLS	10//99-12//99
	Kenosha PMSA, WI	S	19.64 MW	17.58 AW	40850 AAW	WIBLS	10//99-12//99
	La Crosse MSA, WI-MN	S	16.81 MW	15.97 AW	34970 AAW	WIBLS	10//99-12//99
	Madison MSA, WI	S	16.44 MW	17.50 AW	34200 AAW	WIBLS	10//99-12//99
	Milwaukee-Waukesha PMSA, WI	S	20.91 MW	18.91 AW	43500 AAW	WIBLS	10//99-12//99
	Racine PMSA, WI	S	19.54 MW	18.68 AW	40650 AAW	WIBLS	10//99-12//99
	Sheboygan MSA, WI	S	14.82 MW	12.69 AW	30830 AAW	WIBLS	10//99-12//99
	Wyoming	S	15.37 MW	15.36 AW	31960 AAW	WYBLS	10//99-12//99
	Puerto Rico	S	7.88 MW	8.57 AW	17830 AAW	PRBLS	10//99-12//99
	Arecibo PMSA, PR	S	6.52 MW	6.34 AW	13560 AAW	PRBLS	10//99-12//99
	Caguas PMSA, PR	S	7.83 MW	7.32 AW	16280 AAW	PRBLS	10//99-12//99
	Mayaguez MSA, PR	S	8.99 MW	8.54 AW	18710 AAW	PRBLS	10//99-12//99
	Ponce MSA, PR	S	6.52 MW	6.42 AW	13560 AAW	PRBLS	10//99-12//99
	San Juan-Bayamon PMSA, PR	S	8.73 MW	8.01 AW	18150 AAW	PRBLS	10//99-12//99
	Virgin Islands	S	11.9 MW	12.26 AW	25500 AAW	VIBLS	10//99-12//99
	Guam	S	13.26 MW	13.62 AW	28320 AAW	GUBLS	10//99-12//99
Helper							
Brickmason, Blockmason, Stonemason, and Tile and Marble Setter	Alabama	S	9.69 MW	9.65 AW	20080 AAW	ALBLS	10//99-12//99
Brickmason, Blockmason, Stonemason, and Tile and Marble Setter	Arizona	S	9.28 MW	9.64 AW	20050 AAW	AZBLS	10//99-12//99
Brickmason, Blockmason, Stonemason, and Tile and Marble Setter	Arkansas	S	8.99 MW	8.98 AW	18680 AAW	ARBLS	10//99-12//99
Brickmason, Blockmason, Stonemason, and Tile and Marble Setter	California	S	12.62 MW	13.39 AW	27840 AAW	CABLS	10//99-12//99
Brickmason, Blockmason, Stonemason, and Tile and Marble Setter	Colorado	S	11.89 MW	12.12 AW	25210 AAW	COBLS	10//99-12//99
Brickmason, Blockmason, Stonemason, and Tile and Marble Setter	Connecticut	S	16.6 MW	14.58 AW	30320 AAW	CTBLS	10//99-12//99
Brickmason, Blockmason, Stonemason, and Tile and Marble Setter	Delaware	S	9.38 MW	9.25 AW	19250 AAW	DEBLS	10//99-12//99
Brickmason, Blockmason, Stonemason, and Tile and Marble Setter	Florida	S	8.83 MW	9.03 AW	18790 AAW	FLBLS	10//99-12//99
Brickmason, Blockmason, Stonemason, and Tile and Marble Setter	Georgia	S	8.51 MW	8.47 AW	17620 AAW	GABLS	10//99-12//99
Brickmason, Blockmason, Stonemason, and Tile and Marble Setter	Hawaii	S	20.52 MW	19.16 AW	39840 AAW	HIBLS	10//99-12//99
Brickmason, Blockmason, Stonemason, and Tile and Marble Setter	Idaho	S	10.04 MW	12.04 AW	25030 AAW	IDBLS	10//99-12//99
Brickmason, Blockmason, Stonemason, and Tile and Marble Setter	Illinois	S	17.38 MW	17.17 AW	35720 AAW	ILBLS	10//99-12//99
Brickmason, Blockmason, Stonemason, and Tile and Marble Setter	Indiana	S	11.31 MW	12.65 AW	26320 AAW	INBLS	10//99-12//99
Brickmason, Blockmason, Stonemason, and Tile and Marble Setter	Iowa	S	11.04 MW	12.19 AW	25360 AAW	IABLS	10//99-12//99
Brickmason, Blockmason, Stonemason, and Tile and Marble Setter	Kansas	S	11.06 MW	11.57 AW	24060 AAW	KSBLS	10//99-12//99
Brickmason, Blockmason, Stonemason, and Tile and Marble Setter	Kentucky	S	10.33 MW	10.69 AW	22220 AAW	KYBLS	10//99-12//99
Brickmason, Blockmason, Stonemason, and Tile and Marble Setter	Louisiana	S	10.66 MW	10.46 AW	21750 AAW	LABLS	10//99-12//99
Brickmason, Blockmason, Stonemason, and Tile and Marble Setter	Maine	S	9.55 MW	9.65 AW	20070 AAW	MEBLS	10//99-12//99
Brickmason, Blockmason, Stonemason, and Tile and Marble Setter	Maryland	S	10.06 MW	10.39 AW	21620 AAW	MDBLS	10//99-12//99

Helper

Occupation/Type/Industry	Location	Per	Low	Mid	High	Source	Date
Brickmason, Blockmason, Stonemason, and Tile and Marble Setter	Massachusetts	S	21.47 MW	19.78 AW	41140 AAW	MABLS	10//99-12//99
Brickmason, Blockmason, Stonemason, and Tile and Marble Setter	Michigan	S	12.37 MW	13.68 AW	28440 AAW	MIBLS	10//99-12//99
Brickmason, Blockmason, Stonemason, and Tile and Marble Setter	Minnesota	S	17.43 MW	17.31 AW	36010 AAW	MNBLS	10//99-12//99
Brickmason, Blockmason, Stonemason, and Tile and Marble Setter	Mississippi	S	8.24 MW	8.39 AW	17440 AAW	MSBLS	10//99-12//99
Brickmason, Blockmason, Stonemason, and Tile and Marble Setter	Missouri	S	16.71 MW	15.85 AW	32970 AAW	MOBLS	10//99-12//99
Brickmason, Blockmason, Stonemason, and Tile and Marble Setter	Montana	S	13.71 MW	12.99 AW	27020 AAW	MTBLS	10//99-12//99
Brickmason, Blockmason, Stonemason, and Tile and Marble Setter	Nebraska	S	10.55 MW	10.47 AW	21780 AAW	NEBLS	10//99-12//99
Brickmason, Blockmason, Stonemason, and Tile and Marble Setter	Nevada	S	12.37 MW	12.88 AW	26790 AAW	NVBLS	10//99-12//99
Brickmason, Blockmason, Stonemason, and Tile and Marble Setter	New Hampshire	S	11.57 MW	11.36 AW	23630 AAW	NHBLS	10//99-12//99
Brickmason, Blockmason, Stonemason, and Tile and Marble Setter	New Jersey	S	17.26 MW	19.03 AW	39580 AAW	NJBLS	10//99-12//99
Brickmason, Blockmason, Stonemason, and Tile and Marble Setter	New Mexico	S	9.5 MW	9.74 AW	20250 AAW	NMBLS	10//99-12//99
Brickmason, Blockmason, Stonemason, and Tile and Marble Setter	New York	S	11.78 MW	14.96 AW	31120 AAW	NYBLS	10//99-12//99
Brickmason, Blockmason, Stonemason, and Tile and Marble Setter	North Carolina	S	9.56 MW	9.51 AW	19780 AAW	NCBLS	10//99-12//99
Brickmason, Blockmason, Stonemason, and Tile and Marble Setter	North Dakota	S	9.8 MW	9.89 AW	20580 AAW	NDBLS	10//99-12//99
Brickmason, Blockmason, Stonemason, and Tile and Marble Setter	Ohio	S	12.29 MW	13.34 AW	27750 AAW	OHBLS	10//99-12//99
Brickmason, Blockmason, Stonemason, and Tile and Marble Setter	Oklahoma	S	10.26 MW	10.09 AW	20990 AAW	OKBLS	10//99-12//99
Brickmason, Blockmason, Stonemason, and Tile and Marble Setter	Oregon	S	15.71 MW	15.45 AW	32130 AAW	ORBLS	10//99-12//99
Brickmason, Blockmason, Stonemason, and Tile and Marble Setter	Pennsylvania	S	11.16 MW	12.16 AW	25300 AAW	PABLS	10//99-12//99
Brickmason, Blockmason, Stonemason, and Tile and Marble Setter	Rhode Island	S	13.9 MW	15.22 AW	31650 AAW	RIBLS	10//99-12//99
Brickmason, Blockmason, Stonemason, and Tile and Marble Setter	South Carolina	S	9.62 MW	9.80 AW	20380 AAW	SCBLS	10//99-12//99
Brickmason, Blockmason, Stonemason, and Tile and Marble Setter	South Dakota	S	10.35 MW	10.42 AW	21670 AAW	SDBLS	10//99-12//99
Brickmason, Blockmason, Stonemason, and Tile and Marble Setter	Tennessee	S	9.66 MW	9.68 AW	20130 AAW	TNBLS	10//99-12//99
Brickmason, Blockmason, Stonemason, and Tile and Marble Setter	Texas	S	9.04 MW	9.22 AW	19180 AAW	TXBLS	10//99-12//99
Brickmason, Blockmason, Stonemason, and Tile and Marble Setter	Vermont	S	10.77 MW	10.43 AW	21700 AAW	VTBLS	10//99-12//99
Brickmason, Blockmason, Stonemason, and Tile and Marble Setter	Virginia	S	9.45 MW	9.63 AW	20030 AAW	VABLS	10//99-12//99
Brickmason, Blockmason, Stonemason, and Tile and Marble Setter	Washington	S	20.94 MW	17.93 AW	37290 AAW	WABLS	10//99-12//99
Brickmason, Blockmason, Stonemason, and Tile and Marble Setter	West Virginia	S	8.09 MW	9.00 AW	18720 AAW	WVBLS	10//99-12//99
Brickmason, Blockmason, Stonemason, and Tile and Marble Setter	Wisconsin	S	12.49 MW	13.68 AW	28440 AAW	WIBLS	10//99-12//99
Brickmason, Blockmason, Stonemason, and Tile and Marble Setter	Puerto Rico	S	6.16 MW	6.24 AW	12990 AAW	PRBLS	10//99-12//99
Brickmason, Blockmason, Stonemason, and Tile and Marble Setter	Guam	S	8.36 MW	8.27 AW	17190 AAW	GUBLS	10//99-12//99
Carpenter	Alabama	S	8.44 MW	8.74 AW	18180 AAW	ALBLS	10//99-12//99
Carpenter	Alaska	S	9.51 MW	14.48 AW	30110 AAW	AKBLS	10//99-12//99
Carpenter	Arizona	S	8.45 MW	8.82 AW	18340 AAW	AZBLS	10//99-12//99
Carpenter	Arkansas	S	8.7 MW	8.89 AW	18490 AAW	ARBLS	10//99-12//99
Carpenter	California	S	10.02 MW	10.71 AW	22280 AAW	CABLS	10//99-12//99
Carpenter	Colorado	S	10.6 MW	10.43 AW	21700 AAW	COBLS	10//99-12//99
Carpenter	Connecticut	S	11.94 MW	12.06 AW	25080 AAW	CTBLS	10//99-12//99
Carpenter	Delaware	S	9.03 MW	9.03 AW	18770 AAW	DEBLS	10//99-12//99
Carpenter	Florida	S	8.88 MW	9.18 AW	19100 AAW	FLBLS	10//99-12//99
Carpenter	Georgia	S	9.91 MW	10.07 AW	20950 AAW	GABLS	10//99-12//99
Carpenter	Hawaii	S	15.66 MW	16.57 AW	34470 AAW	HIBLS	10//99-12//99

AAW	Average annual wage	AOH	Average offered, high	ASH	Average starting, high	H	Hourly		M	Monthly		S	Special: hourly and annual
AE	Average entry wage	AOL	Average offered, low	ASL	Average starting, low	HI	Highest wage paid		MTC	Median total compensation		TQ	Third quartile wage
AEX	Average experienced wage	APH	Average pay, high range	AW	Average wage paid	HR	High end range		MW	Median wage paid		W	Weekly
AO	Average offered	APL	Average pay, low range	FQ	First quartile wage	LR	Low end range		SQ	Second quartile wage		Y	Yearly

Helper

Occupation/Type/Industry	Location	Per	Low	Mid	High	Source	Date
Carpenter	Idaho	S	8.65 MW	9.35 AW	19440 AAW	IDBLS	10//99-12//99
Carpenter	Illinois	S	10.51 MW	12.15 AW	25280 AAW	ILBLS	10//99-12//99
Carpenter	Indiana	S	10.06 MW	10.08 AW	20970 AAW	INBLS	10//99-12//99
Carpenter	Iowa	S	9.12 MW	9.47 AW	19690 AAW	IABLS	10//99-12//99
Carpenter	Kansas	S	9.25 MW	9.22 AW	19180 AAW	KSBLS	10//99-12//99
Carpenter	Kentucky	S	9.59 MW	9.50 AW	19770 AAW	KYBLS	10//99-12//99
Carpenter	Louisiana	S	9.09 MW	9.05 AW	18820 AAW	LABLS	10//99-12//99
Carpenter	Maine	S	8.38 MW	8.60 AW	17890 AAW	MEBLS	10//99-12//99
Carpenter	Maryland	S	9.92 MW	10.13 AW	21080 AAW	MDBLS	10//99-12//99
Carpenter	Massachusetts	S	12.62 MW	13.03 AW	27090 AAW	MABLS	10//99-12//99
Carpenter	Michigan	S	9.66 MW	10.23 AW	21270 AAW	MIBLS	10//99-12//99
Carpenter	Minnesota	S	11.25 MW	12.22 AW	25420 AAW	MNBLS	10//99-12//99
Carpenter	Mississippi	S	7.94 MW	8.19 AW	17030 AAW	MSBLS	10//99-12//99
Carpenter	Missouri	S	11.31 MW	12.81 AW	26640 AAW	MOBLS	10//99-12//99
Carpenter	Montana	S	10.71 MW	10.38 AW	21600 AAW	MTBLS	10//99-12//99
Carpenter	Nebraska	S	9.06 MW	9.40 AW	19540 AAW	NEBLS	10//99-12//99
Carpenter	Nevada	S	10.49 MW	11.30 AW	23500 AAW	NVBLS	10//99-12//99
Carpenter	New Hampshire	S	10.69 MW	10.55 AW	21950 AAW	NHBLS	10//99-12//99
Carpenter	New Jersey	S	12.12 MW	13.51 AW	28100 AAW	NJBLS	10//99-12//99
Carpenter	New Mexico	S	8.73 MW	8.94 AW	18590 AAW	NMBLS	10//99-12//99
Carpenter	New York	S	9.93 MW	10.48 AW	21790 AAW	NYBLS	10//99-12//99
Carpenter	North Carolina	S	9.3 MW	9.36 AW	19460 AAW	NCBLS	10//99-12//99
Carpenter	North Dakota	S	8.98 MW	9.04 AW	18810 AAW	NDBLS	10//99-12//99
Carpenter	Ohio	S	10.82 MW	11.96 AW	24870 AAW	OHBLS	10//99-12//99
Carpenter	Oklahoma	S	8.82 MW	9.08 AW	18880 AAW	OKBLS	10//99-12//99
Carpenter	Oregon	S	8.98 MW	10.11 AW	21030 AAW	ORBLS	10//99-12//99
Carpenter	Pennsylvania	S	10.28 MW	10.78 AW	22430 AAW	PABLS	10//99-12//99
Carpenter	Rhode Island	S	12.47 MW	13.26 AW	27570 AAW	RIBLS	10//99-12//99
Carpenter	South Carolina	S	9.09 MW	9.21 AW	19160 AAW	SCBLS	10//99-12//99
Carpenter	South Dakota	S	8.2 MW	8.30 AW	17270 AAW	SDBLS	10//99-12//99
Carpenter	Tennessee	S	9.43 MW	9.52 AW	19790 AAW	TNBLS	10//99-12//99
Carpenter	Texas	S	9.05 MW	9.07 AW	18870 AAW	TXBLS	10//99-12//99
Carpenter	Utah	S	8.12 MW	8.54 AW	17770 AAW	UTBLS	10//99-12//99
Carpenter	Vermont	S	8.52 MW	8.95 AW	18620 AAW	VTBLS	10//99-12//99
Carpenter	Virginia	S	9.2 MW	9.14 AW	19000 AAW	VABLS	10//99-12//99
Carpenter	Washington	S	9.38 MW	10.60 AW	22050 AAW	WABLS	10//99-12//99
Carpenter	West Virginia	S	7.99 MW	8.76 AW	18220 AAW	WVBLS	10//99-12//99
Carpenter	Wisconsin	S	10.56 MW	11.04 AW	22960 AAW	WIBLS	10//99-12//99
Carpenter	Wyoming	S	9.23 MW	9.63 AW	20040 AAW	WYBLS	10//99-12//99
Carpenter	Puerto Rico	S	6.04 MW	6.10 AW	12680 AAW	PRBLS	10//99-12//99
Carpenter	Virgin Islands	S	9.94 MW	9.90 AW	20590 AAW	VIBLS	10//99-12//99
Electrician	Alabama	S	8.45 MW	8.60 AW	17890 AAW	ALBLS	10//99-12//99
Electrician	Arizona	S	8.19 MW	8.85 AW	18410 AAW	AZBLS	10//99-12//99
Electrician	Arkansas	S	8.25 MW	9.10 AW	18920 AAW	ARBLS	10//99-12//99
Electrician	California	S	10.52 MW	11.59 AW	24110 AAW	CABLS	10//99-12//99
Electrician	Colorado	S	12.16 MW	12.61 AW	26220 AAW	COBLS	10//99-12//99
Electrician	Connecticut	S	12.34 MW	12.51 AW	26020 AAW	CTBLS	10//99-12//99
Electrician	Delaware	S	9.29 MW	9.46 AW	19670 AAW	DEBLS	10//99-12//99
Electrician	District of Columbia	S	14.33 MW	14.39 AW	29930 AAW	DCBLS	10//99-12//99
Electrician	Florida	S	9.15 MW	9.11 AW	18940 AAW	FLBLS	10//99-12//99
Electrician	Georgia	S	9.76 MW	9.90 AW	20590 AAW	GABLS	10//99-12//99
Electrician	Hawaii	S	14.41 MW	13.63 AW	28360 AAW	HIBLS	10//99-12//99
Electrician	Idaho	S	7.79 MW	8.32 AW	17300 AAW	IDBLS	10//99-12//99
Electrician	Illinois	S	12.06 MW	12.31 AW	25610 AAW	ILBLS	10//99-12//99
Electrician	Indiana	S	9.65 MW	10.89 AW	22660 AAW	INBLS	10//99-12//99
Electrician	Iowa	S	10.75 MW	11.29 AW	23490 AAW	IABLS	10//99-12//99
Electrician	Kansas	S	9.27 MW	9.16 AW	19060 AAW	KSBLS	10//99-12//99
Electrician	Kentucky	S	9.19 MW	9.43 AW	19620 AAW	KYBLS	10//99-12//99
Electrician	Louisiana	S	9.65 MW	9.91 AW	20620 AAW	LABLS	10//99-12//99
Electrician	Maine	S	10.88 MW	10.71 AW	22280 AAW	MEBLS	10//99-12//99
Electrician	Maryland	S	10.03 MW	10.37 AW	21580 AAW	MDBLS	10//99-12//99
Electrician	Massachusetts	S	13.38 MW	14.09 AW	29320 AAW	MABLS	10//99-12//99
Electrician	Michigan	S	10.47 MW	10.72 AW	22290 AAW	MIBLS	10//99-12//99
Electrician	Minnesota	S	11.94 MW	12.01 AW	24980 AAW	MNBLS	10//99-12//99
Electrician	Mississippi	S	8.31 MW	8.37 AW	17420 AAW	MSBLS	10//99-12//99
Electrician	Missouri	S	10.41 MW	11.28 AW	23460 AAW	MOBLS	10//99-12//99
Electrician	Nebraska	S	9.62 MW	9.97 AW	20730 AAW	NEBLS	10//99-12//99
Electrician	Nevada	S	10.94 MW	11.35 AW	23620 AAW	NVBLS	10//99-12//99
Electrician	New Hampshire	S	10.97 MW	11.80 AW	24550 AAW	NHBLS	10//99-12//99
Electrician	New Jersey	S	12.39 MW	12.95 AW	26940 AAW	NJBLS	10//99-12//99
Electrician	New Mexico	S	8.2 MW	8.43 AW	17540 AAW	NMBLS	10//99-12//99

AAW	Average annual wage	AOH	Average offered, high	ASH	Average starting, high	H	Hourly	M	Monthly	S	Special: hourly and annual
AE	Average entry wage	AOL	Average offered, low	ASL	Average starting, low	HI	Highest wage paid	MTC	Median total compensation	TQ	Third quartile wage
AEX	Average experienced wage	APH	Average pay, high range	AW	Average wage paid	HR	High end range	MW	Median wage paid	W	Weekly
AO	Average offered	APL	Average pay, low range	FQ	First quartile wage	LR	Low end range	SQ	Second quartile wage	Y	Yearly

Helper

Occupation/Type/Industry	Location	Per	Low	Mid	High	Source	Date
Electrician	New York	S	9.98 MW	11.25 AW	23400 AAW	NYBLS	10//99-12//99
Electrician	North Carolina	S	9.81 MW	9.97 AW	20740 AAW	NCBLS	10//99-12//99
Electrician	North Dakota	S	10.35 MW	10.77 AW	22400 AAW	NDBLS	10//99-12//99
Electrician	Ohio	S	11.05 MW	11.38 AW	23670 AAW	OHBLS	10//99-12//99
Electrician	Oklahoma	S	8.75 MW	9.73 AW	20240 AAW	OKBLS	10//99-12//99
Electrician	Oregon	S	13.93 MW	13.65 AW	28380 AAW	ORBLS	10//99-12//99
Electrician	Pennsylvania	S	9.8 MW	10.28 AW	21390 AAW	PABLS	10//99-12//99
Electrician	Rhode Island	S	9.62 MW	9.72 AW	20220 AAW	RIBLS	10//99-12//99
Electrician	South Carolina	S	9.09 MW	9.51 AW	19790 AAW	SCBLS	10//99-12//99
Electrician	South Dakota	S	7.98 MW	8.44 AW	17560 AAW	SDBLS	10//99-12//99
Electrician	Tennessee	S	10.06 MW	10.59 AW	22020 AAW	TNBLS	10//99-12//99
Electrician	Texas	S	10.24 MW	10.57 AW	21980 AAW	TXBLS	10//99-12//99
Electrician	Utah	S	12.31 MW	11.85 AW	24650 AAW	UTBLS	10//99-12//99
Electrician	Vermont	S	10.21 MW	10.36 AW	21550 AAW	VTBLS	10//99-12//99
Electrician	Virginia	S	9.74 MW	10.41 AW	21660 AAW	VABLS	10//99-12//99
Electrician	Washington	S	12.06 MW	12.72 AW	26460 AAW	WABLS	10//99-12//99
Electrician	Wisconsin	S	11.24 MW	11.43 AW	23780 AAW	WIBLS	10//99-12//99
Electrician	Wyoming	S	9.71 MW	9.87 AW	20540 AAW	WYBLS	10//99-12//99
Electrician	Puerto Rico	S	6.29 MW	6.57 AW	13670 AAW	PRBLS	10//99-12//99
Electrician	Guam	S	9.39 MW	9.18 AW	19100 AAW	GUBLS	10//99-12//99
Extraction Worker	Alabama	S	6.24 MW	6.55 AW	13630 AAW	ALBLS	10//99-12//99
Extraction Worker	Alaska	S	14.85 MW	14.53 AW	30220 AAW	AKBLS	10//99-12//99
Extraction Worker	Arizona	S	9.04 MW	10.00 AW	20790 AAW	AZBLS	10//99-12//99
Extraction Worker	Arkansas	S	9.22 MW	9.08 AW	18880 AAW	ARBLS	10//99-12//99
Extraction Worker	California	S	8.22 MW	9.42 AW	19590 AAW	CABLS	10//99-12//99
Extraction Worker	Connecticut	S	10.93 MW	10.93 AW	22730 AAW	CTBLS	10//99-12//99
Extraction Worker	Florida	S	7.97 MW	8.22 AW	17110 AAW	FLBLS	10//99-12//99
Extraction Worker	Georgia	S	12.05 MW	12.50 AW	25990 AAW	GABLS	10//99-12//99
Extraction Worker	Idaho	S	9.6 MW	9.53 AW	19820 AAW	IDBLS	10//99-12//99
Extraction Worker	Illinois	S	9.78 MW	10.68 AW	22210 AAW	ILBLS	10//99-12//99
Extraction Worker	Indiana	S	11.71 MW	12.18 AW	25330 AAW	INBLS	10//99-12//99
Extraction Worker	Kansas	S	9.42 MW	9.67 AW	20110 AAW	KSBLS	10//99-12//99
Extraction Worker	Kentucky	S	11.81 MW	11.75 AW	24430 AAW	KYBLS	10//99-12//99
Extraction Worker	Louisiana	S	7.68 MW	7.68 AW	15980 AAW	LABLS	10//99-12//99
Extraction Worker	Maine	S	7.93 MW	8.04 AW	16720 AAW	MEBLS	10//99-12//99
Extraction Worker	Maryland	S	10.72 MW	10.23 AW	21290 AAW	MDBLS	10//99-12//99
Extraction Worker	Massachusetts	S	16.84 MW	16.11 AW	33510 AAW	MABLS	10//99-12//99
Extraction Worker	Michigan	S	11.84 MW	11.81 AW	24570 AAW	MIBLS	10//99-12//99
Extraction Worker	Minnesota	S	9.19 MW	8.74 AW	18180 AAW	MNBLS	10//99-12//99
Extraction Worker	Mississippi	S	8.79 MW	8.28 AW	17210 AAW	MSBLS	10//99-12//99
Extraction Worker	Montana	S	10.41 MW	10.53 AW	21900 AAW	MTBLS	10//99-12//99
Extraction Worker	Nevada	S	10.92 MW	10.87 AW	22600 AAW	NVBLS	10//99-12//99
Extraction Worker	New Hampshire	S	10.44 MW	10.79 AW	22450 AAW	NHBLS	10//99-12//99
Extraction Worker	New Jersey	S	13.17 MW	13.35 AW	27760 AAW	NJBLS	10//99-12//99
Extraction Worker	New Mexico	S	9.44 MW	9.57 AW	19900 AAW	NMBLS	10//99-12//99
Extraction Worker	New York	S	10.04 MW	11.22 AW	23340 AAW	NYBLS	10//99-12//99
Extraction Worker	North Carolina	S	7.39 MW	8.32 AW	17310 AAW	NCBLS	10//99-12//99
Extraction Worker	North Dakota	S	8.25 MW	8.94 AW	18600 AAW	NDBLS	10//99-12//99
Extraction Worker	Oklahoma	S	9.59 MW	9.46 AW	19680 AAW	OKBLS	10//99-12//99
Extraction Worker	Oregon	S	10.44 MW	10.75 AW	22360 AAW	ORBLS	10//99-12//99
Extraction Worker	Pennsylvania	S	12.16 MW	12.89 AW	26810 AAW	PABLS	10//99-12//99
Extraction Worker	South Carolina	S	8.02 MW	8.15 AW	16960 AAW	SCBLS	10//99-12//99
Extraction Worker	South Dakota	S	6.51 MW	7.00 AW	14570 AAW	SDBLS	10//99-12//99
Extraction Worker	Tennessee	S	9.76 MW	9.77 AW	20330 AAW	TNBLS	10//99-12//99
Extraction Worker	Texas	S	9.65 MW	9.70 AW	20170 AAW	TXBLS	10//99-12//99
Extraction Worker	Utah	S	11.41 MW	11.90 AW	24760 AAW	UTBLS	10//99-12//99
Extraction Worker	Virginia	S	15.1 MW	14.72 AW	30610 AAW	VABLS	10//99-12//99
Extraction Worker	Washington	S	13.08 MW	14.75 AW	30680 AAW	WABLS	10//99-12//99
Extraction Worker	West Virginia	S	12.13 MW	11.88 AW	24700 AAW	WVBLS	10//99-12//99
Extraction Worker	Wisconsin	S	11.84 MW	11.77 AW	24480 AAW	WIBLS	10//99-12//99
Extraction Worker	Wyoming	S	12.19 MW	12.13 AW	25220 AAW	WYBLS	10//99-12//99
Extraction Worker	Puerto Rico	S	6.73 MW	7.30 AW	15180 AAW	PRBLS	10//99-12//99
Installation, Maintenance, and Repair Worker	Alabama	S	8.96 MW	9.33 AW	19400 AAW	ALBLS	10//99-12//99
Installation, Maintenance, and Repair Worker	Auburn-Opelika MSA, AL	S	10.75 MW	10.76 AW	22360 AAW	ALBLS	10//99-12//99
Installation, Maintenance, and Repair Worker	Birmingham MSA, AL	S	8.99 MW	8.55 AW	18700 AAW	ALBLS	10//99-12//99
Installation, Maintenance, and Repair Worker	Decatur MSA, AL	S	9.52 MW	8.96 AW	19790 AAW	ALBLS	10//99-12//99

AAW	Average annual wage	AOH	Average offered, high	ASH	Average starting, high	H	Hourly	M	Monthly	S	Special: hourly and annual
AE	Average entry wage	AOL	Average offered, low	ASL	Average starting, low	HI	Highest wage paid	MTC	Median total compensation	TQ	Third quartile wage
AEX	Average experienced wage	APH	Average pay, high range	AW	Average wage paid	HR	High end range	MW	Median wage paid	W	Weekly
AO	Average offered	APL	Average pay, low range	FQ	First quartile wage	LR	Low end range	SQ	Second quartile wage	Y	Yearly

723

Helper

Occupation/Type/Industry	Location	Per	Low	Mid	High	Source	Date
Installation, Maintenance, and Repair Worker	Dothan MSA, AL	S	9.03 MW	8.54 AW	18770 AAW	ALBLS	10//99-12//99
Installation, Maintenance, and Repair Worker	Florence MSA, AL	S	9.43 MW	9.37 AW	19620 AAW	ALBLS	10//99-12//99
Installation, Maintenance, and Repair Worker	Huntsville MSA, AL	S	9.07 MW	9.15 AW	18870 AAW	ALBLS	10//99-12//99
Installation, Maintenance, and Repair Worker	Mobile MSA, AL	S	8.52 MW	7.82 AW	17730 AAW	ALBLS	10//99-12//99
Installation, Maintenance, and Repair Worker	Montgomery MSA, AL	S	8.89 MW	9.25 AW	18490 AAW	ALBLS	10//99-12//99
Installation, Maintenance, and Repair Worker	Tuscaloosa MSA, AL	S	10.26 MW	10.28 AW	21340 AAW	ALBLS	10//99-12//99
Installation, Maintenance, and Repair Worker	Alaska	S	12.06 MW	12.97 AW	26970 AAW	AKBLS	10//99-12//99
Installation, Maintenance, and Repair Worker	Anchorage MSA, AK	S	11.92 MW	10.58 AW	24800 AAW	AKBLS	10//99-12//99
Installation, Maintenance, and Repair Worker	Arizona	S	8.75 MW	9.74 AW	20250 AAW	AZBLS	10//99-12//99
Installation, Maintenance, and Repair Worker	Flagstaff MSA, AZ-UT	S	8.24 MW	7.52 AW	17130 AAW	AZBLS	10//99-12//99
Installation, Maintenance, and Repair Worker	Phoenix-Mesa MSA, AZ	S	9.93 MW	8.98 AW	20650 AAW	AZBLS	10//99-12//99
Installation, Maintenance, and Repair Worker	Tucson MSA, AZ	S	8.87 MW	8.18 AW	18450 AAW	AZBLS	10//99-12//99
Installation, Maintenance, and Repair Worker	Arkansas	S	8.47 MW	9.33 AW	19400 AAW	ARBLS	10//99-12//99
Installation, Maintenance, and Repair Worker	Fayetteville-Springdale-Rogers MSA, AR	S	10.16 MW	9.38 AW	21120 AAW	ARBLS	10//99-12//99
Installation, Maintenance, and Repair Worker	Fort Smith MSA, AR-OK	S	9.31 MW	8.81 AW	19360 AAW	ARBLS	10//99-12//99
Installation, Maintenance, and Repair Worker	Jonesboro MSA, AR	S	7.85 MW	7.69 AW	16330 AAW	ARBLS	10//99-12//99
Installation, Maintenance, and Repair Worker	Little Rock-North Little Rock MSA, AR	S	9.35 MW	8.37 AW	19450 AAW	ARBLS	10//99-12//99
Installation, Maintenance, and Repair Worker	California	S	9.2 MW	10.30 AW	21430 AAW	CABLS	10//99-12//99
Installation, Maintenance, and Repair Worker	Bakersfield MSA, CA	S	9.42 MW	8.13 AW	19590 AAW	CABLS	10//99-12//99
Installation, Maintenance, and Repair Worker	Chico-Paradise MSA, CA	S	10.10 MW	9.03 AW	21000 AAW	CABLS	10//99-12//99
Installation, Maintenance, and Repair Worker	Fresno MSA, CA	S	10.43 MW	9.05 AW	21700 AAW	CABLS	10//99-12//99
Installation, Maintenance, and Repair Worker	Los Angeles-Long Beach PMSA, CA	S	10.12 MW	9.23 AW	21040 AAW	CABLS	10//99-12//99
Installation, Maintenance, and Repair Worker	Merced MSA, CA	S	10.17 MW	9.38 AW	21160 AAW	CABLS	10//99-12//99
Installation, Maintenance, and Repair Worker	Modesto MSA, CA	S	10.63 MW	10.94 AW	22110 AAW	CABLS	10//99-12//99
Installation, Maintenance, and Repair Worker	Oakland PMSA, CA	S	10.69 MW	9.68 AW	22240 AAW	CABLS	10//99-12//99
Installation, Maintenance, and Repair Worker	Orange County PMSA, CA	S	10.23 MW	9.30 AW	21280 AAW	CABLS	10//99-12//99
Installation, Maintenance, and Repair Worker	Redding MSA, CA	S	10.64 MW	10.11 AW	22130 AAW	CABLS	10//99-12//99
Installation, Maintenance, and Repair Worker	Riverside-San Bernardino PMSA, CA	S	9.56 MW	9.13 AW	19880 AAW	CABLS	10//99-12//99
Installation, Maintenance, and Repair Worker	Sacramento PMSA, CA	S	10.64 MW	10.12 AW	22130 AAW	CABLS	10//99-12//99
Installation, Maintenance, and Repair Worker	Salinas MSA, CA	S	12.92 MW	12.96 AW	26870 AAW	CABLS	10//99-12//99
Installation, Maintenance, and Repair Worker	San Diego MSA, CA	S	9.42 MW	7.68 AW	19590 AAW	CABLS	10//99-12//99
Installation, Maintenance, and Repair Worker	San Francisco PMSA, CA	S	14.04 MW	12.24 AW	29190 AAW	CABLS	10//99-12//99
Installation, Maintenance, and Repair Worker	San Jose PMSA, CA	S	9.76 MW	8.51 AW	20290 AAW	CABLS	10//99-12//99

AAW	Average annual wage	AOH	Average offered, high	ASH	Average starting, high	H	Hourly	M	Monthly	S	Special: hourly and annual
AE	Average entry wage	AOL	Average offered, low	ASL	Average starting, low	HI	Highest wage paid	MTC	Median total compensation	TQ	Third quartile wage
AEX	Average experienced wage	APH	Average pay, high range	AW	Average wage paid	HR	High end range	MW	Median wage paid	W	Weekly
AO	Average offered	APL	Average pay, low range	FQ	First quartile wage	LR	Low end range	SQ	Second quartile wage	Y	Yearly

Helper

Occupation/Type/Industry	Location	Per	Low	Mid	High	Source	Date
Installation, Maintenance, and Repair Worker	San Luis Obispo-Atascadero-Paso Robles MSA, CA	S	8.96 MW	7.63 AW	18630 AAW	CABLS	10//99-12//99
Installation, Maintenance, and Repair Worker	Santa Barbara-Santa Maria-Lompoc MSA, CA	S	9.24 MW	7.98 AW	19210 AAW	CABLS	10//99-12//99
Installation, Maintenance, and Repair Worker	Santa Rosa PMSA, CA	S	9.74 MW	9.47 AW	20250 AAW	CABLS	10//99-12//99
Installation, Maintenance, and Repair Worker	Stockton-Lodi MSA, CA	S	10.99 MW	9.94 AW	22850 AAW	CABLS	10//99-12//99
Installation, Maintenance, and Repair Worker	Vallejo-Fairfield-Napa PMSA, CA	S	10.79 MW	9.81 AW	22440 AAW	CABLS	10//99-12//99
Installation, Maintenance, and Repair Worker	Ventura PMSA, CA	S	10.59 MW	10.26 AW	22020 AAW	CABLS	10//99-12//99
Installation, Maintenance, and Repair Worker	Visalia-Tulare-Porterville MSA, CA	S	9.20 MW	8.46 AW	19140 AAW	CABLS	10//99-12//99
Installation, Maintenance, and Repair Worker	Yolo PMSA, CA	S	7.90 MW	6.10 AW	16430 AAW	CABLS	10//99-12//99
Installation, Maintenance, and Repair Worker	Colorado	S	9.49 MW	10.12 AW	21050 AAW	COBLS	10//99-12//99
Installation, Maintenance, and Repair Worker	Boulder-Longmont PMSA, CO	S	9.41 MW	8.81 AW	19580 AAW	COBLS	10//99-12//99
Installation, Maintenance, and Repair Worker	Colorado Springs MSA, CO	S	9.38 MW	9.01 AW	19510 AAW	COBLS	10//99-12//99
Installation, Maintenance, and Repair Worker	Denver PMSA, CO	S	10.44 MW	9.89 AW	21720 AAW	COBLS	10//99-12//99
Installation, Maintenance, and Repair Worker	Fort Collins-Loveland MSA, CO	S	10.95 MW	10.48 AW	22780 AAW	COBLS	10//99-12//99
Installation, Maintenance, and Repair Worker	Grand Junction MSA, CO	S	8.93 MW	7.78 AW	18570 AAW	COBLS	10//99-12//99
Installation, Maintenance, and Repair Worker	Greeley PMSA, CO	S	9.59 MW	8.18 AW	19940 AAW	COBLS	10//99-12//99
Installation, Maintenance, and Repair Worker	Connecticut	S	10.26 MW	10.91 AW	22680 AAW	CTBLS	10//99-12//99
Installation, Maintenance, and Repair Worker	Bridgeport PMSA, CT	S	12.43 MW	10.98 AW	25850 AAW	CTBLS	10//99-12//99
Installation, Maintenance, and Repair Worker	Hartford MSA, CT	S	10.20 MW	10.01 AW	21210 AAW	CTBLS	10//99-12//99
Installation, Maintenance, and Repair Worker	New Haven-Meriden PMSA, CT	S	11.30 MW	9.88 AW	23510 AAW	CTBLS	10//99-12//99
Installation, Maintenance, and Repair Worker	New London-Norwich MSA, CT-RI	S	11.26 MW	11.06 AW	23410 AAW	CTBLS	10//99-12//99
Installation, Maintenance, and Repair Worker	Stamford-Norwalk PMSA, CT	S	10.34 MW	9.95 AW	21500 AAW	CTBLS	10//99-12//99
Installation, Maintenance, and Repair Worker	Waterbury PMSA, CT	S	10.44 MW	9.89 AW	21710 AAW	CTBLS	10//99-12//99
Installation, Maintenance, and Repair Worker	Delaware	S	9.88 MW	11.54 AW	24000 AAW	DEBLS	10//99-12//99
Installation, Maintenance, and Repair Worker	Dover MSA, DE	S	10.35 MW	9.26 AW	21540 AAW	DEBLS	10//99-12//99
Installation, Maintenance, and Repair Worker	Wilmington-Newark PMSA, DE-MD	S	12.02 MW	10.21 AW	25010 AAW	DEBLS	10//99-12//99
Installation, Maintenance, and Repair Worker	District of Columbia	S	14.62 MW	13.80 AW	28700 AAW	DCBLS	10//99-12//99
Installation, Maintenance, and Repair Worker	Washington PMSA, DC-MD-VA-WV	S	9.52 MW	8.62 AW	19800 AAW	DCBLS	10//99-12//99
Installation, Maintenance, and Repair Worker	Florida	S	8.54 MW	9.29 AW	19320 AAW	FLBLS	10//99-12//99
Installation, Maintenance, and Repair Worker	Daytona Beach MSA, FL	S	8.23 MW	7.95 AW	17120 AAW	FLBLS	10//99-12//99
Installation, Maintenance, and Repair Worker	Fort Lauderdale PMSA, FL	S	10.25 MW	9.65 AW	21310 AAW	FLBLS	10//99-12//99

AAW	Average annual wage	AOH	Average offered, high	ASH	Average starting, high	H	Hourly	M	Monthly	S	Special: hourly and annual
AE	Average entry wage	AOL	Average offered, low	ASL	Average starting, low	HI	Highest wage paid	MTC	Median total compensation	TQ	Third quartile wage
AEX	Average experienced wage	APH	Average pay, high range	AW	Average wage paid	HR	High end range	MW	Median wage paid	W	Weekly
AO	Average offered	APL	Average pay, low range	FQ	First quartile wage	LR	Low end range	SQ	Second quartile wage	Y	Yearly

Occupation/Type/Industry	Location	Per	Low	Mid	High	Source	Date
Helper							
Installation, Maintenance, and Repair Worker	Fort Myers-Cape Coral MSA, FL	S	10.66 MW	9.45 AW	22160 AAW	FLBLS	10//99-12//99
Installation, Maintenance, and Repair Worker	Fort Pierce-Port St. Lucie MSA, FL	S	9.38 MW	8.71 AW	19500 AAW	FLBLS	10//99-12//99
Installation, Maintenance, and Repair Worker	Gainesville MSA, FL	S	9.41 MW	9.17 AW	19560 AAW	FLBLS	10//99-12//99
Installation, Maintenance, and Repair Worker	Jacksonville MSA, FL	S	9.50 MW	8.52 AW	19770 AAW	FLBLS	10//99-12//99
Installation, Maintenance, and Repair Worker	Lakeland-Winter Haven MSA, FL	S	9.86 MW	9.57 AW	20510 AAW	FLBLS	10//99-12//99
Installation, Maintenance, and Repair Worker	Melbourne-Titusville-Palm Bay MSA, FL	S	9.55 MW	8.75 AW	19870 AAW	FLBLS	10//99-12//99
Installation, Maintenance, and Repair Worker	Miami PMSA, FL	S	9.18 MW	8.35 AW	19080 AAW	FLBLS	10//99-12//99
Installation, Maintenance, and Repair Worker	Naples MSA, FL	S	11.06 MW	10.03 AW	23010 AAW	FLBLS	10//99-12//99
Installation, Maintenance, and Repair Worker	Ocala MSA, FL	S	8.86 MW	9.07 AW	18440 AAW	FLBLS	10//99-12//99
Installation, Maintenance, and Repair Worker	Orlando MSA, FL	S	10.55 MW	9.61 AW	21940 AAW	FLBLS	10//99-12//99
Installation, Maintenance, and Repair Worker	Panama City MSA, FL	S	8.70 MW	8.31 AW	18090 AAW	FLBLS	10//99-12//99
Installation, Maintenance, and Repair Worker	Pensacola MSA, FL	S	7.48 MW	6.83 AW	15560 AAW	FLBLS	10//99-12//99
Installation, Maintenance, and Repair Worker	Punta Gorda MSA, FL	S	8.00 MW	8.02 AW	16630 AAW	FLBLS	10//99-12//99
Installation, Maintenance, and Repair Worker	Sarasota-Bradenton MSA, FL	S	8.78 MW	8.15 AW	18260 AAW	FLBLS	10//99-12//99
Installation, Maintenance, and Repair Worker	Tallahassee MSA, FL	S	9.66 MW	9.53 AW	20090 AAW	FLBLS	10//99-12//99
Installation, Maintenance, and Repair Worker	Tampa-St. Petersburg-Clearwater MSA, FL	S	8.17 MW	7.75 AW	17000 AAW	FLBLS	10//99-12//99
Installation, Maintenance, and Repair Worker	West Palm Beach-Boca Raton MSA, FL	S	10.20 MW	9.27 AW	21220 AAW	FLBLS	10//99-12//99
Installation, Maintenance, and Repair Worker	Georgia	S	9.18 MW	9.84 AW	20470 AAW	GABLS	10//99-12//99
Installation, Maintenance, and Repair Worker	Albany MSA, GA	S	8.16 MW	8.16 AW	16980 AAW	GABLS	10//99-12//99
Installation, Maintenance, and Repair Worker	Athens MSA, GA	S	8.33 MW	7.55 AW	17330 AAW	GABLS	10//99-12//99
Installation, Maintenance, and Repair Worker	Atlanta MSA, GA	S	10.62 MW	9.86 AW	22090 AAW	GABLS	10//99-12//99
Installation, Maintenance, and Repair Worker	Augusta-Aiken MSA, GA-SC	S	9.36 MW	7.96 AW	19470 AAW	GABLS	10//99-12//99
Installation, Maintenance, and Repair Worker	Columbus MSA, GA-AL	S	10.57 MW	10.10 AW	21980 AAW	GABLS	10//99-12//99
Installation, Maintenance, and Repair Worker	Macon MSA, GA	S	9.61 MW	8.53 AW	19980 AAW	GABLS	10//99-12//99
Installation, Maintenance, and Repair Worker	Savannah MSA, GA	S	8.96 MW	8.44 AW	18640 AAW	GABLS	10//99-12//99
Installation, Maintenance, and Repair Worker	Hawaii	S	10.11 MW	10.83 AW	22520 AAW	HIBLS	10//99-12//99
Installation, Maintenance, and Repair Worker	Honolulu MSA, HI	S	10.82 MW	9.11 AW	22490 AAW	HIBLS	10//99-12//99
Installation, Maintenance, and Repair Worker	Idaho	S	9.23 MW	10.38 AW	21590 AAW	IDBLS	10//99-12//99
Installation, Maintenance, and Repair Worker	Boise City MSA, ID	S	12.13 MW	10.42 AW	25220 AAW	IDBLS	10//99-12//99
Installation, Maintenance, and Repair Worker	Illinois	S	9.85 MW	10.57 AW	21990 AAW	ILBLS	10//99-12//99
Installation, Maintenance, and Repair Worker	Bloomington-Normal MSA, IL	S	8.66 MW	8.20 AW	18010 AAW	ILBLS	10//99-12//99
Installation, Maintenance, and Repair Worker	Champaign-Urbana MSA, IL	S	11.04 MW	10.15 AW	22960 AAW	ILBLS	10//99-12//99

Helper

Occupation/Type/Industry	Location	Per	Low	Mid	High	Source	Date
Installation, Maintenance, and Repair Worker	Chicago PMSA, IL	S	11.08 MW	10.23 AW	23040 AAW	ILBLS	10//99-12//99
Installation, Maintenance, and Repair Worker	Kankakee PMSA, IL	S	9.25 MW	8.31 AW	19240 AAW	ILBLS	10//99-12//99
Installation, Maintenance, and Repair Worker	Peoria-Pekin MSA, IL	S	10.43 MW	9.63 AW	21700 AAW	ILBLS	10//99-12//99
Installation, Maintenance, and Repair Worker	Rockford MSA, IL	S	11.12 MW	10.56 AW	23130 AAW	ILBLS	10//99-12//99
Installation, Maintenance, and Repair Worker	Springfield MSA, IL	S	11.73 MW	9.84 AW	24400 AAW	ILBLS	10//99-12//99
Installation, Maintenance, and Repair Worker	Indiana	S	10.02 MW	10.45 AW	21730 AAW	INBLS	10//99-12//99
Installation, Maintenance, and Repair Worker	Elkhart-Goshen MSA, IN	S	10.29 MW	10.38 AW	21400 AAW	INBLS	10//99-12//99
Installation, Maintenance, and Repair Worker	Evansville-Henderson MSA, IN-KY	S	11.37 MW	10.58 AW	23650 AAW	INBLS	10//99-12//99
Installation, Maintenance, and Repair Worker	Fort Wayne MSA, IN	S	9.66 MW	9.69 AW	20100 AAW	INBLS	10//99-12//99
Installation, Maintenance, and Repair Worker	Gary PMSA, IN	S	11.18 MW	9.63 AW	23250 AAW	INBLS	10//99-12//99
Installation, Maintenance, and Repair Worker	Indianapolis MSA, IN	S	10.34 MW	10.19 AW	21510 AAW	INBLS	10//99-12//99
Installation, Maintenance, and Repair Worker	Kokomo MSA, IN	S	10.86 MW	9.46 AW	22590 AAW	INBLS	10//99-12//99
Installation, Maintenance, and Repair Worker	Lafayette MSA, IN	S	11.22 MW	11.31 AW	23340 AAW	INBLS	10//99-12//99
Installation, Maintenance, and Repair Worker	Muncie MSA, IN	S	9.21 MW	8.56 AW	19160 AAW	INBLS	10//99-12//99
Installation, Maintenance, and Repair Worker	South Bend MSA, IN	S	11.34 MW	10.29 AW	23580 AAW	INBLS	10//99-12//99
Installation, Maintenance, and Repair Worker	Terre Haute MSA, IN	S	9.12 MW	7.94 AW	18980 AAW	INBLS	10//99-12//99
Installation, Maintenance, and Repair Worker	Iowa	S	8.09 MW	8.86 AW	18430 AAW	IABLS	10//99-12//99
Installation, Maintenance, and Repair Worker	Cedar Rapids MSA, IA	S	9.10 MW	7.87 AW	18920 AAW	IABLS	10//99-12//99
Installation, Maintenance, and Repair Worker	Davenport-Moline-Rock Island MSA, IA-IL	S	10.97 MW	10.46 AW	22820 AAW	IABLS	10//99-12//99
Installation, Maintenance, and Repair Worker	Des Moines MSA, IA	S	10.86 MW	10.14 AW	22600 AAW	IABLS	10//99-12//99
Installation, Maintenance, and Repair Worker	Kansas	S	8.1 MW	8.86 AW	18430 AAW	KSBLS	10//99-12//99
Installation, Maintenance, and Repair Worker	Topeka MSA, KS	S	7.99 MW	7.71 AW	16620 AAW	KSBLS	10//99-12//99
Installation, Maintenance, and Repair Worker	Wichita MSA, KS	S	9.32 MW	8.71 AW	19390 AAW	KSBLS	10//99-12//99
Installation, Maintenance, and Repair Worker	Kentucky	S	8.69 MW	9.72 AW	20220 AAW	KYBLS	10//99-12//99
Installation, Maintenance, and Repair Worker	Lexington MSA, KY	S	10.56 MW	9.42 AW	21960 AAW	KYBLS	10//99-12//99
Installation, Maintenance, and Repair Worker	Louisville MSA, KY-IN	S	10.27 MW	9.67 AW	21350 AAW	KYBLS	10//99-12//99
Installation, Maintenance, and Repair Worker	Louisiana	S	8.6 MW	9.25 AW	19240 AAW	LABLS	10//99-12//99
Installation, Maintenance, and Repair Worker	Alexandria MSA, LA	S	9.60 MW	7.94 AW	19980 AAW	LABLS	10//99-12//99
Installation, Maintenance, and Repair Worker	Baton Rouge MSA, LA	S	8.93 MW	8.41 AW	18580 AAW	LABLS	10//99-12//99
Installation, Maintenance, and Repair Worker	Houma MSA, LA	S	8.55 MW	8.15 AW	17780 AAW	LABLS	10//99-12//99
Installation, Maintenance, and Repair Worker	Lafayette MSA, LA	S	9.24 MW	8.71 AW	19220 AAW	LABLS	10//99-12//99
Installation, Maintenance, and Repair Worker	Lake Charles MSA, LA	S	9.55 MW	9.79 AW	19870 AAW	LABLS	10//99-12//99
Installation, Maintenance, and Repair Worker	Monroe MSA, LA	S	8.88 MW	7.86 AW	18460 AAW	LABLS	10//99-12//99
Installation, Maintenance, and Repair Worker	New Orleans MSA, LA	S	10.20 MW	9.22 AW	21210 AAW	LABLS	10//99-12//99

AAW	Average annual wage	AOH	Average offered, high	ASH	Average starting, high	H	Hourly	M	Monthly	S	Special: hourly and annual
AE	Average entry wage	AOL	Average offered, low	ASL	Average starting, low	HI	Highest wage paid	MTC	Median total compensation	TQ	Third quartile wage
AEX	Average experienced wage	APH	Average pay, high range	AW	Average wage paid	HR	High end range	MW	Median wage paid	W	Weekly
AO	Average offered	APL	Average pay, low range	FQ	First quartile wage	LR	Low end range	SQ	Second quartile wage	Y	Yearly

Occupation/Type/Industry	Location	Per	Low	Mid	High	Source	Date
Helper							
Installation, Maintenance, and Repair Worker	Shreveport-Bossier City MSA, LA	S	8.77 MW	8.28 AW	18240 AAW	LABLS	10//99-12//99
Installation, Maintenance, and Repair Worker	Maine	S	9.18 MW	9.35 AW	19450 AAW	MEBLS	10//99-12//99
Installation, Maintenance, and Repair Worker	Portland MSA, ME	S	10.45 MW	9.66 AW	21730 AAW	MEBLS	10//99-12//99
Installation, Maintenance, and Repair Worker	Maryland	S	8.36 MW	9.33 AW	19410 AAW	MDBLS	10//99-12//99
Installation, Maintenance, and Repair Worker	Baltimore PMSA, MD	S	9.20 MW	8.27 AW	19130 AAW	MDBLS	10//99-12//99
Installation, Maintenance, and Repair Worker	Cumberland MSA, MD-WV	S	7.40 MW	6.87 AW	15400 AAW	MDBLS	10//99-12//99
Installation, Maintenance, and Repair Worker	Massachusetts	S	9.62 MW	10.77 AW	22400 AAW	MABLS	10//99-12//99
Installation, Maintenance, and Repair Worker	Barnstable-Yarmouth MSA, MA	S	10.75 MW	10.10 AW	22360 AAW	MABLS	10//99-12//99
Installation, Maintenance, and Repair Worker	Boston PMSA, MA-NH	S	10.80 MW	9.29 AW	22470 AAW	MABLS	10//99-12//99
Installation, Maintenance, and Repair Worker	Brockton PMSA, MA	S	10.63 MW	10.89 AW	22120 AAW	MABLS	10//99-12//99
Installation, Maintenance, and Repair Worker	Lawrence PMSA, MA-NH	S	10.53 MW	9.86 AW	21890 AAW	MABLS	10//99-12//99
Installation, Maintenance, and Repair Worker	Lowell PMSA, MA-NH	S	11.93 MW	10.47 AW	24800 AAW	MABLS	10//99-12//99
Installation, Maintenance, and Repair Worker	New Bedford PMSA, MA	S	10.91 MW	9.82 AW	22690 AAW	MABLS	10//99-12//99
Installation, Maintenance, and Repair Worker	Springfield MSA, MA	S	10.51 MW	9.13 AW	21870 AAW	MABLS	10//99-12//99
Installation, Maintenance, and Repair Worker	Worcester PMSA, MA-CT	S	11.17 MW	10.12 AW	23240 AAW	MABLS	10//99-12//99
Installation, Maintenance, and Repair Worker	Michigan	S	10.38 MW	11.00 AW	22880 AAW	MIBLS	10//99-12//99
Installation, Maintenance, and Repair Worker	Ann Arbor PMSA, MI	S	12.03 MW	11.47 AW	25030 AAW	MIBLS	10//99-12//99
Installation, Maintenance, and Repair Worker	Benton Harbor MSA, MI	S	9.75 MW	9.53 AW	20280 AAW	MIBLS	10//99-12//99
Installation, Maintenance, and Repair Worker	Detroit PMSA, MI	S	11.69 MW	11.14 AW	24310 AAW	MIBLS	10//99-12//99
Installation, Maintenance, and Repair Worker	Flint PMSA, MI	S	9.95 MW	8.63 AW	20700 AAW	MIBLS	10//99-12//99
Installation, Maintenance, and Repair Worker	Grand Rapids-Muskegon-Holland MSA, MI	S	10.72 MW	9.94 AW	22290 AAW	MIBLS	10//99-12//99
Installation, Maintenance, and Repair Worker	Jackson MSA, MI	S	12.09 MW	10.89 AW	25150 AAW	MIBLS	10//99-12//99
Installation, Maintenance, and Repair Worker	Kalamazoo-Battle Creek MSA, MI	S	12.12 MW	11.16 AW	25200 AAW	MIBLS	10//99-12//99
Installation, Maintenance, and Repair Worker	Lansing-East Lansing MSA, MI	S	14.13 MW	11.77 AW	29380 AAW	MIBLS	10//99-12//99
Installation, Maintenance, and Repair Worker	Saginaw-Bay City-Midland MSA, MI	S	11.30 MW	11.64 AW	23510 AAW	MIBLS	10//99-12//99
Installation, Maintenance, and Repair Worker	Minnesota	S	9.42 MW	10.65 AW	22140 AAW	MNBLS	10//99-12//99
Installation, Maintenance, and Repair Worker	Duluth-Superior MSA, MN-WI	S	11.15 MW	11.56 AW	23180 AAW	MNBLS	10//99-12//99
Installation, Maintenance, and Repair Worker	Minneapolis-St. Paul MSA, MN-WI	S	10.84 MW	9.49 AW	22550 AAW	MNBLS	10//99-12//99
Installation, Maintenance, and Repair Worker	Rochester MSA, MN	S	9.31 MW	8.52 AW	19350 AAW	MNBLS	10//99-12//99
Installation, Maintenance, and Repair Worker	St. Cloud MSA, MN	S	8.69 MW	8.45 AW	18080 AAW	MNBLS	10//99-12//99
Installation, Maintenance, and Repair Worker	Mississippi	S	8.19 MW	8.78 AW	18270 AAW	MSBLS	10//99-12//99

Helper

Occupation/Type/Industry	Location	Per	Low	Mid	High	Source	Date
Installation, Maintenance, and Repair Worker	Biloxi-Gulfport-Pascagoula MSA, MS	S	10.40 MW	9.31 AW	21620 AAW	MSBLS	10//99-12//99
Installation, Maintenance, and Repair Worker	Hattiesburg MSA, MS	S	8.24 MW	7.59 AW	17130 AAW	MSBLS	10//99-12//99
Installation, Maintenance, and Repair Worker	Jackson MSA, MS	S	8.43 MW	8.11 AW	17540 AAW	MSBLS	10//99-12//99
Installation, Maintenance, and Repair Worker	Missouri	S	8.74 MW	9.87 AW	20540 AAW	MOBLS	10//99-12//99
Installation, Maintenance, and Repair Worker	Joplin MSA, MO	S	11.47 MW	13.86 AW	23870 AAW	MOBLS	10//99-12//99
Installation, Maintenance, and Repair Worker	Kansas City MSA, MO-KS	S	11.04 MW	10.46 AW	22950 AAW	MOBLS	10//99-12//99
Installation, Maintenance, and Repair Worker	St. Louis MSA, MO-IL	S	10.31 MW	9.78 AW	21450 AAW	MOBLS	10//99-12//99
Installation, Maintenance, and Repair Worker	Springfield MSA, MO	S	8.61 MW	8.39 AW	17900 AAW	MOBLS	10//99-12//99
Installation, Maintenance, and Repair Worker	Montana	S	8.15 MW	9.22 AW	19180 AAW	MTBLS	10//99-12//99
Installation, Maintenance, and Repair Worker	Billings MSA, MT	S	8.62 MW	8.51 AW	17940 AAW	MTBLS	10//99-12//99
Installation, Maintenance, and Repair Worker	Missoula MSA, MT	S	10.93 MW	8.68 AW	22730 AAW	MTBLS	10//99-12//99
Installation, Maintenance, and Repair Worker	Nebraska	S	9.12 MW	10.13 AW	21080 AAW	NEBLS	10//99-12//99
Installation, Maintenance, and Repair Worker	Lincoln MSA, NE	S	9.56 MW	8.61 AW	19890 AAW	NEBLS	10//99-12//99
Installation, Maintenance, and Repair Worker	Omaha MSA, NE-IA	S	11.00 MW	10.12 AW	22890 AAW	NEBLS	10//99-12//99
Installation, Maintenance, and Repair Worker	Nevada	S	10.14 MW	11.22 AW	23340 AAW	NVBLS	10//99-12//99
Installation, Maintenance, and Repair Worker	Las Vegas MSA, NV-AZ	S	10.37 MW	9.42 AW	21560 AAW	NVBLS	10//99-12//99
Installation, Maintenance, and Repair Worker	Reno MSA, NV	S	13.32 MW	12.77 AW	27700 AAW	NVBLS	10//99-12//99
Installation, Maintenance, and Repair Worker	New Hampshire	S	10.5 MW	10.72 AW	22290 AAW	NHBLS	10//99-12//99
Installation, Maintenance, and Repair Worker	Manchester PMSA, NH	S	10.85 MW	10.08 AW	22580 AAW	NHBLS	10//99-12//99
Installation, Maintenance, and Repair Worker	Nashua PMSA, NH	S	10.74 MW	10.09 AW	22330 AAW	NHBLS	10//99-12//99
Installation, Maintenance, and Repair Worker	Portsmouth-Rochester PMSA, NH-ME	S	9.83 MW	9.56 AW	20450 AAW	NHBLS	10//99-12//99
Installation, Maintenance, and Repair Worker	New Jersey	S	10.14 MW	10.68 AW	22200 AAW	NJBLS	10//99-12//99
Installation, Maintenance, and Repair Worker	Atlantic-Cape May PMSA, NJ	S	11.04 MW	11.03 AW	22970 AAW	NJBLS	10//99-12//99
Installation, Maintenance, and Repair Worker	Bergen-Passaic PMSA, NJ	S	10.21 MW	10.10 AW	21240 AAW	NJBLS	10//99-12//99
Installation, Maintenance, and Repair Worker	Jersey City PMSA, NJ	S	10.52 MW	9.44 AW	21880 AAW	NJBLS	10//99-12//99
Installation, Maintenance, and Repair Worker	Middlesex-Somerset-Hunterdon PMSA, NJ	S	10.65 MW	9.47 AW	22140 AAW	NJBLS	10//99-12//99
Installation, Maintenance, and Repair Worker	Monmouth-Ocean PMSA, NJ	S	11.17 MW	11.38 AW	23240 AAW	NJBLS	10//99-12//99
Installation, Maintenance, and Repair Worker	Newark PMSA, NJ	S	11.58 MW	10.74 AW	24080 AAW	NJBLS	10//99-12//99
Installation, Maintenance, and Repair Worker	Trenton PMSA, NJ	S	8.92 MW	8.69 AW	18560 AAW	NJBLS	10//99-12//99
Installation, Maintenance, and Repair Worker	Vineland-Millville-Bridgeton PMSA, NJ	S	9.32 MW	8.63 AW	19380 AAW	NJBLS	10//99-12//99
Installation, Maintenance, and Repair Worker	New Mexico	S	8.66 MW	9.61 AW	19990 AAW	NMBLS	10//99-12//99
Installation, Maintenance, and Repair Worker	Albuquerque MSA, NM	S	9.47 MW	8.63 AW	19690 AAW	NMBLS	10//99-12//99
Installation, Maintenance, and Repair Worker	Las Cruces MSA, NM	S	7.40 MW	6.76 AW	15390 AAW	NMBLS	10//99-12//99

AAW Average annual wage	**AOH** Average offered, high	**ASH** Average starting, high	**H** Hourly	**M** Monthly	**S** Special: hourly and annual
AE Average entry wage	**AOL** Average offered, low	**ASL** Average starting, low	**HI** Highest wage paid	**MTC** Median total compensation	**TQ** Third quartile wage
AEX Average experienced wage	**APH** Average pay, high range	**AW** Average wage paid	**HR** High end range	**MW** Median wage paid	**W** Weekly
AO Average offered	**APL** Average pay, low range	**FQ** First quartile wage	**LR** Low end range	**SQ** Second quartile wage	**Y** Yearly

Helper

Occupation/Type/Industry	Location	Per	Low	Mid	High	Source	Date
Installation, Maintenance, and Repair Worker	New York	S	10.42 MW	10.89 AW	22650 AAW	NYBLS	10//99-12//99
Installation, Maintenance, and Repair Worker	Albany-Schenectady-Troy MSA, NY	S	8.96 MW	8.16 AW	18630 AAW	NYBLS	10//99-12//99
Installation, Maintenance, and Repair Worker	Binghamton MSA, NY	S	9.96 MW	9.36 AW	20720 AAW	NYBLS	10//99-12//99
Installation, Maintenance, and Repair Worker	Buffalo-Niagara Falls MSA, NY	S	11.58 MW	11.57 AW	24100 AAW	NYBLS	10//99-12//99
Installation, Maintenance, and Repair Worker	Dutchess County PMSA, NY	S	10.69 MW	9.64 AW	22240 AAW	NYBLS	10//99-12//99
Installation, Maintenance, and Repair Worker	Elmira MSA, NY	S	10.65 MW	10.08 AW	22140 AAW	NYBLS	10//99-12//99
Installation, Maintenance, and Repair Worker	Nassau-Suffolk PMSA, NY	S	11.01 MW	10.42 AW	22900 AAW	NYBLS	10//99-12//99
Installation, Maintenance, and Repair Worker	New York PMSA, NY	S	12.47 MW	11.60 AW	25940 AAW	NYBLS	10//99-12//99
Installation, Maintenance, and Repair Worker	Newburgh PMSA, NY-PA	S	9.48 MW	9.16 AW	19710 AAW	NYBLS	10//99-12//99
Installation, Maintenance, and Repair Worker	Rochester MSA, NY	S	11.06 MW	11.94 AW	23010 AAW	NYBLS	10//99-12//99
Installation, Maintenance, and Repair Worker	Syracuse MSA, NY	S	8.42 MW	7.21 AW	17500 AAW	NYBLS	10//99-12//99
Installation, Maintenance, and Repair Worker	Utica-Rome MSA, NY	S	11.29 MW	11.74 AW	23490 AAW	NYBLS	10//99-12//99
Installation, Maintenance, and Repair Worker	North Carolina	S	9.86 MW	11.00 AW	22890 AAW	NCBLS	10//99-12//99
Installation, Maintenance, and Repair Worker	Asheville MSA, NC	S	10.31 MW	9.34 AW	21440 AAW	NCBLS	10//99-12//99
Installation, Maintenance, and Repair Worker	Charlotte-Gastonia-Rock Hill MSA, NC-SC	S	10.71 MW	10.55 AW	22270 AAW	NCBLS	10//99-12//99
Installation, Maintenance, and Repair Worker	Fayetteville MSA, NC	S	8.73 MW	8.77 AW	18150 AAW	NCBLS	10//99-12//99
Installation, Maintenance, and Repair Worker	Greensboro--Winston-Salem--High Point MSA, NC	S	9.99 MW	9.77 AW	20780 AAW	NCBLS	10//99-12//99
Installation, Maintenance, and Repair Worker	Greenville MSA, NC	S	7.01 MW	6.51 AW	14570 AAW	NCBLS	10//99-12//99
Installation, Maintenance, and Repair Worker	Hickory-Morganton-Lenoir MSA, NC	S	9.66 MW	9.46 AW	20100 AAW	NCBLS	10//99-12//99
Installation, Maintenance, and Repair Worker	Rocky Mount MSA, NC	S	9.65 MW	8.70 AW	20060 AAW	NCBLS	10//99-12//99
Installation, Maintenance, and Repair Worker	Wilmington MSA, NC	S	9.90 MW	9.18 AW	20590 AAW	NCBLS	10//99-12//99
Installation, Maintenance, and Repair Worker	North Dakota	S	9.25 MW	9.91 AW	20610 AAW	NDBLS	10//99-12//99
Installation, Maintenance, and Repair Worker	Bismarck MSA, ND	S	9.00 MW	8.85 AW	18720 AAW	NDBLS	10//99-12//99
Installation, Maintenance, and Repair Worker	Fargo-Moorhead MSA, ND-MN	S	10.87 MW	10.26 AW	22610 AAW	NDBLS	10//99-12//99
Installation, Maintenance, and Repair Worker	Grand Forks MSA, ND-MN	S	10.52 MW	9.93 AW	21880 AAW	NDBLS	10//99-12//99
Installation, Maintenance, and Repair Worker	Ohio	S	9.91 MW	10.41 AW	21640 AAW	OHBLS	10//99-12//99
Installation, Maintenance, and Repair Worker	Akron PMSA, OH	S	9.43 MW	9.19 AW	19610 AAW	OHBLS	10//99-12//99
Installation, Maintenance, and Repair Worker	Canton-Massillon MSA, OH	S	9.95 MW	8.39 AW	20700 AAW	OHBLS	10//99-12//99
Installation, Maintenance, and Repair Worker	Cincinnati PMSA, OH-KY-IN	S	10.88 MW	10.17 AW	22630 AAW	OHBLS	10//99-12//99
Installation, Maintenance, and Repair Worker	Cleveland-Lorain-Elyria PMSA, OH	S	10.56 MW	9.96 AW	21960 AAW	OHBLS	10//99-12//99
Installation, Maintenance, and Repair Worker	Columbus MSA, OH	S	10.69 MW	9.97 AW	22230 AAW	OHBLS	10//99-12//99

Helper

Occupation/Type/Industry	Location	Per	Low	Mid	High	Source	Date
Installation, Maintenance, and Repair Worker	Dayton-Springfield MSA, OH	S	9.60 MW	8.60 AW	19960 AAW	OHBLS	10//99-12//99
Installation, Maintenance, and Repair Worker	Hamilton-Middletown PMSA, OH	S	12.14 MW	11.98 AW	25250 AAW	OHBLS	10//99-12//99
Installation, Maintenance, and Repair Worker	Lima MSA, OH	S	11.18 MW	10.84 AW	23260 AAW	OHBLS	10//99-12//99
Installation, Maintenance, and Repair Worker	Mansfield MSA, OH	S	11.39 MW	11.05 AW	23690 AAW	OHBLS	10//99-12//99
Installation, Maintenance, and Repair Worker	Steubenville-Weirton MSA, OH-WV	S	9.63 MW	8.17 AW	20030 AAW	OHBLS	10//99-12//99
Installation, Maintenance, and Repair Worker	Toledo MSA, OH	S	10.70 MW	10.35 AW	22250 AAW	OHBLS	10//99-12//99
Installation, Maintenance, and Repair Worker	Youngstown-Warren MSA, OH	S	9.30 MW	8.45 AW	19350 AAW	OHBLS	10//99-12//99
Installation, Maintenance, and Repair Worker	Oklahoma	S	8.54 MW	10.02 AW	20830 AAW	OKBLS	10//99-12//99
Installation, Maintenance, and Repair Worker	Enid MSA, OK	S	7.92 MW	7.88 AW	16470 AAW	OKBLS	10//99-12//99
Installation, Maintenance, and Repair Worker	Lawton MSA, OK	S	11.23 MW	9.52 AW	23370 AAW	OKBLS	10//99-12//99
Installation, Maintenance, and Repair Worker	Oklahoma City MSA, OK	S	11.52 MW	9.33 AW	23960 AAW	OKBLS	10//99-12//99
Installation, Maintenance, and Repair Worker	Tulsa MSA, OK	S	9.12 MW	8.73 AW	18960 AAW	OKBLS	10//99-12//99
Installation, Maintenance, and Repair Worker	Oregon	S	9.91 MW	10.58 AW	22000 AAW	ORBLS	10//99-12//99
Installation, Maintenance, and Repair Worker	Medford-Ashland MSA, OR	S	9.72 MW	10.06 AW	20220 AAW	ORBLS	10//99-12//99
Installation, Maintenance, and Repair Worker	Portland-Vancouver PMSA, OR-WA	S	11.21 MW	10.34 AW	23320 AAW	ORBLS	10//99-12//99
Installation, Maintenance, and Repair Worker	Salem PMSA, OR	S	10.25 MW	9.29 AW	21330 AAW	ORBLS	10//99-12//99
Installation, Maintenance, and Repair Worker	Pennsylvania	S	10.02 MW	10.77 AW	22410 AAW	PABLS	10//99-12//99
Installation, Maintenance, and Repair Worker	Allentown-Bethlehem-Easton MSA, PA	S	11.29 MW	10.58 AW	23470 AAW	PABLS	10//99-12//99
Installation, Maintenance, and Repair Worker	Altoona MSA, PA	S	10.06 MW	9.65 AW	20920 AAW	PABLS	10//99-12//99
Installation, Maintenance, and Repair Worker	Erie MSA, PA	S	9.65 MW	9.23 AW	20060 AAW	PABLS	10//99-12//99
Installation, Maintenance, and Repair Worker	Harrisburg-Lebanon-Carlisle MSA, PA	S	10.10 MW	8.62 AW	21000 AAW	PABLS	10//99-12//99
Installation, Maintenance, and Repair Worker	Johnstown MSA, PA	S	8.88 MW	8.18 AW	18480 AAW	PABLS	10//99-12//99
Installation, Maintenance, and Repair Worker	Lancaster MSA, PA	S	10.44 MW	10.32 AW	21700 AAW	PABLS	10//99-12//99
Installation, Maintenance, and Repair Worker	Philadelphia PMSA, PA-NJ	S	10.49 MW	10.11 AW	21820 AAW	PABLS	10//99-12//99
Installation, Maintenance, and Repair Worker	Pittsburgh MSA, PA	S	11.16 MW	10.39 AW	23220 AAW	PABLS	10//99-12//99
Installation, Maintenance, and Repair Worker	Reading MSA, PA	S	9.52 MW	7.92 AW	19800 AAW	PABLS	10//99-12//99
Installation, Maintenance, and Repair Worker	Scranton--Wilkes-Barre--Hazleton MSA, PA	S	11.66 MW	11.07 AW	24250 AAW	PABLS	10//99-12//99
Installation, Maintenance, and Repair Worker	Williamsport MSA, PA	S	9.72 MW	9.49 AW	20230 AAW	PABLS	10//99-12//99
Installation, Maintenance, and Repair Worker	York MSA, PA	S	11.17 MW	10.70 AW	23240 AAW	PABLS	10//99-12//99
Installation, Maintenance, and Repair Worker	Rhode Island	S	8.49 MW	10.21 AW	21240 AAW	RIBLS	10//99-12//99
Installation, Maintenance, and Repair Worker	Providence-Fall River-Warwick MSA, RI-MA	S	10.13 MW	8.44 AW	21070 AAW	RIBLS	10//99-12//99

AAW Average annual wage	AOH Average offered, high	ASH Average starting, high	H Hourly	M Monthly	S Special: hourly and annual
AE Average entry wage	AOL Average offered, low	ASL Average starting, low	HI Highest wage paid	MTC Median total compensation	TQ Third quartile wage
AEX Average experienced wage	APH Average pay, high range	AW Average wage paid	HR High end range	MW Median wage paid	W Weekly
AO Average offered	APL Average pay, low range	FQ First quartile wage	LR Low end range	SQ Second quartile wage	Y Yearly

Helper

Occupation/Type/Industry	Location	Per	Low	Mid	High	Source	Date
Installation, Maintenance, and Repair Worker	South Carolina	S	8.72 MW	9.92 AW	20630 AAW	SCBLS	10//99-12//99
Installation, Maintenance, and Repair Worker	Charleston-North Charleston MSA, SC	S	9.53 MW	8.74 AW	19810 AAW	SCBLS	10//99-12//99
Installation, Maintenance, and Repair Worker	Columbia MSA, SC	S	10.84 MW	9.68 AW	22540 AAW	SCBLS	10//99-12//99
Installation, Maintenance, and Repair Worker	Florence MSA, SC	S	8.64 MW	7.95 AW	17980 AAW	SCBLS	10//99-12//99
Installation, Maintenance, and Repair Worker	Greenville-Spartanburg-Anderson MSA, SC	S	9.81 MW	9.08 AW	20410 AAW	SCBLS	10//99-12//99
Installation, Maintenance, and Repair Worker	Myrtle Beach MSA, SC	S	10.27 MW	9.67 AW	21350 AAW	SCBLS	10//99-12//99
Installation, Maintenance, and Repair Worker	Sumter MSA, SC	S	8.39 MW	7.87 AW	17450 AAW	SCBLS	10//99-12//99
Installation, Maintenance, and Repair Worker	South Dakota	S	6.9 MW	7.23 AW	15040 AAW	SDBLS	10//99-12//99
Installation, Maintenance, and Repair Worker	Rapid City MSA, SD	S	8.01 MW	7.99 AW	16650 AAW	SDBLS	10//99-12//99
Installation, Maintenance, and Repair Worker	Sioux Falls MSA, SD	S	6.97 MW	6.65 AW	14500 AAW	SDBLS	10//99-12//99
Installation, Maintenance, and Repair Worker	Tennessee	S	9.17 MW	9.63 AW	20020 AAW	TNBLS	10//99-12//99
Installation, Maintenance, and Repair Worker	Chattanooga MSA, TN-GA	S	9.53 MW	9.41 AW	19830 AAW	TNBLS	10//99-12//99
Installation, Maintenance, and Repair Worker	Clarksville-Hopkinsville MSA, TN-KY	S	10.54 MW	12.08 AW	21920 AAW	TNBLS	10//99-12//99
Installation, Maintenance, and Repair Worker	Jackson MSA, TN	S	8.82 MW	8.58 AW	18350 AAW	TNBLS	10//99-12//99
Installation, Maintenance, and Repair Worker	Johnson City-Kingsport-Bristol MSA, TN-VA	S	9.00 MW	8.13 AW	18720 AAW	TNBLS	10//99-12//99
Installation, Maintenance, and Repair Worker	Knoxville MSA, TN	S	9.86 MW	9.50 AW	20510 AAW	TNBLS	10//99-12//99
Installation, Maintenance, and Repair Worker	Memphis MSA, TN-AR-MS	S	10.62 MW	10.14 AW	22100 AAW	MSBLS	10//99-12//99
Installation, Maintenance, and Repair Worker	Nashville MSA, TN	S	10.27 MW	9.74 AW	21370 AAW	TNBLS	10//99-12//99
Installation, Maintenance, and Repair Worker	Texas	S	8.37 MW	8.94 AW	18590 AAW	TXBLS	10//99-12//99
Installation, Maintenance, and Repair Worker	Austin-San Marcos MSA, TX	S	8.86 MW	8.26 AW	18440 AAW	TXBLS	10//99-12//99
Installation, Maintenance, and Repair Worker	Beaumont-Port Arthur MSA, TX	S	9.12 MW	8.31 AW	18970 AAW	TXBLS	10//99-12//99
Installation, Maintenance, and Repair Worker	Brazoria PMSA, TX	S	8.98 MW	8.66 AW	18680 AAW	TXBLS	10//99-12//99
Installation, Maintenance, and Repair Worker	Brownsville-Harlingen-San Benito MSA, TX	S	8.23 MW	7.52 AW	17120 AAW	TXBLS	10//99-12//99
Installation, Maintenance, and Repair Worker	Corpus Christi MSA, TX	S	8.35 MW	7.40 AW	17380 AAW	TXBLS	10//99-12//99
Installation, Maintenance, and Repair Worker	Dallas PMSA, TX	S	8.96 MW	8.66 AW	18640 AAW	TXBLS	10//99-12//99
Installation, Maintenance, and Repair Worker	El Paso MSA, TX	S	8.22 MW	7.73 AW	17100 AAW	TXBLS	10//99-12//99
Installation, Maintenance, and Repair Worker	Fort Worth-Arlington PMSA, TX	S	9.38 MW	8.52 AW	19510 AAW	TXBLS	10//99-12//99
Installation, Maintenance, and Repair Worker	Galveston-Texas City PMSA, TX	S	9.20 MW	9.13 AW	19130 AAW	TXBLS	10//99-12//99
Installation, Maintenance, and Repair Worker	Houston PMSA, TX	S	9.29 MW	8.70 AW	19330 AAW	TXBLS	10//99-12//99
Installation, Maintenance, and Repair Worker	Killeen-Temple MSA, TX	S	7.96 MW	7.37 AW	16560 AAW	TXBLS	10//99-12//99
Installation, Maintenance, and Repair Worker	Laredo MSA, TX	S	7.83 MW	6.58 AW	16280 AAW	TXBLS	10//99-12//99

AAW	Average annual wage	AOH	Average offered, high	ASH	Average starting, high
AE	Average entry wage	AOL	Average offered, low	ASL	Average starting, low
AEX	Average experienced wage	APH	Average pay, high range	AW	Average wage paid
AO	Average offered	APL	Average pay, low range	FQ	First quartile wage

H	Hourly	M	Monthly	S	Special: hourly and annual
HI	Highest wage paid	MTC	Median total compensation	TQ	Third quartile wage
HR	High end range	MW	Median wage paid	W	Weekly
LR	Low end range	SQ	Second quartile wage	Y	Yearly

Helper

Occupation/Type/Industry	Location	Per	Low	Mid	High	Source	Date
Installation, Maintenance, and Repair Worker	Longview-Marshall MSA, TX	S	9.14 MW	8.86 AW	19010 AAW	TXBLS	10//99-12//99
Installation, Maintenance, and Repair Worker	Lubbock MSA, TX	S	8.21 MW	7.66 AW	17070 AAW	TXBLS	10//99-12//99
Installation, Maintenance, and Repair Worker	McAllen-Edinburg-Mission MSA, TX	S	7.27 MW	6.87 AW	15110 AAW	TXBLS	10//99-12//99
Installation, Maintenance, and Repair Worker	Odessa-Midland MSA, TX	S	8.46 MW	8.20 AW	17600 AAW	TXBLS	10//99-12//99
Installation, Maintenance, and Repair Worker	San Angelo MSA, TX	S	8.00 MW	7.83 AW	16640 AAW	TXBLS	10//99-12//99
Installation, Maintenance, and Repair Worker	San Antonio MSA, TX	S	8.74 MW	8.22 AW	18170 AAW	TXBLS	10//99-12//99
Installation, Maintenance, and Repair Worker	Sherman-Denison MSA, TX	S	8.76 MW	8.03 AW	18220 AAW	TXBLS	10//99-12//99
Installation, Maintenance, and Repair Worker	Texarkana MSA, TX-Texarkana, AR	S	8.32 MW	8.33 AW	17310 AAW	TXBLS	10//99-12//99
Installation, Maintenance, and Repair Worker	Tyler MSA, TX	S	7.10 MW	6.39 AW	14760 AAW	TXBLS	10//99-12//99
Installation, Maintenance, and Repair Worker	Victoria MSA, TX	S	7.43 MW	7.25 AW	15460 AAW	TXBLS	10//99-12//99
Installation, Maintenance, and Repair Worker	Waco MSA, TX	S	8.84 MW	8.07 AW	18390 AAW	TXBLS	10//99-12//99
Installation, Maintenance, and Repair Worker	Wichita Falls MSA, TX	S	8.41 MW	7.96 AW	17490 AAW	TXBLS	10//99-12//99
Installation, Maintenance, and Repair Worker	Utah	S	8.58 MW	9.53 AW	19820 AAW	UTBLS	10//99-12//99
Installation, Maintenance, and Repair Worker	Provo-Orem MSA, UT	S	7.89 MW	7.54 AW	16400 AAW	UTBLS	10//99-12//99
Installation, Maintenance, and Repair Worker	Salt Lake City-Ogden MSA, UT	S	9.93 MW	8.93 AW	20640 AAW	UTBLS	10//99-12//99
Installation, Maintenance, and Repair Worker	Vermont	S	8.08 MW	8.75 AW	18210 AAW	VTBLS	10//99-12//99
Installation, Maintenance, and Repair Worker	Burlington MSA, VT	S	9.17 MW	8.40 AW	19060 AAW	VTBLS	10//99-12//99
Installation, Maintenance, and Repair Worker	Virginia	S	8.35 MW	8.91 AW	18540 AAW	VABLS	10//99-12//99
Installation, Maintenance, and Repair Worker	Charlottesville MSA, VA	S	10.66 MW	10.70 AW	22180 AAW	VABLS	10//99-12//99
Installation, Maintenance, and Repair Worker	Danville MSA, VA	S	8.24 MW	8.27 AW	17140 AAW	VABLS	10//99-12//99
Installation, Maintenance, and Repair Worker	Lynchburg MSA, VA	S	9.81 MW	9.63 AW	20400 AAW	VABLS	10//99-12//99
Installation, Maintenance, and Repair Worker	Norfolk-Virginia Beach-Newport News MSA, VA-NC	S	8.60 MW	8.28 AW	17880 AAW	VABLS	10//99-12//99
Installation, Maintenance, and Repair Worker	Richmond-Petersburg MSA, VA	S	8.39 MW	7.36 AW	17460 AAW	VABLS	10//99-12//99
Installation, Maintenance, and Repair Worker	Roanoke MSA, VA	S	8.82 MW	8.19 AW	18340 AAW	VABLS	10//99-12//99
Installation, Maintenance, and Repair Worker	Washington	S	9.89 MW	10.74 AW	22340 AAW	WABLS	10//99-12//99
Installation, Maintenance, and Repair Worker	Bellingham MSA, WA	S	10.98 MW	9.66 AW	22830 AAW	WABLS	10//99-12//99
Installation, Maintenance, and Repair Worker	Bremerton PMSA, WA	S	10.54 MW	9.08 AW	21910 AAW	WABLS	10//99-12//99
Installation, Maintenance, and Repair Worker	Olympia PMSA, WA	S	9.41 MW	8.29 AW	19570 AAW	WABLS	10//99-12//99
Installation, Maintenance, and Repair Worker	Richland-Kennewick-Pasco MSA, WA	S	10.14 MW	9.54 AW	21090 AAW	WABLS	10//99-12//99
Installation, Maintenance, and Repair Worker	Seattle-Bellevue-Everett PMSA, WA	S	11.59 MW	10.82 AW	24100 AAW	WABLS	10//99-12//99
Installation, Maintenance, and Repair Worker	Spokane MSA, WA	S	9.81 MW	7.32 AW	20410 AAW	WABLS	10//99-12//99

AAW	Average annual wage	AOH	Average offered, high	ASH	Average starting, high
AE	Average entry wage	AOL	Average offered, low	ASL	Average starting, low
AEX	Average experienced wage	APH	Average pay, high range	AW	Average wage paid
AO	Average offered	APL	Average pay, low range	FQ	First quartile wage
H	Hourly	M	Monthly	S	Special: hourly and annual
HI	Highest wage paid	MTC	Median total compensation	TQ	Third quartile wage
HR	High end range	MW	Median wage paid	W	Weekly
LR	Low end range	SQ	Second quartile wage	Y	Yearly

Occupation/Type/Industry	Location	Per	Low	Mid	High	Source	Date
Helper							
Installation, Maintenance, and Repair Worker	Tacoma PMSA, WA	S	9.76 MW	9.06 AW	20300 AAW	WABLS	10//99-12//99
Installation, Maintenance, and Repair Worker	Yakima MSA, WA	S	9.96 MW	8.43 AW	20720 AAW	WABLS	10//99-12//99
Installation, Maintenance, and Repair Worker	West Virginia	S	8.25 MW	9.62 AW	20010 AAW	WVBLS	10//99-12//99
Installation, Maintenance, and Repair Worker	Charleston MSA, WV	S	12.05 MW	10.07 AW	25060 AAW	WVBLS	10//99-12//99
Installation, Maintenance, and Repair Worker	Huntington-Ashland MSA, WV-KY-OH	S	11.49 MW	9.68 AW	23900 AAW	WVBLS	10//99-12//99
Installation, Maintenance, and Repair Worker	Parkersburg-Marietta MSA, WV-OH	S	8.43 MW	8.16 AW	17540 AAW	WVBLS	10//99-12//99
Installation, Maintenance, and Repair Worker	Wheeling MSA, WV-OH	S	10.55 MW	7.70 AW	21940 AAW	WVBLS	10//99-12//99
Installation, Maintenance, and Repair Worker	Wisconsin	S	9.56 MW	10.23 AW	21280 AAW	WIBLS	10//99-12//99
Installation, Maintenance, and Repair Worker	Appleton-Oshkosh-Neenah MSA, WI	S	8.58 MW	8.05 AW	17840 AAW	WIBLS	10//99-12//99
Installation, Maintenance, and Repair Worker	Eau Claire MSA, WI	S	10.47 MW	9.37 AW	21770 AAW	WIBLS	10//99-12//99
Installation, Maintenance, and Repair Worker	Green Bay MSA, WI	S	10.48 MW	9.81 AW	21800 AAW	WIBLS	10//99-12//99
Installation, Maintenance, and Repair Worker	Janesville-Beloit MSA, WI	S	10.01 MW	9.66 AW	20830 AAW	WIBLS	10//99-12//99
Installation, Maintenance, and Repair Worker	La Crosse MSA, WI-MN	S	9.03 MW	7.93 AW	18780 AAW	WIBLS	10//99-12//99
Installation, Maintenance, and Repair Worker	Madison MSA, WI	S	10.89 MW	10.32 AW	22650 AAW	WIBLS	10//99-12//99
Installation, Maintenance, and Repair Worker	Milwaukee-Waukesha PMSA, WI	S	10.62 MW	9.83 AW	22100 AAW	WIBLS	10//99-12//99
Installation, Maintenance, and Repair Worker	Racine PMSA, WI	S	10.42 MW	9.96 AW	21680 AAW	WIBLS	10//99-12//99
Installation, Maintenance, and Repair Worker	Sheboygan MSA, WI	S	10.78 MW	10.28 AW	22430 AAW	WIBLS	10//99-12//99
Installation, Maintenance, and Repair Worker	Wyoming	S	10.12 MW	10.63 AW	22110 AAW	WYBLS	10//99-12//99
Installation, Maintenance, and Repair Worker	Casper MSA, WY	S	10.91 MW	11.39 AW	22700 AAW	WYBLS	10//99-12//99
Installation, Maintenance, and Repair Worker	Cheyenne MSA, WY	S	8.36 MW	7.34 AW	17380 AAW	WYBLS	10//99-12//99
Installation, Maintenance, and Repair Worker	Puerto Rico	S	6.9 MW	7.60 AW	15810 AAW	PRBLS	10//99-12//99
Installation, Maintenance, and Repair Worker	Arecibo PMSA, PR	S	5.79 MW	6.03 AW	12050 AAW	PRBLS	10//99-12//99
Installation, Maintenance, and Repair Worker	Caguas PMSA, PR	S	6.51 MW	6.08 AW	13540 AAW	PRBLS	10//99-12//99
Installation, Maintenance, and Repair Worker	Mayaguez MSA, PR	S	6.60 MW	6.03 AW	13720 AAW	PRBLS	10//99-12//99
Installation, Maintenance, and Repair Worker	Ponce MSA, PR	S	8.19 MW	8.39 AW	17030 AAW	PRBLS	10//99-12//99
Installation, Maintenance, and Repair Worker	San Juan-Bayamon PMSA, PR	S	7.84 MW	7.24 AW	16300 AAW	PRBLS	10//99-12//99
Installation, Maintenance, and Repair Worker	Virgin Islands	S	8.48 MW	8.70 AW	18100 AAW	VIBLS	10//99-12//99
Installation, Maintenance, and Repair Worker	Guam	S	7.88 MW	8.10 AW	16850 AAW	GUBLS	10//99-12//99
Painter, Paperhanger, Plasterer, and Stucco Mason	Alabama	S	7.87 MW	8.19 AW	17040 AAW	ALBLS	10//99-12//99
Painter, Paperhanger, Plasterer, and Stucco Mason	Arizona	S	7.82 MW	8.38 AW	17430 AAW	AZBLS	10//99-12//99
Painter, Paperhanger, Plasterer, and Stucco Mason	Arkansas	S	7.84 MW	7.85 AW	16330 AAW	ARBLS	10//99-12//99
Painter, Paperhanger, Plasterer, and Stucco Mason	California	S	8.83 MW	9.68 AW	20140 AAW	CABLS	10//99-12//99
Painter, Paperhanger, Plasterer, and Stucco Mason	Colorado	S	9.01 MW	8.93 AW	18580 AAW	COBLS	10//99-12//99

Helper

Occupation/Type/Industry	Location	Per	Low	Mid	High	Source	Date
Painter, Paperhanger, Plasterer, and Stucco Mason	Connecticut	S	7.86 MW	10.07 AW	20950 AAW	CTBLS	10//99-12//99
Painter, Paperhanger, Plasterer, and Stucco Mason	Florida	S	8.63 MW	9.03 AW	18770 AAW	FLBLS	10//99-12//99
Painter, Paperhanger, Plasterer, and Stucco Mason	Georgia	S	10.18 MW	10.50 AW	21840 AAW	GABLS	10//99-12//99
Painter, Paperhanger, Plasterer, and Stucco Mason	Hawaii	S	10.37 MW	11.60 AW	24130 AAW	HIBLS	10//99-12//99
Painter, Paperhanger, Plasterer, and Stucco Mason	Idaho	S	6.83 MW	7.81 AW	16240 AAW	IDBLS	10//99-12//99
Painter, Paperhanger, Plasterer, and Stucco Mason	Illinois	S	15.29 MW	15.99 AW	33260 AAW	ILBLS	10//99-12//99
Painter, Paperhanger, Plasterer, and Stucco Mason	Indiana	S	9.09 MW	9.32 AW	19390 AAW	INBLS	10//99-12//99
Painter, Paperhanger, Plasterer, and Stucco Mason	Iowa	S	8.23 MW	8.35 AW	17370 AAW	IABLS	10//99-12//99
Painter, Paperhanger, Plasterer, and Stucco Mason	Kansas	S	9.35 MW	9.50 AW	19760 AAW	KSBLS	10//99-12//99
Painter, Paperhanger, Plasterer, and Stucco Mason	Kentucky	S	8.51 MW	8.46 AW	17590 AAW	KYBLS	10//99-12//99
Painter, Paperhanger, Plasterer, and Stucco Mason	Louisiana	S	8.37 MW	8.58 AW	17840 AAW	LABLS	10//99-12//99
Painter, Paperhanger, Plasterer, and Stucco Mason	Maine	S	10.42 MW	10.46 AW	21750 AAW	MEBLS	10//99-12//99
Painter, Paperhanger, Plasterer, and Stucco Mason	Maryland	S	9.41 MW	9.39 AW	19530 AAW	MDBLS	10//99-12//99
Painter, Paperhanger, Plasterer, and Stucco Mason	Massachusetts	S	9.87 MW	10.18 AW	21170 AAW	MABLS	10//99-12//99
Painter, Paperhanger, Plasterer, and Stucco Mason	Michigan	S	9.53 MW	10.49 AW	21830 AAW	MIBLS	10//99-12//99
Painter, Paperhanger, Plasterer, and Stucco Mason	Minnesota	S	12.83 MW	13.84 AW	28790 AAW	MNBLS	10//99-12//99
Painter, Paperhanger, Plasterer, and Stucco Mason	Mississippi	S	7.34 MW	7.31 AW	15210 AAW	MSBLS	10//99-12//99
Painter, Paperhanger, Plasterer, and Stucco Mason	Montana	S	9.9 MW	9.51 AW	19780 AAW	MTBLS	10//99-12//99
Painter, Paperhanger, Plasterer, and Stucco Mason	Nebraska	S	9.11 MW	8.60 AW	17890 AAW	NEBLS	10//99-12//99
Painter, Paperhanger, Plasterer, and Stucco Mason	Nevada	S	9.36 MW	11.60 AW	24120 AAW	NVBLS	10//99-12//99
Painter, Paperhanger, Plasterer, and Stucco Mason	New Jersey	S	11.85 MW	12.59 AW	26180 AAW	NJBLS	10//99-12//99
Painter, Paperhanger, Plasterer, and Stucco Mason	New Mexico	S	7.98 MW	8.21 AW	17070 AAW	NMBLS	10//99-12//99
Painter, Paperhanger, Plasterer, and Stucco Mason	New York	S	9.79 MW	10.59 AW	22030 AAW	NYBLS	10//99-12//99
Painter, Paperhanger, Plasterer, and Stucco Mason	North Carolina	S	9.89 MW	9.61 AW	19980 AAW	NCBLS	10//99-12//99
Painter, Paperhanger, Plasterer, and Stucco Mason	North Dakota	S	9.91 MW	9.66 AW	20090 AAW	NDBLS	10//99-12//99
Painter, Paperhanger, Plasterer, and Stucco Mason	Ohio	S	10.19 MW	10.63 AW	22100 AAW	OHBLS	10//99-12//99
Painter, Paperhanger, Plasterer, and Stucco Mason	Oklahoma	S	7.82 MW	7.95 AW	16540 AAW	OKBLS	10//99-12//99
Painter, Paperhanger, Plasterer, and Stucco Mason	Pennsylvania	S	9.67 MW	10.08 AW	20970 AAW	PABLS	10//99-12//99
Painter, Paperhanger, Plasterer, and Stucco Mason	Rhode Island	S	8.17 MW	8.47 AW	17610 AAW	RIBLS	10//99-12//99
Painter, Paperhanger, Plasterer, and Stucco Mason	South Carolina	S	8.95 MW	9.03 AW	18780 AAW	SCBLS	10//99-12//99
Painter, Paperhanger, Plasterer, and Stucco Mason	South Dakota	S	8.12 MW	8.10 AW	16850 AAW	SDBLS	10//99-12//99
Painter, Paperhanger, Plasterer, and Stucco Mason	Tennessee	S	10.29 MW	10.78 AW	22430 AAW	TNBLS	10//99-12//99
Painter, Paperhanger, Plasterer, and Stucco Mason	Texas	S	7.91 MW	8.07 AW	16780 AAW	TXBLS	10//99-12//99
Painter, Paperhanger, Plasterer, and Stucco Mason	Virginia	S	10.29 MW	9.69 AW	20150 AAW	VABLS	10//99-12//99
Painter, Paperhanger, Plasterer, and Stucco Mason	Washington	S	10.11 MW	10.15 AW	21110 AAW	WABLS	10//99-12//99

AAW Average annual wage	AOH Average offered, high	ASH Average starting, high	H Hourly	M Monthly	S Special: hourly and annual
AE Average entry wage	AOL Average offered, low	ASL Average starting, low	HI Highest wage paid	MTC Median total compensation	TQ Third quartile wage
AEX Average experienced wage	APH Average pay, high range	AW Average wage paid	HR High end range	MW Median wage paid	W Weekly
AO Average offered	APL Average pay, low range	FQ First quartile wage	LR Low end range	SQ Second quartile wage	Y Yearly

Occupation/Type/Industry	Location	Per	Low	Mid	High	Source	Date
Helper							
Painter, Paperhanger, Plasterer, and Stucco Mason	Wisconsin	S	8.99 MW	10.20 AW	21210 AAW	WIBLS	10//99-12//99
Painter, Paperhanger, Plasterer, and Stucco Mason	Wyoming	S	9.36 MW	9.16 AW	19050 AAW	WYBLS	10//99-12//99
Painter, Paperhanger, Plasterer, and Stucco Mason	Puerto Rico	S	6.49 MW	6.90 AW	14360 AAW	PRBLS	10//99-12//99
Painter, Paperhanger, Plasterer, and Stucco Mason	Guam	S	8.48 MW	9.13 AW	18990 AAW	GUBLS	10//99-12//99
Pipelayer, Plumber, Pipefitter, and Steamfitter	Alabama	S	8.49 MW	8.75 AW	18190 AAW	ALBLS	10//99-12//99
Pipelayer, Plumber, Pipefitter, and Steamfitter	Arizona	S	7.98 MW	8.21 AW	17080 AAW	AZBLS	10//99-12//99
Pipelayer, Plumber, Pipefitter, and Steamfitter	Arkansas	S	8.8 MW	9.26 AW	19250 AAW	ARBLS	10//99-12//99
Pipelayer, Plumber, Pipefitter, and Steamfitter	California	S	10.25 MW	10.97 AW	22810 AAW	CABLS	10//99-12//99
Pipelayer, Plumber, Pipefitter, and Steamfitter	Colorado	S	11.11 MW	11.51 AW	23950 AAW	COBLS	10//99-12//99
Pipelayer, Plumber, Pipefitter, and Steamfitter	Connecticut	S	11.18 MW	11.91 AW	24770 AAW	CTBLS	10//99-12//99
Pipelayer, Plumber, Pipefitter, and Steamfitter	Delaware	S	9.39 MW	10.30 AW	21430 AAW	DEBLS	10//99-12//99
Pipelayer, Plumber, Pipefitter, and Steamfitter	District of Columbia	S	9.67 MW	11.42 AW	23760 AAW	DCBLS	10//99-12//99
Pipelayer, Plumber, Pipefitter, and Steamfitter	Florida	S	8.83 MW	8.94 AW	18590 AAW	FLBLS	10//99-12//99
Pipelayer, Plumber, Pipefitter, and Steamfitter	Georgia	S	9.87 MW	9.90 AW	20590 AAW	GABLS	10//99-12//99
Pipelayer, Plumber, Pipefitter, and Steamfitter	Hawaii	S	13.04 MW	14.67 AW	30500 AAW	HIBLS	10//99-12//99
Pipelayer, Plumber, Pipefitter, and Steamfitter	Idaho	S	8.47 MW	9.17 AW	19070 AAW	IDBLS	10//99-12//99
Pipelayer, Plumber, Pipefitter, and Steamfitter	Illinois	S	14.38 MW	15.37 AW	31970 AAW	ILBLS	10//99-12//99
Pipelayer, Plumber, Pipefitter, and Steamfitter	Indiana	S	9.73 MW	10.29 AW	21390 AAW	INBLS	10//99-12//99
Pipelayer, Plumber, Pipefitter, and Steamfitter	Iowa	S	10.19 MW	10.20 AW	21210 AAW	IABLS	10//99-12//99
Pipelayer, Plumber, Pipefitter, and Steamfitter	Kansas	S	9.46 MW	9.83 AW	20450 AAW	KSBLS	10//99-12//99
Pipelayer, Plumber, Pipefitter, and Steamfitter	Kentucky	S	8.71 MW	8.74 AW	18180 AAW	KYBLS	10//99-12//99
Pipelayer, Plumber, Pipefitter, and Steamfitter	Louisiana	S	8.81 MW	9.28 AW	19310 AAW	LABLS	10//99-12//99
Pipelayer, Plumber, Pipefitter, and Steamfitter	Maine	S	8.46 MW	9.32 AW	19380 AAW	MEBLS	10//99-12//99
Pipelayer, Plumber, Pipefitter, and Steamfitter	Maryland	S	10.16 MW	10.63 AW	22110 AAW	MDBLS	10//99-12//99
Pipelayer, Plumber, Pipefitter, and Steamfitter	Massachusetts	S	11.07 MW	11.30 AW	23500 AAW	MABLS	10//99-12//99
Pipelayer, Plumber, Pipefitter, and Steamfitter	Michigan	S	9.68 MW	10.61 AW	22070 AAW	MIBLS	10//99-12//99
Pipelayer, Plumber, Pipefitter, and Steamfitter	Minnesota	S	11.23 MW	12.83 AW	26680 AAW	MNBLS	10//99-12//99
Pipelayer, Plumber, Pipefitter, and Steamfitter	Mississippi	S	8.63 MW	9.27 AW	19290 AAW	MSBLS	10//99-12//99
Pipelayer, Plumber, Pipefitter, and Steamfitter	Missouri	S	11.61 MW	11.86 AW	24670 AAW	MOBLS	10//99-12//99
Pipelayer, Plumber, Pipefitter, and Steamfitter	Nebraska	S	9.42 MW	9.69 AW	20150 AAW	NEBLS	10//99-12//99
Pipelayer, Plumber, Pipefitter, and Steamfitter	Nevada	S	9.85 MW	10.00 AW	20800 AAW	NVBLS	10//99-12//99
Pipelayer, Plumber, Pipefitter, and Steamfitter	New Hampshire	S	11.23 MW	11.52 AW	23960 AAW	NHBLS	10//99-12//99
Pipelayer, Plumber, Pipefitter, and Steamfitter	New Jersey	S	11.11 MW	11.65 AW	24220 AAW	NJBLS	10//99-12//99
Pipelayer, Plumber, Pipefitter, and Steamfitter	New Mexico	S	8.62 MW	10.19 AW	21190 AAW	NMBLS	10//99-12//99
Pipelayer, Plumber, Pipefitter, and Steamfitter	New York	S	11.69 MW	12.80 AW	26620 AAW	NYBLS	10//99-12//99

AAW Average annual wage	**AOH** Average offered, high	**ASH** Average starting, high	**H** Hourly	**M** Monthly	**S** Special: hourly and annual
AE Average entry wage	**AOL** Average offered, low	**ASL** Average starting, low	**HI** Highest wage paid	**MTC** Median total compensation	**TQ** Third quartile wage
AEX Average experienced wage	**APH** Average pay, high range	**AW** Average wage paid	**HR** High end range	**MW** Median wage paid	**W** Weekly
AO Average offered	**APL** Average pay, low range	**FQ** First quartile wage	**LR** Low end range	**SQ** Second quartile wage	**Y** Yearly

Helper

Occupation/Type/Industry	Location	Per	Low	Mid	High	Source	Date
Pipelayer, Plumber, Pipefitter, and Steamfitter	North Carolina	S	9.79 MW	9.89 AW	20570 AAW	NCBLS	10//99-12//99
Pipelayer, Plumber, Pipefitter, and Steamfitter	North Dakota	S	9.82 MW	9.78 AW	20340 AAW	NDBLS	10//99-12//99
Pipelayer, Plumber, Pipefitter, and Steamfitter	Ohio	S	10.07 MW	10.73 AW	22320 AAW	OHBLS	10//99-12//99
Pipelayer, Plumber, Pipefitter, and Steamfitter	Oklahoma	S	9.32 MW	9.33 AW	19410 AAW	OKBLS	10//99-12//99
Pipelayer, Plumber, Pipefitter, and Steamfitter	Oregon	S	11.64 MW	11.68 AW	24280 AAW	ORBLS	10//99-12//99
Pipelayer, Plumber, Pipefitter, and Steamfitter	Pennsylvania	S	10.65 MW	10.70 AW	22260 AAW	PABLS	10//99-12//99
Pipelayer, Plumber, Pipefitter, and Steamfitter	Rhode Island	S	10.56 MW	11.42 AW	23760 AAW	RIBLS	10//99-12//99
Pipelayer, Plumber, Pipefitter, and Steamfitter	South Carolina	S	9.7 MW	10.37 AW	21570 AAW	SCBLS	10//99-12//99
Pipelayer, Plumber, Pipefitter, and Steamfitter	South Dakota	S	8.87 MW	8.89 AW	18500 AAW	SDBLS	10//99-12//99
Pipelayer, Plumber, Pipefitter, and Steamfitter	Tennessee	S	10.09 MW	10.66 AW	22180 AAW	TNBLS	10//99-12//99
Pipelayer, Plumber, Pipefitter, and Steamfitter	Texas	S	8.73 MW	9.03 AW	18780 AAW	TXBLS	10//99-12//99
Pipelayer, Plumber, Pipefitter, and Steamfitter	Utah	S	9.19 MW	9.37 AW	19490 AAW	UTBLS	10//99-12//99
Pipelayer, Plumber, Pipefitter, and Steamfitter	Virginia	S	8.51 MW	8.77 AW	18230 AAW	VABLS	10//99-12//99
Pipelayer, Plumber, Pipefitter, and Steamfitter	Washington	S	11.7 MW	12.00 AW	24960 AAW	WABLS	10//99-12//99
Pipelayer, Plumber, Pipefitter, and Steamfitter	West Virginia	S	9.3 MW	13.52 AW	28120 AAW	WVBLS	10//99-12//99
Pipelayer, Plumber, Pipefitter, and Steamfitter	Wisconsin	S	12 MW	12.92 AW	26870 AAW	WIBLS	10//99-12//99
Pipelayer, Plumber, Pipefitter, and Steamfitter	Wyoming	S	8.99 MW	8.90 AW	18510 AAW	WYBLS	10//99-12//99
Pipelayer, Plumber, Pipefitter, and Steamfitter	Puerto Rico	S	6.38 MW	7.02 AW	14600 AAW	PRBLS	10//99-12//99
Production Worker	Alabama	S	7.27 MW	7.73 AW	16080 AAW	ALBLS	10//99-12//99
Production Worker	Alaska	S	14.84 MW	16.22 AW	33740 AAW	AKBLS	10//99-12//99
Production Worker	Arizona	S	7.51 MW	7.96 AW	16560 AAW	AZBLS	10//99-12//99
Production Worker	Arkansas	S	8.62 MW	8.23 AW	17130 AAW	ARBLS	10//99-12//99
Production Worker	California	S	7.01 MW	8.29 AW	17250 AAW	CABLS	10//99-12//99
Production Worker	Colorado	S	6.62 MW	7.94 AW	16520 AAW	COBLS	10//99-12//99
Production Worker	Connecticut	S	8.21 MW	8.85 AW	18410 AAW	CTBLS	10//99-12//99
Production Worker	Delaware	S	8.65 MW	10.57 AW	21990 AAW	DEBLS	10//99-12//99
Production Worker	District of Columbia	S	9.94 MW	10.22 AW	21260 AAW	DCBLS	10//99-12//99
Production Worker	Florida	S	7.17 MW	7.77 AW	16170 AAW	FLBLS	10//99-12//99
Production Worker	Georgia	S	7.8 MW	8.22 AW	17090 AAW	GABLS	10//99-12//99
Production Worker	Hawaii	S	11.45 MW	10.61 AW	22080 AAW	HIBLS	10//99-12//99
Production Worker	Idaho	S	7.62 MW	7.96 AW	16550 AAW	IDBLS	10//99-12//99
Production Worker	Illinois	S	8.35 MW	9.03 AW	18780 AAW	ILBLS	10//99-12//99
Production Worker	Indiana	S	9.16 MW	9.53 AW	19820 AAW	INBLS	10//99-12//99
Production Worker	Iowa	S	9.51 MW	9.82 AW	20420 AAW	IABLS	10//99-12//99
Production Worker	Kansas	S	9.53 MW	9.48 AW	19720 AAW	KSBLS	10//99-12//99
Production Worker	Kentucky	S	10.24 MW	11.00 AW	22880 AAW	KYBLS	10//99-12//99
Production Worker	Louisiana	S	8.37 MW	8.93 AW	18560 AAW	LABLS	10//99-12//99
Production Worker	Maine	S	9.77 MW	10.81 AW	22480 AAW	MEBLS	10//99-12//99
Production Worker	Maryland	S	9.09 MW	9.35 AW	19450 AAW	MDBLS	10//99-12//99
Production Worker	Massachusetts	S	8.73 MW	9.73 AW	20240 AAW	MABLS	10//99-12//99
Production Worker	Michigan	S	8.58 MW	9.87 AW	20540 AAW	MIBLS	10//99-12//99
Production Worker	Minnesota	S	10 MW	10.29 AW	21410 AAW	MNBLS	10//99-12//99
Production Worker	Mississippi	S	9.02 MW	9.11 AW	18950 AAW	MSBLS	10//99-12//99
Production Worker	Missouri	S	8.86 MW	9.41 AW	19560 AAW	MOBLS	10//99-12//99
Production Worker	Montana	S	6.51 MW	7.33 AW	15250 AAW	MTBLS	10//99-12//99
Production Worker	Nebraska	S	9.07 MW	8.96 AW	18630 AAW	NEBLS	10//99-12//99
Production Worker	Nevada	S	10.23 MW	10.76 AW	22380 AAW	NVBLS	10//99-12//99
Production Worker	New Hampshire	S	8.97 MW	9.36 AW	19480 AAW	NHBLS	10//99-12//99
Production Worker	New Jersey	S	8.45 MW	9.51 AW	19770 AAW	NJBLS	10//99-12//99
Production Worker	New Mexico	S	8.03 MW	8.24 AW	17130 AAW	NMBLS	10//99-12//99
Production Worker	New York	S	9.45 MW	9.37 AW	19500 AAW	NYBLS	10//99-12//99
Production Worker	North Carolina	S	8.29 MW	8.90 AW	18520 AAW	NCBLS	10//99-12//99
Production Worker	North Dakota	S	7.71 MW	7.86 AW	16350 AAW	NDBLS	10//99-12//99

AAW	Average annual wage	AOH	Average offered, high	ASH	Average starting, high	H	Hourly	M	Monthly	S	Special: hourly and annual
AE	Average entry wage	AOL	Average offered, low	ASL	Average starting, low	HI	Highest wage paid	MTC	Median total compensation	TQ	Third quartile wage
AEX	Average experienced wage	APH	Average pay, high range	AW	Average wage paid	HR	High end range	MW	Median wage paid	W	Weekly
AO	Average offered	APL	Average pay, low range	FQ	First quartile wage	LR	Low end range	SQ	Second quartile wage	Y	Yearly

Occupation/Type/Industry	Location	Per	Low	Mid	High	Source	Date
Helper							
Production Worker	Ohio	S	9.13 MW	9.71 AW	20190 AAW	OHBLS	10//99-12//99
Production Worker	Oklahoma	S	6.36 MW	7.06 AW	14680 AAW	OKBLS	10//99-12//99
Production Worker	Oregon	S	7.84 MW	9.07 AW	18870 AAW	ORBLS	10//99-12//99
Production Worker	Pennsylvania	S	8.9 MW	9.71 AW	20190 AAW	PABLS	10//99-12//99
Production Worker	Rhode Island	S	6.76 MW	7.40 AW	15400 AAW	RIBLS	10//99-12//99
Production Worker	South Carolina	S	8 MW	8.52 AW	17730 AAW	SCBLS	10//99-12//99
Production Worker	South Dakota	S	8.21 MW	9.29 AW	19320 AAW	SDBLS	10//99-12//99
Production Worker	Tennessee	S	7.8 MW	8.23 AW	17120 AAW	TNBLS	10//99-12//99
Production Worker	Texas	S	7.75 MW	8.10 AW	16860 AAW	TXBLS	10//99-12//99
Production Worker	Utah	S	10.17 MW	9.90 AW	20590 AAW	UTBLS	10//99-12//99
Production Worker	Vermont	S	8.78 MW	9.48 AW	19730 AAW	VTBLS	10//99-12//99
Production Worker	Virginia	S	8.84 MW	9.21 AW	19160 AAW	VABLS	10//99-12//99
Production Worker	Washington	S	8.63 MW	9.70 AW	20180 AAW	WABLS	10//99-12//99
Production Worker	West Virginia	S	13.69 MW	12.32 AW	25630 AAW	WVBLS	10//99-12//99
Production Worker	Wisconsin	S	9.68 MW	10.05 AW	20900 AAW	WIBLS	10//99-12//99
Production Worker	Wyoming	S	9.77 MW	9.79 AW	20370 AAW	WYBLS	10//99-12//99
Production Worker	Puerto Rico	S	6.46 MW	7.17 AW	14910 AAW	PRBLS	10//99-12//99
Production Worker	Virgin Islands	S	9.46 MW	9.36 AW	19460 AAW	VIBLS	10//99-12//99
Roofer	Alabama	S	7.48 MW	7.60 AW	15800 AAW	ALBLS	10//99-12//99
Roofer	Arizona	S	6.5 MW	6.67 AW	13870 AAW	AZBLS	10//99-12//99
Roofer	Arkansas	S	7.52 MW	7.53 AW	15650 AAW	ARBLS	10//99-12//99
Roofer	California	S	8.26 MW	8.72 AW	18130 AAW	CABLS	10//99-12//99
Roofer	Colorado	S	8.72 MW	8.54 AW	17770 AAW	COBLS	10//99-12//99
Roofer	Connecticut	S	8.6 MW	10.18 AW	21170 AAW	CTBLS	10//99-12//99
Roofer	Delaware	S	10.89 MW	10.71 AW	22270 AAW	DEBLS	10//99-12//99
Roofer	Florida	S	8.22 MW	8.51 AW	17710 AAW	FLBLS	10//99-12//99
Roofer	Georgia	S	8.43 MW	8.51 AW	17710 AAW	GABLS	10//99-12//99
Roofer	Idaho	S	8.17 MW	8.80 AW	18310 AAW	IDBLS	10//99-12//99
Roofer	Illinois	S	10.18 MW	10.65 AW	22160 AAW	ILBLS	10//99-12//99
Roofer	Indiana	S	7.94 MW	8.27 AW	17200 AAW	INBLS	10//99-12//99
Roofer	Iowa	S	9.75 MW	9.90 AW	20580 AAW	IABLS	10//99-12//99
Roofer	Kansas	S	7.83 MW	7.78 AW	16190 AAW	KSBLS	10//99-12//99
Roofer	Kentucky	S	9.35 MW	9.27 AW	19280 AAW	KYBLS	10//99-12//99
Roofer	Louisiana	S	7.89 MW	8.09 AW	16820 AAW	LABLS	10//99-12//99
Roofer	Maine	S	7.91 MW	7.96 AW	16550 AAW	MEBLS	10//99-12//99
Roofer	Maryland	S	9.27 MW	9.27 AW	19270 AAW	MDBLS	10//99-12//99
Roofer	Massachusetts	S	11.58 MW	11.37 AW	23640 AAW	MABLS	10//99-12//99
Roofer	Michigan	S	9.77 MW	10.30 AW	21420 AAW	MIBLS	10//99-12//99
Roofer	Minnesota	S	10.56 MW	11.19 AW	23270 AAW	MNBLS	10//99-12//99
Roofer	Mississippi	S	7.24 MW	7.71 AW	16030 AAW	MSBLS	10//99-12//99
Roofer	Missouri	S	8.32 MW	9.41 AW	19560 AAW	MOBLS	10//99-12//99
Roofer	Nebraska	S	9.28 MW	9.10 AW	18940 AAW	NEBLS	10//99-12//99
Roofer	Nevada	S	10.64 MW	10.28 AW	21380 AAW	NVBLS	10//99-12//99
Roofer	New Hampshire	S	9.62 MW	9.46 AW	19680 AAW	NHBLS	10//99-12//99
Roofer	New Jersey	S	10.45 MW	11.10 AW	23090 AAW	NJBLS	10//99-12//99
Roofer	New Mexico	S	8.21 MW	8.73 AW	18160 AAW	NMBLS	10//99-12//99
Roofer	New York	S	8.83 MW	8.72 AW	18150 AAW	NYBLS	10//99-12//99
Roofer	North Carolina	S	8.39 MW	8.25 AW	17170 AAW	NCBLS	10//99-12//99
Roofer	North Dakota	S	9.4 MW	9.21 AW	19160 AAW	NDBLS	10//99-12//99
Roofer	Ohio	S	8.77 MW	9.69 AW	20150 AAW	OHBLS	10//99-12//99
Roofer	Oklahoma	S	7.99 MW	8.55 AW	17790 AAW	OKBLS	10//99-12//99
Roofer	Oregon	S	8.84 MW	9.09 AW	18910 AAW	ORBLS	10//99-12//99
Roofer	Pennsylvania	S	9.63 MW	10.42 AW	21680 AAW	PABLS	10//99-12//99
Roofer	South Carolina	S	7.99 MW	8.08 AW	16800 AAW	SCBLS	10//99-12//99
Roofer	South Dakota	S	8.25 MW	8.11 AW	16880 AAW	SDBLS	10//99-12//99
Roofer	Tennessee	S	8.51 MW	8.81 AW	18330 AAW	TNBLS	10//99-12//99
Roofer	Texas	S	7.77 MW	7.88 AW	16400 AAW	TXBLS	10//99-12//99
Roofer	Virginia	S	7.95 MW	8.04 AW	16720 AAW	VABLS	10//99-12//99
Roofer	Washington	S	8.96 MW	9.50 AW	19770 AAW	WABLS	10//99-12//99
Roofer	West Virginia	S	7.76 MW	8.07 AW	16780 AAW	WVBLS	10//99-12//99
Roofer	Wisconsin	S	9.54 MW	9.46 AW	19680 AAW	WIBLS	10//99-12//99
Roofer	Wyoming	S	8.4 MW	8.60 AW	17890 AAW	WYBLS	10//99-12//99
Roofer	Puerto Rico	S	6.05 MW	7.17 AW	14910 AAW	PRBLS	10//99-12//99
Herdsman							
Swine, Agriculture	United States	Y	18000 APL	22463 AW	30000 APL	FAJO	1998
Highway Maintenance Worker	Alabama	S	10.14 MW	10.26 AW	21340 AAW	ALBLS	10//99-12//99
	Birmingham MSA, AL	S	11.28 MW	11.11 AW	23470 AAW	ALBLS	10//99-12//99
	Huntsville MSA, AL	S	11.24 MW	10.94 AW	23370 AAW	ALBLS	10//99-12//99
	Mobile MSA, AL	S	10.23 MW	10.07 AW	21290 AAW	ALBLS	10//99-12//99
	Alaska	S	20.03 MW	18.82 AW	39140 AAW	AKBLS	10//99-12//99

AAW	Average annual wage	AOH	Average offered, high	ASH	Average starting, high	H	Hourly	M	Monthly	S	Special: hourly and annual
AE	Average entry wage	AOL	Average offered, low	ASL	Average starting, low	HI	Highest wage paid	MTC	Median total compensation	TQ	Third quartile wage
AEX	Average experienced wage	APH	Average pay, high range	AW	Average wage paid	HR	High end range	MW	Median wage paid	W	Weekly
AO	Average offered	APL	Average pay, low range	FQ	First quartile wage	LR	Low end range	SQ	Second quartile wage	Y	Yearly

Occupation/Type/Industry	Location	Per	Low	Mid	High	Source	Date
Highway Maintenance Worker	Arizona	S	11.19 MW	11.55 AW	24030 AAW	AZBLS	10//99-12//99
	Flagstaff MSA, AZ-UT	S	10.89 MW	10.43 AW	22660 AAW	AZBLS	10//99-12//99
	Phoenix-Mesa MSA, AZ	S	12.67 MW	12.60 AW	26340 AAW	AZBLS	10//99-12//99
	Tucson MSA, AZ	S	11.48 MW	11.50 AW	23880 AAW	AZBLS	10//99-12//99
	Yuma MSA, AZ	S	10.66 MW	10.35 AW	22180 AAW	AZBLS	10//99-12//99
	Arkansas	S	9.59 MW	9.89 AW	20580 AAW	ARBLS	10//99-12//99
	Fayetteville-Springdale-Rogers MSA, AR	S	10.52 MW	10.13 AW	21880 AAW	ARBLS	10//99-12//99
	Fort Smith MSA, AR-OK	S	9.88 MW	9.59 AW	20550 AAW	ARBLS	10//99-12//99
	Jonesboro MSA, AR	S	10.86 MW	10.30 AW	22590 AAW	ARBLS	10//99-12//99
	Little Rock-North Little Rock MSA, AR	S	11.18 MW	10.63 AW	23260 AAW	ARBLS	10//99-12//99
	Pine Bluff MSA, AR	S	10.82 MW	10.20 AW	22510 AAW	ARBLS	10//99-12//99
	California	S	16.16 MW	16.53 AW	34390 AAW	CABLS	10//99-12//99
	Fresno MSA, CA	S	16.52 MW	16.10 AW	34370 AAW	CABLS	10//99-12//99
	Los Angeles-Long Beach PMSA, CA	S	16.71 MW	16.39 AW	34760 AAW	CABLS	10//99-12//99
	Merced MSA, CA	S	14.72 MW	15.14 AW	30610 AAW	CABLS	10//99-12//99
	Oakland PMSA, CA	S	18.18 MW	16.92 AW	37810 AAW	CABLS	10//99-12//99
	Orange County PMSA, CA	S	17.28 MW	17.41 AW	35950 AAW	CABLS	10//99-12//99
	Riverside-San Bernardino PMSA, CA	S	16.29 MW	15.96 AW	33880 AAW	CABLS	10//99-12//99
	Sacramento PMSA, CA	S	15.81 MW	16.09 AW	32880 AAW	CABLS	10//99-12//99
	San Diego MSA, CA	S	14.40 MW	14.66 AW	29950 AAW	CABLS	10//99-12//99
	San Francisco PMSA, CA	S	18.86 MW	18.90 AW	39220 AAW	CABLS	10//99-12//99
	San Jose PMSA, CA	S	17.26 MW	16.50 AW	35890 AAW	CABLS	10//99-12//99
	San Luis Obispo-Atascadero-Paso Robles MSA, CA	S	15.10 MW	15.16 AW	31410 AAW	CABLS	10//99-12//99
	Santa Barbara-Santa Maria-Lompoc MSA, CA	S	16.82 MW	16.54 AW	34990 AAW	CABLS	10//99-12//99
	Stockton-Lodi MSA, CA	S	14.74 MW	14.50 AW	30650 AAW	CABLS	10//99-12//99
	Vallejo-Fairfield-Napa PMSA, CA	S	19.49 MW	19.21 AW	40550 AAW	CABLS	10//99-12//99
	Ventura PMSA, CA	S	16.01 MW	15.61 AW	33300 AAW	CABLS	10//99-12//99
	Visalia-Tulare-Porterville MSA, CA	S	15.26 MW	15.15 AW	31750 AAW	CABLS	10//99-12//99
	Yolo PMSA, CA	S	17.53 MW	17.68 AW	36460 AAW	CABLS	10//99-12//99
	Colorado	S	14.63 MW	14.63 AW	30420 AAW	COBLS	10//99-12//99
	Boulder-Longmont PMSA, CO	S	16.38 MW	15.92 AW	34070 AAW	COBLS	10//99-12//99
	Colorado Springs MSA, CO	S	14.72 MW	13.95 AW	30620 AAW	COBLS	10//99-12//99
	Denver PMSA, CO	S	15.17 MW	15.06 AW	31550 AAW	COBLS	10//99-12//99
	Fort Collins-Loveland MSA, CO	S	13.97 MW	13.70 AW	29060 AAW	COBLS	10//99-12//99
	Connecticut	S	17.29 MW	17.12 AW	35620 AAW	CTBLS	10//99-12//99
	Danbury PMSA, CT	S	16.88 MW	16.76 AW	35120 AAW	CTBLS	10//99-12//99
	Hartford MSA, CT	S	16.91 MW	17.33 AW	35180 AAW	CTBLS	10//99-12//99
	New Haven-Meriden PMSA, CT	S	17.30 MW	17.25 AW	35970 AAW	CTBLS	10//99-12//99
	New London-Norwich MSA, CT-RI	S	16.75 MW	16.71 AW	34840 AAW	CTBLS	10//99-12//99
	Stamford-Norwalk PMSA, CT	S	18.65 MW	18.58 AW	38790 AAW	CTBLS	10//99-12//99
	Waterbury PMSA, CT	S	17.20 MW	17.66 AW	35770 AAW	CTBLS	10//99-12//99
	Delaware	S	12.62 MW	12.59 AW	26200 AAW	DEBLS	10//99-12//99
	Wilmington-Newark PMSA, DE-MD	S	13.12 MW	13.16 AW	27290 AAW	DEBLS	10//99-12//99
	Florida	S	9.38 MW	9.62 AW	20000 AAW	FLBLS	10//99-12//99
	Daytona Beach MSA, FL	S	8.52 MW	8.49 AW	17730 AAW	FLBLS	10//99-12//99
	Fort Lauderdale PMSA, FL	S	9.95 MW	10.03 AW	20690 AAW	FLBLS	10//99-12//99
	Jacksonville MSA, FL	S	8.69 MW	8.32 AW	18080 AAW	FLBLS	10//99-12//99
	Lakeland-Winter Haven MSA, FL	S	9.77 MW	9.47 AW	20320 AAW	FLBLS	10//99-12//99
	Melbourne-Titusville-Palm Bay MSA, FL	S	10.40 MW	10.83 AW	21630 AAW	FLBLS	10//99-12//99
	Miami PMSA, FL	S	10.98 MW	10.05 AW	22840 AAW	FLBLS	10//99-12//99
	Orlando MSA, FL	S	9.10 MW	8.73 AW	18930 AAW	FLBLS	10//99-12//99
	Tallahassee MSA, FL	S	7.06 MW	6.96 AW	14680 AAW	FLBLS	10//99-12//99
	Tampa-St. Petersburg-Clearwater MSA, FL	S	10.33 MW	9.42 AW	21480 AAW	FLBLS	10//99-12//99
	Georgia	S	8.9 MW	9.08 AW	18890 AAW	GABLS	10//99-12//99
	Atlanta MSA, GA	S	9.45 MW	9.10 AW	19650 AAW	GABLS	10//99-12//99
	Augusta-Aiken MSA, GA-SC	S	9.92 MW	9.73 AW	20640 AAW	GABLS	10//99-12//99
	Columbus MSA, GA-AL	S	9.41 MW	8.83 AW	19570 AAW	GABLS	10//99-12//99

AAW	Average annual wage	AOH	Average offered, high	ASH	Average starting, high	H	Hourly	M	Monthly	S	Special: hourly and annual
AE	Average entry wage	AOL	Average offered, low	ASL	Average starting, low	HI	Highest wage paid	MTC	Median total compensation	TQ	Third quartile wage
AEX	Average experienced wage	APH	Average pay, high range	AW	Average wage paid	HR	High end range	MW	Median wage paid	W	Weekly
AO	Average offered	APL	Average pay, low range	FQ	First quartile wage	LR	Low end range	SQ	Second quartile wage	Y	Yearly

Occupation/Type/Industry	Location	Per	Low	Mid	High	Source	Date
Highway Maintenance Worker	Macon MSA, GA	S	9.06 MW	9.35 AW	18840 AAW	GABLS	10//99-12//99
	Savannah MSA, GA	S	8.57 MW	8.71 AW	17830 AAW	GABLS	10//99-12//99
	Idaho	S	12.04 MW	12.54 AW	26070 AAW	IDBLS	10//99-12//99
	Boise City MSA, ID	S	11.90 MW	11.55 AW	24760 AAW	IDBLS	10//99-12//99
	Pocatello MSA, ID	S	13.62 MW	13.25 AW	28320 AAW	IDBLS	10//99-12//99
	Illinois	S	14.9 MW	14.30 AW	29750 AAW	ILBLS	10//99-12//99
	Champaign-Urbana MSA, IL	S	13.28 MW	14.55 AW	27630 AAW	ILBLS	10//99-12//99
	Kankakee PMSA, IL	S	11.05 MW	8.64 AW	22980 AAW	ILBLS	10//99-12//99
	Peoria-Pekin MSA, IL	S	10.46 MW	8.43 AW	21750 AAW	ILBLS	10//99-12//99
	Rockford MSA, IL	S	12.59 MW	13.17 AW	26190 AAW	ILBLS	10//99-12//99
	Indiana	S	10.86 MW	11.18 AW	23250 AAW	INBLS	10//99-12//99
	Elkhart-Goshen MSA, IN	S	10.67 MW	10.31 AW	22190 AAW	INBLS	10//99-12//99
	Evansville-Henderson MSA, IN-KY	S	11.01 MW	11.09 AW	22910 AAW	INBLS	10//99-12//99
	Fort Wayne MSA, IN	S	11.89 MW	11.64 AW	24730 AAW	INBLS	10//99-12//99
	Gary PMSA, IN	S	12.82 MW	12.69 AW	26670 AAW	INBLS	10//99-12//99
	Indianapolis MSA, IN	S	11.03 MW	11.06 AW	22950 AAW	INBLS	10//99-12//99
	Lafayette MSA, IN	S	10.25 MW	10.05 AW	21320 AAW	INBLS	10//99-12//99
	Iowa	S	12.71 MW	12.84 AW	26710 AAW	IABLS	10//99-12//99
	Davenport-Moline-Rock Island MSA, IA-IL	S	13.08 MW	13.87 AW	27210 AAW	IABLS	10//99-12//99
	Des Moines MSA, IA	S	13.40 MW	13.11 AW	27870 AAW	IABLS	10//99-12//99
	Sioux City MSA, IA-NE	S	11.61 MW	10.97 AW	24140 AAW	IABLS	10//99-12//99
	Kansas	S	10.26 MW	10.76 AW	22370 AAW	KSBLS	10//99-12//99
	Wichita MSA, KS	S	11.34 MW	10.74 AW	23580 AAW	KSBLS	10//99-12//99
	Kentucky	S	8.93 MW	9.32 AW	19380 AAW	KYBLS	10//99-12//99
	Lexington MSA, KY	S	9.49 MW	9.38 AW	19730 AAW	KYBLS	10//99-12//99
	Louisville MSA, KY-IN	S	10.83 MW	10.28 AW	22530 AAW	KYBLS	10//99-12//99
	Louisiana	S	8.72 MW	9.60 AW	19980 AAW	LABLS	10//99-12//99
	Baton Rouge MSA, LA	S	9.65 MW	8.51 AW	20070 AAW	LABLS	10//99-12//99
	Lafayette MSA, LA	S	8.21 MW	6.84 AW	17070 AAW	LABLS	10//99-12//99
	Lake Charles MSA, LA	S	12.10 MW	10.54 AW	25180 AAW	LABLS	10//99-12//99
	Monroe MSA, LA	S	8.36 MW	7.93 AW	17380 AAW	LABLS	10//99-12//99
	New Orleans MSA, LA	S	9.85 MW	8.61 AW	20490 AAW	LABLS	10//99-12//99
	Shreveport-Bossier City MSA, LA	S	9.80 MW	9.09 AW	20380 AAW	LABLS	10//99-12//99
	Maine	S	11.05 MW	10.60 AW	22040 AAW	MEBLS	10//99-12//99
	Bangor MSA, ME	S	11.72 MW	11.77 AW	24370 AAW	MEBLS	10//99-12//99
	Lewiston-Auburn MSA, ME	S	11.25 MW	11.34 AW	23410 AAW	MEBLS	10//99-12//99
	Portland MSA, ME	S	12.09 MW	12.11 AW	25140 AAW	MEBLS	10//99-12//99
	Maryland	S	11.65 MW	11.86 AW	24670 AAW	MDBLS	10//99-12//99
	Baltimore PMSA, MD	S	11.95 MW	11.76 AW	24850 AAW	MDBLS	10//99-12//99
	Massachusetts	S	15.39 MW	16.25 AW	33800 AAW	MABLS	10//99-12//99
	Barnstable-Yarmouth MSA, MA	S	14.98 MW	15.02 AW	31160 AAW	MABLS	10//99-12//99
	Boston PMSA, MA-NH	S	17.96 MW	16.68 AW	37350 AAW	MABLS	10//99-12//99
	Brockton PMSA, MA	S	15.37 MW	15.04 AW	31980 AAW	MABLS	10//99-12//99
	Fitchburg-Leominster PMSA, MA	S	15.82 MW	14.79 AW	32900 AAW	MABLS	10//99-12//99
	New Bedford PMSA, MA	S	12.97 MW	12.83 AW	26980 AAW	MABLS	10//99-12//99
	Pittsfield MSA, MA	S	14.32 MW	14.78 AW	29780 AAW	MABLS	10//99-12//99
	Springfield MSA, MA	S	14.79 MW	14.54 AW	30770 AAW	MABLS	10//99-12//99
	Worcester PMSA, MA-CT	S	15.67 MW	15.57 AW	32600 AAW	MABLS	10//99-12//99
	Michigan	S	15.28 MW	15.41 AW	32050 AAW	MIBLS	10//99-12//99
	Ann Arbor PMSA, MI	S	14.87 MW	15.15 AW	30930 AAW	MIBLS	10//99-12//99
	Benton Harbor MSA, MI	S	14.92 MW	14.97 AW	31030 AAW	MIBLS	10//99-12//99
	Detroit PMSA, MI	S	17.22 MW	17.64 AW	35820 AAW	MIBLS	10//99-12//99
	Grand Rapids-Muskegon-Holland MSA, MI	S	15.94 MW	16.21 AW	33150 AAW	MIBLS	10//99-12//99
	Kalamazoo-Battle Creek MSA, MI	S	13.26 MW	13.19 AW	27570 AAW	MIBLS	10//99-12//99
	Lansing-East Lansing MSA, MI	S	16.81 MW	16.66 AW	34970 AAW	MIBLS	10//99-12//99
	Saginaw-Bay City-Midland MSA, MI	S	15.11 MW	15.21 AW	31430 AAW	MIBLS	10//99-12//99
	Duluth-Superior MSA, MN-WI	S	14.56 MW	14.61 AW	30290 AAW	MNBLS	10//99-12//99
	St. Cloud MSA, MN	S	14.82 MW	14.77 AW	30830 AAW	MNBLS	10//99-12//99
	Mississippi	S	8.22 MW	8.47 AW	17630 AAW	MSBLS	10//99-12//99
	Biloxi-Gulfport-Pascagoula MSA, MS	S	8.66 MW	8.43 AW	18010 AAW	MSBLS	10//99-12//99
	Hattiesburg MSA, MS	S	7.27 MW	7.38 AW	15120 AAW	MSBLS	10//99-12//99
	Jackson MSA, MS	S	7.97 MW	7.71 AW	16580 AAW	MSBLS	10//99-12//99
	Missouri	S	11.14 MW	11.42 AW	23750 AAW	MOBLS	10//99-12//99

AAW Average annual wage	**AOH** Average offered, high	**ASH** Average starting, high	**H** Hourly	**M** Monthly	**S** Special: hourly and annual
AE Average entry wage	**AOL** Average offered, low	**ASL** Average starting, low	**HI** Highest wage paid	**MTC** Median total compensation	**TQ** Third quartile wage
AEX Average experienced wage	**APH** Average pay, high range	**AW** Average wage paid	**HR** High end range	**MW** Median wage paid	**W** Weekly
AO Average offered	**APL** Average pay, low range	**FQ** First quartile wage	**LR** Low end range	**SQ** Second quartile wage	**Y** Yearly

Occupation/Type/Industry	Location	Per	Low	Mid	High	Source	Date
Highway Maintenance Worker	St. Louis MSA, MO-IL	S	12.82 MW	13.05 AW	26670 AAW	MOBLS	10//99-12//99
	Montana	S	13.47 MW	13.46 AW	28000 AAW	MTBLS	10//99-12//99
	Missoula MSA, MT	S	13.55 MW	12.87 AW	28170 AAW	MTBLS	10//99-12//99
	Nebraska	S	10.58 MW	10.92 AW	22710 AAW	NEBLS	10//99-12//99
	Omaha MSA, NE-IA	S	13.84 MW	14.00 AW	28780 AAW	NEBLS	10//99-12//99
	Nevada	S	13.59 MW	13.82 AW	28750 AAW	NVBLS	10//99-12//99
	Las Vegas MSA, NV-AZ	S	12.54 MW	11.66 AW	26080 AAW	NVBLS	10//99-12//99
	Reno MSA, NV	S	13.94 MW	13.15 AW	28990 AAW	NVBLS	10//99-12//99
	New Hampshire	S	10.28 MW	10.83 AW	22520 AAW	NHBLS	10//99-12//99
	Manchester PMSA, NH	S	11.14 MW	10.29 AW	23170 AAW	NHBLS	10//99-12//99
	Nashua PMSA, NH	S	12.38 MW	11.66 AW	25750 AAW	NHBLS	10//99-12//99
	Portsmouth-Rochester PMSA, NH-ME	S	12.57 MW	11.87 AW	26150 AAW	NHBLS	10//99-12//99
	New Jersey	S	15.89 MW	16.44 AW	34200 AAW	NJBLS	10//99-12//99
	Atlantic-Cape May PMSA, NJ	S	15.76 MW	14.68 AW	32770 AAW	NJBLS	10//99-12//99
	Bergen-Passaic PMSA, NJ	S	17.60 MW	17.60 AW	36610 AAW	NJBLS	10//99-12//99
	Jersey City PMSA, NJ	S	14.48 MW	14.17 AW	30120 AAW	NJBLS	10//99-12//99
	Middlesex-Somerset-Hunterdon PMSA, NJ	S	17.30 MW	16.82 AW	35990 AAW	NJBLS	10//99-12//99
	Monmouth-Ocean PMSA, NJ	S	14.84 MW	14.63 AW	30870 AAW	NJBLS	10//99-12//99
	Newark PMSA, NJ	S	17.62 MW	17.33 AW	36650 AAW	NJBLS	10//99-12//99
	Trenton PMSA, NJ	S	14.12 MW	14.19 AW	29360 AAW	NJBLS	10//99-12//99
	Vineland-Millville-Bridgeton PMSA, NJ	S	15.49 MW	15.05 AW	32210 AAW	NJBLS	10//99-12//99
	New Mexico	S	10.11 MW	10.16 AW	21130 AAW	NMBLS	10//99-12//99
	New York	S	13.64 MW	14.55 AW	30270 AAW	NYBLS	10//99-12//99
	Albany-Schenectady-Troy MSA, NY	S	13.19 MW	12.85 AW	27440 AAW	NYBLS	10//99-12//99
	Binghamton MSA, NY	S	11.81 MW	12.01 AW	24560 AAW	NYBLS	10//99-12//99
	Buffalo-Niagara Falls MSA, NY	S	14.39 MW	14.46 AW	29940 AAW	NYBLS	10//99-12//99
	Dutchess County PMSA, NY	S	14.13 MW	14.55 AW	29400 AAW	NYBLS	10//99-12//99
	Elmira MSA, NY	S	14.21 MW	14.20 AW	29560 AAW	NYBLS	10//99-12//99
	Glens Falls MSA, NY	S	11.63 MW	11.67 AW	24180 AAW	NYBLS	10//99-12//99
	Jamestown MSA, NY	S	13.73 MW	14.66 AW	28560 AAW	NYBLS	10//99-12//99
	Nassau-Suffolk PMSA, NY	S	15.02 MW	14.41 AW	31230 AAW	NYBLS	10//99-12//99
	Newburgh PMSA, NY-PA	S	15.05 MW	15.25 AW	31300 AAW	NYBLS	10//99-12//99
	Rochester MSA, NY	S	15.32 MW	15.08 AW	31870 AAW	NYBLS	10//99-12//99
	Syracuse MSA, NY	S	13.67 MW	13.98 AW	28440 AAW	NYBLS	10//99-12//99
	Utica-Rome MSA, NY	S	11.96 MW	12.13 AW	24890 AAW	NYBLS	10//99-12//99
	North Carolina	S	9.36 MW	9.80 AW	20390 AAW	NCBLS	10//99-12//99
	Charlotte-Gastonia-Rock Hill MSA, NC-SC	S	10.27 MW	9.88 AW	21370 AAW	NCBLS	10//99-12//99
	Greensboro--Winston-Salem--High Point MSA, NC	S	10.71 MW	9.86 AW	22270 AAW	NCBLS	10//99-12//99
	Raleigh-Durham-Chapel Hill MSA, NC	S	11.02 MW	10.80 AW	22930 AAW	NCBLS	10//99-12//99
	Wilmington MSA, NC	S	10.63 MW	11.00 AW	22100 AAW	NCBLS	10//99-12//99
	North Dakota	S	11.11 MW	11.47 AW	23850 AAW	NDBLS	10//99-12//99
	Bismarck MSA, ND	S	12.88 MW	12.92 AW	26800 AAW	NDBLS	10//99-12//99
	Grand Forks MSA, ND-MN	S	13.27 MW	13.26 AW	27610 AAW	NDBLS	10//99-12//99
	Ohio	S	14.27 MW	13.87 AW	28840 AAW	OHBLS	10//99-12//99
	Akron PMSA, OH	S	13.58 MW	13.66 AW	28240 AAW	OHBLS	10//99-12//99
	Canton-Massillon MSA, OH	S	13.83 MW	14.60 AW	28770 AAW	OHBLS	10//99-12//99
	Cincinnati PMSA, OH-KY-IN	S	13.48 MW	13.83 AW	28040 AAW	OHBLS	10//99-12//99
	Cleveland-Lorain-Elyria PMSA, OH	S	15.28 MW	14.98 AW	31790 AAW	OHBLS	10//99-12//99
	Columbus MSA, OH	S	14.23 MW	14.69 AW	29590 AAW	OHBLS	10//99-12//99
	Dayton-Springfield MSA, OH	S	14.61 MW	14.81 AW	30400 AAW	OHBLS	10//99-12//99
	Hamilton-Middletown PMSA, OH	S	16.75 MW	17.50 AW	34840 AAW	OHBLS	10//99-12//99
	Steubenville-Weirton MSA, OH-WV	S	9.37 MW	9.62 AW	19490 AAW	OHBLS	10//99-12//99
	Toledo MSA, OH	S	15.22 MW	15.48 AW	31650 AAW	OHBLS	10//99-12//99
	Youngstown-Warren MSA, OH	S	15.95 MW	15.89 AW	33180 AAW	OHBLS	10//99-12//99
	Oklahoma	S	9.29 MW	9.21 AW	19150 AAW	OKBLS	10//99-12//99
	Oklahoma City MSA, OK	S	11.12 MW	10.24 AW	23120 AAW	OKBLS	10//99-12//99
	Tulsa MSA, OK	S	9.22 MW	9.36 AW	19180 AAW	OKBLS	10//99-12//99
	Oregon	S	15.14 MW	15.16 AW	31530 AAW	ORBLS	10//99-12//99
	Eugene-Springfield MSA, OR	S	16.20 MW	15.44 AW	33690 AAW	ORBLS	10//99-12//99
	Medford-Ashland MSA, OR	S	12.32 MW	12.54 AW	25620 AAW	ORBLS	10//99-12//99

AAW Average annual wage	AOH Average offered, high	ASH Average starting, high	H Hourly	M Monthly	S Special: hourly and annual
AE Average entry wage	AOL Average offered, low	ASL Average starting, low	HI Highest wage paid	MTC Median total compensation	TQ Third quartile wage
AEX Average experienced wage	APH Average pay, high range	AW Average wage paid	HR High end range	MW Median wage paid	W Weekly
AO Average offered	APL Average pay, low range	FQ First quartile wage	LR Low end range	SQ Second quartile wage	Y Yearly

Occupation/Type/Industry	Location	Per	Low	Mid	High	Source	Date
Highway Maintenance Worker	Portland-Vancouver PMSA,						
	OR-WA	S	16.22 MW	16.21 AW	33750 AAW	ORBLS	10//99-12//99
	Salem PMSA, OR	S	15.54 MW	15.65 AW	32320 AAW	ORBLS	10//99-12//99
	Pennsylvania	S	12.5 MW	12.96 AW	26950 AAW	PABLS	10//99-12//99
	Allentown-Bethlehem-Easton						
	MSA, PA	S	12.91 MW	13.08 AW	26840 AAW	PABLS	10//99-12//99
	Erie MSA, PA	S	13.19 MW	12.10 AW	27440 AAW	PABLS	10//99-12//99
	Harrisburg-Lebanon-Carlisle						
	MSA, PA	S	14.17 MW	13.78 AW	29480 AAW	PABLS	10//99-12//99
	Johnstown MSA, PA	S	10.60 MW	10.02 AW	22040 AAW	PABLS	10//99-12//99
	Lancaster MSA, PA	S	13.84 MW	13.62 AW	28790 AAW	PABLS	10//99-12//99
	Philadelphia PMSA, PA-NJ	S	15.46 MW	15.37 AW	32150 AAW	PABLS	10//99-12//99
	Pittsburgh MSA, PA	S	12.76 MW	12.74 AW	26540 AAW	PABLS	10//99-12//99
	Reading MSA, PA	S	14.04 MW	13.52 AW	29210 AAW	PABLS	10//99-12//99
	Scranton--Wilkes-Barre--						
	Hazleton MSA, PA	S	12.45 MW	11.87 AW	25900 AAW	PABLS	10//99-12//99
	Sharon MSA, PA	S	11.34 MW	10.48 AW	23600 AAW	PABLS	10//99-12//99
	State College MSA, PA	S	12.88 MW	11.19 AW	26780 AAW	PABLS	10//99-12//99
	Williamsport MSA, PA	S	13.39 MW	12.94 AW	27850 AAW	PABLS	10//99-12//99
	York MSA, PA	S	13.40 MW	13.08 AW	27880 AAW	PABLS	10//99-12//99
	Rhode Island	S	14.3 MW	14.02 AW	29160 AAW	RIBLS	10//99-12//99
	Providence-Fall River-						
	Warwick MSA, RI-MA	S	14.98 MW	15.26 AW	31150 AAW	RIBLS	10//99-12//99
	South Carolina	S	9.73 MW	10.73 AW	22330 AAW	SCBLS	10//99-12//99
	Columbia MSA, SC	S	9.85 MW	9.48 AW	20490 AAW	SCBLS	10//99-12//99
	Greenville-Spartanburg-						
	Anderson MSA, SC	S	10.62 MW	10.17 AW	22090 AAW	SCBLS	10//99-12//99
	South Dakota	S	10.34 MW	10.43 AW	21700 AAW	SDBLS	10//99-12//99
	Rapid City MSA, SD	S	11.03 MW	10.36 AW	22950 AAW	SDBLS	10//99-12//99
	Sioux Falls MSA, SD	S	10.40 MW	10.15 AW	21630 AAW	SDBLS	10//99-12//99
	Tennessee	S	9.18 MW	9.36 AW	19460 AAW	TNBLS	10//99-12//99
	Chattanooga MSA, TN-GA	S	8.85 MW	8.38 AW	18410 AAW	TNBLS	10//99-12//99
	Clarksville-Hopkinsville MSA,						
	TN-KY	S	8.20 MW	8.04 AW	17060 AAW	TNBLS	10//99-12//99
	Jackson MSA, TN	S	10.52 MW	10.95 AW	21880 AAW	TNBLS	10//99-12//99
	Johnson City-Kingsport-Bristol						
	MSA, TN-VA	S	10.56 MW	9.99 AW	21970 AAW	TNBLS	10//99-12//99
	Knoxville MSA, TN	S	9.21 MW	8.75 AW	19150 AAW	TNBLS	10//99-12//99
	Memphis MSA, TN-AR-MS	S	10.93 MW	11.34 AW	22740 AAW	MSBLS	10//99-12//99
	Nashville MSA, TN	S	10.91 MW	10.08 AW	22690 AAW	TNBLS	10//99-12//99
	Texas	S	10.53 MW	11.08 AW	23050 AAW	TXBLS	10//99-12//99
	Abilene MSA, TX	S	17.38 MW	18.29 AW	36150 AAW	TXBLS	10//99-12//99
	Amarillo MSA, TX	S	11.33 MW	10.64 AW	23570 AAW	TXBLS	10//99-12//99
	Austin-San Marcos MSA, TX	S	11.54 MW	10.52 AW	24000 AAW	TXBLS	10//99-12//99
	Beaumont-Port Arthur MSA,						
	TX	S	13.70 MW	14.27 AW	28500 AAW	TXBLS	10//99-12//99
	Brazoria PMSA, TX	S	9.18 MW	8.37 AW	19100 AAW	TXBLS	10//99-12//99
	Brownsville-Harlingen-San						
	Benito MSA, TX	S	7.92 MW	7.31 AW	16470 AAW	TXBLS	10//99-12//99
	Corpus Christi MSA, TX	S	8.79 MW	7.84 AW	18280 AAW	TXBLS	10//99-12//99
	El Paso MSA, TX	S	8.23 MW	7.91 AW	17110 AAW	TXBLS	10//99-12//99
	Fort Worth-Arlington PMSA,						
	TX	S	11.08 MW	10.70 AW	23050 AAW	TXBLS	10//99-12//99
	Houston PMSA, TX	S	10.74 MW	10.58 AW	22350 AAW	TXBLS	10//99-12//99
	Killeen-Temple MSA, TX	S	10.26 MW	9.03 AW	21340 AAW	TXBLS	10//99-12//99
	Longview-Marshall MSA, TX	S	13.17 MW	14.05 AW	27400 AAW	TXBLS	10//99-12//99
	Lubbock MSA, TX	S	14.12 MW	13.67 AW	29360 AAW	TXBLS	10//99-12//99
	McAllen-Edinburg-Mission						
	MSA, TX	S	8.56 MW	7.68 AW	17800 AAW	TXBLS	10//99-12//99
	Odessa-Midland MSA, TX	S	11.05 MW	9.58 AW	22980 AAW	TXBLS	10//99-12//99
	San Antonio MSA, TX	S	10.13 MW	9.90 AW	21080 AAW	TXBLS	10//99-12//99
	Texarkana MSA, TX-						
	Texarkana, AR	S	9.61 MW	9.17 AW	19990 AAW	TXBLS	10//99-12//99
	Waco MSA, TX	S	9.44 MW	8.51 AW	19640 AAW	TXBLS	10//99-12//99
	Wichita Falls MSA, TX	S	11.86 MW	11.18 AW	24660 AAW	TXBLS	10//99-12//99
	Utah	S	11.9 MW	12.28 AW	25550 AAW	UTBLS	10//99-12//99
	Provo-Orem MSA, UT	S	11.85 MW	11.25 AW	24640 AAW	UTBLS	10//99-12//99
	Salt Lake City-Ogden MSA,						
	UT	S	12.15 MW	11.54 AW	25270 AAW	UTBLS	10//99-12//99
	Vermont	S	11.96 MW	12.39 AW	25770 AAW	VTBLS	10//99-12//99
	Burlington MSA, VT	S	14.81 MW	14.70 AW	30810 AAW	VTBLS	10//99-12//99
	Virginia	S	12.75 MW	12.56 AW	26120 AAW	VABLS	10//99-12//99

AAW Average annual wage	**AOH** Average offered, high	**ASH** Average starting, high	**H** Hourly	**M** Monthly	**S** Special: hourly and annual
AE Average entry wage	**AOL** Average offered, low	**ASL** Average starting, low	**HI** Highest wage paid	**MTC** Median total compensation	**TQ** Third quartile wage
AEX Average experienced wage	**APH** Average pay, high range	**AW** Average wage paid	**HR** High end range	**MW** Median wage paid	**W** Weekly
AO Average offered	**APL** Average pay, low range	**FQ** First quartile wage	**LR** Low end range	**SQ** Second quartile wage	**Y** Yearly

Occupation/Type/Industry	Location	Per	Low	Mid	High	Source	Date
Highway Maintenance Worker	Washington	S	16.31 MW	16.65 AW	34630 AAW	WABLS	10//99-12//99
	Bellingham MSA, WA	S	14.42 MW	14.66 AW	29990 AAW	WABLS	10//99-12//99
	Bremerton PMSA, WA	S	17.29 MW	17.44 AW	35960 AAW	WABLS	10//99-12//99
	Olympia PMSA, WA	S	15.45 MW	14.31 AW	32140 AAW	WABLS	10//99-12//99
	Richland-Kennewick-Pasco MSA, WA	S	16.31 MW	16.45 AW	33920 AAW	WABLS	10//99-12//99
	Seattle-Bellevue-Everett PMSA, WA	S	18.36 MW	18.35 AW	38200 AAW	WABLS	10//99-12//99
	Spokane MSA, WA	S	16.74 MW	16.61 AW	34810 AAW	WABLS	10//99-12//99
	Tacoma PMSA, WA	S	17.88 MW	17.66 AW	37190 AAW	WABLS	10//99-12//99
	Yakima MSA, WA	S	15.91 MW	15.72 AW	33090 AAW	WABLS	10//99-12//99
	Huntington-Ashland MSA, WV-KY-OH	S	9.79 MW	9.77 AW	20370 AAW	WVBLS	10//99-12//99
	Wisconsin	S	13.82 MW	12.93 AW	26890 AAW	WIBLS	10//99-12//99
	Appleton-Oshkosh-Neenah MSA, WI	S	13.14 MW	14.06 AW	27320 AAW	WIBLS	10//99-12//99
	Eau Claire MSA, WI	S	13.49 MW	14.33 AW	28050 AAW	WIBLS	10//99-12//99
	Kenosha PMSA, WI	S	15.74 MW	16.48 AW	32740 AAW	WIBLS	10//99-12//99
	La Crosse MSA, WI-MN	S	13.25 MW	14.06 AW	27560 AAW	WIBLS	10//99-12//99
	Madison MSA, WI	S	13.67 MW	14.46 AW	28430 AAW	WIBLS	10//99-12//99
	Milwaukee-Waukesha PMSA, WI	S	17.74 MW	17.96 AW	36900 AAW	WIBLS	10//99-12//99
	Wausau MSA, WI	S	15.04 MW	15.27 AW	31280 AAW	WIBLS	10//99-12//99
	Wyoming	S	12.5 MW	12.81 AW	26650 AAW	WYBLS	10//99-12//99
	Puerto Rico	S	6.58 MW	9.17 AW	19060 AAW	PRBLS	10//99-12//99
	Ponce MSA, PR	S	6.60 MW	5.99 AW	13720 AAW	PRBLS	10//99-12//99
	San Juan-Bayamon PMSA, PR	S	11.45 MW	11.79 AW	23820 AAW	PRBLS	10//99-12//99
Histologic Technician							
Medical Laboratory	Atlantic	H	10.70 AE	13.50 AW	15.20 APH	LABMED2	1998
Medical Laboratory	East North Central	H	10.80 AE	13.00 AW	15.60 APH	LABMED2	1998
Medical Laboratory	Far West	H	12.00 AE	15.00 AW	16.40 APH	LABMED2	1998
Medical Laboratory	Northeast	H	11.30 AE	14.90 AW	16.10 APH	LABMED2	1998
Medical Laboratory	West North Central	H	10.10 AE	12.90 AW	14.60 APH	LABMED2	1998
Medical Laboratory	West South Central	H	10.80 AE	13.00 AW	16.00 APH	LABMED2	1998
Historian	Alabama	S	21.79 MW	24.61 AW	51180 AAW	ALBLS	10//99-12//99
	Arkansas	S	18.12 MW	17.35 AW	36100 AAW	ARBLS	10//99-12//99
	California	S	25.61 MW	25.78 AW	53610 AAW	CABLS	10//99-12//99
	Colorado	S	15.95 MW	19.41 AW	40370 AAW	COBLS	10//99-12//99
	Maryland	S	22.35 MW	20.94 AW	43550 AAW	MDBLS	10//99-12//99
	Montana	S	15.4 MW	15.61 AW	32470 AAW	MTBLS	10//99-12//99
	Pennsylvania	S	15.62 MW	16.82 AW	34980 AAW	PABLS	10//99-12//99
	Philadelphia PMSA, PA-NJ	S	16.48 MW	15.44 AW	34280 AAW	PABLS	10//99-12//99
	Texas	S	15.37 MW	16.78 AW	34900 AAW	TXBLS	10//99-12//99
	Houston PMSA, TX	S	16.57 MW	15.30 AW	34460 AAW	TXBLS	10//99-12//99
	Virginia	S	20.99 MW	23.52 AW	48910 AAW	VABLS	10//99-12//99
	Richmond-Petersburg MSA, VA	S	18.32 MW	18.19 AW	38100 AAW	VABLS	10//99-12//99
	Washington	S	21.32 MW	25.32 AW	52670 AAW	WABLS	10//99-12//99
History Teacher							
Postsecondary	Alabama	Y		36880 AAW		ALBLS	10//99-12//99
Postsecondary	Birmingham MSA, AL	Y		33940 AAW		ALBLS	10//99-12//99
Postsecondary	Montgomery MSA, AL	Y		33080 AAW		ALBLS	10//99-12//99
Postsecondary	Arizona	Y		37850 AAW		AZBLS	10//99-12//99
Postsecondary	Phoenix-Mesa MSA, AZ	Y		35400 AAW		AZBLS	10//99-12//99
Postsecondary	Arkansas	Y		44020 AAW		ARBLS	10//99-12//99
Postsecondary	California	Y		54930 AAW		CABLS	10//99-12//99
Postsecondary	Fresno MSA, CA	Y		53760 AAW		CABLS	10//99-12//99
Postsecondary	Los Angeles-Long Beach PMSA, CA	Y		54180 AAW		CABLS	10//99-12//99
Postsecondary	Riverside-San Bernardino PMSA, CA	Y		54620 AAW		CABLS	10//99-12//99
Postsecondary	San Diego MSA, CA	Y		55190 AAW		CABLS	10//99-12//99
Postsecondary	San Francisco PMSA, CA	Y		63790 AAW		CABLS	10//99-12//99
Postsecondary	Colorado	Y		50490 AAW		COBLS	10//99-12//99
Postsecondary	Colorado Springs MSA, CO	Y		59210 AAW		COBLS	10//99-12//99
Postsecondary	Denver PMSA, CO	Y		49500 AAW		COBLS	10//99-12//99
Postsecondary	Connecticut	Y		62820 AAW		CTBLS	10//99-12//99
Postsecondary	Hartford MSA, CT	Y		67570 AAW		CTBLS	10//99-12//99
Postsecondary	District of Columbia	Y		49860 AAW		DCBLS	10//99-12//99

AAW Average annual wage	**AOH** Average offered, high	**ASH** Average starting, high	**H** Hourly	**M** Monthly	**S** Special: hourly and annual
AE Average entry wage	**AOL** Average offered, low	**ASL** Average starting, low	**HI** Highest wage paid	**MTC** Median total compensation	**TQ** Third quartile wage
AEX Average experienced wage	**APH** Average pay, high range	**AW** Average wage paid	**HR** High end range	**MW** Median wage paid	**W** Weekly
AO Average offered	**APL** Average pay, low range	**FQ** First quartile wage	**LR** Low end range	**SQ** Second quartile wage	**Y** Yearly

Occupation/Type/Industry	Location	Per	Low	Mid	High	Source	Date
History Teacher							
Postsecondary	Washington PMSA, DC-MD-VA-WV	Y		52820 AAW		DCBLS	10//99-12//99
Postsecondary	Florida	Y		61330 AAW		FLBLS	10//99-12//99
Postsecondary	Miami PMSA, FL	Y		67470 AAW		FLBLS	10//99-12//99
Postsecondary	Orlando MSA, FL	Y		65990 AAW		FLBLS	10//99-12//99
Postsecondary	Tampa-St. Petersburg-Clearwater MSA, FL	Y		59170 AAW		FLBLS	10//99-12//99
Postsecondary	West Palm Beach-Boca Raton MSA, FL	Y		62170 AAW		FLBLS	10//99-12//99
Postsecondary	Georgia	Y		45060 AAW		GABLS	10//99-12//99
Postsecondary	Atlanta MSA, GA	Y		48260 AAW		GABLS	10//99-12//99
Postsecondary	Savannah MSA, GA	Y		45120 AAW		GABLS	10//99-12//99
Postsecondary	Idaho	Y		42840 AAW		IDBLS	10//99-12//99
Postsecondary	Illinois	Y		56660 AAW		ILBLS	10//99-12//99
Postsecondary	Chicago PMSA, IL	Y		56840 AAW		ILBLS	10//99-12//99
Postsecondary	Indiana	Y		46040 AAW		INBLS	10//99-12//99
Postsecondary	Fort Wayne MSA, IN	Y		48450 AAW		INBLS	10//99-12//99
Postsecondary	Iowa	Y		49400 AAW		IABLS	10//99-12//99
Postsecondary	Des Moines MSA, IA	Y		47630 AAW		IABLS	10//99-12//99
Postsecondary	Kansas	Y		35960 AAW		KSBLS	10//99-12//99
Postsecondary	Kentucky	Y		44200 AAW		KYBLS	10//99-12//99
Postsecondary	Louisiana	Y		48240 AAW		LABLS	10//99-12//99
Postsecondary	Maryland	Y		51820 AAW		MDBLS	10//99-12//99
Postsecondary	Baltimore PMSA, MD	Y		50700 AAW		MDBLS	10//99-12//99
Postsecondary	Massachusetts	Y		54470 AAW		MABLS	10//99-12//99
Postsecondary	Boston PMSA, MA-NH	Y		51110 AAW		MABLS	10//99-12//99
Postsecondary	Brockton PMSA, MA	Y		46040 AAW		MABLS	10//99-12//99
Postsecondary	Springfield MSA, MA	Y		65790 AAW		MABLS	10//99-12//99
Postsecondary	Michigan	Y		52240 AAW		MIBLS	10//99-12//99
Postsecondary	Detroit PMSA, MI	Y		50990 AAW		MIBLS	10//99-12//99
Postsecondary	Kalamazoo-Battle Creek MSA, MI	Y		56180 AAW		MIBLS	10//99-12//99
Postsecondary	Minnesota	Y		55690 AAW		MNBLS	10//99-12//99
Postsecondary	Minneapolis-St. Paul MSA, MN-WI	Y		60610 AAW		MNBLS	10//99-12//99
Postsecondary	St. Cloud MSA, MN	Y		51160 AAW		MNBLS	10//99-12//99
Postsecondary	Mississippi	Y		43440 AAW		MSBLS	10//99-12//99
Postsecondary	Jackson MSA, MS	Y		35250 AAW		MSBLS	10//99-12//99
Postsecondary	Missouri	Y		41310 AAW		MOBLS	10//99-12//99
Postsecondary	Montana	Y		55870 AAW		MTBLS	10//99-12//99
Postsecondary	Omaha MSA, NE-IA	Y		44940 AAW		NEBLS	10//99-12//99
Postsecondary	Nevada	Y		47280 AAW		NVBLS	10//99-12//99
Postsecondary	New Jersey	Y		56550 AAW		NJBLS	10//99-12//99
Postsecondary	Jersey City PMSA, NJ	Y		52930 AAW		NJBLS	10//99-12//99
Postsecondary	Newark PMSA, NJ	Y		56920 AAW		NJBLS	10//99-12//99
Postsecondary	New Mexico	Y		47540 AAW		NMBLS	10//99-12//99
Postsecondary	New York	Y		55590 AAW		NYBLS	10//99-12//99
Postsecondary	Albany-Schenectady-Troy MSA, NY	Y		55660 AAW		NYBLS	10//99-12//99
Postsecondary	New York PMSA, NY	Y		58280 AAW		NYBLS	10//99-12//99
Postsecondary	North Carolina	Y		43740 AAW		NCBLS	10//99-12//99
Postsecondary	Charlotte-Gastonia-Rock Hill MSA, NC-SC	Y		48320 AAW		NCBLS	10//99-12//99
Postsecondary	Greensboro--Winston-Salem--High Point MSA, NC	Y		44750 AAW		NCBLS	10//99-12//99
Postsecondary	Raleigh-Durham-Chapel Hill MSA, NC	Y		41950 AAW		NCBLS	10//99-12//99
Postsecondary	Wilmington MSA, NC	Y		48840 AAW		NCBLS	10//99-12//99
Postsecondary	North Dakota	Y		43280 AAW		NDBLS	10//99-12//99
Postsecondary	Ohio	Y		43730 AAW		OHBLS	10//99-12//99
Postsecondary	Canton-Massillon MSA, OH	Y		42260 AAW		OHBLS	10//99-12//99
Postsecondary	Cincinnati PMSA, OH-KY-IN	Y		42010 AAW		OHBLS	10//99-12//99
Postsecondary	Cleveland-Lorain-Elyria PMSA, OH	Y		44410 AAW		OHBLS	10//99-12//99
Postsecondary	Columbus MSA, OH	Y		42810 AAW		OHBLS	10//99-12//99
Postsecondary	Dayton-Springfield MSA, OH	Y		38350 AAW		OHBLS	10//99-12//99
Postsecondary	Oklahoma	Y		46910 AAW		OKBLS	10//99-12//99
Postsecondary	Oklahoma City MSA, OK	Y		47820 AAW		OKBLS	10//99-12//99
Postsecondary	Oregon	Y		49070 AAW		ORBLS	10//99-12//99
Postsecondary	Portland-Vancouver PMSA, OR-WA	Y		46900 AAW		ORBLS	10//99-12//99

AAW	Average annual wage	AOH	Average offered, high	ASH	Average starting, high	H	Hourly	M	Monthly	S	Special: hourly and annual
AE	Average entry wage	AOL	Average offered, low	ASL	Average starting, low	HI	Highest wage paid	MTC	Median total compensation	TQ	Third quartile wage
AEX	Average experienced wage	APH	Average pay, high range	AW	Average wage paid	HR	High end range	MW	Median wage paid	W	Weekly
AO	Average offered	APL	Average pay, low range	FQ	First quartile wage	LR	Low end range	SQ	Second quartile wage	Y	Yearly

Occupation/Type/Industry	Location	Per	Low	Mid	High	Source	Date
History Teacher							
Postsecondary	Pennsylvania	Y		58830 AAW		PABLS	10//99-12//99
Postsecondary	Allentown-Bethlehem-Easton MSA, PA	Y		53610 AAW		PABLS	10//99-12//99
Postsecondary	Philadelphia PMSA, PA-NJ	Y		64670 AAW		PABLS	10//99-12//99
Postsecondary	Pittsburgh MSA, PA	Y		53650 AAW		PABLS	10//99-12//99
Postsecondary	Reading MSA, PA	Y		55780 AAW		PABLS	10//99-12//99
Postsecondary	Scranton--Wilkes-Barre--Hazleton MSA, PA	Y		50650 AAW		PABLS	10//99-12//99
Postsecondary	Rhode Island	Y		76510 AAW		RIBLS	10//99-12//99
Postsecondary	Providence-Fall River-Warwick MSA, RI-MA	Y		76990 AAW		RIBLS	10//99-12//99
Postsecondary	South Carolina	Y		45310 AAW		SCBLS	10//99-12//99
Postsecondary	Greenville-Spartanburg-Anderson MSA, SC	Y		45750 AAW		SCBLS	10//99-12//99
Postsecondary	South Dakota	Y		40000 AAW		SDBLS	10//99-12//99
Postsecondary	Tennessee	Y		46300 AAW		TNBLS	10//99-12//99
Postsecondary	Johnson City-Kingsport-Bristol MSA, TN-VA	Y		43580 AAW		TNBLS	10//99-12//99
Postsecondary	Memphis MSA, TN-AR-MS	Y		48580 AAW		MSBLS	10//99-12//99
Postsecondary	Nashville MSA, TN	Y		50490 AAW		TNBLS	10//99-12//99
Postsecondary	Texas	Y		46500 AAW		TXBLS	10//99-12//99
Postsecondary	Dallas PMSA, TX	Y		52360 AAW		TXBLS	10//99-12//99
Postsecondary	El Paso MSA, TX	Y		39910 AAW		TXBLS	10//99-12//99
Postsecondary	Houston PMSA, TX	Y		52360 AAW		TXBLS	10//99-12//99
Postsecondary	Killeen-Temple MSA, TX	Y		49570 AAW		TXBLS	10//99-12//99
Postsecondary	Odessa-Midland MSA, TX	Y		44800 AAW		TXBLS	10//99-12//99
Postsecondary	San Antonio MSA, TX	Y		59130 AAW		TXBLS	10//99-12//99
Postsecondary	Vermont	Y		50910 AAW		VTBLS	10//99-12//99
Postsecondary	Virginia	Y		52030 AAW		VABLS	10//99-12//99
Postsecondary	Norfolk-Virginia Beach-Newport News MSA, VA-NC	Y		52820 AAW		VABLS	10//99-12//99
Postsecondary	Richmond-Petersburg MSA, VA	Y		54340 AAW		VABLS	10//99-12//99
Postsecondary	Washington	Y		44830 AAW		WABLS	10//99-12//99
Postsecondary	Seattle-Bellevue-Everett PMSA, WA	Y		49610 AAW		WABLS	10//99-12//99
Postsecondary	Tacoma PMSA, WA	Y		46960 AAW		WABLS	10//99-12//99
Postsecondary	West Virginia	Y		53740 AAW		WVBLS	10//99-12//99
Postsecondary	Milwaukee-Waukesha PMSA, WI	Y		36780 AAW		WIBLS	10//99-12//99
Postsecondary	Wyoming	Y		47240 AAW		WYBLS	10//99-12//99
Postsecondary	Puerto Rico	Y		33430 AAW		PRBLS	10//99-12//99
Postsecondary	San Juan-Bayamon PMSA, PR	Y		35360 AAW		PRBLS	10//99-12//99
Hockey Player							
Professional	United States	Y	150000 APL	1194206 AW	10359852 APH	SPORTS	1999
Hoist and Winch Operator	Alabama	S	11.46 MW	12.29 AW	25570 AAW	ALBLS	10//99-12//99
	Birmingham MSA, AL	S	15.90 MW	16.80 AW	33070 AAW	ALBLS	10//99-12//99
	Arizona	S	13.72 MW	14.23 AW	29600 AAW	AZBLS	10//99-12//99
	Phoenix-Mesa MSA, AZ	S	13.91 MW	14.22 AW	28940 AAW	AZBLS	10//99-12//99
	Arkansas	S	10.15 MW	10.32 AW	21460 AAW	ARBLS	10//99-12//99
	California	S	15.09 MW	15.90 AW	33070 AAW	CABLS	10//99-12//99
	Los Angeles-Long Beach PMSA, CA	S	13.98 MW	12.55 AW	29080 AAW	CABLS	10//99-12//99
	Oakland PMSA, CA	S	18.28 MW	17.12 AW	38030 AAW	CABLS	10//99-12//99
	Orange County PMSA, CA	S	18.27 MW	16.08 AW	38000 AAW	CABLS	10//99-12//99
	San Diego MSA, CA	S	14.37 MW	13.85 AW	29880 AAW	CABLS	10//99-12//99
	San Francisco PMSA, CA	S	18.27 MW	18.23 AW	38010 AAW	CABLS	10//99-12//99
	Colorado	S	11.54 MW	12.81 AW	26650 AAW	COBLS	10//99-12//99
	Denver PMSA, CO	S	12.17 MW	11.40 AW	25310 AAW	COBLS	10//99-12//99
	Connecticut	S	9.51 MW	11.53 AW	23980 AAW	CTBLS	10//99-12//99
	Florida	S	14.82 MW	15.68 AW	32610 AAW	FLBLS	10//99-12//99
	Miami PMSA, FL	S	18.21 MW	17.16 AW	37870 AAW	FLBLS	10//99-12//99
	Georgia	S	13.81 MW	13.40 AW	27870 AAW	GABLS	10//99-12//99
	Atlanta MSA, GA	S	14.12 MW	14.51 AW	29360 AAW	GABLS	10//99-12//99
	Idaho	S	13.14 MW	14.20 AW	29530 AAW	IDBLS	10//99-12//99
	Illinois	S	10.97 MW	11.80 AW	24540 AAW	ILBLS	10//99-12//99
	Indiana	S	14.04 MW	16.04 AW	33370 AAW	INBLS	10//99-12//99
	Indianapolis MSA, IN	S	11.93 MW	12.02 AW	24820 AAW	INBLS	10//99-12//99
	Iowa	S	12.26 MW	13.37 AW	27810 AAW	IABLS	10//99-12//99

AAW Average annual wage	AOH Average offered, high	ASH Average starting, high	H Hourly	M Monthly	S Special: hourly and annual
AE Average entry wage	AOL Average offered, low	ASL Average starting, low	HI Highest wage paid	MTC Median total compensation	TQ Third quartile wage
AEX Average experienced wage	APH Average pay, high range	AW Average wage paid	HR High end range	MW Median wage paid	W Weekly
AO Average offered	APL Average pay, low range	FQ First quartile wage	LR Low end range	SQ Second quartile wage	Y Yearly

Occupation/Type/Industry	Location	Per	Low	Mid	High	Source	Date
Hoist and Winch Operator	Des Moines MSA, IA	S	14.51 MW	14.08 AW	30180 AAW	IABLS	10//99-12//99
	Kansas	S	8.28 MW	10.17 AW	21160 AAW	KSBLS	10//99-12//99
	Kentucky	S	13.28 MW	14.26 AW	29660 AAW	KYBLS	10//99-12//99
	Louisville MSA, KY-IN	S	16.09 MW	13.75 AW	33470 AAW	KYBLS	10//99-12//99
	Louisiana	S	13.83 MW	15.39 AW	32000 AAW	LABLS	10//99-12//99
	Baton Rouge MSA, LA	S	13.83 MW	14.31 AW	28780 AAW	LABLS	10//99-12//99
	Lafayette MSA, LA	S	10.83 MW	11.67 AW	22540 AAW	LABLS	10//99-12//99
	New Orleans MSA, LA	S	18.54 MW	16.79 AW	38570 AAW	LABLS	10//99-12//99
	Maryland	S	13.8 MW	15.39 AW	32010 AAW	MDBLS	10//99-12//99
	Massachusetts	S	16.08 MW	18.65 AW	38790 AAW	MABLS	10//99-12//99
	Boston PMSA, MA-NH	S	18.55 MW	16.06 AW	38580 AAW	MABLS	10//99-12//99
	Michigan	S	16.54 MW	17.04 AW	35440 AAW	MIBLS	10//99-12//99
	Detroit PMSA, MI	S	19.29 MW	17.48 AW	40120 AAW	MIBLS	10//99-12//99
	Grand Rapids-Muskegon-Holland MSA, MI	S	15.37 MW	15.37 AW	31970 AAW	MIBLS	10//99-12//99
	Minnesota	S	15.52 MW	17.68 AW	36780 AAW	MNBLS	10//99-12//99
	Minneapolis-St. Paul MSA, MN-WI	S	22.00 MW	22.75 AW	45760 AAW	MNBLS	10//99-12//99
	Mississippi	S	11.52 MW	12.44 AW	25880 AAW	MSBLS	10//99-12//99
	Biloxi-Gulfport-Pascagoula MSA, MS	S	16.33 MW	14.65 AW	33970 AAW	MSBLS	10//99-12//99
	Missouri	S	10.54 MW	12.85 AW	26740 AAW	MOBLS	10//99-12//99
	Montana	S	14.33 MW	14.34 AW	29830 AAW	MTBLS	10//99-12//99
	Nebraska	S	10.07 MW	10.45 AW	21730 AAW	NEBLS	10//99-12//99
	Omaha MSA, NE-IA	S	11.64 MW	11.92 AW	24220 AAW	NEBLS	10//99-12//99
	New Jersey	S	13.85 MW	14.14 AW	29410 AAW	NJBLS	10//99-12//99
	New York	S	11.36 MW	13.30 AW	27650 AAW	NYBLS	10//99-12//99
	North Carolina	S	9.65 MW	10.89 AW	22660 AAW	NCBLS	10//99-12//99
	Ohio	S	19.88 MW	18.36 AW	38180 AAW	OHBLS	10//99-12//99
	Cincinnati PMSA, OH-KY-IN	S	17.73 MW	17.85 AW	36880 AAW	OHBLS	10//99-12//99
	Cleveland-Lorain-Elyria PMSA, OH	S	21.48 MW	22.33 AW	44670 AAW	OHBLS	10//99-12//99
	Oklahoma	S	12.73 MW	13.16 AW	27380 AAW	OKBLS	10//99-12//99
	Tulsa MSA, OK	S	13.10 MW	12.38 AW	27240 AAW	OKBLS	10//99-12//99
	Oregon	S	15.3 MW	15.29 AW	31800 AAW	ORBLS	10//99-12//99
	Portland-Vancouver PMSA, OR-WA	S	16.61 MW	16.51 AW	34550 AAW	ORBLS	10//99-12//99
	Pennsylvania	S	15.47 MW	18.01 AW	37450 AAW	PABLS	10//99-12//99
	Philadelphia PMSA, PA-NJ	S	15.84 MW	12.71 AW	32950 AAW	PABLS	10//99-12//99
	South Carolina	S	10.52 MW	11.85 AW	24650 AAW	SCBLS	10//99-12//99
	Greenville-Spartanburg-Anderson MSA, SC	S	12.58 MW	10.62 AW	26160 AAW	SCBLS	10//99-12//99
	Tennessee	S	12.12 MW	14.02 AW	29150 AAW	TNBLS	10//99-12//99
	Texas	S	13.47 MW	13.98 AW	29090 AAW	TXBLS	10//99-12//99
	Houston PMSA, TX	S	15.08 MW	14.40 AW	31370 AAW	TXBLS	10//99-12//99
	Utah	S	16.36 MW	15.62 AW	32490 AAW	UTBLS	10//99-12//99
	Virginia	S	15.51 MW	15.02 AW	31240 AAW	VABLS	10//99-12//99
	Washington	S	15.1 MW	16.96 AW	35280 AAW	WABLS	10//99-12//99
	Seattle-Bellevue-Everett PMSA, WA	S	12.80 MW	11.05 AW	26630 AAW	WABLS	10//99-12//99
	Tacoma PMSA, WA	S	21.06 MW	18.73 AW	43800 AAW	WABLS	10//99-12//99
	West Virginia	S	13.12 MW	13.31 AW	27680 AAW	WVBLS	10//99-12//99
	Wisconsin	S	12.05 MW	14.28 AW	29700 AAW	WIBLS	10//99-12//99
	Puerto Rico	S	7.56 MW	7.76 AW	16140 AAW	PRBLS	10//99-12//99
	San Juan-Bayamon PMSA, PR	S	8.47 MW	8.03 AW	17630 AAW	PRBLS	10//99-12//99
Home Appliance Repairer	Alabama	S	11.8 MW	12.23 AW	25430 AAW	ALBLS	10//99-12//99
	Alaska	S	17.46 MW	17.54 AW	36470 AAW	AKBLS	10//99-12//99
	Arizona	S	13.23 MW	14.04 AW	29190 AAW	AZBLS	10//99-12//99
	Arkansas	S	10.64 MW	11.41 AW	23740 AAW	ARBLS	10//99-12//99
	California	S	14.51 MW	15.02 AW	31230 AAW	CABLS	10//99-12//99
	Colorado	S	12.23 MW	13.38 AW	27830 AAW	COBLS	10//99-12//99
	Connecticut	S	15.84 MW	15.50 AW	32250 AAW	CTBLS	10//99-12//99
	Delaware	S	11.36 MW	10.66 AW	22170 AAW	DEBLS	10//99-12//99
	Florida	S	12.72 MW	13.18 AW	27400 AAW	FLBLS	10//99-12//99
	Georgia	S	13.08 MW	13.68 AW	28440 AAW	GABLS	10//99-12//99
	Hawaii	S	14.91 MW	15.47 AW	32180 AAW	HIBLS	10//99-12//99
	Idaho	S	10.2 MW	12.04 AW	25030 AAW	IDBLS	10//99-12//99
	Illinois	S	16.22 MW	17.03 AW	35420 AAW	ILBLS	10//99-12//99
	Indiana	S	16.1 MW	16.16 AW	33600 AAW	INBLS	10//99-12//99
	Iowa	S	10.17 MW	12.46 AW	25910 AAW	IABLS	10//99-12//99
	Kansas	S	13.94 MW	13.19 AW	27430 AAW	KSBLS	10//99-12//99
	Kentucky	S	10.91 MW	10.83 AW	22520 AAW	KYBLS	10//99-12//99

AAW	Average annual wage	AOH	Average offered, high	ASH	Average starting, high	H	Hourly	M	Monthly	S	Special: hourly and annual
AE	Average entry wage	AOL	Average offered, low	ASL	Average starting, low	HI	Highest wage paid	MTC	Median total compensation	TQ	Third quartile wage
AEX	Average experienced wage	APH	Average pay, high range	AW	Average wage paid	HR	High end range	MW	Median wage paid	W	Weekly
AO	Average offered	APL	Average pay, low range	FQ	First quartile wage	LR	Low end range	SQ	Second quartile wage	Y	Yearly

746

Occupation/Type/Industry	Location	Per	Low	Mid	High	Source	Date
Home Appliance Repairer	Louisiana	S	10.65 MW	11.98 AW	24910 AAW	LABLS	10//99-12//99
	Maine	S	12.29 MW	12.52 AW	26040 AAW	MEBLS	10//99-12//99
	Maryland	S	15.47 MW	15.46 AW	32160 AAW	MDBLS	10//99-12//99
	Massachusetts	S	17.57 MW	17.50 AW	36390 AAW	MABLS	10//99-12//99
	Michigan	S	12.98 MW	13.74 AW	28590 AAW	MIBLS	10//99-12//99
	Minnesota	S	17.95 MW	17.35 AW	36080 AAW	MNBLS	10//99-12//99
	Mississippi	S	10.44 MW	11.89 AW	24720 AAW	MSBLS	10//99-12//99
	Missouri	S	9.76 MW	10.90 AW	22680 AAW	MOBLS	10//99-12//99
	Montana	S	11.45 MW	11.55 AW	24030 AAW	MTBLS	10//99-12//99
	Nebraska	S	17.35 MW	16.06 AW	33400 AAW	NEBLS	10//99-12//99
	Nevada	S	14.88 MW	14.66 AW	30490 AAW	NVBLS	10//99-12//99
	New Hampshire	S	16.39 MW	18.26 AW	37990 AAW	NHBLS	10//99-12//99
	New Jersey	S	18.32 MW	17.83 AW	37080 AAW	NJBLS	10//99-12//99
	New Mexico	S	8.49 MW	9.79 AW	20350 AAW	NMBLS	10//99-12//99
	New York	S	14.16 MW	13.68 AW	28460 AAW	NYBLS	10//99-12//99
	North Carolina	S	12.51 MW	12.94 AW	26910 AAW	NCBLS	10//99-12//99
	North Dakota	S	15.97 MW	15.20 AW	31610 AAW	NDBLS	10//99-12//99
	Ohio	S	12.5 MW	13.58 AW	28250 AAW	OHBLS	10//99-12//99
	Oklahoma	S	12.86 MW	13.97 AW	29060 AAW	OKBLS	10//99-12//99
	Oregon	S	13.24 MW	13.44 AW	27940 AAW	ORBLS	10//99-12//99
	Pennsylvania	S	15.34 MW	14.95 AW	31100 AAW	PABLS	10//99-12//99
	Rhode Island	S	15.06 MW	14.85 AW	30880 AAW	RIBLS	10//99-12//99
	South Carolina	S	13.12 MW	13.48 AW	28040 AAW	SCBLS	10//99-12//99
	Tennessee	S	11.36 MW	12.27 AW	25530 AAW	TNBLS	10//99-12//99
	Texas	S	11.85 MW	12.82 AW	26660 AAW	TXBLS	10//99-12//99
	Utah	S	12.84 MW	14.00 AW	29130 AAW	UTBLS	10//99-12//99
	Vermont	S	14.2 MW	13.82 AW	28740 AAW	VTBLS	10//99-12//99
	Virginia	S	12.37 MW	12.65 AW	26320 AAW	VABLS	10//99-12//99
	Washington	S	16.74 MW	17.16 AW	35690 AAW	WABLS	10//99-12//99
	West Virginia	S	7.89 MW	8.45 AW	17580 AAW	WVBLS	10//99-12//99
	Wisconsin	S	14.11 MW	14.38 AW	29910 AAW	WIBLS	10//99-12//99
	Wyoming	S	18.3 MW	16.41 AW	34140 AAW	WYBLS	10//99-12//99
Home Economics Teacher							
Postsecondary	California	Y		57080 AAW		CABLS	10//99-12//99
Postsecondary	Florida	Y		51180 AAW		FLBLS	10//99-12//99
Postsecondary	Georgia	Y		45890 AAW		GABLS	10//99-12//99
Postsecondary	Kansas	Y		49580 AAW		KSBLS	10//99-12//99
Postsecondary	Louisiana	Y		40180 AAW		LABLS	10//99-12//99
Postsecondary	Maine	Y		44600 AAW		MEBLS	10//99-12//99
Postsecondary	Michigan	Y		50210 AAW		MIBLS	10//99-12//99
Postsecondary	Minnesota	Y		56840 AAW		MNBLS	10//99-12//99
Postsecondary	New Hampshire	Y		40800 AAW		NHBLS	10//99-12//99
Postsecondary	North Carolina	Y		43260 AAW		NCBLS	10//99-12//99
Postsecondary	Ohio	Y		40050 AAW		OHBLS	10//99-12//99
Postsecondary	Oklahoma	Y		48030 AAW		OKBLS	10//99-12//99
Postsecondary	Pennsylvania	Y		52710 AAW		PABLS	10//99-12//99
Postsecondary	Tennessee	Y		58800 AAW		TNBLS	10//99-12//99
Postsecondary	Texas	Y		43290 AAW		TXBLS	10//99-12//99
Postsecondary	Washington	Y		37690 AAW		WABLS	10//99-12//99
Postsecondary	West Virginia	Y		54960 AAW		WVBLS	10//99-12//99
Home Health Aide	Alabama	S	7.42 MW	7.57 AW	15740 AAW	ALBLS	10//99-12//99
	Alaska	S	10.3 MW	11.35 AW	23620 AAW	AKBLS	10//99-12//99
	Arizona	S	7.96 MW	8.12 AW	16900 AAW	AZBLS	10//99-12//99
	Arkansas	S	6.42 MW	6.72 AW	13970 AAW	ARBLS	10//99-12//99
	California	S	8.54 MW	9.73 AW	20230 AAW	CABLS	10//99-12//99
	Los Angeles County, CA	Y		20850 AW		LABJ	1999
	Colorado	S	8.3 MW	8.93 AW	18560 AAW	COBLS	10//99-12//99
	Connecticut	S	10.54 MW	11.93 AW	24810 AAW	CTBLS	10//99-12//99
	Delaware	S	9.16 MW	8.79 AW	18280 AAW	DEBLS	10//99-12//99
	District of Columbia	S	7.77 MW	7.84 AW	16320 AAW	DCBLS	10//99-12//99
	Florida	S	8 MW	8.30 AW	17270 AAW	FLBLS	10//99-12//99
	Georgia	S	7.28 MW	7.39 AW	15380 AAW	GABLS	10//99-12//99
	Hawaii	S	8.66 MW	8.33 AW	17330 AAW	HIBLS	10//99-12//99
	Idaho	S	7.74 MW	8.08 AW	16810 AAW	IDBLS	10//99-12//99
	Illinois	S	8.72 MW	8.65 AW	18000 AAW	ILBLS	10//99-12//99
	Indiana	S	8.44 MW	8.50 AW	17690 AAW	INBLS	10//99-12//99
	Iowa	S	7.9 MW	7.99 AW	16630 AAW	IABLS	10//99-12//99
	Kansas	S	7.79 MW	7.94 AW	16510 AAW	KSBLS	10//99-12//99
	Kentucky	S	8.18 MW	8.35 AW	17360 AAW	KYBLS	10//99-12//99
	Louisiana	S	6.92 MW	8.02 AW	16680 AAW	LABLS	10//99-12//99
	Maine	S	7.89 MW	8.13 AW	16920 AAW	MEBLS	10//99-12//99

AAW Average annual wage	AOH Average offered, high	ASH Average starting, high	H Hourly	M Monthly	S Special: hourly and annual
AE Average entry wage	AOL Average offered, low	ASL Average starting, low	HI Highest wage paid	MTC Median total compensation	TQ Third quartile wage
AEX Average experienced wage	APH Average pay, high range	AW Average wage paid	HR High end range	MW Median wage paid	W Weekly
AO Average offered	APL Average pay, low range	FQ First quartile wage	LR Low end range	SQ Second quartile wage	Y Yearly

Occupation/Type/Industry	Location	Per	Low	Mid	High	Source	Date
Home Health Aide	Maryland	S	8.09 MW	8.16 AW	16970 AAW	MDBLS	10//99-12//99
	Massachusetts	S	9.72 MW	9.71 AW	20200 AAW	MABLS	10//99-12//99
	Michigan	S	8.15 MW	8.53 AW	17740 AAW	MIBLS	10//99-12//99
	Minnesota	S	8.9 MW	8.84 AW	18380 AAW	MNBLS	10//99-12//99
	Mississippi	S	7.49 MW	7.88 AW	16380 AAW	MSBLS	10//99-12//99
	Missouri	S	7.37 MW	7.43 AW	15460 AAW	MOBLS	10//99-12//99
	Montana	S	7.6 MW	7.59 AW	15780 AAW	MTBLS	10//99-12//99
	Nebraska	S	8.41 MW	8.37 AW	17410 AAW	NEBLS	10//99-12//99
	Nevada	S	8.87 MW	9.84 AW	20480 AAW	NVBLS	10//99-12//99
	New Hampshire	S	8.66 MW	8.61 AW	17910 AAW	NHBLS	10//99-12//99
	New Jersey	S	8.68 MW	8.82 AW	18350 AAW	NJBLS	10//99-12//99
	New Mexico	S	7.44 MW	7.47 AW	15540 AAW	NMBLS	10//99-12//99
	New York	S	7.97 MW	8.70 AW	18100 AAW	NYBLS	10//99-12//99
	North Carolina	S	7.6 MW	7.71 AW	16030 AAW	NCBLS	10//99-12//99
	North Dakota	S	7.48 MW	7.46 AW	15520 AAW	NDBLS	10//99-12//99
	Ohio	S	7.91 MW	8.20 AW	17060 AAW	OHBLS	10//99-12//99
	Oklahoma	S	8.28 MW	8.53 AW	17740 AAW	OKBLS	10//99-12//99
	Oregon	S	8.03 MW	8.35 AW	17360 AAW	ORBLS	10//99-12//99
	Pennsylvania	S	7.86 MW	8.02 AW	16680 AAW	PABLS	10//99-12//99
	Rhode Island	S	9.14 MW	9.13 AW	18990 AAW	RIBLS	10//99-12//99
	South Carolina	S	7.21 MW	7.35 AW	15290 AAW	SCBLS	10//99-12//99
	South Dakota	S	7.55 MW	7.51 AW	15620 AAW	SDBLS	10//99-12//99
	Tennessee	S	7.86 MW	7.91 AW	16450 AAW	TNBLS	10//99-12//99
	Texas	S	9.74 MW	11.22 AW	23340 AAW	TXBLS	10//99-12//99
	Utah	S	7.82 MW	8.01 AW	16660 AAW	UTBLS	10//99-12//99
	Vermont	S	8.08 MW	8.24 AW	17140 AAW	VTBLS	10//99-12//99
	Virginia	S	7.2 MW	7.45 AW	15490 AAW	VABLS	10//99-12//99
	Washington	S	7.95 MW	8.22 AW	17110 AAW	WABLS	10//99-12//99
	West Virginia	S	6.3 MW	6.45 AW	13420 AAW	WVBLS	10//99-12//99
	Wisconsin	S	8.01 MW	8.18 AW	17010 AAW	WIBLS	10//99-12//99
	Wyoming	S	7.74 MW	7.76 AW	16140 AAW	WYBLS	10//99-12//99
	Puerto Rico	S	6 MW	6.14 AW	12760 AAW	PRBLS	10//99-12//99
Horticulturalist	United States	Y	31200 LR		52000 HR	TQUES	1999
Hospital Administrator	Los Angeles County, CA	Y		230943 AW		LABJ	1999
Host and Hostess							
Restaurant, Lounge, and Coffee Shop	Alabama	S	6.36 MW	6.51 AW	13550 AAW	ALBLS	10//99-12//99
Restaurant, Lounge, and Coffee Shop	Anniston MSA, AL	S	6.13 MW	6.13 AW	12740 AAW	ALBLS	10//99-12//99
Restaurant, Lounge, and Coffee Shop	Auburn-Opelika MSA, AL	S	6.22 MW	6.22 AW	12930 AAW	ALBLS	10//99-12//99
Restaurant, Lounge, and Coffee Shop	Birmingham MSA, AL	S	6.53 MW	6.30 AW	13580 AAW	ALBLS	10//99-12//99
Restaurant, Lounge, and Coffee Shop	Decatur MSA, AL	S	6.54 MW	6.15 AW	13590 AAW	ALBLS	10//99-12//99
Restaurant, Lounge, and Coffee Shop	Dothan MSA, AL	S	5.93 MW	5.97 AW	12330 AAW	ALBLS	10//99-12//99
Restaurant, Lounge, and Coffee Shop	Florence MSA, AL	S	6.42 MW	6.34 AW	13340 AAW	ALBLS	10//99-12//99
Restaurant, Lounge, and Coffee Shop	Gadsden MSA, AL	S	6.07 MW	5.96 AW	12630 AAW	ALBLS	10//99-12//99
Restaurant, Lounge, and Coffee Shop	Huntsville MSA, AL	S	6.79 MW	6.80 AW	14120 AAW	ALBLS	10//99-12//99
Restaurant, Lounge, and Coffee Shop	Mobile MSA, AL	S	6.67 MW	6.53 AW	13880 AAW	ALBLS	10//99-12//99
Restaurant, Lounge, and Coffee Shop	Montgomery MSA, AL	S	6.56 MW	6.46 AW	13640 AAW	ALBLS	10//99-12//99
Restaurant, Lounge, and Coffee Shop	Tuscaloosa MSA, AL	S	6.43 MW	6.41 AW	13380 AAW	ALBLS	10//99-12//99
Restaurant, Lounge, and Coffee Shop	Alaska	S	7.55 MW	7.82 AW	16270 AAW	AKBLS	10//99-12//99
Restaurant, Lounge, and Coffee Shop	Anchorage MSA, AK	S	7.84 MW	7.57 AW	16300 AAW	AKBLS	10//99-12//99
Restaurant, Lounge, and Coffee Shop	Arizona	S	6.36 MW	6.50 AW	13520 AAW	AZBLS	10//99-12//99
Restaurant, Lounge, and Coffee Shop	Flagstaff MSA, AZ-UT	S	6.34 MW	6.13 AW	13180 AAW	AZBLS	10//99-12//99
Restaurant, Lounge, and Coffee Shop	Phoenix-Mesa MSA, AZ	S	6.60 MW	6.49 AW	13720 AAW	AZBLS	10//99-12//99
Restaurant, Lounge, and Coffee Shop	Tucson MSA, AZ	S	6.26 MW	6.20 AW	13020 AAW	AZBLS	10//99-12//99
Restaurant, Lounge, and Coffee Shop	Yuma MSA, AZ	S	6.09 MW	6.20 AW	12660 AAW	AZBLS	10//99-12//99
Restaurant, Lounge, and Coffee Shop	Arkansas	S	6.57 MW	6.70 AW	13940 AAW	ARBLS	10//99-12//99
Restaurant, Lounge, and Coffee Shop	Fayetteville-Springdale-Rogers MSA, AR	S	6.48 MW	6.28 AW	13480 AAW	ARBLS	10//99-12//99
Restaurant, Lounge, and Coffee Shop	Fort Smith MSA, AR-OK	S	6.47 MW	6.41 AW	13460 AAW	ARBLS	10//99-12//99
Restaurant, Lounge, and Coffee Shop	Little Rock-North Little Rock MSA, AR	S	6.81 MW	6.60 AW	14160 AAW	ARBLS	10//99-12//99
Restaurant, Lounge, and Coffee Shop	California	S	6.63 MW	7.18 AW	14930 AAW	CABLS	10//99-12//99
Restaurant, Lounge, and Coffee Shop	Bakersfield MSA, CA	S	6.40 MW	6.15 AW	13310 AAW	CABLS	10//99-12//99
Restaurant, Lounge, and Coffee Shop	Chico-Paradise MSA, CA	S	6.90 MW	6.33 AW	14350 AAW	CABLS	10//99-12//99
Restaurant, Lounge, and Coffee Shop	Fresno MSA, CA	S	6.51 MW	6.25 AW	13540 AAW	CABLS	10//99-12//99
Restaurant, Lounge, and Coffee Shop	Los Angeles-Long Beach PMSA, CA	S	7.16 MW	6.56 AW	14880 AAW	CABLS	10//99-12//99
Restaurant, Lounge, and Coffee Shop	Merced MSA, CA	S	6.82 MW	6.59 AW	14180 AAW	CABLS	10//99-12//99
Restaurant, Lounge, and Coffee Shop	Modesto MSA, CA	S	6.83 MW	6.52 AW	14200 AAW	CABLS	10//99-12//99
Restaurant, Lounge, and Coffee Shop	Oakland PMSA, CA	S	7.58 MW	6.89 AW	15760 AAW	CABLS	10//99-12//99
Restaurant, Lounge, and Coffee Shop	Orange County PMSA, CA	S	6.91 MW	6.58 AW	14380 AAW	CABLS	10//99-12//99

AAW	Average annual wage	AOH	Average offered, high	ASH	Average starting, high	H	Hourly	M	Monthly	S	Special: hourly and annual
AE	Average entry wage	AOL	Average offered, low	ASL	Average starting, low	HI	Highest wage paid	MTC	Median total compensation	TQ	Third quartile wage
AEX	Average experienced wage	APH	Average pay, high range	AW	Average wage paid	HR	High end range	MW	Median wage paid	W	Weekly
AO	Average offered	APL	Average pay, low range	FQ	First quartile wage	LR	Low end range	SQ	Second quartile wage	Y	Yearly

Host and Hostess

Occupation/Type/Industry	Location	Per	Low	Mid	High	Source	Date
Host and Hostess							
Restaurant, Lounge, and Coffee Shop	Redding MSA, CA	S	6.88 MW	6.59 AW	14320 AAW	CABLS	10//99-12//99
Restaurant, Lounge, and Coffee Shop	Riverside-San Bernardino PMSA, CA	S	6.90 MW	6.52 AW	14360 AAW	CABLS	10//99-12//99
Restaurant, Lounge, and Coffee Shop	Sacramento PMSA, CA	S	6.92 MW	6.57 AW	14400 AAW	CABLS	10//99-12//99
Restaurant, Lounge, and Coffee Shop	Salinas MSA, CA	S	7.38 MW	6.90 AW	15350 AAW	CABLS	10//99-12//99
Restaurant, Lounge, and Coffee Shop	San Diego MSA, CA	S	6.96 MW	6.61 AW	14470 AAW	CABLS	10//99-12//99
Restaurant, Lounge, and Coffee Shop	San Francisco PMSA, CA	S	9.05 MW	8.47 AW	18820 AAW	CABLS	10//99-12//99
Restaurant, Lounge, and Coffee Shop	San Jose PMSA, CA	S	7.50 MW	6.76 AW	15590 AAW	CABLS	10//99-12//99
Restaurant, Lounge, and Coffee Shop	San Luis Obispo-Atascadero-Paso Robles MSA, CA	S	7.52 MW	7.15 AW	15650 AAW	CABLS	10//99-12//99
Restaurant, Lounge, and Coffee Shop	Santa Barbara-Santa Maria-Lompoc MSA, CA	S	6.97 MW	6.51 AW	14500 AAW	CABLS	10//99-12//99
Restaurant, Lounge, and Coffee Shop	Santa Cruz-Watsonville PMSA, CA	S	6.75 MW	6.33 AW	14030 AAW	CABLS	10//99-12//99
Restaurant, Lounge, and Coffee Shop	Santa Rosa PMSA, CA	S	6.83 MW	6.42 AW	14210 AAW	CABLS	10//99-12//99
Restaurant, Lounge, and Coffee Shop	Stockton-Lodi MSA, CA	S	6.49 MW	6.34 AW	13500 AAW	CABLS	10//99-12//99
Restaurant, Lounge, and Coffee Shop	Vallejo-Fairfield-Napa PMSA, CA	S	6.81 MW	6.11 AW	14160 AAW	CABLS	10//99-12//99
Restaurant, Lounge, and Coffee Shop	Ventura PMSA, CA	S	7.12 MW	6.73 AW	14810 AAW	CABLS	10//99-12//99
Restaurant, Lounge, and Coffee Shop	Visalia-Tulare-Porterville MSA, CA	S	6.81 MW	6.34 AW	14170 AAW	CABLS	10//99-12//99
Restaurant, Lounge, and Coffee Shop	Yolo PMSA, CA	S	6.77 MW	6.55 AW	14090 AAW	CABLS	10//99-12//99
Restaurant, Lounge, and Coffee Shop	Colorado	S	7.34 MW	7.61 AW	15820 AAW	COBLS	10//99-12//99
Restaurant, Lounge, and Coffee Shop	Boulder-Longmont PMSA, CO	S	7.05 MW	7.18 AW	14660 AAW	COBLS	10//99-12//99
Restaurant, Lounge, and Coffee Shop	Colorado Springs MSA, CO	S	7.43 MW	7.01 AW	15460 AAW	COBLS	10//99-12//99
Restaurant, Lounge, and Coffee Shop	Denver PMSA, CO	S	7.99 MW	7.64 AW	16620 AAW	COBLS	10//99-12//99
Restaurant, Lounge, and Coffee Shop	Fort Collins-Loveland MSA, CO	S	6.52 MW	6.38 AW	13560 AAW	COBLS	10//99-12//99
Restaurant, Lounge, and Coffee Shop	Grand Junction MSA, CO	S	6.89 MW	6.86 AW	14340 AAW	COBLS	10//99-12//99
Restaurant, Lounge, and Coffee Shop	Greeley PMSA, CO	S	6.53 MW	6.41 AW	13580 AAW	COBLS	10//99-12//99
Restaurant, Lounge, and Coffee Shop	Pueblo MSA, CO	S	6.37 MW	6.27 AW	13260 AAW	COBLS	10//99-12//99
Restaurant, Lounge, and Coffee Shop	Connecticut	S	7.69 MW	8.29 AW	17240 AAW	CTBLS	10//99-12//99
Restaurant, Lounge, and Coffee Shop	Bridgeport PMSA, CT	S	7.37 MW	6.82 AW	15340 AAW	CTBLS	10//99-12//99
Restaurant, Lounge, and Coffee Shop	Danbury PMSA, CT	S	8.05 MW	7.98 AW	16750 AAW	CTBLS	10//99-12//99
Restaurant, Lounge, and Coffee Shop	Hartford MSA, CT	S	7.81 MW	7.61 AW	16250 AAW	CTBLS	10//99-12//99
Restaurant, Lounge, and Coffee Shop	New Haven-Meriden PMSA, CT	S	8.05 MW	7.36 AW	16740 AAW	CTBLS	10//99-12//99
Restaurant, Lounge, and Coffee Shop	New London-Norwich MSA, CT-RI	S	8.92 MW	7.99 AW	18550 AAW	CTBLS	10//99-12//99
Restaurant, Lounge, and Coffee Shop	Stamford-Norwalk PMSA, CT	S	10.73 MW	10.13 AW	22320 AAW	CTBLS	10//99-12//99
Restaurant, Lounge, and Coffee Shop	Waterbury PMSA, CT	S	7.92 MW	7.54 AW	16460 AAW	CTBLS	10//99-12//99
Restaurant, Lounge, and Coffee Shop	Delaware	S	6.92 MW	7.40 AW	15380 AAW	DEBLS	10//99-12//99
Restaurant, Lounge, and Coffee Shop	Dover MSA, DE	S	7.19 MW	6.36 AW	14950 AAW	DEBLS	10//99-12//99
Restaurant, Lounge, and Coffee Shop	Wilmington-Newark PMSA, DE-MD	S	7.41 MW	6.87 AW	15400 AAW	DEBLS	10//99-12//99
Restaurant, Lounge, and Coffee Shop	District of Columbia	S	9.95 MW	10.44 AW	21710 AAW	DCBLS	10//99-12//99
Restaurant, Lounge, and Coffee Shop	Washington PMSA, DC-MD-VA-WV	S	8.49 MW	8.31 AW	17660 AAW	DCBLS	10//99-12//99
Restaurant, Lounge, and Coffee Shop	Florida	S	7.04 MW	7.09 AW	14750 AAW	FLBLS	10//99-12//99
Restaurant, Lounge, and Coffee Shop	Daytona Beach MSA, FL	S	6.77 MW	6.65 AW	14090 AAW	FLBLS	10//99-12//99
Restaurant, Lounge, and Coffee Shop	Fort Lauderdale PMSA, FL	S	6.85 MW	6.55 AW	14240 AAW	FLBLS	10//99-12//99
Restaurant, Lounge, and Coffee Shop	Fort Myers-Cape Coral MSA, FL	S	7.00 MW	6.84 AW	14570 AAW	FLBLS	10//99-12//99
Restaurant, Lounge, and Coffee Shop	Fort Pierce-Port St. Lucie MSA, FL	S	7.02 MW	7.00 AW	14600 AAW	FLBLS	10//99-12//99
Restaurant, Lounge, and Coffee Shop	Fort Walton Beach MSA, FL	S	6.28 MW	6.07 AW	13070 AAW	FLBLS	10//99-12//99
Restaurant, Lounge, and Coffee Shop	Gainesville MSA, FL	S	6.71 MW	6.66 AW	13960 AAW	FLBLS	10//99-12//99
Restaurant, Lounge, and Coffee Shop	Jacksonville MSA, FL	S	7.22 MW	7.21 AW	15010 AAW	FLBLS	10//99-12//99
Restaurant, Lounge, and Coffee Shop	Lakeland-Winter Haven MSA, FL	S	6.72 MW	6.42 AW	13970 AAW	FLBLS	10//99-12//99
Restaurant, Lounge, and Coffee Shop	Melbourne-Titusville-Palm Bay MSA, FL	S	6.67 MW	6.62 AW	13860 AAW	FLBLS	10//99-12//99
Restaurant, Lounge, and Coffee Shop	Miami PMSA, FL	S	7.49 MW	7.46 AW	15580 AAW	FLBLS	10//99-12//99
Restaurant, Lounge, and Coffee Shop	Naples MSA, FL	S	7.87 MW	7.61 AW	16370 AAW	FLBLS	10//99-12//99
Restaurant, Lounge, and Coffee Shop	Ocala MSA, FL	S	6.62 MW	6.45 AW	13760 AAW	FLBLS	10//99-12//99
Restaurant, Lounge, and Coffee Shop	Orlando MSA, FL	S	7.28 MW	7.35 AW	15150 AAW	FLBLS	10//99-12//99
Restaurant, Lounge, and Coffee Shop	Panama City MSA, FL	S	6.71 MW	6.56 AW	13950 AAW	FLBLS	10//99-12//99
Restaurant, Lounge, and Coffee Shop	Pensacola MSA, FL	S	6.83 MW	6.61 AW	14210 AAW	FLBLS	10//99-12//99
Restaurant, Lounge, and Coffee Shop	Punta Gorda MSA, FL	S	7.71 MW	7.84 AW	16040 AAW	FLBLS	10//99-12//99
Restaurant, Lounge, and Coffee Shop	Sarasota-Bradenton MSA, FL	S	7.08 MW	7.03 AW	14730 AAW	FLBLS	10//99-12//99
Restaurant, Lounge, and Coffee Shop	Tallahassee MSA, FL	S	6.27 MW	6.04 AW	13040 AAW	FLBLS	10//99-12//99

AAW	Average annual wage	AOH	Average offered, high	ASH	Average starting, high
AE	Average entry wage	AOL	Average offered, low	ASL	Average starting, low
AEX	Average experienced wage	APH	Average pay, high range	AW	Average wage paid
AO	Average offered	APL	Average pay, low range	FQ	First quartile wage

H	Hourly	M	Monthly
HI	Highest wage paid	MTC	Median total compensation
HR	High end range	MW	Median wage paid
LR	Low end range	SQ	Second quartile wage

S	Special: hourly and annual
TQ	Third quartile wage
W	Weekly
Y	Yearly

Occupation/Type/Industry	Location	Per	Low	Mid	High	Source	Date
Host and Hostess							
Restaurant, Lounge, and Coffee Shop	Tampa-St. Petersburg-Clearwater MSA, FL	S	6.81 MW	6.66 AW	14170 AAW	FLBLS	10//99-12//99
Restaurant, Lounge, and Coffee Shop	West Palm Beach-Boca Raton MSA, FL	S	7.46 MW	7.48 AW	15510 AAW	FLBLS	10//99-12//99
Restaurant, Lounge, and Coffee Shop	Georgia	S	6.61 MW	6.83 AW	14200 AAW	GABLS	10//99-12//99
Restaurant, Lounge, and Coffee Shop	Albany MSA, GA	S	6.72 MW	6.47 AW	13970 AAW	GABLS	10//99-12//99
Restaurant, Lounge, and Coffee Shop	Athens MSA, GA	S	6.89 MW	6.89 AW	14340 AAW	GABLS	10//99-12//99
Restaurant, Lounge, and Coffee Shop	Atlanta MSA, GA	S	6.84 MW	6.66 AW	14220 AAW	GABLS	10//99-12//99
Restaurant, Lounge, and Coffee Shop	Augusta-Aiken MSA, GA-SC	S	6.40 MW	6.29 AW	13320 AAW	GABLS	10//99-12//99
Restaurant, Lounge, and Coffee Shop	Columbus MSA, GA-AL	S	6.07 MW	5.98 AW	12630 AAW	GABLS	10//99-12//99
Restaurant, Lounge, and Coffee Shop	Macon MSA, GA	S	6.07 MW	6.02 AW	12620 AAW	GABLS	10//99-12//99
Restaurant, Lounge, and Coffee Shop	Savannah MSA, GA	S	6.87 MW	6.95 AW	14280 AAW	GABLS	10//99-12//99
Restaurant, Lounge, and Coffee Shop	Hawaii	S	8.08 MW	8.77 AW	18240 AAW	HIBLS	10//99-12//99
Restaurant, Lounge, and Coffee Shop	Honolulu MSA, HI	S	8.81 MW	8.13 AW	18320 AAW	HIBLS	10//99-12//99
Restaurant, Lounge, and Coffee Shop	Idaho	S	6.02 MW	6.12 AW	12740 AAW	IDBLS	10//99-12//99
Restaurant, Lounge, and Coffee Shop	Boise City MSA, ID	S	6.20 MW	6.01 AW	12900 AAW	IDBLS	10//99-12//99
Restaurant, Lounge, and Coffee Shop	Pocatello MSA, ID	S	5.97 MW	5.96 AW	12410 AAW	IDBLS	10//99-12//99
Restaurant, Lounge, and Coffee Shop	Illinois	S	6.78 MW	7.12 AW	14810 AAW	ILBLS	10//99-12//99
Restaurant, Lounge, and Coffee Shop	Bloomington-Normal MSA, IL	S	6.39 MW	6.08 AW	13300 AAW	ILBLS	10//99-12//99
Restaurant, Lounge, and Coffee Shop	Champaign-Urbana MSA, IL	S	7.08 MW	6.66 AW	14720 AAW	ILBLS	10//99-12//99
Restaurant, Lounge, and Coffee Shop	Chicago PMSA, IL	S	7.25 MW	6.93 AW	15070 AAW	ILBLS	10//99-12//99
Restaurant, Lounge, and Coffee Shop	Decatur MSA, IL	S	6.91 MW	6.63 AW	14370 AAW	ILBLS	10//99-12//99
Restaurant, Lounge, and Coffee Shop	Kankakee PMSA, IL	S	6.51 MW	6.46 AW	13550 AAW	ILBLS	10//99-12//99
Restaurant, Lounge, and Coffee Shop	Peoria-Pekin MSA, IL	S	6.91 MW	6.68 AW	14370 AAW	ILBLS	10//99-12//99
Restaurant, Lounge, and Coffee Shop	Rockford MSA, IL	S	7.05 MW	7.10 AW	14670 AAW	ILBLS	10//99-12//99
Restaurant, Lounge, and Coffee Shop	Springfield MSA, IL	S	7.32 MW	7.28 AW	15220 AAW	ILBLS	10//99-12//99
Restaurant, Lounge, and Coffee Shop	Indiana	S	6.65 MW	6.85 AW	14250 AAW	INBLS	10//99-12//99
Restaurant, Lounge, and Coffee Shop	Bloomington MSA, IN	S	6.36 MW	6.17 AW	13230 AAW	INBLS	10//99-12//99
Restaurant, Lounge, and Coffee Shop	Elkhart-Goshen MSA, IN	S	6.95 MW	6.87 AW	14460 AAW	INBLS	10//99-12//99
Restaurant, Lounge, and Coffee Shop	Evansville-Henderson MSA, IN-KY	S	6.53 MW	6.11 AW	13580 AAW	INBLS	10//99-12//99
Restaurant, Lounge, and Coffee Shop	Fort Wayne MSA, IN	S	6.92 MW	6.69 AW	14390 AAW	INBLS	10//99-12//99
Restaurant, Lounge, and Coffee Shop	Gary PMSA, IN	S	6.94 MW	7.05 AW	14430 AAW	INBLS	10//99-12//99
Restaurant, Lounge, and Coffee Shop	Indianapolis MSA, IN	S	7.12 MW	6.95 AW	14810 AAW	INBLS	10//99-12//99
Restaurant, Lounge, and Coffee Shop	Kokomo MSA, IN	S	6.65 MW	6.38 AW	13830 AAW	INBLS	10//99-12//99
Restaurant, Lounge, and Coffee Shop	Lafayette MSA, IN	S	6.93 MW	6.90 AW	14410 AAW	INBLS	10//99-12//99
Restaurant, Lounge, and Coffee Shop	Muncie MSA, IN	S	6.40 MW	6.24 AW	13310 AAW	INBLS	10//99-12//99
Restaurant, Lounge, and Coffee Shop	South Bend MSA, IN	S	6.71 MW	6.52 AW	13960 AAW	INBLS	10//99-12//99
Restaurant, Lounge, and Coffee Shop	Terre Haute MSA, IN	S	6.45 MW	6.11 AW	13410 AAW	INBLS	10//99-12//99
Restaurant, Lounge, and Coffee Shop	Iowa	S	6.59 MW	6.76 AW	14060 AAW	IABLS	10//99-12//99
Restaurant, Lounge, and Coffee Shop	Cedar Rapids MSA, IA	S	6.43 MW	6.31 AW	13370 AAW	IABLS	10//99-12//99
Restaurant, Lounge, and Coffee Shop	Davenport-Moline-Rock Island MSA, IA-IL	S	6.99 MW	6.80 AW	14540 AAW	IABLS	10//99-12//99
Restaurant, Lounge, and Coffee Shop	Des Moines MSA, IA	S	6.76 MW	6.68 AW	14070 AAW	IABLS	10//99-12//99
Restaurant, Lounge, and Coffee Shop	Dubuque MSA, IA	S	6.63 MW	6.58 AW	13790 AAW	IABLS	10//99-12//99
Restaurant, Lounge, and Coffee Shop	Iowa City MSA, IA	S	7.15 MW	7.16 AW	14870 AAW	IABLS	10//99-12//99
Restaurant, Lounge, and Coffee Shop	Sioux City MSA, IA-NE	S	6.51 MW	6.48 AW	13530 AAW	IABLS	10//99-12//99
Restaurant, Lounge, and Coffee Shop	Waterloo-Cedar Falls MSA, IA	S	6.91 MW	6.81 AW	14360 AAW	IABLS	10//99-12//99
Restaurant, Lounge, and Coffee Shop	Kansas	S	6.37 MW	6.53 AW	13590 AAW	KSBLS	10//99-12//99
Restaurant, Lounge, and Coffee Shop	Lawrence MSA, KS	S	6.32 MW	6.23 AW	13150 AAW	KSBLS	10//99-12//99
Restaurant, Lounge, and Coffee Shop	Topeka MSA, KS	S	6.30 MW	6.28 AW	13100 AAW	KSBLS	10//99-12//99
Restaurant, Lounge, and Coffee Shop	Wichita MSA, KS	S	6.38 MW	6.31 AW	13280 AAW	KSBLS	10//99-12//99
Restaurant, Lounge, and Coffee Shop	Kentucky	S	6.47 MW	6.81 AW	14170 AAW	KYBLS	10//99-12//99
Restaurant, Lounge, and Coffee Shop	Lexington MSA, KY	S	6.80 MW	6.57 AW	14150 AAW	KYBLS	10//99-12//99
Restaurant, Lounge, and Coffee Shop	Louisville MSA, KY-IN	S	7.18 MW	6.93 AW	14940 AAW	KYBLS	10//99-12//99
Restaurant, Lounge, and Coffee Shop	Owensboro MSA, KY	S	5.91 MW	5.95 AW	12290 AAW	KYBLS	10//99-12//99
Restaurant, Lounge, and Coffee Shop	Louisiana	S	6.25 MW	6.85 AW	14240 AAW	LABLS	10//99-12//99
Restaurant, Lounge, and Coffee Shop	Alexandria MSA, LA	S	6.12 MW	6.02 AW	12730 AAW	LABLS	10//99-12//99
Restaurant, Lounge, and Coffee Shop	Baton Rouge MSA, LA	S	6.78 MW	6.65 AW	14100 AAW	LABLS	10//99-12//99
Restaurant, Lounge, and Coffee Shop	Houma MSA, LA	S	6.02 MW	6.02 AW	12530 AAW	LABLS	10//99-12//99
Restaurant, Lounge, and Coffee Shop	Lafayette MSA, LA	S	6.21 MW	6.18 AW	12930 AAW	LABLS	10//99-12//99
Restaurant, Lounge, and Coffee Shop	Lake Charles MSA, LA	S	6.98 MW	6.56 AW	14520 AAW	LABLS	10//99-12//99
Restaurant, Lounge, and Coffee Shop	Monroe MSA, LA	S	6.24 MW	6.03 AW	12980 AAW	LABLS	10//99-12//99
Restaurant, Lounge, and Coffee Shop	New Orleans MSA, LA	S	7.20 MW	6.52 AW	14970 AAW	LABLS	10//99-12//99
Restaurant, Lounge, and Coffee Shop	Shreveport-Bossier City MSA, LA	S	6.77 MW	6.05 AW	14070 AAW	LABLS	10//99-12//99
Restaurant, Lounge, and Coffee Shop	Maine	S	7.02 MW	7.31 AW	15210 AAW	MEBLS	10//99-12//99
Restaurant, Lounge, and Coffee Shop	Bangor MSA, ME	S	7.67 MW	7.47 AW	15960 AAW	MEBLS	10//99-12//99
Restaurant, Lounge, and Coffee Shop	Lewiston-Auburn MSA, ME	S	7.43 MW	6.65 AW	15450 AAW	MEBLS	10//99-12//99
Restaurant, Lounge, and Coffee Shop	Portland MSA, ME	S	7.35 MW	7.06 AW	15290 AAW	MEBLS	10//99-12//99
Restaurant, Lounge, and Coffee Shop	Maryland	S	7.2 MW	7.39 AW	15380 AAW	MDBLS	10//99-12//99

AAW Average annual wage	**AOH** Average offered, high	**ASH** Average starting, high	**H** Hourly	**M** Monthly	**S** Special: hourly and annual
AE Average entry wage	**AOL** Average offered, low	**ASL** Average starting, low	**HI** Highest wage paid	**MTC** Median total compensation	**TQ** Third quartile wage
AEX Average experienced wage	**APH** Average pay, high range	**AW** Average wage paid	**HR** High end range	**MW** Median wage paid	**W** Weekly
AO Average offered	**APL** Average pay, low range	**FQ** First quartile wage	**LR** Low end range	**SQ** Second quartile wage	**Y** Yearly

Occupation/Type/Industry	Location	Per	Low	Mid	High	Source	Date
Host and Hostess							
Restaurant, Lounge, and Coffee Shop	Baltimore PMSA, MD	S	7.50 MW	7.35 AW	15590 AAW	MDBLS	10//99-12//99
Restaurant, Lounge, and Coffee Shop	Cumberland MSA, MD-WV	S	5.91 MW	6.04 AW	12290 AAW	MDBLS	10//99-12//99
Restaurant, Lounge, and Coffee Shop	Hagerstown PMSA, MD	S	6.80 MW	6.56 AW	14130 AAW	MDBLS	10//99-12//99
Restaurant, Lounge, and Coffee Shop	Massachusetts	S	7.56 MW	7.80 AW	16230 AAW	MABLS	10//99-12//99
Restaurant, Lounge, and Coffee Shop	Barnstable-Yarmouth MSA, MA	S	7.84 MW	7.55 AW	16310 AAW	MABLS	10//99-12//99
Restaurant, Lounge, and Coffee Shop	Boston PMSA, MA-NH	S	7.74 MW	7.49 AW	16100 AAW	MABLS	10//99-12//99
Restaurant, Lounge, and Coffee Shop	Brockton PMSA, MA	S	7.76 MW	7.64 AW	16140 AAW	MABLS	10//99-12//99
Restaurant, Lounge, and Coffee Shop	Fitchburg-Leominster PMSA, MA	S	9.09 MW	9.53 AW	18910 AAW	MABLS	10//99-12//99
Restaurant, Lounge, and Coffee Shop	Lawrence PMSA, MA-NH	S	7.77 MW	7.56 AW	16160 AAW	MABLS	10//99-12//99
Restaurant, Lounge, and Coffee Shop	Lowell PMSA, MA-NH	S	7.84 MW	7.70 AW	16300 AAW	MABLS	10//99-12//99
Restaurant, Lounge, and Coffee Shop	New Bedford PMSA, MA	S	6.72 MW	6.37 AW	13980 AAW	MABLS	10//99-12//99
Restaurant, Lounge, and Coffee Shop	Pittsfield MSA, MA	S	7.61 MW	7.15 AW	15830 AAW	MABLS	10//99-12//99
Restaurant, Lounge, and Coffee Shop	Springfield MSA, MA	S	7.38 MW	6.67 AW	15360 AAW	MABLS	10//99-12//99
Restaurant, Lounge, and Coffee Shop	Worcester PMSA, MA-CT	S	7.76 MW	7.61 AW	16150 AAW	MABLS	10//99-12//99
Restaurant, Lounge, and Coffee Shop	Michigan	S	6.78 MW	6.95 AW	14450 AAW	MIBLS	10//99-12//99
Restaurant, Lounge, and Coffee Shop	Ann Arbor PMSA, MI	S	6.59 MW	6.49 AW	13700 AAW	MIBLS	10//99-12//99
Restaurant, Lounge, and Coffee Shop	Benton Harbor MSA, MI	S	6.67 MW	6.38 AW	13870 AAW	MIBLS	10//99-12//99
Restaurant, Lounge, and Coffee Shop	Detroit PMSA, MI	S	7.37 MW	7.33 AW	15330 AAW	MIBLS	10//99-12//99
Restaurant, Lounge, and Coffee Shop	Flint PMSA, MI	S	6.55 MW	6.19 AW	13630 AAW	MIBLS	10//99-12//99
Restaurant, Lounge, and Coffee Shop	Grand Rapids-Muskegon-Holland MSA, MI	S	6.94 MW	6.67 AW	14440 AAW	MIBLS	10//99-12//99
Restaurant, Lounge, and Coffee Shop	Jackson MSA, MI	S	7.36 MW	6.77 AW	15300 AAW	MIBLS	10//99-12//99
Restaurant, Lounge, and Coffee Shop	Kalamazoo-Battle Creek MSA, MI	S	6.70 MW	6.67 AW	13930 AAW	MIBLS	10//99-12//99
Restaurant, Lounge, and Coffee Shop	Lansing-East Lansing MSA, MI	S	6.35 MW	6.23 AW	13220 AAW	MIBLS	10//99-12//99
Restaurant, Lounge, and Coffee Shop	Saginaw-Bay City-Midland MSA, MI	S	6.24 MW	6.12 AW	12980 AAW	MIBLS	10//99-12//99
Restaurant, Lounge, and Coffee Shop	Minnesota	S	7.25 MW	7.42 AW	15430 AAW	MNBLS	10//99-12//99
Restaurant, Lounge, and Coffee Shop	Duluth-Superior MSA, MN-WI	S	6.51 MW	6.15 AW	13540 AAW	MNBLS	10//99-12//99
Restaurant, Lounge, and Coffee Shop	Minneapolis-St. Paul MSA, MN-WI	S	7.78 MW	7.68 AW	16190 AAW	MNBLS	10//99-12//99
Restaurant, Lounge, and Coffee Shop	Rochester MSA, MN	S	7.07 MW	7.04 AW	14710 AAW	MNBLS	10//99-12//99
Restaurant, Lounge, and Coffee Shop	St. Cloud MSA, MN	S	6.19 MW	6.12 AW	12880 AAW	MNBLS	10//99-12//99
Restaurant, Lounge, and Coffee Shop	Mississippi	S	6.78 MW	7.00 AW	14570 AAW	MSBLS	10//99-12//99
Restaurant, Lounge, and Coffee Shop	Biloxi-Gulfport-Pascagoula MSA, MS	S	6.91 MW	6.93 AW	14370 AAW	MSBLS	10//99-12//99
Restaurant, Lounge, and Coffee Shop	Hattiesburg MSA, MS	S	6.51 MW	6.38 AW	13530 AAW	MSBLS	10//99-12//99
Restaurant, Lounge, and Coffee Shop	Jackson MSA, MS	S	6.77 MW	6.56 AW	14090 AAW	MSBLS	10//99-12//99
Restaurant, Lounge, and Coffee Shop	Missouri	S	6.43 MW	6.92 AW	14400 AAW	MOBLS	10//99-12//99
Restaurant, Lounge, and Coffee Shop	Joplin MSA, MO	S	6.60 MW	6.33 AW	13730 AAW	MOBLS	10//99-12//99
Restaurant, Lounge, and Coffee Shop	Kansas City MSA, MO-KS	S	6.98 MW	6.73 AW	14510 AAW	MOBLS	10//99-12//99
Restaurant, Lounge, and Coffee Shop	St. Louis MSA, MO-IL	S	6.89 MW	6.33 AW	14340 AAW	MOBLS	10//99-12//99
Restaurant, Lounge, and Coffee Shop	Springfield MSA, MO	S	6.64 MW	6.44 AW	13820 AAW	MOBLS	10//99-12//99
Restaurant, Lounge, and Coffee Shop	Montana	S	5.98 MW	6.09 AW	12680 AAW	MTBLS	10//99-12//99
Restaurant, Lounge, and Coffee Shop	Billings MSA, MT	S	5.99 MW	5.97 AW	12460 AAW	MTBLS	10//99-12//99
Restaurant, Lounge, and Coffee Shop	Nebraska	S	6.68 MW	6.84 AW	14230 AAW	NEBLS	10//99-12//99
Restaurant, Lounge, and Coffee Shop	Lincoln MSA, NE	S	6.84 MW	6.75 AW	14220 AAW	NEBLS	10//99-12//99
Restaurant, Lounge, and Coffee Shop	Omaha MSA, NE-IA	S	7.12 MW	7.02 AW	14800 AAW	NEBLS	10//99-12//99
Restaurant, Lounge, and Coffee Shop	Nevada	S	8.33 MW	8.82 AW	18340 AAW	NVBLS	10//99-12//99
Restaurant, Lounge, and Coffee Shop	Las Vegas MSA, NV-AZ	S	9.24 MW	8.94 AW	19230 AAW	NVBLS	10//99-12//99
Restaurant, Lounge, and Coffee Shop	Reno MSA, NV	S	7.21 MW	7.15 AW	15000 AAW	NVBLS	10//99-12//99
Restaurant, Lounge, and Coffee Shop	New Hampshire	S	7.57 MW	7.66 AW	15930 AAW	NHBLS	10//99-12//99
Restaurant, Lounge, and Coffee Shop	Manchester PMSA, NH	S	7.95 MW	7.82 AW	16540 AAW	NHBLS	10//99-12//99
Restaurant, Lounge, and Coffee Shop	Nashua PMSA, NH	S	7.77 MW	7.78 AW	16160 AAW	NHBLS	10//99-12//99
Restaurant, Lounge, and Coffee Shop	Portsmouth-Rochester PMSA, NH-ME	S	7.65 MW	7.55 AW	15910 AAW	NHBLS	10//99-12//99
Restaurant, Lounge, and Coffee Shop	New Jersey	S	7.41 MW	7.80 AW	16220 AAW	NJBLS	10//99-12//99
Restaurant, Lounge, and Coffee Shop	Atlantic-Cape May PMSA, NJ	S	8.10 MW	7.65 AW	16850 AAW	NJBLS	10//99-12//99
Restaurant, Lounge, and Coffee Shop	Bergen-Passaic PMSA, NJ	S	7.79 MW	6.95 AW	16200 AAW	NJBLS	10//99-12//99
Restaurant, Lounge, and Coffee Shop	Jersey City PMSA, NJ	S	7.17 MW	6.86 AW	14910 AAW	NJBLS	10//99-12//99
Restaurant, Lounge, and Coffee Shop	Middlesex-Somerset-Hunterdon PMSA, NJ	S	8.00 MW	7.78 AW	16630 AAW	NJBLS	10//99-12//99
Restaurant, Lounge, and Coffee Shop	Monmouth-Ocean PMSA, NJ	S	7.70 MW	7.35 AW	16020 AAW	NJBLS	10//99-12//99
Restaurant, Lounge, and Coffee Shop	Newark PMSA, NJ	S	8.32 MW	7.73 AW	17310 AAW	NJBLS	10//99-12//99
Restaurant, Lounge, and Coffee Shop	Trenton PMSA, NJ	S	7.93 MW	7.46 AW	16490 AAW	NJBLS	10//99-12//99
Restaurant, Lounge, and Coffee Shop	Vineland-Millville-Bridgeton PMSA, NJ	S	7.49 MW	7.46 AW	15580 AAW	NJBLS	10//99-12//99
Restaurant, Lounge, and Coffee Shop	New Mexico	S	6.43 MW	6.81 AW	14170 AAW	NMBLS	10//99-12//99
Restaurant, Lounge, and Coffee Shop	Albuquerque MSA, NM	S	6.77 MW	6.38 AW	14080 AAW	NMBLS	10//99-12//99

AAW	Average annual wage	AOH	Average offered, high	ASH	Average starting, high
AE	Average entry wage	AOL	Average offered, low	ASL	Average starting, low
AEX	Average experienced wage	APH	Average pay, high range	AW	Average wage paid
AO	Average offered	APL	Average pay, low range	FQ	First quartile wage

H	Hourly	M	Monthly
HI	Highest wage paid	MTC	Median total compensation
HR	High end range	MW	Median wage paid
LR	Low end range	SQ	Second quartile wage

S	Special: hourly and annual
TQ	Third quartile wage
W	Weekly
Y	Yearly

Host and Hostess

Occupation/Type/Industry	Location	Per	Low	Mid	High	Source	Date
Host and Hostess							
Restaurant, Lounge, and Coffee Shop	Las Cruces MSA, NM	S	6.17 MW	6.06 AW	12830 AAW	NMBLS	10//99-12//99
Restaurant, Lounge, and Coffee Shop	Santa Fe MSA, NM	S	7.29 MW	6.89 AW	15150 AAW	NMBLS	10//99-12//99
Restaurant, Lounge, and Coffee Shop	New York	S	7.75 MW	8.58 AW	17850 AAW	NYBLS	10//99-12//99
Restaurant, Lounge, and Coffee Shop	Albany-Schenectady-Troy MSA, NY	S	7.01 MW	6.62 AW	14570 AAW	NYBLS	10//99-12//99
Restaurant, Lounge, and Coffee Shop	Binghamton MSA, NY	S	6.76 MW	6.52 AW	14050 AAW	NYBLS	10//99-12//99
Restaurant, Lounge, and Coffee Shop	Buffalo-Niagara Falls MSA, NY	S	6.79 MW	6.60 AW	14130 AAW	NYBLS	10//99-12//99
Restaurant, Lounge, and Coffee Shop	Dutchess County PMSA, NY	S	6.63 MW	6.04 AW	13790 AAW	NYBLS	10//99-12//99
Restaurant, Lounge, and Coffee Shop	Elmira MSA, NY	S	6.32 MW	6.21 AW	13150 AAW	NYBLS	10//99-12//99
Restaurant, Lounge, and Coffee Shop	Glens Falls MSA, NY	S	7.07 MW	6.76 AW	14710 AAW	NYBLS	10//99-12//99
Restaurant, Lounge, and Coffee Shop	Jamestown MSA, NY	S	6.38 MW	6.24 AW	13270 AAW	NYBLS	10//99-12//99
Restaurant, Lounge, and Coffee Shop	Nassau-Suffolk PMSA, NY	S	7.90 MW	7.47 AW	16430 AAW	NYBLS	10//99-12//99
Restaurant, Lounge, and Coffee Shop	New York PMSA, NY	S	10.62 MW	10.69 AW	22090 AAW	NYBLS	10//99-12//99
Restaurant, Lounge, and Coffee Shop	Newburgh PMSA, NY-PA	S	6.69 MW	6.18 AW	13910 AAW	NYBLS	10//99-12//99
Restaurant, Lounge, and Coffee Shop	Rochester MSA, NY	S	7.31 MW	6.97 AW	15200 AAW	NYBLS	10//99-12//99
Restaurant, Lounge, and Coffee Shop	Syracuse MSA, NY	S	6.73 MW	6.55 AW	14010 AAW	NYBLS	10//99-12//99
Restaurant, Lounge, and Coffee Shop	Utica-Rome MSA, NY	S	7.52 MW	6.27 AW	15630 AAW	NYBLS	10//99-12//99
Restaurant, Lounge, and Coffee Shop	North Carolina	S	6.93 MW	6.95 AW	14450 AAW	NCBLS	10//99-12//99
Restaurant, Lounge, and Coffee Shop	Asheville MSA, NC	S	6.53 MW	6.30 AW	13590 AAW	NCBLS	10//99-12//99
Restaurant, Lounge, and Coffee Shop	Charlotte-Gastonia-Rock Hill MSA, NC-SC	S	7.43 MW	7.51 AW	15450 AAW	NCBLS	10//99-12//99
Restaurant, Lounge, and Coffee Shop	Fayetteville MSA, NC	S	6.56 MW	6.56 AW	13650 AAW	NCBLS	10//99-12//99
Restaurant, Lounge, and Coffee Shop	Goldsboro MSA, NC	S	6.77 MW	6.68 AW	14070 AAW	NCBLS	10//99-12//99
Restaurant, Lounge, and Coffee Shop	Greensboro--Winston-Salem--High Point MSA, NC	S	6.62 MW	6.49 AW	13760 AAW	NCBLS	10//99-12//99
Restaurant, Lounge, and Coffee Shop	Greenville MSA, NC	S	6.04 MW	6.02 AW	12570 AAW	NCBLS	10//99-12//99
Restaurant, Lounge, and Coffee Shop	Hickory-Morganton-Lenoir MSA, NC	S	7.12 MW	7.21 AW	14800 AAW	NCBLS	10//99-12//99
Restaurant, Lounge, and Coffee Shop	Jacksonville MSA, NC	S	5.92 MW	6.04 AW	12310 AAW	NCBLS	10//99-12//99
Restaurant, Lounge, and Coffee Shop	Raleigh-Durham-Chapel Hill MSA, NC	S	7.29 MW	7.20 AW	15160 AAW	NCBLS	10//99-12//99
Restaurant, Lounge, and Coffee Shop	Rocky Mount MSA, NC	S	6.01 MW	6.01 AW	12490 AAW	NCBLS	10//99-12//99
Restaurant, Lounge, and Coffee Shop	Wilmington MSA, NC	S	6.19 MW	6.07 AW	12870 AAW	NCBLS	10//99-12//99
Restaurant, Lounge, and Coffee Shop	North Dakota	S	6.12 MW	6.13 AW	12750 AAW	NDBLS	10//99-12//99
Restaurant, Lounge, and Coffee Shop	Bismarck MSA, ND	S	5.95 MW	6.06 AW	12370 AAW	NDBLS	10//99-12//99
Restaurant, Lounge, and Coffee Shop	Fargo-Moorhead MSA, ND-MN	S	6.13 MW	6.08 AW	12750 AAW	NDBLS	10//99-12//99
Restaurant, Lounge, and Coffee Shop	Grand Forks MSA, ND-MN	S	6.44 MW	6.30 AW	13390 AAW	NDBLS	10//99-12//99
Restaurant, Lounge, and Coffee Shop	Ohio	S	6.53 MW	6.91 AW	14360 AAW	OHBLS	10//99-12//99
Restaurant, Lounge, and Coffee Shop	Akron PMSA, OH	S	8.20 MW	7.38 AW	17050 AAW	OHBLS	10//99-12//99
Restaurant, Lounge, and Coffee Shop	Canton-Massillon MSA, OH	S	6.52 MW	6.27 AW	13560 AAW	OHBLS	10//99-12//99
Restaurant, Lounge, and Coffee Shop	Cincinnati PMSA, OH-KY-IN	S	6.75 MW	6.60 AW	14040 AAW	OHBLS	10//99-12//99
Restaurant, Lounge, and Coffee Shop	Cleveland-Lorain-Elyria PMSA, OH	S	7.16 MW	6.72 AW	14900 AAW	OHBLS	10//99-12//99
Restaurant, Lounge, and Coffee Shop	Columbus MSA, OH	S	6.85 MW	6.59 AW	14250 AAW	OHBLS	10//99-12//99
Restaurant, Lounge, and Coffee Shop	Dayton-Springfield MSA, OH	S	6.62 MW	6.35 AW	13770 AAW	OHBLS	10//99-12//99
Restaurant, Lounge, and Coffee Shop	Hamilton-Middletown PMSA, OH	S	6.56 MW	6.43 AW	13640 AAW	OHBLS	10//99-12//99
Restaurant, Lounge, and Coffee Shop	Lima MSA, OH	S	7.05 MW	6.84 AW	14670 AAW	OHBLS	10//99-12//99
Restaurant, Lounge, and Coffee Shop	Mansfield MSA, OH	S	6.46 MW	6.26 AW	13440 AAW	OHBLS	10//99-12//99
Restaurant, Lounge, and Coffee Shop	Steubenville-Weirton MSA, OH-WV	S	6.72 MW	6.27 AW	13970 AAW	OHBLS	10//99-12//99
Restaurant, Lounge, and Coffee Shop	Toledo MSA, OH	S	6.79 MW	6.67 AW	14130 AAW	OHBLS	10//99-12//99
Restaurant, Lounge, and Coffee Shop	Youngstown-Warren MSA, OH	S	6.57 MW	6.28 AW	13660 AAW	OHBLS	10//99-12//99
Restaurant, Lounge, and Coffee Shop	Oklahoma	S	6.15 MW	6.36 AW	13220 AAW	OKBLS	10//99-12//99
Restaurant, Lounge, and Coffee Shop	Oklahoma City MSA, OK	S	6.57 MW	6.33 AW	13660 AAW	OKBLS	10//99-12//99
Restaurant, Lounge, and Coffee Shop	Tulsa MSA, OK	S	6.14 MW	6.15 AW	12780 AAW	OKBLS	10//99-12//99
Restaurant, Lounge, and Coffee Shop	Oregon	S	7.26 MW	7.47 AW	15530 AAW	ORBLS	10//99-12//99
Restaurant, Lounge, and Coffee Shop	Eugene-Springfield MSA, OR	S	7.18 MW	7.01 AW	14940 AAW	ORBLS	10//99-12//99
Restaurant, Lounge, and Coffee Shop	Medford-Ashland MSA, OR	S	7.20 MW	7.02 AW	14980 AAW	ORBLS	10//99-12//99
Restaurant, Lounge, and Coffee Shop	Portland-Vancouver PMSA, OR-WA	S	7.52 MW	7.30 AW	15630 AAW	ORBLS	10//99-12//99
Restaurant, Lounge, and Coffee Shop	Salem PMSA, OR	S	7.14 MW	6.83 AW	14860 AAW	ORBLS	10//99-12//99
Restaurant, Lounge, and Coffee Shop	Pennsylvania	S	6.65 MW	7.02 AW	14600 AAW	PABLS	10//99-12//99
Restaurant, Lounge, and Coffee Shop	Allentown-Bethlehem-Easton MSA, PA	S	6.98 MW	6.86 AW	14530 AAW	PABLS	10//99-12//99
Restaurant, Lounge, and Coffee Shop	Altoona MSA, PA	S	6.57 MW	6.33 AW	13670 AAW	PABLS	10//99-12//99
Restaurant, Lounge, and Coffee Shop	Erie MSA, PA	S	6.32 MW	6.21 AW	13140 AAW	PABLS	10//99-12//99
Restaurant, Lounge, and Coffee Shop	Harrisburg-Lebanon-Carlisle MSA, PA	S	6.88 MW	6.66 AW	14310 AAW	PABLS	10//99-12//99

Host and Hostess

Occupation/Type/Industry	Location	Per	Low	Mid	High	Source	Date
Restaurant, Lounge, and Coffee Shop	Johnstown MSA, PA	S	6.18 MW	6.11 AW	12850 AAW	PABLS	10//99-12//99
Restaurant, Lounge, and Coffee Shop	Lancaster MSA, PA	S	7.29 MW	7.24 AW	15160 AAW	PABLS	10//99-12//99
Restaurant, Lounge, and Coffee Shop	Philadelphia PMSA, PA-NJ	S	7.55 MW	7.14 AW	15710 AAW	PABLS	10//99-12//99
Restaurant, Lounge, and Coffee Shop	Pittsburgh MSA, PA	S	6.78 MW	6.60 AW	14110 AAW	PABLS	10//99-12//99
Restaurant, Lounge, and Coffee Shop	Reading MSA, PA	S	6.91 MW	6.65 AW	14360 AAW	PABLS	10//99-12//99
Restaurant, Lounge, and Coffee Shop	Scranton--Wilkes-Barre--Hazleton MSA, PA	S	6.35 MW	6.07 AW	13200 AAW	PABLS	10//99-12//99
Restaurant, Lounge, and Coffee Shop	Sharon MSA, PA	S	6.59 MW	6.43 AW	13700 AAW	PABLS	10//99-12//99
Restaurant, Lounge, and Coffee Shop	State College MSA, PA	S	6.45 MW	6.19 AW	13410 AAW	PABLS	10//99-12//99
Restaurant, Lounge, and Coffee Shop	Williamsport MSA, PA	S	6.77 MW	6.25 AW	14070 AAW	PABLS	10//99-12//99
Restaurant, Lounge, and Coffee Shop	York MSA, PA	S	6.99 MW	6.76 AW	14540 AAW	PABLS	10//99-12//99
Restaurant, Lounge, and Coffee Shop	Rhode Island	S	6.77 MW	7.26 AW	15100 AAW	RIBLS	10//99-12//99
Restaurant, Lounge, and Coffee Shop	Providence-Fall River-Warwick MSA, RI-MA	S	7.38 MW	6.85 AW	15350 AAW	RIBLS	10//99-12//99
Restaurant, Lounge, and Coffee Shop	South Carolina	S	6.41 MW	6.89 AW	14330 AAW	SCBLS	10//99-12//99
Restaurant, Lounge, and Coffee Shop	Charleston-North Charleston MSA, SC	S	6.45 MW	5.95 AW	13410 AAW	SCBLS	10//99-12//99
Restaurant, Lounge, and Coffee Shop	Columbia MSA, SC	S	6.49 MW	6.09 AW	13500 AAW	SCBLS	10//99-12//99
Restaurant, Lounge, and Coffee Shop	Florence MSA, SC	S	6.50 MW	6.12 AW	13520 AAW	SCBLS	10//99-12//99
Restaurant, Lounge, and Coffee Shop	Greenville-Spartanburg-Anderson MSA, SC	S	7.09 MW	7.26 AW	14750 AAW	SCBLS	10//99-12//99
Restaurant, Lounge, and Coffee Shop	Myrtle Beach MSA, SC	S	7.53 MW	7.28 AW	15660 AAW	SCBLS	10//99-12//99
Restaurant, Lounge, and Coffee Shop	South Dakota	S	6.73 MW	6.73 AW	14000 AAW	SDBLS	10//99-12//99
Restaurant, Lounge, and Coffee Shop	Rapid City MSA, SD	S	7.11 MW	7.30 AW	14790 AAW	SDBLS	10//99-12//99
Restaurant, Lounge, and Coffee Shop	Sioux Falls MSA, SD	S	6.78 MW	6.89 AW	14100 AAW	SDBLS	10//99-12//99
Restaurant, Lounge, and Coffee Shop	Tennessee	S	6.66 MW	6.81 AW	14160 AAW	TNBLS	10//99-12//99
Restaurant, Lounge, and Coffee Shop	Chattanooga MSA, TN-GA	S	6.90 MW	6.94 AW	14350 AAW	TNBLS	10//99-12//99
Restaurant, Lounge, and Coffee Shop	Clarksville-Hopkinsville MSA, TN-KY	S	6.55 MW	6.37 AW	13610 AAW	TNBLS	10//99-12//99
Restaurant, Lounge, and Coffee Shop	Jackson MSA, TN	S	6.98 MW	6.92 AW	14510 AAW	TNBLS	10//99-12//99
Restaurant, Lounge, and Coffee Shop	Johnson City-Kingsport-Bristol MSA, TN-VA	S	6.45 MW	6.35 AW	13410 AAW	TNBLS	10//99-12//99
Restaurant, Lounge, and Coffee Shop	Knoxville MSA, TN	S	6.97 MW	6.89 AW	14500 AAW	TNBLS	10//99-12//99
Restaurant, Lounge, and Coffee Shop	Memphis MSA, TN-AR-MS	S	6.54 MW	6.33 AW	13590 AAW	MSBLS	10//99-12//99
Restaurant, Lounge, and Coffee Shop	Nashville MSA, TN	S	7.07 MW	6.87 AW	14710 AAW	TNBLS	10//99-12//99
Restaurant, Lounge, and Coffee Shop	Texas	S	6.11 MW	6.32 AW	13150 AAW	TXBLS	10//99-12//99
Restaurant, Lounge, and Coffee Shop	Abilene MSA, TX	S	5.92 MW	6.01 AW	12300 AAW	TXBLS	10//99-12//99
Restaurant, Lounge, and Coffee Shop	Amarillo MSA, TX	S	6.16 MW	6.06 AW	12810 AAW	TXBLS	10//99-12//99
Restaurant, Lounge, and Coffee Shop	Austin-San Marcos MSA, TX	S	6.39 MW	6.21 AW	13280 AAW	TXBLS	10//99-12//99
Restaurant, Lounge, and Coffee Shop	Beaumont-Port Arthur MSA, TX	S	6.60 MW	6.10 AW	13720 AAW	TXBLS	10//99-12//99
Restaurant, Lounge, and Coffee Shop	Brazoria PMSA, TX	S	6.29 MW	6.10 AW	13080 AAW	TXBLS	10//99-12//99
Restaurant, Lounge, and Coffee Shop	Brownsville-Harlingen-San Benito MSA, TX	S	6.01 MW	5.93 AW	12510 AAW	TXBLS	10//99-12//99
Restaurant, Lounge, and Coffee Shop	Bryan-College Station MSA, TX	S	5.81 MW	5.94 AW	12090 AAW	TXBLS	10//99-12//99
Restaurant, Lounge, and Coffee Shop	Corpus Christi MSA, TX	S	6.70 MW	6.44 AW	13930 AAW	TXBLS	10//99-12//99
Restaurant, Lounge, and Coffee Shop	Dallas PMSA, TX	S	6.65 MW	6.50 AW	13820 AAW	TXBLS	10//99-12//99
Restaurant, Lounge, and Coffee Shop	El Paso MSA, TX	S	6.09 MW	6.02 AW	12670 AAW	TXBLS	10//99-12//99
Restaurant, Lounge, and Coffee Shop	Fort Worth-Arlington PMSA, TX	S	6.15 MW	6.07 AW	12790 AAW	TXBLS	10//99-12//99
Restaurant, Lounge, and Coffee Shop	Galveston-Texas City PMSA, TX	S	6.45 MW	6.40 AW	13410 AAW	TXBLS	10//99-12//99
Restaurant, Lounge, and Coffee Shop	Houston PMSA, TX	S	6.19 MW	5.97 AW	12880 AAW	TXBLS	10//99-12//99
Restaurant, Lounge, and Coffee Shop	Killeen-Temple MSA, TX	S	6.22 MW	6.09 AW	12950 AAW	TXBLS	10//99-12//99
Restaurant, Lounge, and Coffee Shop	Laredo MSA, TX	S	6.24 MW	6.05 AW	12980 AAW	TXBLS	10//99-12//99
Restaurant, Lounge, and Coffee Shop	Longview-Marshall MSA, TX	S	6.09 MW	6.07 AW	12660 AAW	TXBLS	10//99-12//99
Restaurant, Lounge, and Coffee Shop	Lubbock MSA, TX	S	6.06 MW	6.01 AW	12610 AAW	TXBLS	10//99-12//99
Restaurant, Lounge, and Coffee Shop	McAllen-Edinburg-Mission MSA, TX	S	6.19 MW	6.26 AW	12880 AAW	TXBLS	10//99-12//99
Restaurant, Lounge, and Coffee Shop	Odessa-Midland MSA, TX	S	6.02 MW	5.95 AW	12520 AAW	TXBLS	10//99-12//99
Restaurant, Lounge, and Coffee Shop	San Angelo MSA, TX	S	6.11 MW	6.09 AW	12710 AAW	TXBLS	10//99-12//99
Restaurant, Lounge, and Coffee Shop	San Antonio MSA, TX	S	6.56 MW	6.36 AW	13640 AAW	TXBLS	10//99-12//99
Restaurant, Lounge, and Coffee Shop	Sherman-Denison MSA, TX	S	6.11 MW	5.99 AW	12720 AAW	TXBLS	10//99-12//99
Restaurant, Lounge, and Coffee Shop	Texarkana, MSA, TX-Texarkana, AR	S	6.09 MW	6.03 AW	12660 AAW	TXBLS	10//99-12//99
Restaurant, Lounge, and Coffee Shop	Tyler MSA, TX	S	6.31 MW	6.27 AW	13130 AAW	TXBLS	10//99-12//99
Restaurant, Lounge, and Coffee Shop	Waco MSA, TX	S	5.97 MW	6.08 AW	12420 AAW	TXBLS	10//99-12//99
Restaurant, Lounge, and Coffee Shop	Wichita Falls MSA, TX	S	6.76 MW	6.85 AW	14060 AAW	TXBLS	10//99-12//99
Restaurant, Lounge, and Coffee Shop	Utah	S	6.82 MW	7.01 AW	14590 AAW	UTBLS	10//99-12//99
Restaurant, Lounge, and Coffee Shop	Provo-Orem MSA, UT	S	7.02 MW	6.82 AW	14600 AAW	UTBLS	10//99-12//99

AAW Average annual wage	AOH Average offered, high	ASH Average starting, high	H Hourly	M Monthly	S Special: hourly and annual
AE Average entry wage	AOL Average offered, low	ASL Average starting, low	HI Highest wage paid	MTC Median total compensation	TQ Third quartile wage
AEX Average experienced wage	APH Average pay, high range	AW Average wage paid	HR High end range	MW Median wage paid	W Weekly
AO Average offered	APL Average pay, low range	FQ First quartile wage	LR Low end range	SQ Second quartile wage	Y Yearly

Occupation/Type/Industry	Location	Per	Low	Mid	High	Source	Date
Host and Hostess							
Restaurant, Lounge, and Coffee Shop	Salt Lake City-Ogden MSA, UT	S	7.09 MW	6.89 AW	14750 AAW	UTBLS	10//99-12//99
Restaurant, Lounge, and Coffee Shop	Vermont	S	7.3 MW	7.45 AW	15490 AAW	VTBLS	10//99-12//99
Restaurant, Lounge, and Coffee Shop	Burlington MSA, VT	S	7.29 MW	6.85 AW	15160 AAW	VTBLS	10//99-12//99
Restaurant, Lounge, and Coffee Shop	Virginia	S	6.55 MW	6.86 AW	14270 AAW	VABLS	10//99-12//99
Restaurant, Lounge, and Coffee Shop	Charlottesville MSA, VA	S	6.74 MW	6.52 AW	14020 AAW	VABLS	10//99-12//99
Restaurant, Lounge, and Coffee Shop	Lynchburg MSA, VA	S	6.77 MW	6.61 AW	14070 AAW	VABLS	10//99-12//99
Restaurant, Lounge, and Coffee Shop	Norfolk-Virginia Beach-Newport News MSA, VA-NC	S	6.46 MW	6.28 AW	13440 AAW	VABLS	10//99-12//99
Restaurant, Lounge, and Coffee Shop	Richmond-Petersburg MSA, VA	S	6.56 MW	6.31 AW	13640 AAW	VABLS	10//99-12//99
Restaurant, Lounge, and Coffee Shop	Roanoke MSA, VA	S	6.61 MW	6.47 AW	13740 AAW	VABLS	10//99-12//99
Restaurant, Lounge, and Coffee Shop	Washington	S	6.64 MW	7.15 AW	14860 AAW	WABLS	10//99-12//99
Restaurant, Lounge, and Coffee Shop	Bellingham MSA, WA	S	6.67 MW	6.37 AW	13870 AAW	WABLS	10//99-12//99
Restaurant, Lounge, and Coffee Shop	Bremerton PMSA, WA	S	6.68 MW	6.35 AW	13890 AAW	WABLS	10//99-12//99
Restaurant, Lounge, and Coffee Shop	Olympia PMSA, WA	S	6.92 MW	6.46 AW	14400 AAW	WABLS	10//99-12//99
Restaurant, Lounge, and Coffee Shop	Richland-Kennewick-Pasco MSA, WA	S	6.88 MW	6.34 AW	14310 AAW	WABLS	10//99-12//99
Restaurant, Lounge, and Coffee Shop	Seattle-Bellevue-Everett PMSA, WA	S	7.64 MW	7.18 AW	15890 AAW	WABLS	10//99-12//99
Restaurant, Lounge, and Coffee Shop	Spokane MSA, WA	S	6.42 MW	6.12 AW	13360 AAW	WABLS	10//99-12//99
Restaurant, Lounge, and Coffee Shop	Tacoma PMSA, WA	S	6.57 MW	6.37 AW	13660 AAW	WABLS	10//99-12//99
Restaurant, Lounge, and Coffee Shop	Yakima MSA, WA	S	6.38 MW	6.13 AW	13270 AAW	WABLS	10//99-12//99
Restaurant, Lounge, and Coffee Shop	West Virginia	S	6.01 MW	6.03 AW	12540 AAW	WVBLS	10//99-12//99
Restaurant, Lounge, and Coffee Shop	Charleston MSA, WV	S	6.21 MW	6.24 AW	12920 AAW	WVBLS	10//99-12//99
Restaurant, Lounge, and Coffee Shop	Huntington-Ashland MSA, WV-KY-OH	S	6.18 MW	6.02 AW	12850 AAW	WVBLS	10//99-12//99
Restaurant, Lounge, and Coffee Shop	Parkersburg-Marietta MSA, WV-OH	S	5.92 MW	5.96 AW	12310 AAW	WVBLS	10//99-12//99
Restaurant, Lounge, and Coffee Shop	Wheeling MSA, WV-OH	S	6.00 MW	6.04 AW	12470 AAW	WVBLS	10//99-12//99
Restaurant, Lounge, and Coffee Shop	Wisconsin	S	6.93 MW	7.17 AW	14920 AAW	WIBLS	10//99-12//99
Restaurant, Lounge, and Coffee Shop	Appleton-Oshkosh-Neenah MSA, WI	S	7.01 MW	7.08 AW	14590 AAW	WIBLS	10//99-12//99
Restaurant, Lounge, and Coffee Shop	Eau Claire MSA, WI	S	6.32 MW	6.24 AW	13150 AAW	WIBLS	10//99-12//99
Restaurant, Lounge, and Coffee Shop	Green Bay MSA, WI	S	7.20 MW	7.11 AW	14970 AAW	WIBLS	10//99-12//99
Restaurant, Lounge, and Coffee Shop	Janesville-Beloit MSA, WI	S	6.50 MW	6.25 AW	13530 AAW	WIBLS	10//99-12//99
Restaurant, Lounge, and Coffee Shop	Kenosha PMSA, WI	S	7.10 MW	7.15 AW	14760 AAW	WIBLS	10//99-12//99
Restaurant, Lounge, and Coffee Shop	La Crosse MSA, WI-MN	S	7.08 MW	6.89 AW	14730 AAW	WIBLS	10//99-12//99
Restaurant, Lounge, and Coffee Shop	Madison MSA, WI	S	7.48 MW	7.56 AW	15560 AAW	WIBLS	10//99-12//99
Restaurant, Lounge, and Coffee Shop	Milwaukee-Waukesha PMSA, WI	S	7.18 MW	6.83 AW	14940 AAW	WIBLS	10//99-12//99
Restaurant, Lounge, and Coffee Shop	Racine PMSA, WI	S	7.70 MW	7.64 AW	16010 AAW	WIBLS	10//99-12//99
Restaurant, Lounge, and Coffee Shop	Wausau MSA, WI	S	7.05 MW	6.95 AW	14670 AAW	WIBLS	10//99-12//99
Restaurant, Lounge, and Coffee Shop	Wyoming	S	6.16 MW	6.56 AW	13650 AAW	WYBLS	10//99-12//99
Restaurant, Lounge, and Coffee Shop	Casper MSA, WY	S	5.78 MW	5.97 AW	12030 AAW	WYBLS	10//99-12//99
Restaurant, Lounge, and Coffee Shop	Cheyenne MSA, WY	S	6.58 MW	6.56 AW	13690 AAW	WYBLS	10//99-12//99
Restaurant, Lounge, and Coffee Shop	Puerto Rico	S	6.1 MW	6.26 AW	13010 AAW	PRBLS	10//99-12//99
Restaurant, Lounge, and Coffee Shop	Mayaguez MSA, PR	S	5.84 MW	6.02 AW	12150 AAW	PRBLS	10//99-12//99
Restaurant, Lounge, and Coffee Shop	San Juan-Bayamon PMSA, PR	S	6.35 MW	6.15 AW	13200 AAW	PRBLS	10//99-12//99
Restaurant, Lounge, and Coffee Shop	Virgin Islands	S	7.51 MW	7.42 AW	15440 AAW	VIBLS	10//99-12//99
Restaurant, Lounge, and Coffee Shop	Guam	S	6.84 MW	6.99 AW	14540 AAW	GUBLS	10//99-12//99
Hotel, Motel, and Resort Desk Clerk	Alabama	S	6.38 MW	6.61 AW	13740 AAW	ALBLS	10//99-12//99
	Anniston MSA, AL	S	6.36 MW	6.11 AW	13230 AAW	ALBLS	10//99-12//99
	Auburn-Opelika MSA, AL	S	5.83 MW	6.03 AW	12120 AAW	ALBLS	10//99-12//99
	Birmingham MSA, AL	S	6.86 MW	6.68 AW	14260 AAW	ALBLS	10//99-12//99
	Dothan MSA, AL	S	6.22 MW	6.15 AW	12930 AAW	ALBLS	10//99-12//99
	Florence MSA, AL	S	6.47 MW	6.31 AW	13460 AAW	ALBLS	10//99-12//99
	Huntsville MSA, AL	S	6.62 MW	6.46 AW	13770 AAW	ALBLS	10//99-12//99
	Mobile MSA, AL	S	6.77 MW	6.52 AW	14090 AAW	ALBLS	10//99-12//99
	Montgomery MSA, AL	S	6.56 MW	6.29 AW	13640 AAW	ALBLS	10//99-12//99
	Tuscaloosa MSA, AL	S	5.97 MW	6.05 AW	12420 AAW	ALBLS	10//99-12//99
	Alaska	S	8.15 MW	8.34 AW	17350 AAW	AKBLS	10//99-12//99
	Anchorage MSA, AK	S	8.42 MW	8.20 AW	17510 AAW	AKBLS	10//99-12//99
	Arizona	S	7.34 MW	7.35 AW	15290 AAW	AZBLS	10//99-12//99
	Flagstaff MSA, AZ-UT	S	7.03 MW	7.02 AW	14630 AAW	AZBLS	10//99-12//99
	Phoenix-Mesa MSA, AZ	S	7.74 MW	7.72 AW	16100 AAW	AZBLS	10//99-12//99
	Tucson MSA, AZ	S	7.43 MW	7.33 AW	15460 AAW	AZBLS	10//99-12//99
	Yuma MSA, AZ	S	7.20 MW	7.37 AW	14970 AAW	AZBLS	10//99-12//99

AAW Average annual wage	**AOH** Average offered, high	**ASH** Average starting, high	**H** Hourly	**M** Monthly	**S** Special: hourly and annual
AE Average entry wage	**AOL** Average offered, low	**ASL** Average starting, low	**HI** Highest wage paid	**MTC** Median total compensation	**TQ** Third quartile wage
AEX Average experienced wage	**APH** Average pay, high range	**AW** Average wage paid	**HR** High end range	**MW** Median wage paid	**W** Weekly
AO Average offered	**APL** Average pay, low range	**FQ** First quartile wage	**LR** Low end range	**SQ** Second quartile wage	**Y** Yearly

Occupation/Type/Industry	Location	Per	Low	Mid	High	Source	Date
Hotel, Motel, and Resort Desk Clerk	Arkansas	S	6.64 MW	6.72 AW	13970 AAW	ARBLS	10//99-12//99
	Fayetteville-Springdale-Rogers MSA, AR	S	6.60 MW	6.57 AW	13740 AAW	ARBLS	10//99-12//99
	Fort Smith MSA, AR-OK	S	6.12 MW	6.08 AW	12720 AAW	ARBLS	10//99-12//99
	Little Rock-North Little Rock MSA, AR	S	7.29 MW	7.44 AW	15170 AAW	ARBLS	10//99-12//99
	Pine Bluff MSA, AR	S	6.36 MW	6.29 AW	13230 AAW	ARBLS	10//99-12//99
	California	S	8.14 MW	8.51 AW	17700 AAW	CABLS	10//99-12//99
	Bakersfield MSA, CA	S	7.33 MW	7.20 AW	15250 AAW	CABLS	10//99-12//99
	Chico-Paradise MSA, CA	S	7.79 MW	7.04 AW	16200 AAW	CABLS	10//99-12//99
	Fresno MSA, CA	S	7.56 MW	7.27 AW	15730 AAW	CABLS	10//99-12//99
	Los Angeles-Long Beach PMSA, CA	S	8.97 MW	8.93 AW	18650 AAW	CABLS	10//99-12//99
	Merced MSA, CA	S	7.00 MW	6.81 AW	14560 AAW	CABLS	10//99-12//99
	Modesto MSA, CA	S	6.85 MW	6.57 AW	14250 AAW	CABLS	10//99-12//99
	Oakland PMSA, CA	S	8.60 MW	8.61 AW	17880 AAW	CABLS	10//99-12//99
	Orange County PMSA, CA	S	7.86 MW	7.57 AW	16350 AAW	CABLS	10//99-12//99
	Redding MSA, CA	S	6.99 MW	6.85 AW	14540 AAW	CABLS	10//99-12//99
	Riverside-San Bernardino PMSA, CA	S	7.78 MW	7.69 AW	16190 AAW	CABLS	10//99-12//99
	Sacramento PMSA, CA	S	7.61 MW	7.52 AW	15820 AAW	CABLS	10//99-12//99
	Salinas MSA, CA	S	8.65 MW	8.41 AW	17990 AAW	CABLS	10//99-12//99
	San Diego MSA, CA	S	8.25 MW	8.15 AW	17160 AAW	CABLS	10//99-12//99
	San Francisco PMSA, CA	S	10.58 MW	10.73 AW	22000 AAW	CABLS	10//99-12//99
	San Jose PMSA, CA	S	9.40 MW	9.64 AW	19540 AAW	CABLS	10//99-12//99
	San Luis Obispo-Atascadero-Paso Robles MSA, CA	S	7.35 MW	6.93 AW	15280 AAW	CABLS	10//99-12//99
	Santa Barbara-Santa Maria-Lompoc MSA, CA	S	7.68 MW	7.37 AW	15970 AAW	CABLS	10//99-12//99
	Santa Cruz-Watsonville PMSA, CA	S	8.04 MW	7.87 AW	16710 AAW	CABLS	10//99-12//99
	Santa Rosa PMSA, CA	S	8.72 MW	8.55 AW	18130 AAW	CABLS	10//99-12//99
	Stockton-Lodi MSA, CA	S	6.81 MW	6.50 AW	14170 AAW	CABLS	10//99-12//99
	Vallejo-Fairfield-Napa PMSA, CA	S	8.17 MW	8.01 AW	17000 AAW	CABLS	10//99-12//99
	Ventura PMSA, CA	S	8.72 MW	7.83 AW	18140 AAW	CABLS	10//99-12//99
	Visalia-Tulare-Porterville MSA, CA	S	6.53 MW	6.15 AW	13590 AAW	CABLS	10//99-12//99
	Yolo PMSA, CA	S	7.37 MW	7.24 AW	15320 AAW	CABLS	10//99-12//99
	Colorado	S	7.91 MW	8.06 AW	16760 AAW	COBLS	10//99-12//99
	Boulder-Longmont PMSA, CO	S	7.79 MW	7.77 AW	16200 AAW	COBLS	10//99-12//99
	Colorado Springs MSA, CO	S	7.48 MW	7.59 AW	15550 AAW	COBLS	10//99-12//99
	Denver PMSA, CO	S	7.95 MW	7.90 AW	16540 AAW	COBLS	10//99-12//99
	Fort Collins-Loveland MSA, CO	S	6.98 MW	6.88 AW	14510 AAW	COBLS	10//99-12//99
	Grand Junction MSA, CO	S	6.80 MW	6.64 AW	14130 AAW	COBLS	10//99-12//99
	Pueblo MSA, CO	S	6.94 MW	6.69 AW	14440 AAW	COBLS	10//99-12//99
	Connecticut	S	8.21 MW	8.38 AW	17430 AAW	CTBLS	10//99-12//99
	Bridgeport PMSA, CT	S	8.42 MW	8.10 AW	17520 AAW	CTBLS	10//99-12//99
	Danbury PMSA, CT	S	9.13 MW	9.19 AW	18990 AAW	CTBLS	10//99-12//99
	Hartford MSA, CT	S	8.14 MW	8.03 AW	16930 AAW	CTBLS	10//99-12//99
	New Haven-Meriden PMSA, CT	S	8.19 MW	8.09 AW	17030 AAW	CTBLS	10//99-12//99
	New London-Norwich MSA, CT-RI	S	8.34 MW	8.22 AW	17350 AAW	CTBLS	10//99-12//99
	Stamford-Norwalk PMSA, CT	S	9.08 MW	8.66 AW	18890 AAW	CTBLS	10//99-12//99
	Waterbury PMSA, CT	S	8.18 MW	8.20 AW	17010 AAW	CTBLS	10//99-12//99
	Delaware	S	7.83 MW	7.92 AW	16470 AAW	DEBLS	10//99-12//99
	Dover MSA, DE	S	6.86 MW	6.60 AW	14270 AAW	DEBLS	10//99-12//99
	Wilmington-Newark PMSA, DE-MD	S	8.12 MW	7.98 AW	16880 AAW	DEBLS	10//99-12//99
	District of Columbia	S	10.88 MW	10.43 AW	21700 AAW	DCBLS	10//99-12//99
	Washington PMSA, DC-MD-VA-WV	S	8.48 MW	8.23 AW	17630 AAW	DCBLS	10//99-12//99
	Florida	S	7.52 MW	7.57 AW	15750 AAW	FLBLS	10//99-12//99
	Daytona Beach MSA, FL	S	7.40 MW	7.45 AW	15400 AAW	FLBLS	10//99-12//99
	Fort Lauderdale PMSA, FL	S	8.03 MW	7.99 AW	16700 AAW	FLBLS	10//99-12//99
	Fort Myers-Cape Coral MSA, FL	S	7.46 MW	7.46 AW	15510 AAW	FLBLS	10//99-12//99
	Fort Pierce-Port St. Lucie MSA, FL	S	7.68 MW	7.67 AW	15980 AAW	FLBLS	10//99-12//99

AAW Average annual wage	**AOH** Average offered, high	**ASH** Average starting, high	**H** Hourly	**M** Monthly	**S** Special: hourly and annual
AE Average entry wage	**AOL** Average offered, low	**ASL** Average starting, low	**HI** Highest wage paid	**MTC** Median total compensation	**TQ** Third quartile wage
AEX Average experienced wage	**APH** Average pay, high range	**AW** Average wage paid	**HR** High end range	**MW** Median wage paid	**W** Weekly
AO Average offered	**APL** Average pay, low range	**FQ** First quartile wage	**LR** Low end range	**SQ** Second quartile wage	**Y** Yearly

Occupation/Type/Industry	Location	Per	Low	Mid	High	Source	Date
Hotel, Motel, and Resort Desk Clerk							
	Fort Walton Beach MSA, FL	S	7.28 MW	7.05 AW	15140 AAW	FLBLS	10//99-12//99
	Jacksonville MSA, FL	S	7.27 MW	7.35 AW	15110 AAW	FLBLS	10//99-12//99
	Lakeland-Winter Haven MSA, FL	S	8.07 MW	7.86 AW	16780 AAW	FLBLS	10//99-12//99
	Melbourne-Titusville-Palm Bay MSA, FL	S	7.52 MW	7.61 AW	15650 AAW	FLBLS	10//99-12//99
	Miami PMSA, FL	S	8.27 MW	8.01 AW	17210 AAW	FLBLS	10//99-12//99
	Naples MSA, FL	S	8.58 MW	8.50 AW	17850 AAW	FLBLS	10//99-12//99
	Ocala MSA, FL	S	6.73 MW	6.63 AW	14010 AAW	FLBLS	10//99-12//99
	Orlando MSA, FL	S	7.60 MW	7.61 AW	15820 AAW	FLBLS	10//99-12//99
	Panama City MSA, FL	S	6.97 MW	6.82 AW	14490 AAW	FLBLS	10//99-12//99
	Pensacola MSA, FL	S	6.79 MW	6.54 AW	14120 AAW	FLBLS	10//99-12//99
	Sarasota-Bradenton MSA, FL	S	7.96 MW	7.83 AW	16550 AAW	FLBLS	10//99-12//99
	Tallahassee MSA, FL	S	6.82 MW	6.72 AW	14180 AAW	FLBLS	10//99-12//99
	Tampa-St. Petersburg-Clearwater MSA, FL	S	7.35 MW	7.27 AW	15300 AAW	FLBLS	10//99-12//99
	West Palm Beach-Boca Raton MSA, FL	S	8.17 MW	8.07 AW	17000 AAW	FLBLS	10//99-12//99
	Georgia	S	8.15 MW	8.20 AW	17050 AAW	GABLS	10//99-12//99
	Albany MSA, GA	S	7.75 MW	7.78 AW	16110 AAW	GABLS	10//99-12//99
	Athens MSA, GA	S	8.45 MW	8.91 AW	17580 AAW	GABLS	10//99-12//99
	Atlanta MSA, GA	S	8.87 MW	9.03 AW	18440 AAW	GABLS	10//99-12//99
	Augusta-Aiken MSA, GA-SC	S	7.01 MW	7.00 AW	14590 AAW	GABLS	10//99-12//99
	Macon MSA, GA	S	7.55 MW	7.25 AW	15700 AAW	GABLS	10//99-12//99
	Savannah MSA, GA	S	8.29 MW	8.40 AW	17250 AAW	GABLS	10//99-12//99
	Hawaii	S	13.48 MW	12.80 AW	26620 AAW	HIBLS	10//99-12//99
	Honolulu MSA, HI	S	12.65 MW	13.41 AW	26310 AAW	HIBLS	10//99-12//99
	Idaho	S	7.06 MW	7.12 AW	14820 AAW	IDBLS	10//99-12//99
	Boise City MSA, ID	S	7.14 MW	7.14 AW	14860 AAW	IDBLS	10//99-12//99
	Pocatello MSA, ID	S	6.60 MW	6.39 AW	13730 AAW	IDBLS	10//99-12//99
	Illinois	S	7.46 MW	7.89 AW	16410 AAW	ILBLS	10//99-12//99
	Bloomington-Normal MSA, IL	S	7.14 MW	6.92 AW	14860 AAW	ILBLS	10//99-12//99
	Champaign-Urbana MSA, IL	S	7.29 MW	7.30 AW	15160 AAW	ILBLS	10//99-12//99
	Chicago PMSA, IL	S	8.50 MW	7.95 AW	17680 AAW	ILBLS	10//99-12//99
	Kankakee PMSA, IL	S	6.36 MW	6.12 AW	13230 AAW	ILBLS	10//99-12//99
	Peoria-Pekin MSA, IL	S	6.68 MW	6.49 AW	13900 AAW	ILBLS	10//99-12//99
	Springfield MSA, IL	S	7.87 MW	7.77 AW	16360 AAW	ILBLS	10//99-12//99
	Indiana	S	7.04 MW	7.06 AW	14690 AAW	INBLS	10//99-12//99
	Bloomington MSA, IN	S	6.98 MW	6.95 AW	14520 AAW	INBLS	10//99-12//99
	Elkhart-Goshen MSA, IN	S	7.27 MW	7.35 AW	15120 AAW	INBLS	10//99-12//99
	Evansville-Henderson MSA, IN-KY	S	6.71 MW	6.51 AW	13970 AAW	INBLS	10//99-12//99
	Fort Wayne MSA, IN	S	7.13 MW	7.12 AW	14830 AAW	INBLS	10//99-12//99
	Gary PMSA, IN	S	6.78 MW	6.70 AW	14090 AAW	INBLS	10//99-12//99
	Indianapolis MSA, IN	S	7.17 MW	7.30 AW	14920 AAW	INBLS	10//99-12//99
	Kokomo MSA, IN	S	6.65 MW	6.77 AW	13830 AAW	INBLS	10//99-12//99
	Lafayette MSA, IN	S	6.87 MW	6.86 AW	14280 AAW	INBLS	10//99-12//99
	Muncie MSA, IN	S	6.68 MW	6.80 AW	13900 AAW	INBLS	10//99-12//99
	South Bend MSA, IN	S	6.92 MW	7.02 AW	14390 AAW	INBLS	10//99-12//99
	Terre Haute MSA, IN	S	7.28 MW	6.91 AW	15150 AAW	INBLS	10//99-12//99
	Iowa	S	7.19 MW	7.10 AW	14770 AAW	IABLS	10//99-12//99
	Cedar Rapids MSA, IA	S	7.19 MW	7.24 AW	14940 AAW	IABLS	10//99-12//99
	Davenport-Moline-Rock Island MSA, IA-IL	S	7.28 MW	7.32 AW	15140 AAW	IABLS	10//99-12//99
	Des Moines MSA, IA	S	7.72 MW	7.80 AW	16060 AAW	IABLS	10//99-12//99
	Dubuque MSA, IA	S	7.26 MW	7.33 AW	15100 AAW	IABLS	10//99-12//99
	Iowa City MSA, IA	S	6.71 MW	6.72 AW	13950 AAW	IABLS	10//99-12//99
	Sioux City MSA, IA-NE	S	6.97 MW	7.07 AW	14500 AAW	IABLS	10//99-12//99
	Waterloo-Cedar Falls MSA, IA	S	6.31 MW	6.16 AW	13120 AAW	IABLS	10//99-12//99
	Kansas	S	6.58 MW	6.68 AW	13890 AAW	KSBLS	10//99-12//99
	Lawrence MSA, KS	S	6.34 MW	6.11 AW	13190 AAW	KSBLS	10//99-12//99
	Topeka MSA, KS	S	6.99 MW	6.79 AW	14530 AAW	KSBLS	10//99-12//99
	Wichita MSA, KS	S	7.03 MW	7.15 AW	14610 AAW	KSBLS	10//99-12//99
	Kentucky	S	6.84 MW	6.89 AW	14330 AAW	KYBLS	10//99-12//99
	Lexington MSA, KY	S	7.02 MW	7.15 AW	14600 AAW	KYBLS	10//99-12//99
	Louisville MSA, KY-IN	S	7.49 MW	7.57 AW	15590 AAW	KYBLS	10//99-12//99
	Owensboro MSA, KY	S	6.09 MW	6.10 AW	12660 AAW	KYBLS	10//99-12//99
	Louisiana	S	6.96 MW	7.05 AW	14670 AAW	LABLS	10//99-12//99
	Alexandria MSA, LA	S	6.33 MW	6.23 AW	13160 AAW	LABLS	10//99-12//99
	Baton Rouge MSA, LA	S	6.62 MW	6.50 AW	13770 AAW	LABLS	10//99-12//99
	Houma MSA, LA	S	7.00 MW	6.60 AW	14550 AAW	LABLS	10//99-12//99

AAW Average annual wage	**AOH** Average offered, high	**ASH** Average starting, high	**H** Hourly	**M** Monthly	**S** Special: hourly and annual
AE Average entry wage	**AOL** Average offered, low	**ASL** Average starting, low	**HI** Highest wage paid	**MTC** Median total compensation	**TQ** Third quartile wage
AEX Average experienced wage	**APH** Average pay, high range	**AW** Average wage paid	**HR** High end range	**MW** Median wage paid	**W** Weekly
AO Average offered	**APL** Average pay, low range	**FQ** First quartile wage	**LR** Low end range	**SQ** Second quartile wage	**Y** Yearly

Occupation/Type/Industry	Location	Per	Low	Mid	High	Source	Date
Hotel, Motel, and Resort Desk Clerk							
	Lafayette MSA, LA	S	6.56 MW	6.42 AW	13650 AAW	LABLS	10//99-12//99
	Lake Charles MSA, LA	S	6.36 MW	6.37 AW	13230 AAW	LABLS	10//99-12//99
	Monroe MSA, LA	S	6.86 MW	6.65 AW	14270 AAW	LABLS	10//99-12//99
	New Orleans MSA, LA	S	7.68 MW	7.68 AW	15970 AAW	LABLS	10//99-12//99
	Shreveport-Bossier City MSA, LA	S	7.04 MW	6.98 AW	14630 AAW	LABLS	10//99-12//99
	Maine	S	7.93 MW	8.03 AW	16700 AAW	MEBLS	10//99-12//99
	Bangor MSA, ME	S	7.80 MW	7.62 AW	16220 AAW	MEBLS	10//99-12//99
	Lewiston-Auburn MSA, ME	S	7.81 MW	7.28 AW	16250 AAW	MEBLS	10//99-12//99
	Portland MSA, ME	S	8.08 MW	7.84 AW	16800 AAW	MEBLS	10//99-12//99
	Maryland	S	7.46 MW	7.49 AW	15590 AAW	MDBLS	10//99-12//99
	Baltimore PMSA, MD	S	7.23 MW	6.92 AW	15050 AAW	MDBLS	10//99-12//99
	Hagerstown PMSA, MD	S	6.99 MW	6.81 AW	14550 AAW	MDBLS	10//99-12//99
	Massachusetts	S	9.12 MW	9.19 AW	19120 AAW	MABLS	10//99-12//99
	Barnstable-Yarmouth MSA, MA	S	8.43 MW	8.36 AW	17530 AAW	MABLS	10//99-12//99
	Boston PMSA, MA-NH	S	9.67 MW	9.61 AW	20110 AAW	MABLS	10//99-12//99
	Fitchburg-Leominster PMSA, MA	S	8.88 MW	9.09 AW	18480 AAW	MABLS	10//99-12//99
	Lawrence PMSA, MA-NH	S	8.59 MW	8.54 AW	17860 AAW	MABLS	10//99-12//99
	Lowell PMSA, MA-NH	S	8.38 MW	8.33 AW	17430 AAW	MABLS	10//99-12//99
	Pittsfield MSA, MA	S	8.19 MW	8.26 AW	17020 AAW	MABLS	10//99-12//99
	Springfield MSA, MA	S	8.94 MW	8.54 AW	18600 AAW	MABLS	10//99-12//99
	Worcester PMSA, MA-CT	S	8.67 MW	8.54 AW	18040 AAW	MABLS	10//99-12//99
	Michigan	S	7.26 MW	7.25 AW	15070 AAW	MIBLS	10//99-12//99
	Ann Arbor PMSA, MI	S	8.30 MW	8.13 AW	17250 AAW	MIBLS	10//99-12//99
	Benton Harbor MSA, MI	S	7.02 MW	7.13 AW	14600 AAW	MIBLS	10//99-12//99
	Detroit PMSA, MI	S	7.62 MW	7.60 AW	15850 AAW	MIBLS	10//99-12//99
	Flint PMSA, MI	S	6.89 MW	6.77 AW	14320 AAW	MIBLS	10//99-12//99
	Grand Rapids-Muskegon-Holland MSA, MI	S	6.81 MW	6.79 AW	14160 AAW	MIBLS	10//99-12//99
	Jackson MSA, MI	S	6.59 MW	6.47 AW	13710 AAW	MIBLS	10//99-12//99
	Kalamazoo-Battle Creek MSA, MI	S	7.02 MW	6.85 AW	14600 AAW	MIBLS	10//99-12//99
	Lansing-East Lansing MSA, MI	S	7.11 MW	7.15 AW	14790 AAW	MIBLS	10//99-12//99
	Saginaw-Bay City-Midland MSA, MI	S	7.13 MW	7.29 AW	14830 AAW	MIBLS	10//99-12//99
	Minnesota	S	7.69 MW	7.75 AW	16120 AAW	MNBLS	10//99-12//99
	Duluth-Superior MSA, MN-WI	S	6.53 MW	6.41 AW	13590 AAW	MNBLS	10//99-12//99
	Minneapolis-St. Paul MSA, MN-WI	S	8.27 MW	8.12 AW	17190 AAW	MNBLS	10//99-12//99
	Rochester MSA, MN	S	7.39 MW	7.51 AW	15370 AAW	MNBLS	10//99-12//99
	St. Cloud MSA, MN	S	6.83 MW	6.92 AW	14200 AAW	MNBLS	10//99-12//99
	Mississippi	S	6.76 MW	7.02 AW	14600 AAW	MSBLS	10//99-12//99
	Biloxi-Gulfport-Pascagoula MSA, MS	S	7.14 MW	6.95 AW	14850 AAW	MSBLS	10//99-12//99
	Hattiesburg MSA, MS	S	5.95 MW	6.00 AW	12380 AAW	MSBLS	10//99-12//99
	Jackson MSA, MS	S	6.72 MW	6.74 AW	13990 AAW	MSBLS	10//99-12//99
	Missouri	S	7.36 MW	7.36 AW	15320 AAW	MOBLS	10//99-12//99
	Columbia MSA, MO	S	7.66 MW	7.65 AW	15930 AAW	MOBLS	10//99-12//99
	Joplin MSA, MO	S	6.67 MW	6.56 AW	13860 AAW	MOBLS	10//99-12//99
	Kansas City MSA, MO-KS	S	7.19 MW	7.12 AW	14960 AAW	MOBLS	10//99-12//99
	St. Louis MSA, MO-IL	S	7.64 MW	7.63 AW	15880 AAW	MOBLS	10//99-12//99
	Montana	S	6.25 MW	6.35 AW	13210 AAW	MTBLS	10//99-12//99
	Billings MSA, MT	S	6.69 MW	6.63 AW	13920 AAW	MTBLS	10//99-12//99
	Great Falls MSA, MT	S	6.25 MW	6.30 AW	13000 AAW	MTBLS	10//99-12//99
	Nebraska	S	7.38 MW	7.22 AW	15020 AAW	NEBLS	10//99-12//99
	Lincoln MSA, NE	S	7.51 MW	7.68 AW	15620 AAW	NEBLS	10//99-12//99
	Omaha MSA, NE-IA	S	7.73 MW	7.79 AW	16070 AAW	NEBLS	10//99-12//99
	Nevada	S	10.25 MW	10.06 AW	20920 AAW	NVBLS	10//99-12//99
	Las Vegas MSA, NV-AZ	S	10.30 MW	10.77 AW	21420 AAW	NVBLS	10//99-12//99
	Reno MSA, NV	S	9.02 MW	8.66 AW	18760 AAW	NVBLS	10//99-12//99
	New Hampshire	S	8.06 MW	8.07 AW	16780 AAW	NHBLS	10//99-12//99
	Manchester PMSA, NH	S	8.93 MW	9.19 AW	18570 AAW	NHBLS	10//99-12//99
	Nashua PMSA, NH	S	8.87 MW	8.99 AW	18440 AAW	NHBLS	10//99-12//99
	Portsmouth-Rochester PMSA, NH-ME	S	7.79 MW	7.79 AW	16190 AAW	NHBLS	10//99-12//99
	New Jersey	S	8.13 MW	8.35 AW	17370 AAW	NJBLS	10//99-12//99
	Atlantic-Cape May PMSA, NJ	S	8.24 MW	7.99 AW	17140 AAW	NJBLS	10//99-12//99
	Bergen-Passaic PMSA, NJ	S	8.74 MW	8.75 AW	18170 AAW	NJBLS	10//99-12//99
	Jersey City PMSA, NJ	S	7.86 MW	7.67 AW	16340 AAW	NJBLS	10//99-12//99

Occupation/Type/Industry	Location	Per	Low	Mid	High	Source	Date
Hotel, Motel, and Resort Desk Clerk	Middlesex-Somerset-Hunterdon PMSA, NJ	S	8.67 MW	8.51 AW	18030 AAW	NJBLS	10//99-12//99
	Monmouth-Ocean PMSA, NJ	S	8.41 MW	8.12 AW	17490 AAW	NJBLS	10//99-12//99
	Newark PMSA, NJ	S	8.71 MW	8.57 AW	18110 AAW	NJBLS	10//99-12//99
	Trenton PMSA, NJ	S	9.18 MW	9.52 AW	19100 AAW	NJBLS	10//99-12//99
	New Mexico	S	6.75 MW	6.87 AW	14290 AAW	NMBLS	10//99-12//99
	Albuquerque MSA, NM	S	7.08 MW	7.18 AW	14720 AAW	NMBLS	10//99-12//99
	Las Cruces MSA, NM	S	5.95 MW	5.97 AW	12380 AAW	NMBLS	10//99-12//99
	Santa Fe MSA, NM	S	7.93 MW	7.85 AW	16500 AAW	NMBLS	10//99-12//99
	New York	S	8.45 MW	9.70 AW	20180 AAW	NYBLS	10//99-12//99
	Albany-Schenectady-Troy MSA, NY	S	7.57 MW	7.65 AW	15750 AAW	NYBLS	10//99-12//99
	Binghamton MSA, NY	S	7.32 MW	7.37 AW	15230 AAW	NYBLS	10//99-12//99
	Buffalo-Niagara Falls MSA, NY	S	7.03 MW	7.10 AW	14620 AAW	NYBLS	10//99-12//99
	Dutchess County PMSA, NY	S	7.73 MW	7.71 AW	16070 AAW	NYBLS	10//99-12//99
	Elmira MSA, NY	S	6.39 MW	6.27 AW	13300 AAW	NYBLS	10//99-12//99
	Glens Falls MSA, NY	S	6.81 MW	6.75 AW	14160 AAW	NYBLS	10//99-12//99
	Jamestown MSA, NY	S	6.16 MW	6.25 AW	12820 AAW	NYBLS	10//99-12//99
	Nassau-Suffolk PMSA, NY	S	8.93 MW	8.94 AW	18570 AAW	NYBLS	10//99-12//99
	New York PMSA, NY	S	13.04 MW	13.61 AW	27110 AAW	NYBLS	10//99-12//99
	Newburgh PMSA, NY-PA	S	7.76 MW	7.66 AW	16150 AAW	NYBLS	10//99-12//99
	Rochester MSA, NY	S	7.63 MW	7.50 AW	15870 AAW	NYBLS	10//99-12//99
	Syracuse MSA, NY	S	7.15 MW	7.20 AW	14880 AAW	NYBLS	10//99-12//99
	Utica-Rome MSA, NY	S	7.12 MW	7.05 AW	14810 AAW	NYBLS	10//99-12//99
	North Carolina	S	7.42 MW	7.39 AW	15370 AAW	NCBLS	10//99-12//99
	Asheville MSA, NC	S	7.83 MW	7.72 AW	16280 AAW	NCBLS	10//99-12//99
	Charlotte-Gastonia-Rock Hill MSA, NC-SC	S	8.05 MW	8.03 AW	16740 AAW	NCBLS	10//99-12//99
	Fayetteville MSA, NC	S	6.53 MW	6.40 AW	13590 AAW	NCBLS	10//99-12//99
	Greensboro--Winston-Salem--High Point MSA, NC	S	7.47 MW	7.51 AW	15540 AAW	NCBLS	10//99-12//99
	Greenville MSA, NC	S	6.50 MW	6.29 AW	13520 AAW	NCBLS	10//99-12//99
	Hickory-Morganton-Lenoir MSA, NC	S	7.43 MW	7.53 AW	15450 AAW	NCBLS	10//99-12//99
	Jacksonville MSA, NC	S	6.53 MW	6.28 AW	13570 AAW	NCBLS	10//99-12//99
	Raleigh-Durham-Chapel Hill MSA, NC	S	7.67 MW	7.72 AW	15960 AAW	NCBLS	10//99-12//99
	Rocky Mount MSA, NC	S	6.75 MW	6.64 AW	14050 AAW	NCBLS	10//99-12//99
	Wilmington MSA, NC	S	7.19 MW	7.24 AW	14960 AAW	NCBLS	10//99-12//99
	North Dakota	S	6.37 MW	6.56 AW	13640 AAW	NDBLS	10//99-12//99
	Bismarck MSA, ND	S	6.73 MW	6.57 AW	13990 AAW	NDBLS	10//99-12//99
	Fargo-Moorhead MSA, ND-MN	S	6.46 MW	6.30 AW	13440 AAW	NDBLS	10//99-12//99
	Grand Forks MSA, ND-MN	S	7.03 MW	7.03 AW	14620 AAW	NDBLS	10//99-12//99
	Ohio	S	7.1 MW	7.13 AW	14820 AAW	OHBLS	10//99-12//99
	Akron PMSA, OH	S	6.84 MW	6.80 AW	14230 AAW	OHBLS	10//99-12//99
	Canton-Massillon MSA, OH	S	7.06 MW	7.21 AW	14680 AAW	OHBLS	10//99-12//99
	Cincinnati PMSA, OH-KY-IN	S	7.75 MW	7.75 AW	16110 AAW	OHBLS	10//99-12//99
	Cleveland-Lorain-Elyria PMSA, OH	S	7.39 MW	7.51 AW	15360 AAW	OHBLS	10//99-12//99
	Columbus MSA, OH	S	7.43 MW	7.42 AW	15440 AAW	OHBLS	10//99-12//99
	Dayton-Springfield MSA, OH	S	6.87 MW	6.85 AW	14290 AAW	OHBLS	10//99-12//99
	Hamilton-Middletown PMSA, OH	S	7.31 MW	6.84 AW	15210 AAW	OHBLS	10//99-12//99
	Lima MSA, OH	S	6.58 MW	6.49 AW	13690 AAW	OHBLS	10//99-12//99
	Mansfield MSA, OH	S	6.63 MW	6.63 AW	13780 AAW	OHBLS	10//99-12//99
	Toledo MSA, OH	S	6.96 MW	6.92 AW	14480 AAW	OHBLS	10//99-12//99
	Youngstown-Warren MSA, OH	S	6.16 MW	6.04 AW	12820 AAW	OHBLS	10//99-12//99
	Oklahoma	S	6.45 MW	6.50 AW	13520 AAW	OKBLS	10//99-12//99
	Lawton MSA, OK	S	5.85 MW	5.94 AW	12180 AAW	OKBLS	10//99-12//99
	Oklahoma City MSA, OK	S	6.57 MW	6.45 AW	13670 AAW	OKBLS	10//99-12//99
	Tulsa MSA, OK	S	7.09 MW	7.30 AW	14760 AAW	OKBLS	10//99-12//99
	Oregon	S	7.68 MW	7.78 AW	16180 AAW	ORBLS	10//99-12//99
	Eugene-Springfield MSA, OR	S	7.74 MW	7.65 AW	16100 AAW	ORBLS	10//99-12//99
	Medford-Ashland MSA, OR	S	7.61 MW	7.48 AW	15830 AAW	ORBLS	10//99-12//99
	Portland-Vancouver PMSA, OR-WA	S	8.12 MW	8.03 AW	16890 AAW	ORBLS	10//99-12//99
	Salem PMSA, OR	S	7.40 MW	7.31 AW	15400 AAW	ORBLS	10//99-12//99
	Pennsylvania	S	7.69 MW	7.74 AW	16100 AAW	PABLS	10//99-12//99

Occupation/Type/Industry	Location	Per	Low	Mid	High	Source	Date
Hotel, Motel, and Resort Desk Clerk	Allentown-Bethlehem-Easton						
	MSA, PA	S	7.79 MW	7.74 AW	16210 AAW	PABLS	10//99-12//99
	Altoona MSA, PA	S	6.42 MW	6.14 AW	13350 AAW	PABLS	10//99-12//99
	Erie MSA, PA	S	6.89 MW	6.80 AW	14340 AAW	PABLS	10//99-12//99
	Harrisburg-Lebanon-Carlisle						
	MSA, PA	S	7.41 MW	7.40 AW	15410 AAW	PABLS	10//99-12//99
	Johnstown MSA, PA	S	6.27 MW	6.21 AW	13040 AAW	PABLS	10//99-12//99
	Lancaster MSA, PA	S	8.01 MW	7.84 AW	16660 AAW	PABLS	10//99-12//99
	Philadelphia PMSA, PA-NJ	S	8.37 MW	8.26 AW	17410 AAW	PABLS	10//99-12//99
	Pittsburgh MSA, PA	S	7.70 MW	7.71 AW	16020 AAW	PABLS	10//99-12//99
	Scranton--Wilkes-Barre--						
	Hazleton MSA, PA	S	7.55 MW	7.56 AW	15710 AAW	PABLS	10//99-12//99
	State College MSA, PA	S	7.06 MW	7.11 AW	14690 AAW	PABLS	10//99-12//99
	Williamsport MSA, PA	S	6.81 MW	6.83 AW	14160 AAW	PABLS	10//99-12//99
	York MSA, PA	S	7.71 MW	7.72 AW	16040 AAW	PABLS	10//99-12//99
	Rhode Island	S	7.76 MW	7.91 AW	16450 AAW	RIBLS	10//99-12//99
	Providence-Fall River-						
	Warwick MSA, RI-MA	S	7.46 MW	7.37 AW	15520 AAW	RIBLS	10//99-12//99
	South Carolina	S	7.48 MW	7.44 AW	15480 AAW	SCBLS	10//99-12//99
	Charleston-North Charleston						
	MSA, SC	S	7.45 MW	7.55 AW	15490 AAW	SCBLS	10//99-12//99
	Columbia MSA, SC	S	7.35 MW	7.41 AW	15290 AAW	SCBLS	10//99-12//99
	Florence MSA, SC	S	7.10 MW	7.31 AW	14760 AAW	SCBLS	10//99-12//99
	Greenville-Spartanburg-						
	Anderson MSA, SC	S	7.38 MW	7.43 AW	15350 AAW	SCBLS	10//99-12//99
	Myrtle Beach MSA, SC	S	7.75 MW	7.74 AW	16120 AAW	SCBLS	10//99-12//99
	Sumter MSA, SC	S	7.06 MW	6.98 AW	14680 AAW	SCBLS	10//99-12//99
	South Dakota	S	7.17 MW	7.05 AW	14670 AAW	SDBLS	10//99-12//99
	Rapid City MSA, SD	S	6.95 MW	7.05 AW	14460 AAW	SDBLS	10//99-12//99
	Sioux Falls MSA, SD	S	7.41 MW	7.55 AW	15420 AAW	SDBLS	10//99-12//99
	Tennessee	S	7.23 MW	7.23 AW	15040 AAW	TNBLS	10//99-12//99
	Chattanooga MSA, TN-GA	S	7.43 MW	7.23 AW	15460 AAW	TNBLS	10//99-12//99
	Clarksville-Hopkinsville MSA,						
	TN-KY	S	6.50 MW	6.34 AW	13520 AAW	TNBLS	10//99-12//99
	Jackson MSA, TN	S	6.32 MW	6.06 AW	13150 AAW	TNBLS	10//99-12//99
	Johnson City-Kingsport-Bristol						
	MSA, TN-VA	S	6.54 MW	6.26 AW	13600 AAW	TNBLS	10//99-12//99
	Knoxville MSA, TN	S	7.86 MW	7.78 AW	16350 AAW	TNBLS	10//99-12//99
	Memphis MSA, TN-AR-MS	S	6.95 MW	6.97 AW	14450 AAW	MSBLS	10//99-12//99
	Nashville MSA, TN	S	7.36 MW	7.47 AW	15300 AAW	TNBLS	10//99-12//99
	Texas	S	6.9 MW	7.00 AW	14560 AAW	TXBLS	10//99-12//99
	Abilene MSA, TX	S	5.93 MW	5.94 AW	12330 AAW	TXBLS	10//99-12//99
	Amarillo MSA, TX	S	6.45 MW	6.40 AW	13410 AAW	TXBLS	10//99-12//99
	Austin-San Marcos MSA, TX	S	6.90 MW	6.80 AW	14360 AAW	TXBLS	10//99-12//99
	Beaumont-Port Arthur MSA,						
	TX	S	6.39 MW	6.15 AW	13300 AAW	TXBLS	10//99-12//99
	Brazoria PMSA, TX	S	7.07 MW	6.82 AW	14710 AAW	TXBLS	10//99-12//99
	Brownsville-Harlingen-San						
	Benito MSA, TX	S	6.06 MW	6.10 AW	12600 AAW	TXBLS	10//99-12//99
	Bryan-College Station MSA,						
	TX	S	6.44 MW	6.35 AW	13390 AAW	TXBLS	10//99-12//99
	Corpus Christi MSA, TX	S	6.96 MW	6.95 AW	14470 AAW	TXBLS	10//99-12//99
	Dallas PMSA, TX	S	7.76 MW	7.78 AW	16140 AAW	TXBLS	10//99-12//99
	El Paso MSA, TX	S	6.69 MW	6.29 AW	13910 AAW	TXBLS	10//99-12//99
	Fort Worth-Arlington PMSA,						
	TX	S	6.97 MW	6.86 AW	14510 AAW	TXBLS	10//99-12//99
	Galveston-Texas City PMSA,						
	TX	S	7.00 MW	6.95 AW	14550 AAW	TXBLS	10//99-12//99
	Houston PMSA, TX	S	7.32 MW	7.44 AW	15230 AAW	TXBLS	10//99-12//99
	Killeen-Temple MSA, TX	S	6.82 MW	6.81 AW	14180 AAW	TXBLS	10//99-12//99
	Laredo MSA, TX	S	6.31 MW	6.17 AW	13120 AAW	TXBLS	10//99-12//99
	Longview-Marshall MSA, TX	S	6.32 MW	6.15 AW	13150 AAW	TXBLS	10//99-12//99
	Lubbock MSA, TX	S	6.39 MW	6.06 AW	13290 AAW	TXBLS	10//99-12//99
	McAllen-Edinburg-Mission						
	MSA, TX	S	6.25 MW	6.12 AW	12990 AAW	TXBLS	10//99-12//99
	Odessa-Midland MSA, TX	S	6.68 MW	6.55 AW	13890 AAW	TXBLS	10//99-12//99
	San Angelo MSA, TX	S	6.23 MW	6.28 AW	12960 AAW	TXBLS	10//99-12//99
	San Antonio MSA, TX	S	7.03 MW	6.90 AW	14630 AAW	TXBLS	10//99-12//99
	Texarkana MSA, TX-						
	Texarkana, AR	S	6.51 MW	6.45 AW	13540 AAW	TXBLS	10//99-12//99
	Tyler MSA, TX	S	7.29 MW	7.32 AW	15160 AAW	TXBLS	10//99-12//99

AAW Average annual wage	**AOH** Average offered, high	**ASH** Average starting, high	**H** Hourly	**M** Monthly	**S** Special: hourly and annual
AE Average entry wage	**AOL** Average offered, low	**ASL** Average starting, low	**HI** Highest wage paid	**MTC** Median total compensation	**TQ** Third quartile wage
AEX Average experienced wage	**APH** Average pay, high range	**AW** Average wage paid	**HR** High end range	**MW** Median wage paid	**W** Weekly
AO Average offered	**APL** Average pay, low range	**FQ** First quartile wage	**LR** Low end range	**SQ** Second quartile wage	**Y** Yearly

Occupation/Type/Industry	Location	Per	Low	Mid	High	Source	Date
Hotel, Motel, and Resort Desk Clerk	Victoria MSA, TX	S	6.78 MW	6.59 AW	14100 AAW	TXBLS	10//99-12//99
	Waco MSA, TX	S	7.11 MW	6.93 AW	14790 AAW	TXBLS	10//99-12//99
	Wichita Falls MSA, TX	S	6.54 MW	6.43 AW	13600 AAW	TXBLS	10//99-12//99
	Utah	S	7.52 MW	7.46 AW	15510 AAW	UTBLS	10//99-12//99
	Provo-Orem MSA, UT	S	7.28 MW	7.43 AW	15150 AAW	UTBLS	10//99-12//99
	Salt Lake City-Ogden MSA, UT	S	7.71 MW	7.77 AW	16040 AAW	UTBLS	10//99-12//99
	Vermont	S	7.88 MW	8.11 AW	16880 AAW	VTBLS	10//99-12//99
	Burlington MSA, VT	S	7.58 MW	7.52 AW	15770 AAW	VTBLS	10//99-12//99
	Virginia	S	7.06 MW	7.19 AW	14960 AAW	VABLS	10//99-12//99
	Charlottesville MSA, VA	S	7.90 MW	7.77 AW	16430 AAW	VABLS	10//99-12//99
	Norfolk-Virginia Beach-Newport News MSA, VA-NC	S	6.98 MW	6.80 AW	14510 AAW	VABLS	10//99-12//99
	Richmond-Petersburg MSA, VA	S	7.01 MW	6.86 AW	14590 AAW	VABLS	10//99-12//99
	Roanoke MSA, VA	S	7.20 MW	7.21 AW	14970 AAW	VABLS	10//99-12//99
	Washington	S	7.85 MW	8.00 AW	16630 AAW	WABLS	10//99-12//99
	Bellingham MSA, WA	S	7.38 MW	7.27 AW	15340 AAW	WABLS	10//99-12//99
	Bremerton PMSA, WA	S	7.70 MW	7.68 AW	16020 AAW	WABLS	10//99-12//99
	Olympia PMSA, WA	S	8.33 MW	8.06 AW	17330 AAW	WABLS	10//99-12//99
	Richland-Kennewick-Pasco MSA, WA	S	7.21 MW	6.98 AW	15000 AAW	WABLS	10//99-12//99
	Seattle-Bellevue-Everett PMSA, WA	S	8.63 MW	8.72 AW	17950 AAW	WABLS	10//99-12//99
	Spokane MSA, WA	S	7.00 MW	6.82 AW	14560 AAW	WABLS	10//99-12//99
	Tacoma PMSA, WA	S	7.45 MW	7.43 AW	15490 AAW	WABLS	10//99-12//99
	Yakima MSA, WA	S	6.93 MW	6.79 AW	14410 AAW	WABLS	10//99-12//99
	West Virginia	S	6.3 MW	6.51 AW	13550 AAW	WVBLS	10//99-12//99
	Charleston MSA, WV	S	7.35 MW	7.21 AW	15300 AAW	WVBLS	10//99-12//99
	Huntington-Ashland MSA, WV-KY-OH	S	6.58 MW	6.38 AW	13690 AAW	WVBLS	10//99-12//99
	Parkersburg-Marietta MSA, WV-OH	S	6.23 MW	6.13 AW	12960 AAW	WVBLS	10//99-12//99
	Wheeling MSA, WV-OH	S	6.60 MW	6.57 AW	13730 AAW	WVBLS	10//99-12//99
	Wisconsin	S	7.42 MW	7.39 AW	15370 AAW	WIBLS	10//99-12//99
	Appleton-Oshkosh-Neenah MSA, WI	S	6.90 MW	6.95 AW	14350 AAW	WIBLS	10//99-12//99
	Eau Claire MSA, WI	S	7.33 MW	7.04 AW	15250 AAW	WIBLS	10//99-12//99
	Green Bay MSA, WI	S	7.82 MW	7.72 AW	16270 AAW	WIBLS	10//99-12//99
	Janesville-Beloit MSA, WI	S	7.13 MW	7.29 AW	14830 AAW	WIBLS	10//99-12//99
	Kenosha PMSA, WI	S	7.73 MW	7.74 AW	16070 AAW	WIBLS	10//99-12//99
	La Crosse MSA, WI-MN	S	6.81 MW	6.63 AW	14170 AAW	WIBLS	10//99-12//99
	Madison MSA, WI	S	7.58 MW	7.65 AW	15760 AAW	WIBLS	10//99-12//99
	Milwaukee-Waukesha PMSA, WI	S	7.82 MW	7.80 AW	16260 AAW	WIBLS	10//99-12//99
	Racine PMSA, WI	S	7.51 MW	7.55 AW	15610 AAW	WIBLS	10//99-12//99
	Sheboygan MSA, WI	S	7.24 MW	7.35 AW	15050 AAW	WIBLS	10//99-12//99
	Wausau MSA, WI	S	7.55 MW	7.68 AW	15710 AAW	WIBLS	10//99-12//99
	Wyoming	S	7.19 MW	7.16 AW	14890 AAW	WYBLS	10//99-12//99
	Casper MSA, WY	S	6.78 MW	6.74 AW	14110 AAW	WYBLS	10//99-12//99
	Cheyenne MSA, WY	S	6.65 MW	6.59 AW	13840 AAW	WYBLS	10//99-12//99
	Puerto Rico	S	6.73 MW	7.05 AW	14660 AAW	PRBLS	10//99-12//99
	Mayaguez MSA, PR	S	5.81 MW	6.02 AW	12070 AAW	PRBLS	10//99-12//99
	Ponce MSA, PR	S	6.68 MW	6.48 AW	13900 AAW	PRBLS	10//99-12//99
	San Juan-Bayamon PMSA, PR	S	7.79 MW	7.74 AW	16200 AAW	PRBLS	10//99-12//99
	Virgin Islands	S	8.2 MW	8.25 AW	17160 AAW	VIBLS	10//99-12//99
	Guam	S	6.78 MW	7.06 AW	14680 AAW	GUBLS	10//99-12//99
Hotwalker (walks horses to cool them)	Louisville, KY	W		200.00 AW		LOUMAG	1999-2000
Household Manager							
Estate-Level	United States	Y	60000 LR		120000 HR	COLBIZ	2000
Single Household	United States	Y	35000 LR		60000 HR	COLBIZ	2000
Housekeeper/Houseman Couple							
Domestic Service	United States	Y	50000 LR		70000 HR	COLBIZ	2000
Managerial, Private Service	United States	Y	60000 LR		120000 HR	COLBIZ	2000

AAW	Average annual wage	AOH	Average offered, high	ASH	Average starting, high	H	Hourly	M	Monthly	S	Special: hourly and annual
AE	Average entry wage	AOL	Average offered, low	ASL	Average starting, low	HI	Highest wage paid	MTC	Median total compensation	TQ	Third quartile wage
AEX	Average experienced wage	APH	Average pay, high range	AW	Average wage paid	HR	High end range	MW	Median wage paid	W	Weekly
AO	Average offered	APL	Average pay, low range	FQ	First quartile wage	LR	Low end range	SQ	Second quartile wage	Y	Yearly

Occupation/Type/Industry	Location	Per	Low	Mid	High	Source	Date
Human Resources Assistant							
Except Payroll and Timekeeping	Alabama	S	11.1 MW	11.55 AW	24020 AAW	ALBLS	10//99-12//99
Except Payroll and Timekeeping	Alaska	S	14.7 MW	15.21 AW	31640 AAW	AKBLS	10//99-12//99
Except Payroll and Timekeeping	Arizona	S	11.32 MW	12.09 AW	25150 AAW	AZBLS	10//99-12//99
Except Payroll and Timekeeping	Arkansas	S	10.44 MW	10.80 AW	22460 AAW	ARBLS	10//99-12//99
Except Payroll and Timekeeping	California	S	13.89 MW	14.38 AW	29910 AAW	CABLS	10//99-12//99
Except Payroll and Timekeeping	Colorado	S	13.27 MW	13.44 AW	27950 AAW	COBLS	10//99-12//99
Except Payroll and Timekeeping	Connecticut	S	14.5 MW	14.44 AW	30030 AAW	CTBLS	10//99-12//99
Except Payroll and Timekeeping	Delaware	S	13.09 MW	13.80 AW	28700 AAW	DEBLS	10//99-12//99
Except Payroll and Timekeeping	Florida	S	11.45 MW	11.87 AW	24690 AAW	FLBLS	10//99-12//99
Except Payroll and Timekeeping	Georgia	S	12 MW	12.22 AW	25410 AAW	GABLS	10//99-12//99
Except Payroll and Timekeeping	Hawaii	S	12.72 MW	13.00 AW	27030 AAW	HIBLS	10//99-12//99
Except Payroll and Timekeeping	Idaho	S	11.26 MW	11.34 AW	23590 AAW	IDBLS	10//99-12//99
Except Payroll and Timekeeping	Illinois	S	12.41 MW	12.67 AW	26360 AAW	ILBLS	10//99-12//99
Except Payroll and Timekeeping	Indiana	S	11.7 MW	11.94 AW	24830 AAW	INBLS	10//99-12//99
Except Payroll and Timekeeping	Iowa	S	12.72 MW	13.22 AW	27500 AAW	IABLS	10//99-12//99
Except Payroll and Timekeeping	Kansas	S	12.03 MW	12.40 AW	25800 AAW	KSBLS	10//99-12//99
Except Payroll and Timekeeping	Kentucky	S	11.45 MW	11.78 AW	24490 AAW	KYBLS	10//99-12//99
Except Payroll and Timekeeping	Louisiana	S	10.82 MW	11.04 AW	22970 AAW	LABLS	10//99-12//99
Except Payroll and Timekeeping	Maine	S	11.93 MW	12.02 AW	25000 AAW	MEBLS	10//99-12//99
Except Payroll and Timekeeping	Maryland	S	13.15 MW	13.43 AW	27940 AAW	MDBLS	10//99-12//99
Except Payroll and Timekeeping	Massachusetts	S	14 MW	14.39 AW	29940 AAW	MABLS	10//99-12//99
Except Payroll and Timekeeping	Michigan	S	12.76 MW	13.19 AW	27440 AAW	MIBLS	10//99-12//99
Except Payroll and Timekeeping	Minnesota	S	13.3 MW	13.61 AW	28320 AAW	MNBLS	10//99-12//99
Except Payroll and Timekeeping	Mississippi	S	10.74 MW	11.11 AW	23110 AAW	MSBLS	10//99-12//99
Except Payroll and Timekeeping	Missouri	S	12.01 MW	12.44 AW	25870 AAW	MOBLS	10//99-12//99
Except Payroll and Timekeeping	Montana	S	10.92 MW	11.66 AW	24250 AAW	MTBLS	10//99-12//99
Except Payroll and Timekeeping	Nebraska	S	11.27 MW	11.74 AW	24420 AAW	NEBLS	10//99-12//99
Except Payroll and Timekeeping	Nevada	S	11.58 MW	12.34 AW	25670 AAW	NVBLS	10//99-12//99
Except Payroll and Timekeeping	New Hampshire	S	12.17 MW	12.52 AW	26040 AAW	NHBLS	10//99-12//99
Except Payroll and Timekeeping	New Jersey	S	14.55 MW	14.95 AW	31110 AAW	NJBLS	10//99-12//99
Except Payroll and Timekeeping	New Mexico	S	11.24 MW	11.19 AW	23280 AAW	NMBLS	10//99-12//99
Except Payroll and Timekeeping	New York	S	13.51 MW	13.90 AW	28910 AAW	NYBLS	10//99-12//99
Except Payroll and Timekeeping	North Carolina	S	12.1 MW	12.50 AW	26000 AAW	NCBLS	10//99-12//99
Except Payroll and Timekeeping	North Dakota	S	11.2 MW	11.43 AW	23780 AAW	NDBLS	10//99-12//99
Except Payroll and Timekeeping	Ohio	S	12.45 MW	12.77 AW	26560 AAW	OHBLS	10//99-12//99
Except Payroll and Timekeeping	Oklahoma	S	10.8 MW	11.20 AW	23300 AAW	OKBLS	10//99-12//99
Except Payroll and Timekeeping	Oregon	S	12.86 MW	12.99 AW	27020 AAW	ORBLS	10//99-12//99
Except Payroll and Timekeeping	Pennsylvania	S	12.73 MW	13.26 AW	27580 AAW	PABLS	10//99-12//99
Except Payroll and Timekeeping	Rhode Island	S	12.27 MW	12.49 AW	25980 AAW	RIBLS	10//99-12//99
Except Payroll and Timekeeping	South Carolina	S	11.25 MW	11.57 AW	24060 AAW	SCBLS	10//99-12//99
Except Payroll and Timekeeping	South Dakota	S	9.72 MW	10.00 AW	20810 AAW	SDBLS	10//99-12//99
Except Payroll and Timekeeping	Tennessee	S	11.62 MW	12.07 AW	25100 AAW	TNBLS	10//99-12//99
Except Payroll and Timekeeping	Texas	S	12.73 MW	13.05 AW	27140 AAW	TXBLS	10//99-12//99
Except Payroll and Timekeeping	Utah	S	11.94 MW	12.40 AW	25780 AAW	UTBLS	10//99-12//99
Except Payroll and Timekeeping	Vermont	S	12.62 MW	12.74 AW	26510 AAW	VTBLS	10//99-12//99
Except Payroll and Timekeeping	Virginia	S	13.06 MW	13.22 AW	27510 AAW	VABLS	10//99-12//99
Except Payroll and Timekeeping	Washington	S	14 MW	14.05 AW	29220 AAW	WABLS	10//99-12//99
Except Payroll and Timekeeping	West Virginia	S	10.97 MW	11.68 AW	24300 AAW	WVBLS	10//99-12//99
Except Payroll and Timekeeping	Wisconsin	S	12.58 MW	12.99 AW	27030 AAW	WIBLS	10//99-12//99
Except Payroll and Timekeeping	Wyoming	S	12.09 MW	12.48 AW	25960 AAW	WYBLS	10//99-12//99
Except Payroll and Timekeeping	Puerto Rico	S	7.8 MW	8.54 AW	17770 AAW	PRBLS	10//99-12//99
Except Payroll and Timekeeping	Virgin Islands	S	11.23 MW	11.18 AW	23260 AAW	VIBLS	10//99-12//99
Except Payroll and Timekeeping	Guam	S	11.17 MW	11.46 AW	23840 AAW	GUBLS	10//99-12//99
Human Resources Manager	United States	Y		80900 AW		TRAVWK2	1999
	Alabama	S	21.71 MW	22.99 AW	47810 AAW	ALBLS	10//99-12//99
	Anniston MSA, AL	S	22.23 MW	20.15 AW	46230 AAW	ALBLS	10//99-12//99
	Auburn-Opelika MSA, AL	S	20.77 MW	20.65 AW	43210 AAW	ALBLS	10//99-12//99
	Birmingham MSA, AL	S	23.52 MW	20.88 AW	48920 AAW	ALBLS	10//99-12//99
	Decatur MSA, AL	S	24.90 MW	25.61 AW	51790 AAW	ALBLS	10//99-12//99
	Dothan MSA, AL	S	23.82 MW	23.81 AW	49540 AAW	ALBLS	10//99-12//99
	Florence MSA, AL	S	21.95 MW	18.05 AW	45660 AAW	ALBLS	10//99-12//99
	Gadsden MSA, AL	S	20.55 MW	19.24 AW	42750 AAW	ALBLS	10//99-12//99
	Huntsville MSA, AL	S	25.01 MW	23.99 AW	52030 AAW	ALBLS	10//99-12//99
	Mobile MSA, AL	S	22.77 MW	21.49 AW	47370 AAW	ALBLS	10//99-12//99
	Montgomery MSA, AL	S	22.56 MW	22.11 AW	46910 AAW	ALBLS	10//99-12//99
	Tuscaloosa MSA, AL	S	23.10 MW	22.31 AW	48040 AAW	ALBLS	10//99-12//99
	Alaska	S	28.47 MW	28.63 AW	59550 AAW	AKBLS	10//99-12//99
	Anchorage MSA, AK	S	28.27 MW	28.58 AW	58790 AAW	AKBLS	10//99-12//99
	Arizona	S	23.73 MW	25.12 AW	52250 AAW	AZBLS	10//99-12//99
	Flagstaff MSA, AZ-UT	S	21.92 MW	20.57 AW	45600 AAW	AZBLS	10//99-12//99
	Phoenix-Mesa MSA, AZ	S	26.14 MW	24.87 AW	54360 AAW	AZBLS	10//99-12//99

AAW Average annual wage	**AOH** Average offered, high	**ASH** Average starting, high	**H** Hourly	**M** Monthly	**S** Special: hourly and annual
AE Average entry wage	**AOL** Average offered, low	**ASL** Average starting, low	**HI** Highest wage paid	**MTC** Median total compensation	**TQ** Third quartile wage
AEX Average experienced wage	**APH** Average pay, high range	**AW** Average wage paid	**HR** High end range	**MW** Median wage paid	**W** Weekly
AO Average offered	**APL** Average pay, low range	**FQ** First quartile wage	**LR** Low end range	**SQ** Second quartile wage	**Y** Yearly

Occupation/Type/Industry	Location	Per	Low	Mid	High	Source	Date
Human Resources Manager	Tucson MSA, AZ	S	20.58 MW	18.91 AW	42800 AAW	AZBLS	10//99-12//99
	Yuma MSA, AZ	S	20.99 MW	20.17 AW	43660 AAW	AZBLS	10//99-12//99
	Arkansas	S	23.77 MW	26.39 AW	54900 AAW	ARBLS	10//99-12//99
	Fayetteville-Springdale-Rogers MSA, AR	S	22.43 MW	20.36 AW	46660 AAW	ARBLS	10//99-12//99
	Fort Smith MSA, AR-OK	S	22.75 MW	20.70 AW	47320 AAW	ARBLS	10//99-12//99
	Little Rock-North Little Rock MSA, AR	S	30.83 MW	28.67 AW	64120 AAW	ARBLS	10//99-12//99
	California	S	27.51 MW	29.17 AW	60670 AAW	CABLS	10//99-12//99
	Bakersfield MSA, CA	S	27.43 MW	27.99 AW	57050 AAW	CABLS	10//99-12//99
	Chico-Paradise MSA, CA	S	22.95 MW	21.92 AW	47730 AAW	CABLS	10//99-12//99
	Fresno MSA, CA	S	24.46 MW	22.98 AW	50880 AAW	CABLS	10//99-12//99
	Los Angeles-Long Beach PMSA, CA	S	29.88 MW	27.54 AW	62150 AAW	CABLS	10//99-12//99
	Merced MSA, CA	S	24.55 MW	23.18 AW	51070 AAW	CABLS	10//99-12//99
	Modesto MSA, CA	S	24.30 MW	22.69 AW	50530 AAW	CABLS	10//99-12//99
	Oakland PMSA, CA	S	30.71 MW	30.30 AW	63870 AAW	CABLS	10//99-12//99
	Orange County PMSA, CA	S	29.15 MW	27.96 AW	60620 AAW	CABLS	10//99-12//99
	Riverside-San Bernardino PMSA, CA	S	24.94 MW	22.45 AW	51870 AAW	CABLS	10//99-12//99
	Sacramento PMSA, CA	S	24.29 MW	20.85 AW	50530 AAW	CABLS	10//99-12//99
	Salinas MSA, CA	S	27.65 MW	25.10 AW	57500 AAW	CABLS	10//99-12//99
	San Diego MSA, CA	S	26.83 MW	26.09 AW	55800 AAW	CABLS	10//99-12//99
	San Francisco PMSA, CA	S	32.71 MW	32.51 AW	68030 AAW	CABLS	10//99-12//99
	San Jose PMSA, CA	S	34.31 MW	33.95 AW	71370 AAW	CABLS	10//99-12//99
	San Luis Obispo-Atascadero-Paso Robles MSA, CA	S	26.60 MW	23.80 AW	55320 AAW	CABLS	10//99-12//99
	Santa Barbara-Santa Maria-Lompoc MSA, CA	S	25.67 MW	23.93 AW	53390 AAW	CABLS	10//99-12//99
	Santa Cruz-Watsonville PMSA, CA	S	25.90 MW	25.59 AW	53870 AAW	CABLS	10//99-12//99
	Santa Rosa PMSA, CA	S	26.69 MW	24.93 AW	55510 AAW	CABLS	10//99-12//99
	Stockton-Lodi MSA, CA	S	25.74 MW	24.37 AW	53540 AAW	CABLS	10//99-12//99
	Vallejo-Fairfield-Napa PMSA, CA	S	26.26 MW	24.98 AW	54620 AAW	CABLS	10//99-12//99
	Ventura PMSA, CA	S	28.91 MW	26.43 AW	60130 AAW	CABLS	10//99-12//99
	Visalia-Tulare-Porterville MSA, CA	S	21.36 MW	20.70 AW	44430 AAW	CABLS	10//99-12//99
	Yolo PMSA, CA	S	30.19 MW	29.10 AW	62790 AAW	CABLS	10//99-12//99
	Yuba City MSA, CA	S	23.76 MW	20.10 AW	49410 AAW	CABLS	10//99-12//99
	Colorado	S	27.29 MW	28.56 AW	59400 AAW	COBLS	10//99-12//99
	Boulder-Longmont PMSA, CO	S	28.35 MW	26.62 AW	58980 AAW	COBLS	10//99-12//99
	Colorado Springs MSA, CO	S	28.99 MW	29.50 AW	60300 AAW	COBLS	10//99-12//99
	Denver PMSA, CO	S	29.66 MW	28.52 AW	61680 AAW	COBLS	10//99-12//99
	Fort Collins-Loveland MSA, CO	S	25.78 MW	24.63 AW	53630 AAW	COBLS	10//99-12//99
	Grand Junction MSA, CO	S	24.14 MW	22.00 AW	50210 AAW	COBLS	10//99-12//99
	Pueblo MSA, CO	S	29.09 MW	29.99 AW	60510 AAW	COBLS	10//99-12//99
	Connecticut	S	30.66 MW	31.83 AW	66200 AAW	CTBLS	10//99-12//99
	Bridgeport PMSA, CT	S	30.21 MW	28.99 AW	62830 AAW	CTBLS	10//99-12//99
	Danbury PMSA, CT	S	31.73 MW	28.28 AW	66000 AAW	CTBLS	10//99-12//99
	Hartford MSA, CT	S	31.17 MW	30.77 AW	64830 AAW	CTBLS	10//99-12//99
	New Haven-Meriden PMSA, CT	S	29.25 MW	26.30 AW	60840 AAW	CTBLS	10//99-12//99
	New London-Norwich MSA, CT-RI	S	28.28 MW	25.64 AW	58830 AAW	CTBLS	10//99-12//99
	Stamford-Norwalk PMSA, CT	S	38.96 MW	38.39 AW	81040 AAW	CTBLS	10//99-12//99
	Waterbury PMSA, CT	S	29.04 MW	28.00 AW	60410 AAW	CTBLS	10//99-12//99
	Delaware	S	28.87 MW	30.13 AW	62670 AAW	DEBLS	10//99-12//99
	Dover MSA, DE	S	27.27 MW	26.24 AW	56720 AAW	DEBLS	10//99-12//99
	Wilmington-Newark PMSA, DE-MD	S	31.79 MW	30.87 AW	66120 AAW	DEBLS	10//99-12//99
	District of Columbia	S	34.64 MW	33.05 AW	68750 AAW	DCBLS	10//99-12//99
	Washington PMSA, DC-MD-VA-WV	S	30.57 MW	31.16 AW	63580 AAW	DCBLS	10//99-12//99
	Florida	S	21.53 MW	23.24 AW	48340 AAW	FLBLS	10//99-12//99
	Daytona Beach MSA, FL	S	21.63 MW	19.61 AW	45000 AAW	FLBLS	10//99-12//99
	Fort Lauderdale PMSA, FL	S	24.20 MW	23.09 AW	50340 AAW	FLBLS	10//99-12//99
	Fort Myers-Cape Coral MSA, FL	S	22.77 MW	20.91 AW	47370 AAW	FLBLS	10//99-12//99
	Fort Pierce-Port St. Lucie MSA, FL	S	20.14 MW	18.63 AW	41890 AAW	FLBLS	10//99-12//99

AAW	Average annual wage	AOH	Average offered, high	ASH	Average starting, high	H	Hourly	M	Monthly	S	Special: hourly and annual
AE	Average entry wage	AOL	Average offered, low	ASL	Average starting, low	HI	Highest wage paid	MTC	Median total compensation	TQ	Third quartile wage
AEX	Average experienced wage	APH	Average pay, high range	AW	Average wage paid	HR	High end range	MW	Median wage paid	W	Weekly
AO	Average offered	APL	Average pay, low range	FQ	First quartile wage	LR	Low end range	SQ	Second quartile wage	Y	Yearly

Occupation/Type/Industry	Location	Per	Low	Mid	High	Source	Date
Human Resources Manager	Fort Walton Beach MSA, FL	S	24.23 MW	24.38 AW	50400 AAW	FLBLS	10//99-12//99
	Gainesville MSA, FL	S	21.31 MW	18.06 AW	44320 AAW	FLBLS	10//99-12//99
	Jacksonville MSA, FL	S	26.19 MW	22.65 AW	54470 AAW	FLBLS	10//99-12//99
	Lakeland-Winter Haven MSA, FL	S	22.53 MW	19.48 AW	46860 AAW	FLBLS	10//99-12//99
	Melbourne-Titusville-Palm Bay MSA, FL	S	26.33 MW	26.66 AW	54780 AAW	FLBLS	10//99-12//99
	Miami PMSA, FL	S	19.76 MW	18.47 AW	41090 AAW	FLBLS	10//99-12//99
	Naples MSA, FL	S	23.96 MW	22.01 AW	49830 AAW	FLBLS	10//99-12//99
	Ocala MSA, FL	S	23.84 MW	24.50 AW	49580 AAW	FLBLS	10//99-12//99
	Orlando MSA, FL	S	24.62 MW	22.73 AW	51220 AAW	FLBLS	10//99-12//99
	Panama City MSA, FL	S	20.33 MW	18.02 AW	42290 AAW	FLBLS	10//99-12//99
	Pensacola MSA, FL	S	21.15 MW	18.25 AW	43980 AAW	FLBLS	10//99-12//99
	Sarasota-Bradenton MSA, FL	S	22.45 MW	20.07 AW	46700 AAW	FLBLS	10//99-12//99
	Tallahassee MSA, FL	S	25.81 MW	24.78 AW	53690 AAW	FLBLS	10//99-12//99
	Tampa-St. Petersburg-Clearwater MSA, FL	S	24.93 MW	22.93 AW	51840 AAW	FLBLS	10//99-12//99
	West Palm Beach-Boca Raton MSA, FL	S	28.00 MW	24.96 AW	58240 AAW	FLBLS	10//99-12//99
	Georgia	S	23.77 MW	26.04 AW	54170 AAW	GABLS	10//99-12//99
	Albany MSA, GA	S	26.10 MW	22.71 AW	54280 AAW	GABLS	10//99-12//99
	Athens MSA, GA	S	25.42 MW	22.95 AW	52880 AAW	GABLS	10//99-12//99
	Atlanta MSA, GA	S	27.07 MW	24.68 AW	56310 AAW	GABLS	10//99-12//99
	Augusta-Aiken MSA, GA-SC	S	28.36 MW	26.50 AW	58980 AAW	GABLS	10//99-12//99
	Columbus MSA, GA-AL	S	23.97 MW	22.26 AW	49850 AAW	GABLS	10//99-12//99
	Macon MSA, GA	S	26.40 MW	25.43 AW	54900 AAW	GABLS	10//99-12//99
	Savannah MSA, GA	S	24.02 MW	20.90 AW	49970 AAW	GABLS	10//99-12//99
	Hawaii	S	26.58 MW	27.59 AW	57390 AAW	HIBLS	10//99-12//99
	Honolulu MSA, HI	S	28.25 MW	27.97 AW	58750 AAW	HIBLS	10//99-12//99
	Idaho	S	24.71 MW	26.41 AW	54920 AAW	IDBLS	10//99-12//99
	Boise City MSA, ID	S	28.48 MW	27.45 AW	59240 AAW	IDBLS	10//99-12//99
	Illinois	S	27.61 MW	30.24 AW	62890 AAW	ILBLS	10//99-12//99
	Bloomington-Normal MSA, IL	S	29.89 MW	25.78 AW	62170 AAW	ILBLS	10//99-12//99
	Champaign-Urbana MSA, IL	S	28.30 MW	26.54 AW	58870 AAW	ILBLS	10//99-12//99
	Chicago PMSA, IL	S	31.78 MW	30.27 AW	66100 AAW	ILBLS	10//99-12//99
	Decatur MSA, IL	S	22.78 MW	21.19 AW	47380 AAW	ILBLS	10//99-12//99
	Kankakee PMSA, IL	S	21.91 MW	19.26 AW	45580 AAW	ILBLS	10//99-12//99
	Peoria-Pekin MSA, IL	S	24.00 MW	22.88 AW	49910 AAW	ILBLS	10//99-12//99
	Rockford MSA, IL	S	23.50 MW	23.27 AW	48870 AAW	ILBLS	10//99-12//99
	Springfield MSA, IL	S	27.11 MW	26.87 AW	56390 AAW	ILBLS	10//99-12//99
	Indiana	S	23.42 MW	25.22 AW	52460 AAW	INBLS	10//99-12//99
	Bloomington MSA, IN	S	24.24 MW	22.46 AW	50430 AAW	INBLS	10//99-12//99
	Elkhart-Goshen MSA, IN	S	24.50 MW	22.92 AW	50970 AAW	INBLS	10//99-12//99
	Evansville-Henderson MSA, IN-KY	S	23.55 MW	22.45 AW	48980 AAW	INBLS	10//99-12//99
	Fort Wayne MSA, IN	S	24.25 MW	22.45 AW	50450 AAW	INBLS	10//99-12//99
	Gary PMSA, IN	S	26.14 MW	24.09 AW	54370 AAW	INBLS	10//99-12//99
	Indianapolis MSA, IN	S	25.88 MW	23.95 AW	53840 AAW	INBLS	10//99-12//99
	Kokomo MSA, IN	S	31.34 MW	30.16 AW	65180 AAW	INBLS	10//99-12//99
	Lafayette MSA, IN	S	24.16 MW	23.43 AW	50250 AAW	INBLS	10//99-12//99
	Muncie MSA, IN	S	27.00 MW	23.99 AW	56160 AAW	INBLS	10//99-12//99
	South Bend MSA, IN	S	23.03 MW	20.14 AW	47910 AAW	INBLS	10//99-12//99
	Terre Haute MSA, IN	S	25.15 MW	23.45 AW	52310 AAW	INBLS	10//99-12//99
	Iowa	S	19.98 MW	22.08 AW	45920 AAW	IABLS	10//99-12//99
	Cedar Rapids MSA, IA	S	24.86 MW	22.83 AW	51710 AAW	IABLS	10//99-12//99
	Davenport-Moline-Rock Island MSA, IA-IL	S	23.87 MW	22.46 AW	49650 AAW	IABLS	10//99-12//99
	Des Moines MSA, IA	S	23.18 MW	21.98 AW	48220 AAW	IABLS	10//99-12//99
	Dubuque MSA, IA	S	22.32 MW	20.79 AW	46430 AAW	IABLS	10//99-12//99
	Iowa City MSA, IA	S	23.54 MW	21.28 AW	48960 AAW	IABLS	10//99-12//99
	Sioux City MSA, IA-NE	S	20.47 MW	19.99 AW	42580 AAW	IABLS	10//99-12//99
	Waterloo-Cedar Falls MSA, IA	S	20.13 MW	17.54 AW	41860 AAW	IABLS	10//99-12//99
	Kansas	S	22.95 MW	25.02 AW	52050 AAW	KSBLS	10//99-12//99
	Lawrence MSA, KS	S	23.92 MW	23.71 AW	49760 AAW	KSBLS	10//99-12//99
	Topeka MSA, KS	S	22.75 MW	20.85 AW	47320 AAW	KSBLS	10//99-12//99
	Wichita MSA, KS	S	25.15 MW	22.40 AW	52320 AAW	KSBLS	10//99-12//99
	Kentucky	S	23.35 MW	24.58 AW	51130 AAW	KYBLS	10//99-12//99
	Lexington MSA, KY	S	26.57 MW	25.70 AW	55270 AAW	KYBLS	10//99-12//99
	Louisville MSA, KY-IN	S	26.59 MW	25.57 AW	55310 AAW	KYBLS	10//99-12//99
	Owensboro MSA, KY	S	21.47 MW	20.03 AW	44650 AAW	KYBLS	10//99-12//99
	Louisiana	S	20.4 MW	22.04 AW	45850 AAW	LABLS	10//99-12//99
	Alexandria MSA, LA	S	18.90 MW	18.70 AW	39310 AAW	LABLS	10//99-12//99

AAW	Average annual wage	AOH	Average offered, high	ASH	Average starting, high	H	Hourly
AE	Average entry wage	AOL	Average offered, low	ASL	Average starting, low	H1	Highest wage paid
AEX	Average experienced wage	APH	Average pay, high range	AW	Average wage paid	HR	High end range
AO	Average offered	APL	Average pay, low range	FQ	First quartile wage	LR	Low end range

M	Monthly	S	Special: hourly and annual
MTC	Median total compensation	TQ	Third quartile wage
MW	Median wage paid	W	Weekly
SQ	Second quartile wage	Y	Yearly

Occupation/Type/Industry	Location	Per	Low	Mid	High	Source	Date
Human Resources Manager	Baton Rouge MSA, LA	S	23.45 MW	22.56 AW	48790 AAW	LABLS	10//99-12//99
	Houma MSA, LA	S	23.05 MW	22.01 AW	47940 AAW	LABLS	10//99-12//99
	Lafayette MSA, LA	S	22.46 MW	20.19 AW	46710 AAW	LABLS	10//99-12//99
	Lake Charles MSA, LA	S	24.83 MW	23.24 AW	51640 AAW	LABLS	10//99-12//99
	Monroe MSA, LA	S	22.98 MW	20.68 AW	47810 AAW	LABLS	10//99-12//99
	New Orleans MSA, LA	S	21.39 MW	19.05 AW	44490 AAW	LABLS	10//99-12//99
	Shreveport-Bossier City MSA, LA	S	20.50 MW	18.56 AW	42650 AAW	LABLS	10//99-12//99
	Maine	S	22.42 MW	23.70 AW	49300 AAW	MEBLS	10//99-12//99
	Bangor MSA, ME	S	24.24 MW	23.31 AW	50430 AAW	MEBLS	10//99-12//99
	Lewiston-Auburn MSA, ME	S	24.23 MW	23.40 AW	50400 AAW	MEBLS	10//99-12//99
	Portland MSA, ME	S	27.29 MW	24.94 AW	56750 AAW	MEBLS	10//99-12//99
	Maryland	S	24.93 MW	26.62 AW	55370 AAW	MDBLS	10//99-12//99
	Baltimore PMSA, MD	S	26.75 MW	24.82 AW	55640 AAW	MDBLS	10//99-12//99
	Hagerstown PMSA, MD	S	23.84 MW	23.16 AW	49590 AAW	MDBLS	10//99-12//99
	Massachusetts	S	30.3 MW	30.87 AW	64210 AAW	MABLS	10//99-12//99
	Barnstable-Yarmouth MSA, MA	S	22.98 MW	22.09 AW	47790 AAW	MABLS	10//99-12//99
	Boston PMSA, MA-NH	S	32.25 MW	32.12 AW	67090 AAW	MABLS	10//99-12//99
	Brockton PMSA, MA	S	26.62 MW	26.96 AW	55380 AAW	MABLS	10//99-12//99
	Fitchburg-Leominster PMSA, MA	S	25.69 MW	23.70 AW	53430 AAW	MABLS	10//99-12//99
	Lowell PMSA, MA-NH	S	29.80 MW	29.97 AW	61980 AAW	MABLS	10//99-12//99
	New Bedford PMSA, MA	S	23.58 MW	23.65 AW	49050 AAW	MABLS	10//99-12//99
	Pittsfield MSA, MA	S	24.05 MW	22.84 AW	50030 AAW	MABLS	10//99-12//99
	Springfield MSA, MA	S	25.23 MW	23.44 AW	52480 AAW	MABLS	10//99-12//99
	Worcester PMSA, MA-CT	S	27.56 MW	26.00 AW	57330 AAW	MABLS	10//99-12//99
	Michigan	S	27.43 MW	28.89 AW	60090 AAW	MIBLS	10//99-12//99
	Ann Arbor PMSA, MI	S	28.19 MW	28.34 AW	58630 AAW	MIBLS	10//99-12//99
	Benton Harbor MSA, MI	S	24.89 MW	23.83 AW	51770 AAW	MIBLS	10//99-12//99
	Detroit PMSA, MI	S	30.70 MW	30.10 AW	63850 AAW	MIBLS	10//99-12//99
	Flint PMSA, MI	S	31.88 MW	31.12 AW	66310 AAW	MIBLS	10//99-12//99
	Grand Rapids-Muskegon-Holland MSA, MI	S	26.61 MW	24.75 AW	55350 AAW	MIBLS	10//99-12//99
	Jackson MSA, MI	S	27.60 MW	25.09 AW	57420 AAW	MIBLS	10//99-12//99
	Kalamazoo-Battle Creek MSA, MI	S	29.07 MW	29.12 AW	60470 AAW	MIBLS	10//99-12//99
	Lansing-East Lansing MSA, MI	S	24.59 MW	23.13 AW	51150 AAW	MIBLS	10//99-12//99
	Saginaw-Bay City-Midland MSA, MI	S	31.39 MW	31.59 AW	65290 AAW	MIBLS	10//99-12//99
	Minnesota	S	29.22 MW	29.28 AW	60890 AAW	MNBLS	10//99-12//99
	Duluth-Superior MSA, MN-WI	S	25.75 MW	24.91 AW	53550 AAW	MNBLS	10//99-12//99
	Minneapolis-St. Paul MSA, MN-WI	S	30.48 MW	30.68 AW	63400 AAW	MNBLS	10//99-12//99
	Rochester MSA, MN	S	26.48 MW	25.50 AW	55070 AAW	MNBLS	10//99-12//99
	St. Cloud MSA, MN	S	28.08 MW	28.72 AW	58410 AAW	MNBLS	10//99-12//99
	Mississippi	S	21.26 MW	22.56 AW	46930 AAW	MSBLS	10//99-12//99
	Biloxi-Gulfport-Pascagoula MSA, MS	S	22.87 MW	21.32 AW	47570 AAW	MSBLS	10//99-12//99
	Hattiesburg MSA, MS	S	19.32 MW	18.47 AW	40190 AAW	MSBLS	10//99-12//99
	Jackson MSA, MS	S	23.22 MW	21.80 AW	48300 AAW	MSBLS	10//99-12//99
	Missouri	S	22.9 MW	24.97 AW	51950 AAW	MOBLS	10//99-12//99
	Columbia MSA, MO	S	20.33 MW	17.07 AW	42280 AAW	MOBLS	10//99-12//99
	Joplin MSA, MO	S	23.47 MW	21.64 AW	48810 AAW	MOBLS	10//99-12//99
	Kansas City MSA, MO-KS	S	26.40 MW	24.12 AW	54900 AAW	MOBLS	10//99-12//99
	St. Joseph MSA, MO	S	22.71 MW	20.73 AW	47240 AAW	MOBLS	10//99-12//99
	St. Louis MSA, MO-IL	S	25.70 MW	23.87 AW	53460 AAW	MOBLS	10//99-12//99
	Springfield MSA, MO	S	22.02 MW	20.99 AW	45800 AAW	MOBLS	10//99-12//99
	Montana	S	21.05 MW	22.96 AW	47760 AAW	MTBLS	10//99-12//99
	Billings MSA, MT	S	21.53 MW	20.29 AW	44780 AAW	MTBLS	10//99-12//99
	Missoula MSA, MT	S	23.61 MW	23.20 AW	49110 AAW	MTBLS	10//99-12//99
	Nebraska	S	23.74 MW	25.19 AW	52400 AAW	NEBLS	10//99-12//99
	Lincoln MSA, NE	S	25.38 MW	24.79 AW	52790 AAW	NEBLS	10//99-12//99
	Omaha MSA, NE-IA	S	26.81 MW	25.51 AW	55760 AAW	NEBLS	10//99-12//99
	Nevada	S	25.03 MW	28.22 AW	58690 AAW	NVBLS	10//99-12//99
	Las Vegas MSA, NV-AZ	S	28.82 MW	25.47 AW	59940 AAW	NVBLS	10//99-12//99
	Reno MSA, NV	S	26.94 MW	24.39 AW	56040 AAW	NVBLS	10//99-12//99
	New Hampshire	S	22.2 MW	23.83 AW	49570 AAW	NHBLS	10//99-12//99
	Manchester PMSA, NH	S	23.43 MW	21.27 AW	48730 AAW	NHBLS	10//99-12//99
	Nashua PMSA, NH	S	26.72 MW	25.98 AW	55570 AAW	NHBLS	10//99-12//99
	Portsmouth-Rochester PMSA, NH-ME	S	23.15 MW	20.81 AW	48150 AAW	NHBLS	10//99-12//99

Occupation/Type/Industry	Location	Per	Low	Mid	High	Source	Date
Human Resources Manager	New Jersey	S	33.75 MW	33.87 AW	70450 AAW	NJBLS	10//99-12//99
	Atlantic-Cape May PMSA, NJ	S	30.18 MW	28.84 AW	62760 AAW	NJBLS	10//99-12//99
	Bergen-Passaic PMSA, NJ	S	34.03 MW	34.33 AW	70790 AAW	NJBLS	10//99-12//99
	Jersey City PMSA, NJ	S	35.91 MW	35.78 AW	74700 AAW	NJBLS	10//99-12//99
	Middlesex-Somerset-Hunterdon PMSA, NJ	S	32.49 MW	31.94 AW	67570 AAW	NJBLS	10//99-12//99
	Monmouth-Ocean PMSA, NJ	S	31.14 MW	30.04 AW	64770 AAW	NJBLS	10//99-12//99
	Newark PMSA, NJ	S	34.92 MW	34.96 AW	72630 AAW	NJBLS	10//99-12//99
	Trenton PMSA, NJ	S	35.85 MW	37.11 AW	74560 AAW	NJBLS	10//99-12//99
	Vineland-Millville-Bridgeton PMSA, NJ	S	33.68 MW	34.64 AW	70050 AAW	NJBLS	10//99-12//99
	New Mexico	S	19.45 MW	21.93 AW	45610 AAW	NMBLS	10//99-12//99
	Albuquerque MSA, NM	S	23.62 MW	21.25 AW	49130 AAW	NMBLS	10//99-12//99
	Las Cruces MSA, NM	S	18.02 MW	17.40 AW	37480 AAW	NMBLS	10//99-12//99
	New York	S	32.58 MW	32.62 AW	67860 AAW	NYBLS	10//99-12//99
	Albany-Schenectady-Troy MSA, NY	S	30.70 MW	30.64 AW	63860 AAW	NYBLS	10//99-12//99
	Binghamton MSA, NY	S	24.07 MW	21.36 AW	50060 AAW	NYBLS	10//99-12//99
	Buffalo-Niagara Falls MSA, NY	S	26.85 MW	25.72 AW	55860 AAW	NYBLS	10//99-12//99
	Dutchess County PMSA, NY	S	25.45 MW	27.55 AW	52930 AAW	NYBLS	10//99-12//99
	Elmira MSA, NY	S	23.91 MW	21.50 AW	49720 AAW	NYBLS	10//99-12//99
	Glens Falls MSA, NY	S	28.23 MW	26.31 AW	58710 AAW	NYBLS	10//99-12//99
	Jamestown MSA, NY	S	23.42 MW	20.05 AW	48720 AAW	NYBLS	10//99-12//99
	Nassau-Suffolk PMSA, NY	S	30.71 MW	30.25 AW	63870 AAW	NYBLS	10//99-12//99
	New York PMSA, NY	S	35.27 MW	35.17 AW	73360 AAW	NYBLS	10//99-12//99
	Newburgh PMSA, NY-PA	S	24.19 MW	23.34 AW	50310 AAW	NYBLS	10//99-12//99
	Rochester MSA, NY	S	30.91 MW	31.56 AW	64290 AAW	NYBLS	10//99-12//99
	Syracuse MSA, NY	S	25.64 MW	24.02 AW	53320 AAW	NYBLS	10//99-12//99
	Utica-Rome MSA, NY	S	27.32 MW	28.82 AW	56830 AAW	NYBLS	10//99-12//99
	North Carolina	S	24.07 MW	25.98 AW	54050 AAW	NCBLS	10//99-12//99
	Asheville MSA, NC	S	21.25 MW	18.83 AW	44210 AAW	NCBLS	10//99-12//99
	Charlotte-Gastonia-Rock Hill MSA, NC-SC	S	27.24 MW	25.05 AW	56670 AAW	NCBLS	10//99-12//99
	Fayetteville MSA, NC	S	22.40 MW	22.13 AW	46590 AAW	NCBLS	10//99-12//99
	Goldsboro MSA, NC	S	20.50 MW	19.78 AW	42640 AAW	NCBLS	10//99-12//99
	Greensboro--Winston-Salem--High Point MSA, NC	S	25.90 MW	24.17 AW	53880 AAW	NCBLS	10//99-12//99
	Greenville MSA, NC	S	26.69 MW	25.21 AW	55510 AAW	NCBLS	10//99-12//99
	Hickory-Morganton-Lenoir MSA, NC	S	23.14 MW	20.32 AW	48130 AAW	NCBLS	10//99-12//99
	Raleigh-Durham-Chapel Hill MSA, NC	S	29.28 MW	28.42 AW	60910 AAW	NCBLS	10//99-12//99
	Rocky Mount MSA, NC	S	26.51 MW	27.81 AW	55140 AAW	NCBLS	10//99-12//99
	Wilmington MSA, NC	S	22.26 MW	20.45 AW	46290 AAW	NCBLS	10//99-12//99
	North Dakota	S	20.31 MW	22.72 AW	47260 AAW	NDBLS	10//99-12//99
	Bismarck MSA, ND	S	23.16 MW	20.92 AW	48160 AAW	NDBLS	10//99-12//99
	Fargo-Moorhead MSA, ND-MN	S	22.77 MW	20.11 AW	47350 AAW	NDBLS	10//99-12//99
	Grand Forks MSA, ND-MN	S	20.72 MW	20.75 AW	43090 AAW	NDBLS	10//99-12//99
	Ohio	S	23.83 MW	25.46 AW	52950 AAW	OHBLS	10//99-12//99
	Akron PMSA, OH	S	26.41 MW	24.77 AW	54930 AAW	OHBLS	10//99-12//99
	Canton-Massillon MSA, OH	S	23.06 MW	20.38 AW	47960 AAW	OHBLS	10//99-12//99
	Cincinnati PMSA, OH-KY-IN	S	26.12 MW	23.75 AW	54320 AAW	OHBLS	10//99-12//99
	Cleveland-Lorain-Elyria PMSA, OH	S	27.04 MW	25.49 AW	56250 AAW	OHBLS	10//99-12//99
	Columbus MSA, OH	S	25.08 MW	23.87 AW	52170 AAW	OHBLS	10//99-12//99
	Dayton-Springfield MSA, OH	S	27.05 MW	27.33 AW	56260 AAW	OHBLS	10//99-12//99
	Hamilton-Middletown PMSA, OH	S	25.87 MW	25.69 AW	53800 AAW	OHBLS	10//99-12//99
	Lima MSA, OH	S	19.52 MW	17.91 AW	40610 AAW	OHBLS	10//99-12//99
	Mansfield MSA, OH	S	23.43 MW	20.44 AW	48730 AAW	OHBLS	10//99-12//99
	Steubenville-Weirton MSA, OH-WV	S	26.12 MW	23.76 AW	54320 AAW	OHBLS	10//99-12//99
	Toledo MSA, OH	S	26.58 MW	23.66 AW	55280 AAW	OHBLS	10//99-12//99
	Youngstown-Warren MSA, OH	S	23.10 MW	21.08 AW	48040 AAW	OHBLS	10//99-12//99
	Oklahoma	S	22.08 MW	23.65 AW	49190 AAW	OKBLS	10//99-12//99
	Oklahoma City MSA, OK	S	24.77 MW	23.22 AW	51520 AAW	OKBLS	10//99-12//99
	Tulsa MSA, OK	S	23.76 MW	22.00 AW	49410 AAW	OKBLS	10//99-12//99
	Oregon	S	23.96 MW	25.74 AW	53530 AAW	ORBLS	10//99-12//99
	Eugene-Springfield MSA, OR	S	23.45 MW	22.79 AW	48770 AAW	ORBLS	10//99-12//99
	Medford-Ashland MSA, OR	S	25.41 MW	25.35 AW	52860 AAW	ORBLS	10//99-12//99

AAW	Average annual wage	AOH	Average offered, high	ASH	Average starting, high	H	Hourly	M	Monthly	S	Special: hourly and annual
AE	Average entry wage	AOL	Average offered, low	ASL	Average starting, low	HI	Highest wage paid	MTC	Median total compensation	TQ	Third quartile wage
AEX	Average experienced wage	APH	Average pay, high range	AW	Average wage paid	HR	High end range	MW	Median wage paid	W	Weekly
AO	Average offered	APL	Average pay, low range	FQ	First quartile wage	LR	Low end range	SQ	Second quartile wage	Y	Yearly

Occupation/Type/Industry	Location	Per	Low	Mid	High	Source	Date
Human Resources Manager	Portland-Vancouver PMSA, OR-WA	S	26.75 MW	24.73 AW	55650 AAW	ORBLS	10//99-12//99
	Salem PMSA, OR	S	25.30 MW	23.91 AW	52610 AAW	ORBLS	10//99-12//99
	Pennsylvania	S	25.96 MW	26.73 AW	55600 AAW	PABLS	10//99-12//99
	Allentown-Bethlehem-Easton MSA, PA	S	31.31 MW	31.43 AW	65130 AAW	PABLS	10//99-12//99
	Altoona MSA, PA	S	24.15 MW	20.77 AW	50230 AAW	PABLS	10//99-12//99
	Erie MSA, PA	S	20.19 MW	19.75 AW	41990 AAW	PABLS	10//99-12//99
	Harrisburg-Lebanon-Carlisle MSA, PA	S	25.58 MW	23.94 AW	53200 AAW	PABLS	10//99-12//99
	Johnstown MSA, PA	S	21.44 MW	19.78 AW	44590 AAW	PABLS	10//99-12//99
	Lancaster MSA, PA	S	25.35 MW	22.29 AW	52730 AAW	PABLS	10//99-12//99
	Philadelphia PMSA, PA-NJ	S	29.78 MW	29.67 AW	61930 AAW	PABLS	10//99-12//99
	Pittsburgh MSA, PA	S	25.61 MW	24.64 AW	53270 AAW	PABLS	10//99-12//99
	Reading MSA, PA	S	22.44 MW	20.64 AW	46680 AAW	PABLS	10//99-12//99
	Scranton--Wilkes-Barre--Hazleton MSA, PA	S	20.61 MW	19.24 AW	42860 AAW	PABLS	10//99-12//99
	Sharon MSA, PA	S	20.60 MW	15.55 AW	42850 AAW	PABLS	10//99-12//99
	State College MSA, PA	S	24.97 MW	23.59 AW	51950 AAW	PABLS	10//99-12//99
	Williamsport MSA, PA	S	20.18 MW	19.18 AW	41970 AAW	PABLS	10//99-12//99
	York MSA, PA	S	23.06 MW	22.47 AW	47970 AAW	PABLS	10//99-12//99
	Rhode Island	S	30.11 MW	30.48 AW	63400 AAW	RIBLS	10//99-12//99
	Providence-Fall River-Warwick MSA, RI-MA	S	28.36 MW	26.60 AW	58980 AAW	RIBLS	10//99-12//99
	South Carolina	S	22.35 MW	23.96 AW	49830 AAW	SCBLS	10//99-12//99
	Charleston-North Charleston MSA, SC	S	24.35 MW	22.12 AW	50650 AAW	SCBLS	10//99-12//99
	Columbia MSA, SC	S	23.85 MW	22.95 AW	49610 AAW	SCBLS	10//99-12//99
	Florence MSA, SC	S	23.69 MW	20.23 AW	49270 AAW	SCBLS	10//99-12//99
	Greenville-Spartanburg-Anderson MSA, SC	S	25.01 MW	23.83 AW	52020 AAW	SCBLS	10//99-12//99
	Myrtle Beach MSA, SC	S	20.46 MW	17.27 AW	42560 AAW	SCBLS	10//99-12//99
	Sumter MSA, SC	S	26.59 MW	23.91 AW	55310 AAW	SCBLS	10//99-12//99
	South Dakota	S	25.32 MW	26.50 AW	55110 AAW	SDBLS	10//99-12//99
	Rapid City MSA, SD	S	26.30 MW	25.13 AW	54700 AAW	SDBLS	10//99-12//99
	Sioux Falls MSA, SD	S	27.30 MW	26.31 AW	56790 AAW	SDBLS	10//99-12//99
	Tennessee	S	23.1 MW	24.50 AW	50970 AAW	TNBLS	10//99-12//99
	Chattanooga MSA, TN-GA	S	24.16 MW	23.05 AW	50240 AAW	TNBLS	10//99-12//99
	Clarksville-Hopkinsville MSA, TN-KY	S	22.63 MW	22.49 AW	47070 AAW	TNBLS	10//99-12//99
	Jackson MSA, TN	S	22.52 MW	19.97 AW	46840 AAW	TNBLS	10//99-12//99
	Johnson City-Kingsport-Bristol MSA, TN-VA	S	24.10 MW	23.46 AW	50120 AAW	TNBLS	10//99-12//99
	Knoxville MSA, TN	S	24.02 MW	21.84 AW	49960 AAW	TNBLS	10//99-12//99
	Memphis MSA, TN-AR-MS	S	26.50 MW	24.65 AW	55110 AAW	MSBLS	10//99-12//99
	Nashville MSA, TN	S	25.06 MW	23.84 AW	52120 AAW	TNBLS	10//99-12//99
	Texas	S	25.31 MW	27.01 AW	56180 AAW	TXBLS	10//99-12//99
	Abilene MSA, TX	S	23.03 MW	20.38 AW	47900 AAW	TXBLS	10//99-12//99
	Amarillo MSA, TX	S	22.30 MW	21.05 AW	46370 AAW	TXBLS	10//99-12//99
	Austin-San Marcos MSA, TX	S	25.95 MW	24.18 AW	53980 AAW	TXBLS	10//99-12//99
	Beaumont-Port Arthur MSA, TX	S	23.54 MW	22.30 AW	48970 AAW	TXBLS	10//99-12//99
	Brazoria PMSA, TX	S	29.40 MW	28.89 AW	61150 AAW	TXBLS	10//99-12//99
	Brownsville-Harlingen-San Benito MSA, TX	S	20.73 MW	18.26 AW	43120 AAW	TXBLS	10//99-12//99
	Bryan-College Station MSA, TX	S	24.64 MW	21.43 AW	51260 AAW	TXBLS	10//99-12//99
	Corpus Christi MSA, TX	S	23.53 MW	20.04 AW	48950 AAW	TXBLS	10//99-12//99
	Dallas PMSA, TX	S	30.23 MW	29.84 AW	62890 AAW	TXBLS	10//99-12//99
	El Paso MSA, TX	S	23.64 MW	21.77 AW	49160 AAW	TXBLS	10//99-12//99
	Fort Worth-Arlington PMSA, TX	S	25.83 MW	24.09 AW	53740 AAW	TXBLS	10//99-12//99
	Houston PMSA, TX	S	28.86 MW	27.17 AW	60030 AAW	TXBLS	10//99-12//99
	Killeen-Temple MSA, TX	S	23.16 MW	21.92 AW	48170 AAW	TXBLS	10//99-12//99
	Laredo MSA, TX	S	18.61 MW	16.11 AW	38710 AAW	TXBLS	10//99-12//99
	Longview-Marshall MSA, TX	S	23.17 MW	22.07 AW	48200 AAW	TXBLS	10//99-12//99
	Lubbock MSA, TX	S	18.46 MW	16.85 AW	38400 AAW	TXBLS	10//99-12//99
	McAllen-Edinburg-Mission MSA, TX	S	22.53 MW	20.66 AW	46870 AAW	TXBLS	10//99-12//99
	Odessa-Midland MSA, TX	S	24.48 MW	20.57 AW	50920 AAW	TXBLS	10//99-12//99
	San Antonio MSA, TX	S	23.18 MW	21.49 AW	48210 AAW	TXBLS	10//99-12//99
	Sherman-Denison MSA, TX	S	26.40 MW	26.08 AW	54910 AAW	TXBLS	10//99-12//99

AAW Average annual wage	**AOH** Average offered, high	**ASH** Average starting, high	**H** Hourly	**M** Monthly	**S** Special: hourly and annual
AE Average entry wage	**AOL** Average offered, low	**ASL** Average starting, low	**HI** Highest wage paid	**MTC** Median total compensation	**TQ** Third quartile wage
AEX Average experienced wage	**APH** Average pay, high range	**AW** Average wage paid	**HR** High end range	**MW** Median wage paid	**W** Weekly
AO Average offered	**APL** Average pay, low range	**FQ** First quartile wage	**LR** Low end range	**SQ** Second quartile wage	**Y** Yearly

Occupation/Type/Industry	Location	Per	Low	Mid	High	Source	Date
Human Resources Manager	Texarkana MSA, TX-						
	Texarkana, AR	S	22.27 MW	19.52 AW	46330 AAW	TXBLS	10//99-12//99
	Tyler MSA, TX	S	24.82 MW	22.69 AW	51620 AAW	TXBLS	10//99-12//99
	Victoria MSA, TX	S	21.00 MW	19.81 AW	43680 AAW	TXBLS	10//99-12//99
	Waco MSA, TX	S	22.57 MW	20.48 AW	46940 AAW	TXBLS	10//99-12//99
	Wichita Falls MSA, TX	S	19.26 MW	16.53 AW	40070 AAW	TXBLS	10//99-12//99
	Utah	S	21.65 MW	23.07 AW	47990 AAW	UTBLS	10//99-12//99
	Provo-Orem MSA, UT	S	24.21 MW	22.84 AW	50360 AAW	UTBLS	10//99-12//99
	Salt Lake City-Ogden MSA, UT	S	23.02 MW	21.48 AW	47890 AAW	UTBLS	10//99-12//99
	Vermont	S	27.06 MW	28.46 AW	59200 AAW	VTBLS	10//99-12//99
	Burlington MSA, VT	S	29.66 MW	29.41 AW	61700 AAW	VTBLS	10//99-12//99
	Virginia	S	28.76 MW	29.06 AW	60440 AAW	VABLS	10//99-12//99
	Charlottesville MSA, VA	S	26.49 MW	27.49 AW	55110 AAW	VABLS	10//99-12//99
	Danville MSA, VA	S	23.08 MW	20.54 AW	48010 AAW	VABLS	10//99-12//99
	Lynchburg MSA, VA	S	24.34 MW	24.36 AW	50620 AAW	VABLS	10//99-12//99
	Norfolk-Virginia Beach-Newport News MSA, VA-NC	S	27.31 MW	26.26 AW	56800 AAW	VABLS	10//99-12//99
	Richmond-Petersburg MSA, VA	S	28.83 MW	26.67 AW	59970 AAW	VABLS	10//99-12//99
	Roanoke MSA, VA	S	25.61 MW	24.34 AW	53260 AAW	VABLS	10//99-12//99
	Washington	S	25.64 MW	26.44 AW	55000 AAW	WABLS	10//99-12//99
	Bellingham MSA, WA	S	23.43 MW	21.50 AW	48730 AAW	WABLS	10//99-12//99
	Bremerton PMSA, WA	S	26.11 MW	27.87 AW	54310 AAW	WABLS	10//99-12//99
	Olympia PMSA, WA	S	24.80 MW	24.19 AW	51590 AAW	WABLS	10//99-12//99
	Richland-Kennewick-Pasco MSA, WA	S	31.79 MW	33.81 AW	66130 AAW	WABLS	10//99-12//99
	Seattle-Bellevue-Everett PMSA, WA	S	28.24 MW	27.77 AW	58740 AAW	WABLS	10//99-12//99
	Spokane MSA, WA	S	24.09 MW	22.61 AW	50110 AAW	WABLS	10//99-12//99
	Tacoma PMSA, WA	S	18.73 MW	17.64 AW	38950 AAW	WABLS	10//99-12//99
	Yakima MSA, WA	S	24.81 MW	22.42 AW	51610 AAW	WABLS	10//99-12//99
	West Virginia	S	20.66 MW	22.82 AW	47480 AAW	WVBLS	10//99-12//99
	Charleston MSA, WV	S	25.23 MW	25.69 AW	52480 AAW	WVBLS	10//99-12//99
	Huntington-Ashland MSA, WV-KY-OH	S	21.45 MW	18.88 AW	44610 AAW	WVBLS	10//99-12//99
	Parkersburg-Marietta MSA, WV-OH	S	24.88 MW	21.93 AW	51760 AAW	WVBLS	10//99-12//99
	Wheeling MSA, WV-OH	S	19.87 MW	16.79 AW	41320 AAW	WVBLS	10//99-12//99
	Wisconsin	S	22.33 MW	23.25 AW	48370 AAW	WIBLS	10//99-12//99
	Appleton-Oshkosh-Neenah MSA, WI	S	22.68 MW	22.85 AW	47170 AAW	WIBLS	10//99-12//99
	Green Bay MSA, WI	S	25.52 MW	24.34 AW	53080 AAW	WIBLS	10//99-12//99
	Janesville-Beloit MSA, WI	S	23.32 MW	22.06 AW	48510 AAW	WIBLS	10//99-12//99
	Kenosha PMSA, WI	S	24.47 MW	22.77 AW	50890 AAW	WIBLS	10//99-12//99
	La Crosse MSA, WI-MN	S	23.94 MW	23.17 AW	49790 AAW	WIBLS	10//99-12//99
	Madison MSA, WI	S	25.03 MW	23.83 AW	52060 AAW	WIBLS	10//99-12//99
	Milwaukee-Waukesha PMSA, WI	S	23.35 MW	22.72 AW	48560 AAW	WIBLS	10//99-12//99
	Racine PMSA, WI	S	23.88 MW	23.13 AW	49680 AAW	WIBLS	10//99-12//99
	Sheboygan MSA, WI	S	23.06 MW	21.88 AW	47970 AAW	WIBLS	10//99-12//99
	Wausau MSA, WI	S	26.53 MW	28.22 AW	55190 AAW	WIBLS	10//99-12//99
	Wyoming	S	21.21 MW	23.68 AW	49250 AAW	WYBLS	10//99-12//99
	Casper MSA, WY	S	20.69 MW	19.54 AW	43030 AAW	WYBLS	10//99-12//99
	Cheyenne MSA, WY	S	21.55 MW	20.53 AW	44830 AAW	WYBLS	10//99-12//99
	Puerto Rico	S	19.41 MW	21.94 AW	45630 AAW	PRBLS	10//99-12//99
	Caguas PMSA, PR	S	25.66 MW	24.11 AW	53380 AAW	PRBLS	10//99-12//99
	Mayaguez MSA, PR	S	21.42 MW	18.37 AW	44550 AAW	PRBLS	10//99-12//99
	Ponce MSA, PR	S	19.07 MW	16.41 AW	39670 AAW	PRBLS	10//99-12//99
	San Juan-Bayamon PMSA, PR	S	22.09 MW	19.50 AW	45940 AAW	PRBLS	10//99-12//99
	Virgin Islands	S	18.89 MW	20.61 AW	42870 AAW	VIBLS	10//99-12//99
	Guam	S	20.85 MW	21.43 AW	44570 AAW	GUBLS	10//99-12//99
Human Resources Top Executive	United States	Y		191800 AW		TRAVWK2	1999
Hydrologist	Alaska	S	23.67 MW	23.24 AW	48330 AAW	AKBLS	10//99-12//99
	Arizona	S	20.72 MW	21.86 AW	45470 AAW	AZBLS	10//99-12//99
	California	S	32.22 MW	32.63 AW	67870 AAW	CABLS	10//99-12//99
	Colorado	S	27.14 MW	27.43 AW	57060 AAW	COBLS	10//99-12//99
	Connecticut	S	20.47 MW	23.06 AW	47970 AAW	CTBLS	10//99-12//99
	Delaware	S	24.91 MW	26.58 AW	55280 AAW	DEBLS	10//99-12//99
	Florida	S	25.85 MW	24.95 AW	51900 AAW	FLBLS	10//99-12//99

AAW	Average annual wage	AOH	Average offered, high	ASH	Average starting, high	H	Hourly	M	Monthly	S	Special: hourly and annual
AE	Average entry wage	AOL	Average offered, low	ASL	Average starting, low	HI	Highest wage paid	MTC	Median total compensation	TQ	Third quartile wage
AEX	Average experienced wage	APH	Average pay, high range	AW	Average wage paid	HR	High end range	MW	Median wage paid	W	Weekly
AO	Average offered	APL	Average pay, low range	FQ	First quartile wage	LR	Low end range	SQ	Second quartile wage	Y	Yearly

Occupation/Type/Industry	Location	Per	Low	Mid	High	Source	Date
Hydrologist	Georgia	S	28.92 MW	29.09 AW	60500 AAW	GABLS	10//99-12//99
	Idaho	S	21.31 MW	22.86 AW	47560 AAW	IDBLS	10//99-12//99
	Illinois	S	29.88 MW	29.01 AW	60340 AAW	ILBLS	10//99-12//99
	Indiana	S	25.67 MW	26.92 AW	55990 AAW	INBLS	10//99-12//99
	Kentucky	S	23.54 MW	23.55 AW	48980 AAW	KYBLS	10//99-12//99
	Louisiana	S	24.73 MW	24.69 AW	51360 AAW	LABLS	10//99-12//99
	Maryland	S	25.93 MW	27.97 AW	58170 AAW	MDBLS	10//99-12//99
	Massachusetts	S	29.07 MW	28.18 AW	58620 AAW	MABLS	10//99-12//99
	Michigan	S	24.52 MW	25.96 AW	53990 AAW	MIBLS	10//99-12//99
	Minnesota	S	28.91 MW	28.04 AW	58320 AAW	MNBLS	10//99-12//99
	Mississippi	S	28.8 MW	28.37 AW	59010 AAW	MSBLS	10//99-12//99
	Missouri	S	26.26 MW	29.48 AW	61320 AAW	MOBLS	10//99-12//99
	Montana	S	16.85 MW	21.55 AW	44830 AAW	MTBLS	10//99-12//99
	Nevada	S	30.08 MW	29.79 AW	61960 AAW	NVBLS	10//99-12//99
	New Hampshire	S	25.01 MW	27.11 AW	56400 AAW	NHBLS	10//99-12//99
	New Jersey	S	27.17 MW	25.44 AW	52910 AAW	NJBLS	10//99-12//99
	New Mexico	S	18.59 MW	20.51 AW	42670 AAW	NMBLS	10//99-12//99
	New York	S	29.45 MW	32.12 AW	66820 AAW	NYBLS	10//99-12//99
	North Carolina	S	21.02 MW	22.23 AW	46250 AAW	NCBLS	10//99-12//99
	Oklahoma	S	25.66 MW	25.14 AW	52290 AAW	OKBLS	10//99-12//99
	Oregon	S	24.47 MW	24.87 AW	51730 AAW	ORBLS	10//99-12//99
	Pennsylvania	S	27.4 MW	26.16 AW	54410 AAW	PABLS	10//99-12//99
	South Carolina	S	19.11 MW	20.05 AW	41700 AAW	SCBLS	10//99-12//99
	South Dakota	S	20.4 MW	20.72 AW	43090 AAW	SDBLS	10//99-12//99
	Tennessee	S	25.71 MW	25.44 AW	52910 AAW	TNBLS	10//99-12//99
	Texas	S	21.88 MW	23.22 AW	48300 AAW	TXBLS	10//99-12//99
	Vermont	S	13.77 MW	19.42 AW	40390 AAW	VTBLS	10//99-12//99
	Virginia	S	29.47 MW	30.46 AW	63350 AAW	VABLS	10//99-12//99
	Washington	S	30.22 MW	30.56 AW	63570 AAW	WABLS	10//99-12//99
	Wisconsin	S	20.81 MW	22.34 AW	46470 AAW	WIBLS	10//99-12//99
	Wyoming	S	23.06 MW	22.52 AW	46840 AAW	WYBLS	10//99-12//99
Industrial Engineer	Alabama	S	24.46 MW	24.50 AW	50960 AAW	ALBLS	10//99-12//99
	Anniston MSA, AL	S	25.33 MW	26.91 AW	52690 AAW	ALBLS	10//99-12//99
	Birmingham MSA, AL	S	24.45 MW	23.99 AW	50860 AAW	ALBLS	10//99-12//99
	Decatur MSA, AL	S	33.10 MW	32.34 AW	68840 AAW	ALBLS	10//99-12//99
	Dothan MSA, AL	S	20.99 MW	19.65 AW	43660 AAW	ALBLS	10//99-12//99
	Florence MSA, AL	S	24.12 MW	23.73 AW	50180 AAW	ALBLS	10//99-12//99
	Huntsville MSA, AL	S	26.95 MW	26.70 AW	56060 AAW	ALBLS	10//99-12//99
	Mobile MSA, AL	S	25.81 MW	27.40 AW	53690 AAW	ALBLS	10//99-12//99
	Montgomery MSA, AL	S	20.30 MW	19.72 AW	42220 AAW	ALBLS	10//99-12//99
	Tuscaloosa MSA, AL	S	24.77 MW	24.88 AW	51510 AAW	ALBLS	10//99-12//99
	Arizona	S	19.55 MW	21.58 AW	44880 AAW	AZBLS	10//99-12//99
	Phoenix-Mesa MSA, AZ	S	21.50 MW	19.38 AW	44720 AAW	AZBLS	10//99-12//99
	Tucson MSA, AZ	S	27.91 MW	26.73 AW	58040 AAW	AZBLS	10//99-12//99
	Arkansas	S	24.09 MW	24.60 AW	51180 AAW	ARBLS	10//99-12//99
	Fayetteville-Springdale-Rogers MSA, AR	S	24.13 MW	24.42 AW	50190 AAW	ARBLS	10//99-12//99
	Fort Smith MSA, AR-OK	S	23.37 MW	22.38 AW	48600 AAW	ARBLS	10//99-12//99
	Little Rock-North Little Rock MSA, AR	S	22.57 MW	22.30 AW	46940 AAW	ARBLS	10//99-12//99
	California	S	30.14 MW	31.07 AW	64620 AAW	CABLS	10//99-12//99
	Bakersfield MSA, CA	S	33.64 MW	35.23 AW	69980 AAW	CABLS	10//99-12//99
	Los Angeles-Long Beach PMSA, CA	S	27.83 MW	27.88 AW	57880 AAW	CABLS	10//99-12//99
	Modesto MSA, CA	S	22.36 MW	21.57 AW	46520 AAW	CABLS	10//99-12//99
	Oakland PMSA, CA	S	30.08 MW	29.77 AW	62570 AAW	CABLS	10//99-12//99
	Orange County PMSA, CA	S	28.43 MW	28.03 AW	59140 AAW	CABLS	10//99-12//99
	Riverside-San Bernardino PMSA, CA	S	25.15 MW	25.14 AW	52320 AAW	CABLS	10//99-12//99
	Sacramento PMSA, CA	S	31.13 MW	32.77 AW	64740 AAW	CABLS	10//99-12//99
	Salinas MSA, CA	S	34.38 MW	32.73 AW	71520 AAW	CABLS	10//99-12//99
	San Diego MSA, CA	S	25.64 MW	24.85 AW	53320 AAW	CABLS	10//99-12//99
	San Francisco PMSA, CA	S	33.78 MW	33.78 AW	70270 AAW	CABLS	10//99-12//99
	San Jose PMSA, CA	S	36.46 MW	35.66 AW	75840 AAW	CABLS	10//99-12//99
	San Luis Obispo-Atascadero-Paso Robles MSA, CA	S	27.57 MW	29.37 AW	57340 AAW	CABLS	10//99-12//99
	Santa Barbara-Santa Maria-Lompoc MSA, CA	S	31.44 MW	34.35 AW	65390 AAW	CABLS	10//99-12//99
	Santa Rosa PMSA, CA	S	37.11 MW	39.98 AW	77190 AAW	CABLS	10//99-12//99
	Stockton-Lodi MSA, CA	S	21.14 MW	22.77 AW	43960 AAW	CABLS	10//99-12//99
	Vallejo-Fairfield-Napa PMSA, CA	S	22.06 MW	19.64 AW	45890 AAW	CABLS	10//99-12//99

AAW Average annual wage	**AOH** Average offered, high	**ASH** Average starting, high	**H** Hourly	**M** Monthly	**S** Special: hourly and annual
AE Average entry wage	**AOL** Average offered, low	**ASL** Average starting, low	**HI** Highest wage paid	**MTC** Median total compensation	**TQ** Third quartile wage
AEX Average experienced wage	**APH** Average pay, high range	**AW** Average wage paid	**HR** High end range	**MW** Median wage paid	**W** Weekly
AO Average offered	**APL** Average pay, low range	**FQ** First quartile wage	**LR** Low end range	**SQ** Second quartile wage	**Y** Yearly

Occupation/Type/Industry	Location	Per	Low	Mid	High	Source	Date
Industrial Engineer	Ventura PMSA, CA	S	28.33 MW	28.22 AW	58920 AAW	CABLS	10//99-12//99
	Colorado	S	24.86 MW	25.84 AW	53750 AAW	COBLS	10//99-12//99
	Boulder-Longmont PMSA, CO	S	24.50 MW	22.83 AW	50970 AAW	COBLS	10//99-12//99
	Colorado Springs MSA, CO	S	26.33 MW	25.01 AW	54760 AAW	COBLS	10//99-12//99
	Denver PMSA, CO	S	25.83 MW	25.36 AW	53730 AAW	COBLS	10//99-12//99
	Fort Collins-Loveland MSA, CO	S	25.12 MW	21.42 AW	52250 AAW	COBLS	10//99-12//99
	Connecticut	S	27.51 MW	28.83 AW	59960 AAW	CTBLS	10//99-12//99
	Bridgeport PMSA, CT	S	30.80 MW	30.48 AW	64050 AAW	CTBLS	10//99-12//99
	Danbury PMSA, CT	S	31.93 MW	29.27 AW	66400 AAW	CTBLS	10//99-12//99
	Hartford MSA, CT	S	27.87 MW	27.51 AW	57960 AAW	CTBLS	10//99-12//99
	New Haven-Meriden PMSA, CT	S	25.18 MW	24.29 AW	52380 AAW	CTBLS	10//99-12//99
	New London-Norwich MSA, CT-RI	S	25.07 MW	23.80 AW	52140 AAW	CTBLS	10//99-12//99
	Stamford-Norwalk PMSA, CT	S	31.83 MW	31.90 AW	66200 AAW	CTBLS	10//99-12//99
	Waterbury PMSA, CT	S	26.46 MW	24.85 AW	55040 AAW	CTBLS	10//99-12//99
	Delaware	S	27.09 MW	26.89 AW	55930 AAW	DEBLS	10//99-12//99
	Wilmington-Newark PMSA, DE-MD	S	26.88 MW	27.10 AW	55900 AAW	DEBLS	10//99-12//99
	Washington PMSA, DC-MD-VA-WV	S	29.49 MW	28.88 AW	61350 AAW	DCBLS	10//99-12//99
	Florida	S	27.1 MW	27.85 AW	57930 AAW	FLBLS	10//99-12//99
	Daytona Beach MSA, FL	S	25.15 MW	25.73 AW	52310 AAW	FLBLS	10//99-12//99
	Fort Lauderdale PMSA, FL	S	33.40 MW	36.54 AW	69470 AAW	FLBLS	10//99-12//99
	Gainesville MSA, FL	S	20.43 MW	20.29 AW	42490 AAW	FLBLS	10//99-12//99
	Jacksonville MSA, FL	S	24.46 MW	24.11 AW	50870 AAW	FLBLS	10//99-12//99
	Lakeland-Winter Haven MSA, FL	S	28.64 MW	26.39 AW	59570 AAW	FLBLS	
	Melbourne-Titusville-Palm Bay MSA, FL	S	26.33 MW	25.47 AW	54760 AAW	FLBLS	10//99-12//99
	Miami PMSA, FL	S	27.27 MW	28.52 AW	56720 AAW	FLBLS	10//99-12//99
	Orlando MSA, FL	S	25.12 MW	24.90 AW	52250 AAW	FLBLS	10//99-12//99
	Pensacola MSA, FL	S	32.57 MW	32.55 AW	67740 AAW	FLBLS	10//99-12//99
	Sarasota-Bradenton MSA, FL	S	24.00 MW	20.56 AW	49930 AAW	FLBLS	10//99-12//99
	Tampa-St. Petersburg-Clearwater MSA, FL	S	27.37 MW	25.98 AW	56920 AAW	FLBLS	10//99-12//99
	West Palm Beach-Boca Raton MSA, FL	S	29.30 MW	29.17 AW	60950 AAW	FLBLS	10//99-12//99
	Georgia	S	26.44 MW	27.62 AW	57450 AAW	GABLS	10//99-12//99
	Athens MSA, GA	S	28.27 MW	28.43 AW	58800 AAW	GABLS	10//99-12//99
	Atlanta MSA, GA	S	28.89 MW	27.81 AW	60080 AAW	GABLS	10//99-12//99
	Columbus MSA, GA-AL	S	24.77 MW	24.38 AW	51510 AAW	GABLS	10//99-12//99
	Hawaii	S	25.52 MW	25.68 AW	53400 AAW	HIBLS	10//99-12//99
	Idaho	S	34.08 MW	34.01 AW	70740 AAW	IDBLS	10//99-12//99
	Boise City MSA, ID	S	36.08 MW	35.57 AW	75040 AAW	IDBLS	10//99-12//99
	Illinois	S	25.61 MW	26.15 AW	54390 AAW	ILBLS	10//99-12//99
	Champaign-Urbana MSA, IL	S	21.56 MW	21.96 AW	44840 AAW	ILBLS	10//99-12//99
	Chicago PMSA, IL	S	27.09 MW	26.23 AW	56350 AAW	ILBLS	10//99-12//99
	Kankakee PMSA, IL	S	25.45 MW	23.52 AW	52940 AAW	ILBLS	10//99-12//99
	Peoria-Pekin MSA, IL	S	28.16 MW	28.45 AW	58570 AAW	ILBLS	10//99-12//99
	Rockford MSA, IL	S	24.18 MW	24.13 AW	50300 AAW	ILBLS	10//99-12//99
	Indiana	S	25.32 MW	25.23 AW	52490 AAW	INBLS	10//99-12//99
	Elkhart-Goshen MSA, IN	S	22.82 MW	21.97 AW	47460 AAW	INBLS	10//99-12//99
	Evansville-Henderson MSA, IN-KY	S	16.64 MW	16.09 AW	34610 AAW	INBLS	10//99-12//99
	Fort Wayne MSA, IN	S	23.36 MW	23.45 AW	48580 AAW	INBLS	10//99-12//99
	Gary PMSA, IN	S	27.10 MW	26.37 AW	56370 AAW	INBLS	10//99-12//99
	Indianapolis MSA, IN	S	24.19 MW	24.24 AW	50320 AAW	INBLS	10//99-12//99
	Kokomo MSA, IN	S	30.16 MW	30.62 AW	62740 AAW	INBLS	10//99-12//99
	Lafayette MSA, IN	S	25.52 MW	24.87 AW	53090 AAW	INBLS	10//99-12//99
	Muncie MSA, IN	S	29.52 MW	25.21 AW	61410 AAW	INBLS	10//99-12//99
	South Bend MSA, IN	S	23.93 MW	24.23 AW	49780 AAW	INBLS	10//99-12//99
	Terre Haute MSA, IN	S	22.31 MW	20.25 AW	46400 AAW	INBLS	10//99-12//99
	Iowa	S	24.11 MW	24.01 AW	49950 AAW	IABLS	10//99-12//99
	Davenport-Moline-Rock Island MSA, IA-IL	S	25.30 MW	24.87 AW	52620 AAW	IABLS	10//99-12//99
	Dubuque MSA, IA	S	20.73 MW	21.86 AW	43110 AAW	IABLS	10//99-12//99
	Kansas	S	23.13 MW	23.16 AW	48180 AAW	KSBLS	10//99-12//99
	Wichita MSA, KS	S	23.51 MW	23.29 AW	48910 AAW	KSBLS	10//99-12//99
	Kentucky	S	25.7 MW	26.17 AW	54430 AAW	KYBLS	10//99-12//99
	Lexington MSA, KY	S	22.03 MW	21.15 AW	45810 AAW	KYBLS	10//99-12//99

AAW	Average annual wage	AOH	Average offered, high	ASH	Average starting, high	H	Hourly
AE	Average entry wage	AOL	Average offered, low	ASL	Average starting, low	HI	Highest wage paid
AEX	Average experienced wage	APH	Average pay, high range	AW	Average wage paid	HR	High end range
AO	Average offered	APL	Average pay, low range	FQ	First quartile wage	LR	Low end range

M	Monthly	S	Special: hourly and annual
MTC	Median total compensation	TQ	Third quartile wage
MW	Median wage paid	W	Weekly
SQ	Second quartile wage	Y	Yearly

Occupation/Type/Industry	Location	Per	Low	Mid	High	Source	Date
Industrial Engineer	Louisiana	s	28.71 MW	31.16 AW	64810 AAW	LABLS	10//99-12//99
	Baton Rouge MSA, LA	s	30.46 MW	29.57 AW	63360 AAW	LABLS	10//99-12//99
	Houma MSA, LA	s	25.13 MW	24.96 AW	52260 AAW	LABLS	10//99-12//99
	Lafayette MSA, LA	s	33.92 MW	29.11 AW	70550 AAW	LABLS	10//99-12//99
	Monroe MSA, LA	s	24.98 MW	20.21 AW	51960 AAW	LABLS	10//99-12//99
	New Orleans MSA, LA	s	33.36 MW	29.88 AW	69390 AAW	LABLS	10//99-12//99
	Shreveport-Bossier City MSA, LA	s	31.01 MW	29.18 AW	64510 AAW	LABLS	10//99-12//99
	Maine	s	25.23 MW	26.08 AW	54250 AAW	MEBLS	10//99-12//99
	Maryland	s	27.26 MW	28.38 AW	59030 AAW	MDBLS	10//99-12//99
	Baltimore PMSA, MD	s	28.30 MW	27.57 AW	58860 AAW	MDBLS	10//99-12//99
	Hagerstown PMSA, MD	s	25.70 MW	24.58 AW	53460 AAW	MDBLS	10//99-12//99
	Massachusetts	s	28.42 MW	28.62 AW	59530 AAW	MABLS	10//99-12//99
	Boston PMSA, MA-NH	s	29.13 MW	28.87 AW	60590 AAW	MABLS	10//99-12//99
	Brockton PMSA, MA	s	25.24 MW	28.50 AW	52500 AAW	MABLS	10//99-12//99
	Fitchburg-Leominster PMSA, MA	s	25.79 MW	26.28 AW	53640 AAW	MABLS	10//99-12//99
	Lawrence PMSA, MA-NH	s	28.81 MW	27.19 AW	59920 AAW	MABLS	10//99-12//99
	Lowell PMSA, MA-NH	s	28.64 MW	29.33 AW	59570 AAW	MABLS	10//99-12//99
	New Bedford PMSA, MA	s	25.57 MW	25.72 AW	53190 AAW	MABLS	10//99-12//99
	Springfield MSA, MA	s	25.11 MW	24.65 AW	52240 AAW	MABLS	10//99-12//99
	Worcester PMSA, MA-CT	s	25.22 MW	25.06 AW	52460 AAW	MABLS	10//99-12//99
	Michigan	s	29.3 MW	29.36 AW	61070 AAW	MIBLS	10//99-12//99
	Ann Arbor PMSA, MI	s	27.85 MW	28.77 AW	57920 AAW	MIBLS	10//99-12//99
	Benton Harbor MSA, MI	s	28.75 MW	29.27 AW	59790 AAW	MIBLS	10//99-12//99
	Detroit PMSA, MI	s	30.90 MW	30.59 AW	64270 AAW	MIBLS	10//99-12//99
	Flint PMSA, MI	s	31.18 MW	31.16 AW	64850 AAW	MIBLS	10//99-12//99
	Grand Rapids-Muskegon-Holland MSA, MI	s	27.08 MW	26.85 AW	56320 AAW	MIBLS	10//99-12//99
	Jackson MSA, MI	s	20.33 MW	19.67 AW	42290 AAW	MIBLS	10//99-12//99
	Kalamazoo-Battle Creek MSA, MI	s	22.21 MW	21.05 AW	46190 AAW	MIBLS	10//99-12//99
	Lansing-East Lansing MSA, MI	s	27.85 MW	27.74 AW	57920 AAW	MIBLS	10//99-12//99
	Saginaw-Bay City-Midland MSA, MI	s	31.76 MW	30.50 AW	66050 AAW	MIBLS	10//99-12//99
	Minnesota	s	27.88 MW	29.34 AW	61030 AAW	MNBLS	10//99-12//99
	Duluth-Superior MSA, MN-WI	s	23.16 MW	23.61 AW	48180 AAW	MNBLS	10//99-12//99
	Minneapolis-St. Paul MSA, MN-WI	s	30.00 MW	28.75 AW	62390 AAW	MNBLS	10//99-12//99
	Mississippi	s	21.94 MW	22.21 AW	46190 AAW	MSBLS	10//99-12//99
	Biloxi-Gulfport-Pascagoula MSA, MS	s	23.51 MW	23.88 AW	48900 AAW	MSBLS	10//99-12//99
	Jackson MSA, MS	s	21.68 MW	20.47 AW	45090 AAW	MSBLS	10//99-12//99
	Missouri	s	23.87 MW	24.96 AW	51920 AAW	MOBLS	10//99-12//99
	Kansas City MSA, MO-KS	s	24.80 MW	24.21 AW	51580 AAW	MOBLS	10//99-12//99
	St. Louis MSA, MO-IL	s	25.84 MW	24.83 AW	53740 AAW	MOBLS	10//99-12//99
	Springfield MSA, MO	s	23.63 MW	24.13 AW	49150 AAW	MOBLS	10//99-12//99
	Montana	s	19.71 MW	19.82 AW	41220 AAW	MTBLS	10//99-12//99
	Nebraska	s	21.98 MW	23.21 AW	48280 AAW	NEBLS	10//99-12//99
	Lincoln MSA, NE	s	23.81 MW	23.38 AW	49520 AAW	NEBLS	10//99-12//99
	Omaha MSA, NE-IA	s	23.15 MW	21.29 AW	48150 AAW	NEBLS	10//99-12//99
	Nevada	s	27.72 MW	28.56 AW	59400 AAW	NVBLS	10//99-12//99
	New Hampshire	s	25.1 MW	25.59 AW	53230 AAW	NHBLS	10//99-12//99
	Manchester PMSA, NH	s	24.06 MW	23.39 AW	50040 AAW	NHBLS	10//99-12//99
	Nashua PMSA, NH	s	27.27 MW	26.44 AW	56730 AAW	NHBLS	10//99-12//99
	Portsmouth-Rochester PMSA, NH-ME	s	26.24 MW	25.21 AW	54570 AAW	NHBLS	10//99-12//99
	New Jersey	s	29.83 MW	30.97 AW	64420 AAW	NJBLS	10//99-12//99
	Bergen-Passaic PMSA, NJ	s	30.26 MW	29.55 AW	62940 AAW	NJBLS	10//99-12//99
	Jersey City PMSA, NJ	s	34.63 MW	31.48 AW	72030 AAW	NJBLS	10//99-12//99
	Middlesex-Somerset-Hunterdon PMSA, NJ	s	34.05 MW	33.22 AW	70820 AAW	NJBLS	10//99-12//99
	Monmouth-Ocean PMSA, NJ	s	28.47 MW	26.06 AW	59230 AAW	NJBLS	10//99-12//99
	Newark PMSA, NJ	s	31.96 MW	30.76 AW	66470 AAW	NJBLS	10//99-12//99
	Trenton PMSA, NJ	s	27.90 MW	28.69 AW	58040 AAW	NJBLS	10//99-12//99
	New Mexico	s	24.67 MW	24.81 AW	51600 AAW	NMBLS	10//99-12//99
	Albuquerque MSA, NM	s	24.89 MW	24.80 AW	51780 AAW	NMBLS	10//99-12//99
	New York	s	26.87 MW	28.04 AW	58320 AAW	NYBLS	10//99-12//99
	Albany-Schenectady-Troy MSA, NY	s	27.71 MW	28.57 AW	57630 AAW	NYBLS	10//99-12//99
	Binghamton MSA, NY	s	28.40 MW	25.93 AW	59080 AAW	NYBLS	10//99-12//99

AAW Average annual wage	AOH Average offered, high	ASH Average starting, high	H Hourly	M Monthly	S Special: hourly and annual
AE Average entry wage	AOL Average offered, low	ASL Average starting, low	HI Highest wage paid	MTC Median total compensation	TQ Third quartile wage
AEX Average experienced wage	APH Average pay, high range	AW Average wage paid	HR High end range	MW Median wage paid	W Weekly
AO Average offered	APL Average pay, low range	FQ First quartile wage	LR Low end range	SQ Second quartile wage	Y Yearly

Occupation/Type/Industry	Location	Per	Low	Mid	High	Source	Date
Industrial Engineer	Buffalo-Niagara Falls MSA, NY	s	26.13 mw	25.58 aw	54350 aaw	NYBLS	10//99-12//99
	Elmira MSA, NY	s	22.11 mw	22.42 aw	46000 aaw	NYBLS	10//99-12//99
	Glens Falls MSA, NY	s	31.23 mw	31.74 aw	64960 aaw	NYBLS	10//99-12//99
	Jamestown MSA, NY	s	18.86 mw	18.65 aw	39220 aaw	NYBLS	10//99-12//99
	Nassau-Suffolk PMSA, NY	s	25.81 mw	25.39 aw	53690 aaw	NYBLS	10//99-12//99
	New York PMSA, NY	s	30.62 mw	29.52 aw	63690 aaw	NYBLS	10//99-12//99
	Newburgh PMSA, NY-PA	s	24.81 mw	20.33 aw	51600 aaw	NYBLS	10//99-12//99
	Rochester MSA, NY	s	28.93 mw	29.19 aw	60180 aaw	NYBLS	10//99-12//99
	Syracuse MSA, NY	s	25.80 mw	25.44 aw	53660 aaw	NYBLS	10//99-12//99
	Utica-Rome MSA, NY	s	20.81 mw	19.85 aw	43290 aaw	NYBLS	10//99-12//99
	North Carolina	s	25.46 mw	25.61 aw	53270 aaw	NCBLS	10//99-12//99
	Asheville MSA, NC	s	20.71 mw	19.87 aw	43070 aaw	NCBLS	10//99-12//99
	Charlotte-Gastonia-Rock Hill MSA, NC-SC	s	26.69 mw	26.76 aw	55510 aaw	NCBLS	10//99-12//99
	Greensboro--Winston-Salem-- High Point MSA, NC	s	24.78 mw	24.60 aw	51550 aaw	NCBLS	10//99-12//99
	Greenville MSA, NC	s	27.88 mw	26.83 aw	57980 aaw	NCBLS	10//99-12//99
	Hickory-Morganton-Lenoir MSA, NC	s	21.85 mw	20.44 aw	45440 aaw	NCBLS	10//99-12//99
	Raleigh-Durham-Chapel Hill MSA, NC	s	28.27 mw	28.52 aw	58800 aaw	NCBLS	10//99-12//99
	Wilmington MSA, NC	s	27.91 mw	28.43 aw	58060 aaw	NCBLS	10//99-12//99
	North Dakota	s	19.92 mw	20.55 aw	42740 aaw	NDBLS	10//99-12//99
	Ohio	s	25.47 mw	25.95 aw	53970 aaw	OHBLS	10//99-12//99
	Akron PMSA, OH	s	25.52 mw	25.04 aw	53090 aaw	OHBLS	10//99-12//99
	Canton-Massillon MSA, OH	s	25.18 mw	26.11 aw	52370 aaw	OHBLS	10//99-12//99
	Cincinnati PMSA, OH-KY-IN	s	25.56 mw	25.38 aw	53170 aaw	OHBLS	10//99-12//99
	Cleveland-Lorain-Elyria PMSA, OH	s	27.46 mw	26.24 aw	57110 aaw	OHBLS	10//99-12//99
	Columbus MSA, OH	s	27.18 mw	26.36 aw	56530 aaw	OHBLS	10//99-12//99
	Dayton-Springfield MSA, OH	s	27.81 mw	28.99 aw	57850 aaw	OHBLS	10//99-12//99
	Hamilton-Middletown PMSA, OH	s	30.91 mw	30.51 aw	64300 aaw	OHBLS	10//99-12//99
	Lima MSA, OH	s	23.58 mw	23.79 aw	49040 aaw	OHBLS	10//99-12//99
	Mansfield MSA, OH	s	24.27 mw	23.47 aw	50470 aaw	OHBLS	10//99-12//99
	Toledo MSA, OH	s	27.24 mw	26.23 aw	56650 aaw	OHBLS	10//99-12//99
	Youngstown-Warren MSA, OH	s	26.17 mw	25.72 aw	54430 aaw	OHBLS	10//99-12//99
	Oklahoma	s	26.32 mw	26.93 aw	56010 aaw	OKBLS	10//99-12//99
	Oklahoma City MSA, OK	s	25.62 mw	25.61 aw	53280 aaw	OKBLS	10//99-12//99
	Tulsa MSA, OK	s	28.25 mw	26.91 aw	58760 aaw	OKBLS	10//99-12//99
	Oregon	s	25.7 mw	26.89 aw	55930 aaw	ORBLS	10//99-12//99
	Eugene-Springfield MSA, OR	s	19.80 mw	19.22 aw	41180 aaw	ORBLS	10//99-12//99
	Portland-Vancouver PMSA, OR-WA	s	27.78 mw	26.22 aw	57770 aaw	ORBLS	10//99-12//99
	Pennsylvania	s	26.68 mw	27.88 aw	57990 aaw	PABLS	10//99-12//99
	Allentown-Bethlehem-Easton MSA, PA	s	27.63 mw	26.35 aw	57480 aaw	PABLS	10//99-12//99
	Altoona MSA, PA	s	24.94 mw	25.77 aw	51870 aaw	PABLS	10//99-12//99
	Erie MSA, PA	s	20.99 mw	19.81 aw	43660 aaw	PABLS	10//99-12//99
	Harrisburg-Lebanon-Carlisle MSA, PA	s	27.11 mw	25.87 aw	56390 aaw	PABLS	10//99-12//99
	Lancaster MSA, PA	s	30.16 mw	30.61 aw	62740 aaw	PABLS	10//99-12//99
	Philadelphia PMSA, PA-NJ	s	29.06 mw	27.05 aw	60450 aaw	PABLS	10//99-12//99
	Pittsburgh MSA, PA	s	28.93 mw	28.35 aw	60180 aaw	PABLS	10//99-12//99
	Reading MSA, PA	s	27.05 mw	26.72 aw	56250 aaw	PABLS	10//99-12//99
	Scranton--Wilkes-Barre-- Hazleton MSA, PA	s	26.79 mw	27.20 aw	55720 aaw	PABLS	10//99-12//99
	York MSA, PA	s	26.40 mw	25.29 aw	54920 aaw	PABLS	10//99-12//99
	Rhode Island	s	30.17 mw	29.91 aw	62220 aaw	RIBLS	10//99-12//99
	Providence-Fall River- Warwick MSA, RI-MA	s	29.78 mw	30.02 aw	61950 aaw	RIBLS	10//99-12//99
	South Carolina	s	31.91 mw	30.90 aw	64270 aaw	SCBLS	10//99-12//99
	Charleston-North Charleston MSA, SC	s	29.18 mw	26.76 aw	60700 aaw	SCBLS	10//99-12//99
	Columbia MSA, SC	s	26.66 mw	26.54 aw	55450 aaw	SCBLS	10//99-12//99
	Florence MSA, SC	s	14.97 mw	12.60 aw	31130 aaw	SCBLS	10//99-12//99
	Greenville-Spartanburg- Anderson MSA, SC	s	28.41 mw	29.38 aw	59090 aaw	SCBLS	10//99-12//99
	Myrtle Beach MSA, SC	s	32.79 mw	31.07 aw	68210 aaw	SCBLS	10//99-12//99
	South Dakota	s	23.86 mw	24.92 aw	51840 aaw	SDBLS	10//99-12//99
	Tennessee	s	22.43 mw	22.52 aw	46840 aaw	TNBLS	10//99-12//99

AAW	Average annual wage	AOH	Average offered, high	ASH	Average starting, high
AE	Average entry wage	AOL	Average offered, low	ASL	Average starting, low
AEX	Average experienced wage	APH	Average pay, high range	AW	Average wage paid
AO	Average offered	APL	Average pay, low range	FQ	First quartile wage

H	Hourly	M	Monthly
HI	Highest wage paid	MTC	Median total compensation
HR	High end range	MW	Median wage paid
LR	Low end range	SQ	Second quartile wage

S	Special: hourly and annual		
TQ	Third quartile wage		
W	Weekly		
Y	Yearly		

Occupation/Type/Industry	Location	Per	Low	Mid	High	Source	Date
Industrial Engineer	Chattanooga MSA, TN-GA	S	22.27 MW	20.87 AW	46330 AAW	TNBLS	10//99-12//99
	Clarksville-Hopkinsville MSA, TN-KY	S	25.08 MW	25.04 AW	52160 AAW	TNBLS	10//99-12//99
	Jackson MSA, TN	S	22.23 MW	20.37 AW	46230 AAW	TNBLS	10//99-12//99
	Johnson City-Kingsport-Bristol MSA, TN-VA	S	23.14 MW	23.80 AW	48130 AAW	TNBLS	10//99-12//99
	Knoxville MSA, TN	S	23.76 MW	23.73 AW	49420 AAW	TNBLS	10//99-12//99
	Memphis MSA, TN-AR-MS	S	24.29 MW	25.17 AW	50520 AAW	MSBLS	10//99-12//99
	Nashville MSA, TN	S	22.97 MW	23.92 AW	47780 AAW	TNBLS	10//99-12//99
	Texas	S	29.33 MW	29.62 AW	61610 AAW	TXBLS	10//99-12//99
	Amarillo MSA, TX	S	31.27 MW	33.29 AW	65050 AAW	TXBLS	10//99-12//99
	Austin-San Marcos MSA, TX	S	26.33 MW	26.23 AW	54760 AAW	TXBLS	10//99-12//99
	Beaumont-Port Arthur MSA, TX	S	33.12 MW	33.00 AW	68890 AAW	TXBLS	10//99-12//99
	Brownsville-Harlingen-San Benito MSA, TX	S	29.95 MW	28.83 AW	62300 AAW	TXBLS	10//99-12//99
	Corpus Christi MSA, TX	S	28.59 MW	29.37 AW	59460 AAW	TXBLS	10//99-12//99
	Dallas PMSA, TX	S	32.59 MW	32.64 AW	67780 AAW	TXBLS	10//99-12//99
	El Paso MSA, TX	S	25.43 MW	24.17 AW	52890 AAW	TXBLS	10//99-12//99
	Fort Worth-Arlington PMSA, TX	S	28.32 MW	27.90 AW	58910 AAW	TXBLS	10//99-12//99
	Houston PMSA, TX	S	29.37 MW	28.38 AW	61100 AAW	TXBLS	10//99-12//99
	Killeen-Temple MSA, TX	S	24.07 MW	27.07 AW	50060 AAW	TXBLS	10//99-12//99
	Lubbock MSA, TX	S	20.78 MW	18.89 AW	43220 AAW	TXBLS	10//99-12//99
	Odessa-Midland MSA, TX	S	35.09 MW	35.92 AW	72980 AAW	TXBLS	10//99-12//99
	San Antonio MSA, TX	S	21.14 MW	20.55 AW	43980 AAW	TXBLS	10//99-12//99
	Sherman-Denison MSA, TX	S	29.06 MW	29.46 AW	60450 AAW	TXBLS	10//99-12//99
	Utah	S	24.56 MW	25.49 AW	53010 AAW	UTBLS	10//99-12//99
	Provo-Orem MSA, UT	S	24.17 MW	24.12 AW	50270 AAW	UTBLS	10//99-12//99
	Salt Lake City-Ogden MSA, UT	S	25.66 MW	24.62 AW	53370 AAW	UTBLS	10//99-12//99
	Vermont	S	23.85 MW	24.00 AW	49920 AAW	VTBLS	10//99-12//99
	Burlington MSA, VT	S	22.09 MW	22.81 AW	45950 AAW	VTBLS	10//99-12//99
	Virginia	S	25.65 MW	26.93 AW	56020 AAW	VABLS	10//99-12//99
	Charlottesville MSA, VA	S	17.40 MW	17.10 AW	36200 AAW	VABLS	10//99-12//99
	Norfolk-Virginia Beach-Newport News MSA, VA-NC	S	26.99 MW	26.28 AW	56130 AAW	VABLS	10//99-12//99
	Richmond-Petersburg MSA, VA	S	27.73 MW	25.93 AW	57670 AAW	VABLS	10//99-12//99
	Roanoke MSA, VA	S	24.37 MW	23.27 AW	50700 AAW	VABLS	10//99-12//99
	Washington	S	28.62 MW	28.71 AW	59720 AAW	WABLS	10//99-12//99
	Seattle-Bellevue-Everett PMSA, WA	S	29.34 MW	29.36 AW	61030 AAW	WABLS	10//99-12//99
	Spokane MSA, WA	S	24.55 MW	24.39 AW	51050 AAW	WABLS	10//99-12//99
	Tacoma PMSA, WA	S	17.44 MW	16.50 AW	36270 AAW	WABLS	10//99-12//99
	West Virginia	S	29.75 MW	29.13 AW	60590 AAW	WVBLS	10//99-12//99
	Parkersburg-Marietta MSA, WV-OH	S	29.27 MW	29.94 AW	60890 AAW	WVBLS	10//99-12//99
	Wisconsin	S	26.41 MW	26.30 AW	54700 AAW	WIBLS	10//99-12//99
	Appleton-Oshkosh-Neenah MSA, WI	S	25.08 MW	24.38 AW	52170 AAW	WIBLS	10//99-12//99
	Eau Claire MSA, WI	S	25.11 MW	24.43 AW	52230 AAW	WIBLS	10//99-12//99
	Green Bay MSA, WI	S	26.78 MW	27.64 AW	55710 AAW	WIBLS	10//99-12//99
	La Crosse MSA, WI-MN	S	22.49 MW	22.58 AW	46780 AAW	WIBLS	10//99-12//99
	Madison MSA, WI	S	23.11 MW	22.81 AW	48060 AAW	WIBLS	10//99-12//99
	Milwaukee-Waukesha PMSA, WI	S	28.48 MW	29.10 AW	59240 AAW	WIBLS	10//99-12//99
	Racine PMSA, WI	S	24.03 MW	24.19 AW	49970 AAW	WIBLS	10//99-12//99
	Sheboygan MSA, WI	S	23.88 MW	24.35 AW	49660 AAW	WIBLS	10//99-12//99
	Wausau MSA, WI	S	20.84 MW	21.90 AW	43350 AAW	WIBLS	10//99-12//99
	Wyoming	S	36.11 MW	33.75 AW	70200 AAW	WYBLS	10//99-12//99
	Puerto Rico	S	19.91 MW	21.56 AW	44850 AAW	PRBLS	10//99-12//99
	Aguadilla MSA, PR	S	18.12 MW	16.53 AW	37680 AAW	PRBLS	10//99-12//99
	Caguas PMSA, PR	S	23.95 MW	24.10 AW	49820 AAW	PRBLS	10//99-12//99
	Mayaguez MSA, PR	S	22.58 MW	22.65 AW	46970 AAW	PRBLS	10//99-12//99
	Ponce MSA, PR	S	19.45 MW	19.39 AW	40460 AAW	PRBLS	10//99-12//99
	San Juan-Bayamon PMSA, PR	S	21.67 MW	19.38 AW	45070 AAW	PRBLS	10//99-12//99
Industrial Engineering Technician	United States	H		18.71 AW		NCS98	1998
	Alabama	S	13.52 MW	15.97 AW	33230 AAW	ALBLS	10//99-12//99
	Birmingham MSA, AL	S	17.11 MW	16.14 AW	35590 AAW	ALBLS	10//99-12//99
	Arizona	S	22.49 MW	22.50 AW	46800 AAW	AZBLS	

AAW Average annual wage	**AOH** Average offered, high	**ASH** Average starting, high	**H** Hourly	**M** Monthly	**S** Special: hourly and annual
AE Average entry wage	**AOL** Average offered, low	**ASL** Average starting, low	**HI** Highest wage paid	**MTC** Median total compensation	**TQ** Third quartile wage
AEX Average experienced wage	**APH** Average pay, high range	**AW** Average wage paid	**HR** High end range	**MW** Median wage paid	**W** Weekly
AO Average offered	**APL** Average pay, low range	**FQ** First quartile wage	**LR** Low end range	**SQ** Second quartile wage	**Y** Yearly

Occupation/Type/Industry	Location	Per	Low	Mid	High	Source	Date
Industrial Engineering Technician	Phoenix-Mesa MSA, AZ	S	23.05 MW	23.20 AW	47930 AAW	AZBLS	10//99-12//99
	Tucson MSA, AZ	S	16.53 MW	15.68 AW	34370 AAW	AZBLS	10//99-12//99
	Arkansas	S	15.25 MW	16.63 AW	34580 AAW	ARBLS	10//99-12//99
	Fayetteville-Springdale-Rogers MSA, AR	S	18.39 MW	16.41 AW	38250 AAW	ARBLS	10//99-12//99
	Fort Smith MSA, AR-OK	S	15.46 MW	16.03 AW	32150 AAW	ARBLS	10//99-12//99
	California	S	21.52 MW	22.75 AW	47330 AAW	CABLS	10//99-12//99
	Bakersfield MSA, CA	S	19.43 MW	20.12 AW	40410 AAW	CABLS	10//99-12//99
	Los Angeles-Long Beach PMSA, CA	S	21.80 MW	19.98 AW	45350 AAW	CABLS	10//99-12//99
	Oakland PMSA, CA	S	22.00 MW	20.30 AW	45750 AAW	CABLS	10//99-12//99
	Orange County PMSA, CA	S	19.81 MW	19.23 AW	41210 AAW	CABLS	10//99-12//99
	Riverside-San Bernardino PMSA, CA	S	24.32 MW	24.72 AW	50580 AAW	CABLS	10//99-12//99
	Sacramento PMSA, CA	S	24.61 MW	23.13 AW	51180 AAW	CABLS	10//99-12//99
	San Diego MSA, CA	S	20.50 MW	19.54 AW	42640 AAW	CABLS	10//99-12//99
	San Francisco PMSA, CA	S	28.08 MW	30.01 AW	58400 AAW	CABLS	10//99-12//99
	San Jose PMSA, CA	S	24.65 MW	23.62 AW	51270 AAW	CABLS	10//99-12//99
	Santa Rosa PMSA, CA	S	22.47 MW	22.74 AW	46730 AAW	CABLS	10//99-12//99
	Vallejo-Fairfield-Napa PMSA, CA	S	29.06 MW	27.19 AW	60440 AAW	CABLS	10//99-12//99
	Ventura PMSA, CA	S	25.51 MW	23.47 AW	53050 AAW	CABLS	10//99-12//99
	Colorado	S	18.17 MW	18.78 AW	39070 AAW	COBLS	10//99-12//99
	Colorado Springs MSA, CO	S	18.37 MW	17.73 AW	38210 AAW	COBLS	10//99-12//99
	Denver PMSA, CO	S	17.80 MW	16.64 AW	37010 AAW	COBLS	10//99-12//99
	Connecticut	S	19.49 MW	22.01 AW	45780 AAW	CTBLS	10//99-12//99
	Bridgeport PMSA, CT	S	17.94 MW	15.78 AW	37320 AAW	CTBLS	10//99-12//99
	Danbury PMSA, CT	S	22.14 MW	20.83 AW	46050 AAW	CTBLS	10//99-12//99
	Hartford MSA, CT	S	27.84 MW	28.66 AW	57910 AAW	CTBLS	10//99-12//99
	New Haven-Meriden PMSA, CT	S	17.40 MW	15.74 AW	36190 AAW	CTBLS	10//99-12//99
	New London-Norwich MSA, CT-RI	S	16.98 MW	15.61 AW	35330 AAW	CTBLS	10//99-12//99
	Delaware	S	14.45 MW	16.52 AW	34370 AAW	DEBLS	10//99-12//99
	Wilmington-Newark PMSA, DE-MD	S	17.51 MW	16.89 AW	36430 AAW	DEBLS	10//99-12//99
	Washington PMSA, DC-MD-VA-WV	S	25.79 MW	26.13 AW	53650 AAW	DCBLS	10//99-12//99
	Florida	S	17.62 MW	19.34 AW	40220 AAW	FLBLS	10//99-12//99
	Fort Lauderdale PMSA, FL	S	32.81 MW	34.91 AW	68240 AAW	FLBLS	10//99-12//99
	Jacksonville MSA, FL	S	22.80 MW	21.63 AW	47430 AAW	FLBLS	10//99-12//99
	Melbourne-Titusville-Palm Bay MSA, FL	S	12.69 MW	12.04 AW	26400 AAW	FLBLS	10//99-12//99
	Orlando MSA, FL	S	18.48 MW	17.63 AW	38440 AAW	FLBLS	10//99-12//99
	Tampa-St. Petersburg-Clearwater MSA, FL	S	15.32 MW	13.25 AW	31870 AAW	FLBLS	10//99-12//99
	West Palm Beach-Boca Raton MSA, FL	S	20.66 MW	22.11 AW	42970 AAW	FLBLS	10//99-12//99
	Georgia	S	18.16 MW	19.03 AW	39580 AAW	GABLS	10//99-12//99
	Athens MSA, GA	S	16.64 MW	13.85 AW	34610 AAW	GABLS	10//99-12//99
	Atlanta MSA, GA	S	20.10 MW	18.53 AW	41810 AAW	GABLS	10//99-12//99
	Illinois	S	20.1 MW	19.74 AW	41050 AAW	ILBLS	10//99-12//99
	Chicago PMSA, IL	S	19.96 MW	20.54 AW	41510 AAW	ILBLS	10//99-12//99
	Peoria-Pekin MSA, IL	S	22.48 MW	23.56 AW	46760 AAW	ILBLS	10//99-12//99
	Rockford MSA, IL	S	17.82 MW	17.89 AW	37070 AAW	ILBLS	10//99-12//99
	Indiana	S	17.44 MW	18.38 AW	38230 AAW	INBLS	10//99-12//99
	Elkhart-Goshen MSA, IN	S	14.80 MW	13.66 AW	30780 AAW	INBLS	10//99-12//99
	Fort Wayne MSA, IN	S	18.43 MW	18.00 AW	38330 AAW	INBLS	10//99-12//99
	Indianapolis MSA, IN	S	21.97 MW	19.29 AW	45700 AAW	INBLS	10//99-12//99
	Lafayette MSA, IN	S	14.97 MW	15.74 AW	31130 AAW	INBLS	10//99-12//99
	Muncie MSA, IN	S	26.37 MW	29.31 AW	54860 AAW	INBLS	10//99-12//99
	Iowa	S	17.16 MW	17.22 AW	35820 AAW	IABLS	10//99-12//99
	Davenport-Moline-Rock Island MSA, IA-IL	S	21.57 MW	20.48 AW	44870 AAW	IABLS	10//99-12//99
	Des Moines MSA, IA	S	14.32 MW	12.49 AW	29780 AAW	IABLS	10//99-12//99
	Kentucky	S	17.89 MW	18.05 AW	37550 AAW	KYBLS	10//99-12//99
	Lexington MSA, KY	S	20.18 MW	21.40 AW	41980 AAW	KYBLS	10//99-12//99
	Louisville MSA, KY-IN	S	19.92 MW	18.65 AW	41440 AAW	KYBLS	10//99-12//99
	Louisiana	S	18.41 MW	21.50 AW	44720 AAW	LABLS	10//99-12//99
	Lafayette MSA, LA	S	17.51 MW	15.69 AW	36420 AAW	LABLS	10//99-12//99
	Maine	S	14.65 MW	15.61 AW	32470 AAW	MEBLS	10//99-12//99
	Portland MSA, ME	S	15.16 MW	15.04 AW	31540 AAW	MEBLS	10//99-12//99

AAW	Average annual wage	AOH	Average offered, high	ASH	Average starting, high	H	Hourly	M	Monthly	S	Special: hourly and annual
AE	Average entry wage	AOL	Average offered, low	ASL	Average starting, low	HI	Highest wage paid	MTC	Median total compensation	TQ	Third quartile wage
AEX	Average experienced wage	APH	Average pay, high range	AW	Average wage paid	HR	High end range	MW	Median wage paid	W	Weekly
AO	Average offered	APL	Average pay, low range	FQ	First quartile wage	LR	Low end range	SQ	Second quartile wage	Y	Yearly

Occupation/Type/Industry	Location	Per	Low	Mid	High	Source	Date
Industrial Engineering Technician	Maryland	S	19.64 MW	20.72 AW	43100 AAW	MDBLS	10//99-12//99
	Baltimore PMSA, MD	S	20.15 MW	19.15 AW	41920 AAW	MDBLS	10//99-12//99
	Massachusetts	S	21.52 MW	23.01 AW	47860 AAW	MABLS	10//99-12//99
	Boston PMSA, MA-NH	S	23.17 MW	21.77 AW	48200 AAW	MABLS	10//99-12//99
	Lawrence PMSA, MA-NH	S	23.13 MW	22.09 AW	48110 AAW	MABLS	10//99-12//99
	Lowell PMSA, MA-NH	S	24.75 MW	23.46 AW	51480 AAW	MABLS	10//99-12//99
	New Bedford PMSA, MA	S	24.16 MW	20.03 AW	50250 AAW	MABLS	10//99-12//99
	Worcester PMSA, MA-CT	S	22.67 MW	21.12 AW	47150 AAW	MABLS	10//99-12//99
	Michigan	S	20.34 MW	22.62 AW	47050 AAW	MIBLS	10//99-12//99
	Ann Arbor PMSA, MI	S	20.65 MW	19.36 AW	42950 AAW	MIBLS	10//99-12//99
	Detroit PMSA, MI	S	25.32 MW	25.28 AW	52660 AAW	MIBLS	10//99-12//99
	Grand Rapids-Muskegon-Holland MSA, MI	S	14.58 MW	12.77 AW	30320 AAW	MIBLS	10//99-12//99
	Kalamazoo-Battle Creek MSA, MI	S	20.98 MW	18.04 AW	43650 AAW	MIBLS	10//99-12//99
	Lansing-East Lansing MSA, MI	S	33.41 MW	36.19 AW	69490 AAW	MIBLS	10//99-12//99
	Minnesota	S	20.25 MW	21.62 AW	44970 AAW	MNBLS	10//99-12//99
	Duluth-Superior MSA, MN-WI	S	16.62 MW	16.29 AW	34560 AAW	MNBLS	10//99-12//99
	Minneapolis-St. Paul MSA, MN-WI	S	22.01 MW	20.45 AW	45770 AAW	MNBLS	10//99-12//99
	Mississippi	S	16.81 MW	18.22 AW	37900 AAW	MSBLS	10//99-12//99
	Missouri	S	16.12 MW	18.47 AW	38410 AAW	MOBLS	10//99-12//99
	Kansas City MSA, MO-KS	S	19.97 MW	17.61 AW	41540 AAW	MOBLS	10//99-12//99
	St. Louis MSA, MO-IL	S	19.73 MW	18.68 AW	41030 AAW	MOBLS	10//99-12//99
	Montana	S	20.5 MW	22.40 AW	46600 AAW	MTBLS	10//99-12//99
	Nebraska	S	14.98 MW	15.89 AW	33050 AAW	NEBLS	10//99-12//99
	Omaha MSA, NE-IA	S	18.68 MW	18.00 AW	38850 AAW	NEBLS	10//99-12//99
	New Hampshire	S	15.28 MW	16.11 AW	33510 AAW	NHBLS	10//99-12//99
	Portsmouth-Rochester PMSA, NH-ME	S	16.14 MW	15.28 AW	33580 AAW	NHBLS	10//99-12//99
	New Jersey	S	21.92 MW	23.12 AW	48090 AAW	NJBLS	10//99-12//99
	Middlesex-Somerset-Hunterdon PMSA, NJ	S	23.97 MW	22.39 AW	49850 AAW	NJBLS	10//99-12//99
	Monmouth-Ocean PMSA, NJ	S	20.52 MW	18.72 AW	42690 AAW	NJBLS	10//99-12//99
	Newark PMSA, NJ	S	22.57 MW	20.98 AW	46950 AAW	NJBLS	10//99-12//99
	New Mexico	S	15.94 MW	16.39 AW	34100 AAW	NMBLS	10//99-12//99
	New York	S	19.95 MW	21.18 AW	44050 AAW	NYBLS	10//99-12//99
	Buffalo-Niagara Falls MSA, NY	S	18.34 MW	16.17 AW	38150 AAW	NYBLS	10//99-12//99
	Glens Falls MSA, NY	S	18.64 MW	20.14 AW	38770 AAW	NYBLS	10//99-12//99
	Jamestown MSA, NY	S	14.55 MW	14.42 AW	30270 AAW	NYBLS	10//99-12//99
	Nassau-Suffolk PMSA, NY	S	20.25 MW	19.31 AW	42130 AAW	NYBLS	10//99-12//99
	New York PMSA, NY	S	24.53 MW	23.46 AW	51020 AAW	NYBLS	10//99-12//99
	Newburgh PMSA, NY-PA	S	18.82 MW	16.66 AW	39140 AAW	NYBLS	10//99-12//99
	Rochester MSA, NY	S	21.96 MW	22.21 AW	45670 AAW	NYBLS	10//99-12//99
	Syracuse MSA, NY	S	17.58 MW	14.92 AW	36560 AAW	NYBLS	10//99-12//99
	North Carolina	S	17.42 MW	19.56 AW	40690 AAW	NCBLS	10//99-12//99
	Asheville MSA, NC	S	17.04 MW	17.24 AW	35450 AAW	NCBLS	10//99-12//99
	Charlotte-Gastonia-Rock Hill MSA, NC-SC	S	20.79 MW	18.65 AW	43240 AAW	NCBLS	10//99-12//99
	Greensboro--Winston-Salem--High Point MSA, NC	S	24.95 MW	20.07 AW	51900 AAW	NCBLS	10//99-12//99
	Hickory-Morganton-Lenoir MSA, NC	S	15.52 MW	15.01 AW	32290 AAW	NCBLS	10//99-12//99
	Raleigh-Durham-Chapel Hill MSA, NC	S	20.06 MW	18.88 AW	41730 AAW	NCBLS	10//99-12//99
	North Dakota	S	15.28 MW	15.44 AW	32110 AAW	NDBLS	10//99-12//99
	Ohio	S	19.59 MW	21.33 AW	44360 AAW	OHBLS	10//99-12//99
	Akron PMSA, OH	S	21.08 MW	19.86 AW	43860 AAW	OHBLS	10//99-12//99
	Canton-Massillon MSA, OH	S	18.24 MW	16.69 AW	37940 AAW	OHBLS	10//99-12//99
	Cleveland-Lorain-Elyria PMSA, OH	S	21.63 MW	19.95 AW	44990 AAW	OHBLS	10//99-12//99
	Columbus MSA, OH	S	19.20 MW	17.65 AW	39930 AAW	OHBLS	10//99-12//99
	Dayton-Springfield MSA, OH	S	23.75 MW	22.47 AW	49400 AAW	OHBLS	10//99-12//99
	Hamilton-Middletown PMSA, OH	S	20.62 MW	20.44 AW	42890 AAW	OHBLS	10//99-12//99
	Lima MSA, OH	S	19.15 MW	18.51 AW	39840 AAW	OHBLS	10//99-12//99
	Toledo MSA, OH	S	21.80 MW	21.28 AW	45340 AAW	OHBLS	10//99-12//99
	Youngstown-Warren MSA, OH	S	20.28 MW	21.86 AW	42180 AAW	OHBLS	10//99-12//99
	Tulsa MSA, OK	S	16.77 MW	15.61 AW	34880 AAW	OKBLS	10//99-12//99
	Oregon	S	19.83 MW	20.90 AW	43480 AAW	ORBLS	10//99-12//99

Occupation/Type/Industry	Location	Per	Low	Mid	High	Source	Date
Industrial Engineering Technician	Portland-Vancouver PMSA, OR-WA	S	20.87 MW	19.95 AW	43420 AAW	ORBLS	10//99-12//99
	Pennsylvania	S	19.99 MW	22.73 AW	47270 AAW	PABLS	10//99-12//99
	Allentown-Bethlehem-Easton MSA, PA	S	20.60 MW	18.35 AW	42850 AAW	PABLS	10//99-12//99
	Altoona MSA, PA	S	20.26 MW	18.33 AW	42140 AAW	PABLS	10//99-12//99
	Erie MSA, PA	S	20.72 MW	19.56 AW	43090 AAW	PABLS	10//99-12//99
	Lancaster MSA, PA	S	18.93 MW	16.83 AW	39380 AAW	PABLS	10//99-12//99
	Philadelphia PMSA, PA-NJ	S	24.88 MW	22.80 AW	51750 AAW	PABLS	10//99-12//99
	Pittsburgh MSA, PA	S	25.22 MW	22.15 AW	52450 AAW	PABLS	10//99-12//99
	Reading MSA, PA	S	19.14 MW	18.48 AW	39810 AAW	PABLS	10//99-12//99
	Scranton--Wilkes-Barre--Hazleton MSA, PA	S	18.47 MW	19.17 AW	38420 AAW	PABLS	10//99-12//99
	Rhode Island	S	16.37 MW	17.55 AW	36500 AAW	RIBLS	10//99-12//99
	Providence-Fall River-Warwick MSA, RI-MA	S	17.41 MW	16.24 AW	36220 AAW	RIBLS	10//99-12//99
	South Carolina	S	18.66 MW	19.14 AW	39800 AAW	SCBLS	10//99-12//99
	Columbia MSA, SC	S	14.25 MW	13.19 AW	29630 AAW	SCBLS	10//99-12//99
	Greenville-Spartanburg-Anderson MSA, SC	S	17.76 MW	17.52 AW	36940 AAW	SCBLS	10//99-12//99
	South Dakota	S	14.3 MW	14.16 AW	29450 AAW	SDBLS	10//99-12//99
	Sioux Falls MSA, SD	S	13.07 MW	12.88 AW	27190 AAW	SDBLS	10//99-12//99
	Tennessee	S	18.52 MW	18.55 AW	38590 AAW	TNBLS	10//99-12//99
	Knoxville MSA, TN	S	16.59 MW	16.36 AW	34500 AAW	TNBLS	10//99-12//99
	Memphis MSA, TN-AR-MS	S	19.93 MW	19.13 AW	41450 AAW	MSBLS	10//99-12//99
	Nashville MSA, TN	S	15.73 MW	15.31 AW	32710 AAW	TNBLS	10//99-12//99
	Texas	S	22.05 MW	22.69 AW	47200 AAW	TXBLS	10//99-12//99
	Austin-San Marcos MSA, TX	S	18.62 MW	17.02 AW	38720 AAW	TXBLS	10//99-12//99
	Corpus Christi MSA, TX	S	24.51 MW	24.80 AW	50980 AAW	TXBLS	10//99-12//99
	El Paso MSA, TX	S	19.11 MW	18.71 AW	39760 AAW	TXBLS	10//99-12//99
	Fort Worth-Arlington PMSA, TX	S	19.93 MW	17.90 AW	41450 AAW	TXBLS	10//99-12//99
	Houston PMSA, TX	S	23.37 MW	23.37 AW	48610 AAW	TXBLS	10//99-12//99
	San Antonio MSA, TX	S	19.67 MW	19.84 AW	40920 AAW	TXBLS	10//99-12//99
	Utah	S	17.46 MW	17.47 AW	36340 AAW	UTBLS	10//99-12//99
	Salt Lake City-Ogden MSA, UT	S	17.59 MW	17.48 AW	36590 AAW	UTBLS	10//99-12//99
	Vermont	S	17.85 MW	18.89 AW	39290 AAW	VTBLS	10//99-12//99
	Burlington MSA, VT	S	21.01 MW	20.89 AW	43700 AAW	VTBLS	10//99-12//99
	Virginia	S	18.58 MW	20.27 AW	42150 AAW	VABLS	10//99-12//99
	Danville MSA, VA	S	16.49 MW	14.93 AW	34300 AAW	VABLS	10//99-12//99
	Norfolk-Virginia Beach-Newport News MSA, VA-NC	S	22.20 MW	20.46 AW	46190 AAW	VABLS	10//99-12//99
	Richmond-Petersburg MSA, VA	S	23.74 MW	22.61 AW	49380 AAW	VABLS	10//99-12//99
	Roanoke MSA, VA	S	16.82 MW	16.40 AW	34980 AAW	VABLS	10//99-12//99
	Spokane MSA, WA	S	20.59 MW	20.76 AW	42830 AAW	WABLS	10//99-12//99
	Tacoma PMSA, WA	S	20.68 MW	20.15 AW	43010 AAW	WABLS	10//99-12//99
	Charleston MSA, WV	S	23.08 MW	23.58 AW	48000 AAW	WVBLS	10//99-12//99
	Wisconsin	S	17.8 MW	18.69 AW	38880 AAW	WIBLS	10//99-12//99
	Madison MSA, WI	S	19.36 MW	17.81 AW	40270 AAW	WIBLS	10//99-12//99
	Milwaukee-Waukesha PMSA, WI	S	19.61 MW	18.17 AW	40780 AAW	WIBLS	10//99-12//99
	Racine PMSA, WI	S	19.42 MW	18.34 AW	40400 AAW	WIBLS	10//99-12//99
	Sheboygan MSA, WI	S	16.12 MW	16.98 AW	33530 AAW	WIBLS	10//99-12//99
	Wausau MSA, WI	S	16.43 MW	16.21 AW	34180 AAW	WIBLS	10//99-12//99
	Puerto Rico	S	10.96 MW	11.32 AW	23540 AAW	PRBLS	10//99-12//99
	San Juan-Bayamon PMSA, PR	S	11.46 MW	11.26 AW	23850 AAW	PRBLS	10//99-12//99
Industrial Machinery Mechanic	Alabama	S	13.79 MW	14.90 AW	31000 AAW	ALBLS	10//99-12//99
	Birmingham MSA, AL	S	17.18 MW	17.26 AW	35740 AAW	ALBLS	10//99-12//99
	Decatur MSA, AL	S	10.89 MW	10.26 AW	22650 AAW	ALBLS	10//99-12//99
	Dothan MSA, AL	S	12.39 MW	12.56 AW	25760 AAW	ALBLS	10//99-12//99
	Florence MSA, AL	S	15.43 MW	15.52 AW	32090 AAW	ALBLS	10//99-12//99
	Mobile MSA, AL	S	15.27 MW	15.27 AW	31750 AAW	ALBLS	10//99-12//99
	Montgomery MSA, AL	S	13.38 MW	13.03 AW	27830 AAW	ALBLS	10//99-12//99
	Tuscaloosa MSA, AL	S	15.28 MW	13.97 AW	31780 AAW	ALBLS	10//99-12//99
	Alaska	S	22.3 MW	22.92 AW	47680 AAW	AKBLS	10//99-12//99
	Anchorage MSA, AK	S	23.29 MW	21.87 AW	48440 AAW	AKBLS	10//99-12//99
	Arizona	S	15.79 MW	16.62 AW	34580 AAW	AZBLS	10//99-12//99
	Phoenix-Mesa MSA, AZ	S	17.38 MW	16.90 AW	36140 AAW	AZBLS	10//99-12//99
	Tucson MSA, AZ	S	14.74 MW	13.37 AW	30670 AAW	AZBLS	10//99-12//99

Occupation/Type/Industry	Location	Per	Low	Mid	High	Source	Date
Industrial Machinery Mechanic	Yuma MSA, AZ	S	14.41 MW	12.73 AW	29980 AAW	AZBLS	10//99-12//99
	Arkansas	S	14.38 MW	14.65 AW	30480 AAW	ARBLS	10//99-12//99
	Fayetteville-Springdale-Rogers MSA, AR	S	13.59 MW	12.85 AW	28260 AAW	ARBLS	10//99-12//99
	Fort Smith MSA, AR-OK	S	14.35 MW	14.31 AW	29850 AAW	ARBLS	10//99-12//99
	Jonesboro MSA, AR	S	13.06 MW	13.31 AW	27160 AAW	ARBLS	10//99-12//99
	Little Rock-North Little Rock MSA, AR	S	13.56 MW	13.88 AW	28200 AAW	ARBLS	10//99-12//99
	California	S	18.8 MW	18.74 AW	38970 AAW	CABLS	10//99-12//99
	Bakersfield MSA, CA	S	21.03 MW	22.93 AW	43740 AAW	CABLS	10//99-12//99
	Chico-Paradise MSA, CA	S	18.53 MW	18.95 AW	38540 AAW	CABLS	10//99-12//99
	Fresno MSA, CA	S	15.85 MW	14.92 AW	32980 AAW	CABLS	10//99-12//99
	Los Angeles-Long Beach PMSA, CA	S	18.27 MW	18.32 AW	38010 AAW	CABLS	10//99-12//99
	Merced MSA, CA	S	16.62 MW	15.73 AW	34560 AAW	CABLS	10//99-12//99
	Modesto MSA, CA	S	17.11 MW	16.75 AW	35600 AAW	CABLS	10//99-12//99
	Oakland PMSA, CA	S	21.10 MW	20.68 AW	43900 AAW	CABLS	10//99-12//99
	Orange County PMSA, CA	S	19.67 MW	19.98 AW	40920 AAW	CABLS	10//99-12//99
	Redding MSA, CA	S	17.85 MW	17.68 AW	37130 AAW	CABLS	10//99-12//99
	Riverside-San Bernardino PMSA, CA	S	19.76 MW	21.73 AW	41090 AAW	CABLS	10//99-12//99
	Sacramento PMSA, CA	S	20.16 MW	19.40 AW	41930 AAW	CABLS	10//99-12//99
	San Diego MSA, CA	S	16.28 MW	16.40 AW	33870 AAW	CABLS	10//99-12//99
	San Francisco PMSA, CA	S	19.67 MW	19.63 AW	40920 AAW	CABLS	10//99-12//99
	San Jose PMSA, CA	S	19.48 MW	19.48 AW	40510 AAW	CABLS	10//99-12//99
	San Luis Obispo-Atascadero-Paso Robles MSA, CA	S	19.93 MW	19.81 AW	41460 AAW	CABLS	10//99-12//99
	Santa Cruz-Watsonville PMSA, CA	S	17.35 MW	15.89 AW	36080 AAW	CABLS	10//99-12//99
	Santa Rosa PMSA, CA	S	14.29 MW	11.84 AW	29720 AAW	CABLS	10//99-12//99
	Stockton-Lodi MSA, CA	S	19.42 MW	19.34 AW	40390 AAW	CABLS	10//99-12//99
	Vallejo-Fairfield-Napa PMSA, CA	S	17.78 MW	17.69 AW	36980 AAW	CABLS	10//99-12//99
	Ventura PMSA, CA	S	15.55 MW	16.57 AW	32350 AAW	CABLS	10//99-12//99
	Visalia-Tulare-Porterville MSA, CA	S	12.09 MW	12.31 AW	25150 AAW	CABLS	10//99-12//99
	Yuba City MSA, CA	S	17.00 MW	15.94 AW	35370 AAW	CABLS	10//99-12//99
	Connecticut	S	19.4 MW	19.32 AW	40190 AAW	CTBLS	10//99-12//99
	Bridgeport PMSA, CT	S	18.78 MW	18.81 AW	39060 AAW	CTBLS	10//99-12//99
	Danbury PMSA, CT	S	21.96 MW	22.14 AW	45670 AAW	CTBLS	10//99-12//99
	Hartford MSA, CT	S	18.74 MW	18.87 AW	38980 AAW	CTBLS	10//99-12//99
	New Haven-Meriden PMSA, CT	S	21.88 MW	23.25 AW	45520 AAW	CTBLS	10//99-12//99
	New London-Norwich MSA, CT-RI	S	19.02 MW	19.42 AW	39550 AAW	CTBLS	10//99-12//99
	Stamford-Norwalk PMSA, CT	S	18.46 MW	18.52 AW	38390 AAW	CTBLS	10//99-12//99
	Delaware	S	23.64 MW	22.35 AW	46490 AAW	DEBLS	10//99-12//99
	Wilmington-Newark PMSA, DE-MD	S	22.72 MW	23.74 AW	47260 AAW	DEBLS	10//99-12//99
	Washington PMSA, DC-MD-VA-WV	S	18.31 MW	17.86 AW	38090 AAW	DCBLS	10//99-12//99
	Florida	S	15.65 MW	16.38 AW	34080 AAW	FLBLS	10//99-12//99
	Daytona Beach MSA, FL	S	17.46 MW	16.52 AW	36310 AAW	FLBLS	10//99-12//99
	Fort Lauderdale PMSA, FL	S	18.01 MW	18.16 AW	37450 AAW	FLBLS	10//99-12//99
	Fort Myers-Cape Coral MSA, FL	S	13.35 MW	12.31 AW	27770 AAW	FLBLS	10//99-12//99
	Gainesville MSA, FL	S	13.40 MW	12.24 AW	27860 AAW	FLBLS	10//99-12//99
	Jacksonville MSA, FL	S	12.43 MW	11.99 AW	25850 AAW	FLBLS	10//99-12//99
	Lakeland-Winter Haven MSA, FL	S	18.49 MW	16.56 AW	38450 AAW	FLBLS	10//99-12//99
	Melbourne-Titusville-Palm Bay MSA, FL	S	15.76 MW	16.48 AW	32780 AAW	FLBLS	10//99-12//99
	Miami PMSA, FL	S	13.89 MW	13.21 AW	28900 AAW	FLBLS	10//99-12//99
	Naples MSA, FL	S	17.12 MW	18.12 AW	35610 AAW	FLBLS	10//99-12//99
	Ocala MSA, FL	S	13.66 MW	11.99 AW	28400 AAW	FLBLS	10//99-12//99
	Orlando MSA, FL	S	15.87 MW	13.29 AW	33020 AAW	FLBLS	10//99-12//99
	Pensacola MSA, FL	S	18.91 MW	19.22 AW	39330 AAW	FLBLS	10//99-12//99
	Sarasota-Bradenton MSA, FL	S	13.26 MW	12.31 AW	27580 AAW	FLBLS	10//99-12//99
	Tallahassee MSA, FL	S	11.27 MW	10.87 AW	23440 AAW	FLBLS	10//99-12//99
	Tampa-St. Petersburg-Clearwater MSA, FL	S	16.96 MW	16.60 AW	35280 AAW	FLBLS	10//99-12//99

AAW Average annual wage	**AOH** Average offered, high	**ASH** Average starting, high	**H** Hourly	**M** Monthly	**S** Special: hourly and annual
AE Average entry wage	**AOL** Average offered, low	**ASL** Average starting, low	**HI** Highest wage paid	**MTC** Median total compensation	**TQ** Third quartile wage
AEX Average experienced wage	**APH** Average pay, high range	**AW** Average wage paid	**HR** High end range	**MW** Median wage paid	**W** Weekly
AO Average offered	**APL** Average pay, low range	**FQ** First quartile wage	**LR** Low end range	**SQ** Second quartile wage	**Y** Yearly

Occupation/Type/Industry	Location	Per	Low	Mid	High	Source	Date
Industrial Machinery Mechanic	West Palm Beach-Boca Raton MSA, FL	S	17.42 MW	17.64 AW	36230 AAW	FLBLS	10//99-12//99
	Georgia	S	14.11 MW	15.39 AW	32020 AAW	GABLS	10//99-12//99
	Albany MSA, GA	S	13.27 MW	13.35 AW	27600 AAW	GABLS	10//99-12//99
	Athens MSA, GA	S	18.13 MW	18.13 AW	37710 AAW	GABLS	10//99-12//99
	Atlanta MSA, GA	S	16.96 MW	17.07 AW	35270 AAW	GABLS	10//99-12//99
	Augusta-Aiken MSA, GA-SC	S	13.84 MW	13.19 AW	28790 AAW	GABLS	10//99-12//99
	Columbus MSA, GA-AL	S	12.30 MW	12.16 AW	25590 AAW	GABLS	10//99-12//99
	Macon MSA, GA	S	18.90 MW	18.99 AW	39310 AAW	GABLS	10//99-12//99
	Hawaii	S	16.07 MW	16.89 AW	35120 AAW	HIBLS	10//99-12//99
	Honolulu MSA, HI	S	16.82 MW	15.62 AW	34990 AAW	HIBLS	10//99-12//99
	Idaho	S	16.64 MW	18.06 AW	37570 AAW	IDBLS	10//99-12//99
	Boise City MSA, ID	S	15.10 MW	14.83 AW	31420 AAW	IDBLS	10//99-12//99
	Illinois	S	17.39 MW	17.02 AW	35400 AAW	ILBLS	10//99-12//99
	Champaign-Urbana MSA, IL	S	14.55 MW	14.76 AW	30270 AAW	ILBLS	10//99-12//99
	Chicago PMSA, IL	S	17.30 MW	17.71 AW	35980 AAW	ILBLS	10//99-12//99
	Rockford MSA, IL	S	18.42 MW	18.06 AW	38310 AAW	ILBLS	10//99-12//99
	Indiana	S	17.66 MW	18.17 AW	37790 AAW	INBLS	10//99-12//99
	Elkhart-Goshen MSA, IN	S	16.01 MW	15.78 AW	33310 AAW	INBLS	10//99-12//99
	Evansville-Henderson MSA, IN-KY	S	15.19 MW	14.80 AW	31600 AAW	INBLS	10//99-12//99
	Fort Wayne MSA, IN	S	17.27 MW	17.04 AW	35920 AAW	INBLS	10//99-12//99
	Gary PMSA, IN	S	16.33 MW	15.48 AW	33960 AAW	INBLS	10//99-12//99
	Indianapolis MSA, IN	S	19.69 MW	16.71 AW	40950 AAW	INBLS	10//99-12//99
	Lafayette MSA, IN	S	19.07 MW	19.19 AW	39670 AAW	INBLS	10//99-12//99
	South Bend MSA, IN	S	15.28 MW	14.92 AW	31790 AAW	INBLS	10//99-12//99
	Terre Haute MSA, IN	S	15.21 MW	13.49 AW	31640 AAW	INBLS	10//99-12//99
	Iowa	S	12.93 MW	13.61 AW	28320 AAW	IABLS	10//99-12//99
	Cedar Rapids MSA, IA	S	16.76 MW	16.67 AW	34860 AAW	IABLS	10//99-12//99
	Davenport-Moline-Rock Island MSA, IA-IL	S	16.65 MW	16.56 AW	34640 AAW	IABLS	10//99-12//99
	Des Moines MSA, IA	S	13.97 MW	13.36 AW	29050 AAW	IABLS	10//99-12//99
	Sioux City MSA, IA-NE	S	13.02 MW	12.48 AW	27080 AAW	IABLS	10//99-12//99
	Waterloo-Cedar Falls MSA, IA	S	13.57 MW	12.10 AW	28230 AAW	IABLS	10//99-12//99
	Kansas	S	14.93 MW	14.60 AW	30360 AAW	KSBLS	10//99-12//99
	Topeka MSA, KS	S	14.80 MW	14.76 AW	30780 AAW	KSBLS	10//99-12//99
	Wichita MSA, KS	S	14.58 MW	14.91 AW	30320 AAW	KSBLS	10//99-12//99
	Kentucky	S	17.01 MW	17.30 AW	35970 AAW	KYBLS	10//99-12//99
	Lexington MSA, KY	S	17.10 MW	16.92 AW	35570 AAW	KYBLS	10//99-12//99
	Louisville MSA, KY-IN	S	15.99 MW	15.90 AW	33270 AAW	KYBLS	10//99-12//99
	Louisiana	S	17.63 MW	17.61 AW	36640 AAW	LABLS	10//99-12//99
	Baton Rouge MSA, LA	S	17.85 MW	18.08 AW	37130 AAW	LABLS	10//99-12//99
	Houma MSA, LA	S	16.37 MW	15.38 AW	34060 AAW	LABLS	10//99-12//99
	Lafayette MSA, LA	S	16.27 MW	14.94 AW	33840 AAW	LABLS	10//99-12//99
	Lake Charles MSA, LA	S	19.31 MW	19.15 AW	40170 AAW	LABLS	10//99-12//99
	Monroe MSA, LA	S	18.72 MW	18.51 AW	38930 AAW	LABLS	10//99-12//99
	New Orleans MSA, LA	S	15.02 MW	13.62 AW	31230 AAW	LABLS	10//99-12//99
	Shreveport-Bossier City MSA, LA	S	18.88 MW	18.89 AW	39270 AAW	LABLS	10//99-12//99
	Maine	S	13.85 MW	14.75 AW	30680 AAW	MEBLS	10//99-12//99
	Portland MSA, ME	S	16.20 MW	15.82 AW	33690 AAW	MEBLS	10//99-12//99
	Maryland	S	16.76 MW	17.61 AW	36630 AAW	MDBLS	10//99-12//99
	Baltimore PMSA, MD	S	17.67 MW	16.76 AW	36750 AAW	MDBLS	10//99-12//99
	Hagerstown PMSA, MD	S	18.65 MW	18.47 AW	38800 AAW	MDBLS	10//99-12//99
	Massachusetts	S	16.66 MW	17.09 AW	35540 AAW	MABLS	10//99-12//99
	Boston PMSA, MA-NH	S	16.89 MW	17.34 AW	35120 AAW	MABLS	10//99-12//99
	Fitchburg-Leominster PMSA, MA	S	18.91 MW	15.14 AW	39330 AAW	MABLS	10//99-12//99
	Lawrence PMSA, MA-NH	S	16.29 MW	15.43 AW	33880 AAW	MABLS	10//99-12//99
	Lowell PMSA, MA-NH	S	22.89 MW	24.07 AW	47610 AAW	MABLS	10//99-12//99
	New Bedford PMSA, MA	S	12.61 MW	12.56 AW	26230 AAW	MABLS	10//99-12//99
	Springfield MSA, MA	S	17.47 MW	15.75 AW	36340 AAW	MABLS	10//99-12//99
	Worcester PMSA, MA-CT	S	17.28 MW	16.20 AW	35940 AAW	MABLS	10//99-12//99
	Michigan	S	26.89 MW	25.96 AW	54000 AAW	MIBLS	10//99-12//99
	Ann Arbor PMSA, MI	S	21.84 MW	23.04 AW	45420 AAW	MIBLS	10//99-12//99
	Detroit PMSA, MI	S	27.84 MW	28.77 AW	57910 AAW	MIBLS	10//99-12//99
	Flint PMSA, MI	S	27.76 MW	27.63 AW	57750 AAW	MIBLS	10//99-12//99
	Grand Rapids-Muskegon-Holland MSA, MI	S	26.78 MW	25.78 AW	55700 AAW	MIBLS	10//99-12//99
	Kalamazoo-Battle Creek MSA, MI	S	23.78 MW	24.31 AW	49470 AAW	MIBLS	10//99-12//99
	Lansing-East Lansing MSA, MI	S	17.43 MW	16.92 AW	36260 AAW	MIBLS	10//99-12//99

AAW Average annual wage	**AOH** Average offered, high	**ASH** Average starting, high	**H** Hourly	**M** Monthly	**S** Special: hourly and annual
AE Average entry wage	**AOL** Average offered, low	**ASL** Average starting, low	**HI** Highest wage paid	**MTC** Median total compensation	**TQ** Third quartile wage
AEX Average experienced wage	**APH** Average pay, high range	**AW** Average wage paid	**HR** High end range	**MW** Median wage paid	**W** Weekly
AO Average offered	**APL** Average pay, low range	**FQ** First quartile wage	**LR** Low end range	**SQ** Second quartile wage	**Y** Yearly

Occupation/Type/Industry	Location	Per	Low	Mid	High	Source	Date
Industrial Machinery Mechanic	Saginaw-Bay City-Midland MSA, MI	S	28.79 MW	30.08 AW	59880 AAW	MIBLS	10//99-12//99
	Minnesota	S	18.17 MW	18.52 AW	38520 AAW	MNBLS	10//99-12//99
	Duluth-Superior MSA, MN-WI	S	16.61 MW	16.28 AW	34560 AAW	MNBLS	10//99-12//99
	Minneapolis-St. Paul MSA, MN-WI	S	20.90 MW	20.51 AW	43480 AAW	MNBLS	10//99-12//99
	Mississippi	S	14.63 MW	15.52 AW	32270 AAW	MSBLS	10//99-12//99
	Biloxi-Gulfport-Pascagoula MSA, MS	S	19.59 MW	20.52 AW	40740 AAW	MSBLS	10//99-12//99
	Jackson MSA, MS	S	12.48 MW	10.98 AW	25950 AAW	MSBLS	10//99-12//99
	Missouri	S	16.35 MW	17.34 AW	36080 AAW	MOBLS	10//99-12//99
	Joplin MSA, MO	S	14.85 MW	13.32 AW	30880 AAW	MOBLS	10//99-12//99
	Kansas City MSA, MO-KS	S	17.06 MW	15.98 AW	35490 AAW	MOBLS	10//99-12//99
	St. Louis MSA, MO-IL	S	19.02 MW	18.15 AW	39550 AAW	MOBLS	10//99-12//99
	Springfield MSA, MO	S	14.11 MW	14.46 AW	29360 AAW	MOBLS	10//99-12//99
	Montana	S	13.99 MW	15.15 AW	31520 AAW	MTBLS	10//99-12//99
	Billings MSA, MT	S	20.65 MW	18.09 AW	42960 AAW	MTBLS	10//99-12//99
	Nebraska	S	12.73 MW	13.49 AW	28070 AAW	NEBLS	10//99-12//99
	Lincoln MSA, NE	S	13.88 MW	14.06 AW	28870 AAW	NEBLS	10//99-12//99
	Omaha MSA, NE-IA	S	16.49 MW	16.59 AW	34290 AAW	NEBLS	10//99-12//99
	Nevada	S	17.45 MW	17.82 AW	37060 AAW	NVBLS	10//99-12//99
	Las Vegas MSA, NV-AZ	S	17.63 MW	16.51 AW	36680 AAW	NVBLS	10//99-12//99
	New Hampshire	S	15.35 MW	15.59 AW	32420 AAW	NHBLS	10//99-12//99
	Manchester PMSA, NH	S	16.37 MW	16.19 AW	34040 AAW	NHBLS	10//99-12//99
	Nashua PMSA, NH	S	16.70 MW	18.10 AW	34730 AAW	NHBLS	10//99-12//99
	Portsmouth-Rochester PMSA, NH-ME	S	17.81 MW	18.36 AW	37040 AAW	NHBLS	10//99-12//99
	New Jersey	S	18.51 MW	18.54 AW	38560 AAW	NJBLS	10//99-12//99
	Bergen-Passaic PMSA, NJ	S	19.16 MW	18.96 AW	39860 AAW	NJBLS	10//99-12//99
	Jersey City PMSA, NJ	S	17.95 MW	17.82 AW	37340 AAW	NJBLS	10//99-12//99
	Middlesex-Somerset-Hunterdon PMSA, NJ	S	18.81 MW	18.91 AW	39130 AAW	NJBLS	10//99-12//99
	Monmouth-Ocean PMSA, NJ	S	18.81 MW	18.83 AW	39130 AAW	NJBLS	10//99-12//99
	Newark PMSA, NJ	S	17.66 MW	17.35 AW	36720 AAW	NJBLS	10//99-12//99
	Trenton PMSA, NJ	S	16.09 MW	15.60 AW	33460 AAW	NJBLS	10//99-12//99
	New Mexico	S	18.65 MW	18.01 AW	37460 AAW	NMBLS	10//99-12//99
	Albuquerque MSA, NM	S	18.19 MW	16.75 AW	37840 AAW	NMBLS	10//99-12//99
	New York	S	17.42 MW	18.29 AW	38030 AAW	NYBLS	10//99-12//99
	Albany-Schenectady-Troy MSA, NY	S	14.16 MW	13.03 AW	29460 AAW	NYBLS	10//99-12//99
	Buffalo-Niagara Falls MSA, NY	S	18.14 MW	18.10 AW	37730 AAW	NYBLS	10//99-12//99
	Dutchess County PMSA, NY	S	15.90 MW	15.93 AW	33070 AAW	NYBLS	10//99-12//99
	Elmira MSA, NY	S	19.54 MW	18.69 AW	40650 AAW	NYBLS	10//99-12//99
	Glens Falls MSA, NY	S	18.77 MW	16.27 AW	39040 AAW	NYBLS	10//99-12//99
	Jamestown MSA, NY	S	11.69 MW	11.93 AW	24310 AAW	NYBLS	10//99-12//99
	Nassau-Suffolk PMSA, NY	S	19.81 MW	19.53 AW	41210 AAW	NYBLS	10//99-12//99
	New York PMSA, NY	S	19.15 MW	19.02 AW	39820 AAW	NYBLS	10//99-12//99
	Newburgh PMSA, NY-PA	S	22.10 MW	21.00 AW	45980 AAW	NYBLS	10//99-12//99
	Rochester MSA, NY	S	15.62 MW	15.26 AW	32490 AAW	NYBLS	10//99-12//99
	Syracuse MSA, NY	S	19.42 MW	19.41 AW	40400 AAW	NYBLS	10//99-12//99
	North Carolina	S	14.23 MW	15.94 AW	33150 AAW	NCBLS	10//99-12//99
	Asheville MSA, NC	S	18.27 MW	18.41 AW	38000 AAW	NCBLS	10//99-12//99
	Charlotte-Gastonia-Rock Hill MSA, NC-SC	S	15.22 MW	13.09 AW	31660 AAW	NCBLS	10//99-12//99
	Hickory-Morganton-Lenoir MSA, NC	S	13.44 MW	13.06 AW	27960 AAW	NCBLS	10//99-12//99
	Raleigh-Durham-Chapel Hill MSA, NC	S	17.97 MW	18.29 AW	37370 AAW	NCBLS	10//99-12//99
	Rocky Mount MSA, NC	S	12.55 MW	11.50 AW	26100 AAW	NCBLS	10//99-12//99
	Wilmington MSA, NC	S	14.16 MW	14.45 AW	29450 AAW	NCBLS	10//99-12//99
	North Dakota	S	13.37 MW	14.94 AW	31070 AAW	NDBLS	10//99-12//99
	Fargo-Moorhead MSA, ND-MN	S	13.13 MW	12.56 AW	27300 AAW	NDBLS	10//99-12//99
	Ohio	S	19.24 MW	20.55 AW	42750 AAW	OHBLS	10//99-12//99
	Akron PMSA, OH	S	15.23 MW	15.33 AW	31690 AAW	OHBLS	10//99-12//99
	Cincinnati PMSA, OH-KY-IN	S	20.65 MW	21.91 AW	42960 AAW	OHBLS	10//99-12//99
	Cleveland-Lorain-Elyria PMSA, OH	S	24.91 MW	28.27 AW	51800 AAW	OHBLS	10//99-12//99
	Columbus MSA, OH	S	16.80 MW	17.24 AW	34940 AAW	OHBLS	10//99-12//99
	Dayton-Springfield MSA, OH	S	21.79 MW	19.38 AW	45320 AAW	OHBLS	10//99-12//99

Occupation/Type/Industry	Location	Per	Low	Mid	High	Source	Date
Industrial Machinery Mechanic	Hamilton-Middletown PMSA, OH	S	15.97 MW	14.97 AW	33210 AAW	OHBLS	10//99-12//99
	Lima MSA, OH	S	18.78 MW	18.96 AW	39060 AAW	OHBLS	10//99-12//99
	Toledo MSA, OH	S	26.47 MW	28.38 AW	55050 AAW	OHBLS	10//99-12//99
	Oklahoma	S	13.06 MW	13.91 AW	28920 AAW	OKBLS	10//99-12//99
	Oklahoma City MSA, OK	S	15.76 MW	14.96 AW	32780 AAW	OKBLS	10//99-12//99
	Tulsa MSA, OK	S	13.92 MW	13.72 AW	28950 AAW	OKBLS	10//99-12//99
	Oregon	S	16.72 MW	17.39 AW	36180 AAW	ORBLS	10//99-12//99
	Corvallis MSA, OR	S	15.14 MW	15.10 AW	31490 AAW	ORBLS	10//99-12//99
	Eugene-Springfield MSA, OR	S	16.28 MW	15.37 AW	33860 AAW	ORBLS	10//99-12//99
	Medford-Ashland MSA, OR	S	14.25 MW	14.52 AW	29640 AAW	ORBLS	10//99-12//99
	Portland-Vancouver PMSA, OR-WA	S	19.21 MW	19.55 AW	39950 AAW	ORBLS	10//99-12//99
	Salem PMSA, OR	S	16.28 MW	16.20 AW	33870 AAW	ORBLS	10//99-12//99
	Pennsylvania	S	15.96 MW	16.60 AW	34530 AAW	PABLS	10//99-12//99
	Allentown-Bethlehem-Easton MSA, PA	S	17.26 MW	17.09 AW	35900 AAW	PABLS	10//99-12//99
	Altoona MSA, PA	S	14.30 MW	14.83 AW	29750 AAW	PABLS	10//99-12//99
	Erie MSA, PA	S	13.70 MW	12.97 AW	28500 AAW	PABLS	10//99-12//99
	Harrisburg-Lebanon-Carlisle MSA, PA	S	17.36 MW	17.96 AW	36100 AAW	PABLS	10//99-12//99
	Johnstown MSA, PA	S	12.45 MW	12.12 AW	25900 AAW	PABLS	10//99-12//99
	Lancaster MSA, PA	S	15.88 MW	15.57 AW	33020 AAW	PABLS	10//99-12//99
	Philadelphia PMSA, PA-NJ	S	17.75 MW	17.66 AW	36920 AAW	PABLS	10//99-12//99
	Pittsburgh MSA, PA	S	16.24 MW	15.44 AW	33780 AAW	PABLS	10//99-12//99
	Reading MSA, PA	S	15.61 MW	15.67 AW	32470 AAW	PABLS	10//99-12//99
	Scranton--Wilkes-Barre--Hazleton MSA, PA	S	13.48 MW	12.92 AW	28040 AAW	PABLS	10//99-12//99
	Sharon MSA, PA	S	15.13 MW	15.13 AW	31470 AAW	PABLS	10//99-12//99
	State College MSA, PA	S	13.99 MW	13.36 AW	29090 AAW	PABLS	10//99-12//99
	York MSA, PA	S	19.43 MW	16.73 AW	40420 AAW	PABLS	10//99-12//99
	Rhode Island	S	14.38 MW	14.86 AW	30900 AAW	RIBLS	10//99-12//99
	Providence-Fall River-Warwick MSA, RI-MA	S	14.48 MW	13.79 AW	30120 AAW	RIBLS	10//99-12//99
	South Carolina	S	13.9 MW	14.80 AW	30780 AAW	SCBLS	10//99-12//99
	Charleston-North Charleston MSA, SC	S	17.88 MW	18.53 AW	37200 AAW	SCBLS	10//99-12//99
	Columbia MSA, SC	S	17.52 MW	16.77 AW	36440 AAW	SCBLS	10//99-12//99
	Florence MSA, SC	S	18.80 MW	16.60 AW	39090 AAW	SCBLS	10//99-12//99
	Greenville-Spartanburg-Anderson MSA, SC	S	13.87 MW	13.53 AW	28850 AAW	SCBLS	10//99-12//99
	Myrtle Beach MSA, SC	S	12.23 MW	13.34 AW	25450 AAW	SCBLS	10//99-12//99
	South Dakota	S	12.84 MW	13.45 AW	27980 AAW	SDBLS	10//99-12//99
	Sioux Falls MSA, SD	S	15.23 MW	15.10 AW	31670 AAW	SDBLS	10//99-12//99
	Tennessee	S	14.94 MW	15.48 AW	32200 AAW	TNBLS	10//99-12//99
	Chattanooga MSA, TN-GA	S	15.01 MW	14.48 AW	31220 AAW	TNBLS	10//99-12//99
	Clarksville-Hopkinsville MSA, TN-KY	S	19.10 MW	17.61 AW	39730 AAW	TNBLS	10//99-12//99
	Johnson City-Kingsport-Bristol MSA, TN-VA	S	15.26 MW	15.14 AW	31740 AAW	TNBLS	10//99-12//99
	Knoxville MSA, TN	S	12.58 MW	12.41 AW	26170 AAW	TNBLS	10//99-12//99
	Memphis MSA, TN-AR-MS	S	20.42 MW	19.91 AW	42470 AAW	MSBLS	10//99-12//99
	Nashville MSA, TN	S	16.73 MW	16.65 AW	34810 AAW	TNBLS	10//99-12//99
	Texas	S	17.35 MW	18.05 AW	37530 AAW	TXBLS	10//99-12//99
	Abilene MSA, TX	S	12.54 MW	12.53 AW	26090 AAW	TXBLS	10//99-12//99
	Amarillo MSA, TX	S	14.96 MW	15.17 AW	31110 AAW	TXBLS	10//99-12//99
	Austin-San Marcos MSA, TX	S	16.57 MW	16.28 AW	34470 AAW	TXBLS	10//99-12//99
	Beaumont-Port Arthur MSA, TX	S	22.92 MW	24.01 AW	47680 AAW	TXBLS	10//99-12//99
	Corpus Christi MSA, TX	S	14.52 MW	14.47 AW	30200 AAW	TXBLS	10//99-12//99
	Dallas PMSA, TX	S	15.68 MW	15.09 AW	32610 AAW	TXBLS	10//99-12//99
	El Paso MSA, TX	S	14.57 MW	12.67 AW	30300 AAW	TXBLS	10//99-12//99
	Fort Worth-Arlington PMSA, TX	S	16.61 MW	16.78 AW	34550 AAW	TXBLS	10//99-12//99
	Galveston-Texas City PMSA, TX	S	19.38 MW	22.71 AW	40300 AAW	TXBLS	10//99-12//99
	Houston PMSA, TX	S	18.14 MW	17.27 AW	37720 AAW	TXBLS	10//99-12//99
	Killeen-Temple MSA, TX	S	14.85 MW	14.02 AW	30890 AAW	TXBLS	10//99-12//99
	Laredo MSA, TX	S	9.11 MW	8.07 AW	18940 AAW	TXBLS	10//99-12//99
	Longview-Marshall MSA, TX	S	13.02 MW	12.28 AW	27070 AAW	TXBLS	10//99-12//99
	Lubbock MSA, TX	S	16.19 MW	17.58 AW	33680 AAW	TXBLS	10//99-12//99

AAW Average annual wage	**AOH** Average offered, high	**ASH** Average starting, high	**H** Hourly	**M** Monthly	**S** Special: hourly and annual
AE Average entry wage	**AOL** Average offered, low	**ASL** Average starting, low	**HI** Highest wage paid	**MTC** Median total compensation	**TQ** Third quartile wage
AEX Average experienced wage	**APH** Average pay, high range	**AW** Average wage paid	**HR** High end range	**MW** Median wage paid	**W** Weekly
AO Average offered	**APL** Average pay, low range	**FQ** First quartile wage	**LR** Low end range	**SQ** Second quartile wage	**Y** Yearly

Occupation/Type/Industry	Location	Per	Low	Mid	High	Source	Date
Industrial Machinery Mechanic	McAllen-Edinburg-Mission MSA, TX	S	12.42 MW	10.55 AW	25840 AAW	TXBLS	10//99-12//99
	San Antonio MSA, TX	S	13.61 MW	13.94 AW	28300 AAW	TXBLS	10//99-12//99
	Sherman-Denison MSA, TX	S	17.84 MW	18.06 AW	37110 AAW	TXBLS	10//99-12//99
	Waco MSA, TX	S	13.66 MW	13.09 AW	28410 AAW	TXBLS	10//99-12//99
	Utah	S	16.75 MW	16.49 AW	34300 AAW	UTBLS	10//99-12//99
	Provo-Orem MSA, UT	S	16.72 MW	16.99 AW	34770 AAW	UTBLS	10//99-12//99
	Vermont	S	16.23 MW	16.50 AW	34320 AAW	VTBLS	10//99-12//99
	Burlington MSA, VT	S	17.38 MW	18.24 AW	36140 AAW	VTBLS	10//99-12//99
	Virginia	S	15.14 MW	15.85 AW	32960 AAW	VABLS	10//99-12//99
	Charlottesville MSA, VA	S	12.56 MW	12.47 AW	26130 AAW	VABLS	10//99-12//99
	Danville MSA, VA	S	9.40 MW	9.06 AW	19540 AAW	VABLS	10//99-12//99
	Lynchburg MSA, VA	S	15.51 MW	15.48 AW	32250 AAW	VABLS	10//99-12//99
	Norfolk-Virginia Beach-Newport News MSA, VA-NC	S	15.03 MW	15.07 AW	31260 AAW	VABLS	10//99-12//99
	Richmond-Petersburg MSA, VA	S	18.92 MW	18.86 AW	39350 AAW	VABLS	10//99-12//99
	Roanoke MSA, VA	S	21.95 MW	19.01 AW	45650 AAW	VABLS	10//99-12//99
	Washington	S	17.13 MW	18.06 AW	37550 AAW	WABLS	10//99-12//99
	Bellingham MSA, WA	S	20.60 MW	20.25 AW	42850 AAW	WABLS	10//99-12//99
	Seattle-Bellevue-Everett PMSA, WA	S	18.41 MW	17.86 AW	38300 AAW	WABLS	10//99-12//99
	Spokane MSA, WA	S	17.46 MW	18.10 AW	36320 AAW	WABLS	10//99-12//99
	Tacoma PMSA, WA	S	19.78 MW	20.16 AW	41130 AAW	WABLS	10//99-12//99
	Yakima MSA, WA	S	15.51 MW	15.39 AW	32260 AAW	WABLS	10//99-12//99
	West Virginia	S	17.95 MW	16.76 AW	34860 AAW	WVBLS	10//99-12//99
	Charleston MSA, WV	S	15.28 MW	17.08 AW	31780 AAW	WVBLS	10//99-12//99
	Huntington-Ashland MSA, WV-KY-OH	S	15.67 MW	14.77 AW	32600 AAW	WVBLS	10//99-12//99
	Parkersburg-Marietta MSA, WV-OH	S	15.25 MW	17.08 AW	31710 AAW	WVBLS	10//99-12//99
	Wheeling MSA, WV-OH	S	18.80 MW	19.10 AW	39100 AAW	WVBLS	10//99-12//99
	Wisconsin	S	18.76 MW	18.78 AW	39070 AAW	WIBLS	10//99-12//99
	Appleton-Oshkosh-Neenah MSA, WI	S	19.16 MW	19.10 AW	39840 AAW	WIBLS	10//99-12//99
	Green Bay MSA, WI	S	20.81 MW	20.97 AW	43280 AAW	WIBLS	10//99-12//99
	Janesville-Beloit MSA, WI	S	18.47 MW	17.68 AW	38430 AAW	WIBLS	10//99-12//99
	Milwaukee-Waukesha PMSA, WI	S	19.77 MW	20.90 AW	41130 AAW	WIBLS	10//99-12//99
	Racine PMSA, WI	S	20.08 MW	20.74 AW	41770 AAW	WIBLS	10//99-12//99
	Wausau MSA, WI	S	17.13 MW	17.24 AW	35620 AAW	WIBLS	10//99-12//99
	Wyoming	S	23.35 MW	21.95 AW	45650 AAW	WYBLS	10//99-12//99
	Casper MSA, WY	S	20.23 MW	21.36 AW	42080 AAW	WYBLS	10//99-12//99
	Puerto Rico	S	10.66 MW	10.98 AW	22840 AAW	PRBLS	10//99-12//99
	Caguas PMSA, PR	S	12.49 MW	12.48 AW	25980 AAW	PRBLS	10//99-12//99
	Mayaguez MSA, PR	S	7.41 MW	7.57 AW	15410 AAW	PRBLS	10//99-12//99
	Ponce MSA, PR	S	9.18 MW	9.53 AW	19100 AAW	PRBLS	10//99-12//99
	San Juan-Bayamon PMSA, PR	S	11.54 MW	11.62 AW	24010 AAW	PRBLS	10//99-12//99
Industrial-Organizational Psychologist	California	S	42.99 MW	42.79 AW	89010 AAW	CABLS	10//99-12//99
	District of Columbia	S	27.56 MW	31.48 AW	65470 AAW	DCBLS	10//99-12//99
	Washington PMSA, DC-MD-VA-WV	S	32.08 MW	30.33 AW	66720 AAW	DCBLS	10//99-12//99
	Florida	S	20.75 MW	30.19 AW	62800 AAW	FLBLS	10//99-12//99
	Georgia	S	24.79 MW	26.36 AW	54840 AAW	GABLS	10//99-12//99
	Idaho	S	19.08 MW	24.80 AW	51580 AAW	IDBLS	10//99-12//99
	Minnesota	S	39.14 MW	38.22 AW	79500 AAW	MNBLS	10//99-12//99
	Minneapolis-St. Paul MSA, MN-WI	S	37.78 MW	38.51 AW	78590 AAW	MNBLS	10//99-12//99
	New York	S	16.03 MW	19.81 AW	41200 AAW	NYBLS	10//99-12//99
	Pennsylvania	S	26.08 MW	25.45 AW	52940 AAW	PABLS	10//99-12//99
	Texas	S	25.59 MW	26.41 AW	54940 AAW	TXBLS	10//99-12//99
	Virginia	S	29.47 MW	30.10 AW	62600 AAW	VABLS	10//99-12//99
Industrial Production Manager	Alabama	S	23.63 MW	25.48 AW	53010 AAW	ALBLS	10//99-12//99
	Anniston MSA, AL	S	25.06 MW	21.94 AW	52130 AAW	ALBLS	10//99-12//99
	Auburn-Opelika MSA, AL	S	24.77 MW	23.17 AW	51520 AAW	ALBLS	10//99-12//99
	Birmingham MSA, AL	S	25.38 MW	24.10 AW	52780 AAW	ALBLS	10//99-12//99
	Decatur MSA, AL	S	29.75 MW	29.61 AW	61890 AAW	ALBLS	10//99-12//99
	Dothan MSA, AL	S	23.90 MW	23.50 AW	49720 AAW	ALBLS	10//99-12//99

AAW Average annual wage	**AOH** Average offered, high	**ASH** Average starting, high	**H** Hourly	**M** Monthly	**S** Special: hourly and annual
AE Average entry wage	**AOL** Average offered, low	**ASL** Average starting, low	**HI** Highest wage paid	**MTC** Median total compensation	**TQ** Third quartile wage
AEX Average experienced wage	**APH** Average pay, high range	**AW** Average wage paid	**HR** High end range	**MW** Median wage paid	**W** Weekly
AO Average offered	**APL** Average pay, low range	**FQ** First quartile wage	**LR** Low end range	**SQ** Second quartile wage	**Y** Yearly

Occupation/Type/Industry	Location	Per	Low	Mid	High	Source	Date
Industrial Production Manager	Florence MSA, AL	S	18.44 MW	14.01 AW	38350 AAW	ALBLS	10//99-12//99
	Gadsden MSA, AL	S	20.08 MW	19.32 AW	41780 AAW	ALBLS	10//99-12//99
	Huntsville MSA, AL	S	30.49 MW	29.26 AW	63410 AAW	ALBLS	10//99-12//99
	Mobile MSA, AL	S	27.35 MW	28.17 AW	56880 AAW	ALBLS	10//99-12//99
	Montgomery MSA, AL	S	23.79 MW	22.91 AW	49480 AAW	ALBLS	10//99-12//99
	Tuscaloosa MSA, AL	S	29.92 MW	30.95 AW	62240 AAW	ALBLS	10//99-12//99
	Alaska	S	25.2 MW	28.91 AW	60140 AAW	AKBLS	10//99-12//99
	Arizona	S	33.71 MW	33.24 AW	69140 AAW	AZBLS	10//99-12//99
	Phoenix-Mesa MSA, AZ	S	34.39 MW	35.03 AW	71530 AAW	AZBLS	10//99-12//99
	Tucson MSA, AZ	S	29.74 MW	27.98 AW	61860 AAW	AZBLS	10//99-12//99
	Arkansas	S	24.65 MW	26.26 AW	54610 AAW	ARBLS	10//99-12//99
	Fayetteville-Springdale-Rogers MSA, AR	S	28.71 MW	27.61 AW	59710 AAW	ARBLS	10//99-12//99
	Fort Smith MSA, AR-OK	S	27.23 MW	25.30 AW	56640 AAW	ARBLS	10//99-12//99
	Jonesboro MSA, AR	S	27.36 MW	24.91 AW	56910 AAW	ARBLS	10//99-12//99
	Little Rock-North Little Rock MSA, AR	S	27.53 MW	26.56 AW	57270 AAW	ARBLS	10//99-12//99
	California	S	31.14 MW	31.40 AW	65300 AAW	CABLS	10//99-12//99
	Bakersfield MSA, CA	S	28.27 MW	25.79 AW	58800 AAW	CABLS	10//99-12//99
	Chico-Paradise MSA, CA	S	23.45 MW	22.61 AW	48770 AAW	CABLS	10//99-12//99
	Fresno MSA, CA	S	25.82 MW	26.09 AW	53710 AAW	CABLS	10//99-12//99
	Los Angeles-Long Beach PMSA, CA	S	29.90 MW	29.67 AW	62190 AAW	CABLS	10//99-12//99
	Merced MSA, CA	S	28.60 MW	29.67 AW	59490 AAW	CABLS	10//99-12//99
	Modesto MSA, CA	S	26.10 MW	25.47 AW	54280 AAW	CABLS	10//99-12//99
	Oakland PMSA, CA	S	33.17 MW	33.18 AW	68990 AAW	CABLS	10//99-12//99
	Orange County PMSA, CA	S	31.08 MW	31.03 AW	64640 AAW	CABLS	10//99-12//99
	Redding MSA, CA	S	22.90 MW	22.71 AW	47630 AAW	CABLS	10//99-12//99
	Riverside-San Bernardino PMSA, CA	S	28.55 MW	27.73 AW	59380 AAW	CABLS	10//99-12//99
	Sacramento PMSA, CA	S	28.15 MW	25.33 AW	58560 AAW	CABLS	10//99-12//99
	Salinas MSA, CA	S	27.82 MW	28.23 AW	57870 AAW	CABLS	10//99-12//99
	San Diego MSA, CA	S	28.92 MW	27.19 AW	60150 AAW	CABLS	10//99-12//99
	San Francisco PMSA, CA	S	33.68 MW	32.65 AW	70050 AAW	CABLS	10//99-12//99
	San Jose PMSA, CA	S	39.07 MW	40.22 AW	81260 AAW	CABLS	10//99-12//99
	San Luis Obispo-Atascadero-Paso Robles MSA, CA	S	29.10 MW	26.27 AW	60520 AAW	CABLS	10//99-12//99
	Santa Barbara-Santa Maria-Lompoc MSA, CA	S	27.68 MW	27.50 AW	57570 AAW	CABLS	10//99-12//99
	Santa Cruz-Watsonville PMSA, CA	S	27.08 MW	27.50 AW	56320 AAW	CABLS	10//99-12//99
	Santa Rosa PMSA, CA	S	28.63 MW	25.41 AW	59540 AAW	CABLS	10//99-12//99
	Stockton-Lodi MSA, CA	S	27.98 MW	27.39 AW	58190 AAW	CABLS	10//99-12//99
	Vallejo-Fairfield-Napa PMSA, CA	S	28.86 MW	28.34 AW	60030 AAW	CABLS	10//99-12//99
	Ventura PMSA, CA	S	30.98 MW	31.35 AW	64430 AAW	CABLS	10//99-12//99
	Visalia-Tulare-Porterville MSA, CA	S	30.17 MW	26.97 AW	62760 AAW	CABLS	10//99-12//99
	Yolo PMSA, CA	S	29.63 MW	27.41 AW	61630 AAW	CABLS	10//99-12//99
	Yuba City MSA, CA	S	23.80 MW	22.29 AW	49490 AAW	CABLS	10//99-12//99
	Colorado	S	28.63 MW	29.34 AW	61020 AAW	COBLS	10//99-12//99
	Boulder-Longmont PMSA, CO	S	33.32 MW	33.77 AW	69300 AAW	COBLS	10//99-12//99
	Colorado Springs MSA, CO	S	34.67 MW	35.16 AW	72110 AAW	COBLS	10//99-12//99
	Denver PMSA, CO	S	28.94 MW	28.45 AW	60200 AAW	COBLS	10//99-12//99
	Fort Collins-Loveland MSA, CO	S	25.19 MW	21.21 AW	52400 AAW	COBLS	10//99-12//99
	Grand Junction MSA, CO	S	24.21 MW	21.79 AW	50360 AAW	COBLS	10//99-12//99
	Greeley PMSA, CO	S	27.40 MW	26.28 AW	57000 AAW	COBLS	10//99-12//99
	Connecticut	S	33.21 MW	33.34 AW	69350 AAW	CTBLS	10//99-12//99
	Bridgeport PMSA, CT	S	34.42 MW	35.00 AW	71590 AAW	CTBLS	10//99-12//99
	Danbury PMSA, CT	S	35.00 MW	34.50 AW	72790 AAW	CTBLS	10//99-12//99
	Hartford MSA, CT	S	33.54 MW	33.46 AW	69770 AAW	CTBLS	10//99-12//99
	New Haven-Meriden PMSA, CT	S	31.25 MW	30.31 AW	65010 AAW	CTBLS	10//99-12//99
	New London-Norwich MSA, CT-RI	S	28.38 MW	29.56 AW	59030 AAW	CTBLS	10//99-12//99
	Stamford-Norwalk PMSA, CT	S	38.71 MW	39.43 AW	80510 AAW	CTBLS	10//99-12//99
	Waterbury PMSA, CT	S	31.44 MW	29.72 AW	65390 AAW	CTBLS	10//99-12//99
	Delaware	S	37.32 MW	36.84 AW	76620 AAW	DEBLS	10//99-12//99
	Dover MSA, DE	S	33.05 MW	32.52 AW	68750 AAW	DEBLS	10//99-12//99
	Wilmington-Newark PMSA, DE-MD	S	38.67 MW	39.06 AW	80430 AAW	DEBLS	10//99-12//99

AAW	Average annual wage	AOH	Average offered, high	ASH	Average starting, high
AE	Average entry wage	AOL	Average offered, low	ASL	Average starting, low
AEX	Average experienced wage	APH	Average pay, high range	AW	Average wage paid
AO	Average offered	APL	Average pay, low range	FQ	First quartile wage

H	Hourly	M	Monthly	S	Special: hourly and annual
HI	Highest wage paid	MTC	Median total compensation	TQ	Third quartile wage
HR	High end range	MW	Median wage paid	W	Weekly
LR	Low end range	SQ	Second quartile wage	Y	Yearly

Occupation/Type/Industry	Location	Per	Low	Mid	High	Source	Date
Industrial Production Manager	District of Columbia	S	28.1 MW	30.65 AW	63760 AAW	DCBLS	10//99-12//99
	Washington PMSA, DC-MD-VA-WV	S	31.01 MW	31.17 AW	64500 AAW	DCBLS	10//99-12//99
	Florida	S	23.94 MW	25.64 AW	53330 AAW	FLBLS	10//99-12//99
	Daytona Beach MSA, FL	S	23.39 MW	22.75 AW	48660 AAW	FLBLS	10//99-12//99
	Fort Lauderdale PMSA, FL	S	25.33 MW	22.46 AW	52680 AAW	FLBLS	10//99-12//99
	Fort Myers-Cape Coral MSA, FL	S	17.01 MW	13.41 AW	35370 AAW	FLBLS	10//99-12//99
	Fort Pierce-Port St. Lucie MSA, FL	S	23.78 MW	22.89 AW	49470 AAW	FLBLS	10//99-12//99
	Gainesville MSA, FL	S	23.18 MW	20.01 AW	48220 AAW	FLBLS	10//99-12//99
	Jacksonville MSA, FL	S	26.66 MW	26.17 AW	55440 AAW	FLBLS	10//99-12//99
	Lakeland-Winter Haven MSA, FL	S	25.81 MW	24.91 AW	53690 AAW	FLBLS	10//99-12//99
	Melbourne-Titusville-Palm Bay MSA, FL	S	25.30 MW	22.60 AW	52620 AAW	FLBLS	10//99-12//99
	Miami PMSA, FL	S	24.63 MW	23.10 AW	51230 AAW	FLBLS	10//99-12//99
	Ocala MSA, FL	S	23.47 MW	19.49 AW	48820 AAW	FLBLS	10//99-12//99
	Orlando MSA, FL	S	27.25 MW	25.18 AW	56690 AAW	FLBLS	10//99-12//99
	Panama City MSA, FL	S	26.94 MW	27.17 AW	56040 AAW	FLBLS	10//99-12//99
	Pensacola MSA, FL	S	28.39 MW	23.81 AW	59050 AAW	FLBLS	10//99-12//99
	Sarasota-Bradenton MSA, FL	S	25.39 MW	24.57 AW	52810 AAW	FLBLS	10//99-12//99
	Tallahassee MSA, FL	S	24.71 MW	23.91 AW	51400 AAW	FLBLS	10//99-12//99
	Tampa-St. Petersburg-Clearwater MSA, FL	S	26.20 MW	24.51 AW	54500 AAW	FLBLS	10//99-12//99
	West Palm Beach-Boca Raton MSA, FL	S	26.99 MW	22.53 AW	56130 AAW	FLBLS	10//99-12//99
	Georgia	S	23.16 MW	25.66 AW	53380 AAW	GABLS	10//99-12//99
	Albany MSA, GA	S	25.93 MW	20.50 AW	53940 AAW	GABLS	10//99-12//99
	Athens MSA, GA	S	26.23 MW	25.09 AW	54570 AAW	GABLS	10//99-12//99
	Atlanta MSA, GA	S	27.09 MW	24.08 AW	56360 AAW	GABLS	10//99-12//99
	Augusta-Aiken MSA, GA-SC	S	31.75 MW	33.67 AW	66030 AAW	GABLS	10//99-12//99
	Columbus MSA, GA-AL	S	26.79 MW	25.79 AW	55730 AAW	GABLS	10//99-12//99
	Macon MSA, GA	S	23.71 MW	21.46 AW	49320 AAW	GABLS	10//99-12//99
	Savannah MSA, GA	S	25.64 MW	24.32 AW	53340 AAW	GABLS	10//99-12//99
	Hawaii	S	25.87 MW	29.10 AW	60530 AAW	HIBLS	10//99-12//99
	Honolulu MSA, HI	S	29.09 MW	27.00 AW	60500 AAW	HIBLS	10//99-12//99
	Idaho	S	23.33 MW	26.20 AW	54510 AAW	IDBLS	10//99-12//99
	Boise City MSA, ID	S	30.00 MW	29.20 AW	62400 AAW	IDBLS	10//99-12//99
	Illinois	S	27.63 MW	28.72 AW	59730 AAW	ILBLS	10//99-12//99
	Bloomington-Normal MSA, IL	S	30.93 MW	29.65 AW	64330 AAW	ILBLS	10//99-12//99
	Champaign-Urbana MSA, IL	S	27.02 MW	25.73 AW	56200 AAW	ILBLS	10//99-12//99
	Chicago PMSA, IL	S	29.30 MW	28.83 AW	60950 AAW	ILBLS	10//99-12//99
	Decatur MSA, IL	S	25.80 MW	24.10 AW	53670 AAW	ILBLS	10//99-12//99
	Kankakee PMSA, IL	S	24.29 MW	24.32 AW	50520 AAW	ILBLS	10//99-12//99
	Peoria-Pekin MSA, IL	S	29.08 MW	26.57 AW	60490 AAW	ILBLS	10//99-12//99
	Rockford MSA, IL	S	27.74 MW	25.71 AW	57690 AAW	ILBLS	10//99-12//99
	Indiana	S	28.97 MW	29.19 AW	60710 AAW	INBLS	10//99-12//99
	Elkhart-Goshen MSA, IN	S	25.02 MW	23.48 AW	52050 AAW	INBLS	10//99-12//99
	Evansville-Henderson MSA, IN-KY	S	24.08 MW	22.55 AW	50080 AAW	INBLS	10//99-12//99
	Fort Wayne MSA, IN	S	29.12 MW	28.22 AW	60570 AAW	INBLS	10//99-12//99
	Gary PMSA, IN	S	33.67 MW	34.50 AW	70030 AAW	INBLS	10//99-12//99
	Indianapolis MSA, IN	S	30.36 MW	30.43 AW	63150 AAW	INBLS	10//99-12//99
	Lafayette MSA, IN	S	29.48 MW	31.88 AW	61310 AAW	INBLS	10//99-12//99
	Muncie MSA, IN	S	30.18 MW	27.33 AW	62780 AAW	INBLS	10//99-12//99
	South Bend MSA, IN	S	27.15 MW	25.55 AW	56480 AAW	INBLS	10//99-12//99
	Terre Haute MSA, IN	S	34.13 MW	32.69 AW	70980 AAW	INBLS	10//99-12//99
	Iowa	S	25.05 MW	27.27 AW	56710 AAW	IABLS	10//99-12//99
	Davenport-Moline-Rock Island MSA, IA-IL	S	27.10 MW	25.95 AW	56360 AAW	IABLS	10//99-12//99
	Des Moines MSA, IA	S	29.59 MW	31.15 AW	61540 AAW	IABLS	10//99-12//99
	Dubuque MSA, IA	S	21.20 MW	19.93 AW	44100 AAW	IABLS	10//99-12//99
	Sioux City MSA, IA-NE	S	25.94 MW	24.68 AW	53950 AAW	IABLS	10//99-12//99
	Waterloo-Cedar Falls MSA, IA	S	30.53 MW	31.32 AW	63510 AAW	IABLS	10//99-12//99
	Kansas	S	27.63 MW	29.53 AW	61420 AAW	KSBLS	10//99-12//99
	Topeka MSA, KS	S	27.90 MW	25.19 AW	58040 AAW	KSBLS	10//99-12//99
	Wichita MSA, KS	S	33.17 MW	32.81 AW	68990 AAW	KSBLS	10//99-12//99
	Kentucky	S	25.73 MW	27.13 AW	56420 AAW	KYBLS	10//99-12//99
	Lexington MSA, KY	S	29.33 MW	31.08 AW	61000 AAW	KYBLS	10//99-12//99
	Louisville MSA, KY-IN	S	27.90 MW	25.29 AW	58030 AAW	KYBLS	10//99-12//99
	Owensboro MSA, KY	S	27.36 MW	26.90 AW	56910 AAW	KYBLS	10//99-12//99

AAW Average annual wage	**AOH** Average offered, high	**ASH** Average starting, high	**H** Hourly	**M** Monthly	**S** Special: hourly and annual
AE Average entry wage	**AOL** Average offered, low	**ASL** Average starting, low	**HI** Highest wage paid	**MTC** Median total compensation	**TQ** Third quartile wage
AEX Average experienced wage	**APH** Average pay, high range	**AW** Average wage paid	**HR** High end range	**MW** Median wage paid	**W** Weekly
AO Average offered	**APL** Average pay, low range	**FQ** First quartile wage	**LR** Low end range	**SQ** Second quartile wage	**Y** Yearly

Occupation/Type/Industry	Location	Per	Low	Mid	High	Source	Date
Industrial Production Manager	Louisiana	S	28.07 MW	28.77 AW	59850 AAW	LABLS	10//99-12//99
	Baton Rouge MSA, LA	S	31.74 MW	31.76 AW	66030 AAW	LABLS	10//99-12//99
	Houma MSA, LA	S	24.70 MW	24.11 AW	51370 AAW	LABLS	10//99-12//99
	Lafayette MSA, LA	S	22.96 MW	21.83 AW	47760 AAW	LABLS	10//99-12//99
	Lake Charles MSA, LA	S	29.58 MW	27.41 AW	61530 AAW	LABLS	10//99-12//99
	Monroe MSA, LA	S	25.63 MW	25.05 AW	53310 AAW	LABLS	10//99-12//99
	New Orleans MSA, LA	S	29.42 MW	28.56 AW	61190 AAW	LABLS	10//99-12//99
	Shreveport-Bossier City MSA, LA	S	28.00 MW	28.44 AW	58250 AAW	LABLS	10//99-12//99
	Maine	S	24.86 MW	26.24 AW	54570 AAW	MEBLS	10//99-12//99
	Lewiston-Auburn MSA, ME	S	22.39 MW	20.67 AW	46570 AAW	MEBLS	10//99-12//99
	Portland MSA, ME	S	23.87 MW	21.59 AW	49660 AAW	MEBLS	10//99-12//99
	Maryland	S	30.66 MW	29.99 AW	62380 AAW	MDBLS	10//99-12//99
	Baltimore PMSA, MD	S	30.98 MW	31.76 AW	64440 AAW	MDBLS	10//99-12//99
	Hagerstown PMSA, MD	S	31.38 MW	31.92 AW	65260 AAW	MDBLS	10//99-12//99
	Massachusetts	S	32.04 MW	31.84 AW	66220 AAW	MABLS	10//99-12//99
	Boston PMSA, MA-NH	S	32.76 MW	33.46 AW	68150 AAW	MABLS	10//99-12//99
	Brockton PMSA, MA	S	27.20 MW	25.10 AW	56580 AAW	MABLS	10//99-12//99
	Fitchburg-Leominster PMSA, MA	S	28.16 MW	26.94 AW	58570 AAW	MABLS	10//99-12//99
	Lawrence PMSA, MA-NH	S	32.71 MW	32.46 AW	68040 AAW	MABLS	10//99-12//99
	Lowell PMSA, MA-NH	S	32.30 MW	30.35 AW	67190 AAW	MABLS	10//99-12//99
	New Bedford PMSA, MA	S	31.44 MW	33.23 AW	65400 AAW	MABLS	10//99-12//99
	Pittsfield MSA, MA	S	27.81 MW	26.05 AW	57850 AAW	MABLS	10//99-12//99
	Springfield MSA, MA	S	28.47 MW	27.67 AW	59230 AAW	MABLS	10//99-12//99
	Worcester PMSA, MA-CT	S	30.31 MW	30.11 AW	63040 AAW	MABLS	10//99-12//99
	Michigan	S	32.1 MW	32.12 AW	66800 AAW	MIBLS	10//99-12//99
	Ann Arbor PMSA, MI	S	33.19 MW	33.51 AW	69040 AAW	MIBLS	10//99-12//99
	Benton Harbor MSA, MI	S	27.56 MW	25.61 AW	57320 AAW	MIBLS	10//99-12//99
	Detroit PMSA, MI	S	34.29 MW	34.55 AW	71320 AAW	MIBLS	10//99-12//99
	Grand Rapids-Muskegon-Holland MSA, MI	S	29.75 MW	28.53 AW	61880 AAW	MIBLS	10//99-12//99
	Jackson MSA, MI	S	29.28 MW	26.41 AW	60910 AAW	MIBLS	10//99-12//99
	Kalamazoo-Battle Creek MSA, MI	S	28.57 MW	27.59 AW	59430 AAW	MIBLS	10//99-12//99
	Lansing-East Lansing MSA, MI	S	32.76 MW	33.44 AW	68140 AAW	MIBLS	10//99-12//99
	Saginaw-Bay City-Midland MSA, MI	S	36.98 MW	38.49 AW	76920 AAW	MIBLS	10//99-12//99
	Minnesota	S	29.99 MW	30.45 AW	63340 AAW	MNBLS	10//99-12//99
	Duluth-Superior MSA, MN-WI	S	25.63 MW	23.49 AW	53300 AAW	MNBLS	10//99-12//99
	Minneapolis-St. Paul MSA, MN-WI	S	32.02 MW	31.87 AW	66610 AAW	MNBLS	10//99-12//99
	St. Cloud MSA, MN	S	27.04 MW	24.02 AW	56240 AAW	MNBLS	10//99-12//99
	Mississippi	S	25.05 MW	26.86 AW	55870 AAW	MSBLS	10//99-12//99
	Biloxi-Gulfport-Pascagoula MSA, MS	S	31.42 MW	35.42 AW	65360 AAW	MSBLS	10//99-12//99
	Jackson MSA, MS	S	27.55 MW	25.86 AW	57310 AAW	MSBLS	10//99-12//99
	Missouri	S	26.72 MW	28.18 AW	58610 AAW	MOBLS	10//99-12//99
	Joplin MSA, MO	S	23.89 MW	22.24 AW	49690 AAW	MOBLS	10//99-12//99
	Kansas City MSA, MO-KS	S	28.14 MW	26.28 AW	58540 AAW	MOBLS	10//99-12//99
	St. Joseph MSA, MO	S	28.22 MW	29.98 AW	58710 AAW	MOBLS	10//99-12//99
	St. Louis MSA, MO-IL	S	30.82 MW	30.06 AW	64110 AAW	MOBLS	10//99-12//99
	Springfield MSA, MO	S	23.95 MW	22.09 AW	49810 AAW	MOBLS	10//99-12//99
	Montana	S	20.25 MW	23.11 AW	48070 AAW	MTBLS	10//99-12//99
	Billings MSA, MT	S	30.60 MW	21.08 AW	63640 AAW	MTBLS	10//99-12//99
	Missoula MSA, MT	S	22.33 MW	19.83 AW	46440 AAW	MTBLS	10//99-12//99
	Nebraska	S	25.6 MW	27.34 AW	56870 AAW	NEBLS	10//99-12//99
	Lincoln MSA, NE	S	27.78 MW	27.31 AW	57790 AAW	NEBLS	10//99-12//99
	Omaha MSA, NE-IA	S	29.11 MW	29.56 AW	60550 AAW	NEBLS	10//99-12//99
	Nevada	S	25.5 MW	27.05 AW	56270 AAW	NVBLS	10//99-12//99
	Las Vegas MSA, NV-AZ	S	27.50 MW	27.58 AW	57200 AAW	NVBLS	10//99-12//99
	Reno MSA, NV	S	25.55 MW	23.54 AW	53130 AAW	NVBLS	10//99-12//99
	New Hampshire	S	29.39 MW	29.32 AW	60990 AAW	NHBLS	10//99-12//99
	Manchester PMSA, NH	S	32.39 MW	32.52 AW	67370 AAW	NHBLS	10//99-12//99
	Nashua PMSA, NH	S	30.10 MW	29.89 AW	62600 AAW	NHBLS	10//99-12//99
	Portsmouth-Rochester PMSA, NH-ME	S	31.71 MW	32.38 AW	65970 AAW	NHBLS	10//99-12//99
	New Jersey	S	37.86 MW	37.42 AW	77840 AAW	NJBLS	10//99-12//99
	Atlantic-Cape May PMSA, NJ	S	33.33 MW	33.69 AW	69320 AAW	NJBLS	10//99-12//99
	Bergen-Passaic PMSA, NJ	S	38.49 MW	38.18 AW	80060 AAW	NJBLS	10//99-12//99
	Jersey City PMSA, NJ	S	43.04 MW	42.71 AW	89530 AAW	NJBLS	10//99-12//99
	Monmouth-Ocean PMSA, NJ	S	34.78 MW	33.41 AW	72350 AAW	NJBLS	10//99-12//99

AAW Average annual wage	AOH Average offered, high	ASH Average starting, high	H Hourly	M Monthly	S Special: hourly and annual
AE Average entry wage	AOL Average offered, low	ASL Average starting, low	HI Highest wage paid	MTC Median total compensation	TQ Third quartile wage
AEX Average experienced wage	APH Average pay, high range	AW Average wage paid	HR High end range	MW Median wage paid	W Weekly
AO Average offered	APL Average pay, low range	FQ First quartile wage	LR Low end range	SQ Second quartile wage	Y Yearly

Occupation/Type/Industry	Location	Per	Low	Mid	High	Source	Date
Industrial Production Manager	Newark PMSA, NJ	S	38.70 MW	39.42 AW	80490 AAW	NJBLS	10//99-12//99
	Trenton PMSA, NJ	S	36.96 MW	36.81 AW	76880 AAW	NJBLS	10//99-12//99
	Vineland-Millville-Bridgeton PMSA, NJ	S	32.71 MW	31.73 AW	68030 AAW	NJBLS	10//99-12//99
	New Mexico	S	24.67 MW	27.30 AW	56770 AAW	NMBLS	10//99-12//99
	Albuquerque MSA, NM	S	30.62 MW	30.85 AW	63690 AAW	NMBLS	10//99-12//99
	Santa Fe MSA, NM	S	18.49 MW	18.61 AW	38460 AAW	NMBLS	10//99-12//99
	New York	S	32.17 MW	32.88 AW	68390 AAW	NYBLS	10//99-12//99
	Albany-Schenectady-Troy MSA, NY	S	31.82 MW	30.75 AW	66180 AAW	NYBLS	10//99-12//99
	Binghamton MSA, NY	S	27.86 MW	28.17 AW	57950 AAW	NYBLS	10//99-12//99
	Buffalo-Niagara Falls MSA, NY	S	29.36 MW	27.38 AW	61070 AAW	NYBLS	10//99-12//99
	Elmira MSA, NY	S	29.12 MW	28.48 AW	60570 AAW	NYBLS	10//99-12//99
	Jamestown MSA, NY	S	24.26 MW	23.38 AW	50460 AAW	NYBLS	10//99-12//99
	Nassau-Suffolk PMSA, NY	S	35.16 MW	33.27 AW	73140 AAW	NYBLS	10//99-12//99
	New York PMSA, NY	S	35.36 MW	35.51 AW	73550 AAW	NYBLS	10//99-12//99
	Newburgh PMSA, NY-PA	S	32.91 MW	32.14 AW	68450 AAW	NYBLS	10//99-12//99
	Rochester MSA, NY	S	33.63 MW	35.05 AW	69960 AAW	NYBLS	10//99-12//99
	Syracuse MSA, NY	S	30.67 MW	30.14 AW	63800 AAW	NYBLS	10//99-12//99
	Utica-Rome MSA, NY	S	24.08 MW	19.42 AW	50080 AAW	NYBLS	10//99-12//99
	North Carolina	S	25.51 MW	27.69 AW	57590 AAW	NCBLS	10//99-12//99
	Asheville MSA, NC	S	26.26 MW	24.82 AW	54610 AAW	NCBLS	10//99-12//99
	Charlotte-Gastonia-Rock Hill MSA, NC-SC	S	28.58 MW	26.79 AW	59450 AAW	NCBLS	10//99-12//99
	Goldsboro MSA, NC	S	25.06 MW	24.73 AW	52120 AAW	NCBLS	10//99-12//99
	Greensboro--Winston-Salem--High Point MSA, NC	S	29.69 MW	28.33 AW	61750 AAW	NCBLS	10//99-12//99
	Greenville MSA, NC	S	26.16 MW	23.72 AW	54410 AAW	NCBLS	10//99-12//99
	Hickory-Morganton-Lenoir MSA, NC	S	24.81 MW	22.61 AW	51600 AAW	NCBLS	10//99-12//99
	Raleigh-Durham-Chapel Hill MSA, NC	S	31.92 MW	31.53 AW	66390 AAW	NCBLS	10//99-12//99
	Rocky Mount MSA, NC	S	24.25 MW	21.82 AW	50440 AAW	NCBLS	10//99-12//99
	Wilmington MSA, NC	S	33.88 MW	36.26 AW	70460 AAW	NCBLS	10//99-12//99
	North Dakota	S	24.56 MW	25.63 AW	53320 AAW	NDBLS	10//99-12//99
	Bismarck MSA, ND	S	23.81 MW	19.99 AW	49530 AAW	NDBLS	10//99-12//99
	Fargo-Moorhead MSA, ND-MN	S	24.26 MW	20.11 AW	50460 AAW	NDBLS	10//99-12//99
	Grand Forks MSA, ND-MN	S	23.84 MW	22.50 AW	49580 AAW	NDBLS	10//99-12//99
	Ohio	S	28.14 MW	29.04 AW	60400 AAW	OHBLS	10//99-12//99
	Akron PMSA, OH	S	26.96 MW	26.00 AW	56070 AAW	OHBLS	10//99-12//99
	Canton-Massillon MSA, OH	S	27.39 MW	26.28 AW	56970 AAW	OHBLS	10//99-12//99
	Cincinnati PMSA, OH-KY-IN	S	29.31 MW	29.32 AW	60960 AAW	OHBLS	10//99-12//99
	Cleveland-Lorain-Elyria PMSA, OH	S	28.92 MW	27.70 AW	60150 AAW	OHBLS	10//99-12//99
	Columbus MSA, OH	S	29.74 MW	26.34 AW	61850 AAW	OHBLS	10//99-12//99
	Dayton-Springfield MSA, OH	S	31.82 MW	32.22 AW	66180 AAW	OHBLS	10//99-12//99
	Hamilton-Middletown PMSA, OH	S	30.19 MW	29.09 AW	62790 AAW	OHBLS	10//99-12//99
	Lima MSA, OH	S	27.69 MW	25.34 AW	57600 AAW	OHBLS	10//99-12//99
	Mansfield MSA, OH	S	26.38 MW	24.61 AW	54880 AAW	OHBLS	10//99-12//99
	Steubenville-Weirton MSA, OH-WV	S	27.89 MW	27.08 AW	58010 AAW	OHBLS	10//99-12//99
	Toledo MSA, OH	S	28.32 MW	27.64 AW	58900 AAW	OHBLS	10//99-12//99
	Youngstown-Warren MSA, OH	S	31.14 MW	31.69 AW	64760 AAW	OHBLS	10//99-12//99
	Oklahoma	S	26 MW	26.80 AW	55740 AAW	OKBLS	10//99-12//99
	Oklahoma City MSA, OK	S	27.91 MW	28.24 AW	58050 AAW	OKBLS	10//99-12//99
	Tulsa MSA, OK	S	26.82 MW	25.83 AW	55780 AAW	OKBLS	10//99-12//99
	Oregon	S	28.42 MW	29.61 AW	61590 AAW	ORBLS	10//99-12//99
	Eugene-Springfield MSA, OR	S	27.94 MW	25.72 AW	58120 AAW	ORBLS	10//99-12//99
	Medford-Ashland MSA, OR	S	23.76 MW	23.77 AW	49420 AAW	ORBLS	10//99-12//99
	Portland-Vancouver PMSA, OR-WA	S	30.32 MW	29.35 AW	63060 AAW	ORBLS	10//99-12//99
	Salem PMSA, OR	S	27.43 MW	25.41 AW	57050 AAW	ORBLS	10//99-12//99
	Pennsylvania	S	28.43 MW	29.15 AW	60630 AAW	PABLS	10//99-12//99
	Allentown-Bethlehem-Easton MSA, PA	S	35.04 MW	35.68 AW	72880 AAW	PABLS	10//99-12//99
	Altoona MSA, PA	S	29.84 MW	32.02 AW	62070 AAW	PABLS	10//99-12//99
	Erie MSA, PA	S	24.94 MW	24.18 AW	51880 AAW	PABLS	10//99-12//99
	Harrisburg-Lebanon-Carlisle MSA, PA	S	32.08 MW	31.55 AW	66720 AAW	PABLS	10//99-12//99

AAW Average annual wage	**AOH** Average offered, high	**ASH** Average starting, high	**H** Hourly	**M** Monthly	**S** Special: hourly and annual
AE Average entry wage	**AOL** Average offered, low	**ASL** Average starting, low	**HI** Highest wage paid	**MTC** Median total compensation	**TQ** Third quartile wage
AEX Average experienced wage	**APH** Average pay, high range	**AW** Average wage paid	**HR** High end range	**MW** Median wage paid	**W** Weekly
AO Average offered	**APL** Average pay, low range	**FQ** First quartile wage	**LR** Low end range	**SQ** Second quartile wage	**Y** Yearly

Occupation/Type/Industry	Location	Per	Low	Mid	High	Source	Date
Industrial Production Manager	Johnstown MSA, PA	S	22.86 MW	21.39 AW	47550 AAW	PABLS	10//99-12//99
	Lancaster MSA, PA	S	29.06 MW	26.11 AW	60450 AAW	PABLS	10//99-12//99
	Philadelphia PMSA, PA-NJ	S	31.40 MW	31.32 AW	65310 AAW	PABLS	10//99-12//99
	Pittsburgh MSA, PA	S	29.36 MW	29.18 AW	61070 AAW	PABLS	10//99-12//99
	Reading MSA, PA	S	30.08 MW	29.72 AW	62580 AAW	PABLS	10//99-12//99
	Scranton--Wilkes-Barre-- Hazleton MSA, PA	S	24.49 MW	24.05 AW	50940 AAW	PABLS	10//99-12//99
	Sharon MSA, PA	S	27.71 MW	27.62 AW	57630 AAW	PABLS	10//99-12//99
	State College MSA, PA	S	24.25 MW	20.91 AW	50430 AAW	PABLS	10//99-12//99
	Williamsport MSA, PA	S	23.07 MW	22.86 AW	47980 AAW	PABLS	10//99-12//99
	York MSA, PA	S	27.28 MW	25.43 AW	56750 AAW	PABLS	10//99-12//99
	Rhode Island	S	32.89 MW	32.87 AW	68370 AAW	RIBLS	10//99-12//99
	Providence-Fall River- Warwick MSA, RI-MA	S	32.34 MW	31.97 AW	67260 AAW	RIBLS	10//99-12//99
	South Carolina	S	27.7 MW	28.19 AW	58630 AAW	SCBLS	10//99-12//99
	Charleston-North Charleston MSA, SC	S	29.80 MW	27.63 AW	61990 AAW	SCBLS	10//99-12//99
	Columbia MSA, SC	S	26.04 MW	25.91 AW	54160 AAW	SCBLS	10//99-12//99
	Florence MSA, SC	S	30.92 MW	32.27 AW	64320 AAW	SCBLS	10//99-12//99
	Greenville-Spartanburg- Anderson MSA, SC	S	27.32 MW	26.17 AW	56830 AAW	SCBLS	10//99-12//99
	Myrtle Beach MSA, SC	S	25.83 MW	23.65 AW	53730 AAW	SCBLS	10//99-12//99
	Sumter MSA, SC	S	26.92 MW	25.61 AW	55990 AAW	SCBLS	10//99-12//99
	South Dakota	S	26.19 MW	28.40 AW	59070 AAW	SDBLS	10//99-12//99
	Rapid City MSA, SD	S	26.19 MW	24.63 AW	54470 AAW	SDBLS	10//99-12//99
	Sioux Falls MSA, SD	S	27.45 MW	26.21 AW	57100 AAW	SDBLS	10//99-12//99
	Tennessee	S	24.06 MW	25.52 AW	53080 AAW	TNBLS	10//99-12//99
	Chattanooga MSA, TN-GA	S	24.47 MW	23.29 AW	50900 AAW	TNBLS	10//99-12//99
	Clarksville-Hopkinsville MSA, TN-KY	S	27.45 MW	25.15 AW	57090 AAW	TNBLS	10//99-12//99
	Jackson MSA, TN	S	21.88 MW	19.76 AW	45510 AAW	TNBLS	10//99-12//99
	Johnson City-Kingsport-Bristol MSA, TN-VA	S	26.14 MW	25.33 AW	54370 AAW	TNBLS	10//99-12//99
	Knoxville MSA, TN	S	26.78 MW	25.14 AW	55690 AAW	TNBLS	10//99-12//99
	Memphis MSA, TN-AR-MS	S	24.59 MW	23.49 AW	51150 AAW	MSBLS	10//99-12//99
	Nashville MSA, TN	S	27.01 MW	24.60 AW	56170 AAW	TNBLS	10//99-12//99
	Texas	S	28.97 MW	29.74 AW	61850 AAW	TXBLS	10//99-12//99
	Amarillo MSA, TX	S	21.91 MW	19.11 AW	45580 AAW	TXBLS	10//99-12//99
	Austin-San Marcos MSA, TX	S	29.09 MW	27.51 AW	60510 AAW	TXBLS	10//99-12//99
	Beaumont-Port Arthur MSA, TX	S	37.69 MW	39.77 AW	78400 AAW	TXBLS	10//99-12//99
	Brazoria PMSA, TX	S	34.35 MW	34.64 AW	71450 AAW	TXBLS	10//99-12//99
	Brownsville-Harlingen-San Benito MSA, TX	S	25.35 MW	23.60 AW	52740 AAW	TXBLS	10//99-12//99
	Corpus Christi MSA, TX	S	27.37 MW	25.20 AW	56920 AAW	TXBLS	10//99-12//99
	Dallas PMSA, TX	S	31.65 MW	32.15 AW	65830 AAW	TXBLS	10//99-12//99
	El Paso MSA, TX	S	25.23 MW	23.09 AW	52480 AAW	TXBLS	10//99-12//99
	Fort Worth-Arlington PMSA, TX	S	29.26 MW	29.09 AW	60860 AAW	TXBLS	10//99-12//99
	Houston PMSA, TX	S	31.56 MW	31.00 AW	65640 AAW	TXBLS	10//99-12//99
	Killeen-Temple MSA, TX	S	20.63 MW	20.48 AW	42900 AAW	TXBLS	10//99-12//99
	Longview-Marshall MSA, TX	S	24.76 MW	24.05 AW	51500 AAW	TXBLS	10//99-12//99
	Lubbock MSA, TX	S	23.22 MW	21.11 AW	48300 AAW	TXBLS	10//99-12//99
	McAllen-Edinburg-Mission MSA, TX	S	24.90 MW	24.53 AW	51780 AAW	TXBLS	10//99-12//99
	Odessa-Midland MSA, TX	S	30.19 MW	28.91 AW	62790 AAW	TXBLS	10//99-12//99
	San Antonio MSA, TX	S	27.33 MW	26.50 AW	56840 AAW	TXBLS	10//99-12//99
	Sherman-Denison MSA, TX	S	30.65 MW	29.90 AW	63750 AAW	TXBLS	10//99-12//99
	Texarkana MSA, TX- Texarkana, AR	S	27.76 MW	28.55 AW	57740 AAW	TXBLS	10//99-12//99
	Tyler MSA, TX	S	23.74 MW	21.87 AW	49370 AAW	TXBLS	10//99-12//99
	Waco MSA, TX	S	23.22 MW	20.98 AW	48300 AAW	TXBLS	10//99-12//99
	Wichita Falls MSA, TX	S	28.01 MW	26.33 AW	58260 AAW	TXBLS	10//99-12//99
	Utah	S	24.09 MW	26.20 AW	54490 AAW	UTBLS	10//99-12//99
	Provo-Orem MSA, UT	S	25.46 MW	22.98 AW	52960 AAW	UTBLS	10//99-12//99
	Salt Lake City-Ogden MSA, UT	S	26.49 MW	24.52 AW	55110 AAW	UTBLS	10//99-12//99
	Vermont	S	33.16 MW	32.98 AW	68610 AAW	VTBLS	10//99-12//99
	Burlington MSA, VT	S	35.34 MW	35.46 AW	73510 AAW	VTBLS	10//99-12//99
	Virginia	S	27.78 MW	28.64 AW	59580 AAW	VABLS	10//99-12//99
	Charlottesville MSA, VA	S	26.62 MW	24.97 AW	55370 AAW	VABLS	10//99-12//99
	Danville MSA, VA	S	26.76 MW	24.96 AW	55670 AAW	VABLS	10//99-12//99

AAW Average annual wage	AOH Average offered, high	ASH Average starting, high	H Hourly	M Monthly	S Special: hourly and annual
AE Average entry wage	AOL Average offered, low	ASL Average starting, low	HI Highest wage paid	MTC Median total compensation	TQ Third quartile wage
AEX Average experienced wage	APH Average pay, high range	AW Average wage paid	HR High end range	MW Median wage paid	W Weekly
AO Average offered	APL Average pay, low range	FQ First quartile wage	LR Low end range	SQ Second quartile wage	Y Yearly

Occupation/Type/Industry	Location	Per	Low	Mid	High	Source	Date
Industrial Production Manager	Lynchburg MSA, VA	S	26.55 MW	24.22 AW	55230 AAW	VABLS	10//99-12//99
	Norfolk-Virginia Beach-Newport News MSA, VA-NC	S	28.85 MW	28.71 AW	60010 AAW	VABLS	10//99-12//99
	Richmond-Petersburg MSA, VA	S	29.21 MW	28.36 AW	60760 AAW	VABLS	10//99-12//99
	Roanoke MSA, VA	S	27.84 MW	29.16 AW	57900 AAW	VABLS	10//99-12//99
	Washington	S	30.36 MW	30.45 AW	63340 AAW	WABLS	10//99-12//99
	Bellingham MSA, WA	S	26.16 MW	24.85 AW	54410 AAW	WABLS	10//99-12//99
	Olympia PMSA, WA	S	22.73 MW	20.66 AW	47280 AAW	WABLS	10//99-12//99
	Richland-Kennewick-Pasco MSA, WA	S	29.89 MW	31.29 AW	62160 AAW	WABLS	10//99-12//99
	Seattle-Bellevue-Everett PMSA, WA	S	32.76 MW	33.61 AW	68140 AAW	WABLS	10//99-12//99
	Spokane MSA, WA	S	26.03 MW	24.54 AW	54150 AAW	WABLS	10//99-12//99
	Tacoma PMSA, WA	S	27.55 MW	25.38 AW	57300 AAW	WABLS	10//99-12//99
	Yakima MSA, WA	S	27.02 MW	25.32 AW	56200 AAW	WABLS	10//99-12//99
	West Virginia	S	23.02 MW	24.58 AW	51130 AAW	WVBLS	10//99-12//99
	Charleston MSA, WV	S	25.94 MW	25.64 AW	53960 AAW	WVBLS	10//99-12//99
	Huntington-Ashland MSA, WV-KY-OH	S	27.03 MW	24.48 AW	56220 AAW	WVBLS	10//99-12//99
	Parkersburg-Marietta MSA, WV-OH	S	23.88 MW	22.35 AW	49670 AAW	WVBLS	10//99-12//99
	Wisconsin	S	25.17 MW	26.70 AW	55530 AAW	WIBLS	10//99-12//99
	Appleton-Oshkosh-Neenah MSA, WI	S	28.20 MW	26.92 AW	58650 AAW	WIBLS	10//99-12//99
	Eau Claire MSA, WI	S	28.98 MW	27.98 AW	60280 AAW	WIBLS	10//99-12//99
	Green Bay MSA, WI	S	26.68 MW	25.04 AW	55500 AAW	WIBLS	10//99-12//99
	Janesville-Beloit MSA, WI	S	32.20 MW	32.48 AW	66970 AAW	WIBLS	10//99-12//99
	Kenosha PMSA, WI	S	30.89 MW	32.57 AW	64250 AAW	WIBLS	10//99-12//99
	La Crosse MSA, WI-MN	S	21.55 MW	19.71 AW	44830 AAW	WIBLS	10//99-12//99
	Madison MSA, WI	S	26.03 MW	24.70 AW	54150 AAW	WIBLS	10//99-12//99
	Milwaukee-Waukesha PMSA, WI	S	28.37 MW	27.67 AW	59010 AAW	WIBLS	10//99-12//99
	Sheboygan MSA, WI	S	26.89 MW	26.80 AW	55930 AAW	WIBLS	10//99-12//99
	Wausau MSA, WI	S	22.81 MW	21.38 AW	47440 AAW	WIBLS	10//99-12//99
	Wyoming	S	20.59 MW	21.37 AW	44440 AAW	WYBLS	10//99-12//99
	Puerto Rico	S	28.96 MW	28.35 AW	58980 AAW	PRBLS	10//99-12//99
	Caguas PMSA, PR	S	29.25 MW	29.06 AW	60840 AAW	PRBLS	10//99-12//99
	Mayaguez MSA, PR	S	24.88 MW	25.00 AW	51750 AAW	PRBLS	10//99-12//99
	Ponce MSA, PR	S	22.50 MW	20.69 AW	46800 AAW	PRBLS	10//99-12//99
	San Juan-Bayamon PMSA, PR	S	28.70 MW	29.62 AW	59700 AAW	PRBLS	10//99-12//99
	Virgin Islands	S	23.51 MW	24.88 AW	51740 AAW	VIBLS	10//99-12//99
Industrial Truck and Tractor Operator	Alabama	S	10.56 MW	11.17 AW	23220 AAW	ALBLS	10//99-12//99
	Anniston MSA, AL	S	11.31 MW	11.17 AW	23520 AAW	ALBLS	10//99-12//99
	Auburn-Opelika MSA, AL	S	9.43 MW	9.53 AW	19610 AAW	ALBLS	10//99-12//99
	Birmingham MSA, AL	S	11.38 MW	10.98 AW	23670 AAW	ALBLS	10//99-12//99
	Decatur MSA, AL	S	12.68 MW	12.74 AW	26370 AAW	ALBLS	10//99-12//99
	Dothan MSA, AL	S	8.99 MW	8.62 AW	18690 AAW	ALBLS	10//99-12//99
	Florence MSA, AL	S	11.01 MW	10.18 AW	22900 AAW	ALBLS	10//99-12//99
	Gadsden MSA, AL	S	10.72 MW	10.52 AW	22300 AAW	ALBLS	10//99-12//99
	Huntsville MSA, AL	S	14.01 MW	14.34 AW	29130 AAW	ALBLS	10//99-12//99
	Mobile MSA, AL	S	10.82 MW	10.62 AW	22510 AAW	ALBLS	10//99-12//99
	Montgomery MSA, AL	S	10.19 MW	10.69 AW	21190 AAW	ALBLS	10//99-12//99
	Tuscaloosa MSA, AL	S	11.63 MW	11.16 AW	24180 AAW	ALBLS	10//99-12//99
	Alaska	S	15.3 MW	15.70 AW	32650 AAW	AKBLS	10//99-12//99
	Anchorage MSA, AK	S	16.21 MW	15.76 AW	33720 AAW	AKBLS	10//99-12//99
	Arizona	S	11.33 MW	12.24 AW	25450 AAW	AZBLS	10//99-12//99
	Phoenix-Mesa MSA, AZ	S	12.64 MW	11.68 AW	26300 AAW	AZBLS	10//99-12//99
	Tucson MSA, AZ	S	10.64 MW	10.49 AW	22130 AAW	AZBLS	10//99-12//99
	Yuma MSA, AZ	S	9.92 MW	9.20 AW	20630 AAW	AZBLS	10//99-12//99
	Arkansas	S	9.99 MW	10.35 AW	21530 AAW	ARBLS	10//99-12//99
	Fayetteville-Springdale-Rogers MSA, AR	S	10.09 MW	9.66 AW	20980 AAW	ARBLS	10//99-12//99
	Fort Smith MSA, AR-OK	S	10.29 MW	10.43 AW	21390 AAW	ARBLS	10//99-12//99
	Jonesboro MSA, AR	S	9.78 MW	9.83 AW	20340 AAW	ARBLS	10//99-12//99
	Little Rock-North Little Rock MSA, AR	S	10.33 MW	9.75 AW	21480 AAW	ARBLS	10//99-12//99
	Pine Bluff MSA, AR	S	11.07 MW	10.37 AW	23030 AAW	ARBLS	10//99-12//99
	California	S	11.5 MW	12.31 AW	25600 AAW	CABLS	10//99-12//99

AAW	Average annual wage	AOH	Average offered, high	ASH	Average starting, high
AE	Average entry wage	AOL	Average offered, low	ASL	Average starting, low
AEX	Average experienced wage	APH	Average pay, high range	AW	Average wage paid
AO	Average offered	APL	Average pay, low range	FQ	First quartile wage

H	Hourly	M	Monthly
HI	Highest wage paid	MTC	Median total compensation
HR	High end range	MW	Median wage paid
LR	Low end range	SQ	Second quartile wage

S	Special: hourly and annual
TQ	Third quartile wage
W	Weekly
Y	Yearly

Occupation/Type/Industry	Location	Per	Low	Mid	High	Source	Date
Industrial Truck and Tractor Operator							
	Bakersfield MSA, CA	S	11.14 MW	11.03 AW	23160 AAW	CABLS	10//99-12//99
	Chico-Paradise MSA, CA	S	13.25 MW	13.59 AW	27550 AAW	CABLS	10//99-12//99
	Fresno MSA, CA	S	10.90 MW	10.79 AW	22680 AAW	CABLS	10//99-12//99
	Los Angeles-Long Beach PMSA, CA	S	11.57 MW	10.63 AW	24070 AAW	CABLS	10//99-12//99
	Merced MSA, CA	S	11.76 MW	11.47 AW	24450 AAW	CABLS	10//99-12//99
	Modesto MSA, CA	S	12.23 MW	11.53 AW	25450 AAW	CABLS	10//99-12//99
	Oakland PMSA, CA	S	13.80 MW	13.39 AW	28700 AAW	CABLS	10//99-12//99
	Orange County PMSA, CA	S	12.68 MW	11.78 AW	26380 AAW	CABLS	10//99-12//99
	Redding MSA, CA	S	12.36 MW	12.39 AW	25720 AAW	CABLS	10//99-12//99
	Riverside-San Bernardino PMSA, CA	S	12.45 MW	11.61 AW	25910 AAW	CABLS	10//99-12//99
	Sacramento PMSA, CA	S	11.79 MW	11.40 AW	24510 AAW	CABLS	10//99-12//99
	Salinas MSA, CA	S	17.14 MW	14.91 AW	35660 AAW	CABLS	10//99-12//99
	San Diego MSA, CA	S	12.37 MW	10.89 AW	25730 AAW	CABLS	10//99-12//99
	San Francisco PMSA, CA	S	15.91 MW	14.54 AW	33090 AAW	CABLS	10//99-12//99
	San Jose PMSA, CA	S	13.45 MW	14.07 AW	27970 AAW	CABLS	10//99-12//99
	San Luis Obispo-Atascadero-Paso Robles MSA, CA	S	12.56 MW	12.42 AW	26130 AAW	CABLS	10//99-12//99
	Santa Barbara-Santa Maria-Lompoc MSA, CA	S	13.43 MW	13.46 AW	27920 AAW	CABLS	10//99-12//99
	Santa Cruz-Watsonville PMSA, CA	S	12.27 MW	11.96 AW	25520 AAW	CABLS	10//99-12//99
	Santa Rosa PMSA, CA	S	12.86 MW	12.47 AW	26740 AAW	CABLS	10//99-12//99
	Stockton-Lodi MSA, CA	S	12.61 MW	12.44 AW	26220 AAW	CABLS	10//99-12//99
	Vallejo-Fairfield-Napa PMSA, CA	S	13.25 MW	13.14 AW	27560 AAW	CABLS	10//99-12//99
	Ventura PMSA, CA	S	10.73 MW	9.76 AW	22330 AAW	CABLS	10//99-12//99
	Visalia-Tulare-Porterville MSA, CA	S	10.28 MW	8.79 AW	21390 AAW	CABLS	10//99-12//99
	Yolo PMSA, CA	S	12.88 MW	11.88 AW	26800 AAW	CABLS	10//99-12//99
	Yuba City MSA, CA	S	11.43 MW	11.30 AW	23780 AAW	CABLS	10//99-12//99
	Colorado	S	11.93 MW	12.28 AW	25540 AAW	COBLS	10//99-12//99
	Boulder-Longmont PMSA, CO	S	11.73 MW	11.94 AW	24410 AAW	COBLS	10//99-12//99
	Colorado Springs MSA, CO	S	11.15 MW	10.67 AW	23200 AAW	COBLS	10//99-12//99
	Denver PMSA, CO	S	12.92 MW	12.60 AW	26880 AAW	COBLS	10//99-12//99
	Fort Collins-Loveland MSA, CO	S	11.13 MW	10.17 AW	23140 AAW	COBLS	10//99-12//99
	Grand Junction MSA, CO	S	11.69 MW	11.05 AW	24320 AAW	COBLS	10//99-12//99
	Greeley PMSA, CO	S	10.53 MW	10.01 AW	21900 AAW	COBLS	10//99-12//99
	Pueblo MSA, CO	S	9.97 MW	9.29 AW	20730 AAW	COBLS	10//99-12//99
	Connecticut	S	13.63 MW	14.04 AW	29200 AAW	CTBLS	10//99-12//99
	Bridgeport PMSA, CT	S	14.07 MW	13.69 AW	29270 AAW	CTBLS	10//99-12//99
	Danbury PMSA, CT	S	14.06 MW	14.31 AW	29240 AAW	CTBLS	10//99-12//99
	Hartford MSA, CT	S	15.04 MW	13.96 AW	31290 AAW	CTBLS	10//99-12//99
	New Haven-Meriden PMSA, CT	S	13.46 MW	13.51 AW	28000 AAW	CTBLS	10//99-12//99
	New London-Norwich MSA, CT-RI	S	11.55 MW	10.50 AW	24020 AAW	CTBLS	10//99-12//99
	Stamford-Norwalk PMSA, CT	S	14.47 MW	14.87 AW	30100 AAW	CTBLS	10//99-12//99
	Waterbury PMSA, CT	S	12.57 MW	12.64 AW	26140 AAW	CTBLS	10//99-12//99
	Delaware	S	12.62 MW	13.31 AW	27670 AAW	DEBLS	10//99-12//99
	Dover MSA, DE	S	12.51 MW	11.03 AW	26030 AAW	DEBLS	10//99-12//99
	Wilmington-Newark PMSA, DE-MD	S	14.50 MW	14.17 AW	30160 AAW	DEBLS	10//99-12//99
	Washington PMSA, DC-MD-VA-WV	S	13.02 MW	12.69 AW	27080 AAW	DCBLS	10//99-12//99
	Florida	S	10.13 MW	11.03 AW	22940 AAW	FLBLS	10//99-12//99
	Daytona Beach MSA, FL	S	10.20 MW	9.52 AW	21210 AAW	FLBLS	10//99-12//99
	Fort Lauderdale PMSA, FL	S	11.43 MW	10.75 AW	23780 AAW	FLBLS	10//99-12//99
	Fort Myers-Cape Coral MSA, FL	S	10.50 MW	10.16 AW	21840 AAW	FLBLS	10//99-12//99
	Fort Pierce-Port St. Lucie MSA, FL	S	8.98 MW	8.44 AW	18680 AAW	FLBLS	10//99-12//99
	Fort Walton Beach MSA, FL	S	14.92 MW	14.11 AW	31030 AAW	FLBLS	10//99-12//99
	Gainesville MSA, FL	S	10.23 MW	9.93 AW	21270 AAW	FLBLS	10//99-12//99
	Jacksonville MSA, FL	S	12.07 MW	10.22 AW	25100 AAW	FLBLS	10//99-12//99
	Lakeland-Winter Haven MSA, FL	S	10.36 MW	9.93 AW	21550 AAW	FLBLS	10//99-12//99
	Melbourne-Titusville-Palm Bay MSA, FL	S	10.22 MW	10.43 AW	21270 AAW	FLBLS	10//99-12//99

Occupation/Type/Industry	Location	Per	Low	Mid	High	Source	Date
Industrial Truck and Tractor Operator							
	Miami PMSA, FL	S	10.46 MW	9.69 AW	21760 AAW	FLBLS	10//99-12//99
	Naples MSA, FL	S	8.70 MW	8.12 AW	18100 AAW	FLBLS	10//99-12//99
	Ocala MSA, FL	S	11.59 MW	10.24 AW	24110 AAW	FLBLS	10//99-12//99
	Orlando MSA, FL	S	11.71 MW	10.60 AW	24360 AAW	FLBLS	10//99-12//99
	Panama City MSA, FL	S	13.03 MW	12.96 AW	27090 AAW	FLBLS	10//99-12//99
	Pensacola MSA, FL	S	9.47 MW	9.10 AW	19700 AAW	FLBLS	10//99-12//99
	Sarasota-Bradenton MSA, FL	S	10.01 MW	9.79 AW	20830 AAW	FLBLS	10//99-12//99
	Tallahassee MSA, FL	S	9.98 MW	10.04 AW	20760 AAW	FLBLS	10//99-12//99
	Tampa-St. Petersburg-Clearwater MSA, FL	S	10.98 MW	10.37 AW	22830 AAW	FLBLS	10//99-12//99
	West Palm Beach-Boca Raton MSA, FL	S	11.54 MW	10.48 AW	23990 AAW	FLBLS	10//99-12//99
	Georgia	S	10.41 MW	10.86 AW	22590 AAW	GABLS	10//99-12//99
	Albany MSA, GA	S	10.58 MW	9.98 AW	22010 AAW	GABLS	10//99-12//99
	Athens MSA, GA	S	10.17 MW	10.14 AW	21160 AAW	GABLS	10//99-12//99
	Atlanta MSA, GA	S	11.55 MW	11.14 AW	24020 AAW	GABLS	10//99-12//99
	Augusta-Aiken MSA, GA-SC	S	10.85 MW	9.95 AW	22580 AAW	GABLS	10//99-12//99
	Columbus MSA, GA-AL	S	9.97 MW	9.72 AW	20730 AAW	GABLS	10//99-12//99
	Macon MSA, GA	S	9.70 MW	9.37 AW	20170 AAW	GABLS	10//99-12//99
	Savannah MSA, GA	S	10.62 MW	10.32 AW	22100 AAW	GABLS	10//99-12//99
	Hawaii	S	12.63 MW	13.86 AW	28830 AAW	HIBLS	10//99-12//99
	Honolulu MSA, HI	S	14.15 MW	12.63 AW	29420 AAW	HIBLS	10//99-12//99
	Idaho	S	10.96 MW	11.13 AW	23140 AAW	IDBLS	10//99-12//99
	Boise City MSA, ID	S	10.84 MW	10.91 AW	22550 AAW	IDBLS	10//99-12//99
	Illinois	S	11.98 MW	12.68 AW	26370 AAW	ILBLS	10//99-12//99
	Bloomington-Normal MSA, IL	S	12.45 MW	12.55 AW	25900 AAW	ILBLS	10//99-12//99
	Champaign-Urbana MSA, IL	S	11.87 MW	11.71 AW	24700 AAW	ILBLS	10//99-12//99
	Chicago PMSA, IL	S	13.05 MW	12.46 AW	27140 AAW	ILBLS	10//99-12//99
	Decatur MSA, IL	S	12.07 MW	11.43 AW	25100 AAW	ILBLS	10//99-12//99
	Kankakee PMSA, IL	S	11.16 MW	10.67 AW	23220 AAW	ILBLS	10//99-12//99
	Peoria-Pekin MSA, IL	S	11.16 MW	10.06 AW	23220 AAW	ILBLS	10//99-12//99
	Rockford MSA, IL	S	12.64 MW	12.57 AW	26290 AAW	ILBLS	10//99-12//99
	Springfield MSA, IL	S	11.22 MW	10.26 AW	23340 AAW	ILBLS	10//99-12//99
	Indiana	S	11.85 MW	12.74 AW	26500 AAW	INBLS	10//99-12//99
	Elkhart-Goshen MSA, IN	S	11.35 MW	11.13 AW	23600 AAW	INBLS	10//99-12//99
	Evansville-Henderson MSA, IN-KY	S	12.60 MW	12.44 AW	26210 AAW	INBLS	10//99-12//99
	Fort Wayne MSA, IN	S	12.79 MW	12.35 AW	26600 AAW	INBLS	10//99-12//99
	Gary PMSA, IN	S	14.26 MW	13.15 AW	29660 AAW	INBLS	10//99-12//99
	Indianapolis MSA, IN	S	13.58 MW	12.44 AW	28250 AAW	INBLS	10//99-12//99
	Kokomo MSA, IN	S	19.18 MW	21.83 AW	39900 AAW	INBLS	10//99-12//99
	Lafayette MSA, IN	S	11.60 MW	11.83 AW	24140 AAW	INBLS	10//99-12//99
	Muncie MSA, IN	S	14.38 MW	15.12 AW	29920 AAW	INBLS	10//99-12//99
	South Bend MSA, IN	S	11.73 MW	11.27 AW	24400 AAW	INBLS	10//99-12//99
	Terre Haute MSA, IN	S	15.04 MW	13.62 AW	31270 AAW	INBLS	10//99-12//99
	Iowa	S	11.74 MW	12.09 AW	25150 AAW	IABLS	10//99-12//99
	Cedar Rapids MSA, IA	S	13.36 MW	13.19 AW	27780 AAW	IABLS	10//99-12//99
	Davenport-Moline-Rock Island MSA, IA-IL	S	11.37 MW	10.04 AW	23640 AAW	IABLS	10//99-12//99
	Des Moines MSA, IA	S	12.54 MW	12.17 AW	26080 AAW	IABLS	10//99-12//99
	Dubuque MSA, IA	S	10.29 MW	10.10 AW	21410 AAW	IABLS	10//99-12//99
	Sioux City MSA, IA-NE	S	10.39 MW	10.20 AW	21610 AAW	IABLS	10//99-12//99
	Waterloo-Cedar Falls MSA, IA	S	12.54 MW	11.84 AW	26080 AAW	IABLS	10//99-12//99
	Kansas	S	10.94 MW	11.68 AW	24290 AAW	KSBLS	10//99-12//99
	Lawrence MSA, KS	S	11.47 MW	11.08 AW	23850 AAW	KSBLS	10//99-12//99
	Topeka MSA, KS	S	12.31 MW	11.98 AW	25610 AAW	KSBLS	10//99-12//99
	Wichita MSA, KS	S	16.44 MW	11.96 AW	34200 AAW	KSBLS	10//99-12//99
	Kentucky	S	11.11 MW	11.56 AW	24050 AAW	KYBLS	10//99-12//99
	Lexington MSA, KY	S	11.27 MW	10.86 AW	23430 AAW	KYBLS	10//99-12//99
	Louisville MSA, KY-IN	S	12.17 MW	11.11 AW	25310 AAW	KYBLS	10//99-12//99
	Owensboro MSA, KY	S	12.68 MW	12.13 AW	26380 AAW	KYBLS	10//99-12//99
	Louisiana	S	10.15 MW	11.12 AW	23120 AAW	LABLS	10//99-12//99
	Alexandria MSA, LA	S	9.55 MW	8.66 AW	19870 AAW	LABLS	10//99-12//99
	Baton Rouge MSA, LA	S	11.12 MW	10.15 AW	23120 AAW	LABLS	10//99-12//99
	Houma MSA, LA	S	9.17 MW	8.91 AW	19070 AAW	LABLS	10//99-12//99
	Lafayette MSA, LA	S	9.33 MW	9.32 AW	19400 AAW	LABLS	10//99-12//99
	Lake Charles MSA, LA	S	8.90 MW	8.57 AW	18510 AAW	LABLS	10//99-12//99
	Monroe MSA, LA	S	12.79 MW	10.45 AW	26590 AAW	LABLS	10//99-12//99
	New Orleans MSA, LA	S	13.66 MW	12.24 AW	28400 AAW	LABLS	10//99-12//99
	Shreveport-Bossier City MSA, LA	S	10.06 MW	9.97 AW	20920 AAW	LABLS	10//99-12//99

AAW Average annual wage	**AOH** Average offered, high	**ASH** Average starting, high	**H** Hourly	**M** Monthly	**S** Special: hourly and annual
AE Average entry wage	**AOL** Average offered, low	**ASL** Average starting, low	**HI** Highest wage paid	**MTC** Median total compensation	**TQ** Third quartile wage
AEX Average experienced wage	**APH** Average pay, high range	**AW** Average wage paid	**HR** High end range	**MW** Median wage paid	**W** Weekly
AO Average offered	**APL** Average pay, low range	**FQ** First quartile wage	**LR** Low end range	**SQ** Second quartile wage	**Y** Yearly

Occupation/Type/Industry	Location	Per	Low	Mid	High	Source	Date
Industrial Truck and Tractor Operator							
	Maine	S	10.53 MW	11.30 AW	23500 AAW	MEBLS	10//99-12//99
	Bangor MSA, ME	S	9.28 MW	9.35 AW	19300 AAW	MEBLS	10//99-12//99
	Lewiston-Auburn MSA, ME	S	10.41 MW	10.39 AW	21660 AAW	MEBLS	10//99-12//99
	Portland MSA, ME	S	11.97 MW	11.34 AW	24900 AAW	MEBLS	10//99-12//99
	Maryland	S	12.55 MW	12.91 AW	26850 AAW	MDBLS	10//99-12//99
	Baltimore PMSA, MD	S	12.87 MW	12.42 AW	26770 AAW	MDBLS	10//99-12//99
	Cumberland MSA, MD-WV	S	14.19 MW	15.18 AW	29510 AAW	MDBLS	10//99-12//99
	Hagerstown PMSA, MD	S	11.67 MW	10.82 AW	24260 AAW	MDBLS	10//99-12//99
	Massachusetts	S	12.86 MW	13.02 AW	27080 AAW	MABLS	10//99-12//99
	Barnstable-Yarmouth MSA, MA	S	14.78 MW	15.08 AW	30750 AAW	MABLS	10//99-12//99
	Boston PMSA, MA-NH	S	13.29 MW	13.29 AW	27650 AAW	MABLS	10//99-12//99
	Brockton PMSA, MA	S	12.34 MW	11.89 AW	25660 AAW	MABLS	10//99-12//99
	Fitchburg-Leominster PMSA, MA	S	13.62 MW	13.02 AW	28330 AAW	MABLS	10//99-12//99
	Lawrence PMSA, MA-NH	S	12.89 MW	12.65 AW	26820 AAW	MABLS	10//99-12//99
	Lowell PMSA, MA-NH	S	12.82 MW	12.45 AW	26670 AAW	MABLS	10//99-12//99
	New Bedford PMSA, MA	S	12.87 MW	13.39 AW	26760 AAW	MABLS	10//99-12//99
	Pittsfield MSA, MA	S	14.17 MW	14.33 AW	29470 AAW	MABLS	10//99-12//99
	Springfield MSA, MA	S	12.61 MW	12.51 AW	26230 AAW	MABLS	10//99-12//99
	Worcester PMSA, MA-CT	S	12.55 MW	12.51 AW	26110 AAW	MABLS	10//99-12//99
	Michigan	S	15.06 MW	16.37 AW	34050 AAW	MIBLS	10//99-12//99
	Ann Arbor PMSA, MI	S	16.49 MW	17.22 AW	34290 AAW	MIBLS	10//99-12//99
	Benton Harbor MSA, MI	S	10.83 MW	10.75 AW	22530 AAW	MIBLS	10//99-12//99
	Detroit PMSA, MI	S	18.23 MW	20.55 AW	37930 AAW	MIBLS	10//99-12//99
	Grand Rapids-Muskegon-Holland MSA, MI	S	13.54 MW	12.36 AW	28160 AAW	MIBLS	10//99-12//99
	Jackson MSA, MI	S	11.24 MW	11.13 AW	23380 AAW	MIBLS	10//99-12//99
	Kalamazoo-Battle Creek MSA, MI	S	16.34 MW	14.85 AW	33980 AAW	MIBLS	10//99-12//99
	Lansing-East Lansing MSA, MI	S	16.11 MW	16.24 AW	33520 AAW	MIBLS	10//99-12//99
	Saginaw-Bay City-Midland MSA, MI	S	18.56 MW	20.91 AW	38610 AAW	MIBLS	10//99-12//99
	Minnesota	S	12.45 MW	12.79 AW	26600 AAW	MNBLS	10//99-12//99
	Duluth-Superior MSA, MN-WI	S	12.24 MW	12.10 AW	25460 AAW	MNBLS	10//99-12//99
	Minneapolis-St. Paul MSA, MN-WI	S	13.46 MW	13.11 AW	27990 AAW	MNBLS	10//99-12//99
	Rochester MSA, MN	S	12.64 MW	12.60 AW	26290 AAW	MNBLS	10//99-12//99
	St. Cloud MSA, MN	S	12.92 MW	12.62 AW	26880 AAW	MNBLS	10//99-12//99
	Mississippi	S	10.02 MW	10.26 AW	21330 AAW	MSBLS	10//99-12//99
	Biloxi-Gulfport-Pascagoula MSA, MS	S	10.66 MW	8.68 AW	22160 AAW	MSBLS	10//99-12//99
	Hattiesburg MSA, MS	S	10.03 MW	9.84 AW	20870 AAW	MSBLS	10//99-12//99
	Jackson MSA, MS	S	11.03 MW	10.52 AW	22950 AAW	MSBLS	10//99-12//99
	Missouri	S	10.72 MW	11.68 AW	24300 AAW	MOBLS	10//99-12//99
	Columbia MSA, MO	S	11.18 MW	11.28 AW	23250 AAW	MOBLS	10//99-12//99
	Joplin MSA, MO	S	13.85 MW	13.72 AW	28800 AAW	MOBLS	10//99-12//99
	Kansas City MSA, MO-KS	S	11.94 MW	11.38 AW	24840 AAW	MOBLS	10//99-12//99
	St. Joseph MSA, MO	S	12.02 MW	12.19 AW	24990 AAW	MOBLS	10//99-12//99
	St. Louis MSA, MO-IL	S	12.74 MW	12.02 AW	26500 AAW	MOBLS	10//99-12//99
	Springfield MSA, MO	S	10.35 MW	9.98 AW	21520 AAW	MOBLS	10//99-12//99
	Montana	S	12.06 MW	11.73 AW	24400 AAW	MTBLS	10//99-12//99
	Billings MSA, MT	S	12.19 MW	11.81 AW	25350 AAW	MTBLS	10//99-12//99
	Missoula MSA, MT	S	10.59 MW	11.29 AW	22030 AAW	MTBLS	10//99-12//99
	Nebraska	S	10.71 MW	11.36 AW	23630 AAW	NEBLS	10//99-12//99
	Lincoln MSA, NE	S	11.89 MW	11.59 AW	24720 AAW	NEBLS	10//99-12//99
	Omaha MSA, NE-IA	S	12.10 MW	11.59 AW	25170 AAW	NEBLS	10//99-12//99
	Nevada	S	12.76 MW	13.39 AW	27860 AAW	NVBLS	10//99-12//99
	Las Vegas MSA, NV-AZ	S	13.41 MW	13.41 AW	27900 AAW	NVBLS	10//99-12//99
	Reno MSA, NV	S	13.22 MW	11.68 AW	27500 AAW	NVBLS	10//99-12//99
	New Hampshire	S	11.8 MW	11.57 AW	24080 AAW	NHBLS	10//99-12//99
	Manchester PMSA, NH	S	12.24 MW	12.51 AW	25470 AAW	NHBLS	10//99-12//99
	Nashua PMSA, NH	S	12.27 MW	11.92 AW	25530 AAW	NHBLS	10//99-12//99
	Portsmouth-Rochester PMSA, NH-ME	S	12.51 MW	12.62 AW	26030 AAW	NHBLS	10//99-12//99
	New Jersey	S	13.17 MW	13.69 AW	28470 AAW	NJBLS	10//99-12//99
	Atlantic-Cape May PMSA, NJ	S	12.11 MW	11.59 AW	25190 AAW	NJBLS	10//99-12//99
	Bergen-Passaic PMSA, NJ	S	13.63 MW	13.47 AW	28350 AAW	NJBLS	10//99-12//99
	Jersey City PMSA, NJ	S	13.14 MW	12.47 AW	27340 AAW	NJBLS	10//99-12//99
	Middlesex-Somerset-Hunterdon PMSA, NJ	S	14.48 MW	13.49 AW	30120 AAW	NJBLS	10//99-12//99

AAW	Average annual wage	AOH	Average offered, high	ASH	Average starting, high
AE	Average entry wage	AOL	Average offered, low	ASL	Average starting, low
AEX	Average experienced wage	APH	Average pay, high range	AW	Average wage paid
AO	Average offered	APL	Average pay, low range	FQ	First quartile wage

H	Hourly	M	Monthly
HI	Highest wage paid	MTC	Median total compensation
HR	High end range	MW	Median wage paid
LR	Low end range	SQ	Second quartile wage

S	Special: hourly and annual
TQ	Third quartile wage
W	Weekly
Y	Yearly

Occupation/Type/Industry	Location	Per	Low	Mid	High	Source	Date
Industrial Truck and Tractor Operator							
	Monmouth-Ocean PMSA, NJ	S	13.15 MW	12.22 AW	27340 AAW	NJBLS	10//99-12//99
	Newark PMSA, NJ	S	13.99 MW	13.39 AW	29090 AAW	NJBLS	10//99-12//99
	Trenton PMSA, NJ	S	13.62 MW	13.37 AW	28330 AAW	NJBLS	10//99-12//99
	Vineland-Millville-Bridgeton PMSA, NJ	S	11.86 MW	11.50 AW	24670 AAW	NJBLS	10//99-12//99
	New Mexico	S	9.5 MW	9.80 AW	20390 AAW	NMBLS	10//99-12//99
	Albuquerque MSA, NM	S	9.83 MW	9.78 AW	20460 AAW	NMBLS	10//99-12//99
	Las Cruces MSA, NM	S	8.91 MW	8.52 AW	18530 AAW	NMBLS	10//99-12//99
	Santa Fe MSA, NM	S	12.68 MW	12.34 AW	26380 AAW	NMBLS	10//99-12//99
	New York	S	12.81 MW	13.78 AW	28670 AAW	NYBLS	10//99-12//99
	Albany-Schenectady-Troy MSA, NY	S	12.19 MW	11.11 AW	25350 AAW	NYBLS	10//99-12//99
	Binghamton MSA, NY	S	10.87 MW	10.75 AW	22620 AAW	NYBLS	10//99-12//99
	Buffalo-Niagara Falls MSA, NY	S	17.54 MW	17.59 AW	36490 AAW	NYBLS	10//99-12//99
	Dutchess County PMSA, NY	S	11.67 MW	10.51 AW	24270 AAW	NYBLS	10//99-12//99
	Elmira MSA, NY	S	12.76 MW	12.60 AW	26540 AAW	NYBLS	10//99-12//99
	Glens Falls MSA, NY	S	13.17 MW	12.80 AW	27390 AAW	NYBLS	10//99-12//99
	Jamestown MSA, NY	S	14.49 MW	14.86 AW	30150 AAW	NYBLS	10//99-12//99
	Nassau-Suffolk PMSA, NY	S	14.89 MW	13.26 AW	30970 AAW	NYBLS	10//99-12//99
	New York PMSA, NY	S	13.05 MW	12.03 AW	27140 AAW	NYBLS	10//99-12//99
	Newburgh PMSA, NY-PA	S	16.70 MW	17.68 AW	34730 AAW	NYBLS	10//99-12//99
	Rochester MSA, NY	S	13.16 MW	12.30 AW	27370 AAW	NYBLS	10//99-12//99
	Syracuse MSA, NY	S	11.57 MW	10.73 AW	24070 AAW	NYBLS	10//99-12//99
	Utica-Rome MSA, NY	S	10.56 MW	10.33 AW	21950 AAW	NYBLS	10//99-12//99
	North Carolina	S	10.93 MW	11.48 AW	23870 AAW	NCBLS	10//99-12//99
	Asheville MSA, NC	S	10.39 MW	10.67 AW	21610 AAW	NCBLS	10//99-12//99
	Charlotte-Gastonia-Rock Hill MSA, NC-SC	S	12.38 MW	11.98 AW	25760 AAW	NCBLS	10//99-12//99
	Goldsboro MSA, NC	S	9.67 MW	9.70 AW	20100 AAW	NCBLS	10//99-12//99
	Greensboro--Winston-Salem-- High Point MSA, NC	S	11.55 MW	10.92 AW	24030 AAW	NCBLS	10//99-12//99
	Greenville MSA, NC	S	9.04 MW	8.70 AW	18810 AAW	NCBLS	10//99-12//99
	Hickory-Morganton-Lenoir MSA, NC	S	11.16 MW	10.94 AW	23210 AAW	NCBLS	10//99-12//99
	Jacksonville MSA, NC	S	10.41 MW	10.73 AW	21650 AAW	NCBLS	10//99-12//99
	Raleigh-Durham-Chapel Hill MSA, NC	S	10.32 MW	10.12 AW	21470 AAW	NCBLS	10//99-12//99
	Rocky Mount MSA, NC	S	10.34 MW	10.23 AW	21510 AAW	NCBLS	10//99-12//99
	Wilmington MSA, NC	S	11.38 MW	10.90 AW	23660 AAW	NCBLS	10//99-12//99
	North Dakota	S	10.63 MW	11.16 AW	23210 AAW	NDBLS	10//99-12//99
	Bismarck MSA, ND	S	13.44 MW	14.58 AW	27960 AAW	NDBLS	10//99-12//99
	Fargo-Moorhead MSA, ND-MN	S	11.89 MW	11.01 AW	24730 AAW	NDBLS	10//99-12//99
	Ohio	S	12.4 MW	13.52 AW	28120 AAW	OHBLS	10//99-12//99
	Akron PMSA, OH	S	14.82 MW	13.27 AW	30830 AAW	OHBLS	10//99-12//99
	Canton-Massillon MSA, OH	S	13.22 MW	12.81 AW	27490 AAW	OHBLS	10//99-12//99
	Cincinnati PMSA, OH-KY-IN	S	12.30 MW	11.34 AW	25580 AAW	OHBLS	10//99-12//99
	Cleveland-Lorain-Elyria PMSA, OH	S	13.91 MW	12.95 AW	28930 AAW	OHBLS	10//99-12//99
	Columbus MSA, OH	S	12.88 MW	12.00 AW	26780 AAW	OHBLS	10//99-12//99
	Dayton-Springfield MSA, OH	S	14.63 MW	12.95 AW	30430 AAW	OHBLS	10//99-12//99
	Hamilton-Middletown PMSA, OH	S	12.19 MW	11.91 AW	25350 AAW	OHBLS	10//99-12//99
	Lima MSA, OH	S	15.17 MW	13.41 AW	31550 AAW	OHBLS	10//99-12//99
	Mansfield MSA, OH	S	15.88 MW	14.70 AW	33030 AAW	OHBLS	10//99-12//99
	Steubenville-Weirton MSA, OH-WV	S	14.34 MW	14.81 AW	29830 AAW	OHBLS	10//99-12//99
	Toledo MSA, OH	S	14.86 MW	13.26 AW	30900 AAW	OHBLS	10//99-12//99
	Youngstown-Warren MSA, OH	S	16.43 MW	15.37 AW	34170 AAW	OHBLS	10//99-12//99
	Oklahoma	S	10.1 MW	10.88 AW	22640 AAW	OKBLS	10//99-12//99
	Enid MSA, OK	S	11.85 MW	10.62 AW	24640 AAW	OKBLS	10//99-12//99
	Lawton MSA, OK	S	9.39 MW	9.30 AW	19530 AAW	OKBLS	10//99-12//99
	Oklahoma City MSA, OK	S	10.55 MW	9.95 AW	21940 AAW	OKBLS	10//99-12//99
	Tulsa MSA, OK	S	12.46 MW	11.71 AW	25910 AAW	OKBLS	10//99-12//99
	Oregon	S	12.26 MW	12.44 AW	25860 AAW	ORBLS	10//99-12//99
	Corvallis MSA, OR	S	13.38 MW	12.86 AW	27830 AAW	ORBLS	10//99-12//99
	Eugene-Springfield MSA, OR	S	11.92 MW	11.92 AW	24790 AAW	ORBLS	10//99-12//99
	Portland-Vancouver PMSA, OR-WA	S	12.95 MW	12.64 AW	26940 AAW	ORBLS	10//99-12//99
	Salem PMSA, OR	S	11.27 MW	10.81 AW	23440 AAW	ORBLS	10//99-12//99

AAW Average annual wage	**AOH** Average offered, high	**ASH** Average starting, high	**H** Hourly	**M** Monthly	**S** Special: hourly and annual
AE Average entry wage	**AOL** Average offered, low	**ASL** Average starting, low	**HI** Highest wage paid	**MTC** Median total compensation	**TQ** Third quartile wage
AEX Average experienced wage	**APH** Average pay, high range	**AW** Average wage paid	**HR** High end range	**MW** Median wage paid	**W** Weekly
AO Average offered	**APL** Average pay, low range	**FQ** First quartile wage	**LR** Low end range	**SQ** Second quartile wage	**Y** Yearly

Occupation/Type/Industry	Location	Per	Low	Mid	High	Source	Date
Industrial Truck and Tractor Operator							
	Pennsylvania	S	12.59 MW	13.01 AW	27050 AAW	PABLS	10//99-12//99
	Allentown-Bethlehem-Easton MSA, PA	S	11.17 MW	10.67 AW	23230 AAW	PABLS	10//99-12//99
	Altoona MSA, PA	S	12.19 MW	12.38 AW	25360 AAW	PABLS	10//99-12//99
	Erie MSA, PA	S	11.53 MW	11.91 AW	23970 AAW	PABLS	10//99-12//99
	Harrisburg-Lebanon-Carlisle MSA, PA	S	13.81 MW	13.24 AW	28730 AAW	PABLS	10//99-12//99
	Johnstown MSA, PA	S	11.49 MW	11.39 AW	23910 AAW	PABLS	10//99-12//99
	Lancaster MSA, PA	S	13.46 MW	13.27 AW	28000 AAW	PABLS	10//99-12//99
	Philadelphia PMSA, PA-NJ	S	13.65 MW	13.37 AW	28400 AAW	PABLS	10//99-12//99
	Pittsburgh MSA, PA	S	13.25 MW	13.03 AW	27550 AAW	PABLS	10//99-12//99
	Reading MSA, PA	S	11.59 MW	11.43 AW	24110 AAW	PABLS	10//99-12//99
	Scranton--Wilkes-Barre--Hazleton MSA, PA	S	13.42 MW	12.86 AW	27910 AAW	PABLS	10//99-12//99
	Sharon MSA, PA	S	14.56 MW	14.51 AW	30280 AAW	PABLS	10//99-12//99
	Williamsport MSA, PA	S	12.15 MW	10.73 AW	25270 AAW	PABLS	10//99-12//99
	York MSA, PA	S	12.79 MW	12.12 AW	26600 AAW	PABLS	10//99-12//99
	Rhode Island	S	11.35 MW	11.71 AW	24360 AAW	RIBLS	10//99-12//99
	Providence-Fall River-Warwick MSA, RI-MA	S	11.91 MW	11.59 AW	24780 AAW	RIBLS	10//99-12//99
	South Carolina	S	10.64 MW	12.03 AW	25030 AAW	SCBLS	10//99-12//99
	Charleston-North Charleston MSA, SC	S	15.66 MW	10.98 AW	32570 AAW	SCBLS	10//99-12//99
	Columbia MSA, SC	S	12.16 MW	11.47 AW	25280 AAW	SCBLS	10//99-12//99
	Florence MSA, SC	S	11.17 MW	10.51 AW	23240 AAW	SCBLS	10//99-12//99
	Greenville-Spartanburg-Anderson MSA, SC	S	11.84 MW	10.82 AW	24620 AAW	SCBLS	10//99-12//99
	Myrtle Beach MSA, SC	S	10.58 MW	10.45 AW	22010 AAW	SCBLS	10//99-12//99
	Sumter MSA, SC	S	9.59 MW	9.65 AW	19940 AAW	SCBLS	10//99-12//99
	South Dakota	S	10.79 MW	10.86 AW	22580 AAW	SDBLS	10//99-12//99
	Rapid City MSA, SD	S	11.44 MW	11.71 AW	23800 AAW	SDBLS	10//99-12//99
	Sioux Falls MSA, SD	S	11.02 MW	10.96 AW	22910 AAW	SDBLS	10//99-12//99
	Tennessee	S	10.93 MW	11.75 AW	24430 AAW	TNBLS	10//99-12//99
	Chattanooga MSA, TN-GA	S	11.11 MW	10.45 AW	23110 AAW	TNBLS	10//99-12//99
	Clarksville-Hopkinsville MSA, TN-KY	S	10.23 MW	10.30 AW	21280 AAW	TNBLS	10//99-12//99
	Jackson MSA, TN	S	10.62 MW	10.64 AW	22090 AAW	TNBLS	10//99-12//99
	Johnson City-Kingsport-Bristol MSA, TN-VA	S	11.33 MW	11.36 AW	23560 AAW	TNBLS	10//99-12//99
	Knoxville MSA, TN	S	11.62 MW	10.77 AW	24180 AAW	TNBLS	10//99-12//99
	Memphis MSA, TN-AR-MS	S	12.08 MW	10.68 AW	25140 AAW	MSBLS	10//99-12//99
	Nashville MSA, TN	S	12.04 MW	11.61 AW	25050 AAW	TNBLS	10//99-12//99
	Texas	S	10.06 MW	10.49 AW	21810 AAW	TXBLS	10//99-12//99
	Abilene MSA, TX	S	9.20 MW	9.28 AW	19140 AAW	TXBLS	10//99-12//99
	Amarillo MSA, TX	S	9.28 MW	8.97 AW	19310 AAW	TXBLS	10//99-12//99
	Austin-San Marcos MSA, TX	S	9.89 MW	9.67 AW	20560 AAW	TXBLS	10//99-12//99
	Beaumont-Port Arthur MSA, TX	S	11.40 MW	11.05 AW	23710 AAW	TXBLS	10//99-12//99
	Brazoria PMSA, TX	S	11.40 MW	10.28 AW	23710 AAW	TXBLS	10//99-12//99
	Brownsville-Harlingen-San Benito MSA, TX	S	7.46 MW	7.23 AW	15520 AAW	TXBLS	10//99-12//99
	Bryan-College Station MSA, TX	S	9.65 MW	9.72 AW	20060 AAW	TXBLS	10//99-12//99
	Dallas PMSA, TX	S	11.82 MW	11.64 AW	24590 AAW	TXBLS	10//99-12//99
	El Paso MSA, TX	S	7.84 MW	7.52 AW	16300 AAW	TXBLS	10//99-12//99
	Fort Worth-Arlington PMSA, TX	S	10.83 MW	10.46 AW	22520 AAW	TXBLS	10//99-12//99
	Galveston-Texas City PMSA, TX	S	13.08 MW	12.02 AW	27210 AAW	TXBLS	10//99-12//99
	Houston PMSA, TX	S	10.59 MW	9.91 AW	22030 AAW	TXBLS	10//99-12//99
	Killeen-Temple MSA, TX	S	11.69 MW	9.67 AW	24320 AAW	TXBLS	10//99-12//99
	Laredo MSA, TX	S	7.98 MW	7.48 AW	16610 AAW	TXBLS	10//99-12//99
	Longview-Marshall MSA, TX	S	10.42 MW	10.24 AW	21670 AAW	TXBLS	10//99-12//99
	Lubbock MSA, TX	S	9.17 MW	8.63 AW	19070 AAW	TXBLS	10//99-12//99
	McAllen-Edinburg-Mission MSA, TX	S	8.21 MW	7.55 AW	17070 AAW	TXBLS	10//99-12//99
	Odessa-Midland MSA, TX	S	10.14 MW	9.62 AW	21090 AAW	TXBLS	10//99-12//99
	San Angelo MSA, TX	S	8.26 MW	7.95 AW	17170 AAW	TXBLS	10//99-12//99
	San Antonio MSA, TX	S	10.37 MW	10.51 AW	21560 AAW	TXBLS	10//99-12//99
	Sherman-Denison MSA, TX	S	12.02 MW	11.19 AW	25000 AAW	TXBLS	10//99-12//99

AAW Average annual wage	AOH Average offered, high	ASH Average starting, high	H Hourly	M Monthly	S Special: hourly and annual
AE Average entry wage	AOL Average offered, low	ASL Average starting, low	HI Highest wage paid	MTC Median total compensation	TQ Third quartile wage
AEX Average experienced wage	APH Average pay, high range	AW Average wage paid	HR High end range	MW Median wage paid	W Weekly
AO Average offered	APL Average pay, low range	FQ First quartile wage	LR Low end range	SQ Second quartile wage	Y Yearly

Occupation/Type/Industry	Location	Per	Low	Mid	High	Source	Date
Industrial Truck and Tractor Operator	Texarkana MSA, TX-Texarkana, AR	S	9.74 MW	9.45 AW	20250 AAW	TXBLS	10//99-12//99
	Tyler MSA, TX	S	14.26 MW	15.24 AW	29660 AAW	TXBLS	10//99-12//99
	Victoria MSA, TX	S	8.64 MW	8.35 AW	17970 AAW	TXBLS	10//99-12//99
	Waco MSA, TX	S	10.18 MW	10.22 AW	21170 AAW	TXBLS	10//99-12//99
	Wichita Falls MSA, TX	S	11.20 MW	10.88 AW	23300 AAW	TXBLS	10//99-12//99
	Utah	S	11.69 MW	11.95 AW	24860 AAW	UTBLS	10//99-12//99
	Provo-Orem MSA, UT	S	11.88 MW	11.45 AW	24710 AAW	UTBLS	10//99-12//99
	Salt Lake City-Ogden MSA, UT	S	11.76 MW	11.66 AW	24450 AAW	UTBLS	10//99-12//99
	Vermont	S	11.29 MW	12.66 AW	26320 AAW	VTBLS	10//99-12//99
	Burlington MSA, VT	S	11.55 MW	11.15 AW	24020 AAW	VTBLS	10//99-12//99
	Virginia	S	10.89 MW	11.55 AW	24020 AAW	VABLS	10//99-12//99
	Charlottesville MSA, VA	S	10.82 MW	10.11 AW	22510 AAW	VABLS	10//99-12//99
	Danville MSA, VA	S	10.05 MW	9.83 AW	20900 AAW	VABLS	10//99-12//99
	Lynchburg MSA, VA	S	12.26 MW	12.73 AW	25500 AAW	VABLS	10//99-12//99
	Norfolk-Virginia Beach-Newport News MSA, VA-NC	S	12.61 MW	12.05 AW	26220 AAW	VABLS	10//99-12//99
	Richmond-Petersburg MSA, VA	S	11.50 MW	11.57 AW	23920 AAW	VABLS	10//99-12//99
	Roanoke MSA, VA	S	10.99 MW	10.57 AW	22860 AAW	VABLS	10//99-12//99
	Washington	S	13.21 MW	13.82 AW	28740 AAW	WABLS	10//99-12//99
	Bellingham MSA, WA	S	13.21 MW	12.69 AW	27490 AAW	WABLS	10//99-12//99
	Bremerton PMSA, WA	S	12.69 MW	11.63 AW	26400 AAW	WABLS	10//99-12//99
	Olympia PMSA, WA	S	13.56 MW	13.74 AW	28210 AAW	WABLS	10//99-12//99
	Richland-Kennewick-Pasco MSA, WA	S	11.32 MW	11.37 AW	23550 AAW	WABLS	10//99-12//99
	Seattle-Bellevue-Everett PMSA, WA	S	14.89 MW	14.53 AW	30970 AAW	WABLS	10//99-12//99
	Spokane MSA, WA	S	14.49 MW	14.38 AW	30150 AAW	WABLS	10//99-12//99
	Tacoma PMSA, WA	S	16.01 MW	14.61 AW	33300 AAW	WABLS	10//99-12//99
	Yakima MSA, WA	S	10.52 MW	10.31 AW	21890 AAW	WABLS	10//99-12//99
	West Virginia	S	11.27 MW	12.75 AW	26530 AAW	WVBLS	10//99-12//99
	Charleston MSA, WV	S	14.79 MW	12.94 AW	30770 AAW	WVBLS	10//99-12//99
	Huntington-Ashland MSA, WV-KY-OH	S	13.70 MW	14.43 AW	28490 AAW	WVBLS	10//99-12//99
	Parkersburg-Marietta MSA, WV-OH	S	11.20 MW	10.13 AW	23300 AAW	WVBLS	10//99-12//99
	Wheeling MSA, WV-OH	S	12.67 MW	11.56 AW	26360 AAW	WVBLS	10//99-12//99
	Wisconsin	S	11.83 MW	12.13 AW	25240 AAW	WIBLS	10//99-12//99
	Appleton-Oshkosh-Neenah MSA, WI	S	13.36 MW	13.87 AW	27780 AAW	WIBLS	10//99-12//99
	Eau Claire MSA, WI	S	12.07 MW	11.97 AW	25100 AAW	WIBLS	10//99-12//99
	Green Bay MSA, WI	S	13.29 MW	12.85 AW	27640 AAW	WIBLS	10//99-12//99
	Janesville-Beloit MSA, WI	S	12.06 MW	11.61 AW	25090 AAW	WIBLS	10//99-12//99
	Kenosha PMSA, WI	S	11.09 MW	10.82 AW	23060 AAW	WIBLS	10//99-12//99
	La Crosse MSA, WI-MN	S	11.65 MW	11.47 AW	24240 AAW	WIBLS	10//99-12//99
	Madison MSA, WI	S	12.15 MW	12.19 AW	25260 AAW	WIBLS	10//99-12//99
	Milwaukee-Waukesha PMSA, WI	S	12.87 MW	12.40 AW	26770 AAW	WIBLS	10//99-12//99
	Racine PMSA, WI	S	10.63 MW	10.26 AW	22120 AAW	WIBLS	10//99-12//99
	Wausau MSA, WI	S	11.31 MW	11.05 AW	23530 AAW	WIBLS	10//99-12//99
	Wyoming	S	14.82 MW	15.07 AW	31340 AAW	WYBLS	10//99-12//99
	Casper MSA, WY	S	11.05 MW	11.29 AW	22970 AAW	WYBLS	10//99-12//99
	Cheyenne MSA, WY	S	10.16 MW	9.50 AW	21130 AAW	WYBLS	10//99-12//99
	Puerto Rico	S	6.91 MW	7.64 AW	15900 AAW	PRBLS	10//99-12//99
	Arecibo PMSA, PR	S	6.62 MW	6.07 AW	13770 AAW	PRBLS	10//99-12//99
	Caguas PMSA, PR	S	7.79 MW	7.30 AW	16200 AAW	PRBLS	10//99-12//99
	Mayaguez MSA, PR	S	6.64 MW	6.09 AW	13800 AAW	PRBLS	10//99-12//99
	Ponce MSA, PR	S	7.71 MW	7.43 AW	16040 AAW	PRBLS	10//99-12//99
	San Juan-Bayamon PMSA, PR	S	7.88 MW	7.22 AW	16390 AAW	PRBLS	10//99-12//99
	Guam	S	10.74 MW	10.71 AW	22280 AAW	GUBLS	10//99-12//99
Information Specialist Human Resources	United States	Y		48400 AW		HRMAG	1999
Information Systems Director City Government	United States	Y		74152 AW		AC&C	1999
County Government	United States	Y		68413 AW		AC&C	1999

Occupation/Type/Industry	Location	Per	Low	Mid	High	Source	Date
Inspector, Tester, Sorter, Sampler, and Weigher							
	Alabama	S	10.33 ₘᵥᵥ	11.84 ₐᵥᵥ	24620 ₐₐᵥᵥ	ALBLS	10//99-12//99
	Alaska	S	21.19 ₘᵥᵥ	20.98 ₐᵥᵥ	43640 ₐₐᵥᵥ	AKBLS	10//99-12//99
	Arizona	S	12.89 ₘᵥᵥ	14.30 ₐᵥᵥ	29740 ₐₐᵥᵥ	AZBLS	10//99-12//99
	Arkansas	S	10.03 ₘᵥᵥ	10.77 ₐᵥᵥ	22400 ₐₐᵥᵥ	ARBLS	10//99-12//99
	California	S	10.98 ₘᵥᵥ	12.43 ₐᵥᵥ	25860 ₐₐᵥᵥ	CABLS	10//99-12//99
	Colorado	S	11.42 ₘᵥᵥ	12.30 ₐᵥᵥ	25580 ₐₐᵥᵥ	COBLS	10//99-12//99
	Connecticut	S	12.93 ₘᵥᵥ	13.93 ₐᵥᵥ	28970 ₐₐᵥᵥ	CTBLS	10//99-12//99
	Delaware	S	13.76 ₘᵥᵥ	14.76 ₐᵥᵥ	30690 ₐₐᵥᵥ	DEBLS	10//99-12//99
	District of Columbia	S	13.28 ₘᵥᵥ	14.69 ₐᵥᵥ	30550 ₐₐᵥᵥ	DCBLS	10//99-12//99
	Florida	S	10.16 ₘᵥᵥ	11.72 ₐᵥᵥ	24370 ₐₐᵥᵥ	FLBLS	10//99-12//99
	Georgia	S	10.33 ₘᵥᵥ	11.45 ₐᵥᵥ	23810 ₐₐᵥᵥ	GABLS	10//99-12//99
	Hawaii	S	13.29 ₘᵥᵥ	14.92 ₐᵥᵥ	31040 ₐₐᵥᵥ	HIBLS	10//99-12//99
	Idaho	S	9.8 ₘᵥᵥ	11.75 ₐᵥᵥ	24440 ₐₐᵥᵥ	IDBLS	10//99-12//99
	Illinois	S	11.78 ₘᵥᵥ	12.87 ₐᵥᵥ	26760 ₐₐᵥᵥ	ILBLS	10//99-12//99
	Indiana	S	12.04 ₘᵥᵥ	13.41 ₐᵥᵥ	27890 ₐₐᵥᵥ	INBLS	10//99-12//99
	Iowa	S	11.82 ₘᵥᵥ	12.65 ₐᵥᵥ	26310 ₐₐᵥᵥ	IABLS	10//99-12//99
	Kansas	S	13.61 ₘᵥᵥ	15.81 ₐᵥᵥ	32870 ₐₐᵥᵥ	KSBLS	10//99-12//99
	Kentucky	S	11.24 ₘᵥᵥ	12.33 ₐᵥᵥ	25660 ₐₐᵥᵥ	KYBLS	10//99-12//99
	Louisiana	S	13.43 ₘᵥᵥ	14.82 ₐᵥᵥ	30820 ₐₐᵥᵥ	LABLS	10//99-12//99
	Maine	S	10.9 ₘᵥᵥ	11.87 ₐᵥᵥ	24690 ₐₐᵥᵥ	MEBLS	10//99-12//99
	Maryland	S	12.53 ₘᵥᵥ	13.53 ₐᵥᵥ	28150 ₐₐᵥᵥ	MDBLS	10//99-12//99
	Massachusetts	S	14.05 ₘᵥᵥ	14.91 ₐᵥᵥ	31010 ₐₐᵥᵥ	MABLS	10//99-12//99
	Michigan	S	13.98 ₘᵥᵥ	15.64 ₐᵥᵥ	32540 ₐₐᵥᵥ	MIBLS	10//99-12//99
	Minnesota	S	13.52 ₘᵥᵥ	14.79 ₐᵥᵥ	30770 ₐₐᵥᵥ	MNBLS	10//99-12//99
	Mississippi	S	10.25 ₘᵥᵥ	11.53 ₐᵥᵥ	23990 ₐₐᵥᵥ	MSBLS	10//99-12//99
	Missouri	S	11.87 ₘᵥᵥ	13.49 ₐᵥᵥ	28050 ₐₐᵥᵥ	MOBLS	10//99-12//99
	Montana	S	13.83 ₘᵥᵥ	13.29 ₐᵥᵥ	27640 ₐₐᵥᵥ	MTBLS	10//99-12//99
	Nebraska	S	11.07 ₘᵥᵥ	11.69 ₐᵥᵥ	24310 ₐₐᵥᵥ	NEBLS	10//99-12//99
	Nevada	S	11.81 ₘᵥᵥ	12.88 ₐᵥᵥ	26780 ₐₐᵥᵥ	NVBLS	10//99-12//99
	New Hampshire	S	11.79 ₘᵥᵥ	12.44 ₐᵥᵥ	25880 ₐₐᵥᵥ	NHBLS	10//99-12//99
	New Jersey	S	13.18 ₘᵥᵥ	14.41 ₐᵥᵥ	29970 ₐₐᵥᵥ	NJBLS	10//99-12//99
	New Mexico	S	12.49 ₘᵥᵥ	13.69 ₐᵥᵥ	28470 ₐₐᵥᵥ	NMBLS	10//99-12//99
	New York	S	11.95 ₘᵥᵥ	13.45 ₐᵥᵥ	27970 ₐₐᵥᵥ	NYBLS	10//99-12//99
	North Carolina	S	10.07 ₘᵥᵥ	10.85 ₐᵥᵥ	22580 ₐₐᵥᵥ	NCBLS	10//99-12//99
	North Dakota	S	11.24 ₘᵥᵥ	12.01 ₐᵥᵥ	24990 ₐₐᵥᵥ	NDBLS	10//99-12//99
	Ohio	S	12.87 ₘᵥᵥ	13.90 ₐᵥᵥ	28910 ₐₐᵥᵥ	OHBLS	10//99-12//99
	Oklahoma	S	12.25 ₘᵥᵥ	12.90 ₐᵥᵥ	26820 ₐₐᵥᵥ	OKBLS	10//99-12//99
	Oregon	S	12.35 ₘᵥᵥ	13.28 ₐᵥᵥ	27630 ₐₐᵥᵥ	ORBLS	10//99-12//99
	Pennsylvania	S	12.56 ₘᵥᵥ	13.28 ₐᵥᵥ	27620 ₐₐᵥᵥ	PABLS	10//99-12//99
	Rhode Island	S	10.2 ₘᵥᵥ	10.99 ₐᵥᵥ	22870 ₐₐᵥᵥ	RIBLS	10//99-12//99
	South Carolina	S	10.91 ₘᵥᵥ	12.23 ₐᵥᵥ	25440 ₐₐᵥᵥ	SCBLS	10//99-12//99
	South Dakota	S	10.54 ₘᵥᵥ	10.63 ₐᵥᵥ	22120 ₐₐᵥᵥ	SDBLS	10//99-12//99
	Tennessee	S	11 ₘᵥᵥ	11.83 ₐᵥᵥ	24600 ₐₐᵥᵥ	TNBLS	10//99-12//99
	Texas	S	11.09 ₘᵥᵥ	12.55 ₐᵥᵥ	26110 ₐₐᵥᵥ	TXBLS	10//99-12//99
	Utah	S	11.51 ₘᵥᵥ	12.78 ₐᵥᵥ	26580 ₐₐᵥᵥ	UTBLS	10//99-12//99
	Vermont	S	11.73 ₘᵥᵥ	12.39 ₐᵥᵥ	25780 ₐₐᵥᵥ	VTBLS	10//99-12//99
	Virginia	S	11.38 ₘᵥᵥ	12.76 ₐᵥᵥ	26540 ₐₐᵥᵥ	VABLS	10//99-12//99
	Washington	S	15 ₘᵥᵥ	15.89 ₐᵥᵥ	33050 ₐₐᵥᵥ	WABLS	10//99-12//99
	West Virginia	S	12.55 ₘᵥᵥ	12.90 ₐᵥᵥ	26820 ₐₐᵥᵥ	WVBLS	10//99-12//99
	Wisconsin	S	11.99 ₘᵥᵥ	12.70 ₐᵥᵥ	26420 ₐₐᵥᵥ	WIBLS	10//99-12//99
	Wyoming	S	12.51 ₘᵥᵥ	14.08 ₐᵥᵥ	29290 ₐₐᵥᵥ	WYBLS	10//99-12//99
	Puerto Rico	S	7.79 ₘᵥᵥ	8.72 ₐᵥᵥ	18150 ₐₐᵥᵥ	PRBLS	10//99-12//99
	Virgin Islands	S	14.97 ₘᵥᵥ	15.26 ₐᵥᵥ	31740 ₐₐᵥᵥ	VIBLS	10//99-12//99
Instructional Coordinator							
	Alabama	S	15.3 ₘᵥᵥ	16.06 ₐᵥᵥ	33400 ₐₐᵥᵥ	ALBLS	10//99-12//99
	Alaska	S	19.35 ₘᵥᵥ	20.79 ₐᵥᵥ	43240 ₐₐᵥᵥ	AKBLS	10//99-12//99
	Arizona	S	17.83 ₘᵥᵥ	18.48 ₐᵥᵥ	38430 ₐₐᵥᵥ	AZBLS	10//99-12//99
	Arkansas	S	17.1 ₘᵥᵥ	16.60 ₐᵥᵥ	34520 ₐₐᵥᵥ	ARBLS	10//99-12//99
	California	S	26.47 ₘᵥᵥ	24.56 ₐᵥᵥ	51090 ₐₐᵥᵥ	CABLS	10//99-12//99
	Connecticut	S	24.54 ₘᵥᵥ	24.99 ₐᵥᵥ	51980 ₐₐᵥᵥ	CTBLS	10//99-12//99
	Delaware	S	19.05 ₘᵥᵥ	21.68 ₐᵥᵥ	45100 ₐₐᵥᵥ	DEBLS	10//99-12//99
	District of Columbia	S	18.03 ₘᵥᵥ	19.01 ₐᵥᵥ	39550 ₐₐᵥᵥ	DCBLS	10//99-12//99
	Florida	S	18.2 ₘᵥᵥ	18.94 ₐᵥᵥ	39390 ₐₐᵥᵥ	FLBLS	10//99-12//99
	Georgia	S	16.04 ₘᵥᵥ	17.19 ₐᵥᵥ	35760 ₐₐᵥᵥ	GABLS	10//99-12//99
	Illinois	S	22.02 ₘᵥᵥ	23.66 ₐᵥᵥ	49210 ₐₐᵥᵥ	ILBLS	10//99-12//99
	Indiana	S	20.45 ₘᵥᵥ	20.94 ₐᵥᵥ	43540 ₐₐᵥᵥ	INBLS	10//99-12//99
	Iowa	S	20.28 ₘᵥᵥ	19.38 ₐᵥᵥ	40310 ₐₐᵥᵥ	IABLS	10//99-12//99
	Kansas	S	21.17 ₘᵥᵥ	23.39 ₐᵥᵥ	48650 ₐₐᵥᵥ	KSBLS	10//99-12//99
	Kentucky	S	17.74 ₘᵥᵥ	19.15 ₐᵥᵥ	39840 ₐₐᵥᵥ	KYBLS	10//99-12//99
	Louisiana	S	17.72 ₘᵥᵥ	17.96 ₐᵥᵥ	37360 ₐₐᵥᵥ	LABLS	10//99-12//99
	Maine	S	19.34 ₘᵥᵥ	19.51 ₐᵥᵥ	40570 ₐₐᵥᵥ	MEBLS	10//99-12//99

AAW	Average annual wage	**AOH**	Average offered, high	**ASH**	Average starting, high	**H**	Hourly	**M**	Monthly	**S** Special: hourly and annual
AE	Average entry wage	**AOL**	Average offered, low	**ASL**	Average starting, low	**HI**	Highest wage paid	**MTC**	Median total compensation	**TQ** Third quartile wage
AEX	Average experienced wage	**APH**	Average pay, high range	**AW**	Average wage paid	**HR**	High end range	**MW**	Median wage paid	**W** Weekly
AO	Average offered	**APL**	Average pay, low range	**FQ**	First quartile wage	**LR**	Low end range	**SQ**	Second quartile wage	**Y** Yearly

Occupation/Type/Industry	Location	Per	Low	Mid	High	Source	Date
Instructional Coordinator	Maryland	S	17.81 MW	20.06 AW	41730 AAW	MDBLS	10//99-12//99
	Massachusetts	S	20.22 MW	21.11 AW	43900 AAW	MABLS	10//99-12//99
	Michigan	S	24.15 MW	23.68 AW	49250 AAW	MIBLS	10//99-12//99
	Minnesota	S	19.91 MW	20.68 AW	43010 AAW	MNBLS	10//99-12//99
	Mississippi	S	15.52 MW	16.24 AW	33790 AAW	MSBLS	10//99-12//99
	Missouri	S	17.69 MW	18.58 AW	38640 AAW	MOBLS	10//99-12//99
	Montana	S	14.28 MW	12.64 AW	26280 AAW	MTBLS	10//99-12//99
	Nebraska	S	27.57 MW	24.58 AW	51120 AAW	NEBLS	10//99-12//99
	Nevada	S	19.82 MW	19.64 AW	40850 AAW	NVBLS	10//99-12//99
	New Hampshire	S	23.19 MW	22.61 AW	47040 AAW	NHBLS	10//99-12//99
	New Jersey	S	25.57 MW	25.84 AW	53740 AAW	NJBLS	10//99-12//99
	New Mexico	S	18.43 MW	18.23 AW	37910 AAW	NMBLS	10//99-12//99
	New York	S	23.6 MW	25.69 AW	53430 AAW	NYBLS	10//99-12//99
	North Carolina	S	16.39 MW	17.09 AW	35550 AAW	NCBLS	10//99-12//99
	North Dakota	S	22.83 MW	21.54 AW	44810 AAW	NDBLS	10//99-12//99
	Ohio	S	21.39 MW	20.99 AW	43650 AAW	OHBLS	10//99-12//99
	Oklahoma	S	19.59 MW	19.08 AW	39690 AAW	OKBLS	10//99-12//99
	Oregon	S	23.15 MW	23.29 AW	48450 AAW	ORBLS	10//99-12//99
	Pennsylvania	S	17.45 MW	19.73 AW	41030 AAW	PABLS	10//99-12//99
	Rhode Island	S	21.79 MW	21.55 AW	44830 AAW	RIBLS	10//99-12//99
	South Carolina	S	17.61 MW	19.35 AW	40260 AAW	SCBLS	10//99-12//99
	South Dakota	S	16.57 MW	17.77 AW	36950 AAW	SDBLS	10//99-12//99
	Tennessee	S	13.38 MW	15.20 AW	31620 AAW	TNBLS	10//99-12//99
	Texas	S	23.52 MW	22.35 AW	46490 AAW	TXBLS	10//99-12//99
	Utah	S	11.16 MW	14.77 AW	30720 AAW	UTBLS	10//99-12//99
	Vermont	S	15.46 MW	16.87 AW	35090 AAW	VTBLS	10//99-12//99
	Virginia	S	21.26 MW	21.11 AW	43910 AAW	VABLS	10//99-12//99
	Washington	S	18.89 MW	19.37 AW	40290 AAW	WABLS	10//99-12//99
	West Virginia	S	23.64 MW	22.99 AW	47810 AAW	WVBLS	10//99-12//99
	Wisconsin	S	17.32 MW	18.78 AW	39070 AAW	WIBLS	10//99-12//99
	Wyoming	S	15.67 MW	17.49 AW	36390 AAW	WYBLS	10//99-12//99
	Puerto Rico	S	8.21 MW	8.46 AW	17610 AAW	PRBLS	10//99-12//99
Instructor							
Agricultural Engineering	United States	Y	34979 APL	43158 AW	54792 APH	RESC	1998-1999
Doctoral Level, Nursing Faculty	United States	Y		42240 AW		AWHONN	1998-1999
Nondoctoral Level, Nursing Faculty	United States	Y		37961 AW		AWHONN	1998-1999
Insulation Worker	Alabama	S	12.02 MW	12.61 AW	26230 AAW	ALBLS	10//99-12//99
	Alaska	S	16.2 MW	17.25 AW	35880 AAW	AKBLS	10//99-12//99
	Arizona	S	9.87 MW	10.91 AW	22690 AAW	AZBLS	10//99-12//99
	Arkansas	S	11.29 MW	11.53 AW	23990 AAW	ARBLS	10//99-12//99
	California	S	13.95 MW	17.62 AW	36660 AAW	CABLS	10//99-12//99
	Colorado	S	12.06 MW	12.78 AW	26580 AAW	COBLS	10//99-12//99
	Connecticut	S	13.6 MW	15.06 AW	31330 AAW	CTBLS	10//99-12//99
	Delaware	S	14.35 MW	14.81 AW	30810 AAW	DEBLS	10//99-12//99
	District of Columbia	S	19.16 MW	20.55 AW	42750 AAW	DCBLS	10//99-12//99
	Florida	S	10.7 MW	11.23 AW	23350 AAW	FLBLS	10//99-12//99
	Georgia	S	11.02 MW	11.56 AW	24050 AAW	GABLS	10//99-12//99
	Idaho	S	9.36 MW	10.02 AW	20830 AAW	IDBLS	10//99-12//99
	Illinois	S	19.98 MW	20.97 AW	43620 AAW	ILBLS	10//99-12//99
	Indiana	S	14.39 MW	15.72 AW	32700 AAW	INBLS	10//99-12//99
	Iowa	S	11.5 MW	12.69 AW	26400 AAW	IABLS	10//99-12//99
	Kentucky	S	11.18 MW	11.37 AW	23640 AAW	KYBLS	10//99-12//99
	Louisiana	S	13.09 MW	12.54 AW	26080 AAW	LABLS	10//99-12//99
	Maine	S	14.14 MW	13.06 AW	27170 AAW	MEBLS	10//99-12//99
	Maryland	S	11.84 MW	12.53 AW	26060 AAW	MDBLS	10//99-12//99
	Massachusetts	S	17.02 MW	19.02 AW	39560 AAW	MABLS	10//99-12//99
	Michigan	S	12.29 MW	15.36 AW	31950 AAW	MIBLS	10//99-12//99
	Minnesota	S	15.45 MW	17.92 AW	37260 AAW	MNBLS	10//99-12//99
	Mississippi	S	13.82 MW	12.70 AW	26420 AAW	MSBLS	10//99-12//99
	Missouri	S	13.76 MW	14.53 AW	30210 AAW	MOBLS	10//99-12//99
	Montana	S	10.53 MW	11.15 AW	23190 AAW	MTBLS	10//99-12//99
	Nebraska	S	10.89 MW	12.79 AW	26610 AAW	NEBLS	10//99-12//99
	Nevada	S	19.93 MW	19.11 AW	39760 AAW	NVBLS	10//99-12//99
	New Hampshire	S	10.99 MW	12.23 AW	25450 AAW	NHBLS	10//99-12//99
	New Jersey	S	22.45 MW	21.91 AW	45580 AAW	NJBLS	10//99-12//99
	New Mexico	S	10.51 MW	11.70 AW	24340 AAW	NMBLS	10//99-12//99
	New York	S	18.59 MW	20.57 AW	42780 AAW	NYBLS	10//99-12//99
	North Carolina	S	11.31 MW	11.65 AW	24220 AAW	NCBLS	10//99-12//99
	North Dakota	S	10.62 MW	12.86 AW	26760 AAW	NDBLS	10//99-12//99
	Ohio	S	12.15 MW	13.73 AW	28560 AAW	OHBLS	10//99-12//99
	Oklahoma	S	11.03 MW	12.32 AW	25630 AAW	OKBLS	10//99-12//99

AAW	Average annual wage	AOH	Average offered, high	ASH	Average starting, high	H	Hourly	M	Monthly	S	Special: hourly and annual
AE	Average entry wage	AOL	Average offered, low	ASL	Average starting, low	HI	Highest wage paid	MTC	Median total compensation	TQ	Third quartile wage
AEX	Average experienced wage	APH	Average pay, high range	AW	Average wage paid	HR	High end range	MW	Median wage paid	W	Weekly
AO	Average offered	APL	Average pay, low range	FQ	First quartile wage	LR	Low end range	SQ	Second quartile wage	Y	Yearly

Occupation/Type/Industry	Location	Per	Low	Mid	High	Source	Date
Insulation Worker	Oregon	S	11.91 MW	13.71 AW	28510 AAW	ORBLS	10//99-12//99
	Pennsylvania	S	13.99 MW	15.08 AW	31380 AAW	PABLS	10//99-12//99
	Rhode Island	S	16.33 MW	15.90 AW	33080 AAW	RIBLS	10//99-12//99
	South Carolina	S	11.52 MW	11.58 AW	24080 AAW	SCBLS	10//99-12//99
	South Dakota	S	8.25 MW	8.40 AW	17470 AAW	SDBLS	10//99-12//99
	Tennessee	S	12.19 MW	12.43 AW	25840 AAW	TNBLS	10//99-12//99
	Texas	S	11.8 MW	11.93 AW	24810 AAW	TXBLS	10//99-12//99
	Vermont	S	9.87 MW	10.39 AW	21610 AAW	VTBLS	10//99-12//99
	Virginia	S	12.84 MW	12.79 AW	26600 AAW	VABLS	10//99-12//99
	Washington	S	16.61 MW	16.42 AW	34140 AAW	WABLS	10//99-12//99
	West Virginia	S	19.53 MW	17.51 AW	36430 AAW	WVBLS	10//99-12//99
	Wisconsin	S	13.16 MW	15.36 AW	31950 AAW	WIBLS	10//99-12//99
	Wyoming	S	11.38 MW	11.86 AW	24660 AAW	WYBLS	10//99-12//99
	Puerto Rico	S	6.26 MW	6.55 AW	13620 AAW	PRBLS	10//99-12//99
Insurance Appraiser							
Auto Damage	Arkansas	S	16.31 MW	19.07 AW	39670 AAW	ARBLS	10//99-12//99
Auto Damage	California	S	21.63 MW	21.70 AW	45130 AAW	CABLS	10//99-12//99
Auto Damage	Colorado	S	17.46 MW	17.66 AW	36720 AAW	COBLS	10//99-12//99
Auto Damage	Connecticut	S	22.93 MW	23.34 AW	48540 AAW	CTBLS	10//99-12//99
Auto Damage	Florida	S	18.89 MW	19.40 AW	40340 AAW	FLBLS	10//99-12//99
Auto Damage	Georgia	S	17.18 MW	17.76 AW	36930 AAW	GABLS	10//99-12//99
Auto Damage	Illinois	S	18.27 MW	19.64 AW	40850 AAW	ILBLS	10//99-12//99
Auto Damage	Indiana	S	20.22 MW	20.00 AW	41590 AAW	INBLS	10//99-12//99
Auto Damage	Iowa	S	17.95 MW	18.62 AW	38740 AAW	IABLS	10//99-12//99
Auto Damage	Kansas	S	17.11 MW	18.18 AW	37820 AAW	KSBLS	10//99-12//99
Auto Damage	Kentucky	S	15.4 MW	17.05 AW	35450 AAW	KYBLS	10//99-12//99
Auto Damage	Louisiana	S	18.77 MW	19.70 AW	40970 AAW	LABLS	10//99-12//99
Auto Damage	Maine	S	18.41 MW	18.22 AW	37900 AAW	MEBLS	10//99-12//99
Auto Damage	Maryland	S	20.1 MW	20.69 AW	43040 AAW	MDBLS	10//99-12//99
Auto Damage	Massachusetts	S	18.43 MW	18.91 AW	39330 AAW	MABLS	10//99-12//99
Auto Damage	Michigan	S	15.13 MW	17.41 AW	36200 AAW	MIBLS	10//99-12//99
Auto Damage	Minnesota	S	18.22 MW	19.06 AW	39650 AAW	MNBLS	10//99-12//99
Auto Damage	Mississippi	S	17.44 MW	17.79 AW	36990 AAW	MSBLS	10//99-12//99
Auto Damage	Nevada	S	12.09 MW	12.91 AW	26860 AAW	NVBLS	10//99-12//99
Auto Damage	New Hampshire	S	22.26 MW	21.75 AW	45230 AAW	NHBLS	10//99-12//99
Auto Damage	New Jersey	S	18.44 MW	19.17 AW	39880 AAW	NJBLS	10//99-12//99
Auto Damage	New Mexico	S	16.56 MW	17.47 AW	36350 AAW	NMBLS	10//99-12//99
Auto Damage	New York	S	19.76 MW	19.18 AW	39900 AAW	NYBLS	10//99-12//99
Auto Damage	North Carolina	S	15.96 MW	16.19 AW	33670 AAW	NCBLS	10//99-12//99
Auto Damage	Ohio	S	20.45 MW	21.24 AW	44180 AAW	OHBLS	10//99-12//99
Auto Damage	Oklahoma	S	16.3 MW	17.91 AW	37260 AAW	OKBLS	10//99-12//99
Auto Damage	Pennsylvania	S	20.38 MW	20.96 AW	43600 AAW	PABLS	10//99-12//99
Auto Damage	South Carolina	S	16.79 MW	18.30 AW	38060 AAW	SCBLS	10//99-12//99
Auto Damage	South Dakota	S	20.06 MW	20.06 AW	41730 AAW	SDBLS	10//99-12//99
Auto Damage	Tennessee	S	16.24 MW	17.81 AW	37050 AAW	TNBLS	10//99-12//99
Auto Damage	Texas	S	20.65 MW	20.57 AW	42780 AAW	TXBLS	10//99-12//99
Auto Damage	Virginia	S	26.97 MW	26.29 AW	54680 AAW	VABLS	10//99-12//99
Auto Damage	Washington	S	20.22 MW	21.10 AW	43890 AAW	WABLS	10//99-12//99
Auto Damage	Wisconsin	S	18.9 MW	20.09 AW	41790 AAW	WIBLS	10//99-12//99
Insurance Claim and Policy Processing Clerk	Alabama	S	12.54 MW	14.01 AW	29140 AAW	ALBLS	10//99-12//99
	Alaska	S	19.78 MW	21.82 AW	45380 AAW	AKBLS	10//99-12//99
	Arizona	S	12.99 MW	15.31 AW	31850 AAW	AZBLS	10//99-12//99
	Arkansas	S	11.9 MW	12.47 AW	25930 AAW	ARBLS	10//99-12//99
	California	S	16.79 MW	19.56 AW	40690 AAW	CABLS	10//99-12//99
	Colorado	S	13.63 MW	14.89 AW	30980 AAW	COBLS	10//99-12//99
	Connecticut	S	14.01 MW	14.68 AW	30530 AAW	CTBLS	10//99-12//99
	Delaware	S	12.7 MW	14.06 AW	29250 AAW	DEBLS	10//99-12//99
	Florida	S	13.86 MW	15.26 AW	31740 AAW	FLBLS	10//99-12//99
	Georgia	S	12.17 MW	13.53 AW	28140 AAW	GABLS	10//99-12//99
	Hawaii	S	11.95 MW	13.64 AW	28360 AAW	HIBLS	10//99-12//99
	Idaho	S	15.96 MW	15.93 AW	33140 AAW	IDBLS	10//99-12//99
	Illinois	S	12.04 MW	13.73 AW	28550 AAW	ILBLS	10//99-12//99
	Indiana	S	12.9 MW	14.50 AW	30160 AAW	INBLS	10//99-12//99
	Iowa	S	12.82 MW	14.20 AW	29540 AAW	IABLS	10//99-12//99
	Kansas	S	14.42 MW	15.85 AW	32980 AAW	KSBLS	10//99-12//99
	Kentucky	S	12.94 MW	14.90 AW	30990 AAW	KYBLS	10//99-12//99
	Louisiana	S	12.66 MW	14.01 AW	29140 AAW	LABLS	10//99-12//99
	Maine	S	10.56 MW	11.15 AW	23180 AAW	MEBLS	10//99-12//99
	Maryland	S	16.99 MW	18.16 AW	37770 AAW	MDBLS	10//99-12//99

AAW	Average annual wage	AOH	Average offered, high	ASH	Average starting, high	H	Hourly	M	Monthly	S	Special: hourly and annual
AE	Average entry wage	AOL	Average offered, low	ASL	Average starting, low	HI	Highest wage paid	MTC	Median total compensation	TQ	Third quartile wage
AEX	Average experienced wage	APH	Average pay, high range	AW	Average wage paid	HR	High end range	MW	Median wage paid	W	Weekly
AO	Average offered	APL	Average pay, low range	FQ	First quartile wage	LR	Low end range	SQ	Second quartile wage	Y	Yearly

Occupation/Type/Industry	Location	Per	Low	Mid	High	Source	Date
Insurance Claim and Policy Processing Clerk	Massachusetts	S	14.66 MW	14.70 AW	30580 AAW	MABLS	10//99-12//99
	Michigan	S	13.64 MW	14.94 AW	31080 AAW	MIBLS	10//99-12//99
	Minnesota	S	13.15 MW	13.64 AW	28370 AAW	MNBLS	10//99-12//99
	Mississippi	S	11.65 MW	12.40 AW	25790 AAW	MSBLS	10//99-12//99
	Missouri	S	13.69 MW	13.61 AW	28300 AAW	MOBLS	10//99-12//99
	Montana	S	12.01 MW	11.91 AW	24780 AAW	MTBLS	10//99-12//99
	Nebraska	S	12.11 MW	12.88 AW	26790 AAW	NEBLS	10//99-12//99
	Nevada	S	12.56 MW	12.80 AW	26620 AAW	NVBLS	10//99-12//99
	New Hampshire	S	15.12 MW	17.23 AW	35830 AAW	NHBLS	10//99-12//99
	New Jersey	S	15.51 MW	16.84 AW	35020 AAW	NJBLS	10//99-12//99
	New Mexico	S	14.43 MW	16.33 AW	33970 AAW	NMBLS	10//99-12//99
	New York	S	16.07 MW	17.57 AW	36540 AAW	NYBLS	10//99-12//99
	North Carolina	S	12.96 MW	14.16 AW	29460 AAW	NCBLS	10//99-12//99
	North Dakota	S	14.35 MW	16.51 AW	34340 AAW	NDBLS	10//99-12//99
	Ohio	S	12.59 MW	13.68 AW	28460 AAW	OHBLS	10//99-12//99
	Oklahoma	S	15.52 MW	17.15 AW	35680 AAW	OKBLS	10//99-12//99
	Oregon	S	12.74 MW	13.04 AW	27120 AAW	ORBLS	10//99-12//99
	Pennsylvania	S	16.55 MW	18.07 AW	37580 AAW	PABLS	10//99-12//99
	Rhode Island	S	12.52 MW	13.06 AW	27160 AAW	RIBLS	10//99-12//99
	South Carolina	S	14.96 MW	16.36 AW	34030 AAW	SCBLS	10//99-12//99
	South Dakota	S	9.5 MW	9.62 AW	20020 AAW	SDBLS	10//99-12//99
	Tennessee	S	10.48 MW	12.83 AW	26690 AAW	TNBLS	10//99-12//99
	Texas	S	14.33 MW	15.40 AW	32040 AAW	TXBLS	10//99-12//99
	Utah	S	10.14 MW	11.02 AW	22930 AAW	UTBLS	10//99-12//99
	Vermont	S	13.47 MW	14.54 AW	30240 AAW	VTBLS	10//99-12//99
	Washington	S	11.88 MW	12.48 AW	25960 AAW	WABLS	10//99-12//99
	West Virginia	S	15.28 MW	17.12 AW	35620 AAW	WVBLS	10//99-12//99
	Wisconsin	S	11.74 MW	12.03 AW	25020 AAW	WIBLS	10//99-12//99
	Wyoming	S	11.61 MW	14.17 AW	29470 AAW	WYBLS	10//99-12//99
	Puerto Rico	S	7.61 MW	7.68 AW	15980 AAW	PRBLS	10//99-12//99
	Guam	S	7.38 MW	7.75 AW	16120 AAW	GUBLS	10//99-12//99
Insurance Clerk Medical Doctor's Office	United States	H		10.81 AEX		MEDEC	2000
Insurance Sales Agent	Alabama	S	18.44 MW	22.15 AW	46080 AAW	ALBLS	10//99-12//99
	Auburn-Opelika MSA, AL	S	19.76 MW	16.90 AW	41110 AAW	ALBLS	10//99-12//99
	Birmingham MSA, AL	S	19.58 MW	17.84 AW	40730 AAW	ALBLS	10//99-12//99
	Decatur MSA, AL	S	25.74 MW	20.47 AW	53540 AAW	ALBLS	10//99-12//99
	Florence MSA, AL	S	18.48 MW	17.95 AW	38440 AAW	ALBLS	10//99-12//99
	Gadsden MSA, AL	S	16.90 MW	13.80 AW	35150 AAW	ALBLS	10//99-12//99
	Huntsville MSA, AL	S	25.28 MW	17.15 AW	52580 AAW	ALBLS	10//99-12//99
	Montgomery MSA, AL	S	21.98 MW	19.82 AW	45720 AAW	ALBLS	10//99-12//99
	Tuscaloosa MSA, AL	S	21.16 MW	17.70 AW	44020 AAW	ALBLS	10//99-12//99
	Alaska	S	15.52 MW	17.51 AW	36430 AAW	AKBLS	10//99-12//99
	Arizona	S	17.16 MW	19.64 AW	40840 AAW	AZBLS	10//99-12//99
	Flagstaff MSA, AZ-UT	S	12.89 MW	11.28 AW	26810 AAW	AZBLS	10//99-12//99
	Phoenix-Mesa MSA, AZ	S	20.12 MW	17.65 AW	41840 AAW	AZBLS	10//99-12//99
	Tucson MSA, AZ	S	16.98 MW	10.65 AW	35320 AAW	AZBLS	10//99-12//99
	Arkansas	S	16.74 MW	22.09 AW	45940 AAW	ARBLS	10//99-12//99
	Fayetteville-Springdale-Rogers MSA, AR	S	31.97 MW	24.87 AW	66490 AAW	ARBLS	10//99-12//99
	Fort Smith MSA, AR-OK	S	14.34 MW	12.43 AW	29820 AAW	ARBLS	10//99-12//99
	Jonesboro MSA, AR	S	9.72 MW	9.63 AW	20210 AAW	ARBLS	10//99-12//99
	Little Rock-North Little Rock MSA, AR	S	24.76 MW	27.75 AW	51490 AAW	ARBLS	10//99-12//99
	California	S	18.71 MW	23.18 AW	48210 AAW	CABLS	10//99-12//99
	Bakersfield MSA, CA	S	28.57 MW	29.04 AW	59420 AAW	CABLS	10//99-12//99
	Chico-Paradise MSA, CA	S	15.24 MW	12.50 AW	31700 AAW	CABLS	10//99-12//99
	Fresno MSA, CA	S	15.79 MW	12.72 AW	32840 AAW	CABLS	10//99-12//99
	Los Angeles-Long Beach PMSA, CA	S	22.14 MW	16.81 AW	46050 AAW	CABLS	10//99-12//99
	Merced MSA, CA	S	24.23 MW	19.25 AW	50390 AAW	CABLS	10//99-12//99
	Oakland PMSA, CA	S	25.41 MW	22.44 AW	52850 AAW	CABLS	10//99-12//99
	Orange County PMSA, CA	S	21.03 MW	18.65 AW	43750 AAW	CABLS	10//99-12//99
	Redding MSA, CA	S	18.83 MW	17.22 AW	39170 AAW	CABLS	10//99-12//99
	Riverside-San Bernardino PMSA, CA	S	35.09 MW	28.29 AW	72990 AAW	CABLS	10//99-12//99
	Sacramento PMSA, CA	S	25.57 MW	19.14 AW	53190 AAW	CABLS	10//99-12//99
	Salinas MSA, CA	S	20.39 MW	18.36 AW	42410 AAW	CABLS	10//99-12//99
	San Diego MSA, CA	S	24.54 MW	20.22 AW	51040 AAW	CABLS	10//99-12//99

AAW	Average annual wage	AOH	Average offered, high	ASH	Average starting, high
AE	Average entry wage	AOL	Average offered, low	ASL	Average starting, low
AEX	Average experienced wage	APH	Average pay, high range	AW	Average wage paid
AO	Average offered	APL	Average pay, low range	FQ	First quartile wage

H	Hourly	M	Monthly
HI	Highest wage paid	MTC	Median total compensation
HR	High end range	MW	Median wage paid
LR	Low end range	SQ	Second quartile wage

S	Special: hourly and annual
TQ	Third quartile wage
W	Weekly
Y	Yearly

Insurance Sales Agent

Occupation/Type/Industry	Location	Per	Low	Mid	High	Source	Date
Insurance Sales Agent	San Francisco PMSA, CA	S	24.22 MW	20.00 AW	50380 AAW	CABLS	10//99-12//99
	San Jose PMSA, CA	S	23.80 MW	24.58 AW	49500 AAW	CABLS	10//99-12//99
	Santa Barbara-Santa Maria-Lompoc MSA, CA	S	27.41 MW	20.29 AW	57000 AAW	CABLS	10//99-12//99
	Santa Rosa PMSA, CA	S	20.87 MW	18.58 AW	43400 AAW	CABLS	10//99-12//99
	Vallejo-Fairfield-Napa PMSA, CA	S	16.11 MW	14.81 AW	33500 AAW	CABLS	10//99-12//99
	Ventura PMSA, CA	S	22.38 MW	22.62 AW	46550 AAW	CABLS	10//99-12//99
	Visalia-Tulare-Porterville MSA, CA	S	21.21 MW	16.35 AW	44110 AAW	CABLS	10//99-12//99
	Yolo PMSA, CA	S	15.73 MW	15.20 AW	32720 AAW	CABLS	10//99-12//99
	Colorado	S	21.25 MW	24.72 AW	51410 AAW	COBLS	10//99-12//99
	Denver PMSA, CO	S	25.73 MW	23.10 AW	53520 AAW	COBLS	10//99-12//99
	Connecticut	S	25.45 MW	27.31 AW	56800 AAW	CTBLS	10//99-12//99
	Bridgeport PMSA, CT	S	21.86 MW	16.73 AW	45460 AAW	CTBLS	10//99-12//99
	Danbury PMSA, CT	S	25.95 MW	23.02 AW	53970 AAW	CTBLS	10//99-12//99
	Hartford MSA, CT	S	26.21 MW	22.49 AW	54520 AAW	CTBLS	10//99-12//99
	New Haven-Meriden PMSA, CT	S	28.71 MW	30.21 AW	59710 AAW	CTBLS	10//99-12//99
	New London-Norwich MSA, CT-RI	S	24.73 MW	24.17 AW	51440 AAW	CTBLS	10//99-12//99
	Delaware	S	14.95 MW	16.66 AW	34660 AAW	DEBLS	10//99-12//99
	Dover MSA, DE	S	14.11 MW	10.90 AW	29360 AAW	DEBLS	10//99-12//99
	Wilmington-Newark PMSA, DE-MD	S	17.21 MW	15.31 AW	35790 AAW	DEBLS	10//99-12//99
	District of Columbia	S	18.89 MW	23.97 AW	49850 AAW	DCBLS	10//99-12//99
	Washington PMSA, DC-MD-VA-WV	S	26.23 MW	23.38 AW	54560 AAW	DCBLS	10//99-12//99
	Florida	S	18.3 MW	22.20 AW	46180 AAW	FLBLS	10//99-12//99
	Daytona Beach MSA, FL	S	14.54 MW	11.80 AW	30240 AAW	FLBLS	10//99-12//99
	Fort Lauderdale PMSA, FL	S	20.03 MW	15.40 AW	41660 AAW	FLBLS	10//99-12//99
	Gainesville MSA, FL	S	16.36 MW	13.93 AW	34020 AAW	FLBLS	10//99-12//99
	Jacksonville MSA, FL	S	22.27 MW	19.60 AW	46330 AAW	FLBLS	10//99-12//99
	Lakeland-Winter Haven MSA, FL	S	23.56 MW	18.61 AW	49000 AAW	FLBLS	10//99-12//99
	Miami PMSA, FL	S	23.96 MW	26.87 AW	49840 AAW	FLBLS	10//99-12//99
	Naples MSA, FL	S	19.00 MW	12.83 AW	39530 AAW	FLBLS	10//99-12//99
	Sarasota-Bradenton MSA, FL	S	23.25 MW	17.44 AW	48360 AAW	FLBLS	10//99-12//99
	West Palm Beach-Boca Raton MSA, FL	S	22.40 MW	16.38 AW	46580 AAW	FLBLS	10//99-12//99
	Georgia	S	16.4 MW	18.19 AW	37840 AAW	GABLS	10//99-12//99
	Athens MSA, GA	S	16.36 MW	16.00 AW	34020 AAW	GABLS	10//99-12//99
	Atlanta MSA, GA	S	17.48 MW	16.30 AW	36360 AAW	GABLS	10//99-12//99
	Augusta-Aiken MSA, GA-SC	S	16.47 MW	15.06 AW	34250 AAW	GABLS	10//99-12//99
	Columbus MSA, GA-AL	S	20.24 MW	17.44 AW	42100 AAW	GABLS	10//99-12//99
	Macon MSA, GA	S	14.63 MW	13.89 AW	30430 AAW	GABLS	10//99-12//99
	Savannah MSA, GA	S	16.77 MW	16.22 AW	34880 AAW	GABLS	10//99-12//99
	Hawaii	S	15.32 MW	21.18 AW	44060 AAW	HIBLS	10//99-12//99
	Honolulu MSA, HI	S	21.64 MW	15.49 AW	45010 AAW	HIBLS	10//99-12//99
	Idaho	S	18.22 MW	20.84 AW	43350 AAW	IDBLS	10//99-12//99
	Illinois	S	16.55 MW	21.17 AW	44030 AAW	ILBLS	10//99-12//99
	Bloomington-Normal MSA, IL	S	26.30 MW	19.81 AW	54700 AAW	ILBLS	10//99-12//99
	Champaign-Urbana MSA, IL	S	20.29 MW	16.00 AW	42210 AAW	ILBLS	10//99-12//99
	Chicago PMSA, IL	S	20.89 MW	16.41 AW	43450 AAW	ILBLS	10//99-12//99
	Decatur MSA, IL	S	20.24 MW	18.62 AW	42090 AAW	ILBLS	10//99-12//99
	Kankakee PMSA, IL	S	15.24 MW	15.25 AW	31700 AAW	ILBLS	10//99-12//99
	Peoria-Pekin MSA, IL	S	24.62 MW	20.58 AW	51200 AAW	ILBLS	10//99-12//99
	Springfield MSA, IL	S	18.29 MW	15.76 AW	38030 AAW	ILBLS	10//99-12//99
	Indiana	S	16.46 MW	20.90 AW	43480 AAW	INBLS	10//99-12//99
	Bloomington MSA, IN	S	16.89 MW	11.67 AW	35130 AAW	INBLS	10//99-12//99
	Elkhart-Goshen MSA, IN	S	23.20 MW	15.23 AW	48250 AAW	INBLS	10//99-12//99
	Evansville-Henderson MSA, IN-KY	S	15.03 MW	8.47 AW	31250 AAW	INBLS	10//99-12//99
	Fort Wayne MSA, IN	S	33.21 MW	25.51 AW	69080 AAW	INBLS	10//99-12//99
	Gary PMSA, IN	S	26.15 MW	19.69 AW	54390 AAW	INBLS	10//99-12//99
	Indianapolis MSA, IN	S	20.20 MW	16.28 AW	42020 AAW	INBLS	10//99-12//99
	Lafayette MSA, IN	S	15.42 MW	8.43 AW	32080 AAW	INBLS	10//99-12//99
	Muncie MSA, IN	S	16.63 MW	13.04 AW	34600 AAW	INBLS	10//99-12//99
	South Bend MSA, IN	S	29.30 MW	33.46 AW	60930 AAW	INBLS	10//99-12//99
	Terre Haute MSA, IN	S	34.17 MW	32.96 AW	71080 AAW	INBLS	10//99-12//99
	Iowa	S	18.02 MW	21.82 AW	45380 AAW	IABLS	10//99-12//99
	Cedar Rapids MSA, IA	S	28.44 MW	28.84 AW	59150 AAW	IABLS	10//99-12//99

AAW Average annual wage	AOH Average offered, high	ASH Average starting, high	H Hourly	M Monthly	S Special: hourly and annual
AE Average entry wage	AOL Average offered, low	ASL Average starting, low	HI Highest wage paid	MTC Median total compensation	TQ Third quartile wage
AEX Average experienced wage	APH Average pay, high range	AW Average wage paid	HR High end range	MW Median wage paid	W Weekly
AO Average offered	APL Average pay, low range	FQ First quartile wage	LR Low end range	SQ Second quartile wage	Y Yearly

Occupation/Type/Industry	Location	Per	Low	Mid	High	Source	Date
Insurance Sales Agent	Davenport-Moline-Rock Island MSA, IA-IL	S	15.87 MW	10.41 AW	33000 AAW	IABLS	10//99-12//99
	Des Moines MSA, IA	S	20.70 MW	19.84 AW	43060 AAW	IABLS	10//99-12//99
	Iowa City MSA, IA	S	12.91 MW	10.69 AW	26840 AAW	IABLS	10//99-12//99
	Kansas	S	8.73 MW	14.61 AW	30390 AAW	KSBLS	10//99-12//99
	Topeka MSA, KS	S	42.24 MW	33.20 AW	87860 AAW	KSBLS	10//99-12//99
	Wichita MSA, KS	S	19.77 MW	15.69 AW	41130 AAW	KSBLS	10//99-12//99
	Kentucky	S	17.12 MW	22.70 AW	47220 AAW	KYBLS	10//99-12//99
	Louisville MSA, KY-IN	S	26.60 MW	19.87 AW	55330 AAW	KYBLS	10//99-12//99
	Owensboro MSA, KY	S	20.36 MW	23.40 AW	42360 AAW	KYBLS	10//99-12//99
	Louisiana	S	14.66 MW	19.00 AW	39520 AAW	LABLS	10//99-12//99
	Alexandria MSA, LA	S	10.68 MW	8.52 AW	22210 AAW	LABLS	10//99-12//99
	Baton Rouge MSA, LA	S	18.36 MW	13.28 AW	38180 AAW	LABLS	10//99-12//99
	Houma MSA, LA	S	25.55 MW	27.27 AW	53150 AAW	LABLS	10//99-12//99
	Lafayette MSA, LA	S	33.59 MW	28.54 AW	69870 AAW	LABLS	10//99-12//99
	Lake Charles MSA, LA	S	18.37 MW	17.87 AW	38210 AAW	LABLS	10//99-12//99
	Monroe MSA, LA	S	11.14 MW	6.42 AW	23170 AAW	LABLS	10//99-12//99
	New Orleans MSA, LA	S	14.98 MW	13.45 AW	31150 AAW	LABLS	10//99-12//99
	Shreveport-Bossier City MSA, LA	S	21.46 MW	16.38 AW	44630 AAW	LABLS	10//99-12//99
	Maine	S	19.3 MW	21.79 AW	45320 AAW	MEBLS	10//99-12//99
	Portland MSA, ME	S	21.81 MW	20.61 AW	45370 AAW	MEBLS	10//99-12//99
	Maryland	S	21.09 MW	24.67 AW	51320 AAW	MDBLS	10//99-12//99
	Baltimore PMSA, MD	S	25.09 MW	17.91 AW	52200 AAW	MDBLS	10//99-12//99
	Cumberland MSA, MD-WV	S	17.44 MW	18.39 AW	36280 AAW	MDBLS	10//99-12//99
	Massachusetts	S	22.31 MW	26.91 AW	55970 AAW	MABLS	10//99-12//99
	Barnstable-Yarmouth MSA, MA	S	19.68 MW	19.22 AW	40940 AAW	MABLS	10//99-12//99
	Boston PMSA, MA-NH	S	28.35 MW	25.15 AW	58970 AAW	MABLS	10//99-12//99
	Lawrence PMSA, MA-NH	S	23.69 MW	19.69 AW	49280 AAW	MABLS	10//99-12//99
	Lowell PMSA, MA-NH	S	29.77 MW	30.29 AW	61910 AAW	MABLS	10//99-12//99
	New Bedford PMSA, MA	S	15.85 MW	10.52 AW	32970 AAW	MABLS	10//99-12//99
	Pittsfield MSA, MA	S	11.28 MW	10.03 AW	23470 AAW	MABLS	10//99-12//99
	Worcester PMSA, MA-CT	S	21.95 MW	19.09 AW	45660 AAW	MABLS	10//99-12//99
	Michigan	S	27.69 MW	32.23 AW	67030 AAW	MIBLS	10//99-12//99
	Ann Arbor PMSA, MI	S	21.26 MW	13.98 AW	44220 AAW	MIBLS	10//99-12//99
	Benton Harbor MSA, MI	S	19.00 MW	18.76 AW	39530 AAW	MIBLS	10//99-12//99
	Detroit PMSA, MI	S	30.23 MW	32.67 AW	62870 AAW	MIBLS	10//99-12//99
	Flint PMSA, MI	S	19.37 MW	15.31 AW	40280 AAW	MIBLS	10//99-12//99
	Grand Rapids-Muskegon-Holland MSA, MI	S	42.26 MW	44.42 AW	87890 AAW	MIBLS	10//99-12//99
	Jackson MSA, MI	S	19.03 MW	12.71 AW	39580 AAW	MIBLS	10//99-12//99
	Kalamazoo-Battle Creek MSA, MI	S	24.16 MW	24.71 AW	50250 AAW	MIBLS	10//99-12//99
	Lansing-East Lansing MSA, MI	S	18.24 MW	17.44 AW	37930 AAW	MIBLS	10//99-12//99
	Saginaw-Bay City-Midland MSA, MI	S	27.23 MW	21.13 AW	56630 AAW	MIBLS	10//99-12//99
	Minnesota	S	19.82 MW	22.98 AW	47790 AAW	MNBLS	10//99-12//99
	Duluth-Superior MSA, MN-WI	S	16.99 MW	14.72 AW	35340 AAW	MNBLS	10//99-12//99
	Minneapolis-St. Paul MSA, MN-WI	S	27.66 MW	24.95 AW	57540 AAW	MNBLS	10//99-12//99
	Rochester MSA, MN	S	22.19 MW	18.59 AW	46160 AAW	MNBLS	10//99-12//99
	St. Cloud MSA, MN	S	22.76 MW	18.61 AW	47330 AAW	MNBLS	10//99-12//99
	Mississippi	S	15.64 MW	19.88 AW	41350 AAW	MSBLS	10//99-12//99
	Hattiesburg MSA, MS	S	15.98 MW	15.25 AW	33230 AAW	MSBLS	10//99-12//99
	Jackson MSA, MS	S	21.26 MW	15.73 AW	44210 AAW	MSBLS	10//99-12//99
	Missouri	S	18.32 MW	22.36 AW	46500 AAW	MOBLS	10//99-12//99
	Columbia MSA, MO	S	34.27 MW	45.22 AW	71270 AAW	MOBLS	10//99-12//99
	Joplin MSA, MO	S	21.74 MW	17.90 AW	45220 AAW	MOBLS	10//99-12//99
	Kansas City MSA, MO-KS	S	21.17 MW	10.68 AW	44020 AAW	MOBLS	10//99-12//99
	St. Louis MSA, MO-IL	S	21.38 MW	17.83 AW	44460 AAW	MOBLS	10//99-12//99
	Montana	S	11.65 MW	21.49 AW	44700 AAW	MTBLS	10//99-12//99
	Billings MSA, MT	S	32.15 MW	16.23 AW	66860 AAW	MTBLS	10//99-12//99
	Nebraska	S	15.36 MW	20.02 AW	41640 AAW	NEBLS	10//99-12//99
	Lincoln MSA, NE	S	15.01 MW	11.99 AW	31230 AAW	NEBLS	10//99-12//99
	Omaha MSA, NE-IA	S	23.57 MW	21.18 AW	49020 AAW	NEBLS	10//99-12//99
	Nevada	S	24.8 MW	26.32 AW	54750 AAW	NVBLS	10//99-12//99
	Las Vegas MSA, NV-AZ	S	26.06 MW	23.20 AW	54200 AAW	NVBLS	10//99-12//99
	Reno MSA, NV	S	26.26 MW	27.47 AW	54610 AAW	NVBLS	10//99-12//99
	Manchester PMSA, NH	S	21.65 MW	21.64 AW	45040 AAW	NHBLS	10//99-12//99
	Nashua PMSA, NH	S	32.65 MW	30.07 AW	67920 AAW	NHBLS	10//99-12//99

AAW Average annual wage	**AOH** Average offered, high	**ASH** Average starting, high	**H** Hourly	**M** Monthly	**S** Special: hourly and annual
AE Average entry wage	**AOL** Average offered, low	**ASL** Average starting, low	**HI** Highest wage paid	**MTC** Median total compensation	**TQ** Third quartile wage
AEX Average experienced wage	**APH** Average pay, high range	**AW** Average wage paid	**HR** High end range	**MW** Median wage paid	**W** Weekly
AO Average offered	**APL** Average pay, low range	**FQ** First quartile wage	**LR** Low end range	**SQ** Second quartile wage	**Y** Yearly

Occupation/Type/Industry	Location	Per	Low	Mid	High	Source	Date
Insurance Sales Agent	Portsmouth-Rochester PMSA, NH-ME	S	17.17 MW	15.30 AW	35710 AAW	NHBLS	10//99-12//99
	New Jersey	S	24.44 MW	28.22 AW	58690 AAW	NJBLS	10//99-12//99
	Jersey City PMSA, NJ	S	20.65 MW	20.76 AW	42960 AAW	NJBLS	10//99-12//99
	Middlesex-Somerset-Hunterdon PMSA, NJ	S	28.86 MW	24.19 AW	60020 AAW	NJBLS	10//99-12//99
	Monmouth-Ocean PMSA, NJ	S	24.46 MW	22.17 AW	50880 AAW	NJBLS	10//99-12//99
	Newark PMSA, NJ	S	32.53 MW	28.01 AW	67660 AAW	NJBLS	10//99-12//99
	Trenton PMSA, NJ	S	28.57 MW	28.89 AW	59420 AAW	NJBLS	10//99-12//99
	Vineland-Millville-Bridgeton PMSA, NJ	S	14.42 MW	14.15 AW	29990 AAW	NJBLS	10//99-12//99
	New Mexico	S	16.04 MW	21.52 AW	44760 AAW	NMBLS	10//99-12//99
	New York	S	24.71 MW	26.60 AW	55330 AAW	NYBLS	10//99-12//99
	Buffalo-Niagara Falls MSA, NY	S	15.83 MW	12.99 AW	32920 AAW	NYBLS	10//99-12//99
	Elmira MSA, NY	S	19.31 MW	18.04 AW	40160 AAW	NYBLS	10//99-12//99
	Nassau-Suffolk PMSA, NY	S	22.90 MW	15.67 AW	47620 AAW	NYBLS	10//99-12//99
	New York PMSA, NY	S	30.49 MW	30.08 AW	63420 AAW	NYBLS	10//99-12//99
	Newburgh PMSA, NY-PA	S	19.98 MW	13.44 AW	41560 AAW	NYBLS	10//99-12//99
	Rochester MSA, NY	S	25.50 MW	21.89 AW	53040 AAW	NYBLS	10//99-12//99
	Syracuse MSA, NY	S	24.61 MW	22.08 AW	51180 AAW	NYBLS	10//99-12//99
	Utica-Rome MSA, NY	S	22.70 MW	19.87 AW	47210 AAW	NYBLS	10//99-12//99
	North Carolina	S	13.61 MW	17.89 AW	37210 AAW	NCBLS	10//99-12//99
	Asheville MSA, NC	S	18.37 MW	13.41 AW	38220 AAW	NCBLS	10//99-12//99
	Charlotte-Gastonia-Rock Hill MSA, NC-SC	S	22.91 MW	18.99 AW	47660 AAW	NCBLS	10//99-12//99
	Fayetteville MSA, NC	S	11.58 MW	8.30 AW	24090 AAW	NCBLS	10//99-12//99
	Greenville MSA, NC	S	16.58 MW	14.81 AW	34490 AAW	NCBLS	10//99-12//99
	Hickory-Morganton-Lenoir MSA, NC	S	15.30 MW	10.37 AW	31820 AAW	NCBLS	10//99-12//99
	Raleigh-Durham-Chapel Hill MSA, NC	S	22.43 MW	18.43 AW	46650 AAW	NCBLS	10//99-12//99
	Rocky Mount MSA, NC	S	15.06 MW	15.39 AW	31310 AAW	NCBLS	10//99-12//99
	Wilmington MSA, NC	S	17.84 MW	12.46 AW	37110 AAW	NCBLS	10//99-12//99
	North Dakota	S	13.59 MW	18.69 AW	38870 AAW	NDBLS	10//99-12//99
	Bismarck MSA, ND	S	16.25 MW	12.09 AW	33800 AAW	NDBLS	10//99-12//99
	Fargo-Moorhead MSA, ND-MN	S	18.93 MW	22.27 AW	39380 AAW	NDBLS	10//99-12//99
	Grand Forks MSA, ND-MN	S	21.63 MW	19.34 AW	44990 AAW	NDBLS	10//99-12//99
	Canton-Massillon MSA, OH	S	35.51 MW	27.16 AW	73870 AAW	OHBLS	10//99-12//99
	Cincinnati PMSA, OH-KY-IN	S	20.57 MW	13.29 AW	42800 AAW	OHBLS	10//99-12//99
	Cleveland-Lorain-Elyria PMSA, OH	S	29.84 MW	24.65 AW	62060 AAW	OHBLS	10//99-12//99
	Dayton-Springfield MSA, OH	S	13.37 MW	10.38 AW	27810 AAW	OHBLS	10//99-12//99
	Hamilton-Middletown PMSA, OH	S	31.39 MW	21.32 AW	65280 AAW	OHBLS	10//99-12//99
	Lima MSA, OH	S	22.28 MW	18.30 AW	46350 AAW	OHBLS	10//99-12//99
	Mansfield MSA, OH	S	16.38 MW	12.24 AW	34070 AAW	OHBLS	10//99-12//99
	Steubenville-Weirton MSA, OH-WV	S	13.49 MW	14.66 AW	28050 AAW	OHBLS	10//99-12//99
	Toledo MSA, OH	S	29.33 MW	21.78 AW	61010 AAW	OHBLS	10//99-12//99
	Youngstown-Warren MSA, OH	S	18.33 MW	18.48 AW	38120 AAW	OHBLS	10//99-12//99
	Oklahoma	S	13.15 MW	16.13 AW	33540 AAW	OKBLS	10//99-12//99
	Lawton MSA, OK	S	15.23 MW	10.21 AW	31670 AAW	OKBLS	10//99-12//99
	Oklahoma City MSA, OK	S	17.07 MW	12.20 AW	35510 AAW	OKBLS	10//99-12//99
	Tulsa MSA, OK	S	22.75 MW	22.02 AW	47320 AAW	OKBLS	10//99-12//99
	Oregon	S	20.5 MW	24.67 AW	51310 AAW	ORBLS	10//99-12//99
	Eugene-Springfield MSA, OR	S	29.17 MW	23.35 AW	60670 AAW	ORBLS	10//99-12//99
	Medford-Ashland MSA, OR	S	24.69 MW	23.51 AW	51340 AAW	ORBLS	10//99-12//99
	Portland-Vancouver PMSA, OR-WA	S	25.46 MW	22.59 AW	52950 AAW	ORBLS	10//99-12//99
	Pennsylvania	S	16.69 MW	19.72 AW	41020 AAW	PABLS	10//99-12//99
	Allentown-Bethlehem-Easton MSA, PA	S	29.65 MW	21.00 AW	61670 AAW	PABLS	10//99-12//99
	Altoona MSA, PA	S	15.42 MW	13.32 AW	32080 AAW	PABLS	10//99-12//99
	Erie MSA, PA	S	15.00 MW	10.55 AW	31200 AAW	PABLS	10//99-12//99
	Harrisburg-Lebanon-Carlisle MSA, PA	S	18.13 MW	15.26 AW	37720 AAW	PABLS	10//99-12//99
	Lancaster MSA, PA	S	22.48 MW	22.61 AW	46760 AAW	PABLS	10//99-12//99
	Philadelphia PMSA, PA-NJ	S	22.95 MW	18.75 AW	47730 AAW	PABLS	10//99-12//99
	Pittsburgh MSA, PA	S	19.43 MW	16.56 AW	40400 AAW	PABLS	10//99-12//99
	Reading MSA, PA	S	19.39 MW	21.58 AW	40320 AAW	PABLS	10//99-12//99

AAW	Average annual wage	AOH	Average offered, high	ASH	Average starting, high	H	Hourly	M	Monthly	S	Special: hourly and annual
AE	Average entry wage	AOL	Average offered, low	ASL	Average starting, low	HI	Highest wage paid	MTC	Median total compensation	TQ	Third quartile wage
AEX	Average experienced wage	APH	Average pay, high range	AW	Average wage paid	HR	High end range	MW	Median wage paid	W	Weekly
AO	Average offered	APL	Average pay, low range	FQ	First quartile wage	LR	Low end range	SQ	Second quartile wage	Y	Yearly

Occupation/Type/Industry	Location	Per	Low	Mid	High	Source	Date
Insurance Sales Agent	Scranton--Wilkes-Barre--						
	Hazleton MSA, PA	S	20.66 MW	18.43 AW	42970 AAW	PABLS	10//99-12//99
	Sharon MSA, PA	S	25.55 MW	28.79 AW	53140 AAW	PABLS	10//99-12//99
	Williamsport MSA, PA	S	16.68 MW	13.21 AW	34700 AAW	PABLS	10//99-12//99
	Rhode Island	S	16.39 MW	23.26 AW	48370 AAW	RIBLS	10//99-12//99
	Providence-Fall River-						
	Warwick MSA, RI-MA	S	28.46 MW	25.86 AW	59200 AAW	RIBLS	10//99-12//99
	South Carolina	S	13.93 MW	17.36 AW	36110 AAW	SCBLS	10//99-12//99
	Charleston-North Charleston						
	MSA, SC	S	19.27 MW	15.48 AW	40090 AAW	SCBLS	10//99-12//99
	Columbia MSA, SC	S	27.78 MW	27.50 AW	57790 AAW	SCBLS	10//99-12//99
	Greenville-Spartanburg-						
	Anderson MSA, SC	S	15.82 MW	12.75 AW	32910 AAW	SCBLS	10//99-12//99
	Myrtle Beach MSA, SC	S	10.06 MW	9.76 AW	20920 AAW	SCBLS	10//99-12//99
	Sumter MSA, SC	S	17.49 MW	14.92 AW	36390 AAW	SCBLS	10//99-12//99
	Tennessee	S	14.7 MW	17.92 AW	37280 AAW	TNBLS	10//99-12//99
	Chattanooga MSA, TN-GA	S	18.38 MW	16.97 AW	38230 AAW	TNBLS	10//99-12//99
	Clarksville-Hopkinsville MSA,						
	TN-KY	S	14.71 MW	12.12 AW	30590 AAW	TNBLS	10//99-12//99
	Jackson MSA, TN	S	12.04 MW	10.16 AW	25040 AAW	TNBLS	10//99-12//99
	Johnson City-Kingsport-Bristol						
	MSA, TN-VA	S	21.76 MW	20.73 AW	45270 AAW	TNBLS	10//99-12//99
	Knoxville MSA, TN	S	30.63 MW	29.04 AW	63710 AAW	TNBLS	10//99-12//99
	Memphis MSA, TN-AR-MS	S	24.69 MW	21.70 AW	51350 AAW	MSBLS	10//99-12//99
	Nashville MSA, TN	S	16.68 MW	13.86 AW	34690 AAW	TNBLS	10//99-12//99
	Texas	S	18.02 MW	22.71 AW	47250 AAW	TXBLS	10//99-12//99
	Brazoria PMSA, TX	S	15.64 MW	17.87 AW	32530 AAW	TXBLS	10//99-12//99
	Brownsville-Harlingen-San						
	Benito MSA, TX	S	11.23 MW	9.36 AW	23350 AAW	TXBLS	10//99-12//99
	Corpus Christi MSA, TX	S	14.38 MW	13.09 AW	29910 AAW	TXBLS	10//99-12//99
	Dallas PMSA, TX	S	18.68 MW	19.06 AW	38840 AAW	TXBLS	10//99-12//99
	Fort Worth-Arlington PMSA,						
	TX	S	24.41 MW	17.05 AW	50770 AAW	TXBLS	10//99-12//99
	Galveston-Texas City PMSA,						
	TX	S	16.81 MW	15.38 AW	34970 AAW	TXBLS	10//99-12//99
	Houston PMSA, TX	S	24.19 MW	19.31 AW	50310 AAW	TXBLS	10//99-12//99
	Odessa-Midland MSA, TX	S	13.48 MW	12.12 AW	28050 AAW	TXBLS	10//99-12//99
	San Angelo MSA, TX	S	28.93 MW	16.04 AW	60170 AAW	TXBLS	10//99-12//99
	San Antonio MSA, TX	S	22.64 MW	18.77 AW	47090 AAW	TXBLS	10//99-12//99
	Sherman-Denison MSA, TX	S	22.68 MW	23.64 AW	47170 AAW	TXBLS	10//99-12//99
	Texarkana MSA, TX-						
	Texarkana, AR	S	17.46 MW	12.91 AW	36320 AAW	TXBLS	10//99-12//99
	Tyler MSA, TX	S	28.56 MW	30.09 AW	59410 AAW	TXBLS	10//99-12//99
	Utah	S	20.58 MW	25.69 AW	53430 AAW	UTBLS	10//99-12//99
	Salt Lake City-Ogden MSA,						
	UT	S	24.57 MW	23.48 AW	51110 AAW	UTBLS	10//99-12//99
	Vermont	S	20.57 MW	22.23 AW	46240 AAW	VTBLS	10//99-12//99
	Burlington MSA, VT	S	23.67 MW	20.19 AW	49220 AAW	VTBLS	10//99-12//99
	Virginia	S	18.23 MW	21.05 AW	43780 AAW	VABLS	10//99-12//99
	Lynchburg MSA, VA	S	13.98 MW	7.31 AW	29070 AAW	VABLS	10//99-12//99
	Norfolk-Virginia Beach-						
	Newport News MSA, VA-						
	NC	S	14.28 MW	11.08 AW	29690 AAW	VABLS	10//99-12//99
	Richmond-Petersburg MSA,						
	VA	S	22.19 MW	19.48 AW	46150 AAW	VABLS	10//99-12//99
	Roanoke MSA, VA	S	16.65 MW	14.13 AW	34630 AAW	VABLS	10//99-12//99
	Washington	S	22.06 MW	24.97 AW	51930 AAW	WABLS	10//99-12//99
	Bremerton PMSA, WA	S	25.39 MW	22.83 AW	52820 AAW	WABLS	10//99-12//99
	Olympia PMSA, WA	S	20.00 MW	18.29 AW	41600 AAW	WABLS	10//99-12//99
	Richland-Kennewick-Pasco						
	MSA, WA	S	12.21 MW	10.47 AW	25400 AAW	WABLS	10//99-12//99
	Seattle-Bellevue-Everett						
	PMSA, WA	S	25.67 MW	22.07 AW	53390 AAW	WABLS	10//99-12//99
	Spokane MSA, WA	S	22.31 MW	19.51 AW	46400 AAW	WABLS	10//99-12//99
	Tacoma PMSA, WA	S	40.30 MW	39.43 AW	83820 AAW	WABLS	10//99-12//99
	West Virginia	S	13.09 MW	17.36 AW	36100 AAW	WVBLS	10//99-12//99
	Huntington-Ashland MSA,						
	WV-KY-OH	S	15.10 MW	9.94 AW	31420 AAW	WVBLS	10//99-12//99
	Parkersburg-Marietta MSA,						
	WV-OH	S	19.09 MW	15.14 AW	39700 AAW	WVBLS	10//99-12//99
	Wheeling MSA, WV-OH	S	15.88 MW	12.62 AW	33030 AAW	WVBLS	10//99-12//99
	Wisconsin	S	21.8 MW	23.07 AW	47980 AAW	WIBLS	10//99-12//99

AAW	Average annual wage	AOH	Average offered, high	ASH	Average starting, high	H	Hourly	M	Monthly	S	Special: hourly and annual
AE	Average entry wage	AOL	Average offered, low	ASL	Average starting, low	HI	Highest wage paid	MTC	Median total compensation	TQ	Third quartile wage
AEX	Average experienced wage	APH	Average pay, high range	AW	Average wage paid	HR	High end range	MW	Median wage paid	W	Weekly
AO	Average offered	APL	Average pay, low range	FQ	First quartile wage	LR	Low end range	SQ	Second quartile wage	Y	Yearly

Occupation/Type/Industry	Location	Per	Low	Mid	High	Source	Date
Insurance Sales Agent	Appleton-Oshkosh-Neenah						
	MSA, WI	S	31.19 MW	25.39 AW	64870 AAW	WIBLS	10//99-12//99
	Eau Claire MSA, WI	S	10.97 MW	10.79 AW	22820 AAW	WIBLS	10//99-12//99
	Janesville-Beloit MSA, WI	S	19.51 MW	15.25 AW	40580 AAW	WIBLS	10//99-12//99
	Kenosha PMSA, WI	S	17.41 MW	12.53 AW	36220 AAW	WIBLS	10//99-12//99
	La Crosse MSA, WI-MN	S	20.69 MW	16.09 AW	43030 AAW	WIBLS	10//99-12//99
	Madison MSA, WI	S	25.87 MW	22.50 AW	53810 AAW	WIBLS	10//99-12//99
	Milwaukee-Waukesha PMSA,						
	WI	S	28.41 MW	26.65 AW	59100 AAW	WIBLS	10//99-12//99
	Racine PMSA, WI	S	25.71 MW	23.69 AW	53480 AAW	WIBLS	10//99-12//99
	Sheboygan MSA, WI	S	24.57 MW	26.10 AW	51100 AAW	WIBLS	10//99-12//99
	Wausau MSA, WI	S	20.44 MW	16.68 AW	42510 AAW	WIBLS	10//99-12//99
	Wyoming	S	14.85 MW	15.05 AW	31310 AAW	WYBLS	10//99-12//99
	Casper MSA, WY	S	17.16 MW	15.10 AW	35700 AAW	WYBLS	10//99-12//99
	Puerto Rico	S	9.25 MW	11.73 AW	24400 AAW	PRBLS	10//99-12//99
	Caguas PMSA, PR	S	10.71 MW	6.64 AW	22290 AAW	PRBLS	10//99-12//99
	San Juan-Bayamon PMSA, PR	S	12.26 MW	9.66 AW	25500 AAW	PRBLS	10//99-12//99
	Virgin Islands	S	10.26 MW	12.75 AW	26510 AAW	VIBLS	10//99-12//99
Insurance Underwriter	Alabama	S	16.64 MW	18.75 AW	39000 AAW	ALBLS	10//99-12//99
	Birmingham MSA, AL	S	20.66 MW	20.01 AW	42960 AAW	ALBLS	10//99-12//99
	Mobile MSA, AL	S	14.72 MW	12.53 AW	30610 AAW	ALBLS	10//99-12//99
	Alaska	S	20.95 MW	21.19 AW	44080 AAW	AKBLS	10//99-12//99
	Anchorage MSA, AK	S	22.13 MW	21.06 AW	46030 AAW	AKBLS	10//99-12//99
	Arizona	S	22.21 MW	23.62 AW	49120 AAW	AZBLS	10//99-12//99
	Phoenix-Mesa MSA, AZ	S	23.87 MW	22.40 AW	49650 AAW	AZBLS	10//99-12//99
	Arkansas	S	21.14 MW	21.44 AW	44590 AAW	ARBLS	10//99-12//99
	Little Rock-North Little Rock						
	MSA, AR	S	22.12 MW	21.95 AW	46020 AAW	ARBLS	10//99-12//99
	California	S	20.18 MW	22.44 AW	46670 AAW	CABLS	10//99-12//99
	Fresno MSA, CA	S	20.49 MW	18.39 AW	42610 AAW	CABLS	10//99-12//99
	Los Angeles-Long Beach						
	PMSA, CA	S	23.69 MW	21.87 AW	49270 AAW	CABLS	10//99-12//99
	Oakland PMSA, CA	S	22.08 MW	19.51 AW	45930 AAW	CABLS	10//99-12//99
	Orange County PMSA, CA	S	20.55 MW	17.15 AW	42750 AAW	CABLS	10//99-12//99
	Riverside-San Bernardino						
	PMSA, CA	S	20.16 MW	18.89 AW	41930 AAW	CABLS	10//99-12//99
	Sacramento PMSA, CA	S	20.90 MW	19.50 AW	43470 AAW	CABLS	10//99-12//99
	Salinas MSA, CA	S	19.85 MW	19.10 AW	41280 AAW	CABLS	10//99-12//99
	San Diego MSA, CA	S	21.41 MW	19.06 AW	44530 AAW	CABLS	10//99-12//99
	San Francisco PMSA, CA	S	25.86 MW	24.20 AW	53800 AAW	CABLS	10//99-12//99
	San Jose PMSA, CA	S	21.67 MW	18.20 AW	45070 AAW	CABLS	10//99-12//99
	Stockton-Lodi MSA, CA	S	18.37 MW	17.90 AW	38210 AAW	CABLS	10//99-12//99
	Colorado	S	17.62 MW	19.79 AW	41160 AAW	COBLS	10//99-12//99
	Denver PMSA, CO	S	21.15 MW	19.15 AW	43990 AAW	COBLS	10//99-12//99
	Connecticut	S	24.12 MW	27.01 AW	56190 AAW	CTBLS	10//99-12//99
	Hartford MSA, CT	S	24.40 MW	22.76 AW	50740 AAW	CTBLS	10//99-12//99
	New Haven-Meriden PMSA,						
	CT	S	23.95 MW	22.05 AW	49810 AAW	CTBLS	10//99-12//99
	Stamford-Norwalk PMSA, CT	S	35.82 MW	32.69 AW	74500 AAW	CTBLS	10//99-12//99
	Delaware	S	21.12 MW	21.98 AW	45710 AAW	DEBLS	10//99-12//99
	Wilmington-Newark PMSA,						
	DE-MD	S	22.28 MW	21.25 AW	46340 AAW	DEBLS	10//99-12//99
	District of Columbia	S	22.97 MW	24.55 AW	51070 AAW	DCBLS	10//99-12//99
	Washington PMSA, DC-MD-						
	VA-WV	S	24.48 MW	23.43 AW	50920 AAW	DCBLS	10//99-12//99
	Florida	S	18.06 MW	19.67 AW	40920 AAW	FLBLS	10//99-12//99
	Fort Lauderdale PMSA, FL	S	23.58 MW	20.16 AW	49050 AAW	FLBLS	10//99-12//99
	Fort Myers-Cape Coral MSA,						
	FL	S	32.09 MW	24.88 AW	66750 AAW	FLBLS	10//99-12//99
	Fort Pierce-Port St. Lucie						
	MSA, FL	S	24.18 MW	24.30 AW	50300 AAW	FLBLS	10//99-12//99
	Gainesville MSA, FL	S	19.95 MW	18.67 AW	41490 AAW	FLBLS	10//99-12//99
	Jacksonville MSA, FL	S	19.69 MW	18.05 AW	40940 AAW	FLBLS	10//99-12//99
	Melbourne-Titusville-Palm						
	Bay MSA, FL	S	12.75 MW	12.13 AW	26530 AAW	FLBLS	10//99-12//99
	Miami PMSA, FL	S	17.14 MW	16.58 AW	35640 AAW	FLBLS	10//99-12//99
	Orlando MSA, FL	S	22.20 MW	19.12 AW	46170 AAW	FLBLS	10//99-12//99
	Sarasota-Bradenton MSA, FL	S	21.55 MW	22.30 AW	44810 AAW	FLBLS	10//99-12//99
	Tampa-St. Petersburg-						
	Clearwater MSA, FL	S	19.41 MW	17.82 AW	40380 AAW	FLBLS	10//99-12//99
	West Palm Beach-Boca Raton						
	MSA, FL	S	17.92 MW	14.29 AW	37280 AAW	FLBLS	10//99-12//99

AAW	Average annual wage	AOH	Average offered, high	ASH	Average starting, high	H	Hourly	M	Monthly	S	Special: hourly and annual
AE	Average entry wage	AOL	Average offered, low	ASL	Average starting, low	HI	Highest wage paid	MTC	Median total compensation	TQ	Third quartile wage
AEX	Average experienced wage	APH	Average pay, high range	AW	Average wage paid	HR	High end range	MW	Median wage paid	W	Weekly
AO	Average offered	APL	Average pay, low range	FQ	First quartile wage	LR	Low end range	SQ	Second quartile wage	Y	Yearly

Occupation/Type/Industry	Location	Per	Low	Mid	High	Source	Date
Insurance Underwriter	Georgia	S	17.79 MW	19.07 AW	39670 AAW	GABLS	10//99-12//99
	Atlanta MSA, GA	S	18.82 MW	17.75 AW	39140 AAW	GABLS	10//99-12//99
	Macon MSA, GA	S	18.50 MW	16.93 AW	38480 AAW	GABLS	10//99-12//99
	Savannah MSA, GA	S	21.66 MW	17.08 AW	45040 AAW	GABLS	10//99-12//99
	Hawaii	S	20.37 MW	20.78 AW	43220 AAW	HIBLS	10//99-12//99
	Honolulu MSA, HI	S	21.15 MW	20.66 AW	43990 AAW	HIBLS	10//99-12//99
	Idaho	S	18.18 MW	17.95 AW	37340 AAW	IDBLS	10//99-12//99
	Boise City MSA, ID	S	19.76 MW	20.61 AW	41100 AAW	IDBLS	10//99-12//99
	Illinois	S	19.84 MW	21.65 AW	45020 AAW	ILBLS	10//99-12//99
	Bloomington-Normal MSA, IL	S	21.93 MW	20.53 AW	45610 AAW	ILBLS	10//99-12//99
	Chicago PMSA, IL	S	22.28 MW	20.32 AW	46350 AAW	ILBLS	10//99-12//99
	Peoria-Pekin MSA, IL	S	21.54 MW	20.62 AW	44810 AAW	ILBLS	10//99-12//99
	Rockford MSA, IL	S	16.02 MW	13.01 AW	33330 AAW	ILBLS	10//99-12//99
	Springfield MSA, IL	S	21.90 MW	19.68 AW	45550 AAW	ILBLS	10//99-12//99
	Indiana	S	19.95 MW	21.47 AW	44660 AAW	INBLS	10//99-12//99
	Fort Wayne MSA, IN	S	22.58 MW	20.89 AW	46970 AAW	INBLS	10//99-12//99
	Indianapolis MSA, IN	S	22.07 MW	20.73 AW	45900 AAW	INBLS	10//99-12//99
	South Bend MSA, IN	S	15.75 MW	14.73 AW	32760 AAW	INBLS	10//99-12//99
	Iowa	S	17.85 MW	18.24 AW	37930 AAW	IABLS	10//99-12//99
	Davenport-Moline-Rock Island MSA, IA-IL	S	17.82 MW	18.06 AW	37070 AAW	IABLS	10//99-12//99
	Des Moines MSA, IA	S	19.27 MW	18.67 AW	40090 AAW	IABLS	10//99-12//99
	Kansas	S	20.01 MW	21.74 AW	45210 AAW	KSBLS	10//99-12//99
	Wichita MSA, KS	S	19.79 MW	18.15 AW	41160 AAW	KSBLS	10//99-12//99
	Kentucky	S	16.77 MW	17.51 AW	36410 AAW	KYBLS	10//99-12//99
	Lexington MSA, KY	S	18.06 MW	17.42 AW	37550 AAW	KYBLS	10//99-12//99
	Louisville MSA, KY-IN	S	16.75 MW	15.87 AW	34840 AAW	KYBLS	10//99-12//99
	Louisiana	S	16.32 MW	18.37 AW	38210 AAW	LABLS	10//99-12//99
	Baton Rouge MSA, LA	S	17.49 MW	15.14 AW	36390 AAW	LABLS	10//99-12//99
	New Orleans MSA, LA	S	20.07 MW	18.14 AW	41740 AAW	LABLS	10//99-12//99
	Shreveport-Bossier City MSA, LA	S	12.89 MW	9.92 AW	26800 AAW	LABLS	10//99-12//99
	Maine	S	19.57 MW	20.14 AW	41890 AAW	MEBLS	10//99-12//99
	Maryland	S	19.49 MW	21.54 AW	44800 AAW	MDBLS	10//99-12//99
	Baltimore PMSA, MD	S	20.62 MW	18.83 AW	42890 AAW	MDBLS	10//99-12//99
	Massachusetts	S	20.98 MW	22.32 AW	46430 AAW	MABLS	10//99-12//99
	Boston PMSA, MA-NH	S	22.79 MW	21.55 AW	47410 AAW	MABLS	10//99-12//99
	Lawrence PMSA, MA-NH	S	28.32 MW	29.60 AW	58910 AAW	MABLS	10//99-12//99
	Pittsfield MSA, MA	S	29.43 MW	24.58 AW	61220 AAW	MABLS	10//99-12//99
	Worcester PMSA, MA-CT	S	21.88 MW	20.01 AW	45510 AAW	MABLS	10//99-12//99
	Michigan	S	19.43 MW	21.32 AW	44340 AAW	MIBLS	10//99-12//99
	Detroit PMSA, MI	S	21.33 MW	19.68 AW	44370 AAW	MIBLS	10//99-12//99
	Flint PMSA, MI	S	19.12 MW	16.87 AW	39770 AAW	MIBLS	10//99-12//99
	Grand Rapids-Muskegon-Holland MSA, MI	S	19.00 MW	18.63 AW	39530 AAW	MIBLS	10//99-12//99
	Lansing-East Lansing MSA, MI	S	21.18 MW	19.78 AW	44060 AAW	MIBLS	10//99-12//99
	Minnesota	S	20.8 MW	22.32 AW	46430 AAW	MNBLS	10//99-12//99
	Minneapolis-St. Paul MSA, MN-WI	S	22.79 MW	21.39 AW	47400 AAW	MNBLS	10//99-12//99
	Mississippi	S	17.04 MW	18.71 AW	38920 AAW	MSBLS	10//99-12//99
	Jackson MSA, MS	S	17.66 MW	16.24 AW	36730 AAW	MSBLS	10//99-12//99
	Missouri	S	18.79 MW	20.81 AW	43280 AAW	MOBLS	10//99-12//99
	Kansas City MSA, MO-KS	S	23.28 MW	20.90 AW	48420 AAW	MOBLS	10//99-12//99
	St. Louis MSA, MO-IL	S	21.58 MW	19.49 AW	44890 AAW	MOBLS	10//99-12//99
	Montana	S	16.62 MW	19.39 AW	40320 AAW	MTBLS	10//99-12//99
	Missoula MSA, MT	S	26.49 MW	23.09 AW	55090 AAW	MTBLS	10//99-12//99
	Nebraska	S	19.11 MW	20.60 AW	42860 AAW	NEBLS	10//99-12//99
	Lincoln MSA, NE	S	20.80 MW	18.38 AW	43270 AAW	NEBLS	10//99-12//99
	Nevada	S	17.27 MW	19.26 AW	40060 AAW	NVBLS	10//99-12//99
	Las Vegas MSA, NV-AZ	S	25.92 MW	25.29 AW	53920 AAW	NVBLS	10//99-12//99
	Reno MSA, NV	S	16.32 MW	17.09 AW	33950 AAW	NVBLS	10//99-12//99
	New Hampshire	S	18.81 MW	20.48 AW	42600 AAW	NHBLS	10//99-12//99
	Manchester PMSA, NH	S	22.05 MW	19.93 AW	45870 AAW	NHBLS	10//99-12//99
	New Jersey	S	22.48 MW	25.21 AW	52430 AAW	NJBLS	10//99-12//99
	Bergen-Passaic PMSA, NJ	S	24.04 MW	21.64 AW	50010 AAW	NJBLS	10//99-12//99
	Jersey City PMSA, NJ	S	28.73 MW	27.73 AW	59750 AAW	NJBLS	10//99-12//99
	Middlesex-Somerset-Hunterdon PMSA, NJ	S	29.67 MW	27.91 AW	61720 AAW	NJBLS	10//99-12//99
	Monmouth-Ocean PMSA, NJ	S	23.53 MW	20.26 AW	48940 AAW	NJBLS	10//99-12//99
	Newark PMSA, NJ	S	26.69 MW	24.70 AW	55510 AAW	NJBLS	10//99-12//99
	Trenton PMSA, NJ	S	25.33 MW	21.83 AW	52680 AAW	NJBLS	10//99-12//99
	New Mexico	S	15.87 MW	18.73 AW	38950 AAW	NMBLS	10//99-12//99

AAW Average annual wage	**AOH** Average offered, high	**ASH** Average starting, high	**H** Hourly	**M** Monthly	**S** Special: hourly and annual
AE Average entry wage	**AOL** Average offered, low	**ASL** Average starting, low	**HI** Highest wage paid	**MTC** Median total compensation	**TQ** Third quartile wage
AEX Average experienced wage	**APH** Average pay, high range	**AW** Average wage paid	**HR** High end range	**MW** Median wage paid	**W** Weekly
AO Average offered	**APL** Average pay, low range	**FQ** First quartile wage	**LR** Low end range	**SQ** Second quartile wage	**Y** Yearly

Occupation/Type/Industry	Location	Per	Low	Mid	High	Source	Date
Insurance Underwriter	Albuquerque MSA, NM	S	18.87 MW	16.14 AW	39250 AAW	NMBLS	10//99-12//99
	New York	S	20.08 MW	23.08 AW	48010 AAW	NYBLS	10//99-12//99
	Albany-Schenectady-Troy MSA, NY	S	23.17 MW	19.73 AW	48190 AAW	NYBLS	10//99-12//99
	Buffalo-Niagara Falls MSA, NY	S	17.57 MW	15.42 AW	36550 AAW	NYBLS	10//99-12//99
	Nassau-Suffolk PMSA, NY	S	21.78 MW	19.57 AW	45290 AAW	NYBLS	10//99-12//99
	New York PMSA, NY	S	26.06 MW	23.56 AW	54210 AAW	NYBLS	10//99-12//99
	Rochester MSA, NY	S	16.88 MW	15.65 AW	35110 AAW	NYBLS	10//99-12//99
	Syracuse MSA, NY	S	19.45 MW	17.66 AW	40450 AAW	NYBLS	10//99-12//99
	North Carolina	S	17.67 MW	19.79 AW	41160 AAW	NCBLS	10//99-12//99
	Charlotte-Gastonia-Rock Hill MSA, NC-SC	S	25.17 MW	23.90 AW	52350 AAW	NCBLS	10//99-12//99
	Greensboro--Winston-Salem--High Point MSA, NC	S	17.42 MW	15.28 AW	36230 AAW	NCBLS	10//99-12//99
	Raleigh-Durham-Chapel Hill MSA, NC	S	19.28 MW	18.22 AW	40100 AAW	NCBLS	10//99-12//99
	Rocky Mount MSA, NC	S	15.17 MW	15.25 AW	31550 AAW	NCBLS	10//99-12//99
	North Dakota	S	13.31 MW	14.69 AW	30560 AAW	NDBLS	10//99-12//99
	Bismarck MSA, ND	S	13.18 MW	12.92 AW	27420 AAW	NDBLS	10//99-12//99
	Fargo-Moorhead MSA, ND-MN	S	15.91 MW	13.47 AW	33080 AAW	NDBLS	10//99-12//99
	Akron PMSA, OH	S	19.24 MW	17.63 AW	40010 AAW	OHBLS	10//99-12//99
	Canton-Massillon MSA, OH	S	23.72 MW	22.30 AW	49350 AAW	OHBLS	10//99-12//99
	Cincinnati PMSA, OH-KY-IN	S	23.51 MW	23.15 AW	48890 AAW	OHBLS	10//99-12//99
	Cleveland-Lorain-Elyria PMSA, OH	S	20.20 MW	18.78 AW	42020 AAW	OHBLS	10//99-12//99
	Columbus MSA, OH	S	21.96 MW	20.21 AW	45680 AAW	OHBLS	10//99-12//99
	Dayton-Springfield MSA, OH	S	15.57 MW	14.39 AW	32390 AAW	OHBLS	10//99-12//99
	Toledo MSA, OH	S	21.35 MW	20.31 AW	44410 AAW	OHBLS	10//99-12//99
	Oklahoma	S	15.39 MW	16.68 AW	34680 AAW	OKBLS	10//99-12//99
	Oklahoma City MSA, OK	S	16.50 MW	15.23 AW	34320 AAW	OKBLS	10//99-12//99
	Tulsa MSA, OK	S	19.34 MW	17.91 AW	40220 AAW	OKBLS	10//99-12//99
	Oregon	S	20.43 MW	21.38 AW	44480 AAW	ORBLS	10//99-12//99
	Portland-Vancouver PMSA, OR-WA	S	21.83 MW	20.72 AW	45410 AAW	ORBLS	10//99-12//99
	Pennsylvania	S	20.73 MW	22.31 AW	46410 AAW	PABLS	10//99-12//99
	Allentown-Bethlehem-Easton MSA, PA	S	20.32 MW	19.47 AW	42270 AAW	PABLS	10//99-12//99
	Harrisburg-Lebanon-Carlisle MSA, PA	S	22.58 MW	21.66 AW	46960 AAW	PABLS	10//99-12//99
	Lancaster MSA, PA	S	18.60 MW	16.25 AW	38700 AAW	PABLS	10//99-12//99
	Philadelphia PMSA, PA-NJ	S	22.59 MW	20.73 AW	46990 AAW	PABLS	10//99-12//99
	Pittsburgh MSA, PA	S	21.82 MW	20.10 AW	45380 AAW	PABLS	10//99-12//99
	Scranton--Wilkes-Barre--Hazleton MSA, PA	S	20.81 MW	21.35 AW	43280 AAW	PABLS	10//99-12//99
	Rhode Island	S	20.24 MW	23.35 AW	48570 AAW	RIBLS	10//99-12//99
	Providence-Fall River-Warwick MSA, RI-MA	S	22.52 MW	19.89 AW	46840 AAW	RIBLS	10//99-12//99
	South Carolina	S	15.65 MW	17.18 AW	35730 AAW	SCBLS	10//99-12//99
	Charleston-North Charleston MSA, SC	S	16.45 MW	15.88 AW	34220 AAW	SCBLS	10//99-12//99
	Columbia MSA, SC	S	15.44 MW	14.88 AW	32120 AAW	SCBLS	10//99-12//99
	Greenville-Spartanburg-Anderson MSA, SC	S	18.79 MW	16.70 AW	39080 AAW	SCBLS	10//99-12//99
	South Dakota	S	18.01 MW	18.38 AW	38220 AAW	SDBLS	10//99-12//99
	Sioux Falls MSA, SD	S	17.66 MW	15.84 AW	36740 AAW	SDBLS	10//99-12//99
	Tennessee	S	21.06 MW	22.63 AW	47080 AAW	TNBLS	10//99-12//99
	Chattanooga MSA, TN-GA	S	22.11 MW	20.66 AW	45980 AAW	TNBLS	10//99-12//99
	Johnson City-Kingsport-Bristol MSA, TN-VA	S	17.39 MW	16.36 AW	36180 AAW	TNBLS	10//99-12//99
	Knoxville MSA, TN	S	29.34 MW	35.81 AW	61030 AAW	TNBLS	10//99-12//99
	Memphis MSA, TN-AR-MS	S	22.70 MW	22.26 AW	47210 AAW	MSBLS	10//99-12//99
	Nashville MSA, TN	S	23.02 MW	21.08 AW	47880 AAW	TNBLS	10//99-12//99
	Texas	S	19.78 MW	21.42 AW	44560 AAW	TXBLS	10//99-12//99
	Austin-San Marcos MSA, TX	S	19.81 MW	18.12 AW	41210 AAW	TXBLS	10//99-12//99
	Dallas PMSA, TX	S	22.69 MW	20.54 AW	47200 AAW	TXBLS	10//99-12//99
	Fort Worth-Arlington PMSA, TX	S	20.26 MW	18.37 AW	42130 AAW	TXBLS	10//99-12//99
	Houston PMSA, TX	S	23.58 MW	20.77 AW	49050 AAW	TXBLS	10//99-12//99
	Killeen-Temple MSA, TX	S	10.08 MW	9.70 AW	20980 AAW	TXBLS	10//99-12//99
	San Antonio MSA, TX	S	21.68 MW	20.89 AW	45100 AAW	TXBLS	10//99-12//99

AAW Average annual wage	**AOH** Average offered, high	**ASH** Average starting, high	**H** Hourly	**M** Monthly	**S** Special: hourly and annual
AE Average entry salaries	**AOL** Average offered, low	**ASL** Average starting, low	**HI** Highest wage paid	**MTC** Median total compensation	**TQ** Third quartile wage
AEX Average experienced wage	**APH** Average pay, high range	**AW** Average wage paid	**HR** High end range	**MW** Median wage paid	**W** Weekly
AO Average offered	**APL** Average pay, low range	**FQ** First quartile wage	**LR** Low end range	**SQ** Second quartile wage	**Y** Yearly

Occupation/Type/Industry	Location	Per	Low	Mid	High	Source	Date
Insurance Underwriter	Tyler MSA, TX	S	19.13 MW	17.94 AW	39780 AAW	TXBLS	10//99-12//99
	Utah	S	20.07 MW	20.63 AW	42900 AAW	UTBLS	10//99-12//99
	Salt Lake City-Ogden MSA, UT	S	22.28 MW	21.70 AW	46340 AAW	UTBLS	10//99-12//99
	Vermont	S	15.99 MW	20.95 AW	43580 AAW	VTBLS	10//99-12//99
	Burlington MSA, VT	S	23.53 MW	16.29 AW	48950 AAW	VTBLS	10//99-12//99
	Virginia	S	21.11 MW	22.24 AW	46270 AAW	VABLS	10//99-12//99
	Norfolk-Virginia Beach-Newport News MSA, VA-NC	S	13.75 MW	12.56 AW	28590 AAW	VABLS	10//99-12//99
	Richmond-Petersburg MSA, VA	S	22.56 MW	20.57 AW	46930 AAW	VABLS	10//99-12//99
	Roanoke MSA, VA	S	20.87 MW	19.71 AW	43410 AAW	VABLS	10//99-12//99
	Washington	S	22.26 MW	23.94 AW	49800 AAW	WABLS	10//99-12//99
	Seattle-Bellevue-Everett PMSA, WA	S	24.62 MW	23.06 AW	51200 AAW	WABLS	10//99-12//99
	West Virginia	S	11.61 MW	13.18 AW	27410 AAW	WVBLS	10//99-12//99
	Charleston MSA, WV	S	15.46 MW	15.30 AW	32160 AAW	WVBLS	10//99-12//99
	Wisconsin	S	19.12 MW	19.80 AW	41190 AAW	WIBLS	10//99-12//99
	Appleton-Oshkosh-Neenah MSA, WI	S	17.59 MW	17.00 AW	36580 AAW	WIBLS	10//99-12//99
	Eau Claire MSA, WI	S	15.23 MW	13.02 AW	31680 AAW	WIBLS	10//99-12//99
	Madison MSA, WI	S	20.30 MW	19.10 AW	42230 AAW	WIBLS	10//99-12//99
	Milwaukee-Waukesha PMSA, WI	S	20.86 MW	20.75 AW	43400 AAW	WIBLS	10//99-12//99
	Wausau MSA, WI	S	20.35 MW	18.48 AW	42330 AAW	WIBLS	10//99-12//99
	Wyoming	S	16.66 MW	18.97 AW	39460 AAW	WYBLS	10//99-12//99
	Puerto Rico	S	14.54 MW	14.38 AW	29900 AAW	PRBLS	10//99-12//99
	San Juan-Bayamon PMSA, PR	S	14.02 MW	14.43 AW	29170 AAW	PRBLS	10//99-12//99
	Guam	S	11.74 MW	13.45 AW	27970 AAW	GUBLS	10//99-12//99
Interior Designer	Alabama	S	12.66 MW	13.95 AW	29010 AAW	ALBLS	10//99-12//99
	Birmingham MSA, AL	S	17.77 MW	16.23 AW	36960 AAW	ALBLS	10//99-12//99
	Tuscaloosa MSA, AL	S	15.76 MW	11.67 AW	32790 AAW	ALBLS	10//99-12//99
	Arizona	S	18.14 MW	22.40 AW	46600 AAW	AZBLS	10//99-12//99
	Phoenix-Mesa MSA, AZ	S	21.63 MW	17.21 AW	45000 AAW	AZBLS	10//99-12//99
	Tucson MSA, AZ	S	22.25 MW	20.46 AW	46280 AAW	AZBLS	10//99-12//99
	Arkansas	S	10.71 MW	14.01 AW	29150 AAW	ARBLS	10//99-12//99
	Jonesboro MSA, AR	S	9.82 MW	9.79 AW	20430 AAW	ARBLS	10//99-12//99
	Little Rock-North Little Rock MSA, AR	S	19.78 MW	17.83 AW	41150 AAW	ARBLS	10//99-12//99
	California	S	17.52 MW	20.82 AW	43310 AAW	CABLS	10//99-12//99
	Los Angeles-Long Beach PMSA, CA	S	17.03 MW	15.35 AW	35420 AAW	CABLS	10//99-12//99
	Oakland PMSA, CA	S	20.31 MW	16.83 AW	42240 AAW	CABLS	10//99-12//99
	Orange County PMSA, CA	S	18.01 MW	17.69 AW	37460 AAW	CABLS	10//99-12//99
	Riverside-San Bernardino PMSA, CA	S	20.35 MW	21.77 AW	42330 AAW	CABLS	10//99-12//99
	Sacramento PMSA, CA	S	15.07 MW	13.48 AW	31350 AAW	CABLS	10//99-12//99
	San Diego MSA, CA	S	21.58 MW	11.70 AW	44890 AAW	CABLS	10//99-12//99
	San Francisco PMSA, CA	S	25.56 MW	21.93 AW	53160 AAW	CABLS	10//99-12//99
	San Jose PMSA, CA	S	21.60 MW	19.97 AW	44930 AAW	CABLS	10//99-12//99
	Santa Barbara-Santa Maria-Lompoc MSA, CA	S	25.71 MW	27.33 AW	53480 AAW	CABLS	10//99-12//99
	Ventura PMSA, CA	S	35.46 MW	30.26 AW	73760 AAW	CABLS	10//99-12//99
	Colorado	S	15.77 MW	16.77 AW	34890 AAW	COBLS	10//99-12//99
	Boulder-Longmont PMSA, CO	S	19.95 MW	19.00 AW	41490 AAW	COBLS	10//99-12//99
	Colorado Springs MSA, CO	S	16.44 MW	13.56 AW	34190 AAW	COBLS	10//99-12//99
	Fort Collins-Loveland MSA, CO	S	18.06 MW	16.67 AW	37560 AAW	COBLS	10//99-12//99
	Connecticut	S	17.73 MW	18.66 AW	38810 AAW	CTBLS	10//99-12//99
	Bridgeport PMSA, CT	S	22.47 MW	21.39 AW	46740 AAW	CTBLS	10//99-12//99
	Danbury PMSA, CT	S	25.66 MW	24.85 AW	53360 AAW	CTBLS	10//99-12//99
	Hartford MSA, CT	S	19.11 MW	18.52 AW	39740 AAW	CTBLS	10//99-12//99
	New Haven-Meriden PMSA, CT	S	16.92 MW	15.78 AW	35200 AAW	CTBLS	10//99-12//99
	Stamford-Norwalk PMSA, CT	S	16.79 MW	16.25 AW	34920 AAW	CTBLS	10//99-12//99
	Delaware	S	14.08 MW	16.69 AW	34700 AAW	DEBLS	10//99-12//99
	District of Columbia	S	20.38 MW	21.78 AW	45310 AAW	DCBLS	10//99-12//99
	Washington PMSA, DC-MD-VA-WV	S	18.73 MW	18.96 AW	38960 AAW	DCBLS	10//99-12//99
	Florida	S	17.78 MW	21.63 AW	44980 AAW	FLBLS	10//99-12//99
	Fort Lauderdale PMSA, FL	S	28.41 MW	23.42 AW	59090 AAW	FLBLS	10//99-12//99

AAW	Average annual wage	AOH	Average offered, high	ASH	Average starting, high	H	Hourly	M	Monthly	S	Special: hourly and annual
AE	Average entry wage	AOL	Average offered, low	ASL	Average starting, low	HI	Highest wage paid	MTC	Median total compensation	TQ	Third quartile wage
AEX	Average experienced wage	APH	Average pay, high range	AW	Average wage paid	HR	High end range	MW	Median wage paid	W	Weekly
AO	Average offered	APL	Average pay, low range	FQ	First quartile wage	LR	Low end range	SQ	Second quartile wage	Y	Yearly

Occupation/Type/Industry	Location	Per	Low	Mid	High	Source	Date
Interior Designer	Jacksonville MSA, FL	S	17.55 MW	17.86 AW	36500 AAW	FLBLS	10//99-12//99
	Melbourne-Titusville-Palm Bay MSA, FL	S	11.72 MW	11.12 AW	24380 AAW	FLBLS	10//99-12//99
	Miami PMSA, FL	S	28.14 MW	19.11 AW	58530 AAW	FLBLS	10//99-12//99
	Naples MSA, FL	S	25.27 MW	25.77 AW	52570 AAW	FLBLS	10//99-12//99
	Orlando MSA, FL	S	17.41 MW	15.45 AW	36210 AAW	FLBLS	10//99-12//99
	Sarasota-Bradenton MSA, FL	S	15.66 MW	17.49 AW	32570 AAW	FLBLS	10//99-12//99
	Tampa-St. Petersburg-Clearwater MSA, FL	S	14.30 MW	13.45 AW	29740 AAW	FLBLS	10//99-12//99
	West Palm Beach-Boca Raton MSA, FL	S	27.58 MW	22.83 AW	57370 AAW	FLBLS	10//99-12//99
	Georgia	S	15.26 MW	16.90 AW	35160 AAW	GABLS	10//99-12//99
	Atlanta MSA, GA	S	18.15 MW	16.07 AW	37750 AAW	GABLS	10//99-12//99
	Macon MSA, GA	S	13.81 MW	12.64 AW	28720 AAW	GABLS	10//99-12//99
	Savannah MSA, GA	S	12.37 MW	11.26 AW	25730 AAW	GABLS	10//99-12//99
	Hawaii	S	17.66 MW	18.52 AW	38520 AAW	HIBLS	10//99-12//99
	Honolulu MSA, HI	S	18.69 MW	18.07 AW	38880 AAW	HIBLS	10//99-12//99
	Idaho	S	11.65 MW	13.26 AW	27590 AAW	IDBLS	10//99-12//99
	Boise City MSA, ID	S	13.61 MW	11.61 AW	28300 AAW	IDBLS	10//99-12//99
	Illinois	S	19.41 MW	21.85 AW	45440 AAW	ILBLS	10//99-12//99
	Chicago PMSA, IL	S	23.11 MW	21.00 AW	48070 AAW	ILBLS	10//99-12//99
	Indiana	S	13.14 MW	14.75 AW	30680 AAW	INBLS	10//99-12//99
	Evansville-Henderson MSA, IN-KY	S	17.75 MW	13.66 AW	36930 AAW	INBLS	10//99-12//99
	Fort Wayne MSA, IN	S	12.90 MW	10.56 AW	26830 AAW	INBLS	10//99-12//99
	Gary PMSA, IN	S	12.05 MW	10.48 AW	25060 AAW	INBLS	10//99-12//99
	Indianapolis MSA, IN	S	16.09 MW	14.58 AW	33470 AAW	INBLS	10//99-12//99
	Terre Haute MSA, IN	S	18.35 MW	18.92 AW	38180 AAW	INBLS	10//99-12//99
	Iowa	S	14.41 MW	14.72 AW	30620 AAW	IABLS	10//99-12//99
	Davenport-Moline-Rock Island MSA, IA-IL	S	13.15 MW	12.72 AW	27360 AAW	IABLS	10//99-12//99
	Des Moines MSA, IA	S	13.56 MW	14.41 AW	28210 AAW	IABLS	10//99-12//99
	Kansas	S	14.13 MW	15.29 AW	31800 AAW	KSBLS	10//99-12//99
	Topeka MSA, KS	S	13.79 MW	12.31 AW	28690 AAW	KSBLS	10//99-12//99
	Wichita MSA, KS	S	15.42 MW	12.60 AW	32080 AAW	KSBLS	10//99-12//99
	Kentucky	S	13.86 MW	17.45 AW	36300 AAW	KYBLS	10//99-12//99
	Louisville MSA, KY-IN	S	18.50 MW	15.68 AW	38470 AAW	KYBLS	10//99-12//99
	Louisiana	S	10.42 MW	11.92 AW	24800 AAW	LABLS	10//99-12//99
	Baton Rouge MSA, LA	S	17.51 MW	16.55 AW	36410 AAW	LABLS	10//99-12//99
	New Orleans MSA, LA	S	13.67 MW	12.46 AW	28430 AAW	LABLS	10//99-12//99
	Maine	S	15.14 MW	17.16 AW	35690 AAW	MEBLS	10//99-12//99
	Portland MSA, ME	S	17.02 MW	16.62 AW	35410 AAW	MEBLS	10//99-12//99
	Maryland	S	20.86 MW	21.09 AW	43860 AAW	MDBLS	10//99-12//99
	Baltimore PMSA, MD	S	22.12 MW	21.91 AW	46020 AAW	MDBLS	10//99-12//99
	Massachusetts	S	15.73 MW	20.29 AW	42200 AAW	MABLS	10//99-12//99
	Boston PMSA, MA-NH	S	20.30 MW	15.78 AW	42220 AAW	MABLS	10//99-12//99
	Springfield MSA, MA	S	13.99 MW	12.56 AW	29110 AAW	MABLS	10//99-12//99
	Michigan	S	11.85 MW	13.48 AW	28040 AAW	MIBLS	10//99-12//99
	Detroit PMSA, MI	S	14.36 MW	11.97 AW	29880 AAW	MIBLS	10//99-12//99
	Flint PMSA, MI	S	10.75 MW	10.83 AW	22350 AAW	MIBLS	10//99-12//99
	Grand Rapids-Muskegon-Holland MSA, MI	S	11.51 MW	6.84 AW	23940 AAW	MIBLS	10//99-12//99
	Kalamazoo-Battle Creek MSA, MI	S	15.68 MW	16.12 AW	32610 AAW	MIBLS	10//99-12//99
	Lansing-East Lansing MSA, MI	S	12.63 MW	11.79 AW	26270 AAW	MIBLS	10//99-12//99
	Saginaw-Bay City-Midland MSA, MI	S	11.80 MW	11.07 AW	24540 AAW	MIBLS	10//99-12//99
	Minnesota	S	15.35 MW	18.33 AW	38120 AAW	MNBLS	10//99-12//99
	Duluth-Superior MSA, MN-WI	S	15.28 MW	14.32 AW	31780 AAW	MNBLS	10//99-12//99
	Minneapolis-St. Paul MSA, MN-WI	S	19.11 MW	15.83 AW	39750 AAW	MNBLS	10//99-12//99
	Mississippi	S	12.99 MW	13.94 AW	28990 AAW	MSBLS	10//99-12//99
	Jackson MSA, MS	S	18.86 MW	17.51 AW	39220 AAW	MSBLS	10//99-12//99
	Missouri	S	14.99 MW	14.14 AW	29410 AAW	MOBLS	10//99-12//99
	Kansas City MSA, MO-KS	S	16.91 MW	16.75 AW	35170 AAW	MOBLS	10//99-12//99
	Montana	S	15.15 MW	14.78 AW	30730 AAW	MTBLS	10//99-12//99
	Nebraska	S	11.29 MW	13.65 AW	28400 AAW	NEBLS	10//99-12//99
	Lincoln MSA, NE	S	14.08 MW	10.58 AW	29280 AAW	NEBLS	10//99-12//99
	Omaha MSA, NE-IA	S	12.35 MW	11.30 AW	25680 AAW	NEBLS	10//99-12//99
	Nevada	S	18.03 MW	18.58 AW	38640 AAW	NVBLS	10//99-12//99
	Las Vegas MSA, NV-AZ	S	18.47 MW	18.05 AW	38420 AAW	NVBLS	10//99-12//99
	Reno MSA, NV	S	20.15 MW	16.47 AW	41920 AAW	NVBLS	10//99-12//99

AAW	Average annual wage	AOH	Average offered, high	ASH	Average starting, high
AE	Average entry wage	AOL	Average offered, low	ASL	Average starting, low
AEX	Average experienced wage	APH	Average pay, high range	AW	Average wage paid
AO	Average offered	APL	Average pay, low range	FQ	First quartile wage

H	Hourly	M	Monthly	S	Special: hourly and annual
HI	Highest wage paid	MTC	Median total compensation	TQ	Third quartile wage
HR	High end range	MW	Median wage paid	W	Weekly
LR	Low end range	SQ	Second quartile wage	Y	Yearly

Occupation/Type/Industry	Location	Per	Low	Mid	High	Source	Date
Interior Designer	New Hampshire	S	19.91 MW	18.89 AW	39300 AAW	NHBLS	10//99-12//99
	Portsmouth-Rochester PMSA, NH-ME	S	16.10 MW	16.25 AW	33480 AAW	NHBLS	10//99-12//99
	New Jersey	S	18.71 MW	22.65 AW	47120 AAW	NJBLS	10//99-12//99
	Atlantic-Cape May PMSA, NJ	S	16.87 MW	15.95 AW	35080 AAW	NJBLS	10//99-12//99
	Monmouth-Ocean PMSA, NJ	S	19.50 MW	18.00 AW	40560 AAW	NJBLS	10//99-12//99
	Newark PMSA, NJ	S	18.57 MW	15.90 AW	38630 AAW	NJBLS	10//99-12//99
	New Mexico	S	15.13 MW	16.68 AW	34690 AAW	NMBLS	10//99-12//99
	New York	S	26.76 MW	25.45 AW	52940 AAW	NYBLS	10//99-12//99
	Buffalo-Niagara Falls MSA, NY	S	15.12 MW	14.70 AW	31450 AAW	NYBLS	10//99-12//99
	Dutchess County PMSA, NY	S	13.41 MW	13.30 AW	27890 AAW	NYBLS	10//99-12//99
	Nassau-Suffolk PMSA, NY	S	16.77 MW	17.24 AW	34870 AAW	NYBLS	10//99-12//99
	New York PMSA, NY	S	29.10 MW	31.02 AW	60530 AAW	NYBLS	10//99-12//99
	Rochester MSA, NY	S	13.31 MW	11.92 AW	27680 AAW	NYBLS	10//99-12//99
	Syracuse MSA, NY	S	13.08 MW	12.88 AW	27200 AAW	NYBLS	10//99-12//99
	North Carolina	S	14.1 MW	15.13 AW	31470 AAW	NCBLS	10//99-12//99
	Charlotte-Gastonia-Rock Hill MSA, NC-SC	S	15.58 MW	14.89 AW	32410 AAW	NCBLS	10//99-12//99
	Greensboro--Winston-Salem-- High Point MSA, NC	S	17.22 MW	16.62 AW	35810 AAW	NCBLS	10//99-12//99
	Hickory-Morganton-Lenoir MSA, NC	S	13.64 MW	12.58 AW	28360 AAW	NCBLS	10//99-12//99
	Raleigh-Durham-Chapel Hill MSA, NC	S	14.20 MW	13.59 AW	29530 AAW	NCBLS	10//99-12//99
	Rocky Mount MSA, NC	S	14.93 MW	14.35 AW	31060 AAW	NCBLS	10//99-12//99
	Wilmington MSA, NC	S	14.42 MW	14.70 AW	30000 AAW	NCBLS	10//99-12//99
	North Dakota	S	13.25 MW	15.21 AW	31630 AAW	NDBLS	10//99-12//99
	Fargo-Moorhead MSA, ND-MN	S	16.14 MW	14.88 AW	33580 AAW	NDBLS	10//99-12//99
	Ohio	S	13.04 MW	14.57 AW	30300 AAW	OHBLS	10//99-12//99
	Akron PMSA, OH	S	14.59 MW	13.50 AW	30340 AAW	OHBLS	10//99-12//99
	Cincinnati PMSA, OH-KY-IN	S	15.64 MW	14.15 AW	32530 AAW	OHBLS	10//99-12//99
	Cleveland-Lorain-Elyria PMSA, OH	S	15.94 MW	16.33 AW	33160 AAW	OHBLS	10//99-12//99
	Columbus MSA, OH	S	16.52 MW	14.89 AW	34360 AAW	OHBLS	10//99-12//99
	Dayton-Springfield MSA, OH	S	14.19 MW	11.40 AW	29510 AAW	OHBLS	10//99-12//99
	Toledo MSA, OH	S	17.99 MW	16.65 AW	37420 AAW	OHBLS	10//99-12//99
	Youngstown-Warren MSA, OH	S	10.84 MW	10.65 AW	22540 AAW	OHBLS	10//99-12//99
	Oklahoma	S	13.5 MW	14.76 AW	30700 AAW	OKBLS	10//99-12//99
	Oklahoma City MSA, OK	S	14.88 MW	14.74 AW	30940 AAW	OKBLS	10//99-12//99
	Tulsa MSA, OK	S	14.91 MW	13.20 AW	31010 AAW	OKBLS	10//99-12//99
	Oregon	S	20.36 MW	19.51 AW	40580 AAW	ORBLS	10//99-12//99
	Eugene-Springfield MSA, OR	S	12.25 MW	11.10 AW	25480 AAW	ORBLS	10//99-12//99
	Portland-Vancouver PMSA, OR-WA	S	20.02 MW	20.61 AW	41640 AAW	ORBLS	10//99-12//99
	Pennsylvania	S	13.77 MW	15.84 AW	32940 AAW	PABLS	10//99-12//99
	Allentown-Bethlehem-Easton MSA, PA	S	15.19 MW	11.67 AW	31600 AAW	PABLS	10//99-12//99
	Harrisburg-Lebanon-Carlisle MSA, PA	S	12.79 MW	10.02 AW	26600 AAW	PABLS	10//99-12//99
	Philadelphia PMSA, PA-NJ	S	18.79 MW	14.31 AW	39080 AAW	PABLS	10//99-12//99
	Pittsburgh MSA, PA	S	17.31 MW	14.62 AW	36010 AAW	PABLS	10//99-12//99
	Scranton--Wilkes-Barre-- Hazleton MSA, PA	S	12.35 MW	11.58 AW	25700 AAW	PABLS	10//99-12//99
	York MSA, PA	S	12.51 MW	13.25 AW	26010 AAW	PABLS	10//99-12//99
	Rhode Island	S	17.55 MW	18.29 AW	38050 AAW	RIBLS	10//99-12//99
	Providence-Fall River- Warwick MSA, RI-MA	S	18.37 MW	17.83 AW	38210 AAW	RIBLS	10//99-12//99
	South Carolina	S	11.09 MW	14.79 AW	30770 AAW	SCBLS	10//99-12//99
	Charleston-North Charleston MSA, SC	S	16.73 MW	12.62 AW	34810 AAW	SCBLS	10//99-12//99
	Columbia MSA, SC	S	14.10 MW	11.21 AW	29320 AAW	SCBLS	10//99-12//99
	Greenville-Spartanburg- Anderson MSA, SC	S	15.97 MW	10.52 AW	33210 AAW	SCBLS	10//99-12//99
	Tennessee	S	13.11 MW	14.26 AW	29670 AAW	TNBLS	10//99-12//99
	Knoxville MSA, TN	S	14.02 MW	11.95 AW	29150 AAW	TNBLS	10//99-12//99
	Memphis MSA, TN-AR-MS	S	16.34 MW	17.01 AW	33980 AAW	MSBLS	10//99-12//99
	Nashville MSA, TN	S	13.60 MW	12.69 AW	28290 AAW	TNBLS	10//99-12//99
	Texas	S	16.9 MW	18.38 AW	38230 AAW	TXBLS	10//99-12//99
	Austin-San Marcos MSA, TX	S	17.15 MW	15.91 AW	35680 AAW	TXBLS	10//99-12//99
	Dallas PMSA, TX	S	21.31 MW	18.46 AW	44330 AAW	TXBLS	10//99-12//99

Occupation/Type/Industry	Location	Per	Low	Mid	High	Source	Date
Interior Designer	Fort Worth-Arlington PMSA, TX	S	15.89 MW	15.53 AW	33050 AAW	TXBLS	10//99-12//99
	Houston PMSA, TX	S	19.99 MW	17.07 AW	41580 AAW	TXBLS	10//99-12//99
	San Antonio MSA, TX	S	15.14 MW	12.04 AW	31500 AAW	TXBLS	10//99-12//99
	Waco MSA, TX	S	11.55 MW	11.53 AW	24020 AAW	TXBLS	10//99-12//99
	Virginia	S	20.44 MW	21.72 AW	45190 AAW	VABLS	10//99-12//99
	Lynchburg MSA, VA	S	10.47 MW	11.04 AW	21780 AAW	VABLS	10//99-12//99
	Norfolk-Virginia Beach-Newport News MSA, VA-NC	S	14.77 MW	14.26 AW	30730 AAW	VABLS	10//99-12//99
	Richmond-Petersburg MSA, VA	S	14.19 MW	11.75 AW	29520 AAW	VABLS	10//99-12//99
	Washington	S	18.14 MW	21.79 AW	45320 AAW	WABLS	10//99-12//99
	Seattle-Bellevue-Everett PMSA, WA	S	22.94 MW	19.11 AW	47720 AAW	WABLS	10//99-12//99
	Spokane MSA, WA	S	25.69 MW	16.49 AW	53440 AAW	WABLS	10//99-12//99
	Tacoma PMSA, WA	S	16.91 MW	15.88 AW	35170 AAW	WABLS	10//99-12//99
	Yakima MSA, WA	S	22.04 MW	19.38 AW	45850 AAW	WABLS	10//99-12//99
	West Virginia	S	10.47 MW	10.72 AW	22300 AAW	WVBLS	10//99-12//99
	Wisconsin	S	12.7 MW	14.39 AW	29940 AAW	WIBLS	10//99-12//99
	Appleton-Oshkosh-Neenah MSA, WI	S	12.99 MW	12.42 AW	27020 AAW	WIBLS	10//99-12//99
	Eau Claire MSA, WI	S	9.15 MW	7.43 AW	19030 AAW	WIBLS	10//99-12//99
	Green Bay MSA, WI	S	16.40 MW	15.97 AW	34110 AAW	WIBLS	10//99-12//99
	Madison MSA, WI	S	14.50 MW	13.74 AW	30160 AAW	WIBLS	10//99-12//99
	Milwaukee-Waukesha PMSA, WI	S	16.55 MW	14.69 AW	34430 AAW	WIBLS	10//99-12//99
	Wausau MSA, WI	S	11.52 MW	9.58 AW	23960 AAW	WIBLS	10//99-12//99
	Wyoming	S	13.21 MW	13.36 AW	27790 AAW	WYBLS	10//99-12//99
	Casper MSA, WY	S	13.76 MW	13.41 AW	28610 AAW	WYBLS	10//99-12//99
	Puerto Rico	S	17.12 MW	17.48 AW	36360 AAW	PRBLS	10//99-12//99
	San Juan-Bayamon PMSA, PR	S	17.55 MW	17.09 AW	36510 AAW	PRBLS	10//99-12//99
Internet Software Architect On-line Enterprise	United States	Y		108400 AW		WSJ1	2000
Internet Worker	Texas	Y		84700 AW		TXMO	1999
Internist, General	Alabama	S	64.42 MW	56.88 AW	118320 AAW	ALBLS	10//99-12//99
	Arizona	S	52.63 MW	54.89 AW	114170 AAW	AZBLS	10//99-12//99
	Phoenix-Mesa MSA, AZ	S	51.04 MW	50.71 AW	106160 AAW	AZBLS	10//99-12//99
	California	S		63.17 AW	131390 AAW	CABLS	10//99-12//99
	Los Angeles-Long Beach PMSA, CA	S	57.28 MW	60.95 AW	119140 AAW	CABLS	10//99-12//99
	Connecticut	S		59.86 AW	124520 AAW	CTBLS	10//99-12//99
	Stamford-Norwalk PMSA, CT	S	68.54 MW		142570 AAW	CTBLS	10//99-12//99
	Washington PMSA, DC-MD-VA-WV	S	66.35 MW		138010 AAW	DCBLS	10//99-12//99
	Florida	S		63.80 AW	132710 AAW	FLBLS	10//99-12//99
	Fort Lauderdale PMSA, FL	S	52.49 MW	51.52 AW	109190 AAW	FLBLS	10//99-12//99
	Jacksonville MSA, FL	S	61.65 MW	67.80 AW	128230 AAW	FLBLS	10//99-12//99
	Melbourne-Titusville-Palm Bay MSA, FL	S	63.59 MW	66.77 AW	132270 AAW	FLBLS	10//99-12//99
	Miami PMSA, FL	S	62.90 MW		130840 AAW	FLBLS	10//99-12//99
	Tampa-St. Petersburg-Clearwater MSA, FL	S	63.53 MW		132150 AAW	FLBLS	10//99-12//99
	West Palm Beach-Boca Raton MSA, FL	S	64.65 MW		134470 AAW	FLBLS	10//99-12//99
	Georgia	S	67.05 MW	61.37 AW	127650 AAW	GABLS	10//99-12//99
	Atlanta MSA, GA	S	61.34 MW	67.46 AW	127590 AAW	GABLS	10//99-12//99
	Illinois	S	43.51 MW	46.51 AW	96740 AAW	ILBLS	10//99-12//99
	Chicago PMSA, IL	S	44.03 MW	45.27 AW	91590 AAW	ILBLS	10//99-12//99
	Indiana	S		62.66 AW	130330 AAW	INBLS	10//99-12//99
	Indianapolis MSA, IN	S	68.34 MW		142160 AAW	INBLS	10//99-12//99
	Iowa	S		51.80 AW	107750 AAW	IABLS	10//99-12//99
	Kansas	S	51.5 MW	53.10 AW	110440 AAW	KSBLS	10//99-12//99
	Kentucky	S		60.16 AW	125130 AAW	KYBLS	10//99-12//99
	Louisiana	S		66.15 AW	137590 AAW	LABLS	10//99-12//99
	Maine	S	64.14 MW	58.88 AW	122470 AAW	MEBLS	10//99-12//99
	Maryland	S	56.77 MW	55.65 AW	115750 AAW	MDBLS	10//99-12//99
	Baltimore PMSA, MD	S	52.45 MW	52.48 AW	109100 AAW	MDBLS	10//99-12//99
	Massachusetts	S	67.05 MW	60.97 AW	126810 AAW	MABLS	10//99-12//99
	Boston PMSA, MA-NH	S	58.02 MW	61.96 AW	120680 AAW	MABLS	10//99-12//99

Occupation/Type/Industry	Location	Per	Low	Mid	High	Source	Date
Internist, General	Michigan	S	65.12 MW	60.23 AW	125290 AAW	MIBLS	10//99-12//99
	Ann Arbor PMSA, MI	S	62.09 MW		129140 AAW	MIBLS	10//99-12//99
	Detroit PMSA, MI	S	58.46 MW	62.51 AW	121590 AAW	MIBLS	10//99-12//99
	Grand Rapids-Muskegon-Holland MSA, MI	S	54.43 MW	58.82 AW	113210 AAW	MIBLS	10//99-12//99
	Lansing-East Lansing MSA, MI	S	60.79 MW	64.70 AW	126450 AAW	MIBLS	10//99-12//99
	Minnesota	S	55.6 MW	55.89 AW	116250 AAW	MNBLS	10//99-12//99
	Minneapolis-St. Paul MSA, MN-WI	S	55.53 MW	55.07 AW	115500 AAW	MNBLS	10//99-12//99
	Mississippi	S		60.40 AW	125620 AAW	MSBLS	10//99-12//99
	Biloxi-Gulfport-Pascagoula MSA, MS	S	50.96 MW	54.18 AW	105990 AAW	MSBLS	10//99-12//99
	Hattiesburg MSA, MS	S	62.79 MW	67.17 AW	130610 AAW	MSBLS	10//99-12//99
	Missouri	S	60.2 MW	56.19 AW	116870 AAW	MOBLS	10//99-12//99
	Kansas City MSA, MO-KS	S	60.73 MW		126320 AAW	MOBLS	10//99-12//99
	St. Louis MSA, MO-IL	S	49.07 MW	59.57 AW	102080 AAW	MOBLS	10//99-12//99
	Montana	S	58.75 MW	55.86 AW	116200 AAW	MTBLS	10//99-12//99
	Nebraska	S	65.98 MW	61.00 AW	126870 AAW	NEBLS	10//99-12//99
	Nevada	S		66.63 AW	138580 AAW	NVBLS	10//99-12//99
	New Hampshire	S	48.15 MW	50.63 AW	105310 AAW	NHBLS	10//99-12//99
	New Mexico	S	50.11 MW	49.94 AW	103870 AAW	NMBLS	10//99-12//99
	Albuquerque MSA, NM	S	48.11 MW	48.26 AW	100060 AAW	NMBLS	10//99-12//99
	New York	S	58.87 MW	48.27 AW	100400 AAW	NYBLS	10//99-12//99
	Nassau-Suffolk PMSA, NY	S	55.30 MW	61.69 AW	115010 AAW	NYBLS	10//99-12//99
	New York PMSA, NY	S	38.14 MW	26.14 AW	79330 AAW	NYBLS	10//99-12//99
	North Carolina	S		60.89 AW	126650 AAW	NCBLS	10//99-12//99
	Greensboro--Winston-Salem--High Point MSA, NC	S	51.30 MW	59.29 AW	106700 AAW	NCBLS	10//99-12//99
	Raleigh-Durham-Chapel Hill MSA, NC	S	65.99 MW		137250 AAW	NCBLS	10//99-12//99
	Wilmington MSA, NC	S	69.14 MW		143820 AAW	NCBLS	10//99-12//99
	North Dakota	S	67.55 MW	63.76 AW	132620 AAW	NDBLS	10//99-12//99
	Ohio	S		62.75 AW	130520 AAW	OHBLS	10//99-12//99
	Cincinnati PMSA, OH-KY-IN	S	61.26 MW		127420 AAW	OHBLS	10//99-12//99
	Cleveland-Lorain-Elyria PMSA, OH	S	51.49 MW	57.68 AW	107110 AAW	OHBLS	10//99-12//99
	Oklahoma	S	64.43 MW	56.46 AW	117440 AAW	OKBLS	10//99-12//99
	Oklahoma City MSA, OK	S	56.93 MW	66.06 AW	118420 AAW	OKBLS	10//99-12//99
	Pennsylvania	S		61.92 AW	128800 AAW	PABLS	10//99-12//99
	Allentown-Bethlehem-Easton MSA, PA	S	55.59 MW	54.98 AW	115630 AAW	PABLS	10//99-12//99
	Erie MSA, PA	S	65.65 MW		136540 AAW	PABLS	10//99-12//99
	Harrisburg-Lebanon-Carlisle MSA, PA	S	56.26 MW	56.88 AW	117020 AAW	PABLS	10//99-12//99
	Philadelphia PMSA, PA-NJ	S	54.75 MW	64.50 AW	113890 AAW	PABLS	10//99-12//99
	Pittsburgh MSA, PA	S	63.60 MW		132290 AAW	PABLS	10//99-12//99
	Rhode Island	S	58.85 MW	55.60 AW	115640 AAW	RIBLS	10//99-12//99
	Providence-Fall River-Warwick MSA, RI-MA	S	55.91 MW	59.34 AW	116290 AAW	RIBLS	10//99-12//99
	South Carolina	S		65.70 AW	136660 AAW	SCBLS	10//99-12//99
	Tennessee	S		62.47 AW	129940 AAW	TNBLS	10//99-12//99
	Johnson City-Kingsport-Bristol MSA, TN-VA	S	61.80 MW	68.45 AW	128550 AAW	TNBLS	10//99-12//99
	Memphis MSA, TN-AR-MS	S	61.46 MW		127850 AAW	MSBLS	10//99-12//99
	Nashville MSA, TN	S	60.38 MW	69.14 AW	125590 AAW	TNBLS	10//99-12//99
	Texas	S		65.54 AW	136320 AAW	TXBLS	10//99-12//99
	Utah	S	68.02 MW	59.97 AW	124730 AAW	UTBLS	10//99-12//99
	Salt Lake City-Ogden MSA, UT	S	59.73 MW	67.68 AW	124230 AAW	UTBLS	10//99-12//99
	Vermont	S	60.89 MW	58.56 AW	121810 AAW	VTBLS	10//99-12//99
	Virginia	S		63.63 AW	132340 AAW	VABLS	10//99-12//99
	Washington	S		65.31 AW	135850 AAW	WABLS	10//99-12//99
	West Virginia	S	68.69 MW	62.60 AW	130210 AAW	WVBLS	10//99-12//99
	Wisconsin	S		67.43 AW	140260 AAW	WIBLS	10//99-12//99
	Madison MSA, WI	S	69.20 MW		143940 AAW	WIBLS	10//99-12//99
	Milwaukee-Waukesha PMSA, WI	S	67.93 MW		141300 AAW	WIBLS	10//99-12//99
	Wyoming	S	54.94 MW	55.51 AW	115470 AAW	WYBLS	10//99-12//99
	Puerto Rico	S	26.08 MW	26.53 AW	55180 AAW	PRBLS	10//99-12//99
	Arecibo PMSA, PR	S	18.67 MW	18.78 AW	38840 AAW	PRBLS	10//99-12//99
	San Juan-Bayamon PMSA, PR	S	30.62 MW	30.52 AW	63700 AAW	PRBLS	10//99-12//99
Interpreter and Translator	Alabama	S	9.62 MW	11.89 AW	24730 AAW	ALBLS	10//99-12//99

AAW	Average annual wage	AOH	Average offered, high	ASH	Average starting, high	H	Hourly	M	Monthly	S	Special: hourly and annual
AE	Average entry wage	AOL	Average offered, low	ASL	Average starting, low	HI	Highest wage paid	MTC	Median total compensation	TQ	Third quartile wage
AEX	Average experienced wage	APH	Average pay, high range	AW	Average wage paid	HR	High end range	MW	Median wage paid	W	Weekly
AO	Average offered	APL	Average pay, low range	FQ	First quartile wage	LR	Low end range	SQ	Second quartile wage	Y	Yearly

Occupation/Type/Industry	Location	Per	Low	Mid	High	Source	Date
Interpreter and Translator	Arizona	S	13.16 MW	13.85 AW	28800 AAW	AZBLS	10//99-12//99
	Arkansas	S	9.9 MW	9.60 AW	19960 AAW	ARBLS	10//99-12//99
	California	S	13.4 MW	14.85 AW	30890 AAW	CABLS	10//99-12//99
	Colorado	S	11.84 MW	11.90 AW	24750 AAW	COBLS	10//99-12//99
	Connecticut	S	18.83 MW	19.79 AW	41170 AAW	CTBLS	10//99-12//99
	Florida	S	10.62 MW	12.36 AW	25710 AAW	FLBLS	10//99-12//99
	Georgia	S	13.28 MW	12.84 AW	26710 AAW	GABLS	10//99-12//99
	Hawaii	S	18.93 MW	18.26 AW	37970 AAW	HIBLS	10//99-12//99
	Idaho	S	6.97 MW	8.18 AW	17020 AAW	IDBLS	10//99-12//99
	Illinois	S	13.06 MW	14.29 AW	29720 AAW	ILBLS	10//99-12//99
	Indiana	S	10.55 MW	12.10 AW	25170 AAW	INBLS	10//99-12//99
	Iowa	S	9.88 MW	11.42 AW	23760 AAW	IABLS	10//99-12//99
	Kansas	S	9.73 MW	10.78 AW	22420 AAW	KSBLS	10//99-12//99
	Kentucky	S	10.45 MW	13.02 AW	27080 AAW	KYBLS	10//99-12//99
	Louisiana	S	15.13 MW	18.55 AW	38580 AAW	LABLS	10//99-12//99
	Maryland	S	16.09 MW	16.17 AW	33630 AAW	MDBLS	10//99-12//99
	Massachusetts	S	12.21 MW	12.54 AW	26080 AAW	MABLS	10//99-12//99
	Minnesota	S	14.96 MW	15.27 AW	31770 AAW	MNBLS	10//99-12//99
	Missouri	S	16.38 MW	18.26 AW	37980 AAW	MOBLS	10//99-12//99
	Nebraska	S	11.3 MW	12.24 AW	25460 AAW	NEBLS	10//99-12//99
	New Jersey	S	10.3 MW	11.86 AW	24670 AAW	NJBLS	10//99-12//99
	New Mexico	S	18.25 MW	19.89 AW	41380 AAW	NMBLS	10//99-12//99
	New York	S	17.44 MW	18.12 AW	37690 AAW	NYBLS	10//99-12//99
	North Carolina	S	12.51 MW	13.47 AW	28030 AAW	NCBLS	10//99-12//99
	Ohio	S	12.4 MW	12.91 AW	26850 AAW	OHBLS	10//99-12//99
	Oklahoma	S	8.31 MW	9.93 AW	20660 AAW	OKBLS	10//99-12//99
	Oregon	S	15.39 MW	15.28 AW	31790 AAW	ORBLS	10//99-12//99
	Pennsylvania	S	12.68 MW	13.63 AW	28350 AAW	PABLS	10//99-12//99
	Rhode Island	S	11.93 MW	12.26 AW	25500 AAW	RIBLS	10//99-12//99
	South Carolina	S	9.62 MW	12.67 AW	26350 AAW	SCBLS	10//99-12//99
	Tennessee	S	10.9 MW	11.04 AW	22960 AAW	TNBLS	10//99-12//99
	Texas	S	11.66 MW	12.39 AW	25760 AAW	TXBLS	10//99-12//99
	Utah	S	9.76 MW	10.61 AW	22060 AAW	UTBLS	10//99-12//99
	Virginia	S	11.26 MW	16.01 AW	33290 AAW	VABLS	10//99-12//99
	Washington	S	15.51 MW	18.91 AW	39330 AAW	WABLS	10//99-12//99
	Wisconsin	S	13.85 MW	14.69 AW	30550 AAW	WIBLS	10//99-12//99
	Puerto Rico	S	12.52 MW	13.35 AW	27770 AAW	PRBLS	10//99-12//99
Interviewer							
Except Eligibility and Loan	Alabama	S	9.42 MW	10.10 AW	21010 AAW	ALBLS	10//99-12//99
Except Eligibility and Loan	Alaska	S	13.07 MW	12.60 AW	26210 AAW	AKBLS	10//99-12//99
Except Eligibility and Loan	Arizona	S	8.45 MW	8.76 AW	18210 AAW	AZBLS	10//99-12//99
Except Eligibility and Loan	Arkansas	S	7.99 MW	8.18 AW	17020 AAW	ARBLS	10//99-12//99
Except Eligibility and Loan	California	S	11.81 MW	12.61 AW	26220 AAW	CABLS	10//99-12//99
Except Eligibility and Loan	Colorado	S	9.44 MW	10.00 AW	20810 AAW	COBLS	10//99-12//99
Except Eligibility and Loan	Connecticut	S	13.27 MW	13.44 AW	27950 AAW	CTBLS	10//99-12//99
Except Eligibility and Loan	Delaware	S	9.79 MW	10.25 AW	21320 AAW	DEBLS	10//99-12//99
Except Eligibility and Loan	District of Columbia	S	10.01 MW	10.47 AW	21770 AAW	DCBLS	10//99-12//99
Except Eligibility and Loan	Florida	S	8.44 MW	8.82 AW	18350 AAW	FLBLS	10//99-12//99
Except Eligibility and Loan	Georgia	S	9 MW	9.41 AW	19570 AAW	GABLS	10//99-12//99
Except Eligibility and Loan	Hawaii	S	12.14 MW	11.28 AW	23470 AAW	HIBLS	10//99-12//99
Except Eligibility and Loan	Idaho	S	7.77 MW	8.02 AW	16690 AAW	IDBLS	10//99-12//99
Except Eligibility and Loan	Illinois	S	9.14 MW	10.01 AW	20830 AAW	ILBLS	10//99-12//99
Except Eligibility and Loan	Indiana	S	9.19 MW	9.34 AW	19430 AAW	INBLS	10//99-12//99
Except Eligibility and Loan	Iowa	S	8.22 MW	8.41 AW	17500 AAW	IABLS	10//99-12//99
Except Eligibility and Loan	Kansas	S	8.28 MW	8.64 AW	17970 AAW	KSBLS	10//99-12//99
Except Eligibility and Loan	Kentucky	S	9.13 MW	9.00 AW	18730 AAW	KYBLS	10//99-12//99
Except Eligibility and Loan	Louisiana	S	8.34 MW	8.71 AW	18120 AAW	LABLS	10//99-12//99
Except Eligibility and Loan	Maine	S	9.72 MW	9.72 AW	20210 AAW	MEBLS	10//99-12//99
Except Eligibility and Loan	Maryland	S	10.09 MW	10.31 AW	21440 AAW	MDBLS	10//99-12//99
Except Eligibility and Loan	Michigan	S	10.07 MW	10.11 AW	21030 AAW	MIBLS	10//99-12//99
Except Eligibility and Loan	Minnesota	S	9.73 MW	9.96 AW	20710 AAW	MNBLS	10//99-12//99
Except Eligibility and Loan	Mississippi	S	9.25 MW	10.14 AW	21090 AAW	MSBLS	10//99-12//99
Except Eligibility and Loan	Missouri	S	8.88 MW	9.11 AW	18940 AAW	MOBLS	10//99-12//99
Except Eligibility and Loan	Montana	S	8.31 MW	9.35 AW	19450 AAW	MTBLS	10//99-12//99
Except Eligibility and Loan	Nebraska	S	8.88 MW	9.96 AW	20730 AAW	NEBLS	10//99-12//99
Except Eligibility and Loan	Nevada	S	10.18 MW	10.40 AW	21640 AAW	NVBLS	10//99-12//99
Except Eligibility and Loan	New Hampshire	S	9.17 MW	9.39 AW	19540 AAW	NHBLS	10//99-12//99
Except Eligibility and Loan	New Jersey	S	10.25 MW	10.73 AW	22320 AAW	NJBLS	10//99-12//99
Except Eligibility and Loan	New York	S	10.54 MW	11.43 AW	23770 AAW	NYBLS	10//99-12//99
Except Eligibility and Loan	North Carolina	S	9.39 MW	9.66 AW	20090 AAW	NCBLS	10//99-12//99
Except Eligibility and Loan	North Dakota	S	8.73 MW	8.81 AW	18330 AAW	NDBLS	10//99-12//99
Except Eligibility and Loan	Ohio	S	9.2 MW	9.57 AW	19900 AAW	OHBLS	10//99-12//99

AAW	Average annual wage	AOH	Average offered, high	ASH	Average starting, high	H	Hourly	M	Monthly	S	Special: hourly and annual
AE	Average entry wage	AOL	Average offered, low	ASL	Average starting, low	HI	Highest wage paid	MTC	Median total compensation	TQ	Third quartile wage
AEX	Average experienced wage	APH	Average pay, high range	AW	Average wage paid	HR	High end range	MW	Median wage paid	W	Weekly
AO	Average offered	APL	Average pay, low range	FQ	First quartile wage	LR	Low end range	SQ	Second quartile wage	Y	Yearly

Occupation/Type/Industry	Location	Per	Low	Mid	High	Source	Date
Interviewer							
Except Eligibility and Loan	Oklahoma	S	8.17 MW	8.53 AW	17730 AAW	OKBLS	10//99-12//99
Except Eligibility and Loan	Oregon	S	9.3 MW	9.60 AW	19960 AAW	ORBLS	10//99-12//99
Except Eligibility and Loan	Pennsylvania	S	9.56 MW	9.90 AW	20600 AAW	PABLS	10//99-12//99
Except Eligibility and Loan	Rhode Island	S	11.9 MW	11.96 AW	24870 AAW	RIBLS	10//99-12//99
Except Eligibility and Loan	South Carolina	S	8.81 MW	9.04 AW	18790 AAW	SCBLS	10//99-12//99
Except Eligibility and Loan	South Dakota	S	7.93 MW	8.08 AW	16810 AAW	SDBLS	10//99-12//99
Except Eligibility and Loan	Tennessee	S	9.03 MW	9.36 AW	19460 AAW	TNBLS	10//99-12//99
Except Eligibility and Loan	Texas	S	11.22 MW	11.25 AW	23400 AAW	TXBLS	10//99-12//99
Except Eligibility and Loan	Utah	S	7.85 MW	8.20 AW	17050 AAW	UTBLS	10//99-12//99
Except Eligibility and Loan	Vermont	S	8.17 MW	8.54 AW	17760 AAW	VTBLS	10//99-12//99
Except Eligibility and Loan	Virginia	S	8.51 MW	9.18 AW	19100 AAW	VABLS	10//99-12//99
Except Eligibility and Loan	Washington	S	11.38 MW	11.38 AW	23660 AAW	WABLS	10//99-12//99
Except Eligibility and Loan	West Virginia	S	9.01 MW	9.04 AW	18800 AAW	WVBLS	10//99-12//99
Except Eligibility and Loan	Wisconsin	S	9.44 MW	10.26 AW	21340 AAW	WIBLS	10//99-12//99
Except Eligibility and Loan	Wyoming	S	8.68 MW	9.92 AW	20630 AAW	WYBLS	10//99-12//99
Except Eligibility and Loan	Puerto Rico	S	6.03 MW	6.09 AW	12660 AAW	PRBLS	10//99-12//99
Inventory Control Manager							
Supply Chain Management	United States	Y		69100 AW		AMSHIP	2000
Investment Banker							
Managing Director	United States	Y			4000000 MTC	BW	2000
Research Director	United States	Y			3000000 MTC	BW	2000
IT Professional							
	United States	Y		70940 AW		INFOWD	2000
	United States	Y		70940 AW		INFOWD	2000
	Colorado	Y		60000 AW		DENBUS	2000
	Colorado	Y		60000 AW		DENBUS	2000
	Colorado	Y		60000 AW		DENBUS	2000
Real Estate and supporting industries	United States	Y		82901 AW		INFOWD	2000
IT Trainer							
2 years experience	Phoenix, AZ	Y		66305 AW		PBJI	2000
Janitor and Cleaner							
Except Maid and Housekeeping Cleaner	Alabama	S	6.68 MW	7.15 AW	14870 AAW	ALBLS	10//99-12//99
Except Maid and Housekeeping Cleaner	Anniston MSA, AL	S	7.58 MW	7.33 AW	15760 AAW	ALBLS	10//99-12//99
Except Maid and Housekeeping Cleaner	Auburn-Opelika MSA, AL	S	6.89 MW	6.62 AW	14330 AAW	ALBLS	10//99-12//99
Except Maid and Housekeeping Cleaner	Birmingham MSA, AL	S	6.96 MW	6.49 AW	14480 AAW	ALBLS	10//99-12//99
Except Maid and Housekeeping Cleaner	Decatur MSA, AL	S	7.87 MW	7.62 AW	16370 AAW	ALBLS	10//99-12//99
Except Maid and Housekeeping Cleaner	Dothan MSA, AL	S	7.25 MW	6.74 AW	15090 AAW	ALBLS	10//99-12//99
Except Maid and Housekeeping Cleaner	Florence MSA, AL	S	7.49 MW	6.95 AW	15570 AAW	ALBLS	10//99-12//99
Except Maid and Housekeeping Cleaner	Gadsden MSA, AL	S	8.11 MW	7.25 AW	16870 AAW	ALBLS	10//99-12//99
Except Maid and Housekeeping Cleaner	Huntsville MSA, AL	S	7.84 MW	7.68 AW	16310 AAW	ALBLS	10//99-12//99
Except Maid and Housekeeping Cleaner	Mobile MSA, AL	S	6.47 MW	6.15 AW	13460 AAW	ALBLS	10//99-12//99
Except Maid and Housekeeping Cleaner	Montgomery MSA, AL	S	7.17 MW	6.62 AW	14920 AAW	ALBLS	10//99-12//99
Except Maid and Housekeeping Cleaner	Tuscaloosa MSA, AL	S	7.93 MW	7.54 AW	16500 AAW	ALBLS	10//99-12//99
Except Maid and Housekeeping Cleaner	Alaska	S	10.44 MW	10.86 AW	22580 AAW	AKBLS	10//99-12//99
Except Maid and Housekeeping Cleaner	Anchorage MSA, AK	S	10.72 MW	10.20 AW	22310 AAW	AKBLS	10//99-12//99
Except Maid and Housekeeping Cleaner	Arizona	S	7.33 MW	7.76 AW	16150 AAW	AZBLS	10//99-12//99
Except Maid and Housekeeping Cleaner	Flagstaff MSA, AZ-UT	S	7.33 MW	6.75 AW	15250 AAW	AZBLS	10//99-12//99
Except Maid and Housekeeping Cleaner	Phoenix-Mesa MSA, AZ	S	7.84 MW	7.43 AW	16310 AAW	AZBLS	10//99-12//99
Except Maid and Housekeeping Cleaner	Tucson MSA, AZ	S	7.71 MW	7.10 AW	16040 AAW	AZBLS	10//99-12//99
Except Maid and Housekeeping Cleaner	Yuma MSA, AZ	S	6.97 MW	6.70 AW	14490 AAW	AZBLS	10//99-12//99
Except Maid and Housekeeping Cleaner	Arkansas	S	6.59 MW	7.00 AW	14560 AAW	ARBLS	10//99-12//99
Except Maid and Housekeeping Cleaner	Fayetteville-Springdale-Rogers MSA, AR	S	7.41 MW	7.22 AW	15400 AAW	ARBLS	10//99-12//99
Except Maid and Housekeeping Cleaner	Fort Smith MSA, AR-OK	S	7.57 MW	7.18 AW	15730 AAW	ARBLS	10//99-12//99
Except Maid and Housekeeping Cleaner	Jonesboro MSA, AR	S	6.88 MW	6.55 AW	14300 AAW	ARBLS	10//99-12//99
Except Maid and Housekeeping Cleaner	Little Rock-North Little Rock MSA, AR	S	6.93 MW	6.43 AW	14420 AAW	ARBLS	10//99-12//99
Except Maid and Housekeeping Cleaner	Pine Bluff MSA, AR	S	6.46 MW	6.28 AW	13430 AAW	ARBLS	10//99-12//99
Except Maid and Housekeeping Cleaner	California	S	7.97 MW	9.03 AW	18770 AAW	CABLS	10//99-12//99
Except Maid and Housekeeping Cleaner	Bakersfield MSA, CA	S	9.35 MW	8.28 AW	19440 AAW	CABLS	10//99-12//99
Except Maid and Housekeeping Cleaner	Chico-Paradise MSA, CA	S	8.48 MW	7.74 AW	17630 AAW	CABLS	10//99-12//99
Except Maid and Housekeeping Cleaner	Fresno MSA, CA	S	8.45 MW	7.21 AW	17580 AAW	CABLS	10//99-12//99
Except Maid and Housekeeping Cleaner	Los Angeles-Long Beach PMSA, CA	S	9.06 MW	7.92 AW	18840 AAW	CABLS	10//99-12//99
Except Maid and Housekeeping Cleaner	Merced MSA, CA	S	8.74 MW	7.93 AW	18170 AAW	CABLS	10//99-12//99
Except Maid and Housekeeping Cleaner	Modesto MSA, CA	S	8.24 MW	6.88 AW	17140 AAW	CABLS	10//99-12//99
Except Maid and Housekeeping Cleaner	Oakland PMSA, CA	S	10.27 MW	9.56 AW	21360 AAW	CABLS	10//99-12//99
Except Maid and Housekeeping Cleaner	Orange County PMSA, CA	S	8.17 MW	6.92 AW	17000 AAW	CABLS	10//99-12//99

AAW	Average annual wage	AOH	Average offered, high	ASH	Average starting, high	H	Hourly	M	Monthly	S	Special: hourly and annual
AE	Average entry wage	AOL	Average offered, low	ASL	Average starting, low	HI	Highest wage paid	MTC	Median total compensation	TQ	Third quartile wage
AEX	Average experienced wage	APH	Average pay, high range	AW	Average wage paid	HR	High end range	MW	Median wage paid	W	Weekly
AO	Average offered	APL	Average pay, low range	FQ	First quartile wage	LR	Low end range	SQ	Second quartile wage	Y	Yearly

Occupation/Type/Industry	Location	Per	Low	Mid	High	Source	Date
Janitor and Cleaner							
Except Maid and Housekeeping Cleaner	Redding MSA, CA	S	9.01 MW	8.11 AW	18750 AAW	CABLS	10//99-12//99
Except Maid and Housekeeping Cleaner	Riverside-San Bernardino PMSA, CA	S	9.12 MW	8.10 AW	18960 AAW	CABLS	10//99-12//99
Except Maid and Housekeeping Cleaner	Sacramento PMSA, CA	S	8.98 MW	8.08 AW	18680 AAW	CABLS	10//99-12//99
Except Maid and Housekeeping Cleaner	Salinas MSA, CA	S	8.69 MW	7.94 AW	18070 AAW	CABLS	10//99-12//99
Except Maid and Housekeeping Cleaner	San Diego MSA, CA	S	8.75 MW	7.74 AW	18200 AAW	CABLS	10//99-12//99
Except Maid and Housekeeping Cleaner	San Francisco PMSA, CA	S	10.00 MW	9.07 AW	20810 AAW	CABLS	10//99-12//99
Except Maid and Housekeeping Cleaner	San Jose PMSA, CA	S	8.94 MW	7.97 AW	18600 AAW	CABLS	10//99-12//99
Except Maid and Housekeeping Cleaner	San Luis Obispo-Atascadero-Paso Robles MSA, CA	S	9.70 MW	9.29 AW	20170 AAW	CABLS	10//99-12//99
Except Maid and Housekeeping Cleaner	Santa Barbara-Santa Maria-Lompoc MSA, CA	S	8.65 MW	7.66 AW	17990 AAW	CABLS	10//99-12//99
Except Maid and Housekeeping Cleaner	Santa Cruz-Watsonville PMSA, CA	S	9.43 MW	8.52 AW	19620 AAW	CABLS	10//99-12//99
Except Maid and Housekeeping Cleaner	Santa Rosa PMSA, CA	S	9.15 MW	8.24 AW	19040 AAW	CABLS	10//99-12//99
Except Maid and Housekeeping Cleaner	Stockton-Lodi MSA, CA	S	8.72 MW	7.99 AW	18140 AAW	CABLS	10//99-12//99
Except Maid and Housekeeping Cleaner	Vallejo-Fairfield-Napa PMSA, CA	S	9.02 MW	8.25 AW	18760 AAW	CABLS	10//99-12//99
Except Maid and Housekeeping Cleaner	Ventura PMSA, CA	S	8.91 MW	7.44 AW	18520 AAW	CABLS	10//99-12//99
Except Maid and Housekeeping Cleaner	Visalia-Tulare-Porterville MSA, CA	S	8.67 MW	7.75 AW	18030 AAW	CABLS	10//99-12//99
Except Maid and Housekeeping Cleaner	Yolo PMSA, CA	S	9.26 MW	8.30 AW	19250 AAW	CABLS	10//99-12//99
Except Maid and Housekeeping Cleaner	Yuba City MSA, CA	S	10.19 MW	9.80 AW	21200 AAW	CABLS	10//99-12//99
Except Maid and Housekeeping Cleaner	Colorado	S	8.07 MW	8.45 AW	17570 AAW	COBLS	10//99-12//99
Except Maid and Housekeeping Cleaner	Boulder-Longmont PMSA, CO	S	8.95 MW	8.36 AW	18610 AAW	COBLS	10//99-12//99
Except Maid and Housekeeping Cleaner	Colorado Springs MSA, CO	S	8.02 MW	7.67 AW	16680 AAW	COBLS	10//99-12//99
Except Maid and Housekeeping Cleaner	Denver PMSA, CO	S	8.47 MW	8.08 AW	17630 AAW	COBLS	10//99-12//99
Except Maid and Housekeeping Cleaner	Fort Collins-Loveland MSA, CO	S	7.86 MW	7.56 AW	16350 AAW	COBLS	10//99-12//99
Except Maid and Housekeeping Cleaner	Grand Junction MSA, CO	S	7.82 MW	7.48 AW	16270 AAW	COBLS	10//99-12//99
Except Maid and Housekeeping Cleaner	Greeley PMSA, CO	S	7.89 MW	7.65 AW	16410 AAW	COBLS	10//99-12//99
Except Maid and Housekeeping Cleaner	Pueblo MSA, CO	S	8.02 MW	7.45 AW	16690 AAW	COBLS	10//99-12//99
Except Maid and Housekeeping Cleaner	Connecticut	S	8.58 MW	9.82 AW	20420 AAW	CTBLS	10//99-12//99
Except Maid and Housekeeping Cleaner	Bridgeport PMSA, CT	S	9.00 MW	7.82 AW	18720 AAW	CTBLS	10//99-12//99
Except Maid and Housekeeping Cleaner	Danbury PMSA, CT	S	9.85 MW	8.89 AW	20490 AAW	CTBLS	10//99-12//99
Except Maid and Housekeeping Cleaner	Hartford MSA, CT	S	9.89 MW	8.90 AW	20580 AAW	CTBLS	10//99-12//99
Except Maid and Housekeeping Cleaner	New Haven-Meriden PMSA, CT	S	10.63 MW	9.68 AW	22120 AAW	CTBLS	10//99-12//99
Except Maid and Housekeeping Cleaner	New London-Norwich MSA, CT-RI	S	9.61 MW	8.69 AW	19990 AAW	CTBLS	10//99-12//99
Except Maid and Housekeeping Cleaner	Stamford-Norwalk PMSA, CT	S	9.85 MW	7.82 AW	20490 AAW	CTBLS	10//99-12//99
Except Maid and Housekeeping Cleaner	Waterbury PMSA, CT	S	10.05 MW	9.37 AW	20900 AAW	CTBLS	10//99-12//99
Except Maid and Housekeeping Cleaner	Delaware	S	7.53 MW	8.72 AW	18130 AAW	DEBLS	10//99-12//99
Except Maid and Housekeeping Cleaner	Dover MSA, DE	S	8.81 MW	8.19 AW	18330 AAW	DEBLS	10//99-12//99
Except Maid and Housekeeping Cleaner	Wilmington-Newark PMSA, DE-MD	S	8.70 MW	7.31 AW	18100 AAW	DEBLS	10//99-12//99
Except Maid and Housekeeping Cleaner	District of Columbia	S	8.18 MW	8.69 AW	18080 AAW	DCBLS	10//99-12//99
Except Maid and Housekeeping Cleaner	Washington PMSA, DC-MD-VA-WV	S	8.23 MW	7.71 AW	17120 AAW	DCBLS	10//99-12//99
Except Maid and Housekeeping Cleaner	Florida	S	7.11 MW	7.51 AW	15620 AAW	FLBLS	10//99-12//99
Except Maid and Housekeeping Cleaner	Daytona Beach MSA, FL	S	7.02 MW	6.52 AW	14610 AAW	FLBLS	10//99-12//99
Except Maid and Housekeeping Cleaner	Fort Lauderdale PMSA, FL	S	8.00 MW	7.49 AW	16650 AAW	FLBLS	10//99-12//99
Except Maid and Housekeeping Cleaner	Fort Myers-Cape Coral MSA, FL	S	7.25 MW	6.58 AW	15070 AAW	FLBLS	10//99-12//99
Except Maid and Housekeeping Cleaner	Fort Pierce-Port St. Lucie MSA, FL	S	8.47 MW	8.03 AW	17610 AAW	FLBLS	10//99-12//99
Except Maid and Housekeeping Cleaner	Fort Walton Beach MSA, FL	S	7.83 MW	7.38 AW	16290 AAW	FLBLS	10//99-12//99
Except Maid and Housekeeping Cleaner	Gainesville MSA, FL	S	7.74 MW	7.62 AW	16110 AAW	FLBLS	10//99-12//99
Except Maid and Housekeeping Cleaner	Jacksonville MSA, FL	S	7.68 MW	7.38 AW	15970 AAW	FLBLS	10//99-12//99
Except Maid and Housekeeping Cleaner	Lakeland-Winter Haven MSA, FL	S	6.96 MW	6.41 AW	14480 AAW	FLBLS	10//99-12//99
Except Maid and Housekeeping Cleaner	Melbourne-Titusville-Palm Bay MSA, FL	S	7.79 MW	7.35 AW	16200 AAW	FLBLS	10//99-12//99
Except Maid and Housekeeping Cleaner	Miami PMSA, FL	S	7.20 MW	6.62 AW	14970 AAW	FLBLS	10//99-12//99
Except Maid and Housekeeping Cleaner	Naples MSA, FL	S	8.11 MW	7.90 AW	16860 AAW	FLBLS	10//99-12//99
Except Maid and Housekeeping Cleaner	Ocala MSA, FL	S	8.47 MW	8.85 AW	17610 AAW	FLBLS	10//99-12//99
Except Maid and Housekeeping Cleaner	Orlando MSA, FL	S	7.60 MW	7.30 AW	15800 AAW	FLBLS	10//99-12//99
Except Maid and Housekeeping Cleaner	Panama City MSA, FL	S	7.69 MW	7.29 AW	15990 AAW	FLBLS	10//99-12//99
Except Maid and Housekeeping Cleaner	Pensacola MSA, FL	S	7.11 MW	6.69 AW	14790 AAW	FLBLS	10//99-12//99
Except Maid and Housekeeping Cleaner	Punta Gorda MSA, FL	S	6.89 MW	6.09 AW	14340 AAW	FLBLS	10//99-12//99
Except Maid and Housekeeping Cleaner	Sarasota-Bradenton MSA, FL	S	8.17 MW	7.85 AW	16990 AAW	FLBLS	10//99-12//99

AAW Average annual wage	AOH Average offered, high	ASH Average starting, high	H Hourly	M Monthly	S Special: hourly and annual
AE Average entry wage	AOL Average offered, low	ASL Average starting, low	HI Highest wage paid	MTC Median total compensation	TQ Third quartile wage
AEX Average experienced wage	APH Average pay, high range	AW Average wage paid	HR High end range	MW Median wage paid	W Weekly
AO Average offered	APL Average pay, low range	FQ First quartile wage	LR Low end range	SQ Second quartile wage	Y Yearly

Occupation/Type/Industry	Location	Per	Low	Mid	High	Source	Date
Janitor and Cleaner							
Except Maid and Housekeeping Cleaner	Tallahassee MSA, FL	S	7.02 MW	6.70 AW	14610 AAW	FLBLS	10//99-12//99
Except Maid and Housekeeping Cleaner	Tampa-St. Petersburg-Clearwater MSA, FL	S	7.47 MW	7.22 AW	15550 AAW	FLBLS	10//99-12//99
Except Maid and Housekeeping Cleaner	West Palm Beach-Boca Raton MSA, FL	S	7.19 MW	6.59 AW	14950 AAW	FLBLS	10//99-12//99
Except Maid and Housekeeping Cleaner	Georgia	S	7.15 MW	7.54 AW	15680 AAW	GABLS	10//99-12//99
Except Maid and Housekeeping Cleaner	Albany MSA, GA	S	6.47 MW	6.25 AW	13460 AAW	GABLS	10//99-12//99
Except Maid and Housekeeping Cleaner	Athens MSA, GA	S	6.63 MW	6.01 AW	13790 AAW	GABLS	10//99-12//99
Except Maid and Housekeeping Cleaner	Atlanta MSA, GA	S	8.07 MW	7.78 AW	16780 AAW	GABLS	10//99-12//99
Except Maid and Housekeeping Cleaner	Augusta-Aiken MSA, GA-SC	S	7.18 MW	6.79 AW	14940 AAW	GABLS	10//99-12//99
Except Maid and Housekeeping Cleaner	Columbus MSA, GA-AL	S	7.10 MW	6.80 AW	14760 AAW	GABLS	10//99-12//99
Except Maid and Housekeeping Cleaner	Macon MSA, GA	S	7.13 MW	6.60 AW	14830 AAW	GABLS	10//99-12//99
Except Maid and Housekeeping Cleaner	Savannah MSA, GA	S	6.85 MW	6.60 AW	14240 AAW	GABLS	10//99-12//99
Except Maid and Housekeeping Cleaner	Hawaii	S	8.66 MW	8.81 AW	18320 AAW	HIBLS	10//99-12//99
Except Maid and Housekeeping Cleaner	Honolulu MSA, HI	S	8.72 MW	8.51 AW	18140 AAW	HIBLS	10//99-12//99
Except Maid and Housekeeping Cleaner	Idaho	S	7.78 MW	8.06 AW	16750 AAW	IDBLS	10//99-12//99
Except Maid and Housekeeping Cleaner	Boise City MSA, ID	S	8.15 MW	8.00 AW	16950 AAW	IDBLS	10//99-12//99
Except Maid and Housekeeping Cleaner	Pocatello MSA, ID	S	7.35 MW	6.89 AW	15280 AAW	IDBLS	10//99-12//99
Except Maid and Housekeeping Cleaner	Illinois	S	8.3 MW	9.46 AW	19690 AAW	ILBLS	10//99-12//99
Except Maid and Housekeeping Cleaner	Bloomington-Normal MSA, IL	S	9.07 MW	8.42 AW	18870 AAW	ILBLS	10//99-12//99
Except Maid and Housekeeping Cleaner	Chicago PMSA, IL	S	9.71 MW	8.46 AW	20200 AAW	ILBLS	10//99-12//99
Except Maid and Housekeeping Cleaner	Decatur MSA, IL	S	9.00 MW	7.14 AW	18720 AAW	ILBLS	10//99-12//99
Except Maid and Housekeeping Cleaner	Kankakee PMSA, IL	S	9.71 MW	8.94 AW	20210 AAW	ILBLS	10//99-12//99
Except Maid and Housekeeping Cleaner	Peoria-Pekin MSA, IL	S	9.51 MW	7.88 AW	19790 AAW	ILBLS	10//99-12//99
Except Maid and Housekeeping Cleaner	Rockford MSA, IL	S	8.57 MW	7.97 AW	17820 AAW	ILBLS	10//99-12//99
Except Maid and Housekeeping Cleaner	Springfield MSA, IL	S	9.16 MW	8.44 AW	19060 AAW	ILBLS	10//99-12//99
Except Maid and Housekeeping Cleaner	Indiana	S	8.32 MW	8.99 AW	18710 AAW	INBLS	10//99-12//99
Except Maid and Housekeeping Cleaner	Bloomington MSA, IN	S	9.72 MW	10.09 AW	20220 AAW	INBLS	10//99-12//99
Except Maid and Housekeeping Cleaner	Elkhart-Goshen MSA, IN	S	9.02 MW	8.32 AW	18750 AAW	INBLS	10//99-12//99
Except Maid and Housekeeping Cleaner	Evansville-Henderson MSA, IN-KY	S	8.36 MW	7.57 AW	17380 AAW	INBLS	10//99-12//99
Except Maid and Housekeeping Cleaner	Fort Wayne MSA, IN	S	8.44 MW	7.93 AW	17560 AAW	INBLS	10//99-12//99
Except Maid and Housekeeping Cleaner	Gary PMSA, IN	S	8.73 MW	8.13 AW	18170 AAW	INBLS	10//99-12//99
Except Maid and Housekeeping Cleaner	Indianapolis MSA, IN	S	9.28 MW	8.57 AW	19310 AAW	INBLS	10//99-12//99
Except Maid and Housekeeping Cleaner	Kokomo MSA, IN	S	13.87 MW	12.11 AW	28850 AAW	INBLS	10//99-12//99
Except Maid and Housekeeping Cleaner	Lafayette MSA, IN	S	8.98 MW	8.58 AW	18690 AAW	INBLS	10//99-12//99
Except Maid and Housekeeping Cleaner	Muncie MSA, IN	S	9.31 MW	8.40 AW	19370 AAW	INBLS	10//99-12//99
Except Maid and Housekeeping Cleaner	South Bend MSA, IN	S	9.35 MW	8.81 AW	19450 AAW	INBLS	10//99-12//99
Except Maid and Housekeeping Cleaner	Terre Haute MSA, IN	S	8.15 MW	7.76 AW	16950 AAW	INBLS	10//99-12//99
Except Maid and Housekeeping Cleaner	Iowa	S	7.99 MW	8.41 AW	17480 AAW	IABLS	10//99-12//99
Except Maid and Housekeeping Cleaner	Cedar Rapids MSA, IA	S	8.35 MW	7.81 AW	17380 AAW	IABLS	10//99-12//99
Except Maid and Housekeeping Cleaner	Davenport-Moline-Rock Island MSA, IA-IL	S	8.62 MW	7.93 AW	17920 AAW	IABLS	10//99-12//99
Except Maid and Housekeeping Cleaner	Des Moines MSA, IA	S	8.80 MW	8.17 AW	18300 AAW	IABLS	10//99-12//99
Except Maid and Housekeeping Cleaner	Dubuque MSA, IA	S	7.85 MW	6.97 AW	16320 AAW	IABLS	10//99-12//99
Except Maid and Housekeeping Cleaner	Sioux City MSA, IA-NE	S	8.48 MW	8.18 AW	17630 AAW	IABLS	10//99-12//99
Except Maid and Housekeeping Cleaner	Waterloo-Cedar Falls MSA, IA	S	7.99 MW	7.37 AW	16620 AAW	IABLS	10//99-12//99
Except Maid and Housekeeping Cleaner	Kansas	S	7.63 MW	8.00 AW	16640 AAW	KSBLS	10//99-12//99
Except Maid and Housekeeping Cleaner	Lawrence MSA, KS	S	8.45 MW	8.09 AW	17570 AAW	KSBLS	10//99-12//99
Except Maid and Housekeeping Cleaner	Topeka MSA, KS	S	7.41 MW	6.79 AW	15400 AAW	KSBLS	10//99-12//99
Except Maid and Housekeeping Cleaner	Wichita MSA, KS	S	8.36 MW	7.69 AW	17380 AAW	KSBLS	10//99-12//99
Except Maid and Housekeeping Cleaner	Kentucky	S	7.35 MW	7.73 AW	16080 AAW	KYBLS	10//99-12//99
Except Maid and Housekeeping Cleaner	Lexington MSA, KY	S	8.12 MW	7.85 AW	16890 AAW	KYBLS	10//99-12//99
Except Maid and Housekeeping Cleaner	Louisville MSA, KY-IN	S	7.99 MW	7.47 AW	16630 AAW	KYBLS	10//99-12//99
Except Maid and Housekeeping Cleaner	Owensboro MSA, KY	S	7.25 MW	6.86 AW	15080 AAW	KYBLS	10//99-12//99
Except Maid and Housekeeping Cleaner	Louisiana	S	6.59 MW	7.15 AW	14870 AAW	LABLS	10//99-12//99
Except Maid and Housekeeping Cleaner	Alexandria MSA, LA	S	7.06 MW	6.63 AW	14680 AAW	LABLS	10//99-12//99
Except Maid and Housekeeping Cleaner	Baton Rouge MSA, LA	S	7.23 MW	6.50 AW	15040 AAW	LABLS	10//99-12//99
Except Maid and Housekeeping Cleaner	Houma MSA, LA	S	6.65 MW	6.39 AW	13840 AAW	LABLS	10//99-12//99
Except Maid and Housekeeping Cleaner	Lafayette MSA, LA	S	7.06 MW	6.61 AW	14690 AAW	LABLS	10//99-12//99
Except Maid and Housekeeping Cleaner	Lake Charles MSA, LA	S	7.56 MW	6.60 AW	15730 AAW	LABLS	10//99-12//99
Except Maid and Housekeeping Cleaner	Monroe MSA, LA	S	6.73 MW	6.05 AW	14010 AAW	LABLS	10//99-12//99
Except Maid and Housekeeping Cleaner	New Orleans MSA, LA	S	7.32 MW	6.68 AW	15230 AAW	LABLS	10//99-12//99
Except Maid and Housekeeping Cleaner	Shreveport-Bossier City MSA, LA	S	6.84 MW	6.51 AW	14230 AAW	LABLS	10//99-12//99
Except Maid and Housekeeping Cleaner	Maine	S	8.26 MW	8.63 AW	17960 AAW	MEBLS	10//99-12//99
Except Maid and Housekeeping Cleaner	Bangor MSA, ME	S	7.81 MW	7.45 AW	16240 AAW	MEBLS	10//99-12//99
Except Maid and Housekeeping Cleaner	Lewiston-Auburn MSA, ME	S	8.08 MW	7.91 AW	16810 AAW	MEBLS	10//99-12//99
Except Maid and Housekeeping Cleaner	Portland MSA, ME	S	8.68 MW	8.20 AW	18050 AAW	MEBLS	10//99-12//99
Except Maid and Housekeeping Cleaner	Maryland	S	7.22 MW	7.93 AW	16480 AAW	MDBLS	10//99-12//99
Except Maid and Housekeeping Cleaner	Baltimore PMSA, MD	S	7.74 MW	7.13 AW	16090 AAW	MDBLS	10//99-12//99

AAW Average annual wage	AOH Average offered, high	ASH Average starting, high	H Hourly	M Monthly	S Special: hourly and annual
AE Average entry wage	AOL Average offered, low	ASL Average starting, low	HI Highest wage paid	MTC Median total compensation	TQ Third quartile wage
AEX Average experienced wage	APH Average pay, high range	AW Average wage paid	HR High end range	MW Median wage paid	W Weekly
AO Average offered	APL Average pay, low range	FQ First quartile wage	LR Low end range	SQ Second quartile wage	Y Yearly

Occupation/Type/Industry	Location	Per	Low	Mid	High	Source	Date
Janitor and Cleaner							
Except Maid and Housekeeping Cleaner	Cumberland MSA, MD-WV	S	7.73 MW	6.83 AW	16080 AAW	MDBLS	10//99-12//99
Except Maid and Housekeeping Cleaner	Hagerstown PMSA, MD	S	8.30 MW	7.79 AW	17260 AAW	MDBLS	10//99-12//99
Except Maid and Housekeeping Cleaner	Massachusetts	S	9.61 MW	10.22 AW	21250 AAW	MABLS	10//99-12//99
Except Maid and Housekeeping Cleaner	Barnstable-Yarmouth MSA, MA	S	10.43 MW	10.09 AW	21690 AAW	MABLS	10//99-12//99
Except Maid and Housekeeping Cleaner	Boston PMSA, MA-NH	S	10.22 MW	9.57 AW	21250 AAW	MABLS	10//99-12//99
Except Maid and Housekeeping Cleaner	Brockton PMSA, MA	S	10.17 MW	9.45 AW	21160 AAW	MABLS	10//99-12//99
Except Maid and Housekeeping Cleaner	Fitchburg-Leominster PMSA, MA	S	10.24 MW	9.86 AW	21290 AAW	MABLS	10//99-12//99
Except Maid and Housekeeping Cleaner	Lawrence PMSA, MA-NH	S	9.47 MW	8.80 AW	19690 AAW	MABLS	10//99-12//99
Except Maid and Housekeeping Cleaner	Lowell PMSA, MA-NH	S	10.79 MW	10.19 AW	22450 AAW	MABLS	10//99-12//99
Except Maid and Housekeeping Cleaner	New Bedford PMSA, MA	S	9.41 MW	8.76 AW	19570 AAW	MABLS	10//99-12//99
Except Maid and Housekeeping Cleaner	Pittsfield MSA, MA	S	9.78 MW	8.86 AW	20340 AAW	MABLS	10//99-12//99
Except Maid and Housekeeping Cleaner	Springfield MSA, MA	S	9.85 MW	9.53 AW	20490 AAW	MABLS	10//99-12//99
Except Maid and Housekeeping Cleaner	Worcester PMSA, MA-CT	S	9.88 MW	9.40 AW	20550 AAW	MABLS	10//99-12//99
Except Maid and Housekeeping Cleaner	Michigan	S	8.76 MW	10.17 AW	21140 AAW	MIBLS	10//99-12//99
Except Maid and Housekeeping Cleaner	Ann Arbor PMSA, MI	S	10.42 MW	9.49 AW	21660 AAW	MIBLS	10//99-12//99
Except Maid and Housekeeping Cleaner	Benton Harbor MSA, MI	S	8.88 MW	8.42 AW	18460 AAW	MIBLS	10//99-12//99
Except Maid and Housekeeping Cleaner	Detroit PMSA, MI	S	10.86 MW	9.21 AW	22580 AAW	MIBLS	10//99-12//99
Except Maid and Housekeeping Cleaner	Flint PMSA, MI	S	11.54 MW	9.16 AW	24000 AAW	MIBLS	10//99-12//99
Except Maid and Housekeeping Cleaner	Grand Rapids-Muskegon-Holland MSA, MI	S	9.19 MW	8.21 AW	19120 AAW	MIBLS	10//99-12//99
Except Maid and Housekeeping Cleaner	Jackson MSA, MI	S	8.95 MW	8.06 AW	18620 AAW	MIBLS	10//99-12//99
Except Maid and Housekeeping Cleaner	Kalamazoo-Battle Creek MSA, MI	S	10.07 MW	9.17 AW	20950 AAW	MIBLS	10//99-12//99
Except Maid and Housekeeping Cleaner	Lansing-East Lansing MSA, MI	S	10.29 MW	8.67 AW	21400 AAW	MIBLS	10//99-12//99
Except Maid and Housekeeping Cleaner	Saginaw-Bay City-Midland MSA, MI	S	9.70 MW	7.83 AW	20170 AAW	MIBLS	10//99-12//99
Except Maid and Housekeeping Cleaner	Minnesota	S	8.75 MW	9.34 AW	19430 AAW	MNBLS	10//99-12//99
Except Maid and Housekeeping Cleaner	Duluth-Superior MSA, MN-WI	S	8.49 MW	7.60 AW	17670 AAW	MNBLS	10//99-12//99
Except Maid and Housekeeping Cleaner	Minneapolis-St. Paul MSA, MN-WI	S	9.64 MW	9.01 AW	20050 AAW	MNBLS	10//99-12//99
Except Maid and Housekeeping Cleaner	Rochester MSA, MN	S	9.59 MW	9.33 AW	19950 AAW	MNBLS	10//99-12//99
Except Maid and Housekeeping Cleaner	St. Cloud MSA, MN	S	8.33 MW	7.83 AW	17320 AAW	MNBLS	10//99-12//99
Except Maid and Housekeeping Cleaner	Mississippi	S	6.46 MW	6.91 AW	14370 AAW	MSBLS	10//99-12//99
Except Maid and Housekeeping Cleaner	Biloxi-Gulfport-Pascagoula MSA, MS	S	7.63 MW	7.02 AW	15870 AAW	MSBLS	10//99-12//99
Except Maid and Housekeeping Cleaner	Hattiesburg MSA, MS	S	6.89 MW	6.38 AW	14330 AAW	MSBLS	10//99-12//99
Except Maid and Housekeeping Cleaner	Jackson MSA, MS	S	6.99 MW	6.55 AW	14530 AAW	MSBLS	10//99-12//99
Except Maid and Housekeeping Cleaner	Missouri	S	7.51 MW	8.06 AW	16760 AAW	MOBLS	10//99-12//99
Except Maid and Housekeeping Cleaner	Columbia MSA, MO	S	7.73 MW	7.29 AW	16070 AAW	MOBLS	10//99-12//99
Except Maid and Housekeeping Cleaner	Joplin MSA, MO	S	7.24 MW	6.79 AW	15070 AAW	MOBLS	10//99-12//99
Except Maid and Housekeeping Cleaner	Kansas City MSA, MO-KS	S	8.52 MW	7.95 AW	17710 AAW	MOBLS	10//99-12//99
Except Maid and Housekeeping Cleaner	St. Joseph MSA, MO	S	9.50 MW	8.49 AW	19760 AAW	MOBLS	10//99-12//99
Except Maid and Housekeeping Cleaner	St. Louis MSA, MO-IL	S	8.13 MW	7.50 AW	16910 AAW	MOBLS	10//99-12//99
Except Maid and Housekeeping Cleaner	Springfield MSA, MO	S	8.44 MW	7.96 AW	17550 AAW	MOBLS	10//99-12//99
Except Maid and Housekeeping Cleaner	Montana	S	7.31 MW	7.81 AW	16240 AAW	MTBLS	10//99-12//99
Except Maid and Housekeeping Cleaner	Billings MSA, MT	S	7.54 MW	6.56 AW	15680 AAW	MTBLS	10//99-12//99
Except Maid and Housekeeping Cleaner	Great Falls MSA, MT	S	7.47 MW	6.90 AW	15530 AAW	MTBLS	10//99-12//99
Except Maid and Housekeeping Cleaner	Missoula MSA, MT	S	7.73 MW	7.54 AW	16080 AAW	MTBLS	10//99-12//99
Except Maid and Housekeeping Cleaner	Nebraska	S	7.86 MW	8.19 AW	17030 AAW	NEBLS	10//99-12//99
Except Maid and Housekeeping Cleaner	Lincoln MSA, NE	S	7.86 MW	7.61 AW	16340 AAW	NEBLS	10//99-12//99
Except Maid and Housekeeping Cleaner	Omaha MSA, NE-IA	S	8.71 MW	8.07 AW	18110 AAW	NEBLS	10//99-12//99
Except Maid and Housekeeping Cleaner	Nevada	S	8.66 MW	8.89 AW	18490 AAW	NVBLS	10//99-12//99
Except Maid and Housekeeping Cleaner	Las Vegas MSA, NV-AZ	S	8.99 MW	8.92 AW	18700 AAW	NVBLS	10//99-12//99
Except Maid and Housekeeping Cleaner	Reno MSA, NV	S	8.34 MW	7.71 AW	17340 AAW	NVBLS	10//99-12//99
Except Maid and Housekeeping Cleaner	New Hampshire	S	8.43 MW	8.90 AW	18500 AAW	NHBLS	10//99-12//99
Except Maid and Housekeeping Cleaner	Manchester PMSA, NH	S	8.45 MW	7.97 AW	17580 AAW	NHBLS	10//99-12//99
Except Maid and Housekeeping Cleaner	Nashua PMSA, NH	S	8.93 MW	8.48 AW	18580 AAW	NHBLS	10//99-12//99
Except Maid and Housekeeping Cleaner	Portsmouth-Rochester PMSA, NH-ME	S	8.89 MW	8.63 AW	18490 AAW	NHBLS	10//99-12//99
Except Maid and Housekeeping Cleaner	New Jersey	S	8.96 MW	9.94 AW	20680 AAW	NJBLS	10//99-12//99
Except Maid and Housekeeping Cleaner	Atlantic-Cape May PMSA, NJ	S	10.51 MW	10.75 AW	21850 AAW	NJBLS	10//99-12//99
Except Maid and Housekeeping Cleaner	Bergen-Passaic PMSA, NJ	S	9.93 MW	8.83 AW	20650 AAW	NJBLS	10//99-12//99
Except Maid and Housekeeping Cleaner	Jersey City PMSA, NJ	S	9.70 MW	9.07 AW	20180 AAW	NJBLS	10//99-12//99
Except Maid and Housekeeping Cleaner	Middlesex-Somerset-Hunterdon PMSA, NJ	S	10.08 MW	8.99 AW	20960 AAW	NJBLS	10//99-12//99
Except Maid and Housekeeping Cleaner	Monmouth-Ocean PMSA, NJ	S	9.07 MW	8.36 AW	18870 AAW	NJBLS	10//99-12//99
Except Maid and Housekeeping Cleaner	Newark PMSA, NJ	S	10.54 MW	9.25 AW	21920 AAW	NJBLS	10//99-12//99
Except Maid and Housekeeping Cleaner	Trenton PMSA, NJ	S	9.85 MW	9.16 AW	20480 AAW	NJBLS	10//99-12//99

Janitor and Cleaner

Occupation/Type/Industry	Location	Per	Low	Mid	High	Source	Date
Except Maid and Housekeeping Cleaner	Vineland-Millville-Bridgeton PMSA, NJ	S	9.78 MW	9.41 AW	20350 AAW	NJBLS	10//99-12//99
Except Maid and Housekeeping Cleaner	New Mexico	S	7.12 MW	7.49 AW	15590 AAW	NMBLS	10//99-12//99
Except Maid and Housekeeping Cleaner	Albuquerque MSA, NM	S	7.47 MW	6.98 AW	15530 AAW	NMBLS	10//99-12//99
Except Maid and Housekeeping Cleaner	Las Cruces MSA, NM	S	7.24 MW	7.01 AW	15060 AAW	NMBLS	10//99-12//99
Except Maid and Housekeeping Cleaner	Santa Fe MSA, NM	S	8.34 MW	8.18 AW	17340 AAW	NMBLS	10//99-12//99
Except Maid and Housekeeping Cleaner	New York	S	10.98 MW	11.27 AW	23450 AAW	NYBLS	10//99-12//99
Except Maid and Housekeeping Cleaner	Albany-Schenectady-Troy MSA, NY	S	9.56 MW	8.62 AW	19880 AAW	NYBLS	10//99-12//99
Except Maid and Housekeeping Cleaner	Binghamton MSA, NY	S	8.33 MW	7.92 AW	17330 AAW	NYBLS	10//99-12//99
Except Maid and Housekeeping Cleaner	Buffalo-Niagara Falls MSA, NY	S	8.72 MW	7.44 AW	18140 AAW	NYBLS	10//99-12//99
Except Maid and Housekeeping Cleaner	Dutchess County PMSA, NY	S	9.70 MW	8.99 AW	20170 AAW	NYBLS	10//99-12//99
Except Maid and Housekeeping Cleaner	Elmira MSA, NY	S	8.46 MW	7.77 AW	17600 AAW	NYBLS	10//99-12//99
Except Maid and Housekeeping Cleaner	Glens Falls MSA, NY	S	9.07 MW	8.48 AW	18860 AAW	NYBLS	10//99-12//99
Except Maid and Housekeeping Cleaner	Jamestown MSA, NY	S	9.34 MW	8.28 AW	19420 AAW	NYBLS	10//99-12//99
Except Maid and Housekeeping Cleaner	Nassau-Suffolk PMSA, NY	S	11.61 MW	10.27 AW	24160 AAW	NYBLS	10//99-12//99
Except Maid and Housekeeping Cleaner	New York PMSA, NY	S	12.37 MW	13.02 AW	25740 AAW	NYBLS	10//99-12//99
Except Maid and Housekeeping Cleaner	Newburgh PMSA, NY-PA	S	9.96 MW	9.44 AW	20720 AAW	NYBLS	10//99-12//99
Except Maid and Housekeeping Cleaner	Rochester MSA, NY	S	8.72 MW	7.92 AW	18130 AAW	NYBLS	10//99-12//99
Except Maid and Housekeeping Cleaner	Syracuse MSA, NY	S	8.85 MW	8.11 AW	18410 AAW	NYBLS	10//99-12//99
Except Maid and Housekeeping Cleaner	Utica-Rome MSA, NY	S	8.55 MW	7.73 AW	17790 AAW	NYBLS	10//99-12//99
Except Maid and Housekeeping Cleaner	North Carolina	S	7.34 MW	7.63 AW	15880 AAW	NCBLS	10//99-12//99
Except Maid and Housekeeping Cleaner	Asheville MSA, NC	S	8.04 MW	7.82 AW	16720 AAW	NCBLS	10//99-12//99
Except Maid and Housekeeping Cleaner	Charlotte-Gastonia-Rock Hill MSA, NC-SC	S	7.74 MW	7.47 AW	16100 AAW	NCBLS	10//99-12//99
Except Maid and Housekeeping Cleaner	Fayetteville MSA, NC	S	7.37 MW	7.18 AW	15320 AAW	NCBLS	10//99-12//99
Except Maid and Housekeeping Cleaner	Goldsboro MSA, NC	S	6.83 MW	6.52 AW	14200 AAW	NCBLS	10//99-12//99
Except Maid and Housekeeping Cleaner	Greensboro--Winston-Salem--High Point MSA, NC	S	7.54 MW	7.30 AW	15690 AAW	NCBLS	10//99-12//99
Except Maid and Housekeeping Cleaner	Greenville MSA, NC	S	7.04 MW	7.02 AW	14640 AAW	NCBLS	10//99-12//99
Except Maid and Housekeeping Cleaner	Hickory-Morganton-Lenoir MSA, NC	S	7.99 MW	7.79 AW	16620 AAW	NCBLS	10//99-12//99
Except Maid and Housekeeping Cleaner	Jacksonville MSA, NC	S	7.44 MW	7.06 AW	15470 AAW	NCBLS	10//99-12//99
Except Maid and Housekeeping Cleaner	Raleigh-Durham-Chapel Hill MSA, NC	S	7.71 MW	7.46 AW	16030 AAW	NCBLS	10//99-12//99
Except Maid and Housekeeping Cleaner	Rocky Mount MSA, NC	S	7.50 MW	6.78 AW	15610 AAW	NCBLS	10//99-12//99
Except Maid and Housekeeping Cleaner	Wilmington MSA, NC	S	7.33 MW	7.12 AW	15240 AAW	NCBLS	10//99-12//99
Except Maid and Housekeeping Cleaner	North Dakota	S	7.8 MW	8.03 AW	16690 AAW	NDBLS	10//99-12//99
Except Maid and Housekeeping Cleaner	Bismarck MSA, ND	S	7.61 MW	7.28 AW	15820 AAW	NDBLS	10//99-12//99
Except Maid and Housekeeping Cleaner	Fargo-Moorhead MSA, ND-MN	S	8.21 MW	7.79 AW	17070 AAW	NDBLS	10//99-12//99
Except Maid and Housekeeping Cleaner	Grand Forks MSA, ND-MN	S	8.71 MW	9.07 AW	18110 AAW	NDBLS	10//99-12//99
Except Maid and Housekeeping Cleaner	Ohio	S	8.06 MW	8.96 AW	18630 AAW	OHBLS	10//99-12//99
Except Maid and Housekeeping Cleaner	Akron PMSA, OH	S	9.00 MW	7.91 AW	18730 AAW	OHBLS	10//99-12//99
Except Maid and Housekeeping Cleaner	Canton-Massillon MSA, OH	S	8.68 MW	8.20 AW	18050 AAW	OHBLS	10//99-12//99
Except Maid and Housekeeping Cleaner	Cincinnati PMSA, OH-KY-IN	S	8.48 MW	7.89 AW	17650 AAW	OHBLS	10//99-12//99
Except Maid and Housekeeping Cleaner	Cleveland-Lorain-Elyria PMSA, OH	S	9.32 MW	8.35 AW	19390 AAW	OHBLS	10//99-12//99
Except Maid and Housekeeping Cleaner	Columbus MSA, OH	S	9.01 MW	8.12 AW	18750 AAW	OHBLS	10//99-12//99
Except Maid and Housekeeping Cleaner	Dayton-Springfield MSA, OH	S	9.74 MW	8.23 AW	20250 AAW	OHBLS	10//99-12//99
Except Maid and Housekeeping Cleaner	Hamilton-Middletown PMSA, OH	S	9.61 MW	9.27 AW	20000 AAW	OHBLS	10//99-12//99
Except Maid and Housekeeping Cleaner	Lima MSA, OH	S	9.53 MW	8.40 AW	19830 AAW	OHBLS	10//99-12//99
Except Maid and Housekeeping Cleaner	Mansfield MSA, OH	S	8.17 MW	7.00 AW	16990 AAW	OHBLS	10//99-12//99
Except Maid and Housekeeping Cleaner	Steubenville-Weirton MSA, OH-WV	S	7.11 MW	6.37 AW	14780 AAW	OHBLS	10//99-12//99
Except Maid and Housekeeping Cleaner	Toledo MSA, OH	S	9.31 MW	8.06 AW	19370 AAW	OHBLS	10//99-12//99
Except Maid and Housekeeping Cleaner	Youngstown-Warren MSA, OH	S	7.98 MW	6.67 AW	16600 AAW	OHBLS	10//99-12//99
Except Maid and Housekeeping Cleaner	Oklahoma	S	7.18 MW	7.51 AW	15610 AAW	OKBLS	10//99-12//99
Except Maid and Housekeeping Cleaner	Enid MSA, OK	S	7.31 MW	6.92 AW	15210 AAW	OKBLS	10//99-12//99
Except Maid and Housekeeping Cleaner	Lawton MSA, OK	S	7.41 MW	7.10 AW	15420 AAW	OKBLS	10//99-12//99
Except Maid and Housekeeping Cleaner	Oklahoma City MSA, OK	S	7.59 MW	7.28 AW	15780 AAW	OKBLS	10//99-12//99
Except Maid and Housekeeping Cleaner	Tulsa MSA, OK	S	7.70 MW	7.31 AW	16020 AAW	OKBLS	10//99-12//99
Except Maid and Housekeeping Cleaner	Oregon	S	8.54 MW	9.22 AW	19180 AAW	ORBLS	10//99-12//99
Except Maid and Housekeeping Cleaner	Corvallis MSA, OR	S	8.91 MW	8.35 AW	18520 AAW	ORBLS	10//99-12//99
Except Maid and Housekeeping Cleaner	Eugene-Springfield MSA, OR	S	8.82 MW	8.05 AW	18350 AAW	ORBLS	10//99-12//99
Except Maid and Housekeeping Cleaner	Medford-Ashland MSA, OR	S	8.67 MW	8.02 AW	18040 AAW	ORBLS	10//99-12//99
Except Maid and Housekeeping Cleaner	Portland-Vancouver PMSA, OR-WA	S	9.41 MW	8.73 AW	19560 AAW	ORBLS	10//99-12//99
Except Maid and Housekeeping Cleaner	Salem PMSA, OR	S	9.61 MW	9.02 AW	19980 AAW	ORBLS	10//99-12//99

AAW Average annual wage	AOH Average offered, high	ASH Average starting, high	H Hourly	M Monthly	S Special: hourly and annual
AE Average entry wage	AOL Average offered, low	ASL Average starting, low	HI Highest wage paid	MTC Median total compensation	TQ Third quartile wage
AEX Average experienced wage	APH Average pay, high range	AW Average wage paid	HR High end range	MW Median wage paid	W Weekly
AO Average offered	APL Average pay, low range	FQ First quartile wage	LR Low end range	SQ Second quartile wage	Y Yearly

Janitor and Cleaner

Occupation/Type/Industry	Location	Per	Low	Mid	High	Source	Date
Except Maid and Housekeeping Cleaner	Pennsylvania	S	8.14 MW	8.84 AW	18380 AAW	PABLS	10//99-12//99
Except Maid and Housekeeping Cleaner	Allentown-Bethlehem-Easton MSA, PA	S	8.89 MW	8.13 AW	18490 AAW	PABLS	10//99-12//99
Except Maid and Housekeeping Cleaner	Altoona MSA, PA	S	8.32 MW	7.74 AW	17300 AAW	PABLS	10//99-12//99
Except Maid and Housekeeping Cleaner	Erie MSA, PA	S	8.36 MW	7.20 AW	17390 AAW	PABLS	10//99-12//99
Except Maid and Housekeeping Cleaner	Harrisburg-Lebanon-Carlisle MSA, PA	S	8.38 MW	7.95 AW	17440 AAW	PABLS	10//99-12//99
Except Maid and Housekeeping Cleaner	Johnstown MSA, PA	S	7.78 MW	6.93 AW	16180 AAW	PABLS	10//99-12//99
Except Maid and Housekeeping Cleaner	Lancaster MSA, PA	S	8.96 MW	8.43 AW	18630 AAW	PABLS	10//99-12//99
Except Maid and Housekeeping Cleaner	Philadelphia PMSA, PA-NJ	S	9.59 MW	8.82 AW	19940 AAW	PABLS	10//99-12//99
Except Maid and Housekeeping Cleaner	Pittsburgh MSA, PA	S	8.78 MW	7.75 AW	18250 AAW	PABLS	10//99-12//99
Except Maid and Housekeeping Cleaner	Reading MSA, PA	S	8.79 MW	8.21 AW	18280 AAW	PABLS	10//99-12//99
Except Maid and Housekeeping Cleaner	Scranton--Wilkes-Barre--Hazleton MSA, PA	S	8.83 MW	8.20 AW	18370 AAW	PABLS	10//99-12//99
Except Maid and Housekeeping Cleaner	Sharon MSA, PA	S	7.78 MW	7.22 AW	16180 AAW	PABLS	10//99-12//99
Except Maid and Housekeeping Cleaner	State College MSA, PA	S	9.49 MW	9.56 AW	19740 AAW	PABLS	10//99-12//99
Except Maid and Housekeeping Cleaner	Williamsport MSA, PA	S	7.40 MW	6.70 AW	15400 AAW	PABLS	10//99-12//99
Except Maid and Housekeeping Cleaner	York MSA, PA	S	8.60 MW	8.27 AW	17900 AAW	PABLS	10//99-12//99
Except Maid and Housekeeping Cleaner	Rhode Island	S	8.69 MW	9.41 AW	19560 AAW	RIBLS	10//99-12//99
Except Maid and Housekeeping Cleaner	Providence-Fall River-Warwick MSA, RI-MA	S	9.38 MW	8.73 AW	19500 AAW	RIBLS	10//99-12//99
Except Maid and Housekeeping Cleaner	South Carolina	S	7.11 MW	7.38 AW	15350 AAW	SCBLS	10//99-12//99
Except Maid and Housekeeping Cleaner	Charleston-North Charleston MSA, SC	S	7.32 MW	6.93 AW	15220 AAW	SCBLS	10//99-12//99
Except Maid and Housekeeping Cleaner	Columbia MSA, SC	S	7.50 MW	7.08 AW	15590 AAW	SCBLS	10//99-12//99
Except Maid and Housekeeping Cleaner	Florence MSA, SC	S	7.33 MW	6.78 AW	15250 AAW	SCBLS	10//99-12//99
Except Maid and Housekeeping Cleaner	Greenville-Spartanburg-Anderson MSA, SC	S	7.30 MW	7.03 AW	15190 AAW	SCBLS	10//99-12//99
Except Maid and Housekeeping Cleaner	Myrtle Beach MSA, SC	S	7.60 MW	7.43 AW	15800 AAW	SCBLS	10//99-12//99
Except Maid and Housekeeping Cleaner	Sumter MSA, SC	S	7.25 MW	7.12 AW	15070 AAW	SCBLS	10//99-12//99
Except Maid and Housekeeping Cleaner	South Dakota	S	7.53 MW	7.66 AW	15940 AAW	SDBLS	10//99-12//99
Except Maid and Housekeeping Cleaner	Rapid City MSA, SD	S	7.56 MW	7.44 AW	15730 AAW	SDBLS	10//99-12//99
Except Maid and Housekeeping Cleaner	Sioux Falls MSA, SD	S	8.00 MW	7.83 AW	16640 AAW	SDBLS	10//99-12//99
Except Maid and Housekeeping Cleaner	Tennessee	S	7.21 MW	7.64 AW	15890 AAW	TNBLS	10//99-12//99
Except Maid and Housekeeping Cleaner	Chattanooga MSA, TN-GA	S	7.57 MW	7.27 AW	15750 AAW	TNBLS	10//99-12//99
Except Maid and Housekeeping Cleaner	Clarksville-Hopkinsville MSA, TN-KY	S	8.03 MW	7.70 AW	16710 AAW	TNBLS	10//99-12//99
Except Maid and Housekeeping Cleaner	Jackson MSA, TN	S	7.44 MW	7.03 AW	15480 AAW	TNBLS	10//99-12//99
Except Maid and Housekeeping Cleaner	Johnson City-Kingsport-Bristol MSA, TN-VA	S	8.21 MW	8.83 AW	17070 AAW	TNBLS	10//99-12//99
Except Maid and Housekeeping Cleaner	Knoxville MSA, TN	S	7.70 MW	7.08 AW	16020 AAW	TNBLS	10//99-12//99
Except Maid and Housekeeping Cleaner	Memphis MSA, TN-AR-MS	S	7.29 MW	6.95 AW	15160 AAW	MSBLS	10//99-12//99
Except Maid and Housekeeping Cleaner	Nashville MSA, TN	S	7.70 MW	7.20 AW	16010 AAW	TNBLS	10//99-12//99
Except Maid and Housekeeping Cleaner	Texas	S	6.63 MW	7.15 AW	14860 AAW	TXBLS	10//99-12//99
Except Maid and Housekeeping Cleaner	Abilene MSA, TX	S	7.67 MW	6.55 AW	15960 AAW	TXBLS	10//99-12//99
Except Maid and Housekeeping Cleaner	Amarillo MSA, TX	S	7.65 MW	7.47 AW	15910 AAW	TXBLS	10//99-12//99
Except Maid and Housekeeping Cleaner	Austin-San Marcos MSA, TX	S	7.35 MW	6.99 AW	15280 AAW	TXBLS	10//99-12//99
Except Maid and Housekeeping Cleaner	Beaumont-Port Arthur MSA, TX	S	7.16 MW	6.66 AW	14890 AAW	TXBLS	10//99-12//99
Except Maid and Housekeeping Cleaner	Brazoria PMSA, TX	S	7.40 MW	7.30 AW	15380 AAW	TXBLS	10//99-12//99
Except Maid and Housekeeping Cleaner	Brownsville-Harlingen-San Benito MSA, TX	S	6.76 MW	6.47 AW	14060 AAW	TXBLS	10//99-12//99
Except Maid and Housekeeping Cleaner	Bryan-College Station MSA, TX	S	6.90 MW	6.53 AW	14360 AAW	TXBLS	10//99-12//99
Except Maid and Housekeeping Cleaner	Corpus Christi MSA, TX	S	6.86 MW	6.53 AW	14270 AAW	TXBLS	10//99-12//99
Except Maid and Housekeeping Cleaner	Dallas PMSA, TX	S	7.02 MW	6.54 AW	14610 AAW	TXBLS	10//99-12//99
Except Maid and Housekeeping Cleaner	El Paso MSA, TX	S	6.99 MW	6.57 AW	14530 AAW	TXBLS	10//99-12//99
Except Maid and Housekeeping Cleaner	Fort Worth-Arlington PMSA, TX	S	7.79 MW	7.28 AW	16200 AAW	TXBLS	10//99-12//99
Except Maid and Housekeeping Cleaner	Galveston-Texas City PMSA, TX	S	7.10 MW	6.86 AW	14780 AAW	TXBLS	10//99-12//99
Except Maid and Housekeeping Cleaner	Houston PMSA, TX	S	7.03 MW	6.39 AW	14610 AAW	TXBLS	10//99-12//99
Except Maid and Housekeeping Cleaner	Killeen-Temple MSA, TX	S	7.14 MW	6.94 AW	14860 AAW	TXBLS	10//99-12//99
Except Maid and Housekeeping Cleaner	Laredo MSA, TX	S	6.84 MW	6.62 AW	14230 AAW	TXBLS	10//99-12//99
Except Maid and Housekeeping Cleaner	Longview-Marshall MSA, TX	S	7.04 MW	6.50 AW	14650 AAW	TXBLS	10//99-12//99
Except Maid and Housekeeping Cleaner	Lubbock MSA, TX	S	7.08 MW	6.46 AW	14730 AAW	TXBLS	10//99-12//99
Except Maid and Housekeeping Cleaner	McAllen-Edinburg-Mission MSA, TX	S	6.70 MW	6.47 AW	13930 AAW	TXBLS	10//99-12//99
Except Maid and Housekeeping Cleaner	Odessa-Midland MSA, TX	S	7.61 MW	6.86 AW	15830 AAW	TXBLS	10//99-12//99
Except Maid and Housekeeping Cleaner	San Angelo MSA, TX	S	6.61 MW	6.04 AW	13740 AAW	TXBLS	10//99-12//99
Except Maid and Housekeeping Cleaner	San Antonio MSA, TX	S	7.46 MW	7.21 AW	15520 AAW	TXBLS	10//99-12//99

AAW Average annual wage	AOH Average offered, high	ASH Average starting, high	H Hourly	M Monthly	S Special: hourly and annual
AE Average entry wage	AOL Average offered, low	ASL Average starting, low	HI Highest wage paid	MTC Median total compensation	TQ Third quartile wage
AEX Average experienced wage	APH Average pay, high range	AW Average wage paid	HR High end range	MW Median wage paid	W Weekly
AO Average offered	APL Average pay, low range	FQ First quartile wage	LR Low end range	SQ Second quartile wage	Y Yearly

Occupation/Type/Industry	Location	Per	Low	Mid	High	Source	Date
Janitor and Cleaner							
Except Maid and Housekeeping Cleaner	Sherman-Denison MSA, TX	S	7.13 MW	6.82 AW	14840 AAW	TXBLS	10//99-12//99
Except Maid and Housekeeping Cleaner	Texarkana MSA, TX- Texarkana, AR	S	6.73 MW	6.37 AW	13990 AAW	TXBLS	10//99-12//99
Except Maid and Housekeeping Cleaner	Tyler MSA, TX	S	7.08 MW	6.72 AW	14720 AAW	TXBLS	10//99-12//99
Except Maid and Housekeeping Cleaner	Victoria MSA, TX	S	6.78 MW	6.52 AW	14110 AAW	TXBLS	10//99-12//99
Except Maid and Housekeeping Cleaner	Waco MSA, TX	S	6.92 MW	6.29 AW	14400 AAW	TXBLS	10//99-12//99
Except Maid and Housekeeping Cleaner	Wichita Falls MSA, TX	S	7.14 MW	6.24 AW	14840 AAW	TXBLS	10//99-12//99
Except Maid and Housekeeping Cleaner	Utah	S	7.53 MW	8.03 AW	16700 AAW	UTBLS	10//99-12//99
Except Maid and Housekeeping Cleaner	Provo-Orem MSA, UT	S	7.77 MW	7.12 AW	16160 AAW	UTBLS	10//99-12//99
Except Maid and Housekeeping Cleaner	Salt Lake City-Ogden MSA, UT	S	7.99 MW	7.64 AW	16630 AAW	UTBLS	10//99-12//99
Except Maid and Housekeeping Cleaner	Vermont	S	8.31 MW	8.94 AW	18600 AAW	VTBLS	10//99-12//99
Except Maid and Housekeeping Cleaner	Burlington MSA, VT	S	8.65 MW	8.23 AW	17980 AAW	VTBLS	10//99-12//99
Except Maid and Housekeeping Cleaner	Virginia	S	7.11 MW	7.61 AW	15840 AAW	VABLS	10//99-12//99
Except Maid and Housekeeping Cleaner	Charlottesville MSA, VA	S	8.14 MW	7.71 AW	16940 AAW	VABLS	10//99-12//99
Except Maid and Housekeeping Cleaner	Danville MSA, VA	S	7.56 MW	7.06 AW	15720 AAW	VABLS	10//99-12//99
Except Maid and Housekeeping Cleaner	Lynchburg MSA, VA	S	7.21 MW	6.83 AW	14990 AAW	VABLS	10//99-12//99
Except Maid and Housekeeping Cleaner	Norfolk-Virginia Beach- Newport News MSA, VA- NC	S	7.44 MW	6.87 AW	15470 AAW	VABLS	10//99-12//99
Except Maid and Housekeeping Cleaner	Richmond-Petersburg MSA, VA	S	7.52 MW	7.13 AW	15640 AAW	VABLS	10//99-12//99
Except Maid and Housekeeping Cleaner	Roanoke MSA, VA	S	7.38 MW	7.02 AW	15340 AAW	VABLS	10//99-12//99
Except Maid and Housekeeping Cleaner	Washington	S	9.02 MW	9.57 AW	19910 AAW	WABLS	10//99-12//99
Except Maid and Housekeeping Cleaner	Bellingham MSA, WA	S	9.12 MW	8.52 AW	18960 AAW	WABLS	10//99-12//99
Except Maid and Housekeeping Cleaner	Bremerton PMSA, WA	S	9.61 MW	9.34 AW	19980 AAW	WABLS	10//99-12//99
Except Maid and Housekeeping Cleaner	Olympia PMSA, WA	S	8.20 MW	7.65 AW	17060 AAW	WABLS	10//99-12//99
Except Maid and Housekeeping Cleaner	Richland-Kennewick-Pasco MSA, WA	S	9.60 MW	8.67 AW	19980 AAW	WABLS	10//99-12//99
Except Maid and Housekeeping Cleaner	Seattle-Bellevue-Everett PMSA, WA	S	9.95 MW	9.36 AW	20690 AAW	WABLS	10//99-12//99
Except Maid and Housekeeping Cleaner	Spokane MSA, WA	S	9.17 MW	8.37 AW	19080 AAW	WABLS	10//99-12//99
Except Maid and Housekeeping Cleaner	Tacoma PMSA, WA	S	9.61 MW	9.45 AW	19990 AAW	WABLS	10//99-12//99
Except Maid and Housekeeping Cleaner	Yakima MSA, WA	S	8.65 MW	8.02 AW	17990 AAW	WABLS	10//99-12//99
Except Maid and Housekeeping Cleaner	West Virginia	S	7.28 MW	7.82 AW	16260 AAW	WVBLS	10//99-12//99
Except Maid and Housekeeping Cleaner	Charleston MSA, WV	S	7.35 MW	6.99 AW	15290 AAW	WVBLS	10//99-12//99
Except Maid and Housekeeping Cleaner	Huntington-Ashland MSA, WV-KY-OH	S	8.00 MW	7.54 AW	16640 AAW	WVBLS	10//99-12//99
Except Maid and Housekeeping Cleaner	Parkersburg-Marietta MSA, WV-OH	S	8.52 MW	8.12 AW	17710 AAW	WVBLS	10//99-12//99
Except Maid and Housekeeping Cleaner	Wheeling MSA, WV-OH	S	7.67 MW	6.65 AW	15950 AAW	WVBLS	10//99-12//99
Except Maid and Housekeeping Cleaner	Wisconsin	S	8.06 MW	8.68 AW	18050 AAW	WIBLS	10//99-12//99
Except Maid and Housekeeping Cleaner	Appleton-Oshkosh-Neenah MSA, WI	S	8.46 MW	7.94 AW	17590 AAW	WIBLS	10//99-12//99
Except Maid and Housekeeping Cleaner	Eau Claire MSA, WI	S	9.09 MW	8.41 AW	18900 AAW	WIBLS	10//99-12//99
Except Maid and Housekeeping Cleaner	Green Bay MSA, WI	S	8.82 MW	8.04 AW	18340 AAW	WIBLS	10//99-12//99
Except Maid and Housekeeping Cleaner	Janesville-Beloit MSA, WI	S	9.00 MW	8.19 AW	18720 AAW	WIBLS	10//99-12//99
Except Maid and Housekeeping Cleaner	Kenosha PMSA, WI	S	9.55 MW	8.52 AW	19870 AAW	WIBLS	10//99-12//99
Except Maid and Housekeeping Cleaner	La Crosse MSA, WI-MN	S	8.51 MW	7.99 AW	17700 AAW	WIBLS	10//99-12//99
Except Maid and Housekeeping Cleaner	Madison MSA, WI	S	9.14 MW	8.59 AW	19010 AAW	WIBLS	10//99-12//99
Except Maid and Housekeeping Cleaner	Milwaukee-Waukesha PMSA, WI	S	8.50 MW	7.88 AW	17680 AAW	WIBLS	10//99-12//99
Except Maid and Housekeeping Cleaner	Racine PMSA, WI	S	8.11 MW	7.54 AW	16880 AAW	WIBLS	10//99-12//99
Except Maid and Housekeeping Cleaner	Sheboygan MSA, WI	S	8.78 MW	8.29 AW	18270 AAW	WIBLS	10//99-12//99
Except Maid and Housekeeping Cleaner	Wausau MSA, WI	S	8.49 MW	8.05 AW	17650 AAW	WIBLS	10//99-12//99
Except Maid and Housekeeping Cleaner	Wyoming	S	7.77 MW	8.24 AW	17150 AAW	WYBLS	10//99-12//99
Except Maid and Housekeeping Cleaner	Casper MSA, WY	S	7.95 MW	7.21 AW	16530 AAW	WYBLS	10//99-12//99
Except Maid and Housekeeping Cleaner	Cheyenne MSA, WY	S	7.75 MW	7.68 AW	16130 AAW	WYBLS	10//99-12//99
Except Maid and Housekeeping Cleaner	Puerto Rico	S	6 MW	6.09 AW	12670 AAW	PRBLS	10//99-12//99
Except Maid and Housekeeping Cleaner	Aguadilla MSA, PR	S	5.95 MW	5.94 AW	12380 AAW	PRBLS	10//99-12//99
Except Maid and Housekeeping Cleaner	Arecibo PMSA, PR	S	5.94 MW	6.01 AW	12360 AAW	PRBLS	10//99-12//99
Except Maid and Housekeeping Cleaner	Caguas PMSA, PR	S	6.38 MW	6.03 AW	13280 AAW	PRBLS	10//99-12//99
Except Maid and Housekeeping Cleaner	Mayaguez MSA, PR	S	6.21 MW	6.02 AW	12920 AAW	PRBLS	10//99-12//99
Except Maid and Housekeeping Cleaner	Ponce MSA, PR	S	6.01 MW	6.00 AW	12490 AAW	PRBLS	10//99-12//99
Except Maid and Housekeeping Cleaner	San Juan-Bayamon PMSA, PR	S	6.04 MW	6.00 AW	12570 AAW	PRBLS	10//99-12//99
Except Maid and Housekeeping Cleaner	Virgin Islands	S	6.76 MW	6.99 AW	14530 AAW	VIBLS	10//99-12//99
Except Maid and Housekeeping Cleaner	Guam	S	6.98 MW	7.89 AW	16410 AAW	GUBLS	10//99-12//99
Jeweler and Precious Stone and Metal Worker	Alabama	S	12.2 MW	12.38 AW	25740 AAW	ALBLS	10//99-12//99
	Mobile MSA, AL	S	11.13 MW	12.20 AW	23150 AAW	ALBLS	10//99-12//99

AAW	Average annual wage	AOH	Average offered, high	ASH	Average starting, high	H	Hourly	M	Monthly	S	Special: hourly and annual
AE	Average entry wage	AOL	Average offered, low	ASL	Average starting, low	HI	Highest wage paid	MTC	Median total compensation	TQ	Third quartile wage
AEX	Average experienced wage	APH	Average pay, high range	AW	Average wage paid	HR	High end range	MW	Median wage paid	W	Weekly
AO	Average offered	APL	Average pay, low range	FQ	First quartile wage	LR	Low end range	SQ	Second quartile wage	Y	Yearly

Occupation/Type/Industry	Location	Per	Low	Mid	High	Source	Date
Jeweler and Precious Stone and Metal Worker							
	Montgomery MSA, AL	S	13.66 MW	12.45 AW	28420 AAW	ALBLS	10//99-12//99
	Alaska	S	10.18 MW	12.68 AW	26380 AAW	AKBLS	10//99-12//99
	Anchorage MSA, AK	S	12.96 MW	10.22 AW	26960 AAW	AKBLS	10//99-12//99
	Arizona	S	11.38 MW	13.49 AW	28050 AAW	AZBLS	10//99-12//99
	Phoenix-Mesa MSA, AZ	S	13.78 MW	14.33 AW	28660 AAW	AZBLS	10//99-12//99
	Arkansas	S	11.76 MW	13.33 AW	27720 AAW	ARBLS	10//99-12//99
	California	S	10.18 MW	10.57 AW	21990 AAW	CABLS	10//99-12//99
	Fresno MSA, CA	S	16.86 MW	16.83 AW	35070 AAW	CABLS	10//99-12//99
	Los Angeles-Long Beach PMSA, CA	S	9.77 MW	8.32 AW	20320 AAW	CABLS	10//99-12//99
	Modesto MSA, CA	S	11.99 MW	11.84 AW	24930 AAW	CABLS	10//99-12//99
	Oakland PMSA, CA	S	10.20 MW	9.87 AW	21220 AAW	CABLS	10//99-12//99
	Orange County PMSA, CA	S	12.49 MW	9.83 AW	25980 AAW	CABLS	10//99-12//99
	Riverside-San Bernardino PMSA, CA	S	11.06 MW	10.99 AW	23010 AAW	CABLS	10//99-12//99
	Sacramento PMSA, CA	S	12.91 MW	12.27 AW	26840 AAW	CABLS	10//99-12//99
	San Francisco PMSA, CA	S	10.48 MW	8.73 AW	21790 AAW	CABLS	10//99-12//99
	Colorado	S	11.46 MW	12.23 AW	25430 AAW	COBLS	10//99-12//99
	Denver PMSA, CO	S	13.48 MW	11.51 AW	28030 AAW	COBLS	10//99-12//99
	Connecticut	S	13.6 MW	15.52 AW	32290 AAW	CTBLS	10//99-12//99
	Danbury PMSA, CT	S	13.97 MW	14.19 AW	29050 AAW	CTBLS	10//99-12//99
	Stamford-Norwalk PMSA, CT	S	17.25 MW	14.19 AW	35880 AAW	CTBLS	10//99-12//99
	Washington PMSA, DC-MD-VA-WV	S	13.01 MW	13.72 AW	27070 AAW	DCBLS	10//99-12//99
	Florida	S	12.13 MW	12.99 AW	27020 AAW	FLBLS	10//99-12//99
	Daytona Beach MSA, FL	S	12.57 MW	11.15 AW	26140 AAW	FLBLS	10//99-12//99
	Fort Lauderdale PMSA, FL	S	12.70 MW	13.18 AW	26420 AAW	FLBLS	10//99-12//99
	Fort Myers-Cape Coral MSA, FL	S	16.95 MW	15.45 AW	35260 AAW	FLBLS	10//99-12//99
	Jacksonville MSA, FL	S	9.49 MW	8.09 AW	19730 AAW	FLBLS	10//99-12//99
	Melbourne-Titusville-Palm Bay MSA, FL	S	13.11 MW	12.80 AW	27260 AAW	FLBLS	10//99-12//99
	Miami PMSA, FL	S	11.40 MW	11.83 AW	23710 AAW	FLBLS	10//99-12//99
	Orlando MSA, FL	S	14.95 MW	13.79 AW	31100 AAW	FLBLS	10//99-12//99
	Tampa-St. Petersburg-Clearwater MSA, FL	S	15.32 MW	11.77 AW	31860 AAW	FLBLS	10//99-12//99
	Georgia	S	12.47 MW	13.10 AW	27250 AAW	GABLS	10//99-12//99
	Atlanta MSA, GA	S	15.26 MW	13.97 AW	31740 AAW	GABLS	10//99-12//99
	Augusta-Aiken MSA, GA-SC	S	11.59 MW	10.47 AW	24100 AAW	GABLS	10//99-12//99
	Hawaii	S	8.81 MW	9.51 AW	19790 AAW	HIBLS	10//99-12//99
	Honolulu MSA, HI	S	9.46 MW	8.75 AW	19680 AAW	HIBLS	10//99-12//99
	Idaho	S	13.14 MW	14.01 AW	29140 AAW	IDBLS	10//99-12//99
	Illinois	S	12.22 MW	12.36 AW	25710 AAW	ILBLS	10//99-12//99
	Champaign-Urbana MSA, IL	S	7.88 MW	6.42 AW	16380 AAW	ILBLS	10//99-12//99
	Chicago PMSA, IL	S	12.73 MW	11.58 AW	26470 AAW	ILBLS	10//99-12//99
	Peoria-Pekin MSA, IL	S	14.09 MW	13.05 AW	29300 AAW	ILBLS	10//99-12//99
	Indiana	S	12.33 MW	13.78 AW	28660 AAW	INBLS	10//99-12//99
	Evansville-Henderson MSA, IN-KY	S	13.04 MW	13.28 AW	27130 AAW	INBLS	10//99-12//99
	Gary PMSA, IN	S	17.01 MW	16.42 AW	35370 AAW	INBLS	10//99-12//99
	Indianapolis MSA, IN	S	15.14 MW	12.60 AW	31490 AAW	INBLS	10//99-12//99
	Iowa	S	12.18 MW	12.59 AW	26180 AAW	IABLS	10//99-12//99
	Waterloo-Cedar Falls MSA, IA	S	12.32 MW	12.15 AW	25620 AAW	IABLS	10//99-12//99
	Kansas	S	12.73 MW	13.12 AW	27290 AAW	KSBLS	10//99-12//99
	Kentucky	S	10.34 MW	10.97 AW	22810 AAW	KYBLS	10//99-12//99
	Louisville MSA, KY-IN	S	10.61 MW	10.23 AW	22070 AAW	KYBLS	10//99-12//99
	New Orleans MSA, LA	S	11.75 MW	12.31 AW	24440 AAW	LABLS	10//99-12//99
	Maine	S	10.9 MW	12.03 AW	25030 AAW	MEBLS	10//99-12//99
	Portland MSA, ME	S	13.23 MW	13.01 AW	27520 AAW	MEBLS	10//99-12//99
	Maryland	S	11.8 MW	13.45 AW	27970 AAW	MDBLS	10//99-12//99
	Baltimore PMSA, MD	S	15.76 MW	15.16 AW	32790 AAW	MDBLS	10//99-12//99
	Barnstable-Yarmouth MSA, MA	S	18.93 MW	17.17 AW	39380 AAW	MABLS	10//99-12//99
	Boston PMSA, MA-NH	S	14.00 MW	11.26 AW	29120 AAW	MABLS	10//99-12//99
	Michigan	S	12.07 MW	12.66 AW	26330 AAW	MIBLS	10//99-12//99
	Ann Arbor PMSA, MI	S	11.45 MW	10.02 AW	23820 AAW	MIBLS	10//99-12//99
	Detroit PMSA, MI	S	14.66 MW	14.01 AW	30490 AAW	MIBLS	10//99-12//99
	Grand Rapids-Muskegon-Holland MSA, MI	S	11.82 MW	11.43 AW	24590 AAW	MIBLS	10//99-12//99
	Lansing-East Lansing MSA, MI	S	17.10 MW	17.47 AW	35570 AAW	MIBLS	10//99-12//99

AAW Average annual wage	**AOH** Average offered, high	**ASH** Average starting, high	**H** Hourly	**M** Monthly	**S** Special: hourly and annual
AE Average entry wage	**AOL** Average offered, low	**ASL** Average starting, low	**HI** Highest wage paid	**MTC** Median total compensation	**TQ** Third quartile wage
AEX Average experienced wage	**APH** Average pay, high range	**AW** Average wage paid	**HR** High end range	**MW** Median wage paid	**W** Weekly
AO Average offered	**APL** Average pay, low range	**FQ** First quartile wage	**LR** Low end range	**SQ** Second quartile wage	**Y** Yearly

Jeweler and Precious Stone and Metal Worker

Occupation/Type/Industry	Location	Per	Low	Mid	High	Source	Date
Jeweler and Precious Stone and Metal Worker	Saginaw-Bay City-Midland MSA, MI	s	11.05 MW	9.91 AW	22990 AAW	MIBLS	10//99-12//99
	Minnesota	s	14.5 MW	14.51 AW	30180 AAW	MNBLS	10//99-12//99
	Minneapolis-St. Paul MSA, MN-WI	s	13.19 MW	11.92 AW	27430 AAW	MNBLS	10//99-12//99
	Mississippi	s	12.67 MW	13.71 AW	28530 AAW	MSBLS	10//99-12//99
	Hattiesburg MSA, MS	s	12.76 MW	12.28 AW	26540 AAW	MSBLS	10//99-12//99
	Missouri	s	11.84 MW	12.28 AW	25540 AAW	MOBLS	10//99-12//99
	Kansas City MSA, MO-KS	s	12.73 MW	12.16 AW	26480 AAW	MOBLS	10//99-12//99
	Montana	s	10.87 MW	11.36 AW	23630 AAW	MTBLS	10//99-12//99
	Nebraska	s	11.58 MW	11.99 AW	24940 AAW	NEBLS	10//99-12//99
	Nevada	s	10.63 MW	13.51 AW	28100 AAW	NVBLS	10//99-12//99
	Las Vegas MSA, NV-AZ	s	14.16 MW	10.63 AW	29450 AAW	NVBLS	10//99-12//99
	New Jersey	s	13.42 MW	14.96 AW	31110 AAW	NJBLS	10//99-12//99
	Bergen-Passaic PMSA, NJ	s	14.45 MW	13.18 AW	30060 AAW	NJBLS	10//99-12//99
	Middlesex-Somerset-Hunterdon PMSA, NJ	s	18.58 MW	18.90 AW	38640 AAW	NJBLS	10//99-12//99
	Newark PMSA, NJ	s	12.29 MW	11.36 AW	25550 AAW	NJBLS	10//99-12//99
	New Mexico	s	9.17 MW	9.63 AW	20030 AAW	NMBLS	10//99-12//99
	Albuquerque MSA, NM	s	9.33 MW	9.30 AW	19410 AAW	NMBLS	10//99-12//99
	Santa Fe MSA, NM	s	12.47 MW	13.01 AW	25930 AAW	NMBLS	10//99-12//99
	New York	s	12.28 MW	14.57 AW	30300 AAW	NYBLS	10//99-12//99
	Buffalo-Niagara Falls MSA, NY	s	14.87 MW	14.75 AW	30930 AAW	NYBLS	10//99-12//99
	Nassau-Suffolk PMSA, NY	s	14.22 MW	12.37 AW	29570 AAW	NYBLS	10//99-12//99
	New York PMSA, NY	s	14.85 MW	12.53 AW	30880 AAW	NYBLS	10//99-12//99
	Newburgh PMSA, NY-PA	s	11.62 MW	11.14 AW	24160 AAW	NYBLS	10//99-12//99
	North Carolina	s	11.58 MW	12.39 AW	25770 AAW	NCBLS	10//99-12//99
	Charlotte-Gastonia-Rock Hill MSA, NC-SC	s	14.17 MW	13.51 AW	29470 AAW	NCBLS	10//99-12//99
	Raleigh-Durham-Chapel Hill MSA, NC	s	13.39 MW	11.82 AW	27840 AAW	NCBLS	10//99-12//99
	North Dakota	s	9.61 MW	10.17 AW	21150 AAW	NDBLS	10//99-12//99
	Ohio	s	9.22 MW	10.83 AW	22530 AAW	OHBLS	10//99-12//99
	Akron PMSA, OH	s	11.60 MW	9.54 AW	24140 AAW	OHBLS	10//99-12//99
	Cincinnati PMSA, OH-KY-IN	s	11.87 MW	11.44 AW	24700 AAW	OHBLS	10//99-12//99
	Cleveland-Lorain-Elyria PMSA, OH	s	10.34 MW	8.13 AW	21500 AAW	OHBLS	10//99-12//99
	Columbus MSA, OH	s	14.01 MW	13.70 AW	29140 AAW	OHBLS	10//99 12//99
	Dayton-Springfield MSA, OH	s	11.98 MW	11.28 AW	24920 AAW	OHBLS	10//99-12//99
	Oklahoma	s	10.39 MW	11.07 AW	23030 AAW	OKBLS	10//99-12//99
	Oklahoma City MSA, OK	s	9.22 MW	8.93 AW	19180 AAW	OKBLS	10//99-12//99
	Tulsa MSA, OK	s	12.37 MW	12.17 AW	25720 AAW	OKBLS	10//99-12//99
	Oregon	s	14.05 MW	15.02 AW	31230 AAW	ORBLS	10//99-12//99
	Portland-Vancouver PMSA, OR-WA	s	13.95 MW	12.88 AW	29020 AAW	ORBLS	10//99-12//99
	Pennsylvania	s	11.82 MW	12.74 AW	26500 AAW	PABLS	10//99-12//99
	Allentown-Bethlehem-Easton MSA, PA	s	13.08 MW	13.75 AW	27210 AAW	PABLS	10//99-12//99
	Johnstown MSA, PA	s	8.83 MW	8.21 AW	18380 AAW	PABLS	10//99-12//99
	Lancaster MSA, PA	s	15.96 MW	14.89 AW	33190 AAW	PABLS	10//99-12//99
	Philadelphia PMSA, PA-NJ	s	14.23 MW	13.30 AW	29600 AAW	PABLS	10//99-12//99
	Pittsburgh MSA, PA	s	10.86 MW	10.15 AW	22590 AAW	PABLS	10//99-12//99
	York MSA, PA	s	15.11 MW	15.22 AW	31420 AAW	PABLS	10//99-12//99
	Rhode Island	s	7.56 MW	8.77 AW	18230 AAW	RIBLS	10//99-12//99
	Providence-Fall River-Warwick MSA, RI-MA	s	10.07 MW	8.70 AW	20950 AAW	RIBLS	10//99-12//99
	South Carolina	s	11.7 MW	13.72 AW	28540 AAW	SCBLS	10//99-12//99
	Charleston-North Charleston MSA, SC	s	15.33 MW	12.67 AW	31880 AAW	SCBLS	10//99-12//99
	Greenville-Spartanburg-Anderson MSA, SC	s	14.89 MW	13.98 AW	30970 AAW	SCBLS	10//99-12//99
	South Dakota	s	9.47 MW	9.24 AW	19230 AAW	SDBLS	10//99-12//99
	Rapid City MSA, SD	s	8.87 MW	9.20 AW	18450 AAW	SDBLS	10//99-12//99
	Tennessee	s	12.24 MW	12.24 AW	25460 AAW	TNBLS	10//99-12//99
	Chattanooga MSA, TN-GA	s	9.93 MW	8.88 AW	20660 AAW	TNBLS	10//99-12//99
	Knoxville MSA, TN	s	14.17 MW	12.73 AW	29460 AAW	TNBLS	10//99-12//99
	Texas	s	10.83 MW	11.94 AW	24830 AAW	TXBLS	10//99-12//99
	Dallas PMSA, TX	s	13.81 MW	13.13 AW	28730 AAW	TXBLS	10//99-12//99
	Fort Worth-Arlington PMSA, TX	s	13.76 MW	11.05 AW	28610 AAW	TXBLS	10//99-12//99

AAW Average annual wage	AOH Average offered, high	ASH Average starting, high	H Hourly	M Monthly	S Special: hourly and annual
AE Average entry wage	AOL Average offered, low	ASL Average starting, low	HI Highest wage paid	MTC Median total compensation	TQ Third quartile wage
AEX Average experienced wage	APH Average pay, high range	AW Average wage paid	HR High end range	MW Median wage paid	W Weekly
AO Average offered	APL Average pay, low range	FQ First quartile wage	LR Low end range	SQ Second quartile wage	Y Yearly

Occupation/Type/Industry	Location	Per	Low	Mid	High	Source	Date
Jeweler and Precious Stone and Metal Worker	Houston PMSA, TX	S	10.32 MW	10.06 AW	21470 AAW	TXBLS	10//99-12//99
	Lubbock MSA, TX	S	13.97 MW	13.59 AW	29050 AAW	TXBLS	10//99-12//99
	Utah	S	11.1 MW	11.86 AW	24670 AAW	UTBLS	10//99-12//99
	Salt Lake City-Ogden MSA, UT	S	11.80 MW	11.03 AW	24540 AAW	UTBLS	10//99-12//99
	Virginia	S	11.2 MW	12.12 AW	25220 AAW	VABLS	10//99-12//99
	Norfolk-Virginia Beach-Newport News MSA, VA-NC	S	13.30 MW	14.58 AW	27670 AAW	VABLS	10//99-12//99
	Richmond-Petersburg MSA, VA	S	11.14 MW	11.04 AW	23170 AAW	VABLS	10//99-12//99
	Washington	S	11.61 MW	13.45 AW	27970 AAW	WABLS	10//99-12//99
	Seattle-Bellevue-Everett PMSA, WA	S	13.46 MW	11.63 AW	27990 AAW	WABLS	10//99-12//99
	Spokane MSA, WA	S	13.67 MW	12.92 AW	28430 AAW	WABLS	10//99-12//99
	Tacoma PMSA, WA	S	14.91 MW	14.94 AW	31010 AAW	WABLS	10//99-12//99
	West Virginia	S	9.88 MW	10.06 AW	20930 AAW	WVBLS	10//99-12//99
	Huntington-Ashland MSA, WV-KY-OH	S	9.16 MW	7.36 AW	19060 AAW	WVBLS	10//99-12//99
	Wisconsin	S	13.78 MW	13.96 AW	29040 AAW	WIBLS	10//99-12//99
	Green Bay MSA, WI	S	17.94 MW	15.25 AW	37310 AAW	WIBLS	10//99-12//99
	Milwaukee-Waukesha PMSA, WI	S	14.30 MW	14.76 AW	29740 AAW	WIBLS	10//99-12//99
	Puerto Rico	S	8.09 MW	8.93 AW	18570 AAW	PRBLS	10//99-12//99
	San Juan-Bayamon PMSA, PR	S	8.53 MW	8.06 AW	17740 AAW	PRBLS	10//99-12//99
Job Printer	Alabama	S	11.09 MW	11.35 AW	23600 AAW	ALBLS	10//99-12//99
	Birmingham MSA, AL	S	12.84 MW	12.63 AW	26710 AAW	ALBLS	10//99-12//99
	Gadsden MSA, AL	S	9.16 MW	10.52 AW	19060 AAW	ALBLS	10//99-12//99
	Alaska	S	15.29 MW	14.70 AW	30570 AAW	AKBLS	10//99-12//99
	Arizona	S	11.78 MW	12.03 AW	25030 AAW	AZBLS	10//99-12//99
	Phoenix-Mesa MSA, AZ	S	12.58 MW	12.53 AW	26170 AAW	AZBLS	10//99-12//99
	Tucson MSA, AZ	S	11.29 MW	10.63 AW	23470 AAW	AZBLS	10//99-12//99
	Arkansas	S	10.4 MW	11.34 AW	23590 AAW	ARBLS	10//99-12//99
	Fayetteville-Springdale-Rogers MSA, AR	S	9.58 MW	9.17 AW	19920 AAW	ARBLS	10//99-12//99
	Jonesboro MSA, AR	S	10.48 MW	9.67 AW	21810 AAW	ARBLS	10//99-12//99
	Little Rock-North Little Rock MSA, AR	S	10.24 MW	9.66 AW	21300 AAW	ARBLS	10//99-12//99
	California	S	12.55 MW	13.38 AW	27840 AAW	CABLS	10//99-12//99
	Fresno MSA, CA	S	9.27 MW	9.44 AW	19290 AAW	CABLS	10//99-12//99
	Los Angeles-Long Beach PMSA, CA	S	13.21 MW	12.08 AW	27470 AAW	CABLS	10//99-12//99
	Orange County PMSA, CA	S	11.68 MW	11.02 AW	24300 AAW	CABLS	10//99-12//99
	Riverside-San Bernardino PMSA, CA	S	14.42 MW	13.91 AW	29990 AAW	CABLS	10//99-12//99
	Sacramento PMSA, CA	S	12.09 MW	10.15 AW	25150 AAW	CABLS	10//99-12//99
	Salinas MSA, CA	S	15.11 MW	15.67 AW	31440 AAW	CABLS	10//99-12//99
	San Diego MSA, CA	S	13.67 MW	12.87 AW	28430 AAW	CABLS	10//99-12//99
	San Francisco PMSA, CA	S	15.17 MW	17.04 AW	31550 AAW	CABLS	10//99-12//99
	San Jose PMSA, CA	S	15.74 MW	16.89 AW	32740 AAW	CABLS	10//99-12//99
	Santa Barbara-Santa Maria-Lompoc MSA, CA	S	13.73 MW	13.90 AW	28560 AAW	CABLS	10//99-12//99
	Stockton-Lodi MSA, CA	S	13.92 MW	13.05 AW	28960 AAW	CABLS	10//99-12//99
	Vallejo-Fairfield-Napa PMSA, CA	S	17.12 MW	17.46 AW	35610 AAW	CABLS	10//99-12//99
	Ventura PMSA, CA	S	16.07 MW	14.55 AW	33420 AAW	CABLS	10//99-12//99
	Colorado	S	16.42 MW	15.44 AW	32120 AAW	COBLS	10//99-12//99
	Boulder-Longmont PMSA, CO	S	13.37 MW	13.74 AW	27820 AAW	COBLS	10//99-12//99
	Colorado Springs MSA, CO	S	14.86 MW	14.66 AW	30900 AAW	COBLS	10//99-12//99
	Denver PMSA, CO	S	17.30 MW	17.66 AW	35970 AAW	COBLS	10//99-12//99
	Connecticut	S	15.51 MW	15.24 AW	31710 AAW	CTBLS	10//99-12//99
	Hartford MSA, CT	S	16.12 MW	17.09 AW	33530 AAW	CTBLS	10//99-12//99
	New Haven-Meriden PMSA, CT	S	14.45 MW	14.35 AW	30050 AAW	CTBLS	10//99-12//99
	Stamford-Norwalk PMSA, CT	S	14.70 MW	14.22 AW	30570 AAW	CTBLS	10//99-12//99
	Waterbury PMSA, CT	S	14.28 MW	13.92 AW	29700 AAW	CTBLS	10//99-12//99
	Delaware	S	15.54 MW	15.72 AW	32690 AAW	DEBLS	10//99-12//99
	Wilmington-Newark PMSA, DE-MD	S	15.79 MW	15.53 AW	32840 AAW	DEBLS	10//99-12//99
	District of Columbia	S	13.32 MW	14.21 AW	29550 AAW	DCBLS	10//99-12//99

AAW	Average annual wage	AOH	Average offered, high	ASH	Average starting, high	H	Hourly	M	Monthly	S	Special: hourly and annual
AE	Average entry wage	AOL	Average offered, low	ASL	Average starting, low	HI	Highest wage paid	MTC	Median total compensation	TQ	Third quartile wage
AEX	Average experienced wage	APH	Average pay, high range	AW	Average wage paid	HR	High end range	MW	Median wage paid	W	Weekly
AO	Average offered	APL	Average pay, low range	FQ	First quartile wage	LR	Low end range	SQ	Second quartile wage	Y	Yearly

Occupation/Type/Industry	Location	Per	Low	Mid	High	Source	Date
Job Printer	Washington PMSA, DC-MD-VA-WV	S	15.06 MW	14.45 AW	31310 AAW	DCBLS	10//99-12//99
	Florida	S	12.27 MW	12.66 AW	26340 AAW	FLBLS	10//99-12//99
	Fort Lauderdale PMSA, FL	S	11.39 MW	9.68 AW	23690 AAW	FLBLS	10//99-12//99
	Jacksonville MSA, FL	S	11.58 MW	11.05 AW	24080 AAW	FLBLS	10//99-12//99
	Melbourne-Titusville-Palm Bay MSA, FL	S	12.35 MW	12.85 AW	25690 AAW	FLBLS	10//99-12//99
	Miami PMSA, FL	S	12.23 MW	12.51 AW	25430 AAW	FLBLS	10//99-12//99
	Orlando MSA, FL	S	11.71 MW	11.98 AW	24360 AAW	FLBLS	10//99-12//99
	Pensacola MSA, FL	S	13.29 MW	13.19 AW	27650 AAW	FLBLS	10//99-12//99
	Sarasota-Bradenton MSA, FL	S	14.44 MW	14.63 AW	30040 AAW	FLBLS	10//99-12//99
	West Palm Beach-Boca Raton MSA, FL	S	15.09 MW	14.70 AW	31380 AAW	FLBLS	10//99-12//99
	Georgia	S	10.97 MW	10.52 AW	21890 AAW	GABLS	10//99-12//99
	Atlanta MSA, GA	S	10.27 MW	9.85 AW	21360 AAW	GABLS	10//99-12//99
	Hawaii	S	14.23 MW	15.43 AW	32090 AAW	HIBLS	10//99-12//99
	Honolulu MSA, HI	S	15.29 MW	14.04 AW	31800 AAW	HIBLS	10//99-12//99
	Idaho	S	10.38 MW	11.10 AW	23090 AAW	IDBLS	10//99-12//99
	Boise City MSA, ID	S	10.70 MW	10.06 AW	22250 AAW	IDBLS	10//99-12//99
	Illinois	S	13.56 MW	14.28 AW	29690 AAW	ILBLS	10//99-12//99
	Chicago PMSA, IL	S	15.36 MW	14.29 AW	31960 AAW	ILBLS	10//99-12//99
	Peoria-Pekin MSA, IL	S	14.91 MW	13.37 AW	31020 AAW	ILBLS	10//99-12//99
	Springfield MSA, IL	S	12.85 MW	13.00 AW	26730 AAW	ILBLS	10//99-12//99
	Indiana	S	13.28 MW	13.49 AW	28050 AAW	INBLS	10//99-12//99
	Elkhart-Goshen MSA, IN	S	12.42 MW	12.58 AW	25840 AAW	INBLS	10//99-12//99
	Fort Wayne MSA, IN	S	14.59 MW	13.72 AW	30350 AAW	INBLS	10//99-12//99
	Gary PMSA, IN	S	15.91 MW	16.39 AW	33090 AAW	INBLS	10//99-12//99
	Indianapolis MSA, IN	S	13.07 MW	12.63 AW	27180 AAW	INBLS	10//99-12//99
	Iowa	S	12.07 MW	12.69 AW	26400 AAW	IABLS	10//99-12//99
	Cedar Rapids MSA, IA	S	12.34 MW	12.16 AW	25660 AAW	IABLS	10//99-12//99
	Des Moines MSA, IA	S	14.30 MW	14.41 AW	29740 AAW	IABLS	10//99-12//99
	Sioux City MSA, IA-NE	S	8.57 MW	7.99 AW	17820 AAW	IABLS	10//99-12//99
	Waterloo-Cedar Falls MSA, IA	S	11.79 MW	11.36 AW	24530 AAW	IABLS	10//99-12//99
	Kansas	S	11.76 MW	11.75 AW	24430 AAW	KSBLS	10//99-12//99
	Kentucky	S	15.07 MW	15.88 AW	33030 AAW	KYBLS	10//99-12//99
	Louisville MSA, KY-IN	S	12.43 MW	12.72 AW	25850 AAW	KYBLS	10//99-12//99
	Louisiana	S	10.93 MW	11.39 AW	23680 AAW	LABLS	10//99-12//99
	Baton Rouge MSA, LA	S	11.56 MW	11.25 AW	24040 AAW	LABLS	10//99-12//99
	Lafayette MSA, LA	S	10.73 MW	11.02 AW	22320 AAW	LABLS	10//99-12//99
	Monroe MSA, LA	S	10.58 MW	10.94 AW	22010 AAW	LABLS	10//99-12//99
	New Orleans MSA, LA	S	11.48 MW	11.08 AW	23880 AAW	LABLS	10//99-12//99
	Shreveport-Bossier City MSA, LA	S	12.98 MW	11.43 AW	26990 AAW	LABLS	10//99-12//99
	Maine	S	12.24 MW	12.64 AW	26300 AAW	MEBLS	10//99-12//99
	Portland MSA, ME	S	12.77 MW	12.40 AW	26560 AAW	MEBLS	10//99-12//99
	Maryland	S	14.55 MW	14.89 AW	30970 AAW	MDBLS	10//99-12//99
	Baltimore PMSA, MD	S	14.08 MW	13.65 AW	29290 AAW	MDBLS	10//99-12//99
	Massachusetts	S	12.17 MW	11.74 AW	24410 AAW	MABLS	10//99-12//99
	Barnstable-Yarmouth MSA, MA	S	17.05 MW	17.47 AW	35470 AAW	MABLS	10//99-12//99
	Boston PMSA, MA-NH	S	10.48 MW	6.75 AW	21800 AAW	MABLS	10//99-12//99
	Brockton PMSA, MA	S	14.80 MW	13.68 AW	30780 AAW	MABLS	10//99-12//99
	Fitchburg-Leominster PMSA, MA	S	14.40 MW	15.41 AW	29940 AAW	MABLS	10//99-12//99
	Lawrence PMSA, MA-NH	S	13.29 MW	12.84 AW	27630 AAW	MABLS	10//99-12//99
	Pittsfield MSA, MA	S	14.06 MW	12.95 AW	29250 AAW	MABLS	10//99-12//99
	Springfield MSA, MA	S	13.54 MW	14.33 AW	28160 AAW	MABLS	10//99-12//99
	Worcester PMSA, MA-CT	S	13.97 MW	13.47 AW	29060 AAW	MABLS	10//99-12//99
	Michigan	S	13.03 MW	14.27 AW	29690 AAW	MIBLS	10//99-12//99
	Ann Arbor PMSA, MI	S	14.48 MW	13.81 AW	30120 AAW	MIBLS	10//99-12//99
	Detroit PMSA, MI	S	15.13 MW	13.45 AW	31470 AAW	MIBLS	10//99-12//99
	Grand Rapids-Muskegon-Holland MSA, MI	S	14.36 MW	13.39 AW	29870 AAW	MIBLS	10//99-12//99
	Jackson MSA, MI	S	11.25 MW	11.08 AW	23400 AAW	MIBLS	10//99-12//99
	Lansing-East Lansing MSA, MI	S	14.64 MW	15.22 AW	30450 AAW	MIBLS	10//99-12//99
	Saginaw-Bay City-Midland MSA, MI	S	10.91 MW	10.41 AW	22690 AAW	MIBLS	10//99-12//99
	Minnesota	S	13.32 MW	13.64 AW	28380 AAW	MNBLS	10//99-12//99
	Duluth-Superior MSA, MN-WI	S	13.26 MW	13.43 AW	27580 AAW	MNBLS	10//99-12//99
	Minneapolis-St. Paul MSA, MN-WI	S	15.34 MW	15.02 AW	31900 AAW	MNBLS	10//99-12//99
	Mississippi	S	12.12 MW	12.84 AW	26700 AAW	MSBLS	10//99-12//99

Occupation/Type/Industry	Location	Per	Low	Mid	High	Source	Date
Job Printer	Jackson MSA, MS	S	12.43 MW	11.33 AW	25860 AAW	MSBLS	10//99-12//99
	Missouri	S	12.12 MW	13.02 AW	27090 AAW	MOBLS	10//99-12//99
	Kansas City MSA, MO-KS	S	14.06 MW	14.23 AW	29230 AAW	MOBLS	10//99-12//99
	St. Louis MSA, MO-IL	S	13.61 MW	12.56 AW	28300 AAW	MOBLS	10//99-12//99
	Springfield MSA, MO	S	11.37 MW	10.19 AW	23640 AAW	MOBLS	10//99-12//99
	Montana	S	13.62 MW	12.64 AW	26280 AAW	MTBLS	10//99-12//99
	Nebraska	S	12.04 MW	12.37 AW	25730 AAW	NEBLS	10//99-12//99
	Nevada	S	14.82 MW	14.38 AW	29920 AAW	NVBLS	10//99-12//99
	Las Vegas MSA, NV-AZ	S	13.57 MW	13.85 AW	28230 AAW	NVBLS	10//99-12//99
	New Hampshire	S	13.98 MW	13.11 AW	27270 AAW	NHBLS	10//99-12//99
	Portsmouth-Rochester PMSA, NH-ME	S	11.27 MW	13.72 AW	23440 AAW	NHBLS	10//99-12//99
	New Jersey	S	17.24 MW	16.18 AW	33660 AAW	NJBLS	10//99-12//99
	Bergen-Passaic PMSA, NJ	S	10.30 MW	9.46 AW	21420 AAW	NJBLS	10//99-12//99
	Jersey City PMSA, NJ	S	15.59 MW	16.34 AW	32430 AAW	NJBLS	10//99-12//99
	Middlesex-Somerset-Hunterdon PMSA, NJ	S	16.55 MW	15.59 AW	34410 AAW	NJBLS	10//99-12//99
	Newark PMSA, NJ	S	18.54 MW	18.40 AW	38570 AAW	NJBLS	10//99-12//99
	New Mexico	S	10.57 MW	11.57 AW	24070 AAW	NMBLS	10//99-12//99
	Albuquerque MSA, NM	S	11.79 MW	10.55 AW	24530 AAW	NMBLS	10//99-12//99
	New York	S	12.21 MW	14.29 AW	29710 AAW	NYBLS	10//99-12//99
	Albany-Schenectady-Troy MSA, NY	S	13.55 MW	13.99 AW	28180 AAW	NYBLS	10//99-12//99
	Nassau-Suffolk PMSA, NY	S	12.92 MW	11.35 AW	26870 AAW	NYBLS	10//99-12//99
	New York PMSA, NY	S	16.83 MW	14.11 AW	35000 AAW	NYBLS	10//99-12//99
	Rochester MSA, NY	S	10.74 MW	10.76 AW	22340 AAW	NYBLS	10//99-12//99
	Syracuse MSA, NY	S	12.36 MW	11.79 AW	25710 AAW	NYBLS	10//99-12//99
	North Carolina	S	10.98 MW	11.62 AW	24180 AAW	NCBLS	10//99-12//99
	Charlotte-Gastonia-Rock Hill MSA, NC-SC	S	11.43 MW	10.64 AW	23770 AAW	NCBLS	10//99-12//99
	Greensboro--Winston-Salem--High Point MSA, NC	S	13.30 MW	12.78 AW	27650 AAW	NCBLS	10//99-12//99
	North Dakota	S	8.84 MW	9.24 AW	19220 AAW	NDBLS	10//99-12//99
	Ohio	S	12.19 MW	12.71 AW	26430 AAW	OHBLS	10//99-12//99
	Akron PMSA, OH	S	16.23 MW	13.42 AW	33750 AAW	OHBLS	10//99-12//99
	Cincinnati PMSA, OH-KY-IN	S	14.87 MW	13.22 AW	30940 AAW	OHBLS	10//99-12//99
	Cleveland-Lorain-Elyria PMSA, OH	S	11.90 MW	12.36 AW	24760 AAW	OHBLS	10//99-12//99
	Columbus MSA, OH	S	13.19 MW	13.06 AW	27440 AAW	OHBLS	10//99-12//99
	Dayton-Springfield MSA, OH	S	12.13 MW	12.61 AW	25220 AAW	OHBLS	10//99-12//99
	Toledo MSA, OH	S	11.77 MW	12.10 AW	24470 AAW	OHBLS	10//99-12//99
	Oklahoma	S	10.27 MW	10.72 AW	22300 AAW	OKBLS	10//99-12//99
	Oklahoma City MSA, OK	S	10.57 MW	10.08 AW	21970 AAW	OKBLS	10//99-12//99
	Tulsa MSA, OK	S	11.77 MW	11.34 AW	24490 AAW	OKBLS	10//99-12//99
	Oregon	S	12.79 MW	13.49 AW	28050 AAW	ORBLS	10//99-12//99
	Eugene-Springfield MSA, OR	S	13.18 MW	9.77 AW	27410 AAW	ORBLS	10//99-12//99
	Portland-Vancouver PMSA, OR-WA	S	15.33 MW	14.99 AW	31890 AAW	ORBLS	10//99-12//99
	Pennsylvania	S	12.86 MW	12.79 AW	26600 AAW	PABLS	10//99-12//99
	Philadelphia PMSA, PA-NJ	S	14.38 MW	13.53 AW	29920 AAW	PABLS	10//99-12//99
	Pittsburgh MSA, PA	S	12.48 MW	12.10 AW	25960 AAW	PABLS	10//99-12//99
	Scranton--Wilkes-Barre--Hazleton MSA, PA	S	13.35 MW	13.66 AW	27760 AAW	PABLS	10//99-12//99
	Rhode Island	S	13.57 MW	14.88 AW	30960 AAW	RIBLS	10//99-12//99
	Providence-Fall River-Warwick MSA, RI-MA	S	13.60 MW	11.79 AW	28280 AAW	RIBLS	10//99-12//99
	South Carolina	S	10.07 MW	10.82 AW	22500 AAW	SCBLS	10//99-12//99
	Charleston-North Charleston MSA, SC	S	9.26 MW	8.67 AW	19260 AAW	SCBLS	10//99-12//99
	Columbia MSA, SC	S	12.36 MW	12.02 AW	25710 AAW	SCBLS	10//99-12//99
	Greenville-Spartanburg-Anderson MSA, SC	S	11.67 MW	9.79 AW	24280 AAW	SCBLS	10//99-12//99
	Tennessee	S	12.54 MW	13.86 AW	28830 AAW	TNBLS	10//99-12//99
	Johnson City-Kingsport-Bristol MSA, TN-VA	S	10.41 MW	9.94 AW	21660 AAW	TNBLS	10//99-12//99
	Knoxville MSA, TN	S	12.58 MW	12.32 AW	26160 AAW	TNBLS	10//99-12//99
	Memphis MSA, TN-AR-MS	S	16.79 MW	17.80 AW	34920 AAW	MSBLS	10//99-12//99
	Nashville MSA, TN	S	11.64 MW	11.09 AW	24200 AAW	TNBLS	10//99-12//99
	Texas	S	12.33 MW	12.46 AW	25910 AAW	TXBLS	10//99-12//99
	Beaumont-Port Arthur MSA, TX	S	10.08 MW	9.12 AW	20970 AAW	TXBLS	10//99-12//99

AAW Average annual wage	AOH Average offered, high	ASH Average starting, high	H Hourly	M Monthly	S Special: hourly and annual
AE Average entry wage	AOL Average offered, low	ASL Average starting, low	HI Highest wage paid	MTC Median total compensation	TQ Third quartile wage
AEX Average experienced wage	APH Average pay, high range	AW Average wage paid	HR High end range	MW Median wage paid	W Weekly
AO Average offered	APL Average pay, low range	FQ First quartile wage	LR Low end range	SQ Second quartile wage	Y Yearly

Occupation/Type/Industry	Location	Per	Low	Mid	High	Source	Date
Job Printer	Brownsville-Harlingen-San Benito MSA, TX	S	7.58 MW	7.44 AW	15760 AAW	TXBLS	10//99-12//99
	Corpus Christi MSA, TX	S	9.68 MW	9.58 AW	20140 AAW	TXBLS	10//99-12//99
	Dallas PMSA, TX	S	14.79 MW	14.55 AW	30770 AAW	TXBLS	10//99-12//99
	Fort Worth-Arlington PMSA, TX	S	12.74 MW	13.72 AW	26500 AAW	TXBLS	10//99-12//99
	Houston PMSA, TX	S	12.42 MW	12.55 AW	25840 AAW	TXBLS	10//99-12//99
	Lubbock MSA, TX	S	10.34 MW	8.49 AW	21510 AAW	TXBLS	10//99-12//99
	San Antonio MSA, TX	S	11.30 MW	10.98 AW	23500 AAW	TXBLS	10//99-12//99
	Waco MSA, TX	S	16.37 MW	14.76 AW	34050 AAW	TXBLS	10//99-12//99
	Utah	S	12.83 MW	13.65 AW	28390 AAW	UTBLS	10//99-12//99
	Salt Lake City-Ogden MSA, UT	S	13.81 MW	12.83 AW	28730 AAW	UTBLS	10//99-12//99
	Vermont	S	13.24 MW	13.44 AW	27960 AAW	VTBLS	10//99-12//99
	Virginia	S	12.47 MW	12.78 AW	26580 AAW	VABLS	10//99-12//99
	Norfolk-Virginia Beach-Newport News MSA, VA-NC	S	11.05 MW	10.50 AW	22990 AAW	VABLS	
	Richmond-Petersburg MSA, VA	S	13.57 MW	13.02 AW	28230 AAW	VABLS	10//99-12//99
	Washington	S	15.03 MW	14.91 AW	31010 AAW	WABLS	10//99-12//99
	Seattle-Bellevue-Everett PMSA, WA	S	15.58 MW	15.56 AW	32400 AAW	WABLS	10//99-12//99
	Spokane MSA, WA	S	13.44 MW	13.07 AW	27950 AAW	WABLS	10//99-12//99
	Tacoma PMSA, WA	S	14.34 MW	14.42 AW	29830 AAW	WABLS	10//99-12//99
	West Virginia	S	9.69 MW	9.83 AW	20450 AAW	WVBLS	10//99-12//99
	Wisconsin	S	12.4 MW	12.85 AW	26720 AAW	WIBLS	10//99-12//99
	Appleton-Oshkosh-Neenah MSA, WI	S	11.93 MW	12.12 AW	24810 AAW	WIBLS	10//99-12//99
	Green Bay MSA, WI	S	9.61 MW	8.69 AW	19980 AAW	WIBLS	10//99-12//99
	Madison MSA, WI	S	13.67 MW	13.43 AW	28430 AAW	WIBLS	10//99-12//99
	Milwaukee-Waukesha PMSA, WI	S	14.15 MW	12.92 AW	29440 AAW	WIBLS	10//99-12//99
	Sheboygan MSA, WI	S	12.99 MW	12.79 AW	27020 AAW	WIBLS	10//99-12//99
	Wyoming	S	8.82 MW	9.68 AW	20130 AAW	WYBLS	10//99-12//99
	Puerto Rico	S	7.64 MW	9.09 AW	18910 AAW	PRBLS	10//99-12//99
	San Juan-Bayamon PMSA, PR	S	8.75 MW	7.39 AW	18200 AAW	PRBLS	10//99-12//99
Judge, Magistrate Judge, and Magistrate	Alabama	S	18.13 MW	22.69 AW	47190 AAW	ALBLS	10//99-12//99
	Birmingham MSA, AL	S	21.58 MW	17.01 AW	44890 AAW	ALBLS	10//99-12//99
	Huntsville MSA, AL	S	27.91 MW	28.25 AW	58050 AAW	ALBLS	10//99-12//99
	Mobile MSA, AL	S	34.69 MW	38.10 AW	72160 AAW	ALBLS	10//99-12//99
	Alaska	S	42.21 MW	40.32 AW	83860 AAW	AKBLS	10//99-12//99
	Arizona	S	38.77 MW	35.04 AW	72870 AAW	AZBLS	10//99-12//99
	Phoenix-Mesa MSA, AZ	S	45.72 MW	47.45 AW	95090 AAW	AZBLS	10//99-12//99
	Arkansas	S	9.49 MW	12.97 AW	26970 AAW	ARBLS	10//99-12//99
	California	S	45.44 MW	39.99 AW	83180 AAW	CABLS	10//99-12//99
	Los Angeles-Long Beach PMSA, CA	S	30.72 MW	21.03 AW	63890 AAW	CABLS	10//99-12//99
	Oakland PMSA, CA	S	40.40 MW	46.04 AW	84040 AAW	CABLS	10//99-12//99
	Riverside-San Bernardino PMSA, CA	S	41.52 MW	46.45 AW	86350 AAW	CABLS	10//99-12//99
	San Francisco PMSA, CA	S	47.55 MW	48.98 AW	98900 AAW	CABLS	10//99-12//99
	Vallejo-Fairfield-Napa PMSA, CA	S	51.60 MW	51.93 AW	107330 AAW	CABLS	10//99-12//99
	Colorado	S	43.33 MW	44.54 AW	92640 AAW	COBLS	10//99-12//99
	Denver PMSA, CO	S	45.91 MW	45.38 AW	95480 AAW	COBLS	10//99-12//99
	Florida	S	58.82 MW	55.24 AW	114910 AAW	FLBLS	10//99-12//99
	Georgia	S	25.19 MW	29.07 AW	60480 AAW	GABLS	10//99-12//99
	Atlanta MSA, GA	S	34.71 MW	32.05 AW	72190 AAW	GABLS	10//99-12//99
	Augusta-Aiken MSA, GA-SC	S	25.25 MW	19.19 AW	52530 AAW	GABLS	10//99-12//99
	Idaho	S	42.87 MW	50.14 AW	104290 AAW	IDBLS	10//99-12//99
	Indiana	S	44.16 MW	33.18 AW	69020 AAW	INBLS	10//99-12//99
	Indianapolis MSA, IN	S	35.50 MW	45.86 AW	73840 AAW	INBLS	10//99-12//99
	Iowa	S	37.68 MW	30.60 AW	63640 AAW	IABLS	10//99-12//99
	Louisiana	S	12.05 MW	12.53 AW	26050 AAW	LABLS	10//99-12//99
	Maryland	S	37.7 MW	32.53 AW	67670 AAW	MDBLS	10//99-12//99
	Michigan	S	32.73 MW	41.02 AW	85330 AAW	MIBLS	10//99-12//99
	Mississippi	S	9.7 MW	16.37 AW	34050 AAW	MSBLS	10//99-12//99
	Jackson MSA, MS	S	39.47 MW	45.87 AW	82110 AAW	MSBLS	10//99-12//99
	Montana	S	19.36 MW	31.60 AW	65720 AAW	MTBLS	10//99-12//99

Occupation/Type/Industry	Location	Per	Low	Mid	High	Source	Date
Judge, Magistrate Judge, and Magistrate							
	Nevada	S	25.33 MW	26.95 AW	56060 AAW	NVBLS	10//99-12//99
	Las Vegas MSA, NV-AZ	S	26.25 MW	21.26 AW	54610 AAW	NVBLS	10//99-12//99
	New Jersey	S	60.05 MW	52.38 AW	108960 AAW	NJBLS	10//99-12//99
	Bergen-Passaic PMSA, NJ	S	55.77 MW	61.02 AW	116000 AAW	NJBLS	10//99-12//99
	Middlesex-Somerset-Hunterdon PMSA, NJ	S	56.11 MW	61.47 AW	116710 AAW	NJBLS	10//99-12//99
	Monmouth-Ocean PMSA, NJ	S	55.13 MW	61.19 AW	114680 AAW	NJBLS	10//99-12//99
	Newark PMSA, NJ	S	50.19 MW	58.33 AW	104390 AAW	NJBLS	10//99-12//99
	Nassau-Suffolk PMSA, NY	S	52.27 MW	61.75 AW	108720 AAW	NYBLS	10//99-12//99
	Ohio	S	23.82 MW	25.37 AW	52760 AAW	OHBLS	10//99-12//99
	Cincinnati PMSA, OH-KY-IN	S	24.12 MW	27.18 AW	50160 AAW	OHBLS	10//99-12//99
	Cleveland-Lorain-Elyria PMSA, OH	S	23.27 MW	20.94 AW	48410 AAW	OHBLS	10//99-12//99
	Columbus MSA, OH	S	20.71 MW	19.80 AW	43080 AAW	OHBLS	10//99-12//99
	Oklahoma	S	30.03 MW	32.71 AW	68040 AAW	OKBLS	10//99-12//99
	Oregon	S	41.1 MW	42.04 AW	87440 AAW	ORBLS	10//99-12//99
	Portland-Vancouver PMSA, OR-WA	S	40.61 MW	40.64 AW	84470 AAW	ORBLS	10//99-12//99
	Pennsylvania	S	36.25 MW	33.87 AW	70440 AAW	PABLS	10//99-12//99
	Philadelphia PMSA, PA-NJ	S	38.93 MW	53.34 AW	80970 AAW	PABLS	10//99-12//99
	South Carolina	S	14.88 MW	21.15 AW	43990 AAW	SCBLS	10//99-12//99
	Charleston-North Charleston MSA, SC	S	15.28 MW	10.25 AW	31780 AAW	SCBLS	10//99-12//99
	Columbia MSA, SC	S	25.60 MW	19.92 AW	53250 AAW	SCBLS	10//99-12//99
	Greenville-Spartanburg-Anderson MSA, SC	S	25.43 MW	17.39 AW	52890 AAW	SCBLS	10//99-12//99
	Tennessee	S	13.3 MW	19.77 AW	41120 AAW	TNBLS	10//99-12//99
	Texas	S	22.88 MW	26.76 AW	55660 AAW	TXBLS	10//99-12//99
	Beaumont-Port Arthur MSA, TX	S	24.28 MW	15.67 AW	50500 AAW	TXBLS	10//99-12//99
	Fort Worth-Arlington PMSA, TX	S	26.52 MW	27.29 AW	55160 AAW	TXBLS	10//99-12//99
	Galveston-Texas City PMSA, TX	S	23.19 MW	15.12 AW	48230 AAW	TXBLS	10//99-12//99
	Houston PMSA, TX	S	33.10 MW	45.20 AW	68850 AAW	TXBLS	10//99-12//99
	Longview-Marshall MSA, TX	S	19.05 MW	15.85 AW	39610 AAW	TXBLS	10//99-12//99
	McAllen-Edinburg-Mission MSA, TX	S	27.43 MW	20.31 AW	57060 AAW	TXBLS	10//99-12//99
	Odessa-Midland MSA, TX	S	31.90 MW	43.86 AW	66360 AAW	TXBLS	10//99-12//99
	Wichita Falls MSA, TX	S	22.39 MW	13.84 AW	46570 AAW	TXBLS	10//99-12//99
	Utah	S	22.39 MW	21.00 AW	43680 AAW	UTBLS	10//99-12//99
	Salt Lake City-Ogden MSA, UT	S	29.64 MW	30.43 AW	61640 AAW	UTBLS	10//99-12//99
	Washington	S	50.27 MW	48.10 AW	100040 AAW	WABLS	10//99-12//99
	Seattle-Bellevue-Everett PMSA, WA	S	50.16 MW	51.45 AW	104330 AAW	WABLS	10//99-12//99
	West Virginia	S	16.71 MW	16.29 AW	33880 AAW	WVBLS	10//99-12//99
Juggler or Mime	Louisville, KY	H	100.00 APL		125.00 APH	LOUMAG	1999-2000
Kindergarten Teacher							
Except Special Education	Alabama	Y		32400 AAW		ALBLS	10//99-12//99
Except Special Education	Anniston MSA, AL	Y		33070 AAW		ALBLS	10//99-12//99
Except Special Education	Birmingham MSA, AL	Y		32320 AAW		ALBLS	10//99-12//99
Except Special Education	Decatur MSA, AL	Y		36740 AAW		ALBLS	10//99-12//99
Except Special Education	Dothan MSA, AL	Y		35600 AAW		ALBLS	10//99-12//99
Except Special Education	Florence MSA, AL	Y		36060 AAW		ALBLS	10//99-12//99
Except Special Education	Huntsville MSA, AL	Y		35910 AAW		ALBLS	10//99-12//99
Except Special Education	Mobile MSA, AL	Y		29390 AAW		ALBLS	10//99-12//99
Except Special Education	Montgomery MSA, AL	Y		30840 AAW		ALBLS	10//99-12//99
Except Special Education	Tuscaloosa MSA, AL	Y		38010 AAW		ALBLS	10//99-12//99
Except Special Education	Alaska	Y		49690 AAW		AKBLS	10//99-12//99
Except Special Education	Arizona	Y		35370 AAW		AZBLS	10//99-12//99
Except Special Education	Flagstaff MSA, AZ-UT	Y		33450 AAW		AZBLS	10//99-12//99
Except Special Education	Phoenix-Mesa MSA, AZ	Y		34570 AAW		AZBLS	10//99-12//99
Except Special Education	Tucson MSA, AZ	Y		41970 AAW		AZBLS	10//99-12//99
Except Special Education	Yuma MSA, AZ	Y		34660 AAW		AZBLS	10//99-12//99
Except Special Education	Arkansas	Y		31470 AAW		ARBLS	10//99-12//99
Except Special Education	Fayetteville-Springdale-Rogers MSA, AR	Y		34580 AAW		ARBLS	10//99-12//99
Except Special Education	Fort Smith MSA, AR-OK	Y		30050 AAW		ARBLS	10//99-12//99

AAW Average annual wage	**AOH** Average offered, high	**ASH** Average starting, high	**H** Hourly	**M** Monthly	**S** Special: hourly and annual
AE Average entry wage	**AOL** Average offered, low	**ASL** Average starting, low	**HI** Highest wage paid	**MTC** Median total compensation	**TQ** Third quartile wage
AEX Average experienced wage	**APH** Average pay, high range	**AW** Average wage paid	**HR** High end range	**MW** Median wage paid	**W** Weekly
AO Average offered	**APL** Average pay, low range	**FQ** First quartile wage	**LR** Low end range	**SQ** Second quartile wage	**Y** Yearly

Occupation/Type/Industry	Location	Per	Low	Mid	High	Source	Date
Kindergarten Teacher							
Except Special Education	Jonesboro MSA, AR	Y		32380 AAW		ARBLS	10//99-12//99
Except Special Education	Little Rock-North Little Rock MSA, AR	Y		32730 AAW		ARBLS	10//99-12//99
Except Special Education	California	Y		41490 AAW		CABLS	10//99-12//99
Except Special Education	Bakersfield MSA, CA	Y		46640 AAW		CABLS	10//99-12//99
Except Special Education	Chico-Paradise MSA, CA	Y		43400 AAW		CABLS	10//99-12//99
Except Special Education	Fresno MSA, CA	Y		42130 AAW		CABLS	10//99-12//99
Except Special Education	Los Angeles-Long Beach PMSA, CA	Y		41210 AAW		CABLS	10//99-12//99
Except Special Education	Merced MSA, CA	Y		41700 AAW		CABLS	10//99-12//99
Except Special Education	Modesto MSA, CA	Y		45600 AAW		CABLS	10//99-12//99
Except Special Education	Oakland PMSA, CA	Y		41860 AAW		CABLS	10//99-12//99
Except Special Education	Orange County PMSA, CA	Y		37910 AAW		CABLS	10//99-12//99
Except Special Education	Redding MSA, CA	Y		41330 AAW		CABLS	10//99-12//99
Except Special Education	Riverside-San Bernardino PMSA, CA	Y		40520 AAW		CABLS	10//99-12//99
Except Special Education	Sacramento PMSA, CA	Y		44650 AAW		CABLS	10//99-12//99
Except Special Education	Salinas MSA, CA	Y		42220 AAW		CABLS	10//99-12//99
Except Special Education	San Diego MSA, CA	Y		44550 AAW		CABLS	10//99-12//99
Except Special Education	San Francisco PMSA, CA	Y		43630 AAW		CABLS	10//99-12//99
Except Special Education	San Jose PMSA, CA	Y		33000 AAW		CABLS	10//99-12//99
Except Special Education	San Luis Obispo-Atascadero-Paso Robles MSA, CA	Y		41490 AAW		CABLS	10//99-12//99
Except Special Education	Santa Barbara-Santa Maria-Lompoc MSA, CA	Y		43700 AAW		CABLS	10//99-12//99
Except Special Education	Santa Cruz-Watsonville PMSA, CA	Y		42400 AAW		CABLS	10//99-12//99
Except Special Education	Santa Rosa PMSA, CA	Y		43320 AAW		CABLS	10//99-12//99
Except Special Education	Stockton-Lodi MSA, CA	Y		42990 AAW		CABLS	10//99-12//99
Except Special Education	Vallejo-Fairfield-Napa PMSA, CA	Y		31970 AAW		CABLS	10//99-12//99
Except Special Education	Ventura PMSA, CA	Y		47910 AAW		CABLS	10//99-12//99
Except Special Education	Visalia-Tulare-Porterville MSA, CA	Y		45310 AAW		CABLS	10//99-12//99
Except Special Education	Yolo PMSA, CA	Y		41290 AAW		CABLS	10//99-12//99
Except Special Education	Colorado	Y		35480 AAW		COBLS	10//99-12//99
Except Special Education	Boulder-Longmont PMSA, CO	Y		34830 AAW		COBLS	10//99-12//99
Except Special Education	Denver PMSA, CO	Y		36590 AAW		COBLS	10//99-12//99
Except Special Education	Connecticut	Y		46100 AAW		CTBLS	10//99-12//99
Except Special Education	Bridgeport PMSA, CT	Y		45770 AAW		CTBLS	10//99-12//99
Except Special Education	Danbury PMSA, CT	Y		44070 AAW		CTBLS	10//99-12//99
Except Special Education	Hartford MSA, CT	Y		44630 AAW		CTBLS	10//99-12//99
Except Special Education	New Haven-Meriden PMSA, CT	Y		47910 AAW		CTBLS	10//99-12//99
Except Special Education	New London-Norwich MSA, CT-RI	Y		49370 AAW		CTBLS	10//99-12//99
Except Special Education	Stamford-Norwalk PMSA, CT	Y		48470 AAW		CTBLS	10//99-12//99
Except Special Education	Waterbury PMSA, CT	Y		49870 AAW		CTBLS	10//99-12//99
Except Special Education	Wilmington-Newark PMSA, DE-MD	Y		40590 AAW		DEBLS	10//99-12//99
Except Special Education	District of Columbia	Y		36770 AAW		DCBLS	10//99-12//99
Except Special Education	Washington PMSA, DC-MD-VA-WV	Y		36890 AAW		DCBLS	10//99-12//99
Except Special Education	Florida	Y		34230 AAW		FLBLS	10//99-12//99
Except Special Education	Fort Pierce-Port St. Lucie MSA, FL	Y		40850 AAW		FLBLS	10//99-12//99
Except Special Education	Jacksonville MSA, FL	Y		40510 AAW		FLBLS	10//99-12//99
Except Special Education	Lakeland-Winter Haven MSA, FL	Y		14400 AAW		FLBLS	10//99-12//99
Except Special Education	Melbourne-Titusville-Palm Bay MSA, FL	Y		19350 AAW		FLBLS	10//99-12//99
Except Special Education	Miami PMSA, FL	Y		26010 AAW		FLBLS	10//99-12//99
Except Special Education	Tampa-St. Petersburg-Clearwater MSA, FL	Y		37710 AAW		FLBLS	10//99-12//99
Except Special Education	West Palm Beach-Boca Raton MSA, FL	Y		18320 AAW		FLBLS	10//99-12//99
Except Special Education	Georgia	Y		35090 AAW		GABLS	10//99-12//99
Except Special Education	Albany MSA, GA	Y		39490 AAW		GABLS	10//99-12//99
Except Special Education	Atlanta MSA, GA	Y		32760 AAW		GABLS	10//99-12//99
Except Special Education	Augusta-Aiken MSA, GA-SC	Y		33260 AAW		GABLS	10//99-12//99
Except Special Education	Columbus MSA, GA-AL	Y		38490 AAW		GABLS	10//99-12//99

AAW	Average annual wage	AOH	Average offered, high	ASH	Average starting, high	H	Hourly
AE	Average entry wage	AOL	Average offered, low	ASL	Average starting, low	HI	Highest wage paid
AEX	Average experienced wage	APH	Average pay, high range	AW	Average wage paid	HR	High end range
AO	Average offered	APL	Average pay, low range	FQ	First quartile wage	LR	Low end range

M	Monthly	S	Special: hourly and annual
MTC	Median total compensation	TQ	Third quartile wage
MW	Median wage paid	W	Weekly
SQ	Second quartile wage	Y	Yearly

Occupation/Type/Industry	Location	Per	Low	Mid	High	Source	Date
Kindergarten Teacher							
Except Special Education	Macon MSA, GA	Y		37660 AAW		GABLS	10//99-12//99
Except Special Education	Savannah MSA, GA	Y		38220 AAW		GABLS	10//99-12//99
Except Special Education	Hawaii	Y		29920 AAW		HIBLS	10//99-12//99
Except Special Education	Honolulu MSA, HI	Y		30850 AAW		HIBLS	10//99-12//99
Except Special Education	Idaho	Y		23590 AAW		IDBLS	10//99-12//99
Except Special Education	Boise City MSA, ID	Y		17090 AAW		IDBLS	10//99-12//99
Except Special Education	Illinois	Y		36380 AAW		ILBLS	10//99-12//99
Except Special Education	Bloomington-Normal MSA, IL	Y		36310 AAW		ILBLS	10//99-12//99
Except Special Education	Champaign-Urbana MSA, IL	Y		37150 AAW		ILBLS	10//99-12//99
Except Special Education	Chicago PMSA, IL	Y		39410 AAW		ILBLS	10//99-12//99
Except Special Education	Kankakee PMSA, IL	Y		38070 AAW		ILBLS	10//99-12//99
Except Special Education	Peoria-Pekin MSA, IL	Y		31940 AAW		ILBLS	10//99-12//99
Except Special Education	Rockford MSA, IL	Y		31960 AAW		ILBLS	10//99-12//99
Except Special Education	Springfield MSA, IL	Y		36910 AAW		ILBLS	10//99-12//99
Except Special Education	Indiana	Y		40430 AAW		INBLS	10//99-12//99
Except Special Education	Elkhart-Goshen MSA, IN	Y		35630 AAW		INBLS	10//99-12//99
Except Special Education	Evansville-Henderson MSA, IN-KY	Y		33720 AAW		INBLS	10//99-12//99
Except Special Education	Fort Wayne MSA, IN	Y		38120 AAW		INBLS	10//99-12//99
Except Special Education	Gary PMSA, IN	Y		38420 AAW		INBLS	10//99-12//99
Except Special Education	Indianapolis MSA, IN	Y		46490 AAW		INBLS	10//99-12//99
Except Special Education	Kokomo MSA, IN	Y		38380 AAW		INBLS	10//99-12//99
Except Special Education	Lafayette MSA, IN	Y		38560 AAW		INBLS	10//99-12//99
Except Special Education	Muncie MSA, IN	Y		38550 AAW		INBLS	10//99-12//99
Except Special Education	Iowa	Y		29370 AAW		IABLS	10//99-12//99
Except Special Education	Cedar Rapids MSA, IA	Y		28390 AAW		IABLS	10//99-12//99
Except Special Education	Davenport-Moline-Rock Island MSA, IA-IL	Y		36990 AAW		IABLS	10//99-12//99
Except Special Education	Des Moines MSA, IA	Y		29110 AAW		IABLS	10//99-12//99
Except Special Education	Dubuque MSA, IA	Y		29610 AAW		IABLS	10//99-12//99
Except Special Education	Kansas	Y		29820 AAW		KSBLS	10//99-12//99
Except Special Education	Lawrence MSA, KS	Y		30610 AAW		KSBLS	10//99-12//99
Except Special Education	Topeka MSA, KS	Y		31630 AAW		KSBLS	10//99-12//99
Except Special Education	Wichita MSA, KS	Y		31200 AAW		KSBLS	10//99-12//99
Except Special Education	Kentucky	Y		33930 AAW		KYBLS	10//99-12//99
Except Special Education	Louisiana	Y		34950 AAW		LABLS	10//99-12//99
Except Special Education	Baton Rouge MSA, LA	Y		33960 AAW		LABLS	10//99-12//99
Except Special Education	Lafayette MSA, LA	Y		30010 AAW		LABLS	10//99-12//99
Except Special Education	Monroe MSA, LA	Y		29500 AAW		LABLS	10//99-12//99
Except Special Education	New Orleans MSA, LA	Y		35110 AAW		LABLS	10//99-12//99
Except Special Education	Maine	Y		34140 AAW		MEBLS	10//99-12//99
Except Special Education	Lewiston-Auburn MSA, ME	Y		37540 AAW		MEBLS	10//99-12//99
Except Special Education	Portland MSA, ME	Y		39280 AAW		MEBLS	10//99-12//99
Except Special Education	Maryland	Y		36510 AAW		MDBLS	10//99-12//99
Except Special Education	Baltimore PMSA, MD	Y		33340 AAW		MDBLS	10//99-12//99
Except Special Education	Hagerstown PMSA, MD	Y		28760 AAW		MDBLS	10//99-12//99
Except Special Education	Massachusetts	Y		40110 AAW		MABLS	10//99-12//99
Except Special Education	Barnstable-Yarmouth MSA, MA	Y		36120 AAW		MABLS	10//99-12//99
Except Special Education	Boston PMSA, MA-NH	Y		41900 AAW		MABLS	10//99-12//99
Except Special Education	Brockton PMSA, MA	Y		40620 AAW		MABLS	10//99-12//99
Except Special Education	Fitchburg-Leominster PMSA, MA	Y		39870 AAW		MABLS	10//99-12//99
Except Special Education	Lowell PMSA, MA-NH	Y		41390 AAW		MABLS	10//99-12//99
Except Special Education	New Bedford PMSA, MA	Y		36740 AAW		MABLS	10//99-12//99
Except Special Education	Pittsfield MSA, MA	Y		41630 AAW		MABLS	10//99-12//99
Except Special Education	Springfield MSA, MA	Y		33850 AAW		MABLS	10//99-12//99
Except Special Education	Worcester PMSA, MA-CT	Y		42080 AAW		MABLS	10//99-12//99
Except Special Education	Michigan	Y		39200 AAW		MIBLS	10//99-12//99
Except Special Education	Ann Arbor PMSA, MI	Y		36280 AAW		MIBLS	10//99-12//99
Except Special Education	Detroit PMSA, MI	Y		36780 AAW		MIBLS	10//99-12//99
Except Special Education	Flint PMSA, MI	Y		40140 AAW		MIBLS	10//99-12//99
Except Special Education	Grand Rapids-Muskegon-Holland MSA, MI	Y		42420 AAW		MIBLS	10//99-12//99
Except Special Education	Kalamazoo-Battle Creek MSA, MI	Y		41730 AAW		MIBLS	10//99-12//99
Except Special Education	Lansing-East Lansing MSA, MI	Y		42670 AAW		MIBLS	10//99-12//99
Except Special Education	Minnesota	Y		38600 AAW		MNBLS	10//99-12//99
Except Special Education	Duluth-Superior MSA, MN-WI	Y		37390 AAW		MNBLS	10//99-12//99
Except Special Education	Minneapolis-St. Paul MSA, MN-WI	Y		40360 AAW		MNBLS	10//99-12//99

AAW	Average annual wage	AOH	Average offered, high	ASH	Average starting, high	H	Hourly	M	Monthly	S	Special: hourly and annual
AE	Average entry wage	AOL	Average offered, low	ASL	Average starting, low	HI	Highest wage paid	MTC	Median total compensation	TQ	Third quartile wage
AEX	Average experienced wage	APH	Average pay, high range	AW	Average wage paid	HR	High end range	MW	Median wage paid	W	Weekly
AO	Average offered	APL	Average pay, low range	FQ	First quartile wage	LR	Low end range	SQ	Second quartile wage	Y	Yearly

Kindergarten Teacher

Occupation/Type/Industry	Location	Per	Low	Mid	High	Source	Date
Kindergarten Teacher							
Except Special Education	St. Cloud MSA, MN	Y		34200 AAW		MNBLS	10//99-12//99
Except Special Education	Mississippi	Y		26520 AAW		MSBLS	10//99-12//99
Except Special Education	Biloxi-Gulfport-Pascagoula MSA, MS	Y		26960 AAW		MSBLS	10//99-12//99
Except Special Education	Hattiesburg MSA, MS	Y		26240 AAW		MSBLS	10//99-12//99
Except Special Education	Jackson MSA, MS	Y		22920 AAW		MSBLS	10//99-12//99
Except Special Education	Missouri	Y		31570 AAW		MOBLS	10//99-12//99
Except Special Education	Joplin MSA, MO	Y		26090 AAW		MOBLS	10//99-12//99
Except Special Education	Kansas City MSA, MO-KS	Y		29620 AAW		MOBLS	10//99-12//99
Except Special Education	St. Louis MSA, MO-IL	Y		34730 AAW		MOBLS	10//99-12//99
Except Special Education	Springfield MSA, MO	Y		29290 AAW		MOBLS	10//99-12//99
Except Special Education	Montana	Y		29310 AAW		MTBLS	10//99-12//99
Except Special Education	Missoula MSA, MT	Y		34860 AAW		MTBLS	10//99-12//99
Except Special Education	Nebraska	Y		30170 AAW		NEBLS	10//99-12//99
Except Special Education	Omaha MSA, NE-IA	Y		31110 AAW		NEBLS	10//99-12//99
Except Special Education	Reno MSA, NV	Y		24860 AAW		NVBLS	10//99-12//99
Except Special Education	New Hampshire	Y		25990 AAW		NHBLS	10//99-12//99
Except Special Education	Manchester PMSA, NH	Y		24800 AAW		NHBLS	10//99-12//99
Except Special Education	Nashua PMSA, NH	Y		23550 AAW		NHBLS	10//99-12//99
Except Special Education	Portsmouth-Rochester PMSA, NH-ME	Y		34450 AAW		NHBLS	10//99-12//99
Except Special Education	New Jersey	Y		45110 AAW		NJBLS	10//99-12//99
Except Special Education	Atlantic-Cape May PMSA, NJ	Y		41050 AAW		NJBLS	10//99-12//99
Except Special Education	Bergen-Passaic PMSA, NJ	Y		44170 AAW		NJBLS	10//99-12//99
Except Special Education	Jersey City PMSA, NJ	Y		44270 AAW		NJBLS	10//99-12//99
Except Special Education	Middlesex-Somerset-Hunterdon PMSA, NJ	Y		41380 AAW		NJBLS	10//99-12//99
Except Special Education	Monmouth-Ocean PMSA, NJ	Y		48080 AAW		NJBLS	10//99-12//99
Except Special Education	Newark PMSA, NJ	Y		45100 AAW		NJBLS	10//99-12//99
Except Special Education	Trenton PMSA, NJ	Y		43010 AAW		NJBLS	10//99-12//99
Except Special Education	Vineland-Millville-Bridgeton PMSA, NJ	Y		46330 AAW		NJBLS	10//99-12//99
Except Special Education	New Mexico	Y		33720 AAW		NMBLS	10//99-12//99
Except Special Education	Las Cruces MSA, NM	Y		30290 AAW		NMBLS	10//99-12//99
Except Special Education	Santa Fe MSA, NM	Y		32120 AAW		NMBLS	10//99-12//99
Except Special Education	New York	Y		44930 AAW		NYBLS	10//99-12//99
Except Special Education	Albany-Schenectady-Troy MSA, NY	Y		39120 AAW		NYBLS	10//99-12//99
Except Special Education	Binghamton MSA, NY	Y		40110 AAW		NYBLS	10//99-12//99
Except Special Education	Buffalo-Niagara Falls MSA, NY	Y		49070 AAW		NYBLS	10//99-12//99
Except Special Education	Dutchess County PMSA, NY	Y		39320 AAW		NYBLS	10//99-12//99
Except Special Education	Glens Falls MSA, NY	Y		40340 AAW		NYBLS	10//99-12//99
Except Special Education	Jamestown MSA, NY	Y		44120 AAW		NYBLS	10//99-12//99
Except Special Education	Nassau-Suffolk PMSA, NY	Y		48300 AAW		NYBLS	10//99-12//99
Except Special Education	New York PMSA, NY	Y		45080 AAW		NYBLS	10//99-12//99
Except Special Education	Newburgh PMSA, NY-PA	Y		49180 AAW		NYBLS	10//99-12//99
Except Special Education	Rochester MSA, NY	Y		46200 AAW		NYBLS	10//99-12//99
Except Special Education	Syracuse MSA, NY	Y		38880 AAW		NYBLS	10//99-12//99
Except Special Education	Utica-Rome MSA, NY	Y		39310 AAW		NYBLS	10//99-12//99
Except Special Education	North Carolina	Y		32650 AAW		NCBLS	10//99-12//99
Except Special Education	Asheville MSA, NC	Y		35870 AAW		NCBLS	10//99-12//99
Except Special Education	Charlotte-Gastonia-Rock Hill MSA, NC-SC	Y		32320 AAW		NCBLS	10//99-12//99
Except Special Education	Greensboro--Winston-Salem--High Point MSA, NC	Y		35540 AAW		NCBLS	10//99-12//99
Except Special Education	Greenville MSA, NC	Y		33000 AAW		NCBLS	10//99-12//99
Except Special Education	Hickory-Morganton-Lenoir MSA, NC	Y		27400 AAW		NCBLS	10//99-12//99
Except Special Education	Raleigh-Durham-Chapel Hill MSA, NC	Y		34150 AAW		NCBLS	10//99-12//99
Except Special Education	Wilmington MSA, NC	Y		33280 AAW		NCBLS	10//99-12//99
Except Special Education	North Dakota	Y		25420 AAW		NDBLS	10//99-12//99
Except Special Education	Fargo-Moorhead MSA, ND-MN	Y		27820 AAW		NDBLS	10//99-12//99
Except Special Education	Grand Forks MSA, ND-MN	Y		33670 AAW		NDBLS	10//99-12//99
Except Special Education	Ohio	Y		37400 AAW		OHBLS	10//99-12//99
Except Special Education	Akron PMSA, OH	Y		35800 AAW		OHBLS	10//99-12//99
Except Special Education	Canton-Massillon MSA, OH	Y		35280 AAW		OHBLS	10//99-12//99
Except Special Education	Cincinnati PMSA, OH-KY-IN	Y		39470 AAW		OHBLS	10//99-12//99

Occupation/Type/Industry	Location	Per	Low	Mid	High	Source	Date
Kindergarten Teacher							
Except Special Education	Cleveland-Lorain-Elyria PMSA, OH	Y		40730 AAW		OHBLS	10//99-12//99
Except Special Education	Columbus MSA, OH	Y		42090 AAW		OHBLS	10//99-12//99
Except Special Education	Dayton-Springfield MSA, OH	Y		38530 AAW		OHBLS	10//99-12//99
Except Special Education	Hamilton-Middletown PMSA, OH	Y		39100 AAW		OHBLS	10//99-12//99
Except Special Education	Lima MSA, OH	Y		36120 AAW		OHBLS	10//99-12//99
Except Special Education	Mansfield MSA, OH	Y		37540 AAW		OHBLS	10//99-12//99
Except Special Education	Steubenville-Weirton MSA, OH-WV	Y		35230 AAW		OHBLS	10//99-12//99
Except Special Education	Toledo MSA, OH	Y		34370 AAW		OHBLS	10//99-12//99
Except Special Education	Youngstown-Warren MSA, OH	Y		35300 AAW		OHBLS	10//99-12//99
Except Special Education	Oklahoma	Y		27810 AAW		OKBLS	10//99-12//99
Except Special Education	Oklahoma City MSA, OK	Y		26480 AAW		OKBLS	10//99-12//99
Except Special Education	Tulsa MSA, OK	Y		29060 AAW		OKBLS	10//99-12//99
Except Special Education	Oregon	Y		36690 AAW		ORBLS	10//99-12//99
Except Special Education	Corvallis MSA, OR	Y		29480 AAW		ORBLS	10//99-12//99
Except Special Education	Eugene-Springfield MSA, OR	Y		38160 AAW		ORBLS	10//99-12//99
Except Special Education	Medford-Ashland MSA, OR	Y		36190 AAW		ORBLS	10//99-12//99
Except Special Education	Portland-Vancouver PMSA, OR-WA	Y		36600 AAW		ORBLS	10//99-12//99
Except Special Education	Salem PMSA, OR	Y		34030 AAW		ORBLS	10//99-12//99
Except Special Education	Pennsylvania	Y		39610 AAW		PABLS	10//99-12//99
Except Special Education	Allentown-Bethlehem-Easton MSA, PA	Y		29870 AAW		PABLS	10//99-12//99
Except Special Education	Altoona MSA, PA	Y		41180 AAW		PABLS	10//99-12//99
Except Special Education	Erie MSA, PA	Y		32940 AAW		PABLS	10//99-12//99
Except Special Education	Harrisburg-Lebanon-Carlisle MSA, PA	Y		34380 AAW		PABLS	10//99-12//99
Except Special Education	Johnstown MSA, PA	Y		40450 AAW		PABLS	10//99-12//99
Except Special Education	Lancaster MSA, PA	Y		45770 AAW		PABLS	10//99-12//99
Except Special Education	Philadelphia PMSA, PA-NJ	Y		43840 AAW		PABLS	10//99-12//99
Except Special Education	Pittsburgh MSA, PA	Y		38110 AAW		PABLS	10//99-12//99
Except Special Education	Reading MSA, PA	Y		45470 AAW		PABLS	10//99-12//99
Except Special Education	Scranton--Wilkes-Barre--Hazleton MSA, PA	Y		40660 AAW		PABLS	10//99-12//99
Except Special Education	Sharon MSA, PA	Y		39760 AAW		PABLS	10//99-12//99
Except Special Education	State College MSA, PA	Y		42180 AAW		PABLS	10//99-12//99
Except Special Education	Williamsport MSA, PA	Y		39120 AAW		PABLS	10//99-12//99
Except Special Education	York MSA, PA	Y		42710 AAW		PABLS	10//99-12//99
Except Special Education	Rhode Island	Y		42040 AAW		RIBLS	10//99-12//99
Except Special Education	Providence-Fall River-Warwick MSA, RI-MA	Y		41840 AAW		RIBLS	10//99-12//99
Except Special Education	South Carolina	Y		33540 AAW		SCBLS	10//99-12//99
Except Special Education	Charleston-North Charleston MSA, SC	Y		32310 AAW		SCBLS	10//99-12//99
Except Special Education	Columbia MSA, SC	Y		31900 AAW		SCBLS	10//99-12//99
Except Special Education	Greenville-Spartanburg-Anderson MSA, SC	Y		34860 AAW		SCBLS	10//99-12//99
Except Special Education	South Dakota	Y		28330 AAW		SDBLS	10//99-12//99
Except Special Education	Tennessee	Y		31750 AAW		TNBLS	10//99-12//99
Except Special Education	Chattanooga MSA, TN-GA	Y		32290 AAW		TNBLS	10//99-12//99
Except Special Education	Jackson MSA, TN	Y		24370 AAW		TNBLS	10//99-12//99
Except Special Education	Johnson City-Kingsport-Bristol MSA, TN-VA	Y		32420 AAW		TNBLS	10//99-12//99
Except Special Education	Knoxville MSA, TN	Y		35090 AAW		TNBLS	10//99-12//99
Except Special Education	Memphis MSA, TN-AR-MS	Y		31770 AAW		MSBLS	10//99-12//99
Except Special Education	Nashville MSA, TN	Y		31640 AAW		TNBLS	10//99-12//99
Except Special Education	Texas	Y		34510 AAW		TXBLS	10//99-12//99
Except Special Education	Abilene MSA, TX	Y		35020 AAW		TXBLS	10//99-12//99
Except Special Education	Austin-San Marcos MSA, TX	Y		34810 AAW		TXBLS	10//99-12//99
Except Special Education	Beaumont-Port Arthur MSA, TX	Y		34370 AAW		TXBLS	10//99-12//99
Except Special Education	Brazoria PMSA, TX	Y		34070 AAW		TXBLS	10//99-12//99
Except Special Education	Brownsville-Harlingen-San Benito MSA, TX	Y		34800 AAW		TXBLS	10//99-12//99
Except Special Education	Corpus Christi MSA, TX	Y		37650 AAW		TXBLS	10//99-12//99
Except Special Education	Dallas PMSA, TX	Y		32860 AAW		TXBLS	10//99-12//99
Except Special Education	El Paso MSA, TX	Y		34900 AAW		TXBLS	10//99-12//99
Except Special Education	Fort Worth-Arlington PMSA, TX	Y		33830 AAW		TXBLS	10//99-12//99

AAW Average annual wage	AOH Average offered, high	ASH Average starting, high	H Hourly	M Monthly	S Special: hourly and annual
AE Average entry wage	AOL Average offered, low	ASL Average starting, low	HI Highest wage paid	MTC Median total compensation	TQ Third quartile wage
AEX Average experienced wage	APH Average pay, high range	AW Average wage paid	HR High end range	MW Median wage paid	W Weekly
AO Average offered	APL Average pay, low range	FQ First quartile wage	LR Low end range	SQ Second quartile wage	Y Yearly

Occupation/Type/Industry	Location	Per	Low	Mid	High	Source	Date
Kindergarten Teacher							
Except Special Education	Galveston-Texas City PMSA, TX	Y		34400 AAW		TXBLS	10//99-12//99
Except Special Education	Houston PMSA, TX	Y		36920 AAW		TXBLS	10//99-12//99
Except Special Education	Killeen-Temple MSA, TX	Y		31590 AAW		TXBLS	10//99-12//99
Except Special Education	Longview-Marshall MSA, TX	Y		32430 AAW		TXBLS	10//99-12//99
Except Special Education	McAllen-Edinburg-Mission MSA, TX	Y		36230 AAW		TXBLS	10//99-12//99
Except Special Education	San Antonio MSA, TX	Y		35070 AAW		TXBLS	10//99-12//99
Except Special Education	Sherman-Denison MSA, TX	Y		33910 AAW		TXBLS	10//99-12//99
Except Special Education	Texarkana MSA, TX-Texarkana, AR	Y		33530 AAW		TXBLS	10//99-12//99
Except Special Education	Victoria MSA, TX	Y		35890 AAW		TXBLS	10//99-12//99
Except Special Education	Waco MSA, TX	Y		31440 AAW		TXBLS	10//99-12//99
Except Special Education	Utah	Y		33490 AAW		UTBLS	10//99-12//99
Except Special Education	Salt Lake City-Ogden MSA, UT	Y		34580 AAW		UTBLS	10//99-12//99
Except Special Education	Vermont	Y		34660 AAW		VTBLS	10//99-12//99
Except Special Education	Burlington MSA, VT	Y		34220 AAW		VTBLS	10//99-12//99
Except Special Education	Virginia	Y		33090 AAW		VABLS	10//99-12//99
Except Special Education	Charlottesville MSA, VA	Y		31180 AAW		VABLS	10//99-12//99
Except Special Education	Norfolk-Virginia Beach-Newport News MSA, VA-NC	Y		28700 AAW		VABLS	10//99-12//99
Except Special Education	Richmond-Petersburg MSA, VA	Y		39930 AAW		VABLS	10//99-12//99
Except Special Education	Washington	Y		35960 AAW		WABLS	10//99-12//99
Except Special Education	Bellingham MSA, WA	Y		33650 AAW		WABLS	10//99-12//99
Except Special Education	Bremerton PMSA, WA	Y		35760 AAW		WABLS	10//99-12//99
Except Special Education	Olympia PMSA, WA	Y		37540 AAW		WABLS	10//99-12//99
Except Special Education	Richland-Kennewick-Pasco MSA, WA	Y		33740 AAW		WABLS	10//99-12//99
Except Special Education	Seattle-Bellevue-Everett PMSA, WA	Y		36080 AAW		WABLS	10//99-12//99
Except Special Education	Spokane MSA, WA	Y		35830 AAW		WABLS	10//99-12//99
Except Special Education	Tacoma PMSA, WA	Y		38180 AAW		WABLS	10//99-12//99
Except Special Education	Yakima MSA, WA	Y		34580 AAW		WABLS	10//99-12//99
Except Special Education	West Virginia	Y		34620 AAW		WVBLS	10//99-12//99
Except Special Education	Huntington-Ashland MSA, WV-KY-OH	Y		33750 AAW		WVBLS	10//99-12//99
Except Special Education	Wheeling MSA, WV-OH	Y		36620 AAW		WVBLS	10//99-12//99
Except Special Education	Wisconsin	Y		35460 AAW		WIBLS	10//99-12//99
Except Special Education	Appleton-Oshkosh-Neenah MSA, WI	Y		38380 AAW		WIBLS	10//99-12//99
Except Special Education	Eau Claire MSA, WI	Y		38250 AAW		WIBLS	10//99-12//99
Except Special Education	Green Bay MSA, WI	Y		33630 AAW		WIBLS	10//99-12//99
Except Special Education	Janesville-Beloit MSA, WI	Y		35150 AAW		WIBLS	10//99-12//99
Except Special Education	Kenosha PMSA, WI	Y		34170 AAW		WIBLS	10//99-12//99
Except Special Education	La Crosse MSA, WI-MN	Y		37440 AAW		WIBLS	10//99-12//99
Except Special Education	Madison MSA, WI	Y		35920 AAW		WIBLS	10//99-12//99
Except Special Education	Milwaukee-Waukesha PMSA, WI	Y		38760 AAW		WIBLS	10//99-12//99
Except Special Education	Sheboygan MSA, WI	Y		37580 AAW		WIBLS	10//99-12//99
Except Special Education	Wyoming	Y		30800 AAW		WYBLS	10//99-12//99
Except Special Education	Caguas PMSA, PR	Y		16360 AAW		PRBLS	10//99-12//99
Except Special Education	San Juan-Bayamon PMSA, PR	Y		18560 AAW		PRBLS	10//99-12//99
Except Special Education	Virgin Islands	Y		23930 AAW		VIBLS	10//99-12//99
Labor Relations Manager	Los Angeles County, CA	Y		86942 AW		LABJ	1999
Labor Relations Specialist							
Human Resources	United States	Y		55300 AW		HRMAG	1999
Labor Relations Supervisor	United States	Y		80600 AW		TRAVWK2	1999
Laboratory Technician							
Medical Doctor's Office	United States	H		13.20 AEX		MEDEC	2000
Laborer							
Manufacturing	Erie County, NY	Y		43177 AW		BUS1BUF	2000
Manufacturing	Monroe County, NY	Y		51872 AW		BUS1BUF	2000
Manufacturing	Niagara County, NY	Y		46829 AW		BUS1BUF	2000
Manufacturing	Wyoming County, NY	Y		29484 AW		BUS1BUF	2000

AAW Average annual wage	**AOH** Average offered, high	**ASH** Average starting, high	**H** Hourly	**M** Monthly	**S** Special: hourly and annual
AE Average entry wage	**AOL** Average offered, low	**ASL** Average starting, low	**HI** Highest wage paid	**MTC** Median total compensation	**TQ** Third quartile wage
AEX Average experienced wage	**APH** Average pay, high range	**AW** Average wage paid	**HR** High end range	**MW** Median wage paid	**W** Weekly
AO Average offered	**APL** Average pay, low range	**FQ** First quartile wage	**LR** Low end range	**SQ** Second quartile wage	**Y** Yearly

Occupation/Type/Industry	Location	Per	Low	Mid	High	Source	Date
Laborer and Freight, Stock, and Material Mover							
Hand	Alabama	S	8.43 MW	8.88 AW	18460 AAW	ALBLS	10//99-12//99
Hand	Alaska	S	11.23 MW	11.84 AW	24630 AAW	AKBLS	10//99-12//99
Hand	Arizona	S	8.44 MW	8.95 AW	18620 AAW	AZBLS	10//99-12//99
Hand	Arkansas	S	7.95 MW	8.29 AW	17250 AAW	ARBLS	10//99-12//99
Hand	California	S	8.8 MW	9.70 AW	20170 AAW	CABLS	10//99-12//99
Hand	Colorado	S	9.5 MW	9.98 AW	20750 AAW	COBLS	10//99-12//99
Hand	Connecticut	S	9.73 MW	10.25 AW	21310 AAW	CTBLS	10//99-12//99
Hand	Delaware	S	10.02 MW	11.41 AW	23730 AAW	DEBLS	10//99-12//99
Hand	District of Columbia	S	8.07 MW	9.32 AW	19380 AAW	DCBLS	10//99-12//99
Hand	Florida	S	8.05 MW	8.37 AW	17400 AAW	FLBLS	10//99-12//99
Hand	Georgia	S	8.44 MW	9.17 AW	19070 AAW	GABLS	10//99-12//99
Hand	Hawaii	S	10.64 MW	12.27 AW	25510 AAW	HIBLS	10//99-12//99
Hand	Idaho	S	8.94 MW	9.66 AW	20090 AAW	IDBLS	10//99-12//99
Hand	Illinois	S	8.81 MW	9.26 AW	19260 AAW	ILBLS	10//99-12//99
Hand	Indiana	S	9.22 MW	9.86 AW	20500 AAW	INBLS	10//99-12//99
Hand	Iowa	S	9.36 MW	9.96 AW	20720 AAW	IABLS	10//99-12//99
Hand	Kansas	S	8.42 MW	8.92 AW	18550 AAW	KSBLS	10//99-12//99
Hand	Kentucky	S	7.9 MW	8.92 AW	18540 AAW	KYBLS	10//99-12//99
Hand	Louisiana	S	8.01 MW	8.90 AW	18510 AAW	LABLS	10//99-12//99
Hand	Maine	S	9.47 MW	9.84 AW	20470 AAW	MEBLS	10//99-12//99
Hand	Maryland	S	8.38 MW	9.13 AW	18990 AAW	MDBLS	10//99-12//99
Hand	Massachusetts	S	10.17 MW	10.62 AW	22090 AAW	MABLS	10//99-12//99
Hand	Michigan	S	10.02 MW	11.67 AW	24270 AAW	MIBLS	10//99-12//99
Hand	Minnesota	S	9.41 MW	10.15 AW	21120 AAW	MNBLS	10//99-12//99
Hand	Mississippi	S	7.95 MW	8.51 AW	17700 AAW	MSBLS	10//99-12//99
Hand	Missouri	S	9.45 MW	9.79 AW	20360 AAW	MOBLS	10//99-12//99
Hand	Montana	S	7.49 MW	8.06 AW	16760 AAW	MTBLS	10//99-12//99
Hand	Nebraska	S	8.9 MW	9.30 AW	19350 AAW	NEBLS	10//99-12//99
Hand	Nevada	S	8.69 MW	9.14 AW	19000 AAW	NVBLS	10//99-12//99
Hand	New Hampshire	S	9.57 MW	9.74 AW	20260 AAW	NHBLS	10//99-12//99
Hand	New Jersey	S	9.13 MW	9.75 AW	20280 AAW	NJBLS	10//99-12//99
Hand	New Mexico	S	7.68 MW	8.71 AW	18120 AAW	NMBLS	10//99-12//99
Hand	New York	S	9.44 MW	10.38 AW	21580 AAW	NYBLS	10//99-12//99
Hand	North Carolina	S	8.38 MW	9.03 AW	18790 AAW	NCBLS	10//99-12//99
Hand	North Dakota	S	8.67 MW	8.91 AW	18540 AAW	NDBLS	10//99-12//99
Hand	Ohio	S	9.22 MW	10.08 AW	20970 AAW	OHBLS	10//99-12//99
Hand	Oklahoma	S	7.56 MW	8.82 AW	18340 AAW	OKBLS	10//99-12//99
Hand	Oregon	S	8.66 MW	9.54 AW	19840 AAW	ORBLS	10//99-12//99
Hand	Pennsylvania	S	9.17 MW	9.71 AW	20200 AAW	PABLS	10//99-12//99
Hand	Rhode Island	S	9.01 MW	9.54 AW	19840 AAW	RIBLS	10//99-12//99
Hand	South Carolina	S	8.16 MW	9.10 AW	18920 AAW	SCBLS	10//99-12//99
Hand	South Dakota	S	7.51 MW	7.65 AW	15920 AAW	SDBLS	10//99-12//99
Hand	Tennessee	S	9.45 MW	10.48 AW	21800 AAW	TNBLS	10//99-12//99
Hand	Texas	S	7.92 MW	8.44 AW	17560 AAW	TXBLS	10//99-12//99
Hand	Utah	S	9.38 MW	9.82 AW	20420 AAW	UTBLS	10//99-12//99
Hand	Vermont	S	9.01 MW	9.13 AW	18990 AAW	VTBLS	10//99-12//99
Hand	Virginia	S	8.44 MW	8.81 AW	18330 AAW	VABLS	10//99-12//99
Hand	Washington	S	9.19 MW	10.06 AW	20920 AAW	WABLS	10//99-12//99
Hand	West Virginia	S	6.23 MW	6.70 AW	13940 AAW	WVBLS	10//99-12//99
Hand	Wisconsin	S	9.26 MW	9.64 AW	20050 AAW	WIBLS	10//99-12//99
Hand	Wyoming	S	8.39 MW	9.60 AW	19970 AAW	WYBLS	10//99-12//99
Hand	Puerto Rico	S	6.17 MW	7.41 AW	15420 AAW	PRBLS	10//99-12//99
Hand	Guam	S	6.75 MW	7.05 AW	14660 AAW	GUBLS	10//99-12//99
Landscape Architect	Arizona	S	15.76 MW	21.04 AW	43770 AAW	AZBLS	10//99-12//99
	Phoenix-Mesa MSA, AZ	S	24.45 MW	21.08 AW	50870 AAW	AZBLS	10//99-12//99
	Tucson MSA, AZ	S	15.50 MW	14.70 AW	32250 AAW	AZBLS	10//99-12//99
	Arkansas	S	17.22 MW	16.33 AW	33970 AAW	ARBLS	10//99-12//99
	California	S	24.54 MW	25.27 AW	52560 AAW	CABLS	10//99-12//99
	Los Angeles-Long Beach PMSA, CA	S	29.45 MW	30.63 AW	61250 AAW	CABLS	10//99-12//99
	Oakland PMSA, CA	S	28.86 MW	29.05 AW	60030 AAW	CABLS	10//99-12//99
	Orange County PMSA, CA	S	30.38 MW	26.57 AW	63190 AAW	CABLS	10//99-12//99
	Riverside-San Bernardino PMSA, CA	S	25.90 MW	26.54 AW	53880 AAW	CABLS	10//99-12//99
	San Diego MSA, CA	S	27.70 MW	28.39 AW	57620 AAW	CABLS	10//99-12//99
	San Francisco PMSA, CA	S	22.31 MW	19.27 AW	46400 AAW	CABLS	10//99-12//99
	San Luis Obispo-Atascadero-Paso Robles MSA, CA	S	21.17 MW	20.03 AW	44030 AAW	CABLS	10//99-12//99
	Colorado	S	18.32 MW	21.22 AW	44130 AAW	COBLS	10//99-12//99

AAW	Average annual wage	AOH	Average offered, high	ASH	Average starting, high	H	Hourly	M	Monthly	S	Special: hourly and annual
AE	Average entry wage	AOL	Average offered, low	ASL	Average starting, low	HI	Highest wage paid	MTC	Median total compensation	TQ	Third quartile wage
AEX	Average experienced wage	APH	Average pay, high range	AW	Average wage paid	HR	High end range	MW	Median wage paid	W	Weekly
AO	Average offered	APL	Average pay, low range	FQ	First quartile wage	LR	Low end range	SQ	Second quartile wage	Y	Yearly

829

Occupation/Type/Industry	Location	Per	Low	Mid	High	Source	Date
Landscape Architect	Denver PMSA, CO	S	24.65 MW	23.20 AW	51270 AAW	COBLS	10//99-12//99
	Fort Collins-Loveland MSA, CO	S	19.56 MW	18.18 AW	40690 AAW	COBLS	10//99-12//99
	Grand Junction MSA, CO	S	20.95 MW	19.18 AW	43580 AAW	COBLS	10//99-12//99
	Connecticut	S	18.39 MW	18.98 AW	39480 AAW	CTBLS	10//99-12//99
	Hartford MSA, CT	S	14.26 MW	11.19 AW	29660 AAW	CTBLS	10//99-12//99
	New Haven-Meriden PMSA, CT	S	20.98 MW	19.96 AW	43640 AAW	CTBLS	10//99-12//99
	District of Columbia	S	25.94 MW	30.21 AW	62830 AAW	DCBLS	10//99-12//99
	Washington PMSA, DC-MD-VA-WV	S	22.29 MW	20.84 AW	46370 AAW	DCBLS	10//99-12//99
	Florida	S	18.95 MW	21.01 AW	43700 AAW	FLBLS	10//99-12//99
	Fort Lauderdale PMSA, FL	S	19.64 MW	17.79 AW	40850 AAW	FLBLS	10//99-12//99
	Fort Myers-Cape Coral MSA, FL	S	13.93 MW	11.45 AW	28980 AAW	FLBLS	10//99-12//99
	Jacksonville MSA, FL	S	28.62 MW	29.25 AW	59520 AAW	FLBLS	10//99-12//99
	Orlando MSA, FL	S	24.36 MW	22.40 AW	50670 AAW	FLBLS	10//99-12//99
	Sarasota-Bradenton MSA, FL	S	21.40 MW	21.37 AW	44520 AAW	FLBLS	10//99-12//99
	Tampa-St. Petersburg-Clearwater MSA, FL	S	20.77 MW	19.11 AW	43210 AAW	FLBLS	10//99-12//99
	West Palm Beach-Boca Raton MSA, FL	S	15.82 MW	14.69 AW	32910 AAW	FLBLS	10//99-12//99
	Georgia	S	16.66 MW	20.20 AW	42010 AAW	GABLS	10//99-12//99
	Athens MSA, GA	S	16.44 MW	14.78 AW	34190 AAW	GABLS	10//99-12//99
	Atlanta MSA, GA	S	20.25 MW	16.65 AW	42110 AAW	GABLS	10//99-12//99
	Hawaii	S	54.83 MW	42.85 AW	89130 AAW	HIBLS	10//99-12//99
	Honolulu MSA, HI	S	47.20 MW	61.90 AW	98170 AAW	HIBLS	10//99-12//99
	Idaho	S	14 MW	16.92 AW	35190 AAW	IDBLS	10//99-12//99
	Illinois	S	13.41 MW	16.60 AW	34530 AAW	ILBLS	10//99-12//99
	Chicago PMSA, IL	S	16.67 MW	13.27 AW	34670 AAW	ILBLS	10//99-12//99
	Indiana	S	16.86 MW	19.06 AW	39640 AAW	INBLS	10//99-12//99
	Fort Wayne MSA, IN	S	15.12 MW	13.52 AW	31460 AAW	INBLS	10//99-12//99
	Indianapolis MSA, IN	S	20.64 MW	17.69 AW	42930 AAW	INBLS	10//99-12//99
	Iowa	S	17.74 MW	19.31 AW	40170 AAW	IABLS	10//99-12//99
	Des Moines MSA, IA	S	21.71 MW	18.97 AW	45150 AAW	IABLS	10//99-12//99
	Kansas	S	18.19 MW	18.08 AW	37610 AAW	KSBLS	10//99-12//99
	Kentucky	S	16.94 MW	18.72 AW	38930 AAW	KYBLS	10//99-12//99
	Lexington MSA, KY	S	17.09 MW	16.10 AW	35540 AAW	KYBLS	10//99-12//99
	Louisville MSA, KY-IN	S	21.30 MW	20.25 AW	44310 AAW	KYBLS	10//99-12//99
	Louisiana	S	14.25 MW	14.41 AW	29980 AAW	LABLS	10//99-12//99
	Baton Rouge MSA, LA	S	13.18 MW	11.55 AW	27420 AAW	LABLS	10//99-12//99
	Maine	S	20.81 MW	20.19 AW	41990 AAW	MEBLS	10//99-12//99
	Maryland	S	18.91 MW	20.03 AW	41660 AAW	MDBLS	10//99-12//99
	Baltimore PMSA, MD	S	21.76 MW	21.71 AW	45260 AAW	MDBLS	10//99-12//99
	Massachusetts	S	20.72 MW	22.11 AW	45980 AAW	MABLS	10//99-12//99
	Boston PMSA, MA-NH	S	22.22 MW	20.53 AW	46210 AAW	MABLS	10//99-12//99
	Michigan	S	19.35 MW	20.39 AW	42400 AAW	MIBLS	10//99-12//99
	Detroit PMSA, MI	S	21.33 MW	20.57 AW	44370 AAW	MIBLS	10//99-12//99
	Grand Rapids-Muskegon-Holland MSA, MI	S	20.34 MW	17.28 AW	42310 AAW	MIBLS	10//99-12//99
	Minnesota	S	20.61 MW	22.52 AW	46850 AAW	MNBLS	10//99-12//99
	Minneapolis-St. Paul MSA, MN-WI	S	22.70 MW	20.90 AW	47210 AAW	MNBLS	10//99-12//99
	Mississippi	S	16.45 MW	18.93 AW	39380 AAW	MSBLS	10//99-12//99
	Jackson MSA, MS	S	19.04 MW	16.19 AW	39600 AAW	MSBLS	10//99-12//99
	Missouri	S	12.7 MW	15.78 AW	32820 AAW	MOBLS	10//99-12//99
	Kansas City MSA, MO-KS	S	19.35 MW	18.00 AW	40240 AAW	MOBLS	10//99-12//99
	Nebraska	S	18.38 MW	20.49 AW	42630 AAW	NEBLS	10//99-12//99
	Omaha MSA, NE-IA	S	21.04 MW	18.70 AW	43770 AAW	NEBLS	10//99-12//99
	Nevada	S	27.04 MW	30.21 AW	62840 AAW	NVBLS	10//99-12//99
	Las Vegas MSA, NV-AZ	S	31.42 MW	29.18 AW	65350 AAW	NVBLS	10//99-12//99
	Reno MSA, NV	S	27.26 MW	24.95 AW	56690 AAW	NVBLS	10//99-12//99
	New Jersey	S	21 MW	21.42 AW	44550 AAW	NJBLS	10//99-12//99
	Bergen-Passaic PMSA, NJ	S	33.17 MW	31.00 AW	69000 AAW	NJBLS	10//99-12//99
	Newark PMSA, NJ	S	19.38 MW	17.87 AW	40320 AAW	NJBLS	10//99-12//99
	Trenton PMSA, NJ	S	23.54 MW	23.45 AW	48960 AAW	NJBLS	10//99-12//99
	New Mexico	S	19.77 MW	21.33 AW	44360 AAW	NMBLS	10//99-12//99
	New York	S	22.74 MW	23.26 AW	48390 AAW	NYBLS	10//99-12//99
	Albany-Schenectady-Troy MSA, NY	S	23.78 MW	23.30 AW	49460 AAW	NYBLS	10//99-12//99
	Nassau-Suffolk PMSA, NY	S	26.92 MW	23.24 AW	56000 AAW	NYBLS	10//99-12//99
	New York PMSA, NY	S	22.45 MW	22.14 AW	46700 AAW	NYBLS	10//99-12//99

Occupation/Type/Industry	Location	Per	Low	Mid	High	Source	Date
Landscape Architect	Syracuse MSA, NY	S	22.15 MW	22.72 AW	46070 AAW	NYBLS	10//99-12//99
	North Carolina	S	18.9 MW	22.12 AW	46010 AAW	NCBLS	10//99-12//99
	Asheville MSA, NC	S	22.31 MW	19.70 AW	46400 AAW	NCBLS	10//99-12//99
	Charlotte-Gastonia-Rock Hill MSA, NC-SC	S	19.43 MW	16.77 AW	40420 AAW	NCBLS	10//99-12//99
	Raleigh-Durham-Chapel Hill MSA, NC	S	26.48 MW	20.81 AW	55080 AAW	NCBLS	10//99-12//99
	Ohio	S	23.01 MW	25.47 AW	52980 AAW	OHBLS	10//99-12//99
	Cleveland-Lorain-Elyria PMSA, OH	S	25.93 MW	25.04 AW	53940 AAW	OHBLS	10//99-12//99
	Columbus MSA, OH	S	18.03 MW	17.19 AW	37510 AAW	OHBLS	10//99-12//99
	Oklahoma	S	15.4 MW	16.93 AW	35220 AAW	OKBLS	10//99-12//99
	Oklahoma City MSA, OK	S	20.33 MW	18.59 AW	42290 AAW	OKBLS	10//99-12//99
	Oregon	S	22.74 MW	23.29 AW	48440 AAW	ORBLS	10//99-12//99
	Eugene-Springfield MSA, OR	S	19.84 MW	18.46 AW	41270 AAW	ORBLS	10//99-12//99
	Portland-Vancouver PMSA, OR-WA	S	23.65 MW	23.15 AW	49200 AAW	ORBLS	10//99-12//99
	Pennsylvania	S	18.42 MW	19.78 AW	41150 AAW	PABLS	10//99-12//99
	Harrisburg-Lebanon-Carlisle MSA, PA	S	26.09 MW	29.84 AW	54260 AAW	PABLS	10//99-12//99
	Lancaster MSA, PA	S	24.91 MW	24.91 AW	51820 AAW	PABLS	10//99-12//99
	Philadelphia PMSA, PA-NJ	S	20.05 MW	19.22 AW	41710 AAW	PABLS	10//99-12//99
	Pittsburgh MSA, PA	S	15.21 MW	12.06 AW	31630 AAW	PABLS	10//99-12//99
	South Carolina	S	17.6 MW	18.67 AW	38840 AAW	SCBLS	10//99-12//99
	Charleston-North Charleston MSA, SC	S	17.86 MW	13.52 AW	37140 AAW	SCBLS	10//99-12//99
	South Dakota	S	15.69 MW	17.52 AW	36440 AAW	SDBLS	10//99-12//99
	Tennessee	S	13.87 MW	17.13 AW	35630 AAW	TNBLS	10//99-12//99
	Knoxville MSA, TN	S	20.97 MW	16.28 AW	43630 AAW	TNBLS	10//99-12//99
	Memphis MSA, TN-AR-MS	S	20.05 MW	17.85 AW	41710 AAW	MSBLS	10//99-12//99
	Nashville MSA, TN	S	15.85 MW	13.14 AW	32960 AAW	TNBLS	10//99-12//99
	Texas	S	20.45 MW	24.28 AW	50500 AAW	TXBLS	10//99-12//99
	Austin-San Marcos MSA, TX	S	24.66 MW	26.03 AW	51290 AAW	TXBLS	10//99-12//99
	Dallas PMSA, TX	S	21.37 MW	19.20 AW	44450 AAW	TXBLS	10//99-12//99
	Houston PMSA, TX	S	21.17 MW	21.85 AW	44040 AAW	TXBLS	10//99-12//99
	San Antonio MSA, TX	S	20.84 MW	18.61 AW	43350 AAW	TXBLS	10//99-12//99
	Utah	S	19.56 MW	22.84 AW	47510 AAW	UTBLS	10//99-12//99
	Vermont	S	16.43 MW	22.41 AW	46610 AAW	VTBLS	10//99-12//99
	Virginia	S	16.02 MW	17.95 AW	37340 AAW	VABLS	10//99-12//99
	Charlottesville MSA, VA	S	15.01 MW	14.99 AW	31220 AAW	VABLS	10//99-12//99
	Norfolk-Virginia Beach-Newport News MSA, VA-NC	S	19.60 MW	17.50 AW	40770 AAW	VABLS	10//99-12//99
	Richmond-Petersburg MSA, VA	S	17.08 MW	17.02 AW	35520 AAW	VABLS	10//99-12//99
	Roanoke MSA, VA	S	17.84 MW	18.21 AW	37100 AAW	VABLS	10//99-12//99
	Washington	S	22.92 MW	23.61 AW	49110 AAW	WABLS	10//99-12//99
	Seattle-Bellevue-Everett PMSA, WA	S	24.00 MW	23.16 AW	49910 AAW	WABLS	10//99-12//99
	Spokane MSA, WA	S	15.47 MW	13.65 AW	32180 AAW	WABLS	10//99-12//99
	Wisconsin	S	17.89 MW	19.73 AW	41030 AAW	WIBLS	10//99-12//99
	Madison MSA, WI	S	17.82 MW	17.36 AW	37050 AAW	WIBLS	10//99-12//99
	Milwaukee-Waukesha PMSA, WI	S	21.82 MW	19.20 AW	45380 AAW	WIBLS	10//99-12//99
	Puerto Rico	S	18.13 MW	19.45 AW	40450 AAW	PRBLS	10//99-12//99
Landscaping and Groundskeeping Worker	Alabama	S	7.5 MW	8.02 AW	16680 AAW	ALBLS	10//99-12//99
	Alaska	S	11.75 MW	13.33 AW	27730 AAW	AKBLS	10//99-12//99
	Arizona	S	7.31 MW	7.93 AW	16500 AAW	AZBLS	10//99-12//99
	Arkansas	S	7.35 MW	7.57 AW	15740 AAW	ARBLS	10//99-12//99
	California	S	8.61 MW	9.84 AW	20470 AAW	CABLS	10//99-12//99
	Colorado	S	8.93 MW	9.47 AW	19690 AAW	COBLS	10//99-12//99
	Connecticut	S	11.55 MW	11.84 AW	24630 AAW	CTBLS	10//99-12//99
	Delaware	S	9.01 MW	9.67 AW	20120 AAW	DEBLS	10//99-12//99
	District of Columbia	S	9.68 MW	10.84 AW	22550 AAW	DCBLS	10//99-12//99
	Florida	S	8.11 MW	8.76 AW	18220 AAW	FLBLS	10//99-12//99
	Georgia	S	7.99 MW	8.25 AW	17150 AAW	GABLS	10//99-12//99
	Hawaii	S	10.65 MW	10.67 AW	22200 AAW	HIBLS	10//99-12//99
	Idaho	S	8.08 MW	8.83 AW	18360 AAW	IDBLS	10//99-12//99
	Illinois	S	9.54 MW	10.20 AW	21210 AAW	ILBLS	10//99-12//99
	Indiana	S	8.15 MW	8.55 AW	17790 AAW	INBLS	10//99-12//99

AAW	Average annual wage	AOH	Average offered, high	ASH	Average starting, high	H	Hourly	M	Monthly	S	Special: hourly and annual
AE	Average entry wage	AOL	Average offered, low	ASL	Average starting, low	HI	Highest wage paid	MTC	Median total compensation	TQ	Third quartile wage
AEX	Average experienced wage	APH	Average pay, high range	AW	Average wage paid	HR	High end range	MW	Median wage paid	W	Weekly
AO	Average offered	APL	Average pay, low range	FQ	First quartile wage	LR	Low end range	SQ	Second quartile wage	Y	Yearly

Occupation/Type/Industry	Location	Per	Low	Mid	High	Source	Date
Landscaping and Groundskeeping Worker	Iowa	S	8.15 MW	8.82 AW	18340 AAW	IABLS	10//99-12//99
	Kansas	S	7.92 MW	8.41 AW	17490 AAW	KSBLS	10//99-12//99
	Kentucky	S	8.62 MW	8.86 AW	18430 AAW	KYBLS	10//99-12//99
	Louisiana	S	7.68 MW	7.99 AW	16620 AAW	LABLS	10//99-12//99
	Maine	S	9.13 MW	9.32 AW	19390 AAW	MEBLS	10//99-12//99
	Maryland	S	8.85 MW	9.26 AW	19270 AAW	MDBLS	10//99-12//99
	Massachusetts	S	10.19 MW	10.88 AW	22640 AAW	MABLS	10//99-12//99
	Michigan	S	8.69 MW	9.45 AW	19660 AAW	MIBLS	10//99-12//99
	Minnesota	S	9.63 MW	10.19 AW	21200 AAW	MNBLS	10//99-12//99
	Mississippi	S	7.59 MW	7.89 AW	16400 AAW	MSBLS	10//99-12//99
	Missouri	S	8.35 MW	8.93 AW	18580 AAW	MOBLS	10//99-12//99
	Montana	S	7.65 MW	8.44 AW	17560 AAW	MTBLS	10//99-12//99
	Nebraska	S	8.36 MW	8.83 AW	18360 AAW	NEBLS	10//99-12//99
	Nevada	S	7.97 MW	8.82 AW	18340 AAW	NVBLS	10//99-12//99
	New Hampshire	S	9.48 MW	10.12 AW	21040 AAW	NHBLS	10//99-12//99
	New Jersey	S	10.17 MW	11.35 AW	23610 AAW	NJBLS	10//99-12//99
	New Mexico	S	7.74 MW	8.03 AW	16710 AAW	NMBLS	10//99-12//99
	New York	S	9.51 MW	10.43 AW	21700 AAW	NYBLS	10//99-12//99
	North Carolina	S	8.39 MW	8.86 AW	18440 AAW	NCBLS	10//99-12//99
	North Dakota	S	7.34 MW	7.75 AW	16120 AAW	NDBLS	10//99-12//99
	Ohio	S	8.69 MW	9.40 AW	19540 AAW	OHBLS	10//99-12//99
	Oklahoma	S	7.62 MW	7.91 AW	16450 AAW	OKBLS	10//99-12//99
	Oregon	S	9.41 MW	9.99 AW	20780 AAW	ORBLS	10//99-12//99
	Pennsylvania	S	8.64 MW	9.29 AW	19330 AAW	PABLS	10//99-12//99
	Rhode Island	S	10.01 MW	10.13 AW	21080 AAW	RIBLS	10//99-12//99
	South Carolina	S	8.03 MW	8.44 AW	17550 AAW	SCBLS	10//99-12//99
	South Dakota	S	7.96 MW	8.32 AW	17300 AAW	SDBLS	10//99-12//99
	Tennessee	S	8.17 MW	8.78 AW	18260 AAW	TNBLS	10//99-12//99
	Texas	S	7.73 MW	8.10 AW	16850 AAW	TXBLS	10//99-12//99
	Utah	S	8.25 MW	8.88 AW	18470 AAW	UTBLS	10//99-12//99
	Vermont	S	8.71 MW	10.11 AW	21030 AAW	VTBLS	10//99-12//99
	Virginia	S	8.29 MW	8.91 AW	18530 AAW	VABLS	10//99-12//99
	Washington	S	9.69 MW	10.44 AW	21720 AAW	WABLS	10//99-12//99
	West Virginia	S	7.08 MW	7.65 AW	15920 AAW	WVBLS	10//99-12//99
	Wisconsin	S	9.01 MW	9.69 AW	20150 AAW	WIBLS	10//99-12//99
	Wyoming	S	8.08 MW	8.94 AW	18590 AAW	WYBLS	10//99-12//99
	Puerto Rico	S	6.08 MW	6.23 AW	12960 AAW	PRBLS	10//99-12//99
	Virgin Islands	S	7.21 MW	7.39 AW	15370 AAW	VIBLS	10//99-12//99
	Guam	S	7.21 MW	7.73 AW	16080 AAW	GUBLS	10//99-12//99
Lathe and Turning Machine Tool Setter, Operator, and Tender							
Metals and Plastics	Alabama	S	16.51 MW	16.42 AW	34150 AAW	ALBLS	10//99-12//99
Metals and Plastics	Birmingham MSA, AL	S	14.31 MW	14.98 AW	29760 AAW	ALBLS	10//99-12//99
Metals and Plastics	Arizona	S	12.93 MW	13.86 AW	28830 AAW	AZBLS	10//99-12//99
Metals and Plastics	Phoenix-Mesa MSA, AZ	S	13.90 MW	12.93 AW	28910 AAW	AZBLS	10//99-12//99
Metals and Plastics	Arkansas	S	11.59 MW	11.73 AW	24400 AAW	ARBLS	10//99-12//99
Metals and Plastics	Fayetteville-Springdale-Rogers MSA, AR	S	14.05 MW	14.82 AW	29220 AAW	ARBLS	10//99-12//99
Metals and Plastics	Fort Smith MSA, AR-OK	S	13.70 MW	14.67 AW	28500 AAW	ARBLS	10//99-12//99
Metals and Plastics	Little Rock-North Little Rock MSA, AR	S	10.17 MW	9.77 AW	21150 AAW	ARBLS	10//99-12//99
Metals and Plastics	California	S	13.87 MW	14.40 AW	29940 AAW	CABLS	10//99-12//99
Metals and Plastics	Fresno MSA, CA	S	14.44 MW	12.66 AW	30040 AAW	CABLS	10//99-12//99
Metals and Plastics	Los Angeles-Long Beach PMSA, CA	S	14.31 MW	14.00 AW	29760 AAW	CABLS	10//99-12//99
Metals and Plastics	Oakland PMSA, CA	S	19.65 MW	19.46 AW	40870 AAW	CABLS	10//99-12//99
Metals and Plastics	Orange County PMSA, CA	S	12.71 MW	13.13 AW	26440 AAW	CABLS	10//99-12//99
Metals and Plastics	Riverside-San Bernardino PMSA, CA	S	11.37 MW	10.63 AW	23650 AAW	CABLS	10//99-12//99
Metals and Plastics	Sacramento PMSA, CA	S	11.01 MW	9.39 AW	22900 AAW	CABLS	10//99-12//99
Metals and Plastics	San Diego MSA, CA	S	13.83 MW	13.18 AW	28770 AAW	CABLS	10//99-12//99
Metals and Plastics	San Francisco PMSA, CA	S	21.42 MW	20.96 AW	44540 AAW	CABLS	10//99-12//99
Metals and Plastics	San Jose PMSA, CA	S	18.84 MW	17.74 AW	39190 AAW	CABLS	10//99-12//99
Metals and Plastics	Santa Barbara-Santa Maria-Lompoc MSA, CA	S	10.54 MW	11.14 AW	21930 AAW	CABLS	10//99-12//99
Metals and Plastics	Ventura PMSA, CA	S	13.07 MW	12.99 AW	27190 AAW	CABLS	10//99-12//99
Metals and Plastics	Colorado	S	15.02 MW	15.67 AW	32590 AAW	COBLS	10//99-12//99
Metals and Plastics	Boulder-Longmont PMSA, CO	S	15.50 MW	15.28 AW	32250 AAW	COBLS	10//99-12//99
Metals and Plastics	Denver PMSA, CO	S	15.69 MW	14.92 AW	32640 AAW	COBLS	10//99-12//99
Metals and Plastics	Connecticut	S	15.29 MW	16.01 AW	33310 AAW	CTBLS	10//99-12//99

AAW Average annual wage	**AOH** Average offered, high	**ASH** Average starting, high	**H** Hourly	**M** Monthly	**S** Special; hourly and annual
AE Average entry wage	**AOL** Average offered, low	**ASL** Average starting, low	**HI** Highest wage paid	**MTC** Median total compensation	**TQ** Third quartile wage
AEX Average experienced wage	**APH** Average pay, high range	**AW** Average wage paid	**HR** High end range	**MW** Median wage paid	**W** Weekly
AO Average offered	**APL** Average pay, low range	**FQ** First quartile wage	**LR** Low end range	**SQ** Second quartile wage	**Y** Yearly

Occupation/Type/Industry	Location	Per	Low	Mid	High	Source	Date
Lathe and Turning Machine Tool Setter, Operator, and Tender							
Metals and Plastics	Bridgeport PMSA, CT	S	14.79 MW	14.66 AW	30750 AAW	CTBLS	10//99-12//99
Metals and Plastics	Danbury PMSA, CT	S	14.75 MW	14.77 AW	30670 AAW	CTBLS	10//99-12//99
Metals and Plastics	Hartford MSA, CT	S	17.06 MW	15.76 AW	35490 AAW	CTBLS	10//99-12//99
Metals and Plastics	New Haven-Meriden PMSA, CT	S	15.20 MW	14.85 AW	31610 AAW	CTBLS	10//99-12//99
Metals and Plastics	Stamford-Norwalk PMSA, CT	S	18.36 MW	18.62 AW	38190 AAW	CTBLS	10//99-12//99
Metals and Plastics	Waterbury PMSA, CT	S	14.38 MW	14.10 AW	29900 AAW	CTBLS	10//99-12//99
Metals and Plastics	Delaware	S	16.6 MW	16.62 AW	34570 AAW	DEBLS	10//99-12//99
Metals and Plastics	Wilmington-Newark PMSA, DE-MD	S	17.05 MW	16.75 AW	35470 AAW	DEBLS	10//99-12//99
Metals and Plastics	Washington PMSA, DC-MD-VA-WV	S	11.34 MW	11.70 AW	23580 AAW	DCBLS	10//99-12//99
Metals and Plastics	Florida	S	12.48 MW	12.92 AW	26880 AAW	FLBLS	10//99-12//99
Metals and Plastics	Daytona Beach MSA, FL	S	11.65 MW	11.62 AW	24230 AAW	FLBLS	10//99-12//99
Metals and Plastics	Fort Lauderdale PMSA, FL	S	12.57 MW	12.34 AW	26150 AAW	FLBLS	10//99-12//99
Metals and Plastics	Jacksonville MSA, FL	S	11.64 MW	11.89 AW	24200 AAW	FLBLS	10//99-12//99
Metals and Plastics	Miami PMSA, FL	S	9.11 MW	8.26 AW	18960 AAW	FLBLS	10//99-12//99
Metals and Plastics	Naples MSA, FL	S	11.90 MW	12.03 AW	24740 AAW	FLBLS	10//99-12//99
Metals and Plastics	Orlando MSA, FL	S	12.83 MW	12.32 AW	26690 AAW	FLBLS	10//99-12//99
Metals and Plastics	Sarasota-Bradenton MSA, FL	S	10.60 MW	10.13 AW	22050 AAW	FLBLS	10//99-12//99
Metals and Plastics	Tampa-St. Petersburg-Clearwater MSA, FL	S	15.17 MW	15.63 AW	31560 AAW	FLBLS	10//99-12//99
Metals and Plastics	West Palm Beach-Boca Raton MSA, FL		16.48 MW	16.91 AW	34270 AAW	FLBLS	10//99-12//99
Metals and Plastics	Georgia	S	14.69 MW	14.53 AW	30220 AAW	GABLS	10//99-12//99
Metals and Plastics	Atlanta MSA, GA	S	14.60 MW	14.27 AW	30380 AAW	GABLS	10//99-12//99
Metals and Plastics	Idaho	S	9.76 MW	10.52 AW	21880 AAW	IDBLS	10//99-12//99
Metals and Plastics	Illinois	S	13.21 MW	14.59 AW	30350 AAW	ILBLS	10//99-12//99
Metals and Plastics	Chicago PMSA, IL	S	14.33 MW	13.43 AW	29810 AAW	ILBLS	10//99-12//99
Metals and Plastics	Decatur MSA, IL	S	12.65 MW	12.48 AW	26310 AAW	ILBLS	10//99-12//99
Metals and Plastics	Peoria-Pekin MSA, IL	S	23.21 MW	23.98 AW	48270 AAW	ILBLS	10//99-12//99
Metals and Plastics	Rockford MSA, IL	S	16.48 MW	15.80 AW	34280 AAW	ILBLS	10//99-12//99
Metals and Plastics	Indiana	S	13.22 MW	13.56 AW	28200 AAW	INBLS	10//99-12//99
Metals and Plastics	Elkhart-Goshen MSA, IN	S	12.56 MW	12.32 AW	26120 AAW	INBLS	10//99-12//99
Metals and Plastics	Fort Wayne MSA, IN	S	14.50 MW	14.77 AW	30170 AAW	INBLS	10//99-12//99
Metals and Plastics	Gary PMSA, IN	S	17.30 MW	18.29 AW	35970 AAW	INBLS	10//99-12//99
Metals and Plastics	Indianapolis MSA, IN	S	13.95 MW	14.17 AW	29010 AAW	INBLS	10//99-12//99
Metals and Plastics	Muncie MSA, IN	S	11.19 MW	10.00 AW	23270 AAW	INBLS	10//99-12//99
Metals and Plastics	South Bend MSA, IN	S	15.42 MW	15.25 AW	32060 AAW	INBLS	10//99-12//99
Metals and Plastics	Iowa	S	14.25 MW	13.85 AW	28810 AAW	IABLS	10//99-12//99
Metals and Plastics	Davenport-Moline-Rock Island MSA, IA-IL	S	13.06 MW	12.74 AW	27170 AAW	IABLS	10//99-12//99
Metals and Plastics	Des Moines MSA, IA	S	14.43 MW	14.94 AW	30020 AAW	IABLS	10//99-12//99
Metals and Plastics	Kansas	S	10.45 MW	11.39 AW	23690 AAW	KSBLS	10//99-12//99
Metals and Plastics	Wichita MSA, KS	S	15.20 MW	14.95 AW	31620 AAW	KSBLS	10//99-12//99
Metals and Plastics	Kentucky	S	11.69 MW	11.57 AW	24060 AAW	KYBLS	10//99-12//99
Metals and Plastics	Lexington MSA, KY	S	11.43 MW	11.68 AW	23780 AAW	KYBLS	10//99-12//99
Metals and Plastics	Louisville MSA, KY-IN	S	11.83 MW	11.90 AW	24600 AAW	KYBLS	10//99-12//99
Metals and Plastics	Louisiana	S	12.99 MW	15.03 AW	31260 AAW	LABLS	10//99-12//99
Metals and Plastics	Baton Rouge MSA, LA	S	18.01 MW	21.76 AW	37470 AAW	LABLS	10//99-12//99
Metals and Plastics	Houma MSA, LA	S	15.34 MW	13.34 AW	31900 AAW	LABLS	10//99-12//99
Metals and Plastics	Shreveport-Bossier City MSA, LA	S	11.17 MW	11.44 AW	23240 AAW	LABLS	10//99-12//99
Metals and Plastics	Maryland	S	12.59 MW	13.64 AW	28360 AAW	MDBLS	10//99-12//99
Metals and Plastics	Baltimore PMSA, MD	S	13.54 MW	12.46 AW	28150 AAW	MDBLS	10//99-12//99
Metals and Plastics	Massachusetts	S	14.81 MW	14.72 AW	30620 AAW	MABLS	10//99-12//99
Metals and Plastics	Boston PMSA, MA-NH	S	16.26 MW	15.68 AW	33810 AAW	MABLS	10//99-12//99
Metals and Plastics	Fitchburg-Leominster PMSA, MA	S	15.28 MW	14.68 AW	31790 AAW	MABLS	10//99-12//99
Metals and Plastics	Lawrence PMSA, MA-NH	S	13.84 MW	14.55 AW	28790 AAW	MABLS	10//99-12//99
Metals and Plastics	Lowell PMSA, MA-NH	S	14.18 MW	14.27 AW	29500 AAW	MABLS	10//99-12//99
Metals and Plastics	Springfield MSA, MA	S	14.27 MW	14.37 AW	29680 AAW	MABLS	10//99-12//99
Metals and Plastics	Worcester PMSA, MA-CT	S	14.31 MW	14.60 AW	29760 AAW	MABLS	10//99-12//99
Metals and Plastics	Michigan	S	16.73 MW	17.15 AW	35680 AAW	MIBLS	10//99-12//99
Metals and Plastics	Ann Arbor PMSA, MI	S	17.21 MW	17.48 AW	35800 AAW	MIBLS	10//99-12//99
Metals and Plastics	Detroit PMSA, MI	S	18.37 MW	18.59 AW	38210 AAW	MIBLS	10//99-12//99
Metals and Plastics	Flint PMSA, MI	S	23.89 MW	24.32 AW	49680 AAW	MIBLS	10//99-12//99
Metals and Plastics	Grand Rapids-Muskegon-Holland MSA, MI	S	22.71 MW	23.96 AW	47230 AAW	MIBLS	10//99-12//99
Metals and Plastics	Jackson MSA, MI	S	10.55 MW	9.96 AW	21940 AAW	MIBLS	10//99-12//99

AAW	Average annual wage	AOH Average offered, high	ASH Average starting, high	H Hourly	M Monthly	S Special: hourly and annual
AE	Average entry wage	AOL Average offered, low	ASL Average starting, low	HI Highest wage paid	MTC Median total compensation	TQ Third quartile wage
AEX	Average experienced wage	APH Average pay, high range	AW Average wage paid	HR High end range	MW Median wage paid	W Weekly
AO	Average offered	APL Average pay, low range	FQ First quartile wage	LR Low end range	SQ Second quartile wage	Y Yearly

Occupation/Type/Industry	Location	Per	Low	Mid	High	Source	Date
Lathe and Turning Machine Tool Setter, Operator, and Tender							
Metals and Plastics	Kalamazoo-Battle Creek MSA, MI	S	13.55 MW	12.83 AW	28180 AAW	MIBLS	10//99-12//99
Metals and Plastics	Lansing-East Lansing MSA, MI	S	14.54 MW	15.01 AW	30240 AAW	MIBLS	10//99-12//99
Metals and Plastics	Saginaw-Bay City-Midland MSA, MI	S	17.16 MW	15.83 AW	35690 AAW	MIBLS	10//99-12//99
Metals and Plastics	Minnesota	S	15.07 MW	15.14 AW	31490 AAW	MNBLS	10//99-12//99
Metals and Plastics	Minneapolis-St. Paul MSA, MN-WI	S	16.28 MW	16.44 AW	33860 AAW	MNBLS	10//99-12//99
Metals and Plastics	Mississippi	S	10.54 MW	10.72 AW	22290 AAW	MSBLS	10//99-12//99
Metals and Plastics	Missouri	S	14.36 MW	14.53 AW	30230 AAW	MOBLS	10//99-12//99
Metals and Plastics	St. Louis MSA, MO-IL	S	17.34 MW	16.13 AW	36060 AAW	MOBLS	10//99-12//99
Metals and Plastics	Nebraska	S	12.32 MW	12.88 AW	26800 AAW	NEBLS	10//99-12//99
Metals and Plastics	Lincoln MSA, NE	S	13.33 MW	13.31 AW	27730 AAW	NEBLS	10//99-12//99
Metals and Plastics	Omaha MSA, NE-IA	S	13.41 MW	11.81 AW	27890 AAW	NEBLS	10//99-12//99
Metals and Plastics	Nevada	S	13.18 MW	12.55 AW	26110 AAW	NVBLS	10//99-12//99
Metals and Plastics	Las Vegas MSA, NV-AZ	S	13.09 MW	13.85 AW	27220 AAW	NVBLS	10//99-12//99
Metals and Plastics	Reno MSA, NV	S	11.78 MW	10.13 AW	24500 AAW	NVBLS	10//99-12//99
Metals and Plastics	New Hampshire	S	12.5 MW	12.95 AW	26940 AAW	NHBLS	10//99-12//99
Metals and Plastics	New Jersey	S	14.38 MW	14.84 AW	30870 AAW	NJBLS	10//99-12//99
Metals and Plastics	Bergen-Passaic PMSA, NJ	S	16.12 MW	16.16 AW	33530 AAW	NJBLS	10//99-12//99
Metals and Plastics	Middlesex-Somerset-Hunterdon PMSA, NJ	S	15.14 MW	13.34 AW	31490 AAW	NJBLS	10//99-12//99
Metals and Plastics	Monmouth-Ocean PMSA, NJ	S	14.58 MW	15.20 AW	30320 AAW	NJBLS	10//99-12//99
Metals and Plastics	Newark PMSA, NJ	S	13.28 MW	11.71 AW	27620 AAW	NJBLS	10//99-12//99
Metals and Plastics	New Mexico	S	11.09 MW	11.11 AW	23110 AAW	NMBLS	10//99-12//99
Metals and Plastics	New York	S	14.68 MW	14.67 AW	30510 AAW	NYBLS	10//99-12//99
Metals and Plastics	Albany-Schenectady-Troy MSA, NY	S	12.53 MW	12.45 AW	26060 AAW	NYBLS	10//99-12//99
Metals and Plastics	Buffalo-Niagara Falls MSA, NY	S	13.93 MW	13.81 AW	28970 AAW	NYBLS	10//99-12//99
Metals and Plastics	Nassau-Suffolk PMSA, NY	S	12.78 MW	10.66 AW	26580 AAW	NYBLS	10//99-12//99
Metals and Plastics	New York PMSA, NY	S	13.81 MW	13.36 AW	28730 AAW	NYBLS	10//99-12//99
Metals and Plastics	Rochester MSA, NY	S	15.26 MW	15.29 AW	31740 AAW	NYBLS	10//99-12//99
Metals and Plastics	Syracuse MSA, NY	S	12.35 MW	12.00 AW	25690 AAW	NYBLS	10//99-12//99
Metals and Plastics	North Carolina	S	14.32 MW	13.95 AW	29020 AAW	NCBLS	10//99-12//99
Metals and Plastics	Asheville MSA, NC	S	13.49 MW	14.03 AW	28050 AAW	NCBLS	10//99-12//99
Metals and Plastics	Charlotte-Gastonia-Rock Hill MSA, NC-SC	S	13.85 MW	13.96 AW	28800 AAW	NCBLS	10//99-12//99
Metals and Plastics	Greensboro--Winston-Salem--High Point MSA, NC	S	12.42 MW	11.71 AW	25840 AAW	NCBLS	10//99-12//99
Metals and Plastics	Hickory-Morganton-Lenoir MSA, NC	S	15.38 MW	15.35 AW	31990 AAW	NCBLS	10//99-12//99
Metals and Plastics	Raleigh-Durham-Chapel Hill MSA, NC	S	12.46 MW	12.35 AW	25920 AAW	NCBLS	10//99-12//99
Metals and Plastics	Ohio	S	14.2 MW	14.33 AW	29810 AAW	OHBLS	10//99-12//99
Metals and Plastics	Akron PMSA, OH	S	13.53 MW	13.30 AW	28150 AAW	OHBLS	10//99-12//99
Metals and Plastics	Canton-Massillon MSA, OH	S	13.45 MW	12.68 AW	27970 AAW	OHBLS	10//99-12//99
Metals and Plastics	Cincinnati PMSA, OH-KY-IN	S	14.28 MW	14.82 AW	29710 AAW	OHBLS	10//99-12//99
Metals and Plastics	Cleveland-Lorain-Elyria PMSA, OH	S	15.78 MW	14.91 AW	32820 AAW	OHBLS	10//99-12//99
Metals and Plastics	Columbus MSA, OH	S	11.22 MW	10.28 AW	23330 AAW	OHBLS	10//99-12//99
Metals and Plastics	Dayton-Springfield MSA, OH	S	15.29 MW	15.08 AW	31800 AAW	OHBLS	10//99-12//99
Metals and Plastics	Hamilton-Middletown PMSA, OH	S	13.39 MW	12.53 AW	27850 AAW	OHBLS	10//99-12//99
Metals and Plastics	Lima MSA, OH	S	12.60 MW	12.27 AW	26210 AAW	OHBLS	10//99-12//99
Metals and Plastics	Mansfield MSA, OH	S	14.89 MW	15.08 AW	30970 AAW	OHBLS	10//99-12//99
Metals and Plastics	Toledo MSA, OH	S	11.85 MW	11.92 AW	24660 AAW	OHBLS	10//99-12//99
Metals and Plastics	Youngstown-Warren MSA, OH	S	12.00 MW	11.35 AW	24960 AAW	OHBLS	10//99-12//99
Metals and Plastics	Oklahoma	S	8.96 MW	9.45 AW	19660 AAW	OKBLS	10//99-12//99
Metals and Plastics	Oklahoma City MSA, OK	S	12.12 MW	12.05 AW	25200 AAW	OKBLS	10//99-12//99
Metals and Plastics	Tulsa MSA, OK	S	11.48 MW	11.34 AW	23880 AAW	OKBLS	10//99-12//99
Metals and Plastics	Oregon	S	16.62 MW	16.67 AW	34670 AAW	ORBLS	10//99-12//99
Metals and Plastics	Portland-Vancouver PMSA, OR-WA	S	18.01 MW	18.83 AW	37460 AAW	ORBLS	10//99-12//99
Metals and Plastics	Pennsylvania	S	13.29 MW	14.45 AW	30050 AAW	PABLS	10//99-12//99
Metals and Plastics	Allentown-Bethlehem-Easton MSA, PA	S	12.89 MW	12.68 AW	26810 AAW	PABLS	10//99-12//99
Metals and Plastics	Erie MSA, PA	S	11.67 MW	11.87 AW	24270 AAW	PABLS	10//99-12//99
Metals and Plastics	Harrisburg-Lebanon-Carlisle MSA, PA	S	13.63 MW	13.07 AW	28350 AAW	PABLS	10//99-12//99

AAW Average annual wage	**AOH** Average offered, high	**ASH** Average starting, high	**H** Hourly	**M** Monthly	**S** Special: hourly and annual
AE Average entry wage	**AOL** Average offered, low	**ASL** Average starting, low	**HI** Highest wage paid	**MTC** Median total compensation	**TQ** Third quartile wage
AEX Average experienced wage	**APH** Average pay, high range	**AW** Average wage paid	**HR** High end range	**MW** Median wage paid	**W** Weekly
AO Average offered	**APL** Average pay, low range	**FQ** First quartile wage	**LR** Low end range	**SQ** Second quartile wage	**Y** Yearly

Occupation/Type/Industry	Location	Per	Low	Mid	High	Source	Date
Lathe and Turning Machine Tool Setter, Operator, and Tender							
Metals and Plastics	Lancaster MSA, PA	S	15.34 MW	14.85 AW	31910 AAW	PABLS	10//99-12//99
Metals and Plastics	Philadelphia PMSA, PA-NJ	S	17.04 MW	17.66 AW	35440 AAW	PABLS	10//99-12//99
Metals and Plastics	Pittsburgh MSA, PA	S	13.15 MW	12.43 AW	27350 AAW	PABLS	10//99-12//99
Metals and Plastics	Reading MSA, PA	S	16.32 MW	15.36 AW	33930 AAW	PABLS	10//99-12//99
Metals and Plastics	Scranton--Wilkes-Barre--Hazleton MSA, PA	S	11.86 MW	12.20 AW	24660 AAW	PABLS	10//99-12//99
Metals and Plastics	York MSA, PA	S	17.37 MW	17.87 AW	36130 AAW	PABLS	10//99-12//99
Metals and Plastics	Rhode Island	S	11.59 MW	12.37 AW	25730 AAW	RIBLS	10//99-12//99
Metals and Plastics	Providence-Fall River-Warwick MSA, RI-MA	S	11.77 MW	10.93 AW	24490 AAW	RIBLS	10//99-12//99
Metals and Plastics	South Carolina	S	14.57 MW	14.33 AW	29800 AAW	SCBLS	10//99-12//99
Metals and Plastics	Columbia MSA, SC	S	10.32 MW	9.73 AW	21460 AAW	SCBLS	10//99-12//99
Metals and Plastics	Greenville-Spartanburg-Anderson MSA, SC	S	14.57 MW	14.59 AW	30310 AAW	SCBLS	10//99-12//99
Metals and Plastics	South Dakota	S	12.13 MW	12.09 AW	25150 AAW	SDBLS	10//99-12//99
Metals and Plastics	Sioux Falls MSA, SD	S	12.30 MW	12.27 AW	25580 AAW	SDBLS	10//99-12//99
Metals and Plastics	Tennessee	S	11.81 MW	12.19 AW	25360 AAW	TNBLS	10//99-12//99
Metals and Plastics	Chattanooga MSA, TN-GA	S	11.61 MW	11.77 AW	24140 AAW	TNBLS	10//99-12//99
Metals and Plastics	Knoxville MSA, TN	S	11.02 MW	11.31 AW	22910 AAW	TNBLS	10//99-12//99
Metals and Plastics	Nashville MSA, TN	S	13.85 MW	14.28 AW	28800 AAW	TNBLS	10//99-12//99
Metals and Plastics	Texas	S	12 MW	12.61 AW	26230 AAW	TXBLS	10//99-12//99
Metals and Plastics	Austin-San Marcos MSA, TX	S	16.50 MW	16.94 AW	34320 AAW	TXBLS	10//99-12//99
Metals and Plastics	Brownsville-Harlingen-San Benito MSA, TX	S	8.20 MW	7.51 AW	17050 AAW	TXBLS	10//99-12//99
Metals and Plastics	Dallas PMSA, TX	S	10.50 MW	10.77 AW	21830 AAW	TXBLS	10//99-12//99
Metals and Plastics	El Paso MSA, TX	S	8.00 MW	7.90 AW	16630 AAW	TXBLS	10//99-12//99
Metals and Plastics	Fort Worth-Arlington PMSA, TX	S	14.96 MW	13.20 AW	31120 AAW	TXBLS	10//99-12//99
Metals and Plastics	Houston PMSA, TX	S	12.82 MW	12.69 AW	26660 AAW	TXBLS	10//99-12//99
Metals and Plastics	Longview-Marshall MSA, TX	S	8.42 MW	6.56 AW	17520 AAW	TXBLS	10//99-12//99
Metals and Plastics	Odessa-Midland MSA, TX	S	11.97 MW	12.07 AW	24890 AAW	TXBLS	10//99-12//99
Metals and Plastics	San Antonio MSA, TX	S	12.30 MW	10.49 AW	25580 AAW	TXBLS	10//99-12//99
Metals and Plastics	Utah	S	13.71 MW	13.53 AW	28140 AAW	UTBLS	10//99-12//99
Metals and Plastics	Vermont	S	14.55 MW	14.43 AW	30010 AAW	VTBLS	10//99-12//99
Metals and Plastics	Burlington MSA, VT	S	13.43 MW	13.73 AW	27940 AAW	VTBLS	10//99-12//99
Metals and Plastics	Virginia	S	12 MW	11.93 AW	24810 AAW	VABLS	10//99-12//99
Metals and Plastics	Washington	S	15.61 MW	16.00 AW	33290 AAW	WABLS	10//99-12//99
Metals and Plastics	Seattle-Bellevue-Everett PMSA, WA	S	17.32 MW	17.04 AW	36020 AAW	WABLS	10//99-12//99
Metals and Plastics	Spokane MSA, WA	S	8.97 MW	8.39 AW	18660 AAW	WABLS	10//99-12//99
Metals and Plastics	West Virginia	S	13.91 MW	12.67 AW	26350 AAW	WVBLS	10//99-12//99
Metals and Plastics	Wisconsin	S	12.48 MW	13.29 AW	27650 AAW	WIBLS	10//99-12//99
Metals and Plastics	Appleton-Oshkosh-Neenah MSA, WI	S	14.95 MW	15.15 AW	31090 AAW	WIBLS	10//99-12//99
Metals and Plastics	Green Bay MSA, WI	S	15.62 MW	15.47 AW	32490 AAW	WIBLS	10//99-12//99
Metals and Plastics	Kenosha PMSA, WI	S	16.97 MW	16.84 AW	35300 AAW	WIBLS	10//99-12//99
Metals and Plastics	Madison MSA, WI	S	12.77 MW	13.25 AW	26570 AAW	WIBLS	10//99-12//99
Metals and Plastics	Milwaukee-Waukesha PMSA, WI	S	13.71 MW	12.68 AW	28520 AAW	WIBLS	10//99-12//99
Metals and Plastics	Racine PMSA, WI	S	12.64 MW	12.74 AW	26280 AAW	WIBLS	10//99-12//99
Metals and Plastics	Wausau MSA, WI	S	13.63 MW	14.03 AW	28340 AAW	WIBLS	10//99-12//99
Metals and Plastics	Puerto Rico	S	9.28 MW	10.43 AW	21690 AAW	PRBLS	10//99-12//99
Metals and Plastics	San Juan-Bayamon PMSA, PR	S	10.30 MW	9.11 AW	21430 AAW	PRBLS	10//99-12//99
Laundry and Dry-Cleaning Worker							
	Alabama	S	6.87 MW	6.97 AW	14490 AAW	ALBLS	10//99-12//99
	Alaska	S	7.91 MW	8.64 AW	17970 AAW	AKBLS	10//99-12//99
	Arizona	S	6.53 MW	6.69 AW	13920 AAW	AZBLS	10//99-12//99
	Arkansas	S	6.67 MW	6.94 AW	14430 AAW	ARBLS	10//99-12//99
	California	S	7.34 MW	7.92 AW	16460 AAW	CABLS	10//99-12//99
	Colorado	S	7.57 MW	7.57 AW	15750 AAW	COBLS	10//99-12//99
	Connecticut	S	8.44 MW	8.72 AW	18150 AAW	CTBLS	10//99-12//99
	Delaware	S	8.43 MW	8.59 AW	17870 AAW	DEBLS	10//99-12//99
	District of Columbia	S	11.82 MW	11.20 AW	23290 AAW	DCBLS	10//99-12//99
	Florida	S	7.04 MW	7.12 AW	14810 AAW	FLBLS	10//99-12//99
	Georgia	S	7.44 MW	7.50 AW	15610 AAW	GABLS	10//99-12//99
	Hawaii	S	8.75 MW	8.98 AW	18680 AAW	HIBLS	10//99-12//99
	Idaho	S	6.98 MW	6.88 AW	14300 AAW	IDBLS	10//99-12//99
	Illinois	S	7.04 MW	7.43 AW	15450 AAW	ILBLS	10//99-12//99
	Indiana	S	6.94 MW	6.94 AW	14440 AAW	INBLS	10//99-12//99

Occupation/Type/Industry	Location	Per	Low	Mid	High	Source	Date
Laundry and Dry-Cleaning Worker	Iowa	S	7.61 MW	7.86 AW	16340 AAW	IABLS	10//99-12//99
	Kansas	S	6.7 MW	6.81 AW	14170 AAW	KSBLS	10//99-12//99
	Kentucky	S	7.6 MW	7.69 AW	16000 AAW	KYBLS	10//99-12//99
	Louisiana	S	6.29 MW	6.45 AW	13420 AAW	LABLS	10//99-12//99
	Maine	S	7.67 MW	7.65 AW	15920 AAW	MEBLS	10//99-12//99
	Maryland	S	7.61 MW	8.81 AW	18320 AAW	MDBLS	10//99-12//99
	Michigan	S	7.69 MW	7.72 AW	16070 AAW	MIBLS	10//99-12//99
	Minnesota	S	9.07 MW	9.08 AW	18900 AAW	MNBLS	10//99-12//99
	Mississippi	S	7.24 MW	7.27 AW	15120 AAW	MSBLS	10//99-12//99
	Missouri	S	6.97 MW	7.38 AW	15340 AAW	MOBLS	10//99-12//99
	Montana	S	6.93 MW	6.99 AW	14550 AAW	MTBLS	10//99-12//99
	Nebraska	S	6.78 MW	7.01 AW	14580 AAW	NEBLS	10//99-12//99
	Nevada	S	7.98 MW	8.13 AW	16920 AAW	NVBLS	10//99-12//99
	New Hampshire	S	7.4 MW	7.56 AW	15730 AAW	NHBLS	10//99-12//99
	New Jersey	S	7.66 MW	7.84 AW	16300 AAW	NJBLS	10//99-12//99
	New Mexico	S	6.41 MW	6.50 AW	13510 AAW	NMBLS	10//99-12//99
	New York	S	7.08 MW	7.92 AW	16460 AAW	NYBLS	10//99-12//99
	North Carolina	S	7.17 MW	7.21 AW	15000 AAW	NCBLS	10//99-12//99
	North Dakota	S	7.3 MW	7.28 AW	15140 AAW	NDBLS	10//99-12//99
	Ohio	S	7.41 MW	7.56 AW	15720 AAW	OHBLS	10//99-12//99
	Oklahoma	S	6.5 MW	6.95 AW	14450 AAW	OKBLS	10//99-12//99
	Oregon	S	7.73 MW	7.94 AW	16510 AAW	ORBLS	10//99-12//99
	Pennsylvania	S	7.7 MW	8.00 AW	16630 AAW	PABLS	10//99-12//99
	Rhode Island	S	7.67 MW	7.75 AW	16120 AAW	RIBLS	10//99-12//99
	South Carolina	S	6.42 MW	6.86 AW	14260 AAW	SCBLS	10//99-12//99
	South Dakota	S	7.49 MW	7.49 AW	15570 AAW	SDBLS	10//99-12//99
	Tennessee	S	6.93 MW	7.08 AW	14730 AAW	TNBLS	10//99-12//99
	Texas	S	6.39 MW	6.82 AW	14180 AAW	TXBLS	10//99-12//99
	Utah	S	7.22 MW	7.24 AW	15050 AAW	UTBLS	10//99-12//99
	Vermont	S	7.82 MW	8.04 AW	16720 AAW	VTBLS	10//99-12//99
	Virginia	S	7.34 MW	7.36 AW	15310 AAW	VABLS	10//99-12//99
	Washington	S	8.25 MW	9.62 AW	20010 AAW	WABLS	10//99-12//99
	West Virginia	S	6.87 MW	7.38 AW	15350 AAW	WVBLS	10//99-12//99
	Wisconsin	S	7.21 MW	7.26 AW	15100 AAW	WIBLS	10//99-12//99
	Wyoming	S	6.22 MW	6.38 AW	13270 AAW	WYBLS	10//99-12//99
	Puerto Rico	S	6.33 MW	6.50 AW	13510 AAW	PRBLS	10//99-12//99
	Virgin Islands	S	7.16 MW	7.06 AW	14670 AAW	VIBLS	10//99-12//99
	Guam	S	6.04 MW	6.14 AW	12780 AAW	GUBLS	10//99-12//99
Law Clerk	Alabama	S	7.65 MW	8.08 AW	16800 AAW	ALBLS	10//99-12//99
	Huntsville MSA, AL	S	7.32 MW	5.89 AW	15220 AAW	ALBLS	10//99-12//99
	Tuscaloosa MSA, AL	S	7.81 MW	7.74 AW	16240 AAW	ALBLS	10//99-12//99
	Alaska	S	15.39 MW	13.96 AW	29030 AAW	AKBLS	10//99-12//99
	Anchorage MSA, AK	S	13.00 MW	14.12 AW	27050 AAW	AKBLS	10//99-12//99
	Arizona	S	16.38 MW	17.99 AW	37410 AAW	AZBLS	10//99-12//99
	Tucson MSA, AZ	S	15.40 MW	14.27 AW	32030 AAW	AZBLS	10//99-12//99
	Arkansas	S	10.77 MW	10.49 AW	21820 AAW	ARBLS	10//99-12//99
	Little Rock-North Little Rock MSA, AR	S	11.34 MW	11.03 AW	23590 AAW	ARBLS	10//99-12//99
	California	S	15.74 MW	17.64 AW	36700 AAW	CABLS	10//99-12//99
	Fresno MSA, CA	S	13.99 MW	13.92 AW	29100 AAW	CABLS	10//99-12//99
	Los Angeles-Long Beach PMSA, CA	S	20.02 MW	15.51 AW	41650 AAW	CABLS	10//99-12//99
	Oakland PMSA, CA	S	16.17 MW	15.97 AW	33640 AAW	CABLS	10//99-12//99
	Orange County PMSA, CA	S	16.55 MW	14.86 AW	34420 AAW	CABLS	10//99-12//99
	Sacramento PMSA, CA	S	14.04 MW	15.07 AW	29200 AAW	CABLS	10//99-12//99
	San Diego MSA, CA	S	18.05 MW	17.42 AW	37540 AAW	CABLS	10//99-12//99
	San Francisco PMSA, CA	S	19.88 MW	16.61 AW	41350 AAW	CABLS	10//99-12//99
	San Jose PMSA, CA	S	21.10 MW	17.45 AW	43890 AAW	CABLS	10//99-12//99
	San Luis Obispo-Atascadero-Paso Robles MSA, CA	S	11.59 MW	13.82 AW	24110 AAW	CABLS	10//99-12//99
	Santa Barbara-Santa Maria-Lompoc MSA, CA	S	12.70 MW	12.61 AW	26420 AAW	CABLS	10//99-12//99
	Colorado	S	12.55 MW	13.18 AW	27410 AAW	COBLS	10//99-12//99
	Denver PMSA, CO	S	13.36 MW	12.72 AW	27800 AAW	COBLS	10//99-12//99
	Connecticut	S	16.81 MW	19.19 AW	39920 AAW	CTBLS	10//99-12//99
	Hartford MSA, CT	S	17.24 MW	15.78 AW	35850 AAW	CTBLS	10//99-12//99
	District of Columbia	S	19.59 MW	20.63 AW	42900 AAW	DCBLS	10//99-12//99
	Washington PMSA, DC-MD-VA-WV	S	17.23 MW	15.25 AW	35830 AAW	DCBLS	10//99-12//99
	Florida	S	13.89 MW	14.94 AW	31080 AAW	FLBLS	10//99-12//99

Occupation/Type/Industry	Location	Per	Low	Mid	High	Source	Date
Law Clerk	Fort Lauderdale PMSA, FL	S	13.93 MW	13.90 AW	28970 AAW	FLBLS	10//99-12//99
	Fort Myers-Cape Coral MSA, FL	S	16.36 MW	12.99 AW	34030 AAW	FLBLS	10//99-12//99
	Miami PMSA, FL	S	19.26 MW	17.37 AW	40070 AAW	FLBLS	10//99-12//99
	Orlando MSA, FL	S	18.31 MW	12.90 AW	38080 AAW	FLBLS	10//99-12//99
	Punta Gorda MSA, FL	S	8.22 MW	7.80 AW	17110 AAW	FLBLS	10//99-12//99
	Tampa-St. Petersburg-Clearwater MSA, FL	S	15.71 MW	15.17 AW	32680 AAW	FLBLS	10//99-12//99
	West Palm Beach-Boca Raton MSA, FL	S	16.01 MW	16.02 AW	33300 AAW	FLBLS	10//99-12//99
	Georgia	S	14.35 MW	14.07 AW	29260 AAW	GABLS	10//99-12//99
	Athens MSA, GA	S	11.17 MW	10.88 AW	23230 AAW	GABLS	10//99-12//99
	Atlanta MSA, GA	S	14.80 MW	14.76 AW	30780 AAW	GABLS	10//99-12//99
	Macon MSA, GA	S	11.98 MW	14.00 AW	24930 AAW	GABLS	10//99-12//99
	Hawaii	S	14.63 MW	13.54 AW	28170 AAW	HIBLS	10//99-12//99
	Honolulu MSA, HI	S	13.23 MW	14.60 AW	27520 AAW	HIBLS	10//99-12//99
	Idaho	S	14.87 MW	15.14 AW	31480 AAW	IDBLS	10//99-12//99
	Illinois	S	11.47 MW	13.23 AW	27530 AAW	ILBLS	10//99-12//99
	Chicago PMSA, IL	S	14.26 MW	12.01 AW	29660 AAW	ILBLS	10//99-12//99
	Indiana	S	13.78 MW	12.93 AW	26900 AAW	INBLS	10//99-12//99
	Bloomington MSA, IN	S	8.56 MW	8.23 AW	17810 AAW	INBLS	10//99-12//99
	Gary PMSA, IN	S	8.57 MW	8.15 AW	17830 AAW	INBLS	10//99-12//99
	Indianapolis MSA, IN	S	13.66 MW	14.19 AW	28400 AAW	INBLS	10//99-12//99
	Iowa	S	11.59 MW	12.98 AW	27000 AAW	IABLS	10//99-12//99
	Des Moines MSA, IA	S	13.28 MW	11.80 AW	27620 AAW	IABLS	10//99-12//99
	Kansas	S	8.92 MW	9.28 AW	19300 AAW	KSBLS	10//99-12//99
	Topeka MSA, KS	S	8.63 MW	8.01 AW	17950 AAW	KSBLS	10//99-12//99
	Kentucky	S	9.58 MW	10.09 AW	20990 AAW	KYBLS	10//99-12//99
	Louisville MSA, KY-IN	S	11.69 MW	11.27 AW	24320 AAW	KYBLS	10//99-12//99
	Louisiana	S	11.55 MW	12.56 AW	26130 AAW	LABLS	10//99-12//99
	Baton Rouge MSA, LA	S	9.47 MW	10.46 AW	19710 AAW	LABLS	10//99-12//99
	Monroe MSA, LA	S	12.10 MW	12.22 AW	25170 AAW	LABLS	10//99-12//99
	New Orleans MSA, LA	S	16.73 MW	17.87 AW	34790 AAW	LABLS	10//99-12//99
	Shreveport-Bossier City MSA, LA	S	10.99 MW	10.88 AW	22860 AAW	LABLS	10//99-12//99
	Maine	S	16.66 MW	16.06 AW	33410 AAW	MEBLS	10//99-12//99
	Maryland	S	14.6 MW	14.15 AW	29430 AAW	MDBLS	10//99-12//99
	Baltimore PMSA, MD	S	12.97 MW	12.71 AW	26980 AAW	MDBLS	10//99-12//99
	Massachusetts	S	12.51 MW	13.01 AW	27060 AAW	MABLS	10//99-12//99
	Boston PMSA, MA-NH	S	12.76 MW	12.49 AW	26540 AAW	MABLS	10//99-12//99
	Michigan	S	8.91 MW	10.23 AW	21280 AAW	MIBLS	10//99-12//99
	Ann Arbor PMSA, MI	S	13.07 MW	11.43 AW	27190 AAW	MIBLS	10//99-12//99
	Detroit PMSA, MI	S	9.46 MW	8.03 AW	19670 AAW	MIBLS	10//99-12//99
	Grand Rapids-Muskegon-Holland MSA, MI	S	13.89 MW	13.25 AW	28900 AAW	MIBLS	10//99-12//99
	Lansing-East Lansing MSA, MI	S	18.07 MW	17.71 AW	37590 AAW	MIBLS	10//99-12//99
	Minnesota	S	12.64 MW	13.66 AW	28410 AAW	MNBLS	10//99-12//99
	Minneapolis-St. Paul MSA, MN-WI	S	13.83 MW	12.72 AW	28760 AAW	MNBLS	10//99-12//99
	Mississippi	S	13.52 MW	14.18 AW	29500 AAW	MSBLS	10//99-12//99
	Missouri	S	11.3 MW	12.29 AW	25550 AAW	MOBLS	10//99-12//99
	Montana	S	12.78 MW	12.75 AW	26510 AAW	MTBLS	10//99-12//99
	Nebraska	S	14.62 MW	14.68 AW	30540 AAW	NEBLS	10//99-12//99
	Lincoln MSA, NE	S	9.60 MW	8.40 AW	19960 AAW	NEBLS	10//99-12//99
	Omaha MSA, NE-IA	S	18.06 MW	18.19 AW	37550 AAW	NEBLS	10//99-12//99
	Nevada	S	18.22 MW	18.31 AW	38080 AAW	NVBLS	10//99-12//99
	Las Vegas MSA, NV-AZ	S	18.15 MW	18.10 AW	37750 AAW	NVBLS	10//99-12//99
	Reno MSA, NV	S	18.95 MW	18.95 AW	39410 AAW	NVBLS	10//99-12//99
	New Jersey	S	16.22 MW	16.30 AW	33910 AAW	NJBLS	10//99-12//99
	Bergen-Passaic PMSA, NJ	S	15.76 MW	15.48 AW	32780 AAW	NJBLS	10//99-12//99
	Jersey City PMSA, NJ	S	17.50 MW	16.16 AW	36400 AAW	NJBLS	10//99-12//99
	Monmouth-Ocean PMSA, NJ	S	15.27 MW	15.70 AW	31760 AAW	NJBLS	10//99-12//99
	Newark PMSA, NJ	S	17.19 MW	17.47 AW	35760 AAW	NJBLS	10//99-12//99
	New Mexico	S	16.63 MW	15.48 AW	32190 AAW	NMBLS	10//99-12//99
	New York	S	15.53 MW	18.68 AW	38850 AAW	NYBLS	10//99-12//99
	Albany-Schenectady-Troy MSA, NY	S	20.27 MW	13.38 AW	42170 AAW	NYBLS	10//99-12//99
	Buffalo-Niagara Falls MSA, NY	S	11.20 MW	11.07 AW	23300 AAW	NYBLS	10//99-12//99
	New York PMSA, NY	S	20.32 MW	17.32 AW	42270 AAW	NYBLS	10//99-12//99
	Rochester MSA, NY	S	20.06 MW	15.31 AW	41730 AAW	NYBLS	10//99-12//99
	North Carolina	S	9.29 MW	10.91 AW	22690 AAW	NCBLS	10//99-12//99

AAW Average annual wage	AOH Average offered, high	ASH Average starting, high	H Hourly	M Monthly	S Special: hourly and annual
AE Average entry wage	AOL Average offered, low	ASL Average starting, low	HI Highest wage paid	MTC Median total compensation	TQ Third quartile wage
AEX Average experienced wage	APH Average pay, high range	AW Average wage paid	HR High end range	MW Median wage paid	W Weekly
AO Average offered	APL Average pay, low range	FQ First quartile wage	LR Low end range	SQ Second quartile wage	Y Yearly

Occupation/Type/Industry	Location	Per	Low	Mid	High	Source	Date
Law Clerk	North Dakota	S	8.38 MW	9.34 AW	19440 AAW	NDBLS	10//99-12//99
	Ohio	S	10.49 MW	11.38 AW	23670 AAW	OHBLS	10//99-12//99
	Akron PMSA, OH	S	9.72 MW	8.43 AW	20220 AAW	OHBLS	10//99-12//99
	Cincinnati PMSA, OH-KY-IN	S	10.99 MW	10.52 AW	22850 AAW	OHBLS	10//99-12//99
	Cleveland-Lorain-Elyria PMSA, OH	S	9.44 MW	8.30 AW	19640 AAW	OHBLS	10//99-12//99
	Columbus MSA, OH	S	11.82 MW	11.51 AW	24580 AAW	OHBLS	10//99-12//99
	Toledo MSA, OH	S	12.68 MW	10.72 AW	26380 AAW	OHBLS	10//99-12//99
	Youngstown-Warren MSA, OH	S	14.40 MW	13.03 AW	29950 AAW	OHBLS	10//99-12//99
	Oklahoma	S	12.14 MW	12.52 AW	26040 AAW	OKBLS	10//99-12//99
	Oklahoma City MSA, OK	S	12.89 MW	12.62 AW	26810 AAW	OKBLS	10//99-12//99
	Tulsa MSA, OK	S	12.37 MW	10.26 AW	25720 AAW	OKBLS	10//99-12//99
	Oregon	S	14.61 MW	15.51 AW	32250 AAW	ORBLS	10//99-12//99
	Portland-Vancouver PMSA, OR-WA	S	15.17 MW	14.10 AW	31560 AAW	ORBLS	10//99-12//99
	Pennsylvania	S	13.21 MW	13.72 AW	28530 AAW	PABLS	10//99-12//99
	Harrisburg-Lebanon-Carlisle MSA, PA	S	13.14 MW	13.30 AW	27330 AAW	PABLS	10//99-12//99
	Philadelphia PMSA, PA-NJ	S	14.21 MW	13.83 AW	29550 AAW	PABLS	10//99-12//99
	Pittsburgh MSA, PA	S	12.32 MW	12.38 AW	25620 AAW	PABLS	10//99-12//99
	Rhode Island	S	18.35 MW	18.66 AW	38810 AAW	RIBLS	10//99-12//99
	Providence-Fall River-Warwick MSA, RI-MA	S	19.11 MW	18.46 AW	39740 AAW	RIBLS	10//99-12//99
	South Carolina	S	11.11 MW	11.69 AW	24320 AAW	SCBLS	10//99-12//99
	Columbia MSA, SC	S	10.36 MW	9.30 AW	21550 AAW	SCBLS	10//99-12//99
	Tennessee	S	8.43 MW	10.28 AW	21380 AAW	TNBLS	10//99-12//99
	Knoxville MSA, TN	S	8.23 MW	7.71 AW	17120 AAW	TNBLS	10//99-12//99
	Nashville MSA, TN	S	14.94 MW	13.43 AW	31080 AAW	TNBLS	10//99-12//99
	Texas	S	12.9 MW	13.46 AW	28000 AAW	TXBLS	10//99-12//99
	Amarillo MSA, TX	S	12.31 MW	10.96 AW	25610 AAW	TXBLS	10//99-12//99
	Dallas PMSA, TX	S	13.49 MW	12.45 AW	28050 AAW	TXBLS	10//99-12//99
	Fort Worth-Arlington PMSA, TX	S	13.24 MW	12.74 AW	27540 AAW	TXBLS	10//99-12//99
	Houston PMSA, TX	S	15.21 MW	15.12 AW	31630 AAW	TXBLS	10//99-12//99
	Lubbock MSA, TX	S	7.93 MW	7.63 AW	16490 AAW	TXBLS	10//99-12//99
	Utah	S	10.78 MW	12.42 AW	25820 AAW	UTBLS	10//99-12//99
	Salt Lake City-Ogden MSA, UT	S	13.93 MW	10.61 AW	28980 AAW	UTBLS	10//99-12//99
	Virginia	S	12.91 MW	14.10 AW	29330 AAW	VABLS	10//99-12//99
	Norfolk-Virginia Beach-Newport News MSA, VA-NC	S	13.95 MW	14.16 AW	29010 AAW	VABLS	10//99-12//99
	Richmond-Petersburg MSA, VA	S	15.19 MW	14.97 AW	31600 AAW	VABLS	10//99-12//99
	Washington	S	8.67 MW	10.34 AW	21510 AAW	WABLS	10//99-12//99
	Seattle-Bellevue-Everett PMSA, WA	S	9.45 MW	8.17 AW	19650 AAW	WABLS	10//99-12//99
	West Virginia	S	10.53 MW	12.76 AW	26550 AAW	WVBLS	10//99-12//99
	Wisconsin	S	12.41 MW	12.46 AW	25920 AAW	WIBLS	10//99-12//99
	Madison MSA, WI	S	10.83 MW	11.76 AW	22530 AAW	WIBLS	10//99-12//99
	Milwaukee-Waukesha PMSA, WI	S	12.92 MW	12.19 AW	26870 AAW	WIBLS	10//99-12//99
	Puerto Rico	S	9.78 MW	10.22 AW	21250 AAW	PRBLS	10//99-12//99
	San Juan-Bayamon PMSA, PR	S	10.50 MW	9.96 AW	21850 AAW	PRBLS	10//99-12//99
Law Teacher							
Postsecondary	Alabama	Y		32560 AAW		ALBLS	10//99-12//99
Postsecondary	California	Y		78440 AAW		CABLS	10//99-12//99
Postsecondary	San Francisco PMSA, CA	Y		95470 AAW		CABLS	10//99-12//99
Postsecondary	Washington PMSA, DC-MD-VA-WV	Y		52370 AAW		DCBLS	10//99-12//99
Postsecondary	Florida	Y		81510 AAW		FLBLS	10//99-12//99
Postsecondary	Illinois	Y		61290 AAW		ILBLS	10//99-12//99
Postsecondary	Chicago PMSA, IL	Y		62940 AAW		ILBLS	10//99-12//99
Postsecondary	Maryland	Y		56950 AAW		MDBLS	10//99-12//99
Postsecondary	Massachusetts	Y		87970 AAW		MABLS	10//99-12//99
Postsecondary	Michigan	Y		70510 AAW		MIBLS	10//99-12//99
Postsecondary	Mississippi	Y		31940 AAW		MSBLS	10//99-12//99
Postsecondary	New Hampshire	Y		66080 AAW		NHBLS	10//99-12//99
Postsecondary	Newark PMSA, NJ	Y		66960 AAW		NJBLS	10//99-12//99
Postsecondary	Ohio	Y		59240 AAW		OHBLS	10//99-12//99
Postsecondary	Dayton-Springfield MSA, OH	Y		25460 AAW		OHBLS	10//99-12//99
Postsecondary	Oklahoma	Y		79090 AAW		OKBLS	10//99-12//99

AAW	Average annual wage	AOH	Average offered, high	ASH	Average starting, high	H	Hourly	M	Monthly	S	Special: hourly and annual
AE	Average entry wage	AOL	Average offered, low	ASL	Average starting, low	HI	Highest wage paid	MTC	Median total compensation	TQ	Third quartile wage
AEX	Average experienced wage	APH	Average pay, high range	AW	Average wage paid	HR	High end range	MW	Median wage paid	W	Weekly
AO	Average offered	APL	Average pay, low range	FQ	First quartile wage	LR	Low end range	SQ	Second quartile wage	Y	Yearly

Occupation/Type/Industry	Location	Per	Low	Mid	High	Source	Date
Law Teacher							
Postsecondary	Pennsylvania	Y		49310 AAW		PABLS	10//99-12//99
Postsecondary	South Carolina	Y		41300 AAW		SCBLS	10//99-12//99
Postsecondary	Tennessee	Y		75600 AAW		TNBLS	10//99-12//99
Postsecondary	Nashville MSA, TN	Y		79700 AAW		TNBLS	10//99-12//99
Postsecondary	Texas	Y		59440 AAW		TXBLS	10//99-12//99
Postsecondary	Fort Worth-Arlington PMSA, TX	Y		45610 AAW		TXBLS	10//99-12//99
Postsecondary	Virginia	Y		70620 AAW		VABLS	10//99-12//99
Lawyer	Alabama	S	47.39 MW	47.34 AW	98460 AAW	ALBLS	10//99-12//99
	Birmingham MSA, AL	S	47.88 MW	45.81 AW	99600 AAW	ALBLS	10//99-12//99
	Decatur MSA, AL	S	25.41 MW	27.45 AW	52850 AAW	ALBLS	10//99-12//99
	Huntsville MSA, AL	S	40.19 MW	44.69 AW	83590 AAW	ALBLS	10//99-12//99
	Montgomery MSA, AL	S	46.15 MW	45.39 AW	95990 AAW	ALBLS	10//99-12//99
	Tuscaloosa MSA, AL	S	60.04 MW	62.82 AW	124890 AAW	ALBLS	10//99-12//99
	Alaska	S	31.26 MW	33.60 AW	69890 AAW	AKBLS	10//99-12//99
	Arizona	S	32.51 MW	33.64 AW	69970 AAW	AZBLS	10//99-12//99
	Flagstaff MSA, AZ-UT	S	38.61 MW	27.60 AW	80300 AAW	AZBLS	10//99-12//99
	Phoenix-Mesa MSA, AZ	S	34.43 MW	34.89 AW	71610 AAW	AZBLS	10//99-12//99
	Tucson MSA, AZ	S	32.76 MW	30.27 AW	68140 AAW	AZBLS	10//99-12//99
	Yuma MSA, AZ	S	28.96 MW	26.76 AW	60230 AAW	AZBLS	10//99-12//99
	Arkansas	S	29.1 MW	34.08 AW	70890 AAW	ARBLS	10//99-12//99
	Fort Smith MSA, AR-OK	S	35.98 MW	36.41 AW	74830 AAW	ARBLS	10//99-12//99
	Little Rock-North Little Rock MSA, AR	S	29.26 MW	27.60 AW	60870 AAW	ARBLS	10//99-12//99
	California	S	51.73 MW	49.43 AW	102820 AAW	CABLS	10//99-12//99
	Bakersfield MSA, CA	S	53.45 MW	56.40 AW	111180 AAW	CABLS	10//99-12//99
	Fresno MSA, CA	S	36.36 MW	35.78 AW	75620 AAW	CABLS	10//99-12//99
	Los Angeles-Long Beach PMSA, CA	S	52.06 MW	57.26 AW	108290 AAW	CABLS	10//99-12//99
	Oakland PMSA, CA	S	42.40 MW	40.87 AW	88200 AAW	CABLS	10//99-12//99
	Orange County PMSA, CA	S	48.02 MW	48.37 AW	99890 AAW	CABLS	10//99-12//99
	Redding MSA, CA	S	39.96 MW	39.58 AW	83120 AAW	CABLS	10//99-12//99
	Riverside-San Bernardino PMSA, CA	S	38.33 MW	39.41 AW	79730 AAW	CABLS	10//99-12//99
	Salinas MSA, CA	S	38.18 MW	37.24 AW	79410 AAW	CABLS	10//99-12//99
	San Diego MSA, CA	S	40.85 MW	39.99 AW	84960 AAW	CABLS	10//99-12//99
	San Francisco PMSA, CA	S	58.55 MW	69.85 AW	121780 AAW	CABLS	10//99-12//99
	San Jose PMSA, CA	S	52.55 MW	52.53 AW	109300 AAW	CABLS	10//99-12//99
	San Luis Obispo-Atascadero-Paso Robles MSA, CA	S	45.24 MW	42.10 AW	94100 AAW	CABLS	10//99-12//99
	Santa Barbara-Santa Maria-Lompoc MSA, CA	S	33.70 MW	33.54 AW	70090 AAW	CABLS	10//99-12//99
	Santa Cruz-Watsonville PMSA, CA	S	39.84 MW	41.17 AW	82870 AAW	CABLS	10//99-12//99
	Santa Rosa PMSA, CA	S	38.46 MW	38.33 AW	80000 AAW	CABLS	10//99-12//99
	Stockton-Lodi MSA, CA	S	38.26 MW	37.91 AW	79580 AAW	CABLS	10//99-12//99
	Ventura PMSA, CA	S	40.12 MW	40.26 AW	83450 AAW	CABLS	10//99-12//99
	Visalia-Tulare-Porterville MSA, CA	S	31.10 MW	29.78 AW	64680 AAW	CABLS	10//99-12//99
	Yuba City MSA, CA	S	39.08 MW	35.44 AW	81290 AAW	CABLS	10//99-12//99
	Colorado	S	38.88 MW	39.21 AW	81560 AAW	COBLS	10//99-12//99
	Denver PMSA, CO	S	42.83 MW	41.11 AW	89080 AAW	COBLS	10//99-12//99
	Pueblo MSA, CO	S	34.90 MW	38.08 AW	72600 AAW	COBLS	10//99-12//99
	Connecticut	S	52.14 MW	51.88 AW	107910 AAW	CTBLS	10//99-12//99
	Bridgeport PMSA, CT	S	44.08 MW	42.71 AW	91680 AAW	CTBLS	10//99-12//99
	Danbury PMSA, CT	S	53.66 MW	46.82 AW	111610 AAW	CTBLS	10//99-12//99
	Hartford MSA, CT	S	50.79 MW	51.23 AW	105630 AAW	CTBLS	10//99-12//99
	New Haven-Meriden PMSA, CT	S	41.69 MW	40.37 AW	86720 AAW	CTBLS	10//99-12//99
	New London-Norwich MSA, CT-RI	S	39.80 MW	39.11 AW	82790 AAW	CTBLS	10//99-12//99
	Delaware	S	35.23 MW	37.43 AW	77850 AAW	DEBLS	10//99-12//99
	Dover MSA, DE	S	36.94 MW	32.64 AW	76820 AAW	DEBLS	10//99-12//99
	Wilmington-Newark PMSA, DE-MD	S	37.94 MW	35.81 AW	78910 AAW	DEBLS	10//99-12//99
	District of Columbia	S	48.15 MW	47.75 AW	99330 AAW	DCBLS	10//99-12//99
	Washington PMSA, DC-MD-VA-WV	S	46.30 MW	46.88 AW	96300 AAW	DCBLS	10//99-12//99
	Jacksonville MSA, FL	S	32.61 MW	30.44 AW	67820 AAW	FLBLS	10//99-12//99
	Lakeland-Winter Haven MSA, FL	S	42.70 MW	47.42 AW	88820 AAW	FLBLS	10//99-12//99

AAW	Average annual wage	AOH	Average offered, high	ASH	Average starting, high	H	Hourly	M	Monthly	S	Special: hourly and annual
AE	Average entry wage	AOL	Average offered, low	ASL	Average starting, low	HI	Highest wage paid	MTC	Median total compensation	TQ	Third quartile wage
AEX	Average experienced wage	APH	Average pay, high range	AW	Average wage paid	HR	High end range	MW	Median wage paid	W	Weekly
AO	Average offered	APL	Average pay, low range	FQ	First quartile wage	LR	Low end range	SQ	Second quartile wage	Y	Yearly

Occupation/Type/Industry	Location	Per	Low	Mid	High	Source	Date
Lawyer	Naples MSA, FL	S	37.32 MW	33.23 AW	77630 AAW	FLBLS	10//99-12//99
	Orlando MSA, FL	S	33.47 MW	32.31 AW	69620 AAW	FLBLS	10//99-12//99
	Punta Gorda MSA, FL	S	41.44 MW	41.66 AW	86200 AAW	FLBLS	10//99-12//99
	Sarasota-Bradenton MSA, FL	S	27.16 MW	24.66 AW	56480 AAW	FLBLS	10//99-12//99
	Tampa-St. Petersburg-Clearwater MSA, FL	S	33.76 MW	32.09 AW	70210 AAW	FLBLS	10//99-12//99
	West Palm Beach-Boca Raton MSA, FL	S	30.23 MW	28.17 AW	62880 AAW	FLBLS	10//99-12//99
	Georgia	S	42.71 MW	43.55 AW	90580 AAW	GABLS	10//99-12//99
	Atlanta MSA, GA	S	44.47 MW	43.33 AW	92500 AAW	GABLS	10//99-12//99
	Columbus MSA, GA-AL	S	43.92 MW	43.86 AW	91350 AAW	GABLS	10//99-12//99
	Macon MSA, GA	S	30.70 MW	28.46 AW	63850 AAW	GABLS	10//99-12//99
	Hawaii	S	31.68 MW	33.34 AW	69340 AAW	HIBLS	10//99-12//99
	Honolulu MSA, HI	S	33.59 MW	30.84 AW	69860 AAW	HIBLS	10//99-12//99
	Idaho	S	26.75 MW	32.55 AW	67710 AAW	IDBLS	10//99-12//99
	Illinois	S	44.74 MW	42.42 AW	88230 AAW	ILBLS	10//99-12//99
	Bloomington-Normal MSA, IL	S	41.31 MW	41.36 AW	85930 AAW	ILBLS	10//99-12//99
	Champaign-Urbana MSA, IL	S	38.51 MW	39.21 AW	80110 AAW	ILBLS	10//99-12//99
	Chicago PMSA, IL	S	43.16 MW	45.64 AW	89760 AAW	ILBLS	10//99-12//99
	Decatur MSA, IL	S	36.96 MW	38.44 AW	76880 AAW	ILBLS	10//99-12//99
	Peoria-Pekin MSA, IL	S	32.39 MW	29.43 AW	67370 AAW	ILBLS	10//99-12//99
	Rockford MSA, IL	S	37.42 MW	36.94 AW	77820 AAW	ILBLS	10//99-12//99
	Springfield MSA, IL	S	28.39 MW	26.69 AW	59050 AAW	ILBLS	10//99-12//99
	Indiana	S	29.28 MW	32.23 AW	67040 AAW	INBLS	10//99-12//99
	Bloomington MSA, IN	S	35.48 MW	36.13 AW	73810 AAW	INBLS	10//99-12//99
	Elkhart-Goshen MSA, IN	S	28.72 MW	21.17 AW	59730 AAW	INBLS	10//99-12//99
	Evansville-Henderson MSA, IN-KY	S	34.25 MW	26.56 AW	71240 AAW	INBLS	10//99-12//99
	Fort Wayne MSA, IN	S	29.85 MW	28.89 AW	62080 AAW	INBLS	10//99-12//99
	Gary PMSA, IN	S	29.59 MW	25.18 AW	61540 AAW	INBLS	10//99-12//99
	Indianapolis MSA, IN	S	32.56 MW	34.24 AW	67730 AAW	INBLS	10//99-12//99
	Lafayette MSA, IN	S	39.70 MW	32.73 AW	82580 AAW	INBLS	10//99-12//99
	South Bend MSA, IN	S	32.19 MW	24.72 AW	66950 AAW	INBLS	10//99-12//99
	Iowa	S	36.48 MW	38.00 AW	79030 AAW	IABLS	10//99-12//99
	Cedar Rapids MSA, IA	S	39.80 MW	38.17 AW	82790 AAW	IABLS	10//99-12//99
	Davenport-Moline-Rock Island MSA, IA-IL	S	30.97 MW	32.09 AW	64410 AAW	IABLS	10//99-12//99
	Des Moines MSA, IA	S	42.28 MW	41.17 AW	87940 AAW	IABLS	10//99-12//99
	Waterloo-Cedar Falls MSA, IA	S	39.58 MW	31.17 AW	82320 AAW	IABLS	10//99-12//99
	Kansas	S	38.58 MW	41.72 AW	86770 AAW	KSBLS	10//99-12//99
	Lawrence MSA, KS	S	26.89 MW	27.39 AW	55920 AAW	KSBLS	10//99-12//99
	Wichita MSA, KS	S	32.74 MW	29.88 AW	68100 AAW	KSBLS	10//99-12//99
	Kentucky	S	33.07 MW	35.08 AW	72960 AAW	KYBLS	10//99-12//99
	Lexington MSA, KY	S	34.83 MW	33.02 AW	72450 AAW	KYBLS	10//99-12//99
	Louisville MSA, KY-IN	S	34.82 MW	33.59 AW	72430 AAW	KYBLS	10//99-12//99
	Louisiana	S	33.69 MW	36.27 AW	75430 AAW	LABLS	10//99-12//99
	Baton Rouge MSA, LA	S	34.92 MW	32.75 AW	72630 AAW	LABLS	10//99-12//99
	Houma MSA, LA	S	15.37 MW	12.83 AW	31960 AAW	LABLS	10//99-12//99
	Lafayette MSA, LA	S	48.98 MW	57.29 AW	101890 AAW	LABLS	10//99-12//99
	Monroe MSA, LA	S	15.97 MW	17.66 AW	33210 AAW	LABLS	10//99-12//99
	New Orleans MSA, LA	S	34.28 MW	32.86 AW	71290 AAW	LABLS	10//99-12//99
	Maine	S	30.94 MW	36.97 AW	76890 AAW	MEBLS	10//99-12//99
	Lewiston-Auburn MSA, ME	S	44.12 MW	37.18 AW	91770 AAW	MEBLS	10//99-12//99
	Portland MSA, ME	S	35.90 MW	32.05 AW	74670 AAW	MEBLS	10//99-12//99
	Maryland	S	32.6 MW	38.33 AW	79720 AAW	MDBLS	10//99-12//99
	Cumberland MSA, MD-WV	S	34.41 MW	31.01 AW	71580 AAW	MDBLS	10//99-12//99
	Hagerstown PMSA, MD	S	20.97 MW	16.82 AW	43620 AAW	MDBLS	10//99-12//99
	Massachusetts	S	56.28 MW	50.56 AW	105170 AAW	MABLS	10//99-12//99
	Boston PMSA, MA-NH	S	52.55 MW	57.91 AW	109290 AAW	MABLS	10//99-12//99
	Brockton PMSA, MA	S	29.25 MW	25.94 AW	60830 AAW	MABLS	10//99-12//99
	Lawrence PMSA, MA-NH	S	39.84 MW	37.42 AW	82870 AAW	MABLS	10//99-12//99
	Lowell PMSA, MA-NH	S	46.01 MW	47.68 AW	95700 AAW	MABLS	10//99-12//99
	Pittsfield MSA, MA	S	53.63 MW	63.92 AW	111560 AAW	MABLS	10//99-12//99
	Springfield MSA, MA	S	30.04 MW	27.81 AW	62490 AAW	MABLS	10//99-12//99
	Worcester PMSA, MA-CT	S	36.25 MW	36.94 AW	75390 AAW	MABLS	10//99-12//99
	Michigan	S	26.89 MW	34.00 AW	70720 AAW	MIBLS	10//99-12//99
	Ann Arbor PMSA, MI	S	34.80 MW	32.14 AW	72380 AAW	MIBLS	10//99-12//99
	Detroit PMSA, MI	S	40.28 MW	38.50 AW	83790 AAW	MIBLS	10//99-12//99
	Grand Rapids-Muskegon-Holland MSA, MI	S	44.21 MW	43.93 AW	91960 AAW	MIBLS	10//99-12//99
	Jackson MSA, MI	S	27.47 MW	29.54 AW	57130 AAW	MIBLS	10//99-12//99

Occupation/Type/Industry	Location	Per	Low	Mid	High	Source	Date
Lawyer	Saginaw-Bay City-Midland						
	MSA, MI	S	24.68 MW	24.67 AW	51340 AAW	MIBLS	10//99-12//99
	Minnesota	S	37.77 MW	39.31 AW	81760 AAW	MNBLS	10//99-12//99
	Duluth-Superior MSA, MN-WI	S	34.19 MW	33.17 AW	71120 AAW	MNBLS	10//99-12//99
	Minneapolis-St. Paul MSA,						
	MN-WI	S	40.09 MW	38.40 AW	83390 AAW	MNBLS	10//99-12//99
	Rochester MSA, MN	S	32.34 MW	29.94 AW	67260 AAW	MNBLS	10//99-12//99
	Mississippi	S	29.31 MW	31.89 AW	66330 AAW	MSBLS	10//99-12//99
	Biloxi-Gulfport-Pascagoula						
	MSA, MS	S	33.81 MW	35.84 AW	70330 AAW	MSBLS	10//99-12//99
	Hattiesburg MSA, MS	S	17.39 MW	15.40 AW	36180 AAW	MSBLS	10//99-12//99
	Jackson MSA, MS	S	33.08 MW	28.59 AW	68800 AAW	MSBLS	10//99-12//99
	Missouri	S	40.25 MW	43.53 AW	90540 AAW	MOBLS	10//99-12//99
	Kansas City MSA, MO-KS	S	45.29 MW	41.27 AW	94200 AAW	MOBLS	10//99-12//99
	St. Louis MSA, MO-IL	S	41.73 MW	41.66 AW	86790 AAW	MOBLS	10//99-12//99
	Montana	S	26.26 MW	31.55 AW	65630 AAW	MTBLS	10//99-12//99
	Billings MSA, MT	S	33.87 MW	27.16 AW	70450 AAW	MTBLS	10//99-12//99
	Great Falls MSA, MT	S	33.74 MW	33.74 AW	70190 AAW	MTBLS	10//99-12//99
	Missoula MSA, MT	S	26.42 MW	23.08 AW	54940 AAW	MTBLS	10//99-12//99
	Nebraska	S	26.93 MW	29.63 AW	61630 AAW	NEBLS	10//99-12//99
	Lincoln MSA, NE	S	24.99 MW	23.21 AW	51970 AAW	NEBLS	10//99-12//99
	Omaha MSA, NE-IA	S	32.01 MW	29.02 AW	66570 AAW	NEBLS	10//99-12//99
	Nevada	S	33.16 MW	37.72 AW	78450 AAW	NVBLS	10//99-12//99
	Las Vegas MSA, NV-AZ	S	34.98 MW	31.53 AW	72770 AAW	NVBLS	10//99-12//99
	New Hampshire	S	54.63 MW	49.18 AW	102290 AAW	NHBLS	10//99-12//99
	Manchester PMSA, NH	S	47.18 MW	47.93 AW	98130 AAW	NHBLS	10//99-12//99
	New Jersey	S	42.48 MW	43.39 AW	90260 AAW	NJBLS	10//99-12//99
	Atlantic-Cape May PMSA, NJ	S	41.00 MW	42.36 AW	85270 AAW	NJBLS	10//99-12//99
	Bergen-Passaic PMSA, NJ	S	41.96 MW	39.63 AW	87280 AAW	NJBLS	10//99-12//99
	Jersey City PMSA, NJ	S	43.37 MW	45.75 AW	90200 AAW	NJBLS	10//99-12//99
	Middlesex-Somerset-						
	Hunterdon PMSA, NJ	S	47.54 MW	42.36 AW	98880 AAW	NJBLS	10//99-12//99
	Newark PMSA, NJ	S	42.91 MW	43.14 AW	89240 AAW	NJBLS	10//99-12//99
	Trenton PMSA, NJ	S	42.18 MW	35.09 AW	87740 AAW	NJBLS	10//99-12//99
	New Mexico	S	32.66 MW	39.26 AW	81650 AAW	NMBLS	10//99-12//99
	Albuquerque MSA, NM	S	41.29 MW	37.48 AW	85890 AAW	NMBLS	10//99-12//99
	Las Cruces MSA, NM	S	35.51 MW	33.92 AW	73860 AAW	NMBLS	10//99-12//99
	New York	S	58.48 MW	52.93 AW	110090 AAW	NYBLS	10//99-12//99
	Albany-Schenectady-Troy						
	MSA, NY	S	32.08 MW	30.41 AW	66730 AAW	NYBLS	10//99-12//99
	Binghamton MSA, NY	S	29.99 MW	25.25 AW	62380 AAW	NYBLS	10//99-12//99
	Buffalo-Niagara Falls MSA,						
	NY	S	33.67 MW	32.08 AW	70030 AAW	NYBLS	10//99-12//99
	New York PMSA, NY	S	56.15 MW	63.58 AW	116790 AAW	NYBLS	10//99-12//99
	Newburgh PMSA, NY-PA	S	32.88 MW	27.90 AW	68390 AAW	NYBLS	10//99-12//99
	Syracuse MSA, NY	S	33.24 MW	30.75 AW	69130 AAW	NYBLS	10//99-12//99
	Utica-Rome MSA, NY	S	30.09 MW	27.91 AW	62590 AAW	NYBLS	10//99-12//99
	North Carolina	S	41.02 MW	41.22 AW	85740 AAW	NCBLS	10//99-12//99
	Fayetteville MSA, NC	S	37.80 MW	33.06 AW	78630 AAW	NCBLS	10//99-12//99
	Greensboro--Winston-Salem--						
	High Point MSA, NC	S	31.14 MW	25.60 AW	64770 AAW	NCBLS	10//99-12//99
	Greenville MSA, NC	S	38.33 MW	34.22 AW	79730 AAW	NCBLS	10//99-12//99
	Hickory-Morganton-Lenoir						
	MSA, NC	S	27.29 MW	27.88 AW	56770 AAW	NCBLS	10//99-12//99
	Rocky Mount MSA, NC	S	37.87 MW	38.37 AW	78770 AAW	NCBLS	10//99-12//99
	Wilmington MSA, NC	S	27.93 MW	27.73 AW	58100 AAW	NCBLS	10//99-12//99
	North Dakota	S	24.2 MW	28.74 AW	59770 AAW	NDBLS	10//99-12//99
	Fargo-Moorhead MSA, ND-						
	MN	S	41.67 MW	31.55 AW	86680 AAW	NDBLS	10//99-12//99
	Grand Forks MSA, ND-MN	S	31.51 MW	25.59 AW	65540 AAW	NDBLS	10//99-12//99
	Ohio	S	34.15 MW	35.23 AW	73280 AAW	OHBLS	10//99-12//99
	Akron PMSA, OH	S	27.52 MW	25.73 AW	57240 AAW	OHBLS	10//99-12//99
	Cincinnati PMSA, OH-KY-IN	S	37.47 MW	36.59 AW	77940 AAW	OHBLS	10//99-12//99
	Cleveland-Lorain-Elyria						
	PMSA, OH	S	39.19 MW	40.16 AW	81510 AAW	OHBLS	10//99-12//99
	Columbus MSA, OH	S	26.36 MW	24.00 AW	54830 AAW	OHBLS	10//99-12//99
	Dayton-Springfield MSA, OH	S	26.96 MW	24.38 AW	56070 AAW	OHBLS	10//99-12//99
	Mansfield MSA, OH	S	35.77 MW	38.42 AW	74400 AAW	OHBLS	10//99-12//99
	Steubenville-Weirton MSA,						
	OH-WV	S	35.88 MW	37.80 AW	74640 AAW	OHBLS	10//99-12//99
	Toledo MSA, OH	S	42.02 MW	33.94 AW	87390 AAW	OHBLS	10//99-12//99
	Youngstown-Warren MSA, OH	S	25.74 MW	19.88 AW	53530 AAW	OHBLS	10//99-12//99

AAW	Average annual wage	AOH	Average offered, high	ASH	Average starting, high
AE	Average entry wage	AOL	Average offered, low	ASL	Average starting, low
AEX	Average experienced wage	APH	Average pay, high range	AW	Average wage paid
AO	Average offered	APL	Average pay, low range	FQ	First quartile wage

H	Hourly	M	Monthly	S	Special: hourly and annual
HI	Highest wage paid	MTC	Median total compensation	TQ	Third quartile wage
HR	High end range	MW	Median wage paid	W	Weekly
LR	Low end range	SQ	Second quartile wage	Y	Yearly

Occupation/Type/Industry	Location	Per	Low	Mid	High	Source	Date
Lawyer	Tulsa MSA, OK	S	32.55 MW	31.36 AW	67700 AAW	OKBLS	10//99-12//99
	Oregon	S	33.54 MW	34.92 AW	72630 AAW	ORBLS	10//99-12//99
	Eugene-Springfield MSA, OR	S	37.15 MW	31.84 AW	77270 AAW	ORBLS	10//99-12//99
	Portland-Vancouver PMSA, OR-WA	S	36.53 MW	36.00 AW	75990 AAW	ORBLS	10//99-12//99
	Pennsylvania	S	40.35 MW	42.90 AW	89240 AAW	PABLS	10//99-12//99
	Allentown-Bethlehem-Easton MSA, PA	S	24.85 MW	24.15 AW	51690 AAW	PABLS	10//99-12//99
	Erie MSA, PA	S	38.42 MW	34.01 AW	79920 AAW	PABLS	10//99-12//99
	Johnstown MSA, PA	S	23.84 MW	16.81 AW	49590 AAW	PABLS	10//99-12//99
	Lancaster MSA, PA	S	39.38 MW	30.90 AW	81920 AAW	PABLS	10//99-12//99
	Philadelphia PMSA, PA-NJ	S	45.18 MW	42.29 AW	93980 AAW	PABLS	10//99-12//99
	Pittsburgh MSA, PA	S	44.71 MW	44.94 AW	92990 AAW	PABLS	10//99-12//99
	Scranton--Wilkes-Barre--Hazleton MSA, PA	S	36.77 MW	29.59 AW	76470 AAW	PABLS	10//99-12//99
	State College MSA, PA	S	45.03 MW	34.25 AW	93670 AAW	PABLS	10//99-12//99
	Williamsport MSA, PA	S	37.03 MW	37.81 AW	77010 AAW	PABLS	10//99-12//99
	Charleston-North Charleston MSA, SC	S	43.60 MW	44.80 AW	90690 AAW	SCBLS	10//99-12//99
	Greenville-Spartanburg-Anderson MSA, SC	S	49.65 MW	57.54 AW	103270 AAW	SCBLS	10//99-12//99
	Myrtle Beach MSA, SC	S	42.05 MW	38.23 AW	87470 AAW	SCBLS	10//99-12//99
	South Dakota	S	24.94 MW	27.86 AW	57950 AAW	SDBLS	10//99-12//99
	Rapid City MSA, SD	S	27.95 MW	23.26 AW	58140 AAW	SDBLS	10//99-12//99
	Sioux Falls MSA, SD	S	33.75 MW	37.47 AW	70200 AAW	SDBLS	10//99-12//99
	Tennessee	S	31.44 MW	34.74 AW	72250 AAW	TNBLS	10//99-12//99
	Chattanooga MSA, TN-GA	S	29.48 MW	28.82 AW	61320 AAW	TNBLS	10//99-12//99
	Clarksville-Hopkinsville MSA, TN-KY	S	27.39 MW	24.49 AW	56960 AAW	TNBLS	10//99-12//99
	Jackson MSA, TN	S	31.26 MW	25.41 AW	65020 AAW	TNBLS	10//99-12//99
	Johnson City-Kingsport-Bristol MSA, TN-VA	S	41.86 MW	47.57 AW	87070 AAW	TNBLS	10//99-12//99
	Knoxville MSA, TN	S	33.60 MW	30.76 AW	69890 AAW	TNBLS	10//99-12//99
	Memphis MSA, TN-AR-MS	S	27.58 MW	16.86 AW	57370 AAW	MSBLS	10//99-12//99
	Nashville MSA, TN	S	43.11 MW	40.35 AW	89660 AAW	TNBLS	10//99-12//99
	Texas	S	33.44 MW	37.73 AW	78470 AAW	TXBLS	10//99-12//99
	Abilene MSA, TX	S	41.45 MW	44.28 AW	86210 AAW	TXBLS	10//99-12//99
	Amarillo MSA, TX	S	40.77 MW	38.38 AW	84810 AAW	TXBLS	10//99-12//99
	Beaumont-Port Arthur MSA, TX	S	37.05 MW	31.72 AW	77060 AAW	TXBLS	10//99-12//99
	Bryan-College Station MSA, TX	S	44.15 MW	51.15 AW	91830 AAW	TXBLS	10//99-12//99
	Corpus Christi MSA, TX	S	40.02 MW	36.67 AW	83250 AAW	TXBLS	10//99-12//99
	Dallas PMSA, TX	S	39.28 MW	34.09 AW	81710 AAW	TXBLS	10//99-12//99
	El Paso MSA, TX	S	46.63 MW	45.59 AW	96990 AAW	TXBLS	10//99-12//99
	Fort Worth-Arlington PMSA, TX	S	43.51 MW	46.42 AW	90510 AAW	TXBLS	10//99-12//99
	Galveston-Texas City PMSA, TX	S	30.74 MW	30.89 AW	63950 AAW	TXBLS	10//99-12//99
	Houston PMSA, TX	S	37.71 MW	33.55 AW	78430 AAW	TXBLS	10//99-12//99
	Laredo MSA, TX	S	42.36 MW	37.42 AW	88110 AAW	TXBLS	10//99-12//99
	Longview-Marshall MSA, TX	S	31.40 MW	25.68 AW	65310 AAW	TXBLS	10//99-12//99
	Lubbock MSA, TX	S	32.97 MW	28.68 AW	68580 AAW	TXBLS	10//99-12//99
	Odessa-Midland MSA, TX	S	44.83 MW	42.22 AW	93240 AAW	TXBLS	10//99-12//99
	San Angelo MSA, TX	S	37.76 MW	35.72 AW	78540 AAW	TXBLS	10//99-12//99
	San Antonio MSA, TX	S	39.64 MW	38.46 AW	82450 AAW	TXBLS	10//99-12//99
	Sherman-Denison MSA, TX	S	37.11 MW	33.86 AW	77180 AAW	TXBLS	10//99-12//99
	Texarkana MSA, TX-Texarkana, AR	S	31.59 MW	30.48 AW	65700 AAW	TXBLS	10//99-12//99
	Tyler MSA, TX	S	36.87 MW	36.92 AW	76690 AAW	TXBLS	10//99-12//99
	Waco MSA, TX	S	29.12 MW	27.47 AW	60570 AAW	TXBLS	10//99-12//99
	Utah	S	29.92 MW	31.53 AW	65580 AAW	UTBLS	10//99-12//99
	Provo-Orem MSA, UT	S	25.84 MW	23.31 AW	53750 AAW	UTBLS	10//99-12//99
	Salt Lake City-Ogden MSA, UT	S	32.93 MW	31.58 AW	68490 AAW	UTBLS	10//99-12//99
	Vermont	S	45.54 MW	48.15 AW	100160 AAW	VTBLS	10//99-12//99
	Virginia	S	36.11 MW	38.53 AW	80130 AAW	VABLS	10//99-12//99
	Charlottesville MSA, VA	S	46.72 MW	52.26 AW	97170 AAW	VABLS	10//99-12//99
	Lynchburg MSA, VA	S	38.30 MW	38.63 AW	79660 AAW	VABLS	10//99-12//99
	Norfolk-Virginia Beach-Newport News MSA, VA-NC	S	33.00 MW	30.97 AW	68640 AAW	VABLS	10//99-12//99

Occupation/Type/Industry	Location	Per	Low	Mid	High	Source	Date
Lawyer	Richmond-Petersburg MSA, VA	S	37.70 MW	33.60 AW	78410 AAW	VABLS	10//99-12//99
	Roanoke MSA, VA	S	36.48 MW	37.44 AW	75880 AAW	VABLS	10//99-12//99
	Washington	S	36.61 MW	39.99 AW	83180 AAW	WABLS	10//99-12//99
	Bremerton PMSA, WA	S	28.80 MW	28.08 AW	59900 AAW	WABLS	10//99-12//99
	Richland-Kennewick-Pasco MSA, WA	S	35.40 MW	34.58 AW	73630 AAW	WABLS	10//99-12//99
	Spokane MSA, WA	S	47.59 MW	45.17 AW	99000 AAW	WABLS	10//99-12//99
	Tacoma PMSA, WA	S	37.99 MW	36.48 AW	79020 AAW	WABLS	10//99-12//99
	Yakima MSA, WA	S	32.20 MW	29.39 AW	66980 AAW	WABLS	10//99-12//99
	West Virginia	S	26.82 MW	28.56 AW	59400 AAW	WVBLS	10//99-12//99
	Charleston MSA, WV	S	26.16 MW	24.49 AW	54420 AAW	WVBLS	10//99-12//99
	Huntington-Ashland MSA, WV-KY-OH	S	26.72 MW	26.44 AW	55580 AAW	WVBLS	10//99-12//99
	Parkersburg-Marietta MSA, WV-OH	S	31.65 MW	30.88 AW	65830 AAW	WVBLS	10//99-12//99
	Wheeling MSA, WV-OH	S	32.26 MW	30.52 AW	67110 AAW	WVBLS	10//99-12//99
	Wisconsin	S	39.48 MW	41.72 AW	86780 AAW	WIBLS	10//99-12//99
	Appleton-Oshkosh-Neenah MSA, WI	S	48.39 MW	50.97 AW	100650 AAW	WIBLS	10//99-12//99
	Eau Claire MSA, WI	S	47.07 MW	48.63 AW	97890 AAW	WIBLS	10//99-12//99
	Green Bay MSA, WI	S	39.48 MW	37.59 AW	82120 AAW	WIBLS	10//99-12//99
	Janesville-Beloit MSA, WI	S	32.16 MW	36.12 AW	66890 AAW	WIBLS	10//99-12//99
	Madison MSA, WI	S	29.76 MW	26.12 AW	61890 AAW	WIBLS	10//99-12//99
	Milwaukee-Waukesha PMSA, WI	S	45.09 MW	42.22 AW	93780 AAW	WIBLS	10//99-12//99
	Racine PMSA, WI	S	28.77 MW	27.81 AW	59850 AAW	WIBLS	10//99-12//99
	Wausau MSA, WI	S	33.10 MW	34.93 AW	68850 AAW	WIBLS	10//99-12//99
	Wyoming	S	20.77 MW	23.84 AW	49600 AAW	WYBLS	10//99-12//99
	Casper MSA, WY	S	36.76 MW	26.91 AW	76450 AAW	WYBLS	10//99-12//99
	Cheyenne MSA, WY	S	21.70 MW	20.68 AW	45150 AAW	WYBLS	10//99-12//99
	Puerto Rico	S	21.3 MW	23.26 AW	48370 AAW	PRBLS	10//99-12//99
	Caguas PMSA, PR	S	12.50 MW	12.41 AW	26000 AAW	PRBLS	10//99-12//99
	Mayaguez MSA, PR	S	15.70 MW	14.56 AW	32660 AAW	PRBLS	10//99-12//99
	Ponce MSA, PR	S	22.60 MW	20.79 AW	47000 AAW	PRBLS	10//99-12//99
	San Juan-Bayamon PMSA, PR	S	24.37 MW	22.93 AW	50690 AAW	PRBLS	10//99-12//99
	Virgin Islands	S	34.65 MW	40.15 AW	83520 AAW	VIBLS	10//99-12//99
	Guam	S	33.69 MW	35.93 AW	74730 AAW	GUBLS	10//99-12//99
Lay-Out Worker							
Metals and Plastics	Alabama	S	13.14 MW	13.46 AW	28000 AAW	ALBLS	10//99-12//99
Metals and Plastics	Arizona	S	12.05 MW	11.83 AW	24600 AAW	AZBLS	10//99-12//99
Metals and Plastics	Arkansas	S	12.45 MW	12.26 AW	25510 AAW	ARBLS	10//99-12//99
Metals and Plastics	California	S	12.42 MW	12.39 AW	25760 AAW	CABLS	10//99-12//99
Metals and Plastics	Connecticut	S	11.89 MW	12.20 AW	25380 AAW	CTBLS	10//99-12//99
Metals and Plastics	Florida	S	9.88 MW	10.33 AW	21490 AAW	FLBLS	10//99-12//99
Metals and Plastics	Georgia	S	14.82 MW	14.23 AW	29600 AAW	GABLS	10//99-12//99
Metals and Plastics	Idaho	S	13.15 MW	13.35 AW	27760 AAW	IDBLS	10//99-12//99
Metals and Plastics	Illinois	S	15.84 MW	16.51 AW	34340 AAW	ILBLS	10//99-12//99
Metals and Plastics	Indiana	S	13.16 MW	13.63 AW	28340 AAW	INBLS	10//99-12//99
Metals and Plastics	Iowa	S	14.24 MW	14.32 AW	29790 AAW	IABLS	10//99-12//99
Metals and Plastics	Kansas	S	14.38 MW	13.43 AW	27930 AAW	KSBLS	10//99-12//99
Metals and Plastics	Kentucky	S	10.63 MW	11.70 AW	24340 AAW	KYBLS	10//99-12//99
Metals and Plastics	Louisiana	S	14.46 MW	14.43 AW	30020 AAW	LABLS	10//99-12//99
Metals and Plastics	Maryland	S	14.18 MW	14.84 AW	30870 AAW	MDBLS	10//99-12//99
Metals and Plastics	Massachusetts	S	17.1 MW	16.72 AW	34780 AAW	MABLS	10//99-12//99
Metals and Plastics	Michigan	S	19.29 MW	20.61 AW	42880 AAW	MIBLS	10//99-12//99
Metals and Plastics	Minnesota	S	16.85 MW	17.52 AW	36440 AAW	MNBLS	10//99-12//99
Metals and Plastics	Mississippi	S	11.3 MW	10.84 AW	22550 AAW	MSBLS	10//99-12//99
Metals and Plastics	Missouri	S	14.04 MW	12.39 AW	25770 AAW	MOBLS	10//99-12//99
Metals and Plastics	Nevada	S	14.72 MW	15.63 AW	32510 AAW	NVBLS	10//99-12//99
Metals and Plastics	New Hampshire	S	14.54 MW	14.62 AW	30410 AAW	NHBLS	10//99-12//99
Metals and Plastics	New Jersey	S	16.92 MW	17.72 AW	36850 AAW	NJBLS	10//99-12//99
Metals and Plastics	New Mexico	S	10.71 MW	10.86 AW	22590 AAW	NMBLS	10//99-12//99
Metals and Plastics	New York	S	10.76 MW	11.05 AW	22980 AAW	NYBLS	10//99-12//99
Metals and Plastics	North Carolina	S	12.48 MW	12.56 AW	26130 AAW	NCBLS	10//99-12//99
Metals and Plastics	Oklahoma	S	12.53 MW	13.26 AW	27580 AAW	OKBLS	10//99-12//99
Metals and Plastics	Oregon	S	14.99 MW	15.87 AW	33010 AAW	ORBLS	10//99-12//99
Metals and Plastics	Pennsylvania	S	15.2 MW	15.76 AW	32780 AAW	PABLS	10//99-12//99
Metals and Plastics	South Carolina	S	14.26 MW	13.42 AW	27920 AAW	SCBLS	10//99-12//99
Metals and Plastics	Tennessee	S	12.29 MW	12.34 AW	25660 AAW	TNBLS	10//99-12//99
Metals and Plastics	Texas	S	9.95 MW	10.40 AW	21630 AAW	TXBLS	10//99-12//99
Metals and Plastics	Utah	S	11.78 MW	11.27 AW	23440 AAW	UTBLS	10//99-12//99

Occupation/Type/Industry	Location	Per	Low	Mid	High	Source	Date
Lay-Out Worker							
Metals and Plastics	Virginia	S	12.21 MW	12.18 AW	25340 AAW	VABLS	10//99-12//99
Metals and Plastics	Washington	S	28.3 MW	22.90 AW	47630 AAW	WABLS	10//99-12//99
Metals and Plastics	West Virginia	S	10.48 MW	13.90 AW	28910 AAW	WVBLS	10//99-12//99
Metals and Plastics	Wisconsin	S	16.05 MW	16.25 AW	33800 AAW	WIBLS	10//99-12//99
Leasing Manager							
Real Estate	United States	Y		131666 AW		TRAVWK4	2000
Legal Assistant	United States	H		17.29 AW		NCS98	1998
Legal Secretary	Alabama	S	12.01 MW	12.76 AW	26540 AAW	ALBLS	10//99-12//99
	Anniston MSA, AL	S	14.19 MW	12.81 AW	29520 AAW	ALBLS	10//99-12//99
	Birmingham MSA, AL	S	14.93 MW	14.95 AW	31050 AAW	ALBLS	10//99-12//99
	Decatur MSA, AL	S	10.25 MW	9.97 AW	21310 AAW	ALBLS	10//99-12//99
	Dothan MSA, AL	S	13.31 MW	13.36 AW	27690 AAW	ALBLS	10//99-12//99
	Florence MSA, AL	S	11.40 MW	11.75 AW	23700 AAW	ALBLS	10//99-12//99
	Huntsville MSA, AL	S	10.67 MW	10.52 AW	22200 AAW	ALBLS	10//99-12//99
	Mobile MSA, AL	S	11.93 MW	11.32 AW	24810 AAW	ALBLS	10//99-12//99
	Montgomery MSA, AL	S	12.95 MW	12.21 AW	26940 AAW	ALBLS	10//99-12//99
	Tuscaloosa MSA, AL	S	11.59 MW	11.06 AW	24110 AAW	ALBLS	10//99-12//99
	Alaska	S	16.99 MW	16.89 AW	35120 AAW	AKBLS	10//99-12//99
	Anchorage MSA, AK	S	17.37 MW	17.73 AW	36130 AAW	AKBLS	10//99-12//99
	Arizona	S	15.51 MW	15.21 AW	31640 AAW	AZBLS	10//99-12//99
	Flagstaff MSA, AZ-UT	S	11.50 MW	11.55 AW	23920 AAW	AZBLS	10//99-12//99
	Phoenix-Mesa MSA, AZ	S	16.08 MW	16.43 AW	33440 AAW	AZBLS	10//99-12//99
	Tucson MSA, AZ	S	14.84 MW	15.00 AW	30860 AAW	AZBLS	10//99-12//99
	Yuma MSA, AZ	S	12.67 MW	12.15 AW	26350 AAW	AZBLS	10//99-12//99
	Arkansas	S	12 MW	11.60 AW	24140 AAW	ARBLS	10//99-12//99
	Fayetteville-Springdale-Rogers MSA, AR	S	12.25 MW	12.52 AW	25470 AAW	ARBLS	10//99-12//99
	Fort Smith MSA, AR-OK	S	11.60 MW	11.16 AW	24130 AAW	ARBLS	10//99-12//99
	Little Rock-North Little Rock MSA, AR	S	12.52 MW	13.02 AW	26030 AAW	ARBLS	10//99-12//99
	California	S	18.15 MW	18.47 AW	38410 AAW	CABLS	10//99-12//99
	Bakersfield MSA, CA	S	14.06 MW	13.84 AW	29250 AAW	CABLS	10//99-12//99
	Chico-Paradise MSA, CA	S	12.37 MW	11.61 AW	25730 AAW	CABLS	10//99-12//99
	Fresno MSA, CA	S	12.51 MW	12.04 AW	26020 AAW	CABLS	10//99-12//99
	Los Angeles-Long Beach PMSA, CA	S	18.51 MW	18.59 AW	38510 AAW	CABLS	10//99-12//99
	Merced MSA, CA	S	14.34 MW	14.62 AW	29830 AAW	CABLS	10//99-12//99
	Oakland PMSA, CA	S	22.19 MW	21.72 AW	46150 AAW	CABLS	10//99-12//99
	Orange County PMSA, CA	S	16.96 MW	16.98 AW	35290 AAW	CABLS	10//99-12//99
	Redding MSA, CA	S	14.75 MW	14.54 AW	30680 AAW	CABLS	10//99-12//99
	Riverside-San Bernardino PMSA, CA	S	15.31 MW	14.12 AW	31850 AAW	CABLS	10//99-12//99
	Sacramento PMSA, CA	S	15.57 MW	15.35 AW	32390 AAW	CABLS	10//99-12//99
	Salinas MSA, CA	S	17.30 MW	17.32 AW	35990 AAW	CABLS	10//99-12//99
	San Diego MSA, CA	S	16.91 MW	16.22 AW	35180 AAW	CABLS	10//99-12//99
	San Francisco PMSA, CA	S	22.42 MW	20.99 AW	46640 AAW	CABLS	10//99-12//99
	San Jose PMSA, CA	S	21.91 MW	20.73 AW	45560 AAW	CABLS	10//99-12//99
	San Luis Obispo-Atascadero-Paso Robles MSA, CA	S	11.55 MW	11.78 AW	24020 AAW	CABLS	10//99-12//99
	Santa Barbara-Santa Maria-Lompoc MSA, CA	S	17.69 MW	16.29 AW	36790 AAW	CABLS	10//99-12//99
	Santa Cruz-Watsonville PMSA, CA	S	15.29 MW	14.76 AW	31810 AAW	CABLS	10//99-12//99
	Santa Rosa PMSA, CA	S	14.52 MW	11.64 AW	30200 AAW	CABLS	10//99-12//99
	Stockton-Lodi MSA, CA	S	15.60 MW	15.44 AW	32440 AAW	CABLS	10//99-12//99
	Vallejo-Fairfield-Napa PMSA, CA	S	16.28 MW	16.24 AW	33850 AAW	CABLS	10//99-12//99
	Ventura PMSA, CA	S	18.49 MW	19.26 AW	38460 AAW	CABLS	10//99-12//99
	Visalia-Tulare-Porterville MSA, CA	S	14.45 MW	15.21 AW	30060 AAW	CABLS	10//99-12//99
	Yuba City MSA, CA	S	14.26 MW	13.53 AW	29670 AAW	CABLS	10//99-12//99
	Colorado	S	13.21 MW	14.15 AW	29430 AAW	COBLS	10//99-12//99
	Boulder-Longmont PMSA, CO	S	15.28 MW	14.98 AW	31770 AAW	COBLS	10//99-12//99
	Colorado Springs MSA, CO	S	14.33 MW	13.45 AW	29800 AAW	COBLS	10//99-12//99
	Denver PMSA, CO	S	14.54 MW	13.38 AW	30230 AAW	COBLS	10//99-12//99
	Greeley PMSA, CO	S	10.63 MW	9.92 AW	22100 AAW	COBLS	10//99-12//99
	Pueblo MSA, CO	S	11.28 MW	11.36 AW	23460 AAW	COBLS	10//99-12//99
	Connecticut	S	16.96 MW	16.41 AW	34140 AAW	CTBLS	10//99-12//99
	Danbury PMSA, CT	S	16.77 MW	16.96 AW	34890 AAW	CTBLS	10//99-12//99

AAW Average annual wage	**AOH** Average offered, high	**ASH** Average starting, high	**H** Hourly	**M** Monthly	**S** Special: hourly and annual
AE Average entry wage	**AOL** Average offered, low	**ASL** Average starting, low	**HI** Highest wage paid	**MTC** Median total compensation	**TQ** Third quartile wage
AEX Average experienced wage	**APH** Average pay, high range	**AW** Average wage paid	**HR** High end range	**MW** Median wage paid	**W** Weekly
AO Average offered	**APL** Average pay, low range	**FQ** First quartile wage	**LR** Low end range	**SQ** Second quartile wage	**Y** Yearly

Occupation/Type/Industry	Location	Per	Low	Mid	High	Source	Date
Legal Secretary	Hartford MSA, CT	s	17.33 MW	17.86 AW	36050 AAW	CTBLS	10//99-12//99
	New London-Norwich MSA, CT-RI	s	13.08 MW	12.85 AW	27200 AAW	CTBLS	10//99-12//99
	Stamford-Norwalk PMSA, CT	s	17.88 MW	17.88 AW	37200 AAW	CTBLS	10//99-12//99
	Delaware	s	15.26 MW	16.62 AW	34580 AAW	DEBLS	10//99-12//99
	Wilmington-Newark PMSA, DE-MD	s	17.22 MW	15.63 AW	35820 AAW	DEBLS	10//99-12//99
	District of Columbia	s	21.31 MW	21.38 AW	44470 AAW	DCBLS	10//99-12//99
	Washington PMSA, DC-MD-VA-WV	s	19.90 MW	19.98 AW	41390 AAW	DCBLS	10//99-12//99
	Florida	s	14.08 MW	14.86 AW	30900 AAW	FLBLS	10//99-12//99
	Daytona Beach MSA, FL	s	11.81 MW	11.30 AW	24570 AAW	FLBLS	10//99-12//99
	Fort Lauderdale PMSA, FL	s	14.80 MW	14.82 AW	30780 AAW	FLBLS	10//99-12//99
	Fort Myers-Cape Coral MSA, FL	s	12.88 MW	12.91 AW	26780 AAW	FLBLS	10//99-12//99
	Fort Pierce-Port St. Lucie MSA, FL	s	16.79 MW	16.00 AW	34910 AAW	FLBLS	10//99-12//99
	Gainesville MSA, FL	s	11.75 MW	11.60 AW	24430 AAW	FLBLS	10//99-12//99
	Jacksonville MSA, FL	s	11.37 MW	11.21 AW	23650 AAW	FLBLS	10//99-12//99
	Lakeland-Winter Haven MSA, FL	s	14.05 MW	13.46 AW	29230 AAW	FLBLS	10//99-12//99
	Melbourne-Titusville-Palm Bay MSA, FL	s	12.42 MW	12.29 AW	25820 AAW	FLBLS	10//99-12//99
	Miami PMSA, FL	s	17.16 MW	18.01 AW	35700 AAW	FLBLS	10//99-12//99
	Naples MSA, FL	s	14.98 MW	15.13 AW	31160 AAW	FLBLS	10//99-12//99
	Orlando MSA, FL	s	15.10 MW	14.88 AW	31410 AAW	FLBLS	10//99-12//99
	Panama City MSA, FL	s	11.03 MW	11.23 AW	22940 AAW	FLBLS	10//99-12//99
	Pensacola MSA, FL	s	11.43 MW	11.33 AW	23770 AAW	FLBLS	10//99-12//99
	Punta Gorda MSA, FL	s	10.68 MW	10.33 AW	22210 AAW	FLBLS	10//99-12//99
	Sarasota-Bradenton MSA, FL	s	13.47 MW	12.64 AW	28010 AAW	FLBLS	10//99-12//99
	Tallahassee MSA, FL	s	12.87 MW	12.13 AW	26760 AAW	FLBLS	10//99-12//99
	Tampa-St. Petersburg-Clearwater MSA, FL	s	15.20 MW	14.65 AW	31610 AAW	FLBLS	10//99-12//99
	West Palm Beach-Boca Raton MSA, FL	s	14.91 MW	14.98 AW	31020 AAW	FLBLS	10//99-12//99
	Georgia	s	14.68 MW	14.83 AW	30850 AAW	GABLS	10//99-12//99
	Athens MSA, GA	s	11.72 MW	10.77 AW	24380 AAW	GABLS	10//99-12//99
	Atlanta MSA, GA	s	16.70 MW	15.97 AW	34740 AAW	GABLS	10//99-12//99
	Augusta-Aiken MSA, GA-SC	s	13.09 MW	12.56 AW	27220 AAW	GABLS	10//99-12//99
	Columbus MSA, GA-AL	s	10.97 MW	10.45 AW	22820 AAW	GABLS	10//99-12//99
	Macon MSA, GA	s	11.14 MW	11.07 AW	23170 AAW	GABLS	10//99-12//99
	Savannah MSA, GA	s	11.65 MW	12.35 AW	24220 AAW	GABLS	10//99-12//99
	Hawaii	s	15.81 MW	16.01 AW	33300 AAW	HIBLS	10//99-12//99
	Honolulu MSA, HI	s	16.31 MW	16.02 AW	33920 AAW	HIBLS	10//99-12//99
	Idaho	s	10.42 MW	10.36 AW	21550 AAW	IDBLS	10//99-12//99
	Boise City MSA, ID	s	10.63 MW	10.93 AW	22110 AAW	IDBLS	10//99-12//99
	Illinois	s	15.96 MW	16.18 AW	33660 AAW	ILBLS	10//99-12//99
	Bloomington-Normal MSA, IL	s	12.34 MW	11.44 AW	25670 AAW	ILBLS	10//99-12//99
	Champaign-Urbana MSA, IL	s	13.30 MW	14.02 AW	27670 AAW	ILBLS	10//99-12//99
	Chicago PMSA, IL	s	17.65 MW	17.29 AW	36720 AAW	ILBLS	10//99-12//99
	Decatur MSA, IL	s	10.10 MW	10.07 AW	21000 AAW	ILBLS	10//99-12//99
	Peoria-Pekin MSA, IL	s	10.58 MW	10.23 AW	22000 AAW	ILBLS	10//99-12//99
	Rockford MSA, IL	s	13.55 MW	14.33 AW	28180 AAW	ILBLS	10//99-12//99
	Springfield MSA, IL	s	11.59 MW	12.66 AW	24110 AAW	ILBLS	10//99-12//99
	Indiana	s	11.91 MW	12.27 AW	25530 AAW	INBLS	10//99-12//99
	Bloomington MSA, IN	s	11.66 MW	11.57 AW	24260 AAW	INBLS	10//99-12//99
	Evansville-Henderson MSA, IN-KY	s	11.65 MW	11.10 AW	24230 AAW	INBLS	10//99-12//99
	Fort Wayne MSA, IN	s	12.45 MW	11.98 AW	25890 AAW	INBLS	10//99-12//99
	Gary PMSA, IN	s	12.51 MW	12.78 AW	26020 AAW	INBLS	10//99-12//99
	Indianapolis MSA, IN	s	13.21 MW	12.85 AW	27470 AAW	INBLS	10//99-12//99
	Lafayette MSA, IN	s	10.79 MW	10.60 AW	22440 AAW	INBLS	10//99-12//99
	Muncie MSA, IN	s	8.65 MW	8.14 AW	17990 AAW	INBLS	10//99-12//99
	South Bend MSA, IN	s	13.19 MW	13.34 AW	27430 AAW	INBLS	10//99-12//99
	Terre Haute MSA, IN	s	11.91 MW	11.82 AW	24770 AAW	INBLS	10//99-12//99
	Iowa	s	10.97 MW	11.31 AW	23510 AAW	IABLS	10//99-12//99
	Cedar Rapids MSA, IA	s	13.26 MW	13.15 AW	27570 AAW	IABLS	10//99-12//99
	Davenport-Moline-Rock Island MSA, IA-IL	s	11.00 MW	10.46 AW	22880 AAW	IABLS	10//99-12//99
	Des Moines MSA, IA	s	13.17 MW	13.45 AW	27400 AAW	IABLS	10//99-12//99
	Dubuque MSA, IA	s	10.60 MW	10.46 AW	22060 AAW	IABLS	10//99-12//99
	Iowa City MSA, IA	s	12.90 MW	12.69 AW	26840 AAW	IABLS	10//99-12//99

AAW Average annual wage	**AOH** Average offered, high	**ASH** Average starting, high	**H** Hourly	**M** Monthly	**S** Special: hourly and annual
AE Average entry wage	**AOL** Average offered, low	**ASL** Average starting, low	**HI** Highest wage paid	**MTC** Median total compensation	**TQ** Third quartile wage
AEX Average experienced wage	**APH** Average pay, high range	**AW** Average wage paid	**HR** High end range	**MW** Median wage paid	**W** Weekly
AO Average offered	**APL** Average pay, low range	**FQ** First quartile wage	**LR** Low end range	**SQ** Second quartile wage	**Y** Yearly

Occupation/Type/Industry	Location	Per	Low	Mid	High	Source	Date
Legal Secretary	Sioux City MSA, IA-NE	S	10.11 MW	10.19 AW	21030 AAW	IABLS	10//99-12//99
	Waterloo-Cedar Falls MSA, IA	S	10.72 MW	10.62 AW	22300 AAW	IABLS	10//99-12//99
	Kansas	S	11.34 MW	11.76 AW	24450 AAW	KSBLS	10//99-12//99
	Wichita MSA, KS	S	12.50 MW	12.55 AW	26000 AAW	KSBLS	10//99-12//99
	Kentucky	S	10.98 MW	11.57 AW	24060 AAW	KYBLS	10//99-12//99
	Lexington MSA, KY	S	13.52 MW	13.34 AW	28130 AAW	KYBLS	10//99-12//99
	Louisville MSA, KY-IN	S	12.41 MW	12.30 AW	25810 AAW	KYBLS	10//99-12//99
	Owensboro MSA, KY	S	11.14 MW	11.07 AW	23170 AAW	KYBLS	10//99-12//99
	Louisiana	S	13.41 MW	13.10 AW	27250 AAW	LABLS	10//99-12//99
	Alexandria MSA, LA	S	12.11 MW	12.49 AW	25190 AAW	LABLS	10//99-12//99
	Baton Rouge MSA, LA	S	12.77 MW	12.87 AW	26550 AAW	LABLS	10//99-12//99
	Lafayette MSA, LA	S	12.56 MW	12.63 AW	26110 AAW	LABLS	10//99-12//99
	Lake Charles MSA, LA	S	8.87 MW	6.96 AW	18440 AAW	LABLS	10//99-12//99
	Monroe MSA, LA	S	10.31 MW	10.32 AW	21440 AAW	LABLS	10//99-12//99
	New Orleans MSA, LA	S	15.10 MW	15.45 AW	31400 AAW	LABLS	10//99-12//99
	Shreveport-Bossier City MSA, LA	S	12.82 MW	12.93 AW	26670 AAW	LABLS	10//99-12//99
	Maine	S	11.65 MW	12.50 AW	25990 AAW	MEBLS	10//99-12//99
	Bangor MSA, ME	S	12.16 MW	12.07 AW	25290 AAW	MEBLS	10//99-12//99
	Lewiston-Auburn MSA, ME	S	12.43 MW	12.16 AW	25850 AAW	MEBLS	10//99-12//99
	Portland MSA, ME	S	13.54 MW	13.11 AW	28160 AAW	MEBLS	10//99-12//99
	Maryland	S	13.35 MW	13.79 AW	28680 AAW	MDBLS	10//99-12//99
	Baltimore PMSA, MD	S	12.90 MW	12.72 AW	26820 AAW	MDBLS	10//99-12//99
	Cumberland MSA, MD-WV	S	11.70 MW	12.39 AW	24330 AAW	MDBLS	10//99-12//99
	Hagerstown PMSA, MD	S	12.39 MW	12.52 AW	25770 AAW	MDBLS	10//99-12//99
	Massachusetts	S	17.37 MW	17.71 AW	36840 AAW	MABLS	10//99-12//99
	Boston PMSA, MA-NH	S	18.86 MW	18.47 AW	39220 AAW	MABLS	10//99-12//99
	Brockton PMSA, MA	S	14.65 MW	14.53 AW	30470 AAW	MABLS	10//99-12//99
	Lawrence PMSA, MA-NH	S	15.54 MW	14.84 AW	32320 AAW	MABLS	10//99-12//99
	Pittsfield MSA, MA	S	15.24 MW	15.82 AW	31710 AAW	MABLS	10//99-12//99
	Springfield MSA, MA	S	14.18 MW	14.03 AW	29500 AAW	MABLS	10//99-12//99
	Worcester PMSA, MA-CT	S	13.14 MW	12.90 AW	27340 AAW	MABLS	10//99-12//99
	Michigan	S	15.19 MW	15.09 AW	31380 AAW	MIBLS	10//99-12//99
	Ann Arbor PMSA, MI	S	13.97 MW	14.04 AW	29070 AAW	MIBLS	10//99-12//99
	Benton Harbor MSA, MI	S	12.34 MW	12.64 AW	25660 AAW	MIBLS	10//99-12//99
	Detroit PMSA, MI	S	16.76 MW	16.42 AW	34860 AAW	MIBLS	10//99-12//99
	Flint PMSA, MI	S	10.63 MW	8.56 AW	22110 AAW	MIBLS	10//99-12//99
	Grand Rapids-Muskegon-Holland MSA, MI	S	14.97 MW	15.48 AW	31140 AAW	MIBLS	10//99-12//99
	Jackson MSA, MI	S	10.69 MW	10.23 AW	22230 AAW	MIBLS	10//99-12//99
	Kalamazoo-Battle Creek MSA, MI	S	12.56 MW	12.25 AW	26120 AAW	MIBLS	10//99-12//99
	Lansing-East Lansing MSA, MI	S	16.20 MW	15.87 AW	33690 AAW	MIBLS	10//99-12//99
	Saginaw-Bay City-Midland MSA, MI	S	11.05 MW	11.15 AW	22980 AAW	MIBLS	10//99-12//99
	Minnesota	S	12.25 MW	13.13 AW	27320 AAW	MNBLS	10//99-12//99
	Duluth-Superior MSA, MN-WI	S	11.74 MW	11.58 AW	24410 AAW	MNBLS	10//99-12//99
	Minneapolis-St. Paul MSA, MN-WI	S	14.28 MW	14.10 AW	29690 AAW	MNBLS	10//99-12//99
	Rochester MSA, MN	S	11.87 MW	11.57 AW	24690 AAW	MNBLS	10//99-12//99
	Mississippi	S	12.43 MW	12.55 AW	26100 AAW	MSBLS	10//99-12//99
	Biloxi-Gulfport-Pascagoula MSA, MS	S	12.85 MW	12.34 AW	26720 AAW	MSBLS	10//99-12//99
	Jackson MSA, MS	S	14.26 MW	14.13 AW	29660 AAW	MSBLS	10//99-12//99
	Missouri	S	13.48 MW	13.20 AW	27460 AAW	MOBLS	10//99-12//99
	Kansas City MSA, MO-KS	S	14.36 MW	14.51 AW	29880 AAW	MOBLS	10//99-12//99
	St. Louis MSA, MO-IL	S	13.82 MW	13.77 AW	28740 AAW	MOBLS	10//99-12//99
	Montana	S	10.35 MW	11.23 AW	23350 AAW	MTBLS	10//99-12//99
	Billings MSA, MT	S	12.68 MW	12.57 AW	26370 AAW	MTBLS	10//99-12//99
	Great Falls MSA, MT	S	13.35 MW	12.35 AW	27760 AAW	MTBLS	10//99-12//99
	Nebraska	S	10.05 MW	10.12 AW	21050 AAW	NEBLS	10//99-12//99
	Lincoln MSA, NE	S	9.89 MW	9.84 AW	20570 AAW	NEBLS	10//99-12//99
	Omaha MSA, NE-IA	S	12.32 MW	11.99 AW	25620 AAW	NEBLS	10//99-12//99
	Nevada	S	14.81 MW	14.34 AW	29830 AAW	NVBLS	10//99-12//99
	Las Vegas MSA, NV-AZ	S	13.79 MW	14.33 AW	28690 AAW	NVBLS	10//99-12//99
	Reno MSA, NV	S	16.77 MW	17.16 AW	34880 AAW	NVBLS	10//99-12//99
	New Hampshire	S	13.31 MW	13.80 AW	28710 AAW	NHBLS	10//99-12//99
	Manchester PMSA, NH	S	15.22 MW	15.06 AW	31650 AAW	NHBLS	10//99-12//99
	Nashua PMSA, NH	S	12.04 MW	11.57 AW	25050 AAW	NHBLS	10//99-12//99
	New Jersey	S	15.94 MW	15.77 AW	32800 AAW	NJBLS	10//99-12//99
	Atlantic-Cape May PMSA, NJ	S	16.39 MW	16.95 AW	34080 AAW	NJBLS	10//99-12//99
	Bergen-Passaic PMSA, NJ	S	14.88 MW	15.02 AW	30960 AAW	NJBLS	10//99-12//99

AAW Average annual wage	**AOH** Average offered, high	**ASH** Average starting, high	**H** Hourly	**M** Monthly	**S** Special: hourly and annual
AE Average entry wage	**AOL** Average offered, low	**ASL** Average starting, low	**HI** Highest wage paid	**MTC** Median total compensation	**TQ** Third quartile wage
AEX Average experienced wage	**APH** Average pay, high range	**AW** Average wage paid	**HR** High end range	**MW** Median wage paid	**W** Weekly
AO Average offered	**APL** Average pay, low range	**FQ** First quartile wage	**LR** Low end range	**SQ** Second quartile wage	**Y** Yearly

Occupation/Type/Industry	Location	Per	Low	Mid	High	Source	Date
Legal Secretary	Jersey City PMSA, NJ	S	15.95 MW	16.10 AW	33170 AAW	NJBLS	10//99-12//99
	Middlesex-Somerset-Hunterdon PMSA, NJ	S	12.96 MW	10.33 AW	26950 AAW	NJBLS	10//99-12//99
	Monmouth-Ocean PMSA, NJ	S	14.96 MW	15.05 AW	31110 AAW	NJBLS	10//99-12//99
	Newark PMSA, NJ	S	17.35 MW	17.58 AW	36080 AAW	NJBLS	10//99-12//99
	Trenton PMSA, NJ	S	17.45 MW	16.76 AW	36290 AAW	NJBLS	10//99-12//99
	Vineland-Millville-Bridgeton PMSA, NJ	S	14.38 MW	14.72 AW	29920 AAW	NJBLS	10//99-12//99
	New Mexico	S	12.86 MW	12.82 AW	26670 AAW	NMBLS	10//99-12//99
	Albuquerque MSA, NM	S	13.67 MW	13.25 AW	28430 AAW	NMBLS	10//99-12//99
	Las Cruces MSA, NM	S	11.22 MW	11.67 AW	23330 AAW	NMBLS	10//99-12//99
	Santa Fe MSA, NM	S	15.21 MW	15.21 AW	31630 AAW	NMBLS	10//99-12//99
	New York	S	18.82 MW	18.39 AW	38250 AAW	NYBLS	10//99-12//99
	Albany-Schenectady-Troy MSA, NY	S	13.42 MW	13.02 AW	27910 AAW	NYBLS	10//99-12//99
	Binghamton MSA, NY	S	10.51 MW	9.99 AW	21870 AAW	NYBLS	10//99-12//99
	Buffalo-Niagara Falls MSA, NY	S	11.91 MW	12.23 AW	24780 AAW	NYBLS	10//99-12//99
	Dutchess County PMSA, NY	S	14.18 MW	14.96 AW	29490 AAW	NYBLS	10//99-12//99
	Elmira MSA, NY	S	10.50 MW	10.46 AW	21840 AAW	NYBLS	10//99-12//99
	Glens Falls MSA, NY	S	10.51 MW	10.26 AW	21860 AAW	NYBLS	10//99-12//99
	Jamestown MSA, NY	S	11.00 MW	10.61 AW	22880 AAW	NYBLS	10//99-12//99
	Nassau-Suffolk PMSA, NY	S	15.48 MW	15.51 AW	32190 AAW	NYBLS	10//99-12//99
	New York PMSA, NY	S	20.87 MW	21.38 AW	43400 AAW	NYBLS	10//99-12//99
	Newburgh PMSA, NY-PA	S	13.75 MW	13.81 AW	28610 AAW	NYBLS	10//99-12//99
	Rochester MSA, NY	S	16.68 MW	17.08 AW	34690 AAW	NYBLS	10//99-12//99
	Syracuse MSA, NY	S	13.05 MW	12.60 AW	27140 AAW	NYBLS	10//99-12//99
	Utica-Rome MSA, NY	S	13.03 MW	12.92 AW	27100 AAW	NYBLS	10//99-12//99
	North Carolina	S	12.87 MW	13.49 AW	28050 AAW	NCBLS	10//99-12//99
	Asheville MSA, NC	S	11.50 MW	11.79 AW	23920 AAW	NCBLS	10//99-12//99
	Charlotte-Gastonia-Rock Hill MSA, NC-SC	S	15.54 MW	15.70 AW	32320 AAW	NCBLS	10//99-12//99
	Fayetteville MSA, NC	S	11.98 MW	11.92 AW	24930 AAW	NCBLS	10//99-12//99
	Goldsboro MSA, NC	S	9.65 MW	9.80 AW	20060 AAW	NCBLS	10//99-12//99
	Greensboro--Winston-Salem--High Point MSA, NC	S	13.49 MW	12.78 AW	28060 AAW	NCBLS	10//99-12//99
	Greenville MSA, NC	S	11.31 MW	11.23 AW	23510 AAW	NCBLS	10//99-12//99
	Raleigh-Durham-Chapel Hill MSA, NC	S	17.93 MW	16.02 AW	37300 AAW	NCBLS	10//99-12//99
	Rocky Mount MSA, NC	S	11.53 MW	11.01 AW	23990 AAW	NCBLS	10//99-12//99
	Wilmington MSA, NC	S	11.54 MW	11.47 AW	24000 AAW	NCBLS	10//99-12//99
	North Dakota	S	10.26 MW	10.61 AW	22070 AAW	NDBLS	10//99-12//99
	Bismarck MSA, ND	S	10.88 MW	11.12 AW	22620 AAW	NDBLS	10//99-12//99
	Fargo-Moorhead MSA, ND-MN	S	12.20 MW	11.95 AW	25380 AAW	NDBLS	10//99-12//99
	Grand Forks MSA, ND-MN	S	9.75 MW	9.34 AW	20270 AAW	NDBLS	10//99-12//99
	Ohio	S	13 MW	12.89 AW	26810 AAW	OHBLS	10//99-12//99
	Akron PMSA, OH	S	12.42 MW	12.52 AW	25840 AAW	OHBLS	10//99-12//99
	Canton-Massillon MSA, OH	S	11.85 MW	11.71 AW	24640 AAW	OHBLS	10//99-12//99
	Cincinnati PMSA, OH-KY-IN	S	12.60 MW	12.28 AW	26210 AAW	OHBLS	10//99-12//99
	Cleveland-Lorain-Elyria PMSA, OH	S	14.60 MW	14.77 AW	30360 AAW	OHBLS	10//99-12//99
	Columbus MSA, OH	S	15.26 MW	15.40 AW	31730 AAW	OHBLS	10//99-12//99
	Hamilton-Middletown PMSA, OH	S	11.46 MW	11.38 AW	23830 AAW	OHBLS	10//99-12//99
	Mansfield MSA, OH	S	11.24 MW	11.21 AW	23370 AAW	OHBLS	10//99-12//99
	Steubenville-Weirton MSA, OH-WV	S	9.62 MW	9.69 AW	20010 AAW	OHBLS	10//99-12//99
	Toledo MSA, OH	S	12.14 MW	12.30 AW	25250 AAW	OHBLS	10//99-12//99
	Oklahoma	S	12.18 MW	12.07 AW	25110 AAW	OKBLS	10//99-12//99
	Enid MSA, OK	S	10.41 MW	10.40 AW	21640 AAW	OKBLS	10//99-12//99
	Lawton MSA, OK	S	10.27 MW	10.35 AW	21360 AAW	OKBLS	10//99-12//99
	Oklahoma City MSA, OK	S	11.99 MW	11.76 AW	24950 AAW	OKBLS	10//99-12//99
	Tulsa MSA, OK	S	13.37 MW	13.42 AW	27810 AAW	OKBLS	10//99-12//99
	Oregon	S	14.91 MW	15.06 AW	31330 AAW	ORBLS	10//99-12//99
	Corvallis MSA, OR	S	13.28 MW	12.79 AW	27620 AAW	ORBLS	10//99-12//99
	Eugene-Springfield MSA, OR	S	11.98 MW	11.36 AW	24910 AAW	ORBLS	10//99-12//99
	Medford-Ashland MSA, OR	S	11.24 MW	11.26 AW	23380 AAW	ORBLS	10//99-12//99
	Portland-Vancouver PMSA, OR-WA	S	16.41 MW	15.91 AW	34120 AAW	ORBLS	10//99-12//99
	Salem PMSA, OR	S	14.03 MW	13.43 AW	29170 AAW	ORBLS	10//99-12//99
	Pennsylvania	S	14.79 MW	15.06 AW	31330 AAW	PABLS	10//99-12//99

AAW	Average annual wage	AOH	Average offered, high	ASH	Average starting, high
AE	Average entry wage	AOL	Average offered, low	ASL	Average starting, low
AEX	Average experienced wage	APH	Average pay, high range	AW	Average wage paid
AO	Average offered	APL	Average pay, low range	FQ	First quartile wage

H	Hourly	M	Monthly
HI	Highest wage paid	MTC	Median total compensation
HR	High end range	MW	Median wage paid
LR	Low end range	SQ	Second quartile wage

S	Special: hourly and annual
TQ	Third quartile wage
W	Weekly
Y	Yearly

Occupation/Type/Industry	Location	Per	Low	Mid	High	Source	Date
Legal Secretary	Allentown-Bethlehem-Easton MSA, PA	S	12.76 MW	12.35 AW	26550 AAW	PABLS	10//99-12//99
	Erie MSA, PA	S	10.01 MW	9.85 AW	20820 AAW	PABLS	10//99-12//99
	Harrisburg-Lebanon-Carlisle MSA, PA	S	12.53 MW	12.15 AW	26070 AAW	PABLS	10//99-12//99
	Lancaster MSA, PA	S	12.17 MW	11.43 AW	25320 AAW	PABLS	10//99-12//99
	Philadelphia PMSA, PA-NJ	S	16.48 MW	16.06 AW	34270 AAW	PABLS	10//99-12//99
	Pittsburgh MSA, PA	S	14.62 MW	14.62 AW	30410 AAW	PABLS	10//99-12//99
	State College MSA, PA	S	12.90 MW	13.25 AW	26840 AAW	PABLS	10//99-12//99
	Williamsport MSA, PA	S	10.43 MW	9.48 AW	21690 AAW	PABLS	10//99-12//99
	Rhode Island	S	15.06 MW	15.32 AW	31870 AAW	RIBLS	10//99-12//99
	Providence-Fall River-Warwick MSA, RI-MA	S	15.49 MW	15.21 AW	32210 AAW	RIBLS	10//99-12//99
	South Carolina	S	12.33 MW	12.62 AW	26240 AAW	SCBLS	10//99-12//99
	Charleston-North Charleston MSA, SC	S	10.79 MW	10.13 AW	22440 AAW	SCBLS	10//99-12//99
	Columbia MSA, SC	S	14.37 MW	14.35 AW	29900 AAW	SCBLS	10//99-12//99
	Florence MSA, SC	S	11.84 MW	12.13 AW	24620 AAW	SCBLS	10//99-12//99
	Greenville-Spartanburg-Anderson MSA, SC	S	12.60 MW	12.43 AW	26210 AAW	SCBLS	10//99-12//99
	Myrtle Beach MSA, SC	S	11.42 MW	11.27 AW	23750 AAW	SCBLS	10//99-12//99
	Sumter MSA, SC	S	10.50 MW	10.10 AW	21840 AAW	SCBLS	10//99-12//99
	South Dakota	S	11.31 MW	11.28 AW	23460 AAW	SDBLS	10//99-12//99
	Rapid City MSA, SD	S	11.46 MW	11.69 AW	23830 AAW	SDBLS	10//99-12//99
	Sioux Falls MSA, SD	S	12.23 MW	12.23 AW	25440 AAW	SDBLS	10//99-12//99
	Tennessee	S	11 MW	10.96 AW	22790 AAW	TNBLS	10//99-12//99
	Clarksville-Hopkinsville MSA, TN-KY	S	10.00 MW	10.17 AW	20800 AAW	TNBLS	10//99-12//99
	Jackson MSA, TN	S	10.79 MW	11.14 AW	22440 AAW	TNBLS	10//99-12//99
	Johnson City-Kingsport-Bristol MSA, TN-VA	S	9.11 MW	8.96 AW	18950 AAW	TNBLS	10//99-12//99
	Knoxville MSA, TN	S	10.82 MW	10.58 AW	22510 AAW	TNBLS	10//99-12//99
	Memphis MSA, TN-AR-MS	S	12.34 MW	12.39 AW	25670 AAW	MSBLS	10//99-12//99
	Nashville MSA, TN	S	12.52 MW	12.91 AW	26030 AAW	TNBLS	10//99-12//99
	Texas	S	14.79 MW	14.80 AW	30780 AAW	TXBLS	10//99-12//99
	Abilene MSA, TX	S	13.81 MW	12.99 AW	28730 AAW	TXBLS	10//99-12//99
	Amarillo MSA, TX	S	11.90 MW	11.45 AW	24740 AAW	TXBLS	10//99-12//99
	Austin-San Marcos MSA, TX	S	16.27 MW	16.76 AW	33840 AAW	TXBLS	10//99-12//99
	Beaumont-Port Arthur MSA, TX	S	12.91 MW	12.98 AW	26850 AAW	TXBLS	10//99-12//99
	Brazoria PMSA, TX	S	16.09 MW	14.62 AW	33470 AAW	TXBLS	10//99-12//99
	Brownsville-Harlingen-San Benito MSA, TX	S	12.37 MW	12.47 AW	25720 AAW	TXBLS	10//99-12//99
	Corpus Christi MSA, TX	S	13.52 MW	13.03 AW	28120 AAW	TXBLS	10//99-12//99
	Dallas PMSA, TX	S	14.57 MW	13.76 AW	30310 AAW	TXBLS	10//99-12//99
	El Paso MSA, TX	S	11.82 MW	11.49 AW	24590 AAW	TXBLS	10//99-12//99
	Fort Worth-Arlington PMSA, TX	S	16.17 MW	16.50 AW	33630 AAW	TXBLS	10//99-12//99
	Galveston-Texas City PMSA, TX	S	14.34 MW	13.41 AW	29830 AAW	TXBLS	10//99-12//99
	Houston PMSA, TX	S	17.48 MW	18.03 AW	36360 AAW	TXBLS	10//99-12//99
	Laredo MSA, TX	S	12.83 MW	11.25 AW	26680 AAW	TXBLS	10//99-12//99
	Longview-Marshall MSA, TX	S	11.19 MW	11.52 AW	23280 AAW	TXBLS	10//99-12//99
	Odessa-Midland MSA, TX	S	12.70 MW	11.30 AW	26410 AAW	TXBLS	10//99-12//99
	San Angelo MSA, TX	S	12.33 MW	11.55 AW	25640 AAW	TXBLS	10//99-12//99
	San Antonio MSA, TX	S	10.98 MW	10.09 AW	22850 AAW	TXBLS	10//99-12//99
	Sherman-Denison MSA, TX	S	10.55 MW	10.84 AW	21950 AAW	TXBLS	10//99-12//99
	Texarkana MSA, TX-Texarkana, AR	S	10.20 MW	9.85 AW	21220 AAW	TXBLS	10//99-12//99
	Tyler MSA, TX	S	14.78 MW	15.10 AW	30750 AAW	TXBLS	10//99-12//99
	Victoria MSA, TX	S	10.92 MW	10.02 AW	22710 AAW	TXBLS	10//99-12//99
	Waco MSA, TX	S	17.31 MW	18.21 AW	36000 AAW	TXBLS	10//99-12//99
	Utah	S	14.18 MW	13.66 AW	28400 AAW	UTBLS	10//99-12//99
	Vermont	S	12.3 MW	12.78 AW	26580 AAW	VTBLS	10//99-12//99
	Burlington MSA, VT	S	12.70 MW	11.84 AW	26420 AAW	VTBLS	10//99-12//99
	Virginia	S	12.84 MW	13.61 AW	28310 AAW	VABLS	10//99-12//99
	Charlottesville MSA, VA	S	11.75 MW	10.55 AW	24440 AAW	VABLS	10//99-12//99
	Danville MSA, VA	S	11.99 MW	10.68 AW	24950 AAW	VABLS	10//99-12//99
	Lynchburg MSA, VA	S	12.70 MW	10.51 AW	26420 AAW	VABLS	10//99-12//99
	Norfolk-Virginia Beach-Newport News MSA, VA-NC	S	12.04 MW	11.51 AW	25050 AAW	VABLS	10//99-12//99

AAW Average annual wage	AOH Average offered, high	ASH Average starting, high	H Hourly	M Monthly	S Special: hourly and annual
AE Average entry wage	AOL Average offered, low	ASL Average starting, low	HI Highest wage paid	MTC Median total compensation	TQ Third quartile wage
AEX Average experienced wage	APH Average pay, high range	AW Average wage paid	HR High end range	MW Median wage paid	W Weekly
AO Average offered	APL Average pay, low range	FQ First quartile wage	LR Low end range	SQ Second quartile wage	Y Yearly

Occupation/Type/Industry	Location	Per	Low	Mid	High	Source	Date
Legal Secretary	Richmond-Petersburg MSA, VA	S	13.91 MW	13.97 AW	28930 AAW	VABLS	10//99-12//99
	Washington	S	16.01 MW	15.88 AW	33030 AAW	WABLS	10//99-12//99
	Richland-Kennewick-Pasco MSA, WA	S	12.80 MW	13.26 AW	26620 AAW	WABLS	10//99-12//99
	Seattle-Bellevue-Everett PMSA, WA	S	17.82 MW	17.94 AW	37060 AAW	WABLS	10//99-12//99
	Spokane MSA, WA	S	13.23 MW	12.76 AW	27530 AAW	WABLS	10//99-12//99
	Tacoma PMSA, WA	S	16.25 MW	15.76 AW	33800 AAW	WABLS	10//99-12//99
	Yakima MSA, WA	S	14.80 MW	14.82 AW	30790 AAW	WABLS	10//99-12//99
	West Virginia	S	10.56 MW	11.73 AW	24390 AAW	WVBLS	10//99-12//99
	Huntington-Ashland MSA, WV-KY-OH	S	10.46 MW	10.25 AW	21760 AAW	WVBLS	10//99-12//99
	Parkersburg-Marietta MSA, WV-OH	S	10.76 MW	11.24 AW	22380 AAW	WVBLS	10//99-12//99
	Wheeling MSA, WV-OH	S	10.02 MW	10.75 AW	20830 AAW	WVBLS	10//99-12//99
	Wisconsin	S	12.78 MW	12.44 AW	25860 AAW	WIBLS	10//99-12//99
	Appleton-Oshkosh-Neenah MSA, WI	S	12.15 MW	11.93 AW	25270 AAW	WIBLS	10//99-12//99
	Eau Claire MSA, WI	S	10.39 MW	10.16 AW	21610 AAW	WIBLS	10//99-12//99
	Green Bay MSA, WI	S	12.22 MW	11.47 AW	25410 AAW	WIBLS	10//99-12//99
	Janesville-Beloit MSA, WI	S	12.39 MW	12.12 AW	25770 AAW	WIBLS	10//99-12//99
	Kenosha PMSA, WI	S	13.48 MW	12.93 AW	28040 AAW	WIBLS	10//99-12//99
	La Crosse MSA, WI-MN	S	10.13 MW	9.66 AW	21070 AAW	WIBLS	10//99-12//99
	Madison MSA, WI	S	13.42 MW	14.31 AW	27920 AAW	WIBLS	10//99-12//99
	Milwaukee-Waukesha PMSA, WI	S	12.40 MW	13.33 AW	25790 AAW	WIBLS	10//99-12//99
	Racine PMSA, WI	S	11.44 MW	11.28 AW	23780 AAW	WIBLS	10//99-12//99
	Wyoming	S	9.54 MW	9.56 AW	19890 AAW	WYBLS	10//99-12//99
	Casper MSA, WY	S	10.49 MW	10.17 AW	21810 AAW	WYBLS	10//99-12//99
	Cheyenne MSA, WY	S	10.86 MW	10.18 AW	22580 AAW	WYBLS	10//99-12//99
	Puerto Rico	S	8.31 MW	8.62 AW	17930 AAW	PRBLS	10//99-12//99
	Aguadilla MSA, PR	S	6.38 MW	6.16 AW	13270 AAW	PRBLS	10//99-12//99
	Arecibo PMSA, PR	S	7.87 MW	7.37 AW	16360 AAW	PRBLS	10//99-12//99
	Ponce MSA, PR	S	8.09 MW	7.81 AW	16820 AAW	PRBLS	10//99-12//99
	San Juan-Bayamon PMSA, PR	S	8.99 MW	8.43 AW	18690 AAW	PRBLS	10//99-12//99
	Virgin Islands	S	14.33 MW	14.54 AW	30240 AAW	VIBLS	10//99-12//99
	Guam	S	11.1 MW	11.37 AW	23650 AAW	GUBLS	10//99-12//99
Legal Support Staffer	United States	Y		40474 AW		BOSBU2	2000
Legislator	Alabama	S	6.18 MW	7.16 AW	14900 AAW	ALBLS	10//99-12//99
	Birmingham MSA, AL	S	9.44 MW	6.41 AW	19630 AAW	ALBLS	10//99-12//99
	Dothan MSA, AL	S	8.05 MW	6.23 AW	16740 AAW	ALBLS	10//99-12//99
	Mobile MSA, AL	S	6.92 MW	6.50 AW	14400 AAW	ALBLS	10//99-12//99
	Montgomery MSA, AL	S	13.06 MW	8.28 AW	27170 AAW	ALBLS	10//99-12//99
	Alaska	S	6.59 MW	8.60 AW	17880 AAW	AKBLS	10//99-12//99
	Arizona	S	6.22 MW	9.79 AW	20360 AAW	AZBLS	10//99-12//99
	Phoenix-Mesa MSA, AZ	S	12.16 MW	6.56 AW	25300 AAW	AZBLS	10//99-12//99
	Arkansas	S	6.31 MW	10.66 AW	22170 AAW	ARBLS	10//99-12//99
	Fayetteville-Springdale-Rogers MSA, AR	S	18.97 MW	22.21 AW	39450 AAW	ARBLS	10//99-12//99
	Little Rock-North Little Rock MSA, AR	S	8.71 MW	6.17 AW	18120 AAW	ARBLS	10//99-12//99
	California	S	19.75 MW	23.95 AW	49820 AAW	CABLS	10//99-12//99
	Los Angeles-Long Beach PMSA, CA	S	24.98 MW	20.43 AW	51960 AAW	CABLS	10//99-12//99
	Oakland PMSA, CA	S	21.19 MW	19.39 AW	44070 AAW	CABLS	10//99-12//99
	Orange County PMSA, CA	S	24.38 MW	20.65 AW	50710 AAW	CABLS	10//99-12//99
	Riverside-San Bernardino PMSA, CA	S	20.36 MW	20.43 AW	42340 AAW	CABLS	10//99-12//99
	Sacramento PMSA, CA	S	29.73 MW	19.61 AW	61830 AAW	CABLS	10//99-12//99
	San Francisco PMSA, CA	S	20.43 MW	19.47 AW	42500 AAW	CABLS	10//99-12//99
	Connecticut	S	17.94 MW	21.08 AW	43850 AAW	CTBLS	10//99-12//99
	Hartford MSA, CT	S	24.81 MW	27.41 AW	51610 AAW	CTBLS	10//99-12//99
	New Haven-Meriden PMSA, CT	S	14.75 MW	6.44 AW	30690 AAW	CTBLS	10//99-12//99
	New London-Norwich MSA, CT-RI	S	13.01 MW	7.45 AW	27060 AAW	CTBLS	10//99-12//99
	Washington PMSA, DC-MD-VA-WV	S	17.20 MW	6.40 AW	35770 AAW	DCBLS	10//99-12//99
	Florida	S	6.45 MW	11.29 AW	23480 AAW	FLBLS	10//99-12//99
	Daytona Beach MSA, FL	S	5.75 MW	5.95 AW	11960 AAW	FLBLS	10//99-12//99

AAW	Average annual wage	AOH	Average offered, high	ASH	Average starting, high	H	Hourly	M	Monthly	S	Special: hourly and annual
AE	Average entry wage	AOL	Average offered, low	ASL	Average starting, low	HI	Highest wage paid	MTC	Median total compensation	TQ	Third quartile wage
AEX	Average experienced wage	APH	Average pay, high range	AW	Average wage paid	HR	High end range	MW	Median wage paid	W	Weekly
AO	Average offered	APL	Average pay, low range	FQ	First quartile wage	LR	Low end range	SQ	Second quartile wage	Y	Yearly

Occupation/Type/Industry	Location	Per	Low	Mid	High	Source	Date
Legislator	Fort Lauderdale PMSA, FL	S	10.20 MW	6.47 AW	21210 AAW	FLBLS	10//99-12//99
	Lakeland-Winter Haven MSA, FL	S	5.75 MW	5.95 AW	11960 AAW	FLBLS	10//99-12//99
	Melbourne-Titusville-Palm Bay MSA, FL	S	7.52 MW	6.66 AW	15650 AAW	FLBLS	10//99-12//99
	Miami PMSA, FL	S	12.37 MW	6.54 AW	25730 AAW	FLBLS	10//99-12//99
	Orlando MSA, FL	S	7.86 MW	6.44 AW	16350 AAW	FLBLS	10//99-12//99
	Pensacola MSA, FL	S	21.67 MW	28.86 AW	45080 AAW	FLBLS	10//99-12//99
	Sarasota-Bradenton MSA, FL	S	8.86 MW	6.19 AW	18430 AAW	FLBLS	10//99-12//99
	Tallahassee MSA, FL	S	24.40 MW	29.67 AW	50750 AAW	FLBLS	10//99-12//99
	West Palm Beach-Boca Raton MSA, FL	S	7.28 MW	6.12 AW	15140 AAW	FLBLS	10//99-12//99
	Georgia	S	22.76 MW	22.16 AW	46100 AAW	GABLS	10//99-12//99
	Idaho	S	10.71 MW	16.82 AW	34980 AAW	IDBLS	10//99-12//99
	Indiana	S	12.76 MW	12.82 AW	26670 AAW	INBLS	10//99-12//99
	Evansville-Henderson MSA, IN-KY	S	12.33 MW	14.22 AW	25650 AAW	INBLS	10//99-12//99
	Gary PMSA, IN	S	14.38 MW	14.68 AW	29900 AAW	INBLS	10//99-12//99
	Indianapolis MSA, IN	S	10.76 MW	10.19 AW	22380 AAW	INBLS	10//99-12//99
	Iowa	S	6.2 MW	8.17 AW	16990 AAW	IABLS	10//99-12//99
	Kansas	S	19 MW	19.41 AW	40380 AAW	KSBLS	10//99-12//99
	Louisville MSA, KY-IN	S	14.48 MW	15.11 AW	30120 AAW	KYBLS	10//99-12//99
	Louisiana	S	6.26 MW	6.72 AW	13970 AAW	LABLS	10//99-12//99
	Houma MSA, LA	S	5.75 MW	5.95 AW	11960 AAW	LABLS	10//99-12//99
	New Orleans MSA, LA	S	7.14 MW	6.26 AW	14850 AAW	LABLS	10//99-12//99
	Shreveport-Bossier City MSA, LA	S	7.34 MW	7.29 AW	15260 AAW	LABLS	10//99-12//99
	Maryland	S	6.7 MW	18.13 AW	37700 AAW	MDBLS	10//99-12//99
	Massachusetts	S	6.29 MW	7.71 AW	16050 AAW	MABLS	10//99-12//99
	Boston PMSA, MA-NH	S	8.08 MW	6.30 AW	16800 AAW	MABLS	10//99-12//99
	Brockton PMSA, MA	S	6.64 MW	6.12 AW	13820 AAW	MABLS	10//99-12//99
	Lawrence PMSA, MA-NH	S	6.37 MW	6.04 AW	13240 AAW	MABLS	10//99-12//99
	Springfield MSA, MA	S	7.40 MW	6.12 AW	15390 AAW	MABLS	10//99-12//99
	Worcester PMSA, MA-CT	S	6.78 MW	6.84 AW	14100 AAW	MABLS	10//99-12//99
	Minnesota	S	6.23 MW	8.02 AW	16670 AAW	MNBLS	10//99-12//99
	Duluth-Superior MSA, MN-WI	S	9.52 MW	6.14 AW	19810 AAW	MNBLS	10//99-12//99
	Minneapolis-St. Paul MSA, MN-WI	S	10.04 MW	6.33 AW	20890 AAW	MNBLS	10//99-12//99
	Rochester MSA, MN	S	11.61 MW	8.76 AW	24140 AAW	MNBLS	10//99-12//99
	Mississippi	S	6.37 MW	8.31 AW	17280 AAW	MSBLS	10//99-12//99
	Hattiesburg MSA, MS	S	9.23 MW	6.30 AW	19200 AAW	MSBLS	10//99-12//99
	Missouri	S	7.93 MW	11.41 AW	23740 AAW	MOBLS	10//99-12//99
	St. Louis MSA, MO-IL	S	7.87 MW	6.22 AW	16360 AAW	MOBLS	10//99-12//99
	Montana	S	12.14 MW	11.89 AW	24730 AAW	MTBLS	10//99-12//99
	Nevada	S	14.82 MW	16.46 AW	34240 AAW	NVBLS	10//99-12//99
	Reno MSA, NV	S	22.21 MW	19.57 AW	46200 AAW	NVBLS	10//99-12//99
	New Hampshire	S	5.95 MW	5.75 AW	11960 AAW	NHBLS	10//99-12//99
	Nashua PMSA, NH	S	5.75 MW	5.95 AW	11960 AAW	NHBLS	10//99-12//99
	New Jersey	S	9.37 MW	12.20 AW	25380 AAW	NJBLS	10//99-12//99
	Newark PMSA, NJ	S	11.87 MW	11.60 AW	24680 AAW	NJBLS	10//99-12//99
	New York	S	6.65 MW	11.68 AW	24300 AAW	NYBLS	10//99-12//99
	Albany-Schenectady-Troy MSA, NY	S	10.39 MW	6.35 AW	21610 AAW	NYBLS	10//99-12//99
	Binghamton MSA, NY	S	8.19 MW	7.14 AW	17030 AAW	NYBLS	10//99-12//99
	Buffalo-Niagara Falls MSA, NY	S	12.16 MW	6.61 AW	25300 AAW	NYBLS	10//99-12//99
	Dutchess County PMSA, NY	S	5.86 MW	5.98 AW	12190 AAW	NYBLS	10//99-12//99
	Elmira MSA, NY	S	5.75 MW	5.95 AW	11960 AAW	NYBLS	10//99-12//99
	Jamestown MSA, NY	S	9.59 MW	7.33 AW	19940 AAW	NYBLS	10//99-12//99
	Nassau-Suffolk PMSA, NY	S	17.83 MW	12.81 AW	37090 AAW	NYBLS	10//99-12//99
	New York PMSA, NY	S	24.38 MW	18.10 AW	50720 AAW	NYBLS	10//99-12//99
	Newburgh PMSA, NY-PA	S	10.08 MW	8.80 AW	20970 AAW	NYBLS	10//99-12//99
	Rochester MSA, NY	S	10.31 MW	7.62 AW	21450 AAW	NYBLS	10//99-12//99
	Utica-Rome MSA, NY	S	5.75 MW	5.95 AW	11960 AAW	NYBLS	10//99-12//99
	Oklahoma	S	8.76 MW	11.44 AW	23800 AAW	OKBLS	10//99-12//99
	Oklahoma City MSA, OK	S	15.50 MW	17.19 AW	32240 AAW	OKBLS	10//99-12//99
	Oregon	S	8.34 MW	12.89 AW	26810 AAW	ORBLS	10//99-12//99
	Pennsylvania	S	6.17 MW	10.92 AW	22710 AAW	PABLS	10//99-12//99
	Allentown-Bethlehem-Easton MSA, PA	S	7.21 MW	6.00 AW	14990 AAW	PABLS	10//99-12//99
	Philadelphia PMSA, PA-NJ	S	19.53 MW	17.69 AW	40620 AAW	PABLS	10//99-12//99
	Reading MSA, PA	S	5.86 MW	5.95 AW	12180 AAW	PABLS	10//99-12//99

AAW Average annual wage	AOH Average offered, high	ASH Average starting, high	H Hourly	M Monthly	S Special: hourly and annual
AE Average entry wage	AOL Average offered, low	ASL Average starting, low	HI Highest wage paid	MTC Median total compensation	TQ Third quartile wage
AEX Average experienced wage	APH Average pay, high range	AW Average wage paid	HR High end range	MW Median wage paid	W Weekly
AO Average offered	APL Average pay, low range	FQ First quartile wage	LR Low end range	SQ Second quartile wage	Y Yearly

Occupation/Type/Industry	Location	Per	Low	Mid	High	Source	Date
Legislator	Scranton--Wilkes-Barre--Hazleton MSA, PA	S	9.60 MW	6.12 AW	19970 AAW	PABLS	10//99-12//99
	State College MSA, PA	S	12.87 MW	9.77 AW	26760 AAW	PABLS	10//99-12//99
	York MSA, PA	S	5.75 MW	5.95 AW	11960 AAW	PABLS	10//99-12//99
	Rhode Island	S	6.42 MW	9.67 AW	20120 AAW	RIBLS	10//99-12//99
	Providence-Fall River-Warwick MSA, RI-MA	S	9.63 MW	6.41 AW	20020 AAW	RIBLS	10//99-12//99
	South Carolina	S	6.2 MW	7.46 AW	15510 AAW	SCBLS	10//99-12//99
	Charleston-North Charleston MSA, SC	S	6.92 MW	6.07 AW	14390 AAW	SCBLS	10//99-12//99
	Columbia MSA, SC	S	7.25 MW	6.50 AW	15070 AAW	SCBLS	10//99-12//99
	Florence MSA, SC	S	5.87 MW	6.01 AW	12200 AAW	SCBLS	10//99-12//99
	Greenville-Spartanburg-Anderson MSA, SC	S	6.33 MW	6.01 AW	13170 AAW	SCBLS	10//99-12//99
	Tennessee	S	6.08 MW	8.86 AW	18430 AAW	TNBLS	10//99-12//99
	Johnson City-Kingsport-Bristol MSA, TN-VA	S	12.39 MW	6.14 AW	25780 AAW	TNBLS	10//99-12//99
	Knoxville MSA, TN	S	6.62 MW	6.72 AW	13760 AAW	TNBLS	10//99-12//99
	Memphis MSA, TN-AR-MS	S	6.37 MW	5.97 AW	13240 AAW	MSBLS	10//99-12//99
	Nashville MSA, TN	S	8.63 MW	6.06 AW	17960 AAW	TNBLS	10//99-12//99
	Texas	S	6.49 MW	9.47 AW	19710 AAW	TXBLS	10//99-12//99
	Austin-San Marcos MSA, TX	S	8.99 MW	6.08 AW	18690 AAW	TXBLS	10//99-12//99
	Beaumont-Port Arthur MSA, TX	S	16.85 MW	6.61 AW	35050 AAW	TXBLS	10//99-12//99
	Corpus Christi MSA, TX	S	12.82 MW	6.71 AW	26660 AAW	TXBLS	10//99-12//99
	Dallas PMSA, TX	S	7.12 MW	6.00 AW	14810 AAW	TXBLS	10//99-12//99
	Utah	S	6.27 MW	10.01 AW	20810 AAW	UTBLS	10//99-12//99
	Washington	S	33.52 MW	39.23 AW	81590 AAW	WABLS	10//99-12//99
	Seattle-Bellevue-Everett PMSA, WA	S	33.14 MW	32.30 AW	68940 AAW	WABLS	10//99-12//99
	Tacoma PMSA, WA	S	18.65 MW	22.68 AW	38790 AAW	WABLS	10//99-12//99
	Wisconsin	S	6.06 MW	7.58 AW	15760 AAW	WIBLS	10//99-12//99
	Appleton-Oshkosh-Neenah MSA, WI	S	6.74 MW	6.04 AW	14010 AAW	WIBLS	10//99-12//99
	Green Bay MSA, WI	S	7.44 MW	6.03 AW	15470 AAW	WIBLS	10//99-12//99
	Janesville-Beloit MSA, WI	S	6.03 MW	5.96 AW	12550 AAW	WIBLS	10//99-12//99
	Kenosha PMSA, WI	S	8.39 MW	6.02 AW	17460 AAW	WIBLS	10//99-12//99
	La Crosse MSA, WI-MN	S	7.46 MW	6.37 AW	15510 AAW	WIBLS	10//99-12//99
	Milwaukee-Waukesha PMSA, WI	S	9.38 MW	6.11 AW	19510 AAW	WIBLS	10//99-12//99
	Racine PMSA, WI	S	6.72 MW	6.00 AW	13970 AAW	WIBLS	10//99-12//99
	Wausau MSA, WI	S	16.21 MW	15.35 AW	33720 AAW	WIBLS	10//99-12//99
Librarian	United States	H		21.86 AW		NCS98	1998
	Alabama	S	18.11 MW	17.56 AW	36510 AAW	ALBLS	10//99-12//99
	Anniston MSA, AL	S	18.45 MW	18.60 AW	38380 AAW	ALBLS	10//99-12//99
	Birmingham MSA, AL	S	18.67 MW	18.86 AW	38830 AAW	ALBLS	10//99-12//99
	Decatur MSA, AL	S	17.97 MW	18.35 AW	37380 AAW	ALBLS	10//99-12//99
	Dothan MSA, AL	S	17.72 MW	18.50 AW	36850 AAW	ALBLS	10//99-12//99
	Florence MSA, AL	S	18.27 MW	18.37 AW	37990 AAW	ALBLS	10//99-12//99
	Gadsden MSA, AL	S	17.14 MW	18.08 AW	35640 AAW	ALBLS	10//99-12//99
	Huntsville MSA, AL	S	19.27 MW	19.97 AW	40090 AAW	ALBLS	10//99-12//99
	Mobile MSA, AL	S	17.72 MW	17.86 AW	36860 AAW	ALBLS	10//99-12//99
	Montgomery MSA, AL	S	16.81 MW	17.47 AW	34970 AAW	ALBLS	10//99-12//99
	Tuscaloosa MSA, AL	S	16.13 MW	13.64 AW	33540 AAW	ALBLS	10//99-12//99
	Alaska	S	22.48 MW	21.81 AW	45360 AAW	AKBLS	10//99-12//99
	Anchorage MSA, AK	S	23.30 MW	23.48 AW	48460 AAW	AKBLS	10//99-12//99
	Arizona	S	16.96 MW	18.22 AW	37900 AAW	AZBLS	10//99-12//99
	Flagstaff MSA, AZ-UT	S	13.09 MW	11.54 AW	27220 AAW	AZBLS	10//99-12//99
	Phoenix-Mesa MSA, AZ	S	19.62 MW	18.46 AW	40800 AAW	AZBLS	10//99-12//99
	Tucson MSA, AZ	S	17.42 MW	16.40 AW	36230 AAW	AZBLS	10//99-12//99
	Yuma MSA, AZ	S	15.93 MW	15.33 AW	33140 AAW	AZBLS	10//99-12//99
	Arkansas	S	16.1 MW	15.92 AW	33110 AAW	ARBLS	10//99-12//99
	Fayetteville-Springdale-Rogers MSA, AR	S	18.74 MW	19.04 AW	38970 AAW	ARBLS	10//99-12//99
	Fort Smith MSA, AR-OK	S	18.32 MW	18.59 AW	38110 AAW	ARBLS	10//99-12//99
	Little Rock-North Little Rock MSA, AR	S	17.80 MW	18.06 AW	37030 AAW	ARBLS	10//99-12//99
	California	S	22.62 MW	23.20 AW	48250 AAW	CABLS	10//99-12//99
	Bakersfield MSA, CA	S	16.25 MW	12.00 AW	33790 AAW	CABLS	10//99-12//99
	Chico-Paradise MSA, CA	S	22.66 MW	22.15 AW	47120 AAW	CABLS	10//99-12//99
	Fresno MSA, CA	S	23.20 MW	22.99 AW	48250 AAW	CABLS	10//99-12//99

AAW Average annual wage	**AOH** Average offered, high	**ASH** Average starting, high	**H** Hourly	**M** Monthly	**S** Special: hourly and annual
AE Average entry wage	**AOL** Average offered, low	**ASL** Average starting, low	**HI** Highest wage paid	**MTC** Median total compensation	**TQ** Third quartile wage
AEX Average experienced wage	**APH** Average pay, high range	**AW** Average wage paid	**HR** High end range	**MW** Median wage paid	**W** Weekly
AO Average offered	**APL** Average pay, low range	**FQ** First quartile wage	**LR** Low end range	**SQ** Second quartile wage	**Y** Yearly

Librarian

Occupation/Type/Industry	Location	Per	Low	Mid	High	Source	Date
Librarian	Los Angeles-Long Beach PMSA, CA	S	24.68 MW	24.14 AW	51330 AAW	CABLS	10//99-12//99
	Merced MSA, CA	S	22.01 MW	20.48 AW	45790 AAW	CABLS	10//99-12//99
	Modesto MSA, CA	S	20.62 MW	18.77 AW	42890 AAW	CABLS	10//99-12//99
	Oakland PMSA, CA	S	23.89 MW	21.30 AW	49690 AAW	CABLS	10//99-12//99
	Orange County PMSA, CA	S	23.51 MW	22.04 AW	48900 AAW	CABLS	10//99-12//99
	Redding MSA, CA	S	22.34 MW	22.74 AW	46460 AAW	CABLS	10//99-12//99
	Riverside-San Bernardino PMSA, CA	S	23.34 MW	22.31 AW	48540 AAW	CABLS	10//99-12//99
	Sacramento PMSA, CA	S	22.78 MW	22.53 AW	47380 AAW	CABLS	10//99-12//99
	Salinas MSA, CA	S	21.12 MW	20.60 AW	43930 AAW	CABLS	10//99-12//99
	San Diego MSA, CA	S	20.79 MW	20.66 AW	43240 AAW	CABLS	10//99-12//99
	San Francisco PMSA, CA	S	23.60 MW	23.01 AW	49090 AAW	CABLS	10//99-12//99
	San Jose PMSA, CA	S	24.88 MW	24.48 AW	51750 AAW	CABLS	10//99-12//99
	San Luis Obispo-Atascadero-Paso Robles MSA, CA	S	20.85 MW	19.59 AW	43370 AAW	CABLS	10//99-12//99
	Santa Barbara-Santa Maria-Lompoc MSA, CA	S	19.50 MW	19.17 AW	40550 AAW	CABLS	10//99-12//99
	Santa Cruz-Watsonville PMSA, CA	S	22.89 MW	21.85 AW	47600 AAW	CABLS	10//99-12//99
	Santa Rosa PMSA, CA	S	24.59 MW	23.87 AW	51150 AAW	CABLS	10//99-12//99
	Stockton-Lodi MSA, CA	S	23.18 MW	23.06 AW	48200 AAW	CABLS	10//99-12//99
	Vallejo-Fairfield-Napa PMSA, CA	S	23.09 MW	23.73 AW	48020 AAW	CABLS	10//99-12//99
	Ventura PMSA, CA	S	24.38 MW	23.39 AW	50710 AAW	CABLS	10//99-12//99
	Visalia-Tulare-Porterville MSA, CA	S	22.49 MW	22.46 AW	46780 AAW	CABLS	10//99-12//99
	Yuba City MSA, CA	S	20.10 MW	20.90 AW	41810 AAW	CABLS	10//99-12//99
	Colorado	S	17.86 MW	18.35 AW	38160 AAW	COBLS	10//99-12//99
	Boulder-Longmont PMSA, CO	S	18.18 MW	18.13 AW	37810 AAW	COBLS	10//99-12//99
	Colorado Springs MSA, CO	S	18.00 MW	16.62 AW	37430 AAW	COBLS	10//99-12//99
	Denver PMSA, CO	S	19.59 MW	18.69 AW	40750 AAW	COBLS	10//99-12//99
	Fort Collins-Loveland MSA, CO	S	17.14 MW	16.86 AW	35660 AAW	COBLS	10//99-12//99
	Connecticut	S	22.04 MW	23.13 AW	48110 AAW	CTBLS	10//99-12//99
	Bridgeport PMSA, CT	S	22.56 MW	21.32 AW	46930 AAW	CTBLS	10//99-12//99
	Danbury PMSA, CT	S	22.73 MW	21.66 AW	47270 AAW	CTBLS	10//99-12//99
	Hartford MSA, CT	S	23.97 MW	22.97 AW	49860 AAW	CTBLS	10//99-12//99
	New Haven-Meriden PMSA, CT	S	23.48 MW	22.21 AW	48840 AAW	CTBLS	10//99-12//99
	New London-Norwich MSA, CT-RI	S	21.31 MW	21.50 AW	44330 AAW	CTBLS	10//99-12//99
	Stamford-Norwalk PMSA, CT	S	22.56 MW	20.77 AW	46920 AAW	CTBLS	10//99-12//99
	Waterbury PMSA, CT	S	21.97 MW	21.43 AW	45690 AAW	CTBLS	10//99-12//99
	Dover MSA, DE	S	19.85 MW	20.42 AW	41290 AAW	DEBLS	10//99-12//99
	Wilmington-Newark PMSA, DE-MD	S	21.52 MW	21.41 AW	44770 AAW	DEBLS	10//99-12//99
	District of Columbia	S	20.85 MW	21.64 AW	45020 AAW	DCBLS	10//99-12//99
	Washington PMSA, DC-MD-VA-WV	S	22.33 MW	21.63 AW	46440 AAW	DCBLS	10//99-12//99
	Florida	S	18.05 MW	19.61 AW	40780 AAW	FLBLS	10//99-12//99
	Daytona Beach MSA, FL	S	18.06 MW	14.01 AW	37570 AAW	FLBLS	10//99-12//99
	Fort Lauderdale PMSA, FL	S	20.23 MW	18.33 AW	42080 AAW	FLBLS	10//99-12//99
	Fort Myers-Cape Coral MSA, FL	S	21.15 MW	18.29 AW	44000 AAW	FLBLS	10//99-12//99
	Jacksonville MSA, FL	S	18.42 MW	16.71 AW	38310 AAW	FLBLS	10//99-12//99
	Miami PMSA, FL	S	18.71 MW	15.97 AW	38910 AAW	FLBLS	10//99-12//99
	Ocala MSA, FL	S	18.40 MW	16.62 AW	38270 AAW	FLBLS	10//99-12//99
	Orlando MSA, FL	S	19.68 MW	18.40 AW	40920 AAW	FLBLS	10//99-12//99
	Pensacola MSA, FL	S	19.36 MW	18.64 AW	40260 AAW	FLBLS	10//99-12//99
	Sarasota-Bradenton MSA, FL	S	19.02 MW	16.67 AW	39560 AAW	FLBLS	10//99-12//99
	Tallahassee MSA, FL	S	22.81 MW	19.65 AW	47450 AAW	FLBLS	10//99-12//99
	Tampa-St. Petersburg-Clearwater MSA, FL	S	21.58 MW	20.08 AW	44880 AAW	FLBLS	10//99-12//99
	West Palm Beach-Boca Raton MSA, FL	S	16.67 MW	16.18 AW	34670 AAW	FLBLS	10//99-12//99
	Georgia	S	21.95 MW	21.76 AW	45260 AAW	GABLS	10//99-12//99
	Atlanta MSA, GA	S	22.03 MW	22.20 AW	45820 AAW	GABLS	10//99-12//99
	Augusta-Aiken MSA, GA-SC	S	19.88 MW	20.59 AW	41340 AAW	GABLS	10//99-12//99
	Cobb County, GA	Y		35635 AW		ATJOCO	1998
	Columbus MSA, GA-AL	S	21.10 MW	20.44 AW	43900 AAW	GABLS	10//99-12//99
	Macon MSA, GA	S	21.52 MW	22.34 AW	44770 AAW	GABLS	10//99-12//99

AAW Average annual wage	AOH Average offered, high	ASH Average starting, high	H Hourly	M Monthly	S Special: hourly and annual
AE Average entry wage	AOL Average offered, low	ASL Average starting, low	HI Highest wage paid	MTC Median total compensation	TQ Third quartile wage
AEX Average experienced wage	APH Average pay, high range	AW Average wage paid	HR High end range	MW Median wage paid	W Weekly
AO Average offered	APL Average pay, low range	FQ First quartile wage	LR Low end range	SQ Second quartile wage	Y Yearly

Occupation/Type/Industry	Location	Per	Low	Mid	High	Source	Date
Librarian	Savannah MSA, GA	S	20.34 MW	17.80 AW	42310 AAW	GABLS	10//99-12//99
	Hawaii	S	22.16 MW	23.02 AW	47880 AAW	HIBLS	10//99-12//99
	Honolulu MSA, HI	S	22.95 MW	22.15 AW	47740 AAW	HIBLS	10//99-12//99
	Idaho	S	17.08 MW	16.47 AW	34250 AAW	IDBLS	10//99-12//99
	Boise City MSA, ID	S	18.31 MW	17.68 AW	38080 AAW	IDBLS	10//99-12//99
	Illinois	S	18.9 MW	18.98 AW	39480 AAW	ILBLS	10//99-12//99
	Bloomington-Normal MSA, IL	S	21.72 MW	21.50 AW	45170 AAW	ILBLS	10//99-12//99
	Chicago PMSA, IL	S	20.89 MW	21.48 AW	43450 AAW	ILBLS	10//99-12//99
	Decatur MSA, IL	S	15.90 MW	17.93 AW	33060 AAW	ILBLS	10//99-12//99
	Kankakee PMSA, IL	S	16.23 MW	17.78 AW	33750 AAW	ILBLS	10//99-12//99
	Rockford MSA, IL	S	19.32 MW	17.35 AW	40180 AAW	ILBLS	10//99-12//99
	Springfield MSA, IL	S	15.23 MW	15.81 AW	31670 AAW	ILBLS	10//99-12//99
	Indiana	S	18.34 MW	19.07 AW	39660 AAW	INBLS	10//99-12//99
	Elkhart-Goshen MSA, IN	S	17.57 MW	14.77 AW	36540 AAW	INBLS	10//99-12//99
	Evansville-Henderson MSA, IN-KY	S	18.53 MW	17.42 AW	38550 AAW	INBLS	10//99-12//99
	Fort Wayne MSA, IN	S	19.84 MW	19.18 AW	41260 AAW	INBLS	10//99-12//99
	Gary PMSA, IN	S	17.91 MW	16.19 AW	37260 AAW	INBLS	10//99-12//99
	Indianapolis MSA, IN	S	19.84 MW	19.03 AW	41270 AAW	INBLS	10//99-12//99
	Kokomo MSA, IN	S	19.76 MW	18.82 AW	41100 AAW	INBLS	10//99-12//99
	Lafayette MSA, IN	S	18.71 MW	18.04 AW	38920 AAW	INBLS	10//99-12//99
	Muncie MSA, IN	S	20.77 MW	22.46 AW	43210 AAW	INBLS	10//99-12//99
	South Bend MSA, IN	S	17.44 MW	16.88 AW	36280 AAW	INBLS	10//99-12//99
	Iowa	S	14.04 MW	14.35 AW	29850 AAW	IABLS	10//99-12//99
	Cedar Rapids MSA, IA	S	15.37 MW	15.86 AW	31960 AAW	IABLS	10//99-12//99
	Davenport-Moline-Rock Island MSA, IA-IL	S	17.75 MW	16.80 AW	36930 AAW	IABLS	10//99-12//99
	Des Moines MSA, IA	S	14.97 MW	14.71 AW	31130 AAW	IABLS	10//99-12//99
	Dubuque MSA, IA	S	17.25 MW	16.85 AW	35880 AAW	IABLS	10//99-12//99
	Sioux City MSA, IA-NE	S	17.11 MW	17.07 AW	35580 AAW	IABLS	10//99-12//99
	Waterloo-Cedar Falls MSA, IA	S	18.43 MW	18.87 AW	38340 AAW	IABLS	10//99-12//99
	Kansas	S	17.78 MW	17.43 AW	36260 AAW	KSBLS	10//99-12//99
	Lawrence MSA, KS	S	16.57 MW	17.17 AW	34460 AAW	KSBLS	10//99-12//99
	Topeka MSA, KS	S	20.00 MW	19.01 AW	41590 AAW	KSBLS	10//99-12//99
	Wichita MSA, KS	S	18.29 MW	18.34 AW	38040 AAW	KSBLS	10//99-12//99
	Kentucky	S	19.84 MW	19.03 AW	39570 AAW	KYBLS	10//99-12//99
	Lexington MSA, KY	S	20.23 MW	20.51 AW	42070 AAW	KYBLS	10//99-12//99
	Louisville MSA, KY-IN	S	20.05 MW	21.82 AW	41700 AAW	KYBLS	10//99-12//99
	Louisiana	S	17.78 MW	18.23 AW	37920 AAW	LABLS	10//99-12//99
	Baton Rouge MSA, LA	S	18.18 MW	18.32 AW	37810 AAW	LABLS	10//99-12//99
	Houma MSA, LA	S	16.44 MW	16.32 AW	34190 AAW	LABLS	10//99-12//99
	Lafayette MSA, LA	S	19.48 MW	18.29 AW	40520 AAW	LABLS	10//99-12//99
	Lake Charles MSA, LA	S	20.13 MW	18.95 AW	41870 AAW	LABLS	10//99-12//99
	Monroe MSA, LA	S	16.03 MW	16.29 AW	33340 AAW	LABLS	10//99-12//99
	New Orleans MSA, LA	S	17.08 MW	17.88 AW	35520 AAW	LABLS	10//99-12//99
	Maine	S	16.17 MW	15.92 AW	33110 AAW	MEBLS	10//99-12//99
	Bangor MSA, ME	S	18.07 MW	17.68 AW	37580 AAW	MEBLS	10//99-12//99
	Lewiston-Auburn MSA, ME	S	16.64 MW	15.96 AW	34610 AAW	MEBLS	10//99-12//99
	Portland MSA, ME	S	17.40 MW	17.40 AW	36190 AAW	MEBLS	10//99-12//99
	Maryland	S	18.8 MW	20.06 AW	41730 AAW	MDBLS	10//99-12//99
	Baltimore PMSA, MD	S	17.87 MW	16.81 AW	37170 AAW	MDBLS	10//99-12//99
	Massachusetts	S	19.52 MW	20.01 AW	41620 AAW	MABLS	10//99-12//99
	Barnstable-Yarmouth MSA, MA	S	17.18 MW	16.81 AW	35730 AAW	MABLS	10//99-12//99
	Boston PMSA, MA-NH	S	20.09 MW	19.49 AW	41780 AAW	MABLS	10//99-12//99
	Brockton PMSA, MA	S	19.94 MW	19.75 AW	41480 AAW	MABLS	10//99-12//99
	Fitchburg-Leominster PMSA, MA	S	18.62 MW	19.35 AW	38730 AAW	MABLS	10//99-12//99
	Lawrence PMSA, MA-NH	S	19.19 MW	18.65 AW	39910 AAW	MABLS	10//99-12//99
	Lowell PMSA, MA-NH	S	21.55 MW	21.68 AW	44830 AAW	MABLS	10//99-12//99
	New Bedford PMSA, MA	S	18.33 MW	18.69 AW	38120 AAW	MABLS	10//99-12//99
	Pittsfield MSA, MA	S	18.12 MW	17.31 AW	37680 AAW	MABLS	10//99-12//99
	Springfield MSA, MA	S	20.97 MW	20.36 AW	43620 AAW	MABLS	10//99-12//99
	Worcester PMSA, MA-CT	S	21.18 MW	20.67 AW	44050 AAW	MABLS	10//99-12//99
	Michigan	S	20.18 MW	21.01 AW	43700 AAW	MIBLS	10//99-12//99
	Ann Arbor PMSA, MI	S	22.42 MW	21.40 AW	46630 AAW	MIBLS	10//99-12//99
	Benton Harbor MSA, MI	S	17.37 MW	16.67 AW	36120 AAW	MIBLS	10//99-12//99
	Detroit PMSA, MI	S	21.69 MW	20.02 AW	45120 AAW	MIBLS	10//99-12//99
	Flint PMSA, MI	S	22.63 MW	22.35 AW	47080 AAW	MIBLS	10//99-12//99
	Grand Rapids-Muskegon-Holland MSA, MI	S	20.65 MW	19.48 AW	42960 AAW	MIBLS	10//99-12//99
	Jackson MSA, MI	S	19.67 MW	19.45 AW	40920 AAW	MIBLS	10//99-12//99

AAW Average annual wage	**AOH** Average offered, high	**ASH** Average starting, high	**H** Hourly	**M** Monthly	**S** Special: hourly and annual
AE Average entry wage	**AOL** Average offered, low	**ASL** Average starting, low	**HI** Highest wage paid	**MTC** Median total compensation	**TQ** Third quartile wage
AEX Average experienced wage	**APH** Average pay, high range	**AW** Average wage paid	**HR** High end range	**MW** Median wage paid	**W** Weekly
AO Average offered	**APL** Average pay, low range	**FQ** First quartile wage	**LR** Low end range	**SQ** Second quartile wage	**Y** Yearly

Occupation/Type/Industry	Location	Per	Low	Mid	High	Source	Date
Librarian	Kalamazoo-Battle Creek MSA, MI	S	21.31 MW	21.24 AW	44320 AAW	MIBLS	10//99-12//99
	Lansing-East Lansing MSA, MI	S	22.33 MW	21.86 AW	46440 AAW	MIBLS	10//99-12//99
	Saginaw-Bay City-Midland MSA, MI	S	20.26 MW	19.25 AW	42150 AAW	MIBLS	10//99-12//99
	Minnesota	S	19.32 MW	19.77 AW	41130 AAW	MNBLS	10//99-12//99
	Duluth-Superior MSA, MN-WI	S	18.10 MW	18.01 AW	37660 AAW	MNBLS	10//99-12//99
	Minneapolis-St. Paul MSA, MN-WI	S	20.56 MW	20.04 AW	42770 AAW	MNBLS	10//99-12//99
	St. Cloud MSA, MN	S	18.42 MW	17.34 AW	38310 AAW	MNBLS	10//99-12//99
	Mississippi	S	15.11 MW	15.08 AW	31370 AAW	MSBLS	10//99-12//99
	Biloxi-Gulfport-Pascagoula MSA, MS	S	16.84 MW	16.64 AW	35020 AAW	MSBLS	10//99-12//99
	Hattiesburg MSA, MS	S	16.23 MW	15.97 AW	33750 AAW	MSBLS	10//99-12//99
	Jackson MSA, MS	S	15.35 MW	15.44 AW	31930 AAW	MSBLS	10//99-12//99
	Missouri	S	16.45 MW	17.46 AW	36320 AAW	MOBLS	10//99-12//99
	Joplin MSA, MO	S	14.02 MW	14.02 AW	29170 AAW	MOBLS	10//99-12//99
	Kansas City MSA, MO-KS	S	17.97 MW	17.67 AW	37380 AAW	MOBLS	10//99-12//99
	St. Joseph MSA, MO	S	14.06 MW	14.44 AW	29240 AAW	MOBLS	10//99-12//99
	St. Louis MSA, MO-IL	S	21.34 MW	20.61 AW	44390 AAW	MOBLS	10//99-12//99
	Springfield MSA, MO	S	17.05 MW	16.27 AW	35470 AAW	MOBLS	10//99-12//99
	Montana	S	15.73 MW	16.44 AW	34200 AAW	MTBLS	10//99-12//99
	Billings MSA, MT	S	17.24 MW	17.53 AW	35850 AAW	MTBLS	10//99-12//99
	Missoula MSA, MT	S	21.74 MW	16.85 AW	45230 AAW	MTBLS	10//99-12//99
	Nebraska	S	14.65 MW	14.13 AW	29380 AAW	NEBLS	10//99-12//99
	Lincoln MSA, NE	S	18.37 MW	17.75 AW	38200 AAW	NEBLS	10//99-12//99
	Omaha MSA, NE-IA	S	16.09 MW	17.14 AW	33460 AAW	NEBLS	10//99-12//99
	Nevada	S	21.99 MW	22.47 AW	46740 AAW	NVBLS	10//99-12//99
	Las Vegas MSA, NV-AZ	S	21.84 MW	21.54 AW	45420 AAW	NVBLS	10//99-12//99
	Reno MSA, NV	S	23.50 MW	22.65 AW	48870 AAW	NVBLS	10//99-12//99
	New Hampshire	S	17.49 MW	17.53 AW	36470 AAW	NHBLS	10//99-12//99
	Manchester PMSA, NH	S	18.29 MW	17.68 AW	38040 AAW	NHBLS	10//99-12//99
	Nashua PMSA, NH	S	19.72 MW	20.74 AW	41010 AAW	NHBLS	10//99-12//99
	Portsmouth-Rochester PMSA, NH-ME	S	19.01 MW	18.67 AW	39540 AAW	NHBLS	10//99-12//99
	New Jersey	S	22.45 MW	23.51 AW	48890 AAW	NJBLS	10//99-12//99
	Atlantic-Cape May PMSA, NJ	S	21.48 MW	19.96 AW	44680 AAW	NJBLS	10//99-12//99
	Bergen-Passaic PMSA, NJ	S	23.70 MW	22.85 AW	49300 AAW	NJBLS	10//99-12//99
	Jersey City PMSA, NJ	S	26.26 MW	25.90 AW	54610 AAW	NJBLS	10//99-12//99
	Middlesex-Somerset-Hunterdon PMSA, NJ	S	23.51 MW	21.66 AW	48890 AAW	NJBLS	10//99-12//99
	Monmouth-Ocean PMSA, NJ	S	22.63 MW	21.73 AW	47070 AAW	NJBLS	10//99-12//99
	Newark PMSA, NJ	S	23.56 MW	22.31 AW	49010 AAW	NJBLS	10//99-12//99
	Trenton PMSA, NJ	S	24.35 MW	23.18 AW	50650 AAW	NJBLS	10//99-12//99
	Vineland-Millville-Bridgeton PMSA, NJ	S	23.81 MW	24.32 AW	49530 AAW	NJBLS	10//99-12//99
	New Mexico	S	15.54 MW	15.92 AW	33120 AAW	NMBLS	10//99-12//99
	Albuquerque MSA, NM	S	16.53 MW	15.81 AW	34380 AAW	NMBLS	10//99-12//99
	Santa Fe MSA, NM	S	18.91 MW	18.04 AW	39330 AAW	NMBLS	10//99-12//99
	New York	S	20.72 MW	21.97 AW	45700 AAW	NYBLS	10//99-12//99
	Albany-Schenectady-Troy MSA, NY	S	21.32 MW	21.83 AW	44350 AAW	NYBLS	10//99-12//99
	Binghamton MSA, NY	S	21.54 MW	21.81 AW	44800 AAW	NYBLS	10//99-12//99
	Buffalo-Niagara Falls MSA, NY	S	21.54 MW	20.17 AW	44800 AAW	NYBLS	10//99-12//99
	Dutchess County PMSA, NY	S	19.15 MW	18.33 AW	39840 AAW	NYBLS	10//99-12//99
	Glens Falls MSA, NY	S	17.55 MW	16.29 AW	36490 AAW	NYBLS	10//99-12//99
	Jamestown MSA, NY	S	21.07 MW	19.86 AW	43830 AAW	NYBLS	10//99-12//99
	Nassau-Suffolk PMSA, NY	S	25.18 MW	23.61 AW	52380 AAW	NYBLS	10//99-12//99
	New York PMSA, NY	S	21.62 MW	20.50 AW	44970 AAW	NYBLS	10//99-12//99
	Newburgh PMSA, NY-PA	S	21.84 MW	21.23 AW	45430 AAW	NYBLS	10//99-12//99
	Rochester MSA, NY	S	21.91 MW	21.45 AW	45580 AAW	NYBLS	10//99-12//99
	Syracuse MSA, NY	S	20.22 MW	19.01 AW	42050 AAW	NYBLS	10//99-12//99
	Utica-Rome MSA, NY	S	19.47 MW	18.98 AW	40490 AAW	NYBLS	10//99-12//99
	North Carolina	S	18.2 MW	18.56 AW	38600 AAW	NCBLS	10//99-12//99
	Asheville MSA, NC	S	15.81 MW	14.97 AW	32880 AAW	NCBLS	10//99-12//99
	Charlotte-Gastonia-Rock Hill MSA, NC-SC	S	18.60 MW	18.69 AW	38690 AAW	NCBLS	10//99-12//99
	Fayetteville MSA, NC	S	18.56 MW	18.45 AW	38600 AAW	NCBLS	10//99-12//99
	Greensboro--Winston-Salem--High Point MSA, NC	S	18.77 MW	18.29 AW	39030 AAW	NCBLS	10//99-12//99

Librarian

Occupation/Type/Industry	Location	Per	Low	Mid	High	Source	Date
Librarian	Hickory-Morganton-Lenoir MSA, NC	S	16.86 MW	16.56 AW	35070 AAW	NCBLS	10//99-12//99
	Raleigh-Durham-Chapel Hill MSA, NC	S	20.58 MW	19.31 AW	42810 AAW	NCBLS	10//99-12//99
	Rocky Mount MSA, NC	S	18.01 MW	17.82 AW	37460 AAW	NCBLS	10//99-12//99
	Wilmington MSA, NC	S	18.43 MW	17.86 AW	38330 AAW	NCBLS	10//99-12//99
	North Dakota	S	13.78 MW	14.39 AW	29940 AAW	NDBLS	10//99-12//99
	Bismarck MSA, ND	S	14.70 MW	14.23 AW	30580 AAW	NDBLS	10//99-12//99
	Fargo-Moorhead MSA, ND-MN	S	17.61 MW	17.45 AW	36630 AAW	NDBLS	10//99-12//99
	Grand Forks MSA, ND-MN	S	16.83 MW	15.15 AW	35000 AAW	NDBLS	10//99-12//99
	Ohio	S	19.05 MW	19.58 AW	40720 AAW	OHBLS	10//99-12//99
	Akron PMSA, OH	S	19.87 MW	20.11 AW	41330 AAW	OHBLS	10//99-12//99
	Canton-Massillon MSA, OH	S	18.34 MW	18.59 AW	38140 AAW	OHBLS	10//99-12//99
	Cincinnati PMSA, OH-KY-IN	S	20.68 MW	20.62 AW	43020 AAW	OHBLS	10//99-12//99
	Cleveland-Lorain-Elyria PMSA, OH	S	21.71 MW	19.94 AW	45150 AAW	OHBLS	10//99-12//99
	Columbus MSA, OH	S	19.37 MW	18.25 AW	40280 AAW	OHBLS	10//99-12//99
	Dayton-Springfield MSA, OH	S	18.55 MW	19.74 AW	38570 AAW	OHBLS	10//99-12//99
	Hamilton-Middletown PMSA, OH	S	18.87 MW	18.97 AW	39250 AAW	OHBLS	10//99-12//99
	Lima MSA, OH	S	19.44 MW	20.56 AW	40440 AAW	OHBLS	10//99-12//99
	Mansfield MSA, OH	S	17.58 MW	15.90 AW	36560 AAW	OHBLS	10//99-12//99
	Steubenville-Weirton MSA, OH-WV	S	15.74 MW	16.67 AW	32730 AAW	OHBLS	10//99-12//99
	Toledo MSA, OH	S	16.64 MW	16.12 AW	34600 AAW	OHBLS	10//99-12//99
	Youngstown-Warren MSA, OH	S	18.16 MW	18.74 AW	37770 AAW	OHBLS	10//99-12//99
	Oklahoma	S	15.72 MW	15.77 AW	32790 AAW	OKBLS	10//99-12//99
	Lawton MSA, OK	S	18.07 MW	17.57 AW	37580 AAW	OKBLS	10//99-12//99
	Oklahoma City MSA, OK	S	16.48 MW	16.43 AW	34270 AAW	OKBLS	10//99-12//99
	Tulsa MSA, OK	S	16.11 MW	15.78 AW	33500 AAW	OKBLS	10//99-12//99
	Oregon	S	20.63 MW	20.74 AW	43150 AAW	ORBLS	10//99-12//99
	Corvallis MSA, OR	S	17.75 MW	16.25 AW	36920 AAW	ORBLS	10//99-12//99
	Eugene-Springfield MSA, OR	S	21.69 MW	21.61 AW	45120 AAW	ORBLS	10//99-12//99
	Medford-Ashland MSA, OR	S	20.84 MW	20.11 AW	43340 AAW	ORBLS	10//99-12//99
	Portland-Vancouver PMSA, OR-WA	S	21.41 MW	20.83 AW	44530 AAW	ORBLS	10//99-12//99
	Salem PMSA, OR	S	20.32 MW	21.23 AW	42270 AAW	ORBLS	10//99-12//99
	Pennsylvania	S	19.95 MW	20.85 AW	43370 AAW	PABLS	10//99-12//99
	Allentown-Bethlehem-Easton MSA, PA	S	21.36 MW	19.44 AW	44420 AAW	PABLS	10//99-12//99
	Altoona MSA, PA	S	19.09 MW	21.67 AW	39710 AAW	PABLS	10//99-12//99
	Erie MSA, PA	S	19.21 MW	19.04 AW	39950 AAW	PABLS	10//99-12//99
	Harrisburg-Lebanon-Carlisle MSA, PA	S	19.25 MW	18.12 AW	40030 AAW	PABLS	10//99-12//99
	Johnstown MSA, PA	S	13.78 MW	12.87 AW	28650 AAW	PABLS	10//99-12//99
	Lancaster MSA, PA	S	20.93 MW	21.39 AW	43540 AAW	PABLS	10//99-12//99
	Philadelphia PMSA, PA-NJ	S	22.58 MW	22.01 AW	46960 AAW	PABLS	10//99-12//99
	Pittsburgh MSA, PA	S	21.41 MW	19.01 AW	44520 AAW	PABLS	10//99-12//99
	Reading MSA, PA	S	22.71 MW	22.91 AW	47240 AAW	PABLS	10//99-12//99
	Scranton--Wilkes-Barre--Hazleton MSA, PA	S	20.59 MW	20.11 AW	42840 AAW	PABLS	10//99-12//99
	Sharon MSA, PA	S	22.33 MW	20.98 AW	46440 AAW	PABLS	10//99-12//99
	York MSA, PA	S	20.85 MW	21.53 AW	43360 AAW	PABLS	10//99-12//99
	Rhode Island	S	19.79 MW	20.30 AW	42220 AAW	RIBLS	10//99-12//99
	Providence-Fall River-Warwick MSA, RI-MA	S	20.51 MW	20.03 AW	42670 AAW	RIBLS	10//99-12//99
	South Carolina	S	17.24 MW	18.08 AW	37610 AAW	SCBLS	10//99-12//99
	Charleston-North Charleston MSA, SC	S	17.19 MW	16.38 AW	35750 AAW	SCBLS	10//99-12//99
	Columbia MSA, SC	S	18.62 MW	16.57 AW	38730 AAW	SCBLS	10//99-12//99
	Florence MSA, SC	S	18.41 MW	18.58 AW	38290 AAW	SCBLS	10//99-12//99
	Greenville-Spartanburg-Anderson MSA, SC	S	17.82 MW	16.80 AW	37060 AAW	SCBLS	10//99-12//99
	Sumter MSA, SC	S	16.29 MW	15.04 AW	33880 AAW	SCBLS	10//99-12//99
	South Dakota	S	13.22 MW	13.99 AW	29090 AAW	SDBLS	10//99-12//99
	Rapid City MSA, SD	S	14.11 MW	12.96 AW	29350 AAW	SDBLS	10//99-12//99
	Sioux Falls MSA, SD	S	17.12 MW	16.22 AW	35610 AAW	SDBLS	10//99-12//99
	Tennessee	S	17.07 MW	17.08 AW	35530 AAW	TNBLS	10//99-12//99
	Chattanooga MSA, TN-GA	S	15.38 MW	14.77 AW	31990 AAW	TNBLS	10//99-12//99
	Clarksville-Hopkinsville MSA, TN-KY	S	17.74 MW	18.17 AW	36910 AAW	TNBLS	10//99-12//99

AAW	Average annual wage	AOH	Average offered, high	ASH	Average starting, high
AE	Average entry wage	AOL	Average offered, low	ASL	Average starting, low
AEX	Average experienced wage	APH	Average pay, high range	AW	Average wage paid
AO	Average offered	APL	Average pay, low range	FQ	First quartile wage

H	Hourly	M	Monthly
HI	Highest wage paid	MTC	Median total compensation
HR	High end range	MW	Median wage paid
LR	Low end range	SQ	Second quartile wage

S	Special: hourly and annual
TQ	Third quartile wage
W	Weekly
Y	Yearly

Occupation/Type/Industry	Location	Per	Low	Mid	High	Source	Date
Librarian	Jackson MSA, TN	S	18.39 MW	18.17 AW	38250 AAW	TNBLS	10//99-12//99
	Johnson City-Kingsport-Bristol MSA, TN-VA	S	17.21 MW	16.65 AW	35790 AAW	TNBLS	10//99-12//99
	Knoxville MSA, TN	S	17.87 MW	17.29 AW	37170 AAW	TNBLS	10//99-12//99
	Memphis MSA, TN-AR-MS	S	18.07 MW	18.59 AW	37580 AAW	MSBLS	10//99-12//99
	Nashville MSA, TN	S	18.03 MW	17.60 AW	37500 AAW	TNBLS	10//99-12//99
	Texas	S	18.77 MW	18.57 AW	38630 AAW	TXBLS	10//99-12//99
	Abilene MSA, TX	S	19.30 MW	20.65 AW	40140 AAW	TXBLS	10//99-12//99
	Austin-San Marcos MSA, TX	S	17.46 MW	17.80 AW	36320 AAW	TXBLS	10//99-12//99
	Beaumont-Port Arthur MSA, TX	S	18.88 MW	18.84 AW	39260 AAW	TXBLS	10//99-12//99
	Brazoria PMSA, TX	S	18.93 MW	18.60 AW	39380 AAW	TXBLS	10//99-12//99
	Brownsville-Harlingen-San Benito MSA, TX	S	19.29 MW	19.49 AW	40110 AAW	TXBLS	10//99-12//99
	Bryan-College Station MSA, TX	S	18.14 MW	17.69 AW	37730 AAW	TXBLS	10//99-12//99
	Corpus Christi MSA, TX	S	17.01 MW	16.50 AW	35380 AAW	TXBLS	10//99-12//99
	Dallas PMSA, TX	S	18.34 MW	18.26 AW	38150 AAW	TXBLS	10//99-12//99
	El Paso MSA, TX	S	19.62 MW	19.53 AW	40810 AAW	TXBLS	10//99-12//99
	Fort Worth-Arlington PMSA, TX	S	19.52 MW	19.79 AW	40600 AAW	TXBLS	10//99-12//99
	Galveston-Texas City PMSA, TX	S	17.65 MW	17.67 AW	36700 AAW	TXBLS	10//99-12//99
	Houston PMSA, TX	S	20.16 MW	20.01 AW	41940 AAW	TXBLS	10//99-12//99
	Killeen-Temple MSA, TX	S	18.48 MW	18.70 AW	38450 AAW	TXBLS	10//99-12//99
	Laredo MSA, TX	S	18.60 MW	17.71 AW	38690 AAW	TXBLS	10//99-12//99
	Longview-Marshall MSA, TX	S	18.33 MW	18.90 AW	38130 AAW	TXBLS	10//99-12//99
	Lubbock MSA, TX	S	16.56 MW	16.70 AW	34440 AAW	TXBLS	10//99-12//99
	McAllen-Edinburg-Mission MSA, TX	S	19.33 MW	19.81 AW	40220 AAW	TXBLS	10//99-12//99
	Odessa-Midland MSA, TX	S	20.78 MW	21.00 AW	43230 AAW	TXBLS	10//99-12//99
	San Angelo MSA, TX	S	15.53 MW	17.00 AW	32310 AAW	TXBLS	10//99-12//99
	San Antonio MSA, TX	S	19.74 MW	19.94 AW	41070 AAW	TXBLS	10//99-12//99
	Sherman-Denison MSA, TX	S	16.69 MW	15.51 AW	34710 AAW	TXBLS	10//99-12//99
	Texarkana MSA, TX-Texarkana, AR	S	15.76 MW	16.94 AW	32780 AAW	TXBLS	10//99-12//99
	Tyler MSA, TX	S	15.94 MW	16.70 AW	33140 AAW	TXBLS	10//99-12//99
	Victoria MSA, TX	S	17.40 MW	19.28 AW	36200 AAW	TXBLS	10//99-12//99
	Waco MSA, TX	S	16.85 MW	17.89 AW	35050 AAW	TXBLS	10//99-12//99
	Wichita Falls MSA, TX	S	16.34 MW	17.16 AW	33990 AAW	TXBLS	10//99-12//99
	Utah	S	17.76 MW	17.59 AW	36580 AAW	UTBLS	10//99-12//99
	Provo-Orem MSA, UT	S	17.33 MW	17.53 AW	36040 AAW	UTBLS	10//99-12//99
	Salt Lake City-Ogden MSA, UT	S	19.21 MW	18.70 AW	39960 AAW	UTBLS	10//99-12//99
	Vermont	S	16.47 MW	16.79 AW	34920 AAW	VTBLS	10//99-12//99
	Burlington MSA, VT	S	17.44 MW	17.42 AW	36280 AAW	VTBLS	10//99-12//99
	Virginia	S	19.26 MW	20.22 AW	42070 AAW	VABLS	10//99-12//99
	Charlottesville MSA, VA	S	21.19 MW	20.82 AW	44080 AAW	VABLS	10//99-12//99
	Danville MSA, VA	S	14.76 MW	14.92 AW	30700 AAW	VABLS	10//99-12//99
	Lynchburg MSA, VA	S	15.53 MW	15.59 AW	32290 AAW	VABLS	10//99-12//99
	Norfolk-Virginia Beach-Newport News MSA, VA-NC	S	19.54 MW	18.51 AW	40650 AAW	VABLS	10//99-12//99
	Richmond-Petersburg MSA, VA	S	22.06 MW	20.88 AW	45890 AAW	VABLS	10//99-12//99
	Roanoke MSA, VA	S	17.31 MW	16.38 AW	36000 AAW	VABLS	10//99-12//99
	Washington	S	21.84 MW	21.43 AW	44570 AAW	WABLS	10//99-12//99
	Bellingham MSA, WA	S	20.45 MW	20.35 AW	42540 AAW	WABLS	10//99-12//99
	Bremerton PMSA, WA	S	20.53 MW	21.05 AW	42700 AAW	WABLS	10//99-12//99
	Olympia PMSA, WA	S	20.72 MW	21.33 AW	43100 AAW	WABLS	10//99-12//99
	Richland-Kennewick-Pasco MSA, WA	S	19.08 MW	19.41 AW	39700 AAW	WABLS	10//99-12//99
	Seattle-Bellevue-Everett PMSA, WA	S	22.95 MW	22.89 AW	47740 AAW	WABLS	10//99-12//99
	Spokane MSA, WA	S	19.94 MW	20.79 AW	41470 AAW	WABLS	10//99-12//99
	Tacoma PMSA, WA	S	21.02 MW	21.93 AW	43720 AAW	WABLS	10//99-12//99
	Yakima MSA, WA	S	21.03 MW	21.79 AW	43730 AAW	WABLS	10//99-12//99
	West Virginia	S	16.18 MW	15.21 AW	31630 AAW	WVBLS	10//99-12//99
	Huntington-Ashland MSA, WV-KY-OH	S	17.59 MW	17.74 AW	36590 AAW	WVBLS	10//99-12//99
	Parkersburg-Marietta MSA, WV-OH	S	14.41 MW	14.98 AW	29970 AAW	WVBLS	10//99-12//99

AAW Average annual wage	**AOH** Average offered, high	**ASH** Average starting, high	**H** Hourly	**M** Monthly	**S** Special: hourly and annual
AE Average entry wage	**AOL** Average offered, low	**ASL** Average starting, low	**HI** Highest wage paid	**MTC** Median total compensation	**TQ** Third quartile wage
AEX Average experienced wage	**APH** Average pay, high range	**AW** Average wage paid	**HR** High end range	**MW** Median wage paid	**W** Weekly
AO Average offered	**APL** Average pay, low range	**FQ** First quartile wage	**LR** Low end range	**SQ** Second quartile wage	**Y** Yearly

Occupation/Type/Industry	Location	Per	Low	Mid	High	Source	Date
Librarian	Wisconsin	S	19.88 MW	19.32 AW	40190 AAW	WIBLS	10//99-12//99
	Appleton-Oshkosh-Neenah MSA, WI	S	19.99 MW	19.03 AW	41580 AAW	WIBLS	10//99-12//99
	Eau Claire MSA, WI	S	18.79 MW	18.63 AW	39070 AAW	WIBLS	10//99-12//99
	Green Bay MSA, WI	S	20.53 MW	20.27 AW	42710 AAW	WIBLS	10//99-12//99
	Janesville-Beloit MSA, WI	S	20.40 MW	20.61 AW	42440 AAW	WIBLS	10//99-12//99
	Kenosha PMSA, WI	S	19.18 MW	18.64 AW	39890 AAW	WIBLS	10//99-12//99
	La Crosse MSA, WI-MN	S	19.07 MW	19.41 AW	39670 AAW	WIBLS	10//99-12//99
	Madison MSA, WI	S	21.03 MW	21.30 AW	43730 AAW	WIBLS	10//99-12//99
	Milwaukee-Waukesha PMSA, WI	S	21.28 MW	20.39 AW	44260 AAW	WIBLS	10//99-12//99
	Racine PMSA, WI	S	19.43 MW	21.51 AW	40420 AAW	WIBLS	10//99-12//99
	Sheboygan MSA, WI	S	21.12 MW	21.70 AW	43920 AAW	WIBLS	10//99-12//99
	Wausau MSA, WI	S	15.95 MW	17.57 AW	33180 AAW	WIBLS	10//99-12//99
	Wyoming	S	16.45 MW	17.19 AW	35750 AAW	WYBLS	10//99-12//99
	Mayaguez MSA, PR	S	11.51 MW	10.99 AW	23940 AAW	PRBLS	10//99-12//99
	San Juan-Bayamon PMSA, PR	S	10.99 MW	10.37 AW	22860 AAW	PRBLS	10//99-12//99
	Virgin Islands	S	13.28 MW	16.13 AW	33540 AAW	VIBLS	10//99-12//99
	Guam	S	13.12 MW	13.30 AW	27650 AAW	GUBLS	10//99-12//99
Beginning Librarian	United States	Y		32160 MW		ALA	2000
Department Head/Senior Manager	United States	Y		50003 MW		ALA	2000
Deputy Director	United States	Y		57210 MW		ALA	2000
Director/Dean	United States	Y		70124 MW		ALA	2000
Female	United States	Y		33956 MW		WOWO2	1998
Male	United States	Y		39312 MW		WOWO2	1998
Manager/Supervisor	United States	Y		41224 MW		ALA	2000
Nonsupervisory	United States	Y		40838 MW		ALA	2000
Librarian/Information Specialist							
Female	United States	Y		43430 MW		WOWO1	1999
Male	United States	Y		42400 MW		WOWO1	1999
Library Assistant, Clerical	Alabama	S	9.39 MW	9.74 AW	20250 AAW	ALBLS	10//99-12//99
	Alaska	S	13.65 MW	13.51 AW	28110 AAW	AKBLS	10//99-12//99
	Arizona	S	9.13 MW	9.34 AW	19420 AAW	AZBLS	10//99-12//99
	Arkansas	S	6.36 MW	6.63 AW	13790 AAW	ARBLS	10//99-12//99
	California	S	11.01 MW	10.88 AW	22630 AAW	CABLS	10//99-12//99
	Colorado	S	8.69 MW	9.06 AW	18840 AAW	COBLS	10//99-12//99
	Connecticut	S	8.94 MW	9.34 AW	19420 AAW	CTBLS	10//99-12//99
	Delaware	S	6.42 MW	7.68 AW	15970 AAW	DEBLS	10//99-12//99
	District of Columbia	S	11.61 MW	11.86 AW	24670 AAW	DCBLS	10//99-12//99
	Florida	S	8.01 MW	8.35 AW	17360 AAW	FLBLS	10//99-12//99
	Georgia	S	8.34 MW	8.84 AW	18380 AAW	GABLS	10//99-12//99
	Hawaii	S	8.52 MW	9.46 AW	19680 AAW	HIBLS	10//99-12//99
	Idaho	S	7.93 MW	8.40 AW	17470 AAW	IDBLS	10//99-12//99
	Illinois	S	9.78 MW	9.97 AW	20740 AAW	ILBLS	10//99-12//99
	Indiana	S	8.21 MW	8.24 AW	17140 AAW	INBLS	10//99-12//99
	Iowa	S	7.62 MW	7.97 AW	16570 AAW	IABLS	10//99-12//99
	Kansas	S	6.32 MW	6.85 AW	14250 AAW	KSBLS	10//99-12//99
	Kentucky	S	7.03 MW	7.27 AW	15120 AAW	KYBLS	10//99-12//99
	Louisiana	S	8.38 MW	9.13 AW	19000 AAW	LABLS	10//99-12//99
	Maine	S	7.53 MW	7.95 AW	16540 AAW	MEBLS	10//99-12//99
	Maryland	S	10.64 MW	10.78 AW	22430 AAW	MDBLS	10//99-12//99
	Massachusetts	S	10.59 MW	10.56 AW	21970 AAW	MABLS	10//99-12//99
	Michigan	S	7.94 MW	8.44 AW	17560 AAW	MIBLS	10//99-12//99
	Minnesota	S	9.07 MW	8.99 AW	18690 AAW	MNBLS	10//99-12//99
	Mississippi	S	6.55 MW	7.01 AW	14580 AAW	MSBLS	10//99-12//99
	Missouri	S	8.96 MW	9.17 AW	19070 AAW	MOBLS	10//99-12//99
	Montana	S	6.1 MW	6.41 AW	13340 AAW	MTBLS	10//99-12//99
	Nebraska	S	6.54 MW	7.04 AW	14650 AAW	NEBLS	10//99-12//99
	Nevada	S	13.2 MW	13.03 AW	27090 AAW	NVBLS	10//99-12//99
	New Hampshire	S	8.43 MW	8.41 AW	17490 AAW	NHBLS	10//99-12//99
	New Jersey	S	9.83 MW	10.10 AW	21010 AAW	NJBLS	10//99-12//99
	New Mexico	S	9.69 MW	9.54 AW	19840 AAW	NMBLS	10//99-12//99
	New York	S	7.9 MW	9.26 AW	19250 AAW	NYBLS	10//99-12//99
	North Carolina	S	9.58 MW	9.74 AW	20260 AAW	NCBLS	10//99-12//99
	Ohio	S	7.89 MW	8.25 AW	17150 AAW	OHBLS	10//99-12//99
	Oklahoma	S	7.55 MW	8.89 AW	18490 AAW	OKBLS	10//99-12//99
	Oregon	S	10.04 MW	10.13 AW	21060 AAW	ORBLS	10//99-12//99
	Pennsylvania	S	8.06 MW	8.70 AW	18090 AAW	PABLS	10//99-12//99
	Rhode Island	S	8.35 MW	9.68 AW	20140 AAW	RIBLS	10//99-12//99
	South Carolina	S	8.02 MW	8.59 AW	17860 AAW	SCBLS	10//99-12//99
	South Dakota	S	6.27 MW	6.73 AW	13990 AAW	SDBLS	10//99-12//99

AAW	Average annual wage	AOH	Average offered, high	ASH	Average starting, high	H	Hourly	M	Monthly	S	Special: hourly and annual
AE	Average entry wage	AOL	Average offered, low	ASL	Average starting, low	HI	Highest wage paid	MTC	Median total compensation	TQ	Third quartile wage
AEX	Average experienced wage	APH	Average pay, high range	AW	Average wage paid	HR	High end range	MW	Median wage paid	W	Weekly
AO	Average offered	APL	Average pay, low range	FQ	First quartile wage	LR	Low end range	SQ	Second quartile wage	Y	Yearly

Occupation/Type/Industry	Location	Per	Low	Mid	High	Source	Date
Library Assistant, Clerical	Tennessee	S	6.5 MW	6.88 AW	14310 AAW	TNBLS	10//99-12//99
	Texas	S	7.87 MW	8.25 AW	17170 AAW	TXBLS	10//99-12//99
	Utah	S	6.27 MW	6.72 AW	13970 AAW	UTBLS	10//99-12//99
	Vermont	S	8.31 MW	8.64 AW	17980 AAW	VTBLS	10//99-12//99
	Virginia	S	10.65 MW	10.72 AW	22300 AAW	VABLS	10//99-12//99
	Washington	S	8.78 MW	9.63 AW	20020 AAW	WABLS	10//99-12//99
	West Virginia	S	6.33 MW	6.47 AW	13450 AAW	WVBLS	10//99-12//99
	Wisconsin	S	9.31 MW	9.39 AW	19530 AAW	WIBLS	10//99-12//99
	Wyoming	S	8.27 MW	8.98 AW	18670 AAW	WYBLS	10//99-12//99
	Puerto Rico	S	6.75 MW	6.97 AW	14500 AAW	PRBLS	10//99-12//99
Library Science Teacher							
Postsecondary	California	Y		47980 AAW		CABLS	10//99-12//99
Postsecondary	Washington PMSA, DC-MD-VA-WV	Y		55710 AAW		DCBLS	10//99-12//99
Postsecondary	Florida	Y		51220 AAW		FLBLS	10//99-12//99
Postsecondary	Georgia	Y		46460 AAW		GABLS	10//99-12//99
Postsecondary	Atlanta MSA, GA	Y		48280 AAW		GABLS	10//99-12//99
Postsecondary	Indiana	Y		48500 AAW		INBLS	10//99-12//99
Postsecondary	Louisiana	Y		46850 AAW		LABLS	10//99-12//99
Postsecondary	Minnesota	Y		51780 AAW		MNBLS	10//99-12//99
Postsecondary	Minneapolis-St. Paul MSA, MN-WI	Y		52670 AAW		MNBLS	10//99-12//99
Postsecondary	Mississippi	Y		36750 AAW		MSBLS	10//99-12//99
Postsecondary	Jackson MSA, MS	Y		35450 AAW		MSBLS	10//99-12//99
Postsecondary	Missouri	Y		51380 AAW		MOBLS	10//99-12//99
Postsecondary	New Jersey	Y		51960 AAW		NJBLS	10//99-12//99
Postsecondary	New York	Y		50950 AAW		NYBLS	10//99-12//99
Postsecondary	Albany-Schenectady-Troy MSA, NY	Y		47390 AAW		NYBLS	10//99-12//99
Postsecondary	New York PMSA, NY	Y		51080 AAW		NYBLS	10//99-12//99
Postsecondary	North Carolina	Y		47680 AAW		NCBLS	10//99-12//99
Postsecondary	Pennsylvania	Y		51550 AAW		PABLS	10//99-12//99
Postsecondary	Tennessee	Y		43050 AAW		TNBLS	10//99-12//99
Postsecondary	Texas	Y		49740 AAW		TXBLS	10//99-12//99
Postsecondary	Houston PMSA, TX	Y		50480 AAW		TXBLS	10//99-12//99
Postsecondary	Virginia	Y		44920 AAW		VABLS	10//99-12//99
Library Technician	Alabama	S	8.8 MW	9.96 AW	20710 AAW	ALBLS	10//99-12//99
	Auburn-Opelika MSA, AL	S	8.15 MW	6.87 AW	16940 AAW	ALBLS	10//99-12//99
	Birmingham MSA, AL	S	9.04 MW	8.20 AW	18810 AAW	ALBLS	10//99-12//99
	Dothan MSA, AL	S	8.49 MW	7.36 AW	17670 AAW	ALBLS	10//99-12//99
	Gadsden MSA, AL	S	12.87 MW	6.61 AW	26780 AAW	ALBLS	10//99-12//99
	Huntsville MSA, AL	S	9.66 MW	9.50 AW	20090 AAW	ALBLS	10//99-12//99
	Mobile MSA, AL	S	10.29 MW	10.02 AW	21390 AAW	ALBLS	10//99-12//99
	Montgomery MSA, AL	S	10.48 MW	11.19 AW	21790 AAW	ALBLS	10//99-12//99
	Alaska	S	14.38 MW	14.15 AW	29430 AAW	AKBLS	10//99-12//99
	Arizona	S	8.68 MW	10.32 AW	21460 AAW	AZBLS	10//99-12//99
	Flagstaff MSA, AZ-UT	S	8.82 MW	8.20 AW	18350 AAW	AZBLS	10//99-12//99
	Phoenix-Mesa MSA, AZ	S	9.61 MW	8.23 AW	19990 AAW	AZBLS	10//99-12//99
	Tucson MSA, AZ	S	16.39 MW	15.58 AW	34100 AAW	AZBLS	10//99-12//99
	Arkansas	S	6.71 MW	7.45 AW	15500 AAW	ARBLS	10//99-12//99
	Fayetteville-Springdale-Rogers MSA, AR	S	7.62 MW	6.69 AW	15850 AAW	ARBLS	10//99-12//99
	Little Rock-North Little Rock MSA, AR	S	8.83 MW	8.49 AW	18360 AAW	ARBLS	10//99-12//99
	California	S	13.78 MW	13.72 AW	28540 AAW	CABLS	10//99-12//99
	Bakersfield MSA, CA	S	12.37 MW	12.19 AW	25740 AAW	CABLS	10//99-12//99
	Chico-Paradise MSA, CA	S	14.64 MW	13.20 AW	30450 AAW	CABLS	10//99-12//99
	Fresno MSA, CA	S	11.31 MW	10.70 AW	23520 AAW	CABLS	10//99-12//99
	Los Angeles-Long Beach PMSA, CA	S	14.39 MW	14.39 AW	29940 AAW	CABLS	10//99-12//99
	Modesto MSA, CA	S	11.35 MW	11.77 AW	23610 AAW	CABLS	10//99-12//99
	Oakland PMSA, CA	S	13.65 MW	13.65 AW	28390 AAW	CABLS	10//99-12//99
	Orange County PMSA, CA	S	14.30 MW	14.00 AW	29740 AAW	CABLS	10//99-12//99
	Riverside-San Bernardino PMSA, CA	S	12.53 MW	12.39 AW	26060 AAW	CABLS	10//99-12//99
	Sacramento PMSA, CA	S	13.62 MW	14.06 AW	28320 AAW	CABLS	10//99-12//99
	Salinas MSA, CA	S	12.08 MW	12.54 AW	25130 AAW	CABLS	10//99-12//99
	San Diego MSA, CA	S	12.48 MW	12.28 AW	25950 AAW	CABLS	10//99-12//99
	San Francisco PMSA, CA	S	15.23 MW	15.48 AW	31670 AAW	CABLS	10//99-12//99
	San Jose PMSA, CA	S	14.50 MW	14.76 AW	30160 AAW	CABLS	10//99-12//99

AAW Average annual wage	AOH Average offered, high	ASH Average starting, high	H Hourly	M Monthly	S Special: hourly and annual
AE Average entry wage	AOL Average offered, low	ASL Average starting, low	HI Highest wage paid	MTC Median total compensation	TQ Third quartile wage
AEX Average experienced wage	APH Average pay, high range	AW Average wage paid	HR High end range	MW Median wage paid	W Weekly
AO Average offered	APL Average pay, low range	FQ First quartile wage	LR Low end range	SQ Second quartile wage	Y Yearly

Occupation/Type/Industry	Location	Per	Low	Mid	High	Source	Date
Library Technician	Santa Barbara-Santa Maria-Lompoc MSA, CA	S	13.35 MW	13.49 AW	27770 AAW	CABLS	10//99-12//99
	Santa Rosa PMSA, CA	S	12.28 MW	11.89 AW	25530 AAW	CABLS	10//99-12//99
	Stockton-Lodi MSA, CA	S	13.18 MW	12.66 AW	27400 AAW	CABLS	10//99-12//99
	Vallejo-Fairfield-Napa PMSA, CA	S	12.14 MW	10.67 AW	25260 AAW	CABLS	10//99-12//99
	Ventura PMSA, CA	S	12.93 MW	12.88 AW	26890 AAW	CABLS	10//99-12//99
	Visalia-Tulare-Porterville MSA, CA	S	12.72 MW	13.28 AW	26460 AAW	CABLS	10//99-12//99
	Yolo PMSA, CA	S	11.66 MW	10.32 AW	24250 AAW	CABLS	10//99-12//99
	Yuba City MSA, CA	S	13.39 MW	14.32 AW	27860 AAW	CABLS	10//99-12//99
	Colorado	S	11.53 MW	11.65 AW	24240 AAW	COBLS	10//99-12//99
	Boulder-Longmont PMSA, CO	S	11.38 MW	10.48 AW	23670 AAW	COBLS	10//99-12//99
	Colorado Springs MSA, CO	S	11.92 MW	11.63 AW	24790 AAW	COBLS	10//99-12//99
	Denver PMSA, CO	S	12.59 MW	12.47 AW	26190 AAW	COBLS	10//99-12//99
	Connecticut	S	12.74 MW	13.24 AW	27530 AAW	CTBLS	10//99-12//99
	Bridgeport PMSA, CT	S	12.17 MW	11.88 AW	25310 AAW	CTBLS	10//99-12//99
	Danbury PMSA, CT	S	10.83 MW	8.43 AW	22530 AAW	CTBLS	10//99-12//99
	Hartford MSA, CT	S	15.48 MW	15.22 AW	32190 AAW	CTBLS	10//99-12//99
	New Haven-Meriden PMSA, CT	S	11.84 MW	11.89 AW	24620 AAW	CTBLS	10//99-12//99
	New London-Norwich MSA, CT-RI	S	13.34 MW	12.27 AW	27750 AAW	CTBLS	10//99-12//99
	Stamford-Norwalk PMSA, CT	S	13.83 MW	13.59 AW	28760 AAW	CTBLS	10//99-12//99
	Waterbury PMSA, CT	S	10.64 MW	9.85 AW	22120 AAW	CTBLS	10//99-12//99
	Delaware	S	10.66 MW	11.00 AW	22880 AAW	DEBLS	10//99-12//99
	Dover MSA, DE	S	9.23 MW	8.36 AW	19190 AAW	DEBLS	10//99-12//99
	Wilmington-Newark PMSA, DE-MD	S	11.79 MW	11.49 AW	24520 AAW	DEBLS	10//99-12//99
	District of Columbia	S	14.31 MW	14.13 AW	29390 AAW	DCBLS	10//99-12//99
	Washington PMSA, DC-MD-VA-WV	S	15.03 MW	14.84 AW	31270 AAW	DCBLS	10//99-12//99
	Florida	S	10.09 MW	10.31 AW	21430 AAW	FLBLS	10//99-12//99
	Fort Lauderdale PMSA, FL	S	10.10 MW	10.03 AW	21010 AAW	FLBLS	10//99-12//99
	Fort Walton Beach MSA, FL	S	8.58 MW	8.16 AW	17850 AAW	FLBLS	10//99-12//99
	Gainesville MSA, FL	S	10.44 MW	10.27 AW	21710 AAW	FLBLS	10//99-12//99
	Jacksonville MSA, FL	S	9.29 MW	8.33 AW	19310 AAW	FLBLS	10//99-12//99
	Lakeland-Winter Haven MSA, FL	S	8.41 MW	8.58 AW	17490 AAW	FLBLS	10//99-12//99
	Melbourne-Titusville-Palm Bay MSA, FL	S	10.26 MW	10.31 AW	21340 AAW	FLBLS	10//99-12//99
	Miami PMSA, FL	S	10.96 MW	11.29 AW	22790 AAW	FLBLS	10//99-12//99
	Ocala MSA, FL	S	9.59 MW	9.70 AW	19940 AAW	FLBLS	10//99-12//99
	Orlando MSA, FL	S	9.62 MW	9.58 AW	20010 AAW	FLBLS	10//99-12//99
	Pensacola MSA, FL	S	10.51 MW	10.24 AW	21870 AAW	FLBLS	10//99-12//99
	Sarasota-Bradenton MSA, FL	S	12.44 MW	10.64 AW	25880 AAW	FLBLS	10//99-12//99
	Tallahassee MSA, FL	S	10.07 MW	9.82 AW	20950 AAW	FLBLS	10//99-12//99
	Tampa-St. Petersburg-Clearwater MSA, FL	S	11.05 MW	11.17 AW	22970 AAW	FLBLS	10//99-12//99
	West Palm Beach-Boca Raton MSA, FL	S	10.21 MW	10.06 AW	21240 AAW	FLBLS	10//99-12//99
	Georgia	S	8.48 MW	10.15 AW	21120 AAW	GABLS	10//99-12//99
	Atlanta MSA, GA	S	11.16 MW	10.89 AW	23220 AAW	GABLS	10//99-12//99
	Augusta-Aiken MSA, GA-SC	S	10.34 MW	10.07 AW	21500 AAW	GABLS	10//99-12//99
	Columbus MSA, GA-AL	S	10.46 MW	10.23 AW	21760 AAW	GABLS	10//99-12//99
	Macon MSA, GA	S	10.86 MW	11.50 AW	22580 AAW	GABLS	10//99-12//99
	Savannah MSA, GA	S	15.85 MW	15.03 AW	32970 AAW	GABLS	10//99-12//99
	Hawaii	S	12.94 MW	13.31 AW	27690 AAW	HIBLS	10//99-12//99
	Honolulu MSA, HI	S	12.82 MW	12.74 AW	26650 AAW	HIBLS	10//99-12//99
	Idaho	S	7.57 MW	7.96 AW	16550 AAW	IDBLS	10//99-12//99
	Boise City MSA, ID	S	9.08 MW	8.08 AW	18880 AAW	IDBLS	10//99-12//99
	Illinois	S	10.77 MW	10.96 AW	22800 AAW	ILBLS	10//99-12//99
	Chicago PMSA, IL	S	11.03 MW	11.17 AW	22940 AAW	ILBLS	10//99-12//99
	Peoria-Pekin MSA, IL	S	8.03 MW	6.62 AW	16710 AAW	ILBLS	10//99-12//99
	Springfield MSA, IL	S	11.27 MW	10.77 AW	23440 AAW	ILBLS	10//99-12//99
	Indiana	S	9.96 MW	10.14 AW	21090 AAW	INBLS	10//99-12//99
	Evansville-Henderson MSA, IN-KY	S	10.39 MW	10.27 AW	21610 AAW	INBLS	10//99-12//99
	Fort Wayne MSA, IN	S	9.92 MW	9.72 AW	20640 AAW	INBLS	10//99-12//99
	Gary PMSA, IN	S	10.81 MW	10.66 AW	22490 AAW	INBLS	10//99-12//99
	Indianapolis MSA, IN	S	11.47 MW	11.22 AW	23870 AAW	INBLS	10//99-12//99
	Muncie MSA, IN	S	8.36 MW	7.61 AW	17390 AAW	INBLS	10//99-12//99

AAW Average annual wage	AOH Average offered, high	ASH Average starting, high	H Hourly	M Monthly	S Special: hourly and annual
AE Average entry wage	AOL Average offered, low	ASL Average starting, low	HI Highest wage paid	MTC Median total compensation	TQ Third quartile wage
AEX Average experienced wage	APH Average pay, high range	AW Average wage paid	HR High end range	MW Median wage paid	W Weekly
AO Average offered	APL Average pay, low range	FQ First quartile wage	LR Low end range	SQ Second quartile wage	Y Yearly

Occupation/Type/Industry	Location	Per	Low	Mid	High	Source	Date
Library Technician	Iowa	S	8.98 MW	9.34 AW	19420 AAW	IABLS	10//99-12//99
	Cedar Rapids MSA, IA	S	8.20 MW	7.94 AW	17050 AAW	IABLS	10//99-12//99
	Davenport-Moline-Rock Island MSA, IA-IL	S	9.43 MW	9.33 AW	19620 AAW	IABLS	10//99-12//99
	Des Moines MSA, IA	S	9.58 MW	9.51 AW	19930 AAW	IABLS	10//99-12//99
	Kansas	S	6.65 MW	7.15 AW	14880 AAW	KSBLS	10//99-12//99
	Lawrence MSA, KS	S	11.15 MW	10.14 AW	23190 AAW	KSBLS	10//99-12//99
	Topeka MSA, KS	S	9.26 MW	8.89 AW	19250 AAW	KSBLS	10//99-12//99
	Wichita MSA, KS	S	7.74 MW	7.85 AW	16100 AAW	KSBLS	10//99-12//99
	Kentucky	S	9.61 MW	9.53 AW	19830 AAW	KYBLS	10//99-12//99
	Lexington MSA, KY	S	10.04 MW	9.95 AW	20890 AAW	KYBLS	10//99-12//99
	Louisville MSA, KY-IN	S	10.50 MW	10.29 AW	21840 AAW	KYBLS	10//99-12//99
	Louisiana	S	8.42 MW	9.50 AW	19750 AAW	LABLS	10//99-12//99
	Baton Rouge MSA, LA	S	11.19 MW	10.40 AW	23270 AAW	LABLS	10//99-12//99
	New Orleans MSA, LA	S	9.89 MW	9.00 AW	20580 AAW	LABLS	10//99-12//99
	Shreveport-Bossier City MSA, LA	S	7.80 MW	7.34 AW	16230 AAW	LABLS	10//99-12//99
	Maine	S	9.12 MW	9.49 AW	19740 AAW	MEBLS	10//99-12//99
	Bangor MSA, ME	S	8.60 MW	8.44 AW	17900 AAW	MEBLS	10//99-12//99
	Lewiston-Auburn MSA, ME	S	12.54 MW	12.47 AW	26090 AAW	MEBLS	10//99-12//99
	Portland MSA, ME	S	10.73 MW	11.41 AW	22320 AAW	MEBLS	10//99-12//99
	Maryland	S	13.86 MW	13.65 AW	28380 AAW	MDBLS	10//99-12//99
	Baltimore PMSA, MD	S	13.19 MW	13.75 AW	27440 AAW	MDBLS	10//99-12//99
	Massachusetts	S	11.28 MW	11.62 AW	24170 AAW	MABLS	10//99-12//99
	Boston PMSA, MA-NH	S	11.96 MW	11.36 AW	24870 AAW	MABLS	10//99-12//99
	Fitchburg-Leominster PMSA, MA	S	10.36 MW	10.48 AW	21550 AAW	MABLS	10//99-12//99
	Pittsfield MSA, MA	S	9.78 MW	10.15 AW	20350 AAW	MABLS	10//99-12//99
	Springfield MSA, MA	S	11.34 MW	11.59 AW	23590 AAW	MABLS	10//99-12//99
	Worcester PMSA, MA-CT	S	11.78 MW	11.62 AW	24510 AAW	MABLS	10//99-12//99
	Michigan	S	11.46 MW	11.76 AW	24460 AAW	MIBLS	10//99-12//99
	Ann Arbor PMSA, MI	S	12.39 MW	12.40 AW	25780 AAW	MIBLS	10//99-12//99
	Benton Harbor MSA, MI	S	12.79 MW	11.68 AW	26600 AAW	MIBLS	10//99-12//99
	Detroit PMSA, MI	S	12.66 MW	12.27 AW	26330 AAW	MIBLS	10//99-12//99
	Flint PMSA, MI	S	11.17 MW	12.07 AW	23240 AAW	MIBLS	10//99-12//99
	Grand Rapids-Muskegon-Holland MSA, MI	S	11.51 MW	10.48 AW	23940 AAW	MIBLS	10//99-12//99
	Jackson MSA, MI	S	9.33 MW	8.65 AW	19410 AAW	MIBLS	10//99-12//99
	Kalamazoo-Battle Creek MSA, MI	S	13.21 MW	13.85 AW	27480 AAW	MIBLS	10//99-12//99
	Saginaw-Bay City-Midland MSA, MI	S	8.29 MW	8.56 AW	17240 AAW	MIBLS	10//99-12//99
	Minnesota	S	11.66 MW	12.10 AW	25160 AAW	MNBLS	10//99-12//99
	Duluth-Superior MSA, MN-WI	S	11.69 MW	12.71 AW	24300 AAW	MNBLS	10//99-12//99
	Minneapolis-St. Paul MSA, MN-WI	S	13.49 MW	12.74 AW	28060 AAW	MNBLS	10//99-12//99
	St. Cloud MSA, MN	S	11.99 MW	11.11 AW	24930 AAW	MNBLS	10//99-12//99
	Mississippi	S	7.73 MW	9.07 AW	18860 AAW	MSBLS	10//99-12//99
	Biloxi-Gulfport-Pascagoula MSA, MS	S	8.21 MW	7.62 AW	17080 AAW	MSBLS	10//99-12//99
	Jackson MSA, MS	S	8.53 MW	8.82 AW	17740 AAW	MSBLS	10//99-12//99
	Missouri	S	9.65 MW	10.01 AW	20820 AAW	MOBLS	10//99-12//99
	St. Louis MSA, MO-IL	S	10.86 MW	11.02 AW	22580 AAW	MOBLS	10//99-12//99
	Springfield MSA, MO	S	10.38 MW	10.28 AW	21590 AAW	MOBLS	10//99-12//99
	Montana	S	8.14 MW	8.53 AW	17740 AAW	MTBLS	10//99-12//99
	Nebraska	S	9.93 MW	10.41 AW	21650 AAW	NEBLS	10//99-12//99
	Lincoln MSA, NE	S	10.19 MW	10.44 AW	21190 AAW	NEBLS	10//99-12//99
	Omaha MSA, NE-IA	S	11.62 MW	12.11 AW	24180 AAW	NEBLS	10//99-12//99
	Nevada	S	13.34 MW	14.15 AW	29440 AAW	NVBLS	10//99-12//99
	Las Vegas MSA, NV-AZ	S	13.70 MW	13.75 AW	28490 AAW	NVBLS	10//99-12//99
	New Hampshire	S	10.57 MW	11.25 AW	23410 AAW	NHBLS	10//99-12//99
	Manchester PMSA, NH	S	10.78 MW	10.34 AW	22420 AAW	NHBLS	10//99-12//99
	Nashua PMSA, NH	S	12.88 MW	11.36 AW	26790 AAW	NHBLS	10//99-12//99
	Portsmouth-Rochester PMSA, NH-ME	S	11.43 MW	10.98 AW	23780 AAW	NHBLS	10//99-12//99
	New Jersey	S	12.47 MW	12.67 AW	26360 AAW	NJBLS	10//99-12//99
	Atlantic-Cape May PMSA, NJ	S	12.26 MW	12.10 AW	25500 AAW	NJBLS	10//99-12//99
	Bergen-Passaic PMSA, NJ	S	10.42 MW	9.02 AW	21680 AAW	NJBLS	10//99-12//99
	Jersey City PMSA, NJ	S	15.32 MW	15.52 AW	31870 AAW	NJBLS	10//99-12//99
	Middlesex-Somerset-Hunterdon PMSA, NJ	S	13.13 MW	13.54 AW	27310 AAW	NJBLS	10//99-12//99
	Monmouth-Ocean PMSA, NJ	S	11.40 MW	10.64 AW	23700 AAW	NJBLS	10//99-12//99

AAW	Average annual wage	AOH	Average offered, high	ASH	Average starting, high
AE	Average entry wage	AOL	Average offered, low	ASL	Average starting, low
AEX	Average experienced wage	APH	Average pay, high range	AW	Average wage paid
AO	Average offered	APL	Average pay, low range	FQ	First quartile wage

H	Hourly	M	Monthly
HI	Highest wage paid	MTC	Median total compensation
HR	High end range	MW	Median wage paid
LR	Low end range	SQ	Second quartile wage

S	Special: hourly and annual
TQ	Third quartile wage
W	Weekly
Y	Yearly

Occupation/Type/Industry	Location	Per	Low	Mid	High	Source	Date
Library Technician	Newark PMSA, NJ	S	12.40 MW	12.33 AW	25790 AAW	NJBLS	10//99-12//99
	Trenton PMSA, NJ	S	14.18 MW	14.71 AW	29490 AAW	NJBLS	10//99-12//99
	New Mexico	S	7.48 MW	8.35 AW	17370 AAW	NMBLS	10//99-12//99
	Albuquerque MSA, NM	S	10.09 MW	9.56 AW	20980 AAW	NMBLS	10//99-12//99
	New York	S	12.52 MW	13.43 AW	27940 AAW	NYBLS	10//99-12//99
	Albany-Schenectady-Troy MSA, NY	S	12.74 MW	11.34 AW	26510 AAW	NYBLS	10//99-12//99
	Binghamton MSA, NY	S	8.96 MW	6.62 AW	18630 AAW	NYBLS	10//99-12//99
	Dutchess County PMSA, NY	S	10.42 MW	10.32 AW	21660 AAW	NYBLS	10//99-12//99
	Glens Falls MSA, NY	S	7.44 MW	6.56 AW	15470 AAW	NYBLS	10//99-12//99
	Jamestown MSA, NY	S	8.92 MW	8.22 AW	18550 AAW	NYBLS	10//99-12//99
	Nassau-Suffolk PMSA, NY	S	15.85 MW	15.75 AW	32970 AAW	NYBLS	10//99-12//99
	New York PMSA, NY	S	14.08 MW	12.90 AW	29290 AAW	NYBLS	10//99-12//99
	Newburgh PMSA, NY-PA	S	10.25 MW	9.78 AW	21320 AAW	NYBLS	10//99-12//99
	Rochester MSA, NY	S	10.85 MW	9.63 AW	22570 AAW	NYBLS	10//99-12//99
	Syracuse MSA, NY	S	12.15 MW	13.83 AW	25280 AAW	NYBLS	10//99-12//99
	Utica-Rome MSA, NY	S	8.14 MW	7.01 AW	16920 AAW	NYBLS	10//99-12//99
	North Carolina	S	10.61 MW	11.51 AW	23940 AAW	NCBLS	10//99-12//99
	Asheville MSA, NC	S	9.89 MW	9.84 AW	20570 AAW	NCBLS	10//99-12//99
	Charlotte-Gastonia-Rock Hill MSA, NC-SC	S	12.56 MW	10.61 AW	26130 AAW	NCBLS	10//99-12//99
	Fayetteville MSA, NC	S	11.63 MW	11.66 AW	24200 AAW	NCBLS	10//99-12//99
	Greensboro--Winston-Salem-- High Point MSA, NC	S	11.57 MW	11.20 AW	24070 AAW	NCBLS	10//99-12//99
	Greenville MSA, NC	S	7.67 MW	6.58 AW	15950 AAW	NCBLS	10//99-12//99
	Hickory-Morganton-Lenoir MSA, NC	S	10.32 MW	10.33 AW	21470 AAW	NCBLS	10//99-12//99
	Raleigh-Durham-Chapel Hill MSA, NC	S	13.92 MW	14.36 AW	28950 AAW	NCBLS	10//99-12//99
	Rocky Mount MSA, NC	S	10.56 MW	10.83 AW	21960 AAW	NCBLS	10//99-12//99
	Wilmington MSA, NC	S	11.82 MW	11.95 AW	24580 AAW	NCBLS	10//99-12//99
	North Dakota	S	9.36 MW	11.38 AW	23660 AAW	NDBLS	10//99-12//99
	Akron PMSA, OH	S	10.73 MW	11.29 AW	22320 AAW	OHBLS	10//99-12//99
	Canton-Massillon MSA, OH	S	10.50 MW	10.25 AW	21830 AAW	OHBLS	10//99-12//99
	Cincinnati PMSA, OH-KY-IN	S	10.30 MW	10.50 AW	21420 AAW	OHBLS	10//99-12//99
	Cleveland-Lorain-Elyria PMSA, OH	S	12.15 MW	11.43 AW	25280 AAW	OHBLS	10//99-12//99
	Columbus MSA, OH	S	11.65 MW	11.26 AW	24230 AAW	OHBLS	10//99-12//99
	Dayton-Springfield MSA, OH	S	10.10 MW	9.99 AW	21010 AAW	OHBLS	10//99-12//99
	Hamilton-Middletown PMSA, OH	S	11.04 MW	10.68 AW	22970 AAW	OHBLS	10//99-12//99
	Toledo MSA, OH	S	10.45 MW	10.27 AW	21740 AAW	OHBLS	10//99-12//99
	Youngstown-Warren MSA, OH	S	13.22 MW	13.52 AW	27500 AAW	OHBLS	10//99-12//99
	Oklahoma	S	7.83 MW	8.27 AW	17190 AAW	OKBLS	10//99-12//99
	Oklahoma City MSA, OK	S	9.73 MW	9.69 AW	20240 AAW	OKBLS	10//99-12//99
	Tulsa MSA, OK	S	7.68 MW	7.70 AW	15980 AAW	OKBLS	10//99-12//99
	Oregon	S	11.62 MW	11.53 AW	23990 AAW	ORBLS	10//99-12//99
	Portland-Vancouver PMSA, OR-WA	S	12.22 MW	12.16 AW	25420 AAW	ORBLS	10//99-12//99
	Salem PMSA, OR	S	11.13 MW	11.18 AW	23150 AAW	ORBLS	10//99-12//99
	Pennsylvania	S	10.14 MW	11.00 AW	22880 AAW	PABLS	10//99-12//99
	Allentown-Bethlehem-Easton MSA, PA	S	10.72 MW	9.95 AW	22300 AAW	PABLS	10//99-12//99
	Altoona MSA, PA	S	8.73 MW	9.19 AW	18160 AAW	PABLS	10//99-12//99
	Erie MSA, PA	S	11.82 MW	12.25 AW	24580 AAW	PABLS	10//99-12//99
	Harrisburg-Lebanon-Carlisle MSA, PA	S	11.01 MW	10.77 AW	22900 AAW	PABLS	10//99-12//99
	Johnstown MSA, PA	S	6.97 MW	6.61 AW	14500 AAW	PABLS	10//99-12//99
	Lancaster MSA, PA	S	10.75 MW	10.11 AW	22360 AAW	PABLS	10//99-12//99
	Philadelphia PMSA, PA-NJ	S	12.37 MW	11.30 AW	25730 AAW	PABLS	10//99-12//99
	Pittsburgh MSA, PA	S	9.38 MW	9.09 AW	19510 AAW	PABLS	10//99-12//99
	Reading MSA, PA	S	12.63 MW	13.84 AW	26260 AAW	PABLS	10//99-12//99
	Scranton--Wilkes-Barre-- Hazleton MSA, PA	S	9.29 MW	9.29 AW	19320 AAW	PABLS	10//99-12//99
	State College MSA, PA	S	8.96 MW	9.33 AW	18640 AAW	PABLS	10//99-12//99
	York MSA, PA	S	8.23 MW	8.11 AW	17130 AAW	PABLS	10//99-12//99
	Rhode Island	S	10.24 MW	10.24 AW	21290 AAW	RIBLS	10//99-12//99
	Providence-Fall River- Warwick MSA, RI-MA	S	10.51 MW	10.65 AW	21860 AAW	RIBLS	10//99-12//99
	South Carolina	S	8.33 MW	9.56 AW	19870 AAW	SCBLS	10//99-12//99
	Charleston-North Charleston MSA, SC	S	9.42 MW	8.22 AW	19590 AAW	SCBLS	10//99-12//99

AAW	Average annual wage	AOH	Average offered, high	ASH	Average starting, high	H	Hourly	M	Monthly	S	Special: hourly and annual
AE	Average entry wage	AOL	Average offered, low	ASL	Average starting, low	HI	Highest wage paid	MTC	Median total compensation	TQ	Third quartile wage
AEX	Average experienced wage	APH	Average pay, high range	AW	Average wage paid	HR	High end range	MW	Median wage paid	W	Weekly
AO	Average offered	APL	Average pay, low range	FQ	First quartile wage	LR	Low end range	SQ	Second quartile wage	Y	Yearly

Occupation/Type/Industry	Location	Per	Low	Mid	High	Source	Date
Library Technician	Columbia MSA, SC	S	13.19 MW	10.84 AW	27440 AAW	SCBLS	10//99-12//99
	Greenville-Spartanburg-Anderson MSA, SC	S	8.51 MW	7.96 AW	17700 AAW	SCBLS	10//99-12//99
	Sumter MSA, SC	S	7.15 MW	6.32 AW	14860 AAW	SCBLS	10//99-12//99
	South Dakota	S	9.57 MW	9.77 AW	20310 AAW	SDBLS	10//99-12//99
	Rapid City MSA, SD	S	11.25 MW	11.47 AW	23410 AAW	SDBLS	10//99-12//99
	Sioux Falls MSA, SD	S	11.46 MW	10.54 AW	23830 AAW	SDBLS	10//99-12//99
	Tennessee	S	8.45 MW	9.17 AW	19070 AAW	TNBLS	10//99-12//99
	Chattanooga MSA, TN-GA	S	11.63 MW	12.16 AW	24180 AAW	TNBLS	10//99-12//99
	Clarksville-Hopkinsville MSA, TN-KY	S	11.16 MW	10.57 AW	23210 AAW	TNBLS	10//99-12//99
	Johnson City-Kingsport-Bristol MSA, TN-VA	S	8.96 MW	8.22 AW	18630 AAW	TNBLS	10//99-12//99
	Knoxville MSA, TN	S	7.83 MW	6.50 AW	16300 AAW	TNBLS	10//99-12//99
	Memphis MSA, TN-AR-MS	S	9.59 MW	8.64 AW	19940 AAW	MSBLS	10//99-12//99
	Nashville MSA, TN	S	8.18 MW	7.43 AW	17010 AAW	TNBLS	10//99-12//99
	Texas	S	8.44 MW	9.15 AW	19030 AAW	TXBLS	10//99-12//99
	Amarillo MSA, TX	S	6.98 MW	6.41 AW	14520 AAW	TXBLS	10//99-12//99
	Austin-San Marcos MSA, TX	S	9.75 MW	9.53 AW	20280 AAW	TXBLS	10//99-12//99
	Beaumont-Port Arthur MSA, TX	S	8.74 MW	8.83 AW	18170 AAW	TXBLS	10//99-12//99
	Brownsville-Harlingen-San Benito MSA, TX	S	7.81 MW	7.26 AW	16240 AAW	TXBLS	10//99-12//99
	Corpus Christi MSA, TX	S	7.60 MW	6.89 AW	15820 AAW	TXBLS	10//99-12//99
	Dallas PMSA, TX	S	10.69 MW	10.56 AW	22230 AAW	TXBLS	10//99-12//99
	El Paso MSA, TX	S	10.35 MW	10.28 AW	21520 AAW	TXBLS	10//99-12//99
	Fort Worth-Arlington PMSA, TX	S	8.88 MW	8.05 AW	18470 AAW	TXBLS	10//99-12//99
	Galveston-Texas City PMSA, TX	S	10.22 MW	8.38 AW	21260 AAW	TXBLS	10//99-12//99
	Houston PMSA, TX	S	11.12 MW	9.47 AW	23120 AAW	TXBLS	10//99-12//99
	Killeen-Temple MSA, TX	S	7.23 MW	6.59 AW	15040 AAW	TXBLS	10//99-12//99
	Longview-Marshall MSA, TX	S	6.73 MW	6.52 AW	14000 AAW	TXBLS	10//99-12//99
	Lubbock MSA, TX	S	6.80 MW	6.49 AW	14150 AAW	TXBLS	10//99-12//99
	McAllen-Edinburg-Mission MSA, TX	S	7.68 MW	7.02 AW	15970 AAW	TXBLS	10//99-12//99
	San Angelo MSA, TX	S	8.54 MW	7.91 AW	17770 AAW	TXBLS	10//99-12//99
	San Antonio MSA, TX	S	8.54 MW	8.35 AW	17770 AAW	TXBLS	10//99-12//99
	Sherman-Denison MSA, TX	S	8.10 MW	7.72 AW	16850 AAW	TXBLS	10//99-12//99
	Waco MSA, TX	S	7.25 MW	7.34 AW	15070 AAW	TXBLS	10//99-12//99
	Utah	S	8.27 MW	8.87 AW	18450 AAW	UTBLS	10//99-12//99
	Provo-Orem MSA, UT	S	8.00 MW	7.54 AW	16640 AAW	UTBLS	10//99-12//99
	Salt Lake City-Ogden MSA, UT	S	9.50 MW	9.37 AW	19760 AAW	UTBLS	10//99-12//99
	Vermont	S	10.13 MW	10.41 AW	21650 AAW	VTBLS	10//99-12//99
	Burlington MSA, VT	S	8.93 MW	8.97 AW	18580 AAW	VTBLS	10//99-12//99
	Virginia	S	11.9 MW	11.86 AW	24670 AAW	VABLS	10//99-12//99
	Charlottesville MSA, VA	S	11.36 MW	11.81 AW	23640 AAW	VABLS	10//99-12//99
	Richmond-Petersburg MSA, VA	S	13.20 MW	12.78 AW	27450 AAW	VABLS	10//99-12//99
	Roanoke MSA, VA	S	8.20 MW	7.22 AW	17050 AAW	VABLS	10//99-12//99
	Washington	S	13.18 MW	13.36 AW	27780 AAW	WABLS	10//99-12//99
	Bellingham MSA, WA	S	12.69 MW	12.47 AW	26400 AAW	WABLS	10//99-12//99
	Olympia PMSA, WA	S	13.07 MW	12.99 AW	27180 AAW	WABLS	10//99-12//99
	Richland-Kennewick-Pasco MSA, WA	S	13.02 MW	12.83 AW	27090 AAW	WABLS	10//99-12//99
	Seattle-Bellevue-Everett PMSA, WA	S	13.90 MW	13.98 AW	28910 AAW	WABLS	10//99-12//99
	Tacoma PMSA, WA	S	13.31 MW	13.12 AW	27690 AAW	WABLS	10//99-12//99
	Yakima MSA, WA	S	9.46 MW	9.59 AW	19680 AAW	WABLS	10//99-12//99
	West Virginia	S	8.33 MW	8.86 AW	18430 AAW	WVBLS	10//99-12//99
	Charleston MSA, WV	S	9.20 MW	8.47 AW	19130 AAW	WVBLS	10//99-12//99
	Huntington-Ashland MSA, WV-KY-OH	S	7.50 MW	7.12 AW	15610 AAW	WVBLS	10//99-12//99
	Wisconsin	S	10.94 MW	10.87 AW	22600 AAW	WIBLS	10//99-12//99
	Appleton-Oshkosh-Neenah MSA, WI	S	10.35 MW	10.60 AW	21520 AAW	WIBLS	10//99-12//99
	Eau Claire MSA, WI	S	11.87 MW	12.46 AW	24700 AAW	WIBLS	10//99-12//99
	Janesville-Beloit MSA, WI	S	11.87 MW	11.77 AW	24690 AAW	WIBLS	10//99-12//99
	Kenosha PMSA, WI	S	11.02 MW	11.67 AW	22920 AAW	WIBLS	10//99-12//99
	La Crosse MSA, WI-MN	S	12.22 MW	12.31 AW	25420 AAW	WIBLS	10//99-12//99
	Madison MSA, WI	S	11.35 MW	10.41 AW	23610 AAW	WIBLS	10//99-12//99

AAW Average annual wage	AOH Average offered, high	ASH Average starting, high	H Hourly	M Monthly	S Special: hourly and annual
AE Average entry wage	AOL Average offered, low	ASL Average starting, low	HI Highest wage paid	MTC Median total compensation	TQ Third quartile wage
AEX Average experienced wage	APH Average pay, high range	AW Average wage paid	HR High end range	MW Median wage paid	W Weekly
AO Average offered	APL Average pay, low range	FQ First quartile wage	LR Low end range	SQ Second quartile wage	Y Yearly

Occupation/Type/Industry	Location	Per	Low	Mid	High	Source	Date
Library Technician	Milwaukee-Waukesha PMSA, WI	S	11.53 MW	11.84 AW	23980 AAW	WIBLS	10//99-12//99
	Sheboygan MSA, WI	S	10.80 MW	10.08 AW	22470 AAW	WIBLS	10//99-12//99
	Wyoming	S	8.26 MW	8.73 AW	18150 AAW	WYBLS	10//99-12//99
	Puerto Rico	S	6.81 MW	7.04 AW	14650 AAW	PRBLS	10//99-12//99
	San Juan-Bayamon PMSA, PR	S	6.89 MW	6.73 AW	14330 AAW	PRBLS	10//99-12//99
	Guam	S	12.01 MW	11.96 AW	24880 AAW	GUBLS	10//99-12//99
Licensed Practical and Licensed Vocational Nurse	Alabama	S	10.89 MW	11.12 AW	23130 AAW	ALBLS	10//99-12//99
	Anniston MSA, AL	S	10.84 MW	10.58 AW	22550 AAW	ALBLS	10//99-12//99
	Auburn-Opelika MSA, AL	S	10.78 MW	10.77 AW	22410 AAW	ALBLS	10//99-12//99
	Birmingham MSA, AL	S	11.62 MW	11.43 AW	24180 AAW	ALBLS	10//99-12//99
	Decatur MSA, AL	S	10.43 MW	10.28 AW	21700 AAW	ALBLS	10//99-12//99
	Dothan MSA, AL	S	11.98 MW	11.54 AW	24920 AAW	ALBLS	10//99-12//99
	Florence MSA, AL	S	10.47 MW	10.45 AW	21780 AAW	ALBLS	10//99-12//99
	Gadsden MSA, AL	S	10.87 MW	10.97 AW	22610 AAW	ALBLS	10//99-12//99
	Huntsville MSA, AL	S	11.07 MW	10.69 AW	23030 AAW	ALBLS	10//99-12//99
	Mobile MSA, AL	S	10.87 MW	10.83 AW	22610 AAW	ALBLS	10//99-12//99
	Montgomery MSA, AL	S	11.57 MW	10.92 AW	24060 AAW	ALBLS	10//99-12//99
	Tuscaloosa MSA, AL	S	10.99 MW	10.94 AW	22850 AAW	ALBLS	10//99-12//99
	Alaska	S	16.24 MW	16.43 AW	34180 AAW	AKBLS	10//99-12//99
	Anchorage MSA, AK	S	16.18 MW	15.94 AW	33650 AAW	AKBLS	10//99-12//99
	Arizona	S	14.22 MW	14.30 AW	29750 AAW	AZBLS	10//99-12//99
	Flagstaff MSA, AZ-UT	S	14.00 MW	14.43 AW	29110 AAW	AZBLS	10//99-12//99
	Phoenix-Mesa MSA, AZ	S	14.33 MW	14.48 AW	29800 AAW	AZBLS	10//99-12//99
	Tucson MSA, AZ	S	14.36 MW	13.70 AW	29860 AAW	AZBLS	10//99-12//99
	Yuma MSA, AZ	S	15.28 MW	15.04 AW	31780 AAW	AZBLS	10//99-12//99
	Arkansas	S	11 MW	11.16 AW	23220 AAW	ARBLS	10//99-12//99
	Fayetteville-Springdale-Rogers MSA, AR	S	11.35 MW	11.27 AW	23610 AAW	ARBLS	10//99-12//99
	Fort Smith MSA, AR-OK	S	11.00 MW	10.86 AW	22880 AAW	ARBLS	10//99-12//99
	Jonesboro MSA, AR	S	11.03 MW	10.63 AW	22940 AAW	ARBLS	10//99-12//99
	Little Rock-North Little Rock MSA, AR	S	12.30 MW	12.19 AW	25580 AAW	ARBLS	10//99-12//99
	Pine Bluff MSA, AR	S	10.88 MW	10.84 AW	22630 AAW	ARBLS	10//99-12//99
	California	S	16.03 MW	17.18 AW	35740 AAW	CABLS	10//99-12//99
	Bakersfield MSA, CA	S	15.38 MW	14.80 AW	31990 AAW	CABLS	10//99-12//99
	Chico-Paradise MSA, CA	S	14.61 MW	14.82 AW	30380 AAW	CABLS	10//99-12//99
	Fresno MSA, CA	S	14.76 MW	14.62 AW	30700 AAW	CABLS	10//99-12//99
	Los Angeles-Long Beach PMSA, CA	S	17.44 MW	15.98 AW	36260 AAW	CABLS	10//99-12//99
	Merced MSA, CA	S	15.32 MW	14.14 AW	31870 AAW	CABLS	10//99-12//99
	Modesto MSA, CA	S	16.26 MW	15.99 AW	33830 AAW	CABLS	10//99-12//99
	Oakland PMSA, CA	S	18.64 MW	18.70 AW	38770 AAW	CABLS	10//99-12//99
	Orange County PMSA, CA	S	17.86 MW	16.65 AW	37150 AAW	CABLS	10//99-12//99
	Redding MSA, CA	S	13.22 MW	13.05 AW	27490 AAW	CABLS	10//99-12//99
	Riverside-San Bernardino PMSA, CA	S	14.80 MW	14.25 AW	30780 AAW	CABLS	10//99-12//99
	Sacramento PMSA, CA	S	17.48 MW	17.06 AW	36350 AAW	CABLS	10//99-12//99
	Salinas MSA, CA	S	17.44 MW	17.24 AW	36270 AAW	CABLS	10//99-12//99
	San Diego MSA, CA	S	17.72 MW	14.99 AW	36850 AAW	CABLS	10//99-12//99
	San Francisco PMSA, CA	S	20.40 MW	19.31 AW	42420 AAW	CABLS	10//99-12//99
	San Jose PMSA, CA	S	18.79 MW	18.53 AW	39090 AAW	CABLS	10//99-12//99
	San Luis Obispo-Atascadero-Paso Robles MSA, CA	S	15.67 MW	14.70 AW	32600 AAW	CABLS	10//99-12//99
	Santa Barbara-Santa Maria-Lompoc MSA, CA	S	15.60 MW	15.34 AW	32440 AAW	CABLS	10//99-12//99
	Santa Cruz-Watsonville PMSA, CA	S	16.19 MW	15.93 AW	33680 AAW	CABLS	10//99-12//99
	Santa Rosa PMSA, CA	S	18.50 MW	16.83 AW	38470 AAW	CABLS	10//99-12//99
	Stockton-Lodi MSA, CA	S	16.91 MW	16.12 AW	35160 AAW	CABLS	10//99-12//99
	Vallejo-Fairfield-Napa PMSA, CA	S	16.21 MW	15.73 AW	33720 AAW	CABLS	10//99-12//99
	Ventura PMSA, CA	S	15.54 MW	15.19 AW	32320 AAW	CABLS	10//99-12//99
	Visalia-Tulare-Porterville MSA, CA	S	15.42 MW	14.94 AW	32080 AAW	CABLS	10//99-12//99
	Yolo PMSA, CA	S	17.22 MW	15.17 AW	35810 AAW	CABLS	10//99-12//99
	Yuba City MSA, CA	S	14.62 MW	14.69 AW	30410 AAW	CABLS	10//99-12//99
	Colorado	S	13.82 MW	14.03 AW	29180 AAW	COBLS	10//99-12//99
	Boulder-Longmont PMSA, CO	S	13.58 MW	13.40 AW	28260 AAW	COBLS	10//99-12//99
	Colorado Springs MSA, CO	S	13.87 MW	13.77 AW	28850 AAW	COBLS	10//99-12//99

AAW Average annual wage	**AOH** Average offered, high	**ASH** Average starting, high	**H** Hourly	**M** Monthly	**S** Special: hourly and annual
AE Average entry wage	**AOL** Average offered, low	**ASL** Average starting, low	**HI** Highest wage paid	**MTC** Median total compensation	**TQ** Third quartile wage
AEX Average experienced wage	**APH** Average pay, high range	**AW** Average wage paid	**HR** High end range	**MW** Median wage paid	**W** Weekly
AO Average offered	**APL** Average pay, low range	**FQ** First quartile wage	**LR** Low end range	**SQ** Second quartile wage	**Y** Yearly

Occupation/Type/Industry	Location	Per	Low	Mid	High	Source	Date
Licensed Practical and Licensed Vocational Nurse	Denver PMSA, CO	S	15.38 MW	14.85 AW	32000 AAW	COBLS	10//99-12//99
	Fort Collins-Loveland MSA, CO	S	13.80 MW	13.07 AW	28700 AAW	COBLS	10//99-12//99
	Grand Junction MSA, CO	S	12.62 MW	12.64 AW	26250 AAW	COBLS	10//99-12//99
	Greeley PMSA, CO	S	14.21 MW	14.37 AW	29560 AAW	COBLS	10//99-12//99
	Pueblo MSA, CO	S	12.65 MW	12.47 AW	26310 AAW	COBLS	10//99-12//99
	Connecticut	S	18.84 MW	18.95 AW	39410 AAW	CTBLS	10//99-12//99
	Bridgeport PMSA, CT	S	19.47 MW	19.76 AW	40490 AAW	CTBLS	10//99-12//99
	Danbury PMSA, CT	S	19.32 MW	18.87 AW	40180 AAW	CTBLS	10//99-12//99
	Hartford MSA, CT	S	18.83 MW	18.77 AW	39170 AAW	CTBLS	10//99-12//99
	New Haven-Meriden PMSA, CT	S	19.75 MW	19.17 AW	41080 AAW	CTBLS	10//99-12//99
	New London-Norwich MSA, CT-RI	S	17.46 MW	17.39 AW	36320 AAW	CTBLS	10//99-12//99
	Stamford-Norwalk PMSA, CT	S	19.44 MW	19.25 AW	40430 AAW	CTBLS	10//99-12//99
	Waterbury PMSA, CT	S	18.13 MW	18.26 AW	37710 AAW	CTBLS	10//99-12//99
	Delaware	S	15.17 MW	15.34 AW	31900 AAW	DEBLS	10//99-12//99
	Dover MSA, DE	S	14.08 MW	14.07 AW	29290 AAW	DEBLS	10//99-12//99
	Wilmington-Newark PMSA, DE-MD	S	15.86 MW	15.71 AW	33000 AAW	DEBLS	10//99-12//99
	District of Columbia	S	15.52 MW	15.91 AW	33100 AAW	DCBLS	10//99-12//99
	Washington PMSA, DC-MD-VA-WV	S	16.07 MW	15.72 AW	33410 AAW	DCBLS	10//99-12//99
	Florida	S	13.56 MW	14.11 AW	29360 AAW	FLBLS	10//99-12//99
	Daytona Beach MSA, FL	S	12.93 MW	12.80 AW	26890 AAW	FLBLS	10//99-12//99
	Fort Lauderdale PMSA, FL	S	15.10 MW	14.13 AW	31400 AAW	FLBLS	10//99-12//99
	Fort Myers-Cape Coral MSA, FL	S	12.43 MW	12.36 AW	25850 AAW	FLBLS	10//99-12//99
	Fort Pierce-Port St. Lucie MSA, FL	S	15.77 MW	15.00 AW	32800 AAW	FLBLS	10//99-12//99
	Fort Walton Beach MSA, FL	S	10.69 MW	10.51 AW	22240 AAW	FLBLS	10//99-12//99
	Gainesville MSA, FL	S	12.97 MW	12.92 AW	26970 AAW	FLBLS	10//99-12//99
	Jacksonville MSA, FL	S	15.46 MW	14.23 AW	32160 AAW	FLBLS	10//99-12//99
	Lakeland-Winter Haven MSA, FL	S	12.39 MW	11.89 AW	25770 AAW	FLBLS	10//99-12//99
	Miami PMSA, FL	S	15.88 MW	15.06 AW	33030 AAW	FLBLS	10//99-12//99
	Naples MSA, FL	S	14.19 MW	13.78 AW	29520 AAW	FLBLS	10//99-12//99
	Ocala MSA, FL	S	14.45 MW	13.21 AW	30060 AAW	FLBLS	10//99-12//99
	Orlando MSA, FL	S	13.49 MW	13.17 AW	28050 AAW	FLBLS	10//99-12//99
	Panama City MSA, FL	S	11.18 MW	10.83 AW	23250 AAW	FLBLS	10//99-12//99
	Pensacola MSA, FL	S	11.36 MW	11.05 AW	23640 AAW	FLBLS	10//99-12//99
	Punta Gorda MSA, FL	S	12.49 MW	12.44 AW	25970 AAW	FLBLS	10//99-12//99
	Sarasota-Bradenton MSA, FL	S	13.32 MW	12.80 AW	27720 AAW	FLBLS	10//99-12//99
	Tallahassee MSA, FL	S	14.53 MW	14.14 AW	30230 AAW	FLBLS	10//99-12//99
	Tampa-St. Petersburg-Clearwater MSA, FL		13.76 MW	13.57 AW	28630 AAW	FLBLS	10//99-12//99
	West Palm Beach-Boca Raton MSA, FL	S	15.06 MW	14.60 AW	31330 AAW	FLBLS	10//99-12//99
	Georgia	S	12.02 MW	12.19 AW	25340 AAW	GABLS	10//99-12//99
	Albany MSA, GA	S	11.50 MW	11.54 AW	23910 AAW	GABLS	10//99-12//99
	Athens MSA, GA	S	11.99 MW	11.96 AW	24950 AAW	GABLS	10//99-12//99
	Atlanta MSA, GA	S	13.07 MW	12.95 AW	27200 AAW	GABLS	10//99-12//99
	Augusta-Aiken MSA, GA-SC	S	13.22 MW	12.97 AW	27500 AAW	GABLS	10//99-12//99
	Columbus MSA, GA-AL	S	11.67 MW	11.40 AW	24260 AAW	GABLS	10//99-12//99
	Macon MSA, GA	S	11.19 MW	11.38 AW	23280 AAW	GABLS	10//99-12//99
	Savannah MSA, GA	S	12.07 MW	11.93 AW	25100 AAW	GABLS	10//99-12//99
	Hawaii	S	14.81 MW	14.83 AW	30850 AAW	HIBLS	10//99-12//99
	Honolulu MSA, HI	S	15.24 MW	15.18 AW	31710 AAW	HIBLS	10//99-12//99
	Idaho	S	12.65 MW	13.09 AW	27230 AAW	IDBLS	10//99-12//99
	Boise City MSA, ID	S	14.19 MW	13.45 AW	29520 AAW	IDBLS	10//99-12//99
	Pocatello MSA, ID	S	11.83 MW	11.61 AW	24610 AAW	IDBLS	10//99-12//99
	Illinois	S	13.06 MW	13.47 AW	28010 AAW	ILBLS	10//99-12//99
	Bloomington-Normal MSA, IL	S	12.74 MW	12.58 AW	26490 AAW	ILBLS	10//99-12//99
	Champaign-Urbana MSA, IL	S	12.21 MW	11.90 AW	25390 AAW	ILBLS	10//99-12//99
	Chicago PMSA, IL	S	14.56 MW	14.49 AW	30290 AAW	ILBLS	10//99-12//99
	Decatur MSA, IL	S	11.03 MW	11.17 AW	22940 AAW	ILBLS	10//99-12//99
	Kankakee PMSA, IL	S	12.62 MW	12.52 AW	26240 AAW	ILBLS	10//99-12//99
	Peoria-Pekin MSA, IL	S	13.15 MW	13.24 AW	27350 AAW	ILBLS	10//99-12//99
	Rockford MSA, IL	S	13.54 MW	13.42 AW	28160 AAW	ILBLS	10//99-12//99
	Springfield MSA, IL	S	12.28 MW	11.80 AW	25550 AAW	ILBLS	10//99-12//99
	Indiana	S	13.19 MW	13.41 AW	27880 AAW	INBLS	10//99-12//99

Occupation/Type/Industry	Location	Per	Low	Mid	High	Source	Date
Licensed Practical and Licensed Vocational Nurse							
	Bloomington MSA, IN	S	12.78 MW	12.43 AW	26580 AAW	INBLS	10//99-12//99
	Elkhart-Goshen MSA, IN	S	13.36 MW	13.11 AW	27780 AAW	INBLS	10//99-12//99
	Evansville-Henderson MSA, IN-KY	S	12.74 MW	12.54 AW	26500 AAW	INBLS	10//99-12//99
	Fort Wayne MSA, IN	S	13.33 MW	13.12 AW	27720 AAW	INBLS	10//99-12//99
	Gary PMSA, IN	S	13.38 MW	13.15 AW	27830 AAW	INBLS	10//99-12//99
	Indianapolis MSA, IN	S	14.91 MW	14.77 AW	31000 AAW	INBLS	10//99-12//99
	Kokomo MSA, IN	S	12.53 MW	12.28 AW	26070 AAW	INBLS	10//99-12//99
	Lafayette MSA, IN	S	13.53 MW	13.32 AW	28140 AAW	INBLS	10//99-12//99
	Muncie MSA, IN	S	12.51 MW	12.17 AW	26020 AAW	INBLS	10//99-12//99
	South Bend MSA, IN	S	13.60 MW	13.45 AW	28280 AAW	INBLS	10//99-12//99
	Iowa	S	12 MW	12.33 AW	25660 AAW	IABLS	10//99-12//99
	Cedar Rapids MSA, IA	S	12.32 MW	12.38 AW	25630 AAW	IABLS	10//99-12//99
	Davenport-Moline-Rock Island MSA, IA-IL	S	11.06 MW	10.91 AW	23010 AAW	IABLS	10//99-12//99
	Dubuque MSA, IA	S	11.41 MW	11.39 AW	23730 AAW	IABLS	10//99-12//99
	Iowa City MSA, IA	S	13.59 MW	13.13 AW	28260 AAW	IABLS	10//99-12//99
	Sioux City MSA, IA-NE	S	11.08 MW	11.60 AW	23040 AAW	IABLS	10//99-12//99
	Waterloo-Cedar Falls MSA, IA	S	11.36 MW	11.34 AW	23620 AAW	IABLS	10//99-12//99
	Kansas	S	12.16 MW	12.49 AW	25980 AAW	KSBLS	10//99-12//99
	Lawrence MSA, KS	S	13.64 MW	13.49 AW	28380 AAW	KSBLS	10//99-12//99
	Topeka MSA, KS	S	12.29 MW	12.03 AW	25570 AAW	KSBLS	10//99-12//99
	Wichita MSA, KS	S	12.89 MW	12.64 AW	26820 AAW	KSBLS	10//99-12//99
	Kentucky	S	12.11 MW	12.41 AW	25810 AAW	KYBLS	10//99-12//99
	Lexington MSA, KY	S	12.79 MW	12.58 AW	26590 AAW	KYBLS	10//99-12//99
	Louisville MSA, KY-IN	S	13.59 MW	13.22 AW	28260 AAW	KYBLS	10//99-12//99
	Owensboro MSA, KY	S	12.13 MW	12.05 AW	25230 AAW	KYBLS	10//99-12//99
	Louisiana	S	11.51 MW	11.82 AW	24590 AAW	LABLS	10//99-12//99
	Alexandria MSA, LA	S	12.05 MW	11.76 AW	25060 AAW	LABLS	10//99-12//99
	Baton Rouge MSA, LA	S	12.34 MW	12.07 AW	25660 AAW	LABLS	10//99-12//99
	Houma MSA, LA	S	11.32 MW	10.54 AW	23550 AAW	LABLS	10//99-12//99
	Lafayette MSA, LA	S	12.16 MW	12.06 AW	25300 AAW	LABLS	10//99-12//99
	Lake Charles MSA, LA	S	11.72 MW	11.26 AW	24390 AAW	LABLS	10//99-12//99
	Monroe MSA, LA	S	10.99 MW	10.95 AW	22850 AAW	LABLS	10//99-12//99
	New Orleans MSA, LA	S	12.45 MW	12.15 AW	25900 AAW	LABLS	10//99-12//99
	Shreveport-Bossier City MSA, LA	S	11.90 MW	11.52 AW	24750 AAW	LABLS	10//99-12//99
	Maine	S	12.9 MW	13.18 AW	27420 AAW	MEBLS	10//99-12//99
	Bangor MSA, ME	S	12.93 MW	12.84 AW	26890 AAW	MEBLS	10//99-12//99
	Lewiston-Auburn MSA, ME	S	12.93 MW	12.88 AW	26890 AAW	MEBLS	10//99-12//99
	Portland MSA, ME	S	13.54 MW	13.29 AW	28150 AAW	MEBLS	10//99-12//99
	Maryland	S	15.92 MW	16.10 AW	33500 AAW	MDBLS	10//99-12//99
	Baltimore PMSA, MD	S	16.08 MW	16.10 AW	33460 AAW	MDBLS	10//99-12//99
	Cumberland MSA, MD-WV	S	12.98 MW	12.52 AW	27000 AAW	MDBLS	10//99-12//99
	Hagerstown PMSA, MD	S	13.44 MW	13.13 AW	27950 AAW	MDBLS	10//99-12//99
	Massachusetts	S	16.74 MW	17.13 AW	35640 AAW	MABLS	10//99-12//99
	Barnstable-Yarmouth MSA, MA	S	15.87 MW	15.15 AW	33000 AAW	MABLS	10//99-12//99
	Boston PMSA, MA-NH	S	17.45 MW	17.08 AW	36300 AAW	MABLS	10//99-12//99
	Brockton PMSA, MA	S	15.96 MW	15.92 AW	33190 AAW	MABLS	10//99-12//99
	Fitchburg-Leominster PMSA, MA	S	15.68 MW	15.51 AW	32610 AAW	MABLS	10//99-12//99
	Lawrence PMSA, MA-NH	S	16.75 MW	16.85 AW	34840 AAW	MABLS	10//99-12//99
	Lowell PMSA, MA-NH	S	16.42 MW	16.31 AW	34160 AAW	MABLS	10//99-12//99
	Pittsfield MSA, MA	S	16.48 MW	17.04 AW	34290 AAW	MABLS	10//99-12//99
	Springfield MSA, MA	S	16.07 MW	15.78 AW	33420 AAW	MABLS	10//99-12//99
	Worcester PMSA, MA-CT	S	16.66 MW	16.24 AW	34650 AAW	MABLS	10//99-12//99
	Michigan	S	14.59 MW	14.66 AW	30490 AAW	MIBLS	10//99-12//99
	Ann Arbor PMSA, MI	S	15.67 MW	15.73 AW	32600 AAW	MIBLS	10//99-12//99
	Benton Harbor MSA, MI	S	13.73 MW	13.29 AW	28570 AAW	MIBLS	10//99-12//99
	Detroit PMSA, MI	S	15.80 MW	15.72 AW	32870 AAW	MIBLS	10//99-12//99
	Flint PMSA, MI	S	14.76 MW	14.92 AW	30700 AAW	MIBLS	10//99-12//99
	Grand Rapids-Muskegon-Holland MSA, MI	S	13.88 MW	13.71 AW	28880 AAW	MIBLS	10//99-12//99
	Jackson MSA, MI	S	13.64 MW	13.37 AW	28370 AAW	MIBLS	10//99-12//99
	Kalamazoo-Battle Creek MSA, MI	S	14.36 MW	14.25 AW	29870 AAW	MIBLS	10//99-12//99
	Lansing-East Lansing MSA, MI	S	15.01 MW	14.52 AW	31220 AAW	MIBLS	10//99-12//99
	Saginaw-Bay City-Midland MSA, MI	S	14.51 MW	14.00 AW	30180 AAW	MIBLS	10//99-12//99
	Minnesota	S	13.3 MW	13.62 AW	28340 AAW	MNBLS	10//99-12//99

AAW	Average annual wage	**AOH**	Average offered, high	**ASH**	Average starting, high	**H**	Hourly	**M**	Monthly
AE	Average entry wage	**AOL**	Average offered, low	**ASL**	Average starting, low	**HI**	Highest wage paid	**MTC**	Median total compensation
AEX	Average experienced wage	**APH**	Average pay, high range	**AW**	Average wage paid	**HR**	High end range	**MW**	Median wage paid
AO	Average offered	**APL**	Average pay, low range	**FQ**	First quartile wage	**LR**	Low end range	**SQ**	Second quartile wage

S	Special: hourly and annual		
TQ	Third quartile wage		
W	Weekly		
Y	Yearly		

Occupation/Type/Industry	Location	Per	Low	Mid	High	Source	Date
Licensed Practical and Licensed Vocational Nurse	Duluth-Superior MSA, MN-WI	S	13.55 MW	13.70 AW	28170 AAW	MNBLS	10//99-12/99
	Minneapolis-St. Paul MSA, MN-WI	S	14.82 MW	14.52 AW	30830 AAW	MNBLS	10//99-12/99
	St. Cloud MSA, MN	S	12.65 MW	12.44 AW	26320 AAW	MNBLS	10//99-12/99
	Mississippi	S	10.81 MW	11.16 AW	23200 AAW	MSBLS	10//99-12/99
	Biloxi-Gulfport-Pascagoula MSA, MS	S	11.20 MW	10.86 AW	23290 AAW	MSBLS	10//99-12/99
	Hattiesburg MSA, MS	S	10.86 MW	10.86 AW	22580 AAW	MSBLS	10//99-12/99
	Jackson MSA, MS	S	11.74 MW	11.37 AW	24410 AAW	MSBLS	10//99-12/99
	Missouri	S	11.94 MW	12.18 AW	25340 AAW	MOBLS	10//99-12/99
	Columbia MSA, MO	S	11.47 MW	11.60 AW	23860 AAW	MOBLS	10//99-12/99
	Joplin MSA, MO	S	10.84 MW	10.82 AW	22540 AAW	MOBLS	10//99-12/99
	Kansas City MSA, MO-KS	S	13.97 MW	13.70 AW	29060 AAW	MOBLS	10//99-12/99
	St. Joseph MSA, MO	S	10.90 MW	10.96 AW	22670 AAW	MOBLS	10//99-12/99
	St. Louis MSA, MO-IL	S	13.60 MW	13.31 AW	28300 AAW	MOBLS	10//99-12/99
	Springfield MSA, MO	S	11.19 MW	10.96 AW	23280 AAW	MOBLS	10//99-12/99
	Montana	S	11.15 MW	11.19 AW	23280 AAW	MTBLS	10//99-12/99
	Billings MSA, MT	S	11.52 MW	11.22 AW	23960 AAW	MTBLS	10//99-12/99
	Great Falls MSA, MT	S	11.56 MW	11.62 AW	24050 AAW	MTBLS	10//99-12/99
	Missoula MSA, MT	S	11.54 MW	11.33 AW	24000 AAW	MTBLS	10//99-12/99
	Nebraska	S	12.07 MW	12.44 AW	25870 AAW	NEBLS	10//99-12/99
	Lincoln MSA, NE	S	13.22 MW	12.28 AW	27500 AAW	NEBLS	10//99-12/99
	Omaha MSA, NE-IA	S	14.20 MW	14.12 AW	29530 AAW	NEBLS	10//99-12/99
	Nevada	S	15.25 MW	15.64 AW	32530 AAW	NVBLS	10//99-12/99
	Las Vegas MSA, NV-AZ	S	15.47 MW	15.08 AW	32180 AAW	NVBLS	10//99-12/99
	Reno MSA, NV	S	15.50 MW	15.27 AW	32230 AAW	NVBLS	10//99-12/99
	New Hampshire	S	13.73 MW	13.92 AW	28940 AAW	NHBLS	10//99-12/99
	Manchester PMSA, NH	S	15.22 MW	14.92 AW	31660 AAW	NHBLS	10//99-12/99
	Nashua PMSA, NH	S	14.28 MW	14.22 AW	29710 AAW	NHBLS	10//99-12/99
	Portsmouth-Rochester PMSA, NH-ME	S	14.50 MW	14.62 AW	30160 AAW	NHBLS	10//99-12/99
	New Jersey	S	16.24 MW	16.62 AW	34580 AAW	NJBLS	10//99-12/99
	Atlantic-Cape May PMSA, NJ	S	15.36 MW	15.20 AW	31950 AAW	NJBLS	10//99-12/99
	Bergen-Passaic PMSA, NJ	S	16.95 MW	16.70 AW	35260 AAW	NJBLS	10//99-12/99
	Jersey City PMSA, NJ	S	16.03 MW	15.65 AW	33340 AAW	NJBLS	10//99-12/99
	Middlesex-Somerset-Hunterdon PMSA, NJ	S	17.20 MW	16.79 AW	35780 AAW	NJBLS	10//99-12/99
	Monmouth-Ocean PMSA, NJ	S	15.32 MW	15.28 AW	31870 AAW	NJBLS	10//99-12/99
	Newark PMSA, NJ	S	17.00 MW	16.60 AW	35360 AAW	NJBLS	10//99-12/99
	Trenton PMSA, NJ	S	15.96 MW	15.87 AW	33210 AAW	NJBLS	10//99-12/99
	Vineland-Millville-Bridgeton PMSA, NJ	S	16.14 MW	15.66 AW	33560 AAW	NJBLS	10//99-12/99
	New Mexico	S	13.48 MW	13.78 AW	28660 AAW	NMBLS	10//99-12/99
	Albuquerque MSA, NM	S	14.06 MW	14.04 AW	29240 AAW	NMBLS	10//99-12/99
	Las Cruces MSA, NM	S	12.37 MW	12.21 AW	25720 AAW	NMBLS	10//99-12/99
	Santa Fe MSA, NM	S	14.66 MW	14.51 AW	30500 AAW	NMBLS	10//99-12/99
	New York	S	14.36 MW	14.81 AW	30800 AAW	NYBLS	10//99-12/99
	Albany-Schenectady-Troy MSA, NY	S	12.94 MW	12.67 AW	26900 AAW	NYBLS	10//99-12/99
	Binghamton MSA, NY	S	12.10 MW	11.91 AW	25160 AAW	NYBLS	10//99-12/99
	Buffalo-Niagara Falls MSA, NY	S	12.52 MW	12.53 AW	26050 AAW	NYBLS	10//99-12/99
	Dutchess County PMSA, NY	S	14.10 MW	13.93 AW	29330 AAW	NYBLS	10//99-12/99
	Elmira MSA, NY	S	11.61 MW	11.23 AW	24140 AAW	NYBLS	10//99-12/99
	Glens Falls MSA, NY	S	10.92 MW	11.03 AW	22710 AAW	NYBLS	10//99-12/99
	Jamestown MSA, NY	S	11.74 MW	11.62 AW	24420 AAW	NYBLS	10//99-12/99
	Nassau-Suffolk PMSA, NY	S	18.06 MW	17.81 AW	37560 AAW	NYBLS	10//99-12/99
	New York PMSA, NY	S	16.26 MW	16.46 AW	33820 AAW	NYBLS	10//99-12/99
	Rochester MSA, NY	S	13.55 MW	13.21 AW	28180 AAW	NYBLS	10//99-12/99
	Syracuse MSA, NY	S	12.02 MW	11.70 AW	25010 AAW	NYBLS	10//99-12/99
	Utica-Rome MSA, NY	S	12.21 MW	11.73 AW	25400 AAW	NYBLS	10//99-12/99
	North Carolina	S	13.31 MW	13.49 AW	28050 AAW	NCBLS	10//99-12/99
	Asheville MSA, NC	S	13.12 MW	12.98 AW	27280 AAW	NCBLS	10//99-12/99
	Charlotte-Gastonia-Rock Hill MSA, NC-SC	S	14.23 MW	14.04 AW	29590 AAW	NCBLS	10//99-12/99
	Fayetteville MSA, NC	S	13.09 MW	12.97 AW	27220 AAW	NCBLS	10//99-12/99
	Goldsboro MSA, NC	S	15.07 MW	13.32 AW	31350 AAW	NCBLS	10//99-12/99
	Greensboro--Winston-Salem--High Point MSA, NC	S	14.03 MW	13.83 AW	29180 AAW	NCBLS	10//99-12/99
	Greenville MSA, NC	S	13.96 MW	13.73 AW	29050 AAW	NCBLS	10//99-12/99

Occupation/Type/Industry	Location	Per	Low	Mid	High	Source	Date
Licensed Practical and Licensed Vocational Nurse							
	Hickory-Morganton-Lenoir MSA, NC	S	13.63 MW	13.82 AW	28350 AAW	NCBLS	10//99-12//99
	Jacksonville MSA, NC	S	11.64 MW	11.27 AW	24200 AAW	NCBLS	10//99-12//99
	Raleigh-Durham-Chapel Hill MSA, NC	S	14.43 MW	14.28 AW	30010 AAW	NCBLS	10//99-12//99
	Rocky Mount MSA, NC	S	12.58 MW	12.70 AW	26160 AAW	NCBLS	10//99-12//99
	Wilmington MSA, NC	S	13.32 MW	13.10 AW	27700 AAW	NCBLS	10//99-12//99
	North Dakota	S	11.77 MW	11.77 AW	24490 AAW	NDBLS	10//99-12//99
	Bismarck MSA, ND	S	11.87 MW	11.92 AW	24680 AAW	NDBLS	10//99-12//99
	Fargo-Moorhead MSA, ND-MN	S	12.34 MW	12.03 AW	25660 AAW	NDBLS	10//99-12//99
	Grand Forks MSA, ND-MN	S	11.75 MW	11.70 AW	24450 AAW	NDBLS	10//99-12//99
	Ohio	S	13.9 MW	14.01 AW	29140 AAW	OHBLS	10//99-12//99
	Akron PMSA, OH	S	14.08 MW	14.00 AW	29280 AAW	OHBLS	10//99-12//99
	Canton-Massillon MSA, OH	S	13.25 MW	13.10 AW	27550 AAW	OHBLS	10//99-12//99
	Cincinnati PMSA, OH-KY-IN	S	15.00 MW	14.92 AW	31200 AAW	OHBLS	10//99-12//99
	Cleveland-Lorain-Elyria PMSA, OH	S	14.66 MW	14.51 AW	30490 AAW	OHBLS	10//99-12//99
	Columbus MSA, OH	S	15.05 MW	14.97 AW	31300 AAW	OHBLS	10//99-12//99
	Dayton-Springfield MSA, OH	S	14.61 MW	14.34 AW	30390 AAW	OHBLS	10//99-12//99
	Hamilton-Middletown PMSA, OH	S	14.78 MW	14.74 AW	30750 AAW	OHBLS	10//99-12//99
	Lima MSA, OH	S	13.05 MW	12.85 AW	27140 AAW	OHBLS	10//99-12//99
	Mansfield MSA, OH	S	13.39 MW	13.19 AW	27850 AAW	OHBLS	10//99-12//99
	Steubenville-Weirton MSA, OH-WV	S	11.65 MW	11.58 AW	24230 AAW	OHBLS	10//99-12//99
	Toledo MSA, OH	S	12.80 MW	12.80 AW	26630 AAW	OHBLS	10//99-12//99
	Youngstown-Warren MSA, OH	S	13.71 MW	13.50 AW	28530 AAW	OHBLS	10//99-12//99
	Oklahoma	S	11.55 MW	11.82 AW	24590 AAW	OKBLS	10//99-12//99
	Enid MSA, OK	S	11.82 MW	11.70 AW	24580 AAW	OKBLS	10//99-12//99
	Lawton MSA, OK	S	10.70 MW	10.45 AW	22260 AAW	OKBLS	10//99-12//99
	Oklahoma City MSA, OK	S	12.16 MW	11.98 AW	25280 AAW	OKBLS	10//99-12//99
	Tulsa MSA, OK	S	13.27 MW	12.49 AW	27600 AAW	OKBLS	10//99-12//99
	Oregon	S	14.78 MW	14.95 AW	31090 AAW	ORBLS	10//99-12//99
	Eugene-Springfield MSA, OR	S	14.02 MW	13.74 AW	29170 AAW	ORBLS	10//99-12//99
	Medford-Ashland MSA, OR	S	15.45 MW	13.89 AW	32150 AAW	ORBLS	10//99-12//99
	Portland-Vancouver PMSA, OR-WA	S	15.58 MW	15.33 AW	32410 AAW	ORBLS	10//99-12//99
	Salem PMSA, OR	S	14.98 MW	15.01 AW	31150 AAW	ORBLS	10//99-12//99
	Pennsylvania	S	13.88 MW	14.39 AW	29930 AAW	PABLS	10//99-12//99
	Allentown-Bethlehem-Easton MSA, PA	S	15.37 MW	15.04 AW	31970 AAW	PABLS	10//99-12//99
	Altoona MSA, PA	S	11.50 MW	11.32 AW	23930 AAW	PABLS	10//99-12//99
	Erie MSA, PA	S	13.87 MW	13.15 AW	28860 AAW	PABLS	10//99-12//99
	Harrisburg-Lebanon-Carlisle MSA, PA	S	14.76 MW	14.69 AW	30690 AAW	PABLS	10//99-12//99
	Johnstown MSA, PA	S	10.74 MW	10.67 AW	22330 AAW	PABLS	10//99-12//99
	Lancaster MSA, PA	S	13.27 MW	12.95 AW	27600 AAW	PABLS	10//99-12//99
	Philadelphia PMSA, PA-NJ	S	16.96 MW	16.71 AW	35280 AAW	PABLS	10//99-12//99
	Pittsburgh MSA, PA	S	13.53 MW	13.19 AW	28140 AAW	PABLS	10//99-12//99
	Reading MSA, PA	S	15.13 MW	14.84 AW	31480 AAW	PABLS	10//99-12//99
	Scranton--Wilkes-Barre--Hazleton MSA, PA	S	12.72 MW	12.46 AW	26460 AAW	PABLS	10//99-12//99
	Sharon MSA, PA	S	12.87 MW	12.79 AW	26770 AAW	PABLS	10//99-12//99
	State College MSA, PA	S	12.95 MW	12.50 AW	26940 AAW	PABLS	10//99-12//99
	Williamsport MSA, PA	S	11.78 MW	11.76 AW	24510 AAW	PABLS	10//99-12//99
	York MSA, PA	S	13.79 MW	13.13 AW	28680 AAW	PABLS	10//99-12//99
	Rhode Island	S	17.15 MW	16.77 AW	34890 AAW	RIBLS	10//99-12//99
	Providence-Fall River-Warwick MSA, RI-MA	S	16.65 MW	16.93 AW	34640 AAW	RIBLS	10//99-12//99
	South Carolina	S	12.28 MW	12.54 AW	26080 AAW	SCBLS	10//99-12//99
	Charleston-North Charleston MSA, SC	S	12.38 MW	12.07 AW	25750 AAW	SCBLS	10//99-12//99
	Columbia MSA, SC	S	12.73 MW	12.51 AW	26480 AAW	SCBLS	10//99-12//99
	Florence MSA, SC	S	12.66 MW	12.65 AW	26340 AAW	SCBLS	10//99-12//99
	Greenville-Spartanburg-Anderson MSA, SC	S	12.44 MW	12.33 AW	25870 AAW	SCBLS	10//99-12//99
	Myrtle Beach MSA, SC	S	11.59 MW	11.35 AW	24110 AAW	SCBLS	10//99-12//99
	Sumter MSA, SC	S	12.25 MW	12.26 AW	25480 AAW	SCBLS	10//99-12//99
	South Dakota	S	11.43 MW	11.59 AW	24100 AAW	SDBLS	10//99-12//99
	Rapid City MSA, SD	S	11.37 MW	11.36 AW	23640 AAW	SDBLS	10//99-12//99

AAW Average annual wage	**AOH** Average offered, high	**ASH** Average starting, high	**H** Hourly	**M** Monthly	**S** Special: hourly and annual
AE Average entry wage	**AOL** Average offered, low	**ASL** Average starting, low	**HI** Highest wage paid	**MTC** Median total compensation	**TQ** Third quartile wage
AEX Average experienced wage	**APH** Average pay, high range	**AW** Average wage paid	**HR** High end range	**MW** Median wage paid	**W** Weekly
AO Average offered	**APL** Average pay, low range	**FQ** First quartile wage	**LR** Low end range	**SQ** Second quartile wage	**Y** Yearly

Occupation/Type/Industry	Location	Per	Low	Mid	High	Source	Date
Licensed Practical and Licensed Vocational Nurse	Sioux Falls MSA, SD	S	12.12 MW	11.72 AW	25200 AAW	SDBLS	10//99-12//99
	Tennessee	S	11.87 MW	12.07 AW	25100 AAW	TNBLS	10//99-12//99
	Chattanooga MSA, TN-GA	S	12.40 MW	12.27 AW	25790 AAW	TNBLS	10//99-12//99
	Clarksville-Hopkinsville MSA, TN-KY	S	11.50 MW	11.42 AW	23920 AAW	TNBLS	10//99-12//99
	Jackson MSA, TN	S	11.85 MW	11.46 AW	24660 AAW	TNBLS	10//99-12//99
	Johnson City-Kingsport-Bristol MSA, TN-VA	S	10.48 MW	10.52 AW	21800 AAW	TNBLS	10//99-12//99
	Knoxville MSA, TN	S	11.57 MW	11.51 AW	24060 AAW	TNBLS	10//99-12//99
	Memphis MSA, TN-AR-MS	S	12.53 MW	12.20 AW	26050 AAW	MSBLS	10//99-12//99
	Nashville MSA, TN	S	13.21 MW	12.91 AW	27480 AAW	TNBLS	10//99-12//99
	Texas	S	13.01 MW	13.74 AW	28570 AAW	TXBLS	10//99-12//99
	Abilene MSA, TX	S	13.21 MW	11.71 AW	27480 AAW	TXBLS	10//99-12//99
	Amarillo MSA, TX	S	13.11 MW	12.37 AW	27260 AAW	TXBLS	10//99-12//99
	Austin-San Marcos MSA, TX	S	14.16 MW	13.41 AW	29450 AAW	TXBLS	10//99-12//99
	Beaumont-Port Arthur MSA, TX	S	12.86 MW	12.11 AW	26760 AAW	TXBLS	10//99-12//99
	Brazoria PMSA, TX	S	13.59 MW	13.20 AW	28260 AAW	TXBLS	10//99-12//99
	Brownsville-Harlingen-San Benito MSA, TX	S	13.84 MW	13.13 AW	28790 AAW	TXBLS	10//99-12//99
	Bryan-College Station MSA, TX	S	12.77 MW	12.57 AW	26560 AAW	TXBLS	10//99-12//99
	Corpus Christi MSA, TX	S	13.31 MW	12.79 AW	27690 AAW	TXBLS	10//99-12//99
	Dallas PMSA, TX	S	15.95 MW	15.34 AW	33170 AAW	TXBLS	10//99-12//99
	El Paso MSA, TX	S	16.99 MW	16.32 AW	35340 AAW	TXBLS	10//99-12//99
	Fort Worth-Arlington PMSA, TX	S	15.47 MW	14.89 AW	32190 AAW	TXBLS	10//99-12//99
	Houston PMSA, TX	S	13.91 MW	13.31 AW	28940 AAW	TXBLS	10//99-12//99
	Killeen-Temple MSA, TX	S	13.27 MW	12.78 AW	27600 AAW	TXBLS	10//99-12//99
	Laredo MSA, TX	S	12.44 MW	12.55 AW	25880 AAW	TXBLS	10//99-12//99
	Longview-Marshall MSA, TX	S	12.04 MW	12.12 AW	25050 AAW	TXBLS	10//99-12//99
	Lubbock MSA, TX	S	12.23 MW	11.97 AW	25440 AAW	TXBLS	10//99-12//99
	McAllen-Edinburg-Mission MSA, TX	S	15.64 MW	14.46 AW	32520 AAW	TXBLS	10//99-12//99
	Odessa-Midland MSA, TX	S	11.52 MW	11.31 AW	23960 AAW	TXBLS	10//99-12//99
	San Angelo MSA, TX	S	12.59 MW	11.60 AW	26180 AAW	TXBLS	10//99-12//99
	San Antonio MSA, TX	S	13.80 MW	12.48 AW	28710 AAW	TXBLS	10//99-12//99
	Sherman-Denison MSA, TX	S	12.89 MW	12.87 AW	26810 AAW	TXBLS	10//99-12//99
	Texarkana MSA, TX-Texarkana, AR	S	11.33 MW	11.08 AW	23560 AAW	TXBLS	10//99-12//99
	Tyler MSA, TX	S	13.14 MW	13.12 AW	27330 AAW	TXBLS	10//99-12//99
	Victoria MSA, TX	S	11.90 MW	11.75 AW	24750 AAW	TXBLS	10//99-12//99
	Waco MSA, TX	S	12.12 MW	11.76 AW	25200 AAW	TXBLS	10//99-12//99
	Wichita Falls MSA, TX	S	12.01 MW	11.38 AW	24970 AAW	TXBLS	10//99-12//99
	Utah	S	12.15 MW	12.73 AW	26480 AAW	UTBLS	10//99-12//99
	Provo-Orem MSA, UT	S	12.53 MW	11.65 AW	26060 AAW	UTBLS	10//99-12//99
	Salt Lake City-Ogden MSA, UT	S	13.62 MW	13.04 AW	28330 AAW	UTBLS	10//99-12//99
	Vermont	S	12.96 MW	13.48 AW	28050 AAW	VTBLS	10//99-12//99
	Burlington MSA, VT	S	14.36 MW	13.74 AW	29870 AAW	VTBLS	10//99-12//99
	Virginia	S	12.59 MW	12.83 AW	26680 AAW	VABLS	10//99-12//99
	Charlottesville MSA, VA	S	13.80 MW	14.11 AW	28700 AAW	VABLS	10//99-12//99
	Danville MSA, VA	S	12.63 MW	11.56 AW	26270 AAW	VABLS	10//99-12//99
	Lynchburg MSA, VA	S	11.57 MW	11.38 AW	24070 AAW	VABLS	10//99-12//99
	Norfolk-Virginia Beach-Newport News MSA, VA-NC	S	11.94 MW	11.87 AW	24830 AAW	VABLS	10//99-12//99
	Richmond-Petersburg MSA, VA	S	13.60 MW	13.79 AW	28280 AAW	VABLS	10//99-12//99
	Roanoke MSA, VA	S	12.79 MW	12.52 AW	26610 AAW	VABLS	10//99-12//99
	Washington	S	14.7 MW	14.84 AW	30870 AAW	WABLS	10//99-12//99
	Bellingham MSA, WA	S	12.94 MW	12.59 AW	26920 AAW	WABLS	10//99-12//99
	Bremerton PMSA, WA	S	15.11 MW	15.03 AW	31420 AAW	WABLS	10//99-12//99
	Olympia PMSA, WA	S	13.16 MW	12.99 AW	27380 AAW	WABLS	10//99-12//99
	Richland-Kennewick-Pasco MSA, WA	S	15.08 MW	14.97 AW	31370 AAW	WABLS	10//99-12//99
	Seattle-Bellevue-Everett PMSA, WA	S	15.38 MW	15.21 AW	31990 AAW	WABLS	10//99-12//99
	Spokane MSA, WA	S	15.26 MW	15.12 AW	31730 AAW	WABLS	10//99-12//99
	Tacoma PMSA, WA	S	15.05 MW	14.94 AW	31310 AAW	WABLS	10//99-12//99
	Yakima MSA, WA	S	14.68 MW	14.64 AW	30540 AAW	WABLS	10//99-12//99

AAW Average annual wage	**AOH** Average offered, high	**ASH** Average starting, high	**H** Hourly	**M** Monthly	**S** Special: hourly and annual
AE Average entry wage	**AOL** Average offered, low	**ASL** Average starting, low	**HI** Highest wage paid	**MTC** Median total compensation	**TQ** Third quartile wage
AEX Average experienced wage	**APH** Average pay, high range	**AW** Average wage paid	**HR** High end range	**MW** Median wage paid	**W** Weekly
AO Average offered	**APL** Average pay, low range	**FQ** First quartile wage	**LR** Low end range	**SQ** Second quartile wage	**Y** Yearly

Occupation/Type/Industry	Location	Per	Low	Mid	High	Source	Date
Licensed Practical and Licensed Vocational Nurse	West Virginia	S	10.75 MW	10.94 AW	22750 AAW	WVBLS	10//99-12//99
	Charleston MSA, WV	S	12.12 MW	11.45 AW	25200 AAW	WVBLS	10//99-12//99
	Huntington-Ashland MSA, WV-KY-OH	S	11.45 MW	11.23 AW	23810 AAW	WVBLS	10//99-12//99
	Parkersburg-Marietta MSA, WV-OH	S	10.56 MW	10.45 AW	21960 AAW	WVBLS	10//99-12//99
	Wheeling MSA, WV-OH	S	10.35 MW	10.04 AW	21540 AAW	WVBLS	10//99-12//99
	Wisconsin	S	13.36 MW	13.70 AW	28500 AAW	WIBLS	10//99-12//99
	Appleton-Oshkosh-Neenah MSA, WI	S	13.05 MW	12.78 AW	27150 AAW	WIBLS	10//99-12//99
	Eau Claire MSA, WI	S	13.01 MW	12.97 AW	27060 AAW	WIBLS	10//99-12//99
	Green Bay MSA, WI	S	12.98 MW	12.86 AW	26990 AAW	WIBLS	10//99-12//99
	Janesville-Beloit MSA, WI	S	12.88 MW	12.88 AW	26790 AAW	WIBLS	10//99-12//99
	Kenosha PMSA, WI	S	13.61 MW	13.59 AW	28310 AAW	WIBLS	10//99-12//99
	La Crosse MSA, WI-MN	S	12.66 MW	12.39 AW	26330 AAW	WIBLS	10//99-12//99
	Madison MSA, WI	S	14.08 MW	13.73 AW	29280 AAW	WIBLS	10//99-12//99
	Milwaukee-Waukesha PMSA, WI	S	14.78 MW	14.61 AW	30740 AAW	WIBLS	10//99-12//99
	Racine PMSA, WI	S	13.19 MW	13.04 AW	27440 AAW	WIBLS	10//99-12//99
	Sheboygan MSA, WI	S	13.50 MW	13.15 AW	28070 AAW	WIBLS	10//99-12//99
	Wausau MSA, WI	S	13.81 MW	14.37 AW	28730 AAW	WIBLS	10//99-12//99
	Wyoming	S	11.21 MW	11.08 AW	23050 AAW	WYBLS	10//99-12//99
	Casper MSA, WY	S	11.46 MW	11.88 AW	23830 AAW	WYBLS	10//99-12//99
	Cheyenne MSA, WY	S	11.83 MW	11.44 AW	24610 AAW	WYBLS	10//99-12//99
	Puerto Rico	S	6.44 MW	6.95 AW	14450 AAW	PRBLS	10//99-12//99
	Arecibo PMSA, PR	S	6.26 MW	6.17 AW	13020 AAW	PRBLS	10//99-12//99
	Caguas PMSA, PR	S	6.37 MW	6.17 AW	13250 AAW	PRBLS	10//99-12//99
	Mayaguez MSA, PR	S	6.47 MW	6.17 AW	13460 AAW	PRBLS	10//99-12//99
	Ponce MSA, PR	S	7.22 MW	7.29 AW	15020 AAW	PRBLS	10//99-12//99
	San Juan-Bayamon PMSA, PR	S	6.99 MW	6.36 AW	14550 AAW	PRBLS	10//99-12//99
Loading Machine Operator							
Underground Mining	Alabama	S	11.79 MW	12.44 AW	25880 AAW	ALBLS	10//99-12//99
Underground Mining	Florida	S	13.22 MW	14.66 AW	30490 AAW	FLBLS	10//99-12//99
Underground Mining	Georgia	S	12.37 MW	12.26 AW	25510 AAW	GABLS	10//99-12//99
Underground Mining	Illinois	S	18.29 MW	18.15 AW	37760 AAW	ILBLS	10//99-12//99
Underground Mining	Indiana	S	14.38 MW	14.45 AW	30050 AAW	INBLS	10//99-12//99
Underground Mining	Kentucky	S	13.45 MW	13.55 AW	28170 AAW	KYBLS	10//99-12//99
Underground Mining	Mississippi	S	8.24 MW	8.90 AW	18510 AAW	MSBLS	10//99-12//99
Underground Mining	North Carolina	S	10.54 MW	10.91 AW	22690 AAW	NCBLS	10//99-12//99
Underground Mining	Oklahoma	S	9.59 MW	9.87 AW	20540 AAW	OKBLS	10//99-12//99
Underground Mining	Pennsylvania	S	16.27 MW	15.36 AW	31950 AAW	PABLS	10//99-12//99
Underground Mining	South Carolina	S	12.8 MW	12.94 AW	26910 AAW	SCBLS	10//99-12//99
Underground Mining	Tennessee	S	11.86 MW	12.16 AW	25300 AAW	TNBLS	10//99-12//99
Underground Mining	Texas	S	8.84 MW	9.73 AW	20240 AAW	TXBLS	10//99-12//99
Underground Mining	Virginia	S	12.64 MW	12.71 AW	26440 AAW	VABLS	10//99-12//99
Underground Mining	West Virginia	S	17.78 MW	16.63 AW	34600 AAW	WVBLS	10//99-12//99
Underground Mining	Wyoming	S	19.56 MW	19.00 AW	39510 AAW	WYBLS	10//99-12//99
Underground Mining	Puerto Rico	S	7.97 MW	8.74 AW	18180 AAW	PRBLS	10//99-12//99
Loan Counselor	Alabama	S	12.47 MW	14.05 AW	29220 AAW	ALBLS	10//99-12//99
	Arizona	S	12.31 MW	15.89 AW	33050 AAW	AZBLS	10//99-12//99
	Arkansas	S	13.41 MW	17.18 AW	35730 AAW	ARBLS	10//99-12//99
	California	S	18.42 MW	20.33 AW	42290 AAW	CABLS	10//99-12//99
	Colorado	S	12.56 MW	13.32 AW	27700 AAW	COBLS	10//99-12//99
	Connecticut	S	17.98 MW	17.67 AW	36760 AAW	CTBLS	10//99-12//99
	Florida	S	27.32 MW	23.36 AW	48580 AAW	FLBLS	10//99-12//99
	Georgia	S	14.5 MW	16.89 AW	35130 AAW	GABLS	10//99-12//99
	Illinois	S	13.52 MW	14.20 AW	29530 AAW	ILBLS	10//99-12//99
	Indiana	S	12.95 MW	13.55 AW	28190 AAW	INBLS	10//99-12//99
	Iowa	S	14.37 MW	15.99 AW	33260 AAW	IABLS	10//99-12//99
	Kansas	S	11.97 MW	12.23 AW	25440 AAW	KSBLS	10//99-12//99
	Kentucky	S	12.65 MW	12.94 AW	26910 AAW	KYBLS	10//99-12//99
	Louisiana	S	11.59 MW	11.06 AW	23010 AAW	LABLS	10//99-12//99
	Maine	S	15.25 MW	15.16 AW	31530 AAW	MEBLS	10//99-12//99
	Maryland	S	13.05 MW	14.51 AW	30190 AAW	MDBLS	10//99-12//99
	Minnesota	S	21.31 MW	22.70 AW	47210 AAW	MNBLS	10//99-12//99
	Mississippi	S	12.78 MW	14.51 AW	30180 AAW	MSBLS	10//99-12//99
	Missouri	S	13.62 MW	13.82 AW	28740 AAW	MOBLS	10//99-12//99
	Nevada	S	17.9 MW	17.20 AW	35770 AAW	NVBLS	10//99-12//99
	New Hampshire	S	16.39 MW	17.71 AW	36840 AAW	NHBLS	10//99-12//99

AAW	Average annual wage	AOH	Average offered, high	ASH	Average starting, high	H	Hourly	M	Monthly	S	Special: hourly and annual
AE	Average entry wage	AOL	Average offered, low	ASL	Average starting, low	HI	Highest wage paid	MTC	Median total compensation	TQ	Third quartile wage
AEX	Average experienced wage	APH	Average pay, high range	AW	Average wage paid	HR	High end range	MW	Median wage paid	W	Weekly
AO	Average offered	APL	Average pay, low range	FQ	First quartile wage	LR	Low end range	SQ	Second quartile wage	Y	Yearly

Occupation/Type/Industry	Location	Per	Low	Mid	High	Source	Date
Loan Counselor	New Jersey	S	12.24 MW	17.01 AW	35380 AAW	NJBLS	10//99-12//99
	New Mexico	S	14.92 MW	14.66 AW	30490 AAW	NMBLS	10//99-12//99
	New York	S	18.15 MW	21.08 AW	43850 AAW	NYBLS	10//99-12//99
	North Carolina	S	13.28 MW	17.91 AW	37260 AAW	NCBLS	10//99-12//99
	Ohio	S	13 MW	14.37 AW	29890 AAW	OHBLS	10//99-12//99
	Oklahoma	S	14.57 MW	14.80 AW	30780 AAW	OKBLS	10//99-12//99
	Oregon	S	13.37 MW	15.39 AW	32010 AAW	ORBLS	10//99-12//99
	Pennsylvania	S	29.05 MW	24.21 AW	50350 AAW	PABLS	10//99-12//99
	South Carolina	S	16.98 MW	16.37 AW	34050 AAW	SCBLS	10//99-12//99
	Tennessee	S	17.26 MW	16.80 AW	34940 AAW	TNBLS	10//99-12//99
	Texas	S	14.47 MW	14.20 AW	29530 AAW	TXBLS	10//99-12//99
	Virginia	S	16.85 MW	17.23 AW	35840 AAW	VABLS	10//99-12//99
	Washington	S	15.43 MW	15.64 AW	32520 AAW	WABLS	10//99-12//99
	West Virginia	S	12.2 MW	13.86 AW	28820 AAW	WVBLS	10//99-12//99
	Wisconsin	S	16.74 MW	17.51 AW	36430 AAW	WIBLS	10//99-12//99
	Puerto Rico	S	17.42 MW	18.30 AW	38070 AAW	PRBLS	10//99-12//99
Loan Interviewer and Clerk	Alabama	S	10.28 MW	10.62 AW	22090 AAW	ALBLS	10//99-12//99
	Alaska	S	13.65 MW	14.21 AW	29560 AAW	AKBLS	10//99-12//99
	Arizona	S	12.89 MW	13.79 AW	28690 AAW	AZBLS	10//99-12//99
	Arkansas	S	10.28 MW	10.45 AW	21730 AAW	ARBLS	10//99-12//99
	California	S	13.31 MW	14.17 AW	29480 AAW	CABLS	10//99-12//99
	Colorado	S	14.51 MW	14.74 AW	30660 AAW	COBLS	10//99-12//99
	Connecticut	S	13.66 MW	15.37 AW	31970 AAW	CTBLS	10//99-12//99
	Delaware	S	10.52 MW	11.44 AW	23800 AAW	DEBLS	10//99-12//99
	Florida	S	11.61 MW	11.89 AW	24730 AAW	FLBLS	10//99-12//99
	Georgia	S	11.83 MW	11.46 AW	23830 AAW	GABLS	10//99-12//99
	Hawaii	S	12.16 MW	12.32 AW	25630 AAW	HIBLS	10//99-12//99
	Idaho	S	10.49 MW	11.15 AW	23200 AAW	IDBLS	10//99-12//99
	Illinois	S	12.94 MW	13.65 AW	28390 AAW	ILBLS	10//99-12//99
	Indiana	S	10.68 MW	11.56 AW	24050 AAW	INBLS	10//99-12//99
	Iowa	S	10.57 MW	11.11 AW	23110 AAW	IABLS	10//99-12//99
	Kansas	S	13.1 MW	12.91 AW	26860 AAW	KSBLS	10//99-12//99
	Kentucky	S	10.38 MW	11.38 AW	23670 AAW	KYBLS	10//99-12//99
	Louisiana	S	8.77 MW	9.93 AW	20650 AAW	LABLS	10//99-12//99
	Maine	S	10.01 MW	10.43 AW	21700 AAW	MEBLS	10//99-12//99
	Maryland	S	13.52 MW	14.01 AW	29130 AAW	MDBLS	10//99-12//99
	Massachusetts	S	12.58 MW	13.14 AW	27330 AAW	MABLS	10//99-12//99
	Michigan	S	12.15 MW	13.26 AW	27570 AAW	MIBLS	10//99-12//99
	Minnesota	S	12.1 MW	12.33 AW	25650 AAW	MNBLS	10//99-12//99
	Mississippi	S	8.17 MW	8.91 AW	18540 AAW	MSBLS	10//99-12//99
	Missouri	S	10.84 MW	11.25 AW	23410 AAW	MOBLS	10//99-12//99
	Montana	S	10.12 MW	11.08 AW	23050 AAW	MTBLS	10//99-12//99
	Nebraska	S	10.58 MW	11.18 AW	23260 AAW	NEBLS	10//99-12//99
	Nevada	S	12.04 MW	13.33 AW	27720 AAW	NVBLS	10//99-12//99
	New Hampshire	S	10.5 MW	11.28 AW	23460 AAW	NHBLS	10//99-12//99
	New Jersey	S	13.34 MW	14.52 AW	30200 AAW	NJBLS	10//99-12//99
	New Mexico	S	10.58 MW	10.91 AW	22680 AAW	NMBLS	10//99-12//99
	New York	S	12.99 MW	13.66 AW	28410 AAW	NYBLS	10//99-12//99
	North Carolina	S	12.34 MW	13.18 AW	27410 AAW	NCBLS	10//99-12//99
	North Dakota	S	11.6 MW	11.16 AW	23200 AAW	NDBLS	10//99-12//99
	Ohio	S	14.17 MW	15.68 AW	32620 AAW	OHBLS	10//99-12//99
	Oklahoma	S	10.23 MW	11.01 AW	22890 AAW	OKBLS	10//99-12//99
	Oregon	S	11.93 MW	12.45 AW	25890 AAW	ORBLS	10//99-12//99
	Pennsylvania	S	11.77 MW	11.94 AW	24830 AAW	PABLS	10//99-12//99
	Rhode Island	S	12.11 MW	12.04 AW	25030 AAW	RIBLS	10//99-12//99
	South Carolina	S	11.51 MW	11.56 AW	24040 AAW	SCBLS	10//99-12//99
	South Dakota	S	9.3 MW	9.25 AW	19250 AAW	SDBLS	10//99-12//99
	Tennessee	S	11.84 MW	11.86 AW	24670 AAW	TNBLS	10//99-12//99
	Texas	S	12.2 MW	12.78 AW	26580 AAW	TXBLS	10//99-12//99
	Utah	S	10.38 MW	11.55 AW	24010 AAW	UTBLS	10//99-12//99
	Vermont	S	10.13 MW	11.66 AW	24250 AAW	VTBLS	10//99-12//99
	Virginia	S	12.18 MW	12.55 AW	26110 AAW	VABLS	10//99-12//99
	Washington	S	13.36 MW	14.17 AW	29470 AAW	WABLS	10//99-12//99
	West Virginia	S	10.3 MW	10.20 AW	21220 AAW	WVBLS	10//99-12//99
	Wisconsin	S	12.34 MW	12.73 AW	26470 AAW	WIBLS	10//99-12//99
	Wyoming	S	9.68 MW	10.05 AW	20910 AAW	WYBLS	10//99-12//99
	Puerto Rico	S	7.03 MW	7.25 AW	15090 AAW	PRBLS	10//99-12//99
	Guam	S	9.27 MW	9.03 AW	18780 AAW	GUBLS	10//99-12//99
Loan Officer	Alabama	S	15.97 MW	18.95 AW	39410 AAW	ALBLS	10//99-12//99
	Anniston MSA, AL	S	17.03 MW	15.83 AW	35430 AAW	ALBLS	10//99-12//99
	Auburn-Opelika MSA, AL	S	24.00 MW	24.17 AW	49920 AAW	ALBLS	10//99-12//99

AAW Average annual wage	**AOH** Average offered, high	**ASH** Average starting, high	**H** Hourly	**M** Monthly	**S** Special: hourly and annual
AE Average entry wage	**AOL** Average offered, low	**ASL** Average starting, low	**HI** Highest wage paid	**MTC** Median total compensation	**TQ** Third quartile wage
AEX Average experienced wage	**APH** Average pay, high range	**AW** Average wage paid	**HR** High end range	**MW** Median wage paid	**W** Weekly
AO Average offered	**APL** Average pay, low range	**FQ** First quartile wage	**LR** Low end range	**SQ** Second quartile wage	**Y** Yearly

Loan Officer

Occupation/Type/Industry	Location	Per	Low	Mid	High	Source	Date
Loan Officer	Birmingham MSA, AL	S	21.56 MW	17.70 AW	44850 AAW	ALBLS	10//99-12//99
	Decatur MSA, AL	S	21.60 MW	16.44 AW	44920 AAW	ALBLS	10//99-12//99
	Florence MSA, AL	S	17.03 MW	12.99 AW	35430 AAW	ALBLS	10//99-12//99
	Gadsden MSA, AL	S	20.70 MW	20.64 AW	43060 AAW	ALBLS	10//99-12//99
	Huntsville MSA, AL	S	25.05 MW	20.59 AW	52110 AAW	ALBLS	10//99-12//99
	Mobile MSA, AL	S	16.52 MW	16.76 AW	34360 AAW	ALBLS	10//99-12//99
	Tuscaloosa MSA, AL	S	18.00 MW	15.77 AW	37440 AAW	ALBLS	10//99-12//99
	Alaska	S	20.56 MW	20.97 AW	43620 AAW	AKBLS	10//99-12//99
	Anchorage MSA, AK	S	17.15 MW	14.25 AW	35670 AAW	AKBLS	10//99-12//99
	Arizona	S	23 MW	23.59 AW	49070 AAW	AZBLS	10//99-12//99
	Flagstaff MSA, AZ-UT	S	19.92 MW	19.10 AW	41440 AAW	AZBLS	10//99-12//99
	Phoenix-Mesa MSA, AZ	S	24.68 MW	24.32 AW	51340 AAW	AZBLS	10//99-12//99
	Tucson MSA, AZ	S	22.41 MW	20.26 AW	46610 AAW	AZBLS	10//99-12//99
	Yuma MSA, AZ	S	30.05 MW	32.51 AW	62510 AAW	AZBLS	10//99-12//99
	Arkansas	S	18.5 MW	19.59 AW	40750 AAW	ARBLS	10//99-12//99
	Fayetteville-Springdale-Rogers MSA, AR	S	21.13 MW	20.02 AW	43950 AAW	ARBLS	10//99-12//99
	Fort Smith MSA, AR-OK	S	17.48 MW	15.83 AW	36350 AAW	ARBLS	10//99-12//99
	Little Rock-North Little Rock MSA, AR	S	19.47 MW	16.20 AW	40490 AAW	ARBLS	10//99-12//99
	California	S	20.34 MW	23.65 AW	49190 AAW	CABLS	10//99-12//99
	Bakersfield MSA, CA	S	21.53 MW	16.03 AW	44780 AAW	CABLS	10//99-12//99
	Chico-Paradise MSA, CA	S	20.14 MW	19.76 AW	41880 AAW	CABLS	10//99-12//99
	Fresno MSA, CA	S	23.63 MW	21.72 AW	49150 AAW	CABLS	10//99-12//99
	Los Angeles-Long Beach PMSA, CA	S	21.35 MW	17.14 AW	44410 AAW	CABLS	10//99-12//99
	Merced MSA, CA	S	20.97 MW	16.95 AW	43610 AAW	CABLS	10//99-12//99
	Modesto MSA, CA	S	23.56 MW	22.27 AW	49010 AAW	CABLS	10//99-12//99
	Oakland PMSA, CA	S	21.63 MW	18.93 AW	44990 AAW	CABLS	10//99-12//99
	Orange County PMSA, CA	S	26.43 MW	24.63 AW	54970 AAW	CABLS	10//99-12//99
	Redding MSA, CA	S	20.20 MW	15.46 AW	42020 AAW	CABLS	10//99-12//99
	Riverside-San Bernardino PMSA, CA	S	20.23 MW	15.88 AW	42070 AAW	CABLS	10//99-12//99
	Sacramento PMSA, CA	S	30.27 MW	23.21 AW	62960 AAW	CABLS	10//99-12//99
	Salinas MSA, CA	S	19.35 MW	17.56 AW	40250 AAW	CABLS	10//99-12//99
	San Diego MSA, CA	S	23.39 MW	20.37 AW	48640 AAW	CABLS	10//99-12//99
	San Francisco PMSA, CA	S	24.96 MW	22.46 AW	51920 AAW	CABLS	10//99-12//99
	San Jose PMSA, CA	S	24.60 MW	22.24 AW	51170 AAW	CABLS	10//99-12//99
	Santa Barbara-Santa Maria-Lompoc MSA, CA	S	20.42 MW	16.84 AW	42470 AAW	CABLS	10//99-12//99
	Santa Rosa PMSA, CA	S	23.12 MW	19.41 AW	48090 AAW	CABLS	10//99-12//99
	Stockton-Lodi MSA, CA	S	21.45 MW	17.38 AW	44610 AAW	CABLS	10//99-12//99
	Vallejo-Fairfield-Napa PMSA, CA	S	21.64 MW	20.23 AW	45010 AAW	CABLS	10//99-12//99
	Ventura PMSA, CA	S	22.50 MW	20.85 AW	46800 AAW	CABLS	10//99-12//99
	Visalia-Tulare-Porterville MSA, CA	S	23.10 MW	21.19 AW	48050 AAW	CABLS	10//99-12//99
	Colorado	S	18.95 MW	21.34 AW	44400 AAW	COBLS	10//99-12//99
	Denver PMSA, CO	S	21.39 MW	19.89 AW	44490 AAW	COBLS	10//99-12//99
	Fort Collins-Loveland MSA, CO	S	18.72 MW	16.52 AW	38940 AAW	COBLS	10//99-12//99
	Grand Junction MSA, CO	S	18.99 MW	18.93 AW	39500 AAW	COBLS	10//99-12//99
	Pueblo MSA, CO	S	20.13 MW	17.95 AW	41870 AAW	COBLS	10//99-12//99
	Connecticut	S	26.21 MW	27.44 AW	57070 AAW	CTBLS	10//99-12//99
	Bridgeport PMSA, CT	S	25.83 MW	19.29 AW	53730 AAW	CTBLS	10//99-12//99
	Hartford MSA, CT	S	29.61 MW	28.82 AW	61600 AAW	CTBLS	10//99-12//99
	New Haven-Meriden PMSA, CT	S	22.46 MW	20.12 AW	46710 AAW	CTBLS	10//99-12//99
	Stamford-Norwalk PMSA, CT	S	26.88 MW	21.65 AW	55910 AAW	CTBLS	10//99-12//99
	Waterbury PMSA, CT	S	28.57 MW	28.74 AW	59430 AAW	CTBLS	10//99-12//99
	Delaware	S	15.93 MW	20.37 AW	42380 AAW	DEBLS	10//99-12//99
	Dover MSA, DE	S	17.47 MW	15.87 AW	36330 AAW	DEBLS	10//99-12//99
	Wilmington-Newark PMSA, DE-MD	S	20.71 MW	15.99 AW	43080 AAW	DEBLS	10//99-12//99
	District of Columbia	S	26.13 MW	26.12 AW	54320 AAW	DCBLS	10//99-12//99
	Washington PMSA, DC-MD-VA-WV	S	21.65 MW	19.80 AW	45030 AAW	DCBLS	10//99-12//99
	Florida	S	16.81 MW	20.45 AW	42540 AAW	FLBLS	10//99-12//99
	Daytona Beach MSA, FL	S	17.54 MW	14.93 AW	36480 AAW	FLBLS	10//99-12//99
	Fort Lauderdale PMSA, FL	S	17.99 MW	15.75 AW	37420 AAW	FLBLS	10//99-12//99
	Fort Myers-Cape Coral MSA, FL	S	26.50 MW	15.81 AW	55120 AAW	FLBLS	10//99-12//99

AAW	Average annual wage	AOH	Average offered, high	ASH	Average starting, high	H	Hourly	M	Monthly	S	Special: hourly and annual
AE	Average entry wage	AOL	Average offered, low	ASL	Average starting, low	HI	Highest wage paid	MTC	Median total compensation	TQ	Third quartile wage
AEX	Average experienced wage	APH	Average pay, high range	AW	Average wage paid	HR	High end range	MW	Median wage paid	W	Weekly
AO	Average offered	APL	Average pay, low range	FQ	First quartile wage	LR	Low end range	SQ	Second quartile wage	Y	Yearly

Occupation/Type/Industry	Location	Per	Low	Mid	High	Source	Date
Loan Officer	Fort Walton Beach MSA, FL	S	22.23 MW	18.89 AW	46240 AAW	FLBLS	10//99-12//99
	Gainesville MSA, FL	S	21.04 MW	19.24 AW	43760 AAW	FLBLS	10//99-12//99
	Jacksonville MSA, FL	S	26.16 MW	19.65 AW	54420 AAW	FLBLS	10//99-12//99
	Lakeland-Winter Haven MSA, FL	S	23.83 MW	20.92 AW	49570 AAW	FLBLS	10//99-12//99
	Melbourne-Titusville-Palm Bay MSA, FL	S	15.20 MW	15.55 AW	31620 AAW	FLBLS	10//99-12//99
	Miami PMSA, FL	S	20.91 MW	17.30 AW	43490 AAW	FLBLS	10//99-12//99
	Naples MSA, FL	S	21.79 MW	23.81 AW	45330 AAW	FLBLS	10//99-12//99
	Ocala MSA, FL	S	17.26 MW	17.79 AW	35910 AAW	FLBLS	10//99-12//99
	Orlando MSA, FL	S	21.01 MW	15.31 AW	43700 AAW	FLBLS	10//99-12//99
	Panama City MSA, FL	S	11.16 MW	10.26 AW	23210 AAW	FLBLS	10//99-12//99
	Pensacola MSA, FL	S	14.87 MW	13.47 AW	30940 AAW	FLBLS	10//99-12//99
	Punta Gorda MSA, FL	S	25.00 MW	27.20 AW	52000 AAW	FLBLS	10//99-12//99
	Sarasota-Bradenton MSA, FL	S	28.76 MW	28.76 AW	59810 AAW	FLBLS	10//99-12//99
	Tallahassee MSA, FL	S	15.89 MW	15.60 AW	33060 AAW	FLBLS	10//99-12//99
	Tampa-St. Petersburg-Clearwater MSA, FL	S	21.20 MW	19.54 AW	44090 AAW	FLBLS	10//99-12//99
	Georgia	S	18.52 MW	21.93 AW	45620 AAW	GABLS	10//99-12//99
	Albany MSA, GA	S	16.39 MW	12.88 AW	34090 AAW	GABLS	10//99-12//99
	Athens MSA, GA	S	19.76 MW	17.85 AW	41090 AAW	GABLS	10//99-12//99
	Atlanta MSA, GA	S	23.75 MW	19.11 AW	49400 AAW	GABLS	10//99-12//99
	Augusta-Aiken MSA, GA-SC	S	20.63 MW	17.55 AW	42910 AAW	GABLS	10//99-12//99
	Columbus MSA, GA-AL	S	16.64 MW	14.57 AW	34610 AAW	GABLS	10//99-12//99
	Macon MSA, GA	S	19.96 MW	19.71 AW	41520 AAW	GABLS	10//99-12//99
	Savannah MSA, GA	S	20.77 MW	20.14 AW	43190 AAW	GABLS	10//99-12//99
	Hawaii	S	16.75 MW	19.33 AW	40210 AAW	HIBLS	10//99-12//99
	Honolulu MSA, HI	S	18.11 MW	16.66 AW	37670 AAW	HIBLS	10//99-12//99
	Idaho	S	16.21 MW	16.68 AW	34690 AAW	IDBLS	10//99-12//99
	Boise City MSA, ID	S	16.66 MW	16.42 AW	34650 AAW	IDBLS	10//99-12//99
	Illinois	S	16.44 MW	18.24 AW	37930 AAW	ILBLS	10//99-12//99
	Bloomington-Normal MSA, IL	S	20.62 MW	16.47 AW	42890 AAW	ILBLS	10//99-12//99
	Champaign-Urbana MSA, IL	S	23.08 MW	21.13 AW	48000 AAW	ILBLS	10//99-12//99
	Chicago PMSA, IL	S	17.36 MW	15.37 AW	36110 AAW	ILBLS	10//99-12//99
	Kankakee PMSA, IL	S	22.81 MW	22.62 AW	47450 AAW	ILBLS	10//99-12//99
	Peoria-Pekin MSA, IL	S	18.33 MW	15.01 AW	38130 AAW	ILBLS	10//99-12//99
	Rockford MSA, IL	S	19.68 MW	17.60 AW	40930 AAW	ILBLS	10//99-12//99
	Springfield MSA, IL	S	18.83 MW	16.92 AW	39160 AAW	ILBLS	10//99-12//99
	Indiana	S	18.7 MW	20.98 AW	43650 AAW	INBLS	10//99-12//99
	Bloomington MSA, IN	S	28.61 MW	25.66 AW	59510 AAW	INBLS	10//99-12//99
	Evansville-Henderson MSA, IN-KY	S	18.23 MW	16.04 AW	37910 AAW	INBLS	10//99-12//99
	Fort Wayne MSA, IN	S	22.06 MW	24.49 AW	45880 AAW	INBLS	10//99-12//99
	Gary PMSA, IN	S	22.93 MW	19.94 AW	47690 AAW	INBLS	10//99-12//99
	Indianapolis MSA, IN	S	22.22 MW	19.84 AW	46210 AAW	INBLS	10//99-12//99
	Kokomo MSA, IN	S	17.86 MW	16.99 AW	37140 AAW	INBLS	10//99-12//99
	Lafayette MSA, IN	S	19.33 MW	19.14 AW	40220 AAW	INBLS	10//99-12//99
	Muncie MSA, IN	S	21.24 MW	15.95 AW	44190 AAW	INBLS	10//99-12//99
	Terre Haute MSA, IN	S	24.93 MW	20.03 AW	51860 AAW	INBLS	10//99-12//99
	Iowa	S	16.83 MW	20.78 AW	43220 AAW	IABLS	10//99-12//99
	Cedar Rapids MSA, IA	S	19.80 MW	16.52 AW	41180 AAW	IABLS	10//99-12//99
	Davenport-Moline-Rock Island MSA, IA-IL	S	16.70 MW	15.10 AW	34730 AAW	IABLS	10//99-12//99
	Des Moines MSA, IA	S	24.72 MW	16.59 AW	51420 AAW	IABLS	10//99-12//99
	Iowa City MSA, IA	S	18.78 MW	17.54 AW	39060 AAW	IABLS	10//99-12//99
	Sioux City MSA, IA-NE	S	14.69 MW	12.83 AW	30550 AAW	IABLS	10//99-12//99
	Waterloo-Cedar Falls MSA, IA	S	23.07 MW	27.68 AW	47990 AAW	IABLS	10//99-12//99
	Kansas	S	19.24 MW	20.80 AW	43260 AAW	KSBLS	10//99-12//99
	Lawrence MSA, KS	S	22.29 MW	22.52 AW	46370 AAW	KSBLS	10//99-12//99
	Wichita MSA, KS	S	21.14 MW	15.75 AW	43970 AAW	KSBLS	10//99-12//99
	Kentucky	S	17.42 MW	19.86 AW	41310 AAW	KYBLS	10//99-12//99
	Lexington MSA, KY	S	21.82 MW	19.57 AW	45380 AAW	KYBLS	10//99-12//99
	Louisville MSA, KY-IN	S	24.14 MW	22.16 AW	50220 AAW	KYBLS	10//99-12//99
	Owensboro MSA, KY	S	18.34 MW	16.96 AW	38140 AAW	KYBLS	10//99-12//99
	Louisiana	S	15.61 MW	16.95 AW	35260 AAW	LABLS	10//99-12//99
	Alexandria MSA, LA	S	16.85 MW	15.66 AW	35050 AAW	LABLS	10//99-12//99
	Baton Rouge MSA, LA	S	14.61 MW	14.96 AW	30380 AAW	LABLS	10//99-12//99
	Houma MSA, LA	S	16.92 MW	16.93 AW	35180 AAW	LABLS	10//99-12//99
	Lake Charles MSA, LA	S	13.82 MW	14.60 AW	28750 AAW	LABLS	10//99-12//99
	Monroe MSA, LA	S	20.14 MW	16.98 AW	41890 AAW	LABLS	10//99-12//99
	New Orleans MSA, LA	S	14.82 MW	14.57 AW	30830 AAW	LABLS	10//99-12//99

Loan Officer

Occupation/Type/Industry	Location	Per	Low	Mid	High	Source	Date
Loan Officer	Shreveport-Bossier City MSA, LA	S	18.93 MW	19.65 AW	39380 AAW	LABLS	10//99-12//99
	Maine	S	18.41 MW	22.14 AW	46040 AAW	MEBLS	10//99-12//99
	Bangor MSA, ME	S	18.87 MW	19.04 AW	39240 AAW	MEBLS	10//99-12//99
	Lewiston-Auburn MSA, ME	S	14.20 MW	13.04 AW	29530 AAW	MEBLS	10//99-12//99
	Portland MSA, ME	S	28.16 MW	19.63 AW	58580 AAW	MEBLS	10//99-12//99
	Maryland	S	16.93 MW	19.30 AW	40140 AAW	MDBLS	10//99-12//99
	Baltimore PMSA, MD	S	21.47 MW	21.30 AW	44650 AAW	MDBLS	10//99-12//99
	Cumberland MSA, MD-WV	S	21.32 MW	19.74 AW	44350 AAW	MDBLS	10//99-12//99
	Massachusetts	S	23.59 MW	26.34 AW	54780 AAW	MABLS	10//99-12//99
	Barnstable-Yarmouth MSA, MA	S	21.82 MW	13.45 AW	45380 AAW	MABLS	10//99-12//99
	Boston PMSA, MA-NH	S	28.58 MW	24.99 AW	59460 AAW	MABLS	10//99-12//99
	Brockton PMSA, MA	S	38.50 MW	34.29 AW	80080 AAW	MABLS	10//99-12//99
	Fitchburg-Leominster PMSA, MA	S	18.99 MW	15.15 AW	39500 AAW	MABLS	10//99-12//99
	Lawrence PMSA, MA-NH	S	24.06 MW	23.17 AW	50050 AAW	MABLS	10//99-12//99
	New Bedford PMSA, MA	S	17.70 MW	17.67 AW	36820 AAW	MABLS	10//99-12//99
	Pittsfield MSA, MA	S	15.90 MW	14.10 AW	33080 AAW	MABLS	10//99-12//99
	Springfield MSA, MA	S	16.59 MW	15.00 AW	34500 AAW	MABLS	10//99-12//99
	Worcester PMSA, MA-CT	S	24.00 MW	24.03 AW	49920 AAW	MABLS	10//99-12//99
	Michigan	S	19.92 MW	24.36 AW	50670 AAW	MIBLS	10//99-12//99
	Benton Harbor MSA, MI	S	26.27 MW	20.95 AW	54630 AAW	MIBLS	10//99-12//99
	Detroit PMSA, MI	S	31.22 MW	30.21 AW	64940 AAW	MIBLS	10//99-12//99
	Flint PMSA, MI	S	16.02 MW	18.23 AW	33320 AAW	MIBLS	10//99-12//99
	Grand Rapids-Muskegon-Holland MSA, MI	S	15.14 MW	12.56 AW	31500 AAW	MIBLS	10//99-12//99
	Kalamazoo-Battle Creek MSA, MI	S	17.54 MW	15.55 AW	36480 AAW	MIBLS	10//99-12//99
	Lansing-East Lansing MSA, MI	S	16.63 MW	14.43 AW	34600 AAW	MIBLS	10//99-12//99
	Saginaw-Bay City-Midland MSA, MI	S	13.71 MW	14.54 AW	28510 AAW	MIBLS	10//99-12//99
	Minnesota	S	19.75 MW	23.08 AW	48000 AAW	MNBLS	10//99-12//99
	Duluth-Superior MSA, MN-WI	S	16.33 MW	14.37 AW	33970 AAW	MNBLS	10//99-12//99
	Minneapolis-St. Paul MSA, MN-WI	S	26.12 MW	24.39 AW	54330 AAW	MNBLS	10//99-12//99
	Rochester MSA, MN	S	25.89 MW	17.90 AW	53840 AAW	MNBLS	10//99-12//99
	St. Cloud MSA, MN	S	26.50 MW	23.51 AW	55110 AAW	MNBLS	10//99-12//99
	Mississippi	S	16.62 MW	19.47 AW	40500 AAW	MSBLS	10//99-12//99
	Biloxi-Gulfport-Pascagoula MSA, MS	S	18.32 MW	17.58 AW	38110 AAW	MSBLS	10//99-12//99
	Hattiesburg MSA, MS	S	20.43 MW	21.30 AW	42490 AAW	MSBLS	10//99-12//99
	Jackson MSA, MS	S	20.39 MW	19.69 AW	42420 AAW	MSBLS	10//99-12//99
	Missouri	S	16.18 MW	17.98 AW	37410 AAW	MOBLS	10//99-12//99
	Columbia MSA, MO	S	23.87 MW	16.85 AW	49650 AAW	MOBLS	10//99-12//99
	Kansas City MSA, MO-KS	S	22.59 MW	19.69 AW	46990 AAW	MOBLS	10//99-12//99
	St. Joseph MSA, MO	S	23.36 MW	21.28 AW	48580 AAW	MOBLS	10//99-12//99
	St. Louis MSA, MO-IL	S	17.18 MW	14.77 AW	35740 AAW	MOBLS	10//99-12//99
	Springfield MSA, MO	S	15.17 MW	13.12 AW	31540 AAW	MOBLS	10//99-12//99
	Montana	S	18.32 MW	19.95 AW	41490 AAW	MTBLS	10//99-12//99
	Billings MSA, MT	S	13.81 MW	11.84 AW	28720 AAW	MTBLS	10//99-12//99
	Missoula MSA, MT	S	19.11 MW	16.87 AW	39740 AAW	MTBLS	10//99-12//99
	Nebraska	S	19.81 MW	22.13 AW	46030 AAW	NEBLS	10//99-12//99
	Lincoln MSA, NE	S	18.77 MW	18.67 AW	39040 AAW	NEBLS	10//99-12//99
	Omaha MSA, NE-IA	S	22.22 MW	19.92 AW	46210 AAW	NEBLS	10//99-12//99
	Nevada	S	15.52 MW	19.33 AW	40210 AAW	NVBLS	10//99-12//99
	Las Vegas MSA, NV-AZ	S	18.85 MW	15.41 AW	39210 AAW	NVBLS	10//99-12//99
	Reno MSA, NV	S	27.97 MW	19.49 AW	58170 AAW	NVBLS	10//99-12//99
	New Hampshire	S	17.69 MW	19.15 AW	39840 AAW	NHBLS	10//99-12//99
	Manchester PMSA, NH	S	21.96 MW	20.41 AW	45680 AAW	NHBLS	10//99-12//99
	Portsmouth-Rochester PMSA, NH-ME	S	14.31 MW	6.29 AW	29770 AAW	NHBLS	10//99-12//99
	New Jersey	S	20.07 MW	22.80 AW	47420 AAW	NJBLS	10//99-12//99
	Atlantic-Cape May PMSA, NJ	S	25.92 MW	20.55 AW	53910 AAW	NJBLS	10//99-12//99
	Bergen-Passaic PMSA, NJ	S	21.78 MW	19.28 AW	45300 AAW	NJBLS	10//99-12//99
	Middlesex-Somerset-Hunterdon PMSA, NJ	S	20.59 MW	19.21 AW	42830 AAW	NJBLS	10//99-12//99
	Monmouth-Ocean PMSA, NJ	S	23.46 MW	22.32 AW	48790 AAW	NJBLS	10//99-12//99
	Newark PMSA, NJ	S	24.53 MW	19.71 AW	51030 AAW	NJBLS	10//99-12//99
	New Mexico	S	16.48 MW	19.20 AW	39940 AAW	NMBLS	10//99-12//99
	Albuquerque MSA, NM	S	21.53 MW	18.29 AW	44790 AAW	NMBLS	10//99-12//99
	Las Cruces MSA, NM	S	18.01 MW	17.50 AW	37470 AAW	NMBLS	10//99-12//99

AAW Average annual wage	AOH Average offered, high	ASH Average starting, high	H Hourly	M Monthly	S Special: hourly and annual
AE Average entry wage	AOL Average offered, low	ASL Average starting, low	HI Highest wage paid	MTC Median total compensation	TQ Third quartile wage
AEX Average experienced wage	APH Average pay, high range	AW Average wage paid	HR High end range	MW Median wage paid	W Weekly
AO Average offered	APL Average pay, low range	FQ First quartile wage	LR Low end range	SQ Second quartile wage	Y Yearly

Occupation/Type/Industry	Location	Per	Low	Mid	High	Source	Date
Loan Officer	Santa Fe MSA, NM	S	16.88 MW	13.32 AW	35100 AAW	NMBLS	10//99-12//99
	New York	S	24.12 MW	28.14 AW	58530 AAW	NYBLS	10//99-12//99
	Buffalo-Niagara Falls MSA, NY	S	20.14 MW	17.49 AW	41890 AAW	NYBLS	10//99-12//99
	Dutchess County PMSA, NY	S	21.16 MW	19.21 AW	44020 AAW	NYBLS	10//99-12//99
	Jamestown MSA, NY	S	21.15 MW	21.62 AW	44000 AAW	NYBLS	10//99-12//99
	Nassau-Suffolk PMSA, NY	S	24.24 MW	20.19 AW	50410 AAW	NYBLS	10//99-12//99
	New York PMSA, NY	S	36.55 MW	30.34 AW	76030 AAW	NYBLS	10//99-12//99
	Newburgh PMSA, NY-PA	S	24.88 MW	23.75 AW	51740 AAW	NYBLS	10//99-12//99
	Rochester MSA, NY	S	18.59 MW	18.33 AW	38670 AAW	NYBLS	10//99-12//99
	Syracuse MSA, NY	S	23.70 MW	23.65 AW	49300 AAW	NYBLS	10//99-12//99
	Utica-Rome MSA, NY	S	17.22 MW	16.28 AW	35820 AAW	NYBLS	10//99-12//99
	North Carolina	S	16.69 MW	20.18 AW	41980 AAW	NCBLS	10//99-12//99
	Asheville MSA, NC	S	15.28 MW	13.47 AW	31780 AAW	NCBLS	10//99-12//99
	Charlotte-Gastonia-Rock Hill MSA, NC-SC	S	20.64 MW	17.20 AW	42940 AAW	NCBLS	10//99-12//99
	Fayetteville MSA, NC	S	15.86 MW	13.84 AW	32980 AAW	NCBLS	10//99-12//99
	Goldsboro MSA, NC	S	18.81 MW	14.92 AW	39130 AAW	NCBLS	10//99-12//99
	Greensboro--Winston-Salem--High Point MSA, NC	S	18.67 MW	16.08 AW	38830 AAW	NCBLS	10//99-12//99
	Hickory-Morganton-Lenoir MSA, NC	S	19.85 MW	17.84 AW	41300 AAW	NCBLS	10//99-12//99
	Raleigh-Durham-Chapel Hill MSA, NC	S	24.12 MW	20.02 AW	50170 AAW	NCBLS	10//99-12//99
	Wilmington MSA, NC	S	24.26 MW	18.47 AW	50460 AAW	NCBLS	10//99-12//99
	North Dakota	S	20.91 MW	21.55 AW	44820 AAW	NDBLS	10//99-12//99
	Bismarck MSA, ND	S	19.87 MW	19.52 AW	41330 AAW	NDBLS	10//99-12//99
	Fargo-Moorhead MSA, ND-MN	S	22.34 MW	22.60 AW	46480 AAW	NDBLS	10//99-12//99
	Grand Forks MSA, ND-MN	S	19.16 MW	16.63 AW	39840 AAW	NDBLS	10//99-12//99
	Ohio	S	16.31 MW	19.97 AW	41530 AAW	OHBLS	10//99-12//99
	Akron PMSA, OH	S	18.55 MW	13.45 AW	38580 AAW	OHBLS	10//99-12//99
	Cincinnati PMSA, OH-KY-IN	S	20.73 MW	16.48 AW	43120 AAW	OHBLS	10//99-12//99
	Cleveland-Lorain-Elyria PMSA, OH	S	20.14 MW	14.96 AW	41900 AAW	OHBLS	10//99-12//99
	Columbus MSA, OH	S	17.92 MW	14.98 AW	37270 AAW	OHBLS	10//99-12//99
	Dayton-Springfield MSA, OH	S	23.22 MW	20.59 AW	48300 AAW	OHBLS	10//99-12//99
	Hamilton-Middletown PMSA, OH	S	19.74 MW	18.19 AW	41060 AAW	OHBLS	10//99-12//99
	Mansfield MSA, OH	S	20.37 MW	18.38 AW	42370 AAW	OHBLS	10//99-12//99
	Steubenville-Weirton MSA, OH-WV	S	13.94 MW	12.75 AW	29000 AAW	OHBLS	10//99-12//99
	Toledo MSA, OH	S	21.20 MW	17.83 AW	44100 AAW	OHBLS	10//99-12//99
	Youngstown-Warren MSA, OH	S	19.82 MW	17.00 AW	41220 AAW	OHBLS	10//99-12//99
	Oklahoma	S	17.47 MW	19.62 AW	40800 AAW	OKBLS	10//99-12//99
	Oklahoma City MSA, OK	S	20.32 MW	15.52 AW	42270 AAW	OKBLS	10//99-12//99
	Tulsa MSA, OK	S	22.44 MW	23.09 AW	46680 AAW	OKBLS	10//99-12//99
	Oregon	S	19.51 MW	21.88 AW	45510 AAW	ORBLS	10//99-12//99
	Corvallis MSA, OR	S	24.77 MW	28.73 AW	51520 AAW	ORBLS	10//99-12//99
	Eugene-Springfield MSA, OR	S	19.34 MW	18.44 AW	40230 AAW	ORBLS	10//99-12//99
	Medford-Ashland MSA, OR	S	23.68 MW	24.10 AW	49260 AAW	ORBLS	10//99-12//99
	Portland-Vancouver PMSA, OR-WA	S	22.30 MW	19.78 AW	46380 AAW	ORBLS	10//99-12//99
	Salem PMSA, OR	S	20.61 MW	18.29 AW	42860 AAW	ORBLS	10//99-12//99
	Pennsylvania	S	18.76 MW	21.38 AW	44470 AAW	PABLS	10//99-12//99
	Allentown-Bethlehem-Easton MSA, PA	S	23.11 MW	22.95 AW	48070 AAW	PABLS	10//99-12//99
	Altoona MSA, PA	S	17.67 MW	15.75 AW	36760 AAW	PABLS	10//99-12//99
	Harrisburg-Lebanon-Carlisle MSA, PA	S	15.98 MW	14.36 AW	33240 AAW	PABLS	10//99-12//99
	Johnstown MSA, PA	S	23.77 MW	22.52 AW	49450 AAW	PABLS	10//99-12//99
	Lancaster MSA, PA	S	23.10 MW	21.91 AW	48050 AAW	PABLS	10//99-12//99
	Philadelphia PMSA, PA-NJ	S	23.79 MW	21.27 AW	49490 AAW	PABLS	10//99-12//99
	Pittsburgh MSA, PA	S	19.29 MW	18.02 AW	40130 AAW	PABLS	10//99-12//99
	Reading MSA, PA	S	17.46 MW	13.23 AW	36320 AAW	PABLS	10//99-12//99
	Scranton--Wilkes-Barre--Hazleton MSA, PA	S	16.91 MW	15.74 AW	35180 AAW	PABLS	10//99-12//99
	Williamsport MSA, PA	S	20.16 MW	16.74 AW	41930 AAW	PABLS	10//99-12//99
	York MSA, PA	S	19.38 MW	18.11 AW	40310 AAW	PABLS	10//99-12//99
	Rhode Island	S	18.01 MW	20.74 AW	43130 AAW	RIBLS	10//99-12//99
	Providence-Fall River-Warwick MSA, RI-MA	S	20.27 MW	17.40 AW	42150 AAW	RIBLS	10//99-12//99

AAW Average annual wage	AOH Average offered, high	ASH Average starting, high	H Hourly	M Monthly	S Special: hourly and annual
AE Average entry wage	AOL Average offered, low	ASL Average starting, low	HI Highest wage paid	MTC Median total compensation	TQ Third quartile wage
AEX Average experienced wage	APH Average pay, high range	AW Average wage paid	HR High end range	MW Median wage paid	W Weekly
AO Average offered	APL Average pay, low range	FQ First quartile wage	LR Low end range	SQ Second quartile wage	Y Yearly

Occupation/Type/Industry	Location	Per	Low	Mid	High	Source	Date
Loan Officer	South Carolina	S	16.93 MW	18.65 AW	38790 AAW	SCBLS	10//99-12//99
	Charleston-North Charleston MSA, SC	S	14.59 MW	12.78 AW	30340 AAW	SCBLS	10//99-12//99
	Columbia MSA, SC	S	19.27 MW	16.76 AW	40080 AAW	SCBLS	10//99-12//99
	Florence MSA, SC	S	19.44 MW	19.34 AW	40440 AAW	SCBLS	10//99-12//99
	Greenville-Spartanburg-Anderson MSA, SC	S	19.78 MW	18.90 AW	41150 AAW	SCBLS	10//99-12//99
	Myrtle Beach MSA, SC	S	19.09 MW	19.17 AW	39710 AAW	SCBLS	10//99-12//99
	South Dakota	S	17.89 MW	18.29 AW	38040 AAW	SDBLS	10//99-12//99
	Sioux Falls MSA, SD	S	18.84 MW	16.84 AW	39190 AAW	SDBLS	10//99-12//99
	Tennessee	S	19.42 MW	23.80 AW	49500 AAW	TNBLS	10//99-12//99
	Chattanooga MSA, TN-GA	S	22.15 MW	20.42 AW	46080 AAW	TNBLS	10//99-12//99
	Clarksville-Hopkinsville MSA, TN-KY	S	14.58 MW	13.22 AW	30320 AAW	TNBLS	10//99-12//99
	Jackson MSA, TN	S	27.07 MW	30.48 AW	56310 AAW	TNBLS	10//99-12//99
	Johnson City-Kingsport-Bristol MSA, TN-VA	S	18.17 MW	16.06 AW	37800 AAW	TNBLS	10//99-12//99
	Knoxville MSA, TN	S	21.95 MW	20.57 AW	45660 AAW	TNBLS	10//99-12//99
	Memphis MSA, TN-AR-MS	S	33.44 MW	25.93 AW	69560 AAW	MSBLS	10//99-12//99
	Nashville MSA, TN	S	26.53 MW	19.96 AW	55190 AAW	TNBLS	10//99-12//99
	Texas	S	17.2 MW	22.28 AW	46340 AAW	TXBLS	10//99-12//99
	Abilene MSA, TX	S	19.13 MW	17.35 AW	39790 AAW	TXBLS	10//99-12//99
	Amarillo MSA, TX	S	14.04 MW	13.37 AW	29210 AAW	TXBLS	10//99-12//99
	Austin-San Marcos MSA, TX	S	18.77 MW	18.57 AW	39050 AAW	TXBLS	10//99-12//99
	Beaumont-Port Arthur MSA, TX	S	13.73 MW	12.93 AW	28550 AAW	TXBLS	10//99-12//99
	Brazoria PMSA, TX	S	17.39 MW	17.07 AW	36160 AAW	TXBLS	10//99-12//99
	Brownsville-Harlingen-San Benito MSA, TX	S	13.02 MW	11.58 AW	27070 AAW	TXBLS	10//99-12//99
	Bryan-College Station MSA, TX	S	19.89 MW	14.86 AW	41370 AAW	TXBLS	10//99-12//99
	Corpus Christi MSA, TX	S	16.40 MW	15.51 AW	34100 AAW	TXBLS	10//99-12//99
	Dallas PMSA, TX	S	27.04 MW	19.10 AW	56250 AAW	TXBLS	10//99-12//99
	El Paso MSA, TX	S	12.39 MW	12.94 AW	25760 AAW	TXBLS	10//99-12//99
	Fort Worth-Arlington PMSA, TX	S	16.29 MW	14.98 AW	33890 AAW	TXBLS	10//99-12//99
	Galveston-Texas City PMSA, TX	S	21.06 MW	20.47 AW	43800 AAW	TXBLS	10//99-12//99
	Houston PMSA, TX	S	24.73 MW	18.77 AW	51430 AAW	TXBLS	10//99-12//99
	Longview-Marshall MSA, TX	S	20.26 MW	20.51 AW	42140 AAW	TXBLS	10//99-12//99
	Lubbock MSA, TX	S	30.01 MW	30.87 AW	62410 AAW	TXBLS	10//99-12//99
	McAllen-Edinburg-Mission MSA, TX	S	16.06 MW	17.47 AW	33410 AAW	TXBLS	10//99-12//99
	Odessa-Midland MSA, TX	S	23.47 MW	18.67 AW	48820 AAW	TXBLS	10//99-12//99
	San Angelo MSA, TX	S	14.29 MW	14.40 AW	29710 AAW	TXBLS	10//99-12//99
	San Antonio MSA, TX	S	20.55 MW	16.90 AW	42730 AAW	TXBLS	10//99-12//99
	Sherman-Denison MSA, TX	S	18.60 MW	21.40 AW	38680 AAW	TXBLS	10//99-12//99
	Waco MSA, TX	S	21.44 MW	21.37 AW	44590 AAW	TXBLS	10//99-12//99
	Wichita Falls MSA, TX	S	28.52 MW	26.44 AW	59320 AAW	TXBLS	10//99-12//99
	Utah	S	14.93 MW	16.50 AW	34320 AAW	UTBLS	10//99-12//99
	Provo-Orem MSA, UT	S	18.81 MW	17.09 AW	39120 AAW	UTBLS	10//99-12//99
	Salt Lake City-Ogden MSA, UT	S	16.00 MW	14.45 AW	33270 AAW	UTBLS	10//99-12//99
	Burlington MSA, VT	S	19.60 MW	18.10 AW	40760 AAW	VTBLS	10//99-12//99
	Virginia	S	19.31 MW	22.25 AW	46280 AAW	VABLS	10//99-12//99
	Norfolk-Virginia Beach-Newport News MSA, VA-NC	S	19.61 MW	17.95 AW	40780 AAW	VABLS	10//99-12//99
	Richmond-Petersburg MSA, VA	S	20.98 MW	17.71 AW	43640 AAW	VABLS	10//99-12//99
	Roanoke MSA, VA	S	28.07 MW	20.09 AW	58380 AAW	VABLS	10//99-12//99
	Washington	S	22.79 MW	24.50 AW	50960 AAW	WABLS	10//99-12//99
	Bellingham MSA, WA	S	24.52 MW	26.55 AW	50990 AAW	WABLS	10//99-12//99
	Olympia PMSA, WA	S	22.83 MW	19.90 AW	47490 AAW	WABLS	10//99-12//99
	Richland-Kennewick-Pasco MSA, WA	S	26.67 MW	25.46 AW	55470 AAW	WABLS	10//99-12//99
	Seattle-Bellevue-Everett PMSA, WA	S	24.34 MW	23.13 AW	50630 AAW	WABLS	10//99-12//99
	Spokane MSA, WA	S	19.29 MW	15.73 AW	40110 AAW	WABLS	10//99-12//99
	Tacoma PMSA, WA	S	30.71 MW	29.38 AW	63880 AAW	WABLS	10//99-12//99
	Yakima MSA, WA	S	31.76 MW	26.25 AW	66050 AAW	WABLS	10//99-12//99
	West Virginia	S	12.75 MW	14.26 AW	29660 AAW	WVBLS	10//99-12//99

AAW	Average annual wage	AOH	Average offered, high	ASH	Average starting, high
AE	Average entry wage	AOL	Average offered, low	ASL	Average starting, low
AEX	Average experienced wage	APH	Average pay, high range	AW	Average wage paid
AO	Average offered	APL	Average pay, low range	FQ	First quartile wage

H	Hourly	M	Monthly
HI	Highest wage paid	MTC	Median total compensation
HR	High end range	MW	Median wage paid
LR	Low end range	SQ	Second quartile wage

S	Special: hourly and annual
TQ	Third quartile wage
W	Weekly
Y	Yearly

Occupation/Type/Industry	Location	Per	Low	Mid	High	Source	Date
Loan Officer	Charleston MSA, WV	S	16.43 MW	14.88 AW	34170 AAW	WVBLS	10//99-12//99
	Huntington-Ashland MSA, WV-KY-OH	S	19.68 MW	16.68 AW	40940 AAW	WVBLS	10//99-12//99
	Parkersburg-Marietta MSA, WV-OH	S	15.39 MW	14.58 AW	32010 AAW	WVBLS	10//99-12//99
	Wheeling MSA, WV-OH	S	20.43 MW	22.87 AW	42500 AAW	WVBLS	10//99-12//99
	Wisconsin	S	20.53 MW	22.95 AW	47750 AAW	WIBLS	10//99-12//99
	Appleton-Oshkosh-Neenah MSA, WI	S	20.89 MW	16.80 AW	43450 AAW	WIBLS	10//99-12//99
	Eau Claire MSA, WI	S	15.84 MW	14.33 AW	32950 AAW	WIBLS	10//99-12//99
	Green Bay MSA, WI	S	22.41 MW	17.74 AW	46620 AAW	WIBLS	10//99-12//99
	Janesville-Beloit MSA, WI	S	14.53 MW	12.83 AW	30230 AAW	WIBLS	10//99-12//99
	Kenosha PMSA, WI	S	28.97 MW	23.13 AW	60250 AAW	WIBLS	10//99-12//99
	La Crosse MSA, WI-MN	S	17.13 MW	13.35 AW	35630 AAW	WIBLS	10//99-12//99
	Madison MSA, WI	S	16.35 MW	15.75 AW	34010 AAW	WIBLS	10//99-12//99
	Milwaukee-Waukesha PMSA, WI	S	26.96 MW	25.21 AW	56080 AAW	WIBLS	10//99-12//99
	Racine PMSA, WI	S	20.88 MW	19.78 AW	43420 AAW	WIBLS	10//99-12//99
	Sheboygan MSA, WI	S	18.17 MW	16.71 AW	37790 AAW	WIBLS	10//99-12//99
	Wausau MSA, WI	S	17.71 MW	15.49 AW	36830 AAW	WIBLS	10//99-12//99
	Wyoming	S	20.08 MW	19.65 AW	40860 AAW	WYBLS	10//99-12//99
	Casper MSA, WY	S	23.84 MW	21.32 AW	49580 AAW	WYBLS	10//99-12//99
	Cheyenne MSA, WY	S	14.23 MW	14.05 AW	29590 AAW	WYBLS	10//99-12//99
	Virgin Islands	S	16.6 MW	17.15 AW	35680 AAW	VIBLS	10//99-12//99
	Guam	S	18.59 MW	18.45 AW	38370 AAW	GUBLS	10//99-12//99
Lobbyist Association	United States	Y		81778 MW		ASMA	1998
Locker Room, Coatroom, and Dressing Room Attendant	Alabama	S	7.02 MW	7.03 AW	14620 AAW	ALBLS	10//99-12//99
	Arizona	S	6.6 MW	7.18 AW	14930 AAW	AZBLS	10//99-12//99
	Arkansas	S	6.92 MW	7.28 AW	15150 AAW	ARBLS	10//99-12//99
	California	S	7.47 MW	8.27 AW	17210 AAW	CABLS	10//99-12//99
	Colorado	S	7.01 MW	7.09 AW	14750 AAW	COBLS	10//99-12//99
	Connecticut	S	9.83 MW	10.22 AW	21250 AAW	CTBLS	10//99-12//99
	Florida	S	7.13 MW	7.30 AW	15190 AAW	FLBLS	10//99-12//99
	Georgia	S	7.58 MW	7.84 AW	16310 AAW	GABLS	10//99-12//99
	Hawaii	S	9 MW	9.15 AW	19040 AAW	HIBLS	10//99-12//99
	Illinois	S	7.59 MW	7.91 AW	16450 AAW	ILBLS	10//99-12//99
	Indiana	S	6.47 MW	6.77 AW	14080 AAW	INBLS	10//99-12//99
	Iowa	S	7.18 MW	7.06 AW	14690 AAW	IABLS	10//99-12//99
	Kansas	S	7.02 MW	7.13 AW	14820 AAW	KSBLS	10//99-12//99
	Kentucky	S	6.82 MW	6.90 AW	14350 AAW	KYBLS	10//99-12//99
	Louisiana	S	6.67 MW	8.22 AW	17090 AAW	LABLS	10//99-12//99
	Maryland	S	7.61 MW	7.73 AW	16090 AAW	MDBLS	10//99-12//99
	Massachusetts	S	8.11 MW	9.03 AW	18790 AAW	MABLS	10//99-12//99
	Michigan	S	7.84 MW	7.95 AW	16540 AAW	MIBLS	10//99-12//99
	Minnesota	S	7.32 MW	7.41 AW	15410 AAW	MNBLS	10//99-12//99
	Mississippi	S	7.2 MW	7.14 AW	14850 AAW	MSBLS	10//99-12//99
	Missouri	S	7.18 MW	7.33 AW	15240 AAW	MOBLS	10//99-12//99
	Montana	S	6.24 MW	6.43 AW	13380 AAW	MTBLS	10//99-12//99
	Nebraska	S	7.67 MW	8.19 AW	17030 AAW	NEBLS	10//99-12//99
	Nevada	S	7.32 MW	7.19 AW	14950 AAW	NVBLS	10//99-12//99
	New Hampshire	S	6.59 MW	7.20 AW	14970 AAW	NHBLS	10//99-12//99
	New Jersey	S	7.61 MW	7.75 AW	16120 AAW	NJBLS	10//99-12//99
	New Mexico	S	6.39 MW	6.48 AW	13480 AAW	NMBLS	10//99-12//99
	New York	S	14.66 MW	13.26 AW	27580 AAW	NYBLS	10//99-12//99
	North Carolina	S	7.57 MW	8.12 AW	16880 AAW	NCBLS	10//99-12//99
	Ohio	S	7.05 MW	7.12 AW	14810 AAW	OHBLS	10//99-12//99
	Oklahoma	S	6.85 MW	7.05 AW	14660 AAW	OKBLS	10//99-12//99
	Oregon	S	7.9 MW	8.06 AW	16770 AAW	ORBLS	10//99-12//99
	Pennsylvania	S	6.4 MW	6.86 AW	14260 AAW	PABLS	10//99-12//99
	South Carolina	S	7.46 MW	7.74 AW	16100 AAW	SCBLS	10//99-12//99
	Tennessee	S	7.53 MW	7.56 AW	15720 AAW	TNBLS	10//99-12//99
	Texas	S	6.82 MW	7.16 AW	14890 AAW	TXBLS	10//99-12//99
	Utah	S	7.92 MW	7.97 AW	16580 AAW	UTBLS	10//99-12//99
	Virginia	S	7.03 MW	7.21 AW	15000 AAW	VABLS	10//99-12//99
	Washington	S	8.19 MW	9.67 AW	20100 AAW	WABLS	10//99-12//99
	West Virginia	S	6.37 MW	6.36 AW	13230 AAW	WVBLS	10//99-12//99
	Wisconsin	S	6.89 MW	7.31 AW	15200 AAW	WIBLS	10//99-12//99
	Wyoming	S	7.19 MW	7.12 AW	14810 AAW	WYBLS	10//99-12//99

Occupation/Type/Industry	Location	Per	Low	Mid	High	Source	Date
Locker Room, Coatroom, and Dressing Room Attendant	Puerto Rico	S	7.79 MW	8.15 AW	16960 AAW	PRBLS	10//99-12//99
Locksmith and Safe Repairer	Alabama	S	9.16 MW	9.95 AW	20690 AAW	ALBLS	10//99-12//99
	Arizona	S	10.72 MW	11.66 AW	24250 AAW	AZBLS	10//99-12//99
	Phoenix-Mesa MSA, AZ	S	11.85 MW	10.85 AW	24650 AAW	AZBLS	10//99-12//99
	California	S	14.09 MW	14.56 AW	30270 AAW	CABLS	10//99-12//99
	Bakersfield MSA, CA	S	15.80 MW	16.38 AW	32860 AAW	CABLS	10//99-12//99
	Los Angeles-Long Beach PMSA, CA	S	16.22 MW	15.29 AW	33730 AAW	CABLS	10//99-12//99
	Oakland PMSA, CA	S	14.44 MW	14.71 AW	30040 AAW	CABLS	10//99-12//99
	Orange County PMSA, CA	S	13.26 MW	11.33 AW	27590 AAW	CABLS	10//99-12//99
	Riverside-San Bernardino PMSA, CA	S	18.94 MW	19.06 AW	39390 AAW	CABLS	10//99-12//99
	San Diego MSA, CA	S	14.37 MW	14.20 AW	29890 AAW	CABLS	10//99-12//99
	San Francisco PMSA, CA	S	15.81 MW	15.40 AW	32880 AAW	CABLS	10//99-12//99
	Santa Rosa PMSA, CA	S	13.87 MW	14.76 AW	28840 AAW	CABLS	10//99-12//99
	Vallejo-Fairfield-Napa PMSA, CA	S	14.65 MW	15.44 AW	30470 AAW	CABLS	10//99-12//99
	Ventura PMSA, CA	S	15.62 MW	15.47 AW	32490 AAW	CABLS	10//99-12//99
	Colorado	S	13.15 MW	13.74 AW	28570 AAW	COBLS	10//99-12//99
	Colorado Springs MSA, CO	S	11.27 MW	10.28 AW	23450 AAW	COBLS	10//99-12//99
	Denver PMSA, CO	S	14.60 MW	13.52 AW	30360 AAW	COBLS	10//99-12//99
	Fort Collins-Loveland MSA, CO	S	11.32 MW	9.66 AW	23550 AAW	COBLS	10//99-12//99
	Connecticut	S	16.76 MW	16.33 AW	33970 AAW	CTBLS	10//99-12//99
	New London-Norwich MSA, CT-RI	S	18.25 MW	20.01 AW	37960 AAW	CTBLS	10//99-12//99
	Delaware	S	14.13 MW	14.99 AW	31170 AAW	DEBLS	10//99-12//99
	Wilmington-Newark PMSA, DE-MD	S	15.08 MW	14.29 AW	31360 AAW	DEBLS	10//99-12//99
	District of Columbia	S	17.76 MW	17.13 AW	35630 AAW	DCBLS	10//99-12//99
	Washington PMSA, DC-MD-VA-WV	S	15.39 MW	15.12 AW	32010 AAW	DCBLS	10//99-12//99
	Florida	S	11.72 MW	12.25 AW	25480 AAW	FLBLS	10//99-12//99
	Jacksonville MSA, FL	S	10.82 MW	10.05 AW	22500 AAW	FLBLS	10//99-12//99
	Lakeland-Winter Haven MSA, FL	S	9.69 MW	8.30 AW	20160 AAW	FLBLS	10//99-12//99
	Melbourne-Titusville-Palm Bay MSA, FL	S	11.62 MW	10.01 AW	24180 AAW	FLBLS	10//99-12//99
	Orlando MSA, FL	S	14.33 MW	11.83 AW	29800 AAW	FLBLS	10//99-12//99
	Sarasota-Bradenton MSA, FL	S	13.95 MW	12.93 AW	29020 AAW	FLBLS	10//99-12//99
	Tampa-St. Petersburg-Clearwater MSA, FL	S	9.85 MW	9.78 AW	20490 AAW	FLBLS	10//99-12//99
	Georgia	S	11.82 MW	12.07 AW	25110 AAW	GABLS	10//99-12//99
	Atlanta MSA, GA	S	12.22 MW	11.82 AW	25410 AAW	GABLS	10//99-12//99
	Columbus MSA, GA-AL	S	10.81 MW	10.46 AW	22470 AAW	GABLS	10//99-12//99
	Hawaii	S	13.63 MW	14.29 AW	29720 AAW	HIBLS	10//99-12//99
	Honolulu MSA, HI	S	14.19 MW	13.61 AW	29510 AAW	HIBLS	10//99-12//99
	Illinois	S	12.12 MW	12.69 AW	26390 AAW	ILBLS	10//99-12//99
	Chicago PMSA, IL	S	12.90 MW	12.75 AW	26840 AAW	ILBLS	10//99-12//99
	Decatur MSA, IL	S	11.61 MW	11.41 AW	24150 AAW	ILBLS	10//99-12//99
	Indiana	S	13.87 MW	14.59 AW	30350 AAW	INBLS	10//99-12//99
	Iowa	S	12.01 MW	12.00 AW	24960 AAW	IABLS	10//99-12//99
	Kansas	S	15.76 MW	16.95 AW	35250 AAW	KSBLS	10//99-12//99
	Kentucky	S	10.85 MW	11.78 AW	24490 AAW	KYBLS	10//99-12//99
	Lexington MSA, KY	S	11.71 MW	11.08 AW	24360 AAW	KYBLS	10//99-12//99
	Louisiana	S	9.06 MW	11.09 AW	23070 AAW	LABLS	10//99-12//99
	Maryland	S	14.77 MW	15.09 AW	31390 AAW	MDBLS	10//99-12//99
	Baltimore PMSA, MD	S	15.37 MW	14.95 AW	31960 AAW	MDBLS	10//99-12//99
	Massachusetts	S	15.29 MW	15.58 AW	32400 AAW	MABLS	10//99-12//99
	Boston PMSA, MA-NH	S	15.79 MW	15.42 AW	32850 AAW	MABLS	10//99-12//99
	Michigan	S	11.24 MW	12.78 AW	26580 AAW	MIBLS	10//99-12//99
	Minnesota	S	10.15 MW	10.73 AW	22310 AAW	MNBLS	10//99-12//99
	Minneapolis-St. Paul MSA, MN-WI	S	12.47 MW	11.99 AW	25930 AAW	MNBLS	10//99-12//99
	Mississippi	S	10.29 MW	11.11 AW	23110 AAW	MSBLS	10//99-12//99
	Biloxi-Gulfport-Pascagoula MSA, MS	S	12.61 MW	10.47 AW	26220 AAW	MSBLS	10//99-12//99
	Jackson MSA, MS	S	14.47 MW	13.23 AW	30100 AAW	MSBLS	10//99-12//99
	Missouri	S	11.4 MW	11.33 AW	23570 AAW	MOBLS	10//99-12//99
	Kansas City MSA, MO-KS	S	13.39 MW	12.69 AW	27850 AAW	MOBLS	10//99-12//99

AAW Average annual wage	**AOH** Average offered, high	**ASH** Average starting, high	**H** Hourly	**M** Monthly	**S** Special: hourly and annual
AE Average entry wage	**AOL** Average offered, low	**ASL** Average starting, low	**HI** Highest wage paid	**MTC** Median total compensation	**TQ** Third quartile wage
AEX Average experienced wage	**APH** Average pay, high range	**AW** Average wage paid	**HR** High end range	**MW** Median wage paid	**W** Weekly
AO Average offered	**APL** Average pay, low range	**FQ** First quartile wage	**LR** Low end range	**SQ** Second quartile wage	**Y** Yearly

Occupation/Type/Industry	Location	Per	Low	Mid	High	Source	Date
Locksmith and Safe Repairer	Montana	S	10.15 MW	11.10 AW	23080 AAW	MTBLS	10//99-12//99
	Nebraska	S	15.63 MW	16.12 AW	33540 AAW	NEBLS	10//99-12//99
	Omaha MSA, NE-IA	S	15.76 MW	15.29 AW	32790 AAW	NEBLS	10//99-12//99
	Nevada	S	13.51 MW	14.21 AW	29570 AAW	NVBLS	10//99-12//99
	Las Vegas MSA, NV-AZ	S	16.74 MW	16.45 AW	34810 AAW	NVBLS	10//99-12//99
	New Jersey	S	16.88 MW	17.92 AW	37280 AAW	NJBLS	10//99-12//99
	Bergen-Passaic PMSA, NJ	S	15.29 MW	14.90 AW	31810 AAW	NJBLS	10//99-12//99
	Monmouth-Ocean PMSA, NJ	S	24.30 MW	20.71 AW	50540 AAW	NJBLS	10//99-12//99
	New Mexico	S	8.54 MW	10.03 AW	20860 AAW	NMBLS	10//99-12//99
	Albuquerque MSA, NM	S	11.32 MW	11.03 AW	23560 AAW	NMBLS	10//99-12//99
	New York	S	11.57 MW	12.52 AW	26050 AAW	NYBLS	10//99-12//99
	Albany-Schenectady-Troy MSA, NY	S	12.62 MW	12.41 AW	26240 AAW	NYBLS	10//99-12//99
	Nassau-Suffolk PMSA, NY	S	14.07 MW	13.26 AW	29260 AAW	NYBLS	10//99-12//99
	New York PMSA, NY	S	11.94 MW	10.49 AW	24830 AAW	NYBLS	10//99-12//99
	North Carolina	S	11.48 MW	12.37 AW	25740 AAW	NCBLS	10//99-12//99
	Greenville MSA, NC	S	9.50 MW	9.64 AW	19750 AAW	NCBLS	10//99-12//99
	Raleigh-Durham-Chapel Hill MSA, NC	S	12.33 MW	12.59 AW	25650 AAW	NCBLS	10//99-12//99
	Ohio	S	12.14 MW	12.57 AW	26150 AAW	OHBLS	10//99-12//99
	Akron PMSA, OH	S	15.75 MW	15.03 AW	32760 AAW	OHBLS	10//99-12//99
	Cincinnati PMSA, OH-KY-IN	S	11.94 MW	10.37 AW	24840 AAW	OHBLS	10//99-12//99
	Columbus MSA, OH	S	10.97 MW	10.98 AW	22810 AAW	OHBLS	10//99-12//99
	Oregon	S	11.25 MW	12.38 AW	25760 AAW	ORBLS	10//99-12//99
	Eugene-Springfield MSA, OR	S	10.94 MW	11.06 AW	22760 AAW	ORBLS	10//99-12//99
	Portland-Vancouver PMSA, OR-WA	S	12.16 MW	11.32 AW	25290 AAW	ORBLS	10//99-12//99
	Salem PMSA, OR	S	13.20 MW	11.43 AW	27460 AAW	ORBLS	10//99-12//99
	Pennsylvania	S	15.01 MW	16.12 AW	33520 AAW	PABLS	10//99-12//99
	Philadelphia PMSA, PA-NJ	S	16.19 MW	16.69 AW	33680 AAW	PABLS	10//99-12//99
	Rhode Island	S	15.6 MW	15.55 AW	32350 AAW	RIBLS	10//99-12//99
	Providence-Fall River-Warwick MSA, RI-MA	S	15.88 MW	15.84 AW	33030 AAW	RIBLS	10//99-12//99
	South Carolina	S	14.72 MW	15.13 AW	31480 AAW	SCBLS	10//99-12//99
	Myrtle Beach MSA, SC	S	14.98 MW	16.28 AW	31170 AAW	SCBLS	10//99-12//99
	Tennessee	S	14.28 MW	13.72 AW	28530 AAW	TNBLS	10//99-12//99
	Texas	S	10.25 MW	10.83 AW	22520 AAW	TXBLS	10//99-12//99
	Austin-San Marcos MSA, TX	S	12.14 MW	11.32 AW	25250 AAW	TXBLS	10//99-12//99
	Dallas PMSA, TX	S	15.66 MW	14.39 AW	32580 AAW	TXBLS	10//99-12//99
	Houston PMSA, TX	S	8.00 MW	7.21 AW	16640 AAW	TXBLS	10//99-12//99
	San Antonio MSA, TX	S	11.83 MW	11.83 AW	24600 AAW	TXBLS	10//99-12//99
	Utah	S	9.97 MW	11.44 AW	23800 AAW	UTBLS	10//99-12//99
	Virginia	S	13.49 MW	13.71 AW	28510 AAW	VABLS	10//99-12//99
	Lynchburg MSA, VA	S	11.83 MW	10.67 AW	24600 AAW	VABLS	10//99-12//99
	Norfolk-Virginia Beach-Newport News MSA, VA-NC	S	12.81 MW	11.71 AW	26650 AAW	VABLS	10//99-12//99
	Washington	S	13.72 MW	13.97 AW	29050 AAW	WABLS	10//99-12//99
	Bremerton PMSA, WA	S	9.17 MW	6.76 AW	19060 AAW	WABLS	10//99-12//99
	Seattle-Bellevue-Everett PMSA, WA	S	14.99 MW	14.79 AW	31180 AAW	WABLS	10//99-12//99
	Wisconsin	S	11.57 MW	12.41 AW	25820 AAW	WIBLS	10//99-12//99
	Puerto Rico	S	7.6 MW	8.92 AW	18560 AAW	PRBLS	10//99-12//99
Locomotive Engineer	Alabama	S	20.62 MW	21.03 AW	43740 AAW	ALBLS	10//99-12//99
	Arizona	S	17.7 MW	18.72 AW	38940 AAW	AZBLS	10//99-12//99
	Arkansas	S	19.01 MW	20.26 AW	42140 AAW	ARBLS	10//99-12//99
	California	S	26.42 MW	28.99 AW	60300 AAW	CABLS	10//99-12//99
	Colorado	S	14.58 MW	15.06 AW	31320 AAW	COBLS	10//99-12//99
	Florida	S	22.27 MW	24.15 AW	50240 AAW	FLBLS	10//99-12//99
	Georgia	S	13.86 MW	15.43 AW	32090 AAW	GABLS	10//99-12//99
	Idaho	S	20.38 MW	20.87 AW	43410 AAW	IDBLS	10//99-12//99
	Illinois	S	21.95 MW	23.81 AW	49520 AAW	ILBLS	10//99-12//99
	Indiana	S	18.62 MW	19.15 AW	39840 AAW	INBLS	10//99-12//99
	Iowa	S	22.35 MW	21.96 AW	45670 AAW	IABLS	10//99-12//99
	Kansas	S	21.44 MW	23.53 AW	48940 AAW	KSBLS	10//99-12//99
	Kentucky	S	22.26 MW	24.53 AW	51010 AAW	KYBLS	10//99-12//99
	Louisiana	S	20.81 MW	23.04 AW	47930 AAW	LABLS	10//99-12//99
	Maryland	S	23.47 MW	24.16 AW	50250 AAW	MDBLS	10//99-12//99
	Minnesota	S	25.84 MW	25.62 AW	53280 AAW	MNBLS	10//99-12//99
	Montana	S	23.39 MW	25.78 AW	53610 AAW	MTBLS	10//99-12//99
	Nebraska	S	18.93 MW	20.18 AW	41980 AAW	NEBLS	10//99-12//99
	New Hampshire	S	14.97 MW	15.90 AW	33070 AAW	NHBLS	10//99-12//99

AAW Average annual wage	**AOH** Average offered, high	**ASH** Average starting, high	**H** Hourly	**M** Monthly	**S** Special: hourly and annual
AE Average entry wage	**AOL** Average offered, low	**ASL** Average starting, low	**HI** Highest wage paid	**MTC** Median total compensation	**TQ** Third quartile wage
AEX Average experienced wage	**APH** Average pay, high range	**AW** Average wage paid	**HR** High end range	**MW** Median wage paid	**W** Weekly
AO Average offered	**APL** Average pay, low range	**FQ** First quartile wage	**LR** Low end range	**SQ** Second quartile wage	**Y** Yearly

Occupation/Type/Industry	Location	Per	Low	Mid	High	Source	Date
Locomotive Engineer	New Jersey	S	22.86 MW	22.04 AW	45840 AAW	NJBLS	10//99-12//99
	New York	S	19.51 MW	20.44 AW	42510 AAW	NYBLS	10//99-12//99
	North Carolina	S	13.01 MW	13.64 AW	28370 AAW	NCBLS	10//99-12//99
	North Dakota	S	23.56 MW	24.72 AW	51420 AAW	NDBLS	10//99-12//99
	Oklahoma	S	20.49 MW	21.07 AW	43820 AAW	OKBLS	10//99-12//99
	Oregon	S	19.61 MW	21.82 AW	45390 AAW	ORBLS	10//99-12//99
	South Carolina	S	19.67 MW	20.48 AW	42610 AAW	SCBLS	10//99-12//99
	Tennessee	S	14.18 MW	16.72 AW	34770 AAW	TNBLS	10//99-12//99
	Texas	S	25.12 MW	27.10 AW	56370 AAW	TXBLS	10//99-12//99
	Utah	S	21.01 MW	22.22 AW	46210 AAW	UTBLS	10//99-12//99
	Virginia	S	23.17 MW	23.19 AW	48240 AAW	VABLS	10//99-12//99
	Wisconsin	S	28.46 MW	27.08 AW	56330 AAW	WIBLS	10//99-12//99
Locomotive Firer	Arkansas	S	22.85 MW	23.72 AW	49330 AAW	ARBLS	10//99-12//99
	Illinois	S	26.7 MW	25.92 AW	53920 AAW	ILBLS	10//99-12//99
	Wisconsin	S	24.85 MW	25.14 AW	52300 AAW	WIBLS	10//99-12//99
Lodging Manager	Alabama	S	14.37 MW	14.71 AW	30590 AAW	ALBLS	10//99-12//99
	Auburn-Opelika MSA, AL	S	11.36 MW	10.17 AW	23630 AAW	ALBLS	10//99-12//99
	Birmingham MSA, AL	S	16.36 MW	17.75 AW	34020 AAW	ALBLS	10//99-12//99
	Huntsville MSA, AL	S	16.80 MW	17.71 AW	34940 AAW	ALBLS	10//99-12//99
	Mobile MSA, AL	S	15.63 MW	15.36 AW	32510 AAW	ALBLS	10//99-12//99
	Alaska	S	17.96 MW	17.02 AW	35390 AAW	AKBLS	10//99-12//99
	Arizona	S	14.93 MW	15.10 AW	31410 AAW	AZBLS	10//99-12//99
	Flagstaff MSA, AZ-UT	S	18.07 MW	18.33 AW	37590 AAW	AZBLS	10//99-12//99
	Phoenix-Mesa MSA, AZ	S	15.43 MW	15.67 AW	32100 AAW	AZBLS	10//99-12//99
	Arkansas	S	14.45 MW	14.29 AW	29720 AAW	ARBLS	10//99-12//99
	Fayetteville-Springdale-Rogers MSA, AR	S	13.55 MW	14.19 AW	28170 AAW	ARBLS	10//99-12//99
	Fort Smith MSA, AR-OK	S	11.69 MW	10.33 AW	24320 AAW	ARBLS	10//99-12//99
	California	S	20.38 MW	20.07 AW	41740 AAW	CABLS	10//99-12//99
	Fresno MSA, CA	S	12.37 MW	11.29 AW	25730 AAW	CABLS	10//99-12//99
	Los Angeles-Long Beach PMSA, CA	S	21.51 MW	22.97 AW	44750 AAW	CABLS	10//99-12//99
	Oakland PMSA, CA	S	18.61 MW	16.66 AW	38710 AAW	CABLS	10//99-12//99
	Riverside-San Bernardino PMSA, CA	S	18.38 MW	16.74 AW	38240 AAW	CABLS	10//99-12//99
	Sacramento PMSA, CA	S	19.32 MW	20.13 AW	40190 AAW	CABLS	10//99-12//99
	Salinas MSA, CA	S	18.27 MW	17.00 AW	37990 AAW	CABLS	10//99-12//99
	San Diego MSA, CA	S	23.24 MW	26.92 AW	48330 AAW	CABLS	10//99-12//99
	San Francisco PMSA, CA	S	20.31 MW	19.77 AW	42250 AAW	CABLS	10//99-12//99
	San Jose PMSA, CA	S	17.62 MW	16.06 AW	36650 AAW	CABLS	10//99-12//99
	Ventura PMSA, CA	S	12.52 MW	12.44 AW	26040 AAW	CABLS	10//99-12//99
	Colorado	S	13.19 MW	16.00 AW	33290 AAW	COBLS	10//99-12//99
	Connecticut	S	13.49 MW	17.13 AW	35640 AAW	CTBLS	10//99-12//99
	Hartford MSA, CT	S	14.31 MW	12.10 AW	29770 AAW	CTBLS	10//99-12//99
	New Haven-Meriden PMSA, CT	S	12.22 MW	12.13 AW	25430 AAW	CTBLS	10//99-12//99
	New London-Norwich MSA, CT-RI	S	14.42 MW	12.67 AW	30000 AAW	CTBLS	10//99-12//99
	Stamford-Norwalk PMSA, CT	S	28.89 MW	30.28 AW	60080 AAW	CTBLS	10//99-12//99
	District of Columbia	S	16.97 MW	20.62 AW	42890 AAW	DCBLS	10//99-12//99
	Washington PMSA, DC-MD-VA-WV	S	17.66 MW	15.53 AW	36720 AAW	DCBLS	10//99-12//99
	Florida	S	15.13 MW	17.46 AW	36310 AAW	FLBLS	10//99-12//99
	Daytona Beach MSA, FL	S	15.97 MW	15.76 AW	33220 AAW	FLBLS	10//99-12//99
	Fort Lauderdale PMSA, FL	S	27.04 MW	24.26 AW	56250 AAW	FLBLS	10//99-12//99
	Fort Myers-Cape Coral MSA, FL	S	13.15 MW	13.54 AW	27350 AAW	FLBLS	10//99-12//99
	Fort Pierce-Port St. Lucie MSA, FL	S	14.20 MW	13.66 AW	29550 AAW	FLBLS	10//99-12//99
	Gainesville MSA, FL	S	13.47 MW	12.06 AW	28020 AAW	FLBLS	10//99-12//99
	Jacksonville MSA, FL	S	16.47 MW	15.56 AW	34260 AAW	FLBLS	10//99-12//99
	Miami PMSA, FL	S	21.61 MW	18.25 AW	44950 AAW	FLBLS	10//99-12//99
	Naples MSA, FL	S	15.96 MW	13.17 AW	33190 AAW	FLBLS	10//99-12//99
	Orlando MSA, FL	S	24.59 MW	22.78 AW	51140 AAW	FLBLS	10//99-12//99
	Panama City MSA, FL	S	15.38 MW	13.44 AW	31990 AAW	FLBLS	10//99-12//99
	Pensacola MSA, FL	S	15.79 MW	12.60 AW	32830 AAW	FLBLS	10//99-12//99
	Sarasota-Bradenton MSA, FL	S	19.34 MW	15.73 AW	40230 AAW	FLBLS	10//99-12//99
	Tallahassee MSA, FL	S	21.08 MW	21.65 AW	43850 AAW	FLBLS	10//99-12//99
	Tampa-St. Petersburg-Clearwater MSA, FL	S	20.52 MW	15.94 AW	42680 AAW	FLBLS	10//99-12//99

Occupation/Type/Industry	Location	Per	Low	Mid	High	Source	Date
Lodging Manager	West Palm Beach-Boca Raton						
	MSA, FL	S	18.10 MW	15.62 AW	37650 AAW	FLBLS	10//99-12//99
	Georgia	S	12.91 MW	14.00 AW	29110 AAW	GABLS	10//99-12//99
	Atlanta MSA, GA	S	14.36 MW	13.06 AW	29870 AAW	GABLS	10//99-12//99
	Augusta-Aiken MSA, GA-SC	S	13.65 MW	13.41 AW	28400 AAW	GABLS	10//99-12//99
	Macon MSA, GA	S	14.17 MW	13.80 AW	29470 AAW	GABLS	10//99-12//99
	Savannah MSA, GA	S	11.26 MW	11.55 AW	23420 AAW	GABLS	10//99-12//99
	Idaho	S	11.83 MW	13.20 AW	27450 AAW	IDBLS	10//99-12//99
	Illinois	S	16.4 MW	17.83 AW	37080 AAW	ILBLS	10//99-12//99
	Chicago PMSA, IL	S	19.89 MW	19.64 AW	41370 AAW	ILBLS	10//99-12//99
	Springfield MSA, IL	S	21.99 MW	22.67 AW	45730 AAW	ILBLS	10//99-12//99
	Indiana	S	12.66 MW	14.10 AW	29330 AAW	INBLS	10//99-12//99
	Evansville-Henderson MSA,						
	IN-KY	S	13.51 MW	12.46 AW	28100 AAW	INBLS	10//99-12//99
	Gary PMSA, IN	S	14.03 MW	14.20 AW	29180 AAW	INBLS	10//99-12//99
	Iowa	S	10.84 MW	12.11 AW	25190 AAW	IABLS	10//99-12//99
	Cedar Rapids MSA, IA	S	12.13 MW	12.07 AW	25230 AAW	IABLS	10//99-12//99
	Davenport-Moline-Rock Island						
	MSA, IA-IL	S	17.25 MW	15.68 AW	35870 AAW	IABLS	10//99-12//99
	Kansas	S	10.55 MW	11.99 AW	24930 AAW	KSBLS	10//99-12//99
	Topeka MSA, KS	S	10.94 MW	10.30 AW	22750 AAW	KSBLS	10//99-12//99
	Wichita MSA, KS	S	11.68 MW	9.90 AW	24290 AAW	KSBLS	10//99-12//99
	Kentucky	S	13.14 MW	13.82 AW	28750 AAW	KYBLS	10//99-12//99
	Lexington MSA, KY	S	10.28 MW	10.34 AW	21390 AAW	KYBLS	10//99-12//99
	Louisville MSA, KY-IN	S	15.52 MW	15.25 AW	32280 AAW	KYBLS	10//99-12//99
	Louisiana	S	14.76 MW	15.73 AW	32720 AAW	LABLS	10//99-12//99
	Baton Rouge MSA, LA	S	16.02 MW	17.00 AW	33310 AAW	LABLS	10//99-12//99
	Lake Charles MSA, LA	S	13.36 MW	10.75 AW	27790 AAW	LABLS	10//99-12//99
	New Orleans MSA, LA	S	16.56 MW	14.54 AW	34440 AAW	LABLS	10//99-12//99
	Shreveport-Bossier City MSA,						
	LA	S	16.08 MW	15.80 AW	33440 AAW	LABLS	10//99-12//99
	Maine	S	9.79 MW	11.25 AW	23400 AAW	MEBLS	10//99-12//99
	Bangor MSA, ME	S	10.98 MW	9.83 AW	22850 AAW	MEBLS	10//99-12//99
	Maryland	S	15.32 MW	17.94 AW	37320 AAW	MDBLS	10//99-12//99
	Massachusetts	S	15.79 MW	17.68 AW	36770 AAW	MABLS	10//99-12//99
	Barnstable-Yarmouth MSA,						
	MA	S	16.58 MW	14.78 AW	34490 AAW	MABLS	10//99-12//99
	Boston PMSA, MA-NH	S	18.53 MW	16.20 AW	38530 AAW	MABLS	10//99-12//99
	Springfield MSA, MA	S	13.64 MW	13.64 AW	28370 AAW	MABLS	10//99-12//99
	Minnesota	S	12.55 MW	13.30 AW	27670 AAW	MNBLS	10//99-12//99
	Duluth-Superior MSA, MN-WI	S	14.71 MW	12.89 AW	30590 AAW	MNBLS	10//99-12//99
	Minneapolis-St. Paul MSA,						
	MN-WI	S	15.57 MW	13.85 AW	32380 AAW	MNBLS	10//99-12//99
	Rochester MSA, MN	S	17.33 MW	15.54 AW	36040 AAW	MNBLS	10//99-12//99
	Mississippi	S	14.39 MW	16.57 AW	34470 AAW	MSBLS	10//99-12//99
	Jackson MSA, MS	S	14.32 MW	14.30 AW	29780 AAW	MSBLS	10//99-12//99
	Missouri	S	13.14 MW	13.92 AW	28960 AAW	MOBLS	10//99-12//99
	Kansas City MSA, MO-KS	S	14.16 MW	12.37 AW	29460 AAW	MOBLS	10//99-12//99
	St. Louis MSA, MO-IL	S	19.73 MW	16.84 AW	41040 AAW	MOBLS	10//99-12//99
	Springfield MSA, MO	S	14.35 MW	14.71 AW	29850 AAW	MOBLS	10//99-12//99
	Nebraska	S	12.55 MW	12.81 AW	26640 AAW	NEBLS	10//99-12//99
	Lincoln MSA, NE	S	11.56 MW	11.55 AW	24040 AAW	NEBLS	10//99-12//99
	Omaha MSA, NE-IA	S	15.77 MW	16.12 AW	32800 AAW	NEBLS	10//99-12//99
	Nevada	S	17.97 MW	21.27 AW	44240 AAW	NVBLS	10//99-12//99
	Las Vegas MSA, NV-AZ	S	23.54 MW	19.63 AW	48960 AAW	NVBLS	10//99-12//99
	Reno MSA, NV	S	17.10 MW	13.20 AW	35570 AAW	NVBLS	10//99-12//99
	New Hampshire	S	13.84 MW	14.69 AW	30550 AAW	NHBLS	10//99-12//99
	Portsmouth-Rochester PMSA,						
	NH-ME	S	13.04 MW	10.38 AW	27120 AAW	NHBLS	10//99-12//99
	New Jersey	S	20.34 MW	21.95 AW	45650 AAW	NJBLS	10//99-12//99
	Atlantic-Cape May PMSA, NJ	S	19.88 MW	22.08 AW	41360 AAW	NJBLS	10//99-12//99
	Bergen-Passaic PMSA, NJ	S	21.87 MW	19.46 AW	45500 AAW	NJBLS	10//99-12//99
	Middlesex-Somerset-						
	Hunterdon PMSA, NJ	S	22.27 MW	18.07 AW	46310 AAW	NJBLS	10//99-12//99
	Monmouth-Ocean PMSA, NJ	S	20.96 MW	22.61 AW	43600 AAW	NJBLS	10//99-12//99
	Newark PMSA, NJ	S	25.06 MW	24.86 AW	52120 AAW	NJBLS	10//99-12//99
	New Mexico	S	10.67 MW	13.14 AW	27330 AAW	NMBLS	10//99-12//99
	Albuquerque MSA, NM	S	13.70 MW	12.77 AW	28500 AAW	NMBLS	10//99-12//99
	New York	S	16.05 MW	18.25 AW	37960 AAW	NYBLS	10//99-12//99
	Buffalo-Niagara Falls MSA,						
	NY	S	15.62 MW	13.84 AW	32480 AAW	NYBLS	10//99-12//99
	Dutchess County PMSA, NY	S	12.15 MW	12.13 AW	25270 AAW	NYBLS	10//99-12//99

AAW Average annual wage	**AOH** Average offered, high	**ASH** Average starting, high	**H** Hourly	**M** Monthly	**S** Special: hourly and annual
AE Average entry wage	**AOL** Average offered, low	**ASL** Average starting, low	**HI** Highest wage paid	**MTC** Median total compensation	**TQ** Third quartile wage
AEX Average experienced wage	**APH** Average pay, high range	**AW** Average wage paid	**HR** High end range	**MW** Median wage paid	**W** Weekly
AO Average offered	**APL** Average pay, low range	**FQ** First quartile wage	**LR** Low end range	**SQ** Second quartile wage	**Y** Yearly

Occupation/Type/Industry	Location	Per	Low	Mid	High	Source	Date
Lodging Manager	Glens Falls MSA, NY	S	15.65 MW	14.86 AW	32540 AAW	NYBLS	10//99-12//99
	Nassau-Suffolk PMSA, NY	S	22.71 MW	16.68 AW	47230 AAW	NYBLS	10//99-12//99
	New York PMSA, NY	S	21.33 MW	19.69 AW	44360 AAW	NYBLS	10//99-12//99
	Newburgh PMSA, NY-PA	S	19.02 MW	20.46 AW	39560 AAW	NYBLS	10//99-12//99
	Rochester MSA, NY	S	19.80 MW	16.51 AW	41170 AAW	NYBLS	10//99-12//99
	Syracuse MSA, NY	S	25.77 MW	29.55 AW	53600 AAW	NYBLS	10//99-12//99
	North Carolina	S	13.09 MW	14.30 AW	29730 AAW	NCBLS	10//99-12//99
	Charlotte-Gastonia-Rock Hill MSA, NC-SC	S	16.95 MW	15.47 AW	35260 AAW	NCBLS	10//99-12//99
	Greensboro--Winston-Salem--High Point MSA, NC	S	18.38 MW	15.51 AW	38240 AAW	NCBLS	10//99-12//99
	Hickory-Morganton-Lenoir MSA, NC	S	13.34 MW	14.42 AW	27750 AAW	NCBLS	10//99-12//99
	Raleigh-Durham-Chapel Hill MSA, NC	S	14.08 MW	12.93 AW	29290 AAW	NCBLS	10//99-12//99
	Rocky Mount MSA, NC	S	10.60 MW	10.75 AW	22040 AAW	NCBLS	10//99-12//99
	Wilmington MSA, NC	S	12.97 MW	11.49 AW	26980 AAW	NCBLS	10//99-12//99
	North Dakota	S	9.85 MW	10.10 AW	21010 AAW	NDBLS	10//99-12//99
	Ohio	S	14.61 MW	18.87 AW	39260 AAW	OHBLS	10//99-12//99
	Cincinnati PMSA, OH-KY-IN	S	16.99 MW	15.75 AW	35340 AAW	OHBLS	10//99-12//99
	Cleveland-Lorain-Elyria PMSA, OH	S	19.21 MW	16.70 AW	39950 AAW	OHBLS	10//99-12//99
	Columbus MSA, OH	S	27.19 MW	24.49 AW	56560 AAW	OHBLS	10//99-12//99
	Dayton-Springfield MSA, OH	S	16.56 MW	17.85 AW	34450 AAW	OHBLS	10//99-12//99
	Oklahoma	S	12.65 MW	14.93 AW	31050 AAW	OKBLS	10//99-12//99
	Tulsa MSA, OK	S	14.47 MW	12.48 AW	30110 AAW	OKBLS	10//99-12//99
	Oregon	S	15.93 MW	17.15 AW	35670 AAW	ORBLS	10//99-12//99
	Medford-Ashland MSA, OR	S	14.15 MW	12.70 AW	29430 AAW	ORBLS	10//99-12//99
	Portland-Vancouver PMSA, OR-WA	S	15.36 MW	14.65 AW	31960 AAW	ORBLS	10//99-12//99
	Salem PMSA, OR	S	15.72 MW	15.17 AW	32700 AAW	ORBLS	10//99-12//99
	Pennsylvania	S	23.27 MW	24.04 AW	50010 AAW	PABLS	10//99-12//99
	Allentown-Bethlehem-Easton MSA, PA	S	17.43 MW	14.39 AW	36250 AAW	PABLS	10//99-12//99
	Erie MSA, PA	S	12.37 MW	8.20 AW	25730 AAW	PABLS	10//99-12//99
	Lancaster MSA, PA	S	22.64 MW	20.13 AW	47080 AAW	PABLS	10//99-12//99
	Philadelphia PMSA, PA-NJ	S	25.32 MW	24.04 AW	52670 AAW	PABLS	10//99-12//99
	Pittsburgh MSA, PA	S	27.06 MW	27.58 AW	56290 AAW	PABLS	10//99-12//99
	Scranton--Wilkes-Barre--Hazleton MSA, PA	S	13.38 MW	12.45 AW	27830 AAW	PABLS	10//99-12//99
	Rhode Island	S	14.31 MW	18.37 AW	38210 AAW	RIBLS	10//99-12//99
	Providence-Fall River-Warwick MSA, RI-MA	S	18.32 MW	13.38 AW	38100 AAW	RIBLS	10//99-12//99
	South Carolina	S	12.12 MW	14.02 AW	29170 AAW	SCBLS	10//99-12//99
	Charleston-North Charleston MSA, SC	S	23.20 MW	17.90 AW	48260 AAW	SCBLS	10//99-12//99
	Greenville-Spartanburg-Anderson MSA, SC	S	10.88 MW	10.15 AW	22630 AAW	SCBLS	10//99-12//99
	South Dakota	S	18.52 MW	18.38 AW	38240 AAW	SDBLS	10//99-12//99
	Rapid City MSA, SD	S	17.80 MW	17.57 AW	37010 AAW	SDBLS	10//99-12//99
	Sioux Falls MSA, SD	S	18.12 MW	18.05 AW	37690 AAW	SDBLS	10//99-12//99
	Tennessee	S	13.36 MW	15.11 AW	31420 AAW	TNBLS	10//99-12//99
	Chattanooga MSA, TN-GA	S	18.59 MW	15.21 AW	38660 AAW	TNBLS	10//99-12//99
	Clarksville-Hopkinsville MSA, TN-KY	S	14.09 MW	14.10 AW	29300 AAW	TNBLS	10//99-12//99
	Johnson City-Kingsport-Bristol MSA, TN-VA	S	12.27 MW	12.24 AW	25530 AAW	TNBLS	10//99-12//99
	Knoxville MSA, TN	S	9.31 MW	7.79 AW	19360 AAW	TNBLS	10//99-12//99
	Memphis MSA, TN-AR-MS	S	17.68 MW	17.41 AW	36780 AAW	MSBLS	10//99-12//99
	Nashville MSA, TN	S	17.98 MW	16.55 AW	37400 AAW	TNBLS	10//99-12//99
	Texas	S	10.58 MW	12.34 AW	25680 AAW	TXBLS	10//99-12//99
	Brownsville-Harlingen-San Benito MSA, TX	S	12.80 MW	14.34 AW	26630 AAW	TXBLS	10//99-12//99
	Bryan-College Station MSA, TX	S	12.85 MW	12.63 AW	26720 AAW	TXBLS	10//99-12//99
	Corpus Christi MSA, TX	S	20.93 MW	18.24 AW	43530 AAW	TXBLS	10//99-12//99
	Dallas PMSA, TX	S	12.30 MW	10.14 AW	25590 AAW	TXBLS	10//99-12//99
	El Paso MSA, TX	S	14.81 MW	11.01 AW	30810 AAW	TXBLS	10//99-12//99
	Fort Worth-Arlington PMSA, TX	S	18.23 MW	15.58 AW	37910 AAW	TXBLS	10//99-12//99
	Houston PMSA, TX	S	10.60 MW	10.02 AW	22040 AAW	TXBLS	10//99-12//99
	Killeen-Temple MSA, TX	S	12.02 MW	14.38 AW	25000 AAW	TXBLS	10//99-12//99

AAW	Average annual wage	AOH	Average offered, high	ASH	Average starting, high	H	Hourly	M	Monthly	S	Special: hourly and annual
AE	Average entry wage	AOL	Average offered, low	ASL	Average starting, low	HI	Highest wage paid	MTC	Median total compensation	TQ	Third quartile wage
AEX	Average experienced wage	APH	Average pay, high range	AW	Average wage paid	HR	High end range	MW	Median wage paid	W	Weekly
AO	Average offered	APL	Average pay, low range	FQ	First quartile wage	LR	Low end range	SQ	Second quartile wage	Y	Yearly

Occupation/Type/Industry	Location	Per	Low	Mid	High	Source	Date
Lodging Manager	McAllen-Edinburg-Mission MSA, TX	S	15.25 MW	14.52 AW	31720 AAW	TXBLS	10//99-12//99
	Odessa-Midland MSA, TX	S	9.57 MW	9.48 AW	19910 AAW	TXBLS	10//99-12//99
	San Antonio MSA, TX	S	10.95 MW	9.75 AW	22780 AAW	TXBLS	10//99-12//99
	Waco MSA, TX	S	11.99 MW	12.07 AW	24940 AAW	TXBLS	10//99-12//99
	Utah	S	17.6 MW	19.27 AW	40080 AAW	UTBLS	10//99-12//99
	Salt Lake City-Ogden MSA, UT	S	19.39 MW	16.50 AW	40330 AAW	UTBLS	10//99-12//99
	Vermont	S	26.45 MW	33.20 AW	69060 AAW	VTBLS	10//99-12//99
	Virginia	S	13.06 MW	15.07 AW	31350 AAW	VABLS	10//99-12//99
	Charlottesville MSA, VA	S	10.72 MW	9.96 AW	22300 AAW	VABLS	10//99-12//99
	Roanoke MSA, VA	S	15.26 MW	15.25 AW	31740 AAW	VABLS	10//99-12//99
	Washington	S	14.37 MW	16.97 AW	35310 AAW	WABLS	10//99-12//99
	Seattle-Bellevue-Everett PMSA, WA	S	19.05 MW	12.92 AW	39620 AAW	WABLS	10//99-12//99
	Tacoma PMSA, WA	S	16.35 MW	17.56 AW	34010 AAW	WABLS	10//99-12//99
	West Virginia	S	14.57 MW	14.70 AW	30570 AAW	WVBLS	10//99-12//99
	Huntington-Ashland MSA, WV-KY-OH	S	14.69 MW	14.25 AW	30560 AAW	WVBLS	10//99-12//99
	Wisconsin	S	13.48 MW	15.03 AW	31250 AAW	WIBLS	10//99-12//99
	Green Bay MSA, WI	S	14.94 MW	13.06 AW	31080 AAW	WIBLS	10//99-12//99
	Milwaukee-Waukesha PMSA, WI	S	15.29 MW	14.17 AW	31810 AAW	WIBLS	10//99-12//99
	Wyoming	S	12.06 MW	12.63 AW	26260 AAW	WYBLS	10//99-12//99
	Cheyenne MSA, WY	S	10.82 MW	9.80 AW	22500 AAW	WYBLS	10//99-12//99
	Puerto Rico	S	15.28 MW	15.92 AW	33100 AAW	PRBLS	10//99-12//99
	San Juan-Bayamon PMSA, PR	S	19.09 MW	19.40 AW	39700 AAW	PRBLS	10//99-12//99
	Virgin Islands	S	19.67 MW	22.28 AW	46330 AAW	VIBLS	10//99-12//99
Log Grader and Scaler	Alabama	S	12.16 MW	13.04 AW	27120 AAW	ALBLS	10//99-12//99
	Alaska	S	12.95 MW	18.03 AW	37500 AAW	AKBLS	10//99-12//99
	Arkansas	S	10.79 MW	10.20 AW	21220 AAW	ARBLS	10//99-12//99
	California	S	14.87 MW	14.21 AW	29550 AAW	CABLS	10//99-12//99
	Florida	S	10.12 MW	10.98 AW	22850 AAW	FLBLS	10//99-12//99
	Georgia	S	9.45 MW	9.97 AW	20740 AAW	GABLS	10//99-12//99
	Idaho	S	14.55 MW	14.19 AW	29510 AAW	IDBLS	10//99-12//99
	Indiana	S	15.52 MW	17.97 AW	37370 AAW	INBLS	10//99-12//99
	Iowa	S	16.8 MW	16.37 AW	34050 AAW	IABLS	10//99-12//99
	Kentucky	S	11.19 MW	11.17 AW	23240 AAW	KYBLS	10//99-12//99
	Louisiana	S	10.8 MW	10.94 AW	22750 AAW	LABLS	10//99-12//99
	Maine	S	12.47 MW	12.88 AW	26790 AAW	MEBLS	10//99-12//99
	Maryland	S	9.31 MW	11.93 AW	24810 AAW	MDBLS	10//99-12//99
	Michigan	S	11.4 MW	11.83 AW	24610 AAW	MIBLS	10//99-12//99
	Mississippi	S	11.99 MW	11.90 AW	24760 AAW	MSBLS	10//99-12//99
	Missouri	S	10.04 MW	11.85 AW	24650 AAW	MOBLS	10//99-12//99
	Montana	S	12.99 MW	13.37 AW	27810 AAW	MTBLS	10//99-12//99
	New Hampshire	S	12.83 MW	13.38 AW	27820 AAW	NHBLS	10//99-12//99
	New York	S	11.6 MW	13.65 AW	28400 AAW	NYBLS	10//99-12//99
	North Carolina	S	12.3 MW	12.15 AW	25270 AAW	NCBLS	10//99-12//99
	Ohio	S	11.8 MW	14.08 AW	29280 AAW	OHBLS	10//99-12//99
	Pennsylvania	S	11.57 MW	12.61 AW	26240 AAW	PABLS	10//99-12//99
	South Carolina	S	8.75 MW	10.77 AW	22410 AAW	SCBLS	10//99-12//99
	Tennessee	S	10.39 MW	11.41 AW	23730 AAW	TNBLS	10//99-12//99
	Texas	S	11.02 MW	11.79 AW	24520 AAW	TXBLS	10//99-12//99
	Virginia	S	9.89 MW	10.75 AW	22350 AAW	VABLS	10//99-12//99
	Washington	S	16.83 MW	17.78 AW	36980 AAW	WABLS	10//99-12//99
	West Virginia	S	10.46 MW	10.83 AW	22520 AAW	WVBLS	10//99-12//99
	Wisconsin	S	11.53 MW	14.06 AW	29250 AAW	WIBLS	10//99-12//99
Logging Equipment Operator	Alabama	S	10.74 MW	10.90 AW	22680 AAW	ALBLS	10//99-12//99
	Alaska	S	18.07 MW	17.91 AW	37250 AAW	AKBLS	10//99-12//99
	Arizona	S	8.68 MW	8.89 AW	18480 AAW	AZBLS	10//99-12//99
	Arkansas	S	11.19 MW	11.82 AW	24590 AAW	ARBLS	10//99-12//99
	California	S	14.6 MW	14.53 AW	30210 AAW	CABLS	10//99-12//99
	Colorado	S	10.32 MW	10.81 AW	22490 AAW	COBLS	10//99-12//99
	Florida	S	10.52 MW	10.65 AW	22150 AAW	FLBLS	10//99-12//99
	Georgia	S	9.8 MW	10.27 AW	21370 AAW	GABLS	10//99-12//99
	Idaho	S	16.58 MW	17.02 AW	35410 AAW	IDBLS	10//99-12//99
	Illinois	S	10.32 MW	10.34 AW	21510 AAW	ILBLS	10//99-12//99
	Indiana	S	9.82 MW	9.53 AW	19830 AAW	INBLS	10//99-12//99
	Iowa	S	9.91 MW	10.97 AW	22810 AAW	IABLS	10//99-12//99
	Kentucky	S	8.42 MW	9.29 AW	19320 AAW	KYBLS	10//99-12//99
	Louisiana	S	10.88 MW	10.79 AW	22440 AAW	LABLS	10//99-12//99

AAW Average annual wage	**AOH** Average offered, high	**ASH** Average starting, high	**H** Hourly	**M** Monthly	**S** Special: hourly and annual
AE Average entry wage	**AOL** Average offered, low	**ASL** Average starting, low	**HI** Highest wage paid	**MTC** Median total compensation	**TQ** Third quartile wage
AEX Average experienced wage	**APH** Average pay, high range	**AW** Average wage paid	**HR** High end range	**MW** Median wage paid	**W** Weekly
AO Average offered	**APL** Average pay, low range	**FQ** First quartile wage	**LR** Low end range	**SQ** Second quartile wage	**Y** Yearly

Occupation/Type/Industry	Location	Per	Low	Mid	High	Source	Date
Logging Equipment Operator	Maine	s	10.82 MW	11.48 AW	23890 AAW	MEBLS	10//99-12//99
	Maryland	s	8.78 MW	10.07 AW	20950 AAW	MDBLS	10//99-12//99
	Michigan	s	11.03 MW	11.26 AW	23430 AAW	MIBLS	10//99-12//99
	Minnesota	s	12.84 MW	12.39 AW	25770 AAW	MNBLS	10//99-12//99
	Mississippi	s	10.19 MW	10.56 AW	21970 AAW	MSBLS	10//99-12//99
	Missouri	s	9.9 MW	10.11 AW	21030 AAW	MOBLS	10//99-12//99
	Montana	s	14.61 MW	14.46 AW	30080 AAW	MTBLS	10//99-12//99
	New Hampshire	s	12.07 MW	13.67 AW	28440 AAW	NHBLS	10//99-12//99
	New Mexico	s	10.58 MW	10.92 AW	22700 AAW	NMBLS	10//99-12//99
	New York	s	10.7 MW	11.43 AW	23770 AAW	NYBLS	10//99-12//99
	North Carolina	s	10.87 MW	11.29 AW	23480 AAW	NCBLS	10//99-12//99
	Ohio	s	10.38 MW	10.56 AW	21970 AAW	OHBLS	10//99-12//99
	Oklahoma	s	13.84 MW	13.73 AW	28550 AAW	OKBLS	10//99-12//99
	Oregon	s	14.99 MW	16.00 AW	33280 AAW	ORBLS	10//99-12//99
	Pennsylvania	s	9.62 MW	9.88 AW	20550 AAW	PABLS	10//99-12//99
	South Carolina	s	10.24 MW	10.39 AW	21610 AAW	SCBLS	10//99-12//99
	Tennessee	s	10.32 MW	10.91 AW	22700 AAW	TNBLS	10//99-12//99
	Texas	s	12.67 MW	12.77 AW	26550 AAW	TXBLS	10//99-12//99
	Utah	s	9.26 MW	9.59 AW	19940 AAW	UTBLS	10//99-12//99
	Vermont	s	11.48 MW	11.66 AW	24240 AAW	VTBLS	10//99-12//99
	Virginia	s	9.23 MW	9.64 AW	20040 AAW	VABLS	10//99-12//99
	Washington	s	17.76 MW	17.81 AW	37050 AAW	WABLS	10//99-12//99
	West Virginia	s	9.07 MW	9.74 AW	20260 AAW	WVBLS	10//99-12//99
	Wisconsin	s	10.53 MW	11.52 AW	23970 AAW	WIBLS	10//99-12//99
	Wyoming	s	14.9 MW	14.54 AW	30240 AAW	WYBLS	10//99-12//99
Logistics Manager	United States	Y		75154 AW		MATMAN	1999
Machine Feeder and Offbearer	Alabama	s	8.98 MW	10.11 AW	21030 AAW	ALBLS	10//99-12//99
	Birmingham MSA, AL	s	13.89 MW	15.22 AW	28890 AAW	ALBLS	10//99-12//99
	Decatur MSA, AL	s	9.93 MW	8.21 AW	20660 AAW	ALBLS	10//99-12//99
	Dothan MSA, AL	s	9.12 MW	9.08 AW	18970 AAW	ALBLS	10//99-12//99
	Huntsville MSA, AL	s	9.94 MW	8.79 AW	20670 AAW	ALBLS	10//99-12//99
	Mobile MSA, AL	s	9.83 MW	8.38 AW	20460 AAW	ALBLS	10//99-12//99
	Montgomery MSA, AL	s	8.42 MW	7.50 AW	17510 AAW	ALBLS	10//99-12//99
	Alaska	s	11.39 MW	11.78 AW	24490 AAW	AKBLS	10//99-12//99
	Arizona	s	8.43 MW	8.54 AW	17770 AAW	AZBLS	10//99-12//99
	Phoenix-Mesa MSA, AZ	s	9.02 MW	9.06 AW	18770 AAW	AZBLS	10//99-12//99
	Arkansas	s	8.42 MW	9.47 AW	19700 AAW	ARBLS	10//99-12//99
	Fayetteville-Springdale-Rogers MSA, AR	s	8.97 MW	8.15 AW	18650 AAW	ARBLS	10//99-12//99
	Fort Smith MSA, AR-OK	s	8.07 MW	7.74 AW	16780 AAW	ARBLS	10//99-12//99
	Little Rock-North Little Rock MSA, AR	s	9.62 MW	9.30 AW	20000 AAW	ARBLS	10//99-12//99
	California	s	8.39 MW	9.52 AW	19800 AAW	CABLS	10//99-12//99
	Bakersfield MSA, CA	s	9.04 MW	7.45 AW	18800 AAW	CABLS	10//99-12//99
	Fresno MSA, CA	s	8.84 MW	8.34 AW	18390 AAW	CABLS	10//99-12//99
	Los Angeles-Long Beach PMSA, CA	s	8.58 MW	7.64 AW	17840 AAW	CABLS	10//99-12//99
	Merced MSA, CA	s	11.77 MW	11.59 AW	24490 AAW	CABLS	10//99-12//99
	Modesto MSA, CA	s	9.82 MW	9.88 AW	20420 AAW	CABLS	10//99-12//99
	Oakland PMSA, CA	s	11.04 MW	9.32 AW	22970 AAW	CABLS	10//99-12//99
	Orange County PMSA, CA	s	10.38 MW	9.07 AW	21580 AAW	CABLS	10//99-12//99
	Redding MSA, CA	s	11.99 MW	12.83 AW	24940 AAW	CABLS	10//99-12//99
	Riverside-San Bernardino PMSA, CA	s	8.66 MW	8.05 AW	18020 AAW	CABLS	10//99-12//99
	Sacramento PMSA, CA	s	9.74 MW	8.31 AW	20260 AAW	CABLS	10//99-12//99
	Salinas MSA, CA	s	12.23 MW	12.31 AW	25440 AAW	CABLS	10//99-12//99
	San Diego MSA, CA	s	8.12 MW	7.61 AW	16900 AAW	CABLS	10//99-12//99
	San Francisco PMSA, CA	s	8.75 MW	7.61 AW	18200 AAW	CABLS	10//99-12//99
	San Jose PMSA, CA	s	11.92 MW	12.09 AW	24800 AAW	CABLS	10//99-12//99
	Santa Barbara-Santa Maria-Lompoc MSA, CA	s	7.59 MW	6.57 AW	15790 AAW	CABLS	10//99-12//99
	Santa Cruz-Watsonville PMSA, CA	s	12.97 MW	12.94 AW	26970 AAW	CABLS	10//99-12//99
	Santa Rosa PMSA, CA	s	8.58 MW	8.22 AW	17840 AAW	CABLS	10//99-12//99
	Stockton-Lodi MSA, CA	s	10.91 MW	10.42 AW	22680 AAW	CABLS	10//99-12//99
	Vallejo-Fairfield-Napa PMSA, CA	s	10.19 MW	9.57 AW	21190 AAW	CABLS	10//99-12//99
	Ventura PMSA, CA	s	7.60 MW	6.61 AW	15800 AAW	CABLS	10//99-12//99
	Visalia-Tulare-Porterville MSA, CA	s	8.25 MW	7.68 AW	17160 AAW	CABLS	10//99-12//99
	Colorado	s	10.43 MW	10.38 AW	21600 AAW	COBLS	10//99-12//99

Occupation/Type/Industry	Location	Per	Low	Mid	High	Source	Date
Machine Feeder and Offbearer	Denver PMSA, CO	S	11.08 MW	11.25 AW	23040 AAW	COBLS	10//99-12//99
	Greeley PMSA, CO	S	9.91 MW	10.45 AW	20620 AAW	COBLS	10//99-12//99
	Connecticut	S	9.71 MW	10.15 AW	21110 AAW	CTBLS	10//99-12//99
	Bridgeport PMSA, CT	S	8.87 MW	8.01 AW	18460 AAW	CTBLS	10//99-12//99
	Hartford MSA, CT	S	11.53 MW	11.94 AW	23980 AAW	CTBLS	10//99-12//99
	New Haven-Meriden PMSA, CT	S	9.51 MW	8.98 AW	19780 AAW	CTBLS	10//99-12//99
	New London-Norwich MSA, CT-RI	S	11.85 MW	11.69 AW	24640 AAW	CTBLS	10//99-12//99
	Stamford-Norwalk PMSA, CT	S	10.44 MW	9.61 AW	21710 AAW	CTBLS	10//99-12//99
	Waterbury PMSA, CT	S	8.51 MW	8.36 AW	17700 AAW	CTBLS	10//99-12//99
	Delaware	S	12.77 MW	12.51 AW	26020 AAW	DEBLS	10//99-12//99
	Wilmington-Newark PMSA, DE-MD	S	12.37 MW	12.74 AW	25730 AAW	DEBLS	10//99-12//99
	Washington PMSA, DC-MD-VA-WV	S	9.96 MW	9.37 AW	20720 AAW	DCBLS	10//99-12//99
	Florida	S	7.95 MW	8.33 AW	17320 AAW	FLBLS	10//99-12//99
	Daytona Beach MSA, FL	S	9.02 MW	7.90 AW	18770 AAW	FLBLS	10//99-12//99
	Fort Lauderdale PMSA, FL	S	7.43 MW	7.51 AW	15460 AAW	FLBLS	10//99-12//99
	Jacksonville MSA, FL	S	8.90 MW	8.41 AW	18510 AAW	FLBLS	10//99-12//99
	Lakeland-Winter Haven MSA, FL	S	9.24 MW	8.48 AW	19220 AAW	FLBLS	10//99-12//99
	Melbourne-Titusville-Palm Bay MSA, FL	S	9.88 MW	8.96 AW	20540 AAW	FLBLS	10//99-12//99
	Miami PMSA, FL	S	7.56 MW	6.58 AW	15720 AAW	FLBLS	10//99-12//99
	Orlando MSA, FL	S	9.52 MW	8.32 AW	19810 AAW	FLBLS	10//99-12//99
	Tampa-St. Petersburg-Clearwater MSA, FL	S	8.17 MW	7.94 AW	17000 AAW	FLBLS	10//99-12//99
	Georgia	S	8.79 MW	9.04 AW	18800 AAW	GABLS	10//99-12//99
	Athens MSA, GA	S	9.72 MW	10.50 AW	20210 AAW	GABLS	10//99-12//99
	Atlanta MSA, GA	S	9.82 MW	9.16 AW	20420 AAW	GABLS	10//99-12//99
	Augusta-Aiken MSA, GA-SC	S	10.50 MW	10.44 AW	21830 AAW	GABLS	10//99-12//99
	Columbus MSA, GA-AL	S	8.98 MW	8.28 AW	18680 AAW	GABLS	10//99-12//99
	Macon MSA, GA	S	8.75 MW	7.79 AW	18200 AAW	GABLS	10//99-12//99
	Savannah MSA, GA	S	10.86 MW	11.07 AW	22600 AAW	GABLS	10//99-12//99
	Hawaii	S	8.06 MW	9.60 AW	19960 AAW	HIBLS	10//99-12//99
	Honolulu MSA, HI	S	9.63 MW	8.00 AW	20030 AAW	HIBLS	10//99-12//99
	Idaho	S	9.55 MW	9.84 AW	20470 AAW	IDBLS	10//99-12//99
	Boise City MSA, ID	S	8.35 MW	8.19 AW	17380 AAW	IDBLS	10//99-12//99
	Illinois	S	9.84 MW	10.27 AW	21370 AAW	ILBLS	10//99-12//99
	Champaign-Urbana MSA, IL	S	9.21 MW	9.31 AW	19160 AAW	ILBLS	10//99-12//99
	Chicago PMSA, IL	S	10.49 MW	10.09 AW	21810 AAW	ILBLS	10//99-12//99
	Rockford MSA, IL	S	10.22 MW	10.41 AW	21250 AAW	ILBLS	10//99-12//99
	Indiana	S	9.95 MW	10.49 AW	21810 AAW	INBLS	10//99-12//99
	Elkhart-Goshen MSA, IN	S	9.61 MW	9.71 AW	19990 AAW	INBLS	10//99-12//99
	Evansville-Henderson MSA, IN-KY	S	9.99 MW	9.46 AW	20780 AAW	INBLS	10//99-12//99
	Fort Wayne MSA, IN	S	9.89 MW	9.49 AW	20560 AAW	INBLS	10//99-12//99
	Gary PMSA, IN	S	14.80 MW	15.95 AW	30780 AAW	INBLS	10//99-12//99
	Indianapolis MSA, IN	S	9.63 MW	9.15 AW	20030 AAW	INBLS	10//99-12//99
	Kokomo MSA, IN	S	8.42 MW	8.34 AW	17510 AAW	INBLS	10//99-12//99
	Lafayette MSA, IN	S	9.41 MW	9.18 AW	19580 AAW	INBLS	10//99-12//99
	Muncie MSA, IN	S	11.23 MW	9.99 AW	23360 AAW	INBLS	10//99-12//99
	South Bend MSA, IN	S	8.67 MW	8.66 AW	18040 AAW	INBLS	10//99-12//99
	Terre Haute MSA, IN	S	10.56 MW	11.08 AW	21960 AAW	INBLS	10//99-12//99
	Iowa	S	9.89 MW	10.78 AW	22430 AAW	IABLS	10//99-12//99
	Cedar Rapids MSA, IA	S	14.20 MW	12.63 AW	29530 AAW	IABLS	10//99-12//99
	Davenport-Moline-Rock Island MSA, IA-IL	S	8.20 MW	7.20 AW	17060 AAW	IABLS	10//99-12//99
	Des Moines MSA, IA	S	13.55 MW	13.33 AW	28190 AAW	IABLS	10//99-12//99
	Sioux City MSA, IA-NE	S	12.11 MW	12.05 AW	25190 AAW	IABLS	10//99-12//99
	Waterloo-Cedar Falls MSA, IA	S	11.08 MW	11.16 AW	23040 AAW	IABLS	10//99-12//99
	Kansas	S	10.76 MW	10.57 AW	21990 AAW	KSBLS	10//99-12//99
	Wichita MSA, KS	S	9.76 MW	9.71 AW	20290 AAW	KSBLS	10//99-12//99
	Kentucky	S	8.79 MW	9.34 AW	19430 AAW	KYBLS	10//99-12//99
	Lexington MSA, KY	S	11.08 MW	11.57 AW	23040 AAW	KYBLS	10//99-12//99
	Louisville MSA, KY-IN	S	9.13 MW	8.54 AW	18990 AAW	KYBLS	10//99-12//99
	Owensboro MSA, KY	S	9.55 MW	9.30 AW	19870 AAW	KYBLS	10//99-12//99
	Louisiana	S	9.24 MW	9.42 AW	19590 AAW	LABLS	10//99-12//99
	Lafayette MSA, LA	S	7.76 MW	7.77 AW	16140 AAW	LABLS	10//99-12//99
	New Orleans MSA, LA	S	9.26 MW	8.99 AW	19250 AAW	LABLS	10//99-12//99
	Maine	S	8.73 MW	9.17 AW	19070 AAW	MEBLS	10//99-12//99

AAW Average annual wage	**AOH** Average offered, high	**ASH** Average starting, high	**H** Hourly	**M** Monthly	**S** Special: hourly and annual
AE Average entry wage	**AOL** Average offered, low	**ASL** Average starting, low	**HI** Highest wage paid	**MTC** Median total compensation	**TQ** Third quartile wage
AEX Average experienced wage	**APH** Average pay, high range	**AW** Average wage paid	**HR** High end range	**MW** Median wage paid	**W** Weekly
AO Average offered.	**APL** Average pay, low range	**FQ** First quartile wage	**LR** Low end range	**SQ** Second quartile wage	**Y** Yearly

Occupation/Type/Industry	Location	Per	Low	Mid	High	Source	Date
Machine Feeder and Offbearer	Lewiston-Auburn MSA, ME	S	10.41 MW	11.40 AW	21650 AAW	MEBLS	10//99-12//99
	Maryland	S	9.89 MW	10.36 AW	21560 AAW	MDBLS	10//99-12//99
	Baltimore PMSA, MD	S	10.34 MW	9.80 AW	21500 AAW	MDBLS	10//99-12//99
	Massachusetts	S	10.68 MW	10.77 AW	22400 AAW	MABLS	10//99-12//99
	Boston PMSA, MA-NH	S	12.04 MW	11.45 AW	25040 AAW	MABLS	10//99-12//99
	Brockton PMSA, MA	S	9.11 MW	9.06 AW	18950 AAW	MABLS	10//99-12//99
	Fitchburg-Leominster PMSA, MA	S	10.38 MW	10.04 AW	21580 AAW	MABLS	10//99-12//99
	Lawrence PMSA, MA-NH	S	10.62 MW	10.88 AW	22080 AAW	MABLS	10//99-12//99
	Lowell PMSA, MA-NH	S	11.55 MW	11.28 AW	24030 AAW	MABLS	10//99-12//99
	New Bedford PMSA, MA	S	9.37 MW	9.04 AW	19480 AAW	MABLS	10//99-12//99
	Springfield MSA, MA	S	10.09 MW	9.95 AW	20980 AAW	MABLS	10//99-12//99
	Worcester PMSA, MA-CT	S	10.86 MW	10.86 AW	22590 AAW	MABLS	10//99-12//99
	Michigan	S	12.7 MW	14.26 AW	29650 AAW	MIBLS	10//99-12//99
	Benton Harbor MSA, MI	S	7.39 MW	6.70 AW	15380 AAW	MIBLS	10//99-12//99
	Detroit PMSA, MI	S	12.87 MW	12.82 AW	26760 AAW	MIBLS	10//99-12//99
	Grand Rapids-Muskegon-Holland MSA, MI	S	16.91 MW	20.76 AW	35180 AAW	MIBLS	10//99-12//99
	Kalamazoo-Battle Creek MSA, MI	S	10.19 MW	8.96 AW	21200 AAW	MIBLS	10//99-12//99
	Lansing-East Lansing MSA, MI	S	10.37 MW	8.86 AW	21570 AAW	MIBLS	10//99-12//99
	Minnesota	S	10.37 MW	10.50 AW	21850 AAW	MNBLS	10//99-12//99
	Minneapolis-St. Paul MSA, MN-WI	S	10.67 MW	10.18 AW	22190 AAW	MNBLS	10//99-12//99
	St. Cloud MSA, MN	S	10.67 MW	11.09 AW	22200 AAW	MNBLS	10//99-12//99
	Mississippi	S	8.92 MW	9.00 AW	18720 AAW	MSBLS	10//99-12//99
	Jackson MSA, MS	S	8.84 MW	8.26 AW	18390 AAW	MSBLS	10//99-12//99
	Missouri	S	9.97 MW	10.58 AW	22010 AAW	MOBLS	10//99-12//99
	Kansas City MSA, MO-KS	S	12.16 MW	12.26 AW	25300 AAW	MOBLS	10//99-12//99
	St. Louis MSA, MO-IL	S	10.38 MW	9.83 AW	21590 AAW	MOBLS	10//99-12//99
	Montana	S	10.06 MW	10.34 AW	21500 AAW	MTBLS	10//99-12//99
	Nebraska	S	9.94 MW	10.12 AW	21050 AAW	NEBLS	10//99-12//99
	Lincoln MSA, NE	S	10.28 MW	9.99 AW	21380 AAW	NEBLS	10//99-12//99
	Omaha MSA, NE-IA	S	10.38 MW	10.40 AW	21590 AAW	NEBLS	10//99-12//99
	Reno MSA, NV	S	9.12 MW	8.71 AW	18970 AAW	NVBLS	10//99-12//99
	New Hampshire	S	9.92 MW	10.38 AW	21600 AAW	NHBLS	10//99-12//99
	Manchester PMSA, NH	S	8.24 MW	8.34 AW	17150 AAW	NHBLS	10//99-12//99
	Nashua PMSA, NH	S	12.14 MW	12.39 AW	25250 AAW	NHBLS	10//99-12//99
	Portsmouth-Rochester PMSA, NH-ME	S	12.54 MW	12.86 AW	26080 AAW	NHBLS	10//99-12//99
	New Jersey	S	9.15 MW	9.72 AW	20210 AAW	NJBLS	10//99-12//99
	Bergen-Passaic PMSA, NJ	S	9.81 MW	9.43 AW	20410 AAW	NJBLS	10//99-12//99
	Jersey City PMSA, NJ	S	7.95 MW	7.77 AW	16530 AAW	NJBLS	10//99-12//99
	Middlesex-Somerset-Hunterdon PMSA, NJ	S	9.62 MW	9.21 AW	20000 AAW	NJBLS	10//99-12//99
	Monmouth-Ocean PMSA, NJ	S	8.41 MW	7.85 AW	17490 AAW	NJBLS	10//99-12//99
	Newark PMSA, NJ	S	9.44 MW	8.36 AW	19640 AAW	NJBLS	10//99-12//99
	Trenton PMSA, NJ	S	9.84 MW	9.70 AW	20460 AAW	NJBLS	10//99-12//99
	New Mexico	S	7.56 MW	7.78 AW	16180 AAW	NMBLS	10//99-12//99
	New York	S	8.52 MW	9.20 AW	19140 AAW	NYBLS	10//99-12//99
	Albany-Schenectady-Troy MSA, NY	S	11.00 MW	9.79 AW	22880 AAW	NYBLS	10//99-12//99
	Binghamton MSA, NY	S	10.22 MW	10.33 AW	21260 AAW	NYBLS	10//99-12//99
	Buffalo-Niagara Falls MSA, NY	S	11.19 MW	9.79 AW	23270 AAW	NYBLS	10//99-12//99
	Glens Falls MSA, NY	S	12.35 MW	13.76 AW	25690 AAW	NYBLS	10//99-12//99
	Nassau-Suffolk PMSA, NY	S	8.72 MW	9.21 AW	18140 AAW	NYBLS	10//99-12//99
	New York PMSA, NY	S	8.21 MW	7.20 AW	17070 AAW	NYBLS	10//99-12//99
	Rochester MSA, NY	S	8.64 MW	8.23 AW	17980 AAW	NYBLS	10//99-12//99
	Syracuse MSA, NY	S	9.59 MW	9.16 AW	19940 AAW	NYBLS	10//99-12//99
	Utica-Rome MSA, NY	S	9.63 MW	9.62 AW	20030 AAW	NYBLS	10//99-12//99
	North Carolina	S	8.84 MW	9.17 AW	19070 AAW	NCBLS	10//99-12//99
	Asheville MSA, NC	S	8.91 MW	8.63 AW	18530 AAW	NCBLS	10//99-12//99
	Charlotte-Gastonia-Rock Hill MSA, NC-SC	S	10.36 MW	9.46 AW	21540 AAW	NCBLS	10//99-12//99
	Fayetteville MSA, NC	S	11.60 MW	8.78 AW	24130 AAW	NCBLS	10//99-12//99
	Greensboro--Winston-Salem--High Point MSA, NC	S	9.40 MW	9.29 AW	19550 AAW	NCBLS	10//99-12//99
	Hickory-Morganton-Lenoir MSA, NC	S	9.35 MW	9.04 AW	19440 AAW	NCBLS	10//99-12//99
	Raleigh-Durham-Chapel Hill MSA, NC	S	8.86 MW	8.43 AW	18440 AAW	NCBLS	10//99-12//99

AAW	Average annual wage	AOH	Average offered, high	ASH	Average starting, high	H	Hourly	M	Monthly	S	Special: hourly and annual
AE	Average entry wage	AOL	Average offered, low	ASL	Average starting, low	HI	Highest wage paid	MTC	Median total compensation	TQ	Third quartile wage
AEX	Average experienced wage	APH	Average pay, high range	AW	Average wage paid	HR	High end range	MW	Median wage paid	W	Weekly
AO	Average offered	APL	Average pay, low range	FQ	First quartile wage	LR	Low end range	SQ	Second quartile wage	Y	Yearly

Occupation/Type/Industry	Location	Per	Low	Mid	High	Source	Date
Machine Feeder and Offbearer	North Dakota	S	8.44 MW	8.90 AW	18520 AAW	NDBLS	10//99-12//99
	Grand Forks MSA, ND-MN	S	10.65 MW	11.22 AW	22150 AAW	NDBLS	10//99-12//99
	Ohio	S	10.94 MW	11.18 AW	23260 AAW	OHBLS	10//99-12//99
	Akron PMSA, OH	S	11.32 MW	12.42 AW	23540 AAW	OHBLS	10//99-12//99
	Canton-Massillon MSA, OH	S	10.08 MW	9.90 AW	20960 AAW	OHBLS	10//99-12//99
	Cincinnati PMSA, OH-KY-IN	S	10.30 MW	9.75 AW	21410 AAW	OHBLS	10//99-12//99
	Cleveland-Lorain-Elyria PMSA, OH	S	11.12 MW	10.78 AW	23120 AAW	OHBLS	10//99-12//99
	Columbus MSA, OH	S	11.13 MW	10.51 AW	23160 AAW	OHBLS	10//99-12//99
	Hamilton-Middletown PMSA, OH	S	15.17 MW	14.87 AW	31550 AAW	OHBLS	10//99-12//99
	Lima MSA, OH	S	8.86 MW	9.14 AW	18430 AAW	OHBLS	10//99-12//99
	Mansfield MSA, OH	S	11.37 MW	11.28 AW	23660 AAW	OHBLS	10//99-12//99
	Steubenville-Weirton MSA, OH-WV	S	12.64 MW	12.02 AW	26290 AAW	OHBLS	10//99-12//99
	Toledo MSA, OH	S	11.25 MW	11.15 AW	23410 AAW	OHBLS	10//99-12//99
	Oklahoma	S	8.83 MW	10.08 AW	20960 AAW	OKBLS	10//99-12//99
	Oklahoma City MSA, OK	S	8.85 MW	8.05 AW	18410 AAW	OKBLS	10//99-12//99
	Tulsa MSA, OK	S	9.26 MW	8.73 AW	19270 AAW	OKBLS	10//99-12//99
	Oregon	S	10.94 MW	11.61 AW	24150 AAW	ORBLS	10//99-12//99
	Corvallis MSA, OR	S	11.20 MW	10.49 AW	23290 AAW	ORBLS	10//99-12//99
	Eugene-Springfield MSA, OR	S	10.67 MW	10.26 AW	22190 AAW	ORBLS	10//99-12//99
	Medford-Ashland MSA, OR	S	10.78 MW	10.94 AW	22430 AAW	ORBLS	10//99-12//99
	Portland-Vancouver PMSA, OR-WA	S	12.45 MW	11.01 AW	25890 AAW	ORBLS	10//99-12//99
	Salem PMSA, OR	S	7.96 MW	7.86 AW	16560 AAW	ORBLS	10//99-12//99
	Pennsylvania	S	10.26 MW	11.00 AW	22890 AAW	PABLS	10//99-12//99
	Allentown-Bethlehem-Easton MSA, PA	S	10.50 MW	9.89 AW	21830 AAW	PABLS	10//99-12//99
	Erie MSA, PA	S	8.86 MW	8.58 AW	18430 AAW	PABLS	10//99-12//99
	Harrisburg-Lebanon-Carlisle MSA, PA	S	11.99 MW	11.11 AW	24940 AAW	PABLS	10//99-12//99
	Johnstown MSA, PA	S	8.42 MW	8.00 AW	17500 AAW	PABLS	10//99-12//99
	Lancaster MSA, PA	S	11.10 MW	11.25 AW	23080 AAW	PABLS	10//99-12//99
	Philadelphia PMSA, PA-NJ	S	11.08 MW	10.46 AW	23050 AAW	PABLS	10//99-12//99
	Pittsburgh MSA, PA	S	13.64 MW	14.07 AW	28360 AAW	PABLS	10//99-12//99
	Reading MSA, PA	S	11.83 MW	12.13 AW	24600 AAW	PABLS	10//99-12//99
	Scranton--Wilkes-Barre--Hazleton MSA, PA	S	9.07 MW	8.93 AW	18870 AAW	PABLS	10//99-12//99
	Sharon MSA, PA	S	14.34 MW	14.66 AW	29820 AAW	PABLS	10//99-12//99
	State College MSA, PA	S	9.39 MW	8.30 AW	19530 AAW	PABLS	10//99-12//99
	Williamsport MSA, PA	S	9.34 MW	8.37 AW	19430 AAW	PABLS	10//99-12//99
	York MSA, PA	S	9.35 MW	9.15 AW	19450 AAW	PABLS	10//99-12//99
	Rhode Island	S	9.75 MW	10.21 AW	21240 AAW	RIBLS	10//99-12//99
	Providence-Fall River-Warwick MSA, RI-MA	S	10.28 MW	9.91 AW	21390 AAW	RIBLS	10//99-12//99
	South Carolina	S	9.1 MW	9.42 AW	19590 AAW	SCBLS	
	Charleston-North Charleston MSA, SC	S	10.43 MW	9.62 AW	21700 AAW	SCBLS	10//99-12//99
	Columbia MSA, SC	S	10.05 MW	9.92 AW	20900 AAW	SCBLS	10//99-12//99
	Greenville-Spartanburg-Anderson MSA, SC	S	9.72 MW	9.28 AW	20210 AAW	SCBLS	10//99-12//99
	South Dakota	S	8.47 MW	8.51 AW	17700 AAW	SDBLS	10//99-12//99
	Sioux Falls MSA, SD	S	9.23 MW	9.49 AW	19200 AAW	SDBLS	10//99-12//99
	Tennessee	S	9.27 MW	9.57 AW	19900 AAW	TNBLS	10//99-12//99
	Chattanooga MSA, TN-GA	S	9.41 MW	9.07 AW	19570 AAW	TNBLS	10//99-12//99
	Jackson MSA, TN	S	10.92 MW	11.47 AW	22710 AAW	TNBLS	10//99-12//99
	Johnson City-Kingsport-Bristol MSA, TN-VA	S	10.17 MW	9.53 AW	21150 AAW	TNBLS	10//99-12//99
	Knoxville MSA, TN	S	10.72 MW	10.65 AW	22300 AAW	TNBLS	10//99-12//99
	Memphis MSA, TN-AR-MS	S	9.32 MW	9.13 AW	19390 AAW	MSBLS	10//99-12//99
	Nashville MSA, TN	S	10.44 MW	10.17 AW	21720 AAW	TNBLS	10//99-12//99
	Texas	S	8.63 MW	8.82 AW	18350 AAW	TXBLS	10//99-12//99
	Amarillo MSA, TX	S	7.02 MW	7.20 AW	14590 AAW	TXBLS	10//99-12//99
	Austin-San Marcos MSA, TX	S	8.49 MW	8.19 AW	17660 AAW	TXBLS	10//99-12//99
	Dallas PMSA, TX	S	9.47 MW	9.42 AW	19700 AAW	TXBLS	10//99-12//99
	El Paso MSA, TX	S	7.06 MW	6.52 AW	14690 AAW	TXBLS	10//99-12//99
	Fort Worth-Arlington PMSA, TX	S	9.33 MW	9.27 AW	19410 AAW	TXBLS	10//99-12//99
	Houston PMSA, TX	S	7.79 MW	7.43 AW	16190 AAW	TXBLS	10//99-12//99
	Longview-Marshall MSA, TX	S	7.22 MW	6.94 AW	15020 AAW	TXBLS	10//99-12//99

AAW Average annual wage	**AOH** Average offered, high	**ASH** Average starting, high	**H** Hourly	**M** Monthly	**S** Special: hourly and annual
AE Average entry wage	**AOL** Average offered, low	**ASL** Average starting, low	**HI** Highest wage paid	**MTC** Median total compensation	**TQ** Third quartile wage
AEX Average experienced wage	**APH** Average pay, high range	**AW** Average wage paid	**HR** High end range	**MW** Median wage paid	**W** Weekly
AO Average offered	**APL** Average pay, low range	**FQ** First quartile wage	**LR** Low end range	**SQ** Second quartile wage	**Y** Yearly

Occupation/Type/Industry	Location	Per	Low	Mid	High	Source	Date
Machine Feeder and Offbearer	McAllen-Edinburg-Mission MSA, TX	S	8.85 MW	8.80 AW	18400 AAW	TXBLS	10//99-12//99
	San Angelo MSA, TX	S	8.99 MW	7.95 AW	18710 AAW	TXBLS	10//99-12//99
	San Antonio MSA, TX	S	8.18 MW	8.21 AW	17020 AAW	TXBLS	10//99-12//99
	Texarkana MSA, TX-Texarkana, AR	S	9.07 MW	9.24 AW	18870 AAW	TXBLS	10//99-12//99
	Tyler MSA, TX	S	8.43 MW	7.80 AW	17520 AAW	TXBLS	10//99-12//99
	Waco MSA, TX	S	9.97 MW	9.88 AW	20740 AAW	TXBLS	10//99-12//99
	Utah	S	8.83 MW	9.10 AW	18940 AAW	UTBLS	10//99-12//99
	Salt Lake City-Ogden MSA, UT	S	9.06 MW	8.72 AW	18840 AAW	UTBLS	10//99-12//99
	Vermont	S	8.63 MW	8.88 AW	18470 AAW	VTBLS	10//99-12//99
	Virginia	S	9.15 MW	9.88 AW	20550 AAW	VABLS	10//99-12//99
	Lynchburg MSA, VA	S	8.96 MW	8.39 AW	18640 AAW	VABLS	10//99-12//99
	Norfolk-Virginia Beach-Newport News MSA, VA-NC	S	11.15 MW	10.01 AW	23200 AAW	VABLS	10//99-12//99
	Richmond-Petersburg MSA, VA	S	11.38 MW	11.19 AW	23670 AAW	VABLS	10//99-12//99
	Roanoke MSA, VA	S	9.02 MW	9.03 AW	18760 AAW	VABLS	10//99-12//99
	Washington	S	10.97 MW	11.24 AW	23380 AAW	WABLS	10//99-12//99
	Bellingham MSA, WA	S	11.41 MW	10.14 AW	23730 AAW	WABLS	10//99-12//99
	Richland-Kennewick-Pasco MSA, WA	S	8.26 MW	8.70 AW	17190 AAW	WABLS	10//99-12//99
	Seattle-Bellevue-Everett PMSA, WA	S	11.26 MW	10.85 AW	23420 AAW	WABLS	10//99-12//99
	Tacoma PMSA, WA	S	10.79 MW	10.92 AW	22440 AAW	WABLS	10//99-12//99
	Yakima MSA, WA	S	10.70 MW	10.42 AW	22260 AAW	WABLS	10//99-12//99
	West Virginia	S	7.53 MW	8.48 AW	17650 AAW	WVBLS	10//99-12//99
	Charleston MSA, WV	S	8.75 MW	7.52 AW	18210 AAW	WVBLS	10//99-12//99
	Huntington-Ashland MSA, WV-KY-OH	S	10.85 MW	9.59 AW	22570 AAW	WVBLS	10//99-12//99
	Parkersburg-Marietta MSA, WV-OH	S	8.01 MW	7.74 AW	16670 AAW	WVBLS	10//99-12//99
	Wheeling MSA, WV-OH	S	9.91 MW	6.61 AW	20600 AAW	WVBLS	10//99-12//99
	Wisconsin	S	9.48 MW	9.75 AW	20290 AAW	WIBLS	10//99-12//99
	Appleton-Oshkosh-Neenah MSA, WI	S	10.73 MW	9.90 AW	22320 AAW	WIBLS	10//99-12//99
	Eau Claire MSA, WI	S	10.81 MW	12.08 AW	22490 AAW	WIBLS	10//99-12//99
	Green Bay MSA, WI	S	8.69 MW	8.47 AW	18080 AAW	WIBLS	10//99-12//99
	Janesville-Beloit MSA, WI	S	9.80 MW	8.86 AW	20390 AAW	WIBLS	10//99-12//99
	La Crosse MSA, WI-MN	S	9.60 MW	8.69 AW	19960 AAW	WIBLS	10//99-12//99
	Madison MSA, WI	S	10.42 MW	10.27 AW	21670 AAW	WIBLS	10//99-12//99
	Milwaukee-Waukesha PMSA, WI	S	10.95 MW	10.95 AW	22770 AAW	WIBLS	10//99-12//99
	Racine PMSA, WI	S	8.62 MW	8.56 AW	17920 AAW	WIBLS	10//99-12//99
	Sheboygan MSA, WI	S	8.92 MW	8.81 AW	18540 AAW	WIBLS	10//99-12//99
	Wausau MSA, WI	S	8.67 MW	8.55 AW	18040 AAW	WIBLS	10//99-12//99
	Puerto Rico	S	6.4 MW	6.77 AW	14090 AAW	PRBLS	10//99-12//99
	Arecibo PMSA, PR	S	5.95 MW	6.03 AW	12370 AAW	PRBLS	10//99-12//99
	Caguas PMSA, PR	S	7.20 MW	6.05 AW	14980 AAW	PRBLS	10//99-12//99
	Mayaguez MSA, PR	S	6.95 MW	6.75 AW	14450 AAW	PRBLS	10//99-12//99
	Ponce MSA, PR	S	6.73 MW	6.56 AW	14010 AAW	PRBLS	10//99-12//99
	San Juan-Bayamon PMSA, PR	S	6.54 MW	6.29 AW	13610 AAW	PRBLS	10//99-12//99
Machinist	Alabama	S	13.96 MW	14.02 AW	29160 AAW	ALBLS	10//99-12//99
	Anniston MSA, AL	S	12.38 MW	11.16 AW	25760 AAW	ALBLS	10//99-12//99
	Auburn-Opelika MSA, AL	S	11.08 MW	8.41 AW	23050 AAW	ALBLS	10//99-12//99
	Birmingham MSA, AL	S	13.44 MW	13.46 AW	27960 AAW	ALBLS	10//99-12//99
	Decatur MSA, AL	S	16.45 MW	15.73 AW	34210 AAW	ALBLS	10//99-12//99
	Dothan MSA, AL	S	9.29 MW	8.70 AW	19330 AAW	ALBLS	10//99-12//99
	Florence MSA, AL	S	15.95 MW	15.80 AW	33170 AAW	ALBLS	10//99-12//99
	Gadsden MSA, AL	S	11.13 MW	11.05 AW	23160 AAW	ALBLS	10//99-12//99
	Huntsville MSA, AL	S	14.91 MW	14.66 AW	31020 AAW	ALBLS	10//99-12//99
	Mobile MSA, AL	S	16.03 MW	16.62 AW	33340 AAW	ALBLS	10//99-12//99
	Montgomery MSA, AL	S	11.37 MW	10.65 AW	23650 AAW	ALBLS	10//99-12//99
	Tuscaloosa MSA, AL	S	12.04 MW	12.41 AW	25030 AAW	ALBLS	10//99-12//99
	Alaska	S	20.9 MW	20.55 AW	42740 AAW	AKBLS	10//99-12//99
	Anchorage MSA, AK	S	23.88 MW	24.10 AW	49680 AAW	AKBLS	10//99-12//99
	Arizona	S	15.54 MW	15.50 AW	32250 AAW	AZBLS	10//99-12//99
	Flagstaff MSA, AZ-UT	S	13.77 MW	13.41 AW	28640 AAW	AZBLS	10//99-12//99
	Phoenix-Mesa MSA, AZ	S	15.52 MW	15.58 AW	32290 AAW	AZBLS	10//99-12//99
	Tucson MSA, AZ	S	16.13 MW	16.20 AW	33540 AAW	AZBLS	10//99-12//99

AAW	Average annual wage	AOH	Average offered, high	ASH	Average starting, high
AE	Average entry wage	AOL	Average offered, low	ASL	Average starting, low
AEX	Average experienced wage	APH	Average pay, high range	AW	Average wage paid
AO	Average offered	APL	Average pay, low range	FQ	First quartile wage

H	Hourly	M	Monthly
HI	Highest wage paid	MTC	Median total compensation
HR	High end range	MW	Median wage paid
LR	Low end range	SQ	Second quartile wage

S	Special: hourly and annual
TQ	Third quartile wage
W	Weekly
Y	Yearly

Occupation/Type/Industry	Location	Per	Low	Mid	High	Source	Date
Machinist	Arkansas	S	12.88 MW	13.36 AW	27780 AAW	ARBLS	10//99-12//99
	Fayetteville-Springdale-Rogers MSA, AR	S	12.31 MW	11.99 AW	25600 AAW	ARBLS	10//99-12//99
	Fort Smith MSA, AR-OK	S	11.97 MW	11.61 AW	24890 AAW	ARBLS	10//99-12//99
	Jonesboro MSA, AR	S	13.92 MW	13.40 AW	28950 AAW	ARBLS	10//99-12//99
	Little Rock-North Little Rock MSA, AR	S	14.06 MW	14.20 AW	29250 AAW	ARBLS	10//99-12//99
	California	S	14.45 MW	15.13 AW	31460 AAW	CABLS	10//99-12//99
	Bakersfield MSA, CA	S	12.64 MW	10.96 AW	26290 AAW	CABLS	10//99-12//99
	Chico-Paradise MSA, CA	S	13.73 MW	12.70 AW	28560 AAW	CABLS	10//99-12//99
	Fresno MSA, CA	S	12.31 MW	11.65 AW	25610 AAW	CABLS	10//99-12//99
	Los Angeles-Long Beach PMSA, CA	S	14.13 MW	13.60 AW	29390 AAW	CABLS	10//99-12//99
	Merced MSA, CA	S	12.62 MW	12.52 AW	26240 AAW	CABLS	10//99-12//99
	Modesto MSA, CA	S	14.35 MW	14.79 AW	29850 AAW	CABLS	10//99-12//99
	Oakland PMSA, CA	S	19.46 MW	19.61 AW	40470 AAW	CABLS	10//99-12//99
	Orange County PMSA, CA	S	15.82 MW	15.06 AW	32910 AAW	CABLS	10//99-12//99
	Redding MSA, CA	S	14.93 MW	14.83 AW	31050 AAW	CABLS	10//99-12//99
	Riverside-San Bernardino PMSA, CA	S	13.11 MW	12.34 AW	27280 AAW	CABLS	10//99-12//99
	Sacramento PMSA, CA	S	16.61 MW	16.93 AW	34550 AAW	CABLS	10//99-12//99
	Salinas MSA, CA	S	11.11 MW	10.46 AW	23110 AAW	CABLS	10//99-12//99
	San Diego MSA, CA	S	14.32 MW	13.69 AW	29780 AAW	CABLS	10//99-12//99
	San Francisco PMSA, CA	S	18.06 MW	18.41 AW	37570 AAW	CABLS	10//99-12//99
	San Jose PMSA, CA	S	17.15 MW	17.67 AW	35680 AAW	CABLS	10//99-12//99
	San Luis Obispo-Atascadero-Paso Robles MSA, CA	S	19.73 MW	20.72 AW	41040 AAW	CABLS	10//99-12//99
	Santa Barbara-Santa Maria-Lompoc MSA, CA	S	17.95 MW	17.84 AW	37340 AAW	CABLS	10//99-12//99
	Santa Cruz-Watsonville PMSA, CA	S	12.05 MW	11.82 AW	25060 AAW	CABLS	10//99-12//99
	Santa Rosa PMSA, CA	S	15.20 MW	14.94 AW	31620 AAW	CABLS	10//99-12//99
	Stockton-Lodi MSA, CA	S	21.05 MW	19.90 AW	43770 AAW	CABLS	10//99-12//99
	Vallejo-Fairfield-Napa PMSA, CA	S	16.65 MW	16.43 AW	34620 AAW	CABLS	10//99-12//99
	Ventura PMSA, CA	S	13.67 MW	13.22 AW	28440 AAW	CABLS	10//99-12//99
	Visalia-Tulare-Porterville MSA, CA	S	13.83 MW	13.59 AW	28760 AAW	CABLS	10//99-12//99
	Yolo PMSA, CA	S	13.46 MW	13.59 AW	27990 AAW	CABLS	10//99-12//99
	Yuba City MSA, CA	S	12.91 MW	12.99 AW	26860 AAW	CABLS	10//99-12//99
	Colorado	S	15.01 MW	15.11 AW	31420 AAW	COBLS	10//99-12//99
	Boulder-Longmont PMSA, CO	S	15.59 MW	15.73 AW	32430 AAW	COBLS	10//99-12//99
	Colorado Springs MSA, CO	S	12.66 MW	11.97 AW	26330 AAW	COBLS	10//99-12//99
	Denver PMSA, CO	S	15.62 MW	15.21 AW	32490 AAW	COBLS	10//99-12//99
	Fort Collins-Loveland MSA, CO	S	15.61 MW	15.59 AW	32470 AAW	COBLS	10//99-12//99
	Greeley PMSA, CO	S	12.64 MW	12.38 AW	26290 AAW	COBLS	10//99-12//99
	Connecticut	S	15.79 MW	15.86 AW	32980 AAW	CTBLS	10//99-12//99
	Bridgeport PMSA, CT	S	17.69 MW	17.84 AW	36790 AAW	CTBLS	10//99-12//99
	Danbury PMSA, CT	S	17.18 MW	18.11 AW	35740 AAW	CTBLS	10//99-12//99
	Hartford MSA, CT	S	16.16 MW	16.46 AW	33600 AAW	CTBLS	10//99-12//99
	New Haven-Meriden PMSA, CT	S	15.59 MW	15.44 AW	32420 AAW	CTBLS	10//99-12//99
	New London-Norwich MSA, CT-RI	S	15.82 MW	15.41 AW	32910 AAW	CTBLS	10//99-12//99
	Stamford-Norwalk PMSA, CT	S	14.01 MW	13.14 AW	29130 AAW	CTBLS	10//99-12//99
	Waterbury PMSA, CT	S	13.68 MW	11.49 AW	28440 AAW	CTBLS	10//99-12//99
	Wilmington-Newark PMSA, DE-MD	S	19.20 MW	19.08 AW	39940 AAW	DEBLS	10//99-12//99
	District of Columbia	S	19.4 MW	19.02 AW	39570 AAW	DCBLS	10//99-12//99
	Washington PMSA, DC-MD-VA-WV	S	17.36 MW	17.15 AW	36100 AAW	DCBLS	10//99-12//99
	Florida	S	11.73 MW	12.99 AW	27020 AAW	FLBLS	10//99-12//99
	Daytona Beach MSA, FL	S	11.48 MW	10.52 AW	23870 AAW	FLBLS	10//99-12//99
	Fort Lauderdale PMSA, FL	S	14.62 MW	14.60 AW	30420 AAW	FLBLS	10//99-12//99
	Fort Pierce-Port St. Lucie MSA, FL	S	10.97 MW	10.02 AW	22820 AAW	FLBLS	10//99-12//99
	Fort Walton Beach MSA, FL	S	12.46 MW	8.03 AW	25910 AAW	FLBLS	10//99-12//99
	Gainesville MSA, FL	S	10.88 MW	10.60 AW	22630 AAW	FLBLS	10//99-12//99
	Jacksonville MSA, FL	S	13.24 MW	12.39 AW	27530 AAW	FLBLS	10//99-12//99
	Lakeland-Winter Haven MSA, FL	S	14.63 MW	14.28 AW	30440 AAW	FLBLS	10//99-12//99

AAW	Average annual wage	**AOH**	Average offered, high	**ASH**	Average starting, high	**H** Hourly	**M** Monthly	**S** Special: hourly and annual
AE	Average entry wage	**AOL**	Average offered, low	**ASL**	Average starting, low	**HI** Highest wage paid	**MTC** Median total compensation	**TQ** Third quartile wage
AEX	Average experienced wage	**APH**	Average pay, high range	**AW**	Average wage paid	**HR** High end range	**MW** Median wage paid	**W** Weekly
AO	Average offered	**APL**	Average pay, low range	**FQ**	First quartile wage	**LR** Low end range	**SQ** Second quartile wage	**Y** Yearly

Occupation/Type/Industry	Location	Per	Low	Mid	High	Source	Date
Machinist	Melbourne-Titusville-Palm						
	Bay MSA, FL	S	13.07 MW	12.44 AW	27190 AAW	FLBLS	10//99-12//99
	Miami PMSA, FL	S	11.11 MW	10.68 AW	23110 AAW	FLBLS	10//99-12//99
	Naples MSA, FL	S	12.51 MW	11.93 AW	26010 AAW	FLBLS	10//99-12//99
	Ocala MSA, FL	S	10.41 MW	10.01 AW	21660 AAW	FLBLS	10//99-12//99
	Orlando MSA, FL	S	14.84 MW	13.11 AW	30860 AAW	FLBLS	10//99-12//99
	Panama City MSA, FL	S	15.56 MW	14.57 AW	32370 AAW	FLBLS	10//99-12//99
	Pensacola MSA, FL	S	10.98 MW	9.94 AW	22830 AAW	FLBLS	10//99-12//99
	Sarasota-Bradenton MSA, FL	S	14.31 MW	14.51 AW	29760 AAW	FLBLS	10//99-12//99
	Tallahassee MSA, FL	S	15.51 MW	13.42 AW	32270 AAW	FLBLS	10//99-12//99
	Tampa-St. Petersburg-						
	Clearwater MSA, FL	S	13.01 MW	11.52 AW	27060 AAW	FLBLS	10//99-12//99
	West Palm Beach-Boca Raton						
	MSA, FL	S	15.10 MW	15.54 AW	31410 AAW	FLBLS	10//99-12//99
	Georgia	S	12.95 MW	13.37 AW	27810 AAW	GABLS	10//99-12//99
	Athens MSA, GA	S	14.88 MW	15.07 AW	30950 AAW	GABLS	10//99-12//99
	Atlanta MSA, GA	S	13.59 MW	13.22 AW	28270 AAW	GABLS	10//99-12//99
	Augusta-Aiken MSA, GA-SC	S	13.94 MW	12.76 AW	28990 AAW	GABLS	10//99-12//99
	Columbus MSA, GA-AL	S	12.97 MW	12.36 AW	26970 AAW	GABLS	10//99-12//99
	Macon MSA, GA	S	14.98 MW	14.78 AW	31170 AAW	GABLS	10//99-12//99
	Savannah MSA, GA	S	12.82 MW	12.43 AW	26660 AAW	GABLS	10//99-12//99
	Hawaii	S	16.38 MW	18.35 AW	38160 AAW	HIBLS	10//99-12//99
	Honolulu MSA, HI	S	18.47 MW	16.29 AW	38420 AAW	HIBLS	10//99-12//99
	Idaho	S	13.18 MW	14.11 AW	29350 AAW	IDBLS	10//99-12//99
	Boise City MSA, ID	S	14.01 MW	13.51 AW	29140 AAW	IDBLS	10//99-12//99
	Pocatello MSA, ID	S	12.84 MW	12.45 AW	26710 AAW	IDBLS	10//99-12//99
	Illinois	S	14.65 MW	14.93 AW	31040 AAW	ILBLS	10//99-12//99
	Bloomington-Normal MSA, IL	S	12.50 MW	12.88 AW	26000 AAW	ILBLS	10//99-12//99
	Champaign-Urbana MSA, IL	S	14.19 MW	14.61 AW	29520 AAW	ILBLS	10//99-12//99
	Chicago PMSA, IL	S	14.79 MW	14.58 AW	30760 AAW	ILBLS	10//99-12//99
	Decatur MSA, IL	S	14.57 MW	12.88 AW	30300 AAW	ILBLS	10//99-12//99
	Kankakee PMSA, IL	S	10.52 MW	9.88 AW	21880 AAW	ILBLS	10//99-12//99
	Peoria-Pekin MSA, IL	S	15.92 MW	14.63 AW	33120 AAW	ILBLS	10//99-12//99
	Rockford MSA, IL	S	14.87 MW	14.51 AW	30940 AAW	ILBLS	10//99-12//99
	Indiana	S	14.89 MW	14.88 AW	30940 AAW	INBLS	10//99-12//99
	Bloomington MSA, IN	S	12.70 MW	13.54 AW	26410 AAW	INBLS	10//99-12//99
	Elkhart-Goshen MSA, IN	S	11.68 MW	11.31 AW	24300 AAW	INBLS	10//99-12//99
	Evansville-Henderson MSA,						
	IN-KY	S	14.21 MW	13.98 AW	29550 AAW	INBLS	10//99-12//99
	Fort Wayne MSA, IN	S	15.56 MW	15.50 AW	32360 AAW	INBLS	10//99-12//99
	Gary PMSA, IN	S	17.11 MW	17.94 AW	35580 AAW	INBLS	10//99-12//99
	Indianapolis MSA, IN	S	15.27 MW	15.34 AW	31760 AAW	INBLS	10//99-12//99
	Kokomo MSA, IN	S	16.26 MW	16.88 AW	33830 AAW	INBLS	10//99-12//99
	Lafayette MSA, IN	S	13.29 MW	13.92 AW	27640 AAW	INBLS	10//99-12//99
	Muncie MSA, IN	S	15.79 MW	12.95 AW	32850 AAW	INBLS	10//99-12//99
	South Bend MSA, IN	S	15.30 MW	15.15 AW	31830 AAW	INBLS	10//99-12//99
	Terre Haute MSA, IN	S	13.33 MW	13.68 AW	27720 AAW	INBLS	10//99-12//99
	Iowa	S	11.85 MW	13.14 AW	27330 AAW	IABLS	10//99-12//99
	Cedar Rapids MSA, IA	S	16.18 MW	15.48 AW	33660 AAW	IABLS	10//99-12//99
	Davenport-Moline-Rock Island						
	MSA, IA-IL	S	15.25 MW	13.35 AW	31710 AAW	IABLS	10//99-12//99
	Des Moines MSA, IA	S	10.75 MW	10.13 AW	22360 AAW	IABLS	10//99-12//99
	Dubuque MSA, IA	S	13.39 MW	13.64 AW	27840 AAW	IABLS	10//99-12//99
	Waterloo-Cedar Falls MSA, IA	S	17.69 MW	16.84 AW	36790 AAW	IABLS	10//99-12//99
	Kansas	S	14.06 MW	14.01 AW	29130 AAW	KSBLS	10//99-12//99
	Topeka MSA, KS	S	13.83 MW	12.70 AW	28780 AAW	KSBLS	10//99-12//99
	Wichita MSA, KS	S	13.49 MW	13.70 AW	28060 AAW	KSBLS	10//99-12//99
	Kentucky	S	14.4 MW	14.56 AW	30280 AAW	KYBLS	10//99-12//99
	Lexington MSA, KY	S	12.75 MW	12.53 AW	26520 AAW	KYBLS	10//99-12//99
	Louisville MSA, KY-IN	S	15.29 MW	15.31 AW	31800 AAW	KYBLS	10//99-12//99
	Owensboro MSA, KY	S	11.68 MW	11.81 AW	24300 AAW	KYBLS	10//99-12//99
	Louisiana	S	14.08 MW	14.09 AW	29300 AAW	LABLS	10//99-12//99
	Alexandria MSA, LA	S	9.98 MW	9.79 AW	20760 AAW	LABLS	10//99-12//99
	Baton Rouge MSA, LA	S	16.33 MW	15.95 AW	33970 AAW	LABLS	10//99-12//99
	Houma MSA, LA	S	13.73 MW	13.96 AW	28550 AAW	LABLS	10//99-12//99
	Lafayette MSA, LA	S	13.59 MW	13.21 AW	28270 AAW	LABLS	10//99-12//99
	Lake Charles MSA, LA	S	14.25 MW	14.92 AW	29640 AAW	LABLS	10//99-12//99
	Monroe MSA, LA	S	16.20 MW	16.12 AW	33690 AAW	LABLS	10//99-12//99
	New Orleans MSA, LA	S	13.75 MW	13.80 AW	28600 AAW	LABLS	10//99-12//99
	Shreveport-Bossier City MSA,						
	LA	S	13.19 MW	13.52 AW	27440 AAW	LABLS	10//99-12//99
	Maine	S	14.46 MW	14.29 AW	29720 AAW	MEBLS	10//99-12//99

Occupation/Type/Industry	Location	Per	Low	Mid	High	Source	Date
Machinist	Maryland	S	14.75 MW	15.51 AW	32250 AAW	MDBLS	10//99-12//99
	Baltimore PMSA, MD	S	14.60 MW	13.97 AW	30380 AAW	MDBLS	10//99-12//99
	Hagerstown PMSA, MD	S	11.42 MW	10.59 AW	23750 AAW	MDBLS	10//99-12//99
	Massachusetts	S	17.09 MW	17.07 AW	35510 AAW	MABLS	10//99-12//99
	Barnstable-Yarmouth MSA, MA	S	15.21 MW	16.46 AW	31640 AAW	MABLS	10//99-12//99
	Boston PMSA, MA-NH	S	17.85 MW	17.98 AW	37130 AAW	MABLS	10//99-12//99
	Brockton PMSA, MA	S	14.22 MW	13.00 AW	29570 AAW	MABLS	10//99-12//99
	Fitchburg-Leominster PMSA, MA	S	18.92 MW	18.65 AW	39360 AAW	MABLS	10//99-12//99
	Lawrence PMSA, MA-NH	S	16.98 MW	17.59 AW	35320 AAW	MABLS	10//99-12//99
	Lowell PMSA, MA-NH	S	13.51 MW	12.20 AW	28110 AAW	MABLS	10//99-12//99
	Pittsfield MSA, MA	S	11.66 MW	11.89 AW	24260 AAW	MABLS	10//99-12//99
	Springfield MSA, MA	S	17.44 MW	15.90 AW	36270 AAW	MABLS	10//99-12//99
	Worcester PMSA, MA-CT	S	16.72 MW	16.99 AW	34790 AAW	MABLS	10//99-12//99
	Michigan	S	13.99 MW	14.70 AW	30580 AAW	MIBLS	10//99-12//99
	Ann Arbor PMSA, MI	S	15.35 MW	14.95 AW	31930 AAW	MIBLS	10//99-12//99
	Benton Harbor MSA, MI	S	14.98 MW	15.38 AW	31170 AAW	MIBLS	10//99-12//99
	Detroit PMSA, MI	S	14.52 MW	13.84 AW	30210 AAW	MIBLS	10//99-12//99
	Flint PMSA, MI	S	18.07 MW	15.74 AW	37590 AAW	MIBLS	10//99-12//99
	Grand Rapids-Muskegon-Holland MSA, MI	S	14.70 MW	14.14 AW	30580 AAW	MIBLS	10//99-12//99
	Jackson MSA, MI	S	15.63 MW	15.91 AW	32510 AAW	MIBLS	10//99-12//99
	Kalamazoo-Battle Creek MSA, MI	S	10.89 MW	10.00 AW	22660 AAW	MIBLS	10//99-12//99
	Lansing-East Lansing MSA, MI	S	15.83 MW	14.99 AW	32930 AAW	MIBLS	10//99-12//99
	Saginaw-Bay City-Midland MSA, MI	S	16.50 MW	14.77 AW	34320 AAW	MIBLS	10//99-12//99
	Minnesota	S	15.19 MW	15.72 AW	32700 AAW	MNBLS	10//99-12//99
	Duluth-Superior MSA, MN-WI	S	14.00 MW	14.31 AW	29110 AAW	MNBLS	10//99-12//99
	Minneapolis-St. Paul MSA, MN-WI	S	16.56 MW	16.10 AW	34440 AAW	MNBLS	10//99-12//99
	Rochester MSA, MN	S	11.69 MW	11.84 AW	24310 AAW	MNBLS	10//99-12//99
	St. Cloud MSA, MN	S	13.44 MW	12.29 AW	27950 AAW	MNBLS	10//99-12//99
	Mississippi	S	12 MW	12.03 AW	25020 AAW	MSBLS	10//99-12//99
	Jackson MSA, MS	S	12.23 MW	12.53 AW	25430 AAW	MSBLS	10//99-12//99
	Missouri	S	14.41 MW	14.98 AW	31160 AAW	MOBLS	10//99-12//99
	Joplin MSA, MO	S	12.02 MW	12.09 AW	25010 AAW	MOBLS	10//99-12//99
	Kansas City MSA, MO-KS	S	15.11 MW	15.11 AW	31430 AAW	MOBLS	10//99-12//99
	St. Joseph MSA, MO	S	11.63 MW	12.21 AW	24190 AAW	MOBLS	10//99-12//99
	St. Louis MSA, MO-IL	S	16.87 MW	15.96 AW	35090 AAW	MOBLS	10//99-12//99
	Springfield MSA, MO	S	13.00 MW	13.31 AW	27030 AAW	MOBLS	10//99-12//99
	Montana	S	14.49 MW	14.11 AW	29350 AAW	MTBLS	10//99-12//99
	Billings MSA, MT	S	15.05 MW	15.29 AW	31300 AAW	MTBLS	10//99-12//99
	Missoula MSA, MT	S	12.58 MW	12.94 AW	26160 AAW	MTBLS	10//99-12//99
	Nebraska	S	11.29 MW	11.61 AW	24150 AAW	NEBLS	10//99-12//99
	Lincoln MSA, NE	S	13.04 MW	13.55 AW	27130 AAW	NEBLS	10//99-12//99
	Nevada	S	15.16 MW	16.76 AW	34860 AAW	NVBLS	10//99-12//99
	Las Vegas MSA, NV-AZ	S	14.30 MW	14.16 AW	29750 AAW	NVBLS	10//99-12//99
	New Hampshire	S	14.42 MW	14.48 AW	30110 AAW	NHBLS	10//99-12//99
	Manchester PMSA, NH	S	14.93 MW	14.46 AW	31050 AAW	NHBLS	10//99-12//99
	Nashua PMSA, NH	S	14.58 MW	14.73 AW	30320 AAW	NHBLS	10//99-12//99
	New Jersey	S	15.67 MW	16.05 AW	33390 AAW	NJBLS	10//99-12//99
	Atlantic-Cape May PMSA, NJ	S	17.42 MW	13.30 AW	36230 AAW	NJBLS	10//99-12//99
	Bergen-Passaic PMSA, NJ	S	16.28 MW	15.94 AW	33860 AAW	NJBLS	10//99-12//99
	Jersey City PMSA, NJ	S	18.20 MW	16.88 AW	37850 AAW	NJBLS	10//99-12//99
	Middlesex-Somerset-Hunterdon PMSA, NJ	S	16.07 MW	15.70 AW	33420 AAW	NJBLS	10//99-12//99
	Monmouth-Ocean PMSA, NJ	S	17.19 MW	16.78 AW	35760 AAW	NJBLS	10//99-12//99
	Newark PMSA, NJ	S	15.18 MW	14.56 AW	31580 AAW	NJBLS	10//99-12//99
	Trenton PMSA, NJ	S	15.38 MW	15.12 AW	32000 AAW	NJBLS	10//99-12//99
	Vineland-Millville-Bridgeton PMSA, NJ	S	17.39 MW	18.32 AW	36170 AAW	NJBLS	10//99-12//99
	New Mexico	S	13.13 MW	13.75 AW	28610 AAW	NMBLS	10//99-12//99
	Albuquerque MSA, NM	S	13.70 MW	13.73 AW	28490 AAW	NMBLS	10//99-12//99
	Las Cruces MSA, NM	S	20.50 MW	20.09 AW	42640 AAW	NMBLS	10//99-12//99
	New York	S	13.93 MW	14.50 AW	30150 AAW	NYBLS	10//99-12//99
	Albany-Schenectady-Troy MSA, NY	S	18.55 MW	17.85 AW	38590 AAW	NYBLS	10//99-12//99
	Binghamton MSA, NY	S	10.14 MW	9.55 AW	21090 AAW	NYBLS	10//99-12//99
	Buffalo-Niagara Falls MSA, NY	S	15.22 MW	14.52 AW	31660 AAW	NYBLS	10//99-12//99

AAW	Average annual wage	AOH	Average offered, high	ASH	Average starting, high
AE	Average entry wage	AOL	Average offered, low	ASL	Average starting, low
AEX	Average experienced wage	APH	Average pay, high range	AW	Average wage paid
AO	Average offered	APL	Average pay, low range	FQ	First quartile wage

H	Hourly	M	Monthly
HI	Highest wage paid	MTC	Median total compensation
HR	High end range	MW	Median wage paid
LR	Low end range	SQ	Second quartile wage

S	Special: hourly and annual
TQ	Third quartile wage
W	Weekly
Y	Yearly

Occupation/Type/Industry	Location	Per	Low	Mid	High	Source	Date
Machinist	Dutchess County PMSA, NY	S	12.82 MW	12.43 AW	26670 AAW	NYBLS	10//99-12//99
	Elmira MSA, NY	S	14.38 MW	15.85 AW	29900 AAW	NYBLS	10//99-12//99
	Glens Falls MSA, NY	S	16.21 MW	15.99 AW	33720 AAW	NYBLS	10//99-12//99
	Jamestown MSA, NY	S	9.91 MW	9.99 AW	20600 AAW	NYBLS	10//99-12//99
	Nassau-Suffolk PMSA, NY	S	15.22 MW	15.08 AW	31650 AAW	NYBLS	10//99-12//99
	New York PMSA, NY	S	14.95 MW	14.47 AW	31090 AAW	NYBLS	10//99-12//99
	Newburgh PMSA, NY-PA	S	13.18 MW	13.54 AW	27410 AAW	NYBLS	10//99-12//99
	Rochester MSA, NY	S	13.41 MW	13.15 AW	27890 AAW	NYBLS	10//99-12//99
	Syracuse MSA, NY	S	14.60 MW	14.01 AW	30370 AAW	NYBLS	10//99-12//99
	Utica-Rome MSA, NY	S	12.16 MW	13.53 AW	25280 AAW	NYBLS	10//99-12//99
	North Carolina	S	14.04 MW	14.20 AW	29540 AAW	NCBLS	10//99-12//99
	Asheville MSA, NC	S	14.42 MW	12.51 AW	30000 AAW	NCBLS	10//99-12//99
	Charlotte-Gastonia-Rock Hill MSA, NC-SC	S	14.85 MW	14.78 AW	30890 AAW	NCBLS	10//99-12//99
	Fayetteville MSA, NC	S	12.93 MW	12.36 AW	26890 AAW	NCBLS	10//99-12//99
	Greensboro--Winston-Salem--High Point MSA, NC	S	12.72 MW	12.27 AW	26460 AAW	NCBLS	10//99-12//99
	Raleigh-Durham-Chapel Hill MSA, NC	S	15.33 MW	15.16 AW	31890 AAW	NCBLS	10//99-12//99
	Rocky Mount MSA, NC	S	14.27 MW	14.21 AW	29680 AAW	NCBLS	10//99-12//99
	Wilmington MSA, NC	S	14.07 MW	13.55 AW	29270 AAW	NCBLS	10//99-12//99
	North Dakota	S	13.31 MW	12.98 AW	27010 AAW	NDBLS	10//99-12//99
	Bismarck MSA, ND	S	11.96 MW	11.65 AW	24880 AAW	NDBLS	10//99-12//99
	Fargo-Moorhead MSA, ND-MN	S	13.67 MW	14.04 AW	28430 AAW	NDBLS	10//99-12//99
	Grand Forks MSA, ND-MN	S	11.36 MW	11.49 AW	23630 AAW	NDBLS	10//99-12//99
	Ohio	S	13.79 MW	14.22 AW	29580 AAW	OHBLS	10//99-12//99
	Akron PMSA, OH	S	13.93 MW	13.82 AW	28970 AAW	OHBLS	10//99-12//99
	Canton-Massillon MSA, OH	S	12.27 MW	11.88 AW	25520 AAW	OHBLS	10//99-12//99
	Cincinnati PMSA, OH-KY-IN	S	13.57 MW	13.10 AW	28220 AAW	OHBLS	10//99-12//99
	Cleveland-Lorain-Elyria PMSA, OH	S	14.76 MW	14.64 AW	30700 AAW	OHBLS	10//99-12//99
	Columbus MSA, OH	S	13.96 MW	14.16 AW	29030 AAW	OHBLS	10//99-12//99
	Dayton-Springfield MSA, OH	S	14.44 MW	13.75 AW	30030 AAW	OHBLS	10//99-12//99
	Hamilton-Middletown PMSA, OH	S	16.40 MW	15.51 AW	34120 AAW	OHBLS	10//99-12//99
	Lima MSA, OH	S	13.34 MW	13.00 AW	27750 AAW	OHBLS	10//99-12//99
	Mansfield MSA, OH	S	17.89 MW	13.26 AW	37210 AAW	OHBLS	10//99-12//99
	Steubenville-Weirton MSA, OH-WV	S	17.74 MW	18.03 AW	36900 AAW	OHBLS	10//99-12//99
	Youngstown-Warren MSA, OH	S	14.04 MW	13.03 AW	29200 AAW	OHBLS	10//99-12//99
	Oklahoma	S	13.69 MW	13.79 AW	28680 AAW	OKBLS	10//99-12//99
	Enid MSA, OK	S	10.89 MW	10.19 AW	22660 AAW	OKBLS	10//99-12//99
	Oklahoma City MSA, OK	S	14.52 MW	14.15 AW	30200 AAW	OKBLS	10//99-12//99
	Tulsa MSA, OK	S	14.51 MW	14.46 AW	30170 AAW	OKBLS	10//99-12//99
	Oregon	S	16.44 MW	16.55 AW	34420 AAW	ORBLS	10//99-12//99
	Corvallis MSA, OR	S	15.09 MW	15.26 AW	31400 AAW	ORBLS	10//99-12//99
	Eugene-Springfield MSA, OR	S	12.52 MW	11.60 AW	26040 AAW	ORBLS	10//99-12//99
	Medford-Ashland MSA, OR	S	13.77 MW	12.84 AW	28640 AAW	ORBLS	10//99-12//99
	Portland-Vancouver PMSA, OR-WA	S	17.04 MW	17.33 AW	35450 AAW	ORBLS	10//99-12//99
	Salem PMSA, OR	S	15.36 MW	15.28 AW	31950 AAW	ORBLS	10//99-12//99
	Pennsylvania	S	14.31 MW	14.23 AW	29600 AAW	PABLS	10//99-12//99
	Allentown-Bethlehem-Easton MSA, PA	S	13.75 MW	13.13 AW	28610 AAW	PABLS	10//99-12//99
	Altoona MSA, PA	S	13.19 MW	12.12 AW	27440 AAW	PABLS	10//99-12//99
	Erie MSA, PA	S	12.95 MW	12.89 AW	26930 AAW	PABLS	10//99-12//99
	Harrisburg-Lebanon-Carlisle MSA, PA	S	11.56 MW	8.46 AW	24050 AAW	PABLS	10//99-12//99
	Johnstown MSA, PA	S	12.22 MW	12.78 AW	25410 AAW	PABLS	10//99-12//99
	Lancaster MSA, PA	S	13.29 MW	13.04 AW	27640 AAW	PABLS	10//99-12//99
	Philadelphia PMSA, PA-NJ	S	15.07 MW	14.95 AW	31350 AAW	PABLS	10//99-12//99
	Pittsburgh MSA, PA	S	14.30 MW	14.47 AW	29740 AAW	PABLS	10//99-12//99
	Reading MSA, PA	S	15.29 MW	15.06 AW	31810 AAW	PABLS	10//99-12//99
	Scranton--Wilkes-Barre--Hazleton MSA, PA	S	13.75 MW	14.52 AW	28590 AAW	PABLS	10//99-12//99
	Sharon MSA, PA	S	16.29 MW	15.31 AW	33880 AAW	PABLS	10//99-12//99
	State College MSA, PA	S	12.19 MW	12.58 AW	25340 AAW	PABLS	10//99-12//99
	Williamsport MSA, PA	S	13.88 MW	14.25 AW	28870 AAW	PABLS	10//99-12//99
	York MSA, PA	S	13.20 MW	13.58 AW	27460 AAW	PABLS	10//99-12//99
	Rhode Island	S	9.68 MW	11.49 AW	23900 AAW	RIBLS	10//99-12//99

AAW Average annual wage	AOH Average offered, high	ASH Average starting, high	H Hourly	M Monthly	S Special: hourly and annual
AE Average entry wage	AOL Average offered, low	ASL Average starting, low	HI Highest wage paid	MTC Median total compensation	TQ Third quartile wage
AEX Average experienced wage	APH Average pay, high range	AW Average wage paid	HR High end range	MW Median wage paid	W Weekly
AO Average offered	APL Average pay, low range	FQ First quartile wage	LR Low end range	SQ Second quartile wage	Y Yearly

Occupation/Type/Industry	Location	Per	Low	Mid	High	Source	Date
Machinist	Providence-Fall River-						
	Warwick MSA, RI-MA	S	11.51 mw	9.92 aw	23930 aaw	RIBLS	10//99-12//99
	South Carolina	S	15.03 mw	14.91 aw	31010 aaw	SCBLS	10//99-12//99
	Charleston-North Charleston						
	MSA, SC	S	13.42 mw	13.44 aw	27920 aaw	SCBLS	10//99-12//99
	Columbia MSA, SC	S	11.54 mw	9.10 aw	24010 aaw	SCBLS	10//99-12//99
	Florence MSA, SC	S	10.89 mw	10.14 aw	22660 aaw	SCBLS	10//99-12//99
	Greenville-Spartanburg-						
	Anderson MSA, SC	S	15.86 mw	15.98 aw	33000 aaw	SCBLS	10//99-12//99
	Myrtle Beach MSA, SC	S	10.86 mw	10.96 aw	22580 aaw	SCBLS	10//99-12//99
	Sumter MSA, SC	S	9.57 mw	7.88 aw	19910 aaw	SCBLS	10//99-12//99
	South Dakota	S	11.01 mw	11.23 aw	23360 aaw	SDBLS	10//99-12//99
	Rapid City MSA, SD	S	11.24 mw	11.02 aw	23390 aaw	SDBLS	10//99-12//99
	Sioux Falls MSA, SD	S	12.66 mw	13.11 aw	26330 aaw	SDBLS	10//99-12//99
	Tennessee	S	14.09 mw	15.01 aw	31220 aaw	TNBLS	10//99-12//99
	Chattanooga MSA, TN-GA	S	15.04 mw	14.48 aw	31290 aaw	TNBLS	10//99-12//99
	Clarksville-Hopkinsville MSA,						
	TN-KY	S	13.53 mw	13.99 aw	28130 aaw	TNBLS	10//99-12//99
	Jackson MSA, TN	S	13.89 mw	14.30 aw	28890 aaw	TNBLS	10//99-12//99
	Johnson City-Kingsport-Bristol						
	MSA, TN-VA	S	13.04 mw	13.19 aw	27120 aaw	TNBLS	10//99-12//99
	Knoxville MSA, TN	S	12.22 mw	11.03 aw	25410 aaw	TNBLS	10//99-12//99
	Memphis MSA, TN-AR-MS	S	14.70 mw	13.69 aw	30580 aaw	MSBLS	10//99-12//99
	Nashville MSA, TN	S	16.78 mw	17.11 aw	34890 aaw	TNBLS	10//99-12//99
	Texas	S	12.84 mw	13.36 aw	27780 aaw	TXBLS	10//99-12//99
	Abilene MSA, TX	S	11.00 mw	10.76 aw	22890 aaw	TXBLS	10//99-12//99
	Amarillo MSA, TX	S	11.92 mw	10.79 aw	24790 aaw	TXBLS	10//99-12//99
	Austin-San Marcos MSA, TX	S	13.88 mw	14.11 aw	28880 aaw	TXBLS	10//99-12//99
	Beaumont-Port Arthur MSA,						
	TX	S	14.56 mw	14.41 aw	30280 aaw	TXBLS	10//99-12//99
	Brazoria PMSA, TX	S	12.23 mw	12.20 aw	25450 aaw	TXBLS	10//99-12//99
	Brownsville-Harlingen-San						
	Benito MSA, TX	S	7.96 mw	7.58 aw	16550 aaw	TXBLS	10//99-12//99
	Bryan-College Station MSA,						
	TX	S	13.15 mw	13.94 aw	27350 aaw	TXBLS	10//99-12//99
	Corpus Christi MSA, TX	S	16.14 mw	16.01 aw	33570 aaw	TXBLS	10//99-12//99
	Dallas PMSA, TX	S	12.58 mw	11.80 aw	26160 aaw	TXBLS	10//99-12//99
	El Paso MSA, TX	S	10.39 mw	9.26 aw	21620 aaw	TXBLS	10//99-12//99
	Fort Worth-Arlington PMSA,						
	TX	S	13.80 mw	13.59 aw	28700 aaw	TXBLS	10//99-12//99
	Galveston-Texas City PMSA,						
	TX	S	16.94 mw	16.86 aw	35220 aaw	TXBLS	10//99-12//99
	Houston PMSA, TX	S	15.12 mw	15.37 aw	31440 aaw	TXBLS	10//99-12//99
	Killeen-Temple MSA, TX	S	12.20 mw	11.34 aw	25370 aaw	TXBLS	10//99-12//99
	Longview-Marshall MSA, TX	S	11.87 mw	11.65 aw	24700 aaw	TXBLS	10//99-12//99
	Lubbock MSA, TX	S	11.21 mw	10.40 aw	23320 aaw	TXBLS	10//99-12//99
	McAllen-Edinburg-Mission						
	MSA, TX	S	9.61 mw	8.82 aw	19990 aaw	TXBLS	10//99-12//99
	Odessa-Midland MSA, TX	S	11.72 mw	11.08 aw	24370 aaw	TXBLS	10//99-12//99
	San Angelo MSA, TX	S	10.17 mw	11.19 aw	21150 aaw	TXBLS	10//99-12//99
	San Antonio MSA, TX	S	10.46 mw	9.96 aw	21750 aaw	TXBLS	10//99-12//99
	Sherman-Denison MSA, TX	S	13.08 mw	12.79 aw	27200 aaw	TXBLS	10//99-12//99
	Tyler MSA, TX	S	14.96 mw	15.10 aw	31120 aaw	TXBLS	10//99-12//99
	Waco MSA, TX	S	14.65 mw	11.28 aw	30460 aaw	TXBLS	10//99-12//99
	Wichita Falls MSA, TX	S	13.87 mw	13.92 aw	28850 aaw	TXBLS	10//99-12//99
	Utah	S	14.68 mw	15.26 aw	31740 aaw	UTBLS	10//99-12//99
	Provo-Orem MSA, UT	S	16.62 mw	17.06 aw	34580 aaw	UTBLS	10//99-12//99
	Salt Lake City-Ogden MSA,						
	UT	S	15.51 mw	14.89 aw	32270 aaw	UTBLS	10//99-12//99
	Vermont	S	12.77 mw	13.01 aw	27060 aaw	VTBLS	10//99-12//99
	Burlington MSA, VT	S	13.29 mw	13.15 aw	27640 aaw	VTBLS	10//99-12//99
	Virginia	S	15.14 mw	15.06 aw	31330 aaw	VABLS	10//99-12//99
	Danville MSA, VA	S	11.67 mw	12.41 aw	24280 aaw	VABLS	10//99-12//99
	Lynchburg MSA, VA	S	18.16 mw	18.78 aw	37770 aaw	VABLS	10//99-12//99
	Norfolk-Virginia Beach-						
	Newport News MSA, VA-						
	NC	S	14.73 mw	14.83 aw	30640 aaw	VABLS	10//99-12//99
	Richmond-Petersburg MSA,						
	VA	S	17.77 mw	18.01 aw	36960 aaw	VABLS	10//99-12//99
	Roanoke MSA, VA	S	13.61 mw	13.72 aw	28300 aaw	VABLS	10//99-12//99
	Washington	S	18.62 mw	18.51 aw	38500 aaw	WABLS	10//99-12//99
	Bellingham MSA, WA	S	16.24 mw	15.15 aw	33780 aaw	WABLS	10//99-12//99

AAW Average annual wage	**AOH** Average offered, high	**ASH** Average starting, high	**H** Hourly	**M** Monthly	**S** Special: hourly and annual
AE Average entry wage	**AOL** Average offered, low	**ASL** Average starting, low	**HI** Highest wage paid	**MTC** Median total compensation	**TQ** Third quartile wage
AEX Average experienced wage	**APH** Average pay, high range	**AW** Average wage paid	**HR** High end range	**MW** Median wage paid	**W** Weekly
AO Average offered	**APL** Average pay, low range	**FQ** First quartile wage	**LR** Low end range	**SQ** Second quartile wage	**Y** Yearly

Occupation/Type/Industry	Location	Per	Low	Mid	High	Source	Date
Machinist	Richland-Kennewick-Pasco MSA, WA	S	14.81 MW	15.14 AW	30810 AAW	WABLS	10//99-12//99
	Seattle-Bellevue-Everett PMSA, WA	S	19.70 MW	20.05 AW	40980 AAW	WABLS	10//99-12//99
	Spokane MSA, WA	S	13.75 MW	14.00 AW	28590 AAW	WABLS	10//99-12//99
	Tacoma PMSA, WA	S	17.52 MW	17.35 AW	36430 AAW	WABLS	10//99-12//99
	Yakima MSA, WA	S	14.91 MW	15.06 AW	31000 AAW	WABLS	10//99-12//99
	West Virginia	S	11.8 MW	12.36 AW	25700 AAW	WVBLS	10//99-12//99
	Charleston MSA, WV	S	10.40 MW	9.73 AW	21630 AAW	WVBLS	10//99-12//99
	Huntington-Ashland MSA, WV-KY-OH	S	14.29 MW	12.65 AW	29730 AAW	WVBLS	10//99-12//99
	Parkersburg-Marietta MSA, WV-OH	S	9.84 MW	9.72 AW	20480 AAW	WVBLS	10//99-12//99
	Wheeling MSA, WV-OH	S	14.88 MW	13.36 AW	30940 AAW	WVBLS	10//99-12//99
	Wisconsin	S	14.76 MW	15.06 AW	31320 AAW	WIBLS	10//99-12//99
	Appleton-Oshkosh-Neenah MSA, WI	S	15.55 MW	15.53 AW	32350 AAW	WIBLS	10//99-12//99
	Eau Claire MSA, WI	S	13.16 MW	12.68 AW	27370 AAW	WIBLS	10//99-12//99
	Janesville-Beloit MSA, WI	S	15.47 MW	15.37 AW	32170 AAW	WIBLS	10//99-12//99
	Kenosha PMSA, WI	S	13.39 MW	13.93 AW	27850 AAW	WIBLS	10//99-12//99
	La Crosse MSA, WI-MN	S	13.84 MW	13.77 AW	28790 AAW	WIBLS	10//99-12//99
	Madison MSA, WI	S	14.28 MW	14.25 AW	29700 AAW	WIBLS	10//99-12//99
	Milwaukee-Waukesha PMSA, WI	S	14.88 MW	14.44 AW	30960 AAW	WIBLS	10//99-12//99
	Racine PMSA, WI	S	12.21 MW	12.19 AW	25410 AAW	WIBLS	10//99-12//99
	Sheboygan MSA, WI	S	12.68 MW	13.91 AW	26380 AAW	WIBLS	10//99-12//99
	Wausau MSA, WI	S	12.36 MW	11.98 AW	25700 AAW	WIBLS	10//99-12//99
	Wyoming	S	12.9 MW	13.60 AW	28290 AAW	WYBLS	10//99-12//99
	Casper MSA, WY	S	10.32 MW	9.32 AW	21470 AAW	WYBLS	10//99-12//99
	Puerto Rico	S	8.08 MW	9.18 AW	19100 AAW	PRBLS	10//99-12//99
	Mayaguez MSA, PR	S	8.18 MW	8.33 AW	17010 AAW	PRBLS	10//99-12//99
	San Juan-Bayamon PMSA, PR	S	9.58 MW	8.32 AW	19920 AAW	PRBLS	10//99-12//99
	Guam	S	11.27 MW	12.28 AW	25550 AAW	GUBLS	10//99-12//99
Automobile Industry	Fort Wayne, IN	Y		38365 AW		SITSEL	2000
Automobile Industry	Grand Rapids, MI	Y		41781 AW		SITSEL	2000
Automobile Industry	St. Louis, MO	Y		39753 AW		SITSEL	2000
Automobile Industry	Greenville, SC	Y		36063 AW		SITSEL	2000
Maid and Housekeeping Cleaner	Alabama	S	6.09 MW	6.35 AW	13220 AAW	ALBLS	10//99-12//99
	Anniston MSA, AL	S	6.35 MW	6.07 AW	13200 AAW	ALBLS	10//99-12//99
	Auburn-Opelika MSA, AL	S	5.98 MW	5.99 AW	12440 AAW	ALBLS	10//99-12//99
	Birmingham MSA, AL	S	6.44 MW	6.08 AW	13400 AAW	ALBLS	10//99-12//99
	Decatur MSA, AL	S	6.34 MW	6.12 AW	13190 AAW	ALBLS	10//99-12//99
	Dothan MSA, AL	S	6.20 MW	6.08 AW	12900 AAW	ALBLS	10//99-12//99
	Florence MSA, AL	S	6.36 MW	6.12 AW	13230 AAW	ALBLS	10//99-12//99
	Gadsden MSA, AL	S	7.25 MW	6.50 AW	15070 AAW	ALBLS	10//99-12//99
	Huntsville MSA, AL	S	6.06 MW	6.00 AW	12610 AAW	ALBLS	10//99-12//99
	Mobile MSA, AL	S	6.35 MW	6.14 AW	13220 AAW	ALBLS	10//99-12//99
	Montgomery MSA, AL	S	6.22 MW	6.05 AW	12930 AAW	ALBLS	10//99-12//99
	Tuscaloosa MSA, AL	S	6.42 MW	6.25 AW	13350 AAW	ALBLS	10//99-12//99
	Alaska	S	8.63 MW	9.09 AW	18900 AAW	AKBLS	10//99-12//99
	Anchorage MSA, AK	S	9.39 MW	9.25 AW	19530 AAW	AKBLS	10//99-12//99
	Arizona	S	6.51 MW	6.66 AW	13850 AAW	AZBLS	10//99-12//99
	Flagstaff MSA, AZ-UT	S	6.37 MW	6.11 AW	13260 AAW	AZBLS	10//99-12//99
	Phoenix-Mesa MSA, AZ	S	6.85 MW	6.77 AW	14250 AAW	AZBLS	10//99-12//99
	Tucson MSA, AZ	S	6.40 MW	6.24 AW	13300 AAW	AZBLS	10//99-12//99
	Yuma MSA, AZ	S	6.18 MW	6.15 AW	12860 AAW	AZBLS	10//99-12//99
	Arkansas	S	6.13 MW	6.30 AW	13090 AAW	ARBLS	10//99-12//99
	Fayetteville-Springdale-Rogers MSA, AR	S	6.39 MW	6.27 AW	13290 AAW	ARBLS	10//99-12//99
	Fort Smith MSA, AR-OK	S	6.35 MW	6.23 AW	13210 AAW	ARBLS	10//99-12//99
	Jonesboro MSA, AR	S	6.97 MW	6.40 AW	14500 AAW	ARBLS	10//99-12//99
	Little Rock-North Little Rock MSA, AR	S	6.44 MW	6.31 AW	13390 AAW	ARBLS	10//99-12//99
	Pine Bluff MSA, AR	S	5.84 MW	5.99 AW	12150 AAW	ARBLS	10//99-12//99
	California	S	7.26 MW	7.82 AW	16260 AAW	CABLS	10//99-12//99
	Bakersfield MSA, CA	S	6.82 MW	6.47 AW	14190 AAW	CABLS	10//99-12//99
	Chico-Paradise MSA, CA	S	7.13 MW	6.94 AW	14840 AAW	CABLS	10//99-12//99
	Fresno MSA, CA	S	7.06 MW	6.78 AW	14690 AAW	CABLS	10//99-12//99
	Los Angeles-Long Beach PMSA, CA	S	7.80 MW	7.35 AW	16210 AAW	CABLS	10//99-12//99
	Merced MSA, CA	S	7.02 MW	6.70 AW	14590 AAW	CABLS	10//99-12//99
	Modesto MSA, CA	S	6.99 MW	6.24 AW	14540 AAW	CABLS	10//99-12//99

AAW	Average annual wage	AOH	Average offered, high	ASH	Average starting, high	H	Hourly	M	Monthly	S	Special: hourly and annual
AE	Average entry wage	AOL	Average offered, low	ASL	Average starting, low	HI	Highest wage paid	MTC	Median total compensation	TQ	Third quartile wage
AEX	Average experienced wage	APH	Average pay, high range	AW	Average wage paid	HR	High end range	MW	Median wage paid	W	Weekly
AO	Average offered	APL	Average pay, low range	FQ	First quartile wage	LR	Low end range	SQ	Second quartile wage	Y	Yearly

Maid and Housekeeping Cleaner

Occupation/Type/Industry	Location	Per	Low	Mid	High	Source	Date
Maid and Housekeeping Cleaner	Oakland PMSA, CA	S	8.37 MW	7.99 AW	17420 AAW	CABLS	10//99-12//99
	Orange County PMSA, CA	S	7.28 MW	7.04 AW	15140 AAW	CABLS	10//99-12//99
	Redding MSA, CA	S	6.79 MW	6.50 AW	14110 AAW	CABLS	10//99-12//99
	Riverside-San Bernardino PMSA, CA	S	7.21 MW	6.61 AW	14990 AAW	CABLS	10//99-12//99
	Sacramento PMSA, CA	S	7.37 MW	6.85 AW	15320 AAW	CABLS	10//99-12//99
	Salinas MSA, CA	S	7.70 MW	7.24 AW	16020 AAW	CABLS	10//99-12//99
	San Diego MSA, CA	S	7.43 MW	7.03 AW	15450 AAW	CABLS	10//99-12//99
	San Francisco PMSA, CA	S	9.90 MW	10.08 AW	20580 AAW	CABLS	10//99-12//99
	San Jose PMSA, CA	S	8.57 MW	7.85 AW	17820 AAW	CABLS	10//99-12//99
	San Luis Obispo-Atascadero-Paso Robles MSA, CA	S	7.12 MW	6.63 AW	14810 AAW	CABLS	10//99-12//99
	Santa Barbara-Santa Maria-Lompoc MSA, CA	S	6.89 MW	6.55 AW	14330 AAW	CABLS	10//99-12//99
	Santa Cruz-Watsonville PMSA, CA	S	7.86 MW	7.40 AW	16340 AAW	CABLS	10//99-12//99
	Santa Rosa PMSA, CA	S	7.56 MW	7.31 AW	15720 AAW	CABLS	10//99-12//99
	Stockton-Lodi MSA, CA	S	7.74 MW	7.37 AW	16100 AAW	CABLS	10//99-12//99
	Vallejo-Fairfield-Napa PMSA, CA	S	8.77 MW	8.02 AW	18240 AAW	CABLS	10//99-12//99
	Ventura PMSA, CA	S	7.43 MW	6.82 AW	15450 AAW	CABLS	10//99-12//99
	Visalia-Tulare-Porterville MSA, CA	S	7.26 MW	6.57 AW	15110 AAW	CABLS	10//99-12//99
	Yolo PMSA, CA	S	7.46 MW	7.15 AW	15510 AAW	CABLS	10//99-12//99
	Yuba City MSA, CA	S	7.34 MW	7.28 AW	15260 AAW	CABLS	10//99-12//99
	Colorado	S	7.22 MW	7.42 AW	15440 AAW	COBLS	10//99-12//99
	Boulder-Longmont PMSA, CO	S	7.55 MW	7.61 AW	15690 AAW	COBLS	10//99-12//99
	Colorado Springs MSA, CO	S	6.98 MW	6.88 AW	14520 AAW	COBLS	10//99-12//99
	Denver PMSA, CO	S	7.12 MW	7.06 AW	14810 AAW	COBLS	10//99-12//99
	Fort Collins-Loveland MSA, CO	S	7.10 MW	6.94 AW	14760 AAW	COBLS	10//99-12//99
	Grand Junction MSA, CO	S	6.59 MW	6.28 AW	13710 AAW	COBLS	10//99-12//99
	Greeley PMSA, CO	S	6.48 MW	6.31 AW	13490 AAW	COBLS	10//99-12//99
	Pueblo MSA, CO	S	6.47 MW	6.27 AW	13450 AAW	COBLS	10//99-12//99
	Connecticut	S	8.32 MW	8.69 AW	18070 AAW	CTBLS	10//99-12//99
	Bridgeport PMSA, CT	S	9.45 MW	9.21 AW	19650 AAW	CTBLS	10//99-12//99
	Danbury PMSA, CT	S	9.19 MW	8.67 AW	19120 AAW	CTBLS	10//99-12//99
	Hartford MSA, CT	S	8.99 MW	8.65 AW	18700 AAW	CTBLS	10//99-12//99
	New Haven-Meriden PMSA, CT	S	8.13 MW	7.80 AW	16920 AAW	CTBLS	10//99-12//99
	New London-Norwich MSA, CT-RI	S	7.95 MW	7.78 AW	16540 AAW	CTBLS	10//99-12//99
	Stamford-Norwalk PMSA, CT	S	8.71 MW	8.51 AW	18120 AAW	CTBLS	10//99-12//99
	Waterbury PMSA, CT	S	9.04 MW	8.63 AW	18800 AAW	CTBLS	10//99-12//99
	Delaware	S	7.27 MW	7.45 AW	15500 AAW	DEBLS	10//99-12//99
	Dover MSA, DE	S	6.86 MW	6.47 AW	14280 AAW	DEBLS	10//99-12//99
	Wilmington-Newark PMSA, DE-MD	S	7.59 MW	7.41 AW	15790 AAW	DEBLS	10//99-12//99
	District of Columbia	S	10.76 MW	10.33 AW	21490 AAW	DCBLS	10//99-12//99
	Washington PMSA, DC-MD-VA-WV	S	8.55 MW	8.04 AW	17790 AAW	DCBLS	10//99-12//99
	Florida	S	6.95 MW	7.07 AW	14710 AAW	FLBLS	10//99-12//99
	Daytona Beach MSA, FL	S	6.78 MW	6.48 AW	14110 AAW	FLBLS	10//99-12//99
	Fort Lauderdale PMSA, FL	S	7.41 MW	7.24 AW	15400 AAW	FLBLS	10//99-12//99
	Fort Myers-Cape Coral MSA, FL	S	7.03 MW	7.03 AW	14620 AAW	FLBLS	10//99-12//99
	Fort Pierce-Port St. Lucie MSA, FL	S	7.34 MW	7.35 AW	15260 AAW	FLBLS	10//99-12//99
	Fort Walton Beach MSA, FL	S	6.93 MW	7.01 AW	14420 AAW	FLBLS	10//99-12//99
	Gainesville MSA, FL	S	6.62 MW	6.45 AW	13780 AAW	FLBLS	10//99-12//99
	Jacksonville MSA, FL	S	6.97 MW	6.99 AW	14500 AAW	FLBLS	10//99-12//99
	Lakeland-Winter Haven MSA, FL	S	6.39 MW	6.19 AW	13300 AAW	FLBLS	10//99-12//99
	Melbourne-Titusville-Palm Bay MSA, FL	S	6.97 MW	6.80 AW	14490 AAW	FLBLS	10//99-12//99
	Miami PMSA, FL	S	7.06 MW	6.95 AW	14680 AAW	FLBLS	10//99-12//99
	Naples MSA, FL	S	7.18 MW	6.99 AW	14930 AAW	FLBLS	10//99-12//99
	Ocala MSA, FL	S	6.28 MW	6.29 AW	13070 AAW	FLBLS	10//99-12//99
	Orlando MSA, FL	S	7.21 MW	7.16 AW	15000 AAW	FLBLS	10//99-12//99
	Panama City MSA, FL	S	6.75 MW	6.56 AW	14030 AAW	FLBLS	10//99-12//99
	Pensacola MSA, FL	S	6.36 MW	6.14 AW	13230 AAW	FLBLS	10//99-12//99
	Punta Gorda MSA, FL	S	6.76 MW	6.46 AW	14060 AAW	FLBLS	10//99-12//99

AAW Average annual wage	AOH Average offered, high	ASH Average starting, high	H Hourly	M Monthly	S Special: hourly and annual
AE Average entry wage	AOL Average offered, low	ASL Average starting, low	HI Highest wage paid	MTC Median total compensation	TQ Third quartile wage
AEX Average experienced wage	APH Average pay, high range	AW Average wage paid	HR High end range	MW Median wage paid	W Weekly
AO Average offered	APL Average pay, low range	FQ First quartile wage	LR Low end range	SQ Second quartile wage	Y Yearly

Maid and Housekeeping Cleaner

Occupation/Type/Industry	Location	Per	Low	Mid	High	Source	Date
Maid and Housekeeping Cleaner	Sarasota-Bradenton MSA, FL	S	7.62 MW	7.59 AW	15850 AAW	FLBLS	10//99-12//99
	Tallahassee MSA, FL	S	6.40 MW	6.31 AW	13310 AAW	FLBLS	10//99-12//99
	Tampa-St. Petersburg-Clearwater MSA, FL	S	6.95 MW	6.93 AW	14460 AAW	FLBLS	10//99-12//99
	West Palm Beach-Boca Raton MSA, FL	S	7.56 MW	7.52 AW	15720 AAW	FLBLS	10//99-12//99
	Georgia	S	6.61 MW	6.80 AW	14150 AAW	GABLS	10//99-12//99
	Albany MSA, GA	S	6.31 MW	6.16 AW	13130 AAW	GABLS	10//99-12//99
	Athens MSA, GA	S	6.78 MW	6.67 AW	14100 AAW	GABLS	10//99-12//99
	Atlanta MSA, GA	S	7.06 MW	7.02 AW	14690 AAW	GABLS	10//99-12//99
	Augusta-Aiken MSA, GA-SC	S	6.83 MW	6.55 AW	14210 AAW	GABLS	10//99-12//99
	Columbus MSA, GA-AL	S	6.44 MW	6.35 AW	13400 AAW	GABLS	10//99-12//99
	Macon MSA, GA	S	6.30 MW	6.09 AW	13100 AAW	GABLS	10//99-12//99
	Savannah MSA, GA	S	6.48 MW	6.27 AW	13480 AAW	GABLS	10//99-12//99
	Hawaii	S	11.27 MW	10.96 AW	22790 AAW	HIBLS	10//99-12//99
	Honolulu MSA, HI	S	10.82 MW	11.23 AW	22510 AAW	HIBLS	10//99-12//99
	Idaho	S	6.48 MW	6.67 AW	13880 AAW	IDBLS	10//99-12//99
	Boise City MSA, ID	S	7.01 MW	6.90 AW	14590 AAW	IDBLS	10//99-12//99
	Pocatello MSA, ID	S	5.96 MW	5.93 AW	12410 AAW	IDBLS	10//99-12//99
	Illinois	S	7.02 MW	7.29 AW	15170 AAW	ILBLS	10//99-12//99
	Bloomington-Normal MSA, IL	S	6.75 MW	6.55 AW	14050 AAW	ILBLS	10//99-12//99
	Champaign-Urbana MSA, IL	S	6.91 MW	6.70 AW	14370 AAW	ILBLS	10//99-12//99
	Chicago PMSA, IL	S	7.60 MW	7.37 AW	15810 AAW	ILBLS	10//99-12//99
	Decatur MSA, IL	S	6.75 MW	6.76 AW	14040 AAW	ILBLS	10//99-12//99
	Kankakee PMSA, IL	S	7.23 MW	7.24 AW	15030 AAW	ILBLS	10//99-12//99
	Peoria-Pekin MSA, IL	S	7.04 MW	7.08 AW	14650 AAW	ILBLS	10//99-12//99
	Rockford MSA, IL	S	7.00 MW	6.63 AW	14560 AAW	ILBLS	10//99-12//99
	Springfield MSA, IL	S	6.82 MW	6.68 AW	14190 AAW	ILBLS	10//99-12//99
	Indiana	S	6.85 MW	7.01 AW	14580 AAW	INBLS	10//99-12//99
	Bloomington MSA, IN	S	7.13 MW	7.19 AW	14840 AAW	INBLS	10//99-12//99
	Elkhart-Goshen MSA, IN	S	7.32 MW	7.26 AW	15230 AAW	INBLS	10//99-12//99
	Evansville-Henderson MSA, IN-KY	S	6.88 MW	6.50 AW	14310 AAW	INBLS	10//99-12//99
	Fort Wayne MSA, IN	S	6.86 MW	6.77 AW	14270 AAW	INBLS	10//99-12//99
	Gary PMSA, IN	S	7.15 MW	6.86 AW	14860 AAW	INBLS	10//99-12//99
	Indianapolis MSA, IN	S	7.06 MW	7.00 AW	14690 AAW	INBLS	10//99-12//99
	Kokomo MSA, IN	S	6.50 MW	6.35 AW	13520 AAW	INBLS	10//99-12//99
	Lafayette MSA, IN	S	6.90 MW	6.70 AW	14360 AAW	INBLS	10//99-12//99
	Muncie MSA, IN	S	6.75 MW	6.60 AW	14040 AAW	INBLS	10//99-12//99
	South Bend MSA, IN	S	7.25 MW	6.95 AW	15070 AAW	INBLS	10//99-12//99
	Terre Haute MSA, IN	S	6.57 MW	6.26 AW	13670 AAW	INBLS	10//99-12//99
	Iowa	S	7.02 MW	7.07 AW	14720 AAW	IABLS	10//99-12//99
	Cedar Rapids MSA, IA	S	7.30 MW	7.34 AW	15190 AAW	IABLS	10//99-12//99
	Davenport-Moline-Rock Island MSA, IA-IL	S	6.87 MW	6.57 AW	14280 AAW	IABLS	10//99-12//99
	Des Moines MSA, IA	S	7.44 MW	7.47 AW	15470 AAW	IABLS	10//99-12//99
	Dubuque MSA, IA	S	6.87 MW	6.80 AW	14280 AAW	IABLS	10//99-12//99
	Iowa City MSA, IA	S	8.33 MW	8.05 AW	17330 AAW	IABLS	10//99-12//99
	Sioux City MSA, IA-NE	S	7.10 MW	7.17 AW	14770 AAW	IABLS	10//99-12//99
	Waterloo-Cedar Falls MSA, IA	S	6.88 MW	6.96 AW	14300 AAW	IABLS	10//99-12//99
	Kansas	S	6.73 MW	6.82 AW	14180 AAW	KSBLS	10//99-12//99
	Lawrence MSA, KS	S	6.66 MW	6.56 AW	13860 AAW	KSBLS	10//99-12//99
	Topeka MSA, KS	S	6.70 MW	6.58 AW	13940 AAW	KSBLS	10//99-12//99
	Wichita MSA, KS	S	7.11 MW	7.18 AW	14790 AAW	KSBLS	10//99-12//99
	Kentucky	S	6.56 MW	6.80 AW	14130 AAW	KYBLS	10//99-12//99
	Lexington MSA, KY	S	6.99 MW	6.97 AW	14530 AAW	KYBLS	10//99-12//99
	Louisville MSA, KY-IN	S	7.18 MW	7.18 AW	14930 AAW	KYBLS	10//99-12//99
	Owensboro MSA, KY	S	6.19 MW	6.12 AW	12880 AAW	KYBLS	10//99-12//99
	Louisiana	S	6.17 MW	6.32 AW	13150 AAW	LABLS	10//99-12//99
	Alexandria MSA, LA	S	6.14 MW	6.12 AW	12770 AAW	LABLS	10//99-12//99
	Baton Rouge MSA, LA	S	6.35 MW	6.23 AW	13200 AAW	LABLS	10//99-12//99
	Houma MSA, LA	S	6.67 MW	6.57 AW	13870 AAW	LABLS	10//99-12//99
	Lafayette MSA, LA	S	5.99 MW	6.05 AW	12460 AAW	LABLS	10//99-12//99
	Lake Charles MSA, LA	S	6.15 MW	6.16 AW	12800 AAW	LABLS	10//99-12//99
	Monroe MSA, LA	S	5.84 MW	5.97 AW	12150 AAW	LABLS	10//99-12//99
	New Orleans MSA, LA	S	6.51 MW	6.30 AW	13540 AAW	LABLS	10//99-12//99
	Shreveport-Bossier City MSA, LA	S	6.27 MW	6.08 AW	13040 AAW	LABLS	10//99-12//99
	Maine	S	7.55 MW	7.61 AW	15820 AAW	MEBLS	10//99-12//99
	Bangor MSA, ME	S	6.86 MW	6.53 AW	14270 AAW	MEBLS	10//99-12//99
	Lewiston-Auburn MSA, ME	S	7.31 MW	7.46 AW	15190 AAW	MEBLS	10//99-12//99
	Portland MSA, ME	S	8.07 MW	8.05 AW	16780 AAW	MEBLS	10//99-12//99

Occupation/Type/Industry	Location	Per	Low	Mid	High	Source	Date
Maid and Housekeeping Cleaner	Maryland	S	7.59 MW	7.85 AW	16330 AAW	MDBLS	10//99-12//99
	Baltimore PMSA, MD	S	7.81 MW	7.77 AW	16250 AAW	MDBLS	10//99-12//99
	Cumberland MSA, MD-WV	S	7.29 MW	6.75 AW	15170 AAW	MDBLS	10//99-12//99
	Hagerstown PMSA, MD	S	7.70 MW	7.65 AW	16020 AAW	MDBLS	10//99-12//99
	Massachusetts	S	8.12 MW	8.45 AW	17580 AAW	MABLS	10//99-12//99
	Barnstable-Yarmouth MSA, MA	S	8.20 MW	7.97 AW	17050 AAW	MABLS	10//99-12//99
	Boston PMSA, MA-NH	S	8.75 MW	8.40 AW	18200 AAW	MABLS	10//99-12//99
	Brockton PMSA, MA	S	8.66 MW	8.20 AW	18010 AAW	MABLS	10//99-12//99
	Fitchburg-Leominster PMSA, MA	S	7.53 MW	7.47 AW	15670 AAW	MABLS	10//99-12//99
	Lawrence PMSA, MA-NH	S	8.46 MW	8.24 AW	17600 AAW	MABLS	10//99-12//99
	Lowell PMSA, MA-NH	S	7.67 MW	7.60 AW	15960 AAW	MABLS	10//99-12//99
	New Bedford PMSA, MA	S	7.70 MW	7.39 AW	16010 AAW	MABLS	10//99-12//99
	Pittsfield MSA, MA	S	7.41 MW	7.16 AW	15410 AAW	MABLS	10//99-12//99
	Springfield MSA, MA	S	7.83 MW	7.65 AW	16280 AAW	MABLS	10//99-12//99
	Worcester PMSA, MA-CT	S	7.80 MW	7.67 AW	16210 AAW	MABLS	10//99-12//99
	Michigan	S	7.45 MW	7.59 AW	15780 AAW	MIBLS	10//99-12//99
	Ann Arbor PMSA, MI	S	7.93 MW	7.87 AW	16500 AAW	MIBLS	10//99-12//99
	Benton Harbor MSA, MI	S	6.54 MW	6.38 AW	13600 AAW	MIBLS	10//99-12//99
	Detroit PMSA, MI	S	8.20 MW	8.04 AW	17050 AAW	MIBLS	10//99-12//99
	Flint PMSA, MI	S	7.41 MW	6.88 AW	15410 AAW	MIBLS	10//99-12//99
	Grand Rapids-Muskegon-Holland MSA, MI	S	7.18 MW	6.95 AW	14940 AAW	MIBLS	10//99-12//99
	Jackson MSA, MI	S	7.57 MW	7.43 AW	15750 AAW	MIBLS	10//99-12//99
	Kalamazoo-Battle Creek MSA, MI	S	7.62 MW	6.92 AW	15840 AAW	MIBLS	10//99-12//99
	Lansing-East Lansing MSA, MI	S	6.78 MW	6.51 AW	14110 AAW	MIBLS	10//99-12//99
	Saginaw-Bay City-Midland MSA, MI	S	6.71 MW	6.50 AW	13950 AAW	MIBLS	10//99-12//99
	Minnesota	S	7.83 MW	8.05 AW	16750 AAW	MNBLS	10//99-12//99
	Duluth-Superior MSA, MN-WI	S	7.29 MW	6.74 AW	15160 AAW	MNBLS	10//99-12//99
	Minneapolis-St. Paul MSA, MN-WI	S	8.60 MW	8.32 AW	17890 AAW	MNBLS	10//99-12//99
	Rochester MSA, MN	S	7.09 MW	7.06 AW	14750 AAW	MNBLS	10//99-12//99
	St. Cloud MSA, MN	S	6.84 MW	6.46 AW	14220 AAW	MNBLS	10//99-12//99
	Mississippi	S	6.25 MW	6.46 AW	13440 AAW	MSBLS	10//99-12//99
	Biloxi-Gulfport-Pascagoula MSA, MS	S	6.70 MW	6.51 AW	13940 AAW	MSBLS	10//99-12//99
	Hattiesburg MSA, MS	S	6.23 MW	6.11 AW	12960 AAW	MSBLS	10//99-12//99
	Jackson MSA, MS	S	6.56 MW	6.32 AW	13650 AAW	MSBLS	10//99-12//99
	Missouri	S	6.7 MW	6.88 AW	14320 AAW	MOBLS	10//99-12//99
	Columbia MSA, MO	S	7.17 MW	7.33 AW	14900 AAW	MOBLS	10//99-12//99
	Joplin MSA, MO	S	6.37 MW	6.33 AW	13260 AAW	MOBLS	10//99-12//99
	Kansas City MSA, MO-KS	S	7.15 MW	7.12 AW	14860 AAW	MOBLS	10//99-12//99
	St. Joseph MSA, MO	S	7.17 MW	6.71 AW	14920 AAW	MOBLS	10//99-12//99
	St. Louis MSA, MO-IL	S	6.99 MW	6.74 AW	14540 AAW	MOBLS	10//99-12//99
	Springfield MSA, MO	S	6.58 MW	6.37 AW	13690 AAW	MOBLS	10//99-12//99
	Montana	S	6.26 MW	6.45 AW	13410 AAW	MTBLS	10//99-12//99
	Billings MSA, MT	S	6.84 MW	6.75 AW	14230 AAW	MTBLS	10//99-12//99
	Great Falls MSA, MT	S	6.46 MW	6.30 AW	13440 AAW	MTBLS	10//99-12//99
	Missoula MSA, MT	S	6.52 MW	6.39 AW	13560 AAW	MTBLS	10//99-12//99
	Nebraska	S	6.84 MW	6.96 AW	14480 AAW	NEBLS	10//99-12//99
	Lincoln MSA, NE	S	6.96 MW	7.02 AW	14480 AAW	NEBLS	10//99-12//99
	Omaha MSA, NE-IA	S	7.33 MW	7.41 AW	15250 AAW	NEBLS	10//99-12//99
	Nevada	S	8.86 MW	8.66 AW	18020 AAW	NVBLS	10//99-12//99
	Las Vegas MSA, NV-AZ	S	8.98 MW	9.24 AW	18680 AAW	NVBLS	10//99-12//99
	Reno MSA, NV	S	7.35 MW	7.30 AW	15290 AAW	NVBLS	10//99-12//99
	New Hampshire	S	7.64 MW	7.71 AW	16030 AAW	NHBLS	10//99-12//99
	Manchester PMSA, NH	S	8.16 MW	7.96 AW	16980 AAW	NHBLS	10//99-12//99
	Nashua PMSA, NH	S	7.79 MW	7.78 AW	16200 AAW	NHBLS	10//99-12//99
	Portsmouth-Rochester PMSA, NH-ME	S	7.64 MW	7.67 AW	15890 AAW	NHBLS	10//99-12//99
	New Jersey	S	7.74 MW	7.98 AW	16610 AAW	NJBLS	10//99-12//99
	Atlantic-Cape May PMSA, NJ	S	7.87 MW	7.15 AW	16380 AAW	NJBLS	10//99-12//99
	Bergen-Passaic PMSA, NJ	S	7.78 MW	7.50 AW	16180 AAW	NJBLS	10//99-12//99
	Jersey City PMSA, NJ	S	7.65 MW	7.47 AW	15910 AAW	NJBLS	10//99-12//99
	Middlesex-Somerset-Hunterdon PMSA, NJ	S	8.15 MW	7.97 AW	16950 AAW	NJBLS	10//99-12//99
	Monmouth-Ocean PMSA, NJ	S	7.72 MW	7.65 AW	16060 AAW	NJBLS	10//99-12//99
	Newark PMSA, NJ	S	8.48 MW	8.25 AW	17640 AAW	NJBLS	10//99-12//99
	Trenton PMSA, NJ	S	8.72 MW	8.43 AW	18130 AAW	NJBLS	10//99-12//99

AAW Average annual wage	AOH Average offered, high	ASH Average starting, high	H Hourly	M Monthly	S Special: hourly and annual
AE Average entry wage	AOL Average offered, low	ASL Average starting, low	HI Highest wage paid	MTC Median total compensation	TQ Third quartile wage
AEX Average experienced wage	APH Average pay, high range	AW Average wage paid	HR High end range	MW Median wage paid	W Weekly
AO Average offered	APL Average pay, low range	FQ First quartile wage	LR Low end range	SQ Second quartile wage	Y Yearly

Occupation/Type/Industry	Location	Per	Low	Mid	High	Source	Date
Maid and Housekeeping Cleaner	New Mexico	S	6.42 MW	6.69 AW	13910 AAW	NMBLS	10//99-12//99
	Albuquerque MSA, NM	S	6.63 MW	6.49 AW	13800 AAW	NMBLS	10//99-12//99
	Las Cruces MSA, NM	S	6.24 MW	6.13 AW	12980 AAW	NMBLS	10//99-12//99
	Santa Fe MSA, NM	S	7.69 MW	7.59 AW	15990 AAW	NMBLS	10//99-12//99
	New York	S	8.8 MW	9.71 AW	20200 AAW	NYBLS	
	Albany-Schenectady-Troy MSA, NY	S	7.34 MW	7.29 AW	15260 AAW	NYBLS	10//99-12//99
	Binghamton MSA, NY	S	6.78 MW	6.18 AW	14090 AAW	NYBLS	10//99-12//99
	Buffalo-Niagara Falls MSA, NY	S	7.38 MW	6.83 AW	15340 AAW	NYBLS	10//99-12//99
	Dutchess County PMSA, NY	S	8.40 MW	7.74 AW	17480 AAW	NYBLS	10//99-12//99
	Elmira MSA, NY	S	7.44 MW	6.95 AW	15480 AAW	NYBLS	10//99-12//99
	Glens Falls MSA, NY	S	6.81 MW	6.54 AW	14160 AAW	NYBLS	10//99-12//99
	Jamestown MSA, NY	S	6.76 MW	6.51 AW	14070 AAW	NYBLS	10//99-12//99
	Nassau-Suffolk PMSA, NY	S	9.89 MW	9.62 AW	20560 AAW	NYBLS	10//99-12//99
	New York PMSA, NY	S	11.53 MW	11.84 AW	23980 AAW	NYBLS	10//99-12//99
	Newburgh PMSA, NY-PA	S	7.47 MW	6.93 AW	15540 AAW	NYBLS	10//99-12//99
	Rochester MSA, NY	S	6.99 MW	6.68 AW	14540 AAW	NYBLS	10//99-12//99
	Syracuse MSA, NY	S	6.92 MW	6.61 AW	14390 AAW	NYBLS	10//99-12//99
	Utica-Rome MSA, NY	S	6.95 MW	6.72 AW	14460 AAW	NYBLS	10//99-12//99
	North Carolina	S	6.92 MW	7.06 AW	14680 AAW	NCBLS	10//99-12//99
	Asheville MSA, NC	S	7.13 MW	7.08 AW	14830 AAW	NCBLS	10//99-12//99
	Charlotte-Gastonia-Rock Hill MSA, NC-SC	S	7.24 MW	7.22 AW	15060 AAW	NCBLS	10//99-12//99
	Fayetteville MSA, NC	S	6.42 MW	6.08 AW	13360 AAW	NCBLS	10//99-12//99
	Goldsboro MSA, NC	S	6.73 MW	6.52 AW	14000 AAW	NCBLS	10//99-12//99
	Greensboro--Winston-Salem-- High Point MSA, NC	S	6.97 MW	6.83 AW	14500 AAW	NCBLS	10//99-12//99
	Greenville MSA, NC	S	6.38 MW	6.29 AW	13280 AAW	NCBLS	10//99-12//99
	Hickory-Morganton-Lenoir MSA, NC	S	7.16 MW	7.19 AW	14900 AAW	NCBLS	10//99-12//99
	Jacksonville MSA, NC	S	6.37 MW	6.31 AW	13250 AAW	NCBLS	10//99-12//99
	Raleigh-Durham-Chapel Hill MSA, NC	S	7.42 MW	7.43 AW	15430 AAW	NCBLS	10//99-12//99
	Rocky Mount MSA, NC	S	6.29 MW	6.08 AW	13090 AAW	NCBLS	10//99-12//99
	Wilmington MSA, NC	S	6.88 MW	6.77 AW	14310 AAW	NCBLS	10//99-12//99
	North Dakota	S	6.41 MW	6.56 AW	13640 AAW	NDBLS	10//99-12//99
	Bismarck MSA, ND	S	6.16 MW	6.07 AW	12800 AAW	NDBLS	10//99-12//99
	Fargo-Moorhead MSA, ND-MN	S	6.82 MW	6.57 AW	14190 AAW	NDBLS	10//99-12//99
	Grand Forks MSA, ND-MN	S	7.00 MW	7.02 AW	14560 AAW	NDBLS	10//99-12//99
	Ohio	S	7.16 MW	7.27 AW	15120 AAW	OHBLS	10//99-12//99
	Canton-Massillon MSA, OH	S	6.80 MW	6.61 AW	14140 AAW	OHBLS	10//99-12//99
	Cincinnati PMSA, OH-KY-IN	S	7.57 MW	7.55 AW	15740 AAW	OHBLS	10//99-12//99
	Cleveland-Lorain-Elyria PMSA, OH	S	7.50 MW	7.41 AW	15600 AAW	OHBLS	10//99-12//99
	Columbus MSA, OH	S	7.36 MW	7.28 AW	15300 AAW	OHBLS	10//99-12//99
	Dayton-Springfield MSA, OH	S	7.33 MW	7.10 AW	15250 AAW	OHBLS	10//99-12//99
	Hamilton-Middletown PMSA, OH	S	7.54 MW	7.51 AW	15680 AAW	OHBLS	10//99-12//99
	Lima MSA, OH	S	7.01 MW	6.84 AW	14580 AAW	OHBLS	10//99-12//99
	Mansfield MSA, OH	S	7.10 MW	7.10 AW	14770 AAW	OHBLS	10//99-12//99
	Steubenville-Weirton MSA, OH-WV	S	6.04 MW	6.05 AW	12560 AAW	OHBLS	10//99-12//99
	Toledo MSA, OH	S	7.36 MW	7.36 AW	15310 AAW	OHBLS	10//99-12//99
	Youngstown-Warren MSA, OH	S	7.42 MW	7.04 AW	15430 AAW	OHBLS	10//99-12//99
	Oklahoma	S	6.32 MW	6.53 AW	13580 AAW	OKBLS	10//99-12//99
	Enid MSA, OK	S	6.11 MW	6.02 AW	12710 AAW	OKBLS	10//99-12//99
	Lawton MSA, OK	S	6.92 MW	6.37 AW	14400 AAW	OKBLS	10//99-12//99
	Oklahoma City MSA, OK	S	6.61 MW	6.33 AW	13740 AAW	OKBLS	10//99-12//99
	Tulsa MSA, OK	S	6.74 MW	6.65 AW	14030 AAW	OKBLS	10//99-12//99
	Oregon	S	7.39 MW	7.68 AW	15980 AAW	ORBLS	10//99-12//99
	Corvallis MSA, OR	S	7.74 MW	7.74 AW	16100 AAW	ORBLS	10//99-12//99
	Eugene-Springfield MSA, OR	S	7.49 MW	6.90 AW	15570 AAW	ORBLS	10//99-12//99
	Medford-Ashland MSA, OR	S	7.64 MW	7.19 AW	15890 AAW	ORBLS	10//99-12//99
	Portland-Vancouver PMSA, OR-WA	S	7.91 MW	7.66 AW	16460 AAW	ORBLS	10//99-12//99
	Salem PMSA, OR	S	8.33 MW	7.89 AW	17320 AAW	ORBLS	10//99-12//99
	Pennsylvania	S	7.48 MW	7.66 AW	15940 AAW	PABLS	10//99-12//99
	Allentown-Bethlehem-Easton MSA, PA	S	7.66 MW	7.52 AW	15930 AAW	PABLS	10//99-12//99
	Altoona MSA, PA	S	6.64 MW	6.09 AW	13820 AAW	PABLS	10//99-12//99

AAW Average annual wage	**AOH** Average offered, high	**ASH** Average starting, high	**H** Hourly	**M** Monthly	**S** Special: hourly and annual
AE Average entry wage	**AOL** Average offered, low	**ASL** Average starting, low	**HI** Highest wage paid	**MTC** Median total compensation	**TQ** Third quartile wage
AEX Average experienced wage	**APH** Average pay, high range	**AW** Average wage paid	**HR** High end range	**MW** Median wage paid	**W** Weekly
AO Average offered	**APL** Average pay, low range	**FQ** First quartile wage	**LR** Low end range	**SQ** Second quartile wage	**Y** Yearly

Occupation/Type/Industry	Location	Per	Low	Mid	High	Source	Date
Maid and Housekeeping Cleaner	Erie MSA, PA	S	6.76 MW	6.49 AW	14070 AAW	PABLS	10//99-12//99
	Harrisburg-Lebanon-Carlisle MSA, PA	S	7.99 MW	8.04 AW	16610 AAW	PABLS	10//99-12//99
	Johnstown MSA, PA	S	6.58 MW	6.26 AW	13680 AAW	PABLS	10//99-12//99
	Lancaster MSA, PA	S	7.71 MW	7.62 AW	16040 AAW	PABLS	10//99-12//99
	Philadelphia PMSA, PA-NJ	S	8.33 MW	8.14 AW	17330 AAW	PABLS	10//99-12//99
	Pittsburgh MSA, PA	S	7.54 MW	7.32 AW	15680 AAW	PABLS	10//99-12//99
	Reading MSA, PA	S	7.26 MW	7.13 AW	15110 AAW	PABLS	10//99-12//99
	Scranton--Wilkes-Barre-- Hazleton MSA, PA	S	7.39 MW	7.31 AW	15370 AAW	PABLS	10//99-12//99
	Sharon MSA, PA	S	6.63 MW	6.42 AW	13800 AAW	PABLS	10//99-12//99
	State College MSA, PA	S	7.20 MW	6.94 AW	14970 AAW	PABLS	10//99-12//99
	Williamsport MSA, PA	S	6.52 MW	6.30 AW	13560 AAW	PABLS	10//99-12//99
	York MSA, PA	S	6.90 MW	6.84 AW	14360 AAW	PABLS	10//99-12//99
	Rhode Island	S	7.92 MW	8.28 AW	17230 AAW	RIBLS	10//99-12//99
	Providence-Fall River- Warwick MSA, RI-MA	S	8.29 MW	7.85 AW	17250 AAW	RIBLS	10//99-12//99
	South Carolina	S	6.63 MW	6.93 AW	14400 AAW	SCBLS	10//99-12//99
	Charleston-North Charleston MSA, SC	S	6.52 MW	6.29 AW	13560 AAW	SCBLS	10//99-12//99
	Columbia MSA, SC	S	7.38 MW	6.57 AW	15350 AAW	SCBLS	10//99-12//99
	Florence MSA, SC	S	6.14 MW	6.01 AW	12760 AAW	SCBLS	10//99-12//99
	Greenville-Spartanburg- Anderson MSA, SC	S	6.99 MW	6.86 AW	14530 AAW	SCBLS	10//99-12//99
	Myrtle Beach MSA, SC	S	7.30 MW	7.11 AW	15190 AAW	SCBLS	10//99-12//99
	Sumter MSA, SC	S	6.76 MW	6.64 AW	14060 AAW	SCBLS	10//99-12//99
	South Dakota	S	6.43 MW	6.60 AW	13730 AAW	SDBLS	10//99-12//99
	Rapid City MSA, SD	S	6.51 MW	6.33 AW	13530 AAW	SDBLS	10//99-12//99
	Sioux Falls MSA, SD	S	7.23 MW	7.14 AW	15040 AAW	SDBLS	10//99-12//99
	Tennessee	S	6.58 MW	6.79 AW	14120 AAW	TNBLS	10//99-12//99
	Chattanooga MSA, TN-GA	S	6.82 MW	6.54 AW	14180 AAW	TNBLS	10//99-12//99
	Clarksville-Hopkinsville MSA, TN-KY	S	6.72 MW	6.35 AW	13970 AAW	TNBLS	10//99-12//99
	Jackson MSA, TN	S	6.30 MW	6.07 AW	13110 AAW	TNBLS	10//99-12//99
	Johnson City-Kingsport-Bristol MSA, TN-VA	S	6.44 MW	6.13 AW	13400 AAW	TNBLS	10//99-12//99
	Knoxville MSA, TN	S	7.06 MW	7.07 AW	14680 AAW	TNBLS	10//99-12//99
	Memphis MSA, TN-AR-MS	S	6.57 MW	6.24 AW	13660 AAW	MSBLS	10//99-12//99
	Nashville MSA, TN	S	7.13 MW	6.97 AW	14840 AAW	TNBLS	10//99-12//99
	Texas	S	6.18 MW	6.40 AW	13320 AAW	TXBLS	10//99-12//99
	Abilene MSA, TX	S	6.10 MW	5.99 AW	12690 AAW	TXBLS	10//99-12//99
	Amarillo MSA, TX	S	6.53 MW	6.40 AW	13570 AAW	TXBLS	10//99-12//99
	Austin-San Marcos MSA, TX	S	6.82 MW	6.61 AW	14200 AAW	TXBLS	10//99-12//99
	Beaumont-Port Arthur MSA, TX	S	6.02 MW	6.00 AW	12530 AAW	TXBLS	10//99-12//99
	Brazoria PMSA, TX	S	6.56 MW	6.11 AW	13640 AAW	TXBLS	10//99-12//99
	Brownsville-Harlingen-San Benito MSA, TX	S	6.02 MW	6.05 AW	12510 AAW	TXBLS	10//99-12//99
	Bryan-College Station MSA, TX	S	6.12 MW	6.11 AW	12720 AAW	TXBLS	10//99-12//99
	Corpus Christi MSA, TX	S	6.21 MW	6.08 AW	12920 AAW	TXBLS	10//99-12//99
	Dallas PMSA, TX	S	6.51 MW	6.28 AW	13540 AAW	TXBLS	10//99-12//99
	El Paso MSA, TX	S	6.17 MW	6.07 AW	12840 AAW	TXBLS	10//99-12//99
	Fort Worth-Arlington PMSA, TX	S	7.05 MW	6.80 AW	14660 AAW	TXBLS	10//99-12//99
	Galveston-Texas City PMSA, TX	S	6.35 MW	6.06 AW	13200 AAW	TXBLS	10//99-12//99
	Houston PMSA, TX	S	6.34 MW	6.19 AW	13180 AAW	TXBLS	10//99-12//99
	Killeen-Temple MSA, TX	S	6.24 MW	6.13 AW	12980 AAW	TXBLS	10//99-12//99
	Laredo MSA, TX	S	6.16 MW	5.98 AW	12810 AAW	TXBLS	10//99-12//99
	Longview-Marshall MSA, TX	S	6.00 MW	6.01 AW	12470 AAW	TXBLS	10//99-12//99
	Lubbock MSA, TX	S	6.22 MW	6.07 AW	12940 AAW	TXBLS	10//99-12//99
	McAllen-Edinburg-Mission MSA, TX	S	5.94 MW	6.00 AW	12350 AAW	TXBLS	10//99-12//99
	Odessa-Midland MSA, TX	S	6.17 MW	6.10 AW	12830 AAW	TXBLS	10//99-12//99
	San Angelo MSA, TX	S	6.01 MW	6.07 AW	12500 AAW	TXBLS	10//99-12//99
	San Antonio MSA, TX	S	6.25 MW	6.10 AW	13000 AAW	TXBLS	10//99-12//99
	Sherman-Denison MSA, TX	S	6.84 MW	6.44 AW	14220 AAW	TXBLS	10//99-12//99
	Texarkana MSA, TX- Texarkana, AR	S	6.25 MW	6.11 AW	13010 AAW	TXBLS	10//99-12//99
	Tyler MSA, TX	S	6.42 MW	6.21 AW	13350 AAW	TXBLS	10//99-12//99
	Victoria MSA, TX	S	7.06 MW	6.03 AW	14680 AAW	TXBLS	10//99-12//99

AAW	Average annual wage	AOH	Average offered, high	ASH	Average starting, high	H	Hourly	M	Monthly	S	Special: hourly and annual
AE	Average entry wage	AOL	Average offered, low	ASL	Average starting, low	HI	Highest wage paid	MTC	Median total compensation	TQ	Third quartile wage
AEX	Average experienced wage	APH	Average pay, high range	AW	Average wage paid	HR	High end range	MW	Median wage paid	W	Weekly
AO	Average offered	APL	Average pay, low range	FQ	First quartile wage	LR	Low end range	SQ	Second quartile wage	Y	Yearly

Occupation/Type/Industry	Location	Per	Low	Mid	High	Source	Date
Maid and Housekeeping Cleaner	Waco MSA, TX	S	6.10 MW	6.01 AW	12680 AAW	TXBLS	10//99-12//99
	Wichita Falls MSA, TX	S	6.06 MW	5.98 AW	12600 AAW	TXBLS	10//99-12//99
	Utah	S	6.86 MW	7.08 AW	14720 AAW	UTBLS	10//99-12//99
	Provo-Orem MSA, UT	S	7.03 MW	6.88 AW	14610 AAW	UTBLS	10//99-12//99
	Salt Lake City-Ogden MSA, UT	S	7.08 MW	6.96 AW	14730 AAW	UTBLS	10//99-12//99
	Vermont	S	7.2 MW	7.42 AW	15430 AAW	VTBLS	10//99-12//99
	Burlington MSA, VT	S	7.57 MW	7.46 AW	15750 AAW	VTBLS	10//99-12//99
	Virginia	S	6.78 MW	7.05 AW	14670 AAW	VABLS	10//99-12//99
	Charlottesville MSA, VA	S	7.44 MW	7.35 AW	15470 AAW	VABLS	10//99-12//99
	Danville MSA, VA	S	6.32 MW	6.14 AW	13140 AAW	VABLS	10//99-12//99
	Lynchburg MSA, VA	S	6.47 MW	6.14 AW	13470 AAW	VABLS	10//99-12//99
	Norfolk-Virginia Beach-Newport News MSA, VA-NC	S	6.58 MW	6.29 AW	13690 AAW	VABLS	10//99-12//99
	Richmond-Petersburg MSA, VA	S	6.85 MW	6.69 AW	14250 AAW	VABLS	10//99-12//99
	Roanoke MSA, VA	S	7.03 MW	6.88 AW	14630 AAW	VABLS	10//99-12//99
	Washington	S	7.52 MW	7.87 AW	16370 AAW	WABLS	10//99-12//99
	Bellingham MSA, WA	S	7.74 MW	7.13 AW	16100 AAW	WABLS	10//99-12//99
	Bremerton PMSA, WA	S	7.93 MW	7.44 AW	16500 AAW	WABLS	10//99-12//99
	Olympia PMSA, WA	S	8.29 MW	7.79 AW	17230 AAW	WABLS	10//99-12//99
	Richland-Kennewick-Pasco MSA, WA	S	6.80 MW	6.45 AW	14150 AAW	WABLS	10//99-12//99
	Seattle-Bellevue-Everett PMSA, WA	S	8.21 MW	7.99 AW	17080 AAW	WABLS	10//99-12//99
	Spokane MSA, WA	S	7.30 MW	6.75 AW	15180 AAW	WABLS	10//99-12//99
	Tacoma PMSA, WA	S	8.26 MW	7.68 AW	17190 AAW	WABLS	10//99-12//99
	Yakima MSA, WA	S	6.90 MW	6.62 AW	14350 AAW	WABLS	10//99-12//99
	West Virginia	S	6.39 MW	6.57 AW	13670 AAW	WVBLS	10//99-12//99
	Charleston MSA, WV	S	6.92 MW	6.66 AW	14400 AAW	WVBLS	10//99-12//99
	Huntington-Ashland MSA, WV-KY-OH	S	6.55 MW	6.08 AW	13630 AAW	WVBLS	10//99-12//99
	Parkersburg-Marietta MSA, WV-OH	S	6.71 MW	6.58 AW	13970 AAW	WVBLS	10//99-12//99
	Wheeling MSA, WV-OH	S	6.59 MW	6.37 AW	13700 AAW	WVBLS	10//99-12//99
	Wisconsin	S	7.31 MW	7.37 AW	15330 AAW	WIBLS	10//99-12//99
	Appleton-Oshkosh-Neenah MSA, WI	S	7.67 MW	7.47 AW	15950 AAW	WIBLS	10//99-12//99
	Eau Claire MSA, WI	S	7.10 MW	6.91 AW	14770 AAW	WIBLS	10//99-12//99
	Green Bay MSA, WI	S	7.50 MW	7.49 AW	15600 AAW	WIBLS	10//99-12//99
	Janesville-Beloit MSA, WI	S	7.22 MW	7.25 AW	15020 AAW	WIBLS	10//99-12//99
	Kenosha PMSA, WI	S	7.70 MW	7.39 AW	16020 AAW	WIBLS	10//99-12//99
	La Crosse MSA, WI-MN	S	7.29 MW	7.17 AW	15160 AAW	WIBLS	10//99-12//99
	Madison MSA, WI	S	7.57 MW	7.56 AW	15740 AAW	WIBLS	10//99-12//99
	Milwaukee-Waukesha PMSA, WI	S	7.46 MW	7.45 AW	15520 AAW	WIBLS	10//99-12//99
	Racine PMSA, WI	S	7.41 MW	7.32 AW	15410 AAW	WIBLS	10//99-12//99
	Sheboygan MSA, WI	S	7.05 MW	6.66 AW	14670 AAW	WIBLS	10//99-12//99
	Wausau MSA, WI	S	7.20 MW	7.32 AW	14980 AAW	WIBLS	10//99-12//99
	Wyoming	S	6.79 MW	7.09 AW	14760 AAW	WYBLS	10//99-12//99
	Casper MSA, WY	S	6.35 MW	6.14 AW	13210 AAW	WYBLS	10//99-12//99
	Cheyenne MSA, WY	S	6.51 MW	6.31 AW	13540 AAW	WYBLS	10//99-12//99
	Puerto Rico	S	6.22 MW	6.56 AW	13650 AAW	PRBLS	10//99-12//99
	Aguadilla MSA, PR	S	5.80 MW	5.93 AW	12060 AAW	PRBLS	10//99-12//99
	Arecibo PMSA, PR	S	5.81 MW	5.92 AW	12070 AAW	PRBLS	10//99-12//99
	Mayaguez MSA, PR	S	5.84 MW	5.96 AW	12150 AAW	PRBLS	10//99-12//99
	Ponce MSA, PR	S	5.99 MW	6.10 AW	12450 AAW	PRBLS	10//99-12//99
	San Juan-Bayamon PMSA, PR	S	6.74 MW	6.35 AW	14010 AAW	PRBLS	10//99-12//99
	Virgin Islands	S	6.83 MW	6.85 AW	14250 AAW	VIBLS	10//99-12//99
	Guam	S	6.31 MW	6.52 AW	13560 AAW	GUBLS	10//99-12//99
Mail Carrier							
Postal	United States	Y		34840 AW		DENE	1999
Mail Clerk and Mail Machine Operator							
Except Postal Service	Alabama	S	8.01 MW	8.36 AW	17390 AAW	ALBLS	10//99-12//99
Except Postal Service	Alaska	S	9.27 MW	9.58 AW	19930 AAW	AKBLS	10//99-12//99
Except Postal Service	Arizona	S	8.34 MW	8.57 AW	17830 AAW	AZBLS	10//99-12//99
Except Postal Service	Arkansas	S	6.7 MW	7.43 AW	15440 AAW	ARBLS	10//99-12//99
Except Postal Service	California	S	9.05 MW	9.91 AW	20610 AAW	CABLS	10//99-12//99

AAW	Average annual wage	AOH	Average offered, high	ASH	Average starting, high	H	Hourly	M	Monthly	S	Special: hourly and annual
AE	Average entry wage	AOL	Average offered, low	ASL	Average starting, low	HI	Highest wage paid	MTC	Median total compensation	TQ	Third quartile wage
AEX	Average experienced wage	APH	Average pay, high range	AW	Average wage paid	HR	High end range	MW	Median wage paid	W	Weekly
AO	Average offered	APL	Average pay, low range	FQ	First quartile wage	LR	Low end range	SQ	Second quartile wage	Y	Yearly

Occupation/Type/Industry	Location	Per	Low	Mid	High	Source	Date
Mail Clerk and Mail Machine Operator							
Except Postal Service	Colorado	S	9.3 MW	9.54 AW	19850 AAW	COBLS	10//99-12//99
Except Postal Service	Connecticut	S	9.09 MW	9.74 AW	20260 AAW	CTBLS	10//99-12//99
Except Postal Service	Delaware	S	8.62 MW	8.85 AW	18400 AAW	DEBLS	10//99-12//99
Except Postal Service	District of Columbia	S	11.3 MW	11.74 AW	24420 AAW	DCBLS	10//99-12//99
Except Postal Service	Florida	S	8.19 MW	8.59 AW	17870 AAW	FLBLS	10//99-12//99
Except Postal Service	Georgia	S	8.98 MW	9.32 AW	19390 AAW	GABLS	10//99-12//99
Except Postal Service	Hawaii	S	9.98 MW	10.24 AW	21290 AAW	HIBLS	10//99-12//99
Except Postal Service	Idaho	S	8.57 MW	9.01 AW	18750 AAW	IDBLS	10//99-12//99
Except Postal Service	Illinois	S	8.32 MW	8.72 AW	18130 AAW	ILBLS	10//99-12//99
Except Postal Service	Indiana	S	9.6 MW	10.14 AW	21080 AAW	INBLS	10//99-12//99
Except Postal Service	Iowa	S	8.29 MW	8.92 AW	18560 AAW	IABLS	10//99-12//99
Except Postal Service	Kansas	S	8.12 MW	8.32 AW	17310 AAW	KSBLS	10//99-12//99
Except Postal Service	Kentucky	S	8.33 MW	8.91 AW	18540 AAW	KYBLS	10//99-12//99
Except Postal Service	Louisiana	S	6.76 MW	7.60 AW	15800 AAW	LABLS	10//99-12//99
Except Postal Service	Maine	S	8.41 MW	8.64 AW	17980 AAW	MEBLS	10//99-12//99
Except Postal Service	Maryland	S	8.86 MW	9.40 AW	19550 AAW	MDBLS	10//99-12//99
Except Postal Service	Massachusetts	S	10.77 MW	11.21 AW	23320 AAW	MABLS	10//99-12//99
Except Postal Service	Michigan	S	8.68 MW	9.34 AW	19420 AAW	MIBLS	10//99-12//99
Except Postal Service	Minnesota	S	9.32 MW	9.58 AW	19930 AAW	MNBLS	10//99-12//99
Except Postal Service	Mississippi	S	8.13 MW	8.52 AW	17720 AAW	MSBLS	10//99-12//99
Except Postal Service	Missouri	S	8.13 MW	8.73 AW	18150 AAW	MOBLS	10//99-12//99
Except Postal Service	Montana	S	7.78 MW	8.26 AW	17180 AAW	MTBLS	10//99-12//99
Except Postal Service	Nebraska	S	8.12 MW	8.32 AW	17300 AAW	NEBLS	10//99-12//99
Except Postal Service	Nevada	S	8.72 MW	9.38 AW	19510 AAW	NVBLS	10//99-12//99
Except Postal Service	New Hampshire	S	8.62 MW	9.25 AW	19240 AAW	NHBLS	10//99-12//99
Except Postal Service	New Jersey	S	9.55 MW	9.92 AW	20640 AAW	NJBLS	10//99-12//99
Except Postal Service	New Mexico	S	7.94 MW	8.31 AW	17280 AAW	NMBLS	10//99-12//99
Except Postal Service	New York	S	9.1 MW	9.56 AW	19880 AAW	NYBLS	10//99-12//99
Except Postal Service	North Carolina	S	8.92 MW	9.43 AW	19620 AAW	NCBLS	10//99-12//99
Except Postal Service	North Dakota	S	7.71 MW	8.04 AW	16720 AAW	NDBLS	10//99-12//99
Except Postal Service	Ohio	S	8.56 MW	9.27 AW	19290 AAW	OHBLS	10//99-12//99
Except Postal Service	Oklahoma	S	8.02 MW	8.29 AW	17250 AAW	OKBLS	10//99-12//99
Except Postal Service	Oregon	S	8.69 MW	9.23 AW	19190 AAW	ORBLS	10//99-12//99
Except Postal Service	Pennsylvania	S	8.89 MW	9.20 AW	19140 AAW	PABLS	10//99-12//99
Except Postal Service	Rhode Island	S	9.64 MW	10.13 AW	21070 AAW	RIBLS	10//99-12//99
Except Postal Service	South Carolina	S	8.28 MW	8.58 AW	17850 AAW	SCBLS	10//99-12//99
Except Postal Service	South Dakota	S	9.48 MW	9.65 AW	20080 AAW	SDBLS	10//99-12//99
Except Postal Service	Tennessee	S	8.6 MW	9.15 AW	19030 AAW	TNBLS	10//99-12//99
Except Postal Service	Texas	S	8.43 MW	8.81 AW	18330 AAW	TXBLS	10//99-12//99
Except Postal Service	Utah	S	8.15 MW	8.73 AW	18160 AAW	UTBLS	10//99-12//99
Except Postal Service	Vermont	S	9.17 MW	9.18 AW	19090 AAW	VTBLS	10//99-12//99
Except Postal Service	Virginia	S	9.41 MW	10.29 AW	21400 AAW	VABLS	10//99-12//99
Except Postal Service	Washington	S	8.8 MW	9.76 AW	20310 AAW	WABLS	10//99-12//99
Except Postal Service	West Virginia	S	7.81 MW	8.17 AW	17000 AAW	WVBLS	10//99-12//99
Except Postal Service	Wisconsin	S	8.99 MW	9.16 AW	19050 AAW	WIBLS	10//99-12//99
Except Postal Service	Wyoming	S	7.18 MW	7.78 AW	16190 AAW	WYBLS	10//99-12//99
Except Postal Service	Puerto Rico	S	7.44 MW	7.91 AW	16460 AAW	PRBLS	10//99-12//99
Except Postal Service	Virgin Islands	S	9.47 MW	9.23 AW	19200 AAW	VIBLS	10//99-12//99
Maintenance and Repair Worker							
General	Alabama	S	11.43 MW	12.28 AW	25540 AAW	ALBLS	10//99-12//99
General	Alaska	S	16.41 MW	17.50 AW	36390 AAW	AKBLS	10//99-12//99
General	Arizona	S	11.01 MW	12.12 AW	25210 AAW	AZBLS	10//99-12//99
General	Arkansas	S	10.6 MW	11.18 AW	23260 AAW	ARBLS	10//99-12//99
General	California	S	12.51 MW	13.75 AW	28590 AAW	CABLS	10//99-12//99
General	Colorado	S	11.32 MW	12.16 AW	25300 AAW	COBLS	10//99-12//99
General	Connecticut	S	14.03 MW	14.48 AW	30120 AAW	CTBLS	10//99-12//99
General	Delaware	S	13.1 MW	14.24 AW	29630 AAW	DEBLS	10//99-12//99
General	District of Columbia	S	14.14 MW	14.46 AW	30080 AAW	DCBLS	10//99-12//99
General	Florida	S	10.19 MW	11.13 AW	23140 AAW	FLBLS	10//99-12//99
General	Georgia	S	11.66 MW	12.22 AW	25410 AAW	GABLS	10//99-12//99
General	Hawaii	S	13.69 MW	14.32 AW	29780 AAW	HIBLS	10//99-12//99
General	Idaho	S	11.06 MW	11.56 AW	24050 AAW	IDBLS	10//99-12//99
General	Illinois	S	13.81 MW	14.36 AW	29880 AAW	ILBLS	10//99-12//99
General	Indiana	S	12.34 MW	13.09 AW	27220 AAW	INBLS	10//99-12//99
General	Iowa	S	11.39 MW	11.85 AW	24640 AAW	IABLS	10//99-12//99
General	Kansas	S	11.16 MW	12.06 AW	25090 AAW	KSBLS	10//99-12//99
General	Kentucky	S	11.62 MW	12.70 AW	26410 AAW	KYBLS	10//99-12//99
General	Louisiana	S	10.85 MW	11.95 AW	24860 AAW	LABLS	10//99-12//99
General	Maine	S	12.17 MW	13.93 AW	28980 AAW	MEBLS	10//99-12//99

AAW	Average annual wage	AOH	Average offered, high	ASH	Average starting, high	H	Hourly	M	Monthly	S	Special: hourly and annual
AE	Average entry wage	AOL	Average offered, low	ASL	Average starting, low	HI	Highest wage paid	MTC	Median total compensation	TQ	Third quartile wage
AEX	Average experienced wage	APH	Average pay, high range	AW	Average wage paid	HR	High end range	MW	Median wage paid	W	Weekly
AO	Average offered	APL	Average pay, low range	FQ	First quartile wage	LR	Low end range	SQ	Second quartile wage	Y	Yearly

Occupation/Type/Industry	Location	Per	Low	Mid	High	Source	Date
Maintenance and Repair Worker							
General	Maryland	S	12.47 MW	13.02 AW	27080 AAW	MDBLS	10//99-12//99
General	Massachusetts	S	14.24 MW	14.78 AW	30740 AAW	MABLS	10//99-12//99
General	Michigan	S	12.83 MW	13.83 AW	28770 AAW	MIBLS	10//99-12//99
General	Minnesota	S	13.16 MW	13.48 AW	28040 AAW	MNBLS	10//99-12//99
General	Mississippi	S	10.26 MW	11.21 AW	23320 AAW	MSBLS	10//99-12//99
General	Missouri	S	11.34 MW	12.51 AW	26020 AAW	MOBLS	10//99-12//99
General	Montana	S	9.81 MW	10.48 AW	21800 AAW	MTBLS	10//99-12//99
General	Nebraska	S	11 MW	11.52 AW	23970 AAW	NEBLS	10//99-12//99
General	Nevada	S	13.29 MW	14.34 AW	29830 AAW	NVBLS	10//99-12//99
General	New Hampshire	S	11.84 MW	12.44 AW	25870 AAW	NHBLS	10//99-12//99
General	New Jersey	S	15.24 MW	15.48 AW	32200 AAW	NJBLS	10//99-12//99
General	New Mexico	S	9.97 MW	10.79 AW	22440 AAW	NMBLS	10//99-12//99
General	New York	S	14.07 MW	14.39 AW	29930 AAW	NYBLS	10//99-12//99
General	North Carolina	S	12.24 MW	13.04 AW	27130 AAW	NCBLS	10//99-12//99
General	North Dakota	S	10.49 MW	10.92 AW	22720 AAW	NDBLS	10//99-12//99
General	Ohio	S	12.09 MW	12.72 AW	26460 AAW	OHBLS	10//99-12//99
General	Oklahoma	S	10.18 MW	11.25 AW	23400 AAW	OKBLS	10//99-12//99
General	Oregon	S	12.03 MW	12.89 AW	26820 AAW	ORBLS	10//99-12//99
General	Pennsylvania	S	13.06 MW	13.37 AW	27810 AAW	PABLS	10//99-12//99
General	Rhode Island	S	12.29 MW	12.81 AW	26640 AAW	RIBLS	10//99-12//99
General	South Carolina	S	11.55 MW	12.85 AW	26720 AAW	SCBLS	10//99-12//99
General	South Dakota	S	9.87 MW	10.16 AW	21140 AAW	SDBLS	10//99-12//99
General	Tennessee	S	11.78 MW	12.62 AW	26250 AAW	TNBLS	10//99-12//99
General	Texas	S	10.44 MW	11.51 AW	23940 AAW	TXBLS	10//99-12//99
General	Utah	S	11.38 MW	12.21 AW	25390 AAW	UTBLS	10//99-12//99
General	Vermont	S	10.98 MW	11.52 AW	23950 AAW	VTBLS	10//99-12//99
General	Virginia	S	11.45 MW	12.22 AW	25420 AAW	VABLS	10//99-12//99
General	Washington	S	13.89 MW	14.16 AW	29450 AAW	WABLS	10//99-12//99
General	West Virginia	S	10.15 MW	11.38 AW	23680 AAW	WVBLS	10//99-12//99
General	Wisconsin	S	12.56 MW	13.04 AW	27130 AAW	WIBLS	10//99-12//99
General	Wyoming	S	11.31 MW	13.59 AW	28270 AAW	WYBLS	10//99-12//99
General	Puerto Rico	S	6.97 MW	8.14 AW	16940 AAW	PRBLS	10//99-12//99
General	Virgin Islands	S	8.18 MW	8.74 AW	18180 AAW	VIBLS	10//99-12//99
General	Guam	S	9.18 MW	9.68 AW	20140 AAW	GUBLS	10//99-12//99
Maintenance Worker							
Machinery	Alabama	S	12.17 MW	13.35 AW	27760 AAW	ALBLS	10//99-12//99
Machinery	Alaska	S	18.59 MW	19.73 AW	41030 AAW	AKBLS	10//99-12//99
Machinery	Arizona	S	15.03 MW	15.89 AW	33050 AAW	AZBLS	10//99-12//99
Machinery	Arkansas	S	11.87 MW	12.43 AW	25860 AAW	ARBLS	10//99-12//99
Machinery	California	S	15.53 MW	15.87 AW	33020 AAW	CABLS	10//99-12//99
Machinery	Connecticut	S	15.41 MW	15.76 AW	32770 AAW	CTBLS	10//99-12//99
Machinery	Delaware	S	16.99 MW	16.81 AW	34960 AAW	DEBLS	10//99-12//99
Machinery	District of Columbia	S	11.98 MW	12.64 AW	26300 AAW	DCBLS	10//99-12//99
Machinery	Florida	S	12.3 MW	13.15 AW	27350 AAW	FLBLS	10//99-12//99
Machinery	Georgia	S	12.33 MW	13.06 AW	27160 AAW	GABLS	10//99-12//99
Machinery	Hawaii	S	18.9 MW	19.03 AW	39590 AAW	HIBLS	10//99-12//99
Machinery	Idaho	S	10.94 MW	11.34 AW	23580 AAW	IDBLS	10//99-12//99
Machinery	Illinois	S	15.81 MW	16.30 AW	33910 AAW	ILBLS	10//99-12//99
Machinery	Indiana	S	15.44 MW	16.03 AW	33340 AAW	INBLS	10//99-12//99
Machinery	Iowa	S	13.53 MW	13.96 AW	29040 AAW	IABLS	10//99-12//99
Machinery	Kansas	S	13.79 MW	14.01 AW	29140 AAW	KSBLS	10//99-12//99
Machinery	Kentucky	S	13.88 MW	14.58 AW	30320 AAW	KYBLS	10//99-12//99
Machinery	Louisiana	S	12.89 MW	14.97 AW	31140 AAW	LABLS	10//99-12//99
Machinery	Maine	S	16.59 MW	16.58 AW	34500 AAW	MEBLS	10//99-12//99
Machinery	Maryland	S	13.36 MW	13.85 AW	28800 AAW	MDBLS	10//99-12//99
Machinery	Massachusetts	S	15.21 MW	15.21 AW	31640 AAW	MABLS	10//99-12//99
Machinery	Michigan	S	16.99 MW	18.45 AW	38380 AAW	MIBLS	10//99-12//99
Machinery	Minnesota	S	15.19 MW	15.34 AW	31910 AAW	MNBLS	10//99-12//99
Machinery	Mississippi	S	11.56 MW	12.45 AW	25900 AAW	MSBLS	10//99-12//99
Machinery	Missouri	S	12.89 MW	13.57 AW	28220 AAW	MOBLS	10//99-12//99
Machinery	Montana	S	14.39 MW	14.49 AW	30130 AAW	MTBLS	10//99-12//99
Machinery	Nebraska	S	13.47 MW	13.81 AW	28730 AAW	NEBLS	10//99-12//99
Machinery	Nevada	S	17.39 MW	16.49 AW	34300 AAW	NVBLS	10//99-12//99
Machinery	New Hampshire	S	13.89 MW	13.37 AW	27810 AAW	NHBLS	10//99-12//99
Machinery	New Jersey	S	16.11 MW	16.16 AW	33610 AAW	NJBLS	10//99-12//99
Machinery	New Mexico	S	11.91 MW	12.80 AW	26610 AAW	NMBLS	10//99-12//99
Machinery	New York	S	15.17 MW	15.64 AW	32540 AAW	NYBLS	10//99-12//99
Machinery	North Carolina	S	13.29 MW	14.65 AW	30480 AAW	NCBLS	10//99-12//99
Machinery	North Dakota	S	13.62 MW	14.67 AW	30520 AAW	NDBLS	10//99-12//99
Machinery	Ohio	S	16.54 MW	17.54 AW	36480 AAW	OHBLS	10//99-12//99
Machinery	Oklahoma	S	13.64 MW	14.46 AW	30080 AAW	OKBLS	10//99-12//99

AAW	Average annual wage	AOH	Average offered, high	ASH	Average starting, high	H	Hourly	M	Monthly	S	Special: hourly and annual
AE	Average entry wage	AOL	Average offered, low	ASL	Average starting, low	HI	Highest wage paid	MTC	Median total compensation	TQ	Third quartile wage
AEX	Average experienced wage	APH	Average pay, high range	AW	Average wage paid	HR	High end range	MW	Median wage paid	W	Weekly
AO	Average offered	APL	Average pay, low range	FQ	First quartile wage	LR	Low end range	SQ	Second quartile wage	Y	Yearly

Occupation/Type/Industry	Location	Per	Low	Mid	High	Source	Date
Maintenance Worker							
Machinery	Oregon	S	15.37 MW	15.82 AW	32900 AAW	ORBLS	10//99-12//99
Machinery	Pennsylvania	S	14.58 MW	14.84 AW	30870 AAW	PABLS	10//99-12//99
Machinery	Rhode Island	S	12.72 MW	13.38 AW	27820 AAW	RIBLS	10//99-12//99
Machinery	South Carolina	S	14.76 MW	15.11 AW	31440 AAW	SCBLS	10//99-12//99
Machinery	South Dakota	S	10.22 MW	10.98 AW	22840 AAW	SDBLS	10//99-12//99
Machinery	Tennessee	S	14.4 MW	15.62 AW	32490 AAW	TNBLS	10//99-12//99
Machinery	Texas	S	13.79 MW	14.93 AW	31060 AAW	TXBLS	10//99-12//99
Machinery	Utah	S	14.41 MW	14.64 AW	30450 AAW	UTBLS	10//99-12//99
Machinery	Vermont	S	13.13 MW	13.26 AW	27580 AAW	VTBLS	10//99-12//99
Machinery	Virginia	S	13.91 MW	13.94 AW	28990 AAW	VABLS	10//99-12//99
Machinery	Washington	S	17.74 MW	18.05 AW	37550 AAW	WABLS	10//99-12//99
Machinery	West Virginia	S	14.99 MW	15.01 AW	31230 AAW	WVBLS	10//99-12//99
Machinery	Wisconsin	S	13.81 MW	14.61 AW	30380 AAW	WIBLS	10//99-12//99
Machinery	Wyoming	S	20.34 MW	19.26 AW	40050 AAW	WYBLS	10//99-12//99
Machinery	Puerto Rico	S	8.44 MW	9.34 AW	19440 AAW	PRBLS	10//99-12//99
Makeup Artist							
Theatrical and Performance	California	S	17.85 MW	17.30 AW	35990 AAW	CABLS	10//99-12//99
Theatrical and Performance	Florida	S	11.29 MW	11.10 AW	23080 AAW	FLBLS	10//99-12//99
Theatrical and Performance	Maryland	S	9.41 MW	9.20 AW	19130 AAW	MDBLS	10//99-12//99
Theatrical and Performance	New York	S	7.64 MW	12.30 AW	25570 AAW	NYBLS	10//99-12//99
Theatrical and Performance	Texas	S	7.82 MW	8.59 AW	17860 AAW	TXBLS	10//99-12//99
Theatrical and Performance	Washington	S	12.22 MW	13.31 AW	27680 AAW	WABLS	10//99-12//99
Theatrical and Performance	Puerto Rico	S	9.98 MW	10.63 AW	22100 AAW	PRBLS	10//99-12//99
Mall Manager							
Shopping Center	United States	Y	54000 APL	74000 AW	80000 APH	SCW2	2000
Shopping Mall	United States	Y	39000 APL	66000 AW	78000 APH	SCW	1999
Mall Security Officer							
Shopping Center	United States	Y	33000 APL	40000 AW	47000 APH	SCW2	2000
Shopping Mall	United States	Y	25000 APL	39000 AW	49000 APH	SCW	1999
Managed Care Executive							
Hospital	United States	Y		110100 MW		HHN	2000
Management Analyst							
	Alabama	S	24.63 MW	24.41 AW	50780 AAW	ALBLS	10//99-12//99
	Birmingham MSA, AL	S	25.62 MW	25.73 AW	53280 AAW	ALBLS	10//99-12//99
	Huntsville MSA, AL	S	26.67 MW	26.35 AW	55470 AAW	ALBLS	10//99-12//99
	Mobile MSA, AL	S	22.94 MW	22.79 AW	47720 AAW	ALBLS	10//99-12//99
	Montgomery MSA, AL	S	24.55 MW	23.52 AW	51070 AAW	ALBLS	10//99-12//99
	Alaska	S	24.49 MW	26.99 AW	56130 AAW	AKBLS	10//99-12//99
	Arizona	S	23.04 MW	23.97 AW	49860 AAW	AZBLS	10//99-12//99
	Flagstaff MSA, AZ-UT	S	22.54 MW	22.01 AW	46880 AAW	AZBLS	10//99-12//99
	Phoenix-Mesa MSA, AZ	S	24.23 MW	23.18 AW	50400 AAW	AZBLS	10//99-12//99
	Tucson MSA, AZ	S	26.43 MW	24.92 AW	54970 AAW	AZBLS	10//99-12//99
	Yuma MSA, AZ	S	18.65 MW	19.02 AW	38800 AAW	AZBLS	10//99-12//99
	Arkansas	S	16.46 MW	18.00 AW	37430 AAW	ARBLS	10//99-12//99
	Fayetteville-Springdale-Rogers MSA, AR	S	21.61 MW	21.66 AW	44950 AAW	ARBLS	10//99-12//99
	Fort Smith MSA, AR-OK	S	26.58 MW	26.01 AW	55290 AAW	ARBLS	10//99-12//99
	Little Rock-North Little Rock MSA, AR	S	17.52 MW	16.22 AW	36440 AAW	ARBLS	10//99-12//99
	California	S	28.57 MW	30.26 AW	62940 AAW	CABLS	10//99-12//99
	Fresno MSA, CA	S	24.39 MW	23.31 AW	50730 AAW	CABLS	10//99-12//99
	Los Angeles-Long Beach PMSA, CA	S	31.10 MW	29.30 AW	64680 AAW	CABLS	10//99-12//99
	Oakland PMSA, CA	S	31.91 MW	29.51 AW	66370 AAW	CABLS	10//99-12//99
	Orange County PMSA, CA	S	33.75 MW	32.14 AW	70190 AAW	CABLS	10//99-12//99
	Riverside-San Bernardino PMSA, CA	S	23.89 MW	23.86 AW	49680 AAW	CABLS	10//99-12//99
	Sacramento PMSA, CA	S	26.76 MW	24.55 AW	55660 AAW	CABLS	10//99-12//99
	San Diego MSA, CA	S	25.28 MW	24.27 AW	52580 AAW	CABLS	10//99-12//99
	San Francisco PMSA, CA	S	29.04 MW	28.73 AW	60410 AAW	CABLS	10//99-12//99
	San Jose PMSA, CA	S	30.05 MW	29.78 AW	62510 AAW	CABLS	10//99-12//99
	San Luis Obispo-Atascadero-Paso Robles MSA, CA	S	23.73 MW	23.63 AW	49350 AAW	CABLS	10//99-12//99
	Santa Barbara-Santa Maria-Lompoc MSA, CA	S	27.70 MW	26.45 AW	57610 AAW	CABLS	10//99-12//99
	Santa Cruz-Watsonville PMSA, CA	S	41.24 MW	46.89 AW	85770 AAW	CABLS	10//99-12//99
	Santa Rosa PMSA, CA	S	29.76 MW	28.79 AW	61900 AAW	CABLS	10//99-12//99

AAW	Average annual wage	AOH	Average offered, high	ASH	Average starting, high	H	Hourly
AE	Average entry wage	AOL	Average offered, low	ASL	Average starting, low	HI	Highest wage paid
AEX	Average experienced wage	APH	Average pay, high range	AW	Average wage paid	HR	High end range
AO	Average offered	APL	Average pay, low range	FQ	First quartile wage	LR	Low end range

M Monthly · S Special: hourly and annual · MTC Median total compensation · TQ Third quartile wage · MW Median wage paid · W Weekly · SQ Second quartile wage · Y Yearly

Occupation/Type/Industry	Location	Per	Low	Mid	High	Source	Date
Management Analyst	Vallejo-Fairfield-Napa PMSA, CA	S	26.21 MW	25.21 AW	54520 AAW	CABLS	10//99-12//99
	Yolo PMSA, CA	S	22.99 MW	22.86 AW	47810 AAW	CABLS	10//99-12//99
	Colorado	S	28.4 MW	32.46 AW	67520 AAW	COBLS	10//99-12//99
	Connecticut	S	26.97 MW	31.03 AW	64550 AAW	CTBLS	10//99-12//99
	Bridgeport PMSA, CT	S	40.44 MW	31.72 AW	84110 AAW	CTBLS	10//99-12//99
	Hartford MSA, CT	S	29.02 MW	26.78 AW	60360 AAW	CTBLS	10//99-12//99
	New Haven-Meriden PMSA, CT	S	25.66 MW	24.41 AW	53380 AAW	CTBLS	10//99-12//99
	New London-Norwich MSA, CT-RI	S	26.38 MW	27.87 AW	54880 AAW	CTBLS	10//99-12//99
	Stamford-Norwalk PMSA, CT	S	34.42 MW	27.06 AW	71600 AAW	CTBLS	10//99-12//99
	Waterbury PMSA, CT	S	27.28 MW	25.70 AW	56750 AAW	CTBLS	10//99-12//99
	Delaware	S	23.28 MW	24.89 AW	51770 AAW	DEBLS	10//99-12//99
	Wilmington-Newark PMSA, DE-MD	S	25.34 MW	23.94 AW	52710 AAW	DEBLS	10//99-12//99
	Washington PMSA, DC-MD-VA-WV	S	29.39 MW	28.88 AW	61120 AAW	DCBLS	10//99-12//99
	Florida	S	23.05 MW	25.16 AW	52330 AAW	FLBLS	10//99-12//99
	Daytona Beach MSA, FL	S	18.71 MW	18.76 AW	38910 AAW	FLBLS	10//99-12//99
	Fort Lauderdale PMSA, FL	S	23.52 MW	23.13 AW	48910 AAW	FLBLS	10//99-12//99
	Fort Myers-Cape Coral MSA, FL	S	27.33 MW	29.90 AW	56850 AAW	FLBLS	10//99-12//99
	Fort Pierce-Port St. Lucie MSA, FL	S	25.43 MW	22.91 AW	52890 AAW	FLBLS	10//99-12//99
	Jacksonville MSA, FL	S	21.26 MW	19.73 AW	44220 AAW	FLBLS	10//99-12//99
	Lakeland-Winter Haven MSA, FL	S	19.28 MW	18.67 AW	40100 AAW	FLBLS	10//99-12//99
	Melbourne-Titusville-Palm Bay MSA, FL	S	26.41 MW	25.64 AW	54940 AAW	FLBLS	10//99-12//99
	Miami PMSA, FL	S	27.69 MW	22.54 AW	57600 AAW	FLBLS	10//99-12//99
	Naples MSA, FL	S	33.87 MW	29.02 AW	70440 AAW	FLBLS	10//99-12//99
	Ocala MSA, FL	S	18.84 MW	17.17 AW	39190 AAW	FLBLS	10//99-12//99
	Orlando MSA, FL	S	21.02 MW	22.13 AW	43720 AAW	FLBLS	10//99-12//99
	Sarasota-Bradenton MSA, FL	S	20.96 MW	19.25 AW	43600 AAW	FLBLS	10//99-12//99
	Tampa-St. Petersburg-Clearwater MSA, FL	S	26.73 MW	26.27 AW	55590 AAW	FLBLS	10//99-12//99
	West Palm Beach-Boca Raton MSA, FL	S	26.82 MW	25.40 AW	55780 AAW	FLBLS	10//99-12//99
	Georgia	S	25.3 MW	27.40 AW	56990 AAW	GABLS	10//99-12//99
	Atlanta MSA, GA	S	27.80 MW	25.63 AW	57820 AAW	GABLS	10//99-12//99
	Columbus MSA, GA-AL	S	24.20 MW	23.76 AW	50330 AAW	GABLS	10//99-12//99
	Savannah MSA, GA	S	20.21 MW	20.02 AW	42040 AAW	GABLS	10//99-12//99
	Hawaii	S	24.11 MW	25.78 AW	53630 AAW	HIBLS	10//99-12//99
	Honolulu MSA, HI	S	25.29 MW	23.78 AW	52590 AAW	HIBLS	10//99-12//99
	Illinois	S	21.58 MW	23.05 AW	47950 AAW	ILBLS	10//99-12//99
	Champaign-Urbana MSA, IL	S	25.84 MW	24.82 AW	53750 AAW	ILBLS	10//99-12//99
	Chicago PMSA, IL	S	22.96 MW	21.43 AW	47760 AAW	ILBLS	10//99-12//99
	Peoria-Pekin MSA, IL	S	23.62 MW	21.39 AW	49130 AAW	ILBLS	10//99-12//99
	Rockford MSA, IL	S	24.22 MW	21.96 AW	50380 AAW	ILBLS	10//99-12//99
	Springfield MSA, IL	S	22.92 MW	21.02 AW	47670 AAW	ILBLS	10//99-12//99
	Indiana	S	20.93 MW	25.24 AW	52510 AAW	INBLS	10//99-12//99
	Bloomington MSA, IN	S	39.97 MW	47.44 AW	83140 AAW	INBLS	10//99-12//99
	Elkhart-Goshen MSA, IN	S	12.58 MW	10.30 AW	26180 AAW	INBLS	10//99-12//99
	Evansville-Henderson MSA, IN-KY	S	16.17 MW	13.27 AW	33640 AAW	INBLS	10//99-12//99
	Fort Wayne MSA, IN	S	17.50 MW	16.90 AW	36400 AAW	INBLS	10//99-12//99
	Indianapolis MSA, IN	S	25.13 MW	21.74 AW	52260 AAW	INBLS	10//99-12//99
	Lafayette MSA, IN	S	30.87 MW	19.57 AW	64220 AAW	INBLS	10//99-12//99
	Muncie MSA, IN	S	22.62 MW	15.84 AW	47040 AAW	INBLS	10//99-12//99
	South Bend MSA, IN	S	23.77 MW	21.17 AW	49440 AAW	INBLS	10//99-12//99
	Terre Haute MSA, IN	S	28.76 MW	26.28 AW	59820 AAW	INBLS	10//99-12//99
	Iowa	S	21.8 MW	22.34 AW	46460 AAW	IABLS	10//99-12//99
	Cedar Rapids MSA, IA	S	21.86 MW	20.90 AW	45470 AAW	IABLS	10//99-12//99
	Des Moines MSA, IA	S	22.24 MW	22.14 AW	46250 AAW	IABLS	10//99-12//99
	Iowa City MSA, IA	S	22.26 MW	21.33 AW	46290 AAW	IABLS	10//99-12//99
	Kansas	S	20.93 MW	26.02 AW	54110 AAW	KSBLS	10//99-12//99
	Lawrence MSA, KS	S	27.29 MW	23.50 AW	56770 AAW	KSBLS	10//99-12//99
	Wichita MSA, KS	S	32.02 MW	24.85 AW	66590 AAW	KSBLS	10//99-12//99
	Kentucky	S	18.25 MW	19.28 AW	40110 AAW	KYBLS	10//99-12//99
	Lexington MSA, KY	S	17.89 MW	14.89 AW	37200 AAW	KYBLS	10//99-12//99
	Louisville MSA, KY-IN	S	16.97 MW	10.68 AW	35300 AAW	KYBLS	10//99-12//99

AAW Average annual wage	AOH Average offered, high	ASH Average starting, high	H Hourly	M Monthly	S Special: hourly and annual
AE Average entry wage	AOL Average offered, low	ASL Average starting, low	HI Highest wage paid	MTC Median total compensation	TQ Third quartile wage
AEX Average experienced wage	APH Average pay, high range	AW Average wage paid	HR High end range	MW Median wage paid	W Weekly
AO Average offered	APL Average pay, low range	FQ First quartile wage	LR Low end range	SQ Second quartile wage	Y Yearly

Occupation/Type/Industry	Location	Per	Low	Mid	High	Source	Date
Management Analyst	Louisiana	s	20.76 MW	22.12 AW	46020 AAW	LABLS	10//99-12//99
	Baton Rouge MSA, LA	s	24.00 MW	21.18 AW	49930 AAW	LABLS	10//99-12//99
	Lafayette MSA, LA	s	17.31 MW	17.05 AW	36000 AAW	LABLS	10//99-12//99
	Lake Charles MSA, LA	s	20.79 MW	20.51 AW	43230 AAW	LABLS	10//99-12//99
	Monroe MSA, LA	s	18.82 MW	18.48 AW	39160 AAW	LABLS	10//99-12//99
	New Orleans MSA, LA	s	22.61 MW	22.00 AW	47030 AAW	LABLS	10//99-12//99
	Shreveport-Bossier City MSA, LA	s	19.65 MW	19.04 AW	40870 AAW	LABLS	10//99-12//99
	Maine	s	22.96 MW	24.11 AW	50150 AAW	MEBLS	10//99-12//99
	Portland MSA, ME	s	22.78 MW	19.78 AW	47390 AAW	MEBLS	10//99-12//99
	Maryland	s	27.44 MW	27.89 AW	58020 AAW	MDBLS	10//99-12//99
	Baltimore PMSA, MD	s	28.14 MW	26.87 AW	58520 AAW	MDBLS	10//99-12//99
	Massachusetts	s	31.77 MW	35.30 AW	73420 AAW	MABLS	10//99-12//99
	Barnstable-Yarmouth MSA, MA	s	31.75 MW	30.69 AW	66030 AAW	MABLS	10//99-12//99
	Boston PMSA, MA-NH	s	36.18 MW	32.44 AW	75260 AAW	MABLS	10//99-12//99
	Lowell PMSA, MA-NH	s	30.50 MW	30.34 AW	63450 AAW	MABLS	10//99-12//99
	Worcester PMSA, MA-CT	s	29.09 MW	28.31 AW	60500 AAW	MABLS	10//99-12//99
	Michigan	s	28.24 MW	30.55 AW	63550 AAW	MIBLS	10//99-12//99
	Ann Arbor PMSA, MI	s	34.52 MW	31.15 AW	71810 AAW	MIBLS	10//99-17//99
	Detroit PMSA, MI	s	28.96 MW	27.91 AW	60230 AAW	MIBLS	10//99-12//99
	Flint PMSA, MI	s	33.34 MW	30.66 AW	69340 AAW	MIBLS	10//99-12//99
	Grand Rapids-Muskegon-Holland MSA, MI	s	28.21 MW	25.31 AW	58680 AAW	MIBLS	10//99-12//99
	Lansing-East Lansing MSA, MI	s	23.44 MW	20.87 AW	48760 AAW	MIBLS	10//99-12//99
	Saginaw-Bay City-Midland MSA, MI	s	26.01 MW	24.52 AW	54100 AAW	MIBLS	10//99-12//99
	Minnesota	s	25.72 MW	27.13 AW	56430 AAW	MNBLS	10//99-12//99
	Duluth-Superior MSA, MN-WI	s	26.48 MW	25.20 AW	55080 AAW	MNBLS	10//99-12//99
	Minneapolis-St. Paul MSA, MN-WI	s	27.08 MW	25.79 AW	56320 AAW	MNBLS	10//99-12//99
	Rochester MSA, MN	s	26.09 MW	25.37 AW	54260 AAW	MNBLS	10//99-12//99
	St. Cloud MSA, MN	s	32.12 MW	35.37 AW	66810 AAW	MNBLS	10//99-12//99
	Mississippi	s	19.72 MW	21.04 AW	43770 AAW	MSBLS	10//99-12//99
	Biloxi-Gulfport-Pascagoula MSA, MS	s	22.18 MW	21.13 AW	46140 AAW	MSBLS	10//99-12//99
	Missouri	s	21.41 MW	23.38 AW	48620 AAW	MOBLS	10//99-12//99
	Kansas City MSA, MO-KS	s	25.75 MW	22.97 AW	53560 AAW	MOBLS	10//99-12//99
	St. Louis MSA, MO-IL	s	23.88 MW	21.42 AW	49670 AAW	MOBLS	10//99-12//99
	Springfield MSA, MO	s	21.90 MW	20.12 AW	45550 AAW	MOBLS	10//99-12//99
	Montana	s	21.26 MW	23.21 AW	48280 AAW	MTBLS	10//99-12//99
	Missoula MSA, MT	s	26.86 MW	26.34 AW	55860 AAW	MTBLS	10//99-12//99
	Nebraska	s	24.88 MW	28.73 AW	59750 AAW	NEBLS	10//99-12//99
	Lincoln MSA, NE	s	26.13 MW	25.03 AW	54360 AAW	NEBLS	10//99-12//99
	Omaha MSA, NE-IA	s	29.85 MW	25.12 AW	62080 AAW	NEBLS	10//99-12//99
	Nevada	s	24.12 MW	24.76 AW	51500 AAW	NVBLS	10//99-12//99
	Las Vegas MSA, NV-AZ	s	25.31 MW	25.06 AW	52640 AAW	NVBLS	10//99-12//99
	Reno MSA, NV	s	26.01 MW	24.36 AW	54100 AAW	NVBLS	10//99-12//99
	New Hampshire	s	37.4 MW	38.25 AW	79550 AAW	NHBLS	10//99-12//99
	Nashua PMSA, NH	s	28.60 MW	24.33 AW	59490 AAW	NHBLS	10//99-12//99
	New Jersey	s	28.29 MW	29.32 AW	60990 AAW	NJBLS	10//99-12//99
	Bergen-Passaic PMSA, NJ	s	26.98 MW	25.20 AW	56130 AAW	NJBLS	10//99-12//99
	Jersey City PMSA, NJ	s	19.66 MW	21.20 AW	40890 AAW	NJBLS	10//99-12//99
	Middlesex-Somerset-Hunterdon PMSA, NJ	s	27.59 MW	25.44 AW	57380 AAW	NJBLS	10//99-12//99
	Newark PMSA, NJ	s	30.26 MW	28.26 AW	62940 AAW	NJBLS	10//99-12//99
	Vineland-Millville-Bridgeton PMSA, NJ	s	26.18 MW	26.32 AW	54450 AAW	NJBLS	10//99-12//99
	New Mexico	s	22.08 MW	23.46 AW	48790 AAW	NMBLS	10//99-12//99
	Albuquerque MSA, NM	s	22.38 MW	21.23 AW	46550 AAW	NMBLS	10//99-12//99
	Santa Fe MSA, NM	s	23.79 MW	22.88 AW	49490 AAW	NMBLS	10//99-12//99
	New York	s	25.83 MW	29.04 AW	60400 AAW	NYBLS	10//99-12//99
	Albany-Schenectady-Troy MSA, NY	s	24.97 MW	24.73 AW	51940 AAW	NYBLS	10//99-12//99
	Binghamton MSA, NY	s	24.76 MW	23.75 AW	51510 AAW	NYBLS	10//99-12//99
	Buffalo-Niagara Falls MSA, NY	s	22.15 MW	20.32 AW	46080 AAW	NYBLS	10//99-12//99
	Dutchess County PMSA, NY	s	25.18 MW	24.93 AW	52370 AAW	NYBLS	10//99-12//99
	Nassau-Suffolk PMSA, NY	s	24.46 MW	20.85 AW	50880 AAW	NYBLS	10//99-12//99
	New York PMSA, NY	s	31.37 MW	26.91 AW	65240 AAW	NYBLS	10//99-12//99
	Newburgh PMSA, NY-PA	s	20.65 MW	19.89 AW	42960 AAW	NYBLS	10//99-12//99
	Rochester MSA, NY	s	26.52 MW	26.70 AW	55170 AAW	NYBLS	10//99-12//99

AAW Average annual wage	AOH Average offered, high	ASH Average starting, high	H Hourly	M Monthly	S Special: hourly and annual
AE Average entry wage	AOL Average offered, low	ASL Average starting, low	HI Highest wage paid	MTC Median total compensation	TQ Third quartile wage
AEX Average experienced wage	APH Average pay, high range	AW Average wage paid	HR High end range	MW Median wage paid	W Weekly
AO Average offered	APL Average pay, low range	FQ First quartile wage	LR Low end range	SQ Second quartile wage	Y Yearly

Occupation/Type/Industry	Location	Per	Low	Mid	High	Source	Date
Management Analyst	Syracuse MSA, NY	S	24.52 MW	25.32 AW	51010 AAW	NYBLS	10//99-12//99
	Utica-Rome MSA, NY	S	17.81 MW	16.71 AW	37040 AAW	NYBLS	10//99-12//99
	North Carolina	S	24.76 MW	27.08 AW	56320 AAW	NCBLS	10//99-12//99
	Charlotte-Gastonia-Rock Hill MSA, NC-SC	S	27.43 MW	22.89 AW	57050 AAW	NCBLS	10//99-12//99
	Greensboro--Winston-Salem-- High Point MSA, NC	S	26.02 MW	23.99 AW	54120 AAW	NCBLS	10//99-12//99
	Greenville MSA, NC	S	21.28 MW	21.95 AW	44260 AAW	NCBLS	10//99-12//99
	Raleigh-Durham-Chapel Hill MSA, NC	S	28.38 MW	28.84 AW	59020 AAW	NCBLS	10//99-12//99
	Rocky Mount MSA, NC	S	24.05 MW	24.49 AW	50030 AAW	NCBLS	10//99-12//99
	Wilmington MSA, NC	S	19.53 MW	16.12 AW	40620 AAW	NCBLS	10//99-12//99
	North Dakota	S	18.64 MW	17.83 AW	37080 AAW	NDBLS	10//99-12//99
	Bismarck MSA, ND	S	20.69 MW	18.82 AW	43030 AAW	NDBLS	10//99-12//99
	Ohio	S	25 MW	26.27 AW	54630 AAW	OHBLS	10//99-12//99
	Akron PMSA, OH	S	23.80 MW	23.37 AW	49510 AAW	OHBLS	10//99-12//99
	Cincinnati PMSA, OH-KY-IN	S	26.28 MW	23.70 AW	54660 AAW	OHBLS	10//99-12//99
	Cleveland-Lorain-Elyria PMSA, OH	S	26.04 MW	24.98 AW	54160 AAW	OHBLS	10//99-12//99
	Dayton-Springfield MSA, OH	S	23.90 MW	23.57 AW	49710 AAW	OHBLS	10//99-12//99
	Hamilton-Middletown PMSA, OH	S	21.92 MW	21.33 AW	45600 AAW	OHBLS	10//99-12//99
	Toledo MSA, OH	S	33.65 MW	31.20 AW	70000 AAW	OHBLS	10//99-12//99
	Youngstown-Warren MSA, OH	S	24.37 MW	24.78 AW	50690 AAW	OHBLS	10//99-12//99
	Oklahoma	S	21.87 MW	21.92 AW	45590 AAW	OKBLS	10//99-12//99
	Lawton MSA, OK	S	15.60 MW	14.72 AW	32440 AAW	OKBLS	10//99-12//99
	Tulsa MSA, OK	S	22.98 MW	22.22 AW	47810 AAW	OKBLS	10//99-12//99
	Oregon	S	26.21 MW	29.12 AW	60580 AAW	ORBLS	10//99-12//99
	Eugene-Springfield MSA, OR	S	28.76 MW	29.55 AW	59810 AAW	ORBLS	10//99-12//99
	Medford-Ashland MSA, OR	S	27.84 MW	26.16 AW	57900 AAW	ORBLS	10//99-12//99
	Portland-Vancouver PMSA, OR-WA	S	28.84 MW	25.27 AW	59990 AAW	ORBLS	10//99-12//99
	Pennsylvania	S	24.75 MW	25.43 AW	52890 AAW	PABLS	10//99-12//99
	Allentown-Bethlehem-Easton MSA, PA	S	18.87 MW	18.61 AW	39250 AAW	PABLS	10//99-12//99
	Harrisburg-Lebanon-Carlisle MSA, PA	S	23.06 MW	22.51 AW	47970 AAW	PABLS	10//99-12//99
	Lancaster MSA, PA	S	26.93 MW	22.53 AW	56020 AAW	PABLS	10//99-12//99
	Philadelphia PMSA, PA-NJ	S	26.61 MW	25.39 AW	55350 AAW	PABLS	10//99-12//99
	Pittsburgh MSA, PA	S	25.21 MW	25.70 AW	52440 AAW	PABLS	10//99-12//99
	Scranton--Wilkes-Barre-- Hazleton MSA, PA	S	30.57 MW	35.12 AW	63580 AAW	PABLS	10//99-12//99
	York MSA, PA	S	24.44 MW	21.36 AW	50840 AAW	PABLS	10//99-12//99
	Rhode Island	S	25.62 MW	26.86 AW	55870 AAW	RIBLS	10//99-12//99
	Providence-Fall River- Warwick MSA, RI-MA	S	27.65 MW	26.40 AW	57510 AAW	RIBLS	10//99-12//99
	South Carolina	S	20.82 MW	21.36 AW	44430 AAW	SCBLS	10//99-12//99
	Charleston-North Charleston MSA, SC	S	19.98 MW	19.52 AW	41560 AAW	SCBLS	10//99-12//99
	Columbia MSA, SC	S	19.56 MW	19.79 AW	40680 AAW	SCBLS	10//99-12//99
	Greenville-Spartanburg- Anderson MSA, SC	S	19.09 MW	16.36 AW	39700 AAW	SCBLS	10//99-12//99
	Myrtle Beach MSA, SC	S	21.50 MW	23.31 AW	44730 AAW	SCBLS	10//99-12//99
	Sumter MSA, SC	S	30.19 MW	30.76 AW	62790 AAW	SCBLS	10//99-12//99
	South Dakota	S	24.79 MW	27.41 AW	57020 AAW	SDBLS	10//99-12//99
	Rapid City MSA, SD	S	25.71 MW	23.18 AW	53470 AAW	SDBLS	10//99-12//99
	Tennessee	S	24.73 MW	24.90 AW	51800 AAW	TNBLS	10//99-12//99
	Johnson City-Kingsport-Bristol MSA, TN-VA	S	21.64 MW	22.65 AW	45000 AAW	TNBLS	10//99-12//99
	Memphis MSA, TN-AR-MS	S	24.76 MW	23.80 AW	51500 AAW	MSBLS	10//99-12//99
	Nashville MSA, TN	S	23.48 MW	22.65 AW	48840 AAW	TNBLS	10//99-12//99
	Texas	S	25.86 MW	29.02 AW	60360 AAW	TXBLS	10//99-12//99
	Amarillo MSA, TX	S	24.98 MW	25.57 AW	51970 AAW	TXBLS	10//99-12//99
	Beaumont-Port Arthur MSA, TX	S	29.71 MW	28.07 AW	61790 AAW	TXBLS	10//99-12//99
	Corpus Christi MSA, TX	S	30.89 MW	30.41 AW	64250 AAW	TXBLS	10//99-12//99
	Dallas PMSA, TX	S	31.55 MW	28.34 AW	65630 AAW	TXBLS	10//99-12//99
	El Paso MSA, TX	S	23.00 MW	21.04 AW	47850 AAW	TXBLS	10//99-12//99
	Fort Worth-Arlington PMSA, TX	S	24.43 MW	22.94 AW	50810 AAW	TXBLS	10//99-12//99
	Galveston-Texas City PMSA, TX	S	25.99 MW	25.21 AW	54060 AAW	TXBLS	10//99-12//99

AAW	Average annual wage	**AOH**	Average offered, high	**ASH**	Average starting, high	**H**	Hourly	**M**	Monthly	**S**	Special: hourly and annual
AE	Average entry wage	**AOL**	Average offered, low	**ASL**	Average starting, low	**HI**	Highest wage paid	**MTC**	Median total compensation	**TQ**	Third quartile wage
AEX	Average experienced wage	**APH**	Average pay, high range	**AW**	Average wage paid	**HR**	High end range	**MW**	Median wage paid	**W**	Weekly
AO	Average offered	**APL**	Average pay, low range	**FQ**	First quartile wage	**LR**	Low end range	**SQ**	Second quartile wage	**Y**	Yearly

Occupation/Type/Industry	Location	Per	Low	Mid	High	Source	Date
Management Analyst	Houston PMSA, TX	S	32.34 MW	29.40 AW	67270 AAW	TXBLS	10//99-12//99
	Laredo MSA, TX	S	19.88 MW	18.45 AW	41350 AAW	TXBLS	10//99-12//99
	Longview-Marshall MSA, TX	S	29.54 MW	29.43 AW	61430 AAW	TXBLS	10//99-12//99
	Odessa-Midland MSA, TX	S	26.86 MW	24.19 AW	55870 AAW	TXBLS	10//99-12//99
	San Antonio MSA, TX	S	25.59 MW	23.82 AW	53230 AAW	TXBLS	10//99-12//99
	Texarkana MSA, TX- Texarkana, AR	S	23.56 MW	23.67 AW	49010 AAW	TXBLS	10//99-12//99
	Waco MSA, TX	S	24.01 MW	23.72 AW	49950 AAW	TXBLS	10//99-12//99
	Wichita Falls MSA, TX	S	30.11 MW	26.93 AW	62620 AAW	TXBLS	10//99-12//99
	Utah	S	24.16 MW	25.20 AW	52420 AAW	UTBLS	10//99-12//99
	Provo-Orem MSA, UT	S	27.49 MW	26.99 AW	57180 AAW	UTBLS	10//99-12//99
	Salt Lake City-Ogden MSA, UT	S	24.40 MW	23.69 AW	50750 AAW	UTBLS	10//99-12//99
	Vermont	S	24.8 MW	26.25 AW	54600 AAW	VTBLS	10//99-12//99
	Burlington MSA, VT	S	24.20 MW	22.27 AW	50340 AAW	VTBLS	10//99-12//99
	Virginia	S	26.45 MW	28.36 AW	58990 AAW	VABLS	10//99-12//99
	Charlottesville MSA, VA	S	21.74 MW	17.11 AW	45220 AAW	VABLS	10//99-12//99
	Danville MSA, VA	S	18.80 MW	15.98 AW	39100 AAW	VABLS	10//99-12//99
	Lynchburg MSA, VA	S	19.97 MW	19.27 AW	41530 AAW	VABLS	10//99-12//99
	Norfolk-Virginia Beach-Newport News MSA, VA-NC	S	26.56 MW	24.23 AW	55250 AAW	VABLS	10//99-12//99
	Richmond-Petersburg MSA, VA	S	24.24 MW	21.69 AW	50410 AAW	VABLS	10//99-12//99
	Washington	S	28.06 MW	32.15 AW	66880 AAW	WABLS	10//99-12//99
	Richland-Kennewick-Pasco MSA, WA	S	33.10 MW	27.64 AW	68840 AAW	WABLS	10//99-12//99
	Seattle-Bellevue-Everett PMSA, WA	S	32.25 MW	28.23 AW	67090 AAW	WABLS	10//99-12//99
	Tacoma PMSA, WA	S	26.03 MW	23.46 AW	54140 AAW	WABLS	10//99-12//99
	West Virginia	S	26.07 MW	27.51 AW	57220 AAW	WVBLS	10//99-12//99
	Charleston MSA, WV	S	28.30 MW	25.19 AW	58870 AAW	WVBLS	10//99-12//99
	Huntington-Ashland MSA, WV-KY-OH	S	23.23 MW	23.53 AW	48320 AAW	WVBLS	10//99-12//99
	Wisconsin	S	24.8 MW	25.75 AW	53570 AAW	WIBLS	10//99-12//99
	Appleton-Oshkosh-Neenah MSA, WI	S	22.14 MW	20.61 AW	46050 AAW	WIBLS	10//99-12//99
	Eau Claire MSA, WI	S	21.44 MW	21.08 AW	44600 AAW	WIBLS	10//99-12//99
	Green Bay MSA, WI	S	25.02 MW	23.19 AW	52040 AAW	WIBLS	10//99-12//99
	Milwaukee-Waukesha PMSA, WI	S	26.62 MW	26.46 AW	55370 AAW	WIBLS	10//99-12//99
	Wausau MSA, WI	S	24.99 MW	22.07 AW	51970 AAW	WIBLS	10//99-12//99
	Wyoming	S	23.52 MW	30.22 AW	62860 AAW	WYBLS	10//99-12//99
	Puerto Rico	S	17.74 MW	19.73 AW	41030 AAW	PRBLS	10//99-12//99
	San Juan-Bayamon PMSA, PR	S	17.76 MW	15.61 AW	36930 AAW	PRBLS	10//99-12//99
Manager							
Bicycle Store	United States	Y	20000 APL		45000 APH	BICRET	2000
Business/Management Degree	United States	Y	34870 AE			CSM1	2000
Computer-aided Design, Apparel Industry	United States	Y		56019 AW		BOBBIN	1999
Computer Reseller	United States	Y		70500 MW		CORES	1999
Engineering, Corrosion	United States	Y		81400 AW		MATPER	1999
Female, Logistics	United States	Y	60000 FQ	75000 SQ	90000 TQ	TRAFWD	2000
New Car Sales, Auto Dealership	United States	Y		83245 AW		WARD1	1999
Purchasing, Electronics	United States	Y		109900 AW		ELBUY	2000
Service and Body Shop, Auto Dealership	United States	Y		58904 AW		WARD1	1999
Strategic Planning, On-line Enterprise	United States	Y		115300 AW		WSJ1	2000
Swine, Agriculture	United States	Y	25000 APL	33022 AW	50000 APL	FAJO	1998
Transportation, Fleet with 25-99 vehicles	United States	Y		48000 AW		TFM	1999
Transportation, Fleet with 500+ vehicles	United States	Y		62000 AW		TFM	1999
Used Car Sales, Auto Dealership	United States	Y		80023 AW		WARD1	1999
Manager of Data Processing							
IBM AS/400 Computers	United States	Y		61400 AW		NV&A	1999
Manager of Information Systems							
IBM AS/400 Computers	United States	Y		89500 AW		NV&A	1999
Manager of Operations							
IBM AS/400 Computers	United States	Y		53100 AW		NV&A	1999
Managing Editor							
Magazine	United States	Y		57000 AW		FOLIO	2000

Occupation/Type/Industry	Location	Per	Low	Mid	High	Source	Date
Manicurist and Pedicurist	Alabama	s	7.29 MW	7.72 AW	16050 AAW	ALBLS	10//99-12//99
	Arizona	s	6.64 MW	7.29 AW	15160 AAW	AZBLS	10//99-12//99
	Phoenix-Mesa MSA, AZ	s	7.18 MW	7.04 AW	14920 AAW	AZBLS	10//99-12//99
	Arkansas	s	6.96 MW	9.03 AW	18790 AAW	ARBLS	10//99-12//99
	Little Rock-North Little Rock MSA, AR	s	10.16 MW	9.27 AW	21130 AAW	ARBLS	10//99-12//99
	California	s	6.48 MW	6.78 AW	14110 AAW	CABLS	10//99-12//99
	Los Angeles-Long Beach PMSA, CA	s	6.89 MW	6.48 AW	14340 AAW	CABLS	10//99-12//99
	Oakland PMSA, CA	s	6.88 MW	6.45 AW	14300 AAW	CABLS	10//99-12//99
	Orange County PMSA, CA	s	6.67 MW	6.50 AW	13870 AAW	CABLS	10//99-12//99
	Redding MSA, CA	s	8.04 MW	8.09 AW	16710 AAW	CABLS	10//99-12//99
	Riverside-San Bernardino PMSA, CA	s	6.71 MW	6.55 AW	13960 AAW	CABLS	10//99-12//99
	Salinas MSA, CA	s	6.23 MW	6.25 AW	12960 AAW	CABLS	10//99-12//99
	San Diego MSA, CA	s	6.49 MW	6.47 AW	13490 AAW	CABLS	10//99-12//99
	San Francisco PMSA, CA	s	7.59 MW	7.08 AW	15790 AAW	CABLS	10//99-12//99
	San Jose PMSA, CA	s	7.51 MW	6.06 AW	15620 AAW	CABLS	10//99-12//99
	Santa Rosa PMSA, CA	s	8.95 MW	9.35 AW	18620 AAW	CABLS	10//99-12//99
	Stockton-Lodi MSA, CA	s	6.26 MW	6.28 AW	13010 AAW	CABLS	10//99-12//99
	Vallejo-Fairfield-Napa PMSA, CA	s	6.85 MW	6.66 AW	14240 AAW	CABLS	10//99-12//99
	Colorado	s	7.54 MW	7.96 AW	16560 AAW	COBLS	10//99-12//99
	Boulder-Longmont PMSA, CO	s	6.98 MW	6.22 AW	14520 AAW	COBLS	10//99-12//99
	Denver PMSA, CO	s	8.31 MW	7.92 AW	17280 AAW	COBLS	10//99-12//99
	Connecticut	s	6.4 MW	7.11 AW	14790 AAW	CTBLS	10//99-12//99
	Hartford MSA, CT	s	6.38 MW	6.34 AW	13270 AAW	CTBLS	10//99-12//99
	New Haven-Meriden PMSA, CT	s	9.08 MW	10.11 AW	18890 AAW	CTBLS	10//99-12//99
	Stamford-Norwalk PMSA, CT	s	7.65 MW	6.09 AW	15910 AAW	CTBLS	10//99-12//99
	Waterbury PMSA, CT	s	5.98 MW	5.94 AW	12440 AAW	CTBLS	10//99-12//99
	Delaware	s	8.57 MW	9.35 AW	19450 AAW	DEBLS	10//99-12//99
	Wilmington-Newark PMSA, DE-MD	s	8.73 MW	8.22 AW	18150 AAW	DEBLS	10//99-12//99
	Washington PMSA, DC-MD-VA-WV	s	9.61 MW	8.19 AW	20000 AAW	DCBLS	10//99-12//99
	Florida	s	6.68 MW	7.59 AW	15790 AAW	FLBLS	10//99-12//99
	Daytona Beach MSA, FL	s	8.01 MW	6.49 AW	16660 AAW	FLBLS	10//99-12//99
	Fort Lauderdale PMSA, FL	s	6.38 MW	6.33 AW	13270 AAW	FLBLS	10//99-12//99
	Fort Myers-Cape Coral MSA, FL	s	8.05 MW	7.94 AW	16750 AAW	FLBLS	10//99-12//99
	Fort Pierce-Port St. Lucie MSA, FL	s	6.89 MW	6.89 AW	14320 AAW	FLBLS	10//99-12//99
	Fort Walton Beach MSA, FL	s	6.38 MW	6.40 AW	13270 AAW	FLBLS	10//99-12//99
	Jacksonville MSA, FL	s	7.70 MW	7.31 AW	16020 AAW	FLBLS	10//99-12//99
	Miami PMSA, FL	s	7.65 MW	6.05 AW	15910 AAW	FLBLS	10//99-12//99
	Naples MSA, FL	s	8.33 MW	8.04 AW	17330 AAW	FLBLS	10//99-12//99
	Ocala MSA, FL	s	6.40 MW	6.42 AW	13310 AAW	FLBLS	10//99-12//99
	Orlando MSA, FL	s	7.20 MW	7.02 AW	14970 AAW	FLBLS	10//99-12//99
	Punta Gorda MSA, FL	s	6.72 MW	6.20 AW	13970 AAW	FLBLS	10//99-12//99
	Sarasota-Bradenton MSA, FL	s	8.82 MW	7.71 AW	18340 AAW	FLBLS	10//99-12//99
	Tampa-St. Petersburg-Clearwater MSA, FL	s	6.95 MW	6.72 AW	14450 AAW	FLBLS	10//99-12//99
	West Palm Beach-Boca Raton MSA, FL	s	9.90 MW	10.91 AW	20590 AAW	FLBLS	10//99-12//99
	Georgia	s	6.34 MW	8.18 AW	17010 AAW	GABLS	10//99-12//99
	Hawaii	s	6.26 MW	6.76 AW	14060 AAW	HIBLS	10//99-12//99
	Illinois	s	7.65 MW	8.32 AW	17300 AAW	ILBLS	10//99-12//99
	Bloomington-Normal MSA, IL	s	8.52 MW	8.02 AW	17710 AAW	ILBLS	10//99-12//99
	Chicago PMSA, IL	s	8.48 MW	7.73 AW	17640 AAW	ILBLS	10//99-12//99
	Indiana	s	6.37 MW	7.21 AW	15000 AAW	INBLS	10//99-12//99
	Iowa	s	7.75 MW	8.03 AW	16700 AAW	IABLS	10//99-12//99
	Davenport-Moline-Rock Island MSA, IA-IL	s	6.83 MW	6.90 AW	14210 AAW	IABLS	10//99-12//99
	Des Moines MSA, IA	s	7.65 MW	7.60 AW	15910 AAW	IABLS	10//99-12//99
	Kansas	s	7.52 MW	8.30 AW	17260 AAW	KSBLS	10//99-12//99
	Kentucky	s	7.52 MW	7.64 AW	15900 AAW	KYBLS	10//99-12//99
	Louisville MSA, KY-IN	s	8.01 MW	7.61 AW	16670 AAW	KYBLS	10//99-12//99
	Louisiana	s	6.36 MW	6.72 AW	13970 AAW	LABLS	10//99-12//99
	Baton Rouge MSA, LA	s	7.83 MW	8.02 AW	16280 AAW	LABLS	10//99-12//99
	New Orleans MSA, LA	s	6.64 MW	6.29 AW	13800 AAW	LABLS	10//99-12//99
	Maine	s	6.46 MW	7.55 AW	15710 AAW	MEBLS	10//99-12//99

AAW	Average annual wage	AOH	Average offered, high	ASH	Average starting, high	H	Hourly	M	Monthly	S	Special: hourly and annual
AE	Average entry wage	AOL	Average offered, low	ASL	Average starting, low	HI	Highest wage paid	MTC	Median total compensation	TQ	Third quartile wage
AEX	Average experienced wage	APH	Average pay, high range	AW	Average wage paid	HR	High end range	MW	Median wage paid	W	Weekly
AO	Average offered	APL	Average pay, low range	FQ	First quartile wage	LR	Low end range	SQ	Second quartile wage	Y	Yearly

Occupation/Type/Industry	Location	Per	Low	Mid	High	Source	Date
Manicurist and Pedicurist	Maryland	S	6.55 MW	8.58 AW	17850 AAW	MDBLS	10//99-12//99
	Baltimore PMSA, MD	S	7.71 MW	6.01 AW	16040 AAW	MDBLS	10//99-12//99
	Massachusetts	S	7.99 MW	8.10 AW	16840 AAW	MABLS	10//99-12//99
	Boston PMSA, MA-NH	S	8.29 MW	8.28 AW	17240 AAW	MABLS	10//99-12//99
	Lawrence PMSA, MA-NH	S	6.75 MW	6.43 AW	14030 AAW	MABLS	10//99-12//99
	Springfield MSA, MA	S	7.47 MW	7.11 AW	15530 AAW	MABLS	10//99-12//99
	Worcester PMSA, MA-CT	S	8.15 MW	6.45 AW	16950 AAW	MABLS	10//99-12//99
	Michigan	S	7.34 MW	7.64 AW	15890 AAW	MIBLS	10//99-12//99
	Detroit PMSA, MI	S	7.67 MW	7.44 AW	15950 AAW	MIBLS	10//99-12//99
	Minnesota	S	8.21 MW	9.24 AW	19220 AAW	MNBLS	10//99-12//99
	Minneapolis-St. Paul MSA, MN-WI	S	9.59 MW	8.43 AW	19960 AAW	MNBLS	10//99-12//99
	Mississippi	S	8.1 MW	9.02 AW	18760 AAW	MSBLS	10//99-12//99
	Jackson MSA, MS	S	9.22 MW	8.35 AW	19180 AAW	MSBLS	10//99-12//99
	Missouri	S	10.73 MW	9.44 AW	19640 AAW	MOBLS	10//99-12//99
	Kansas City MSA, MO-KS	S	8.82 MW	7.90 AW	18340 AAW	MOBLS	10//99-12//99
	St. Louis MSA, MO-IL	S	9.57 MW	10.81 AW	19890 AAW	MOBLS	10//99-12//99
	Nebraska	S	9.6 MW	9.99 AW	20770 AAW	NEBLS	10//99-12//99
	Omaha MSA, NE-IA	S	9.88 MW	9.48 AW	20560 AAW	NEBLS	10//99-12//99
	Nevada	S	7.44 MW	7.58 AW	15770 AAW	NVBLS	10//99-12//99
	Las Vegas MSA, NV-AZ	S	7.35 MW	6.76 AW	15300 AAW	NVBLS	10//99-12//99
	New Hampshire	S	6.91 MW	7.31 AW	15210 AAW	NHBLS	10//99-12//99
	Nashua PMSA, NH	S	7.45 MW	7.59 AW	15490 AAW	NHBLS	10//99-12//99
	Portsmouth-Rochester PMSA, NH-ME	S	9.26 MW	7.96 AW	19260 AAW	NHBLS	10//99-12//99
	New Jersey	S	6.99 MW	8.02 AW	16690 AAW	NJBLS	10//99-12//99
	Atlantic-Cape May PMSA, NJ	S	8.17 MW	8.48 AW	16990 AAW	NJBLS	10//99-12//99
	Bergen-Passaic PMSA, NJ	S	8.39 MW	6.88 AW	17450 AAW	NJBLS	10//99-12//99
	Middlesex-Somerset-Hunterdon PMSA, NJ	S	7.14 MW	6.39 AW	14860 AAW	NJBLS	10//99-12//99
	Monmouth-Ocean PMSA, NJ	S	6.70 MW	6.48 AW	13930 AAW	NJBLS	10//99-12//99
	Newark PMSA, NJ	S	9.43 MW	8.47 AW	19610 AAW	NJBLS	10//99-12//99
	Trenton PMSA, NJ	S	9.18 MW	8.36 AW	19100 AAW	NJBLS	10//99-12//99
	New York	S	6.28 MW	6.86 AW	14260 AAW	NYBLS	10//99-12//99
	Albany-Schenectady-Troy MSA, NY	S	6.62 MW	6.03 AW	13760 AAW	NYBLS	10//99-12//99
	New York PMSA, NY	S	7.06 MW	6.19 AW	14690 AAW	NYBLS	10//99-12//99
	Rochester MSA, NY	S	6.21 MW	6.07 AW	12920 AAW	NYBLS	10//99-12//99
	North Carolina	S	7.19 MW	7.56 AW	15720 AAW	NCBLS	10//99-12//99
	Charlotte-Gastonia-Rock Hill MSA, NC-SC	S	10.54 MW	9.93 AW	21930 AAW	NCBLS	10//99-12//99
	Greensboro--Winston-Salem--High Point MSA, NC	S	6.84 MW	6.11 AW	14230 AAW	NCBLS	10//99-12//99
	Raleigh-Durham-Chapel Hill MSA, NC	S	7.61 MW	7.68 AW	15840 AAW	NCBLS	10//99-12//99
	Ohio	S	8.16 MW	9.37 AW	19480 AAW	OHBLS	10//99-12//99
	Akron PMSA, OH	S	7.13 MW	6.77 AW	14830 AAW	OHBLS	10//99-12//99
	Canton-Massillon MSA, OH	S	7.10 MW	6.59 AW	14770 AAW	OHBLS	10//99-12//99
	Cincinnati PMSA, OH-KY-IN	S	9.06 MW	8.67 AW	18840 AAW	OHBLS	10//99-12//99
	Columbus MSA, OH	S	10.17 MW	10.55 AW	21150 AAW	OHBLS	10//99-12//99
	Toledo MSA, OH	S	7.56 MW	7.38 AW	15730 AAW	OHBLS	10//99-12//99
	Youngstown-Warren MSA, OH	S	6.45 MW	6.12 AW	13410 AAW	OHBLS	10//99-12//99
	Oklahoma	S	6.16 MW	6.42 AW	13350 AAW	OKBLS	10//99-12//99
	Oregon	S	6.91 MW	8.37 AW	17400 AAW	ORBLS	10//99-12//99
	Portland-Vancouver PMSA, OR-WA	S	8.21 MW	6.83 AW	17070 AAW	ORBLS	10//99-12//99
	Pennsylvania	S	6.64 MW	8.95 AW	18610 AAW	PABLS	10//99-12//99
	Allentown-Bethlehem-Easton MSA, PA	S	6.64 MW	6.07 AW	13800 AAW	PABLS	10//99-12//99
	Erie MSA, PA	S	5.95 MW	5.96 AW	12380 AAW	PABLS	10//99-12//99
	Johnstown MSA, PA	S	7.44 MW	6.19 AW	15470 AAW	PABLS	10//99-12//99
	Philadelphia PMSA, PA-NJ	S	10.47 MW	8.30 AW	21770 AAW	PABLS	10//99-12//99
	Pittsburgh MSA, PA	S	8.13 MW	6.59 AW	16920 AAW	PABLS	10//99-12//99
	York MSA, PA	S	6.89 MW	6.75 AW	14340 AAW	PABLS	10//99-12//99
	Rhode Island	S	8.04 MW	8.29 AW	17250 AAW	RIBLS	10//99-12//99
	Providence-Fall River-Warwick MSA, RI-MA	S	8.48 MW	8.16 AW	17630 AAW	RIBLS	10//99-12//99
	South Carolina	S	7.4 MW	8.01 AW	16650 AAW	SCBLS	10//99-12//99
	Charleston-North Charleston MSA, SC	S	7.86 MW	7.77 AW	16340 AAW	SCBLS	10//99-12//99
	Tennessee	S	7.4 MW	8.64 AW	17980 AAW	TNBLS	10//99-12//99
	Knoxville MSA, TN	S	10.03 MW	10.01 AW	20860 AAW	TNBLS	10//99-12//99

Occupation/Type/Industry	Location	Per	Low	Mid	High	Source	Date
Manicurist and Pedicurist	Memphis MSA, TN-AR-MS	S	10.35 MW	8.21 AW	21530 AAW	MSBLS	10//99-12//99
	Nashville MSA, TN	S	7.77 MW	7.22 AW	16150 AAW	TNBLS	10//99-12//99
	Texas	S	6.39 MW	7.54 AW	15680 AAW	TXBLS	10//99-12//99
	Abilene MSA, TX	S	6.45 MW	6.04 AW	13410 AAW	TXBLS	10//99-12//99
	Corpus Christi MSA, TX	S	6.16 MW	6.18 AW	12800 AAW	TXBLS	10//99-12//99
	Dallas PMSA, TX	S	6.91 MW	6.00 AW	14370 AAW	TXBLS	10//99-12//99
	El Paso MSA, TX	S	7.45 MW	6.81 AW	15490 AAW	TXBLS	10//99-12//99
	Houston PMSA, TX	S	10.30 MW	10.32 AW	21430 AAW	TXBLS	10//99-12//99
	Killeen-Temple MSA, TX	S	7.69 MW	6.53 AW	15990 AAW	TXBLS	10//99-12//99
	McAllen-Edinburg-Mission MSA, TX	S	5.87 MW	5.92 AW	12210 AAW	TXBLS	10//99-12//99
	San Antonio MSA, TX	S	7.62 MW	6.70 AW	15860 AAW	TXBLS	10//99-12//99
	Virginia	S	7.28 MW	8.65 AW	17990 AAW	VABLS	10//99-12//99
	Norfolk-Virginia Beach-Newport News MSA, VA-NC	S	8.42 MW	6.51 AW	17510 AAW	VABLS	10//99-12//99
	Roanoke MSA, VA	S	6.35 MW	6.06 AW	13210 AAW	VABLS	10//99-12//99
	Washington	S	7.07 MW	8.55 AW	17780 AAW	WABLS	10//99-12//99
	Seattle-Bellevue-Everett PMSA, WA	S	8.64 MW	6.90 AW	17970 AAW	WABLS	10//99-12//99
	Spokane MSA, WA	S	7.16 MW	6.62 AW	14890 AAW	WABLS	10//99-12//99
	West Virginia	S	6.91 MW	7.52 AW	15640 AAW	WVBLS	10//99-12//99
	Wisconsin	S	7.65 MW	8.64 AW	17980 AAW	WIBLS	10//99-12//99
	Milwaukee-Waukesha PMSA, WI	S	8.15 MW	7.68 AW	16960 AAW	WIBLS	10//99-12//99
	Wyoming	S	9.65 MW	9.62 AW	20000 AAW	WYBLS	10//99-12//99
	Puerto Rico	S	6.01 MW	6.11 AW	12710 AAW	PRBLS	10//99-12//99
	San Juan-Bayamon PMSA, PR	S	6.27 MW	6.03 AW	13040 AAW	PRBLS	10//99-12//99
Manual Cutter							
Garment Company, $10-25 Million in Sales	Los Angeles, CA	H		11.45 AW		CAAPN	1998
Manufactured Building and Mobile Home Installer							
	Alabama	S	6.69 MW	10.42 AW	21670 AAW	ALBLS	10//99-12//99
	Arizona	S	11.23 MW	12.13 AW	25230 AAW	AZBLS	10//99-12//99
	Phoenix-Mesa MSA, AZ	S	13.53 MW	12.86 AW	28130 AAW	AZBLS	10//99-12//99
	Arkansas	S	12.35 MW	13.08 AW	27200 AAW	ARBLS	10//99-12//99
	California	S	13.13 MW	13.18 AW	27400 AAW	CABLS	10//99-12//99
	Colorado	S	9.94 MW	10.16 AW	21130 AAW	COBLS	10//99-12//99
	Florida	S	9.75 MW	11.13 AW	23140 AAW	FLBLS	10//99-12//99
	Georgia	S	7.8 MW	8.81 AW	18320 AAW	GABLS	10//99-12//99
	Atlanta MSA, GA	S	7.25 MW	7.40 AW	15090 AAW	GABLS	10//99-12//99
	Idaho	S	10.16 MW	10.71 AW	22280 AAW	IDBLS	10//99-12//99
	Illinois	S	10.12 MW	10.09 AW	20990 AAW	ILBLS	10//99-12//99
	Indiana	S	12.01 MW	13.26 AW	27570 AAW	INBLS	10//99-12//99
	Elkhart-Goshen MSA, IN	S	15.66 MW	13.73 AW	32570 AAW	INBLS	10//99-12//99
	Iowa	S	10.7 MW	11.60 AW	24120 AAW	IABLS	10//99-12//99
	Kansas	S	10.46 MW	11.76 AW	24470 AAW	KSBLS	10//99-12//99
	Kentucky	S	8.45 MW	9.95 AW	20690 AAW	KYBLS	10//99-12//99
	Louisville MSA, KY-IN	S	12.63 MW	12.13 AW	26270 AAW	KYBLS	10//99-12//99
	Louisiana	S	13.31 MW	14.15 AW	29430 AAW	LABLS	10//99-12//99
	Maine	S	9.38 MW	10.12 AW	21050 AAW	MEBLS	10//99-12//99
	Michigan	S	11.77 MW	12.11 AW	25180 AAW	MIBLS	10//99-12//99
	Detroit PMSA, MI	S	12.31 MW	11.99 AW	25610 AAW	MIBLS	10//99-12//99
	Minnesota	S	11.23 MW	11.40 AW	23710 AAW	MNBLS	10//99-12//99
	Mississippi	S	9.44 MW	10.01 AW	20810 AAW	MSBLS	10//99-12//99
	Missouri	S	10.25 MW	11.81 AW	24570 AAW	MOBLS	10//99-12//99
	St. Louis MSA, MO-IL	S	14.10 MW	14.58 AW	29330 AAW	MOBLS	10//99-12//99
	Nebraska	S	9.46 MW	9.34 AW	19430 AAW	NEBLS	10//99-12//99
	Omaha MSA, NE-IA	S	10.41 MW	10.26 AW	21650 AAW	NEBLS	10//99-12//99
	New Hampshire	S	14.95 MW	14.24 AW	29620 AAW	NHBLS	10//99-12//99
	New Mexico	S	10.68 MW	11.71 AW	24360 AAW	NMBLS	10//99-12//99
	New York	S	11.42 MW	11.51 AW	23940 AAW	NYBLS	10//99-12//99
	North Carolina	S	10.91 MW	11.44 AW	23800 AAW	NCBLS	10//99-12//99
	North Dakota	S	9.41 MW	9.54 AW	19840 AAW	NDBLS	10//99-12//99
	Ohio	S	10.73 MW	11.26 AW	23420 AAW	OHBLS	10//99-12//99
	Oklahoma	S	10.95 MW	12.27 AW	25520 AAW	OKBLS	10//99-12//99
	Oregon	S	10.78 MW	11.41 AW	23730 AAW	ORBLS	10//99-12//99
	Portland-Vancouver PMSA, OR-WA	S	11.17 MW	10.59 AW	23240 AAW	ORBLS	10//99-12//99
	Pennsylvania	S	10.49 MW	10.79 AW	22450 AAW	PABLS	10//99-12//99
	South Carolina	S	9.17 MW	10.06 AW	20930 AAW	SCBLS	10//99-12//99

Occupation/Type/Industry	Location	Per	Low	Mid	High	Source	Date
Manufactured Building and Mobile Home Installer	South Dakota	S	9.5 MW	9.34 AW	19430 AAW	SDBLS	10//99-12//99
	Sioux Falls MSA, SD	S	10.03 MW	9.98 AW	20850 AAW	SDBLS	10//99-12//99
	Tennessee	S	9.53 MW	9.64 AW	20040 AAW	TNBLS	10//99-12//99
	Texas	S	9.42 MW	9.81 AW	20400 AAW	TXBLS	10//99-12//99
	Fort Worth-Arlington PMSA, TX	S	8.42 MW	8.35 AW	17520 AAW	TXBLS	
	Texarkana MSA, TX-Texarkana, AR	S	8.97 MW	9.39 AW	18660 AAW	TXBLS	10//99-12//99
	Virginia	S	10.04 MW	10.00 AW	20810 AAW	VABLS	10//99-12//99
	West Virginia	S	7.52 MW	7.61 AW	15830 AAW	WVBLS	10//99-12//99
	Huntington-Ashland MSA, WV-KY-OH	S	9.55 MW	9.32 AW	19870 AAW	WVBLS	10//99-12//99
	Wisconsin	S	10.49 MW	11.05 AW	22980 AAW	WIBLS	10//99-12//99
	Wyoming	S	9.8 MW	9.82 AW	20420 AAW	WYBLS	10//99-12//99
Marine Engineer and Naval Architect	Alabama	S	29.81 MW	30.15 AW	62710 AAW	ALBLS	10//99-12//99
	California	S	26.67 MW	27.45 AW	57100 AAW	CABLS	10//99-12//99
	Florida	S	24.41 MW	28.07 AW	58390 AAW	FLBLS	10//99-12//99
	Georgia	S	17.23 MW	20.60 AW	42860 AAW	GABLS	10//99-12//99
	Hawaii	S	30.7 MW	32.90 AW	68440 AAW	HIBLS	10//99-12//99
	Indiana	S	25.37 MW	27.04 AW	56230 AAW	INBLS	10//99-12//99
	Louisiana	S	28.27 MW	28.60 AW	59480 AAW	LABLS	10//99-12//99
	Massachusetts	S	26.41 MW	26.52 AW	55170 AAW	MABLS	10//99-12//99
	New Jersey	S	33.11 MW	31.16 AW	64820 AAW	NJBLS	10//99-12//99
	New York	S	23.11 MW	25.69 AW	53430 AAW	NYBLS	10//99-12//99
	Texas	S	24.79 MW	26.29 AW	54670 AAW	TXBLS	10//99-12//99
	Virginia	S	30.96 MW	29.91 AW	62210 AAW	VABLS	10//99-12//99
	Washington	S	30.26 MW	30.14 AW	62690 AAW	WABLS	10//99-12//99
Market Research Analyst	Alabama	S	26.68 MW	27.77 AW	57760 AAW	ALBLS	10//99-12//99
	Alaska	S	17.71 MW	17.27 AW	35920 AAW	AKBLS	10//99-12//99
	Arizona	S	21.8 MW	23.73 AW	49360 AAW	AZBLS	10//99-12//99
	Arkansas	S	16.91 MW	18.41 AW	38290 AAW	ARBLS	10//99-12//99
	California	S	26.41 MW	31.10 AW	64690 AAW	CABLS	10//99-12//99
	Connecticut	S	25.17 MW	26.28 AW	54660 AAW	CTBLS	10//99-12//99
	Delaware	S	14.56 MW	20.66 AW	42970 AAW	DEBLS	10//99-12//99
	Florida	S	19.93 MW	21.22 AW	44140 AAW	FLBLS	10//99-12//99
	Georgia	S	22.74 MW	24.34 AW	50620 AAW	GABLS	10//99-12//99
	Hawaii	S	19.53 MW	20.87 AW	43420 AAW	HIBLS	10//99-12//99
	Illinois	S	18.57 MW	21.31 AW	44330 AAW	ILBLS	10//99-12//99
	Indiana	S	17.93 MW	20.80 AW	43260 AAW	INBLS	10//99-12//99
	Iowa	S	14.84 MW	18.24 AW	37930 AAW	IABLS	10//99-12//99
	Kansas	S	23.08 MW	24.38 AW	50710 AAW	KSBLS	10//99-12//99
	Louisiana	S	19.9 MW	20.49 AW	42610 AAW	LABLS	10//99-12//99
	Maine	S	18.85 MW	19.61 AW	40780 AAW	MEBLS	10//99-12//99
	Maryland	S	21.93 MW	24.86 AW	51700 AAW	MDBLS	10//99-12//99
	Massachusetts	S	25 MW	26.55 AW	55220 AAW	MABLS	10//99-12//99
	Michigan	S	24.99 MW	28.80 AW	59910 AAW	MIBLS	10//99-12//99
	Minnesota	S	29.73 MW	30.94 AW	64350 AAW	MNBLS	10//99-12//99
	Mississippi	S	20.7 MW	20.53 AW	42710 AAW	MSBLS	10//99-12//99
	Missouri	S	18.01 MW	18.81 AW	39130 AAW	MOBLS	10//99-12//99
	Montana	S	21.07 MW	23.08 AW	48000 AAW	MTBLS	10//99-12//99
	Nebraska	S	13.33 MW	16.01 AW	33310 AAW	NEBLS	10//99-12//99
	Nevada	S	19.22 MW	20.88 AW	43430 AAW	NVBLS	10//99-12//99
	New Hampshire	S	21.07 MW	27.43 AW	57050 AAW	NHBLS	10//99-12//99
	New Jersey	S	27.86 MW	29.57 AW	61510 AAW	NJBLS	10//99-12//99
	New Mexico	S	18.01 MW	20.04 AW	41690 AAW	NMBLS	10//99-12//99
	New York	S	22.7 MW	24.53 AW	51030 AAW	NYBLS	10//99-12//99
	North Carolina	S	21.21 MW	21.59 AW	44900 AAW	NCBLS	10//99-12//99
	North Dakota	S	22.87 MW	27.18 AW	56530 AAW	NDBLS	10//99-12//99
	Ohio	S	21.3 MW	24.59 AW	51150 AAW	OHBLS	10//99-12//99
	Oklahoma	S	14.24 MW	17.24 AW	35850 AAW	OKBLS	10//99-12//99
	Oregon	S	21.82 MW	23.17 AW	48190 AAW	ORBLS	10//99-12//99
	Pennsylvania	S	20.02 MW	22.39 AW	46570 AAW	PABLS	10//99-12//99
	Rhode Island	S	22.94 MW	24.46 AW	50880 AAW	RIBLS	10//99-12//99
	South Carolina	S	13.97 MW	15.11 AW	31430 AAW	SCBLS	10//99-12//99
	South Dakota	S	16.18 MW	17.29 AW	35970 AAW	SDBLS	10//99-12//99
	Tennessee	S	17.94 MW	20.62 AW	42890 AAW	TNBLS	10//99-12//99
	Texas	S	24.93 MW	26.72 AW	55570 AAW	TXBLS	10//99-12//99
	Utah	S	28.49 MW	28.18 AW	58610 AAW	UTBLS	10//99-12//99

AAW Average annual wage	**AOH** Average offered, high	**ASH** Average starting, high	**H** Hourly	**M** Monthly	**S** Special: hourly and annual
AE Average entry wage	**AOL** Average offered, low	**ASL** Average starting, low	**HI** Highest wage paid	**MTC** Median total compensation	**TQ** Third quartile wage
AEX Average experienced wage	**APH** Average pay, high range	**AW** Average wage paid	**HR** High end range	**MW** Median wage paid	**W** Weekly
AO Average offered	**APL** Average pay, low range	**FQ** First quartile wage	**LR** Low end range	**SQ** Second quartile wage	**Y** Yearly

Occupation/Type/Industry	Location	Per	Low	Mid	High	Source	Date
Market Research Analyst	Vermont	s	18.31 MW	22.28 AW	46340 AAW	VTBLS	10//99-12//99
	Virginia	s	23.58 MW	26.35 AW	54810 AAW	VABLS	10//99-12//99
	Washington	s	26.28 MW	28.46 AW	59210 AAW	WABLS	10//99-12//99
	West Virginia	s	14.6 MW	19.02 AW	39570 AAW	WVBLS	10//99-12//99
	Wisconsin	s	17.47 MW	20.90 AW	43470 AAW	WIBLS	10//99-12//99
	Puerto Rico	s	18.36 MW	19.80 AW	41190 AAW	PRBLS	10//99-12//99
Marketing Manager	Alabama	s	24.27 MW	25.89 AW	53850 AAW	ALBLS	10//99-12//99
	Anniston MSA, AL	s	27.20 MW	24.87 AW	56570 AAW	ALBLS	10//99-12//99
	Birmingham MSA, AL	s	27.46 MW	25.72 AW	57120 AAW	ALBLS	10//99-12//99
	Decatur MSA, AL	s	28.50 MW	25.45 AW	59270 AAW	ALBLS	10//99-12//99
	Dothan MSA, AL	s	18.36 MW	15.82 AW	38190 AAW	ALBLS	10//99-12//99
	Mobile MSA, AL	s	19.67 MW	16.33 AW	40910 AAW	ALBLS	10//99-12//99
	Montgomery MSA, AL	s	29.07 MW	27.02 AW	60470 AAW	ALBLS	10//99-12//99
	Tuscaloosa MSA, AL	s	25.03 MW	19.76 AW	52060 AAW	ALBLS	10//99-12//99
	Alaska	s	22.94 MW	27.44 AW	57080 AAW	AKBLS	10//99-12//99
	Anchorage MSA, AK	s	27.93 MW	23.72 AW	58090 AAW	AKBLS	10//99-12//99
	Arizona	s	27.79 MW	29.92 AW	62240 AAW	AZBLS	10//99-12//99
	Flagstaff MSA, AZ-UT	s	23.65 MW	19.56 AW	49200 AAW	AZBLS	10//99-12//99
	Phoenix-Mesa MSA, AZ	s	30.56 MW	28.45 AW	63560 AAW	AZBLS	10//99-12//99
	Tucson MSA, AZ	s	25.19 MW	22.10 AW	52390 AAW	AZBLS	10//99-12//99
	Arkansas	s	26.32 MW	29.00 AW	60320 AAW	ARBLS	10//99-12//99
	Fayetteville-Springdale-Rogers MSA, AR	s	25.29 MW	20.41 AW	52600 AAW	ARBLS	10//99-12//99
	Fort Smith MSA, AR-OK	s	25.01 MW	23.96 AW	52030 AAW	ARBLS	10//99-12//99
	Jonesboro MSA, AR	s	25.63 MW	25.08 AW	53320 AAW	ARBLS	10//99-12//99
	Little Rock-North Little Rock MSA, AR	s	32.17 MW	30.06 AW	66910 AAW	ARBLS	10//99-12//99
	California	s	37.52 MW	38.74 AW	80580 AAW	CABLS	10//99-12//99
	Bakersfield MSA, CA	s	37.05 MW	36.86 AW	77070 AAW	CABLS	10//99-12//99
	Fresno MSA, CA	s	26.31 MW	24.85 AW	54730 AAW	CABLS	10//99-12//99
	Los Angeles-Long Beach PMSA, CA	s	36.14 MW	35.75 AW	75180 AAW	CABLS	10//99-12//99
	Modesto MSA, CA	s	34.15 MW	36.12 AW	71030 AAW	CABLS	10//99-12//99
	Oakland PMSA, CA	s	38.90 MW	38.20 AW	80920 AAW	CABLS	10//99-12//99
	Orange County PMSA, CA	s	39.53 MW	38.62 AW	82220 AAW	CABLS	10//99-12//99
	Riverside-San Bernardino PMSA, CA	s	31.04 MW	30.18 AW	64570 AAW	CABLS	10//99-12//99
	Sacramento PMSA, CA	s	37.52 MW	33.55 AW	78050 AAW	CABLS	10//99-12//99
	Salinas MSA, CA	s	31.93 MW	31.49 AW	66420 AAW	CABLS	10//99-12//99
	San Diego MSA, CA	s	37.58 MW	35.15 AW	78170 AAW	CABLS	10//99-12//99
	San Francisco PMSA, CA	s	40.04 MW	37.79 AW	83280 AAW	CABLS	10//99-12//99
	San Jose PMSA, CA	s	47.98 MW	49.08 AW	99800 AAW	CABLS	10//99-12//99
	San Luis Obispo-Atascadero-Paso Robles MSA, CA	s	24.04 MW	19.84 AW	49990 AAW	CABLS	10//99-12//99
	Santa Barbara-Santa Maria-Lompoc MSA, CA	s	38.21 MW	39.00 AW	79470 AAW	CABLS	10//99-12//99
	Santa Cruz-Watsonville PMSA, CA	s	41.88 MW	41.68 AW	87110 AAW	CABLS	10//99-12//99
	Santa Rosa PMSA, CA	s	32.26 MW	28.55 AW	67100 AAW	CABLS	10//99-12//99
	Stockton-Lodi MSA, CA	s	30.73 MW	28.70 AW	63930 AAW	CABLS	10//99-12//99
	Vallejo-Fairfield-Napa PMSA, CA	s	29.06 MW	29.14 AW	60440 AAW	CABLS	10//99-12//99
	Ventura PMSA, CA	s	32.86 MW	34.06 AW	68350 AAW	CABLS	10//99-12//99
	Visalia-Tulare-Porterville MSA, CA	s	27.38 MW	21.25 AW	56950 AAW	CABLS	10//99-12//99
	Yolo PMSA, CA	s	45.08 MW	57.08 AW	93760 AAW	CABLS	10//99-12//99
	Colorado	s	33.57 MW	34.74 AW	72270 AAW	COBLS	10//99-12//99
	Denver PMSA, CO	s	36.41 MW	35.34 AW	75740 AAW	COBLS	10//99-12//99
	Connecticut	s	41.03 MW	42.21 AW	87790 AAW	CTBLS	10//99-12//99
	Bridgeport PMSA, CT	s	37.63 MW	37.85 AW	78270 AAW	CTBLS	10//99-12//99
	Danbury PMSA, CT	s	41.52 MW	42.89 AW	86360 AAW	CTBLS	10//99-12//99
	Hartford MSA, CT	s	39.90 MW	39.88 AW	82980 AAW	CTBLS	10//99-12//99
	New Haven-Meriden PMSA, CT	s	38.48 MW	35.69 AW	80040 AAW	CTBLS	10//99-12//99
	New London-Norwich MSA, CT-RI	s	39.21 MW	36.68 AW	81550 AAW	CTBLS	10//99-12//99
	Stamford-Norwalk PMSA, CT	s	46.67 MW	46.67 AW	97060 AAW	CTBLS	10//99-12//99
	Waterbury PMSA, CT	s	46.80 MW	52.43 AW	97350 AAW	CTBLS	10//99-12//99
	Delaware	s	36.62 MW	36.37 AW	75650 AAW	DEBLS	10//99-12//99
	Dover MSA, DE	s	29.62 MW	27.05 AW	61600 AAW	DEBLS	10//99-12//99
	Wilmington-Newark PMSA, DE-MD	s	37.80 MW	37.76 AW	78620 AAW	DEBLS	10//99-12//99

AAW	Average annual wage	AOH	Average offered, high	ASH	Average starting, high	H	Hourly	M	Monthly	S	Special: hourly and annual
AE	Average entry wage	AOL	Average offered, low	ASL	Average starting, low	HI	Highest wage paid	MTC	Median total compensation	TQ	Third quartile wage
AEX	Average experienced wage	APH	Average pay, high range	AW	Average wage paid	HR	High end range	MW	Median wage paid	W	Weekly
AO	Average offered	APL	Average pay, low range	FQ	First quartile wage	LR	Low end range	SQ	Second quartile wage	Y	Yearly

Occupation/Type/Industry	Location	Per	Low	Mid	High	Source	Date
Marketing Manager	District of Columbia	S	31.79 MW	32.89 AW	68410 AAW	DCBLS	10//99-12//99
	Washington PMSA, DC-MD-VA-WV	S	35.59 MW	34.38 AW	74030 AAW	DCBLS	10//99-12//99
	Florida	S	26.54 MW	30.18 AW	62780 AAW	FLBLS	10//99-12//99
	Daytona Beach MSA, FL	S	28.75 MW	23.83 AW	59810 AAW	FLBLS	10//99-12//99
	Fort Lauderdale PMSA, FL	S	25.98 MW	24.08 AW	54030 AAW	FLBLS	10//99-12//99
	Fort Myers-Cape Coral MSA, FL	S	21.60 MW	20.05 AW	44920 AAW	FLBLS	10//99-12//99
	Fort Pierce-Port St. Lucie MSA, FL	S	27.27 MW	26.39 AW	56730 AAW	FLBLS	10//99-12//99
	Fort Walton Beach MSA, FL	S	28.61 MW	22.18 AW	59510 AAW	FLBLS	10//99-12//99
	Gainesville MSA, FL	S	29.65 MW	28.75 AW	61670 AAW	FLBLS	10//99-12//99
	Jacksonville MSA, FL	S	31.21 MW	26.34 AW	64920 AAW	FLBLS	10//99-12//99
	Lakeland-Winter Haven MSA, FL	S	26.73 MW	24.02 AW	55590 AAW	FLBLS	10//99-12//99
	Melbourne-Titusville-Palm Bay MSA, FL	S	32.59 MW	34.62 AW	67780 AAW	FLBLS	10//99-12//99
	Miami PMSA, FL	S	32.74 MW	29.62 AW	68100 AAW	FLBLS	10//99-12//99
	Naples MSA, FL	S	19.68 MW	16.59 AW	40940 AAW	FLBLS	10//99-12//99
	Ocala MSA, FL	S	18.86 MW	15.98 AW	39230 AAW	FLBLS	10//99-12//99
	Orlando MSA, FL	S	35.14 MW	30.64 AW	73090 AAW	FLBLS	10//99-12//99
	Panama City MSA, FL	S	28.25 MW	29.99 AW	58760 AAW	FLBLS	10//99-12//99
	Pensacola MSA, FL	S	22.94 MW	23.24 AW	47720 AAW	FLBLS	10//99-12//99
	Sarasota-Bradenton MSA, FL	S	20.26 MW	16.19 AW	42150 AAW	FLBLS	10//99-12//99
	Tallahassee MSA, FL	S	23.13 MW	18.34 AW	48120 AAW	FLBLS	10//99-12//99
	Tampa-St. Petersburg-Clearwater MSA, FL	S	30.35 MW	26.76 AW	63140 AAW	FLBLS	10//99-12//99
	West Palm Beach-Boca Raton MSA, FL	S	33.03 MW	31.47 AW	68690 AAW	FLBLS	10//99-12//99
	Georgia	S	35.33 MW	35.38 AW	73600 AAW	GABLS	10//99-12//99
	Atlanta MSA, GA	S	36.83 MW	37.45 AW	76600 AAW	GABLS	10//99-12//99
	Augusta-Aiken MSA, GA-SC	S	33.08 MW	30.01 AW	68800 AAW	GABLS	10//99-12//99
	Columbus MSA, GA-AL	S	28.48 MW	28.84 AW	59240 AAW	GABLS	10//99-12//99
	Macon MSA, GA	S	28.50 MW	27.70 AW	59290 AAW	GABLS	10//99-12//99
	Savannah MSA, GA	S	25.23 MW	19.99 AW	52490 AAW	GABLS	10//99-12//99
	Hawaii	S	31.51 MW	35.47 AW	73790 AAW	HIBLS	10//99-12//99
	Honolulu MSA, HI	S	35.58 MW	30.61 AW	74000 AAW	HIBLS	10//99-12//99
	Idaho	S	26.87 MW	33.11 AW	68860 AAW	IDBLS	10//99-12//99
	Boise City MSA, ID	S	33.56 MW	27.11 AW	69800 AAW	IDBLS	10//99-12//99
	Illinois	S	31.43 MW	32.49 AW	67580 AAW	ILBLS	10//99-12//99
	Bloomington-Normal MSA, IL	S	40.88 MW	40.27 AW	85030 AAW	ILBLS	10//99-12//99
	Champaign-Urbana MSA, IL	S	26.32 MW	22.95 AW	54750 AAW	ILBLS	10//99-12//99
	Chicago PMSA, IL	S	33.51 MW	32.49 AW	69700 AAW	ILBLS	10//99-12//99
	Kankakee PMSA, IL	S	25.46 MW	26.90 AW	52950 AAW	ILBLS	10//99-12//99
	Peoria-Pekin MSA, IL	S	28.03 MW	22.84 AW	58300 AAW	ILBLS	10//99-12//99
	Rockford MSA, IL	S	26.71 MW	27.64 AW	55570 AAW	ILBLS	10//99-12//99
	Springfield MSA, IL	S	24.14 MW	24.16 AW	50200 AAW	ILBLS	10//99-12//99
	Indiana	S	27.22 MW	30.18 AW	62770 AAW	INBLS	10//99-12//99
	Elkhart-Goshen MSA, IN	S	32.78 MW	32.91 AW	68180 AAW	INBLS	10//99-12//99
	Evansville-Henderson MSA, IN-KY	S	24.92 MW	24.14 AW	51830 AAW	INBLS	10//99-12//99
	Fort Wayne MSA, IN	S	27.45 MW	25.23 AW	57090 AAW	INBLS	10//99-12//99
	Gary PMSA, IN	S	34.14 MW	27.63 AW	71020 AAW	INBLS	10//99-12//99
	Indianapolis MSA, IN	S	28.94 MW	27.12 AW	60190 AAW	INBLS	10//99-12//99
	Kokomo MSA, IN	S	31.24 MW	31.75 AW	64970 AAW	INBLS	10//99-12//99
	Lafayette MSA, IN	S	34.97 MW	36.74 AW	72730 AAW	INBLS	10//99-12//99
	South Bend MSA, IN	S	33.65 MW	30.56 AW	69980 AAW	INBLS	10//99-12//99
	Terre Haute MSA, IN	S	26.94 MW	24.65 AW	56040 AAW	INBLS	10//99-12//99
	Iowa	S	25.49 MW	27.17 AW	56510 AAW	IABLS	10//99-12//99
	Davenport-Moline-Rock Island MSA, IA-IL	S	25.20 MW	21.13 AW	52410 AAW	IABLS	10//99-12//99
	Des Moines MSA, IA	S	26.83 MW	25.76 AW	55820 AAW	IABLS	10//99-12//99
	Dubuque MSA, IA	S	21.77 MW	20.40 AW	45290 AAW	IABLS	10//99-12//99
	Iowa City MSA, IA	S	20.67 MW	20.13 AW	42990 AAW	IABLS	10//99-12//99
	Sioux City MSA, IA-NE	S	25.92 MW	25.21 AW	53910 AAW	IABLS	10//99-12//99
	Waterloo-Cedar Falls MSA, IA	S	26.33 MW	26.82 AW	54760 AAW	IABLS	10//99-12//99
	Kansas	S	26.71 MW	28.28 AW	58820 AAW	KSBLS	10//99-12//99
	Lawrence MSA, KS	S	20.86 MW	19.91 AW	43380 AAW	KSBLS	10//99-12//99
	Topeka MSA, KS	S	22.73 MW	16.74 AW	47270 AAW	KSBLS	10//99-12//99
	Wichita MSA, KS	S	27.97 MW	27.22 AW	58180 AAW	KSBLS	10//99-12//99
	Kentucky	S	25.67 MW	27.35 AW	56880 AAW	KYBLS	10//99-12//99
	Lexington MSA, KY	S	25.70 MW	25.54 AW	53460 AAW	KYBLS	10//99-12//99

AAW Average annual wage	AOH Average offered, high	ASH Average starting, high	H Hourly	M Monthly	S Special: hourly and annual
AE Average entry wage	AOL Average offered, low	ASL Average starting, low	HI Highest wage paid	MTC Median total compensation	TQ Third quartile wage
AEX Average experienced wage	APH Average pay, high range	AW Average wage paid	HR High end range	MW Median wage paid	W Weekly
AO Average offered	APL Average pay, low range	FQ First quartile wage	LR Low end range	SQ Second quartile wage	Y Yearly

Occupation/Type/Industry	Location	Per	Low	Mid	High	Source	Date
Marketing Manager	Louisville MSA, KY-IN	S	28.97 MW	28.44 AW	60260 AAW	KYBLS	10//99-12//99
	Louisiana	S	22.4 MW	25.43 AW	52880 AAW	LABLS	10//99-12//99
	Alexandria MSA, LA	S	31.58 MW	32.36 AW	65680 AAW	LABLS	10//99-12//99
	Baton Rouge MSA, LA	S	24.96 MW	20.58 AW	51910 AAW	LABLS	10//99-12//99
	Houma MSA, LA	S	22.05 MW	22.53 AW	45870 AAW	LABLS	10//99-12//99
	Lafayette MSA, LA	S	23.05 MW	20.07 AW	47940 AAW	LABLS	10//99-12//99
	Lake Charles MSA, LA	S	23.18 MW	20.13 AW	48220 AAW	LABLS	10//99-12//99
	New Orleans MSA, LA	S	24.68 MW	23.08 AW	51330 AAW	LABLS	10//99-12//99
	Shreveport-Bossier City MSA, LA	S	23.36 MW	22.56 AW	48590 AAW	LABLS	10//99-12//99
	Maine	S	25.18 MW	28.18 AW	58620 AAW	MEBLS	10//99-12//99
	Bangor MSA, ME	S	26.59 MW	21.19 AW	55300 AAW	MEBLS	10//99-12//99
	Lewiston-Auburn MSA, ME	S	22.68 MW	19.02 AW	47180 AAW	MEBLS	10//99-12//99
	Portland MSA, ME	S	31.84 MW	29.01 AW	66220 AAW	MEBLS	10//99-12//99
	Maryland	S	27.26 MW	30.97 AW	64410 AAW	MDBLS	10//99-12//99
	Baltimore PMSA, MD	S	31.78 MW	27.78 AW	66110 AAW	MDBLS	10//99-12//99
	Massachusetts	S	37.4 MW	38.46 AW	79990 AAW	MABLS	10//99-12//99
	Boston PMSA, MA-NH	S	40.74 MW	39.87 AW	84740 AAW	MABLS	10//99-12//99
	Brockton PMSA, MA	S	35.48 MW	34.56 AW	73800 AAW	MABLS	10//99-12//99
	Fitchburg-Leominster PMSA, MA	S	32.56 MW	33.81 AW	67720 AAW	MABLS	10//99-12//99
	Lawrence PMSA, MA-NH	S	36.58 MW	34.28 AW	76090 AAW	MABLS	10//99-12//99
	Lowell PMSA, MA-NH	S	38.35 MW	36.91 AW	79760 AAW	MABLS	10//99-12//99
	New Bedford PMSA, MA	S	29.63 MW	25.33 AW	61630 AAW	MABLS	10//99-12//99
	Pittsfield MSA, MA	S	24.98 MW	24.60 AW	51950 AAW	MABLS	10//99-12//99
	Worcester PMSA, MA-CT	S	31.88 MW	31.09 AW	66310 AAW	MABLS	10//99-12//99
	Michigan	S	32.45 MW	34.94 AW	72680 AAW	MIBLS	10//99-12//99
	Ann Arbor PMSA, MI	S	35.61 MW	33.78 AW	74070 AAW	MIBLS	10//99-12//99
	Benton Harbor MSA, MI	S	28.09 MW	25.59 AW	58420 AAW	MIBLS	10//99-12//99
	Detroit PMSA, MI	S	37.69 MW	36.18 AW	78410 AAW	MIBLS	10//99-12//99
	Flint PMSA, MI	S	34.88 MW	36.61 AW	72560 AAW	MIBLS	10//99-12//99
	Grand Rapids-Muskegon-Holland MSA, MI	S	29.26 MW	28.86 AW	60870 AAW	MIBLS	10//99-12//99
	Kalamazoo-Battle Creek MSA, MI	S	36.06 MW	33.64 AW	75010 AAW	MIBLS	10//99-12//99
	Lansing-East Lansing MSA, MI	S	28.44 MW	24.92 AW	59150 AAW	MIBLS	10//99-12//99
	Saginaw-Bay City-Midland MSA, MI	S	32.50 MW	27.17 AW	67600 AAW	MIBLS	10//99-12//99
	Minnesota	S	37.45 MW	37.97 AW	78980 AAW	MNBLS	10//99-12//99
	Duluth-Superior MSA, MN-WI	S	24.80 MW	22.84 AW	51590 AAW	MNBLS	10//99-12//99
	Minneapolis-St. Paul MSA, MN-WI	S	38.82 MW	38.20 AW	80740 AAW	MNBLS	10//99-12//99
	Rochester MSA, MN	S	37.71 MW	37.48 AW	78430 AAW	MNBLS	10//99-12//99
	St. Cloud MSA, MN	S	34.15 MW	29.83 AW	71040 AAW	MNBLS	10//99-12//99
	Mississippi	S	23.93 MW	25.99 AW	54070 AAW	MSBLS	10//99-12//99
	Biloxi-Gulfport-Pascagoula MSA, MS	S	32.29 MW	29.55 AW	67160 AAW	MSBLS	10//99-12//99
	Jackson MSA, MS	S	26.44 MW	24.45 AW	54990 AAW	MSBLS	10//99-12//99
	Missouri	S	31.03 MW	32.57 AW	67750 AAW	MOBLS	10//99-12//99
	Columbia MSA, MO	S	30.41 MW	27.05 AW	63260 AAW	MOBLS	10//99-12//99
	Joplin MSA, MO	S	31.30 MW	26.77 AW	65090 AAW	MOBLS	10//99-12//99
	Kansas City MSA, MO-KS	S	29.12 MW	25.92 AW	60560 AAW	MOBLS	10//99-12//99
	St. Joseph MSA, MO	S	26.12 MW	22.96 AW	54330 AAW	MOBLS	10//99-12//99
	St. Louis MSA, MO-IL	S	34.40 MW	33.48 AW	71550 AAW	MOBLS	10//99-12//99
	Springfield MSA, MO	S	27.04 MW	26.04 AW	56250 AAW	MOBLS	10//99-12//99
	Montana	S	20.77 MW	23.39 AW	48650 AAW	MTBLS	10//99-12//99
	Billings MSA, MT	S	23.74 MW	23.50 AW	49380 AAW	MTBLS	10//99-12//99
	Nebraska	S	21.68 MW	23.01 AW	47860 AAW	NEBLS	10//99-12//99
	Lincoln MSA, NE	S	21.39 MW	21.42 AW	44500 AAW	NEBLS	10//99-12//99
	Omaha MSA, NE-IA	S	23.00 MW	21.31 AW	47850 AAW	NEBLS	10//99-12//99
	Nevada	S	27.49 MW	31.47 AW	65460 AAW	NVBLS	10//99-12//99
	Las Vegas MSA, NV-AZ	S	32.52 MW	28.19 AW	67630 AAW	NVBLS	10//99-12//99
	Reno MSA, NV	S	29.39 MW	27.10 AW	61130 AAW	NVBLS	10//99-12//99
	New Hampshire	S	30.86 MW	33.98 AW	70690 AAW	NHBLS	10//99-12//99
	Manchester PMSA, NH	S	32.92 MW	30.87 AW	68470 AAW	NHBLS	10//99-12//99
	Nashua PMSA, NH	S	38.06 MW	37.23 AW	79170 AAW	NHBLS	10//99-12//99
	Portsmouth-Rochester PMSA, NH-ME	S	32.78 MW	31.52 AW	68190 AAW	NHBLS	10//99-12//99
	New Jersey	S	37.79 MW	40.29 AW	83790 AAW	NJBLS	10//99-12//99
	Atlantic-Cape May PMSA, NJ	S	32.09 MW	30.58 AW	66750 AAW	NJBLS	10//99-12//99
	Bergen-Passaic PMSA, NJ	S	43.42 MW	39.91 AW	90310 AAW	NJBLS	10//99-12//99
	Jersey City PMSA, NJ	S	38.01 MW	33.22 AW	79060 AAW	NJBLS	10//99-12//99

AAW Average annual wage	AOH Average offered, high	ASH Average starting, high	H Hourly	M Monthly	S Special: hourly and annual
AE Average entry wage	AOL Average offered, low	ASL Average starting, low	HI Highest wage paid	MTC Median total compensation	TQ Third quartile wage
AEX Average experienced wage	APH Average pay, high range	AW Average wage paid	HR High end range	MW Median wage paid	W Weekly
AO Average offered	APL Average pay, low range	FQ First quartile wage	LR Low end range	SQ Second quartile wage	Y Yearly

Marketing Manager

Occupation/Type/Industry	Location	Per	Low	Mid	High	Source	Date
Marketing Manager	Middlesex-Somerset-Hunterdon PMSA, NJ	S	43.65 MW	45.49 AW	90800 AAW	NJBLS	10//99-12//99
	Monmouth-Ocean PMSA, NJ	S	39.20 MW	36.44 AW	81530 AAW	NJBLS	10//99-12//99
	Newark PMSA, NJ	S	39.13 MW	37.85 AW	81380 AAW	NJBLS	10//99-12//99
	Trenton PMSA, NJ	S	43.15 MW	44.08 AW	89760 AAW	NJBLS	10//99-12//99
	New Mexico	S	25.84 MW	28.78 AW	59860 AAW	NMBLS	10//99-12//99
	Albuquerque MSA, NM	S	29.76 MW	27.91 AW	61900 AAW	NMBLS	10//99-12//99
	Santa Fe MSA, NM	S	23.66 MW	20.89 AW	49220 AAW	NMBLS	10//99-12//99
	New York	S	38.57 MW	40.94 AW	85150 AAW	NYBLS	10//99-12//99
	Albany-Schenectady-Troy MSA, NY	S	32.58 MW	30.27 AW	67770 AAW	NYBLS	10//99-12//99
	Binghamton MSA, NY	S	26.31 MW	22.05 AW	54730 AAW	NYBLS	10//99-12//99
	Buffalo-Niagara Falls MSA, NY	S	32.67 MW	29.97 AW	67960 AAW	NYBLS	10//99-12//99
	Glens Falls MSA, NY	S	35.75 MW	36.11 AW	74350 AAW	NYBLS	10//99-12//99
	Nassau-Suffolk PMSA, NY	S	41.46 MW	38.67 AW	86240 AAW	NYBLS	10//99-12//99
	New York PMSA, NY	S	43.73 MW	42.03 AW	90950 AAW	NYBLS	10//99-12//99
	Newburgh PMSA, NY-PA	S	26.60 MW	25.91 AW	55330 AAW	NYBLS	10//99-12//99
	Rochester MSA, NY	S	33.34 MW	31.38 AW	69340 AAW	NYBLS	10//99-12//99
	Syracuse MSA, NY	S	42.67 MW	41.19 AW	88750 AAW	NYBLS	10//99-12//99
	Utica-Rome MSA, NY	S	23.08 MW	19.93 AW	48010 AAW	NYBLS	10//99-12//99
	North Carolina	S	35.94 MW	37.32 AW	77620 AAW	NCBLS	10//99-12//99
	Asheville MSA, NC	S	24.94 MW	23.24 AW	51880 AAW	NCBLS	10//99-12//99
	Charlotte-Gastonia-Rock Hill MSA, NC-SC	S	34.87 MW	32.77 AW	72520 AAW	NCBLS	10//99-12//99
	Fayetteville MSA, NC	S	21.15 MW	18.90 AW	43990 AAW	NCBLS	10//99-12//99
	Goldsboro MSA, NC	S	19.14 MW	17.53 AW	39810 AAW	NCBLS	10//99-12//99
	Greensboro--Winston-Salem--High Point MSA, NC	S	40.71 MW	36.78 AW	84670 AAW	NCBLS	10//99-12//99
	Hickory-Morganton-Lenoir MSA, NC	S	33.89 MW	29.43 AW	70480 AAW	NCBLS	10//99-12//99
	Raleigh-Durham-Chapel Hill MSA, NC	S	41.41 MW	41.25 AW	86130 AAW	NCBLS	10//99-12//99
	Rocky Mount MSA, NC	S	34.23 MW	30.66 AW	71190 AAW	NCBLS	10//99-12//99
	Wilmington MSA, NC	S	25.35 MW	24.49 AW	52740 AAW	NCBLS	10//99-12//99
	North Dakota	S	24.11 MW	24.59 AW	51150 AAW	NDBLS	10//99-12//99
	Bismarck MSA, ND	S	28.35 MW	35.66 AW	58970 AAW	NDBLS	10//99-12//99
	Fargo-Moorhead MSA, ND-MN	S	26.16 MW	25.91 AW	54410 AAW	NDBLS	10//99-12//99
	Grand Forks MSA, ND-MN	S	17.77 MW	16.68 AW	36950 AAW	NDBLS	10//99-12//99
	Ohio	S	29.67 MW	31.49 AW	65500 AAW	OHBLS	10//99-12//99
	Akron PMSA, OH	S	33.82 MW	33.30 AW	70350 AAW	OHBLS	10//99-12//99
	Canton-Massillon MSA, OH	S	22.98 MW	19.02 AW	47810 AAW	OHBLS	10//99-12//99
	Cincinnati PMSA, OH-KY-IN	S	32.13 MW	28.89 AW	66830 AAW	OHBLS	10//99-12//99
	Cleveland-Lorain-Elyria PMSA, OH	S	32.63 MW	31.11 AW	67860 AAW	OHBLS	10//99-12//99
	Columbus MSA, OH	S	29.97 MW	27.28 AW	62340 AAW	OHBLS	10//99-12//99
	Dayton-Springfield MSA, OH	S	36.37 MW	36.05 AW	75650 AAW	OHBLS	10//99-12//99
	Hamilton-Middletown PMSA, OH	S	40.23 MW	38.47 AW	83670 AAW	OHBLS	10//99-12//99
	Lima MSA, OH	S	30.26 MW	29.44 AW	62940 AAW	OHBLS	10//99-12//99
	Mansfield MSA, OH	S	27.57 MW	26.98 AW	57340 AAW	OHBLS	10//99-12//99
	Toledo MSA, OH	S	29.61 MW	30.09 AW	61590 AAW	OHBLS	10//99-12//99
	Youngstown-Warren MSA, OH	S	26.91 MW	19.57 AW	55960 AAW	OHBLS	10//99-12//99
	Oklahoma	S	24 MW	25.80 AW	53660 AAW	OKBLS	10//99-12//99
	Oklahoma City MSA, OK	S	23.79 MW	21.23 AW	49480 AAW	OKBLS	10//99-12//99
	Tulsa MSA, OK	S	29.41 MW	28.47 AW	61170 AAW	OKBLS	10//99-12//99
	Oregon	S	32.63 MW	34.37 AW	71490 AAW	ORBLS	10//99-12//99
	Eugene-Springfield MSA, OR	S	27.30 MW	25.34 AW	56790 AAW	ORBLS	10//99-12//99
	Medford-Ashland MSA, OR	S	27.73 MW	24.30 AW	57690 AAW	ORBLS	10//99-12//99
	Portland-Vancouver PMSA, OR-WA	S	35.68 MW	34.04 AW	74220 AAW	ORBLS	10//99-12//99
	Salem PMSA, OR	S	37.03 MW	45.16 AW	77020 AAW	ORBLS	10//99-12//99
	Pennsylvania	S	31.88 MW	32.13 AW	66830 AAW	PABLS	10//99-12//99
	Allentown-Bethlehem-Easton MSA, PA	S	31.95 MW	27.04 AW	66460 AAW	PABLS	10//99-12//99
	Altoona MSA, PA	S	33.33 MW	27.82 AW	69330 AAW	PABLS	10//99-12//99
	Erie MSA, PA	S	21.70 MW	22.40 AW	45130 AAW	PABLS	10//99-12//99
	Harrisburg-Lebanon-Carlisle MSA, PA	S	29.32 MW	25.51 AW	60980 AAW	PABLS	10//99-12//99
	Johnstown MSA, PA	S	30.15 MW	25.26 AW	62710 AAW	PABLS	10//99-12//99
	Lancaster MSA, PA	S	33.06 MW	34.57 AW	68770 AAW	PABLS	10//99-12//99

Marketing Manager

Occupation/Type/Industry	Location	Per	Low	Mid	High	Source	Date
Marketing Manager	Philadelphia PMSA, PA-NJ	S	35.01 MW	34.92 AW	72810 AAW	PABLS	10//99-12//99
	Pittsburgh MSA, PA	S	29.76 MW	28.83 AW	61900 AAW	PABLS	10//99-12//99
	Reading MSA, PA	S	28.95 MW	26.76 AW	60210 AAW	PABLS	10//99-12//99
	Scranton--Wilkes-Barre-- Hazleton MSA, PA	S	27.54 MW	25.89 AW	57270 AAW	PABLS	10//99-12//99
	State College MSA, PA	S	23.49 MW	24.16 AW	48860 AAW	PABLS	10//99-12//99
	Williamsport MSA, PA	S	32.10 MW	26.59 AW	66770 AAW	PABLS	10//99-12//99
	York MSA, PA	S	33.36 MW	34.96 AW	69390 AAW	PABLS	10//99-12//99
	Rhode Island	S	30.05 MW	31.68 AW	65900 AAW	RIBLS	10//99-12//99
	Providence-Fall River- Warwick MSA, RI-MA	S	30.57 MW	28.13 AW	63580 AAW	RIBLS	10//99-12//99
	South Carolina	S	20.89 MW	26.09 AW	54270 AAW	SCBLS	10//99-12//99
	Charleston-North Charleston MSA, SC	S	23.26 MW	21.71 AW	48370 AAW	SCBLS	10//99-12//99
	Columbia MSA, SC	S	28.07 MW	24.05 AW	58380 AAW	SCBLS	10//99-12//99
	Florence MSA, SC	S	30.63 MW	22.42 AW	63710 AAW	SCBLS	10//99-12//99
	Greenville-Spartanburg- Anderson MSA, SC	S	25.07 MW	17.92 AW	52150 AAW	SCBLS	10//99-12//99
	Myrtle Beach MSA, SC	S	19.28 MW	18.78 AW	40090 AAW	SCBLS	10//99-12//99
	South Dakota	S	31.5 MW	34.95 AW	72690 AAW	SDBLS	10//99-12//99
	Rapid City MSA, SD	S	30.20 MW	29.32 AW	62810 AAW	SDBLS	10//99-12//99
	Sioux Falls MSA, SD	S	31.10 MW	30.91 AW	64690 AAW	SDBLS	10//99-12//99
	Tennessee	S	25.68 MW	29.02 AW	60350 AAW	TNBLS	10//99-12//99
	Chattanooga MSA, TN-GA	S	25.28 MW	23.50 AW	52590 AAW	TNBLS	10//99-12//99
	Clarksville-Hopkinsville MSA, TN-KY	S	26.64 MW	24.75 AW	55410 AAW	TNBLS	10//99-12//99
	Johnson City-Kingsport-Bristol MSA, TN-VA	S	27.71 MW	28.46 AW	57640 AAW	TNBLS	10//99-12//99
	Knoxville MSA, TN	S	25.23 MW	20.94 AW	52480 AAW	TNBLS	10//99-12//99
	Memphis MSA, TN-AR-MS	S	32.45 MW	30.51 AW	67500 AAW	MSBLS	10//99-12//99
	Nashville MSA, TN	S	28.11 MW	23.40 AW	58470 AAW	TNBLS	10//99-12//99
	Texas	S	30.62 MW	32.40 AW	67400 AAW	TXBLS	10//99-12//99
	Abilene MSA, TX	S	21.73 MW	20.04 AW	45190 AAW	TXBLS	10//99-12//99
	Amarillo MSA, TX	S	23.83 MW	22.09 AW	49570 AAW	TXBLS	10//99-12//99
	Austin-San Marcos MSA, TX	S	28.63 MW	26.76 AW	59550 AAW	TXBLS	10//99-12//99
	Beaumont-Port Arthur MSA, TX	S	28.65 MW	24.85 AW	59590 AAW	TXBLS	10//99-12//99
	Brazoria PMSA, TX	S	29.39 MW	24.14 AW	61140 AAW	TXBLS	10//99-12//99
	Bryan-College Station MSA, TX	S	23.50 MW	20.48 AW	48890 AAW	TXBLS	10//99-12//99
	Dallas PMSA, TX	S	37.70 MW	36.54 AW	78420 AAW	TXBLS	10//99-12//99
	El Paso MSA, TX	S	30.74 MW	22.73 AW	63940 AAW	TXBLS	10//99-12//99
	Fort Worth-Arlington PMSA, TX	S	33.16 MW	30.34 AW	68980 AAW	TXBLS	10//99-12//99
	Galveston-Texas City PMSA, TX	S	30.85 MW	30.44 AW	64160 AAW	TXBLS	10//99-12//99
	Houston PMSA, TX	S	32.62 MW	30.31 AW	67840 AAW	TXBLS	10//99-12//99
	Longview-Marshall MSA, TX	S	28.81 MW	30.85 AW	59920 AAW	TXBLS	10//99-12//99
	Odessa-Midland MSA, TX	S	23.14 MW	15.71 AW	48140 AAW	TXBLS	10//99-12//99
	San Antonio MSA, TX	S	28.98 MW	29.13 AW	60290 AAW	TXBLS	10//99-12//99
	Sherman-Denison MSA, TX	S	36.33 MW	38.85 AW	75560 AAW	TXBLS	10//99-12//99
	Texarkana MSA, TX- Texarkana, AR	S	24.53 MW	21.21 AW	51020 AAW	TXBLS	10//99-12//99
	Tyler MSA, TX	S	27.82 MW	24.67 AW	57860 AAW	TXBLS	10//99-12//99
	Waco MSA, TX	S	33.92 MW	31.45 AW	70550 AAW	TXBLS	10//99-12//99
	Wichita Falls MSA, TX	S	34.16 MW	33.47 AW	71040 AAW	TXBLS	10//99-12//99
	Utah	S	30.93 MW	32.25 AW	67070 AAW	UTBLS	10//99-12//99
	Provo-Orem MSA, UT	S	34.60 MW	33.20 AW	71960 AAW	UTBLS	10//99-12//99
	Salt Lake City-Ogden MSA, UT	S	32.89 MW	31.72 AW	68410 AAW	UTBLS	10//99-12//99
	Vermont	S	30.03 MW	32.53 AW	67670 AAW	VTBLS	10//99-12//99
	Burlington MSA, VT	S	35.31 MW	34.98 AW	73440 AAW	VTBLS	10//99-12//99
	Virginia	S	36.5 MW	37.25 AW	77470 AAW	VABLS	10//99-12//99
	Charlottesville MSA, VA	S	32.70 MW	26.92 AW	68020 AAW	VABLS	10//99-12//99
	Norfolk-Virginia Beach- Newport News MSA, VA-NC	S	30.30 MW	26.70 AW	63030 AAW	VABLS	10//99-12//99
	Richmond-Petersburg MSA, VA	S	30.05 MW	27.23 AW	62510 AAW	VABLS	10//99-12//99
	Roanoke MSA, VA	S	28.29 MW	27.61 AW	58840 AAW	VABLS	10//99-12//99
	Washington	S	36.26 MW	36.28 AW	75450 AAW	WABLS	10//99-12//99
	Bellingham MSA, WA	S	24.48 MW	24.01 AW	50920 AAW	WABLS	10//99-12//99

AAW Average annual wage	AOH Average offered, high	ASH Average starting, high	H Hourly	M Monthly	S Special: hourly and annual
AE Average entry wage	AOL Average offered, low	ASL Average starting, low	HI Highest wage paid	MTC Median total compensation	TQ Third quartile wage
AEX Average experienced wage	APH Average pay, high range	AW Average wage paid	HR High end range	MW Median wage paid	W Weekly
AO Average offered	APL Average pay, low range	FQ First quartile wage	LR Low end range	SQ Second quartile wage	Y Yearly

Occupation/Type/Industry	Location	Per	Low	Mid	High	Source	Date
Marketing Manager	Olympia PMSA, WA	S	27.00 MW	24.47 AW	56160 AAW	WABLS	10//99-12//99
	Richland-Kennewick-Pasco MSA, WA	S	37.04 MW	37.72 AW	77040 AAW	WABLS	10//99-12//99
	Seattle-Bellevue-Everett PMSA, WA	S	37.39 MW	37.58 AW	77770 AAW	WABLS	10//99-12//99
	Spokane MSA, WA	S	28.66 MW	25.05 AW	59610 AAW	WABLS	10//99-12//99
	Tacoma PMSA, WA	S	29.60 MW	29.94 AW	61580 AAW	WABLS	10//99-12//99
	Yakima MSA, WA	S	35.58 MW	35.43 AW	74000 AAW	WABLS	10//99-12//99
	West Virginia	S	22.3 MW	26.96 AW	56070 AAW	WVBLS	10//99-12//99
	Charleston MSA, WV	S	32.80 MW	30.74 AW	68220 AAW	WVBLS	10//99-12//99
	Huntington-Ashland MSA, WV-KY-OH	S	32.21 MW	32.42 AW	66990 AAW	WVBLS	10//99-12//99
	Parkersburg-Marietta MSA, WV-OH	S	27.38 MW	19.27 AW	56960 AAW	WVBLS	10//99-12//99
	Wheeling MSA, WV-OH	S	16.17 MW	15.68 AW	33630 AAW	WVBLS	10//99-12//99
	Wisconsin	S	30.1 MW	32.20 AW	66970 AAW	WIBLS	10//99-12//99
	Appleton-Oshkosh-Neenah MSA, WI	S	31.26 MW	28.64 AW	65030 AAW	WIBLS	10//99-12//99
	Green Bay MSA, WI	S	32.68 MW	30.12 AW	67980 AAW	WIBLS	10//99-12//99
	Janesville-Beloit MSA, WI	S	38.24 MW	38.34 AW	79530 AAW	WIBLS	10//99-12//99
	La Crosse MSA, WI-MN	S	26.63 MW	28.08 AW	55380 AAW	WIBLS	10//99-12//99
	Madison MSA, WI	S	27.88 MW	26.68 AW	57980 AAW	WIBLS	10//99-12//99
	Milwaukee-Waukesha PMSA, WI	S	35.63 MW	34.22 AW	74100 AAW	WIBLS	10//99-12//99
	Racine PMSA, WI	S	32.78 MW	31.17 AW	68170 AAW	WIBLS	10//99-12//99
	Sheboygan MSA, WI	S	27.11 MW	29.34 AW	56380 AAW	WIBLS	10//99-12//99
	Wausau MSA, WI	S	23.85 MW	21.51 AW	49610 AAW	WIBLS	10//99-12//99
	Wyoming	S	21 MW	24.60 AW	51160 AAW	WYBLS	10//99-12//99
	Puerto Rico	S	26.82 MW	27.86 AW	57940 AAW	PRBLS	10//99-12//99
	San Juan-Bayamon PMSA, PR	S	27.62 MW	26.55 AW	57450 AAW	PRBLS	10//99-12//99
	Guam	S	17.25 MW	20.88 AW	43440 AAW	GUBLS	10//99-12//99
Divisional	United States	Y		70793 MW		TRAVWK3	1999
National	United States	Y		80040 MW		TRAVWK3	1999
Regional	United States	Y		66962 MW		TRAVWK3	1999
Marriage and Family Therapist	Alabama	S	17.84 MW	18.16 AW	37780 AAW	ALBLS	10//99-12//99
	Arizona	S	14.43 MW	14.24 AW	29610 AAW	AZBLS	10//99-12//99
	California	S	19.25 MW	18.92 AW	39360 AAW	CABLS	10//99-12//99
	Colorado	S	15.44 MW	16.29 AW	33880 AAW	COBLS	10//99-12//99
	Connecticut	S	16.68 MW	18.09 AW	37630 AAW	CTBLS	10//99-12//99
	Florida	S	14.41 MW	14.22 AW	29580 AAW	FLBLS	10//99-12//99
	Georgia	S	16.73 MW	17.16 AW	35700 AAW	GABLS	10//99-12//99
	Idaho	S	19.37 MW	18.51 AW	38490 AAW	IDBLS	10//99-12//99
	Illinois	S	12.71 MW	14.84 AW	30870 AAW	ILBLS	10//99-12//99
	Indiana	S	16.13 MW	18.10 AW	37660 AAW	INBLS	10//99-12//99
	Iowa	S	13.53 MW	15.11 AW	31430 AAW	IABLS	10//99-12//99
	Kansas	S	20.01 MW	25.10 AW	52210 AAW	KSBLS	10//99-12//99
	Louisiana	S	13.46 MW	15.46 AW	32150 AAW	LABLS	10//99-12//99
	Massachusetts	S	14.12 MW	14.79 AW	30750 AAW	MABLS	10//99-12//99
	Michigan	S	22.02 MW	26.81 AW	55760 AAW	MIBLS	10//99-12//99
	Minnesota	S	17.44 MW	18.51 AW	38500 AAW	MNBLS	10//99-12//99
	Mississippi	S	12.28 MW	12.32 AW	25620 AAW	MSBLS	10//99-12//99
	Missouri	S	14.46 MW	16.38 AW	34060 AAW	MOBLS	10//99-12//99
	Nebraska	S	15.1 MW	16.60 AW	34520 AAW	NEBLS	10//99-12//99
	New Hampshire	S	11.86 MW	12.61 AW	26230 AAW	NHBLS	10//99-12//99
	New Jersey	S	17.66 MW	19.07 AW	39650 AAW	NJBLS	10//99-12//99
	New York	S	14.29 MW	14.63 AW	30440 AAW	NYBLS	10//99-12//99
	North Carolina	S	14.85 MW	16.44 AW	34200 AAW	NCBLS	10//99-12//99
	Oklahoma	S	17.85 MW	18.15 AW	37740 AAW	OKBLS	10//99-12//99
	Oregon	S	15.9 MW	18.82 AW	39150 AAW	ORBLS	10//99-12//99
	Pennsylvania	S	12.32 MW	14.62 AW	30400 AAW	PABLS	10//99-12//99
	South Carolina	S	14.91 MW	15.55 AW	32340 AAW	SCBLS	10//99-12//99
	South Dakota	S	12.02 MW	12.21 AW	25390 AAW	SDBLS	10//99-12//99
	Tennessee	S	14.88 MW	18.92 AW	39340 AAW	TNBLS	10//99-12//99
	Texas	S	14.9 MW	15.49 AW	32220 AAW	TXBLS	10//99-12//99
	Utah	S	20.3 MW	19.54 AW	40650 AAW	UTBLS	10//99-12//99
	Virginia	S	12.49 MW	13.35 AW	27770 AAW	VABLS	10//99-12//99
	Washington	S	13.36 MW	14.92 AW	31040 AAW	WABLS	10//99-12//99
	West Virginia	S	13.92 MW	13.76 AW	28610 AAW	WVBLS	10//99-12//99
	Wisconsin	S	11.44 MW	12.42 AW	25840 AAW	WIBLS	10//99-12//99
Mascot Pro Sports Team	United States	H		300 AW		MENHEL	1999

AAW	Average annual wage	AOH	Average offered, high	ASH	Average starting, high	H	Hourly	M	Monthly	S	Special: hourly and annual
AE	Average entry wage	AOL	Average offered, low	ASL	Average starting, low	HI	Highest wage paid	MTC	Median total compensation	TQ	Third quartile wage
AEX	Average experienced wage	APH	Average pay, high range	AW	Average wage paid	HR	High end range	MW	Median wage paid	W	Weekly
AO	Average offered	APL	Average pay, low range	FQ	First quartile wage	LR	Low end range	SQ	Second quartile wage	Y	Yearly

Occupation/Type/Industry	Location	Per	Low	Mid	High	Source	Date
Massage Therapist	Alabama	S	8.17 MW	9.04 AW	18800 AAW	ALBLS	10//99-12//99
	Arizona	S	22.71 MW	20.15 AW	41900 AAW	AZBLS	10//99-12//99
	Arkansas	S	8.72 MW	8.10 AW	16840 AAW	ARBLS	10//99-12//99
	California	S	12.87 MW	15.15 AW	31520 AAW	CABLS	10//99-12//99
	Connecticut	S	15.99 MW	17.43 AW	36260 AAW	CTBLS	10//99-12//99
	District of Columbia	S	10.35 MW	11.10 AW	23090 AAW	DCBLS	10//99-12//99
	Florida	S	10.76 MW	12.21 AW	25390 AAW	FLBLS	10//99-12//99
	Georgia	S	17.22 MW	17.86 AW	37150 AAW	GABLS	10//99-12//99
	Hawaii	S	6.7 MW	13.16 AW	27360 AAW	HIBLS	10//99-12//99
	Idaho	S	8.47 MW	8.83 AW	18360 AAW	IDBLS	10//99-12//99
	Illinois	S	15.56 MW	15.13 AW	31470 AAW	ILBLS	10//99-12//99
	Indiana	S	6.59 MW	13.26 AW	27580 AAW	INBLS	10//99-12//99
	Iowa	S	6.3 MW	7.75 AW	16130 AAW	IABLS	10//99-12//99
	Kansas	S	9.95 MW	12.18 AW	25340 AAW	KSBLS	10//99-12//99
	Kentucky	S	11.48 MW	11.20 AW	23300 AAW	KYBLS	10//99-12//99
	Louisiana	S	10.45 MW	11.22 AW	23330 AAW	LABLS	10//99-12//99
	Maryland	S	7.41 MW	8.41 AW	17490 AAW	MDBLS	10//99-12//99
	Massachusetts	S	12.51 MW	12.88 AW	26780 AAW	MABLS	10//99-12//99
	Minnesota	S	16.07 MW	16.32 AW	33940 AAW	MNBLS	10//99-12//99
	Mississippi	S	14.65 MW	14.47 AW	30100 AAW	MSBLS	10//99-12//99
	New Hampshire	S	14.42 MW	13.10 AW	27240 AAW	NHBLS	10//99-12//99
	New Jersey	S	21.05 MW	21.09 AW	43870 AAW	NJBLS	10//99-12//99
	New Mexico	S	27.25 MW	27.04 AW	56250 AAW	NMBLS	10//99-12//99
	New York	S	28.02 MW	22.34 AW	46480 AAW	NYBLS	10//99-12//99
	North Carolina	S	20.16 MW	18.61 AW	38720 AAW	NCBLS	10//99-12//99
	Pennsylvania	S	6.33 MW	6.66 AW	13850 AAW	PABLS	10//99-12//99
	Rhode Island	S	8.41 MW	9.39 AW	19540 AAW	RIBLS	10//99-12//99
	South Carolina	S	10.58 MW	13.10 AW	27250 AAW	SCBLS	10//99-12//99
	South Dakota	S	10.9 MW	10.12 AW	21040 AAW	SDBLS	10//99-12//99
	Tennessee	S	7.57 MW	8.00 AW	16630 AAW	TNBLS	10//99-12//99
	Utah	S	6.58 MW	7.63 AW	15870 AAW	UTBLS	10//99-12//99
	Virginia	S	8.73 MW	9.28 AW	19290 AAW	VABLS	10//99-12//99
	Washington	S	10.37 MW	12.38 AW	25760 AAW	WABLS	10//99-12//99
	West Virginia	S	7.94 MW	9.28 AW	19310 AAW	WVBLS	10//99-12//99
	Wisconsin	S	14.54 MW	13.59 AW	28270 AAW	WIBLS	10//99-12//99
	Wyoming	S	24.12 MW	22.91 AW	47660 AAW	WYBLS	10//99-12//99
	Guam	S	7.52 MW	7.64 AW	15900 AAW	GUBLS	10//99-12//99
Materials Engineer	Alabama	S	28.77 MW	29.85 AW	62080 AAW	ALBLS	10//99-12//99
	Arizona	S	25.52 MW	25.73 AW	53520 AAW	AZBLS	10//99-12//99
	Arkansas	S	25.47 MW	26.09 AW	54270 AAW	ARBLS	10//99-12//99
	California	S	30.46 MW	30.31 AW	63040 AAW	CABLS	10//99-12//99
	Colorado	S	28.61 MW	28.26 AW	58780 AAW	COBLS	10//99-12//99
	Connecticut	S	28.61 MW	28.16 AW	58570 AAW	CTBLS	10//99-12//99
	Florida	S	24.99 MW	25.39 AW	52820 AAW	FLBLS	10//99-12//99
	Georgia	S	25.12 MW	26.63 AW	55390 AAW	GABLS	10//99-12//99
	Illinois	S	25.84 MW	27.52 AW	57230 AAW	ILBLS	10//99-12//99
	Indiana	S	28.26 MW	27.80 AW	57820 AAW	INBLS	10//99-12//99
	Iowa	S	28.09 MW	27.96 AW	58160 AAW	IABLS	10//99-12//99
	Kansas	S	22.76 MW	28.69 AW	59670 AAW	KSBLS	10//99-12//99
	Kentucky	S	26.72 MW	27.04 AW	56230 AAW	KYBLS	10//99-12//99
	Louisiana	S	25.96 MW	26.18 AW	54460 AAW	LABLS	10//99-12//99
	Maine	S	26.55 MW	27.32 AW	56830 AAW	MEBLS	10//99-12//99
	Maryland	S	32.21 MW	32.09 AW	66750 AAW	MDBLS	10//99-12//99
	Massachusetts	S	30.32 MW	30.19 AW	62790 AAW	MABLS	10//99-12//99
	Michigan	S	27.84 MW	27.65 AW	57510 AAW	MIBLS	10//99-12//99
	Minnesota	S	29.63 MW	29.25 AW	60840 AAW	MNBLS	10//99-12//99
	Mississippi	S	22.78 MW	23.11 AW	48070 AAW	MSBLS	10//99-12//99
	Nebraska	S	24.39 MW	24.41 AW	50770 AAW	NEBLS	10//99-12//99
	Nevada	S	29.56 MW	28.11 AW	58470 AAW	NVBLS	10//99-12//99
	New Hampshire	S	24 MW	24.53 AW	51020 AAW	NHBLS	10//99-12//99
	New Jersey	S	27.27 MW	28.75 AW	59800 AAW	NJBLS	10//99-12//99
	New York	S	29.14 MW	30.15 AW	62720 AAW	NYBLS	10//99-12//99
	North Carolina	S	27.1 MW	28.16 AW	58580 AAW	NCBLS	10//99-12//99
	Ohio	S	28.56 MW	28.43 AW	59130 AAW	OHBLS	10//99-12//99
	Oklahoma	S	24.21 MW	25.07 AW	52140 AAW	OKBLS	10//99-12//99
	Oregon	S	28.29 MW	28.31 AW	58890 AAW	ORBLS	10//99-12//99
	Pennsylvania	S	26.32 MW	26.37 AW	54850 AAW	PABLS	10//99-12//99
	Rhode Island	S	29.24 MW	27.66 AW	57540 AAW	RIBLS	10//99-12//99
	South Carolina	S	26.02 MW	26.56 AW	55240 AAW	SCBLS	10//99-12//99
	Tennessee	S	28.32 MW	27.51 AW	57210 AAW	TNBLS	10//99-12//99
	Texas	S	29.43 MW	29.98 AW	62350 AAW	TXBLS	10//99-12//99
	Utah	S	29.78 MW	31.13 AW	64740 AAW	UTBLS	10//99-12//99

AAW Average annual wage	**AOH** Average offered, high	**ASH** Average starting, high	**H** Hourly	**M** Monthly	**S** Special: hourly and annual
AE Average entry wage	**AOL** Average offered, low	**ASL** Average starting, low	**HI** Highest wage paid	**MTC** Median total compensation	**TQ** Third quartile wage
AEX Average experienced wage	**APH** Average pay, high range	**AW** Average wage paid	**HR** High end range	**MW** Median wage paid	**W** Weekly
AO Average offered	**APL** Average pay, low range	**FQ** First quartile wage	**LR** Low end range	**SQ** Second quartile wage	**Y** Yearly

Occupation/Type/Industry	Location	Per	Low	Mid	High	Source	Date
Materials Engineer	Virginia	S	26.95 MW	27.77 AW	57760 AAW	VABLS	10//99-12//99
	West Virginia	S	28.31 MW	29.12 AW	60580 AAW	WVBLS	10//99-12//99
	Wisconsin	S	24.66 MW	25.50 AW	53030 AAW	WIBLS	10//99-12//99
Materials Scientist	Alabama	S	27.58 MW	27.97 AW	58180 AAW	ALBLS	10//99-12//99
	Huntsville MSA, AL	S	33.42 MW	34.90 AW	69510 AAW	ALBLS	10//99-12//99
	Arizona	S	29.38 MW	30.65 AW	63740 AAW	AZBLS	10//99-12//99
	Tucson MSA, AZ	S	32.37 MW	31.78 AW	67330 AAW	AZBLS	10//99-12//99
	California	S	26.95 MW	28.09 AW	58440 AAW	CABLS	10//99-12//99
	Los Angeles-Long Beach PMSA, CA	S	25.23 MW	23.56 AW	52470 AAW	CABLS	10//99-12//99
	Oakland PMSA, CA	S	27.59 MW	25.90 AW	57380 AAW	CABLS	10//99-12//99
	Orange County PMSA, CA	S	28.72 MW	28.33 AW	59740 AAW	CABLS	10//99-12//99
	San Diego MSA, CA	S	34.35 MW	35.15 AW	71440 AAW	CABLS	10//99-12//99
	San Francisco PMSA, CA	S	34.57 MW	34.49 AW	71900 AAW	CABLS	10//99-12//99
	San Jose PMSA, CA	S	29.87 MW	30.05 AW	62120 AAW	CABLS	10//99-12//99
	Colorado	S	23.81 MW	25.05 AW	52100 AAW	COBLS	10//99-12//99
	Connecticut	S	26.8 MW	28.59 AW	59470 AAW	CTBLS	10//99-12//99
	District of Columbia	S	24.64 MW	28.23 AW	58720 AAW	DCBLS	10//99-12//99
	Washington PMSA, DC-MD-VA-WV	S	32.58 MW	30.64 AW	67770 AAW	DCBLS	10//99-12//99
	Florida	S	33.24 MW	34.33 AW	71410 AAW	FLBLS	10//99-12//99
	Georgia	S	21.8 MW	23.94 AW	49800 AAW	GABLS	10//99-12//99
	Illinois	S	28.22 MW	31.97 AW	66500 AAW	ILBLS	10//99-12//99
	Chicago PMSA, IL	S	31.90 MW	27.39 AW	66350 AAW	ILBLS	10//99-12//99
	Indiana	S	24.91 MW	24.15 AW	50230 AAW	INBLS	10//99-12//99
	Massachusetts	S	37.09 MW	36.83 AW	76620 AAW	MABLS	10//99-12//99
	Boston PMSA, MA-NH	S	34.59 MW	35.44 AW	71950 AAW	MABLS	10//99-12//99
	Worcester PMSA, MA-CT	S	40.59 MW	41.21 AW	84430 AAW	MABLS	10//99-12//99
	Michigan	S	23.21 MW	25.39 AW	52810 AAW	MIBLS	10//99-12//99
	Detroit PMSA, MI	S	27.76 MW	24.53 AW	57750 AAW	MIBLS	10//99-12//99
	Grand Rapids-Muskegon-Holland MSA, MI	S	23.58 MW	23.03 AW	49060 AAW	MIBLS	10//99-12//99
	Minnesota	S	31.51 MW	30.02 AW	62440 AAW	MNBLS	10//99-12//99
	Minneapolis-St. Paul MSA, MN-WI	S	30.02 MW	31.51 AW	62440 AAW	MNBLS	10//99-12//99
	New Jersey	S	32.85 MW	37.33 AW	77640 AAW	NJBLS	10//99-12//99
	Bergen-Passaic PMSA, NJ	S	38.38 MW	33.66 AW	79840 AAW	NJBLS	10//99-12//99
	New York	S	26.59 MW	29.88 AW	62150 AAW	NYBLS	10//99-12//99
	Buffalo-Niagara Falls MSA, NY	S	23.38 MW	23.44 AW	48630 AAW	NYBLS	10//99-12//99
	New York PMSA, NY	S	46.97 MW	56.37 AW	97690 AAW	NYBLS	10//99-12//99
	Rochester MSA, NY	S	24.98 MW	24.13 AW	51960 AAW	NYBLS	10//99-12//99
	North Carolina	S	34.74 MW	32.67 AW	67940 AAW	NCBLS	10//99-12//99
	Ohio	S	16.14 MW	19.76 AW	41110 AAW	OHBLS	10//99-12//99
	Oklahoma	S	44.66 MW	45.21 AW	94040 AAW	OKBLS	10//99-12//99
	Oregon	S	28.56 MW	28.11 AW	58460 AAW	ORBLS	10//99-12//99
	Pennsylvania	S	28.1 MW	28.12 AW	58480 AAW	PABLS	10//99-12//99
	Philadelphia PMSA, PA-NJ	S	28.61 MW	26.38 AW	59500 AAW	PABLS	10//99-12//99
	Pittsburgh MSA, PA	S	31.20 MW	30.99 AW	64890 AAW	PABLS	10//99-12//99
	South Carolina	S	33.55 MW	33.29 AW	69250 AAW	SCBLS	10//99-12//99
	Greenville-Spartanburg-Anderson MSA, SC	S	33.68 MW	33.76 AW	70060 AAW	SCBLS	10//99-12//99
	Texas	S	27.86 MW	25.99 AW	54050 AAW	TXBLS	10//99-12//99
	Houston PMSA, TX	S	32.15 MW	30.30 AW	66870 AAW	TXBLS	10//99-12//99
	Virginia	S	19.65 MW	20.87 AW	43400 AAW	VABLS	10//99-12//99
	Washington	S	25.06 MW	24.58 AW	51140 AAW	WABLS	10//99-12//99
	Seattle-Bellevue-Everett PMSA, WA	S	25.53 MW	25.57 AW	53100 AAW	WABLS	10//99-12//99
	Wisconsin	S	20.73 MW	22.20 AW	46180 AAW	WIBLS	10//99-12//99
Mathematical Science Teacher							
Postsecondary	Alabama	Y		41230 AAW		ALBLS	10//99-12//99
Postsecondary	Birmingham MSA, AL	Y		45560 AAW		ALBLS	10//99-12//99
Postsecondary	Montgomery MSA, AL	Y		36980 AAW		ALBLS	10//99-12//99
Postsecondary	Arizona	Y		32930 AAW		AZBLS	10//99-12//99
Postsecondary	Phoenix-Mesa MSA, AZ	Y		32940 AAW		AZBLS	10//99-12//99
Postsecondary	Arkansas	Y		41140 AAW		ARBLS	10//99-12//99
Postsecondary	California	Y		56090 AAW		CABLS	10//99-12//99
Postsecondary	Fresno MSA, CA	Y		54920 AAW		CABLS	10//99-12//99
Postsecondary	Los Angeles-Long Beach PMSA, CA	Y		56720 AAW		CABLS	10//99-12//99

AAW	Average annual wage	AOH	Average offered, high	ASH	Average starting, high
AE	Average entry wage	AOL	Average offered, low	ASL	Average starting, low
AEX	Average experienced wage	APH	Average pay, high range	AW	Average wage paid
AO	Average offered	APL	Average pay, low range	FQ	First quartile wage

H	Hourly
HI	Highest wage paid
HR	High end range
LR	Low end range

M	Monthly
MTC	Median total compensation
MW	Median wage paid
SQ	Second quartile wage

S	Special: hourly and annual
TQ	Third quartile wage
W	Weekly
Y	Yearly

Occupation/Type/Industry	Location	Per	Low	Mid	High	Source	Date
Mathematical Science Teacher							
Postsecondary	Riverside-San Bernardino PMSA, CA	Y		52710 AAW		CABLS	10//99-12//99
Postsecondary	Sacramento PMSA, CA	Y		47690 AAW		CABLS	10//99-12//99
Postsecondary	San Diego MSA, CA	Y		53740 AAW		CABLS	10//99-12//99
Postsecondary	San Francisco PMSA, CA	Y		66980 AAW		CABLS	10//99-12//99
Postsecondary	Colorado	Y		49660 AAW		COBLS	10//99-12//99
Postsecondary	Denver PMSA, CO	Y		50100 AAW		COBLS	10//99-12//99
Postsecondary	Connecticut	Y		62330 AAW		CTBLS	10//99-12//99
Postsecondary	Hartford MSA, CT	Y		68310 AAW		CTBLS	10//99-12//99
Postsecondary	New Haven-Meriden PMSA, CT	Y		59210 AAW		CTBLS	10//99-12//99
Postsecondary	District of Columbia	Y		46180 AAW		DCBLS	10//99-12//99
Postsecondary	Washington PMSA, DC-MD-VA-WV	Y		49090 AAW		DCBLS	10//99-12//99
Postsecondary	Florida	Y		51130 AAW		FLBLS	10//99-12//99
Postsecondary	Fort Lauderdale PMSA, FL	Y		52820 AAW		FLBLS	10//99-12//99
Postsecondary	Gainesville MSA, FL	Y		72250 AAW		FLBLS	10//99-12//99
Postsecondary	Jacksonville MSA, FL	Y		54450 AAW		FLBLS	10//99-12//99
Postsecondary	Melbourne-Titusville-Palm Bay MSA, FL	Y		45050 AAW		FLBLS	10//99-12//99
Postsecondary	Miami PMSA, FL	Y		62830 AAW		FLBLS	10//99-12//99
Postsecondary	Orlando MSA, FL	Y		38990 AAW		FLBLS	10//99-12//99
Postsecondary	Pensacola MSA, FL	Y		56890 AAW		FLBLS	10//99-12//99
Postsecondary	Tampa-St. Petersburg-Clearwater MSA, FL	Y		48260 AAW		FLBLS	10//99-12//99
Postsecondary	West Palm Beach-Boca Raton MSA, FL	Y		54590 AAW		FLBLS	10//99-12//99
Postsecondary	Georgia	Y		44430 AAW		GABLS	10//99-12//99
Postsecondary	Atlanta MSA, GA	Y		45800 AAW		GABLS	10//99-12//99
Postsecondary	Savannah MSA, GA	Y		45030 AAW		GABLS	10//99-12//99
Postsecondary	Idaho	Y		48480 AAW		IDBLS	10//99-12//99
Postsecondary	Illinois	Y		47100 AAW		ILBLS	10//99-12//99
Postsecondary	Chicago PMSA, IL	Y		46960 AAW		ILBLS	10//99-12//99
Postsecondary	Indiana	Y		47340 AAW		INBLS	10//99-12//99
Postsecondary	Gary PMSA, IN	Y		45160 AAW		INBLS	10//99-12//99
Postsecondary	Indianapolis MSA, IN	Y		38030 AAW		INBLS	10//99-12//99
Postsecondary	South Bend MSA, IN	Y		45380 AAW		INBLS	10//99-12//99
Postsecondary	Iowa	Y		54080 AAW		IABLS	10//99-12//99
Postsecondary	Des Moines MSA, IA	Y		48780 AAW		IABLS	10//99-12//99
Postsecondary	Kansas	Y		36050 AAW		KSBLS	10//99-12//99
Postsecondary	Kentucky	Y		40720 AAW		KYBLS	10//99-12//99
Postsecondary	Louisiana	Y		43950 AAW		LABLS	10//99-12//99
Postsecondary	Maine	Y		46190 AAW		MEBLS	10//99-12//99
Postsecondary	Portland MSA, ME	Y		53540 AAW		MEBLS	10//99-12//99
Postsecondary	Maryland	Y		50830 AAW		MDBLS	10//99-12//99
Postsecondary	Baltimore PMSA, MD	Y		50880 AAW		MDBLS	10//99-12//99
Postsecondary	Massachusetts	Y		52580 AAW		MABLS	10//99-12//99
Postsecondary	Boston PMSA, MA-NH	Y		52190 AAW		MABLS	10//99-12//99
Postsecondary	Springfield MSA, MA	Y		60550 AAW		MABLS	10//99-12//99
Postsecondary	Worcester PMSA, MA-CT	Y		51030 AAW		MABLS	10//99-12//99
Postsecondary	Michigan	Y		53530 AAW		MIBLS	10//99-12//99
Postsecondary	Detroit PMSA, MI	Y		49800 AAW		MIBLS	10//99-12//99
Postsecondary	Kalamazoo-Battle Creek MSA, MI	Y		61510 AAW		MIBLS	10//99-12//99
Postsecondary	Minnesota	Y		56460 AAW		MNBLS	10//99-12//99
Postsecondary	Duluth-Superior MSA, MN-WI	Y		53240 AAW		MNBLS	10//99-12//99
Postsecondary	Minneapolis-St. Paul MSA, MN-WI	Y		63340 AAW		MNBLS	10//99-12//99
Postsecondary	St. Cloud MSA, MN	Y		54850 AAW		MNBLS	10//99-12//99
Postsecondary	Mississippi	Y		40110 AAW		MSBLS	10//99-12//99
Postsecondary	Jackson MSA, MS	Y		27830 AAW		MSBLS	10//99-12//99
Postsecondary	Missouri	Y		37790 AAW		MOBLS	10//99-12//99
Postsecondary	Montana	Y		52900 AAW		MTBLS	10//99-12//99
Postsecondary	Nebraska	Y		54830 AAW		NEBLS	10//99-12//99
Postsecondary	Omaha MSA, NE-IA	Y		44430 AAW		NEBLS	10//99-12//99
Postsecondary	Nevada	Y		39730 AAW		NVBLS	10//99-12//99
Postsecondary	Las Vegas MSA, NV-AZ	Y		46030 AAW		NVBLS	10//99-12//99
Postsecondary	New Hampshire	Y		57970 AAW		NHBLS	10//99-12//99
Postsecondary	New Jersey	Y		60260 AAW		NJBLS	10//99-12//99
Postsecondary	Bergen-Passaic PMSA, NJ	Y		54330 AAW		NJBLS	10//99-12//99
Postsecondary	Jersey City PMSA, NJ	Y		68630 AAW		NJBLS	10//99-12//99

AAW Average annual wage	**AOH** Average offered, high	**ASH** Average starting, high	**H** Hourly	**M** Monthly	**S** Special: hourly and annual
AE Average entry wage	**AOL** Average offered, low	**ASL** Average starting, low	**HI** Highest wage paid	**MTC** Median total compensation	**TQ** Third quartile wage
AEX Average experienced wage	**APH** Average pay, high range	**AW** Average wage paid	**HR** High end range	**MW** Median wage paid	**W** Weekly
AO Average offered	**APL** Average pay, low range	**FQ** First quartile wage	**LR** Low end range	**SQ** Second quartile wage	**Y** Yearly

Mathematical Science Teacher

Occupation/Type/Industry	Location	Per	Low	Mid	High	Source	Date
Postsecondary	Monmouth-Ocean PMSA, NJ	Y		51680 AAW		NJBLS	10//99-12//99
Postsecondary	Newark PMSA, NJ	Y		62440 AAW		NJBLS	10//99-12//99
Postsecondary	New Mexico	Y		47070 AAW		NMBLS	10//99-12//99
Postsecondary	New York	Y		56090 AAW		NYBLS	10//99-12//99
Postsecondary	Albany-Schenectady-Troy MSA, NY	Y		49600 AAW		NYBLS	10//99-12//99
Postsecondary	Buffalo-Niagara Falls MSA, NY	Y		52810 AAW		NYBLS	10//99-12//99
Postsecondary	Nassau-Suffolk PMSA, NY	Y		65220 AAW		NYBLS	10//99-12//99
Postsecondary	New York PMSA, NY	Y		61770 AAW		NYBLS	10//99-12//99
Postsecondary	North Carolina	Y		45500 AAW		NCBLS	10//99-12//99
Postsecondary	Asheville MSA, NC	Y		45850 AAW		NCBLS	10//99-12//99
Postsecondary	Charlotte-Gastonia-Rock Hill MSA, NC-SC	Y		36770 AAW		NCBLS	10//99-12//99
Postsecondary	Greensboro--Winston-Salem--High Point MSA, NC	Y		45990 AAW		NCBLS	10//99-12//99
Postsecondary	Hickory-Morganton-Lenoir MSA, NC	Y		35920 AAW		NCBLS	10//99-12//99
Postsecondary	Raleigh-Durham-Chapel Hill MSA, NC	Y		54400 AAW		NCBLS	10//99-12//99
Postsecondary	North Dakota	Y		43350 AAW		NDBLS	10//99-12//99
Postsecondary	Ohio	Y		43700 AAW		OHBLS	10//99-12//99
Postsecondary	Canton-Massillon MSA, OH	Y		38450 AAW		OHBLS	10//99-12//99
Postsecondary	Cincinnati PMSA, OH-KY-IN	Y		41420 AAW		OHBLS	10//99-12//99
Postsecondary	Cleveland-Lorain-Elyria PMSA, OH	Y		46050 AAW		OHBLS	10//99-12//99
Postsecondary	Columbus MSA, OH	Y		45150 AAW		OHBLS	10//99-12//99
Postsecondary	Dayton-Springfield MSA, OH	Y		32960 AAW		OHBLS	10//99-12//99
Postsecondary	Toledo MSA, OH	Y		40360 AAW		OHBLS	10//99-12//99
Postsecondary	Oklahoma	Y		41040 AAW		OKBLS	10//99-12//99
Postsecondary	Oklahoma City MSA, OK	Y		38490 AAW		OKBLS	10//99-12//99
Postsecondary	Oregon	Y		47990 AAW		ORBLS	10//99-12//99
Postsecondary	Portland-Vancouver PMSA, OR-WA	Y		46070 AAW		ORBLS	10//99-12//99
Postsecondary	Pennsylvania	Y		58000 AAW		PABLS	10//99-12//99
Postsecondary	Allentown-Bethlehem-Easton MSA, PA	Y		49670 AAW		PABLS	10//99-12//99
Postsecondary	Erie MSA, PA	Y		54680 AAW		PABLS	10//99-12//99
Postsecondary	Lancaster MSA, PA	Y		56280 AAW		PABLS	10//99-12//99
Postsecondary	Philadelphia PMSA, PA-NJ	Y		60300 AAW		PABLS	10//99-12//99
Postsecondary	Pittsburgh MSA, PA	Y		60660 AAW		PABLS	10//99-12//99
Postsecondary	Reading MSA, PA	Y		48230 AAW		PABLS	10//99-12//99
Postsecondary	Scranton--Wilkes-Barre--Hazleton MSA, PA	Y		52400 AAW		PABLS	10//99-12//99
Postsecondary	Rhode Island	Y		76410 AAW		RIBLS	10//99-12//99
Postsecondary	Providence-Fall River-Warwick MSA, RI-MA	Y		76010 AAW		RIBLS	10//99-12//99
Postsecondary	South Carolina	Y		47580 AAW		SCBLS	10//99-12//99
Postsecondary	Greenville-Spartanburg-Anderson MSA, SC	Y		50720 AAW		SCBLS	10//99-12//99
Postsecondary	Sumter MSA, SC	Y		44940 AAW		SCBLS	10//99-12//99
Postsecondary	South Dakota	Y		40310 AAW		SDBLS	10//99-12//99
Postsecondary	Tennessee	Y		45130 AAW		TNBLS	10//99-12//99
Postsecondary	Johnson City-Kingsport-Bristol MSA, TN-VA	Y		37120 AAW		TNBLS	10//99-12//99
Postsecondary	Memphis MSA, TN-AR-MS	Y		51150 AAW		MSBLS	10//99-12//99
Postsecondary	Nashville MSA, TN	Y		52130 AAW		TNBLS	10//99-12//99
Postsecondary	Texas	Y		42620 AAW		TXBLS	10//99-12//99
Postsecondary	Dallas PMSA, TX	Y		44350 AAW		TXBLS	10//99-12//99
Postsecondary	El Paso MSA, TX	Y		35190 AAW		TXBLS	10//99-12//99
Postsecondary	Houston PMSA, TX	Y		51540 AAW		TXBLS	10//99-12//99
Postsecondary	Killeen-Temple MSA, TX	Y		34850 AAW		TXBLS	10//99-12//99
Postsecondary	Longview-Marshall MSA, TX	Y		33360 AAW		TXBLS	10//99-12//99
Postsecondary	Odessa-Midland MSA, TX	Y		41460 AAW		TXBLS	10//99-12//99
Postsecondary	San Antonio MSA, TX	Y		49370 AAW		TXBLS	10//99-12//99
Postsecondary	Vermont	Y		50800 AAW		VTBLS	10//99-12//99
Postsecondary	Burlington MSA, VT	Y		52170 AAW		VTBLS	10//99-12//99
Postsecondary	Virginia	Y		44710 AAW		VABLS	10//99-12//99
Postsecondary	Richmond-Petersburg MSA, VA	Y		47040 AAW		VABLS	10//99-12//99
Postsecondary	Washington	Y		45220 AAW		WABLS	10//99-12//99

AAW	Average annual wage	AOH	Average offered, high	ASH	Average starting, high	H	Hourly	M	Monthly	S	Special: hourly and annual
AE	Average entry wage	AOL	Average offered, low	ASL	Average starting, low	HI	Highest wage paid	MTC	Median total compensation	TQ	Third quartile wage
AEX	Average experienced wage	APH	Average pay, high range	AW	Average wage paid	HR	High end range	MW	Median wage paid	W	Weekly
AO	Average offered	APL	Average pay, low range	FQ	First quartile wage	LR	Low end range	SQ	Second quartile wage	Y	Yearly

Occupation/Type/Industry	Location	Per	Low	Mid	High	Source	Date
Mathematical Science Teacher							
Postsecondary	Seattle-Bellevue-Everett PMSA, WA	Y		50430 AAW		WABLS	10//99-12//99
Postsecondary	Tacoma PMSA, WA	Y		45980 AAW		WABLS	10//99-12//99
Postsecondary	West Virginia	Y		50210 AAW		WVBLS	10//99-12//99
Postsecondary	Milwaukee-Waukesha PMSA, WI	Y		34690 AAW		WIBLS	10//99-12//99
Postsecondary	Wyoming	Y		44850 AAW		WYBLS	10//99-12//99
Postsecondary	Puerto Rico	Y		32380 AAW		PRBLS	10//99-12//99
Postsecondary	Arecibo PMSA, PR	Y		31170 AAW		PRBLS	10//99-12//99
Postsecondary	San Juan-Bayamon PMSA, PR	Y		33450 AAW		PRBLS	10//99-12//99
Mathematical Technician	California	S	16.06 MW	16.29 AW	33890 AAW	CABLS	10//99-12//99
	Connecticut	S	20.79 MW	25.45 AW	52940 AAW	CTBLS	10//99-12//99
	Hartford MSA, CT	S	25.59 MW	19.40 AW	53220 AAW	CTBLS	10//99-12//99
	Washington PMSA, DC-MD-VA-WV	S	21.91 MW	20.82 AW	45580 AAW	DCBLS	10//99-12//99
	Orlando MSA, FL	S	30.84 MW	35.39 AW	64140 AAW	FLBLS	10//99-12//99
	Tampa-St. Petersburg-Clearwater MSA, FL	S	27.72 MW	20.74 AW	57650 AAW	FLBLS	10//99-12//99
	Georgia	S	13.23 MW	13.83 AW	28770 AAW	GABLS	10//99-12//99
	Atlanta MSA, GA	S	13.85 MW	13.22 AW	28800 AAW	GABLS	10//99-12//99
	Maryland	S	17.39 MW	17.23 AW	35830 AAW	MDBLS	10//99-12//99
	New Jersey	S	13.11 MW	13.51 AW	28090 AAW	NJBLS	10//99-12//99
	New York	S	33.6 MW	28.98 AW	60280 AAW	NYBLS	10//99-12//99
	South Carolina	S	13.89 MW	13.68 AW	28450 AAW	SCBLS	10//99-12//99
	Texas	S	19.2 MW	21.79 AW	45320 AAW	TXBLS	10//99-12//99
	Dallas PMSA, TX	S	21.38 MW	19.20 AW	44460 AAW	TXBLS	10//99-12//99
	Virginia	S	23.77 MW	24.01 AW	49930 AAW	VABLS	10//99-12//99
	Washington	S	16.19 MW	18.06 AW	37560 AAW	WABLS	10//99-12//99
	Seattle-Bellevue-Everett PMSA, WA	S	16.92 MW	15.28 AW	35190 AAW	WABLS	10//99-12//99
	Wisconsin	S	14.86 MW	16.08 AW	33440 AAW	WIBLS	10//99-12//99
Mathematician	California	S	34.34 MW	34.71 AW	72190 AAW	CABLS	10//99-12//99
	Colorado	S	38.72 MW	38.11 AW	79270 AAW	COBLS	10//99-12//99
	Colorado Springs MSA, CO	S	39.90 MW	40.31 AW	83000 AAW	COBLS	10//99-12//99
	Connecticut	S	37.68 MW	38.16 AW	79370 AAW	CTBLS	10//99-12//99
	Florida	S	29.92 MW	29.38 AW	61110 AAW	FLBLS	10//99-12//99
	Maryland	S	33.48 MW	34.24 AW	71220 AAW	MDBLS	10//99-12//99
	Massachusetts	S	37.17 MW	35.76 AW	74380 AAW	MABLS	10//99-12//99
	New Jersey	S	32.22 MW	32.35 AW	67290 AAW	NJBLS	10//99-12//99
	New Mexico	S	33.96 MW	33.29 AW	69250 AAW	NMBLS	10//99-12//99
	New York	S	20.76 MW	28.61 AW	59510 AAW	NYBLS	10//99-12//99
	Texas	S	35.86 MW	34.82 AW	72430 AAW	TXBLS	10//99-12//99
	Washington	S	38.14 MW	37.09 AW	77140 AAW	WABLS	10//99-12//99
Meat, Poultry, and Fish Cutter and Trimmer	Alabama	S	7.58 MW	7.47 AW	15530 AAW	ALBLS	10//99-12//99
	Alaska	S	7.38 MW	7.82 AW	16260 AAW	AKBLS	10//99-12//99
	Arizona	S	11.87 MW	12.51 AW	26010 AAW	AZBLS	10//99-12//99
	Arkansas	S	7.91 MW	7.97 AW	16580 AAW	ARBLS	10//99-12//99
	California	S	8.37 MW	9.03 AW	18770 AAW	CABLS	10//99-12//99
	Bakersfield MSA, CA	S	8.83 MW	8.02 AW	18370 AAW	CABLS	10//99-12//99
	Los Angeles-Long Beach PMSA, CA	S	9.65 MW	9.83 AW	20070 AAW	CABLS	10//99-12//99
	Modesto MSA, CA	S	8.23 MW	7.78 AW	17120 AAW	CABLS	10//99-12//99
	Oakland PMSA, CA	S	12.81 MW	13.03 AW	26650 AAW	CABLS	10//99-12//99
	Orange County PMSA, CA	S	10.16 MW	10.22 AW	21140 AAW	CABLS	10//99-12//99
	Redding MSA, CA	S	8.46 MW	7.71 AW	17600 AAW	CABLS	10//99-12//99
	Riverside-San Bernardino PMSA, CA	S	10.21 MW	10.22 AW	21240 AAW	CABLS	10//99-12//99
	Sacramento PMSA, CA	S	12.52 MW	12.70 AW	26040 AAW	CABLS	10//99-12//99
	Salinas MSA, CA	S	11.93 MW	11.42 AW	24800 AAW	CABLS	10//99-12//99
	San Diego MSA, CA	S	9.24 MW	8.91 AW	19220 AAW	CABLS	10//99-12//99
	San Francisco PMSA, CA	S	11.50 MW	10.62 AW	23910 AAW	CABLS	10//99-12//99
	San Jose PMSA, CA	S	11.22 MW	11.20 AW	23340 AAW	CABLS	10//99-12//99
	Santa Barbara-Santa Maria-Lompoc MSA, CA	S	11.29 MW	11.50 AW	23470 AAW	CABLS	10//99-12//99
	Santa Rosa PMSA, CA	S	10.39 MW	8.77 AW	21610 AAW	CABLS	10//99-12//99
	Stockton-Lodi MSA, CA	S	8.93 MW	8.30 AW	18570 AAW	CABLS	10//99-12//99

AAW	Average annual wage	AOH	Average offered, high	ASH	Average starting, high
AE	Average entry wage	AOL	Average offered, low	ASL	Average starting, low
AEX	Average experienced wage	APH	Average pay, high range	AW	Average wage paid
AO	Average offered	APL	Average pay, low range	FQ	First quartile wage

H	Hourly	M	Monthly
HI	Highest wage paid	MTC	Median total compensation
HR	High end range	MW	Median wage paid
LR	Low end range	SQ	Second quartile wage

S	Special: hourly and annual
TQ	Third quartile wage
W	Weekly
Y	Yearly

Meat, Poultry, and Fish Cutter and Trimmer

Occupation/Type/Industry	Location	Per	Low	Mid	High	Source	Date
	Vallejo-Fairfield-Napa PMSA, CA	S	12.14 MW	10.98 AW	25240 AAW	CABLS	10//99-12//99
	Ventura PMSA, CA	S	7.79 MW	6.53 AW	16200 AAW	CABLS	10//99-12//99
	Colorado	S	9.81 MW	9.65 AW	20070 AAW	COBLS	10//99-12//99
	Denver PMSA, CO	S	10.04 MW	9.96 AW	20890 AAW	COBLS	10//99-12//99
	Connecticut	S	8.02 MW	9.63 AW	20030 AAW	CTBLS	10//99-12//99
	Hartford MSA, CT	S	11.47 MW	10.57 AW	23860 AAW	CTBLS	10//99-12//99
	Delaware	S	7.71 MW	7.85 AW	16320 AAW	DEBLS	10//99-12//99
	Washington PMSA, DC-MD-VA-WV	S	8.21 MW	7.74 AW	17080 AAW	DCBLS	10//99-12//99
	Florida	S	7.69 MW	7.86 AW	16350 AAW	FLBLS	10//99-12//99
	Fort Lauderdale PMSA, FL	S	9.92 MW	9.70 AW	20620 AAW	FLBLS	10//99-12//99
	Fort Myers-Cape Coral MSA, FL	S	9.14 MW	9.23 AW	19020 AAW	FLBLS	10//99-12//99
	Jacksonville MSA, FL	S	7.62 MW	7.52 AW	15840 AAW	FLBLS	10//99-12//99
	Miami PMSA, FL	S	7.37 MW	6.97 AW	15330 AAW	FLBLS	10//99-12//99
	Orlando MSA, FL	S	9.94 MW	9.20 AW	20670 AAW	FLBLS	10//99-12//99
	Tampa-St. Petersburg-Clearwater MSA, FL	S	7.61 MW	7.40 AW	15820 AAW	FLBLS	10//99-12//99
	Georgia	S	7.69 MW	7.65 AW	15910 AAW	GABLS	10//99-12//99
	Atlanta MSA, GA	S	8.51 MW	8.73 AW	17690 AAW	GABLS	10//99-12//99
	Hawaii	S	12.35 MW	12.11 AW	25180 AAW	HIBLS	10//99-12//99
	Honolulu MSA, HI	S	12.30 MW	12.61 AW	25580 AAW	HIBLS	10//99-12//99
	Idaho	S	9.24 MW	8.86 AW	18430 AAW	IDBLS	10//99-12//99
	Illinois	S	8.1 MW	8.50 AW	17680 AAW	ILBLS	10//99-12//99
	Chicago PMSA, IL	S	8.43 MW	8.03 AW	17540 AAW	ILBLS	10//99-12//99
	Peoria-Pekin MSA, IL	S	8.88 MW	9.06 AW	18480 AAW	ILBLS	10//99-12//99
	Indiana	S	7.89 MW	7.98 AW	16600 AAW	INBLS	10//99-12//99
	Evansville-Henderson MSA, IN-KY	S	6.89 MW	6.81 AW	14330 AAW	INBLS	10//99-12//99
	Iowa	S	9.83 MW	10.15 AW	21110 AAW	IABLS	10//99-12//99
	Des Moines MSA, IA	S	8.77 MW	8.96 AW	18240 AAW	IABLS	10//99-12//99
	Kansas	S	8.46 MW	8.41 AW	17490 AAW	KSBLS	10//99-12//99
	Kentucky	S	8.2 MW	8.43 AW	17540 AAW	KYBLS	10//99-12//99
	Louisiana	S	7.35 MW	7.32 AW	15230 AAW	LABLS	10//99-12//99
	Houma MSA, LA	S	6.62 MW	6.05 AW	13780 AAW	LABLS	10//99-12//99
	Lafayette MSA, LA	S	6.14 MW	6.03 AW	12780 AAW	LABLS	10//99-12//99
	New Orleans MSA, LA	S	8.40 MW	8.58 AW	17480 AAW	LABLS	10//99-12//99
	Maine	S	8.04 MW	8.25 AW	17160 AAW	MEBLS	10//99-12//99
	Portland MSA, ME	S	8.55 MW	8.46 AW	17790 AAW	MEBLS	10//99-12//99
	Maryland	S	7.25 MW	7.16 AW	14890 AAW	MDBLS	10//99-12//99
	Baltimore PMSA, MD	S	6.98 MW	6.73 AW	14530 AAW	MDBLS	10//99-12//99
	Massachusetts	S	9.1 MW	9.96 AW	20720 AAW	MABLS	10//99-12//99
	Boston PMSA, MA-NH	S	9.78 MW	9.71 AW	20340 AAW	MABLS	10//99-12//99
	New Bedford PMSA, MA	S	10.40 MW	8.00 AW	21640 AAW	MABLS	10//99-12//99
	Worcester PMSA, MA-CT	S	9.35 MW	8.32 AW	19450 AAW	MABLS	10//99-12//99
	Michigan	S	9.08 MW	8.98 AW	18680 AAW	MIBLS	10//99-12//99
	Detroit PMSA, MI	S	9.07 MW	9.29 AW	18870 AAW	MIBLS	10//99-12//99
	Minnesota	S	9.58 MW	9.55 AW	19860 AAW	MNBLS	10//99-12//99
	Minneapolis-St. Paul MSA, MN-WI	S	9.34 MW	9.12 AW	19420 AAW	MNBLS	10//99-12//99
	Mississippi	S	7.19 MW	7.12 AW	14820 AAW	MSBLS	10//99-12//99
	Biloxi-Gulfport-Pascagoula MSA, MS	S	6.06 MW	6.12 AW	12610 AAW	MSBLS	10//99-12//99
	Kansas City MSA, MO-KS	S	7.31 MW	7.22 AW	15190 AAW	MOBLS	10//99-12//99
	Montana	S	10.58 MW	10.52 AW	21890 AAW	MTBLS	10//99-12//99
	Nebraska	S	9.51 MW	9.40 AW	19540 AAW	NEBLS	10//99-12//99
	Nevada	S	10.19 MW	10.55 AW	21940 AAW	NVBLS	10//99-12//99
	Las Vegas MSA, NV-AZ	S	10.32 MW	9.91 AW	21470 AAW	NVBLS	10//99-12//99
	Reno MSA, NV	S	9.06 MW	8.70 AW	18850 AAW	NVBLS	10//99-12//99
	New Hampshire	S	7.91 MW	8.17 AW	17000 AAW	NHBLS	10//99-12//99
	New Jersey	S	10.2 MW	10.62 AW	22090 AAW	NJBLS	10//99-12//99
	Jersey City PMSA, NJ	S	12.25 MW	14.39 AW	25480 AAW	NJBLS	10//99-12//99
	Trenton PMSA, NJ	S	12.88 MW	14.06 AW	26780 AAW	NJBLS	10//99-12//99
	New York	S	12.9 MW	13.32 AW	27700 AAW	NYBLS	10//99-12//99
	New York PMSA, NY	S	14.14 MW	13.62 AW	29420 AAW	NYBLS	10//99-12//99
	North Carolina	S	7.75 MW	7.76 AW	16150 AAW	NCBLS	10//99-12//99
	Greensboro--Winston-Salem--High Point MSA, NC	S	9.27 MW	8.70 AW	19280 AAW	NCBLS	10//99-12//99
	North Dakota	S	6.27 MW	6.28 AW	13060 AAW	NDBLS	10//99-12//99
	Ohio	S	9.4 MW	9.22 AW	19180 AAW	OHBLS	10//99-12//99

AAW Average annual wage	AOH Average offered, high	ASH Average starting, high	H Hourly	M Monthly	S Special: hourly and annual
AE Average entry wage	AOL Average offered, low	ASL Average starting, low	HI Highest wage paid	MTC Median total compensation	TQ Third quartile wage
AEX Average experienced wage	APH Average pay, high range	AW Average wage paid	HR High end range	MW Median wage paid	W Weekly
AO Average offered	APL Average pay, low range	FQ First quartile wage	LR Low end range	SQ Second quartile wage	Y Yearly

Occupation/Type/Industry	Location	Per	Low	Mid	High	Source	Date
Meat, Poultry, and Fish Cutter and Trimmer	Canton-Massillon MSA, OH	s	9.32 MW	9.52 AW	19380 AAW	OHBLS	10//99-12//99
	Cincinnati PMSA, OH-KY-IN	s	8.60 MW	8.17 AW	17880 AAW	OHBLS	10//99-12//99
	Columbus MSA, OH	s	9.51 MW	9.11 AW	19780 AAW	OHBLS	10//99-12//99
	Lima MSA, OH	s	8.32 MW	8.11 AW	17310 AAW	OHBLS	10//99-12//99
	Toledo MSA, OH	s	10.26 MW	10.02 AW	21330 AAW	OHBLS	10//99-12//99
	Oklahoma	s	8.03 MW	8.41 AW	17490 AAW	OKBLS	10//99-12//99
	Oklahoma City MSA, OK	s	8.50 MW	8.53 AW	17690 AAW	OKBLS	10//99-12//99
	Tulsa MSA, OK	s	8.57 MW	8.15 AW	17820 AAW	OKBLS	10//99-12//99
	Oregon	s	8.72 MW	10.02 AW	20840 AAW	ORBLS	10//99-12//99
	Eugene-Springfield MSA, OR	s	9.78 MW	9.28 AW	20350 AAW	ORBLS	10//99-12//99
	Portland-Vancouver PMSA, OR-WA	s	11.38 MW	11.67 AW	23680 AAW	ORBLS	10//99-12//99
	Pennsylvania	s	9.78 MW	9.81 AW	20400 AAW	PABLS	10//99-12//99
	Allentown-Bethlehem-Easton MSA, PA	s	9.40 MW	9.95 AW	19560 AAW	PABLS	10//99-12//99
	Lancaster MSA, PA	s	9.92 MW	9.85 AW	20630 AAW	PABLS	10//99-12//99
	Philadelphia PMSA, PA-NJ	s	9.50 MW	9.27 AW	19770 AAW	PABLS	10//99-12//99
	Pittsburgh MSA, PA	s	9.98 MW	9.49 AW	20750 AAW	PABLS	10//99-12//99
	Scranton--Wilkes-Barre--Hazleton MSA, PA	s	8.38 MW	8.27 AW	17430 AAW	PABLS	10//99-12//99
	South Carolina	s	7.82 MW	7.86 AW	16340 AAW	SCBLS	10//99-12//99
	South Dakota	s	10.79 MW	10.39 AW	21620 AAW	SDBLS	10//99-12//99
	Sioux Falls MSA, SD	s	11.08 MW	11.07 AW	23040 AAW	SDBLS	10//99-12//99
	Tennessee	s	8.57 MW	10.96 AW	22790 AAW	TNBLS	10//99-12//99
	Johnson City-Kingsport-Bristol MSA, TN-VA	s	9.42 MW	8.27 AW	19600 AAW	TNBLS	10//99-12//99
	Texas	s	7.89 MW	8.14 AW	16930 AAW	TXBLS	10//99-12//99
	Dallas PMSA, TX	s	7.69 MW	6.92 AW	16000 AAW	TXBLS	10//99-12//99
	El Paso MSA, TX	s	8.37 MW	8.36 AW	17420 AAW	TXBLS	10//99-12//99
	Fort Worth-Arlington PMSA, TX	s	9.53 MW	9.42 AW	19810 AAW	TXBLS	10//99-12//99
	Houston PMSA, TX	s	8.61 MW	6.60 AW	17910 AAW	TXBLS	10//99-12//99
	McAllen-Edinburg-Mission MSA, TX	s	6.02 MW	5.95 AW	12520 AAW	TXBLS	10//99-12//99
	Vermont	s	7.6 MW	8.15 AW	16960 AAW	VTBLS	10//99-12//99
	Burlington MSA, VT	s	8.64 MW	7.37 AW	17970 AAW	VTBLS	10//99-12//99
	Virginia	s	8.11 MW	8.05 AW	16750 AAW	VABLS	10//99-12//99
	Norfolk-Virginia Beach-Newport News MSA, VA-NC	s	7.42 MW	7.39 AW	15430 AAW	VABLS	10//99-12//99
	Richmond-Petersburg MSA, VA	s	8.79 MW	8.39 AW	18280 AAW	VABLS	10//99-12//99
	Washington	s	8.44 MW	9.33 AW	19400 AAW	WABLS	10//99-12//99
	Bellingham MSA, WA	s	9.21 MW	8.23 AW	19150 AAW	WABLS	10//99-12//99
	Seattle-Bellevue-Everett PMSA, WA	s	11.69 MW	10.27 AW	24310 AAW	WABLS	10//99-12//99
	Tacoma PMSA, WA	s	8.91 MW	8.08 AW	18540 AAW	WABLS	10//99-12//99
	Wisconsin	s	8.92 MW	9.17 AW	19080 AAW	WIBLS	10//99-12//99
	Green Bay MSA, WI	s	10.54 MW	10.73 AW	21930 AAW	WIBLS	10//99-12//99
	Milwaukee-Waukesha PMSA, WI	s	11.10 MW	11.93 AW	23090 AAW	WIBLS	10//99-12//99
	Wyoming	s	8.48 MW	8.87 AW	18440 AAW	WYBLS	10//99-12//99
	San Juan-Bayamon PMSA, PR	s	7.50 MW	7.30 AW	15590 AAW	PRBLS	10//99-12//99
Mechanical Door Repairer	California	s	14.76 MW	15.43 AW	32100 AAW	CABLS	10//99-12//99
	Colorado	s	16.37 MW	16.63 AW	34580 AAW	COBLS	10//99-12//99
	Florida	s	9.34 MW	10.24 AW	21290 AAW	FLBLS	10//99-12//99
	Georgia	s	15.65 MW	15.37 AW	31970 AAW	GABLS	10//99-12//99
	Iowa	s	11.85 MW	11.83 AW	24620 AAW	IABLS	10//99-12//99
	Kentucky	s	11.05 MW	12.14 AW	25260 AAW	KYBLS	10//99-12//99
	Maryland	s	12.3 MW	12.47 AW	25940 AAW	MDBLS	10//99-12//99
	Massachusetts	s	18.99 MW	18.96 AW	39430 AAW	MABLS	10//99-12//99
	Michigan	s	13.17 MW	13.62 AW	28330 AAW	MIBLS	10//99-12//99
	Minnesota	s	16.08 MW	15.97 AW	33220 AAW	MNBLS	10//99-12//99
	Montana	s	11.19 MW	11.58 AW	24090 AAW	MTBLS	10//99-12//99
	Nebraska	s	13.13 MW	13.98 AW	29070 AAW	NEBLS	10//99-12//99
	Nevada	s	14.48 MW	14.88 AW	30940 AAW	NVBLS	10//99-12//99
	New Jersey	s	20.11 MW	21.51 AW	44750 AAW	NJBLS	10//99-12//99
	New York	s	13.21 MW	14.28 AW	29700 AAW	NYBLS	10//99-12//99
	North Carolina	s	14.49 MW	14.21 AW	29560 AAW	NCBLS	10//99-12//99
	North Dakota	s	10.99 MW	11.09 AW	23060 AAW	NDBLS	10//99-12//99

AAW	Average annual wage	AOH	Average offered, high	ASH	Average starting, high
AE	Average entry wage	AOL	Average offered, low	ASL	Average starting, low
AEX	Average experienced wage	APH	Average pay, high range	AW	Average wage paid
AO	Average offered	APL	Average pay, low range	FQ	First quartile wage

H	Hourly	M	Monthly	S	Special: hourly and annual
HI	Highest wage paid	MTC	Median total compensation	TQ	Third quartile wage
HR	High end range	MW	Median wage paid	W	Weekly
LR	Low end range	SQ	Second quartile wage	Y	Yearly

Occupation/Type/Industry	Location	Per	Low	Mid	High	Source	Date
Mechanical Door Repairer	Ohio	S	14.94 MW	14.85 AW	30900 AAW	OHBLS	10//99-12//99
	Oklahoma	S	10.53 MW	10.85 AW	22560 AAW	OKBLS	10//99-12//99
	Pennsylvania	S	14.96 MW	14.87 AW	30930 AAW	PABLS	10//99-12//99
	South Carolina	S	15.25 MW	15.84 AW	32950 AAW	SCBLS	10//99-12//99
	Texas	S	12.33 MW	12.73 AW	26480 AAW	TXBLS	10//99-12//99
	Virginia	S	10.49 MW	13.66 AW	28420 AAW	VABLS	10//99-12//99
	Washington	S	16.26 MW	18.44 AW	38350 AAW	WABLS	10//99-12//99
	Wisconsin	S	10.24 MW	10.29 AW	21400 AAW	WIBLS	10//99-12//99
Mechanical Drafter	Alabama	S	16.26 MW	18.08 AW	37610 AAW	ALBLS	10//99-12//99
	Birmingham MSA, AL	S	18.34 MW	16.11 AW	38150 AAW	ALBLS	10//99-12//99
	Florence MSA, AL	S	15.78 MW	15.81 AW	32820 AAW	ALBLS	10//99-12//99
	Huntsville MSA, AL	S	25.65 MW	24.97 AW	53340 AAW	ALBLS	10//99-12//99
	Mobile MSA, AL	S	20.23 MW	19.45 AW	42070 AAW	ALBLS	10//99-12//99
	Alaska	S	22.67 MW	21.21 AW	44120 AAW	AKBLS	10//99-12//99
	Anchorage MSA, AK	S	22.22 MW	23.63 AW	46210 AAW	AKBLS	10//99-12//99
	Arizona	S	16.05 MW	16.37 AW	34060 AAW	AZBLS	10//99-12//99
	Phoenix-Mesa MSA, AZ	S	16.42 MW	16.38 AW	34150 AAW	AZBLS	10//99-12//99
	Tucson MSA, AZ	S	19.59 MW	18.12 AW	40740 AAW	AZBLS	10//99-12//99
	Arkansas	S	13.28 MW	14.59 AW	30340 AAW	ARBLS	10//99-12//99
	Fayetteville-Springdale-Rogers MSA, AR	S	15.79 MW	15.37 AW	32850 AAW	ARBLS	10//99-12//99
	Fort Smith MSA, AR-OK	S	15.23 MW	12.64 AW	31680 AAW	ARBLS	10//99-12//99
	Little Rock-North Little Rock MSA, AR	S	14.69 MW	13.37 AW	30550 AAW	ARBLS	10//99-12//99
	California	S	18.28 MW	19.58 AW	40720 AAW	CABLS	10//99-12//99
	Bakersfield MSA, CA	S	20.04 MW	17.94 AW	41680 AAW	CABLS	10//99-12//99
	Fresno MSA, CA	S	14.24 MW	12.78 AW	29630 AAW	CABLS	10//99-12//99
	Los Angeles-Long Beach PMSA, CA	S	19.18 MW	17.24 AW	39890 AAW	CABLS	10//99-12//99
	Modesto MSA, CA	S	17.70 MW	16.62 AW	36820 AAW	CABLS	10//99-12//99
	Oakland PMSA, CA	S	22.46 MW	22.39 AW	46720 AAW	CABLS	10//99-12//99
	Orange County PMSA, CA	S	17.75 MW	17.09 AW	36920 AAW	CABLS	10//99-12//99
	Riverside-San Bernardino PMSA, CA	S	17.15 MW	17.48 AW	35680 AAW	CABLS	10//99-12//99
	Sacramento PMSA, CA	S	15.79 MW	15.59 AW	32840 AAW	CABLS	10//99-12//99
	San Diego MSA, CA	S	16.92 MW	15.54 AW	35200 AAW	CABLS	10//99-12//99
	San Francisco PMSA, CA	S	22.59 MW	22.60 AW	46990 AAW	CABLS	10//99-12//99
	San Jose PMSA, CA	S	24.55 MW	24.25 AW	51070 AAW	CABLS	10//99-12//99
	San Luis Obispo-Atascadero-Paso Robles MSA, CA	S	16.90 MW	16.99 AW	35150 AAW	CABLS	10//99-12//99
	Santa Barbara-Santa Maria-Lompoc MSA, CA	S	24.76 MW	21.90 AW	51500 AAW	CABLS	10//99-12//99
	Vallejo-Fairfield-Napa PMSA, CA	S	16.24 MW	14.16 AW	33780 AAW	CABLS	10//99-12//99
	Ventura PMSA, CA	S	20.21 MW	18.99 AW	42030 AAW	CABLS	10//99-12//99
	Visalia-Tulare-Porterville MSA, CA	S	15.90 MW	16.85 AW	33080 AAW	CABLS	10//99-12//99
	Colorado	S	18.9 MW	19.45 AW	40460 AAW	COBLS	10//99-12//99
	Boulder-Longmont PMSA, CO	S	23.95 MW	22.00 AW	49820 AAW	COBLS	10//99-12//99
	Denver PMSA, CO	S	19.79 MW	19.41 AW	41150 AAW	COBLS	10//99-12//99
	Fort Collins-Loveland MSA, CO	S	19.28 MW	18.60 AW	40110 AAW	COBLS	10//99-12//99
	Connecticut	S	20.19 MW	20.56 AW	42750 AAW	CTBLS	10//99-12//99
	Bridgeport PMSA, CT	S	20.68 MW	22.10 AW	43010 AAW	CTBLS	10//99-12//99
	Hartford MSA, CT	S	20.31 MW	19.72 AW	42240 AAW	CTBLS	10//99-12//99
	New Haven-Meriden PMSA, CT	S	21.42 MW	21.58 AW	44550 AAW	CTBLS	10//99-12//99
	Stamford-Norwalk PMSA, CT	S	19.17 MW	19.15 AW	39860 AAW	CTBLS	10//99-12//99
	Waterbury PMSA, CT	S	17.38 MW	17.05 AW	36140 AAW	CTBLS	10//99-12//99
	Delaware	S	17.67 MW	18.40 AW	38280 AAW	DEBLS	10//99-12//99
	Wilmington-Newark PMSA, DE-MD	S	18.74 MW	18.18 AW	38970 AAW	DEBLS	10//99-12//99
	Washington PMSA, DC-MD-VA-WV	S	21.93 MW	20.55 AW	45620 AAW	DCBLS	10//99-12//99
	Florida	S	16.86 MW	17.17 AW	35710 AAW	FLBLS	10//99-12//99
	Daytona Beach MSA, FL	S	22.88 MW	17.99 AW	47600 AAW	FLBLS	10//99-12//99
	Fort Lauderdale PMSA, FL	S	15.87 MW	16.17 AW	33010 AAW	FLBLS	10//99-12//99
	Fort Walton Beach MSA, FL	S	16.82 MW	17.64 AW	34990 AAW	FLBLS	10//99-12//99
	Gainesville MSA, FL	S	13.53 MW	12.67 AW	28150 AAW	FLBLS	10//99-12//99
	Jacksonville MSA, FL	S	15.66 MW	14.84 AW	32580 AAW	FLBLS	10//99-12//99
	Lakeland-Winter Haven MSA, FL	S	16.00 MW	15.91 AW	33280 AAW	FLBLS	10//99-12//99

Mechanical Drafter

Occupation/Type/Industry	Location	Per	Low	Mid	High	Source	Date
Mechanical Drafter	Melbourne-Titusville-Palm Bay MSA, FL	S	17.42 MW	17.71 AW	36230 AAW	FLBLS	10//99-12//99
	Miami PMSA, FL	S	15.96 MW	14.73 AW	33200 AAW	FLBLS	10//99-12//99
	Ocala MSA, FL	S	11.84 MW	11.95 AW	24620 AAW	FLBLS	10//99-12//99
	Orlando MSA, FL	S	16.96 MW	17.06 AW	35270 AAW	FLBLS	10//99-12//99
	Sarasota-Bradenton MSA, FL	S	18.48 MW	17.41 AW	38440 AAW	FLBLS	10//99-12//99
	Tampa-St. Petersburg-Clearwater MSA, FL	S	17.89 MW	17.19 AW	37210 AAW	FLBLS	10//99-12//99
	West Palm Beach-Boca Raton MSA, FL	S	20.11 MW	20.16 AW	41820 AAW	FLBLS	10//99-12//99
	Georgia	S	18.73 MW	19.87 AW	41330 AAW	GABLS	10//99-12//99
	Atlanta MSA, GA	S	20.67 MW	19.71 AW	43000 AAW	GABLS	10//99-12//99
	Augusta-Aiken MSA, GA-SC	S	16.53 MW	12.56 AW	34380 AAW	GABLS	10//99-12//99
	Idaho	S	15.49 MW	17.21 AW	35800 AAW	IDBLS	10//99-12//99
	Boise City MSA, ID	S	15.20 MW	14.92 AW	31610 AAW	IDBLS	10//99-12//99
	Pocatello MSA, ID	S	14.38 MW	14.53 AW	29900 AAW	IDBLS	10//99-12//99
	Illinois	S	17.41 MW	17.76 AW	36930 AAW	ILBLS	10//99-12//99
	Chicago PMSA, IL	S	18.14 MW	17.90 AW	37720 AAW	ILBLS	10//99-12//99
	Peoria-Pekin MSA, IL	S	22.04 MW	23.74 AW	45850 AAW	ILBLS	10//99-12//99
	Rockford MSA, IL	S	18.63 MW	17.70 AW	38760 AAW	ILBLS	10//99-12//99
	Springfield MSA, IL	S	15.40 MW	15.11 AW	32030 AAW	ILBLS	10//99-12//99
	Indiana	S	15.83 MW	17.01 AW	35380 AAW	INBLS	10//99-12//99
	Elkhart-Goshen MSA, IN	S	13.51 MW	14.64 AW	28100 AAW	INBLS	10//99-12//99
	Evansville-Henderson MSA, IN-KY	S	14.78 MW	14.74 AW	30750 AAW	INBLS	10//99-12//99
	Fort Wayne MSA, IN	S	20.81 MW	21.60 AW	43290 AAW	INBLS	10//99-12//99
	Gary PMSA, IN	S	21.58 MW	22.77 AW	44890 AAW	INBLS	10//99-12//99
	Indianapolis MSA, IN	S	15.10 MW	14.78 AW	31410 AAW	INBLS	10//99-12//99
	Kokomo MSA, IN	S	23.45 MW	20.48 AW	48780 AAW	INBLS	10//99-12//99
	Muncie MSA, IN	S	15.37 MW	15.50 AW	31970 AAW	INBLS	10//99-12//99
	South Bend MSA, IN	S	14.41 MW	14.24 AW	29980 AAW	INBLS	10//99-12//99
	Iowa	S	16.28 MW	16.15 AW	33580 AAW	IABLS	10//99-12//99
	Cedar Rapids MSA, IA	S	18.26 MW	18.54 AW	37980 AAW	IABLS	10//99-12//99
	Davenport-Moline-Rock Island MSA, IA-IL	S	12.82 MW	12.34 AW	26670 AAW	IABLS	10//99-12//99
	Des Moines MSA, IA	S	14.48 MW	13.21 AW	30110 AAW	IABLS	10//99-12//99
	Kansas	S	14.75 MW	15.05 AW	31310 AAW	KSBLS	10//99-12//99
	Wichita MSA, KS	S	14.83 MW	14.90 AW	30850 AAW	KSBLS	10//99-12//99
	Kentucky	S	14.84 MW	15.47 AW	32180 AAW	KYBLS	10//99-12//99
	Lexington MSA, KY	S	15.04 MW	15.12 AW	31280 AAW	KYBLS	10//99-12//99
	Louisville MSA, KY-IN	S	16.42 MW	15.70 AW	34160 AAW	KYBLS	10//99-12//99
	Louisiana	S	18.87 MW	19.35 AW	40260 AAW	LABLS	10//99-12//99
	Baton Rouge MSA, LA	S	23.31 MW	23.35 AW	48480 AAW	LABLS	10//99-12//99
	Lafayette MSA, LA	S	12.26 MW	11.49 AW	25500 AAW	LABLS	10//99-12//99
	Monroe MSA, LA	S	15.23 MW	13.72 AW	31680 AAW	LABLS	10//99-12//99
	New Orleans MSA, LA	S	20.91 MW	21.06 AW	43500 AAW	LABLS	10//99-12//99
	Shreveport-Bossier City MSA, LA	S	13.13 MW	13.89 AW	27300 AAW	LABLS	10//99-12//99
	Maine	S	16.59 MW	17.08 AW	35520 AAW	MEBLS	10//99-12//99
	Portland MSA, ME	S	17.79 MW	18.11 AW	37010 AAW	MEBLS	10//99-12//99
	Maryland	S	18.65 MW	19.39 AW	40320 AAW	MDBLS	10//99-12//99
	Baltimore PMSA, MD	S	16.55 MW	16.02 AW	34430 AAW	MDBLS	10//99-12//99
	Massachusetts	S	18.85 MW	19.15 AW	39820 AAW	MABLS	10//99-12//99
	Boston PMSA, MA-NH	S	19.30 MW	19.05 AW	40150 AAW	MABLS	10//99-12//99
	Brockton PMSA, MA	S	17.88 MW	16.34 AW	37180 AAW	MABLS	10//99-12//99
	Fitchburg-Leominster PMSA, MA	S	22.89 MW	22.83 AW	47610 AAW	MABLS	10//99-12//99
	Lawrence PMSA, MA-NH	S	17.80 MW	16.58 AW	37020 AAW	MABLS	10//99-12//99
	Lowell PMSA, MA-NH	S	21.37 MW	21.05 AW	44460 AAW	MABLS	10//99-12//99
	Springfield MSA, MA	S	17.28 MW	17.03 AW	35940 AAW	MABLS	10//99-12//99
	Worcester PMSA, MA-CT	S	16.65 MW	16.03 AW	34640 AAW	MABLS	10//99-12//99
	Michigan	S	21.91 MW	24.74 AW	51470 AAW	MIBLS	10//99-12//99
	Ann Arbor PMSA, MI	S	18.53 MW	18.92 AW	38550 AAW	MIBLS	10//99-12//99
	Benton Harbor MSA, MI	S	14.42 MW	12.92 AW	30000 AAW	MIBLS	10//99-12//99
	Detroit PMSA, MI	S	27.83 MW	24.97 AW	57890 AAW	MIBLS	10//99-12//99
	Flint PMSA, MI	S	29.24 MW	28.50 AW	60810 AAW	MIBLS	10//99-12//99
	Grand Rapids-Muskegon-Holland MSA, MI	S	21.09 MW	19.45 AW	43860 AAW	MIBLS	10//99-12//99
	Jackson MSA, MI	S	20.22 MW	20.74 AW	42070 AAW	MIBLS	10//99-12//99
	Kalamazoo-Battle Creek MSA, MI	S	19.35 MW	18.94 AW	40250 AAW	MIBLS	10//99-12//99
	Lansing-East Lansing MSA, MI	S	19.66 MW	19.50 AW	40890 AAW	MIBLS	10//99-12//99

AAW	Average annual wage	AOH	Average offered, high	ASH	Average starting, high
AE	Average entry wage	AOL	Average offered, low	ASL	Average starting, low
AEX	Average experienced wage	APH	Average pay, high range	AW	Average wage paid
AO	Average offered	APL	Average pay, low range	FQ	First quartile wage

H	Hourly	M	Monthly
HI	Highest wage paid	MTC	Median total compensation
HR	High end range	MW	Median wage paid
LR	Low end range	SQ	Second quartile wage

S	Special: hourly and annual
TQ	Third quartile wage
W	Weekly
Y	Yearly

Occupation/Type/Industry	Location	Per	Low	Mid	High	Source	Date
Mechanical Drafter	Saginaw-Bay City-Midland MSA, MI	S	13.96 MW	12.65 AW	29030 AAW	MIBLS	10//99-12//99
	Minnesota	S	17.43 MW	17.91 AW	37260 AAW	MNBLS	10//99-12//99
	Duluth-Superior MSA, MN-WI	S	13.52 MW	13.25 AW	28120 AAW	MNBLS	10//99-12//99
	Minneapolis-St. Paul MSA, MN-WI	S	18.77 MW	18.29 AW	39050 AAW	MNBLS	10//99-12//99
	St. Cloud MSA, MN	S	16.57 MW	17.17 AW	34470 AAW	MNBLS	10//99-12//99
	Mississippi	S	14.84 MW	15.50 AW	32230 AAW	MSBLS	10//99-12//99
	Biloxi-Gulfport-Pascagoula MSA, MS	S	15.47 MW	14.41 AW	32180 AAW	MSBLS	10//99-12//99
	Jackson MSA, MS	S	10.92 MW	11.21 AW	22710 AAW	MSBLS	10//99-12//99
	Missouri	S	15.93 MW	17.03 AW	35420 AAW	MOBLS	10//99-12//99
	Kansas City MSA, MO-KS	S	17.73 MW	15.98 AW	36880 AAW	MOBLS	10//99-12//99
	St. Louis MSA, MO-IL	S	16.99 MW	16.03 AW	35330 AAW	MOBLS	10//99-12//99
	Montana	S	11.51 MW	12.62 AW	26250 AAW	MTBLS	10//99-12//99
	Nebraska	S	10.86 MW	11.75 AW	24430 AAW	NEBLS	10//99-12//99
	Omaha MSA, NE-IA	S	12.24 MW	10.38 AW	25460 AAW	NEBLS	10//99-12//99
	Nevada	S	19.67 MW	21.25 AW	44200 AAW	NVBLS	10//99-12//99
	Las Vegas MSA, NV-AZ	S	18.17 MW	18.05 AW	37780 AAW	NVBLS	10//99-12//99
	Reno MSA, NV	S	19.64 MW	18.72 AW	40850 AAW	NVBLS	10//99-12//99
	New Hampshire	S	16.2 MW	18.17 AW	37800 AAW	NHBLS	10//99-12//99
	Nashua PMSA, NH	S	18.65 MW	18.03 AW	38790 AAW	NHBLS	10//99-12//99
	Portsmouth-Rochester PMSA, NH-ME	S	16.13 MW	15.35 AW	33550 AAW	NHBLS	10//99-12//99
	New Jersey	S	17.92 MW	18.69 AW	38870 AAW	NJBLS	10//99-12//99
	Bergen-Passaic PMSA, NJ	S	18.06 MW	17.61 AW	37570 AAW	NJBLS	10//99-12//99
	Middlesex-Somerset-Hunterdon PMSA, NJ	S	18.78 MW	18.40 AW	39070 AAW	NJBLS	10//99-12//99
	Monmouth-Ocean PMSA, NJ	S	17.82 MW	16.99 AW	37070 AAW	NJBLS	10//99-12//99
	Newark PMSA, NJ	S	20.36 MW	18.93 AW	42340 AAW	NJBLS	10//99-12//99
	Trenton PMSA, NJ	S	17.61 MW	17.99 AW	36620 AAW	NJBLS	10//99-12//99
	New Mexico	S	12.79 MW	12.83 AW	26690 AAW	NMBLS	10//99-12//99
	Albuquerque MSA, NM	S	12.68 MW	13.03 AW	26370 AAW	NMBLS	10//99-12//99
	New York	S	18.87 MW	19.41 AW	40380 AAW	NYBLS	10//99-12//99
	Albany-Schenectady-Troy MSA, NY	S	18.02 MW	18.48 AW	37480 AAW	NYBLS	10//99-12//99
	Binghamton MSA, NY	S	15.56 MW	15.55 AW	32370 AAW	NYBLS	10//99-12//99
	Buffalo-Niagara Falls MSA, NY	S	18.07 MW	17.55 AW	37580 AAW	NYBLS	10//99-12//99
	Dutchess County PMSA, NY	S	15.61 MW	17.36 AW	32480 AAW	NYBLS	10//99-12//99
	Elmira MSA, NY	S	13.53 MW	13.51 AW	28140 AAW	NYBLS	10//99-12//99
	Nassau-Suffolk PMSA, NY	S	21.43 MW	20.95 AW	44580 AAW	NYBLS	10//99-12//99
	New York PMSA, NY	S	21.43 MW	22.42 AW	44580 AAW	NYBLS	10//99-12//99
	Newburgh PMSA, NY-PA	S	20.83 MW	22.19 AW	43330 AAW	NYBLS	10//99-12//99
	Rochester MSA, NY	S	18.87 MW	18.37 AW	39260 AAW	NYBLS	10//99-12//99
	Syracuse MSA, NY	S	16.42 MW	15.65 AW	34140 AAW	NYBLS	10//99-12//99
	Utica-Rome MSA, NY	S	15.59 MW	13.49 AW	32430 AAW	NYBLS	10//99-12//99
	North Carolina	S	17.09 MW	18.32 AW	38100 AAW	NCBLS	10//99-12//99
	Asheville MSA, NC	S	16.92 MW	16.66 AW	35190 AAW	NCBLS	10//99-12//99
	Charlotte-Gastonia-Rock Hill MSA, NC-SC	S	20.59 MW	19.68 AW	42820 AAW	NCBLS	10//99-12//99
	Greensboro--Winston-Salem--High Point MSA, NC	S	18.84 MW	17.71 AW	39180 AAW	NCBLS	10//99-12//99
	Hickory-Morganton-Lenoir MSA, NC	S	15.68 MW	15.51 AW	32610 AAW	NCBLS	10//99-12//99
	Raleigh-Durham-Chapel Hill MSA, NC	S	17.66 MW	16.65 AW	36740 AAW	NCBLS	10//99-12//99
	North Dakota	S	11.7 MW	11.73 AW	24400 AAW	NDBLS	10//99-12//99
	Fargo-Moorhead MSA, ND-MN	S	12.16 MW	11.93 AW	25290 AAW	NDBLS	10//99-12//99
	Ohio	S	16.84 MW	17.71 AW	36830 AAW	OHBLS	10//99-12//99
	Akron PMSA, OH	S	16.09 MW	15.93 AW	33460 AAW	OHBLS	10//99-12//99
	Canton-Massillon MSA, OH	S	20.25 MW	20.43 AW	42120 AAW	OHBLS	10//99-12//99
	Cincinnati PMSA, OH-KY-IN	S	17.20 MW	17.44 AW	35770 AAW	OHBLS	10//99-12//99
	Cleveland-Lorain-Elyria PMSA, OH	S	18.26 MW	17.84 AW	37980 AAW	OHBLS	10//99-12//99
	Columbus MSA, OH	S	17.38 MW	16.51 AW	36150 AAW	OHBLS	10//99-12//99
	Hamilton-Middletown PMSA, OH	S	23.09 MW	22.89 AW	48020 AAW	OHBLS	10//99-12//99
	Lima MSA, OH	S	12.50 MW	12.41 AW	26000 AAW	OHBLS	10//99-12//99
	Mansfield MSA, OH	S	14.79 MW	13.53 AW	30770 AAW	OHBLS	10//99-12//99
	Toledo MSA, OH	S	16.54 MW	15.69 AW	34400 AAW	OHBLS	10//99-12//99

AAW	Average annual wage	AOH	Average offered, high	ASH	Average starting, high	H	Hourly	M	Monthly	S	Special: hourly and annual
AE	Average entry wage	AOL	Average offered, low	ASL	Average starting, low	HI	Highest wage paid	MTC	Median total compensation	TQ	Third quartile wage
AEX	Average experienced wage	APH	Average pay, high range	AW	Average wage paid	HR	High end range	MW	Median wage paid	W	Weekly
AO	Average offered	APL	Average pay, low range	FQ	First quartile wage	LR	Low end range	SQ	Second quartile wage	Y	Yearly

Occupation/Type/Industry	Location	Per	Low	Mid	High	Source	Date
Mechanical Drafter	Youngstown-Warren MSA, OH	S	14.00 MW	13.54 AW	29120 AAW	OHBLS	10//99-12//99
	Oklahoma	S	18.08 MW	18.01 AW	37460 AAW	OKBLS	10//99-12//99
	Oklahoma City MSA, OK	S	14.93 MW	14.14 AW	31050 AAW	OKBLS	10//99-12//99
	Tulsa MSA, OK	S	19.33 MW	19.52 AW	40210 AAW	OKBLS	10//99-12//99
	Oregon	S	15.8 MW	16.35 AW	34010 AAW	ORBLS	10//99-12//99
	Eugene-Springfield MSA, OR	S	15.71 MW	15.14 AW	32680 AAW	ORBLS	10//99-12//99
	Medford-Ashland MSA, OR	S	14.62 MW	14.96 AW	30410 AAW	ORBLS	10//99-12//99
	Portland-Vancouver PMSA, OR-WA	S	16.83 MW	16.27 AW	35010 AAW	ORBLS	10//99-12//99
	Salem PMSA, OR	S	16.11 MW	16.87 AW	33500 AAW	ORBLS	10//99-12//99
	Pennsylvania	S	16.38 MW	17.07 AW	35500 AAW	PABLS	10//99-12//99
	Allentown-Bethlehem-Easton MSA, PA	S	18.55 MW	18.85 AW	38570 AAW	PABLS	10//99-12//99
	Erie MSA, PA	S	14.28 MW	13.14 AW	29700 AAW	PABLS	10//99-12//99
	Harrisburg-Lebanon-Carlisle MSA, PA	S	19.16 MW	18.78 AW	39840 AAW	PABLS	10//99-12//99
	Johnstown MSA, PA	S	11.99 MW	11.60 AW	24940 AAW	PABLS	10//99-12//99
	Lancaster MSA, PA	S	15.78 MW	15.07 AW	32830 AAW	PABLS	10//99-12//99
	Philadelphia PMSA, PA-NJ	S	18.44 MW	18.24 AW	38360 AAW	PABLS	10//99-12//99
	Pittsburgh MSA, PA	S	17.89 MW	17.32 AW	37210 AAW	PABLS	10//99-12//99
	Reading MSA, PA	S	17.52 MW	17.37 AW	36450 AAW	PABLS	10//99-12//99
	Scranton--Wilkes-Barre--Hazleton MSA, PA	S	14.45 MW	13.50 AW	30050 AAW	PABLS	10//99-12//99
	Sharon MSA, PA	S	15.27 MW	14.35 AW	31770 AAW	PABLS	10//99-12//99
	Williamsport MSA, PA	S	14.25 MW	13.02 AW	29630 AAW	PABLS	10//99-12//99
	York MSA, PA	S	16.03 MW	15.58 AW	33340 AAW	PABLS	10//99-12//99
	Rhode Island	S	17.5 MW	17.02 AW	35400 AAW	RIBLS	10//99-12//99
	Providence-Fall River-Warwick MSA, RI-MA	S	16.25 MW	15.56 AW	33800 AAW	RIBLS	10//99-12//99
	South Carolina	S	18.69 MW	21.28 AW	44270 AAW	SCBLS	10//99-12//99
	Charleston-North Charleston MSA, SC	S	16.76 MW	16.30 AW	34860 AAW	SCBLS	10//99-12//99
	Columbia MSA, SC	S	19.03 MW	16.65 AW	39590 AAW	SCBLS	10//99-12//99
	Greenville-Spartanburg-Anderson MSA, SC	S	24.20 MW	23.76 AW	50340 AAW	SCBLS	10//99-12//99
	South Dakota	S	13.29 MW	14.00 AW	29120 AAW	SDBLS	10//99-12//99
	Sioux Falls MSA, SD	S	13.16 MW	12.54 AW	27380 AAW	SDBLS	10//99-12//99
	Tennessee	S	16.18 MW	17.85 AW	37120 AAW	TNBLS	10//99-12//99
	Chattanooga MSA, TN-GA	S	14.61 MW	14.26 AW	30380 AAW	TNBLS	10//99-12//99
	Johnson City-Kingsport-Bristol MSA, TN-VA	S	14.29 MW	12.82 AW	29720 AAW	TNBLS	10//99-12//99
	Knoxville MSA, TN	S	18.78 MW	16.22 AW	39060 AAW	TNBLS	10//99-12//99
	Memphis MSA, TN-AR-MS	S	18.75 MW	16.75 AW	39010 AAW	MSBLS	10//99-12//99
	Nashville MSA, TN	S	18.40 MW	18.56 AW	38270 AAW	TNBLS	10//99-12//99
	Texas	S	17.21 MW	17.91 AW	37250 AAW	TXBLS	10//99-12//99
	Austin-San Marcos MSA, TX	S	18.70 MW	18.46 AW	38900 AAW	TXBLS	10//99-12//99
	Beaumont-Port Arthur MSA, TX	S	17.21 MW	14.70 AW	35800 AAW	TXBLS	10//99-12//99
	Dallas PMSA, TX	S	16.30 MW	16.77 AW	33900 AAW	TXBLS	10//99-12//99
	El Paso MSA, TX	S	9.11 MW	9.33 AW	18940 AAW	TXBLS	10//99-12//99
	Fort Worth-Arlington PMSA, TX	S	19.55 MW	19.40 AW	40660 AAW	TXBLS	10//99-12//99
	Galveston-Texas City PMSA, TX	S	24.69 MW	22.62 AW	51350 AAW	TXBLS	10//99-12//99
	Houston PMSA, TX	S	19.86 MW	18.75 AW	41310 AAW	TXBLS	10//99-12//99
	Killeen-Temple MSA, TX	S	16.51 MW	16.01 AW	34340 AAW	TXBLS	10//99-12//99
	Lubbock MSA, TX	S	12.93 MW	12.92 AW	26890 AAW	TXBLS	10//99-12//99
	San Antonio MSA, TX	S	15.31 MW	15.18 AW	31850 AAW	TXBLS	10//99-12//99
	Texarkana MSA, TX-Texarkana, AR	S	11.89 MW	11.97 AW	24730 AAW	TXBLS	10//99-12//99
	Tyler MSA, TX	S	16.35 MW	15.66 AW	34000 AAW	TXBLS	10//99-12//99
	Waco MSA, TX	S	13.05 MW	13.09 AW	27150 AAW	TXBLS	10//99-12//99
	Utah	S	15.07 MW	16.21 AW	33720 AAW	UTBLS	10//99-12//99
	Salt Lake City-Ogden MSA, UT	S	16.53 MW	15.54 AW	34380 AAW	UTBLS	10//99-12//99
	Vermont	S	16.2 MW	16.18 AW	33660 AAW	VTBLS	10//99-12//99
	Virginia	S	18.49 MW	18.68 AW	38850 AAW	VABLS	10//99-12//99
	Lynchburg MSA, VA	S	12.41 MW	12.02 AW	25810 AAW	VABLS	10//99-12//99
	Richmond-Petersburg MSA, VA	S	20.28 MW	21.74 AW	42180 AAW	VABLS	10//99-12//99
	Washington	S	15.33 MW	15.60 AW	32440 AAW	WABLS	10//99-12//99

AAW	Average annual wage	AOH	Average offered, high	ASH	Average starting, high	H	Hourly	M	Monthly	S	Special: hourly and annual
AE	Average entry wage	AOL	Average offered, low	ASL	Average starting, low	HI	Highest wage paid	MTC	Median total compensation	TQ	Third quartile wage
AEX	Average experienced wage	APH	Average pay, high range	AW	Average wage paid	HR	High end range	MW	Median wage paid	W	Weekly
AO	Average offered	APL	Average pay, low range	FQ	First quartile wage	LR	Low end range	SQ	Second quartile wage	Y	Yearly

Occupation/Type/Industry	Location	Per	Low	Mid	High	Source	Date
Mechanical Drafter	Seattle-Bellevue-Everett						
	PMSA, WA	S	16.29 MW	15.71 AW	33870 AAW	WABLS	10//99-12//99
	Spokane MSA, WA	S	13.84 MW	13.90 AW	28790 AAW	WABLS	10//99-12//99
	Tacoma PMSA, WA	S	15.21 MW	16.91 AW	31630 AAW	WABLS	10//99-12//99
	Yakima MSA, WA	S	11.58 MW	11.02 AW	24090 AAW	WABLS	10//99-12//99
	West Virginia	S	15.92 MW	17.75 AW	36910 AAW	WVBLS	10//99-12//99
	Charleston MSA, WV	S	16.00 MW	15.65 AW	33290 AAW	WVBLS	10//99-12//99
	Huntington-Ashland MSA, WV-KY-OH	S	15.30 MW	14.38 AW	31810 AAW	WVBLS	10//99-12//99
	Parkersburg-Marietta MSA, WV-OH	S	15.24 MW	14.69 AW	31700 AAW	WVBLS	10//99-12//99
	Wisconsin	S	16.47 MW	17.03 AW	35420 AAW	WIBLS	10//99-12//99
	Appleton-Oshkosh-Neenah MSA, WI	S	16.81 MW	15.98 AW	34970 AAW	WIBLS	10//99-12//99
	Eau Claire MSA, WI	S	16.28 MW	16.17 AW	33860 AAW	WIBLS	10//99-12//99
	Green Bay MSA, WI	S	17.59 MW	16.42 AW	36580 AAW	WIBLS	10//99-12//99
	Janesville-Beloit MSA, WI	S	16.66 MW	16.51 AW	34660 AAW	WIBLS	10//99-12//99
	Kenosha PMSA, WI	S	15.90 MW	15.64 AW	33070 AAW	WIBLS	10//99-12//99
	Madison MSA, WI	S	15.26 MW	13.87 AW	31740 AAW	WIBLS	10//99-12//99
	Milwaukee-Waukesha PMSA, WI	S	18.01 MW	17.78 AW	37470 AAW	WIBLS	10//99-12//99
	Racine PMSA, WI	S	17.31 MW	16.99 AW	36000 AAW	WIBLS	10//99-12//99
	Puerto Rico	S	15.14 MW	14.31 AW	29770 AAW	PRBLS	10//99-12//99
	San Juan-Bayamon PMSA, PR	S	14.17 MW	15.05 AW	29480 AAW	PRBLS	10//99-12//99
Mechanical Engineer	Alabama	S	27.32 MW	27.64 AW	57490 AAW	ALBLS	10//99-12//99
	Anniston MSA, AL	S	25.67 MW	25.16 AW	53400 AAW	ALBLS	10//99-12//99
	Birmingham MSA, AL	S	28.38 MW	25.57 AW	59020 AAW	ALBLS	10//99-12//99
	Decatur MSA, AL	S	29.27 MW	30.42 AW	60890 AAW	ALBLS	10//99-12//99
	Dothan MSA, AL	S	28.40 MW	29.54 AW	59070 AAW	ALBLS	10//99-12//99
	Florence MSA, AL	S	28.10 MW	26.65 AW	58450 AAW	ALBLS	10//99-12//99
	Huntsville MSA, AL	S	28.85 MW	29.58 AW	60010 AAW	ALBLS	10//99-12//99
	Mobile MSA, AL	S	28.38 MW	29.31 AW	59040 AAW	ALBLS	10//99-12//99
	Alaska	S	29.8 MW	28.98 AW	60270 AAW	AKBLS	10//99-12//99
	Anchorage MSA, AK	S	28.95 MW	29.71 AW	60220 AAW	AKBLS	10//99-12//99
	Arizona	S	28.75 MW	27.97 AW	58180 AAW	AZBLS	10//99-12//99
	Phoenix-Mesa MSA, AZ	S	28.17 MW	28.99 AW	58600 AAW	AZBLS	10//99-12//99
	Tucson MSA, AZ	S	27.33 MW	27.44 AW	56840 AAW	AZBLS	10//99-12//99
	Arkansas	S	24.04 MW	24.60 AW	51180 AAW	ARBLS	10//99-12//99
	Fayetteville-Springdale-Rogers MSA, AR	S	22.61 MW	22.38 AW	47020 AAW	ARBLS	10//99-12//99
	Fort Smith MSA, AR-OK	S	22.71 MW	22.61 AW	47250 AAW	ARBLS	10//99-12//99
	Little Rock-North Little Rock MSA, AR	S	22.41 MW	21.66 AW	46620 AAW	ARBLS	10//99-12//99
	California	S	30.72 MW	30.07 AW	62540 AAW	CABLS	10//99-12//99
	Chico-Paradise MSA, CA	S	18.27 MW	18.00 AW	38000 AAW	CABLS	10//99-12//99
	Fresno MSA, CA	S	24.52 MW	22.96 AW	51000 AAW	CABLS	10//99-12//99
	Los Angeles-Long Beach PMSA, CA	S	31.12 MW	31.36 AW	64730 AAW	CABLS	10//99-12//99
	Modesto MSA, CA	S	24.51 MW	23.99 AW	50980 AAW	CABLS	10//99-12//99
	Oakland PMSA, CA	S	30.91 MW	32.29 AW	64300 AAW	CABLS	10//99-12//99
	Orange County PMSA, CA	S	28.16 MW	28.60 AW	58560 AAW	CABLS	10//99-12//99
	Redding MSA, CA	S	25.66 MW	23.39 AW	53370 AAW	CABLS	10//99-12//99
	Riverside-San Bernardino PMSA, CA	S	22.22 MW	21.53 AW	46210 AAW	CABLS	10//99-12//99
	Sacramento PMSA, CA	S	28.60 MW	28.60 AW	59490 AAW	CABLS	10//99-12//99
	Salinas MSA, CA	S	28.63 MW	26.29 AW	59540 AAW	CABLS	10//99-12//99
	San Diego MSA, CA	S	30.47 MW	30.61 AW	63370 AAW	CABLS	10//99-12//99
	San Francisco PMSA, CA	S	30.98 MW	32.40 AW	64440 AAW	CABLS	10//99-12//99
	San Jose PMSA, CA	S	32.70 MW	32.97 AW	68010 AAW	CABLS	10//99-12//99
	San Luis Obispo-Atascadero-Paso Robles MSA, CA	S	23.51 MW	22.80 AW	48900 AAW	CABLS	10//99-12//99
	Santa Barbara-Santa Maria-Lompoc MSA, CA	S	31.18 MW	32.50 AW	64860 AAW	CABLS	10//99-12//99
	Santa Cruz-Watsonville PMSA, CA	S	28.28 MW	31.21 AW	58820 AAW	CABLS	10//99-12//99
	Santa Rosa PMSA, CA	S	30.90 MW	31.20 AW	64280 AAW	CABLS	10//99-12//99
	Stockton-Lodi MSA, CA	S	25.92 MW	24.97 AW	53910 AAW	CABLS	10//99-12//99
	Vallejo-Fairfield-Napa PMSA, CA	S	27.94 MW	30.19 AW	58120 AAW	CABLS	10//99-12//99
	Ventura PMSA, CA	S	28.32 MW	28.47 AW	58910 AAW	CABLS	10//99-12//99
	Visalia-Tulare-Porterville MSA, CA	S	22.06 MW	22.18 AW	45890 AAW	CABLS	10//99-12//99

AAW Average annual wage	**AOH** Average offered, high	**ASH** Average starting, high	**H** Hourly	**M** Monthly	**S** Special: hourly and annual
AE Average entry wage	**AOL** Average offered, low	**ASL** Average starting, low	**HI** Highest wage paid	**MTC** Median total compensation	**TQ** Third quartile wage
AEX Average experienced wage	**APH** Average pay, high range	**AW** Average wage paid	**HR** High end range	**MW** Median wage paid	**W** Weekly
AO Average offered	**APL** Average pay, low range	**FQ** First quartile wage	**LR** Low end range	**SQ** Second quartile wage	**Y** Yearly

Occupation/Type/Industry	Location	Per	Low	Mid	High	Source	Date
Mechanical Engineer	Yolo PMSA, CA	s	24.90 MW	22.89 AW	51800 AAW	CABLS	10//99-12//99
	Colorado	s	26.72 MW	27.38 AW	56940 AAW	COBLS	10//99-12//99
	Boulder-Longmont PMSA, CO	s	29.49 MW	30.29 AW	61340 AAW	COBLS	10//99-12//99
	Colorado Springs MSA, CO	s	22.86 MW	19.35 AW	47550 AAW	COBLS	10//99-12//99
	Denver PMSA, CO	s	27.99 MW	27.71 AW	58220 AAW	COBLS	10//99-12//99
	Fort Collins-Loveland MSA, CO	s	23.95 MW	21.74 AW	49810 AAW	COBLS	10//99-12//99
	Connecticut	s	28.9 MW	28.65 AW	59590 AAW	CTBLS	10//99-12//99
	Bridgeport PMSA, CT	s	29.40 MW	30.89 AW	61150 AAW	CTBLS	10//99-12//99
	Danbury PMSA, CT	s	30.27 MW	31.27 AW	62950 AAW	CTBLS	10//99-12//99
	Hartford MSA, CT	s	28.71 MW	28.21 AW	59710 AAW	CTBLS	10//99-12//99
	New Haven-Meriden PMSA, CT	s	27.18 MW	25.91 AW	56530 AAW	CTBLS	10//99-12//99
	New London-Norwich MSA, CT-RI	s	28.85 MW	28.57 AW	60020 AAW	CTBLS	10//99-12//99
	Stamford-Norwalk PMSA, CT	s	27.49 MW	27.25 AW	57180 AAW	CTBLS	10//99-12//99
	Waterbury PMSA, CT	s	28.52 MW	30.18 AW	59320 AAW	CTBLS	10//99-12//99
	Delaware	s	29.9 MW	29.56 AW	61480 AAW	DEBLS	10//99-12//99
	Wilmington-Newark PMSA, DE-MD	s	30.00 MW	30.08 AW	62410 AAW	DEBLS	10//99-12//99
	Washington PMSA, DC-MD-VA-WV	s	29.65 MW	30.36 AW	61660 AAW	DCBLS	10//99-12//99
	Florida	s	26.95 MW	26.62 AW	55370 AAW	FLBLS	10//99-12//99
	Daytona Beach MSA, FL	s	26.32 MW	25.75 AW	54750 AAW	FLBLS	10//99-12//99
	Fort Lauderdale PMSA, FL	s	21.44 MW	21.13 AW	44590 AAW	FLBLS	10//99-12//99
	Fort Myers-Cape Coral MSA, FL	s	25.70 MW	24.96 AW	53450 AAW	FLBLS	10//99-12//99
	Fort Walton Beach MSA, FL	s	25.99 MW	26.81 AW	54060 AAW	FLBLS	10//99-12//99
	Gainesville MSA, FL	s	25.30 MW	24.37 AW	52620 AAW	FLBLS	10//99-12//99
	Jacksonville MSA, FL	s	25.50 MW	25.32 AW	53030 AAW	FLBLS	10//99-12//99
	Lakeland-Winter Haven MSA, FL	s	23.62 MW	22.67 AW	49130 AAW	FLBLS	10//99-12//99
	Melbourne-Titusville-Palm Bay MSA, FL	s	25.64 MW	24.93 AW	53330 AAW	FLBLS	10//99-12//99
	Miami PMSA, FL	s	21.30 MW	20.16 AW	44310 AAW	FLBLS	10//99-12//99
	Orlando MSA, FL	s	27.48 MW	28.71 AW	57160 AAW	FLBLS	10//99-12//99
	Pensacola MSA, FL	s	29.07 MW	29.83 AW	60470 AAW	FLBLS	10//99-12//99
	Sarasota-Bradenton MSA, FL	s	23.82 MW	23.23 AW	49540 AAW	FLBLS	10//99-12//99
	Tampa-St. Petersburg-Clearwater MSA, FL	s	25.37 MW	24.77 AW	52770 AAW	FLBLS	10//99-12//99
	West Palm Beach-Boca Raton MSA, FL	s	32.83 MW	32.23 AW	68280 AAW	FLBLS	10//99-12//99
	Georgia	s	25.06 MW	26.14 AW	54370 AAW	GABLS	10//99-12//99
	Athens MSA, GA	s	26.81 MW	27.13 AW	55760 AAW	GABLS	10//99-12//99
	Atlanta MSA, GA	s	26.27 MW	25.06 AW	54640 AAW	GABLS	10//99-12//99
	Augusta-Aiken MSA, GA-SC	s	35.91 MW	37.13 AW	74700 AAW	GABLS	10//99-12//99
	Columbus MSA, GA-AL	s	25.02 MW	24.05 AW	52040 AAW	GABLS	10//99-12//99
	Macon MSA, GA	s	27.71 MW	28.76 AW	57630 AAW	GABLS	10//99-12//99
	Savannah MSA, GA	s	25.51 MW	27.24 AW	53050 AAW	GABLS	10//99-12//99
	Hawaii	s	27.21 MW	28.05 AW	58350 AAW	HIBLS	10//99-12//99
	Honolulu MSA, HI	s	28.33 MW	27.62 AW	58920 AAW	HIBLS	10//99-12//99
	Idaho	s	26.57 MW	27.16 AW	56500 AAW	IDBLS	10//99-12//99
	Boise City MSA, ID	s	24.68 MW	23.26 AW	51330 AAW	IDBLS	10//99-12//99
	Illinois	s	25.12 MW	26.30 AW	54710 AAW	ILBLS	10//99-12//99
	Champaign-Urbana MSA, IL	s	24.52 MW	23.65 AW	50990 AAW	ILBLS	10//99-12//99
	Chicago PMSA, IL	s	26.79 MW	25.38 AW	55720 AAW	ILBLS	10//99-12//99
	Kankakee PMSA, IL	s	25.11 MW	24.05 AW	52220 AAW	ILBLS	10//99-12//99
	Peoria-Pekin MSA, IL	s	28.62 MW	28.23 AW	59530 AAW	ILBLS	10//99-12//99
	Rockford MSA, IL	s	24.03 MW	22.67 AW	49980 AAW	ILBLS	10//99-12//99
	Springfield MSA, IL	s	30.69 MW	30.33 AW	63840 AAW	ILBLS	10//99-12//99
	Indiana	s	24.32 MW	25.45 AW	52940 AAW	INBLS	10//99-12//99
	Elkhart-Goshen MSA, IN	s	24.03 MW	23.03 AW	49980 AAW	INBLS	10//99-12//99
	Evansville-Henderson MSA, IN-KY	s	25.22 MW	24.42 AW	52460 AAW	INBLS	10//99-12//99
	Fort Wayne MSA, IN	s	23.68 MW	22.74 AW	49250 AAW	INBLS	10//99-12//99
	Gary PMSA, IN	s	29.41 MW	30.95 AW	61170 AAW	INBLS	10//99-12//99
	Indianapolis MSA, IN	s	25.93 MW	24.61 AW	53940 AAW	INBLS	10//99-12//99
	Kokomo MSA, IN	s	29.96 MW	31.32 AW	62320 AAW	INBLS	10//99-12//99
	Lafayette MSA, IN	s	27.15 MW	23.68 AW	56470 AAW	INBLS	10//99-12//99
	Muncie MSA, IN	s	24.65 MW	24.10 AW	51280 AAW	INBLS	10//99-12//99
	South Bend MSA, IN	s	25.15 MW	23.07 AW	52320 AAW	INBLS	10//99-12//99
	Terre Haute MSA, IN	s	24.43 MW	23.82 AW	50820 AAW	INBLS	10//99-12//99

AAW	Average annual wage	AOH	Average offered, high	ASH	Average starting, high	H	Hourly	M	Monthly	S	Special: hourly and annual
AE	Average entry wage	AOL	Average offered, low	ASL	Average starting, low	HI	Highest wage paid	MTC	Median total compensation	TQ	Third quartile wage
AEX	Average experienced wage	APH	Average pay, high range	AW	Average wage paid	HR	High end range	MW	Median wage paid	W	Weekly
AO	Average offered	APL	Average pay, low range	FQ	First quartile wage	LR	Low end range	SQ	Second quartile wage	Y	Yearly

Occupation/Type/Industry	Location	Per	Low	Mid	High	Source	Date
Mechanical Engineer	Iowa	S	24.31 MW	25.61 AW	53270 AAW	IABLS	10//99-12//99
	Davenport-Moline-Rock Island MSA, IA-IL	S	23.96 MW	23.74 AW	49840 AAW	IABLS	10//99-12//99
	Des Moines MSA, IA	S	23.85 MW	23.21 AW	49610 AAW	IABLS	10//99-12//99
	Kansas	S	25.3 MW	25.81 AW	53690 AAW	KSBLS	10//99-12//99
	Topeka MSA, KS	S	28.48 MW	28.42 AW	59230 AAW	KSBLS	10//99-12//99
	Wichita MSA, KS	S	27.49 MW	27.99 AW	57180 AAW	KSBLS	10//99-12//99
	Kentucky	S	24.65 MW	25.50 AW	53050 AAW	KYBLS	10//99-12//99
	Lexington MSA, KY	S	24.10 MW	23.43 AW	50130 AAW	KYBLS	10//99-12//99
	Louisville MSA, KY-IN	S	26.56 MW	25.57 AW	55250 AAW	KYBLS	10//99-12//99
	Louisiana	S	25.35 MW	26.23 AW	54560 AAW	LABLS	10//99-12//99
	Baton Rouge MSA, LA	S	19.92 MW	13.48 AW	41440 AAW	LABLS	10//99-12//99
	Houma MSA, LA	S	25.38 MW	24.74 AW	52800 AAW	LABLS	10//99-12//99
	Lake Charles MSA, LA	S	28.93 MW	30.78 AW	60170 AAW	LABLS	10//99-12//99
	Monroe MSA, LA	S	25.95 MW	25.98 AW	53980 AAW	LABLS	10//99-12//99
	New Orleans MSA, LA	S	28.68 MW	28.13 AW	59660 AAW	LABLS	10//99-12//99
	Shreveport-Bossier City MSA, LA	S	27.78 MW	27.03 AW	57780 AAW	LABLS	10//99-12//99
	Maine	S	26.91 MW	27.50 AW	57200 AAW	MEBLS	10//99-12//99
	Portland MSA, ME	S	28.45 MW	27.48 AW	59180 AAW	MEBLS	10//99-12//99
	Maryland	S	28.49 MW	27.86 AW	57950 AAW	MDBLS	10//99-12//99
	Baltimore PMSA, MD	S	26.05 MW	26.33 AW	54190 AAW	MDBLS	10//99-12//99
	Massachusetts	S	30.27 MW	29.94 AW	62270 AAW	MABLS	10//99-12//99
	Boston PMSA, MA-NH	S	30.85 MW	31.65 AW	64180 AAW	MABLS	10//99-12//99
	Brockton PMSA, MA	S	25.63 MW	24.06 AW	53310 AAW	MABLS	10//99-12//99
	Fitchburg-Leominster PMSA, MA	S	26.60 MW	25.06 AW	55330 AAW	MABLS	10//99-12//99
	Lawrence PMSA, MA-NH	S	27.09 MW	26.29 AW	56350 AAW	MABLS	10//99-12//99
	Lowell PMSA, MA-NH	S	30.51 MW	29.29 AW	63470 AAW	MABLS	10//99-12//99
	New Bedford PMSA, MA	S	25.08 MW	24.55 AW	52160 AAW	MABLS	10//99-12//99
	Pittsfield MSA, MA	S	27.23 MW	26.99 AW	56640 AAW	MABLS	10//99-12//99
	Springfield MSA, MA	S	25.87 MW	23.95 AW	53810 AAW	MABLS	10//99-12//99
	Worcester PMSA, MA-CT	S	27.00 MW	26.09 AW	56160 AAW	MABLS	10//99-12//99
	Michigan	S	27 MW	27.50 AW	57200 AAW	MIBLS	10//99-12//99
	Ann Arbor PMSA, MI	S	28.04 MW	27.74 AW	58330 AAW	MIBLS	10//99-12//99
	Benton Harbor MSA, MI	S	25.98 MW	23.37 AW	54050 AAW	MIBLS	10//99-12//99
	Detroit PMSA, MI	S	28.83 MW	29.29 AW	59960 AAW	MIBLS	10//99-12//99
	Flint PMSA, MI	S	26.76 MW	27.28 AW	55650 AAW	MIBLS	10//99-12//99
	Grand Rapids-Muskegon-Holland MSA, MI	S	24.90 MW	23.59 AW	51800 AAW	MIBLS	10//99-12//99
	Jackson MSA, MI	S	22.85 MW	20.80 AW	47530 AAW	MIBLS	10//99-12//99
	Kalamazoo-Battle Creek MSA, MI	S	26.81 MW	27.14 AW	55750 AAW	MIBLS	10//99-12//99
	Lansing-East Lansing MSA, MI	S	23.83 MW	23.27 AW	49560 AAW	MIBLS	10//99-12//99
	Saginaw-Bay City-Midland MSA, MI	S	26.06 MW	24.72 AW	54190 AAW	MIBLS	10//99-12//99
	Minnesota	S	25.37 MW	26.34 AW	54790 AAW	MNBLS	10//99-12//99
	Duluth-Superior MSA, MN-WI	S	24.57 MW	23.34 AW	51110 AAW	MNBLS	10//99-12//99
	Minneapolis-St. Paul MSA, MN-WI	S	27.06 MW	26.39 AW	56280 AAW	MNBLS	10//99-12//99
	Rochester MSA, MN	S	23.90 MW	23.32 AW	49720 AAW	MNBLS	10//99-12//99
	St. Cloud MSA, MN	S	23.18 MW	21.25 AW	48210 AAW	MNBLS	10//99-12//99
	Mississippi	S	24.45 MW	25.15 AW	52310 AAW	MSBLS	10//99-12//99
	Biloxi-Gulfport-Pascagoula MSA, MS	S	26.30 MW	26.16 AW	54700 AAW	MSBLS	10//99-12//99
	Jackson MSA, MS	S	25.58 MW	24.60 AW	53210 AAW	MSBLS	10//99-12//99
	Missouri	S	25.04 MW	25.64 AW	53340 AAW	MOBLS	10//99-12//99
	Kansas City MSA, MO-KS	S	26.16 MW	26.23 AW	54410 AAW	MOBLS	10//99-12//99
	St. Louis MSA, MO-IL	S	26.08 MW	25.58 AW	54240 AAW	MOBLS	10//99-12//99
	Montana	S	22.68 MW	23.39 AW	48650 AAW	MTBLS	10//99-12//99
	Billings MSA, MT	S	23.84 MW	23.35 AW	49590 AAW	MTBLS	10//99-12//99
	Nebraska	S	23.15 MW	24.23 AW	50390 AAW	NEBLS	10//99-12//99
	Lincoln MSA, NE	S	24.76 MW	24.45 AW	51490 AAW	NEBLS	10//99-12//99
	Omaha MSA, NE-IA	S	24.01 MW	22.28 AW	49940 AAW	NEBLS	10//99-12//99
	Nevada	S	26.88 MW	28.27 AW	58790 AAW	NVBLS	10//99-12//99
	Las Vegas MSA, NV-AZ	S	29.20 MW	26.90 AW	60740 AAW	NVBLS	10//99-12//99
	Reno MSA, NV	S	28.32 MW	29.76 AW	58900 AAW	NVBLS	10//99-12//99
	New Hampshire	S	24.27 MW	25.32 AW	52670 AAW	NHBLS	10//99-12//99
	Manchester PMSA, NH	S	25.80 MW	24.96 AW	53660 AAW	NHBLS	10//99-12//99
	Nashua PMSA, NH	S	24.94 MW	23.80 AW	51870 AAW	NHBLS	10//99-12//99
	Portsmouth-Rochester PMSA, NH-ME	S	26.58 MW	26.15 AW	55290 AAW	NHBLS	10//99-12//99

AAW Average annual wage	**AOH** Average offered, high	**ASH** Average starting, high	**H** Hourly	**M** Monthly	**S** Special: hourly and annual
AE Average entry wage	**AOL** Average offered, low	**ASL** Average starting, low	**HI** Highest wage paid	**MTC** Median total compensation	**TQ** Third quartile wage
AEX Average experienced wage	**APH** Average pay, high range	**AW** Average wage paid	**HR** High end range	**MW** Median wage paid	**W** Weekly
AO Average offered	**APL** Average pay, low range	**FQ** First quartile wage	**LR** Low end range	**SQ** Second quartile wage	**Y** Yearly

Occupation/Type/Industry	Location	Per	Low	Mid	High	Source	Date
Mechanical Engineer	New Jersey	S	29.39 MW	28.68 AW	59650 AAW	NJBLS	10//99-12//99
	Bergen-Passaic PMSA, NJ	S	27.97 MW	27.46 AW	58180 AAW	NJBLS	10//99-12//99
	Middlesex-Somerset- Hunterdon PMSA, NJ	S	28.83 MW	29.25 AW	59960 AAW	NJBLS	10//99-12//99
	Monmouth-Ocean PMSA, NJ	S	29.91 MW	30.32 AW	62220 AAW	NJBLS	10//99-12//99
	Newark PMSA, NJ	S	28.86 MW	29.51 AW	60030 AAW	NJBLS	10//99-12//99
	Trenton PMSA, NJ	S	26.62 MW	25.73 AW	55360 AAW	NJBLS	10//99-12//99
	Vineland-Millville-Bridgeton PMSA, NJ	S	25.29 MW	25.71 AW	52600 AAW	NJBLS	10//99-12//99
	New Mexico	S	30.79 MW	29.28 AW	60900 AAW	NMBLS	10//99-12//99
	Albuquerque MSA, NM	S	28.74 MW	30.60 AW	59770 AAW	NMBLS	10//99-12//99
	New York	S	25.31 MW	26.55 AW	55220 AAW	NYBLS	10//99-12//99
	Albany-Schenectady-Troy MSA, NY	S	26.54 MW	25.85 AW	55200 AAW	NYBLS	10//99-12//99
	Binghamton MSA, NY	S	21.29 MW	19.92 AW	44280 AAW	NYBLS	10//99-12//99
	Buffalo-Niagara Falls MSA, NY	S	25.84 MW	24.96 AW	53740 AAW	NYBLS	10//99-12//99
	Dutchess County PMSA, NY	S	27.68 MW	26.95 AW	57570 AAW	NYBLS	10//99-12//99
	Elmira MSA, NY	S	24.45 MW	23.32 AW	50860 AAW	NYBLS	10//99-12//99
	Glens Falls MSA, NY	S	24.95 MW	23.55 AW	51900 AAW	NYBLS	10//99-12//99
	Jamestown MSA, NY	S	22.12 MW	20.17 AW	46010 AAW	NYBLS	10//99-12//99
	Nassau-Suffolk PMSA, NY	S	29.72 MW	29.65 AW	61820 AAW	NYBLS	10//99-12//99
	New York PMSA, NY	S	27.20 MW	25.66 AW	56570 AAW	NYBLS	10//99-12//99
	Newburgh PMSA, NY-PA	S	25.56 MW	24.06 AW	53160 AAW	NYBLS	10//99-12//99
	Rochester MSA, NY	S	28.02 MW	27.37 AW	58280 AAW	NYBLS	10//99-12//99
	Syracuse MSA, NY	S	24.43 MW	23.63 AW	50820 AAW	NYBLS	10//99-12//99
	Utica-Rome MSA, NY	S	25.06 MW	22.43 AW	52120 AAW	NYBLS	10//99-12//99
	North Carolina	S	25.45 MW	26.72 AW	55570 AAW	NCBLS	10//99-12//99
	Asheville MSA, NC	S	26.10 MW	25.24 AW	54300 AAW	NCBLS	10//99-12//99
	Charlotte-Gastonia-Rock Hill MSA, NC-SC	S	27.59 MW	26.29 AW	57390 AAW	NCBLS	10//99-12//99
	Greensboro--Winston-Salem-- High Point MSA, NC	S	28.57 MW	29.26 AW	59430 AAW	NCBLS	10//99-12//99
	Hickory-Morganton-Lenoir MSA, NC	S	22.93 MW	20.57 AW	47680 AAW	NCBLS	10//99-12//99
	Raleigh-Durham-Chapel Hill MSA, NC	S	26.45 MW	24.41 AW	55020 AAW	NCBLS	10//99-12//99
	Rocky Mount MSA, NC	S	26.47 MW	25.71 AW	55060 AAW	NCBLS	10//99-12//99
	Wilmington MSA, NC	S	27.73 MW	28.40 AW	57680 AAW	NCBLS	10//99-12//99
	North Dakota	S	22.97 MW	23.72 AW	49330 AAW	NDBLS	10//99-12//99
	Ohio	S	24.31 MW	25.31 AW	52640 AAW	OHBLS	10//99-12//99
	Akron PMSA, OH	S	25.63 MW	24.92 AW	53310 AAW	OHBLS	10//99-12//99
	Canton-Massillon MSA, OH	S	25.35 MW	24.57 AW	52720 AAW	OHBLS	10//99-12//99
	Cincinnati PMSA, OH-KY-IN	S	26.14 MW	24.84 AW	54380 AAW	OHBLS	10//99-12//99
	Cleveland-Lorain-Elyria PMSA, OH	S	25.32 MW	24.23 AW	52670 AAW	OHBLS	10//99-12//99
	Columbus MSA, OH	S	26.20 MW	25.79 AW	54500 AAW	OHBLS	10//99-12//99
	Dayton-Springfield MSA, OH	S	26.55 MW	26.88 AW	55230 AAW	OHBLS	10//99-12//99
	Lima MSA, OH	S	20.90 MW	20.99 AW	43470 AAW	OHBLS	10//99-12//99
	Mansfield MSA, OH	S	20.76 MW	19.49 AW	43180 AAW	OHBLS	10//99-12//99
	Toledo MSA, OH	S	23.54 MW	22.25 AW	48960 AAW	OHBLS	10//99-12//99
	Youngstown-Warren MSA, OH	S	23.64 MW	22.91 AW	49170 AAW	OHBLS	10//99-12//99
	Oklahoma	S	28.25 MW	27.41 AW	57020 AAW	OKBLS	10//99-12//99
	Oklahoma City MSA, OK	S	26.76 MW	27.71 AW	55660 AAW	OKBLS	10//99-12//99
	Tulsa MSA, OK	S	28.33 MW	29.27 AW	58930 AAW	OKBLS	10//99-12//99
	Oregon	S	25.6 MW	28.79 AW	59880 AAW	ORBLS	10//99-12//99
	Eugene-Springfield MSA, OR	S	23.93 MW	22.91 AW	49770 AAW	ORBLS	10//99-12//99
	Portland-Vancouver PMSA, OR-WA	S	30.23 MW	28.19 AW	62870 AAW	ORBLS	10//99-12//99
	Salem PMSA, OR	S	21.15 MW	19.19 AW	43990 AAW	ORBLS	10//99-12//99
	Pennsylvania	S	24.79 MW	26.08 AW	54240 AAW	PABLS	10//99-12//99
	Allentown-Bethlehem-Easton MSA, PA	S	25.55 MW	23.85 AW	53140 AAW	PABLS	10//99-12//99
	Altoona MSA, PA	S	26.36 MW	25.79 AW	54830 AAW	PABLS	10//99-12//99
	Erie MSA, PA	S	23.38 MW	23.03 AW	48620 AAW	PABLS	10//99-12//99
	Harrisburg-Lebanon-Carlisle MSA, PA	S	25.62 MW	24.71 AW	53300 AAW	PABLS	10//99-12//99
	Johnstown MSA, PA	S	23.82 MW	22.51 AW	49540 AAW	PABLS	10//99-12//99
	Lancaster MSA, PA	S	27.02 MW	25.55 AW	56200 AAW	PABLS	10//99-12//99
	Philadelphia PMSA, PA-NJ	S	26.75 MW	25.58 AW	55650 AAW	PABLS	10//99-12//99
	Pittsburgh MSA, PA	S	28.33 MW	28.77 AW	58930 AAW	PABLS	10//99-12//99
	Reading MSA, PA	S	25.64 MW	24.41 AW	53340 AAW	PABLS	10//99-12//99

AAW Average annual wage	**AOH** Average offered, high	**ASH** Average starting, high	**H** Hourly	**M** Monthly	**S** Special: hourly and annual
AE Average entry wage	**AOL** Average offered, low	**ASL** Average starting, low	**HI** Highest wage paid	**MTC** Median total compensation	**TQ** Third quartile wage
AEX Average experienced wage	**APH** Average pay, high range	**AW** Average wage paid	**HR** High end range	**MW** Median wage paid	**W** Weekly
AO Average offered	**APL** Average pay, low range	**FQ** First quartile wage	**LR** Low end range	**SQ** Second quartile wage	**Y** Yearly

Occupation/Type/Industry	Location	Per	Low	Mid	High	Source	Date
Mechanical Engineer	Scranton--Wilkes-Barre--Hazleton MSA, PA	S	24.19 MW	23.29 AW	50310 AAW	PABLS	10//99-12//99
	Sharon MSA, PA	S	23.85 MW	21.45 AW	49610 AAW	PABLS	10//99-12//99
	State College MSA, PA	S	25.32 MW	24.31 AW	52670 AAW	PABLS	10//99-12//99
	York MSA, PA	S	24.73 MW	23.82 AW	51440 AAW	PABLS	10//99-12//99
	Rhode Island	S	29.47 MW	28.56 AW	59410 AAW	RIBLS	10//99-12//99
	Providence-Fall River-Warwick MSA, RI-MA	S	27.47 MW	28.24 AW	57140 AAW	RIBLS	10//99-12//99
	South Carolina	S	28.88 MW	28.93 AW	60180 AAW	SCBLS	10//99-12//99
	Charleston-North Charleston MSA, SC	S	25.10 MW	27.68 AW	52210 AAW	SCBLS	10//99-12//99
	Columbia MSA, SC	S	29.20 MW	29.48 AW	60730 AAW	SCBLS	10//99-12//99
	Florence MSA, SC	S	26.66 MW	24.72 AW	55450 AAW	SCBLS	10//99-12//99
	Greenville-Spartanburg-Anderson MSA, SC	S	26.53 MW	25.76 AW	55180 AAW	SCBLS	10//99-12//99
	South Dakota	S	21.59 MW	23.19 AW	48240 AAW	SDBLS	10//99-12//99
	Sioux Falls MSA, SD	S	21.78 MW	21.70 AW	45310 AAW	SDBLS	10//99-12//99
	Tennessee	S	24.57 MW	25.59 AW	53220 AAW	TNBLS	10//99-12//99
	Chattanooga MSA, TN-GA	S	26.84 MW	28.25 AW	55820 AAW	TNBLS	10//99-12//99
	Johnson City-Kingsport-Bristol MSA, TN-VA	S	25.10 MW	24.27 AW	52210 AAW	TNBLS	10//99-12//99
	Knoxville MSA, TN	S	24.87 MW	23.71 AW	51720 AAW	TNBLS	10//99-12//99
	Memphis MSA, TN-AR-MS	S	26.03 MW	25.07 AW	54140 AAW	MSBLS	10//99-12//99
	Nashville MSA, TN	S	24.39 MW	22.98 AW	50720 AAW	TNBLS	10//99-12//99
	Texas	S	32.36 MW	30.43 AW	63290 AAW	TXBLS	10//99-12//99
	Austin-San Marcos MSA, TX	S	26.67 MW	26.07 AW	55460 AAW	TXBLS	10//99-12//99
	Beaumont-Port Arthur MSA, TX	S	28.99 MW	30.24 AW	60300 AAW	TXBLS	10//99-12//99
	Brazoria PMSA, TX	S	31.85 MW	35.48 AW	66250 AAW	TXBLS	10//99-12//99
	Brownsville-Harlingen-San Benito MSA, TX	S	25.64 MW	25.39 AW	53330 AAW	TXBLS	10//99-12//99
	Corpus Christi MSA, TX	S	27.69 MW	28.79 AW	57600 AAW	TXBLS	10//99-12//99
	Dallas PMSA, TX	S	29.23 MW	30.22 AW	60790 AAW	TXBLS	10//99-12//99
	El Paso MSA, TX	S	25.69 MW	26.47 AW	53440 AAW	TXBLS	10//99-12//99
	Fort Worth-Arlington PMSA, TX	S	26.80 MW	25.99 AW	55740 AAW	TXBLS	10//99-12//99
	Galveston-Texas City PMSA, TX	S	30.74 MW	34.11 AW	63930 AAW	TXBLS	10//99-12//99
	Houston PMSA, TX	S	32.56 MW	35.75 AW	67720 AAW	TXBLS	10//99-12//99
	Lubbock MSA, TX	S	25.18 MW	25.27 AW	52370 AAW	TXBLS	10//99-12//99
	Odessa-Midland MSA, TX	S	26.59 MW	24.41 AW	55300 AAW	TXBLS	10//99-12//99
	San Antonio MSA, TX	S	28.12 MW	27.73 AW	58500 AAW	TXBLS	10//99-12//99
	Tyler MSA, TX	S	28.64 MW	29.95 AW	59570 AAW	TXBLS	10//99-12//99
	Waco MSA, TX	S	25.88 MW	24.55 AW	53820 AAW	TXBLS	10//99-12//99
	Wichita Falls MSA, TX	S	26.52 MW	27.23 AW	55160 AAW	TXBLS	10//99-12//99
	Utah	S	26.61 MW	26.87 AW	55890 AAW	UTBLS	10//99-12//99
	Salt Lake City-Ogden MSA, UT	S	26.45 MW	25.57 AW	55010 AAW	UTBLS	10//99-12//99
	Vermont	S	24.25 MW	25.69 AW	53430 AAW	VTBLS	10//99-12//99
	Burlington MSA, VT	S	27.14 MW	25.47 AW	56450 AAW	VTBLS	10//99-12//99
	Virginia	S	26.01 MW	26.76 AW	55650 AAW	VABLS	10//99-12//99
	Charlottesville MSA, VA	S	25.80 MW	24.99 AW	53670 AAW	VABLS	10//99-12//99
	Norfolk-Virginia Beach-Newport News MSA, VA-NC	S	25.74 MW	25.31 AW	53540 AAW	VABLS	10//99-12//99
	Richmond-Petersburg MSA, VA	S	26.41 MW	25.84 AW	54940 AAW	VABLS	10//99-12//99
	Roanoke MSA, VA	S	21.53 MW	20.48 AW	44770 AAW	VABLS	10//99-12//99
	Bellingham MSA, WA	S	31.00 MW	33.74 AW	64470 AAW	WABLS	10//99-12//99
	Spokane MSA, WA	S	24.70 MW	23.76 AW	51380 AAW	WABLS	10//99-12//99
	Tacoma PMSA, WA	S	26.40 MW	26.09 AW	54920 AAW	WABLS	10//99-12//99
	Yakima MSA, WA	S	20.13 MW	17.13 AW	41860 AAW	WABLS	10//99-12//99
	West Virginia	S	22.36 MW	22.76 AW	47340 AAW	WVBLS	10//99-12//99
	Huntington-Ashland MSA, WV-KY-OH	S	25.17 MW	24.78 AW	52360 AAW	WVBLS	10//99-12//99
	Parkersburg-Marietta MSA, WV-OH	S	24.30 MW	23.00 AW	50540 AAW	WVBLS	10//99-12//99
	Wisconsin	S	24.22 MW	25.30 AW	52620 AAW	WIBLS	10//99-12//99
	Appleton-Oshkosh-Neenah MSA, WI	S	24.56 MW	23.41 AW	51080 AAW	WIBLS	10//99-12//99
	Eau Claire MSA, WI	S	27.15 MW	25.86 AW	56460 AAW	WIBLS	10//99-12//99
	Green Bay MSA, WI	S	28.01 MW	27.33 AW	58270 AAW	WIBLS	10//99-12//99

Occupation/Type/Industry	Location	Per	Low	Mid	High	Source	Date
Mechanical Engineer	Janesville-Beloit MSA, WI	S	26.08 MW	25.13 AW	54250 AAW	WIBLS	10//99-12//99
	Kenosha PMSA, WI	S	23.02 MW	22.08 AW	47890 AAW	WIBLS	10//99-12//99
	Madison MSA, WI	S	25.51 MW	24.83 AW	53060 AAW	WIBLS	10//99-12//99
	Milwaukee-Waukesha PMSA, WI	S	26.24 MW	25.18 AW	54580 AAW	WIBLS	10//99-12//99
	Racine PMSA, WI	S	23.94 MW	23.26 AW	49800 AAW	WIBLS	10//99-12//99
	Sheboygan MSA, WI	S	24.90 MW	23.87 AW	51780 AAW	WIBLS	10//99-12//99
	Wausau MSA, WI	S	22.17 MW	21.06 AW	46120 AAW	WIBLS	10//99-12//99
	Wyoming	S	25.33 MW	25.39 AW	52820 AAW	WYBLS	10//99-12//99
	Puerto Rico	S	20.33 MW	21.44 AW	44600 AAW	PRBLS	10//99-12//99
	Ponce MSA, PR	S	20.78 MW	21.35 AW	43230 AAW	PRBLS	10//99-12//99
	San Juan-Bayamon PMSA, PR	S	21.90 MW	20.58 AW	45560 AAW	PRBLS	10//99-12//99
	Guam	S	21.82 MW	21.24 AW	44180 AAW	GUBLS	10//99-12//99
Mechanical Engineering Technician	United States	H		19.29 AW		NCS98	1998
	Alabama	S	19.26 MW	20.16 AW	41930 AAW	ALBLS	10//99-12//99
	Birmingham MSA, AL	S	24.31 MW	20.42 AW	50560 AAW	ALBLS	10//99-12//99
	Huntsville MSA, AL	S	17.41 MW	17.14 AW	36210 AAW	ALBLS	10//99-12//99
	Mobile MSA, AL	S	24.79 MW	25.65 AW	51560 AAW	ALBLS	10//99-12//99
	Arizona	S	18.22 MW	23.89 AW	49690 AAW	AZBLS	10//99-12//99
	Phoenix-Mesa MSA, AZ	S	24.19 MW	18.44 AW	50320 AAW	AZBLS	10//99-12//99
	Tucson MSA, AZ	S	17.10 MW	16.15 AW	35560 AAW	AZBLS	10//99-12//99
	Arkansas	S	21.03 MW	22.40 AW	46600 AAW	ARBLS	10//99-12//99
	Fayetteville-Springdale-Rogers MSA, AR	S	16.40 MW	15.15 AW	34110 AAW	ARBLS	10//99-12//99
	Little Rock-North Little Rock MSA, AR	S	18.96 MW	16.77 AW	39430 AAW	ARBLS	10//99-12//99
	California	S	17.86 MW	20.02 AW	41640 AAW	CABLS	10//99-12//99
	Los Angeles-Long Beach PMSA, CA	S	17.75 MW	16.11 AW	36920 AAW	CABLS	10//99-12//99
	Oakland PMSA, CA	S	17.51 MW	16.23 AW	36410 AAW	CABLS	10//99-12//99
	Orange County PMSA, CA	S	19.96 MW	18.82 AW	41510 AAW	CABLS	10//99-12//99
	Riverside-San Bernardino PMSA, CA	S	18.33 MW	18.45 AW	38120 AAW	CABLS	10//99-12//99
	San Diego MSA, CA	S	17.18 MW	16.03 AW	35730 AAW	CABLS	10//99-12//99
	San Francisco PMSA, CA	S	17.03 MW	15.90 AW	35420 AAW	CABLS	10//99-12//99
	San Jose PMSA, CA	S	19.88 MW	18.63 AW	41350 AAW	CABLS	10//99-12//99
	San Luis Obispo-Atascadero-Paso Robles MSA, CA	S	24.89 MW	27.32 AW	51770 AAW	CABLS	10//99-12//99
	Santa Barbara-Santa Maria-Lompoc MSA, CA	S	13.87 MW	14.04 AW	28850 AAW	CABLS	10//99-12//99
	Santa Rosa PMSA, CA	S	20.63 MW	20.30 AW	42910 AAW	CABLS	10//99-12//99
	Vallejo-Fairfield-Napa PMSA, CA	S	19.77 MW	18.68 AW	41120 AAW	CABLS	10//99-12//99
	Ventura PMSA, CA	S	17.12 MW	16.72 AW	35610 AAW	CABLS	10//99-12//99
	Colorado	S	16.18 MW	17.00 AW	35360 AAW	COBLS	10//99-12//99
	Boulder-Longmont PMSA, CO	S	17.48 MW	17.83 AW	36360 AAW	COBLS	10//99-12//99
	Denver PMSA, CO	S	18.12 MW	17.58 AW	37700 AAW	COBLS	10//99-12//99
	Connecticut	S	17.47 MW	17.77 AW	36970 AAW	CTBLS	10//99-12//99
	Bridgeport PMSA, CT	S	23.81 MW	23.40 AW	49530 AAW	CTBLS	10//99-12//99
	Danbury PMSA, CT	S	18.69 MW	18.85 AW	38880 AAW	CTBLS	10//99-12//99
	Hartford MSA, CT	S	16.39 MW	15.56 AW	34080 AAW	CTBLS	10//99-12//99
	New Haven-Meriden PMSA, CT	S	20.12 MW	19.79 AW	41840 AAW	CTBLS	10//99-12//99
	New London-Norwich MSA, CT-RI	S	16.48 MW	15.12 AW	34280 AAW	CTBLS	10//99-12//99
	Delaware	S	18.16 MW	18.02 AW	37490 AAW	DEBLS	10//99-12//99
	Wilmington-Newark PMSA, DE-MD	S	17.65 MW	17.39 AW	36700 AAW	DEBLS	10//99-12//99
	Washington PMSA, DC-MD-VA-WV	S	18.72 MW	18.67 AW	38940 AAW	DCBLS	10//99-12//99
	Florida	S	17.09 MW	17.35 AW	36090 AAW	FLBLS	10//99-12//99
	Fort Lauderdale PMSA, FL	S	17.17 MW	18.19 AW	35720 AAW	FLBLS	10//99-12//99
	Jacksonville MSA, FL	S	23.36 MW	21.72 AW	48580 AAW	FLBLS	10//99-12//99
	Melbourne-Titusville-Palm Bay MSA, FL	S	16.79 MW	16.77 AW	34920 AAW	FLBLS	10//99-12//99
	Miami PMSA, FL	S	14.57 MW	14.77 AW	30300 AAW	FLBLS	10//99-12//99
	Orlando MSA, FL	S	15.92 MW	15.77 AW	33120 AAW	FLBLS	10//99-12//99
	Tampa-St. Petersburg-Clearwater MSA, FL	S	18.29 MW	18.42 AW	38030 AAW	FLBLS	10//99-12//99

AAW Average annual wage	**AOH** Average offered, high	**ASH** Average starting, high	**H** Hourly	**M** Monthly	**S** Special: hourly and annual
AE Average entry wage	**AOL** Average offered, low	**ASL** Average starting, low	**HI** Highest wage paid	**MTC** Median total compensation	**TQ** Third quartile wage
AEX Average experienced wage	**APH** Average pay, high range	**AW** Average wage paid	**HR** High end range	**MW** Median wage paid	**W** Weekly
AO Average offered	**APL** Average pay, low range	**FQ** First quartile wage	**LR** Low end range	**SQ** Second quartile wage	**Y** Yearly

Occupation/Type/Industry	Location	Per	Low	Mid	High	Source	Date
Mechanical Engineering Technician							
	West Palm Beach-Boca Raton MSA, FL	S	17.69 MW	17.18 AW	36800 AAW	FLBLS	10//99-12//99
	Georgia	S	18.02 MW	20.80 AW	43260 AAW	GABLS	10//99-12//99
	Atlanta MSA, GA	S	21.87 MW	19.10 AW	45490 AAW	GABLS	10//99-12//99
	Macon MSA, GA	S	17.50 MW	17.48 AW	36410 AAW	GABLS	10//99-12//99
	Hawaii	S	19.12 MW	19.18 AW	39890 AAW	HIBLS	10//99-12//99
	Honolulu MSA, HI	S	19.49 MW	19.30 AW	40550 AAW	HIBLS	10//99-12//99
	Idaho	S	17.32 MW	17.91 AW	37250 AAW	IDBLS	10//99-12//99
	Boise City MSA, ID	S	17.03 MW	16.48 AW	35410 AAW	IDBLS	10//99-12//99
	Illinois	S	18.79 MW	19.00 AW	39510 AAW	ILBLS	10//99-12//99
	Champaign-Urbana MSA, IL	S	22.24 MW	20.31 AW	46250 AAW	ILBLS	10//99-12//99
	Chicago PMSA, IL	S	19.30 MW	18.92 AW	40150 AAW	ILBLS	10//99-12//99
	Peoria-Pekin MSA, IL	S	17.62 MW	18.43 AW	36640 AAW	ILBLS	10//99-12//99
	Rockford MSA, IL	S	19.20 MW	19.00 AW	39930 AAW	ILBLS	10//99-12//99
	Springfield MSA, IL	S	16.95 MW	17.62 AW	35250 AAW	ILBLS	10//99-12//99
	Indiana	S	17.81 MW	17.69 AW	36800 AAW	INBLS	10//99-12//99
	Elkhart-Goshen MSA, IN	S	14.50 MW	14.66 AW	30150 AAW	INBLS	10//99-12//99
	Evansville-Henderson MSA, IN-KY	S	13.54 MW	12.42 AW	28170 AAW	INBLS	10//99-12//99
	Fort Wayne MSA, IN	S	20.46 MW	19.99 AW	42560 AAW	INBLS	10//99-12//99
	Indianapolis MSA, IN	S	18.38 MW	18.60 AW	38230 AAW	INBLS	10//99-12//99
	Lafayette MSA, IN	S	17.98 MW	16.15 AW	37410 AAW	INBLS	10//99-12//99
	Iowa	S	19.92 MW	20.77 AW	43200 AAW	IABLS	10//99-12//99
	Davenport-Moline-Rock Island MSA, IA-IL	S	18.63 MW	18.19 AW	38760 AAW	IABLS	10//99-12//99
	Kansas	S	16.5 MW	16.86 AW	35070 AAW	KSBLS	10//99-12//99
	Kentucky	S	14.53 MW	15.91 AW	33080 AAW	KYBLS	10//99-12//99
	Lexington MSA, KY	S	16.08 MW	15.00 AW	33440 AAW	KYBLS	10//99-12//99
	Louisville MSA, KY-IN	S	14.43 MW	13.16 AW	30010 AAW	KYBLS	10//99-12//99
	Louisiana	S	21.72 MW	21.98 AW	45720 AAW	LABLS	10//99-12//99
	New Orleans MSA, LA	S	22.29 MW	22.02 AW	46370 AAW	LABLS	10//99-12//99
	Maine	S	15.34 MW	15.98 AW	33230 AAW	MEBLS	10//99-12//99
	Maryland	S	18.25 MW	18.61 AW	38710 AAW	MDBLS	10//99-12//99
	Baltimore PMSA, MD	S	19.04 MW	19.36 AW	39600 AAW	MDBLS	10//99-12//99
	Massachusetts	S	19.41 MW	20.29 AW	42210 AAW	MABLS	10//99-12//99
	Boston PMSA, MA-NH	S	20.97 MW	19.78 AW	43610 AAW	MABLS	10//99-12//99
	Worcester PMSA, MA-CT	S	21.42 MW	20.13 AW	44560 AAW	MABLS	10//99-12//99
	Michigan	S	19.81 MW	20.21 AW	42030 AAW	MIBLS	10//99-12//99
	Ann Arbor PMSA, MI	S	24.19 MW	24.63 AW	50320 AAW	MIBLS	10//99-12//99
	Detroit PMSA, MI	S	21.28 MW	21.18 AW	44260 AAW	MIBLS	10//99-12//99
	Grand Rapids-Muskegon-Holland MSA, MI	S	22.49 MW	23.13 AW	46770 AAW	MIBLS	10//99-12//99
	Jackson MSA, MI	S	20.94 MW	19.77 AW	43550 AAW	MIBLS	10//99-12//99
	Kalamazoo-Battle Creek MSA, MI	S	21.24 MW	21.26 AW	44180 AAW	MIBLS	10//99-12//99
	Lansing-East Lansing MSA, MI	S	18.16 MW	16.61 AW	37780 AAW	MIBLS	10//99-12//99
	Saginaw-Bay City-Midland MSA, MI	S	17.67 MW	18.32 AW	36740 AAW	MIBLS	10//99-12//99
	Minnesota	S	20.2 MW	20.62 AW	42900 AAW	MNBLS	10//99-12//99
	Minneapolis-St. Paul MSA, MN-WI	S	21.46 MW	21.05 AW	44640 AAW	MNBLS	10//99-12//99
	Rochester MSA, MN	S	14.55 MW	13.89 AW	30270 AAW	MNBLS	10//99-12//99
	Mississippi	S	11.63 MW	12.53 AW	26070 AAW	MSBLS	10//99-12//99
	Missouri	S	20.6 MW	23.95 AW	49810 AAW	MOBLS	10//99-12//99
	Kansas City MSA, MO-KS	S	18.83 MW	18.12 AW	39160 AAW	MOBLS	10//99-12//99
	St. Louis MSA, MO-IL	S	25.13 MW	21.07 AW	52270 AAW	MOBLS	10//99-12//99
	Springfield MSA, MO	S	14.62 MW	13.10 AW	30420 AAW	MOBLS	10//99-12//99
	Montana	S	16.78 MW	17.52 AW	36440 AAW	MTBLS	10//99-12//99
	Nebraska	S	18.58 MW	20.08 AW	41770 AAW	NEBLS	10//99-12//99
	Lincoln MSA, NE	S	17.74 MW	18.13 AW	36900 AAW	NEBLS	10//99-12//99
	Nevada	S	22.44 MW	22.04 AW	45850 AAW	NVBLS	10//99-12//99
	Las Vegas MSA, NV-AZ	S	23.81 MW	24.56 AW	49510 AAW	NVBLS	10//99-12//99
	New Hampshire	S	16.75 MW	16.81 AW	34970 AAW	NHBLS	10//99-12//99
	Nashua PMSA, NH	S	16.40 MW	16.37 AW	34110 AAW	NHBLS	10//99-12//99
	Portsmouth-Rochester PMSA, NH-ME	S	16.32 MW	16.18 AW	33940 AAW	NHBLS	10//99-12//99
	New Jersey	S	23.85 MW	23.84 AW	49580 AAW	NJBLS	10//99-12//99
	Bergen-Passaic PMSA, NJ	S	27.53 MW	29.56 AW	57270 AAW	NJBLS	10//99-12//99
	Middlesex-Somerset-Hunterdon PMSA, NJ	S	22.95 MW	21.13 AW	47730 AAW	NJBLS	10//99-12//99
	Newark PMSA, NJ	S	21.24 MW	22.80 AW	44180 AAW	NJBLS	10//99-12//99

AAW Average annual wage	**AOH** Average offered, high	**ASH** Average starting, high	**H** Hourly	**M** Monthly	**S** Special: hourly and annual
AE Average entry wage	**AOL** Average offered, low	**ASL** Average starting, low	**HI** Highest wage paid	**MTC** Median total compensation	**TQ** Third quartile wage
AEX Average experienced wage	**APH** Average pay, high range	**AW** Average wage paid	**HR** High end range	**MW** Median wage paid	**W** Weekly
AO Average offered	**APL** Average pay, low range	**FQ** First quartile wage	**LR** Low end range	**SQ** Second quartile wage	**Y** Yearly

Occupation/Type/Industry	Location	Per	Low	Mid	High	Source	Date
Mechanical Engineering Technician							
	New Mexico	S	18.93 MW	18.94 AW	39380 AAW	NMBLS	10//99-12//99
	Albuquerque MSA, NM	S	19.19 MW	19.11 AW	39910 AAW	NMBLS	10//99-12//99
	New York	S	18.72 MW	19.07 AW	39670 AAW	NYBLS	10//99-12//99
	Albany-Schenectady-Troy MSA, NY	S	21.74 MW	19.47 AW	45220 AAW	NYBLS	10//99-12//99
	Binghamton MSA, NY	S	14.80 MW	14.43 AW	30780 AAW	NYBLS	10//99-12//99
	Buffalo-Niagara Falls MSA, NY	S	20.21 MW	19.41 AW	42030 AAW	NYBLS	10//99-12//99
	Elmira MSA, NY	S	20.18 MW	20.40 AW	41980 AAW	NYBLS	10//99-12//99
	Nassau-Suffolk PMSA, NY	S	19.25 MW	18.85 AW	40040 AAW	NYBLS	10//99-12//99
	New York PMSA, NY	S	18.63 MW	18.57 AW	38740 AAW	NYBLS	10//99-12//99
	Rochester MSA, NY	S	19.66 MW	19.80 AW	40890 AAW	NYBLS	10//99-12//99
	Syracuse MSA, NY	S	17.24 MW	16.70 AW	35850 AAW	NYBLS	10//99-12//99
	North Carolina	S	17.15 MW	18.44 AW	38360 AAW	NCBLS	10//99-12//99
	Charlotte-Gastonia-Rock Hill MSA, NC-SC	S	19.19 MW	18.48 AW	39910 AAW	NCBLS	10//99-12//99
	Greensboro--Winston-Salem-- High Point MSA, NC	S	19.33 MW	18.92 AW	40200 AAW	NCBLS	10//99-12//99
	Hickory-Morganton-Lenoir MSA, NC	S	17.68 MW	16.37 AW	36770 AAW	NCBLS	10//99-12//99
	Raleigh-Durham-Chapel Hill MSA, NC	S	16.24 MW	15.65 AW	33790 AAW	NCBLS	10//99-12//99
	North Dakota	S	12.12 MW	12.72 AW	26460 AAW	NDBLS	10//99-12//99
	Fargo-Moorhead MSA, ND-MN	S	12.75 MW	12.09 AW	26520 AAW	NDBLS	10//99-12//99
	Ohio	S	17.47 MW	17.97 AW	37390 AAW	OHBLS	10//99-12//99
	Akron PMSA, OH	S	22.97 MW	21.72 AW	47790 AAW	OHBLS	10//99-12//99
	Canton-Massillon MSA, OH	S	19.47 MW	19.37 AW	40500 AAW	OHBLS	10//99-12//99
	Cincinnati PMSA, OH-KY-IN	S	21.26 MW	21.61 AW	44220 AAW	OHBLS	10//99-12//99
	Cleveland-Lorain-Elyria PMSA, OH	S	18.92 MW	18.77 AW	39340 AAW	OHBLS	10//99-12//99
	Dayton-Springfield MSA, OH	S	16.89 MW	15.94 AW	35140 AAW	OHBLS	10//99-12//99
	Lima MSA, OH	S	15.35 MW	14.42 AW	31930 AAW	OHBLS	10//99-12//99
	Mansfield MSA, OH	S	13.56 MW	13.18 AW	28200 AAW	OHBLS	10//99-12//99
	Toledo MSA, OH	S	18.46 MW	16.52 AW	38390 AAW	OHBLS	10//99-12//99
	Youngstown-Warren MSA, OH	S	10.88 MW	9.89 AW	22630 AAW	OHBLS	10//99-12//99
	Oklahoma City MSA, OK	S	18.08 MW	15.87 AW	37600 AAW	OKBLS	10//99-12//99
	Tulsa MSA, OK	S	20.80 MW	18.90 AW	43260 AAW	OKBLS	10//99-12//99
	Oregon	S	18.98 MW	19.72 AW	41030 AAW	ORBLS	10//99-12//99
	Eugene-Springfield MSA, OR	S	17.41 MW	16.23 AW	36220 AAW	ORBLS	10//99-12//99
	Portland-Vancouver PMSA, OR-WA	S	20.11 MW	19.24 AW	41830 AAW	ORBLS	10//99-12//99
	Pennsylvania	S	18.87 MW	19.63 AW	40820 AAW	PABLS	10//99-12//99
	Allentown-Bethlehem-Easton MSA, PA	S	18.59 MW	17.83 AW	38660 AAW	PABLS	10//99-12//99
	Harrisburg-Lebanon-Carlisle MSA, PA	S	19.90 MW	19.42 AW	41390 AAW	PABLS	10//99-12//99
	Lancaster MSA, PA	S	20.43 MW	18.67 AW	42500 AAW	PABLS	10//99-12//99
	Philadelphia PMSA, PA-NJ	S	20.23 MW	19.39 AW	42080 AAW	PABLS	10//99-12//99
	Pittsburgh MSA, PA	S	23.84 MW	24.73 AW	49600 AAW	PABLS	10//99-12//99
	Reading MSA, PA	S	15.73 MW	15.81 AW	32710 AAW	PABLS	10//99-12//99
	York MSA, PA	S	20.28 MW	18.24 AW	42190 AAW	PABLS	10//99-12//99
	Rhode Island	S	19.75 MW	21.87 AW	45500 AAW	RIBLS	10//99-12//99
	Providence-Fall River-Warwick MSA, RI-MA	S	20.75 MW	20.13 AW	43150 AAW	RIBLS	10//99-12//99
	South Carolina	S	16.69 MW	18.64 AW	38770 AAW	SCBLS	10//99-12//99
	Charleston-North Charleston MSA, SC	S	15.28 MW	13.04 AW	31780 AAW	SCBLS	10//99-12//99
	Columbia MSA, SC	S	23.30 MW	23.90 AW	48470 AAW	SCBLS	10//99-12//99
	Greenville-Spartanburg-Anderson MSA, SC	S	15.58 MW	15.74 AW	32400 AAW	SCBLS	10//99-12//99
	South Dakota	S	14.75 MW	14.68 AW	30520 AAW	SDBLS	10//99-12//99
	Tennessee	S	16.32 MW	16.92 AW	35200 AAW	TNBLS	10//99-12//99
	Chattanooga MSA, TN-GA	S	16.84 MW	15.80 AW	35020 AAW	TNBLS	10//99-12//99
	Knoxville MSA, TN	S	15.79 MW	14.80 AW	32830 AAW	TNBLS	10//99-12//99
	Memphis MSA, TN-AR-MS	S	16.77 MW	15.41 AW	34890 AAW	MSBLS	10//99-12//99
	Nashville MSA, TN	S	18.63 MW	18.10 AW	38760 AAW	TNBLS	10//99-12//99
	Texas	S	18.25 MW	18.87 AW	39240 AAW	TXBLS	10//99-12//99
	Austin-San Marcos MSA, TX	S	18.83 MW	16.35 AW	39160 AAW	TXBLS	10//99-12//99
	Beaumont-Port Arthur MSA, TX	S	18.93 MW	16.75 AW	39370 AAW	TXBLS	10//99-12//99

AAW	Average annual wage	AOH	Average offered, high	ASH	Average starting, high
AE	Average entry wage	AOL	Average offered, low	ASL	Average starting, low
AEX	Average experienced wage	APH	Average pay, high range	AW	Average wage paid
AO	Average offered	APL	Average pay, low range	FQ	First quartile wage

H	Hourly	M	Monthly
HI	Highest wage paid	MTC	Median total compensation
HR	High end range	MW	Median wage paid
LR	Low end range	SQ	Second quartile wage

S	Special: hourly and annual
TQ	Third quartile wage
W	Weekly
Y	Yearly

Occupation/Type/Industry	Location	Per	Low	Mid	High	Source	Date
Mechanical Engineering Technician	Dallas PMSA, TX	S	18.24 MW	18.36 AW	37940 AAW	TXBLS	10//99-12//99
	El Paso MSA, TX	S	19.12 MW	19.00 AW	39780 AAW	TXBLS	10//99-12//99
	Fort Worth-Arlington PMSA, TX	S	17.55 MW	16.62 AW	36500 AAW	TXBLS	10//99-12//99
	Houston PMSA, TX	S	18.75 MW	17.79 AW	38990 AAW	TXBLS	10//99-12//99
	Lubbock MSA, TX	S	20.67 MW	19.30 AW	43000 AAW	TXBLS	10//99-12//99
	San Antonio MSA, TX	S	14.76 MW	13.35 AW	30700 AAW	TXBLS	10//99-12//99
	Sherman-Denison MSA, TX	S	21.14 MW	20.51 AW	43970 AAW	TXBLS	10//99-12//99
	Tyler MSA, TX	S	18.64 MW	18.79 AW	38770 AAW	TXBLS	10//99-12//99
	Waco MSA, TX	S	19.70 MW	19.01 AW	40980 AAW	TXBLS	10//99-12//99
	Utah	S	17.16 MW	16.90 AW	35160 AAW	UTBLS	10//99-12//99
	Salt Lake City-Ogden MSA, UT	S	16.63 MW	16.96 AW	34590 AAW	UTBLS	10//99-12//99
	Vermont	S	16.4 MW	15.55 AW	32340 AAW	VTBLS	10//99-12//99
	Burlington MSA, VT	S	18.15 MW	18.64 AW	37760 AAW	VTBLS	10//99-12//99
	Virginia	S	18.93 MW	18.77 AW	39040 AAW	VABLS	10//99-12//99
	Richmond-Petersburg MSA, VA	S	18.55 MW	18.15 AW	38580 AAW	VABLS	10//99-12//99
	Roanoke MSA, VA	S	18.66 MW	20.36 AW	38810 AAW	VABLS	10//99-12//99
	Washington	S	16.34 MW	16.90 AW	35150 AAW	WABLS	10//99-12//99
	Bremerton PMSA, WA	S	12.52 MW	12.35 AW	26050 AAW	WABLS	10//99-12//99
	Seattle-Bellevue-Everett PMSA, WA	S	18.22 MW	17.99 AW	37890 AAW	WABLS	10//99-12//99
	Spokane MSA, WA	S	15.85 MW	15.64 AW	32970 AAW	WABLS	10//99-12//99
	West Virginia	S	20.22 MW	21.61 AW	44940 AAW	WVBLS	10//99-12//99
	Charleston MSA, WV	S	22.29 MW	20.79 AW	46350 AAW	WVBLS	10//99-12//99
	Huntington-Ashland MSA, WV-KY-OH	S	16.32 MW	14.41 AW	33950 AAW	WVBLS	10//99-12//99
	Wisconsin	S	19.38 MW	20.30 AW	42220 AAW	WIBLS	10//99-12//99
	Appleton-Oshkosh-Neenah MSA, WI	S	18.46 MW	17.85 AW	38400 AAW	WIBLS	10//99-12//99
	Green Bay MSA, WI	S	22.77 MW	22.75 AW	47370 AAW	WIBLS	10//99-12//99
	Madison MSA, WI	S	17.87 MW	17.15 AW	37160 AAW	WIBLS	10//99-12//99
	Milwaukee-Waukesha PMSA, WI	S	22.03 MW	22.07 AW	45830 AAW	WIBLS	10//99-12//99
	Wausau MSA, WI	S	19.22 MW	19.90 AW	39980 AAW	WIBLS	10//99-12//99
	Puerto Rico	S	14.44 MW	14.61 AW	30400 AAW	PRBLS	10//99-12//99
	San Juan-Bayamon PMSA, PR	S	13.81 MW	13.79 AW	28730 AAW	PRBLS	10//99-12//99
Medical and Clinical Laboratory Technician	Alabama	S	11.55 MW	12.25 AW	25480 AAW	ALBLS	10//99-12//99
	Anniston MSA, AL	S	11.72 MW	11.82 AW	24380 AAW	ALBLS	10//99-12//99
	Auburn-Opelika MSA, AL	S	14.25 MW	13.57 AW	29650 AAW	ALBLS	10//99-12//99
	Birmingham MSA, AL	S	12.66 MW	11.51 AW	26330 AAW	ALBLS	10//99-12//99
	Decatur MSA, AL	S	10.96 MW	11.05 AW	22800 AAW	ALBLS	10//99-12//99
	Dothan MSA, AL	S	11.07 MW	10.77 AW	23030 AAW	ALBLS	10//99-12//99
	Florence MSA, AL	S	11.53 MW	11.44 AW	23990 AAW	ALBLS	10//99-12//99
	Gadsden MSA, AL	S	11.34 MW	11.15 AW	23590 AAW	ALBLS	10//99-12//99
	Huntsville MSA, AL	S	13.59 MW	13.33 AW	28260 AAW	ALBLS	10//99-12//99
	Mobile MSA, AL	S	13.93 MW	11.14 AW	28980 AAW	ALBLS	10//99-12//99
	Montgomery MSA, AL	S	10.21 MW	10.85 AW	21230 AAW	ALBLS	10//99-12//99
	Alaska	S	15.59 MW	16.76 AW	34850 AAW	AKBLS	10//99-12//99
	Anchorage MSA, AK	S	13.99 MW	14.57 AW	29100 AAW	AKBLS	10//99-12//99
	Arizona	S	10.82 MW	11.54 AW	24000 AAW	AZBLS	10//99-12//99
	Phoenix-Mesa MSA, AZ	S	11.53 MW	10.78 AW	23970 AAW	AZBLS	10//99-12//99
	Tucson MSA, AZ	S	11.53 MW	11.52 AW	23980 AAW	AZBLS	10//99-12//99
	Yuma MSA, AZ	S	11.35 MW	10.66 AW	23600 AAW	AZBLS	10//99-12//99
	Arkansas	S	11.4 MW	12.07 AW	25100 AAW	ARBLS	10//99-12//99
	Fayetteville-Springdale-Rogers MSA, AR	S	11.27 MW	10.53 AW	23450 AAW	ARBLS	10//99-12//99
	Fort Smith MSA, AR-OK	S	11.71 MW	10.56 AW	24360 AAW	ARBLS	10//99-12//99
	Little Rock-North Little Rock MSA, AR	S	12.72 MW	12.46 AW	26450 AAW	ARBLS	10//99-12//99
	California	S	13.8 MW	15.24 AW	31690 AAW	CABLS	10//99-12//99
	Bakersfield MSA, CA	S	14.57 MW	10.98 AW	30310 AAW	CABLS	10//99-12//99
	Chico-Paradise MSA, CA	S	13.69 MW	12.59 AW	28480 AAW	CABLS	10//99-12//99
	Fresno MSA, CA	S	13.67 MW	11.93 AW	28430 AAW	CABLS	10//99-12//99
	Los Angeles-Long Beach PMSA, CA	S	14.10 MW	12.89 AW	29320 AAW	CABLS	10//99-12//99
	Modesto MSA, CA	S	14.23 MW	13.83 AW	29610 AAW	CABLS	10//99-12//99
	Oakland PMSA, CA	S	15.57 MW	15.10 AW	32390 AAW	CABLS	10//99-12//99

Occupation/Type/Industry	Location	Per	Low	Mid	High	Source	Date
Medical and Clinical Laboratory Technician	Orange County PMSA, CA	S	14.02 MW	12.76 AW	29160 AAW	CABLS	10//99-12//99
	Riverside-San Bernardino PMSA, CA	S	16.69 MW	15.28 AW	34720 AAW	CABLS	10//99-12//99
	Sacramento PMSA, CA	S	15.46 MW	14.65 AW	32160 AAW	CABLS	10//99-12//99
	Salinas MSA, CA	S	18.67 MW	18.80 AW	38830 AAW	CABLS	10//99-12//99
	San Diego MSA, CA	S	15.40 MW	14.28 AW	32030 AAW	CABLS	10//99-12//99
	San Francisco PMSA, CA	S	16.82 MW	15.79 AW	34990 AAW	CABLS	10//99-12//99
	San Jose PMSA, CA	S	25.18 MW	25.24 AW	52370 AAW	CABLS	10//99-12//99
	San Luis Obispo-Atascadero-Paso Robles MSA, CA	S	15.54 MW	13.14 AW	32330 AAW	CABLS	10//99-12//99
	Santa Barbara-Santa Maria-Lompoc MSA, CA	S	14.15 MW	11.69 AW	29440 AAW	CABLS	10//99-12//99
	Santa Rosa PMSA, CA	S	15.29 MW	12.24 AW	31810 AAW	CABLS	10//99-12//99
	Stockton-Lodi MSA, CA	S	14.14 MW	12.66 AW	29400 AAW	CABLS	10//99-12//99
	Vallejo-Fairfield-Napa PMSA, CA	S	19.09 MW	19.11 AW	39700 AAW	CABLS	10//99-12//99
	Yuba City MSA, CA	S	15.65 MW	13.86 AW	32550 AAW	CABLS	10//99-12//99
	Colorado	S	15.8	15.67 AW	32600 AAW	COBLS	10//99-12//99
	Boulder-Longmont PMSA, CO	S	13.19 MW	12.40 AW	27430 AAW	COBLS	10//99-12//99
	Colorado Springs MSA, CO	S	13.55 MW	14.14 AW	28180 AAW	COBLS	10//99-12//99
	Denver PMSA, CO	S	16.36 MW	16.60 AW	34040 AAW	COBLS	10//99-12//99
	Fort Collins-Loveland MSA, CO	S	14.13 MW	13.54 AW	29390 AAW	COBLS	10//99-12//99
	Connecticut	S	15.07 MW	16.42 AW	34140 AAW	CTBLS	10//99-12//99
	Bridgeport PMSA, CT	S	15.16 MW	14.55 AW	31530 AAW	CTBLS	10//99-12//99
	Hartford MSA, CT	S	15.58 MW	13.98 AW	32410 AAW	CTBLS	10//99-12//99
	Stamford-Norwalk PMSA, CT	S	18.88 MW	17.69 AW	39280 AAW	CTBLS	10//99-12//99
	Delaware	S	12.37 MW	12.31 AW	25610 AAW	DEBLS	10//99-12//99
	Dover MSA, DE	S	10.10 MW	9.06 AW	21000 AAW	DEBLS	10//99-12//99
	District of Columbia	S	14.29 MW	15.04 AW	31290 AAW	DCBLS	10//99-12//99
	Washington PMSA, DC-MD-VA-WV	S	14.67 MW	13.87 AW	30510 AAW	DCBLS	10//99-12//99
	Florida	S	11.22 MW	11.97 AW	24890 AAW	FLBLS	10//99-12//99
	Daytona Beach MSA, FL	S	11.89 MW	11.45 AW	24740 AAW	FLBLS	10//99-12//99
	Fort Lauderdale PMSA, FL	S	12.07 MW	11.47 AW	25120 AAW	FLBLS	10//99-12//99
	Fort Myers-Cape Coral MSA, FL	S	12.26 MW	11.62 AW	25500 AAW	FLBLS	10//99-12//99
	Fort Pierce-Port St. Lucie MSA, FL	S	16.34 MW	16.67 AW	33980 AAW	FLBLS	10//99-12//99
	Gainesville MSA, FL	S	11.19 MW	10.36 AW	23280 AAW	FLBLS	10//99-12//99
	Jacksonville MSA, FL	S	11.45 MW	11.16 AW	23810 AAW	FLBLS	10//99-12//99
	Lakeland-Winter Haven MSA, FL	S	12.11 MW	11.91 AW	25200 AAW	FLBLS	10//99-12//99
	Melbourne-Titusville-Palm Bay MSA, FL	S	12.86 MW	10.69 AW	26750 AAW	FLBLS	10//99-12//99
	Miami PMSA, FL	S	11.06 MW	11.27 AW	23010 AAW	FLBLS	10//99-12//99
	Naples MSA, FL	S	11.96 MW	12.50 AW	24870 AAW	FLBLS	10//99-12//99
	Orlando MSA, FL	S	11.17 MW	10.33 AW	23240 AAW	FLBLS	10//99-12//99
	Panama City MSA, FL	S	13.11 MW	13.17 AW	27260 AAW	FLBLS	10//99-12//99
	Pensacola MSA, FL	S	10.51 MW	9.67 AW	21870 AAW	FLBLS	10//99-12//99
	Sarasota-Bradenton MSA, FL	S	11.39 MW	10.50 AW	23680 AAW	FLBLS	10//99-12//99
	Tallahassee MSA, FL	S	9.81 MW	9.98 AW	20410 AAW	FLBLS	10//99-12//99
	Tampa-St. Petersburg-Clearwater MSA, FL	S	11.98 MW	11.36 AW	24920 AAW	FLBLS	10//99-12//99
	West Palm Beach-Boca Raton MSA, FL	S	14.93 MW	15.23 AW	31060 AAW	FLBLS	10//99-12//99
	Georgia	S	10.47 MW	10.73 AW	22310 AAW	GABLS	10//99-12//99
	Albany MSA, GA	S	10.56 MW	9.02 AW	21970 AAW	GABLS	10//99-12//99
	Athens MSA, GA	S	11.28 MW	11.36 AW	23470 AAW	GABLS	10//99-12//99
	Atlanta MSA, GA	S	10.51 MW	10.73 AW	21860 AAW	GABLS	10//99-12//99
	Augusta-Aiken MSA, GA-SC	S	10.44 MW	9.83 AW	21710 AAW	GABLS	10//99-12//99
	Columbus MSA, GA-AL	S	12.41 MW	10.16 AW	25810 AAW	GABLS	10//99-12//99
	Macon MSA, GA	S	10.96 MW	10.93 AW	22790 AAW	GABLS	10//99-12//99
	Hawaii	S	15.33 MW	16.07 AW	33420 AAW	HIBLS	10//99-12//99
	Honolulu MSA, HI	S	16.14 MW	15.39 AW	33580 AAW	HIBLS	10//99-12//99
	Idaho	S	14.12 MW	13.81 AW	28720 AAW	IDBLS	10//99-12//99
	Boise City MSA, ID	S	14.22 MW	14.45 AW	29590 AAW	IDBLS	10//99-12//99
	Illinois	S	14.63 MW	15.10 AW	31400 AAW	ILBLS	10//99-12//99
	Bloomington-Normal MSA, IL	S	11.86 MW	10.59 AW	24670 AAW	ILBLS	10//99-12//99
	Champaign-Urbana MSA, IL	S	10.98 MW	10.42 AW	22830 AAW	ILBLS	10//99-12//99
	Chicago PMSA, IL	S	15.81 MW	15.70 AW	32890 AAW	ILBLS	10//99-12//99

AAW Average annual wage	AOH Average offered, high	ASH Average starting, high	H Hourly	M Monthly	S Special: hourly and annual
AE Average entry wage	AOL Average offered, low	ASL Average starting, low	HI Highest wage paid	MTC Median total compensation	TQ Third quartile wage
AEX Average experienced wage	APH Average pay, high range	AW Average wage paid	HR High end range	MW Median wage paid	W Weekly
AO Average offered	APL Average pay, low range	FQ First quartile wage	LR Low end range	SQ Second quartile wage	Y Yearly

Occupation/Type/Industry	Location	Per	Low	Mid	High	Source	Date
Medical and Clinical Laboratory Technician							
	Peoria-Pekin MSA, IL	S	12.44 MW	12.06 AW	25870 AAW	ILBLS	10//99-12//99
	Springfield MSA, IL	S	15.00 MW	14.64 AW	31200 AAW	ILBLS	10//99-12//99
	Indiana	S	12.33 MW	12.60 AW	26210 AAW	INBLS	10//99-12//99
	Bloomington MSA, IN	S	13.38 MW	13.83 AW	27840 AAW	INBLS	10//99-12//99
	Elkhart-Goshen MSA, IN	S	13.01 MW	13.24 AW	27060 AAW	INBLS	10//99-12//99
	Evansville-Henderson MSA, IN-KY		10.69 MW	10.02 AW	22230 AAW	INBLS	10//99-12//99
	Fort Wayne MSA, IN	S	12.90 MW	12.45 AW	26830 AAW	INBLS	10//99-12//99
	Gary PMSA, IN	S	14.18 MW	14.50 AW	29500 AAW	INBLS	10//99-12//99
	Indianapolis MSA, IN	S	12.63 MW	12.70 AW	26260 AAW	INBLS	10//99-12//99
	Kokomo MSA, IN	S	12.08 MW	11.76 AW	25130 AAW	INBLS	10//99-12//99
	Lafayette MSA, IN	S	11.70 MW	11.06 AW	24340 AAW	INBLS	10//99-12//99
	South Bend MSA, IN	S	14.03 MW	13.08 AW	29180 AAW	INBLS	10//99-12//99
	Iowa	S	12.45 MW	12.98 AW	26990 AAW	IABLS	10//99-12//99
	Davenport-Moline-Rock Island MSA, IA-IL	S	12.11 MW	11.59 AW	25190 AAW	IABLS	10//99-12//99
	Des Moines MSA, IA	S	14.51 MW	12.69 AW	30170 AAW	IABLS	10//99-12//99
	Dubuque MSA, IA	S	11.03 MW	11.04 AW	22930 AAW	IABLS	10//99-12//99
	Sioux City MSA, IA-NE	S	12.79 MW	13.64 AW	26610 AAW	IABLS	10//99-12//99
	Kansas	S	12 MW	12.58 AW	26160 AAW	KSBLS	10//99-12//99
	Topeka MSA, KS	S	11.77 MW	11.01 AW	24480 AAW	KSBLS	10//99-12//99
	Wichita MSA, KS	S	13.45 MW	12.99 AW	27970 AAW	KSBLS	10//99-12//99
	Kentucky	S	12.3 MW	12.51 AW	26020 AAW	KYBLS	10//99-12//99
	Lexington MSA, KY	S	11.69 MW	11.49 AW	24310 AAW	KYBLS	10//99-12//99
	Louisville MSA, KY-IN	S	12.60 MW	12.30 AW	26210 AAW	KYBLS	10//99-12//99
	Louisiana	S	11 MW	11.93 AW	24810 AAW	LABLS	10//99-12//99
	Alexandria MSA, LA	S	10.76 MW	9.82 AW	22370 AAW	LABLS	10//99-12//99
	Baton Rouge MSA, LA	S	12.52 MW	10.62 AW	26050 AAW	LABLS	10//99-12//99
	Houma MSA, LA	S	13.28 MW	11.99 AW	27620 AAW	LABLS	10//99-12//99
	Lafayette MSA, LA	S	10.97 MW	9.80 AW	22820 AAW	LABLS	10//99-12//99
	Lake Charles MSA, LA	S	11.18 MW	10.73 AW	23260 AAW	LABLS	10//99-12//99
	Monroe MSA, LA	S	10.53 MW	10.45 AW	21900 AAW	LABLS	10//99-12//99
	New Orleans MSA, LA	S	12.02 MW	11.18 AW	25000 AAW	LABLS	10//99-12//99
	Shreveport-Bossier City MSA, LA		12.70 MW	12.46 AW	26420 AAW	LABLS	10//99-12//99
	Maine	S	12.78 MW	12.99 AW	27020 AAW	MEBLS	10//99-12//99
	Bangor MSA, ME	S	14.69 MW	14.38 AW	30550 AAW	MEBLS	10//99-12//99
	Portland MSA, ME	S	13.29 MW	12.99 AW	27640 AAW	MEBLS	10//99-12//99
	Maryland	S	13.21 MW	14.05 AW	29220 AAW	MDBLS	10//99-12//99
	Baltimore PMSA, MD	S	13.63 MW	12.79 AW	28340 AAW	MDBLS	10//99-12//99
	Cumberland MSA, MD-WV	S	13.04 MW	11.85 AW	27120 AAW	MDBLS	10//99-12//99
	Massachusetts	S	14.99 MW	16.30 AW	33900 AAW	MABLS	10//99-12//99
	Boston PMSA, MA-NH	S	16.99 MW	15.15 AW	35340 AAW	MABLS	10//99-12//99
	Brockton PMSA, MA	S	16.68 MW	17.39 AW	34700 AAW	MABLS	10//99-12//99
	Lowell PMSA, MA-NH	S	15.24 MW	14.69 AW	31710 AAW	MABLS	10//99-12//99
	Springfield MSA, MA	S	15.32 MW	14.00 AW	31860 AAW	MABLS	10//99-12//99
	Worcester PMSA, MA-CT	S	14.17 MW	14.37 AW	29480 AAW	MABLS	10//99-12//99
	Michigan	S	14.05 MW	14.53 AW	30230 AAW	MIBLS	10//99-12//99
	Ann Arbor PMSA, MI	S	14.44 MW	13.76 AW	30040 AAW	MIBLS	10//99-12//99
	Detroit PMSA, MI	S	15.26 MW	14.49 AW	31740 AAW	MIBLS	10//99-12//99
	Flint PMSA, MI	S	12.30 MW	12.33 AW	25590 AAW	MIBLS	10//99-12//99
	Grand Rapids-Muskegon-Holland MSA, MI	S	14.19 MW	13.84 AW	29510 AAW	MIBLS	10//99-12//99
	Kalamazoo-Battle Creek MSA, MI	S	14.58 MW	13.67 AW	30330 AAW	MIBLS	10//99-12//99
	Lansing-East Lansing MSA, MI	S	12.61 MW	12.26 AW	26230 AAW	MIBLS	10//99-12//99
	Saginaw-Bay City-Midland MSA, MI	S	12.62 MW	12.50 AW	26260 AAW	MIBLS	10//99-12//99
	Minnesota	S	13.83 MW	14.07 AW	29260 AAW	MNBLS	10//99-12//99
	Duluth-Superior MSA, MN-WI	S	13.90 MW	13.82 AW	28900 AAW	MNBLS	10//99-12//99
	Minneapolis-St. Paul MSA, MN-WI	S	14.43 MW	14.11 AW	30010 AAW	MNBLS	10//99-12//99
	Mississippi	S	11.36 MW	11.74 AW	24410 AAW	MSBLS	10//99-12//99
	Biloxi-Gulfport-Pascagoula MSA, MS	S	13.52 MW	12.20 AW	28120 AAW	MSBLS	10//99-12//99
	Hattiesburg MSA, MS	S	9.19 MW	8.34 AW	19120 AAW	MSBLS	10//99-12//99
	Jackson MSA, MS	S	12.16 MW	12.05 AW	25290 AAW	MSBLS	10//99-12//99
	Missouri	S	11.13 MW	11.91 AW	24770 AAW	MOBLS	10//99-12//99
	Columbia MSA, MO	S	9.64 MW	8.99 AW	20050 AAW	MOBLS	10//99-12//99
	Kansas City MSA, MO-KS	S	12.97 MW	12.75 AW	26990 AAW	MOBLS	10//99-12//99
	St. Louis MSA, MO-IL	S	12.14 MW	11.74 AW	25240 AAW	MOBLS	10//99-12//99

AAW Average annual wage	**AOH** Average offered, high	**ASH** Average starting, high	**H** Hourly	**M** Monthly	**S** Special: hourly and annual
AE Average entry wage	**AOL** Average offered, low	**ASL** Average starting, low	**HI** Highest wage paid	**MTC** Median total compensation	**TQ** Third quartile wage
AEX Average experienced wage	**APH** Average pay, high range	**AW** Average wage paid	**HR** High end range	**MW** Median wage paid	**W** Weekly
AO Average offered	**APL** Average pay, low range	**FQ** First quartile wage	**LR** Low end range	**SQ** Second quartile wage	**Y** Yearly

Occupation/Type/Industry	Location	Per	Low	Mid	High	Source	Date
Medical and Clinical Laboratory Technician							
	Montana	S	12.27 MW	12.56 AW	26110 AAW	MTBLS	10//99-12//99
	Missoula MSA, MT	S	11.58 MW	11.07 AW	24090 AAW	MTBLS	10//99-12//99
	Nebraska	S	11.85 MW	12.44 AW	25880 AAW	NEBLS	10//99-12//99
	Lincoln MSA, NE	S	12.52 MW	11.55 AW	26040 AAW	NEBLS	10//99-12//99
	Omaha MSA, NE-IA	S	13.03 MW	12.36 AW	27100 AAW	NEBLS	10//99-12//99
	Nevada	S	11.86 MW	13.33 AW	27730 AAW	NVBLS	10//99-12//99
	Las Vegas MSA, NV-AZ	S	12.89 MW	11.06 AW	26810 AAW	NVBLS	10//99-12//99
	Reno MSA, NV	S	12.58 MW	11.54 AW	26160 AAW	NVBLS	10//99-12//99
	New Hampshire	S	14.08 MW	13.55 AW	28190 AAW	NHBLS	10//99-12//99
	Manchester PMSA, NH	S	13.12 MW	13.75 AW	27290 AAW	NHBLS	10//99-12//99
	Portsmouth-Rochester PMSA, NH-ME	S	15.15 MW	15.00 AW	31520 AAW	NHBLS	10//99-12//99
	New Jersey	S	14.64 MW	15.69 AW	32630 AAW	NJBLS	10//99-12//99
	Atlantic-Cape May PMSA, NJ	S	18.71 MW	17.85 AW	38920 AAW	NJBLS	10//99-12//99
	Bergen-Passaic PMSA, NJ	S	15.26 MW	13.93 AW	31740 AAW	NJBLS	10//99-12//99
	Jersey City PMSA, NJ	S	17.28 MW	17.17 AW	35950 AAW	NJBLS	10//99-12//99
	Middlesex-Somerset-Hunterdon PMSA, NJ	S	13.93 MW	13.61 AW	28980 AAW	NJBLS	10//99-12//99
	Monmouth-Ocean PMSA, NJ	S	17.98 MW	17.26 AW	37390 AAW	NJBLS	10//99-12//99
	Newark PMSA, NJ	S	16.72 MW	15.47 AW	34780 AAW	NJBLS	10//99-12//99
	Trenton PMSA, NJ	S	15.53 MW	16.31 AW	32310 AAW	NJBLS	10//99-12//99
	New Mexico	S	12.02 MW	13.15 AW	27350 AAW	NMBLS	10//99-12//99
	Albuquerque MSA, NM	S	12.04 MW	11.65 AW	25040 AAW	NMBLS	10//99-12//99
	Las Cruces MSA, NM	S	8.73 MW	7.24 AW	18170 AAW	NMBLS	10//99-12//99
	New York	S	14.4 MW	15.76 AW	32790 AAW	NYBLS	10//99-12//99
	Albany-Schenectady-Troy MSA, NY	S	13.43 MW	13.02 AW	27940 AAW	NYBLS	10//99-12//99
	Binghamton MSA, NY	S	12.44 MW	10.70 AW	25880 AAW	NYBLS	10//99-12//99
	Buffalo-Niagara Falls MSA, NY	S	13.37 MW	13.27 AW	27800 AAW	NYBLS	10//99-12//99
	Dutchess County PMSA, NY	S	15.94 MW	16.09 AW	33160 AAW	NYBLS	10//99-12//99
	Glens Falls MSA, NY	S	14.40 MW	13.74 AW	29960 AAW	NYBLS	10//99-12//99
	Nassau-Suffolk PMSA, NY	S	15.43 MW	14.31 AW	32100 AAW	NYBLS	10//99-12//99
	New York PMSA, NY	S	17.16 MW	15.39 AW	35690 AAW	NYBLS	10//99-12//99
	Newburgh PMSA, NY-PA	S	22.16 MW	16.05 AW	46100 AAW	NYBLS	10//99-12//99
	Rochester MSA, NY	S	13.70 MW	12.82 AW	28500 AAW	NYBLS	10//99-12//99
	Syracuse MSA, NY	S	13.57 MW	13.23 AW	28230 AAW	NYBLS	10//99-12//99
	Utica-Rome MSA, NY	S	13.50 MW	13.36 AW	28090 AAW	NYBLS	10//99-12//99
	North Carolina	S	11.62 MW	12.30 AW	25590 AAW	NCBLS	10//99-12//99
	Asheville MSA, NC	S	13.61 MW	13.71 AW	28310 AAW	NCBLS	10//99-12//99
	Charlotte-Gastonia-Rock Hill MSA, NC-SC	S	13.70 MW	12.86 AW	28490 AAW	NCBLS	10//99-12//99
	Fayetteville MSA, NC	S	11.44 MW	11.25 AW	23800 AAW	NCBLS	10//99-12//99
	Goldsboro MSA, NC	S	17.36 MW	14.80 AW	36120 AAW	NCBLS	10//99-12//99
	Greensboro--Winston-Salem--High Point MSA, NC	S	11.01 MW	10.28 AW	22900 AAW	NCBLS	10//99-12//99
	Greenville MSA, NC	S	11.99 MW	11.56 AW	24940 AAW	NCBLS	10//99-12//99
	Hickory-Morganton-Lenoir MSA, NC	S	13.74 MW	12.85 AW	28580 AAW	NCBLS	10//99-12//99
	Jacksonville MSA, NC	S	13.10 MW	11.35 AW	27240 AAW	NCBLS	10//99-12//99
	Raleigh-Durham-Chapel Hill MSA, NC	S	13.73 MW	12.85 AW	28560 AAW	NCBLS	10//99-12//99
	Rocky Mount MSA, NC	S	11.11 MW	10.19 AW	23110 AAW	NCBLS	10//99-12//99
	Wilmington MSA, NC	S	12.93 MW	11.33 AW	26890 AAW	NCBLS	10//99-12//99
	North Dakota	S	11.53 MW	11.86 AW	24670 AAW	NDBLS	10//99-12//99
	Bismarck MSA, ND	S	11.81 MW	11.65 AW	24560 AAW	NDBLS	10//99-12//99
	Fargo-Moorhead MSA, ND-MN	S	12.00 MW	11.28 AW	24960 AAW	NDBLS	10//99-12//99
	Ohio	S	13.48 MW	13.84 AW	28790 AAW	OHBLS	10//99-12//99
	Akron PMSA, OH	S	16.89 MW	14.08 AW	35120 AAW	OHBLS	10//99-12//99
	Canton-Massillon MSA, OH	S	13.66 MW	13.56 AW	28420 AAW	OHBLS	10//99-12//99
	Cincinnati PMSA, OH-KY-IN	S	13.96 MW	13.84 AW	29030 AAW	OHBLS	10//99-12//99
	Cleveland-Lorain-Elyria PMSA, OH	S	14.64 MW	14.67 AW	30450 AAW	OHBLS	10//99-12//99
	Columbus MSA, OH	S	13.21 MW	13.24 AW	27490 AAW	OHBLS	10//99-12//99
	Dayton-Springfield MSA, OH	S	12.64 MW	12.46 AW	26290 AAW	OHBLS	10//99-12//99
	Hamilton-Middletown PMSA, OH	S	13.57 MW	14.01 AW	28220 AAW	OHBLS	10//99-12//99
	Lima MSA, OH	S	12.44 MW	11.85 AW	25870 AAW	OHBLS	10//99-12//99
	Toledo MSA, OH	S	12.64 MW	12.09 AW	26280 AAW	OHBLS	10//99-12//99
	Youngstown-Warren MSA, OH	S	12.55 MW	12.11 AW	26090 AAW	OHBLS	10//99-12//99

AAW	Average annual wage	AOH	Average offered, high	ASH	Average starting, high	H	Hourly	M	Monthly	S	Special: hourly and annual
AE	Average entry wage	AOL	Average offered, low	ASL	Average starting, low	HI	Highest wage paid	MTC	Median total compensation	TQ	Third quartile wage
AEX	Average experienced wage	APH	Average pay, high range	AW	Average wage paid	HR	High end range	MW	Median wage paid	W	Weekly
AO	Average offered	APL	Average pay, low range	FQ	First quartile wage	LR	Low end range	SQ	Second quartile wage	Y	Yearly

Occupation/Type/Industry	Location	Per	Low	Mid	High	Source	Date
Medical and Clinical Laboratory Technician							
	Oklahoma	S	10.05 MW	10.56 AW	21970 AAW	OKBLS	10//99-12//99
	Oklahoma City MSA, OK	S	10.88 MW	10.28 AW	22620 AAW	OKBLS	10//99-12//99
	Tulsa MSA, OK	S	10.60 MW	10.57 AW	22040 AAW	OKBLS	10//99-12//99
	Oregon	S	13.56 MW	14.42 AW	30000 AAW	ORBLS	10//99-12//99
	Eugene-Springfield MSA, OR	S	13.95 MW	13.28 AW	29020 AAW	ORBLS	10//99-12//99
	Portland-Vancouver PMSA, OR-WA	S	14.13 MW	13.34 AW	29390 AAW	ORBLS	10//99-12//99
	Salem PMSA, OR	S	13.85 MW	12.98 AW	28800 AAW	ORBLS	10//99-12//99
	Pennsylvania	S	14.59 MW	14.48 AW	30110 AAW	PABLS	10//99-12//99
	Allentown-Bethlehem-Easton MSA, PA	S	15.44 MW	14.98 AW	32120 AAW	PABLS	10//99-12//99
	Altoona MSA, PA	S	11.40 MW	11.26 AW	23720 AAW	PABLS	10//99-12//99
	Erie MSA, PA	S	12.90 MW	12.89 AW	26820 AAW	PABLS	10//99-12//99
	Johnstown MSA, PA	S	14.56 MW	14.69 AW	30290 AAW	PABLS	10//99-12//99
	Philadelphia PMSA, PA-NJ	S	15.14 MW	15.07 AW	31480 AAW	PABLS	10//99-12//99
	Pittsburgh MSA, PA	S	14.07 MW	14.20 AW	29260 AAW	PABLS	10//99-12//99
	Reading MSA, PA	S	15.27 MW	14.76 AW	31760 AAW	PABLS	10//99-12//99
	Scranton--Wilkes-Barre--Hazleton MSA, PA	S	12.74 MW	12.43 AW	26490 AAW	PABLS	10//99-12//99
	Sharon MSA, PA	S	14.86 MW	15.05 AW	30910 AAW	PABLS	10//99-12//99
	York MSA, PA	S	14.19 MW	14.28 AW	29510 AAW	PABLS	10//99-12//99
	Rhode Island	S	16.81 MW	17.35 AW	36100 AAW	RIBLS	10//99-12//99
	Providence-Fall River-Warwick MSA, RI-MA	S	17.15 MW	16.63 AW	35680 AAW	RIBLS	10//99-12//99
	South Carolina	S	12.4 MW	13.35 AW	27760 AAW	SCBLS	10//99-12//99
	Charleston-North Charleston MSA, SC	S	13.64 MW	12.44 AW	28380 AAW	SCBLS	10//99-12//99
	Columbia MSA, SC	S	14.32 MW	13.53 AW	29790 AAW	SCBLS	10//99-12//99
	Florence MSA, SC	S	11.81 MW	11.62 AW	24560 AAW	SCBLS	10//99-12//99
	Greenville-Spartanburg-Anderson MSA, SC	S	13.00 MW	12.74 AW	27040 AAW	SCBLS	10//99-12//99
	Myrtle Beach MSA, SC	S	12.44 MW	11.97 AW	25880 AAW	SCBLS	10//99-12//99
	South Dakota	S	11.51 MW	11.61 AW	24160 AAW	SDBLS	10//99-12//99
	Rapid City MSA, SD	S	12.04 MW	11.77 AW	25040 AAW	SDBLS	10//99-12//99
	Sioux Falls MSA, SD	S	11.67 MW	11.66 AW	24270 AAW	SDBLS	10//99-12//99
	Tennessee	S	11.88 MW	12.02 AW	24990 AAW	TNBLS	10//99-12//99
	Chattanooga MSA, TN-GA	S	12.30 MW	11.12 AW	25580 AAW	TNBLS	10//99-12//99
	Clarksville-Hopkinsville MSA, TN-KY	S	11.92 MW	11.34 AW	24800 AAW	TNBLS	10//99-12//99
	Jackson MSA, TN	S	10.45 MW	9.94 AW	21730 AAW	TNBLS	10//99-12//99
	Johnson City-Kingsport-Bristol MSA, TN-VA	S	11.02 MW	10.92 AW	22920 AAW	TNBLS	10//99-12//99
	Knoxville MSA, TN	S	11.86 MW	11.71 AW	24680 AAW	TNBLS	10//99-12//99
	Memphis MSA, TN-AR-MS	S	12.16 MW	11.75 AW	25300 AAW	MSBLS	10//99-12//99
	Nashville MSA, TN	S	12.39 MW	12.43 AW	25770 AAW	TNBLS	10//99-12//99
	Texas	S	12.07 MW	12.62 AW	26240 AAW	TXBLS	10//99-12//99
	Abilene MSA, TX	S	11.66 MW	10.88 AW	24260 AAW	TXBLS	10//99-12//99
	Amarillo MSA, TX	S	9.05 MW	8.23 AW	18820 AAW	TXBLS	10//99-12//99
	Austin-San Marcos MSA, TX	S	12.94 MW	12.71 AW	26920 AAW	TXBLS	10//99-12//99
	Beaumont-Port Arthur MSA, TX	S	13.65 MW	12.31 AW	28380 AAW	TXBLS	10//99-12//99
	Brownsville-Harlingen-San Benito MSA, TX	S	11.87 MW	10.40 AW	24690 AAW	TXBLS	10//99-12//99
	Bryan-College Station MSA, TX	S	13.61 MW	13.04 AW	28310 AAW	TXBLS	10//99-12//99
	Corpus Christi MSA, TX	S	10.31 MW	8.41 AW	21450 AAW	TXBLS	10//99-12//99
	Dallas PMSA, TX	S	13.38 MW	13.04 AW	27830 AAW	TXBLS	10//99-12//99
	El Paso MSA, TX	S	13.71 MW	14.56 AW	28520 AAW	TXBLS	10//99-12//99
	Fort Worth-Arlington PMSA, TX	S	13.76 MW	13.63 AW	28620 AAW	TXBLS	10//99-12//99
	Houston PMSA, TX	S	13.50 MW	11.99 AW	28090 AAW	TXBLS	10//99-12//99
	Lubbock MSA, TX	S	11.09 MW	10.57 AW	23080 AAW	TXBLS	10//99-12//99
	McAllen-Edinburg-Mission MSA, TX	S	11.83 MW	11.89 AW	24600 AAW	TXBLS	10//99-12//99
	Odessa-Midland MSA, TX	S	11.16 MW	11.98 AW	23200 AAW	TXBLS	10//99-12//99
	San Angelo MSA, TX	S	8.59 MW	7.66 AW	17870 AAW	TXBLS	10//99-12//99
	San Antonio MSA, TX	S	11.84 MW	11.60 AW	24630 AAW	TXBLS	10//99-12//99
	Sherman-Denison MSA, TX	S	11.45 MW	11.88 AW	23820 AAW	TXBLS	10//99-12//99
	Tyler MSA, TX	S	10.73 MW	9.79 AW	22320 AAW	TXBLS	10//99-12//99
	Waco MSA, TX	S	11.81 MW	11.36 AW	24560 AAW	TXBLS	10//99-12//99
	Wichita Falls MSA, TX	S	12.09 MW	10.45 AW	25150 AAW	TXBLS	10//99-12//99

Occupation/Type/Industry	Location	Per	Low	Mid	High	Source	Date
Medical and Clinical Laboratory Technician	Utah	S	9.9 MW	10.86 AW	22590 AAW	UTBLS	10//99-12//99
	Salt Lake City-Ogden MSA, UT	S	11.03 MW	10.07 AW	22950 AAW	UTBLS	10//99-12//99
	Vermont	S	13.1 MW	14.14 AW	29410 AAW	VTBLS	10//99-12//99
	Virginia	S	11.9 MW	12.74 AW	26490 AAW	VABLS	10//99-12//99
	Charlottesville MSA, VA	S	12.77 MW	11.48 AW	26550 AAW	VABLS	10//99-12//99
	Danville MSA, VA	S	10.01 MW	9.37 AW	20810 AAW	VABLS	10//99-12//99
	Lynchburg MSA, VA	S	13.67 MW	13.10 AW	28420 AAW	VABLS	10//99-12//99
	Norfolk-Virginia Beach-Newport News MSA, VA-NC	S	11.39 MW	11.13 AW	23690 AAW	VABLS	10//99-12//99
	Richmond-Petersburg MSA, VA	S	12.99 MW	12.38 AW	27030 AAW	VABLS	10//99-12//99
	Roanoke MSA, VA	S	11.79 MW	12.24 AW	24520 AAW	VABLS	10//99-12//99
	Washington	S	13.33 MW	14.27 AW	29680 AAW	WABLS	10//99-12//99
	Bremerton PMSA, WA	S	14.09 MW	13.39 AW	29310 AAW	WABLS	10//99-12//99
	Olympia PMSA, WA	S	14.55 MW	13.18 AW	30270 AAW	WABLS	10//99-12//99
	Richland-Kennewick-Pasco MSA, WA	S	11.58 MW	10.52 AW	24080 AAW	WABLS	10//99-12//99
	Seattle-Bellevue-Everett PMSA, WA	S	14.17 MW	13.28 AW	29470 AAW	WABLS	10//99-12//99
	Spokane MSA, WA	S	16.35 MW	15.37 AW	34000 AAW	WABLS	10//99-12//99
	Tacoma PMSA, WA	S	13.04 MW	12.91 AW	27120 AAW	WABLS	10//99-12//99
	Yakima MSA, WA	S	13.72 MW	13.55 AW	28540 AAW	WABLS	10//99-12//99
	West Virginia	S	10.94 MW	11.32 AW	23550 AAW	WVBLS	10//99-12//99
	Charleston MSA, WV	S	10.79 MW	10.36 AW	22430 AAW	WVBLS	10//99-12//99
	Huntington-Ashland MSA, WV-KY-OH	S	14.25 MW	13.84 AW	29640 AAW	WVBLS	10//99-12//99
	Parkersburg-Marietta MSA, WV-OH	S	12.87 MW	12.97 AW	26770 AAW	WVBLS	10//99-12//99
	Wheeling MSA, WV-OH	S	11.49 MW	11.45 AW	23910 AAW	WVBLS	10//99-12//99
	Wisconsin	S	13.31 MW	13.51 AW	28100 AAW	WIBLS	10//99-12//99
	Appleton-Oshkosh-Neenah MSA, WI	S	14.13 MW	13.76 AW	29390 AAW	WIBLS	10//99-12//99
	Eau Claire MSA, WI	S	13.65 MW	13.44 AW	28390 AAW	WIBLS	10//99-12//99
	Green Bay MSA, WI	S	13.86 MW	13.69 AW	28830 AAW	WIBLS	10//99-12//99
	La Crosse MSA, WI-MN	S	11.20 MW	11.78 AW	23300 AAW	WIBLS	10//99-12//99
	Madison MSA, WI	S	13.62 MW	13.41 AW	28340 AAW	WIBLS	10//99-12//99
	Milwaukee-Waukesha PMSA, WI	S	13.72 MW	13.57 AW	28550 AAW	WIBLS	10//99-12//99
	Racine PMSA, WI	S	14.06 MW	13.82 AW	29250 AAW	WIBLS	10//99-12//99
	Wyoming	S	13.28 MW	13.09 AW	27230 AAW	WYBLS	10//99-12//99
	Cheyenne MSA, WY	S	9.15 MW	8.79 AW	19040 AAW	WYBLS	10//99-12//99
	Puerto Rico	S	6.79 MW	7.48 AW	15560 AAW	PRBLS	10//99-12//99
	Arecibo PMSA, PR	S	10.33 MW	11.52 AW	21490 AAW	PRBLS	10//99-12//99
	Mayaguez MSA, PR	S	5.84 MW	6.02 AW	12140 AAW	PRBLS	10//99-12//99
	Ponce MSA, PR	S	6.99 MW	7.05 AW	14540 AAW	PRBLS	10//99-12//99
	San Juan-Bayamon PMSA, PR	S	7.34 MW	6.90 AW	15280 AAW	PRBLS	10//99-12//99
	Virgin Islands	S	10.18 MW	10.46 AW	21750 AAW	VIBLS	10//99-12//99
Medical and Clinical Laboratory Technologist	Alabama	S	16.48 MW	16.78 AW	34900 AAW	ALBLS	10//99-12//99
	Alaska	S	23.14 MW	23.41 AW	48690 AAW	AKBLS	10//99-12//99
	Arizona	S	18.4 MW	19.04 AW	39600 AAW	AZBLS	10//99-12//99
	Arkansas	S	17.39 MW	17.52 AW	36440 AAW	ARBLS	10//99-12//99
	California	S	23.63 MW	23.74 AW	49380 AAW	CABLS	10//99-12//99
	Colorado	S	18.54 MW	18.64 AW	38760 AAW	COBLS	10//99-12//99
	Connecticut	S	21.91 MW	22.18 AW	46130 AAW	CTBLS	10//99-12//99
	Delaware	S	20.06 MW	21.00 AW	43680 AAW	DEBLS	10//99-12//99
	District of Columbia	S	16.12 MW	16.48 AW	34280 AAW	DCBLS	10//99-12//99
	Florida	S	18.21 MW	18.24 AW	37940 AAW	FLBLS	10//99-12//99
	Georgia	S	17.81 MW	17.57 AW	36540 AAW	GABLS	10//99-12//99
	Hawaii	S	21.29 MW	21.70 AW	45140 AAW	HIBLS	10//99-12//99
	Idaho	S	18.95 MW	19.09 AW	39710 AAW	IDBLS	10//99-12//99
	Illinois	S	17.06 MW	17.38 AW	36140 AAW	ILBLS	10//99-12//99
	Indiana	S	16.94 MW	16.89 AW	35130 AAW	INBLS	10//99-12//99
	Iowa	S	15.72 MW	15.86 AW	32990 AAW	IABLS	10//99-12//99
	Kansas	S	16.91 MW	17.34 AW	36060 AAW	KSBLS	10//99-12//99
	Kentucky	S	17.59 MW	17.76 AW	36940 AAW	KYBLS	10//99-12//99
	Louisiana	S	17.64 MW	17.79 AW	37000 AAW	LABLS	10//99-12//99
	Maine	S	17.43 MW	17.41 AW	36210 AAW	MEBLS	10//99-12//99

AAW Average annual wage	AOH Average offered, high	ASH Average starting, high	H Hourly	M Monthly	S Special: hourly and annual
AE Average entry wage	AOL Average offered, low	ASL Average starting, low	HI Highest wage paid	MTC Median total compensation	TQ Third quartile wage
AEX Average experienced wage	APH Average pay, high range	AW Average wage paid	HR High end range	MW Median wage paid	W Weekly
AO Average offered	APL Average pay, low range	FQ First quartile wage	LR Low end range	SQ Second quartile wage	Y Yearly

Occupation/Type/Industry	Location	Per	Low	Mid	High	Source	Date
Medical and Clinical Laboratory Technologist	Maryland	S	18.76 MW	18.41 AW	38290 AAW	MDBLS	10//99-12//99
	Massachusetts	S	19.52 MW	19.61 AW	40780 AAW	MABLS	10//99-12//99
	Michigan	S	18.67 MW	18.60 AW	38680 AAW	MIBLS	10//99-12//99
	Minnesota	S	19.66 MW	19.58 AW	40720 AAW	MNBLS	10//99-12//99
	Mississippi	S	16.87 MW	17.37 AW	36130 AAW	MSBLS	10//99-12//99
	Missouri	S	18.31 MW	18.17 AW	37790 AAW	MOBLS	10//99-12//99
	Montana	S	17.48 MW	18.13 AW	37710 AAW	MTBLS	10//99-12//99
	Nebraska	S	17.5 MW	17.35 AW	36080 AAW	NEBLS	10//99-12//99
	Nevada	S	20.73 MW	20.64 AW	42920 AAW	NVBLS	10//99-12//99
	New Hampshire	S	17.79 MW	17.69 AW	36790 AAW	NHBLS	10//99-12//99
	New Jersey	S	20.45 MW	21.35 AW	44410 AAW	NJBLS	10//99-12//99
	New Mexico	S	15.11 MW	15.47 AW	32170 AAW	NMBLS	10//99-12//99
	New York	S	19.54 MW	20.19 AW	42000 AAW	NYBLS	10//99-12//99
	North Carolina	S	16.52 MW	17.37 AW	36130 AAW	NCBLS	10//99-12//99
	North Dakota	S	15.66 MW	15.99 AW	33250 AAW	NDBLS	10//99-12//99
	Ohio	S	18.94 MW	19.33 AW	40200 AAW	OHBLS	10//99-12//99
	Oklahoma	S	16.75 MW	16.61 AW	34560 AAW	OKBLS	10//99-12//99
	Oregon	S	20.34 MW	19.92 AW	41440 AAW	ORBLS	10//99-12//99
	Pennsylvania	S	18.21 MW	18.61 AW	38710 AAW	PABLS	10//99-12//99
	Rhode Island	S	20.74 MW	21.72 AW	45170 AAW	RIBLS	10//99-12//99
	South Carolina	S	17.2 MW	17.22 AW	35820 AAW	SCBLS	10//99-12//99
	South Dakota	S	15.67 MW	15.79 AW	32850 AAW	SDBLS	10//99-12//99
	Tennessee	S	17.37 MW	17.20 AW	35780 AAW	TNBLS	10//99-12//99
	Texas	S	16.57 MW	17.36 AW	36110 AAW	TXBLS	10//99-12//99
	Utah	S	18.62 MW	19.12 AW	39770 AAW	UTBLS	10//99-12//99
	Vermont	S	19.62 MW	20.50 AW	42640 AAW	VTBLS	10//99-12//99
	Virginia	S	16.71 MW	17.08 AW	35520 AAW	VABLS	10//99-12//99
	Washington	S	20.43 MW	20.44 AW	42520 AAW	WABLS	10//99-12//99
	West Virginia	S	17.21 MW	17.22 AW	35810 AAW	WVBLS	10//99-12//99
	Wisconsin	S	18.22 MW	18.14 AW	37730 AAW	WIBLS	10//99-12//99
	Wyoming	S	17.07 MW	17.17 AW	35710 AAW	WYBLS	10//99-12//99
	Puerto Rico	S	10.36 MW	10.80 AW	22470 AAW	PRBLS	10//99-12//99
Medical and Health Services Manager	Alabama	S	24.13 MW	25.23 AW	52470 AAW	ALBLS	10//99-12//99
	Anniston MSA, AL	S	18.43 MW	18.31 AW	38330 AAW	ALBLS	10//99-12//99
	Birmingham MSA, AL	S	27.47 MW	26.53 AW	57140 AAW	ALBLS	10//99-12//99
	Decatur MSA, AL	S	21.97 MW	21.48 AW	45710 AAW	ALBLS	10//99-12//99
	Dothan MSA, AL	S	19.82 MW	19.02 AW	41220 AAW	ALBLS	10//99-12//99
	Florence MSA, AL	S	23.34 MW	24.13 AW	48550 AAW	ALBLS	10//99-12//99
	Gadsden MSA, AL	S	25.72 MW	23.31 AW	53500 AAW	ALBLS	10//99-12//99
	Huntsville MSA, AL	S	27.18 MW	27.46 AW	56540 AAW	ALBLS	10//99-12//99
	Mobile MSA, AL	S	24.36 MW	24.25 AW	50660 AAW	ALBLS	10//99-12//99
	Montgomery MSA, AL	S	30.18 MW	26.39 AW	62780 AAW	ALBLS	10//99-12//99
	Tuscaloosa MSA, AL	S	22.87 MW	23.07 AW	47570 AAW	ALBLS	10//99-12//99
	Alaska	S	24.73 MW	25.63 AW	53320 AAW	AKBLS	10//99-12//99
	Anchorage MSA, AK	S	24.12 MW	20.99 AW	50170 AAW	AKBLS	10//99-12//99
	Arizona	S	25.63 MW	27.90 AW	58030 AAW	AZBLS	10//99-12//99
	Flagstaff MSA, AZ-UT	S	34.89 MW	32.00 AW	72570 AAW	AZBLS	10//99-12//99
	Phoenix-Mesa MSA, AZ	S	28.58 MW	25.65 AW	59440 AAW	AZBLS	10//99-12//99
	Tucson MSA, AZ	S	24.84 MW	23.70 AW	51670 AAW	AZBLS	10//99-12//99
	Yuma MSA, AZ	S	29.17 MW	30.30 AW	60680 AAW	AZBLS	10//99-12//99
	Arkansas	S	24.97 MW	27.10 AW	56370 AAW	ARBLS	10//99-12//99
	Fayetteville-Springdale-Rogers MSA, AR	S	22.16 MW	21.05 AW	46090 AAW	ARBLS	10//99-12//99
	Fort Smith MSA, AR-OK	S	29.36 MW	28.06 AW	61070 AAW	ARBLS	10//99-12//99
	Jonesboro MSA, AR	S	18.85 MW	19.24 AW	39210 AAW	ARBLS	10//99-12//99
	Little Rock-North Little Rock MSA, AR	S	33.29 MW	31.30 AW	69240 AAW	ARBLS	10//99-12//99
	California	S	31 MW	32.19 AW	66960 AAW	CABLS	10//99-12//99
	Bakersfield MSA, CA	S	23.87 MW	22.04 AW	49640 AAW	CABLS	10//99-12//99
	Chico-Paradise MSA, CA	S	29.00 MW	25.98 AW	60320 AAW	CABLS	10//99-12//99
	Fresno MSA, CA	S	42.12 MW	39.63 AW	87600 AAW	CABLS	10//99-12//99
	Los Angeles-Long Beach PMSA, CA	S	32.07 MW	30.87 AW	66700 AAW	CABLS	10//99-12//99
	Merced MSA, CA	S	29.19 MW	29.53 AW	60720 AAW	CABLS	10//99-12//99
	Modesto MSA, CA	S	29.19 MW	27.17 AW	60720 AAW	CABLS	10//99-12//99
	Oakland PMSA, CA	S	33.89 MW	32.18 AW	70490 AAW	CABLS	10//99-12//99
	Orange County PMSA, CA	S	29.19 MW	28.43 AW	60720 AAW	CABLS	10//99-12//99
	Redding MSA, CA	S	23.12 MW	21.04 AW	48100 AAW	CABLS	10//99-12//99

Occupation/Type/Industry	Location	Per	Low	Mid	High	Source	Date
Medical and Health Services Manager	Riverside-San Bernardino PMSA, CA	S	31.51 MW	31.03 AW	65540 AAW	CABLS	10//99-12//99
	Sacramento PMSA, CA	S	34.80 MW	33.59 AW	72390 AAW	CABLS	10//99-12//99
	Salinas MSA, CA	S	38.75 MW	44.19 AW	80590 AAW	CABLS	10//99-12//99
	San Diego MSA, CA	S	31.22 MW	30.72 AW	64940 AAW	CABLS	10//99-12//99
	San Francisco PMSA, CA	S	35.65 MW	33.33 AW	74160 AAW	CABLS	10//99-12//99
	San Jose PMSA, CA	S	38.10 MW	38.23 AW	79260 AAW	CABLS	10//99-12//99
	San Luis Obispo-Atascadero-Paso Robles MSA, CA	S	28.32 MW	27.98 AW	58910 AAW	CABLS	10//99-12//99
	Santa Barbara-Santa Maria-Lompoc MSA, CA	S	29.03 MW	30.09 AW	60370 AAW	CABLS	10//99-12//99
	Santa Cruz-Watsonville PMSA, CA	S	26.11 MW	24.65 AW	54300 AAW	CABLS	10//99-12//99
	Santa Rosa PMSA, CA	S	26.47 MW	25.11 AW	55050 AAW	CABLS	10//99-12//99
	Stockton-Lodi MSA, CA	S	27.75 MW	29.46 AW	57710 AAW	CABLS	10//99-12//99
	Vallejo-Fairfield-Napa PMSA, CA	S	34.82 MW	32.96 AW	72430 AAW	CABLS	10//99-12//99
	Ventura PMSA, CA	S	25.89 MW	20.93 AW	53860 AAW	CABLS	10//99-12//99
	Visalia-Tulare-Porterville MSA, CA	S	29.65 MW	30.26 AW	61670 AAW	CABLS	10//99-12//99
	Yolo PMSA, CA	S	33.46 MW	26.09 AW	69610 AAW	CABLS	10//99-12//99
	Colorado	S	25.68 MW	28.31 AW	58880 AAW	COBLS	10//99-12//99
	Boulder-Longmont PMSA, CO	S	22.57 MW	21.83 AW	46940 AAW	COBLS	10//99-12//99
	Colorado Springs MSA, CO	S	24.78 MW	23.55 AW	51540 AAW	COBLS	10//99-12//99
	Denver PMSA, CO	S	31.03 MW	27.70 AW	64530 AAW	COBLS	10//99-12//99
	Fort Collins-Loveland MSA, CO	S	33.46 MW	26.58 AW	69600 AAW	COBLS	10//99-12//99
	Grand Junction MSA, CO	S	28.42 MW	25.40 AW	59120 AAW	COBLS	10//99-12//99
	Pueblo MSA, CO	S	29.15 MW	30.38 AW	60630 AAW	COBLS	10//99-12//99
	Connecticut	S	31.02 MW	33.51 AW	69700 AAW	CTBLS	10//99-12//99
	Bridgeport PMSA, CT	S	36.73 MW	32.63 AW	76400 AAW	CTBLS	10//99-12//99
	Danbury PMSA, CT	S	29.03 MW	25.67 AW	60380 AAW	CTBLS	10//99-12//99
	Hartford MSA, CT	S	32.33 MW	30.28 AW	67250 AAW	CTBLS	10//99-12//99
	New Haven-Meriden PMSA, CT	S	32.18 MW	31.69 AW	66940 AAW	CTBLS	10//99-12//99
	New London-Norwich MSA, CT-RI	S	30.83 MW	29.87 AW	64130 AAW	CTBLS	10//99-12//99
	Stamford-Norwalk PMSA, CT	S	36.30 MW	32.04 AW	75510 AAW	CTBLS	10//99-12//99
	Waterbury PMSA, CT	S	45.60 MW	38.27 AW	94850 AAW	CTBLS	10//99-12//99
	Delaware	S	26.09 MW	28.75 AW	59800 AAW	DEBLS	10//99-12//99
	Wilmington-Newark PMSA, DE-MD	S	29.30 MW	25.39 AW	60950 AAW	DEBLS	10//99-12//99
	District of Columbia	S	27.73 MW	29.61 AW	61590 AAW	DCBLS	10//99-12//99
	Washington PMSA, DC-MD-VA-WV	S	29.86 MW	28.45 AW	62110 AAW	DCBLS	10//99-12//99
	Florida	S	24.86 MW	27.05 AW	56270 AAW	FLBLS	10//99-12//99
	Daytona Beach MSA, FL	S	25.93 MW	23.80 AW	53940 AAW	FLBLS	10//99-12//99
	Fort Lauderdale PMSA, FL	S	27.48 MW	25.99 AW	57160 AAW	FLBLS	10//99-12//99
	Fort Myers-Cape Coral MSA, FL	S	22.32 MW	20.39 AW	46420 AAW	FLBLS	10//99-12//99
	Fort Pierce-Port St. Lucie MSA, FL	S	25.59 MW	21.38 AW	53230 AAW	FLBLS	10//99-12//99
	Fort Walton Beach MSA, FL	S	21.14 MW	18.91 AW	43970 AAW	FLBLS	10//99-12//99
	Gainesville MSA, FL	S	30.89 MW	27.18 AW	64260 AAW	FLBLS	10//99-12//99
	Jacksonville MSA, FL	S	27.56 MW	25.57 AW	57320 AAW	FLBLS	10//99-12//99
	Lakeland-Winter Haven MSA, FL	S	25.13 MW	24.71 AW	52270 AAW	FLBLS	10//99-12//99
	Melbourne-Titusville-Palm Bay MSA, FL	S	26.93 MW	24.67 AW	56020 AAW	FLBLS	10//99-12//99
	Miami PMSA, FL	S	32.68 MW	32.24 AW	67980 AAW	FLBLS	10//99-12//99
	Naples MSA, FL	S	22.82 MW	20.55 AW	47460 AAW	FLBLS	10//99-12//99
	Ocala MSA, FL	S	26.17 MW	27.85 AW	54430 AAW	FLBLS	10//99-12//99
	Orlando MSA, FL	S	25.89 MW	24.00 AW	53850 AAW	FLBLS	10//99-12//99
	Pensacola MSA, FL	S	24.30 MW	23.37 AW	50550 AAW	FLBLS	10//99-12//99
	Punta Gorda MSA, FL	S	24.61 MW	24.25 AW	51200 AAW	FLBLS	10//99-12//99
	Sarasota-Bradenton MSA, FL	S	24.97 MW	23.28 AW	51940 AAW	FLBLS	10//99-12//99
	Tampa-St. Petersburg-Clearwater MSA, FL	S	25.07 MW	22.62 AW	52140 AAW	FLBLS	10//99-12//99
	West Palm Beach-Boca Raton MSA, FL	S	25.53 MW	23.94 AW	53100 AAW	FLBLS	10//99-12//99
	Georgia	S	25.19 MW	26.39 AW	54900 AAW	GABLS	10//99-12//99

AAW Average annual wage	AOH Average offered, high	ASH Average starting, high	H Hourly	M Monthly	S Special: hourly and annual
AE Average entry wage	AOL Average offered, low	ASL Average starting, low	HI Highest wage paid	MTC Median total compensation	TQ Third quartile wage
AEX Average experienced wage	APH Average pay, high range	AW Average wage paid	HR High end range	MW Median wage paid	W Weekly
AO Average offered	APL Average pay, low range	FQ First quartile wage	LR Low end range	SQ Second quartile wage	Y Yearly

Occupation/Type/Industry	Location	Per	Low	Mid	High	Source	Date
Medical and Health Services Manager							
	Albany MSA, GA	S	19.73 MW	16.34 AW	41050 AAW	GABLS	10//99-12//99
	Athens MSA, GA	S	26.28 MW	24.28 AW	54670 AAW	GABLS	10//99-12//99
	Atlanta MSA, GA	S	27.78 MW	25.98 AW	57780 AAW	GABLS	10//99-12//99
	Augusta-Aiken MSA, GA-SC	S	25.39 MW	24.52 AW	52820 AAW	GABLS	10//99-12//99
	Columbus MSA, GA-AL	S	28.72 MW	27.08 AW	59740 AAW	GABLS	10//99-12//99
	Macon MSA, GA	S	25.52 MW	25.55 AW	53070 AAW	GABLS	10//99-12//99
	Savannah MSA, GA	S	19.78 MW	18.13 AW	41150 AAW	GABLS	10//99-12//99
	Hawaii	S	31.12 MW	30.99 AW	64470 AAW	HIBLS	10//99-12//99
	Honolulu MSA, HI	S	31.48 MW	31.69 AW	65480 AAW	HIBLS	10//99-12//99
	Idaho	S	25.97 MW	26.45 AW	55020 AAW	IDBLS	10//99-12//99
	Boise City MSA, ID	S	27.92 MW	28.22 AW	58080 AAW	IDBLS	10//99-12//99
	Pocatello MSA, ID	S	20.42 MW	18.79 AW	42470 AAW	IDBLS	10//99-12//99
	Illinois	S	25.29 MW	27.69 AW	57600 AAW	ILBLS	10//99-12//99
	Bloomington-Normal MSA, IL	S	26.64 MW	23.75 AW	55410 AAW	ILBLS	10//99-12//99
	Champaign-Urbana MSA, IL	S	25.72 MW	25.27 AW	53510 AAW	ILBLS	10//99-12//99
	Chicago PMSA, IL	S	28.48 MW	26.34 AW	59230 AAW	ILBLS	10//99-12//99
	Kankakee PMSA, IL	S	22.87 MW	20.83 AW	47570 AAW	ILBLS	10//99-12//99
	Peoria-Pekin MSA, IL	S	37.78 MW	30.53 AW	78580 AAW	ILBLS	10//99-12//99
	Rockford MSA, IL	S	20.07 MW	20.32 AW	41750 AAW	ILBLS	10//99-12//99
	Springfield MSA, IL	S	25.33 MW	28.24 AW	52680 AAW	ILBLS	10//99-12//99
	Indiana	S	22.44 MW	23.51 AW	48900 AAW	INBLS	10//99-12//99
	Bloomington MSA, IN	S	17.86 MW	18.93 AW	37150 AAW	INBLS	10//99-12//99
	Elkhart-Goshen MSA, IN	S	25.24 MW	24.82 AW	52500 AAW	INBLS	10//99-12//99
	Evansville-Henderson MSA, IN-KY	S	18.90 MW	19.00 AW	39320 AAW	INBLS	10//99-12//99
	Fort Wayne MSA, IN	S	19.98 MW	19.34 AW	41550 AAW	INBLS	10//99-12//99
	Gary PMSA, IN	S	27.18 MW	26.05 AW	56530 AAW	INBLS	10//99-12//99
	Indianapolis MSA, IN	S	26.05 MW	24.15 AW	54190 AAW	INBLS	10//99-12//99
	Kokomo MSA, IN	S	23.32 MW	21.35 AW	48500 AAW	INBLS	10//99-12//99
	Lafayette MSA, IN	S	25.36 MW	20.47 AW	52750 AAW	INBLS	10//99-12//99
	Muncie MSA, IN	S	19.58 MW	16.94 AW	40730 AAW	INBLS	10//99-12//99
	South Bend MSA, IN	S	18.27 MW	17.32 AW	38010 AAW	INBLS	10//99-12//99
	Terre Haute MSA, IN	S	20.73 MW	20.25 AW	43120 AAW	INBLS	10//99-12//99
	Iowa	S	21.26 MW	22.37 AW	46530 AAW	IABLS	10//99-12//99
	Cedar Rapids MSA, IA	S	23.12 MW	23.41 AW	48090 AAW	IABLS	10//99-12//99
	Des Moines MSA, IA	S	22.77 MW	20.49 AW	47360 AAW	IABLS	10//99-12//99
	Sioux City MSA, IA-NE	S	23.66 MW	22.68 AW	49210 AAW	IABLS	10//99-12//99
	Waterloo-Cedar Falls MSA, IA	S	19.92 MW	20.78 AW	41440 AAW	IABLS	10//99-12//99
	Kansas	S	22.51 MW	23.90 AW	49700 AAW	KSBLS	10//99-12//99
	Lawrence MSA, KS	S	33.92 MW	32.23 AW	70550 AAW	KSBLS	10//99-12//99
	Topeka MSA, KS	S	21.81 MW	20.77 AW	45370 AAW	KSBLS	10//99-12//99
	Wichita MSA, KS	S	23.29 MW	21.36 AW	48440 AAW	KSBLS	10//99-12//99
	Kentucky	S	22.54 MW	23.69 AW	49270 AAW	KYBLS	10//99-12//99
	Lexington MSA, KY	S	22.12 MW	20.35 AW	46000 AAW	KYBLS	10//99-12//99
	Louisville MSA, KY-IN	S	24.17 MW	23.12 AW	50280 AAW	KYBLS	10//99-12//99
	Owensboro MSA, KY	S	21.89 MW	20.38 AW	45540 AAW	KYBLS	10//99-12//99
	Louisiana	S	22.83 MW	24.41 AW	50770 AAW	LABLS	10//99-12//99
	Alexandria MSA, LA	S	25.68 MW	24.25 AW	53410 AAW	LABLS	10//99-12//99
	Baton Rouge MSA, LA	S	29.90 MW	25.76 AW	62200 AAW	LABLS	10//99-12//99
	Lafayette MSA, LA	S	23.40 MW	21.47 AW	48670 AAW	LABLS	10//99-12//99
	Lake Charles MSA, LA	S	20.77 MW	20.67 AW	43200 AAW	LABLS	10//99-12//99
	Monroe MSA, LA	S	23.48 MW	23.93 AW	48830 AAW	LABLS	10//99-12//99
	New Orleans MSA, LA	S	25.08 MW	23.80 AW	52160 AAW	LABLS	10//99-12//99
	Shreveport-Bossier City MSA, LA	S	20.45 MW	19.24 AW	42540 AAW	LABLS	10//99-12//99
	Maine	S	24.49 MW	26.70 AW	55530 AAW	MEBLS	10//99-12//99
	Bangor MSA, ME	S	22.08 MW	21.04 AW	45920 AAW	MEBLS	10//99-12//99
	Lewiston-Auburn MSA, ME	S	22.31 MW	22.47 AW	46410 AAW	MEBLS	10//99-12//99
	Portland MSA, ME	S	29.66 MW	26.75 AW	61690 AAW	MEBLS	10//99-12//99
	Maryland	S	26.48 MW	28.03 AW	58310 AAW	MDBLS	10//99-12//99
	Baltimore PMSA, MD	S	28.09 MW	25.94 AW	58420 AAW	MDBLS	10//99-12//99
	Cumberland MSA, MD-WV	S	24.45 MW	25.31 AW	50850 AAW	MDBLS	10//99-12//99
	Hagerstown PMSA, MD	S	23.55 MW	23.09 AW	48990 AAW	MDBLS	10//99-12//99
	Massachusetts	S	27.51 MW	29.31 AW	60970 AAW	MABLS	10//99-12//99
	Barnstable-Yarmouth MSA, MA	S	18.40 MW	17.88 AW	38260 AAW	MABLS	10//99-12//99
	Boston PMSA, MA-NH	S	31.10 MW	29.18 AW	64690 AAW	MABLS	10//99-12//99
	Brockton PMSA, MA	S	27.94 MW	27.90 AW	58120 AAW	MABLS	10//99-12//99
	Fitchburg-Leominster PMSA, MA	S	29.11 MW	28.83 AW	60540 AAW	MABLS	10//99-12//99
	Lawrence PMSA, MA-NH	S	26.29 MW	26.78 AW	54680 AAW	MABLS	10//99-12//99

AAW Average annual wage	AOH Average offered, high	ASH Average starting, high	H Hourly	M Monthly	S Special: hourly and annual
AE Average entry wage	AOL Average offered, low	ASL Average starting, low	HI Highest wage paid	MTC Median total compensation	TQ Third quartile wage
AEX Average experienced wage	APH Average pay, high range	AW Average wage paid	HR High end range	MW Median wage paid	W Weekly
AO Average offered	APL Average pay, low range	FQ First quartile wage	LR Low end range	SQ Second quartile wage	Y Yearly

Occupation/Type/Industry	Location	Per	Low	Mid	High	Source	Date
Medical and Health Services Manager							
	Lowell PMSA, MA-NH	S	25.95 MW	25.45 AW	53980 AAW	MABLS	10//99-12//99
	New Bedford PMSA, MA	S	39.01 MW	29.52 AW	81150 AAW	MABLS	10//99-12//99
	Springfield MSA, MA	S	25.85 MW	24.99 AW	53770 AAW	MABLS	10//99-12//99
	Worcester PMSA, MA-CT	S	24.81 MW	24.61 AW	51600 AAW	MABLS	10//99-12//99
	Michigan	S	25.39 MW	27.52 AW	57240 AAW	MIBLS	10//99-12//99
	Ann Arbor PMSA, MI	S	24.17 MW	20.89 AW	50270 AAW	MIBLS	10//99-12//99
	Benton Harbor MSA, MI	S	28.47 MW	27.11 AW	59220 AAW	MIBLS	10//99-12//99
	Detroit PMSA, MI	S	30.31 MW	28.29 AW	63040 AAW	MIBLS	10//99-12//99
	Flint PMSA, MI	S	27.66 MW	28.06 AW	57520 AAW	MIBLS	10//99-12//99
	Grand Rapids-Muskegon-Holland MSA, MI	S	24.33 MW	22.47 AW	50610 AAW	MIBLS	10//99-12//99
	Jackson MSA, MI	S	23.62 MW	22.77 AW	49140 AAW	MIBLS	10//99-12//99
	Kalamazoo-Battle Creek MSA, MI	S	24.10 MW	22.96 AW	50140 AAW	MIBLS	10//99-12//99
	Lansing-East Lansing MSA, MI	S	29.55 MW	26.10 AW	61470 AAW	MIBLS	10//99-12//99
	Saginaw-Bay City-Midland MSA, MI	S	34.71 MW	30.95 AW	72190 AAW	MIBLS	10//99-12//99
	Minnesota	S	25.9 MW	28.17 AW	58600 AAW	MNBLS	10//99-12//99
	Duluth-Superior MSA, MN-WI	S	27.32 MW	24.82 AW	56820 AAW	MNBLS	10//99-12//99
	Minneapolis-St. Paul MSA, MN-WI	S	30.78 MW	27.60 AW	64020 AAW	MNBLS	10//99-12//99
	St. Cloud MSA, MN	S	25.77 MW	20.94 AW	53610 AAW	MNBLS	10//99-12//99
	Mississippi	S	23.85 MW	26.26 AW	54620 AAW	MSBLS	10//99-12//99
	Biloxi-Gulfport-Pascagoula MSA, MS	S	29.77 MW	26.03 AW	61920 AAW	MSBLS	10//99-12//99
	Hattiesburg MSA, MS	S	28.61 MW	26.05 AW	59500 AAW	MSBLS	10//99-12//99
	Jackson MSA, MS	S	24.37 MW	22.26 AW	50690 AAW	MSBLS	10//99-12//99
	Missouri	S	23.46 MW	26.76 AW	55670 AAW	MOBLS	10//99-12//99
	Columbia MSA, MO	S	27.30 MW	22.24 AW	56780 AAW	MOBLS	10//99-12//99
	Joplin MSA, MO	S	41.74 MW	35.88 AW	86830 AAW	MOBLS	10//99-12//99
	Kansas City MSA, MO-KS	S	26.45 MW	24.37 AW	55010 AAW	MOBLS	10//99-12//99
	St. Joseph MSA, MO	S	29.52 MW	28.10 AW	61400 AAW	MOBLS	10//99-12//99
	St. Louis MSA, MO-IL	S	28.72 MW	24.44 AW	59740 AAW	MOBLS	10//99-12//99
	Springfield MSA, MO	S	23.66 MW	23.92 AW	49210 AAW	MOBLS	10//99-12//99
	Montana	S	22.41 MW	22.61 AW	47030 AAW	MTBLS	10//99-12//99
	Billings MSA, MT	S	28.32 MW	25.57 AW	58910 AAW	MTBLS	10//99-12//99
	Great Falls MSA, MT	S	14.67 MW	14.49 AW	30520 AAW	MTBLS	10//99-12//99
	Missoula MSA, MT	S	20.81 MW	21.86 AW	43270 AAW	MTBLS	10//99-12//99
	Nebraska	S	22.71 MW	23.54 AW	48960 AAW	NEBLS	10//99-12//99
	Lincoln MSA, NE	S	23.63 MW	22.36 AW	49140 AAW	NEBLS	10//99-12//99
	Omaha MSA, NE-IA	S	27.10 MW	25.54 AW	56360 AAW	NEBLS	10//99-12//99
	Nevada	S	30.22 MW	32.27 AW	67130 AAW	NVBLS	10//99-12//99
	Las Vegas MSA, NV-AZ	S	32.65 MW	30.67 AW	67900 AAW	NVBLS	10//99-12//99
	Reno MSA, NV	S	31.56 MW	31.28 AW	65650 AAW	NVBLS	10//99-12//99
	New Hampshire	S	26.58 MW	27.62 AW	57450 AAW	NHBLS	10//99-12//99
	Manchester PMSA, NH	S	32.74 MW	30.82 AW	68090 AAW	NHBLS	10//99-12//99
	Nashua PMSA, NH	S	25.58 MW	27.03 AW	53200 AAW	NHBLS	10//99-12//99
	Portsmouth-Rochester PMSA, NH-ME	S	25.33 MW	24.85 AW	52690 AAW	NHBLS	10//99-12//99
	New Jersey	S	32.52 MW	35.12 AW	73040 AAW	NJBLS	10//99-12//99
	Bergen-Passaic PMSA, NJ	S	37.89 MW	37.46 AW	78800 AAW	NJBLS	10//99-12//99
	Jersey City PMSA, NJ	S	34.89 MW	35.87 AW	72560 AAW	NJBLS	10//99-12//99
	Middlesex-Somerset-Hunterdon PMSA, NJ	S	33.64 MW	31.52 AW	69970 AAW	NJBLS	10//99-12//99
	Monmouth-Ocean PMSA, NJ	S	35.15 MW	37.03 AW	73110 AAW	NJBLS	10//99-12//99
	Newark PMSA, NJ	S	33.80 MW	32.75 AW	70300 AAW	NJBLS	10//99-12//99
	Trenton PMSA, NJ	S	31.66 MW	26.24 AW	65860 AAW	NJBLS	10//99-12//99
	Vineland-Millville-Bridgeton PMSA, NJ	S	28.03 MW	26.22 AW	58300 AAW	NJBLS	10//99-12//99
	New Mexico	S	24.44 MW	26.58 AW	55280 AAW	NMBLS	10//99-12//99
	Albuquerque MSA, NM	S	27.41 MW	25.33 AW	57010 AAW	NMBLS	10//99-12//99
	Las Cruces MSA, NM	S	18.42 MW	18.25 AW	38310 AAW	NMBLS	10//99-12//99
	New York	S	29.14 MW	31.86 AW	66260 AAW	NYBLS	10//99-12//99
	Albany-Schenectady-Troy MSA, NY	S	29.24 MW	27.49 AW	60820 AAW	NYBLS	10//99-12//99
	Binghamton MSA, NY	S	22.58 MW	21.98 AW	46960 AAW	NYBLS	10//99-12//99
	Buffalo-Niagara Falls MSA, NY	S	27.14 MW	24.16 AW	56460 AAW	NYBLS	10//99-12//99
	Dutchess County PMSA, NY	S	30.67 MW	27.55 AW	63790 AAW	NYBLS	10//99-12//99
	Elmira MSA, NY	S	26.55 MW	25.18 AW	55230 AAW	NYBLS	10//99-12//99
	Glens Falls MSA, NY	S	21.93 MW	20.50 AW	45610 AAW	NYBLS	10//99-12//99

AAW	Average annual wage	AOH	Average offered, high	ASH	Average starting, high
AE	Average entry wage	AOL	Average offered, low	ASL	Average starting, low
AEX	Average experienced wage	APH	Average pay, high range	AW	Average wage paid
AO	Average offered	APL	Average pay, low range	FQ	First quartile wage

H	Hourly	M	Monthly
HI	Highest wage paid	MTC	Median total compensation
HR	High end range	MW	Median wage paid
LR	Low end range	SQ	Second quartile wage

S	Special: hourly and annual
TQ	Third quartile wage
W	Weekly
Y	Yearly

Occupation/Type/Industry	Location	Per	Low	Mid	High	Source	Date
Medical and Health Services Manager	Jamestown MSA, NY	S	25.46 MW	26.13 AW	52960 AAW	NYBLS	10//99-12//99
	Nassau-Suffolk PMSA, NY	S	37.32 MW	34.34 AW	77630 AAW	NYBLS	10//99-12//99
	New York PMSA, NY	S	34.63 MW	32.45 AW	72040 AAW	NYBLS	10//99-12//99
	Newburgh PMSA, NY-PA	S	30.55 MW	27.08 AW	63550 AAW	NYBLS	10//99-12//99
	Rochester MSA, NY	S	26.74 MW	23.71 AW	55620 AAW	NYBLS	10//99-12//99
	Syracuse MSA, NY	S	26.03 MW	24.18 AW	54140 AAW	NYBLS	10//99-12//99
	Utica-Rome MSA, NY	S	26.83 MW	25.50 AW	55810 AAW	NYBLS	10//99-12//99
	North Carolina	S	25.27 MW	26.52 AW	55170 AAW	NCBLS	10//99-12//99
	Charlotte-Gastonia-Rock Hill MSA, NC-SC	S	30.09 MW	30.18 AW	62590 AAW	NCBLS	10//99-12//99
	Greensboro--Winston-Salem-- High Point MSA, NC	S	26.36 MW	25.42 AW	54840 AAW	NCBLS	10//99-12//99
	Hickory-Morganton-Lenoir MSA, NC	S	26.70 MW	26.38 AW	55540 AAW	NCBLS	10//99-12//99
	Raleigh-Durham-Chapel Hill MSA, NC	S	27.22 MW	25.75 AW	56620 AAW	NCBLS	10//99-12//99
	Rocky Mount MSA, NC	S	24.00 MW	21.50 AW	49930 AAW	NCBLS	10//99-12//99
	Wilmington MSA, NC	S	26.07 MW	24.08 AW	54230 AAW	NCBLS	10//99-12//99
	North Dakota	S	20.11 MW	19.14 AW	39800 AAW	NDBLS	10//99-12//99
	Bismarck MSA, ND	S	22.32 MW	22.21 AW	46430 AAW	NDBLS	10//99-12//99
	Fargo-Moorhead MSA, ND-MN	S	26.34 MW	26.72 AW	54790 AAW	NDBLS	10//99-12//99
	Ohio	S	23.98 MW	25.50 AW	53030 AAW	OHBLS	10//99-12//99
	Akron PMSA, OH	S	22.34 MW	20.13 AW	46460 AAW	OHBLS	10//99-12//99
	Canton-Massillon MSA, OH	S	23.71 MW	20.21 AW	49320 AAW	OHBLS	10//99-12//99
	Cincinnati PMSA, OH-KY-IN	S	26.17 MW	24.37 AW	54430 AAW	OHBLS	10//99-12//99
	Cleveland-Lorain-Elyria PMSA, OH	S	27.36 MW	25.77 AW	56910 AAW	OHBLS	10//99-12//99
	Columbus MSA, OH	S	27.63 MW	26.75 AW	57470 AAW	OHBLS	10//99-12//99
	Dayton-Springfield MSA, OH	S	23.93 MW	23.06 AW	49780 AAW	OHBLS	10//99-12//99
	Hamilton-Middletown PMSA, OH	S	25.63 MW	25.32 AW	53310 AAW	OHBLS	10//99-12//99
	Mansfield MSA, OH	S	22.10 MW	22.08 AW	45970 AAW	OHBLS	10//99-12//99
	Steubenville-Weirton MSA, OH-WV	S	23.58 MW	21.44 AW	49060 AAW	OHBLS	10//99-12//99
	Toledo MSA, OH	S	27.06 MW	23.91 AW	56290 AAW	OHBLS	10//99-12//99
	Youngstown-Warren MSA, OH	S	21.09 MW	20.79 AW	43870 AAW	OHBLS	10//99-12//99
	Oklahoma	S	24.78 MW	26.78 AW	55710 AAW	OKBLS	10//99-12//99
	Enid MSA, OK	S	24.70 MW	22.72 AW	51380 AAW	OKBLS	10//99-12//99
	Oklahoma City MSA, OK	S	26.03 MW	24.44 AW	54140 AAW	OKBLS	10//99-12//99
	Tulsa MSA, OK	S	32.37 MW	30.19 AW	67320 AAW	OKBLS	10//99-12//99
	Oregon	S	30.33 MW	32.53 AW	67650 AAW	ORBLS	10//99-12//99
	Eugene-Springfield MSA, OR	S	33.90 MW	31.40 AW	70510 AAW	ORBLS	10//99-12//99
	Medford-Ashland MSA, OR	S	26.75 MW	27.31 AW	55640 AAW	ORBLS	10//99-12//99
	Portland-Vancouver PMSA, OR-WA	S	35.81 MW	33.76 AW	74490 AAW	ORBLS	10//99-12//99
	Salem PMSA, OR	S	28.75 MW	27.54 AW	59810 AAW	ORBLS	10//99-12//99
	Pennsylvania	S	26.75 MW	28.69 AW	59670 AAW	PABLS	10//99-12//99
	Allentown-Bethlehem-Easton MSA, PA	S	36.71 MW	30.33 AW	76360 AAW	PABLS	10//99-12//99
	Altoona MSA, PA	S	22.57 MW	20.20 AW	46950 AAW	PABLS	10//99-12//99
	Erie MSA, PA	S	23.14 MW	22.69 AW	48140 AAW	PABLS	10//99-12//99
	Harrisburg-Lebanon-Carlisle MSA, PA	S	32.18 MW	31.19 AW	66940 AAW	PABLS	10//99-12//99
	Johnstown MSA, PA	S	22.17 MW	20.88 AW	46110 AAW	PABLS	10//99-12//99
	Lancaster MSA, PA	S	21.21 MW	20.61 AW	44110 AAW	PABLS	10//99-12//99
	Philadelphia PMSA, PA-NJ	S	29.73 MW	28.04 AW	61840 AAW	PABLS	10//99-12//99
	Pittsburgh MSA, PA	S	28.32 MW	25.94 AW	58920 AAW	PABLS	10//99-12//99
	Reading MSA, PA	S	26.28 MW	27.95 AW	54670 AAW	PABLS	10//99-12//99
	Scranton--Wilkes-Barre-- Hazleton MSA, PA	S	25.78 MW	24.35 AW	53620 AAW	PABLS	10//99-12//99
	Sharon MSA, PA	S	21.12 MW	21.62 AW	43920 AAW	PABLS	10//99-12//99
	Williamsport MSA, PA	S	19.22 MW	22.52 AW	39970 AAW	PABLS	10//99-12//99
	York MSA, PA	S	25.52 MW	23.06 AW	53090 AAW	PABLS	10//99-12//99
	Rhode Island	S	27.03 MW	31.09 AW	64660 AAW	RIBLS	10//99-12//99
	Providence-Fall River- Warwick MSA, RI-MA	S	29.57 MW	25.91 AW	61510 AAW	RIBLS	10//99-12//99
	South Carolina	S	27.02 MW	28.37 AW	59020 AAW	SCBLS	10//99-12//99
	Charleston-North Charleston MSA, SC	S	33.36 MW	36.45 AW	69380 AAW	SCBLS	10//99-12//99
	Columbia MSA, SC	S	26.36 MW	25.86 AW	54830 AAW	SCBLS	10//99-12//99

AAW Average annual wage	**AOH** Average offered, high	**ASH** Average starting, high	**H** Hourly	**M** Monthly	**S** Special: hourly and annual
AE Average entry wage	**AOL** Average offered, low	**ASL** Average starting, low	**HI** Highest wage paid	**MTC** Median total compensation	**TQ** Third quartile wage
AEX Average experienced wage	**APH** Average pay, high range	**AW** Average wage paid	**HR** High end range	**MW** Median wage paid	**W** Weekly
AO Average offered	**APL** Average pay, low range	**FQ** First quartile wage	**LR** Low end range	**SQ** Second quartile wage	**Y** Yearly

Occupation/Type/Industry	Location	Per	Low	Mid	High	Source	Date
Medical and Health Services Manager	Florence MSA, SC	S	29.70 MW	32.10 AW	61770 AAW	SCBLS	10//99-12//99
	Greenville-Spartanburg-Anderson MSA, SC	S	34.22 MW	34.74 AW	71170 AAW	SCBLS	10//99-12//99
	Myrtle Beach MSA, SC	S	24.07 MW	22.65 AW	50070 AAW	SCBLS	10//99-12//99
	Sumter MSA, SC	S	20.43 MW	19.40 AW	42490 AAW	SCBLS	10//99-12//99
	South Dakota	S	26.33 MW	28.51 AW	59310 AAW	SDBLS	10//99-12//99
	Rapid City MSA, SD	S	31.77 MW	31.76 AW	66080 AAW	SDBLS	10//99-12//99
	Sioux Falls MSA, SD	S	32.85 MW	32.98 AW	68330 AAW	SDBLS	10//99-12//99
	Tennessee	S	25.17 MW	30.97 AW	64420 AAW	TNBLS	10//99-12//99
	Chattanooga MSA, TN-GA	S	29.15 MW	25.11 AW	60620 AAW	TNBLS	10//99-12//99
	Clarksville-Hopkinsville MSA, TN-KY	S	23.29 MW	22.34 AW	48450 AAW	TNBLS	10//99-12//99
	Jackson MSA, TN	S	24.87 MW	24.83 AW	51720 AAW	TNBLS	10//99-12//99
	Johnson City-Kingsport-Bristol MSA, TN-VA	S	25.41 MW	22.13 AW	52860 AAW	TNBLS	10//99-12//99
	Knoxville MSA, TN	S	24.16 MW	23.43 AW	50250 AAW	TNBLS	10//99-12//99
	Nashville MSA, TN	S	30.68 MW	26.26 AW	63820 AAW	TNBLS	10//99-12//99
	Texas	S	24.15 MW	24.77 AW	51520 AAW	TXBLS	10//99-12//99
	Abilene MSA, TX	S	28.67 MW	29.99 AW	59630 AAW	TXBLS	10//99-12//99
	Amarillo MSA, TX	S	24.94 MW	23.80 AW	51870 AAW	TXBLS	10//99-12//99
	Austin-San Marcos MSA, TX	S	24.48 MW	23.59 AW	50910 AAW	TXBLS	10//99-12//99
	Beaumont-Port Arthur MSA, TX	S	19.66 MW	18.83 AW	40890 AAW	TXBLS	10//99-12//99
	Brazoria PMSA, TX	S	26.84 MW	25.00 AW	55820 AAW	TXBLS	10//99-12//99
	Brownsville-Harlingen-San Benito MSA, TX	S	22.64 MW	22.07 AW	47100 AAW	TXBLS	10//99-12//99
	Bryan-College Station MSA, TX	S	21.47 MW	20.45 AW	44670 AAW	TXBLS	10//99-12//99
	Corpus Christi MSA, TX	S	31.20 MW	26.31 AW	64890 AAW	TXBLS	10//99-12//99
	Dallas PMSA, TX	S	26.31 MW	26.86 AW	54720 AAW	TXBLS	10//99-12//99
	El Paso MSA, TX	S	25.83 MW	28.19 AW	53730 AAW	TXBLS	10//99-12//99
	Fort Worth-Arlington PMSA, TX	S	26.62 MW	25.39 AW	55380 AAW	TXBLS	10//99-12//99
	Galveston-Texas City PMSA, TX	S	27.73 MW	23.51 AW	57680 AAW	TXBLS	10//99-12//99
	Houston PMSA, TX	S	24.24 MW	22.10 AW	50410 AAW	TXBLS	10//99-12//99
	Laredo MSA, TX	S	24.85 MW	23.27 AW	51680 AAW	TXBLS	10//99-12//99
	Lubbock MSA, TX	S	28.37 MW	28.96 AW	59020 AAW	TXBLS	10//99-12//99
	McAllen-Edinburg-Mission MSA, TX	S	23.19 MW	24.61 AW	48230 AAW	TXBLS	10//99-12//99
	Odessa-Midland MSA, TX	S	16.06 MW	16.17 AW	33400 AAW	TXBLS	10//99-12//99
	San Angelo MSA, TX	S	26.54 MW	25.08 AW	55200 AAW	TXBLS	10//99-12//99
	San Antonio MSA, TX	S	23.82 MW	22.95 AW	49540 AAW	TXBLS	10//99-12//99
	Sherman-Denison MSA, TX	S	15.05 MW	12.70 AW	31310 AAW	TXBLS	10//99-12//99
	Tyler MSA, TX	S	28.88 MW	25.24 AW	60080 AAW	TXBLS	10//99-12//99
	Victoria MSA, TX	S	25.21 MW	24.25 AW	52440 AAW	TXBLS	10//99-12//99
	Waco MSA, TX	S	24.28 MW	23.11 AW	50510 AAW	TXBLS	10//99-12//99
	Wichita Falls MSA, TX	S	19.62 MW	22.45 AW	40800 AAW	TXBLS	10//99-12//99
	Utah	S	26.95 MW	27.78 AW	57780 AAW	UTBLS	10//99-12//99
	Provo-Orem MSA, UT	S	32.25 MW	29.89 AW	67080 AAW	UTBLS	
	Salt Lake City-Ogden MSA, UT	S	27.65 MW	27.41 AW	57510 AAW	UTBLS	10//99-12//99
	Vermont	S	31.2 MW	31.52 AW	65550 AAW	VTBLS	10//99-12//99
	Burlington MSA, VT	S	38.25 MW	38.92 AW	79550 AAW	VTBLS	10//99-12//99
	Virginia	S	24.44 MW	25.97 AW	54010 AAW	VABLS	10//99-12//99
	Charlottesville MSA, VA	S	25.66 MW	23.17 AW	53380 AAW	VABLS	10//99-12//99
	Danville MSA, VA	S	17.76 MW	18.54 AW	36930 AAW	VABLS	10//99-12//99
	Lynchburg MSA, VA	S	28.46 MW	25.69 AW	59200 AAW	VABLS	10//99-12//99
	Norfolk-Virginia Beach-Newport News MSA, VA-NC	S	25.07 MW	24.49 AW	52140 AAW	VABLS	10//99-12//99
	Richmond-Petersburg MSA, VA	S	25.52 MW	22.92 AW	53090 AAW	VABLS	10//99-12//99
	Roanoke MSA, VA	S	22.60 MW	23.10 AW	47000 AAW	VABLS	10//99-12//99
	Washington	S	27.18 MW	31.57 AW	65660 AAW	WABLS	10//99-12//99
	Bellingham MSA, WA	S	23.76 MW	24.50 AW	49430 AAW	WABLS	10//99-12//99
	Bremerton PMSA, WA	S	26.85 MW	25.66 AW	55850 AAW	WABLS	10//99-12//99
	Seattle-Bellevue-Everett PMSA, WA	S	35.77 MW	31.23 AW	74410 AAW	WABLS	10//99-12//99
	Spokane MSA, WA	S	33.12 MW	27.43 AW	68890 AAW	WABLS	10//99-12//99
	Tacoma PMSA, WA	S	27.54 MW	25.49 AW	57290 AAW	WABLS	10//99-12//99

Occupation/Type/Industry	Location	Per	Low	Mid	High	Source	Date
Medical and Health Services Manager	Yakima MSA, WA	S	32.89 MW	28.68 AW	68420 AAW	WABLS	10//99-12//99
	West Virginia	S	19.46 MW	21.13 AW	43950 AAW	WVBLS	10//99-12//99
	Charleston MSA, WV	S	24.17 MW	20.36 AW	50270 AAW	WVBLS	10//99-12//99
	Huntington-Ashland MSA, WV-KY-OH	S	24.69 MW	22.14 AW	51360 AAW	WVBLS	10//99-12//99
	Parkersburg-Marietta MSA, WV-OH	S	18.50 MW	18.50 AW	38470 AAW	WVBLS	10//99-12//99
	Wheeling MSA, WV-OH	S	23.51 MW	21.39 AW	48900 AAW	WVBLS	10//99-12//99
	Wisconsin	S	24.48 MW	26.34 AW	54790 AAW	WIBLS	10//99-12//99
	Appleton-Oshkosh-Neenah MSA, WI	S	24.16 MW	24.55 AW	50260 AAW	WIBLS	10//99-12//99
	Eau Claire MSA, WI	S	23.06 MW	18.36 AW	47960 AAW	WIBLS	10//99-12//99
	Green Bay MSA, WI	S	23.69 MW	24.26 AW	49280 AAW	WIBLS	10//99-12//99
	Janesville-Beloit MSA, WI	S	20.44 MW	22.72 AW	42510 AAW	WIBLS	10//99-12//99
	Kenosha PMSA, WI	S	21.72 MW	20.28 AW	45170 AAW	WIBLS	10//99-12//99
	La Crosse MSA, WI-MN	S	19.48 MW	21.52 AW	40510 AAW	WIBLS	10//99-12//99
	Madison MSA, WI	S	31.04 MW	25.45 AW	64560 AAW	WIBLS	10//99-12//99
	Milwaukee-Waukesha PMSA, WI	S	26.87 MW	24.60 AW	55900 AAW	WIBLS	10//99-12//99
	Sheboygan MSA, WI	S	18.59 MW	18.02 AW	38670 AAW	WIBLS	10//99-12//99
	Wausau MSA, WI	S	25.77 MW	25.27 AW	53600 AAW	WIBLS	10//99-12//99
	Wyoming	S	20.13 MW	20.01 AW	41620 AAW	WYBLS	10//99-12//99
	Cheyenne MSA, WY	S	21.59 MW	18.57 AW	44910 AAW	WYBLS	10//99-12//99
	Puerto Rico	S	18.99 MW	24.13 AW	50190 AAW	PRBLS	10//99-12//99
	Arecibo PMSA, PR	S	23.68 MW	28.47 AW	49260 AAW	PRBLS	10//99-12//99
	Caguas PMSA, PR	S	25.09 MW	19.47 AW	52190 AAW	PRBLS	10//99-12//99
	Mayaguez MSA, PR	S	15.35 MW	15.07 AW	31920 AAW	PRBLS	10//99-12//99
	San Juan-Bayamon PMSA, PR	S	26.63 MW	20.24 AW	55390 AAW	PRBLS	10//99-12//99
	Guam	S	22.04 MW	24.03 AW	49980 AAW	GUBLS	10//99-12//99
Medical and Public Health Social Worker	Alabama	S	14.78 MW	15.24 AW	31690 AAW	ALBLS	10//99-12//99
	Alaska	S	14.85 MW	16.34 AW	33990 AAW	AKBLS	10//99-12//99
	Arizona	S	15.11 MW	16.43 AW	34170 AAW	AZBLS	10//99-12//99
	Arkansas	S	14.6 MW	15.14 AW	31480 AAW	ARBLS	10//99-12//99
	California	S	19.35 MW	20.67 AW	43000 AAW	CABLS	10//99-12//99
	Colorado	S	15.7 MW	16.70 AW	34750 AAW	COBLS	10//99-12//99
	Connecticut	S	20.14 MW	21.81 AW	45370 AAW	CTBLS	10//99-12//99
	Delaware	S	13.14 MW	13.69 AW	28470 AAW	DEBLS	10//99-12//99
	District of Columbia	S	16.88 MW	17.53 AW	36470 AAW	DCBLS	10//99-12//99
	Florida	S	13.91 MW	15.38 AW	31990 AAW	FLBLS	10//99-12//99
	Georgia	S	14.66 MW	14.82 AW	30830 AAW	GABLS	10//99-12//99
	Hawaii	S	18.17 MW	18.45 AW	38370 AAW	HIBLS	10//99-12//99
	Idaho	S	15.04 MW	15.27 AW	31750 AAW	IDBLS	10//99-12//99
	Illinois	S	14.9 MW	15.31 AW	31840 AAW	ILBLS	10//99-12//99
	Indiana	S	15.08 MW	15.35 AW	31940 AAW	INBLS	10//99-12//99
	Iowa	S	13.13 MW	14.16 AW	29460 AAW	IABLS	10//99-12//99
	Kansas	S	14.95 MW	15.51 AW	32260 AAW	KSBLS	10//99-12//99
	Kentucky	S	12.54 MW	12.91 AW	26850 AAW	KYBLS	10//99-12//99
	Louisiana	S	13.44 MW	14.35 AW	29850 AAW	LABLS	10//99-12//99
	Maine	S	16.94 MW	17.15 AW	35670 AAW	MEBLS	10//99-12//99
	Maryland	S	18.24 MW	18.10 AW	37650 AAW	MDBLS	10//99-12//99
	Massachusetts	S	18.32 MW	18.93 AW	39380 AAW	MABLS	10//99-12//99
	Michigan	S	17.59 MW	18.02 AW	37470 AAW	MIBLS	10//99-12//99
	Minnesota	S	15.62 MW	16.80 AW	34930 AAW	MNBLS	10//99-12//99
	Mississippi	S	15.88 MW	16.73 AW	34790 AAW	MSBLS	10//99-12//99
	Missouri	S	16.27 MW	17.01 AW	35390 AAW	MOBLS	10//99-12//99
	Montana	S	13.35 MW	13.26 AW	27580 AAW	MTBLS	10//99-12//99
	Nebraska	S	14.03 MW	14.80 AW	30780 AAW	NEBLS	10//99-12//99
	Nevada	S	20.56 MW	20.42 AW	42470 AAW	NVBLS	10//99-12//99
	New Hampshire	S	16.32 MW	16.75 AW	34840 AAW	NHBLS	10//99-12//99
	New Jersey	S	16.66 MW	16.10 AW	33490 AAW	NJBLS	10//99-12//99
	New Mexico	S	11.67 MW	14.63 AW	30430 AAW	NMBLS	10//99-12//99
	New York	S	18.78 MW	18.97 AW	39450 AAW	NYBLS	10//99-12//99
	North Carolina	S	16.49 MW	17.61 AW	36640 AAW	NCBLS	10//99-12//99
	North Dakota	S	12.74 MW	13.02 AW	27080 AAW	NDBLS	10//99-12//99
	Ohio	S	16.01 MW	16.63 AW	34580 AAW	OHBLS	10//99-12//99
	Oklahoma	S	13.92 MW	14.33 AW	29800 AAW	OKBLS	10//99-12//99
	Oregon	S	19.87 MW	19.45 AW	40460 AAW	ORBLS	10//99-12//99
	Pennsylvania	S	15.32 MW	15.89 AW	33060 AAW	PABLS	10//99-12//99
	Rhode Island	S	15.78 MW	16.81 AW	34970 AAW	RIBLS	10//99-12//99

AAW	Average annual wage	AOH	Average offered, high	ASH	Average starting, high
AE	Average entry wage	AOL	Average offered, low	ASL	Average starting, low
AEX	Average experienced wage	APH	Average pay, high range	AW	Average wage paid
AO	Average offered	APL	Average pay, low range	FQ	First quartile wage

H	Hourly	M	Monthly
HI	Highest wage paid	MTC	Median total compensation
HR	High end range	MW	Median wage paid
LR	Low end range	SQ	Second quartile wage

S	Special: hourly and annual
TQ	Third quartile wage
W	Weekly
Y	Yearly

Occupation/Type/Industry	Location	Per	Low	Mid	High	Source	Date
Medical and Public Health Social Worker							
	South Carolina	S	14.83 MW	16.59 AW	34510 AAW	SCBLS	10//99-12//99
	South Dakota	S	14.19 MW	15.03 AW	31270 AAW	SDBLS	10//99-12//99
	Tennessee	S	14.38 MW	14.86 AW	30900 AAW	TNBLS	10//99-12//99
	Texas	S	14.73 MW	15.60 AW	32450 AAW	TXBLS	10//99-12//99
	Utah	S	15.89 MW	16.64 AW	34610 AAW	UTBLS	10//99-12//99
	Vermont	S	16.66 MW	17.23 AW	35830 AAW	VTBLS	10//99-12//99
	Virginia	S	15.4 MW	16.35 AW	34010 AAW	VABLS	10//99-12//99
	Washington	S	17.53 MW	17.80 AW	37010 AAW	WABLS	10//99-12//99
	West Virginia	S	11.73 MW	11.98 AW	24930 AAW	WVBLS	10//99-12//99
	Wisconsin	S	15.91 MW	17.17 AW	35700 AAW	WIBLS	10//99-12//99
	Wyoming	S	14.15 MW	16.24 AW	33780 AAW	WYBLS	10//99-12//99
	Puerto Rico	S	8.54 MW	8.96 AW	18640 AAW	PRBLS	10//99-12//99
Medical Appliance Technician	Alabama	S	12.97 MW	14.82 AW	30830 AAW	ALBLS	10//99-12//99
	Arizona	S	12.02 MW	12.53 AW	26050 AAW	AZBLS	10//99-12//99
	California	S	9.96 MW	13.13 AW	27310 AAW	CABLS	10//99-12//99
	Colorado	S	9.87 MW	10.47 AW	21780 AAW	COBLS	10//99-12//99
	Connecticut	S	10.73 MW	10.83 AW	22520 AAW	CTBLS	10//99-12//99
	Florida	S	8.84 MW	11.39 AW	23690 AAW	FLBLS	10//99-12//99
	Georgia	S	8.28 MW	9.20 AW	19140 AAW	GABLS	10//99-12//99
	Idaho	S	9.78 MW	11.06 AW	23000 AAW	IDBLS	10//99-12//99
	Indiana	S	10.54 MW	11.83 AW	24610 AAW	INBLS	10//99-12//99
	Maine	S	17.4 MW	17.27 AW	35930 AAW	MEBLS	10//99-12//99
	Maryland	S	11.35 MW	13.38 AW	27830 AAW	MDBLS	10//99-12//99
	Massachusetts	S	14.8 MW	14.90 AW	31000 AAW	MABLS	10//99-12//99
	Michigan	S	19.49 MW	21.65 AW	45040 AAW	MIBLS	10//99-12//99
	Mississippi	S	14 MW	14.04 AW	29210 AAW	MSBLS	10//99-12//99
	Missouri	S	10.71 MW	11.83 AW	24610 AAW	MOBLS	10//99-12//99
	New Jersey	S	15.25 MW	16.43 AW	34170 AAW	NJBLS	10//99-12//99
	New York	S	12.44 MW	13.45 AW	27970 AAW	NYBLS	10//99-12//99
	Ohio	S	12.12 MW	13.13 AW	27320 AAW	OHBLS	10//99-12//99
	Oklahoma	S	10.21 MW	11.08 AW	23050 AAW	OKBLS	10//99-12//99
	Oregon	S	13.24 MW	14.75 AW	30680 AAW	ORBLS	10//99-12//99
	Pennsylvania	S	13.43 MW	15.55 AW	32330 AAW	PABLS	10//99-12//99
	Tennessee	S	14.03 MW	16.23 AW	33770 AAW	TNBLS	10//99-12//99
	Texas	S	11.47 MW	13.26 AW	27580 AAW	TXBLS	10//99-12//99
	Virginia	S	13.92 MW	18.43 AW	38330 AAW	VABLS	10//99-12//99
	Washington	S	11.13 MW	11.81 AW	24560 AAW	WABLS	10//99-12//99
	Wisconsin	S	10.73 MW	13.96 AW	29030 AAW	WIBLS	10//99-12//99
Medical Assistant	Alabama	S	9.69 MW	10.12 AW	21060 AAW	ALBLS	10//99-12//99
	Alaska	S	14.56 MW	16.37 AW	34050 AAW	AKBLS	10//99-12//99
	Arizona	S	9.58 MW	9.92 AW	20640 AAW	AZBLS	10//99-12//99
	Arkansas	S	8.77 MW	8.46 AW	17590 AAW	ARBLS	10//99-12//99
	California	S	12.62 MW	12.73 AW	26470 AAW	CABLS	10//99-12//99
	Colorado	S	10.74 MW	10.94 AW	22750 AAW	COBLS	10//99-12//99
	Connecticut	S	12.56 MW	12.93 AW	26900 AAW	CTBLS	10//99-12//99
	Delaware	S	9.99 MW	10.55 AW	21950 AAW	DEBLS	10//99-12//99
	District of Columbia	S	11.41 MW	11.52 AW	23960 AAW	DCBLS	10//99-12//99
	Florida	S	9.98 MW	10.32 AW	21470 AAW	FLBLS	10//99-12//99
	Georgia	S	10.56 MW	10.59 AW	22020 AAW	GABLS	10//99-12//99
	Hawaii	S	12.14 MW	12.20 AW	25370 AAW	HIBLS	10//99-12//99
	Idaho	S	10.44 MW	10.49 AW	21810 AAW	IDBLS	10//99-12//99
	Illinois	S	9.31 MW	9.78 AW	20330 AAW	ILBLS	10//99-12//99
	Indiana	S	9.98 MW	10.28 AW	21390 AAW	INBLS	10//99-12//99
	Iowa	S	9.8 MW	10.01 AW	20820 AAW	IABLS	10//99-12//99
	Kansas	S	9.29 MW	9.44 AW	19640 AAW	KSBLS	10//99-12//99
	Kentucky	S	9.79 MW	10.27 AW	21370 AAW	KYBLS	10//99-12//99
	Louisiana	S	9.03 MW	9.26 AW	19270 AAW	LABLS	10//99-12//99
	Maine	S	11.56 MW	11.63 AW	24200 AAW	MEBLS	10//99-12//99
	Maryland	S	11.74 MW	11.91 AW	24780 AAW	MDBLS	10//99-12//99
	Massachusetts	S	12.02 MW	12.10 AW	25160 AAW	MABLS	10//99-12//99
	Michigan	S	10.37 MW	10.52 AW	21880 AAW	MIBLS	10//99-12//99
	Minnesota	S	11.62 MW	11.43 AW	23770 AAW	MNBLS	10//99-12//99
	Mississippi	S	8.92 MW	8.77 AW	18230 AAW	MSBLS	10//99-12//99
	Missouri	S	9.95 MW	9.99 AW	20770 AAW	MOBLS	10//99-12//99
	Montana	S	9.93 MW	10.39 AW	21610 AAW	MTBLS	10//99-12//99
	Nebraska	S	9.86 MW	9.98 AW	20760 AAW	NEBLS	10//99-12//99
	Nevada	S	11.26 MW	12.12 AW	25200 AAW	NVBLS	10//99-12//99
	New Hampshire	S	10.33 MW	10.46 AW	21770 AAW	NHBLS	10//99-12//99
	New Jersey	S	11.6 MW	11.93 AW	24810 AAW	NJBLS	10//99-12//99

Occupation/Type/Industry	Location	Per	Low	Mid	High	Source	Date
Medical Assistant	New Mexico	S	9.27 MW	9.17 AW	19060 AAW	NMBLS	10//99-12//99
	New York	S	10.6 MW	10.75 AW	22350 AAW	NYBLS	10//99-12//99
	North Carolina	S	11.24 MW	11.60 AW	24120 AAW	NCBLS	10//99-12//99
	North Dakota	S	8.74 MW	8.97 AW	18650 AAW	NDBLS	10//99-12//99
	Ohio	S	10.04 MW	10.23 AW	21280 AAW	OHBLS	10//99-12//99
	Oklahoma	S	8.45 MW	8.90 AW	18520 AAW	OKBLS	10//99-12//99
	Oregon	S	11.87 MW	11.78 AW	24500 AAW	ORBLS	10//99-12//99
	Pennsylvania	S	10.65 MW	10.87 AW	22610 AAW	PABLS	10//99-12//99
	Rhode Island	S	10.16 MW	10.28 AW	21380 AAW	RIBLS	10//99-12//99
	South Carolina	S	9.41 MW	10.21 AW	21230 AAW	SCBLS	10//99-12//99
	South Dakota	S	9.4 MW	9.41 AW	19570 AAW	SDBLS	10//99-12//99
	Tennessee	S	9.94 MW	10.11 AW	21020 AAW	TNBLS	10//99-12//99
	Texas	S	9.29 MW	9.45 AW	19650 AAW	TXBLS	10//99-12//99
	Utah	S	8.73 MW	8.80 AW	18310 AAW	UTBLS	10//99-12//99
	Vermont	S	12.12 MW	12.02 AW	25000 AAW	VTBLS	10//99-12//99
	Virginia	S	9.35 MW	9.94 AW	20680 AAW	VABLS	10//99-12//99
	Washington	S	12.54 MW	12.62 AW	26250 AAW	WABLS	10//99-12//99
	West Virginia	S	6.75 MW	7.16 AW	14900 AAW	WVBLS	10//99-12//99
	Wisconsin	S	10.91 MW	11.32 AW	23540 AAW	WIBLS	10//99-12//99
	Wyoming	S	8.58 MW	8.93 AW	18580 AAW	WYBLS	10//99-12//99
	Puerto Rico	S	7.87 MW	9.30 AW	19350 AAW	PRBLS	10//99-12//99
	Virgin Islands	S	9.21 MW	9.83 AW	20440 AAW	VIBLS	10//99-12//99
	Guam	S	9.89 MW	10.20 AW	21210 AAW	GUBLS	10//99-12//99
Medical Director							
Behavioral Health Organization	United States	Y	104352 APL	133801 AW	148427 APH	ADAW	2000
Hospital	United States	Y		173300 MW		HHN	2000
Medical Equipment Preparer	Alabama	S	7.96 MW	8.47 AW	17620 AAW	ALBLS	10//99-12//99
	Alaska	S	14.53 MW	14.61 AW	30400 AAW	AKBLS	10//99-12//99
	Arizona	S	8.37 MW	9.45 AW	19660 AAW	AZBLS	10//99-12//99
	Arkansas	S	8.98 MW	10.57 AW	21980 AAW	ARBLS	10//99-12//99
	California	S	10.58 MW	11.26 AW	23410 AAW	CABLS	10//99-12//99
	Colorado	S	11.27 MW	11.55 AW	24030 AAW	COBLS	10//99-12//99
	Connecticut	S	12.16 MW	12.33 AW	25650 AAW	CTBLS	10//99-12//99
	Delaware	S	11.8 MW	12.43 AW	25860 AAW	DEBLS	10//99-12//99
	District of Columbia	S	10.83 MW	10.87 AW	22600 AAW	DCBLS	10//99-12//99
	Florida	S	8.81 MW	9.01 AW	18740 AAW	FLBLS	10//99-12//99
	Georgia	S	9.27 MW	9.10 AW	18930 AAW	GABLS	10//99-12//99
	Hawaii	S	10.58 MW	10.79 AW	22450 AAW	HIBLS	10//99-12//99
	Illinois	S	8.74 MW	9.06 AW	18840 AAW	ILBLS	10//99-12//99
	Indiana	S	8.9 MW	9.25 AW	19230 AAW	INBLS	10//99-12//99
	Iowa	S	8.22 MW	8.31 AW	17280 AAW	IABLS	10//99-12//99
	Kansas	S	8.11 MW	10.17 AW	21150 AAW	KSBLS	10//99-12//99
	Kentucky	S	9.91 MW	9.84 AW	20470 AAW	KYBLS	10//99-12//99
	Louisiana	S	8.44 MW	8.92 AW	18540 AAW	LABLS	10//99-12//99
	Maine	S	9.98 MW	9.98 AW	20750 AAW	MEBLS	10//99-12//99
	Maryland	S	12.91 MW	11.91 AW	24780 AAW	MDBLS	10//99-12//99
	Massachusetts	S	11.12 MW	11.30 AW	23510 AAW	MABLS	10//99-12//99
	Michigan	S	10.66 MW	10.97 AW	22820 AAW	MIBLS	10//99-12//99
	Minnesota	S	10.48 MW	10.19 AW	21190 AAW	MNBLS	10//99-12//99
	Mississippi	S	8.25 MW	8.46 AW	17600 AAW	MSBLS	10//99-12//99
	Missouri	S	9 MW	10.42 AW	21680 AAW	MOBLS	10//99-12//99
	Montana	S	8.5 MW	8.58 AW	17850 AAW	MTBLS	10//99-12//99
	Nebraska	S	9.37 MW	9.31 AW	19360 AAW	NEBLS	10//99-12//99
	Nevada	S	11.73 MW	11.66 AW	24250 AAW	NVBLS	10//99-12//99
	New Hampshire	S	11.22 MW	10.84 AW	22550 AAW	NHBLS	10//99-12//99
	New Jersey	S	10.88 MW	11.30 AW	23510 AAW	NJBLS	10//99-12//99
	New Mexico	S	9.81 MW	9.78 AW	20350 AAW	NMBLS	10//99-12//99
	New York	S	10.72 MW	11.16 AW	23220 AAW	NYBLS	10//99-12//99
	North Carolina	S	9.77 MW	10.14 AW	21090 AAW	NCBLS	10//99-12//99
	Ohio	S	10 MW	10.43 AW	21700 AAW	OHBLS	10//99-12//99
	Oklahoma	S	8.38 MW	8.73 AW	18170 AAW	OKBLS	10//99-12//99
	Oregon	S	12.52 MW	12.60 AW	26200 AAW	ORBLS	10//99-12//99
	Pennsylvania	S	11.58 MW	13.17 AW	27400 AAW	PABLS	10//99-12//99
	Rhode Island	S	10.3 MW	10.77 AW	22400 AAW	RIBLS	10//99-12//99
	South Carolina	S	8.31 MW	10.13 AW	21070 AAW	SCBLS	10//99-12//99
	Tennessee	S	9.75 MW	9.93 AW	20650 AAW	TNBLS	10//99-12//99
	Texas	S	7.77 MW	8.07 AW	16770 AAW	TXBLS	10//99-12//99
	Utah	S	8.62 MW	8.92 AW	18560 AAW	UTBLS	10//99-12//99
	Vermont	S	10.15 MW	10.53 AW	21900 AAW	VTBLS	10//99-12//99
	Virginia	S	9.2 MW	9.17 AW	19070 AAW	VABLS	10//99-12//99
	Washington	S	10.98 MW	11.05 AW	22990 AAW	WABLS	10//99-12//99

Occupation/Type/Industry	Location	Per	Low	Mid	High	Source	Date
Medical Equipment Preparer	West Virginia	S	9.84 MW	10.17 AW	21160 AAW	WVBLS	10//99-12//99
	Wisconsin	S	8.47 MW	8.84 AW	18380 AAW	WIBLS	10//99-12//99
	Wyoming	S	9.24 MW	9.43 AW	19610 AAW	WYBLS	10//99-12//99
Medical Equipment Repairer	Alabama	S	14.75 MW	15.30 AW	31830 AAW	ALBLS	10//99-12//99
	Arizona	S	12.17 MW	13.72 AW	28540 AAW	AZBLS	10//99-12//99
	Arkansas	S	12.5 MW	15.38 AW	31990 AAW	ARBLS	10//99-12//99
	California	S	16.88 MW	18.78 AW	39060 AAW	CABLS	10//99-12//99
	Colorado	S	18.71 MW	18.76 AW	39030 AAW	COBLS	10//99-12//99
	Connecticut	S	20.71 MW	21.15 AW	43980 AAW	CTBLS	10//99-12//99
	Florida	S	15.44 MW	16.71 AW	34760 AAW	FLBLS	10//99-12//99
	Georgia	S	15.56 MW	16.30 AW	33910 AAW	GABLS	10//99-12//99
	Hawaii	S	22.41 MW	25.47 AW	52980 AAW	HIBLS	10//99-12//99
	Illinois	S	17.31 MW	16.86 AW	35060 AAW	ILBLS	10//99-12//99
	Indiana	S	16.84 MW	16.76 AW	34870 AAW	INBLS	10//99-12//99
	Iowa	S	17.25 MW	18.43 AW	38340 AAW	IABLS	10//99-12//99
	Kansas	S	15.76 MW	16.31 AW	33920 AAW	KSBLS	10//99-12//99
	Kentucky	S	12.97 MW	12.81 AW	26630 AAW	KYBLS	10//99-12//99
	Louisiana	S	14.26 MW	15.09 AW	31400 AAW	LABLS	10//99-12//99
	Maryland	S	17.4 MW	17.33 AW	36050 AAW	MDBLS	10//99-12//99
	Massachusetts	S	15.72 MW	16.96 AW	35270 AAW	MABLS	10//99-12//99
	Michigan	S	15.94 MW	16.24 AW	33770 AAW	MIBLS	10//99-12//99
	Minnesota	S	16.57 MW	16.25 AW	33800 AAW	MNBLS	10//99-12//99
	Mississippi	S	15.18 MW	16.17 AW	33640 AAW	MSBLS	10//99-12//99
	Missouri	S	17.8 MW	18.41 AW	38290 AAW	MOBLS	10//99-12//99
	Montana	S	14.76 MW	14.44 AW	30040 AAW	MTBLS	10//99-12//99
	Nebraska	S	13.37 MW	13.96 AW	29030 AAW	NEBLS	10//99-12//99
	Nevada	S	15.23 MW	14.97 AW	31130 AAW	NVBLS	10//99-12//99
	New Hampshire	S	15.97 MW	16.42 AW	34160 AAW	NHBLS	10//99-12//99
	New Jersey	S	19.15 MW	20.88 AW	43430 AAW	NJBLS	10//99-12//99
	New Mexico	S	13.27 MW	13.60 AW	28280 AAW	NMBLS	10//99-12//99
	New York	S	14.45 MW	15.51 AW	32260 AAW	NYBLS	10//99-12//99
	North Carolina	S	16.14 MW	17.49 AW	36370 AAW	NCBLS	10//99-12//99
	Ohio	S	20.15 MW	20.00 AW	41590 AAW	OHBLS	10//99-12//99
	Oklahoma	S	18.6 MW	18.38 AW	38220 AAW	OKBLS	10//99-12//99
	Oregon	S	16.54 MW	17.08 AW	35530 AAW	ORBLS	10//99-12//99
	Pennsylvania	S	16.96 MW	17.39 AW	36180 AAW	PABLS	10//99-12//99
	Rhode Island	S	15.18 MW	16.05 AW	33390 AAW	RIBLS	10//99-12//99
	South Carolina	S	15.69 MW	15.45 AW	32130 AAW	SCBLS	10//99-12//99
	South Dakota	S	12.97 MW	14.13 AW	29380 AAW	SDBLS	10//99-12//99
	Tennessee	S	16.63 MW	17.16 AW	35700 AAW	TNBLS	10//99-12//99
	Texas	S	13.61 MW	14.25 AW	29630 AAW	TXBLS	10//99-12//99
	Utah	S	12.64 MW	13.42 AW	27910 AAW	UTBLS	10//99-12//99
	Virginia	S	16.68 MW	16.99 AW	35340 AAW	VABLS	10//99-12//99
	Washington	S	17.35 MW	17.34 AW	36060 AAW	WABLS	10//99-12//99
	West Virginia	S	17.03 MW	15.59 AW	32420 AAW	WVBLS	10//99-12//99
	Wisconsin	S	19.02 MW	19.63 AW	40820 AAW	WIBLS	10//99-12//99
	Puerto Rico	S	10.79 MW	14.45 AW	30060 AAW	PRBLS	10//99-12//99
Medical Laboratory Technician	Atlantic	H	10.00 AE	12.10 AW	14.70 APH	LABMED2	1998
	East North Central	H	10.50 AE	13.00 AW	15.00 APH	LABMED2	1998
	Far West	H	10.60 AE	13.00 AW	16.10 APH	LABMED2	1998
	Northeast	H	11.40 AE	13.60 AW	15.50 APH	LABMED2	1998
	West North Central	H	10.40 AE	12.50 AW	14.40 APH	LABMED2	1998
	West South Central	H	10.30 AE	12.60 AW	14.30 APH	LABMED2	1998
Medical Receptionist	San Diego County, CA	Y		21427 AW		ERDGE	1998
Medical Record and Health Information Technician	Alabama	S	9.7 MW	10.14 AW	21080 AAW	ALBLS	10//99-12//99
	Arizona	S	10.93 MW	11.54 AW	24010 AAW	AZBLS	10//99-12//99
	Arkansas	S	10.48 MW	10.75 AW	22360 AAW	ARBLS	10//99-12//99
	California	S	12.59 MW	12.92 AW	26870 AAW	CABLS	10//99-12//99
	Connecticut	S	13.39 MW	14.71 AW	30600 AAW	CTBLS	10//99-12//99
	Delaware	S	11.24 MW	11.32 AW	23540 AAW	DEBLS	10//99-12//99
	District of Columbia	S	12.01 MW	12.64 AW	26280 AAW	DCBLS	10//99-12//99
	Florida	S	10.03 MW	11.03 AW	22950 AAW	FLBLS	10//99-12//99
	Georgia	S	10.15 MW	10.74 AW	22340 AAW	GABLS	10//99-12//99
	Hawaii	S	12.89 MW	13.39 AW	27850 AAW	HIBLS	10//99-12//99
	Idaho	S	9.75 MW	10.01 AW	20820 AAW	IDBLS	10//99-12//99
	Illinois	S	9.88 MW	10.71 AW	22270 AAW	ILBLS	10//99-12//99
	Indiana	S	9.84 MW	10.46 AW	21760 AAW	INBLS	10//99-12//99
	Iowa	S	10.12 MW	11.01 AW	22910 AAW	IABLS	10//99-12//99

AAW Average annual wage	AOH Average offered, high	ASH Average starting, high	H Hourly	M Monthly	S Special: hourly and annual
AE Average entry wage	AOL Average offered, low	ASL Average starting, low	HI Highest wage paid	MTC Median total compensation	TQ Third quartile wage
AEX Average experienced wage	APH Average pay, high range	AW Average wage paid	HR High end range	MW Median wage paid	W Weekly
AO Average offered	APL Average pay, low range	FQ First quartile wage	LR Low end range	SQ Second quartile wage	Y Yearly

Occupation/Type/Industry	Location	Per	Low	Mid	High	Source	Date
Medical Record and Health Information Technician	Kansas	S	9.02 MW	10.12 AW	21050 AAW	KSBLS	10//99-12//99
	Kentucky	S	9.82 MW	10.21 AW	21230 AAW	KYBLS	10//99-12//99
	Louisiana	S	9.05 MW	9.77 AW	20320 AAW	LABLS	10//99-12//99
	Maine	S	9.74 MW	10.42 AW	21670 AAW	MEBLS	10//99-12//99
	Maryland	S	11.76 MW	12.40 AW	25780 AAW	MDBLS	10//99-12//99
	Massachusetts	S	11.18 MW	11.69 AW	24310 AAW	MABLS	10//99-12//99
	Michigan	S	10.79 MW	11.48 AW	23870 AAW	MIBLS	10//99-12//99
	Minnesota	S	10.3 MW	10.94 AW	22760 AAW	MNBLS	10//99-12//99
	Mississippi	S	9.17 MW	9.83 AW	20440 AAW	MSBLS	10//99-12//99
	Missouri	S	8.96 MW	9.59 AW	19960 AAW	MOBLS	10//99-12//99
	Montana	S	9.09 MW	10.02 AW	20830 AAW	MTBLS	10//99-12//99
	Nebraska	S	10.51 MW	11.62 AW	24170 AAW	NEBLS	10//99-12//99
	Nevada	S	11.31 MW	12.36 AW	25720 AAW	NVBLS	10//99-12//99
	New Hampshire	S	11.22 MW	11.49 AW	23890 AAW	NHBLS	10//99-12//99
	New Jersey	S	12.58 MW	13.25 AW	27560 AAW	NJBLS	10//99-12//99
	New Mexico	S	9.55 MW	10.02 AW	20830 AAW	NMBLS	10//99-12//99
	New York	S	12.54 MW	12.53 AW	26070 AAW	NYBLS	10//99-12//99
	North Carolina	S	9.65 MW	10.15 AW	21110 AAW	NCBLS	10//99-12//99
	North Dakota	S	9.05 MW	9.40 AW	19560 AAW	NDBLS	10//99-12//99
	Ohio	S	10.48 MW	11.32 AW	23540 AAW	OHBLS	10//99-12//99
	Oklahoma	S	8.8 MW	9.46 AW	19670 AAW	OKBLS	10//99-12//99
	Oregon	S	10.6 MW	11.46 AW	23840 AAW	ORBLS	10//99-12//99
	Pennsylvania	S	10.11 MW	10.67 AW	22190 AAW	PABLS	10//99-12//99
	Rhode Island	S	9.93 MW	10.88 AW	22620 AAW	RIBLS	10//99-12//99
	South Carolina	S	10.33 MW	11.68 AW	24300 AAW	SCBLS	10//99-12//99
	South Dakota	S	9.83 MW	10.69 AW	22240 AAW	SDBLS	10//99-12//99
	Tennessee	S	9.7 MW	10.19 AW	21200 AAW	TNBLS	10//99-12//99
	Texas	S	9 MW	9.92 AW	20620 AAW	TXBLS	10//99-12//99
	Utah	S	8.89 MW	9.20 AW	19130 AAW	UTBLS	10//99-12//99
	Vermont	S	14.15 MW	15.40 AW	32040 AAW	VTBLS	10//99-12//99
	Virginia	S	10.02 MW	10.48 AW	21790 AAW	VABLS	10//99-12//99
	Washington	S	11.8 MW	12.07 AW	25100 AAW	WABLS	10//99-12//99
	West Virginia	S	8.22 MW	8.61 AW	17910 AAW	WVBLS	10//99-12//99
	Wisconsin	S	9.4 MW	9.86 AW	20510 AAW	WIBLS	10//99-12//99
	Wyoming	S	10 MW	10.40 AW	21630 AAW	WYBLS	10//99-12//99
	Puerto Rico	S	6.6 MW	6.89 AW	14340 AAW	PRBLS	10//99-12//99
	Guam	S	11.22 MW	11.20 AW	23290 AAW	GUBLS	10//99-12//99
Medical Records Technician							
Hospital	Florida	H			13.77 HI	BJTAMP	2000
Medical Scientist							
Except Epidemiologist	Alabama	S	20.2 MW	22.38 AW	46550 AAW	ALBLS	10//99-12//99
Except Epidemiologist	Arizona	S	24.55 MW	25.52 AW	53080 AAW	AZBLS	10//99-12//99
Except Epidemiologist	Phoenix-Mesa MSA, AZ	S	25.96 MW	24.71 AW	54000 AAW	AZBLS	10//99-12//99
Except Epidemiologist	Arkansas	S	23.88 MW	25.56 AW	53160 AAW	ARBLS	10//99-12//99
Except Epidemiologist	Little Rock-North Little Rock MSA, AR	S	21.03 MW	20.98 AW	43740 AAW	ARBLS	10//99-12//99
Except Epidemiologist	California	S	20.75 MW	24.76 AW	51500 AAW	CABLS	10//99-12//99
Except Epidemiologist	Oakland PMSA, CA	S	35.42 MW	37.02 AW	73680 AAW	CABLS	10//99-12//99
Except Epidemiologist	Riverside-San Bernardino PMSA, CA	S	20.16 MW	19.55 AW	41930 AAW	CABLS	10//99-12//99
Except Epidemiologist	San Diego MSA, CA	S	34.00 MW	33.40 AW	70720 AAW	CABLS	10//99-12//99
Except Epidemiologist	San Francisco PMSA, CA	S	43.02 MW	40.89 AW	89480 AAW	CABLS	10//99-12//99
Except Epidemiologist	San Jose PMSA, CA	S	34.96 MW	34.42 AW	72710 AAW	CABLS	10//99-12//99
Except Epidemiologist	Santa Barbara-Santa Maria-Lompoc MSA, CA	S	28.73 MW	26.25 AW	59750 AAW	CABLS	10//99-12//99
Except Epidemiologist	Colorado	S	24.06 MW	28.28 AW	58820 AAW	COBLS	10//99-12//99
Except Epidemiologist	Denver PMSA, CO	S	29.67 MW	24.64 AW	61710 AAW	COBLS	10//99-12//99
Except Epidemiologist	Connecticut	S	21.32 MW	26.04 AW	54160 AAW	CTBLS	10//99-12//99
Except Epidemiologist	New Haven-Meriden PMSA, CT	S	26.40 MW	20.85 AW	54920 AAW	CTBLS	10//99-12//99
Except Epidemiologist	District of Columbia	S	32.03 MW	34.23 AW	71200 AAW	DCBLS	10//99-12//99
Except Epidemiologist	Washington PMSA, DC-MD-VA-WV	S	32.71 MW	31.55 AW	68030 AAW	DCBLS	10//99-12//99
Except Epidemiologist	Florida	S	26.29 MW	28.21 AW	58680 AAW	FLBLS	10//99-12//99
Except Epidemiologist	Fort Lauderdale PMSA, FL	S	25.16 MW	24.75 AW	52330 AAW	FLBLS	10//99-12//99
Except Epidemiologist	Miami PMSA, FL	S	25.48 MW	25.09 AW	52990 AAW	FLBLS	10//99-12//99
Except Epidemiologist	Orlando MSA, FL	S	27.64 MW	24.96 AW	57490 AAW	FLBLS	10//99-12//99
Except Epidemiologist	Tampa-St. Petersburg-Clearwater MSA, FL	S	32.54 MW	30.12 AW	67670 AAW	FLBLS	10//99-12//99

AAW	Average annual wage	AOH	Average offered, high	ASH	Average starting, high	H	Hourly	M	Monthly	S	Special: hourly and annual
AE	Average entry wage	AOL	Average offered, low	ASL	Average starting, low	HI	Highest wage paid	MTC	Median total compensation	TQ	Third quartile wage
AEX	Average experienced wage	APH	Average pay, high range	AW	Average wage paid	HR	High end range	MW	Median wage paid	W	Weekly
AO	Average offered	APL	Average pay, low range	FQ	First quartile wage	LR	Low end range	SQ	Second quartile wage	Y	Yearly

Occupation/Type/Industry	Location	Per	Low	Mid	High	Source	Date
Medical Scientist							
Except Epidemiologist	Georgia	S	20.55 MW	23.80 AW	49490 AAW	GABLS	10//99-12//99
Except Epidemiologist	Atlanta MSA, GA	S	23.11 MW	20.20 AW	48080 AAW	GABLS	10//99-12//99
Except Epidemiologist	Illinois	S	26.01 MW	28.66 AW	59610 AAW	ILBLS	10//99-12//99
Except Epidemiologist	Chicago PMSA, IL	S	30.70 MW	30.69 AW	63860 AAW	ILBLS	10//99-12//99
Except Epidemiologist	Baltimore PMSA, MD	S	25.76 MW	24.65 AW	53570 AAW	MDBLS	10//99-12//99
Except Epidemiologist	Massachusetts	S	33.56 MW	34.91 AW	72600 AAW	MABLS	10//99-12//99
Except Epidemiologist	Boston PMSA, MA-NH	S	34.89 MW	33.24 AW	72560 AAW	MABLS	10//99-12//99
Except Epidemiologist	Minnesota	S	22.31 MW	22.79 AW	47390 AAW	MNBLS	10//99-12//99
Except Epidemiologist	Minneapolis-St. Paul MSA, MN-WI	S	21.71 MW	21.64 AW	45160 AAW	MNBLS	10//99-12//99
Except Epidemiologist	Mississippi	S	15.93 MW	18.38 AW	38220 AAW	MSBLS	10//99-12//99
Except Epidemiologist	Nebraska	S	14.62 MW	16.79 AW	34910 AAW	NEBLS	10//99-12//99
Except Epidemiologist	Omaha MSA, NE-IA	S	14.87 MW	13.84 AW	30920 AAW	NEBLS	10//99-12//99
Except Epidemiologist	New Mexico	S	28.27 MW	31.20 AW	64900 AAW	NMBLS	10//99-12//99
Except Epidemiologist	Albuquerque MSA, NM	S	31.22 MW	28.33 AW	64950 AAW	NMBLS	10//99-12//99
Except Epidemiologist	New York	S	20.8 MW	23.47 AW	48810 AAW	NYBLS	10//99-12//99
Except Epidemiologist	Nassau-Suffolk PMSA, NY	S	25.75 MW	23.89 AW	53560 AAW	NYBLS	10//99-12//99
Except Epidemiologist	New York PMSA, NY	S	22.93 MW	20.30 AW	47690 AAW	NYBLS	10//99-12//99
Except Epidemiologist	North Carolina	S	24.84 MW	26.26 AW	54610 AAW	NCBLS	10//99-12//99
Except Epidemiologist	Raleigh-Durham-Chapel Hill MSA, NC	S	27.22 MW	25.46 AW	56620 AAW	NCBLS	10//99-12//99
Except Epidemiologist	North Dakota	S	27.25 MW	28.90 AW	60120 AAW	NDBLS	10//99-12//99
Except Epidemiologist	Oregon	S	19.9 MW	22.09 AW	45940 AAW	ORBLS	10//99-12//99
Except Epidemiologist	Portland-Vancouver PMSA, OR-WA	S	21.78 MW	19.89 AW	45300 AAW	ORBLS	10//99-12//99
Except Epidemiologist	Pennsylvania	S	16.75 MW	21.46 AW	44630 AAW	PABLS	10//99-12//99
Except Epidemiologist	Philadelphia PMSA, PA-NJ	S	19.57 MW	16.21 AW	40710 AAW	PABLS	10//99-12//99
Except Epidemiologist	Tennessee	S	19.13 MW	20.69 AW	43030 AAW	TNBLS	10//99-12//99
Except Epidemiologist	Memphis MSA, TN-AR-MS	S	20.44 MW	18.82 AW	42510 AAW	MSBLS	10//99-12//99
Except Epidemiologist	Texas	S	21.13 MW	23.53 AW	48940 AAW	TXBLS	10//99-12//99
Except Epidemiologist	Austin-San Marcos MSA, TX	S	24.16 MW	23.09 AW	50250 AAW	TXBLS	10//99-12//99
Except Epidemiologist	Dallas PMSA, TX	S	19.78 MW	16.23 AW	41140 AAW	TXBLS	10//99-12//99
Except Epidemiologist	Houston PMSA, TX	S	23.14 MW	21.64 AW	48130 AAW	TXBLS	10//99-12//99
Except Epidemiologist	San Antonio MSA, TX	S	30.88 MW	28.70 AW	64240 AAW	TXBLS	10//99-12//99
Except Epidemiologist	Virginia	S	27.41 MW	29.51 AW	61380 AAW	VABLS	10//99-12//99
Except Epidemiologist	Richmond-Petersburg MSA, VA	S	50.67 MW	52.54 AW	105400 AAW	VABLS	10//99-12//99
Except Epidemiologist	Washington	S	27.13 MW	28.52 AW	59330 AAW	WABLS	10//99-12//99
Except Epidemiologist	Seattle-Bellevue-Everett PMSA, WA	S	28.41 MW	27.99 AW	59100 AAW	WABLS	10//99-12//99
Except Epidemiologist	Tacoma PMSA, WA	S	33.14 MW	25.73 AW	68940 AAW	WABLS	10//99-12//99
Except Epidemiologist	Wisconsin	S	21.25 MW	26.62 AW	55360 AAW	WIBLS	10//99-12//99
Except Epidemiologist	Madison MSA, WI	S	29.06 MW	22.28 AW	60450 AAW	WIBLS	10//99-12//99
Medical Secretary	Alabama	S	8.08 MW	8.33 AW	17340 AAW	ALBLS	10//99-12//99
	Anniston MSA, AL	S	7.74 MW	7.18 AW	16100 AAW	ALBLS	10//99-12//99
	Auburn-Opelika MSA, AL	S	8.49 MW	8.53 AW	17670 AAW	ALBLS	10//99-12//99
	Birmingham MSA, AL	S	8.06 MW	6.86 AW	16770 AAW	ALBLS	10//99-12//99
	Decatur MSA, AL	S	10.49 MW	10.33 AW*	21820 AAW	ALBLS	10//99-12//99
	Dothan MSA, AL	S	9.03 MW	8.96 AW	18790 AAW	ALBLS	10//99-12//99
	Florence MSA, AL	S	8.12 MW	8.02 AW	16890 AAW	ALBLS	10//99-12//99
	Huntsville MSA, AL	S	9.10 MW	9.00 AW	18920 AAW	ALBLS	10//99-12//99
	Mobile MSA, AL	S	8.50 MW	8.22 AW	17670 AAW	ALBLS	10//99-12//99
	Montgomery MSA, AL	S	9.58 MW	9.61 AW	19930 AAW	ALBLS	10//99-12//99
	Tuscaloosa MSA, AL	S	9.51 MW	9.56 AW	19780 AAW	ALBLS	10//99-12//99
	Alaska	S	13.5 MW	13.50 AW	28070 AAW	AKBLS	10//99-12//99
	Anchorage MSA, AK	S	13.21 MW	14.25 AW	27470 AAW	AKBLS	10//99-12//99
	Arizona	S	10.5 MW	10.53 AW	21900 AAW	AZBLS	10//99-12//99
	Phoenix-Mesa MSA, AZ	S	10.55 MW	10.44 AW	21940 AAW	AZBLS	10//99-12//99
	Tucson MSA, AZ	S	10.94 MW	11.34 AW	22760 AAW	AZBLS	10//99-12//99
	Yuma MSA, AZ	S	9.91 MW	9.82 AW	20600 AAW	AZBLS	10//99-12//99
	Arkansas	S	9.3 MW	9.58 AW	19930 AAW	ARBLS	10//99-12//99
	Fayetteville-Springdale-Rogers MSA, AR	S	9.09 MW	9.12 AW	18910 AAW	ARBLS	10//99-12//99
	Little Rock-North Little Rock MSA, AR	S	10.40 MW	10.20 AW	21630 AAW	ARBLS	10//99-12//99
	California	S	13.17 MW	13.91 AW	28920 AAW	CABLS	10//99-12//99
	Bakersfield MSA, CA	S	11.22 MW	11.04 AW	23340 AAW	CABLS	10//99-12//99
	Chico-Paradise MSA, CA	S	12.73 MW	13.99 AW	26470 AAW	CABLS	10//99-12//99
	Fresno MSA, CA	S	11.82 MW	12.18 AW	24580 AAW	CABLS	10//99-12//99
	Los Angeles-Long Beach PMSA, CA	S	13.56 MW	12.93 AW	28210 AAW	CABLS	10//99-12//99

AAW	Average annual wage	AOH	Average offered, high	ASH	Average starting, high	H	Hourly	M	Monthly	S	Special: hourly and annual
AE	Average entry wage	AOL	Average offered, low	ASL	Average starting, low	HI	Highest wage paid	MTC	Median total compensation	TQ	Third quartile wage
AEX	Average experienced wage	APH	Average pay, high range	AW	Average wage paid	HR	High end range	MW	Median wage paid	W	Weekly
AO	Average offered	APL	Average pay, low range	FQ	First quartile wage	LR	Low end range	SQ	Second quartile wage	Y	Yearly

Occupation/Type/Industry	Location	Per	Low	Mid	High	Source	Date
Medical Secretary	Merced MSA, CA	S	9.48 MW	9.10 AW	19720 AAW	CABLS	10//99-12//99
	Modesto MSA, CA	S	10.91 MW	9.38 AW	22690 AAW	CABLS	10//99-12//99
	Oakland PMSA, CA	S	15.08 MW	14.77 AW	31360 AAW	CABLS	10//99-12//99
	Orange County PMSA, CA	S	12.35 MW	11.36 AW	25700 AAW	CABLS	10//99-12//99
	Redding MSA, CA	S	9.68 MW	9.60 AW	20140 AAW	CABLS	10//99-12//99
	Riverside-San Bernardino PMSA, CA	S	11.68 MW	12.05 AW	24300 AAW	CABLS	10//99-12//99
	Sacramento PMSA, CA	S	12.00 MW	10.48 AW	24970 AAW	CABLS	10//99-12//99
	Salinas MSA, CA	S	13.54 MW	12.33 AW	28170 AAW	CABLS	10//99-12//99
	San Diego MSA, CA	S	12.51 MW	12.54 AW	26010 AAW	CABLS	10//99-12//99
	San Francisco PMSA, CA	S	17.89 MW	17.27 AW	37210 AAW	CABLS	10//99-12//99
	San Jose PMSA, CA	S	16.80 MW	17.60 AW	34940 AAW	CABLS	10//99-12//99
	San Luis Obispo-Atascadero-Paso Robles MSA, CA	S	10.69 MW	11.08 AW	22230 AAW	CABLS	10//99-12//99
	Santa Barbara-Santa Maria-Lompoc MSA, CA	S	12.93 MW	12.76 AW	26890 AAW	CABLS	10//99-12//99
	Santa Cruz-Watsonville PMSA, CA	S	12.16 MW	12.04 AW	25290 AAW	CABLS	10//99-12//99
	Santa Rosa PMSA, CA	S	14.64 MW	13.23 AW	30450 AAW	CABLS	10//99-12//99
	Stockton-Lodi MSA, CA	S	9.61 MW	9.59 AW	19980 AAW	CABLS	10//99-12//99
	Vallejo-Fairfield-Napa PMSA, CA	S	15.04 MW	15.03 AW	31280 AAW	CABLS	10//99-12//99
	Ventura PMSA, CA	S	13.29 MW	11.86 AW	27640 AAW	CABLS	10//99-12//99
	Visalia-Tulare-Porterville MSA, CA	S	11.05 MW	11.06 AW	22980 AAW	CABLS	10//99-12//99
	Yuba City MSA, CA	S	12.25 MW	12.58 AW	25480 AAW	CABLS	10//99-12//99
	Colorado	S	11.12 MW	11.41 AW	23720 AAW	COBLS	10//99-12//99
	Boulder-Longmont PMSA, CO	S	11.73 MW	11.43 AW	24390 AAW	COBLS	10//99-12//99
	Colorado Springs MSA, CO	S	10.80 MW	10.78 AW	22470 AAW	COBLS	10//99-12//99
	Denver PMSA, CO	S	12.25 MW	11.52 AW	25490 AAW	COBLS	10//99-12//99
	Fort Collins-Loveland MSA, CO	S	10.88 MW	10.55 AW	22630 AAW	COBLS	10//99-12//99
	Grand Junction MSA, CO	S	10.52 MW	10.17 AW	21890 AAW	COBLS	10//99-12//99
	Pueblo MSA, CO	S	9.29 MW	9.45 AW	19330 AAW	COBLS	10//99-12//99
	Connecticut	S	13.78 MW	13.79 AW	28690 AAW	CTBLS	10//99-12//99
	Bridgeport PMSA, CT	S	14.21 MW	14.39 AW	29560 AAW	CTBLS	10//99-12//99
	Danbury PMSA, CT	S	13.24 MW	13.11 AW	27540 AAW	CTBLS	10//99-12//99
	Hartford MSA, CT	S	13.13 MW	12.92 AW	27310 AAW	CTBLS	10//99-12//99
	New Haven-Meriden PMSA, CT	S	15.55 MW	15.52 AW	32340 AAW	CTBLS	10//99-12//99
	New London-Norwich MSA, CT-RI	S	12.01 MW	11.73 AW	24990 AAW	CTBLS	10//99-12//99
	Stamford-Norwalk PMSA, CT	S	14.44 MW	14.83 AW	30040 AAW	CTBLS	10//99-12//99
	Waterbury PMSA, CT	S	11.89 MW	11.30 AW	24720 AAW	CTBLS	10//99-12//99
	Delaware	S	10.95 MW	11.30 AW	23510 AAW	DEBLS	10//99-12//99
	Dover MSA, DE	S	9.33 MW	9.52 AW	19400 AAW	DEBLS	10//99-12//99
	Wilmington-Newark PMSA, DE-MD	S	12.50 MW	12.68 AW	25990 AAW	DEBLS	10//99-12//99
	District of Columbia	S	13.14 MW	13.40 AW	27860 AAW	DCBLS	10//99-12//99
	Washington PMSA, DC-MD-VA-WV	S	12.76 MW	12.79 AW	26540 AAW	DCBLS	10//99-12//99
	Florida	S	10.44 MW	10.61 AW	22070 AAW	FLBLS	10//99-12//99
	Daytona Beach MSA, FL	S	10.17 MW	10.32 AW	21160 AAW	FLBLS	10//99-12//99
	Fort Lauderdale PMSA, FL	S	11.54 MW	11.14 AW	24000 AAW	FLBLS	10//99-12//99
	Fort Myers-Cape Coral MSA, FL	S	9.96 MW	9.93 AW	20720 AAW	FLBLS	10//99-12//99
	Fort Pierce-Port St. Lucie MSA, FL	S	11.11 MW	10.75 AW	23110 AAW	FLBLS	10//99-12//99
	Fort Walton Beach MSA, FL	S	10.39 MW	11.02 AW	21610 AAW	FLBLS	10//99-12//99
	Gainesville MSA, FL	S	9.55 MW	9.74 AW	19870 AAW	FLBLS	10//99-12//99
	Jacksonville MSA, FL	S	11.99 MW	11.62 AW	24950 AAW	FLBLS	10//99-12//99
	Lakeland-Winter Haven MSA, FL	S	8.88 MW	8.65 AW	18480 AAW	FLBLS	10//99-12//99
	Melbourne-Titusville-Palm Bay MSA, FL	S	9.67 MW	9.37 AW	20100 AAW	FLBLS	10//99-12//99
	Miami PMSA, FL	S	11.39 MW	11.44 AW	23690 AAW	FLBLS	10//99-12//99
	Naples MSA, FL	S	11.45 MW	10.65 AW	23820 AAW	FLBLS	10//99-12//99
	Ocala MSA, FL	S	11.32 MW	11.27 AW	23540 AAW	FLBLS	10//99-12//99
	Orlando MSA, FL	S	10.14 MW	10.05 AW	21100 AAW	FLBLS	10//99-12//99
	Panama City MSA, FL	S	9.69 MW	9.93 AW	20160 AAW	FLBLS	10//99-12//99
	Pensacola MSA, FL	S	11.34 MW	10.14 AW	23580 AAW	FLBLS	10//99-12//99
	Punta Gorda MSA, FL	S	9.77 MW	9.55 AW	20330 AAW	FLBLS	10//99-12//99

AAW	Average annual wage	AOH	Average offered, high	ASH	Average starting, high	H	Hourly	M	Monthly	S	Special: hourly and annual
AE	Average entry wage	AOL	Average offered, low	ASL	Average starting, low	HI	Highest wage paid	MTC	Median total compensation	TQ	Third quartile wage
AEX	Average experienced wage	APH	Average pay, high range	AW	Average wage paid	HR	High end range	MW	Median wage paid	W	Weekly
AO	Average offered	APL	Average pay, low range	FQ	First quartile wage	LR	Low end range	SQ	Second quartile wage	Y	Yearly

Occupation/Type/Industry	Location	Per	Low	Mid	High	Source	Date
Medical Secretary	Sarasota-Bradenton MSA, FL	S	10.30 MW	10.30 AW	21430 AAW	FLBLS	10//99-12//99
	Tallahassee MSA, FL	S	9.14 MW	9.43 AW	19020 AAW	FLBLS	10//99-12//99
	Tampa-St. Petersburg-Clearwater MSA, FL	S	10.14 MW	10.19 AW	21090 AAW	FLBLS	10//99-12//99
	West Palm Beach-Boca Raton MSA, FL	S	11.84 MW	11.57 AW	24630 AAW	FLBLS	10//99-12//99
	Georgia	S	10.76 MW	10.76 AW	22380 AAW	GABLS	10//99-12//99
	Albany MSA, GA	S	10.27 MW	8.52 AW	21360 AAW	GABLS	10//99-12//99
	Athens MSA, GA	S	9.55 MW	8.24 AW	19870 AAW	GABLS	10//99-12//99
	Atlanta MSA, GA	S	11.55 MW	11.50 AW	24020 AAW	GABLS	10//99-12//99
	Augusta-Aiken MSA, GA-SC	S	10.08 MW	10.38 AW	20970 AAW	GABLS	10//99-12//99
	Columbus MSA, GA-AL	S	9.07 MW	8.48 AW	18860 AAW	GABLS	10//99-12//99
	Macon MSA, GA	S	10.91 MW	10.88 AW	22700 AAW	GABLS	10//99-12//99
	Savannah MSA, GA	S	10.26 MW	10.01 AW	21350 AAW	GABLS	10//99-12//99
	Hawaii	S	13.32 MW	13.33 AW	27720 AAW	HIBLS	10//99-12//99
	Honolulu MSA, HI	S	15.55 MW	15.52 AW	32350 AAW	HIBLS	10//99-12//99
	Idaho	S	9.51 MW	9.61 AW	19990 AAW	IDBLS	10//99-12//99
	Boise City MSA, ID	S	10.99 MW	10.81 AW	22860 AAW	IDBLS	10//99-12//99
	Pocatello MSA, ID	S	9.17 MW	8.77 AW	19070 AAW	IDBLS	10//99-12//99
	Illinois	S	10.91 MW	13.61 AW	28310 AAW	ILBLS	10//99-12//99
	Bloomington-Normal MSA, IL	S	9.52 MW	10.36 AW	19810 AAW	ILBLS	10//99-12//99
	Champaign-Urbana MSA, IL	S	11.26 MW	11.27 AW	23410 AAW	ILBLS	10//99-12//99
	Chicago PMSA, IL	S	15.58 MW	11.64 AW	32410 AAW	ILBLS	10//99-12//99
	Decatur MSA, IL	S	8.91 MW	9.60 AW	18520 AAW	ILBLS	10//99-12//99
	Kankakee PMSA, IL	S	9.90 MW	9.97 AW	20590 AAW	ILBLS	10//99-12//99
	Peoria-Pekin MSA, IL	S	9.95 MW	9.79 AW	20700 AAW	ILBLS	10//99-12//99
	Rockford MSA, IL	S	10.38 MW	10.34 AW	21600 AAW	ILBLS	10//99-12//99
	Springfield MSA, IL	S	11.54 MW	11.42 AW	24010 AAW	ILBLS	10//99-12//99
	Indiana	S	10.25 MW	10.56 AW	21960 AAW	INBLS	10//99-12//99
	Bloomington MSA, IN	S	11.58 MW	10.57 AW	24090 AAW	INBLS	10//99-12//99
	Elkhart-Goshen MSA, IN	S	10.74 MW	10.64 AW	22330 AAW	INBLS	10//99-12//99
	Evansville-Henderson MSA, IN-KY	S	11.02 MW	10.25 AW	22920 AAW	INBLS	10//99-12//99
	Fort Wayne MSA, IN	S	10.97 MW	10.58 AW	22810 AAW	INBLS	10//99-12//99
	Gary PMSA, IN	S	9.24 MW	8.84 AW	19220 AAW	INBLS	10//99-12//99
	Indianapolis MSA, IN	S	10.51 MW	10.47 AW	21860 AAW	INBLS	10//99-12//99
	Kokomo MSA, IN	S	17.44 MW	20.92 AW	36270 AAW	INBLS	10//99-12//99
	Lafayette MSA, IN	S	11.44 MW	10.54 AW	23790 AAW	INBLS	10//99-12//99
	Muncie MSA, IN	S	10.40 MW	9.72 AW	21640 AAW	INBLS	10//99-12//99
	South Bend MSA, IN	S	11.39 MW	10.55 AW	23690 AAW	INBLS	10//99-12//99
	Terre Haute MSA, IN	S	12.60 MW	11.30 AW	26200 AAW	INBLS	10//99-12//99
	Iowa	S	9.81 MW	10.11 AW	21030 AAW	IABLS	10//99-12//99
	Cedar Rapids MSA, IA	S	9.65 MW	9.70 AW	20070 AAW	IABLS	10//99-12//99
	Davenport-Moline-Rock Island MSA, IA-IL	S	9.48 MW	9.52 AW	19720 AAW	IABLS	10//99-12//99
	Des Moines MSA, IA	S	11.48 MW	11.53 AW	23880 AAW	IABLS	10//99-12//99
	Dubuque MSA, IA	S	9.74 MW	10.13 AW	20270 AAW	IABLS	10//99-12//99
	Iowa City MSA, IA	S	10.31 MW	10.43 AW	21440 AAW	IABLS	10//99-12//99
	Waterloo-Cedar Falls MSA, IA	S	8.01 MW	6.64 AW	16670 AAW	IABLS	10//99-12//99
	Kansas	S	9.68 MW	10.07 AW	20940 AAW	KSBLS	10//99-12//99
	Topeka MSA, KS	S	10.25 MW	9.29 AW	21320 AAW	KSBLS	10//99-12//99
	Wichita MSA, KS	S	10.37 MW	10.10 AW	21570 AAW	KSBLS	10//99-12//99
	Kentucky	S	9.28 MW	9.42 AW	19600 AAW	KYBLS	10//99-12//99
	Lexington MSA, KY	S	9.94 MW	9.78 AW	20670 AAW	KYBLS	10//99-12//99
	Louisville MSA, KY-IN	S	10.31 MW	10.47 AW	21450 AAW	KYBLS	10//99-12//99
	Owensboro MSA, KY	S	8.38 MW	8.03 AW	17420 AAW	KYBLS	10//99-12//99
	Louisiana	S	8.77 MW	9.24 AW	19220 AAW	LABLS	10//99-12//99
	Baton Rouge MSA, LA	S	10.43 MW	9.58 AW	21690 AAW	LABLS	10//99-12//99
	Houma MSA, LA	S	9.43 MW	9.45 AW	19620 AAW	LABLS	10//99-12//99
	Lafayette MSA, LA	S	9.52 MW	8.72 AW	19800 AAW	LABLS	10//99-12//99
	Lake Charles MSA, LA	S	9.23 MW	9.09 AW	19200 AAW	LABLS	10//99-12//99
	New Orleans MSA, LA	S	8.97 MW	8.36 AW	18660 AAW	LABLS	10//99-12//99
	Shreveport-Bossier City MSA, LA	S	9.75 MW	9.77 AW	20280 AAW	LABLS	10//99-12//99
	Maine	S	10.76 MW	10.79 AW	22450 AAW	MEBLS	10//99-12//99
	Bangor MSA, ME	S	10.26 MW	10.14 AW	21350 AAW	MEBLS	10//99-12//99
	Lewiston-Auburn MSA, ME	S	9.83 MW	9.79 AW	20440 AAW	MEBLS	10//99-12//99
	Portland MSA, ME	S	11.58 MW	11.42 AW	24080 AAW	MEBLS	10//99-12//99
	Maryland	S	11.13 MW	11.31 AW	23520 AAW	MDBLS	10//99-12//99
	Baltimore PMSA, MD	S	11.22 MW	11.32 AW	23330 AAW	MDBLS	10//99-12//99
	Hagerstown PMSA, MD	S	10.00 MW	10.02 AW	20800 AAW	MDBLS	10//99-12//99
	Massachusetts	S	12.48 MW	13.10 AW	27250 AAW	MABLS	10//99-12//99

Occupation/Type/Industry	Location	Per	Low	Mid	High	Source	Date
Medical Secretary	Barnstable-Yarmouth MSA, MA	S	11.73 MW	11.31 AW	24390 AAW	MABLS	10//99-12//99
	Boston PMSA, MA-NH	S	13.70 MW	13.10 AW	28500 AAW	MABLS	10//99-12//99
	Brockton PMSA, MA	S	13.26 MW	12.84 AW	27590 AAW	MABLS	10//99-12//99
	Fitchburg-Leominster PMSA, MA	S	12.82 MW	11.94 AW	26670 AAW	MABLS	10//99-12//99
	Lawrence PMSA, MA-NH	S	11.04 MW	11.17 AW	22970 AAW	MABLS	10//99-12//99
	Lowell PMSA, MA-NH	S	11.78 MW	11.53 AW	24500 AAW	MABLS	10//99-12//99
	New Bedford PMSA, MA	S	11.43 MW	11.19 AW	23780 AAW	MABLS	10//99-12//99
	Pittsfield MSA, MA	S	11.30 MW	11.12 AW	23500 AAW	MABLS	10//99-12//99
	Springfield MSA, MA	S	12.58 MW	12.56 AW	26170 AAW	MABLS	10//99-12//99
	Worcester PMSA, MA-CT	S	12.08 MW	11.74 AW	25120 AAW	MABLS	10//99-12//99
	Michigan	S	11.05 MW	11.33 AW	23570 AAW	MIBLS	10//99-12//99
	Ann Arbor PMSA, MI	S	13.29 MW	12.42 AW	27640 AAW	MIBLS	10//99-12//99
	Benton Harbor MSA, MI	S	11.52 MW	12.48 AW	23950 AAW	MIBLS	10//99-12//99
	Detroit PMSA, MI	S	11.86 MW	11.77 AW	24670 AAW	MIBLS	10//99-12//99
	Flint PMSA, MI	S	11.59 MW	11.28 AW	24120 AAW	MIBLS	10//99-12//99
	Grand Rapids-Muskegon-Holland MSA, MI	S	11.00 MW	10.16 AW	22890 AAW	MIBLS	10//99-12//99
	Jackson MSA, MI	S	9.87 MW	9.86 AW	20520 AAW	MIBLS	10//99-12//99
	Kalamazoo-Battle Creek MSA, MI	S	10.65 MW	10.80 AW	22150 AAW	MIBLS	10//99-12//99
	Lansing-East Lansing MSA, MI	S	11.44 MW	11.00 AW	23780 AAW	MIBLS	10//99-12//99
	Saginaw-Bay City-Midland MSA, MI	S	10.59 MW	10.87 AW	22020 AAW	MIBLS	10//99-12//99
	Minnesota	S	11.13 MW	11.33 AW	23560 AAW	MNBLS	10//99-12//99
	Duluth-Superior MSA, MN-WI	S	10.81 MW	10.92 AW	22480 AAW	MNBLS	10//99-12//99
	Minneapolis-St. Paul MSA, MN-WI	S	12.10 MW	11.77 AW	25160 AAW	MNBLS	10//99-12//99
	St. Cloud MSA, MN	S	10.32 MW	10.13 AW	21470 AAW	MNBLS	10//99-12//99
	Mississippi	S	9.77 MW	9.90 AW	20580 AAW	MSBLS	10//99-12//99
	Biloxi-Gulfport-Pascagoula MSA, MS	S	8.86 MW	9.13 AW	18430 AAW	MSBLS	10//99-12//99
	Hattiesburg MSA, MS	S	8.67 MW	8.31 AW	18040 AAW	MSBLS	10//99-12//99
	Jackson MSA, MS	S	10.80 MW	11.11 AW	22460 AAW	MSBLS	10//99-12//99
	Missouri	S	10.02 MW	10.22 AW	21260 AAW	MOBLS	10//99-12//99
	Kansas City MSA, MO-KS	S	11.31 MW	11.48 AW	23520 AAW	MOBLS	10//99-12//99
	St. Louis MSA, MO-IL	S	10.71 MW	10.50 AW	22270 AAW	MOBLS	10//99-12//99
	Montana	S	9.9 MW	10.19 AW	21190 AAW	MTBLS	10//99-12//99
	Billings MSA, MT	S	11.37 MW	11.72 AW	23640 AAW	MTBLS	10//99-12//99
	Missoula MSA, MT	S	9.87 MW	10.37 AW	20540 AAW	MTBLS	10//99-12//99
	Nebraska	S	10 MW	10.12 AW	21050 AAW	NEBLS	10//99-12//99
	Lincoln MSA, NE	S	11.03 MW	11.01 AW	22930 AAW	NEBLS	10//99-12//99
	Omaha MSA, NE-IA	S	11.13 MW	11.14 AW	23150 AAW	NEBLS	10//99-12//99
	Nevada	S	11.9 MW	12.05 AW	25070 AAW	NVBLS	10//99-12//99
	Las Vegas MSA, NV-AZ	S	12.07 MW	11.84 AW	25110 AAW	NVBLS	10//99-12//99
	Reno MSA, NV	S	11.59 MW	11.53 AW	24100 AAW	NVBLS	10//99-12//99
	New Hampshire	S	11.38 MW	11.59 AW	24110 AAW	NHBLS	10//99-12//99
	Manchester PMSA, NH	S	12.23 MW	11.73 AW	25430 AAW	NHBLS	10//99-12//99
	Nashua PMSA, NH	S	14.42 MW	14.61 AW	29990 AAW	NHBLS	10//99-12//99
	Portsmouth-Rochester PMSA, NH-ME	S	10.44 MW	10.64 AW	21710 AAW	NHBLS	10//99-12//99
	New Jersey	S	12.92 MW	13.34 AW	27740 AAW	NJBLS	10//99-12//99
	Atlantic-Cape May PMSA, NJ	S	11.17 MW	10.99 AW	23240 AAW	NJBLS	10//99-12//99
	Bergen-Passaic PMSA, NJ	S	13.86 MW	13.21 AW	28820 AAW	NJBLS	10//99-12//99
	Jersey City PMSA, NJ	S	14.37 MW	14.23 AW	29890 AAW	NJBLS	10//99-12//99
	Middlesex-Somerset-Hunterdon PMSA, NJ	S	13.72 MW	12.87 AW	28540 AAW	NJBLS	10//99-12//99
	Monmouth-Ocean PMSA, NJ	S	11.47 MW	11.22 AW	23860 AAW	NJBLS	10//99-12//99
	Newark PMSA, NJ	S	15.52 MW	14.99 AW	32290 AAW	NJBLS	10//99-12//99
	Trenton PMSA, NJ	S	13.65 MW	13.07 AW	28390 AAW	NJBLS	10//99-12//99
	New Mexico	S	9.85 MW	9.94 AW	20670 AAW	NMBLS	10//99-12//99
	Albuquerque MSA, NM	S	10.29 MW	10.21 AW	21400 AAW	NMBLS	10//99-12//99
	Las Cruces MSA, NM	S	8.69 MW	8.16 AW	18070 AAW	NMBLS	10//99-12//99
	Santa Fe MSA, NM	S	10.71 MW	10.34 AW	22290 AAW	NMBLS	10//99-12//99
	New York	S	12.5 MW	13.14 AW	27330 AAW	NYBLS	10//99-12//99
	Albany-Schenectady-Troy MSA, NY	S	11.29 MW	10.98 AW	23480 AAW	NYBLS	10//99-12//99
	Binghamton MSA, NY	S	8.96 MW	8.88 AW	18630 AAW	NYBLS	10//99-12//99
	Buffalo-Niagara Falls MSA, NY	S	10.93 MW	10.27 AW	22720 AAW	NYBLS	10//99-12//99
	Dutchess County PMSA, NY	S	11.33 MW	11.06 AW	23560 AAW	NYBLS	10//99-12//99

Occupation/Type/Industry	Location	Per	Low	Mid	High	Source	Date
Medical Secretary	Elmira MSA, NY	S	11.73 MW	10.21 AW	24390 AAW	NYBLS	10//99-12//99
	Glens Falls MSA, NY	S	11.06 MW	11.83 AW	23000 AAW	NYBLS	10//99-12//99
	Jamestown MSA, NY	S	8.12 MW	8.00 AW	16880 AAW	NYBLS	10//99-12//99
	Nassau-Suffolk PMSA, NY	S	14.41 MW	13.64 AW	29960 AAW	NYBLS	10//99-12//99
	New York PMSA, NY	S	15.06 MW	14.89 AW	31330 AAW	NYBLS	10//99-12//99
	Newburgh PMSA, NY-PA	S	12.20 MW	12.44 AW	25380 AAW	NYBLS	10//99-12//99
	Rochester MSA, NY	S	10.66 MW	10.03 AW	22160 AAW	NYBLS	10//99-12//99
	Syracuse MSA, NY	S	10.35 MW	9.96 AW	21530 AAW	NYBLS	10//99-12//99
	Utica-Rome MSA, NY	S	9.62 MW	9.59 AW	20000 AAW	NYBLS	10//99-12//99
	North Carolina	S	10.28 MW	10.51 AW	21860 AAW	NCBLS	10//99-12//99
	Asheville MSA, NC	S	10.88 MW	10.58 AW	22620 AAW	NCBLS	10//99-12//99
	Charlotte-Gastonia-Rock Hill MSA, NC-SC	S	11.83 MW	11.35 AW	24600 AAW	NCBLS	10//99-12//99
	Goldsboro MSA, NC	S	9.65 MW	9.82 AW	20080 AAW	NCBLS	10//99-12//99
	Greensboro--Winston-Salem--High Point MSA, NC	S	10.32 MW	10.26 AW	21470 AAW	NCBLS	10//99-12//99
	Greenville MSA, NC	S	9.12 MW	8.70 AW	18960 AAW	NCBLS	10//99-12//99
	Hickory-Morganton-Lenoir MSA, NC	S	10.13 MW	9.52 AW	21070 AAW	NCBLS	10//99-12//99
	Jacksonville MSA, NC	S	8.12 MW	8.02 AW	16890 AAW	NCBLS	10//99-12//99
	Raleigh-Durham-Chapel Hill MSA, NC	S	10.88 MW	10.68 AW	22640 AAW	NCBLS	10//99-12//99
	Rocky Mount MSA, NC	S	9.44 MW	9.30 AW	19630 AAW	NCBLS	10//99-12//99
	Wilmington MSA, NC	S	9.51 MW	9.59 AW	19780 AAW	NCBLS	10//99-12//99
	North Dakota	S	8.93 MW	8.85 AW	18410 AAW	NDBLS	10//99-12//99
	Bismarck MSA, ND	S	8.62 MW	8.64 AW	17930 AAW	NDBLS	10//99-12//99
	Fargo-Moorhead MSA, ND-MN	S	9.75 MW	9.72 AW	20290 AAW	NDBLS	10//99-12//99
	Grand Forks MSA, ND-MN	S	8.86 MW	8.80 AW	18430 AAW	NDBLS	10//99-12//99
	Ohio	S	10.27 MW	10.42 AW	21660 AAW	OHBLS	10//99-12//99
	Canton-Massillon MSA, OH	S	9.58 MW	9.81 AW	19920 AAW	OHBLS	10//99-12//99
	Cincinnati PMSA, OH-KY-IN	S	10.88 MW	10.68 AW	22630 AAW	OHBLS	10//99-12//99
	Cleveland-Lorain-Elyria PMSA, OH	S	10.87 MW	10.64 AW	22600 AAW	OHBLS	10//99-12//99
	Columbus MSA, OH	S	10.94 MW	10.63 AW	22750 AAW	OHBLS	10//99-12//99
	Dayton-Springfield MSA, OH	S	10.79 MW	10.27 AW	22450 AAW	OHBLS	10//99-12//99
	Hamilton-Middletown PMSA, OH	S	10.58 MW	10.22 AW	22010 AAW	OHBLS	10//99-12//99
	Lima MSA, OH	S	9.22 MW	9.38 AW	19180 AAW	OHBLS	10//99-12//99
	Mansfield MSA, OH	S	9.70 MW	10.47 AW	20180 AAW	OHBLS	10//99-12//99
	Steubenville-Weirton MSA, OH-WV	S	10.01 MW	9.84 AW	20820 AAW	OHBLS	10//99-12//99
	Toledo MSA, OH	S	10.68 MW	10.75 AW	22210 AAW	OHBLS	10//99-12//99
	Youngstown-Warren MSA, OH	S	8.40 MW	8.13 AW	17480 AAW	OHBLS	10//99-12//99
	Oklahoma	S	9.24 MW	9.94 AW	20680 AAW	OKBLS	10//99-12//99
	Enid MSA, OK	S	8.75 MW	8.48 AW	18210 AAW	OKBLS	10//99-12//99
	Lawton MSA, OK	S	8.39 MW	8.18 AW	17450 AAW	OKBLS	10//99-12//99
	Oklahoma City MSA, OK	S	10.95 MW	10.72 AW	22770 AAW	OKBLS	10//99-12//99
	Tulsa MSA, OK	S	10.01 MW	9.90 AW	20820 AAW	OKBLS	10//99-12//99
	Oregon	S	11.7 MW	11.73 AW	24400 AAW	ORBLS	10//99-12//99
	Eugene-Springfield MSA, OR	S	11.95 MW	11.86 AW	24850 AAW	ORBLS	10//99-12//99
	Medford-Ashland MSA, OR	S	10.84 MW	11.22 AW	22540 AAW	ORBLS	10//99-12//99
	Portland-Vancouver PMSA, OR-WA	S	12.10 MW	11.91 AW	25170 AAW	ORBLS	10//99-12//99
	Salem PMSA, OR	S	12.43 MW	12.11 AW	25860 AAW	ORBLS	10//99-12//99
	Pennsylvania	S	10.48 MW	10.71 AW	22270 AAW	PABLS	10//99-12//99
	Allentown-Bethlehem-Easton MSA, PA	S	10.85 MW	10.58 AW	22570 AAW	PABLS	10//99-12//99
	Altoona MSA, PA	S	9.27 MW	9.68 AW	19280 AAW	PABLS	10//99-12//99
	Erie MSA, PA	S	10.00 MW	9.83 AW	20800 AAW	PABLS	10//99-12//99
	Harrisburg-Lebanon-Carlisle MSA, PA	S	10.47 MW	10.14 AW	21770 AAW	PABLS	10//99-12//99
	Johnstown MSA, PA	S	9.62 MW	9.54 AW	20010 AAW	PABLS	10//99-12//99
	Lancaster MSA, PA	S	10.52 MW	10.67 AW	21880 AAW	PABLS	10//99-12//99
	Philadelphia PMSA, PA-NJ	S	11.68 MW	11.26 AW	24300 AAW	PABLS	10//99-12//99
	Pittsburgh MSA, PA	S	9.50 MW	9.89 AW	19750 AAW	PABLS	10//99-12//99
	Scranton--Wilkes-Barre--Hazleton MSA, PA	S	9.68 MW	9.69 AW	20130 AAW	PABLS	10//99-12//99
	Sharon MSA, PA	S	9.98 MW	9.87 AW	20760 AAW	PABLS	10//99-12//99
	State College MSA, PA	S	11.31 MW	11.36 AW	23520 AAW	PABLS	10//99-12//99
	York MSA, PA	S	10.77 MW	10.93 AW	22410 AAW	PABLS	10//99-12//99
	Rhode Island	S	11.94 MW	11.93 AW	24810 AAW	RIBLS	10//99-12//99

AAW	Average annual wage	AOH	Average offered, high	ASH	Average starting, high	H	Hourly	M	Monthly	S	Special: hourly and annual
AE	Average entry wage	AOL	Average offered, low	ASL	Average starting, low	HI	Highest wage paid	MTC	Median total compensation	TQ	Third quartile wage
AEX	Average experienced wage	APH	Average pay, high range	AW	Average wage paid	HR	High end range	MW	Median wage paid	W	Weekly
AO	Average offered	APL	Average pay, low range	FQ	First quartile wage	LR	Low end range	SQ	Second quartile wage	Y	Yearly

Occupation/Type/Industry	Location	Per	Low	Mid	High	Source	Date
Medical Secretary	Providence-Fall River- Warwick MSA, RI-MA	S	11.90 MW	11.81 AW	24750 AAW	RIBLS	10//99-12//99
	South Carolina	S	10.05 MW	10.16 AW	21140 AAW	SCBLS	10//99-12//99
	Charleston-North Charleston MSA, SC	S	9.96 MW	9.99 AW	20710 AAW	SCBLS	10//99-12//99
	Columbia MSA, SC	S	10.90 MW	10.68 AW	22680 AAW	SCBLS	10//99-12//99
	Greenville-Spartanburg- Anderson MSA, SC	S	10.19 MW	10.18 AW	21190 AAW	SCBLS	10//99-12//99
	Myrtle Beach MSA, SC	S	9.69 MW	9.82 AW	20160 AAW	SCBLS	10//99-12//99
	Sumter MSA, SC	S	10.58 MW	10.01 AW	22020 AAW	SCBLS	10//99-12//99
	South Dakota	S	9.74 MW	9.81 AW	20410 AAW	SDBLS	10//99-12//99
	Rapid City MSA, SD	S	10.04 MW	9.97 AW	20890 AAW	SDBLS	10//99-12//99
	Sioux Falls MSA, SD	S	10.99 MW	10.70 AW	22870 AAW	SDBLS	10//99-12//99
	Tennessee	S	10.58 MW	11.11 AW	23110 AAW	TNBLS	10//99-12//99
	Chattanooga MSA, TN-GA	S	11.51 MW	11.20 AW	23950 AAW	TNBLS	10//99-12//99
	Clarksville-Hopkinsville MSA, TN-KY	S	8.34 MW	8.04 AW	17350 AAW	TNBLS	10//99-12//99
	Jackson MSA, TN	S	9.22 MW	9.19 AW	19180 AAW	TNBLS	10//99-12//99
	Johnson City-Kingsport-Bristol MSA, TN-VA	S	8.25 MW	7.86 AW	17150 AAW	TNBLS	10//99-12//99
	Knoxville MSA, TN	S	9.40 MW	9.45 AW	19560 AAW	TNBLS	10//99-12//99
	Memphis MSA, TN-AR-MS	S	13.47 MW	12.39 AW	28020 AAW	MSBLS	10//99-12//99
	Nashville MSA, TN	S	11.49 MW	10.98 AW	23890 AAW	TNBLS	10//99-12//99
	Texas	S	10.24 MW	10.85 AW	22570 AAW	TXBLS	10//99-12//99
	Abilene MSA, TX	S	9.39 MW	8.49 AW	19520 AAW	TXBLS	10//99-12//99
	Amarillo MSA, TX	S	9.39 MW	9.59 AW	19530 AAW	TXBLS	10//99-12//99
	Austin-San Marcos MSA, TX	S	10.79 MW	10.81 AW	22450 AAW	TXBLS	10//99-12//99
	Beaumont-Port Arthur MSA, TX	S	9.05 MW	9.33 AW	18820 AAW	TXBLS	10//99-12//99
	Brazoria PMSA, TX	S	10.92 MW	11.16 AW	22710 AAW	TXBLS	10//99-12//99
	Brownsville-Harlingen-San Benito MSA, TX	S	8.20 MW	7.37 AW	17060 AAW	TXBLS	10//99-12//99
	Bryan-College Station MSA, TX	S	9.59 MW	9.28 AW	19950 AAW	TXBLS	10//99-12//99
	Corpus Christi MSA, TX	S	9.03 MW	8.64 AW	18790 AAW	TXBLS	10//99-12//99
	Dallas PMSA, TX	S	13.10 MW	11.86 AW	27260 AAW	TXBLS	10//99-12//99
	El Paso MSA, TX	S	9.33 MW	9.01 AW	19410 AAW	TXBLS	10//99-12//99
	Fort Worth-Arlington PMSA, TX	S	12.32 MW	12.07 AW	25630 AAW	TXBLS	10//99-12//99
	Galveston-Texas City PMSA, TX	S	10.36 MW	9.87 AW	21540 AAW	TXBLS	10//99-12//99
	Houston PMSA, TX	S	11.42 MW	10.89 AW	23750 AAW	TXBLS	10//99-12//99
	Killeen-Temple MSA, TX	S	9.16 MW	9.11 AW	19040 AAW	TXBLS	10//99-12//99
	Longview-Marshall MSA, TX	S	9.93 MW	10.31 AW	20660 AAW	TXBLS	10//99-12//99
	Lubbock MSA, TX	S	9.91 MW	10.04 AW	20620 AAW	TXBLS	10//99-12//99
	McAllen-Edinburg-Mission MSA, TX	S	9.26 MW	9.76 AW	19270 AAW	TXBLS	10//99-12//99
	Odessa-Midland MSA, TX	S	8.58 MW	8.48 AW	17840 AAW	TXBLS	10//99-12//99
	San Angelo MSA, TX	S	11.11 MW	12.16 AW	23120 AAW	TXBLS	10//99-12//99
	San Antonio MSA, TX	S	9.31 MW	8.95 AW	19360 AAW	TXBLS	10//99-12//99
	Sherman-Denison MSA, TX	S	10.05 MW	10.19 AW	20900 AAW	TXBLS	10//99-12//99
	Texarkana MSA, TX- Texarkana, AR	S	10.28 MW	9.97 AW	21380 AAW	TXBLS	10//99-12//99
	Tyler MSA, TX	S	9.66 MW	9.61 AW	20100 AAW	TXBLS	10//99-12//99
	Victoria MSA, TX	S	8.60 MW	6.87 AW	17880 AAW	TXBLS	10//99-12//99
	Waco MSA, TX	S	10.40 MW	10.48 AW	21640 AAW	TXBLS	10//99-12//99
	Wichita Falls MSA, TX	S	9.42 MW	9.56 AW	19600 AAW	TXBLS	10//99-12//99
	Utah	S	10.68 MW	10.90 AW	22670 AAW	UTBLS	10//99-12//99
	Salt Lake City-Ogden MSA, UT	S	11.84 MW	11.37 AW	24620 AAW	UTBLS	10//99-12//99
	Vermont	S	11.69 MW	11.72 AW	24390 AAW	VTBLS	10//99-12//99
	Burlington MSA, VT	S	11.57 MW	11.71 AW	24060 AAW	VTBLS	10//99-12//99
	Virginia	S	10.77 MW	10.97 AW	22820 AAW	VABLS	10//99-12//99
	Charlottesville MSA, VA	S	11.60 MW	11.76 AW	24120 AAW	VABLS	10//99-12//99
	Danville MSA, VA	S	11.12 MW	11.81 AW	23130 AAW	VABLS	10//99-12//99
	Lynchburg MSA, VA	S	11.15 MW	11.35 AW	23190 AAW	VABLS	10//99-12//99
	Norfolk-Virginia Beach- Newport News MSA, VA- NC	S	9.66 MW	9.54 AW	20090 AAW	VABLS	10//99-12//99
	Richmond-Petersburg MSA, VA	S	11.16 MW	10.89 AW	23210 AAW	VABLS	10//99-12//99
	Roanoke MSA, VA	S	9.81 MW	9.73 AW	20400 AAW	VABLS	10//99-12//99

AAW	Average annual wage	**AOH**	Average offered, high	**ASH**	Average starting, high	**H**	Hourly	
AE	Average entry wage	**AOL**	Average offered, low	**ASL**	Average starting, low	**HI**	Highest wage paid	
AEX	Average experienced wage	**APH**	Average pay, high range	**AW**	Average wage paid	**HR**	High end range	
AO	Average offered	**APL**	Average pay, low range	**FQ**	First quartile wage	**LR**	Low end range	

M	Monthly	**S**	Special: hourly and annual
MTC	Median total compensation	**TQ**	Third quartile wage
MW	Median wage paid	**W**	Weekly
SQ	Second quartile wage	**Y**	Yearly

Occupation/Type/Industry	Location	Per	Low	Mid	High	Source	Date
Medical Secretary	Washington	S	11.14 MW	11.32 AW	23540 AAW	WABLS	10//99-12//99
	Bellingham MSA, WA	S	11.40 MW	10.69 AW	23700 AAW	WABLS	10//99-12//99
	Bremerton PMSA, WA	S	11.31 MW	11.03 AW	23520 AAW	WABLS	10//99-12//99
	Olympia PMSA, WA	S	13.44 MW	12.16 AW	27950 AAW	WABLS	10//99-12//99
	Richland-Kennewick-Pasco MSA, WA	S	11.24 MW	10.39 AW	23370 AAW	WABLS	10//99-12//99
	Seattle-Bellevue-Everett PMSA, WA	S	11.24 MW	11.14 AW	23390 AAW	WABLS	10//99-12//99
	Spokane MSA, WA	S	11.36 MW	10.83 AW	23620 AAW	WABLS	10//99-12//99
	Yakima MSA, WA	S	11.49 MW	11.76 AW	23900 AAW	WABLS	10//99-12//99
	West Virginia	S	8.97 MW	9.15 AW	19030 AAW	WVBLS	10//99-12//99
	Charleston MSA, WV	S	9.78 MW	9.42 AW	20340 AAW	WVBLS	10//99-12//99
	Huntington-Ashland MSA, WV-KY-OH	S	9.01 MW	8.57 AW	18750 AAW	WVBLS	10//99-12//99
	Parkersburg-Marietta MSA, WV-OH		9.40 MW	9.06 AW	19550 AAW	WVBLS	10//99-12//99
	Wheeling MSA, WV-OH	S	8.64 MW	8.56 AW	17980 AAW	WVBLS	10//99-12//99
	Wisconsin	S	10.2 MW	10.43 AW	21690 AAW	WIBLS	10//99-12//99
	Appleton-Oshkosh-Neenah MSA, WI	S	9.47 MW	9.87 AW	19690 AAW	WIBLS	10//99-12//99
	Eau Claire MSA, WI	S	10.32 MW	10.40 AW	21460 AAW	WIBLS	10//99-12//99
	Green Bay MSA, WI	S	9.92 MW	9.80 AW	20630 AAW	WIBLS	10//99-12//99
	Janesville-Beloit MSA, WI	S	9.84 MW	9.78 AW	20460 AAW	WIBLS	10//99-12//99
	Kenosha PMSA, WI	S	10.78 MW	10.28 AW	22420 AAW	WIBLS	10//99-12//99
	La Crosse MSA, WI-MN	S	10.14 MW	10.21 AW	21100 AAW	WIBLS	10//99-12//99
	Madison MSA, WI	S	11.25 MW	11.13 AW	23400 AAW	WIBLS	10//99-12//99
	Milwaukee-Waukesha PMSA, WI	S	10.77 MW	10.26 AW	22390 AAW	WIBLS	10//99-12//99
	Racine PMSA, WI	S	11.62 MW	11.54 AW	24160 AAW	WIBLS	10//99-12//99
	Sheboygan MSA, WI	S	9.14 MW	9.44 AW	19000 AAW	WIBLS	10//99-12//99
	Wausau MSA, WI	S	10.76 MW	10.34 AW	22380 AAW	WIBLS	10//99-12//99
	Wyoming	S	8.71 MW	9.10 AW	18920 AAW	WYBLS	10//99-12//99
	Casper MSA, WY	S	7.73 MW	7.69 AW	16080 AAW	WYBLS	10//99-12//99
	Cheyenne MSA, WY	S	8.74 MW	8.42 AW	18170 AAW	WYBLS	10//99-12//99
	Puerto Rico	S	6.79 MW	8.19 AW	17040 AAW	PRBLS	10//99-12//99
	Aguadilla MSA, PR	S	5.79 MW	5.92 AW	12040 AAW	PRBLS	10//99-12//99
	Caguas PMSA, PR	S	6.66 MW	6.32 AW	13850 AAW	PRBLS	10//99-12//99
	Mayaguez MSA, PR	S	6.91 MW	6.72 AW	14380 AAW	PRBLS	10//99-12//99
	San Juan-Bayamon PMSA, PR	S	9.52 MW	8.65 AW	19810 AAW	PRBLS	10//99-12//99
Medical Technician							
Emergency	Los Angeles County, CA	Y		28474 AW		LABJ	1999
Medical Transcriptionist	Alabama	S	10.95 MW	10.86 AW	22590 AAW	ALBLS	10//99-12//99
	Alaska	S	15.85 MW	15.88 AW	33020 AAW	AKBLS	10//99-12//99
	Arizona	S	11.92 MW	12.28 AW	25550 AAW	AZBLS	10//99-12//99
	Arkansas	S	9.91 MW	10.12 AW	21050 AAW	ARBLS	10//99-12//99
	California	S	14.58 MW	14.19 AW	29510 AAW	CABLS	10//99-12//99
	Colorado	S	12.05 MW	12.38 AW	25740 AAW	COBLS	10//99-12//99
	Connecticut	S	13.95 MW	13.98 AW	29070 AAW	CTBLS	10//99-12//99
	Delaware	S	11.73 MW	11.55 AW	24030 AAW	DEBLS	10//99-12//99
	Florida	S	11.37 MW	11.47 AW	23860 AAW	FLBLS	10//99-12//99
	Georgia	S	10.01 MW	10.33 AW	21490 AAW	GABLS	10//99-12//99
	Hawaii	S	15.86 MW	16.37 AW	34050 AAW	HIBLS	10//99-12//99
	Idaho	S	11.35 MW	11.05 AW	22980 AAW	IDBLS	10//99-12//99
	Illinois	S	10.74 MW	11.19 AW	23280 AAW	ILBLS	10//99-12//99
	Indiana	S	11.04 MW	10.95 AW	22780 AAW	INBLS	10//99-12//99
	Iowa	S	10.19 MW	10.50 AW	21840 AAW	IABLS	10//99-12//99
	Kansas	S	10.37 MW	10.52 AW	21880 AAW	KSBLS	10//99-12//99
	Kentucky	S	11.25 MW	11.09 AW	23070 AAW	KYBLS	10//99-12//99
	Louisiana	S	9.71 MW	9.73 AW	20230 AAW	LABLS	10//99-12//99
	Maine	S	11.07 MW	11.23 AW	23350 AAW	MEBLS	10//99-12//99
	Maryland	S	15.9 MW	15.77 AW	32810 AAW	MDBLS	10//99-12//99
	Massachusetts	S	12.74 MW	12.85 AW	26720 AAW	MABLS	10//99-12//99
	Michigan	S	11.63 MW	11.43 AW	23760 AAW	MIBLS	10//99-12//99
	Minnesota	S	12.78 MW	12.80 AW	26630 AAW	MNBLS	10//99-12//99
	Mississippi	S	9.54 MW	9.52 AW	19790 AAW	MSBLS	10//99-12//99
	Missouri	S	11.09 MW	11.26 AW	23420 AAW	MOBLS	10//99-12//99
	Montana	S	9.99 MW	10.01 AW	20810 AAW	MTBLS	10//99-12//99
	Nebraska	S	9.82 MW	10.02 AW	20840 AAW	NEBLS	10//99-12//99
	Nevada	S	14.04 MW	13.58 AW	28250 AAW	NVBLS	10//99-12//99
	New Hampshire	S	12.38 MW	12.44 AW	25860 AAW	NHBLS	10//99-12//99
	New Jersey	S	13.33 MW	13.53 AW	28140 AAW	NJBLS	10//99-12//99

AAW	Average annual wage	AOH	Average offered, high	ASH	Average starting, high	H	Hourly	M	Monthly	S	Special: hourly and annual
AE	Average entry wage	AOL	Average offered, low	ASL	Average starting, low	HI	Highest wage paid	MTC	Median total compensation	TQ	Third quartile wage
AEX	Average experienced wage	APH	Average pay, high range	AW	Average wage paid	HR	High end range	MW	Median wage paid	W	Weekly
AO	Average offered	APL	Average pay, low range	FQ	First quartile wage	LR	Low end range	SQ	Second quartile wage	Y	Yearly

959

Occupation/Type/Industry	Location	Per	Low	Mid	High	Source	Date
Medical Transcriptionist	New Mexico	S	10.18 MW	10.49 AW	21820 AAW	NMBLS	10//99-12//99
	New York	S	11.53 MW	11.76 AW	24460 AAW	NYBLS	10//99-12//99
	North Carolina	S	12.15 MW	12.38 AW	25740 AAW	NCBLS	10//99-12//99
	North Dakota	S	9.24 MW	9.64 AW	20060 AAW	NDBLS	10//99-12//99
	Ohio	S	11.74 MW	11.55 AW	24030 AAW	OHBLS	10//99-12//99
	Oklahoma	S	10.63 MW	10.62 AW	22090 AAW	OKBLS	10//99-12//99
	Oregon	S	12.77 MW	12.78 AW	26570 AAW	ORBLS	10//99-12//99
	Pennsylvania	S	10.93 MW	11.13 AW	23150 AAW	PABLS	10//99-12//99
	Rhode Island	S	12.06 MW	12.10 AW	25160 AAW	RIBLS	10//99-12//99
	South Carolina	S	10.93 MW	11.28 AW	23470 AAW	SCBLS	10//99-12//99
	South Dakota	S	11.05 MW	10.88 AW	22620 AAW	SDBLS	10//99-12//99
	Tennessee	S	11.23 MW	11.19 AW	23270 AAW	TNBLS	10//99-12//99
	Texas	S	10.68 MW	10.70 AW	22260 AAW	TXBLS	10//99-12//99
	Utah	S	11.06 MW	11.09 AW	23070 AAW	UTBLS	10//99-12//99
	Vermont	S	11.23 MW	11.31 AW	23510 AAW	VTBLS	10//99-12//99
	Virginia	S	10.53 MW	11.34 AW	23580 AAW	VABLS	10//99-12//99
	Washington	S	14.01 MW	14.37 AW	29880 AAW	WABLS	10//99-12//99
	West Virginia	S	8.46 MW	9.27 AW	19290 AAW	WVBLS	10//99-12//99
	Wisconsin	S	11.45 MW	11.47 AW	23860 AAW	WIBLS	10//99-12//99
	Wyoming	S	9.98 MW	10.38 AW	21580 AAW	WYBLS	10//99-12//99
	Puerto Rico	S	7.92 MW	7.94 AW	16520 AAW	PRBLS	10//99-12//99
Meeting and Convention Planner	Alabama	S	15.59 MW	15.36 AW	31940 AAW	ALBLS	10//99-12//99
	Birmingham MSA, AL	S	15.45 MW	15.69 AW	32140 AAW	ALBLS	10//99-12//99
	Huntsville MSA, AL	S	15.38 MW	15.05 AW	32000 AAW	ALBLS	10//99-12//99
	Alaska	S	16.35 MW	18.48 AW	38450 AAW	AKBLS	10//99-12//99
	Anchorage MSA, AK	S	18.34 MW	16.42 AW	38140 AAW	AKBLS	10//99-12//99
	Arizona	S	15.62 MW	16.13 AW	33550 AAW	AZBLS	10//99-12//99
	Phoenix-Mesa MSA, AZ	S	16.42 MW	15.77 AW	34160 AAW	AZBLS	10//99-12//99
	Tucson MSA, AZ	S	17.89 MW	16.65 AW	37220 AAW	AZBLS	10//99-12//99
	Arkansas	S	10.65 MW	11.84 AW	24630 AAW	ARBLS	10//99-12//99
	California	S	17.46 MW	17.66 AW	36740 AAW	CABLS	10//99-12//99
	Los Angeles-Long Beach PMSA, CA	S	16.52 MW	16.23 AW	34360 AAW	CABLS	10//99-12//99
	Modesto MSA, CA	S	13.69 MW	13.27 AW	28470 AAW	CABLS	10//99-12//99
	Oakland PMSA, CA	S	18.93 MW	18.68 AW	39360 AAW	CABLS	10//99-12//99
	Orange County PMSA, CA	S	18.06 MW	15.98 AW	37560 AAW	CABLS	10//99-12//99
	Riverside-San Bernardino PMSA, CA	S	18.26 MW	16.91 AW	37990 AAW	CABLS	10//99-12//99
	Sacramento PMSA, CA	S	17.07 MW	18.44 AW	35510 AAW	CABLS	10//99-12//99
	Salinas MSA, CA	S	19.82 MW	18.11 AW	41220 AAW	CABLS	10//99-12//99
	San Diego MSA, CA	S	18.05 MW	17.64 AW	37540 AAW	CABLS	10//99-12//99
	San Francisco PMSA, CA	S	17.77 MW	16.92 AW	36960 AAW	CABLS	10//99-12//99
	San Jose PMSA, CA	S	18.93 MW	18.85 AW	39380 AAW	CABLS	10//99-12//99
	Santa Barbara-Santa Maria-Lompoc MSA, CA	S	15.68 MW	16.54 AW	32610 AAW	CABLS	10//99-12//99
	Santa Rosa PMSA, CA	S	13.36 MW	12.94 AW	27780 AAW	CABLS	10//99-12//99
	Ventura PMSA, CA	S	16.76 MW	17.67 AW	34870 AAW	CABLS	10//99-12//99
	Visalia-Tulare-Porterville MSA, CA	S	15.98 MW	15.35 AW	33240 AAW	CABLS	10//99-12//99
	Colorado	S	16.89 MW	18.10 AW	37650 AAW	COBLS	10//99-12//99
	Boulder-Longmont PMSA, CO	S	16.99 MW	16.84 AW	35340 AAW	COBLS	10//99-12//99
	Colorado Springs MSA, CO	S	17.07 MW	15.72 AW	35510 AAW	COBLS	10//99-12//99
	Denver PMSA, CO	S	18.51 MW	17.48 AW	38510 AAW	COBLS	10//99-12//99
	Connecticut	S	18.13 MW	18.80 AW	39100 AAW	CTBLS	10//99-12//99
	Hartford MSA, CT	S	17.78 MW	16.86 AW	36980 AAW	CTBLS	10//99-12//99
	New Haven-Meriden PMSA, CT	S	16.32 MW	15.84 AW	33950 AAW	CTBLS	10//99-12//99
	Stamford-Norwalk PMSA, CT	S	19.93 MW	18.59 AW	41460 AAW	CTBLS	10//99-12//99
	Delaware	S	22.48 MW	21.79 AW	45330 AAW	DEBLS	10//99-12//99
	Wilmington-Newark PMSA, DE-MD	S	21.17 MW	22.48 AW	44040 AAW	DEBLS	10//99-12//99
	District of Columbia	S	22.14 MW	22.81 AW	47450 AAW	DCBLS	10//99-12//99
	Washington PMSA, DC-MD-VA-WV	S	21.01 MW	19.51 AW	43700 AAW	DCBLS	10//99-12//99
	Florida	S	13.86 MW	14.10 AW	29330 AAW	FLBLS	10//99-12//99
	Daytona Beach MSA, FL	S	13.10 MW	10.57 AW	27250 AAW	FLBLS	10//99-12//99
	Fort Lauderdale PMSA, FL	S	18.38 MW	16.57 AW	38240 AAW	FLBLS	10//99-12//99
	Fort Myers-Cape Coral MSA, FL	S	13.39 MW	13.00 AW	27840 AAW	FLBLS	10//99-12//99
	Jacksonville MSA, FL	S	14.72 MW	14.51 AW	30620 AAW	FLBLS	10//99-12//99
	Miami PMSA, FL	S	15.60 MW	14.71 AW	32450 AAW	FLBLS	10//99-12//99
	Naples MSA, FL	S	10.91 MW	11.19 AW	22690 AAW	FLBLS	10//99-12//99

AAW	Average annual wage	AOH	Average offered, high	ASH	Average starting, high	H	Hourly	M	Monthly	S	Special: hourly and annual
AE	Average entry wage	AOL	Average offered, low	ASL	Average starting, low	HI	Highest wage paid	MTC	Median total compensation	TQ	Third quartile wage
AEX	Average experienced wage	APH	Average pay, high range	AW	Average wage paid	HR	High end range	MW	Median wage paid	W	Weekly
AO	Average offered	APL	Average pay, low range	FQ	First quartile wage	LR	Low end range	SQ	Second quartile wage	Y	Yearly

Occupation/Type/Industry	Location	Per	Low	Mid	High	Source	Date
Meeting and Convention Planner	Orlando MSA, FL	s	12.79 MW	12.08 AW	26600 AAW	FLBLS	10//99-12//99
	Pensacola MSA, FL	s	9.23 MW	7.94 AW	19190 AAW	FLBLS	10//99-12//99
	Sarasota-Bradenton MSA, FL	s	12.73 MW	11.65 AW	26470 AAW	FLBLS	10//99-12//99
	Tallahassee MSA, FL	s	12.49 MW	12.39 AW	25970 AAW	FLBLS	10//99-12//99
	Tampa-St. Petersburg-Clearwater MSA, FL	s	16.01 MW	16.07 AW	33290 AAW	FLBLS	10//99-12//99
	West Palm Beach-Boca Raton MSA, FL	s	15.87 MW	15.07 AW	33000 AAW	FLBLS	10//99-12//99
	Georgia	s	13.1 MW	14.89 AW	30980 AAW	GABLS	10//99-12//99
	Atlanta MSA, GA	s	13.90 MW	12.64 AW	28920 AAW	GABLS	10//99-12//99
	Hawaii	s	20.47 MW	20.18 AW	41980 AAW	HIBLS	10//99-12//99
	Honolulu MSA, HI	s	17.17 MW	18.25 AW	35710 AAW	HIBLS	10//99-12//99
	Idaho	s	13.91 MW	14.46 AW	30080 AAW	IDBLS	10//99-12//99
	Boise City MSA, ID	s	14.74 MW	14.19 AW	30650 AAW	IDBLS	10//99-12//99
	Illinois	s	19.18 MW	19.44 AW	40440 AAW	ILBLS	10//99-12//99
	Chicago PMSA, IL	s	19.91 MW	19.44 AW	41410 AAW	ILBLS	10//99-12//99
	Springfield MSA, IL	s	15.44 MW	14.53 AW	32100 AAW	ILBLS	10//99-12//99
	Indiana	s	14.61 MW	16.97 AW	35310 AAW	INBLS	10//99-12//99
	Gary PMSA, IN	s	16.96 MW	15.54 AW	35280 AAW	INBLS	10//99-12//99
	Indianapolis MSA, IN	s	18.36 MW	15.50 AW	38190 AAW	INBLS	10//99-12//99
	Iowa	s	12.77 MW	14.30 AW	29740 AAW	IABLS	10//99-12//99
	Davenport-Moline-Rock Island MSA, IA-IL	s	16.30 MW	14.89 AW	33910 AAW	IABLS	10//99-12//99
	Des Moines MSA, IA	s	14.57 MW	14.22 AW	30300 AAW	IABLS	10//99-12//99
	Kansas	s	13.21 MW	16.07 AW	33420 AAW	KSBLS	10//99-12//99
	Topeka MSA, KS	s	16.64 MW	15.25 AW	34610 AAW	KSBLS	10//99-12//99
	Kentucky	s	12.43 MW	13.63 AW	28350 AAW	KYBLS	10//99-12//99
	Louisville MSA, KY-IN	s	12.18 MW	10.72 AW	25330 AAW	KYBLS	10//99-12//99
	Louisiana	s	12.08 MW	13.38 AW	27820 AAW	LABLS	10//99-12//99
	Lafayette MSA, LA	s	7.51 MW	6.26 AW	15620 AAW	LABLS	10//99-12//99
	New Orleans MSA, LA	s	14.27 MW	12.00 AW	29680 AAW	LABLS	10//99-12//99
	Maine	s	12.94 MW	14.18 AW	29500 AAW	MEBLS	10//99-12//99
	Maryland	s	16.13 MW	16.65 AW	34630 AAW	MDBLS	10//99-12//99
	Baltimore PMSA, MD	s	15.28 MW	14.57 AW	31780 AAW	MDBLS	10//99-12//99
	Massachusetts	s	17.26 MW	18.53 AW	38540 AAW	MABLS	10//99-12//99
	Boston PMSA, MA-NH	s	18.57 MW	17.26 AW	38630 AAW	MABLS	10//99-12//99
	Springfield MSA, MA	s	20.60 MW	21.37 AW	42850 AAW	MABLS	10//99-12//99
	Michigan	s	15.44 MW	16.59 AW	34500 AAW	MIBLS	10//99-12//99
	Ann Arbor PMSA, MI	s	14.68 MW	13.92 AW	30540 AAW	MIBLS	10//99-12//99
	Detroit PMSA, MI	s	18.12 MW	16.89 AW	37690 AAW	MIBLS	10//99-12//99
	Lansing-East Lansing MSA, MI	s	20.29 MW	19.15 AW	42190 AAW	MIBLS	10//99-12//99
	Saginaw-Bay City-Midland MSA, MI	s	11.76 MW	10.02 AW	24460 AAW	MIBLS	10//99-12//99
	Minnesota	s	15.01 MW	15.72 AW	32700 AAW	MNBLS	10//99-12//99
	Minneapolis-St. Paul MSA, MN-WI	s	15.69 MW	15.00 AW	32630 AAW	MNBLS	10//99-12//99
	Mississippi	s	17.15 MW	18.23 AW	37910 AAW	MSBLS	10//99-12//99
	Missouri	s	15.66 MW	16.20 AW	33700 AAW	MOBLS	10//99-12//99
	Kansas City MSA, MO-KS	s	17.83 MW	16.02 AW	37090 AAW	MOBLS	10//99-12//99
	St. Louis MSA, MO-IL	s	16.04 MW	15.42 AW	33360 AAW	MOBLS	10//99-12//99
	Montana	s	12.09 MW	13.38 AW	27830 AAW	MTBLS	10//99-12//99
	Nebraska	s	12.63 MW	13.30 AW	27670 AAW	NEBLS	10//99-12//99
	Omaha MSA, NE-IA	s	13.59 MW	12.55 AW	28270 AAW	NEBLS	10//99-12//99
	Nevada	s	14.99 MW	15.77 AW	32790 AAW	NVBLS	10//99-12//99
	Las Vegas MSA, NV-AZ	s	16.63 MW	16.08 AW	34590 AAW	NVBLS	10//99-12//99
	Reno MSA, NV	s	13.44 MW	12.51 AW	27950 AAW	NVBLS	10//99-12//99
	New Hampshire	s	17.8 MW	17.15 AW	35670 AAW	NHBLS	10//99-12//99
	New Jersey	s	20.38 MW	26.45 AW	55010 AAW	NJBLS	10//99-12//99
	Atlantic-Cape May PMSA, NJ	s	17.02 MW	17.00 AW	35400 AAW	NJBLS	10//99-12//99
	Middlesex-Somerset-Hunterdon PMSA, NJ	s	20.37 MW	18.62 AW	42380 AAW	NJBLS	10//99-12//99
	Trenton PMSA, NJ	s	23.67 MW	20.19 AW	49240 AAW	NJBLS	10//99-12//99
	New Mexico	s	16.01 MW	16.69 AW	34710 AAW	NMBLS	10//99-12//99
	Albuquerque MSA, NM	s	17.62 MW	17.63 AW	36650 AAW	NMBLS	10//99-12//99
	New York	s	19.03 MW	20.66 AW	42980 AAW	NYBLS	10//99-12//99
	Albany-Schenectady-Troy MSA, NY	s	19.12 MW	18.18 AW	39770 AAW	NYBLS	10//99-12//99
	Buffalo-Niagara Falls MSA, NY	s	18.94 MW	19.12 AW	39390 AAW	NYBLS	10//99-12//99
	Nassau-Suffolk PMSA, NY	s	22.47 MW	23.65 AW	46740 AAW	NYBLS	10//99-12//99
	New York PMSA, NY	s	22.40 MW	19.68 AW	46590 AAW	NYBLS	10//99-12//99
	Rochester MSA, NY	s	13.22 MW	12.47 AW	27490 AAW	NYBLS	10//99-12//99

AAW	Average annual wage	AOH	Average offered, high	ASH	Average starting, high
AE	Average entry wage	AOL	Average offered, low	ASL	Average starting, low
AEX	Average experienced wage	APH	Average pay, high range	AW	Average wage paid
AO	Average offered	APL	Average pay, low range	FQ	First quartile wage

H	Hourly	
HI	Highest wage paid	
HR	High end range	
LR	Low end range	

M	Monthly	
MTC	Median total compensation	
MW	Median wage paid	
SQ	Second quartile wage	

S	Special: hourly and annual
TQ	Third quartile wage
W	Weekly
Y	Yearly

Occupation/Type/Industry	Location	Per	Low	Mid	High	Source	Date
Meeting and Convention Planner	North Carolina	S	14.67 MW	15.48 AW	32200 AAW	NCBLS	10//99-12//99
	Charlotte-Gastonia-Rock Hill MSA, NC-SC	S	14.92 MW	15.01 AW	31040 AAW	NCBLS	10//99-12//99
	Greensboro--Winston-Salem-- High Point MSA, NC	S	15.29 MW	14.87 AW	31800 AAW	NCBLS	10//99-12//99
	Raleigh-Durham-Chapel Hill MSA, NC	S	16.21 MW	14.58 AW	33720 AAW	NCBLS	10//99-12//99
	North Dakota	S	11.44 MW	12.25 AW	25490 AAW	NDBLS	10//99-12//99
	Ohio	S	16.12 MW	16.98 AW	35310 AAW	OHBLS	10//99-12//99
	Akron PMSA, OH	S	11.58 MW	11.52 AW	24090 AAW	OHBLS	10//99-12//99
	Cincinnati PMSA, OH-KY-IN	S	16.59 MW	15.43 AW	34510 AAW	OHBLS	10//99-12//99
	Columbus MSA, OH	S	16.82 MW	15.65 AW	34980 AAW	OHBLS	10//99-12//99
	Dayton-Springfield MSA, OH	S	19.39 MW	20.72 AW	40330 AAW	OHBLS	10//99-12//99
	Oklahoma	S	11.02 MW	14.91 AW	31020 AAW	OKBLS	10//99-12//99
	Oklahoma City MSA, OK	S	15.96 MW	17.57 AW	33190 AAW	OKBLS	10//99-12//99
	Tulsa MSA, OK	S	17.62 MW	17.50 AW	36650 AAW	OKBLS	10//99-12//99
	Oregon	S	15.55 MW	16.35 AW	34000 AAW	ORBLS	10//99-12//99
	Portland-Vancouver PMSA, OR-WA	S	16.83 MW	16.55 AW	35010 AAW	ORBLS	10//99-12//99
	Pennsylvania	S	15.89 MW	16.48 AW	34290 AAW	PABLS	10//99-12//99
	Harrisburg-Lebanon-Carlisle MSA, PA	S	22.62 MW	21.72 AW	47040 AAW	PABLS	10//99-12//99
	Lancaster MSA, PA	S	17.05 MW	16.74 AW	35460 AAW	PABLS	10//99-12//99
	Philadelphia PMSA, PA-NJ	S	17.26 MW	16.55 AW	35900 AAW	PABLS	10//99-12//99
	Pittsburgh MSA, PA	S	15.71 MW	15.61 AW	32670 AAW	PABLS	10//99-12//99
	Rhode Island	S	17.75 MW	18.61 AW	38720 AAW	RIBLS	10//99-12//99
	South Carolina	S	15.89 MW	18.21 AW	37870 AAW	SCBLS	10//99-12//99
	Charleston-North Charleston MSA, SC	S	17.00 MW	16.32 AW	35370 AAW	SCBLS	10//99-12//99
	Columbia MSA, SC	S	25.25 MW	21.18 AW	52520 AAW	SCBLS	10//99-12//99
	Greenville-Spartanburg- Anderson MSA, SC	S	10.88 MW	10.22 AW	22640 AAW	SCBLS	10//99-12//99
	Myrtle Beach MSA, SC	S	16.15 MW	14.12 AW	33590 AAW	SCBLS	10//99-12//99
	South Dakota	S	12.56 MW	13.12 AW	27300 AAW	SDBLS	10//99-12//99
	Tennessee	S	17.09 MW	17.89 AW	37210 AAW	TNBLS	10//99-12//99
	Chattanooga MSA, TN-GA	S	19.42 MW	15.92 AW	40390 AAW	TNBLS	10//99-12//99
	Knoxville MSA, TN	S	13.62 MW	12.60 AW	28340 AAW	TNBLS	10//99-12//99
	Memphis MSA, TN-AR-MS	S	17.17 MW	17.83 AW	35710 AAW	MSBLS	10//99-12//99
	Nashville MSA, TN	S	19.52 MW	18.54 AW	40610 AAW	TNBLS	10//99-12//99
	Texas	S	15.75 MW	16.55 AW	34430 AAW	TXBLS	10//99-12//99
	Austin-San Marcos MSA, TX	S	17.47 MW	17.00 AW	36330 AAW	TXBLS	10//99-12//99
	Bryan-College Station MSA, TX	S	10.45 MW	9.76 AW	21740 AAW	TXBLS	10//99-12//99
	Dallas PMSA, TX	S	18.82 MW	17.95 AW	39140 AAW	TXBLS	10//99-12//99
	Fort Worth-Arlington PMSA, TX	S	16.16 MW	14.77 AW	33620 AAW	TXBLS	10//99-12//99
	Galveston-Texas City PMSA, TX	S	16.19 MW	15.85 AW	33670 AAW	TXBLS	10//99-12//99
	Houston PMSA, TX	S	17.50 MW	16.80 AW	36390 AAW	TXBLS	10//99-12//99
	San Antonio MSA, TX	S	14.84 MW	14.95 AW	30860 AAW	TXBLS	10//99-12//99
	Utah	S	13.72 MW	14.55 AW	30270 AAW	UTBLS	10//99-12//99
	Salt Lake City-Ogden MSA, UT	S	14.07 MW	13.40 AW	29260 AAW	UTBLS	10//99-12//99
	Vermont	S	12.68 MW	13.79 AW	28680 AAW	VTBLS	10//99-12//99
	Burlington MSA, VT	S	14.86 MW	14.74 AW	30910 AAW	VTBLS	10//99-12//99
	Virginia	S	16.29 MW	17.93 AW	37290 AAW	VABLS	10//99-12//99
	Norfolk-Virginia Beach- Newport News MSA, VA- NC	S	14.56 MW	13.12 AW	30290 AAW	VABLS	10//99-12//99
	Richmond-Petersburg MSA, VA	S	16.80 MW	16.10 AW	34930 AAW	VABLS	10//99-12//99
	Washington	S	14.1 MW	15.72 AW	32710 AAW	WABLS	10//99-12//99
	Seattle-Bellevue-Everett PMSA, WA	S	15.78 MW	13.81 AW	32820 AAW	WABLS	10//99-12//99
	Spokane MSA, WA	S	14.30 MW	13.01 AW	29730 AAW	WABLS	10//99-12//99
	West Virginia	S	10.69 MW	12.21 AW	25400 AAW	WVBLS	10//99-12//99
	Charleston MSA, WV	S	12.20 MW	10.54 AW	25370 AAW	WVBLS	10//99-12//99
	Wisconsin	S	15.37 MW	16.10 AW	33490 AAW	WIBLS	10//99-12//99
	Eau Claire MSA, WI	S	13.29 MW	12.58 AW	27640 AAW	WIBLS	10//99-12//99
	Madison MSA, WI	S	18.63 MW	18.82 AW	38750 AAW	WIBLS	10//99-12//99
	Milwaukee-Waukesha PMSA, WI	S	18.08 MW	16.52 AW	37610 AAW	WIBLS	10//99-12//99

AAW	Average annual wage	AOH	Average offered, high	ASH	Average starting, high	H	Hourly	M	Monthly	S	Special: hourly and annual
AE	Average entry wage	AOL	Average offered, low	ASL	Average starting, low	HI	Highest wage paid	MTC	Median total compensation	TQ	Third quartile wage
AEX	Average experienced wage	APH	Average pay, high range	AW	Average wage paid	HR	High end range	MW	Median wage paid	W	Weekly
AO	Average offered	APL	Average pay, low range	FQ	First quartile wage	LR	Low end range	SQ	Second quartile wage	Y	Yearly

Occupation/Type/Industry	Location	Per	Low	Mid	High	Source	Date
Meeting and Convention Planner	Puerto Rico	S	19.01 MW	17.43 AW	36250 AAW	PRBLS	10//99-12//99
	San Juan-Bayamon PMSA, PR	S	19.21 MW	19.84 AW	39950 AAW	PRBLS	10//99-12//99
	Virgin Islands	S	12.78 MW	14.99 AW	31180 AAW	VIBLS	10//99-12//99
Meetings Manager							
Association	United States	Y		54500 MW		ASMA	1998
Mental Health and Substance Abuse Social Worker	Alabama	S	11.3 MW	12.50 AW	26000 AAW	ALBLS	10//99-12//99
	Birmingham MSA, AL	S	11.94 MW	11.21 AW	24840 AAW	ALBLS	10//99-12//99
	Montgomery MSA, AL	S	11.76 MW	8.44 AW	24460 AAW	ALBLS	10//99-12//99
	Tuscaloosa MSA, AL	S	18.03 MW	18.39 AW	37490 AAW	ALBLS	10//99-12//99
	Alaska	S	13.13 MW	13.89 AW	28890 AAW	AKBLS	10//99-12//99
	Anchorage MSA, AK	S	14.92 MW	14.22 AW	31030 AAW	AKBLS	10//99-12//99
	Arizona	S	11.88 MW	13.27 AW	27600 AAW	AZBLS	10//99-12//99
	Flagstaff MSA, AZ-UT	S	15.64 MW	15.30 AW	32530 AAW	AZBLS	10//99-12//99
	Phoenix-Mesa MSA, AZ	S	13.67 MW	12.26 AW	28440 AAW	AZBLS	10//99-12//99
	Arkansas	S	13.12 MW	13.45 AW	27980 AAW	ARBLS	10//99-12//99
	Fort Smith MSA, AR-OK	S	12.74 MW	10.62 AW	26500 AAW	ARBLS	10//99-12//99
	Little Rock-North Little Rock MSA, AR	S	13.72 MW	13.89 AW	28530 AAW	ARBLS	10//99-12//99
	California	S	15.99 MW	16.67 AW	34680 AAW	CABLS	10//99-12//99
	Bakersfield MSA, CA	S	17.68 MW	18.61 AW	36780 AAW	CABLS	10//99-12//99
	Fresno MSA, CA	S	17.28 MW	16.12 AW	35940 AAW	CABLS	10//99-12//99
	Los Angeles-Long Beach PMSA, CA	S	16.68 MW	17.12 AW	34700 AAW	CABLS	10//99-12//99
	Oakland PMSA, CA	S	19.09 MW	19.54 AW	39710 AAW	CABLS	10//99-12//99
	Riverside-San Bernardino PMSA, CA	S	14.36 MW	12.15 AW	29870 AAW	CABLS	10//99-12//99
	Salinas MSA, CA	S	13.80 MW	13.58 AW	28700 AAW	CABLS	10//99-12//99
	San Diego MSA, CA	S	14.45 MW	13.37 AW	30060 AAW	CABLS	10//99-12//99
	San Francisco PMSA, CA	S	18.00 MW	16.77 AW	37430 AAW	CABLS	10//99-12//99
	Santa Barbara-Santa Maria-Lompoc MSA, CA	S	12.47 MW	12.39 AW	25940 AAW	CABLS	10//99-12//99
	Colorado	S	13.45 MW	14.87 AW	30920 AAW	COBLS	10//99-12//99
	Connecticut	S	22.1 MW	20.92 AW	43520 AAW	CTBLS	10//99-12//99
	Bridgeport PMSA, CT	S	18.77 MW	21.97 AW	39040 AAW	CTBLS	10//99-12//99
	Hartford MSA, CT	S	22.87 MW	23.66 AW	47560 AAW	CTBLS	10//99-12//99
	New Haven-Meriden PMSA, CT	S	15.99 MW	14.41 AW	33260 AAW	CTBLS	10//99-12//99
	New London-Norwich MSA, CT-RI	S	18.43 MW	16.35 AW	38330 AAW	CTBLS	10//99-12//99
	Delaware	S	17.24 MW	16.90 AW	35150 AAW	DEBLS	10//99-12//99
	Wilmington-Newark PMSA, DE-MD	S	16.80 MW	17.08 AW	34950 AAW	DEBLS	10//99-12//99
	District of Columbia	S	19.81 MW	23.62 AW	49120 AAW	DCBLS	10//99-12//99
	Washington PMSA, DC-MD-VA-WV	S	22.35 MW	22.36 AW	46480 AAW	DCBLS	10//99-12//99
	Florida	S	12.31 MW	12.81 AW	26650 AAW	FLBLS	10//99-12//99
	Fort Lauderdale PMSA, FL	S	15.01 MW	14.27 AW	31210 AAW	FLBLS	10//99-12//99
	Gainesville MSA, FL	S	12.34 MW	12.28 AW	25670 AAW	FLBLS	10//99-12//99
	Jacksonville MSA, FL	S	15.41 MW	13.25 AW	32040 AAW	FLBLS	10//99-12//99
	Melbourne-Titusville-Palm Bay MSA, FL	S	12.80 MW	12.07 AW	26630 AAW	FLBLS	10//99-12//99
	Miami PMSA, FL	S	12.93 MW	12.40 AW	26900 AAW	FLBLS	10//99-12//99
	Orlando MSA, FL	S	12.45 MW	12.18 AW	25900 AAW	FLBLS	10//99-12//99
	Sarasota-Bradenton MSA, FL	S	10.57 MW	10.24 AW	21980 AAW	FLBLS	10//99-12//99
	Tampa-St. Petersburg-Clearwater MSA, FL	S	11.88 MW	11.20 AW	24710 AAW	FLBLS	10//99-12//99
	West Palm Beach-Boca Raton MSA, FL	S	14.35 MW	14.16 AW	29840 AAW	FLBLS	10//99-12//99
	Georgia	S	15.13 MW	15.79 AW	32830 AAW	GABLS	10//99-12//99
	Atlanta MSA, GA	S	14.89 MW	14.76 AW	30970 AAW	GABLS	10//99-12//99
	Hawaii	S	19.16 MW	18.99 AW	39500 AAW	HIBLS	10//99-12//99
	Honolulu MSA, HI	S	19.22 MW	19.23 AW	39990 AAW	HIBLS	10//99-12//99
	Idaho	S	13.78 MW	14.00 AW	29110 AAW	IDBLS	10//99-12//99
	Boise City MSA, ID	S	15.18 MW	15.05 AW	31570 AAW	IDBLS	10//99-12//99
	Illinois	S	13.05 MW	14.09 AW	29310 AAW	ILBLS	10//99-12//99
	Champaign-Urbana MSA, IL	S	12.33 MW	10.10 AW	25640 AAW	ILBLS	10//99-12//99
	Chicago PMSA, IL	S	14.06 MW	13.39 AW	29240 AAW	ILBLS	10//99-12//99
	Peoria-Pekin MSA, IL	S	21.11 MW	18.68 AW	43910 AAW	ILBLS	10//99-12//99
	Indiana	S	14.49 MW	14.39 AW	29940 AAW	INBLS	10//99-12//99

AAW Average annual wage	AOH Average offered, high	ASH Average starting, high	H Hourly	M Monthly	S Special: hourly and annual
AE Average entry wage	AOL Average offered, low	ASL Average starting, low	HI Highest wage paid	MTC Median total compensation	TQ Third quartile wage
AEX Average experienced wage	APH Average pay, high range	AW Average wage paid	HR High end range	MW Median wage paid	W Weekly
AO Average offered	APL Average pay, low range	FQ First quartile wage	LR Low end range	SQ Second quartile wage	Y Yearly

Occupation/Type/Industry	Location	Per	Low	Mid	High	Source	Date
Mental Health and Substance Abuse Social Worker	Evansville-Henderson MSA, IN-KY	S	12.24 MW	12.12 AW	25470 AAW	INBLS	10//99-12//99
	Fort Wayne MSA, IN	S	12.64 MW	12.70 AW	26300 AAW	INBLS	10//99-12//99
	Gary PMSA, IN	S	16.51 MW	15.92 AW	34340 AAW	INBLS	10//99-12//99
	Indianapolis MSA, IN	S	15.89 MW	15.64 AW	33050 AAW	INBLS	10//99-12//99
	South Bend MSA, IN	S	15.89 MW	15.85 AW	33040 AAW	INBLS	10//99-12//99
	Iowa	S	11.86 MW	12.87 AW	26760 AAW	IABLS	10//99-12//99
	Des Moines MSA, IA	S	12.11 MW	11.10 AW	25180 AAW	IABLS	10//99-12//99
	Kansas	S	13.72 MW	14.42 AW	29990 AAW	KSBLS	10//99-12//99
	Topeka MSA, KS	S	13.64 MW	13.22 AW	28370 AAW	KSBLS	10//99-12//99
	Kentucky	S	11.52 MW	12.33 AW	25650 AAW	KYBLS	10//99-12//99
	Lexington MSA, KY	S	11.78 MW	11.89 AW	24490 AAW	KYBLS	10//99-12//99
	Louisville MSA, KY-IN	S	12.60 MW	11.46 AW	26210 AAW	KYBLS	10//99-12//99
	Louisiana	S	13.54 MW	13.95 AW	29010 AAW	LABLS	10//99-12//99
	Monroe MSA, LA	S	11.90 MW	11.76 AW	24760 AAW	LABLS	10//99-12//99
	New Orleans MSA, LA	S	16.69 MW	16.87 AW	34730 AAW	LABLS	10//99-12//99
	Maine	S	14.98 MW	15.36 AW	31950 AAW	MEBLS	10//99-12//99
	Bangor MSA, ME	S	16.47 MW	15.72 AW	34260 AAW	MEBLS	10//99-12//99
	Portland MSA, ME	S	17.43 MW	16.80 AW	36250 AAW	MEBLS	10//99-12//99
	Maryland	S	18.15 MW	17.97 AW	37370 AAW	MDBLS	10//99-12//99
	Baltimore PMSA, MD	S	17.78 MW	18.19 AW	36980 AAW	MDBLS	10//99-12//99
	Massachusetts	S	13.35 MW	14.85 AW	30890 AAW	MABLS	10//99-12//99
	Boston PMSA, MA-NH	S	14.74 MW	13.49 AW	30650 AAW	MABLS	10//99-12//99
	Lowell PMSA, MA-NH	S	16.95 MW	13.24 AW	35260 AAW	MABLS	10//99-12//99
	Michigan	S	16.32 MW	16.66 AW	34640 AAW	MIBLS	10//99-12//99
	Detroit PMSA, MI	S	18.70 MW	18.23 AW	38890 AAW	MIBLS	10//99-12//99
	Flint PMSA, MI	S	16.42 MW	16.22 AW	34150 AAW	MIBLS	10//99-12//99
	Grand Rapids-Muskegon-Holland MSA, MI	S	14.54 MW	13.98 AW	30240 AAW	MIBLS	10//99-12//99
	Kalamazoo-Battle Creek MSA, MI	S	16.45 MW	15.55 AW	34220 AAW	MIBLS	10//99-12//99
	Lansing-East Lansing MSA, MI	S	13.84 MW	13.86 AW	28790 AAW	MIBLS	10//99-12//99
	Minnesota	S	16.78 MW	17.79 AW	37000 AAW	MNBLS	10//99-12//99
	Duluth-Superior MSA, MN-WI	S	15.25 MW	14.82 AW	31720 AAW	MNBLS	10//99-12//99
	Minneapolis-St. Paul MSA, MN-WI	S	17.39 MW	16.33 AW	36180 AAW	MNBLS	10//99-12//99
	Mississippi	S	9.88 MW	10.50 AW	21840 AAW	MSBLS	10//99-12//99
	Missouri	S	16.44 MW	16.52 AW	34360 AAW	MOBLS	10//99-12//99
	St. Louis MSA, MO-IL	S	17.55 MW	17.68 AW	36510 AAW	MOBLS	10//99-12//99
	Montana	S	11.02 MW	11.19 AW	23280 AAW	MTBLS	10//99-12//99
	Nebraska	S	10.71 MW	11.87 AW	24690 AAW	NEBLS	10//99-12//99
	Lincoln MSA, NE	S	13.48 MW	13.58 AW	28030 AAW	NEBLS	10//99-12//99
	Omaha MSA, NE-IA	S	11.94 MW	10.61 AW	24840 AAW	NEBLS	10//99-12//99
	Nevada	S	17.59 MW	16.90 AW	35140 AAW	NVBLS	10//99-12//99
	Las Vegas MSA, NV-AZ	S	17.03 MW	17.70 AW	35430 AAW	NVBLS	10//99-12//99
	New Hampshire	S	15.87 MW	16.09 AW	33470 AAW	NHBLS	10//99-12//99
	Manchester PMSA, NH	S	15.69 MW	15.51 AW	32630 AAW	NHBLS	10//99-12//99
	New Jersey	S	18.71 MW	18.54 AW	38560 AAW	NJBLS	10//99-12//99
	Atlantic-Cape May PMSA, NJ	S	12.39 MW	12.38 AW	25760 AAW	NJBLS	10//99-12//99
	Bergen-Passaic PMSA, NJ	S	15.06 MW	12.69 AW	31330 AAW	NJBLS	10//99-12//99
	Jersey City PMSA, NJ	S	20.20 MW	19.83 AW	42030 AAW	NJBLS	10//99-12//99
	Middlesex-Somerset-Hunterdon PMSA, NJ	S	14.81 MW	12.58 AW	30800 AAW	NJBLS	10//99-12//99
	Monmouth-Ocean PMSA, NJ	S	21.37 MW	22.55 AW	44450 AAW	NJBLS	10//99-12//99
	Newark PMSA, NJ	S	17.99 MW	17.06 AW	37420 AAW	NJBLS	10//99-12//99
	Trenton PMSA, NJ	S	23.24 MW	23.50 AW	48350 AAW	NJBLS	10//99-12//99
	Vineland-Millville-Bridgeton PMSA, NJ	S	16.54 MW	17.07 AW	34410 AAW	NJBLS	10//99-12//99
	New Mexico	S	12.42 MW	13.86 AW	28840 AAW	NMBLS	10//99-12//99
	Albuquerque MSA, NM	S	17.64 MW	20.04 AW	36700 AAW	NMBLS	10//99-12//99
	Las Cruces MSA, NM	S	12.55 MW	12.42 AW	26090 AAW	NMBLS	10//99-12//99
	New York	S	17.79 MW	18.18 AW	37820 AAW	NYBLS	10//99-12//99
	Albany-Schenectady-Troy MSA, NY	S	13.34 MW	12.68 AW	27750 AAW	NYBLS	10//99-12//99
	Binghamton MSA, NY	S	16.64 MW	15.95 AW	34620 AAW	NYBLS	10//99-12//99
	Buffalo-Niagara Falls MSA, NY	S	15.44 MW	14.41 AW	32120 AAW	NYBLS	10//99-12//99
	Dutchess County PMSA, NY	S	21.96 MW	22.92 AW	45680 AAW	NYBLS	10//99-12//99
	Nassau-Suffolk PMSA, NY	S	18.68 MW	18.04 AW	38860 AAW	NYBLS	10//99-12//99
	New York PMSA, NY	S	18.71 MW	19.22 AW	38920 AAW	NYBLS	10//99-12//99
	Rochester MSA, NY	S	16.61 MW	17.25 AW	34540 AAW	NYBLS	10//99-12//99

AAW Average annual wage	**AOH** Average offered, high	**ASH** Average starting, high	**H** Hourly	**M** Monthly	**S** Special: hourly and annual
AE Average entry wage	**AOL** Average offered, low	**ASL** Average starting, low	**HI** Highest wage paid	**MTC** Median total compensation	**TQ** Third quartile wage
AEX Average experienced wage	**APH** Average pay, high range	**AW** Average wage paid	**HR** High end range	**MW** Median wage paid	**W** Weekly
AO Average offered	**APL** Average pay, low range	**FQ** First quartile wage	**LR** Low end range	**SQ** Second quartile wage	**Y** Yearly

Mental Health and Substance Abuse Social Worker

Occupation/Type/Industry	Location	Per	Low	Mid	High	Source	Date
Mental Health and Substance Abuse Social Worker	Syracuse MSA, NY	S	17.92 MW	18.55 AW	37280 AAW	NYBLS	10//99-12//99
	North Carolina	S	12.84 MW	13.40 AW	27880 AAW	NCBLS	10//99-12//99
	Charlotte-Gastonia-Rock Hill MSA, NC-SC	S	13.60 MW	13.33 AW	28290 AAW	NCBLS	10//99-12//99
	Greensboro--Winston-Salem-- High Point MSA, NC	S	17.13 MW	17.98 AW	35620 AAW	NCBLS	10//99-12//99
	Hickory-Morganton-Lenoir MSA, NC	S	15.55 MW	15.40 AW	32340 AAW	NCBLS	10//99-12//99
	Raleigh-Durham-Chapel Hill MSA, NC	S	10.51 MW	9.74 AW	21850 AAW	NCBLS	10//99-12//99
	North Dakota	S	14.59 MW	15.47 AW	32180 AAW	NDBLS	10//99-12//99
	Ohio	S	13.43 MW	13.92 AW	28960 AAW	OHBLS	10//99-12//99
	Akron PMSA, OH	S	14.28 MW	13.54 AW	29700 AAW	OHBLS	10//99-12//99
	Canton-Massillon MSA, OH	S	15.99 MW	15.48 AW	33250 AAW	OHBLS	10//99-12//99
	Cincinnati PMSA, OH-KY-IN	S	12.76 MW	12.35 AW	26540 AAW	OHBLS	10//99-12//99
	Cleveland-Lorain-Elyria PMSA, OH	S	15.08 MW	15.15 AW	31360 AAW	OHBLS	10//99-12//99
	Columbus MSA, OH	S	14.62 MW	13.35 AW	30400 AAW	OHBLS	10//99-12//99
	Hamilton-Middletown PMSA, OH	S	11.10 MW	10.72 AW	23080 AAW	OHBLS	10//99-12//99
	Mansfield MSA, OH	S	11.91 MW	12.00 AW	24780 AAW	OHBLS	10//99-12//99
	Toledo MSA, OH	S	12.22 MW	12.29 AW	25420 AAW	OHBLS	10//99-12//99
	Youngstown-Warren MSA, OH	S	22.82 MW	20.76 AW	47460 AAW	OHBLS	10//99-12//99
	Oklahoma	S	11.78 MW	12.06 AW	25090 AAW	OKBLS	10//99-12//99
	Tulsa MSA, OK	S	13.01 MW	13.08 AW	27050 AAW	OKBLS	10//99-12//99
	Oregon	S	12.37 MW	13.27 AW	27600 AAW	ORBLS	10//99-12//99
	Eugene-Springfield MSA, OR	S	11.43 MW	11.67 AW	23770 AAW	ORBLS	10//99-12//99
	Portland-Vancouver PMSA, OR-WA	S	11.13 MW	9.50 AW	23160 AAW	ORBLS	10//99-12//99
	Pennsylvania	S	12.67 MW	13.64 AW	28380 AAW	PABLS	10//99-12//99
	Harrisburg-Lebanon-Carlisle MSA, PA	S	15.81 MW	14.08 AW	32890 AAW	PABLS	10//99-12//99
	Philadelphia PMSA, PA-NJ	S	14.73 MW	13.06 AW	30640 AAW	PABLS	10//99-12//99
	Pittsburgh MSA, PA	S	11.32 MW	10.46 AW	23540 AAW	PABLS	10//99-12//99
	Reading MSA, PA	S	18.99 MW	18.17 AW	39500 AAW	PABLS	10//99-12//99
	Scranton--Wilkes-Barre-- Hazleton MSA, PA	S	15.68 MW	14.88 AW	32620 AAW	PABLS	10//99-12//99
	Rhode Island	S	11.92 MW	14.05 AW	29210 AAW	RIBLS	10//99-12//99
	Providence-Fall River- Warwick MSA, RI-MA	S	13.27 MW	12.50 AW	27610 AAW	RIBLS	10//99-12//99
	South Carolina	S	13.87 MW	14.24 AW	29610 AAW	SCBLS	10//99-12//99
	Columbia MSA, SC	S	14.80 MW	14.86 AW	30790 AAW	SCBLS	10//99-12//99
	South Dakota	S	13.02 MW	13.50 AW	28070 AAW	SDBLS	10//99-12//99
	Rapid City MSA, SD	S	14.87 MW	14.22 AW	30920 AAW	SDBLS	10//99-12//99
	Sioux Falls MSA, SD	S	13.11 MW	12.66 AW	27270 AAW	SDBLS	10//99-12//99
	Tennessee	S	10.91 MW	11.36 AW	23630 AAW	TNBLS	10//99-12//99
	Chattanooga MSA, TN-GA	S	12.53 MW	12.31 AW	26060 AAW	TNBLS	10//99-12//99
	Jackson MSA, TN	S	10.96 MW	10.04 AW	22810 AAW	TNBLS	10//99-12//99
	Knoxville MSA, TN	S	9.11 MW	8.22 AW	18950 AAW	TNBLS	10//99-12//99
	Memphis MSA, TN-AR-MS	S	10.89 MW	10.42 AW	22650 AAW	MSBLS	10//99-12//99
	Nashville MSA, TN	S	12.96 MW	13.12 AW	26960 AAW	TNBLS	10//99-12//99
	Texas	S	11.55 MW	12.17 AW	25310 AAW	TXBLS	10//99-12//99
	Dallas PMSA, TX	S	13.65 MW	13.23 AW	28390 AAW	TXBLS	10//99-12//99
	Fort Worth-Arlington PMSA, TX	S	10.64 MW	10.08 AW	22140 AAW	TXBLS	10//99-12//99
	Houston PMSA, TX	S	14.23 MW	13.36 AW	29590 AAW	TXBLS	10//99-12//99
	Killeen-Temple MSA, TX	S	11.69 MW	10.52 AW	24310 AAW	TXBLS	10//99-12//99
	San Antonio MSA, TX	S	10.91 MW	8.62 AW	22690 AAW	TXBLS	10//99-12//99
	Utah	S	15.73 MW	15.68 AW	32610 AAW	UTBLS	10//99-12//99
	Provo-Orem MSA, UT	S	16.40 MW	16.29 AW	34110 AAW	UTBLS	10//99-12//99
	Virginia	S	18.91 MW	20.07 AW	41740 AAW	VABLS	10//99-12//99
	Charlottesville MSA, VA	S	15.30 MW	15.26 AW	31820 AAW	VABLS	10//99-12//99
	Norfolk-Virginia Beach- Newport News MSA, VA- NC	S	19.32 MW	17.83 AW	40190 AAW	VABLS	10//99-12//99
	Richmond-Petersburg MSA, VA	S	17.21 MW	15.09 AW	35800 AAW	VABLS	10//99-12//99
	Washington	S	14.25 MW	14.98 AW	31160 AAW	WABLS	10//99-12//99
	Seattle-Bellevue-Everett PMSA, WA	S	14.94 MW	13.24 AW	31080 AAW	WABLS	10//99-12//99
	Spokane MSA, WA	S	13.81 MW	13.74 AW	28720 AAW	WABLS	10//99-12//99

AAW Average annual wage	AOH Average offered, high	ASH Average starting, high	H Hourly	M Monthly	S Special: hourly and annual
AE Average entry wage	AOL Average offered, low	ASL Average starting, low	HI Highest wage paid	MTC Median total compensation	TQ Third quartile wage
AEX Average experienced wage	APH Average pay, high range	AW Average wage paid	HR High end range	MW Median wage paid	W Weekly
AO Average offered	APL Average pay, low range	FQ First quartile wage	LR Low end range	SQ Second quartile wage	Y Yearly

Occupation/Type/Industry	Location	Per	Low	Mid	High	Source	Date
Mental Health and Substance Abuse Social Worker	Tacoma PMSA, WA	S	15.96 MW	15.86 AW	33190 AAW	WABLS	10//99-12//99
	Yakima MSA, WA	S	13.05 MW	11.66 AW	27140 AAW	WABLS	10//99-12//99
	West Virginia	S	8.33 MW	8.43 AW	17520 AAW	WVBLS	10//99-12//99
	Charleston MSA, WV	S	8.66 MW	8.21 AW	18010 AAW	WVBLS	10//99-12//99
	Huntington-Ashland MSA, WV-KY-OH	S	10.16 MW	9.82 AW	21140 AAW	WVBLS	10//99-12//99
	Wisconsin	S	15.32 MW	15.38 AW	31990 AAW	WIBLS	10//99-12//99
	Green Bay MSA, WI	S	15.32 MW	15.29 AW	31860 AAW	WIBLS	10//99-12//99
	Madison MSA, WI	S	17.94 MW	18.09 AW	37320 AAW	WIBLS	10//99-12//99
	Milwaukee-Waukesha PMSA, WI	S	15.27 MW	15.23 AW	31760 AAW	WIBLS	10//99-12//99
	Wyoming	S	14.55 MW	14.58 AW	30320 AAW	WYBLS	10//99-12//99
Mental Health Counselor	Alabama	S	11.49 MW	12.09 AW	25150 AAW	ALBLS	10//99-12//99
	Anniston MSA, AL	S	9.07 MW	9.02 AW	18880 AAW	ALBLS	10//99-12//99
	Birmingham MSA, AL	S	12.84 MW	12.47 AW	26710 AAW	ALBLS	10//99-12//99
	Huntsville MSA, AL	S	9.48 MW	8.37 AW	19720 AAW	ALBLS	10//99-12//99
	Montgomery MSA, AL	S	17.06 MW	15.68 AW	35490 AAW	ALBLS	10//99-12//99
	Alaska	S	17.92 MW	17.28 AW	35950 AAW	AKBLS	10//99-12//99
	Arizona	S	12.43 MW	13.56 AW	28200 AAW	AZBLS	10//99-12//99
	Phoenix-Mesa MSA, AZ	S	13.58 MW	12.33 AW	28240 AAW	AZBLS	10//99-12//99
	Arkansas	S	15.29 MW	15.57 AW	32390 AAW	ARBLS	10//99-12//99
	Little Rock-North Little Rock MSA, AR	S	15.52 MW	15.30 AW	32290 AAW	ARBLS	10//99-12//99
	California	S	11.81 MW	13.37 AW	27820 AAW	CABLS	10//99-12//99
	Bakersfield MSA, CA	S	15.95 MW	15.83 AW	33170 AAW	CABLS	10//99-12//99
	Chico-Paradise MSA, CA	S	16.30 MW	15.59 AW	33910 AAW	CABLS	10//99-12//99
	Los Angeles-Long Beach PMSA, CA	S	15.61 MW	12.81 AW	32480 AAW	CABLS	10//99-12//99
	Oakland PMSA, CA	S	10.60 MW	10.20 AW	22040 AAW	CABLS	10//99-12//99
	Orange County PMSA, CA	S	12.18 MW	11.80 AW	25340 AAW	CABLS	10//99-12//99
	Sacramento PMSA, CA	S	17.42 MW	14.91 AW	36230 AAW	CABLS	10//99-12//99
	San Francisco PMSA, CA	S	12.49 MW	13.45 AW	25970 AAW	CABLS	10//99-12//99
	San Jose PMSA, CA	S	15.35 MW	15.06 AW	31940 AAW	CABLS	10//99-12//99
	Santa Barbara-Santa Maria-Lompoc MSA, CA	S	11.33 MW	10.35 AW	23560 AAW	CABLS	10//99-12//99
	Santa Cruz-Watsonville PMSA, CA	S	11.09 MW	10.12 AW	23060 AAW	CABLS	10//99-12//99
	Stockton-Lodi MSA, CA	S	14.29 MW	13.58 AW	29710 AAW	CABLS	10//99-12//99
	Colorado	S	10.98 MW	13.62 AW	28330 AAW	COBLS	10//99-12//99
	Denver PMSA, CO	S	13.13 MW	10.66 AW	27310 AAW	COBLS	10//99-12//99
	Connecticut	S	14.49 MW	16.02 AW	33330 AAW	CTBLS	10//99-12//99
	Bridgeport PMSA, CT	S	16.70 MW	16.82 AW	34740 AAW	CTBLS	10//99-12//99
	Hartford MSA, CT	S	23.24 MW	22.36 AW	48340 AAW	CTBLS	10//99-12//99
	New Haven-Meriden PMSA, CT	S	13.08 MW	12.36 AW	27200 AAW	CTBLS	10//99-12//99
	New London-Norwich MSA, CT-RI	S	11.97 MW	11.22 AW	24900 AAW	CTBLS	10//99-12//99
	Stamford-Norwalk PMSA, CT	S	12.91 MW	12.41 AW	26860 AAW	CTBLS	10//99-12//99
	Waterbury PMSA, CT	S	12.58 MW	12.30 AW	26170 AAW	CTBLS	10//99-12//99
	Delaware	S	15.46 MW	16.12 AW	33520 AAW	DEBLS	10//99-12//99
	Wilmington-Newark PMSA, DE-MD	S	16.12 MW	15.46 AW	33520 AAW	DEBLS	10//99-12//99
	Washington PMSA, DC-MD-VA-WV	S	14.35 MW	13.54 AW	29850 AAW	DCBLS	10//99-12//99
	Florida	S	12.77 MW	13.70 AW	28500 AAW	FLBLS	10//99-12//99
	Fort Lauderdale PMSA, FL	S	16.34 MW	15.66 AW	33980 AAW	FLBLS	10//99-12//99
	Gainesville MSA, FL	S	16.73 MW	15.20 AW	34800 AAW	FLBLS	10//99-12//99
	Jacksonville MSA, FL	S	10.87 MW	10.20 AW	22600 AAW	FLBLS	10//99-12//99
	Melbourne-Titusville-Palm Bay MSA, FL	S	15.93 MW	13.20 AW	33140 AAW	FLBLS	10//99-12//99
	Miami PMSA, FL	S	13.70 MW	13.26 AW	28490 AAW	FLBLS	10//99-12//99
	Naples MSA, FL	S	14.05 MW	12.95 AW	29230 AAW	FLBLS	10//99-12//99
	Orlando MSA, FL	S	14.41 MW	14.36 AW	29980 AAW	FLBLS	10//99-12//99
	Panama City MSA, FL	S	14.25 MW	14.54 AW	29640 AAW	FLBLS	10//99-12//99
	Sarasota-Bradenton MSA, FL	S	13.70 MW	12.99 AW	28490 AAW	FLBLS	10//99-12//99
	Tallahassee MSA, FL	S	14.06 MW	14.34 AW	29250 AAW	FLBLS	10//99-12//99
	Tampa-St. Petersburg-Clearwater MSA, FL	S	11.01 MW	10.56 AW	22910 AAW	FLBLS	10//99-12//99
	West Palm Beach-Boca Raton MSA, FL	S	15.02 MW	14.17 AW	31230 AAW	FLBLS	10//99-12//99

AAW	Average annual wage	AOH	Average offered, high	ASH	Average starting, high	H	Hourly	M	Monthly	S	Special: hourly and annual
AE	Average entry wage	AOL	Average offered, low	ASL	Average starting, low	HI	Highest wage paid	MTC	Median total compensation	TQ	Third quartile wage
AEX	Average experienced wage	APH	Average pay, high range	AW	Average wage paid	HR	High end range	MW	Median wage paid	W	Weekly
AO	Average offered	APL	Average pay, low range	FQ	First quartile wage	LR	Low end range	SQ	Second quartile wage	Y	Yearly

Occupation/Type/Industry	Location	Per	Low	Mid	High	Source	Date
Mental Health Counselor	Georgia	S	11.17 MW	11.87 AW	24690 AAW	GABLS	10//99-12//99
	Atlanta MSA, GA	S	10.91 MW	10.37 AW	22700 AAW	GABLS	10//99-12//99
	Augusta-Aiken MSA, GA-SC	S	9.25 MW	8.07 AW	19240 AAW	GABLS	10//99-12//99
	Idaho	S	12.14 MW	15.12 AW	31460 AAW	IDBLS	10//99-12//99
	Illinois	S	12.59 MW	13.36 AW	27780 AAW	ILBLS	10//99-12//99
	Chicago PMSA, IL	S	13.22 MW	12.57 AW	27510 AAW	ILBLS	10//99-12//99
	Peoria-Pekin MSA, IL	S	12.81 MW	11.48 AW	26640 AAW	ILBLS	10//99-12//99
	Rockford MSA, IL	S	16.03 MW	17.36 AW	33350 AAW	ILBLS	10//99-12//99
	Springfield MSA, IL	S	13.35 MW	13.05 AW	27760 AAW	ILBLS	10//99-12//99
	Indiana	S	12.09 MW	12.97 AW	26970 AAW	INBLS	10//99-12//99
	Gary PMSA, IN	S	12.09 MW	11.57 AW	25150 AAW	INBLS	10//99-12//99
	Indianapolis MSA, IN	S	15.16 MW	14.55 AW	31540 AAW	INBLS	10//99-12//99
	Kansas	S	11.5 MW	13.20 AW	27460 AAW	KSBLS	10//99-12//99
	Kentucky	S	10.46 MW	11.40 AW	23710 AAW	KYBLS	10//99-12//99
	Lexington MSA, KY	S	10.00 MW	9.63 AW	20800 AAW	KYBLS	10//99-12//99
	Louisville MSA, KY-IN	S	11.11 MW	10.24 AW	23100 AAW	KYBLS	10//99-12//99
	Louisiana	S	11.4 MW	12.58 AW	26160 AAW	LABLS	10//99-12//99
	Baton Rouge MSA, LA	S	17.57 MW	16.44 AW	36550 AAW	LABLS	10//99-12//99
	Houma MSA, LA	S	14.37 MW	14.89 AW	29900 AAW	LABLS	10//99-12//99
	Lafayette MSA, LA	S	19.41 MW	21.92 AW	40380 AAW	LABLS	10//99-12//99
	New Orleans MSA, LA	S	11.31 MW	9.29 AW	23530 AAW	LABLS	10//99-12//99
	Shreveport-Bossier City MSA, LA	S	14.39 MW	14.59 AW	29930 AAW	LABLS	10//99-12//99
	Maine	S	13.36 MW	18.57 AW	38630 AAW	MEBLS	10//99-12//99
	Maryland	S	12.98 MW	14.33 AW	29810 AAW	MDBLS	10//99-12//99
	Baltimore PMSA, MD	S	15.11 MW	13.22 AW	31430 AAW	MDBLS	10//99-12//99
	Massachusetts	S	13.12 MW	14.82 AW	30820 AAW	MABLS	10//99-12//99
	Boston PMSA, MA-NH	S	13.71 MW	12.77 AW	28510 AAW	MABLS	10//99-12//99
	Lawrence PMSA, MA-NH	S	12.86 MW	11.83 AW	26750 AAW	MABLS	10//99-12//99
	Worcester PMSA, MA-CT	S	11.30 MW	10.75 AW	23490 AAW	MABLS	10//99-12//99
	Michigan	S	17.13 MW	17.21 AW	35800 AAW	MIBLS	10//99-12//99
	Ann Arbor PMSA, MI	S	18.02 MW	17.49 AW	37490 AAW	MIBLS	10//99-12//99
	Detroit PMSA, MI	S	15.66 MW	15.22 AW	32570 AAW	MIBLS	10//99-12//99
	Grand Rapids-Muskegon-Holland MSA, MI	S	19.12 MW	18.40 AW	39760 AAW	MIBLS	10//99-12//99
	Minnesota	S	16.12 MW	17.92 AW	37270 AAW	MNBLS	10//99-12//99
	Minneapolis-St. Paul MSA, MN-WI	S	18.05 MW	15.84 AW	37540 AAW	MNBLS	10//99-12//99
	Rochester MSA, MN	S	14.11 MW	10.85 AW	29340 AAW	MNBLS	10//99-12//99
	Mississippi	S	12.21 MW	12.75 AW	26530 AAW	MSBLS	10//99-12//99
	Jackson MSA, MS	S	11.95 MW	11.19 AW	24860 AAW	MSBLS	10//99-12//99
	Missouri	S	14.85 MW	15.57 AW	32390 AAW	MOBLS	10//99-12//99
	Kansas City MSA, MO-KS	S	17.28 MW	16.51 AW	35950 AAW	MOBLS	10//99-12//99
	St. Joseph MSA, MO	S	18.79 MW	20.89 AW	39080 AAW	MOBLS	10//99-12//99
	St. Louis MSA, MO-IL	S	17.42 MW	16.09 AW	36240 AAW	MOBLS	10//99-12//99
	Montana	S	11.35 MW	10.92 AW	22720 AAW	MTBLS	10//99-12//99
	Nebraska	S	16.12 MW	15.79 AW	32840 AAW	NEBLS	10//99-12//99
	Lincoln MSA, NE	S	15.38 MW	15.41 AW	31980 AAW	NEBLS	10//99-12//99
	Omaha MSA, NE-IA	S	17.14 MW	17.74 AW	35650 AAW	NEBLS	10//99-12//99
	Nevada	S	19.17 MW	19.04 AW	39600 AAW	NVBLS	10//99-12//99
	New Hampshire	S	14.66 MW	15.62 AW	32490 AAW	NHBLS	10//99-12//99
	New Jersey	S	11.53 MW	11.84 AW	24620 AAW	NJBLS	10//99-12//99
	Bergen-Passaic PMSA, NJ	S	13.73 MW	12.99 AW	28560 AAW	NJBLS	10//99-12//99
	Newark PMSA, NJ	S	11.39 MW	11.43 AW	23690 AAW	NJBLS	10//99-12//99
	Vineland-Millville-Bridgeton PMSA, NJ	S	13.71 MW	12.73 AW	28510 AAW	NJBLS	10//99-12//99
	New York	S	12.88 MW	14.60 AW	30370 AAW	NYBLS	10//99-12//99
	Albany-Schenectady-Troy MSA, NY	S	12.87 MW	11.42 AW	26770 AAW	NYBLS	10//99-12//99
	Buffalo-Niagara Falls MSA, NY	S	12.52 MW	10.44 AW	26040 AAW	NYBLS	10//99-12//99
	Dutchess County PMSA, NY	S	19.16 MW	18.91 AW	39850 AAW	NYBLS	10//99-12//99
	Nassau-Suffolk PMSA, NY	S	13.25 MW	12.40 AW	27570 AAW	NYBLS	10//99-12//99
	New York PMSA, NY	S	16.00 MW	13.27 AW	33290 AAW	NYBLS	10//99-12//99
	Rochester MSA, NY	S	11.55 MW	11.67 AW	24020 AAW	NYBLS	10//99-12//99
	North Carolina	S	13.86 MW	14.56 AW	30280 AAW	NCBLS	10//99-12//99
	Charlotte-Gastonia-Rock Hill MSA, NC-SC	S	16.34 MW	15.71 AW	34000 AAW	NCBLS	10//99-12//99
	Greensboro--Winston-Salem--High Point MSA, NC	S	13.07 MW	12.47 AW	27180 AAW	NCBLS	10//99-12//99
	Hickory-Morganton-Lenoir MSA, NC	S	15.97 MW	15.62 AW	33210 AAW	NCBLS	10//99-12//99

AAW	Average annual wage	AOH	Average offered, high	ASH	Average starting, high
AE	Average entry wage	AOL	Average offered, low	ASL	Average starting, low
AEX	Average experienced wage	APH	Average pay, high range	AW	Average wage paid
AO	Average offered	APL	Average pay, low range	FQ	First quartile wage

H	Hourly	M	Monthly	S	Special: hourly and annual
HI	Highest wage paid	MTC	Median total compensation	TQ	Third quartile wage
HR	High end range	MW	Median wage paid	W	Weekly
LR	Low end range	SQ	Second quartile wage	Y	Yearly

Occupation/Type/Industry	Location	Per	Low	Mid	High	Source	Date
Mental Health Counselor	Raleigh-Durham-Chapel Hill MSA, NC	S	17.33 MW	17.76 AW	36040 AAW	NCBLS	10//99-12//99
	Ohio	S	15.16 MW	15.94 AW	33160 AAW	OHBLS	10//99-12//99
	Cincinnati PMSA, OH-KY-IN	S	13.88 MW	12.85 AW	28860 AAW	OHBLS	10//99-12//99
	Cleveland-Lorain-Elyria PMSA, OH	S	15.05 MW	15.21 AW	31290 AAW	OHBLS	10//99-12//99
	Columbus MSA, OH	S	17.21 MW	16.05 AW	35790 AAW	OHBLS	10//99-12//99
	Dayton-Springfield MSA, OH	S	18.20 MW	17.60 AW	37860 AAW	OHBLS	10//99-12//99
	Toledo MSA, OH	S	24.20 MW	24.86 AW	50340 AAW	OHBLS	10//99-12//99
	Oklahoma	S	12.18 MW	12.76 AW	26530 AAW	OKBLS	10//99-12//99
	Oklahoma City MSA, OK	S	14.19 MW	13.44 AW	29520 AAW	OKBLS	10//99-12//99
	Tulsa MSA, OK	S	11.84 MW	12.00 AW	24630 AAW	OKBLS	10//99-12//99
	Oregon	S	12.76 MW	14.21 AW	29550 AAW	ORBLS	10//99-12//99
	Portland-Vancouver PMSA, OR-WA	S	15.41 MW	13.32 AW	32050 AAW	ORBLS	10//99-12//99
	Pennsylvania	S	10.34 MW	10.65 AW	22140 AAW	PABLS	10//99-12//99
	Allentown-Bethlehem-Easton MSA, PA	S	10.52 MW	9.99 AW	21890 AAW	PABLS	10//99-12//99
	Harrisburg-Lebanon-Carlisle MSA, PA	S	9.62 MW	9.58 AW	20010 AAW	PABLS	10//99-12//99
	Philadelphia PMSA, PA-NJ	S	11.25 MW	10.49 AW	23400 AAW	PABLS	10//99-12//99
	Pittsburgh MSA, PA	S	14.70 MW	12.88 AW	30580 AAW	PABLS	10//99-12//99
	Scranton--Wilkes-Barre-- Hazleton MSA, PA	S	9.34 MW	9.12 AW	19430 AAW	PABLS	10//99-12//99
	Sharon MSA, PA	S	11.39 MW	11.43 AW	23700 AAW	PABLS	10//99-12//99
	Rhode Island	S	11.58 MW	11.80 AW	24540 AAW	RIBLS	10//99-12//99
	Providence-Fall River- Warwick MSA, RI-MA	S	14.83 MW	13.09 AW	30850 AAW	RIBLS	10//99-12//99
	South Carolina	S	11.97 MW	13.51 AW	28110 AAW	SCBLS	10//99-12//99
	Columbia MSA, SC	S	15.03 MW	15.13 AW	31270 AAW	SCBLS	10//99-12//99
	South Dakota	S	15.61 MW	15.77 AW	32800 AAW	SDBLS	10//99-12//99
	Tennessee	S	12.06 MW	12.72 AW	26470 AAW	TNBLS	10//99-12//99
	Johnson City-Kingsport-Bristol MSA, TN-VA	S	19.01 MW	19.86 AW	39540 AAW	TNBLS	10//99-12//99
	Knoxville MSA, TN	S	10.71 MW	9.99 AW	22280 AAW	TNBLS	10//99-12//99
	Memphis MSA, TN-AR-MS	S	15.82 MW	16.13 AW	32910 AAW	MSBLS	10//99-12//99
	Nashville MSA, TN	S	12.76 MW	12.93 AW	26550 AAW	TNBLS	10//99-12//99
	Texas	S	14.47 MW	14.62 AW	30400 AAW	TXBLS	10//99-12//99
	Austin-San Marcos MSA, TX	S	17.27 MW	17.83 AW	35920 AAW	TXBLS	10//99-12//99
	Corpus Christi MSA, TX	S	15.57 MW	15.39 AW	32390 AAW	TXBLS	10//99-12//99
	Dallas PMSA, TX	S	13.49 MW	12.43 AW	28050 AAW	TXBLS	10//99-12//99
	Houston PMSA, TX	S	19.06 MW	18.82 AW	39640 AAW	TXBLS	10//99-12//99
	San Antonio MSA, TX	S	12.48 MW	11.81 AW	25970 AAW	TXBLS	10//99-12//99
	Vermont	S	20.64 MW	21.12 AW	43940 AAW	VTBLS	10//99-12//99
	Burlington MSA, VT	S	15.51 MW	15.40 AW	32270 AAW	VTBLS	10//99-12//99
	Virginia	S	12.92 MW	14.37 AW	29880 AAW	VABLS	10//99-12//99
	Lynchburg MSA, VA	S	11.56 MW	10.83 AW	24050 AAW	VABLS	10//99-12//99
	Norfolk-Virginia Beach- Newport News MSA, VA-NC	S	11.03 MW	10.46 AW	22930 AAW	VABLS	10//99-12//99
	Washington	S	15.44 MW	15.67 AW	32580 AAW	WABLS	10//99-12//99
	Bellingham MSA, WA	S	17.03 MW	16.72 AW	35420 AAW	WABLS	10//99-12//99
	Richland-Kennewick-Pasco MSA, WA	S	16.02 MW	15.65 AW	33320 AAW	WABLS	10//99-12//99
	Seattle-Bellevue-Everett PMSA, WA	S	16.91 MW	17.08 AW	35170 AAW	WABLS	10//99-12//99
	Spokane MSA, WA	S	16.45 MW	16.11 AW	34220 AAW	WABLS	10//99-12//99
	Tacoma PMSA, WA	S	12.90 MW	13.00 AW	26830 AAW	WABLS	10//99-12//99
	Yakima MSA, WA	S	13.43 MW	12.79 AW	27920 AAW	WABLS	10//99-12//99
	West Virginia	S	10.47 MW	11.46 AW	23830 AAW	WVBLS	10//99-12//99
	Huntington-Ashland MSA, WV-KY-OH	S	12.31 MW	12.24 AW	25610 AAW	WVBLS	10//99-12//99
	Janesville-Beloit MSA, WI	S	21.59 MW	23.11 AW	44910 AAW	WIBLS	10//99-12//99
	Wyoming	S	15.59 MW	15.95 AW	33170 AAW	WYBLS	10//99-12//99
	Puerto Rico	S	10.13 MW	11.21 AW	23320 AAW	PRBLS	10//99-12//99
	San Juan-Bayamon PMSA, PR	S	10.21 MW	9.88 AW	21230 AAW	PRBLS	10//99-12//99
Merchandise Displayer and Window Trimmer	Alabama	S	8.2 MW	9.15 AW	19030 AAW	ALBLS	10//99-12//99
	Alaska	S	10.84 MW	11.03 AW	22950 AAW	AKBLS	10//99-12//99
	Arizona	S	7.74 MW	8.61 AW	17910 AAW	AZBLS	10//99-12//99
	Arkansas	S	8.28 MW	8.51 AW	17710 AAW	ARBLS	10//99-12//99

AAW Average annual wage	**AOH** Average offered, high	**ASH** Average starting, high	**H** Hourly	**M** Monthly	**S** Special: hourly and annual
AE Average entry wage	**AOL** Average offered, low	**ASL** Average starting, low	**HI** Highest wage paid	**MTC** Median total compensation	**TQ** Third quartile wage
AEX Average experienced wage	**APH** Average pay, high range	**AW** Average wage paid	**HR** High end range	**MW** Median wage paid	**W** Weekly
AO Average offered	**APL** Average pay, low range	**FQ** First quartile wage	**LR** Low end range	**SQ** Second quartile wage	**Y** Yearly

Occupation/Type/Industry	Location	Per	Low	Mid	High	Source	Date
Merchandise Displayer and Window Trimmer	California	S	9.7 MW	10.74 AW	22330 AAW	CABLS	10//99-12//99
	Colorado	S	9.23 MW	10.10 AW	21020 AAW	COBLS	10//99-12//99
	Connecticut	S	11.05 MW	11.48 AW	23880 AAW	CTBLS	10//99-12//99
	Delaware	S	10.64 MW	11.14 AW	23170 AAW	DEBLS	10//99-12//99
	District of Columbia	S	11.56 MW	12.43 AW	25860 AAW	DCBLS	10//99-12//99
	Florida	S	9.37 MW	9.91 AW	20610 AAW	FLBLS	10//99-12//99
	Georgia	S	10.16 MW	10.55 AW	21950 AAW	GABLS	10//99-12//99
	Hawaii	S	11.16 MW	12.79 AW	26610 AAW	HIBLS	10//99-12//99
	Idaho	S	8.37 MW	9.81 AW	20400 AAW	IDBLS	10//99-12//99
	Illinois	S	9.17 MW	9.94 AW	20670 AAW	ILBLS	10//99-12//99
	Indiana	S	9.06 MW	9.37 AW	19500 AAW	INBLS	10//99-12//99
	Iowa	S	8.13 MW	8.26 AW	17180 AAW	IABLS	10//99-12//99
	Kansas	S	8.95 MW	9.22 AW	19180 AAW	KSBLS	10//99-12//99
	Kentucky	S	9.62 MW	9.96 AW	20720 AAW	KYBLS	10//99-12//99
	Louisiana	S	9.38 MW	9.50 AW	19770 AAW	LABLS	10//99-12//99
	Maine	S	8.09 MW	9.73 AW	20230 AAW	MEBLS	10//99-12//99
	Maryland	S	10.87 MW	11.35 AW	23610 AAW	MDBLS	10//99-12//99
	Massachusetts	S	10.66 MW	11.95 AW	24860 AAW	MABLS	10//99-12//99
	Michigan	S	8.32 MW	9.00 AW	18710 AAW	MIBLS	10//99-12//99
	Minnesota	S	9.64 MW	10.36 AW	21540 AAW	MNBLS	10//99-12//99
	Mississippi	S	9.31 MW	9.64 AW	20050 AAW	MSBLS	10//99-12//99
	Missouri	S	6.95 MW	8.31 AW	17290 AAW	MOBLS	10//99-12//99
	Montana	S	7.87 MW	8.66 AW	18020 AAW	MTBLS	10//99-12//99
	Nebraska	S	8.62 MW	8.79 AW	18280 AAW	NEBLS	10//99-12//99
	Nevada	S	8.94 MW	9.43 AW	19620 AAW	NVBLS	10//99-12//99
	New Hampshire	S	9.7 MW	11.08 AW	23050 AAW	NHBLS	10//99-12//99
	New Jersey	S	10.68 MW	11.51 AW	23930 AAW	NJBLS	10//99-12//99
	New Mexico	S	8.6 MW	8.86 AW	18420 AAW	NMBLS	10//99-12//99
	New York	S	10.4 MW	12.49 AW	25970 AAW	NYBLS	10//99-12//99
	North Carolina	S	9.48 MW	9.83 AW	20450 AAW	NCBLS	10//99-12//99
	North Dakota	S	8.13 MW	8.50 AW	17670 AAW	NDBLS	10//99-12//99
	Ohio	S	10.1 MW	10.64 AW	22140 AAW	OHBLS	10//99-12//99
	Oklahoma	S	8.17 MW	8.52 AW	17710 AAW	OKBLS	10//99-12//99
	Oregon	S	10.19 MW	11.30 AW	23500 AAW	ORBLS	10//99-12//99
	Pennsylvania	S	8.22 MW	9.75 AW	20280 AAW	PABLS	10//99-12//99
	Rhode Island	S	9.77 MW	10.43 AW	21700 AAW	RIBLS	10//99-12//99
	South Carolina	S	8.21 MW	8.71 AW	18130 AAW	SCBLS	10//99-12//99
	South Dakota	S	8.19 MW	8.38 AW	17440 AAW	SDBLS	10//99-12//99
	Tennessee	S	9.23 MW	9.32 AW	19390 AAW	TNBLS	10//99-12//99
	Texas	S	9.29 MW	10.63 AW	22120 AAW	TXBLS	10//99-12//99
	Utah	S	9.83 MW	11.77 AW	24470 AAW	UTBLS	10//99-12//99
	Vermont	S	7.7 MW	8.40 AW	17470 AAW	VTBLS	10//99-12//99
	Virginia	S	9.63 MW	10.05 AW	20900 AAW	VABLS	10//99-12//99
	Washington	S	10.02 MW	11.12 AW	23130 AAW	WABLS	10//99-12//99
	West Virginia	S	7.56 MW	8.41 AW	17500 AAW	WVBLS	10//99-12//99
	Wisconsin	S	9.95 MW	10.16 AW	21130 AAW	WIBLS	10//99-12//99
	Puerto Rico	S	6.89 MW	7.57 AW	15740 AAW	PRBLS	10//99-12//99
	Guam	S	7.43 MW	7.45 AW	15500 AAW	GUBLS	10//99-12//99
Metal-Refining Furnace Operator and Tender	Alabama	S	13.34 MW	14.40 AW	29960 AAW	ALBLS	10//99-12//99
	Arizona	S	11.44 MW	11.78 AW	24500 AAW	AZBLS	10//99-12//99
	Arkansas	S	12.68 MW	13.17 AW	27390 AAW	ARBLS	10//99-12//99
	California	S	12.38 MW	12.69 AW	26390 AAW	CABLS	10//99-12//99
	Colorado	S	13.91 MW	13.90 AW	28910 AAW	COBLS	10//99-12//99
	Connecticut	S	14.16 MW	13.66 AW	28400 AAW	CTBLS	10//99-12//99
	Florida	S	11.4 MW	11.96 AW	24890 AAW	FLBLS	10//99-12//99
	Georgia	S	12.06 MW	12.44 AW	25870 AAW	GABLS	10//99-12//99
	Illinois	S	11.56 MW	11.88 AW	24710 AAW	ILBLS	10//99-12//99
	Indiana	S	13.67 MW	15.35 AW	31920 AAW	INBLS	10//99-12//99
	Iowa	S	12.25 MW	12.53 AW	26060 AAW	IABLS	10//99-12//99
	Kansas	S	11.73 MW	11.84 AW	24620 AAW	KSBLS	10//99-12//99
	Kentucky	S	11.95 MW	13.21 AW	27480 AAW	KYBLS	10//99-12//99
	Louisiana	S	9.72 MW	9.61 AW	20000 AAW	LABLS	10//99-12//99
	Massachusetts	S	13.57 MW	13.59 AW	28260 AAW	MABLS	10//99-12//99
	Michigan	S	13.46 MW	14.24 AW	29620 AAW	MIBLS	10//99-12//99
	Minnesota	S	15.04 MW	14.73 AW	30640 AAW	MNBLS	10//99-12//99
	Mississippi	S	11.06 MW	10.89 AW	22650 AAW	MSBLS	10//99-12//99
	Missouri	S	13.73 MW	13.45 AW	27980 AAW	MOBLS	10//99-12//99
	New Jersey	S	13.25 MW	13.94 AW	28990 AAW	NJBLS	10//99-12//99
	New York	S	14.12 MW	14.86 AW	30910 AAW	NYBLS	10//99-12//99

AAW	Average annual wage	AOH	Average offered, high	ASH	Average starting, high
AE	Average entry wage	AOL	Average offered, low	ASL	Average starting, low
AEX	Average experienced wage	APH	Average pay, high range	AW	Average wage paid
AO	Average offered	APL	Average pay, low range	FQ	First quartile wage

H	Hourly	M	Monthly
HI	Highest wage paid	MTC	Median total compensation
HR	High end range	MW	Median wage paid
LR	Low end range	SQ	Second quartile wage

S	Special: hourly and annual
TQ	Third quartile wage
W	Weekly
Y	Yearly

Occupation/Type/Industry	Location	Per	Low	Mid	High	Source	Date
Metal-Refining Furnace Operator and Tender	North Carolina	S	13.42 MW	12.99 AW	27020 AAW	NCBLS	10//99-12//99
	Ohio	S	13.46 MW	14.88 AW	30950 AAW	OHBLS	10//99-12//99
	Oklahoma	S	10.29 MW	10.88 AW	22640 AAW	OKBLS	10//99-12//99
	Oregon	S	15.1 MW	15.19 AW	31590 AAW	ORBLS	10//99-12//99
	Pennsylvania	S	13.19 MW	13.93 AW	28970 AAW	PABLS	10//99-12//99
	Rhode Island	S	12.52 MW	13.07 AW	27180 AAW	RIBLS	10//99-12//99
	South Carolina	S	14.3 MW	14.65 AW	30480 AAW	SCBLS	10//99-12//99
	Tennessee	S	12.05 MW	12.74 AW	26500 AAW	TNBLS	10//99-12//99
	Texas	S	10.75 MW	11.04 AW	22960 AAW	TXBLS	10//99-12//99
	Utah	S	13.89 MW	15.80 AW	32860 AAW	UTBLS	10//99-12//99
	Virginia	S	12.11 MW	11.68 AW	24290 AAW	VABLS	10//99-12//99
	Washington	S	15.11 MW	15.16 AW	31530 AAW	WABLS	10//99-12//99
	West Virginia	S	17 MW	17.09 AW	35540 AAW	WVBLS	10//99-12//99
	Wisconsin	S	13.05 MW	13.60 AW	28290 AAW	WIBLS	10//99-12//99
Metallurgist							
Foundry	United States	Y	58200 MW	56900 AW		MODCAS	1999
Meteorologist	United States	Y		57000 AW		SCWO	1999
Meter Reader							
Utilities	Alabama	S	11.43 MW	12.35 AW	25680 AAW	ALBLS	10//99-12//99
Utilities	Anniston MSA, AL	S	12.70 MW	10.58 AW	26420 AAW	ALBLS	10//99-12//99
Utilities	Auburn-Opelika MSA, AL	S	14.51 MW	14.19 AW	30180 AAW	ALBLS	10//99-12//99
Utilities	Birmingham MSA, AL	S	14.59 MW	13.41 AW	30350 AAW	ALBLS	10//99-12//99
Utilities	Florence MSA, AL	S	16.10 MW	17.65 AW	33500 AAW	ALBLS	10//99-12//99
Utilities	Mobile MSA, AL	S	11.20 MW	10.06 AW	23290 AAW	ALBLS	10//99-12//99
Utilities	Alaska	S	27.88 MW	26.02 AW	54110 AAW	AKBLS	10//99-12//99
Utilities	Anchorage MSA, AK	S	28.43 MW	30.10 AW	59130 AAW	AKBLS	10//99-12//99
Utilities	Arizona	S	14.84 MW	15.00 AW	31190 AAW	AZBLS	10//99-12//99
Utilities	Tucson MSA, AZ	S	12.29 MW	11.30 AW	25570 AAW	AZBLS	10//99-12//99
Utilities	Arkansas	S	9.12 MW	9.52 AW	19810 AAW	ARBLS	10//99-12//99
Utilities	Fort Smith MSA, AR-OK	S	10.64 MW	10.76 AW	22130 AAW	ARBLS	10//99-12//99
Utilities	Little Rock-North Little Rock MSA, AR	S	9.91 MW	9.65 AW	20610 AAW	ARBLS	10//99-12//99
Utilities	California	S	16.89 MW	16.57 AW	34470 AAW	CABLS	10//99-12//99
Utilities	Bakersfield MSA, CA	S	17.77 MW	18.17 AW	36970 AAW	CABLS	10//99-12//99
Utilities	Merced MSA, CA	S	15.85 MW	16.01 AW	32960 AAW	CABLS	10//99-12//99
Utilities	Oakland PMSA, CA	S	16.30 MW	17.66 AW	33900 AAW	CABLS	10//99-12//99
Utilities	Orange County PMSA, CA	S	16.22 MW	16.85 AW	33740 AAW	CABLS	10//99-12//99
Utilities	Riverside-San Bernardino PMSA, CA	S	15.45 MW	15.01 AW	32140 AAW	CABLS	10//99-12//99
Utilities	Sacramento PMSA, CA	S	16.01 MW	17.08 AW	33300 AAW	CABLS	10//99-12//99
Utilities	San Francisco PMSA, CA	S	18.48 MW	19.94 AW	38450 AAW	CABLS	10//99-12//99
Utilities	Ventura PMSA, CA	S	16.68 MW	17.08 AW	34690 AAW	CABLS	10//99-12//99
Utilities	Colorado	S	14.22 MW	15.53 AW	32310 AAW	COBLS	10//99-12//99
Utilities	Denver PMSA, CO	S	16.62 MW	15.04 AW	34580 AAW	COBLS	10//99-12//99
Utilities	Fort Collins-Loveland MSA, CO	S	14.20 MW	12.91 AW	29540 AAW	COBLS	10//99-12//99
Utilities	Pueblo MSA, CO	S	14.98 MW	14.34 AW	31150 AAW	COBLS	10//99-12//99
Utilities	Connecticut	S	18.15 MW	17.55 AW	36490 AAW	CTBLS	10//99-12//99
Utilities	Hartford MSA, CT	S	17.57 MW	18.67 AW	36540 AAW	CTBLS	10//99-12//99
Utilities	New London-Norwich MSA, CT-RI	S	17.66 MW	18.15 AW	36740 AAW	CTBLS	10//99-12//99
Utilities	Delaware	S	14.76 MW	14.00 AW	29130 AAW	DEBLS	10//99-12//99
Utilities	Wilmington-Newark PMSA, DE-MD	S	14.78 MW	15.33 AW	30730 AAW	DEBLS	10//99-12//99
Utilities	Washington PMSA, DC-MD-VA-WV	S	14.98 MW	15.59 AW	31170 AAW	DCBLS	10//99-12//99
Utilities	Florida	S	10.46 MW	11.05 AW	22980 AAW	FLBLS	10//99-12//99
Utilities	Daytona Beach MSA, FL	S	9.99 MW	9.97 AW	20780 AAW	FLBLS	10//99-12//99
Utilities	Fort Lauderdale PMSA, FL	S	10.76 MW	10.74 AW	22380 AAW	FLBLS	10//99-12//99
Utilities	Fort Walton Beach MSA, FL	S	9.49 MW	9.52 AW	19740 AAW	FLBLS	10//99-12//99
Utilities	Jacksonville MSA, FL	S	11.66 MW	10.96 AW	24260 AAW	FLBLS	10//99-12//99
Utilities	Lakeland-Winter Haven MSA, FL	S	10.57 MW	10.25 AW	21990 AAW	FLBLS	10//99-12//99
Utilities	Melbourne-Titusville-Palm Bay MSA, FL	S	10.83 MW	10.25 AW	22520 AAW	FLBLS	10//99-12//99
Utilities	Orlando MSA, FL	S	11.14 MW	10.57 AW	23180 AAW	FLBLS	10//99-12//99
Utilities	Pensacola MSA, FL	S	9.47 MW	9.36 AW	19700 AAW	FLBLS	10//99-12//99
Utilities	Sarasota-Bradenton MSA, FL	S	9.68 MW	9.40 AW	20140 AAW	FLBLS	10//99-12//99

Occupation/Type/Industry	Location	Per	Low	Mid	High	Source	Date
Meter Reader							
Utilities	Tampa-St. Petersburg-Clearwater MSA, FL	S	12.78 MW	12.29 AW	26580 AAW	FLBLS	10//99-12//99
Utilities	West Palm Beach-Boca Raton MSA, FL	S	12.32 MW	12.42 AW	25630 AAW	FLBLS	10//99-12//99
Utilities	Georgia	S	11.24 MW	11.23 AW	23350 AAW	GABLS	10//99-12//99
Utilities	Atlanta MSA, GA	S	11.82 MW	11.86 AW	24590 AAW	GABLS	10//99-12//99
Utilities	Augusta-Aiken MSA, GA-SC	S	11.07 MW	10.26 AW	23030 AAW	GABLS	10//99-12//99
Utilities	Columbus MSA, GA-AL	S	9.34 MW	8.32 AW	19430 AAW	GABLS	10//99-12//99
Utilities	Macon MSA, GA	S	11.02 MW	11.86 AW	22910 AAW	GABLS	10//99-12//99
Utilities	Savannah MSA, GA	S	12.91 MW	13.77 AW	26840 AAW	GABLS	10//99-12//99
Utilities	Hawaii	S	16.39 MW	15.86 AW	32990 AAW	HIBLS	10//99-12//99
Utilities	Idaho	S	11.65 MW	12.75 AW	26520 AAW	IDBLS	10//99-12//99
Utilities	Boise City MSA, ID	S	15.55 MW	15.89 AW	32350 AAW	IDBLS	10//99-12//99
Utilities	Illinois	S	12.87 MW	13.70 AW	28490 AAW	ILBLS	10//99-12//99
Utilities	Chicago PMSA, IL	S	14.79 MW	13.55 AW	30750 AAW	ILBLS	10//99-12//99
Utilities	Kankakee PMSA, IL	S	13.37 MW	12.43 AW	27800 AAW	ILBLS	10//99-12//99
Utilities	Indiana	S	11.2 MW	11.63 AW	24190 AAW	INBLS	10//99-12//99
Utilities	Elkhart-Goshen MSA, IN	S	12.02 MW	12.05 AW	24990 AAW	INBLS	10//99-12//99
Utilities	Evansville-Henderson MSA, IN-KY	S	10.61 MW	10.58 AW	22060 AAW	INBLS	10//99-12//99
Utilities	Gary PMSA, IN	S	9.90 MW	9.07 AW	20590 AAW	INBLS	10//99-12//99
Utilities	Indianapolis MSA, IN	S	13.58 MW	14.64 AW	28240 AAW	INBLS	10//99-12//99
Utilities	Iowa	S	13.11 MW	12.81 AW	26640 AAW	IABLS	10//99-12//99
Utilities	Davenport-Moline-Rock Island MSA, IA-IL	S	14.55 MW	13.65 AW	30270 AAW	IABLS	10//99-12//99
Utilities	Des Moines MSA, IA	S	16.25 MW	17.62 AW	33790 AAW	IABLS	10//99-12//99
Utilities	Sioux City MSA, IA-NE	S	16.47 MW	16.17 AW	34250 AAW	IABLS	10//99-12//99
Utilities	Kansas	S	13.13 MW	13.26 AW	27580 AAW	KSBLS	10//99-12//99
Utilities	Wichita MSA, KS	S	11.94 MW	10.55 AW	24840 AAW	KSBLS	10//99-12//99
Utilities	Kentucky	S	10.38 MW	11.59 AW	24110 AAW	KYBLS	10//99-12//99
Utilities	Lexington MSA, KY	S	13.88 MW	14.66 AW	28880 AAW	KYBLS	10//99-12//99
Utilities	Louisville MSA, KY-IN	S	14.05 MW	14.74 AW	29220 AAW	KYBLS	10//99-12//99
Utilities	Louisiana	S	8.62 MW	9.21 AW	19150 AAW	LABLS	10//99-12//99
Utilities	Baton Rouge MSA, LA	S	11.08 MW	11.84 AW	23050 AAW	LABLS	10//99-12//99
Utilities	Houma MSA, LA	S	9.21 MW	9.30 AW	19160 AAW	LABLS	10//99-12//99
Utilities	Lake Charles MSA, LA	S	8.81 MW	8.09 AW	18320 AAW	LABLS	10//99-12//99
Utilities	New Orleans MSA, LA	S	8.29 MW	7.87 AW	17230 AAW	LABLS	10//99-12//99
Utilities	Shreveport-Bossier City MSA, LA	S	9.44 MW	9.32 AW	19640 AAW	LABLS	10//99-12//99
Utilities	Maine	S	13.06 MW	12.80 AW	26620 AAW	MEBLS	10//99-12//99
Utilities	Maryland	S	14.98 MW	15.19 AW	31590 AAW	MDBLS	10//99-12//99
Utilities	Baltimore PMSA, MD	S	15.87 MW	15.77 AW	33020 AAW	MDBLS	10//99-12//99
Utilities	Massachusetts	S	15.45 MW	15.49 AW	32230 AAW	MABLS	10//99-12//99
Utilities	Barnstable-Yarmouth MSA, MA	S	15.16 MW	15.08 AW	31530 AAW	MABLS	10//99-12//99
Utilities	Boston PMSA, MA-NH	S	16.59 MW	16.17 AW	34500 AAW	MABLS	10//99-12//99
Utilities	Brockton PMSA, MA	S	16.56 MW	17.80 AW	34440 AAW	MABLS	10//99-12//99
Utilities	Springfield MSA, MA	S	16.33 MW	17.47 AW	33960 AAW	MABLS	10//99-12//99
Utilities	Worcester PMSA, MA-CT	S	15.43 MW	15.54 AW	32090 AAW	MABLS	10//99-12//99
Utilities	Michigan	S	14.52 MW	14.67 AW	30510 AAW	MIBLS	10//99-12//99
Utilities	Benton Harbor MSA, MI	S	12.30 MW	11.47 AW	25590 AAW	MIBLS	10//99-12//99
Utilities	Detroit PMSA, MI	S	14.98 MW	14.99 AW	31170 AAW	MIBLS	10//99-12//99
Utilities	Grand Rapids-Muskegon-Holland MSA, MI	S	13.60 MW	13.55 AW	28280 AAW	MIBLS	10//99-12//99
Utilities	Saginaw-Bay City-Midland MSA, MI	S	13.16 MW	12.33 AW	27370 AAW	MIBLS	10//99-12//99
Utilities	Minnesota	S	13.39 MW	14.69 AW	30550 AAW	MNBLS	10//99-12//99
Utilities	Duluth-Superior MSA, MN-WI	S	15.44 MW	16.16 AW	32110 AAW	MNBLS	10//99-12//99
Utilities	Minneapolis-St. Paul MSA, MN-WI	S	15.16 MW	13.30 AW	31530 AAW	MNBLS	10//99-12//99
Utilities	Mississippi	S	9.49 MW	9.93 AW	20650 AAW	MSBLS	10//99-12//99
Utilities	Biloxi-Gulfport-Pascagoula MSA, MS	S	10.99 MW	9.81 AW	22860 AAW	MSBLS	10//99-12//99
Utilities	Hattiesburg MSA, MS	S	7.54 MW	6.97 AW	15690 AAW	MSBLS	10//99-12//99
Utilities	Jackson MSA, MS	S	10.90 MW	10.52 AW	22680 AAW	MSBLS	10//99-12//99
Utilities	Missouri	S	13.83 MW	13.08 AW	27200 AAW	MOBLS	10//99-12//99
Utilities	Kansas City MSA, MO-KS	S	12.77 MW	14.09 AW	26570 AAW	MOBLS	10//99-12//99
Utilities	Montana	S	12.3 MW	11.56 AW	24050 AAW	MTBLS	10//99-12//99
Utilities	Nebraska	S	10.65 MW	10.49 AW	21820 AAW	NEBLS	10//99-12//99
Utilities	Nevada	S	16.69 MW	16.67 AW	34670 AAW	NVBLS	10//99-12//99
Utilities	Las Vegas MSA, NV-AZ	S	15.34 MW	15.34 AW	31900 AAW	NVBLS	10//99-12//99

AAW	Average annual wage	AOH	Average offered, high	ASH	Average starting, high	H	Hourly
AE	Average entry wage	AOL	Average offered, low	ASL	Average starting, low	HI	Highest wage paid
AEX	Average experienced wage	APH	Average pay, high range	AW	Average wage paid	HR	High end range
AO	Average offered	APL	Average pay, low range	FQ	First quartile wage	LR	Low end range

M	Monthly	S	Special: hourly and annual
MTC	Median total compensation	TQ	Third quartile wage
MW	Median wage paid	W	Weekly
SQ	Second quartile wage	Y	Yearly

Meter Reader

Occupation/Type/Industry	Location	Per	Low	Mid	High	Source	Date
Utilities	New Hampshire	S	16.31 MW	15.69 AW	32630 AAW	NHBLS	10//99-12//99
Utilities	Portsmouth-Rochester PMSA, NH-ME	S	15.73 MW	15.74 AW	32720 AAW	NHBLS	10//99-12//99
Utilities	New Jersey	S	18.71 MW	18.73 AW	38960 AAW	NJBLS	10//99-12//99
Utilities	Atlantic-Cape May PMSA, NJ	S	18.74 MW	18.53 AW	38970 AAW	NJBLS	10//99-12//99
Utilities	Bergen-Passaic PMSA, NJ	S	18.60 MW	18.86 AW	38690 AAW	NJBLS	10//99-12//99
Utilities	Middlesex-Somerset-Hunterdon PMSA, NJ	S	20.87 MW	20.39 AW	43410 AAW	NJBLS	10//99-12//99
Utilities	Monmouth-Ocean PMSA, NJ	S	19.72 MW	19.05 AW	41020 AAW	NJBLS	10//99-12//99
Utilities	Newark PMSA, NJ	S	18.51 MW	18.46 AW	38500 AAW	NJBLS	10//99-12//99
Utilities	New Mexico	S	10.76 MW	11.81 AW	24550 AAW	NMBLS	10//99-12//99
Utilities	Albuquerque MSA, NM	S	14.27 MW	13.05 AW	29690 AAW	NMBLS	10//99-12//99
Utilities	New York	S	17.95 MW	17.34 AW	36080 AAW	NYBLS	10//99-12//99
Utilities	Buffalo-Niagara Falls MSA, NY	S	15.63 MW	17.45 AW	32520 AAW	NYBLS	10//99-12//99
Utilities	Jamestown MSA, NY	S	15.47 MW	16.70 AW	32180 AAW	NYBLS	10//99-12//99
Utilities	New York PMSA, NY	S	18.05 MW	18.58 AW	37550 AAW	NYBLS	10//99-12//99
Utilities	Rochester MSA, NY	S	13.65 MW	12.57 AW	28400 AAW	NYBLS	10//99-12//99
Utilities	North Carolina	S	10.31 MW	11.08 AW	23050 AAW	NCBLS	10//99-12//99
Utilities	Charlotte-Gastonia-Rock Hill MSA, NC-SC	S	11.89 MW	11.05 AW	24720 AAW	NCBLS	10//99-12//99
Utilities	Fayetteville MSA, NC	S	11.03 MW	10.93 AW	22950 AAW	NCBLS	10//99-12//99
Utilities	Goldsboro MSA, NC	S	11.56 MW	11.28 AW	24040 AAW	NCBLS	10//99-12//99
Utilities	Greensboro--Winston-Salem--High Point MSA, NC	S	12.35 MW	11.83 AW	25680 AAW	NCBLS	10//99-12//99
Utilities	Hickory-Morganton-Lenoir MSA, NC	S	9.98 MW	8.99 AW	20760 AAW	NCBLS	10//99-12//99
Utilities	Raleigh-Durham-Chapel Hill MSA, NC	S	12.33 MW	11.12 AW	25660 AAW	NCBLS	10//99-12//99
Utilities	Wilmington MSA, NC	S	10.71 MW	10.29 AW	22280 AAW	NCBLS	10//99-12//99
Utilities	North Dakota	S	10.62 MW	10.95 AW	22770 AAW	NDBLS	10//99-12//99
Utilities	Grand Forks MSA, ND-MN	S	15.45 MW	13.44 AW	32140 AAW	NDBLS	10//99-12//99
Utilities	Ohio	S	12.61 MW	12.84 AW	26700 AAW	OHBLS	10//99-12//99
Utilities	Akron PMSA, OH	S	13.94 MW	14.38 AW	29000 AAW	OHBLS	10//99-12//99
Utilities	Cincinnati PMSA, OH-KY-IN	S	13.80 MW	13.82 AW	28700 AAW	OHBLS	10//99-12//99
Utilities	Cleveland-Lorain-Elyria PMSA, OH	S	13.99 MW	14.86 AW	29110 AAW	OHBLS	10//99-12//99
Utilities	Columbus MSA, OH	S	13.73 MW	13.81 AW	28560 AAW	OHBLS	10//99-12//99
Utilities	Lima MSA, OH	S	13.82 MW	14.49 AW	28750 AAW	OHBLS	10//99-12//99
Utilities	Mansfield MSA, OH	S	12.92 MW	12.62 AW	26870 AAW	OHBLS	10//99-12//99
Utilities	Youngstown-Warren MSA, OH	S	12.91 MW	13.07 AW	26860 AAW	OHBLS	10//99-12//99
Utilities	Oklahoma	S	10.34 MW	10.47 AW	21780 AAW	OKBLS	10//99-12//99
Utilities	Oklahoma City MSA, OK	S	11.02 MW	11.39 AW	22920 AAW	OKBLS	10//99-12//99
Utilities	Tulsa MSA, OK	S	10.84 MW	10.97 AW	22540 AAW	OKBLS	10//99-12//99
Utilities	Oregon	S	13.09 MW	13.67 AW	28430 AAW	ORBLS	10//99-12//99
Utilities	Medford-Ashland MSA, OR	S	11.97 MW	11.61 AW	24900 AAW	ORBLS	10//99-12//99
Utilities	Portland-Vancouver PMSA, OR-WA	S	16.01 MW	15.38 AW	33310 AAW	ORBLS	10//99-12//99
Utilities	Salem PMSA, OR	S	15.68 MW	15.98 AW	32610 AAW	ORBLS	10//99-12//99
Utilities	Pennsylvania	S	17.15 MW	16.14 AW	33580 AAW	PABLS	10//99-12//99
Utilities	Allentown-Bethlehem-Easton MSA, PA	S	17.12 MW	17.79 AW	35610 AAW	PABLS	10//99-12//99
Utilities	Harrisburg-Lebanon-Carlisle MSA, PA	S	16.50 MW	17.40 AW	34310 AAW	PABLS	10//99-12//99
Utilities	Philadelphia PMSA, PA-NJ	S	16.46 MW	17.58 AW	34240 AAW	PABLS	10//99-12//99
Utilities	Pittsburgh MSA, PA	S	16.01 MW	15.96 AW	33300 AAW	PABLS	10//99-12//99
Utilities	Reading MSA, PA	S	16.26 MW	17.62 AW	33830 AAW	PABLS	10//99-12//99
Utilities	Scranton--Wilkes-Barre--Hazleton MSA, PA	S	15.81 MW	17.53 AW	32880 AAW	PABLS	10//99-12//99
Utilities	York MSA, PA	S	15.16 MW	16.29 AW	31540 AAW	PABLS	10//99-12//99
Utilities	Rhode Island	S	16.5 MW	16.71 AW	34750 AAW	RIBLS	10//99-12//99
Utilities	Providence-Fall River-Warwick MSA, RI-MA	S	13.03 MW	11.66 AW	27090 AAW	RIBLS	10//99-12//99
Utilities	South Carolina	S	9.25 MW	10.35 AW	21520 AAW	SCBLS	10//99-12//99
Utilities	Charleston-North Charleston MSA, SC	S	12.63 MW	11.64 AW	26280 AAW	SCBLS	10//99-12//99
Utilities	Columbia MSA, SC	S	8.67 MW	8.03 AW	18020 AAW	SCBLS	10//99-12//99
Utilities	Greenville-Spartanburg-Anderson MSA, SC	S	12.64 MW	12.13 AW	26290 AAW	SCBLS	10//99-12//99
Utilities	Myrtle Beach MSA, SC	S	11.08 MW	10.23 AW	23060 AAW	SCBLS	10//99-12//99
Utilities	South Dakota	S	11.49 MW	11.77 AW	24490 AAW	SDBLS	10//99-12//99

Occupation/Type/Industry	Location	Per	Low	Mid	High	Source	Date
Meter Reader							
Utilities	Tennessee	S	12.24 MW	12.19 AW	25360 AAW	TNBLS	10//99-12//99
Utilities	Johnson City-Kingsport-Bristol MSA, TN-VA	S	10.07 MW	9.35 AW	20940 AAW	TNBLS	10//99-12//99
Utilities	Knoxville MSA, TN	S	14.14 MW	14.62 AW	29420 AAW	TNBLS	10//99-12//99
Utilities	Memphis MSA, TN-AR-MS	S	10.73 MW	10.15 AW	22330 AAW	MSBLS	10//99-12//99
Utilities	Nashville MSA, TN	S	12.46 MW	12.57 AW	25910 AAW	TNBLS	10//99-12//99
Utilities	Texas	S	9.81 MW	10.22 AW	21260 AAW	TXBLS	10//99-12//99
Utilities	Amarillo MSA, TX	S	10.39 MW	10.03 AW	21610 AAW	TXBLS	10//99-12//99
Utilities	Austin-San Marcos MSA, TX	S	9.71 MW	9.83 AW	20200 AAW	TXBLS	10//99-12//99
Utilities	Beaumont-Port Arthur MSA, TX	S	11.62 MW	10.44 AW	24180 AAW	TXBLS	10//99-12//99
Utilities	Brazoria PMSA, TX	S	9.17 MW	9.23 AW	19070 AAW	TXBLS	10//99-12//99
Utilities	Brownsville-Harlingen-San Benito MSA, TX	S	10.21 MW	9.72 AW	21240 AAW	TXBLS	10//99-12//99
Utilities	Corpus Christi MSA, TX	S	9.18 MW	8.52 AW	19090 AAW	TXBLS	10//99-12//99
Utilities	Dallas PMSA, TX	S	10.69 MW	10.39 AW	22240 AAW	TXBLS	10//99-12//99
Utilities	El Paso MSA, TX	S	10.14 MW	9.87 AW	21090 AAW	TXBLS	10//99-12//99
Utilities	Fort Worth-Arlington PMSA, TX	S	11.60 MW	11.42 AW	24130 AAW	TXBLS	10//99-12//99
Utilities	Galveston-Texas City PMSA, TX	S	11.47 MW	10.58 AW	23870 AAW	TXBLS	10//99-12//99
Utilities	Houston PMSA, TX	S	9.94 MW	9.39 AW	20670 AAW	TXBLS	10//99-12//99
Utilities	Killeen-Temple MSA, TX	S	9.07 MW	8.64 AW	18860 AAW	TXBLS	10//99-12//99
Utilities	Longview-Marshall MSA, TX	S	11.28 MW	12.09 AW	23460 AAW	TXBLS	10//99-12//99
Utilities	Lubbock MSA, TX	S	11.21 MW	11.25 AW	23320 AAW	TXBLS	10//99-12//99
Utilities	McAllen-Edinburg-Mission MSA, TX	S	8.97 MW	8.29 AW	18650 AAW	TXBLS	10//99-12//99
Utilities	San Antonio MSA, TX	S	12.52 MW	12.60 AW	26040 AAW	TXBLS	10//99-12//99
Utilities	Tyler MSA, TX	S	10.74 MW	10.39 AW	22340 AAW	TXBLS	10//99-12//99
Utilities	Wichita Falls MSA, TX	S	10.20 MW	10.12 AW	21210 AAW	TXBLS	10//99-12//99
Utilities	Utah	S	12.38 MW	13.06 AW	27170 AAW	UTBLS	10//99-12//99
Utilities	Provo-Orem MSA, UT	S	12.24 MW	12.15 AW	25450 AAW	UTBLS	10//99-12//99
Utilities	Salt Lake City-Ogden MSA, UT	S	13.80 MW	13.26 AW	28710 AAW	UTBLS	10//99-12//99
Utilities	Vermont	S	12.91 MW	13.53 AW	28150 AAW	VTBLS	10//99-12//99
Utilities	Virginia	S	10.83 MW	12.74 AW	26500 AAW	VABLS	10//99-12//99
Utilities	Danville MSA, VA	S	10.41 MW	9.98 AW	21650 AAW	VABLS	10//99-12//99
Utilities	Norfolk-Virginia Beach-Newport News MSA, VA-NC	S	15.51 MW	17.41 AW	32260 AAW	VABLS	10//99-12//99
Utilities	Richmond-Petersburg MSA, VA	S	12.98 MW	11.12 AW	26990 AAW	VABLS	10//99-12//99
Utilities	Roanoke MSA, VA	S	12.12 MW	11.09 AW	25210 AAW	VABLS	10//99-12//99
Utilities	Washington	S	15.28 MW	15.29 AW	31810 AAW	WABLS	10//99-12//99
Utilities	Bremerton PMSA, WA	S	15.50 MW	14.43 AW	32230 AAW	WABLS	10//99-12//99
Utilities	Richland-Kennewick-Pasco MSA, WA	S	15.51 MW	15.30 AW	32270 AAW	WABLS	10//99-12//99
Utilities	Seattle-Bellevue-Everett PMSA, WA	S	14.47 MW	14.67 AW	30100 AAW	WABLS	10//99-12//99
Utilities	Tacoma PMSA, WA	S	15.68 MW	15.82 AW	32610 AAW	WABLS	10//99-12//99
Utilities	West Virginia	S	9.32 MW	10.87 AW	22600 AAW	WVBLS	10//99-12//99
Utilities	Charleston MSA, WV	S	13.05 MW	14.81 AW	27150 AAW	WVBLS	10//99-12//99
Utilities	Huntington-Ashland MSA, WV-KY-OH	S	10.55 MW	9.88 AW	21940 AAW	WVBLS	10//99-12//99
Utilities	Wheeling MSA, WV-OH	S	13.62 MW	14.65 AW	28330 AAW	WVBLS	10//99-12//99
Utilities	Wisconsin	S	14.73 MW	14.15 AW	29420 AAW	WIBLS	10//99-12//99
Utilities	Green Bay MSA, WI	S	16.45 MW	15.56 AW	34210 AAW	WIBLS	10//99-12//99
Utilities	Milwaukee-Waukesha PMSA, WI	S	15.11 MW	15.01 AW	31430 AAW	WIBLS	10//99-12//99
Utilities	Wyoming	S	12.82 MW	13.86 AW	28820 AAW	WYBLS	10//99-12//99
Microbiologist	Alaska	S	21.63 MW	21.67 AW	45070 AAW	AKBLS	10//99-12//99
	California	S	28.47 MW	29.05 AW	60420 AAW	CABLS	10//99-12//99
	Los Angeles-Long Beach PMSA, CA	S	27.24 MW	25.99 AW	56650 AAW	CABLS	10//99-12//99
	Oakland PMSA, CA	S	27.62 MW	25.28 AW	57450 AAW	CABLS	10//99-12//99
	Orange County PMSA, CA	S	23.21 MW	20.75 AW	48280 AAW	CABLS	10//99-12//99
	Riverside-San Bernardino PMSA, CA	S	27.62 MW	27.35 AW	57450 AAW	CABLS	10//99-12//99
	San Diego MSA, CA	S	29.50 MW	28.21 AW	61360 AAW	CABLS	10//99-12//99
	San Francisco PMSA, CA	S	31.81 MW	32.27 AW	66160 AAW	CABLS	10//99-12//99
	San Jose PMSA, CA	S	32.14 MW	31.65 AW	66850 AAW	CABLS	10//99-12//99

AAW	Average annual wage	AOH	Average offered, high	ASH	Average starting, high
AE	Average entry wage	AOL	Average offered, low	ASL	Average starting, low
AEX	Average experienced wage	APH	Average pay, high range	AW	Average wage paid
AO	Average offered	APL	Average pay, low range	FQ	First quartile wage

H	Hourly	M	Monthly
HI	Highest wage paid	MTC	Median total compensation
HR	High end range	MW	Median wage paid
LR	Low end range	SQ	Second quartile wage

S	Special: hourly and annual
TQ	Third quartile wage
W	Weekly
Y	Yearly

Occupation/Type/Industry	Location	Per	Low	Mid	High	Source	Date
Microbiologist	Colorado	S	24.12 MW	22.95 AW	47730 AAW	COBLS	10//99-12//99
	Connecticut	S	29.1 MW	29.53 AW	61420 AAW	CTBLS	10//99-12//99
	Delaware	S	25.52 MW	30.87 AW	64210 AAW	DEBLS	10//99-12//99
	Wilmington-Newark PMSA, DE-MD	S	31.58 MW	26.10 AW	65690 AAW	DEBLS	10//99-12//99
	Washington PMSA, DC-MD-VA-WV	S	26.72 MW	27.13 AW	55580 AAW	DCBLS	10//99-12//99
	Florida	S	20.4 MW	23.45 AW	48780 AAW	FLBLS	10//99-12//99
	Melbourne-Titusville-Palm Bay MSA, FL	S	20.81 MW	19.73 AW	43280 AAW	FLBLS	10//99-12//99
	Miami PMSA, FL	S	23.83 MW	19.92 AW	49560 AAW	FLBLS	10//99-12//99
	Tampa-St. Petersburg-Clearwater MSA, FL	S	24.04 MW	20.73 AW	50000 AAW	FLBLS	10//99-12//99
	Georgia	S	22.05 MW	23.93 AW	49780 AAW	GABLS	10//99-12//99
	Atlanta MSA, GA	S	23.92 MW	22.00 AW	49750 AAW	GABLS	10//99-12//99
	Idaho	S	17.13 MW	20.33 AW	42290 AAW	IDBLS	10//99-12//99
	Illinois	S	21.31 MW	22.98 AW	47800 AAW	ILBLS	10//99-12//99
	Chicago PMSA, IL	S	23.12 MW	22.14 AW	48090 AAW	ILBLS	10//99-12//99
	Indiana	S	20.06 MW	21.03 AW	43750 AAW	INBLS	10//99-12//99
	Evansville-Henderson MSA, IN-KY	S	19.16 MW	19.25 AW	39850 AAW	INBLS	10//99-12//99
	Indianapolis MSA, IN	S	21.30 MW	20.39 AW	44300 AAW	INBLS	10//99-12//99
	Iowa	S	25.68 MW	27.46 AW	57110 AAW	IABLS	10//99-12//99
	Kansas	S	19.34 MW	19.82 AW	41230 AAW	KSBLS	10//99-12//99
	Kentucky	S	18.21 MW	18.20 AW	37850 AAW	KYBLS	10//99-12//99
	Louisiana	S	25.65 MW	26.41 AW	54920 AAW	LABLS	10//99-12//99
	Maine	S	20.68 MW	26.09 AW	54270 AAW	MEBLS	10//99-12//99
	Baltimore PMSA, MD	S	23.30 MW	22.27 AW	48470 AAW	MDBLS	10//99-12//99
	Massachusetts	S	25.46 MW	29.67 AW	61710 AAW	MABLS	10//99-12//99
	Boston PMSA, MA-NH	S	29.88 MW	25.44 AW	62150 AAW	MABLS	10//99-12//99
	Minnesota	S	20.02 MW	20.54 AW	42720 AAW	MNBLS	10//99-12//99
	Minneapolis-St. Paul MSA, MN-WI	S	20.65 MW	20.19 AW	42940 AAW	MNBLS	10//99-12//99
	Mississippi	S	19.9 MW	21.66 AW	45050 AAW	MSBLS	10//99-12//99
	Missouri	S	18.07 MW	19.36 AW	40270 AAW	MOBLS	10//99-12//99
	Kansas City MSA, MO-KS	S	20.62 MW	20.01 AW	42880 AAW	MOBLS	10//99-12//99
	St. Louis MSA, MO-IL	S	19.83 MW	18.89 AW	41240 AAW	MOBLS	10//99-12//99
	Montana	S	17.4 MW	18.08 AW	37610 AAW	MTBLS	10//99-12//99
	Nebraska	S	16.2 MW	17.31 AW	36010 AAW	NEBLS	10//99-12//99
	Omaha MSA, NE-IA	S	16.28 MW	15.36 AW	33850 AAW	NEBLS	10//99-12//99
	New Hampshire	S	20.96 MW	21.24 AW	44180 AAW	NHBLS	10//99-12//99
	New Jersey	S	21.39 MW	22.70 AW	47220 AAW	NJBLS	10//99-12//99
	Middlesex-Somerset-Hunterdon PMSA, NJ	S	22.96 MW	20.18 AW	47760 AAW	NJBLS	10//99-12//99
	Monmouth-Ocean PMSA, NJ	S	22.17 MW	23.24 AW	46120 AAW	NJBLS	10//99-12//99
	Newark PMSA, NJ	S	22.50 MW	20.83 AW	46800 AAW	NJBLS	10//99-12//99
	Trenton PMSA, NJ	S	23.76 MW	23.59 AW	49410 AAW	NJBLS	10//99-12//99
	New York	S	19.86 MW	23.64 AW	49160 AAW	NYBLS	10//99-12//99
	Nassau-Suffolk PMSA, NY	S	23.19 MW	19.46 AW	48240 AAW	NYBLS	10//99-12//99
	New York PMSA, NY	S	23.57 MW	19.96 AW	49020 AAW	NYBLS	10//99-12//99
	North Carolina	S	31.64 MW	31.02 AW	64520 AAW	NCBLS	10//99-12//99
	Raleigh-Durham-Chapel Hill MSA, NC	S	31.42 MW	32.44 AW	65350 AAW	NCBLS	10//99-12//99
	Ohio	S	17.76 MW	18.52 AW	38530 AAW	OHBLS	10//99-12//99
	Cincinnati PMSA, OH-KY-IN	S	20.52 MW	19.84 AW	42690 AAW	OHBLS	10//99-12//99
	Columbus MSA, OH	S	13.54 MW	12.45 AW	28160 AAW	OHBLS	10//99-12//99
	Dayton-Springfield MSA, OH	S	18.05 MW	17.95 AW	37540 AAW	OHBLS	10//99-12//99
	Oklahoma	S	19.26 MW	20.93 AW	43530 AAW	OKBLS	10//99-12//99
	Oregon	S	20.98 MW	21.77 AW	45280 AAW	ORBLS	10//99-12//99
	Corvallis MSA, OR	S	21.79 MW	21.73 AW	45330 AAW	ORBLS	10//99-12//99
	Portland-Vancouver PMSA, OR-WA	S	21.10 MW	19.51 AW	43900 AAW	ORBLS	10//99-12//99
	Pennsylvania	S	21.9 MW	23.96 AW	49830 AAW	PABLS	10//99-12//99
	Philadelphia PMSA, PA-NJ	S	25.03 MW	24.19 AW	52060 AAW	PABLS	10//99-12//99
	South Carolina	S	18.9 MW	20.83 AW	43330 AAW	SCBLS	10//99-12//99
	Tennessee	S	18.98 MW	19.01 AW	39530 AAW	TNBLS	10//99-12//99
	Knoxville MSA, TN	S	18.45 MW	18.58 AW	38380 AAW	TNBLS	10//99-12//99
	Nashville MSA, TN	S	18.90 MW	18.91 AW	39320 AAW	TNBLS	10//99-12//99
	Texas	S	21.65 MW	24.53 AW	51030 AAW	TXBLS	10//99-12//99
	Dallas PMSA, TX	S	19.54 MW	19.46 AW	40650 AAW	TXBLS	10//99-12//99
	Houston PMSA, TX	S	22.21 MW	22.69 AW	46190 AAW	TXBLS	10//99-12//99
	San Antonio MSA, TX	S	19.21 MW	18.03 AW	39950 AAW	TXBLS	10//99-12//99

AAW	Average annual wage	AOH	Average offered, high	ASH	Average starting, high	H	Hourly	M	Monthly	S	Special: hourly and annual
AE	Average entry wage	AOL	Average offered, low	ASL	Average starting, low	HI	Highest wage paid	MTC	Median total compensation	TQ	Third quartile wage
AEX	Average experienced wage	APH	Average pay, high range	AW	Average wage paid	HR	High end range	MW	Median wage paid	W	Weekly
AO	Average offered	APL	Average pay, low range	FQ	First quartile wage	LR	Low end range	SQ	Second quartile wage	Y	Yearly

Occupation/Type/Industry	Location	Per	Low	Mid	High	Source	Date
Microbiologist	Utah	S	16.4 MW	18.02 AW	37480 AAW	UTBLS	10//99-12//99
	Virginia	S	19.17 MW	21.78 AW	45300 AAW	VABLS	10//99-12//99
	Norfolk-Virginia Beach-Newport News MSA, VA-NC	S	25.30 MW	21.15 AW	52620 AAW	VABLS	10//99-12//99
	Washington	S	21.89 MW	23.30 AW	48460 AAW	WABLS	10//99-12//99
	Seattle-Bellevue-Everett PMSA, WA	S	23.50 MW	22.25 AW	48880 AAW	WABLS	10//99-12//99
	West Virginia	S	18.51 MW	22.76 AW	47330 AAW	WVBLS	10//99-12//99
	Wisconsin	S	20.25 MW	21.16 AW	44010 AAW	WIBLS	10//99-12//99
	Madison MSA, WI	S	19.50 MW	18.89 AW	40560 AAW	WIBLS	10//99-12//99
	Milwaukee-Waukesha PMSA, WI	S	21.67 MW	20.45 AW	45070 AAW	WIBLS	10//99-12//99
	Puerto Rico	S	16.18 MW	17.93 AW	37300 AAW	PRBLS	10//99-12//99
	Caguas PMSA, PR	S	16.20 MW	16.21 AW	33700 AAW	PRBLS	10//99-12//99
	San Juan-Bayamon PMSA, PR	S	18.60 MW	16.49 AW	38700 AAW	PRBLS	10//99-12//99
Middle School Teacher							
Except Special and Vocational Education	Alabama	Y		36690 AAW		ALBLS	10//99-12//99
Except Special and Vocational Education	Alaska	Y		45270 AAW		AKBLS	10//99-12//99
Except Special and Vocational Education	Arizona	Y		36460 AAW		AZBLS	10//99-12//99
Except Special and Vocational Education	Arkansas	Y		32100 AAW		ARBLS	10//99-12//99
Except Special and Vocational Education	California	Y		44810 AAW		CABLS	10//99-12//99
Except Special and Vocational Education	Colorado	Y		38090 AAW		COBLS	10//99-12//99
Except Special and Vocational Education	Connecticut	Y		50900 AAW		CTBLS	10//99-12//99
Except Special and Vocational Education	Delaware	Y		43580 AAW		DEBLS	10//99-12//99
Except Special and Vocational Education	Florida	Y		38110 AAW		FLBLS	10//99-12//99
Except Special and Vocational Education	Georgia	Y		40290 AAW		GABLS	10//99-12//99
Except Special and Vocational Education	Illinois	Y		42370 AAW		ILBLS	10//99-12//99
Except Special and Vocational Education	Indiana	Y		40870 AAW		INBLS	10//99-12//99
Except Special and Vocational Education	Iowa	Y		32120 AAW		IABLS	10//99-12//99
Except Special and Vocational Education	Kansas	Y		33030 AAW		KSBLS	10//99-12//99
Except Special and Vocational Education	Kentucky	Y		34660 AAW		KYBLS	10//99-12//99
Except Special and Vocational Education	Louisiana	Y		20000 AAW		LABLS	10//99-12//99
Except Special and Vocational Education	Maine	Y		35480 AAW		MEBLS	10//99-12//99
Except Special and Vocational Education	Maryland	Y		39730 AAW		MDBLS	10//99-12//99
Except Special and Vocational Education	Massachusetts	Y		41980 AAW		MABLS	10//99-12//99
Except Special and Vocational Education	Michigan	Y		44690 AAW		MIBLS	10//99-12//99
Except Special and Vocational Education	Minnesota	Y		39700 AAW		MNBLS	10//99-12//99
Except Special and Vocational Education	Mississippi	Y		31110 AAW		MSBLS	10//99-12//99
Except Special and Vocational Education	Missouri	Y		34730 AAW		MOBLS	10//99-12//99
Except Special and Vocational Education	Montana	Y		22580 AAW		MTBLS	10//99-12//99
Except Special and Vocational Education	Nebraska	Y		34820 AAW		NEBLS	10//99-12//99
Except Special and Vocational Education	Nevada	Y		42610 AAW		NVBLS	10//99-12//99
Except Special and Vocational Education	New Hampshire	Y		34280 AAW		NHBLS	10//99-12//99
Except Special and Vocational Education	New Jersey	Y		49040 AAW		NJBLS	10//99-12//99
Except Special and Vocational Education	New Mexico	Y		31060 AAW		NMBLS	10//99-12//99
Except Special and Vocational Education	New York	Y		48970 AAW		NYBLS	10//99-12//99
Except Special and Vocational Education	North Carolina	Y		34260 AAW		NCBLS	10//99-12//99
Except Special and Vocational Education	Ohio	Y		40320 AAW		OHBLS	10//99-12//99
Except Special and Vocational Education	Oklahoma	Y		32160 AAW		OKBLS	10//99-12//99
Except Special and Vocational Education	Oregon	Y		41470 AAW		ORBLS	10//99-12//99
Except Special and Vocational Education	Pennsylvania	Y		46110 AAW		PABLS	10//99-12//99
Except Special and Vocational Education	Rhode Island	Y		40510 AAW		RIBLS	10//99-12//99
Except Special and Vocational Education	South Carolina	Y		36470 AAW		SCBLS	10//99-12//99
Except Special and Vocational Education	South Dakota	Y		29700 AAW		SDBLS	10//99-12//99
Except Special and Vocational Education	Tennessee	Y		31500 AAW		TNBLS	10//99-12//99
Except Special and Vocational Education	Texas	Y		36340 AAW		TXBLS	10//99-12//99
Except Special and Vocational Education	Utah	Y		35370 AAW		UTBLS	10//99-12//99
Except Special and Vocational Education	Vermont	Y		38600 AAW		VTBLS	10//99-12//99
Except Special and Vocational Education	Virginia	Y		34650 AAW		VABLS	10//99-12//99
Except Special and Vocational Education	Washington	Y		42130 AAW		WABLS	10//99-12//99
Except Special and Vocational Education	West Virginia	Y		34790 AAW		WVBLS	10//99-12//99
Except Special and Vocational Education	Wisconsin	Y		41790 AAW		WIBLS	10//99-12//99
Except Special and Vocational Education	Wyoming	Y		35160 AAW		WYBLS	10//99-12//99
Except Special and Vocational Education	Puerto Rico	Y		19600 AAW		PRBLS	10//99-12//99
Except Special and Vocational Education	Guam	Y		20840 AAW		GUBLS	10//99-12//99
Milking Couple							
Dairy, Agriculture	United States	Y	22000 APL	29833 AW	44000 APL	FAJO	1998

AAW	Average annual wage	AOH	Average offered, high	ASH	Average starting, high
AE	Average entry wage	AOL	Average offered, low	ASL	Average starting, low
AEX	Average experienced wage	APH	Average pay, high range	AW	Average wage paid
AO	Average offered	APL	Average pay, low range	FQ	First quartile wage

H	Hourly	M	Monthly	S	Special: hourly and annual
HI	Highest wage paid	MTC	Median total compensation	TQ	Third quartile wage
HR	High end range	MW	Median wage paid	W	Weekly
LR	Low end range	SQ	Second quartile wage	Y	Yearly

Occupation/Type/Industry	Location	Per	Low	Mid	High	Source	Date
Milling and Planing Machine							
Setter, Operator, and Tender							
Metals and Plastics	Alabama	S	20.15 MW	19.91 AW	41410 AAW	ALBLS	10//99-12//99
Metals and Plastics	Birmingham MSA, AL	S	21.27 MW	22.29 AW	44250 AAW	ALBLS	10//99-12//99
Metals and Plastics	Arizona	S	12.19 MW	12.81 AW	26640 AAW	AZBLS	10//99-12//99
Metals and Plastics	Phoenix-Mesa MSA, AZ	S	12.61 MW	12.01 AW	26240 AAW	AZBLS	10//99-12//99
Metals and Plastics	Arkansas	S	10.79 MW	12.44 AW	25870 AAW	ARBLS	10//99-12//99
Metals and Plastics	Fayetteville-Springdale-Rogers MSA, AR	S	8.96 MW	8.79 AW	18650 AAW	ARBLS	10//99-12//99
Metals and Plastics	California	S	12.39 MW	13.22 AW	27500 AAW	CABLS	10//99-12//99
Metals and Plastics	Los Angeles-Long Beach PMSA, CA	S	12.44 MW	13.37 AW	25880 AAW	CABLS	10//99-12//99
Metals and Plastics	Oakland PMSA, CA	S	10.32 MW	8.86 AW	21460 AAW	CABLS	10//99-12//99
Metals and Plastics	Orange County PMSA, CA	S	16.62 MW	13.78 AW	34570 AAW	CABLS	10//99-12//99
Metals and Plastics	Riverside-San Bernardino PMSA, CA	S	16.35 MW	18.28 AW	34010 AAW	CABLS	10//99-12//99
Metals and Plastics	San Diego MSA, CA	S	10.00 MW	8.11 AW	20810 AAW	CABLS	10//99-12//99
Metals and Plastics	San Jose PMSA, CA	S	11.26 MW	11.10 AW	23420 AAW	CABLS	10//99-12//99
Metals and Plastics	Santa Barbara-Santa Maria-Lompoc MSA, CA	S	11.46 MW	9.97 AW	23830 AAW	CABLS	10//99-12//99
Metals and Plastics	Ventura PMSA, CA	S	10.44 MW	10.60 AW	21710 AAW	CABLS	10//99-12//99
Metals and Plastics	Connecticut	S	15.32 MW	15.07 AW	31360 AAW	CTBLS	10//99-12//99
Metals and Plastics	Bridgeport PMSA, CT	S	19.85 MW	19.64 AW	41280 AAW	CTBLS	10//99-12//99
Metals and Plastics	Hartford MSA, CT	S	14.24 MW	14.47 AW	29630 AAW	CTBLS	10//99-12//99
Metals and Plastics	New Haven-Meriden PMSA, CT	S	15.29 MW	15.37 AW	31800 AAW	CTBLS	10//99-12//99
Metals and Plastics	Waterbury PMSA, CT	S	13.18 MW	10.66 AW	27410 AAW	CTBLS	10//99-12//99
Metals and Plastics	Florida	S	13.39 MW	13.70 AW	28510 AAW	FLBLS	10//99-12//99
Metals and Plastics	Fort Lauderdale PMSA, FL	S	13.73 MW	13.20 AW	28550 AAW	FLBLS	10//99-12//99
Metals and Plastics	Jacksonville MSA, FL	S	14.93 MW	14.77 AW	31060 AAW	FLBLS	10//99-12//99
Metals and Plastics	Orlando MSA, FL	S	13.49 MW	12.38 AW	28060 AAW	FLBLS	10//99-12//99
Metals and Plastics	Tampa-St. Petersburg-Clearwater MSA, FL	S	11.07 MW	11.45 AW	23030 AAW	FLBLS	10//99-12//99
Metals and Plastics	West Palm Beach-Boca Raton MSA, FL	S	17.33 MW	17.25 AW	36050 AAW	FLBLS	10//99-12//99
Metals and Plastics	Georgia	S	12.22 MW	12.30 AW	25590 AAW	GABLS	10//99-12//99
Metals and Plastics	Atlanta MSA, GA	S	14.60 MW	14.68 AW	30360 AAW	GABLS	10//99-12//99
Metals and Plastics	Augusta-Aiken MSA, GA-SC	S	10.98 MW	9.80 AW	22850 AAW	GABLS	10//99-12//99
Metals and Plastics	Idaho	S	12.26 MW	12.28 AW	25550 AAW	IDBLS	10//99-12//99
Metals and Plastics	Illinois	S	11.47 MW	11.92 AW	24790 AAW	ILBLS	10//99-12//99
Metals and Plastics	Chicago PMSA, IL	S	11.44 MW	11.29 AW	23790 AAW	ILBLS	10//99-12//99
Metals and Plastics	Rockford MSA, IL	S	18.58 MW	15.85 AW	38650 AAW	ILBLS	10//99-12//99
Metals and Plastics	Indiana	S	13.44 MW	13.82 AW	28750 AAW	INBLS	10//99-12//99
Metals and Plastics	Elkhart-Goshen MSA, IN	S	13.26 MW	11.73 AW	27580 AAW	INBLS	10//99-12//99
Metals and Plastics	Fort Wayne MSA, IN	S	14.98 MW	15.43 AW	31170 AAW	INBLS	10//99-12//99
Metals and Plastics	Indianapolis MSA, IN	S	14.11 MW	14.41 AW	29350 AAW	INBLS	10//99-12//99
Metals and Plastics	South Bend MSA, IN	S	10.94 MW	11.27 AW	22760 AAW	INBLS	10//99-12//99
Metals and Plastics	Iowa	S	12.71 MW	14.85 AW	30880 AAW	IABLS	10//99-12//99
Metals and Plastics	Des Moines MSA, IA	S	11.32 MW	10.36 AW	23540 AAW	IABLS	10//99-12//99
Metals and Plastics	Kansas	S	15.74 MW	15.14 AW	31490 AAW	KSBLS	10//99-12//99
Metals and Plastics	Wichita MSA, KS	S	16.61 MW	17.44 AW	34550 AAW	KSBLS	10//99-12//99
Metals and Plastics	Kentucky	S	10.79 MW	11.35 AW	23610 AAW	KYBLS	10//99-12//99
Metals and Plastics	Lexington MSA, KY	S	10.68 MW	9.97 AW	22220 AAW	KYBLS	10//99-12//99
Metals and Plastics	Louisiana	S	13.87 MW	11.97 AW	24900 AAW	LABLS	10//99-12//99
Metals and Plastics	New Orleans MSA, LA	S	11.64 MW	13.07 AW	24220 AAW	LABLS	10//99-12//99
Metals and Plastics	Maryland	S	10.65 MW	11.75 AW	24450 AAW	MDBLS	10//99-12//99
Metals and Plastics	Baltimore PMSA, MD	S	14.29 MW	13.17 AW	29720 AAW	MDBLS	10//99-12//99
Metals and Plastics	Massachusetts	S	14.78 MW	14.66 AW	30500 AAW	MABLS	10//99-12//99
Metals and Plastics	Boston PMSA, MA-NH	S	16.02 MW	15.67 AW	33310 AAW	MABLS	10//99-12//99
Metals and Plastics	Lowell PMSA, MA-NH	S	11.53 MW	11.23 AW	23990 AAW	MABLS	10//99-12//99
Metals and Plastics	Springfield MSA, MA	S	14.89 MW	15.03 AW	30980 AAW	MABLS	10//99-12//99
Metals and Plastics	Worcester PMSA, MA-CT	S	13.12 MW	13.37 AW	27300 AAW	MABLS	10//99-12//99
Metals and Plastics	Michigan	S	16.83 MW	17.71 AW	36840 AAW	MIBLS	10//99-12//99
Metals and Plastics	Ann Arbor PMSA, MI	S	14.52 MW	13.60 AW	30210 AAW	MIBLS	10//99-12//99
Metals and Plastics	Detroit PMSA, MI	S	19.23 MW	18.81 AW	40000 AAW	MIBLS	10//99-12//99
Metals and Plastics	Flint PMSA, MI	S	19.89 MW	22.53 AW	41370 AAW	MIBLS	10//99-12//99
Metals and Plastics	Grand Rapids-Muskegon-Holland MSA, MI	S	24.63 MW	27.97 AW	51240 AAW	MIBLS	10//99-12//99
Metals and Plastics	Kalamazoo-Battle Creek MSA, MI	S	24.92 MW	28.41 AW	51840 AAW	MIBLS	10//99-12//99
Metals and Plastics	Minnesota	S	15.85 MW	15.89 AW	33050 AAW	MNBLS	10//99-12//99

AAW Average annual wage	AOH Average offered, high	ASH Average starting, high	H Hourly	M Monthly	S Special: hourly and annual
AE Average entry wage	AOL Average offered, low	ASL Average starting, low	HI Highest wage paid	MTC Median total compensation	TQ Third quartile wage
AEX Average experienced wage	APH Average pay, high range	AW Average wage paid	HR High end range	MW Median wage paid	W Weekly
AO Average offered	APL Average pay, low range	FQ First quartile wage	LR Low end range	SQ Second quartile wage	Y Yearly

Occupation/Type/Industry	Location	Per	Low	Mid	High	Source	Date
Milling and Planing Machine Setter, Operator, and Tender							
Metals and Plastics	Minneapolis-St. Paul MSA, MN-WI	S	16.17 MW	16.15 AW	33630 AAW	MNBLS	10//99-12//99
Metals and Plastics	Mississippi	S	11.73 MW	11.57 AW	24060 AAW	MSBLS	10//99-12//99
Metals and Plastics	Missouri	S	8.02 MW	8.85 AW	18420 AAW	MOBLS	10//99-12//99
Metals and Plastics	Nebraska	S	17.15 MW	16.78 AW	34900 AAW	NEBLS	10//99-12//99
Metals and Plastics	Nevada	S	10.01 MW	11.57 AW	24070 AAW	NVBLS	10//99-12//99
Metals and Plastics	New Hampshire	S	11.06 MW	11.32 AW	23560 AAW	NHBLS	10//99-12//99
Metals and Plastics	New Jersey	S	15.12 MW	14.64 AW	30450 AAW	NJBLS	10//99-12//99
Metals and Plastics	New York	S	9.42 MW	10.28 AW	21390 AAW	NYBLS	10//99-12//99
Metals and Plastics	Albany-Schenectady-Troy MSA, NY	S	10.91 MW	10.26 AW	22690 AAW	NYBLS	10//99-12//99
Metals and Plastics	Buffalo-Niagara Falls MSA, NY	S	14.40 MW	13.33 AW	29950 AAW	NYBLS	10//99-12//99
Metals and Plastics	Nassau-Suffolk PMSA, NY	S	11.09 MW	10.53 AW	23080 AAW	NYBLS	10//99-12//99
Metals and Plastics	Rochester MSA, NY	S	8.67 MW	8.30 AW	18030 AAW	NYBLS	10//99-12//99
Metals and Plastics	Syracuse MSA, NY	S	10.61 MW	10.24 AW	22060 AAW	NYBLS	10//99-12//99
Metals and Plastics	North Carolina	S	11.1 MW	11.49 AW	23900 AAW	NCBLS	10//99-12//99
Metals and Plastics	Charlotte-Gastonia-Rock Hill MSA, NC-SC	S	11.66 MW	10.68 AW	24250 AAW	NCBLS	10//99-12//99
Metals and Plastics	Greensboro--Winston-Salem--High Point MSA, NC	S	10.79 MW	11.33 AW	22440 AAW	NCBLS	10//99-12//99
Metals and Plastics	Raleigh-Durham-Chapel Hill MSA, NC	S	10.89 MW	10.57 AW	22650 AAW	NCBLS	10//99-12//99
Metals and Plastics	Ohio	S	10.75 MW	12.39 AW	25780 AAW	OHBLS	10//99-12//99
Metals and Plastics	Akron PMSA, OH	S	14.33 MW	13.92 AW	29810 AAW	OHBLS	10//99-12//99
Metals and Plastics	Canton-Massillon MSA, OH	S	15.72 MW	15.81 AW	32700 AAW	OHBLS	10//99-12//99
Metals and Plastics	Dayton-Springfield MSA, OH	S	15.53 MW	15.40 AW	32290 AAW	OHBLS	10//99-12//99
Metals and Plastics	Toledo MSA, OH	S	12.26 MW	12.25 AW	25490 AAW	OHBLS	10//99-12//99
Metals and Plastics	Youngstown-Warren MSA, OH	S	17.92 MW	15.63 AW	37270 AAW	OHBLS	10//99-12//99
Metals and Plastics	Oklahoma	S	10.41 MW	10.84 AW	22550 AAW	OKBLS	10//99-12//99
Metals and Plastics	Oklahoma City MSA, OK	S	12.03 MW	11.48 AW	25030 AAW	OKBLS	10//99-12//99
Metals and Plastics	Tulsa MSA, OK	S	12.04 MW	12.37 AW	25040 AAW	OKBLS	10//99-12//99
Metals and Plastics	Oregon	S	14.55 MW	16.48 AW	34270 AAW	ORBLS	10//99-12//99
Metals and Plastics	Portland-Vancouver PMSA, OR-WA	S	16.31 MW	14.23 AW	33920 AAW	ORBLS	10//99-12//99
Metals and Plastics	Pennsylvania	S	13.14 MW	13.21 AW	27480 AAW	PABLS	10//99-12//99
Metals and Plastics	Allentown-Bethlehem-Easton MSA, PA	S	12.83 MW	13.90 AW	26690 AAW	PABLS	10//99-12//99
Metals and Plastics	Erie MSA, PA	S	11.28 MW	11.37 AW	23470 AAW	PABLS	10//99-12//99
Metals and Plastics	Harrisburg-Lebanon-Carlisle MSA, PA	S	11.59 MW	11.97 AW	24110 AAW	PABLS	10//99-12//99
Metals and Plastics	Lancaster MSA, PA	S	13.23 MW	13.12 AW	27520 AAW	PABLS	10//99-12//99
Metals and Plastics	Philadelphia PMSA, PA-NJ	S	16.87 MW	15.86 AW	35090 AAW	PABLS	10//99-12//99
Metals and Plastics	Pittsburgh MSA, PA	S	11.39 MW	10.17 AW	23690 AAW	PABLS	10//99-12//99
Metals and Plastics	Reading MSA, PA	S	14.62 MW	14.89 AW	30410 AAW	PABLS	10//99-12//99
Metals and Plastics	York MSA, PA	S	15.40 MW	15.31 AW	32020 AAW	PABLS	10//99-12//99
Metals and Plastics	Rhode Island	S	10.45 MW	11.95 AW	24850 AAW	RIBLS	10//99-12//99
Metals and Plastics	Providence-Fall River-Warwick MSA, RI-MA	S	12.01 MW	10.68 AW	24980 AAW	RIBLS	10//99-12//99
Metals and Plastics	South Carolina	S	12.34 MW	11.99 AW	24930 AAW	SCBLS	10//99-12//99
Metals and Plastics	Charleston-North Charleston MSA, SC	S	12.42 MW	12.64 AW	25830 AAW	SCBLS	10//99-12//99
Metals and Plastics	Greenville-Spartanburg-Anderson MSA, SC	S	12.33 MW	12.51 AW	25650 AAW	SCBLS	10//99-12//99
Metals and Plastics	South Dakota	S	10.74 MW	10.47 AW	21780 AAW	SDBLS	10//99-12//99
Metals and Plastics	Tennessee	S	11.01 MW	12.40 AW	25800 AAW	TNBLS	10//99-12//99
Metals and Plastics	Chattanooga MSA, TN-GA	S	11.22 MW	11.00 AW	23330 AAW	TNBLS	10//99-12//99
Metals and Plastics	Johnson City-Kingsport-Bristol MSA, TN-VA	S	10.36 MW	10.59 AW	21550 AAW	TNBLS	10//99-12//99
Metals and Plastics	Knoxville MSA, TN	S	10.83 MW	11.11 AW	22520 AAW	TNBLS	10//99-12//99
Metals and Plastics	Memphis MSA, TN-AR-MS	S	12.39 MW	12.34 AW	25770 AAW	MSBLS	10//99-12//99
Metals and Plastics	Nashville MSA, TN	S	13.32 MW	12.23 AW	27710 AAW	TNBLS	10//99-12//99
Metals and Plastics	Texas	S	10.52 MW	11.97 AW	24890 AAW	TXBLS	10//99-12//99
Metals and Plastics	Austin-San Marcos MSA, TX	S	15.23 MW	15.61 AW	31690 AAW	TXBLS	10//99-12//99
Metals and Plastics	Dallas PMSA, TX	S	9.64 MW	9.15 AW	20040 AAW	TXBLS	10//99-12//99
Metals and Plastics	Fort Worth-Arlington PMSA, TX	S	18.90 MW	20.57 AW	39310 AAW	TXBLS	10//99-12//99
Metals and Plastics	Houston PMSA, TX	S	10.84 MW	9.50 AW	22550 AAW	TXBLS	10//99-12//99
Metals and Plastics	San Antonio MSA, TX	S	9.55 MW	9.64 AW	19860 AAW	TXBLS	10//99-12//99
Metals and Plastics	Utah	S	11.3 MW	11.60 AW	24130 AAW	UTBLS	10//99-12//99

AAW	Average annual wage	AOH	Average offered, high	ASH	Average starting, high
AE	Average entry wage	AOL	Average offered, low	ASL	Average starting, low
AEX	Average experienced wage	APH	Average pay, high range	AW	Average wage paid
AO	Average offered	APL	Average pay, low range	FQ	First quartile wage

H	Hourly	M	Monthly
HI	Highest wage paid	MTC	Median total compensation
HR	High end range	MW	Median wage paid
LR	Low end range	SQ	Second quartile wage

S	Special: hourly and annual
TQ	Third quartile wage
W	Weekly
Y	Yearly

Occupation/Type/Industry	Location	Per	Low	Mid	High	Source	Date
Milling and Planing Machine Setter, Operator, and Tender							
Metals and Plastics	Virginia	S	12.33 MW	12.34 AW	25660 AAW	VABLS	10//99-12//99
Metals and Plastics	Roanoke MSA, VA	S	12.29 MW	12.26 AW	25570 AAW	VABLS	10//99-12//99
Metals and Plastics	Washington	S	14.26 MW	15.17 AW	31540 AAW	WABLS	10//99-12//99
Metals and Plastics	Seattle-Bellevue-Everett PMSA, WA	S	15.32 MW	14.58 AW	31860 AAW	WABLS	10//99-12//99
Metals and Plastics	Wisconsin	S	13.13 MW	13.79 AW	28680 AAW	WIBLS	10//99-12//99
Metals and Plastics	Appleton-Oshkosh-Neenah MSA, WI	S	14.26 MW	13.69 AW	29660 AAW	WIBLS	10//99-12//99
Metals and Plastics	Green Bay MSA, WI	S	14.86 MW	14.83 AW	30910 AAW	WIBLS	10//99-12//99
Metals and Plastics	Madison MSA, WI	S	14.56 MW	14.82 AW	30280 AAW	WIBLS	10//99-12//99
Metals and Plastics	Milwaukee-Waukesha PMSA, WI	S	15.56 MW	15.75 AW	32360 AAW	WIBLS	10//99-12//99
Millwright	Alabama	S	13.36 MW	13.77 AW	28640 AAW	ALBLS	10//99-12//99
	Anniston MSA, AL	S	13.33 MW	13.05 AW	27720 AAW	ALBLS	10//99-12//99
	Birmingham MSA, AL	S	13.92 MW	13.91 AW	28950 AAW	ALBLS	10//99-12//99
	Gadsden MSA, AL	S	18.07 MW	18.37 AW	37590 AAW	ALBLS	10//99-12//99
	Mobile MSA, AL	S	13.43 MW	12.96 AW	27930 AAW	ALBLS	10//99-12//99
	Tuscaloosa MSA, AL	S	17.66 MW	17.71 AW	36740 AAW	ALBLS	10//99-12//99
	Arizona	S	17.14 MW	17.77 AW	36960 AAW	AZBLS	10//99-12//99
	Phoenix-Mesa MSA, AZ	S	18.68 MW	18.21 AW	38860 AAW	AZBLS	10//99-12//99
	Arkansas	S	16.6 MW	17.70 AW	36820 AAW	ARBLS	10//99-12//99
	Fayetteville-Springdale-Rogers MSA, AR	S	14.39 MW	14.50 AW	29930 AAW	ARBLS	10//99-12//99
	Little Rock-North Little Rock MSA, AR	S	15.44 MW	14.84 AW	32120 AAW	ARBLS	10//99-12//99
	California	S	19.1 MW	20.01 AW	41630 AAW	CABLS	10//99-12//99
	Fresno MSA, CA	S	17.02 MW	15.26 AW	35400 AAW	CABLS	10//99-12//99
	Los Angeles-Long Beach PMSA, CA	S	22.96 MW	21.94 AW	47760 AAW	CABLS	10//99-12//99
	Modesto MSA, CA	S	21.50 MW	21.42 AW	44730 AAW	CABLS	10//99-12//99
	Oakland PMSA, CA	S	19.76 MW	18.58 AW	41110 AAW	CABLS	10//99-12//99
	Redding MSA, CA	S	18.11 MW	18.25 AW	37670 AAW	CABLS	10//99-12//99
	Riverside-San Bernardino PMSA, CA	S	18.83 MW	18.80 AW	39170 AAW	CABLS	10//99-12//99
	San Jose PMSA, CA	S	20.18 MW	20.80 AW	41970 AAW	CABLS	10//99-12//99
	Stockton-Lodi MSA, CA	S	17.39 MW	18.04 AW	36170 AAW	CABLS	10//99-12//99
	Vallejo-Fairfield-Napa PMSA, CA	S	16.80 MW	15.19 AW	34940 AAW	CABLS	10//99-12//99
	Ventura PMSA, CA	S	20.56 MW	21.88 AW	42770 AAW	CABLS	10//99-12//99
	Colorado	S	17.56 MW	16.28 AW	33860 AAW	COBLS	10//99-12//99
	Denver PMSA, CO	S	17.63 MW	18.00 AW	36660 AAW	COBLS	10//99-12//99
	Connecticut	S	18.7 MW	18.50 AW	38470 AAW	CTBLS	10//99-12//99
	Hartford MSA, CT	S	17.64 MW	18.23 AW	36700 AAW	CTBLS	10//99-12//99
	New Haven-Meriden PMSA, CT	S	19.39 MW	20.54 AW	40330 AAW	CTBLS	10//99-12//99
	Delaware	S	22.06 MW	21.64 AW	45010 AAW	DEBLS	10//99-12//99
	Wilmington-Newark PMSA, DE-MD	S	25.23 MW	24.94 AW	52480 AAW	DEBLS	10//99-12//99
	Washington PMSA, DC-MD-VA-WV	S	18.42 MW	18.34 AW	38310 AAW	DCBLS	10//99-12//99
	Florida	S	13.08 MW	13.90 AW	28920 AAW	FLBLS	10//99-12//99
	Fort Lauderdale PMSA, FL	S	15.94 MW	15.76 AW	33150 AAW	FLBLS	10//99-12//99
	Jacksonville MSA, FL	S	13.97 MW	14.25 AW	29060 AAW	FLBLS	10//99-12//99
	Lakeland-Winter Haven MSA, FL	S	15.19 MW	15.29 AW	31600 AAW	FLBLS	10//99-12//99
	Melbourne-Titusville-Palm Bay MSA, FL	S	15.08 MW	14.54 AW	31360 AAW	FLBLS	10//99-12//99
	Orlando MSA, FL	S	11.05 MW	11.18 AW	22980 AAW	FLBLS	10//99-12//99
	Tallahassee MSA, FL	S	16.12 MW	16.26 AW	33530 AAW	FLBLS	10//99-12//99
	Tampa-St. Petersburg-Clearwater MSA, FL	S	16.93 MW	17.70 AW	35220 AAW	FLBLS	10//99-12//99
	Georgia	S	16.49 MW	18.00 AW	37430 AAW	GABLS	10//99-12//99
	Atlanta MSA, GA	S	16.74 MW	15.44 AW	34830 AAW	GABLS	10//99-12//99
	Columbus MSA, GA-AL	S	16.71 MW	15.02 AW	34750 AAW	GABLS	10//99-12//99
	Savannah MSA, GA	S	18.69 MW	19.35 AW	38880 AAW	GABLS	10//99-12//99
	Idaho	S	15.69 MW	15.94 AW	33150 AAW	IDBLS	10//99-12//99
	Boise City MSA, ID	S	16.27 MW	16.94 AW	33830 AAW	IDBLS	10//99-12//99
	Illinois	S	19.83 MW	20.57 AW	42780 AAW	ILBLS	10//99-12//99
	Chicago PMSA, IL	S	21.47 MW	21.77 AW	44650 AAW	ILBLS	10//99-12//99

AAW Average annual wage	**AOH** Average offered, high	**ASH** Average starting, high	**H** Hourly	**M** Monthly	**S** Special: hourly and annual
AE Average entry wage	**AOL** Average offered, low	**ASL** Average starting, low	**HI** Highest wage paid	**MTC** Median total compensation	**TQ** Third quartile wage
AEX Average experienced wage	**APH** Average pay, high range	**AW** Average wage paid	**HR** High end range	**MW** Median wage paid	**W** Weekly
AO Average offered	**APL** Average pay, low range	**FQ** First quartile wage	**LR** Low end range	**SQ** Second quartile wage	**Y** Yearly

Occupation/Type/Industry	Location	Per	Low	Mid	High	Source	Date
Millwright	Indiana	s	20.78 ᴍᴡ	20.21 ᴀᴡ	42040 ᴀᴀᴡ	INBLS	10//99-12//99
	Evansville-Henderson MSA, IN-KY	s	21.13 ᴍᴡ	20.17 ᴀᴡ	43950 ᴀᴀᴡ	INBLS	10//99-12//99
	Fort Wayne MSA, IN	s	18.16 ᴍᴡ	17.91 ᴀᴡ	37770 ᴀᴀᴡ	INBLS	10//99-12//99
	Gary PMSA, IN	s	16.95 ᴍᴡ	16.37 ᴀᴡ	35250 ᴀᴀᴡ	INBLS	10//99-12//99
	Indianapolis MSA, IN	s	22.49 ᴍᴡ	22.11 ᴀᴡ	46780 ᴀᴀᴡ	INBLS	10//99-12//99
	South Bend MSA, IN	s	17.21 ᴍᴡ	17.11 ᴀᴡ	35790 ᴀᴀᴡ	INBLS	10//99-12//99
	Iowa	s	18.33 ᴍᴡ	17.81 ᴀᴡ	37040 ᴀᴀᴡ	IABLS	10//99-12//99
	Cedar Rapids MSA, IA	s	19.53 ᴍᴡ	20.16 ᴀᴡ	40620 ᴀᴀᴡ	IABLS	10//99-12//99
	Davenport-Moline-Rock Island MSA, IA-IL	s	19.11 ᴍᴡ	19.08 ᴀᴡ	39750 ᴀᴀᴡ	IABLS	10//99-12//99
	Kansas	s	15.9 ᴍᴡ	17.77 ᴀᴡ	36970 ᴀᴀᴡ	KSBLS	10//99-12//99
	Topeka MSA, KS	s	18.79 ᴍᴡ	18.91 ᴀᴡ	39080 ᴀᴀᴡ	KSBLS	10//99-12//99
	Kentucky	s	19.18 ᴍᴡ	18.51 ᴀᴡ	38490 ᴀᴀᴡ	KYBLS	10//99-12//99
	Lexington MSA, KY	s	17.58 ᴍᴡ	17.25 ᴀᴡ	36560 ᴀᴀᴡ	KYBLS	10//99-12//99
	Louisville MSA, KY-IN	s	19.97 ᴍᴡ	21.45 ᴀᴡ	41530 ᴀᴀᴡ	KYBLS	10//99-12//99
	Louisiana	s	15.36 ᴍᴡ	15.46 ᴀᴡ	32150 ᴀᴀᴡ	LABLS	10//99-12//99
	Baton Rouge MSA, LA	s	16.64 ᴍᴡ	16.97 ᴀᴡ	34600 ᴀᴀᴡ	LABLS	10//99-12//99
	Houma MSA, LA	s	15.83 ᴍᴡ	14.29 ᴀᴡ	32920 ᴀᴀᴡ	LABLS	10//99-12//99
	Lafayette MSA, LA	s	14.22 ᴍᴡ	14.69 ᴀᴡ	29580 ᴀᴀᴡ	LABLS	10//99-12//99
	Lake Charles MSA, LA	s	16.90 ᴍᴡ	17.78 ᴀᴡ	35150 ᴀᴀᴡ	LABLS	10//99-12//99
	Monroe MSA, LA	s	13.57 ᴍᴡ	12.83 ᴀᴡ	28220 ᴀᴀᴡ	LABLS	10//99-12//99
	New Orleans MSA, LA	s	16.23 ᴍᴡ	16.41 ᴀᴡ	33770 ᴀᴀᴡ	LABLS	10//99-12//99
	Maine	s	18.49 ᴍᴡ	18.55 ᴀᴡ	38590 ᴀᴀᴡ	MEBLS	10//99-12//99
	Portland MSA, ME	s	20.59 ᴍᴡ	20.25 ᴀᴡ	42840 ᴀᴀᴡ	MEBLS	10//99-12//99
	Maryland	s	18.4 ᴍᴡ	18.33 ᴀᴡ	38130 ᴀᴀᴡ	MDBLS	10//99-12//99
	Baltimore PMSA, MD	s	17.85 ᴍᴡ	17.95 ᴀᴡ	37120 ᴀᴀᴡ	MDBLS	10//99-12//99
	Massachusetts	s	17.02 ᴍᴡ	17.44 ᴀᴡ	36280 ᴀᴀᴡ	MABLS	10//99-12//99
	Boston PMSA, MA-NH	s	17.58 ᴍᴡ	16.71 ᴀᴡ	36560 ᴀᴀᴡ	MABLS	10//99-12//99
	Lowell PMSA, MA-NH	s	15.90 ᴍᴡ	15.08 ᴀᴡ	33070 ᴀᴀᴡ	MABLS	10//99-12//99
	Pittsfield MSA, MA	s	16.75 ᴍᴡ	16.77 ᴀᴡ	34830 ᴀᴀᴡ	MABLS	10//99-12//99
	Springfield MSA, MA	s	17.20 ᴍᴡ	16.70 ᴀᴡ	35780 ᴀᴀᴡ	MABLS	10//99-12//99
	Michigan	s	23.03 ᴍᴡ	22.63 ᴀᴡ	47070 ᴀᴀᴡ	MIBLS	10//99-12//99
	Benton Harbor MSA, MI	s	23.37 ᴍᴡ	23.28 ᴀᴡ	48610 ᴀᴀᴡ	MIBLS	10//99-12//99
	Detroit PMSA, MI	s	23.50 ᴍᴡ	23.53 ᴀᴡ	48880 ᴀᴀᴡ	MIBLS	10//99-12//99
	Grand Rapids-Muskegon-Holland MSA, MI	s	20.12 ᴍᴡ	19.70 ᴀᴡ	41850 ᴀᴀᴡ	MIBLS	10//99-12//99
	Jackson MSA, MI	s	19.07 ᴍᴡ	19.62 ᴀᴡ	39660 ᴀᴀᴡ	MIBLS	10//99-12//99
	Kalamazoo-Battle Creek MSA, MI	s	21.23 ᴍᴡ	22.18 ᴀᴡ	44150 ᴀᴀᴡ	MIBLS	10//99-12//99
	Minnesota	s	21.67 ᴍᴡ	20.30 ᴀᴡ	42220 ᴀᴀᴡ	MNBLS	10//99-12//99
	Minneapolis-St. Paul MSA, MN-WI	s	21.04 ᴍᴡ	22.60 ᴀᴡ	43750 ᴀᴀᴡ	MNBLS	10//99-12//99
	Mississippi	s	14.98 ᴍᴡ	15.28 ᴀᴡ	31780 ᴀᴀᴡ	MSBLS	10//99-12//99
	Biloxi-Gulfport-Pascagoula MSA, MS	s	16.03 ᴍᴡ	15.41 ᴀᴡ	33350 ᴀᴀᴡ	MSBLS	10//99-12//99
	Jackson MSA, MS	s	14.76 ᴍᴡ	14.71 ᴀᴡ	30710 ᴀᴀᴡ	MSBLS	10//99-12//99
	Missouri	s	19.6 ᴍᴡ	19.69 ᴀᴡ	40960 ᴀᴀᴡ	MOBLS	10//99-12//99
	Kansas City MSA, MO-KS	s	19.94 ᴍᴡ	22.11 ᴀᴡ	41470 ᴀᴀᴡ	MOBLS	10//99-12//99
	St. Louis MSA, MO-IL	s	19.74 ᴍᴡ	18.34 ᴀᴡ	41060 ᴀᴀᴡ	MOBLS	10//99-12//99
	Montana	s	16.74 ᴍᴡ	20.17 ᴀᴡ	41940 ᴀᴀᴡ	MTBLS	10//99-12//99
	Nebraska	s	13.19 ᴍᴡ	13.26 ᴀᴡ	27580 ᴀᴀᴡ	NEBLS	10//99-12//99
	Nevada	s	17.32 ᴍᴡ	17.73 ᴀᴡ	36880 ᴀᴀᴡ	NVBLS	10//99-12//99
	Las Vegas MSA, NV-AZ	s	18.17 ᴍᴡ	19.15 ᴀᴡ	37790 ᴀᴀᴡ	NVBLS	10//99-12//99
	New Hampshire	s	15.5 ᴍᴡ	15.76 ᴀᴡ	32770 ᴀᴀᴡ	NHBLS	10//99-12//99
	Nashua PMSA, NH	s	15.88 ᴍᴡ	14.88 ᴀᴡ	33030 ᴀᴀᴡ	NHBLS	10//99-12//99
	New Jersey	s	22.53 ᴍᴡ	23.28 ᴀᴡ	48420 ᴀᴀᴡ	NJBLS	10//99-12//99
	Bergen-Passaic PMSA, NJ	s	20.62 ᴍᴡ	20.53 ᴀᴡ	42880 ᴀᴀᴡ	NJBLS	10//99-12//99
	Middlesex-Somerset-Hunterdon PMSA, NJ	s	24.16 ᴍᴡ	23.90 ᴀᴡ	50250 ᴀᴀᴡ	NJBLS	10//99-12//99
	New Mexico	s	11.51 ᴍᴡ	11.87 ᴀᴡ	24700 ᴀᴀᴡ	NMBLS	10//99-12//99
	New York	s	19.72 ᴍᴡ	19.38 ᴀᴡ	40310 ᴀᴀᴡ	NYBLS	10//99-12//99
	Albany-Schenectady-Troy MSA, NY	s	18.95 ᴍᴡ	18.86 ᴀᴡ	39420 ᴀᴀᴡ	NYBLS	10//99-12//99
	Buffalo-Niagara Falls MSA, NY	s	19.98 ᴍᴡ	21.47 ᴀᴡ	41570 ᴀᴀᴡ	NYBLS	10//99-12//99
	Jamestown MSA, NY	s	18.70 ᴍᴡ	18.70 ᴀᴡ	38900 ᴀᴀᴡ	NYBLS	10//99-12//99
	Nassau-Suffolk PMSA, NY	s	19.01 ᴍᴡ	19.09 ᴀᴡ	39530 ᴀᴀᴡ	NYBLS	10//99-12//99
	New York PMSA, NY	s	19.47 ᴍᴡ	19.44 ᴀᴡ	40500 ᴀᴀᴡ	NYBLS	10//99-12//99
	Syracuse MSA, NY	s	18.25 ᴍᴡ	18.53 ᴀᴡ	37970 ᴀᴀᴡ	NYBLS	10//99-12//99
	Utica-Rome MSA, NY	s	15.65 ᴍᴡ	15.44 ᴀᴡ	32550 ᴀᴀᴡ	NYBLS	10//99-12//99
	North Carolina	s	15.32 ᴍᴡ	16.36 ᴀᴡ	34020 ᴀᴀᴡ	NCBLS	10//99-12//99

Millwright

Occupation/Type/Industry	Location	Per	Low	Mid	High	Source	Date
Millwright	Asheville MSA, NC	S	14.25 MW	14.31 AW	29630 AAW	NCBLS	10//99-12//99
	Greensboro--Winston-Salem--High Point MSA, NC	S	20.85 MW	18.07 AW	43380 AAW	NCBLS	10//99-12//99
	Hickory-Morganton-Lenoir MSA, NC	S	14.64 MW	14.30 AW	30440 AAW	NCBLS	10//99-12//99
	Raleigh-Durham-Chapel Hill MSA, NC	S	14.57 MW	14.78 AW	30300 AAW	NCBLS	10//99-12//99
	Rocky Mount MSA, NC	S	13.30 MW	13.60 AW	27670 AAW	NCBLS	10//99-12//99
	North Dakota	S	15.36 MW	15.72 AW	32700 AAW	NDBLS	10//99-12//99
	Fargo-Moorhead MSA, ND-MN	S	15.14 MW	15.32 AW	31490 AAW	NDBLS	10//99-12//99
	Ohio	S	21.78 MW	21.09 AW	43860 AAW	OHBLS	10//99-12//99
	Akron PMSA, OH	S	19.76 MW	21.56 AW	41090 AAW	OHBLS	10//99-12//99
	Canton-Massillon MSA, OH	S	18.79 MW	18.30 AW	39080 AAW	OHBLS	10//99-12//99
	Cincinnati PMSA, OH-KY-IN	S	20.01 MW	20.55 AW	41630 AAW	OHBLS	10//99-12//99
	Cleveland-Lorain-Elyria PMSA, OH	S	22.36 MW	22.95 AW	46510 AAW	OHBLS	10//99-12//99
	Columbus MSA, OH	S	16.76 MW	15.74 AW	34860 AAW	OHBLS	10//99-12//99
	Toledo MSA, OH	S	22.97 MW	23.50 AW	47770 AAW	OHBLS	10//99-12//99
	Youngstown-Warren MSA, OH	S	24.46 MW	25.19 AW	50890 AAW	OHBLS	10//99-12//99
	Oklahoma	S	16.09 MW	15.84 AW	32950 AAW	OKBLS	10//99-12//99
	Oklahoma City MSA, OK	S	15.91 MW	15.73 AW	33080 AAW	OKBLS	10//99-12//99
	Tulsa MSA, OK	S	19.33 MW	21.86 AW	40210 AAW	OKBLS	10//99-12//99
	Oregon	S	18.59 MW	19.78 AW	41150 AAW	ORBLS	10//99-12//99
	Eugene-Springfield MSA, OR	S	22.94 MW	20.79 AW	47720 AAW	ORBLS	10//99-12//99
	Pennsylvania	S	16.76 MW	16.91 AW	35180 AAW	PABLS	10//99-12//99
	Allentown-Bethlehem-Easton MSA, PA	S	15.94 MW	15.51 AW	33150 AAW	PABLS	10//99-12//99
	Erie MSA, PA	S	14.97 MW	14.94 AW	31130 AAW	PABLS	10//99-12//99
	Harrisburg-Lebanon-Carlisle MSA, PA	S	16.02 MW	17.18 AW	33330 AAW	PABLS	10//99-12//99
	Johnstown MSA, PA	S	15.43 MW	14.94 AW	32100 AAW	PABLS	10//99-12//99
	Lancaster MSA, PA	S	17.27 MW	16.48 AW	35920 AAW	PABLS	10//99-12//99
	Philadelphia PMSA, PA-NJ	S	17.29 MW	17.22 AW	35950 AAW	PABLS	10//99-12//99
	Pittsburgh MSA, PA	S	18.17 MW	18.63 AW	37790 AAW	PABLS	10//99-12//99
	Reading MSA, PA	S	17.79 MW	17.93 AW	37000 AAW	PABLS	10//99-12//99
	Scranton--Wilkes-Barre--Hazleton MSA, PA	S	18.03 MW	18.26 AW	37510 AAW	PABLS	10//99-12//99
	Sharon MSA, PA	S	14.56 MW	14.21 AW	30290 AAW	PABLS	10//99-12//99
	York MSA, PA	S	16.94 MW	17.39 AW	35240 AAW	PABLS	10//99-12//99
	Rhode Island	S	15.02 MW	15.80 AW	32860 AAW	RIBLS	10//99-12//99
	Providence-Fall River-Warwick MSA, RI-MA	S	14.07 MW	13.34 AW	29270 AAW	RIBLS	10//99-12//99
	South Carolina	S	17.85 MW	18.36 AW	38200 AAW	SCBLS	10//99-12//99
	Charleston-North Charleston MSA, SC	S	18.05 MW	18.90 AW	37540 AAW	SCBLS	10//99-12//99
	Greenville-Spartanburg-Anderson MSA, SC	S	19.48 MW	18.40 AW	40530 AAW	SCBLS	10//99-12//99
	South Dakota	S	12.97 MW	13.25 AW	27570 AAW	SDBLS	10//99-12//99
	Tennessee	S	15.06 MW	15.20 AW	31620 AAW	TNBLS	10//99-12//99
	Chattanooga MSA, TN-GA	S	15.11 MW	15.05 AW	31440 AAW	TNBLS	10//99-12//99
	Jackson MSA, TN	S	13.00 MW	12.59 AW	27030 AAW	TNBLS	10//99-12//99
	Johnson City-Kingsport-Bristol MSA, TN-VA	S	13.76 MW	13.16 AW	28610 AAW	TNBLS	10//99-12//99
	Knoxville MSA, TN	S	16.33 MW	15.46 AW	33970 AAW	TNBLS	10//99-12//99
	Memphis MSA, TN-AR-MS	S	16.21 MW	16.07 AW	33720 AAW	MSBLS	10//99-12//99
	Nashville MSA, TN	S	17.90 MW	18.13 AW	37230 AAW	TNBLS	10//99-12//99
	Texas	S	16.27 MW	16.74 AW	34830 AAW	TXBLS	10//99-12//99
	Austin-San Marcos MSA, TX	S	16.00 MW	16.43 AW	33280 AAW	TXBLS	10//99-12//99
	Beaumont-Port Arthur MSA, TX	S	17.10 MW	16.43 AW	35560 AAW	TXBLS	10//99-12//99
	Dallas PMSA, TX	S	17.22 MW	16.63 AW	35810 AAW	TXBLS	10//99-12//99
	Fort Worth-Arlington PMSA, TX	S	16.86 MW	15.79 AW	35060 AAW	TXBLS	10//99-12//99
	Houston PMSA, TX	S	17.20 MW	17.36 AW	35770 AAW	TXBLS	10//99-12//99
	San Antonio MSA, TX	S	18.70 MW	18.56 AW	38900 AAW	TXBLS	10//99-12//99
	Sherman-Denison MSA, TX	S	13.04 MW	12.64 AW	27130 AAW	TXBLS	10//99-12//99
	Texarkana MSA, TX-Texarkana, AR	S	14.31 MW	14.12 AW	29770 AAW	TXBLS	10//99-12//99
	Utah	S	17.39 MW	16.01 AW	33300 AAW	UTBLS	10//99-12//99
	Salt Lake City-Ogden MSA, UT	S	15.87 MW	17.34 AW	33000 AAW	UTBLS	10//99-12//99

AAW Average annual wage	**AOH** Average offered, high	**ASH** Average starting, high	**H** Hourly	**M** Monthly	**S** Special: hourly and annual
AE Average entry wage	**AOL** Average offered, low	**ASL** Average starting, low	**HI** Highest wage paid	**MTC** Median total compensation	**TQ** Third quartile wage
AEX Average experienced wage	**APH** Average pay, high range	**AW** Average wage paid	**HR** High end range	**MW** Median wage paid	**W** Weekly
AO Average offered	**APL** Average pay, low range	**FQ** First quartile wage	**LR** Low end range	**SQ** Second quartile wage	**Y** Yearly

Occupation/Type/Industry	Location	Per	Low	Mid	High	Source	Date
Millwright	Vermont	S	18.37 MW	18.92 AW	39340 AAW	VTBLS	10//99-12//99
	Virginia	S	15.81 MW	16.88 AW	35100 AAW	VABLS	10//99-12//99
	Danville MSA, VA	S	11.81 MW	11.50 AW	24560 AAW	VABLS	10//99-12//99
	Lynchburg MSA, VA	S	16.44 MW	17.43 AW	34200 AAW	VABLS	10//99-12//99
	Norfolk-Virginia Beach-Newport News MSA, VA-NC	S	20.58 MW	22.50 AW	42800 AAW	VABLS	10//99-12//99
	Richmond-Petersburg MSA, VA	S	16.45 MW	15.34 AW	34220 AAW	VABLS	10//99-12//99
	Washington	S	21.55 MW	21.50 AW	44720 AAW	WABLS	10//99-12//99
	Seattle-Bellevue-Everett PMSA, WA	S	24.28 MW	23.68 AW	50500 AAW	WABLS	10//99-12//99
	Tacoma PMSA, WA	S	18.36 MW	17.75 AW	38190 AAW	WABLS	10//99-12//99
	Yakima MSA, WA	S	17.45 MW	17.52 AW	36300 AAW	WABLS	10//99-12//99
	West Virginia	S	17.46 MW	16.70 AW	34730 AAW	WVBLS	10//99-12//99
	Huntington-Ashland MSA, WV-KY-OH	S	17.24 MW	15.90 AW	35870 AAW	WVBLS	10//99-12//99
	Parkersburg-Marietta MSA, WV-OH	S	22.48 MW	23.41 AW	46750 AAW	WVBLS	10//99-12//99
	Wisconsin	S	20.24 MW	20.04 AW	41680 AAW	WIBLS	10//99-12//99
	Appleton-Oshkosh-Neenah MSA, WI	S	20.34 MW	19.62 AW	42300 AAW	WIBLS	10//99-12//99
	Milwaukee-Waukesha PMSA, WI	S	21.56 MW	22.05 AW	44840 AAW	WIBLS	10//99-12//99
	Racine PMSA, WI	S	18.16 MW	17.26 AW	37770 AAW	WIBLS	10//99-12//99
	Wausau MSA, WI	S	17.12 MW	17.56 AW	35600 AAW	WIBLS	10//99-12//99
	Wyoming	S	14.55 MW	14.87 AW	30940 AAW	WYBLS	10//99-12//99
	Puerto Rico	S	13.44 MW	14.80 AW	30790 AAW	PRBLS	10//99-12//99
	San Juan-Bayamon PMSA, PR	S	15.01 MW	14.03 AW	31210 AAW	PRBLS	10//99-12//99
Mine Cutting and Channeling Machine Operator	Alabama	S	18.06 MW	16.58 AW	34490 AAW	ALBLS	10//99-12//99
	Florida	S	14.42 MW	16.46 AW	34230 AAW	FLBLS	10//99-12//99
	Georgia	S	12.21 MW	12.09 AW	25140 AAW	GABLS	10//99-12//99
	Illinois	S	18.97 MW	18.29 AW	38050 AAW	ILBLS	10//99-12//99
	Indiana	S	14.58 MW	14.65 AW	30470 AAW	INBLS	10//99-12//99
	Kentucky	S	13.39 MW	13.68 AW	28450 AAW	KYBLS	10//99-12//99
	Nevada	S	19.62 MW	20.86 AW	43390 AAW	NVBLS	10//99-12//99
	Ohio	S	10.96 MW	13.22 AW	27500 AAW	OHBLS	10//99-12//99
	Pennsylvania	S	18.3 MW	17.58 AW	36560 AAW	PABLS	10//99-12//99
	Tennessee	S	13.67 MW	15.24 AW	31710 AAW	TNBLS	10//99-12//99
	Virginia	S	12.95 MW	13.69 AW	28480 AAW	VABLS	10//99-12//99
	Washington	S	15.2 MW	15.83 AW	32920 AAW	WABLS	10//99-12//99
	West Virginia	S	18.69 MW	18.20 AW	37870 AAW	WVBLS	10//99-12//99
Mining and Geological Engineer							
Including Mining Safety Engineer	Alabama	S	27.4 MW	26.81 AW	55770 AAW	ALBLS	10//99-12//99
Including Mining Safety Engineer	Alaska	S	31.06 MW	31.13 AW	64750 AAW	AKBLS	10//99-12//99
Including Mining Safety Engineer	Arizona	S	24.81 MW	26.28 AW	54660 AAW	AZBLS	10//99-12//99
Including Mining Safety Engineer	California	S	32.96 MW	37.13 AW	77240 AAW	CABLS	10//99-12//99
Including Mining Safety Engineer	Colorado	S	30.26 MW	31.93 AW	66420 AAW	COBLS	10//99-12//99
Including Mining Safety Engineer	Florida	S	28.21 MW	27.41 AW	57020 AAW	FLBLS	10//99-12//99
Including Mining Safety Engineer	Idaho	S	24.09 MW	26.47 AW	55060 AAW	IDBLS	10//99-12//99
Including Mining Safety Engineer	Illinois	S	25.65 MW	26.84 AW	55820 AAW	ILBLS	10//99-12//99
Including Mining Safety Engineer	Indiana	S	26.17 MW	25.92 AW	53910 AAW	INBLS	10//99-12//99
Including Mining Safety Engineer	Iowa	S	20.45 MW	21.86 AW	45470 AAW	IABLS	10//99-12//99
Including Mining Safety Engineer	Kentucky	S	19.59 MW	21.48 AW	44670 AAW	KYBLS	10//99-12//99
Including Mining Safety Engineer	Louisiana	S	27.02 MW	28.40 AW	59070 AAW	LABLS	10//99-12//99
Including Mining Safety Engineer	Massachusetts	S	25.33 MW	26.60 AW	55330 AAW	MABLS	10//99-12//99
Including Mining Safety Engineer	Minnesota	S	25.98 MW	29.13 AW	60600 AAW	MNBLS	10//99-12//99
Including Mining Safety Engineer	Missouri	S	19.54 MW	20.33 AW	42280 AAW	MOBLS	10//99-12//99
Including Mining Safety Engineer	Montana	S	25.93 MW	26.28 AW	54650 AAW	MTBLS	10//99-12//99
Including Mining Safety Engineer	Nevada	S	28.78 MW	28.93 AW	60180 AAW	NVBLS	10//99-12//99
Including Mining Safety Engineer	New Jersey	S	34.27 MW	35.54 AW	73930 AAW	NJBLS	10//99-12//99
Including Mining Safety Engineer	New York	S	19.83 MW	20.93 AW	43540 AAW	NYBLS	10//99-12//99
Including Mining Safety Engineer	Ohio	S	24.74 MW	24.62 AW	51210 AAW	OHBLS	10//99-12//99
Including Mining Safety Engineer	Oklahoma	S	25.98 MW	36.14 AW	75160 AAW	OKBLS	10//99-12//99
Including Mining Safety Engineer	Pennsylvania	S	26.12 MW	24.57 AW	51100 AAW	PABLS	10//99-12//99
Including Mining Safety Engineer	South Carolina	S	23.23 MW	22.97 AW	47770 AAW	SCBLS	10//99-12//99
Including Mining Safety Engineer	Texas	S	33.66 MW	33.20 AW	69060 AAW	TXBLS	10//99-12//99
Including Mining Safety Engineer	Virginia	S	27.91 MW	28.44 AW	59150 AAW	VABLS	10//99-12//99
Including Mining Safety Engineer	Washington	S	26.59 MW	27.13 AW	56440 AAW	WABLS	10//99-12//99

AAW	Average annual wage	AOH	Average offered, high	ASH	Average starting, high	H	Hourly	M	Monthly	S	Special: hourly and annual
AE	Average entry wage	AOL	Average offered, low	ASL	Average starting, low	HI	Highest wage paid	MTC	Median total compensation	TQ	Third quartile wage
AEX	Average experienced wage	APH	Average pay, high range	AW	Average wage paid	HR	High end range	MW	Median wage paid	W	Weekly
AO	Average offered	APL	Average pay, low range	FQ	First quartile wage	LR	Low end range	SQ	Second quartile wage	Y	Yearly

Occupation/Type/Industry	Location	Per	Low	Mid	High	Source	Date
Mining and Geological Engineer							
Including Mining Safety Engineer	West Virginia	S	20.81 MW	24.84 AW	51670 AAW	WVBLS	10//99-12//99
Including Mining Safety Engineer	Wisconsin	S	28.41 MW	25.10 AW	52210 AAW	WIBLS	10//99-12//99
Including Mining Safety Engineer	Wyoming	S	27.57 MW	28.37 AW	59010 AAW	WYBLS	10//99-12//99
Mixing and Blending Machine Setter, Operator, and Tender	Alabama	S	14.39 MW	13.78 AW	28670 AAW	ALBLS	10//99-12//99
	Birmingham MSA, AL	S	13.19 MW	13.80 AW	27440 AAW	ALBLS	10//99-12//99
	Decatur MSA, AL	S	12.24 MW	11.77 AW	25470 AAW	ALBLS	10//99-12//99
	Florence MSA, AL	S	10.06 MW	9.80 AW	20930 AAW	ALBLS	10//99-12//99
	Huntsville MSA, AL	S	18.85 MW	19.15 AW	39200 AAW	ALBLS	10//99-12//99
	Mobile MSA, AL	S	9.13 MW	8.07 AW	19000 AAW	ALBLS	10//99-12//99
	Arizona	S	9.63 MW	10.31 AW	21440 AAW	AZBLS	10//99-12//99
	Phoenix-Mesa MSA, AZ	S	10.22 MW	9.56 AW	21250 AAW	AZBLS	10//99-12//99
	Arkansas	S	10.23 MW	10.18 AW	21180 AAW	ARBLS	10//99-12//99
	Fayetteville-Springdale-Rogers MSA, AR	S	9.35 MW	9.06 AW	19450 AAW	ARBLS	10//99-12//99
	Fort Smith MSA, AR-OK	S	9.82 MW	9.23 AW	20420 AAW	ARBLS	10//99-12//99
	Little Rock-North Little Rock MSA, AR	S	9.61 MW	8.46 AW	19990 AAW	ARBLS	10//99-12//99
	California	S	12.41 MW	12.77 AW	26560 AAW	CABLS	10//99-12//99
	Fresno MSA, CA	S	11.40 MW	9.73 AW	23710 AAW	CABLS	10//99-12//99
	Los Angeles-Long Beach PMSA, CA	S	12.26 MW	10.99 AW	25510 AAW	CABLS	10//99-12//99
	Oakland PMSA, CA	S	14.60 MW	15.21 AW	30360 AAW	CABLS	10//99-12//99
	Orange County PMSA, CA	S	11.44 MW	10.83 AW	23800 AAW	CABLS	10//99-12//99
	Riverside-San Bernardino PMSA, CA	S	11.09 MW	11.20 AW	23070 AAW	CABLS	10//99-12//99
	Salinas MSA, CA	S	11.54 MW	10.09 AW	24010 AAW	CABLS	10//99-12//99
	San Diego MSA, CA	S	14.55 MW	14.69 AW	30260 AAW	CABLS	10//99-12//99
	San Francisco PMSA, CA	S	16.82 MW	17.25 AW	34990 AAW	CABLS	10//99-12//99
	San Jose PMSA, CA	S	14.64 MW	15.08 AW	30440 AAW	CABLS	10//99-12//99
	Santa Rosa PMSA, CA	S	11.23 MW	11.35 AW	23360 AAW	CABLS	10//99-12//99
	Stockton-Lodi MSA, CA	S	13.74 MW	13.27 AW	28580 AAW	CABLS	10//99-12//99
	Vallejo-Fairfield-Napa PMSA, CA	S	13.44 MW	12.23 AW	27960 AAW	CABLS	10//99-12//99
	Ventura PMSA, CA	S	10.80 MW	10.06 AW	22470 AAW	CABLS	10//99-12//99
	Visalia-Tulare-Porterville MSA, CA	S	15.29 MW	15.32 AW	31800 AAW	CABLS	10//99-12//99
	Yolo PMSA, CA	S	13.91 MW	14.67 AW	28930 AAW	CABLS	10//99-12//99
	Colorado	S	11.88 MW	11.84 AW	24620 AAW	COBLS	10//99-12//99
	Denver PMSA, CO	S	11.95 MW	11.97 AW	24850 AAW	COBLS	10//99-12//99
	Fort Collins-Loveland MSA, CO	S	10.77 MW	11.07 AW	22400 AAW	COBLS	10//99-12//99
	Connecticut	S	11.33 MW	12.22 AW	25410 AAW	CTBLS	10//99-12//99
	Bridgeport PMSA, CT	S	12.09 MW	11.63 AW	25140 AAW	CTBLS	10//99-12//99
	Hartford MSA, CT	S	13.70 MW	12.47 AW	28490 AAW	CTBLS	10//99-12//99
	New Haven-Meriden PMSA, CT	S	14.40 MW	13.20 AW	29950 AAW	CTBLS	10//99-12//99
	New London-Norwich MSA, CT-RI	S	12.49 MW	12.59 AW	25970 AAW	CTBLS	10//99-12//99
	Delaware	S	14.17 MW	13.75 AW	28590 AAW	DEBLS	10//99-12//99
	Wilmington-Newark PMSA, DE-MD	S	14.11 MW	14.40 AW	29350 AAW	DEBLS	10//99-12//99
	Washington PMSA, DC-MD-VA-WV	S	10.53 MW	10.21 AW	21900 AAW	DCBLS	10//99-12//99
	Florida	S	10.83 MW	11.15 AW	23190 AAW	FLBLS	10//99-12//99
	Daytona Beach MSA, FL	S	8.92 MW	9.01 AW	18550 AAW	FLBLS	10//99-12//99
	Fort Lauderdale PMSA, FL	S	13.36 MW	12.22 AW	27790 AAW	FLBLS	10//99-12//99
	Fort Myers-Cape Coral MSA, FL	S	9.73 MW	9.74 AW	20240 AAW	FLBLS	10//99-12//99
	Fort Pierce-Port St. Lucie MSA, FL	S	9.43 MW	9.33 AW	19620 AAW	FLBLS	10//99-12//99
	Jacksonville MSA, FL	S	14.19 MW	14.77 AW	29510 AAW	FLBLS	10//99-12//99
	Lakeland-Winter Haven MSA, FL	S	12.25 MW	12.34 AW	25470 AAW	FLBLS	10//99-12//99
	Melbourne-Titusville-Palm Bay MSA, FL	S	10.26 MW	10.64 AW	21350 AAW	FLBLS	10//99-12//99
	Miami PMSA, FL	S	10.87 MW	10.88 AW	22620 AAW	FLBLS	10//99-12//99
	Orlando MSA, FL	S	9.90 MW	9.46 AW	20590 AAW	FLBLS	10//99-12//99
	Tampa-St. Petersburg-Clearwater MSA, FL	S	10.62 MW	9.54 AW	22080 AAW	FLBLS	10//99-12//99

AAW Average annual wage	**AOH** Average offered, high	**ASH** Average starting, high	**H** Hourly	**M** Monthly	**S** Special: hourly and annual
AE Average entry wage	**AOL** Average offered, low	**ASL** Average starting, low	**HI** Highest wage paid	**MTC** Median total compensation	**TQ** Third quartile wage
AEX Average experienced wage	**APH** Average pay, high range	**AW** Average wage paid	**HR** High end range	**MW** Median wage paid	**W** Weekly
AO Average offered	**APL** Average pay, low range	**FQ** First quartile wage	**LR** Low end range	**SQ** Second quartile wage	**Y** Yearly

Occupation/Type/Industry	Location	Per	Low	Mid	High	Source	Date
Mixing and Blending Machine Setter, Operator, and Tender	West Palm Beach-Boca Raton MSA, FL	S	10.61 MW	11.11 AW	22080 AAW	FLBLS	10//99-12//99
	Georgia	S	11.42 MW	11.70 AW	24330 AAW	GABLS	10//99-12//99
	Albany MSA, GA	S	9.96 MW	9.74 AW	20720 AAW	GABLS	10//99-12//99
	Athens MSA, GA	S	11.95 MW	12.06 AW	24860 AAW	GABLS	10//99-12//99
	Atlanta MSA, GA	S	12.73 MW	12.32 AW	26480 AAW	GABLS	10//99-12//99
	Augusta-Aiken MSA, GA-SC	S	12.96 MW	13.49 AW	26960 AAW	GABLS	10//99-12//99
	Macon MSA, GA	S	10.28 MW	10.75 AW	21380 AAW	GABLS	10//99-12//99
	Savannah MSA, GA	S	8.44 MW	8.69 AW	17550 AAW	GABLS	10//99-12//99
	Idaho	S	10.74 MW	11.12 AW	23120 AAW	IDBLS	10//99-12//99
	Boise City MSA, ID	S	10.62 MW	11.02 AW	22080 AAW	IDBLS	10//99-12//99
	Illinois	S	11.91 MW	12.34 AW	25670 AAW	ILBLS	10//99-12//99
	Chicago PMSA, IL	S	12.94 MW	12.67 AW	26910 AAW	ILBLS	10//99-12//99
	Rockford MSA, IL	S	14.22 MW	14.25 AW	29580 AAW	ILBLS	10//99-12//99
	Indiana	S	14	14.12 AW	29370 AAW	INBLS	10//99-12//99
	Elkhart-Goshen MSA, IN	S	12.97 MW	13.50 AW	26970 AAW	INBLS	10//99-12//99
	Evansville-Henderson MSA, IN-KY	S	9.03 MW	9.02 AW	18790 AAW	INBLS	10//99-12//99
	Fort Wayne MSA, IN	S	13.11 MW	11.47 AW	27260 AAW	INBLS	10//99-12//99
	Gary PMSA, IN	S	19.46 MW	19.27 AW	40480 AAW	INBLS	10//99-12//99
	Indianapolis MSA, IN	S	14.36 MW	14.08 AW	29880 AAW	INBLS	10//99-12//99
	Lafayette MSA, IN	S	12.55 MW	12.31 AW	26110 AAW	INBLS	10//99-12//99
	South Bend MSA, IN	S	9.33 MW	8.48 AW	19400 AAW	INBLS	10//99-12//99
	Terre Haute MSA, IN	S	13.75 MW	14.59 AW	28610 AAW	INBLS	10//99-12//99
	Iowa	S	12.84 MW	12.68 AW	26380 AAW	IABLS	10//99-12//99
	Davenport-Moline-Rock Island MSA, IA-IL	S	13.32 MW	13.32 AW	27700 AAW	IABLS	10//99-12//99
	Kansas	S	10.99 MW	11.20 AW	23290 AAW	KSBLS	10//99-12//99
	Wichita MSA, KS	S	10.21 MW	9.68 AW	21240 AAW	KSBLS	10//99-12//99
	Kentucky	S	12.02 MW	12.08 AW	25120 AAW	KYBLS	10//99-12//99
	Lexington MSA, KY	S	13.49 MW	12.22 AW	28060 AAW	KYBLS	10//99-12//99
	Louisville MSA, KY-IN	S	11.54 MW	11.73 AW	24000 AAW	KYBLS	10//99-12//99
	Louisiana	S	10.31 MW	10.90 AW	22670 AAW	LABLS	10//99-12//99
	Baton Rouge MSA, LA	S	14.01 MW	15.51 AW	29150 AAW	LABLS	10//99-12//99
	New Orleans MSA, LA	S	11.07 MW	10.33 AW	23030 AAW	LABLS	10//99-12//99
	Maine	S	15.48 MW	15.80 AW	32870 AAW	MEBLS	10//99-12//99
	Portland MSA, ME	S	17.06 MW	16.95 AW	35480 AAW	MEBLS	10//99-12//99
	Maryland	S	12.24 MW	12.92 AW	26870 AAW	MDBLS	10//99-12//99
	Baltimore PMSA, MD	S	12.83 MW	12.08 AW	26680 AAW	MDBLS	10//99-12//99
	Hagerstown PMSA, MD	S	14.08 MW	13.80 AW	29280 AAW	MDBLS	10//99-12//99
	Massachusetts	S	12.97 MW	13.28 AW	27620 AAW	MABLS	10//99-12//99
	Boston PMSA, MA-NH	S	13.81 MW	13.73 AW	28720 AAW	MABLS	10//99-12//99
	Brockton PMSA, MA	S	10.87 MW	10.98 AW	22600 AAW	MABLS	10//99-12//99
	Fitchburg-Leominster PMSA, MA	S	11.52 MW	10.92 AW	23970 AAW	MABLS	10//99-12//99
	Lawrence PMSA, MA-NH	S	14.56 MW	14.87 AW	30270 AAW	MABLS	10//99-12//99
	Springfield MSA, MA	S	15.90 MW	15.03 AW	33070 AAW	MABLS	10//99-12//99
	Worcester PMSA, MA-CT	S	12.14 MW	12.11 AW	25240 AAW	MABLS	10//99-12//99
	Michigan	S	13.6	13.77 AW	28650 AAW	MIBLS	10//99-12//99
	Detroit PMSA, MI	S	13.82 MW	13.93 AW	28740 AAW	MIBLS	10//99-12//99
	Flint PMSA, MI	S	19.54 MW	21.48 AW	40650 AAW	MIBLS	10//99-12//99
	Grand Rapids-Muskegon-Holland MSA, MI	S	12.37 MW	12.02 AW	25730 AAW	MIBLS	10//99-12//99
	Jackson MSA, MI	S	14.35 MW	14.64 AW	29860 AAW	MIBLS	10//99-12//99
	Kalamazoo-Battle Creek MSA, MI	S	15.16 MW	15.26 AW	31540 AAW	MIBLS	10//99-12//99
	Saginaw-Bay City-Midland MSA, MI	S	13.69 MW	14.24 AW	28470 AAW	MIBLS	10//99-12//99
	Minnesota	S	14.56 MW	14.13 AW	29380 AAW	MNBLS	10//99-12//99
	Duluth-Superior MSA, MN-WI	S	11.12 MW	8.41 AW	23130 AAW	MNBLS	10//99-12//99
	Minneapolis-St. Paul MSA, MN-WI	S	14.39 MW	14.82 AW	29930 AAW	MNBLS	10//99-12//99
	Mississippi	S	11.39 MW	11.89 AW	24740 AAW	MSBLS	10//99-12//99
	Biloxi-Gulfport-Pascagoula MSA, MS	S	19.81 MW	22.80 AW	41210 AAW	MSBLS	10//99-12//99
	Jackson MSA, MS	S	9.70 MW	9.72 AW	20180 AAW	MSBLS	10//99-12//99
	Missouri	S	14.73 MW	14.72 AW	30620 AAW	MOBLS	10//99-12//99
	Kansas City MSA, MO-KS	S	12.11 MW	11.18 AW	25190 AAW	MOBLS	10//99-12//99
	St. Joseph MSA, MO	S	10.69 MW	11.24 AW	22240 AAW	MOBLS	10//99-12//99
	St. Louis MSA, MO-IL	S	15.21 MW	15.08 AW	31640 AAW	MOBLS	10//99-12//99
	Montana	S	11.85 MW	13.97 AW	29050 AAW	MTBLS	10//99-12//99

AAW	Average annual wage	AOH	Average offered, high	ASH	Average starting, high
AE	Average entry wage	AOL	Average offered, low	ASL	Average starting, low
AEX	Average experienced wage	APH	Average pay, high range	AW	Average wage paid
AO	Average offered	APL	Average pay, low range	FQ	First quartile wage

H	Hourly	M	Monthly
HI	Highest wage paid	MTC	Median total compensation
HR	High end range	MW	Median wage paid
LR	Low end range	SQ	Second quartile wage

S	Special: hourly and annual
TQ	Third quartile wage
W	Weekly
Y	Yearly

Occupation/Type/Industry	Location	Per	Low	Mid	High	Source	Date
Mixing and Blending Machine Setter, Operator, and Tender	Nebraska	S	9.17 MW	10.21 AW	21230 AAW	NEBLS	10//99-12//99
	Omaha MSA, NE-IA	S	9.97 MW	8.27 AW	20730 AAW	NEBLS	10//99-12//99
	Nevada	S	11.39 MW	11.61 AW	24150 AAW	NVBLS	10//99-12//99
	Las Vegas MSA, NV-AZ	S	10.72 MW	10.65 AW	22300 AAW	NVBLS	10//99-12//99
	Reno MSA, NV	S	13.51 MW	12.81 AW	28100 AAW	NVBLS	10//99-12//99
	New Hampshire	S	11.48 MW	11.78 AW	24510 AAW	NHBLS	10//99-12//99
	Manchester PMSA, NH	S	12.47 MW	13.65 AW	25940 AAW	NHBLS	10//99-12//99
	New Jersey	S	12.91 MW	13.73 AW	28560 AAW	NJBLS	10//99-12//99
	Bergen-Passaic PMSA, NJ	S	13.11 MW	11.99 AW	27270 AAW	NJBLS	10//99-12//99
	Jersey City PMSA, NJ	S	12.88 MW	11.78 AW	26800 AAW	NJBLS	10//99-12//99
	Middlesex-Somerset-Hunterdon PMSA, NJ	S	17.10 MW	16.99 AW	35570 AAW	NJBLS	10//99-12//99
	Monmouth-Ocean PMSA, NJ	S	12.25 MW	11.21 AW	25480 AAW	NJBLS	10//99-12//99
	Newark PMSA, NJ	S	10.43 MW	9.57 AW	21690 AAW	NJBLS	10//99-12//99
	New Mexico	S	9.29 MW	9.14 AW	19010 AAW	NMBLS	10//99-12//99
	Albuquerque MSA, NM	S	10.27 MW	10.91 AW	21360 AAW	NMBLS	10//99-12//99
	New York	S	12.09 MW	12.59 AW	26190 AAW	NYBLS	10//99-12//99
	Albany-Schenectady-Troy MSA, NY	S	14.80 MW	15.12 AW	30780 AAW	NYBLS	10//99-12//99
	Binghamton MSA, NY	S	12.06 MW	12.07 AW	25080 AAW	NYBLS	10//99-12//99
	Buffalo-Niagara Falls MSA, NY	S	14.40 MW	14.54 AW	29950 AAW	NYBLS	10//99-12//99
	Dutchess County PMSA, NY	S	8.98 MW	8.71 AW	18670 AAW	NYBLS	10//99-12//99
	Nassau-Suffolk PMSA, NY	S	10.30 MW	9.45 AW	21420 AAW	NYBLS	10//99-12//99
	New York PMSA, NY	S	10.65 MW	10.15 AW	22150 AAW	NYBLS	10//99-12//99
	Newburgh PMSA, NY-PA	S	12.04 MW	10.95 AW	25040 AAW	NYBLS	10//99-12//99
	Rochester MSA, NY	S	18.10 MW	18.51 AW	37660 AAW	NYBLS	10//99-12//99
	Syracuse MSA, NY	S	12.76 MW	11.72 AW	26550 AAW	NYBLS	10//99-12//99
	Utica-Rome MSA, NY	S	9.67 MW	8.76 AW	20120 AAW	NYBLS	10//99-12//99
	North Carolina	S	12.47 MW	12.82 AW	26660 AAW	NCBLS	10//99-12//99
	Asheville MSA, NC	S	11.64 MW	11.87 AW	24200 AAW	NCBLS	10//99-12//99
	Charlotte-Gastonia-Rock Hill MSA, NC-SC	S	12.36 MW	11.96 AW	25710 AAW	NCBLS	10//99-12//99
	Greensboro--Winston-Salem--High Point MSA, NC	S	15.34 MW	15.21 AW	31920 AAW	NCBLS	10//99-12//99
	Hickory-Morganton-Lenoir MSA, NC	S	9.93 MW	9.85 AW	20660 AAW	NCBLS	10//99-12//99
	Raleigh-Durham-Chapel Hill MSA, NC	S	12.91 MW	12.93 AW	26850 AAW	NCBLS	10//99-12//99
	North Dakota	S	9.45 MW	9.51 AW	19790 AAW	NDBLS	10//99-12//99
	Ohio	S	11.98 MW	12.33 AW	25650 AAW	OHBLS	10//99-12//99
	Akron PMSA, OH	S	13.26 MW	13.13 AW	27570 AAW	OHBLS	10//99-12//99
	Canton-Massillon MSA, OH	S	11.96 MW	11.82 AW	24880 AAW	OHBLS	10//99-12//99
	Cleveland-Lorain-Elyria PMSA, OH	S	13.12 MW	13.89 AW	27290 AAW	OHBLS	10//99-12//99
	Columbus MSA, OH	S	12.06 MW	11.42 AW	25090 AAW	OHBLS	10//99-12//99
	Dayton-Springfield MSA, OH	S	10.83 MW	10.85 AW	22520 AAW	OHBLS	10//99-12//99
	Hamilton-Middletown PMSA, OH	S	13.76 MW	14.75 AW	28610 AAW	OHBLS	10//99-12//99
	Mansfield MSA, OH	S	10.50 MW	10.37 AW	21840 AAW	OHBLS	10//99-12//99
	Toledo MSA, OH	S	10.80 MW	10.42 AW	22470 AAW	OHBLS	10//99-12//99
	Youngstown-Warren MSA, OH	S	9.88 MW	9.18 AW	20560 AAW	OHBLS	10//99-12//99
	Oklahoma	S	10.17 MW	10.21 AW	21240 AAW	OKBLS	10//99-12//99
	Oklahoma City MSA, OK	S	9.88 MW	9.95 AW	20540 AAW	OKBLS	10//99-12//99
	Tulsa MSA, OK	S	11.52 MW	11.43 AW	23970 AAW	OKBLS	10//99-12//99
	Oregon	S	14.46 MW	13.96 AW	29030 AAW	ORBLS	10//99-12//99
	Portland-Vancouver PMSA, OR-WA	S	13.87 MW	14.62 AW	28850 AAW	ORBLS	10//99-12//99
	Salem PMSA, OR	S	14.34 MW	12.77 AW	29830 AAW	ORBLS	10//99-12//99
	Pennsylvania	S	12.25 MW	12.59 AW	26180 AAW	PABLS	10//99-12//99
	Allentown-Bethlehem-Easton MSA, PA	S	13.93 MW	12.87 AW	28980 AAW	PABLS	10//99-12//99
	Altoona MSA, PA	S	16.11 MW	15.53 AW	33520 AAW	PABLS	10//99-12//99
	Erie MSA, PA	S	8.50 MW	7.76 AW	17690 AAW	PABLS	10//99-12//99
	Harrisburg-Lebanon-Carlisle MSA, PA	S	12.17 MW	12.18 AW	25320 AAW	PABLS	10//99-12//99
	Lancaster MSA, PA	S	12.38 MW	12.40 AW	25750 AAW	PABLS	10//99-12//99
	Philadelphia PMSA, PA-NJ	S	13.60 MW	13.62 AW	28290 AAW	PABLS	10//99-12//99
	Pittsburgh MSA, PA	S	12.69 MW	12.80 AW	26390 AAW	PABLS	10//99-12//99
	Reading MSA, PA	S	11.53 MW	11.66 AW	23980 AAW	PABLS	10//99-12//99

Occupation/Type/Industry	Location	Per	Low	Mid	High	Source	Date
Mixing and Blending Machine Setter, Operator, and Tender	Scranton--Wilkes-Barre--Hazleton MSA, PA	S	12.78 MW	13.88 AW	26580 AAW	PABLS	10//99-12//99
	York MSA, PA	S	11.75 MW	11.93 AW	24450 AAW	PABLS	10//99-12//99
	Rhode Island	S	17.57 MW	15.81 AW	32880 AAW	RIBLS	10//99-12//99
	Providence-Fall River-Warwick MSA, RI-MA	S	15.82 MW	17.49 AW	32900 AAW	RIBLS	10//99-12//99
	South Carolina	S	12.17 MW	12.60 AW	26210 AAW	SCBLS	10//99-12//99
	Columbia MSA, SC	S	12.33 MW	12.37 AW	25650 AAW	SCBLS	10//99-12//99
	Florence MSA, SC	S	9.98 MW	9.68 AW	20750 AAW	SCBLS	10//99-12//99
	Greenville-Spartanburg-Anderson MSA, SC	S	13.41 MW	13.65 AW	27890 AAW	SCBLS	10//99-12//99
	South Dakota	S	10.96 MW	10.55 AW	21940 AAW	SDBLS	10//99-12//99
	Rapid City MSA, SD	S	10.09 MW	9.38 AW	20990 AAW	SDBLS	10//99-12//99
	Tennessee	S	12.8 MW	12.98 AW	27010 AAW	TNBLS	10//99-12//99
	Chattanooga MSA, TN-GA	S	11.35 MW	11.55 AW	23600 AAW	TNBLS	10//99-12//99
	Clarksville-Hopkinsville MSA, TN-KY	S	11.95 MW	12.15 AW	24860 AAW	TNBLS	10//99-12//99
	Johnson City-Kingsport-Bristol MSA, TN-VA	S	13.78 MW	14.20 AW	28670 AAW	TNBLS	10//99-12//99
	Knoxville MSA, TN	S	10.41 MW	10.11 AW	21650 AAW	TNBLS	10//99-12//99
	Memphis MSA, TN-AR-MS	S	11.61 MW	11.03 AW	24160 AAW	MSBLS	10//99-12//99
	Nashville MSA, TN	S	13.98 MW	14.11 AW	29070 AAW	TNBLS	10//99-12//99
	Texas	S	10.76 MW	11.95 AW	24850 AAW	TXBLS	10//99-12//99
	Abilene MSA, TX	S	10.32 MW	9.59 AW	21470 AAW	TXBLS	10//99-12//99
	Austin-San Marcos MSA, TX	S	8.97 MW	8.51 AW	18650 AAW	TXBLS	10//99-12//99
	Dallas PMSA, TX	S	12.24 MW	11.79 AW	25460 AAW	TXBLS	10//99-12//99
	El Paso MSA, TX	S	8.61 MW	8.65 AW	17920 AAW	TXBLS	10//99-12//99
	Fort Worth-Arlington PMSA, TX	S	11.56 MW	10.89 AW	24050 AAW	TXBLS	10//99-12//99
	Galveston-Texas City PMSA, TX	S	20.29 MW	13.55 AW	42200 AAW	TXBLS	10//99-12//99
	Houston PMSA, TX	S	13.15 MW	11.54 AW	27350 AAW	TXBLS	10//99-12//99
	Longview-Marshall MSA, TX	S	6.40 MW	6.21 AW	13300 AAW	TXBLS	10//99-12//99
	Lubbock MSA, TX	S	8.94 MW	9.07 AW	18590 AAW	TXBLS	10//99-12//99
	Odessa-Midland MSA, TX	S	14.86 MW	15.47 AW	30900 AAW	TXBLS	10//99-12//99
	San Antonio MSA, TX	S	10.66 MW	11.05 AW	22160 AAW	TXBLS	10//99-12//99
	Sherman-Denison MSA, TX	S	14.79 MW	17.61 AW	30760 AAW	TXBLS	10//99-12//99
	Texarkana MSA, TX-Texarkana, AR	S	14.31 MW	14.96 AW	29760 AAW	TXBLS	10//99-12//99
	Tyler MSA, TX	S	11.54 MW	10.70 AW	24000 AAW	TXBLS	10//99-12//99
	Utah	S	10.21 MW	10.96 AW	22810 AAW	UTBLS	10//99-12//99
	Provo-Orem MSA, UT	S	9.80 MW	9.68 AW	20390 AAW	UTBLS	10//99-12//99
	Salt Lake City-Ogden MSA, UT	S	12.34 MW	12.08 AW	25660 AAW	UTBLS	10//99-12//99
	Vermont	S	14.72 MW	14.35 AW	29850 AAW	VTBLS	10//99-12//99
	Burlington MSA, VT	S	13.94 MW	14.15 AW	28980 AAW	VTBLS	10//99-12//99
	Virginia	S	12.37 MW	12.53 AW	26070 AAW	VABLS	10//99-12//99
	Lynchburg MSA, VA	S	13.43 MW	14.34 AW	27940 AAW	VABLS	10//99-12//99
	Norfolk-Virginia Beach-Newport News MSA, VA-NC	S	13.18 MW	13.99 AW	27410 AAW	VABLS	10//99-12//99
	Richmond-Petersburg MSA, VA	S	11.34 MW	10.96 AW	23590 AAW	VABLS	10//99-12//99
	Roanoke MSA, VA	S	17.45 MW	18.34 AW	36290 AAW	VABLS	10//99-12//99
	Washington	S	12.37 MW	13.01 AW	27070 AAW	WABLS	10//99-12//99
	Seattle-Bellevue-Everett PMSA, WA	S	12.16 MW	12.06 AW	25290 AAW	WABLS	10//99-12//99
	Spokane MSA, WA	S	12.39 MW	13.65 AW	25770 AAW	WABLS	10//99-12//99
	Tacoma PMSA, WA	S	12.68 MW	12.63 AW	26370 AAW	WABLS	10//99-12//99
	West Virginia	S	10.32 MW	10.53 AW	21900 AAW	WVBLS	10//99-12//99
	Charleston MSA, WV	S	9.92 MW	8.82 AW	20630 AAW	WVBLS	10//99-12//99
	Huntington-Ashland MSA, WV-KY-OH	S	10.00 MW	10.78 AW	20790 AAW	WVBLS	10//99-12//99
	Parkersburg-Marietta MSA, WV-OH	S	11.58 MW	12.00 AW	24080 AAW	WVBLS	10//99-12//99
	Wisconsin	S	12.61 MW	13.36 AW	27800 AAW	WIBLS	10//99-12//99
	Appleton-Oshkosh-Neenah MSA, WI	S	16.84 MW	17.64 AW	35020 AAW	WIBLS	10//99-12//99
	Eau Claire MSA, WI	S	11.96 MW	12.02 AW	24880 AAW	WIBLS	10//99-12//99
	Green Bay MSA, WI	S	11.90 MW	11.69 AW	24750 AAW	WIBLS	10//99-12//99
	La Crosse MSA, WI-MN	S	10.37 MW	11.52 AW	21570 AAW	WIBLS	10//99-12//99

AAW Average annual wage	**AOH** Average offered, high	**ASH** Average starting, high	**H** Hourly	**M** Monthly	**S** Special: hourly and annual
AE Average entry wage	**AOL** Average offered, low	**ASL** Average starting, low	**HI** Highest wage paid	**MTC** Median total compensation	**TQ** Third quartile wage
AEX Average experienced wage	**APH** Average pay, high range	**AW** Average wage paid	**HR** High end range	**MW** Median wage paid	**W** Weekly
AO Average offered	**APL** Average pay, low range	**FQ** First quartile wage	**LR** Low end range	**SQ** Second quartile wage	**Y** Yearly

Occupation/Type/Industry	Location	Per	Low	Mid	High	Source	Date
Mixing and Blending Machine Setter, Operator, and Tender	Madison MSA, WI	S	11.38 MW	11.03 AW	23680 AAW	WIBLS	10//99-12//99
	Milwaukee-Waukesha PMSA, WI	S	12.43 MW	11.56 AW	25850 AAW	WIBLS	10//99-12//99
	Wausau MSA, WI	S	12.59 MW	12.47 AW	26190 AAW	WIBLS	10//99-12//99
	Wyoming	S	10.43 MW	11.60 AW	24130 AAW	WYBLS	10//99-12//99
	Puerto Rico	S	11.54 MW	11.25 AW	23390 AAW	PRBLS	10//99-12//99
	Caguas PMSA, PR	S	10.10 MW	11.13 AW	21000 AAW	PRBLS	10//99-12//99
	Mayaguez MSA, PR	S	11.46 MW	11.74 AW	23830 AAW	PRBLS	10//99-12//99
	San Juan-Bayamon PMSA, PR	S	11.55 MW	11.69 AW	24030 AAW	PRBLS	10//99-12//99
	Virgin Islands	S	12.33 MW	12.41 AW	25820 AAW	VIBLS	10//99-12//99
Mobile Heavy Equipment Mechanic							
Except Engine	Alabama	S	14.95 MW	15.13 AW	31460 AAW	ALBLS	10//99-12//99
Except Engine	Alaska	S	21.88 MW	22.08 AW	45940 AAW	AKBLS	10//99-12//99
Except Engine	Arizona	S	15.82 MW	15.84 AW	32950 AAW	AZBLS	10//99-12//99
Except Engine	Arkansas	S	13.66 MW	13.44 AW	27960 AAW	ARBLS	10//99-12//99
Except Engine	California	S	18.68 MW	19.37 AW	40300 AAW	CABLS	10//99-12//99
Except Engine	Colorado	S	16.13 MW	16.27 AW	33850 AAW	COBLS	10//99-12//99
Except Engine	Connecticut	S	18.76 MW	18.67 AW	38840 AAW	CTBLS	10//99-12//99
Except Engine	Delaware	S	15.22 MW	15.36 AW	31940 AAW	DEBLS	10//99-12//99
Except Engine	Florida	S	13.41 MW	14.03 AW	29170 AAW	FLBLS	10//99-12//99
Except Engine	Georgia	S	14.62 MW	15.00 AW	31190 AAW	GABLS	10//99-12//99
Except Engine	Hawaii	S	21.73 MW	21.88 AW	45510 AAW	HIBLS	10//99-12//99
Except Engine	Idaho	S	15.75 MW	16.13 AW	33550 AAW	IDBLS	10//99-12//99
Except Engine	Illinois	S	19.22 MW	19.45 AW	40470 AAW	ILBLS	10//99-12//99
Except Engine	Indiana	S	16.13 MW	16.34 AW	33980 AAW	INBLS	10//99-12//99
Except Engine	Iowa	S	15.88 MW	16.36 AW	34020 AAW	IABLS	10//99-12//99
Except Engine	Kansas	S	13.63 MW	13.79 AW	28670 AAW	KSBLS	10//99-12//99
Except Engine	Kentucky	S	14.74 MW	14.90 AW	30980 AAW	KYBLS	10//99-12//99
Except Engine	Louisiana	S	15.06 MW	15.25 AW	31730 AAW	LABLS	10//99-12//99
Except Engine	Maine	S	14.45 MW	14.63 AW	30430 AAW	MEBLS	10//99-12//99
Except Engine	Maryland	S	16.15 MW	16.20 AW	33690 AAW	MDBLS	10//99-12//99
Except Engine	Massachusetts	S	17.53 MW	18.20 AW	37860 AAW	MABLS	10//99-12//99
Except Engine	Michigan	S	16.5 MW	16.73 AW	34800 AAW	MIBLS	10//99-12//99
Except Engine	Minnesota	S	17.88 MW	17.42 AW	36230 AAW	MNBLS	10//99-12//99
Except Engine	Mississippi	S	13.05 MW	13.55 AW	28190 AAW	MSBLS	10//99-12//99
Except Engine	Missouri	S	15.45 MW	15.59 AW	32430 AAW	MOBLS	10//99-12//99
Except Engine	Montana	S	15.88 MW	15.87 AW	33000 AAW	MTBLS	10//99-12//99
Except Engine	Nebraska	S	14.68 MW	14.67 AW	30520 AAW	NEBLS	10//99-12//99
Except Engine	Nevada	S	18.83 MW	19.29 AW	40120 AAW	NVBLS	10//99-12//99
Except Engine	New Hampshire	S	15.9 MW	15.83 AW	32920 AAW	NHBLS	10//99-12//99
Except Engine	New Jersey	S	18.19 MW	19.52 AW	40610 AAW	NJBLS	10//99-12//99
Except Engine	New Mexico	S	15.44 MW	15.68 AW	32610 AAW	NMBLS	10//99-12//99
Except Engine	New York	S	16.2 MW	16.59 AW	34520 AAW	NYBLS	10//99-12//99
Except Engine	North Carolina	S	13.79 MW	14.10 AW	29330 AAW	NCBLS	10//99-12//99
Except Engine	North Dakota	S	15.12 MW	15.61 AW	32470 AAW	NDBLS	10//99-12//99
Except Engine	Ohio	S	15.1 MW	15.37 AW	31970 AAW	OHBLS	10//99-12//99
Except Engine	Oklahoma	S	12.76 MW	13.34 AW	27740 AAW	OKBLS	10//99-12//99
Except Engine	Oregon	S	16.06 MW	16.55 AW	34410 AAW	ORBLS	10//99-12//99
Except Engine	Pennsylvania	S	15.33 MW	15.54 AW	32320 AAW	PABLS	10//99-12//99
Except Engine	Rhode Island	S	16.03 MW	16.59 AW	34500 AAW	RIBLS	10//99-12//99
Except Engine	South Carolina	S	14.66 MW	16.20 AW	33700 AAW	SCBLS	10//99-12//99
Except Engine	South Dakota	S	14.59 MW	14.91 AW	31010 AAW	SDBLS	10//99-12//99
Except Engine	Tennessee	S	14.12 MW	14.14 AW	29400 AAW	TNBLS	10//99-12//99
Except Engine	Texas	S	13.44 MW	14.11 AW	29350 AAW	TXBLS	10//99-12//99
Except Engine	Utah	S	17.41 MW	17.26 AW	35900 AAW	UTBLS	10//99-12//99
Except Engine	Vermont	S	14.86 MW	14.80 AW	30790 AAW	VTBLS	10//99-12//99
Except Engine	Virginia	S	14.08 MW	14.76 AW	30700 AAW	VABLS	10//99-12//99
Except Engine	Washington	S	18.72 MW	18.69 AW	38880 AAW	WABLS	10//99-12//99
Except Engine	West Virginia	S	17.39 MW	17.12 AW	35610 AAW	WVBLS	10//99-12//99
Except Engine	Wisconsin	S	16.36 MW	16.40 AW	34120 AAW	WIBLS	10//99-12//99
Except Engine	Wyoming	S	19.02 MW	18.55 AW	38590 AAW	WYBLS	10//99-12//99
Except Engine	Puerto Rico	S	8.09 MW	8.69 AW	18080 AAW	PRBLS	10//99-12//99
Except Engine	Virgin Islands	S	14.73 MW	14.62 AW	30400 AAW	VIBLS	10//99-12//99
Except Engine	Guam	S	13.66 MW	14.81 AW	30810 AAW	GUBLS	10//99-12//99
Model	Arizona	S	10.01 MW	11.14 AW	23180 AAW	AZBLS	10//99-12//99
	California	S	7.75 MW	8.78 AW	18270 AAW	CABLS	10//99-12//99
	Los Angeles-Long Beach PMSA, CA	S	11.68 MW	12.05 AW	24300 AAW	CABLS	10//99-12//99

Occupation/Type/Industry	Location	Per	Low	Mid	High	Source	Date
Model	Orange County PMSA, CA	S	7.65 MW	7.48 AW	15900 AAW	CABLS	10//99-12//99
	Florida	S	7.28 MW	10.48 AW	21810 AAW	FLBLS	10//99-12//99
	Illinois	S	7.32 MW	7.43 AW	15460 AAW	ILBLS	10//99-12//99
	Indiana	S	8.3 MW	9.05 AW	18830 AAW	INBLS	10//99-12//99
	Maryland	S	7.78 MW	9.25 AW	19240 AAW	MDBLS	10//99-12//99
	Minnesota	S	6.36 MW	6.74 AW	14020 AAW	MNBLS	10//99-12//99
	Minneapolis-St. Paul MSA, MN-WI	S	6.35 MW	6.24 AW	13220 AAW	MNBLS	10//99-12//99
	St. Cloud MSA, MN	S	9.34 MW	8.72 AW	19430 AAW	MNBLS	10//99-12//99
	New York	S	12.27 MW	15.51 AW	32260 AAW	NYBLS	10//99-12//99
	New York PMSA, NY	S	13.03 MW	13.14 AW	27090 AAW	NYBLS	10//99-12//99
	North Carolina	S	7.68 MW	7.77 AW	16160 AAW	NCBLS	10//99-12//99
	Texas	S	14.16 MW	13.38 AW	27830 AAW	TXBLS	10//99-12//99
	Washington	S	9.55 MW	9.90 AW	20590 AAW	WABLS	10//99-12//99
	Seattle-Bellevue-Everett PMSA, WA	S	10.34 MW	9.64 AW	21510 AAW	WABLS	10//99-12//99
Model Maker							
Metals and Plastics	Alabama	S	9.45 MW	11.08 AW	23050 AAW	ALBLS	10//99-12//99
Metals and Plastics	Arkansas	S	15.42 MW	18.13 AW	37700 AAW	ARBLS	10//99-12//99
Metals and Plastics	California	S	16.2 MW	17.55 AW	36490 AAW	CABLS	10//99-12//99
Metals and Plastics	Colorado	S	18.23 MW	17.06 AW	35490 AAW	COBLS	10//99-12//99
Metals and Plastics	Florida	S	18.02 MW	16.86 AW	35070 AAW	FLBLS	10//99-12//99
Metals and Plastics	Georgia	S	8.9 MW	10.14 AW	21080 AAW	GABLS	10//99-12//99
Metals and Plastics	Illinois	S	16.02 MW	15.54 AW	32330 AAW	ILBLS	10//99-12//99
Metals and Plastics	Indiana	S	21.9 MW	22.03 AW	45830 AAW	INBLS	10//99-12//99
Metals and Plastics	Iowa	S	7.93 MW	8.91 AW	18540 AAW	IABLS	10//99-12//99
Metals and Plastics	Kansas	S	13.99 MW	13.96 AW	29030 AAW	KSBLS	10//99-12//99
Metals and Plastics	Kentucky	S	19.66 MW	19.63 AW	40840 AAW	KYBLS	10//99-12//99
Metals and Plastics	Massachusetts	S	13.76 MW	12.61 AW	26230 AAW	MABLS	10//99-12//99
Metals and Plastics	Michigan	S	27.34 MW	25.67 AW	53400 AAW	MIBLS	10//99-12//99
Metals and Plastics	Minnesota	S	15.47 MW	16.28 AW	33850 AAW	MNBLS	10//99-12//99
Metals and Plastics	Missouri	S	17.5 MW	16.68 AW	34690 AAW	MOBLS	10//99-12//99
Metals and Plastics	Nebraska	S	10.14 MW	10.42 AW	21670 AAW	NEBLS	10//99-12//99
Metals and Plastics	New Jersey	S	16.28 MW	23.97 AW	49860 AAW	NJBLS	10//99-12//99
Metals and Plastics	New York	S	6.52 MW	11.14 AW	23180 AAW	NYBLS	10//99-12//99
Metals and Plastics	North Carolina	S	6.93 MW	7.69 AW	16000 AAW	NCBLS	10//99-12//99
Metals and Plastics	Ohio	S	19.14 MW	19.99 AW	41590 AAW	OHBLS	10//99-12//99
Metals and Plastics	Pennsylvania	S	15.97 MW	15.60 AW	32450 AAW	PABLS	10//99-12//99
Metals and Plastics	Rhode Island	S	18.39 MW	18.40 AW	38270 AAW	RIBLS	10//99-12//99
Metals and Plastics	Tennessee	S	12.97 MW	13.83 AW	28760 AAW	TNBLS	10//99-12//99
Metals and Plastics	Texas	S	13.95 MW	14.96 AW	31130 AAW	TXBLS	10//99-12//99
Metals and Plastics	Utah	S	15.99 MW	17.70 AW	36810 AAW	UTBLS	10//99-12//99
Metals and Plastics	Virginia	S	13.41 MW	13.91 AW	28930 AAW	VABLS	10//99-12//99
Metals and Plastics	Washington	S	24.71 MW	24.67 AW	51310 AAW	WABLS	10//99-12//99
Metals and Plastics	Wisconsin	S	17.26 MW	17.18 AW	35730 AAW	WIBLS	10//99-12//99
Wood	Alabama	S	11.52 MW	10.65 AW	22150 AAW	ALBLS	10//99-12//99
Wood	Arkansas	S	7.94 MW	8.03 AW	16700 AAW	ARBLS	10//99-12//99
Wood	California	S	12.35 MW	13.23 AW	27530 AAW	CABLS	10//99-12//99
Wood	Florida	S	9.97 MW	10.84 AW	22540 AAW	FLBLS	10//99-12//99
Wood	Illinois	S	10.19 MW	11.28 AW	23450 AAW	ILBLS	10//99-12//99
Wood	Indiana	S	11.16 MW	12.51 AW	26020 AAW	INBLS	10//99-12//99
Wood	Iowa	S	14.92 MW	14.21 AW	29570 AAW	IABLS	10//99-12//99
Wood	Michigan	S	25.16 MW	24.25 AW	50440 AAW	MIBLS	10//99-12//99
Wood	Mississippi	S	8.02 MW	8.39 AW	17440 AAW	MSBLS	10//99-12//99
Wood	New Jersey	S	14.46 MW	13.79 AW	28670 AAW	NJBLS	10//99-12//99
Wood	New York	S	14.68 MW	15.14 AW	31500 AAW	NYBLS	10//99-12//99
Wood	North Carolina	S	11.6 MW	11.44 AW	23800 AAW	NCBLS	10//99-12//99
Wood	Pennsylvania	S	11.74 MW	11.59 AW	24100 AAW	PABLS	10//99-12//99
Wood	South Carolina	S	9.03 MW	9.85 AW	20490 AAW	SCBLS	10//99-12//99
Wood	Tennessee	S	9.82 MW	9.69 AW	20160 AAW	TNBLS	10//99-12//99
Wood	Texas	S	12.53 MW	11.67 AW	24270 AAW	TXBLS	10//99-12//99
Wood	Vermont	S	8.23 MW	9.77 AW	20320 AAW	VTBLS	10//99-12//99
Wood	Virginia	S	11.71 MW	13.22 AW	27500 AAW	VABLS	10//99-12//99
Molder, Shaper, and Caster							
Except Metals and Plastics	Alabama	S	9.09 MW	9.03 AW	18790 AAW	ALBLS	10//99-12//99
Except Metals and Plastics	Arizona	S	9.89 MW	9.98 AW	20760 AAW	AZBLS	10//99-12//99
Except Metals and Plastics	Phoenix-Mesa MSA, AZ	S	10.06 MW	9.93 AW	20930 AAW	AZBLS	10//99-12//99
Except Metals and Plastics	Tucson MSA, AZ	S	9.77 MW	10.98 AW	20330 AAW	AZBLS	10//99-12//99
Except Metals and Plastics	Arkansas	S	9.02 MW	8.72 AW	18130 AAW	ARBLS	10//99-12//99
Except Metals and Plastics	Fayetteville-Springdale-Rogers MSA, AR	S	9.49 MW	8.86 AW	19740 AAW	ARBLS	10//99-12//99

AAW	Average annual wage	**AOH**	Average offered, high	**ASH**	Average starting, high	**H**	Hourly	**M**	Monthly
AE	Average entry wage	**AOL**	Average offered, low	**ASL**	Average starting, low	**HI**	Highest wage paid	**MTC**	Median total compensation
AEX	Average experienced wage	**APH**	Average pay, high range	**AW**	Average wage paid	**HR**	High end range	**MW**	Median wage paid
AO	Average offered	**APL**	Average pay, low range	**FQ**	First quartile wage	**LR**	Low end range	**SQ**	Second quartile wage

S	Special: hourly and annual	**TQ**	Third quartile wage
		W	Weekly
		Y	Yearly

Occupation/Type/Industry	Location	Per	Low	Mid	High	Source	Date
Molder, Shaper, and Caster							
Except Metals and Plastics	California	S	10.37 MW	13.12 AW	27280 AAW	CABLS	10//99-12//99
Except Metals and Plastics	Los Angeles-Long Beach PMSA, CA	S	9.88 MW	8.70 AW	20550 AAW	CABLS	10//99-12//99
Except Metals and Plastics	Oakland PMSA, CA	S	11.12 MW	10.44 AW	23130 AAW	CABLS	10//99-12//99
Except Metals and Plastics	Orange County PMSA, CA	S	21.08 MW	16.85 AW	43850 AAW	CABLS	10//99-12//99
Except Metals and Plastics	San Francisco PMSA, CA	S	11.76 MW	11.08 AW	24460 AAW	CABLS	10//99-12//99
Except Metals and Plastics	Ventura PMSA, CA	S	8.89 MW	7.86 AW	18480 AAW	CABLS	10//99-12//99
Except Metals and Plastics	Colorado	S	13.41 MW	13.63 AW	28350 AAW	COBLS	10//99-12//99
Except Metals and Plastics	Colorado Springs MSA, CO	S	16.53 MW	15.23 AW	34370 AAW	COBLS	10//99-12//99
Except Metals and Plastics	Denver PMSA, CO	S	13.16 MW	13.62 AW	27380 AAW	COBLS	10//99-12//99
Except Metals and Plastics	Connecticut	S	16.26 MW	15.35 AW	31920 AAW	CTBLS	10//99-12//99
Except Metals and Plastics	Hartford MSA, CT	S	12.89 MW	13.83 AW	26810 AAW	CTBLS	10//99-12//99
Except Metals and Plastics	Florida	S	9.09 MW	9.11 AW	18950 AAW	FLBLS	10//99-12//99
Except Metals and Plastics	Jacksonville MSA, FL	S	14.68 MW	13.24 AW	30540 AAW	FLBLS	10//99-12//99
Except Metals and Plastics	Georgia	S	9.68 MW	9.72 AW	20220 AAW	GABLS	10//99-12//99
Except Metals and Plastics	Athens MSA, GA	S	8.32 MW	7.87 AW	17300 AAW	GABLS	10//99-12//99
Except Metals and Plastics	Atlanta MSA, GA	S	9.62 MW	9.64 AW	20010 AAW	GABLS	10//99-12//99
Except Metals and Plastics	Hawaii	S	10.49 MW	11.79 AW	24530 AAW	HIBLS	10//99-12//99
Except Metals and Plastics	Idaho	S	7.69 MW	7.73 AW	16080 AAW	IDBLS	10//99-12//99
Except Metals and Plastics	Illinois	S	11.84 MW	12.28 AW	25550 AAW	ILBLS	10//99-12//99
Except Metals and Plastics	Chicago PMSA, IL	S	11.60 MW	11.16 AW	24120 AAW	ILBLS	10//99-12//99
Except Metals and Plastics	Indiana	S	11.92 MW	11.58 AW	24080 AAW	INBLS	10//99-12//99
Except Metals and Plastics	Elkhart-Goshen MSA, IN	S	13.02 MW	12.78 AW	27080 AAW	INBLS	10//99-12//99
Except Metals and Plastics	Evansville-Henderson MSA, IN-KY	S	9.78 MW	8.49 AW	20350 AAW	INBLS	10//99-12//99
Except Metals and Plastics	Gary PMSA, IN	S	9.76 MW	8.92 AW	20310 AAW	INBLS	10//99-12//99
Except Metals and Plastics	Indianapolis MSA, IN	S	10.34 MW	10.19 AW	21510 AAW	INBLS	10//99-12//99
Except Metals and Plastics	Iowa	S	10.63 MW	11.17 AW	23230 AAW	IABLS	10//99-12//99
Except Metals and Plastics	Kansas	S	12.15 MW	11.01 AW	22900 AAW	KSBLS	10//99-12//99
Except Metals and Plastics	Wichita MSA, KS	S	10.69 MW	11.32 AW	22230 AAW	KSBLS	10//99-12//99
Except Metals and Plastics	Kentucky	S	7.6 MW	8.44 AW	17550 AAW	KYBLS	10//99-12//99
Except Metals and Plastics	Louisville MSA, KY-IN	S	12.20 MW	12.78 AW	25370 AAW	KYBLS	10//99-12//99
Except Metals and Plastics	Louisiana	S	7.44 MW	7.75 AW	16120 AAW	LABLS	10//99-12//99
Except Metals and Plastics	Maine	S	7.57 MW	7.70 AW	16020 AAW	MEBLS	10//99-12//99
Except Metals and Plastics	Maryland	S	8.09 MW	8.78 AW	18250 AAW	MDBLS	10//99-12//99
Except Metals and Plastics	Baltimore PMSA, MD	S	8.67 MW	7.99 AW	18030 AAW	MDBLS	10//99-12//99
Except Metals and Plastics	Massachusetts	S	14.87 MW	14.87 AW	30930 AAW	MABLS	10//99-12//99
Except Metals and Plastics	Boston PMSA, MA-NH	S	10.97 MW	10.09 AW	22810 AAW	MABLS	10//99-12//99
Except Metals and Plastics	Michigan	S	11.81 MW	13.62 AW	28320 AAW	MIBLS	10//99-12//99
Except Metals and Plastics	Detroit PMSA, MI	S	14.19 MW	12.42 AW	29510 AAW	MIBLS	10//99-12//99
Except Metals and Plastics	Minnesota	S	14.47 MW	14.00 AW	29110 AAW	MNBLS	10//99-12//99
Except Metals and Plastics	Minneapolis-St. Paul MSA, MN-WI	S	14.46 MW	14.86 AW	30080 AAW	MNBLS	10//99-12//99
Except Metals and Plastics	Mississippi	S	8.18 MW	10.84 AW	22550 AAW	MSBLS	10//99-12//99
Except Metals and Plastics	Missouri	S	10.95 MW	11.71 AW	24360 AAW	MOBLS	10//99-12//99
Except Metals and Plastics	Nebraska	S	8 MW	8.73 AW	18150 AAW	NEBLS	10//99-12//99
Except Metals and Plastics	Nevada	S	7.67 MW	7.69 AW	15990 AAW	NVBLS	10//99-12//99
Except Metals and Plastics	Reno MSA, NV	S	7.69 MW	7.67 AW	15990 AAW	NVBLS	10//99-12//99
Except Metals and Plastics	New Hampshire	S	8.08 MW	8.35 AW	17370 AAW	NHBLS	10//99-12//99
Except Metals and Plastics	Portsmouth-Rochester PMSA, NH-ME	S	8.50 MW	8.17 AW	17680 AAW	NHBLS	10//99-12//99
Except Metals and Plastics	New Jersey	S	13.69 MW	13.32 AW	27710 AAW	NJBLS	10//99-12//99
Except Metals and Plastics	Bergen-Passaic PMSA, NJ	S	12.64 MW	13.85 AW	26290 AAW	NJBLS	10//99-12//99
Except Metals and Plastics	Jersey City PMSA, NJ	S	9.84 MW	9.83 AW	20460 AAW	NJBLS	10//99-12//99
Except Metals and Plastics	Middlesex-Somerset-Hunterdon PMSA, NJ	S	15.27 MW	15.28 AW	31760 AAW	NJBLS	10//99-12//99
Except Metals and Plastics	Monmouth-Ocean PMSA, NJ	S	11.62 MW	11.98 AW	24180 AAW	NJBLS	10//99-12//99
Except Metals and Plastics	Newark PMSA, NJ	S	15.91 MW	15.09 AW	33090 AAW	NJBLS	10//99-12//99
Except Metals and Plastics	Vineland-Millville-Bridgeton PMSA, NJ	S	12.87 MW	13.84 AW	26780 AAW	NJBLS	10//99-12//99
Except Metals and Plastics	New Mexico	S	11.98 MW	11.42 AW	23750 AAW	NMBLS	10//99-12//99
Except Metals and Plastics	New York	S	9.95 MW	10.43 AW	21700 AAW	NYBLS	10//99-12//99
Except Metals and Plastics	Albany-Schenectady-Troy MSA, NY	S	19.72 MW	19.50 AW	41030 AAW	NYBLS	10//99-12//99
Except Metals and Plastics	Buffalo-Niagara Falls MSA, NY	S	9.82 MW	9.44 AW	20420 AAW	NYBLS	10//99-12//99
Except Metals and Plastics	Nassau-Suffolk PMSA, NY	S	11.30 MW	10.43 AW	23500 AAW	NYBLS	10//99-12//99
Except Metals and Plastics	New York PMSA, NY	S	10.46 MW	10.09 AW	21760 AAW	NYBLS	10//99-12//99
Except Metals and Plastics	Syracuse MSA, NY	S	9.51 MW	9.63 AW	19780 AAW	NYBLS	10//99-12//99
Except Metals and Plastics	North Carolina	S	9.14 MW	9.88 AW	20540 AAW	NCBLS	10//99-12//99

AAW Average annual wage	AOH Average offered, high	ASH Average starting, high	H Hourly	M Monthly	S Special: hourly and annual
AE Average entry wage	AOL Average offered, low	ASL Average starting, low	HI Highest wage paid	MTC Median total compensation	TQ Third quartile wage
AEX Average experienced wage	APH Average pay, high range	AW Average wage paid	HR High end range	MW Median wage paid	W Weekly
AO Average offered	APL Average pay, low range	FQ First quartile wage	LR Low end range	SQ Second quartile wage	Y Yearly

Occupation/Type/Industry	Location	Per	Low	Mid	High	Source	Date
Molder, Shaper, and Caster							
Except Metals and Plastics	Charlotte-Gastonia-Rock Hill MSA, NC-SC	S	11.11 MW	11.36 AW	23110 AAW	NCBLS	10//99-12//99
Except Metals and Plastics	Greensboro--Winston-Salem-- High Point MSA, NC	S	7.80 MW	7.67 AW	16220 AAW	NCBLS	10//99-12//99
Except Metals and Plastics	Ohio	S	11.88 MW	12.76 AW	26550 AAW	OHBLS	10//99-12//99
Except Metals and Plastics	Canton-Massillon MSA, OH	S	10.15 MW	9.86 AW	21120 AAW	OHBLS	10//99-12//99
Except Metals and Plastics	Cincinnati PMSA, OH-KY-IN	S	10.44 MW	10.05 AW	21700 AAW	OHBLS	10//99-12//99
Except Metals and Plastics	Cleveland-Lorain-Elyria PMSA, OH	S	9.54 MW	9.76 AW	19830 AAW	OHBLS	10//99-12//99
Except Metals and Plastics	Dayton-Springfield MSA, OH	S	13.30 MW	13.03 AW	27670 AAW	OHBLS	10//99-12//99
Except Metals and Plastics	Youngstown-Warren MSA, OH	S	9.04 MW	8.71 AW	18790 AAW	OHBLS	10//99-12//99
Except Metals and Plastics	Oklahoma	S	9.22 MW	9.29 AW	19320 AAW	OKBLS	10//99-12//99
Except Metals and Plastics	Oklahoma City MSA, OK	S	10.22 MW	9.66 AW	21250 AAW	OKBLS	10//99-12//99
Except Metals and Plastics	Oregon	S	11.15 MW	12.15 AW	25270 AAW	ORBLS	10//99-12//99
Except Metals and Plastics	Eugene-Springfield MSA, OR	S	10.73 MW	9.90 AW	22320 AAW	ORBLS	10//99-12//99
Except Metals and Plastics	Portland-Vancouver PMSA, OR-WA	S	13.14 MW	13.43 AW	27330 AAW	ORBLS	10//99-12//99
Except Metals and Plastics	Pennsylvania	S	11.83 MW	12.26 AW	25510 AAW	PABLS	10//99-12//99
Except Metals and Plastics	Johnstown MSA, PA	S	10.64 MW	10.71 AW	22130 AAW	PABLS	10//99-12//99
Except Metals and Plastics	Philadelphia PMSA, PA-NJ	S	10.30 MW	9.60 AW	21430 AAW	PABLS	10//99-12//99
Except Metals and Plastics	Pittsburgh MSA, PA	S	12.26 MW	12.22 AW	25490 AAW	PABLS	10//99-12//99
Except Metals and Plastics	Reading MSA, PA	S	12.94 MW	12.71 AW	26910 AAW	PABLS	10//99-12//99
Except Metals and Plastics	Scranton--Wilkes-Barre-- Hazleton MSA, PA	S	11.49 MW	11.77 AW	23900 AAW	PABLS	10//99-12//99
Except Metals and Plastics	York MSA, PA	S	9.83 MW	9.53 AW	20450 AAW	PABLS	10//99-12//99
Except Metals and Plastics	Rhode Island	S	8.38 MW	9.17 AW	19070 AAW	RIBLS	10//99-12//99
Except Metals and Plastics	Providence-Fall River- Warwick MSA, RI-MA	S	9.17 MW	8.38 AW	19070 AAW	RIBLS	10//99-12//99
Except Metals and Plastics	South Carolina	S	11.44 MW	13.06 AW	27170 AAW	SCBLS	10//99-12//99
Except Metals and Plastics	Charleston-North Charleston MSA, SC	S	11.73 MW	9.15 AW	24400 AAW	SCBLS	10//99-12//99
Except Metals and Plastics	Greenville-Spartanburg- Anderson MSA, SC	S	14.47 MW	11.51 AW	30090 AAW	SCBLS	10//99-12//99
Except Metals and Plastics	Tennessee	S	8.38 MW	9.38 AW	19520 AAW	TNBLS	10//99-12//99
Except Metals and Plastics	Texas	S	7.23 MW	8.46 AW	17590 AAW	TXBLS	10//99-12//99
Except Metals and Plastics	Austin-San Marcos MSA, TX	S	7.40 MW	7.45 AW	15380 AAW	TXBLS	10//99-12//99
Except Metals and Plastics	Dallas PMSA, TX	S	10.13 MW	9.71 AW	21070 AAW	TXBLS	10//99-12//99
Except Metals and Plastics	Fort Worth-Arlington PMSA, TX	S	10.81 MW	11.21 AW	22490 AAW	TXBLS	10//99-12//99
Except Metals and Plastics	Houston PMSA, TX	S	6.01 MW	6.00 AW	12500 AAW	TXBLS	10//99-12//99
Except Metals and Plastics	Longview-Marshall MSA, TX	S	9.12 MW	6.59 AW	18970 AAW	TXBLS	10//99-12//99
Except Metals and Plastics	Lubbock MSA, TX	S	6.87 MW	6.46 AW	14290 AAW	TXBLS	10//99-12//99
Except Metals and Plastics	San Antonio MSA, TX	S	6.48 MW	6.36 AW	13480 AAW	TXBLS	10//99-12//99
Except Metals and Plastics	Utah	S	9.38 MW	9.57 AW	19900 AAW	UTBLS	10//99-12//99
Except Metals and Plastics	Vermont	S	11.56 MW	11.22 AW	23340 AAW	VTBLS	10//99-12//99
Except Metals and Plastics	Virginia	S	6.9 MW	7.41 AW	15410 AAW	VABLS	10//99-12//99
Except Metals and Plastics	Norfolk-Virginia Beach- Newport News MSA, VA-NC	S	8.36 MW	7.25 AW	17390 AAW	VABLS	10//99-12//99
Except Metals and Plastics	Washington	S	10.91 MW	12.37 AW	25740 AAW	WABLS	10//99-12//99
Except Metals and Plastics	Seattle-Bellevue-Everett PMSA, WA	S	13.49 MW	11.04 AW	28050 AAW	WABLS	10//99-12//99
Except Metals and Plastics	Tacoma PMSA, WA	S	15.59 MW	15.25 AW	32430 AAW	WABLS	10//99-12//99
Except Metals and Plastics	Wisconsin	S	11.59 MW	11.28 AW	23460 AAW	WIBLS	10//99-12//99
Except Metals and Plastics	Wyoming	S	10.58 MW	10.87 AW	22600 AAW	WYBLS	10//99-12//99
Molding, Coremaking, and Casting Machine Setter, Operator, and Tender							
Metals and Plastics	Alabama	S	8.31 MW	10.08 AW	20960 AAW	ALBLS	10//99-12//99
Metals and Plastics	Birmingham MSA, AL	S	12.19 MW	9.29 AW	25350 AAW	ALBLS	10//99-12//99
Metals and Plastics	Decatur MSA, AL	S	11.69 MW	10.61 AW	24310 AAW	ALBLS	10//99-12//99
Metals and Plastics	Mobile MSA, AL	S	9.80 MW	9.62 AW	20380 AAW	ALBLS	10//99-12//99
Metals and Plastics	Arizona	S	14.7 MW	15.12 AW	31450 AAW	AZBLS	10//99-12//99
Metals and Plastics	Phoenix-Mesa MSA, AZ	S	15.50 MW	15.84 AW	32240 AAW	AZBLS	10//99-12//99
Metals and Plastics	Tucson MSA, AZ	S	11.99 MW	10.72 AW	24940 AAW	AZBLS	10//99-12//99
Metals and Plastics	Arkansas	S	10.43 MW	10.76 AW	22390 AAW	ARBLS	10//99-12//99
Metals and Plastics	Fayetteville-Springdale-Rogers MSA, AR	S	11.06 MW	11.34 AW	23000 AAW	ARBLS	10//99-12//99
Metals and Plastics	Pine Bluff MSA, AR	S	11.98 MW	12.11 AW	24930 AAW	ARBLS	10//99-12//99
Metals and Plastics	California	S	8.27 MW	9.45 AW	19650 AAW	CABLS	10//99-12//99

Occupation/Type/Industry	Location	Per	Low	Mid	High	Source	Date
Molding, Coremaking, and Casting Machine Setter, Operator, and Tender							
Metals and Plastics	Los Angeles-Long Beach PMSA, CA	S	9.31 MW	8.47 AW	19370 AAW	CABLS	10//99-12//99
Metals and Plastics	Oakland PMSA, CA	S	14.08 MW	9.92 AW	29290 AAW	CABLS	10//99-12//99
Metals and Plastics	Orange County PMSA, CA	S	8.51 MW	7.32 AW	17690 AAW	CABLS	10//99-12//99
Metals and Plastics	Riverside-San Bernardino PMSA, CA	S	10.56 MW	8.89 AW	21960 AAW	CABLS	10//99-12//99
Metals and Plastics	Sacramento PMSA, CA	S	9.12 MW	9.07 AW	18980 AAW	CABLS	10//99-12//99
Metals and Plastics	San Diego MSA, CA	S	8.68 MW	7.68 AW	18050 AAW	CABLS	10//99-12//99
Metals and Plastics	San Francisco PMSA, CA	S	9.17 MW	8.04 AW	19080 AAW	CABLS	10//99-12//99
Metals and Plastics	San Jose PMSA, CA	S	8.79 MW	7.77 AW	18280 AAW	CABLS	10//99-12//99
Metals and Plastics	Santa Barbara-Santa Maria-Lompoc MSA, CA	S	10.17 MW	10.68 AW	21150 AAW	CABLS	10//99-12//99
Metals and Plastics	Santa Cruz-Watsonville PMSA, CA		14.52 MW	14.76 AW	30210 AAW	CABLS	10//99-12//99
Metals and Plastics	Santa Rosa PMSA, CA	S	10.93 MW	10.05 AW	22740 AAW	CABLS	10//99-12//99
Metals and Plastics	Stockton-Lodi MSA, CA	S	12.22 MW	11.58 AW	25420 AAW	CABLS	10//99-12//99
Metals and Plastics	Ventura PMSA, CA	S	7.73 MW	6.46 AW	16070 AAW	CABLS	10//99-12//99
Metals and Plastics	Colorado	S	8.99 MW	9.76 AW	20310 AAW	COBLS	10//99-12//99
Metals and Plastics	Denver PMSA, CO	S	9.67 MW	9.25 AW	20100 AAW	COBLS	10//99-12//99
Metals and Plastics	Fort Collins-Loveland MSA, CO	S	9.16 MW	7.80 AW	19060 AAW	COBLS	10//99-12//99
Metals and Plastics	Connecticut	S	13.09 MW	13.26 AW	27580 AAW	CTBLS	10//99-12//99
Metals and Plastics	Bridgeport PMSA, CT	S	13.38 MW	13.29 AW	27840 AAW	CTBLS	10//99-12//99
Metals and Plastics	Hartford MSA, CT	S	14.13 MW	13.38 AW	29400 AAW	CTBLS	10//99-12//99
Metals and Plastics	New Haven-Meriden PMSA, CT	S	7.94 MW	7.75 AW	16520 AAW	CTBLS	10//99-12//99
Metals and Plastics	New London-Norwich MSA, CT-RI	S	10.94 MW	10.80 AW	22760 AAW	CTBLS	10//99-12//99
Metals and Plastics	Stamford-Norwalk PMSA, CT	S	7.64 MW	7.38 AW	15880 AAW	CTBLS	10//99-12//99
Metals and Plastics	Waterbury PMSA, CT	S	16.63 MW	18.05 AW	34590 AAW	CTBLS	10//99-12//99
Metals and Plastics	Florida	S	7.76 MW	8.37 AW	17410 AAW	FLBLS	10//99-12//99
Metals and Plastics	Fort Lauderdale PMSA, FL	S	9.00 MW	8.60 AW	18720 AAW	FLBLS	10//99-12//99
Metals and Plastics	Jacksonville MSA, FL	S	10.66 MW	11.12 AW	22180 AAW	FLBLS	10//99-12//99
Metals and Plastics	Miami PMSA, FL	S	7.71 MW	7.66 AW	16040 AAW	FLBLS	10//99-12//99
Metals and Plastics	Orlando MSA, FL	S	11.31 MW	10.19 AW	23520 AAW	FLBLS	10//99-12//99
Metals and Plastics	Sarasota-Bradenton MSA, FL	S	8.61 MW	7.78 AW	17900 AAW	FLBLS	10//99-12//99
Metals and Plastics	Tampa-St. Petersburg-Clearwater MSA, FL	S	7.02 MW	7.03 AW	14600 AAW	FLBLS	10//99-12//99
Metals and Plastics	Georgia	S	7.87 MW	8.76 AW	18220 AAW	GABLS	10//99-12//99
Metals and Plastics	Atlanta MSA, GA	S	8.68 MW	7.71 AW	18050 AAW	GABLS	10//99-12//99
Metals and Plastics	Idaho	S	7.56 MW	7.70 AW	16020 AAW	IDBLS	10//99-12//99
Metals and Plastics	Boise City MSA, ID	S	8.05 MW	7.77 AW	16740 AAW	IDBLS	10//99-12//99
Metals and Plastics	Illinois	S	10.21 MW	10.76 AW	22370 AAW	ILBLS	10//99-12//99
Metals and Plastics	Chicago PMSA, IL	S	10.53 MW	10.49 AW	21900 AAW	ILBLS	10//99-12//99
Metals and Plastics	Rockford MSA, IL	S	9.42 MW	8.79 AW	19600 AAW	ILBLS	10//99-12//99
Metals and Plastics	Indiana	S	10.11 MW	11.17 AW	23230 AAW	INBLS	10//99-12//99
Metals and Plastics	Elkhart-Goshen MSA, IN	S	12.40 MW	11.80 AW	25790 AAW	INBLS	10//99-12//99
Metals and Plastics	Evansville-Henderson MSA, IN-KY	S	8.47 MW	7.93 AW	17610 AAW	INBLS	10//99-12//99
Metals and Plastics	Fort Wayne MSA, IN	S	12.41 MW	12.55 AW	25820 AAW	INBLS	10//99-12//99
Metals and Plastics	Indianapolis MSA, IN	S	10.14 MW	9.59 AW	21100 AAW	INBLS	10//99-12//99
Metals and Plastics	South Bend MSA, IN	S	9.12 MW	8.23 AW	18970 AAW	INBLS	10//99-12//99
Metals and Plastics	Iowa	S	9.82 MW	10.19 AW	21200 AAW	IABLS	10//99-12//99
Metals and Plastics	Des Moines MSA, IA	S	13.07 MW	13.87 AW	27180 AAW	IABLS	10//99-12//99
Metals and Plastics	Kansas	S	9.28 MW	9.82 AW	20430 AAW	KSBLS	10//99-12//99
Metals and Plastics	Kentucky	S	10.09 MW	10.61 AW	22070 AAW	KYBLS	10//99-12//99
Metals and Plastics	Lexington MSA, KY	S	10.65 MW	10.59 AW	22150 AAW	KYBLS	10//99-12//99
Metals and Plastics	Louisville MSA, KY-IN	S	8.47 MW	8.12 AW	17630 AAW	KYBLS	10//99-12//99
Metals and Plastics	Owensboro MSA, KY	S	10.40 MW	9.83 AW	21620 AAW	KYBLS	10//99-12//99
Metals and Plastics	Louisiana	S	14.07 MW	12.13 AW	25220 AAW	LABLS	10//99-12//99
Metals and Plastics	Shreveport-Bossier City MSA, LA	S	6.50 MW	6.22 AW	13510 AAW	LABLS	10//99-12//99
Metals and Plastics	Maine	S	10.02 MW	10.35 AW	21530 AAW	MEBLS	10//99-12//99
Metals and Plastics	Maryland	S	9.1 MW	10.06 AW	20920 AAW	MDBLS	10//99-12//99
Metals and Plastics	Baltimore PMSA, MD	S	9.66 MW	9.20 AW	20090 AAW	MDBLS	10//99-12//99
Metals and Plastics	Hagerstown PMSA, MD	S	10.09 MW	8.77 AW	20980 AAW	MDBLS	10//99-12//99
Metals and Plastics	Massachusetts	S	10.1 MW	10.96 AW	22800 AAW	MABLS	10//99-12//99
Metals and Plastics	Boston PMSA, MA-NH	S	11.47 MW	11.23 AW	23850 AAW	MABLS	10//99-12//99

AAW	Average annual wage	**AOH**	Average offered, high	**ASH**	Average starting, high	**H**	Hourly
AE	Average entry wage	**AOL**	Average offered, low	**ASL**	Average starting, low	**HI**	Highest wage paid
AEX	Average experienced wage	**APH**	Average pay, high range	**AW**	Average wage paid	**HR**	High end range
AO	Average offered	**APL**	Average pay, low range	**FQ**	First quartile wage	**LR**	Low end range

M	Monthly	**S**	Special: hourly and annual
MTC	Median total compensation	**TQ**	Third quartile wage
MW	Median wage paid	**W**	Weekly
SQ	Second quartile wage	**Y**	Yearly

Occupation/Type/Industry	Location	Per	Low	Mid	High	Source	Date
Molding, Coremaking, and Casting Machine Setter, Operator, and Tender							
Metals and Plastics	Fitchburg-Leominster PMSA, MA	S	9.27 MW	8.03 AW	19270 AAW	MABLS	10//99-12//99
Metals and Plastics	Lowell PMSA, MA-NH	S	10.96 MW	10.29 AW	22800 AAW	MABLS	10//99-12//99
Metals and Plastics	New Bedford PMSA, MA	S	13.44 MW	13.85 AW	27960 AAW	MABLS	10//99-12//99
Metals and Plastics	Springfield MSA, MA	S	11.59 MW	11.37 AW	24110 AAW	MABLS	10//99-12//99
Metals and Plastics	Worcester PMSA, MA-CT	S	10.18 MW	9.35 AW	21170 AAW	MABLS	10//99-12//99
Metals and Plastics	Michigan	S	10.35 MW	11.89 AW	24730 AAW	MIBLS	10//99-12//99
Metals and Plastics	Benton Harbor MSA, MI	S	9.71 MW	9.84 AW	20190 AAW	MIBLS	10//99-12//99
Metals and Plastics	Detroit PMSA, MI	S	11.20 MW	9.76 AW	23290 AAW	MIBLS	10//99-12//99
Metals and Plastics	Grand Rapids-Muskegon-Holland MSA, MI	S	11.13 MW	10.07 AW	23150 AAW	MIBLS	10//99-12//99
Metals and Plastics	Kalamazoo-Battle Creek MSA, MI	S	11.88 MW	11.05 AW	24700 AAW	MIBLS	10//99-12//99
Metals and Plastics	Saginaw-Bay City-Midland MSA, MI	S	17.89 MW	21.67 AW	37210 AAW	MIBLS	10//99-12//99
Metals and Plastics	Minnesota	S	11.63 MW	11.78 AW	24490 AAW	MNBLS	10//99-12//99
Metals and Plastics	Minneapolis-St. Paul MSA, MN-WI	S	11.85 MW	11.44 AW	24650 AAW	MNBLS	10//99-12//99
Metals and Plastics	Mississippi	S	9.19 MW	9.39 AW	19530 AAW	MSBLS	10//99-12//99
Metals and Plastics	Jackson MSA, MS	S	8.19 MW	6.24 AW	17040 AAW	MSBLS	10//99-12//99
Metals and Plastics	Missouri	S	8.66 MW	9.22 AW	19180 AAW	MOBLS	10//99-12//99
Metals and Plastics	Kansas City MSA, MO-KS	S	10.37 MW	10.10 AW	21570 AAW	MOBLS	10//99-12//99
Metals and Plastics	St. Louis MSA, MO-IL	S	9.16 MW	8.42 AW	19050 AAW	MOBLS	10//99-12//99
Metals and Plastics	Nebraska	S	10.33 MW	11.55 AW	24020 AAW	NEBLS	10//99-12//99
Metals and Plastics	Lincoln MSA, NE	S	16.45 MW	17.62 AW	34210 AAW	NEBLS	10//99-12//99
Metals and Plastics	Omaha MSA, NE-IA	S	10.60 MW	10.99 AW	22050 AAW	NEBLS	10//99-12//99
Metals and Plastics	Nevada	S	10.39 MW	13.15 AW	27360 AAW	NVBLS	10//99-12//99
Metals and Plastics	Las Vegas MSA, NV-AZ	S	13.88 MW	12.41 AW	28880 AAW	NVBLS	10//99-12//99
Metals and Plastics	New Hampshire	S	9.88 MW	10.13 AW	21070 AAW	NHBLS	10//99-12//99
Metals and Plastics	Nashua PMSA, NH	S	11.19 MW	10.42 AW	23280 AAW	NHBLS	10//99-12//99
Metals and Plastics	New Jersey	S	7.81 MW	8.72 AW	18140 AAW	NJBLS	10//99-12//99
Metals and Plastics	Bergen-Passaic PMSA, NJ	S	10.02 MW	10.17 AW	20850 AAW	NJBLS	10//99-12//99
Metals and Plastics	Jersey City PMSA, NJ	S	7.42 MW	7.40 AW	15440 AAW	NJBLS	10//99-12//99
Metals and Plastics	Monmouth-Ocean PMSA, NJ	S	8.53 MW	6.43 AW	17730 AAW	NJBLS	10//99-12//99
Metals and Plastics	Newark PMSA, NJ	S	7.75 MW	6.88 AW	16130 AAW	NJBLS	10//99-12//99
Metals and Plastics	New Mexico	S	9.73 MW	12.23 AW	25430 AAW	NMBLS	10//99-12//99
Metals and Plastics	Albuquerque MSA, NM	S	12.23 MW	9.73 AW	25430 AAW	NMBLS	10//99-12//99
Metals and Plastics	New York	S	9.18 MW	10.16 AW	21140 AAW	NYBLS	10//99-12//99
Metals and Plastics	Albany-Schenectady-Troy MSA, NY	S	9.06 MW	9.30 AW	18840 AAW	NYBLS	10//99-12//99
Metals and Plastics	Binghamton MSA, NY	S	7.21 MW	7.12 AW	15000 AAW	NYBLS	10//99-12//99
Metals and Plastics	Buffalo-Niagara Falls MSA, NY	S	9.58 MW	9.52 AW	19930 AAW	NYBLS	10//99-12//99
Metals and Plastics	Glens Falls MSA, NY	S	14.04 MW	14.30 AW	29210 AAW	NYBLS	10//99-12//99
Metals and Plastics	Nassau-Suffolk PMSA, NY	S	8.27 MW	7.84 AW	17200 AAW	NYBLS	10//99-12//99
Metals and Plastics	New York PMSA, NY	S	10.47 MW	8.20 AW	21780 AAW	NYBLS	10//99-12//99
Metals and Plastics	Rochester MSA, NY	S	12.59 MW	10.23 AW	26200 AAW	NYBLS	10//99-12//99
Metals and Plastics	Syracuse MSA, NY	S	11.23 MW	10.22 AW	23360 AAW	NYBLS	10//99-12//99
Metals and Plastics	North Carolina	S	10 MW	10.75 AW	22360 AAW	NCBLS	10//99-12//99
Metals and Plastics	Charlotte-Gastonia-Rock Hill MSA, NC-SC	S	11.07 MW	10.51 AW	23030 AAW	NCBLS	10//99-12//99
Metals and Plastics	Greensboro--Winston-Salem--High Point MSA, NC	S	10.30 MW	9.63 AW	21420 AAW	NCBLS	10//99-12//99
Metals and Plastics	Hickory-Morganton-Lenoir MSA, NC	S	6.88 MW	7.00 AW	14310 AAW	NCBLS	10//99-12//99
Metals and Plastics	Raleigh-Durham-Chapel Hill MSA, NC	S	12.49 MW	12.53 AW	25990 AAW	NCBLS	10//99-12//99
Metals and Plastics	Ohio	S	11.43 MW	13.28 AW	27620 AAW	OHBLS	10//99-12//99
Metals and Plastics	Akron PMSA, OH	S	11.52 MW	11.53 AW	23960 AAW	OHBLS	10//99-12//99
Metals and Plastics	Cincinnati PMSA, OH-KY-IN	S	10.30 MW	10.35 AW	21420 AAW	OHBLS	10//99-12//99
Metals and Plastics	Cleveland-Lorain-Elyria PMSA, OH	S	17.01 MW	16.19 AW	35380 AAW	OHBLS	10//99-12//99
Metals and Plastics	Columbus MSA, OH	S	11.26 MW	10.27 AW	23430 AAW	OHBLS	10//99-12//99
Metals and Plastics	Dayton-Springfield MSA, OH	S	9.65 MW	8.36 AW	20060 AAW	OHBLS	10//99-12//99
Metals and Plastics	Toledo MSA, OH	S	14.71 MW	11.89 AW	30590 AAW	OHBLS	10//99-12//99
Metals and Plastics	Youngstown-Warren MSA, OH	S	11.85 MW	11.62 AW	24660 AAW	OHBLS	10//99-12//99
Metals and Plastics	Oklahoma	S	9.49 MW	9.66 AW	20090 AAW	OKBLS	10//99-12//99
Metals and Plastics	Oklahoma City MSA, OK	S	10.02 MW	9.63 AW	20840 AAW	OKBLS	10//99-12//99
Metals and Plastics	Tulsa MSA, OK	S	10.01 MW	8.02 AW	20810 AAW	OKBLS	10//99-12//99

Occupation/Type/Industry	Location	Per	Low	Mid	High	Source	Date
Molding, Coremaking, and Casting Machine Setter, Operator, and Tender							
Metals and Plastics	Oregon	S	14.01 MW	13.31 AW	27690 AAW	ORBLS	10//99-12//99
Metals and Plastics	Portland-Vancouver PMSA, OR-WA	S	13.41 MW	14.19 AW	27890 AAW	ORBLS	10//99-12//99
Metals and Plastics	Pennsylvania	S	12.15 MW	12.74 AW	26500 AAW	PABLS	10//99-12//99
Metals and Plastics	Erie MSA, PA	S	10.11 MW	11.25 AW	21040 AAW	PABLS	10//99-12//99
Metals and Plastics	Harrisburg-Lebanon-Carlisle MSA, PA	S	14.41 MW	13.54 AW	29980 AAW	PABLS	10//99-12//99
Metals and Plastics	Lancaster MSA, PA	S	12.36 MW	12.17 AW	25720 AAW	PABLS	10//99-12//99
Metals and Plastics	Philadelphia PMSA, PA-NJ	S	12.55 MW	12.41 AW	26100 AAW	PABLS	10//99-12//99
Metals and Plastics	Pittsburgh MSA, PA	S	16.90 MW	15.30 AW	35160 AAW	PABLS	10//99-12//99
Metals and Plastics	Reading MSA, PA	S	13.76 MW	13.81 AW	28620 AAW	PABLS	10//99-12//99
Metals and Plastics	York MSA, PA	S	9.95 MW	9.42 AW	20700 AAW	PABLS	10//99-12//99
Metals and Plastics	Rhode Island	S	10.35 MW	11.40 AW	23720 AAW	RIBLS	10//99-12//99
Metals and Plastics	Providence-Fall River-Warwick MSA, RI-MA	S	11.55 MW	10.46 AW	24030 AAW	RIBLS	10//99-12//99
Metals and Plastics	South Carolina	S	9.76 MW	11.07 AW	23020 AAW	SCBLS	10//99-12//99
Metals and Plastics	Greenville-Spartanburg-Anderson MSA, SC	S	9.82 MW	9.24 AW	20420 AAW	SCBLS	10//99-12//99
Metals and Plastics	South Dakota	S	8.63 MW	8.81 AW	18330 AAW	SDBLS	10//99-12//99
Metals and Plastics	Rapid City MSA, SD	S	9.00 MW	9.15 AW	18710 AAW	SDBLS	10//99-12//99
Metals and Plastics	Tennessee	S	9.72 MW	10.24 AW	21300 AAW	TNBLS	10//99-12//99
Metals and Plastics	Chattanooga MSA, TN-GA	S	11.00 MW	11.16 AW	22880 AAW	TNBLS	10//99-12//99
Metals and Plastics	Johnson City-Kingsport-Bristol MSA, TN-VA	S	8.40 MW	7.65 AW	17470 AAW	TNBLS	10//99-12//99
Metals and Plastics	Knoxville MSA, TN	S	8.68 MW	8.39 AW	18060 AAW	TNBLS	10//99-12//99
Metals and Plastics	Memphis MSA, TN-AR-MS	S	12.14 MW	10.99 AW	25250 AAW	MSBLS	10//99-12//99
Metals and Plastics	Nashville MSA, TN	S	11.30 MW	10.32 AW	23500 AAW	TNBLS	10//99-12//99
Metals and Plastics	Texas	S	7.86 MW	8.53 AW	17740 AAW	TXBLS	10//99-12//99
Metals and Plastics	Austin-San Marcos MSA, TX	S	7.64 MW	7.68 AW	15890 AAW	TXBLS	10//99-12//99
Metals and Plastics	Dallas PMSA, TX	S	9.30 MW	7.98 AW	19340 AAW	TXBLS	10//99-12//99
Metals and Plastics	El Paso MSA, TX	S	7.59 MW	7.65 AW	15800 AAW	TXBLS	10//99-12//99
Metals and Plastics	Fort Worth-Arlington PMSA, TX	S	8.34 MW	7.91 AW	17360 AAW	TXBLS	10//99-12//99
Metals and Plastics	Houston PMSA, TX	S	9.42 MW	9.23 AW	19600 AAW	TXBLS	10//99-12//99
Metals and Plastics	Longview-Marshall MSA, TX	S	6.10 MW	6.03 AW	12690 AAW	TXBLS	10//99-12//99
Metals and Plastics	Utah	S	10.47 MW	10.99 AW	22850 AAW	UTBLS	10//99-12//99
Metals and Plastics	Provo-Orem MSA, UT	S	13.39 MW	12.38 AW	27860 AAW	UTBLS	10//99-12//99
Metals and Plastics	Salt Lake City-Ogden MSA, UT	S	10.48 MW	10.34 AW	21800 AAW	UTBLS	10//99-12//99
Metals and Plastics	Vermont	S	11.48 MW	12.34 AW	25670 AAW	VTBLS	10//99-12//99
Metals and Plastics	Virginia	S	9.73 MW	10.73 AW	22310 AAW	VABLS	10//99-12//99
Metals and Plastics	Norfolk-Virginia Beach-Newport News MSA, VA-NC	S	11.67 MW	13.74 AW	24270 AAW	VABLS	10//99-12//99
Metals and Plastics	Washington	S	10.37 MW	10.82 AW	22500 AAW	WABLS	10//99-12//99
Metals and Plastics	Seattle-Bellevue-Everett PMSA, WA	S	10.75 MW	9.64 AW	22350 AAW	WABLS	10//99-12//99
Metals and Plastics	Tacoma PMSA, WA	S	10.45 MW	10.75 AW	21740 AAW	WABLS	10//99-12//99
Metals and Plastics	Wisconsin	S	12.25 MW	12.64 AW	26300 AAW	WIBLS	10//99-12//99
Metals and Plastics	Madison MSA, WI	S	12.39 MW	12.42 AW	25770 AAW	WIBLS	10//99-12//99
Metals and Plastics	Milwaukee-Waukesha PMSA, WI	S	14.04 MW	13.78 AW	29210 AAW	WIBLS	10//99-12//99
Metals and Plastics	Racine PMSA, WI	S	10.38 MW	10.37 AW	21580 AAW	WIBLS	10//99-12//99
Metals and Plastics	Puerto Rico	S	7.48 MW	7.40 AW	15390 AAW	PRBLS	10//99-12//99
Metals and Plastics	San Juan-Bayamon PMSA, PR	S	7.14 MW	7.36 AW	14850 AAW	PRBLS	10//99-12//99
Molding Supervisor							
Foundry	United States	Y	40000 MW	41700 AW		MODCAS	1999
Motion Picture Projectionist	Alabama	S	6.28 MW	6.50 AW	13510 AAW	ALBLS	10//99-12//99
	Alaska	S	6.62 MW	7.60 AW	15810 AAW	AKBLS	10//99-12//99
	Arkansas	S	7.05 MW	7.50 AW	15600 AAW	ARBLS	10//99-12//99
	California	S	8.91 MW	14.31 AW	29770 AAW	CABLS	10//99-12//99
	Colorado	S	11.38 MW	11.20 AW	23290 AAW	COBLS	10//99-12//99
	Connecticut	S	9.74 MW	11.57 AW	24070 AAW	CTBLS	10//99-12//99
	Delaware	S	7.28 MW	10.32 AW	21470 AAW	DEBLS	10//99-12//99
	Florida	S	7.22 MW	8.14 AW	16920 AAW	FLBLS	10//99-12//99
	Georgia	S	6.33 MW	6.88 AW	14310 AAW	GABLS	10//99-12//99
	Hawaii	S	14.86 MW	14.85 AW	30900 AAW	HIBLS	10//99-12//99

Occupation/Type/Industry	Location	Per	Low	Mid	High	Source	Date
Motion Picture Projectionist	Idaho	S	6.18 MW	7.10 AW	14770 AAW	IDBLS	10//99-12//99
	Indiana	S	6.62 MW	8.26 AW	17190 AAW	INBLS	10//99-12//99
	Iowa	S	6.18 MW	6.44 AW	13400 AAW	IABLS	10//99-12//99
	Kansas	S	6.99 MW	7.00 AW	14550 AAW	KSBLS	10//99-12//99
	Kentucky	S	6.55 MW	7.25 AW	15080 AAW	KYBLS	10//99-12//99
	Louisiana	S	6.02 MW	6.56 AW	13630 AAW	LABLS	10//99-12//99
	Maryland	S	8.14 MW	9.16 AW	19060 AAW	MDBLS	10//99-12//99
	Massachusetts	S	11.76 MW	11.62 AW	24180 AAW	MABLS	10//99-12//99
	Michigan	S	6.66 MW	9.42 AW	19600 AAW	MIBLS	10//99-12//99
	Minnesota	S	6.64 MW	7.26 AW	15090 AAW	MNBLS	10//99-12//99
	Mississippi	S	6.38 MW	6.74 AW	14020 AAW	MSBLS	10//99-12//99
	Missouri	S	6.46 MW	7.91 AW	16460 AAW	MOBLS	10//99-12//99
	Montana	S	6.06 MW	6.40 AW	13320 AAW	MTBLS	10//99-12//99
	Nebraska	S	6.04 MW	7.47 AW	15530 AAW	NEBLS	10//99-12//99
	Nevada	S	6.22 MW	6.53 AW	13580 AAW	NVBLS	10//99-12//99
	New Jersey	S	10.53 MW	12.32 AW	25630 AAW	NJBLS	10//99-12//99
	New York	S	16.24 MW	16.59 AW	34520 AAW	NYBLS	10//99-12//99
	North Carolina	S	6.23 MW	6.70 AW	13930 AAW	NCBLS	10//99-12//99
	North Dakota	S	6.47 MW	6.54 AW	13610 AAW	NDBLS	10//99-12//99
	Ohio	S	6.53 MW	8.03 AW	16700 AAW	OHBLS	10//99-12//99
	Oklahoma	S	6.25 MW	6.59 AW	13700 AAW	OKBLS	10//99-12//99
	Oregon	S	7.45 MW	9.00 AW	18710 AAW	ORBLS	10//99-12//99
	Pennsylvania	S	7.03 MW	7.44 AW	15470 AAW	PABLS	10//99-12//99
	Rhode Island	S	7.9 MW	9.23 AW	19210 AAW	RIBLS	10//99-12//99
	Tennessee	S	6.1 MW	7.47 AW	15530 AAW	TNBLS	10//99-12//99
	Texas	S	6.43 MW	7.02 AW	14600 AAW	TXBLS	10//99-12//99
	Virginia	S	6.73 MW	6.90 AW	14360 AAW	VABLS	10//99-12//99
	Washington	S	9.32 MW	9.57 AW	19900 AAW	WABLS	10//99-12//99
	Wisconsin	S	6.46 MW	7.28 AW	15150 AAW	WIBLS	10//99-12//99
	Puerto Rico	S	6.22 MW	6.33 AW	13160 AAW	PRBLS	10//99-12//99
Motorboat Mechanic	Alabama	S	7.48 MW	8.81 AW	18320 AAW	ALBLS	10//99-12//99
	Alaska	S	15.42 MW	15.35 AW	31920 AAW	AKBLS	10//99-12//99
	Arizona	S	12.85 MW	12.51 AW	26030 AAW	AZBLS	10//99-12//99
	Arkansas	S	9.83 MW	10.44 AW	21700 AAW	ARBLS	10//99-12//99
	California	S	13.09 MW	14.38 AW	29910 AAW	CABLS	10//99-12//99
	Colorado	S	14.82 MW	14.62 AW	30420 AAW	COBLS	10//99-12//99
	Connecticut	S	16.58 MW	17.01 AW	35390 AAW	CTBLS	10//99-12//99
	Florida	S	14.95 MW	15.59 AW	32430 AAW	FLBLS	10//99-12//99
	Georgia	S	15.19 MW	15.33 AW	31880 AAW	GABLS	10//99-12//99
	Hawaii	S	11.28 MW	12.49 AW	25980 AAW	HIBLS	10//99-12//99
	Idaho	S	10.29 MW	10.25 AW	21330 AAW	IDBLS	10//99-12//99
	Illinois	S	10.64 MW	11.44 AW	23790 AAW	ILBLS	10//99-12//99
	Indiana	S	12.2 MW	11.99 AW	24940 AAW	INBLS	10//99-12//99
	Iowa	S	8.51 MW	9.96 AW	20720 AAW	IABLS	10//99-12//99
	Kansas	S	10.28 MW	11.54 AW	24010 AAW	KSBLS	10//99-12//99
	Kentucky	S	9.72 MW	10.73 AW	22320 AAW	KYBLS	10//99-12//99
	Louisiana	S	13.19 MW	14.95 AW	31100 AAW	LABLS	10//99-12//99
	Maine	S	14.59 MW	14.34 AW	29820 AAW	MEBLS	10//99-12//99
	Maryland	S	15.65 MW	17.02 AW	35410 AAW	MDBLS	10//99-12//99
	Massachusetts	S	15.59 MW	15.59 AW	32420 AAW	MABLS	10//99-12//99
	Michigan	S	13.18 MW	13.13 AW	27300 AAW	MIBLS	10//99-12//99
	Minnesota	S	12.62 MW	12.99 AW	27010 AAW	MNBLS	10//99-12//99
	Mississippi	S	12.19 MW	13.41 AW	27900 AAW	MSBLS	10//99-12//99
	Missouri	S	14.08 MW	13.44 AW	27960 AAW	MOBLS	10//99-12//99
	Montana	S	14.8 MW	13.80 AW	28700 AAW	MTBLS	10//99-12//99
	Nebraska	S	8.77 MW	8.85 AW	18410 AAW	NEBLS	10//99-12//99
	Nevada	S	11.04 MW	11.17 AW	23230 AAW	NVBLS	10//99-12//99
	New Hampshire	S	12.02 MW	12.11 AW	25190 AAW	NHBLS	10//99-12//99
	New Jersey	S	12.76 MW	12.75 AW	26520 AAW	NJBLS	10//99-12//99
	New York	S	13.9 MW	14.23 AW	29600 AAW	NYBLS	10//99-12//99
	North Carolina	S	13.65 MW	14.06 AW	29250 AAW	NCBLS	10//99-12//99
	Ohio	S	13.01 MW	13.16 AW	27360 AAW	OHBLS	10//99-12//99
	Oklahoma	S	10.59 MW	11.81 AW	24570 AAW	OKBLS	10//99-12//99
	Oregon	S	12.9 MW	12.85 AW	26730 AAW	ORBLS	10//99-12//99
	Pennsylvania	S	9.94 MW	10.62 AW	22100 AAW	PABLS	10//99-12//99
	Rhode Island	S	16.61 MW	16.20 AW	33710 AAW	RIBLS	10//99-12//99
	South Carolina	S	11.71 MW	11.81 AW	24570 AAW	SCBLS	10//99-12//99
	South Dakota	S	11.05 MW	10.55 AW	21950 AAW	SDBLS	10//99-12//99
	Tennessee	S	12.98 MW	13.47 AW	28020 AAW	TNBLS	10//99-12//99
	Texas	S	11.37 MW	13.08 AW	27210 AAW	TXBLS	10//99-12//99
	Utah	S	13.25 MW	14.71 AW	30610 AAW	UTBLS	10//99-12//99
	Vermont	S	12.24 MW	12.02 AW	25010 AAW	VTBLS	10//99-12//99

AAW Average annual wage	AOH Average offered, high	ASH Average starting, high	H Hourly	M Monthly	S Special: hourly and annual
AE Average entry wage	AOL Average offered, low	ASL Average starting, low	HI Highest wage paid	MTC Median total compensation	TQ Third quartile wage
AEX Average experienced wage	APH Average pay, high range	AW Average wage paid	HR High end range	MW Median wage paid	W Weekly
AO Average offered	APL Average pay, low range	FQ First quartile wage	LR Low end range	SQ Second quartile wage	Y Yearly

Occupation/Type/Industry	Location	Per	Low	Mid	High	Source	Date
Motorboat Mechanic	Virginia	S	9.86 MW	10.59 AW	22030 AAW	VABLS	10//99-12//99
	Washington	S	14.9 MW	15.27 AW	31750 AAW	WABLS	10//99-12//99
	West Virginia	S	8.02 MW	8.42 AW	17520 AAW	WVBLS	10//99-12//99
	Wisconsin	S	11.39 MW	11.62 AW	24170 AAW	WIBLS	10//99-12//99
	Puerto Rico	S	8.22 MW	9.91 AW	20610 AAW	PRBLS	10//99-12//99
	Virgin Islands	S	12.65 MW	13.04 AW	27130 AAW	VIBLS	10//99-12//99
Motorboat Operator	Alabama	S	14.62 MW	15.29 AW	31810 AAW	ALBLS	10//99-12//99
	California	S	19.47 MW	19.85 AW	41300 AAW	CABLS	10//99-12//99
	Connecticut	S	6.91 MW	7.54 AW	15680 AAW	CTBLS	10//99-12//99
	Hawaii	S	15.81 MW	16.49 AW	34300 AAW	HIBLS	10//99-12//99
	Illinois	S	14.14 MW	12.83 AW	26680 AAW	ILBLS	10//99-12//99
	Louisiana	S	12.46 MW	12.86 AW	26740 AAW	LABLS	10//99-12//99
	Michigan	S	10.53 MW	12.79 AW	26600 AAW	MIBLS	10//99-12//99
	New York	S	12.79 MW	13.00 AW	27040 AAW	NYBLS	10//99-12//99
	Pennsylvania	S	17.68 MW	17.52 AW	36450 AAW	PABLS	10//99-12//99
	Texas	S	17.91 MW	16.60 AW	34520 AAW	TXBLS	10//99-12//99
	Virginia	S	16.38 MW	16.10 AW	33490 AAW	VABLS	10//99-12//99
Motorcycle Mechanic	Alabama	S	10.7 MW	10.90 AW	22670 AAW	ALBLS	10//99-12//99
	Birmingham MSA, AL	S	12.44 MW	12.67 AW	25880 AAW	ALBLS	10//99-12//99
	Montgomery MSA, AL	S	9.91 MW	9.63 AW	20600 AAW	ALBLS	10//99-12//99
	Alaska	S	11.05 MW	11.96 AW	24870 AAW	AKBLS	10//99-12//99
	Arizona	S	11.55 MW	12.78 AW	26580 AAW	AZBLS	10//99-12//99
	Phoenix-Mesa MSA, AZ	S	13.84 MW	13.92 AW	28790 AAW	AZBLS	10//99-12//99
	Arkansas	S	9.98 MW	10.07 AW	20940 AAW	ARBLS	10//99-12//99
	Little Rock-North Little Rock MSA, AR	S	10.61 MW	11.41 AW	22070 AAW	ARBLS	10//99-12//99
	California	S	14.01 MW	14.55 AW	30260 AAW	CABLS	10//99-12//99
	Los Angeles-Long Beach PMSA, CA	S	14.97 MW	14.62 AW	31130 AAW	CABLS	10//99-12//99
	Orange County PMSA, CA	S	14.38 MW	14.25 AW	29910 AAW	CABLS	10//99-12//99
	Riverside-San Bernardino PMSA, CA	S	15.15 MW	14.01 AW	31520 AAW	CABLS	10//99-12//99
	Sacramento PMSA, CA	S	13.74 MW	13.89 AW	28580 AAW	CABLS	10//99-12//99
	San Diego MSA, CA	S	15.52 MW	15.22 AW	32280 AAW	CABLS	10//99-12//99
	San Francisco PMSA, CA	S	17.06 MW	15.56 AW	35490 AAW	CABLS	10//99-12//99
	San Jose PMSA, CA	S	14.14 MW	13.12 AW	29420 AAW	CABLS	10//99-12//99
	Ventura PMSA, CA	S	16.04 MW	13.84 AW	33360 AAW	CABLS	10//99-12//99
	Colorado	S	12.02 MW	12.51 AW	26030 AAW	COBLS	10//99-12//99
	Denver PMSA, CO	S	13.31 MW	12.77 AW	27680 AAW	COBLS	10//99-12//99
	Grand Junction MSA, CO	S	9.93 MW	11.02 AW	20650 AAW	COBLS	10//99-12//99
	Connecticut	S	12.47 MW	12.81 AW	26640 AAW	CTBLS	10//99-12//99
	Hartford MSA, CT	S	11.02 MW	10.35 AW	22920 AAW	CTBLS	10//99-12//99
	Washington PMSA, DC-MD-VA-WV	S	13.14 MW	12.91 AW	27330 AAW	DCBLS	10//99-12//99
	Florida	S	10.29 MW	10.87 AW	22610 AAW	FLBLS	10//99-12//99
	Daytona Beach MSA, FL	S	8.49 MW	6.75 AW	17670 AAW	FLBLS	10//99-12//99
	Jacksonville MSA, FL	S	11.09 MW	9.92 AW	23060 AAW	FLBLS	10//99-12//99
	Miami PMSA, FL	S	11.46 MW	10.95 AW	23830 AAW	FLBLS	10//99-12//99
	Tampa-St. Petersburg-Clearwater MSA, FL	S	10.70 MW	10.27 AW	22260 AAW	FLBLS	10//99-12//99
	Georgia	S	11.05 MW	11.72 AW	24370 AAW	GABLS	10//99-12//99
	Atlanta MSA, GA	S	14.06 MW	13.84 AW	29250 AAW	GABLS	10//99-12//99
	Augusta-Aiken MSA, GA-SC	S	12.60 MW	11.69 AW	26210 AAW	GABLS	10//99-12//99
	Idaho	S	12.65 MW	13.30 AW	27660 AAW	IDBLS	10//99-12//99
	Boise City MSA, ID	S	13.76 MW	12.95 AW	28620 AAW	IDBLS	10//99-12//99
	Illinois	S	14.77 MW	14.54 AW	30250 AAW	ILBLS	10//99-12//99
	Chicago PMSA, IL	S	15.85 MW	16.34 AW	32970 AAW	ILBLS	10//99-12//99
	Indiana	S	13.14 MW	12.91 AW	26850 AAW	INBLS	10//99-12//99
	Gary PMSA, IN	S	10.74 MW	9.41 AW	22330 AAW	INBLS	10//99-12//99
	Indianapolis MSA, IN	S	14.41 MW	15.00 AW	29970 AAW	INBLS	10//99-12//99
	Iowa	S	10.31 MW	10.27 AW	21360 AAW	IABLS	10//99-12//99
	Kansas	S	11.1 MW	11.09 AW	23070 AAW	KSBLS	10//99-12//99
	Wichita MSA, KS	S	10.05 MW	10.38 AW	20910 AAW	KSBLS	10//99-12//99
	Kentucky	S	8.08 MW	8.70 AW	18090 AAW	KYBLS	10//99-12//99
	Lexington MSA, KY	S	9.48 MW	8.03 AW	19720 AAW	KYBLS	10//99-12//99
	Louisville MSA, KY-IN	S	9.03 MW	8.08 AW	18780 AAW	KYBLS	10//99-12//99
	Louisiana	S	10.08 MW	10.83 AW	22520 AAW	LABLS	10//99-12//99
	Maine	S	9.28 MW	10.20 AW	21210 AAW	MEBLS	10//99-12//99
	Maryland	S	12.81 MW	13.40 AW	27870 AAW	MDBLS	10//99-12//99
	Massachusetts	S	12.43 MW	12.72 AW	26470 AAW	MABLS	10//99-12//99
	Boston PMSA, MA-NH	S	12.55 MW	12.55 AW	26110 AAW	MABLS	10//99-12//99

AAW	Average annual wage	AOH	Average offered, high	ASH	Average starting, high	H	Hourly	M	Monthly	S	Special: hourly and annual
AE	Average entry wage	AOL	Average offered, low	ASL	Average starting, low	HI	Highest wage paid	MTC	Median total compensation	TQ	Third quartile wage
AEX	Average experienced wage	APH	Average pay, high range	AW	Average wage paid	HR	High end range	MW	Median wage paid	W	Weekly
AO	Average offered	APL	Average pay, low range	FQ	First quartile wage	LR	Low end range	SQ	Second quartile wage	Y	Yearly

Occupation/Type/Industry	Location	Per	Low	Mid	High	Source	Date
Motorcycle Mechanic	Springfield MSA, MA	S	12.74 MW	13.57 AW	26510 AAW	MABLS	10//99-12//99
	Michigan	S	12.09 MW	13.47 AW	28030 AAW	MIBLS	10//99-12//99
	Detroit PMSA, MI	S	15.22 MW	14.99 AW	31650 AAW	MIBLS	10//99-12//99
	Saginaw-Bay City-Midland MSA, MI	S	11.50 MW	10.76 AW	23930 AAW	MIBLS	10//99-12//99
	Minnesota	S	11.62 MW	11.48 AW	23870 AAW	MNBLS	10//99-12//99
	Minneapolis-St. Paul MSA, MN-WI	S	11.72 MW	11.67 AW	24370 AAW	MNBLS	10//99-12//99
	Mississippi	S	10.52 MW	10.89 AW	22660 AAW	MSBLS	10//99-12//99
	Biloxi-Gulfport-Pascagoula MSA, MS	S	9.26 MW	9.12 AW	19270 AAW	MSBLS	10//99-12//99
	Missouri	S	9.54 MW	9.82 AW	20420 AAW	MOBLS	10//99-12//99
	Kansas City MSA, MO-KS	S	9.92 MW	9.71 AW	20630 AAW	MOBLS	10//99-12//99
	St. Louis MSA, MO-IL	S	11.15 MW	10.07 AW	23200 AAW	MOBLS	10//99-12//99
	Montana	S	8.73 MW	9.81 AW	20400 AAW	MTBLS	10//99-12//99
	Billings MSA, MT	S	11.03 MW	10.75 AW	22940 AAW	MTBLS	10//99-12//99
	Nebraska	S	10.59 MW	10.91 AW	22690 AAW	NEBLS	10//99-12//99
	Nevada	S	14.71 MW	14.78 AW	30750 AAW	NVBLS	10//99-12//99
	Las Vegas MSA, NV-AZ	S	16.01 MW	14.95 AW	33290 AAW	NVBLS	10//99-12//99
	Reno MSA, NV	S	13.78 MW	14.61 AW	28670 AAW	NVBLS	10//99-12//99
	New Hampshire	S	12.96 MW	12.63 AW	26270 AAW	NHBLS	10//99-12//99
	Manchester PMSA, NH	S	12.33 MW	12.89 AW	25650 AAW	NHBLS	10//99-12//99
	New Jersey	S	11.28 MW	12.38 AW	25750 AAW	NJBLS	10//99-12//99
	Bergen-Passaic PMSA, NJ	S	13.36 MW	13.93 AW	27780 AAW	NJBLS	10//99-12//99
	Middlesex-Somerset-Hunterdon PMSA, NJ	S	11.91 MW	11.02 AW	24780 AAW	NJBLS	10//99-12//99
	New Mexico	S	10.24 MW	11.69 AW	24310 AAW	NMBLS	10//99-12//99
	Albuquerque MSA, NM	S	13.93 MW	13.97 AW	28980 AAW	NMBLS	10//99-12//99
	New York	S	11.36 MW	11.75 AW	24440 AAW	NYBLS	10//99-12//99
	Buffalo-Niagara Falls MSA, NY	S	11.85 MW	12.39 AW	24650 AAW	NYBLS	10//99-12//99
	Jamestown MSA, NY	S	10.65 MW	10.87 AW	22160 AAW	NYBLS	10//99-12//99
	Nassau-Suffolk PMSA, NY	S	10.84 MW	10.97 AW	22540 AAW	NYBLS	10//99-12//99
	New York PMSA, NY	S	15.48 MW	16.96 AW	32200 AAW	NYBLS	10//99-12//99
	Rochester MSA, NY	S	11.03 MW	10.87 AW	22950 AAW	NYBLS	10//99-12//99
	Syracuse MSA, NY	S	9.79 MW	9.20 AW	20350 AAW	NYBLS	10//99-12//99
	North Carolina	S	10.53 MW	10.91 AW	22690 AAW	NCBLS	10//99-12//99
	Fayetteville MSA, NC	S	12.12 MW	11.55 AW	25210 AAW	NCBLS	10//99-12//99
	Greensboro--Winston-Salem--High Point MSA, NC	S	11.46 MW	10.33 AW	23840 AAW	NCBLS	10//99-12//99
	Raleigh-Durham-Chapel Hill MSA, NC	S	8.99 MW	6.88 AW	18690 AAW	NCBLS	10//99-12//99
	Wilmington MSA, NC	S	12.44 MW	12.37 AW	25880 AAW	NCBLS	10//99-12//99
	North Dakota	S	10.86 MW	11.46 AW	23840 AAW	NDBLS	10//99-12//99
	Ohio	S	10.57 MW	11.26 AW	23410 AAW	OHBLS	10//99-12//99
	Canton-Massillon MSA, OH	S	10.63 MW	11.00 AW	22110 AAW	OHBLS	10//99-12//99
	Cleveland-Lorain-Elyria PMSA, OH	S	11.92 MW	12.28 AW	24790 AAW	OHBLS	10//99-12//99
	Columbus MSA, OH	S	15.44 MW	15.58 AW	32120 AAW	OHBLS	10//99-12//99
	Hamilton-Middletown PMSA, OH	S	13.87 MW	14.59 AW	28850 AAW	OHBLS	10//99-12//99
	Youngstown-Warren MSA, OH	S	9.86 MW	9.73 AW	20510 AAW	OHBLS	10//99-12//99
	Oklahoma	S	10.5 MW	11.11 AW	23100 AAW	OKBLS	10//99-12//99
	Tulsa MSA, OK	S	10.72 MW	10.75 AW	22290 AAW	OKBLS	10//99-12//99
	Oregon	S	12.07 MW	12.57 AW	26150 AAW	ORBLS	10//99-12//99
	Portland-Vancouver PMSA, OR-WA	S	13.07 MW	12.15 AW	27180 AAW	ORBLS	10//99-12//99
	Pennsylvania	S	10.74 MW	11.40 AW	23710 AAW	PABLS	10//99-12//99
	Lancaster MSA, PA	S	11.88 MW	11.39 AW	24720 AAW	PABLS	10//99-12//99
	Philadelphia PMSA, PA-NJ	S	13.34 MW	12.49 AW	27760 AAW	PABLS	10//99-12//99
	Pittsburgh MSA, PA	S	10.13 MW	10.21 AW	21060 AAW	PABLS	10//99-12//99
	Rhode Island	S	10.57 MW	11.35 AW	23600 AAW	RIBLS	10//99-12//99
	Providence-Fall River-Warwick MSA, RI-MA	S	11.35 MW	10.58 AW	23620 AAW	RIBLS	10//99-12//99
	South Carolina	S	11.65 MW	12.55 AW	26100 AAW	SCBLS	10//99-12//99
	Greenville-Spartanburg-Anderson MSA, SC	S	12.44 MW	11.77 AW	25870 AAW	SCBLS	10//99-12//99
	South Dakota	S	10.68 MW	11.34 AW	23580 AAW	SDBLS	10//99-12//99
	Tennessee	S	11.71 MW	11.57 AW	24080 AAW	TNBLS	10//99-12//99
	Knoxville MSA, TN	S	11.11 MW	10.61 AW	23110 AAW	TNBLS	10//99-12//99
	Memphis MSA, TN-AR-MS	S	12.23 MW	12.25 AW	25440 AAW	MSBLS	10//99-12//99
	Nashville MSA, TN	S	11.07 MW	10.55 AW	23020 AAW	TNBLS	10//99-12//99

AAW Average annual wage	**AOH** Average offered, high	**ASH** Average starting, high	**H** Hourly	**M** Monthly	**S** Special: hourly and annual
AE Average entry wage	**AOL** Average offered, low	**ASL** Average starting, low	**HI** Highest wage paid	**MTC** Median total compensation	**TQ** Third quartile wage
AEX Average experienced wage	**APH** Average pay, high range	**AW** Average wage paid	**HR** High end range	**MW** Median wage paid	**W** Weekly
AO Average offered	**APL** Average pay, low range	**FQ** First quartile wage	**LR** Low end range	**SQ** Second quartile wage	**Y** Yearly

Occupation/Type/Industry	Location	Per	Low	Mid	High	Source	Date
Motorcycle Mechanic	Texas	S	11.39 MW	12.25 AW	25480 AAW	TXBLS	10//99-12//99
	Austin-San Marcos MSA, TX	S	14.19 MW	13.85 AW	29510 AAW	TXBLS	10//99-12//99
	Dallas PMSA, TX	S	13.84 MW	13.15 AW	28780 AAW	TXBLS	10//99-12//99
	Fort Worth-Arlington PMSA, TX	S	11.90 MW	10.99 AW	24760 AAW	TXBLS	10//99-12//99
	Houston PMSA, TX	S	13.35 MW	12.24 AW	27770 AAW	TXBLS	10//99-12//99
	Killeen-Temple MSA, TX	S	12.12 MW	13.02 AW	25210 AAW	TXBLS	10//99-12//99
	Longview-Marshall MSA, TX	S	18.71 MW	17.95 AW	38910 AAW	TXBLS	10//99-12//99
	Waco MSA, TX	S	11.61 MW	11.73 AW	24140 AAW	TXBLS	10//99-12//99
	Wichita Falls MSA, TX	S	8.32 MW	7.91 AW	17300 AAW	TXBLS	10//99-12//99
	Utah	S	14.05 MW	13.47 AW	28020 AAW	UTBLS	10//99-12//99
	Provo-Orem MSA, UT	S	13.97 MW	14.01 AW	29060 AAW	UTBLS	10//99-12//99
	Vermont	S	12.45 MW	12.37 AW	25740 AAW	VTBLS	10//99-12//99
	Virginia	S	10.72 MW	11.30 AW	23500 AAW	VABLS	10//99-12//99
	Norfolk-Virginia Beach-Newport News MSA, VA-NC	S	9.20 MW	7.90 AW	19140 AAW	VABLS	10//99-12//99
	Richmond-Petersburg MSA, VA	S	12.13 MW	11.67 AW	25240 AAW	VABLS	10//99-12//99
	Washington	S	12.63 MW	13.51 AW	28110 AAW	WABLS	10//99-12//99
	Seattle-Bellevue-Everett PMSA, WA	S	15.05 MW	13.17 AW	31300 AAW	WABLS	10//99-12//99
	West Virginia	S	7.84 MW	8.05 AW	16730 AAW	WVBLS	10//99-12//99
	Wisconsin	S	11.68 MW	12.07 AW	25100 AAW	WIBLS	10//99-12//99
	Milwaukee-Waukesha PMSA, WI	S	14.00 MW	13.85 AW	29130 AAW	WIBLS	10//99-12//99
	Wyoming	S	12.35 MW	12.90 AW	26820 AAW	WYBLS	10//99-12//99
Movie Critic	United States	W		572 AW		MENHEL	1999
Multi-Media Artist and Animator	Alabama	S	15.61 MW	15.89 AW	33050 AAW	ALBLS	10//99-12//99
	Arizona	S	17.91 MW	19.63 AW	40840 AAW	AZBLS	10//99-12//99
	Arkansas	S	7.81 MW	8.81 AW	18330 AAW	ARBLS	10//99-12//99
	California	S	23.89 MW	24.40 AW	50750 AAW	CABLS	10//99-12//99
	Colorado	S	16.43 MW	17.24 AW	35860 AAW	COBLS	10//99-12//99
	Connecticut	S	22.36 MW	26.98 AW	56110 AAW	CTBLS	10//99-12//99
	District of Columbia	S	23.08 MW	22.06 AW	45890 AAW	DCBLS	10//99-12//99
	Florida	S	16.15 MW	17.49 AW	36370 AAW	FLBLS	10//99-12//99
	Georgia	S	16.61 MW	20.16 AW	41930 AAW	GABLS	10//99-12//99
	Hawaii	S	17 MW	24.64 AW	51240 AAW	HIBLS	10//99-12//99
	Illinois	S	14.78 MW	15.84 AW	32950 AAW	ILBLS	10//99-12//99
	Indiana	S	15.65 MW	16.97 AW	35290 AAW	INBLS	10//99-12//99
	Iowa	S	13.06 MW	14.65 AW	30470 AAW	IABLS	10//99-12//99
	Kansas	S	12.78 MW	13.05 AW	27140 AAW	KSBLS	10//99-12//99
	Kentucky	S	12.72 MW	14.60 AW	30370 AAW	KYBLS	10//99-12//99
	Louisiana	S	13.16 MW	14.75 AW	30670 AAW	LABLS	10//99-12//99
	Maryland	S	19.54 MW	21.34 AW	44390 AAW	MDBLS	10//99-12//99
	Massachusetts	S	18.31 MW	19.84 AW	41270 AAW	MABLS	10//99-12//99
	Michigan	S	22.53 MW	22.68 AW	47180 AAW	MIBLS	10//99-12//99
	Minnesota	S	20.61 MW	20.71 AW	43080 AAW	MNBLS	10//99-12//99
	Missouri	S	16.03 MW	18.26 AW	37980 AAW	MOBLS	10//99-12//99
	Nebraska	S	11.85 MW	12.47 AW	25930 AAW	NEBLS	10//99-12//99
	Nevada	S	16.34 MW	16.77 AW	34880 AAW	NVBLS	10//99-12//99
	New Hampshire	S	20.17 MW	20.44 AW	42510 AAW	NHBLS	10//99-12//99
	New Jersey	S	16.1 MW	19.99 AW	41580 AAW	NJBLS	10//99-12//99
	New Mexico	S	18.57 MW	18.19 AW	37830 AAW	NMBLS	10//99-12//99
	New York	S	19.8 MW	23.41 AW	48680 AAW	NYBLS	10//99-12//99
	North Carolina	S	16.74 MW	18.23 AW	37930 AAW	NCBLS	10//99-12//99
	North Dakota	S	11.07 MW	10.30 AW	21420 AAW	NDBLS	10//99-12//99
	Ohio	S	15.41 MW	16.30 AW	33900 AAW	OHBLS	10//99-12//99
	Oklahoma	S	12.38 MW	14.36 AW	29870 AAW	OKBLS	10//99-12//99
	Pennsylvania	S	17.99 MW	18.82 AW	39140 AAW	PABLS	10//99-12//99
	Rhode Island	S	16.98 MW	18.48 AW	38440 AAW	RIBLS	10//99-12//99
	South Carolina	S	14.12 MW	17.32 AW	36030 AAW	SCBLS	10//99-12//99
	South Dakota	S	12.17 MW	12.86 AW	26750 AAW	SDBLS	10//99-12//99
	Tennessee	S	14.37 MW	16.20 AW	33690 AAW	TNBLS	10//99-12//99
	Texas	S	21.04 MW	22.52 AW	46840 AAW	TXBLS	10//99-12//99
	Utah	S	19.2 MW	19.49 AW	40540 AAW	UTBLS	10//99-12//99
	Vermont	S	23.92 MW	25.35 AW	52720 AAW	VTBLS	10//99-12//99
	Virginia	S	20.42 MW	20.64 AW	42930 AAW	VABLS	10//99-12//99
	Washington	S	15.52 MW	16.16 AW	33620 AAW	WABLS	10//99-12//99
	Wisconsin	S	17.1 MW	18.28 AW	38030 AAW	WIBLS	10//99-12//99
	Puerto Rico	S	17.99 MW	18.27 AW	38000 AAW	PRBLS	10//99-12//99

Occupation/Type/Industry	Location	Per	Low	Mid	High	Source	Date
Multiple Machine Tool Setter, Operator, and Tender							
Metals and Plastics	Alabama	S	11.14 MW	11.71 AW	24360 AAW	ALBLS	10//99-12//99
Metals and Plastics	Arizona	S	9.57 MW	9.93 AW	20660 AAW	AZBLS	10//99-12//99
Metals and Plastics	Arkansas	S	10.73 MW	10.94 AW	22750 AAW	ARBLS	10//99-12//99
Metals and Plastics	California	S	10.89 MW	12.06 AW	25090 AAW	CABLS	10//99-12//99
Metals and Plastics	Colorado	S	11.19 MW	11.42 AW	23760 AAW	COBLS	10//99-12//99
Metals and Plastics	Connecticut	S	14.17 MW	14.18 AW	29500 AAW	CTBLS	10//99-12//99
Metals and Plastics	Florida	S	11.74 MW	12.68 AW	26370 AAW	FLBLS	10//99-12//99
Metals and Plastics	Georgia	S	11.72 MW	11.86 AW	24670 AAW	GABLS	10//99-12//99
Metals and Plastics	Idaho	S	9.04 MW	9.61 AW	19990 AAW	IDBLS	10//99-12//99
Metals and Plastics	Illinois	S	11.91 MW	12.44 AW	25870 AAW	ILBLS	10//99-12//99
Metals and Plastics	Indiana	S	12.97 MW	14.36 AW	29870 AAW	INBLS	10//99-12//99
Metals and Plastics	Iowa	S	10.86 MW	11.51 AW	23940 AAW	IABLS	10//99-12//99
Metals and Plastics	Kansas	S	11.36 MW	11.85 AW	24640 AAW	KSBLS	10//99-12//99
Metals and Plastics	Kentucky	S	11.54 MW	11.39 AW	23680 AAW	KYBLS	10//99-12//99
Metals and Plastics	Louisiana	S	10.64 MW	12.38 AW	25750 AAW	LABLS	10//99-12//99
Metals and Plastics	Maine	S	10.16 MW	10.50 AW	21830 AAW	MEBLS	10//99-12//99
Metals and Plastics	Maryland	S	12.84 MW	12.96 AW	26950 AAW	MDBLS	10//99-12//99
Metals and Plastics	Massachusetts	S	11.73 MW	13.11 AW	27270 AAW	MABLS	10//99-12//99
Metals and Plastics	Michigan	S	14.9 MW	16.32 AW	33950 AAW	MIBLS	10//99-12//99
Metals and Plastics	Minnesota	S	15.93 MW	16.04 AW	33370 AAW	MNBLS	10//99-12//99
Metals and Plastics	Mississippi	S	11.18 MW	11.41 AW	23730 AAW	MSBLS	10//99-12//99
Metals and Plastics	Missouri	S	10.47 MW	10.97 AW	22830 AAW	MOBLS	10//99-12//99
Metals and Plastics	Montana	S	9.93 MW	10.56 AW	21970 AAW	MTBLS	10//99-12//99
Metals and Plastics	Nebraska	S	12.12 MW	12.30 AW	25590 AAW	NEBLS	10//99-12//99
Metals and Plastics	Nevada	S	10.73 MW	11.45 AW	23820 AAW	NVBLS	10//99-12//99
Metals and Plastics	New Hampshire	S	10.58 MW	10.96 AW	22810 AAW	NHBLS	10//99-12//99
Metals and Plastics	New Jersey	S	11.13 MW	11.92 AW	24780 AAW	NJBLS	10//99-12//99
Metals and Plastics	New Mexico	S	9.59 MW	9.56 AW	19880 AAW	NMBLS	10//99-12//99
Metals and Plastics	New York	S	10.69 MW	12.00 AW	24970 AAW	NYBLS	10//99-12//99
Metals and Plastics	North Carolina	S	12.36 MW	12.50 AW	26010 AAW	NCBLS	10//99-12//99
Metals and Plastics	North Dakota	S	10.3 MW	11.15 AW	23200 AAW	NDBLS	10//99-12//99
Metals and Plastics	Oklahoma	S	10.91 MW	11.40 AW	23720 AAW	OKBLS	10//99-12//99
Metals and Plastics	Oregon	S	12.68 MW	12.69 AW	26390 AAW	ORBLS	10//99-12//99
Metals and Plastics	Pennsylvania	S	12.16 MW	12.05 AW	25070 AAW	PABLS	10//99-12//99
Metals and Plastics	Rhode Island	S	11.25 MW	11.69 AW	24320 AAW	RIBLS	10//99-12//99
Metals and Plastics	South Carolina	S	12.27 MW	13.01 AW	27070 AAW	SCBLS	10//99-12//99
Metals and Plastics	South Dakota	S	10.43 MW	10.49 AW	21820 AAW	SDBLS	10//99-12//99
Metals and Plastics	Tennessee	S	10.53 MW	10.97 AW	22830 AAW	TNBLS	10//99-12//99
Metals and Plastics	Texas	S	10.43 MW	11.22 AW	23330 AAW	TXBLS	10//99-12//99
Metals and Plastics	Utah	S	10.39 MW	10.89 AW	22660 AAW	UTBLS	10//99-12//99
Metals and Plastics	Vermont	S	12.34 MW	12.65 AW	26300 AAW	VTBLS	10//99-12//99
Metals and Plastics	Virginia	S	12.05 MW	11.74 AW	24420 AAW	VABLS	10//99-12//99
Metals and Plastics	Washington	S	11.69 MW	12.36 AW	25700 AAW	WABLS	10//99-12//99
Metals and Plastics	West Virginia	S	12.17 MW	11.62 AW	24180 AAW	WVBLS	10//99-12//99
Metals and Plastics	Wisconsin	S	13.17 MW	13.72 AW	28550 AAW	WIBLS	10//99-12//99
Metals and Plastics	Puerto Rico	S	7.07 MW	7.41 AW	15420 AAW	PRBLS	10//99-12//99
Music Director and Composer	Alabama	Y		20370 AAW		ALBLS	10//99-12//99
	Arizona	Y		27200 AAW		AZBLS	10//99-12//99
	California	Y		35720 AAW		CABLS	10//99-12//99
	Los Angeles-Long Beach PMSA, CA	Y		44700 AAW		CABLS	10//99-12//99
	San Diego MSA, CA	Y		24980 AAW		CABLS	10//99-12//99
	San Francisco PMSA, CA	Y		44600 AAW		CABLS	10//99-12//99
	San Luis Obispo-Atascadero-Paso Robles MSA, CA	Y		25990 AAW		CABLS	10//99-12//99
	Connecticut	Y		37130 AAW		CTBLS	10//99-12//99
	Hartford MSA, CT	Y		38030 AAW		CTBLS	10//99-12//99
	District of Columbia	Y		60870 AAW		DCBLS	10//99-12//99
	Florida	Y		25510 AAW		FLBLS	10//99-12//99
	Fort Lauderdale PMSA, FL	Y		26660 AAW		FLBLS	10//99-12//99
	Fort Myers-Cape Coral MSA, FL	Y		24820 AAW		FLBLS	10//99-12//99
	Orlando MSA, FL	Y		27690 AAW		FLBLS	10//99-12//99
	Tampa-St. Petersburg-Clearwater MSA, FL	Y		25120 AAW		FLBLS	10//99-12//99
	Georgia	Y		35600 AAW		GABLS	10//99-12//99
	Atlanta MSA, GA	Y		42810 AAW		GABLS	10//99-12//99
	Illinois	Y		27780 AAW		ILBLS	10//99-12//99
	Chicago PMSA, IL	Y		25570 AAW		ILBLS	10//99-12//99

AAW Average annual wage	**AOH** Average offered, high	**ASH** Average starting, high	**H** Hourly	**M** Monthly	**S** Special: hourly and annual
AE Average entry wage	**AOL** Average offered, low	**ASL** Average starting, low	**HI** Highest wage paid	**MTC** Median total compensation	**TQ** Third quartile wage
AEX Average experienced wage	**APH** Average pay, high range	**AW** Average wage paid	**HR** High end range	**MW** Median wage paid	**W** Weekly
AO Average offered	**APL** Average pay, low range	**FQ** First quartile wage	**LR** Low end range	**SQ** Second quartile wage	**Y** Yearly

Occupation/Type/Industry	Location	Per	Low	Mid	High	Source	Date
Music Director and Composer	Indiana	Y		29500 AAW		INBLS	10//99-12//99
	Iowa	Y		39250 AAW		IABLS	10//99-12//99
	Louisiana	Y		37860 AAW		LABLS	10//99-12//99
	Maryland	Y		36510 AAW		MDBLS	10//99-12//99
	Baltimore PMSA, MD	Y		33370 AAW		MDBLS	10//99-12//99
	Massachusetts	Y		39070 AAW		MABLS	10//99-12//99
	Boston PMSA, MA-NH	Y		40570 AAW		MABLS	10//99-12//99
	Detroit PMSA, MI	Y		23220 AAW		MIBLS	10//99-12//99
	Minnesota	Y		37310 AAW		MNBLS	10//99-12//99
	Minneapolis-St. Paul MSA, MN-WI	Y		29880 AAW		MNBLS	10//99-12//99
	Missouri	Y		41360 AAW		MOBLS	10//99-12//99
	New Jersey	Y		43820 AAW		NJBLS	10//99-12//99
	New York	Y		42600 AAW		NYBLS	10//99-12//99
	Nassau-Suffolk PMSA, NY	Y		19570 AAW		NYBLS	10//99-12//99
	New York PMSA, NY	Y		69570 AAW		NYBLS	10//99-12//99
	North Carolina	Y		36230 AAW		NCBLS	10//99-12//99
	Raleigh-Durham-Chapel Hill MSA, NC	Y		37630 AAW		NCBLS	10//99-12//99
	Columbus MSA, OH	Y		38040 AAW		OHBLS	10//99-12//99
	Oklahoma	Y		33280 AAW		OKBLS	10//99-12//99
	Oregon	Y		30330 AAW		ORBLS	10//99-12//99
	Corvallis MSA, OR	Y		34780 AAW		ORBLS	10//99-12//99
	Medford-Ashland MSA, OR	Y		34700 AAW		ORBLS	10//99-12//99
	Portland-Vancouver PMSA, OR-WA	Y		29810 AAW		ORBLS	10//99-12//99
	Pennsylvania	Y		74030 AAW		PABLS	10//99-12//99
	Philadelphia PMSA, PA-NJ	Y		90870 AAW		PABLS	10//99-12//99
	Tennessee	Y		55120 AAW		TNBLS	10//99-12//99
	Knoxville MSA, TN	Y		52620 AAW		TNBLS	10//99-12//99
	Texas	Y		24250 AAW		TXBLS	10//99-12//99
	Virginia	Y		42750 AAW		VABLS	10//99-12//99
	Washington	Y		38320 AAW		WABLS	10//99-12//99
	Puerto Rico	Y		21950 AAW		PRBLS	10//99-12//99
	San Juan-Bayamon PMSA, PR	Y		20610 AAW		PRBLS	10//99-12//99
Musical Instrument Repairer and Tuner	Alabama	S	12.18 MW	11.79 AW	24520 AAW	ALBLS	10//99-12//99
	California	S	11.3 MW	11.17 AW	23230 AAW	CABLS	10//99-12//99
	Florida	S	10.86 MW	12.72 AW	26450 AAW	FLBLS	10//99-12//99
	Georgia	S	13.95 MW	12.72 AW	26460 AAW	GABLS	10//99-12//99
	Illinois	S	10.31 MW	11.25 AW	23400 AAW	ILBLS	10//99-12//99
	Indiana	S	12.22 MW	12.84 AW	26710 AAW	INBLS	10//99-12//99
	Iowa	S	17.16 MW	17.31 AW	36010 AAW	IABLS	10//99-12//99
	Kansas	S	10.67 MW	11.93 AW	24820 AAW	KSBLS	10//99-12//99
	Kentucky	S	10.46 MW	10.69 AW	22230 AAW	KYBLS	10//99-12//99
	Louisiana	S	11.14 MW	11.27 AW	23440 AAW	LABLS	10//99-12//99
	Maryland	S	13.18 MW	14.64 AW	30440 AAW	MDBLS	10//99-12//99
	Massachusetts	S	15.93 MW	16.49 AW	34290 AAW	MABLS	10//99-12//99
	Michigan	S	16.13 MW	16.34 AW	33990 AAW	MIBLS	10//99-12//99
	Minnesota	S	11.8 MW	12.98 AW	27000 AAW	MNBLS	10//99-12//99
	Mississippi	S	8.77 MW	9.50 AW	19760 AAW	MSBLS	10//99-12//99
	Missouri	S	13.13 MW	13.43 AW	27930 AAW	MOBLS	10//99-12//99
	New Jersey	S	11.63 MW	12.83 AW	26690 AAW	NJBLS	10//99-12//99
	New York	S	12.82 MW	12.81 AW	26650 AAW	NYBLS	10//99-12//99
	North Carolina	S	13.93 MW	13.20 AW	27450 AAW	NCBLS	10//99-12//99
	Ohio	S	12.21 MW	11.88 AW	24700 AAW	OHBLS	10//99-12//99
	Oregon	S	9.61 MW	10.88 AW	22640 AAW	ORBLS	10//99-12//99
	Pennsylvania	S	14.59 MW	14.73 AW	30630 AAW	PABLS	10//99-12//99
	Rhode Island	S	9.24 MW	9.22 AW	19180 AAW	RIBLS	10//99-12//99
	South Carolina	S	6.93 MW	8.59 AW	17860 AAW	SCBLS	10//99-12//99
	Tennessee	S	9.66 MW	9.89 AW	20580 AAW	TNBLS	10//99-12//99
	Texas	S	15.15 MW	16.43 AW	34180 AAW	TXBLS	10//99-12//99
	Virginia	S	12.09 MW	12.15 AW	25260 AAW	VABLS	10//99-12//99
	Washington	S	14.02 MW	15.80 AW	32860 AAW	WABLS	10//99-12//99
	Wisconsin	S	11.4 MW	13.39 AW	27850 AAW	WIBLS	10//99-12//99
Musician and Singer	Alabama	Y		36190 AAW		ALBLS	10//99-12//99
	California	Y		37090 AAW		CABLS	10//99-12//99
	Oakland PMSA, CA	Y		51250 AAW		CABLS	10//99-12//99
	Orange County PMSA, CA	Y		35270 AAW		CABLS	10//99-12//99
	San Francisco PMSA, CA	Y		67740 AAW		CABLS	10//99-12//99

AAW	Average annual wage	AOH	Average offered, high	ASH	Average starting, high	H	Hourly	M	Monthly	S	Special: hourly and annual
AE	Average entry wage	AOL	Average offered, low	ASL	Average starting, low	HI	Highest wage paid	MTC	Median total compensation	TQ	Third quartile wage
AEX	Average experienced wage	APH	Average pay, high range	AW	Average wage paid	HR	High end range	MW	Median wage paid	W	Weekly
AO	Average offered	APL	Average pay, low range	FQ	First quartile wage	LR	Low end range	SQ	Second quartile wage	Y	Yearly

Occupation/Type/Industry	Location	Per	Low	Mid	High	Source	Date
Musician and Singer	Santa Barbara-Santa Maria-Lompoc MSA, CA	Y		25760 AAW		CABLS	10//99-12//99
	Delaware	Y		75000 AAW		DEBLS	10//99-12//99
	District of Columbia	Y		34310 AAW		DCBLS	10//99-12//99
	Washington PMSA, DC-MD-VA-WV	Y		41660 AAW		DCBLS	10//99-12//99
	Florida	Y		34480 AAW		FLBLS	10//99-12//99
	Fort Lauderdale PMSA, FL	Y		44400 AAW		FLBLS	10//99-12//99
	Jacksonville MSA, FL	Y		29500 AAW		FLBLS	10//99-12//99
	Miami PMSA, FL	Y		30110 AAW		FLBLS	10//99-12//99
	Orlando MSA, FL	Y		63070 AAW		FLBLS	10//99-12//99
	Georgia	Y		43900 AAW		GABLS	10//99-12//99
	Hawaii	Y		35090 AAW		HIBLS	10//99-12//99
	Honolulu MSA, HI	Y		31960 AAW		HIBLS	10//99-12//99
	Indiana	Y		22700 AAW		INBLS	10//99-12//99
	Fort Wayne MSA, IN	Y		17110 AAW		INBLS	10//99-12//99
	Wichita MSA, KS	Y		19780 AAW		KSBLS	10//99-12//99
	Kentucky	Y		32570 AAW		KYBLS	10//99-12//99
	Louisiana	Y		15230 AAW		LABLS	10//99-12//99
	Massachusetts	Y		21680 AAW		MABLS	10//99-12//99
	Springfield MSA, MA	Y		19760 AAW		MABLS	10//99-12//99
	Detroit PMSA, MI	Y		52730 AAW		MIBLS	10//99-12//99
	Kalamazoo-Battle Creek MSA, MI	Y		34530 AAW		MIBLS	10//99-12//99
	Minnesota	Y		46550 AAW		MNBLS	10//99-12//99
	Minneapolis-St. Paul MSA, MN-WI	Y		47010 AAW		MNBLS	10//99-12//99
	Missouri	Y		40780 AAW		MOBLS	10//99-12//99
	Kansas City MSA, MO-KS	Y		19290 AAW		MOBLS	10//99-12//99
	Montana	Y		39850 AAW		MTBLS	10//99-12//99
	Nebraska	Y		30270 AAW		NEBLS	10//99-12//99
	Lincoln MSA, NE	Y		35000 AAW		NEBLS	10//99-12//99
	Nevada	Y		39510 AAW		NVBLS	10//99-12//99
	Las Vegas MSA, NV-AZ	Y		39140 AAW		NVBLS	10//99-12//99
	New Jersey	Y		60370 AAW		NJBLS	10//99-12//99
	New York	Y		38730 AAW		NYBLS	10//99-12//99
	New York PMSA, NY	Y		41950 AAW		NYBLS	10//99-12//99
	Charlotte-Gastonia-Rock Hill MSA, NC-SC	Y		65090 AAW		NCBLS	10//99-12//99
	Cleveland-Lorain-Elyria PMSA, OH	Y		27790 AAW		OHBLS	10//99-12//99
	Columbus MSA, OH	Y		63270 AAW		OHBLS	10//99-12//99
	Toledo MSA, OH	Y		26430 AAW		OHBLS	10//99-12//99
	Oklahoma	Y		35630 AAW		OKBLS	10//99-12//99
	Oregon	Y		30840 AAW		ORBLS	10//99-12//99
	Portland-Vancouver PMSA, OR-WA	Y		34260 AAW		ORBLS	10//99-12//99
	Pennsylvania	Y		42510 AAW		PABLS	10//99-12//99
	Pittsburgh MSA, PA	Y		23500 AAW		PABLS	10//99-12//99
	South Carolina	Y		26360 AAW		SCBLS	10//99-12//99
	Tennessee	Y		33530 AAW		TNBLS	10//99-12//99
	Texas	Y		32740 AAW		TXBLS	10//99-12//99
	Fort Worth-Arlington PMSA, TX	Y		32810 AAW		TXBLS	10//99-12//99
	Houston PMSA, TX	Y		19220 AAW		TXBLS	10//99-12//99
	San Antonio MSA, TX	Y		37260 AAW		TXBLS	10//99-12//99
	Virginia	Y		46190 AAW		VABLS	10//99-12//99
	Richmond-Petersburg MSA, VA	Y		31530 AAW		VABLS	10//99-12//99
	Seattle-Bellevue-Everett PMSA, WA	Y		52400 AAW		WABLS	10//99-12//99
	Wisconsin	Y		29860 AAW		WIBLS	10//99-12//99
	Puerto Rico	Y		23600 AAW		PRBLS	10//99-12//99
Musician, Composer	United States	H		39.48 AW		NCS98	1998
Natural Sciences Manager	Alabama	S	35.7 MW	36.06 AW	75010 AAW	ALBLS	10//99-12//99
	Alaska	S	29.71 MW	29.67 AW	61710 AAW	AKBLS	10//99-12//99
	Arizona	S	26.89 MW	27.58 AW	57360 AAW	AZBLS	10//99-12//99
	Arkansas	S	29.87 MW	30.34 AW	63110 AAW	ARBLS	10//99-12//99
	California	S	33.99 MW	35.36 AW	73540 AAW	CABLS	10//99-12//99
	Colorado	S	33.84 MW	34.70 AW	72170 AAW	COBLS	10//99-12//99
	Connecticut	S	49.74 MW	49.20 AW	102340 AAW	CTBLS	10//99-12//99

AAW Average annual wage	AOH Average offered, high	ASH Average starting, high	H Hourly	M Monthly	S Special: hourly and annual
AE Average entry wage	AOL Average offered, low	ASL Average starting, low	HI Highest wage paid	MTC Median total compensation	TQ Third quartile wage
AEX Average experienced wage	APH Average pay, high range	AW Average wage paid	HR High end range	MW Median wage paid	W Weekly
AO Average offered	APL Average pay, low range	FQ First quartile wage	LR Low end range	SQ Second quartile wage	Y Yearly

Occupation/Type/Industry	Location	Per	Low	Mid	High	Source	Date
Natural Sciences Manager	Delaware	S	41.85 MW	40.27 AW	83760 AAW	DEBLS	10//99-12//99
	Florida	S	32.95 MW	33.97 AW	70660 AAW	FLBLS	10//99-12//99
	Georgia	S	33.09 MW	34.27 AW	71280 AAW	GABLS	10//99-12//99
	Idaho	S	26.35 MW	27.39 AW	56980 AAW	IDBLS	10//99-12//99
	Illinois	S	33.29 MW	35.21 AW	73230 AAW	ILBLS	10//99-12//99
	Indiana	S	22.28 MW	23.29 AW	48430 AAW	INBLS	10//99-12//99
	Iowa	S	29.12 MW	28.70 AW	59690 AAW	IABLS	10//99-12//99
	Kansas	S	30.43 MW	32.77 AW	68160 AAW	KSBLS	10//99-12//99
	Kentucky	S	25.91 MW	28.02 AW	58290 AAW	KYBLS	10//99-12//99
	Louisiana	S	28.42 MW	30.86 AW	64180 AAW	LABLS	10//99-12//99
	Maine	S	23.63 MW	25.09 AW	52190 AAW	MEBLS	10//99-12//99
	Maryland	S	39.83 MW	38.07 AW	79180 AAW	MDBLS	10//99-12//99
	Massachusetts	S	42.15 MW	41.26 AW	85810 AAW	MABLS	10//99-12//99
	Michigan	S	33.68 MW	36.46 AW	75830 AAW	MIBLS	10//99-12//99
	Minnesota	S	40.03 MW	41.62 AW	86560 AAW	MNBLS	10//99-12//99
	Mississippi	S	30.8 MW	30.87 AW	64210 AAW	MSBLS	10//99-12//99
	Missouri	S	33.24 MW	34.44 AW	71630 AAW	MOBLS	10//99-12//99
	Montana	S	24.28 MW	25.81 AW	53690 AAW	MTBLS	10//99-12//99
	Nebraska	S	30.32 MW	30.68 AW	63810 AAW	NEBLS	10//99-12//99
	Nevada	S	29.08 MW	28.95 AW	60220 AAW	NVBLS	10//99-12//99
	New Hampshire	S	31.96 MW	32.76 AW	68130 AAW	NHBLS	10//99-12//99
	New Jersey	S	43.74 MW	44.73 AW	93040 AAW	NJBLS	10//99-12//99
	New Mexico	S	27.46 MW	27.58 AW	57360 AAW	NMBLS	10//99-12//99
	New York	S	37.13 MW	39.17 AW	81480 AAW	NYBLS	10//99-12//99
	North Carolina	S	37.23 MW	36.79 AW	76510 AAW	NCBLS	10//99-12//99
	North Dakota	S	30.86 MW	31.35 AW	65220 AAW	NDBLS	10//99-12//99
	Ohio	S	31.06 MW	30.44 AW	63310 AAW	OHBLS	10//99-12//99
	Oklahoma	S	21.74 MW	26.63 AW	55390 AAW	OKBLS	10//99-12//99
	Oregon	S	25.99 MW	27.84 AW	57910 AAW	ORBLS	10//99-12//99
	Pennsylvania	S	37.78 MW	38.07 AW	79180 AAW	PABLS	10//99-12//99
	Rhode Island	S	26.74 MW	30.27 AW	62970 AAW	RIBLS	10//99-12//99
	South Carolina	S	40.03 MW	40.05 AW	83300 AAW	SCBLS	10//99-12//99
	South Dakota	S	29.96 MW	31.82 AW	66180 AAW	SDBLS	10//99-12//99
	Tennessee	S	29.61 MW	29.90 AW	62190 AAW	TNBLS	10//99-12//99
	Texas	S	32.51 MW	34.20 AW	71130 AAW	TXBLS	10//99-12//99
	Utah	S	27.73 MW	31.09 AW	64660 AAW	UTBLS	10//99-12//99
	Vermont	S	22.05 MW	23.87 AW	49650 AAW	VTBLS	10//99-12//99
	Virginia	S	40.17 MW	38.81 AW	80720 AAW	VABLS	10//99-12//99
	Washington	S	34.87 MW	36.82 AW	76580 AAW	WABLS	10//99-12//99
	West Virginia	S	29.54 MW	32.08 AW	66730 AAW	WVBLS	10//99-12//99
	Wisconsin	S	32.46 MW	33.50 AW	69680 AAW	WIBLS	10//99-12//99
	Wyoming	S	25.55 MW	25.88 AW	53830 AAW	WYBLS	10//99-12//99
	Puerto Rico	S	27.09 MW	29.33 AW	61010 AAW	PRBLS	10//99-12//99
Naval Architect	United States	H		30.54 AW		NCS98	1998
Network Administrator							
Groupware/Collaboration	United States	Y		58000 AW		ENT	2000
Information Technology	Atlanta, GA	Y		65146 AW		ATBUS	3//00
Internet Infrastructure	United States	Y		55700 AW		ENT	2000
Novell NetWare	United States	Y		54800 AW		ENT	2000
UNIX	United States	Y		57600 AW		ENT	2000
Windows NT/2000	United States	Y		53400 AW		ENT	2000
Network and Computer Systems Administrator	Alabama	S	19.04 MW	19.48 AW	40530 AAW	ALBLS	10//99-12//99
	Birmingham MSA, AL	S	20.06 MW	19.80 AW	41720 AAW	ALBLS	10//99-12//99
	Dothan MSA, AL	S	21.31 MW	20.81 AW	44330 AAW	ALBLS	10//99-12//99
	Florence MSA, AL	S	17.61 MW	16.60 AW	36620 AAW	ALBLS	10//99-12//99
	Huntsville MSA, AL	S	19.77 MW	20.00 AW	41120 AAW	ALBLS	10//99-12//99
	Mobile MSA, AL	S	17.60 MW	17.40 AW	36620 AAW	ALBLS	10//99-12//99
	Montgomery MSA, AL	S	21.18 MW	19.85 AW	44060 AAW	ALBLS	10//99-12//99
	Alaska	S	23.35 MW	23.67 AW	49230 AAW	AKBLS	10//99-12//99
	Anchorage MSA, AK	S	24.21 MW	24.36 AW	50360 AAW	AKBLS	10//99-12//99
	Arizona	S	22.56 MW	24.08 AW	50080 AAW	AZBLS	10//99-12//99
	Flagstaff MSA, AZ-UT	S	17.26 MW	15.16 AW	35900 AAW	AZBLS	10//99-12//99
	Phoenix-Mesa MSA, AZ	S	24.66 MW	22.88 AW	51290 AAW	AZBLS	10//99-12//99
	Tucson MSA, AZ	S	20.55 MW	18.48 AW	42740 AAW	AZBLS	10//99-12//99
	Arkansas	S	17.23 MW	18.18 AW	37810 AAW	ARBLS	10//99-12//99
	Fayetteville-Springdale-Rogers MSA, AR	S	17.73 MW	17.26 AW	36880 AAW	ARBLS	10//99-12//99
	Fort Smith MSA, AR-OK	S	20.33 MW	17.55 AW	42280 AAW	ARBLS	10//99-12//99

AAW	Average annual wage	AOH	Average offered, high	ASH	Average starting, high	**H**	Hourly	**M**	Monthly	**S**	Special: hourly and annual
AE	Average entry wage	AOL	Average offered, low	ASL	Average starting, low	**HI**	Highest wage paid	MTC	Median total compensation	TQ	Third quartile wage
AEX	Average experienced wage	APH	Average pay, high range	AW	Average wage paid	**HR**	High end range	MW	Median wage paid	W	Weekly
AO	Average offered	APL	Average pay, low range	FQ	First quartile wage	**LR**	Low end range	SQ	Second quartile wage	Y	Yearly

Occupation/Type/Industry	Location	Per	Low	Mid	High	Source	Date
Network and Computer Systems Administrator							
	Little Rock-North Little Rock MSA, AR	s	19.48 mw	17.88 aw	40510 aaw	ARBLS	10//99-12//99
	California	s	24.4 mw	25.26 aw	52530 aaw	CABLS	10//99-12//99
	Bakersfield MSA, CA	s	20.61 mw	20.08 aw	42880 aaw	CABLS	10//99-12//99
	Chico-Paradise MSA, CA	s	26.19 mw	27.27 aw	54480 aaw	CABLS	10//99-12//99
	Fresno MSA, CA	s	23.22 mw	23.78 aw	48290 aaw	CABLS	10//99-12//99
	Los Angeles-Long Beach PMSA, CA	s	23.76 mw	22.95 aw	49430 aaw	CABLS	10//99-12//99
	Merced MSA, CA	s	21.32 mw	20.44 aw	44350 aaw	CABLS	10//99-12//99
	Modesto MSA, CA	s	18.44 mw	18.91 aw	38360 aaw	CABLS	10//99-12//99
	Oakland PMSA, CA	s	27.01 mw	26.77 aw	56190 aaw	CABLS	10//99-12//99
	Orange County PMSA, CA	s	24.72 mw	24.18 aw	51410 aaw	CABLS	10//99-12//99
	Riverside-San Bernardino PMSA, CA	s	22.14 mw	20.98 aw	46050 aaw	CABLS	10//99-12//99
	Sacramento PMSA, CA	s	23.50 mw	21.58 aw	48880 aaw	CABLS	10//99-12//99
	Salinas MSA, CA	s	21.07 mw	21.42 aw	43830 aaw	CABLS	10//99-12//99
	San Diego MSA, CA	s	23.93 mw	23.73 aw	49760 aaw	CABLS	10//99-12//99
	San Francisco PMSA, CA	s	27.89 mw	27.36 aw	58010 aaw	CABLS	10//99-12//99
	San Jose PMSA, CA	s	28.85 mw	27.74 aw	60000 aaw	CABLS	10//99-12//99
	San Luis Obispo-Atascadero-Paso Robles MSA, CA	s	21.10 mw	19.18 aw	43880 aaw	CABLS	10//99-12//99
	Santa Barbara-Santa Maria-Lompoc MSA, CA	s	20.78 mw	19.29 aw	43220 aaw	CABLS	10//99-12//99
	Santa Cruz-Watsonville PMSA, CA	s	25.45 mw	24.70 aw	52940 aaw	CABLS	10//99-12//99
	Santa Rosa PMSA, CA	s	23.08 mw	22.59 aw	48000 aaw	CABLS	10//99-12//99
	Stockton-Lodi MSA, CA	s	27.25 mw	23.00 aw	56680 aaw	CABLS	10//99-12//99
	Vallejo-Fairfield-Napa PMSA, CA	s	22.31 mw	22.26 aw	46410 aaw	CABLS	10//99-12//99
	Ventura PMSA, CA	s	24.81 mw	24.29 aw	51610 aaw	CABLS	10//99-12//99
	Visalia-Tulare-Porterville MSA, CA	s	21.06 mw	19.46 aw	43810 aaw	CABLS	10//99-12//99
	Yolo PMSA, CA	s	26.86 mw	25.63 aw	55880 aaw	CABLS	10//99-12//99
	Colorado	s	24.58 mw	27.67 aw	57560 aaw	COBLS	10//99-12//99
	Boulder-Longmont PMSA, CO	s	26.18 mw	25.82 aw	54460 aaw	COBLS	10//99-12//99
	Denver PMSA, CO	s	25.45 mw	24.36 aw	52940 aaw	COBLS	10//99-12//99
	Fort Collins-Loveland MSA, CO	s	25.28 mw	20.65 aw	52590 aaw	COBLS	10//99-12//99
	Greeley PMSA, CO	s	21.68 mw	19.72 aw	45090 aaw	COBLS	10//99-12//99
	Pueblo MSA, CO	s	21.55 mw	21.00 aw	44820 aaw	COBLS	10//99-12//99
	Connecticut	s	26.29 mw	27.64 aw	57490 aaw	CTBLS	10//99-12//99
	Bridgeport PMSA, CT	s	31.16 mw	30.18 aw	64820 aaw	CTBLS	10//99-12//99
	Danbury PMSA, CT	s	26.00 mw	25.12 aw	54080 aaw	CTBLS	10//99-12//99
	Hartford MSA, CT	s	25.61 mw	24.88 aw	53260 aaw	CTBLS	10//99-12//99
	New Haven-Meriden PMSA, CT	s	26.89 mw	25.40 aw	55920 aaw	CTBLS	10//99-12//99
	New London-Norwich MSA, CT-RI	s	27.48 mw	27.40 aw	57160 aaw	CTBLS	10//99-12//99
	Stamford-Norwalk PMSA, CT	s	30.76 mw	28.85 aw	63970 aaw	CTBLS	10//99-12//99
	Waterbury PMSA, CT	s	25.36 mw	25.15 aw	52740 aaw	CTBLS	10//99-12//99
	Delaware	s	24.28 mw	25.18 aw	52380 aaw	DEBLS	10//99-12//99
	Dover MSA, DE	s	22.24 mw	19.82 aw	46250 aaw	DEBLS	10//99-12//99
	Wilmington-Newark PMSA, DE-MD	s	25.42 mw	24.56 aw	52870 aaw	DEBLS	10//99-12//99
	District of Columbia	s	25.31 mw	26.48 aw	55070 aaw	DCBLS	10//99-12//99
	Washington PMSA, DC-MD-VA-WV	s	25.10 mw	24.38 aw	52200 aaw	DCBLS	10//99-12//99
	Florida	s	22.17 mw	23.04 aw	47920 aaw	FLBLS	10//99-12//99
	Daytona Beach MSA, FL	s	21.35 mw	21.92 aw	44400 aaw	FLBLS	10//99-12//99
	Fort Lauderdale PMSA, FL	s	22.45 mw	21.38 aw	46700 aaw	FLBLS	10//99-12//99
	Fort Myers-Cape Coral MSA, FL	s	21.52 mw	22.68 aw	44770 aaw	FLBLS	10//99-12//99
	Fort Pierce-Port St. Lucie MSA, FL	s	21.30 mw	20.15 aw	44300 aaw	FLBLS	10//99-12//99
	Fort Walton Beach MSA, FL	s	23.57 mw	23.86 aw	49020 aaw	FLBLS	10//99-12//99
	Gainesville MSA, FL	s	22.17 mw	21.29 aw	46110 aaw	FLBLS	10//99-12//99
	Jacksonville MSA, FL	s	24.05 mw	22.75 aw	50030 aaw	FLBLS	10//99-12//99
	Lakeland-Winter Haven MSA, FL	s	19.07 mw	18.19 aw	39660 aaw	FLBLS	10//99-12//99
	Melbourne-Titusville-Palm Bay MSA, FL	s	23.42 mw	23.23 aw	48720 aaw	FLBLS	10//99-12//99

AAW	Average annual wage	AOH	Average offered, high	ASH	Average starting, high	H	Hourly	M	Monthly	S	Special: hourly and annual
AE	Average entry wage	AOL	Average offered, low	ASL	Average starting, low	HI	Highest wage paid	MTC	Median total compensation	TQ	Third quartile wage
AEX	Average experienced wage	APH	Average pay, high range	AW	Average wage paid	HR	High end range	MW	Median wage paid	W	Weekly
AO	Average offered	APL	Average pay, low range	FQ	First quartile wage	LR	Low end range	SQ	Second quartile wage	Y	Yearly

Occupation/Type/Industry	Location	Per	Low	Mid	High	Source	Date
Network and Computer Systems Administrator	Miami PMSA, FL	S	23.18 MW	23.10 AW	48200 AAW	FLBLS	10//99-12//99
	Ocala MSA, FL	S	22.40 MW	23.38 AW	46590 AAW	FLBLS	10//99-12//99
	Orlando MSA, FL	S	23.08 MW	21.85 AW	48020 AAW	FLBLS	10//99-12//99
	Pensacola MSA, FL	S	19.32 MW	18.72 AW	40190 AAW	FLBLS	10//99-12//99
	Sarasota-Bradenton MSA, FL	S	25.83 MW	19.35 AW	53730 AAW	FLBLS	10//99-12//99
	Tallahassee MSA, FL	S	23.09 MW	21.87 AW	48020 AAW	FLBLS	10//99-12//99
	Tampa-St. Petersburg-Clearwater MSA, FL	S	23.14 MW	21.66 AW	48130 AAW	FLBLS	10//99-12//99
	West Palm Beach-Boca Raton MSA, FL	S	24.72 MW	23.69 AW	51420 AAW	FLBLS	10//99-12//99
	Georgia	S	23.72 MW	24.85 AW	51700 AAW	GABLS	10//99-12//99
	Albany MSA, GA	S	18.63 MW	18.95 AW	38740 AAW	GABLS	10//99-12//99
	Atlanta MSA, GA	S	25.25 MW	23.94 AW	52520 AAW	GABLS	10//99-12//99
	Augusta-Aiken MSA, GA-SC	S	21.79 MW	21.75 AW	45330 AAW	GABLS	10//99-12//99
	Columbus MSA, GA-AL	S	25.53 MW	24.85 AW	53110 AAW	GABLS	10//99-12//99
	Macon MSA, GA	S	23.07 MW	22.86 AW	47980 AAW	GABLS	10//99-12//99
	Savannah MSA, GA	S	19.70 MW	20.14 AW	40980 AAW	GABLS	10//99-12//99
	Hawaii	S	22.3 MW	22.20 AW	46170 AAW	HIBLS	10//99-12//99
	Honolulu MSA, HI	S	22.08 MW	22.15 AW	45940 AAW	HIBLS	10//99-12//99
	Idaho	S	17.16 MW	18.78 AW	39060 AAW	IDBLS	10//99-12//99
	Boise City MSA, ID	S	17.83 MW	16.50 AW	37080 AAW	IDBLS	10//99-12//99
	Illinois	S	24.87 MW	25.95 AW	53980 AAW	ILBLS	10//99-12//99
	Bloomington-Normal MSA, IL	S	27.45 MW	26.19 AW	57100 AAW	ILBLS	10//99-12//99
	Champaign-Urbana MSA, IL	S	22.70 MW	20.37 AW	47220 AAW	ILBLS	10//99-12//99
	Chicago PMSA, IL	S	26.80 MW	25.62 AW	55740 AAW	ILBLS	10//99-12//99
	Peoria-Pekin MSA, IL	S	17.84 MW	18.73 AW	37110 AAW	ILBLS	10//99-12//99
	Rockford MSA, IL	S	20.89 MW	20.34 AW	43450 AAW	ILBLS	10//99-12//99
	Springfield MSA, IL	S	21.38 MW	19.85 AW	44480 AAW	ILBLS	10//99-12//99
	Indiana	S	20.51 MW	21.02 AW	43730 AAW	INBLS	10//99-12//99
	Bloomington MSA, IN	S	18.86 MW	18.73 AW	39220 AAW	INBLS	10//99-12//99
	Elkhart-Goshen MSA, IN	S	21.92 MW	19.72 AW	45590 AAW	INBLS	10//99-12//99
	Evansville-Henderson MSA, IN-KY	S	19.45 MW	18.95 AW	40450 AAW	INBLS	10//99-12//99
	Fort Wayne MSA, IN	S	21.64 MW	21.54 AW	45000 AAW	INBLS	10//99-12//99
	Gary PMSA, IN	S	20.02 MW	18.26 AW	41640 AAW	INBLS	10//99-12//99
	Indianapolis MSA, IN	S	22.06 MW	21.93 AW	45880 AAW	INBLS	10//99-12//99
	Lafayette MSA, IN	S	19.83 MW	20.50 AW	41240 AAW	INBLS	10//99-12//99
	Muncie MSA, IN	S	20.74 MW	18.48 AW	43140 AAW	INBLS	10//99-12//99
	South Bend MSA, IN	S	17.55 MW	16.89 AW	36510 AAW	INBLS	10//99-12//99
	Terre Haute MSA, IN	S	14.61 MW	12.55 AW	30400 AAW	INBLS	10//99-12//99
	Iowa	S	19.43 MW	20.67 AW	42990 AAW	IABLS	10//99-12//99
	Cedar Rapids MSA, IA	S	19.37 MW	17.87 AW	40290 AAW	IABLS	10//99-12//99
	Davenport-Moline-Rock Island MSA, IA-IL	S	21.25 MW	20.15 AW	44200 AAW	IABLS	10//99-12//99
	Iowa City MSA, IA	S	17.75 MW	16.88 AW	36920 AAW	IABLS	10//99-12//99
	Waterloo-Cedar Falls MSA, IA	S	20.14 MW	20.16 AW	41890 AAW	IABLS	10//99-12//99
	Kansas	S	18.31 MW	19.40 AW	40360 AAW	KSBLS	10//99-12//99
	Lawrence MSA, KS	S	21.91 MW	23.45 AW	45570 AAW	KSBLS	10//99-12//99
	Topeka MSA, KS	S	18.66 MW	16.89 AW	38810 AAW	KSBLS	10//99-12//99
	Wichita MSA, KS	S	22.03 MW	20.82 AW	45830 AAW	KSBLS	10//99-12//99
	Kentucky	S	18.51 MW	19.53 AW	40620 AAW	KYBLS	10//99-12//99
	Lexington MSA, KY	S	21.71 MW	19.54 AW	45160 AAW	KYBLS	10//99-12//99
	Louisville MSA, KY-IN	S	20.44 MW	19.66 AW	42520 AAW	KYBLS	10//99-12//99
	Owensboro MSA, KY	S	19.15 MW	18.72 AW	39830 AAW	KYBLS	10//99-12//99
	Louisiana	S	20.66 MW	21.33 AW	44360 AAW	LABLS	10//99-12//99
	Baton Rouge MSA, LA	S	21.70 MW	20.64 AW	45140 AAW	LABLS	10//99-12//99
	Lafayette MSA, LA	S	18.92 MW	19.34 AW	39360 AAW	LABLS	10//99-12//99
	Lake Charles MSA, LA	S	24.13 MW	25.46 AW	50190 AAW	LABLS	10//99-12//99
	New Orleans MSA, LA	S	20.07 MW	18.14 AW	41750 AAW	LABLS	10//99-12//99
	Shreveport-Bossier City MSA, LA	S	20.67 MW	21.04 AW	43000 AAW	LABLS	10//99-12//99
	Maine	S	19.75 MW	20.22 AW	42060 AAW	MEBLS	10//99-12//99
	Bangor MSA, ME	S	19.56 MW	16.70 AW	40690 AAW	MEBLS	10//99-12//99
	Lewiston-Auburn MSA, ME	S	20.32 MW	21.17 AW	42260 AAW	MEBLS	10//99-12//99
	Portland MSA, ME	S	20.66 MW	20.29 AW	42970 AAW	MEBLS	10//99-12//99
	Maryland	S	23.06 MW	23.69 AW	49260 AAW	MDBLS	10//99-12//99
	Baltimore PMSA, MD	S	22.77 MW	21.71 AW	47360 AAW	MDBLS	10//99-12//99
	Massachusetts	S	26.07 MW	26.89 AW	55940 AAW	MABLS	10//99-12//99
	Boston PMSA, MA-NH	S	27.69 MW	26.83 AW	57600 AAW	MABLS	10//99-12//99
	Brockton PMSA, MA	S	23.04 MW	20.79 AW	47920 AAW	MABLS	10//99-12//99
	Lawrence PMSA, MA-NH	S	25.82 MW	26.62 AW	53700 AAW	MABLS	10//99-12//99

AAW Average annual wage	**AOH** Average offered, high	**ASH** Average starting, high	**H** Hourly	**M** Monthly	**S** Special: hourly and annual
AE Average entry wage	**AOL** Average offered, low	**ASL** Average starting, low	**HI** Highest wage paid	**MTC** Median total compensation	**TQ** Third quartile wage
AEX Average experienced wage	**APH** Average pay, high range	**AW** Average wage paid	**HR** High end range	**MW** Median wage paid	**W** Weekly
AO Average offered	**APL** Average pay, low range	**FQ** First quartile wage	**LR** Low end range	**SQ** Second quartile wage	**Y** Yearly

Occupation/Type/Industry	Location	Per	Low	Mid	High	Source	Date
Network and Computer Systems Administrator	Lowell PMSA, MA-NH	S	25.44 MW	25.78 AW	52910 AAW	MABLS	10//99-12//99
	Pittsfield MSA, MA	S	19.82 MW	15.68 AW	41230 AAW	MABLS	10//99-12//99
	Springfield MSA, MA	S	22.68 MW	22.33 AW	47180 AAW	MABLS	10//99-12//99
	Worcester PMSA, MA-CT	S	22.95 MW	22.61 AW	47740 AAW	MABLS	10//99-12//99
	Michigan	S	23.04 MW	23.53 AW	48940 AAW	MIBLS	10//99-12//99
	Ann Arbor PMSA, MI	S	21.82 MW	22.79 AW	45380 AAW	MIBLS	10//99-12//99
	Benton Harbor MSA, MI	S	22.75 MW	22.88 AW	47310 AAW	MIBLS	10//99-12//99
	Detroit PMSA, MI	S	24.93 MW	24.32 AW	51840 AAW	MIBLS	10//99-12//99
	Flint PMSA, MI	S	23.23 MW	23.04 AW	48310 AAW	MIBLS	10//99-12//99
	Grand Rapids-Muskegon-Holland MSA, MI	S	22.55 MW	21.04 AW	46900 AAW	MIBLS	10//99-12//99
	Jackson MSA, MI	S	22.36 MW	22.90 AW	46510 AAW	MIBLS	10//99-12//99
	Kalamazoo-Battle Creek MSA, MI	S	20.35 MW	20.26 AW	42320 AAW	MIBLS	10//99-12//99
	Lansing-East Lansing MSA, MI	S	22.69 MW	22.21 AW	47200 AAW	MIBLS	10//99-12//99
	Saginaw-Bay City-Midland MSA, MI	S	21.38 MW	20.10 AW	44460 AAW	MIBLS	10//99-12//99
	Minnesota	S	21.93 MW	23.16 AW	48170 AAW	MNBLS	10//99-12//99
	Duluth-Superior MSA, MN-WI	S	21.40 MW	19.10 AW	44520 AAW	MNBLS	10//99-12//99
	Minneapolis-St. Paul MSA, MN-WI	S	23.29 MW	22.19 AW	48440 AAW	MNBLS	10//99-12//99
	Rochester MSA, MN	S	23.49 MW	23.14 AW	48850 AAW	MNBLS	10//99-12//99
	St. Cloud MSA, MN	S	31.62 MW	24.88 AW	65770 AAW	MNBLS	10//99-12//99
	Mississippi	S	17.31 MW	18.21 AW	37880 AAW	MSBLS	10//99-12//99
	Biloxi-Gulfport-Pascagoula MSA, MS	S	21.24 MW	18.57 AW	44180 AAW	MSBLS	10//99-12//99
	Missouri	S	22.33 MW	22.45 AW	46700 AAW	MOBLS	10//99-12//99
	Columbia MSA, MO	S	19.04 MW	17.59 AW	39600 AAW	MOBLS	10//99-12//99
	Joplin MSA, MO	S	18.82 MW	16.10 AW	39150 AAW	MOBLS	10//99-12//99
	Kansas City MSA, MO-KS	S	19.48 MW	18.32 AW	40510 AAW	MOBLS	10//99-12//99
	St. Louis MSA, MO-IL	S	23.70 MW	24.09 AW	49300 AAW	MOBLS	10//99-12//99
	Springfield MSA, MO	S	23.18 MW	23.78 AW	48210 AAW	MOBLS	10//99-12//99
	Montana	S	16.77 MW	17.89 AW	37220 AAW	MTBLS	10//99-12//99
	Billings MSA, MT	S	17.69 MW	16.26 AW	36800 AAW	MTBLS	10//99-12//99
	Great Falls MSA, MT	S	20.57 MW	20.25 AW	42790 AAW	MTBLS	10//99-12//99
	Missoula MSA, MT	S	20.77 MW	21.57 AW	43210 AAW	MTBLS	10//99-12//99
	Nebraska	S	21.92 MW	23.04 AW	47920 AAW	NEBLS	10//99-12//99
	Lincoln MSA, NE	S	21.29 MW	20.24 AW	44280 AAW	NEBLS	10//99-12//99
	Omaha MSA, NE-IA	S	23.97 MW	23.29 AW	49850 AAW	NEBLS	10//99-12//99
	Nevada	S	21.01 MW	21.14 AW	43970 AAW	NVBLS	10//99-12//99
	Las Vegas MSA, NV-AZ	S	21.03 MW	21.29 AW	43750 AAW	NVBLS	10//99-12//99
	Reno MSA, NV	S	21.05 MW	20.11 AW	43780 AAW	NVBLS	10//99-12//99
	New Hampshire	S	20.44 MW	20.94 AW	43560 AAW	NHBLS	10//99-12//99
	Manchester PMSA, NH	S	21.46 MW	21.51 AW	44630 AAW	NHBLS	10//99-12//99
	Nashua PMSA, NH	S	23.93 MW	21.99 AW	49770 AAW	NHBLS	10//99-12//99
	Portsmouth-Rochester PMSA, NH-ME	S	22.10 MW	21.49 AW	45970 AAW	NHBLS	10//99-12//99
	New Jersey	S	26.34 MW	29.39 AW	61140 AAW	NJBLS	10//99-12//99
	Atlantic-Cape May PMSA, NJ	S	25.53 MW	25.69 AW	53100 AAW	NJBLS	10//99-12//99
	Bergen-Passaic PMSA, NJ	S	28.24 MW	26.69 AW	58740 AAW	NJBLS	10//99-12//99
	Jersey City PMSA, NJ	S	28.66 MW	26.02 AW	59620 AAW	NJBLS	10//99-12//99
	Monmouth-Ocean PMSA, NJ	S	23.15 MW	20.79 AW	48140 AAW	NJBLS	10//99-12//99
	Newark PMSA, NJ	S	26.13 MW	24.28 AW	54360 AAW	NJBLS	10//99-12//99
	Trenton PMSA, NJ	S	27.11 MW	25.92 AW	56400 AAW	NJBLS	10//99-12//99
	Vineland-Millville-Bridgeton PMSA, NJ	S	23.20 MW	21.32 AW	48260 AAW	NJBLS	10//99-12//99
	New Mexico	S	19.94 MW	20.52 AW	42680 AAW	NMBLS	10//99-12//99
	Albuquerque MSA, NM	S	21.82 MW	21.00 AW	45380 AAW	NMBLS	10//99-12//99
	Santa Fe MSA, NM	S	19.96 MW	18.96 AW	41510 AAW	NMBLS	10//99-12//99
	New York	S	25.76 MW	26.82 AW	55780 AAW	NYBLS	10//99-12//99
	Albany-Schenectady-Troy MSA, NY	S	22.00 MW	21.49 AW	45760 AAW	NYBLS	10//99-12//99
	Binghamton MSA, NY	S	23.36 MW	24.02 AW	48580 AAW	NYBLS	10//99-12//99
	Buffalo-Niagara Falls MSA, NY	S	26.78 MW	25.43 AW	55700 AAW	NYBLS	10//99-12//99
	Dutchess County PMSA, NY	S	29.31 MW	27.65 AW	60970 AAW	NYBLS	10//99-12//99
	Elmira MSA, NY	S	16.89 MW	16.06 AW	35130 AAW	NYBLS	10//99-12//99
	Nassau-Suffolk PMSA, NY	S	24.35 MW	23.39 AW	50650 AAW	NYBLS	10//99-12//99
	New York PMSA, NY	S	29.78 MW	29.00 AW	61950 AAW	NYBLS	10//99-12//99
	Newburgh PMSA, NY-PA	S	23.85 MW	23.60 AW	49610 AAW	NYBLS	10//99-12//99
	Rochester MSA, NY	S	22.96 MW	22.89 AW	47750 AAW	NYBLS	10//99-12//99

AAW Average annual wage	**AOH** Average offered, high	**ASH** Average starting, high	**H** Hourly	**M** Monthly	**S** Special: hourly and annual
AE Average entry salaries	**AOL** Average offered, low	**ASL** Average starting, low	**HI** Highest wage paid	**MTC** Median total compensation	**TQ** Third quartile wage
AEX Average experienced wage	**APH** Average pay, high range	**AW** Average wage paid	**HR** High end range	**MW** Median wage paid	**W** Weekly
AO Average offered	**APL** Average pay, low range	**FQ** First quartile wage	**LR** Low end range	**SQ** Second quartile wage	**Y** Yearly

Occupation/Type/Industry	Location	Per	Low	Mid	High	Source	Date
Network and Computer Systems Administrator	Syracuse MSA, NY	S	23.98 MW	22.10 AW	49870 AAW	NYBLS	10//99-12//99
	Utica-Rome MSA, NY	S	26.85 MW	26.78 AW	55860 AAW	NYBLS	10//99-12//99
	North Carolina	S	22.85 MW	24.19 AW	50310 AAW	NCBLS	10//99-12//99
	Asheville MSA, NC	S	24.43 MW	26.09 AW	50820 AAW	NCBLS	10//99-12//99
	Charlotte-Gastonia-Rock Hill MSA, NC-SC	S	26.28 MW	24.66 AW	54660 AAW	NCBLS	10//99-12//99
	Greensboro--Winston-Salem-- High Point MSA, NC	S	20.91 MW	20.02 AW	43490 AAW	NCBLS	10//99-12//99
	Greenville MSA, NC	S	25.42 MW	24.22 AW	52870 AAW	NCBLS	10//99-12//99
	Hickory-Morganton-Lenoir MSA, NC	S	22.30 MW	22.75 AW	46380 AAW	NCBLS	10//99-12//99
	Raleigh-Durham-Chapel Hill MSA, NC	S	25.37 MW	24.34 AW	52770 AAW	NCBLS	10//99-12//99
	Rocky Mount MSA, NC	S	18.99 MW	17.40 AW	39510 AAW	NCBLS	10//99-12//99
	Wilmington MSA, NC	S	20.71 MW	18.56 AW	43080 AAW	NCBLS	10//99-12//99
	North Dakota	S	15.34 MW	16.25 AW	33790 AAW	NDBLS	10//99-12//99
	Bismarck MSA, ND	S	15.08 MW	15.06 AW	31360 AAW	NDBLS	10//99-12//99
	Fargo-Moorhead MSA, ND-MN	S	19.16 MW	18.72 AW	39850 AAW	NDBLS	10//99-12//99
	Ohio	S	21.16 MW	22.11 AW	46000 AAW	OHBLS	10//99-12//99
	Akron PMSA, OH	S	23.73 MW	22.54 AW	49360 AAW	OHBLS	10//99-12//99
	Canton-Massillon MSA, OH	S	20.11 MW	19.75 AW	41830 AAW	OHBLS	10//99-12//99
	Cincinnati PMSA, OH-KY-IN	S	22.53 MW	20.92 AW	46870 AAW	OHBLS	10//99-12//99
	Cleveland-Lorain-Elyria PMSA, OH	S	23.64 MW	22.59 AW	49180 AAW	OHBLS	10//99-12//99
	Columbus MSA, OH	S	23.27 MW	22.97 AW	48410 AAW	OHBLS	10//99-12//99
	Dayton-Springfield MSA, OH	S	21.67 MW	21.37 AW	45070 AAW	OHBLS	10//99-12//99
	Hamilton-Middletown PMSA, OH	S	21.55 MW	19.03 AW	44820 AAW	OHBLS	10//99-12//99
	Lima MSA, OH	S	19.65 MW	19.21 AW	40880 AAW	OHBLS	10//99-12//99
	Mansfield MSA, OH	S	23.68 MW	24.15 AW	49250 AAW	OHBLS	10//99-12//99
	Steubenville-Weirton MSA, OH-WV	S	19.55 MW	19.78 AW	40670 AAW	OHBLS	10//99-12//99
	Toledo MSA, OH	S	19.19 MW	19.13 AW	39920 AAW	OHBLS	10//99-12//99
	Youngstown-Warren MSA, OH	S	20.37 MW	19.19 AW	42360 AAW	OHBLS	10//99-12//99
	Oklahoma	S	19.54 MW	20.71 AW	43070 AAW	OKBLS	10//99-12//99
	Oklahoma City MSA, OK	S	22.07 MW	22.24 AW	45910 AAW	OKBLS	10//99-12//99
	Tulsa MSA, OK	S	20.23 MW	18.11 AW	42080 AAW	OKBLS	10//99-12//99
	Oregon	S	21.24 MW	22.42 AW	46630 AAW	ORBLS	10//99-12//99
	Corvallis MSA, OR	S	18.26 MW	18.89 AW	37980 AAW	ORBLS	10//99-12//99
	Eugene-Springfield MSA, OR	S	19.65 MW	18.35 AW	40880 AAW	ORBLS	10//99-12//99
	Medford-Ashland MSA, OR	S	22.28 MW	20.49 AW	46350 AAW	ORBLS	10//99-12//99
	Portland-Vancouver PMSA, OR-WA	S	23.76 MW	22.58 AW	49410 AAW	ORBLS	10//99-12//99
	Salem PMSA, OR	S	19.83 MW	19.32 AW	41240 AAW	ORBLS	10//99-12//99
	Pennsylvania	S	21.21 MW	22.18 AW	46130 AAW	PABLS	10//99-12//99
	Allentown-Bethlehem-Easton MSA, PA	S	22.83 MW	21.37 AW	47500 AAW	PABLS	10//99-12//99
	Altoona MSA, PA	S	15.99 MW	12.84 AW	33250 AAW	PABLS	10//99-12//99
	Harrisburg-Lebanon-Carlisle MSA, PA	S	20.15 MW	20.07 AW	41920 AAW	PABLS	10//99-12//99
	Johnstown MSA, PA	S	23.95 MW	25.62 AW	49810 AAW	PABLS	10//99-12//99
	Lancaster MSA, PA	S	24.32 MW	23.94 AW	50590 AAW	PABLS	10//99-12//99
	Philadelphia PMSA, PA-NJ	S	25.90 MW	25.17 AW	53880 AAW	PABLS	10//99-12//99
	Pittsburgh MSA, PA	S	18.48 MW	16.92 AW	38430 AAW	PABLS	10//99-12//99
	Reading MSA, PA	S	23.26 MW	22.38 AW	48370 AAW	PABLS	10//99-12//99
	Scranton--Wilkes-Barre-- Hazleton MSA, PA	S	19.20 MW	16.76 AW	39940 AAW	PABLS	10//99-12//99
	State College MSA, PA	S	20.97 MW	22.21 AW	43610 AAW	PABLS	10//99-12//99
	Williamsport MSA, PA	S	18.25 MW	17.02 AW	37950 AAW	PABLS	10//99-12//99
	York MSA, PA	S	19.66 MW	18.35 AW	40900 AAW	PABLS	10//99-12//99
	Rhode Island	S	24.97 MW	25.77 AW	53610 AAW	RIBLS	10//99-12//99
	Providence-Fall River-Warwick MSA, RI-MA	S	25.53 MW	24.60 AW	53090 AAW	RIBLS	10//99-12//99
	South Carolina	S	20.11 MW	21.16 AW	44010 AAW	SCBLS	10//99-12//99
	Charleston-North Charleston MSA, SC	S	17.15 MW	16.47 AW	35670 AAW	SCBLS	10//99-12//99
	Columbia MSA, SC	S	21.35 MW	21.01 AW	44400 AAW	SCBLS	10//99-12//99
	Florence MSA, SC	S	22.64 MW	23.63 AW	47090 AAW	SCBLS	10//99-12//99
	Greenville-Spartanburg-Anderson MSA, SC	S	24.45 MW	22.47 AW	50850 AAW	SCBLS	10//99-12//99

Occupation/Type/Industry	Location	Per	Low	Mid	High	Source	Date
Network and Computer Systems Administrator							
	Myrtle Beach MSA, SC	S	24.51 MW	27.32 AW	50990 AAW	SCBLS	10//99-12//99
	South Dakota	S	19.32 MW	19.35 AW	40250 AAW	SDBLS	10//99-12//99
	Rapid City MSA, SD	S	19.12 MW	18.76 AW	39780 AAW	SDBLS	10//99-12//99
	Sioux Falls MSA, SD	S	20.61 MW	20.47 AW	42860 AAW	SDBLS	10//99-12//99
	Tennessee	S	19.65 MW	20.21 AW	42030 AAW	TNBLS	10//99-12//99
	Chattanooga MSA, TN-GA	S	20.72 MW	20.81 AW	43100 AAW	TNBLS	10//99-12//99
	Clarksville-Hopkinsville MSA, TN-KY	S	17.88 MW	18.51 AW	37180 AAW	TNBLS	10//99-12//99
	Johnson City-Kingsport-Bristol MSA, TN-VA	S	16.56 MW	15.97 AW	34450 AAW	TNBLS	10//99-12//99
	Knoxville MSA, TN	S	18.46 MW	17.55 AW	38390 AAW	TNBLS	10//99-12//99
	Memphis MSA, TN-AR-MS	S	21.57 MW	21.25 AW	44860 AAW	MSBLS	10//99-12//99
	Nashville MSA, TN	S	20.83 MW	19.79 AW	43330 AAW	TNBLS	10//99-12//99
	Texas	S	23.08 MW	24.78 AW	51530 AAW	TXBLS	10//99-12//99
	Abilene MSA, TX	S	18.74 MW	17.05 AW	38970 AAW	TXBLS	10//99-12//99
	Amarillo MSA, TX	S	17.82 MW	18.10 AW	37070 AAW	TXBLS	10//99-12//99
	Austin-San Marcos MSA, TX	S	33.11 MW	29.66 AW	68870 AAW	TXBLS	10//99-12//99
	Beaumont-Port Arthur MSA, TX	S	22.05 MW	19.65 AW	45870 AAW	TXBLS	10//99-12//99
	Brazoria PMSA, TX	S	22.74 MW	20.82 AW	47290 AAW	TXBLS	10//99-12//99
	Brownsville-Harlingen-San Benito MSA, TX	S	18.66 MW	18.17 AW	38820 AAW	TXBLS	10//99-12//99
	Bryan-College Station MSA, TX	S	17.28 MW	16.59 AW	35950 AAW	TXBLS	10//99-12//99
	Corpus Christi MSA, TX	S	17.66 MW	17.61 AW	36720 AAW	TXBLS	10//99-12//99
	Dallas PMSA, TX	S	26.50 MW	25.34 AW	55120 AAW	TXBLS	10//99-12//99
	El Paso MSA, TX	S	18.58 MW	17.71 AW	38650 AAW	TXBLS	10//99-12//99
	Fort Worth-Arlington PMSA, TX	S	23.71 MW	21.14 AW	49310 AAW	TXBLS	10//99-12//99
	Galveston-Texas City PMSA, TX	S	22.53 MW	21.13 AW	46860 AAW	TXBLS	10//99-12//99
	Houston PMSA, TX	S	23.58 MW	23.03 AW	49040 AAW	TXBLS	10//99-12//99
	Killeen-Temple MSA, TX	S	23.91 MW	19.08 AW	49730 AAW	TXBLS	10//99-12//99
	Laredo MSA, TX	S	22.17 MW	22.62 AW	46110 AAW	TXBLS	10//99-12//99
	Longview-Marshall MSA, TX	S	21.47 MW	20.77 AW	44660 AAW	TXBLS	10//99-12//99
	Lubbock MSA, TX	S	21.56 MW	19.67 AW	44840 AAW	TXBLS	10//99-12//99
	McAllen-Edinburg-Mission MSA, TX	S	15.13 MW	14.44 AW	31480 AAW	TXBLS	10//99-12//99
	Odessa-Midland MSA, TX	S	19.46 MW	18.96 AW	40480 AAW	TXBLS	10//99-12//99
	San Angelo MSA, TX	S	14.97 MW	13.04 AW	31130 AAW	TXBLS	10//99-12//99
	San Antonio MSA, TX	S	18.73 MW	17.41 AW	38960 AAW	TXBLS	10//99-12//99
	Texarkana MSA, TX-Texarkana, AR	S	22.75 MW	22.79 AW	47320 AAW	TXBLS	10//99-12//99
	Tyler MSA, TX	S	18.58 MW	18.74 AW	38640 AAW	TXBLS	10//99-12//99
	Victoria MSA, TX	S	14.94 MW	15.51 AW	31080 AAW	TXBLS	10//99-12//99
	Waco MSA, TX	S	19.64 MW	18.42 AW	40850 AAW	TXBLS	10//99-12//99
	Wichita Falls MSA, TX	S	17.49 MW	16.39 AW	36380 AAW	TXBLS	10//99-12//99
	Utah	S	22.03 MW	22.91 AW	47660 AAW	UTBLS	10//99-12//99
	Provo-Orem MSA, UT	S	23.16 MW	22.97 AW	48170 AAW	UTBLS	10//99-12//99
	Salt Lake City-Ogden MSA, UT	S	22.76 MW	21.59 AW	47340 AAW	UTBLS	10//99-12//99
	Vermont	S	19.41 MW	20.06 AW	41720 AAW	VTBLS	10//99-12//99
	Burlington MSA, VT	S	20.59 MW	19.40 AW	42820 AAW	VTBLS	10//99-12//99
	Virginia	S	23.88 MW	24.56 AW	51080 AAW	VABLS	10//99-12//99
	Charlottesville MSA, VA	S	23.90 MW	23.76 AW	49710 AAW	VABLS	10//99-12//99
	Lynchburg MSA, VA	S	21.95 MW	21.35 AW	45650 AAW	VABLS	10//99-12//99
	Norfolk-Virginia Beach-Newport News MSA, VA-NC	S	21.69 MW	20.93 AW	45120 AAW	VABLS	10//99-12//99
	Richmond-Petersburg MSA, VA	S	25.86 MW	25.07 AW	53800 AAW	VABLS	10//99-12//99
	Roanoke MSA, VA	S	22.08 MW	21.09 AW	45940 AAW	VABLS	10//99-12//99
	Washington	S	23.79 MW	24.02 AW	49970 AAW	WABLS	10//99-12//99
	Bellingham MSA, WA	S	25.34 MW	22.05 AW	52710 AAW	WABLS	10//99-12//99
	Bremerton PMSA, WA	S	21.41 MW	21.83 AW	44520 AAW	WABLS	10//99-12//99
	Olympia PMSA, WA	S	20.25 MW	19.87 AW	42130 AAW	WABLS	10//99-12//99
	Richland-Kennewick-Pasco MSA, WA	S	20.14 MW	19.17 AW	41900 AAW	WABLS	10//99-12//99
	Seattle-Bellevue-Everett PMSA, WA	S	24.55 MW	24.25 AW	51070 AAW	WABLS	10//99-12//99
	Spokane MSA, WA	S	19.87 MW	19.29 AW	41330 AAW	WABLS	10//99-12//99

Occupation/Type/Industry	Location	Per	Low	Mid	High	Source	Date
Network and Computer Systems Administrator	Tacoma PMSA, WA	S	25.06 MW	24.66 AW	52120 AAW	WABLS	10//99-12//99
	Yakima MSA, WA	S	20.62 MW	18.86 AW	42890 AAW	WABLS	10//99-12//99
	West Virginia	S	20.07 MW	19.82 AW	41220 AAW	WVBLS	10//99-12//99
	Charleston MSA, WV	S	18.90 MW	18.80 AW	39310 AAW	WVBLS	10//99-12//99
	Huntington-Ashland MSA, WV-KY-OH	S	17.25 MW	16.79 AW	35880 AAW	WVBLS	10//99-12//99
	Wheeling MSA, WV-OH	S	14.76 MW	13.33 AW	30710 AAW	WVBLS	10//99-12//99
	Wisconsin	S	20.68 MW	21.19 AW	44080 AAW	WIBLS	10//99-12//99
	Appleton-Oshkosh-Neenah MSA, WI	S	18.75 MW	19.07 AW	39000 AAW	WIBLS	10//99-12//99
	Green Bay MSA, WI	S	19.19 MW	19.50 AW	39910 AAW	WIBLS	10//99-12//99
	Janesville-Beloit MSA, WI	S	27.13 MW	21.13 AW	56430 AAW	WIBLS	10//99-12//99
	Kenosha PMSA, WI	S	20.62 MW	20.74 AW	42900 AAW	WIBLS	10//99-12//99
	La Crosse MSA, WI-MN	S	20.20 MW	18.76 AW	42020 AAW	WIBLS	10//99-12//99
	Madison MSA, WI	S	25.19 MW	25.42 AW	52390 AAW	WIBLS	10//99-12//99
	Milwaukee-Waukesha PMSA, WI	S	24.25 MW	22.80 AW	50430 AAW	WIBLS	10//99-12//99
	Racine PMSA, WI	S	22.64 MW	22.32 AW	47090 AAW	WIBLS	10//99-12//99
	Wausau MSA, WI	S	17.19 MW	16.47 AW	35750 AAW	WIBLS	10//99-12//99
	Wyoming	S	16 MW	17.29 AW	35950 AAW	WYBLS	10//99-12//99
	Puerto Rico	S	15.81 MW	16.45 AW	34210 AAW	PRBLS	10//99-12//99
	San Juan-Bayamon PMSA, PR	S	16.56 MW	15.96 AW	34450 AAW	PRBLS	10//99-12//99
Network System and Data Communications Analyst	Alabama	S	23.69 MW	23.43 AW	48740 AAW	ALBLS	10//99-12//99
	Alaska	S	23.91 MW	23.57 AW	49020 AAW	AKBLS	10//99-12//99
	Arizona	S	23.73 MW	24.60 AW	51170 AAW	AZBLS	10//99-12//99
	Arkansas	S	16.41 MW	17.34 AW	36080 AAW	ARBLS	10//99-12//99
	California	S	26.67 MW	32.38 AW	67360 AAW	CABLS	10//99-12//99
	Colorado	S	26.91 MW	28.06 AW	58360 AAW	COBLS	10//99-12//99
	Connecticut	S	27.07 MW	29.62 AW	61600 AAW	CTBLS	10//99-12//99
	Delaware	S	26.2 MW	27.42 AW	57030 AAW	DEBLS	10//99-12//99
	District of Columbia	S	29.02 MW	27.69 AW	57590 AAW	DCBLS	10//99-12//99
	Florida	S	20.82 MW	24.41 AW	50770 AAW	FLBLS	10//99-12//99
	Georgia	S	21.74 MW	24.04 AW	50010 AAW	GABLS	10//99-12//99
	Hawaii	S	22.93 MW	22.52 AW	46850 AAW	HIBLS	10//99-12//99
	Idaho	S	21.01 MW	22.66 AW	47130 AAW	IDBLS	10//99-12//99
	Illinois	S	24.78 MW	26.52 AW	55170 AAW	ILBLS	10//99-12//99
	Indiana	S	16.31 MW	18.79 AW	39090 AAW	INBLS	10//99-12//99
	Iowa	S	21.8 MW	22.56 AW	46930 AAW	IABLS	10//99-12//99
	Kansas	S	23.63 MW	24.11 AW	50160 AAW	KSBLS	10//99-12//99
	Kentucky	S	19.66 MW	20.33 AW	42280 AAW	KYBLS	10//99-12//99
	Louisiana	S	20.35 MW	23.46 AW	48790 AAW	LABLS	10//99-12//99
	Maine	S	17.89 MW	17.52 AW	36450 AAW	MEBLS	10//99-12//99
	Maryland	S	26.26 MW	26.46 AW	55030 AAW	MDBLS	10//99-12//99
	Massachusetts	S	26.7 MW	28.10 AW	58440 AAW	MABLS	10//99-12//99
	Michigan	S	25.14 MW	26.45 AW	55010 AAW	MIBLS	10//99-12//99
	Minnesota	S	26.65 MW	27.82 AW	57860 AAW	MNBLS	10//99-12//99
	Mississippi	S	17.07 MW	20.24 AW	42100 AAW	MSBLS	10//99-12//99
	Missouri	S	22.26 MW	24.51 AW	50990 AAW	MOBLS	10//99-12//99
	Montana	S	18.54 MW	20.53 AW	42700 AAW	MTBLS	10//99-12//99
	Nebraska	S	19.04 MW	19.92 AW	41430 AAW	NEBLS	10//99-12//99
	Nevada	S	21.01 MW	21.72 AW	45180 AAW	NVBLS	10//99-12//99
	New Hampshire	S	22.12 MW	26.51 AW	55150 AAW	NHBLS	10//99-12//99
	New Jersey	S	30.36 MW	30.18 AW	62780 AAW	NJBLS	10//99-12//99
	New Mexico	S	23.36 MW	23.10 AW	48040 AAW	NMBLS	10//99-12//99
	New York	S	24.71 MW	25.86 AW	53790 AAW	NYBLS	10//99-12//99
	North Carolina	S	25.8 MW	26.86 AW	55870 AAW	NCBLS	10//99-12//99
	North Dakota	S	18.81 MW	19.51 AW	40580 AAW	NDBLS	10//99-12//99
	Ohio	S	25.89 MW	26.76 AW	55650 AAW	OHBLS	10//99-12//99
	Oklahoma	S	20.55 MW	22.15 AW	46080 AAW	OKBLS	10//99-12//99
	Oregon	S	24.19 MW	24.69 AW	51360 AAW	ORBLS	10//99-12//99
	Pennsylvania	S	27.22 MW	28.61 AW	59510 AAW	PABLS	10//99-12//99
	Rhode Island	S	22.06 MW	23.49 AW	48860 AAW	RIBLS	10//99-12//99
	South Carolina	S	25.67 MW	26.24 AW	54580 AAW	SCBLS	10//99-12//99
	South Dakota	S	21.17 MW	22.08 AW	45920 AAW	SDBLS	10//99-12//99
	Tennessee	S	21.95 MW	23.37 AW	48620 AAW	TNBLS	10//99-12//99
	Texas	S	24.73 MW	25.00 AW	51990 AAW	TXBLS	10//99-12//99
	Utah	S	22.72 MW	23.02 AW	47880 AAW	UTBLS	10//99-12//99
	Vermont	S	15.85 MW	17.42 AW	36230 AAW	VTBLS	10//99-12//99
	Virginia	S	28.38 MW	30.17 AW	62740 AAW	VABLS	10//99-12//99

AAW Average annual wage	**AOH** Average offered, high	**ASH** Average starting, high	**H** Hourly	**M** Monthly	**S** Special: hourly and annual
AE Average entry wage	**AOL** Average offered, low	**ASL** Average starting, low	**HI** Highest wage paid	**MTC** Median total compensation	**TQ** Third quartile wage
AEX Average experienced wage	**APH** Average pay, high range	**AW** Average wage paid	**HR** High end range	**MW** Median wage paid	**W** Weekly
AO Average offered	**APL** Average pay, low range	**FQ** First quartile wage	**LR** Low end range	**SQ** Second quartile wage	**Y** Yearly

Occupation/Type/Industry	Location	Per	Low	Mid	High	Source	Date
Network System and Data Communications Analyst	Washington	S	29.04 MW	28.29 AW	58830 AAW	WABLS	10//99-12//99
	West Virginia	S	22.85 MW	23.12 AW	48090 AAW	WVBLS	10//99-12//99
	Wisconsin	S	17.74 MW	19.64 AW	40840 AAW	WIBLS	10//99-12//99
	Wyoming	S	24.8 MW	23.73 AW	49360 AAW	WYBLS	10//99-12//99
	Puerto Rico	S	14.73 MW	16.79 AW	34920 AAW	PRBLS	10//99-12//99
New Accounts Clerk	Alabama	S	8.77 MW	8.88 AW	18470 AAW	ALBLS	10//99-12//99
	Alaska	S	12.98 MW	12.69 AW	26400 AAW	AKBLS	10//99-12//99
	Arizona	S	10.23 MW	10.71 AW	22280 AAW	AZBLS	10//99-12//99
	Arkansas	S	9.6 MW	9.68 AW	20140 AAW	ARBLS	10//99-12//99
	California	S	12.39 MW	12.70 AW	26420 AAW	CABLS	10//99-12//99
	Colorado	S	10.33 MW	10.59 AW	22030 AAW	COBLS	10//99-12//99
	Connecticut	S	11.99 MW	12.25 AW	25470 AAW	CTBLS	10//99-12//99
	District of Columbia	S	11.95 MW	12.34 AW	25670 AAW	DCBLS	10//99-12//99
	Florida	S	10.1 MW	10.51 AW	21860 AAW	FLBLS	10//99-12//99
	Georgia	S	10.19 MW	10.20 AW	21220 AAW	GABLS	10//99-12//99
	Hawaii	S	11.6 MW	11.89 AW	24730 AAW	HIBLS	10//99-12//99
	Idaho	S	10.93 MW	10.95 AW	22780 AAW	IDBLS	10//99-12//99
	Illinois	S	10.59 MW	10.88 AW	22630 AAW	ILBLS	10//99-12//99
	Indiana	S	9.96 MW	10.22 AW	21270 AAW	INBLS	10//99-12//99
	Iowa	S	9.52 MW	9.74 AW	20270 AAW	IABLS	10//99-12//99
	Kansas	S	9.67 MW	9.96 AW	20730 AAW	KSBLS	10//99-12//99
	Kentucky	S	9.6 MW	9.81 AW	20410 AAW	KYBLS	10//99-12//99
	Louisiana	S	9.46 MW	9.35 AW	19460 AAW	LABLS	10//99-12//99
	Maine	S	10.33 MW	10.90 AW	22670 AAW	MEBLS	10//99-12//99
	Maryland	S	11.49 MW	11.49 AW	23910 AAW	MDBLS	10//99-12//99
	Massachusetts	S	11.36 MW	11.40 AW	23710 AAW	MABLS	10//99-12//99
	Michigan	S	11.65 MW	11.61 AW	24150 AAW	MIBLS	10//99-12//99
	Minnesota	S	10.23 MW	10.49 AW	21810 AAW	MNBLS	10//99-12//99
	Mississippi	S	9.73 MW	9.61 AW	20000 AAW	MSBLS	10//99-12//99
	Missouri	S	10.19 MW	10.27 AW	21370 AAW	MOBLS	10//99-12//99
	Montana	S	8.63 MW	8.82 AW	18350 AAW	MTBLS	10//99-12//99
	Nebraska	S	10.34 MW	10.55 AW	21940 AAW	NEBLS	10//99-12//99
	Nevada	S	11.76 MW	11.83 AW	24610 AAW	NVBLS	10//99-12//99
	New Hampshire	S	10.2 MW	10.06 AW	20930 AAW	NHBLS	10//99-12//99
	New Jersey	S	11.86 MW	12.03 AW	25010 AAW	NJBLS	10//99-12//99
	New Mexico	S	9.09 MW	9.29 AW	19330 AAW	NMBLS	10//99-12//99
	New York	S	11.65 MW	11.67 AW	24260 AAW	NYBLS	10//99-12//99
	North Carolina	S	10.59 MW	10.56 AW	21960 AAW	NCBLS	10//99-12//99
	North Dakota	S	8.86 MW	9.70 AW	20180 AAW	NDBLS	10//99-12//99
	Ohio	S	10.26 MW	10.51 AW	21860 AAW	OHBLS	10//99-12//99
	Oklahoma	S	9.76 MW	9.80 AW	20380 AAW	OKBLS	10//99-12//99
	Oregon	S	10.98 MW	11.02 AW	22910 AAW	ORBLS	10//99-12//99
	Pennsylvania	S	10.9 MW	10.63 AW	22110 AAW	PABLS	10//99-12//99
	Rhode Island	S	12.15 MW	12.51 AW	26020 AAW	RIBLS	10//99-12//99
	South Carolina	S	10.14 MW	10.22 AW	21270 AAW	SCBLS	10//99-12//99
	South Dakota	S	9.4 MW	9.07 AW	18860 AAW	SDBLS	10//99-12//99
	Tennessee	S	9.78 MW	10.03 AW	20860 AAW	TNBLS	10//99-12//99
	Texas	S	10.28 MW	10.54 AW	21920 AAW	TXBLS	10//99-12//99
	Utah	S	10.47 MW	10.79 AW	22440 AAW	UTBLS	10//99-12//99
	Vermont	S	10.87 MW	11.20 AW	23290 AAW	VTBLS	10//99-12//99
	Virginia	S	10.2 MW	10.36 AW	21550 AAW	VABLS	10//99-12//99
	Washington	S	11.17 MW	11.67 AW	24280 AAW	WABLS	10//99-12//99
	West Virginia	S	8.99 MW	9.44 AW	19620 AAW	WVBLS	10//99-12//99
	Wisconsin	S	10.7 MW	10.84 AW	22540 AAW	WIBLS	10//99-12//99
	Wyoming	S	10.28 MW	10.10 AW	21000 AAW	WYBLS	10//99-12//99
	Puerto Rico	S	8.59 MW	9.66 AW	20100 AAW	PRBLS	10//99-12//99
	Guam	S	10.11 MW	10.07 AW	20940 AAW	GUBLS	10//99-12//99
New Car Manager Auto Dealership	United States	Y		79211 MW		WARD2	1999
New Car Salesperson Auto Dealership	United States	Y		45000 MW		WARD2	1999
News Analyst, Reporter and Correspondent	Alabama	S	12.18 MW	13.76 AW	28620 AAW	ALBLS	10//99-12//99
	Birmingham MSA, AL	S	17.13 MW	14.35 AW	35630 AAW	ALBLS	10//99-12//99
	Mobile MSA, AL	S	15.23 MW	14.34 AW	31680 AAW	ALBLS	10//99-12//99
	Tuscaloosa MSA, AL	S	10.35 MW	10.75 AW	21540 AAW	ALBLS	10//99-12//99
	Alaska	S	14.61 MW	15.62 AW	32490 AAW	AKBLS	10//99-12//99

AAW Average annual wage	**AOH** Average offered, high	**ASH** Average starting, high	**H** Hourly	**M** Monthly	**S** Special: hourly and annual
AE Average entry wage	**AOL** Average offered, low	**ASL** Average starting, low	**HI** Highest wage paid	**MTC** Median total compensation	**TQ** Third quartile wage
AEX Average experienced wage	**APH** Average pay, high range	**AW** Average wage paid	**HR** High end range	**MW** Median wage paid	**W** Weekly
AO Average offered	**APL** Average pay, low range	**FQ** First quartile wage	**LR** Low end range	**SQ** Second quartile wage	**Y** Yearly

Occupation/Type/Industry	Location	Per	Low	Mid	High	Source	Date
News Analyst, Reporter and Correspondent							
	Anchorage MSA, AK	S	17.21 MW	15.96 AW	35800 AAW	AKBLS	10//99-12//99
	Arizona	S	17.59 MW	18.62 AW	38740 AAW	AZBLS	10//99-12//99
	Phoenix-Mesa MSA, AZ	S	19.60 MW	19.29 AW	40770 AAW	AZBLS	10//99-12//99
	Tucson MSA, AZ	S	17.29 MW	15.97 AW	35970 AAW	AZBLS	10//99-12//99
	Arkansas	S	10.77 MW	12.03 AW	25020 AAW	ARBLS	10//99-12//99
	Fayetteville-Springdale-Rogers MSA, AR	S	11.58 MW	11.31 AW	24090 AAW	ARBLS	10//99-12//99
	Little Rock-North Little Rock MSA, AR	S	16.85 MW	14.92 AW	35050 AAW	ARBLS	10//99-12//99
	California	S	16.18 MW	21.37 AW	44450 AAW	CABLS	10//99-12//99
	Bakersfield MSA, CA	S	19.71 MW	16.46 AW	40990 AAW	CABLS	10//99-12//99
	Fresno MSA, CA	S	16.58 MW	14.00 AW	34480 AAW	CABLS	10//99-12//99
	Los Angeles-Long Beach PMSA, CA	S	26.03 MW	24.30 AW	54130 AAW	CABLS	10//99-12//99
	Modesto MSA, CA	S	13.03 MW	12.22 AW	27100 AAW	CABLS	10//99-12//99
	Oakland PMSA, CA	S	18.79 MW	15.53 AW	39080 AAW	CABLS	10//99-12//99
	Orange County PMSA, CA	S	17.67 MW	15.70 AW	36760 AAW	CABLS	10//99-12//99
	Riverside-San Bernardino PMSA, CA	S	17.06 MW	13.56 AW	35490 AAW	CABLS	10//99-12//99
	Sacramento PMSA, CA	S	16.40 MW	12.92 AW	34120 AAW	CABLS	10//99-12//99
	Salinas MSA, CA	S	17.86 MW	15.77 AW	37160 AAW	CABLS	10//99-12//99
	San Diego MSA, CA	S	18.81 MW	11.10 AW	39120 AAW	CABLS	10//99-12//99
	San Francisco PMSA, CA	S	23.94 MW	25.36 AW	49800 AAW	CABLS	10//99-12//99
	San Jose PMSA, CA	S	25.95 MW	24.78 AW	53970 AAW	CABLS	10//99-12//99
	San Luis Obispo-Atascadero-Paso Robles MSA, CA	S	11.21 MW	11.01 AW	23320 AAW	CABLS	10//99-12//99
	Santa Barbara-Santa Maria-Lompoc MSA, CA	S	12.02 MW	11.18 AW	25010 AAW	CABLS	10//99-12//99
	Vallejo-Fairfield-Napa PMSA, CA	S	12.07 MW	11.83 AW	25110 AAW	CABLS	10//99-12//99
	Visalia-Tulare-Porterville MSA, CA	S	19.33 MW	16.29 AW	40200 AAW	CABLS	10//99-12//99
	Colorado	S	13.5 MW	17.51 AW	36430 AAW	COBLS	10//99-12//99
	Boulder-Longmont PMSA, CO	S	19.84 MW	17.23 AW	41260 AAW	COBLS	10//99-12//99
	Denver PMSA, CO	S	24.47 MW	23.53 AW	50900 AAW	COBLS	10//99-12//99
	Grand Junction MSA, CO	S	15.14 MW	12.93 AW	31490 AAW	COBLS	10//99-12//99
	Connecticut	S	13.95 MW	16.08 AW	33450 AAW	CTBLS	10//99-12//99
	Danbury PMSA, CT	S	15.04 MW	15.02 AW	31290 AAW	CTBLS	10//99-12//99
	Hartford MSA, CT	S	15.34 MW	13.02 AW	31900 AAW	CTBLS	10//99-12//99
	New Haven-Meriden PMSA, CT	S	17.74 MW	14.93 AW	36910 AAW	CTBLS	10//99-12//99
	Stamford-Norwalk PMSA, CT	S	17.25 MW	15.79 AW	35880 AAW	CTBLS	10//99-12//99
	Waterbury PMSA, CT	S	12.19 MW	10.36 AW	25350 AAW	CTBLS	10//99-12//99
	Delaware	S	12.81 MW	16.17 AW	33620 AAW	DEBLS	10//99-12//99
	Wilmington-Newark PMSA, DE-MD	S	16.88 MW	14.07 AW	35120 AAW	DEBLS	10//99-12//99
	District of Columbia	S	20.06 MW	23.39 AW	48660 AAW	DCBLS	10//99-12//99
	Washington PMSA, DC-MD-VA-WV	S	22.37 MW	19.40 AW	46540 AAW	DCBLS	10//99-12//99
	Florida	S	16.39 MW	20.61 AW	42860 AAW	FLBLS	10//99-12//99
	Fort Lauderdale PMSA, FL	S	19.85 MW	14.94 AW	41290 AAW	FLBLS	10//99-12//99
	Fort Myers-Cape Coral MSA, FL	S	17.21 MW	11.76 AW	35810 AAW	FLBLS	10//99-12//99
	Lakeland-Winter Haven MSA, FL	S	13.62 MW	14.39 AW	28330 AAW	FLBLS	10//99-12//99
	Pensacola MSA, FL	S	19.83 MW	14.82 AW	41240 AAW	FLBLS	10//99-12//99
	Tallahassee MSA, FL	S	24.66 MW	16.01 AW	51280 AAW	FLBLS	10//99-12//99
	Tampa-St. Petersburg-Clearwater MSA, FL	S	17.54 MW	13.62 AW	36480 AAW	FLBLS	10//99-12//99
	Georgia	S	11.3 MW	11.87 AW	24680 AAW	GABLS	10//99-12//99
	Atlanta MSA, GA	S	12.10 MW	11.63 AW	25180 AAW	GABLS	10//99-12//99
	Augusta-Aiken MSA, GA-SC	S	12.73 MW	10.70 AW	26470 AAW	GABLS	10//99-12//99
	Columbus MSA, GA-AL	S	13.28 MW	12.99 AW	27620 AAW	GABLS	10//99-12//99
	Macon MSA, GA	S	13.20 MW	11.83 AW	27450 AAW	GABLS	10//99-12//99
	Savannah MSA, GA	S	13.17 MW	12.22 AW	27400 AAW	GABLS	10//99-12//99
	Hawaii	S	20.25 MW	24.14 AW	50210 AAW	HIBLS	10//99-12//99
	Honolulu MSA, HI	S	25.09 MW	21.15 AW	52180 AAW	HIBLS	10//99-12//99
	Idaho	S	10.62 MW	12.47 AW	25930 AAW	IDBLS	10//99-12//99
	Boise City MSA, ID	S	15.56 MW	12.26 AW	32360 AAW	IDBLS	10//99-12//99
	Illinois	S	10.04 MW	12.20 AW	25370 AAW	ILBLS	10//99-12//99
	Chicago PMSA, IL	S	11.85 MW	8.37 AW	24650 AAW	ILBLS	10//99-12//99

Occupation/Type/Industry	Location	Per	Low	Mid	High	Source	Date
News Analyst, Reporter and Correspondent	Kankakee PMSA, IL	S	16.50 MW	15.75 AW	34330 AAW	ILBLS	10//99-12//99
	Peoria-Pekin MSA, IL	S	14.58 MW	11.13 AW	30330 AAW	ILBLS	10//99-12//99
	Rockford MSA, IL	S	14.27 MW	13.36 AW	29680 AAW	ILBLS	10//99-12//99
	Indiana	S	11.05 MW	12.30 AW	25590 AAW	INBLS	10//99-12//99
	Evansville-Henderson MSA, IN-KY	S	14.04 MW	13.13 AW	29210 AAW	INBLS	10//99-12//99
	Fort Wayne MSA, IN	S	13.73 MW	12.48 AW	28550 AAW	INBLS	10//99-12//99
	Gary PMSA, IN	S	12.55 MW	12.58 AW	26110 AAW	INBLS	10//99-12//99
	Indianapolis MSA, IN	S	12.93 MW	11.55 AW	26890 AAW	INBLS	10//99-12//99
	Lafayette MSA, IN	S	12.05 MW	10.88 AW	25060 AAW	INBLS	10//99-12//99
	Iowa	S	9.9 MW	12.76 AW	26530 AAW	IABLS	10//99-12//99
	Davenport-Moline-Rock Island MSA, IA-IL	S	15.82 MW	12.81 AW	32900 AAW	IABLS	10//99-12//99
	Des Moines MSA, IA	S	18.15 MW	15.40 AW	37750 AAW	IABLS	10//99-12//99
	Dubuque MSA, IA	S	10.09 MW	10.81 AW	20990 AAW	IABLS	10//99-12//99
	Sioux City MSA, IA-NE	S	13.67 MW	10.01 AW	28430 AAW	IABLS	10//99-12//99
	Kansas	S	10.38 MW	12.10 AW	25180 AAW	KSBLS	10//99-12//99
	Topeka MSA, KS	S	14.78 MW	13.20 AW	30730 AAW	KSBLS	10//99-12//99
	Wichita MSA, KS	S	14.86 MW	11.68 AW	30900 AAW	KSBLS	10//99-12//99
	Kentucky	S	11.44 MW	15.02 AW	31250 AAW	KYBLS	10//99-12//99
	Lexington MSA, KY	S	18.91 MW	14.98 AW	39330 AAW	KYBLS	10//99-12//99
	Louisville MSA, KY-IN	S	17.74 MW	13.69 AW	36890 AAW	KYBLS	10//99-12//99
	Louisiana	S	13.05 MW	15.95 AW	33170 AAW	LABLS	10//99-12//99
	Baton Rouge MSA, LA	S	17.57 MW	15.73 AW	36550 AAW	LABLS	10//99-12//99
	Lafayette MSA, LA	S	16.13 MW	14.14 AW	33550 AAW	LABLS	10//99-12//99
	New Orleans MSA, LA	S	16.85 MW	9.78 AW	35040 AAW	LABLS	10//99-12//99
	Maine	S	10.98 MW	12.96 AW	26960 AAW	MEBLS	10//99-12//99
	Maryland	S	13.32 MW	18.33 AW	38120 AAW	MDBLS	10//99-12//99
	Baltimore PMSA, MD	S	18.09 MW	13.75 AW	37640 AAW	MDBLS	10//99-12//99
	Massachusetts	S	14.96 MW	16.89 AW	35120 AAW	MABLS	10//99-12//99
	Boston PMSA, MA-NH	S	17.69 MW	14.99 AW	36790 AAW	MABLS	10//99-12//99
	Springfield MSA, MA	S	15.11 MW	14.32 AW	31430 AAW	MABLS	10//99-12//99
	Michigan	S	15.33 MW	19.64 AW	40850 AAW	MIBLS	10//99-12//99
	Ann Arbor PMSA, MI	S	19.26 MW	17.17 AW	40050 AAW	MIBLS	10//99-12//99
	Detroit PMSA, MI	S	26.49 MW	25.40 AW	55110 AAW	MIBLS	10//99-12//99
	Flint PMSA, MI	S	21.55 MW	22.90 AW	44830 AAW	MIBLS	10//99-12//99
	Grand Rapids-Muskegon-Holland MSA, MI	S	11.80 MW	9.89 AW	24540 AAW	MIBLS	10//99-12//99
	Kalamazoo-Battle Creek MSA, MI	S	19.16 MW	16.06 AW	39850 AAW	MIBLS	10//99-12//99
	Saginaw-Bay City-Midland MSA, MI	S	16.80 MW	16.15 AW	34950 AAW	MIBLS	10//99-12//99
	Minnesota	S	11.37 MW	15.98 AW	33240 AAW	MNBLS	10//99-12//99
	Minneapolis-St. Paul MSA, MN-WI	S	20.62 MW	17.91 AW	42890 AAW	MNBLS	10//99-12//99
	St. Cloud MSA, MN	S	19.85 MW	17.42 AW	41280 AAW	MNBLS	10//99-12//99
	Mississippi	S	11.46 MW	12.27 AW	25510 AAW	MSBLS	10//99-12//99
	Biloxi-Gulfport-Pascagoula MSA, MS	S	15.15 MW	14.46 AW	31500 AAW	MSBLS	10//99-12//99
	Jackson MSA, MS	S	15.24 MW	14.07 AW	31690 AAW	MSBLS	10//99-12//99
	Missouri	S	11.2 MW	15.31 AW	31850 AAW	MOBLS	10//99-12//99
	St. Louis MSA, MO-IL	S	17.42 MW	13.44 AW	36240 AAW	MOBLS	10//99-12//99
	Springfield MSA, MO	S	19.66 MW	13.97 AW	40880 AAW	MOBLS	10//99-12//99
	Montana	S	11.76 MW	13.19 AW	27440 AAW	MTBLS	10//99-12//99
	Billings MSA, MT	S	13.27 MW	13.21 AW	27600 AAW	MTBLS	10//99-12//99
	Nebraska	S	9.44 MW	10.28 AW	21380 AAW	NEBLS	10//99-12//99
	Omaha MSA, NE-IA	S	12.33 MW	10.93 AW	25640 AAW	NEBLS	10//99-12//99
	Nevada	S	15.2 MW	16.47 AW	34260 AAW	NVBLS	10//99-12//99
	Las Vegas MSA, NV-AZ	S	17.42 MW	16.37 AW	36240 AAW	NVBLS	10//99-12//99
	Reno MSA, NV	S	15.16 MW	14.04 AW	31540 AAW	NVBLS	10//99-12//99
	New Hampshire	S	11.14 MW	14.86 AW	30910 AAW	NHBLS	10//99-12//99
	Portsmouth-Rochester PMSA, NH-ME	S	12.32 MW	11.07 AW	25620 AAW	NHBLS	10//99-12//99
	New Jersey	S	13.18 MW	16.00 AW	33280 AAW	NJBLS	10//99-12//99
	Bergen-Passaic PMSA, NJ	S	18.59 MW	14.33 AW	38660 AAW	NJBLS	10//99-12//99
	Jersey City PMSA, NJ	S	16.87 MW	15.11 AW	35080 AAW	NJBLS	10//99-12//99
	Middlesex-Somerset-Hunterdon PMSA, NJ	S	14.84 MW	11.96 AW	30860 AAW	NJBLS	10//99-12//99
	Monmouth-Ocean PMSA, NJ	S	15.72 MW	13.50 AW	32690 AAW	NJBLS	10//99-12//99
	Newark PMSA, NJ	S	15.42 MW	12.30 AW	32080 AAW	NJBLS	10//99-12//99
	New Mexico	S	10.67 MW	12.64 AW	26290 AAW	NMBLS	10//99-12//99

AAW Average annual wage	**AOH** Average offered, high	**ASH** Average starting, high	**H** Hourly	**M** Monthly	**S** Special: hourly and annual
AE Average entry wage	**AOL** Average offered, low	**ASL** Average starting, low	**HI** Highest wage paid	**MTC** Median total compensation	**TQ** Third quartile wage
AEX Average experienced wage	**APH** Average pay, high range	**AW** Average wage paid	**HR** High end range	**MW** Median wage paid	**W** Weekly
AO Average offered	**APL** Average pay, low range	**FQ** First quartile wage	**LR** Low end range	**SQ** Second quartile wage	**Y** Yearly

Occupation/Type/Industry	Location	Per	Low	Mid	High	Source	Date
News Analyst, Reporter and Correspondent	Albuquerque MSA, NM	S	15.28 MW	13.01 AW	31790 AAW	NMBLS	10//99-12//99
	Santa Fe MSA, NM	S	12.48 MW	10.69 AW	25950 AAW	NMBLS	10//99-12//99
	New York	S	15.93 MW	21.52 AW	44750 AAW	NYBLS	10//99-12//99
	Albany-Schenectady-Troy MSA, NY	S	19.08 MW	16.38 AW	39680 AAW	NYBLS	10//99-12//99
	Binghamton MSA, NY	S	15.25 MW	12.45 AW	31720 AAW	NYBLS	10//99-12//99
	Buffalo-Niagara Falls MSA, NY	S	21.59 MW	18.28 AW	44900 AAW	NYBLS	10//99-12//99
	Glens Falls MSA, NY	S	15.87 MW	13.40 AW	33000 AAW	NYBLS	10//99-12//99
	Nassau-Suffolk PMSA, NY	S	19.25 MW	16.73 AW	40030 AAW	NYBLS	10//99-12//99
	New York PMSA, NY	S	25.19 MW	17.60 AW	52390 AAW	NYBLS	10//99-12//99
	Rochester MSA, NY	S	14.94 MW	13.06 AW	31070 AAW	NYBLS	10//99-12//99
	Syracuse MSA, NY	S	15.30 MW	10.53 AW	31810 AAW	NYBLS	10//99-12//99
	Utica-Rome MSA, NY	S	17.62 MW	12.02 AW	36650 AAW	NYBLS	10//99-12//99
	North Carolina	S	13.91 MW	16.25 AW	33800 AAW	NCBLS	10//99-12//99
	Charlotte-Gastonia-Rock Hill MSA, NC-SC	S	20.80 MW	17.77 AW	43270 AAW	NCBLS	10//99-12//99
	Greensboro--Winston-Salem--High Point MSA, NC	S	17.01 MW	14.78 AW	35390 AAW	NCBLS	10//99-12//99
	Raleigh-Durham-Chapel Hill MSA, NC	S	19.94 MW	18.16 AW	41470 AAW	NCBLS	10//99-12//99
	North Dakota	S	11.21 MW	11.68 AW	24300 AAW	NDBLS	10//99-12//99
	Bismarck MSA, ND	S	14.97 MW	13.45 AW	31140 AAW	NDBLS	10//99-12//99
	Fargo-Moorhead MSA, ND-MN	S	12.84 MW	11.83 AW	26710 AAW	NDBLS	10//99-12//99
	Grand Forks MSA, ND-MN	S	12.20 MW	12.51 AW	25380 AAW	NDBLS	10//99-12//99
	Ohio	S	11.82 MW	14.29 AW	29730 AAW	OHBLS	10//99-12//99
	Akron PMSA, OH	S	11.72 MW	11.03 AW	24390 AAW	OHBLS	10//99-12//99
	Canton-Massillon MSA, OH	S	14.23 MW	13.00 AW	29600 AAW	OHBLS	10//99-12//99
	Cincinnati PMSA, OH-KY-IN	S	19.36 MW	17.78 AW	40270 AAW	OHBLS	10//99-12//99
	Cleveland-Lorain-Elyria PMSA, OH	S	16.46 MW	12.60 AW	34240 AAW	OHBLS	10//99-12//99
	Columbus MSA, OH	S	13.85 MW	11.73 AW	28800 AAW	OHBLS	10//99-12//99
	Dayton-Springfield MSA, OH	S	14.59 MW	11.25 AW	30350 AAW	OHBLS	10//99-12//99
	Hamilton-Middletown PMSA, OH	S	12.30 MW	12.34 AW	25590 AAW	OHBLS	10//99-12//99
	Lima MSA, OH	S	11.89 MW	10.65 AW	24740 AAW	OHBLS	10//99-12//99
	Mansfield MSA, OH	S	11.55 MW	11.53 AW	24020 AAW	OHBLS	10//99-12//99
	Toledo MSA, OH	S	15.78 MW	13.59 AW	32830 AAW	OHBLS	10//99-12//99
	Youngstown-Warren MSA, OH	S	13.44 MW	12.79 AW	27960 AAW	OHBLS	10//99-12//99
	Oklahoma	S	9.9 MW	11.33 AW	23570 AAW	OKBLS	10//99-12//99
	Oklahoma City MSA, OK	S	13.68 MW	11.27 AW	28450 AAW	OKBLS	10//99-12//99
	Tulsa MSA, OK	S	10.22 MW	9.72 AW	21250 AAW	OKBLS	10//99-12//99
	Oregon	S	10.45 MW	12.62 AW	26240 AAW	ORBLS	10//99-12//99
	Eugene-Springfield MSA, OR	S	12.18 MW	9.63 AW	25330 AAW	ORBLS	10//99-12//99
	Pennsylvania	S	13.19 MW	15.28 AW	31770 AAW	PABLS	10//99-12//99
	Allentown-Bethlehem-Easton MSA, PA	S	18.32 MW	18.87 AW	38110 AAW	PABLS	10//99-12//99
	Erie MSA, PA	S	13.32 MW	11.48 AW	27700 AAW	PABLS	10//99-12//99
	Harrisburg-Lebanon-Carlisle MSA, PA	S	15.41 MW	15.48 AW	32040 AAW	PABLS	10//99-12//99
	Johnstown MSA, PA	S	13.19 MW	10.50 AW	27440 AAW	PABLS	10//99-12//99
	Lancaster MSA, PA	S	15.10 MW	15.08 AW	31420 AAW	PABLS	10//99-12//99
	Philadelphia PMSA, PA-NJ	S	17.67 MW	12.91 AW	36760 AAW	PABLS	10//99-12//99
	Pittsburgh MSA, PA	S	12.13 MW	11.38 AW	25230 AAW	PABLS	10//99-12//99
	Scranton--Wilkes-Barre--Hazleton MSA, PA	S	17.82 MW	15.88 AW	37060 AAW	PABLS	10//99-12//99
	Rhode Island	S	16.64 MW	20.72 AW	43100 AAW	RIBLS	10//99-12//99
	Providence-Fall River-Warwick MSA, RI-MA	S	19.89 MW	16.06 AW	41360 AAW	RIBLS	10//99-12//99
	South Carolina	S	12.9 MW	14.65 AW	30480 AAW	SCBLS	10//99-12//99
	Charleston-North Charleston MSA, SC	S	12.60 MW	10.51 AW	26220 AAW	SCBLS	10//99-12//99
	Columbia MSA, SC	S	18.49 MW	16.85 AW	38450 AAW	SCBLS	10//99-12//99
	Greenville-Spartanburg-Anderson MSA, SC	S	16.09 MW	14.62 AW	33460 AAW	SCBLS	10//99-12//99
	South Dakota	S	10.41 MW	11.10 AW	23090 AAW	SDBLS	10//99-12//99
	Tennessee	S	13.55 MW	16.21 AW	33720 AAW	TNBLS	10//99-12//99
	Chattanooga MSA, TN-GA	S	16.17 MW	13.31 AW	33640 AAW	TNBLS	10//99-12//99
	Johnson City-Kingsport-Bristol MSA, TN-VA	S	16.15 MW	11.98 AW	33590 AAW	TNBLS	10//99-12//99

AAW Average annual wage	**AOH** Average offered, high	**ASH** Average starting, high	**H** Hourly	**M** Monthly	**S** Special: hourly and annual
AE Average entry wage	**AOL** Average offered, low	**ASL** Average starting, low	**HI** Highest wage paid	**MTC** Median total compensation	**TQ** Third quartile wage
AEX Average experienced wage	**APH** Average pay, high range	**AW** Average wage paid	**HR** High end range	**MW** Median wage paid	**W** Weekly
AO Average offered	**APL** Average pay, low range	**FQ** First quartile wage	**LR** Low end range	**SQ** Second quartile wage	**Y** Yearly

Occupation/Type/Industry	Location	Per	Low	Mid	High	Source	Date
News Analyst, Reporter and Correspondent							
	Knoxville MSA, TN	S	16.27 MW	16.66 AW	33840 AAW	TNBLS	10//99-12//99
	Memphis MSA, TN-AR-MS	S	19.52 MW	20.31 AW	40600 AAW	MSBLS	10//99-12//99
	Nashville MSA, TN	S	17.72 MW	14.01 AW	36850 AAW	TNBLS	10//99-12//99
	Texas	S	11.86 MW	14.80 AW	30770 AAW	TXBLS	10//99-12//99
	Amarillo MSA, TX	S	12.00 MW	11.23 AW	24960 AAW	TXBLS	10//99-12//99
	Austin-San Marcos MSA, TX	S	17.81 MW	16.54 AW	37040 AAW	TXBLS	10//99-12//99
	Beaumont-Port Arthur MSA, TX	S	12.61 MW	10.34 AW	26240 AAW	TXBLS	10//99-12//99
	Brownsville-Harlingen-San Benito MSA, TX	S	10.34 MW	9.87 AW	21500 AAW	TXBLS	10//99-12//99
	Dallas PMSA, TX	S	15.12 MW	12.28 AW	31440 AAW	TXBLS	10//99-12//99
	El Paso MSA, TX	S	17.02 MW	15.26 AW	35400 AAW	TXBLS	10//99-12//99
	Houston PMSA, TX	S	16.35 MW	12.39 AW	34010 AAW	TXBLS	10//99-12//99
	Lubbock MSA, TX	S	16.46 MW	11.65 AW	34230 AAW	TXBLS	10//99-12//99
	San Antonio MSA, TX	S	17.73 MW	16.20 AW	36870 AAW	TXBLS	10//99-12//99
	Utah	S	16 MW	17.99 AW	37410 AAW	UTBLS	10//99-12//99
	Salt Lake City-Ogden MSA, UT	S	19.49 MW	17.70 AW	40540 AAW	UTBLS	10//99-12//99
	Virginia	S	12.7 MW	16.39 AW	34100 AAW	VABLS	10//99-12//99
	Norfolk-Virginia Beach-Newport News MSA, VA-NC	S	18.74 MW	14.03 AW	38980 AAW	VABLS	10//99-12//99
	Richmond-Petersburg MSA, VA	S	19.00 MW	17.50 AW	39520 AAW	VABLS	10//99-12//99
	Roanoke MSA, VA	S	16.36 MW	13.55 AW	34020 AAW	VABLS	10//99-12//99
	Washington	S	16.99 MW	19.26 AW	40060 AAW	WABLS	10//99-12//99
	Bellingham MSA, WA	S	14.03 MW	12.94 AW	29180 AAW	WABLS	10//99-12//99
	Richland-Kennewick-Pasco MSA, WA	S	16.61 MW	13.46 AW	34540 AAW	WABLS	10//99-12//99
	Seattle-Bellevue-Everett PMSA, WA	S	21.60 MW	19.96 AW	44930 AAW	WABLS	10//99-12//99
	Spokane MSA, WA	S	20.82 MW	19.22 AW	43310 AAW	WABLS	10//99-12//99
	West Virginia	S	9.85 MW	12.52 AW	26050 AAW	WVBLS	10//99-12//99
	Huntington-Ashland MSA, WV-KY-OH	S	15.84 MW	12.61 AW	32940 AAW	WVBLS	10//99-12//99
	Wisconsin	S	12.9 MW	14.89 AW	30970 AAW	WIBLS	10//99-12//99
	Green Bay MSA, WI	S	16.51 MW	14.81 AW	34330 AAW	WIBLS	10//99-12//99
	La Crosse MSA, WI-MN	S	16.71 MW	12.76 AW	34750 AAW	WIBLS	10//99-12//99
	Madison MSA, WI	S	14.14 MW	13.59 AW	29420 AAW	WIBLS	10//99-12//99
	Milwaukee-Waukesha PMSA, WI	S	16.88 MW	13.73 AW	35100 AAW	WIBLS	10//99-12//99
	Wyoming	S	9.5 MW	10.49 AW	21820 AAW	WYBLS	10//99-12//99
	Casper MSA, WY	S	12.88 MW	10.86 AW	26790 AAW	WYBLS	10//99-12//99
	Puerto Rico	S	13.25 MW	14.42 AW	30000 AAW	PRBLS	10//99-12//99
	San Juan-Bayamon PMSA, PR	S	15.07 MW	13.78 AW	31340 AAW	PRBLS	10//99-12//99
	Virgin Islands	S	13.94 MW	15.39 AW	32010 AAW	VIBLS	10//99-12//99
Nonfarm Animal Caretaker	Alabama	S	7.7 MW	8.30 AW	17270 AAW	ALBLS	10//99-12//99
	Alaska	S	7.5 MW	8.94 AW	18590 AAW	AKBLS	10//99-12//99
	Arizona	S	6.67 MW	6.85 AW	14250 AAW	AZBLS	10//99-12//99
	Arkansas	S	7.12 MW	7.80 AW	16220 AAW	ARBLS	10//99-12//99
	California	S	7.68 MW	8.88 AW	18480 AAW	CABLS	10//99-12//99
	Colorado	S	8.52 MW	9.40 AW	19550 AAW	COBLS	10//99-12//99
	Connecticut	S	8.03 MW	8.96 AW	18640 AAW	CTBLS	10//99-12//99
	Delaware	S	11.19 MW	10.22 AW	21250 AAW	DEBLS	10//99-12//99
	District of Columbia	S	7.63 MW	8.14 AW	16930 AAW	DCBLS	10//99-12//99
	Florida	S	7.07 MW	7.40 AW	15400 AAW	FLBLS	10//99-12//99
	Georgia	S	7.91 MW	8.65 AW	17990 AAW	GABLS	10//99-12//99
	Hawaii	S	9.81 MW	9.78 AW	20340 AAW	HIBLS	10//99-12//99
	Idaho	S	6.3 MW	6.79 AW	14130 AAW	IDBLS	10//99-12//99
	Illinois	S	7.2 MW	7.95 AW	16540 AAW	ILBLS	10//99-12//99
	Indiana	S	7.13 MW	7.53 AW	15670 AAW	INBLS	10//99-12//99
	Iowa	S	6.1 MW	6.67 AW	13880 AAW	IABLS	10//99-12//99
	Kansas	S	7.38 MW	7.56 AW	15720 AAW	KSBLS	10//99-12//99
	Kentucky	S	7.28 MW	7.86 AW	16350 AAW	KYBLS	10//99-12//99
	Louisiana	S	6.85 MW	7.21 AW	14990 AAW	LABLS	10//99-12//99
	Maine	S	7.36 MW	7.54 AW	15680 AAW	MEBLS	10//99-12//99
	Maryland	S	8.28 MW	8.78 AW	18260 AAW	MDBLS	10//99-12//99
	Massachusetts	S	7.74 MW	8.27 AW	17200 AAW	MABLS	10//99-12//99
	Michigan	S	8.07 MW	8.94 AW	18600 AAW	MIBLS	10//99-12//99
	Minnesota	S	7.78 MW	7.88 AW	16380 AAW	MNBLS	10//99-12//99

AAW	Average annual wage	AOH	Average offered, high	ASH	Average starting, high
AE	Average entry wage	AOL	Average offered, low	ASL	Average starting, low
AEX	Average experienced wage	APH	Average pay, high range	AW	Average wage paid
AO	Average offered	APL	Average pay, low range	FQ	First quartile wage

H	Hourly	M	Monthly
HI	Highest wage paid	MTC	Median total compensation
HR	High end range	MW	Median wage paid
LR	Low end range	SQ	Second quartile wage

S	Special: hourly and annual
TQ	Third quartile wage
W	Weekly
Y	Yearly

Occupation/Type/Industry	Location	Per	Low	Mid	High	Source	Date
Nonfarm Animal Caretaker	Mississippi	S	6.61 MW	7.06 AW	14690 AAW	MSBLS	10//99-12//99
	Missouri	S	7.04 MW	7.80 AW	16220 AAW	MOBLS	10//99-12//99
	Montana	S	6.42 MW	7.06 AW	14690 AAW	MTBLS	10//99-12//99
	Nebraska	S	8.68 MW	10.06 AW	20920 AAW	NEBLS	10//99-12//99
	Nevada	S	7.96 MW	9.31 AW	19370 AAW	NVBLS	10//99-12//99
	New Hampshire	S	7.37 MW	8.40 AW	17460 AAW	NHBLS	10//99-12//99
	New Jersey	S	7.52 MW	7.88 AW	16390 AAW	NJBLS	10//99-12//99
	New Mexico	S	8.01 MW	8.59 AW	17860 AAW	NMBLS	10//99-12//99
	New York	S	7.95 MW	8.80 AW	18300 AAW	NYBLS	10//99-12//99
	North Carolina	S	7.65 MW	8.30 AW	17270 AAW	NCBLS	10//99-12//99
	North Dakota	S	6.73 MW	7.66 AW	15930 AAW	NDBLS	10//99-12//99
	Ohio	S	7.13 MW	7.83 AW	16290 AAW	OHBLS	10//99-12//99
	Oklahoma	S	7.65 MW	8.09 AW	16820 AAW	OKBLS	10//99-12//99
	Oregon	S	7.92 MW	10.23 AW	21290 AAW	ORBLS	10//99-12//99
	Pennsylvania	S	6.79 MW	7.86 AW	16350 AAW	PABLS	10//99-12//99
	Rhode Island	S	8.58 MW	9.34 AW	19430 AAW	RIBLS	10//99-12//99
	South Carolina	S	7.11 MW	7.51 AW	15620 AAW	SCBLS	10//99-12//99
	South Dakota	S	8.22 MW	8.55 AW	17780 AAW	SDBLS	10//99-12//99
	Tennessee	S	7.8 MW	8.16 AW	16980 AAW	TNBLS	10//99-12//99
	Texas	S	7.15 MW	7.60 AW	15820 AAW	TXBLS	10//99-12//99
	Utah	S	7.47 MW	8.39 AW	17460 AAW	UTBLS	10//99-12//99
	Vermont	S	7.71 MW	8.19 AW	17030 AAW	VTBLS	10//99-12//99
	Virginia	S	7.11 MW	8.23 AW	17120 AAW	VABLS	10//99-12//99
	Washington	S	8.01 MW	9.28 AW	19290 AAW	WABLS	10//99-12//99
	West Virginia	S	6.61 MW	7.31 AW	15210 AAW	WVBLS	10//99-12//99
	Wisconsin	S	7.55 MW	8.03 AW	16710 AAW	WIBLS	10//99-12//99
	Wyoming	S	9.18 MW	9.01 AW	18740 AAW	WYBLS	10//99-12//99
	Puerto Rico	S	5.99 MW	5.90 AW	12270 AAW	PRBLS	10//99-12//99
Nuclear Engineer	California	S	39.36 MW	38.55 AW	80190 AAW	CABLS	10//99-12//99
	Colorado	S	49.19 MW	45.51 AW	94670 AAW	COBLS	10//99-12//99
	Connecticut	S	33.41 MW	32.91 AW	68460 AAW	CTBLS	10//99-12//99
	Florida	S	33.05 MW	32.51 AW	67630 AAW	FLBLS	10//99-12//99
	Illinois	S	40.23 MW	39.05 AW	81230 AAW	ILBLS	10//99-12//99
	Massachusetts	S	61.9 MW	55.83 AW	116130 AAW	MABLS	10//99-12//99
	New Jersey	S	35.77 MW	34.67 AW	72110 AAW	NJBLS	10//99-12//99
	New York	S	35.13 MW	32.33 AW	67240 AAW	NYBLS	10//99-12//99
	Oklahoma	S	45.99 MW	43.75 AW	91010 AAW	OKBLS	10//99-12//99
	South Carolina	S	36.12 MW	34.86 AW	72500 AAW	SCBLS	10//99-12//99
	Texas	S	35.58 MW	32.81 AW	68240 AAW	TXBLS	10//99-12//99
	Washington	S	32.85 MW	32.23 AW	67030 AAW	WABLS	10//99-12//99
Nuclear Medicine Technologist	Alabama	S	18.07 MW	18.23 AW	37920 AAW	ALBLS	10//99-12//99
	Alaska	S	23.26 MW	23.08 AW	48010 AAW	AKBLS	10//99-12//99
	Arizona	S	19.43 MW	20.24 AW	42100 AAW	AZBLS	10//99-12//99
	Arkansas	S	17.95 MW	18.19 AW	37840 AAW	ARBLS	10//99-12//99
	California	S	25 MW	26.14 AW	54370 AAW	CABLS	10//99-12//99
	Colorado	S	18.63 MW	18.70 AW	38900 AAW	COBLS	10//99-12//99
	Connecticut	S	22.7 MW	23.39 AW	48650 AAW	CTBLS	10//99-12//99
	Delaware	S	19.82 MW	19.32 AW	40190 AAW	DEBLS	10//99-12//99
	District of Columbia	S	19.8 MW	20.15 AW	41900 AAW	DCBLS	10//99-12//99
	Florida	S	19.22 MW	20.07 AW	41750 AAW	FLBLS	10//99-12//99
	Georgia	S	18.2 MW	18.16 AW	37780 AAW	GABLS	10//99-12//99
	Hawaii	S	23.04 MW	23.09 AW	48030 AAW	HIBLS	10//99-12//99
	Illinois	S	19.43 MW	19.82 AW	41230 AAW	ILBLS	10//99-12//99
	Indiana	S	18.75 MW	18.89 AW	39300 AAW	INBLS	10//99-12//99
	Iowa	S	17.13 MW	16.97 AW	35300 AAW	IABLS	10//99-12//99
	Kansas	S	18.65 MW	18.90 AW	39300 AAW	KSBLS	10//99-12//99
	Kentucky	S	17.89 MW	18.14 AW	37730 AAW	KYBLS	10//99-12//99
	Louisiana	S	19.15 MW	19.41 AW	40370 AAW	LABLS	10//99-12//99
	Maine	S	17.65 MW	17.79 AW	37000 AAW	MEBLS	10//99-12//99
	Maryland	S	22.24 MW	21.91 AW	45570 AAW	MDBLS	10//99-12//99
	Massachusetts	S	21.01 MW	21.87 AW	45490 AAW	MABLS	10//99-12//99
	Michigan	S	19.13 MW	19.34 AW	40220 AAW	MIBLS	10//99-12//99
	Minnesota	S	19.86 MW	20.00 AW	41610 AAW	MNBLS	10//99-12//99
	Mississippi	S	18.06 MW	17.70 AW	36810 AAW	MSBLS	10//99-12//99
	Missouri	S	19.5 MW	19.99 AW	41570 AAW	MOBLS	10//99-12//99
	Montana	S	19.27 MW	19.48 AW	40520 AAW	MTBLS	10//99-12//99
	Nebraska	S	18.4 MW	18.82 AW	39150 AAW	NEBLS	10//99-12//99
	Nevada	S	20.93 MW	20.91 AW	43500 AAW	NVBLS	10//99-12//99
	New Hampshire	S	19.39 MW	19.37 AW	40290 AAW	NHBLS	10//99-12//99
	New Jersey	S	23.72 MW	24.09 AW	50120 AAW	NJBLS	10//99-12//99
	New Mexico	S	19.47 MW	20.47 AW	42590 AAW	NMBLS	10//99-12//99

Occupation/Type/Industry	Location	Per	Low	Mid	High	Source	Date
Nuclear Medicine Technologist	New York	S	21.51 MW	23.11 AW	48060 AAW	NYBLS	10//99-12//99
	North Carolina	S	18.74 MW	19.00 AW	39510 AAW	NCBLS	10//99-12//99
	North Dakota	S	18.14 MW	17.95 AW	37330 AAW	NDBLS	10//99-12//99
	Ohio	S	18.06 MW	18.10 AW	37640 AAW	OHBLS	10//99-12//99
	Oklahoma	S	20 MW	20.31 AW	42240 AAW	OKBLS	10//99-12//99
	Oregon	S	19.93 MW	20.36 AW	42360 AAW	ORBLS	10//99-12//99
	Pennsylvania	S	18.52 MW	18.78 AW	39060 AAW	PABLS	10//99-12//99
	Rhode Island	S	20.57 MW	21.81 AW	45360 AAW	RIBLS	10//99-12//99
	South Carolina	S	19.58 MW	20.49 AW	42630 AAW	SCBLS	10//99-12//99
	South Dakota	S	17.31 MW	17.79 AW	37000 AAW	SDBLS	10//99-12//99
	Tennessee	S	18.69 MW	18.78 AW	39070 AAW	TNBLS	10//99-12//99
	Texas	S	18.67 MW	19.00 AW	39520 AAW	TXBLS	10//99-12//99
	Utah	S	18.97 MW	19.03 AW	39580 AAW	UTBLS	10//99-12//99
	Vermont	S	17.67 MW	18.04 AW	37520 AAW	VTBLS	10//99-12//99
	Virginia	S	19.05 MW	19.18 AW	39900 AAW	VABLS	10//99-12//99
	Washington	S	21.36 MW	21.36 AW	44420 AAW	WABLS	10//99-12//99
	West Virginia	S	17.69 MW	18.02 AW	37470 AAW	WVBLS	10//99-12//99
	Wisconsin	S	19.53 MW	20.11 AW	41830 AAW	WIBLS	10//99-12//99
	Puerto Rico	S	10.38 MW	10.65 AW	22160 AAW	PRBLS	10//99-12//99
Nuclear Power Reactor Operator	Georgia	S	24.53 MW	23.95 AW	49820 AAW	GABLS	10//99-12//99
	Virginia	S	25.32 MW	25.84 AW	53740 AAW	VABLS	10//99-12//99
Nuclear Technician	California	S	30.67 MW	30.41 AW	63240 AAW	CABLS	10//99-12//99
	Illinois	S	21.69 MW	22.84 AW	47500 AAW	ILBLS	10//99-12//99
	New Jersey	S	23.79 MW	24.40 AW	50740 AAW	NJBLS	10//99-12//99
	North Carolina	S	27.57 MW	27.11 AW	56390 AAW	NCBLS	10//99-12//99
	Pennsylvania	S	24.49 MW	23.75 AW	49400 AAW	PABLS	10//99-12//99
	Texas	S	20.27 MW	22.32 AW	46420 AAW	TXBLS	10//99-12//99
	Virginia	S	31.64 MW	31.14 AW	64760 AAW	VABLS	10//99-12//99
Numerical Control Tool Programmer	United States	H		17.32 AW		NCS98	1998
Numerical Tool and Process Control Programmer	Alabama	S	13.47 MW	15.41 AW	32050 AAW	ALBLS	10//99-12//99
	Huntsville MSA, AL	S	11.94 MW	11.55 AW	24840 AAW	ALBLS	10//99-12//99
	Arizona	S	18.2 MW	17.05 AW	35470 AAW	AZBLS	10//99-12//99
	Phoenix-Mesa MSA, AZ	S	17.95 MW	19.09 AW	37330 AAW	AZBLS	10//99-12//99
	Arkansas	S	17.59 MW	17.53 AW	36460 AAW	ARBLS	10//99-12//99
	California	S	19.78 MW	20.21 AW	42030 AAW	CABLS	10//99-12//99
	Fresno MSA, CA	S	18.73 MW	18.91 AW	38950 AAW	CABLS	10//99-12//99
	Los Angeles-Long Beach PMSA, CA	S	22.91 MW	21.29 AW	47650 AAW	CABLS	10//99-12//99
	Oakland PMSA, CA	S	21.87 MW	20.63 AW	45490 AAW	CABLS	10//99-12//99
	Orange County PMSA, CA	S	17.27 MW	17.48 AW	35930 AAW	CABLS	10//99-12//99
	Riverside-San Bernardino PMSA, CA	S	16.62 MW	16.23 AW	34570 AAW	CABLS	10//99-12//99
	Sacramento PMSA, CA	S	16.07 MW	12.68 AW	33420 AAW	CABLS	10//99-12//99
	San Diego MSA, CA	S	20.96 MW	19.39 AW	43600 AAW	CABLS	10//99-12//99
	San Francisco PMSA, CA	S	22.00 MW	20.99 AW	45760 AAW	CABLS	10//99-12//99
	San Jose PMSA, CA	S	21.76 MW	23.08 AW	45270 AAW	CABLS	10//99-12//99
	Santa Rosa PMSA, CA	S	18.40 MW	17.74 AW	38280 AAW	CABLS	10//99-12//99
	Ventura PMSA, CA	S	18.76 MW	18.81 AW	39020 AAW	CABLS	10//99-12//99
	Colorado	S	19.56 MW	20.46 AW	42570 AAW	COBLS	10//99-12//99
	Boulder-Longmont PMSA, CO	S	19.26 MW	19.25 AW	40060 AAW	COBLS	10//99-12//99
	Colorado Springs MSA, CO	S	19.35 MW	18.01 AW	40240 AAW	COBLS	10//99-12//99
	Denver PMSA, CO	S	21.77 MW	20.71 AW	45290 AAW	COBLS	10//99-12//99
	Connecticut	S	20.24 MW	21.04 AW	43760 AAW	CTBLS	10//99-12//99
	Bridgeport PMSA, CT	S	21.83 MW	20.54 AW	45400 AAW	CTBLS	10//99-12//99
	Hartford MSA, CT	S	20.73 MW	20.06 AW	43120 AAW	CTBLS	10//99-12//99
	New Haven-Meriden PMSA, CT	S	23.62 MW	22.93 AW	49120 AAW	CTBLS	10//99-12//99
	Waterbury PMSA, CT	S	20.71 MW	20.22 AW	43070 AAW	CTBLS	10//99-12//99
	Florida	S	16.37 MW	16.99 AW	35330 AAW	FLBLS	10//99-12//99
	Fort Lauderdale PMSA, FL	S	14.41 MW	14.63 AW	29970 AAW	FLBLS	10//99-12//99
	Miami PMSA, FL	S	15.20 MW	15.96 AW	31620 AAW	FLBLS	10//99-12//99
	Orlando MSA, FL	S	22.32 MW	22.75 AW	46430 AAW	FLBLS	10//99-12//99
	Tampa-St. Petersburg-Clearwater MSA, FL	S	17.77 MW	16.48 AW	36960 AAW	FLBLS	10//99-12//99
	Georgia	S	11.17 MW	12.51 AW	26020 AAW	GABLS	10//99-12//99
	Atlanta MSA, GA	S	12.15 MW	10.22 AW	25280 AAW	GABLS	10//99-12//99

AAW	Average annual wage	AOH	Average offered, high	ASH	Average starting, high
AE	Average entry wage	AOL	Average offered, low	ASL	Average starting, low
AEX	Average experienced wage	APH	Average pay, high range	AW	Average wage paid
AO	Average offered	APL	Average pay, low range	FQ	First quartile wage

H	Hourly	
HI	Highest wage paid	
HR	High end range	
LR	Low end range	

M	Monthly	S	Special: hourly and annual
MTC	Median total compensation	TQ	Third quartile wage
MW	Median wage paid	W	Weekly
SQ	Second quartile wage	Y	Yearly

Occupation/Type/Industry	Location	Per	Low	Mid	High	Source	Date
Numerical Tool and Process Control Programmer	Idaho	S	12.13 MW	12.00 AW	24950 AAW	IDBLS	10//99-12//99
	Illinois	S	15 MW	15.86 AW	33000 AAW	ILBLS	10//99-12//99
	Chicago PMSA, IL	S	16.09 MW	15.24 AW	33460 AAW	ILBLS	10//99-12//99
	Rockford MSA, IL	S	20.01 MW	19.69 AW	41620 AAW	ILBLS	10//99-12//99
	Indiana	S	14.51 MW	16.02 AW	33330 AAW	INBLS	10//99-12//99
	Evansville-Henderson MSA, IN-KY	S	11.49 MW	11.43 AW	23910 AAW	INBLS	10//99-12//99
	Fort Wayne MSA, IN	S	13.79 MW	14.15 AW	28680 AAW	INBLS	10//99-12//99
	Indianapolis MSA, IN	S	22.96 MW	21.40 AW	47750 AAW	INBLS	10//99-12//99
	Iowa	S	19.78 MW	19.13 AW	39780 AAW	IABLS	10//99-12//99
	Kansas	S	16.44 MW	16.50 AW	34310 AAW	KSBLS	10//99-12//99
	Wichita MSA, KS	S	17.50 MW	17.69 AW	36390 AAW	KSBLS	10//99-12//99
	Kentucky	S	15.46 MW	15.60 AW	32440 AAW	KYBLS	10//99-12//99
	Louisville MSA, KY-IN	S	16.57 MW	16.21 AW	34470 AAW	KYBLS	10//99-12//99
	Louisiana	S	17.15 MW	16.18 AW	33660 AAW	LABLS	10//99-12//99
	Maryland	S	18.49 MW	16.56 AW	34450 AAW	MDBLS	10//99-12//99
	Baltimore PMSA, MD	S	17.91 MW	19.08 AW	37260 AAW	MDBLS	10//99-12//99
	Hagerstown PMSA, MD	S	11.86 MW	10.43 AW	24670 AAW	MDBLS	10//99-12//99
	Massachusetts	S	19.45 MW	19.83 AW	41250 AAW	MABLS	10//99-12//99
	Boston PMSA, MA-NH	S	20.28 MW	20.02 AW	42190 AAW	MABLS	10//99-12//99
	Lawrence PMSA, MA-NH	S	18.12 MW	17.95 AW	37680 AAW	MABLS	10//99-12//99
	Lowell PMSA, MA-NH	S	17.62 MW	17.75 AW	36650 AAW	MABLS	10//99-12//99
	Springfield MSA, MA	S	19.20 MW	19.16 AW	39930 AAW	MABLS	10//99-12//99
	Worcester PMSA, MA-CT	S	24.22 MW	24.29 AW	50380 AAW	MABLS	10//99-12//99
	Michigan	S	19.97 MW	19.13 AW	39780 AAW	MIBLS	10//99-12//99
	Ann Arbor PMSA, MI	S	14.56 MW	10.74 AW	30280 AAW	MIBLS	10//99-12//99
	Detroit PMSA, MI	S	22.83 MW	22.97 AW	47490 AAW	MIBLS	10//99-12//99
	Grand Rapids-Muskegon-Holland MSA, MI	S	21.50 MW	21.24 AW	44730 AAW	MIBLS	10//99-12//99
	Minnesota	S	20.3 MW	20.94 AW	43550 AAW	MNBLS	10//99-12//99
	Minneapolis-St. Paul MSA, MN-WI	S	21.24 MW	20.51 AW	44170 AAW	MNBLS	10//99-12//99
	Mississippi	S	14.39 MW	14.85 AW	30890 AAW	MSBLS	10//99-12//99
	Biloxi-Gulfport-Pascagoula MSA, MS	S	15.62 MW	15.15 AW	32480 AAW	MSBLS	10//99-12//99
	Missouri	S	15.16 MW	17.48 AW	36360 AAW	MOBLS	10//99-12//99
	Kansas City MSA, MO-KS	S	16.09 MW	15.91 AW	33480 AAW	MOBLS	10//99-12//99
	St. Louis MSA, MO-IL	S	22.41 MW	21.34 AW	46620 AAW	MOBLS	10//99-12//99
	New Hampshire	S	17.73 MW	17.62 AW	36640 AAW	NHBLS	10//99-12//99
	Nashua PMSA, NH	S	16.10 MW	12.88 AW	33480 AAW	NHBLS	10//99-12//99
	Portsmouth-Rochester PMSA, NH-ME	S	16.80 MW	17.86 AW	34940 AAW	NHBLS	10//99-12//99
	New Jersey	S	22.55 MW	22.94 AW	47720 AAW	NJBLS	10//99-12//99
	Bergen-Passaic PMSA, NJ	S	20.89 MW	20.41 AW	43460 AAW	NJBLS	10//99-12//99
	Newark PMSA, NJ	S	20.09 MW	18.40 AW	41780 AAW	NJBLS	10//99-12//99
	New York	S	17.05 MW	16.04 AW	33370 AAW	NYBLS	10//99-12//99
	Nassau-Suffolk PMSA, NY	S	22.39 MW	21.04 AW	46560 AAW	NYBLS	10//99-12//99
	New York PMSA, NY	S	19.46 MW	19.73 AW	40480 AAW	NYBLS	10//99-12//99
	Rochester MSA, NY	S	20.29 MW	18.75 AW	42190 AAW	NYBLS	10//99-12//99
	Syracuse MSA, NY	S	16.77 MW	16.65 AW	34890 AAW	NYBLS	10//99-12//99
	North Carolina	S	11.93 MW	11.55 AW	24020 AAW	NCBLS	10//99-12//99
	Asheville MSA, NC	S	16.03 MW	15.43 AW	33330 AAW	NCBLS	10//99-12//99
	Charlotte-Gastonia-Rock Hill MSA, NC-SC	S	13.30 MW	13.09 AW	27660 AAW	NCBLS	10//99-12//99
	Greensboro--Winston-Salem--High Point MSA, NC	S	13.67 MW	13.52 AW	28440 AAW	NCBLS	10//99-12//99
	Ohio	S	15.35 MW	15.66 AW	32580 AAW	OHBLS	10//99-12//99
	Akron PMSA, OH	S	16.80 MW	15.95 AW	34930 AAW	OHBLS	10//99-12//99
	Cincinnati PMSA, OH-KY-IN	S	15.73 MW	15.25 AW	32720 AAW	OHBLS	10//99-12//99
	Cleveland-Lorain-Elyria PMSA, OH	S	17.87 MW	18.16 AW	37160 AAW	OHBLS	10//99-12//99
	Columbus MSA, OH	S	12.26 MW	10.61 AW	25490 AAW	OHBLS	10//99-12//99
	Dayton-Springfield MSA, OH	S	19.21 MW	18.75 AW	39950 AAW	OHBLS	10//99-12//99
	Hamilton-Middletown PMSA, OH	S	13.24 MW	13.29 AW	27540 AAW	OHBLS	10//99-12//99
	Mansfield MSA, OH	S	12.59 MW	12.23 AW	26180 AAW	OHBLS	10//99-12//99
	Youngstown-Warren MSA, OH	S	12.86 MW	12.51 AW	26750 AAW	OHBLS	10//99-12//99
	Oklahoma	S	15.07 MW	14.20 AW	29540 AAW	OKBLS	10//99-12//99
	Oklahoma City MSA, OK	S	18.41 MW	18.98 AW	38300 AAW	OKBLS	10//99-12//99
	Tulsa MSA, OK	S	16.98 MW	16.39 AW	35320 AAW	OKBLS	10//99-12//99
	Oregon	S	20.32 MW	21.54 AW	44810 AAW	ORBLS	10//99-12//99

AAW Average annual wage	**AOH** Average offered, high	**ASH** Average starting, high	**H** Hourly	**M** Monthly	**S** Special: hourly and annual
AE Average entry wage	**AOL** Average offered, low	**ASL** Average starting, low	**HI** Highest wage paid	**MTC** Median total compensation	**TQ** Third quartile wage
AEX Average experienced wage	**APH** Average pay, high range	**AW** Average wage paid	**HR** High end range	**MW** Median wage paid	**W** Weekly
AO Average offered	**APL** Average pay, low range	**FQ** First quartile wage	**LR** Low end range	**SQ** Second quartile wage	**Y** Yearly

Occupation/Type/Industry	Location	Per	Low	Mid	High	Source	Date
Numerical Tool and Process Control Programmer	Portland-Vancouver PMSA, OR-WA	S	22.53 MW	21.16 AW	46860 AAW	ORBLS	10//99-12//99
	Pennsylvania	S	19.78 MW	18.91 AW	39330 AAW	PABLS	10//99-12//99
	Erie MSA, PA	S	13.09 MW	13.41 AW	27230 AAW	PABLS	10//99-12//99
	Harrisburg-Lebanon-Carlisle MSA, PA	S	15.20 MW	15.35 AW	31620 AAW	PABLS	10//99-12//99
	Lancaster MSA, PA	S	16.92 MW	17.76 AW	35200 AAW	PABLS	10//99-12//99
	Philadelphia PMSA, PA-NJ	S	23.69 MW	24.03 AW	49280 AAW	PABLS	10//99-12//99
	Pittsburgh MSA, PA	S	17.07 MW	16.70 AW	35510 AAW	PABLS	10//99-12//99
	York MSA, PA	S	20.99 MW	21.23 AW	43660 AAW	PABLS	10//99-12//99
	Providence-Fall River-Warwick MSA, RI-MA	S	16.24 MW	13.59 AW	33790 AAW	RIBLS	10//99-12//99
	South Carolina	S	17.49 MW	17.38 AW	36150 AAW	SCBLS	10//99-12//99
	Greenville-Spartanburg-Anderson MSA, SC	S	18.04 MW	18.20 AW	37530 AAW	SCBLS	10//99-12//99
	South Dakota	S	15.55 MW	15.98 AW	33250 AAW	SDBLS	10//99-12//99
	Tennessee	S	16.61 MW	16.29 AW	33880 AAW	TNBLS	10//99-12//99
	Johnson City-Kingsport-Bristol MSA, TN-VA	S	15.25 MW	15.86 AW	31720 AAW	TNBLS	10//99-12//99
	Knoxville MSA, TN	S	19.08 MW	19.15 AW	39690 AAW	TNBLS	10//99-12//99
	Memphis MSA, TN-AR-MS	S	15.16 MW	15.25 AW	31530 AAW	MSBLS	10//99-12//99
	Nashville MSA, TN	S	18.25 MW	18.41 AW	37950 AAW	TNBLS	10//99-12//99
	Texas	S	15.88 MW	16.03 AW	33350 AAW	TXBLS	10//99-12//99
	Austin-San Marcos MSA, TX	S	17.92 MW	17.08 AW	37280 AAW	TXBLS	10//99-12//99
	Beaumont-Port Arthur MSA, TX	S	14.06 MW	14.31 AW	29240 AAW	TXBLS	10//99-12//99
	Dallas PMSA, TX	S	13.35 MW	14.42 AW	27770 AAW	TXBLS	10//99-12//99
	Fort Worth-Arlington PMSA, TX	S	16.77 MW	15.74 AW	34890 AAW	TXBLS	10//99-12//99
	Houston PMSA, TX	S	17.68 MW	18.71 AW	36780 AAW	TXBLS	10//99-12//99
	San Antonio MSA, TX	S	16.08 MW	17.43 AW	33450 AAW	TXBLS	10//99-12//99
	Virginia	S	17.57 MW	17.34 AW	36060 AAW	VABLS	10//99-12//99
	Washington	S	21 MW	22.93 AW	47690 AAW	WABLS	10//99-12//99
	Seattle-Bellevue-Everett PMSA, WA	S	22.98 MW	21.03 AW	47800 AAW	WABLS	10//99-12//99
	Wisconsin	S	20.06 MW	20.77 AW	43200 AAW	WIBLS	10//99-12//99
	Appleton-Oshkosh-Neenah MSA, WI	S	18.07 MW	17.50 AW	37590 AAW	WIBLS	10//99-12//99
	Madison MSA, WI	S	15.80 MW	15.58 AW	32870 AAW	WIBLS	10//99-12//99
	Milwaukee-Waukesha PMSA, WI	S	22.23 MW	22.25 AW	46250 AAW	WIBLS	10//99-12//99
	Racine PMSA, WI	S	19.00 MW	18.61 AW	39530 AAW	WIBLS	10//99-12//99
Nurse							
Hospital Staff	East North Central	Y		38692 AW		NUR2	10//99
Hospital Staff	East South Central	Y		35852 AW		NUR2	10//99
Hospital Staff	Middle Atlantic	Y		41944 AW		NUR2	10//99
Hospital Staff	Mountain	Y		39916 AW		NUR2	10//99
Hospital Staff	New England	Y		39410 AW		NUR2	10//99
Hospital Staff	Pacific	Y		41552 AW		NUR2	10//99
Hospital Staff	South Atlantic	Y		38673 AW		NUR2	10//99
Hospital Staff	West North Central	Y		34204 AW		NUR2	10//99
Hospital Staff	West South Central	Y		37406 AW		NUR2	10//99
Licensed Practical	United States	H		12.92 AW		NCS98	1998
Licensed, Practical	Florida	H			14.31 HI	BJTAMP	2000
Licensed, Practical, Family Practice	United States	Y		24259 AW		MEDEC1	1999
Licensed, Practical, Internal Medicine	United States	Y		26411 AW		MEDEC1	1999
Licensed Practical, Medical Doctor's Office	United States	H		11.90 AEX		MEDEC	2000
Licensed, Practical, Obstetrics-gynecology	United States	Y		25098 AW		MEDEC1	1999
Licensed, Practical, Pediatrics	United States	Y		25523 AW		MEDEC1	1999
Operating Room	Florida	H			22.78 HI	BJTAMP	2000
Nurse Manager/Executive	East North Central	Y		61272 AW		NURMAN	2000
	East North Central	Y		52000 AW		NURMAN2	4//99-5//99
	East South Central	Y		48000 AW		NURMAN2	4//99-5//99
	East South Central	Y		55744 AW		NURMAN	2000
	Middle Atlantic	Y		53000 AW		NURMAN2	4//99-5//99
	Middle Atlantic	Y		64457 AW		NURMAN	2000
	Mountain	Y		62216 AW		NURMAN	2000
	Mountain	Y		50000 AW		NURMAN2	4//99-5//99
	New England	Y		65452 AW		NURMAN	2000

Occupation/Type/Industry	Location	Per	Low	Mid	High	Source	Date
Nurse Manager/Executive	New England	Y		57000 AW		NURMAN2	4//99-5//99
	Pacific	Y		55000 AW		NURMAN2	4//99-5//99
	Pacific	Y		73087 AW		NURMAN	2000
	South Atlantic	Y		63365 AW		NURMAN	2000
	South Atlantic	Y		53000 AW		NURMAN2	4//99-5//99
	West North Central	Y		59024 AW		NURMAN	2000
	West North Central	Y		48000 AW		NURMAN2	4//99-5//99
	West South Central	Y		63351 AW		NURMAN	2000
	West South Central	Y		51000 AW		NURMAN2	4//99-5//99
Nurse Practitioner	United States	Y	54100 AOL	62000 AO	76000 AOH	NURMAN3	1998
	San Diego County, CA	Y		61960 AW		ERDGE	1998
Medical Doctor's Office	United States	H		26.90 AEX		MEDEC	2000
Nursing Aide, Orderly, and Attendant	Alabama	S	7.22 MW	7.27 AW	15120 AAW	ALBLS	10//99-12//99
	Anniston MSA, AL	S	7.11 MW	7.21 AW	14790 AAW	ALBLS	10//99-12//99
	Auburn-Opelika MSA, AL	S	6.86 MW	6.74 AW	14260 AAW	ALBLS	10//99-12//99
	Birmingham MSA, AL	S	7.64 MW	7.63 AW	15900 AAW	ALBLS	10//99-12//99
	Decatur MSA, AL	S	6.71 MW	6.68 AW	13950 AAW	ALBLS	10//99-12//99
	Dothan MSA, AL	S	7.28 MW	7.38 AW	15130 AAW	ALBLS	10//99-12//99
	Florence MSA, AL	S	7.16 MW	7.26 AW	14890 AAW	ALBLS	10//99-12//99
	Gadsden MSA, AL	S	7.42 MW	7.51 AW	15420 AAW	ALBLS	10//99-12//99
	Huntsville MSA, AL	S	6.90 MW	6.69 AW	14360 AAW	ALBLS	10//99-12//99
	Mobile MSA, AL	S	6.87 MW	6.67 AW	14280 AAW	ALBLS	10//99-12//99
	Montgomery MSA, AL	S	7.68 MW	7.69 AW	15970 AAW	ALBLS	10//99-12//99
	Tuscaloosa MSA, AL	S	7.92 MW	7.66 AW	16470 AAW	ALBLS	10//99-12//99
	Alaska	S	11.81 MW	11.92 AW	24800 AAW	AKBLS	10//99-12//99
	Anchorage MSA, AK	S	11.30 MW	11.30 AW	23500 AAW	AKBLS	10//99-12//99
	Arizona	S	8.4 MW	8.48 AW	17640 AAW	AZBLS	10//99-12//99
	Flagstaff MSA, AZ-UT	S	8.05 MW	7.89 AW	16740 AAW	AZBLS	10//99-12//99
	Phoenix-Mesa MSA, AZ	S	8.73 MW	8.76 AW	18150 AAW	AZBLS	10//99-12//99
	Tucson MSA, AZ	S	8.54 MW	8.17 AW	17750 AAW	AZBLS	10//99-12//99
	Yuma MSA, AZ	S	8.14 MW	8.24 AW	16930 AAW	AZBLS	10//99-12//99
	Arkansas	S	6.67 MW	6.82 AW	14190 AAW	ARBLS	10//99-12//99
	Fayetteville-Springdale-Rogers MSA, AR	S	7.18 MW	7.16 AW	14930 AAW	ARBLS	10//99-12//99
	Fort Smith MSA, AR-OK	S	6.79 MW	6.61 AW	14130 AAW	ARBLS	10//99-12//99
	Jonesboro MSA, AR	S	6.81 MW	6.64 AW	14170 AAW	ARBLS	10//99-12//99
	Little Rock-North Little Rock MSA, AR	S	7.86 MW	7.73 AW	16340 AAW	ARBLS	10//99-12//99
	Pine Bluff MSA, AR	S	6.69 MW	6.58 AW	13900 AAW	ARBLS	10//99-12//99
	California	S	8.4 MW	8.78 AW	18260 AAW	CABLS	10//99-12//99
	Bakersfield MSA, CA	S	8.31 MW	7.98 AW	17280 AAW	CABLS	10//99-12//99
	Chico-Paradise MSA, CA	S	8.37 MW	8.15 AW	17400 AAW	CABLS	10//99-12//99
	Fresno MSA, CA	S	7.71 MW	7.56 AW	16040 AAW	CABLS	10//99-12//99
	Los Angeles-Long Beach PMSA, CA	S	8.49 MW	8.19 AW	17660 AAW	CABLS	10//99-12//99
	Merced MSA, CA	S	7.92 MW	7.75 AW	16470 AAW	CABLS	10//99-12//99
	Modesto MSA, CA	S	8.90 MW	8.51 AW	18510 AAW	CABLS	10//99-12//99
	Oakland PMSA, CA	S	9.14 MW	9.03 AW	19000 AAW	CABLS	10//99-12//99
	Orange County PMSA, CA	S	8.80 MW	8.32 AW	18300 AAW	CABLS	10//99-12//99
	Redding MSA, CA	S	7.85 MW	7.67 AW	16330 AAW	CABLS	10//99-12//99
	Riverside-San Bernardino PMSA, CA	S	8.03 MW	7.84 AW	16690 AAW	CABLS	10//99-12//99
	Sacramento PMSA, CA	S	8.86 MW	8.68 AW	18420 AAW	CABLS	10//99-12//99
	Salinas MSA, CA	S	9.14 MW	8.26 AW	19000 AAW	CABLS	10//99-12//99
	San Diego MSA, CA	S	8.32 MW	7.96 AW	17300 AAW	CABLS	10//99-12//99
	San Francisco PMSA, CA	S	10.89 MW	10.49 AW	22650 AAW	CABLS	10//99-12//99
	San Jose PMSA, CA	S	10.39 MW	9.96 AW	21600 AAW	CABLS	10//99-12//99
	San Luis Obispo-Atascadero-Paso Robles MSA, CA	S	7.77 MW	7.62 AW	16160 AAW	CABLS	10//99-12//99
	Santa Barbara-Santa Maria-Lompoc MSA, CA	S	8.05 MW	7.95 AW	16740 AAW	CABLS	10//99-12//99
	Santa Cruz-Watsonville PMSA, CA	S	8.17 MW	7.94 AW	16990 AAW	CABLS	10//99-12//99
	Santa Rosa PMSA, CA	S	9.61 MW	9.45 AW	19990 AAW	CABLS	10//99-12//99
	Stockton-Lodi MSA, CA	S	8.59 MW	8.30 AW	17870 AAW	CABLS	10//99-12//99
	Vallejo-Fairfield-Napa PMSA, CA	S	8.82 MW	8.56 AW	18350 AAW	CABLS	10//99-12//99
	Ventura PMSA, CA	S	8.64 MW	8.55 AW	17960 AAW	CABLS	10//99-12//99

AAW Average annual wage	AOH Average offered, high	ASH Average starting, high	H Hourly	M Monthly	S Special: hourly and annual
AE Average entry wage	AOL Average offered, low	ASL Average starting, low	HI Highest wage paid	MTC Median total compensation	TQ Third quartile wage
AEX Average experienced wage	APH Average pay, high range	AW Average wage paid	HR High end range	MW Median wage paid	W Weekly
AO Average offered	APL Average pay, low range	FQ First quartile wage	LR Low end range	SQ Second quartile wage	Y Yearly

Occupation/Type/Industry	Location	Per	Low	Mid	High	Source	Date
Nursing Aide, Orderly, and Attendant							
	Visalia-Tulare-Porterville MSA, CA	S	8.53 MW	8.01 AW	17750 AAW	CABLS	10//99-12//99
	Yuba City MSA, CA	S	8.63 MW	8.58 AW	17940 AAW	CABLS	10//99-12//99
	Colorado	S	8.84 MW	8.84 AW	18390 AAW	COBLS	10//99-12//99
	Boulder-Longmont PMSA, CO	S	9.25 MW	9.28 AW	19240 AAW	COBLS	10//99-12//99
	Colorado Springs MSA, CO	S	8.50 MW	8.30 AW	17680 AAW	COBLS	10//99-12//99
	Denver PMSA, CO	S	9.43 MW	9.50 AW	19610 AAW	COBLS	10//99-12//99
	Fort Collins-Loveland MSA, CO	S	8.54 MW	8.27 AW	17770 AAW	COBLS	10//99-12//99
	Grand Junction MSA, CO	S	7.90 MW	7.87 AW	16440 AAW	COBLS	10//99-12//99
	Greeley PMSA, CO	S	8.65 MW	8.50 AW	17980 AAW	COBLS	10//99-12//99
	Connecticut	S	11.15 MW	11.20 AW	23290 AAW	CTBLS	10//99-12//99
	Bridgeport PMSA, CT	S	11.14 MW	11.17 AW	23170 AAW	CTBLS	10//99-12//99
	Danbury PMSA, CT	S	10.99 MW	10.92 AW	22850 AAW	CTBLS	10//99-12//99
	Hartford MSA, CT	S	11.52 MW	11.45 AW	23970 AAW	CTBLS	10//99-12//99
	New Haven-Meriden PMSA, CT	S	11.13 MW	11.05 AW	23160 AAW	CTBLS	10//99-12//99
	New London-Norwich MSA, CT-RI	S	10.26 MW	10.11 AW	21340 AAW	CTBLS	10//99-12//99
	Stamford-Norwalk PMSA, CT	S	11.34 MW	11.31 AW	23590 AAW	CTBLS	10//99-12//99
	Waterbury PMSA, CT	S	10.65 MW	10.64 AW	22160 AAW	CTBLS	10//99-12//99
	Delaware	S	9.1 MW	9.04 AW	18810 AAW	DEBLS	10//99-12//99
	Dover MSA, DE	S	9.17 MW	8.62 AW	19070 AAW	DEBLS	10//99-12//99
	Wilmington-Newark PMSA, DE-MD	S	9.30 MW	9.36 AW	19340 AAW	DEBLS	10//99-12//99
	District of Columbia	S	8.85 MW	9.29 AW	19330 AAW	DCBLS	10//99-12//99
	Washington PMSA, DC-MD-VA-WV	S	9.31 MW	8.88 AW	19370 AAW	DCBLS	10//99-12//99
	Florida	S	8.14 MW	8.30 AW	17260 AAW	FLBLS	10//99-12//99
	Daytona Beach MSA, FL	S	8.13 MW	8.11 AW	16920 AAW	FLBLS	10//99-12//99
	Fort Lauderdale PMSA, FL	S	8.46 MW	8.36 AW	17590 AAW	FLBLS	10//99-12//99
	Fort Myers-Cape Coral MSA, FL	S	7.76 MW	7.75 AW	16130 AAW	FLBLS	10//99-12//99
	Fort Pierce-Port St. Lucie MSA, FL	S	8.21 MW	7.80 AW	17080 AAW	FLBLS	10//99-12//99
	Fort Walton Beach MSA, FL	S	7.56 MW	7.55 AW	15720 AAW	FLBLS	10//99-12//99
	Gainesville MSA, FL	S	8.06 MW	7.88 AW	16760 AAW	FLBLS	10//99-12//99
	Jacksonville MSA, FL	S	8.21 MW	8.13 AW	17080 AAW	FLBLS	10//99-12//99
	Lakeland-Winter Haven MSA, FL	S	8.31 MW	8.04 AW	17280 AAW	FLBLS	10//99-12//99
	Melbourne-Titusville-Palm Bay MSA, FL	S	7.97 MW	7.90 AW	16580 AAW	FLBLS	10//99-12//99
	Miami PMSA, FL	S	8.53 MW	8.33 AW	17730 AAW	FLBLS	10//99-12//99
	Naples MSA, FL	S	8.40 MW	8.18 AW	17470 AAW	FLBLS	10//99-12//99
	Ocala MSA, FL	S	7.83 MW	7.82 AW	16280 AAW	FLBLS	10//99-12//99
	Orlando MSA, FL	S	8.18 MW	8.00 AW	17010 AAW	FLBLS	10//99-12//99
	Pensacola MSA, FL	S	7.62 MW	7.56 AW	15840 AAW	FLBLS	10//99-12//99
	Punta Gorda MSA, FL	S	8.04 MW	8.03 AW	16720 AAW	FLBLS	10//99-12//99
	Sarasota-Bradenton MSA, FL	S	8.53 MW	8.45 AW	17740 AAW	FLBLS	10//99-12//99
	Tallahassee MSA, FL	S	7.99 MW	7.94 AW	16610 AAW	FLBLS	10//99-12//99
	Tampa-St. Petersburg-Clearwater MSA, FL	S	8.57 MW	8.42 AW	17830 AAW	FLBLS	10//99-12//99
	West Palm Beach-Boca Raton MSA, FL	S	8.42 MW	8.25 AW	17510 AAW	FLBLS	10//99-12//99
	Georgia	S	7.25 MW	7.40 AW	15400 AAW	GABLS	10//99-12//99
	Albany MSA, GA	S	7.09 MW	6.98 AW	14760 AAW	GABLS	10//99-12//99
	Athens MSA, GA	S	7.18 MW	6.85 AW	14930 AAW	GABLS	10//99-12//99
	Atlanta MSA, GA	S	7.89 MW	7.84 AW	16400 AAW	GABLS	10//99-12//99
	Augusta-Aiken MSA, GA-SC	S	8.19 MW	8.00 AW	17030 AAW	GABLS	10//99-12//99
	Columbus MSA, GA-AL	S	7.48 MW	7.46 AW	15550 AAW	GABLS	10//99-12//99
	Macon MSA, GA	S	6.96 MW	6.67 AW	14480 AAW	GABLS	10//99-12//99
	Savannah MSA, GA	S	6.24 MW	6.09 AW	12990 AAW	GABLS	10//99-12//99
	Hawaii	S	10.6 MW	10.45 AW	21730 AAW	HIBLS	10//99-12//99
	Honolulu MSA, HI	S	10.42 MW	10.62 AW	21670 AAW	HIBLS	10//99-12//99
	Idaho	S	7.69 MW	7.67 AW	15950 AAW	IDBLS	10//99-12//99
	Boise City MSA, ID	S	8.33 MW	8.20 AW	17320 AAW	IDBLS	10//99-12//99
	Pocatello MSA, ID	S	7.50 MW	7.58 AW	15600 AAW	IDBLS	10//99-12//99
	Illinois	S	7.99 MW	8.22 AW	17100 AAW	ILBLS	10//99-12//99
	Bloomington-Normal MSA, IL	S	7.82 MW	7.78 AW	16270 AAW	ILBLS	10//99-12//99
	Champaign-Urbana MSA, IL	S	7.78 MW	7.67 AW	16190 AAW	ILBLS	10//99-12//99
	Chicago PMSA, IL	S	8.52 MW	8.21 AW	17710 AAW	ILBLS	10//99-12//99

AAW Average annual wage	AOH Average offered, high	ASH Average starting, high	H Hourly	M Monthly	S Special: hourly and annual
AE Average entry wage	AOL Average offered, low	ASL Average starting, low	HI Highest wage paid	MTC Median total compensation	TQ Third quartile wage
AEX Average experienced wage	APH Average pay, high range	AW Average wage paid	HR High end range	MW Median wage paid	W Weekly
AO Average offered	APL Average pay, low range	FQ First quartile wage	LR Low end range	SQ Second quartile wage	Y Yearly

Occupation/Type/Industry	Location	Per	Low	Mid	High	Source	Date
Nursing Aide, Orderly, and Attendant	Decatur MSA, IL	S	7.99 MW	7.89 AW	16610 AAW	ILBLS	10//99-12//99
	Kankakee PMSA, IL	S	8.82 MW	8.54 AW	18350 AAW	ILBLS	10//99-12//99
	Peoria-Pekin MSA, IL	S	8.36 MW	8.21 AW	17390 AAW	ILBLS	10//99-12//99
	Rockford MSA, IL	S	8.37 MW	8.32 AW	17410 AAW	ILBLS	10//99-12//99
	Springfield MSA, IL	S	7.59 MW	7.59 AW	15800 AAW	ILBLS	10//99-12//99
	Indiana	S	8.12 MW	8.21 AW	17080 AAW	INBLS	10//99-12//99
	Bloomington MSA, IN	S	8.12 MW	7.91 AW	16890 AAW	INBLS	10//99-12//99
	Elkhart-Goshen MSA, IN	S	8.17 MW	8.32 AW	16990 AAW	INBLS	10//99-12//99
	Evansville-Henderson MSA, IN-KY	S	7.97 MW	7.91 AW	16580 AAW	INBLS	10//99-12//99
	Fort Wayne MSA, IN	S	8.64 MW	8.76 AW	17970 AAW	INBLS	10//99-12//99
	Gary PMSA, IN	S	7.85 MW	7.80 AW	16320 AAW	INBLS	10//99-12//99
	Indianapolis MSA, IN	S	8.64 MW	8.54 AW	17970 AAW	INBLS	10//99-12//99
	Kokomo MSA, IN	S	8.09 MW	7.95 AW	16830 AAW	INBLS	10//99-12//99
	Lafayette MSA, IN	S	8.75 MW	8.27 AW	18200 AAW	INBLS	10//99-12//99
	Muncie MSA, IN	S	7.81 MW	7.77 AW	16240 AAW	INBLS	10//99-12//99
	South Bend MSA, IN	S	8.37 MW	8.40 AW	17410 AAW	INBLS	10//99-12//99
	Terre Haute MSA, IN	S	8.34 MW	7.96 AW	17340 AAW	INBLS	10//99-12//99
	Iowa	S	8.13 MW	8.25 AW	17170 AAW	IABLS	10//99-12//99
	Cedar Rapids MSA, IA	S	8.78 MW	8.83 AW	18270 AAW	IABLS	10//99-12//99
	Davenport-Moline-Rock Island MSA, IA-IL	S	8.41 MW	8.16 AW	17490 AAW	IABLS	10//99-12//99
	Des Moines MSA, IA	S	9.24 MW	9.27 AW	19210 AAW	IABLS	10//99-12//99
	Dubuque MSA, IA	S	8.14 MW	8.00 AW	16930 AAW	IABLS	10//99-12//99
	Sioux City MSA, IA-NE	S	8.16 MW	8.17 AW	16980 AAW	IABLS	10//99-12//99
	Waterloo-Cedar Falls MSA, IA	S	8.36 MW	8.15 AW	17390 AAW	IABLS	10//99-12//99
	Kansas	S	7.89 MW	7.94 AW	16520 AAW	KSBLS	10//99-12//99
	Lawrence MSA, KS	S	8.29 MW	8.16 AW	17240 AAW	KSBLS	10//99-12//99
	Topeka MSA, KS	S	8.27 MW	8.07 AW	17210 AAW	KSBLS	10//99-12//99
	Wichita MSA, KS	S	8.26 MW	8.22 AW	17170 AAW	KSBLS	10//99-12//99
	Kentucky	S	7.71 MW	7.75 AW	16110 AAW	KYBLS	10//99-12//99
	Lexington MSA, KY	S	8.44 MW	8.35 AW	17550 AAW	KYBLS	10//99-12//99
	Louisville MSA, KY-IN	S	8.39 MW	8.46 AW	17450 AAW	KYBLS	10//99-12//99
	Owensboro MSA, KY	S	7.38 MW	7.34 AW	15350 AAW	KYBLS	10//99-12//99
	Louisiana	S	6.17 MW	6.36 AW	13230 AAW	LABLS	10//99-12//99
	Alexandria MSA, LA	S	6.62 MW	6.22 AW	13770 AAW	LABLS	10//99-12//99
	Baton Rouge MSA, LA	S	6.39 MW	6.27 AW	13290 AAW	LABLS	10//99-12//99
	Houma MSA, LA	S	6.38 MW	6.28 AW	13260 AAW	LABLS	10//99-12//99
	Lafayette MSA, LA	S	6.12 MW	6.06 AW	12730 AAW	LABLS	10//99-12//99
	Lake Charles MSA, LA	S	5.96 MW	5.98 AW	12400 AAW	LABLS	10//99-12//99
	Monroe MSA, LA	S	6.47 MW	6.31 AW	13450 AAW	LABLS	10//99-12//99
	New Orleans MSA, LA	S	6.43 MW	6.12 AW	13370 AAW	LABLS	10//99-12//99
	Shreveport-Bossier City MSA, LA	S	6.53 MW	6.33 AW	13590 AAW	LABLS	10//99-12//99
	Maine	S	8.23 MW	8.38 AW	17430 AAW	MEBLS	10//99-12//99
	Bangor MSA, ME	S	8.21 MW	8.08 AW	17080 AAW	MEBLS	10//99-12//99
	Lewiston-Auburn MSA, ME	S	8.40 MW	8.31 AW	17460 AAW	MEBLS	10//99-12//99
	Portland MSA, ME	S	9.42 MW	9.55 AW	19580 AAW	MEBLS	10//99-12//99
	Maryland	S	9.12 MW	9.36 AW	19480 AAW	MDBLS	10//99-12//99
	Baltimore PMSA, MD	S	9.33 MW	9.23 AW	19410 AAW	MDBLS	10//99-12//99
	Cumberland MSA, MD-WV	S	8.75 MW	8.72 AW	18190 AAW	MDBLS	10//99-12//99
	Hagerstown PMSA, MD	S	9.55 MW	9.56 AW	19870 AAW	MDBLS	10//99-12//99
	Massachusetts	S	9.93 MW	10.11 AW	21030 AAW	MABLS	10//99-12//99
	Barnstable-Yarmouth MSA, MA	S	10.57 MW	10.22 AW	21990 AAW	MABLS	10//99-12//99
	Boston PMSA, MA-NH	S	10.26 MW	10.05 AW	21350 AAW	MABLS	10//99-12//99
	Brockton PMSA, MA	S	10.42 MW	10.21 AW	21670 AAW	MABLS	10//99-12//99
	Fitchburg-Leominster PMSA, MA	S	9.71 MW	9.56 AW	20200 AAW	MABLS	10//99-12//99
	Lawrence PMSA, MA-NH	S	10.20 MW	10.20 AW	21210 AAW	MABLS	10//99-12//99
	Lowell PMSA, MA-NH	S	10.26 MW	9.90 AW	21330 AAW	MABLS	10//99-12//99
	New Bedford PMSA, MA	S	9.32 MW	9.07 AW	19380 AAW	MABLS	10//99-12//99
	Pittsfield MSA, MA	S	9.12 MW	8.43 AW	18980 AAW	MABLS	10//99-12//99
	Springfield MSA, MA	S	9.46 MW	9.39 AW	19670 AAW	MABLS	10//99-12//99
	Worcester PMSA, MA-CT	S	10.10 MW	9.94 AW	21010 AAW	MABLS	10//99-12//99
	Michigan	S	9.15 MW	9.18 AW	19100 AAW	MIBLS	10//99-12//99
	Ann Arbor PMSA, MI	S	9.88 MW	9.79 AW	20550 AAW	MIBLS	10//99-12//99
	Benton Harbor MSA, MI	S	8.04 MW	8.07 AW	16710 AAW	MIBLS	10//99-12//99
	Detroit PMSA, MI	S	9.68 MW	9.56 AW	20140 AAW	MIBLS	10//99-12//99
	Flint PMSA, MI	S	8.00 MW	7.96 AW	16630 AAW	MIBLS	10//99-12//99

AAW Average annual wage	**AOH** Average offered, high	**ASH** Average starting, high	**H** Hourly	**M** Monthly	**S** Special: hourly and annual
AE Average entry wage	**AOL** Average offered, low	**ASL** Average starting, low	**HI** Highest wage paid	**MTC** Median total compensation	**TQ** Third quartile wage
AEX Average experienced wage	**APH** Average pay, high range	**AW** Average wage paid	**HR** High end range	**MW** Median wage paid	**W** Weekly
AO Average offered	**APL** Average pay, low range	**FQ** First quartile wage	**LR** Low end range	**SQ** Second quartile wage	**Y** Yearly

Occupation/Type/Industry	Location	Per	Low	Mid	High	Source	Date
Nursing Aide, Orderly, and Attendant							
	Grand Rapids-Muskegon-Holland MSA, MI	S	9.25 MW	9.23 AW	19230 AAW	MIBLS	10//99-12//99
	Jackson MSA, MI	S	8.78 MW	8.90 AW	18260 AAW	MIBLS	10//99-12//99
	Kalamazoo-Battle Creek MSA, MI	S	8.82 MW	8.71 AW	18340 AAW	MIBLS	10//99-12//99
	Lansing-East Lansing MSA, MI	S	9.15 MW	9.23 AW	19040 AAW	MIBLS	10//99-12//99
	Saginaw-Bay City-Midland MSA, MI	S	8.48 MW	8.43 AW	17640 AAW	MIBLS	10//99-12//99
	Minnesota	S	9.66 MW	9.76 AW	20300 AAW	MNBLS	10//99-12//99
	Duluth-Superior MSA, MN-WI	S	9.43 MW	9.42 AW	19610 AAW	MNBLS	10//99-12//99
	Minneapolis-St. Paul MSA, MN-WI	S	10.80 MW	10.82 AW	22470 AAW	MNBLS	10//99-12//99
	Rochester MSA, MN	S	9.49 MW	9.44 AW	19730 AAW	MNBLS	10//99-12//99
	St. Cloud MSA, MN	S	8.63 MW	8.51 AW	17940 AAW	MNBLS	10//99-12//99
	Mississippi	S	6.81 MW	7.13 AW	14830 AAW	MSBLS	10//99-12//99
	Biloxi-Gulfport-Pascagoula MSA, MS	S	7.90 MW	7.58 AW	16430 AAW	MSBLS	10//99-12//99
	Hattiesburg MSA, MS	S	6.58 MW	6.48 AW	13690 AAW	MSBLS	10//99-12//99
	Jackson MSA, MS	S	7.60 MW	7.42 AW	15820 AAW	MSBLS	10//99-12//99
	Missouri	S	7.51 MW	7.58 AW	15760 AAW	MOBLS	10//99-12//99
	Joplin MSA, MO	S	7.49 MW	7.56 AW	15570 AAW	MOBLS	10//99-12//99
	Kansas City MSA, MO-KS	S	8.50 MW	8.35 AW	17680 AAW	MOBLS	10//99-12//99
	St. Joseph MSA, MO	S	6.42 MW	6.15 AW	13360 AAW	MOBLS	10//99-12//99
	St. Louis MSA, MO-IL	S	7.93 MW	7.83 AW	16490 AAW	MOBLS	10//99-12//99
	Springfield MSA, MO	S	7.65 MW	7.60 AW	15920 AAW	MOBLS	10//99-12//99
	Montana	S	7.71 MW	7.75 AW	16120 AAW	MTBLS	10//99-12//99
	Billings MSA, MT	S	8.13 MW	8.10 AW	16900 AAW	MTBLS	10//99-12//99
	Great Falls MSA, MT	S	7.64 MW	7.56 AW	15900 AAW	MTBLS	10//99-12//99
	Missoula MSA, MT	S	7.85 MW	7.80 AW	16320 AAW	MTBLS	10//99-12//99
	Nebraska	S	8.4 MW	8.44 AW	17550 AAW	NEBLS	10//99-12//99
	Lincoln MSA, NE	S	9.18 MW	9.03 AW	19100 AAW	NEBLS	10//99-12//99
	Omaha MSA, NE-IA	S	9.20 MW	9.36 AW	19140 AAW	NEBLS	10//99-12//99
	Nevada	S	9.59 MW	9.57 AW	19900 AAW	NVBLS	10//99-12//99
	Las Vegas MSA, NV-AZ	S	9.36 MW	9.39 AW	19480 AAW	NVBLS	10//99-12//99
	Reno MSA, NV	S	9.77 MW	9.82 AW	20320 AAW	NVBLS	10//99-12//99
	New Hampshire	S	9.78 MW	9.78 AW	20330 AAW	NHBLS	10//99-12//99
	Manchester PMSA, NH	S	10.27 MW	10.60 AW	21370 AAW	NHBLS	10//99-12//99
	Nashua PMSA, NH	S	10.41 MW	10.14 AW	21650 AAW	NHBLS	10//99-12//99
	Portsmouth-Rochester PMSA, NH-ME	S	9.60 MW	9.65 AW	19970 AAW	NHBLS	10//99-12//99
	New Jersey	S	10.11 MW	10.49 AW	21810 AAW	NJBLS	10//99-12//99
	Atlantic-Cape May PMSA, NJ	S	10.14 MW	9.69 AW	21090 AAW	NJBLS	10//99-12//99
	Bergen-Passaic PMSA, NJ	S	10.85 MW	10.60 AW	22570 AAW	NJBLS	10//99-12//99
	Jersey City PMSA, NJ	S	10.00 MW	9.88 AW	20790 AAW	NJBLS	10//99-12//99
	Middlesex-Somerset-Hunterdon PMSA, NJ	S	11.01 MW	10.40 AW	22910 AAW	NJBLS	10//99-12//99
	Monmouth-Ocean PMSA, NJ	S	9.61 MW	9.50 AW	20000 AAW	NJBLS	10//99-12//99
	Newark PMSA, NJ	S	10.44 MW	10.19 AW	21720 AAW	NJBLS	10//99-12//99
	Trenton PMSA, NJ	S	10.46 MW	9.95 AW	21760 AAW	NJBLS	10//99-12//99
	New Mexico	S	7.42 MW	7.61 AW	15820 AAW	NMBLS	10//99-12//99
	Albuquerque MSA, NM	S	8.50 MW	8.25 AW	17690 AAW	NMBLS	10//99-12//99
	Las Cruces MSA, NM	S	6.80 MW	6.53 AW	14140 AAW	NMBLS	10//99-12//99
	Santa Fe MSA, NM	S	7.79 MW	7.73 AW	16200 AAW	NMBLS	10//99-12//99
	New York	S	10.92 MW	10.71 AW	22270 AAW	NYBLS	10//99-12//99
	Albany-Schenectady-Troy MSA, NY	S	9.09 MW	9.05 AW	18900 AAW	NYBLS	10//99-12//99
	Binghamton MSA, NY	S	8.16 MW	8.06 AW	16970 AAW	NYBLS	10//99-12//99
	Buffalo-Niagara Falls MSA, NY	S	8.74 MW	8.52 AW	18180 AAW	NYBLS	10//99-12//99
	Dutchess County PMSA, NY	S	10.02 MW	9.88 AW	20840 AAW	NYBLS	10//99-12//99
	Elmira MSA, NY	S	8.57 MW	8.07 AW	17830 AAW	NYBLS	10//99-12//99
	Glens Falls MSA, NY	S	9.12 MW	8.73 AW	18960 AAW	NYBLS	10//99-12//99
	Jamestown MSA, NY	S	7.72 MW	7.73 AW	16070 AAW	NYBLS	10//99-12//99
	Nassau-Suffolk PMSA, NY	S	12.89 MW	13.00 AW	26800 AAW	NYBLS	10//99-12//99
	New York PMSA, NY	S	11.58 MW	12.06 AW	24090 AAW	NYBLS	10//99-12//99
	Rochester MSA, NY	S	8.81 MW	8.82 AW	18330 AAW	NYBLS	10//99-12//99
	Syracuse MSA, NY	S	8.50 MW	8.32 AW	17680 AAW	NYBLS	10//99-12//99
	Utica-Rome MSA, NY	S	8.03 MW	7.79 AW	16690 AAW	NYBLS	10//99-12//99
	North Carolina	S	7.88 MW	8.01 AW	16660 AAW	NCBLS	10//99-12//99
	Asheville MSA, NC	S	8.16 MW	8.03 AW	16970 AAW	NCBLS	10//99-12//99

AAW	Average annual wage	AOH	Average offered, high	ASH	Average starting, high	H	Hourly	M	Monthly	S	Special: hourly and annual
AE	Average entry wage	AOL	Average offered, low	ASL	Average starting, low	HI	Highest wage paid	MTC	Median total compensation	TQ	Third quartile wage
AEX	Average experienced wage	APH	Average pay, high range	AW	Average wage paid	HR	High end range	MW	Median wage paid	W	Weekly
AO	Average offered	APL	Average pay, low range	FQ	First quartile wage	LR	Low end range	SQ	Second quartile wage	Y	Yearly

Occupation/Type/Industry	Location	Per	Low	Mid	High	Source	Date
Nursing Aide, Orderly, and Attendant							
	Charlotte-Gastonia-Rock Hill MSA, NC-SC	S	8.94 MW	8.90 AW	18590 AAW	NCBLS	10//99-12//99
	Fayetteville MSA, NC	S	8.72 MW	8.52 AW	18130 AAW	NCBLS	10//99-12//99
	Goldsboro MSA, NC	S	7.32 MW	7.03 AW	15230 AAW	NCBLS	10//99-12//99
	Greensboro--Winston-Salem-- High Point MSA, NC	S	8.05 MW	7.92 AW	16740 AAW	NCBLS	10//99-12//99
	Hickory-Morganton-Lenoir MSA, NC	S	8.14 MW	8.08 AW	16930 AAW	NCBLS	10//99-12//99
	Jacksonville MSA, NC	S	6.92 MW	6.73 AW	14400 AAW	NCBLS	10//99-12//99
	Raleigh-Durham-Chapel Hill MSA, NC	S	8.29 MW	8.03 AW	17230 AAW	NCBLS	10//99-12//99
	Rocky Mount MSA, NC	S	7.46 MW	7.42 AW	15520 AAW	NCBLS	10//99-12//99
	Wilmington MSA, NC	S	7.48 MW	7.46 AW	15560 AAW	NCBLS	10//99-12//99
	North Dakota	S	7.58 MW	7.54 AW	15690 AAW	NDBLS	10//99-12//99
	Bismarck MSA, ND	S	7.67 MW	7.72 AW	15960 AAW	NDBLS	10//99-12//99
	Fargo-Moorhead MSA, ND-MN	S	8.44 MW	8.17 AW	17560 AAW	NDBLS	10//99-12//99
	Grand Forks MSA, ND-MN	S	8.35 MW	8.26 AW	17380 AAW	NDBLS	10//99-12//99
	Ohio	S	8.3 MW	8.48 AW	17630 AAW	OHBLS	10//99-12//99
	Akron PMSA, OH	S	8.22 MW	8.14 AW	17100 AAW	OHBLS	10//99-12//99
	Canton-Massillon MSA, OH	S	8.34 MW	8.42 AW	17350 AAW	OHBLS	10//99-12//99
	Cincinnati PMSA, OH-KY-IN	S	8.60 MW	8.54 AW	17890 AAW	OHBLS	10//99-12//99
	Cleveland-Lorain-Elyria PMSA, OH	S	8.80 MW	8.58 AW	18310 AAW	OHBLS	10//99-12//99
	Columbus MSA, OH	S	9.00 MW	8.81 AW	18720 AAW	OHBLS	10//99-12//99
	Dayton-Springfield MSA, OH	S	8.80 MW	8.61 AW	18310 AAW	OHBLS	10//99-12//99
	Hamilton-Middletown PMSA, OH	S	8.48 MW	8.47 AW	17640 AAW	OHBLS	10//99-12//99
	Lima MSA, OH	S	7.95 MW	7.81 AW	16530 AAW	OHBLS	10//99-12//99
	Mansfield MSA, OH	S	8.54 MW	8.19 AW	17760 AAW	OHBLS	10//99-12//99
	Steubenville-Weirton MSA, OH-WV	S	6.91 MW	7.03 AW	14370 AAW	OHBLS	10//99-12//99
	Toledo MSA, OH	S	8.44 MW	8.28 AW	17560 AAW	OHBLS	10//99-12//99
	Youngstown-Warren MSA, OH	S	7.87 MW	7.81 AW	16380 AAW	OHBLS	10//99-12//99
	Oklahoma	S	6.8 MW	6.96 AW	14470 AAW	OKBLS	10//99-12//99
	Enid MSA, OK	S	6.60 MW	6.42 AW	13730 AAW	OKBLS	10//99-12//99
	Lawton MSA, OK	S	6.66 MW	6.36 AW	13840 AAW	OKBLS	10//99-12//99
	Oklahoma City MSA, OK	S	7.36 MW	7.29 AW	15300 AAW	OKBLS	10//99-12//99
	Tulsa MSA, OK	S	7.24 MW	7.31 AW	15070 AAW	OKBLS	10//99-12//99
	Oregon	S	8.75 MW	8.92 AW	18550 AAW	ORBLS	10//99-12//99
	Corvallis MSA, OR	S	8.82 MW	8.80 AW	18350 AAW	ORBLS	10//99-12//99
	Eugene-Springfield MSA, OR	S	9.36 MW	9.11 AW	19470 AAW	ORBLS	10//99-12//99
	Medford-Ashland MSA, OR	S	8.31 MW	8.25 AW	17290 AAW	ORBLS	10//99-12//99
	Portland-Vancouver PMSA, OR-WA	S	9.04 MW	9.00 AW	18810 AAW	ORBLS	10//99-12//99
	Salem PMSA, OR	S	9.71 MW	9.53 AW	20190 AAW	ORBLS	10//99-12//99
	Pennsylvania	S	8.98 MW	9.10 AW	18930 AAW	PABLS	10//99-12//99
	Allentown-Bethlehem-Easton MSA, PA	S	9.24 MW	9.31 AW	19210 AAW	PABLS	10//99-12//99
	Altoona MSA, PA	S	8.97 MW	9.05 AW	18650 AAW	PABLS	10//99-12//99
	Erie MSA, PA	S	9.28 MW	8.75 AW	19300 AAW	PABLS	10//99-12//99
	Harrisburg-Lebanon-Carlisle MSA, PA	S	10.02 MW	9.92 AW	20840 AAW	PABLS	10//99-12//99
	Johnstown MSA, PA	S	8.67 MW	8.19 AW	18030 AAW	PABLS	10//99-12//99
	Lancaster MSA, PA	S	9.74 MW	9.69 AW	20260 AAW	PABLS	10//99-12//99
	Philadelphia PMSA, PA-NJ	S	9.74 MW	9.52 AW	20270 AAW	PABLS	10//99-12//99
	Pittsburgh MSA, PA	S	8.89 MW	8.80 AW	18480 AAW	PABLS	10//99-12//99
	Reading MSA, PA	S	9.43 MW	9.23 AW	19610 AAW	PABLS	10//99-12//99
	Scranton--Wilkes-Barre--Hazleton MSA, PA	S	8.50 MW	8.26 AW	17680 AAW	PABLS	10//99-12//99
	Sharon MSA, PA	S	8.14 MW	8.03 AW	16930 AAW	PABLS	10//99-12//99
	State College MSA, PA	S	8.71 MW	8.87 AW	18120 AAW	PABLS	10//99-12//99
	Williamsport MSA, PA	S	7.76 MW	7.68 AW	16140 AAW	PABLS	10//99-12//99
	York MSA, PA	S	9.10 MW	8.88 AW	18930 AAW	PABLS	10//99-12//99
	Rhode Island	S	9.12 MW	9.31 AW	19370 AAW	RIBLS	10//99-12//99
	Providence-Fall River-Warwick MSA, RI-MA	S	9.36 MW	9.21 AW	19470 AAW	RIBLS	10//99-12//99
	South Carolina	S	7.42 MW	7.49 AW	15580 AAW	SCBLS	10//99-12//99
	Charleston-North Charleston MSA, SC	S	7.29 MW	7.18 AW	15160 AAW	SCBLS	10//99-12//99
	Columbia MSA, SC	S	8.12 MW	7.82 AW	16880 AAW	SCBLS	10//99-12//99

AAW	Average annual wage	AOH	Average offered, high	ASH	Average starting, high	H	Hourly	M	Monthly	S	Special: hourly and annual
AE	Average entry wage	AOL	Average offered, low	ASL	Average starting, low	HI	Highest wage paid	MTC	Median total compensation	TQ	Third quartile wage
AEX	Average experienced wage	APH	Average pay, high range	AW	Average wage paid	HR	High end range	MW	Median wage paid	W	Weekly
AO	Average offered	APL	Average pay, low range	FQ	First quartile wage	LR	Low end range	SQ	Second quartile wage	Y	Yearly

Occupation/Type/Industry	Location	Per	Low	Mid	High	Source	Date
Nursing Aide, Orderly, and Attendant	Florence MSA, SC	S	6.97 MW	6.80 AW	14490 AAW	SCBLS	10//99-12//99
	Greenville-Spartanburg-Anderson MSA, SC	S	7.58 MW	7.61 AW	15760 AAW	SCBLS	10//99-12//99
	Myrtle Beach MSA, SC	S	6.78 MW	6.88 AW	14090 AAW	SCBLS	10//99-12//99
	Sumter MSA, SC	S	8.26 MW	7.48 AW	17180 AAW	SCBLS	10//99-12//99
	South Dakota	S	7.73 MW	7.75 AW	16120 AAW	SDBLS	10//99-12//99
	Rapid City MSA, SD	S	7.90 MW	7.90 AW	16430 AAW	SDBLS	10//99-12//99
	Sioux Falls MSA, SD	S	8.63 MW	8.53 AW	17950 AAW	SDBLS	10//99-12//99
	Tennessee	S	7.72 MW	7.82 AW	16270 AAW	TNBLS	10//99-12//99
	Chattanooga MSA, TN-GA	S	8.15 MW	7.98 AW	16950 AAW	TNBLS	10//99-12//99
	Clarksville-Hopkinsville MSA, TN-KY	S	7.69 MW	7.57 AW	16000 AAW	TNBLS	10//99-12//99
	Jackson MSA, TN	S	7.26 MW	7.47 AW	15100 AAW	TNBLS	10//99-12//99
	Johnson City-Kingsport-Bristol MSA, TN-VA	S	7.51 MW	7.34 AW	15620 AAW	TNBLS	10//99-12//99
	Knoxville MSA, TN	S	7.80 MW	7.78 AW	16230 AAW	TNBLS	10//99-12//99
	Memphis MSA, TN-AR-MS	S	8.19 MW	7.90 AW	17030 AAW	MSBLS	10//99-12//99
	Nashville MSA, TN	S	8.11 MW	7.93 AW	16870 AAW	TNBLS	10//99-12//99
	Texas	S	6.77 MW	7.04 AW	14640 AAW	TXBLS	10//99-12//99
	Abilene MSA, TX	S	6.57 MW	6.36 AW	13670 AAW	TXBLS	10//99-12//99
	Amarillo MSA, TX	S	8.12 MW	7.69 AW	16890 AAW	TXBLS	10//99-12//99
	Austin-San Marcos MSA, TX	S	8.04 MW	7.86 AW	16720 AAW	TXBLS	10//99-12//99
	Beaumont-Port Arthur MSA, TX	S	6.16 MW	6.05 AW	12810 AAW	TXBLS	10//99-12//99
	Brazoria PMSA, TX	S	6.76 MW	6.76 AW	14060 AAW	TXBLS	10//99-12//99
	Brownsville-Harlingen-San Benito MSA, TX	S	6.08 MW	6.15 AW	12650 AAW	TXBLS	10//99-12//99
	Bryan-College Station MSA, TX	S	7.16 MW	7.22 AW	14900 AAW	TXBLS	10//99-12//99
	Corpus Christi MSA, TX	S	6.37 MW	6.23 AW	13260 AAW	TXBLS	10//99-12//99
	Dallas PMSA, TX	S	7.72 MW	7.42 AW	16060 AAW	TXBLS	10//99-12//99
	El Paso MSA, TX	S	6.93 MW	6.60 AW	14410 AAW	TXBLS	10//99-12//99
	Fort Worth-Arlington PMSA, TX	S	7.51 MW	7.53 AW	15630 AAW	TXBLS	10//99-12//99
	Galveston-Texas City PMSA, TX	S	7.42 MW	7.47 AW	15440 AAW	TXBLS	10//99-12//99
	Houston PMSA, TX	S	6.90 MW	6.50 AW	14350 AAW	TXBLS	10//99-12//99
	Killeen-Temple MSA, TX	S	7.28 MW	7.13 AW	15150 AAW	TXBLS	10//99-12//99
	Laredo MSA, TX	S	6.65 MW	6.48 AW	13830 AAW	TXBLS	10//99-12//99
	Longview-Marshall MSA, TX	S	6.75 MW	6.55 AW	14040 AAW	TXBLS	10//99-12//99
	Lubbock MSA, TX	S	6.49 MW	6.36 AW	13500 AAW	TXBLS	10//99-12//99
	McAllen-Edinburg-Mission MSA, TX	S	6.14 MW	6.15 AW	12760 AAW	TXBLS	10//99-12//99
	Odessa-Midland MSA, TX	S	6.69 MW	6.56 AW	13920 AAW	TXBLS	10//99-12//99
	San Angelo MSA, TX	S	6.99 MW	6.90 AW	14540 AAW	TXBLS	10//99-12//99
	San Antonio MSA, TX	S	7.36 MW	7.39 AW	15300 AAW	TXBLS	10//99-12//99
	Sherman-Denison MSA, TX	S	7.33 MW	7.40 AW	15240 AAW	TXBLS	10//99-12//99
	Texarkana MSA, TX-Texarkana, AR	S	7.35 MW	7.20 AW	15300 AAW	TXBLS	10//99-12//99
	Tyler MSA, TX	S	6.86 MW	6.29 AW	14260 AAW	TXBLS	10//99-12//99
	Victoria MSA, TX	S	7.06 MW	7.12 AW	14690 AAW	TXBLS	10//99-12//99
	Waco MSA, TX	S	7.56 MW	7.02 AW	15730 AAW	TXBLS	10//99-12//99
	Wichita Falls MSA, TX	S	6.47 MW	6.27 AW	13470 AAW	TXBLS	10//99-12//99
	Utah	S	7.99 MW	8.16 AW	16980 AAW	UTBLS	10//99-12//99
	Provo-Orem MSA, UT	S	7.99 MW	7.80 AW	16620 AAW	UTBLS	10//99-12//99
	Salt Lake City-Ogden MSA, UT	S	8.38 MW	8.16 AW	17440 AAW	UTBLS	10//99-12//99
	Vermont	S	8.21 MW	8.46 AW	17600 AAW	VTBLS	10//99-12//99
	Burlington MSA, VT	S	8.90 MW	8.74 AW	18500 AAW	VTBLS	10//99-12//99
	Virginia	S	7.75 MW	7.94 AW	16510 AAW	VABLS	10//99-12//99
	Charlottesville MSA, VA	S	9.85 MW	9.87 AW	20480 AAW	VABLS	10//99-12//99
	Danville MSA, VA	S	7.29 MW	7.46 AW	15170 AAW	VABLS	10//99-12//99
	Lynchburg MSA, VA	S	7.19 MW	7.17 AW	14940 AAW	VABLS	10//99-12//99
	Norfolk-Virginia Beach-Newport News MSA, VA-NC	S	7.65 MW	7.49 AW	15910 AAW	VABLS	10//99-12//99
	Richmond-Petersburg MSA, VA	S	8.49 MW	8.20 AW	17670 AAW	VABLS	10//99-12//99
	Roanoke MSA, VA	S	8.20 MW	8.01 AW	17060 AAW	VABLS	10//99-12//99
	Washington	S	8.85 MW	9.02 AW	18760 AAW	WABLS	10//99-12//99
	Bellingham MSA, WA	S	8.17 MW	8.06 AW	17000 AAW	WABLS	10//99-12//99

AAW Average annual wage	**AOH** Average offered, high	**ASH** Average starting, high	**H** Hourly	**M** Monthly	**S** Special: hourly and annual
AE Average entry salary	**AOL** Average offered, low	**ASL** Average starting, low	**HI** Highest wage paid	**MTC** Median total compensation	**TQ** Third quartile wage
AEX Average experienced wage	**APH** Average pay, high range	**AW** Average wage paid	**HR** High end range	**MW** Median wage paid	**W** Weekly
AO Average offered	**APL** Average pay, low range	**FQ** First quartile wage	**LR** Low end range	**SQ** Second quartile wage	**Y** Yearly

Occupation/Type/Industry	Location	Per	Low	Mid	High	Source	Date
Nursing Aide, Orderly, and Attendant	Bremerton PMSA, WA	S	9.26 MW	8.51 AW	19260 AAW	WABLS	10//99-12//99
	Olympia PMSA, WA	S	8.94 MW	8.56 AW	18590 AAW	WABLS	10//99-12//99
	Richland-Kennewick-Pasco MSA, WA	S	8.65 MW	8.37 AW	17990 AAW	WABLS	10//99-12//99
	Seattle-Bellevue-Everett PMSA, WA	S	10.08 MW	10.14 AW	20960 AAW	WABLS	10//99-12//99
	Spokane MSA, WA	S	8.04 MW	7.91 AW	16730 AAW	WABLS	10//99-12//99
	Tacoma PMSA, WA	S	8.76 MW	8.47 AW	18230 AAW	WABLS	10//99-12//99
	Yakima MSA, WA	S	8.20 MW	8.03 AW	17060 AAW	WABLS	10//99-12//99
	West Virginia	S	6.82 MW	7.13 AW	14840 AAW	WVBLS	10//99-12//99
	Charleston MSA, WV	S	7.21 MW	6.91 AW	14990 AAW	WVBLS	10//99-12//99
	Huntington-Ashland MSA, WV-KY-OH	S	7.14 MW	6.62 AW	14850 AAW	WVBLS	10//99-12//99
	Parkersburg-Marietta MSA, WV-OH	S	7.02 MW	6.71 AW	14610 AAW	WVBLS	10//99-12//99
	Wheeling MSA, WV-OH	S	7.66 MW	7.36 AW	15920 AAW	WVBLS	10//99-12//99
	Wisconsin	S	8.9 MW	9.04 AW	18800 AAW	WIBLS	10//99-12//99
	Appleton-Oshkosh-Neenah MSA, WI	S	9.52 MW	9.51 AW	19800 AAW	WIBLS	10//99-12//99
	Eau Claire MSA, WI	S	9.18 MW	8.89 AW	19100 AAW	WIBLS	10//99-12//99
	Green Bay MSA, WI	S	9.15 MW	9.30 AW	19030 AAW	WIBLS	10//99-12//99
	Janesville-Beloit MSA, WI	S	9.12 MW	9.23 AW	18960 AAW	WIBLS	10//99-12//99
	Kenosha PMSA, WI	S	8.20 MW	8.05 AW	17060 AAW	WIBLS	10//99-12//99
	La Crosse MSA, WI-MN	S	8.99 MW	9.02 AW	18690 AAW	WIBLS	10//99-12//99
	Madison MSA, WI	S	9.56 MW	9.36 AW	19880 AAW	WIBLS	10//99-12//99
	Milwaukee-Waukesha PMSA, WI	S	9.12 MW	9.12 AW	18960 AAW	WIBLS	10//99-12//99
	Racine PMSA, WI	S	9.63 MW	9.32 AW	20030 AAW	WIBLS	10//99-12//99
	Sheboygan MSA, WI	S	8.77 MW	8.87 AW	18250 AAW	WIBLS	10//99-12//99
	Wausau MSA, WI	S	8.94 MW	9.16 AW	18600 AAW	WIBLS	10//99-12//99
	Wyoming	S	7.73 MW	7.74 AW	16090 AAW	WYBLS	10//99-12//99
	Cheyenne MSA, WY	S	8.56 MW	8.48 AW	17800 AAW	WYBLS	10//99-12//99
	Puerto Rico	S	6.09 MW	6.37 AW	13250 AAW	PRBLS	10//99-12//99
	San Juan-Bayamon PMSA, PR	S	6.25 MW	6.10 AW	12990 AAW	PRBLS	10//99-12//99
	Guam	S	10.42 MW	10.22 AW	21250 AAW	GUBLS	10//99-12//99
Nursing Home Administrator	United States	Y		68940 AW		MLTC	1999
Nursing Instructor and Teacher							
Postsecondary	Alabama	Y		42910 AAW		ALBLS	10//99-12//99
Postsecondary	Birmingham MSA, AL	Y		45530 AAW		ALBLS	10//99-12//99
Postsecondary	Huntsville MSA, AL	Y		43140 AAW		ALBLS	10//99-12//99
Postsecondary	Mobile MSA, AL	Y		44000 AAW		ALBLS	10//99-12//99
Postsecondary	Montgomery MSA, AL	Y		41440 AAW		ALBLS	10//99-12//99
Postsecondary	Arizona	Y		44550 AAW		AZBLS	10//99-12//99
Postsecondary	Phoenix-Mesa MSA, AZ	Y		50380 AAW		AZBLS	10//99-12//99
Postsecondary	Arkansas	Y		40210 AAW		ARBLS	10//99-12//99
Postsecondary	California	Y		52910 AAW		CABLS	10//99-12//99
Postsecondary	Fresno MSA, CA	Y		50750 AAW		CABLS	10//99-12//99
Postsecondary	Los Angeles-Long Beach PMSA, CA	Y		54710 AAW		CABLS	10//99-12//99
Postsecondary	Oakland PMSA, CA	Y		53180 AAW		CABLS	10//99-12//99
Postsecondary	Orange County PMSA, CA	Y		51840 AAW		CABLS	10//99-12//99
Postsecondary	Riverside-San Bernardino PMSA, CA	Y		56040 AAW		CABLS	10//99-12//99
Postsecondary	Sacramento PMSA, CA	Y		55210 AAW		CABLS	10//99-12//99
Postsecondary	Salinas MSA, CA	Y		56600 AAW		CABLS	10//99-12//99
Postsecondary	San Diego MSA, CA	Y		49720 AAW		CABLS	10//99-12//99
Postsecondary	San Francisco PMSA, CA	Y		52210 AAW		CABLS	10//99-12//99
Postsecondary	San Jose PMSA, CA	Y		58820 AAW		CABLS	10//99-12//99
Postsecondary	Santa Cruz-Watsonville PMSA, CA	Y		53850 AAW		CABLS	10//99-12//99
Postsecondary	Colorado	Y		40840 AAW		COBLS	10//99-12//99
Postsecondary	Denver PMSA, CO	Y		46310 AAW		COBLS	10//99-12//99
Postsecondary	Fort Collins-Loveland MSA, CO	Y		33670 AAW		COBLS	10//99-12//99
Postsecondary	Connecticut	Y		59960 AAW		CTBLS	10//99-12//99
Postsecondary	Hartford MSA, CT	Y		59230 AAW		CTBLS	10//99-12//99
Postsecondary	New Haven-Meriden PMSA, CT	Y		59130 AAW		CTBLS	10//99-12//99
Postsecondary	District of Columbia	Y		47060 AAW		DCBLS	10//99-12//99

Occupation/Type/Industry	Location	Per	Low	Mid	High	Source	Date
Nursing Instructor and Teacher							
Postsecondary	Washington PMSA, DC-MD-VA-WV	Y		51770 AAW		DCBLS	10//99-12//99
Postsecondary	Florida	Y		54300 AAW		FLBLS	10//99-12//99
Postsecondary	Fort Lauderdale PMSA, FL	Y		59430 AAW		FLBLS	10//99-12//99
Postsecondary	Gainesville MSA, FL	Y		56470 AAW		FLBLS	10//99-12//99
Postsecondary	Jacksonville MSA, FL	Y		46600 AAW		FLBLS	10//99-12//99
Postsecondary	Melbourne-Titusville-Palm Bay MSA, FL	Y		47410 AAW		FLBLS	10//99-12//99
Postsecondary	Miami PMSA, FL	Y		54640 AAW		FLBLS	10//99-12//99
Postsecondary	Orlando MSA, FL	Y		49690 AAW		FLBLS	10//99-12//99
Postsecondary	Pensacola MSA, FL	Y		56970 AAW		FLBLS	10//99-12//99
Postsecondary	Tallahassee MSA, FL	Y		59030 AAW		FLBLS	10//99-12//99
Postsecondary	Tampa-St. Petersburg-Clearwater MSA, FL	Y		59690 AAW		FLBLS	10//99-12//99
Postsecondary	West Palm Beach-Boca Raton MSA, FL	Y		57660 AAW		FLBLS	10//99-12//99
Postsecondary	Georgia	Y		47500 AAW		GABLS	10//99-12//99
Postsecondary	Atlanta MSA, GA	Y		51270 AAW		GABLS	10//99-12//99
Postsecondary	Savannah MSA, GA	Y		53780 AAW		GABLS	10//99-12//99
Postsecondary	Hawaii	Y		62800 AAW		HIBLS	10//99-12//99
Postsecondary	Honolulu MSA, HI	Y		61770 AAW		HIBLS	10//99-12//99
Postsecondary	Idaho	Y		46230 AAW		IDBLS	10//99-12//99
Postsecondary	Illinois	Y		46090 AAW		ILBLS	10//99-12//99
Postsecondary	Chicago PMSA, IL	Y		46470 AAW		ILBLS	10//99-12//99
Postsecondary	Indiana	Y		40660 AAW		INBLS	10//99-12//99
Postsecondary	Evansville-Henderson MSA, IN-KY	Y		40420 AAW		INBLS	10//99-12//99
Postsecondary	Fort Wayne MSA, IN	Y		43550 AAW		INBLS	10//99-12//99
Postsecondary	Gary PMSA, IN	Y		44600 AAW		INBLS	10//99-12//99
Postsecondary	Indianapolis MSA, IN	Y		40940 AAW		INBLS	10//99-12//99
Postsecondary	Lafayette MSA, IN	Y		38020 AAW		INBLS	10//99-12//99
Postsecondary	South Bend MSA, IN	Y		37730 AAW		INBLS	10//99-12//99
Postsecondary	Iowa	Y		45120 AAW		IABLS	10//99-12//99
Postsecondary	Cedar Rapids MSA, IA	Y		42180 AAW		IABLS	10//99-12//99
Postsecondary	Des Moines MSA, IA	Y		41940 AAW		IABLS	10//99-12//99
Postsecondary	Kansas	Y		39760 AAW		KSBLS	10//99-12//99
Postsecondary	Kentucky	Y		38910 AAW		KYBLS	10//99-12//99
Postsecondary	Louisville MSA, KY-IN	Y		38890 AAW		KYBLS	10//99-12//99
Postsecondary	Louisiana	Y		40030 AAW		LABLS	10//99-12//99
Postsecondary	New Orleans MSA, LA	Y		39330 AAW		LABLS	10//99-12//99
Postsecondary	Shreveport-Bossier City MSA, LA	Y		38620 AAW		LABLS	10//99-12//99
Postsecondary	Maine	Y		45680 AAW		MEBLS	10//99-12//99
Postsecondary	Maryland	Y		54040 AAW		MDBLS	10//99-12//99
Postsecondary	Baltimore PMSA, MD	Y		53670 AAW		MDBLS	10//99-12//99
Postsecondary	Massachusetts	Y		44320 AAW		MABLS	10//99-12//99
Postsecondary	Boston PMSA, MA-NH	Y		41550 AAW		MABLS	10//99-12//99
Postsecondary	Fitchburg-Leominster PMSA, MA	Y		42160 AAW		MABLS	10//99-12//99
Postsecondary	Springfield MSA, MA	Y		55380 AAW		MABLS	10//99-12//99
Postsecondary	Worcester PMSA, MA-CT	Y		46120 AAW		MABLS	10//99-12//99
Postsecondary	Michigan	Y		52100 AAW		MIBLS	10//99-12//99
Postsecondary	Detroit PMSA, MI	Y		55570 AAW		MIBLS	10//99-12//99
Postsecondary	Flint PMSA, MI	Y		50770 AAW		MIBLS	10//99-12//99
Postsecondary	Grand Rapids-Muskegon-Holland MSA, MI	Y		50190 AAW		MIBLS	10//99-12//99
Postsecondary	Kalamazoo-Battle Creek MSA, MI	Y		51550 AAW		MIBLS	10//99-12//99
Postsecondary	Saginaw-Bay City-Midland MSA, MI	Y		40680 AAW		MIBLS	10//99-12//99
Postsecondary	Minnesota	Y		48700 AAW		MNBLS	10//99-12//99
Postsecondary	Duluth-Superior MSA, MN-WI	Y		45150 AAW		MNBLS	10//99-12//99
Postsecondary	Minneapolis-St. Paul MSA, MN-WI	Y		54400 AAW		MNBLS	10//99-12//99
Postsecondary	Mississippi	Y		44840 AAW		MSBLS	10//99-12//99
Postsecondary	Missouri	Y		40300 AAW		MOBLS	10//99-12//99
Postsecondary	Kansas City MSA, MO-KS	Y		44520 AAW		MOBLS	10//99-12//99
Postsecondary	Montana	Y		43400 AAW		MTBLS	10//99-12//99
Postsecondary	Nebraska	Y		48930 AAW		NEBLS	10//99-12//99
Postsecondary	Lincoln MSA, NE	Y		56930 AAW		NEBLS	10//99-12//99
Postsecondary	Omaha MSA, NE-IA	Y		48040 AAW		NEBLS	10//99-12//99

AAW	Average annual wage	AOH	Average offered, high	ASH	Average starting, high	H	Hourly	M	Monthly	S	Special: hourly and annual
AE	Average entry wage	AOL	Average offered, low	ASL	Average starting, low	HI	Highest wage paid	MTC	Median total compensation	TQ	Third quartile wage
AEX	Average experienced wage	APH	Average pay, high range	AW	Average wage paid	HR	High end range	MW	Median wage paid	W	Weekly
AO	Average offered	APL	Average pay, low range	FQ	First quartile wage	LR	Low end range	SQ	Second quartile wage	Y	Yearly

Occupation/Type/Industry	Location	Per	Low	Mid	High	Source	Date
Nursing Instructor and Teacher							
Postsecondary	Nevada	Y		45530 AAW		NVBLS	10//99-12//99
Postsecondary	New Hampshire	Y		41480 AAW		NHBLS	10//99-12//99
Postsecondary	New Jersey	Y		52220 AAW		NJBLS	10//99-12//99
Postsecondary	Bergen-Passaic PMSA, NJ	Y		51580 AAW		NJBLS	10//99-12//99
Postsecondary	Jersey City PMSA, NJ	Y		51040 AAW		NJBLS	10//99-12//99
Postsecondary	Middlesex-Somerset-Hunterdon PMSA, NJ	Y		56370 AAW		NJBLS	10//99-12//99
Postsecondary	Newark PMSA, NJ	Y		55820 AAW		NJBLS	10//99-12//99
Postsecondary	Trenton PMSA, NJ	Y		54710 AAW		NJBLS	10//99-12//99
Postsecondary	New Mexico	Y		45470 AAW		NMBLS	10//99-12//99
Postsecondary	New York	Y		53670 AAW		NYBLS	10//99-12//99
Postsecondary	Albany-Schenectady-Troy MSA, NY	Y		45360 AAW		NYBLS	10//99-12//99
Postsecondary	Buffalo-Niagara Falls MSA, NY	Y		51860 AAW		NYBLS	10//99-12//99
Postsecondary	New York PMSA, NY	Y		63030 AAW		NYBLS	10//99-12//99
Postsecondary	Utica-Rome MSA, NY	Y		44250 AAW		NYBLS	10//99-12//99
Postsecondary	North Carolina	Y		46010 AAW		NCBLS	10//99-12//99
Postsecondary	Charlotte-Gastonia-Rock Hill MSA, NC-SC	Y		39800 AAW		NCBLS	10//99-12//99
Postsecondary	Greensboro--Winston-Salem--High Point MSA, NC	Y		45460 AAW		NCBLS	10//99-12//99
Postsecondary	Hickory-Morganton-Lenoir MSA, NC	Y		38830 AAW		NCBLS	10//99-12//99
Postsecondary	Raleigh-Durham-Chapel Hill MSA, NC	Y		53560 AAW		NCBLS	10//99-12//99
Postsecondary	Wilmington MSA, NC	Y		48520 AAW		NCBLS	10//99-12//99
Postsecondary	North Dakota	Y		40590 AAW		NDBLS	10//99-12//99
Postsecondary	Ohio	Y		40410 AAW		OHBLS	10//99-12//99
Postsecondary	Cincinnati PMSA, OH-KY-IN	Y		41830 AAW		OHBLS	10//99-12//99
Postsecondary	Cleveland-Lorain-Elyria PMSA, OH	Y		38520 AAW		OHBLS	10//99-12//99
Postsecondary	Columbus MSA, OH	Y		39580 AAW		OHBLS	10//99-12//99
Postsecondary	Dayton-Springfield MSA, OH	Y		38830 AAW		OHBLS	10//99-12//99
Postsecondary	Toledo MSA, OH	Y		39380 AAW		OHBLS	10//99-12//99
Postsecondary	Youngstown-Warren MSA, OH	Y		44230 AAW		OHBLS	10//99-12//99
Postsecondary	Oklahoma	Y		41160 AAW		OKBLS	10//99-12//99
Postsecondary	Oklahoma City MSA, OK	Y		43160 AAW		OKBLS	10//99-12//99
Postsecondary	Oregon	Y		48080 AAW		ORBLS	10//99-12//99
Postsecondary	Portland-Vancouver PMSA, OR-WA	Y		47040 AAW		ORBLS	10//99-12//99
Postsecondary	Pennsylvania	Y		51530 AAW		PABLS	10//99-12//99
Postsecondary	Allentown-Bethlehem-Easton MSA, PA	Y		46860 AAW		PABLS	10//99-12//99
Postsecondary	Erie MSA, PA	Y		44910 AAW		PABLS	10//99-12//99
Postsecondary	Harrisburg-Lebanon-Carlisle MSA, PA	Y		47120 AAW		PABLS	10//99-12//99
Postsecondary	Philadelphia PMSA, PA-NJ	Y		55050 AAW		PABLS	10//99-12//99
Postsecondary	Pittsburgh MSA, PA	Y		49620 AAW		PABLS	10//99-12//99
Postsecondary	Scranton--Wilkes-Barre--Hazleton MSA, PA	Y		51070 AAW		PABLS	10//99-12//99
Postsecondary	York MSA, PA	Y		47370 AAW		PABLS	10//99-12//99
Postsecondary	Providence-Fall River-Warwick MSA, RI-MA	Y		58780 AAW		RIBLS	10//99-12//99
Postsecondary	South Carolina	Y		44640 AAW		SCBLS	10//99-12//99
Postsecondary	Charleston-North Charleston MSA, SC	Y		38570 AAW		SCBLS	10//99-12//99
Postsecondary	Greenville-Spartanburg-Anderson MSA, SC	Y		45440 AAW		SCBLS	10//99-12//99
Postsecondary	South Dakota	Y		35710 AAW		SDBLS	10//99-12//99
Postsecondary	Tennessee	Y		49660 AAW		TNBLS	10//99-12//99
Postsecondary	Memphis MSA, TN-AR-MS	Y		47430 AAW		MSBLS	10//99-12//99
Postsecondary	Texas	Y		42140 AAW		TXBLS	10//99-12//99
Postsecondary	Dallas PMSA, TX	Y		44940 AAW		TXBLS	10//99-12//99
Postsecondary	El Paso MSA, TX	Y		40830 AAW		TXBLS	10//99-12//99
Postsecondary	Fort Worth-Arlington PMSA, TX	Y		51420 AAW		TXBLS	10//99-12//99
Postsecondary	Houston PMSA, TX	Y		43000 AAW		TXBLS	10//99-12//99
Postsecondary	Killeen-Temple MSA, TX	Y		41390 AAW		TXBLS	10//99-12//99
Postsecondary	Longview-Marshall MSA, TX	Y		40820 AAW		TXBLS	10//99-12//99
Postsecondary	Odessa-Midland MSA, TX	Y		40230 AAW		TXBLS	10//99-12//99

AAW	Average annual wage	AOH	Average offered, high	ASH	Average starting, high	H	Hourly	M	Monthly	S	Special: hourly and annual
AE	Average entry wage	AOL	Average offered, low	ASL	Average starting, low	HI	Highest wage paid	MTC	Median total compensation	TQ	Third quartile wage
AEX	Average experienced wage	APH	Average pay, high range	AW	Average wage paid	HR	High end range	MW	Median wage paid	W	Weekly
AO	Average offered	APL	Average pay, low range	FQ	First quartile wage	LR	Low end range	SQ	Second quartile wage	Y	Yearly

Occupation/Type/Industry	Location	Per	Low	Mid	High	Source	Date
Nursing Instructor and Teacher							
Postsecondary	San Antonio MSA, TX	Y		43220 AAW		TXBLS	10//99-12//99
Postsecondary	Virginia	Y		48370 AAW		VABLS	10//99-12//99
Postsecondary	Norfolk-Virginia Beach-Newport News MSA, VA-NC	Y		48260 AAW		VABLS	10//99-12//99
Postsecondary	Richmond-Petersburg MSA, VA	Y		49230 AAW		VABLS	10//99-12//99
Postsecondary	Washington	Y		46460 AAW		WABLS	10//99-12//99
Postsecondary	Seattle-Bellevue-Everett PMSA, WA	Y		51910 AAW		WABLS	10//99-12//99
Postsecondary	Tacoma PMSA, WA	Y		47530 AAW		WABLS	10//99-12//99
Postsecondary	West Virginia	Y		53410 AAW		WVBLS	10//99-12//99
Postsecondary	Wisconsin	Y		44620 AAW		WIBLS	10//99-12//99
Postsecondary	Milwaukee-Waukesha PMSA, WI	Y		42290 AAW		WIBLS	10//99-12//99
Postsecondary	Wyoming	Y		35800 AAW		WYBLS	10//99-12//99
Postsecondary	Puerto Rico	Y		26320 AAW		PRBLS	10//99-12//99
Postsecondary	San Juan-Bayamon PMSA, PR	Y		25030 AAW		PRBLS	10//99-12//99
Nursing Services Director							
Hospital	United States	Y		102300 AW		MODHE	1999
Hospital	North Central	Y		99400 AW		MODHE	1999
Hospital	Northeast	Y		104400 AW		MODHE	1999
Hospital	South Central	Y		103500 AW		MODHE	1999
Hospital	Southeast	Y		99900 AW		MODHE	1999
Hospital	West	Y		115400 AW		MODHE	1999
Hospital	West Central	Y		112500 AW		MODHE	1999
Obstetrician and Gynecologist	Arizona	S		67.73 AW	140870 AAW	AZBLS	10//99-12//99
	California	S		65.95 AW	137170 AAW	CABLS	10//99-12//99
	Los Angeles-Long Beach PMSA, CA	S	56.90 MW		118350 AAW	CABLS	10//99-12//99
	Connecticut	S		64.56 AW	134280 AAW	CTBLS	10//99-12//99
	Bridgeport PMSA, CT	S	62.16 MW		129300 AAW	CTBLS	10//99-12//99
	Florida	S		69.72 AW	145020 AAW	FLBLS	10//99-12//99
	Miami PMSA, FL	S	62.23 MW	64.80 AW	129450 AAW	FLBLS	10//99-12//99
	Georgia	S		64.84 AW	134880 AAW	GABLS	10//99-12//99
	Chicago PMSA, IL	S	60.04 MW	62.75 AW	124890 AAW	ILBLS	10//99-12//99
	Indiana	S		65.26 AW	135750 AAW	INBLS	10//99-12//99
	Gary PMSA, IN	S	70.00 MW		145600 AAW	INBLS	10//99-12//99
	Kansas	S		66.67 AW	138680 AAW	KSBLS	10//99-12//99
	Kentucky	S		67.75 AW	140930 AAW	KYBLS	10//99-12//99
	Maine	S		68.96 AW	143430 AAW	MEBLS	10//99-12//99
	Maryland	S	50.22 MW	50.15 AW	104300 AAW	MDBLS	10//99-12//99
	Baltimore PMSA, MD	S	50.41 MW	50.31 AW	104860 AAW	MDBLS	10//99-12//99
	Massachusetts	S		67.06 AW	139480 AAW	MABLS	10//99-12//99
	Boston PMSA, MA-NH	S	65.80 MW		136870 AAW	MABLS	10//99-12//99
	Michigan	S		67.09 AW	139540 AAW	MIBLS	10//99-12//99
	Minnesota	S		67.69 AW	140790 AAW	MNBLS	10//99-12//99
	Minneapolis-St. Paul MSA, MN-WI	S	67.43 MW		140260 AAW	MNBLS	10//99-12//99
	Mississippi	S		68.81 AW	143110 AAW	MSBLS	10//99-12//99
	Missouri	S	52.13 MW	53.44 AW	111150 AAW	MOBLS	10//99-12//99
	New Jersey	S		63.33 AW	131730 AAW	NJBLS	10//99-12//99
	New Mexico	S		61.28 AW	127450 AAW	NMBLS	10//99-12//99
	New York	S		67.84 AW	141100 AAW	NYBLS	10//99-12//99
	North Carolina	S		63.72 AW	132530 AAW	NCBLS	10//99-12//99
	Charlotte-Gastonia-Rock Hill MSA, NC-SC	S	63.90 MW		132900 AAW	NCBLS	10//99-12//99
	North Dakota	S	64.07 MW	61.57 AW	128070 AAW	NDBLS	10//99-12//99
	Ohio	S		69.04 AW	143610 AAW	OHBLS	10//99-12//99
	Cincinnati PMSA, OH-KY-IN	S	68.37 MW		142210 AAW	OHBLS	10//99-12//99
	Oklahoma	S		69.07 AW	143660 AAW	OKBLS	10//99-12//99
	Pennsylvania	S		66.49 AW	138300 AAW	PABLS	10//99-12//99
	Pittsburgh MSA, PA	S	69.58 MW		144730 AAW	PABLS	10//99-12//99
	South Carolina	S	64.3 MW	59.57 AW	123900 AAW	SCBLS	10//99-12//99
	Greenville-Spartanburg-Anderson MSA, SC	S	54.68 MW	54.09 AW	113740 AAW	SCBLS	10//99-12//99
	Tennessee	S		68.94 AW	143390 AAW	TNBLS	10//99-12//99
	Texas	S	54.86 MW	57.86 AW	120350 AAW	TXBLS	10//99-12//99
	Houston PMSA, TX	S	54.31 MW	52.25 AW	112970 AAW	TXBLS	10//99-12//99
	Utah	S		62.90 AW	130830 AAW	UTBLS	10//99-12//99

AAW	Average annual wage	AOH	Average offered, high	ASH	Average starting, high
AE	Average entry wage	AOL	Average offered, low	ASL	Average starting, low
AEX	Average experienced wage	APH	Average pay, high range	AW	Average wage paid
AO	Average offered	APL	Average pay, low range	FQ	First quartile wage

H	Hourly
HI	Highest wage paid
HR	High end range
LR	Low end range

M	Monthly	S	Special: hourly and annual
MTC	Median total compensation	TQ	Third quartile wage
MW	Median wage paid	W	Weekly
SQ	Second quartile wage	Y	Yearly

Occupation/Type/Industry	Location	Per	Low	Mid	High	Source	Date
Obstetrician and Gynecologist	Salt Lake City-Ogden MSA, UT	S	66.36 MW		138030 AAW	UTBLS	10//99-12//99
	Washington	S		67.66 AW	140720 AAW	WABLS	10//99-12//99
	West Virginia	S		69.35 AW	144250 AAW	WVBLS	10//99-12//99
	Wisconsin	S		61.62 AW	128170 AAW	WIBLS	10//99-12//99
	Puerto Rico	S	25.95 MW	26.16 AW	54410 AAW	PRBLS	10//99-12//99
	Arecibo PMSA, PR	S	23.72 MW	24.08 AW	49340 AAW	PRBLS	10//99-12//99
Occupational Health and Safety Specialist and Technician	Alabama	S	19.31 MW	19.78 AW	41140 AAW	ALBLS	10//99-12//99
	Alaska	S	27.48 MW	26.05 AW	54180 AAW	AKBLS	10//99-12//99
	Arizona	S	15.29 MW	16.49 AW	34300 AAW	AZBLS	10//99-12//99
	Arkansas	S	16.98 MW	17.27 AW	35920 AAW	ARBLS	10//99-12//99
	California	S	25.74 MW	25.19 AW	52390 AAW	CABLS	10//99-12//99
	Colorado	S	24.8 MW	24.34 AW	50620 AAW	COBLS	10//99-12//99
	Connecticut	S	23.3 MW	22.28 AW	46330 AAW	CTBLS	10//99-12//99
	Delaware	S	23.22 MW	24.25 AW	50450 AAW	DEBLS	10//99-12//99
	Florida	S	20.07 MW	20.87 AW	43410 AAW	FLBLS	10//99-12//99
	Georgia	S	20.18 MW	21.30 AW	44300 AAW	GABLS	10//99-12//99
	Hawaii	S	16.24 MW	17.84 AW	37110 AAW	HIBLS	10//99-12//99
	Illinois	S	19.44 MW	20.08 AW	41770 AAW	ILBLS	10//99-12//99
	Indiana	S	18.54 MW	19.94 AW	41470 AAW	INBLS	10//99-12//99
	Iowa	S	16.98 MW	17.18 AW	35730 AAW	IABLS	10//99-12//99
	Kansas	S	15.84 MW	16.42 AW	34160 AAW	KSBLS	10//99-12//99
	Kentucky	S	20.02 MW	20.95 AW	43580 AAW	KYBLS	10//99-12//99
	Louisiana	S	17.67 MW	18.71 AW	38920 AAW	LABLS	10//99-12//99
	Maine	S	18.3 MW	18.15 AW	37760 AAW	MEBLS	10//99-12//99
	Maryland	S	21.99 MW	22.43 AW	46650 AAW	MDBLS	10//99-12//99
	Massachusetts	S	22.9 MW	23.55 AW	48980 AAW	MABLS	10//99-12//99
	Michigan	S	19.57 MW	20.33 AW	42290 AAW	MIBLS	10//99-12//99
	Minnesota	S	20.22 MW	21.27 AW	44240 AAW	MNBLS	10//99-12//99
	Mississippi	S	12.87 MW	14.02 AW	29160 AAW	MSBLS	10//99-12//99
	Missouri	S	19.45 MW	20.68 AW	43010 AAW	MOBLS	10//99-12//99
	Montana	S	16.56 MW	18.90 AW	39300 AAW	MTBLS	10//99-12//99
	Nebraska	S	21.58 MW	20.30 AW	42230 AAW	NEBLS	10//99-12//99
	Nevada	S	19.35 MW	19.80 AW	41190 AAW	NVBLS	10//99-12//99
	New Hampshire	S	21.41 MW	21.84 AW	45430 AAW	NHBLS	10//99-12//99
	New Jersey	S	22.2 MW	22.38 AW	46560 AAW	NJBLS	10//99-12//99
	New Mexico	S	15.35 MW	16.49 AW	34310 AAW	NMBLS	10//99-12//99
	New York	S	20.61 MW	21.27 AW	44230 AAW	NYBLS	10//99-12//99
	North Carolina	S	17.65 MW	17.81 AW	37050 AAW	NCBLS	10//99-12//99
	North Dakota	S	16.9 MW	22.05 AW	45860 AAW	NDBLS	10//99-12//99
	Ohio	S	17.96 MW	19.01 AW	39550 AAW	OHBLS	10//99-12//99
	Oklahoma	S	25.61 MW	26.25 AW	54600 AAW	OKBLS	10//99-12//99
	Oregon	S	21.3 MW	21.52 AW	44750 AAW	ORBLS	10//99-12//99
	Pennsylvania	S	14.8 MW	16.26 AW	33810 AAW	PABLS	10//99-12//99
	Rhode Island	S	21.43 MW	21.17 AW	44030 AAW	RIBLS	10//99-12//99
	South Carolina	S	17.35 MW	19.18 AW	39890 AAW	SCBLS	10//99-12//99
	South Dakota	S	18.88 MW	19.74 AW	41050 AAW	SDBLS	10//99-12//99
	Tennessee	S	17.47 MW	19.32 AW	40180 AAW	TNBLS	10//99-12//99
	Texas	S	17.53 MW	19.26 AW	40060 AAW	TXBLS	10//99-12//99
	Utah	S	21.38 MW	22.01 AW	45780 AAW	UTBLS	10//99-12//99
	Vermont	S	14.2 MW	17.03 AW	35420 AAW	VTBLS	10//99-12//99
	Virginia	S	18.53 MW	19.64 AW	40850 AAW	VABLS	10//99-12//99
	Washington	S	22.76 MW	23.48 AW	48830 AAW	WABLS	10//99-12//99
	West Virginia	S	25.56 MW	24.62 AW	51210 AAW	WVBLS	10//99-12//99
	Wisconsin	S	16.25 MW	16.37 AW	34060 AAW	WIBLS	10//99-12//99
	Wyoming	S	22.18 MW	21.33 AW	44370 AAW	WYBLS	10//99-12//99
	Puerto Rico	S	10.47 MW	12.31 AW	25600 AAW	PRBLS	10//99-12//99
Occupational Therapist	United States	H		22.68 AW		NCS98	1998
	Alabama	S	24.21 MW	25.31 AW	52650 AAW	ALBLS	10//99-12//99
	Alaska	S	24.21 MW	25.20 AW	52420 AAW	AKBLS	10//99-12//99
	Arizona	S	20.95 MW	22.27 AW	46310 AAW	AZBLS	10//99-12//99
	Arkansas	S	24.29 MW	25.66 AW	53370 AAW	ARBLS	10//99-12//99
	California	S	29.91 MW	29.40 AW	61160 AAW	CABLS	10//99-12//99
	Colorado	S	21.22 MW	22.24 AW	46270 AAW	COBLS	10//99-12//99
	Connecticut	S	26.13 MW	27.63 AW	57470 AAW	CTBLS	10//99-12//99
	Delaware	S	24.91 MW	26.32 AW	54740 AAW	DEBLS	10//99-12//99
	District of Columbia	S	22.79 MW	23.27 AW	48410 AAW	DCBLS	10//99-12//99
	Florida	S	23.49 MW	23.67 AW	49220 AAW	FLBLS	10//99-12//99
	Georgia	S	27.7 MW	27.49 AW	57190 AAW	GABLS	10//99-12//99

AAW Average annual wage	**AOH** Average offered, high	**ASH** Average starting, high	**H** Hourly	**M** Monthly	**S** Special: hourly and annual
AE Average entry wage	**AOL** Average offered, low	**ASL** Average starting, low	**HI** Highest wage paid	**MTC** Median total compensation	**TQ** Third quartile wage
AEX Average experienced wage	**APH** Average pay, high range	**AW** Average wage paid	**HR** High end range	**MW** Median wage paid	**W** Weekly
AO Average offered	**APL** Average pay, low range	**FQ** First quartile wage	**LR** Low end range	**SQ** Second quartile wage	**Y** Yearly

Occupation/Type/Industry	Location	Per	Low	Mid	High	Source	Date
Occupational Therapist	Hawaii	S	23.65 MW	24.40 AW	50740 AAW	HIBLS	10//99-12//99
	Idaho	S	21.31 MW	20.87 AW	43410 AAW	IDBLS	10//99-12//99
	Illinois	S	23.04 MW	23.53 AW	48940 AAW	ILBLS	10//99-12//99
	Indiana	S	23.53 MW	24.13 AW	50180 AAW	INBLS	10//99-12//99
	Iowa	S	20.62 MW	21.27 AW	44250 AAW	IABLS	10//99-12//99
	Kansas	S	22.63 MW	23.36 AW	48590 AAW	KSBLS	10//99-12//99
	Kentucky	S	23.28 MW	24.36 AW	50660 AAW	KYBLS	10//99-12//99
	Louisiana	S	23.76 MW	25.78 AW	53630 AAW	LABLS	10//99-12//99
	Maine	S	21.52 MW	22.35 AW	46500 AAW	MEBLS	10//99-12//99
	Maryland	S	24.2 MW	26.03 AW	54140 AAW	MDBLS	10//99-12//99
	Massachusetts	S	23.8 MW	24.89 AW	51780 AAW	MABLS	10//99-12//99
	Michigan	S	21.8 MW	23.04 AW	47920 AAW	MIBLS	10//99-12//99
	Minnesota	S	21.49 MW	21.35 AW	44400 AAW	MNBLS	10//99-12//99
	Mississippi	S	26.57 MW	28.60 AW	59480 AAW	MSBLS	10//99-12//99
	Missouri	S	23.28 MW	23.94 AW	49790 AAW	MOBLS	10//99-12//99
	Montana	S	22.26 MW	23.14 AW	48130 AAW	MTBLS	10//99-12//99
	Nebraska	S	21.44 MW	21.81 AW	45360 AAW	NEBLS	10//99-12//99
	Nevada	S	29.76 MW	28.75 AW	59810 AAW	NVBLS	10//99-12//99
	New Hampshire	S	22.51 MW	22.77 AW	47360 AAW	NHBLS	10//99-12//99
	New Jersey	S	25.41 MW	27.32 AW	56820 AAW	NJBLS	10//99-12//99
	New Mexico	S	20.16 MW	20.77 AW	43200 AAW	NMBLS	10//99-12//99
	New York	S	22.8 MW	25.00 AW	52000 AAW	NYBLS	10//99-12//99
	North Carolina	S	24.06 MW	25.12 AW	52250 AAW	NCBLS	10//99-12//99
	North Dakota	S	19.52 MW	19.43 AW	40410 AAW	NDBLS	10//99-12//99
	Ohio	S	23.34 MW	24.36 AW	50670 AAW	OHBLS	10//99-12//99
	Oklahoma	S	19.01 MW	19.64 AW	40850 AAW	OKBLS	10//99-12//99
	Oregon	S	22.57 MW	22.29 AW	46360 AAW	ORBLS	10//99-12//99
	Pennsylvania	S	24.97 MW	26.65 AW	55420 AAW	PABLS	10//99-12//99
	Rhode Island	S	24.82 MW	25.68 AW	53420 AAW	RIBLS	10//99-12//99
	South Carolina	S	24.75 MW	27.13 AW	56420 AAW	SCBLS	10//99-12//99
	South Dakota	S	21.52 MW	21.49 AW	44690 AAW	SDBLS	10//99-12//99
	Tennessee	S	24.4 MW	25.57 AW	53180 AAW	TNBLS	10//99-12//99
	Texas	S	23.34 MW	25.43 AW	52890 AAW	TXBLS	10//99-12//99
	Utah	S	22.92 MW	22.81 AW	47450 AAW	UTBLS	10//99-12//99
	Vermont	S	21.63 MW	22.68 AW	47170 AAW	VTBLS	10//99-12//99
	Virginia	S	24.24 MW	26.46 AW	55040 AAW	VABLS	10//99-12//99
	Washington	S	23.14 MW	23.73 AW	49370 AAW	WABLS	10//99-12//99
	West Virginia	S	22.65 MW	23.78 AW	49450 AAW	WVBLS	10//99-12//99
	Wisconsin	S	20.84 MW	21.21 AW	44110 AAW	WIBLS	10//99-12//99
	Wyoming	S	22.27 MW	22.56 AW	46930 AAW	WYBLS	10//99-12//99
	Puerto Rico	S	10.51 MW	12.37 AW	25730 AAW	PRBLS	10//99-12//99
Occupational Therapist Aide	Alabama	S	9.71 MW	12.77 AW	26550 AAW	ALBLS	10//99-12//99
	Arizona	S	16.15 MW	15.28 AW	31790 AAW	AZBLS	10//99-12//99
	Arkansas	S	9.01 MW	10.32 AW	21470 AAW	ARBLS	10//99-12//99
	California	S	12.98 MW	16.08 AW	33460 AAW	CABLS	10//99-12//99
	Colorado	S	8.23 MW	8.55 AW	17780 AAW	COBLS	10//99-12//99
	Connecticut	S	12.45 MW	12.92 AW	26880 AAW	CTBLS	10//99-12//99
	Florida	S	9.72 MW	11.01 AW	22900 AAW	FLBLS	10//99-12//99
	Georgia	S	6.88 MW	7.54 AW	15680 AAW	GABLS	10//99-12//99
	Idaho	S	7.81 MW	9.05 AW	18820 AAW	IDBLS	10//99-12//99
	Illinois	S	8.66 MW	9.15 AW	19030 AAW	ILBLS	10//99-12//99
	Indiana	S	7.75 MW	9.85 AW	20500 AAW	INBLS	10//99-12//99
	Iowa	S	11.4 MW	11.50 AW	23910 AAW	IABLS	10//99-12//99
	Kansas	S	13.61 MW	12.89 AW	26810 AAW	KSBLS	10//99-12//99
	Kentucky	S	7.23 MW	8.58 AW	17840 AAW	KYBLS	10//99-12//99
	Louisiana	S	7.13 MW	8.02 AW	16680 AAW	LABLS	10//99-12//99
	Massachusetts	S	16.45 MW	15.86 AW	32980 AAW	MABLS	10//99-12//99
	Michigan	S	9.01 MW	10.44 AW	21720 AAW	MIBLS	10//99-12//99
	Minnesota	S	10.69 MW	12.04 AW	25050 AAW	MNBLS	10//99-12//99
	Mississippi	S	6.67 MW	9.85 AW	20500 AAW	MSBLS	10//99-12//99
	Missouri	S	8.14 MW	9.86 AW	20510 AAW	MOBLS	10//99-12//99
	Nebraska	S	9.61 MW	9.69 AW	20150 AAW	NEBLS	10//99-12//99
	New Jersey	S	9.66 MW	10.59 AW	22020 AAW	NJBLS	10//99-12//99
	New Mexico	S	7.9 MW	8.00 AW	16640 AAW	NMBLS	10//99-12//99
	New York	S	10.29 MW	10.97 AW	22820 AAW	NYBLS	10//99-12//99
	North Carolina	S	13.85 MW	13.69 AW	28470 AAW	NCBLS	10//99-12//99
	Ohio	S	10.48 MW	15.65 AW	32550 AAW	OHBLS	10//99-12//99
	Oklahoma	S	7.58 MW	7.42 AW	15440 AAW	OKBLS	10//99-12//99
	Oregon	S	12 MW	12.87 AW	26770 AAW	ORBLS	10//99-12//99
	Pennsylvania	S	6.88 MW	7.83 AW	16290 AAW	PABLS	10//99-12//99
	South Carolina	S	7.03 MW	8.10 AW	16850 AAW	SCBLS	10//99-12//99
	Tennessee	S	8.61 MW	9.60 AW	19970 AAW	TNBLS	10//99-12//99

Occupation/Type/Industry	Location	Per	Low	Mid	High	Source	Date
Occupational Therapist Aide	Texas	s	8.69 MW	8.62 AW	17930 AAW	TXBLS	10//99-12//99
	Utah	s	9 MW	8.82 AW	18340 AAW	UTBLS	10//99-12//99
	Washington	s	13.93 MW	13.24 AW	27540 AAW	WABLS	10//99-12//99
	West Virginia	s	9.4 MW	9.99 AW	20780 AAW	WVBLS	10//99-12//99
	Wisconsin	s	9.06 MW	9.39 AW	19530 AAW	WIBLS	10//99-12//99
Occupational Therapist Assistant	Alabama	s	18.38 MW	17.67 AW	36760 AAW	ALBLS	10//99-12//99
	Arizona	s	16.29 MW	16.41 AW	34140 AAW	AZBLS	10//99-12//99
	Arkansas	s	12.32 MW	13.31 AW	27680 AAW	ARBLS	10//99-12//99
	California	s	18.73 MW	18.52 AW	38510 AAW	CABLS	10//99-12//99
	Colorado	s	14.2 MW	14.48 AW	30110 AAW	COBLS	10//99-12//99
	Connecticut	s	17.39 MW	17.30 AW	35990 AAW	CTBLS	10//99-12//99
	Florida	s	18.61 MW	18.57 AW	38620 AAW	FLBLS	10//99-12//99
	Georgia	s	15.48 MW	16.05 AW	33380 AAW	GABLS	10//99-12//99
	Hawaii	s	13.56 MW	14.20 AW	29540 AAW	HIBLS	10//99-12//99
	Idaho	s	18.05 MW	17.59 AW	36580 AAW	IDBLS	10//99-12//99
	Illinois	s	15.35 MW	15.92 AW	33110 AAW	ILBLS	10//99-12//99
	Indiana	s	15.78 MW	16.68 AW	34690 AAW	INBLS	10//99-12//99
	Iowa	s	16.25 MW	16.45 AW	34210 AAW	IABLS	10//99-12//99
	Kansas	s	14.89 MW	15.14 AW	31490 AAW	KSBLS	10//99-12//99
	Kentucky	s	15.56 MW	15.37 AW	31960 AAW	KYBLS	10//99-12//99
	Louisiana	s	18.64 MW	18.46 AW	38410 AAW	LABLS	10//99-12//99
	Maine	s	13.09 MW	13.19 AW	27440 AAW	MEBLS	10//99-12//99
	Maryland	s	14.15 MW	13.78 AW	28660 AAW	MDBLS	10//99-12//99
	Massachusetts	s	15.93 MW	16.54 AW	34400 AAW	MABLS	10//99-12//99
	Michigan	s	12.22 MW	12.89 AW	26810 AAW	MIBLS	10//99-12//99
	Minnesota	s	15.91 MW	15.92 AW	33110 AAW	MNBLS	10//99-12//99
	Mississippi	s	15.66 MW	15.42 AW	32070 AAW	MSBLS	10//99-12//99
	Missouri	s	17.6 MW	17.65 AW	36710 AAW	MOBLS	10//99-12//99
	Nebraska	s	6.56 MW	9.79 AW	20360 AAW	NEBLS	10//99-12//99
	Nevada	s	14.08 MW	13.60 AW	28280 AAW	NVBLS	10//99-12//99
	New Hampshire	s	14.99 MW	15.43 AW	32090 AAW	NHBLS	10//99-12//99
	New Jersey	s	15.65 MW	16.46 AW	34230 AAW	NJBLS	10//99-12//99
	New Mexico	s	9.94 MW	12.80 AW	26620 AAW	NMBLS	10//99-12//99
	New York	s	15.74 MW	15.74 AW	32730 AAW	NYBLS	10//99-12//99
	North Carolina	s	14.6 MW	13.89 AW	28880 AAW	NCBLS	10//99-12//99
	North Dakota	s	12.5 MW	13.73 AW	28570 AAW	NDBLS	10//99-12//99
	Ohio	s	16.76 MW	17.28 AW	35950 AAW	OHBLS	10//99-12//99
	Oklahoma	s	16.14 MW	16.24 AW	33770 AAW	OKBLS	10//99-12//99
	Oregon	s	15.53 MW	15.68 AW	32610 AAW	ORBLS	10//99-12//99
	Pennsylvania	s	14.44 MW	14.52 AW	30210 AAW	PABLS	10//99-12//99
	Rhode Island	s	14.92 MW	15.24 AW	31690 AAW	RIBLS	10//99-12//99
	South Carolina	s	16.52 MW	16.74 AW	34820 AAW	SCBLS	10//99-12//99
	South Dakota	s	10.8 MW	10.79 AW	22440 AAW	SDBLS	10//99-12//99
	Tennessee	s	15.32 MW	14.83 AW	30840 AAW	TNBLS	10//99-12//99
	Texas	s	16.44 MW	16.58 AW	34480 AAW	TXBLS	10//99-12//99
	Utah	s	13.32 MW	13.63 AW	28340 AAW	UTBLS	10//99-12//99
	Vermont	s	15.25 MW	15.16 AW	31530 AAW	VTBLS	10//99-12//99
	Virginia	s	15.04 MW	15.77 AW	32800 AAW	VABLS	10//99-12//99
	Washington	s	15.65 MW	15.82 AW	32900 AAW	WABLS	10//99-12//99
	West Virginia	s	17.61 MW	17.50 AW	36400 AAW	WVBLS	10//99-12//99
	Wisconsin	s	14.95 MW	14.87 AW	30920 AAW	WIBLS	10//99-12//99
	Wyoming	s	13.61 MW	14.56 AW	30290 AAW	WYBLS	10//99-12//99
	Puerto Rico	s	7.88 MW	8.67 AW	18040 AAW	PRBLS	10//99-12//99
Office Clerk							
General	Alabama	s	8.67 MW	9.15 AW	19030 AAW	ALBLS	10//99-12//99
General	Anniston MSA, AL	s	8.67 MW	8.37 AW	18040 AAW	ALBLS	10//99-12//99
General	Auburn-Opelika MSA, AL	s	7.88 MW	7.59 AW	16400 AAW	ALBLS	10//99-12//99
General	Birmingham MSA, AL	s	9.65 MW	9.29 AW	20080 AAW	ALBLS	10//99-12//99
General	Decatur MSA, AL	s	10.61 MW	10.94 AW	22070 AAW	ALBLS	10//99-12//99
General	Dothan MSA, AL	s	8.74 MW	7.97 AW	18170 AAW	ALBLS	10//99-12//99
General	Florence MSA, AL	s	8.36 MW	8.23 AW	17380 AAW	ALBLS	10//99-12//99
General	Gadsden MSA, AL	s	8.83 MW	8.36 AW	18360 AAW	ALBLS	10//99-12//99
General	Huntsville MSA, AL	s	9.29 MW	8.46 AW	19320 AAW	ALBLS	10//99-12//99
General	Mobile MSA, AL	s	8.31 MW	7.93 AW	17280 AAW	ALBLS	10//99-12//99
General	Montgomery MSA, AL	s	9.61 MW	9.26 AW	19980 AAW	ALBLS	10//99-12//99
General	Tuscaloosa MSA, AL	s	8.12 MW	7.75 AW	16900 AAW	ALBLS	10//99-12//99
General	Alaska	s	11.57 MW	12.05 AW	25070 AAW	AKBLS	10//99-12//99
General	Anchorage MSA, AK	s	12.10 MW	11.64 AW	25160 AAW	AKBLS	10//99-12//99
General	Arizona	s	8.97 MW	9.72 AW	20220 AAW	AZBLS	10//99-12//99
General	Flagstaff MSA, AZ-UT	s	9.27 MW	9.41 AW	19280 AAW	AZBLS	10//99-12//99
General	Phoenix-Mesa MSA, AZ	s	9.99 MW	9.24 AW	20780 AAW	AZBLS	10//99-12//99

AAW Average annual wage	**AOH** Average offered, high	**ASH** Average starting, high	**H** Hourly	**M** Monthly	**S** Special: hourly and annual
AE Average entry wage	**AOL** Average offered, low	**ASL** Average starting, low	**HI** Highest wage paid	**MTC** Median total compensation	**TQ** Third quartile wage
AEX Average experienced wage	**APH** Average pay, high range	**AW** Average wage paid	**HR** High end range	**MW** Median wage paid	**W** Weekly
AO Average offered	**APL** Average pay, low range	**FQ** First quartile wage	**LR** Low end range	**SQ** Second quartile wage	**Y** Yearly

Occupation/Type/Industry	Location	Per	Low	Mid	High	Source	Date
Office Clerk							
General	Tucson MSA, AZ	S	9.61 MW	8.72 AW	19980 AAW	AZBLS	10//99-12//99
General	Yuma MSA, AZ	S	9.38 MW	8.92 AW	19500 AAW	AZBLS	10//99-12//99
General	Arkansas	S	7.91 MW	8.36 AW	17390 AAW	ARBLS	10//99-12//99
General	Fayetteville-Springdale-Rogers MSA, AR	S	7.86 MW	7.56 AW	16350 AAW	ARBLS	10//99-12//99
General	Fort Smith MSA, AR-OK	S	9.81 MW	8.37 AW	20400 AAW	ARBLS	10//99-12//99
General	Jonesboro MSA, AR	S	7.92 MW	7.21 AW	16480 AAW	ARBLS	10//99-12//99
General	Little Rock-North Little Rock MSA, AR	S	8.83 MW	8.42 AW	18360 AAW	ARBLS	10//99-12//99
General	Pine Bluff MSA, AR	S	7.43 MW	7.24 AW	15450 AAW	ARBLS	10//99-12//99
General	California	S	10.81 MW	11.31 AW	23520 AAW	CABLS	10//99-12//99
General	Bakersfield MSA, CA	S	9.56 MW	9.00 AW	19890 AAW	CABLS	10//99-12//99
General	Chico-Paradise MSA, CA	S	8.71 MW	8.03 AW	18110 AAW	CABLS	10//99-12//99
General	Fresno MSA, CA	S	10.55 MW	10.17 AW	21940 AAW	CABLS	10//99-12//99
General	Los Angeles-Long Beach PMSA, CA	S	11.38 MW	10.92 AW	23670 AAW	CABLS	10//99-12//99
General	Merced MSA, CA	S	9.72 MW	9.79 AW	20220 AAW	CABLS	10//99-12//99
General	Modesto MSA, CA	S	9.63 MW	9.34 AW	20040 AAW	CABLS	10//99-12//99
General	Oakland PMSA, CA	S	12.02 MW	11.46 AW	25010 AAW	CABLS	10//99-12//99
General	Orange County PMSA, CA	S	11.70 MW	11.46 AW	24340 AAW	CABLS	10//99-12//99
General	Redding MSA, CA	S	9.54 MW	8.86 AW	19850 AAW	CABLS	10//99-12//99
General	Riverside-San Bernardino PMSA, CA	S	10.64 MW	10.30 AW	22130 AAW	CABLS	10//99-12//99
General	Sacramento PMSA, CA	S	11.41 MW	11.41 AW	23730 AAW	CABLS	10//99-12//99
General	Salinas MSA, CA	S	10.81 MW	9.92 AW	22480 AAW	CABLS	10//99-12//99
General	San Diego MSA, CA	S	11.23 MW	10.88 AW	23360 AAW	CABLS	10//99-12//99
General	San Francisco PMSA, CA	S	12.69 MW	12.44 AW	26400 AAW	CABLS	10//99-12//99
General	San Jose PMSA, CA	S	12.17 MW	11.52 AW	25300 AAW	CABLS	10//99-12//99
General	San Luis Obispo-Atascadero-Paso Robles MSA, CA	S	10.29 MW	10.31 AW	21400 AAW	CABLS	10//99-12//99
General	Santa Barbara-Santa Maria-Lompoc MSA, CA	S	10.29 MW	9.99 AW	21400 AAW	CABLS	10//99-12//99
General	Santa Cruz-Watsonville PMSA, CA	S	10.84 MW	10.39 AW	22550 AAW	CABLS	10//99-12//99
General	Santa Rosa PMSA, CA	S	10.56 MW	10.09 AW	21970 AAW	CABLS	10//99-12//99
General	Stockton-Lodi MSA, CA	S	9.60 MW	9.36 AW	19960 AAW	CABLS	10//99-12//99
General	Vallejo-Fairfield-Napa PMSA, CA	S	11.73 MW	11.69 AW	24400 AAW	CABLS	10//99-12//99
General	Ventura PMSA, CA	S	11.89 MW	10.90 AW	24730 AAW	CABLS	10//99-12//99
General	Visalia-Tulare-Porterville MSA, CA	S	8.90 MW	8.55 AW	18510 AAW	CABLS	10//99-12//99
General	Yolo PMSA, CA	S	10.32 MW	9.55 AW	21470 AAW	CABLS	10//99-12//99
General	Yuba City MSA, CA	S	11.76 MW	11.48 AW	24450 AAW	CABLS	10//99-12//99
General	Colorado	S	10.21 MW	10.70 AW	22270 AAW	COBLS	10//99-12//99
General	Boulder-Longmont PMSA, CO	S	11.19 MW	11.03 AW	23280 AAW	COBLS	10//99-12//99
General	Colorado Springs MSA, CO	S	11.26 MW	10.23 AW	23420 AAW	COBLS	10//99-12//99
General	Denver PMSA, CO	S	11.12 MW	10.54 AW	23120 AAW	COBLS	10//99-12//99
General	Fort Collins-Loveland MSA, CO	S	8.27 MW	8.12 AW	17210 AAW	COBLS	10//99-12//99
General	Grand Junction MSA, CO	S	9.74 MW	9.26 AW	20260 AAW	COBLS	10//99-12//99
General	Greeley PMSA, CO	S	9.16 MW	8.91 AW	19050 AAW	COBLS	10//99-12//99
General	Pueblo MSA, CO	S	8.81 MW	8.77 AW	18330 AAW	COBLS	10//99-12//99
General	Connecticut	S	10.79 MW	11.22 AW	23340 AAW	CTBLS	10//99-12//99
General	Bridgeport PMSA, CT	S	11.03 MW	10.95 AW	22930 AAW	CTBLS	10//99-12//99
General	Danbury PMSA, CT	S	11.09 MW	10.39 AW	23060 AAW	CTBLS	10//99-12//99
General	Hartford MSA, CT	S	11.15 MW	10.93 AW	23190 AAW	CTBLS	10//99-12//99
General	New Haven-Meriden PMSA, CT	S	11.01 MW	10.51 AW	22900 AAW	CTBLS	10//99-12//99
General	New London-Norwich MSA, CT-RI	S	10.84 MW	10.17 AW	22540 AAW	CTBLS	10//99-12//99
General	Stamford-Norwalk PMSA, CT	S	12.44 MW	12.31 AW	25880 AAW	CTBLS	10//99-12//99
General	Waterbury PMSA, CT	S	10.73 MW	10.52 AW	22310 AAW	CTBLS	10//99-12//99
General	Delaware	S	9.69 MW	10.32 AW	21470 AAW	DEBLS	10//99-12//99
General	Dover MSA, DE	S	8.49 MW	7.94 AW	17660 AAW	DEBLS	10//99-12//99
General	Wilmington-Newark PMSA, DE-MD	S	10.79 MW	9.96 AW	22430 AAW	DEBLS	10//99-12//99
General	District of Columbia	S	10.86 MW	12.03 AW	25030 AAW	DCBLS	10//99-12//99
General	Washington PMSA, DC-MD-VA-WV	S	11.40 MW	10.61 AW	23700 AAW	DCBLS	10//99-12//99
General	Florida	S	9.24 MW	9.56 AW	19880 AAW	FLBLS	10//99-12//99
General	Daytona Beach MSA, FL	S	8.80 MW	8.66 AW	18290 AAW	FLBLS	10//99-12//99

AAW	Average annual wage	AOH	Average offered, high	ASH	Average starting, high	H	Hourly	M	Monthly	S	Special: hourly and annual
AE	Average entry wage	AOL	Average offered, low	ASL	Average starting, low	HI	Highest wage paid	MTC	Median total compensation	TQ	Third quartile wage
AEX	Average experienced wage	APH	Average pay, high range	AW	Average wage paid	HR	High end range	MW	Median wage paid	W	Weekly
AO	Average offered	APL	Average pay, low range	FQ	First quartile wage	LR	Low end range	SQ	Second quartile wage	Y	Yearly

Office Clerk

Occupation/Type/Industry	Location	Per	Low	Mid	High	Source	Date
Office Clerk							
General	Fort Lauderdale PMSA, FL	S	10.32 MW	10.10 AW	21460 AAW	FLBLS	10//99-12//99
General	Fort Myers-Cape Coral MSA, FL	S	9.37 MW	9.30 AW	19480 AAW	FLBLS	10//99-12//99
General	Fort Pierce-Port St. Lucie MSA, FL	S	8.83 MW	8.29 AW	18360 AAW	FLBLS	10//99-12//99
General	Fort Walton Beach MSA, FL	S	8.50 MW	8.12 AW	17680 AAW	FLBLS	10//99-12//99
General	Gainesville MSA, FL	S	9.97 MW	9.87 AW	20740 AAW	FLBLS	10//99-12//99
General	Jacksonville MSA, FL	S	9.14 MW	8.97 AW	19010 AAW	FLBLS	10//99-12//99
General	Lakeland-Winter Haven MSA, FL	S	9.36 MW	8.40 AW	19480 AAW	FLBLS	10//99-12//99
General	Melbourne-Titusville-Palm Bay MSA, FL	S	9.46 MW	8.69 AW	19680 AAW	FLBLS	10//99-12//99
General	Miami PMSA, FL	S	10.14 MW	9.60 AW	21090 AAW	FLBLS	10//99-12//99
General	Naples MSA, FL	S	10.15 MW	9.93 AW	21100 AAW	FLBLS	10//99-12//99
General	Ocala MSA, FL	S	8.23 MW	7.89 AW	17130 AAW	FLBLS	10//99-12//99
General	Orlando MSA, FL	S	9.25 MW	8.97 AW	19230 AAW	FLBLS	10//99-12//99
General	Panama City MSA, FL	S	8.78 MW	8.08 AW	18270 AAW	FLBLS	10//99-12//99
General	Pensacola MSA, FL	S	8.38 MW	8.00 AW	17430 AAW	FLBLS	10//99-12//99
General	Punta Gorda MSA, FL	S	7.25 MW	6.69 AW	15080 AAW	FLBLS	10//99-12//99
General	Sarasota-Bradenton MSA, FL	S	8.03 MW	7.77 AW	16700 AAW	FLBLS	10//99-12//99
General	Tallahassee MSA, FL	S	9.56 MW	9.57 AW	19880 AAW	FLBLS	10//99-12//99
General	Tampa-St. Petersburg-Clearwater MSA, FL	S	9.58 MW	9.23 AW	19920 AAW	FLBLS	10//99-12//99
General	West Palm Beach-Boca Raton MSA, FL	S	10.32 MW	9.91 AW	21470 AAW	FLBLS	10//99-12//99
General	Georgia	S	9.42 MW	11.18 AW	23260 AAW	GABLS	10//99-12//99
General	Albany MSA, GA	S	8.62 MW	8.33 AW	17930 AAW	GABLS	10//99-12//99
General	Atlanta MSA, GA	S	12.36 MW	9.85 AW	25720 AAW	GABLS	10//99-12//99
General	Augusta-Aiken MSA, GA-SC	S	9.57 MW	8.59 AW	19910 AAW	GABLS	10//99-12//99
General	Columbus MSA, GA-AL	S	9.03 MW	9.14 AW	18790 AAW	GABLS	10//99-12//99
General	Macon MSA, GA	S	8.51 MW	8.18 AW	17700 AAW	GABLS	10//99-12//99
General	Savannah MSA, GA	S	9.55 MW	9.44 AW	19860 AAW	GABLS	10//99-12//99
General	Hawaii	S	10.94 MW	11.47 AW	23860 AAW	HIBLS	10//99-12//99
General	Honolulu MSA, HI	S	11.07 MW	10.57 AW	23030 AAW	HIBLS	10//99-12//99
General	Idaho	S	9.13 MW	9.73 AW	20240 AAW	IDBLS	10//99-12//99
General	Boise City MSA, ID	S	9.54 MW	9.53 AW	19850 AAW	IDBLS	10//99-12//99
General	Pocatello MSA, ID	S	9.01 MW	8.30 AW	18750 AAW	IDBLS	10//99-12//99
General	Illinois	S	9.8 MW	10.08 AW	20970 AAW	ILBLS	10//99-12//99
General	Bloomington-Normal MSA, IL	S	11.53 MW	10.72 AW	23990 AAW	ILBLS	10//99-12//99
General	Champaign-Urbana MSA, IL	S	9.99 MW	9.80 AW	20770 AAW	ILBLS	10//99-12//99
General	Chicago PMSA, IL	S	10.50 MW	10.16 AW	21830 AAW	ILBLS	10//99-12//99
General	Decatur MSA, IL	S	8.45 MW	8.43 AW	17580 AAW	ILBLS	10//99-12//99
General	Kankakee PMSA, IL	S	9.47 MW	9.30 AW	19690 AAW	ILBLS	10//99-12//99
General	Peoria-Pekin MSA, IL	S	9.40 MW	8.86 AW	19560 AAW	ILBLS	10//99-12//99
General	Rockford MSA, IL	S	9.80 MW	9.47 AW	20380 AAW	ILBLS	10//99-12//99
General	Indiana	S	8.87 MW	9.11 AW	18950 AAW	INBLS	10//99-12//99
General	Bloomington MSA, IN	S	8.26 MW	7.98 AW	17190 AAW	INBLS	10//99-12//99
General	Elkhart-Goshen MSA, IN	S	9.56 MW	9.50 AW	19890 AAW	INBLS	10//99-12//99
General	Evansville-Henderson MSA, IN-KY	S	8.83 MW	8.72 AW	18370 AAW	INBLS	10//99-12//99
General	Fort Wayne MSA, IN	S	9.37 MW	9.33 AW	19490 AAW	INBLS	10//99-12//99
General	Gary PMSA, IN	S	9.03 MW	8.35 AW	18780 AAW	INBLS	10//99-12//99
General	Indianapolis MSA, IN	S	9.22 MW	8.99 AW	19190 AAW	INBLS	10//99-12//99
General	Kokomo MSA, IN	S	11.90 MW	9.45 AW	24750 AAW	INBLS	10//99-12//99
General	Lafayette MSA, IN	S	8.32 MW	7.92 AW	17310 AAW	INBLS	10//99-12//99
General	Muncie MSA, IN	S	8.11 MW	8.08 AW	16860 AAW	INBLS	10//99-12//99
General	South Bend MSA, IN	S	9.13 MW	8.75 AW	18980 AAW	INBLS	10//99-12//99
General	Terre Haute MSA, IN	S	8.61 MW	8.22 AW	17900 AAW	INBLS	10//99-12//99
General	Iowa	S	9.32 MW	9.66 AW	20080 AAW	IABLS	10//99-12//99
General	Cedar Rapids MSA, IA	S	10.01 MW	9.87 AW	20820 AAW	IABLS	10//99-12//99
General	Davenport-Moline-Rock Island MSA, IA-IL	S	9.34 MW	9.14 AW	19420 AAW	IABLS	10//99-12//99
General	Des Moines MSA, IA	S	10.63 MW	10.28 AW	22120 AAW	IABLS	10//99-12//99
General	Dubuque MSA, IA	S	7.97 MW	7.51 AW	16570 AAW	IABLS	10//99-12//99
General	Iowa City MSA, IA	S	11.23 MW	10.74 AW	23370 AAW	IABLS	10//99-12//99
General	Sioux City MSA, IA-NE	S	8.36 MW	7.66 AW	17380 AAW	IABLS	10//99-12//99
General	Waterloo-Cedar Falls MSA, IA	S	9.60 MW	9.07 AW	19970 AAW	IABLS	10//99-12//99
General	Kansas	S	9.15 MW	9.43 AW	19620 AAW	KSBLS	10//99-12//99
General	Lawrence MSA, KS	S	9.40 MW	9.43 AW	19550 AAW	KSBLS	10//99-12//99
General	Topeka MSA, KS	S	10.04 MW	9.88 AW	20880 AAW	KSBLS	10//99-12//99
General	Wichita MSA, KS	S	9.06 MW	8.68 AW	18840 AAW	KSBLS	10//99-12//99

AAW Average annual wage	**AOH** Average offered, high	**ASH** Average starting, high	**H** Hourly	**M** Monthly	**S** Special: hourly and annual
AE Average entry wage	**AOL** Average offered, low	**ASL** Average starting, low	**HI** Highest wage paid	**MTC** Median total compensation	**TQ** Third quartile wage
AEX Average experienced wage	**APH** Average pay, high range	**AW** Average wage paid	**HR** High end range	**MW** Median wage paid	**W** Weekly
AO Average offered	**APL** Average pay, low range	**FQ** First quartile wage	**LR** Low end range	**SQ** Second quartile wage	**Y** Yearly

Office Clerk

Occupation/Type/Industry	Location	Per	Low	Mid	High	Source	Date
Office Clerk							
General	Kentucky	S	8.7 MW	9.05 AW	18820 AAW	KYBLS	10//99-12//99
General	Lexington MSA, KY	S	9.69 MW	8.95 AW	20150 AAW	KYBLS	10//99-12//99
General	Louisville MSA, KY-IN	S	9.50 MW	9.26 AW	19760 AAW	KYBLS	10//99-12//99
General	Owensboro MSA, KY	S	9.56 MW	8.99 AW	19880 AAW	KYBLS	10//99-12//99
General	Louisiana	S	8.15 MW	8.74 AW	18170 AAW	LABLS	10//99-12//99
General	Alexandria MSA, LA	S	7.77 MW	7.48 AW	16160 AAW	LABLS	10//99-12//99
General	Baton Rouge MSA, LA	S	8.81 MW	8.16 AW	18310 AAW	LABLS	10//99-12//99
General	Houma MSA, LA	S	8.91 MW	8.05 AW	18530 AAW	LABLS	10//99-12//99
General	Lafayette MSA, LA	S	8.16 MW	7.41 AW	16980 AAW	LABLS	10//99-12//99
General	Lake Charles MSA, LA	S	9.09 MW	8.19 AW	18910 AAW	LABLS	10//99-12//99
General	Monroe MSA, LA	S	8.13 MW	7.46 AW	16900 AAW	LABLS	10//99-12//99
General	New Orleans MSA, LA	S	9.31 MW	8.69 AW	19370 AAW	LABLS	10//99-12//99
General	Shreveport-Bossier City MSA, LA	S	8.75 MW	8.69 AW	18200 AAW	LABLS	10//99-12//99
General	Maine	S	9.66 MW	9.91 AW	20610 AAW	MEBLS	10//99-12//99
General	Bangor MSA, ME	S	9.18 MW	8.76 AW	19100 AAW	MEBLS	10//99-12//99
General	Lewiston-Auburn MSA, ME	S	9.01 MW	9.03 AW	18750 AAW	MEBLS	10//99-12//99
General	Portland MSA, ME	S	10.27 MW	10.13 AW	21360 AAW	MEBLS	10//99-12//99
General	Maryland	S	10.27 MW	10.88 AW	22640 AAW	MDBLS	10//99-12//99
General	Baltimore PMSA, MD	S	10.90 MW	10.39 AW	22670 AAW	MDBLS	10//99-12//99
General	Cumberland MSA, MD-WV	S	9.93 MW	10.92 AW	20660 AAW	MDBLS	10//99-12//99
General	Hagerstown PMSA, MD	S	10.15 MW	9.77 AW	21110 AAW	MDBLS	10//99-12//99
General	Massachusetts	S	11.4 MW	11.88 AW	24710 AAW	MABLS	10//99-12//99
General	Barnstable-Yarmouth MSA, MA	S	11.23 MW	10.45 AW	23360 AAW	MABLS	10//99-12//99
General	Boston PMSA, MA-NH	S	12.33 MW	11.82 AW	25650 AAW	MABLS	10//99-12//99
General	Brockton PMSA, MA	S	10.49 MW	10.09 AW	21810 AAW	MABLS	10//99-12//99
General	Fitchburg-Leominster PMSA, MA	S	11.37 MW	10.60 AW	23640 AAW	MABLS	10//99-12//99
General	Lawrence PMSA, MA-NH	S	10.41 MW	10.11 AW	21650 AAW	MABLS	10//99-12//99
General	Lowell PMSA, MA-NH	S	11.40 MW	11.10 AW	23710 AAW	MABLS	10//99-12//99
General	New Bedford PMSA, MA	S	9.79 MW	9.41 AW	20350 AAW	MABLS	10//99-12//99
General	Pittsfield MSA, MA	S	9.83 MW	8.92 AW	20450 AAW	MABLS	10//99-12//99
General	Springfield MSA, MA	S	11.10 MW	10.95 AW	23090 AAW	MABLS	10//99-12//99
General	Worcester PMSA, MA-CT	S	10.80 MW	10.27 AW	22460 AAW	MABLS	10//99-12//99
General	Michigan	S	10.16 MW	11.05 AW	22990 AAW	MIBLS	10//99-12//99
General	Ann Arbor PMSA, MI	S	10.14 MW	9.93 AW	21090 AAW	MIBLS	10//99-12//99
General	Benton Harbor MSA, MI	S	9.77 MW	9.41 AW	20330 AAW	MIBLS	10//99-12//99
General	Detroit PMSA, MI	S	12.21 MW	10.77 AW	25400 AAW	MIBLS	10//99-12//99
General	Flint PMSA, MI	S	10.13 MW	9.09 AW	21070 AAW	MIBLS	10//99-12//99
General	Grand Rapids-Muskegon-Holland MSA, MI	S	10.49 MW	10.12 AW	21820 AAW	MIBLS	10//99-12//99
General	Jackson MSA, MI	S	10.15 MW	9.76 AW	21100 AAW	MIBLS	10//99-12//99
General	Kalamazoo-Battle Creek MSA, MI	S	9.84 MW	9.72 AW	20460 AAW	MIBLS	10//99-12//99
General	Lansing-East Lansing MSA, MI	S	10.14 MW	9.53 AW	21100 AAW	MIBLS	10//99-12//99
General	Saginaw-Bay City-Midland MSA, MI	S	9.30 MW	8.93 AW	19340 AAW	MIBLS	10//99-12//99
General	Minnesota	S	10.79 MW	11.18 AW	23260 AAW	MNBLS	10//99-12//99
General	Duluth-Superior MSA, MN-WI	S	10.28 MW	9.59 AW	21390 AAW	MNBLS	10//99-12//99
General	Minneapolis-St. Paul MSA, MN-WI	S	11.78 MW	11.48 AW	24510 AAW	MNBLS	10//99-12//99
General	Rochester MSA, MN	S	11.40 MW	10.52 AW	23720 AAW	MNBLS	10//99-12//99
General	St. Cloud MSA, MN	S	10.10 MW	9.57 AW	21010 AAW	MNBLS	10//99-12//99
General	Mississippi	S	8.08 MW	8.47 AW	17620 AAW	MSBLS	10//99-12//99
General	Biloxi-Gulfport-Pascagoula MSA, MS	S	9.30 MW	8.47 AW	19330 AAW	MSBLS	10//99-12//99
General	Hattiesburg MSA, MS	S	8.10 MW	7.90 AW	16850 AAW	MSBLS	10//99-12//99
General	Jackson MSA, MS	S	8.42 MW	7.96 AW	17510 AAW	MSBLS	10//99-12//99
General	Missouri	S	9.37 MW	9.93 AW	20650 AAW	MOBLS	10//99-12//99
General	Columbia MSA, MO	S	9.98 MW	9.72 AW	20750 AAW	MOBLS	10//99-12//99
General	Joplin MSA, MO	S	8.13 MW	8.02 AW	16910 AAW	MOBLS	10//99-12//99
General	Kansas City MSA, MO-KS	S	10.58 MW	10.25 AW	22000 AAW	MOBLS	10//99-12//99
General	St. Joseph MSA, MO	S	8.69 MW	8.51 AW	18070 AAW	MOBLS	10//99-12//99
General	St. Louis MSA, MO-IL	S	10.38 MW	9.76 AW	21590 AAW	MOBLS	10//99-12//99
General	Springfield MSA, MO	S	8.59 MW	8.23 AW	17870 AAW	MOBLS	10//99-12//99
General	Montana	S	8.29 MW	8.98 AW	18680 AAW	MTBLS	10//99-12//99
General	Billings MSA, MT	S	7.77 MW	7.51 AW	16150 AAW	MTBLS	10//99-12//99
General	Great Falls MSA, MT	S	8.69 MW	8.62 AW	18080 AAW	MTBLS	10//99-12//99
General	Missoula MSA, MT	S	8.52 MW	8.18 AW	17730 AAW	MTBLS	10//99-12//99
General	Nebraska	S	8.43 MW	9.05 AW	18820 AAW	NEBLS	10//99-12//99

AAW	Average annual wage	AOH	Average offered, high	ASH	Average starting, high
AE	Average entry wage	AOL	Average offered, low	ASL	Average starting, low
AEX	Average experienced wage	APH	Average pay, high range	AW	Average wage paid
AO	Average offered	APL	Average pay, low range	FQ	First quartile wage

H	Hourly	M	Monthly	S	Special: hourly and annual
HI	Highest wage paid	MTC	Median total compensation	TQ	Third quartile wage
HR	High end range	MW	Median wage paid	W	Weekly
LR	Low end range	SQ	Second quartile wage	Y	Yearly

Occupation/Type/Industry	Location	Per	Low	Mid	High	Source	Date
Office Clerk							
General	Lincoln MSA, NE	S	9.49 MW	8.80 AW	19750 AAW	NEBLS	10//99-12//99
General	Omaha MSA, NE-IA	S	9.45 MW	9.17 AW	19670 AAW	NEBLS	10//99-12//99
General	Nevada	S	8.97 MW	9.32 AW	19390 AAW	NVBLS	10//99-12//99
General	Las Vegas MSA, NV-AZ	S	9.26 MW	8.90 AW	19260 AAW	NVBLS	10//99-12//99
General	Reno MSA, NV	S	9.50 MW	9.05 AW	19750 AAW	NVBLS	10//99-12//99
General	New Hampshire	S	10.05 MW	10.50 AW	21840 AAW	NHBLS	10//99-12//99
General	Manchester PMSA, NH	S	10.98 MW	10.40 AW	22830 AAW	NHBLS	10//99-12//99
General	Nashua PMSA, NH	S	11.13 MW	10.42 AW	23140 AAW	NHBLS	10//99-12//99
General	Portsmouth-Rochester PMSA, NH-ME	S	9.60 MW	9.59 AW	19970 AAW	NHBLS	10//99-12//99
General	New Jersey	S	10.52 MW	11.03 AW	22940 AAW	NJBLS	10//99-12//99
General	Atlantic-Cape May PMSA, NJ	S	10.31 MW	10.14 AW	21450 AAW	NJBLS	10//99-12//99
General	Bergen-Passaic PMSA, NJ	S	11.18 MW	10.61 AW	23250 AAW	NJBLS	10//99-12//99
General	Jersey City PMSA, NJ	S	11.75 MW	11.42 AW	24450 AAW	NJBLS	10//99-12//99
General	Middlesex-Somerset-Hunterdon PMSA, NJ	S	11.34 MW	10.88 AW	23580 AAW	NJBLS	10//99-12//99
General	Monmouth-Ocean PMSA, NJ	S	10.53 MW	10.13 AW	21900 AAW	NJBLS	10//99-12//99
General	Newark PMSA, NJ	S	11.55 MW	11.09 AW	24010 AAW	NJBLS	10//99-12//99
General	Trenton PMSA, NJ	S	10.91 MW	10.45 AW	22700 AAW	NJBLS	10//99-12//99
General	Vineland-Millville-Bridgeton PMSA, NJ	S	9.82 MW	9.36 AW	20430 AAW	NJBLS	10//99-12//99
General	New Mexico	S	7.89 MW	8.38 AW	17440 AAW	NMBLS	10//99-12//99
General	Albuquerque MSA, NM	S	8.67 MW	8.04 AW	18030 AAW	NMBLS	10//99-12//99
General	Las Cruces MSA, NM	S	7.28 MW	6.99 AW	15130 AAW	NMBLS	10//99-12//99
General	Santa Fe MSA, NM	S	9.30 MW	9.07 AW	19340 AAW	NMBLS	10//99-12//99
General	New York	S	11.1 MW	11.43 AW	23770 AAW	NYBLS	10//99-12//99
General	Albany-Schenectady-Troy MSA, NY	S	11.25 MW	11.25 AW	23400 AAW	NYBLS	10//99-12//99
General	Binghamton MSA, NY	S	9.23 MW	8.22 AW	19210 AAW	NYBLS	10//99-12//99
General	Buffalo-Niagara Falls MSA, NY	S	9.51 MW	9.40 AW	19790 AAW	NYBLS	10//99-12//99
General	Dutchess County PMSA, NY	S	10.18 MW	9.74 AW	21180 AAW	NYBLS	10//99-12//99
General	Elmira MSA, NY	S	9.23 MW	8.38 AW	19190 AAW	NYBLS	10//99-12//99
General	Glens Falls MSA, NY	S	10.55 MW	9.58 AW	21940 AAW	NYBLS	10//99-12//99
General	Jamestown MSA, NY	S	8.43 MW	8.07 AW	17540 AAW	NYBLS	10//99-12//99
General	Nassau-Suffolk PMSA, NY	S	11.51 MW	10.92 AW	23940 AAW	NYBLS	10//99-12//99
General	New York PMSA, NY	S	12.22 MW	11.92 AW	25420 AAW	NYBLS	10//99-12//99
General	Newburgh PMSA, NY-PA	S	9.61 MW	9.23 AW	19990 AAW	NYBLS	10//99-12//99
General	Rochester MSA, NY	S	10.48 MW	9.66 AW	21790 AAW	NYBLS	10//99-12//99
General	Syracuse MSA, NY	S	11.04 MW	10.27 AW	22960 AAW	NYBLS	10//99-12//99
General	Utica-Rome MSA, NY	S	9.85 MW	8.80 AW	20500 AAW	NYBLS	10//99-12//99
General	North Carolina	S	9.69 MW	9.96 AW	20710 AAW	NCBLS	10//99-12//99
General	Asheville MSA, NC	S	10.31 MW	10.10 AW	21440 AAW	NCBLS	10//99-12//99
General	Charlotte-Gastonia-Rock Hill MSA, NC-SC	S	10.22 MW	9.85 AW	21250 AAW	NCBLS	10//99-12//99
General	Fayetteville MSA, NC	S	9.61 MW	9.48 AW	20000 AAW	NCBLS	10//99-12//99
General	Goldsboro MSA, NC	S	8.09 MW	7.45 AW	16820 AAW	NCBLS	10//99-12//99
General	Greensboro--Winston-Salem--High Point MSA, NC	S	9.88 MW	9.72 AW	20550 AAW	NCBLS	10//99-12//99
General	Greenville MSA, NC	S	8.52 MW	7.99 AW	17720 AAW	NCBLS	10//99-12//99
General	Hickory-Morganton-Lenoir MSA, NC	S	10.00 MW	9.69 AW	20800 AAW	NCBLS	10//99-12//99
General	Jacksonville MSA, NC	S	8.21 MW	7.78 AW	17080 AAW	NCBLS	10//99-12//99
General	Raleigh-Durham-Chapel Hill MSA, NC	S	10.64 MW	10.50 AW	22120 AAW	NCBLS	10//99-12//99
General	Rocky Mount MSA, NC	S	9.37 MW	9.11 AW	19480 AAW	NCBLS	10//99-12//99
General	Wilmington MSA, NC	S	9.63 MW	9.33 AW	20040 AAW	NCBLS	10//99-12//99
General	North Dakota	S	7.36 MW	7.88 AW	16380 AAW	NDBLS	10//99-12//99
General	Bismarck MSA, ND	S	7.56 MW	7.32 AW	15720 AAW	NDBLS	10//99-12//99
General	Fargo-Moorhead MSA, ND-MN	S	9.47 MW	9.33 AW	19690 AAW	NDBLS	10//99-12//99
General	Grand Forks MSA, ND-MN	S	8.44 MW	7.97 AW	17560 AAW	NDBLS	10//99-12//99
General	Ohio	S	9.43 MW	9.87 AW	20520 AAW	OHBLS	10//99-12//99
General	Akron PMSA, OH	S	9.80 MW	9.49 AW	20390 AAW	OHBLS	10//99-12//99
General	Canton-Massillon MSA, OH	S	9.95 MW	9.68 AW	20690 AAW	OHBLS	10//99-12//99
General	Cincinnati PMSA, OH-KY-IN	S	9.80 MW	9.26 AW	20380 AAW	OHBLS	10//99-12//99
General	Cleveland-Lorain-Elyria PMSA, OH	S	10.49 MW	10.07 AW	21820 AAW	OHBLS	10//99-12//99
General	Columbus MSA, OH	S	10.20 MW	9.82 AW	21220 AAW	OHBLS	10//99-12//99
General	Hamilton-Middletown PMSA, OH	S	9.55 MW	8.30 AW	19870 AAW	OHBLS	10//99-12//99

Occupation/Type/Industry	Location	Per	Low	Mid	High	Source	Date
Office Clerk							
General	Lima MSA, OH	S	8.51 MW	8.32 AW	17690 AAW	OHBLS	10//99-12//99
General	Mansfield MSA, OH	S	9.56 MW	9.51 AW	19880 AAW	OHBLS	10//99-12//99
General	Steubenville-Weirton MSA, OH-WV	S	7.77 MW	7.30 AW	16160 AAW	OHBLS	10//99-12//99
General	Toledo MSA, OH	S	9.34 MW	8.85 AW	19430 AAW	OHBLS	10//99-12//99
General	Youngstown-Warren MSA, OH	S	9.15 MW	8.58 AW	19030 AAW	OHBLS	10//99-12//99
General	Oklahoma	S	8.12 MW	8.56 AW	17810 AAW	OKBLS	10//99-12//99
General	Enid MSA, OK	S	7.73 MW	6.87 AW	16070 AAW	OKBLS	10//99-12//99
General	Lawton MSA, OK	S	8.91 MW	8.53 AW	18520 AAW	OKBLS	10//99-12//99
General	Oklahoma City MSA, OK	S	8.33 MW	7.86 AW	17330 AAW	OKBLS	10//99-12//99
General	Tulsa MSA, OK	S	9.36 MW	9.01 AW	19460 AAW	OKBLS	10//99-12//99
General	Oregon	S	10.81 MW	11.11 AW	23100 AAW	ORBLS	10//99-12//99
General	Corvallis MSA, OR	S	11.02 MW	9.94 AW	22920 AAW	ORBLS	10//99-12//99
General	Eugene-Springfield MSA, OR	S	11.04 MW	10.66 AW	22960 AAW	ORBLS	10//99-12//99
General	Medford-Ashland MSA, OR	S	9.59 MW	9.09 AW	19950 AAW	ORBLS	10//99-12//99
General	Portland-Vancouver PMSA, OR-WA	S	11.48 MW	11.26 AW	23880 AAW	ORBLS	10//99-12//99
General	Salem PMSA, OR	S	10.75 MW	10.50 AW	22370 AAW	ORBLS	10//99-12//99
General	Pennsylvania	S	9.48 MW	9.97 AW	20740 AAW	PABLS	10//99-12//99
General	Allentown-Bethlehem-Easton MSA, PA	S	9.86 MW	9.48 AW	20510 AAW	PABLS	10//99-12//99
General	Altoona MSA, PA	S	9.32 MW	8.52 AW	19380 AAW	PABLS	10//99-12//99
General	Erie MSA, PA	S	8.85 MW	8.15 AW	18410 AAW	PABLS	10//99-12//99
General	Harrisburg-Lebanon-Carlisle MSA, PA	S	11.12 MW	10.48 AW	23140 AAW	PABLS	10//99-12//99
General	Johnstown MSA, PA	S	8.72 MW	8.28 AW	18140 AAW	PABLS	10//99-12//99
General	Lancaster MSA, PA	S	10.13 MW	9.80 AW	21070 AAW	PABLS	10//99-12//99
General	Philadelphia PMSA, PA-NJ	S	10.53 MW	10.07 AW	21910 AAW	PABLS	10//99-12//99
General	Pittsburgh MSA, PA	S	9.36 MW	8.94 AW	19460 AAW	PABLS	10//99-12//99
General	Reading MSA, PA	S	10.18 MW	9.64 AW	21170 AAW	PABLS	10//99-12//99
General	Scranton--Wilkes-Barre--Hazleton MSA, PA	S	9.69 MW	8.62 AW	20140 AAW	PABLS	10//99-12//99
General	Sharon MSA, PA	S	7.72 MW	7.51 AW	16050 AAW	PABLS	10//99-12//99
General	State College MSA, PA	S	8.99 MW	8.41 AW	18690 AAW	PABLS	10//99-12//99
General	Williamsport MSA, PA	S	9.27 MW	8.11 AW	19270 AAW	PABLS	10//99-12//99
General	York MSA, PA	S	9.92 MW	9.61 AW	20630 AAW	PABLS	10//99-12//99
General	Rhode Island	S	9.79 MW	10.27 AW	21370 AAW	RIBLS	10//99-12//99
General	Providence-Fall River-Warwick MSA, RI-MA	S	10.35 MW	9.89 AW	21530 AAW	RIBLS	10//99-12//99
General	South Carolina	S	8.79 MW	9.49 AW	19750 AAW	SCBLS	10//99-12//99
General	Charleston-North Charleston MSA, SC	S	9.02 MW	8.41 AW	18770 AAW	SCBLS	10//99-12//99
General	Columbia MSA, SC	S	9.63 MW	9.08 AW	20020 AAW	SCBLS	10//99-12//99
General	Florence MSA, SC	S	9.42 MW	8.97 AW	19590 AAW	SCBLS	10//99-12//99
General	Greenville-Spartanburg-Anderson MSA, SC	S	9.63 MW	8.79 AW	20020 AAW	SCBLS	10//99-12//99
General	Myrtle Beach MSA, SC	S	9.29 MW	8.48 AW	19320 AAW	SCBLS	10//99-12//99
General	Sumter MSA, SC	S	9.19 MW	8.13 AW	19120 AAW	SCBLS	10//99-12//99
General	South Dakota	S	7.42 MW	7.50 AW	15600 AAW	SDBLS	10//99-12//99
General	Rapid City MSA, SD	S	8.16 MW	7.95 AW	16970 AAW	SDBLS	10//99-12//99
General	Sioux Falls MSA, SD	S	8.18 MW	8.01 AW	17010 AAW	SDBLS	10//99-12//99
General	Tennessee	S	9.22 MW	9.62 AW	20010 AAW	TNBLS	10//99-12//99
General	Chattanooga MSA, TN-GA	S	9.16 MW	9.08 AW	19050 AAW	TNBLS	10//99-12//99
General	Clarksville-Hopkinsville MSA, TN-KY	S	8.65 MW	8.11 AW	17980 AAW	TNBLS	10//99-12//99
General	Jackson MSA, TN	S	8.54 MW	8.58 AW	17750 AAW	TNBLS	10//99-12//99
General	Johnson City-Kingsport-Bristol MSA, TN-VA	S	8.41 MW	8.03 AW	17500 AAW	TNBLS	10//99-12//99
General	Knoxville MSA, TN	S	10.02 MW	9.38 AW	20840 AAW	TNBLS	10//99-12//99
General	Memphis MSA, TN-AR-MS	S	10.04 MW	9.57 AW	20890 AAW	MSBLS	10//99-12//99
General	Nashville MSA, TN	S	10.16 MW	9.68 AW	21140 AAW	TNBLS	10//99-12//99
General	Texas	S	9.42 MW	9.88 AW	20540 AAW	TXBLS	10//99-12//99
General	Abilene MSA, TX	S	9.32 MW	8.70 AW	19390 AAW	TXBLS	10//99-12//99
General	Amarillo MSA, TX	S	7.89 MW	7.34 AW	16400 AAW	TXBLS	10//99-12//99
General	Austin-San Marcos MSA, TX	S	10.17 MW	9.80 AW	21150 AAW	TXBLS	10//99-12//99
General	Beaumont-Port Arthur MSA, TX	S	9.07 MW	8.58 AW	18860 AAW	TXBLS	10//99-12//99
General	Brazoria PMSA, TX	S	9.97 MW	9.63 AW	20740 AAW	TXBLS	10//99-12//99
General	Brownsville-Harlingen-San Benito MSA, TX	S	7.70 MW	7.22 AW	16020 AAW	TXBLS	10//99-12//99

Office Clerk

Occupation/Type/Industry	Location	Per	Low	Mid	High	Source	Date
Office Clerk							
General	Bryan-College Station MSA, TX	S	7.03 MW	6.47 AW	14630 AAW	TXBLS	10//99-12//99
General	Corpus Christi MSA, TX	S	9.28 MW	9.27 AW	19300 AAW	TXBLS	10//99-12//99
General	Dallas PMSA, TX	S	11.04 MW	10.62 AW	22970 AAW	TXBLS	10//99-12//99
General	El Paso MSA, TX	S	8.01 MW	7.64 AW	16660 AAW	TXBLS	10//99-12//99
General	Fort Worth-Arlington PMSA, TX	S	9.97 MW	9.43 AW	20730 AAW	TXBLS	10//99-12//99
General	Galveston-Texas City PMSA, TX	S	9.41 MW	9.19 AW	19570 AAW	TXBLS	10//99-12//99
General	Houston PMSA, TX	S	10.98 MW	10.50 AW	22830 AAW	TXBLS	10//99-12//99
General	Killeen-Temple MSA, TX	S	8.33 MW	7.87 AW	17330 AAW	TXBLS	10//99-12//99
General	Laredo MSA, TX	S	7.85 MW	6.98 AW	16330 AAW	TXBLS	10//99-12//99
General	Longview-Marshall MSA, TX	S	8.11 MW	7.60 AW	16860 AAW	TXBLS	10//99-12//99
General	Lubbock MSA, TX	S	8.05 MW	7.44 AW	16750 AAW	TXBLS	10//99-12//99
General	McAllen-Edinburg-Mission MSA, TX	S	7.50 MW	6.89 AW	15590 AAW	TXBLS	10//99-12//99
General	Odessa-Midland MSA, TX	S	8.97 MW	8.38 AW	18660 AAW	TXBLS	10//99-12//99
General	San Angelo MSA, TX	S	9.37 MW	8.91 AW	19490 AAW	TXBLS	10//99-12//99
General	San Antonio MSA, TX	S	8.68 MW	8.07 AW	18060 AAW	TXBLS	10//99-12//99
General	Sherman-Denison MSA, TX	S	8.37 MW	8.44 AW	17410 AAW	TXBLS	10//99-12//99
General	Texarkana MSA, TX-Texarkana, AR	S	8.44 MW	8.19 AW	17540 AAW	TXBLS	10//99-12//99
General	Tyler MSA, TX	S	8.33 MW	7.65 AW	17330 AAW	TXBLS	10//99-12//99
General	Victoria MSA, TX	S	7.55 MW	6.74 AW	15710 AAW	TXBLS	10//99-12//99
General	Waco MSA, TX	S	8.24 MW	7.80 AW	17130 AAW	TXBLS	10//99-12//99
General	Wichita Falls MSA, TX	S	8.34 MW	8.16 AW	17340 AAW	TXBLS	10//99-12//99
General	Utah	S	9.34 MW	9.50 AW	19770 AAW	UTBLS	10//99-12//99
General	Provo-Orem MSA, UT	S	9.08 MW	9.25 AW	18880 AAW	UTBLS	10//99-12//99
General	Salt Lake City-Ogden MSA, UT	S	9.83 MW	9.55 AW	20440 AAW	UTBLS	10//99-12//99
General	Vermont	S	8.5 MW	8.83 AW	18370 AAW	VTBLS	10//99-12//99
General	Burlington MSA, VT	S	8.14 MW	6.73 AW	16930 AAW	VTBLS	10//99-12//99
General	Virginia	S	9.5 MW	9.96 AW	20710 AAW	VABLS	10//99-12//99
General	Charlottesville MSA, VA	S	9.55 MW	9.26 AW	19870 AAW	VABLS	10//99-12//99
General	Danville MSA, VA	S	8.80 MW	8.24 AW	18300 AAW	VABLS	10//99-12//99
General	Lynchburg MSA, VA	S	9.18 MW	9.05 AW	19090 AAW	VABLS	10//99-12//99
General	Norfolk-Virginia Beach-Newport News MSA, VA-NC	S	9.32 MW	8.83 AW	19390 AAW	VABLS	10//99-12//99
General	Richmond-Petersburg MSA, VA	S	10.01 MW	9.82 AW	20830 AAW	VABLS	10//99-12//99
General	Roanoke MSA, VA	S	8.89 MW	8.45 AW	18500 AAW	VABLS	10//99-12//99
General	Washington	S	10.63 MW	10.77 AW	22410 AAW	WABLS	10//99-12//99
General	Bellingham MSA, WA	S	9.67 MW	9.24 AW	20120 AAW	WABLS	10//99-12//99
General	Bremerton PMSA, WA	S	9.51 MW	9.26 AW	19770 AAW	WABLS	10//99-12//99
General	Richland-Kennewick-Pasco MSA, WA	S	9.53 MW	9.34 AW	19810 AAW	WABLS	10//99-12//99
General	Seattle-Bellevue-Everett PMSA, WA	S	11.27 MW	11.10 AW	23440 AAW	WABLS	10//99-12//99
General	Spokane MSA, WA	S	10.39 MW	10.01 AW	21610 AAW	WABLS	10//99-12//99
General	Tacoma PMSA, WA	S	10.64 MW	10.66 AW	22130 AAW	WABLS	10//99-12//99
General	Yakima MSA, WA	S	10.72 MW	10.83 AW	22300 AAW	WABLS	10//99-12//99
General	West Virginia	S	7.57 MW	8.19 AW	17030 AAW	WVBLS	10//99-12//99
General	Charleston MSA, WV	S	9.38 MW	8.15 AW	19500 AAW	WVBLS	10//99-12//99
General	Huntington-Ashland MSA, WV-KY-OH	S	8.09 MW	7.74 AW	16820 AAW	WVBLS	10//99-12//99
General	Parkersburg-Marietta MSA, WV-OH	S	8.62 MW	8.04 AW	17940 AAW	WVBLS	10//99-12//99
General	Wheeling MSA, WV-OH	S	7.89 MW	7.04 AW	16410 AAW	WVBLS	10//99-12//99
General	Wisconsin	S	9.81 MW	10.14 AW	21090 AAW	WIBLS	10//99-12//99
General	Appleton-Oshkosh-Neenah MSA, WI	S	10.23 MW	10.10 AW	21270 AAW	WIBLS	10//99-12//99
General	Eau Claire MSA, WI	S	9.05 MW	8.81 AW	18820 AAW	WIBLS	10//99-12//99
General	Green Bay MSA, WI	S	10.62 MW	9.97 AW	22090 AAW	WIBLS	10//99-12//99
General	Janesville-Beloit MSA, WI	S	9.22 MW	9.24 AW	19180 AAW	WIBLS	10//99-12//99
General	Kenosha PMSA, WI	S	9.55 MW	9.44 AW	19860 AAW	WIBLS	10//99-12//99
General	La Crosse MSA, WI-MN	S	10.17 MW	10.07 AW	21150 AAW	WIBLS	10//99-12//99
General	Madison MSA, WI	S	11.64 MW	11.41 AW	24200 AAW	WIBLS	10//99-12//99
General	Milwaukee-Waukesha PMSA, WI	S	10.29 MW	9.90 AW	21390 AAW	WIBLS	10//99-12//99
General	Racine PMSA, WI	S	10.08 MW	9.85 AW	20970 AAW	WIBLS	10//99-12//99

AAW Average annual wage	**AOH** Average offered, high	**ASH** Average starting, high	**H** Hourly	**M** Monthly	**S** Special: hourly and annual
AE Average entry wage	**AOL** Average offered, low	**ASL** Average starting, low	**HI** Highest wage paid	**MTC** Median total compensation	**TQ** Third quartile wage
AEX Average experienced wage	**APH** Average pay, high range	**AW** Average wage paid	**HR** High end range	**MW** Median wage paid	**W** Weekly
AO Average offered	**APL** Average pay, low range	**FQ** First quartile wage	**LR** Low end range	**SQ** Second quartile wage	**Y** Yearly

Occupation/Type/Industry	Location	Per	Low	Mid	High	Source	Date
Office Clerk							
General	Sheboygan MSA, WI	S	9.36 MW	8.73 AW	19470 AAW	WIBLS	10//99-12//99
General	Wausau MSA, WI	S	9.30 MW	9.24 AW	19330 AAW	WIBLS	10//99-12//99
General	Wyoming	S	8.1 MW	8.55 AW	17790 AAW	WYBLS	10//99-12//99
General	Casper MSA, WY	S	8.27 MW	7.94 AW	17210 AAW	WYBLS	10//99-12//99
General	Cheyenne MSA, WY	S	9.04 MW	8.68 AW	18810 AAW	WYBLS	10//99-12//99
General	Puerto Rico	S	6.35 MW	6.99 AW	14540 AAW	PRBLS	10//99-12//99
General	Aguadilla MSA, PR	S	5.84 MW	5.98 AW	12150 AAW	PRBLS	10//99-12//99
General	Arecibo PMSA, PR	S	6.35 MW	6.13 AW	13200 AAW	PRBLS	10//99-12//99
General	Caguas PMSA, PR	S	6.16 MW	6.08 AW	12810 AAW	PRBLS	10//99-12//99
General	Mayaguez MSA, PR	S	6.93 MW	6.37 AW	14420 AAW	PRBLS	10//99-12//99
General	Ponce MSA, PR	S	6.84 MW	6.31 AW	14220 AAW	PRBLS	10//99-12//99
General	San Juan-Bayamon PMSA, PR	S	7.18 MW	6.43 AW	14940 AAW	PRBLS	10//99-12//99
General	Virgin Islands	S	7.69 MW	7.72 AW	16070 AAW	VIBLS	10//99-12//99
General	Guam	S	7.43 MW	7.85 AW	16320 AAW	GUBLS	10//99-12//99
Office Machine Operator							
Except Computer	Alabama	S	7.99 MW	8.48 AW	17640 AAW	ALBLS	10//99-12//99
Except Computer	Alaska	S	9.2 MW	9.66 AW	20090 AAW	AKBLS	10//99-12//99
Except Computer	Arizona	S	8.1 MW	8.72 AW	18140 AAW	AZBLS	10//99-12//99
Except Computer	Arkansas	S	7.66 MW	8.15 AW	16950 AAW	ARBLS	10//99-12//99
Except Computer	California	S	10.26 MW	10.91 AW	22690 AAW	CABLS	10//99-12//99
Except Computer	Colorado	S	9.52 MW	9.78 AW	20340 AAW	COBLS	10//99-12//99
Except Computer	Connecticut	S	11.11 MW	11.43 AW	23780 AAW	CTBLS	10//99-12//99
Except Computer	Delaware	S	9.6 MW	10.58 AW	22010 AAW	DEBLS	10//99-12//99
Except Computer	District of Columbia	S	12.38 MW	12.19 AW	25350 AAW	DCBLS	10//99-12//99
Except Computer	Florida	S	9.43 MW	9.60 AW	19970 AAW	FLBLS	10//99-12//99
Except Computer	Georgia	S	10.08 MW	10.50 AW	21830 AAW	GABLS	10//99-12//99
Except Computer	Hawaii	S	8.69 MW	9.37 AW	19490 AAW	HIBLS	10//99-12//99
Except Computer	Idaho	S	8.76 MW	8.95 AW	18610 AAW	IDBLS	10//99-12//99
Except Computer	Illinois	S	11.1 MW	12.10 AW	25160 AAW	ILBLS	10//99-12//99
Except Computer	Indiana	S	9.21 MW	9.50 AW	19760 AAW	INBLS	10//99-12//99
Except Computer	Iowa	S	9.75 MW	9.97 AW	20740 AAW	IABLS	10//99-12//99
Except Computer	Kansas	S	8.84 MW	9.16 AW	19040 AAW	KSBLS	10//99-12//99
Except Computer	Kentucky	S	8.17 MW	8.49 AW	17650 AAW	KYBLS	10//99-12//99
Except Computer	Louisiana	S	8.38 MW	8.86 AW	18430 AAW	LABLS	10//99-12//99
Except Computer	Maine	S	8.92 MW	9.20 AW	19130 AAW	MEBLS	10//99-12//99
Except Computer	Maryland	S	10.76 MW	10.67 AW	22190 AAW	MDBLS	10//99-12//99
Except Computer	Massachusetts	S	10.5 MW	11.11 AW	23120 AAW	MABLS	10//99-12//99
Except Computer	Michigan	S	10.34 MW	11.98 AW	24920 AAW	MIBLS	10//99-12//99
Except Computer	Minnesota	S	10.66 MW	10.88 AW	22630 AAW	MNBLS	10//99-12//99
Except Computer	Mississippi	S	8.02 MW	8.46 AW	17590 AAW	MSBLS	10//99-12//99
Except Computer	Missouri	S	8.47 MW	10.10 AW	21000 AAW	MOBLS	10//99-12//99
Except Computer	Montana	S	8.38 MW	8.82 AW	18350 AAW	MTBLS	10//99-12//99
Except Computer	Nebraska	S	9.18 MW	10.01 AW	20820 AAW	NEBLS	10//99-12//99
Except Computer	Nevada	S	9.39 MW	9.68 AW	20130 AAW	NVBLS	10//99-12//99
Except Computer	New Hampshire	S	9.98 MW	10.32 AW	21460 AAW	NHBLS	10//99-12//99
Except Computer	New Jersey	S	11.03 MW	11.64 AW	24210 AAW	NJBLS	10//99-12//99
Except Computer	New Mexico	S	9.88 MW	9.99 AW	20780 AAW	NMBLS	10//99-12//99
Except Computer	New York	S	9.67 MW	10.59 AW	22040 AAW	NYBLS	10//99-12//99
Except Computer	North Carolina	S	9.69 MW	9.84 AW	20470 AAW	NCBLS	10//99-12//99
Except Computer	North Dakota	S	9.28 MW	9.42 AW	19600 AAW	NDBLS	10//99-12//99
Except Computer	Ohio	S	9.48 MW	10.03 AW	20860 AAW	OHBLS	10//99-12//99
Except Computer	Oklahoma	S	8.77 MW	9.53 AW	19830 AAW	OKBLS	10//99-12//99
Except Computer	Oregon	S	9.7 MW	10.23 AW	21270 AAW	ORBLS	10//99-12//99
Except Computer	Pennsylvania	S	10.71 MW	10.93 AW	22730 AAW	PABLS	10//99-12//99
Except Computer	Rhode Island	S	9.93 MW	10.08 AW	20970 AAW	RIBLS	10//99-12//99
Except Computer	South Carolina	S	7.99 MW	8.93 AW	18570 AAW	SCBLS	10//99-12//99
Except Computer	South Dakota	S	8.43 MW	8.50 AW	17680 AAW	SDBLS	10//99-12//99
Except Computer	Tennessee	S	9.14 MW	9.54 AW	19830 AAW	TNBLS	10//99-12//99
Except Computer	Texas	S	9.55 MW	9.87 AW	20530 AAW	TXBLS	10//99-12//99
Except Computer	Utah	S	8.62 MW	9.34 AW	19430 AAW	UTBLS	10//99-12//99
Except Computer	Vermont	S	8.36 MW	9.35 AW	19450 AAW	VTBLS	10//99-12//99
Except Computer	Virginia	S	9.27 MW	9.67 AW	20120 AAW	VABLS	10//99-12//99
Except Computer	Washington	S	10.33 MW	10.77 AW	22390 AAW	WABLS	10//99-12//99
Except Computer	West Virginia	S	9.95 MW	11.19 AW	23280 AAW	WVBLS	10//99-12//99
Except Computer	Wisconsin	S	9.45 MW	9.88 AW	20550 AAW	WIBLS	10//99-12//99
Except Computer	Wyoming	S	8.03 MW	8.46 AW	17590 AAW	WYBLS	10//99-12//99
Except Computer	Puerto Rico	S	6.9 MW	7.74 AW	16090 AAW	PRBLS	10//99-12//99

AAW	Average annual wage	AOH	Average offered, high	ASH	Average starting, high	H	Hourly
AE	Average entry wage	AOL	Average offered, low	ASL	Average starting, low	HI	Highest wage paid
AEX	Average experienced wage	APH	Average pay, high range	AW	Average wage paid	HR	High end range
AO	Average offered	APL	Average pay, low range	FQ	First quartile wage	LR	Low end range

M	Monthly	S	Special: hourly and annual
MTC	Median total compensation	TQ	Third quartile wage
MW	Median wage paid	W	Weekly
SQ	Second quartile wage	Y	Yearly

Occupation/Type/Industry	Location	Per	Low	Mid	High	Source	Date
Operating Engineer and Other Construction Equipment Operator	Alabama	S	11.95 MW	12.42 AW	25840 AAW	ALBLS	10//99-12//99
	Alaska	S	26.63 MW	26.13 AW	54350 AAW	AKBLS	10//99-12//99
	Arizona	S	15.15 MW	15.16 AW	31520 AAW	AZBLS	10//99-12//99
	Arkansas	S	10.63 MW	11.21 AW	23310 AAW	ARBLS	10//99-12//99
	California	S	23.55 MW	23.77 AW	49440 AAW	CABLS	10//99-12//99
	Colorado	S	16.46 MW	16.66 AW	34660 AAW	COBLS	10//99-12//99
	Connecticut	S	19.58 MW	19.66 AW	40900 AAW	CTBLS	10//99-12//99
	Delaware	S	15.54 MW	15.90 AW	33060 AAW	DEBLS	10//99-12//99
	District of Columbia	S	17.79 MW	17.91 AW	37250 AAW	DCBLS	10//99-12//99
	Florida	S	11.56 MW	12.15 AW	25260 AAW	FLBLS	10//99-12//99
	Georgia	S	12.16 MW	12.66 AW	26330 AAW	GABLS	10//99-12//99
	Hawaii	S	28.1 MW	25.79 AW	53630 AAW	HIBLS	10//99-12//99
	Idaho	S	15.39 MW	16.40 AW	34110 AAW	IDBLS	10//99-12//99
	Illinois	S	22.67 MW	22.18 AW	46140 AAW	ILBLS	10//99-12//99
	Indiana	S	16.66 MW	17.85 AW	37130 AAW	INBLS	10//99-12//99
	Iowa	S	13.95 MW	14.56 AW	30290 AAW	IABLS	10//99-12//99
	Kansas	S	11.83 MW	13.04 AW	27120 AAW	KSBLS	10//99-12//99
	Kentucky	S	15.35 MW	15.64 AW	32520 AAW	KYBLS	10//99-12//99
	Louisiana	S	12.18 MW	12.53 AW	26060 AAW	LABLS	10//99-12//99
	Maine	S	11.68 MW	12.39 AW	25760 AAW	MEBLS	10//99-12//99
	Maryland	S	14.72 MW	15.08 AW	31360 AAW	MDBLS	10//99-12//99
	Massachusetts	S	19.15 MW	21.11 AW	43900 AAW	MABLS	10//99-12//99
	Michigan	S	17.87 MW	18.01 AW	37450 AAW	MIBLS	10//99-12//99
	Minnesota	S	19.13 MW	18.71 AW	38910 AAW	MNBLS	10//99-12//99
	Mississippi	S	11.36 MW	11.69 AW	24320 AAW	MSBLS	10//99-12//99
	Missouri	S	17.87 MW	17.72 AW	36860 AAW	MOBLS	10//99-12//99
	Montana	S	15.27 MW	15.40 AW	32030 AAW	MTBLS	10//99-12//99
	Nebraska	S	13.99 MW	14.55 AW	30260 AAW	NEBLS	10//99-12//99
	Nevada	S	19.26 MW	20.97 AW	43610 AAW	NVBLS	10//99-12//99
	New Hampshire	S	15.28 MW	15.76 AW	32780 AAW	NHBLS	10//99-12//99
	New Jersey	S	19.93 MW	21.82 AW	45390 AAW	NJBLS	10//99-12//99
	New Mexico	S	12.55 MW	13.49 AW	28050 AAW	NMBLS	10//99-12//99
	New York	S	19.27 MW	20.81 AW	43280 AAW	NYBLS	10//99-12//99
	North Carolina	S	11.82 MW	12.15 AW	25270 AAW	NCBLS	10//99-12//99
	North Dakota	S	14.97 MW	15.35 AW	31930 AAW	NDBLS	10//99-12//99
	Ohio	S	18.14 MW	18.12 AW	37690 AAW	OHBLS	10//99-12//99
	Oklahoma	S	10.69 MW	11.18 AW	23260 AAW	OKBLS	10//99-12//99
	Oregon	S	18.57 MW	18.93 AW	39380 AAW	ORBLS	10//99-12//99
	Pennsylvania	S	15.42 MW	16.00 AW	33280 AAW	PABLS	10//99-12//99
	Rhode Island	S	19.41 MW	19.30 AW	40150 AAW	RIBLS	10//99-12//99
	South Carolina	S	11.11 MW	11.86 AW	24670 AAW	SCBLS	10//99-12//99
	South Dakota	S	12.33 MW	12.58 AW	26160 AAW	SDBLS	10//99-12//99
	Tennessee	S	12.17 MW	12.57 AW	26140 AAW	TNBLS	10//99-12//99
	Texas	S	11.87 MW	12.80 AW	26630 AAW	TXBLS	10//99-12//99
	Utah	S	14.83 MW	15.12 AW	31440 AAW	UTBLS	10//99-12//99
	Vermont	S	11.4 MW	11.96 AW	24880 AAW	VTBLS	10//99-12//99
	Virginia	S	12.29 MW	12.71 AW	26430 AAW	VABLS	10//99-12//99
	Washington	S	21.41 MW	21.28 AW	44250 AAW	WABLS	10//99-12//99
	West Virginia	S	16.08 MW	16.07 AW	33420 AAW	WVBLS	10//99-12//99
	Wisconsin	S	20.03 MW	19.18 AW	39900 AAW	WIBLS	10//99-12//99
	Wyoming	S	13.19 MW	14.23 AW	29590 AAW	WYBLS	10//99-12//99
	Puerto Rico	S	8.24 MW	8.85 AW	18410 AAW	PRBLS	10//99-12//99
	Virgin Islands	S	12.17 MW	12.41 AW	25800 AAW	VIBLS	10//99-12//99
	Guam	S	12.79 MW	13.35 AW	27760 AAW	GUBLS	10//99-12//99
Operations Analyst	United States	H		27.92 AW		NCS98	1998
Operations Manager Purchasing, Electronics	United States	Y		73900 AW		ELBUY	2000
Operations Research Analyst	Alabama	S	27.66 MW	26.81 AW	55760 AAW	ALBLS	10//99-12//99
	Arizona	S	21.84 MW	21.47 AW	44670 AAW	AZBLS	10//99-12//99
	Arkansas	S	15.93 MW	18.27 AW	38000 AAW	ARBLS	10//99-12//99
	California	S	29.31 MW	35.99 AW	74860 AAW	CABLS	10//99-12//99
	Colorado	S	25.67 MW	25.83 AW	53720 AAW	COBLS	10//99-12//99
	Connecticut	S	22.48 MW	23.34 AW	48550 AAW	CTBLS	10//99-12//99
	Florida	S	21.73 MW	22.08 AW	45930 AAW	FLBLS	10//99-12//99
	Georgia	S	24.67 MW	27.04 AW	56240 AAW	GABLS	10//99-12//99
	Hawaii	S	20.37 MW	21.49 AW	44700 AAW	HIBLS	10//99-12//99
	Illinois	S	23.56 MW	27.18 AW	56530 AAW	ILBLS	10//99-12//99

AAW Average annual wage	**AOH** Average offered, high	**ASH** Average starting, high	**H** Hourly	**M** Monthly	**S** Special: hourly and annual
AE Average entry wage	**AOL** Average offered, low	**ASL** Average starting, low	**HI** Highest wage paid	**MTC** Median total compensation	**TQ** Third quartile wage
AEX Average experienced wage	**APH** Average pay, high range	**AW** Average wage paid	**HR** High end range	**MW** Median wage paid	**W** Weekly
AO Average offered	**APL** Average pay, low range	**FQ** First quartile wage	**LR** Low end range	**SQ** Second quartile wage	**Y** Yearly

Occupation/Type/Industry	Location	Per	Low	Mid	High	Source	Date
Operations Research Analyst	Indiana	S	21.78 MW	22.22 AW	46220 AAW	INBLS	10//99-12//99
	Iowa	S	17.72 MW	18.77 AW	39050 AAW	IABLS	10//99-12//99
	Kansas	S	25.27 MW	27.26 AW	56710 AAW	KSBLS	10//99-12//99
	Kentucky	S	22.98 MW	23.58 AW	49050 AAW	KYBLS	10//99-12//99
	Louisiana	S	19.27 MW	21.15 AW	44000 AAW	LABLS	10//99-12//99
	Maine	S	21.25 MW	20.62 AW	42880 AAW	MEBLS	10//99-12//99
	Maryland	S	29.73 MW	29.26 AW	60850 AAW	MDBLS	10//99-12//99
	Massachusetts	S	21.3 MW	23.63 AW	49160 AAW	MABLS	10//99-12//99
	Michigan	S	26.18 MW	27.35 AW	56890 AAW	MIBLS	10//99-12//99
	Minnesota	S	22.3 MW	24.26 AW	50460 AAW	MNBLS	10//99-12//99
	Mississippi	S	16.24 MW	17.29 AW	35970 AAW	MSBLS	10//99-12//99
	Missouri	S	19.96 MW	22.04 AW	45840 AAW	MOBLS	10//99-12//99
	Montana	S	20.3 MW	20.19 AW	42000 AAW	MTBLS	10//99-12//99
	Nebraska	S	21.37 MW	22.31 AW	46410 AAW	NEBLS	10//99-12//99
	Nevada	S	23.72 MW	24.71 AW	51400 AAW	NVBLS	10//99-12//99
	New Hampshire	S	27.66 MW	28.11 AW	58470 AAW	NHBLS	10//99-12//99
	New Jersey	S	22.36 MW	25.95 AW	53970 AAW	NJBLS	10//99-12//99
	New Mexico	S	28.88 MW	27.77 AW	57760 AAW	NMBLS	10//99-12//99
	New York	S	26.67 MW	30.45 AW	63340 AAW	NYBLS	10//99-12//99
	North Carolina	S	19.09 MW	20.78 AW	43230 AAW	NCBLS	10//99-12//99
	Ohio	S	21.01 MW	22.09 AW	45950 AAW	OHBLS	10//99-12//99
	Oklahoma	S	17.54 MW	18.83 AW	39160 AAW	OKBLS	10//99-12//99
	Oregon	S	23.1 MW	23.52 AW	48920 AAW	ORBLS	10//99-12//99
	Pennsylvania	S	18.66 MW	20.39 AW	42410 AAW	PABLS	10//99-12//99
	Rhode Island	S	22.69 MW	23.79 AW	49490 AAW	RIBLS	10//99-12//99
	South Carolina	S	22.57 MW	23.42 AW	48720 AAW	SCBLS	10//99-12//99
	Tennessee	S	18.37 MW	20.21 AW	42030 AAW	TNBLS	10//99-12//99
	Texas	S	20.92 MW	24.96 AW	51920 AAW	TXBLS	10//99-12//99
	Vermont	S	20.38 MW	21.86 AW	45470 AAW	VTBLS	10//99-12//99
	Virginia	S	28.16 MW	29.17 AW	60680 AAW	VABLS	10//99-12//99
	Washington	S	23.44 MW	25.02 AW	52030 AAW	WABLS	10//99-12//99
	West Virginia	S	21.86 MW	20.69 AW	43030 AAW	WVBLS	10//99-12//99
	Wisconsin	S	24.27 MW	25.85 AW	53770 AAW	WIBLS	10//99-12//99
	Puerto Rico	S	18.95 MW	18.12 AW	37700 AAW	PRBLS	10//99-12//99
Ophthalmic Laboratory Technician	Alabama	S	8.21 MW	9.11 AW	18940 AAW	ALBLS	10//99-12//99
	Arizona	S	9.26 MW	9.73 AW	20240 AAW	AZBLS	10//99-12//99
	Phoenix-Mesa MSA, AZ	S	9.71 MW	9.21 AW	20200 AAW	AZBLS	10//99-12//99
	California	S	10.05 MW	10.85 AW	22570 AAW	CABLS	10//99-12//99
	Los Angeles-Long Beach PMSA, CA	S	11.32 MW	10.56 AW	23550 AAW	CABLS	10//99-12//99
	Oakland PMSA, CA	S	12.89 MW	12.40 AW	26820 AAW	CABLS	10//99-12//99
	Orange County PMSA, CA	S	10.09 MW	8.83 AW	20990 AAW	CABLS	10//99-12//99
	San Francisco PMSA, CA	S	10.70 MW	10.06 AW	22250 AAW	CABLS	10//99-12//99
	Santa Barbara-Santa Maria-Lompoc MSA, CA	S	10.42 MW	9.89 AW	21670 AAW	CABLS	10//99-12//99
	Ventura PMSA, CA	S	14.32 MW	14.17 AW	29780 AAW	CABLS	10//99-12//99
	Colorado	S	9.09 MW	10.13 AW	21070 AAW	COBLS	10//99-12//99
	Denver PMSA, CO	S	10.91 MW	10.06 AW	22690 AAW	COBLS	10//99-12//99
	Connecticut	S	12.54 MW	12.96 AW	26960 AAW	CTBLS	10//99-12//99
	Hartford MSA, CT	S	10.92 MW	10.06 AW	22700 AAW	CTBLS	10//99-12//99
	Waterbury PMSA, CT	S	15.21 MW	16.36 AW	31640 AAW	CTBLS	10//99-12//99
	Washington PMSA, DC-MD-VA-WV	S	10.40 MW	9.73 AW	21630 AAW	DCBLS	10//99-12//99
	Florida	S	8.68 MW	9.53 AW	19830 AAW	FLBLS	10//99-12//99
	Daytona Beach MSA, FL	S	10.47 MW	10.09 AW	21780 AAW	FLBLS	10//99-12//99
	Fort Lauderdale PMSA, FL	S	10.43 MW	10.44 AW	21690 AAW	FLBLS	10//99-12//99
	Jacksonville MSA, FL	S	9.64 MW	8.63 AW	20060 AAW	FLBLS	10//99-12//99
	Miami PMSA, FL	S	8.72 MW	8.18 AW	18130 AAW	FLBLS	10//99-12//99
	Orlando MSA, FL	S	10.61 MW	8.88 AW	22060 AAW	FLBLS	10//99-12//99
	Sarasota-Bradenton MSA, FL	S	8.74 MW	8.58 AW	18170 AAW	FLBLS	10//99-12//99
	Tampa-St. Petersburg-Clearwater MSA, FL	S	9.70 MW	8.90 AW	20180 AAW	FLBLS	10//99-12//99
	West Palm Beach-Boca Raton MSA, FL	S	9.76 MW	9.54 AW	20290 AAW	FLBLS	10//99-12//99
	Georgia	S	14.85 MW	15.26 AW	31740 AAW	GABLS	10//99-12//99
	Athens MSA, GA	S	8.72 MW	8.97 AW	18140 AAW	GABLS	10//99-12//99
	Augusta-Aiken MSA, GA-SC	S	8.08 MW	8.58 AW	16800 AAW	GABLS	10//99-12//99
	Macon MSA, GA	S	7.89 MW	7.66 AW	16420 AAW	GABLS	10//99-12//99
	Savannah MSA, GA	S	8.82 MW	8.83 AW	18340 AAW	GABLS	10//99-12//99
	Hawaii	S	9.63 MW	12.37 AW	25730 AAW	HIBLS	10//99-12//99

AAW	Average annual wage	AOH	Average offered, high	ASH Average starting, high H Hourly M Monthly S Special: hourly and annual
AE	Average entry wage	AOL	Average offered, low	ASL Average starting, low HI Highest wage paid MTC Median total compensation TQ Third quartile wage
AEX	Average experienced wage	APH	Average pay, high range	AW Average wage paid HR High end range MW Median wage paid W Weekly
AO	Average offered	APL	Average pay, low range	FQ First quartile wage LR Low end range SQ Second quartile wage Y Yearly

Ophthalmic Laboratory Technician

Occupation/Type/Industry	Location	Per	Low	Mid	High	Source	Date
Ophthalmic Laboratory Technician	Honolulu MSA, HI	S	11.52 MW	8.92 AW	23950 AAW	HIBLS	10//99-12//99
	Idaho	S	10.93 MW	11.32 AW	23540 AAW	IDBLS	10//99-12//99
	Boise City MSA, ID	S	12.55 MW	13.39 AW	26100 AAW	IDBLS	10//99-12//99
	Illinois	S	10.92 MW	11.21 AW	23310 AAW	ILBLS	10//99-12//99
	Chicago PMSA, IL	S	11.16 MW	10.87 AW	23200 AAW	ILBLS	10//99-12//99
	Indiana	S	10.18 MW	10.35 AW	21530 AAW	INBLS	10//99-12//99
	Evansville-Henderson MSA, IN-KY	S	11.09 MW	11.76 AW	23080 AAW	INBLS	10//99-12//99
	Indianapolis MSA, IN	S	9.42 MW	9.12 AW	19590 AAW	INBLS	10//99-12//99
	Iowa	S	8.7 MW	9.06 AW	18840 AAW	IABLS	10//99-12//99
	Des Moines MSA, IA	S	8.85 MW	8.50 AW	18420 AAW	IABLS	10//99-12//99
	Kansas	S	10.14 MW	10.08 AW	20960 AAW	KSBLS	10//99-12//99
	Topeka MSA, KS	S	10.11 MW	9.95 AW	21030 AAW	KSBLS	10//99-12//99
	Kentucky	S	9.8 MW	10.07 AW	20940 AAW	KYBLS	10//99-12//99
	Lexington MSA, KY	S	9.35 MW	9.16 AW	19450 AAW	KYBLS	10//99-12//99
	Louisville MSA, KY-IN	S	10.38 MW	10.01 AW	21580 AAW	KYBLS	10//99-12//99
	Louisiana	S	8.15 MW	8.80 AW	18310 AAW	LABLS	10//99-12//99
	Maine	S	9.5 MW	9.90 AW	20600 AAW	MEBLS	10//99-12//99
	Maryland	S	9.94 MW	11.10 AW	23090 AAW	MDBLS	10//99-12//99
	Massachusetts	S	11.01 MW	12.34 AW	25660 AAW	MABLS	10//99-12//99
	Boston PMSA, MA-NH	S	13.41 MW	12.22 AW	27890 AAW	MABLS	10//99-12//99
	Fitchburg-Leominster PMSA, MA	S	12.12 MW	10.04 AW	25210 AAW	MABLS	10//99-12//99
	Lawrence PMSA, MA-NH	S	11.99 MW	10.68 AW	24930 AAW	MABLS	10//99-12//99
	New Bedford PMSA, MA	S	10.26 MW	9.06 AW	21340 AAW	MABLS	10//99-12//99
	Michigan	S	10.95 MW	11.57 AW	24070 AAW	MIBLS	10//99-12//99
	Detroit PMSA, MI	S	12.62 MW	11.53 AW	26260 AAW	MIBLS	10//99-12//99
	Flint PMSA, MI	S	12.87 MW	13.54 AW	26770 AAW	MIBLS	10//99-12//99
	Minnesota	S	9.18 MW	9.70 AW	20170 AAW	MNBLS	10//99-12//99
	Minneapolis-St. Paul MSA, MN-WI	S	11.90 MW	12.08 AW	24750 AAW	MNBLS	10//99-12//99
	St. Cloud MSA, MN	S	9.07 MW	8.65 AW	18870 AAW	MNBLS	10//99-12//99
	Mississippi	S	9.25 MW	9.17 AW	19080 AAW	MSBLS	10//99-12//99
	Biloxi-Gulfport-Pascagoula MSA, MS	S	10.20 MW	10.05 AW	21220 AAW	MSBLS	10//99-12//99
	Jackson MSA, MS	S	8.52 MW	8.46 AW	17710 AAW	MSBLS	10//99-12//99
	Missouri	S	9.45 MW	10.19 AW	21190 AAW	MOBLS	10//99-12//99
	Montana	S	11.83 MW	11.32 AW	23550 AAW	MTBLS	10//99-12//99
	Nevada	S	9.15 MW	9.80 AW	20390 AAW	NVBLS	10//99-12//99
	Las Vegas MSA, NV-AZ	S	9.90 MW	9.46 AW	20580 AAW	NVBLS	10//99-12//99
	New Hampshire	S	10.63 MW	11.97 AW	24900 AAW	NHBLS	10//99-12//99
	Manchester PMSA, NH	S	10.25 MW	9.72 AW	21310 AAW	NHBLS	10//99-12//99
	New Jersey	S	10.69 MW	12.51 AW	26010 AAW	NJBLS	10//99-12//99
	Bergen-Passaic PMSA, NJ	S	12.70 MW	10.94 AW	26420 AAW	NJBLS	10//99-12//99
	Monmouth-Ocean PMSA, NJ	S	12.00 MW	10.30 AW	24950 AAW	NJBLS	10//99-12//99
	Newark PMSA, NJ	S	13.24 MW	11.19 AW	27530 AAW	NJBLS	10//99-12//99
	New Mexico	S	9.58 MW	9.58 AW	19940 AAW	NMBLS	10//99-12//99
	New York	S	8.72 MW	9.72 AW	20230 AAW	NYBLS	10//99-12//99
	Buffalo-Niagara Falls MSA, NY	S	9.30 MW	8.75 AW	19340 AAW	NYBLS	10//99-12//99
	Nassau-Suffolk PMSA, NY	S	11.05 MW	9.92 AW	22980 AAW	NYBLS	10//99-12//99
	New York PMSA, NY	S	8.57 MW	8.20 AW	17840 AAW	NYBLS	10//99-12//99
	Syracuse MSA, NY	S	9.72 MW	9.12 AW	20220 AAW	NYBLS	10//99-12//99
	North Carolina	S	9.06 MW	10.01 AW	20830 AAW	NCBLS	10//99-12//99
	Asheville MSA, NC	S	9.25 MW	9.05 AW	19250 AAW	NCBLS	10//99-12//99
	Charlotte-Gastonia-Rock Hill MSA, NC-SC	S	8.24 MW	8.09 AW	17150 AAW	NCBLS	10//99-12//99
	Ohio	S	8.91 MW	10.29 AW	21410 AAW	OHBLS	10//99-12//99
	Cincinnati PMSA, OH-KY-IN	S	13.39 MW	10.47 AW	27860 AAW	OHBLS	10//99-12//99
	Cleveland-Lorain-Elyria PMSA, OH	S	10.53 MW	10.21 AW	21910 AAW	OHBLS	10//99-12//99
	Dayton-Springfield MSA, OH	S	9.62 MW	8.57 AW	20020 AAW	OHBLS	10//99-12//99
	Youngstown-Warren MSA, OH	S	8.30 MW	7.99 AW	17260 AAW	OHBLS	10//99-12//99
	Oklahoma	S	9.29 MW	9.76 AW	20290 AAW	OKBLS	10//99-12//99
	Oklahoma City MSA, OK	S	7.34 MW	7.53 AW	15270 AAW	OKBLS	10//99-12//99
	Tulsa MSA, OK	S	10.47 MW	9.77 AW	21770 AAW	OKBLS	10//99-12//99
	Oregon	S	10.5 MW	10.75 AW	22360 AAW	ORBLS	10//99-12//99
	Eugene-Springfield MSA, OR	S	9.27 MW	8.77 AW	19280 AAW	ORBLS	10//99-12//99
	Portland-Vancouver PMSA, OR-WA	S	10.80 MW	10.36 AW	22470 AAW	ORBLS	10//99-12//99
	Pennsylvania	S	9.82 MW	10.49 AW	21820 AAW	PABLS	10//99-12//99

Occupation/Type/Industry	Location	Per	Low	Mid	High	Source	Date
Ophthalmic Laboratory Technician							
	Lancaster MSA, PA	S	11.83 MW	10.60 AW	24610 AAW	PABLS	10//99-12//99
	Philadelphia PMSA, PA-NJ	S	10.60 MW	9.74 AW	22060 AAW	PABLS	10//99-12//99
	Pittsburgh MSA, PA	S	11.91 MW	11.44 AW	24770 AAW	PABLS	10//99-12//99
	Scranton--Wilkes-Barre--Hazleton MSA, PA	S	9.44 MW	9.08 AW	19640 AAW	PABLS	10//99-12//99
	Providence-Fall River-Warwick MSA, RI-MA	S	8.48 MW	7.66 AW	17650 AAW	RIBLS	10//99-12//99
	South Carolina	S	8.92 MW	8.91 AW	18530 AAW	SCBLS	10//99-12//99
	Columbia MSA, SC	S	8.47 MW	8.12 AW	17610 AAW	SCBLS	10//99-12//99
	Greenville-Spartanburg-Anderson MSA, SC	S	9.05 MW	8.96 AW	18820 AAW	SCBLS	10//99-12//99
	Tennessee	S	7.4 MW	7.76 AW	16140 AAW	TNBLS	10//99-12//99
	Chattanooga MSA, TN-GA	S	9.86 MW	9.72 AW	20520 AAW	TNBLS	10//99-12//99
	Johnson City-Kingsport-Bristol MSA, TN-VA	S	9.13 MW	9.37 AW	18990 AAW	TNBLS	10//99-12//99
	Memphis MSA, TN-AR-MS	S	9.21 MW	9.21 AW	19150 AAW	MSBLS	10//99-12//99
	Nashville MSA, TN	S	7.27 MW	6.99 AW	15130 AAW	TNBLS	10//99-12//99
	Texas	S	8.18 MW	8.82 AW	18340 AAW	TXBLS	10//99-12//99
	Austin-San Marcos MSA, TX	S	9.52 MW	9.70 AW	19800 AAW	TXBLS	10//99-12//99
	Brownsville-Harlingen-San Benito MSA, TX	S	7.34 MW	7.34 AW	15270 AAW	TXBLS	10//99-12//99
	Corpus Christi MSA, TX	S	8.28 MW	8.51 AW	17210 AAW	TXBLS	10//99-12//99
	Dallas PMSA, TX	S	9.50 MW	8.34 AW	19750 AAW	TXBLS	10//99-12//99
	El Paso MSA, TX	S	7.32 MW	7.37 AW	15240 AAW	TXBLS	10//99-12//99
	San Antonio MSA, TX	S	8.84 MW	8.27 AW	18390 AAW	TXBLS	10//99-12//99
	Utah	S	10.75 MW	10.27 AW	21360 AAW	UTBLS	10//99-12//99
	Salt Lake City-Ogden MSA, UT	S	10.44 MW	10.95 AW	21720 AAW	UTBLS	10//99-12//99
	Vermont	S	11.02 MW	16.03 AW	33340 AAW	VTBLS	10//99-12//99
	Virginia	S	8.92 MW	9.51 AW	19790 AAW	VABLS	10//99-12//99
	Norfolk-Virginia Beach-Newport News MSA, VA-NC	S	10.13 MW	9.10 AW	21060 AAW	VABLS	10//99-12//99
	Richmond-Petersburg MSA, VA	S	9.50 MW	9.27 AW	19770 AAW	VABLS	10//99-12//99
	Washington	S	11.33 MW	12.68 AW	26380 AAW	WABLS	10//99-12//99
	Bellingham MSA, WA	S	9.40 MW	8.89 AW	19560 AAW	WABLS	10//99-12//99
	Seattle-Bellevue-Everett PMSA, WA	S	11.85 MW	11.35 AW	24660 AAW	WABLS	10//99-12//99
	West Virginia	S	8.75 MW	8.85 AW	18410 AAW	WVBLS	10//99-12//99
	Huntington-Ashland MSA, WV-KY-OH	S	8.29 MW	7.94 AW	17240 AAW	WVBLS	10//99-12//99
	Wisconsin	S	9.78 MW	10.67 AW	22190 AAW	WIBLS	10//99-12//99
	Madison MSA, WI	S	11.69 MW	10.73 AW	24320 AAW	WIBLS	10//99-12//99
	Milwaukee-Waukesha PMSA, WI	S	9.75 MW	8.82 AW	20280 AAW	WIBLS	10//99-12//99
	Puerto Rico	S	7.51 MW	7.73 AW	16080 AAW	PRBLS	10//99-12//99
	San Juan-Bayamon PMSA, PR	S	7.33 MW	6.91 AW	15250 AAW	PRBLS	10//99-12//99
Optician, Dispensing	Alabama	S	10.52 MW	11.39 AW	23690 AAW	ALBLS	10//99-12//99
	Alaska	S	12.73 MW	13.64 AW	28360 AAW	AKBLS	10//99-12//99
	Arizona	S	10.94 MW	11.36 AW	23630 AAW	AZBLS	10//99-12//99
	Arkansas	S	10.45 MW	10.67 AW	22190 AAW	ARBLS	10//99-12//99
	California	S	11.29 MW	12.20 AW	25390 AAW	CABLS	10//99-12//99
	Colorado	S	12.84 MW	13.57 AW	28230 AAW	COBLS	10//99-12//99
	Connecticut	S	18.29 MW	17.18 AW	35740 AAW	CTBLS	10//99-12//99
	Delaware	S	11.6 MW	11.17 AW	23230 AAW	DEBLS	10//99-12//99
	District of Columbia	S	16.47 MW	20.52 AW	42690 AAW	DCBLS	10//99-12//99
	Florida	S	12.89 MW	13.48 AW	28030 AAW	FLBLS	10//99-12//99
	Georgia	S	10.01 MW	10.68 AW	22220 AAW	GABLS	10//99-12//99
	Hawaii	S	14.47 MW	14.39 AW	29940 AAW	HIBLS	10//99-12//99
	Idaho	S	8.29 MW	8.97 AW	18660 AAW	IDBLS	10//99-12//99
	Illinois	S	10.53 MW	11.47 AW	23850 AAW	ILBLS	10//99-12//99
	Indiana	S	10.29 MW	10.63 AW	22100 AAW	INBLS	10//99-12//99
	Iowa	S	10.11 MW	10.77 AW	22400 AAW	IABLS	10//99-12//99
	Kansas	S	9.79 MW	10.02 AW	20850 AAW	KSBLS	10//99-12//99
	Kentucky	S	11.92 MW	12.87 AW	26770 AAW	KYBLS	10//99-12//99
	Louisiana	S	9.6 MW	12.37 AW	25730 AAW	LABLS	10//99-12//99
	Maine	S	10.79 MW	10.92 AW	22720 AAW	MEBLS	10//99-12//99
	Maryland	S	10.92 MW	12.06 AW	25090 AAW	MDBLS	10//99-12//99
	Massachusetts	S	15.08 MW	19.23 AW	39990 AAW	MABLS	10//99-12//99

AAW Average annual wage	**AOH** Average offered, high	**ASH** Average starting, high	**H** Hourly	**M** Monthly	**S** Special: hourly and annual
AE Average entry salaries	**AOL** Average offered, low	**ASL** Average starting, low	**HI** Highest wage paid	**MTC** Median total compensation	**TQ** Third quartile wage
AEX Average experienced wage	**APH** Average pay, high range	**AW** Average wage paid	**HR** High end range	**MW** Median wage paid	**W** Weekly
AO Average offered	**APL** Average pay, low range	**FQ** First quartile wage	**LR** Low end range	**SQ** Second quartile wage	**Y** Yearly

Occupation/Type/Industry	Location	Per	Low	Mid	High	Source	Date
Optician, Dispensing	Michigan	S	10.21 MW	11.51 AW	23940 AAW	MIBLS	10//99-12//99
	Minnesota	S	10.97 MW	11.44 AW	23790 AAW	MNBLS	10//99-12//99
	Mississippi	S	9.39 MW	10.22 AW	21260 AAW	MSBLS	10//99-12//99
	Missouri	S	10.04 MW	11.71 AW	24350 AAW	MOBLS	10//99-12//99
	Montana	S	11.45 MW	11.37 AW	23650 AAW	MTBLS	10//99-12//99
	Nebraska	S	9.21 MW	9.25 AW	19240 AAW	NEBLS	10//99-12//99
	Nevada	S	14.85 MW	14.52 AW	30210 AAW	NVBLS	10//99-12//99
	New Hampshire	S	11.92 MW	12.87 AW	26780 AAW	NHBLS	10//99-12//99
	New Jersey	S	18.33 MW	18.90 AW	39320 AAW	NJBLS	10//99-12//99
	New Mexico	S	9.89 MW	10.72 AW	22300 AAW	NMBLS	10//99-12//99
	New York	S	14.93 MW	15.54 AW	32320 AAW	NYBLS	10//99-12//99
	North Carolina	S	13.16 MW	13.80 AW	28700 AAW	NCBLS	10//99-12//99
	North Dakota	S	8.76 MW	9.77 AW	20310 AAW	NDBLS	10//99-12//99
	Ohio	S	11.75 MW	12.48 AW	25950 AAW	OHBLS	10//99-12//99
	Oklahoma	S	8.18 MW	8.58 AW	17850 AAW	OKBLS	10//99-12//99
	Oregon	S	10.83 MW	11.36 AW	23630 AAW	ORBLS	10//99-12//99
	Pennsylvania	S	9.97 MW	10.75 AW	22360 AAW	PABLS	10//99-12//99
	South Carolina	S	13.4 MW	13.62 AW	28340 AAW	SCBLS	10//99-12//99
	South Dakota	S	10.13 MW	10.57 AW	21980 AAW	SDBLS	10//99-12//99
	Tennessee	S	10.87 MW	11.63 AW	24180 AAW	TNBLS	10//99-12//99
	Texas	S	9.74 MW	10.53 AW	21910 AAW	TXBLS	10//99-12//99
	Utah	S	8.7 MW	9.06 AW	18850 AAW	UTBLS	10//99-12//99
	Vermont	S	12.02 MW	11.72 AW	24380 AAW	VTBLS	10//99-12//99
	Virginia	S	13.07 MW	13.56 AW	28210 AAW	VABLS	10//99-12//99
	Washington	S	13.09 MW	13.68 AW	28450 AAW	WABLS	10//99-12//99
	West Virginia	S	9.46 MW	9.55 AW	19870 AAW	WVBLS	10//99-12//99
	Wisconsin	S	9.69 MW	10.62 AW	22100 AAW	WIBLS	10//99-12//99
	Wyoming	S	9.11 MW	10.74 AW	22330 AAW	WYBLS	10//99-12//99
	Puerto Rico	S	7.87 MW	8.67 AW	18030 AAW	PRBLS	10//99-12//99
Optometrist	United States	H		38.14 AW		NCS98	1998
	Alabama	S	25.25 MW	24.69 AW	51360 AAW	ALBLS	10//99-12//99
	Huntsville MSA, AL	S	34.59 MW	32.03 AW	71950 AAW	ALBLS	10//99-12//99
	California	S	39.19 MW	39.51 AW	82170 AAW	CABLS	10//99-12//99
	Fresno MSA, CA	S	34.69 MW	36.69 AW	72150 AAW	CABLS	
	Los Angeles-Long Beach PMSA, CA	S	34.72 MW	34.14 AW	72210 AAW	CABLS	10//99-12//99
	Modesto MSA, CA	S	50.65 MW	42.05 AW	105350 AAW	CABLS	10//99-12//99
	Oakland PMSA, CA	S	39.07 MW	39.22 AW	81270 AAW	CABLS	10//99-12//99
	Riverside-San Bernardino PMSA, CA	S	41.07 MW	40.90 AW	85420 AAW	CABLS	
	Sacramento PMSA, CA	S	38.50 MW	39.09 AW	80090 AAW	CABLS	
	San Diego MSA, CA	S	38.18 MW	38.98 AW	79420 AAW	CABLS	
	San Francisco PMSA, CA	S	46.27 MW	41.93 AW	96250 AAW	CABLS	10//99-12//99
	San Jose PMSA, CA	S	45.23 MW	48.50 AW	94080 AAW	CABLS	10//99-12//99
	San Luis Obispo-Atascadero-Paso Robles MSA, CA	S	44.63 MW	48.42 AW	92830 AAW	CABLS	
	Vallejo-Fairfield-Napa PMSA, CA	S	41.31 MW	40.12 AW	85930 AAW	CABLS	10//99-12//99
	Connecticut	S	35.59 MW	35.46 AW	73750 AAW	CTBLS	10//99-12//99
	Delaware	S	39.48 MW	42.88 AW	89180 AAW	DEBLS	10//99-12//99
	Wilmington-Newark PMSA, DE-MD	S	43.29 MW	39.52 AW	90030 AAW	DEBLS	
	Washington PMSA, DC-MD-VA-WV	S	26.78 MW	22.82 AW	55700 AAW	DCBLS	10//99-12//99
	Florida	S	41.22 MW	42.68 AW	88780 AAW	FLBLS	10//99-12//99
	Hawaii	S	25.69 MW	32.49 AW	67580 AAW	HIBLS	10//99-12//99
	Idaho	S	33.42 MW	35.70 AW	74260 AAW	IDBLS	10//99-12//99
	Boise City MSA, ID	S	27.57 MW	20.09 AW	57340 AAW	IDBLS	10//99-12//99
	Illinois	S	36.29 MW	35.65 AW	74140 AAW	ILBLS	10//99-12//99
	Chicago PMSA, IL	S	31.21 MW	29.41 AW	64930 AAW	ILBLS	10//99-12//99
	Indiana	S	39.28 MW	40.88 AW	85030 AAW	INBLS	10//99-12//99
	Elkhart-Goshen MSA, IN	S	45.27 MW	42.40 AW	94170 AAW	INBLS	10//99-12//99
	Fort Wayne MSA, IN	S	32.71 MW	26.41 AW	68030 AAW	INBLS	10//99-12//99
	Iowa	S	35.65 MW	31.09 AW	64670 AAW	IABLS	10//99-12//99
	Kansas	S	51.69 MW	50.59 AW	105220 AAW	KSBLS	10//99-12//99
	Wichita MSA, KS	S	54.51 MW	62.37 AW	113380 AAW	KSBLS	10//99-12//99
	Baton Rouge MSA, LA	S	36.35 MW	44.05 AW	75610 AAW	LABLS	10//99-12//99
	New Orleans MSA, LA	S	47.38 MW	48.69 AW	98550 AAW	LABLS	10//99-12//99
	Maine	S	46.73 MW	41.11 AW	85520 AAW	MEBLS	10//99-12//99
	Maryland	S	40.06 MW	38.19 AW	79440 AAW	MDBLS	10//99-12//99
	Baltimore PMSA, MD	S	41.40 MW	42.77 AW	86110 AAW	MDBLS	10//99-12//99
	Massachusetts	S	31.02 MW	33.53 AW	69740 AAW	MABLS	10//99-12//99

AAW Average annual wage	**AOH** Average offered, high	**ASH** Average starting, high	**H** Hourly	**M** Monthly	**S** Special: hourly and annual
AE Average entry wage	**AOL** Average offered, low	**ASL** Average starting, low	**HI** Highest wage paid	**MTC** Median total compensation	**TQ** Third quartile wage
AEX Average experienced wage	**APH** Average pay, high range	**AW** Average wage paid	**HR** High end range	**MW** Median wage paid	**W** Weekly
AO Average offered	**APL** Average pay, low range	**FQ** First quartile wage	**LR** Low end range	**SQ** Second quartile wage	**Y** Yearly

Occupation/Type/Industry	Location	Per	Low	Mid	High	Source	Date
Optometrist	Boston PMSA, MA-NH	S	33.85 mw	30.71 aw	70400 aaw	MABLS	10//99-12//99
	Michigan	S	43.38 mw	41.18 aw	85650 aaw	MIBLS	10//99-12//99
	Ann Arbor PMSA, MI	S	40.35 mw	39.23 aw	83930 aaw	MIBLS	10//99-12//99
	Detroit PMSA, MI	S	43.40 mw	45.91 aw	90270 aaw	MIBLS	10//99-12//99
	Saginaw-Bay City-Midland MSA, MI	S	55.56 mw	60.93 aw	115550 aaw	MIBLS	10//99-12//99
	Minnesota	S	31.8 mw	28.14 aw	58520 aaw	MNBLS	10//99-12//99
	Minneapolis-St. Paul MSA, MN-WI	S	35.53 mw	36.62 aw	73900 aaw	MNBLS	10//99-12//99
	Mississippi	S	60.19 mw	52.60 aw	109410 aaw	MSBLS	10//99-12//99
	Missouri	S	41.22 mw	41.55 aw	86430 aaw	MOBLS	10//99-12//99
	Kansas City MSA, MO-KS	S	48.42 mw	48.18 aw	100710 aaw	MOBLS	10//99-12//99
	St. Louis MSA, MO-IL	S	38.75 mw	34.71 aw	80590 aaw	MOBLS	10//99-12//99
	Nebraska	S	38.6 mw	43.62 aw	90740 aaw	NEBLS	10//99-12//99
	Omaha MSA, NE-IA	S	37.79 mw	26.95 aw	78610 aaw	NEBLS	10//99-12//99
	Nevada	S	43.04 mw	47.09 aw	97950 aaw	NVBLS	10//99-12//99
	Las Vegas MSA, NV-AZ	S	55.20 mw		114810 aaw	NVBLS	10//99-12//99
	New Hampshire	S	23.89 mw	23.01 aw	47850 aaw	NHBLS	10//99-12//99
	New Jersey	S	37.01 mw	36.02 aw	74910 aaw	NJBLS	10//99-12//99
	Bergen-Passaic PMSA, NJ	S	38.43 mw	39.13 aw	79930 aaw	NJBLS	10//99-12//99
	Newark PMSA, NJ	S	32.72 mw	34.93 aw	68060 aaw	NJBLS	10//99-12//99
	New Mexico	S	35.29 mw	35.50 aw	73840 aaw	NMBLS	10//99-12//99
	Albuquerque MSA, NM	S	30.26 mw	26.79 aw	62950 aaw	NMBLS	10//99-12//99
	Buffalo-Niagara Falls MSA, NY	S	45.91 mw	47.40 aw	95500 aaw	NYBLS	10//99-12//99
	North Carolina	S	46.22 mw	45.39 aw	94410 aaw	NCBLS	10//99-12//99
	Charlotte-Gastonia-Rock Hill MSA, NC-SC	S	52.24 mw	59.84 aw	108650 aaw	NCBLS	10//99-12//99
	North Dakota	S	29.93 mw	27.42 aw	57030 aaw	NDBLS	10//99-12//99
	Cincinnati PMSA, OH-KY-IN	S	49.92 mw	52.29 aw	103820 aaw	OHBLS	10//99-12//99
	Columbus MSA, OH	S	36.88 mw	38.10 aw	76710 aaw	OHBLS	10//99-12//99
	Oklahoma	S	66.93 mw	53.91 aw	112130 aaw	OKBLS	10//99-12//99
	Oregon	S	15.71 mw	20.27 aw	42160 aaw	ORBLS	10//99-12//99
	Portland-Vancouver PMSA, OR-WA	S	18.32 mw	15.63 aw	38110 aaw	ORBLS	10//99-12//99
	Pennsylvania	S	15.82 mw	20.25 aw	42120 aaw	PABLS	10//99-12//99
	Harrisburg-Lebanon-Carlisle MSA, PA	S	32.46 mw	37.11 aw	67520 aaw	PABLS	10//99-12//99
	South Carolina	S	26.03 mw	30.74 aw	63930 aaw	SCBLS	10//99-12//99
	Greenville-Spartanburg-Anderson MSA, SC	S	34.72 mw	35.85 aw	72210 aaw	SCBLS	10//99-12//99
	South Dakota	S	43.2 mw	43.77 aw	91040 aaw	SDBLS	10//99-12//99
	Tennessee	S	38.3 mw	39.48 aw	82120 aaw	TNBLS	10//99-12//99
	Memphis MSA, TN-AR-MS	S	45.96 mw	40.45 aw	95590 aaw	MSBLS	10//99-12//99
	Texas	S	42.21 mw	42.12 aw	87600 aaw	TXBLS	10//99-12//99
	Austin-San Marcos MSA, TX	S	37.09 mw	39.13 aw	77140 aaw	TXBLS	10//99-12//99
	Houston PMSA, TX	S	38.90 mw	40.60 aw	80920 aaw	TXBLS	10//99-12//99
	Virginia	S	24.92 mw	29.14 aw	60610 aaw	VABLS	10//99-12//99
	Norfolk-Virginia Beach-Newport News MSA, VA-NC	S	30.35 mw	30.43 aw	63120 aaw	VABLS	10//99-12//99
	Richmond-Petersburg MSA, VA	S	56.59 mw	56.72 aw	117710 aaw	VABLS	10//99-12//99
	Washington	S	38.61 mw	42.52 aw	88450 aaw	WABLS	10//99-12//99
	Seattle-Bellevue-Everett PMSA, WA	S	35.52 mw	36.91 aw	73890 aaw	WABLS	10//99-12//99
	Wisconsin	S	43.67 mw	41.37 aw	86040 aaw	WIBLS	10//99-12//99
	Madison MSA, WI	S	47.00 mw	48.95 aw	97750 aaw	WIBLS	10//99-12//99
	Puerto Rico	S	23.71 mw	22.76 aw	47330 aaw	PRBLS	10//99-12//99
Order Clerk	Alabama	S	8.25 mw	9.05 aw	18830 aaw	ALBLS	10//99-12//99
	Anniston MSA, AL	S	8.84 mw	8.04 aw	18380 aaw	ALBLS	10//99-12//99
	Auburn-Opelika MSA, AL	S	7.41 mw	6.23 aw	15410 aaw	ALBLS	10//99-12//99
	Birmingham MSA, AL	S	8.51 mw	7.85 aw	17700 aaw	ALBLS	10//99-12//99
	Decatur MSA, AL	S	11.77 mw	11.09 aw	24480 aaw	ALBLS	10//99-12//99
	Dothan MSA, AL	S	11.85 mw	11.77 aw	24650 aaw	ALBLS	10//99-12//99
	Florence MSA, AL	S	6.91 mw	6.52 aw	14370 aaw	ALBLS	10//99-12//99
	Gadsden MSA, AL	S	9.45 mw	8.38 aw	19650 aaw	ALBLS	10//99-12//99
	Huntsville MSA, AL	S	9.63 mw	9.49 aw	20030 aaw	ALBLS	10//99-12//99
	Mobile MSA, AL	S	9.20 mw	8.06 aw	19130 aaw	ALBLS	10//99-12//99
	Montgomery MSA, AL	S	11.77 mw	12.00 aw	24470 aaw	ALBLS	10//99-12//99
	Tuscaloosa MSA, AL	S	7.38 mw	7.26 aw	15340 aaw	ALBLS	10//99-12//99
	Alaska	S	12.9 mw	14.09 aw	29300 aaw	AKBLS	10//99-12//99

Occupation/Type/Industry	Location	Per	Low	Mid	High	Source	Date
Order Clerk	Anchorage MSA, AK	S	12.77 MW	12.22 AW	26560 AAW	AKBLS	10//99-12//99
	Arizona	S	9.92 MW	10.39 AW	21600 AAW	AZBLS	10//99-12//99
	Phoenix-Mesa MSA, AZ	S	10.50 MW	10.02 AW	21850 AAW	AZBLS	10//99-12//99
	Tucson MSA, AZ	S	9.62 MW	8.85 AW	20000 AAW	AZBLS	10//99-12//99
	Yuma MSA, AZ	S	10.23 MW	9.33 AW	21280 AAW	AZBLS	10//99-12//99
	Arkansas	S	8.89 MW	9.23 AW	19190 AAW	ARBLS	10//99-12//99
	Fayetteville-Springdale-Rogers MSA, AR	S	7.06 MW	6.78 AW	14690 AAW	ARBLS	10//99-12//99
	Fort Smith MSA, AR-OK	S	10.29 MW	11.09 AW	21410 AAW	ARBLS	10//99-12//99
	Jonesboro MSA, AR	S	10.36 MW	9.83 AW	21550 AAW	ARBLS	10//99-12//99
	Little Rock-North Little Rock MSA, AR	S	10.08 MW	9.72 AW	20960 AAW	ARBLS	10//99-12//99
	Pine Bluff MSA, AR	S	10.22 MW	7.74 AW	21260 AAW	ARBLS	10//99-12//99
	California	S	11.47 MW	12.41 AW	25810 AAW	CABLS	10//99-12//99
	Bakersfield MSA, CA	S	13.36 MW	10.96 AW	27790 AAW	CABLS	10//99-12//99
	Chico-Paradise MSA, CA	S	9.33 MW	7.55 AW	19400 AAW	CABLS	10//99-12//99
	Fresno MSA, CA	S	11.14 MW	11.20 AW	23180 AAW	CABLS	10//99-12//99
	Los Angeles-Long Beach PMSA, CA	S	11.69 MW	10.60 AW	24320 AAW	CABLS	10//99-12//99
	Merced MSA, CA	S	12.42 MW	11.65 AW	25830 AAW	CABLS	10//99-12//99
	Modesto MSA, CA	S	11.04 MW	9.79 AW	22960 AAW	CABLS	10//99-12//99
	Oakland PMSA, CA	S	14.63 MW	13.81 AW	30430 AAW	CABLS	10//99-12//99
	Orange County PMSA, CA	S	13.47 MW	12.41 AW	28030 AAW	CABLS	10//99-12//99
	Redding MSA, CA	S	12.49 MW	12.45 AW	25980 AAW	CABLS	10//99-12//99
	Riverside-San Bernardino PMSA, CA	S	12.15 MW	10.68 AW	25270 AAW	CABLS	10//99-12//99
	Sacramento PMSA, CA	S	12.59 MW	12.45 AW	26190 AAW	CABLS	10//99-12//99
	Salinas MSA, CA	S	12.51 MW	12.29 AW	26010 AAW	CABLS	10//99-12//99
	San Diego MSA, CA	S	10.61 MW	9.95 AW	22070 AAW	CABLS	10//99-12//99
	San Francisco PMSA, CA	S	14.65 MW	14.36 AW	30460 AAW	CABLS	10//99-12//99
	San Jose PMSA, CA	S	14.41 MW	14.26 AW	29970 AAW	CABLS	10//99-12//99
	San Luis Obispo-Atascadero-Paso Robles MSA, CA	S	11.79 MW	10.16 AW	24510 AAW	CABLS	10//99-12//99
	Santa Barbara-Santa Maria-Lompoc MSA, CA	S	10.54 MW	9.89 AW	21930 AAW	CABLS	10//99-12//99
	Santa Cruz-Watsonville PMSA, CA	S	10.76 MW	9.71 AW	22390 AAW	CABLS	10//99-12//99
	Santa Rosa PMSA, CA	S	13.38 MW	13.21 AW	27820 AAW	CABLS	10//99-12//99
	Stockton-Lodi MSA, CA	S	10.60 MW	10.36 AW	22060 AAW	CABLS	10//99-12//99
	Vallejo-Fairfield-Napa PMSA, CA	S	11.90 MW	12.39 AW	24750 AAW	CABLS	10//99-12//99
	Ventura PMSA, CA	S	14.83 MW	13.82 AW	30850 AAW	CABLS	10//99-12//99
	Visalia-Tulare-Porterville MSA, CA	S	9.84 MW	8.93 AW	20470 AAW	CABLS	10//99-12//99
	Yolo PMSA, CA	S	9.95 MW	9.65 AW	20700 AAW	CABLS	10//99-12//99
	Yuba City MSA, CA	S	10.99 MW	10.44 AW	22870 AAW	CABLS	10//99-12//99
	Colorado	S	11.34 MW	12.04 AW	25040 AAW	COBLS	10//99-12//99
	Boulder-Longmont PMSA, CO	S	12.32 MW	12.05 AW	25630 AAW	COBLS	10//99-12//99
	Colorado Springs MSA, CO	S	10.63 MW	9.72 AW	22120 AAW	COBLS	10//99-12//99
	Denver PMSA, CO	S	12.54 MW	12.01 AW	26070 AAW	COBLS	10//99-12//99
	Connecticut	S	12.67 MW	13.29 AW	27630 AAW	CTBLS	10//99-12//99
	Bridgeport PMSA, CT	S	14.65 MW	13.54 AW	30460 AAW	CTBLS	10//99-12//99
	Danbury PMSA, CT	S	16.33 MW	13.81 AW	33970 AAW	CTBLS	10//99-12//99
	Hartford MSA, CT	S	12.77 MW	12.41 AW	26560 AAW	CTBLS	10//99-12//99
	New Haven-Meriden PMSA, CT	S	12.41 MW	11.92 AW	25820 AAW	CTBLS	10//99-12//99
	New London-Norwich MSA, CT-RI	S	10.34 MW	8.92 AW	21500 AAW	CTBLS	10//99-12//99
	Stamford-Norwalk PMSA, CT	S	14.61 MW	13.83 AW	30380 AAW	CTBLS	10//99-12//99
	Waterbury PMSA, CT	S	10.90 MW	11.00 AW	22680 AAW	CTBLS	10//99-12//99
	Delaware	S	12.18 MW	12.76 AW	26550 AAW	DEBLS	10//99-12//99
	Dover MSA, DE	S	8.30 MW	8.03 AW	17260 AAW	DEBLS	10//99-12//99
	Wilmington-Newark PMSA, DE-MD	S	13.48 MW	13.01 AW	28040 AAW	DEBLS	10//99-12//99
	District of Columbia	S	11.15 MW	11.91 AW	24780 AAW	DCBLS	10//99-12//99
	Washington PMSA, DC-MD-VA-WV	S	12.11 MW	11.16 AW	25180 AAW	DCBLS	10//99-12//99
	Florida	S	10.65 MW	11.02 AW	22920 AAW	FLBLS	10//99-12//99
	Daytona Beach MSA, FL	S	9.29 MW	9.19 AW	19320 AAW	FLBLS	10//99-12//99
	Fort Lauderdale PMSA, FL	S	11.02 MW	10.84 AW	22930 AAW	FLBLS	10//99-12//99
	Fort Myers-Cape Coral MSA, FL	S	12.74 MW	13.57 AW	26490 AAW	FLBLS	10//99-12//99

AAW	Average annual wage	AOH	Average offered, high	ASH	Average starting, high	H	Hourly	M	Monthly	S	Special: hourly and annual
AE	Average entry wage	AOL	Average offered, low	ASL	Average starting, low	HI	Highest wage paid	MTC	Median total compensation	TQ	Third quartile wage
AEX	Average experienced wage	APH	Average pay, high range	AW	Average wage paid	HR	High end range	MW	Median wage paid	W	Weekly
AO	Average offered	APL	Average pay, low range	FQ	First quartile wage	LR	Low end range	SQ	Second quartile wage	Y	Yearly

1042

Order Clerk

Occupation/Type/Industry	Location	Per	Low	Mid	High	Source	Date
Order Clerk	Fort Pierce-Port St. Lucie MSA, FL	S	9.47 MW	9.54 AW	19700 AAW	FLBLS	10//99-12//99
	Fort Walton Beach MSA, FL	S	9.54 MW	8.43 AW	19850 AAW	FLBLS	10//99-12//99
	Gainesville MSA, FL	S	8.16 MW	7.89 AW	16970 AAW	FLBLS	10//99-12//99
	Jacksonville MSA, FL	S	10.66 MW	10.32 AW	22180 AAW	FLBLS	10//99-12//99
	Lakeland-Winter Haven MSA, FL	S	10.69 MW	10.96 AW	22230 AAW	FLBLS	10//99-12//99
	Melbourne-Titusville-Palm Bay MSA, FL	S	7.53 MW	7.00 AW	15660 AAW	FLBLS	10//99-12//99
	Miami PMSA, FL	S	11.39 MW	11.29 AW	23680 AAW	FLBLS	10//99-12//99
	Naples MSA, FL	S	12.92 MW	11.46 AW	26880 AAW	FLBLS	10//99-12//99
	Ocala MSA, FL	S	9.00 MW	8.75 AW	18720 AAW	FLBLS	10//99-12//99
	Orlando MSA, FL	S	11.94 MW	10.75 AW	24830 AAW	FLBLS	10//99-12//99
	Panama City MSA, FL	S	8.90 MW	8.62 AW	18520 AAW	FLBLS	10//99-12//99
	Pensacola MSA, FL	S	7.60 MW	7.46 AW	15810 AAW	FLBLS	10//99-12//99
	Sarasota-Bradenton MSA, FL	S	11.69 MW	12.01 AW	24310 AAW	FLBLS	10//99-12//99
	Tallahassee MSA, FL	S	10.23 MW	9.91 AW	21290 AAW	FLBLS	10//99-12//99
	Tampa-St. Petersburg-Clearwater MSA, FL	S	11.18 MW	10.97 AW	23260 AAW	FLBLS	10//99-12//99
	West Palm Beach-Boca Raton MSA, FL	S	10.74 MW	11.02 AW	22340 AAW	FLBLS	10//99-12//99
	Georgia	S	11.05 MW	11.49 AW	23900 AAW	GABLS	10//99-12//99
	Albany MSA, GA	S	10.45 MW	10.05 AW	21730 AAW	GABLS	10//99-12//99
	Athens MSA, GA	S	8.21 MW	7.71 AW	17080 AAW	GABLS	10//99-12//99
	Atlanta MSA, GA	S	12.26 MW	11.80 AW	25500 AAW	GABLS	10//99-12//99
	Augusta-Aiken MSA, GA-SC	S	9.10 MW	8.60 AW	18920 AAW	GABLS	10//99-12//99
	Columbus MSA, GA-AL	S	9.50 MW	9.16 AW	19750 AAW	GABLS	10//99-12//99
	Macon MSA, GA	S	9.78 MW	10.19 AW	20340 AAW	GABLS	10//99-12//99
	Savannah MSA, GA	S	9.43 MW	9.28 AW	19610 AAW	GABLS	10//99-12//99
	Hawaii	S	11.53 MW	11.73 AW	24390 AAW	HIBLS	10//99-12//99
	Honolulu MSA, HI	S	11.62 MW	11.39 AW	24160 AAW	HIBLS	10//99-12//99
	Idaho	S	8.01 MW	8.53 AW	17740 AAW	IDBLS	10//99-12//99
	Boise City MSA, ID	S	10.21 MW	9.94 AW	21240 AAW	IDBLS	10//99-12//99
	Illinois	S	10.66 MW	11.56 AW	24050 AAW	ILBLS	10//99-12//99
	Bloomington-Normal MSA, IL	S	13.21 MW	11.09 AW	27470 AAW	ILBLS	10//99-12//99
	Champaign-Urbana MSA, IL	S	10.26 MW	8.66 AW	21340 AAW	ILBLS	10//99-12//99
	Chicago PMSA, IL	S	11.76 MW	10.76 AW	24460 AAW	ILBLS	10//99-12//99
	Decatur MSA, IL	S	9.32 MW	6.64 AW	19380 AAW	ILBLS	10//99-12//99
	Kankakee PMSA, IL	S	13.39 MW	13.68 AW	27860 AAW	ILBLS	10//99-12//99
	Peoria-Pekin MSA, IL	S	10.45 MW	9.94 AW	21740 AAW	ILBLS	10//99-12//99
	Rockford MSA, IL	S	12.48 MW	12.10 AW	25950 AAW	ILBLS	10//99-12//99
	Springfield MSA, IL	S	13.50 MW	13.49 AW	28090 AAW	ILBLS	10//99-12//99
	Indiana	S	10.32 MW	10.83 AW	22530 AAW	INBLS	10//99-12//99
	Elkhart-Goshen MSA, IN	S	11.45 MW	10.88 AW	23810 AAW	INBLS	10//99-12//99
	Evansville-Henderson MSA, IN-KY	S	11.36 MW	11.04 AW	23640 AAW	INBLS	10//99-12//99
	Fort Wayne MSA, IN	S	10.81 MW	10.58 AW	22480 AAW	INBLS	10//99-12//99
	Gary PMSA, IN	S	9.52 MW	8.68 AW	19810 AAW	INBLS	10//99-12//99
	Indianapolis MSA, IN	S	11.50 MW	11.17 AW	23920 AAW	INBLS	10//99-12//99
	Kokomo MSA, IN	S	12.17 MW	12.38 AW	25310 AAW	INBLS	10//99-12//99
	Lafayette MSA, IN	S	11.42 MW	10.58 AW	23760 AAW	INBLS	10//99-12//99
	Muncie MSA, IN	S	8.44 MW	8.71 AW	17560 AAW	INBLS	10//99-12//99
	South Bend MSA, IN	S	11.87 MW	11.77 AW	24690 AAW	INBLS	10//99-12//99
	Terre Haute MSA, IN	S	10.05 MW	9.72 AW	20900 AAW	INBLS	10//99-12//99
	Iowa	S	9.88 MW	10.58 AW	22010 AAW	IABLS	10//99-12//99
	Cedar Rapids MSA, IA	S	12.49 MW	11.37 AW	25970 AAW	IABLS	10//99-12//99
	Davenport-Moline-Rock Island MSA, IA-IL	S	9.44 MW	9.26 AW	19640 AAW	IABLS	10//99-12//99
	Des Moines MSA, IA	S	12.80 MW	10.94 AW	26630 AAW	IABLS	10//99-12//99
	Dubuque MSA, IA	S	8.13 MW	7.57 AW	16910 AAW	IABLS	10//99-12//99
	Iowa City MSA, IA	S	12.75 MW	12.92 AW	26530 AAW	IABLS	10//99-12//99
	Sioux City MSA, IA-NE	S	9.45 MW	9.10 AW	19650 AAW	IABLS	10//99-12//99
	Waterloo-Cedar Falls MSA, IA	S	11.15 MW	10.68 AW	23180 AAW	IABLS	10//99-12//99
	Kansas	S	10.39 MW	11.19 AW	23280 AAW	KSBLS	10//99-12//99
	Lawrence MSA, KS	S	8.81 MW	8.40 AW	18320 AAW	KSBLS	10//99-12//99
	Topeka MSA, KS	S	12.10 MW	12.23 AW	25160 AAW	KSBLS	10//99-12//99
	Wichita MSA, KS	S	11.16 MW	10.09 AW	23210 AAW	KSBLS	10//99-12//99
	Kentucky	S	9.64 MW	10.29 AW	21410 AAW	KYBLS	10//99-12//99
	Lexington MSA, KY	S	9.50 MW	8.50 AW	19770 AAW	KYBLS	10//99-12//99
	Louisville MSA, KY-IN	S	11.67 MW	11.23 AW	24270 AAW	KYBLS	10//99-12//99
	Owensboro MSA, KY	S	10.42 MW	9.67 AW	21680 AAW	KYBLS	10//99-12//99
	Louisiana	S	10.25 MW	11.62 AW	24160 AAW	LABLS	10//99-12//99

AAW Average annual wage	AOH Average offered, high	ASH Average starting, high	H Hourly	M Monthly	S Special: hourly and annual
AE Average entry wage	AOL Average offered, low	ASL Average starting, low	HI Highest wage paid	MTC Median total compensation	TQ Third quartile wage
AEX Average experienced wage	APH Average pay, high range	AW Average wage paid	HR High end range	MW Median wage paid	W Weekly
AO Average offered	APL Average pay, low range	FQ First quartile wage	LR Low end range	SQ Second quartile wage	Y Yearly

Occupation/Type/Industry	Location	Per	Low	Mid	High	Source	Date
Order Clerk	Alexandria MSA, LA	S	10.86 MW	9.81 AW	22590 AAW	LABLS	10//99-12//99
	Baton Rouge MSA, LA	S	12.83 MW	13.48 AW	26680 AAW	LABLS	10//99-12//99
	Houma MSA, LA	S	14.64 MW	14.62 AW	30440 AAW	LABLS	10//99-12//99
	Lafayette MSA, LA	S	9.02 MW	8.19 AW	18760 AAW	LABLS	10//99-12//99
	Lake Charles MSA, LA	S	8.96 MW	8.82 AW	18640 AAW	LABLS	10//99-12//99
	Monroe MSA, LA	S	8.79 MW	8.06 AW	18290 AAW	LABLS	10//99-12//99
	New Orleans MSA, LA	S	12.88 MW	10.62 AW	26780 AAW	LABLS	10//99-12//99
	Shreveport-Bossier City MSA, LA	S	10.16 MW	10.96 AW	21120 AAW	LABLS	10//99-12//99
	Maine	S	10.33 MW	10.61 AW	22070 AAW	MEBLS	10//99-12//99
	Bangor MSA, ME	S	11.23 MW	10.60 AW	23350 AAW	MEBLS	10//99-12//99
	Lewiston-Auburn MSA, ME	S	11.34 MW	10.66 AW	23590 AAW	MEBLS	10//99-12//99
	Portland MSA, ME	S	12.16 MW	12.03 AW	25300 AAW	MEBLS	10//99-12//99
	Maryland	S	11.66 MW	12.07 AW	25100 AAW	MDBLS	10//99-12//99
	Baltimore PMSA, MD	S	11.77 MW	11.79 AW	24490 AAW	MDBLS	10//99-12//99
	Cumberland MSA, MD-WV	S	8.82 MW	9.18 AW	18350 AAW	MDBLS	10//99-12//99
	Hagerstown PMSA, MD	S	9.77 MW	8.14 AW	20320 AAW	MDBLS	10//99-12//99
	Barnstable-Yarmouth MSA, MA	S	10.71 MW	10.71 AW	22280 AAW	MABLS	10//99-12//99
	Boston PMSA, MA-NH	S	13.38 MW	13.28 AW	27830 AAW	MABLS	10//99-12//99
	Brockton PMSA, MA	S	10.48 MW	9.19 AW	21800 AAW	MABLS	10//99-12//99
	Fitchburg-Leominster PMSA, MA	S	13.86 MW	13.72 AW	28830 AAW	MABLS	10//99-12//99
	Lawrence PMSA, MA-NH	S	12.47 MW	12.08 AW	25930 AAW	MABLS	10//99-12//99
	Lowell PMSA, MA-NH	S	15.14 MW	15.44 AW	31490 AAW	MABLS	10//99-12//99
	New Bedford PMSA, MA	S	10.85 MW	11.42 AW	22560 AAW	MABLS	10//99-12//99
	Pittsfield MSA, MA	S	10.10 MW	9.27 AW	21010 AAW	MABLS	10//99-12//99
	Springfield MSA, MA	S	11.84 MW	10.20 AW	24620 AAW	MABLS	10//99-12//99
	Worcester PMSA, MA-CT	S	13.69 MW	12.27 AW	28480 AAW	MABLS	10//99-12//99
	Michigan	S	11.21 MW	11.80 AW	24530 AAW	MIBLS	10//99-12//99
	Ann Arbor PMSA, MI	S	11.89 MW	11.35 AW	24730 AAW	MIBLS	10//99-12//99
	Benton Harbor MSA, MI	S	11.41 MW	10.41 AW	23740 AAW	MIBLS	10//99-12//99
	Detroit PMSA, MI	S	12.28 MW	11.80 AW	25540 AAW	MIBLS	10//99-12//99
	Flint PMSA, MI	S	12.04 MW	10.93 AW	25030 AAW	MIBLS	10//99-12//99
	Grand Rapids-Muskegon-Holland MSA, MI	S	11.18 MW	11.37 AW	23260 AAW	MIBLS	10//99-12//99
	Jackson MSA, MI	S	11.18 MW	10.33 AW	23250 AAW	MIBLS	10//99-12//99
	Kalamazoo-Battle Creek MSA, MI	S	11.72 MW	11.25 AW	24370 AAW	MIBLS	10//99-12//99
	Lansing-East Lansing MSA, MI	S	9.76 MW	9.07 AW	20310 AAW	MIBLS	10//99-12//99
	Saginaw-Bay City-Midland MSA, MI	S	12.13 MW	10.64 AW	25230 AAW	MIBLS	10//99-12//99
	Minnesota	S	10.94 MW	11.30 AW	23500 AAW	MNBLS	10//99-12//99
	Duluth-Superior MSA, MN-WI	S	10.09 MW	9.28 AW	20990 AAW	MNBLS	10//99-12//99
	Minneapolis-St. Paul MSA, MN-WI	S	12.01 MW	11.57 AW	24980 AAW	MNBLS	10//99-12//99
	Rochester MSA, MN	S	10.77 MW	9.93 AW	22400 AAW	MNBLS	10//99-12//99
	St. Cloud MSA, MN	S	9.25 MW	9.26 AW	19240 AAW	MNBLS	10//99-12//99
	Mississippi	S	9.56 MW	10.20 AW	21210 AAW	MSBLS	10//99-12//99
	Biloxi-Gulfport-Pascagoula MSA, MS	S	10.89 MW	9.14 AW	22650 AAW	MSBLS	10//99-12//99
	Hattiesburg MSA, MS	S	9.99 MW	10.36 AW	20780 AAW	MSBLS	10//99-12//99
	Jackson MSA, MS	S	10.71 MW	9.84 AW	22280 AAW	MSBLS	10//99-12//99
	Missouri	S	11.09 MW	11.70 AW	24340 AAW	MOBLS	10//99-12//99
	Columbia MSA, MO	S	11.70 MW	10.94 AW	24340 AAW	MOBLS	10//99-12//99
	Joplin MSA, MO	S	11.26 MW	10.60 AW	23420 AAW	MOBLS	10//99-12//99
	Kansas City MSA, MO-KS	S	12.84 MW	12.36 AW	26720 AAW	MOBLS	10//99-12//99
	St. Joseph MSA, MO	S	9.57 MW	9.41 AW	19910 AAW	MOBLS	10//99-12//99
	St. Louis MSA, MO-IL	S	11.61 MW	11.04 AW	24160 AAW	MOBLS	10//99-12//99
	Springfield MSA, MO	S	9.29 MW	8.96 AW	19330 AAW	MOBLS	10//99-12//99
	Montana	S	9.01 MW	9.70 AW	20170 AAW	MTBLS	10//99-12//99
	Billings MSA, MT	S	9.09 MW	8.72 AW	18900 AAW	MTBLS	10//99-12//99
	Great Falls MSA, MT	S	9.22 MW	8.39 AW	19190 AAW	MTBLS	10//99-12//99
	Missoula MSA, MT	S	10.10 MW	8.87 AW	21000 AAW	MTBLS	10//99-12//99
	Nebraska	S	8.09 MW	9.05 AW	18820 AAW	NEBLS	10//99-12//99
	Lincoln MSA, NE	S	9.51 MW	9.40 AW	19770 AAW	NEBLS	10//99-12//99
	Omaha MSA, NE-IA	S	10.56 MW	9.66 AW	21960 AAW	NEBLS	10//99-12//99
	Nevada	S	9.36 MW	10.69 AW	22240 AAW	NVBLS	10//99-12//99
	Las Vegas MSA, NV-AZ	S	10.22 MW	8.87 AW	21260 AAW	NVBLS	10//99-12//99
	Reno MSA, NV	S	11.83 MW	10.30 AW	24600 AAW	NVBLS	10//99-12//99
	New Hampshire	S	11.05 MW	11.29 AW	23480 AAW	NHBLS	10//99-12//99
	Manchester PMSA, NH	S	12.95 MW	12.82 AW	26940 AAW	NHBLS	10//99-12//99

AAW Average annual wage	**AOH** Average offered, high	**ASH** Average starting, high	**H** Hourly	**M** Monthly	**S** Special: hourly and annual
AE Average entry wage	**AOL** Average offered, low	**ASL** Average starting, low	**HI** Highest wage paid	**MTC** Median total compensation	**TQ** Third quartile wage
AEX Average experienced wage	**APH** Average pay, high range	**AW** Average wage paid	**HR** High end range	**MW** Median wage paid	**W** Weekly
AO Average offered	**APL** Average pay, low range	**FQ** First quartile wage	**LR** Low end range	**SQ** Second quartile wage	**Y** Yearly

Occupation/Type/Industry	Location	Per	Low	Mid	High	Source	Date
Order Clerk	Nashua PMSA, NH	S	11.82 MW	11.33 AW	24580 AAW	NHBLS	10//99-12//99
	Portsmouth-Rochester PMSA, NH-ME	S	11.23 MW	10.43 AW	23350 AAW	NHBLS	10//99-12//99
	New Jersey	S	12.68 MW	13.21 AW	27470 AAW	NJBLS	10//99-12//99
	Atlantic-Cape May PMSA, NJ	S	13.01 MW	11.65 AW	27070 AAW	NJBLS	10//99-12//99
	Bergen-Passaic PMSA, NJ	S	12.86 MW	11.99 AW	26760 AAW	NJBLS	10//99-12//99
	Jersey City PMSA, NJ	S	11.69 MW	11.40 AW	24320 AAW	NJBLS	10//99-12//99
	Middlesex-Somerset-Hunterdon PMSA, NJ	S	14.31 MW	13.49 AW	29760 AAW	NJBLS	10//99-12//99
	Monmouth-Ocean PMSA, NJ	S	12.53 MW	11.90 AW	26060 AAW	NJBLS	10//99-12//99
	Newark PMSA, NJ	S	13.24 MW	13.01 AW	27530 AAW	NJBLS	10//99-12//99
	Trenton PMSA, NJ	S	12.07 MW	12.17 AW	25120 AAW	NJBLS	10//99-12//99
	Vineland-Millville-Bridgeton PMSA, NJ	S	14.01 MW	12.55 AW	29140 AAW	NJBLS	10//99-12//99
	New Mexico	S	9.31 MW	10.02 AW	20830 AAW	NMBLS	10//99-12//99
	Albuquerque MSA, NM	S	9.42 MW	9.14 AW	19590 AAW	NMBLS	10//99-12//99
	Las Cruces MSA, NM	S	10.95 MW	10.14 AW	22780 AAW	NMBLS	10//99-12//99
	Santa Fe MSA, NM	S	13.51 MW	12.78 AW	28100 AAW	NMBLS	10//99-12//99
	New York	S	11.66 MW	12.24 AW	25470 AAW	NYBLS	10//99-12//99
	Albany-Schenectady-Troy MSA, NY	S	12.17 MW	10.95 AW	25320 AAW	NYBLS	10//99-12//99
	Binghamton MSA, NY	S	11.72 MW	10.55 AW	24370 AAW	NYBLS	10//99-12//99
	Buffalo-Niagara Falls MSA, NY	S	11.33 MW	11.30 AW	23570 AAW	NYBLS	10//99-12//99
	Dutchess County PMSA, NY	S	11.71 MW	11.97 AW	24360 AAW	NYBLS	10//99-12//99
	Elmira MSA, NY	S	10.17 MW	9.86 AW	21140 AAW	NYBLS	10//99-12//99
	Glens Falls MSA, NY	S	10.11 MW	9.79 AW	21030 AAW	NYBLS	10//99-12//99
	Jamestown MSA, NY	S	9.56 MW	8.36 AW	19880 AAW	NYBLS	10//99-12//99
	Nassau-Suffolk PMSA, NY	S	12.48 MW	11.17 AW	25950 AAW	NYBLS	10//99-12//99
	New York PMSA, NY	S	12.76 MW	12.91 AW	26530 AAW	NYBLS	10//99-12//99
	Newburgh PMSA, NY-PA	S	11.53 MW	11.38 AW	23990 AAW	NYBLS	10//99-12//99
	Rochester MSA, NY	S	10.75 MW	10.05 AW	22350 AAW	NYBLS	10//99-12//99
	Syracuse MSA, NY	S	12.86 MW	12.26 AW	26750 AAW	NYBLS	10//99-12//99
	Utica-Rome MSA, NY	S	10.60 MW	10.52 AW	22050 AAW	NYBLS	10//99-12//99
	North Carolina	S	10.22 MW	10.76 AW	22380 AAW	NCBLS	10//99-12//99
	Asheville MSA, NC	S	9.18 MW	8.97 AW	19090 AAW	NCBLS	10//99-12//99
	Charlotte-Gastonia-Rock Hill MSA, NC-SC	S	11.25 MW	10.73 AW	23410 AAW	NCBLS	10//99-12//99
	Fayetteville MSA, NC	S	8.46 MW	8.87 AW	17610 AAW	NCBLS	10//99-12//99
	Goldsboro MSA, NC	S	9.30 MW	8.20 AW	19330 AAW	NCBLS	10//99-12//99
	Greensboro--Winston-Salem--High Point MSA, NC	S	11.40 MW	10.64 AW	23710 AAW	NCBLS	10//99-12//99
	Greenville MSA, NC	S	11.42 MW	11.63 AW	23760 AAW	NCBLS	10//99-12//99
	Hickory-Morganton-Lenoir MSA, NC	S	10.57 MW	10.36 AW	21980 AAW	NCBLS	10//99-12//99
	Raleigh-Durham-Chapel Hill MSA, NC	S	11.04 MW	10.65 AW	22960 AAW	NCBLS	10//99-12//99
	Rocky Mount MSA, NC	S	11.95 MW	12.03 AW	24860 AAW	NCBLS	10//99-12//99
	Wilmington MSA, NC	S	9.30 MW	8.68 AW	19350 AAW	NCBLS	10//99-12//99
	North Dakota	S	9.71 MW	10.21 AW	21240 AAW	NDBLS	10//99-12//99
	Bismarck MSA, ND	S	9.59 MW	8.11 AW	19950 AAW	NDBLS	10//99-12//99
	Fargo-Moorhead MSA, ND-MN	S	10.57 MW	9.98 AW	21990 AAW	NDBLS	10//99-12//99
	Grand Forks MSA, ND-MN	S	10.27 MW	11.11 AW	21360 AAW	NDBLS	10//99-12//99
	Ohio	S	10.6 MW	11.10 AW	23090 AAW	OHBLS	10//99-12//99
	Akron PMSA, OH	S	11.81 MW	11.45 AW	24550 AAW	OHBLS	10//99-12//99
	Canton-Massillon MSA, OH	S	10.26 MW	9.55 AW	21340 AAW	OHBLS	10//99-12//99
	Cincinnati PMSA, OH-KY-IN	S	10.90 MW	10.25 AW	22680 AAW	OHBLS	10//99-12//99
	Cleveland-Lorain-Elyria PMSA, OH	S	11.08 MW	10.75 AW	23050 AAW	OHBLS	10//99-12//99
	Columbus MSA, OH	S	11.25 MW	10.96 AW	23400 AAW	OHBLS	10//99-12//99
	Hamilton-Middletown PMSA, OH	S	13.78 MW	13.24 AW	28660 AAW	OHBLS	10//99-12//99
	Lima MSA, OH	S	8.51 MW	8.19 AW	17700 AAW	OHBLS	10//99-12//99
	Mansfield MSA, OH	S	13.55 MW	13.19 AW	28190 AAW	OHBLS	10//99-12//99
	Toledo MSA, OH	S	11.73 MW	11.43 AW	24400 AAW	OHBLS	10//99-12//99
	Youngstown-Warren MSA, OH	S	9.34 MW	9.21 AW	19430 AAW	OHBLS	10//99-12//99
	Oklahoma	S	8.07 MW	9.45 AW	19660 AAW	OKBLS	10//99-12//99
	Enid MSA, OK	S	7.72 MW	7.77 AW	16070 AAW	OKBLS	10//99-12//99
	Lawton MSA, OK	S	7.46 MW	6.91 AW	15520 AAW	OKBLS	10//99-12//99
	Oklahoma City MSA, OK	S	9.38 MW	8.40 AW	19510 AAW	OKBLS	10//99-12//99
	Tulsa MSA, OK	S	8.85 MW	7.38 AW	18410 AAW	OKBLS	10//99-12//99

AAW Average annual wage	**AOH** Average offered, high	**ASH** Average starting, high	**H** Hourly	**M** Monthly	**S** Special: hourly and annual
AE Average entry wage	**AOL** Average offered, low	**ASL** Average starting, low	**HI** Highest wage paid	**MTC** Median total compensation	**TQ** Third quartile wage
AEX Average experienced wage	**APH** Average pay, high range	**AW** Average wage paid	**HR** High end range	**MW** Median wage paid	**W** Weekly
AO Average offered	**APL** Average pay, low range	**FQ** First quartile wage	**LR** Low end range	**SQ** Second quartile wage	**Y** Yearly

Order Clerk

Occupation/Type/Industry	Location	Per	Low	Mid	High	Source	Date
Order Clerk	Oregon	S	11.97 MW	12.46 AW	25910 AAW	ORBLS	10//99-12//99
	Eugene-Springfield MSA, OR	S	10.65 MW	9.56 AW	22150 AAW	ORBLS	10//99-12//99
	Medford-Ashland MSA, OR	S	11.09 MW	10.41 AW	23070 AAW	ORBLS	10//99-12//99
	Portland-Vancouver PMSA, OR-WA	S	13.00 MW	12.54 AW	27040 AAW	ORBLS	10//99-12//99
	Salem PMSA, OR	S	11.26 MW	10.38 AW	23410 AAW	ORBLS	10//99-12//99
	Pennsylvania	S	11.3 MW	11.70 AW	24330 AAW	PABLS	10//99-12//99
	Allentown-Bethlehem-Easton MSA, PA	S	11.96 MW	11.73 AW	24870 AAW	PABLS	10//99-12//99
	Altoona MSA, PA	S	9.49 MW	9.52 AW	19730 AAW	PABLS	10//99-12//99
	Erie MSA, PA	S	10.69 MW	10.58 AW	22230 AAW	PABLS	10//99-12//99
	Harrisburg-Lebanon-Carlisle MSA, PA	S	10.38 MW	10.93 AW	21590 AAW	PABLS	10//99-12//99
	Johnstown MSA, PA	S	9.69 MW	9.45 AW	20160 AAW	PABLS	10//99-12//99
	Lancaster MSA, PA	S	11.12 MW	10.31 AW	23130 AAW	PABLS	10//99-12//99
	Philadelphia PMSA, PA-NJ	S	12.74 MW	12.39 AW	26500 AAW	PABLS	10//99-12//99
	Pittsburgh MSA, PA	S	11.24 MW	11.11 AW	23380 AAW	PABLS	10//99-12//99
	Reading MSA, PA	S	10.98 MW	10.75 AW	22850 AAW	PABLS	10//99-12//99
	Scranton--Wilkes-Barre--Hazleton MSA, PA	S	11.78 MW	11.26 AW	24510 AAW	PABLS	10//99-12//99
	Sharon MSA, PA	S	9.14 MW	8.45 AW	19020 AAW	PABLS	10//99-12//99
	State College MSA, PA	S	9.66 MW	9.94 AW	20090 AAW	PABLS	10//99-12//99
	Williamsport MSA, PA	S	10.50 MW	10.40 AW	21840 AAW	PABLS	10//99-12//99
	York MSA, PA	S	12.05 MW	11.95 AW	25070 AAW	PABLS	10//99-12//99
	Rhode Island	S	10.43 MW	11.61 AW	24150 AAW	RIBLS	10//99-12//99
	Providence-Fall River-Warwick MSA, RI-MA	S	12.33 MW	11.22 AW	25640 AAW	RIBLS	10//99-12//99
	South Carolina	S	10.93 MW	11.79 AW	24530 AAW	SCBLS	10//99-12//99
	Charleston-North Charleston MSA, SC	S	10.98 MW	10.98 AW	22830 AAW	SCBLS	10//99-12//99
	Columbia MSA, SC	S	11.65 MW	10.86 AW	24230 AAW	SCBLS	10//99-12//99
	Florence MSA, SC	S	12.58 MW	11.82 AW	26170 AAW	SCBLS	10//99-12//99
	Greenville-Spartanburg-Anderson MSA, SC	S	13.25 MW	12.24 AW	27560 AAW	SCBLS	10//99-12//99
	Myrtle Beach MSA, SC	S	9.07 MW	7.70 AW	18860 AAW	SCBLS	10//99-12//99
	Sumter MSA, SC	S	8.93 MW	9.06 AW	18570 AAW	SCBLS	10//99-12//99
	South Dakota	S	8.9 MW	8.87 AW	18450 AAW	SDBLS	10//99-12//99
	Rapid City MSA, SD	S	8.74 MW	8.35 AW	18180 AAW	SDBLS	10//99-12//99
	Sioux Falls MSA, SD	S	9.43 MW	9.19 AW	19620 AAW	SDBLS	10//99-12//99
	Tennessee	S	10.11 MW	10.34 AW	21510 AAW	TNBLS	10//99-12//99
	Chattanooga MSA, TN-GA	S	11.13 MW	11.35 AW	23150 AAW	TNBLS	10//99-12//99
	Clarksville-Hopkinsville MSA, TN-KY	S	8.14 MW	8.12 AW	16930 AAW	TNBLS	10//99-12//99
	Jackson MSA, TN	S	9.65 MW	9.26 AW	20070 AAW	TNBLS	10//99-12//99
	Johnson City-Kingsport-Bristol MSA, TN-VA	S	11.14 MW	10.68 AW	23180 AAW	TNBLS	10//99-12//99
	Knoxville MSA, TN	S	9.70 MW	9.50 AW	20170 AAW	TNBLS	10//99-12//99
	Memphis MSA, TN-AR-MS	S	10.28 MW	10.19 AW	21390 AAW	MSBLS	10//99-12//99
	Nashville MSA, TN	S	11.43 MW	11.25 AW	23770 AAW	TNBLS	10//99-12//99
	Texas	S	10.24 MW	11.07 AW	23030 AAW	TXBLS	10//99-12//99
	Abilene MSA, TX	S	9.86 MW	9.14 AW	20510 AAW	TXBLS	10//99-12//99
	Amarillo MSA, TX	S	8.75 MW	8.98 AW	18200 AAW	TXBLS	10//99-12//99
	Austin-San Marcos MSA, TX	S	9.48 MW	8.41 AW	19720 AAW	TXBLS	10//99-12//99
	Beaumont-Port Arthur MSA, TX	S	7.93 MW	7.34 AW	16480 AAW	TXBLS	10//99-12//99
	Brazoria PMSA, TX	S	9.63 MW	8.22 AW	20030 AAW	TXBLS	10//99-12//99
	Brownsville-Harlingen-San Benito MSA, TX	S	8.93 MW	8.51 AW	18580 AAW	TXBLS	10//99-12//99
	Bryan-College Station MSA, TX	S	10.92 MW	9.88 AW	22720 AAW	TXBLS	10//99-12//99
	Corpus Christi MSA, TX	S	9.94 MW	9.79 AW	20680 AAW	TXBLS	10//99-12//99
	Dallas PMSA, TX	S	11.91 MW	11.13 AW	24770 AAW	TXBLS	10//99-12//99
	El Paso MSA, TX	S	9.53 MW	8.40 AW	19820 AAW	TXBLS	10//99-12//99
	Fort Worth-Arlington PMSA, TX	S	11.68 MW	9.71 AW	24300 AAW	TXBLS	10//99-12//99
	Galveston-Texas City PMSA, TX	S	8.54 MW	7.80 AW	17760 AAW	TXBLS	10//99-12//99
	Houston PMSA, TX	S	11.79 MW	11.35 AW	24520 AAW	TXBLS	10//99-12//99
	Killeen-Temple MSA, TX	S	10.58 MW	9.75 AW	22000 AAW	TXBLS	10//99-12//99
	Laredo MSA, TX	S	8.98 MW	9.05 AW	18680 AAW	TXBLS	10//99-12//99
	Longview-Marshall MSA, TX	S	8.84 MW	8.29 AW	18380 AAW	TXBLS	10//99-12//99
	Lubbock MSA, TX	S	8.19 MW	7.82 AW	17040 AAW	TXBLS	10//99-12//99

AAW	Average annual wage	AOH	Average offered, high	ASH	Average starting, high	H	Hourly	M	Monthly	S	Special: hourly and annual
AE	Average entry wage	AOL	Average offered, low	ASL	Average starting, low	HI	Highest wage paid	MTC	Median total compensation	TQ	Third quartile wage
AEX	Average experienced wage	APH	Average pay, high range	AW	Average wage paid	HR	High end range	MW	Median wage paid	W	Weekly
AO	Average offered	APL	Average pay, low range	FQ	First quartile wage	LR	Low end range	SQ	Second quartile wage	Y	Yearly

Occupation/Type/Industry	Location	Per	Low	Mid	High	Source	Date
Order Clerk	McAllen-Edinburg-Mission MSA, TX	S	9.37 MW	9.05 AW	19480 AAW	TXBLS	10//99-12//99
	Odessa-Midland MSA, TX	S	10.61 MW	10.19 AW	22060 AAW	TXBLS	10//99-12//99
	San Angelo MSA, TX	S	13.67 MW	14.59 AW	28430 AAW	TXBLS	10//99-12//99
	San Antonio MSA, TX	S	9.71 MW	9.07 AW	20190 AAW	TXBLS	10//99-12//99
	Sherman-Denison MSA, TX	S	11.17 MW	11.80 AW	23230 AAW	TXBLS	10//99-12//99
	Texarkana MSA, TX-Texarkana, AR	S	8.84 MW	8.23 AW	18380 AAW	TXBLS	10//99-12//99
	Tyler MSA, TX	S	7.59 MW	6.50 AW	15780 AAW	TXBLS	10//99-12//99
	Victoria MSA, TX	S	12.62 MW	13.67 AW	26250 AAW	TXBLS	10//99-12//99
	Waco MSA, TX	S	10.85 MW	9.53 AW	22580 AAW	TXBLS	10//99-12//99
	Wichita Falls MSA, TX	S	10.61 MW	9.93 AW	22060 AAW	TXBLS	10//99-12//99
	Utah	S	10.11 MW	10.45 AW	21730 AAW	UTBLS	10//99-12//99
	Provo-Orem MSA, UT	S	9.36 MW	9.04 AW	19460 AAW	UTBLS	10//99-12//99
	Salt Lake City-Ogden MSA, UT	S	10.88 MW	10.49 AW	22620 AAW	UTBLS	10//99-12//99
	Vermont	S	10.04 MW	10.69 AW	22240 AAW	VTBLS	10//99-12//99
	Burlington MSA, VT	S	9.76 MW	9.25 AW	20300 AAW	VTBLS	10//99-12//99
	Virginia	S	8.99 MW	9.79 AW	20370 AAW	VABLS	10//99-12//99
	Charlottesville MSA, VA	S	9.86 MW	9.79 AW	20510 AAW	VABLS	10//99-12//99
	Danville MSA, VA	S	9.42 MW	9.56 AW	19590 AAW	VABLS	10//99-12//99
	Lynchburg MSA, VA	S	8.72 MW	7.70 AW	18130 AAW	VABLS	10//99-12//99
	Norfolk-Virginia Beach-Newport News MSA, VA-NC	S	8.52 MW	6.53 AW	17720 AAW	VABLS	10//99-12//99
	Richmond-Petersburg MSA, VA	S	12.38 MW	11.77 AW	25750 AAW	VABLS	10//99-12//99
	Roanoke MSA, VA	S	10.64 MW	10.06 AW	22140 AAW	VABLS	10//99-12//99
	Washington	S	12.23 MW	12.56 AW	26130 AAW	WABLS	10//99-12//99
	Bellingham MSA, WA	S	12.55 MW	11.99 AW	26110 AAW	WABLS	10//99-12//99
	Bremerton PMSA, WA	S	12.06 MW	11.50 AW	25090 AAW	WABLS	10//99-12//99
	Olympia PMSA, WA	S	12.32 MW	10.74 AW	25630 AAW	WABLS	10//99-12//99
	Richland-Kennewick-Pasco MSA, WA	S	11.26 MW	10.59 AW	23430 AAW	WABLS	10//99-12//99
	Seattle-Bellevue-Everett PMSA, WA	S	13.20 MW	12.74 AW	27450 AAW	WABLS	10//99-12//99
	Spokane MSA, WA	S	10.81 MW	10.69 AW	22490 AAW	WABLS	10//99-12//99
	Tacoma PMSA, WA	S	11.63 MW	11.62 AW	24200 AAW	WABLS	10//99-12//99
	Yakima MSA, WA	S	10.74 MW	10.76 AW	22350 AAW	WABLS	10//99-12//99
	West Virginia	S	7.78 MW	8.66 AW	18000 AAW	WVBLS	10//99-12//99
	Charleston MSA, WV	S	8.54 MW	7.75 AW	17770 AAW	WVBLS	10//99-12//99
	Huntington-Ashland MSA, WV-KY-OH	S	8.88 MW	7.60 AW	18470 AAW	WVBLS	10//99-12//99
	Parkersburg-Marietta MSA, WV-OH	S	7.72 MW	7.42 AW	16050 AAW	WVBLS	10//99-12//99
	Wheeling MSA, WV-OH	S	7.77 MW	7.69 AW	16170 AAW	WVBLS	10//99-12//99
	Wisconsin	S	11.67 MW	12.50 AW	26000 AAW	WIBLS	10//99-12//99
	Appleton-Oshkosh-Neenah MSA, WI	S	11.82 MW	11.16 AW	24590 AAW	WIBLS	10//99-12//99
	Green Bay MSA, WI	S	14.04 MW	12.87 AW	29210 AAW	WIBLS	10//99-12//99
	Janesville-Beloit MSA, WI	S	11.28 MW	9.79 AW	23470 AAW	WIBLS	10//99-12//99
	La Crosse MSA, WI-MN	S	11.61 MW	11.78 AW	24140 AAW	WIBLS	10//99-12//99
	Madison MSA, WI	S	11.79 MW	11.81 AW	24530 AAW	WIBLS	10//99-12//99
	Milwaukee-Waukesha PMSA, WI	S	14.39 MW	13.65 AW	29940 AAW	WIBLS	10//99-12//99
	Racine PMSA, WI	S	10.78 MW	11.09 AW	22410 AAW	WIBLS	10//99-12//99
	Sheboygan MSA, WI	S	12.55 MW	12.91 AW	26110 AAW	WIBLS	10//99-12//99
	Wausau MSA, WI	S	9.74 MW	9.76 AW	20270 AAW	WIBLS	10//99-12//99
	Wyoming	S	8.89 MW	9.59 AW	19940 AAW	WYBLS	10//99-12//99
	Casper MSA, WY	S	15.19 MW	14.85 AW	31580 AAW	WYBLS	10//99-12//99
	Puerto Rico	S	7.43 MW	7.58 AW	15770 AAW	PRBLS	10//99-12//99
	Arecibo PMSA, PR	S	6.15 MW	6.04 AW	12790 AAW	PRBLS	10//99-12//99
	Caguas PMSA, PR	S	7.88 MW	7.81 AW	16390 AAW	PRBLS	10//99-12//99
	Mayaguez MSA, PR	S	5.89 MW	6.02 AW	12240 AAW	PRBLS	10//99-12//99
	Ponce MSA, PR	S	6.49 MW	6.43 AW	13500 AAW	PRBLS	10//99-12//99
	San Juan-Bayamon PMSA, PR	S	7.82 MW	7.78 AW	16270 AAW	PRBLS	10//99-12//99
	Guam	S	8.93 MW	9.45 AW	19660 AAW	GUBLS	10//99-12//99
Orthotist and Prosthetist	California	S	16.56 MW	18.43 AW	38330 AAW	CABLS	10//99-12//99
	Colorado	S	15.75 MW	17.14 AW	35650 AAW	COBLS	10//99-12//99
	Florida	S	14.01 MW	14.55 AW	30250 AAW	FLBLS	10//99-12//99
	Georgia	S	14.58 MW	16.25 AW	33810 AAW	GABLS	10//99-12//99
	Illinois	S	16.83 MW	20.30 AW	42220 AAW	ILBLS	10//99-12//99

AAW Average annual wage	AOH Average offered, high	ASH Average starting, high	H Hourly	M Monthly	S Special: hourly and annual
AE Average entry wage	AOL Average offered, low	ASL Average starting, low	HI Highest wage paid	MTC Median total compensation	TQ Third quartile wage
AEX Average experienced wage	APH Average pay, high range	AW Average wage paid	HR High end range	MW Median wage paid	W Weekly
AO Average offered	APL Average pay, low range	FQ First quartile wage	LR Low end range	SQ Second quartile wage	Y Yearly

Occupation/Type/Industry	Location	Per	Low	Mid	High	Source	Date
Orthotist and Prosthetist	Indiana	S	12.09 MW	19.32 AW	40190 AAW	INBLS	10//99-12//99
	Iowa	S	16.87 MW	24.04 AW	50010 AAW	IABLS	10//99-12//99
	Kansas	S	22.59 MW	23.20 AW	48260 AAW	KSBLS	10//99-12//99
	Louisiana	S	15.27 MW	17.16 AW	35690 AAW	LABLS	10//99-12//99
	Michigan	S	22.7 MW	22.35 AW	46490 AAW	MIBLS	10//99-12//99
	Minnesota	S	27.31 MW	26.00 AW	54090 AAW	MNBLS	10//99-12//99
	Mississippi	S	14.48 MW	13.78 AW	28670 AAW	MSBLS	10//99-12//99
	New Hampshire	S	22.55 MW	20.38 AW	42390 AAW	NHBLS	10//99-12//99
	New Mexico	S	18.75 MW	18.66 AW	38820 AAW	NMBLS	10//99-12//99
	New York	S	35.14 MW	29.29 AW	60930 AAW	NYBLS	10//99-12//99
	North Carolina	S	24.21 MW	23.55 AW	48980 AAW	NCBLS	10//99-12//99
	Oregon	S	16.13 MW	20.28 AW	42190 AAW	ORBLS	10//99-12//99
	Pennsylvania	S	8.48 MW	10.85 AW	22570 AAW	PABLS	10//99-12//99
	Texas	S	23.69 MW	22.98 AW	47810 AAW	TXBLS	10//99-12//99
	Virginia	S	25.01 MW	25.46 AW	52960 AAW	VABLS	10//99-12//99
	Washington	S	22.76 MW	23.54 AW	48960 AAW	WABLS	10//99-12//99
	Wisconsin	S	14.99 MW	19.47 AW	40500 AAW	WIBLS	10//99-12//99
Outdoor Power Equipment and Other Small Engine Mechanic	Alabama	S	7.82 MW	8.61 AW	17910 AAW	ALBLS	10//99-12//99
	Birmingham MSA, AL	S	8.31 MW	7.89 AW	17280 AAW	ALBLS	10//99-12//99
	Dothan MSA, AL	S	6.33 MW	6.26 AW	13170 AAW	ALBLS	10//99-12//99
	Florence MSA, AL	S	6.39 MW	6.06 AW	13290 AAW	ALBLS	10//99-12//99
	Huntsville MSA, AL	S	11.03 MW	10.29 AW	22950 AAW	ALBLS	10//99-12//99
	Mobile MSA, AL	S	13.23 MW	11.42 AW	27510 AAW	ALBLS	10//99-12//99
	Montgomery MSA, AL	S	13.49 MW	13.33 AW	28050 AAW	ALBLS	10//99-12//99
	Alaska	S	12.26 MW	14.09 AW	29300 AAW	AKBLS	10//99-12//99
	Arizona	S	11.22 MW	11.19 AW	23280 AAW	AZBLS	10//99-12//99
	Phoenix-Mesa MSA, AZ	S	11.55 MW	11.71 AW	24020 AAW	AZBLS	10//99-12//99
	Tucson MSA, AZ	S	10.34 MW	10.14 AW	21500 AAW	AZBLS	10//99-12//99
	Arkansas	S	8.71 MW	8.66 AW	18010 AAW	ARBLS	10//99-12//99
	Little Rock-North Little Rock MSA, AR	S	7.09 MW	6.23 AW	14750 AAW	ARBLS	10//99-12//99
	California	S	12.15 MW	12.37 AW	25730 AAW	CABLS	10//99-12//99
	Fresno MSA, CA	S	12.45 MW	11.68 AW	25900 AAW	CABLS	10//99-12//99
	Los Angeles-Long Beach PMSA, CA	S	13.93 MW	14.48 AW	28980 AAW	CABLS	10//99-12//99
	Modesto MSA, CA	S	12.67 MW	12.48 AW	26340 AAW	CABLS	10//99-12//99
	Oakland PMSA, CA	S	12.30 MW	11.92 AW	25590 AAW	CABLS	10//99-12//99
	Orange County PMSA, CA	S	11.96 MW	10.88 AW	24880 AAW	CABLS	10//99-12//99
	Redding MSA, CA	S	11.97 MW	12.50 AW	24890 AAW	CABLS	10//99-12//99
	Riverside-San Bernardino PMSA, CA	S	14.74 MW	14.87 AW	30660 AAW	CABLS	10//99-12//99
	Sacramento PMSA, CA	S	14.09 MW	14.28 AW	29320 AAW	CABLS	10//99-12//99
	San Diego MSA, CA	S	11.69 MW	11.72 AW	24320 AAW	CABLS	10//99-12//99
	San Jose PMSA, CA	S	11.88 MW	11.94 AW	24710 AAW	CABLS	10//99-12//99
	Santa Rosa PMSA, CA	S	13.50 MW	13.37 AW	28080 AAW	CABLS	10//99-12//99
	Stockton-Lodi MSA, CA	S	12.34 MW	11.86 AW	25670 AAW	CABLS	10//99-12//99
	Yolo PMSA, CA	S	11.21 MW	11.24 AW	23320 AAW	CABLS	10//99-12//99
	Colorado	S	12.17 MW	12.37 AW	25730 AAW	COBLS	10//99-12//99
	Boulder-Longmont PMSA, CO	S	11.89 MW	13.59 AW	24720 AAW	COBLS	10//99-12//99
	Denver PMSA, CO	S	13.56 MW	12.71 AW	28210 AAW	COBLS	10//99-12//99
	Connecticut	S	14.6 MW	15.16 AW	31530 AAW	CTBLS	10//99-12//99
	Danbury PMSA, CT	S	14.01 MW	12.98 AW	29140 AAW	CTBLS	10//99-12//99
	Hartford MSA, CT	S	13.87 MW	14.13 AW	28840 AAW	CTBLS	10//99-12//99
	Stamford-Norwalk PMSA, CT	S	19.23 MW	19.16 AW	40010 AAW	CTBLS	10//99-12//99
	Delaware	S	10.94 MW	11.06 AW	23000 AAW	DEBLS	10//99-12//99
	Washington PMSA, DC-MD-VA-WV	S	12.51 MW	11.66 AW	26010 AAW	DCBLS	10//99-12//99
	Florida	S	11.76 MW	12.25 AW	25480 AAW	FLBLS	10//99-12//99
	Fort Lauderdale PMSA, FL	S	12.81 MW	12.90 AW	26650 AAW	FLBLS	10//99-12//99
	Fort Myers-Cape Coral MSA, FL	S	11.50 MW	10.90 AW	23910 AAW	FLBLS	10//99-12//99
	Jacksonville MSA, FL	S	11.29 MW	10.65 AW	23480 AAW	FLBLS	10//99-12//99
	Lakeland-Winter Haven MSA, FL	S	11.18 MW	10.57 AW	23260 AAW	FLBLS	10//99-12//99
	Melbourne-Titusville-Palm Bay MSA, FL	S	9.20 MW	7.78 AW	19130 AAW	FLBLS	10//99-12//99
	Miami PMSA, FL	S	12.86 MW	12.29 AW	26760 AAW	FLBLS	10//99-12//99
	Orlando MSA, FL	S	14.62 MW	14.36 AW	30410 AAW	FLBLS	10//99-12//99
	Sarasota-Bradenton MSA, FL	S	11.48 MW	10.59 AW	23880 AAW	FLBLS	10//99-12//99

AAW	Average annual wage	AOH	Average offered, high	ASH	Average starting, high	H	Hourly	M	Monthly	S	Special: hourly and annual
AE	Average entry wage	AOL	Average offered, low	ASL	Average starting, low	HI	Highest wage paid	MTC	Median total compensation	TQ	Third quartile wage
AEX	Average experienced wage	APH	Average pay, high range	AW	Average wage paid	HR	High end range	MW	Median wage paid	W	Weekly
AO	Average offered	APL	Average pay, low range	FQ	First quartile wage	LR	Low end range	SQ	Second quartile wage	Y	Yearly

Occupation/Type/Industry	Location	Per	Low	Mid	High	Source	Date
Outdoor Power Equipment and Other Small Engine Mechanic	Tampa-St. Petersburg-Clearwater MSA, FL	S	12.04 MW	11.57 AW	25040 AAW	FLBLS	10//99-12/99
	West Palm Beach-Boca Raton MSA, FL	S	11.84 MW	12.08 AW	24630 AAW	FLBLS	10//99-12/99
	Georgia	S	9.53 MW	10.29 AW	21410 AAW	GABLS	10//99-12/99
	Atlanta MSA, GA	S	11.09 MW	9.34 AW	23070 AAW	GABLS	10//99-12/99
	Hawaii	S	14.01 MW	14.16 AW	29450 AAW	HIBLS	10//99-12/99
	Honolulu MSA, HI	S	14.32 MW	14.19 AW	29780 AAW	HIBLS	10//99-12/99
	Idaho	S	11.86 MW	13.15 AW	27350 AAW	IDBLS	10//99-12/99
	Boise City MSA, ID	S	13.32 MW	13.12 AW	27710 AAW	IDBLS	10//99-12/99
	Illinois	S	11.84 MW	13.24 AW	27530 AAW	ILBLS	10//99-12/99
	Chicago PMSA, IL	S	12.71 MW	12.05 AW	26430 AAW	ILBLS	10//99-12/99
	Rockford MSA, IL	S	9.75 MW	9.42 AW	20280 AAW	ILBLS	10//99-12/99
	Indiana	S	11.89 MW	11.75 AW	24430 AAW	INBLS	10//99-12/99
	Bloomington MSA, IN	S	12.53 MW	12.55 AW	26060 AAW	INBLS	10//99-12/99
	Fort Wayne MSA, IN	S	10.43 MW	10.88 AW	21690 AAW	INBLS	10//99-12/99
	Indianapolis MSA, IN	S	13.18 MW	12.96 AW	27420 AAW	INBLS	10//99-12/99
	Terre Haute MSA, IN	S	12.63 MW	14.05 AW	26260 AAW	INBLS	10//99-12/99
	Iowa	S	11.63 MW	11.23 AW	23350 AAW	IABLS	10//99-12/99
	Kansas	S	11.09 MW	11.70 AW	24340 AAW	KSBLS	10//99-12/99
	Kentucky	S	7.78 MW	8.58 AW	17850 AAW	KYBLS	10//99-12/99
	Louisville MSA, KY-IN	S	9.95 MW	9.30 AW	20710 AAW	KYBLS	10//99-12/99
	Louisiana	S	10.42 MW	10.71 AW	22280 AAW	LABLS	10//99-12/99
	Baton Rouge MSA, LA	S	12.21 MW	14.04 AW	25390 AAW	LABLS	10//99-12/99
	Houma MSA, LA	S	10.39 MW	9.40 AW	21600 AAW	LABLS	10//99-12/99
	Lafayette MSA, LA	S	9.57 MW	9.73 AW	19890 AAW	LABLS	10//99-12/99
	Shreveport-Bossier City MSA, LA	S	8.51 MW	8.20 AW	17700 AAW	LABLS	10//99-12/99
	Maine	S	10.39 MW	10.73 AW	22320 AAW	MEBLS	10//99-12/99
	Portland MSA, ME	S	11.51 MW	11.61 AW	23930 AAW	MEBLS	10//99-12/99
	Maryland	S	12.04 MW	12.25 AW	25490 AAW	MDBLS	10//99-12/99
	Baltimore PMSA, MD	S	12.62 MW	12.35 AW	26240 AAW	MDBLS	10//99-12/99
	Cumberland MSA, MD-WV	S	13.95 MW	14.96 AW	29010 AAW	MDBLS	10//99-12/99
	Massachusetts	S	12.4 MW	12.32 AW	25620 AAW	MABLS	10//99-12/99
	Boston PMSA, MA-NH	S	12.46 MW	12.67 AW	25910 AAW	MABLS	10//99-12/99
	Lawrence PMSA, MA-NH	S	10.45 MW	10.04 AW	21740 AAW	MABLS	10//99-12/99
	Springfield MSA, MA	S	12.18 MW	12.57 AW	25340 AAW	MABLS	10//99-12/99
	Worcester PMSA, MA-CT	S	11.87 MW	11.41 AW	24690 AAW	MABLS	10//99-12/99
	Michigan	S	8.6 MW	10.17 AW	21150 AAW	MIBLS	10//99-12/99
	Ann Arbor PMSA, MI	S	9.94 MW	8.37 AW	20680 AAW	MIBLS	10//99-12/99
	Benton Harbor MSA, MI	S	10.76 MW	10.71 AW	22390 AAW	MIBLS	10//99-12/99
	Detroit PMSA, MI	S	14.16 MW	15.01 AW	29450 AAW	MIBLS	10//99-12/99
	Grand Rapids-Muskegon-Holland MSA, MI	S	15.16 MW	16.06 AW	31540 AAW	MIBLS	10//99-12/99
	Lansing-East Lansing MSA, MI	S	12.83 MW	14.22 AW	26690 AAW	MIBLS	10//99-12/99
	Minnesota	S	10.32 MW	10.88 AW	22640 AAW	MNBLS	10//99-12/99
	Minneapolis-St. Paul MSA, MN-WI	S	11.79 MW	11.90 AW	24520 AAW	MNBLS	10//99-12/99
	St. Cloud MSA, MN	S	13.14 MW	12.47 AW	27320 AAW	MNBLS	10//99-12/99
	Mississippi	S	10.13 MW	10.62 AW	22090 AAW	MSBLS	10//99-12/99
	Biloxi-Gulfport-Pascagoula MSA, MS	S	10.78 MW	11.44 AW	22410 AAW	MSBLS	10//99-12/99
	Missouri	S	10.16 MW	10.77 AW	22410 AAW	MOBLS	10//99-12/99
	Kansas City MSA, MO-KS	S	10.36 MW	10.05 AW	21540 AAW	MOBLS	10//99-12/99
	St. Louis MSA, MO-IL	S	11.10 MW	10.31 AW	23090 AAW	MOBLS	10//99-12/99
	Montana	S	7.8 MW	7.97 AW	16570 AAW	MTBLS	10//99-12/99
	Billings MSA, MT	S	6.97 MW	6.38 AW	14490 AAW	MTBLS	10//99-12/99
	Nebraska	S	10.04 MW	10.19 AW	21190 AAW	NEBLS	10//99-12/99
	Omaha MSA, NE-IA	S	10.16 MW	9.93 AW	21140 AAW	NEBLS	10//99-12/99
	Nevada	S	11.4 MW	11.65 AW	24230 AAW	NVBLS	10//99-12/99
	Las Vegas MSA, NV-AZ	S	11.42 MW	11.23 AW	23760 AAW	NVBLS	10//99-12/99
	New Hampshire	S	12.05 MW	11.97 AW	24910 AAW	NHBLS	10//99-12/99
	Portsmouth-Rochester PMSA, NH-ME	S	11.89 MW	12.09 AW	24730 AAW	NHBLS	10//99-12/99
	New Jersey	S	15.62 MW	16.01 AW	33310 AAW	NJBLS	10//99-12/99
	Middlesex-Somerset-Hunterdon PMSA, NJ	S	16.48 MW	16.08 AW	34270 AAW	NJBLS	10//99-12/99
	Monmouth-Ocean PMSA, NJ	S	15.94 MW	15.29 AW	33160 AAW	NJBLS	10//99-12/99
	Newark PMSA, NJ	S	15.00 MW	14.61 AW	31210 AAW	NJBLS	10//99-12/99
	New Mexico	S	9.71 MW	10.07 AW	20940 AAW	NMBLS	10//99-12/99
	Albuquerque MSA, NM	S	10.35 MW	10.12 AW	21520 AAW	NMBLS	10//99-12/99

AAW Average annual wage	**AOH** Average offered, high	**ASH** Average starting, high	**H** Hourly	**M** Monthly	**S** Special: hourly and annual
AE Average entry wage	**AOL** Average offered, low	**ASL** Average starting, low	**HI** Highest wage paid	**MTC** Median total compensation	**TQ** Third quartile wage
AEX Average experienced wage	**APH** Average pay, high range	**AW** Average wage paid	**HR** High end range	**MW** Median wage paid	**W** Weekly
AO Average offered	**APL** Average pay, low range	**FQ** First quartile wage	**LR** Low end range	**SQ** Second quartile wage	**Y** Yearly

1049

Occupation/Type/Industry	Location	Per	Low	Mid	High	Source	Date
Outdoor Power Equipment and Other Small Engine Mechanic	New York	S	10.65 MW	11.44 AW	23800 AAW	NYBLS	10//99-12//99
	Albany-Schenectady-Troy MSA, NY	S	11.51 MW	11.67 AW	23940 AAW	NYBLS	10//99-12//99
	Buffalo-Niagara Falls MSA, NY	S	10.97 MW	11.05 AW	22810 AAW	NYBLS	10//99-12//99
	Nassau-Suffolk PMSA, NY	S	11.32 MW	9.93 AW	23540 AAW	NYBLS	10//99-12//99
	New York PMSA, NY	S	12.08 MW	11.43 AW	25130 AAW	NYBLS	10//99-12//99
	Rochester MSA, NY	S	13.18 MW	11.83 AW	27420 AAW	NYBLS	10//99-12//99
	Utica-Rome MSA, NY	S	9.14 MW	9.24 AW	19000 AAW	NYBLS	10//99-12//99
	North Carolina	S	10.98 MW	11.46 AW	23850 AAW	NCBLS	10//99-12//99
	Charlotte-Gastonia-Rock Hill MSA, NC-SC	S	12.36 MW	11.79 AW	25710 AAW	NCBLS	10//99-12//99
	Fayetteville MSA, NC	S	6.27 MW	6.14 AW	13040 AAW	NCBLS	10//99-12//99
	Greensboro--Winston-Salem--High Point MSA, NC	S	13.33 MW	12.12 AW	27740 AAW	NCBLS	10//99-12//99
	Raleigh-Durham-Chapel Hill MSA, NC	S	12.06 MW	11.88 AW	25090 AAW	NCBLS	10//99-12//99
	North Dakota	S	9.18 MW	9.66 AW	20090 AAW	NDBLS	10//99-12//99
	Bismarck MSA, ND	S	8.28 MW	9.02 AW	17220 AAW	NDBLS	10//99-12//99
	Ohio	S	10.94 MW	11.23 AW	23350 AAW	OHBLS	10//99-12//99
	Cincinnati PMSA, OH-KY-IN	S	9.76 MW	9.08 AW	20290 AAW	OHBLS	10//99-12//99
	Cleveland-Lorain-Elyria PMSA, OH	S	13.43 MW	12.87 AW	27920 AAW	OHBLS	10//99-12//99
	Dayton-Springfield MSA, OH	S	13.81 MW	13.61 AW	28720 AAW	OHBLS	10//99-12//99
	Lima MSA, OH	S	11.12 MW	11.59 AW	23130 AAW	OHBLS	10//99-12//99
	Toledo MSA, OH	S	8.70 MW	8.78 AW	18100 AAW	OHBLS	10//99-12//99
	Youngstown-Warren MSA, OH	S	11.25 MW	9.96 AW	23390 AAW	OHBLS	10//99-12//99
	Oklahoma	S	9.94 MW	10.26 AW	21340 AAW	OKBLS	10//99-12//99
	Oklahoma City MSA, OK	S	11.29 MW	10.28 AW	23490 AAW	OKBLS	10//99-12//99
	Oregon	S	11.31 MW	11.99 AW	24940 AAW	ORBLS	10//99-12//99
	Portland-Vancouver PMSA, OR-WA	S	12.43 MW	12.23 AW	25850 AAW	ORBLS	10//99-12//99
	Salem PMSA, OR	S	13.48 MW	13.94 AW	28040 AAW	ORBLS	10//99-12//99
	Pennsylvania	S	12.13 MW	13.13 AW	27310 AAW	PABLS	10//99-12//99
	Allentown-Bethlehem-Easton MSA, PA	S	11.23 MW	11.51 AW	23350 AAW	PABLS	10//99-12//99
	Harrisburg-Lebanon-Carlisle MSA, PA	S	14.22 MW	13.92 AW	29570 AAW	PABLS	10//99-12//99
	Johnstown MSA, PA	S	10.51 MW	10.15 AW	21870 AAW	PABLS	10//99-12//99
	Lancaster MSA, PA	S	11.26 MW	10.79 AW	23430 AAW	PABLS	10//99-12//99
	Philadelphia PMSA, PA-NJ	S	17.08 MW	18.02 AW	35520 AAW	PABLS	10//99-12//99
	Pittsburgh MSA, PA	S	12.25 MW	11.12 AW	25480 AAW	PABLS	10//99-12//99
	Scranton--Wilkes-Barre--Hazleton MSA, PA	S	15.61 MW	17.69 AW	32460 AAW	PABLS	10//99-12//99
	York MSA, PA	S	11.58 MW	11.26 AW	24090 AAW	PABLS	10//99-12//99
	Rhode Island	S	12.38 MW	12.22 AW	25420 AAW	RIBLS	10//99-12//99
	South Carolina	S	8.87 MW	9.53 AW	19810 AAW	SCBLS	10//99-12//99
	Charleston-North Charleston MSA, SC	S	12.17 MW	12.46 AW	25300 AAW	SCBLS	10//99-12//99
	Greenville-Spartanburg-Anderson MSA, SC	S	9.62 MW	9.52 AW	20000 AAW	SCBLS	10//99-12//99
	South Dakota	S	7.99 MW	8.37 AW	17410 AAW	SDBLS	10//99-12//99
	Tennessee	S	10.1 MW	10.08 AW	20960 AAW	TNBLS	10//99-12//99
	Chattanooga MSA, TN-GA	S	10.90 MW	10.69 AW	22670 AAW	TNBLS	10//99-12//99
	Clarksville-Hopkinsville MSA, TN-KY	S	8.05 MW	7.68 AW	16740 AAW	TNBLS	10//99-12//99
	Memphis MSA, TN-AR-MS	S	10.38 MW	10.21 AW	21590 AAW	MSBLS	10//99-12//99
	Texas	S	10.12 MW	10.54 AW	21920 AAW	TXBLS	10//99-12//99
	Austin-San Marcos MSA, TX	S	9.64 MW	8.39 AW	20050 AAW	TXBLS	10//99-12//99
	Beaumont-Port Arthur MSA, TX	S	9.74 MW	9.67 AW	20260 AAW	TXBLS	10//99-12//99
	Dallas PMSA, TX	S	12.70 MW	12.24 AW	26420 AAW	TXBLS	10//99-12//99
	El Paso MSA, TX	S	9.50 MW	9.75 AW	19760 AAW	TXBLS	10//99-12//99
	Fort Worth-Arlington PMSA, TX	S	11.30 MW	11.47 AW	23500 AAW	TXBLS	10//99-12//99
	Houston PMSA, TX	S	9.07 MW	8.13 AW	18860 AAW	TXBLS	10//99-12//99
	San Antonio MSA, TX	S	11.38 MW	11.56 AW	23670 AAW	TXBLS	10//99-12//99
	Utah	S	12.67 MW	12.52 AW	26030 AAW	UTBLS	10//99-12//99
	Salt Lake City-Ogden MSA, UT	S	12.95 MW	12.99 AW	26930 AAW	UTBLS	10//99-12//99
	Vermont	S	10.12 MW	10.59 AW	22020 AAW	VTBLS	10//99-12//99

AAW Average annual wage	**AOH** Average offered, high	**ASH** Average starting, high	**H** Hourly	**M** Monthly	**S** Special: hourly and annual
AE Average entry wage	**AOL** Average offered, low	**ASL** Average starting, low	**HI** Highest wage paid	**MTC** Median total compensation	**TQ** Third quartile wage
AEX Average experienced wage	**APH** Average pay, high range	**AW** Average wage paid	**HR** High end range	**MW** Median wage paid	**W** Weekly
AO Average offered	**APL** Average pay, low range	**FQ** First quartile wage	**LR** Low end range	**SQ** Second quartile wage	**Y** Yearly

Occupation/Type/Industry	Location	Per	Low	Mid	High	Source	Date
Outdoor Power Equipment and Other Small Engine Mechanic	Virginia	S	10.02 MW	10.28 AW	21370 AAW	VABLS	10//99-12//99
	Lynchburg MSA, VA	S	10.46 MW	10.51 AW	21760 AAW	VABLS	10//99-12//99
	Norfolk-Virginia Beach-Newport News MSA, VA-NC	S	9.96 MW	9.84 AW	20720 AAW	VABLS	10//99-12//99
	Richmond-Petersburg MSA, VA	S	10.65 MW	10.36 AW	22150 AAW	VABLS	10//99-12//99
	Washington	S	11.76 MW	11.60 AW	24140 AAW	WABLS	10//99-12//99
	Bellingham MSA, WA	S	12.27 MW	12.13 AW	25520 AAW	WABLS	10//99-12//99
	Olympia PMSA, WA	S	12.20 MW	12.36 AW	25380 AAW	WABLS	10//99-12//99
	Seattle-Bellevue-Everett PMSA, WA	S	10.28 MW	8.37 AW	21380 AAW	WABLS	10//99-12//99
	Spokane MSA, WA	S	13.63 MW	12.87 AW	28360 AAW	WABLS	10//99-12//99
	Tacoma PMSA, WA	S	11.58 MW	10.71 AW	24090 AAW	WABLS	10//99-12//99
	West Virginia	S	7.96 MW	8.16 AW	16970 AAW	WVBLS	10//99-12//99
	Parkersburg-Marietta MSA, WV-OH	S	8.73 MW	9.13 AW	18160 AAW	WVBLS	10//99-12//99
	Wisconsin	S	12.05 MW	13.16 AW	27370 AAW	WIBLS	10//99-12//99
	Eau Claire MSA, WI	S	10.58 MW	10.27 AW	22000 AAW	WIBLS	10//99-12//99
	Green Bay MSA, WI	S	12.43 MW	12.49 AW	25850 AAW	WIBLS	10//99-12//99
	Milwaukee-Waukesha PMSA, WI	S	12.70 MW	13.47 AW	26420 AAW	WIBLS	10//99-12//99
	Puerto Rico	S	10.01 MW	11.06 AW	23000 AAW	PRBLS	10//99-12//99
	San Juan-Bayamon PMSA, PR	S	11.02 MW	10.06 AW	22930 AAW	PRBLS	10//99-12//99
Owner/Manager Funeral Parlor	United States	Y	53000 APL		72000 APH	NYT1	1999
Packaging and Filling Machine Operator and Tender	Alabama	S	9.32 MW	9.31 AW	19360 AAW	ALBLS	10//99-12//99
	Birmingham MSA, AL	S	10.21 MW	10.11 AW	21250 AAW	ALBLS	10//99-12//99
	Decatur MSA, AL	S	9.94 MW	11.21 AW	20680 AAW	ALBLS	10//99-12//99
	Dothan MSA, AL	S	8.30 MW	7.40 AW	17260 AAW	ALBLS	10//99-12//99
	Florence MSA, AL	S	10.76 MW	10.15 AW	22380 AAW	ALBLS	10//99-12//99
	Huntsville MSA, AL	S	7.58 MW	7.63 AW	15780 AAW	ALBLS	10//99-12//99
	Mobile MSA, AL	S	9.64 MW	10.12 AW	20040 AAW	ALBLS	10//99-12//99
	Montgomery MSA, AL	S	9.07 MW	9.43 AW	18860 AAW	ALBLS	10//99-12//99
	Alaska	S	10.66 MW	11.42 AW	23750 AAW	AKBLS	10//99-12//99
	Anchorage MSA, AK	S	10.43 MW	8.30 AW	21700 AAW	AKBLS	10//99-12//99
	Arizona	S	7.91 MW	8.37 AW	17410 AAW	AZBLS	10//99-12//99
	Phoenix-Mesa MSA, AZ	S	8.51 MW	8.22 AW	17710 AAW	AZBLS	10//99-12//99
	Tucson MSA, AZ	S	7.10 MW	7.17 AW	14780 AAW	AZBLS	10//99-12//99
	Arkansas	S	7.74 MW	7.86 AW	16350 AAW	ARBLS	10//99-12//99
	Fayetteville-Springdale-Rogers MSA, AR	S	7.95 MW	7.87 AW	16530 AAW	ARBLS	10//99-12//99
	Fort Smith MSA, AR-OK	S	7.60 MW	7.66 AW	15820 AAW	ARBLS	10//99-12//99
	Little Rock-North Little Rock MSA, AR	S	7.74 MW	7.39 AW	16090 AAW	ARBLS	10//99-12//99
	California	S	8.27 MW	9.86 AW	20510 AAW	CABLS	10//99-12//99
	Bakersfield MSA, CA	S	10.30 MW	9.62 AW	21420 AAW	CABLS	10//99-12//99
	Chico-Paradise MSA, CA	S	6.99 MW	6.38 AW	14540 AAW	CABLS	10//99-12//99
	Fresno MSA, CA	S	10.70 MW	8.27 AW	22250 AAW	CABLS	10//99-12//99
	Los Angeles-Long Beach PMSA, CA	S	9.78 MW	7.76 AW	20340 AAW	CABLS	10//99-12//99
	Merced MSA, CA	S	13.93 MW	14.72 AW	28970 AAW	CABLS	10//99-12//99
	Modesto MSA, CA	S	11.27 MW	11.50 AW	23440 AAW	CABLS	10//99-12//99
	Oakland PMSA, CA	S	11.78 MW	9.63 AW	24510 AAW	CABLS	10//99-12//99
	Orange County PMSA, CA	S	9.45 MW	7.20 AW	19660 AAW	CABLS	10//99-12//99
	Redding MSA, CA	S	8.76 MW	8.78 AW	18220 AAW	CABLS	10//99-12//99
	Riverside-San Bernardino PMSA, CA	S	7.74 MW	7.24 AW	16100 AAW	CABLS	10//99-12//99
	Sacramento PMSA, CA	S	11.87 MW	11.82 AW	24690 AAW	CABLS	10//99-12//99
	Salinas MSA, CA	S	8.33 MW	6.71 AW	17330 AAW	CABLS	10//99-12//99
	San Diego MSA, CA	S	8.35 MW	7.85 AW	17360 AAW	CABLS	10//99-12//99
	San Francisco PMSA, CA	S	9.88 MW	9.32 AW	20550 AAW	CABLS	10//99-12//99
	San Jose PMSA, CA	S	10.34 MW	10.11 AW	21500 AAW	CABLS	10//99-12//99
	San Luis Obispo-Atascadero-Paso Robles MSA, CA	S	9.32 MW	8.93 AW	19390 AAW	CABLS	10//99-12//99
	Santa Cruz-Watsonville PMSA, CA	S	8.21 MW	7.80 AW	17070 AAW	CABLS	10//99-12//99
	Santa Rosa PMSA, CA	S	10.20 MW	9.29 AW	21210 AAW	CABLS	10//99-12//99

Occupation/Type/Industry	Location	Per	Low	Mid	High	Source	Date
Packaging and Filling Machine Operator and Tender	Stockton-Lodi MSA, CA	S	12.46 MW	12.43 AW	25920 AAW	CABLS	10//99-12//99
	Vallejo-Fairfield-Napa PMSA, CA	S	10.37 MW	9.72 AW	21570 AAW	CABLS	10//99-12//99
	Ventura PMSA, CA	S	11.54 MW	9.87 AW	24000 AAW	CABLS	10//99-12//99
	Visalia-Tulare-Porterville MSA, CA	S	6.72 MW	6.41 AW	13980 AAW	CABLS	10//99-12//99
	Yolo PMSA, CA	S	11.77 MW	11.14 AW	24490 AAW	CABLS	10//99-12//99
	Colorado	S	9.98 MW	10.53 AW	21900 AAW	COBLS	10//99-12//99
	Colorado Springs MSA, CO	S	10.49 MW	9.64 AW	21810 AAW	COBLS	10//99-12//99
	Denver PMSA, CO	S	11.44 MW	10.60 AW	23800 AAW	COBLS	10//99-12//99
	Fort Collins-Loveland MSA, CO	S	11.50 MW	10.25 AW	23930 AAW	COBLS	10//99-12//99
	Grand Junction MSA, CO	S	9.69 MW	8.11 AW	20160 AAW	COBLS	10//99-12//99
	Greeley PMSA, CO	S	8.69 MW	9.09 AW	18080 AAW	COBLS	10//99-12//99
	Connecticut	S	8.47 MW	9.61 AW	19980 AAW	CTBLS	10//99-12//99
	Bridgeport PMSA, CT	S	8.06 MW	7.69 AW	16770 AAW	CTBLS	10//99-12//99
	Hartford MSA, CT	S	9.51 MW	8.27 AW	19780 AAW	CTBLS	10//99-12//99
	New Haven-Meriden PMSA, CT	S	9.80 MW	9.55 AW	20390 AAW	CTBLS	10//99-12//99
	New London-Norwich MSA, CT-RI	S	8.11 MW	7.96 AW	16880 AAW	CTBLS	10//99-12//99
	Stamford-Norwalk PMSA, CT	S	9.84 MW	8.33 AW	20460 AAW	CTBLS	10//99-12//99
	Waterbury PMSA, CT	S	9.21 MW	8.63 AW	19150 AAW	CTBLS	10//99-12//99
	Delaware	S	12.83 MW	12.84 AW	26710 AAW	DEBLS	10//99-12//99
	Wilmington-Newark PMSA, DE-MD	S	12.78 MW	12.39 AW	26570 AAW	DEBLS	10//99-12//99
	Washington PMSA, DC-MD-VA-WV	S	8.82 MW	7.87 AW	18350 AAW	DCBLS	10//99-12//99
	Florida	S	7.25 MW	7.55 AW	15700 AAW	FLBLS	10//99-12//99
	Daytona Beach MSA, FL	S	7.66 MW	7.60 AW	15930 AAW	FLBLS	10//99-12//99
	Fort Lauderdale PMSA, FL	S	7.77 MW	7.47 AW	16170 AAW	FLBLS	10//99-12//99
	Fort Myers-Cape Coral MSA, FL	S	9.58 MW	9.60 AW	19920 AAW	FLBLS	10//99-12//99
	Fort Pierce-Port St. Lucie MSA, FL	S	9.45 MW	9.58 AW	19660 AAW	FLBLS	10//99-12//99
	Jacksonville MSA, FL	S	11.64 MW	10.88 AW	24220 AAW	FLBLS	10//99-12//99
	Lakeland-Winter Haven MSA, FL	S	8.73 MW	9.09 AW	18150 AAW	FLBLS	10//99-12//99
	Miami PMSA, FL	S	8.03 MW	7.75 AW	16700 AAW	FLBLS	10//99-12//99
	Orlando MSA, FL	S	9.04 MW	8.48 AW	18810 AAW	FLBLS	10//99-12//99
	Sarasota-Bradenton MSA, FL	S	7.10 MW	6.98 AW	14770 AAW	FLBLS	10//99-12//99
	Tampa-St. Petersburg-Clearwater MSA, FL	S	7.44 MW	7.19 AW	15480 AAW	FLBLS	10//99-12//99
	West Palm Beach-Boca Raton MSA, FL	S	7.12 MW	6.92 AW	14810 AAW	FLBLS	10//99-12//99
	Georgia	S	8.48 MW	9.66 AW	20100 AAW	GABLS	10//99-12//99
	Athens MSA, GA	S	7.86 MW	7.67 AW	16350 AAW	GABLS	10//99-12//99
	Atlanta MSA, GA	S	10.18 MW	9.65 AW	21170 AAW	GABLS	10//99-12//99
	Augusta-Aiken MSA, GA-SC	S	13.00 MW	12.50 AW	27030 AAW	GABLS	10//99-12//99
	Columbus MSA, GA-AL	S	9.30 MW	8.27 AW	19340 AAW	GABLS	10//99-12//99
	Macon MSA, GA	S	7.82 MW	7.74 AW	16270 AAW	GABLS	10//99-12//99
	Savannah MSA, GA	S	8.36 MW	6.96 AW	17380 AAW	GABLS	10//99-12//99
	Hawaii	S	10.82 MW	10.44 AW	21720 AAW	HIBLS	10//99-12//99
	Honolulu MSA, HI	S	10.53 MW	10.83 AW	21900 AAW	HIBLS	10//99-12//99
	Idaho	S	8.61 MW	8.76 AW	18210 AAW	IDBLS	10//99-12//99
	Boise City MSA, ID	S	11.82 MW	11.92 AW	24590 AAW	IDBLS	10//99-12//99
	Illinois	S	9.67 MW	10.61 AW	22070 AAW	ILBLS	10//99-12//99
	Chicago PMSA, IL	S	10.50 MW	9.61 AW	21840 AAW	ILBLS	10//99-12//99
	Peoria-Pekin MSA, IL	S	9.71 MW	8.30 AW	20190 AAW	ILBLS	10//99-12//99
	Rockford MSA, IL	S	10.61 MW	10.79 AW	22070 AAW	ILBLS	10//99-12//99
	Indiana	S	9.14 MW	9.63 AW	20030 AAW	INBLS	10//99-12//99
	Elkhart-Goshen MSA, IN	S	10.92 MW	10.26 AW	22710 AAW	INBLS	10//99-12//99
	Evansville-Henderson MSA, IN-KY	S	9.76 MW	9.79 AW	20300 AAW	INBLS	10//99-12//99
	Fort Wayne MSA, IN	S	10.95 MW	11.57 AW	22780 AAW	INBLS	10//99-12//99
	Gary PMSA, IN	S	9.22 MW	8.43 AW	19180 AAW	INBLS	10//99-12//99
	Indianapolis MSA, IN	S	11.66 MW	11.72 AW	24240 AAW	INBLS	10//99-12//99
	Muncie MSA, IN	S	7.01 MW	7.27 AW	14580 AAW	INBLS	10//99-12//99
	South Bend MSA, IN	S	7.20 MW	7.33 AW	14980 AAW	INBLS	10//99-12//99
	Terre Haute MSA, IN	S	13.50 MW	13.57 AW	28070 AAW	INBLS	10//99-12//99
	Iowa	S	10.09 MW	10.16 AW	21120 AAW	IABLS	10//99-12//99

AAW Average annual wage	AOH Average offered, high	ASH Average starting, high	H Hourly	M Monthly	S Special: hourly and annual
AE Average entry wage	AOL Average offered, low	ASL Average starting, low	HI Highest wage paid	MTC Median total compensation	TQ Third quartile wage
AEX Average experienced wage	APH Average pay, high range	AW Average wage paid	HR High end range	MW Median wage paid	W Weekly
AO Average offered	APL Average pay, low range	FQ First quartile wage	LR Low end range	SQ Second quartile wage	Y Yearly

Occupation/Type/Industry	Location	Per	Low	Mid	High	Source	Date
Packaging and Filling Machine Operator and Tender							
	Des Moines MSA, IA	S	10.00 MW	9.82 AW	20800 AAW	IABLS	10//99-12//99
	Sioux City MSA, IA-NE	S	8.42 MW	8.24 AW	17520 AAW	IABLS	10//99-12//99
	Waterloo-Cedar Falls MSA, IA	S	10.35 MW	9.72 AW	21530 AAW	IABLS	10//99-12//99
	Kansas	S	10.6 MW	11.22 AW	23340 AAW	KSBLS	10//99-12//99
	Wichita MSA, KS	S	12.04 MW	12.14 AW	25040 AAW	KSBLS	10//99-12//99
	Kentucky	S	11.48 MW	11.66 AW	24260 AAW	KYBLS	10//99-12//99
	Lexington MSA, KY	S	12.60 MW	14.02 AW	26210 AAW	KYBLS	10//99-12//99
	Louisville MSA, KY-IN	S	11.66 MW	11.17 AW	24250 AAW	KYBLS	10//99-12//99
	Louisiana	S	9.44 MW	9.66 AW	20100 AAW	LABLS	10//99-12//99
	Baton Rouge MSA, LA	S	11.64 MW	11.76 AW	24200 AAW	LABLS	10//99-12//99
	Monroe MSA, LA	S	8.30 MW	6.58 AW	17260 AAW	LABLS	10//99-12//99
	New Orleans MSA, LA	S	8.70 MW	8.27 AW	18110 AAW	LABLS	10//99-12//99
	Maine	S	10.46 MW	11.24 AW	23380 AAW	MEBLS	10//99-12//99
	Portland MSA, ME	S	10.58 MW	11.71 AW	22010 AAW	MEBLS	10//99-12//99
	Maryland	S	10.82 MW	11.31 AW	23520 AAW	MDBLS	10//99-12//99
	Baltimore PMSA, MD	S	10.14 MW	10.44 AW	21080 AAW	MDBLS	10//99-12//99
	Hagerstown PMSA, MD	S	10.91 MW	10.72 AW	22700 AAW	MDBLS	10//99-12//99
	Massachusetts	S	9.05 MW	9.63 AW	20040 AAW	MABLS	10//99-12//99
	Boston PMSA, MA-NH	S	9.52 MW	8.93 AW	19800 AAW	MABLS	10//99-12//99
	Lawrence PMSA, MA-NH	S	10.05 MW	9.62 AW	20900 AAW	MABLS	10//99-12//99
	Lowell PMSA, MA-NH	S	7.76 MW	7.63 AW	16140 AAW	MABLS	10//99-12//99
	Springfield MSA, MA	S	10.82 MW	10.81 AW	22510 AAW	MABLS	10//99-12//99
	Worcester PMSA, MA-CT	S	9.60 MW	8.33 AW	19960 AAW	MABLS	10//99-12//99
	Michigan	S	8.91 MW	10.81 AW	22490 AAW	MIBLS	10//99-12//99
	Ann Arbor PMSA, MI	S	11.92 MW	9.96 AW	24800 AAW	MIBLS	10//99-12//99
	Detroit PMSA, MI	S	10.24 MW	8.31 AW	21290 AAW	MIBLS	10//99-12//99
	Grand Rapids-Muskegon-Holland MSA, MI	S	11.32 MW	10.70 AW	23550 AAW	MIBLS	10//99-12//99
	Jackson MSA, MI	S	11.27 MW	11.56 AW	23440 AAW	MIBLS	10//99-12//99
	Kalamazoo-Battle Creek MSA, MI	S	14.27 MW	10.53 AW	29690 AAW	MIBLS	10//99-12//99
	Lansing-East Lansing MSA, MI	S	9.06 MW	8.59 AW	18840 AAW	MIBLS	10//99-12//99
	Saginaw-Bay City-Midland MSA, MI	S	8.31 MW	7.80 AW	17290 AAW	MIBLS	10//99-12//99
	Minnesota	S	11.29 MW	11.82 AW	24580 AAW	MNBLS	10//99-12//99
	Minneapolis-St. Paul MSA, MN-WI	S	12.77 MW	12.73 AW	26560 AAW	MNBLS	10//99-12//99
	St. Cloud MSA, MN	S	10.55 MW	10.23 AW	21950 AAW	MNBLS	10//99-12//99
	Mississippi	S	8.47 MW	8.87 AW	18450 AAW	MSBLS	10//99-12//99
	Jackson MSA, MS	S	8.26 MW	7.71 AW	17170 AAW	MSBLS	10//99-12//99
	Missouri	S	9.49 MW	11.03 AW	22950 AAW	MOBLS	10//99-12//99
	Joplin MSA, MO	S	6.30 MW	6.19 AW	13100 AAW	MOBLS	10//99-12//99
	Kansas City MSA, MO-KS	S	10.68 MW	9.71 AW	22220 AAW	MOBLS	10//99-12//99
	St. Joseph MSA, MO	S	8.24 MW	7.88 AW	17130 AAW	MOBLS	10//99-12//99
	St. Louis MSA, MO-IL	S	11.72 MW	11.13 AW	24370 AAW	MOBLS	10//99-12//99
	Springfield MSA, MO	S	8.56 MW	6.75 AW	17800 AAW	MOBLS	10//99-12//99
	Montana	S	8.98 MW	8.88 AW	18470 AAW	MTBLS	10//99-12//99
	Great Falls MSA, MT	S	9.40 MW	8.57 AW	19550 AAW	MTBLS	10//99-12//99
	Missoula MSA, MT	S	7.94 MW	7.56 AW	16520 AAW	MTBLS	10//99-12//99
	Nebraska	S	9.08 MW	9.01 AW	18750 AAW	NEBLS	10//99-12//99
	Lincoln MSA, NE	S	8.42 MW	8.61 AW	17520 AAW	NEBLS	10//99-12//99
	Nevada	S	7.83 MW	8.31 AW	17290 AAW	NVBLS	10//99-12//99
	Las Vegas MSA, NV-AZ	S	8.55 MW	7.74 AW	17780 AAW	NVBLS	10//99-12//99
	Reno MSA, NV	S	8.18 MW	7.82 AW	17020 AAW	NVBLS	10//99-12//99
	New Hampshire	S	11.52 MW	12.29 AW	25560 AAW	NHBLS	10//99-12//99
	Nashua PMSA, NH	S	10.34 MW	9.92 AW	21510 AAW	NHBLS	10//99-12//99
	New Jersey	S	9.63 MW	10.62 AW	22100 AAW	NJBLS	10//99-12//99
	Atlantic-Cape May PMSA, NJ	S	9.80 MW	9.79 AW	20380 AAW	NJBLS	10//99-12//99
	Bergen-Passaic PMSA, NJ	S	10.33 MW	10.18 AW	21490 AAW	NJBLS	10//99-12//99
	Jersey City PMSA, NJ	S	12.59 MW	12.06 AW	26190 AAW	NJBLS	10//99-12//99
	Middlesex-Somerset-Hunterdon PMSA, NJ	S	11.43 MW	9.56 AW	23760 AAW	NJBLS	10//99-12//99
	Monmouth-Ocean PMSA, NJ	S	9.99 MW	10.51 AW	20780 AAW	NJBLS	10//99-12//99
	Newark PMSA, NJ	S	9.01 MW	7.58 AW	18750 AAW	NJBLS	10//99-12//99
	Trenton PMSA, NJ	S	9.41 MW	8.60 AW	19560 AAW	NJBLS	10//99-12//99
	Vineland-Millville-Bridgeton PMSA, NJ	S	9.38 MW	8.98 AW	19500 AAW	NJBLS	10//99-12//99
	New Mexico	S	7.57 MW	7.97 AW	16570 AAW	NMBLS	10//99-12//99
	Albuquerque MSA, NM	S	8.58 MW	7.97 AW	17840 AAW	NMBLS	10//99-12//99
	New York	S	8.28 MW	9.69 AW	20160 AAW	NYBLS	10//99-12//99

AAW Average annual wage	AOH Average offered, high	ASH Average starting, high	H Hourly	M Monthly	S Special: hourly and annual
AE Average entry wage	AOL Average offered, low	ASL Average starting, low	HI Highest wage paid	MTC Median total compensation	TQ Third quartile wage
AEX Average experienced wage	APH Average pay, high range	AW Average wage paid	HR High end range	MW Median wage paid	W Weekly
AO Average offered	APL Average pay, low range	FQ First quartile wage	LR Low end range	SQ Second quartile wage	Y Yearly

Occupation/Type/Industry	Location	Per	Low	Mid	High	Source	Date
Packaging and Filling Machine Operator and Tender							
	Albany-Schenectady-Troy MSA, NY	S	9.74 MW	9.73 AW	20270 AAW	NYBLS	10//99-12//99
	Binghamton MSA, NY	S	10.85 MW	10.89 AW	22570 AAW	NYBLS	10//99-12//99
	Buffalo-Niagara Falls MSA, NY	S	8.74 MW	8.53 AW	18170 AAW	NYBLS	10//99-12//99
	Elmira MSA, NY	S	9.74 MW	8.53 AW	20260 AAW	NYBLS	10//99-12//99
	Glens Falls MSA, NY	S	15.16 MW	15.25 AW	31530 AAW	NYBLS	10//99-12//99
	Nassau-Suffolk PMSA, NY	S	7.33 MW	7.05 AW	15260 AAW	NYBLS	10//99-12//99
	New York PMSA, NY	S	10.77 MW	8.45 AW	22400 AAW	NYBLS	10//99-12//99
	Newburgh PMSA, NY-PA	S	8.41 MW	8.81 AW	17480 AAW	NYBLS	10//99-12//99
	Rochester MSA, NY	S	10.62 MW	10.13 AW	22090 AAW	NYBLS	10//99-12//99
	Syracuse MSA, NY	S	10.61 MW	9.73 AW	22060 AAW	NYBLS	10//99-12//99
	Utica-Rome MSA, NY	S	7.35 MW	6.91 AW	15290 AAW	NYBLS	10//99-12//99
	North Carolina	S	10.41 MW	11.58 AW	24080 AAW	NCBLS	10//99-12//99
	Asheville MSA, NC	S	8.70 MW	8.94 AW	18100 AAW	NCBLS	10//99-12//99
	Charlotte-Gastonia-Rock Hill MSA, NC-SC	S	11.33 MW	11.44 AW	23560 AAW	NCBLS	10//99-12//99
	Fayetteville MSA, NC	S	6.10 MW	6.12 AW	12700 AAW	NCBLS	10//99-12//99
	Goldsboro MSA, NC	S	7.14 MW	7.25 AW	14840 AAW	NCBLS	10//99-12//99
	Greensboro--Winston-Salem--High Point MSA, NC	S	14.21 MW	10.64 AW	29550 AAW	NCBLS	10//99-12//99
	Greenville MSA, NC	S	10.01 MW	7.60 AW	20820 AAW	NCBLS	10//99-12//99
	Hickory-Morganton-Lenoir MSA, NC	S	9.16 MW	9.07 AW	19060 AAW	NCBLS	10//99-12//99
	Raleigh-Durham-Chapel Hill MSA, NC	S	11.01 MW	11.35 AW	22910 AAW	NCBLS	10//99-12//99
	Wilmington MSA, NC	S	8.73 MW	7.23 AW	18160 AAW	NCBLS	10//99-12//99
	North Dakota	S	7.59 MW	7.81 AW	16240 AAW	NDBLS	10//99-12//99
	Bismarck MSA, ND	S	8.01 MW	7.87 AW	16650 AAW	NDBLS	10//99-12//99
	Ohio	S	9.81 MW	10.48 AW	21800 AAW	OHBLS	10//99-12//99
	Akron PMSA, OH	S	11.72 MW	12.10 AW	24380 AAW	OHBLS	10//99-12//99
	Canton-Massillon MSA, OH	S	9.54 MW	9.73 AW	19850 AAW	OHBLS	10//99-12//99
	Cincinnati PMSA, OH-KY-IN	S	11.84 MW	10.74 AW	24620 AAW	OHBLS	10//99-12//99
	Cleveland-Lorain-Elyria PMSA, OH	S	10.92 MW	11.24 AW	22700 AAW	OHBLS	10//99-12//99
	Dayton-Springfield MSA, OH	S	14.10 MW	10.59 AW	29330 AAW	OHBLS	10//99-12//99
	Lima MSA, OH	S	10.27 MW	10.23 AW	21350 AAW	OHBLS	10//99-12//99
	Mansfield MSA, OH	S	8.77 MW	8.73 AW	18240 AAW	OHBLS	10//99-12//99
	Toledo MSA, OH	S	12.60 MW	13.68 AW	26200 AAW	OHBLS	10//99-12//99
	Youngstown-Warren MSA, OH	S	10.26 MW	9.02 AW	21340 AAW	OHBLS	10//99-12//99
	Oklahoma	S	7.39 MW	7.84 AW	16300 AAW	OKBLS	10//99-12//99
	Oklahoma City MSA, OK	S	9.33 MW	9.51 AW	19400 AAW	OKBLS	10//99-12//99
	Tulsa MSA, OK	S	7.96 MW	7.53 AW	16550 AAW	OKBLS	10//99-12//99
	Oregon	S	10.25 MW	10.98 AW	22830 AAW	ORBLS	10//99-12//99
	Eugene-Springfield MSA, OR	S	12.67 MW	13.32 AW	26340 AAW	ORBLS	10//99-12//99
	Portland-Vancouver PMSA, OR-WA	S	11.56 MW	10.89 AW	24050 AAW	ORBLS	10//99-12//99
	Salem PMSA, OR	S	10.79 MW	10.75 AW	22440 AAW	ORBLS	10//99-12//99
	Pennsylvania	S	11.54 MW	11.85 AW	24640 AAW	PABLS	10//99-12//99
	Allentown-Bethlehem-Easton MSA, PA	S	12.39 MW	11.63 AW	25780 AAW	PABLS	10//99-12//99
	Altoona MSA, PA	S	14.78 MW	15.04 AW	30740 AAW	PABLS	10//99-12//99
	Erie MSA, PA	S	9.76 MW	9.57 AW	20310 AAW	PABLS	10//99-12//99
	Harrisburg-Lebanon-Carlisle MSA, PA	S	14.00 MW	13.55 AW	29110 AAW	PABLS	10//99-12//99
	Johnstown MSA, PA	S	10.38 MW	10.65 AW	21600 AAW	PABLS	10//99-12//99
	Lancaster MSA, PA	S	12.87 MW	12.61 AW	26780 AAW	PABLS	10//99-12//99
	Philadelphia PMSA, PA-NJ	S	12.16 MW	12.18 AW	25290 AAW	PABLS	10//99-12//99
	Pittsburgh MSA, PA	S	13.14 MW	13.92 AW	27330 AAW	PABLS	10//99-12//99
	Reading MSA, PA	S	11.65 MW	11.41 AW	24230 AAW	PABLS	10//99-12//99
	Scranton--Wilkes-Barre--Hazleton MSA, PA	S	10.29 MW	10.34 AW	21390 AAW	PABLS	10//99-12//99
	Williamsport MSA, PA	S	10.94 MW	11.42 AW	22760 AAW	PABLS	10//99-12//99
	York MSA, PA	S	10.57 MW	11.07 AW	21990 AAW	PABLS	10//99-12//99
	Rhode Island	S	11.05 MW	10.54 AW	21920 AAW	RIBLS	10//99-12//99
	Providence-Fall River-Warwick MSA, RI-MA	S	10.42 MW	10.93 AW	21670 AAW	RIBLS	10//99-12//99
	South Carolina	S	9.99 MW	10.99 AW	22860 AAW	SCBLS	10//99-12//99
	Columbia MSA, SC	S	11.14 MW	11.54 AW	23180 AAW	SCBLS	10//99-12//99
	Florence MSA, SC	S	9.48 MW	9.39 AW	19720 AAW	SCBLS	10//99-12//99

AAW Average annual wage	**AOH** Average offered, high	**ASH** Average starting, high	**H** Hourly	**M** Monthly	**S** Special: hourly and annual
AE Average entry wage	**AOL** Average offered, low	**ASL** Average starting, low	**HI** Highest wage paid	**MTC** Median total compensation	**TQ** Third quartile wage
AEX Average experienced wage	**APH** Average pay, high range	**AW** Average wage paid	**HR** High end range	**MW** Median wage paid	**W** Weekly
AO Average offered	**APL** Average pay, low range	**FQ** First quartile wage	**LR** Low end range	**SQ** Second quartile wage	**Y** Yearly

Occupation/Type/Industry	Location	Per	Low	Mid	High	Source	Date
Packaging and Filling Machine Operator and Tender							
	Greenville-Spartanburg-Anderson MSA, SC	S	11.98 MW	10.38 AW	24920 AAW	SCBLS	10//99-12//99
	Myrtle Beach MSA, SC	S	8.68 MW	8.06 AW	18050 AAW	SCBLS	10//99-12//99
	Sumter MSA, SC	S	8.48 MW	8.44 AW	17640 AAW	SCBLS	10//99-12//99
	South Dakota	S	9.6 MW	9.71 AW	20190 AAW	SDBLS	10//99-12//99
	Rapid City MSA, SD	S	9.22 MW	8.83 AW	19170 AAW	SDBLS	10//99-12//99
	Sioux Falls MSA, SD	S	9.84 MW	9.81 AW	20480 AAW	SDBLS	10//99-12//99
	Tennessee	S	10.16 MW	10.52 AW	21880 AAW	TNBLS	10//99-12//99
	Chattanooga MSA, TN-GA	S	11.13 MW	10.23 AW	23150 AAW	TNBLS	10//99-12//99
	Clarksville-Hopkinsville MSA, TN-KY	S	6.70 MW	6.28 AW	13950 AAW	TNBLS	10//99-12//99
	Johnson City-Kingsport-Bristol MSA, TN-VA	S	9.07 MW	9.27 AW	18860 AAW	TNBLS	10//99-12//99
	Knoxville MSA, TN	S	8.66 MW	8.44 AW	18010 AAW	TNBLS	10//99-12//99
	Memphis MSA, TN-AR-MS	S	13.08 MW	13.40 AW	27210 AAW	MSBLS	10//99-12//99
	Nashville MSA, TN	S	9.88 MW	9.93 AW	20550 AAW	TNBLS	10//99-12//99
	Texas	S	8.12 MW	9.20 AW	19140 AAW	TXBLS	10//99-12//99
	Abilene MSA, TX	S	10.77 MW	10.71 AW	22390 AAW	TXBLS	10//99-12//99
	Austin-San Marcos MSA, TX	S	8.53 MW	8.02 AW	17750 AAW	TXBLS	10//99-12//99
	Brownsville-Harlingen-San Benito MSA, TX	S	6.07 MW	5.99 AW	12620 AAW	TXBLS	10//99-12//99
	Corpus Christi MSA, TX	S	6.09 MW	6.00 AW	12660 AAW	TXBLS	10//99-12//99
	Dallas PMSA, TX	S	10.28 MW	9.81 AW	21390 AAW	TXBLS	10//99-12//99
	El Paso MSA, TX	S	8.67 MW	8.11 AW	18030 AAW	TXBLS	10//99-12//99
	Fort Worth-Arlington PMSA, TX	S	8.97 MW	8.75 AW	18660 AAW	TXBLS	10//99-12//99
	Galveston-Texas City PMSA, TX	S	6.38 MW	6.40 AW	13280 AAW	TXBLS	10//99-12//99
	Houston PMSA, TX	S	9.62 MW	7.82 AW	20000 AAW	TXBLS	10//99-12//99
	Longview-Marshall MSA, TX	S	6.41 MW	6.15 AW	13320 AAW	TXBLS	10//99-12//99
	Lubbock MSA, TX	S	6.65 MW	6.23 AW	13840 AAW	TXBLS	10//99-12//99
	McAllen-Edinburg-Mission MSA, TX	S	8.40 MW	7.76 AW	17470 AAW	TXBLS	10//99-12//99
	San Antonio MSA, TX	S	8.94 MW	8.15 AW	18600 AAW	TXBLS	10//99-12//99
	Sherman-Denison MSA, TX	S	11.89 MW	10.47 AW	24730 AAW	TXBLS	10//99-12//99
	Tyler MSA, TX	S	7.00 MW	6.45 AW	14560 AAW	TXBLS	10//99-12//99
	Waco MSA, TX	S	7.66 MW	7.50 AW	15920 AAW	TXBLS	10//99-12//99
	Utah	S	8.96 MW	8.96 AW	18630 AAW	UTBLS	10//99-12//99
	Vermont	S	9.08 MW	9.64 AW	20050 AAW	VTBLS	10//99-12//99
	Burlington MSA, VT	S	12.02 MW	12.32 AW	25000 AAW	VTBLS	10//99-12//99
	Virginia	S	10.27 MW	11.53 AW	23980 AAW	VABLS	10//99-12//99
	Norfolk-Virginia Beach-Newport News MSA, VA-NC	S	10.86 MW	9.69 AW	22580 AAW	VABLS	10//99-12//99
	Richmond-Petersburg MSA, VA	S	13.00 MW	12.70 AW	27050 AAW	VABLS	10//99-12//99
	Roanoke MSA, VA	S	11.25 MW	10.26 AW	23390 AAW	VABLS	10//99-12//99
	Washington	S	10.38 MW	10.70 AW	22260 AAW	WABLS	10//99-12//99
	Bellingham MSA, WA	S	10.19 MW	10.63 AW	21190 AAW	WABLS	10//99-12//99
	Seattle-Bellevue-Everett PMSA, WA	S	11.97 MW	13.04 AW	24900 AAW	WABLS	10//99-12//99
	Spokane MSA, WA	S	10.64 MW	9.80 AW	22140 AAW	WABLS	10//99-12//99
	Tacoma PMSA, WA	S	8.40 MW	8.01 AW	17460 AAW	WABLS	10//99-12//99
	Yakima MSA, WA	S	9.17 MW	8.16 AW	19080 AAW	WABLS	10//99-12//99
	West Virginia	S	7.24 MW	8.06 AW	16770 AAW	WVBLS	10//99-12//99
	Parkersburg-Marietta MSA, WV-OH	S	9.00 MW	7.85 AW	18710 AAW	WVBLS	10//99-12//99
	Wheeling MSA, WV-OH	S	10.17 MW	10.16 AW	21150 AAW	WVBLS	10//99-12//99
	Wisconsin	S	9.71 MW	10.23 AW	21290 AAW	WIBLS	10//99-12//99
	Appleton-Oshkosh-Neenah MSA, WI	S	13.56 MW	12.95 AW	28210 AAW	WIBLS	10//99-12//99
	Eau Claire MSA, WI	S	10.90 MW	11.28 AW	22670 AAW	WIBLS	10//99-12//99
	Green Bay MSA, WI	S	8.35 MW	6.52 AW	17370 AAW	WIBLS	10//99-12//99
	Madison MSA, WI	S	10.94 MW	10.24 AW	22760 AAW	WIBLS	10//99-12//99
	Milwaukee-Waukesha PMSA, WI	S	9.46 MW	9.31 AW	19670 AAW	WIBLS	10//99-12//99
	Racine PMSA, WI	S	8.30 MW	8.03 AW	17260 AAW	WIBLS	10//99-12//99
	Wyoming	S	9.66 MW	10.34 AW	21520 AAW	WYBLS	10//99-12//99
	Puerto Rico	S	6.49 MW	7.40 AW	15390 AAW	PRBLS	10//99-12//99
	Caguas PMSA, PR	S	7.63 MW	7.29 AW	15870 AAW	PRBLS	10//99-12//99
	Mayaguez MSA, PR	S	6.20 MW	6.06 AW	12890 AAW	PRBLS	10//99-12//99

AAW Average annual wage	**AOH** Average offered, high	**ASH** Average starting, high	**H** Hourly	**M** Monthly	**S** Special: hourly and annual
AE Average entry wage	**AOL** Average offered, low	**ASL** Average starting, low	**HI** Highest wage paid	**MTC** Median total compensation	**TQ** Third quartile wage
AEX Average experienced wage	**APH** Average pay, high range	**AW** Average wage paid	**HR** High end range	**MW** Median wage paid	**W** Weekly
AO Average offered	**APL** Average pay, low range	**FQ** First quartile wage	**LR** Low end range	**SQ** Second quartile wage	**Y** Yearly

Occupation/Type/Industry	Location	Per	Low	Mid	High	Source	Date
Packaging and Filling Machine Operator and Tender	San Juan-Bayamon PMSA, PR	S	7.50 MW	6.50 AW	15600 AAW	PRBLS	10//99-12//99
Packer and Packager							
Hand	Alabama	S	6.64 MW	7.18 AW	14930 AAW	ALBLS	10//99-12//99
Hand	Alaska	S	8.34 MW	9.10 AW	18930 AAW	AKBLS	10//99-12//99
Hand	Arizona	S	6.35 MW	6.96 AW	14480 AAW	AZBLS	10//99-12//99
Hand	Arkansas	S	7.49 MW	7.68 AW	15980 AAW	ARBLS	10//99-12//99
Hand	California	S	7.04 MW	7.92 AW	16470 AAW	CABLS	10//99-12//99
Hand	Colorado	S	6.78 MW	7.33 AW	15250 AAW	COBLS	10//99-12//99
Hand	Connecticut	S	7.43 MW	8.16 AW	16970 AAW	CTBLS	10//99-12//99
Hand	Delaware	S	7.02 MW	8.34 AW	17350 AAW	DEBLS	10//99-12//99
Hand	District of Columbia	S	7.58 MW	8.81 AW	18320 AAW	DCBLS	10//99-12//99
Hand	Florida	S	6.44 MW	6.67 AW	13870 AAW	FLBLS	10//99-12//99
Hand	Georgia	S	7.25 MW	7.57 AW	15750 AAW	GABLS	10//99-12//99
Hand	Hawaii	S	7.75 MW	8.35 AW	17360 AAW	HIBLS	10//99-12//99
Hand	Idaho	S	6.37 MW	6.90 AW	14340 AAW	IDBLS	10//99-12//99
Hand	Illinois	S	7.84 MW	8.15 AW	16950 AAW	ILBLS	10//99-12//99
Hand	Indiana	S	8.5 MW	8.68 AW	18050 AAW	INBLS	10//99-12//99
Hand	Iowa	S	7.8 MW	8.21 AW	17080 AAW	IABLS	10//99-12//99
Hand	Kansas	S	7.34 MW	7.79 AW	16200 AAW	KSBLS	10//99-12//99
Hand	Kentucky	S	7.91 MW	8.19 AW	17030 AAW	KYBLS	10//99-12//99
Hand	Louisiana	S	6.26 MW	6.86 AW	14270 AAW	LABLS	10//99-12//99
Hand	Maine	S	7.25 MW	7.54 AW	15690 AAW	MEBLS	10//99-12//99
Hand	Maryland	S	7.59 MW	8.11 AW	16870 AAW	MDBLS	10//99-12//99
Hand	Massachusetts	S	7.58 MW	8.47 AW	17620 AAW	MABLS	10//99-12//99
Hand	Michigan	S	6.65 MW	7.71 AW	16030 AAW	MIBLS	10//99-12//99
Hand	Minnesota	S	8.3 MW	8.61 AW	17900 AAW	MNBLS	10//99-12//99
Hand	Mississippi	S	7.06 MW	7.54 AW	15670 AAW	MSBLS	10//99-12//99
Hand	Missouri	S	6.93 MW	7.55 AW	15710 AAW	MOBLS	10//99-12//99
Hand	Montana	S	6.7 MW	7.58 AW	15780 AAW	MTBLS	10//99-12//99
Hand	Nebraska	S	7.58 MW	7.94 AW	16510 AAW	NEBLS	10//99-12//99
Hand	Nevada	S	6.97 MW	7.42 AW	15430 AAW	NVBLS	10//99-12//99
Hand	New Hampshire	S	7.45 MW	7.72 AW	16060 AAW	NHBLS	10//99-12//99
Hand	New Jersey	S	7.56 MW	8.09 AW	16830 AAW	NJBLS	10//99-12//99
Hand	New Mexico	S	6.19 MW	6.55 AW	13630 AAW	NMBLS	10//99-12//99
Hand	New York	S	7.45 MW	8.31 AW	17290 AAW	NYBLS	10//99-12//99
Hand	North Carolina	S	7.47 MW	7.76 AW	16130 AAW	NCBLS	10//99-12//99
Hand	North Dakota	S	6.79 MW	7.13 AW	14830 AAW	NDBLS	10//99-12//99
Hand	Ohio	S	7.47 MW	8.09 AW	16830 AAW	OHBLS	10//99-12//99
Hand	Oklahoma	S	7.3 MW	7.54 AW	15680 AAW	OKBLS	10//99-12//99
Hand	Oregon	S	7.58 MW	8.56 AW	17810 AAW	ORBLS	10//99-12//99
Hand	Pennsylvania	S	8.11 MW	8.70 AW	18090 AAW	PABLS	10//99-12//99
Hand	Rhode Island	S	6.67 MW	7.43 AW	15450 AAW	RIBLS	10//99-12//99
Hand	South Carolina	S	7.45 MW	7.66 AW	15940 AAW	SCBLS	10//99-12//99
Hand	South Dakota	S	7.52 MW	7.67 AW	15950 AAW	SDBLS	10//99-12//99
Hand	Tennessee	S	7.42 MW	7.78 AW	16180 AAW	TNBLS	10//99-12//99
Hand	Texas	S	6.44 MW	7.15 AW	14880 AAW	TXBLS	10//99-12//99
Hand	Utah	S	7.02 MW	7.50 AW	15600 AAW	UTBLS	10//99-12//99
Hand	Vermont	S	7.48 MW	7.86 AW	16350 AAW	VTBLS	10//99-12//99
Hand	Virginia	S	6.7 MW	7.35 AW	15290 AAW	VABLS	10//99-12//99
Hand	Washington	S	7.56 MW	8.21 AW	17080 AAW	WABLS	10//99-12//99
Hand	West Virginia	S	6.41 MW	7.14 AW	14860 AAW	WVBLS	10//99-12//99
Hand	Wisconsin	S	8.38 MW	8.93 AW	18580 AAW	WIBLS	10//99-12//99
Hand	Wyoming	S	6.31 MW	6.88 AW	14310 AAW	WYBLS	10//99-12//99
Hand	Puerto Rico	S	6.05 MW	6.47 AW	13460 AAW	PRBLS	10//99-12//99
Hand	Guam	S	5.97 MW	6.00 AW	12480 AAW	GUBLS	10//99-12//99
Painter							
Construction and Maintenance	Alabama	S	11.9 MW	11.98 AW	24920 AAW	ALBLS	10//99-12//99
Construction and Maintenance	Birmingham MSA, AL	S	12.43 MW	12.40 AW	25860 AAW	ALBLS	10//99-12//99
Construction and Maintenance	Decatur MSA, AL	S	10.51 MW	10.17 AW	21870 AAW	ALBLS	10//99-12//99
Construction and Maintenance	Dothan MSA, AL	S	10.01 MW	10.16 AW	20810 AAW	ALBLS	10//99-12//99
Construction and Maintenance	Florence MSA, AL	S	11.63 MW	11.64 AW	24180 AAW	ALBLS	10//99-12//99
Construction and Maintenance	Huntsville MSA, AL	S	12.21 MW	11.73 AW	25400 AAW	ALBLS	10//99-12//99
Construction and Maintenance	Mobile MSA, AL	S	11.98 MW	11.89 AW	24920 AAW	ALBLS	10//99-12//99
Construction and Maintenance	Montgomery MSA, AL	S	10.75 MW	10.58 AW	22360 AAW	ALBLS	10//99-12//99
Construction and Maintenance	Tuscaloosa MSA, AL	S	12.25 MW	12.43 AW	25480 AAW	ALBLS	10//99-12//99
Construction and Maintenance	Alaska	S	15.56 MW	17.93 AW	37300 AAW	AKBLS	10//99-12//99
Construction and Maintenance	Anchorage MSA, AK	S	17.24 MW	13.99 AW	35850 AAW	AKBLS	10//99-12//99
Construction and Maintenance	Arizona	S	11.84 MW	12.35 AW	25680 AAW	AZBLS	10//99-12//99
Construction and Maintenance	Flagstaff MSA, AZ-UT	S	10.95 MW	10.05 AW	22780 AAW	AZBLS	10//99-12//99

Painter

Occupation/Type/Industry	Location	Per	Low	Mid	High	Source	Date
Construction and Maintenance	Phoenix-Mesa MSA, AZ	S	12.74 MW	12.18 AW	26510 AAW	AZBLS	10//99-12//99
Construction and Maintenance	Tucson MSA, AZ	S	11.36 MW	10.88 AW	23630 AAW	AZBLS	10//99-12//99
Construction and Maintenance	Yuma MSA, AZ	S	10.71 MW	10.24 AW	22270 AAW	AZBLS	10//99-12//99
Construction and Maintenance	Arkansas	S	11.35 MW	11.51 AW	23940 AAW	ARBLS	10//99-12//99
Construction and Maintenance	Fayetteville-Springdale-Rogers MSA, AR	S	11.16 MW	10.98 AW	23210 AAW	ARBLS	10//99-12//99
Construction and Maintenance	Jonesboro MSA, AR	S	11.05 MW	11.80 AW	22980 AAW	ARBLS	10//99-12//99
Construction and Maintenance	Little Rock-North Little Rock MSA, AR	S	12.10 MW	11.99 AW	25160 AAW	ARBLS	10//99-12//99
Construction and Maintenance	California	S	13.46 MW	14.38 AW	29900 AAW	CABLS	10//99-12//99
Construction and Maintenance	Bakersfield MSA, CA	S	11.83 MW	11.15 AW	24610 AAW	CABLS	10//99-12//99
Construction and Maintenance	Chico-Paradise MSA, CA	S	12.59 MW	12.67 AW	26180 AAW	CABLS	10//99-12//99
Construction and Maintenance	Los Angeles-Long Beach PMSA, CA	S	12.91 MW	12.26 AW	26850 AAW	CABLS	10//99-12//99
Construction and Maintenance	Merced MSA, CA	S	13.75 MW	13.26 AW	28600 AAW	CABLS	10//99-12//99
Construction and Maintenance	Modesto MSA, CA	S	13.49 MW	13.41 AW	28050 AAW	CABLS	10//99-12//99
Construction and Maintenance	Oakland PMSA, CA	S	18.15 MW	17.94 AW	37760 AAW	CABLS	10//99-12//99
Construction and Maintenance	Orange County PMSA, CA	S	13.22 MW	12.40 AW	27490 AAW	CABLS	10//99-12//99
Construction and Maintenance	Redding MSA, CA	S	15.32 MW	12.89 AW	31870 AAW	CABLS	10//99-12//99
Construction and Maintenance	Riverside-San Bernardino PMSA, CA	S	12.07 MW	10.37 AW	25100 AAW	CABLS	10//99-12//99
Construction and Maintenance	Sacramento PMSA, CA	S	14.18 MW	13.16 AW	29500 AAW	CABLS	10//99-12//99
Construction and Maintenance	Salinas MSA, CA	S	17.28 MW	17.83 AW	35940 AAW	CABLS	10//99-12//99
Construction and Maintenance	San Diego MSA, CA	S	15.46 MW	15.34 AW	32150 AAW	CABLS	10//99-12//99
Construction and Maintenance	San Francisco PMSA, CA	S	16.02 MW	14.97 AW	33330 AAW	CABLS	10//99-12//99
Construction and Maintenance	San Jose PMSA, CA	S	18.18 MW	18.37 AW	37810 AAW	CABLS	10//99-12//99
Construction and Maintenance	San Luis Obispo-Atascadero-Paso Robles MSA, CA	S	13.62 MW	12.67 AW	28330 AAW	CABLS	10//99-12//99
Construction and Maintenance	Santa Barbara-Santa Maria-Lompoc MSA, CA	S	14.22 MW	14.35 AW	29570 AAW	CABLS	10//99-12//99
Construction and Maintenance	Santa Cruz-Watsonville PMSA, CA	S	12.46 MW	12.08 AW	25910 AAW	CABLS	10//99-12//99
Construction and Maintenance	Santa Rosa PMSA, CA	S	13.10 MW	10.21 AW	27250 AAW	CABLS	10//99-12//99
Construction and Maintenance	Stockton-Lodi MSA, CA	S	13.24 MW	12.68 AW	27530 AAW	CABLS	10//99-12//99
Construction and Maintenance	Vallejo-Fairfield-Napa PMSA, CA	S	19.30 MW	19.77 AW	40150 AAW	CABLS	10//99-12//99
Construction and Maintenance	Ventura PMSA, CA	S	14.37 MW	13.06 AW	29900 AAW	CABLS	10//99-12//99
Construction and Maintenance	Visalia-Tulare-Porterville MSA, CA	S	13.40 MW	11.21 AW	27870 AAW	CABLS	10//99-12//99
Construction and Maintenance	Yolo PMSA, CA	S	16.99 MW	16.25 AW	35340 AAW	CABLS	10//99-12//99
Construction and Maintenance	Yuba City MSA, CA	S	14.41 MW	13.07 AW	29980 AAW	CABLS	10//99-12//99
Construction and Maintenance	Colorado	S	12.09 MW	12.39 AW	25770 AAW	COBLS	10//99-12//99
Construction and Maintenance	Boulder-Longmont PMSA, CO	S	12.26 MW	12.15 AW	25510 AAW	COBLS	10//99-12//99
Construction and Maintenance	Denver PMSA, CO	S	12.08 MW	11.92 AW	25130 AAW	COBLS	10//99-12//99
Construction and Maintenance	Fort Collins-Loveland MSA, CO	S	10.97 MW	10.10 AW	22810 AAW	COBLS	10//99-12//99
Construction and Maintenance	Grand Junction MSA, CO	S	12.68 MW	11.79 AW	26380 AAW	COBLS	10//99-12//99
Construction and Maintenance	Connecticut	S	12.12 MW	12.74 AW	26490 AAW	CTBLS	10//99-12//99
Construction and Maintenance	Danbury PMSA, CT	S	11.09 MW	10.41 AW	23060 AAW	CTBLS	10//99-12//99
Construction and Maintenance	Hartford MSA, CT	S	12.09 MW	11.70 AW	25140 AAW	CTBLS	10//99-12//99
Construction and Maintenance	New Haven-Meriden PMSA, CT	S	12.69 MW	13.27 AW	26390 AAW	CTBLS	10//99-12//99
Construction and Maintenance	New London-Norwich MSA, CT-RI	S	13.13 MW	13.17 AW	27310 AAW	CTBLS	10//99-12//99
Construction and Maintenance	Stamford-Norwalk PMSA, CT	S	16.61 MW	17.26 AW	34560 AAW	CTBLS	10//99-12//99
Construction and Maintenance	Waterbury PMSA, CT	S	12.95 MW	13.25 AW	26930 AAW	CTBLS	10//99-12//99
Construction and Maintenance	Delaware	S	16.21 MW	17.13 AW	35620 AAW	DEBLS	10//99-12//99
Construction and Maintenance	Dover MSA, DE	S	17.53 MW	14.71 AW	36460 AAW	DEBLS	10//99-12//99
Construction and Maintenance	Wilmington-Newark PMSA, DE-MD	S	18.64 MW	19.48 AW	38760 AAW	DEBLS	10//99-12//99
Construction and Maintenance	District of Columbia	S	15.5 MW	15.88 AW	33040 AAW	DCBLS	10//99-12//99
Construction and Maintenance	Washington PMSA, DC-MD-VA-WV	S	13.05 MW	12.85 AW	27150 AAW	DCBLS	10//99-12//99
Construction and Maintenance	Florida	S	11.03 MW	11.24 AW	23380 AAW	FLBLS	10//99-12//99
Construction and Maintenance	Daytona Beach MSA, FL	S	8.40 MW	7.86 AW	17460 AAW	FLBLS	10//99-12//99
Construction and Maintenance	Fort Lauderdale PMSA, FL	S	11.90 MW	11.87 AW	24750 AAW	FLBLS	10//99-12//99
Construction and Maintenance	Fort Myers-Cape Coral MSA, FL	S	11.14 MW	11.18 AW	23180 AAW	FLBLS	10//99-12//99
Construction and Maintenance	Fort Pierce-Port St. Lucie MSA, FL	S	10.32 MW	10.01 AW	21460 AAW	FLBLS	10//99-12//99
Construction and Maintenance	Fort Walton Beach MSA, FL	S	10.19 MW	9.93 AW	21190 AAW	FLBLS	10//99-12//99

AAW Average annual wage	AOH Average offered, high	ASH Average starting, high	H Hourly	M Monthly	S Special: hourly and annual
AE Average entry wage	AOL Average offered, low	ASL Average starting, low	HI Highest wage paid	MTC Median total compensation	TQ Third quartile wage
AEX Average experienced wage	APH Average pay, high range	AW Average wage paid	HR High end range	MW Median wage paid	W Weekly
AO Average offered	APL Average pay, low range	FQ First quartile wage	LR Low end range	SQ Second quartile wage	Y Yearly

Painter

Occupation/Type/Industry	Location	Per	Low	Mid	High	Source	Date
Construction and Maintenance	Gainesville MSA, FL	S	11.35 MW	11.43 AW	23600 AAW	FLBLS	10//99-12//99
Construction and Maintenance	Jacksonville MSA, FL	S	10.27 MW	10.35 AW	21370 AAW	FLBLS	10//99-12//99
Construction and Maintenance	Lakeland-Winter Haven MSA, FL	S	13.97 MW	13.93 AW	29060 AAW	FLBLS	10//99-12//99
Construction and Maintenance	Melbourne-Titusville-Palm Bay MSA, FL	S	14.35 MW	14.60 AW	29860 AAW	FLBLS	10//99-12//99
Construction and Maintenance	Miami PMSA, FL	S	11.67 MW	11.60 AW	24280 AAW	FLBLS	10//99-12//99
Construction and Maintenance	Naples MSA, FL	S	11.91 MW	12.11 AW	24770 AAW	FLBLS	10//99-12//99
Construction and Maintenance	Ocala MSA, FL	S	10.47 MW	10.84 AW	21780 AAW	FLBLS	10//99-12//99
Construction and Maintenance	Orlando MSA, FL	S	11.43 MW	11.55 AW	23770 AAW	FLBLS	10//99-12//99
Construction and Maintenance	Panama City MSA, FL	S	7.65 MW	7.42 AW	15920 AAW	FLBLS	10//99-12//99
Construction and Maintenance	Pensacola MSA, FL	S	9.17 MW	8.75 AW	19080 AAW	FLBLS	10//99-12//99
Construction and Maintenance	Punta Gorda MSA, FL	S	10.38 MW	10.09 AW	21580 AAW	FLBLS	10//99-12//99
Construction and Maintenance	Sarasota-Bradenton MSA, FL	S	10.54 MW	10.10 AW	21920 AAW	FLBLS	10//99-12//99
Construction and Maintenance	Tallahassee MSA, FL	S	10.17 MW	9.98 AW	21140 AAW	FLBLS	10//99-12//99
Construction and Maintenance	Tampa-St. Petersburg-Clearwater MSA, FL	S	10.82 MW	10.54 AW	22510 AAW	FLBLS	10//99-12//99
Construction and Maintenance	West Palm Beach-Boca Raton MSA, FL	S	14.91 MW	15.36 AW	31000 AAW	FLBLS	10//99-12//99
Construction and Maintenance	Georgia	S	14.05 MW	14.51 AW	30180 AAW	GABLS	10//99-12//99
Construction and Maintenance	Atlanta MSA, GA	S	15.66 MW	14.88 AW	32580 AAW	GABLS	10//99-12//99
Construction and Maintenance	Augusta-Aiken MSA, GA-SC	S	14.01 MW	12.41 AW	29130 AAW	GABLS	10//99-12//99
Construction and Maintenance	Columbus MSA, GA-AL	S	10.09 MW	9.65 AW	20990 AAW	GABLS	10//99-12//99
Construction and Maintenance	Macon MSA, GA	S	14.59 MW	14.67 AW	30350 AAW	GABLS	10//99-12//99
Construction and Maintenance	Savannah MSA, GA	S	17.27 MW	17.81 AW	35930 AAW	GABLS	10//99-12//99
Construction and Maintenance	Hawaii	S	20.09 MW	19.73 AW	41050 AAW	HIBLS	10//99-12//99
Construction and Maintenance	Honolulu MSA, HI	S	20.25 MW	20.99 AW	42120 AAW	HIBLS	10//99-12//99
Construction and Maintenance	Idaho	S	13.04 MW	13.63 AW	28350 AAW	IDBLS	10//99-12//99
Construction and Maintenance	Boise City MSA, ID	S	13.23 MW	12.79 AW	27510 AAW	IDBLS	10//99-12//99
Construction and Maintenance	Illinois	S	14.39 MW	15.27 AW	31770 AAW	ILBLS	10//99-12//99
Construction and Maintenance	Bloomington-Normal MSA, IL	S	21.94 MW	23.74 AW	45640 AAW	ILBLS	10//99-12//99
Construction and Maintenance	Chicago PMSA, IL	S	15.57 MW	14.75 AW	32380 AAW	ILBLS	10//99-12//99
Construction and Maintenance	Peoria-Pekin MSA, IL	S	14.99 MW	15.33 AW	31170 AAW	ILBLS	10//99-12//99
Construction and Maintenance	Rockford MSA, IL	S	11.87 MW	8.17 AW	24680 AAW	ILBLS	10//99-12//99
Construction and Maintenance	Springfield MSA, IL	S	20.01 MW	15.00 AW	41630 AAW	ILBLS	10//99-12//99
Construction and Maintenance	Indiana	S	14.75 MW	15.38 AW	31980 AAW	INBLS	10//99-12//99
Construction and Maintenance	Bloomington MSA, IN	S	6.63 MW	6.18 AW	13800 AAW	INBLS	10//99-12//99
Construction and Maintenance	Elkhart-Goshen MSA, IN	S	13.54 MW	12.72 AW	28170 AAW	INBLS	10//99-12//99
Construction and Maintenance	Evansville-Henderson MSA, IN-KY	S	15.54 MW	13.13 AW	32320 AAW	INBLS	10//99-12//99
Construction and Maintenance	Fort Wayne MSA, IN	S	15.05 MW	12.90 AW	31310 AAW	INBLS	10//99-12//99
Construction and Maintenance	Gary PMSA, IN	S	19.47 MW	19.55 AW	40500 AAW	INBLS	10//99-12//99
Construction and Maintenance	Indianapolis MSA, IN	S	16.08 MW	17.33 AW	33440 AAW	INBLS	10//99-12//99
Construction and Maintenance	Kokomo MSA, IN	S	19.89 MW	22.29 AW	41380 AAW	INBLS	10//99-12//99
Construction and Maintenance	Lafayette MSA, IN	S	16.53 MW	17.28 AW	34370 AAW	INBLS	10//99-12//99
Construction and Maintenance	South Bend MSA, IN	S	15.30 MW	14.98 AW	31820 AAW	INBLS	10//99-12//99
Construction and Maintenance	Terre Haute MSA, IN	S	16.86 MW	18.27 AW	35070 AAW	INBLS	10//99-12//99
Construction and Maintenance	Iowa	S	13.12 MW	13.69 AW	28470 AAW	IABLS	10//99-12//99
Construction and Maintenance	Cedar Rapids MSA, IA	S	15.92 MW	16.47 AW	33120 AAW	IABLS	10//99-12//99
Construction and Maintenance	Davenport-Moline-Rock Island MSA, IA-IL	S	13.21 MW	11.88 AW	27490 AAW	IABLS	10//99-12//99
Construction and Maintenance	Des Moines MSA, IA	S	15.02 MW	16.31 AW	31250 AAW	IABLS	10//99-12//99
Construction and Maintenance	Dubuque MSA, IA	S	12.17 MW	11.80 AW	25310 AAW	IABLS	10//99-12//99
Construction and Maintenance	Iowa City MSA, IA	S	13.44 MW	13.19 AW	27960 AAW	IABLS	10//99-12//99
Construction and Maintenance	Sioux City MSA, IA-NE	S	11.93 MW	12.74 AW	24810 AAW	IABLS	10//99-12//99
Construction and Maintenance	Waterloo-Cedar Falls MSA, IA	S	10.81 MW	10.22 AW	22480 AAW	IABLS	10//99-12//99
Construction and Maintenance	Kansas	S	11.75 MW	12.75 AW	26520 AAW	KSBLS	10//99-12//99
Construction and Maintenance	Lawrence MSA, KS	S	13.36 MW	13.55 AW	27780 AAW	KSBLS	10//99-12//99
Construction and Maintenance	Topeka MSA, KS	S	17.29 MW	17.69 AW	35960 AAW	KSBLS	10//99-12//99
Construction and Maintenance	Wichita MSA, KS	S	13.11 MW	12.18 AW	27260 AAW	KSBLS	10//99-12//99
Construction and Maintenance	Kentucky	S	10.76 MW	11.05 AW	22980 AAW	KYBLS	10//99-12//99
Construction and Maintenance	Lexington MSA, KY	S	9.53 MW	9.74 AW	19810 AAW	KYBLS	10//99-12//99
Construction and Maintenance	Louisville MSA, KY-IN	S	11.80 MW	11.76 AW	24550 AAW	KYBLS	10//99-12//99
Construction and Maintenance	Louisiana	S	11.87 MW	11.98 AW	24920 AAW	LABLS	10//99-12//99
Construction and Maintenance	Alexandria MSA, LA	S	12.57 MW	10.68 AW	26140 AAW	LABLS	10//99-12//99
Construction and Maintenance	Baton Rouge MSA, LA	S	12.84 MW	12.32 AW	26700 AAW	LABLS	10//99-12//99
Construction and Maintenance	Houma MSA, LA	S	11.53 MW	11.90 AW	23990 AAW	LABLS	10//99-12//99
Construction and Maintenance	Lafayette MSA, LA	S	10.90 MW	10.65 AW	22670 AAW	LABLS	10//99-12//99
Construction and Maintenance	Lake Charles MSA, LA	S	11.94 MW	12.15 AW	24840 AAW	LABLS	10//99-12//99
Construction and Maintenance	Monroe MSA, LA	S	11.16 MW	9.90 AW	23210 AAW	LABLS	10//99-12//99
Construction and Maintenance	New Orleans MSA, LA	S	12.46 MW	12.19 AW	25920 AAW	LABLS	10//99-12//99

AAW Average annual wage	AOH Average offered, high	ASH Average starting, high	H Hourly	M Monthly	S Special: hourly and annual
AE Average entry wage	AOL Average offered, low	ASL Average starting, low	HI Highest wage paid	MTC Median total compensation	TQ Third quartile wage
AEX Average experienced wage	APH Average pay, high range	AW Average wage paid	HR High end range	MW Median wage paid	W Weekly
AO Average offered	APL Average pay, low range	FQ First quartile wage	LR Low end range	SQ Second quartile wage	Y Yearly

Painter

Occupation/Type/Industry	Location	Per	Low	Mid	High	Source	Date
Construction and Maintenance	Shreveport-Bossier City MSA, LA	S	11.50 MW	11.00 AW	23930 AAW	LABLS	10//99-12//99
Construction and Maintenance	Maine	S	13.73 MW	12.71 AW	26440 AAW	MEBLS	10//99-12//99
Construction and Maintenance	Bangor MSA, ME	S	9.85 MW	9.76 AW	20480 AAW	MEBLS	10//99-12//99
Construction and Maintenance	Lewiston-Auburn MSA, ME	S	9.00 MW	8.98 AW	18730 AAW	MEBLS	10//99-12//99
Construction and Maintenance	Portland MSA, ME	S	9.90 MW	9.96 AW	20590 AAW	MEBLS	10//99-12//99
Construction and Maintenance	Maryland	S	12.83 MW	13.25 AW	27560 AAW	MDBLS	10//99-12//99
Construction and Maintenance	Baltimore PMSA, MD	S	14.63 MW	13.29 AW	30440 AAW	MDBLS	10//99-12//99
Construction and Maintenance	Hagerstown PMSA, MD	S	9.11 MW	8.82 AW	18950 AAW	MDBLS	10//99-12//99
Construction and Maintenance	Massachusetts	S	14.45 MW	16.06 AW	33410 AAW	MABLS	10//99-12//99
Construction and Maintenance	Barnstable-Yarmouth MSA, MA	S	11.82 MW	11.61 AW	24590 AAW	MABLS	10//99-12//99
Construction and Maintenance	Boston PMSA, MA-NH	S	16.85 MW	15.04 AW	35060 AAW	MABLS	10//99-12//99
Construction and Maintenance	Brockton PMSA, MA	S	14.50 MW	14.21 AW	30170 AAW	MABLS	10//99-12//99
Construction and Maintenance	Fitchburg-Leominster PMSA, MA	S	18.22 MW	15.74 AW	37900 AAW	MABLS	10//99-12//99
Construction and Maintenance	Lawrence PMSA, MA-NH	S	14.89 MW	14.63 AW	30970 AAW	MABLS	10//99-12//99
Construction and Maintenance	Pittsfield MSA, MA	S	11.17 MW	10.57 AW	23230 AAW	MABLS	10//99-12//99
Construction and Maintenance	Springfield MSA, MA	S	12.47 MW	12.48 AW	25930 AAW	MABLS	10//99-12//99
Construction and Maintenance	Worcester PMSA, MA-CT	S	13.82 MW	13.25 AW	28740 AAW	MABLS	10//99-12//99
Construction and Maintenance	Michigan	S	14.2 MW	15.14 AW	31500 AAW	MIBLS	10//99-12//99
Construction and Maintenance	Ann Arbor PMSA, MI	S	16.41 MW	17.49 AW	34130 AAW	MIBLS	10//99-12//99
Construction and Maintenance	Benton Harbor MSA, MI	S	12.31 MW	10.47 AW	25610 AAW	MIBLS	10//99-12//99
Construction and Maintenance	Detroit PMSA, MI	S	15.23 MW	13.36 AW	31680 AAW	MIBLS	10//99-12//99
Construction and Maintenance	Flint PMSA, MI	S	19.38 MW	19.51 AW	40320 AAW	MIBLS	10//99-12//99
Construction and Maintenance	Grand Rapids-Muskegon-Holland MSA, MI	S	14.31 MW	13.46 AW	29760 AAW	MIBLS	10//99-12//99
Construction and Maintenance	Jackson MSA, MI	S	14.65 MW	14.96 AW	30480 AAW	MIBLS	10//99-12//99
Construction and Maintenance	Kalamazoo-Battle Creek MSA, MI	S	13.49 MW	13.24 AW	28070 AAW	MIBLS	10//99-12//99
Construction and Maintenance	Lansing-East Lansing MSA, MI	S	14.01 MW	13.24 AW	29140 AAW	MIBLS	10//99-12//99
Construction and Maintenance	Saginaw-Bay City-Midland MSA, MI	S	15.66 MW	16.65 AW	32560 AAW	MIBLS	10//99-12//99
Construction and Maintenance	Minnesota	S	22.54 MW	20.06 AW	41720 AAW	MNBLS	10//99-12//99
Construction and Maintenance	Duluth-Superior MSA, MN-WI	S	18.19 MW	19.43 AW	37840 AAW	MNBLS	10//99-12//99
Construction and Maintenance	Minneapolis-St. Paul MSA, MN-WI	S	21.49 MW	23.30 AW	44700 AAW	MNBLS	10//99-12//99
Construction and Maintenance	Rochester MSA, MN	S	24.98 MW	29.11 AW	51960 AAW	MNBLS	10//99-12//99
Construction and Maintenance	St. Cloud MSA, MN	S	12.34 MW	11.63 AW	25670 AAW	MNBLS	10//99-12//99
Construction and Maintenance	Mississippi	S	12.47 MW	12.57 AW	26140 AAW	MSBLS	10//99-12//99
Construction and Maintenance	Biloxi-Gulfport-Pascagoula MSA, MS	S	13.51 MW	13.31 AW	28100 AAW	MSBLS	10//99-12//99
Construction and Maintenance	Hattiesburg MSA, MS	S	11.15 MW	11.71 AW	23200 AAW	MSBLS	10//99-12//99
Construction and Maintenance	Jackson MSA, MS	S	11.52 MW	11.66 AW	23970 AAW	MSBLS	10//99-12//99
Construction and Maintenance	Missouri	S	19.27 MW	18.14 AW	37730 AAW	MOBLS	10//99-12//99
Construction and Maintenance	Columbia MSA, MO	S	10.95 MW	9.95 AW	22770 AAW	MOBLS	10//99-12//99
Construction and Maintenance	Kansas City MSA, MO-KS	S	14.51 MW	13.28 AW	30180 AAW	MOBLS	10//99-12//99
Construction and Maintenance	St. Joseph MSA, MO	S	12.18 MW	10.03 AW	25330 AAW	MOBLS	10//99-12//99
Construction and Maintenance	St. Louis MSA, MO-IL	S	20.18 MW	22.17 AW	41980 AAW	MOBLS	10//99-12//99
Construction and Maintenance	Springfield MSA, MO	S	11.61 MW	10.67 AW	24150 AAW	MOBLS	10//99-12//99
Construction and Maintenance	Montana	S	13.9 MW	13.57 AW	28220 AAW	MTBLS	10//99-12//99
Construction and Maintenance	Billings MSA, MT	S	13.67 MW	14.87 AW	28440 AAW	MTBLS	10//99-12//99
Construction and Maintenance	Great Falls MSA, MT	S	14.40 MW	14.56 AW	29950 AAW	MTBLS	10//99-12//99
Construction and Maintenance	Missoula MSA, MT	S	13.06 MW	13.21 AW	27170 AAW	MTBLS	10//99-12//99
Construction and Maintenance	Nebraska	S	10.87 MW	11.25 AW	23400 AAW	NEBLS	10//99-12//99
Construction and Maintenance	Lincoln MSA, NE	S	10.74 MW	10.95 AW	22330 AAW	NEBLS	10//99-12//99
Construction and Maintenance	Omaha MSA, NE-IA	S	12.63 MW	12.50 AW	26270 AAW	NEBLS	10//99-12//99
Construction and Maintenance	Nevada	S	14.16 MW	15.66 AW	32560 AAW	NVBLS	10//99-12//99
Construction and Maintenance	Las Vegas MSA, NV-AZ	S	15.46 MW	13.50 AW	32170 AAW	NVBLS	10//99-12//99
Construction and Maintenance	Reno MSA, NV	S	16.16 MW	16.21 AW	33610 AAW	NVBLS	10//99-12//99
Construction and Maintenance	New Hampshire	S	11.88 MW	11.69 AW	24310 AAW	NHBLS	10//99-12//99
Construction and Maintenance	Manchester PMSA, NH	S	12.43 MW	12.41 AW	25850 AAW	NHBLS	10//99-12//99
Construction and Maintenance	Nashua PMSA, NH	S	10.68 MW	11.24 AW	22210 AAW	NHBLS	10//99-12//99
Construction and Maintenance	Portsmouth-Rochester PMSA, NH-ME	S	12.19 MW	12.20 AW	25350 AAW	NHBLS	10//99-12//99
Construction and Maintenance	New Jersey	S	14.46 MW	16.42 AW	34150 AAW	NJBLS	10//99-12//99
Construction and Maintenance	Atlantic-Cape May PMSA, NJ	S	15.75 MW	15.06 AW	32760 AAW	NJBLS	10//99-12//99
Construction and Maintenance	Bergen-Passaic PMSA, NJ	S	14.51 MW	14.51 AW	30180 AAW	NJBLS	10//99-12//99
Construction and Maintenance	Middlesex-Somerset-Hunterdon PMSA, NJ	S	13.61 MW	12.11 AW	28310 AAW	NJBLS	10//99-12//99
Construction and Maintenance	Monmouth-Ocean PMSA, NJ	S	16.30 MW	14.41 AW	33910 AAW	NJBLS	10//99-12//99

AAW	Average annual wage	AOH	Average offered, high	ASH	Average starting, high	H	Hourly	M	Monthly	S	Special: hourly and annual
AE	Average entry wage	AOL	Average offered, low	ASL	Average starting, low	HI	Highest wage paid	MTC	Median total compensation	TQ	Third quartile wage
AEX	Average experienced wage	APH	Average pay, high range	AW	Average wage paid	HR	High end range	MW	Median wage paid	W	Weekly
AO	Average offered	APL	Average pay, low range	FQ	First quartile wage	LR	Low end range	SQ	Second quartile wage	Y	Yearly

Occupation/Type/Industry	Location	Per	Low	Mid	High	Source	Date
Painter							
Construction and Maintenance	Trenton PMSA, NJ	S	16.10 MW	15.05 AW	33500 AAW	NJBLS	10//99-12//99
Construction and Maintenance	Vineland-Millville-Bridgeton PMSA, NJ	S	12.95 MW	12.28 AW	26940 AAW	NJBLS	10//99-12//99
Construction and Maintenance	New Mexico	S	12.39 MW	12.52 AW	26030 AAW	NMBLS	10//99-12//99
Construction and Maintenance	Albuquerque MSA, NM	S	13.14 MW	13.42 AW	27330 AAW	NMBLS	10//99-12//99
Construction and Maintenance	Santa Fe MSA, NM	S	13.91 MW	12.34 AW	28920 AAW	NMBLS	10//99-12//99
Construction and Maintenance	New York	S	17.03 MW	19.37 AW	40290 AAW	NYBLS	10//99-12//99
Construction and Maintenance	Albany-Schenectady-Troy MSA, NY	S	17.20 MW	18.33 AW	35780 AAW	NYBLS	10//99-12//99
Construction and Maintenance	Binghamton MSA, NY	S	11.72 MW	11.97 AW	24380 AAW	NYBLS	10//99-12//99
Construction and Maintenance	Buffalo-Niagara Falls MSA, NY	S	20.74 MW	22.08 AW	43150 AAW	NYBLS	10//99-12//99
Construction and Maintenance	Dutchess County PMSA, NY	S	14.20 MW	13.95 AW	29530 AAW	NYBLS	10//99-12//99
Construction and Maintenance	Glens Falls MSA, NY	S	11.63 MW	10.40 AW	24200 AAW	NYBLS	10//99-12//99
Construction and Maintenance	Nassau-Suffolk PMSA, NY	S	21.43 MW	22.04 AW	44580 AAW	NYBLS	10//99-12//99
Construction and Maintenance	New York PMSA, NY	S	22.42 MW	23.06 AW	46630 AAW	NYBLS	10//99-12//99
Construction and Maintenance	Newburgh PMSA, NY-PA	S	12.08 MW	11.85 AW	25130 AAW	NYBLS	10//99-12//99
Construction and Maintenance	Rochester MSA, NY	S	13.78 MW	12.91 AW	28650 AAW	NYBLS	10//99-12//99
Construction and Maintenance	Syracuse MSA, NY	S	11.19 MW	10.24 AW	23280 AAW	NYBLS	10//99-12//99
Construction and Maintenance	Utica-Rome MSA, NY	S	9.82 MW	8.41 AW	20420 AAW	NYBLS	10//99-12//99
Construction and Maintenance	North Carolina	S	10.51 MW	11.02 AW	22920 AAW	NCBLS	10//99-12//99
Construction and Maintenance	Asheville MSA, NC	S	10.31 MW	10.09 AW	21450 AAW	NCBLS	10//99-12//99
Construction and Maintenance	Charlotte-Gastonia-Rock Hill MSA, NC-SC	S	10.92 MW	10.85 AW	22720 AAW	NCBLS	10//99-12//99
Construction and Maintenance	Fayetteville MSA, NC	S	11.25 MW	11.71 AW	23400 AAW	NCBLS	10//99-12//99
Construction and Maintenance	Goldsboro MSA, NC	S	10.88 MW	11.19 AW	22620 AAW	NCBLS	10//99-12//99
Construction and Maintenance	Greensboro--Winston-Salem--High Point MSA, NC	S	11.23 MW	10.36 AW	23350 AAW	NCBLS	10//99-12//99
Construction and Maintenance	Greenville MSA, NC	S	11.37 MW	9.97 AW	23650 AAW	NCBLS	10//99-12//99
Construction and Maintenance	Hickory-Morganton-Lenoir MSA, NC	S	11.06 MW	10.80 AW	23010 AAW	NCBLS	10//99-12//99
Construction and Maintenance	Jacksonville MSA, NC	S	10.61 MW	10.23 AW	22080 AAW	NCBLS	10//99-12//99
Construction and Maintenance	Raleigh-Durham-Chapel Hill MSA, NC	S	10.83 MW	10.33 AW	22520 AAW	NCBLS	10//99-12//99
Construction and Maintenance	Rocky Mount MSA, NC	S	8.52 MW	8.01 AW	17720 AAW	NCBLS	10//99-12//99
Construction and Maintenance	Wilmington MSA, NC	S	10.71 MW	9.87 AW	22270 AAW	NCBLS	10//99-12//99
Construction and Maintenance	North Dakota	S	12.59 MW	13.62 AW	28330 AAW	NDBLS	10//99-12//99
Construction and Maintenance	Fargo-Moorhead MSA, ND-MN	S	14.36 MW	13.15 AW	29860 AAW	NDBLS	10//99-12//99
Construction and Maintenance	Grand Forks MSA, ND-MN	S	11.02 MW	11.09 AW	22910 AAW	NDBLS	10//99-12//99
Construction and Maintenance	Ohio	S	14.66 MW	15.08 AW	31370 AAW	OHBIO	10//99-12//99
Construction and Maintenance	Akron PMSA, OH	S	13.58 MW	12.86 AW	28240 AAW	OHBLS	10//99-12//99
Construction and Maintenance	Canton-Massillon MSA, OH	S	11.55 MW	10.08 AW	24030 AAW	OHBLS	10//99-12//99
Construction and Maintenance	Cincinnati PMSA, OH-KY-IN	S	14.87 MW	14.78 AW	30920 AAW	OHBLS	10//99-12//99
Construction and Maintenance	Cleveland-Lorain-Elyria PMSA, OH	S	18.12 MW	18.54 AW	37690 AAW	OHBLS	10//99-12//99
Construction and Maintenance	Columbus MSA, OH	S	14.41 MW	14.73 AW	29970 AAW	OHBLS	10//99-12//99
Construction and Maintenance	Dayton-Springfield MSA, OH	S	11.50 MW	10.74 AW	23910 AAW	OHBLS	10//99-12//99
Construction and Maintenance	Hamilton-Middletown PMSA, OH	S	15.25 MW	14.72 AW	31730 AAW	OHBLS	10//99-12//99
Construction and Maintenance	Lima MSA, OH	S	13.92 MW	14.37 AW	28950 AAW	OHBLS	10//99-12//99
Construction and Maintenance	Mansfield MSA, OH	S	13.38 MW	12.19 AW	27830 AAW	OHBLS	10//99-12//99
Construction and Maintenance	Youngstown-Warren MSA, OH	S	15.47 MW	13.64 AW	32180 AAW	OHBLS	10//99-12//99
Construction and Maintenance	Oklahoma	S	11.77 MW	12.15 AW	25270 AAW	OKBLS	10//99-12//99
Construction and Maintenance	Lawton MSA, OK	S	11.43 MW	11.85 AW	23770 AAW	OKBLS	10//99-12//99
Construction and Maintenance	Oklahoma City MSA, OK	S	13.14 MW	12.67 AW	27340 AAW	OKBLS	10//99-12//99
Construction and Maintenance	Tulsa MSA, OK	S.	11.56 MW	11.20 AW	24050 AAW	OKBLS	10//99-12//99
Construction and Maintenance	Oregon	S	14.1 MW	13.66 AW	28420 AAW	ORBLS	10//99-12//99
Construction and Maintenance	Corvallis MSA, OR	S	10.80 MW	9.42 AW	22470 AAW	ORBLS	10//99-12//99
Construction and Maintenance	Eugene-Springfield MSA, OR	S	12.63 MW	12.52 AW	26270 AAW	ORBLS	10//99-12//99
Construction and Maintenance	Portland-Vancouver PMSA, OR-WA	S	13.84 MW	14.27 AW	28780 AAW	ORBLS	10//99-12//99
Construction and Maintenance	Salem PMSA, OR	S	12.10 MW	11.06 AW	25170 AAW	ORBLS	10//99-12//99
Construction and Maintenance	Pennsylvania	S	15.01 MW	15.06 AW	31320 AAW	PABLS	10//99-12//99
Construction and Maintenance	Allentown-Bethlehem-Easton MSA, PA	S	13.84 MW	13.01 AW	28790 AAW	PABLS	10//99-12//99
Construction and Maintenance	Altoona MSA, PA	S	10.32 MW	9.80 AW	21460 AAW	PABLS	10//99-12//99
Construction and Maintenance	Erie MSA, PA	S	10.33 MW	10.69 AW	21480 AAW	PABLS	10//99-12//99
Construction and Maintenance	Harrisburg-Lebanon-Carlisle MSA, PA	S	17.11 MW	18.26 AW	35580 AAW	PABLS	10//99-12//99
Construction and Maintenance	Johnstown MSA, PA	S	10.52 MW	8.80 AW	21890 AAW	PABLS	10//99-12//99

Painter

Occupation/Type/Industry	Location	Per	Low	Mid	High	Source	Date
Construction and Maintenance	Lancaster MSA, PA	S	12.51 MW	11.89 AW	26010 AAW	PABLS	10//99-12//99
Construction and Maintenance	Philadelphia PMSA, PA-NJ	S	15.49 MW	14.84 AW	32220 AAW	PABLS	10//99-12//99
Construction and Maintenance	Pittsburgh MSA, PA	S	17.20 MW	18.50 AW	35780 AAW	PABLS	10//99-12//99
Construction and Maintenance	Reading MSA, PA	S	13.12 MW	13.33 AW	27290 AAW	PABLS	10//99-12//99
Construction and Maintenance	Scranton--Wilkes-Barre--Hazleton MSA, PA	S	16.88 MW	18.23 AW	35110 AAW	PABLS	10//99-12//99
Construction and Maintenance	Sharon MSA, PA	S	12.80 MW	11.03 AW	26630 AAW	PABLS	10//99-12//99
Construction and Maintenance	Williamsport MSA, PA	S	12.63 MW	12.44 AW	26270 AAW	PABLS	10//99-12//99
Construction and Maintenance	York MSA, PA	S	12.77 MW	12.92 AW	26560 AAW	PABLS	10//99-12//99
Construction and Maintenance	Rhode Island	S	11.86 MW	12.25 AW	25470 AAW	RIBLS	10//99-12//99
Construction and Maintenance	Providence-Fall River-Warwick MSA, RI-MA	S	13.75 MW	13.07 AW	28590 AAW	RIBLS	10//99-12//99
Construction and Maintenance	South Carolina	S	10.35 MW	10.98 AW	22840 AAW	SCBLS	10//99-12//99
Construction and Maintenance	Charleston-North Charleston MSA, SC	S	11.98 MW	12.11 AW	24920 AAW	SCBLS	10//99-12//99
Construction and Maintenance	Columbia MSA, SC	S	10.33 MW	10.05 AW	21480 AAW	SCBLS	10//99-12//99
Construction and Maintenance	Florence MSA, SC	S	8.94 MW	9.41 AW	18590 AAW	SCBLS	10//99-12//99
Construction and Maintenance	Greenville-Spartanburg-Anderson MSA, SC	S	10.74 MW	10.27 AW	22350 AAW	SCBLS	10//99-12//99
Construction and Maintenance	Myrtle Beach MSA, SC	S	9.04 MW	9.44 AW	18810 AAW	SCBLS	10//99-12//99
Construction and Maintenance	Sumter MSA, SC	S	13.66 MW	13.85 AW	28410 AAW	SCBLS	10//99-12//99
Construction and Maintenance	South Dakota	S	10.14 MW	11.02 AW	22910 AAW	SDBLS	10//99-12//99
Construction and Maintenance	Rapid City MSA, SD	S	12.05 MW	11.21 AW	25070 AAW	SDBLS	10//99-12//99
Construction and Maintenance	Sioux Falls MSA, SD	S	10.10 MW	9.70 AW	21000 AAW	SDBLS	10//99-12//99
Construction and Maintenance	Tennessee	S	12.31 MW	12.80 AW	26620 AAW	TNBLS	10//99-12//99
Construction and Maintenance	Chattanooga MSA, TN-GA	S	13.43 MW	13.67 AW	27940 AAW	TNBLS	10//99-12//99
Construction and Maintenance	Clarksville-Hopkinsville MSA, TN-KY	S	12.47 MW	12.54 AW	25940 AAW	TNBLS	10//99-12//99
Construction and Maintenance	Johnson City-Kingsport-Bristol MSA, TN-VA	S	8.81 MW	8.26 AW	18320 AAW	TNBLS	10//99-12//99
Construction and Maintenance	Knoxville MSA, TN	S	11.31 MW	11.44 AW	23530 AAW	TNBLS	10//99-12//99
Construction and Maintenance	Memphis MSA, TN-AR-MS	S	13.05 MW	12.63 AW	27140 AAW	MSBLS	10//99-12//99
Construction and Maintenance	Nashville MSA, TN	S	14.06 MW	12.97 AW	29240 AAW	TNBLS	10//99-12//99
Construction and Maintenance	Texas	S	11.25 MW	11.42 AW	23750 AAW	TXBLS	10//99-12//99
Construction and Maintenance	Amarillo MSA, TX	S	11.70 MW	11.96 AW	24340 AAW	TXBLS	10//99-12//99
Construction and Maintenance	Austin-San Marcos MSA, TX	S	11.32 MW	11.44 AW	23550 AAW	TXBLS	10//99-12//99
Construction and Maintenance	Beaumont-Port Arthur MSA, TX	S	11.59 MW	11.66 AW	24110 AAW	TXBLS	10//99-12//99
Construction and Maintenance	Brazoria PMSA, TX	S	12.41 MW	12.26 AW	25800 AAW	TXBLS	10//99-12//99
Construction and Maintenance	Brownsville-Harlingen-San Benito MSA, TX	S	8.57 MW	8.21 AW	17820 AAW	TXBLS	10//99-12//99
Construction and Maintenance	Corpus Christi MSA, TX	S	11.16 MW	10.27 AW	23220 AAW	TXBLS	10//99-12//99
Construction and Maintenance	Dallas PMSA, TX	S	11.23 MW	11.10 AW	23360 AAW	TXBLS	10//99-12//99
Construction and Maintenance	El Paso MSA, TX	S	9.77 MW	9.62 AW	20330 AAW	TXBLS	10//99-12//99
Construction and Maintenance	Fort Worth-Arlington PMSA, TX	S	12.15 MW	11.80 AW	25270 AAW	TXBLS	10//99-12//99
Construction and Maintenance	Galveston-Texas City PMSA, TX	S	13.00 MW	12.98 AW	27040 AAW	TXBLS	10//99-12//99
Construction and Maintenance	Houston PMSA, TX	S	12.25 MW	11.91 AW	25480 AAW	TXBLS	10//99-12//99
Construction and Maintenance	Killeen-Temple MSA, TX	S	11.12 MW	10.55 AW	23140 AAW	TXBLS	10//99-12//99
Construction and Maintenance	Longview-Marshall MSA, TX	S	11.73 MW	11.93 AW	24390 AAW	TXBLS	10//99-12//99
Construction and Maintenance	Lubbock MSA, TX	S	9.10 MW	9.37 AW	18920 AAW	TXBLS	10//99-12//99
Construction and Maintenance	McAllen-Edinburg-Mission MSA, TX	S	7.33 MW	7.34 AW	15240 AAW	TXBLS	10//99-12//99
Construction and Maintenance	Odessa-Midland MSA, TX	S	11.99 MW	12.01 AW	24950 AAW	TXBLS	10//99-12//99
Construction and Maintenance	San Angelo MSA, TX	S	9.06 MW	8.44 AW	18840 AAW	TXBLS	10//99-12//99
Construction and Maintenance	San Antonio MSA, TX	S	9.36 MW	9.22 AW	19460 AAW	TXBLS	10//99-12//99
Construction and Maintenance	Sherman-Denison MSA, TX	S	12.89 MW	12.51 AW	26820 AAW	TXBLS	10//99-12//99
Construction and Maintenance	Tyler MSA, TX	S	11.41 MW	11.42 AW	23740 AAW	TXBLS	10//99-12//99
Construction and Maintenance	Victoria MSA, TX	S	10.60 MW	11.06 AW	22040 AAW	TXBLS	10//99-12//99
Construction and Maintenance	Wichita Falls MSA, TX	S	10.43 MW	10.11 AW	21680 AAW	TXBLS	10//99-12//99
Construction and Maintenance	Utah	S	12.62 MW	12.79 AW	26590 AAW	UTBLS	10//99-12//99
Construction and Maintenance	Provo-Orem MSA, UT	S	13.28 MW	13.05 AW	27620 AAW	UTBLS	10//99-12//99
Construction and Maintenance	Salt Lake City-Ogden MSA, UT	S	12.69 MW	12.59 AW	26400 AAW	UTBLS	10//99-12//99
Construction and Maintenance	Vermont	S	9.97 MW	10.24 AW	21290 AAW	VTBLS	10//99-12//99
Construction and Maintenance	Burlington MSA, VT	S	10.84 MW	10.36 AW	22550 AAW	VTBLS	10//99-12//99
Construction and Maintenance	Virginia	S	12.57 MW	12.69 AW	26400 AAW	VABLS	10//99-12//99
Construction and Maintenance	Charlottesville MSA, VA	S	12.22 MW	12.22 AW	25410 AAW	VABLS	10//99-12//99
Construction and Maintenance	Lynchburg MSA, VA	S	10.76 MW	11.34 AW	22380 AAW	VABLS	10//99-12//99

AAW	Average annual wage	AOH	Average offered, high	ASH	Average starting, high	H	Hourly	M	Monthly	S	Special: hourly and annual
AE	Average entry wage	AOL	Average offered, low	ASL	Average starting, low	HI	Highest wage paid	MTC	Median total compensation	TQ	Third quartile wage
AEX	Average experienced wage	APH	Average pay, high range	AW	Average wage paid	HR	High end range	MW	Median wage paid	W	Weekly
AO	Average offered	APL	Average pay, low range	FQ	First quartile wage	LR	Low end range	SQ	Second quartile wage	Y	Yearly

Occupation/Type/Industry	Location	Per	Low	Mid	High	Source	Date
Painter							
Construction and Maintenance	Norfolk-Virginia Beach-Newport News MSA, VA-NC	S	13.06 MW	13.84 AW	27170 AAW	VABLS	10//99-12//99
Construction and Maintenance	Richmond-Petersburg MSA, VA	S	12.53 MW	12.43 AW	26070 AAW	VABLS	10//99-12//99
Construction and Maintenance	Roanoke MSA, VA	S	10.41 MW	9.78 AW	21660 AAW	VABLS	10//99-12//99
Construction and Maintenance	Washington	S	16.79 MW	16.71 AW	34760 AAW	WABLS	10//99-12//99
Construction and Maintenance	Bellingham MSA, WA	S	18.97 MW	21.70 AW	39470 AAW	WABLS	10//99-12//99
Construction and Maintenance	Olympia PMSA, WA	S	12.89 MW	12.76 AW	26810 AAW	WABLS	10//99-12//99
Construction and Maintenance	Richland-Kennewick-Pasco MSA, WA	S	12.78 MW	10.17 AW	26580 AAW	WABLS	10//99-12//99
Construction and Maintenance	Seattle-Bellevue-Everett PMSA, WA	S	18.13 MW	18.48 AW	37720 AAW	WABLS	10//99-12//99
Construction and Maintenance	Spokane MSA, WA	S	15.04 MW	13.20 AW	31290 AAW	WABLS	10//99-12//99
Construction and Maintenance	Tacoma PMSA, WA	S	11.91 MW	10.19 AW	24780 AAW	WABLS	10//99-12//99
Construction and Maintenance	Yakima MSA, WA	S	14.79 MW	14.76 AW	30770 AAW	WABLS	10//99-12//99
Construction and Maintenance	West Virginia	S	13.75 MW	13.57 AW	28230 AAW	WVBLS	10//99-12//99
Construction and Maintenance	Charleston MSA, WV	S	16.22 MW	17.66 AW	33730 AAW	WVBLS	10//99-12//99
Construction and Maintenance	Huntington-Ashland MSA, WV-KY-OH	S	9.93 MW	9.25 AW	20650 AAW	WVBLS	10//99-12//99
Construction and Maintenance	Parkersburg-Marietta MSA, WV-OH	S	13.76 MW	13.61 AW	28610 AAW	WVBLS	10//99-12//99
Construction and Maintenance	Wheeling MSA, WV-OH	S	12.38 MW	11.68 AW	25750 AAW	WVBLS	10//99-12//99
Construction and Maintenance	Wisconsin	S	14.93 MW	16.34 AW	33990 AAW	WIBLS	10//99-12//99
Construction and Maintenance	Appleton-Oshkosh-Neenah MSA, WI	S	12.17 MW	12.50 AW	25310 AAW	WIBLS	10//99-12//99
Construction and Maintenance	Eau Claire MSA, WI	S	14.28 MW	14.52 AW	29700 AAW	WIBLS	10//99-12//99
Construction and Maintenance	Green Bay MSA, WI	S	13.21 MW	11.73 AW	27470 AAW	WIBLS	10//99-12//99
Construction and Maintenance	Janesville-Beloit MSA, WI	S	9.72 MW	9.50 AW	20230 AAW	WIBLS	10//99-12//99
Construction and Maintenance	La Crosse MSA, WI-MN	S	11.96 MW	11.92 AW	24870 AAW	WIBLS	10//99-12//99
Construction and Maintenance	Madison MSA, WI	S	18.02 MW	18.39 AW	37480 AAW	WIBLS	10//99-12//99
Construction and Maintenance	Milwaukee-Waukesha PMSA, WI	S	17.86 MW	17.18 AW	37140 AAW	WIBLS	10//99-12//99
Construction and Maintenance	Racine PMSA, WI	S	13.71 MW	12.80 AW	28510 AAW	WIBLS	10//99-12//99
Construction and Maintenance	Sheboygan MSA, WI	S	10.62 MW	10.26 AW	22090 AAW	WIBLS	10//99-12//99
Construction and Maintenance	Wausau MSA, WI	S	13.62 MW	13.22 AW	28330 AAW	WIBLS	10//99-12//99
Construction and Maintenance	Wyoming	S	11.25 MW	12.46 AW	25920 AAW	WYBLS	10//99-12//99
Construction and Maintenance	Casper MSA, WY	S	10.06 MW	9.95 AW	20930 AAW	WYBLS	10//99-12//99
Construction and Maintenance	Cheyenne MSA, WY	S	10.95 MW	10.14 AW	22770 AAW	WYBLS	10//99-12//99
Construction and Maintenance	Puerto Rico	S	6.16 MW	6.42 AW	13350 AAW	PRBLS	10//99-12//99
Construction and Maintenance	Arecibo PMSA, PR	S	5.89 MW	6.02 AW	12260 AAW	PRBLS	10//99-12//99
Construction and Maintenance	Caguas PMSA, PR	S	6.95 MW	7.14 AW	14460 AAW	PRBLS	10//99-12//99
Construction and Maintenance	Mayaguez MSA, PR	S	5.89 MW	6.00 AW	12240 AAW	PRBLS	10//99-12//99
Construction and Maintenance	Ponce MSA, PR	S	6.24 MW	6.16 AW	12980 AAW	PRBLS	10//99-12//99
Construction and Maintenance	San Juan-Bayamon PMSA, PR	S	6.51 MW	6.16 AW	13530 AAW	PRBLS	10//99-12//99
Construction and Maintenance	Virgin Islands	S	11.53 MW	11.23 AW	23360 AAW	VIBLS	10//99-12//99
Construction and Maintenance	Guam	S	12.23 MW	12.32 AW	25630 AAW	GUBLS	10//99-12//99
Production, Manufacturing	United States	Y		31675 AW		WARD3	1998
Transportation Equipment	Alabama	S	12.71 MW	13.47 AW	28020 AAW	ALBLS	10//99-12//99
Transportation Equipment	Arizona	S	14.65 MW	17.28 AW	35940 AAW	AZBLS	10//99-12//99
Transportation Equipment	Arkansas	S	11.29 MW	12.34 AW	25670 AAW	ARBLS	10//99-12//99
Transportation Equipment	California	S	13.15 MW	15.08 AW	31370 AAW	CABLS	10//99-12//99
Transportation Equipment	Connecticut	S	14.17 MW	14.47 AW	30100 AAW	CTBLS	10//99-12//99
Transportation Equipment	Delaware	S	15.66 MW	14.82 AW	30820 AAW	DEBLS	10//99-12//99
Transportation Equipment	Florida	S	11.68 MW	13.22 AW	27510 AAW	FLBLS	10//99-12//99
Transportation Equipment	Georgia	S	14.3 MW	15.14 AW	31480 AAW	GABLS	10//99-12//99
Transportation Equipment	Hawaii	S	18.12 MW	17.18 AW	35740 AAW	HIBLS	10//99-12//99
Transportation Equipment	Idaho	S	15.14 MW	15.38 AW	31990 AAW	IDBLS	10//99-12//99
Transportation Equipment	Illinois	S	15.91 MW	17.78 AW	36990 AAW	ILBLS	10//99-12//99
Transportation Equipment	Indiana	S	15.89 MW	15.75 AW	32760 AAW	INBLS	10//99-12//99
Transportation Equipment	Iowa	S	12.25 MW	13.53 AW	28150 AAW	IABLS	10//99-12//99
Transportation Equipment	Kansas	S	15.68 MW	16.04 AW	33370 AAW	KSBLS	10//99-12//99
Transportation Equipment	Louisiana	S	11.59 MW	13.29 AW	27630 AAW	LABLS	10//99-12//99
Transportation Equipment	Maryland	S	18.16 MW	20.56 AW	42760 AAW	MDBLS	10//99-12//99
Transportation Equipment	Massachusetts	S	17.31 MW	16.23 AW	33760 AAW	MABLS	10//99-12//99
Transportation Equipment	Michigan	S	21.65 MW	20.54 AW	42720 AAW	MIBLS	10//99-12//99
Transportation Equipment	Minnesota	S	12.94 MW	15.83 AW	32930 AAW	MNBLS	10//99-12//99
Transportation Equipment	Missouri	S	18.6 MW	18.06 AW	37570 AAW	MOBLS	10//99-12//99
Transportation Equipment	Nebraska	S	11.03 MW	12.55 AW	26110 AAW	NEBLS	10//99-12//99
Transportation Equipment	Nevada	S	14.5 MW	14.99 AW	31170 AAW	NVBLS	10//99-12//99
Transportation Equipment	New Jersey	S	16.62 MW	19.07 AW	39660 AAW	NJBLS	10//99-12//99

AAW Average annual wage	**AOH** Average offered, high	**ASH** Average starting, high	**H** Hourly	**M** Monthly	**S** Special: hourly and annual
AE Average entry wage	**AOL** Average offered, low	**ASL** Average starting, low	**HI** Highest wage paid	**MTC** Median total compensation	**TQ** Third quartile wage
AEX Average experienced wage	**APH** Average pay, high range	**AW** Average wage paid	**HR** High end range	**MW** Median wage paid	**W** Weekly
AO Average offered	**APL** Average pay, low range	**FQ** First quartile wage	**LR** Low end range	**SQ** Second quartile wage	**Y** Yearly

Occupation/Type/Industry	Location	Per	Low	Mid	High	Source	Date
Painter							
Transportation Equipment	New York	S	12.42 MW	13.74 AW	28580 AAW	NYBLS	10//99-12//99
Transportation Equipment	North Carolina	S	13.56 MW	14.62 AW	30400 AAW	NCBLS	10//99-12//99
Transportation Equipment	North Dakota	S	11.17 MW	12.05 AW	25060 AAW	NDBLS	10//99-12//99
Transportation Equipment	Ohio	S	16.04 MW	16.94 AW	35240 AAW	OHBLS	10//99-12//99
Transportation Equipment	Oklahoma	S	12.03 MW	11.96 AW	24880 AAW	OKBLS	10//99-12//99
Transportation Equipment	Oregon	S	15.27 MW	16.01 AW	33310 AAW	ORBLS	10//99-12//99
Transportation Equipment	Pennsylvania	S	13.47 MW	13.51 AW	28100 AAW	PABLS	10//99-12//99
Transportation Equipment	Rhode Island	S	12.31 MW	12.97 AW	26970 AAW	RIBLS	10//99-12//99
Transportation Equipment	South Carolina	S	11.79 MW	13.68 AW	28450 AAW	SCBLS	10//99-12//99
Transportation Equipment	South Dakota	S	12.64 MW	13.96 AW	29040 AAW	SDBLS	10//99-12//99
Transportation Equipment	Tennessee	S	15.25 MW	15.34 AW	31900 AAW	TNBLS	10//99-12//99
Transportation Equipment	Texas	S	13.46 MW	15.11 AW	31420 AAW	TXBLS	10//99-12//99
Transportation Equipment	Vermont	S	13.89 MW	13.06 AW	27170 AAW	VTBLS	10//99-12//99
Transportation Equipment	Virginia	S	16.94 MW	16.69 AW	34720 AAW	VABLS	10//99-12//99
Transportation Equipment	West Virginia	S	12.8 MW	13.37 AW	27810 AAW	WVBLS	10//99-12//99
Transportation Equipment	Wisconsin	S	13.25 MW	14.39 AW	29930 AAW	WIBLS	10//99-12//99
Transportation Equipment	Wyoming	S	12.9 MW	13.05 AW	27140 AAW	WYBLS	10//99-12//99
Transportation Equipment	Puerto Rico	S	8.46 MW	10.25 AW	21320 AAW	PRBLS	10//99-12//99
Painting, Coating, and Decorating Worker							
	Alabama	S	9.72 MW	11.15 AW	23190 AAW	ALBLS	10//99-12//99
	Birmingham MSA, AL	S	12.46 MW	10.71 AW	25920 AAW	ALBLS	10//99-12//99
	Mobile MSA, AL	S	7.21 MW	7.19 AW	15000 AAW	ALBLS	10//99-12//99
	Arizona	S	9.58 MW	10.67 AW	22190 AAW	AZBLS	10//99-12//99
	Phoenix-Mesa MSA, AZ	S	11.09 MW	10.29 AW	23070 AAW	AZBLS	10//99-12//99
	Tucson MSA, AZ	S	8.19 MW	7.66 AW	17030 AAW	AZBLS	10//99-12//99
	Arkansas	S	9.24 MW	9.03 AW	18780 AAW	ARBLS	10//99-12//99
	California	S	10.1 MW	11.07 AW	23010 AAW	CABLS	10//99-12//99
	Bakersfield MSA, CA	S	12.08 MW	11.52 AW	25130 AAW	CABLS	10//99-12//99
	Chico-Paradise MSA, CA	S	7.73 MW	6.39 AW	16090 AAW	CABLS	10//99-12//99
	Los Angeles-Long Beach PMSA, CA	S	9.92 MW	9.12 AW	20640 AAW	CABLS	10//99-12//99
	Oakland PMSA, CA	S	11.87 MW	10.63 AW	24690 AAW	CABLS	10//99-12//99
	Orange County PMSA, CA	S	12.66 MW	12.49 AW	26340 AAW	CABLS	10//99-12//99
	Riverside-San Bernardino PMSA, CA	S	10.84 MW	10.73 AW	22560 AAW	CABLS	10//99-12//99
	Sacramento PMSA, CA	S	8.41 MW	6.75 AW	17490 AAW	CABLS	10//99-12//99
	San Diego MSA, CA	S	10.76 MW	10.43 AW	22370 AAW	CABLS	10//99-12//99
	San Francisco PMSA, CA	S	12.73 MW	11.82 AW	26480 AAW	CABLS	10//99-12//99
	San Jose PMSA, CA	S	13.89 MW	12.42 AW	28890 AAW	CABLS	10//99-12//99
	Vallejo-Fairfield-Napa PMSA, CA	S	10.04 MW	9.44 AW	20890 AAW	CABLS	10//99-12//99
	Ventura PMSA, CA	S	10.08 MW	7.65 AW	20970 AAW	CABLS	10//99-12//99
	Visalia-Tulare-Porterville MSA, CA	S	10.04 MW	8.27 AW	20890 AAW	CABLS	10//99-12//99
	Colorado	S	10.73 MW	10.72 AW	22300 AAW	COBLS	10//99-12//99
	Boulder-Longmont PMSA, CO	S	8.04 MW	7.33 AW	16720 AAW	COBLS	10//99-12//99
	Colorado Springs MSA, CO	S	11.17 MW	10.71 AW	23240 AAW	COBLS	10//99-12//99
	Denver PMSA, CO	S	11.51 MW	11.40 AW	23940 AAW	COBLS	10//99-12//99
	Fort Collins-Loveland MSA, CO	S	11.24 MW	11.19 AW	23380 AAW	COBLS	10//99-12//99
	Greeley PMSA, CO	S	10.62 MW	11.16 AW	22080 AAW	COBLS	10//99-12//99
	Connecticut	S	10.57 MW	11.20 AW	23290 AAW	CTBLS	10//99-12//99
	Bridgeport PMSA, CT	S	12.07 MW	11.33 AW	25110 AAW	CTBLS	10//99-12//99
	Hartford MSA, CT	S	10.67 MW	9.72 AW	22200 AAW	CTBLS	10//99-12//99
	Washington PMSA, DC-MD-VA-WV	S	14.33 MW	14.39 AW	29800 AAW	DCBLS	10//99-12//99
	Florida	S	9 MW	9.44 AW	19640 AAW	FLBLS	10//99-12//99
	Daytona Beach MSA, FL	S	9.28 MW	8.48 AW	19310 AAW	FLBLS	10//99-12//99
	Fort Lauderdale PMSA, FL	S	10.00 MW	9.59 AW	20800 AAW	FLBLS	10//99-12//99
	Miami PMSA, FL	S	8.50 MW	7.36 AW	17690 AAW	FLBLS	10//99-12//99
	Tampa-St. Petersburg-Clearwater MSA, FL	S	10.26 MW	11.09 AW	21350 AAW	FLBLS	10//99-12//99
	Georgia	S	9.25 MW	10.07 AW	20950 AAW	GABLS	10//99-12//99
	Atlanta MSA, GA	S	11.65 MW	11.40 AW	24220 AAW	GABLS	10//99-12//99
	Hawaii	S	10.17 MW	11.04 AW	22970 AAW	HIBLS	10//99-12//99
	Honolulu MSA, HI	S	10.93 MW	10.08 AW	22730 AAW	HIBLS	10//99-12//99
	Idaho	S	11.35 MW	11.80 AW	24540 AAW	IDBLS	10//99-12//99
	Boise City MSA, ID	S	10.90 MW	10.27 AW	22670 AAW	IDBLS	10//99-12//99
	Illinois	S	10.63 MW	11.13 AW	23150 AAW	ILBLS	10//99-12//99
	Chicago PMSA, IL	S	10.82 MW	10.31 AW	22510 AAW	ILBLS	10//99-12//99

AAW Average annual wage	**AOH** Average offered, high	**ASH** Average starting, high	**H** Hourly	**M** Monthly	**S** Special: hourly and annual
AE Average entry wage	**AOL** Average offered, low	**ASL** Average starting, low	**HI** Highest wage paid	**MTC** Median total compensation	**TQ** Third quartile wage
AEX Average experienced wage	**APH** Average pay, high range	**AW** Average wage paid	**HR** High end range	**MW** Median wage paid	**W** Weekly
AO Average offered	**APL** Average pay, low range	**FQ** First quartile wage	**LR** Low end range	**SQ** Second quartile wage	**Y** Yearly

Occupation/Type/Industry	Location	Per	Low	Mid	High	Source	Date
Painting, Coating, and Decorating Worker	Indiana	S	8.9 MW	9.91 AW	20600 AAW	INBLS	10//99-12//99
	Elkhart-Goshen MSA, IN	S	10.25 MW	10.07 AW	21320 AAW	INBLS	10//99-12//99
	Evansville-Henderson MSA, IN-KY	S	9.95 MW	9.47 AW	20690 AAW	INBLS	10//99-12//99
	Fort Wayne MSA, IN	S	11.00 MW	10.20 AW	22870 AAW	INBLS	10//99-12//99
	Lafayette MSA, IN	S	8.98 MW	8.53 AW	18670 AAW	INBLS	10//99-12//99
	South Bend MSA, IN	S	10.28 MW	10.20 AW	21390 AAW	INBLS	10//99-12//99
	Terre Haute MSA, IN	S	10.16 MW	8.20 AW	21120 AAW	INBLS	10//99-12//99
	Iowa	S	10.1 MW	10.66 AW	22170 AAW	IABLS	10//99-12//99
	Davenport-Moline-Rock Island MSA, IA-IL	S	14.25 MW	13.41 AW	29630 AAW	IABLS	10//99-12//99
	Kansas	S	8.11 MW	8.69 AW	18070 AAW	KSBLS	10//99-12//99
	Kentucky	S	9.64 MW	10.76 AW	22380 AAW	KYBLS	10//99-12//99
	Lexington MSA, KY	S	12.36 MW	10.40 AW	25720 AAW	KYBLS	10//99-12//99
	Louisville MSA, KY-IN	S	10.33 MW	9.65 AW	21490 AAW	KYBLS	10//99-12//99
	Louisiana	S	8.86 MW	9.50 AW	19770 AAW	LABLS	10//99-12//99
	Lake Charles MSA, LA	S	8.82 MW	7.84 AW	18340 AAW	LABLS	10//99-12//99
	New Orleans MSA, LA	S	9.64 MW	9.31 AW	20040 AAW	LABLS	10//99-12//99
	Shreveport-Bossier City MSA, LA	S	12.45 MW	10.11 AW	25890 AAW	LABLS	10//99-12//99
	Maine	S	8.48 MW	8.67 AW	18040 AAW	MEBLS	10//99-12//99
	Maryland	S	10.16 MW	10.71 AW	22280 AAW	MDBLS	10//99-12//99
	Baltimore PMSA, MD	S	10.38 MW	10.01 AW	21590 AAW	MDBLS	10//99-12//99
	Massachusetts	S	9.97 MW	10.60 AW	22050 AAW	MABLS	10//99-12//99
	Boston PMSA, MA-NH	S	10.34 MW	9.89 AW	21510 AAW	MABLS	10//99-12//99
	Fitchburg-Leominster PMSA, MA	S	9.14 MW	8.38 AW	19000 AAW	MABLS	10//99-12//99
	Michigan	S	10.67 MW	12.45 AW	25900 AAW	MIBLS	10//99-12//99
	Ann Arbor PMSA, MI	S	8.17 MW	7.76 AW	17000 AAW	MIBLS	10//99-12//99
	Detroit PMSA, MI	S	13.49 MW	10.62 AW	28060 AAW	MIBLS	10//99-12//99
	Grand Rapids-Muskegon-Holland MSA, MI	S	11.58 MW	11.75 AW	24080 AAW	MIBLS	10//99-12//99
	Minnesota	S	11.2 MW	11.83 AW	24600 AAW	MNBLS	10//99-12//99
	Minneapolis-St. Paul MSA, MN-WI	S	12.30 MW	11.32 AW	25590 AAW	MNBLS	10//99-12//99
	St. Cloud MSA, MN	S	7.61 MW	6.88 AW	15830 AAW	MNBLS	10//99-12//99
	Mississippi	S	8.01 MW	8.29 AW	17250 AAW	MSBLS	10//99-12//99
	Missouri	S	8.79 MW	9.43 AW	19610 AAW	MOBLS	10//99-12//99
	Kansas City MSA, MO-KS	S	8.93 MW	8.52 AW	18570 AAW	MOBLS	10//99-12//99
	St. Louis MSA, MO-IL	S	11.26 MW	11.14 AW	23420 AAW	MOBLS	10//99-12//99
	Montana	S	7.73 MW	8.50 AW	17690 AAW	MTBLS	10//99-12//99
	Nebraska	S	9.14 MW	9.49 AW	19750 AAW	NEBLS	10//99-12//99
	Omaha MSA, NE-IA	S	9.68 MW	9.54 AW	20130 AAW	NEBLS	10//99-12//99
	Nevada	S	10.78 MW	11.55 AW	24020 AAW	NVBLS	10//99-12//99
	Las Vegas MSA, NV-AZ	S	11.57 MW	10.76 AW	24070 AAW	NVBLS	10//99-12//99
	Reno MSA, NV	S	9.96 MW	9.74 AW	20720 AAW	NVBLS	10//99-12//99
	New Hampshire	S	9.99 MW	11.49 AW	23900 AAW	NHBLS	10//99-12//99
	New Jersey	S	10.59 MW	12.00 AW	24960 AAW	NJBLS	10//99-12//99
	Bergen-Passaic PMSA, NJ	S	12.50 MW	9.11 AW	25990 AAW	NJBLS	10//99-12//99
	Middlesex-Somerset-Hunterdon PMSA, NJ	S	8.53 MW	7.97 AW	17740 AAW	NJBLS	10//99-12//99
	Monmouth-Ocean PMSA, NJ	S	9.38 MW	8.96 AW	19510 AAW	NJBLS	10//99-12//99
	Newark PMSA, NJ	S	12.07 MW	10.82 AW	25100 AAW	NJBLS	10//99-12//99
	New Mexico	S	11.64 MW	10.58 AW	22000 AAW	NMBLS	10//99-12//99
	Albuquerque MSA, NM	S	11.43 MW	12.26 AW	23780 AAW	NMBLS	10//99-12//99
	New York	S	10.67 MW	10.95 AW	22780 AAW	NYBLS	10//99-12//99
	Buffalo-Niagara Falls MSA, NY	S	10.34 MW	10.95 AW	21510 AAW	NYBLS	10//99-12//99
	Nassau-Suffolk PMSA, NY	S	9.55 MW	8.33 AW	19870 AAW	NYBLS	10//99-12//99
	New York PMSA, NY	S	12.28 MW	11.83 AW	25540 AAW	NYBLS	10//99-12//99
	Syracuse MSA, NY	S	10.06 MW	9.84 AW	20930 AAW	NYBLS	10//99-12//99
	North Carolina	S	9.49 MW	9.99 AW	20790 AAW	NCBLS	10//99-12//99
	Charlotte-Gastonia-Rock Hill MSA, NC-SC	S	9.85 MW	9.60 AW	20490 AAW	NCBLS	10//99-12//99
	Greensboro--Winston-Salem--High Point MSA, NC	S	8.80 MW	8.44 AW	18310 AAW	NCBLS	10//99-12//99
	Greenville MSA, NC	S	7.54 MW	6.63 AW	15680 AAW	NCBLS	10//99-12//99
	Hickory-Morganton-Lenoir MSA, NC	S	9.81 MW	9.25 AW	20400 AAW	NCBLS	10//99-12//99
	Raleigh-Durham-Chapel Hill MSA, NC	S	16.23 MW	20.65 AW	33760 AAW	NCBLS	10//99-12//99

AAW	Average annual wage	AOH	Average offered, high	ASH	Average starting, high	H	Hourly	M	Monthly	S	Special: hourly and annual
AE	Average entry wage	AOL	Average offered, low	ASL	Average starting, low	HI	Highest wage paid	MTC	Median total compensation	TQ	Third quartile wage
AEX	Average experienced wage	APH	Average pay, high range	AW	Average wage paid	HR	High end range	MW	Median wage paid	W	Weekly
AO	Average offered	APL	Average pay, low range	FQ	First quartile wage	LR	Low end range	SQ	Second quartile wage	Y	Yearly

Occupation/Type/Industry	Location	Per	Low	Mid	High	Source	Date
Painting, Coating, and Decorating Worker	North Dakota	s	7.64 MW	8.33 AW	17330 AAW	NDBLS	10//99-12//99
	Fargo-Moorhead MSA, ND-MN	s	9.06 MW	6.84 AW	18830 AAW	NDBLS	10//99-12//99
	Ohio	s	8.62 MW	9.49 AW	19750 AAW	OHBLS	10//99-12//99
	Akron PMSA, OH	s	7.75 MW	6.86 AW	16130 AAW	OHBLS	10//99-12//99
	Cincinnati PMSA, OH-KY-IN	s	10.21 MW	9.58 AW	21240 AAW	OHBLS	10//99-12//99
	Cleveland-Lorain-Elyria PMSA, OH	s	8.89 MW	8.05 AW	18490 AAW	OHBLS	10//99-12//99
	Columbus MSA, OH	s	10.32 MW	9.37 AW	21470 AAW	OHBLS	10//99-12//99
	Toledo MSA, OH	s	8.40 MW	7.79 AW	17460 AAW	OHBLS	10//99-12//99
	Youngstown-Warren MSA, OH	s	8.16 MW	8.69 AW	16980 AAW	OHBLS	10//99-12//99
	Oklahoma	s	8.46 MW	9.36 AW	19470 AAW	OKBLS	10//99-12//99
	Oklahoma City MSA, OK	s	8.97 MW	8.06 AW	18670 AAW	OKBLS	10//99-12//99
	Tulsa MSA, OK	s	9.88 MW	8.45 AW	20550 AAW	OKBLS	10//99-12//99
	Oregon	s	12.34 MW	11.97 AW	24890 AAW	ORBLS	10//99-12//99
	Medford-Ashland MSA, OR	s	10.60 MW	10.62 AW	22050 AAW	ORBLS	10//99-12//99
	Portland-Vancouver PMSA, OR-WA	s	12.46 MW	13.16 AW	25910 AAW	ORBLS	10//99-12//99
	Pennsylvania	s	9.24 MW	9.79 AW	20360 AAW	PABLS	10//99-12//99
	Lancaster MSA, PA	s	10.83 MW	8.52 AW	22540 AAW	PABLS	10//99-12//99
	Philadelphia PMSA, PA-NJ	s	10.53 MW	10.71 AW	21900 AAW	PABLS	10//99-12//99
	Pittsburgh MSA, PA	s	9.90 MW	10.04 AW	20580 AAW	PABLS	10//99-12//99
	Scranton--Wilkes-Barre--Hazleton MSA, PA	s	10.53 MW	10.33 AW	21900 AAW	PABLS	10//99-12//99
	York MSA, PA	s	9.33 MW	8.19 AW	19400 AAW	PABLS	10//99-12//99
	Rhode Island	s	8.73 MW	8.95 AW	18610 AAW	RIBLS	10//99-12//99
	Providence-Fall River-Warwick MSA, RI-MA	s	9.36 MW	9.07 AW	19470 AAW	RIBLS	10//99-12//99
	South Carolina	s	8.16 MW	8.99 AW	18690 AAW	SCBLS	10//99-12//99
	Columbia MSA, SC	s	10.12 MW	9.01 AW	21050 AAW	SCBLS	10//99-12//99
	Greenville-Spartanburg-Anderson MSA, SC	s	8.30 MW	7.96 AW	17250 AAW	SCBLS	10//99-12//99
	South Dakota	s	8.2 MW	8.55 AW	17790 AAW	SDBLS	10//99-12//99
	Tennessee	s	9.86 MW	10.27 AW	21370 AAW	TNBLS	10//99-12//99
	Knoxville MSA, TN	s	10.11 MW	10.09 AW	21030 AAW	TNBLS	10//99-12//99
	Memphis MSA, TN-AR-MS	s	10.86 MW	9.01 AW	22580 AAW	MSBLS	10//99-12//99
	Nashville MSA, TN	s	12.17 MW	12.30 AW	25320 AAW	TNBLS	10//99-12//99
	Texas	s	8.5 MW	9.50 AW	19760 AAW	TXBLS	10//99-12//99
	Dallas PMSA, TX	s	9.53 MW	9.14 AW	19830 AAW	TXBLS	10//99-12//99
	Fort Worth-Arlington PMSA, TX	s	8.45 MW	7.59 AW	17570 AAW	TXBLS	10//99-12//99
	Houston PMSA, TX	s	10.35 MW	9.79 AW	21520 AAW	TXBLS	10//99-12//99
	Longview-Marshall MSA, TX	s	6.21 MW	6.01 AW	12920 AAW	TXBLS	10//99-12//99
	San Antonio MSA, TX	s	11.59 MW	9.51 AW	24110 AAW	TXBLS	10//99-12//99
	Utah	s	8.72 MW	9.44 AW	19640 AAW	UTBLS	10//99-12//99
	Salt Lake City-Ogden MSA, UT	s	9.48 MW	8.76 AW	19720 AAW	UTBLS	10//99-12//99
	Vermont	s	10.5 MW	10.49 AW	21830 AAW	VTBLS	10//99-12//99
	Virginia	s	8.72 MW	9.92 AW	20620 AAW	VABLS	10//99-12//99
	Norfolk-Virginia Beach-Newport News MSA, VA-NC	s	8.55 MW	6.87 AW	17780 AAW	VABLS	10//99-12//99
	Washington	s	10.56 MW	11.43 AW	23780 AAW	WABLS	10//99-12//99
	Seattle-Bellevue-Everett PMSA, WA	s	11.31 MW	10.67 AW	23520 AAW	WABLS	10//99-12//99
	Spokane MSA, WA	s	10.19 MW	8.86 AW	21200 AAW	WABLS	10//99-12//99
	Tacoma PMSA, WA	s	12.19 MW	12.64 AW	25350 AAW	WABLS	10//99-12//99
	West Virginia	s	7.69 MW	8.37 AW	17410 AAW	WVBLS	10//99-12//99
	Parkersburg-Marietta MSA, WV-OH	s	8.87 MW	8.38 AW	18450 AAW	WVBLS	10//99-12//99
	Wisconsin	s	8.87 MW	9.54 AW	19850 AAW	WIBLS	10//99-12//99
	Appleton-Oshkosh-Neenah MSA, WI	s	8.90 MW	9.19 AW	18520 AAW	WIBLS	10//99-12//99
	Madison MSA, WI	s	9.99 MW	9.21 AW	20780 AAW	WIBLS	10//99-12//99
	Milwaukee-Waukesha PMSA, WI	s	11.60 MW	11.69 AW	24120 AAW	WIBLS	10//99-12//99
	Racine PMSA, WI	s	9.41 MW	9.05 AW	19570 AAW	WIBLS	10//99-12//99
	Puerto Rico	s	6.59 MW	7.12 AW	14820 AAW	PRBLS	10//99-12//99
	San Juan-Bayamon PMSA, PR	s	6.86 MW	6.35 AW	14270 AAW	PRBLS	10//99-12//99

AAW	Average annual wage	AOH	Average offered, high	ASH	Average starting, high	H	Hourly	M	Monthly	S	Special: hourly and annual
AE	Average entry wage	AOL	Average offered, low	ASL	Average starting, low	HI	Highest wage paid	MTC	Median total compensation	TQ	Third quartile wage
AEX	Average experienced wage	APH	Average pay, high range	AW	Average wage paid	HR	High end range	MW	Median wage paid	W	Weekly
AO	Average offered	APL	Average pay, low range	FQ	First quartile wage	LR	Low end range	SQ	Second quartile wage	Y	Yearly

Occupation/Type/Industry	Location	Per	Low	Mid	High	Source	Date
Paper Goods Machine Setter, Operator, and Tender	Alabama	S	11.26 MW	11.32 AW	23550 AAW	ALBLS	10//99-12//99
	Arizona	S	9.01 MW	9.48 AW	19730 AAW	AZBLS	10//99-12//99
	Arkansas	S	15.36 MW	15.69 AW	32630 AAW	ARBLS	10//99-12//99
	California	S	14.19 MW	13.97 AW	29060 AAW	CABLS	10//99-12//99
	Colorado	S	12.16 MW	12.20 AW	25370 AAW	COBLS	10//99-12//99
	Connecticut	S	10.89 MW	10.88 AW	22640 AAW	CTBLS	10//99-12//99
	Florida	S	11.88 MW	11.86 AW	24660 AAW	FLBLS	10//99-12//99
	Georgia	S	11.45 MW	12.09 AW	25160 AAW	GABLS	10//99-12//99
	Idaho	S	12.09 MW	12.09 AW	25140 AAW	IDBLS	10//99-12//99
	Illinois	S	12.5 MW	12.71 AW	26440 AAW	ILBLS	10//99-12//99
	Indiana	S	12.82 MW	12.79 AW	26610 AAW	INBLS	10//99-12//99
	Iowa	S	12.74 MW	12.85 AW	26730 AAW	IABLS	10//99-12//99
	Kansas	S	12.76 MW	13.47 AW	28020 AAW	KSBLS	10//99-12//99
	Kentucky	S	12.82 MW	13.80 AW	28710 AAW	KYBLS	10//99-12//99
	Louisiana	S	17.33 MW	18.51 AW	38500 AAW	LABLS	10//99-12//99
	Maine	S	14.66 MW	14.05 AW	29230 AAW	MEBLS	10//99-12//99
	Maryland	S	12.25 MW	12.46 AW	25920 AAW	MDBLS	10//99-12//99
	Massachusetts	S	13.01 MW	12.71 AW	26430 AAW	MABLS	10//99-12//99
	Michigan	S	13.23 MW	12.75 AW	26510 AAW	MIBLS	10//99-12//99
	Minnesota	S	13.2 MW	13.69 AW	28470 AAW	MNBLS	10//99-12//99
	Mississippi	S	12.21 MW	12.93 AW	26900 AAW	MSBLS	10//99-12//99
	Missouri	S	10.49 MW	10.52 AW	21880 AAW	MOBLS	10//99-12//99
	Nebraska	S	12.25 MW	12.18 AW	25330 AAW	NEBLS	10//99-12//99
	Nevada	S	11.23 MW	11.44 AW	23790 AAW	NVBLS	10//99-12//99
	New Hampshire	S	12.28 MW	12.17 AW	25310 AAW	NHBLS	10//99-12//99
	New Jersey	S	12.25 MW	12.80 AW	26630 AAW	NJBLS	10//99-12//99
	New York	S	12.58 MW	12.58 AW	26160 AAW	NYBLS	10//99-12//99
	North Carolina	S	11.98 MW	12.08 AW	25130 AAW	NCBLS	10//99-12//99
	Ohio	S	12.3 MW	12.54 AW	26080 AAW	OHBLS	10//99-12//99
	Oklahoma	S	11.89 MW	12.91 AW	26850 AAW	OKBLS	10//99-12//99
	Oregon	S	14.04 MW	14.16 AW	29460 AAW	ORBLS	10//99-12//99
	Pennsylvania	S	13.82 MW	13.79 AW	28690 AAW	PABLS	10//99-12//99
	Rhode Island	S	12.39 MW	12.79 AW	26600 AAW	RIBLS	10//99-12//99
	South Carolina	S	11.95 MW	13.77 AW	28650 AAW	SCBLS	10//99-12//99
	Tennessee	S	11.9 MW	13.91 AW	28940 AAW	TNBLS	10//99-12//99
	Texas	S	12.68 MW	12.69 AW	26390 AAW	TXBLS	10//99-12//99
	Utah	S	12.1 MW	12.00 AW	24960 AAW	UTBLS	10//99-12//99
	Vermont	S	12.58 MW	12.65 AW	26300 AAW	VTBLS	10//99-12//99
	Virginia	S	12.41 MW	12.48 AW	25960 AAW	VABLS	10//99-12//99
	Washington	S	15.7 MW	15.61 AW	32470 AAW	WABLS	10//99-12//99
	West Virginia	S	14.53 MW	13.41 AW	27890 AAW	WVBLS	10//99-12//99
	Wisconsin	S	14.65 MW	15.03 AW	31260 AAW	WIBLS	10//99-12//99
	Puerto Rico	S	6.48 MW	6.91 AW	14380 AAW	PRBLS	10//99-12//99
Paperhanger	Alabama	S	11.51 MW	11.73 AW	24400 AAW	ALBLS	10//99-12//99
	California	S	16.62 MW	17.95 AW	37330 AAW	CABLS	10//99-12//99
	Oakland PMSA, CA	S	24.28 MW	24.68 AW	50500 AAW	CABLS	10//99-12//99
	Washington PMSA, DC-MD-VA-WV	S	17.65 MW	17.80 AW	36720 AAW	DCBLS	10//99-12//99
	Florida	S	11.25 MW	11.14 AW	23160 AAW	FLBLS	10//99-12//99
	Georgia	S	9.6 MW	10.01 AW	20830 AAW	GABLS	10//99-12//99
	Illinois	S	23.11 MW	20.36 AW	42340 AAW	ILBLS	10//99-12//99
	Chicago PMSA, IL	S	18.94 MW	22.65 AW	39400 AAW	ILBLS	10//99-12//99
	Peoria-Pekin MSA, IL	S	28.88 MW	30.34 AW	60070 AAW	ILBLS	10//99-12//99
	Indiana	S	17.51 MW	16.93 AW	35200 AAW	INBLS	10//99-12//99
	Indianapolis MSA, IN	S	17.30 MW	17.74 AW	35980 AAW	INBLS	10//99-12//99
	Kentucky	S	10.88 MW	12.54 AW	26070 AAW	KYBLS	10//99-12//99
	Louisville MSA, KY-IN	S	12.73 MW	11.77 AW	26490 AAW	KYBLS	10//99-12//99
	Maine	S	10.66 MW	11.44 AW	23800 AAW	MEBLS	10//99-12//99
	Maryland	S	18.24 MW	17.61 AW	36620 AAW	MDBLS	10//99-12//99
	Baltimore PMSA, MD	S	18.73 MW	19.08 AW	38960 AAW	MDBLS	10//99-12//99
	Massachusetts	S	19.35 MW	18.27 AW	37990 AAW	MABLS	10//99-12//99
	Springfield MSA, MA	S	18.16 MW	16.65 AW	37770 AAW	MABLS	10//99-12//99
	Minnesota	S	26.77 MW	25.48 AW	52990 AAW	MNBLS	10//99-12//99
	Rochester MSA, MN	S	27.51 MW	30.27 AW	57230 AAW	MNBLS	10//99-12//99
	Mississippi	S	14.28 MW	13.87 AW	28840 AAW	MSBLS	10//99-12//99
	Missouri	S	19.93 MW	18.55 AW	38580 AAW	MOBLS	10//99-12//99
	Nebraska	S	9.97 MW	10.73 AW	22310 AAW	NEBLS	10//99-12//99
	Omaha MSA, NE-IA	S	12.75 MW	12.64 AW	26530 AAW	NEBLS	10//99-12//99
	Nevada	S	22.85 MW	21.58 AW	44880 AAW	NVBLS	10//99-12//99
	New Jersey	S	14.81 MW	16.10 AW	33490 AAW	NJBLS	10//99-12//99

AAW Average annual wage	**AOH** Average offered, high	**ASH** Average starting, high	**H** Hourly	**M** Monthly	**S** Special: hourly and annual
AE Average entry wage	**AOL** Average offered, low	**ASL** Average starting, low	**HI** Highest wage paid	**MTC** Median total compensation	**TQ** Third quartile wage
AEX Average experienced wage	**APH** Average pay, high range	**AW** Average wage paid	**HR** High end range	**MW** Median wage paid	**W** Weekly
AO Average offered	**APL** Average pay, low range	**FQ** First quartile wage	**LR** Low end range	**SQ** Second quartile wage	**Y** Yearly

Occupation/Type/Industry	Location	Per	Low	Mid	High	Source	Date
Paperhanger	New York	S	15.87 MW	16.60 AW	34530 AAW	NYBLS	10//99-12//99
	Albany-Schenectady-Troy MSA, NY	S	17.64 MW	17.87 AW	36690 AAW	NYBLS	10//99-12//99
	Buffalo-Niagara Falls MSA, NY	S	11.85 MW	10.42 AW	24640 AAW	NYBLS	10//99-12//99
	Nassau-Suffolk PMSA, NY	S	18.93 MW	13.01 AW	39370 AAW	NYBLS	10//99-12//99
	New York PMSA, NY	S	16.96 MW	16.12 AW	35270 AAW	NYBLS	10//99-12//99
	Rochester MSA, NY	S	15.66 MW	15.51 AW	32580 AAW	NYBLS	10//99-12//99
	North Carolina	S	8.96 MW	9.14 AW	19010 AAW	NCBLS	10//99-12//99
	Ohio	S	19.46 MW	19.48 AW	40520 AAW	OHBLS	10//99-12//99
	Cleveland-Lorain-Elyria PMSA, OH	S	18.44 MW	18.69 AW	38360 AAW	OHBLS	10//99-12//99
	Oklahoma	S	11.21 MW	11.84 AW	24620 AAW	OKBLS	10//99-12//99
	Oklahoma City MSA, OK	S	11.24 MW	10.73 AW	23370 AAW	OKBLS	10//99-12//99
	Oregon	S	16.97 MW	16.62 AW	34560 AAW	ORBLS	10//99-12//99
	Portland-Vancouver PMSA, OR-WA	S	15.66 MW	15.50 AW	32560 AAW	ORBLS	10//99-12//99
	Pennsylvania	S	15.32 MW	14.94 AW	31070 AAW	PABLS	10//99-12//99
	Philadelphia PMSA, PA-NJ	S	16.70 MW	16.88 AW	34730 AAW	PABLS	10//99-12//99
	South Carolina	S	10.85 MW	10.77 AW	22400 AAW	SCBLS	10//99-12//99
	Tennessee	S	12.15 MW	12.27 AW	25530 AAW	TNBLS	10//99-12//99
	Texas	S	11.18 MW	11.37 AW	23650 AAW	TXBLS	10//99-12//99
	Houston PMSA, TX	S	11.80 MW	11.98 AW	24540 AAW	TXBLS	10//99-12//99
	Virginia	S	18.97 MW	18.46 AW	38390 AAW	VABLS	10//99-12//99
	West Virginia	S	19.25 MW	19.26 AW	40060 AAW	WVBLS	10//99-12//99
	Wisconsin	S	18.52 MW	17.45 AW	36300 AAW	WIBLS	10//99-12//99
Paralegal and Legal Assistant	Alabama	S	13.14 MW	15.65 AW	32550 AAW	ALBLS	10//99-12//99
	Birmingham MSA, AL	S	18.24 MW	18.91 AW	37940 AAW	ALBLS	10//99-12//99
	Decatur MSA, AL	S	15.60 MW	15.33 AW	32440 AAW	ALBLS	10//99-12//99
	Huntsville MSA, AL	S	11.82 MW	11.77 AW	24580 AAW	ALBLS	10//99-12//99
	Montgomery MSA, AL	S	16.83 MW	14.90 AW	35010 AAW	ALBLS	10//99-12//99
	Alaska	S	15.37 MW	15.91 AW	33080 AAW	AKBLS	10//99-12//99
	Anchorage MSA, AK	S	19.41 MW	18.55 AW	40370 AAW	AKBLS	10//99-12//99
	Arizona	S	17.34 MW	17.32 AW	36020 AAW	AZBLS	10//99-12//99
	Flagstaff MSA, AZ-UT	S	17.58 MW	17.16 AW	36560 AAW	AZBLS	10//99-12//99
	Phoenix-Mesa MSA, AZ	S	17.76 MW	17.74 AW	36950 AAW	AZBLS	10//99-12//99
	Tucson MSA, AZ	S	14.28 MW	14.28 AW	29710 AAW	AZBLS	10//99-12//99
	Arkansas	S	12.67 MW	13.12 AW	27290 AAW	ARBLS	10//99-12//99
	Fayetteville-Springdale-Rogers MSA, AR	S	10.23 MW	8.14 AW	21280 AAW	ARBLS	10//99-12//99
	Fort Smith MSA, AR-OK	S	11.26 MW	9.78 AW	23430 AAW	ARBLS	10//99-12//99
	Little Rock-North Little Rock MSA, AR	S	13.85 MW	13.04 AW	28810 AAW	ARBLS	10//99-12//99
	California	S	22.62 MW	22.48 AW	46760 AAW	CABLS	10//99-12//99
	Bakersfield MSA, CA	S	17.27 MW	16.05 AW	35910 AAW	CABLS	10//99-12//99
	Fresno MSA, CA	S	19.06 MW	18.72 AW	39630 AAW	CABLS	10//99-12//99
	Los Angeles-Long Beach PMSA, CA	S	26.18 MW	25.80 AW	54450 AAW	CABLS	10//99-12//99
	Modesto MSA, CA	S	21.00 MW	20.53 AW	43670 AAW	CABLS	10//99-12//99
	Oakland PMSA, CA	S	22.48 MW	21.76 AW	46760 AAW	CABLS	10//99-12//99
	Orange County PMSA, CA	S	19.97 MW	19.68 AW	41530 AAW	CABLS	10//99-12//99
	Riverside-San Bernardino PMSA, CA	S	15.23 MW	13.29 AW	31680 AAW	CABLS	10//99-12//99
	Sacramento PMSA, CA	S	19.24 MW	19.29 AW	40020 AAW	CABLS	10//99-12//99
	Salinas MSA, CA	S	17.15 MW	15.78 AW	35680 AAW	CABLS	10//99-12//99
	San Diego MSA, CA	S	20.63 MW	20.34 AW	42910 AAW	CABLS	10//99-12//99
	San Francisco PMSA, CA	S	19.45 MW	18.98 AW	40450 AAW	CABLS	10//99-12//99
	San Jose PMSA, CA	S	22.57 MW	21.65 AW	46950 AAW	CABLS	10//99-12//99
	San Luis Obispo-Atascadero-Paso Robles MSA, CA	S	17.08 MW	16.26 AW	35520 AAW	CABLS	10//99-12//99
	Santa Barbara-Santa Maria-Lompoc MSA, CA	S	19.87 MW	19.26 AW	41320 AAW	CABLS	10//99-12//99
	Stockton-Lodi MSA, CA	S	18.17 MW	17.93 AW	37800 AAW	CABLS	10//99-12//99
	Vallejo-Fairfield-Napa PMSA, CA	S	19.47 MW	19.25 AW	40490 AAW	CABLS	10//99-12//99
	Ventura PMSA, CA	S	20.74 MW	20.78 AW	43130 AAW	CABLS	10//99-12//99
	Visalia-Tulare-Porterville MSA, CA	S	15.55 MW	13.48 AW	32340 AAW	CABLS	10//99-12//99
	Colorado Springs MSA, CO	S	14.86 MW	14.80 AW	30910 AAW	COBLS	10//99-12//99
	Denver PMSA, CO	S	19.74 MW	19.45 AW	41060 AAW	COBLS	10//99-12//99
	Fort Collins-Loveland MSA, CO	S	12.55 MW	12.43 AW	26110 AAW	COBLS	10//99-12//99

AAW	Average annual wage	AOH	Average offered, high	ASH	Average starting, high	H	Hourly	M	Monthly	S	Special: hourly and annual
AE	Average entry wage	AOL	Average offered, low	ASL	Average starting, low	HI	Highest wage paid	MTC	Median total compensation	TQ	Third quartile wage
AEX	Average experienced wage	APH	Average pay, high range	AW	Average wage paid	HR	High end range	MW	Median wage paid	W	Weekly
AO	Average offered	APL	Average pay, low range	FQ	First quartile wage	LR	Low end range	SQ	Second quartile wage	Y	Yearly

Occupation/Type/Industry	Location	Per	Low	Mid	High	Source	Date
Paralegal and Legal Assistant	Pueblo MSA, CO	S	11.74 MW	11.89 AW	24420 AAW	COBLS	10//99-12//99
	Connecticut	S	19.97 MW	19.53 AW	40630 AAW	CTBLS	10//99-12//99
	Danbury PMSA, CT	S	21.63 MW	21.47 AW	44990 AAW	CTBLS	10//99-12//99
	New Haven-Meriden PMSA, CT	S	21.68 MW	19.54 AW	45090 AAW	CTBLS	10//99-12//99
	New London-Norwich MSA, CT-RI	S	17.48 MW	16.56 AW	36360 AAW	CTBLS	10//99-12//99
	Stamford-Norwalk PMSA, CT	S	24.83 MW	22.79 AW	51650 AAW	CTBLS	10//99-12//99
	Waterbury PMSA, CT	S	14.62 MW	14.74 AW	30420 AAW	CTBLS	10//99-12//99
	Delaware	S	14.76 MW	14.91 AW	31010 AAW	DEBLS	10//99-12//99
	Dover MSA, DE	S	13.45 MW	13.51 AW	27980 AAW	DEBLS	10//99-12//99
	Wilmington-Newark PMSA, DE-MD	S	15.09 MW	14.87 AW	31380 AAW	DEBLS	10//99-12//99
	District of Columbia	S	18.21 MW	18.85 AW	39210 AAW	DCBLS	10//99-12//99
	Washington PMSA, DC-MD-VA-WV	S	17.22 MW	15.93 AW	35820 AAW	DCBLS	10//99-12//99
	Fort Lauderdale PMSA, FL	S	15.60 MW	15.05 AW	32450 AAW	FLBLS	10//99-12//99
	Jacksonville MSA, FL	S	16.61 MW	15.89 AW	34540 AAW	FLBLS	10//99-12//99
	Lakeland-Winter Haven MSA, FL	S	17.51 MW	17.28 AW	36420 AAW	FLBLS	10//99-12//99
	Miami PMSA, FL	S	22.18 MW	23.07 AW	46140 AAW	FLBLS	10//99-12//99
	Naples MSA, FL	S	19.07 MW	19.18 AW	39650 AAW	FLBLS	10//99-12//99
	Ocala MSA, FL	S	12.77 MW	12.67 AW	26560 AAW	FLBLS	10//99-12//99
	Orlando MSA, FL	S	18.45 MW	16.84 AW	38380 AAW	FLBLS	10//99-12//99
	Panama City MSA, FL	S	13.95 MW	12.20 AW	29010 AAW	FLBLS	10//99-12//99
	Pensacola MSA, FL	S	14.38 MW	14.58 AW	29910 AAW	FLBLS	10//99-12//99
	Punta Gorda MSA, FL	S	13.84 MW	13.97 AW	28780 AAW	FLBLS	10//99-12//99
	Sarasota-Bradenton MSA, FL	S	15.50 MW	13.88 AW	32230 AAW	FLBLS	10//99-12//99
	Tampa-St. Petersburg-Clearwater MSA, FL	S	20.14 MW	15.97 AW	41890 AAW	FLBLS	10//99-12//99
	West Palm Beach-Boca Raton MSA, FL	S	15.20 MW	14.74 AW	31620 AAW	FLBLS	10//99-12//99
	Georgia	S	16.92 MW	18.49 AW	38460 AAW	GABLS	10//99-12//99
	Atlanta MSA, GA	S	19.12 MW	17.76 AW	39760 AAW	GABLS	10//99-12//99
	Columbus MSA, GA-AL	S	15.69 MW	12.87 AW	32640 AAW	GABLS	10//99-12//99
	Macon MSA, GA	S	12.54 MW	11.86 AW	26080 AAW	GABLS	10//99-12//99
	Savannah MSA, GA	S	17.97 MW	16.77 AW	37370 AAW	GABLS	10//99-12//99
	Hawaii	S	15.22 MW	15.47 AW	32170 AAW	HIBLS	10//99-12//99
	Honolulu MSA, HI	S	16.04 MW	15.85 AW	33360 AAW	HIBLS	10//99-12//99
	Idaho	S	16.95 MW	17.12 AW	35600 AAW	IDBLS	10//99-12//99
	Boise City MSA, ID	S	17.47 MW	17.45 AW	36340 AAW	IDBLS	10//99-12//99
	Illinois	S	16.16 MW	17.31 AW	36000 AAW	ILBLS	10//99-12//99
	Champaign-Urbana MSA, IL	S	15.16 MW	15.25 AW	31530 AAW	ILBLS	10//99-12//99
	Chicago PMSA, IL	S	17.40 MW	16.27 AW	36190 AAW	ILBLS	10//99-12//99
	Peoria-Pekin MSA, IL	S	20.28 MW	22.48 AW	42190 AAW	ILBLS	10//99-12//99
	Springfield MSA, IL	S	17.20 MW	18.67 AW	35780 AAW	ILBLS	10//99-12//99
	Indiana	S	15.14 MW	15.80 AW	32860 AAW	INBLS	10//99-12//99
	Evansville-Henderson MSA, IN-KY	S	12.47 MW	10.71 AW	25940 AAW	INBLS	10//99-12//99
	Fort Wayne MSA, IN	S	14.69 MW	14.82 AW	30560 AAW	INBLS	10//99-12//99
	Gary PMSA, IN	S	17.33 MW	17.26 AW	36040 AAW	INBLS	10//99-12//99
	Indianapolis MSA, IN	S	18.73 MW	17.53 AW	38970 AAW	INBLS	10//99-12//99
	Lafayette MSA, IN	S	17.27 MW	16.13 AW	35910 AAW	INBLS	10//99-12//99
	Muncie MSA, IN	S	13.48 MW	13.25 AW	28030 AAW	INBLS	10//99-12//99
	South Bend MSA, IN	S	13.75 MW	14.36 AW	28590 AAW	INBLS	10//99-12//99
	Terre Haute MSA, IN	S	16.90 MW	16.72 AW	35160 AAW	INBLS	10//99-12//99
	Iowa	S	16.6 MW	16.40 AW	34120 AAW	IABLS	10//99-12//99
	Cedar Rapids MSA, IA	S	17.27 MW	16.06 AW	35930 AAW	IABLS	10//99-12//99
	Davenport-Moline-Rock Island MSA, IA-IL	S	14.57 MW	14.33 AW	30310 AAW	IABLS	10//99-12//99
	Des Moines MSA, IA	S	18.19 MW	18.60 AW	37840 AAW	IABLS	10//99-12//99
	Dubuque MSA, IA	S	14.30 MW	14.50 AW	29750 AAW	IABLS	10//99-12//99
	Sioux City MSA, IA-NE	S	16.60 MW	14.77 AW	34530 AAW	IABLS	10//99-12//99
	Waterloo-Cedar Falls MSA, IA	S	13.74 MW	12.75 AW	28590 AAW	IABLS	10//99-12//99
	Kansas	S	14.42 MW	15.27 AW	31750 AAW	KSBLS	10//99-12//99
	Lawrence MSA, KS	S	12.73 MW	12.54 AW	26490 AAW	KSBLS	10//99-12//99
	Topeka MSA, KS	S	13.31 MW	12.52 AW	27690 AAW	KSBLS	10//99-12//99
	Wichita MSA, KS	S	17.87 MW	17.67 AW	37160 AAW	KSBLS	10//99-12//99
	Kentucky	S	13.28 MW	14.29 AW	29730 AAW	KYBLS	10//99-12//99
	Lexington MSA, KY	S	15.70 MW	15.13 AW	32660 AAW	KYBLS	10//99-12//99
	Louisville MSA, KY-IN	S	16.40 MW	17.23 AW	34110 AAW	KYBLS	10//99-12//99
	Owensboro MSA, KY	S	17.38 MW	18.54 AW	36150 AAW	KYBLS	10//99-12//99

Occupation/Type/Industry	Location	Per	Low	Mid	High	Source	Date
Paralegal and Legal Assistant	Baton Rouge MSA, LA	S	15.90 MW	15.78 AW	33080 AAW	LABLS	10//99-12//99
	Lafayette MSA, LA	S	15.17 MW	15.25 AW	31540 AAW	LABLS	10//99-12//99
	Monroe MSA, LA	S	12.25 MW	10.24 AW	25490 AAW	LABLS	10//99-12//99
	New Orleans MSA, LA	S	18.78 MW	18.52 AW	39060 AAW	LABLS	10//99-12//99
	Shreveport-Bossier City MSA, LA	S	12.37 MW	12.13 AW	25730 AAW	LABLS	10//99-12//99
	Maine	S	13.87 MW	13.99 AW	29100 AAW	MEBLS	10//99-12//99
	Bangor MSA, ME	S	13.62 MW	13.51 AW	28340 AAW	MEBLS	10//99-12//99
	Lewiston-Auburn MSA, ME	S	14.09 MW	14.33 AW	29300 AAW	MEBLS	10//99-12//99
	Portland MSA, ME	S	16.12 MW	15.50 AW	33520 AAW	MEBLS	10//99-12//99
	Maryland	S	19.77 MW	20.46 AW	42550 AAW	MDBLS	10//99-12//99
	Baltimore PMSA, MD	S	20.97 MW	20.51 AW	43610 AAW	MDBLS	10//99-12//99
	Cumberland MSA, MD-WV	S	12.27 MW	12.25 AW	25520 AAW	MDBLS	10//99-12//99
	Massachusetts	S	19.54 MW	20.39 AW	42410 AAW	MABLS	10//99-12//99
	Boston PMSA, MA-NH	S	21.84 MW	20.89 AW	45430 AAW	MABLS	10//99-12//99
	Lowell PMSA, MA-NH	S	19.32 MW	19.25 AW	40180 AAW	MABLS	10//99-12//99
	Springfield MSA, MA	S	16.16 MW	15.68 AW	33620 AAW	MABLS	10//99-12//99
	Worcester PMSA, MA-CT	S	19.99 MW	20.34 AW	41580 AAW	MABLS	10//99-12//99
	Michigan	S	16.4 MW	17.42 AW	36220 AAW	MIBLS	10//99-12//99
	Ann Arbor PMSA, MI	S	20.28 MW	23.37 AW	42180 AAW	MIBLS	10//99-12//99
	Detroit PMSA, MI	S	19.84 MW	19.27 AW	41280 AAW	MIBLS	10//99-12//99
	Grand Rapids-Muskegon-Holland MSA, MI	S	17.66 MW	17.91 AW	36740 AAW	MIBLS	10//99-12//99
	Kalamazoo-Battle Creek MSA, MI	S	14.28 MW	13.92 AW	29710 AAW	MIBLS	10//99-12//99
	Minnesota	S	17.92 MW	18.12 AW	37690 AAW	MNBLS	10//99-12//99
	Duluth-Superior MSA, MN-WI	S	15.16 MW	17.12 AW	31530 AAW	MNBLS	10//99-12//99
	Minneapolis-St. Paul MSA, MN-WI	S	18.29 MW	18.05 AW	38040 AAW	MNBLS	10//99-12//99
	Rochester MSA, MN	S	17.36 MW	16.19 AW	36110 AAW	MNBLS	10//99-12//99
	St. Cloud MSA, MN	S	17.11 MW	16.40 AW	35600 AAW	MNBLS	10//99-12//99
	Mississippi	S	14.84 MW	18.08 AW	37600 AAW	MSBLS	10//99-12//99
	Biloxi-Gulfport-Pascagoula MSA, MS	S	13.49 MW	13.15 AW	28050 AAW	MSBLS	10//99-12//99
	Jackson MSA, MS	S	15.55 MW	15.16 AW	32340 AAW	MSBLS	10//99-12//99
	Missouri	S	15.79 MW	16.78 AW	34910 AAW	MOBLS	10//99-12//99
	Joplin MSA, MO	S	14.17 MW	14.91 AW	29470 AAW	MOBLS	10//99-12//99
	Kansas City MSA, MO-KS	S	15.83 MW	15.19 AW	32940 AAW	MOBLS	10//99-12//99
	St. Louis MSA, MO-IL	S	19.54 MW	17.26 AW	40640 AAW	MOBLS	10//99-12//99
	Montana	S	13.18 MW	13.04 AW	27130 AAW	MTBLS	10//99-12//99
	Billings MSA, MT	S	12.73 MW	13.54 AW	26480 AAW	MTBLS	10//99-12//99
	Great Falls MSA, MT	S	12.98 MW	12.65 AW	26990 AAW	MTBLS	10//99-12//99
	Nebraska	S	14.86 MW	15.07 AW	31350 AAW	NEBLS	10//99-12//99
	Lincoln MSA, NE	S	15.20 MW	14.36 AW	31610 AAW	NEBLS	10//99-12//99
	Omaha MSA, NE-IA	S	14.89 MW	14.66 AW	30960 AAW	NEBLS	10//99-12//99
	Nevada	S	19.06 MW	19.59 AW	40740 AAW	NVBLS	10//99-12//99
	Las Vegas MSA, NV-AZ	S	19.48 MW	18.87 AW	40520 AAW	NVBLS	10//99-12//99
	Reno MSA, NV	S	18.73 MW	18.80 AW	38960 AAW	NVBLS	10//99-12//99
	New Hampshire	S	17.2 MW	17.08 AW	35530 AAW	NHBLS	10//99-12//99
	Manchester PMSA, NH	S	19.53 MW	18.67 AW	40620 AAW	NHBLS	10//99-12//99
	New Jersey	S	16.1 MW	17.08 AW	35530 AAW	NJBLS	10//99-12//99
	Atlantic-Cape May PMSA, NJ	S	20.81 MW	20.38 AW	43270 AAW	NJBLS	10//99-12//99
	Bergen-Passaic PMSA, NJ	S	18.22 MW	16.11 AW	37900 AAW	NJBLS	10//99-12//99
	Jersey City PMSA, NJ	S	18.12 MW	15.78 AW	37690 AAW	NJBLS	10//99-12//99
	Monmouth-Ocean PMSA, NJ	S	18.06 MW	18.20 AW	37560 AAW	NJBLS	10//99-12//99
	Newark PMSA, NJ	S	16.94 MW	15.91 AW	35230 AAW	NJBLS	10//99-12//99
	Trenton PMSA, NJ	S	20.78 MW	19.61 AW	43230 AAW	NJBLS	10//99-12//99
	New Mexico	S	15.69 MW	16.23 AW	33760 AAW	NMBLS	10//99-12//99
	Albuquerque MSA, NM	S	17.04 MW	16.72 AW	35430 AAW	NMBLS	10//99-12//99
	Santa Fe MSA, NM	S	15.88 MW	15.43 AW	33030 AAW	NMBLS	10//99-12//99
	New York	S	16.96 MW	19.15 AW	39830 AAW	NYBLS	10//99-12//99
	Albany-Schenectady-Troy MSA, NY	S	18.24 MW	18.33 AW	37930 AAW	NYBLS	10//99-12//99
	Binghamton MSA, NY	S	14.41 MW	14.51 AW	29970 AAW	NYBLS	10//99-12//99
	Buffalo-Niagara Falls MSA, NY	S	17.54 MW	15.45 AW	36480 AAW	NYBLS	10//99-12//99
	Nassau-Suffolk PMSA, NY	S	18.94 MW	18.36 AW	39390 AAW	NYBLS	10//99-12//99
	New York PMSA, NY	S	19.49 MW	17.24 AW	40530 AAW	NYBLS	10//99-12//99
	Rochester MSA, NY	S	18.08 MW	16.82 AW	37610 AAW	NYBLS	10//99-12//99
	Syracuse MSA, NY	S	14.16 MW	13.39 AW	29440 AAW	NYBLS	10//99-12//99
	Utica-Rome MSA, NY	S	17.97 MW	18.13 AW	37380 AAW	NYBLS	10//99-12//99
	North Carolina	S	15.13 MW	16.20 AW	33700 AAW	NCBLS	10//99-12//99

AAW	Average annual wage	AOH	Average offered, high	ASH	Average starting, high
AE	Average entry wage	AOL	Average offered, low	ASL	Average starting, low
AEX	Average experienced wage	APH	Average pay, high range	AW	Average wage paid
AO	Average offered	APL	Average pay, low range	FQ	First quartile wage

H	Hourly	M	Monthly
HI	Highest wage paid	MTC	Median total compensation
HR	High end range	MW	Median wage paid
LR	Low end range	SQ	Second quartile wage

S	Special: hourly and annual
TQ	Third quartile wage
W	Weekly
Y	Yearly

Occupation/Type/Industry	Location	Per	Low	Mid	High	Source	Date
Paralegal and Legal Assistant	Asheville MSA, NC	S	15.67 mw	14.60 aw	32590 aaw	NCBLS	10//99-12//99
	Charlotte-Gastonia-Rock Hill MSA, NC-SC	S	21.27 mw	22.44 aw	44240 aaw	NCBLS	10//99-12//99
	Fayetteville MSA, NC	S	11.85 mw	11.82 aw	24660 aaw	NCBLS	10//99-12//99
	Goldsboro MSA, NC	S	11.37 mw	10.58 aw	23650 aaw	NCBLS	10//99-12//99
	Greenville MSA, NC	S	15.43 mw	15.81 aw	32090 aaw	NCBLS	10//99-12//99
	Raleigh-Durham-Chapel Hill MSA, NC	S	17.29 mw	15.76 aw	35970 aaw	NCBLS	10//99-12//99
	Rocky Mount MSA, NC	S	15.16 mw	14.65 aw	31530 aaw	NCBLS	10//99-12//99
	Wilmington MSA, NC	S	18.12 mw	17.44 aw	37680 aaw	NCBLS	10//99-12//99
	North Dakota	S	14.37 mw	14.91 aw	31010 aaw	NDBLS	10//99-12//99
	Fargo-Moorhead MSA, ND-MN	S	16.96 mw	15.99 aw	35270 aaw	NDBLS	10//99-12//99
	Ohio	S	16.17 mw	16.89 aw	35120 aaw	OHBLS	10//99-12//99
	Akron PMSA, OH	S	15.76 mw	15.55 aw	32780 aaw	OHBLS	10//99-12//99
	Canton-Massillon MSA, OH	S	13.84 mw	13.08 aw	28790 aaw	OHBLS	10//99-12//99
	Cleveland-Lorain-Elyria PMSA, OH	S	18.30 mw	18.07 aw	38070 aaw	OHBLS	10//99-12//99
	Columbus MSA, OH	S	16.02 mw	15.69 aw	33320 aaw	OHBLS	10//99-12//99
	Dayton-Springfield MSA, OH	S	19.07 mw	16.74 aw	39660 aaw	OHBLS	10//99-12//99
	Hamilton-Middletown PMSA, OH	S	17.58 mw	17.65 aw	36560 aaw	OHBLS	10//99-12//99
	Steubenville-Weirton MSA, OH-WV	S	13.44 mw	14.43 aw	27950 aaw	OHBLS	10//99-12//99
	Toledo MSA, OH	S	17.90 mw	16.01 aw	37240 aaw	OHBLS	10//99-12//99
	Oklahoma	S	17.3 mw	18.39 aw	38250 aaw	OKBLS	10//99-12//99
	Lawton MSA, OK	S	16.84 mw	18.41 aw	35020 aaw	OKBLS	10//99-12//99
	Oklahoma City MSA, OK	S	24.13 mw	21.22 aw	50180 aaw	OKBLS	10//99-12//99
	Tulsa MSA, OK	S	14.81 mw	12.70 aw	30790 aaw	OKBLS	10//99-12//99
	Oregon	S	18.54 mw	18.24 aw	37940 aaw	ORBLS	10//99-12//99
	Corvallis MSA, OR	S	11.82 mw	11.99 aw	24580 aaw	ORBLS	10//99-12//99
	Eugene-Springfield MSA, OR	S	16.38 mw	16.91 aw	34070 aaw	ORBLS	10//99-12//99
	Portland-Vancouver PMSA, OR-WA	S	19.02 mw	19.01 aw	39560 aaw	ORBLS	10//99-12//99
	Pennsylvania	S	15.64 mw	16.62 aw	34570 aaw	PABLS	10//99-12//99
	Allentown-Bethlehem-Easton MSA, PA	S	13.77 mw	13.64 aw	28640 aaw	PABLS	10//99-12//99
	Erie MSA, PA	S	13.70 mw	13.44 aw	28500 aaw	PABLS	10//99-12//99
	Lancaster MSA, PA	S	14.17 mw	12.50 aw	29470 aaw	PABLS	10//99-12//99
	Philadelphia PMSA, PA-NJ	S	17.64 mw	16.22 aw	36680 aaw	PABLS	10//99-12//99
	Pittsburgh MSA, PA	S	16.10 mw	17.04 aw	33490 aaw	PABLS	10//99-12//99
	Scranton--Wilkes-Barre--Hazleton MSA, PA	S	15.27 mw	15.29 aw	31760 aaw	PABLS	10//99-12//99
	Williamsport MSA, PA	S	11.22 mw	11.38 aw	23330 aaw	PABLS	10//99-12//99
	York MSA, PA	S	12.35 mw	11.49 aw	25680 aaw	PABLS	10//99-12//99
	Rhode Island	S	18.3 mw	19.23 aw	39990 aaw	RIBLS	10//99-12//99
	Providence-Fall River-Warwick MSA, RI-MA	S	18.94 mw	18.11 aw	39390 aaw	RIBLS	10//99-12//99
	South Carolina	S	14.02 mw	14.72 aw	30610 aaw	SCBLS	10//99-12//99
	Charleston-North Charleston MSA, SC	S	13.55 mw	14.08 aw	28180 aaw	SCBLS	10//99-12//99
	Columbia MSA, SC	S	13.79 mw	13.56 aw	28680 aaw	SCBLS	10//99-12//99
	Florence MSA, SC	S	12.84 mw	12.35 aw	26710 aaw	SCBLS	10//99-12//99
	Greenville-Spartanburg-Anderson MSA, SC	S	20.10 mw	20.41 aw	41820 aaw	SCBLS	10//99-12//99
	Myrtle Beach MSA, SC	S	13.29 mw	12.78 aw	27640 aaw	SCBLS	10//99-12//99
	Sumter MSA, SC	S	20.32 mw	21.70 aw	42270 aaw	SCBLS	10//99-12//99
	South Dakota	S	12.64 mw	12.41 aw	25820 aaw	SDBLS	10//99-12//99
	Rapid City MSA, SD	S	10.31 mw	8.34 aw	21450 aaw	SDBLS	10//99-12//99
	Sioux Falls MSA, SD	S	12.94 mw	13.83 aw	26910 aaw	SDBLS	10//99-12//99
	Tennessee	S	13.09 mw	13.93 aw	28970 aaw	TNBLS	10//99-12//99
	Chattanooga MSA, TN-GA	S	12.63 mw	11.19 aw	26280 aaw	TNBLS	10//99-12//99
	Clarksville-Hopkinsville MSA, TN-KY	S	11.06 mw	10.98 aw	23010 aaw	TNBLS	10//99-12//99
	Jackson MSA, TN	S	13.38 mw	12.87 aw	27820 aaw	TNBLS	10//99-12//99
	Johnson City-Kingsport-Bristol MSA, TN-VA	S	13.77 mw	13.00 aw	28640 aaw	TNBLS	10//99-12//99
	Knoxville MSA, TN	S	13.65 mw	12.69 aw	28380 aaw	TNBLS	10//99-12//99
	Memphis MSA, TN-AR-MS	S	12.50 mw	11.85 aw	26000 aaw	MSBLS	10//99-12//99
	Nashville MSA, TN	S	17.05 mw	16.47 aw	35470 aaw	TNBLS	10//99-12//99
	Texas	S	15.03 mw	16.28 aw	33850 aaw	TXBLS	10//99-12//99
	Abilene MSA, TX	S	15.16 mw	15.18 aw	31540 aaw	TXBLS	10//99-12//99

Occupation/Type/Industry	Location	Per	Low	Mid	High	Source	Date
Paralegal and Legal Assistant	Amarillo MSA, TX	S	22.57 MW	23.57 AW	46950 AAW	TXBLS	10//99-12//99
	Austin-San Marcos MSA, TX	S	13.84 MW	13.11 AW	28790 AAW	TXBLS	10//99-12//99
	Beaumont-Port Arthur MSA, TX	S	15.50 MW	15.20 AW	32250 AAW	TXBLS	10//99-12//99
	Bryan-College Station MSA, TX	S	14.53 MW	14.67 AW	30220 AAW	TXBLS	10//99-12//99
	Dallas PMSA, TX	S	16.26 MW	14.74 AW	33830 AAW	TXBLS	10//99-12//99
	El Paso MSA, TX	S	13.78 MW	12.69 AW	28660 AAW	TXBLS	10//99-12//99
	Fort Worth-Arlington PMSA, TX	S	18.89 MW	18.49 AW	39280 AAW	TXBLS	10//99-12//99
	Houston PMSA, TX	S	18.23 MW	17.63 AW	37920 AAW	TXBLS	10//99-12//99
	Laredo MSA, TX	S	16.06 MW	15.28 AW	33400 AAW	TXBLS	10//99-12//99
	Longview-Marshall MSA, TX	S	13.62 MW	13.02 AW	28330 AAW	TXBLS	10//99-12//99
	Lubbock MSA, TX	S	15.33 MW	15.27 AW	31890 AAW	TXBLS	10//99-12//99
	Odessa-Midland MSA, TX	S	17.27 MW	16.00 AW	35930 AAW	TXBLS	10//99-12//99
	San Antonio MSA, TX	S	18.25 MW	17.26 AW	37960 AAW	TXBLS	10//99-12//99
	Sherman-Denison MSA, TX	S	13.47 MW	13.93 AW	28010 AAW	TXBLS	10//99-12//99
	Texarkana MSA, TX-Texarkana, AR	S	13.00 MW	12.40 AW	27040 AAW	TXBLS	10//99-12//99
	Victoria MSA, TX	S	15.01 MW	14.86 AW	31230 AAW	TXBLS	10//99-12//99
	Waco MSA, TX	S	12.01 MW	10.93 AW	24980 AAW	TXBLS	10//99-12//99
	Wichita Falls MSA, TX	S	9.43 MW	9.53 AW	19620 AAW	TXBLS	10//99-12//99
	Salt Lake City-Ogden MSA, UT	S	16.60 MW	15.88 AW	34530 AAW	UTBLS	10//99-12//99
	Vermont	S	19.03 MW	19.25 AW	40040 AAW	VTBLS	10//99-12//99
	Burlington MSA, VT	S	17.23 MW	17.04 AW	35830 AAW	VTBLS	10//99-12//99
	Virginia	S	14.1 MW	14.84 AW	30860 AAW	VABLS	10//99-12//99
	Charlottesville MSA, VA	S	14.65 MW	12.51 AW	30470 AAW	VABLS	10//99-12//99
	Norfolk-Virginia Beach-Newport News MSA, VA-NC	S	18.72 MW	18.31 AW	38950 AAW	VABLS	10//99-12//99
	Richmond-Petersburg MSA, VA	S	13.72 MW	13.29 AW	28540 AAW	VABLS	10//99-12//99
	Roanoke MSA, VA	S	13.39 MW	13.26 AW	27860 AAW	VABLS	10//99-12//99
	Washington	S	17.92 MW	18.22 AW	37900 AAW	WABLS	10//99-12//99
	Bellingham MSA, WA	S	19.63 MW	19.44 AW	40830 AAW	WABLS	10//99-12//99
	Bremerton PMSA, WA	S	17.94 MW	16.00 AW	37310 AAW	WABLS	10//99-12//99
	Olympia PMSA, WA	S	17.56 MW	17.29 AW	36520 AAW	WABLS	10//99-12//99
	Richland-Kennewick-Pasco MSA, WA	S	25.03 MW	28.15 AW	52070 AAW	WABLS	10//99-12//99
	Seattle-Bellevue-Everett PMSA, WA	S	18.07 MW	17.83 AW	37590 AAW	WABLS	10//99-12//99
	Spokane MSA, WA	S	18.39 MW	18.45 AW	38250 AAW	WABLS	10//99-12//99
	Tacoma PMSA, WA	S	20.13 MW	19.83 AW	41880 AAW	WABLS	10//99-12//99
	West Virginia	S	13.03 MW	13.51 AW	28100 AAW	WVBLS	10//99-12//99
	Charleston MSA, WV	S	13.55 MW	13.43 AW	28190 AAW	WVBLS	10//99-12//99
	Huntington-Ashland MSA, WV-KY-OH	S	11.25 MW	11.23 AW	23400 AAW	WVBLS	10//99-12//99
	Parkersburg-Marietta MSA, WV-OH	S	11.25 MW	10.76 AW	23400 AAW	WVBLS	10//99-12//99
	Wheeling MSA, WV-OH	S	14.12 MW	14.57 AW	29370 AAW	WVBLS	10//99-12//99
	Wisconsin	S	15.54 MW	16.40 AW	34110 AAW	WIBLS	10//99-12//99
	Appleton-Oshkosh-Neenah MSA, WI	S	15.16 MW	15.25 AW	31530 AAW	WIBLS	10//99-12//99
	Eau Claire MSA, WI	S	14.35 MW	13.17 AW	29840 AAW	WIBLS	10//99-12//99
	Green Bay MSA, WI	S	13.44 MW	12.58 AW	27950 AAW	WIBLS	10//99-12//99
	La Crosse MSA, WI-MN	S	12.23 MW	12.19 AW	25450 AAW	WIBLS	10//99-12//99
	Madison MSA, WI	S	16.82 MW	16.14 AW	34980 AAW	WIBLS	10//99-12//99
	Milwaukee-Waukesha PMSA, WI	S	17.73 MW	16.92 AW	36880 AAW	WIBLS	10//99-12//99
	Wyoming	S	12.52 MW	13.07 AW	27180 AAW	WYBLS	10//99-12//99
	Casper MSA, WY	S	14.26 MW	13.91 AW	29670 AAW	WYBLS	10//99-12//99
	Cheyenne MSA, WY	S	11.94 MW	11.70 AW	24840 AAW	WYBLS	10//99-12//99
	Puerto Rico	S	6.7 MW	9.56 AW	19880 AAW	PRBLS	10//99-12//99
	San Juan-Bayamon PMSA, PR	S	9.08 MW	6.60 AW	18880 AAW	PRBLS	10//99-12//99
	Virgin Islands	S	15.78 MW	20.72 AW	43090 AAW	VIBLS	10//99-12//99
	Guam	S	16.5 MW	17.02 AW	35400 AAW	GUBLS	10//99-12//99
Pari-mutuel Window Teller	Louisville, KY	H	13.00 APL		19.00 APH	LOUMAG	1999-2000
Parking Enforcement Worker	Alabama	S	9.9 MW	10.20 AW	21220 AAW	ALBLS	10//99-12//99
	California	S	15.51 MW	15.68 AW	32610 AAW	CABLS	10//99-12//99
	Connecticut	S	10.35 MW	11.45 AW	23820 AAW	CTBLS	10//99-12//99

AAW Average annual wage	**AOH** Average offered, high	**ASH** Average starting, high	**H** Hourly	**M** Monthly	**S** Special: hourly and annual
AE Average entry wage	**AOL** Average offered, low	**ASL** Average starting, low	**HI** Highest wage paid	**MTC** Median total compensation	**TQ** Third quartile wage
AEX Average experienced wage	**APH** Average pay, high range	**AW** Average wage paid	**HR** High end range	**MW** Median wage paid	**W** Weekly
AO Average offered	**APL** Average pay, low range	**FQ** First quartile wage	**LR** Low end range	**SQ** Second quartile wage	**Y** Yearly

Occupation/Type/Industry	Location	Per	Low	Mid	High	Source	Date
Parking Enforcement Worker	Delaware	S	12.1 MW	12.51 AW	26020 AAW	DEBLS	10//99-12//99
	Florida	S	10.87 MW	10.82 AW	22510 AAW	FLBLS	10//99-12//99
	Georgia	S	10.52 MW	11.47 AW	23860 AAW	GABLS	10//99-12//99
	Illinois	S	12.87 MW	13.04 AW	27120 AAW	ILBLS	10//99-12//99
	Indiana	S	9.49 MW	9.43 AW	19620 AAW	INBLS	10//99-12//99
	Iowa	S	12.43 MW	12.02 AW	25010 AAW	IABLS	10//99-12//99
	Louisiana	S	12.04 MW	12.38 AW	25740 AAW	LABLS	10//99-12//99
	Maine	S	11.89 MW	11.59 AW	24100 AAW	MEBLS	10//99-12//99
	Maryland	S	9.82 MW	9.99 AW	20780 AAW	MDBLS	10//99-12//99
	Massachusetts	S	10.94 MW	11.77 AW	24490 AAW	MABLS	10//99-12//99
	Michigan	S	12.09 MW	11.66 AW	24250 AAW	MIBLS	10//99-12//99
	Minnesota	S	12.38 MW	12.49 AW	25990 AAW	MNBLS	10//99-12//99
	Mississippi	S	8.26 MW	8.99 AW	18700 AAW	MSBLS	10//99-12//99
	Missouri	S	11.33 MW	11.65 AW	24240 AAW	MOBLS	10//99-12//99
	New Hampshire	S	10.14 MW	9.88 AW	20550 AAW	NHBLS	10//99-12//99
	New Jersey	S	11.67 MW	11.90 AW	24750 AAW	NJBLS	10//99-12//99
	New York	S	12.84 MW	12.97 AW	26980 AAW	NYBLS	10//99-12//99
	North Carolina	S	9.29 MW	9.36 AW	19470 AAW	NCBLS	10//99-12//99
	Ohio	S	10.33 MW	10.51 AW	21870 AAW	OHBLS	10//99-12//99
	Oklahoma	S	11.79 MW	11.07 AW	23030 AAW	OKBLS	10//99-12//99
	Oregon	S	13.75 MW	13.54 AW	28160 AAW	ORBLS	10//99-12//99
	Pennsylvania	S	11.36 MW	11.70 AW	24330 AAW	PABLS	10//99-12//99
	South Carolina	S	8.21 MW	8.25 AW	17150 AAW	SCBLS	10//99-12//99
	Tennessee	S	11.89 MW	11.64 AW	24210 AAW	TNBLS	10//99-12//99
	Texas	S	8.71 MW	9.12 AW	18960 AAW	TXBLS	10//99-12//99
	Virginia	S	12.28 MW	12.21 AW	25400 AAW	VABLS	10//99-12//99
	Washington	S	16.29 MW	16.05 AW	33380 AAW	WABLS	10//99-12//99
	West Virginia	S	7.08 MW	7.52 AW	15630 AAW	WVBLS	10//99-12//99
	Wisconsin	S	13.6 MW	12.90 AW	26820 AAW	WIBLS	10//99-12//99
Parking Lot Attendant	Alabama	S	6.78 MW	7.50 AW	15600 AAW	ALBLS	10//99-12//99
	Birmingham MSA, AL	S	7.84 MW	7.16 AW	16320 AAW	ALBLS	10//99-12//99
	Huntsville MSA, AL	S	6.97 MW	6.92 AW	14500 AAW	ALBLS	10//99-12//99
	Mobile MSA, AL	S	6.06 MW	6.07 AW	12590 AAW	ALBLS	10//99-12//99
	Alaska	S	7.95 MW	8.23 AW	17110 AAW	AKBLS	10//99-12//99
	Anchorage MSA, AK	S	8.14 MW	7.91 AW	16920 AAW	AKBLS	10//99-12//99
	Arizona	S	6.63 MW	7.74 AW	16100 AAW	AZBLS	10//99-12//99
	Phoenix-Mesa MSA, AZ	S	7.90 MW	6.70 AW	16420 AAW	AZBLS	10//99-12//99
	Tucson MSA, AZ	S	6.83 MW	6.33 AW	14200 AAW	AZBLS	10//99-12//99
	Arkansas	S	6.02 MW	6.34 AW	13200 AAW	ARBLS	10//99-12//99
	Little Rock-North Little Rock MSA, AR	S	6.64 MW	6.40 AW	13810 AAW	ARBLS	10//99-12//99
	California	S	6.7 MW	7.37 AW	15340 AAW	CABLS	10//99-12//99
	Fresno MSA, CA	S	6.34 MW	6.08 AW	13180 AAW	CABLS	10//99-12//99
	Los Angeles-Long Beach PMSA, CA	S	6.89 MW	6.55 AW	14330 AAW	CABLS	10//99-12//99
	Oakland PMSA, CA	S	7.71 MW	6.71 AW	16040 AAW	CABLS	10//99-12//99
	Orange County PMSA, CA	S	6.85 MW	6.60 AW	14240 AAW	CABLS	10//99-12//99
	Riverside-San Bernardino PMSA, CA	S	7.06 MW	6.70 AW	14680 AAW	CABLS	10//99-12//99
	Sacramento PMSA, CA	S	7.61 MW	6.75 AW	15820 AAW	CABLS	10//99-12//99
	San Diego MSA, CA	S	7.50 MW	6.67 AW	15590 AAW	CABLS	10//99-12//99
	San Francisco PMSA, CA	S	9.40 MW	8.16 AW	19550 AAW	CABLS	10//99-12//99
	San Jose PMSA, CA	S	7.38 MW	7.21 AW	15360 AAW	CABLS	10//99-12//99
	Santa Barbara-Santa Maria-Lompoc MSA, CA	S	6.96 MW	6.82 AW	14480 AAW	CABLS	10//99-12//99
	Santa Rosa PMSA, CA	S	8.87 MW	8.36 AW	18440 AAW	CABLS	10//99-12//99
	Colorado	S	8.01 MW	7.99 AW	16620 AAW	COBLS	10//99-12//99
	Colorado Springs MSA, CO	S	7.57 MW	7.03 AW	15750 AAW	COBLS	10//99-12//99
	Denver PMSA, CO	S	7.94 MW	7.88 AW	16510 AAW	COBLS	10//99-12//99
	Connecticut	S	7.67 MW	7.73 AW	16070 AAW	CTBLS	10//99-12//99
	Bridgeport PMSA, CT	S	8.57 MW	7.95 AW	17830 AAW	CTBLS	10//99-12//99
	Hartford MSA, CT	S	7.74 MW	7.69 AW	16090 AAW	CTBLS	10//99-12//99
	Stamford-Norwalk PMSA, CT	S	8.48 MW	8.44 AW	17640 AAW	CTBLS	10//99-12//99
	Delaware	S	7.36 MW	7.54 AW	15690 AAW	DEBLS	10//99-12//99
	Wilmington-Newark PMSA, DE-MD	S	7.62 MW	7.41 AW	15840 AAW	DEBLS	10//99-12//99
	District of Columbia	S	8.76 MW	9.23 AW	19210 AAW	DCBLS	10//99-12//99
	Washington PMSA, DC-MD-VA-WV	S	8.61 MW	8.10 AW	17910 AAW	DCBLS	10//99-12//99
	Florida	S	6.42 MW	6.77 AW	14080 AAW	FLBLS	10//99-12//99
	Fort Lauderdale PMSA, FL	S	6.38 MW	6.31 AW	13260 AAW	FLBLS	10//99-12//99

AAW Average annual wage	**AOH** Average offered, high	**ASH** Average starting, high	**H** Hourly	**M** Monthly	**S** Special: hourly and annual
AE Average entry wage	**AOL** Average offered, low	**ASL** Average starting, low	**HI** Highest wage paid	**MTC** Median total compensation	**TQ** Third quartile wage
AEX Average experienced wage	**APH** Average pay, high range	**AW** Average wage paid	**HR** High end range	**MW** Median wage paid	**W** Weekly
AO Average offered	**APL** Average pay, low range	**FQ** First quartile wage	**LR** Low end range	**SQ** Second quartile wage	**Y** Yearly

Occupation/Type/Industry	Location	Per	Low	Mid	High	Source	Date
Parking Lot Attendant	Fort Myers-Cape Coral MSA, FL	S	6.84 MW	6.42 AW	14230 AAW	FLBLS	10//99-12//99
	Jacksonville MSA, FL	S	7.38 MW	6.79 AW	15350 AAW	FLBLS	10//99-12//99
	Miami PMSA, FL	S	6.71 MW	6.54 AW	13950 AAW	FLBLS	10//99-12//99
	Orlando MSA, FL	S	7.09 MW	6.21 AW	14750 AAW	FLBLS	10//99-12//99
	Pensacola MSA, FL	S	6.20 MW	6.33 AW	12890 AAW	FLBLS	10//99-12//99
	Tampa-St. Petersburg-Clearwater MSA, FL	S	7.07 MW	6.65 AW	14700 AAW	FLBLS	10//99-12//99
	West Palm Beach-Boca Raton MSA, FL	S	7.17 MW	6.59 AW	14910 AAW	FLBLS	10//99-12//99
	Georgia	S	6.77 MW	7.17 AW	14910 AAW	GABLS	10//99-12//99
	Atlanta MSA, GA	S	7.24 MW	6.87 AW	15070 AAW	GABLS	10//99-12//99
	Savannah MSA, GA	S	6.34 MW	5.90 AW	13190 AAW	GABLS	10//99-12//99
	Hawaii	S	6.7 MW	7.15 AW	14880 AAW	HIBLS	10//99-12//99
	Honolulu MSA, HI	S	7.02 MW	6.59 AW	14600 AAW	HIBLS	10//99-12//99
	Idaho	S	6.71 MW	6.97 AW	14490 AAW	IDBLS	10//99-12//99
	Boise City MSA, ID	S	7.38 MW	7.30 AW	15360 AAW	IDBLS	10//99-12//99
	Illinois	S	7.91 MW	7.86 AW	16340 AAW	ILBLS	10//99-12//99
	Chicago PMSA, IL	S	7.87 MW	7.96 AW	16380 AAW	ILBLS	10//99-12//99
	Indiana	S	6.74 MW	7.30 AW	15180 AAW	INBLS	10//99-12//99
	Evansville-Henderson MSA, IN-KY	S	7.35 MW	6.46 AW	15300 AAW	INBLS	10//99-12//99
	Fort Wayne MSA, IN	S	8.08 MW	8.05 AW	16810 AAW	INBLS	10//99-12//99
	Gary PMSA, IN	S	6.19 MW	6.15 AW	12880 AAW	INBLS	10//99-12//99
	Indianapolis MSA, IN	S	7.46 MW	7.14 AW	15520 AAW	INBLS	10//99-12//99
	Iowa	S	6.4 MW	6.79 AW	14130 AAW	IABLS	10//99-12//99
	Cedar Rapids MSA, IA	S	6.56 MW	6.06 AW	13640 AAW	IABLS	10//99-12//99
	Des Moines MSA, IA	S	6.49 MW	6.13 AW	13500 AAW	IABLS	10//99-12//99
	Kansas	S	6.5 MW	7.13 AW	14840 AAW	KSBLS	10//99-12//99
	Wichita MSA, KS	S	7.35 MW	6.66 AW	15280 AAW	KSBLS	10//99-12//99
	Kentucky	S	6.66 MW	7.46 AW	15520 AAW	KYBLS	10//99-12//99
	Lexington MSA, KY	S	5.96 MW	5.99 AW	12400 AAW	KYBLS	10//99-12//99
	Louisville MSA, KY-IN	S	8.69 MW	8.55 AW	18080 AAW	KYBLS	10//99-12//99
	Louisiana	S	6.29 MW	6.92 AW	14380 AAW	LABLS	10//99-12//99
	Baton Rouge MSA, LA	S	6.49 MW	6.24 AW	13490 AAW	LABLS	10//99-12//99
	New Orleans MSA, LA	S	7.12 MW	6.34 AW	14800 AAW	LABLS	10//99-12//99
	Shreveport-Bossier City MSA, LA	S	6.55 MW	6.11 AW	13620 AAW	LABLS	10//99-12//99
	Maine	S	7.34 MW	7.60 AW	15820 AAW	MEBLS	10//99-12//99
	Portland MSA, ME	S	7.99 MW	7.80 AW	16630 AAW	MEBLS	10//99-12//99
	Maryland	S	6.89 MW	7.11 AW	14800 AAW	MDBLS	10//99-12//99
	Baltimore PMSA, MD	S	6.95 MW	6.74 AW	14460 AAW	MDBLS	10//99-12//99
	Massachusetts	S	7.63 MW	7.96 AW	16550 AAW	MABLS	10//99-12//99
	Boston PMSA, MA-NH	S	7.95 MW	7.63 AW	16540 AAW	MABLS	10//99-12//99
	Worcester PMSA, MA-CT	S	7.85 MW	7.78 AW	16340 AAW	MABLS	10//99-12//99
	Michigan	S	6.4 MW	6.89 AW	14330 AAW	MIBLS	10//99-12//99
	Detroit PMSA, MI	S	6.76 MW	6.35 AW	14060 AAW	MIBLS	10//99-12//99
	Grand Rapids-Muskegon-Holland MSA, MI	S	6.32 MW	6.08 AW	13150 AAW	MIBLS	10//99-12//99
	Saginaw-Bay City-Midland MSA, MI	S	7.07 MW	6.51 AW	14700 AAW	MIBLS	10//99-12//99
	Minnesota	S	7.74 MW	7.80 AW	16230 AAW	MNBLS	10//99-12//99
	Minneapolis-St. Paul MSA, MN-WI	S	7.71 MW	7.69 AW	16030 AAW	MNBLS	10//99-12//99
	Mississippi	S	6.2 MW	6.53 AW	13580 AAW	MSBLS	10//99-12//99
	Biloxi-Gulfport-Pascagoula MSA, MS	S	6.18 MW	6.13 AW	12860 AAW	MSBLS	10//99-12//99
	Missouri	S	6.04 MW	6.38 AW	13270 AAW	MOBLS	10//99-12//99
	Kansas City MSA, MO-KS	S	6.26 MW	5.88 AW	13010 AAW	MOBLS	10//99-12//99
	Montana	S	6.71 MW	7.07 AW	14700 AAW	MTBLS	10//99-12//99
	Nebraska	S	7.3 MW	7.46 AW	15510 AAW	NEBLS	10//99-12//99
	Omaha MSA, NE-IA	S	7.37 MW	7.23 AW	15330 AAW	NEBLS	10//99-12//99
	Nevada	S	7.12 MW	7.24 AW	15050 AAW	NVBLS	10//99-12//99
	Las Vegas MSA, NV-AZ	S	7.44 MW	7.37 AW	15470 AAW	NVBLS	10//99-12//99
	Reno MSA, NV	S	6.39 MW	6.06 AW	13280 AAW	NVBLS	10//99-12//99
	New Hampshire	S	6.83 MW	7.18 AW	14930 AAW	NHBLS	10//99-12//99
	Portsmouth-Rochester PMSA, NH-ME	S	6.96 MW	6.79 AW	14480 AAW	NHBLS	10//99-12//99
	New Jersey	S	6.59 MW	7.36 AW	15310 AAW	NJBLS	10//99-12//99
	Atlantic-Cape May PMSA, NJ	S	7.56 MW	6.63 AW	15730 AAW	NJBLS	10//99-12//99
	Bergen-Passaic PMSA, NJ	S	7.28 MW	6.47 AW	15150 AAW	NJBLS	10//99-12//99
	Jersey City PMSA, NJ	S	7.17 MW	6.61 AW	14920 AAW	NJBLS	10//99-12//99

AAW	Average annual wage	AOH	Average offered, high	ASH	Average starting, high	H	Hourly	M	Monthly	S	Special: hourly and annual
AE	Average entry wage	AOL	Average offered, low	ASL	Average starting, low	HI	Highest wage paid	MTC	Median total compensation	TQ	Third quartile wage
AEX	Average experienced wage	APH	Average pay, high range	AW	Average wage paid	HR	High end range	MW	Median wage paid	W	Weekly
AO	Average offered	APL	Average pay, low range	FQ	First quartile wage	LR	Low end range	SQ	Second quartile wage	Y	Yearly

Occupation/Type/Industry	Location	Per	Low	Mid	High	Source	Date
Parking Lot Attendant	Middlesex-Somerset-						
	Hunterdon PMSA, NJ	S	7.21 MW	6.98 AW	14990 AAW	NJBLS	10//99-12//99
	Monmouth-Ocean PMSA, NJ	S	10.07 MW	9.87 AW	20940 AAW	NJBLS	10//99-12//99
	Newark PMSA, NJ	S	6.84 MW	6.32 AW	14230 AAW	NJBLS	10//99-12//99
	New Mexico	S	7.54 MW	7.62 AW	15860 AAW	NMBLS	10//99-12//99
	Albuquerque MSA, NM	S	7.39 MW	7.50 AW	15380 AAW	NMBLS	10//99-12//99
	Santa Fe MSA, NM	S	6.31 MW	6.05 AW	13110 AAW	NMBLS	10//99-12//99
	New York	S	7.55 MW	7.72 AW	16060 AAW	NYBLS	10//99-12//99
	Albany-Schenectady-Troy						
	MSA, NY	S	7.12 MW	6.12 AW	14820 AAW	NYBLS	10//99-12//99
	Binghamton MSA, NY	S	7.58 MW	7.38 AW	15760 AAW	NYBLS	10//99-12//99
	Buffalo-Niagara Falls MSA,						
	NY	S	7.48 MW	6.52 AW	15570 AAW	NYBLS	10//99-12//99
	Nassau-Suffolk PMSA, NY	S	7.62 MW	6.63 AW	15850 AAW	NYBLS	10//99-12//99
	New York PMSA, NY	S	7.75 MW	7.61 AW	16110 AAW	NYBLS	10//99-12//99
	Rochester MSA, NY	S	8.22 MW	7.62 AW	17090 AAW	NYBLS	10//99-12//99
	Syracuse MSA, NY	S	7.90 MW	7.15 AW	16420 AAW	NYBLS	10//99-12//99
	North Carolina	S	7.33 MW	7.47 AW	15540 AAW	NCBLS	10//99-12//99
	Asheville MSA, NC	S	7.31 MW	7.25 AW	15210 AAW	NCBLS	10//99-12//99
	Greensboro--Winston-Salem--						
	High Point MSA, NC	S	6.33 MW	5.97 AW	13170 AAW	NCBLS	10//99-12//99
	North Dakota	S	6.31 MW	6.48 AW	13480 AAW	NDBLS	10//99-12//99
	Fargo-Moorhead MSA, ND-						
	MN	S	6.42 MW	6.19 AW	13350 AAW	NDBLS	10//99-12//99
	Ohio	S	6.66 MW	7.09 AW	14740 AAW	OHBLS	10//99-12//99
	Akron PMSA, OH	S	6.88 MW	6.45 AW	14310 AAW	OHBLS	10//99-12//99
	Canton-Massillon MSA, OH	S	6.30 MW	5.98 AW	13100 AAW	OHBLS	10//99-12//99
	Cincinnati PMSA, OH-KY-IN	S	7.12 MW	6.65 AW	14810 AAW	OHBLS	10//99-12//99
	Cleveland-Lorain-Elyria						
	PMSA, OH	S	7.45 MW	7.00 AW	15500 AAW	OHBLS	10//99-12//99
	Columbus MSA, OH	S	6.96 MW	6.66 AW	14480 AAW	OHBLS	10//99-12//99
	Dayton-Springfield MSA, OH	S	6.40 MW	6.09 AW	13310 AAW	OHBLS	10//99-12//99
	Toledo MSA, OH	S	6.91 MW	6.57 AW	14380 AAW	OHBLS	10//99-12//99
	Youngstown-Warren MSA, OH	S	6.15 MW	5.89 AW	12790 AAW	OHBLS	10//99-12//99
	Oklahoma	S	6.43 MW	6.64 AW	13800 AAW	OKBLS	10//99-12//99
	Oklahoma City MSA, OK	S	6.83 MW	6.45 AW	14200 AAW	OKBLS	10//99-12//99
	Tulsa MSA, OK	S	6.32 MW	6.35 AW	13150 AAW	OKBLS	10//99-12//99
	Oregon	S	7.65 MW	7.71 AW	16050 AAW	ORBLS	10//99-12//99
	Pennsylvania	S	6.66 MW	7.13 AW	14830 AAW	PABLS	10//99-12//99
	Allentown-Bethlehem-Easton						
	MSA, PA	S	6.93 MW	6.84 AW	14410 AAW	PABLS	10//99-12//99
	Erie MSA, PA	S	6.38 MW	6.23 AW	13270 AAW	PABLS	10//99-12//99
	Harrisburg-Lebanon-Carlisle						
	MSA, PA	S	7.90 MW	7.01 AW	16420 AAW	PABLS	10//99-12//99
	Philadelphia PMSA, PA-NJ	S	6.92 MW	6.65 AW	14390 AAW	PABLS	10//99-12//99
	Pittsburgh MSA, PA	S	8.05 MW	7.08 AW	16740 AAW	PABLS	10//99-12//99
	Scranton--Wilkes-Barre--						
	Hazleton MSA, PA	S	6.68 MW	6.44 AW	13890 AAW	PABLS	10//99-12//99
	State College MSA, PA	S	6.64 MW	6.49 AW	13800 AAW	PABLS	10//99-12//99
	Rhode Island	S	7.13 MW	7.51 AW	15620 AAW	RIBLS	10//99-12//99
	Providence-Fall River-						
	Warwick MSA, RI-MA	S	7.81 MW	7.39 AW	16250 AAW	RIBLS	10//99-12//99
	South Carolina	S	6.04 MW	7.22 AW	15020 AAW	SCBLS	10//99-12//99
	Charleston-North Charleston						
	MSA, SC	S	5.93 MW	5.92 AW	12340 AAW	SCBLS	10//99-12//99
	South Dakota	S	7.53 MW	7.60 AW	15800 AAW	SDBLS	10//99-12//99
	Sioux Falls MSA, SD	S	8.05 MW	8.21 AW	16750 AAW	SDBLS	10//99-12//99
	Tennessee	S	6.64 MW	7.33 AW	15240 AAW	TNBLS	10//99-12//99
	Knoxville MSA, TN	S	8.72 MW	8.73 AW	18140 AAW	TNBLS	10//99-12//99
	Memphis MSA, TN-AR-MS	S	7.65 MW	6.59 AW	15910 AAW	MSBLS	10//99-12//99
	Nashville MSA, TN	S	6.57 MW	6.19 AW	13660 AAW	TNBLS	10//99-12//99
	Texas	S	6.24 MW	6.85 AW	14250 AAW	TXBLS	10//99-12//99
	Austin-San Marcos MSA, TX	S	6.42 MW	6.29 AW	13360 AAW	TXBLS	10//99-12//99
	Dallas PMSA, TX	S	7.54 MW	6.48 AW	15680 AAW	TXBLS	10//99-12//99
	El Paso MSA, TX	S	6.78 MW	6.29 AW	14100 AAW	TXBLS	10//99-12//99
	Fort Worth-Arlington PMSA,						
	TX	S	6.36 MW	5.93 AW	13220 AAW	TXBLS	10//99-12//99
	Houston PMSA, TX	S	6.65 MW	6.26 AW	13840 AAW	TXBLS	10//99-12//99
	San Antonio MSA, TX	S	6.45 MW	6.06 AW	13420 AAW	TXBLS	10//99-12//99
	Utah	S	6.92 MW	7.29 AW	15170 AAW	UTBLS	10//99-12//99
	Salt Lake City-Ogden MSA,						
	UT	S	7.28 MW	6.90 AW	15140 AAW	UTBLS	10//99-12//99

Occupation/Type/Industry	Location	Per	Low	Mid	High	Source	Date
Parking Lot Attendant	Vermont	S	8.46 MW	8.36 AW	17390 AAW	VTBLS	10//99-12//99
	Virginia	S	6.61 MW	6.72 AW	13980 AAW	VABLS	10//99-12//99
	Lynchburg MSA, VA	S	7.66 MW	6.45 AW	15920 AAW	VABLS	10//99-12//99
	Norfolk-Virginia Beach- Newport News MSA, VA- NC	S	7.02 MW	7.30 AW	14610 AAW	VABLS	
	Richmond-Petersburg MSA, VA	S	6.13 MW	6.10 AW	12750 AAW	VABLS	10//99-12//99
	Washington	S	8.33 MW	8.81 AW	18330 AAW	WABLS	10//99-12//99
	Seattle-Bellevue-Everett PMSA, WA	S	9.24 MW	8.68 AW	19220 AAW	WABLS	10//99-12//99
	Tacoma PMSA, WA	S	8.37 MW	8.50 AW	17410 AAW	WABLS	10//99-12//99
	West Virginia	S	6.05 MW	6.21 AW	12920 AAW	WVBLS	10//99-12//99
	Wisconsin	S	8.07 MW	8.49 AW	17650 AAW	WIBLS	10//99-12//99
	Milwaukee-Waukesha PMSA, WI	S	8.79 MW	8.24 AW	18290 AAW	WIBLS	10//99-12//99
	Wyoming	S	6.59 MW	6.75 AW	14040 AAW	WYBLS	10//99-12//99
	Puerto Rico	S	5.93 MW	5.87 AW	12200 AAW	PRBLS	10//99-12//99
	San Juan-Bayamon PMSA, PR	S	5.87 MW	5.92 AW	12210 AAW	PRBLS	10//99-12//99
	Virgin Islands	S	6.37 MW	6.56 AW	13640 AAW	VIBLS	10//99-12//99
Parts Salesperson	Alabama	S	10.18 MW	11.37 AW	23640 AAW	ALBLS	10//99-12//99
	Alaska	S	12.92 MW	13.27 AW	27610 AAW	AKBLS	10//99-12//99
	Arizona	S	10.99 MW	12.56 AW	26130 AAW	AZBLS	10//99-12//99
	Arkansas	S	8.76 MW	9.80 AW	20380 AAW	ARBLS	10//99-12//99
	California	S	11.86 MW	13.73 AW	28570 AAW	CABLS	10//99-12//99
	Colorado	S	10.96 MW	12.25 AW	25480 AAW	COBLS	10//99-12//99
	Connecticut	S	12.26 MW	13.10 AW	27260 AAW	CTBLS	10//99-12//99
	Delaware	S	10.19 MW	11.05 AW	22990 AAW	DEBLS	10//99-12//99
	Florida	S	11.64 MW	13.06 AW	27160 AAW	FLBLS	10//99-12//99
	Georgia	S	12.1 MW	13.15 AW	27350 AAW	GABLS	10//99-12//99
	Hawaii	S	11.97 MW	13.16 AW	27370 AAW	HIBLS	10//99-12//99
	Idaho	S	10.65 MW	11.22 AW	23330 AAW	IDBLS	10//99-12//99
	Illinois	S	12.27 MW	13.84 AW	28780 AAW	ILBLS	10//99-12//99
	Indiana	S	10.7 MW	11.32 AW	23550 AAW	INBLS	10//99-12//99
	Iowa	S	10.98 MW	11.83 AW	24610 AAW	IABLS	10//99-12//99
	Kansas	S	9.65 MW	10.30 AW	21430 AAW	KSBLS	10//99-12//99
	Kentucky	S	9.49 MW	10.24 AW	21310 AAW	KYBLS	10//99-12//99
	Louisiana	S	9.96 MW	10.84 AW	22550 AAW	LABLS	10//99-12//99
	Maine	S	10.36 MW	10.76 AW	22380 AAW	MEBLS	10//99-12//99
	Maryland	S	10.98 MW	12.20 AW	25370 AAW	MDBLS	10//99-12//99
	Massachusetts	S	12.75 MW	13.96 AW	29030 AAW	MABLS	10//99-12//99
	Michigan	S	12.19 MW	13.55 AW	28190 AAW	MIBLS	10//99-12//99
	Minnesota	S	12.23 MW	13.12 AW	27300 AAW	MNBLS	10//99-12//99
	Mississippi	S	10.07 MW	10.41 AW	21660 AAW	MSBLS	10//99-12//99
	Missouri	S	9.61 MW	11.00 AW	22870 AAW	MOBLS	10//99-12//99
	Montana	S	10.34 MW	10.74 AW	22330 AAW	MTBLS	10//99-12//99
	Nebraska	S	10.76 MW	11.59 AW	24110 AAW	NEBLS	10//99-12//99
	Nevada	S	10.85 MW	12.53 AW	26060 AAW	NVBLS	10//99-12//99
	New Hampshire	S	11.68 MW	12.53 AW	26070 AAW	NHBLS	10//99-12//99
	New Jersey	S	13.18 MW	14.43 AW	30020 AAW	NJBLS	10//99-12//99
	New Mexico	S	9.87 MW	11.01 AW	22900 AAW	NMBLS	10//99-12//99
	New York	S	10.72 MW	11.94 AW	24840 AAW	NYBLS	10//99-12//99
	North Carolina	S	10.41 MW	11.45 AW	23810 AAW	NCBLS	10//99-12//99
	North Dakota	S	10.08 MW	10.95 AW	22780 AAW	NDBLS	10//99-12//99
	Ohio	S	10.38 MW	11.28 AW	23460 AAW	OHBLS	10//99-12//99
	Oklahoma	S	8.68 MW	10.47 AW	21780 AAW	OKBLS	10//99-12//99
	Oregon	S	12.49 MW	13.07 AW	27190 AAW	ORBLS	10//99-12//99
	Pennsylvania	S	10.26 MW	11.26 AW	23410 AAW	PABLS	10//99-12//99
	Rhode Island	S	10.89 MW	11.85 AW	24650 AAW	RIBLS	10//99-12//99
	South Carolina	S	10.07 MW	10.80 AW	22460 AAW	SCBLS	10//99-12//99
	South Dakota	S	10.02 MW	10.55 AW	21930 AAW	SDBLS	10//99-12//99
	Tennessee	S	11.06 MW	12.04 AW	25050 AAW	TNBLS	10//99-12//99
	Texas	S	9.77 MW	11.55 AW	24030 AAW	TXBLS	10//99-12//99
	Utah	S	11.4 MW	12.75 AW	26510 AAW	UTBLS	10//99-12//99
	Vermont	S	10.57 MW	11.20 AW	23290 AAW	VTBLS	10//99-12//99
	Virginia	S	10.65 MW	11.56 AW	24050 AAW	VABLS	10//99-12//99
	Washington	S	11.74 MW	12.33 AW	25640 AAW	WABLS	10//99-12//99
	West Virginia	S	8.52 MW	9.29 AW	19320 AAW	WVBLS	10//99-12//99
	Wisconsin	S	11.76 MW	12.79 AW	26590 AAW	WIBLS	10//99-12//99
	Wyoming	S	9.51 MW	10.18 AW	21170 AAW	WYBLS	10//99-12//99
	Puerto Rico	S	6.31 MW	6.93 AW	14410 AAW	PRBLS	10//99-12//99
	Virgin Islands	S	7.8 MW	7.91 AW	16440 AAW	VIBLS	10//99-12//99

AAW	Average annual wage	AOH	Average offered, high	ASH	Average starting, high	H	Hourly			M	Monthly		S	Special: hourly and annual
AE	Average entry wage	AOL	Average offered, low	ASL	Average starting, low	HI	Highest wage paid		MTC	Median total compensation	TQ	Third quartile wage
AEX	Average experienced wage	APH	Average pay, high range	AW	Average wage paid	HR	High end range		MW	Median wage paid	W	Weekly
AO	Average offered	APL	Average pay, low range	FQ	First quartile wage	LR	Low end range		SQ	Second quartile wage	Y	Yearly

Occupation/Type/Industry	Location	Per	Low	Mid	High	Source	Date
Parts Salesperson	Guam	S	8.51 MW	9.07 AW	18860 AAW	GUBLS	10//99-12//99
Patient Care Executive							
Hospital	United States	Y		106300 MW		HHN	2000
Patternmaker							
Metals and Plastics	Alabama	S	15.37 MW	15.37 AW	31980 AAW	ALBLS	10//99-12//99
Metals and Plastics	Arizona	S	14.44 MW	14.38 AW	29920 AAW	AZBLS	10//99-12//99
Metals and Plastics	Arkansas	S	14.66 MW	13.54 AW	28160 AAW	ARBLS	10//99-12//99
Metals and Plastics	California	S	9.67 MW	10.61 AW	22060 AAW	CABLS	10//99-12//99
Metals and Plastics	Colorado	S	22.1 MW	21.17 AW	44020 AAW	COBLS	10//99-12//99
Metals and Plastics	Connecticut	S	16.02 MW	17.77 AW	36950 AAW	CTBLS	10//99-12//99
Metals and Plastics	Florida	S	11.47 MW	12.42 AW	25840 AAW	FLBLS	10//99-12//99
Metals and Plastics	Illinois	S	9.99 MW	10.73 AW	22320 AAW	ILBLS	10//99-12//99
Metals and Plastics	Indiana	S	18.27 MW	17.84 AW	37100 AAW	INBLS	10//99-12//99
Metals and Plastics	Iowa	S	13.9 MW	16.59 AW	34510 AAW	IABLS	10//99-12//99
Metals and Plastics	Kansas	S	18.8 MW	18.53 AW	38540 AAW	KSBLS	10//99-12//99
Metals and Plastics	Massachusetts	S	18.23 MW	17.43 AW	36240 AAW	MABLS	10//99-12//99
Metals and Plastics	Michigan	S	20.46 MW	18.73 AW	38970 AAW	MIBLS	10//99-12//99
Metals and Plastics	Minnesota	S	18.5 MW	18.14 AW	37740 AAW	MNBLS	10//99-12//99
Metals and Plastics	Mississippi	S	7.09 MW	7.99 AW	16620 AAW	MSBLS	10//99-12//99
Metals and Plastics	Missouri	S	8.39 MW	11.33 AW	23580 AAW	MOBLS	10//99-12//99
Metals and Plastics	New Jersey	S	12.62 MW	13.34 AW	27740 AAW	NJBLS	10//99-12//99
Metals and Plastics	New York	S	16.17 MW	17.55 AW	36500 AAW	NYBLS	10//99-12//99
Metals and Plastics	North Carolina	S	14.15 MW	16.40 AW	34120 AAW	NCBLS	10//99-12//99
Metals and Plastics	Ohio	S	14.96 MW	16.00 AW	33280 AAW	OHBLS	10//99-12//99
Metals and Plastics	Pennsylvania	S	11.73 MW	11.92 AW	24800 AAW	PABLS	10//99-12//99
Metals and Plastics	Tennessee	S	11.91 MW	11.64 AW	24220 AAW	TNBLS	10//99-12//99
Metals and Plastics	Texas	S	9.04 MW	10.42 AW	21670 AAW	TXBLS	10//99-12//99
Metals and Plastics	Utah	S	19.23 MW	19.44 AW	40430 AAW	UTBLS	10//99-12//99
Metals and Plastics	Washington	S	13.47 MW	13.83 AW	28770 AAW	WABLS	10//99-12//99
Metals and Plastics	Wisconsin	S	12.95 MW	14.90 AW	31000 AAW	WIBLS	10//99-12//99
Wood	Alabama	S	12.55 MW	12.87 AW	26780 AAW	ALBLS	10//99-12//99
Wood	Florida	S	13.35 MW	13.95 AW	29020 AAW	FLBLS	10//99-12//99
Wood	Illinois	S	14.72 MW	13.64 AW	28370 AAW	ILBLS	10//99-12//99
Wood	Indiana	S	20.36 MW	19.74 AW	41070 AAW	INBLS	10//99-12//99
Wood	Kansas	S	12.69 MW	14.35 AW	29850 AAW	KSBLS	10//99-12//99
Wood	Massachusetts	S	22.07 MW	20.65 AW	42950 AAW	MABLS	10//99-12//99
Wood	Michigan	S	22.87 MW	21.51 AW	44740 AAW	MIBLS	10//99-12//99
Wood	Minnesota	S	12.14 MW	12.55 AW	26100 AAW	MNBLS	10//99-12//99
Wood	Mississippi	S	10.2 MW	10.51 AW	21860 AAW	MSBLS	10//99-12//99
Wood	Missouri	S	8.96 MW	11.04 AW	22960 AAW	MOBLS	10//99-12//99
Wood	New Jersey	S	16.73 MW	16.55 AW	34430 AAW	NJBLS	10//99-12//99
Wood	New York	S	11.89 MW	11.95 AW	24860 AAW	NYBLS	10//99-12//99
Wood	North Carolina	S	10.38 MW	11.33 AW	23570 AAW	NCBLS	10//99-12//99
Wood	Ohio	S	18.99 MW	18.57 AW	38620 AAW	OHBLS	10//99-12//99
Wood	Oklahoma	S	13.62 MW	15.51 AW	32260 AAW	OKBLS	10//99-12//99
Wood	Oregon	S	24.14 MW	23.30 AW	48460 AAW	ORBLS	10//99-12//99
Wood	Pennsylvania	S	13.53 MW	12.93 AW	26880 AAW	PABLS	10//99-12//99
Wood	South Carolina	S	11.28 MW	11.09 AW	23080 AAW	SCBLS	10//99-12//99
Wood	Tennessee	S	6.96 MW	6.99 AW	14540 AAW	TNBLS	10//99-12//99
Wood	Utah	S	10.95 MW	11.62 AW	24170 AAW	UTBLS	10//99-12//99
Wood	Virginia	S	15.45 MW	16.04 AW	33360 AAW	VABLS	10//99-12//99
Wood	Washington	S	16.08 MW	16.46 AW	34230 AAW	WABLS	10//99-12//99
Wood	Wisconsin	S	18.24 MW	17.46 AW	36310 AAW	WIBLS	10//99-12//99
Paving, Surfacing, and Tamping Equipment Operator							
	Alabama	S	10.82 MW	11.04 AW	22960 AAW	ALBLS	10//99-12//99
	Alaska	S	21.61 MW	21.09 AW	43870 AAW	AKBLS	10//99-12//99
	Arizona	S	12.86 MW	13.32 AW	27700 AAW	AZBLS	10//99-12//99
	Arkansas	S	10.07 MW	10.43 AW	21690 AAW	ARBLS	10//99-12//99
	California	S	17.98 MW	18.70 AW	38900 AAW	CABLS	10//99-12//99
	Colorado	S	13.84 MW	13.64 AW	28360 AAW	COBLS	10//99-12//99
	Connecticut	S	17.29 MW	16.08 AW	33450 AAW	CTBLS	10//99-12//99
	Delaware	S	13.51 MW	14.51 AW	30180 AAW	DEBLS	10//99-12//99
	Florida	S	10.24 MW	10.58 AW	22010 AAW	FLBLS	10//99-12//99
	Georgia	S	10.52 MW	10.62 AW	22090 AAW	GABLS	10//99-12//99
	Hawaii	S	27.8 MW	24.95 AW	51900 AAW	HIBLS	10//99-12//99
	Idaho	S	13.05 MW	13.08 AW	27210 AAW	IDBLS	10//99-12//99
	Illinois	S	20.31 MW	18.12 AW	37700 AAW	ILBLS	10//99-12//99
	Indiana	S	16.77 MW	17.20 AW	35770 AAW	INBLS	10//99-12//99
	Iowa	S	12.7 MW	12.65 AW	26320 AAW	IABLS	10//99-12//99

Occupation/Type/Industry	Location	Per	Low	Mid	High	Source	Date
Paving, Surfacing, and Tamping Equipment Operator	Kansas	S	10.06 MW	10.45 AW	21730 AAW	KSBLS	10//99-12//99
	Kentucky	S	11.84 MW	12.57 AW	26140 AAW	KYBLS	10//99-12//99
	Louisiana	S	9.4 MW	10.19 AW	21200 AAW	LABLS	10//99-12//99
	Maine	S	10.34 MW	10.57 AW	21990 AAW	MEBLS	10//99-12//99
	Maryland	S	11.93 MW	12.29 AW	25550 AAW	MDBLS	10//99-12//99
	Massachusetts	S	14.7 MW	15.58 AW	32410 AAW	MABLS	10//99-12//99
	Michigan	S	14.96 MW	14.81 AW	30800 AAW	MIBLS	10//99-12//99
	Minnesota	S	17.39 MW	16.87 AW	35090 AAW	MNBLS	10//99-12//99
	Mississippi	S	9.24 MW	9.38 AW	19520 AAW	MSBLS	10//99-12//99
	Missouri	S	13.64 MW	14.31 AW	29770 AAW	MOBLS	10//99-12//99
	Montana	S	12.4 MW	13.20 AW	27470 AAW	MTBLS	10//99-12//99
	Nebraska	S	12.57 MW	13.15 AW	27350 AAW	NEBLS	10//99-12//99
	Nevada	S	18.66 MW	20.75 AW	43150 AAW	NVBLS	10//99-12//99
	New Hampshire	S	13.07 MW	13.59 AW	28260 AAW	NHBLS	10//99-12//99
	New Jersey	S	18.56 MW	18.98 AW	39470 AAW	NJBLS	10//99-12//99
	New Mexico	S	10.62 MW	10.55 AW	21940 AAW	NMBLS	10//99-12//99
	New York	S	15.53 MW	17.52 AW	36450 AAW	NYBLS	10//99-12//99
	North Carolina	S	10.31 MW	10.94 AW	22760 AAW	NCBLS	10//99-12//99
	North Dakota	S	13.98 MW	13.77 AW	28640 AAW	NDBLS	10//99-12//99
	Ohio	S	13.05 MW	14.09 AW	29310 AAW	OHBLS	10//99-12//99
	Oklahoma	S	9.85 MW	10.50 AW	21840 AAW	OKBLS	10//99-12//99
	Oregon	S	15.55 MW	16.68 AW	34690 AAW	ORBLS	10//99-12//99
	Pennsylvania	S	11.76 MW	13.14 AW	27320 AAW	PABLS	10//99-12//99
	Rhode Island	S	17.68 MW	17.25 AW	35890 AAW	RIBLS	10//99-12//99
	South Carolina	S	10.41 MW	10.92 AW	22710 AAW	SCBLS	10//99-12//99
	South Dakota	S	12.29 MW	12.65 AW	26310 AAW	SDBLS	10//99-12//99
	Tennessee	S	10.82 MW	10.93 AW	22720 AAW	TNBLS	10//99-12//99
	Texas	S	10.09 MW	10.41 AW	21660 AAW	TXBLS	10//99-12//99
	Utah	S	14.22 MW	14.43 AW	30020 AAW	UTBLS	10//99-12//99
	Virginia	S	10.91 MW	11.44 AW	23800 AAW	VABLS	10//99-12//99
	Washington	S	15.43 MW	16.39 AW	34090 AAW	WABLS	10//99-12//99
	West Virginia	S	11.99 MW	13.11 AW	27260 AAW	WVBLS	10//99-12//99
	Wisconsin	S	13.66 MW	13.76 AW	28610 AAW	WIBLS	10//99-12//99
	Wyoming	S	13.82 MW	14.04 AW	29200 AAW	WYBLS	10//99-12//99
	Puerto Rico	S	8.03 MW	10.65 AW	22150 AAW	PRBLS	10//99-12//99
Payroll and Timekeeping Clerk	Alabama	S	10.84 MW	11.31 AW	23520 AAW	ALBLS	10//99-12//99
	Anniston MSA, AL	S	9.82 MW	9.98 AW	20420 AAW	ALBLS	10//99-12//99
	Auburn-Opelika MSA, AL	S	12.23 MW	12.50 AW	25440 AAW	ALBLS	10//99-12//99
	Birmingham MSA, AL	S	11.90 MW	11.36 AW	24760 AAW	ALBLS	10//99-12//99
	Decatur MSA, AL	S	11.78 MW	11.23 AW	24500 AAW	ALBLS	10//99-12//99
	Dothan MSA, AL	S	11.19 MW	10.69 AW	23270 AAW	ALBLS	10//99-12//99
	Florence MSA, AL	S	10.68 MW	10.09 AW	22210 AAW	ALBLS	10//99-12//99
	Gadsden MSA, AL	S	10.73 MW	9.68 AW	22310 AAW	ALBLS	10//99-12//99
	Huntsville MSA, AL	S	12.51 MW	12.57 AW	26010 AAW	ALBLS	10//99-12//99
	Mobile MSA, AL	S	10.69 MW	10.50 AW	22240 AAW	ALBLS	10//99-12//99
	Montgomery MSA, AL	S	11.37 MW	10.95 AW	23640 AAW	ALBLS	10//99-12//99
	Tuscaloosa MSA, AL	S	11.20 MW	11.19 AW	23300 AAW	ALBLS	10//99-12//99
	Alaska	S	15.48 MW	15.57 AW	32390 AAW	AKBLS	10//99-12//99
	Anchorage MSA, AK	S	14.95 MW	14.94 AW	31090 AAW	AKBLS	10//99-12//99
	Arizona	S	11.36 MW	11.64 AW	24210 AAW	AZBLS	10//99-12//99
	Flagstaff MSA, AZ-UT	S	11.50 MW	11.26 AW	23920 AAW	AZBLS	10//99-12//99
	Phoenix-Mesa MSA, AZ	S	11.80 MW	11.55 AW	24550 AAW	AZBLS	10//99-12//99
	Tucson MSA, AZ	S	11.21 MW	10.64 AW	23310 AAW	AZBLS	10//99-12//99
	Yuma MSA, AZ	S	10.60 MW	9.69 AW	22050 AAW	AZBLS	10//99-12//99
	Arkansas	S	10.46 MW	10.76 AW	22390 AAW	ARBLS	10//99-12//99
	Fayetteville-Springdale-Rogers MSA, AR	S	11.01 MW	10.54 AW	22900 AAW	ARBLS	10//99-12//99
	Fort Smith MSA, AR-OK	S	10.39 MW	10.45 AW	21610 AAW	ARBLS	10//99-12//99
	Jonesboro MSA, AR	S	10.86 MW	10.62 AW	22580 AAW	ARBLS	10//99-12//99
	Little Rock-North Little Rock MSA, AR	S	11.66 MW	11.28 AW	24260 AAW	ARBLS	10//99-12//99
	California	S	14.47 MW	14.75 AW	30670 AAW	CABLS	10//99-12//99
	Bakersfield MSA, CA	S	12.32 MW	12.10 AW	25620 AAW	CABLS	10//99-12//99
	Chico-Paradise MSA, CA	S	12.41 MW	12.00 AW	25820 AAW	CABLS	10//99-12//99
	Fresno MSA, CA	S	11.89 MW	11.23 AW	24730 AAW	CABLS	10//99-12//99
	Los Angeles-Long Beach PMSA, CA	S	14.74 MW	14.70 AW	30660 AAW	CABLS	10//99-12//99
	Merced MSA, CA	S	11.88 MW	11.93 AW	24710 AAW	CABLS	10//99-12//99
	Modesto MSA, CA	S	12.06 MW	11.99 AW	25090 AAW	CABLS	10//99-12//99
	Oakland PMSA, CA	S	15.64 MW	15.50 AW	32540 AAW	CABLS	10//99-12//99

AAW	Average annual wage	AOH	Average offered, high	ASH	Average starting, high	H	Hourly			M	Monthly	S	Special: hourly and annual
AE	Average entry wage	AOL	Average offered, low	ASL	Average starting, low	HI	Highest wage paid			MTC	Median total compensation	TQ	Third quartile wage
AEX	Average experienced wage	APH	Average pay, high range	AW	Average wage paid	HR	High end range			MW	Median wage paid	W	Weekly
AO	Average offered	APL	Average pay, low range	FQ	First quartile wage	LR	Low end range			SQ	Second quartile wage	Y	Yearly

Occupation/Type/Industry	Location	Per	Low	Mid	High	Source	Date
Payroll and Timekeeping Clerk	Orange County PMSA, CA	S	15.83 MW	15.80 AW	32920 AAW	CABLS	10//99-12//99
	Redding MSA, CA	S	12.97 MW	12.86 AW	26970 AAW	CABLS	10//99-12//99
	Riverside-San Bernardino PMSA, CA	S	13.42 MW	12.97 AW	27920 AAW	CABLS	10//99-12//99
	Sacramento PMSA, CA	S	13.60 MW	13.49 AW	28280 AAW	CABLS	10//99-12//99
	Salinas MSA, CA	S	12.50 MW	12.24 AW	26010 AAW	CABLS	10//99-12//99
	San Diego MSA, CA	S	14.34 MW	14.17 AW	29830 AAW	CABLS	10//99-12//99
	San Francisco PMSA, CA	S	17.26 MW	15.81 AW	35900 AAW	CABLS	10//99-12//99
	San Jose PMSA, CA	S	16.44 MW	15.90 AW	34190 AAW	CABLS	10//99-12//99
	San Luis Obispo-Atascadero-Paso Robles MSA, CA	S	13.30 MW	13.81 AW	27670 AAW	CABLS	10//99-12//99
	Santa Barbara-Santa Maria-Lompoc MSA, CA	S	14.17 MW	13.72 AW	29470 AAW	CABLS	10//99-12//99
	Santa Cruz-Watsonville PMSA, CA	S	14.87 MW	14.30 AW	30930 AAW	CABLS	10//99-12//99
	Santa Rosa PMSA, CA	S	16.87 MW	16.18 AW	35090 AAW	CABLS	10//99-12//99
	Stockton-Lodi MSA, CA	S	13.28 MW	12.97 AW	27610 AAW	CABLS	10//99-12//99
	Vallejo-Fairfield-Napa PMSA, CA	S	14.22 MW	14.17 AW	29570 AAW	CABLS	10//99-12//99
	Ventura PMSA, CA	S	14.31 MW	14.40 AW	29760 AAW	CABLS	10//99-12//99
	Visalia-Tulare-Porterville MSA, CA	S	11.29 MW	11.00 AW	23480 AAW	CABLS	10//99-12//99
	Yolo PMSA, CA	S	14.87 MW	14.89 AW	30930 AAW	CABLS	10//99-12//99
	Yuba City MSA, CA	S	13.11 MW	13.30 AW	27270 AAW	CABLS	10//99-12//99
	Colorado	S	12.93 MW	14.40 AW	29960 AAW	COBLS	10//99-12//99
	Boulder-Longmont PMSA, CO	S	13.38 MW	13.16 AW	27840 AAW	COBLS	10//99-12//99
	Colorado Springs MSA, CO	S	12.05 MW	11.91 AW	25060 AAW	COBLS	10//99-12//99
	Fort Collins-Loveland MSA, CO	S	12.48 MW	12.30 AW	25950 AAW	COBLS	10//99-12//99
	Greeley PMSA, CO	S	11.42 MW	11.31 AW	23750 AAW	COBLS	10//99-12//99
	Connecticut	S	14.19 MW	14.64 AW	30440 AAW	CTBLS	10//99-12//99
	Bridgeport PMSA, CT	S	14.96 MW	14.77 AW	31120 AAW	CTBLS	10//99-12//99
	Danbury PMSA, CT	S	15.98 MW	15.97 AW	33240 AAW	CTBLS	10//99-12//99
	Hartford MSA, CT	S	15.15 MW	15.09 AW	31520 AAW	CTBLS	10//99-12//99
	New Haven-Meriden PMSA, CT	S	14.99 MW	14.70 AW	31190 AAW	CTBLS	10//99-12//99
	New London-Norwich MSA, CT-RI	S	13.16 MW	12.98 AW	27380 AAW	CTBLS	10//99-12//99
	Stamford-Norwalk PMSA, CT	S	14.13 MW	13.34 AW	29380 AAW	CTBLS	10//99-12//99
	Waterbury PMSA, CT	S	13.68 MW	13.70 AW	28460 AAW	CTBLS	10//99-12//99
	Delaware	S	12.64 MW	12.39 AW	25760 AAW	DEBLS	10//99-12//99
	Dover MSA, DE	S	12.71 MW	11.98 AW	26430 AAW	DEBLS	10//99-12//99
	Wilmington-Newark PMSA, DE-MD	S	13.30 MW	13.72 AW	27660 AAW	DEBLS	10//99-12//99
	District of Columbia	S	15.34 MW	15.70 AW	32650 AAW	DCBLS	10//99-12//99
	Washington PMSA, DC-MD-VA-WV	S	14.10 MW	13.98 AW	29320 AAW	DCBLS	10//99-12//99
	Florida	S	11.55 MW	11.93 AW	24810 AAW	FLBLS	10//99-12//99
	Daytona Beach MSA, FL	S	11.53 MW	11.33 AW	23970 AAW	FLBLS	10//99-12//99
	Fort Lauderdale PMSA, FL	S	13.05 MW	12.37 AW	27140 AAW	FLBLS	10//99-12//99
	Fort Myers-Cape Coral MSA, FL	S	11.21 MW	10.99 AW	23310 AAW	FLBLS	10//99-12//99
	Fort Pierce-Port St. Lucie MSA, FL	S	11.38 MW	11.11 AW	23680 AAW	FLBLS	10//99-12//99
	Fort Walton Beach MSA, FL	S	9.40 MW	9.56 AW	19550 AAW	FLBLS	10//99-12//99
	Gainesville MSA, FL	S	11.45 MW	11.01 AW	23820 AAW	FLBLS	10//99-12//99
	Jacksonville MSA, FL	S	11.68 MW	11.23 AW	24280 AAW	FLBLS	10//99-12//99
	Lakeland-Winter Haven MSA, FL	S	10.98 MW	10.60 AW	22840 AAW	FLBLS	10//99-12//99
	Melbourne-Titusville-Palm Bay MSA, FL	S	11.96 MW	11.99 AW	24880 AAW	FLBLS	10//99-12//99
	Miami PMSA, FL	S	12.39 MW	11.99 AW	25780 AAW	FLBLS	10//99-12//99
	Naples MSA, FL	S	11.53 MW	11.50 AW	23990 AAW	FLBLS	10//99-12//99
	Ocala MSA, FL	S	10.60 MW	10.41 AW	22040 AAW	FLBLS	10//99-12//99
	Orlando MSA, FL	S	11.73 MW	11.34 AW	24400 AAW	FLBLS	10//99-12//99
	Panama City MSA, FL	S	11.44 MW	10.65 AW	23790 AAW	FLBLS	10//99-12//99
	Pensacola MSA, FL	S	12.45 MW	12.89 AW	25900 AAW	FLBLS	10//99-12//99
	Punta Gorda MSA, FL	S	10.49 MW	10.86 AW	21810 AAW	FLBLS	10//99-12//99
	Sarasota-Bradenton MSA, FL	S	11.76 MW	11.31 AW	24450 AAW	FLBLS	10//99-12//99
	Tallahassee MSA, FL	S	11.90 MW	11.77 AW	24760 AAW	FLBLS	10//99-12//99
	Tampa-St. Petersburg-Clearwater MSA, FL	S	11.62 MW	11.15 AW	24160 AAW	FLBLS	10//99-12//99

AAW	Average annual wage	AOH	Average offered, high	ASH	Average starting, high
AE	Average entry wage	AOL	Average offered, low	ASL	Average starting, low
AEX	Average experienced wage	APH	Average pay, high range	AW	Average wage paid
AO	Average offered	APL	Average pay, low range	FQ	First quartile wage

H	Hourly	M	Monthly
HI	Highest wage paid	MTC	Median total compensation
HR	High end range	MW	Median wage paid
LR	Low end range	SQ	Second quartile wage

S	Special: hourly and annual
TQ	Third quartile wage
W	Weekly
Y	Yearly

Occupation/Type/Industry	Location	Per	Low	Mid	High	Source	Date
Payroll and Timekeeping Clerk	West Palm Beach-Boca Raton						
	MSA, FL	S	12.60 MW	12.49 AW	26210 AAW	FLBLS	10//99-12//99
	Georgia	S	11.54 MW	11.87 AW	24680 AAW	GABLS	10//99-12//99
	Albany MSA, GA	S	11.27 MW	11.33 AW	23440 AAW	GABLS	10//99-12//99
	Athens MSA, GA	S	10.32 MW	10.06 AW	21460 AAW	GABLS	10//99-12//99
	Atlanta MSA, GA	S	12.58 MW	12.14 AW	26180 AAW	GABLS	10//99-12//99
	Augusta-Aiken MSA, GA-SC	S	10.80 MW	10.79 AW	22460 AAW	GABLS	10//99-12//99
	Columbus MSA, GA-AL	S	11.23 MW	11.09 AW	23350 AAW	GABLS	10//99-12//99
	Macon MSA, GA	S	10.87 MW	10.67 AW	22600 AAW	GABLS	10//99-12//99
	Savannah MSA, GA	S	10.92 MW	10.51 AW	22710 AAW	GABLS	10//99-12//99
	Hawaii	S	13.35 MW	13.46 AW	28000 AAW	HIBLS	10//99-12//99
	Honolulu MSA, HI	S	13.49 MW	13.46 AW	28050 AAW	HIBLS	10//99-12//99
	Idaho	S	11.42 MW	11.57 AW	24070 AAW	IDBLS	10//99-12//99
	Boise City MSA, ID	S	11.86 MW	11.82 AW	24670 AAW	IDBLS	10//99-12//99
	Illinois	S	12.5 MW	12.99 AW	27010 AAW	ILBLS	10//99-12//99
	Bloomington-Normal MSA, IL	S	12.85 MW	12.45 AW	26720 AAW	ILBLS	10//99-12//99
	Champaign-Urbana MSA, IL	S	11.99 MW	11.85 AW	24930 AAW	ILBLS	10//99-12//99
	Chicago PMSA, IL	S	13.36 MW	12.83 AW	27790 AAW	ILBLS	10//99-12//99
	Decatur MSA, IL	S	11.28 MW	10.97 AW	23470 AAW	ILBLS	10//99-12//99
	Kankakee PMSA, IL	S	12.64 MW	12.01 AW	26300 AAW	ILBLS	10//99-12//99
	Peoria-Pekin MSA, IL	S	11.80 MW	11.56 AW	24540 AAW	ILBLS	10//99-12//99
	Rockford MSA, IL	S	13.74 MW	14.10 AW	28580 AAW	ILBLS	10//99-12//99
	Springfield MSA, IL	S	12.61 MW	12.00 AW	26240 AAW	ILBLS	10//99-12//99
	Indiana	S	11.82 MW	12.22 AW	25410 AAW	INBLS	10//99-12//99
	Bloomington MSA, IN	S	11.81 MW	11.84 AW	24560 AAW	INBLS	10//99-12//99
	Elkhart-Goshen MSA, IN	S	12.02 MW	11.89 AW	25000 AAW	INBLS	10//99-12//99
	Evansville-Henderson MSA, IN-KY	S	11.72 MW	11.19 AW	24370 AAW	INBLS	10//99-12//99
	Fort Wayne MSA, IN	S	11.87 MW	11.74 AW	24680 AAW	INBLS	10//99-12//99
	Gary PMSA, IN	S	11.64 MW	11.45 AW	24220 AAW	INBLS	10//99-12//99
	Indianapolis MSA, IN	S	13.25 MW	12.80 AW	27560 AAW	INBLS	10//99-12//99
	Kokomo MSA, IN	S	12.19 MW	11.74 AW	25350 AAW	INBLS	10//99-12//99
	Lafayette MSA, IN	S	11.84 MW	11.50 AW	24630 AAW	INBLS	10//99-12//99
	Muncie MSA, IN	S	11.65 MW	11.17 AW	24230 AAW	INBLS	10//99-12//99
	South Bend MSA, IN	S	11.56 MW	11.38 AW	24050 AAW	INBLS	10//99-12//99
	Terre Haute MSA, IN	S	11.67 MW	11.32 AW	24260 AAW	INBLS	10//99-12//99
	Iowa	S	11.11 MW	11.48 AW	23890 AAW	IABLS	10//99-12//99
	Cedar Rapids MSA, IA	S	11.57 MW	11.10 AW	24060 AAW	IABLS	10//99-12//99
	Davenport-Moline-Rock Island MSA, IA-IL	S	12.23 MW	11.93 AW	25450 AAW	IABLS	10//99-12//99
	Des Moines MSA, IA	S	12.19 MW	11.97 AW	25350 AAW	IABLS	10//99-12//99
	Dubuque MSA, IA	S	10.80 MW	10.53 AW	22450 AAW	IABLS	10//99-12//99
	Sioux City MSA, IA-NE	S	11.20 MW	11.11 AW	23310 AAW	IABLS	10//99-12//99
	Waterloo-Cedar Falls MSA, IA	S	13.34 MW	11.81 AW	27750 AAW	IABLS	10//99-12//99
	Kansas	S	11.57 MW	11.99 AW	24930 AAW	KSBLS	10//99-12//99
	Lawrence MSA, KS	S	13.00 MW	13.57 AW	27040 AAW	KSBLS	10//99-12//99
	Topeka MSA, KS	S	12.05 MW	11.18 AW	25060 AAW	KSBLS	10//99-12//99
	Wichita MSA, KS	S	12.78 MW	11.86 AW	26580 AAW	KSBLS	10//99-12//99
	Kentucky	S	11.3 MW	11.50 AW	23920 AAW	KYBLS	10//99-12//99
	Lexington MSA, KY	S	11.63 MW	11.34 AW	24200 AAW	KYBLS	10//99-12//99
	Louisville MSA, KY-IN	S	11.43 MW	11.28 AW	23780 AAW	KYBLS	10//99-12//99
	Owensboro MSA, KY	S	11.72 MW	11.95 AW	24370 AAW	KYBLS	10//99-12//99
	Louisiana	S	10.78 MW	11.46 AW	23830 AAW	LABLS	10//99-12//99
	Alexandria MSA, LA	S	9.94 MW	9.87 AW	20680 AAW	LABLS	10//99-12//99
	Baton Rouge MSA, LA	S	11.88 MW	11.45 AW	24710 AAW	LABLS	10//99-12//99
	Houma MSA, LA	S	11.59 MW	11.27 AW	24100 AAW	LABLS	10//99-12//99
	Lafayette MSA, LA	S	10.54 MW	10.48 AW	21930 AAW	LABLS	10//99-12//99
	Lake Charles MSA, LA	S	11.18 MW	9.90 AW	23250 AAW	LABLS	10//99-12//99
	Monroe MSA, LA	S	10.82 MW	10.68 AW	22510 AAW	LABLS	10//99-12//99
	New Orleans MSA, LA	S	12.07 MW	11.05 AW	25100 AAW	LABLS	10//99-12//99
	Shreveport-Bossier City MSA, LA	S	11.07 MW	10.50 AW	23030 AAW	LABLS	10//99-12//99
	Maine	S	11.65 MW	11.67 AW	24280 AAW	MEBLS	10//99-12//99
	Bangor MSA, ME	S	11.17 MW	11.18 AW	23230 AAW	MEBLS	10//99-12//99
	Lewiston-Auburn MSA, ME	S	10.56 MW	10.74 AW	21960 AAW	MEBLS	10//99-12//99
	Portland MSA, ME	S	11.96 MW	11.93 AW	24870 AAW	MEBLS	10//99-12//99
	Maryland	S	12.69 MW	12.92 AW	26880 AAW	MDBLS	10//99-12//99
	Baltimore PMSA, MD	S	12.88 MW	12.41 AW	26790 AAW	MDBLS	10//99-12//99
	Cumberland MSA, MD-WV	S	10.63 MW	9.63 AW	22120 AAW	MDBLS	10//99-12//99
	Hagerstown PMSA, MD	S	12.40 MW	11.34 AW	25790 AAW	MDBLS	10//99-12//99
	Massachusetts	S	13.75 MW	14.14 AW	29410 AAW	MABLS	10//99-12//99

AAW Average annual wage	AOH Average offered, high	ASH Average starting, high	H Hourly	M Monthly	S Special: hourly and annual
AE Average entry wage	AOL Average offered, low	ASL Average starting, low	HI Highest wage paid	MTC Median total compensation	TQ Third quartile wage
AEX Average experienced wage	APH Average pay, high range	AW Average wage paid	HR High end range	MW Median wage paid	W Weekly
AO Average offered	APL Average pay, low range	FQ First quartile wage	LR Low end range	SQ Second quartile wage	Y Yearly

Occupation/Type/Industry	Location	Per	Low	Mid	High	Source	Date
Payroll and Timekeeping Clerk	Barnstable-Yarmouth MSA, MA	S	13.86 MW	13.85 AW	28820 AAW	MABLS	10//99-12//99
	Boston PMSA, MA-NH	S	14.57 MW	14.23 AW	30310 AAW	MABLS	10//99-12//99
	Brockton PMSA, MA	S	14.14 MW	14.01 AW	29410 AAW	MABLS	10//99-12//99
	Fitchburg-Leominster PMSA, MA	S	12.55 MW	12.55 AW	26110 AAW	MABLS	10//99-12//99
	Lawrence PMSA, MA-NH	S	12.88 MW	12.70 AW	26790 AAW	MABLS	10//99-12//99
	Lowell PMSA, MA-NH	S	14.38 MW	13.82 AW	29910 AAW	MABLS	10//99-12//99
	New Bedford PMSA, MA	S	12.80 MW	12.52 AW	26630 AAW	MABLS	10//99-12//99
	Pittsfield MSA, MA	S	14.87 MW	14.30 AW	30940 AAW	MABLS	10//99-12//99
	Springfield MSA, MA	S	13.16 MW	12.84 AW	27380 AAW	MABLS	10//99-12//99
	Worcester PMSA, MA-CT	S	13.97 MW	13.33 AW	29060 AAW	MABLS	10//99-12//99
	Michigan	S	12.73 MW	13.10 AW	27250 AAW	MIBLS	10//99-12//99
	Ann Arbor PMSA, MI	S	13.49 MW	13.22 AW	28060 AAW	MIBLS	10//99-12//99
	Benton Harbor MSA, MI	S	11.92 MW	11.48 AW	24800 AAW	MIBLS	10//99-12//99
	Detroit PMSA, MI	S	13.77 MW	13.37 AW	28640 AAW	MIBLS	10//99-12//99
	Flint PMSA, MI	S	13.87 MW	13.78 AW	28850 AAW	MIBLS	10//99-12//99
	Grand Rapids-Muskegon-Holland MSA, MI	S	12.41 MW	12.21 AW	25820 AAW	MIBLS	10//99-12//99
	Jackson MSA, MI	S	13.35 MW	12.34 AW	27760 AAW	MIBLS	10//99-12//99
	Kalamazoo-Battle Creek MSA, MI	S	12.96 MW	12.43 AW	26950 AAW	MIBLS	10//99-12//99
	Lansing-East Lansing MSA, MI	S	13.75 MW	12.97 AW	28590 AAW	MIBLS	10//99-12//99
	Saginaw-Bay City-Midland MSA, MI	S	11.95 MW	11.74 AW	24860 AAW	MIBLS	10//99-12//99
	Minnesota	S	13.35 MW	13.59 AW	28270 AAW	MNBLS	10//99-12//99
	Duluth-Superior MSA, MN-WI	S	12.55 MW	12.70 AW	26100 AAW	MNBLS	10//99-12//99
	Minneapolis-St. Paul MSA, MN-WI	S	14.38 MW	14.07 AW	29900 AAW	MNBLS	10//99-12//99
	Rochester MSA, MN	S	12.46 MW	12.02 AW	25910 AAW	MNBLS	10//99-12//99
	St. Cloud MSA, MN	S	11.24 MW	10.83 AW	23370 AAW	MNBLS	10//99-12//99
	Mississippi	S	10.53 MW	10.77 AW	22400 AAW	MSBLS	10//99-12//99
	Biloxi-Gulfport-Pascagoula MSA, MS	S	11.54 MW	11.37 AW	24010 AAW	MSBLS	10//99-12//99
	Hattiesburg MSA, MS	S	9.68 MW	9.43 AW	20140 AAW	MSBLS	10//99-12//99
	Jackson MSA, MS	S	11.50 MW	11.17 AW	23910 AAW	MSBLS	10//99-12//99
	Missouri	S	11.18 MW	11.82 AW	24590 AAW	MOBLS	10//99-12//99
	Columbia MSA, MO	S	11.49 MW	10.95 AW	23900 AAW	MOBLS	10//99-12//99
	Joplin MSA, MO	S	10.63 MW	9.99 AW	22110 AAW	MOBLS	10//99-12//99
	Kansas City MSA, MO-KS	S	12.90 MW	12.57 AW	26830 AAW	MOBLS	10//99-12//99
	St. Louis MSA, MO-IL	S	12.34 MW	11.80 AW	25670 AAW	MOBLS	10//99-12//99
	Springfield MSA, MO	S	10.53 MW	9.83 AW	21900 AAW	MOBLS	10//99-12//99
	Montana	S	10.4 MW	10.76 AW	22370 AAW	MTBLS	10//99-12//99
	Billings MSA, MT	S	10.84 MW	10.26 AW	22540 AAW	MTBLS	10//99-12//99
	Missoula MSA, MT	S	11.00 MW	11.13 AW	22880 AAW	MTBLS	10//99-12//99
	Nebraska	S	10.92 MW	11.36 AW	23620 AAW	NEBLS	10//99-12//99
	Lincoln MSA, NE	S	11.56 MW	11.15 AW	24050 AAW	NEBLS	10//99-12//99
	Omaha MSA, NE-IA	S	12.56 MW	11.85 AW	26120 AAW	NEBLS	10//99-12//99
	Nevada	S	11.61 MW	12.07 AW	25100 AAW	NVBLS	10//99-12//99
	Las Vegas MSA, NV-AZ	S	11.84 MW	11.34 AW	24620 AAW	NVBLS	10//99-12//99
	Reno MSA, NV	S	12.63 MW	12.21 AW	26280 AAW	NVBLS	10//99-12//99
	New Hampshire	S	12.39 MW	12.68 AW	26380 AAW	NHBLS	10//99-12//99
	Manchester PMSA, NH	S	12.30 MW	11.74 AW	25580 AAW	NHBLS	10//99-12//99
	Nashua PMSA, NH	S	13.57 MW	13.14 AW	28220 AAW	NHBLS	10//99-12//99
	Portsmouth-Rochester PMSA, NH-ME	S	12.52 MW	12.54 AW	26040 AAW	NHBLS	10//99-12//99
	New Jersey	S	14.11 MW	14.48 AW	30110 AAW	NJBLS	10//99-12//99
	Atlantic-Cape May PMSA, NJ	S	12.00 MW	11.60 AW	24960 AAW	NJBLS	10//99-12//99
	Bergen-Passaic PMSA, NJ	S	14.93 MW	14.07 AW	31050 AAW	NJBLS	10//99-12//99
	Jersey City PMSA, NJ	S	14.56 MW	13.73 AW	30290 AAW	NJBLS	10//99-12//99
	Middlesex-Somerset-Hunterdon PMSA, NJ	S	15.47 MW	15.54 AW	32180 AAW	NJBLS	10//99-12//99
	Monmouth-Ocean PMSA, NJ	S	13.71 MW	13.33 AW	28510 AAW	NJBLS	10//99-12//99
	Newark PMSA, NJ	S	15.26 MW	15.19 AW	31740 AAW	NJBLS	10//99-12//99
	Trenton PMSA, NJ	S	13.87 MW	13.67 AW	28850 AAW	NJBLS	10//99-12//99
	Vineland-Millville-Bridgeton PMSA, NJ	S	12.29 MW	11.87 AW	25570 AAW	NJBLS	10//99-12//99
	New Mexico	S	11.08 MW	11.45 AW	23810 AAW	NMBLS	10//99-12//99
	Albuquerque MSA, NM	S	12.23 MW	11.86 AW	25440 AAW	NMBLS	10//99-12//99
	Las Cruces MSA, NM	S	9.79 MW	9.69 AW	20360 AAW	NMBLS	10//99-12//99
	Santa Fe MSA, NM	S	12.51 MW	11.96 AW	26010 AAW	NMBLS	10//99-12//99
	New York	S	13.83 MW	14.34 AW	29820 AAW	NYBLS	10//99-12//99

AAW Average annual wage	**AOH** Average offered, high	**ASH** Average starting, high	**H** Hourly	**M** Monthly	**S** Special: hourly and annual
AE Average entry wage	**AOL** Average offered, low	**ASL** Average starting, low	**HI** Highest wage paid	**MTC** Median total compensation	**TQ** Third quartile wage
AEX Average experienced wage	**APH** Average pay, high range	**AW** Average wage paid	**HR** High end range	**MW** Median wage paid	**W** Weekly
AO Average offered	**APL** Average pay, low range	**FQ** First quartile wage	**LR** Low end range	**SQ** Second quartile wage	**Y** Yearly

Occupation/Type/Industry	Location	Per	Low	Mid	High	Source	Date
Payroll and Timekeeping Clerk	Albany-Schenectady-Troy MSA, NY	S	13.59 MW	13.37 AW	28280 AAW	NYBLS	10//99-12//99
	Binghamton MSA, NY	S	11.61 MW	11.18 AW	24160 AAW	NYBLS	10//99-12//99
	Buffalo-Niagara Falls MSA, NY	S	11.99 MW	11.76 AW	24940 AAW	NYBLS	10//99-12//99
	Dutchess County PMSA, NY	S	13.72 MW	13.45 AW	28540 AAW	NYBLS	10//99-12//99
	Elmira MSA, NY	S	12.32 MW	12.40 AW	25620 AAW	NYBLS	10//99-12//99
	Glens Falls MSA, NY	S	13.61 MW	12.99 AW	28320 AAW	NYBLS	10//99-12//99
	Jamestown MSA, NY	S	11.19 MW	10.72 AW	23270 AAW	NYBLS	10//99-12//99
	Nassau-Suffolk PMSA, NY	S	14.86 MW	14.52 AW	30910 AAW	NYBLS	10//99-12//99
	New York PMSA, NY	S	15.87 MW	15.53 AW	33000 AAW	NYBLS	10//99-12//99
	Newburgh PMSA, NY-PA	S	13.67 MW	13.37 AW	28430 AAW	NYBLS	10//99-12//99
	Rochester MSA, NY	S	13.29 MW	12.61 AW	27630 AAW	NYBLS	10//99-12//99
	Syracuse MSA, NY	S	12.57 MW	12.32 AW	26140 AAW	NYBLS	10//99-12//99
	Utica-Rome MSA, NY	S	12.65 MW	12.56 AW	26300 AAW	NYBLS	10//99-12//99
	North Carolina	S	11.47 MW	11.83 AW	24610 AAW	NCBLS	10//99-12//99
	Asheville MSA, NC	S	11.28 MW	11.46 AW	23460 AAW	NCBLS	10//99-12//99
	Charlotte-Gastonia-Rock Hill MSA, NC-SC	S	12.08 MW	11.83 AW	25130 AAW	NCBLS	10//99-12//99
	Fayetteville MSA, NC	S	10.94 MW	9.94 AW	22760 AAW	NCBLS	10//99-12//99
	Goldsboro MSA, NC	S	11.45 MW	11.34 AW	23810 AAW	NCBLS	10//99-12//99
	Greensboro--Winston-Salem--High Point MSA, NC	S	12.39 MW	11.72 AW	25760 AAW	NCBLS	10//99-12//99
	Greenville MSA, NC	S	11.50 MW	11.51 AW	23920 AAW	NCBLS	10//99-12//99
	Hickory-Morganton-Lenoir MSA, NC	S	11.45 MW	10.80 AW	23810 AAW	NCBLS	10//99-12//99
	Raleigh-Durham-Chapel Hill MSA, NC	S	12.84 MW	12.59 AW	26710 AAW	NCBLS	10//99-12//99
	Rocky Mount MSA, NC	S	11.44 MW	11.44 AW	23790 AAW	NCBLS	10//99-12//99
	Wilmington MSA, NC	S	10.36 MW	9.71 AW	21540 AAW	NCBLS	10//99-12//99
	North Dakota	S	10.84 MW	11.37 AW	23640 AAW	NDBLS	10//99-12//99
	Bismarck MSA, ND	S	13.08 MW	11.43 AW	27210 AAW	NDBLS	10//99-12//99
	Fargo-Moorhead MSA, ND-MN	S	11.81 MW	11.72 AW	24570 AAW	NDBLS	10//99-12//99
	Grand Forks MSA, ND-MN	S	11.09 MW	10.91 AW	23070 AAW	NDBLS	10//99-12//99
	Ohio	S	12.75 MW	13.14 AW	27340 AAW	OHBLS	10//99-12//99
	Akron PMSA, OH	S	12.67 MW	12.73 AW	26350 AAW	OHBLS	10//99-12//99
	Canton-Massillon MSA, OH	S	11.49 MW	11.36 AW	23900 AAW	OHBLS	10//99-12//99
	Cincinnati PMSA, OH-KY-IN	S	14.65 MW	14.49 AW	30480 AAW	OHBLS	10//99-12//99
	Cleveland-Lorain-Elyria PMSA, OH	S	13.48 MW	13.24 AW	28030 AAW	OHBLS	10//99-12//99
	Columbus MSA, OH	S	13.77 MW	13.09 AW	28640 AAW	OHBLS	10//99-12//99
	Dayton-Springfield MSA, OH	S	12.14 MW	11.75 AW	25240 AAW	OHBLS	10//99-12//99
	Hamilton-Middletown PMSA, OH	S	11.31 MW	11.96 AW	23530 AAW	OHBLS	10//99-12//99
	Lima MSA, OH	S	10.84 MW	10.87 AW	22540 AAW	OHBLS	10//99-12//99
	Mansfield MSA, OH	S	12.27 MW	12.26 AW	25510 AAW	OHBLS	10//99-12//99
	Steubenville-Weirton MSA, OH-WV	S	12.11 MW	11.70 AW	25180 AAW	OHBLS	10//99-12//99
	Toledo MSA, OH	S	12.86 MW	12.51 AW	26760 AAW	OHBLS	10//99-12//99
	Youngstown-Warren MSA, OH	S	12.34 MW	11.96 AW	25660 AAW	OHBLS	10//99-12//99
	Oklahoma	S	11 MW	11.52 AW	23970 AAW	OKBLS	10//99-12//99
	Enid MSA, OK	S	8.55 MW	8.27 AW	17790 AAW	OKBLS	10//99-12//99
	Lawton MSA, OK	S	10.37 MW	10.72 AW	21580 AAW	OKBLS	10//99-12//99
	Oklahoma City MSA, OK	S	11.71 MW	11.49 AW	24360 AAW	OKBLS	10//99-12//99
	Tulsa MSA, OK	S	12.99 MW	12.11 AW	27020 AAW	OKBLS	10//99-12//99
	Oregon	S	13.17 MW	13.47 AW	28010 AAW	ORBLS	10//99-12//99
	Corvallis MSA, OR	S	13.52 MW	13.95 AW	28120 AAW	ORBLS	10//99-12//99
	Eugene-Springfield MSA, OR	S	13.17 MW	12.60 AW	27390 AAW	ORBLS	10//99-12//99
	Medford-Ashland MSA, OR	S	12.70 MW	12.57 AW	26410 AAW	ORBLS	10//99-12//99
	Portland-Vancouver PMSA, OR-WA	S	14.02 MW	13.65 AW	29170 AAW	ORBLS	10//99-12//99
	Salem PMSA, OR	S	12.58 MW	12.36 AW	26160 AAW	ORBLS	10//99-12//99
	Pennsylvania	S	11.76 MW	12.10 AW	25160 AAW	PABLS	10//99-12//99
	Allentown-Bethlehem-Easton MSA, PA	S	11.79 MW	11.45 AW	24520 AAW	PABLS	10//99-12//99
	Altoona MSA, PA	S	10.69 MW	10.26 AW	22230 AAW	PABLS	10//99-12//99
	Erie MSA, PA	S	11.60 MW	11.59 AW	24120 AAW	PABLS	10//99-12//99
	Harrisburg-Lebanon-Carlisle MSA, PA	S	12.18 MW	11.75 AW	25330 AAW	PABLS	10//99-12//99
	Johnstown MSA, PA	S	10.55 MW	10.34 AW	21950 AAW	PABLS	10//99-12//99
	Lancaster MSA, PA	S	12.18 MW	11.58 AW	25340 AAW	PABLS	10//99-12//99

AAW Average annual wage	**AOH** Average offered, high	**ASH** Average starting, high	**H** Hourly	**M** Monthly	**S** Special: hourly and annual
AE Average entry wage	**AOL** Average offered, low	**ASL** Average starting, low	**HI** Highest wage paid	**MTC** Median total compensation	**TQ** Third quartile wage
AEX Average experienced wage	**APH** Average pay, high range	**AW** Average wage paid	**HR** High end range	**MW** Median wage paid	**W** Weekly
AO Average offered	**APL** Average pay, low range	**FQ** First quartile wage	**LR** Low end range	**SQ** Second quartile wage	**Y** Yearly

Occupation/Type/Industry	Location	Per	Low	Mid	High	Source	Date
Payroll and Timekeeping Clerk	Philadelphia PMSA, PA-NJ	S	13.35 MW	12.98 AW	27760 AAW	PABLS	10//99-12//99
	Pittsburgh MSA, PA	S	12.20 MW	11.84 AW	25370 AAW	PABLS	10//99-12//99
	Reading MSA, PA	S	11.62 MW	11.19 AW	24170 AAW	PABLS	10//99-12//99
	Scranton--Wilkes-Barre-- Hazleton MSA, PA	S	11.61 MW	11.43 AW	24140 AAW	PABLS	10//99-12//99
	Sharon MSA, PA	S	12.08 MW	11.61 AW	25120 AAW	PABLS	10//99-12//99
	State College MSA, PA	S	12.08 MW	11.54 AW	25120 AAW	PABLS	10//99-12//99
	Williamsport MSA, PA	S	11.41 MW	11.27 AW	23740 AAW	PABLS	10//99-12//99
	York MSA, PA	S	10.17 MW	10.25 AW	21140 AAW	PABLS	10//99-12//99
	Rhode Island	S	12.82 MW	12.98 AW	26990 AAW	RIBLS	10//99-12//99
	Providence-Fall River- Warwick MSA, RI-MA	S	12.73 MW	12.46 AW	26480 AAW	RIBLS	10//99-12//99
	South Carolina	S	11.32 MW	11.58 AW	24090 AAW	SCBLS	10//99-12//99
	Charleston-North Charleston MSA, SC	S	12.82 MW	12.49 AW	26670 AAW	SCBLS	10//99-12//99
	Columbia MSA, SC	S	11.94 MW	11.35 AW	24840 AAW	SCBLS	10//99-12//99
	Florence MSA, SC	S	10.12 MW	9.78 AW	21040 AAW	SCBLS	10//99-12//99
	Greenville-Spartanburg- Anderson MSA, SC	S	11.94 MW	11.61 AW	24840 AAW	SCBLS	10//99-12//99
	Myrtle Beach MSA, SC	S	10.72 MW	10.73 AW	22310 AAW	SCBLS	10//99-12//99
	Sumter MSA, SC	S	10.22 MW	10.39 AW	21270 AAW	SCBLS	10//99-12//99
	South Dakota	S	9.95 MW	10.05 AW	20910 AAW	SDBLS	10//99-12//99
	Rapid City MSA, SD	S	10.45 MW	10.40 AW	21740 AAW	SDBLS	10//99-12//99
	Sioux Falls MSA, SD	S	10.48 MW	10.31 AW	21790 AAW	SDBLS	10//99-12//99
	Tennessee	S	11.67 MW	12.12 AW	25210 AAW	TNBLS	10//99-12//99
	Chattanooga MSA, TN-GA	S	11.79 MW	11.44 AW	24520 AAW	TNBLS	10//99-12//99
	Clarksville-Hopkinsville MSA, TN-KY	S	11.69 MW	11.45 AW	24320 AAW	TNBLS	10//99-12//99
	Jackson MSA, TN	S	10.89 MW	10.87 AW	22660 AAW	TNBLS	10//99-12//99
	Johnson City-Kingsport-Bristol MSA, TN-VA	S	11.44 MW	11.19 AW	23790 AAW	TNBLS	10//99-12//99
	Knoxville MSA, TN	S	11.58 MW	11.39 AW	24090 AAW	TNBLS	10//99-12//99
	Memphis MSA, TN-AR-MS	S	12.51 MW	11.89 AW	26010 AAW	MSBLS	10//99-12//99
	Nashville MSA, TN	S	12.96 MW	12.14 AW	26950 AAW	TNBLS	10//99-12//99
	Texas	S	11.63 MW	12.03 AW	25020 AAW	TXBLS	10//99-12//99
	Abilene MSA, TX	S	10.31 MW	9.13 AW	21440 AAW	TXBLS	10//99-12//99
	Amarillo MSA, TX	S	11.42 MW	10.94 AW	23760 AAW	TXBLS	10//99-12//99
	Austin-San Marcos MSA, TX	S	12.45 MW	12.28 AW	25890 AAW	TXBLS	10//99-12//99
	Beaumont-Port Arthur MSA, TX	S	13.21 MW	10.78 AW	27480 AAW	TXBLS	10//99-12//99
	Brazoria PMSA, TX	S	11.83 MW	12.17 AW	24610 AAW	TXBLS	10//99-12//99
	Brownsville-Harlingen-San Benito MSA, TX	S	8.45 MW	8.10 AW	17580 AAW	TXBLS	10//99-12//99
	Bryan-College Station MSA, TX	S	11.97 MW	11.27 AW	24890 AAW	TXBLS	10//99-12//99
	Corpus Christi MSA, TX	S	11.40 MW	11.44 AW	23710 AAW	TXBLS	10//99-12//99
	Dallas PMSA, TX	S	13.36 MW	12.79 AW	27800 AAW	TXBLS	10//99-12//99
	El Paso MSA, TX	S	9.96 MW	9.79 AW	20720 AAW	TXBLS	10//99-12//99
	Fort Worth-Arlington PMSA, TX	S	12.17 MW	11.68 AW	25310 AAW	TXBLS	10//99-12//99
	Galveston-Texas City PMSA, TX	S	11.08 MW	10.68 AW	23050 AAW	TXBLS	10//99-12//99
	Houston PMSA, TX	S	13.20 MW	12.75 AW	27460 AAW	TXBLS	10//99-12//99
	Killeen-Temple MSA, TX	S	11.16 MW	10.52 AW	23210 AAW	TXBLS	10//99-12//99
	Laredo MSA, TX	S	9.99 MW	9.64 AW	20780 AAW	TXBLS	10//99-12//99
	Longview-Marshall MSA, TX	S	11.17 MW	11.25 AW	23240 AAW	TXBLS	10//99-12//99
	Lubbock MSA, TX	S	10.30 MW	9.94 AW	21430 AAW	TXBLS	10//99-12//99
	McAllen-Edinburg-Mission MSA, TX	S	10.02 MW	9.96 AW	20840 AAW	TXBLS	10//99-12//99
	Odessa-Midland MSA, TX	S	11.32 MW	10.69 AW	23540 AAW	TXBLS	10//99-12//99
	San Angelo MSA, TX	S	11.66 MW	10.38 AW	24250 AAW	TXBLS	10//99-12//99
	San Antonio MSA, TX	S	10.37 MW	10.15 AW	21560 AAW	TXBLS	10//99-12//99
	Sherman-Denison MSA, TX	S	10.79 MW	10.41 AW	22430 AAW	TXBLS	10//99-12//99
	Texarkana MSA, TX- Texarkana, AR	S	10.74 MW	10.54 AW	22350 AAW	TXBLS	10//99-12//99
	Tyler MSA, TX	S	10.92 MW	10.20 AW	22720 AAW	TXBLS	10//99-12//99
	Victoria MSA, TX	S	11.22 MW	10.76 AW	23340 AAW	TXBLS	10//99-12//99
	Waco MSA, TX	S	11.46 MW	11.00 AW	23830 AAW	TXBLS	10//99-12//99
	Wichita Falls MSA, TX	S	11.81 MW	11.56 AW	24570 AAW	TXBLS	10//99-12//99
	Utah	S	11.06 MW	11.70 AW	24340 AAW	UTBLS	10//99-12//99
	Provo-Orem MSA, UT	S	10.96 MW	10.07 AW	22800 AAW	UTBLS	10//99-12//99

AAW	Average annual wage	AOH	Average offered, high	ASH	Average starting, high	H	Hourly	M	Monthly	S	Special: hourly and annual
AE	Average entry wage	AOL	Average offered, low	ASL	Average starting, low	HI	Highest wage paid	MTC	Median total compensation	TQ	Third quartile wage
AEX	Average experienced wage	APH	Average pay, high range	AW	Average wage paid	HR	High end range	MW	Median wage paid	W	Weekly
AO	Average offered	APL	Average pay, low range	FQ	First quartile wage	LR	Low end range	SQ	Second quartile wage	Y	Yearly

Occupation/Type/Industry	Location	Per	Low	Mid	High	Source	Date
Payroll and Timekeeping Clerk	Salt Lake City-Ogden MSA, UT	S	11.87 MW	11.17 AW	24690 AAW	UTBLS	10//99-12//99
	Vermont	S	11.91 MW	12.12 AW	25210 AAW	VTBLS	10//99-12//99
	Burlington MSA, VT	S	12.73 MW	12.62 AW	26470 AAW	VTBLS	10//99-12//99
	Virginia	S	12.05 MW	12.55 AW	26110 AAW	VABLS	10//99-12//99
	Charlottesville MSA, VA	S	12.88 MW	12.03 AW	26780 AAW	VABLS	10//99-12//99
	Danville MSA, VA	S	10.76 MW	10.46 AW	22380 AAW	VABLS	10//99-12//99
	Lynchburg MSA, VA	S	12.36 MW	11.76 AW	25710 AAW	VABLS	10//99-12//99
	Norfolk-Virginia Beach-Newport News MSA, VA-NC	S	12.16 MW	11.61 AW	25290 AAW	VABLS	10//99-12//99
	Richmond-Petersburg MSA, VA	S	12.47 MW	12.27 AW	25930 AAW	VABLS	10//99-12//99
	Roanoke MSA, VA	S	12.11 MW	11.15 AW	25180 AAW	VABLS	10//99-12//99
	Washington	S	13.68 MW	13.88 AW	28870 AAW	WABLS	10//99-12//99
	Bellingham MSA, WA	S	13.06 MW	12.56 AW	27160 AAW	WABLS	10//99-12//99
	Bremerton PMSA, WA	S	11.98 MW	11.98 AW	24910 AAW	WABLS	10//99-12//99
	Olympia PMSA, WA	S	13.30 MW	13.44 AW	27660 AAW	WABLS	10//99-12//99
	Richland-Kennewick-Pasco MSA, WA	S	12.84 MW	12.17 AW	26710 AAW	WABLS	10//99-12//99
	Seattle-Bellevue-Everett PMSA, WA	S	14.41 MW	14.18 AW	29970 AAW	WABLS	10//99-12//99
	Spokane MSA, WA	S	13.32 MW	13.39 AW	27710 AAW	WABLS	10//99-12//99
	Tacoma PMSA, WA	S	13.84 MW	13.52 AW	28790 AAW	WABLS	10//99-12//99
	Yakima MSA, WA	S	13.24 MW	13.32 AW	27540 AAW	WABLS	10//99-12//99
	West Virginia	S	10.66 MW	11.34 AW	23580 AAW	WVBLS	10//99-12//99
	Charleston MSA, WV	S	12.73 MW	11.47 AW	26470 AAW	WVBLS	10//99-12//99
	Huntington-Ashland MSA, WV-KY-OH	S	11.04 MW	10.96 AW	22960 AAW	WVBLS	10//99-12//99
	Parkersburg-Marietta MSA, WV-OH	S	10.31 MW	9.87 AW	21440 AAW	WVBLS	10//99-12//99
	Wheeling MSA, WV-OH	S	11.74 MW	10.66 AW	24410 AAW	WVBLS	10//99-12//99
	Wisconsin	S	11.8 MW	12.16 AW	25300 AAW	WIBLS	10//99-12//99
	Appleton-Oshkosh-Neenah MSA, WI	S	11.63 MW	11.22 AW	24180 AAW	WIBLS	10//99-12//99
	Eau Claire MSA, WI	S	11.26 MW	11.04 AW	23410 AAW	WIBLS	10//99-12//99
	Green Bay MSA, WI	S	12.60 MW	12.26 AW	26210 AAW	WIBLS	10//99-12//99
	Janesville-Beloit MSA, WI	S	12.24 MW	12.16 AW	25450 AAW	WIBLS	10//99-12//99
	Kenosha PMSA, WI	S	13.39 MW	12.75 AW	27850 AAW	WIBLS	10//99-12//99
	La Crosse MSA, WI-MN	S	11.03 MW	10.84 AW	22950 AAW	WIBLS	10//99-12//99
	Madison MSA, WI	S	12.71 MW	12.12 AW	26430 AAW	WIBLS	10//99-12//99
	Milwaukee-Waukesha PMSA, WI	S	12.69 MW	12.34 AW	26400 AAW	WIBLS	10//99-12//99
	Racine PMSA, WI	S	12.60 MW	12.57 AW	26210 AAW	WIBLS	10//99-12//99
	Sheboygan MSA, WI	S	12.36 MW	11.51 AW	25700 AAW	WIBLS	10//99-12//99
	Wausau MSA, WI	S	11.20 MW	11.10 AW	23290 AAW	WIBLS	10//99-12//99
	Wyoming	S	11.22 MW	11.66 AW	24260 AAW	WYBLS	10//99-12//99
	Casper MSA, WY	S	10.72 MW	11.04 AW	22290 AAW	WYBLS	10//99-12//99
	Cheyenne MSA, WY	S	12.36 MW	11.99 AW	25700 AAW	WYBLS	10//99-12//99
	Puerto Rico	S	7.87 MW	8.60 AW	17880 AAW	PRBLS	10//99-12//99
	Aguadilla MSA, PR	S	7.32 MW	6.55 AW	15220 AAW	PRBLS	10//99-12//99
	Caguas PMSA, PR	S	8.53 MW	7.72 AW	17740 AAW	PRBLS	10//99-12//99
	Mayaguez MSA, PR	S	7.75 MW	6.68 AW	16110 AAW	PRBLS	10//99-12//99
	Ponce MSA, PR	S	8.45 MW	8.16 AW	17570 AAW	PRBLS	10//99-12//99
	San Juan-Bayamon PMSA, PR	S	8.80 MW	8.03 AW	18300 AAW	PRBLS	10//99-12//99
	Virgin Islands	S	9.18 MW	10.23 AW	21290 AAW	VIBLS	10//99-12//99
	Guam	S	11.57 MW	11.49 AW	23910 AAW	GUBLS	10//99-12//99
Pediatrician							
General	Alabama	S		61.65 AW	128240 AAW	ALBLS	10//99-12//99
General	Arizona	S	61.8 MW	58.52 AW	121720 AAW	AZBLS	10//99-12//99
General	California	S	45.41 MW	40.65 AW	84550 AAW	CABLS	10//99-12//99
General	Sacramento PMSA, CA	S	48.29 MW	49.63 AW	100450 AAW	CABLS	10//99-12//99
General	Connecticut	S	47.18 MW	46.20 AW	96100 AAW	CTBLS	10//99-12//99
General	Bridgeport PMSA, CT	S	47.95 MW	48.72 AW	99740 AAW	CTBLS	10//99-12//99
General	Stamford-Norwalk PMSA, CT	S	37.57 MW	33.76 AW	78140 AAW	CTBLS	10//99-12//99
General	Florida	S	63.03 MW	58.96 AW	122640 AAW	FLBLS	10//99-12//99
General	Lakeland-Winter Haven MSA, FL	S	59.58 MW	63.08 AW	123920 AAW	FLBLS	10//99-12//99
General	Tampa-St. Petersburg-Clearwater MSA, FL	S	56.55 MW	54.51 AW	117630 AAW	FLBLS	10//99-12//99
General	Georgia	S	52.21 MW	50.47 AW	104980 AAW	GABLS	10//99-12//99
General	Illinois	S	40.03 MW	41.85 AW	87040 AAW	ILBLS	10//99-12//99

AAW	Average annual wage	AOH	Average offered, high	ASH	Average starting, high	H	Hourly	M	Monthly	S	Special: hourly and annual
AE	Average entry wage	AOL	Average offered, low	ASL	Average starting, low	HI	Highest wage paid	MTC	Median total compensation	TQ	Third quartile wage
AEX	Average experienced wage	APH	Average pay, high range	AW	Average wage paid	HR	High end range	MW	Median wage paid	W	Weekly
AO	Average offered	APL	Average pay, low range	FQ	First quartile wage	LR	Low end range	SQ	Second quartile wage	Y	Yearly

Occupation/Type/Industry	Location	Per	Low	Mid	High	Source	Date
Pediatrician							
General	Chicago PMSA, IL	S	44.74 MW	48.49 AW	93050 AAW	ILBLS	10//99-12//99
General	Kentucky	S		64.74 AW	134670 AAW	KYBLS	10//99-12//99
General	Maine	S	54.39 MW	51.75 AW	107650 AAW	MEBLS	10//99-12//99
General	Bangor MSA, ME	S	49.55 MW	48.65 AW	103060 AAW	MEBLS	10//99-12//99
General	Maryland	S	45.75 MW	44.77 AW	93130 AAW	MDBLS	10//99-12//99
General	Baltimore PMSA, MD	S	44.65 MW	45.60 AW	92860 AAW	MDBLS	10//99-12//99
General	Massachusetts	S	49.95 MW	48.71 AW	101310 AAW	MABLS	10//99-12//99
General	Boston PMSA, MA-NH	S	52.90 MW	54.77 AW	110040 AAW	MABLS	10//99-12//99
General	Springfield MSA, MA	S	41.14 MW	41.83 AW	85580 AAW	MABLS	10//99-12//99
General	Michigan	S	51.08 MW	49.98 AW	103960 AAW	MIBLS	10//99-12//99
General	Detroit PMSA, MI	S	50.52 MW	51.24 AW	105080 AAW	MIBLS	10//99-12//99
General	Minnesota	S	54.88 MW	54.54 AW	113440 AAW	MNBLS	10//99-12//99
General	Minneapolis-St. Paul MSA, MN-WI	S	54.41 MW	54.71 AW	113160 AAW	MNBLS	10//99-12//99
General	Missouri	S	58.62 MW	57.53 AW	119660 AAW	MOBLS	10//99-12//99
General	St. Louis MSA, MO-IL	S	60.55 MW	64.82 AW	125940 AAW	MOBLS	10//99-12//99
General	Montana	S	50.16 MW	49.28 AW	102490 AAW	MTBLS	10//99-12//99
General	Nevada	S	65.49 MW	62.77 AW	130570 AAW	NVBLS	10//99-12//99
General	New Hampshire	S	40.72 MW	41.23 AW	85760 AAW	NHBLS	10//99-12//99
General	New Mexico	S	65.36 MW	60.50 AW	125830 AAW	NMBLS	10//99-12//99
General	New York	S	55.07 MW	54.66 AW	113680 AAW	NYBLS	10//99-12//99
General	New York PMSA, NY	S	56.00 MW	57.17 AW	116490 AAW	NYBLS	10//99-12//99
General	North Carolina	S		58.94 AW	122590 AAW	NCBLS	10//99-12//99
General	Charlotte-Gastonia-Rock Hill MSA, NC-SC	S	33.72 MW	25.34 AW	70140 AAW	NCBLS	10//99-12//99
General	Wilmington MSA, NC	S	61.27 MW	63.77 AW	127440 AAW	NCBLS	10//99-12//99
General	Ohio	S	53.91 MW	53.19 AW	110640 AAW	OHBLS	10//99-12//99
General	Cincinnati PMSA, OH-KY-IN	S	57.42 MW	60.91 AW	119420 AAW	OHBLS	10//99-12//99
General	Cleveland-Lorain-Elyria PMSA, OH	S	55.84 MW	59.42 AW	116150 AAW	OHBLS	10//99-12//99
General	Columbus MSA, OH	S	54.92 MW	56.31 AW	114230 AAW	OHBLS	10//99-12//99
General	Dayton-Springfield MSA, OH	S	48.77 MW	49.84 AW	101440 AAW	OHBLS	10//99-12//99
General	Oklahoma	S	62.98 MW	57.58 AW	119770 AAW	OKBLS	10//99-12//99
General	Oklahoma City MSA, OK	S	54.17 MW	60.04 AW	112680 AAW	OKBLS	10//99-12//99
General	Pennsylvania	S	60.4 MW	56.50 AW	117520 AAW	PABLS	10//99-12//99
General	Philadelphia PMSA, PA-NJ	S	55.21 MW	57.92 AW	114840 AAW	PABLS	10//99-12//99
General	Pittsburgh MSA, PA	S	58.13 MW	63.02 AW	120900 AAW	PABLS	10//99-12//99
General	Rhode Island	S		61.84 AW	128640 AAW	RIBLS	10//99-12//99
General	South Carolina	S	61.67 MW	57.37 AW	119330 AAW	SCBLS	10//99-12//99
General	Greenville-Spartanburg-Anderson MSA, SC	S	60.19 MW	64.35 AW	125200 AAW	SCBLS	10//99-12//99
General	Tennessee	S	43.07 MW	50.38 AW	104780 AAW	TNBLS	10//99-12//99
General	Memphis MSA, TN-AR-MS	S	63.23 MW	69.92 AW	131520 AAW	MSBLS	10//99-12//99
General	Texas	S		60.56 AW	125960 AAW	TXBLS	10//99-12//99
General	Brownsville-Harlingen-San Benito MSA, TX	S	52.53 MW	60.82 AW	109260 AAW	TXBLS	10//99-12//99
General	Houston PMSA, TX	S	63.38 MW		131830 AAW	TXBLS	10//99-12//99
General	Utah	S	51.75 MW	51.64 AW	107400 AAW	UTBLS	10//99-12//99
General	Salt Lake City-Ogden MSA, UT	S	49.50 MW	48.80 AW	102950 AAW	UTBLS	10//99-12//99
General	Virginia	S	60.53 MW	58.25 AW	121150 AAW	VABLS	10//99-12//99
General	Washington	S	59.65 MW	56.43 AW	117370 AAW	WABLS	10//99-12//99
General	Seattle-Bellevue-Everett PMSA, WA	S	57.68 MW	61.43 AW	119970 AAW	WABLS	10//99-12//99
General	Wisconsin	S	61.09 MW	57.40 AW	119390 AAW	WIBLS	10//99-12//99
General	Green Bay MSA, WI	S	57.41 MW	59.05 AW	119410 AAW	WIBLS	10//99-12//99
General	Milwaukee-Waukesha PMSA, WI	S	54.27 MW	55.06 AW	112880 AAW	WIBLS	10//99-12//99
General	Wyoming	S	51.58 MW	52.82 AW	109870 AAW	WYBLS	10//99-12//99
General	Puerto Rico	S	26.39 MW	27.08 AW	56320 AAW	PRBLS	10//99-12//99
General	San Juan-Bayamon PMSA, PR	S	33.41 MW	32.61 AW	69480 AAW	PRBLS	10//99-12//99
Personal and Home Care Aide	Alabama	S	6.27 MW	6.40 AW	13310 AAW	ALBLS	10//99-12//99
	Alaska	S	10.31 MW	11.26 AW	23420 AAW	AKBLS	10//99-12//99
	Arizona	S	7.67 MW	7.66 AW	15940 AAW	AZBLS	10//99-12//99
	Arkansas	S	6.29 MW	6.52 AW	13570 AAW	ARBLS	10//99-12//99
	California	S	7.72 MW	8.23 AW	17120 AAW	CABLS	10//99-12//99
	Colorado	S	6.98 MW	7.07 AW	14700 AAW	COBLS	10//99-12//99
	Connecticut	S	9.3 MW	9.88 AW	20540 AAW	CTBLS	10//99-12//99
	Delaware	S	7.04 MW	7.68 AW	15980 AAW	DEBLS	10//99-12//99
	District of Columbia	S	7.65 MW	7.58 AW	15770 AAW	DCBLS	10//99-12//99
	Florida	S	7.72 MW	7.86 AW	16360 AAW	FLBLS	10//99-12//99

AAW	Average annual wage	AOH	Average offered, high	ASH	Average starting, high	H	Hourly	M	Monthly	S	Special: hourly and annual
AE	Average entry wage	AOL	Average offered, low	ASL	Average starting, low	HI	Highest wage paid	MTC	Median total compensation	TQ	Third quartile wage
AEX	Average experienced wage	APH	Average pay, high range	AW	Average wage paid	HR	High end range	MW	Median wage paid	W	Weekly
AO	Average offered	APL	Average pay, low range	FQ	First quartile wage	LR	Low end range	SQ	Second quartile wage	Y	Yearly

Occupation/Type/Industry	Location	Per	Low	Mid	High	Source	Date
Personal and Home Care Aide	Georgia	S	6.95 MW	7.36 AW	15310 AAW	GABLS	10//99-12//99
	Hawaii	S	8.81 MW	7.98 AW	16590 AAW	HIBLS	10//99-12//99
	Idaho	S	6.42 MW	6.48 AW	13480 AAW	IDBLS	10//99-12//99
	Illinois	S	6.78 MW	7.34 AW	15280 AAW	ILBLS	10//99-12//99
	Indiana	S	7.72 MW	7.77 AW	16150 AAW	INBLS	10//99-12//99
	Iowa	S	7.73 MW	7.78 AW	16190 AAW	IABLS	10//99-12//99
	Kansas	S	7.67 MW	7.52 AW	15630 AAW	KSBLS	10//99-12//99
	Kentucky	S	6.3 MW	6.67 AW	13880 AAW	KYBLS	10//99-12//99
	Louisiana	S	6.14 MW	6.39 AW	13290 AAW	LABLS	10//99-12//99
	Maine	S	6.99 MW	7.12 AW	14810 AAW	MEBLS	10//99-12//99
	Maryland	S	7.65 MW	7.72 AW	16050 AAW	MDBLS	10//99-12//99
	Massachusetts	S	9.17 MW	9.25 AW	19240 AAW	MABLS	10//99-12//99
	Michigan	S	7.62 MW	7.64 AW	15890 AAW	MIBLS	10//99-12//99
	Minnesota	S	8.41 MW	8.63 AW	17940 AAW	MNBLS	10//99-12//99
	Mississippi	S	5.95 MW	6.23 AW	12960 AAW	MSBLS	10//99-12//99
	Missouri	S	6.88 MW	6.94 AW	14430 AAW	MOBLS	10//99-12//99
	Montana	S	6.39 MW	6.37 AW	13260 AAW	MTBLS	10//99-12//99
	Nebraska	S	7.46 MW	7.47 AW	15540 AAW	NEBLS	10//99-12//99
	Nevada	S	6.91 MW	7.04 AW	14650 AAW	NVBLS	10//99-12//99
	New Hampshire	S	7.45 MW	7.48 AW	15570 AAW	NHBLS	10//99-12//99
	New Jersey	S	8.39 MW	8.65 AW	17990 AAW	NJBLS	10//99-12//99
	New Mexico	S	6.62 MW	6.92 AW	14380 AAW	NMBLS	10//99-12//99
	New York	S	7.84 MW	8.27 AW	17190 AAW	NYBLS	10//99-12//99
	North Carolina	S	7.11 MW	7.23 AW	15050 AAW	NCBLS	10//99-12//99
	North Dakota	S	7.35 MW	7.20 AW	14970 AAW	NDBLS	10//99-12//99
	Ohio	S	7.69 MW	7.70 AW	16020 AAW	OHBLS	10//99-12//99
	Oklahoma	S	6.8 MW	6.91 AW	14360 AAW	OKBLS	10//99-12//99
	Oregon	S	7.73 MW	7.81 AW	16240 AAW	ORBLS	10//99-12//99
	Pennsylvania	S	7.79 MW	8.07 AW	16790 AAW	PABLS	10//99-12//99
	Rhode Island	S	12.35 MW	11.68 AW	24290 AAW	RIBLS	10//99-12//99
	South Carolina	S	7.77 MW	7.86 AW	16340 AAW	SCBLS	10//99-12//99
	South Dakota	S	7.43 MW	7.40 AW	15390 AAW	SDBLS	10//99-12//99
	Tennessee	S	6.95 MW	7.25 AW	15090 AAW	TNBLS	10//99-12//99
	Texas	S	6.04 MW	6.20 AW	12900 AAW	TXBLS	10//99-12//99
	Vermont	S	6.68 MW	7.22 AW	15020 AAW	VTBLS	10//99-12//99
	Virginia	S	6.35 MW	6.91 AW	14380 AAW	VABLS	10//99-12//99
	Washington	S	7.61 MW	7.75 AW	16110 AAW	WABLS	10//99-12//99
	West Virginia	S	6.29 MW	6.47 AW	13450 AAW	WVBLS	10//99-12//99
	Wisconsin	S	7.57 MW	7.56 AW	15730 AAW	WIBLS	10//99-12//99
Personal Financial Advisor	Alabama	S	17.74 MW	24.36 AW	50670 AAW	ALBLS	10//99-12//99
	Birmingham MSA, AL	S	23.94 MW	16.35 AW	49790 AAW	ALBLS	10//99-12//99
	Mobile MSA, AL	S	19.08 MW	17.56 AW	39690 AAW	ALBLS	10//99-12//99
	Montgomery MSA, AL	S	23.46 MW	18.53 AW	48800 AAW	ALBLS	10//99-12//99
	Arizona	S	31.92 MW	34.32 AW	71390 AAW	AZBLS	10//99-12//99
	Phoenix-Mesa MSA, AZ	S	33.79 MW	34.55 AW	70290 AAW	AZBLS	10//99-12//99
	Tucson MSA, AZ	S	41.47 MW	37.37 AW	86260 AAW	AZBLS	10//99-12//99
	Arkansas	S	16.38 MW	22.73 AW	47280 AAW	ARBLS	10//99-12//99
	Little Rock-North Little Rock MSA, AR	S	25.52 MW	19.72 AW	53080 AAW	ARBLS	10//99-12//99
	California	S	31 MW	37.99 AW	79020 AAW	CABLS	10//99-12//99
	Los Angeles-Long Beach PMSA, CA	S	50.95 MW	57.72 AW	105970 AAW	CABLS	10//99-12//99
	Oakland PMSA, CA	S	21.70 MW	17.92 AW	45130 AAW	CABLS	10//99-12//99
	Orange County PMSA, CA	S	42.02 MW	32.52 AW	87410 AAW	CABLS	10//99-12//99
	Sacramento PMSA, CA	S	24.02 MW	20.51 AW	49950 AAW	CABLS	10//99-12//99
	San Diego MSA, CA	S	36.76 MW	30.86 AW	76460 AAW	CABLS	10//99-12//99
	San Francisco PMSA, CA	S	39.35 MW	37.03 AW	81850 AAW	CABLS	10//99-12//99
	Santa Rosa PMSA, CA	S	38.56 MW	19.25 AW	80200 AAW	CABLS	10//99-12//99
	Colorado	S	27.69 MW	31.96 AW	66470 AAW	COBLS	10//99-12//99
	Denver PMSA, CO	S	28.79 MW	26.02 AW	59890 AAW	COBLS	10//99-12//99
	Connecticut	S	27.79 MW	32.37 AW	67340 AAW	CTBLS	10//99-12//99
	Hartford MSA, CT	S	32.11 MW	25.59 AW	66790 AAW	CTBLS	10//99-12//99
	New Haven-Meriden PMSA, CT	S	36.44 MW	31.44 AW	75800 AAW	CTBLS	10//99-12//99
	New London-Norwich MSA, CT-RI	S	30.64 MW	25.76 AW	63730 AAW	CTBLS	10//99-12//99
	Stamford-Norwalk PMSA, CT	S	31.23 MW	30.91 AW	64970 AAW	CTBLS	10//99-12//99
	Florida	S	18.39 MW	21.29 AW	44270 AAW	FLBLS	10//99-12//99
	Daytona Beach MSA, FL	S	14.99 MW	12.06 AW	31180 AAW	FLBLS	10//99-12//99
	Fort Myers-Cape Coral MSA, FL	S	20.90 MW	19.32 AW	43460 AAW	FLBLS	10//99-12//99

AAW	Average annual wage	AOH	Average offered, high	ASH	Average starting, high	H	Hourly	M	Monthly	S	Special: hourly and annual
AE	Average entry wage	AOL	Average offered, low	ASL	Average starting, low	HI	Highest wage paid	MTC	Median total compensation	TQ	Third quartile wage
AEX	Average experienced wage	APH	Average pay, high range	AW	Average wage paid	HR	High end range	MW	Median wage paid	W	Weekly
AO	Average offered	APL	Average pay, low range	FQ	First quartile wage	LR	Low end range	SQ	Second quartile wage	Y	Yearly

Occupation/Type/Industry	Location	Per	Low	Mid	High	Source	Date
Personal Financial Advisor	Lakeland-Winter Haven MSA, FL	S	17.12 MW	14.73 AW	35610 AAW	FLBLS	10//99-12//99
	Miami PMSA, FL	S	28.63 MW	24.58 AW	59540 AAW	FLBLS	10//99-12//99
	Orlando MSA, FL	S	26.44 MW	26.23 AW	55000 AAW	FLBLS	10//99-12//99
	West Palm Beach-Boca Raton MSA, FL	S	25.11 MW	23.67 AW	52230 AAW	FLBLS	10//99-12//99
	Georgia	S	25.1 MW	27.52 AW	57250 AAW	GABLS	10//99-12//99
	Atlanta MSA, GA	S	27.43 MW	24.95 AW	57050 AAW	GABLS	10//99-12//99
	Hawaii	S	18.68 MW	19.31 AW	40150 AAW	HIBLS	10//99-12//99
	Illinois	S	24.53 MW	29.33 AW	61010 AAW	ILBLS	10//99-12//99
	Chicago PMSA, IL	S	29.92 MW	24.74 AW	62240 AAW	ILBLS	10//99-12//99
	Rockford MSA, IL	S	24.16 MW	23.54 AW	50250 AAW	ILBLS	10//99-12//99
	Indiana	S	27.05 MW	32.16 AW	66900 AAW	INBLS	10//99-12//99
	Bloomington MSA, IN	S	46.63 MW	45.97 AW	96990 AAW	INBLS	10//99-12//99
	Evansville-Henderson MSA, IN-KY	S	21.28 MW	18.71 AW	44260 AAW	INBLS	10//99-12//99
	Fort Wayne MSA, IN	S	24.36 MW	22.40 AW	50670 AAW	INBLS	10//99-12//99
	Gary PMSA, IN	S	28.04 MW	29.80 AW	58330 AAW	INBLS	10//99-12//99
	Indianapolis MSA, IN	S	38.81 MW	37.92 AW	80730 AAW	INBLS	10//99-12//99
	Lafayette MSA, IN	S	34.81 MW	42.78 AW	72400 AAW	INBLS	10//99-12//99
	Terre Haute MSA, IN	S	20.83 MW	18.62 AW	43320 AAW	INBLS	10//99-12//99
	Iowa	S	20.74 MW	29.07 AW	60480 AAW	IABLS	10//99-12//99
	Cedar Rapids MSA, IA	S	24.27 MW	19.36 AW	50470 AAW	IABLS	10//99-12//99
	Davenport-Moline-Rock Island MSA, IA-IL	S	16.30 MW	15.29 AW	33890 AAW	IABLS	10//99-12//99
	Lawrence MSA, KS	S	35.63 MW	26.42 AW	74110 AAW	KSBLS	10//99-12//99
	Topeka MSA, KS	S	27.19 MW	29.49 AW	56550 AAW	KSBLS	10//99-12//99
	Wichita MSA, KS	S	47.98 MW	56.51 AW	99800 AAW	KSBLS	10//99-12//99
	Kentucky	S	22.95 MW	31.71 AW	65960 AAW	KYBLS	10//99-12//99
	Lexington MSA, KY	S	33.86 MW	34.77 AW	70420 AAW	KYBLS	10//99-12//99
	Louisville MSA, KY-IN	S	32.77 MW	24.53 AW	68170 AAW	KYBLS	10//99-12//99
	Louisiana	S	13.18 MW	18.07 AW	37580 AAW	LABLS	10//99-12//99
	New Orleans MSA, LA	S	26.03 MW	16.36 AW	54140 AAW	LABLS	10//99-12//99
	Shreveport-Bossier City MSA, LA	S	12.58 MW	12.65 AW	26160 AAW	LABLS	10//99-12//99
	Maine	S	26.32 MW	30.77 AW	63990 AAW	MEBLS	10//99-12//99
	Maryland	S	12.74 MW	18.00 AW	37430 AAW	MDBLS	10//99-12//99
	Baltimore PMSA, MD	S	22.48 MW	13.48 AW	46750 AAW	MDBLS	10//99-12//99
	Massachusetts	S	36.96 MW	38.54 AW	80170 AAW	MABLS	10//99-12//99
	Boston PMSA, MA-NH	S	39.70 MW	41.02 AW	82580 AAW	MABLS	10//99-12//99
	Worcester PMSA, MA-CT	S	50.05 MW	62.29 AW	104100 AAW	MABLS	10//99-12//99
	Michigan	S	26.88 MW	33.00 AW	68630 AAW	MIBLS	10//99-12//99
	Ann Arbor PMSA, MI	S	33.93 MW	36.03 AW	70570 AAW	MIBLS	10//99-12//99
	Detroit PMSA, MI	S	32.00 MW	26.21 AW	66560 AAW	MIBLS	10//99-12//99
	Lansing-East Lansing MSA, MI	S	31.05 MW	25.53 AW	64580 AAW	MIBLS	10//99-12//99
	Saginaw-Bay City-Midland MSA, MI	S	45.41 MW	46.80 AW	94450 AAW	MIBLS	10//99-12//99
	Minnesota	S	14.31 MW	17.81 AW	37040 AAW	MNBLS	10//99-12//99
	Minneapolis-St. Paul MSA, MN-WI	S	17.47 MW	13.11 AW	36330 AAW	MNBLS	10//99-12//99
	Rochester MSA, MN	S	20.16 MW	16.53 AW	41930 AAW	MNBLS	10//99-12//99
	Mississippi	S	21.25 MW	22.73 AW	47280 AAW	MSBLS	10//99-12//99
	Jackson MSA, MS	S	26.63 MW	23.82 AW	55390 AAW	MSBLS	10//99-12//99
	Montana	S	23.48 MW	27.40 AW	57000 AAW	MTBLS	10//99-12//99
	Billings MSA, MT	S	28.78 MW	25.29 AW	59860 AAW	MTBLS	10//99-12//99
	Omaha MSA, NE-IA	S	17.65 MW	15.89 AW	36720 AAW	NEBLS	10//99-12//99
	Nevada	S	30.41 MW	31.17 AW	64830 AAW	NVBLS	10//99-12//99
	Las Vegas MSA, NV-AZ	S	28.40 MW	25.16 AW	59080 AAW	NVBLS	10//99-12//99
	Reno MSA, NV	S	37.70 MW	37.35 AW	78410 AAW	NVBLS	10//99-12//99
	New Hampshire	S	22.25 MW	31.90 AW	66350 AAW	NHBLS	10//99-12//99
	Manchester PMSA, NH	S	36.30 MW	36.00 AW	75510 AAW	NHBLS	10//99-12//99
	New Jersey	S	48.05 MW	43.38 AW	90220 AAW	NJBLS	10//99-12//99
	Bergen-Passaic PMSA, NJ	S	37.03 MW	45.42 AW	77020 AAW	NJBLS	10//99-12//99
	Jersey City PMSA, NJ	S	44.59 MW	48.14 AW	92740 AAW	NJBLS	10//99-12//99
	Newark PMSA, NJ	S	42.79 MW	47.11 AW	89010 AAW	NJBLS	10//99-12//99
	New Mexico	S	16.23 MW	23.53 AW	48950 AAW	NMBLS	10//99-12//99
	Albuquerque MSA, NM	S	20.52 MW	15.19 AW	42680 AAW	NMBLS	10//99-12//99
	Santa Fe MSA, NM	S	35.61 MW	31.06 AW	74070 AAW	NMBLS	10//99-12//99
	New York	S	30.43 MW	36.73 AW	76390 AAW	NYBLS	10//99-12//99
	Binghamton MSA, NY	S	31.22 MW	25.55 AW	64950 AAW	NYBLS	10//99-12//99
	Buffalo-Niagara Falls MSA, NY	S	42.57 MW	45.45 AW	88540 AAW	NYBLS	10//99-12//99

Occupation/Type/Industry	Location	Per	Low	Mid	High	Source	Date
Personal Financial Advisor	Nassau-Suffolk PMSA, NY	S	27.96 MW	28.47 AW	58150 AAW	NYBLS	10//99-12//99
	New York PMSA, NY	S	37.68 MW	30.60 AW	78370 AAW	NYBLS	10//99-12//99
	Utica-Rome MSA, NY	S	44.66 MW	42.57 AW	92900 AAW	NYBLS	10//99-12//99
	North Carolina	S	22.81 MW	26.78 AW	55700 AAW	NCBLS	10//99-12//99
	Asheville MSA, NC	S	47.39 MW	52.43 AW	98570 AAW	NCBLS	10//99-12//99
	Charlotte-Gastonia-Rock Hill MSA, NC-SC	S	27.15 MW	26.34 AW	56480 AAW	NCBLS	10//99-12//99
	Hickory-Morganton-Lenoir MSA, NC	S	23.71 MW	27.27 AW	49310 AAW	NCBLS	10//99-12//99
	Raleigh-Durham-Chapel Hill MSA, NC	S	24.70 MW	24.10 AW	51370 AAW	NCBLS	10//99-12//99
	Cincinnati PMSA, OH-KY-IN	S	24.15 MW	24.46 AW	50220 AAW	OHBLS	10//99-12//99
	Cleveland-Lorain-Elyria PMSA, OH	S	26.57 MW	19.04 AW	55260 AAW	OHBLS	10//99-12//99
	Youngstown-Warren MSA, OH	S	21.90 MW	25.06 AW	45560 AAW	OHBLS	10//99-12//99
	Oklahoma	S	13.08 MW	14.36 AW	29880 AAW	OKBLS	10//99-12//99
	Oklahoma City MSA, OK	S	13.92 MW	13.37 AW	28950 AAW	OKBLS	10//99-12//99
	Tulsa MSA, OK	S	12.63 MW	10.72 AW	26270 AAW	OKBLS	10//99-12//99
	Pennsylvania	S	22.32 MW	23.79 AW	49480 AAW	PABLS	10//99-12//99
	Harrisburg-Lebanon-Carlisle MSA, PA	S	32.05 MW	31.21 AW	66650 AAW	PABLS	10//99-12//99
	Lancaster MSA, PA	S	27.43 MW	24.46 AW	57050 AAW	PABLS	10//99-12//99
	Philadelphia PMSA, PA-NJ	S	26.67 MW	23.99 AW	55480 AAW	PABLS	10//99-12//99
	Pittsburgh MSA, PA	S	18.16 MW	12.19 AW	37780 AAW	PABLS	10//99-12//99
	York MSA, PA	S	24.76 MW	23.34 AW	51510 AAW	PABLS	10//99-12//99
	Rhode Island	S	25.99 MW	25.87 AW	53810 AAW	RIBLS	10//99-12//99
	Providence-Fall River-Warwick MSA, RI-MA	S	19.51 MW	16.58 AW	40570 AAW	RIBLS	10//99-12//99
	South Carolina	S	17.76 MW	16.65 AW	34630 AAW	SCBLS	10//99-12//99
	Columbia MSA, SC	S	16.12 MW	18.17 AW	33530 AAW	SCBLS	10//99-12//99
	Greenville-Spartanburg-Anderson MSA, SC	S	19.58 MW	12.77 AW	40730 AAW	SCBLS	10//99-12//99
	South Dakota	S	26.77 MW	26.99 AW	56140 AAW	SDBLS	10//99-12//99
	Tennessee	S	28.04 MW	28.26 AW	58780 AAW	TNBLS	10//99-12//99
	Clarksville-Hopkinsville MSA, TN-KY	S	36.88 MW	20.76 AW	76700 AAW	TNBLS	10//99-12//99
	Knoxville MSA, TN	S	29.01 MW	28.18 AW	60330 AAW	TNBLS	10//99-12//99
	Texas	S	21.26 MW	28.62 AW	59530 AAW	TXBLS	10//99-12//99
	Austin-San Marcos MSA, TX	S	25.13 MW	20.83 AW	52270 AAW	TXBLS	10//99-12//99
	Beaumont-Port Arthur MSA, TX	S	25.31 MW	23.35 AW	52650 AAW	TXBLS	10//99-12//99
	Dallas PMSA, TX	S	23.26 MW	18.90 AW	48370 AAW	TXBLS	10//99-12//99
	Fort Worth-Arlington PMSA, TX	S	33.28 MW	23.84 AW	69230 AAW	TXBLS	10//99-12//99
	Galveston-Texas City PMSA, TX	S	19.47 MW	12.12 AW	40490 AAW	TXBLS	10//99-12//99
	Houston PMSA, TX	S	29.47 MW	21.01 AW	61300 AAW	TXBLS	10//99-12//99
	Longview-Marshall MSA, TX	S	16.31 MW	10.41 AW	33920 AAW	TXBLS	10//99-12//99
	Odessa-Midland MSA, TX	S	32.16 MW	26.16 AW	66900 AAW	TXBLS	10//99-12//99
	San Antonio MSA, TX	S	31.29 MW	23.74 AW	65090 AAW	TXBLS	10//99-12//99
	Texarkana MSA, TX-Texarkana, AR	S	18.60 MW	15.98 AW	38680 AAW	TXBLS	10//99-12//99
	Wichita Falls MSA, TX	S	22.34 MW	22.49 AW	46470 AAW	TXBLS	10//99-12//99
	Vermont	S	23.61 MW	33.23 AW	69130 AAW	VTBLS	10//99-12//99
	Virginia	S	32.07 MW	34.85 AW	72490 AAW	VABLS	10//99-12//99
	Richmond-Petersburg MSA, VA	S	36.58 MW	35.89 AW	76080 AAW	VABLS	10//99-12//99
	Washington	S	27.94 MW	34.91 AW	72610 AAW	WABLS	10//99-12//99
	Seattle-Bellevue-Everett PMSA, WA	S	28.82 MW	18.97 AW	59950 AAW	WABLS	10//99-12//99
	Spokane MSA, WA	S	24.75 MW	19.94 AW	51480 AAW	WABLS	10//99-12//99
	Wisconsin	S	17.16 MW	21.07 AW	43820 AAW	WIBLS	10//99-12//99
	Madison MSA, WI	S	27.77 MW	25.54 AW	57770 AAW	WIBLS	10//99-12//99
	Milwaukee-Waukesha PMSA, WI	S	20.54 MW	16.83 AW	42710 AAW	WIBLS	10//99-12//99
Personnel and Labor Relations Manager	United States	Y		43212 AW		TRAVWK2	1999
Pest Control Worker	Alabama	S	9.13 MW	9.43 AW	19610 AAW	ALBLS	10//99-12//99
	Alaska	S	15.98 MW	17.19 AW	35760 AAW	AKBLS	10//99-12//99
	Arizona	S	10.04 MW	10.51 AW	21860 AAW	AZBLS	10//99-12//99

AAW Average annual wage	**AOH** Average offered, high	**ASH** Average starting, high	**H** Hourly	**M** Monthly	**S** Special: hourly and annual
AE Average entry wage	**AOL** Average offered, low	**ASL** Average starting, low	**HI** Highest wage paid	**MTC** Median total compensation	**TQ** Third quartile wage
AEX Average experienced wage	**APH** Average pay, high range	**AW** Average wage paid	**HR** High end range	**MW** Median wage paid	**W** Weekly
AO Average offered	**APL** Average pay, low range	**FQ** First quartile wage	**LR** Low end range	**SQ** Second quartile wage	**Y** Yearly

Occupation/Type/Industry	Location	Per	Low	Mid	High	Source	Date
Pest Control Worker	Arkansas	S	9.9 MW	9.45 AW	19660 AAW	ARBLS	10//99-12//99
	California	S	13.03 MW	13.77 AW	28640 AAW	CABLS	10//99-12//99
	Colorado	S	13.71 MW	12.24 AW	25450 AAW	COBLS	10//99-12//99
	Connecticut	S	13.16 MW	14.56 AW	30280 AAW	CTBLS	10//99-12//99
	Florida	S	10.48 MW	10.67 AW	22190 AAW	FLBLS	10//99-12//99
	Georgia	S	11.64 MW	11.74 AW	24410 AAW	GABLS	10//99-12//99
	Hawaii	S	11.39 MW	12.53 AW	26070 AAW	HIBLS	10//99-12//99
	Idaho	S	12.91 MW	13.46 AW	27990 AAW	IDBLS	10//99-12//99
	Illinois	S	11.45 MW	12.30 AW	25580 AAW	ILBLS	10//99-12//99
	Indiana	S	10.93 MW	10.93 AW	22730 AAW	INBLS	10//99-12//99
	Iowa	S	9.56 MW	10.50 AW	21830 AAW	IABLS	10//99-12//99
	Kansas	S	9.59 MW	10.16 AW	21140 AAW	KSBLS	10//99-12//99
	Kentucky	S	8.31 MW	8.95 AW	18620 AAW	KYBLS	10//99-12//99
	Louisiana	S	10.56 MW	10.28 AW	21390 AAW	LABLS	10//99-12//99
	Maryland	S	11.02 MW	11.75 AW	24440 AAW	MDBLS	10//99-12//99
	Massachusetts	S	12.32 MW	13.66 AW	28410 AAW	MABLS	10//99-12//99
	Michigan	S	10.91 MW	11.33 AW	23560 AAW	MIBLS	10//99-12//99
	Minnesota	S	13.07 MW	12.90 AW	26830 AAW	MNBLS	10//99-12//99
	Mississippi	S	10.5 MW	10.78 AW	22420 AAW	MSBLS	10//99-12//99
	Montana	S	8.34 MW	10.14 AW	21100 AAW	MTBLS	10//99-12//99
	Nevada	S	11.5 MW	12.35 AW	25690 AAW	NVBLS	10//99-12//99
	New Jersey	S	13.31 MW	13.47 AW	28020 AAW	NJBLS	10//99-12//99
	New Mexico	S	10.32 MW	10.90 AW	22670 AAW	NMBLS	10//99-12//99
	New York	S	12.07 MW	11.52 AW	23970 AAW	NYBLS	10//99-12//99
	North Carolina	S	10.49 MW	9.99 AW	20790 AAW	NCBLS	10//99-12//99
	Ohio	S	11.06 MW	11.14 AW	23160 AAW	OHBLS	10//99-12//99
	Oklahoma	S	10.99 MW	11.18 AW	23250 AAW	OKBLS	10//99-12//99
	Oregon	S	11.66 MW	11.64 AW	24220 AAW	ORBLS	10//99-12//99
	Pennsylvania	S	12.34 MW	13.39 AW	27860 AAW	PABLS	10//99-12//99
	Rhode Island	S	10.06 MW	10.17 AW	21160 AAW	RIBLS	10//99-12//99
	South Carolina	S	10.77 MW	11.84 AW	24630 AAW	SCBLS	10//99-12//99
	Tennessee	S	11.16 MW	11.54 AW	24010 AAW	TNBLS	10//99-12//99
	Texas	S	10.69 MW	10.90 AW	22680 AAW	TXBLS	10//99-12//99
	Virginia	S	10.71 MW	10.65 AW	22150 AAW	VABLS	10//99-12//99
	Washington	S	11.28 MW	12.06 AW	25090 AAW	WABLS	10//99-12//99
	West Virginia	S	11.07 MW	10.70 AW	22250 AAW	WVBLS	10//99-12//99
	Wisconsin	S	15.65 MW	15.98 AW	33240 AAW	WIBLS	10//99-12//99
	Puerto Rico	S	5.87 MW	6.17 AW	12830 AAW	PRBLS	10//99-12//99
	Guam	S	10.23 MW	11.82 AW	24580 AAW	GUBLS	10//99-12//99
Pesticide Handler, Sprayer, and Applicator	Alabama	S	11.32 MW	11.35 AW	23600 AAW	ALBLS	10//99-12//99
	Arkansas	S	7.22 MW	7.46 AW	15520 AAW	ARBLS	10//99-12//99
	California	S	10.9 MW	11.83 AW	24610 AAW	CABLS	10//99-12//99
	Colorado	S	10.53 MW	12.11 AW	25190 AAW	COBLS	10//99-12//99
	Connecticut	S	11.4 MW	12.47 AW	25940 AAW	CTBLS	10//99-12//99
	Florida	S	11.04 MW	11.20 AW	23290 AAW	FLBLS	10//99-12//99
	Georgia	S	10.65 MW	11.25 AW	23400 AAW	GABLS	10//99-12//99
	Idaho	S	9.87 MW	9.86 AW	20510 AAW	IDBLS	10//99-12//99
	Illinois	S	12.16 MW	13.05 AW	27150 AAW	ILBLS	10//99-12//99
	Indiana	S	11 MW	11.47 AW	23860 AAW	INBLS	10//99-12//99
	Iowa	S	9.77 MW	10.52 AW	21870 AAW	IABLS	10//99-12//99
	Kansas	S	10.16 MW	10.29 AW	21400 AAW	KSBLS	10//99-12//99
	Kentucky	S	10.35 MW	10.67 AW	22190 AAW	KYBLS	10//99-12//99
	Louisiana	S	9.45 MW	9.65 AW	20070 AAW	LABLS	10//99-12//99
	Maine	S	14.03 MW	16.45 AW	34210 AAW	MEBLS	10//99-12//99
	Maryland	S	10.45 MW	10.96 AW	22800 AAW	MDBLS	10//99-12//99
	Massachusetts	S	13.77 MW	13.99 AW	29110 AAW	MABLS	10//99-12//99
	Michigan	S	11.24 MW	11.37 AW	23650 AAW	MIBLS	10//99-12//99
	Minnesota	S	11.8 MW	12.26 AW	25500 AAW	MNBLS	10//99-12//99
	Mississippi	S	8.5 MW	8.87 AW	18440 AAW	MSBLS	10//99-12//99
	Missouri	S	10.68 MW	11.27 AW	23440 AAW	MOBLS	10//99-12//99
	Montana	S	8.26 MW	9.21 AW	19160 AAW	MTBLS	10//99-12//99
	Nebraska	S	9.73 MW	10.83 AW	22530 AAW	NEBLS	10//99-12//99
	New Jersey	S	11.33 MW	11.70 AW	24330 AAW	NJBLS	10//99-12//99
	New Mexico	S	10.9 MW	10.57 AW	21990 AAW	NMBLS	10//99-12//99
	New York	S	12.42 MW	15.32 AW	31860 AAW	NYBLS	10//99-12//99
	North Carolina	S	10.33 MW	10.50 AW	21830 AAW	NCBLS	10//99-12//99
	North Dakota	S	8.36 MW	9.27 AW	19290 AAW	NDBLS	10//99-12//99
	Ohio	S	10.12 MW	10.14 AW	21080 AAW	OHBLS	10//99-12//99
	Oklahoma	S	8.39 MW	8.95 AW	18610 AAW	OKBLS	10//99-12//99
	Oregon	S	11.74 MW	11.66 AW	24260 AAW	ORBLS	10//99-12//99

AAW Average annual wage	**AOH** Average offered, high	**ASH** Average starting, high	**H** Hourly	**M** Monthly	**S** Special: hourly and annual
AE Average entry wage	**AOL** Average offered, low	**ASL** Average starting, low	**HI** Highest wage paid	**MTC** Median total compensation	**TQ** Third quartile wage
AEX Average experienced wage	**APH** Average pay, high range	**AW** Average wage paid	**HR** High end range	**MW** Median wage paid	**W** Weekly
AO Average offered	**APL** Average pay, low range	**FQ** First quartile wage	**LR** Low end range	**SQ** Second quartile wage	**Y** Yearly

Occupation/Type/Industry	Location	Per	Low	Mid	High	Source	Date
Pesticide Handler, Sprayer, and Applicator	Pennsylvania	S	11.39 MW	11.85 AW	24660 AAW	PABLS	10//99-12/99
	South Carolina	S	9.7 MW	9.88 AW	20560 AAW	SCBLS	10//99-12/99
	South Dakota	S	8.86 MW	9.45 AW	19670 AAW	SDBLS	10//99-12/99
	Tennessee	S	11.11 MW	11.46 AW	23830 AAW	TNBLS	10//99-12/99
	Texas	S	11.08 MW	11.35 AW	23600 AAW	TXBLS	10//99-12/99
	Vermont	S	9.71 MW	10.41 AW	21640 AAW	VTBLS	10//99-12/99
	Virginia	S	11.07 MW	11.21 AW	23310 AAW	VABLS	10//99-12/99
	Washington	S	11.97 MW	12.29 AW	25560 AAW	WABLS	10//99-12/99
	West Virginia	S	11.68 MW	12.27 AW	25520 AAW	WVBLS	10//99-12/99
	Wisconsin	S	10.86 MW	10.99 AW	22860 AAW	WIBLS	10//99-12/99
	Wyoming	S	9.42 MW	9.07 AW	18870 AAW	WYBLS	10//99-12/99
	Puerto Rico	S	8.98 MW	8.80 AW	18300 AAW	PRBLS	10//99-12/99
Petroleum Engineer	Alaska	S	23.06 MW	26.55 AW	55220 AAW	AKBLS	10//99-12/99
	Arkansas	S	29.01 MW	28.90 AW	60110 AAW	ARBLS	10//99-12/99
	California	S	33.94 MW	33.96 AW	70630 AAW	CABLS	10//99-12/99
	Los Angeles County, CA	Y		78629 AW		LABJ	1999
	Colorado	S	39.01 MW	38.13 AW	79310 AAW	COBLS	10//99-12/99
	Illinois	S	30.91 MW	30.63 AW	63710 AAW	ILBLS	10//99-12/99
	Kansas	S	27.58 MW	30.49 AW	63420 AAW	KSBLS	10//99-12/99
	Kentucky	S	31.09 MW	31.08 AW	64660 AAW	KYBLS	10//99-12/99
	Louisiana	S	34.3 MW	33.96 AW	70630 AAW	LABLS	10//99-12/99
	Michigan	S	30.18 MW	30.06 AW	62520 AAW	MIBLS	10//99-12/99
	Mississippi	S	31.2 MW	30.76 AW	63980 AAW	MSBLS	10//99-12/99
	Montana	S	30.64 MW	29.68 AW	61740 AAW	MTBLS	10//99-12/99
	New Mexico	S	31.56 MW	31.86 AW	66280 AAW	NMBLS	10//99-12/99
	New York	S	28.33 MW	29.22 AW	60780 AAW	NYBLS	10//99-12/99
	Oklahoma	S	33.19 MW	32.83 AW	68280 AAW	OKBLS	10//99-12/99
	Pennsylvania	S	33.44 MW	31.86 AW	66260 AAW	PABLS	10//99-12/99
	Texas	S	38.81 MW	37.19 AW	77350 AAW	TXBLS	10//99-12/99
	Virginia	S	34.28 MW	33.75 AW	70200 AAW	VABLS	10//99-12/99
	West Virginia	S	35.9 MW	33.88 AW	70470 AAW	WVBLS	10//99-12/99
	Wyoming	S	30.31 MW	30.48 AW	63390 AAW	WYBLS	10//99-12/99
Petroleum Pump System Operator, Refinery Operator, and Gauger	Alabama	S	19.98 MW	19.96 AW	41520 AAW	ALBLS	10//99-12/99
	Alaska	S	30.86 MW	30.00 AW	62390 AAW	AKBLS	10//99-12/99
	Arizona	S	14.71 MW	14.22 AW	29580 AAW	AZBLS	10//99-12/99
	Arkansas	S	14.22 MW	16.71 AW	34750 AAW	ARBLS	10//99-12/99
	California	S	22.75 MW	22.24 AW	46270 AAW	CABLS	10//99-12/99
	Colorado	S	21.63 MW	21.97 AW	45700 AAW	COBLS	10//99-12/99
	Connecticut	S	18.67 MW	20.14 AW	41890 AAW	CTBLS	10//99-12/99
	Delaware	S	20.6 MW	19.80 AW	41190 AAW	DEBLS	10//99-12/99
	Florida	S	17.25 MW	17.79 AW	37010 AAW	FLBLS	10//99-12/99
	Georgia	S	15 MW	17.61 AW	36630 AAW	GABLS	10//99-12/99
	Kansas	S	18.78 MW	17.70 AW	36820 AAW	KSBLS	10//99-12/99
	Kentucky	S	21.38 MW	19.68 AW	40940 AAW	KYBLS	10//99-12/99
	Louisiana	S	21.02 MW	20.59 AW	42820 AAW	LABLS	10//99-12/99
	Massachusetts	S	18.44 MW	19.75 AW	41080 AAW	MABLS	10//99-12/99
	Michigan	S	18.9 MW	18.37 AW	38200 AAW	MIBLS	10//99-12/99
	Montana	S	24.07 MW	23.43 AW	48730 AAW	MTBLS	10//99-12/99
	Nebraska	S	16 MW	17.01 AW	35370 AAW	NEBLS	10//99-12/99
	New Jersey	S	24.54 MW	25.55 AW	53150 AAW	NJBLS	10//99-12/99
	New Mexico	S	22.33 MW	22.06 AW	45890 AAW	NMBLS	10//99-12/99
	New York	S	19.93 MW	19.53 AW	40610 AAW	NYBLS	10//99-12/99
	North Carolina	S	20.88 MW	19.78 AW	41140 AAW	NCBLS	10//99-12/99
	Oklahoma	S	20.87 MW	18.62 AW	38740 AAW	OKBLS	10//99-12/99
	Pennsylvania	S	21.68 MW	20.74 AW	43140 AAW	PABLS	10//99-12/99
	Tennessee	S	15.58 MW	15.69 AW	32640 AAW	TNBLS	10//99-12/99
	Texas	S	22.25 MW	21.33 AW	44360 AAW	TXBLS	10//99-12/99
	Virginia	S	16.54 MW	17.09 AW	35540 AAW	VABLS	10//99-12/99
	Washington	S	20.48 MW	19.71 AW	40990 AAW	WABLS	10//99-12/99
	West Virginia	S	18.24 MW	17.87 AW	37160 AAW	WVBLS	10//99-12/99
	Wisconsin	S	20.46 MW	19.83 AW	41240 AAW	WIBLS	10//99-12/99
	Wyoming	S	21.87 MW	22.06 AW	45880 AAW	WYBLS	10//99-12/99
	Puerto Rico	S	14.16 MW	15.11 AW	31420 AAW	PRBLS	10//99-12/99
Pharmaceutical Sales Representative	United States	Y	40000 ASL	50000 ASH		KRTBN	2000

Occupation/Type/Industry	Location	Per	Low	Mid	High	Source	Date
Pharmacist	United States	H		27.87 AW		NCS98	1998
	Alabama	S	30.92 MW	29.68 AW	61740 AAW	ALBLS	10//99-12//99
	Anniston MSA, AL	S	28.99 MW	30.80 AW	60300 AAW	ALBLS	10//99-12//99
	Auburn-Opelika MSA, AL	S	28.60 MW	26.68 AW	59490 AAW	ALBLS	10//99-12//99
	Birmingham MSA, AL	S	29.39 MW	30.79 AW	61130 AAW	ALBLS	10//99-12//99
	Decatur MSA, AL	S	27.98 MW	27.68 AW	58200 AAW	ALBLS	10//99-12//99
	Dothan MSA, AL	S	29.42 MW	31.57 AW	61190 AAW	ALBLS	10//99-12//99
	Florence MSA, AL	S	30.24 MW	33.00 AW	62900 AAW	ALBLS	10//99-12//99
	Gadsden MSA, AL	S	30.80 MW	30.86 AW	64050 AAW	ALBLS	10//99-12//99
	Huntsville MSA, AL	S	30.42 MW	31.67 AW	63270 AAW	ALBLS	10//99-12//99
	Mobile MSA, AL	S	30.85 MW	32.66 AW	64160 AAW	ALBLS	10//99-12//99
	Montgomery MSA, AL	S	29.19 MW	30.22 AW	60720 AAW	ALBLS	10//99-12//99
	Tuscaloosa MSA, AL	S	28.58 MW	30.72 AW	59440 AAW	ALBLS	10//99-12//99
	Alaska	S	33.32 MW	32.55 AW	67700 AAW	AKBLS	10//99-12//99
	Anchorage MSA, AK	S	31.84 MW	32.66 AW	66230 AAW	AKBLS	10//99-12//99
	Arizona	S	32.57 MW	30.77 AW	63990 AAW	AZBLS	10//99-12//99
	Flagstaff MSA, AZ-UT	S	30.47 MW	33.70 AW	63370 AAW	AZBLS	10//99-12//99
	Phoenix-Mesa MSA, AZ	S	30.91 MW	32.70 AW	64300 AAW	AZBLS	10//99-12//99
	Tucson MSA, AZ	S	30.78 MW	32.36 AW	64010 AAW	AZBLS	10//99-12//99
	Yuma MSA, AZ	S	30.16 MW	31.45 AW	62740 AAW	AZBLS	10//99-12//99
	Arkansas	S	27.78 MW	27.16 AW	56490 AAW	ARBLS	10//99-12//99
	Fayetteville-Springdale-Rogers MSA, AR	S	29.69 MW	30.50 AW	61760 AAW	ARBLS	10//99-12//99
	Fort Smith MSA, AR-OK	S	29.17 MW	30.97 AW	60680 AAW	ARBLS	10//99-12//99
	Jonesboro MSA, AR	S	25.46 MW	26.20 AW	52970 AAW	ARBLS	10//99-12//99
	Little Rock-North Little Rock MSA, AR	S	27.78 MW	28.13 AW	57770 AAW	ARBLS	10//99-12//99
	Pine Bluff MSA, AR	S	29.35 MW	30.24 AW	61040 AAW	ARBLS	10//99-12//99
	California	S	36.39 MW	33.54 AW	69760 AAW	CABLS	10//99-12//99
	Bakersfield MSA, CA	S	34.80 MW	36.63 AW	72380 AAW	CABLS	10//99-12//99
	Chico-Paradise MSA, CA	S	33.29 MW	36.17 AW	69240 AAW	CABLS	10//99-12//99
	Fresno MSA, CA	S	34.34 MW	36.49 AW	71420 AAW	CABLS	10//99-12//99
	Los Angeles-Long Beach PMSA, CA	S	33.50 MW	35.90 AW	69680 AAW	CABLS	10//99-12//99
	Merced MSA, CA	S	33.39 MW	35.12 AW	69450 AAW	CABLS	10//99-12//99
	Modesto MSA, CA	S	35.47 MW	37.84 AW	73780 AAW	CABLS	10//99-12//99
	Oakland PMSA, CA	S	34.81 MW	37.49 AW	72410 AAW	CABLS	10//99-12//99
	Orange County PMSA, CA	S	34.27 MW	36.12 AW	71280 AAW	CABLS	10//99-12//99
	Redding MSA, CA	S	34.67 MW	37.52 AW	72110 AAW	CABLS	10//99-12//99
	Riverside-San Bernardino PMSA, CA	S	33.92 MW	36.95 AW	70560 AAW	CABLS	10//99-12//99
	Sacramento PMSA, CA	S	32.31 MW	36.34 AW	67210 AAW	CABLS	10//99-12//99
	Salinas MSA, CA	S	33.92 MW	35.99 AW	70560 AAW	CABLS	10//99-12//99
	San Diego County, CA	Y		75949 AW		ERDGE	1998
	San Diego MSA, CA	S	33.45 MW	36.22 AW	69580 AAW	CABLS	10//99-12//99
	San Francisco PMSA, CA	S	32.56 MW	36.21 AW	67730 AAW	CABLS	10//99-12//99
	San Jose PMSA, CA	S	33.82 MW	37.02 AW	70340 AAW	CABLS	10//99-12//99
	San Luis Obispo-Atascadero-Paso Robles MSA, CA	S	30.74 MW	34.05 AW	63950 AAW	CABLS	10//99-12//99
	Santa Barbara-Santa Maria-Lompoc MSA, CA	S	32.17 MW	35.46 AW	66900 AAW	CABLS	10//99-12//99
	Santa Cruz-Watsonville PMSA, CA	S	32.94 MW	36.99 AW	68510 AAW	CABLS	10//99-12//99
	Santa Rosa PMSA, CA	S	33.22 MW	36.57 AW	69090 AAW	CABLS	10//99-12//99
	Stockton-Lodi MSA, CA	S	32.67 MW	35.89 AW	67960 AAW	CABLS	10//99-12//99
	Vallejo-Fairfield-Napa PMSA, CA	S	31.63 MW	35.01 AW	65790 AAW	CABLS	10//99-12//99
	Ventura PMSA, CA	S	33.81 MW	36.80 AW	70330 AAW	CABLS	10//99-12//99
	Visalia-Tulare-Porterville MSA, CA	S	34.00 MW	36.74 AW	70720 AAW	CABLS	10//99-12//99
	Yolo PMSA, CA	S	34.13 MW	36.70 AW	70990 AAW	CABLS	10//99-12//99
	Yuba City MSA, CA	S	33.79 MW	37.26 AW	70290 AAW	CABLS	10//99-12//99
	Colorado	S	32.02 MW	30.68 AW	63810 AAW	COBLS	10//99-12//99
	Boulder-Longmont PMSA, CO	S	29.55 MW	31.36 AW	61470 AAW	COBLS	10//99-12//99
	Colorado Springs MSA, CO	S	30.89 MW	31.68 AW	64250 AAW	COBLS	10//99-12//99
	Denver PMSA, CO	S	31.15 MW	32.56 AW	64800 AAW	COBLS	10//99-12//99
	Fort Collins-Loveland MSA, CO	S	30.02 MW	31.10 AW	62440 AAW	COBLS	10//99-12//99
	Grand Junction MSA, CO	S	31.44 MW	33.30 AW	65390 AAW	COBLS	10//99-12//99
	Greeley PMSA, CO	S	30.62 MW	32.38 AW	63690 AAW	COBLS	10//99-12//99
	Pueblo MSA, CO	S	27.57 MW	27.88 AW	57350 AAW	COBLS	10//99-12//99
	Connecticut	S	34.02 MW	32.03 AW	66630 AAW	CTBLS	10//99-12//99

Pharmacist

Occupation/Type/Industry	Location	Per	Low	Mid	High	Source	Date
Pharmacist	Bridgeport PMSA, CT	S	31.53 MW	34.25 AW	65590 AAW	CTBLS	10//99-12//99
	Danbury PMSA, CT	S	32.33 MW	35.23 AW	67250 AAW	CTBLS	10//99-12//99
	Hartford MSA, CT	S	32.13 MW	34.26 AW	66830 AAW	CTBLS	10//99-12//99
	New Haven-Meriden PMSA, CT	S	31.41 MW	32.63 AW	65340 AAW	CTBLS	10//99-12//99
	New London-Norwich MSA, CT-RI	S	33.32 MW	34.53 AW	69310 AAW	CTBLS	10//99-12//99
	Stamford-Norwalk PMSA, CT	S	32.96 MW	35.96 AW	68550 AAW	CTBLS	10//99-12//99
	Waterbury PMSA, CT	S	31.39 MW	33.45 AW	65300 AAW	CTBLS	10//99-12//99
	Delaware	S	33.28 MW	30.79 AW	64050 AAW	DEBLS	10//99-12//99
	Wilmington-Newark PMSA, DE-MD	S	32.03 MW	34.76 AW	66620 AAW	DEBLS	10//99-12//99
	District of Columbia	S	30.34 MW	28.74 AW	59790 AAW	DCBLS	10//99-12//99
	Washington PMSA, DC-MD-VA-WV	S	30.28 MW	31.77 AW	62980 AAW	DCBLS	10//99-12//99
	Florida	S	34.57 MW	32.13 AW	66840 AAW	FLBLS	10//99-12//99
	Daytona Beach MSA, FL	S	32.60 MW	34.63 AW	67800 AAW	FLBLS	10//99-12//99
	Fort Lauderdale PMSA, FL	S	31.12 MW	33.81 AW	64740 AAW	FLBLS	10//99-12//99
	Fort Myers-Cape Coral MSA, FL	S	33.71 MW	35.68 AW	70120 AAW	FLBLS	10//99-12//99
	Fort Pierce-Port St. Lucie MSA, FL	S	34.44 MW	36.45 AW	71630 AAW	FLBLS	10//99-12//99
	Fort Walton Beach MSA, FL	S	31.86 MW	33.40 AW	66260 AAW	FLBLS	10//99-12//99
	Gainesville MSA, FL	S	30.80 MW	32.83 AW	64070 AAW	FLBLS	10//99-12//99
	Jacksonville MSA, FL	S	31.53 MW	35.96 AW	65590 AAW	FLBLS	10//99-12//99
	Lakeland-Winter Haven MSA, FL	S	32.27 MW	34.52 AW	67110 AAW	FLBLS	10//99-12//99
	Melbourne-Titusville-Palm Bay MSA, FL	S	33.69 MW	34.44 AW	70070 AAW	FLBLS	10//99-12//99
	Miami PMSA, FL	S	32.35 MW	34.24 AW	67280 AAW	FLBLS	10//99-12//99
	Naples MSA, FL	S	35.19 MW	37.43 AW	73190 AAW	FLBLS	10//99-12//99
	Ocala MSA, FL	S	33.15 MW	35.74 AW	68940 AAW	FLBLS	10//99-12//99
	Orlando MSA, FL	S	32.48 MW	34.21 AW	67560 AAW	FLBLS	10//99-12//99
	Panama City MSA, FL	S	31.83 MW	34.08 AW	66200 AAW	FLBLS	10//99-12//99
	Pensacola MSA, FL	S	32.04 MW	33.66 AW	66640 AAW	FLBLS	10//99-12//99
	Punta Gorda MSA, FL	S	28.20 MW	32.52 AW	58660 AAW	FLBLS	10//99-12//99
	Sarasota-Bradenton MSA, FL	S	32.85 MW	35.16 AW	68330 AAW	FLBLS	10//99-12//99
	Tallahassee MSA, FL	S	32.12 MW	33.36 AW	66810 AAW	FLBLS	10//99-12//99
	Tampa-St. Petersburg-Clearwater MSA, FL	S	31.92 MW	34.88 AW	66390 AAW	FLBLS	10//99-12//99
	West Palm Beach-Boca Raton MSA, FL	S	31.95 MW	34.74 AW	66460 AAW	FLBLS	10//99-12//99
	Georgia	S	29.69 MW	29.30 AW	60940 AAW	GABLS	10//99-12//99
	Albany MSA, GA	S	29.60 MW	31.22 AW	61570 AAW	GABLS	10//99-12//99
	Athens MSA, GA	S	28.51 MW	28.92 AW	59290 AAW	GABLS	10//99-12//99
	Atlanta MSA, GA	S	28.15 MW	28.32 AW	58540 AAW	GABLS	10//99-12//99
	Augusta-Aiken MSA, GA-SC	S	30.37 MW	30.99 AW	63160 AAW	GABLS	10//99-12//99
	Columbus MSA, GA-AL	S	31.29 MW	32.47 AW	65090 AAW	GABLS	10//99-12//99
	Macon MSA, GA	S	28.14 MW	27.25 AW	58530 AAW	GABLS	10//99-12//99
	Savannah MSA, GA	S	31.54 MW	33.37 AW	65610 AAW	GABLS	10//99-12//99
	Hawaii	S	33.85 MW	32.49 AW	67580 AAW	HIBLS	10//99-12//99
	Honolulu MSA, HI	S	32.35 MW	33.62 AW	67290 AAW	HIBLS	10//99-12//99
	Idaho	S	29.73 MW	28.71 AW	59720 AAW	IDBLS	10//99-12//99
	Boise City MSA, ID	S	29.43 MW	29.93 AW	61220 AAW	IDBLS	10//99-12//99
	Pocatello MSA, ID	S	30.64 MW	31.50 AW	63740 AAW	IDBLS	10//99-12//99
	Illinois	S	32.59 MW	30.66 AW	63770 AAW	ILBLS	10//99-12//99
	Bloomington-Normal MSA, IL	S	33.20 MW	32.65 AW	69050 AAW	ILBLS	10//99-12//99
	Champaign-Urbana MSA, IL	S	29.38 MW	32.56 AW	61110 AAW	ILBLS	10//99-12//99
	Chicago PMSA, IL	S	30.76 MW	32.98 AW	63990 AAW	ILBLS	10//99-12//99
	Decatur MSA, IL	S	31.42 MW	33.34 AW	65340 AAW	ILBLS	10//99-12//99
	Kankakee PMSA, IL	S	28.10 MW	30.88 AW	58450 AAW	ILBLS	10//99-12//99
	Peoria-Pekin MSA, IL	S	30.46 MW	32.87 AW	63360 AAW	ILBLS	10//99-12//99
	Rockford MSA, IL	S	30.38 MW	33.06 AW	63200 AAW	ILBLS	10//99-12//99
	Springfield MSA, IL	S	29.70 MW	29.92 AW	61770 AAW	ILBLS	10//99-12//99
	Indiana	S	32.73 MW	31.34 AW	65190 AAW	INBLS	10//99-12//99
	Bloomington MSA, IN	S	32.08 MW	34.32 AW	66740 AAW	INBLS	10//99-12//99
	Elkhart-Goshen MSA, IN	S	32.71 MW	35.20 AW	68050 AAW	INBLS	10//99-12//99
	Evansville-Henderson MSA, IN-KY	S	29.84 MW	31.31 AW	62060 AAW	INBLS	10//99-12//99
	Fort Wayne MSA, IN	S	31.46 MW	32.46 AW	65440 AAW	INBLS	10//99-12//99
	Gary PMSA, IN	S	31.70 MW	34.55 AW	65940 AAW	INBLS	10//99-12//99
	Indianapolis MSA, IN	S	31.10 MW	32.38 AW	64690 AAW	INBLS	10//99-12//99

AAW Average annual wage	AOH Average offered, high	ASH Average starting, high	H Hourly	M Monthly	S Special: hourly and annual
AE Average entry wage	AOL Average offered, low	ASL Average starting, low	HI Highest wage paid	MTC Median total compensation	TQ Third quartile wage
AEX Average experienced wage	APH Average pay, high range	AW Average wage paid	HR High end range	MW Median wage paid	W Weekly
AO Average offered	APL Average pay, low range	FQ First quartile wage	LR Low end range	SQ Second quartile wage	Y Yearly

Occupation/Type/Industry	Location	Per	Low	Mid	High	Source	Date
Pharmacist	Kokomo MSA, IN	S	31.13 MW	31.82 AW	64750 AAW	INBLS	10//99-12//99
	Lafayette MSA, IN	S	31.42 MW	32.66 AW	65340 AAW	INBLS	10//99-12//99
	Muncie MSA, IN	S	32.53 MW	31.67 AW	67660 AAW	INBLS	10//99-12//99
	South Bend MSA, IN	S	32.24 MW	33.62 AW	67050 AAW	INBLS	10//99-12//99
	Terre Haute MSA, IN	S	30.51 MW	32.39 AW	63460 AAW	INBLS	10//99-12//99
	Iowa	S	28.94 MW	27.86 AW	57950 AAW	IABLS	10//99-12//99
	Cedar Rapids MSA, IA	S	28.37 MW	28.09 AW	59010 AAW	IABLS	10//99-12//99
	Davenport-Moline-Rock Island MSA, IA-IL	S	30.12 MW	31.66 AW	62640 AAW	IABLS	10//99-12//99
	Des Moines MSA, IA	S	24.69 MW	25.13 AW	51360 AAW	IABLS	10//99-12//99
	Dubuque MSA, IA	S	28.18 MW	29.47 AW	58620 AAW	IABLS	10//99-12//99
	Iowa City MSA, IA	S	27.02 MW	28.66 AW	56190 AAW	IABLS	10//99-12//99
	Sioux City MSA, IA-NE	S	28.31 MW	29.79 AW	58880 AAW	IABLS	10//99-12//99
	Waterloo-Cedar Falls MSA, IA	S	31.12 MW	31.25 AW	64740 AAW	IABLS	10//99-12//99
	Kansas	S	31.65 MW	30.53 AW	63500 AAW	KSBLS	10//99-12//99
	Lawrence MSA, KS	S	27.29 MW	28.99 AW	56760 AAW	KSBLS	10//99-12//99
	Topeka MSA, KS	S	30.60 MW	31.23 AW	63640 AAW	KSBLS	10//99-12//99
	Wichita MSA, KS	S	31.33 MW	32.76 AW	65160 AAW	KSBLS	10//99-12//99
	Kentucky	S	32.29 MW	29.90 AW	62200 AAW	KYBLS	10//99-12//99
	Lexington MSA, KY	S	28.49 MW	30.56 AW	59260 AAW	KYBLS	10//99-12//99
	Louisville MSA, KY-IN	S	31.76 MW	34.18 AW	66060 AAW	KYBLS	10//99-12//99
	Owensboro MSA, KY	S	30.60 MW	32.73 AW	63660 AAW	KYBLS	10//99-12//99
	Louisiana	S	28.05 MW	27.31 AW	56800 AAW	LABLS	10//99-12//99
	Alexandria MSA, LA	S	27.69 MW	28.27 AW	57590 AAW	LABLS	10//99-12//99
	Baton Rouge MSA, LA	S	28.79 MW	29.88 AW	59880 AAW	LABLS	10//99-12//99
	Houma MSA, LA	S	27.46 MW	28.14 AW	57120 AAW	LABLS	10//99-12//99
	Lafayette MSA, LA	S	24.62 MW	24.24 AW	51220 AAW	LABLS	10//99-12//99
	Lake Charles MSA, LA	S	28.82 MW	30.41 AW	59950 AAW	LABLS	10//99-12//99
	Monroe MSA, LA	S	25.38 MW	24.38 AW	52800 AAW	LABLS	10//99-12//99
	New Orleans MSA, LA	S	27.67 MW	28.43 AW	57560 AAW	LABLS	10//99-12//99
	Shreveport-Bossier City MSA, LA	S	30.27 MW	32.08 AW	62960 AAW	LABLS	10//99-12//99
	Maine	S	31.95 MW	30.84 AW	64150 AAW	MEBLS	10//99-12//99
	Bangor MSA, ME	S	31.19 MW	33.59 AW	64870 AAW	MEBLS	10//99-12//99
	Lewiston-Auburn MSA, ME	S	30.24 MW	32.46 AW	62900 AAW	MEBLS	10//99-12//99
	Portland MSA, ME	S	30.82 MW	31.29 AW	64100 AAW	MEBLS	10//99-12//99
	Maryland	S	32.5 MW	31.22 AW	64930 AAW	MDBLS	10//99-12//99
	Baltimore PMSA, MD	S	30.98 MW	32.24 AW	64430 AAW	MDBLS	10//99-12//99
	Cumberland MSA, MD-WV	S	31.32 MW	33.64 AW	65140 AAW	MDBLS	10//99-12//99
	Hagerstown PMSA, MD	S	29.51 MW	31.35 AW	61370 AAW	MDBLS	10//99-12//99
	Massachusetts	S	31.25 MW	29.50 AW	61370 AAW	MABLS	10//99-12//99
	Barnstable-Yarmouth MSA, MA	S	27.75 MW	30.70 AW	57730 AAW	MABLS	10//99-12//99
	Boston PMSA, MA-NH	S	29.35 MW	31.17 AW	61050 AAW	MABLS	10//99-12//99
	Brockton PMSA, MA	S	29.12 MW	29.74 AW	60580 AAW	MABLS	10//99-12//99
	Fitchburg-Leominster PMSA, MA	S	30.19 MW	31.15 AW	62790 AAW	MABLS	10//99-12//99
	Lawrence PMSA, MA-NH	S	29.80 MW	30.94 AW	61980 AAW	MABLS	10//99-12//99
	Lowell PMSA, MA-NH	S	29.92 MW	31.37 AW	62240 AAW	MABLS	10//99-12//99
	New Bedford PMSA, MA	S	27.66 MW	32.43 AW	57530 AAW	MABLS	10//99-12//99
	Pittsfield MSA, MA	S	30.88 MW	32.64 AW	64220 AAW	MABLS	10//99-12//99
	Springfield MSA, MA	S	30.73 MW	33.23 AW	63910 AAW	MABLS	10//99-12//99
	Worcester PMSA, MA-CT	S	30.90 MW	31.91 AW	64270 AAW	MABLS	10//99-12//99
	Michigan	S	31.98 MW	30.94 AW	64350 AAW	MIBLS	10//99-12//99
	Ann Arbor PMSA, MI	S	29.38 MW	30.17 AW	61110 AAW	MIBLS	10//99-12//99
	Benton Harbor MSA, MI	S	31.59 MW	33.36 AW	65710 AAW	MIBLS	10//99-12//99
	Detroit PMSA, MI	S	31.99 MW	32.21 AW	66530 AAW	MIBLS	10//99-12//99
	Flint PMSA, MI	S	29.57 MW	30.68 AW	61510 AAW	MIBLS	10//99-12//99
	Grand Rapids-Muskegon-Holland MSA, MI	S	30.88 MW	32.73 AW	64230 AAW	MIBLS	10//99-12//99
	Jackson MSA, MI	S	30.45 MW	32.23 AW	63350 AAW	MIBLS	10//99-12//99
	Kalamazoo-Battle Creek MSA, MI	S	29.98 MW	32.01 AW	62370 AAW	MIBLS	10//99-12//99
	Lansing-East Lansing MSA, MI	S	29.98 MW	32.18 AW	62350 AAW	MIBLS	10//99-12//99
	Saginaw-Bay City-Midland MSA, MI	S	29.91 MW	32.70 AW	62200 AAW	MIBLS	10//99-12//99
	Minnesota	S	31.94 MW	30.25 AW	62910 AAW	MNBLS	10//99-12//99
	Duluth-Superior MSA, MN-WI	S	28.75 MW	32.50 AW	59810 AAW	MNBLS	10//99-12//99
	Minneapolis-St. Paul MSA, MN-WI	S	31.45 MW	33.06 AW	65410 AAW	MNBLS	10//99-12//99
	Rochester MSA, MN	S	31.55 MW	32.65 AW	65630 AAW	MNBLS	10//99-12//99
	St. Cloud MSA, MN	S	29.65 MW	32.00 AW	61680 AAW	MNBLS	10//99-12//99

Occupation/Type/Industry	Location	Per	Low	Mid	High	Source	Date
Pharmacist	Mississippi	S	27.06 MW	27.70 AW	57610 AAW	MSBLS	10//99-12//99
	Biloxi-Gulfport-Pascagoula MSA, MS	S	26.79 MW	27.97 AW	55730 AAW	MSBLS	10//99-12//99
	Hattiesburg MSA, MS	S	26.75 MW	28.45 AW	55640 AAW	MSBLS	10//99-12//99
	Jackson MSA, MS	S	28.40 MW	28.25 AW	59070 AAW	MSBLS	10//99-12//99
	Missouri	S	31.7 MW	29.64 AW	61660 AAW	MOBLS	10//99-12//99
	Columbia MSA, MO	S	29.80 MW	31.95 AW	61980 AAW	MOBLS	10//99-12//99
	Joplin MSA, MO	S	27.95 MW	31.75 AW	58140 AAW	MOBLS	10//99-12//99
	Kansas City MSA, MO-KS	S	29.63 MW	31.56 AW	61640 AAW	MOBLS	10//99-12//99
	St. Louis MSA, MO-IL	S	28.98 MW	31.52 AW	60290 AAW	MOBLS	10//99-12//99
	Springfield MSA, MO	S	32.39 MW	34.45 AW	67380 AAW	MOBLS	10//99-12//99
	Montana	S	28.71 MW	27.38 AW	56950 AAW	MTBLS	10//99-12//99
	Billings MSA, MT	S	29.85 MW	31.29 AW	62080 AAW	MTBLS	10//99-12//99
	Great Falls MSA, MT	S	27.31 MW	28.30 AW	56800 AAW	MTBLS	10//99-12//99
	Missoula MSA, MT	S	21.70 MW	22.70 AW	45130 AAW	MTBLS	10//99-12//99
	Nebraska	S	28.61 MW	27.37 AW	56920 AAW	NEBLS	10//99-12//99
	Lincoln MSA, NE	S	29.02 MW	31.26 AW	60350 AAW	NEBLS	10//99-12//99
	Omaha MSA, NE-IA	S	27.56 MW	29.16 AW	57330 AAW	NEBLS	10//99-12//99
	Nevada	S	34.91 MW	32.45 AW	67500 AAW	NVBLS	10//99-12//99
	Las Vegas MSA, NV-AZ	S	32.94 MW	35.34 AW	68520 AAW	NVBLS	10//99-12//99
	Reno MSA, NV	S	31.53 MW	33.99 AW	65580 AAW	NVBLS	10//99-12//99
	New Hampshire	S	32.41 MW	30.49 AW	63420 AAW	NHBLS	10//99-12//99
	Manchester PMSA, NH	S	30.63 MW	32.14 AW	63710 AAW	NHBLS	10//99-12//99
	Nashua PMSA, NH	S	29.63 MW	32.31 AW	61630 AAW	NHBLS	10//99-12//99
	Portsmouth-Rochester PMSA, NH-ME	S	31.43 MW	33.39 AW	65370 AAW	NHBLS	10//99-12//99
	New Jersey	S	31.94 MW	30.35 AW	63130 AAW	NJBLS	10//99-12//99
	Atlantic-Cape May PMSA, NJ	S	31.62 MW	33.82 AW	65770 AAW	NJBLS	10//99-12//99
	Bergen-Passaic PMSA, NJ	S	31.44 MW	33.36 AW	65390 AAW	NJBLS	10//99-12//99
	Jersey City PMSA, NJ	S	30.75 MW	32.46 AW	63950 AAW	NJBLS	10//99-12//99
	Middlesex-Somerset- Hunterdon PMSA, NJ	S	29.81 MW	31.28 AW	62010 AAW	NJBLS	10//99-12//99
	Monmouth-Ocean PMSA, NJ	S	29.44 MW	30.61 AW	61240 AAW	NJBLS	10//99-12//99
	Newark PMSA, NJ	S	29.62 MW	31.14 AW	61610 AAW	NJBLS	10//99-12//99
	Trenton PMSA, NJ	S	29.70 MW	31.42 AW	61770 AAW	NJBLS	10//99-12//99
	Vineland-Millville-Bridgeton PMSA, NJ	S	30.62 MW	32.60 AW	63690 AAW	NJBLS	10//99-12//99
	New Mexico	S	32.79 MW	30.76 AW	63980 AAW	NMBLS	10//99-12//99
	Albuquerque MSA, NM	S	29.25 MW	31.43 AW	60830 AAW	NMBLS	10//99-12//99
	Las Cruces MSA, NM	S	32.71 MW	32.41 AW	68040 AAW	NMBLS	10//99-12//99
	Santa Fe MSA, NM	S	31.67 MW	33.24 AW	65870 AAW	NMBLS	10//99-12//99
	New York	S	29.4 MW	27.57 AW	57340 AAW	NYBLS	10//99-12//99
	Albany-Schenectady-Troy MSA, NY	S	29.33 MW	30.68 AW	61010 AAW	NYBLS	10//99-12//99
	Binghamton MSA, NY	S	28.40 MW	30.61 AW	59080 AAW	NYBLS	10//99-12//99
	Buffalo-Niagara Falls MSA, NY	S	30.25 MW	31.78 AW	62910 AAW	NYBLS	10//99-12//99
	Dutchess County PMSA, NY	S	31.31 MW	31.48 AW	65120 AAW	NYBLS	10//99-12//99
	Elmira MSA, NY	S	33.29 MW	33.57 AW	69230 AAW	NYBLS	10//99-12//99
	Glens Falls MSA, NY	S	30.31 MW	31.69 AW	63050 AAW	NYBLS	10//99-12//99
	Jamestown MSA, NY	S	29.68 MW	31.85 AW	61730 AAW	NYBLS	10//99-12//99
	Nassau-Suffolk PMSA, NY	S	28.09 MW	30.82 AW	58420 AAW	NYBLS	10//99-12//99
	New York PMSA, NY	S	25.28 MW	25.46 AW	52570 AAW	NYBLS	10//99-12//99
	Newburgh PMSA, NY-PA	S	30.33 MW	32.36 AW	63080 AAW	NYBLS	10//99-12//99
	Rochester MSA, NY	S	29.99 MW	31.41 AW	62380 AAW	NYBLS	10//99-12//99
	Syracuse MSA, NY	S	32.28 MW	34.15 AW	67130 AAW	NYBLS	10//99-12//99
	Utica-Rome MSA, NY	S	30.05 MW	32.28 AW	62510 AAW	NYBLS	10//99-12//99
	North Carolina	S	31.56 MW	29.67 AW	61710 AAW	NCBLS	10//99-12//99
	Asheville MSA, NC	S	30.57 MW	32.83 AW	63580 AAW	NCBLS	10//99-12//99
	Charlotte-Gastonia-Rock Hill MSA, NC-SC	S	30.19 MW	32.36 AW	62790 AAW	NCBLS	10//99-12//99
	Fayetteville MSA, NC	S	30.08 MW	32.41 AW	62570 AAW	NCBLS	10//99-12//99
	Goldsboro MSA, NC	S	32.04 MW	34.52 AW	66640 AAW	NCBLS	10//99-12//99
	Greensboro--Winston-Salem-- High Point MSA, NC	S	30.20 MW	32.62 AW	62820 AAW	NCBLS	10//99-12//99
	Hickory-Morganton-Lenoir MSA, NC	S	29.03 MW	28.61 AW	60390 AAW	NCBLS	10//99-12//99
	Jacksonville MSA, NC	S	32.10 MW	32.69 AW	66770 AAW	NCBLS	10//99-12//99
	Raleigh-Durham-Chapel Hill MSA, NC	S	29.45 MW	31.07 AW	61250 AAW	NCBLS	10//99-12//99
	Rocky Mount MSA, NC	S	30.26 MW	32.71 AW	62950 AAW	NCBLS	10//99-12//99
	Wilmington MSA, NC	S	30.05 MW	31.73 AW	62510 AAW	NCBLS	10//99-12//99

AAW Average annual wage	**AOH** Average offered, high	**ASH** Average starting, high	**H** Hourly	**M** Monthly	**S** Special: hourly and annual
AE Average entry wage	**AOL** Average offered, low	**ASL** Average starting, low	**HI** Highest wage paid	**MTC** Median total compensation	**TQ** Third quartile wage
AEX Average experienced wage	**APH** Average pay, high range	**AW** Average wage paid	**HR** High end range	**MW** Median wage paid	**W** Weekly
AO Average offered	**APL** Average pay, low range	**FQ** First quartile wage	**LR** Low end range	**SQ** Second quartile wage	**Y** Yearly

Occupation/Type/Industry	Location	Per	Low	Mid	High	Source	Date
Pharmacist	North Dakota	S	24 MW	24.59 AW	51150 AAW	NDBLS	10//99-12//99
	Bismarck MSA, ND	S	25.15 MW	23.89 AW	52320 AAW	NDBLS	10//99-12//99
	Fargo-Moorhead MSA, ND-MN	S	26.26 MW	26.12 AW	54610 AAW	NDBLS	10//99-12//99
	Grand Forks MSA, ND-MN	S	26.48 MW	25.49 AW	55070 AAW	NDBLS	10//99-12//99
	Ohio	S	32.41 MW	30.05 AW	62490 AAW	OHBLS	10//99-12//99
	Canton-Massillon MSA, OH	S	30.49 MW	32.43 AW	63420 AAW	OHBLS	10//99-12//99
	Cincinnati PMSA, OH-KY-IN	S	29.59 MW	31.76 AW	61540 AAW	OHBLS	10//99-12//99
	Cleveland-Lorain-Elyria PMSA, OH	S	31.91 MW	33.54 AW	66360 AAW	OHBLS	10//99-12//99
	Columbus MSA, OH	S	27.72 MW	31.02 AW	57650 AAW	OHBLS	10//99-12//99
	Dayton-Springfield MSA, OH	S	31.51 MW	33.71 AW	65540 AAW	OHBLS	10//99-12//99
	Hamilton-Middletown PMSA, OH	S	31.14 MW	33.01 AW	64780 AAW	OHBLS	10//99-12//99
	Lima MSA, OH	S	28.99 MW	30.60 AW	60300 AAW	OHBLS	10//99-12//99
	Mansfield MSA, OH	S	31.31 MW	33.16 AW	65130 AAW	OHBLS	10//99-12//99
	Steubenville-Weirton MSA, OH-WV	S	31.09 MW	32.39 AW	64670 AAW	OHBLS	10//99-12//99
	Toledo MSA, OH	S	27.71 MW	30.32 AW	57640 AAW	OHBLS	10//99-12//99
	Youngstown-Warren MSA, OH	S	30.94 MW	32.76 AW	64350 AAW	OHBLS	10//99-12//99
	Oklahoma	S	29.07 MW	28.11 AW	58460 AAW	OKBLS	10//99-12//99
	Enid MSA, OK	S	27.79 MW	28.94 AW	57810 AAW	OKBLS	10//99-12//99
	Lawton MSA, OK	S	24.58 MW	23.84 AW	51130 AAW	OKBLS	10//99-12//99
	Oklahoma City MSA, OK	S	26.83 MW	26.17 AW	55810 AAW	OKBLS	10//99-12//99
	Tulsa MSA, OK	S	31.68 MW	32.69 AW	65890 AAW	OKBLS	10//99-12//99
	Oregon	S	32.86 MW	30.91 AW	64280 AAW	ORBLS	10//99-12//99
	Corvallis MSA, OR	S	27.66 MW	30.39 AW	57530 AAW	ORBLS	10//99-12//99
	Eugene-Springfield MSA, OR	S	30.40 MW	33.18 AW	63240 AAW	ORBLS	10//99-12//99
	Medford-Ashland MSA, OR	S	31.73 MW	33.90 AW	66000 AAW	ORBLS	10//99-12//99
	Portland-Vancouver PMSA, OR-WA	S	31.15 MW	32.90 AW	64790 AAW	ORBLS	10//99-12//99
	Salem PMSA, OR	S	31.42 MW	32.44 AW	65340 AAW	ORBLS	10//99-12//99
	Pennsylvania	S	29.5 MW	27.93 AW	58090 AAW	PABLS	10//99-12//99
	Allentown-Bethlehem-Easton MSA, PA	S	27.53 MW	29.99 AW	57260 AAW	PABLS	10//99-12//99
	Altoona MSA, PA	S	28.40 MW	29.37 AW	59070 AAW	PABLS	10//99-12//99
	Erie MSA, PA	S	27.93 MW	28.46 AW	58090 AAW	PABLS	10//99-12//99
	Harrisburg-Lebanon-Carlisle MSA, PA	S	29.82 MW	32.77 AW	62020 AAW	PABLS	10//99-12//99
	Johnstown MSA, PA	S	30.35 MW	32.56 AW	63140 AAW	PABLS	10//99-12//99
	Lancaster MSA, PA	S	31.84 MW	33.79 AW	66230 AAW	PABLS	10//99-12//99
	Philadelphia PMSA, PA-NJ	S	29.41 MW	31.15 AW	61180 AAW	PABLS	10//99-12//99
	Pittsburgh MSA, PA	S	23.68 MW	23.77 AW	49260 AAW	PABLS	10//99-12//99
	Reading MSA, PA	S	31.79 MW	32.92 AW	66120 AAW	PABLS	10//99-12//99
	Scranton--Wilkes-Barre--Hazleton MSA, PA	S	27.42 MW	30.13 AW	57030 AAW	PABLS	10//99-12//99
	Sharon MSA, PA	S	24.52 MW	26.93 AW	51010 AAW	PABLS	10//99-12//99
	State College MSA, PA	S	27.60 MW	30.06 AW	57410 AAW	PABLS	10//99-12//99
	Williamsport MSA, PA	S	31.69 MW	34.47 AW	65920 AAW	PABLS	10//99-12//99
	York MSA, PA	S	31.36 MW	33.15 AW	65230 AAW	PABLS	10//99-12//99
	Rhode Island	S	32.94 MW	30.73 AW	63910 AAW	RIBLS	10//99-12//99
	Providence-Fall River-Warwick MSA, RI-MA	S	30.89 MW	33.12 AW	64250 AAW	RIBLS	10//99-12//99
	South Carolina	S	30.69 MW	28.79 AW	59890 AAW	SCBLS	10//99-12//99
	Charleston-North Charleston MSA, SC	S	28.35 MW	30.25 AW	58960 AAW	SCBLS	10//99-12//99
	Columbia MSA, SC	S	28.07 MW	29.59 AW	58390 AAW	SCBLS	10//99-12//99
	Florence MSA, SC	S	25.49 MW	25.82 AW	53020 AAW	SCBLS	10//99-12//99
	Greenville-Spartanburg-Anderson MSA, SC	S	30.13 MW	32.82 AW	62660 AAW	SCBLS	10//99-12//99
	Myrtle Beach MSA, SC	S	29.52 MW	31.24 AW	61410 AAW	SCBLS	10//99-12//99
	South Dakota	S	27.71 MW	27.78 AW	57790 AAW	SDBLS	10//99-12//99
	Rapid City MSA, SD	S	31.15 MW	33.42 AW	64780 AAW	SDBLS	10//99-12//99
	Sioux Falls MSA, SD	S	29.71 MW	30.25 AW	61800 AAW	SDBLS	10//99-12//99
	Tennessee	S	31.9 MW	29.48 AW	61320 AAW	TNBLS	10//99-12//99
	Chattanooga MSA, TN-GA	S	31.14 MW	32.60 AW	64780 AAW	TNBLS	10//99-12//99
	Clarksville-Hopkinsville MSA, TN-KY	S	28.50 MW	30.07 AW	59270 AAW	TNBLS	10//99-12//99
	Jackson MSA, TN	S	30.87 MW	32.89 AW	64210 AAW	TNBLS	10//99-12//99
	Johnson City-Kingsport-Bristol MSA, TN-VA	S	31.54 MW	32.21 AW	65600 AAW	TNBLS	10//99-12//99
	Knoxville MSA, TN	S	30.91 MW	33.66 AW	64290 AAW	TNBLS	10//99-12//99

Occupation/Type/Industry	Location	Per	Low	Mid	High	Source	Date
Pharmacist	Memphis MSA, TN-AR-MS	S	30.21 MW	31.48 AW	62830 AAW	MSBLS	10//99-12//99
	Nashville MSA, TN	S	30.26 MW	32.96 AW	62950 AAW	TNBLS	10//99-12//99
	Texas	S	32.55 MW	30.97 AW	64410 AAW	TXBLS	10//99-12//99
	Abilene MSA, TX	S	28.11 MW	31.16 AW	58470 AAW	TXBLS	10//99-12//99
	Amarillo MSA, TX	S	30.76 MW	32.22 AW	63990 AAW	TXBLS	10//99-12//99
	Austin-San Marcos MSA, TX	S	30.47 MW	31.80 AW	63390 AAW	TXBLS	10//99-12//99
	Beaumont-Port Arthur MSA, TX	S	30.07 MW	31.11 AW	62550 AAW	TXBLS	10//99-12//99
	Brazoria PMSA, TX	S	31.47 MW	32.05 AW	65450 AAW	TXBLS	10//99-12//99
	Brownsville-Harlingen-San Benito MSA, TX	S	31.05 MW	32.11 AW	64590 AAW	TXBLS	
	Bryan-College Station MSA, TX	S	31.25 MW	31.07 AW	64990 AAW	TXBLS	
	Corpus Christi MSA, TX	S	31.70 MW	33.92 AW	65940 AAW	TXBLS	10//99-12//99
	Dallas PMSA, TX	S	31.75 MW	33.32 AW	66030 AAW	TXBLS	10//99-12//99
	El Paso MSA, TX	S	32.45 MW	33.40 AW	67500 AAW	TXBLS	
	Fort Worth-Arlington PMSA, TX	S	31.29 MW	33.05 AW	65080 AAW	TXBLS	
	Galveston-Texas City PMSA, TX	S	30.83 MW	32.69 AW	64130 AAW	TXBLS	10//99-12//99
	Houston PMSA, TX	S	31.44 MW	32.79 AW	65400 AAW	TXBLS	10//99-12//99
	Killeen-Temple MSA, TX	S	31.25 MW	32.98 AW	64990 AAW	TXBLS	10//99-12//99
	Laredo MSA, TX	S	31.15 MW	33.10 AW	64790 AAW	TXBLS	10//99-12//99
	Longview-Marshall MSA, TX	S	31.92 MW	33.21 AW	66400 AAW	TXBLS	10//99-12//99
	Lubbock MSA, TX	S	29.14 MW	31.67 AW	60600 AAW	TXBLS	10//99-12//99
	McAllen-Edinburg-Mission MSA, TX	S	32.83 MW	33.58 AW	68280 AAW	TXBLS	10//99-12//99
	Odessa-Midland MSA, TX	S	32.84 MW	35.41 AW	68300 AAW	TXBLS	10//99-12//99
	San Angelo MSA, TX	S	31.21 MW	33.01 AW	64910 AAW	TXBLS	10//99-12//99
	San Antonio MSA, TX	S	29.99 MW	31.22 AW	62390 AAW	TXBLS	10//99-12//99
	Sherman-Denison MSA, TX	S	23.12 MW	28.20 AW	48090 AAW	TXBLS	10//99-12//99
	Texarkana MSA, TX-Texarkana, AR	S	30.46 MW	31.15 AW	63360 AAW	TXBLS	10//99-12//99
	Tyler MSA, TX	S	31.10 MW	32.01 AW	64690 AAW	TXBLS	10//99-12//99
	Victoria MSA, TX	S	28.77 MW	30.66 AW	59830 AAW	TXBLS	10//99-12//99
	Waco MSA, TX	S	28.77 MW	31.35 AW	59840 AAW	TXBLS	10//99-12//99
	Wichita Falls MSA, TX	S	29.89 MW	31.14 AW	62160 AAW	TXBLS	10//99-12//99
	Utah	S	33.23 MW	31.61 AW	65750 AAW	UTBLS	10//99-12//99
	Provo-Orem MSA, UT	S	32.03 MW	33.44 AW	66630 AAW	UTBLS	10//99-12//99
	Salt Lake City-Ogden MSA, UT	S	30.60 MW	32.88 AW	63650 AAW	UTBLS	10//99-12//99
	Vermont	S	33.35 MW	31.58 AW	65680 AAW	VTBLS	10//99-12//99
	Burlington MSA, VT	S	32.01 MW	33.69 AW	66570 AAW	VTBLS	10//99-12//99
	Virginia	S	32.5 MW	30.76 AW	63980 AAW	VABLS	10//99-12//99
	Charlottesville MSA, VA	S	31.68 MW	33.22 AW	65890 AAW	VABLS	10//99-12//99
	Danville MSA, VA	S	31.48 MW	33.29 AW	65480 AAW	VABLS	10//99-12//99
	Lynchburg MSA, VA	S	30.53 MW	32.04 AW	63500 AAW	VABLS	10//99-12//99
	Norfolk-Virginia Beach-Newport News MSA, VA-NC	S	31.97 MW	33.86 AW	66490 AAW	VABLS	10//99-12//99
	Richmond-Petersburg MSA, VA	S	30.26 MW	32.32 AW	62950 AAW	VABLS	10//99-12//99
	Roanoke MSA, VA	S	31.19 MW	32.44 AW	64880 AAW	VABLS	10//99-12//99
	Washington	S	32.59 MW	30.83 AW	64120 AAW	WABLS	10//99-12//99
	Bellingham MSA, WA	S	29.31 MW	32.39 AW	60960 AAW	WABLS	10//99-12//99
	Bremerton PMSA, WA	S	31.56 MW	32.37 AW	65650 AAW	WABLS	10//99-12//99
	Olympia PMSA, WA	S	31.11 MW	31.85 AW	64700 AAW	WABLS	10//99-12//99
	Richland-Kennewick-Pasco MSA, WA	S	30.24 MW	31.91 AW	62900 AAW	WABLS	10//99-12//99
	Seattle-Bellevue-Everett PMSA, WA	S	30.53 MW	32.50 AW	63510 AAW	WABLS	10//99-12//99
	Spokane MSA, WA	S	30.60 MW	32.35 AW	63650 AAW	WABLS	10//99-12//99
	Tacoma PMSA, WA	S	31.17 MW	33.33 AW	64830 AAW	WABLS	10//99-12//99
	Yakima MSA, WA	S	31.91 MW	33.30 AW	66360 AAW	WABLS	10//99-12//99
	West Virginia	S	32.56 MW	31.29 AW	65080 AAW	WVBLS	10//99-12//99
	Charleston MSA, WV	S	32.57 MW	35.22 AW	67740 AAW	WVBLS	10//99-12//99
	Huntington-Ashland MSA, WV-KY-OH	S	30.70 MW	32.17 AW	63850 AAW	WVBLS	10//99-12//99
	Parkersburg-Marietta MSA, WV-OH	S	33.54 MW	33.43 AW	69750 AAW	WVBLS	10//99-12//99
	Wheeling MSA, WV-OH	S	31.31 MW	30.14 AW	65120 AAW	WVBLS	10//99-12//99
	Wisconsin	S	34.88 MW	32.31 AW	67200 AAW	WIBLS	10//99-12//99

AAW	Average annual wage	AOH	Average offered, high	ASH	Average starting, high	H	Hourly	M	Monthly	S	Special: hourly and annual
AE	Average entry wage	AOL	Average offered, low	ASL	Average starting, low	HI	Highest wage paid	MTC	Median total compensation	TQ	Third quartile wage
AEX	Average experienced wage	APH	Average pay, high range	AW	Average wage paid	HR	High end range	MW	Median wage paid	W	Weekly
AO	Average offered	APL	Average pay, low range	FQ	First quartile wage	LR	Low end range	SQ	Second quartile wage	Y	Yearly

Occupation/Type/Industry	Location	Per	Low	Mid	High	Source	Date
Pharmacist	Appleton-Oshkosh-Neenah						
	MSA, WI	S	33.32 MW	35.19 AW	69310 AAW	WIBLS	10//99-12//99
	Eau Claire MSA, WI	S	32.53 MW	34.39 AW	67660 AAW	WIBLS	10//99-12//99
	Green Bay MSA, WI	S	33.55 MW	34.85 AW	69790 AAW	WIBLS	10//99-12//99
	Janesville-Beloit MSA, WI	S	31.80 MW	34.24 AW	66130 AAW	WIBLS	10//99-12//99
	Kenosha PMSA, WI	S	33.36 MW	36.67 AW	69400 AAW	WIBLS	10//99-12//99
	La Crosse MSA, WI-MN	S	31.87 MW	31.89 AW	66290 AAW	WIBLS	10//99-12//99
	Madison MSA, WI	S	31.93 MW	34.72 AW	66410 AAW	WIBLS	10//99-12//99
	Milwaukee-Waukesha PMSA,						
	WI	S	31.36 MW	34.40 AW	65220 AAW	WIBLS	10//99-12//99
	Racine PMSA, WI	S	34.03 MW	36.99 AW	70790 AAW	WIBLS	10//99-12//99
	Sheboygan MSA, WI	S	31.83 MW	33.48 AW	66200 AAW	WIBLS	10//99-12//99
	Wausau MSA, WI	S	30.17 MW	31.82 AW	62760 AAW	WIBLS	10//99-12//99
	Wyoming	S	28.27 MW	28.17 AW	58590 AAW	WYBLS	10//99-12//99
	Casper MSA, WY	S	30.82 MW	32.23 AW	64110 AAW	WYBLS	10//99-12//99
	Cheyenne MSA, WY	S	27.59 MW	27.92 AW	57390 AAW	WYBLS	10//99-12//99
	Puerto Rico	S	16.01 MW	16.47 AW	34260 AAW	PRBLS	10//99-12//99
	Arecibo PMSA, PR	S	15.88 MW	16.39 AW	33020 AAW	PRBLS	10//99-12//99
	Caguas PMSA, PR	S	19.66 MW	18.55 AW	40880 AAW	PRBLS	10//99-12//99
	Mayaguez MSA, PR	S	17.06 MW	16.55 AW	35490 AAW	PRBLS	10//99-12//99
	Ponce MSA, PR	S	17.11 MW	15.71 AW	35600 AAW	PRBLS	10//99-12//99
	San Juan-Bayamon PMSA, PR	S	16.20 MW	15.85 AW	33700 AAW	PRBLS	10//99-12//99
	Virgin Islands	S	25.91 MW	27.12 AW	56410 AAW	VIBLS	10//99-12//99
	Guam	S	32.35 MW	31.41 AW	65330 AAW	GUBLS	10//99-12//99
Chain Store	United States	Y	59761 AE	62285 AW		DRTOP	1998
Chain Store, Female	United States	Y		61392 AW		WOWO2	1998
Chain Store, Male	United States	Y		63564 AW		WOWO2	1998
Female	United States	Y		57460 MW		WOWO1	1999
HMO	United States	Y	56883 AE	65151 AW		DRTOP	1998
Hospital	United States	Y	50410 AE	56302 AW		DRTOP	1998
Hospital	Florida	H	23.92 AE		35.08 HI	BJTAMP	2000
Hospital, Female	United States	Y		56950 AW		WOWO2	1998
Hospital, Male	United States	Y		60950 AW		WOWO2	1998
Independent, Female	United States	Y		53667 AW		WOWO2	1998
Independent, Male	United States	Y		57399 AW		WOWO2	1998
Independent Retailer	United States	Y	49633 AE	56302 AW		DRTOP	1998
Male	United States	Y		63544 MW		WOWO1	1999
Mass Merchant Store	United States	Y	59456 AE	63817 AW		DRTOP	1998
Supermarket	United States	Y	59235 AE	56302 AW		DRTOP	1998
Pharmacy Aide	Alabama	S	7.48 MW	7.58 AW	15770 AAW	ALBLS	10//99-12//99
	Alaska	S	11.61 MW	11.64 AW	24200 AAW	AKBLS	10//99-12//99
	Arizona	S	8.65 MW	8.84 AW	18390 AAW	AZBLS	10//99-12//99
	Arkansas	S	7.5 MW	7.53 AW	15670 AAW	ARBLS	10//99-12//99
	California	S	10.63 MW	10.69 AW	22230 AAW	CABLS	10//99-12//99
	Colorado	S	9.62 MW	9.54 AW	19840 AAW	COBLS	10//99-12//99
	Connecticut	S	9.28 MW	9.53 AW	19820 AAW	CTBLS	10//99-12//99
	Delaware	S	9.29 MW	9.14 AW	19010 AAW	DEBLS	10//99-12//99
	District of Columbia	S	10.27 MW	10.40 AW	21640 AAW	DCBLS	10//99-12//99
	Florida	S	7.89 MW	8.17 AW	17000 AAW	FLBLS	10//99-12//99
	Georgia	S	7.8 MW	8.17 AW	16990 AAW	GABLS	10//99-12//99
	Idaho	S	8.41 MW	8.87 AW	18460 AAW	IDBLS	10//99-12//99
	Illinois	S	9.37 MW	9.56 AW	19890 AAW	ILBLS	10//99-12//99
	Indiana	S	8.39 MW	8.48 AW	17640 AAW	INBLS	10//99-12//99
	Iowa	S	9.25 MW	8.99 AW	18710 AAW	IABLS	10//99-12//99
	Kansas	S	8.02 MW	8.03 AW	16690 AAW	KSBLS	10//99-12//99
	Kentucky	S	8.19 MW	8.41 AW	17490 AAW	KYBLS	10//99-12//99
	Louisiana	S	7 MW	7.18 AW	14930 AAW	LABLS	10//99-12//99
	Maine	S	8.85 MW	9.16 AW	19060 AAW	MEBLS	10//99-12//99
	Maryland	S	9.1 MW	9.17 AW	19080 AAW	MDBLS	10//99-12//99
	Massachusetts	S	10.2 MW	10.16 AW	21130 AAW	MABLS	10//99-12//99
	Michigan	S	8.28 MW	8.52 AW	17730 AAW	MIBLS	10//99-12//99
	Minnesota	S	9.71 MW	9.82 AW	20430 AAW	MNBLS	10//99-12//99
	Mississippi	S	7.23 MW	7.37 AW	15320 AAW	MSBLS	10//99-12//99
	Missouri	S	8.55 MW	8.62 AW	17930 AAW	MOBLS	10//99-12//99
	Montana	S	8.63 MW	8.93 AW	18580 AAW	MTBLS	10//99-12//99
	Nebraska	S	9.15 MW	9.32 AW	19390 AAW	NEBLS	10//99-12//99
	Nevada	S	10.7 MW	10.43 AW	21700 AAW	NVBLS	10//99-12//99
	New Hampshire	S	8.91 MW	9.18 AW	19090 AAW	NHBLS	10//99-12//99
	New Jersey	S	8.98 MW	9.07 AW	18860 AAW	NJBLS	10//99-12//99
	New Mexico	S	8.4 MW	8.56 AW	17810 AAW	NMBLS	10//99-12//99
	New York	S	8.21 MW	9.37 AW	19480 AAW	NYBLS	10//99-12//99
	North Carolina	S	8.79 MW	9.36 AW	19470 AAW	NCBLS	10//99-12//99

AAW	Average annual wage	AOH	Average offered, high	ASH	Average starting, high	H	Hourly	M	Monthly	S	Special: hourly and annual
AE	Average entry wage	AOL	Average offered, low	ASL	Average starting, low	HI	Highest wage paid	MTC	Median total compensation	TQ	Third quartile wage
AEX	Average experienced wage	APH	Average pay, high range	AW	Average wage paid	HR	High end range	MW	Median wage paid	W	Weekly
AO	Average offered	APL	Average pay, low range	FQ	First quartile wage	LR	Low end range	SQ	Second quartile wage	Y	Yearly

Occupation/Type/Industry	Location	Per	Low	Mid	High	Source	Date
Pharmacy Aide	North Dakota	S	6.83 MW	7.72 AW	16060 AAW	NDBLS	10//99-12//99
	Ohio	S	8.79 MW	9.01 AW	18740 AAW	OHBLS	10//99-12//99
	Oklahoma	S	7.25 MW	7.37 AW	15320 AAW	OKBLS	10//99-12//99
	Oregon	S	11.24 MW	11.18 AW	23250 AAW	ORBLS	10//99-12//99
	Pennsylvania	S	9.53 MW	9.41 AW	19580 AAW	PABLS	10//99-12//99
	Rhode Island	S	7.61 MW	8.71 AW	18120 AAW	RIBLS	10//99-12//99
	South Carolina	S	7.49 MW	7.97 AW	16570 AAW	SCBLS	10//99-12//99
	South Dakota	S	7.57 MW	7.63 AW	15860 AAW	SDBLS	10//99-12//99
	Tennessee	S	8.39 MW	8.63 AW	17960 AAW	TNBLS	10//99-12//99
	Texas	S	7.33 MW	7.70 AW	16020 AAW	TXBLS	10//99-12//99
	Utah	S	8.82 MW	8.95 AW	18610 AAW	UTBLS	10//99-12//99
	Vermont	S	7.57 MW	7.99 AW	16610 AAW	VTBLS	10//99-12//99
	Virginia	S	8.15 MW	8.57 AW	17830 AAW	VABLS	10//99-12//99
	Washington	S	10.35 MW	10.53 AW	21900 AAW	WABLS	10//99-12//99
	West Virginia	S	7.73 MW	8.08 AW	16800 AAW	WVBLS	10//99-12//99
	Wisconsin	S	9.52 MW	9.46 AW	19680 AAW	WIBLS	10//99-12//99
	Wyoming	S	9.67 MW	9.44 AW	19630 AAW	WYBLS	10//99-12//99
	Puerto Rico	S	6.18 MW	6.38 AW	13270 AAW	PRBLS	10//99-12//99
	Virgin Islands	S	9.08 MW	8.83 AW	18380 AAW	VIBLS	10//99-12//99
Pharmacy Technician	Alabama	S	7.79 MW	8.18 AW	17020 AAW	ALBLS	10//99-12//99
	Alaska	S	12.86 MW	13.45 AW	27980 AAW	AKBLS	10//99-12//99
	Arizona	S	9.24 MW	9.50 AW	19750 AAW	AZBLS	10//99-12//99
	Arkansas	S	7.96 MW	8.42 AW	17510 AAW	ARBLS	10//99-12//99
	California	S	12.65 MW	12.83 AW	26680 AAW	CABLS	10//99-12//99
	Colorado	S	11.24 MW	11.04 AW	22960 AAW	COBLS	10//99-12//99
	Connecticut	S	9.43 MW	10.12 AW	21060 AAW	CTBLS	10//99-12//99
	Delaware	S	7.43 MW	7.91 AW	16450 AAW	DEBLS	10//99-12//99
	District of Columbia	S	10.4 MW	10.78 AW	22420 AAW	DCBLS	10//99-12//99
	Florida	S	8.7 MW	9.21 AW	19160 AAW	FLBLS	10//99-12//99
	Georgia	S	8.3 MW	8.59 AW	17860 AAW	GABLS	10//99-12//99
	Hawaii	S	11.93 MW	11.89 AW	24740 AAW	HIBLS	10//99-12//99
	Idaho	S	9.9 MW	9.95 AW	20690 AAW	IDBLS	10//99-12//99
	Illinois	S	8.86 MW	9.41 AW	19580 AAW	ILBLS	10//99-12//99
	Indiana	S	8.83 MW	8.94 AW	18590 AAW	INBLS	10//99-12//99
	Iowa	S	8.88 MW	9.38 AW	19520 AAW	IABLS	10//99-12//99
	Kansas	S	8.68 MW	9.10 AW	18940 AAW	KSBLS	10//99-12//99
	Kentucky	S	8.68 MW	9.45 AW	19650 AAW	KYBLS	10//99-12//99
	Louisiana	S	7.67 MW	8.08 AW	16810 AAW	LABLS	10//99-12//99
	Maine	S	8.16 MW	8.68 AW	18050 AAW	MEBLS	10//99-12//99
	Maryland	S	10.11 MW	10.13 AW	21080 AAW	MDBLS	10//99-12//99
	Massachusetts	S	8.76 MW	9.23 AW	19190 AAW	MABLS	10//99-12//99
	Michigan	S	9.25 MW	9.40 AW	19550 AAW	MIBLS	10//99-12//99
	Minnesota	S	9.74 MW	10.01 AW	20820 AAW	MNBLS	10//99-12//99
	Mississippi	S	8.16 MW	8.54 AW	17760 AAW	MSBLS	10//99-12//99
	Missouri	S	8.46 MW	9.29 AW	19320 AAW	MOBLS	10//99-12//99
	Montana	S	9.48 MW	9.61 AW	19990 AAW	MTBLS	10//99-12//99
	Nebraska	S	9.08 MW	9.19 AW	19120 AAW	NEBLS	10//99-12//99
	Nevada	S	11.06 MW	11.09 AW	23070 AAW	NVBLS	10//99-12//99
	New Hampshire	S	9.1 MW	9.11 AW	18940 AAW	NHBLS	10//99-12//99
	New Jersey	S	9.79 MW	10.14 AW	21090 AAW	NJBLS	10//99-12//99
	New Mexico	S	8.86 MW	9.09 AW	18900 AAW	NMBLS	10//99-12//99
	New York	S	9.63 MW	10.00 AW	20800 AAW	NYBLS	10//99-12//99
	North Carolina	S	8.1 MW	8.39 AW	17440 AAW	NCBLS	10//99-12//99
	North Dakota	S	9.16 MW	9.02 AW	18760 AAW	NDBLS	10//99-12//99
	Ohio	S	8.77 MW	9.28 AW	19300 AAW	OHBLS	10//99-12//99
	Oklahoma	S	8.3 MW	8.78 AW	18250 AAW	OKBLS	10//99-12//99
	Oregon	S	11.23 MW	10.93 AW	22730 AAW	ORBLS	10//99-12//99
	Pennsylvania	S	8.17 MW	8.56 AW	17800 AAW	PABLS	10//99-12//99
	Rhode Island	S	8.65 MW	9.05 AW	18820 AAW	RIBLS	10//99-12//99
	South Carolina	S	8.26 MW	9.15 AW	19040 AAW	SCBLS	10//99-12//99
	South Dakota	S	10.14 MW	10.15 AW	21100 AAW	SDBLS	10//99-12//99
	Tennessee	S	8.2 MW	8.61 AW	17900 AAW	TNBLS	10//99-12//99
	Texas	S	8.55 MW	8.87 AW	18440 AAW	TXBLS	10//99-12//99
	Utah	S	10.58 MW	11.03 AW	22950 AAW	UTBLS	10//99-12//99
	Vermont	S	9.38 MW	9.80 AW	20390 AAW	VTBLS	10//99-12//99
	Virginia	S	8.56 MW	9.14 AW	19010 AAW	VABLS	10//99-12//99
	Washington	S	12.05 MW	11.92 AW	24780 AAW	WABLS	10//99-12//99
	West Virginia	S	8.11 MW	8.73 AW	18150 AAW	WVBLS	10//99-12//99
	Wisconsin	S	8.95 MW	9.20 AW	19130 AAW	WIBLS	10//99-12//99
	Wyoming	S	9.91 MW	9.92 AW	20630 AAW	WYBLS	10//99-12//99
	Puerto Rico	S	7.69 MW	8.07 AW	16780 AAW	PRBLS	10//99-12//99
	Guam	S	11.11 MW	11.14 AW	23180 AAW	GUBLS	10//99-12//99

AAW Average annual wage	**AOH** Average offered, high	**ASH** Average starting, high	**H** Hourly	**M** Monthly	**S** Special: hourly and annual
AE Average entry wage	**AOL** Average offered, low	**ASL** Average starting, low	**HI** Highest wage paid	**MTC** Median total compensation	**TQ** Third quartile wage
AEX Average experienced wage	**APH** Average pay, high range	**AW** Average wage paid	**HR** High end range	**MW** Median wage paid	**W** Weekly
AO Average offered	**APL** Average pay, low range	**FQ** First quartile wage	**LR** Low end range	**SQ** Second quartile wage	**Y** Yearly

Occupation/Type/Industry	Location	Per	Low	Mid	High	Source	Date
Philosophy and Religion Teacher							
Postsecondary	Alabama	Y		33630 AAW		ALBLS	10//99-12//99
Postsecondary	Birmingham MSA, AL	Y		32260 AAW		ALBLS	10//99-12//99
Postsecondary	Arizona	Y		35120 AAW		AZBLS	10//99-12//99
Postsecondary	California	Y		56520 AAW		CABLS	10//99-12//99
Postsecondary	Los Angeles-Long Beach PMSA, CA	Y		51850 AAW		CABLS	10//99-12//99
Postsecondary	Orange County PMSA, CA	Y		63750 AAW		CABLS	10//99-12//99
Postsecondary	Riverside-San Bernardino PMSA, CA	Y		53580 AAW		CABLS	10//99-12//99
Postsecondary	Sacramento PMSA, CA	Y		46510 AAW		CABLS	10//99-12//99
Postsecondary	San Francisco PMSA, CA	Y		63700 AAW		CABLS	10//99-12//99
Postsecondary	Colorado	Y		49800 AAW		COBLS	10//99-12//99
Postsecondary	Denver PMSA, CO	Y		49190 AAW		COBLS	10//99-12//99
Postsecondary	Connecticut	Y		54920 AAW		CTBLS	10//99-12//99
Postsecondary	District of Columbia	Y		48590 AAW		DCBLS	10//99-12//99
Postsecondary	Washington PMSA, DC-MD-VA-WV	Y		50240 AAW		DCBLS	10//99-12//99
Postsecondary	Florida	Y		51110 AAW		FLBLS	10//99-12//99
Postsecondary	Miami PMSA, FL	Y		57360 AAW		FLBLS	10//99-12//99
Postsecondary	Tampa-St. Petersburg-Clearwater MSA, FL	Y		63210 AAW		FLBLS	10//99-12//99
Postsecondary	West Palm Beach-Boca Raton MSA, FL	Y		37870 AAW		FLBLS	10//99-12//99
Postsecondary	Georgia	Y		45340 AAW		GABLS	10//99-12//99
Postsecondary	Atlanta MSA, GA	Y		45300 AAW		GABLS	10//99-12//99
Postsecondary	Illinois	Y		47250 AAW		ILBLS	10//99-12//99
Postsecondary	Chicago PMSA, IL	Y		52780 AAW		ILBLS	10//99-12//99
Postsecondary	Indiana	Y		45580 AAW		INBLS	10//99-12//99
Postsecondary	Fort Wayne MSA, IN	Y		59460 AAW		INBLS	10//99-12//99
Postsecondary	Gary PMSA, IN	Y		42030 AAW		INBLS	10//99-12//99
Postsecondary	Iowa	Y		46870 AAW		IABLS	10//99-12//99
Postsecondary	Kansas	Y		35590 AAW		KSBLS	10//99-12//99
Postsecondary	Kentucky	Y		45950 AAW		KYBLS	10//99-12//99
Postsecondary	Louisiana	Y		66540 AAW		LABLS	10//99-12//99
Postsecondary	Maryland	Y		55880 AAW		MDBLS	10//99-12//99
Postsecondary	Baltimore PMSA, MD	Y		54880 AAW		MDBLS	10//99-12//99
Postsecondary	Massachusetts	Y		49930 AAW		MABLS	10//99-12//99
Postsecondary	Boston PMSA, MA-NH	Y		48240 AAW		MABLS	10//99-12//99
Postsecondary	Springfield MSA, MA	Y		63030 AAW		MABLS	10//99-12//99
Postsecondary	Worcester PMSA, MA-CT	Y		49860 AAW		MABLS	10//99-12//99
Postsecondary	Michigan	Y		47370 AAW		MIBLS	10//99-12//99
Postsecondary	Detroit PMSA, MI	Y		44170 AAW		MIBLS	10//99-12//99
Postsecondary	Grand Rapids-Muskegon-Holland MSA, MI	Y		38500 AAW		MIBLS	10//99-12//99
Postsecondary	Kalamazoo-Battle Creek MSA, MI	Y		56690 AAW		MIBLS	10//99-12//99
Postsecondary	Minnesota	Y		47450 AAW		MNBLS	10//99-12//99
Postsecondary	Minneapolis-St. Paul MSA, MN-WI	Y		46290 AAW		MNBLS	10//99-12//99
Postsecondary	St. Cloud MSA, MN	Y		48130 AAW		MNBLS	10//99-12//99
Postsecondary	Mississippi	Y		41450 AAW		MSBLS	10//99-12//99
Postsecondary	Jackson MSA, MS	Y		38820 AAW		MSBLS	10//99-12//99
Postsecondary	Missouri	Y		42390 AAW		MOBLS	10//99-12//99
Postsecondary	Montana	Y		69930 AAW		MTBLS	10//99-12//99
Postsecondary	Nebraska	Y		43340 AAW		NEBLS	10//99-12//99
Postsecondary	Nevada	Y		39710 AAW		NVBLS	10//99-12//99
Postsecondary	New Hampshire	Y		50900 AAW		NHBLS	10//99-12//99
Postsecondary	New Jersey	Y		59240 AAW		NJBLS	10//99-12//99
Postsecondary	Bergen-Passaic PMSA, NJ	Y		60540 AAW		NJBLS	10//99-12//99
Postsecondary	Newark PMSA, NJ	Y		55890 AAW		NJBLS	10//99-12//99
Postsecondary	New Mexico	Y		46420 AAW		NMBLS	10//99-12//99
Postsecondary	New York	Y		49760 AAW		NYBLS	10//99-12//99
Postsecondary	New York PMSA, NY	Y		49880 AAW		NYBLS	10//99-12//99
Postsecondary	North Carolina	Y		44720 AAW		NCBLS	10//99-12//99
Postsecondary	Charlotte-Gastonia-Rock Hill MSA, NC-SC	Y		49170 AAW		NCBLS	10//99-12//99
Postsecondary	Greensboro--Winston-Salem--High Point MSA, NC	Y		45090 AAW		NCBLS	10//99-12//99
Postsecondary	Raleigh-Durham-Chapel Hill MSA, NC	Y		45200 AAW		NCBLS	10//99-12//99
Postsecondary	Ohio	Y		43700 AAW		OHBLS	10//99-12//99

AAW Average annual wage	**AOH** Average offered, high	**ASH** Average starting, high	**H** Hourly	**M** Monthly	**S** Special: hourly and annual
AE Average entry wage	**AOL** Average offered, low	**ASL** Average starting, low	**HI** Highest wage paid	**MTC** Median total compensation	**TQ** Third quartile wage
AEX Average experienced wage	**APH** Average pay, high range	**AW** Average wage paid	**HR** High end range	**MW** Median wage paid	**W** Weekly
AO Average offered	**APL** Average pay, low range	**FQ** First quartile wage	**LR** Low end range	**SQ** Second quartile wage	**Y** Yearly

Occupation/Type/Industry	Location	Per	Low	Mid	High	Source	Date
Philosophy and Religion Teacher							
Postsecondary	Canton-Massillon MSA, OH	Y		41890 AAW		OHBLS	10//99-12//99
Postsecondary	Cincinnati PMSA, OH-KY-IN	Y		41480 AAW		OHBLS	10//99-12//99
Postsecondary	Cleveland-Lorain-Elyria PMSA, OH	Y		45560 AAW		OHBLS	10//99-12//99
Postsecondary	Columbus MSA, OH	Y		41220 AAW		OHBLS	10//99-12//99
Postsecondary	Dayton-Springfield MSA, OH	Y		42770 AAW		OHBLS	10//99-12//99
Postsecondary	Youngstown-Warren MSA, OH	Y		51350 AAW		OHBLS	10//99-12//99
Postsecondary	Oklahoma	Y		44010 AAW		OKBLS	10//99-12//99
Postsecondary	Oklahoma City MSA, OK	Y		42590 AAW		OKBLS	10//99-12//99
Postsecondary	Tulsa MSA, OK	Y		50300 AAW		OKBLS	10//99-12//99
Postsecondary	Oregon	Y		42310 AAW		ORBLS	10//99-12//99
Postsecondary	Portland-Vancouver PMSA, OR-WA	Y		44860 AAW		ORBLS	10//99-12//99
Postsecondary	Pennsylvania	Y		53670 AAW		PABLS	10//99-12//99
Postsecondary	Allentown-Bethlehem-Easton MSA, PA	Y		47240 AAW		PABLS	10//99-12//99
Postsecondary	Philadelphia PMSA, PA-NJ	Y		58180 AAW		PABLS	10//99-12//99
Postsecondary	Pittsburgh MSA, PA	Y		55750 AAW		PABLS	10//99-12//99
Postsecondary	Reading MSA, PA	Y		44390 AAW		PABLS	10//99-12//99
Postsecondary	Scranton--Wilkes-Barre--Hazleton MSA, PA	Y		43150 AAW		PABLS	10//99-12//99
Postsecondary	Rhode Island	Y		68330 AAW		RIBLS	10//99-12//99
Postsecondary	Providence-Fall River-Warwick MSA, RI-MA	Y		69950 AAW		RIBLS	10//99-12//99
Postsecondary	South Carolina	Y		46640 AAW		SCBLS	10//99-12//99
Postsecondary	Greenville-Spartanburg-Anderson MSA, SC	Y		46780 AAW		SCBLS	10//99-12//99
Postsecondary	Tennessee	Y		43060 AAW		TNBLS	10//99-12//99
Postsecondary	Johnson City-Kingsport-Bristol MSA, TN-VA	Y		41050 AAW		TNBLS	10//99-12//99
Postsecondary	Memphis MSA, TN-AR-MS	Y		47620 AAW		MSBLS	10//99-12//99
Postsecondary	Nashville MSA, TN	Y		46910 AAW		TNBLS	10//99-12//99
Postsecondary	Texas	Y		47190 AAW		TXBLS	10//99-12//99
Postsecondary	Fort Worth-Arlington PMSA, TX	Y		46020 AAW		TXBLS	10//99-12//99
Postsecondary	Houston PMSA, TX	Y		51380 AAW		TXBLS	10//99-12//99
Postsecondary	San Antonio MSA, TX	Y		48510 AAW		TXBLS	10//99-12//99
Postsecondary	Vermont	Y		54890 AAW		VTBLS	10//99-12//99
Postsecondary	Virginia	Y		44850 AAW		VABLS	10//99-12//99
Postsecondary	Norfolk-Virginia Beach-Newport News MSA, VA-NC	Y		47160 AAW		VABLS	10//99-12//99
Postsecondary	Washington	Y		43950 AAW		WABLS	10//99-12//99
Postsecondary	Seattle-Bellevue-Everett PMSA, WA	Y		45050 AAW		WABLS	10//99-12//99
Postsecondary	Tacoma PMSA, WA	Y		47180 AAW		WABLS	10//99-12//99
Postsecondary	West Virginia	Y		52210 AAW		WVBLS	10//99-12//99
Postsecondary	Wisconsin	Y		45720 AAW		WIBLS	10//99-12//99
Postsecondary	Milwaukee-Waukesha PMSA, WI	Y		47910 AAW		WIBLS	10//99-12//99
Postsecondary	Puerto Rico	Y		35340 AAW		PRBLS	10//99-12//99
Postsecondary	San Juan-Bayamon PMSA, PR	Y		38260 AAW		PRBLS	10//99-12//99
Phlebotomist							
Medical Laboratory	Atlantic	H	7.00 AE	8.30 AW	14.70 APH	LABMED2	1998
Medical Laboratory	East North Central	H	7.80 AE	9.10 AW	15.00 APH	LABMED2	1998
Medical Laboratory	Far West	H	8.50 AE	10.00 AW	16.10 APH	LABMED2	1998
Medical Laboratory	Northeast	H	8.10 AE	10.00 AW	15.50 APH	LABMED2	1998
Medical Laboratory	West North Central	H	7.20 AE	8.50 AW	14.40 APH	LABMED2	1998
Medical Laboratory	West South Central	H	6.50 AE	7.90 AW	14.30 APH	LABMED2	1998
Photographer							
	United States	H		16.94 AW		NCS98	1998
	Alabama	S	8.79 MW	10.25 AW	21320 AAW	ALBLS	10//99-12//99
	Auburn-Opelika MSA, AL	S	6.24 MW	6.05 AW	12990 AAW	ALBLS	10//99-12//99
	Birmingham MSA, AL	S	11.71 MW	9.68 AW	24350 AAW	ALBLS	10//99-12//99
	Decatur MSA, AL	S	13.40 MW	13.40 AW	27870 AAW	ALBLS	10//99-12//99
	Florence MSA, AL	S	9.38 MW	8.74 AW	19520 AAW	ALBLS	10//99-12//99
	Huntsville MSA, AL	S	11.59 MW	10.71 AW	24100 AAW	ALBLS	10//99-12//99
	Mobile MSA, AL	S	9.72 MW	8.34 AW	20210 AAW	ALBLS	10//99-12//99
	Montgomery MSA, AL	S	10.71 MW	8.32 AW	22280 AAW	ALBLS	10//99-12//99
	Tuscaloosa MSA, AL	S	7.33 MW	6.92 AW	15250 AAW	ALBLS	10//99-12//99
	Alaska	S	12.25 MW	13.04 AW	27110 AAW	AKBLS	10//99-12//99

AAW	Average annual wage	AOH	Average offered, high	ASH	Average starting, high	H	Hourly	M	Monthly	S	Special: hourly and annual
AE	Average entry wage	AOL	Average offered, low	ASL	Average starting, low	HI	Highest wage paid	MTC	Median total compensation	TQ	Third quartile wage
AEX	Average experienced wage	APH	Average pay, high range	AW	Average wage paid	HR	High end range	MW	Median wage paid	W	Weekly
AO	Average offered	APL	Average pay, low range	FQ	First quartile wage	LR	Low end range	SQ	Second quartile wage	Y	Yearly

Occupation/Type/Industry	Location	Per	Low	Mid	High	Source	Date
Photographer	Anchorage MSA, AK	S	13.06 MW	12.47 AW	27160 AAW	AKBLS	10//99-12//99
	Arizona	S	10.26 MW	12.79 AW	26610 AAW	AZBLS	10//99-12//99
	Phoenix-Mesa MSA, AZ	S	13.18 MW	10.50 AW	27410 AAW	AZBLS	10//99-12//99
	Tucson MSA, AZ	S	12.03 MW	9.99 AW	25030 AAW	AZBLS	10//99-12//99
	Arkansas	S	7.74 MW	8.60 AW	17890 AAW	ARBLS	10//99-12//99
	Fayetteville-Springdale-Rogers MSA, AR	S	10.50 MW	8.15 AW	21840 AAW	ARBLS	10//99-12//99
	Fort Smith MSA, AR-OK	S	8.60 MW	8.91 AW	17880 AAW	ARBLS	10//99-12//99
	Little Rock-North Little Rock MSA, AR	S	8.37 MW	6.86 AW	17410 AAW	ARBLS	10//99-12//99
	California	S	10.45 MW	14.72 AW	30620 AAW	CABLS	10//99-12//99
	Fresno MSA, CA	S	11.89 MW	8.85 AW	24740 AAW	CABLS	10//99-12//99
	Los Angeles-Long Beach PMSA, CA	S	22.74 MW	17.62 AW	47300 AAW	CABLS	10//99-12//99
	Modesto MSA, CA	S	8.32 MW	7.92 AW	17310 AAW	CABLS	10//99-12//99
	Oakland PMSA, CA	S	9.93 MW	8.08 AW	20650 AAW	CABLS	10//99-12//99
	Orange County PMSA, CA	S	15.22 MW	12.23 AW	31650 AAW	CABLS	10//99-12//99
	Riverside-San Bernardino PMSA, CA	S	11.64 MW	9.35 AW	24210 AAW	CABLS	10//99-12//99
	Sacramento PMSA, CA	S	11.06 MW	9.17 AW	23010 AAW	CABLS	10//99-12//99
	Salinas MSA, CA	S	11.41 MW	10.74 AW	23740 AAW	CABLS	10//99-12//99
	San Diego MSA, CA	S	11.21 MW	9.72 AW	23330 AAW	CABLS	10//99-12//99
	San Francisco PMSA, CA	S	13.87 MW	13.94 AW	28840 AAW	CABLS	10//99-12//99
	San Jose PMSA, CA	S	13.62 MW	9.69 AW	28330 AAW	CABLS	10//99-12//99
	Santa Barbara-Santa Maria-Lompoc MSA, CA	S	12.55 MW	9.82 AW	26110 AAW	CABLS	10//99-12//99
	Santa Cruz-Watsonville PMSA, CA	S	13.85 MW	12.53 AW	28810 AAW	CABLS	10//99-12//99
	Santa Rosa PMSA, CA	S	9.76 MW	8.85 AW	20310 AAW	CABLS	10//99-12//99
	Stockton-Lodi MSA, CA	S	10.36 MW	8.14 AW	21550 AAW	CABLS	10//99-12//99
	Vallejo-Fairfield-Napa PMSA, CA	S	10.74 MW	10.07 AW	22330 AAW	CABLS	10//99-12//99
	Ventura PMSA, CA	S	11.20 MW	10.19 AW	23300 AAW	CABLS	10//99-12//99
	Yolo PMSA, CA	S	16.52 MW	16.84 AW	34370 AAW	CABLS	10//99-12//99
	Colorado	S	8.76 MW	10.76 AW	22380 AAW	COBLS	10//99-12//99
	Colorado Springs MSA, CO	S	9.31 MW	8.75 AW	19360 AAW	COBLS	10//99-12//99
	Denver PMSA, CO	S	11.12 MW	9.08 AW	23120 AAW	COBLS	10//99-12//99
	Fort Collins-Loveland MSA, CO	S	11.30 MW	11.30 AW	23500 AAW	COBLS	10//99-12//99
	Connecticut	S	11.44 MW	13.89 AW	28880 AAW	CTBLS	10//99-12//99
	Bridgeport PMSA, CT	S	13.16 MW	12.16 AW	27370 AAW	CTBLS	10//99-12//99
	Danbury PMSA, CT	S	13.40 MW	8.98 AW	27870 AAW	CTBLS	10//99-12//99
	Hartford MSA, CT	S	13.59 MW	11.69 AW	28270 AAW	CTBLS	10//99-12//99
	New Haven-Meriden PMSA, CT	S	15.30 MW	15.06 AW	31830 AAW	CTBLS	10//99-12//99
	New London-Norwich MSA, CT-RI	S	12.78 MW	8.64 AW	26570 AAW	CTBLS	10//99-12//99
	Stamford-Norwalk PMSA, CT	S	18.37 MW	16.72 AW	38210 AAW	CTBLS	10//99-12//99
	Waterbury PMSA, CT	S	10.20 MW	8.20 AW	21220 AAW	CTBLS	10//99-12//99
	Delaware	S	14.24 MW	15.34 AW	31910 AAW	DEBLS	10//99-12//99
	Dover MSA, DE	S	11.52 MW	9.80 AW	23960 AAW	DEBLS	10//99-12//99
	Wilmington-Newark PMSA, DE-MD	S	20.57 MW	22.76 AW	42800 AAW	DEBLS	10//99-12//99
	District of Columbia	S	14.21 MW	16.79 AW	34930 AAW	DCBLS	10//99-12//99
	Washington PMSA, DC-MD-VA-WV	S	13.67 MW	11.38 AW	28430 AAW	DCBLS	10//99-12//99
	Florida	S	10.38 MW	11.91 AW	24770 AAW	FLBLS	10//99-12//99
	Daytona Beach MSA, FL	S	11.42 MW	11.00 AW	23760 AAW	FLBLS	10//99-12//99
	Fort Lauderdale PMSA, FL	S	11.11 MW	10.33 AW	23100 AAW	FLBLS	10//99-12//99
	Fort Myers-Cape Coral MSA, FL	S	8.64 MW	8.65 AW	17960 AAW	FLBLS	10//99-12//99
	Fort Walton Beach MSA, FL	S	8.15 MW	7.59 AW	16950 AAW	FLBLS	10//99-12//99
	Gainesville MSA, FL	S	10.12 MW	8.99 AW	21050 AAW	FLBLS	10//99-12//99
	Jacksonville MSA, FL	S	11.92 MW	10.89 AW	24800 AAW	FLBLS	10//99-12//99
	Lakeland-Winter Haven MSA, FL	S	10.10 MW	8.32 AW	21000 AAW	FLBLS	10//99-12//99
	Melbourne-Titusville-Palm Bay MSA, FL	S	11.41 MW	8.57 AW	23730 AAW	FLBLS	10//99-12//99
	Miami PMSA, FL	S	15.54 MW	14.11 AW	32330 AAW	FLBLS	10//99-12//99
	Ocala MSA, FL	S	10.44 MW	10.77 AW	21710 AAW	FLBLS	10//99-12//99
	Orlando MSA, FL	S	10.96 MW	9.73 AW	22790 AAW	FLBLS	10//99-12//99
	Pensacola MSA, FL	S	10.35 MW	8.25 AW	21520 AAW	FLBLS	10//99-12//99

AAW	Average annual wage	AOH	Average offered, high	ASH	Average starting, high	H	Hourly	M	Monthly	S	Special: hourly and annual
AE	Average entry wage	AOL	Average offered, low	ASL	Average starting, low	HI	Highest wage paid	MTC	Median total compensation	TQ	Third quartile wage
AEX	Average experienced wage	APH	Average pay, high range	AW	Average wage paid	HR	High end range	MW	Median wage paid	W	Weekly
AO	Average offered	APL	Average pay, low range	FQ	First quartile wage	LR	Low end range	SQ	Second quartile wage	Y	Yearly

Occupation/Type/Industry	Location	Per	Low	Mid	High	Source	Date
Photographer	Sarasota-Bradenton MSA, FL	S	10.69 MW	9.52 AW	22240 AAW	FLBLS	10//99-12//99
	Tallahassee MSA, FL	S	12.66 MW	10.36 AW	26330 AAW	FLBLS	10//99-12//99
	Tampa-St. Petersburg-Clearwater MSA, FL	S	12.14 MW	12.05 AW	25240 AAW	FLBLS	10//99-12//99
	West Palm Beach-Boca Raton MSA, FL	S	14.10 MW	11.53 AW	29330 AAW	FLBLS	10//99-12//99
	Georgia	S	12.08 MW	11.86 AW	24670 AAW	GABLS	10//99-12//99
	Atlanta MSA, GA	S	12.34 MW	11.55 AW	25660 AAW	GABLS	10//99-12//99
	Augusta-Aiken MSA, GA-SC	S	11.59 MW	10.80 AW	24100 AAW	GABLS	10//99-12//99
	Columbus MSA, GA-AL	S	9.71 MW	9.04 AW	20200 AAW	GABLS	10//99-12//99
	Savannah MSA, GA	S	12.18 MW	11.42 AW	25330 AAW	GABLS	10//99-12//99
	Hawaii	S	9.03 MW	11.13 AW	23160 AAW	HIBLS	10//99-12//99
	Honolulu MSA, HI	S	11.05 MW	8.48 AW	22980 AAW	HIBLS	10//99-12//99
	Idaho	S	8.93 MW	10.52 AW	21880 AAW	IDBLS	10//99-12//99
	Boise City MSA, ID	S	12.73 MW	9.67 AW	26470 AAW	IDBLS	10//99-12//99
	Illinois	S	12.96 MW	13.16 AW	27360 AAW	ILBLS	10//99-12//99
	Bloomington-Normal MSA, IL	S	13.19 MW	12.75 AW	27430 AAW	ILBLS	10//99-12//99
	Chicago PMSA, IL	S	13.38 MW	13.19 AW	27820 AAW	ILBLS	10//99-12//99
	Rockford MSA, IL	S	12.95 MW	11.67 AW	26940 AAW	ILBLS	10//99-12//99
	Indiana	S	8.46 MW	9.79 AW	20370 AAW	INBLS	10//99-12//99
	Elkhart-Goshen MSA, IN	S	10.71 MW	10.79 AW	22270 AAW	INBLS	10//99-12//99
	Evansville-Henderson MSA, IN-KY	S	12.19 MW	10.89 AW	25360 AAW	INBLS	10//99-12//99
	Fort Wayne MSA, IN	S	10.59 MW	9.60 AW	22030 AAW	INBLS	10//99-12//99
	Gary PMSA, IN	S	8.10 MW	6.71 AW	16840 AAW	INBLS	10//99-12//99
	Indianapolis MSA, IN	S	11.11 MW	10.14 AW	23110 AAW	INBLS	10//99-12//99
	Lafayette MSA, IN	S	11.61 MW	9.19 AW	24150 AAW	INBLS	10//99-12//99
	South Bend MSA, IN	S	13.71 MW	10.44 AW	28510 AAW	INBLS	10//99-12//99
	Terre Haute MSA, IN	S	10.28 MW	8.25 AW	21370 AAW	INBLS	10//99-12//99
	Iowa	S	8.95 MW	10.73 AW	22320 AAW	IABLS	10//99-12//99
	Cedar Rapids MSA, IA	S	13.23 MW	11.89 AW	27520 AAW	IABLS	10//99-12//99
	Davenport-Moline-Rock Island MSA, IA-IL	S	10.56 MW	10.15 AW	21970 AAW	IABLS	10//99-12//99
	Des Moines MSA, IA	S	12.19 MW	10.93 AW	25360 AAW	IABLS	10//99-12//99
	Sioux City MSA, IA-NE	S	12.77 MW	11.03 AW	26560 AAW	IABLS	10//99-12//99
	Kansas	S	9.35 MW	9.94 AW	20680 AAW	KSBLS	10//99-12//99
	Topeka MSA, KS	S	9.45 MW	7.88 AW	19660 AAW	KSBLS	10//99-12//99
	Wichita MSA, KS	S	10.04 MW	9.80 AW	20880 AAW	KSBLS	10//99-12//99
	Kentucky	S	10.94 MW	11.95 AW	24860 AAW	KYBLS	10//99-12//99
	Lexington MSA, KY	S	12.58 MW	12.29 AW	26160 AAW	KYBLS	10//99-12//99
	Louisville MSA, KY-IN	S	12.67 MW	11.52 AW	26350 AAW	KYBLS	10//99-12//99
	Owensboro MSA, KY	S	8.04 MW	6.50 AW	16720 AAW	KYBLS	10//99-12//99
	Louisiana	S	8.4 MW	10.28 AW	21380 AAW	LABLS	10//99-12//99
	Baton Rouge MSA, LA	S	11.55 MW	8.52 AW	24020 AAW	LABLS	10//99-12//99
	Lafayette MSA, LA	S	8.72 MW	7.14 AW	18140 AAW	LABLS	10//99-12//99
	Monroe MSA, LA	S	8.74 MW	8.71 AW	18170 AAW	LABLS	10//99-12//99
	New Orleans MSA, LA	S	10.43 MW	8.54 AW	21700 AAW	LABLS	10//99-12//99
	Shreveport-Bossier City MSA, LA	S	10.66 MW	9.35 AW	22180 AAW	LABLS	10//99-12//99
	Maine	S	11.93 MW	14.13 AW	29380 AAW	MEBLS	10//99-12//99
	Portland MSA, ME	S	17.66 MW	16.93 AW	36720 AAW	MEBLS	10//99-12//99
	Maryland	S	8.23 MW	10.27 AW	21360 AAW	MDBLS	10//99-12//99
	Baltimore PMSA, MD	S	11.34 MW	8.70 AW	23590 AAW	MDBLS	10//99-12//99
	Cumberland MSA, MD-WV	S	10.15 MW	6.73 AW	21110 AAW	MDBLS	10//99-12//99
	Hagerstown PMSA, MD	S	16.54 MW	14.71 AW	34410 AAW	MDBLS	10//99-12//99
	Massachusetts	S	10.7 MW	13.46 AW	27990 AAW	MABLS	10//99-12//99
	Boston PMSA, MA-NH	S	13.28 MW	11.48 AW	27610 AAW	MABLS	10//99-12//99
	Lowell PMSA, MA-NH	S	14.32 MW	10.12 AW	29780 AAW	MABLS	10//99-12//99
	Springfield MSA, MA	S	13.19 MW	8.87 AW	27430 AAW	MABLS	10//99-12//99
	Michigan	S	9.48 MW	12.83 AW	26680 AAW	MIBLS	10//99-12//99
	Benton Harbor MSA, MI	S	16.69 MW	12.79 AW	34720 AAW	MIBLS	10//99-12//99
	Detroit PMSA, MI	S	15.57 MW	10.03 AW	32390 AAW	MIBLS	10//99-12//99
	Grand Rapids-Muskegon-Holland MSA, MI	S	12.12 MW	11.27 AW	25200 AAW	MIBLS	10//99-12//99
	Jackson MSA, MI	S	10.77 MW	9.34 AW	22400 AAW	MIBLS	10//99-12//99
	Kalamazoo-Battle Creek MSA, MI	S	17.31 MW	15.22 AW	36010 AAW	MIBLS	10//99-12//99
	Lansing-East Lansing MSA, MI	S	11.02 MW	8.36 AW	22920 AAW	MIBLS	10//99-12//99
	Saginaw-Bay City-Midland MSA, MI	S	13.23 MW	10.64 AW	27520 AAW	MIBLS	10//99-12//99
	Minnesota	S	10.04 MW	14.69 AW	30550 AAW	MNBLS	10//99-12//99

Occupation/Type/Industry	Location	Per	Low	Mid	High	Source	Date
Photographer	Minneapolis-St. Paul MSA, MN-WI	S	17.25 MW	14.07 AW	35880 AAW	MNBLS	10//99-12//99
	Mississippi	S	9.72 MW	9.88 AW	20540 AAW	MSBLS	10//99-12//99
	Biloxi-Gulfport-Pascagoula MSA, MS	S	9.62 MW	8.39 AW	20010 AAW	MSBLS	10//99-12//99
	Jackson MSA, MS	S	11.48 MW	10.90 AW	23890 AAW	MSBLS	10//99-12//99
	Missouri	S	9.53 MW	11.54 AW	24010 AAW	MOBLS	10//99-12//99
	Joplin MSA, MO	S	8.87 MW	7.98 AW	18440 AAW	MOBLS	10//99-12//99
	Kansas City MSA, MO-KS	S	9.94 MW	8.77 AW	20680 AAW	MOBLS	10//99-12//99
	St. Louis MSA, MO-IL	S	13.28 MW	11.74 AW	27620 AAW	MOBLS	10//99-12//99
	Springfield MSA, MO	S	9.08 MW	7.96 AW	18880 AAW	MOBLS	10//99-12//99
	Montana	S	8.25 MW	9.73 AW	20250 AAW	MTBLS	10//99-12//99
	Nebraska	S	10.85 MW	11.68 AW	24290 AAW	NEBLS	10//99-12//99
	Lincoln MSA, NE	S	8.84 MW	7.87 AW	18390 AAW	NEBLS	10//99-12//99
	Omaha MSA, NE-IA	S	11.43 MW	8.88 AW	23760 AAW	NEBLS	10//99-12//99
	Nevada	S	7.49 MW	9.93 AW	20650 AAW	NVBLS	10//99-12//99
	Las Vegas MSA, NV-AZ	S	9.80 MW	6.93 AW	20390 AAW	NVBLS	10//99-12//99
	Reno MSA, NV	S	13.59 MW	12.56 AW	28270 AAW	NVBLS	10//99-12//99
	New Hampshire	S	10.13 MW	12.82 AW	26660 AAW	NHBLS	10//99-12//99
	Manchester PMSA, NH	S	12.12 MW	9.52 AW	25210 AAW	NHBLS	10//99-12//99
	New Jersey	S	11.45 MW	13.02 AW	27080 AAW	NJBLS	10//99-12//99
	Atlantic-Cape May PMSA, NJ	S	11.66 MW	10.79 AW	24250 AAW	NJBLS	10//99-12//99
	Bergen-Passaic PMSA, NJ	S	13.91 MW	12.59 AW	28930 AAW	NJBLS	10//99-12//99
	Jersey City PMSA, NJ	S	16.98 MW	15.64 AW	35310 AAW	NJBLS	10//99-12//99
	Middlesex-Somerset-Hunterdon PMSA, NJ	S	12.40 MW	9.09 AW	25790 AAW	NJBLS	10//99-12//99
	Monmouth-Ocean PMSA, NJ	S	12.39 MW	10.22 AW	25770 AAW	NJBLS	10//99-12//99
	Newark PMSA, NJ	S	13.53 MW	11.90 AW	28150 AAW	NJBLS	10//99-12//99
	Trenton PMSA, NJ	S	16.22 MW	15.05 AW	33730 AAW	NJBLS	10//99-12//99
	New Mexico	S	9.01 MW	10.53 AW	21900 AAW	NMBLS	10//99-12//99
	Albuquerque MSA, NM	S	12.63 MW	12.15 AW	26270 AAW	NMBLS	10//99-12//99
	New York	S	10.67 MW	14.99 AW	31180 AAW	NYBLS	10//99-12//99
	Albany-Schenectady-Troy MSA, NY	S	14.80 MW	11.48 AW	30790 AAW	NYBLS	10//99-12//99
	Binghamton MSA, NY	S	9.98 MW	8.22 AW	20760 AAW	NYBLS	10//99-12//99
	Buffalo-Niagara Falls MSA, NY	S	11.04 MW	8.66 AW	22970 AAW	NYBLS	10//99-12//99
	Dutchess County PMSA, NY	S	10.34 MW	8.33 AW	21500 AAW	NYBLS	10//99-12//99
	Glens Falls MSA, NY	S	10.30 MW	9.20 AW	21420 AAW	NYBLS	10//99-12//99
	Nassau-Suffolk PMSA, NY	S	13.94 MW	11.80 AW	29000 AAW	NYBLS	10//99-12//99
	New York PMSA, NY	S	18.84 MW	14.86 AW	39190 AAW	NYBLS	10//99-12//99
	Newburgh PMSA, NY-PA	S	12.35 MW	7.91 AW	25680 AAW	NYBLS	10//99-12//99
	Rochester MSA, NY	S	13.12 MW	10.21 AW	27280 AAW	NYBLS	10//99-12//99
	Syracuse MSA, NY	S	10.58 MW	9.33 AW	22020 AAW	NYBLS	10//99-12//99
	Utica-Rome MSA, NY	S	8.77 MW	8.29 AW	18250 AAW	NYBLS	10//99-12//99
	North Carolina	S	10.16 MW	11.40 AW	23720 AAW	NCBLS	10//99-12//99
	Charlotte-Gastonia-Rock Hill MSA, NC-SC	S	13.89 MW	11.73 AW	28900 AAW	NCBLS	10//99-12//99
	Greensboro--Winston-Salem--High Point MSA, NC	S	11.06 MW	10.10 AW	23010 AAW	NCBLS	10//99-12//99
	Raleigh-Durham-Chapel Hill MSA, NC	S	13.19 MW	13.56 AW	27430 AAW	NCBLS	10//99-12//99
	North Dakota	S	8.77 MW	10.41 AW	21650 AAW	NDBLS	10//99-12//99
	Fargo-Moorhead MSA, ND-MN	S	9.25 MW	8.10 AW	19240 AAW	NDBLS	10//99-12//99
	Ohio	S	8.88 MW	10.72 AW	22300 AAW	OHBLS	10//99-12//99
	Akron PMSA, OH	S	8.91 MW	7.72 AW	18540 AAW	OHBLS	10//99-12//99
	Canton-Massillon MSA, OH	S	9.58 MW	8.17 AW	19920 AAW	OHBLS	10//99-12//99
	Cincinnati PMSA, OH-KY-IN	S	12.31 MW	8.73 AW	25600 AAW	OHBLS	10//99-12//99
	Cleveland-Lorain-Elyria PMSA, OH	S	12.62 MW	10.24 AW	26250 AAW	OHBLS	10//99-12//99
	Columbus MSA, OH	S	12.13 MW	10.34 AW	25220 AAW	OHBLS	10//99-12//99
	Dayton-Springfield MSA, OH	S	9.97 MW	8.38 AW	20740 AAW	OHBLS	10//99-12//99
	Hamilton-Middletown PMSA, OH	S	10.96 MW	9.86 AW	22810 AAW	OHBLS	10//99-12//99
	Toledo MSA, OH	S	12.68 MW	10.59 AW	26370 AAW	OHBLS	10//99-12//99
	Youngstown-Warren MSA, OH	S	10.91 MW	10.77 AW	22700 AAW	OHBLS	10//99-12//99
	Oklahoma	S	8.61 MW	9.59 AW	19950 AAW	OKBLS	10//99-12//99
	Oklahoma City MSA, OK	S	10.50 MW	9.27 AW	21850 AAW	OKBLS	10//99-12//99
	Tulsa MSA, OK	S	9.28 MW	8.15 AW	19300 AAW	OKBLS	10//99-12//99
	Oregon	S	10.14 MW	11.82 AW	24580 AAW	ORBLS	10//99-12//99
	Medford-Ashland MSA, OR	S	9.15 MW	8.11 AW	19040 AAW	ORBLS	10//99-12//99

AAW Average annual wage	**AOH** Average offered, high	**ASH** Average starting, high	**H** Hourly	**M** Monthly	**S** Special: hourly and annual
AE Average entry wage	**AOL** Average offered, low	**ASL** Average starting, low	**HI** Highest wage paid	**MTC** Median total compensation	**TQ** Third quartile wage
AEX Average experienced wage	**APH** Average pay, high range	**AW** Average wage paid	**HR** High end range	**MW** Median wage paid	**W** Weekly
AO Average offered	**APL** Average pay, low range	**FQ** First quartile wage	**LR** Low end range	**SQ** Second quartile wage	**Y** Yearly

Photographer

Occupation/Type/Industry	Location	Per	Low	Mid	High	Source	Date
Photographer	Portland-Vancouver PMSA, OR-WA	S	15.94 MW	11.86 AW	33150 AAW	ORBLS	10//99-12//99
	Salem PMSA, OR	S	9.69 MW	8.27 AW	20140 AAW	ORBLS	10//99-12//99
	Pennsylvania	S	10.61 MW	11.94 AW	24830 AAW	PABLS	10//99-12//99
	Allentown-Bethlehem-Easton MSA, PA	S	14.96 MW	14.54 AW	31120 AAW	PABLS	10//99-12//99
	Erie MSA, PA	S	11.13 MW	9.71 AW	23140 AAW	PABLS	10//99-12//99
	Harrisburg-Lebanon-Carlisle MSA, PA	S	14.30 MW	12.82 AW	29740 AAW	PABLS	10//99-12//99
	Johnstown MSA, PA	S	14.28 MW	13.47 AW	29690 AAW	PABLS	10//99-12//99
	Lancaster MSA, PA	S	13.70 MW	10.57 AW	28490 AAW	PABLS	10//99-12//99
	Philadelphia PMSA, PA-NJ	S	12.95 MW	12.12 AW	26940 AAW	PABLS	10//99-12//99
	Pittsburgh MSA, PA	S	9.70 MW	8.10 AW	20180 AAW	PABLS	10//99-12//99
	Scranton--Wilkes-Barre-- Hazleton MSA, PA	S	12.84 MW	12.15 AW	26710 AAW	PABLS	10//99-12//99
	York MSA, PA	S	12.56 MW	11.23 AW	26120 AAW	PABLS	10//99-12//99
	Rhode Island	S	10.43 MW	13.23 AW	27510 AAW	RIBLS	10//99-12//99
	Providence-Fall River- Warwick MSA, RI-MA	S	12.26 MW	9.95 AW	25490 AAW	RIBLS	10//99-12//99
	South Carolina	S	8.58 MW	13.08 AW	27220 AAW	SCBLS	10//99-12//99
	Columbia MSA, SC	S	8.89 MW	7.95 AW	18490 AAW	SCBLS	10//99-12//99
	Greenville-Spartanburg- Anderson MSA, SC	S	13.33 MW	12.02 AW	27730 AAW	SCBLS	10//99-12//99
	Myrtle Beach MSA, SC	S	8.84 MW	7.81 AW	18380 AAW	SCBLS	10//99-12//99
	South Dakota	S	10.13 MW	10.87 AW	22610 AAW	SDBLS	10//99-12//99
	Sioux Falls MSA, SD	S	11.53 MW	11.18 AW	23980 AAW	SDBLS	10//99-12//99
	Tennessee	S	9.78 MW	11.73 AW	24410 AAW	TNBLS	10//99-12//99
	Chattanooga MSA, TN-GA	S	13.15 MW	8.27 AW	27350 AAW	TNBLS	10//99-12//99
	Jackson MSA, TN	S	15.74 MW	16.26 AW	32730 AAW	TNBLS	10//99-12//99
	Knoxville MSA, TN	S	10.88 MW	11.07 AW	22630 AAW	TNBLS	10//99-12//99
	Memphis MSA, TN-AR-MS	S	12.48 MW	10.22 AW	25960 AAW	MSBLS	10//99-12//99
	Nashville MSA, TN	S	16.27 MW	14.74 AW	33840 AAW	TNBLS	10//99-12//99
	Texas	S	9.55 MW	11.16 AW	23200 AAW	TXBLS	10//99-12//99
	Amarillo MSA, TX	S	9.21 MW	8.67 AW	19150 AAW	TXBLS	10//99-12//99
	Austin-San Marcos MSA, TX	S	11.89 MW	11.22 AW	24730 AAW	TXBLS	10//99-12//99
	Beaumont-Port Arthur MSA, TX	S	10.84 MW	11.36 AW	22550 AAW	TXBLS	10//99-12//99
	Corpus Christi MSA, TX	S	10.38 MW	10.24 AW	21580 AAW	TXBLS	10//99-12//99
	Dallas PMSA, TX	S	12.48 MW	10.50 AW	25950 AAW	TXBLS	10//99-12//99
	El Paso MSA, TX	S	9.54 MW	8.40 AW	19850 AAW	TXBLS	10//99-12//99
	Fort Worth-Arlington PMSA, TX	S	11.58 MW	10.49 AW	24080 AAW	TXBLS	10//99-12//99
	Galveston-Texas City PMSA, TX	S	8.91 MW	7.97 AW	18530 AAW	TXBLS	10//99-12//99
	Houston PMSA, TX	S	12.33 MW	11.12 AW	25650 AAW	TXBLS	10//99-12//99
	Longview-Marshall MSA, TX	S	6.86 MW	6.03 AW	14270 AAW	TXBLS	10//99-12//99
	McAllen-Edinburg-Mission MSA, TX	S	7.14 MW	6.33 AW	14850 AAW	TXBLS	10//99-12//99
	Odessa-Midland MSA, TX	S	9.10 MW	8.41 AW	18920 AAW	TXBLS	10//99-12//99
	San Antonio MSA, TX	S	10.11 MW	8.11 AW	21030 AAW	TXBLS	10//99-12//99
	Tyler MSA, TX	S	9.95 MW	8.64 AW	20690 AAW	TXBLS	10//99-12//99
	Waco MSA, TX	S	9.82 MW	9.46 AW	20420 AAW	TXBLS	10//99-12//99
	Wichita Falls MSA, TX	S	8.77 MW	7.93 AW	18230 AAW	TXBLS	10//99-12//99
	Utah	S	9.77 MW	10.08 AW	20970 AAW	UTBLS	10//99-12//99
	Provo-Orem MSA, UT	S	8.48 MW	8.43 AW	17640 AAW	UTBLS	10//99-12//99
	Salt Lake City-Ogden MSA, UT	S	10.09 MW	9.80 AW	20990 AAW	UTBLS	10//99-12//99
	Vermont	S	10.32 MW	13.09 AW	27230 AAW	VTBLS	10//99-12//99
	Virginia	S	9.02 MW	11.24 AW	23380 AAW	VABLS	10//99-12//99
	Danville MSA, VA	S	13.55 MW	10.36 AW	28190 AAW	VABLS	10//99-12//99
	Norfolk-Virginia Beach- Newport News MSA, VA-NC	S	11.73 MW	10.28 AW	24400 AAW	VABLS	10//99-12//99
	Richmond-Petersburg MSA, VA	S	13.61 MW	12.79 AW	28320 AAW	VABLS	10//99-12//99
	Roanoke MSA, VA	S	11.22 MW	10.71 AW	23340 AAW	VABLS	10//99-12//99
	Washington	S	11.88 MW	14.52 AW	30200 AAW	WABLS	10//99-12//99
	Bellingham MSA, WA	S	13.55 MW	10.28 AW	28170 AAW	WABLS	10//99-12//99
	Richland-Kennewick-Pasco MSA, WA	S	16.28 MW	17.48 AW	33870 AAW	WABLS	10//99-12//99
	Seattle-Bellevue-Everett PMSA, WA	S	12.70 MW	9.73 AW	26410 AAW	WABLS	10//99-12//99

AAW Average annual wage	**AOH** Average offered, high	**ASH** Average starting, high	**H** Hourly	**M** Monthly	**S** Special: hourly and annual
AE Average entry wage	**AOL** Average offered, low	**ASL** Average starting, low	**HI** Highest wage paid	**MTC** Median total compensation	**TQ** Third quartile wage
AEX Average experienced wage	**APH** Average pay, high range	**AW** Average wage paid	**HR** High end range	**MW** Median wage paid	**W** Weekly
AO Average offered	**APL** Average pay, low range	**FQ** First quartile wage	**LR** Low end range	**SQ** Second quartile wage	**Y** Yearly

Occupation/Type/Industry	Location	Per	Low	Mid	High	Source	Date
Photographer	Spokane MSA, WA	S	12.94 MW	10.70 AW	26910 AAW	WABLS	10//99-12//99
	Tacoma PMSA, WA	S	19.31 MW	17.82 AW	40170 AAW	WABLS	10//99-12//99
	West Virginia	S	10.15 MW	11.27 AW	23430 AAW	WVBLS	10//99-12//99
	Huntington-Ashland MSA, WV-KY-OH	S	11.20 MW	8.61 AW	23290 AAW	WVBLS	10//99-12//99
	Wheeling MSA, WV-OH	S	9.28 MW	7.35 AW	19300 AAW	WVBLS	10//99-12//99
	Wisconsin	S	9.24 MW	11.41 AW	23720 AAW	WIBLS	10//99-12//99
	Appleton-Oshkosh-Neenah MSA, WI	S	11.06 MW	9.57 AW	23010 AAW	WIBLS	10//99-12//99
	Eau Claire MSA, WI	S	11.55 MW	9.93 AW	24020 AAW	WIBLS	10//99-12//99
	Green Bay MSA, WI	S	13.29 MW	12.36 AW	27650 AAW	WIBLS	10//99-12//99
	Janesville-Beloit MSA, WI	S	13.74 MW	10.94 AW	28590 AAW	WIBLS	10//99-12//99
	La Crosse MSA, WI-MN	S	11.48 MW	8.39 AW	23880 AAW	WIBLS	10//99-12//99
	Madison MSA, WI	S	10.11 MW	9.44 AW	21020 AAW	WIBLS	10//99-12//99
	Milwaukee-Waukesha PMSA, WI	S	12.02 MW	9.17 AW	25010 AAW	WIBLS	10//99-12//99
	Racine PMSA, WI	S	12.48 MW	8.43 AW	25950 AAW	WIBLS	10//99-12//99
	Sheboygan MSA, WI	S	7.23 MW	7.18 AW	15030 AAW	WIBLS	10//99-12//99
	Wausau MSA, WI	S	11.13 MW	9.81 AW	23140 AAW	WIBLS	10//99-12//99
	Wyoming	S	8.41 MW	9.68 AW	20140 AAW	WYBLS	10//99-12//99
	Puerto Rico	S	8.46 MW	9.79 AW	20370 AAW	PRBLS	10//99-12//99
	San Juan-Bayamon PMSA, PR	S	11.49 MW	11.19 AW	23910 AAW	PRBLS	10//99-12//99
	Virgin Islands	S	11.84 MW	12.02 AW	25010 AAW	VIBLS	10//99-12//99
Centerfold	United States	Y		250000 AW		MENHEL	1999
Photographic Process Worker	Alabama	S	7.65 MW	7.97 AW	16580 AAW	ALBLS	10//99-12//99
	Arizona	S	10.41 MW	11.64 AW	24220 AAW	AZBLS	10//99-12//99
	Phoenix-Mesa MSA, AZ	S	12.91 MW	11.49 AW	26860 AAW	AZBLS	10//99-12//99
	Arkansas	S	6.93 MW	7.84 AW	16310 AAW	ARBLS	10//99-12//99
	California	S	12.3 MW	13.70 AW	28500 AAW	CABLS	10//99-12//99
	Los Angeles-Long Beach PMSA, CA	S	15.67 MW	13.81 AW	32600 AAW	CABLS	10//99-12//99
	Oakland PMSA, CA	S	13.66 MW	12.70 AW	28400 AAW	CABLS	10//99-12//99
	Orange County PMSA, CA	S	10.78 MW	9.98 AW	22410 AAW	CABLS	10//99-12//99
	Riverside-San Bernardino PMSA, CA	S	10.90 MW	10.27 AW	22680 AAW	CABLS	10//99-12//99
	San Diego MSA, CA	S	13.99 MW	12.99 AW	29100 AAW	CABLS	10//99-12//99
	San Francisco PMSA, CA	S	17.22 MW	16.20 AW	35820 AAW	CABLS	10//99-12//99
	San Jose PMSA, CA	S	14.07 MW	12.06 AW	29280 AAW	CABLS	10//99-12//99
	Visalia-Tulare-Porterville MSA, CA	S	9.39 MW	9.62 AW	19520 AAW	CABLS	10//99-12//99
	Colorado	S	11.12 MW	11.70 AW	24340 AAW	COBLS	10//99-12//99
	Colorado Springs MSA, CO	S	12.56 MW	11.85 AW	26130 AAW	COBLS	10//99-12//99
	Denver PMSA, CO	S	11.19 MW	10.59 AW	23280 AAW	COBLS	10//99-12//99
	Connecticut	S	8.79 MW	9.76 AW	20290 AAW	CTBLS	10//99-12//99
	Hartford MSA, CT	S	8.90 MW	8.10 AW	18510 AAW	CTBLS	10//99-12//99
	New London-Norwich MSA, CT-RI	S	10.23 MW	9.73 AW	21270 AAW	CTBLS	10//99-12//99
	Washington PMSA, DC-MD-VA-WV	S	10.23 MW	10.09 AW	21280 AAW	DCBLS	10//99-12//99
	Florida	S	8.32 MW	9.88 AW	20550 AAW	FLBLS	10//99-12//99
	Jacksonville MSA, FL	S	11.39 MW	9.47 AW	23690 AAW	FLBLS	10//99-12//99
	Miami PMSA, FL	S	9.52 MW	8.91 AW	19800 AAW	FLBLS	10//99-12//99
	Orlando MSA, FL	S	14.86 MW	11.97 AW	30920 AAW	FLBLS	10//99-12//99
	Georgia	S	9.84 MW	9.84 AW	20460 AAW	GABLS	10//99-12//99
	Atlanta MSA, GA	S	10.04 MW	9.99 AW	20880 AAW	GABLS	10//99-12//99
	Illinois	S	8.56 MW	9.73 AW	20250 AAW	ILBLS	10//99-12//99
	Chicago PMSA, IL	S	10.23 MW	8.82 AW	21280 AAW	ILBLS	10//99-12//99
	Indiana	S	12.06 MW	12.36 AW	25710 AAW	INBLS	10//99-12//99
	Fort Wayne MSA, IN	S	13.03 MW	13.36 AW	27110 AAW	INBLS	10//99-12//99
	South Bend MSA, IN	S	9.04 MW	8.45 AW	18800 AAW	INBLS	10//99-12//99
	Iowa	S	6.42 MW	7.91 AW	16460 AAW	IABLS	10//99-12//99
	Kansas	S	8.75 MW	8.84 AW	18380 AAW	KSBLS	10//99-12//99
	Kentucky	S	10.07 MW	10.63 AW	22100 AAW	KYBLS	10//99-12//99
	Louisiana	S	7.74 MW	8.00 AW	16640 AAW	LABLS	10//99-12//99
	New Orleans MSA, LA	S	8.44 MW	7.85 AW	17560 AAW	LABLS	10//99-12//99
	Maryland	S	10.38 MW	11.42 AW	23750 AAW	MDBLS	10//99-12//99
	Baltimore PMSA, MD	S	12.49 MW	11.24 AW	25970 AAW	MDBLS	10//99-12//99
	Massachusetts	S	12.47 MW	13.36 AW	27790 AAW	MABLS	10//99-12//99
	Boston PMSA, MA-NH	S	15.29 MW	16.31 AW	31800 AAW	MABLS	10//99-12//99
	Springfield MSA, MA	S	11.06 MW	9.57 AW	23010 AAW	MABLS	10//99-12//99
	Worcester PMSA, MA-CT	S	10.38 MW	9.84 AW	21590 AAW	MABLS	10//99-12//99
	Michigan	S	10.3 MW	11.76 AW	24470 AAW	MIBLS	10//99-12//99

AAW Average annual wage	**AOH** Average offered, high	**ASH** Average starting, high	**H** Hourly	**M** Monthly	**S** Special: hourly and annual
AE Average entry wage	**AOL** Average offered, low	**ASL** Average starting, low	**HI** Highest wage paid	**MTC** Median total compensation	**TQ** Third quartile wage
AEX Average experienced wage	**APH** Average pay, high range	**AW** Average wage paid	**HR** High end range	**MW** Median wage paid	**W** Weekly
AO Average offered	**APL** Average pay, low range	**FQ** First quartile wage	**LR** Low end range	**SQ** Second quartile wage	**Y** Yearly

Occupation/Type/Industry	Location	Per	Low	Mid	High	Source	Date
Photographic Process Worker	Detroit PMSA, MI	S	12.38 MW	10.61 AW	25750 AAW	MIBLS	10//99-12//99
	Kalamazoo-Battle Creek MSA, MI	S	9.73 MW	9.70 AW	20230 AAW	MIBLS	10//99-12//99
	Minnesota	S	9.71 MW	10.46 AW	21750 AAW	MNBLS	10//99-12//99
	Minneapolis-St. Paul MSA, MN-WI	S	11.79 MW	11.37 AW	24510 AAW	MNBLS	10//99-12//99
	Mississippi	S	6.13 MW	6.66 AW	13850 AAW	MSBLS	10//99-12//99
	Jackson MSA, MS	S	9.43 MW	9.73 AW	19620 AAW	MSBLS	10//99-12//99
	Kansas City MSA, MO-KS	S	12.21 MW	11.43 AW	25410 AAW	MOBLS	10//99-12//99
	Montana	S	10.05 MW	11.69 AW	24320 AAW	MTBLS	10//99-12//99
	Nebraska	S	10.83 MW	12.19 AW	25340 AAW	NEBLS	10//99-12//99
	Omaha MSA, NE-IA	S	14.56 MW	11.68 AW	30280 AAW	NEBLS	10//99-12//99
	Nevada	S	15.07 MW	15.69 AW	32640 AAW	NVBLS	10//99-12//99
	Las Vegas MSA, NV-AZ	S	15.96 MW	15.15 AW	33190 AAW	NVBLS	10//99-12//99
	New Jersey	S	14.17 MW	14.60 AW	30380 AAW	NJBLS	10//99-12//99
	Bergen-Passaic PMSA, NJ	S	14.93 MW	14.45 AW	31050 AAW	NJBLS	10//99-12//99
	Newark PMSA, NJ	S	14.35 MW	14.89 AW	29850 AAW	NJBLS	10//99-12//99
	New Mexico	S	10.21 MW	11.18 AW	23260 AAW	NMBLS	10//99-12//99
	Albuquerque MSA, NM	S	10.67 MW	9.01 AW	22190 AAW	NMBLS	10//99-12//99
	New York	S	12.54 MW	13.82 AW	28750 AAW	NYBLS	10//99-12//99
	Nassau-Suffolk PMSA, NY	S	11.54 MW	11.62 AW	24000 AAW	NYBLS	10//99-12//99
	New York PMSA, NY	S	14.43 MW	13.61 AW	30010 AAW	NYBLS	10//99-12//99
	Rochester MSA, NY	S	9.90 MW	9.99 AW	20590 AAW	NYBLS	10//99-12//99
	Syracuse MSA, NY	S	10.46 MW	10.04 AW	21760 AAW	NYBLS	10//99-12//99
	North Carolina	S	8.44 MW	9.23 AW	19200 AAW	NCBLS	10//99-12//99
	Charlotte-Gastonia-Rock Hill MSA, NC-SC	S	9.73 MW	10.44 AW	20230 AAW	NCBLS	10//99-12//99
	Greensboro--Winston-Salem-- High Point MSA, NC	S	10.57 MW	10.13 AW	21990 AAW	NCBLS	10//99-12//99
	Ohio	S	12.22 MW	11.72 AW	24370 AAW	OHBLS	10//99-12//99
	Akron PMSA, OH	S	10.19 MW	9.54 AW	21190 AAW	OHBLS	10//99-12//99
	Canton-Massillon MSA, OH	S	12.18 MW	12.66 AW	25330 AAW	OHBLS	10//99-12//99
	Cincinnati PMSA, OH-KY-IN	S	11.17 MW	12.30 AW	23230 AAW	OHBLS	10//99-12//99
	Cleveland-Lorain-Elyria PMSA, OH	S	13.09 MW	12.76 AW	27230 AAW	OHBLS	10//99-12//99
	Columbus MSA, OH	S	12.36 MW	12.30 AW	25700 AAW	OHBLS	10//99-12//99
	Dayton-Springfield MSA, OH	S	11.54 MW	11.03 AW	24010 AAW	OHBLS	10//99-12//99
	Oklahoma	S	8.29 MW	11.25 AW	23400 AAW	OKBLS	10//99-12//99
	Oregon	S	8.35 MW	9.21 AW	19160 AAW	ORBLS	10//99-12//99
	Pennsylvania	S	10.5 MW	12.53 AW	26070 AAW	PABLS	10//99-12//99
	Philadelphia PMSA, PA-NJ	S	13.61 MW	11.46 AW	28320 AAW	PABLS	10//99-12//99
	Pittsburgh MSA, PA	S	11.44 MW	9.90 AW	23790 AAW	PABLS	10//99-12//99
	Rhode Island	S	9.62 MW	10.12 AW	21050 AAW	RIBLS	10//99-12//99
	Providence-Fall River- Warwick MSA, RI-MA	S	10.27 MW	9.48 AW	21370 AAW	RIBLS	10//99-12//99
	South Carolina	S	10.37 MW	11.25 AW	23390 AAW	SCBLS	10//99-12//99
	Greenville-Spartanburg- Anderson MSA, SC	S	12.27 MW	11.19 AW	25520 AAW	SCBLS	10//99-12//99
	Chattanooga MSA, TN-GA	S	10.77 MW	10.57 AW	22410 AAW	TNBLS	10//99-12//99
	Memphis MSA, TN-AR-MS	S	10.14 MW	9.88 AW	21100 AAW	MSBLS	10//99-12//99
	Nashville MSA, TN	S	15.71 MW	15.98 AW	32680 AAW	TNBLS	10//99-12//99
	Texas	S	7.7 MW	9.27 AW	19290 AAW	TXBLS	10//99-12//99
	Austin-San Marcos MSA, TX	S	8.45 MW	7.20 AW	17580 AAW	TXBLS	10//99-12//99
	Bryan-College Station MSA, TX	S	6.54 MW	6.60 AW	13610 AAW	TXBLS	10//99-12//99
	Dallas PMSA, TX	S	10.89 MW	8.36 AW	22650 AAW	TXBLS	10//99-12//99
	Houston PMSA, TX	S	9.29 MW	7.41 AW	19330 AAW	TXBLS	10//99-12//99
	San Antonio MSA, TX	S	11.28 MW	9.89 AW	23460 AAW	TXBLS	10//99-12//99
	Utah	S	7.9 MW	8.14 AW	16940 AAW	UTBLS	10//99-12//99
	Salt Lake City-Ogden MSA, UT	S	8.09 MW	7.89 AW	16830 AAW	UTBLS	10//99-12//99
	Virginia	S	9.75 MW	9.53 AW	19820 AAW	VABLS	10//99-12//99
	Norfolk-Virginia Beach- Newport News MSA, VA-NC	S	7.80 MW	7.26 AW	16230 AAW	VABLS	10//99-12//99
	Richmond-Petersburg MSA, VA	S	10.30 MW	10.51 AW	21430 AAW	VABLS	10//99-12//99
	Washington	S	10.25 MW	10.94 AW	22750 AAW	WABLS	10//99-12//99
	Seattle-Bellevue-Everett PMSA, WA	S	11.65 MW	10.63 AW	24230 AAW	WABLS	10//99-12//99
	Spokane MSA, WA	S	9.40 MW	8.81 AW	19550 AAW	WABLS	10//99-12//99
	West Virginia	S	7.04 MW	8.07 AW	16790 AAW	WVBLS	10//99-12//99

AAW	Average annual wage	AOH	Average offered, high	ASH	Average starting, high	H	Hourly	M	Monthly	S	Special: hourly and annual
AE	Average entry wage	AOL	Average offered, low	ASL	Average starting, low	HI	Highest wage paid	MTC	Median total compensation	TQ	Third quartile wage
AEX	Average experienced wage	APH	Average pay, high range	AW	Average wage paid	HR	High end range	MW	Median wage paid	W	Weekly
AO	Average offered	APL	Average pay, low range	FQ	First quartile wage	LR	Low end range	SQ	Second quartile wage	Y	Yearly

Occupation/Type/Industry	Location	Per	Low	Mid	High	Source	Date
Photographic Process Worker	Wisconsin	S	12.38 MW	14.54 AW	30240 AAW	WIBLS	10//99-12//99
	Madison MSA, WI	S	11.25 MW	9.51 AW	23390 AAW	WIBLS	10//99-12//99
	Milwaukee-Waukesha PMSA, WI	S	13.86 MW	12.81 AW	28820 AAW	WIBLS	10//99-12//99
	Wyoming	S	11.54 MW	10.69 AW	22240 AAW	WYBLS	10//99-12//99
	Puerto Rico	S	8.23 MW	8.36 AW	17380 AAW	PRBLS	10//99-12//99
	San Juan-Bayamon PMSA, PR	S	8.47 MW	8.49 AW	17620 AAW	PRBLS	10//99-12//99
Photographic Processing Machine Operator	Arizona	S	8.5 MW	8.84 AW	18380 AAW	AZBLS	10//99-12//99
	Arkansas	S	8.07 MW	8.57 AW	17820 AAW	ARBLS	10//99-12//99
	California	S	10.86 MW	11.77 AW	24480 AAW	CABLS	10//99-12//99
	Colorado	S	9.78 MW	10.22 AW	21250 AAW	COBLS	10//99-12//99
	Connecticut	S	11.11 MW	11.56 AW	24040 AAW	CTBLS	10//99-12//99
	District of Columbia	S	11.47 MW	12.34 AW	25660 AAW	DCBLS	10//99-12//99
	Florida	S	7.57 MW	7.94 AW	16510 AAW	FLBLS	10//99-12//99
	Georgia	S	7.94 MW	7.96 AW	16560 AAW	GABLS	10//99-12//99
	Hawaii	S	8.38 MW	9.22 AW	19170 AAW	HIBLS	10//99-12//99
	Idaho	S	8.33 MW	8.93 AW	18580 AAW	IDBLS	10//99-12//99
	Illinois	S	8.71 MW	9.22 AW	19180 AAW	ILBLS	10//99-12//99
	Indiana	S	8.33 MW	9.07 AW	18860 AAW	INBLS	10//99-12//99
	Iowa	S	7.94 MW	8.77 AW	18230 AAW	IABLS	10//99-12//99
	Kansas	S	7.9 MW	8.91 AW	18540 AAW	KSBLS	10//99-12//99
	Kentucky	S	8.04 MW	8.60 AW	17890 AAW	KYBLS	10//99-12//99
	Louisiana	S	7.67 MW	8.59 AW	17860 AAW	LABLS	10//99-12//99
	Maine	S	8.53 MW	8.89 AW	18490 AAW	MEBLS	10//99-12//99
	Maryland	S	7.97 MW	8.37 AW	17410 AAW	MDBLS	10//99-12//99
	Massachusetts	S	10.13 MW	11.40 AW	23710 AAW	MABLS	10//99-12//99
	Michigan	S	8.61 MW	9.13 AW	18990 AAW	MIBLS	10//99-12//99
	Minnesota	S	8.47 MW	9.26 AW	19250 AAW	MNBLS	10//99-12//99
	Mississippi	S	7.63 MW	7.93 AW	16490 AAW	MSBLS	10//99-12//99
	Missouri	S	8.38 MW	9.24 AW	19230 AAW	MOBLS	10//99-12//99
	Montana	S	8.06 MW	9.08 AW	18890 AAW	MTBLS	10//99-12//99
	Nebraska	S	10.57 MW	11.53 AW	23990 AAW	NEBLS	10//99-12//99
	Nevada	S	8.28 MW	8.94 AW	18600 AAW	NVBLS	10//99-12//99
	New Hampshire	S	8.39 MW	8.55 AW	17780 AAW	NHBLS	10//99-12//99
	New Jersey	S	11.03 MW	12.67 AW	26340 AAW	NJBLS	10//99-12//99
	New Mexico	S	7.76 MW	8.67 AW	18040 AAW	NMBLS	10//99-12//99
	New York	S	10.28 MW	11.17 AW	23230 AAW	NYBLS	10//99-12//99
	North Carolina	S	8.11 MW	8.47 AW	17610 AAW	NCBLS	10//99-12//99
	North Dakota	S	8.29 MW	8.58 AW	17850 AAW	NDBLS	10//99-12//99
	Ohio	S	8.54 MW	8.78 AW	18250 AAW	OHBLS	10//99-12//99
	Oklahoma	S	8.02 MW	8.27 AW	17200 AAW	OKBLS	10//99-12//99
	Oregon	S	9.05 MW	9.83 AW	20450 AAW	ORBLS	10//99-12//99
	Pennsylvania	S	8.25 MW	8.81 AW	18320 AAW	PABLS	10//99-12//99
	Rhode Island	S	12.03 MW	10.78 AW	22410 AAW	RIBLS	10//99-12//99
	South Carolina	S	7.98 MW	8.34 AW	17350 AAW	SCBLS	10//99-12//99
	South Dakota	S	7.95 MW	8.08 AW	16810 AAW	SDBLS	10//99-12//99
	Tennessee	S	8.42 MW	9.02 AW	18760 AAW	TNBLS	10//99-12//99
	Texas	S	8.74 MW	8.80 AW	18310 AAW	TXBLS	10//99-12//99
	Vermont	S	8.58 MW	10.03 AW	20860 AAW	VTBLS	10//99-12//99
	Virginia	S	7.98 MW	8.79 AW	18280 AAW	VABLS	10//99-12//99
	Washington	S	8.74 MW	10.11 AW	21020 AAW	WABLS	10//99-12//99
	West Virginia	S	8 MW	8.19 AW	17040 AAW	WVBLS	10//99-12//99
	Wisconsin	S	9.41 MW	9.50 AW	19750 AAW	WIBLS	10//99-12//99
	Wyoming	S	6.49 MW	6.88 AW	14320 AAW	WYBLS	10//99-12//99
	Puerto Rico	S	6.42 MW	6.81 AW	14170 AAW	PRBLS	10//99-12//99
Physical Therapist	United States	H		23.48 AW		NCS98	1998
	Alabama	S	26.78 MW	27.05 AW	56270 AAW	ALBLS	10//99-12//99
	Alaska	S	26.41 MW	26.60 AW	55340 AAW	AKBLS	10//99-12//99
	Arizona	S	25.63 MW	27.80 AW	57830 AAW	AZBLS	10//99-12//99
	Arkansas	S	26.31 MW	27.84 AW	57900 AAW	ARBLS	10//99-12//99
	California	S	32.53 MW	31.60 AW	65720 AAW	CABLS	10//99-12//99
	Colorado	S	23.32 MW	24.54 AW	51040 AAW	COBLS	10//99-12//99
	Connecticut	S	28.83 MW	29.74 AW	61860 AAW	CTBLS	10//99-12//99
	Delaware	S	29.33 MW	30.29 AW	63000 AAW	DEBLS	10//99-12//99
	District of Columbia	S	27 MW	26.34 AW	54800 AAW	DCBLS	10//99-12//99
	Florida	S	25.95 MW	26.64 AW	55410 AAW	FLBLS	10//99-12//99
	Georgia	S	29.11 MW	28.03 AW	58310 AAW	GABLS	10//99-12//99
	Hawaii	S	27.41 MW	27.58 AW	57360 AAW	HIBLS	10//99-12//99
	Idaho	S	24.5 MW	25.51 AW	53060 AAW	IDBLS	10//99-12//99

AAW Average annual wage	**AOH** Average offered, high	**ASH** Average starting, high	**H** Hourly	**M** Monthly	**S** Special: hourly and annual
AE Average entry wage	**AOL** Average offered, low	**ASL** Average starting, low	**HI** Highest wage paid	**MTC** Median total compensation	**TQ** Third quartile wage
AEX Average experienced wage	**APH** Average pay, high range	**AW** Average wage paid	**HR** High end range	**MW** Median wage paid	**W** Weekly
AO Average offered	**APL** Average pay, low range	**FQ** First quartile wage	**LR** Low end range	**SQ** Second quartile wage	**Y** Yearly

Occupation/Type/Industry	Location	Per	Low	Mid	High	Source	Date
Physical Therapist	Illinois	S	27.82 MW	26.83 AW	55800 AAW	ILBLS	10//99-12//99
	Indiana	S	27.94 MW	28.10 AW	58450 AAW	INBLS	10//99-12//99
	Iowa	S	24.43 MW	25.04 AW	52070 AAW	IABLS	10//99-12//99
	Kansas	S	24.22 MW	25.03 AW	52070 AAW	KSBLS	10//99-12//99
	Kentucky	S	25.32 MW	27.73 AW	57680 AAW	KYBLS	10//99-12//99
	Louisiana	S	29.3 MW	30.70 AW	63860 AAW	LABLS	10//99-12//99
	Maine	S	22.99 MW	24.05 AW	50010 AAW	MEBLS	10//99-12//99
	Maryland	S	26.85 MW	27.43 AW	57050 AAW	MDBLS	10//99-12//99
	Massachusetts	S	25.75 MW	26.65 AW	55420 AAW	MABLS	10//99-12//99
	Michigan	S	26.85 MW	28.46 AW	59190 AAW	MIBLS	10//99-12//99
	Minnesota	S	24.01 MW	24.99 AW	51980 AAW	MNBLS	10//99-12//99
	Mississippi	S	31.32 MW	30.94 AW	64360 AAW	MSBLS	10//99-12//99
	Missouri	S	25.46 MW	25.67 AW	53400 AAW	MOBLS	10//99-12//99
	Montana	S	23.85 MW	24.70 AW	51370 AAW	MTBLS	10//99-12//99
	Nebraska	S	23.76 MW	24.96 AW	51910 AAW	NEBLS	10//99-12//99
	Nevada	S	28.39 MW	29.29 AW	60920 AAW	NVBLS	10//99-12//99
	New Hampshire	S	22.85 MW	23.39 AW	48640 AAW	NHBLS	10//99-12//99
	New Jersey	S	30.28 MW	30.68 AW	63810 AAW	NJBLS	10//99-12//99
	New Mexico	S	24.67 MW	26.41 AW	54930 AAW	NMBLS	10//99-12//99
	New York	S	25.1 MW	28.78 AW	59870 AAW	NYBLS	10//99-12//99
	North Carolina	S	25.14 MW	26.22 AW	54530 AAW	NCBLS	10//99-12//99
	North Dakota	S	23.7 MW	24.02 AW	49960 AAW	NDBLS	10//99-12//99
	Ohio	S	26.56 MW	27.53 AW	57260 AAW	OHBLS	10//99-12//99
	Oklahoma	S	25.87 MW	25.90 AW	53870 AAW	OKBLS	10//99-12//99
	Oregon	S	24.29 MW	25.88 AW	53820 AAW	ORBLS	10//99-12//99
	Pennsylvania	S	29.56 MW	29.49 AW	61330 AAW	PABLS	10//99-12//99
	Rhode Island	S	29.82 MW	28.73 AW	59770 AAW	RIBLS	10//99-12//99
	South Carolina	S	28.7 MW	31.23 AW	64960 AAW	SCBLS	10//99-12//99
	South Dakota	S	23.71 MW	24.41 AW	50780 AAW	SDBLS	10//99-12//99
	Tennessee	S	26.29 MW	27.17 AW	56510 AAW	TNBLS	10//99-12//99
	Texas	S	28.35 MW	28.68 AW	59660 AAW	TXBLS	10//99-12//99
	Utah	S	24.98 MW	25.76 AW	53590 AAW	UTBLS	10//99-12//99
	Vermont	S	21.7 MW	22.44 AW	46680 AAW	VTBLS	10//99-12//99
	Virginia	S	28.22 MW	28.16 AW	58580 AAW	VABLS	10//99-12//99
	Washington	S	24.39 MW	25.99 AW	54070 AAW	WABLS	10//99-12//99
	West Virginia	S	27.87 MW	27.25 AW	56680 AAW	WVBLS	10//99-12//99
	Wisconsin	S	26.66 MW	26.81 AW	55770 AAW	WIBLS	10//99-12//99
	Wyoming	S	24.8 MW	27.84 AW	57910 AAW	WYBLS	10//99-12//99
	Puerto Rico	S	9.95 MW	11.00 AW	22880 AAW	PRBLS	10//99-12//99
	Virgin Islands	S	20.37 MW	28.64 AW	59570 AAW	VIBLS	10//99-12//99
Hospital	Florida	H			29.71 HI	BJTAMP	2000
Physical Therapist Aide	Alabama	S	7.35 MW	7.56 AW	15720 AAW	ALBLS	10//99-12//99
	Alaska	S	11.8 MW	11.60 AW	24130 AAW	AKBLS	10//99-12//99
	Arizona	S	8.91 MW	9.04 AW	18800 AAW	AZBLS	10//99-12//99
	Arkansas	S	7.33 MW	7.96 AW	16560 AAW	ARBLS	10//99-12//99
	California	S	9.63 MW	10.48 AW	21800 AAW	CABLS	10//99-12//99
	Colorado	S	8.67 MW	9.74 AW	20260 AAW	COBLS	10//99-12//99
	Connecticut	S	10.08 MW	10.42 AW	21670 AAW	CTBLS	10//99-12//99
	Delaware	S	9.69 MW	9.65 AW	20070 AAW	DEBLS	10//99-12//99
	Florida	S	9.54 MW	10.04 AW	20880 AAW	FLBLS	10//99-12//99
	Georgia	S	7.16 MW	7.63 AW	15870 AAW	GABLS	10//99-12//99
	Hawaii	S	12.65 MW	12.11 AW	25180 AAW	HIBLS	10//99-12//99
	Idaho	S	7.76 MW	7.77 AW	16160 AAW	IDBLS	10//99-12//99
	Illinois	S	9.46 MW	9.80 AW	20390 AAW	ILBLS	10//99-12//99
	Indiana	S	9.66 MW	11.70 AW	24330 AAW	INBLS	10//99-12//99
	Iowa	S	9.24 MW	9.38 AW	19510 AAW	IABLS	10//99-12//99
	Kansas	S	8.11 MW	9.74 AW	20250 AAW	KSBLS	10//99-12//99
	Kentucky	S	8.86 MW	10.30 AW	21430 AAW	KYBLS	10//99-12//99
	Louisiana	S	7.17 MW	7.39 AW	15370 AAW	LABLS	10//99-12//99
	Maine	S	8.41 MW	8.83 AW	18360 AAW	MEBLS	10//99-12//99
	Maryland	S	8.39 MW	9.82 AW	20420 AAW	MDBLS	10//99-12//99
	Massachusetts	S	11.51 MW	12.45 AW	25900 AAW	MABLS	10//99-12//99
	Michigan	S	10.08 MW	10.36 AW	21540 AAW	MIBLS	10//99-12//99
	Minnesota	S	9.68 MW	9.77 AW	20320 AAW	MNBLS	10//99-12//99
	Mississippi	S	10.34 MW	12.89 AW	26810 AAW	MSBLS	10//99-12//99
	Missouri	S	9.14 MW	9.31 AW	19350 AAW	MOBLS	10//99-12//99
	Montana	S	7.3 MW	7.35 AW	15290 AAW	MTBLS	10//99-12//99
	Nebraska	S	7.67 MW	7.90 AW	16430 AAW	NEBLS	10//99-12//99
	Nevada	S	8.09 MW	8.56 AW	17810 AAW	NVBLS	10//99-12//99
	New Hampshire	S	9.78 MW	10.26 AW	21340 AAW	NHBLS	10//99-12//99
	New Jersey	S	10.01 MW	10.27 AW	21370 AAW	NJBLS	10//99-12//99
	New Mexico	S	8.9 MW	11.41 AW	23740 AAW	NMBLS	10//99-12//99

AAW	Average annual wage	AOH	Average offered, high	ASH	Average starting, high
AE	Average entry wage	AOL	Average offered, low	ASL	Average starting, low
AEX	Average experienced wage	APH	Average pay, high range	AW	Average wage paid
AO	Average offered	APL	Average pay, low range	FQ	First quartile wage

H	Hourly	M	Monthly
HI	Highest wage paid	MTC	Median total compensation
HR	High end range	MW	Median wage paid
LR	Low end range	SQ	Second quartile wage

S	Special: hourly and annual
TQ	Third quartile wage
W	Weekly
Y	Yearly

Occupation/Type/Industry	Location	Per	Low	Mid	High	Source	Date
Physical Therapist Aide	New York	S	9.15 MW	9.70 AW	20170 AAW	NYBLS	10//99-12//99
	North Carolina	S	9.68 MW	10.42 AW	21680 AAW	NCBLS	10//99-12//99
	North Dakota	S	8.44 MW	8.54 AW	17750 AAW	NDBLS	10//99-12//99
	Ohio	S	9.43 MW	10.14 AW	21090 AAW	OHBLS	10//99-12//99
	Oklahoma	S	7.84 MW	8.35 AW	17370 AAW	OKBLS	10//99-12//99
	Oregon	S	9.47 MW	9.30 AW	19350 AAW	ORBLS	10//99-12//99
	Pennsylvania	S	9.55 MW	9.85 AW	20480 AAW	PABLS	10//99-12//99
	Rhode Island	S	13.83 MW	14.78 AW	30730 AAW	RIBLS	10//99-12//99
	South Carolina	S	10.47 MW	18.20 AW	37850 AAW	SCBLS	10//99-12//99
	South Dakota	S	8.28 MW	8.63 AW	17940 AAW	SDBLS	10//99-12//99
	Tennessee	S	8.32 MW	8.73 AW	18160 AAW	TNBLS	10//99-12//99
	Texas	S	7.92 MW	8.80 AW	18300 AAW	TXBLS	10//99-12//99
	Utah	S	7.53 MW	7.95 AW	16540 AAW	UTBLS	10//99-12//99
	Virginia	S	7.81 MW	8.28 AW	17210 AAW	VABLS	10//99-12//99
	Washington	S	9.67 MW	9.76 AW	20300 AAW	WABLS	10//99-12//99
	West Virginia	S	7.28 MW	8.06 AW	16760 AAW	WVBLS	10//99-12//99
	Wisconsin	S	9.29 MW	9.37 AW	19490 AAW	WIBLS	10//99-12//99
	Wyoming	S	7.89 MW	8.07 AW	16780 AAW	WYBLS	10//99-12//99
	Puerto Rico	S	8.03 MW	8.30 AW	17270 AAW	PRBLS	10//99-12//99
	Virgin Islands	S	7.54 MW	7.40 AW	15390 AAW	VIBLS	10//99-12//99
Physical Therapist Assistant	Alabama	S	17.6 MW	16.86 AW	35070 AAW	ALBLS	10//99-12//99
	Alaska	S	18.27 MW	17.89 AW	37200 AAW	AKBLS	10//99-12//99
	Arizona	S	14.43 MW	14.85 AW	30890 AAW	AZBLS	10//99-12//99
	Arkansas	S	14.67 MW	14.01 AW	29150 AAW	ARBLS	10//99-12//99
	California	S	18.79 MW	18.92 AW	39360 AAW	CABLS	10//99-12//99
	Colorado	S	14.23 MW	14.43 AW	30010 AAW	COBLS	10//99-12//99
	Connecticut	S	13.25 MW	13.95 AW	29020 AAW	CTBLS	10//99-12//99
	Delaware	S	14.41 MW	13.75 AW	28600 AAW	DEBLS	10//99-12//99
	District of Columbia	S	15.29 MW	15.20 AW	31620 AAW	DCBLS	10//99-12//99
	Florida	S	17.74 MW	17.90 AW	37240 AAW	FLBLS	10//99-12//99
	Georgia	S	15.91 MW	15.91 AW	33090 AAW	GABLS	10//99-12//99
	Hawaii	S	16.77 MW	16.99 AW	35340 AAW	HIBLS	10//99-12//99
	Idaho	S	14.27 MW	13.22 AW	27490 AAW	IDBLS	10//99-12//99
	Illinois	S	14.95 MW	14.61 AW	30390 AAW	ILBLS	10//99-12//99
	Indiana	S	16.35 MW	16.84 AW	35020 AAW	INBLS	10//99-12//99
	Iowa	S	12.99 MW	12.98 AW	27010 AAW	IABLS	10//99-12//99
	Kansas	S	13.78 MW	13.63 AW	28340 AAW	KSBLS	10//99-12//99
	Kentucky	S	15 MW	14.97 AW	31130 AAW	KYBLS	10//99-12//99
	Louisiana	S	8.04 MW	11.01 AW	22910 AAW	LABLS	10//99-12//99
	Maine	S	15 MW	14.79 AW	30770 AAW	MEBLS	10//99-12//99
	Maryland	S	15.59 MW	15.93 AW	33140 AAW	MDBLS	10//99-12//99
	Massachusetts	S	16.16 MW	15.95 AW	33170 AAW	MABLS	10//99-12//99
	Michigan	S	14.25 MW	14.20 AW	29530 AAW	MIBLS	10//99-12//99
	Minnesota	S	15.64 MW	16.27 AW	33840 AAW	MNBLS	10//99-12//99
	Mississippi	S	14.94 MW	14.69 AW	30560 AAW	MSBLS	10//99-12//99
	Montana	S	12.09 MW	11.70 AW	24340 AAW	MTBLS	10//99-12//99
	Nebraska	S	8.33 MW	9.96 AW	20720 AAW	NEBLS	10//99-12//99
	Nevada	S	14.2 MW	14.47 AW	30090 AAW	NVBLS	10//99-12//99
	New Hampshire	S	15.48 MW	15.48 AW	32200 AAW	NHBLS	10//99-12//99
	New Jersey	S	17.69 MW	16.97 AW	35290 AAW	NJBLS	10//99-12//99
	New Mexico	S	15 MW	14.92 AW	31030 AAW	NMBLS	10//99-12//99
	New York	S	17.66 MW	17.66 AW	36720 AAW	NYBLS	10//99-12//99
	North Carolina	S	17.19 MW	17.09 AW	35540 AAW	NCBLS	10//99-12//99
	North Dakota	S	10.57 MW	10.58 AW	22010 AAW	NDBLS	10//99-12//99
	Oklahoma	S	14.56 MW	14.48 AW	30110 AAW	OKBLS	10//99-12//99
	Oregon	S	16.79 MW	16.95 AW	35250 AAW	ORBLS	10//99-12//99
	Pennsylvania	S	14.2 MW	13.85 AW	28810 AAW	PABLS	10//99-12//99
	Rhode Island	S	15.67 MW	16.02 AW	33320 AAW	RIBLS	10//99-12//99
	South Carolina	S	19.16 MW	21.02 AW	43730 AAW	SCBLS	10//99-12//99
	South Dakota	S	10.37 MW	11.01 AW	22900 AAW	SDBLS	10//99-12//99
	Tennessee	S	15.24 MW	15.28 AW	31790 AAW	TNBLS	10//99-12//99
	Texas	S	17.9 MW	18.38 AW	38220 AAW	TXBLS	10//99-12//99
	Utah	S	13.84 MW	13.77 AW	28630 AAW	UTBLS	10//99-12//99
	Vermont	S	12.44 MW	12.55 AW	26100 AAW	VTBLS	10//99-12//99
	Virginia	S	15.77 MW	16.62 AW	34570 AAW	VABLS	10//99-12//99
	Washington	S	15.46 MW	15.81 AW	32880 AAW	WABLS	10//99-12//99
	West Virginia	S	10.28 MW	11.64 AW	24200 AAW	WVBLS	10//99-12//99
	Wisconsin	S	15.84 MW	16.02 AW	33310 AAW	WIBLS	10//99-12//99
	Wyoming	S	14.52 MW	14.41 AW	29960 AAW	WYBLS	10//99-12//99
	Puerto Rico	S	7.13 MW	7.11 AW	14800 AAW	PRBLS	10//99-12//99
Physical Therapy Aide	United States	Y	28782 AE			CARWO1	2000

AAW	Average annual wage	AOH	Average offered, high	ASH	Average starting, high	H	Hourly	M	Monthly	S	Special: hourly and annual
AE	Average entry wage	AOL	Average offered, low	ASL	Average starting, low	HI	Highest wage paid	MTC	Median total compensation	TQ	Third quartile wage
AEX	Average experienced wage	APH	Average pay, high range	AW	Average wage paid	HR	High end range	MW	Median wage paid	W	Weekly
AO	Average offered	APL	Average pay, low range	FQ	First quartile wage	LR	Low end range	SQ	Second quartile wage	Y	Yearly

Occupation/Type/Industry	Location	Per	Low	Mid	High	Source	Date
Physician	United States	H		37.20 AW		NCS98	1998
Cardiology	United States	Y		206000 AW		MEDEC2	1998-1999
Cardiology, Noninvasive, Group Practice	United States	Y		278900 AW		MEDEC3	1998
Critical Care	United States	Y	150254 APL	201260 MW	237638 HI	CCA	1999
Family Practice	United States	Y		136000 AW		MEDEC2	1998-1999
Family Practice (without OB), Group Practice	United States	Y		138277 AW		MEDEC3	1998
Gastroenterology, Group Practice	United States	Y		240278 AW		MEDEC3	1998
General Surgery, Group Practice	United States	Y		225653 AW		MEDEC3	1998
Internal Medicine	United States	Y		139000 AW		MEDEC2	1998-1999
Internal Medicine, Group Practice	United States	Y		141147 AW		MEDEC3	1998
Neurology, Group Practice	United States	Y		160601 AW		MEDEC3	1998
Obstetrics-gynecology	United States	Y		211000 AW		MEDEC2	1998-1999
Obstetrics/Gynecology, Group Practice	United States	Y		216307 AW		MEDEC3	1998
Oncology	United States	Y		201000 AW		MEDEC2	1998-1999
Orthopedic Surgery, Group Practice	United States	Y		312356 AW		MEDEC3	1998
Pediatrics	United States	Y		132000 AW		MEDEC2	1998-1999
Pediatrics	Los Angeles County, CA	Y		186718 AW		LABJ	1999
Pediatrics, Group Practice	United States	Y		135000 AW		MEDEC3	1998
Radiology	United States	Y		197000 AW		MEDEC2	1998-1999
Urology, Group Practice	United States	Y		240000 AW		MEDEC3	1998
Physician Assistant	Birmingham MSA, AL	S	21.76 MW	24.32 AW	45270 AAW	ALBLS	10//99-12//99
	Dothan MSA, AL	S	17.91 MW	11.89 AW	37250 AAW	ALBLS	10//99-12//99
	Mobile MSA, AL	S	12.26 MW	6.02 AW	25500 AAW	ALBLS	10//99-12//99
	Alaska	S	37.15 MW	35.85 AW	74570 AAW	AKBLS	10//99-12//99
	Arizona	S	21.16 MW	21.30 AW	44310 AAW	AZBLS	10//99-12//99
	Phoenix-Mesa MSA, AZ	S	21.67 MW	21.84 AW	45080 AAW	AZBLS	10//99-12//99
	Tucson MSA, AZ	S	17.76 MW	13.34 AW	36940 AAW	AZBLS	10//99-12//99
	Yuma MSA, AZ	S	18.90 MW	13.55 AW	39320 AAW	AZBLS	10//99-12//99
	Arkansas	S	10.07 MW	13.78 AW	28670 AAW	ARBLS	10//99-12//99
	Little Rock-North Little Rock MSA, AR	S	11.70 MW	10.31 AW	24340 AAW	ARBLS	10//99-12//99
	California	S	29.35 MW	25.99 AW	54060 AAW	CABLS	10//99-12//99
	Bakersfield MSA, CA	S	22.88 MW	23.42 AW	47580 AAW	CABLS	10//99-12//99
	Chico-Paradise MSA, CA	S	33.06 MW	35.24 AW	68770 AAW	CABLS	10//99-12//99
	Fresno MSA, CA	S	32.43 MW	33.75 AW	67450 AAW	CABLS	10//99-12//99
	Los Angeles-Long Beach PMSA, CA	S	24.35 MW	22.24 AW	50660 AAW	CABLS	10//99-12//99
	Merced MSA, CA	S	32.31 MW	35.31 AW	67210 AAW	CABLS	10//99-12//99
	Modesto MSA, CA	S	28.53 MW	30.22 AW	59340 AAW	CABLS	10//99-12//99
	Oakland PMSA, CA	S	30.77 MW	34.14 AW	64000 AAW	CABLS	10//99-12//99
	Orange County PMSA, CA	S	23.69 MW	22.84 AW	49270 AAW	CABLS	10//99-12//99
	Riverside-San Bernardino PMSA, CA	S	30.42 MW	34.60 AW	63270 AAW	CABLS	10//99-12//99
	Salinas MSA, CA	S	34.93 MW	36.94 AW	72660 AAW	CABLS	10//99-12//99
	San Diego County, CA	Y		54000 AW		ERDGE	1998
	San Diego MSA, CA	S	31.56 MW	34.68 AW	65640 AAW	CABLS	10//99-12//99
	San Francisco PMSA, CA	S	22.38 MW	25.90 AW	46540 AAW	CABLS	10//99-12//99
	San Jose PMSA, CA	S	29.50 MW	33.99 AW	61370 AAW	CABLS	10//99-12//99
	Santa Cruz-Watsonville PMSA, CA	S	16.39 MW	12.11 AW	34090 AAW	CABLS	10//99-12//99
	Vallejo-Fairfield-Napa PMSA, CA	S	18.45 MW	13.77 AW	38380 AAW	CABLS	10//99-12//99
	Colorado	S	27.04 MW	26.12 AW	54320 AAW	COBLS	10//99-12//99
	Colorado Springs MSA, CO	S	27.82 MW	28.42 AW	57860 AAW	COBLS	10//99-12//99
	Fort Collins-Loveland MSA, CO	S	29.04 MW	29.41 AW	60400 AAW	COBLS	10//99-12//99
	Grand Junction MSA, CO	S	24.30 MW	24.53 AW	50530 AAW	COBLS	10//99-12//99
	Greeley PMSA, CO	S	29.97 MW	31.84 AW	62330 AAW	COBLS	10//99-12//99
	Pueblo MSA, CO	S	25.13 MW	24.93 AW	52260 AAW	COBLS	10//99-12//99
	Connecticut	S	33.05 MW	30.74 AW	63940 AAW	CTBLS	10//99-12//99
	Bridgeport PMSA, CT	S	28.05 MW	32.63 AW	58340 AAW	CTBLS	10//99-12//99
	Danbury PMSA, CT	S	30.20 MW	33.83 AW	62820 AAW	CTBLS	10//99-12//99
	Hartford MSA, CT	S	31.25 MW	33.72 AW	65000 AAW	CTBLS	10//99-12//99
	New Haven-Meriden PMSA, CT	S	32.90 MW	33.55 AW	68430 AAW	CTBLS	10//99-12//99
	New London-Norwich MSA, CT-RI	S	31.32 MW	33.38 AW	65150 AAW	CTBLS	10//99-12//99
	Stamford-Norwalk PMSA, CT	S	30.77 MW	32.54 AW	64000 AAW	CTBLS	10//99-12//99
	Waterbury PMSA, CT	S	26.30 MW	28.60 AW	54700 AAW	CTBLS	10//99-12//99
	Delaware	S	38.1 MW	35.42 AW	73680 AAW	DEBLS	10//99-12//99

Occupation/Type/Industry	Location	Per	Low	Mid	High	Source	Date
Physician Assistant	Wilmington-Newark PMSA, DE-MD	S	37.46 MW	39.98 AW	77920 AAW	DEBLS	10//99-12//99
	District of Columbia	S	28.02 MW	25.73 AW	53510 AAW	DCBLS	10//99-12//99
	Washington PMSA, DC-MD-VA-WV	S	22.34 MW	20.84 AW	46470 AAW	DCBLS	10//99-12//99
	Florida	S	26.04 MW	24.42 AW	50800 AAW	FLBLS	10//99-12//99
	Fort Myers-Cape Coral MSA, FL	S	27.60 MW	27.51 AW	57400 AAW	FLBLS	10//99-12//99
	Fort Pierce-Port St. Lucie MSA, FL	S	27.00 MW	27.49 AW	56170 AAW	FLBLS	10//99-12//99
	Fort Walton Beach MSA, FL	S	24.42 MW	24.54 AW	50780 AAW	FLBLS	10//99-12//99
	Gainesville MSA, FL	S	26.65 MW	28.86 AW	55430 AAW	FLBLS	10//99-12//99
	Jacksonville MSA, FL	S	31.96 MW	33.82 AW	66480 AAW	FLBLS	10//99-12//99
	Lakeland-Winter Haven MSA, FL	S	18.52 MW	12.82 AW	38520 AAW	FLBLS	10//99-12//99
	Melbourne-Titusville-Palm Bay MSA, FL	S	30.43 MW	32.67 AW	63300 AAW	FLBLS	10//99-12//99
	Miami PMSA, FL	S	20.41 MW	12.01 AW	42460 AAW	FLBLS	10//99-12//99
	Naples MSA, FL	S	31.52 MW	35.91 AW	65570 AAW	FLBLS	10//99-12//99
	Orlando MSA, FL	S	28.01 MW	32.72 AW	58260 AAW	FLBLS	10//99-12//99
	Pensacola MSA, FL	S	30.44 MW	29.37 AW	63320 AAW	FLBLS	10//99-12//99
	Sarasota-Bradenton MSA, FL	S	16.05 MW	13.41 AW	33370 AAW	FLBLS	10//99-12//99
	Tampa-St. Petersburg-Clearwater MSA, FL	S	21.43 MW	20.14 AW	44580 AAW	FLBLS	10//99-12//99
	West Palm Beach-Boca Raton MSA, FL	S	19.45 MW	15.19 AW	40460 AAW	FLBLS	10//99-12//99
	Georgia	S	28.78 MW	26.79 AW	55720 AAW	GABLS	10//99-12//99
	Albany MSA, GA	S	29.31 MW	31.16 AW	60970 AAW	GABLS	10//99-12//99
	Atlanta MSA, GA	S	27.87 MW	31.28 AW	57970 AAW	GABLS	10//99-12//99
	Augusta-Aiken MSA, GA-SC	S	22.96 MW	25.00 AW	47760 AAW	GABLS	10//99-12//99
	Hawaii	S	11.55 MW	17.35 AW	36090 AAW	HIBLS	10//99-12//99
	Honolulu MSA, HI	S	16.68 MW	11.39 AW	34690 AAW	HIBLS	10//99-12//99
	Idaho	S	24.32 MW	24.03 AW	49990 AAW	IDBLS	10//99-12//99
	Boise City MSA, ID	S	35.10 MW	33.69 AW	73010 AAW	IDBLS	10//99-12//99
	Illinois	S	21.7 MW	21.35 AW	44420 AAW	ILBLS	10//99-12//99
	Bloomington-Normal MSA, IL	S	21.02 MW	22.47 AW	43720 AAW	ILBLS	10//99-12//99
	Chicago PMSA, IL	S	21.84 MW	21.86 AW	45430 AAW	ILBLS	10//99-12//99
	Peoria-Pekin MSA, IL	S	24.07 MW	24.33 AW	50070 AAW	ILBLS	10//99-12//99
	Springfield MSA, IL	S	19.69 MW	21.11 AW	40950 AAW	ILBLS	10//99-12//99
	Indiana	S	15.64 MW	19.65 AW	40880 AAW	INBLS	10//99-12//99
	Evansville-Henderson MSA, IN-KY	S	19.95 MW	15.48 AW	41490 AAW	INBLS	10//99-12//99
	Fort Wayne MSA, IN	S	23.46 MW	27.64 AW	48800 AAW	INBLS	10//99-12//99
	Gary PMSA, IN	S	18.77 MW	15.29 AW	39030 AAW	INBLS	10//99-12//99
	Indianapolis MSA, IN	S	18.11 MW	13.26 AW	37680 AAW	INBLS	10//99-12//99
	Muncie MSA, IN	S	23.44 MW	20.83 AW	48750 AAW	INBLS	10//99-12//99
	Iowa	S	26.4 MW	25.66 AW	53370 AAW	IABLS	10//99-12//99
	Des Moines MSA, IA	S	28.28 MW	29.95 AW	58830 AAW	IABLS	10//99-12//99
	Dubuque MSA, IA	S	20.71 MW	19.40 AW	43090 AAW	IABLS	10//99-12//99
	Iowa City MSA, IA	S	20.13 MW	23.66 AW	41880 AAW	IABLS	10//99-12//99
	Sioux City MSA, IA-NE	S	23.92 MW	25.21 AW	49760 AAW	IABLS	10//99-12//99
	Waterloo-Cedar Falls MSA, IA	S	26.31 MW	29.25 AW	54730 AAW	IABLS	10//99-12//99
	Kansas	S	29.65 MW	28.11 AW	58460 AAW	KSBLS	10//99-12//99
	Topeka MSA, KS	S	19.54 MW	21.37 AW	40630 AAW	KSBLS	10//99-12//99
	Wichita MSA, KS	S	26.87 MW	27.50 AW	55880 AAW	KSBLS	10//99-12//99
	Kentucky	S	29.42 MW	28.82 AW	59940 AAW	KYBLS	10//99-12//99
	Lexington MSA, KY	S	26.79 MW	24.28 AW	55720 AAW	KYBLS	10//99-12//99
	Louisville MSA, KY-IN	S	24.16 MW	23.59 AW	50260 AAW	KYBLS	10//99-12//99
	Owensboro MSA, KY	S	36.59 MW	37.88 AW	76110 AAW	KYBLS	10//99-12//99
	Louisiana	S	10.9 MW	14.42 AW	30000 AAW	LABLS	10//99-12//99
	Baton Rouge MSA, LA	S	14.68 MW	11.03 AW	30520 AAW	LABLS	10//99-12//99
	Lake Charles MSA, LA	S	16.23 MW	12.55 AW	33760 AAW	LABLS	10//99-12//99
	New Orleans MSA, LA	S	11.76 MW	9.88 AW	24460 AAW	LABLS	10//99-12//99
	Shreveport-Bossier City MSA, LA	S	18.63 MW	14.01 AW	38750 AAW	LABLS	10//99-12//99
	Maine	S	31.42 MW	30.95 AW	64380 AAW	MEBLS	10//99-12//99
	Bangor MSA, ME	S	30.45 MW	32.26 AW	63340 AAW	MEBLS	10//99-12//99
	Portland MSA, ME	S	31.99 MW	29.87 AW	66550 AAW	MEBLS	10//99-12//99
	Baltimore PMSA, MD	S	19.36 MW	19.81 AW	40280 AAW	MDBLS	10//99-12//99
	Hagerstown PMSA, MD	S	22.49 MW	23.63 AW	46770 AAW	MDBLS	10//99-12//99
	Massachusetts	S	18.86 MW	21.40 AW	44500 AAW	MABLS	10//99-12//99
	Boston PMSA, MA-NH	S	24.52 MW	25.75 AW	51000 AAW	MABLS	10//99-12//99

AAW Average annual wage	**AOH** Average offered, high	**ASH** Average starting, high	**H** Hourly	**M** Monthly	**S** Special: hourly and annual
AE Average entry wage	**AOL** Average offered, low	**ASL** Average starting, low	**HI** Highest wage paid	**MTC** Median total compensation	**TQ** Third quartile wage
AEX Average experienced wage	**APH** Average pay, high range	**AW** Average wage paid	**HR** High end range	**MW** Median wage paid	**W** Weekly
AO Average offered	**APL** Average pay, low range	**FQ** First quartile wage	**LR** Low end range	**SQ** Second quartile wage	**Y** Yearly

Occupation/Type/Industry	Location	Per	Low	Mid	High	Source	Date
Physician Assistant	Fitchburg-Leominster PMSA, MA	S	24.43 MW	26.16 AW	50810 AAW	MABLS	10//99-12//99
	Lawrence PMSA, MA-NH	S	18.94 MW	12.81 AW	39390 AAW	MABLS	10//99-12//99
	Lowell PMSA, MA-NH	S	18.62 MW	18.20 AW	38730 AAW	MABLS	10//99-12//99
	Worcester PMSA, MA-CT	S	15.25 MW	13.40 AW	31730 AAW	MABLS	10//99-12//99
	Michigan	S	28.13 MW	24.78 AW	51540 AAW	MIBLS	10//99-12//99
	Ann Arbor PMSA, MI	S	25.12 MW	25.67 AW	52250 AAW	MIBLS	10//99-12//99
	Detroit PMSA, MI	S	20.66 MW	13.64 AW	42970 AAW	MIBLS	10//99-12//99
	Flint PMSA, MI	S	30.52 MW	30.37 AW	63490 AAW	MIBLS	10//99-12//99
	Grand Rapids-Muskegon-Holland MSA, MI	S	27.26 MW	29.98 AW	56690 AAW	MIBLS	10//99-12//99
	Kalamazoo-Battle Creek MSA, MI	S	25.05 MW	27.49 AW	52100 AAW	MIBLS	10//99-12//99
	Lansing-East Lansing MSA, MI	S	30.74 MW	31.88 AW	63930 AAW	MIBLS	10//99-12//99
	Saginaw-Bay City-Midland MSA, MI	S	31.33 MW	33.62 AW	65160 AAW	MIBLS	10//99-12//99
	Minnesota	S	28.24 MW	26.65 AW	55430 AAW	MNBLS	10//99-12//99
	Minneapolis-St. Paul MSA, MN-WI	S	27.00 MW	29.62 AW	56150 AAW	MNBLS	10//99-12//99
	St. Cloud MSA, MN	S	22.67 MW	23.20 AW	47150 AAW	MNBLS	10//99-12//99
	Mississippi	S	13.96 MW	18.47 AW	38410 AAW	MSBLS	10//99-12//99
	Missouri	S	23.49 MW	25.50 AW	53030 AAW	MOBLS	10//99-12//99
	St. Louis MSA, MO-IL	S	22.10 MW	23.18 AW	45970 AAW	MOBLS	10//99-12//99
	Montana	S	26.97 MW	28.02 AW	58280 AAW	MTBLS	10//99-12//99
	Nebraska	S	29.16 MW	29.00 AW	60330 AAW	NEBLS	10//99-12//99
	Lincoln MSA, NE	S	27.18 MW	29.18 AW	56540 AAW	NEBLS	10//99-12//99
	Omaha MSA, NE-IA	S	23.86 MW	22.98 AW	49620 AAW	NEBLS	10//99-12//99
	Nevada	S	23.23 MW	25.22 AW	52460 AAW	NVBLS	10//99-12//99
	Las Vegas MSA, NV-AZ	S	26.05 MW	28.47 AW	54180 AAW	NVBLS	10//99-12//99
	New Hampshire	S	28.92 MW	25.86 AW	53790 AAW	NHBLS	10//99-12//99
	Manchester PMSA, NH	S	27.25 MW	29.94 AW	56670 AAW	NHBLS	10//99-12//99
	Nashua PMSA, NH	S	31.24 MW	33.50 AW	64970 AAW	NHBLS	10//99-12//99
	Middlesex-Somerset-Hunterdon PMSA, NJ	S	18.66 MW	15.67 AW	38810 AAW	NJBLS	10//99-12//99
	Newark PMSA, NJ	S	22.51 MW	16.45 AW	46830 AAW	NJBLS	10//99-12//99
	New Mexico	S	22.69 MW	20.76 AW	43190 AAW	NMBLS	10//99-12//99
	Albuquerque MSA, NM	S	21.48 MW	23.36 AW	44680 AAW	NMBLS	10//99-12//99
	New York	S	32.5 MW	30.36 AW	63140 AAW	NYBLS	10//99-12//99
	Albany-Schenectady-Troy MSA, NY	S	30.64 MW	31.80 AW	63730 AAW	NYBLS	10//99-12//99
	Binghamton MSA, NY	S	31.43 MW	31.67 AW	65380 AAW	NYBLS	10//99-12//99
	Buffalo-Niagara Falls MSA, NY	S	28.57 MW	29.20 AW	59420 AAW	NYBLS	10//99-12//99
	Dutchess County PMSA, NY	S	26.30 MW	26.58 AW	54700 AAW	NYBLS	10//99-12//99
	Glens Falls MSA, NY	S	31.94 MW	33.85 AW	66430 AAW	NYBLS	10//99-12//99
	Jamestown MSA, NY	S	27.77 MW	27.79 AW	57760 AAW	NYBLS	10//99-12//99
	Nassau-Suffolk PMSA, NY	S	29.69 MW	33.37 AW	61750 AAW	NYBLS	10//99-12//99
	New York PMSA, NY	S	32.11 MW	33.69 AW	66800 AAW	NYBLS	10//99-12//99
	Newburgh PMSA, NY-PA	S	29.01 MW	31.85 AW	60330 AAW	NYBLS	10//99-12//99
	Rochester MSA, NY	S	28.51 MW	31.68 AW	59300 AAW	NYBLS	10//99-12//99
	Syracuse MSA, NY	S	27.75 MW	29.01 AW	57720 AAW	NYBLS	10//99-12//99
	Utica-Rome MSA, NY	S	27.95 MW	30.28 AW	58130 AAW	NYBLS	10//99-12//99
	North Carolina	S	28.43 MW	26.53 AW	55190 AAW	NCBLS	10//99-12//99
	Asheville MSA, NC	S	29.26 MW	29.86 AW	60870 AAW	NCBLS	10//99-12//99
	Charlotte-Gastonia-Rock Hill MSA, NC-SC	S	27.58 MW	28.69 AW	57360 AAW	NCBLS	10//99-12//99
	Fayetteville MSA, NC	S	29.77 MW	31.06 AW	61920 AAW	NCBLS	10//99-12//99
	Greensboro--Winston-Salem--High Point MSA, NC	S	25.67 MW	25.90 AW	53390 AAW	NCBLS	10//99-12//99
	Greenville MSA, NC	S	30.85 MW	31.44 AW	64170 AAW	NCBLS	10//99-12//99
	Hickory-Morganton-Lenoir MSA, NC	S	29.44 MW	30.90 AW	61240 AAW	NCBLS	10//99-12//99
	Jacksonville MSA, NC	S	27.77 MW	25.27 AW	57760 AAW	NCBLS	10//99-12//99
	Raleigh-Durham-Chapel Hill MSA, NC	S	30.09 MW	31.30 AW	62580 AAW	NCBLS	10//99-12//99
	North Dakota	S	29.42 MW	28.89 AW	60080 AAW	NDBLS	10//99-12//99
	Fargo-Moorhead MSA, ND-MN	S	28.77 MW	29.21 AW	59840 AAW	NDBLS	10//99-12//99
	Ohio	S	28.81 MW	28.10 AW	58450 AAW	OHBLS	10//99-12//99
	Cincinnati PMSA, OH-KY-IN	S	28.04 MW	28.43 AW	58320 AAW	OHBLS	10//99-12//99
	Cleveland-Lorain-Elyria PMSA, OH	S	28.14 MW	28.46 AW	58540 AAW	OHBLS	10//99-12//99

AAW	Average annual wage	AOH	Average offered, high	ASH	Average starting, high
AE	Average entry wage	AOL	Average offered, low	ASL	Average starting, low
AEX	Average experienced wage	APH	Average pay, high range	AW	Average wage paid
AO	Average offered	APL	Average pay, low range	FQ	First quartile wage

H	Hourly
HI	Highest wage paid
HR	High end range
LR	Low end range

M	Monthly
MTC	Median total compensation
MW	Median wage paid
SQ	Second quartile wage

S	Special: hourly and annual
TQ	Third quartile wage
W	Weekly
Y	Yearly

Occupation/Type/Industry	Location	Per	Low	Mid	High	Source	Date
Physician Assistant	Columbus MSA, OH	S	27.77 MW	28.33 AW	57770 AAW	OHBLS	10//99-12//99
	Dayton-Springfield MSA, OH	S	28.62 MW	31.11 AW	59540 AAW	OHBLS	10//99-12//99
	Toledo MSA, OH	S	27.65 MW	29.45 AW	57520 AAW	OHBLS	10//99-12//99
	Oklahoma	S	13.71 MW	19.64 AW	40850 AAW	OKBLS	10//99-12//99
	Oklahoma City MSA, OK	S	30.66 MW	32.85 AW	63770 AAW	OKBLS	10//99-12//99
	Oregon	S	26.25 MW	23.94 AW	49790 AAW	ORBLS	10//99-12//99
	Eugene-Springfield MSA, OR	S	32.42 MW	34.29 AW	67440 AAW	ORBLS	10//99-12//99
	Portland-Vancouver PMSA, OR-WA	S	24.17 MW	26.80 AW	50260 AAW	ORBLS	10//99-12//99
	Salem PMSA, OR	S	22.18 MW	19.26 AW	46140 AAW	ORBLS	10//99-12//99
	Pennsylvania	S	24.32 MW	24.29 AW	50520 AAW	PABLS	10//99-12//99
	Allentown-Bethlehem-Easton MSA, PA	S	27.81 MW	30.03 AW	57840 AAW	PABLS	10//99-12//99
	Altoona MSA, PA	S	29.68 MW	29.96 AW	61720 AAW	PABLS	10//99-12//99
	Erie MSA, PA	S	15.95 MW	10.40 AW	33170 AAW	PABLS	10//99-12//99
	Harrisburg-Lebanon-Carlisle MSA, PA	S	21.27 MW	22.81 AW	44240 AAW	PABLS	10//99-12//99
	Johnstown MSA, PA	S	24.61 MW	23.46 AW	51180 AAW	PABLS	10//99-12//99
	Lancaster MSA, PA	S	28.64 MW	29.45 AW	59580 AAW	PABLS	10//99-12//99
	Philadelphia PMSA, PA-NJ	S	22.65 MW	22.08 AW	47110 AAW	PABLS	10//99-12//99
	Pittsburgh MSA, PA	S	25.84 MW	25.63 AW	53750 AAW	PABLS	10//99-12//99
	Reading MSA, PA	S	29.03 MW	29.90 AW	60380 AAW	PABLS	10//99-12//99
	Scranton--Wilkes-Barre--Hazleton MSA, PA	S	19.83 MW	21.05 AW	41250 AAW	PABLS	10//99-12//99
	Sharon MSA, PA	S	22.35 MW	22.32 AW	46490 AAW	PABLS	10//99-12//99
	Williamsport MSA, PA	S	24.46 MW	26.02 AW	50880 AAW	PABLS	10//99-12//99
	York MSA, PA	S	23.93 MW	22.86 AW	49760 AAW	PABLS	10//99-12//99
	Rhode Island	S	33.35 MW	30.74 AW	63950 AAW	RIBLS	10//99-12//99
	Providence-Fall River-Warwick MSA, RI-MA	S	30.56 MW	33.22 AW	63560 AAW	RIBLS	10//99-12//99
	South Carolina	S	18.31 MW	19.49 AW	40540 AAW	SCBLS	10//99-12//99
	Charleston-North Charleston MSA, SC	S	18.70 MW	13.09 AW	38900 AAW	SCBLS	10//99-12//99
	Columbia MSA, SC	S	20.22 MW	18.86 AW	42060 AAW	SCBLS	10//99-12//99
	Florence MSA, SC	S	8.67 MW	7.76 AW	18040 AAW	SCBLS	10//99-12//99
	South Dakota	S	30.94 MW	29.44 AW	61230 AAW	SDBLS	10//99-12//99
	Rapid City MSA, SD	S	31.57 MW	33.25 AW	65670 AAW	SDBLS	10//99-12//99
	Tennessee	S	20.65 MW	20.39 AW	42400 AAW	TNBLS	10//99-12//99
	Johnson City-Kingsport-Bristol MSA, TN-VA	S	28.68 MW	30.72 AW	59650 AAW	TNBLS	10//99-12//99
	Knoxville MSA, TN	S	19.70 MW	22.04 AW	40970 AAW	TNBLS	10//99-12//99
	Memphis MSA, TN-AR-MS	S	14.89 MW	11.16 AW	30980 AAW	MSBLS	10//99-12//99
	Nashville MSA, TN	S	22.17 MW	21.96 AW	46110 AAW	TNBLS	10//99-12//99
	Texas	S	21.75 MW	22.58 AW	46960 AAW	TXBLS	10//99-12//99
	Amarillo MSA, TX	S	24.03 MW	23.99 AW	49970 AAW	TXBLS	10//99-12//99
	Austin-San Marcos MSA, TX	S	16.19 MW	11.65 AW	33670 AAW	TXBLS	10//99-12//99
	Beaumont-Port Arthur MSA, TX	S	18.35 MW	15.40 AW	38170 AAW	TXBLS	10//99-12//99
	Brazoria PMSA, TX	S	29.46 MW	31.76 AW	61280 AAW	TXBLS	10//99-12//99
	Brownsville-Harlingen-San Benito MSA, TX	S	30.44 MW	33.15 AW	63320 AAW	TXBLS	10//99-12//99
	Corpus Christi MSA, TX	S	20.64 MW	16.80 AW	42930 AAW	TXBLS	10//99-12//99
	Dallas PMSA, TX	S	22.24 MW	21.28 AW	46260 AAW	TXBLS	10//99-12//99
	El Paso MSA, TX	S	16.02 MW	11.58 AW	33320 AAW	TXBLS	10//99-12//99
	Fort Worth-Arlington PMSA, TX	S	16.32 MW	10.67 AW	33940 AAW	TXBLS	10//99-12//99
	Houston PMSA, TX	S	25.30 MW	28.90 AW	52630 AAW	TXBLS	10//99-12//99
	Killeen-Temple MSA, TX	S	31.97 MW	32.25 AW	66500 AAW	TXBLS	10//99-12//99
	Longview-Marshall MSA, TX	S	22.25 MW	24.62 AW	46280 AAW	TXBLS	10//99-12//99
	Lubbock MSA, TX	S	21.92 MW	11.84 AW	45590 AAW	TXBLS	10//99-12//99
	McAllen-Edinburg-Mission MSA, TX	S	30.56 MW	31.40 AW	63560 AAW	TXBLS	10//99-12//99
	San Antonio MSA, TX	S	26.96 MW	19.65 AW	56080 AAW	TXBLS	10//99-12//99
	Utah	S	31.9 MW	32.26 AW	67090 AAW	UTBLS	10//99-12//99
	Provo-Orem MSA, UT	S	47.77 MW	61.90 AW	99360 AAW	UTBLS	10//99-12//99
	Salt Lake City-Ogden MSA, UT	S	29.32 MW	30.84 AW	60980 AAW	UTBLS	10//99-12//99
	Vermont	S	35.9 MW	33.89 AW	70500 AAW	VTBLS	10//99-12//99
	Virginia	S	13.34 MW	16.38 AW	34070 AAW	VABLS	10//99-12//99
	Norfolk-Virginia Beach-Newport News MSA, VA-NC	S	12.73 MW	7.73 AW	26470 AAW	VABLS	10//99-12//99

AAW Average annual wage	AOH Average offered, high	ASH Average starting, high	H Hourly	M Monthly	S Special: hourly and annual
AE Average entry wage	AOL Average offered, low	ASL Average starting, low	HI Highest wage paid	MTC Median total compensation	TQ Third quartile wage
AEX Average experienced wage	APH Average pay, high range	AW Average wage paid	HR High end range	MW Median wage paid	W Weekly
AO Average offered	APL Average pay, low range	FQ First quartile wage	LR Low end range	SQ Second quartile wage	Y Yearly

Occupation/Type/Industry	Location	Per	Low	Mid	High	Source	Date
Physician Assistant	Richmond-Petersburg MSA, VA	S	17.54 MW	13.34 AW	36490 AAW	VABLS	10//99-12//99
	Washington	S	28.58 MW	25.92 AW	53910 AAW	WABLS	10//99-12//99
	Bellingham MSA, WA	S	28.01 MW	28.38 AW	58260 AAW	WABLS	10//99-12//99
	Olympia PMSA, WA	S	26.75 MW	25.87 AW	55640 AAW	WABLS	10//99-12//99
	Richland-Kennewick-Pasco MSA, WA	S	29.45 MW	29.96 AW	61260 AAW	WABLS	10//99-12//99
	Seattle-Bellevue-Everett PMSA, WA	S	24.77 MW	28.37 AW	51520 AAW	WABLS	10//99-12//99
	Spokane MSA, WA	S	29.14 MW	29.65 AW	60610 AAW	WABLS	10//99-12//99
	Tacoma PMSA, WA	S	24.14 MW	25.87 AW	50210 AAW	WABLS	10//99-12//99
	Yakima MSA, WA	S	27.89 MW	30.24 AW	58010 AAW	WABLS	10//99-12//99
	West Virginia	S	20.39 MW	17.62 AW	36650 AAW	WVBLS	10//99-12//99
	Huntington-Ashland MSA, WV-KY-OH	S	12.96 MW	7.93 AW	26950 AAW	WVBLS	10//99-12//99
	Wisconsin	S	26.52 MW	26.78 AW	55700 AAW	WIBLS	10//99-12//99
	Appleton-Oshkosh-Neenah MSA, WI	S	31.90 MW	34.10 AW	66360 AAW	WIBLS	10//99-12//99
	Green Bay MSA, WI	S	36.40 MW	38.39 AW	75710 AAW	WIBLS	10//99-12//99
	Milwaukee-Waukesha PMSA, WI	S	24.16 MW	22.84 AW	50250 AAW	WIBLS	10//99-12//99
	Wyoming	S	29.39 MW	26.96 AW	56070 AAW	WYBLS	10//99-12//99
	Puerto Rico	S	8.43 MW	10.30 AW	21420 AAW	PRBLS	10//99-12//99
	San Juan-Bayamon PMSA, PR	S	9.24 MW	7.94 AW	19220 AAW	PRBLS	10//99-12//99
Medical Doctor's Office	United States	H		28.80 AEX		MEDEC	2000
Physicians' Assistant	United States	H		26.75 AW		NCS98	1998
Physicist	Arizona	S	25.24 MW	27.34 AW	56870 AAW	AZBLS	10//99-12//99
	California	S	36.93 MW	36.04 AW	74950 AAW	CABLS	10//99-12//99
	Los Angeles-Long Beach PMSA, CA	S	35.92 MW	37.07 AW	74700 AAW	CABLS	10//99-12//99
	San Francisco PMSA, CA	S	36.01 MW	36.96 AW	74890 AAW	CABLS	10//99-12//99
	Colorado	S	33.93 MW	35.13 AW	73060 AAW	COBLS	10//99-12//99
	Denver PMSA, CO	S	32.76 MW	32.45 AW	68150 AAW	COBLS	10//99-12//99
	Connecticut	S	44.48 MW	43.25 AW	89960 AAW	CTBLS	10//99-12//99
	Washington PMSA, DC-MD-VA-WV	S	39.38 MW	39.09 AW	81920 AAW	DCBLS	10//99-12//99
	Florida	S	37.43 MW	36.93 AW	76810 AAW	FLBLS	10//99-12//99
	Miami PMSA, FL	S	37.18 MW	38.37 AW	77330 AAW	FLBLS	10//99-12//99
	Tampa-St. Petersburg-Clearwater MSA, FL	S	36.65 MW	38.44 AW	76230 AAW	FLBLS	10//99-12//99
	Georgia	S	35.24 MW	34.85 AW	72490 AAW	GABLS	10//99-12//99
	Atlanta MSA, GA	S	36.26 MW	37.05 AW	75420 AAW	GABLS	10//99-12//99
	Illinois	S	36.15 MW	35.55 AW	73940 AAW	ILBLS	10//99-12//99
	Indiana	S	33.14 MW	36.35 AW	75610 AAW	INBLS	10//99-12//99
	Iowa	S	30.6 MW	31.97 AW	66510 AAW	IABLS	10//99-12//99
	Louisiana	S	26.22 MW	26.37 AW	54840 AAW	LABLS	10//99-12//99
	Massachusetts	S	36.51 MW	35.67 AW	74180 AAW	MABLS	10//99-12//99
	Boston PMSA, MA-NH	S	33.13 MW	35.89 AW	68910 AAW	MABLS	10//99-12//99
	Michigan	S	35.32 MW	34.97 AW	72730 AAW	MIBLS	10//99-12//99
	Detroit PMSA, MI	S	36.36 MW	37.89 AW	75630 AAW	MIBLS	10//99-12//99
	Mississippi	S	30.43 MW	28.95 AW	60210 AAW	MSBLS	10//99-12//99
	Missouri	S	36.22 MW	34.66 AW	72080 AAW	MOBLS	10//99-12//99
	Nebraska	S	46.11 MW	41.54 AW	86410 AAW	NEBLS	10//99-12//99
	New Jersey	S	35.11 MW	37.02 AW	77000 AAW	NJBLS	10//99-12//99
	New Mexico	S	37.33 MW	37.40 AW	77790 AAW	NMBLS	10//99-12//99
	Albuquerque MSA, NM	S	37.47 MW	37.41 AW	77940 AAW	NMBLS	10//99-12//99
	New York	S	37.19 MW	41.90 AW	87160 AAW	NYBLS	10//99-12//99
	New York PMSA, NY	S	27.58 MW	24.96 AW	57360 AAW	NYBLS	10//99-12//99
	North Carolina	S	30.88 MW	31.33 AW	65170 AAW	NCBLS	10//99-12//99
	Raleigh-Durham-Chapel Hill MSA, NC	S	31.42 MW	30.88 AW	65360 AAW	NCBLS	10//99-12//99
	Ohio	S	33.64 MW	35.40 AW	73630 AAW	OHBLS	10//99-12//99
	Cincinnati PMSA, OH-KY-IN	S	41.28 MW	43.59 AW	85860 AAW	OHBLS	10//99-12//99
	Cleveland-Lorain-Elyria PMSA, OH	S	34.24 MW	32.93 AW	71230 AAW	OHBLS	10//99-12//99
	Pennsylvania	S	37.06 MW	36.57 AW	76070 AAW	PABLS	10//99-12//99
	Tennessee	S	32.26 MW	32.52 AW	67640 AAW	TNBLS	10//99-12//99
	Texas	S	36.84 MW	36.39 AW	75700 AAW	TXBLS	10//99-12//99
	Virginia	S	38.01 MW	39.27 AW	81690 AAW	VABLS	10//99-12//99

AAW Average annual wage	**AOH** Average offered, high	**ASH** Average starting, high	**H** Hourly	**M** Monthly	**S** Special: hourly and annual
AE Average entry wage	**AOL** Average offered, low	**ASL** Average starting, low	**HI** Highest wage paid	**MTC** Median total compensation	**TQ** Third quartile wage
AEX Average experienced wage	**APH** Average pay, high range	**AW** Average wage paid	**HR** High end range	**MW** Median wage paid	**W** Weekly
AO Average offered	**APL** Average pay, low range	**FQ** First quartile wage	**LR** Low end range	**SQ** Second quartile wage	**Y** Yearly

Occupation/Type/Industry	Location	Per	Low	Mid	High	Source	Date
Physicist	Norfolk-Virginia Beach-Newport News MSA, VA-NC	S	33.58 mw	31.46 aw	69850 aaw	VABLS	10//99-12//99
	Wisconsin	S	34.38 mw	37.56 aw	78120 aaw	WIBLS	10//99-12//99
	Madison MSA, WI	S	32.25 mw	31.50 aw	67090 aaw	WIBLS	10//99-12//99
Physics Teacher							
Postsecondary	Alabama	Y		58390 aaw		ALBLS	10//99-12//99
Postsecondary	Birmingham MSA, AL	Y		56320 aaw		ALBLS	10//99-12//99
Postsecondary	California	Y		58840 aaw		CABLS	10//99-12//99
Postsecondary	Los Angeles-Long Beach PMSA, CA	Y		56220 aaw		CABLS	10//99-12//99
Postsecondary	Riverside-San Bernardino PMSA, CA	Y		57900 aaw		CABLS	10//99-12//99
Postsecondary	San Diego MSA, CA	Y		62470 aaw		CABLS	10//99-12//99
Postsecondary	San Francisco PMSA, CA	Y		56730 aaw		CABLS	10//99-12//99
Postsecondary	Colorado	Y		63090 aaw		COBLS	10//99-12//99
Postsecondary	Denver PMSA, CO	Y		64450 aaw		COBLS	10//99-12//99
Postsecondary	Connecticut	Y		63730 aaw		CTBLS	10//99-12//99
Postsecondary	District of Columbia	Y		59210 aaw		DCBLS	10//99-12//99
Postsecondary	Washington PMSA, DC-MD-VA-WV	Y		69430 aaw		DCBLS	10//99-12//99
Postsecondary	Florida	Y		65590 aaw		FLBLS	10//99-12//99
Postsecondary	Miami PMSA, FL	Y		61570 aaw		FLBLS	10//99-12//99
Postsecondary	Georgia	Y		56320 aaw		GABLS	10//99-12//99
Postsecondary	Hawaii	Y		74490 aaw		HIBLS	10//99-12//99
Postsecondary	Honolulu MSA, HI	Y		73760 aaw		HIBLS	10//99-12//99
Postsecondary	Indiana	Y		57230 aaw		INBLS	10//99-12//99
Postsecondary	Indianapolis MSA, IN	Y		57600 aaw		INBLS	10//99-12//99
Postsecondary	Iowa	Y		62270 aaw		IABLS	10//99-12//99
Postsecondary	Kansas	Y		54620 aaw		KSBLS	10//99-12//99
Postsecondary	Kentucky	Y		54000 aaw		KYBLS	10//99-12//99
Postsecondary	Louisiana	Y		48980 aaw		LABLS	10//99-12//99
Postsecondary	Portland MSA, ME	Y		52960 aaw		MEBLS	10//99-12//99
Postsecondary	Maryland	Y		69630 aaw		MDBLS	10//99-12//99
Postsecondary	Baltimore PMSA, MD	Y		62880 aaw		MDBLS	10//99-12//99
Postsecondary	Massachusetts	Y		65240 aaw		MABLS	10//99-12//99
Postsecondary	Boston PMSA, MA-NH	Y		66840 aaw		MABLS	10//99-12//99
Postsecondary	Springfield MSA, MA	Y		71290 aaw		MABLS	10//99-12//99
Postsecondary	Michigan	Y		65740 aaw		MIBLS	10//99-12//99
Postsecondary	Detroit PMSA, MI	Y		63880 aaw		MIBLS	10//99-12//99
Postsecondary	Kalamazoo-Battle Creek MSA, MI	Y		55660 aaw		MIBLS	10//99-12//99
Postsecondary	Minnesota	Y		61830 aaw		MNBLS	10//99-12//99
Postsecondary	Mississippi	Y		44280 aaw		MSBLS	10//99-12//99
Postsecondary	Jackson MSA, MS	Y		35630 aaw		MSBLS	10//99-12//99
Postsecondary	Nevada	Y		56870 aaw		NVBLS	10//99-12//99
Postsecondary	New Hampshire	Y		69650 aaw		NHBLS	10//99-12//99
Postsecondary	New Jersey	Y		69810 aaw		NJBLS	10//99-12//99
Postsecondary	Jersey City PMSA, NJ	Y		61880 aaw		NJBLS	10//99-12//99
Postsecondary	New Mexico	Y		52730 aaw		NMBLS	10//99-12//99
Postsecondary	New York	Y		64460 aaw		NYBLS	10//99-12//99
Postsecondary	Albany-Schenectady-Troy MSA, NY	Y		64370 aaw		NYBLS	10//99-12//99
Postsecondary	New York PMSA, NY	Y		67360 aaw		NYBLS	10//99-12//99
Postsecondary	North Carolina	Y		61150 aaw		NCBLS	10//99-12//99
Postsecondary	Greensboro--Winston-Salem--High Point MSA, NC	Y		53770 aaw		NCBLS	10//99-12//99
Postsecondary	Raleigh-Durham-Chapel Hill MSA, NC	Y		68020 aaw		NCBLS	10//99-12//99
Postsecondary	North Dakota	Y		45160 aaw		NDBLS	10//99-12//99
Postsecondary	Ohio	Y		55070 aaw		OHBLS	10//99-12//99
Postsecondary	Cleveland-Lorain-Elyria PMSA, OH	Y		59300 aaw		OHBLS	10//99-12//99
Postsecondary	Columbus MSA, OH	Y		58100 aaw		OHBLS	10//99-12//99
Postsecondary	Dayton-Springfield MSA, OH	Y		45370 aaw		OHBLS	10//99-12//99
Postsecondary	Oklahoma	Y		51420 aaw		OKBLS	10//99-12//99
Postsecondary	Oregon	Y		56440 aaw		ORBLS	10//99-12//99
Postsecondary	Portland-Vancouver PMSA, OR-WA	Y		56630 aaw		ORBLS	10//99-12//99
Postsecondary	Pennsylvania	Y		62990 aaw		PABLS	10//99-12//99
Postsecondary	Allentown-Bethlehem-Easton MSA, PA	Y		52300 aaw		PABLS	10//99-12//99

AAW	Average annual wage	AOH	Average offered, high	ASH	Average starting, high	H	Hourly	M	Monthly	S	Special: hourly and annual
AE	Average entry wage	AOL	Average offered, low	ASL	Average starting, low	HI	Highest wage paid	MTC	Median total compensation	TQ	Third quartile wage
AEX	Average experienced wage	APH	Average pay, high range	AW	Average wage paid	HR	High end range	MW	Median wage paid	W	Weekly
AO	Average offered	APL	Average pay, low range	FQ	First quartile wage	LR	Low end range	SQ	Second quartile wage	Y	Yearly

Occupation/Type/Industry	Location	Per	Low	Mid	High	Source	Date
Physics Teacher							
Postsecondary	Lancaster MSA, PA	Y		67620 AAW		PABLS	10//99-12//99
Postsecondary	Philadelphia PMSA, PA-NJ	Y		65260 AAW		PABLS	10//99-12//99
Postsecondary	Pittsburgh MSA, PA	Y		62690 AAW		PABLS	10//99-12//99
Postsecondary	Scranton--Wilkes-Barre--						
	Hazleton MSA, PA	Y		64670 AAW		PABLS	10//99-12//99
Postsecondary	Rhode Island	Y		79930 AAW		RIBLS	10//99-12//99
Postsecondary	Providence-Fall River-						
	Warwick MSA, RI-MA	Y		79090 AAW		RIBLS	10//99-12//99
Postsecondary	South Carolina	Y		46990 AAW		SCBLS	10//99-12//99
Postsecondary	Tennessee	Y		55190 AAW		TNBLS	10//99-12//99
Postsecondary	Memphis MSA, TN-AR-MS	Y		54140 AAW		MSBLS	10//99-12//99
Postsecondary	Nashville MSA, TN	Y		59440 AAW		TNBLS	10//99-12//99
Postsecondary	Texas	Y		57970 AAW		TXBLS	10//99-12//99
Postsecondary	El Paso MSA, TX	Y		44120 AAW		TXBLS	10//99-12//99
Postsecondary	Fort Worth-Arlington PMSA,						
	TX	Y		61840 AAW		TXBLS	10//99-12//99
Postsecondary	Houston PMSA, TX	Y		70670 AAW		TXBLS	10//99-12//99
Postsecondary	San Antonio MSA, TX	Y		62340 AAW		TXBLS	10//99-12//99
Postsecondary	Virginia	Y		72070 AAW		VABLS	10//99-12//99
Postsecondary	Washington	Y		55980 AAW		WABLS	10//99-12//99
Postsecondary	Tacoma PMSA, WA	Y		49190 AAW		WABLS	10//99-12//99
Postsecondary	West Virginia	Y		61450 AAW		WVBLS	10//99-12//99
Postsecondary	Puerto Rico	Y		34850 AAW		PRBLS	10//99-12//99
Postsecondary	San Juan-Bayamon PMSA, PR	Y		34870 AAW		PRBLS	10//99-12//99
Pile-Driver Operator	Alabama	S	11.26 MW	11.31 AW	23530 AAW	ALBLS	10//99-12//99
	California	S	28.9	27.03 AW	56220 AAW	CABLS	10//99-12//99
	Colorado	S	13.05 MW	15.56 AW	32370 AAW	COBLS	10//99-12//99
	Florida	S	18.2	17.47 AW	36330 AAW	FLBLS	10//99-12//99
	Kentucky	S	12.22 MW	12.28 AW	25550 AAW	KYBLS	10//99-12//99
	Louisiana	S	16.01 MW	17.86 AW	37160 AAW	LABLS	10//99-12//99
	Maryland	S	16.18 MW	17.62 AW	36640 AAW	MDBLS	10//99-12//99
	Massachusetts	S	26.47 MW	27.02 AW	56210 AAW	MABLS	10//99-12//99
	New Jersey	S	23.7	23.61 AW	49110 AAW	NJBLS	10//99-12//99
	New York	S	21.92 MW	23.01 AW	47860 AAW	NYBLS	10//99-12//99
	North Carolina	S	11.68 MW	12.09 AW	25140 AAW	NCBLS	10//99-12//99
	Oklahoma	S	13.13 MW	12.56 AW	26120 AAW	OKBLS	10//99-12//99
	Pennsylvania	S	24.66 MW	24.63 AW	51230 AAW	PABLS	10//99-12//99
	South Carolina	S	10.06 MW	10.64 AW	22130 AAW	SCBLS	10//99-12//99
	Texas	S	14.42 MW	14.53 AW	30210 AAW	TXBLS	10//99-12//99
	Virginia	S	12.36 MW	14.38 AW	29910 AAW	VABLS	10//99-12//99
	Washington	S	22.23 MW	21.67 AW	45080 AAW	WABLS	10//99-12//99
Pilot							
Airline	United States	Y		91750 AW		DENE	1999
Pipelayer	Alabama	S	10.29 MW	11.29 AW	23480 AAW	ALBLS	10//99-12//99
	Arizona	S	11.6	11.84 AW	24620 AAW	AZBLS	10//99-12//99
	Arkansas	S	9.95 MW	10.35 AW	21530 AAW	ARBLS	10//99-12//99
	California	S	17.81 MW	18.21 AW	37880 AAW	CABLS	10//99-12//99
	Colorado	S	12.35 MW	12.83 AW	26690 AAW	COBLS	10//99-12//99
	Connecticut	S	17.83 MW	17.23 AW	35830 AAW	CTBLS	10//99-12//99
	Delaware	S	13.21 MW	13.62 AW	28330 AAW	DEBLS	10//99-12//99
	Florida	S	9.93 MW	10.23 AW	21280 AAW	FLBLS	10//99-12//99
	Georgia	S	10.87 MW	11.24 AW	23370 AAW	GABLS	10//99-12//99
	Hawaii	S	16.13 MW	19.11 AW	39750 AAW	HIBLS	10//99-12//99
	Idaho	S	12.24 MW	12.16 AW	25300 AAW	IDBLS	10//99-12//99
	Illinois	S	21.14 MW	19.37 AW	40290 AAW	ILBLS	10//99-12//99
	Indiana	S	14.44 MW	14.62 AW	30410 AAW	INBLS	10//99-12//99
	Iowa	S	13.07 MW	13.22 AW	27500 AAW	IABLS	10//99-12//99
	Kansas	S	13.48 MW	13.48 AW	28050 AAW	KSBLS	10//99-12//99
	Kentucky	S	11.25 MW	12.21 AW	25390 AAW	KYBLS	10//99-12//99
	Louisiana	S	9.42 MW	10.20 AW	21220 AAW	LABLS	10//99-12//99
	Maine	S	10.59 MW	10.71 AW	22280 AAW	MEBLS	10//99-12//99
	Maryland	S	11.76 MW	12.68 AW	26370 AAW	MDBLS	10//99-12//99
	Massachusetts	S	19.69 MW	20.47 AW	42580 AAW	MABLS	10//99-12//99
	Michigan	S	14.25 MW	14.49 AW	30140 AAW	MIBLS	10//99-12//99
	Minnesota	S	17.96 MW	17.57 AW	36540 AAW	MNBLS	10//99-12//99
	Mississippi	S	9.16 MW	9.89 AW	20560 AAW	MSBLS	10//99-12//99
	Missouri	S	15.43 MW	16.00 AW	33280 AAW	MOBLS	10//99-12//99
	Montana	S	13.9	15.44 AW	32110 AAW	MTBLS	10//99-12//99
	Nebraska	S	13.14 MW	13.54 AW	28160 AAW	NEBLS	10//99-12//99

AAW	Average annual wage	AOH	Average offered, high	ASH	Average starting, high	H	Hourly	M	Monthly	S	Special: hourly and annual
AE	Average entry wage	AOL	Average offered, low	ASL	Average starting, low	HI	Highest wage paid	MTC	Median total compensation	TQ	Third quartile wage
AEX	Average experienced wage	APH	Average pay, high range	AW	Average wage paid	HR	High end range	MW	Median wage paid	W	Weekly
AO	Average offered	APL	Average pay, low range	FQ	First quartile wage	LR	Low end range	SQ	Second quartile wage	Y	Yearly

Occupation/Type/Industry	Location	Per	Low	Mid	High	Source	Date
Pipelayer	Nevada	S	14.56 MW	15.30 AW	31820 AAW	NVBLS	10//99-12//99
	New Hampshire	S	14.63 MW	15.83 AW	32930 AAW	NHBLS	10//99-12//99
	New Jersey	S	20.57 MW	19.70 AW	40980 AAW	NJBLS	10//99-12//99
	New Mexico	S	9.01 MW	9.59 AW	19960 AAW	NMBLS	10//99-12//99
	New York	S	21.56 MW	20.93 AW	43530 AAW	NYBLS	10//99-12//99
	North Carolina	S	10.34 MW	10.59 AW	22030 AAW	NCBLS	10//99-12//99
	North Dakota	S	10.59 MW	12.05 AW	25070 AAW	NDBLS	10//99-12//99
	Ohio	S	16.61 MW	16.55 AW	34430 AAW	OHBLS	10//99-12//99
	Oklahoma	S	10.66 MW	12.35 AW	25680 AAW	OKBLS	10//99-12//99
	Oregon	S	16.3 MW	16.88 AW	35110 AAW	ORBLS	10//99-12//99
	Pennsylvania	S	14.32 MW	15.04 AW	31270 AAW	PABLS	10//99-12//99
	Rhode Island	S	19.37 MW	19.21 AW	39950 AAW	RIBLS	10//99-12//99
	South Carolina	S	9.95 MW	10.60 AW	22050 AAW	SCBLS	10//99-12//99
	South Dakota	S	10.47 MW	11.16 AW	23210 AAW	SDBLS	10//99-12//99
	Tennessee	S	11.17 MW	11.34 AW	23580 AAW	TNBLS	10//99-12//99
	Texas	S	10.05 MW	10.77 AW	22410 AAW	TXBLS	10//99-12//99
	Vermont	S	12.12 MW	12.12 AW	25210 AAW	VTBLS	10//99-12//99
	Virginia	S	10.7 MW	11.15 AW	23180 AAW	VABLS	10//99-12//99
	Washington	S	20.9 MW	20.07 AW	41740 AAW	WABLS	10//99-12//99
	West Virginia	S	15.02 MW	15.71 AW	32680 AAW	WVBLS	10//99-12//99
	Wisconsin	S	19.3 MW	19.13 AW	39790 AAW	WIBLS	10//99-12//99
	Wyoming	S	11.8 MW	12.20 AW	25370 AAW	WYBLS	10//99-12//99
	Puerto Rico	S	8.2 MW	8.66 AW	18000 AAW	PRBLS	10//99-12//99
Plasterer and Stucco Mason	Alabama	S	11.1 MW	11.47 AW	23850 AAW	ALBLS	10//99-12//99
	Birmingham MSA, AL	S	11.99 MW	11.90 AW	24930 AAW	ALBLS	10//99-12//99
	Alaska	S	25.83 MW	24.10 AW	50120 AAW	AKBLS	10//99-12//99
	Arizona	S	12.45 MW	12.56 AW	26120 AAW	AZBLS	10//99-12//99
	Phoenix-Mesa MSA, AZ	S	12.57 MW	12.51 AW	26140 AAW	AZBLS	10//99-12//99
	Tucson MSA, AZ	S	12.80 MW	12.96 AW	26610 AAW	AZBLS	10//99-12//99
	Yuma MSA, AZ	S	10.94 MW	10.70 AW	22760 AAW	AZBLS	10//99-12//99
	Arkansas	S	12.9 MW	12.79 AW	26600 AAW	ARBLS	10//99-12//99
	California	S	14.22 MW	16.33 AW	33960 AAW	CABLS	10//99-12//99
	Bakersfield MSA, CA	S	17.58 MW	17.91 AW	36560 AAW	CABLS	10//99-12//99
	Fresno MSA, CA	S	14.44 MW	14.19 AW	30040 AAW	CABLS	10//99-12//99
	Los Angeles-Long Beach PMSA, CA	S	14.43 MW	12.33 AW	30010 AAW	CABLS	10//99-12//99
	Modesto MSA, CA	S	16.92 MW	15.48 AW	35200 AAW	CABLS	10//99-12//99
	Oakland PMSA, CA	S	22.14 MW	21.15 AW	46040 AAW	CABLS	10//99-12//99
	Orange County PMSA, CA	S	16.54 MW	15.32 AW	34390 AAW	CABLS	10//99-12//99
	Riverside-San Bernardino PMSA, CA	S	12.69 MW	12.13 AW	26400 AAW	CABLS	10//99-12//99
	Sacramento PMSA, CA	S	18.75 MW	15.74 AW	39000 AAW	CABLS	10//99-12//99
	Salinas MSA, CA	S	19.06 MW	21.07 AW	39650 AAW	CABLS	10//99-12//99
	San Diego MSA, CA	S	16.27 MW	15.78 AW	33840 AAW	CABLS	10//99-12//99
	San Francisco PMSA, CA	S	24.81 MW	24.93 AW	51600 AAW	CABLS	10//99-12//99
	San Jose PMSA, CA	S	15.51 MW	13.39 AW	32260 AAW	CABLS	10//99-12//99
	San Luis Obispo-Atascadero-Paso Robles MSA, CA	S	16.85 MW	16.48 AW	35050 AAW	CABLS	
	Santa Cruz-Watsonville PMSA, CA	S	17.53 MW	18.29 AW	36460 AAW	CABLS	10//99-12//99
	Santa Rosa PMSA, CA	S	20.20 MW	21.24 AW	42020 AAW	CABLS	10//99-12//99
	Stockton-Lodi MSA, CA	S	12.48 MW	12.27 AW	25950 AAW	CABLS	10//99-12//99
	Vallejo-Fairfield-Napa PMSA, CA	S	21.07 MW	20.56 AW	43830 AAW	CABLS	10//99-12//99
	Colorado	S	13.89 MW	13.39 AW	27850 AAW	COBLS	10//99-12//99
	Denver PMSA, CO	S	14.10 MW	14.38 AW	29340 AAW	COBLS	10//99-12//99
	Fort Collins-Loveland MSA, CO	S	12.80 MW	13.31 AW	26620 AAW	COBLS	10//99-12//99
	Connecticut	S	21.47 MW	18.32 AW	38100 AAW	CTBLS	10//99-12//99
	Delaware	S	16.75 MW	15.79 AW	32850 AAW	DEBLS	10//99-12//99
	Wilmington-Newark PMSA, DE-MD	S	15.82 MW	16.95 AW	32910 AAW	DEBLS	10//99-12//99
	Washington PMSA, DC-MD-VA-WV	S	12.92 MW	11.95 AW	26870 AAW	DCBLS	10//99-12//99
	Florida	S	13.83 MW	13.39 AW	27860 AAW	FLBLS	10//99-12//99
	Daytona Beach MSA, FL	S	11.99 MW	12.31 AW	24940 AAW	FLBLS	10//99-12//99
	Fort Lauderdale PMSA, FL	S	13.80 MW	14.87 AW	28710 AAW	FLBLS	10//99-12//99
	Fort Myers-Cape Coral MSA, FL	S	15.38 MW	15.72 AW	31990 AAW	FLBLS	10//99-12//99
	Jacksonville MSA, FL	S	12.21 MW	11.94 AW	25400 AAW	FLBLS	10//99-12//99
	Melbourne-Titusville-Palm Bay MSA, FL	S	14.02 MW	14.58 AW	29170 AAW	FLBLS	10//99-12//99

AAW Average annual wage	AOH Average offered, high	ASH Average starting, high	H Hourly	M Monthly	S Special: hourly and annual
AE Average entry wage	AOL Average offered, low	ASL Average starting, low	HI Highest wage paid	MTC Median total compensation	TQ Third quartile wage
AEX Average experienced wage	APH Average pay, high range	AW Average wage paid	HR High end range	MW Median wage paid	W Weekly
AO Average offered	APL Average pay, low range	FQ First quartile wage	LR Low end range	SQ Second quartile wage	Y Yearly

Occupation/Type/Industry	Location	Per	Low	Mid	High	Source	Date
Plasterer and Stucco Mason	Miami PMSA, FL	S	14.75 MW	13.98 AW	30670 AAW	FLBLS	10//99-12//99
	Naples MSA, FL	S	14.48 MW	14.79 AW	30120 AAW	FLBLS	10//99-12//99
	Orlando MSA, FL	S	12.87 MW	14.17 AW	26760 AAW	FLBLS	10//99-12//99
	Panama City MSA, FL	S	12.39 MW	12.48 AW	25770 AAW	FLBLS	10//99-12//99
	Pensacola MSA, FL	S	13.12 MW	12.77 AW	27290 AAW	FLBLS	10//99-12//99
	Sarasota-Bradenton MSA, FL	S	12.97 MW	12.81 AW	26990 AAW	FLBLS	10//99-12//99
	Tampa-St. Petersburg-Clearwater MSA, FL	S	10.89 MW	11.08 AW	22640 AAW	FLBLS	10//99-12//99
	West Palm Beach-Boca Raton MSA, FL	S	17.23 MW	17.36 AW	35850 AAW	FLBLS	10//99-12//99
	Georgia	S	12 MW	12.74 AW	26500 AAW	GABLS	10//99-12//99
	Atlanta MSA, GA	S	12.86 MW	12.26 AW	26740 AAW	GABLS	10//99-12//99
	Hawaii	S	20.04 MW	20.18 AW	41970 AAW	HIBLS	10//99-12//99
	Idaho	S	14.23 MW	14.13 AW	29390 AAW	IDBLS	10//99-12//99
	Boise City MSA, ID	S	14.14 MW	14.21 AW	29410 AAW	IDBLS	10//99-12//99
	Illinois	S	22.59 MW	21.12 AW	43930 AAW	ILBLS	10//99-12//99
	Chicago PMSA, IL	S	21.24 MW	22.92 AW	44180 AAW	ILBLS	10//99-12//99
	Indiana	S	16.14 MW	16.69 AW	34720 AAW	INBLS	10//99-12//99
	Indianapolis MSA, IN	S	17.30 MW	17.30 AW	35990 AAW	INBLS	10//99-12//99
	Iowa	S	18.14 MW	17.70 AW	36810 AAW	IABLS	10//99-12//99
	Kansas	S	16.26 MW	16.40 AW	34120 AAW	KSBLS	10//99-12//99
	Kentucky	S	13.25 MW	13.76 AW	28620 AAW	KYBLS	10//99-12//99
	Louisiana	S	13.35 MW	13.53 AW	28150 AAW	LABLS	10//99-12//99
	Alexandria MSA, LA	S	13.35 MW	13.65 AW	27770 AAW	LABLS	10//99-12//99
	Baton Rouge MSA, LA	S	11.37 MW	11.31 AW	23640 AAW	LABLS	10//99-12//99
	Lafayette MSA, LA	S	15.49 MW	14.70 AW	32210 AAW	LABLS	10//99-12//99
	New Orleans MSA, LA	S	12.39 MW	12.63 AW	25760 AAW	LABLS	10//99-12//99
	Maine	S	6.43 MW	8.09 AW	16830 AAW	MEBLS	10//99-12//99
	Maryland	S	12.47 MW	13.33 AW	27720 AAW	MDBLS	10//99-12//99
	Baltimore PMSA, MD	S	16.33 MW	16.43 AW	33970 AAW	MDBLS	10//99-12//99
	Massachusetts	S	21.96 MW	23.96 AW	49830 AAW	MABLS	10//99-12//99
	Boston PMSA, MA-NH	S	26.35 MW	25.29 AW	54820 AAW	MABLS	10//99-12//99
	Brockton PMSA, MA	S	19.81 MW	21.36 AW	41210 AAW	MABLS	10//99-12//99
	Michigan	S	19.25 MW	18.87 AW	39250 AAW	MIBLS	10//99-12//99
	Detroit PMSA, MI	S	18.33 MW	18.36 AW	38120 AAW	MIBLS	10//99-12//99
	Grand Rapids-Muskegon-Holland MSA, MI	S	20.91 MW	22.19 AW	43490 AAW	MIBLS	10//99-12//99
	Kalamazoo-Battle Creek MSA, MI	S	15.72 MW	14.10 AW	32700 AAW	MIBLS	10//99-12//99
	Saginaw-Bay City-Midland MSA, MI	S	19.90 MW	21.81 AW	41400 AAW	MIBLS	10//99-12//99
	Minnesota	S	19.72 MW	21.65 AW	45040 AAW	MNBLS	10//99-12//99
	Minneapolis-St. Paul MSA, MN-WI	S	22.57 MW	19.99 AW	46950 AAW	MNBLS	10//99-12//99
	Rochester MSA, MN	S	14.94 MW	12.17 AW	31070 AAW	MNBLS	10//99-12//99
	Mississippi	S	12.2 MW	12.35 AW	25690 AAW	MSBLS	10//99-12//99
	Jackson MSA, MS	S	11.92 MW	11.86 AW	24800 AAW	MSBLS	10//99-12//99
	Missouri	S	16.43 MW	16.90 AW	35150 AAW	MOBLS	10//99-12//99
	Kansas City MSA, MO-KS	S	17.22 MW	17.93 AW	35810 AAW	MOBLS	10//99-12//99
	Nebraska	S	15.94 MW	14.95 AW	31100 AAW	NEBLS	10//99-12//99
	Lincoln MSA, NE	S	11.01 MW	11.26 AW	22900 AAW	NEBLS	10//99-12//99
	Nevada	S	16.06 MW	16.32 AW	33950 AAW	NVBLS	10//99-12//99
	Las Vegas MSA, NV-AZ	S	15.94 MW	15.62 AW	33160 AAW	NVBLS	10//99-12//99
	Reno MSA, NV	S	15.73 MW	16.01 AW	32720 AAW	NVBLS	10//99-12//99
	New Jersey	S	15.08 MW	15.65 AW	32550 AAW	NJBLS	10//99-12//99
	Bergen-Passaic PMSA, NJ	S	16.13 MW	15.80 AW	33550 AAW	NJBLS	10//99-12//99
	Newark PMSA, NJ	S	13.67 MW	13.71 AW	28440 AAW	NJBLS	10//99-12//99
	Vineland-Millville-Bridgeton PMSA, NJ	S	16.33 MW	16.04 AW	33960 AAW	NJBLS	10//99-12//99
	New Mexico	S	11.94 MW	13.35 AW	27760 AAW	NMBLS	10//99-12//99
	Albuquerque MSA, NM	S	13.68 MW	11.95 AW	28460 AAW	NMBLS	10//99-12//99
	Las Cruces MSA, NM	S	10.35 MW	10.07 AW	21520 AAW	NMBLS	10//99-12//99
	Santa Fe MSA, NM	S	14.29 MW	14.65 AW	29720 AAW	NMBLS	10//99-12//99
	New York	S	24.05 MW	23.92 AW	49750 AAW	NYBLS	10//99-12//99
	Nassau-Suffolk PMSA, NY	S	24.49 MW	25.36 AW	50950 AAW	NYBLS	10//99-12//99
	New York PMSA, NY	S	25.04 MW	24.79 AW	52090 AAW	NYBLS	10//99-12//99
	North Carolina	S	12.61 MW	12.52 AW	26040 AAW	NCBLS	10//99-12//99
	Charlotte-Gastonia-Rock Hill MSA, NC-SC	S	14.27 MW	13.81 AW	29680 AAW	NCBLS	10//99-12//99
	Greensboro--Winston-Salem--High Point MSA, NC	S	11.14 MW	10.29 AW	23170 AAW	NCBLS	10//99-12//99
	Jacksonville MSA, NC	S	14.02 MW	12.76 AW	29170 AAW	NCBLS	10//99-12//99

AAW Average annual wage	**AOH** Average offered, high	**ASH** Average starting, high	**H** Hourly	**M** Monthly	**S** Special: hourly and annual
AE Average entry wage	**AOL** Average offered, low	**ASL** Average starting, low	**HI** Highest wage paid	**MTC** Median total compensation	**TQ** Third quartile wage
AEX Average experienced wage	**APH** Average pay, high range	**AW** Average wage paid	**HR** High end range	**MW** Median wage paid	**W** Weekly
AO Average offered	**APL** Average pay, low range	**FQ** First quartile wage	**LR** Low end range	**SQ** Second quartile wage	**Y** Yearly

Plasterer and Stucco Mason

Occupation/Type/Industry	Location	Per	Low	Mid	High	Source	Date
Plasterer and Stucco Mason	Ohio	S	17.54 MW	17.73 AW	36880 AAW	OHBLS	10//99-12//99
	Akron PMSA, OH	S	17.45 MW	18.66 AW	36290 AAW	OHBLS	10//99-12//99
	Cincinnati PMSA, OH-KY-IN	S	17.06 MW	17.75 AW	35480 AAW	OHBLS	10//99-12//99
	Columbus MSA, OH	S	14.76 MW	14.00 AW	30700 AAW	OHBLS	10//99-12//99
	Dayton-Springfield MSA, OH	S	14.46 MW	13.64 AW	30070 AAW	OHBLS	10//99-12//99
	Hamilton-Middletown PMSA, OH	S	16.43 MW	16.60 AW	34170 AAW	OHBLS	10//99-12//99
	Toledo MSA, OH	S	22.34 MW	23.23 AW	46470 AAW	OHBLS	10//99-12//99
	Youngstown-Warren MSA, OH	S	18.81 MW	19.38 AW	39120 AAW	OHBLS	10//99-12//99
	Oklahoma	S	15.23 MW	14.78 AW	30750 AAW	OKBLS	10//99-12//99
	Tulsa MSA, OK	S	14.88 MW	15.08 AW	30940 AAW	OKBLS	10//99-12//99
	Oregon	S	14.82 MW	16.64 AW	34610 AAW	ORBLS	10//99-12//99
	Eugene-Springfield MSA, OR	S	20.92 MW	20.34 AW	43520 AAW	ORBLS	10//99-12//99
	Portland-Vancouver PMSA, OR-WA	S	17.81 MW	17.08 AW	37050 AAW	ORBLS	10//99-12//99
	Pennsylvania	S	15.12 MW	16.09 AW	33460 AAW	PABLS	10//99-12//99
	Allentown-Bethlehem-Easton MSA, PA	S	18.55 MW	20.83 AW	38570 AAW	PABLS	10//99-12//99
	Harrisburg-Lebanon-Carlisle MSA, PA	S	14.27 MW	13.39 AW	29680 AAW	PABLS	10//99-12//99
	Philadelphia PMSA, PA-NJ	S	16.56 MW	15.38 AW	34450 AAW	PABLS	10//99-12//99
	Pittsburgh MSA, PA	S	14.20 MW	11.59 AW	29540 AAW	PABLS	10//99-12//99
	Rhode Island	S	14.5 MW	14.89 AW	30980 AAW	RIBLS	10//99-12//99
	Providence-Fall River-Warwick MSA, RI-MA	S	15.77 MW	15.54 AW	32800 AAW	RIBLS	10//99-12//99
	South Carolina	S	11.37 MW	11.14 AW	23170 AAW	SCBLS	10//99-12//99
	Columbia MSA, SC	S	12.45 MW	12.44 AW	25890 AAW	SCBLS	10//99-12//99
	South Dakota	S	14.82 MW	14.53 AW	30210 AAW	SDBLS	10//99-12//99
	Tennessee	S	13.73 MW	13.18 AW	27410 AAW	TNBLS	10//99-12//99
	Chattanooga MSA, TN-GA	S	14.64 MW	14.82 AW	30450 AAW	TNBLS	10//99-12//99
	Memphis MSA, TN-AR-MS	S	11.58 MW	11.32 AW	24090 AAW	MSBLS	10//99-12//99
	Nashville MSA, TN	S	14.53 MW	14.95 AW	30230 AAW	TNBLS	10//99-12//99
	Texas	S	13.38 MW	13.34 AW	27740 AAW	TXBLS	10//99-12//99
	Austin-San Marcos MSA, TX	S	14.16 MW	14.64 AW	29460 AAW	TXBLS	10//99-12//99
	Dallas PMSA, TX	S	13.71 MW	12.53 AW	28520 AAW	TXBLS	10//99-12//99
	El Paso MSA, TX	S	9.08 MW	8.96 AW	18880 AAW	TXBLS	10//99-12//99
	Houston PMSA, TX	S	13.85 MW	13.97 AW	28800 AAW	TXBLS	10//99-12//99
	San Antonio MSA, TX	S	14.01 MW	14.50 AW	29140 AAW	TXBLS	10//99-12//99
	Victoria MSA, TX	S	8.66 MW	7.83 AW	18020 AAW	TXBLS	10//99-12//99
	Utah	S	13.13 MW	13.04 AW	27120 AAW	UTBLS	10//99-12//99
	Provo-Orem MSA, UT	S	15.02 MW	15.00 AW	31250 AAW	UTBLS	10//99-12//99
	Virginia	S	12.11 MW	12.68 AW	26370 AAW	VABLS	10//99-12//99
	Charlottesville MSA, VA	S	12.72 MW	12.47 AW	26450 AAW	VABLS	10//99-12//99
	Norfolk-Virginia Beach-Newport News MSA, VA-NC	S	12.72 MW	12.65 AW	26460 AAW	VABLS	10//99-12//99
	Richmond-Petersburg MSA, VA	S	14.03 MW	13.42 AW	29170 AAW	VABLS	10//99-12//99
	Washington	S	21.78 MW	20.56 AW	42760 AAW	WABLS	10//99-12//99
	Seattle-Bellevue-Everett PMSA, WA	S	21.49 MW	22.56 AW	44700 AAW	WABLS	10//99-12//99
	Spokane MSA, WA	S	17.91 MW	17.99 AW	37240 AAW	WABLS	10//99-12//99
	Wisconsin	S	14.41 MW	14.22 AW	29580 AAW	WIBLS	10//99-12//99
	Green Bay MSA, WI	S	12.12 MW	11.72 AW	25210 AAW	WIBLS	10//99-12//99
	Madison MSA, WI	S	13.45 MW	13.72 AW	27980 AAW	WIBLS	10//99-12//99
	Milwaukee-Waukesha PMSA, WI	S	21.83 MW	23.19 AW	45400 AAW	WIBLS	10//99-12//99
	Puerto Rico	S	7.11 MW	7.99 AW	16620 AAW	PRBLS	10//99-12//99
	San Juan-Bayamon PMSA, PR	S	8.58 MW	7.66 AW	17860 AAW	PRBLS	10//99-12//99
	Guam	S	9.63 MW	9.64 AW	20050 AAW	GUBLS	10//99-12//99
Plating and Coating Machine Setter, Operator, and Tender							
Metals and Plastics	Alabama	S	12.04 MW	11.62 AW	24170 AAW	ALBLS	10//99-12//99
Metals and Plastics	Anniston MSA, AL	S	12.58 MW	13.96 AW	26170 AAW	ALBLS	10//99-12//99
Metals and Plastics	Birmingham MSA, AL	S	12.66 MW	13.78 AW	26330 AAW	ALBLS	10//99-12//99
Metals and Plastics	Huntsville MSA, AL	S	11.32 MW	10.73 AW	23540 AAW	ALBLS	10//99-12//99
Metals and Plastics	Arizona	S	9.93 MW	10.41 AW	21650 AAW	AZBLS	10//99-12//99
Metals and Plastics	Phoenix-Mesa MSA, AZ	S	10.48 MW	10.00 AW	21800 AAW	AZBLS	10//99-12//99
Metals and Plastics	Tucson MSA, AZ	S	10.53 MW	10.09 AW	21900 AAW	AZBLS	10//99-12//99
Metals and Plastics	Arkansas	S	10.22 MW	10.89 AW	22650 AAW	ARBLS	10//99-12//99
Metals and Plastics	California	S	9.75 MW	10.59 AW	22030 AAW	CABLS	10//99-12//99

AAW	Average annual wage	AOH	Average offered, high	ASH	Average starting, high	H	Hourly	M	Monthly	S	Special: hourly and annual
AE	Average entry wage	AOL	Average offered, low	ASL	Average starting, low	HI	Highest wage paid	MTC	Median total compensation	TQ	Third quartile wage
AEX	Average experienced wage	APH	Average pay, high range	AW	Average wage paid	HR	High end range	MW	Median wage paid	W	Weekly
AO	Average offered	APL	Average pay, low range	FQ	First quartile wage	LR	Low end range	SQ	Second quartile wage	Y	Yearly

Occupation/Type/Industry	Location	Per	Low	Mid	High	Source	Date
Plating and Coating Machine Setter, Operator, and Tender							
Metals and Plastics	Bakersfield MSA, CA	S	13.39 MW	14.22 AW	27850 AAW	CABLS	10//99-12//99
Metals and Plastics	Fresno MSA, CA	S	9.49 MW	8.94 AW	19730 AAW	CABLS	10//99-12//99
Metals and Plastics	Los Angeles-Long Beach PMSA, CA	S	10.06 MW	9.70 AW	20930 AAW	CABLS	10//99-12//99
Metals and Plastics	Oakland PMSA, CA	S	13.20 MW	11.53 AW	27460 AAW	CABLS	10//99-12//99
Metals and Plastics	Orange County PMSA, CA	S	10.25 MW	9.71 AW	21320 AAW	CABLS	10//99-12//99
Metals and Plastics	Riverside-San Bernardino PMSA, CA	S	16.09 MW	10.38 AW	33460 AAW	CABLS	10//99-12//99
Metals and Plastics	Sacramento PMSA, CA	S	11.67 MW	11.09 AW	24280 AAW	CABLS	10//99-12//99
Metals and Plastics	San Diego MSA, CA	S	9.77 MW	9.31 AW	20330 AAW	CABLS	10//99-12//99
Metals and Plastics	San Francisco PMSA, CA	S	13.33 MW	12.14 AW	27730 AAW	CABLS	10//99-12//99
Metals and Plastics	San Jose PMSA, CA	S	10.24 MW	9.51 AW	21290 AAW	CABLS	10//99-12//99
Metals and Plastics	Santa Cruz-Watsonville PMSA, CA	S	11.21 MW	10.51 AW	23320 AAW	CABLS	10//99-12//99
Metals and Plastics	Ventura PMSA, CA	S	9.83 MW	9.02 AW	20450 AAW	CABLS	10//99-12//99
Metals and Plastics	Colorado	S	10.08 MW	10.57 AW	21980 AAW	COBLS	10//99-12//99
Metals and Plastics	Boulder-Longmont PMSA, CO	S	10.70 MW	10.00 AW	22260 AAW	COBLS	10//99-12//99
Metals and Plastics	Colorado Springs MSA, CO	S	9.20 MW	8.84 AW	19140 AAW	COBLS	10//99-12//99
Metals and Plastics	Denver PMSA, CO	S	11.07 MW	10.92 AW	23020 AAW	COBLS	10//99-12//99
Metals and Plastics	Connecticut	S	12.43 MW	12.59 AW	26180 AAW	CTBLS	10//99-12//99
Metals and Plastics	Bridgeport PMSA, CT	S	14.50 MW	14.02 AW	30160 AAW	CTBLS	10//99-12//99
Metals and Plastics	Hartford MSA, CT	S	12.52 MW	12.73 AW	26040 AAW	CTBLS	10//99-12//99
Metals and Plastics	New Haven-Meriden PMSA, CT	S	13.26 MW	13.68 AW	27580 AAW	CTBLS	10//99-12//99
Metals and Plastics	New London-Norwich MSA, CT-RI	S	10.97 MW	11.44 AW	22820 AAW	CTBLS	10//99-12//99
Metals and Plastics	Stamford-Norwalk PMSA, CT	S	9.40 MW	8.64 AW	19550 AAW	CTBLS	10//99-12//99
Metals and Plastics	Waterbury PMSA, CT	S	11.58 MW	11.01 AW	24080 AAW	CTBLS	10//99-12//99
Metals and Plastics	Washington PMSA, DC-MD-VA-WV	S	14.00 MW	11.62 AW	29110 AAW	DCBLS	10//99-12//99
Metals and Plastics	Florida	S	9.42 MW	10.11 AW	21040 AAW	FLBLS	10//99-12//99
Metals and Plastics	Daytona Beach MSA, FL	S	10.71 MW	10.07 AW	22270 AAW	FLBLS	10//99-12//99
Metals and Plastics	Fort Lauderdale PMSA, FL	S	10.47 MW	9.90 AW	21780 AAW	FLBLS	10//99-12//99
Metals and Plastics	Jacksonville MSA, FL	S	11.53 MW	10.50 AW	23980 AAW	FLBLS	10//99-12//99
Metals and Plastics	Miami PMSA, FL	S	8.97 MW	8.39 AW	18650 AAW	FLBLS	10//99-12//99
Metals and Plastics	Orlando MSA, FL	S	10.41 MW	9.24 AW	21650 AAW	FLBLS	10//99-12//99
Metals and Plastics	Tampa-St. Petersburg-Clearwater MSA, FL	S	9.59 MW	8.71 AW	19940 AAW	FLBLS	10//99-12//99
Metals and Plastics	West Palm Beach-Boca Raton MSA, FL	S	11.59 MW	10.93 AW	24110 AAW	FLBLS	10//99-12//99
Metals and Plastics	Georgia	S	10.33 MW	10.64 AW	22130 AAW	GABLS	10//99-12//99
Metals and Plastics	Atlanta MSA, GA	S	10.82 MW	10.57 AW	22510 AAW	GABLS	10//99-12//99
Metals and Plastics	Idaho	S	8.26 MW	9.29 AW	19320 AAW	IDBLS	10//99-12//99
Metals and Plastics	Illinois	S	10.71 MW	10.93 AW	22740 AAW	ILBLS	10//99-12//99
Metals and Plastics	Chicago PMSA, IL	S	10.79 MW	10.65 AW	22450 AAW	ILBLS	10//99-12//99
Metals and Plastics	Rockford MSA, IL	S	11.36 MW	11.45 AW	23620 AAW	ILBLS	10//99-12//99
Metals and Plastics	Indiana	S	11.51 MW	12.14 AW	25260 AAW	INBLS	10//99-12//99
Metals and Plastics	Elkhart-Goshen MSA, IN	S	13.80 MW	14.06 AW	28710 AAW	INBLS	10//99-12//99
Metals and Plastics	Evansville-Henderson MSA, IN-KY	S	14.32 MW	12.64 AW	29790 AAW	INBLS	10//99-12//99
Metals and Plastics	Fort Wayne MSA, IN	S	10.36 MW	10.16 AW	21540 AAW	INBLS	10//99-12//99
Metals and Plastics	Gary PMSA, IN	S	16.56 MW	14.91 AW	34450 AAW	INBLS	10//99-12//99
Metals and Plastics	Indianapolis MSA, IN	S	11.69 MW	11.20 AW	24310 AAW	INBLS	10//99-12//99
Metals and Plastics	South Bend MSA, IN	S	10.06 MW	9.73 AW	20920 AAW	INBLS	10//99-12//99
Metals and Plastics	Iowa	S	11.17 MW	10.79 AW	22450 AAW	IABLS	10//99-12//99
Metals and Plastics	Davenport-Moline-Rock Island MSA, IA-IL	S	11.11 MW	9.42 AW	23110 AAW	IABLS	10//99-12//99
Metals and Plastics	Kansas	S	11.78 MW	15.10 AW	31410 AAW	KSBLS	10//99-12//99
Metals and Plastics	Kentucky	S	10.4 MW	10.92 AW	22710 AAW	KYBLS	10//99-12//99
Metals and Plastics	Lexington MSA, KY	S	9.91 MW	9.94 AW	20610 AAW	KYBLS	10//99-12//99
Metals and Plastics	Louisville MSA, KY-IN	S	12.13 MW	10.99 AW	25230 AAW	KYBLS	10//99-12//99
Metals and Plastics	Louisiana	S	7.87 MW	8.33 AW	17320 AAW	LABLS	10//99-12//99
Metals and Plastics	Maine	S	10.61 MW	11.20 AW	23290 AAW	MEBLS	10//99-12//99
Metals and Plastics	Maryland	S	11.44 MW	12.08 AW	25120 AAW	MDBLS	10//99-12//99
Metals and Plastics	Baltimore PMSA, MD	S	12.31 MW	11.70 AW	25600 AAW	MDBLS	10//99-12//99
Metals and Plastics	Massachusetts	S	11.45 MW	12.35 AW	25690 AAW	MABLS	10//99-12//99
Metals and Plastics	Boston PMSA, MA-NH	S	12.56 MW	11.59 AW	26120 AAW	MABLS	10//99-12//99
Metals and Plastics	Brockton PMSA, MA	S	11.58 MW	10.58 AW	24090 AAW	MABLS	10//99-12//99
Metals and Plastics	Lawrence PMSA, MA-NH	S	11.08 MW	10.35 AW	23050 AAW	MABLS	10//99-12//99
Metals and Plastics	Lowell PMSA, MA-NH	S	12.44 MW	11.68 AW	25870 AAW	MABLS	10//99-12//99

AAW	Average annual wage	**AOH**	Average offered, high	**ASH**	Average starting, high	**H**	Hourly	**M**	Monthly	**S**	Special: hourly and annual
AE	Average entry wage	**AOL**	Average offered, low	**ASL**	Average starting, low	**HI**	Highest wage paid	**MTC**	Median total compensation	**TQ**	Third quartile wage
AEX	Average experienced wage	**APH**	Average pay, high range	**AW**	Average wage paid	**HR**	High end range	**MW**	Median wage paid	**W**	Weekly
AO	Average offered	**APL**	Average pay, low range	**FQ**	First quartile wage	**LR**	Low end range	**SQ**	Second quartile wage	**Y**	Yearly

Occupation/Type/Industry	Location	Per	Low	Mid	High	Source	Date
Plating and Coating Machine Setter, Operator, and Tender							
Metals and Plastics	New Bedford PMSA, MA	S	11.68 MW	11.23 AW	24290 AAW	MABLS	10//99-12//99
Metals and Plastics	Springfield MSA, MA	S	12.92 MW	11.72 AW	26860 AAW	MABLS	10//99-12//99
Metals and Plastics	Worcester PMSA, MA-CT	S	11.38 MW	10.14 AW	23660 AAW	MABLS	10//99-12//99
Metals and Plastics	Michigan	S	11.18 MW	11.77 AW	24480 AAW	MIBLS	10//99-12//99
Metals and Plastics	Ann Arbor PMSA, MI	S	13.80 MW	12.93 AW	28700 AAW	MIBLS	10//99-12//99
Metals and Plastics	Benton Harbor MSA, MI	S	10.29 MW	9.32 AW	21410 AAW	MIBLS	10//99-12//99
Metals and Plastics	Detroit PMSA, MI	S	11.41 MW	10.65 AW	23730 AAW	MIBLS	10//99-12//99
Metals and Plastics	Flint PMSA, MI	S	13.11 MW	12.39 AW	27270 AAW	MIBLS	10//99-12//99
Metals and Plastics	Grand Rapids-Muskegon-Holland MSA, MI	S	12.04 MW	11.88 AW	25040 AAW	MIBLS	10//99-12//99
Metals and Plastics	Kalamazoo-Battle Creek MSA, MI	S	12.49 MW	12.54 AW	25980 AAW	MIBLS	10//99-12//99
Metals and Plastics	Saginaw-Bay City-Midland MSA, MI	S	14.93 MW	13.62 AW	31060 AAW	MIBLS	10//99-12//99
Metals and Plastics	Minnesota	S	12.86 MW	12.94 AW	26920 AAW	MNBLS	10//99-12//99
Metals and Plastics	Minneapolis-St. Paul MSA, MN-WI	S	13.49 MW	13.71 AW	28060 AAW	MNBLS	10//99-12//99
Metals and Plastics	Mississippi	S	11.38 MW	12.02 AW	24990 AAW	MSBLS	10//99-12//99
Metals and Plastics	Missouri	S	10.12 MW	10.58 AW	22000 AAW	MOBLS	10//99-12//99
Metals and Plastics	Kansas City MSA, MO-KS	S	11.03 MW	9.77 AW	22940 AAW	MOBLS	10//99-12//99
Metals and Plastics	St. Louis MSA, MO-IL	S	10.30 MW	9.70 AW	21430 AAW	MOBLS	10//99-12//99
Metals and Plastics	Nebraska	S	12.53 MW	15.01 AW	31220 AAW	NEBLS	10//99-12//99
Metals and Plastics	Lincoln MSA, NE	S	17.52 MW	16.29 AW	36440 AAW	NEBLS	10//99-12//99
Metals and Plastics	Nevada	S	9.93 MW	10.26 AW	21340 AAW	NVBLS	10//99-12//99
Metals and Plastics	Las Vegas MSA, NV-AZ	S	9.91 MW	9.39 AW	20620 AAW	NVBLS	10//99-12//99
Metals and Plastics	Reno MSA, NV	S	10.72 MW	10.10 AW	22290 AAW	NVBLS	10//99-12//99
Metals and Plastics	New Hampshire	S	10.25 MW	10.74 AW	22330 AAW	NHBLS	10//99-12//99
Metals and Plastics	Manchester PMSA, NH	S	10.55 MW	10.29 AW	21940 AAW	NHBLS	10//99-12//99
Metals and Plastics	Nashua PMSA, NH	S	10.65 MW	10.44 AW	22150 AAW	NHBLS	10//99-12//99
Metals and Plastics	Portsmouth-Rochester PMSA, NH-ME	S	9.51 MW	8.18 AW	19780 AAW	NHBLS	10//99-12//99
Metals and Plastics	New Jersey	S	10.86 MW	10.92 AW	22720 AAW	NJBLS	10//99-12//99
Metals and Plastics	Bergen-Passaic PMSA, NJ	S	10.18 MW	10.40 AW	21180 AAW	NJBLS	10//99-12//99
Metals and Plastics	Middlesex-Somerset-Hunterdon PMSA, NJ	S	11.53 MW	11.15 AW	23980 AAW	NJBLS	10//99-12//99
Metals and Plastics	Monmouth-Ocean PMSA, NJ	S	10.06 MW	10.09 AW	20930 AAW	NJBLS	10//99-12//99
Metals and Plastics	Newark PMSA, NJ	S	10.49 MW	10.10 AW	21820 AAW	NJBLS	10//99-12//99
Metals and Plastics	Albuquerque MSA, NM	S	8.71 MW	9.08 AW	18120 AAW	NMBLS	10//99-12//99
Metals and Plastics	New York	S	10.39 MW	10.84 AW	22540 AAW	NYBLS	10//99-12//99
Metals and Plastics	Albany-Schenectady-Troy MSA, NY	S	12.49 MW	12.00 AW	25980 AAW	NYBLS	10//99-12//99
Metals and Plastics	Binghamton MSA, NY	S	9.70 MW	9.42 AW	20170 AAW	NYBLS	10//99-12//99
Metals and Plastics	Buffalo-Niagara Falls MSA, NY	S	12.80 MW	12.19 AW	26620 AAW	NYBLS	10//99-12//99
Metals and Plastics	New York PMSA, NY	S	9.88 MW	10.07 AW	20560 AAW	NYBLS	10//99-12//99
Metals and Plastics	Rochester MSA, NY	S	11.21 MW	10.09 AW	23320 AAW	NYBLS	10//99-12//99
Metals and Plastics	Syracuse MSA, NY	S	9.92 MW	8.84 AW	20640 AAW	NYBLS	10//99-12//99
Metals and Plastics	North Carolina	S	11.3 MW	11.80 AW	24540 AAW	NCBLS	10//99-12//99
Metals and Plastics	Asheville MSA, NC	S	10.76 MW	10.42 AW	22370 AAW	NCBLS	10//99-12//99
Metals and Plastics	Charlotte-Gastonia-Rock Hill MSA, NC-SC	S	11.69 MW	11.10 AW	24320 AAW	NCBLS	10//99-12//99
Metals and Plastics	Greensboro--Winston-Salem--High Point MSA, NC	S	12.10 MW	10.61 AW	25170 AAW	NCBLS	10//99-12//99
Metals and Plastics	Hickory-Morganton-Lenoir MSA, NC	S	11.22 MW	10.41 AW	23330 AAW	NCBLS	10//99-12//99
Metals and Plastics	Raleigh-Durham-Chapel Hill MSA, NC	S	12.05 MW	12.23 AW	25070 AAW	NCBLS	10//99-12//99
Metals and Plastics	Ohio	S	11.53 MW	12.52 AW	26040 AAW	OHBLS	10//99-12//99
Metals and Plastics	Canton-Massillon MSA, OH	S	11.30 MW	11.47 AW	23500 AAW	OHBLS	10//99-12//99
Metals and Plastics	Cincinnati PMSA, OH-KY-IN	S	12.07 MW	11.84 AW	25100 AAW	OHBLS	10//99-12//99
Metals and Plastics	Cleveland-Lorain-Elyria PMSA, OH	S	11.77 MW	10.56 AW	24480 AAW	OHBLS	10//99-12//99
Metals and Plastics	Columbus MSA, OH	S	13.88 MW	12.29 AW	28870 AAW	OHBLS	10//99-12//99
Metals and Plastics	Dayton-Springfield MSA, OH	S	11.52 MW	10.44 AW	23970 AAW	OHBLS	10//99-12//99
Metals and Plastics	Hamilton-Middletown PMSA, OH	S	16.40 MW	16.08 AW	34110 AAW	OHBLS	10//99-12//99
Metals and Plastics	Lima MSA, OH	S	11.66 MW	11.74 AW	24250 AAW	OHBLS	10//99-12//99
Metals and Plastics	Toledo MSA, OH	S	13.47 MW	11.73 AW	28020 AAW	OHBLS	10//99-12//99
Metals and Plastics	Youngstown-Warren MSA, OH	S	13.05 MW	12.46 AW	27140 AAW	OHBLS	10//99-12//99
Metals and Plastics	Oklahoma	S	11.14 MW	12.16 AW	25300 AAW	OKBLS	10//99-12//99

AAW	Average annual wage	AOH	Average offered, high	ASH	Average starting, high	H	Hourly	M	Monthly	S	Special: hourly and annual
AE	Average entry wage	AOL	Average offered, low	ASL	Average starting, low	HI	Highest wage paid	MTC	Median total compensation	TQ	Third quartile wage
AEX	Average experienced wage	APH	Average pay, high range	AW	Average wage paid	HR	High end range	MW	Median wage paid	W	Weekly
AO	Average offered	APL	Average pay, low range	FQ	First quartile wage	LR	Low end range	SQ	Second quartile wage	Y	Yearly

Occupation/Type/Industry	Location	Per	Low	Mid	High	Source	Date
Plating and Coating Machine							
Setter, Operator, and Tender							
Metals and Plastics	Tulsa MSA, OK	S	10.96 MW	9.16 AW	22800 AAW	OKBLS	10//99-12//99
Metals and Plastics	Oregon	S	9.67 MW	10.62 AW	22100 AAW	ORBLS	10//99-12//99
Metals and Plastics	Portland-Vancouver PMSA, OR-WA	S	10.63 MW	9.56 AW	22120 AAW	ORBLS	10//99-12//99
Metals and Plastics	Pennsylvania	S	11.15 MW	11.64 AW	24210 AAW	PABLS	10//99-12//99
Metals and Plastics	Allentown-Bethlehem-Easton MSA, PA	S	14.88 MW	15.25 AW	30960 AAW	PABLS	10//99-12//99
Metals and Plastics	Erie MSA, PA	S	9.44 MW	8.49 AW	19630 AAW	PABLS	10//99-12//99
Metals and Plastics	Harrisburg-Lebanon-Carlisle MSA, PA	S	13.87 MW	13.20 AW	28850 AAW	PABLS	10//99-12//99
Metals and Plastics	Lancaster MSA, PA	S	15.38 MW	16.83 AW	31990 AAW	PABLS	10//99-12//99
Metals and Plastics	Philadelphia PMSA, PA-NJ	S	12.03 MW	11.42 AW	25020 AAW	PABLS	10//99-12//99
Metals and Plastics	Pittsburgh MSA, PA	S	10.80 MW	10.47 AW	22460 AAW	PABLS	10//99-12//99
Metals and Plastics	Scranton--Wilkes-Barre--Hazleton MSA, PA	S	10.94 MW	10.29 AW	22760 AAW	PABLS	10//99-12//99
Metals and Plastics	Sharon MSA, PA	S	13.60 MW	13.37 AW	28290 AAW	PABLS	10//99-12//99
Metals and Plastics	York MSA, PA	S	9.78 MW	9.85 AW	20350 AAW	PABLS	10//99-12//99
Metals and Plastics	Rhode Island	S	10.21 MW	10.60 AW	22050 AAW	RIBLS	10//99-12//99
Metals and Plastics	Providence-Fall River-Warwick MSA, RI-MA	S	10.99 MW	10.56 AW	22870 AAW	RIBLS	10//99-12//99
Metals and Plastics	South Carolina	S	11.7 MW	12.50 AW	26000 AAW	SCBLS	10//99-12//99
Metals and Plastics	Greenville-Spartanburg-Anderson MSA, SC	S	11.54 MW	11.54 AW	23990 AAW	SCBLS	10//99-12//99
Metals and Plastics	Sumter MSA, SC	S	10.22 MW	10.02 AW	21250 AAW	SCBLS	10//99-12//99
Metals and Plastics	South Dakota	S	10.28 MW	10.38 AW	21580 AAW	SDBLS	10//99-12//99
Metals and Plastics	Tennessee	S	9.54 MW	9.47 AW	19700 AAW	TNBLS	10//99-12//99
Metals and Plastics	Chattanooga MSA, TN-GA	S	8.51 MW	8.41 AW	17700 AAW	TNBLS	10//99-12//99
Metals and Plastics	Memphis MSA, TN-AR-MS	S	11.28 MW	11.62 AW	23460 AAW	MSBLS	10//99-12//99
Metals and Plastics	Nashville MSA, TN	S	9.56 MW	9.27 AW	19890 AAW	TNBLS	10//99-12//99
Metals and Plastics	Texas	S	10.06 MW	10.76 AW	22370 AAW	TXBLS	10//99-12//99
Metals and Plastics	Austin-San Marcos MSA, TX	S	8.30 MW	7.73 AW	17260 AAW	TXBLS	10//99-12//99
Metals and Plastics	Dallas PMSA, TX	S	11.40 MW	11.14 AW	23710 AAW	TXBLS	10//99-12//99
Metals and Plastics	El Paso MSA, TX	S	10.60 MW	10.10 AW	22040 AAW	TXBLS	10//99-12//99
Metals and Plastics	Fort Worth-Arlington PMSA, TX	S	13.03 MW	11.44 AW	27110 AAW	TXBLS	10//99-12//99
Metals and Plastics	Houston PMSA, TX	S	10.22 MW	9.83 AW	21260 AAW	TXBLS	10//99-12//99
Metals and Plastics	Longview-Marshall MSA, TX	S	11.88 MW	10.76 AW	24710 AAW	TXBLS	10//99-12//99
Metals and Plastics	San Antonio MSA, TX	S	9.89 MW	9.49 AW	20570 AAW	TXBLS	10//99-12//99
Metals and Plastics	Vermont	S	11.27 MW	11.65 AW	24220 AAW	VTBLS	10//99-12//99
Metals and Plastics	Burlington MSA, VT	S	11.34 MW	10.97 AW	23580 AAW	VTBLS	10//99-12//99
Metals and Plastics	Virginia	S	11.22 MW	11.44 AW	23800 AAW	VABLS	10//99-12//99
Metals and Plastics	Charlottesville MSA, VA	S	12.32 MW	12.72 AW	25620 AAW	VABLS	10//99-12//99
Metals and Plastics	Norfolk-Virginia Beach-Newport News MSA, VA-NC	S	9.92 MW	9.66 AW	20640 AAW	VABLS	10//99-12//99
Metals and Plastics	Richmond-Petersburg MSA, VA	S	10.61 MW	9.83 AW	22070 AAW	VABLS	10//99-12//99
Metals and Plastics	Washington	S	13.53 MW	14.38 AW	29910 AAW	WABLS	10//99-12//99
Metals and Plastics	Seattle-Bellevue-Everett PMSA, WA	S	14.66 MW	13.88 AW	30480 AAW	WABLS	10//99-12//99
Metals and Plastics	Tacoma PMSA, WA	S	13.28 MW	12.58 AW	27630 AAW	WABLS	10//99-12//99
Metals and Plastics	West Virginia	S	16.26 MW	17.46 AW	36320 AAW	WVBLS	10//99-12//99
Metals and Plastics	Wisconsin	S	10.96 MW	11.14 AW	23170 AAW	WIBLS	10//99-12//99
Metals and Plastics	Green Bay MSA, WI	S	12.10 MW	11.15 AW	25170 AAW	WIBLS	10//99-12//99
Metals and Plastics	Milwaukee-Waukesha PMSA, WI	S	11.50 MW	11.35 AW	23910 AAW	WIBLS	10//99-12//99
Metals and Plastics	Racine PMSA, WI	S	9.13 MW	9.22 AW	18990 AAW	WIBLS	10//99-12//99
Metals and Plastics	Puerto Rico	S	7.16 MW	7.50 AW	15610 AAW	PRBLS	10//99-12//99
Plumber, Pipefitter, and							
Steamfitter	Alabama	S	14.57 MW	14.92 AW	31040 AAW	ALBLS	10//99-12//99
	Auburn-Opelika MSA, AL	S	14.17 MW	13.64 AW	29480 AAW	ALBLS	10//99-12//99
	Birmingham MSA, AL	S	15.88 MW	15.96 AW	33020 AAW	ALBLS	10//99-12//99
	Decatur MSA, AL	S	18.62 MW	17.91 AW	38720 AAW	ALBLS	10//99-12//99
	Dothan MSA, AL	S	11.29 MW	11.26 AW	23490 AAW	ALBLS	10//99-12//99
	Florence MSA, AL	S	19.22 MW	19.32 AW	39980 AAW	ALBLS	10//99-12//99
	Huntsville MSA, AL	S	14.56 MW	13.48 AW	30280 AAW	ALBLS	10//99-12//99
	Mobile MSA, AL	S	14.47 MW	14.58 AW	30110 AAW	ALBLS	10//99-12//99
	Montgomery MSA, AL	S	11.47 MW	10.37 AW	23870 AAW	ALBLS	10//99-12//99
	Tuscaloosa MSA, AL	S	15.59 MW	14.94 AW	32430 AAW	ALBLS	10//99-12//99

AAW	Average annual wage	AOH	Average offered, high	ASH	Average starting, high
AE	Average entry wage	AOL	Average offered, low	ASL	Average starting, low
AEX	Average experienced wage	APH	Average pay, high range	AW	Average wage paid
AO	Average offered	APL	Average pay, low range	FQ	First quartile wage

H	Hourly	M	Monthly
HI	Highest wage paid	MTC	Median total compensation
HR	High end range	MW	Median wage paid
LR	Low end range	SQ	Second quartile wage

S	Special: hourly and annual
TQ	Third quartile wage
W	Weekly
Y	Yearly

Plumber, Pipefitter, and Steamfitter

Occupation/Type/Industry	Location	Per	Low	Mid	High	Source	Date
Plumber, Pipefitter, and Steamfitter	Alaska	S	29.89 MW	27.69 AW	57590 AAW	AKBLS	10//99-12//99
	Anchorage MSA, AK	S	28.67 MW	31.34 AW	59620 AAW	AKBLS	10//99-12//99
	Arizona	S	15.65 MW	16.53 AW	34390 AAW	AZBLS	10//99-12//99
	Flagstaff MSA, AZ-UT	S	15.61 MW	14.43 AW	32470 AAW	AZBLS	10//99-12//99
	Phoenix-Mesa MSA, AZ	S	17.35 MW	16.67 AW	36100 AAW	AZBLS	10//99-12//99
	Tucson MSA, AZ	S	14.68 MW	13.42 AW	30530 AAW	AZBLS	10//99-12//99
	Yuma MSA, AZ	S	12.60 MW	11.73 AW	26200 AAW	AZBLS	10//99-12//99
	Arkansas	S	13.05 MW	13.59 AW	28260 AAW	ARBLS	10//99-12//99
	Fayetteville-Springdale-Rogers MSA, AR	S	12.88 MW	12.51 AW	26790 AAW	ARBLS	10//99-12//99
	Fort Smith MSA, AR-OK	S	13.68 MW	13.90 AW	28460 AAW	ARBLS	10//99-12//99
	Little Rock-North Little Rock MSA, AR	S	15.07 MW	15.17 AW	31330 AAW	ARBLS	10//99-12//99
	Pine Bluff MSA, AR	S	15.19 MW	14.33 AW	31590 AAW	ARBLS	10//99-12//99
	California	S	18.88 MW	19.85 AW	41280 AAW	CABLS	10//99-12//99
	Bakersfield MSA, CA	S	15.98 MW	15.99 AW	33240 AAW	CABLS	10//99-12//99
	Chico-Paradise MSA, CA	S	15.70 MW	13.78 AW	32660 AAW	CABLS	10//99-12//99
	Fresno MSA, CA	S	20.24 MW	20.57 AW	42090 AAW	CABLS	10//99-12//99
	Los Angeles-Long Beach PMSA, CA	S	19.49 MW	19.18 AW	40530 AAW	CABLS	10//99-12//99
	Merced MSA, CA	S	15.70 MW	14.64 AW	32660 AAW	CABLS	10//99-12//99
	Modesto MSA, CA	S	18.40 MW	16.49 AW	38270 AAW	CABLS	10//99-12//99
	Oakland PMSA, CA	S	23.85 MW	23.27 AW	49600 AAW	CABLS	10//99-12//99
	Orange County PMSA, CA	S	18.77 MW	17.46 AW	39040 AAW	CABLS	10//99-12//99
	Redding MSA, CA	S	14.51 MW	14.52 AW	30190 AAW	CABLS	10//99-12//99
	Riverside-San Bernardino PMSA, CA	S	16.87 MW	17.16 AW	35100 AAW	CABLS	10//99-12//99
	Sacramento PMSA, CA	S	18.09 MW	17.53 AW	37630 AAW	CABLS	10//99-12//99
	Salinas MSA, CA	S	22.68 MW	22.35 AW	47180 AAW	CABLS	10//99-12//99
	San Diego MSA, CA	S	18.84 MW	17.41 AW	39190 AAW	CABLS	10//99-12//99
	San Francisco PMSA, CA	S	25.24 MW	24.04 AW	52500 AAW	CABLS	10//99-12//99
	San Jose PMSA, CA	S	23.89 MW	24.13 AW	49690 AAW	CABLS	10//99-12//99
	San Luis Obispo-Atascadero-Paso Robles MSA, CA	S	19.53 MW	18.98 AW	40620 AAW	CABLS	10//99-12//99
	Santa Barbara-Santa Maria-Lompoc MSA, CA	S	23.53 MW	22.00 AW	48930 AAW	CABLS	10//99-12//99
	Santa Cruz-Watsonville PMSA, CA	S	20.16 MW	19.23 AW	41940 AAW	CABLS	10//99-12//99
	Santa Rosa PMSA, CA	S	18.05 MW	17.14 AW	37530 AAW	CABLS	10//99-12//99
	Stockton-Lodi MSA, CA	S	19.19 MW	18.67 AW	39920 AAW	CABLS	10//99-12//99
	Vallejo-Fairfield-Napa PMSA, CA	S	21.06 MW	20.29 AW	43810 AAW	CABLS	10//99-12//99
	Ventura PMSA, CA	S	17.25 MW	17.60 AW	35880 AAW	CABLS	10//99-12//99
	Visalia-Tulare-Porterville MSA, CA	S	15.18 MW	13.73 AW	31580 AAW	CABLS	10//99-12//99
	Yolo PMSA, CA	S	20.58 MW	19.59 AW	42810 AAW	CABLS	10//99-12//99
	Yuba City MSA, CA	S	24.59 MW	25.92 AW	51140 AAW	CABLS	10//99-12//99
	Colorado	S	16.01 MW	16.73 AW	34800 AAW	COBLS	10//99-12//99
	Boulder-Longmont PMSA, CO	S	19.17 MW	20.03 AW	39870 AAW	COBLS	10//99-12//99
	Colorado Springs MSA, CO	S	16.73 MW	16.68 AW	34800 AAW	COBLS	10//99-12//99
	Denver PMSA, CO	S	16.47 MW	15.42 AW	34250 AAW	COBLS	10//99-12//99
	Fort Collins-Loveland MSA, CO	S	17.54 MW	16.90 AW	36490 AAW	COBLS	10//99-12//99
	Grand Junction MSA, CO	S	15.63 MW	14.18 AW	32500 AAW	COBLS	10//99-12//99
	Greeley PMSA, CO	S	14.68 MW	14.20 AW	30540 AAW	COBLS	10//99-12//99
	Pueblo MSA, CO	S	16.27 MW	16.02 AW	33840 AAW	COBLS	10//99-12//99
	Connecticut	S	18.67 MW	18.79 AW	39080 AAW	CTBLS	10//99-12//99
	Bridgeport PMSA, CT	S	18.13 MW	18.11 AW	37710 AAW	CTBLS	10//99-12//99
	Danbury PMSA, CT	S	16.94 MW	16.93 AW	35240 AAW	CTBLS	10//99-12//99
	Hartford MSA, CT	S	17.86 MW	18.21 AW	37150 AAW	CTBLS	10//99-12//99
	New Haven-Meriden PMSA, CT	S	18.75 MW	20.12 AW	39010 AAW	CTBLS	10//99-12//99
	New London-Norwich MSA, CT-RI	S	19.36 MW	20.09 AW	40270 AAW	CTBLS	10//99-12//99
	Stamford-Norwalk PMSA, CT	S	19.65 MW	19.47 AW	40860 AAW	CTBLS	10//99-12//99
	Waterbury PMSA, CT	S	20.90 MW	18.87 AW	43460 AAW	CTBLS	10//99-12//99
	Delaware	S	20.71 MW	19.85 AW	41280 AAW	DEBLS	10//99-12//99
	Dover MSA, DE	S	15.58 MW	14.73 AW	32400 AAW	DEBLS	10//99-12//99
	Wilmington-Newark PMSA, DE-MD	S	20.56 MW	21.83 AW	42770 AAW	DEBLS	10//99-12//99
	District of Columbia	S	18.23 MW	18.84 AW	39180 AAW	DCBLS	10//99-12//99

AAW Average annual wage	**AOH** Average offered, high	**ASH** Average starting, high	**H** Hourly	**M** Monthly	**S** Special: hourly and annual
AE Average entry wage	**AOL** Average offered, low	**ASL** Average starting, low	**HI** Highest wage paid	**MTC** Median total compensation	**TQ** Third quartile wage
AEX Average experienced wage	**APH** Average pay, high range	**AW** Average wage paid	**HR** High end range	**MW** Median wage paid	**W** Weekly
AO Average offered	**APL** Average pay, low range	**FQ** First quartile wage	**LR** Low end range	**SQ** Second quartile wage	**Y** Yearly

Occupation/Type/Industry	Location	Per	Low	Mid	High	Source	Date
Plumber, Pipefitter, and Steamfitter							
	Washington PMSA, DC-MD-VA-WV	S	17.89 MW	17.33 AW	37210 AAW	DCBLS	10//99-12//99
	Florida	S	13.29 MW	13.94 AW	29000 AAW	FLBLS	10//99-12//99
	Daytona Beach MSA, FL	S	12.62 MW	12.16 AW	26250 AAW	FLBLS	10//99-12//99
	Fort Lauderdale PMSA, FL	S	15.29 MW	14.64 AW	31810 AAW	FLBLS	10//99-12//99
	Fort Myers-Cape Coral MSA, FL	S	15.01 MW	15.35 AW	31210 AAW	FLBLS	10//99-12//99
	Fort Pierce-Port St. Lucie MSA, FL	S	11.70 MW	11.47 AW	24330 AAW	FLBLS	10//99-12//99
	Fort Walton Beach MSA, FL	S	11.93 MW	11.46 AW	24820 AAW	FLBLS	10//99-12//99
	Gainesville MSA, FL	S	12.65 MW	12.43 AW	26320 AAW	FLBLS	10//99-12//99
	Jacksonville MSA, FL	S	14.46 MW	14.37 AW	30080 AAW	FLBLS	10//99-12//99
	Lakeland-Winter Haven MSA, FL	S	11.89 MW	11.75 AW	24730 AAW	FLBLS	10//99-12//99
	Melbourne-Titusville-Palm Bay MSA, FL	S	13.56 MW	12.62 AW	28210 AAW	FLBLS	10//99-12//99
	Miami PMSA, FL	S	14.36 MW	13.51 AW	29870 AAW	FLBLS	10//99-12//99
	Naples MSA, FL	S	14.43 MW	14.05 AW	30010 AAW	FLBLS	10//99-12//99
	Ocala MSA, FL	S	13.86 MW	12.94 AW	28820 AAW	FLBLS	10//99-12//99
	Orlando MSA, FL	S	13.94 MW	13.84 AW	28990 AAW	FLBLS	10//99-12//99
	Panama City MSA, FL	S	12.69 MW	11.94 AW	26400 AAW	FLBLS	10//99-12//99
	Pensacola MSA, FL	S	13.94 MW	13.77 AW	29000 AAW	FLBLS	10//99-12//99
	Punta Gorda MSA, FL	S	13.69 MW	13.24 AW	28470 AAW	FLBLS	10//99-12//99
	Sarasota-Bradenton MSA, FL	S	12.94 MW	12.75 AW	26910 AAW	FLBLS	10//99-12//99
	Tallahassee MSA, FL	S	13.28 MW	12.78 AW	27630 AAW	FLBLS	10//99-12//99
	Tampa-St. Petersburg-Clearwater MSA, FL	S	12.87 MW	12.61 AW	26770 AAW	FLBLS	10//99-12//99
	West Palm Beach-Boca Raton MSA, FL	S	14.54 MW	14.65 AW	30250 AAW	FLBLS	10//99-12//99
	Georgia	S	14.84 MW	15.42 AW	32060 AAW	GABLS	10//99-12//99
	Albany MSA, GA	S	17.55 MW	16.28 AW	36510 AAW	GABLS	10//99-12//99
	Athens MSA, GA	S	14.45 MW	13.24 AW	30050 AAW	GABLS	10//99-12//99
	Atlanta MSA, GA	S	15.87 MW	15.30 AW	33000 AAW	GABLS	10//99-12//99
	Augusta-Aiken MSA, GA-SC	S	16.81 MW	15.64 AW	34960 AAW	GABLS	10//99-12//99
	Columbus MSA, GA-AL	S	12.70 MW	12.58 AW	26420 AAW	GABLS	10//99-12//99
	Macon MSA, GA	S	14.64 MW	14.37 AW	30440 AAW	GABLS	10//99-12//99
	Savannah MSA, GA	S	15.65 MW	15.38 AW	32560 AAW	GABLS	10//99-12//99
	Hawaii	S	20.3 MW	21.61 AW	44950 AAW	HIBLS	10//99-12//99
	Honolulu MSA, HI	S	21.90 MW	20.94 AW	45560 AAW	HIBLS	10//99-12//99
	Idaho	S	17.77 MW	17.59 AW	36590 AAW	IDBLS	10//99-12//99
	Boise City MSA, ID	S	17.58 MW	17.99 AW	36570 AAW	IDBLS	10//99-12//99
	Pocatello MSA, ID	S	15.43 MW	14.35 AW	32090 AAW	IDBLS	10//99-12//99
	Illinois	S	27.1 MW	25.58 AW	53210 AAW	ILBLS	10//99-12//99
	Bloomington-Normal MSA, IL	S	22.12 MW	22.92 AW	46000 AAW	ILBLS	10//99-12//99
	Champaign-Urbana MSA, IL	S	29.95 MW	33.03 AW	62290 AAW	ILBLS	10//99-12//99
	Chicago PMSA, IL	S	26.43 MW	28.65 AW	54970 AAW	ILBLS	10//99-12//99
	Decatur MSA, IL	S	26.65 MW	27.21 AW	55440 AAW	ILBLS	10//99-12//99
	Kankakee PMSA, IL	S	23.58 MW	25.05 AW	49040 AAW	ILBLS	10//99-12//99
	Peoria-Pekin MSA, IL	S	22.75 MW	22.78 AW	47310 AAW	ILBLS	10//99-12//99
	Rockford MSA, IL	S	24.69 MW	26.89 AW	51360 AAW	ILBLS	10//99-12//99
	Springfield MSA, IL	S	22.87 MW	22.33 AW	47560 AAW	ILBLS	10//99-12//99
	Indiana	S	19.24 MW	19.54 AW	40640 AAW	INBLS	10//99-12//99
	Elkhart-Goshen MSA, IN	S	18.62 MW	19.14 AW	38720 AAW	INBLS	10//99-12//99
	Evansville-Henderson MSA, IN-KY	S	21.37 MW	22.84 AW	44450 AAW	INBLS	10//99-12//99
	Fort Wayne MSA, IN	S	17.62 MW	17.41 AW	36650 AAW	INBLS	10//99-12//99
	Gary PMSA, IN	S	24.53 MW	24.14 AW	51030 AAW	INBLS	10//99-12//99
	Indianapolis MSA, IN	S	18.70 MW	16.15 AW	38900 AAW	INBLS	10//99-12//99
	Kokomo MSA, IN	S	21.58 MW	23.02 AW	44890 AAW	INBLS	10//99-12//99
	Lafayette MSA, IN	S	15.19 MW	14.35 AW	31580 AAW	INBLS	10//99-12//99
	Muncie MSA, IN	S	20.93 MW	21.68 AW	43540 AAW	INBLS	10//99-12//99
	South Bend MSA, IN	S	18.55 MW	18.64 AW	38590 AAW	INBLS	10//99-12//99
	Iowa	S	16.13 MW	17.35 AW	36090 AAW	IABLS	10//99-12//99
	Cedar Rapids MSA, IA	S	23.12 MW	23.20 AW	48090 AAW	IABLS	10//99-12//99
	Davenport-Moline-Rock Island MSA, IA-IL	S	22.98 MW	23.32 AW	47800 AAW	IABLS	10//99-12//99
	Des Moines MSA, IA	S	18.19 MW	16.54 AW	37840 AAW	IABLS	10//99-12//99
	Dubuque MSA, IA	S	15.46 MW	13.33 AW	32170 AAW	IABLS	10//99-12//99
	Iowa City MSA, IA	S	18.88 MW	16.39 AW	39270 AAW	IABLS	10//99-12//99
	Sioux City MSA, IA-NE	S	13.83 MW	13.05 AW	28760 AAW	IABLS	10//99-12//99
	Waterloo-Cedar Falls MSA, IA	S	18.67 MW	19.91 AW	38830 AAW	IABLS	10//99-12//99

AAW	Average annual wage	AOH	Average offered, high	ASH	Average starting, high
AE	Average entry wage	AOL	Average offered, low	ASL	Average starting, low
AEX	Average experienced wage	APH	Average pay, high range	AW	Average wage paid
AO	Average offered	APL	Average pay, low range	FQ	First quartile wage

H	Hourly	M	Monthly
HI	Highest wage paid	MTC	Median total compensation
HR	High end range	MW	Median wage paid
LR	Low end range	SQ	Second quartile wage

S	Special: hourly and annual
TQ	Third quartile wage
W	Weekly
Y	Yearly

Occupation/Type/Industry	Location	Per	Low	Mid	High	Source	Date
Plumber, Pipefitter, and Steamfitter	Kansas	S	16.27 MW	17.79 AW	37000 AAW	KSBLS	10//99-12//99
	Lawrence MSA, KS	S	19.53 MW	18.79 AW	40620 AAW	KSBLS	10//99-12//99
	Topeka MSA, KS	S	20.07 MW	18.34 AW	41730 AAW	KSBLS	10//99-12//99
	Wichita MSA, KS	S	19.66 MW	18.61 AW	40900 AAW	KSBLS	10//99-12//99
	Kentucky	S	17.5 MW	17.88 AW	37180 AAW	KYBLS	10//99-12//99
	Lexington MSA, KY	S	16.64 MW	15.89 AW	34600 AAW	KYBLS	10//99-12//99
	Louisville MSA, KY-IN	S	17.94 MW	18.19 AW	37320 AAW	KYBLS	10//99-12//99
	Owensboro MSA, KY	S	16.04 MW	14.65 AW	33350 AAW	KYBLS	10//99-12//99
	Louisiana	S	15.57 MW	16.09 AW	33480 AAW	LABLS	10//99-12//99
	Alexandria MSA, LA	S	13.54 MW	12.43 AW	28150 AAW	LABLS	10//99-12//99
	Baton Rouge MSA, LA	S	16.58 MW	16.19 AW	34490 AAW	LABLS	10//99-12//99
	Houma MSA, LA	S	14.31 MW	14.47 AW	29770 AAW	LABLS	10//99-12//99
	Lafayette MSA, LA	S	18.31 MW	15.35 AW	38080 AAW	LABLS	10//99-12//99
	Lake Charles MSA, LA	S	16.03 MW	15.65 AW	33350 AAW	LABLS	10//99-12//99
	Monroe MSA, LA	S	13.86 MW	13.40 AW	28820 AAW	LABLS	10//99-12//99
	New Orleans MSA, LA	S	16.43 MW	15.96 AW	34170 AAW	LABLS	10//99-12//99
	Shreveport-Bossier City MSA, LA	S	17.21 MW	13.92 AW	35800 AAW	LABLS	10//99-12//99
	Maine	S	15.16 MW	15.29 AW	31800 AAW	MEBLS	10//99-12//99
	Bangor MSA, ME	S	15.04 MW	14.96 AW	31290 AAW	MEBLS	10//99-12//99
	Lewiston-Auburn MSA, ME	S	15.46 MW	16.33 AW	32160 AAW	MEBLS	10//99-12//99
	Portland MSA, ME	S	14.92 MW	13.82 AW	31040 AAW	MEBLS	10//99-12//99
	Maryland	S	16.42 MW	17.04 AW	35440 AAW	MDBLS	10//99-12//99
	Baltimore PMSA, MD	S	16.22 MW	16.09 AW	33740 AAW	MDBLS	10//99-12//99
	Hagerstown PMSA, MD	S	15.32 MW	13.58 AW	31860 AAW	MDBLS	10//99-12//99
	Massachusetts	S	20.42 MW	21.45 AW	44610 AAW	MABLS	10//99-12//99
	Barnstable-Yarmouth MSA, MA	S	20.44 MW	18.73 AW	42510 AAW	MABLS	10//99-12//99
	Boston PMSA, MA-NH	S	23.58 MW	23.73 AW	49040 AAW	MABLS	10//99-12//99
	Brockton PMSA, MA	S	23.61 MW	21.45 AW	49100 AAW	MABLS	10//99-12//99
	Fitchburg-Leominster PMSA, MA	S	20.84 MW	21.24 AW	43350 AAW	MABLS	10//99-12//99
	Lawrence PMSA, MA-NH	S	19.40 MW	19.43 AW	40350 AAW	MABLS	10//99-12//99
	Lowell PMSA, MA-NH	S	15.80 MW	15.99 AW	32870 AAW	MABLS	10//99-12//99
	New Bedford PMSA, MA	S	18.58 MW	19.78 AW	38640 AAW	MABLS	10//99-12//99
	Pittsfield MSA, MA	S	20.78 MW	20.03 AW	43230 AAW	MABLS	10//99-12//99
	Springfield MSA, MA	S	18.63 MW	18.84 AW	38750 AAW	MABLS	10//99-12//99
	Worcester PMSA, MA-CT	S	16.87 MW	16.50 AW	35080 AAW	MABLS	10//99-12//99
	Michigan	S	22.32 MW	21.92 AW	45600 AAW	MIBLS	10//99-12//99
	Ann Arbor PMSA, MI	S	20.33 MW	20.98 AW	42280 AAW	MIBLS	10//99-12//99
	Benton Harbor MSA, MI	S	19.61 MW	19.77 AW	40790 AAW	MIBLS	10//99-12//99
	Detroit PMSA, MI	S	24.39 MW	24.01 AW	50740 AAW	MIBLS	10//99-12//99
	Flint PMSA, MI	S	22.07 MW	23.01 AW	45920 AAW	MIBLS	10//99-12//99
	Grand Rapids-Muskegon-Holland MSA, MI	S	18.54 MW	18.34 AW	38560 AAW	MIBLS	10//99-12//99
	Jackson MSA, MI	S	19.38 MW	19.22 AW	40310 AAW	MIBLS	10//99-12//99
	Kalamazoo-Battle Creek MSA, MI	S	20.58 MW	21.75 AW	42810 AAW	MIBLS	10//99-12//99
	Lansing-East Lansing MSA, MI	S	22.08 MW	22.47 AW	45920 AAW	MIBLS	10//99-12//99
	Saginaw-Bay City-Midland MSA, MI	S	20.87 MW	22.62 AW	43410 AAW	MIBLS	10//99-12//99
	Minnesota	S	22.4 MW	22.30 AW	46390 AAW	MNBLS	10//99-12//99
	Duluth-Superior MSA, MN-WI	S	21.08 MW	20.74 AW	43850 AAW	MNBLS	10//99-12//99
	Minneapolis-St. Paul MSA, MN-WI	S	25.00 MW	25.10 AW	52000 AAW	MNBLS	10//99-12//99
	Rochester MSA, MN	S	23.25 MW	23.97 AW	48360 AAW	MNBLS	10//99-12//99
	St. Cloud MSA, MN	S	16.61 MW	16.26 AW	34550 AAW	MNBLS	10//99-12//99
	Mississippi	S	14.18 MW	14.28 AW	29710 AAW	MSBLS	10//99-12//99
	Biloxi-Gulfport-Pascagoula MSA, MS	S	15.34 MW	15.27 AW	31910 AAW	MSBLS	10//99-12//99
	Hattiesburg MSA, MS	S	12.24 MW	11.79 AW	25450 AAW	MSBLS	10//99-12//99
	Jackson MSA, MS	S	13.03 MW	12.67 AW	27110 AAW	MSBLS	10//99-12//99
	Missouri	S	19.66 MW	20.19 AW	41990 AAW	MOBLS	10//99-12//99
	Kansas City MSA, MO-KS	S	20.36 MW	20.03 AW	42350 AAW	MOBLS	10//99-12//99
	St. Louis MSA, MO-IL	S	23.07 MW	22.97 AW	47990 AAW	MOBLS	10//99-12//99
	Springfield MSA, MO	S	19.07 MW	19.05 AW	39660 AAW	MOBLS	10//99-12//99
	Montana	S	19.33 MW	18.71 AW	38920 AAW	MTBLS	10//99-12//99
	Billings MSA, MT	S	20.32 MW	21.81 AW	42270 AAW	MTBLS	10//99-12//99
	Great Falls MSA, MT	S	18.86 MW	20.04 AW	39220 AAW	MTBLS	10//99-12//99
	Nebraska	S	18.47 MW	19.23 AW	39990 AAW	NEBLS	10//99-12//99
	Lincoln MSA, NE	S	16.33 MW	15.90 AW	33970 AAW	NEBLS	10//99-12//99

AAW	Average annual wage	AOH	Average offered, high	ASH	Average starting, high	H	Hourly	M	Monthly	S	Special: hourly and annual
AE	Average entry wage	AOL	Average offered, low	ASL	Average starting, low	HI	Highest wage paid	MTC	Median total compensation	TQ	Third quartile wage
AEX	Average experienced wage	APH	Average pay, high range	AW	Average wage paid	HR	High end range	MW	Median wage paid	W	Weekly
AO	Average offered	APL	Average pay, low range	FQ	First quartile wage	LR	Low end range	SQ	Second quartile wage	Y	Yearly

Occupation/Type/Industry	Location	Per	Low	Mid	High	Source	Date
Plumber, Pipefitter, and Steamfitter	Omaha MSA, NE-IA	S	21.96 MW	21.59 AW	45670 AAW	NEBLS	10//99-12//99
	Nevada	S	19.63 MW	21.31 AW	44320 AAW	NVBLS	10//99-12//99
	Las Vegas MSA, NV-AZ	S	21.51 MW	19.96 AW	44750 AAW	NVBLS	10//99-12//99
	Reno MSA, NV	S	20.72 MW	19.36 AW	43100 AAW	NVBLS	10//99-12//99
	New Hampshire	S	15.39 MW	15.82 AW	32910 AAW	NHBLS	10//99-12//99
	Manchester PMSA, NH	S	16.74 MW	15.96 AW	34810 AAW	NHBLS	10//99-12//99
	Nashua PMSA, NH	S	16.06 MW	15.83 AW	33400 AAW	NHBLS	10//99-12//99
	Portsmouth-Rochester PMSA, NH-ME	S	14.66 MW	13.95 AW	30500 AAW	NHBLS	10//99-12//99
	New Jersey	S	19.79 MW	20.90 AW	43470 AAW	NJBLS	10//99-12//99
	Atlantic-Cape May PMSA, NJ	S	22.20 MW	20.21 AW	46170 AAW	NJBLS	10//99-12//99
	Bergen-Passaic PMSA, NJ	S	20.87 MW	19.41 AW	43410 AAW	NJBLS	10//99-12//99
	Middlesex-Somerset-Hunterdon PMSA, NJ	S	21.44 MW	19.91 AW	44590 AAW	NJBLS	10//99-12//99
	Monmouth-Ocean PMSA, NJ	S	18.30 MW	16.13 AW	38050 AAW	NJBLS	10//99-12//99
	Trenton PMSA, NJ	S	20.72 MW	20.38 AW	43110 AAW	NJBLS	10//99-12//99
	New Mexico	S	14.28 MW	15.67 AW	32590 AAW	NMBLS	10//99-12//99
	Albuquerque MSA, NM	S	16.47 MW	14.92 AW	34260 AAW	NMBLS	10//99-12//99
	Las Cruces MSA, NM	S	13.58 MW	11.14 AW	28240 AAW	NMBLS	10//99-12//99
	Santa Fe MSA, NM	S	18.43 MW	17.49 AW	38330 AAW	NMBLS	10//99-12//99
	New York	S	21.5 MW	22.10 AW	45970 AAW	NYBLS	10//99-12//99
	Albany-Schenectady-Troy MSA, NY	S	20.87 MW	21.42 AW	43410 AAW	NYBLS	10//99-12//99
	Binghamton MSA, NY	S	22.40 MW	22.71 AW	46590 AAW	NYBLS	10//99-12//99
	Buffalo-Niagara Falls MSA, NY	S	22.11 MW	22.84 AW	45990 AAW	NYBLS	10//99-12//99
	Dutchess County PMSA, NY	S	19.14 MW	18.66 AW	39810 AAW	NYBLS	10//99-12//99
	Elmira MSA, NY	S	20.14 MW	21.83 AW	41880 AAW	NYBLS	10//99-12//99
	Glens Falls MSA, NY	S	17.96 MW	17.42 AW	37350 AAW	NYBLS	10//99-12//99
	Jamestown MSA, NY	S	18.02 MW	16.20 AW	37480 AAW	NYBLS	10//99-12//99
	Nassau-Suffolk PMSA, NY	S	21.02 MW	18.90 AW	43720 AAW	NYBLS	10//99-12//99
	New York PMSA, NY	S	23.64 MW	23.13 AW	49170 AAW	NYBLS	10//99-12//99
	Newburgh PMSA, NY-PA	S	16.27 MW	15.48 AW	33840 AAW	NYBLS	10//99-12//99
	Rochester MSA, NY	S	19.31 MW	19.22 AW	40160 AAW	NYBLS	10//99-12//99
	Syracuse MSA, NY	S	19.61 MW	20.69 AW	40790 AAW	NYBLS	10//99-12//99
	Utica-Rome MSA, NY	S	17.35 MW	16.94 AW	36100 AAW	NYBLS	10//99-12//99
	North Carolina	S	13.8 MW	14.05 AW	29230 AAW	NCBLS	10//99-12//99
	Asheville MSA, NC	S	13.20 MW	13.54 AW	27460 AAW	NCBLS	10//99-12//99
	Charlotte-Gastonia-Rock Hill MSA, NC-SC	S	14.83 MW	14.61 AW	30850 AAW	NCBLS	10//99-12//99
	Fayetteville MSA, NC	S	13.92 MW	13.57 AW	28960 AAW	NCBLS	10//99-12//99
	Goldsboro MSA, NC	S	12.41 MW	11.71 AW	25810 AAW	NCBLS	10//99-12//99
	Greensboro--Winston-Salem--High Point MSA, NC	S	15.83 MW	15.56 AW	32930 AAW	NCBLS	10//99-12//99
	Greenville MSA, NC	S	13.95 MW	14.11 AW	29010 AAW	NCBLS	10//99-12//99
	Hickory-Morganton-Lenoir MSA, NC	S	13.38 MW	12.54 AW	27820 AAW	NCBLS	10//99-12//99
	Jacksonville MSA, NC	S	12.84 MW	12.06 AW	26700 AAW	NCBLS	10//99-12//99
	Raleigh-Durham-Chapel Hill MSA, NC	S	14.34 MW	14.54 AW	29830 AAW	NCBLS	10//99-12//99
	Rocky Mount MSA, NC	S	13.36 MW	13.63 AW	27800 AAW	NCBLS	10//99-12//99
	Wilmington MSA, NC	S	15.03 MW	16.27 AW	31270 AAW	NCBLS	10//99-12//99
	North Dakota	S	16.1 MW	16.21 AW	33710 AAW	NDBLS	10//99-12//99
	Bismarck MSA, ND	S	18.40 MW	16.43 AW	38260 AAW	NDBLS	10//99-12//99
	Fargo-Moorhead MSA, ND-MN	S	16.76 MW	17.87 AW	34870 AAW	NDBLS	10//99-12//99
	Grand Forks MSA, ND-MN	S	14.72 MW	13.66 AW	30610 AAW	NDBLS	10//99-12//99
	Ohio	S	19.82 MW	19.71 AW	41000 AAW	OHBLS	10//99-12//99
	Akron PMSA, OH	S	18.54 MW	17.58 AW	38560 AAW	OHBLS	10//99-12//99
	Canton-Massillon MSA, OH	S	18.38 MW	16.86 AW	38220 AAW	OHBLS	10//99-12//99
	Cincinnati PMSA, OH-KY-IN	S	17.41 MW	16.82 AW	36210 AAW	OHBLS	10//99-12//99
	Cleveland-Lorain-Elyria PMSA, OH	S	22.51 MW	22.54 AW	46820 AAW	OHBLS	10//99-12//99
	Columbus MSA, OH	S	20.45 MW	20.41 AW	42530 AAW	OHBLS	10//99-12//99
	Dayton-Springfield MSA, OH	S	18.81 MW	19.96 AW	39130 AAW	OHBLS	10//99-12//99
	Hamilton-Middletown PMSA, OH	S	16.68 MW	15.19 AW	34700 AAW	OHBLS	10//99-12//99
	Lima MSA, OH	S	16.65 MW	15.73 AW	34630 AAW	OHBLS	10//99-12//99
	Mansfield MSA, OH	S	18.59 MW	20.49 AW	38660 AAW	OHBLS	10//99-12//99
	Toledo MSA, OH	S	21.26 MW	22.05 AW	44220 AAW	OHBLS	10//99-12//99
	Youngstown-Warren MSA, OH	S	18.86 MW	19.24 AW	39220 AAW	OHBLS	10//99-12//99

AAW Average annual wage	**AOH** Average offered, high	**ASH** Average starting, high	**H** Hourly	**M** Monthly	**S** Special: hourly and annual
AE Average entry wage	**AOL** Average offered, low	**ASL** Average starting, low	**HI** Highest wage paid	**MTC** Median total compensation	**TQ** Third quartile wage
AEX Average experienced wage	**APH** Average pay, high range	**AW** Average wage paid	**HR** High end range	**MW** Median wage paid	**W** Weekly
AO Average offered	**APL** Average pay, low range	**FQ** First quartile wage	**LR** Low end range	**SQ** Second quartile wage	**Y** Yearly

Occupation/Type/Industry	Location	Per	Low	Mid	High	Source	Date
Plumber, Pipefitter, and							
Steamfitter	Oklahoma	S	14.47 MW	14.77 AW	30720 AAW	OKBLS	10//99-12//99
	Enid MSA, OK	S	14.64 MW	14.78 AW	30450 AAW	OKBLS	10//99-12//99
	Lawton MSA, OK	S	13.40 MW	13.04 AW	27880 AAW	OKBLS	10//99-12//99
	Oklahoma City MSA, OK	S	15.73 MW	15.17 AW	32720 AAW	OKBLS	10//99-12//99
	Tulsa MSA, OK	S	15.65 MW	15.71 AW	32540 AAW	OKBLS	10//99-12//99
	Oregon	S	22.52 MW	22.80 AW	47420 AAW	ORBLS	10//99-12//99
	Corvallis MSA, OR	S	18.49 MW	19.31 AW	38460 AAW	ORBLS	10//99-12//99
	Eugene-Springfield MSA, OR	S	21.93 MW	21.57 AW	45610 AAW	ORBLS	10//99-12//99
	Medford-Ashland MSA, OR	S	18.86 MW	18.19 AW	39240 AAW	ORBLS	10//99-12//99
	Portland-Vancouver PMSA, OR-WA	S	24.17 MW	23.94 AW	50270 AAW	ORBLS	10//99-12//99
	Pennsylvania	S	18.76 MW	20.20 AW	42010 AAW	PABLS	10//99-12//99
	Allentown-Bethlehem-Easton MSA, PA	S	19.42 MW	18.38 AW	40400 AAW	PABLS	10//99-12//99
	Altoona MSA, PA	S	17.95 MW	17.78 AW	37330 AAW	PABLS	10//99-12//99
	Erie MSA, PA	S	19.59 MW	19.58 AW	40750 AAW	PABLS	10//99-12//99
	Harrisburg-Lebanon-Carlisle MSA, PA	S	18.14 MW	16.18 AW	37720 AAW	PABLS	10//99-12//99
	Johnstown MSA, PA	S	15.59 MW	13.69 AW	32430 AAW	PABLS	10//99-12//99
	Lancaster MSA, PA	S	15.36 MW	14.77 AW	31940 AAW	PABLS	10//99-12//99
	Philadelphia PMSA, PA-NJ	S	22.23 MW	20.08 AW	46230 AAW	PABLS	10//99-12//99
	Pittsburgh MSA, PA	S	20.13 MW	19.89 AW	41880 AAW	PABLS	10//99-12//99
	Reading MSA, PA	S	17.94 MW	16.70 AW	37320 AAW	PABLS	10//99-12//99
	Scranton--Wilkes-Barre--Hazleton MSA, PA	S	19.12 MW	18.17 AW	39760 AAW	PABLS	10//99-12//99
	Sharon MSA, PA	S	16.07 MW	15.92 AW	33420 AAW	PABLS	10//99-12//99
	State College MSA, PA	S	15.28 MW	13.52 AW	31780 AAW	PABLS	10//99-12//99
	Williamsport MSA, PA	S	14.48 MW	13.69 AW	30130 AAW	PABLS	10//99-12//99
	York MSA, PA	S	16.68 MW	16.10 AW	34680 AAW	PABLS	10//99-12//99
	Rhode Island	S	15.5 MW	16.40 AW	34120 AAW	RIBLS	10//99-12//99
	Providence-Fall River-Warwick MSA, RI-MA	S	16.69 MW	16.10 AW	34720 AAW	RIBLS	10//99-12//99
	South Carolina	S	14.53 MW	15.09 AW	31380 AAW	SCBLS	10//99-12//99
	Charleston-North Charleston MSA, SC	S	13.66 MW	13.47 AW	28420 AAW	SCBLS	10//99-12//99
	Columbia MSA, SC	S	17.34 MW	15.94 AW	36070 AAW	SCBLS	10//99-12//99
	Florence MSA, SC	S	13.79 MW	14.42 AW	28680 AAW	SCBLS	10//99-12//99
	Greenville-Spartanburg-Anderson MSA, SC	S	14.69 MW	14.91 AW	30550 AAW	SCBLS	10//99-12//99
	Myrtle Beach MSA, SC	S	10.63 MW	10.22 AW	22120 AAW	SCBLS	10//99-12//99
	Sumter MSA, SC	S	13.50 MW	13.41 AW	28070 AAW	SCBLS	10//99-12//99
	South Dakota	S	14.57 MW	14.66 AW	30490 AAW	SDBLS	10//99-12//99
	Rapid City MSA, SD	S	15.47 MW	15.43 AW	32180 AAW	SDBLS	10//99-12//99
	Sioux Falls MSA, SD	S	15.73 MW	15.44 AW	32710 AAW	SDBLS	10//99-12//99
	Tennessee	S	15.48 MW	16.04 AW	33350 AAW	TNBLS	10//99-12//99
	Chattanooga MSA, TN-GA	S	15.74 MW	16.59 AW	32740 AAW	TNBLS	10//99-12//99
	Clarksville-Hopkinsville MSA, TN-KY	S	13.35 MW	13.32 AW	27760 AAW	TNBLS	10//99-12//99
	Jackson MSA, TN	S	15.15 MW	15.23 AW	31510 AAW	TNBLS	10//99-12//99
	Johnson City-Kingsport-Bristol MSA, TN-VA	S	14.28 MW	13.83 AW	29700 AAW	TNBLS	10//99-12//99
	Knoxville MSA, TN	S	16.23 MW	15.60 AW	33750 AAW	TNBLS	10//99-12//99
	Memphis MSA, TN-AR-MS	S	16.87 MW	17.40 AW	35090 AAW	MSBLS	10//99-12//99
	Nashville MSA, TN	S	16.11 MW	15.10 AW	33500 AAW	TNBLS	10//99-12//99
	Texas	S	15.57 MW	15.66 AW	32570 AAW	TXBLS	10//99-12//99
	Abilene MSA, TX	S	13.62 MW	12.46 AW	28320 AAW	TXBLS	10//99-12//99
	Amarillo MSA, TX	S	15.51 MW	16.16 AW	32270 AAW	TXBLS	10//99-12//99
	Austin-San Marcos MSA, TX	S	15.34 MW	15.89 AW	31910 AAW	TXBLS	10//99-12//99
	Beaumont-Port Arthur MSA, TX	S	17.82 MW	18.55 AW	37070 AAW	TXBLS	10//99-12//99
	Brazoria PMSA, TX	S	15.38 MW	16.32 AW	31990 AAW	TXBLS	10//99-12//99
	Brownsville-Harlingen-San Benito MSA, TX	S	12.84 MW	12.48 AW	26710 AAW	TXBLS	10//99-12//99
	Bryan-College Station MSA, TX	S	15.23 MW	15.14 AW	31670 AAW	TXBLS	10//99-12//99
	Corpus Christi MSA, TX	S	15.55 MW	14.76 AW	32350 AAW	TXBLS	10//99-12//99
	Dallas PMSA, TX	S	15.81 MW	15.86 AW	32890 AAW	TXBLS	10//99-12//99
	El Paso MSA, TX	S	12.19 MW	11.72 AW	25360 AAW	TXBLS	10//99-12//99
	Fort Worth-Arlington PMSA, TX	S	16.16 MW	16.64 AW	33610 AAW	TXBLS	10//99-12//99

AAW Average annual wage	**AOH** Average offered, high	**ASH** Average starting, high	**H** Hourly	**M** Monthly	**S** Special: hourly and annual
AE Average entry wage	**AOL** Average offered, low	**ASL** Average starting, low	**HI** Highest wage paid	**MTC** Median total compensation	**TQ** Third quartile wage
AEX Average experienced wage	**APH** Average pay, high range	**AW** Average wage paid	**HR** High end range	**MW** Median wage paid	**W** Weekly
AO Average offered	**APL** Average pay, low range	**FQ** First quartile wage	**LR** Low end range	**SQ** Second quartile wage	**Y** Yearly

Occupation/Type/Industry	Location	Per	Low	Mid	High	Source	Date
Plumber, Pipefitter, and Steamfitter							
	Galveston-Texas City PMSA, TX	S	17.42 MW	17.79 AW	36230 AAW	TXBLS	10//99-12//99
	Houston PMSA, TX	S	16.98 MW	16.51 AW	35330 AAW	TXBLS	10//99-12//99
	Killeen-Temple MSA, TX	S	13.62 MW	14.02 AW	28330 AAW	TXBLS	10//99-12//99
	Laredo MSA, TX	S	12.37 MW	12.14 AW	25720 AAW	TXBLS	10//99-12//99
	Longview-Marshall MSA, TX	S	14.59 MW	15.16 AW	30350 AAW	TXBLS	10//99-12//99
	Lubbock MSA, TX	S	13.75 MW	13.09 AW	28610 AAW	TXBLS	10//99-12//99
	McAllen-Edinburg-Mission MSA, TX	S	9.28 MW	8.07 AW	19300 AAW	TXBLS	10//99-12//99
	Odessa-Midland MSA, TX	S	12.30 MW	11.76 AW	25580 AAW	TXBLS	10//99-12//99
	San Angelo MSA, TX	S	15.59 MW	15.68 AW	32420 AAW	TXBLS	10//99-12//99
	San Antonio MSA, TX	S	15.16 MW	14.70 AW	31530 AAW	TXBLS	10//99-12//99
	Sherman-Denison MSA, TX	S	11.03 MW	9.67 AW	22940 AAW	TXBLS	10//99-12//99
	Texarkana MSA, TX-Texarkana, AR	S	14.92 MW	14.90 AW	31030 AAW	TXBLS	10//99-12//99
	Tyler MSA, TX	S	14.98 MW	14.29 AW	31160 AAW	TXBLS	10//99-12//99
	Victoria MSA, TX	S	13.94 MW	14.30 AW	28990 AAW	TXBLS	10//99-12//99
	Waco MSA, TX	S	17.08 MW	17.76 AW	35520 AAW	TXBLS	10//99-12//99
	Wichita Falls MSA, TX	S	15.70 MW	15.60 AW	32650 AAW	TXBLS	10//99-12//99
	Utah	S	16.89 MW	16.98 AW	35320 AAW	UTBLS	10//99-12//99
	Provo-Orem MSA, UT	S	15.22 MW	14.36 AW	31660 AAW	UTBLS	10//99-12//99
	Salt Lake City-Ogden MSA, UT	S	17.58 MW	17.49 AW	36570 AAW	UTBLS	10//99-12//99
	Vermont	S	14.43 MW	15.14 AW	31480 AAW	VTBLS	10//99-12//99
	Burlington MSA, VT	S	17.97 MW	16.91 AW	37390 AAW	VTBLS	10//99-12//99
	Virginia	S	15.01 MW	15.16 AW	31530 AAW	VABLS	10//99-12//99
	Charlottesville MSA, VA	S	13.10 MW	12.86 AW	27240 AAW	VABLS	10//99-12//99
	Danville MSA, VA	S	10.13 MW	10.04 AW	21060 AAW	VABLS	10//99-12//99
	Lynchburg MSA, VA	S	14.72 MW	13.82 AW	30620 AAW	VABLS	10//99-12//99
	Norfolk-Virginia Beach-Newport News MSA, VA-NC	S	15.07 MW	15.13 AW	31340 AAW	VABLS	10//99-12//99
	Richmond-Petersburg MSA, VA	S	16.16 MW	15.76 AW	33610 AAW	VABLS	10//99-12//99
	Roanoke MSA, VA	S	10.01 MW	9.54 AW	20810 AAW	VABLS	10//99-12//99
	Washington	S	21.01 MW	22.16 AW	46080 AAW	WABLS	10//99-12//99
	Bellingham MSA, WA	S	23.06 MW	22.98 AW	47970 AAW	WABLS	10//99-12//99
	Olympia PMSA, WA	S	19.38 MW	18.74 AW	40310 AAW	WABLS	10//99-12//99
	Richland-Kennewick-Pasco MSA, WA	S	26.23 MW	28.12 AW	54560 AAW	WABLS	10//99-12//99
	Seattle-Bellevue-Everett PMSA, WA	S	23.38 MW	22.96 AW	48620 AAW	WABLS	10//99-12//99
	Spokane MSA, WA	S	16.93 MW	17.02 AW	35210 AAW	WABLS	10//99-12//99
	Tacoma PMSA, WA	S	19.22 MW	19.11 AW	39970 AAW	WABLS	10//99-12//99
	Yakima MSA, WA	S	20.79 MW	21.60 AW	43230 AAW	WABLS	10//99-12//99
	West Virginia	S	19.32 MW	18.45 AW	38370 AAW	WVBLS	10//99-12//99
	Charleston MSA, WV	S	19.52 MW	20.13 AW	40600 AAW	WVBLS	10//99-12//99
	Huntington-Ashland MSA, WV-KY-OH	S	20.44 MW	21.61 AW	42510 AAW	WVBLS	10//99-12//99
	Parkersburg-Marietta MSA, WV-OH	S	21.55 MW	22.30 AW	44820 AAW	WVBLS	10//99-12//99
	Wheeling MSA, WV-OH	S	16.88 MW	17.67 AW	35100 AAW	WVBLS	10//99-12//99
	Wisconsin	S	22.59 MW	22.59 AW	46980 AAW	WIBLS	10//99-12//99
	Appleton-Oshkosh-Neenah MSA, WI	S	22.39 MW	22.13 AW	46560 AAW	WIBLS	10//99-12//99
	Eau Claire MSA, WI	S	19.85 MW	20.25 AW	41280 AAW	WIBLS	10//99-12//99
	Green Bay MSA, WI	S	22.50 MW	22.54 AW	46800 AAW	WIBLS	10//99-12//99
	Janesville-Beloit MSA, WI	S	23.63 MW	24.55 AW	49160 AAW	WIBLS	10//99-12//99
	Kenosha PMSA, WI	S	23.92 MW	23.49 AW	49760 AAW	WIBLS	10//99-12//99
	La Crosse MSA, WI-MN	S	19.96 MW	20.07 AW	41520 AAW	WIBLS	10//99-12//99
	Madison MSA, WI	S	23.17 MW	23.55 AW	48180 AAW	WIBLS	10//99-12//99
	Milwaukee-Waukesha PMSA, WI	S	26.61 MW	28.50 AW	55350 AAW	WIBLS	10//99-12//99
	Racine PMSA, WI	S	23.51 MW	23.68 AW	48910 AAW	WIBLS	10//99-12//99
	Sheboygan MSA, WI	S	19.38 MW	20.10 AW	40310 AAW	WIBLS	10//99-12//99
	Wausau MSA, WI	S	20.12 MW	20.26 AW	41850 AAW	WIBLS	10//99-12//99
	Wyoming	S	15.47 MW	15.74 AW	32750 AAW	WYBLS	10//99-12//99
	Casper MSA, WY	S	15.26 MW	15.08 AW	31740 AAW	WYBLS	10//99-12//99
	Cheyenne MSA, WY	S	18.11 MW	17.81 AW	37660 AAW	WYBLS	10//99-12//99
	Puerto Rico	S	6.86 MW	7.24 AW	15050 AAW	PRBLS	10//99-12//99
	Caguas PMSA, PR	S	7.72 MW	7.66 AW	16050 AAW	PRBLS	10//99-12//99

AAW Average annual wage	AOH Average offered, high	ASH Average starting, high	H Hourly	M Monthly	S Special: hourly and annual
AE Average entry wage	AOL Average offered, low	ASL Average starting, low	HI Highest wage paid	MTC Median total compensation	TQ Third quartile wage
AEX Average experienced wage	APH Average pay, high range	AW Average wage paid	HR High end range	MW Median wage paid	W Weekly
AO Average offered	APL Average pay, low range	FQ First quartile wage	LR Low end range	SQ Second quartile wage	Y Yearly

Occupation/Type/Industry	Location	Per	Low	Mid	High	Source	Date
Plumber, Pipefitter, and Steamfitter	Mayaguez MSA, PR	S	7.55 mw	7.20 aw	15710 aaw	PRBLS	10//99-12//99
	Ponce MSA, PR	S	6.96 mw	6.98 aw	14470 aaw	PRBLS	10//99-12//99
	San Juan-Bayamon PMSA, PR	S	7.32 mw	6.94 aw	15230 aaw	PRBLS	10//99-12//99
	Guam	S	12.88 mw	13.32 aw	27710 aaw	GUBLS	10//99-12//99
Podiatrist	Arizona	S	42.5 mw	37.39 aw	77770 aaw	AZBLS	10//99-12//99
	California	S	48.64 mw	45.11 aw	93830 aaw	CABLS	10//99-12//99
	San Diego MSA, CA	S	51.34 mw	51.79 aw	106790 aaw	CABLS	10//99-12//99
	Connecticut	S	58.23 mw	53.93 aw	112170 aaw	CTBLS	10//99-12//99
	District of Columbia	S	35.54 mw	33.26 aw	69170 aaw	DCBLS	10//99-12//99
	Washington PMSA, DC-MD-VA-WV	S	53.83 mw	62.44 aw	111970 aaw	DCBLS	10//99-12//99
	Florida	S	58.29 mw	51.68 aw	107490 aaw	FLBLS	10//99-12//99
	Fort Lauderdale PMSA, FL	S	47.58 mw	52.25 aw	98970 aaw	FLBLS	10//99-12//99
	Illinois	S	42.56 mw	35.60 aw	74040 aaw	ILBLS	10//99-12//99
	Indiana	S		57.56 aw	119720 aaw	INBLS	10//99-12//99
	Iowa	S		65.74 aw	136740 aaw	IABLS	10//99-12//99
	Massachusetts	S	51.14 mw	48.56 aw	101010 aaw	MABLS	10//99-12//99
	Boston PMSA, MA-NH	S	51.00 mw	53.08 aw	106070 aaw	MABLS	10//99-12//99
	Minnesota	S	33.69 mw	35.33 aw	73490 aaw	MNBLS	10//99-12//99
	Minneapolis-St. Paul MSA, MN-WI	S	32.05 mw	30.29 aw	66670 aaw	MNBLS	10//99-12//99
	New Jersey	S	59.4 mw	51.38 aw	106880 aaw	NJBLS	10//99-12//99
	New York	S	47.69 mw	46.54 aw	96800 aaw	NYBLS	10//99-12//99
	Nassau-Suffolk PMSA, NY	S	49.74 mw	51.59 aw	103460 aaw	NYBLS	10//99-12//99
	Rochester MSA, NY	S	52.25 mw	43.54 aw	108690 aaw	NYBLS	10//99-12//99
	North Carolina	S	66.88 mw	62.97 aw	130970 aaw	NCBLS	10//99-12//99
	Pennsylvania	S	36.87 mw	37.30 aw	77590 aaw	PABLS	10//99-12//99
	Philadelphia PMSA, PA-NJ	S	39.18 mw	39.28 aw	81490 aaw	PABLS	10//99-12//99
	Rhode Island	S	52.4 mw	51.79 aw	107730 aaw	RIBLS	10//99-12//99
	Texas	S		61.25 aw	127390 aaw	TXBLS	10//99-12//99
	Wisconsin	S	52.57 mw	53.06 aw	110360 aaw	WIBLS	10//99-12//99
Police and Sheriff's Patrol Officer	Alabama	S	13.37 mw	13.91 aw	28940 aaw	ALBLS	10//99-12//99
	Anniston MSA, AL	S	12.26 mw	12.16 aw	25500 aaw	ALBLS	10//99-12//99
	Auburn-Opelika MSA, AL	S	13.28 mw	12.93 aw	27620 aaw	ALBLS	10//99-12//99
	Birmingham MSA, AL	S	15.77 mw	15.60 aw	32800 aaw	ALBLS	10//99-12//99
	Decatur MSA, AL	S	14.71 mw	14.03 aw	30590 aaw	ALBLS	10//99-12//99
	Dothan MSA, AL	S	12.14 mw	11.70 aw	25250 aaw	ALBLS	10//99-12//99
	Florence MSA, AL	S	14.90 mw	14.69 aw	30980 aaw	ALBLS	10//99-12//99
	Huntsville MSA, AL	S	15.64 mw	15.26 aw	32520 aaw	ALBLS	10//99-12//99
	Mobile MSA, AL	S	13.56 mw	12.76 aw	28210 aaw	ALBLS	10//99-12//99
	Tuscaloosa MSA, AL	S	13.30 mw	12.74 aw	27660 aaw	ALBLS	10//99-12//99
	Alaska	S	23.26 mw	22.32 aw	46420 aaw	AKBLS	10//99-12//99
	Arizona	S	18.95 mw	18.91 aw	39340 aaw	AZBLS	10//99-12//99
	Flagstaff MSA, AZ-UT	S	15.95 mw	15.31 aw	33180 aaw	AZBLS	10//99-12//99
	Phoenix-Mesa MSA, AZ	S	20.41 mw	21.24 aw	42460 aaw	AZBLS	10//99-12//99
	Tucson MSA, AZ	S	17.36 mw	16.68 aw	36110 aaw	AZBLS	10//99-12//99
	Arkansas	S	12.22 mw	12.80 aw	26630 aaw	ARBLS	10//99-12//99
	Fayetteville-Springdale-Rogers MSA, AR	S	12.66 mw	12.11 aw	26320 aaw	ARBLS	10//99-12//99
	Fort Smith MSA, AR-OK	S	13.52 mw	12.86 aw	28120 aaw	ARBLS	10//99-12//99
	Little Rock-North Little Rock MSA, AR	S	14.59 mw	14.48 aw	30340 aaw	ARBLS	10//99-12//99
	California	S	23.97 mw	24.49 aw	50950 aaw	CABLS	10//99-12//99
	Bakersfield MSA, CA	S	24.13 mw	24.70 aw	50180 aaw	CABLS	10//99-12//99
	Los Angeles-Long Beach PMSA, CA	S	22.73 mw	20.70 aw	47270 aaw	CABLS	10//99-12//99
	Merced MSA, CA	S	21.07 mw	20.97 aw	43830 aaw	CABLS	10//99-12//99
	Oakland PMSA, CA	S	30.15 mw	30.96 aw	62700 aaw	CABLS	10//99-12//99
	Orange County PMSA, CA	S	26.38 mw	27.97 aw	54860 aaw	CABLS	10//99-12//99
	Redding MSA, CA	S	25.19 mw	25.36 aw	52390 aaw	CABLS	10//99-12//99
	Riverside-San Bernardino PMSA, CA	S	23.70 mw	23.80 aw	49300 aaw	CABLS	10//99-12//99
	Sacramento PMSA, CA	S	24.10 mw	23.57 aw	50140 aaw	CABLS	10//99-12//99
	Salinas MSA, CA	S	21.50 mw	21.76 aw	44730 aaw	CABLS	10//99-12//99
	San Diego MSA, CA	S	24.24 mw	24.34 aw	50430 aaw	CABLS	10//99-12//99
	San Francisco PMSA, CA	S	29.72 mw	29.98 aw	61830 aaw	CABLS	10//99-12//99
	San Jose PMSA, CA	S	24.38 mw	23.01 aw	50700 aaw	CABLS	10//99-12//99
	San Luis Obispo-Atascadero-Paso Robles MSA, CA	S	22.46 mw	21.36 aw	46720 aaw	CABLS	10//99-12//99

AAW Average annual wage	**AOH** Average offered, high	**ASH** Average starting, high	**H** Hourly	**M** Monthly	**S** Special: hourly and annual
AE Average entry wage	**AOL** Average offered, low	**ASL** Average starting, low	**HI** Highest wage paid	**MTC** Median total compensation	**TQ** Third quartile wage
AEX Average experienced wage	**APH** Average pay, high range	**AW** Average wage paid	**HR** High end range	**MW** Median wage paid	**W** Weekly
AO Average offered	**APL** Average pay, low range	**FQ** First quartile wage	**LR** Low end range	**SQ** Second quartile wage	**Y** Yearly

Occupation/Type/Industry	Location	Per	Low	Mid	High	Source	Date
Police and Sheriff's Patrol Officer	Santa Barbara-Santa Maria-Lompoc MSA, CA	S	23.55 MW	21.99 AW	48980 AAW	CABLS	10//99-12//99
	Santa Cruz-Watsonville PMSA, CA	S	23.53 MW	21.82 AW	48940 AAW	CABLS	10//99-12//99
	Santa Rosa PMSA, CA	S	25.74 MW	25.17 AW	53530 AAW	CABLS	10//99-12//99
	Stockton-Lodi MSA, CA	S	21.90 MW	23.09 AW	45540 AAW	CABLS	10//99-12//99
	Vallejo-Fairfield-Napa PMSA, CA	S	26.67 MW	26.02 AW	55470 AAW	CABLS	10//99-12//99
	Ventura PMSA, CA	S	23.49 MW	22.17 AW	48860 AAW	CABLS	10//99-12//99
	Visalia-Tulare-Porterville MSA, CA	S	23.33 MW	23.20 AW	48530 AAW	CABLS	10//99-12//99
	Yuba City MSA, CA	S	22.85 MW	21.09 AW	47530 AAW	CABLS	10//99-12//99
	Colorado	S	19.65 MW	19.65 AW	40880 AAW	COBLS	10//99-12//99
	Boulder-Longmont PMSA, CO	S	21.72 MW	21.75 AW	45180 AAW	COBLS	10//99-12//99
	Denver PMSA, CO	S	20.89 MW	21.04 AW	43440 AAW	COBLS	10//99-12//99
	Fort Collins-Loveland MSA, CO	S	21.89 MW	21.61 AW	45540 AAW	COBLS	10//99-12//99
	Grand Junction MSA, CO	S	17.60 MW	17.85 AW	36600 AAW	COBLS	10//99-12//99
	Greeley PMSA, CO	S	15.23 MW	15.25 AW	31690 AAW	COBLS	10//99-12//99
	Pueblo MSA, CO	S	19.14 MW	18.66 AW	39810 AAW	COBLS	10//99-12//99
	Connecticut	S	21.71 MW	21.47 AW	44650 AAW	CTBLS	10//99-12//99
	Bridgeport PMSA, CT	S	21.01 MW	21.34 AW	43700 AAW	CTBLS	10//99-12//99
	Danbury PMSA, CT	S	21.30 MW	21.75 AW	44310 AAW	CTBLS	10//99-12//99
	Hartford MSA, CT	S	21.21 MW	21.34 AW	44110 AAW	CTBLS	10//99-12//99
	New Haven-Meriden PMSA, CT	S	21.63 MW	21.45 AW	44990 AAW	CTBLS	10//99-12//99
	New London-Norwich MSA, CT-RI	S	20.68 MW	20.35 AW	43010 AAW	CTBLS	10//99-12//99
	Stamford-Norwalk PMSA, CT	S	23.14 MW	23.71 AW	48140 AAW	CTBLS	10//99-12//99
	Delaware	S	19.55 MW	19.76 AW	41110 AAW	DEBLS	10//99-12//99
	Wilmington-Newark PMSA, DE-MD	S	19.76 MW	19.53 AW	41100 AAW	DEBLS	10//99-12//99
	Washington PMSA, DC-MD-VA-WV	S	19.75 MW	19.38 AW	41070 AAW	DCBLS	10//99-12//99
	Florida	S	16.54 MW	17.78 AW	36980 AAW	FLBLS	10//99-12//99
	Daytona Beach MSA, FL	S	13.65 MW	13.14 AW	28400 AAW	FLBLS	10//99-12//99
	Fort Lauderdale PMSA, FL	S	20.53 MW	20.37 AW	42710 AAW	FLBLS	10//99-12//99
	Fort Myers-Cape Coral MSA, FL	S	15.31 MW	14.93 AW	31840 AAW	FLBLS	10//99-12//99
	Fort Pierce-Port St. Lucie MSA, FL	S	15.18 MW	14.41 AW	31580 AAW	FLBLS	10//99-12//99
	Gainesville MSA, FL	S	14.70 MW	14.41 AW	30580 AAW	FLBLS	10//99-12//99
	Jacksonville MSA, FL	S	14.18 MW	13.35 AW	29480 AAW	FLBLS	10//99-12//99
	Lakeland-Winter Haven MSA, FL	S	14.58 MW	14.23 AW	30330 AAW	FLBLS	10//99-12//99
	Melbourne-Titusville-Palm Bay MSA, FL	S	15.52 MW	15.14 AW	32290 AAW	FLBLS	10//99-12//99
	Miami PMSA, FL	S	21.20 MW	20.67 AW	44090 AAW	FLBLS	10//99-12//99
	Ocala MSA, FL	S	17.95 MW	16.71 AW	37330 AAW	FLBLS	10//99-12//99
	Orlando MSA, FL	S	14.87 MW	13.92 AW	30930 AAW	FLBLS	10//99-12//99
	Panama City MSA, FL	S	11.66 MW	10.48 AW	24240 AAW	FLBLS	10//99-12//99
	Pensacola MSA, FL	S	14.36 MW	13.41 AW	29870 AAW	FLBLS	10//99-12//99
	Sarasota-Bradenton MSA, FL	S	17.29 MW	16.52 AW	35970 AAW	FLBLS	10//99-12//99
	Tallahassee MSA, FL	S	15.89 MW	15.31 AW	33050 AAW	FLBLS	10//99-12//99
	Tampa-St. Petersburg-Clearwater MSA, FL	S	19.90 MW	19.35 AW	41400 AAW	FLBLS	10//99-12//99
	West Palm Beach-Boca Raton MSA, FL	S	19.33 MW	18.70 AW	40210 AAW	FLBLS	10//99-12//99
	Georgia	S	13.45 MW	13.95 AW	29020 AAW	GABLS	10//99-12//99
	Athens MSA, GA	S	13.02 MW	12.26 AW	27070 AAW	GABLS	10//99-12//99
	Atlanta MSA, GA	S	15.54 MW	15.33 AW	32320 AAW	GABLS	10//99-12//99
	Augusta-Aiken MSA, GA-SC	S	12.88 MW	12.56 AW	26790 AAW	GABLS	10//99-12//99
	Columbus MSA, GA-AL	S	13.34 MW	13.01 AW	27760 AAW	GABLS	10//99-12//99
	Macon MSA, GA	S	13.15 MW	12.84 AW	27350 AAW	GABLS	10//99-12//99
	Savannah MSA, GA	S	15.22 MW	15.22 AW	31670 AAW	GABLS	10//99-12//99
	Idaho	S	14.19 MW	14.73 AW	30630 AAW	IDBLS	10//99-12//99
	Boise City MSA, ID	S	17.97 MW	16.98 AW	37380 AAW	IDBLS	10//99-12//99
	Illinois	S	20.39 MW	20.51 AW	42650 AAW	ILBLS	10//99-12//99
	Bloomington-Normal MSA, IL	S	16.44 MW	15.82 AW	34200 AAW	ILBLS	10//99-12//99
	Champaign-Urbana MSA, IL	S	20.06 MW	19.63 AW	41730 AAW	ILBLS	10//99-12//99
	Decatur MSA, IL	S	19.07 MW	18.59 AW	39660 AAW	ILBLS	10//99-12//99
	Kankakee PMSA, IL	S	16.20 MW	15.11 AW	33700 AAW	ILBLS	10//99-12//99

AAW Average annual wage	AOH Average offered, high	ASH Average starting, high	H Hourly	M Monthly	S Special: hourly and annual
AE Average entry wage	AOL Average offered, low	ASL Average starting, low	HI Highest wage paid	MTC Median total compensation	TQ Third quartile wage
AEX Average experienced wage	APH Average pay, high range	AW Average wage paid	HR High end range	MW Median wage paid	W Weekly
AO Average offered	APL Average pay, low range	FQ First quartile wage	LR Low end range	SQ Second quartile wage	Y Yearly

Occupation/Type/Industry	Location	Per	Low	Mid	High	Source	Date
Police and Sheriff's Patrol Officer	Peoria-Pekin MSA, IL	S	18.48 MW	18.79 AW	38450 AAW	ILBLS	10//99-12//99
	Rockford MSA, IL	S	17.79 MW	16.54 AW	37010 AAW	ILBLS	10//99-12//99
	Springfield MSA, IL	S	17.70 MW	18.15 AW	36810 AAW	ILBLS	10//99-12//99
	Indiana	S	15.01 MW	15.03 AW	31260 AAW	INBLS	10//99-12//99
	Bloomington MSA, IN	S	16.02 MW	16.58 AW	33320 AAW	INBLS	10//99-12//99
	Elkhart-Goshen MSA, IN	S	14.99 MW	14.89 AW	31180 AAW	INBLS	10//99-12//99
	Evansville-Henderson MSA, IN-KY	S	16.02 MW	16.11 AW	33320 AAW	INBLS	10//99-12//99
	Fort Wayne MSA, IN	S	15.84 MW	15.35 AW	32940 AAW	INBLS	10//99-12//99
	Gary PMSA, IN	S	16.21 MW	16.53 AW	33720 AAW	INBLS	10//99-12//99
	Indianapolis MSA, IN	S	15.81 MW	15.77 AW	32880 AAW	INBLS	10//99-12//99
	Kokomo MSA, IN	S	15.10 MW	14.99 AW	31410 AAW	INBLS	10//99-12//99
	Lafayette MSA, IN	S	16.11 MW	17.23 AW	33510 AAW	INBLS	10//99-12//99
	South Bend MSA, IN	S	15.90 MW	15.81 AW	33080 AAW	INBLS	10//99-12//99
	Terre Haute MSA, IN	S	13.83 MW	14.17 AW	28770 AAW	INBLS	10//99-12//99
	Iowa	S	16.07 MW	16.00 AW	33280 AAW	IABLS	10//99-12//99
	Cedar Rapids MSA, IA	S	16.52 MW	17.12 AW	34360 AAW	IABLS	10//99-12//99
	Davenport-Moline-Rock Island MSA, IA-IL	S	16.84 MW	16.81 AW	35030 AAW	IABLS	10//99-12//99
	Des Moines MSA, IA	S	18.94 MW	19.24 AW	39400 AAW	IABLS	10//99-12//99
	Iowa City MSA, IA	S	18.15 MW	18.47 AW	37740 AAW	IABLS	10//99-12//99
	Waterloo-Cedar Falls MSA, IA	S	16.44 MW	16.92 AW	34200 AAW	IABLS	10//99-12//99
	Kansas	S	13.3 MW	14.28 AW	29710 AAW	KSBLS	10//99-12//99
	Wichita MSA, KS	S	12.56 MW	12.35 AW	26120 AAW	KSBLS	10//99-12//99
	Kentucky	S	13.49 MW	13.59 AW	28280 AAW	KYBLS	10//99-12//99
	Lexington MSA, KY	S	13.99 MW	14.09 AW	29100 AAW	KYBLS	10//99-12//99
	Louisville MSA, KY-IN	S	14.40 MW	14.38 AW	29940 AAW	KYBLS	10//99-12//99
	Louisiana	S	10.83 MW	11.05 AW	22980 AAW	LABLS	10//99-12//99
	Alexandria MSA, LA	S	11.24 MW	10.70 AW	23380 AAW	LABLS	10//99-12//99
	Baton Rouge MSA, LA	S	11.65 MW	11.24 AW	24230 AAW	LABLS	10//99-12//99
	Houma MSA, LA	S	11.41 MW	10.96 AW	23720 AAW	LABLS	10//99-12//99
	Lafayette MSA, LA	S	9.49 MW	9.02 AW	19740 AAW	LABLS	10//99-12//99
	Lake Charles MSA, LA	S	9.60 MW	9.24 AW	19960 AAW	LABLS	10//99-12//99
	Monroe MSA, LA	S	12.15 MW	12.18 AW	25270 AAW	LABLS	10//99-12//99
	New Orleans MSA, LA	S	11.54 MW	11.70 AW	24000 AAW	LABLS	10//99-12//99
	Shreveport-Bossier City MSA, LA	S	14.04 MW	14.32 AW	29200 AAW	LABLS	10//99-12//99
	Maine	S	13.32 MW	13.13 AW	27300 AAW	MEBLS	10//99-12//99
	Bangor MSA, ME	S	12.44 MW	12.33 AW	25860 AAW	MEBLS	10//99-12//99
	Portland MSA, ME	S	14.85 MW	14.86 AW	30900 AAW	MEBLS	10//99-12//99
	Maryland	S	19.88 MW	20.77 AW	43200 AAW	MDBLS	10//99-12//99
	Baltimore PMSA, MD	S	21.55 MW	21.28 AW	44830 AAW	MDBLS	10//99-12//99
	Cumberland MSA, MD-WV	S	13.42 MW	13.96 AW	27910 AAW	MDBLS	10//99-12//99
	Hagerstown PMSA, MD	S	16.15 MW	16.85 AW	33600 AAW	MDBLS	10//99-12//99
	Massachusetts	S	18.93 MW	19.68 AW	40940 AAW	MABLS	10//99-12//99
	Barnstable-Yarmouth MSA, MA	S	19.98 MW	19.89 AW	41560 AAW	MABLS	10//99-12//99
	Boston PMSA, MA-NH	S	20.37 MW	19.17 AW	42360 AAW	MABLS	10//99-12//99
	Brockton PMSA, MA	S	20.10 MW	19.53 AW	41820 AAW	MABLS	10//99-12//99
	Fitchburg-Leominster PMSA, MA	S	17.88 MW	17.25 AW	37180 AAW	MABLS	10//99-12//99
	Lawrence PMSA, MA-NH	S	17.59 MW	17.81 AW	36590 AAW	MABLS	10//99-12//99
	New Bedford PMSA, MA	S	18.27 MW	16.24 AW	38010 AAW	MABLS	10//99-12//99
	Pittsfield MSA, MA	S	18.82 MW	18.52 AW	39140 AAW	MABLS	10//99-12//99
	Springfield MSA, MA	S	17.97 MW	16.97 AW	37370 AAW	MABLS	10//99-12//99
	Worcester PMSA, MA-CT	S	19.93 MW	19.52 AW	41450 AAW	MABLS	10//99-12//99
	Michigan	S	19.69 MW	19.02 AW	39550 AAW	MIBLS	10//99-12//99
	Ann Arbor PMSA, MI	S	19.19 MW	19.04 AW	39920 AAW	MIBLS	10//99-12//99
	Benton Harbor MSA, MI	S	15.73 MW	15.69 AW	32730 AAW	MIBLS	10//99-12//99
	Detroit PMSA, MI	S	19.81 MW	20.72 AW	41210 AAW	MIBLS	10//99-12//99
	Flint PMSA, MI	S	18.99 MW	18.88 AW	39490 AAW	MIBLS	10//99-12//99
	Grand Rapids-Muskegon-Holland MSA, MI	S	19.61 MW	19.77 AW	40780 AAW	MIBLS	10//99-12//99
	Jackson MSA, MI	S	17.50 MW	18.33 AW	36400 AAW	MIBLS	10//99-12//99
	Kalamazoo-Battle Creek MSA, MI	S	17.65 MW	18.44 AW	36710 AAW	MIBLS	10//99-12//99
	Lansing-East Lansing MSA, MI	S	17.61 MW	18.34 AW	36630 AAW	MIBLS	10//99-12//99
	Saginaw-Bay City-Midland MSA, MI	S	18.76 MW	19.07 AW	39010 AAW	MIBLS	10//99-12//99
	Minnesota	S	18.83 MW	18.77 AW	39030 AAW	MNBLS	10//99-12//99
	Duluth-Superior MSA, MN-WI	S	16.84 MW	17.79 AW	35020 AAW	MNBLS	10//99-12//99

AAW	Average annual wage	AOH	Average offered, high	ASH	Average starting, high	H	Hourly	M	Monthly	S	Special: hourly and annual
AE	Average entry wage	AOL	Average offered, low	ASL	Average starting, low	HI	Highest wage paid	MTC	Median total compensation	TQ	Third quartile wage
AEX	Average experienced wage	APH	Average pay, high range	AW	Average wage paid	HR	High end range	MW	Median wage paid	W	Weekly
AO	Average offered	APL	Average pay, low range	FQ	First quartile wage	LR	Low end range	SQ	Second quartile wage	Y	Yearly

Occupation/Type/Industry	Location	Per	Low	Mid	High	Source	Date
Police and Sheriff's Patrol Officer	Minneapolis-St. Paul MSA, MN-WI	S	20.23 MW	20.90 AW	42070 AAW	MNBLS	10//99-12//99
	St. Cloud MSA, MN	S	15.10 MW	15.65 AW	31400 AAW	MNBLS	10//99-12//99
	Mississippi	S	11.43 MW	11.38 AW	23680 AAW	MSBLS	10//99-12//99
	Biloxi-Gulfport-Pascagoula MSA, MS	S	12.25 MW	12.15 AW	25480 AAW	MSBLS	10//99-12//99
	Hattiesburg MSA, MS	S	11.41 MW	11.11 AW	23730 AAW	MSBLS	10//99-12//99
	Jackson MSA, MS	S	12.30 MW	12.10 AW	25580 AAW	MSBLS	10//99-12//99
	Missouri	S	12.18 MW	12.67 AW	26360 AAW	MOBLS	10//99-12//99
	Kansas City MSA, MO-KS	S	14.51 MW	14.34 AW	30170 AAW	MOBLS	10//99-12//99
	St. Louis MSA, MO-IL	S	14.46 MW	13.39 AW	30070 AAW	MOBLS	10//99-12//99
	Montana	S	13.95 MW	14.37 AW	29890 AAW	MTBLS	10//99-12//99
	Nebraska	S	15.5	16.41 AW	34130 AAW	NEBLS	10//99-12//99
	Lincoln MSA, NE	S	16.82 MW	16.93 AW	34980 AAW	NEBLS	10//99-12//99
	Omaha MSA, NE-IA	S	19.49 MW	20.08 AW	40540 AAW	NEBLS	10//99-12//99
	Nevada	S	21.46 MW	21.43 AW	44580 AAW	NVBLS	10//99-12//99
	New Hampshire	S	16.06 MW	15.98 AW	33240 AAW	NHBLS	10//99-12//99
	Manchester PMSA, NH	S	17.91 MW	18.41 AW	37250 AAW	NHBLS	10//99-12//99
	Nashua PMSA, NH	S	17.61 MW	18.46 AW	36620 AAW	NHBLS	10//99-12//99
	Portsmouth-Rochester PMSA, NH-ME	S	16.33 MW	16.38 AW	33960 AAW	NHBLS	10//99-12//99
	New Jersey	S	28.03 MW	26.51 AW	55140 AAW	NJBLS	10//99-12//99
	Atlantic-Cape May PMSA, NJ	S	22.02 MW	22.55 AW	45810 AAW	NJBLS	10//99-12//99
	Bergen-Passaic PMSA, NJ	S	28.46 MW	31.40 AW	59190 AAW	NJBLS	10//99-12//99
	Jersey City PMSA, NJ	S	27.84 MW	29.66 AW	57910 AAW	NJBLS	10//99-12//99
	Middlesex-Somerset-Hunterdon PMSA, NJ	S	26.87 MW	28.22 AW	55890 AAW	NJBLS	10//99-12//99
	Monmouth-Ocean PMSA, NJ	S	26.33 MW	27.60 AW	54760 AAW	NJBLS	10//99-12//99
	Newark PMSA, NJ	S	27.41 MW	29.50 AW	57010 AAW	NJBLS	10//99-12//99
	Trenton PMSA, NJ	S	26.76 MW	28.25 AW	55660 AAW	NJBLS	10//99-12//99
	Vineland-Millville-Bridgeton PMSA, NJ	S	18.93 MW	19.94 AW	39380 AAW	NJBLS	10//99-12//99
	New Mexico	S	15.07 MW	15.07 AW	31350 AAW	NMBLS	10//99-12//99
	Las Cruces MSA, NM	S	15.63 MW	15.39 AW	32510 AAW	NMBLS	10//99-12//99
	Santa Fe MSA, NM	S	12.82 MW	12.51 AW	26670 AAW	NMBLS	10//99-12//99
	New York	S	22.5	21.47 AW	44650 AAW	NYBLS	10//99-12//99
	Albany-Schenectady-Troy MSA, NY	S	18.27 MW	17.06 AW	38010 AAW	NYBLS	10//99-12//99
	Binghamton MSA, NY	S	17.53 MW	18.59 AW	36460 AAW	NYBLS	10//99-12//99
	Buffalo-Niagara Falls MSA, NY	S	20.51 MW	21.53 AW	42650 AAW	NYBLS	10//99-12//99
	Dutchess County PMSA, NY	S	19.10 MW	19.62 AW	39740 AAW	NYBLS	10//99-12//99
	Elmira MSA, NY	S	21.18 MW	22.05 AW	44050 AAW	NYBLS	10//99-12//99
	Glens Falls MSA, NY	S	15.31 MW	15.48 AW	31840 AAW	NYBLS	10//99-12//99
	Jamestown MSA, NY	S	14.40 MW	15.00 AW	29950 AAW	NYBLS	10//99-12//99
	Nassau-Suffolk PMSA, NY	S	24.99 MW	25.29 AW	51970 AAW	NYBLS	10//99-12//99
	Newburgh PMSA, NY-PA	S	18.49 MW	18.97 AW	38460 AAW	NYBLS	10//99-12//99
	Rochester MSA, NY	S	17.73 MW	16.35 AW	36890 AAW	NYBLS	10//99-12//99
	Syracuse MSA, NY	S	17.18 MW	17.93 AW	35740 AAW	NYBLS	10//99-12//99
	Utica-Rome MSA, NY	S	15.85 MW	15.56 AW	32970 AAW	NYBLS	10//99-12//99
	North Carolina	S	13.65 MW	14.63 AW	30430 AAW	NCBLS	10//99-12//99
	Asheville MSA, NC	S	14.52 MW	13.28 AW	30200 AAW	NCBLS	10//99-12//99
	Charlotte-Gastonia-Rock Hill MSA, NC-SC	S	16.21 MW	15.59 AW	33710 AAW	NCBLS	10//99-12//99
	Goldsboro MSA, NC	S	12.40 MW	11.78 AW	25800 AAW	NCBLS	10//99-12//99
	Greensboro--Winston-Salem--High Point MSA, NC	S	15.52 MW	14.79 AW	32270 AAW	NCBLS	10//99-12//99
	Hickory-Morganton-Lenoir MSA, NC	S	12.93 MW	12.28 AW	26880 AAW	NCBLS	10//99-12//99
	Raleigh-Durham-Chapel Hill MSA, NC	S	16.21 MW	15.53 AW	33720 AAW	NCBLS	10//99-12//99
	Rocky Mount MSA, NC	S	13.21 MW	12.79 AW	27470 AAW	NCBLS	10//99-12//99
	Wilmington MSA, NC	S	13.57 MW	12.53 AW	28220 AAW	NCBLS	10//99-12//99
	North Dakota	S	14.18 MW	14.35 AW	29850 AAW	NDBLS	10//99-12//99
	Fargo-Moorhead MSA, ND-MN	S	15.18 MW	15.37 AW	31570 AAW	NDBLS	10//99-12//99
	Grand Forks MSA, ND-MN	S	17.12 MW	17.26 AW	35600 AAW	NDBLS	10//99-12//99
	Ohio	S	18.22 MW	17.69 AW	36790 AAW	OHBLS	10//99-12//99
	Akron PMSA, OH	S	17.34 MW	17.92 AW	36070 AAW	OHBLS	10//99-12//99
	Canton-Massillon MSA, OH	S	15.04 MW	15.86 AW	31280 AAW	OHBLS	10//99-12//99
	Cincinnati PMSA, OH-KY-IN	S	18.47 MW	18.71 AW	38410 AAW	OHBLS	10//99-12//99

AAW	Average annual wage	AOH	Average offered, high	ASH	Average starting, high	H	Hourly	M	Monthly	S	Special: hourly and annual
AE	Average entry wage	AOL	Average offered, low	ASL	Average starting, low	HI	Highest wage paid	MTC	Median total compensation	TQ	Third quartile wage
AEX	Average experienced wage	APH	Average pay, high range	AW	Average wage paid	HR	High end range	MW	Median wage paid	W	Weekly
AO	Average offered	APL	Average pay, low range	FQ	First quartile wage	LR	Low end range	SQ	Second quartile wage	Y	Yearly

Occupation/Type/Industry	Location	Per	Low	Mid	High	Source	Date
Police and Sheriff's Patrol Officer	Cleveland-Lorain-Elyria						
	PMSA, OH	S	18.64 MW	19.12 AW	38780 AAW	OHBLS	10//99-12//99
	Columbus MSA, OH	S	19.63 MW	21.29 AW	40830 AAW	OHBLS	10//99-12//99
	Dayton-Springfield MSA, OH	S	18.37 MW	18.86 AW	38200 AAW	OHBLS	10//99-12//99
	Hamilton-Middletown PMSA,						
	OH	S	17.89 MW	18.60 AW	37220 AAW	OHBLS	10//99-12//99
	Lima MSA, OH	S	15.64 MW	15.96 AW	32530 AAW	OHBLS	10//99-12//99
	Mansfield MSA, OH	S	16.24 MW	16.81 AW	33770 AAW	OHBLS	10//99-12//99
	Steubenville-Weirton MSA,						
	OH-WV	S	13.87 MW	13.27 AW	28860 AAW	OHBLS	10//99-12//99
	Toledo MSA, OH	S	17.13 MW	16.67 AW	35640 AAW	OHBLS	10//99-12//99
	Youngstown-Warren MSA, OH	S	15.28 MW	15.80 AW	31790 AAW	OHBLS	10//99-12//99
	Oklahoma	S	12.53 MW	13.62 AW	28320 AAW	OKBLS	10//99-12//99
	Oklahoma City MSA, OK	S	16.86 MW	17.40 AW	35070 AAW	OKBLS	10//99-12//99
	Tulsa MSA, OK	S	12.48 MW	12.21 AW	25950 AAW	OKBLS	10//99-12//99
	Oregon	S	20.04 MW	20.22 AW	42060 AAW	ORBLS	10//99-12//99
	Medford-Ashland MSA, OR	S	18.95 MW	19.08 AW	39430 AAW	ORBLS	10//99-12//99
	Portland-Vancouver PMSA,						
	OR-WA	S	23.14 MW	22.65 AW	48140 AAW	ORBLS	10//99-12//99
	Salem PMSA, OR	S	18.73 MW	19.45 AW	38960 AAW	ORBLS	10//99-12//99
	Pennsylvania	S	20.09 MW	19.41 AW	40380 AAW	PABLS	10//99-12//99
	Allentown-Bethlehem-Easton						
	MSA, PA	S	18.32 MW	18.62 AW	38100 AAW	PABLS	10//99-12//99
	Altoona MSA, PA	S	16.94 MW	17.35 AW	35240 AAW	PABLS	10//99-12//99
	Erie MSA, PA	S	21.26 MW	22.11 AW	44210 AAW	PABLS	10//99-12//99
	Harrisburg-Lebanon-Carlisle						
	MSA, PA	S	19.78 MW	20.01 AW	41130 AAW	PABLS	10//99-12//99
	Johnstown MSA, PA	S	13.51 MW	11.22 AW	28090 AAW	PABLS	10//99-12//99
	Lancaster MSA, PA	S	19.14 MW	19.01 AW	39820 AAW	PABLS	10//99-12//99
	Philadelphia PMSA, PA-NJ	S	22.57 MW	22.87 AW	46940 AAW	PABLS	10//99-12//99
	Pittsburgh MSA, PA	S	19.04 MW	19.48 AW	39610 AAW	PABLS	10//99-12//99
	Reading MSA, PA	S	17.92 MW	17.90 AW	37270 AAW	PABLS	10//99-12//99
	Scranton--Wilkes-Barre--						
	Hazleton MSA, PA	S	15.05 MW	14.84 AW	31290 AAW	PABLS	10//99-12//99
	Sharon MSA, PA	S	17.03 MW	16.65 AW	35430 AAW	PABLS	10//99-12//99
	State College MSA, PA	S	22.45 MW	23.31 AW	46690 AAW	PABLS	10//99-12//99
	Williamsport MSA, PA	S	18.46 MW	19.92 AW	38400 AAW	PABLS	10//99-12//99
	York MSA, PA	S	19.90 MW	20.32 AW	41390 AAW	PABLS	10//99-12//99
	Rhode Island	S	19.31 MW	19.33 AW	40200 AAW	RIBLS	10//99-12//99
	Providence-Fall River-						
	Warwick MSA, RI-MA	S	19.58 MW	19.41 AW	40730 AAW	RIBLS	10//99-12//99
	South Carolina	S	12.97 MW	13.62 AW	28320 AAW	SCBLS	10//99-12//99
	Charleston-North Charleston						
	MSA, SC	S	14.40 MW	13.54 AW	29950 AAW	SCBLS	10//99-12//99
	Columbia MSA, SC	S	14.59 MW	13.82 AW	30340 AAW	SCBLS	10//99-12//99
	Florence MSA, SC	S	13.37 MW	12.52 AW	27800 AAW	SCBLS	10//99-12//99
	Greenville-Spartanburg-						
	Anderson MSA, SC	S	14.08 MW	13.52 AW	29280 AAW	SCBLS	10//99-12//99
	Myrtle Beach MSA, SC	S	12.45 MW	12.05 AW	25890 AAW	SCBLS	10//99-12//99
	South Dakota	S	14.09 MW	14.31 AW	29760 AAW	SDBLS	10//99-12//99
	Tennessee	S	14.19 MW	14.58 AW	30320 AAW	TNBLS	10//99-12//99
	Chattanooga MSA, TN-GA	S	14.16 MW	13.48 AW	29460 AAW	TNBLS	10//99-12//99
	Clarksville-Hopkinsville MSA,						
	TN-KY	S	12.98 MW	12.77 AW	26990 AAW	TNBLS	10//99-12//99
	Johnson City-Kingsport-Bristol						
	MSA, TN-VA	S	13.28 MW	12.54 AW	27630 AAW	TNBLS	10//99-12//99
	Knoxville MSA, TN	S	13.68 MW	13.23 AW	28460 AAW	TNBLS	10//99-12//99
	Memphis MSA, TN-AR-MS	S	16.39 MW	17.32 AW	34090 AAW	MSBLS	10//99-12//99
	Nashville MSA, TN	S	15.26 MW	15.34 AW	31740 AAW	TNBLS	10//99-12//99
	Texas	S	17.34 MW	17.33 AW	36040 AAW	TXBLS	10//99-12//99
	Austin-San Marcos MSA, TX	S	18.26 MW	18.50 AW	37990 AAW	TXBLS	10//99-12//99
	Beaumont-Port Arthur MSA,						
	TX	S	16.77 MW	16.52 AW	34880 AAW	TXBLS	10//99-12//99
	Brazoria PMSA, TX	S	14.16 MW	14.21 AW	29450 AAW	TXBLS	10//99-12//99
	Bryan-College Station MSA,						
	TX	S	16.96 MW	16.60 AW	35280 AAW	TXBLS	10//99-12//99
	Corpus Christi MSA, TX	S	20.73 MW	22.47 AW	43120 AAW	TXBLS	10//99-12//99
	Dallas PMSA, TX	S	20.00 MW	20.05 AW	41610 AAW	TXBLS	10//99-12//99
	El Paso MSA, TX	S	16.59 MW	16.33 AW	34510 AAW	TXBLS	10//99-12//99
	Fort Worth-Arlington PMSA,						
	TX	S	17.48 MW	17.06 AW	36370 AAW	TXBLS	10//99-12//99

AAW	Average annual wage	AOH	Average offered, high	ASH	Average starting, high	H	Hourly	M	Monthly	S	Special: hourly and annual
AE	Average entry wage	AOL	Average offered, low	ASL	Average starting, low	HI	Highest wage paid	MTC	Median total compensation	TQ	Third quartile wage
AEX	Average experienced wage	APH	Average pay, high range	AW	Average wage paid	HR	High end range	MW	Median wage paid	W	Weekly
AO	Average offered	APL	Average pay, low range	FQ	First quartile wage	LR	Low end range	SQ	Second quartile wage	Y	Yearly

Occupation/Type/Industry	Location	Per	Low	Mid	High	Source	Date
Police and Sheriff's Patrol Officer	Galveston-Texas City PMSA, TX	S	15.42 MW	14.99 AW	32070 AAW	TXBLS	10//99-12//99
	Houston PMSA, TX	S	18.69 MW	18.53 AW	38880 AAW	TXBLS	10//99-12//99
	Killeen-Temple MSA, TX	S	14.88 MW	14.97 AW	30940 AAW	TXBLS	10//99-12//99
	Longview-Marshall MSA, TX	S	12.30 MW	11.74 AW	25580 AAW	TXBLS	10//99-12//99
	McAllen-Edinburg-Mission MSA, TX	S	14.67 MW	14.84 AW	30520 AAW	TXBLS	10//99-12//99
	Odessa-Midland MSA, TX	S	16.84 MW	16.71 AW	35030 AAW	TXBLS	10//99-12//99
	San Angelo MSA, TX	S	20.41 MW	20.08 AW	42450 AAW	TXBLS	10//99-12//99
	San Antonio MSA, TX	S	16.56 MW	17.49 AW	34450 AAW	TXBLS	10//99-12//99
	Sherman-Denison MSA, TX	S	16.18 MW	16.58 AW	33660 AAW	TXBLS	10//99-12//99
	Texarkana MSA, TX-Texarkana, AR	S	13.26 MW	13.68 AW	27570 AAW	TXBLS	10//99-12//99
	Tyler MSA, TX	S	17.66 MW	18.07 AW	36740 AAW	TXBLS	10//99-12//99
	Waco MSA, TX	S	12.54 MW	11.56 AW	26080 AAW	TXBLS	10//99-12//99
	Wichita Falls MSA, TX	S	11.54 MW	11.63 AW	24000 AAW	TXBLS	10//99-12//99
	Utah	S	16 MW	16.05 AW	33380 AAW	UTBLS	10//99-12//99
	Provo-Orem MSA, UT	S	15.59 MW	15.62 AW	32430 AAW	UTBLS	10//99-12//99
	Salt Lake City-Ogden MSA, UT	S	16.76 MW	16.89 AW	34870 AAW	UTBLS	10//99-12//99
	Vermont	S	13.35 MW	14.25 AW	29630 AAW	VTBLS	10//99-12//99
	Burlington MSA, VT	S	15.42 MW	15.07 AW	32080 AAW	VTBLS	10//99-12//99
	Virginia	S	16 MW	17.30 AW	35980 AAW	VABLS	10//99-12//99
	Charlottesville MSA, VA	S	14.60 MW	14.01 AW	30360 AAW	VABLS	10//99-12//99
	Danville MSA, VA	S	15.34 MW	13.55 AW	31910 AAW	VABLS	10//99-12//99
	Lynchburg MSA, VA	S	14.39 MW	13.24 AW	29930 AAW	VABLS	10//99-12//99
	Norfolk-Virginia Beach-Newport News MSA, VA-NC	S	16.10 MW	15.58 AW	33490 AAW	VABLS	10//99-12//99
	Richmond-Petersburg MSA, VA	S	16.83 MW	15.32 AW	35010 AAW	VABLS	10//99-12//99
	Washington	S	22.42 MW	22.19 AW	46160 AAW	WABLS	10//99-12//99
	Bellingham MSA, WA	S	23.74 MW	22.57 AW	49390 AAW	WABLS	10//99-12//99
	Bremerton PMSA, WA	S	20.80 MW	21.85 AW	43270 AAW	WABLS	10//99-12//99
	Olympia PMSA, WA	S	22.05 MW	22.91 AW	45870 AAW	WABLS	10//99-12//99
	Richland-Kennewick-Pasco MSA, WA	S	20.83 MW	21.45 AW	43320 AAW	WABLS	10//99-12//99
	Seattle-Bellevue-Everett PMSA, WA	S	23.40 MW	23.32 AW	48660 AAW	WABLS	10//99-12//99
	Tacoma PMSA, WA	S	21.39 MW	21.57 AW	44480 AAW	WABLS	10//99-12//99
	Yakima MSA, WA	S	23.61 MW	23.54 AW	49110 AAW	WABLS	10//99-12//99
	West Virginia	S	12.33 MW	12.51 AW	26030 AAW	WVBLS	10//99-12//99
	Charleston MSA, WV	S	13.67 MW	13.70 AW	28430 AAW	WVBLS	10//99-12//99
	Huntington-Ashland MSA, WV-KY-OH	S	12.17 MW	12.00 AW	25310 AAW	WVBLS	10//99-12//99
	Parkersburg-Marietta MSA, WV-OH	S	12.73 MW	13.12 AW	26480 AAW	WVBLS	10//99-12//99
	Wheeling MSA, WV-OH	S	12.64 MW	12.02 AW	26300 AAW	WVBLS	10//99-12//99
	Wisconsin	S	17.96 MW	17.07 AW	35500 AAW	WIBLS	10//99-12//99
	Appleton-Oshkosh-Neenah MSA, WI	S	17.24 MW	18.32 AW	35860 AAW	WIBLS	10//99-12//99
	Eau Claire MSA, WI	S	14.98 MW	15.57 AW	31150 AAW	WIBLS	10//99-12//99
	Green Bay MSA, WI	S	19.11 MW	18.92 AW	39760 AAW	WIBLS	10//99-12//99
	Janesville-Beloit MSA, WI	S	18.91 MW	19.20 AW	39330 AAW	WIBLS	10//99-12//99
	Kenosha PMSA, WI	S	19.11 MW	19.45 AW	39740 AAW	WIBLS	10//99-12//99
	La Crosse MSA, WI-MN	S	18.26 MW	18.69 AW	37970 AAW	WIBLS	10//99-12//99
	Madison MSA, WI	S	18.74 MW	18.62 AW	38970 AAW	WIBLS	10//99-12//99
	Racine PMSA, WI	S	20.65 MW	20.56 AW	42950 AAW	WIBLS	10//99-12//99
	Wausau MSA, WI	S	17.23 MW	18.26 AW	35850 AAW	WIBLS	10//99-12//99
	Wyoming	S	14.17 MW	14.36 AW	29870 AAW	WYBLS	10//99-12//99
	Cheyenne MSA, WY	S	13.99 MW	13.52 AW	29100 AAW	WYBLS	10//99-12//99
	Caguas PMSA, PR	S	6.49 MW	6.41 AW	13510 AAW	PRBLS	10//99-12//99
	Mayaguez MSA, PR	S	5.99 MW	5.90 AW	12450 AAW	PRBLS	10//99-12//99
	Ponce MSA, PR	S	6.87 MW	6.69 AW	14280 AAW	PRBLS	10//99-12//99
	San Juan-Bayamon PMSA, PR	S	7.58 MW	7.61 AW	15770 AAW	PRBLS	10//99-12//99
Police, Detective Public Service	United States	H		19.57 AW		NCS98	1998
Police, Fire, and Ambulance Dispatcher	Alabama	S	10.31 MW	10.65 AW	22140 AAW	ALBLS	10//99-12//99
	Birmingham MSA, AL	S	11.65 MW	11.77 AW	24240 AAW	ALBLS	10//99-12//99

AAW	Average annual wage	AOH	Average offered, high	ASH	Average starting, high
AE	Average entry wage	AOL	Average offered, low	ASL	Average starting, low
AEX	Average experienced wage	APH	Average pay, high range	AW	Average wage paid
AO	Average offered	APL	Average pay, low range	FQ	First quartile wage

H	Hourly	M	Monthly
HI	Highest wage paid	MTC	Median total compensation
HR	High end range	MW	Median wage paid
LR	Low end range	SQ	Second quartile wage

S	Special: hourly and annual
TQ	Third quartile wage
W	Weekly
Y	Yearly

Occupation/Type/Industry	Location	Per	Low	Mid	High	Source	Date
Police, Fire, and Ambulance Dispatcher							
	Decatur MSA, AL	S	11.03 MW	10.84 AW	22930 AAW	ALBLS	10//99-12//99
	Dothan MSA, AL	S	10.60 MW	9.97 AW	22040 AAW	ALBLS	10//99-12//99
	Huntsville MSA, AL	S	11.60 MW	11.31 AW	24130 AAW	ALBLS	10//99-12//99
	Mobile MSA, AL	S	11.39 MW	11.02 AW	23680 AAW	ALBLS	10//99-12//99
	Montgomery MSA, AL	S	11.41 MW	11.20 AW	23740 AAW	ALBLS	10//99-12//99
	Tuscaloosa MSA, AL	S	11.29 MW	11.15 AW	23490 AAW	ALBLS	10//99-12//99
	Alaska	S	15.61 MW	14.83 AW	30840 AAW	AKBLS	10//99-12//99
	Arizona	S	12.9 MW	12.76 AW	26540 AAW	AZBLS	10//99-12//99
	Flagstaff MSA, AZ-UT	S	11.93 MW	11.35 AW	24820 AAW	AZBLS	10//99-12//99
	Phoenix-Mesa MSA, AZ	S	14.38 MW	14.80 AW	29910 AAW	AZBLS	10//99-12//99
	Tucson MSA, AZ	S	9.57 MW	9.69 AW	19910 AAW	AZBLS	10//99-12//99
	Arkansas	S	8.49 MW	8.70 AW	18100 AAW	ARBLS	10//99-12//99
	Fayetteville-Springdale-Rogers MSA, AR	S	11.06 MW	10.97 AW	23000 AAW	ARBLS	10//99-12//99
	Little Rock-North Little Rock MSA, AR	S	9.78 MW	9.55 AW	20350 AAW	ARBLS	10//99-12//99
	California	S	16.83 MW	17.07 AW	35510 AAW	CABLS	10//99-12//99
	Fresno MSA, CA	S	15.15 MW	14.58 AW	31500 AAW	CABLS	10//99-12//99
	Los Angeles-Long Beach PMSA, CA	S	17.26 MW	17.30 AW	35900 AAW	CABLS	10//99-12//99
	Merced MSA, CA	S	13.31 MW	12.98 AW	27690 AAW	CABLS	10//99-12//99
	Oakland PMSA, CA	S	20.02 MW	19.96 AW	41640 AAW	CABLS	10//99-12//99
	Orange County PMSA, CA	S	20.05 MW	20.32 AW	41710 AAW	CABLS	10//99-12//99
	Redding MSA, CA	S	15.62 MW	15.18 AW	32490 AAW	CABLS	10//99-12//99
	Riverside-San Bernardino PMSA, CA	S	15.73 MW	15.57 AW	32710 AAW	CABLS	10//99-12//99
	Sacramento PMSA, CA	S	16.91 MW	16.74 AW	35170 AAW	CABLS	10//99-12//99
	San Diego MSA, CA	S	17.60 MW	17.99 AW	36600 AAW	CABLS	10//99-12//99
	San Francisco PMSA, CA	S	18.54 MW	18.82 AW	38570 AAW	CABLS	10//99-12//99
	San Jose PMSA, CA	S	19.04 MW	18.68 AW	39600 AAW	CABLS	10//99-12//99
	San Luis Obispo-Atascadero-Paso Robles MSA, CA	S	15.94 MW	15.90 AW	33160 AAW	CABLS	10//99-12//99
	Santa Rosa PMSA, CA	S	20.12 MW	20.07 AW	41840 AAW	CABLS	10//99-12//99
	Ventura PMSA, CA	S	16.97 MW	16.45 AW	35300 AAW	CABLS	10//99-12//99
	Visalia-Tulare-Porterville MSA, CA	S	15.19 MW	14.16 AW	31590 AAW	CABLS	10//99-12//99
	Colorado	S	14.59 MW	14.50 AW	30160 AAW	COBLS	10//99-12//99
	Boulder-Longmont PMSA, CO	S	14.20 MW	14.27 AW	29540 AAW	COBLS	10//99-12//99
	Denver PMSA, CO	S	15.80 MW	15.64 AW	32870 AAW	COBLS	10//99-12//99
	Fort Collins-Loveland MSA, CO	S	16.28 MW	16.10 AW	33870 AAW	COBLS	10//99-12//99
	Pueblo MSA, CO	S	14.42 MW	14.49 AW	29990 AAW	COBLS	10//99-12//99
	Connecticut	S	14.25 MW	14.33 AW	29810 AAW	CTBLS	10//99-12//99
	Bridgeport PMSA, CT	S	12.40 MW	12.32 AW	25790 AAW	CTBLS	10//99-12//99
	Danbury PMSA, CT	S	12.92 MW	12.54 AW	26870 AAW	CTBLS	10//99-12//99
	Hartford MSA, CT	S	14.30 MW	14.41 AW	29730 AAW	CTBLS	10//99-12//99
	New Haven-Meriden PMSA, CT	S	15.39 MW	15.25 AW	32000 AAW	CTBLS	10//99-12//99
	New London-Norwich MSA, CT-RI	S	13.77 MW	13.91 AW	28640 AAW	CTBLS	10//99-12//99
	Stamford-Norwalk PMSA, CT	S	16.42 MW	16.62 AW	34150 AAW	CTBLS	10//99-12//99
	Waterbury PMSA, CT	S	16.54 MW	15.89 AW	34400 AAW	CTBLS	10//99-12//99
	Delaware	S	13.75 MW	13.51 AW	28100 AAW	DEBLS	10//99-12//99
	Wilmington-Newark PMSA, DE-MD	S	14.62 MW	14.81 AW	30410 AAW	DEBLS	10//99-12//99
	Washington PMSA, DC-MD-VA-WV	S	14.07 MW	13.29 AW	29260 AAW	DCBLS	10//99-12//99
	Florida	S	11.2 MW	11.65 AW	24230 AAW	FLBLS	10//99-12//99
	Daytona Beach MSA, FL	S	10.77 MW	10.96 AW	22390 AAW	FLBLS	10//99-12//99
	Fort Lauderdale PMSA, FL	S	12.39 MW	12.18 AW	25770 AAW	FLBLS	10//99-12//99
	Fort Myers-Cape Coral MSA, FL	S	12.49 MW	12.00 AW	25980 AAW	FLBLS	10//99-12//99
	Fort Pierce-Port St. Lucie MSA, FL	S	11.82 MW	11.33 AW	24590 AAW	FLBLS	10//99-12//99
	Fort Walton Beach MSA, FL	S	9.55 MW	9.48 AW	19860 AAW	FLBLS	10//99-12//99
	Gainesville MSA, FL	S	11.36 MW	10.63 AW	23630 AAW	FLBLS	10//99-12//99
	Jacksonville MSA, FL	S	10.84 MW	10.40 AW	22550 AAW	FLBLS	10//99-12//99
	Lakeland-Winter Haven MSA, FL	S	10.35 MW	10.11 AW	21520 AAW	FLBLS	10//99-12//99
	Melbourne-Titusville-Palm Bay MSA, FL	S	10.59 MW	10.48 AW	22030 AAW	FLBLS	10//99-12//99

Occupation/Type/Industry	Location	Per	Low	Mid	High	Source	Date
Police, Fire, and Ambulance Dispatcher							
	Miami PMSA, FL	S	13.48 MW	13.12 AW	28050 AAW	FLBLS	10//99-12//99
	Orlando MSA, FL	S	12.13 MW	11.65 AW	25230 AAW	FLBLS	10//99-12//99
	Panama City MSA, FL	S	9.73 MW	9.70 AW	20230 AAW	FLBLS	10//99-12//99
	Pensacola MSA, FL	S	10.23 MW	10.02 AW	21280 AAW	FLBLS	10//99-12//99
	Sarasota-Bradenton MSA, FL	S	11.11 MW	10.61 AW	23110 AAW	FLBLS	10//99-12//99
	Tallahassee MSA, FL	S	10.42 MW	10.29 AW	21680 AAW	FLBLS	10//99-12//99
	Tampa-St. Petersburg-Clearwater MSA, FL	S	12.19 MW	11.53 AW	25340 AAW	FLBLS	10//99-12//99
	West Palm Beach-Boca Raton MSA, FL	S	12.99 MW	12.73 AW	27020 AAW	FLBLS	10//99-12//99
	Georgia	S	9.7 MW	9.97 AW	20740 AAW	GABLS	10//99-12//99
	Atlanta MSA, GA	S	11.67 MW	11.36 AW	24280 AAW	GABLS	10//99-12//99
	Augusta-Aiken MSA, GA-SC	S	9.16 MW	9.46 AW	19060 AAW	GABLS	10//99-12//99
	Columbus MSA, GA-AL	S	8.65 MW	8.63 AW	17990 AAW	GABLS	10//99-12//99
	Macon MSA, GA	S	9.62 MW	9.52 AW	20000 AAW	GABLS	10//99-12//99
	Hawaii	S	14.94 MW	14.68 AW	30530 AAW	HIBLS	10//99-12//99
	Idaho	S	10.79 MW	10.72 AW	22290 AAW	IDBLS	10//99-12//99
	Boise City MSA, ID	S	13.16 MW	13.34 AW	27370 AAW	IDBLS	10//99-12//99
	Illinois	S	12.42 MW	13.32 AW	27700 AAW	ILBLS	10//99-12//99
	Chicago PMSA, IL	S	14.75 MW	14.17 AW	30670 AAW	ILBLS	10//99-12//99
	Peoria-Pekin MSA, IL	S	11.89 MW	11.75 AW	24730 AAW	ILBLS	10//99-12//99
	Rockford MSA, IL	S	12.73 MW	12.25 AW	26480 AAW	ILBLS	10//99-12//99
	Springfield MSA, IL	S	11.08 MW	10.53 AW	23040 AAW	ILBLS	10//99-12//99
	Indiana	S	10.47 MW	10.39 AW	21600 AAW	INBLS	10//99-12//99
	Evansville-Henderson MSA, IN-KY	S	10.90 MW	10.33 AW	22660 AAW	INBLS	10//99-12//99
	Fort Wayne MSA, IN	S	10.60 MW	10.95 AW	22050 AAW	INBLS	10//99-12//99
	Gary PMSA, IN	S	10.44 MW	10.96 AW	21710 AAW	INBLS	10//99-12//99
	Indianapolis MSA, IN	S	11.10 MW	11.27 AW	23090 AAW	INBLS	10//99-12//99
	Iowa	S	10.83 MW	11.37 AW	23640 AAW	IABLS	10//99-12//99
	Davenport-Moline-Rock Island MSA, IA-IL	S	12.84 MW	12.31 AW	26700 AAW	IABLS	10//99-12//99
	Des Moines MSA, IA	S	14.61 MW	14.81 AW	30390 AAW	IABLS	10//99-12//99
	Kansas	S	9.9 MW	10.19 AW	21200 AAW	KSBLS	10//99-12//99
	Wichita MSA, KS	S	10.93 MW	10.50 AW	22740 AAW	KSBLS	10//99-12//99
	Kentucky	S	10.04 MW	10.25 AW	21320 AAW	KYBLS	10//99-12//99
	Lexington MSA, KY	S	10.82 MW	10.25 AW	22500 AAW	KYBLS	10//99-12//99
	Louisville MSA, KY-IN	S	10.88 MW	10.79 AW	22640 AAW	KYBLS	10//99-12//99
	Louisiana	S	8.24 MW	8.44 AW	17550 AAW	LABLS	10//99-12//99
	Baton Rouge MSA, LA	S	9.57 MW	9.51 AW	19900 AAW	LABLS	10//99-12//99
	Lafayette MSA, LA	S	8.45 MW	9.05 AW	17570 AAW	LABLS	10//99-12//99
	Lake Charles MSA, LA	S	8.30 MW	8.39 AW	17260 AAW	LABLS	10//99-12//99
	New Orleans MSA, LA	S	9.54 MW	9.22 AW	19830 AAW	LABLS	10//99-12//99
	Shreveport-Bossier City MSA, LA	S	8.16 MW	7.94 AW	16970 AAW	LABLS	10//99-12//99
	Maine	S	11.05 MW	10.81 AW	22490 AAW	MEBLS	10//99-12//99
	Bangor MSA, ME	S	11.77 MW	11.93 AW	24490 AAW	MEBLS	10//99-12//99
	Portland MSA, ME	S	11.14 MW	11.06 AW	23170 AAW	MEBLS	10//99-12//99
	Maryland	S	13.29 MW	14.36 AW	29870 AAW	MDBLS	10//99-12//99
	Baltimore PMSA, MD	S	14.82 MW	14.09 AW	30830 AAW	MDBLS	10//99-12//99
	Massachusetts	S	13.12 MW	13.07 AW	27180 AAW	MABLS	10//99-12//99
	Barnstable-Yarmouth MSA, MA	S	14.16 MW	14.22 AW	29440 AAW	MABLS	10//99-12//99
	Boston PMSA, MA-NH	S	14.13 MW	14.25 AW	29390 AAW	MABLS	10//99-12//99
	Brockton PMSA, MA	S	13.02 MW	12.82 AW	27080 AAW	MABLS	10//99-12//99
	Fitchburg-Leominster PMSA, MA	S	10.53 MW	9.99 AW	21900 AAW	MABLS	10//99-12//99
	Lawrence PMSA, MA-NH	S	12.35 MW	12.59 AW	25690 AAW	MABLS	10//99-12//99
	New Bedford PMSA, MA	S	11.79 MW	11.80 AW	24530 AAW	MABLS	10//99-12//99
	Pittsfield MSA, MA	S	11.88 MW	11.47 AW	24720 AAW	MABLS	10//99-12//99
	Springfield MSA, MA	S	11.63 MW	11.82 AW	24190 AAW	MABLS	10//99-12//99
	Worcester PMSA, MA-CT	S	12.44 MW	12.73 AW	25880 AAW	MABLS	10//99-12//99
	Michigan	S	13.9 MW	14.10 AW	29320 AAW	MIBLS	10//99-12//99
	Ann Arbor PMSA, MI	S	12.66 MW	12.61 AW	26340 AAW	MIBLS	10//99-12//99
	Benton Harbor MSA, MI	S	12.45 MW	12.65 AW	25890 AAW	MIBLS	10//99-12//99
	Detroit PMSA, MI	S	14.94 MW	14.70 AW	31070 AAW	MIBLS	10//99-12//99
	Grand Rapids-Muskegon-Holland MSA, MI	S	16.39 MW	16.13 AW	34090 AAW	MIBLS	10//99-12//99
	Kalamazoo-Battle Creek MSA, MI	S	13.10 MW	13.27 AW	27240 AAW	MIBLS	10//99-12//99

AAW Average annual wage	**AOH** Average offered, high	**ASH** Average starting, high	**H** Hourly	**M** Monthly	**S** Special: hourly and annual
AE Average entry wage	**AOL** Average offered, low	**ASL** Average starting, low	**HI** Highest wage paid	**MTC** Median total compensation	**TQ** Third quartile wage
AEX Average experienced wage	**APH** Average pay, high range	**AW** Average wage paid	**HR** High end range	**MW** Median wage paid	**W** Weekly
AO Average offered	**APL** Average pay, low range	**FQ** First quartile wage	**LR** Low end range	**SQ** Second quartile wage	**Y** Yearly

Occupation/Type/Industry	Location	Per	Low	Mid	High	Source	Date
Police, Fire, and Ambulance Dispatcher	Saginaw-Bay City-Midland						
	MSA, MI	S	14.33 MW	14.62 AW	29800 AAW	MIBLS	10//99-12//99
	Minnesota	S	14.23 MW	14.16 AW	29450 AAW	MNBLS	10//99-12//99
	Duluth-Superior MSA, MN-WI	S	13.32 MW	14.27 AW	27700 AAW	MNBLS	10//99-12//99
	Minneapolis-St. Paul MSA,						
	MN-WI	S	16.44 MW	16.27 AW	34190 AAW	MNBLS	10//99-12//99
	St. Cloud MSA, MN	S	13.94 MW	14.20 AW	29000 AAW	MNBLS	10//99-12//99
	Mississippi	S	8.5 MW	8.74 AW	18170 AAW	MSBLS	10//99-12//99
	Biloxi-Gulfport-Pascagoula						
	MSA, MS	S	8.81 MW	8.37 AW	18330 AAW	MSBLS	10//99-12//99
	Hattiesburg MSA, MS	S	8.03 MW	8.04 AW	16700 AAW	MSBLS	10//99-12//99
	Jackson MSA, MS	S	10.79 MW	10.99 AW	22430 AAW	MSBLS	10//99-12//99
	Missouri	S	10.96 MW	11.34 AW	23590 AAW	MOBLS	10//99-12//99
	Kansas City MSA, MO-KS	S	12.57 MW	12.35 AW	26140 AAW	MOBLS	10//99-12//99
	St. Louis MSA, MO-IL	S	13.26 MW	12.64 AW	27580 AAW	MOBLS	10//99-12//99
	Montana	S	9.79 MW	9.84 AW	20470 AAW	MTBLS	10//99-12//99
	Nebraska	S	9.98 MW	10.35 AW	21520 AAW	NEBLS	10//99-12//99
	Omaha MSA, NE-IA	S	12.27 MW	12.12 AW	25520 AAW	NEBLS	10//99-12//99
	Nevada	S	14.53 MW	14.97 AW	31140 AAW	NVBLS	10//99-12//99
	Las Vegas MSA, NV-AZ	S	13.58 MW	12.92 AW	28240 AAW	NVBLS	10//99-12//99
	New Hampshire	S	11.92 MW	12.12 AW	25200 AAW	NHBLS	10//99-12//99
	Manchester PMSA, NH	S	12.62 MW	12.35 AW	26250 AAW	NHBLS	10//99-12//99
	Nashua PMSA, NH	S	14.21 MW	13.62 AW	29560 AAW	NHBLS	10//99-12//99
	Portsmouth-Rochester PMSA,						
	NH-ME	S	13.05 MW	13.10 AW	27150 AAW	NHBLS	10//99-12//99
	New Jersey	S	13.42 MW	13.52 AW	28110 AAW	NJBLS	10//99-12//99
	Atlantic-Cape May PMSA, NJ	S	13.51 MW	13.84 AW	28100 AAW	NJBLS	10//99-12//99
	Bergen-Passaic PMSA, NJ	S	11.81 MW	11.77 AW	24570 AAW	NJBLS	10//99-12//99
	Jersey City PMSA, NJ	S	14.23 MW	13.71 AW	29590 AAW	NJBLS	10//99-12//99
	Middlesex-Somerset-						
	Hunterdon PMSA, NJ	S	14.09 MW	13.69 AW	29310 AAW	NJBLS	10//99-12//99
	Monmouth-Ocean PMSA, NJ	S	12.34 MW	12.41 AW	25660 AAW	NJBLS	10//99-12//99
	Newark PMSA, NJ	S	14.51 MW	14.32 AW	30180 AAW	NJBLS	10//99-12//99
	Trenton PMSA, NJ	S	15.33 MW	14.79 AW	31880 AAW	NJBLS	10//99-12//99
	Vineland-Millville-Bridgeton						
	PMSA, NJ	S	10.80 MW	10.19 AW	22470 AAW	NJBLS	10//99-12//99
	New Mexico	S	9.98 MW	9.99 AW	20770 AAW	NMBLS	10//99-12//99
	Albuquerque MSA, NM	S	10.56 MW	10.28 AW	21960 AAW	NMBLS	10//99-12//99
	New York	S	13.29 MW	13.40 AW	27880 AAW	NYBLS	10//99-12//99
	Albany-Schenectady-Troy						
	MSA, NY	S	13.64 MW	13.49 AW	28360 AAW	NYBLS	10//99-12//99
	Buffalo-Niagara Falls MSA,						
	NY	S	12.42 MW	10.90 AW	25830 AAW	NYBLS	10//99-12//99
	Dutchess County PMSA, NY	S	14.92 MW	14.88 AW	31020 AAW	NYBLS	10//99-12//99
	Nassau-Suffolk PMSA, NY	S	14.50 MW	14.39 AW	30170 AAW	NYBLS	10//99-12//99
	Newburgh PMSA, NY-PA	S	11.52 MW	11.42 AW	23970 AAW	NYBLS	10//99-12//99
	Rochester MSA, NY	S	12.07 MW	12.21 AW	25110 AAW	NYBLS	10//99-12//99
	Syracuse MSA, NY	S	15.00 MW	15.10 AW	31200 AAW	NYBLS	10//99-12//99
	Utica-Rome MSA, NY	S	10.31 MW	9.39 AW	21450 AAW	NYBLS	10//99-12//99
	North Carolina	S	10.5 MW	10.65 AW	22160 AAW	NCBLS	10//99-12//99
	Asheville MSA, NC	S	10.45 MW	10.63 AW	21740 AAW	NCBLS	10//99-12//99
	Charlotte-Gastonia-Rock Hill						
	MSA, NC-SC	S	11.64 MW	11.86 AW	24210 AAW	NCBLS	10//99-12//99
	Greensboro--Winston-Salem--						
	High Point MSA, NC	S	12.30 MW	12.44 AW	25580 AAW	NCBLS	10//99-12//99
	Hickory-Morganton-Lenoir						
	MSA, NC	S	10.13 MW	10.06 AW	21070 AAW	NCBLS	10//99-12//99
	Raleigh-Durham-Chapel Hill						
	MSA, NC	S	12.41 MW	12.00 AW	25810 AAW	NCBLS	10//99-12//99
	Wilmington MSA, NC	S	11.56 MW	11.51 AW	24040 AAW	NCBLS	10//99-12//99
	North Dakota	S	10.42 MW	10.42 AW	21680 AAW	NDBLS	10//99-12//99
	Bismarck MSA, ND	S	12.10 MW	11.92 AW	25170 AAW	NDBLS	10//99-12//99
	Fargo-Moorhead MSA, ND-						
	MN	S	11.62 MW	11.69 AW	24170 AAW	NDBLS	10//99-12//99
	Ohio	S	12.92 MW	12.82 AW	26660 AAW	OHBLS	10//99-12//99
	Akron PMSA, OH	S	11.86 MW	12.53 AW	24660 AAW	OHBLS	10//99-12//99
	Canton-Massillon MSA, OH	S	11.37 MW	10.60 AW	23640 AAW	OHBLS	10//99-12//99
	Cincinnati PMSA, OH-KY-IN	S	13.61 MW	13.58 AW	28300 AAW	OHBLS	10//99-12//99
	Lima MSA, OH	S	13.24 MW	13.00 AW	27540 AAW	OHBLS	10//99-12//99
	Toledo MSA, OH	S	14.39 MW	13.70 AW	29920 AAW	OHBLS	10//99-12//99
	Oklahoma	S	8.08 MW	8.67 AW	18040 AAW	OKBLS	

AAW	Average annual wage	AOH	Average offered, high	ASH	Average starting, high	H	Hourly	M	Monthly	S	Special: hourly and annual
AE	Average entry wage	AOL	Average offered, low	ASL	Average starting, low	HI	Highest wage paid	MTC	Median total compensation	TQ	Third quartile wage
AEX	Average experienced wage	APH	Average pay, high range	AW	Average wage paid	HR	High end range	MW	Median wage paid	W	Weekly
AO	Average offered	APL	Average pay, low range	FQ	First quartile wage	LR	Low end range	SQ	Second quartile wage	Y	Yearly

Occupation/Type/Industry	Location	Per	Low	Mid	High	Source	Date
Police, Fire, and Ambulance Dispatcher	Oklahoma City MSA, OK	S	11.37 MW	11.05 AW	23650 AAW	OKBLS	10//99-12//99
	Tulsa MSA, OK	S	9.61 MW	9.20 AW	19980 AAW	OKBLS	10//99-12//99
	Oregon	S	15.09 MW	15.76 AW	32780 AAW	ORBLS	10//99-12//99
	Portland-Vancouver PMSA, OR-WA	S	18.39 MW	17.73 AW	38250 AAW	ORBLS	10//99-12//99
	Pennsylvania	S	12.09 MW	12.64 AW	26290 AAW	PABLS	10//99-12//99
	Allentown-Bethlehem-Easton MSA, PA	S	12.01 MW	11.42 AW	24970 AAW	PABLS	10//99-12//99
	Altoona MSA, PA	S	12.34 MW	13.20 AW	25660 AAW	PABLS	10//99-12//99
	Harrisburg-Lebanon-Carlisle MSA, PA	S	12.57 MW	12.82 AW	26140 AAW	PABLS	10//99-12//99
	Philadelphia PMSA, PA-NJ	S	14.17 MW	14.30 AW	29470 AAW	PABLS	10//99-12//99
	Pittsburgh MSA, PA	S	11.39 MW	10.85 AW	23680 AAW	PABLS	10//99-12//99
	Scranton--Wilkes-Barre--Hazleton MSA, PA	S	11.11 MW	10.59 AW	23110 AAW	PABLS	10//99-12//99
	Rhode Island	S	15.3 MW	15.06 AW	31320 AAW	RIBLS	10//99-12//99
	Providence-Fall River-Warwick MSA, RI-MA	S	14.43 MW	14.40 AW	30010 AAW	RIBLS	10//99-12//99
	South Carolina	S	10.06 MW	10.17 AW	21150 AAW	SCBLS	10//99-12//99
	Charleston-North Charleston MSA, SC	S	10.51 MW	10.39 AW	21850 AAW	SCBLS	10//99-12//99
	Columbia MSA, SC	S	10.94 MW	10.96 AW	22750 AAW	SCBLS	10//99-12//99
	Greenville-Spartanburg-Anderson MSA, SC	S	10.57 MW	10.26 AW	21980 AAW	SCBLS	10//99-12//99
	South Dakota	S	9.06 MW	9.35 AW	19460 AAW	SDBLS	10//99-12//99
	Tennessee	S	10.01 MW	10.70 AW	22250 AAW	TNBLS	10//99-12//99
	Chattanooga MSA, TN-GA	S	9.84 MW	9.79 AW	20470 AAW	TNBLS	10//99-12//99
	Clarksville-Hopkinsville MSA, TN-KY	S	11.21 MW	11.34 AW	23310 AAW	TNBLS	10//99-12//99
	Johnson City-Kingsport-Bristol MSA, TN-VA	S	9.95 MW	9.58 AW	20700 AAW	TNBLS	10//99-12//99
	Knoxville MSA, TN	S	11.94 MW	11.34 AW	24830 AAW	TNBLS	10//99-12//99
	Memphis MSA, TN-AR-MS	S	14.25 MW	14.05 AW	29640 AAW	MSBLS	10//99-12//99
	Nashville MSA, TN	S	12.20 MW	11.62 AW	25370 AAW	TNBLS	10//99-12//99
	Texas	S	10.29 MW	10.62 AW	22100 AAW	TXBLS	10//99-12//99
	Austin-San Marcos MSA, TX	S	11.44 MW	11.39 AW	23790 AAW	TXBLS	10//99-12//99
	Beaumont-Port Arthur MSA, TX	S	11.87 MW	11.42 AW	24680 AAW	TXBLS	10//99-12//99
	Brazoria PMSA, TX	S	10.25 MW	10.13 AW	21310 AAW	TXBLS	10//99-12//99
	Brownsville-Harlingen-San Benito MSA, TX	S	9.25 MW	8.89 AW	19250 AAW	TXBLS	10//99-12//99
	Bryan-College Station MSA, TX	S	11.33 MW	11.19 AW	23570 AAW	TXBLS	10//99-12//99
	Corpus Christi MSA, TX	S	10.38 MW	10.42 AW	21580 AAW	TXBLS	10//99-12//99
	Dallas PMSA, TX	S	12.48 MW	11.55 AW	25960 AAW	TXBLS	10//99-12//99
	El Paso MSA, TX	S	11.73 MW	11.88 AW	24400 AAW	TXBLS	10//99-12//99
	Fort Worth-Arlington PMSA, TX	S	12.35 MW	11.96 AW	25680 AAW	TXBLS	10//99-12//99
	Galveston-Texas City PMSA, TX	S	11.24 MW	10.85 AW	23370 AAW	TXBLS	10//99-12//99
	Houston PMSA, TX	S	12.36 MW	12.16 AW	25710 AAW	TXBLS	10//99-12//99
	Killeen-Temple MSA, TX	S	8.50 MW	8.25 AW	17670 AAW	TXBLS	10//99-12//99
	Laredo MSA, TX	S	11.66 MW	11.88 AW	24250 AAW	TXBLS	10//99-12//99
	Longview-Marshall MSA, TX	S	9.03 MW	9.16 AW	18780 AAW	TXBLS	10//99-12//99
	Lubbock MSA, TX	S	10.49 MW	10.16 AW	21810 AAW	TXBLS	10//99-12//99
	McAllen-Edinburg-Mission MSA, TX	S	9.27 MW	9.22 AW	19270 AAW	TXBLS	10//99-12//99
	Odessa-Midland MSA, TX	S	10.73 MW	10.70 AW	22320 AAW	TXBLS	10//99-12//99
	San Antonio MSA, TX	S	10.31 MW	10.02 AW	21440 AAW	TXBLS	10//99-12//99
	Sherman-Denison MSA, TX	S	10.79 MW	11.15 AW	22440 AAW	TXBLS	10//99-12//99
	Texarkana MSA, TX-Texarkana, AR	S	8.93 MW	8.49 AW	18570 AAW	TXBLS	10//99-12//99
	Tyler MSA, TX	S	9.89 MW	9.66 AW	20560 AAW	TXBLS	10//99-12//99
	Waco MSA, TX	S	9.03 MW	8.93 AW	18790 AAW	TXBLS	10//99-12//99
	Wichita Falls MSA, TX	S	7.88 MW	7.28 AW	16390 AAW	TXBLS	10//99-12//99
	Utah	S	12.28 MW	12.52 AW	26030 AAW	UTBLS	10//99-12//99
	Provo-Orem MSA, UT	S	12.06 MW	12.17 AW	25080 AAW	UTBLS	10//99-12//99
	Salt Lake City-Ogden MSA, UT	S	13.23 MW	12.78 AW	27530 AAW	UTBLS	10//99-12//99
	Vermont	S	12.02 MW	12.59 AW	26200 AAW	VTBLS	10//99-12//99
	Burlington MSA, VT	S	13.28 MW	12.44 AW	27620 AAW	VTBLS	10//99-12//99

Occupation/Type/Industry	Location	Per	Low	Mid	High	Source	Date
Police, Fire, and Ambulance Dispatcher	Virginia	S	11 MW	11.63 AW	24190 AAW	VABLS	10//99-12//99
	Charlottesville MSA, VA	S	11.54 MW	10.97 AW	24010 AAW	VABLS	10//99-12//99
	Lynchburg MSA, VA	S	9.81 MW	9.73 AW	20400 AAW	VABLS	10//99-12//99
	Norfolk-Virginia Beach-Newport News MSA, VA-NC	S	12.57 MW	11.88 AW	26150 AAW	VABLS	10//99-12//99
	Richmond-Petersburg MSA, VA	S	13.26 MW	12.72 AW	27570 AAW	VABLS	10//99-12//99
	Roanoke MSA, VA	S	12.13 MW	11.91 AW	25240 AAW	VABLS	10//99-12//99
	Washington	S	15.32 MW	15.54 AW	32320 AAW	WABLS	10//99-12//99
	Seattle-Bellevue-Everett PMSA, WA	S	15.38 MW	14.35 AW	31990 AAW	WABLS	10//99-12//99
	Spokane MSA, WA	S	17.46 MW	16.90 AW	36310 AAW	WABLS	10//99-12//99
	Tacoma PMSA, WA	S	16.49 MW	16.28 AW	34310 AAW	WABLS	10//99-12//99
	Yakima MSA, WA	S	14.70 MW	14.40 AW	30580 AAW	WABLS	10//99-12//99
	West Virginia	S	8.03 MW	8.13 AW	16920 AAW	WVBLS	10//99-12//99
	Charleston MSA, WV	S	8.69 MW	8.69 AW	18080 AAW	WVBLS	10//99-12//99
	Huntington-Ashland MSA, WV-KY-OH	S	8.46 MW	8.35 AW	17590 AAW	WVBLS	10//99-12//99
	Parkersburg-Marietta MSA, WV-OH	S	9.55 MW	9.24 AW	19870 AAW	WVBLS	10//99-12//99
	Wheeling MSA, WV-OH	S	8.44 MW	8.05 AW	17570 AAW	WVBLS	10//99-12//99
	Wisconsin	S	13.71 MW	13.97 AW	29060 AAW	WIBLS	10//99-12//99
	Appleton-Oshkosh-Neenah MSA, WI	S	14.04 MW	14.16 AW	29210 AAW	WIBLS	10//99-12//99
	Eau Claire MSA, WI	S	14.67 MW	14.87 AW	30520 AAW	WIBLS	10//99-12//99
	Green Bay MSA, WI	S	15.25 MW	15.24 AW	31710 AAW	WIBLS	10//99-12//99
	Kenosha PMSA, WI	S	13.46 MW	13.22 AW	28000 AAW	WIBLS	10//99-12//99
	Milwaukee-Waukesha PMSA, WI	S	14.91 MW	14.49 AW	31000 AAW	WIBLS	10//99-12//99
	Racine PMSA, WI	S	13.82 MW	12.54 AW	28750 AAW	WIBLS	10//99-12//99
	Wyoming	S	10.35 MW	10.49 AW	21810 AAW	WYBLS	10//99-12//99
	Puerto Rico	S	6.67 MW	9.40 AW	19540 AAW	PRBLS	10//99-12//99
	San Juan-Bayamon PMSA, PR	S	12.51 MW	13.32 AW	26020 AAW	PRBLS	10//99-12//99
Policeperson, Detective							
Supervisory	United States	H		24.14 AW		NCS98	1998
Political Science Teacher							
Postsecondary	Alabama	Y		45340 AAW		ALBLS	10//99-12//99
Postsecondary	Arizona	Y		30680 AAW		AZBLS	10//99-12//99
Postsecondary	Arkansas	Y		49770 AAW		ARBLS	10//99-12//99
Postsecondary	California	Y		56750 AAW		CABLS	10//99-12//99
Postsecondary	Colorado	Y		56280 AAW		COBLS	10//99-12//99
Postsecondary	Connecticut	Y		62480 AAW		CTBLS	10//99-12//99
Postsecondary	District of Columbia	Y		52370 AAW		DCBLS	10//99-12//99
Postsecondary	Florida	Y		61270 AAW		FLBLS	10//99-12//99
Postsecondary	Georgia	Y		48000 AAW		GABLS	10//99-12//99
Postsecondary	Illinois	Y		51340 AAW		ILBLS	10//99-12//99
Postsecondary	Indiana	Y		52130 AAW		INBLS	10//99-12//99
Postsecondary	Iowa	Y		52180 AAW		IABLS	10//99-12//99
Postsecondary	Kansas	Y		48430 AAW		KSBLS	10//99-12//99
Postsecondary	Kentucky	Y		52100 AAW		KYBLS	10//99-12//99
Postsecondary	Louisiana	Y		48870 AAW		LABLS	10//99-12//99
Postsecondary	Maryland	Y		60340 AAW		MDBLS	10//99-12//99
Postsecondary	Massachusetts	Y		59640 AAW		MABLS	10//99-12//99
Postsecondary	Michigan	Y		59780 AAW		MIBLS	10//99-12//99
Postsecondary	Minnesota	Y		63220 AAW		MNBLS	10//99-12//99
Postsecondary	Mississippi	Y		40170 AAW		MSBLS	10//99-12//99
Postsecondary	Missouri	Y		49660 AAW		MOBLS	10//99-12//99
Postsecondary	Montana	Y		64790 AAW		MTBLS	10//99-12//99
Postsecondary	Nevada	Y		48810 AAW		NVBLS	10//99-12//99
Postsecondary	New Hampshire	Y		59700 AAW		NHBLS	10//99-12//99
Postsecondary	New Jersey	Y		62930 AAW		NJBLS	10//99-12//99
Postsecondary	New York	Y		54040 AAW		NYBLS	10//99-12//99
Postsecondary	North Carolina	Y		45700 AAW		NCBLS	10//99-12//99
Postsecondary	Ohio	Y		48000 AAW		OHBLS	10//99-12//99
Postsecondary	Oklahoma	Y		43920 AAW		OKBLS	10//99-12//99
Postsecondary	Oregon	Y		53160 AAW		ORBLS	10//99-12//99
Postsecondary	Pennsylvania	Y		59630 AAW		PABLS	10//99-12//99
Postsecondary	South Carolina	Y		48220 AAW		SCBLS	10//99-12//99

AAW Average annual wage	**AOH** Average offered, high	**ASH** Average starting, high	**H** Hourly	**M** Monthly	**S** Special: hourly and annual
AE Average entry wage	**AOL** Average offered, low	**ASL** Average starting, low	**HI** Highest wage paid	**MTC** Median total compensation	**TQ** Third quartile wage
AEX Average experienced wage	**APH** Average pay, high range	**AW** Average wage paid	**HR** High end range	**MW** Median wage paid	**W** Weekly
AO Average offered	**APL** Average pay, low range	**FQ** First quartile wage	**LR** Low end range	**SQ** Second quartile wage	**Y** Yearly

Occupation/Type/Industry	Location	Per	Low	Mid	High	Source	Date
Political Science Teacher							
Postsecondary	Tennessee	Y		52820 AAW		TNBLS	10//99-12//99
Postsecondary	Texas	Y		46650 AAW		TXBLS	10//99-12//99
Postsecondary	Virginia	Y		53430 AAW		VABLS	10//99-12//99
Postsecondary	Washington	Y		51610 AAW		WABLS	10//99-12//99
Postsecondary	West Virginia	Y		53200 AAW		WVBLS	10//99-12//99
Postsecondary	Wyoming	Y		45830 AAW		WYBLS	10//99-12//99
Postsecondary	Puerto Rico	Y		45210 AAW		PRBLS	10//99-12//99
Political Scientist	California	S	15.5 MW	18.43 AW	38340 AAW	CABLS	10//99-12//99
	Connecticut	S	24.5 MW	32.49 AW	67580 AAW	CTBLS	10//99-12//99
	Maryland	S	21.38 MW	26.23 AW	54560 AAW	MDBLS	10//99-12//99
	New York	S	42.68 MW	47.52 AW	98840 AAW	NYBLS	10//99-12//99
Postal Service Clerk	Alabama	S	18.58 MW	18.31 AW	38090 AAW	ALBLS	10//99-12//99
	Alaska	S	18.61 MW	18.36 AW	38180 AAW	AKBLS	10//99-12//99
	Arkansas	S	18.47 MW	18.21 AW	37880 AAW	ARBLS	10//99-12//99
	California	S	18.62 MW	18.31 AW	38090 AAW	CABLS	10//99-12//99
	Colorado	S	18.68 MW	18.43 AW	38340 AAW	COBLS	10//99-12//99
	Connecticut	S	18.6 MW	18.32 AW	38110 AAW	CTBLS	10//99-12//99
	Florida	S	18.86 MW	18.61 AW	38720 AAW	FLBLS	10//99-12//99
	Georgia	S	18.48 MW	18.21 AW	37880 AAW	GABLS	10//99-12//99
	Idaho	S	18.41 MW	18.13 AW	37710 AAW	IDBLS	10//99-12//99
	Illinois	S	18.85 MW	18.64 AW	38760 AAW	ILBLS	10//99-12//99
	Indiana	S	18.65 MW	18.39 AW	38250 AAW	INBLS	10//99-12//99
	Iowa	S	19.02 MW	18.87 AW	39250 AAW	IABLS	10//99-12//99
	Kansas	S	18.67 MW	18.41 AW	38300 AAW	KSBLS	10//99-12//99
	Kentucky	S	18.33 MW	18.07 AW	37590 AAW	KYBLS	10//99-12//99
	Louisiana	S	18.71 MW	18.46 AW	38400 AAW	LABLS	10//99-12//99
	Maine	S	18.32 MW	18.03 AW	37500 AAW	MEBLS	10//99-12//99
	Maryland	S	18.63 MW	18.38 AW	38220 AAW	MDBLS	10//99-12//99
	Massachusetts	S	18.72 MW	18.46 AW	38390 AAW	MABLS	10//99-12//99
	Michigan	S	18.62 MW	18.36 AW	38190 AAW	MIBLS	10//99-12//99
	Minnesota	S	19.03 MW	18.86 AW	39230 AAW	MNBLS	10//99-12//99
	Mississippi	S	18.26 MW	18.01 AW	37450 AAW	MSBLS	10//99-12//99
	Missouri	S	18.8 MW	18.58 AW	38650 AAW	MOBLS	10//99-12//99
	Montana	S	18.35 MW	18.09 AW	37620 AAW	MTBLS	10//99-12//99
	Nebraska	S	18.32 MW	18.07 AW	37580 AAW	NEBLS	10//99-12//99
	Nevada	S	18.61 MW	18.33 AW	38130 AAW	NVBLS	10//99-12//99
	New Hampshire	S	18.53 MW	18.27 AW	38010 AAW	NHBLS	10//99-12//99
	New Jersey	S	18.59 MW	18.34 AW	38140 AAW	NJBLS	10//99-12//99
	New Mexico	S	18.41 MW	18.16 AW	37760 AAW	NMBLS	10//99-12//99
	New York	S	18.66 MW	18.41 AW	38280 AAW	NYBLS	10//99-12//99
	North Carolina	S	18.6 MW	18.34 AW	38150 AAW	NCBLS	10//99-12//99
	North Dakota	S	18.53 MW	18.27 AW	38000 AAW	NDBLS	10//99-12//99
	Ohio	S	18.69 MW	18.42 AW	38320 AAW	OHBLS	10//99-12//99
	Oklahoma	S	18.91 MW	18.72 AW	38940 AAW	OKBLS	10//99-12//99
	Oregon	S	18.47 MW	18.20 AW	37860 AAW	ORBLS	10//99-12//99
	Pennsylvania	S	18.72 MW	18.48 AW	38440 AAW	PABLS	10//99-12//99
	South Carolina	S	18.49 MW	18.23 AW	37920 AAW	SCBLS	10//99-12//99
	South Dakota	S	18.67 MW	18.44 AW	38350 AAW	SDBLS	10//99-12//99
	Tennessee	S	18.57 MW	18.09 AW	37620 AAW	TNBLS	10//99-12//99
	Texas	S	18.7 MW	18.45 AW	38380 AAW	TXBLS	10//99-12//99
	Utah	S	18.36 MW	18.10 AW	37650 AAW	UTBLS	10//99-12//99
	Vermont	S	18.67 MW	18.42 AW	38310 AAW	VTBLS	10//99-12//99
	Virginia	S	18.53 MW	18.26 AW	37980 AAW	VABLS	10//99-12//99
	Washington	S	18.44 MW	18.18 AW	37820 AAW	WABLS	10//99-12//99
	West Virginia	S	18.1 MW	17.89 AW	37220 AAW	WVBLS	10//99-12//99
	Wisconsin	S	18.36 MW	18.11 AW	37660 AAW	WIBLS	10//99-12//99
	Wyoming	S	18.66 MW	18.34 AW	38140 AAW	WYBLS	10//99-12//99
Postal Service Mail Carrier	Alabama	S	17.55 MW	16.93 AW	35220 AAW	ALBLS	10//99-12//99
	Arkansas	S	17.51 MW	16.92 AW	35190 AAW	ARBLS	10//99-12//99
	California	S	18.64 MW	18.25 AW	37970 AAW	CABLS	10//99-12//99
	Colorado	S	18.17 MW	17.63 AW	36660 AAW	COBLS	10//99-12//99
	Denver PMSA, CO	S	17.95 MW	18.35 AW	37330 AAW	COBLS	10//99-12//99
	Connecticut	S	18.47 MW	17.98 AW	37410 AAW	CTBLS	10//99-12//99
	Washington PMSA, DC-MD-VA-WV	S	17.91 MW	18.40 AW	37250 AAW	DCBLS	10//99-12//99
	Florida	S	18.44 MW	17.85 AW	37120 AAW	FLBLS	10//99-12//99
	Georgia	S	17.7 MW	17.00 AW	35360 AAW	GABLS	10//99-12//99
	Atlanta MSA, GA	S	17.18 MW	17.91 AW	35730 AAW	GABLS	10//99-12//99
	Idaho	S	17.53 MW	16.73 AW	34790 AAW	IDBLS	10//99-12//99

AAW Average annual wage	**AOH** Average offered, high	**ASH** Average starting, high	**H** Hourly	**M** Monthly	**S** Special: hourly and annual
AE Average entry wage	**AOL** Average offered, low	**ASL** Average starting, low	**HI** Highest wage paid	**MTC** Median total compensation	**TQ** Third quartile wage
AEX Average experienced wage	**APH** Average pay, high range	**AW** Average wage paid	**HR** High end range	**MW** Median wage paid	**W** Weekly
AO Average offered	**APL** Average pay, low range	**FQ** First quartile wage	**LR** Low end range	**SQ** Second quartile wage	**Y** Yearly

Occupation/Type/Industry	Location	Per	Low	Mid	High	Source	Date
Postal Service Mail Carrier	Illinois	S	18.24 MW	17.73 AW	36870 AAW	ILBLS	10//99-12//99
	Indiana	S	18.02 MW	17.27 AW	35930 AAW	INBLS	10//99-12//99
	Iowa	S	18.05 MW	17.38 AW	36150 AAW	IABLS	10//99-12//99
	Kansas	S	17.91 MW	17.27 AW	35920 AAW	KSBLS	10//99-12//99
	Kentucky	S	17.76 MW	17.01 AW	35390 AAW	KYBLS	10//99-12//99
	Louisiana	S	17.93 MW	17.37 AW	36120 AAW	LABLS	10//99-12//99
	New Orleans MSA, LA	S	17.89 MW	18.28 AW	37200 AAW	LABLS	10//99-12//99
	Maine	S	17.49 MW	16.84 AW	35030 AAW	MEBLS	10//99-12//99
	Maryland	S	18.27 MW	17.73 AW	36870 AAW	MDBLS	10//99-12//99
	Massachusetts	S	18.52 MW	18.05 AW	37550 AAW	MABLS	10//99-12//99
	Michigan	S	18.14 MW	17.48 AW	36360 AAW	MIBLS	10//99-12//99
	Minnesota	S	18.11 MW	17.43 AW	36260 AAW	MNBLS	10//99-12//99
	Minneapolis-St. Paul MSA, MN-WI	S	17.78 MW	18.38 AW	36990 AAW	MNBLS	10//99-12//99
	Mississippi	S	17.18 MW	16.73 AW	34790 AAW	MSBLS	10//99-12//99
	Missouri	S	18.15 MW	17.44 AW	36270 AAW	MOBLS	10//99-12//99
	Kansas City MSA, MO-KS	S	17.75 MW	18.34 AW	36920 AAW	MOBLS	10//99-12//99
	St. Louis MSA, MO-IL	S	17.94 MW	18.52 AW	37310 AAW	MOBLS	10//99-12//99
	Montana	S	17.74 MW	16.85 AW	35060 AAW	MTBLS	10//99-12//99
	Nebraska	S	17.69 MW	17.11 AW	35600 AAW	NEBLS	10//99-12//99
	New Hampshire	S	17.99 MW	17.29 AW	35970 AAW	NHBLS	10//99-12//99
	New Jersey	S	18.47 MW	18.07 AW	37590 AAW	NJBLS	10//99-12//99
	Newark PMSA, NJ	S	17.99 MW	18.33 AW	37420 AAW	NJBLS	10//99-12//99
	New Mexico	S	18.2 MW	17.58 AW	36560 AAW	NMBLS	10//99-12//99
	New York	S	18.31 MW	17.85 AW	37140 AAW	NYBLS	10//99-12//99
	Albany-Schenectady-Troy MSA, NY	S	17.60 MW	18.16 AW	36610 AAW	NYBLS	10//99-12//99
	New York PMSA, NY	S	18.14 MW	18.44 AW	37730 AAW	NYBLS	10//99-12//99
	North Carolina	S	17.51 MW	16.68 AW	34700 AAW	NCBLS	10//99-12//99
	Greensboro--Winston-Salem--High Point MSA, NC	S	17.22 MW	17.96 AW	35820 AAW	NCBLS	10//99-12//99
	Hickory-Morganton-Lenoir MSA, NC	S	16.35 MW	17.24 AW	34000 AAW	NCBLS	10//99-12//99
	North Dakota	S	17.71 MW	17.07 AW	35510 AAW	NDBLS	10//99-12//99
	Ohio	S	18.32 MW	17.74 AW	36900 AAW	OHBLS	10//99-12//99
	Oklahoma	S	17.75 MW	17.31 AW	36010 AAW	OKBLS	10//99-12//99
	Oregon	S	18.23 MW	17.55 AW	36500 AAW	ORBLS	10//99-12//99
	Pennsylvania	S	18.5 MW	17.95 AW	37330 AAW	PABLS	10//99-12//99
	Philadelphia PMSA, PA-NJ	S	18.29 MW	18.68 AW	38040 AAW	PABLS	10//99-12//99
	South Carolina	S	17.56 MW	16.77 AW	34880 AAW	SCBLS	10//99-12//99
	Greenville-Spartanburg-Anderson MSA, SC	S	16.79 MW	17.64 AW	34920 AAW	SCBLS	10//99-12//99
	South Dakota	S	17.73 MW	16.95 AW	35260 AAW	SDBLS	10//99-12//99
	Tennessee	S	17.69 MW	17.10 AW	35570 AAW	TNBLS	10//99-12//99
	Johnson City-Kingsport-Bristol MSA, TN-VA	S	16.86 MW	17.51 AW	35070 AAW	TNBLS	10//99-12//99
	Nashville MSA, TN	S	17.34 MW	17.88 AW	36070 AAW	TNBLS	10//99-12//99
	Texas	S	18.1 MW	17.53 AW	36460 AAW	TXBLS	10//99-12//99
	Utah	S	17.87 MW	17.24 AW	35850 AAW	UTBLS	10//99-12//99
	Vermont	S	17.14 MW	16.32 AW	33950 AAW	VTBLS	10//99-12//99
	Virginia	S	18.01 MW	17.39 AW	36170 AAW	VABLS	10//99-12//99
	Lynchburg MSA, VA	S	16.89 MW	17.78 AW	35130 AAW	VABLS	10//99-12//99
	Norfolk-Virginia Beach-Newport News MSA, VA-NC	S	18.10 MW	18.53 AW	37650 AAW	VABLS	10//99-12//99
	Washington	S	18.11 MW	17.45 AW	36310 AAW	WABLS	10//99-12//99
	West Virginia	S	17.71 MW	16.92 AW	35200 AAW	WVBLS	10//99-12//99
	Huntington-Ashland MSA, WV-KY-OH	S	17.01 MW	17.73 AW	35380 AAW	WVBLS	10//99-12//99
	Wisconsin	S	17.9 MW	17.10 AW	35570 AAW	WIBLS	10//99-12//99
	Wyoming	S	18.2 MW	17.66 AW	36730 AAW	WYBLS	10//99-12//99
Postal Service Mail Sorter, Processor, and Processing Machine Operator	Alabama	S	14.16 MW	13.29 AW	27650 AAW	ALBLS	10//99-12//99
	Arkansas	S	12.62 MW	12.55 AW	26100 AAW	ARBLS	10//99-12//99
	California	S	14.04 MW	14.25 AW	29650 AAW	CABLS	10//99-12//99
	Florida	S	15.42 MW	14.43 AW	30020 AAW	FLBLS	10//99-12//99
	Kansas	S	14.52 MW	14.09 AW	29310 AAW	KSBLS	10//99-12//99
	Kentucky	S	12.56 MW	13.16 AW	27380 AAW	KYBLS	10//99-12//99
	Maryland	S	17.01 MW	15.40 AW	32040 AAW	MDBLS	10//99-12//99
	Massachusetts	S	17 MW	15.88 AW	33020 AAW	MABLS	10//99-12//99

AAW Average annual wage	AOH Average offered, high	ASH Average starting, high	H Hourly	M Monthly	S Special: hourly and annual
AE Average entry wage	AOL Average offered, low	ASL Average starting, low	HI Highest wage paid	MTC Median total compensation	TQ Third quartile wage
AEX Average experienced wage	APH Average pay, high range	AW Average wage paid	HR High end range	MW Median wage paid	W Weekly
AO Average offered	APL Average pay, low range	FQ First quartile wage	LR Low end range	SQ Second quartile wage	Y Yearly

Occupation/Type/Industry	Location	Per	Low	Mid	High	Source	Date
Postal Service Mail Sorter, Processor, and Processing Machine Operator	Minnesota	S	13.61 MW	14.58 AW	30330 AAW	MNBLS	10//99-12//99
	Mississippi	S	11.86 MW	12.65 AW	26310 AAW	MSBLS	10//99-12//99
	Missouri	S	13.79 MW	13.79 AW	28680 AAW	MOBLS	10//99-12//99
	Montana	S	10.69 MW	11.27 AW	23440 AAW	MTBLS	10//99-12//99
	New Jersey	S	17.42 MW	15.87 AW	33000 AAW	NJBLS	10//99-12//99
	New York	S	16.53 MW	15.26 AW	31750 AAW	NYBLS	10//99-12//99
	North Carolina	S	14.42 MW	14.27 AW	29690 AAW	NCBLS	10//99-12//99
	North Dakota	S	11.13 MW	12.16 AW	25300 AAW	NDBLS	10//99-12//99
	Pennsylvania	S	16.22 MW	14.73 AW	30630 AAW	PABLS	10//99-12//99
	South Carolina	S	13.5 MW	13.39 AW	27850 AAW	SCBLS	10//99-12//99
	South Dakota	S	11.64 MW	12.52 AW	26050 AAW	SDBLS	10//99-12//99
	Tennessee	S	15.51 MW	14.84 AW	30870 AAW	TNBLS	10//99-12//99
	Texas	S	14.63 MW	14.27 AW	29670 AAW	TXBLS	10//99-12//99
	Virginia	S	16.03 MW	15.03 AW	31250 AAW	VABLS	10//99-12//99
	West Virginia	S	11.94 MW	12.28 AW	25540 AAW	WVBLS	10//99-12//99
	Wyoming	S	9.71 MW	10.98 AW	22850 AAW	WYBLS	10//99-12//99
Postmaster and Mail Superintendent	Alabama	S	21.34 MW	21.82 AW	45380 AAW	ALBLS	10//99-12//99
	Alaska	S	17.94 MW	17.83 AW	37090 AAW	AKBLS	10//99-12//99
	Arizona	S	22.57 MW	23.04 AW	47930 AAW	AZBLS	10//99-12//99
	Arkansas	S	20 MW	20.25 AW	42120 AAW	ARBLS	10//99-12//99
	California	S	24.14 MW	24.55 AW	51050 AAW	CABLS	10//99-12//99
	Colorado	S	20.68 MW	21.22 AW	44150 AAW	COBLS	10//99-12//99
	Connecticut	S	24.62 MW	24.89 AW	51780 AAW	CTBLS	10//99-12//99
	Delaware	S	23.74 MW	23.99 AW	49890 AAW	DEBLS	10//99-12//99
	Florida	S	25.06 MW	25.36 AW	52750 AAW	FLBLS	10//99-12//99
	Georgia	S	22.8 MW	23.15 AW	48150 AAW	GABLS	10//99-12//99
	Hawaii	S	23.14 MW	23.30 AW	48470 AAW	HIBLS	10//99-12//99
	Idaho	S	20.29 MW	20.86 AW	43400 AAW	IDBLS	10//99-12//99
	Illinois	S	20.97 MW	21.79 AW	45330 AAW	ILBLS	10//99-12//99
	Indiana	S	21.12 MW	21.60 AW	44930 AAW	INBLS	10//99-12//99
	Iowa	S	20.02 MW	20.23 AW	42090 AAW	IABLS	10//99-12//99
	Kansas	S	19.46 MW	19.36 AW	40270 AAW	KSBLS	10//99-12//99
	Kentucky	S	19.9 MW	20.12 AW	41850 AAW	KYBLS	10//99-12//99
	Louisiana	S	21.37 MW	22.19 AW	46160 AAW	LABLS	10//99-12//99
	Maine	S	20.26 MW	20.63 AW	42910 AAW	MEBLS	10//99-12//99
	Maryland	S	22.38 MW	22.68 AW	47170 AAW	MDBLS	10//99-12//99
	Massachusetts	S	24.85 MW	25.04 AW	52090 AAW	MABLS	10//99-12//99
	Michigan	S	22.66 MW	22.80 AW	47420 AAW	MIBLS	10//99-12//99
	Minnesota	S	21.02 MW	21.41 AW	44530 AAW	MNBLS	10//99-12//99
	Mississippi	S	21.2 MW	21.90 AW	45540 AAW	MSBLS	10//99-12//99
	Missouri	S	20.01 MW	20.25 AW	42120 AAW	MOBLS	10//99-12//99
	Montana	S	19.19 MW	19.10 AW	39730 AAW	MTBLS	10//99-12//99
	Nebraska	S	19.65 MW	19.79 AW	41170 AAW	NEBLS	10//99-12//99
	Nevada	S	20.16 MW	20.96 AW	43600 AAW	NVBLS	10//99-12//99
	New Hampshire	S	22.43 MW	22.38 AW	46560 AAW	NHBLS	10//99-12//99
	New Jersey	S	25.8 MW	25.84 AW	53760 AAW	NJBLS	10//99-12//99
	New Mexico	S	19.01 MW	19.01 AW	39540 AAW	NMBLS	10//99-12//99
	New York	S	22.53 MW	22.89 AW	47610 AAW	NYBLS	10//99-12//99
	North Carolina	S	22.84 MW	23.05 AW	47950 AAW	NCBLS	10//99-12//99
	North Dakota	S	18.55 MW	17.93 AW	37300 AAW	NDBLS	10//99-12//99
	Ohio	S	21.53 MW	22.23 AW	46240 AAW	OHBLS	10//99-12//99
	Oklahoma	S	20.61 MW	21.05 AW	43790 AAW	OKBLS	10//99-12//99
	Oregon	S	20.98 MW	21.68 AW	45100 AAW	ORBLS	10//99-12//99
	Pennsylvania	S	21.07 MW	21.68 AW	45100 AAW	PABLS	10//99-12//99
	Rhode Island	S	23.87 MW	24.70 AW	51370 AAW	RIBLS	10//99-12//99
	South Carolina	S	23.18 MW	23.16 AW	48170 AAW	SCBLS	10//99-12//99
	South Dakota	S	19.05 MW	18.74 AW	38980 AAW	SDBLS	10//99-12//99
	Tennessee	S	22.66 MW	22.80 AW	47430 AAW	TNBLS	10//99-12//99
	Texas	S	21.45 MW	21.92 AW	45590 AAW	TXBLS	10//99-12//99
	Utah	S	20.97 MW	21.94 AW	45630 AAW	UTBLS	10//99-12//99
	Vermont	S	20.16 MW	20.63 AW	42910 AAW	VTBLS	10//99-12//99
	Virginia	S	20.9 MW	21.34 AW	44390 AAW	VABLS	10//99-12//99
	Washington	S	21.27 MW	22.14 AW	46050 AAW	WABLS	10//99-12//99
	West Virginia	S	19.62 MW	19.82 AW	41230 AAW	WVBLS	10//99-12//99
	Wisconsin	S	21.93 MW	22.25 AW	46280 AAW	WIBLS	10//99-12//99
	Wyoming	S	19.11 MW	19.18 AW	39890 AAW	WYBLS	10//99-12//99

AAW Average annual wage	AOH Average offered, high	ASH Average starting, high	H Hourly	M Monthly	S Special: hourly and annual
AE Average entry wage	AOL Average offered, low	ASL Average starting, low	HI Highest wage paid	MTC Median total compensation	TQ Third quartile wage
AEX Average experienced wage	APH Average pay, high range	AW Average wage paid	HR High end range	MW Median wage paid	W Weekly
AO Average offered	APL Average pay, low range	FQ First quartile wage	LR Low end range	SQ Second quartile wage	Y Yearly

Occupation/Type/Industry	Location	Per	Low	Mid	High	Source	Date
Pourer and Caster							
Metal	Alabama	S	12.87 MW	13.04 AW	27120 AAW	ALBLS	10//99-12//99
Metal	Anniston MSA, AL	S	9.64 MW	9.77 AW	20060 AAW	ALBLS	10//99-12//99
Metal	Birmingham MSA, AL	S	13.93 MW	13.72 AW	28980 AAW	ALBLS	10//99-12//99
Metal	Arizona	S	13.26 MW	12.93 AW	26880 AAW	AZBLS	10//99-12//99
Metal	Phoenix-Mesa MSA, AZ	S	11.95 MW	11.56 AW	24860 AAW	AZBLS	10//99-12//99
Metal	Arkansas	S	12.55 MW	14.34 AW	29820 AAW	ARBLS	10//99-12//99
Metal	California	S	10.41 MW	11.91 AW	24770 AAW	CABLS	10//99-12//99
Metal	Los Angeles-Long Beach PMSA, CA	S	10.73 MW	9.50 AW	22310 AAW	CABLS	10//99-12//99
Metal	Oakland PMSA, CA	S	14.81 MW	14.95 AW	30810 AAW	CABLS	10//99-12//99
Metal	Orange County PMSA, CA	S	9.52 MW	8.98 AW	19800 AAW	CABLS	10//99-12//99
Metal	Riverside-San Bernardino PMSA, CA	S	13.37 MW	10.47 AW	27820 AAW	CABLS	10//99-12//99
Metal	Connecticut	S	11.01 MW	10.98 AW	22840 AAW	CTBLS	10//99-12//99
Metal	Florida	S	11.87 MW	11.65 AW	24230 AAW	FLBLS	10//99-12//99
Metal	Jacksonville MSA, FL	S	12.48 MW	12.36 AW	25960 AAW	FLBLS	10//99-12//99
Metal	Georgia	S	11.29 MW	11.14 AW	23170 AAW	GABLS	10//99-12//99
Metal	Illinois	S	11.78 MW	12.50 AW	25990 AAW	ILBLS	10//99-12//99
Metal	Chicago PMSA, IL	S	11.75 MW	11.52 AW	24430 AAW	ILBLS	10//99-12//99
Metal	Indiana	S	15.62 MW	15.41 AW	32050 AAW	INBLS	10//99-12//99
Metal	Evansville-Henderson MSA, IN-KY	S	15.74 MW	17.31 AW	32730 AAW	INBLS	10//99-12//99
Metal	Fort Wayne MSA, IN	S	11.17 MW	10.73 AW	23230 AAW	INBLS	10//99-12//99
Metal	Indianapolis MSA, IN	S	14.54 MW	13.32 AW	30250 AAW	INBLS	10//99-12//99
Metal	Iowa	S	10.91 MW	10.84 AW	22550 AAW	IABLS	10//99-12//99
Metal	Kansas	S	10.89 MW	11.23 AW	23350 AAW	KSBLS	10//99-12//99
Metal	Kentucky	S	13.38 MW	14.21 AW	29560 AAW	KYBLS	10//99-12//99
Metal	Maryland	S	13.96 MW	12.17 AW	25320 AAW	MDBLS	10//99-12//99
Metal	Massachusetts	S	12.2 MW	11.96 AW	24880 AAW	MABLS	10//99-12//99
Metal	Boston PMSA, MA-NH	S	14.56 MW	14.05 AW	30280 AAW	MABLS	10//99-12//99
Metal	Michigan	S	12.25 MW	13.18 AW	27420 AAW	MIBLS	10//99-12//99
Metal	Benton Harbor MSA, MI	S	9.62 MW	9.70 AW	20020 AAW	MIBLS	10//99-12//99
Metal	Detroit PMSA, MI	S	15.53 MW	15.82 AW	32290 AAW	MIBLS	10//99-12//99
Metal	Grand Rapids-Muskegon-Holland MSA, MI	S	11.24 MW	10.51 AW	23380 AAW	MIBLS	10//99-12//99
Metal	Minnesota	S	13.57 MW	13.21 AW	27480 AAW	MNBLS	10//99-12//99
Metal	Minneapolis-St. Paul MSA, MN-WI	S	14.04 MW	14.20 AW	29210 AAW	MNBLS	10//99-12//99
Metal	Mississippi	S	10.93 MW	11.51 AW	23940 AAW	MSBLS	10//99-12//99
Metal	Missouri	S	12.56 MW	13.00 AW	27030 AAW	MOBLS	10//99-12//99
Metal	St. Louis MSA, MO-IL	S	12.62 MW	12.45 AW	26260 AAW	MOBLS	10//99-12//99
Metal	Nebraska	S	11.39 MW	11.57 AW	24070 AAW	NEBLS	10//99-12//99
Metal	New Hampshire	S	12.91 MW	13.94 AW	28990 AAW	NHBLS	10//99-12//99
Metal	New Jersey	S	12.46 MW	14.38 AW	29900 AAW	NJBLS	10//99-12//99
Metal	Bergen-Passaic PMSA, NJ	S	10.75 MW	10.58 AW	22350 AAW	NJBLS	10//99-12//99
Metal	Newark PMSA, NJ	S	11.35 MW	11.47 AW	23610 AAW	NJBLS	10//99-12//99
Metal	New York	S	11.35 MW	12.20 AW	25380 AAW	NYBLS	10//99-12//99
Metal	Syracuse MSA, NY	S	15.90 MW	17.82 AW	33080 AAW	NYBLS	10//99-12//99
Metal	North Carolina	S	12.95 MW	13.54 AW	28150 AAW	NCBLS	10//99-12//99
Metal	Ohio	S	11.86 MW	13.06 AW	27160 AAW	OHBLS	10//99-12//99
Metal	Akron PMSA, OH	S	12.32 MW	11.80 AW	25630 AAW	OHBLS	10//99-12//99
Metal	Canton-Massillon MSA, OH	S	9.59 MW	10.12 AW	19960 AAW	OHBLS	10//99-12//99
Metal	Cincinnati PMSA, OH-KY-IN	S	13.51 MW	12.68 AW	28100 AAW	OHBLS	10//99-12//99
Metal	Cleveland-Lorain-Elyria PMSA, OH	S	15.46 MW	12.98 AW	32160 AAW	OHBLS	10//99-12//99
Metal	Columbus MSA, OH	S	14.84 MW	13.19 AW	30860 AAW	OHBLS	10//99-12//99
Metal	Dayton-Springfield MSA, OH	S	12.46 MW	12.86 AW	25920 AAW	OHBLS	10//99-12//99
Metal	Mansfield MSA, OH	S	12.09 MW	11.18 AW	25150 AAW	OHBLS	10//99-12//99
Metal	Youngstown-Warren MSA, OH	S	10.93 MW	10.20 AW	22740 AAW	OHBLS	10//99-12//99
Metal	Pennsylvania	S	13.19 MW	13.57 AW	28230 AAW	PABLS	10//99-12//99
Metal	Allentown-Bethlehem-Easton MSA, PA	S	12.88 MW	12.99 AW	26800 AAW	PABLS	10//99-12//99
Metal	Harrisburg-Lebanon-Carlisle MSA, PA	S	16.60 MW	15.98 AW	34520 AAW	PABLS	10//99-12//99
Metal	Lancaster MSA, PA	S	11.92 MW	12.21 AW	24780 AAW	PABLS	10//99-12//99
Metal	Pittsburgh MSA, PA	S	14.05 MW	13.31 AW	29210 AAW	PABLS	10//99-12//99
Metal	Reading MSA, PA	S	13.30 MW	13.46 AW	27670 AAW	PABLS	10//99-12//99
Metal	Rhode Island	S	9.95 MW	10.32 AW	21460 AAW	RIBLS	10//99-12//99
Metal	Providence-Fall River-Warwick MSA, RI-MA	S	10.36 MW	9.97 AW	21540 AAW	RIBLS	10//99-12//99
Metal	South Carolina	S	16.83 MW	14.25 AW	29640 AAW	SCBLS	10//99-12//99

AAW	Average annual wage	AOH	Average offered, high	ASH	Average starting, high
AE	Average entry wage	AOL	Average offered, low	ASL	Average starting, low
AEX	Average experienced wage	APH	Average pay, high range	AW	Average wage paid
AO	Average offered	APL	Average pay, low range	FQ	First quartile wage

H	Hourly	M	Monthly	S	Special: hourly and annual
HI	Highest wage paid	MTC	Median total compensation	TQ	Third quartile wage
HR	High end range	MW	Median wage paid	W	Weekly
LR	Low end range	SQ	Second quartile wage	Y	Yearly

Occupation/Type/Industry	Location	Per	Low	Mid	High	Source	Date
Pourer and Caster							
Metal	Tennessee	S	10.35 MW	10.48 AW	21790 AAW	TNBLS	10//99-12//99
Metal	Chattanooga MSA, TN-GA	S	10.83 MW	11.11 AW	22530 AAW	TNBLS	10//99-12//99
Metal	Texas	S	10.06 MW	10.45 AW	21730 AAW	TXBLS	10//99-12//99
Metal	Dallas PMSA, TX	S	10.00 MW	10.00 AW	20800 AAW	TXBLS	10//99-12//99
Metal	Houston PMSA, TX	S	9.96 MW	9.56 AW	20730 AAW	TXBLS	10//99-12//99
Metal	Virginia	S	12.06 MW	11.44 AW	23790 AAW	VABLS	10//99-12//99
Metal	Lynchburg MSA, VA	S	11.70 MW	12.49 AW	24330 AAW	VABLS	10//99-12//99
Metal	Washington	S	12.89 MW	12.99 AW	27020 AAW	WABLS	10//99-12//99
Metal	Seattle-Bellevue-Everett PMSA, WA	S	12.17 MW	12.62 AW	25320 AAW	WABLS	10//99-12//99
Metal	West Virginia	S	13.35 MW	14.66 AW	30500 AAW	WVBLS	10//99-12//99
Metal	Huntington-Ashland MSA, WV-KY-OH	S	16.15 MW	15.55 AW	33600 AAW	WVBLS	10//99-12//99
Metal	Wisconsin	S	13.95 MW	13.59 AW	28280 AAW	WIBLS	10//99-12//99
Metal	Milwaukee-Waukesha PMSA, WI	S	13.01 MW	12.46 AW	27070 AAW	WIBLS	10//99-12//99
Metal	Racine PMSA, WI	S	12.28 MW	11.64 AW	25540 AAW	WIBLS	10//99-12//99
Metal	Sheboygan MSA, WI	S	15.12 MW	15.24 AW	31440 AAW	WIBLS	10//99-12//99
Power Distributor and Dispatcher	Alabama	S	22.19 MW	21.73 AW	45200 AAW	ALBLS	10//99-12//99
	Alaska	S	28.39 MW	28.84 AW	59990 AAW	AKBLS	10//99-12//99
	Arkansas	S	22.43 MW	23.15 AW	48150 AAW	ARBLS	10//99-12//99
	California	S	29.67 MW	28.18 AW	58610 AAW	CABLS	10//99-12//99
	Los Angeles-Long Beach PMSA, CA	S	27.12 MW	28.23 AW	56400 AAW	CABLS	10//99-12//99
	Riverside-San Bernardino PMSA, CA	S	25.20 MW	24.26 AW	52410 AAW	CABLS	10//99-12//99
	Colorado	S	24.11 MW	23.96 AW	49830 AAW	COBLS	10//99-12//99
	Fort Collins-Loveland MSA, CO	S	24.54 MW	24.72 AW	51050 AAW	COBLS	10//99-12//99
	Connecticut	S	26.4 MW	26.90 AW	55950 AAW	CTBLS	10//99-12//99
	Delaware	S	19.68 MW	20.06 AW	41730 AAW	DEBLS	10//99-12//99
	Washington PMSA, DC-MD-VA-WV	S	21.93 MW	21.08 AW	45610 AAW	DCBLS	10//99-12//99
	Florida	S	21.91 MW	22.37 AW	46530 AAW	FLBLS	10//99-12//99
	Orlando MSA, FL	S	22.78 MW	22.57 AW	47380 AAW	FLBLS	10//99-12//99
	West Palm Beach-Boca Raton MSA, FL	S	23.30 MW	22.16 AW	48450 AAW	FLBLS	10//99-12//99
	Georgia	S	21.58 MW	21.49 AW	44690 AAW	GABLS	10//99-12//99
	Atlanta MSA, GA	S	21.92 MW	22.35 AW	45590 AAW	GABLS	10//99-12//99
	Idaho	S	26.43 MW	26.89 AW	55930 AAW	IDBLS	10//99-12//99
	Illinois	S	23.92 MW	25.55 AW	53150 AAW	ILBLS	10//99-12//99
	Chicago PMSA, IL	S	25.76 MW	23.63 AW	53580 AAW	ILBLS	10//99-12//99
	Indiana	S	20.88 MW	21.48 AW	44670 AAW	INBLS	10//99-12//99
	Evansville-Henderson MSA, IN-KY	S	19.61 MW	18.66 AW	40780 AAW	INBLS	10//99-12//99
	Gary PMSA, IN	S	19.68 MW	18.83 AW	40930 AAW	INBLS	10//99-12//99
	Indianapolis MSA, IN	S	26.84 MW	25.72 AW	55820 AAW	INBLS	10//99-12//99
	Iowa	S	21.98 MW	22.00 AW	45760 AAW	IABLS	10//99-12//99
	Kansas	S	22.25 MW	20.17 AW	41960 AAW	KSBLS	10//99-12//99
	Wichita MSA, KS	S	19.05 MW	21.78 AW	39630 AAW	KSBLS	10//99-12//99
	Kentucky	S	21.16 MW	21.53 AW	44780 AAW	KYBLS	10//99-12//99
	Maine	S	19.71 MW	20.35 AW	42320 AAW	MEBLS	10//99-12//99
	Maryland	S	19.52 MW	20.48 AW	42600 AAW	MDBLS	10//99-12//99
	Massachusetts	S	23.42 MW	23.91 AW	49740 AAW	MABLS	10//99-12//99
	Boston PMSA, MA-NH	S	23.16 MW	23.30 AW	48170 AAW	MABLS	10//99-12//99
	Michigan	S	22.62 MW	22.75 AW	47320 AAW	MIBLS	10//99-12//99
	Minnesota	S	19.96 MW	21.06 AW	43800 AAW	MNBLS	10//99-12//99
	Minneapolis-St. Paul MSA, MN-WI	S	24.75 MW	23.95 AW	51470 AAW	MNBLS	10//99-12//99
	Mississippi	S	13.83 MW	15.62 AW	32490 AAW	MSBLS	10//99-12//99
	Biloxi-Gulfport-Pascagoula MSA, MS	S	21.80 MW	19.62 AW	45350 AAW	MSBLS	10//99-12//99
	Missouri	S	22.63 MW	22.12 AW	46010 AAW	MOBLS	10//99-12//99
	Montana	S	25.08 MW	25.14 AW	52290 AAW	MTBLS	10//99-12//99
	Nebraska	S	22.47 MW	22.50 AW	46790 AAW	NEBLS	10//99-12//99
	Nevada	S	29.18 MW	28.38 AW	59020 AAW	NVBLS	10//99-12//99
	Las Vegas MSA, NV-AZ	S	28.38 MW	29.18 AW	59030 AAW	NVBLS	10//99-12//99
	New Hampshire	S	16.37 MW	19.42 AW	40380 AAW	NHBLS	10//99-12//99
	New Jersey	S	24.68 MW	25.16 AW	52330 AAW	NJBLS	10//99-12//99
	New York	S	18.62 MW	20.00 AW	41590 AAW	NYBLS	10//99-12//99
	Syracuse MSA, NY	S	15.06 MW	13.49 AW	31330 AAW	NYBLS	10//99-12//99

AAW	Average annual wage	AOH	Average offered, high	ASH	Average starting, high	H	Hourly	M	Monthly	S	Special: hourly and annual
AE	Average entry wage	AOL	Average offered, low	ASL	Average starting, low	HI	Highest wage paid	MTC	Median total compensation	TQ	Third quartile wage
AEX	Average experienced wage	APH	Average pay, high range	AW	Average wage paid	HR	High end range	MW	Median wage paid	W	Weekly
AO	Average offered	APL	Average pay, low range	FQ	First quartile wage	LR	Low end range	SQ	Second quartile wage	Y	Yearly

Occupation/Type/Industry	Location	Per	Low	Mid	High	Source	Date
Power Distributor and Dispatcher	North Carolina	S	19.76 MW	19.24 AW	40020 AAW	NCBLS	10//99-12//99
	North Dakota	S	29.34 MW	27.53 AW	57250 AAW	NDBLS	10//99-12//99
	Ohio	S	22.26 MW	21.85 AW	45440 AAW	OHBLS	10//99-12//99
	Cleveland-Lorain-Elyria PMSA, OH	S	20.22 MW	21.60 AW	42050 AAW	OHBLS	10//99-12//99
	Columbus MSA, OH	S	21.45 MW	20.44 AW	44620 AAW	OHBLS	10//99-12//99
	Oklahoma	S	18.8 MW	18.12 AW	37690 AAW	OKBLS	10//99-12//99
	Oregon	S	25.03 MW	25.64 AW	53330 AAW	ORBLS	10//99-12//99
	Portland-Vancouver PMSA, OR-WA	S	27.51 MW	26.97 AW	57210 AAW	ORBLS	10//99-12//99
	Pennsylvania	S	24.08 MW	24.73 AW	51430 AAW	PABLS	10//99-12//99
	South Carolina	S	22.33 MW	21.16 AW	44020 AAW	SCBLS	10//99-12//99
	South Dakota	S	23.06 MW	22.27 AW	46310 AAW	SDBLS	10//99-12//99
	Tennessee	S	22.11 MW	21.82 AW	45380 AAW	TNBLS	10//99-12//99
	Johnson City-Kingsport-Bristol MSA, TN-VA	S	21.14 MW	20.13 AW	43980 AAW	TNBLS	10//99-12//99
	Knoxville MSA, TN	S	20.05 MW	20.59 AW	41710 AAW	TNBLS	10//99-12//99
	Texas	S	19.32 MW	19.86 AW	41310 AAW	TXBLS	10//99-12//99
	Beaumont-Port Arthur MSA, TX	S	27.64 MW	29.04 AW	57500 AAW	TXBLS	10//99-12//99
	Houston PMSA, TX	S	21.48 MW	21.80 AW	44680 AAW	TXBLS	10//99-12//99
	San Antonio MSA, TX	S	11.76 MW	11.48 AW	24460 AAW	TXBLS	10//99-12//99
	Utah	S	23.48 MW	23.65 AW	49200 AAW	UTBLS	10//99-12//99
	Vermont	S	27.44 MW	26.32 AW	54750 AAW	VTBLS	10//99-12//99
	Virginia	S	20.73 MW	20.98 AW	43650 AAW	VABLS	10//99-12//99
	Norfolk-Virginia Beach-Newport News MSA, VA-NC	S	18.62 MW	19.24 AW	38720 AAW	VABLS	10//99-12//99
	Richmond-Petersburg MSA, VA	S	21.97 MW	21.31 AW	45690 AAW	VABLS	10//99-12//99
	Washington	S	26.47 MW	26.81 AW	55760 AAW	WABLS	10//99-12//99
	Richland-Kennewick-Pasco MSA, WA	S	25.14 MW	24.96 AW	52290 AAW	WABLS	10//99-12//99
	Seattle-Bellevue-Everett PMSA, WA	S	28.22 MW	28.35 AW	58700 AAW	WABLS	10//99-12//99
	West Virginia	S	18.88 MW	19.42 AW	40390 AAW	WVBLS	10//99-12//99
	Wisconsin	S	21.05 MW	21.82 AW	45390 AAW	WIBLS	10//99-12//99
	Wyoming	S	19.88 MW	19.92 AW	41430 AAW	WYBLS	10//99-12//99
Power Plant Operator	Alaska	S	25.45 MW	25.13 AW	52260 AAW	AKBLS	10//99-12//99
	Arizona	S	24.5 MW	24.12 AW	50180 AAW	AZBLS	10//99-12//99
	Arkansas	S	24.46 MW	24.40 AW	50750 AAW	ARBLS	10//99-12//99
	California	S	21.75 MW	21.49 AW	44690 AAW	CABLS	10//99-12//99
	Fresno MSA, CA	S	23.36 MW	23.95 AW	48590 AAW	CABLS	10//99-12//99
	Los Angeles-Long Beach PMSA, CA	S	20.94 MW	20.94 AW	43540 AAW	CABLS	10//99-12//99
	Oakland PMSA, CA	S	22.24 MW	22.20 AW	46270 AAW	CABLS	10//99-12//99
	San Jose PMSA, CA	S	20.85 MW	20.49 AW	43360 AAW	CABLS	10//99-12//99
	Colorado	S	21.92 MW	20.78 AW	43210 AAW	COBLS	10//99-12//99
	Connecticut	S	20.96 MW	21.08 AW	43840 AAW	CTBLS	10//99-12//99
	Florida	S	19.26 MW	19.38 AW	40320 AAW	FLBLS	10//99-12//99
	Lakeland-Winter Haven MSA, FL	S	17.99 MW	17.86 AW	37430 AAW	FLBLS	10//99-12//99
	Orlando MSA, FL	S	19.02 MW	19.03 AW	39550 AAW	FLBLS	10//99-12//99
	Tampa-St. Petersburg-Clearwater MSA, FL	S	22.36 MW	23.22 AW	46510 AAW	FLBLS	10//99-12//99
	West Palm Beach-Boca Raton MSA, FL	S	18.47 MW	18.54 AW	38410 AAW	FLBLS	10//99-12//99
	Georgia	S	19.66 MW	20.53 AW	42710 AAW	GABLS	10//99-12//99
	Idaho	S	24.23 MW	23.82 AW	49540 AAW	IDBLS	10//99-12//99
	Illinois	S	21.4 MW	21.26 AW	44220 AAW	ILBLS	10//99-12//99
	Chicago PMSA, IL	S	19.28 MW	19.32 AW	40100 AAW	ILBLS	10//99-12//99
	Indiana	S	20.33 MW	20.43 AW	42490 AAW	INBLS	10//99-12//99
	Gary PMSA, IN	S	21.10 MW	21.40 AW	43880 AAW	INBLS	10//99-12//99
	Iowa	S	18.96 MW	19.12 AW	39770 AAW	IABLS	10//99-12//99
	Kansas	S	18.77 MW	17.81 AW	37050 AAW	KSBLS	10//99-12//99
	Kentucky	S	19.7 MW	19.96 AW	41510 AAW	KYBLS	10//99-12//99
	Louisiana	S	20.71 MW	20.28 AW	42170 AAW	LABLS	10//99-12//99
	New Orleans MSA, LA	S	21.57 MW	22.41 AW	44860 AAW	LABLS	10//99-12//99
	Massachusetts	S	19.3 MW	19.71 AW	41000 AAW	MABLS	10//99-12//99
	Boston PMSA, MA-NH	S	19.81 MW	19.39 AW	41210 AAW	MABLS	10//99-12//99
	Springfield MSA, MA	S	22.45 MW	21.84 AW	46710 AAW	MABLS	10//99-12//99
	Michigan	S	19.37 MW	19.32 AW	40190 AAW	MIBLS	10//99-12//99

Occupation/Type/Industry	Location	Per	Low	Mid	High	Source	Date
Power Plant Operator	Minnesota	S	23.69 MW	23.29 AW	48440 AAW	MNBLS	10//99-12//99
	Minneapolis-St. Paul MSA, MN-WI	S	23.89 MW	24.53 AW	49690 AAW	MNBLS	10//99-12//99
	Mississippi	S	20.26 MW	19.96 AW	41520 AAW	MSBLS	10//99-12//99
	Missouri	S	23.17 MW	21.51 AW	44730 AAW	MOBLS	10//99-12//99
	St. Louis MSA, MO-IL	S	24.15 MW	24.81 AW	50230 AAW	MOBLS	10//99-12//99
	Nebraska	S	16.69 MW	18.05 AW	37550 AAW	NEBLS	10//99-12//99
	Nevada	S	23.21 MW	22.13 AW	46020 AAW	NVBLS	10//99-12//99
	Las Vegas MSA, NV-AZ	S	24.59 MW	25.44 AW	51140 AAW	NVBLS	10//99-12//99
	New Hampshire	S	17.43 MW	18.10 AW	37650 AAW	NHBLS	10//99-12//99
	New Jersey	S	23.56 MW	23.36 AW	48600 AAW	NJBLS	10//99-12//99
	New Mexico	S	22.85 MW	22.39 AW	46570 AAW	NMBLS	10//99-12//99
	New York	S	20.37 MW	22.19 AW	46150 AAW	NYBLS	10//99-12//99
	Buffalo-Niagara Falls MSA, NY	S	18.21 MW	18.47 AW	37870 AAW	NYBLS	10//99-12//99
	Nassau-Suffolk PMSA, NY	S	25.87 MW	27.30 AW	53800 AAW	NYBLS	10//99-12//99
	New York PMSA, NY	S	22.23 MW	21.45 AW	46230 AAW	NYBLS	10//99-12//99
	North Carolina	S	22.59 MW	21.34 AW	44390 AAW	NCBLS	10//99-12//99
	Ohio	S	20.65 MW	20.57 AW	42790 AAW	OHBLS	10//99-12//99
	Cleveland-Lorain-Elyria PMSA, OH	S	20.95 MW	20.79 AW	43580 AAW	OHBLS	10//99-12//99
	Oklahoma	S	21.07 MW	20.30 AW	42220 AAW	OKBLS	10//99-12//99
	Oregon	S	19.03 MW	20.26 AW	42130 AAW	ORBLS	10//99-12//99
	Pennsylvania	S	22.26 MW	20.89 AW	43450 AAW	PABLS	10//99-12//99
	Harrisburg-Lebanon-Carlisle MSA, PA	S	22.73 MW	23.87 AW	47270 AAW	PABLS	10//99-12//99
	Philadelphia PMSA, PA-NJ	S	21.56 MW	23.05 AW	44850 AAW	PABLS	10//99-12//99
	Pittsburgh MSA, PA	S	21.58 MW	22.91 AW	44890 AAW	PABLS	10//99-12//99
	Reading MSA, PA	S	20.89 MW	22.03 AW	43440 AAW	PABLS	10//99-12//99
	South Carolina	S	22.33 MW	23.88 AW	49670 AAW	SCBLS	10//99-12//99
	Texas	S	22.69 MW	20.47 AW	42580 AAW	TXBLS	10//99-12//99
	Fort Worth-Arlington PMSA, TX	S	18.95 MW	21.55 AW	39420 AAW	TXBLS	10//99-12//99
	Houston PMSA, TX	S	21.64 MW	23.66 AW	45020 AAW	TXBLS	10//99-12//99
	San Antonio MSA, TX	S	16.23 MW	13.45 AW	33760 AAW	TXBLS	10//99-12//99
	Utah	S	19.61 MW	19.57 AW	40690 AAW	UTBLS	10//99-12//99
	Provo-Orem MSA, UT	S	15.73 MW	15.48 AW	32720 AAW	UTBLS	10//99-12//99
	Salt Lake City-Ogden MSA, UT	S	21.05 MW	22.07 AW	43780 AAW	UTBLS	10//99-12//99
	Virginia	S	15.69 MW	17.41 AW	36210 AAW	VABLS	10//99-12//99
	Richmond-Petersburg MSA, VA	S	18.75 MW	21.56 AW	39000 AAW	VABLS	10//99-12//99
	Washington	S	23.29 MW	25.35 AW	52720 AAW	WABLS	10//99-12//99
	West Virginia	S	20.97 MW	19.75 AW	41080 AAW	WVBLS	10//99-12//99
	Wisconsin	S	22.07 MW	20.20 AW	42020 AAW	WIBLS	10//99-12//99
	Milwaukee-Waukesha PMSA, WI	S	21.51 MW	22.70 AW	44740 AAW	WIBLS	10//99-12//99
	Puerto Rico	S	11.75 MW	10.91 AW	22700 AAW	PRBLS	10//99-12//99
	San Juan-Bayamon PMSA, PR	S	11.59 MW	11.96 AW	24110 AAW	PRBLS	10//99-12//99
Prepress Technician and Worker	Alabama	S	10.18 MW	10.84 AW	22540 AAW	ALBLS	10//99-12//99
	Alaska	S	22.27 MW	18.41 AW	38300 AAW	AKBLS	10//99-12//99
	Arizona	S	12.47 MW	13.17 AW	27390 AAW	AZBLS	10//99-12//99
	Arkansas	S	10.58 MW	10.91 AW	22690 AAW	ARBLS	10//99-12//99
	California	S	17.03 MW	17.33 AW	36040 AAW	CABLS	10//99-12//99
	Colorado	S	15.5 MW	15.94 AW	33150 AAW	COBLS	10//99-12//99
	Connecticut	S	16.17 MW	16.81 AW	34970 AAW	CTBLS	10//99-12//99
	Delaware	S	18.24 MW	17.24 AW	35860 AAW	DEBLS	10//99-12//99
	Florida	S	11.91 MW	12.34 AW	25680 AAW	FLBLS	10//99-12//99
	Georgia	S	13.43 MW	13.77 AW	28650 AAW	GABLS	10//99-12//99
	Hawaii	S	11.49 MW	11.96 AW	24870 AAW	HIBLS	10//99-12//99
	Idaho	S	10.8 MW	12.09 AW	25140 AAW	IDBLS	10//99-12//99
	Indiana	S	12.72 MW	13.28 AW	27630 AAW	INBLS	10//99-12//99
	Iowa	S	11.44 MW	12.42 AW	25840 AAW	IABLS	10//99-12//99
	Kansas	S	12.97 MW	14.06 AW	29230 AAW	KSBLS	10//99-12//99
	Kentucky	S	11.99 MW	13.60 AW	28280 AAW	KYBLS	10//99-12//99
	Louisiana	S	11 MW	10.89 AW	22650 AAW	LABLS	10//99-12//99
	Maine	S	11.12 MW	12.13 AW	25240 AAW	MEBLS	10//99-12//99
	Maryland	S	14.78 MW	15.13 AW	31470 AAW	MDBLS	10//99-12//99
	Massachusetts	S	16.2 MW	16.40 AW	34110 AAW	MABLS	10//99-12//99
	Michigan	S	13.57 MW	14.08 AW	29300 AAW	MIBLS	10//99-12//99
	Minnesota	S	15.21 MW	15.43 AW	32090 AAW	MNBLS	10//99-12//99
	Mississippi	S	11.26 MW	11.60 AW	24120 AAW	MSBLS	10//99-12//99

AAW	Average annual wage	AOH	Average offered, high	ASH	Average starting, high	H	Hourly	M	Monthly	S	Special: hourly and annual
AE	Average entry wage	AOL	Average offered, low	ASL	Average starting, low	HI	Highest wage paid	MTC	Median total compensation	TQ	Third quartile wage
AEX	Average experienced wage	APH	Average pay, high range	AW	Average wage paid	HR	High end range	MW	Median wage paid	W	Weekly
AO	Average offered	APL	Average pay, low range	FQ	First quartile wage	LR	Low end range	SQ	Second quartile wage	Y	Yearly

Occupation/Type/Industry	Location	Per	Low	Mid	High	Source	Date
Prepress Technician and Worker	Missouri	S	11.72 MW	12.85 AW	26730 AAW	MOBLS	10//99-12//99
	Montana	S	12.2 MW	13.28 AW	27630 AAW	MTBLS	10//99-12//99
	Nebraska	S	11.14 MW	11.57 AW	24060 AAW	NEBLS	10//99-12//99
	Nevada	S	12.17 MW	12.17 AW	25320 AAW	NVBLS	10//99-12//99
	New Hampshire	S	13.27 MW	13.71 AW	28510 AAW	NHBLS	10//99-12//99
	New Jersey	S	15.81 MW	16.13 AW	33560 AAW	NJBLS	10//99-12//99
	New Mexico	S	11.52 MW	11.68 AW	24300 AAW	NMBLS	10//99-12//99
	New York	S	15.99 MW	16.42 AW	34160 AAW	NYBLS	10//99-12//99
	North Carolina	S	12.56 MW	12.93 AW	26890 AAW	NCBLS	10//99-12//99
	North Dakota	S	10 MW	9.99 AW	20780 AAW	NDBLS	10//99-12//99
	Ohio	S	13.65 MW	14.15 AW	29440 AAW	OHBLS	10//99-12//99
	Oklahoma	S	10.93 MW	11.33 AW	23570 AAW	OKBLS	10//99-12//99
	Oregon	S	15.89 MW	16.40 AW	34110 AAW	ORBLS	10//99-12//99
	Pennsylvania	S	15.73 MW	15.83 AW	32930 AAW	PABLS	10//99-12//99
	Rhode Island	S	13.21 MW	14.75 AW	30680 AAW	RIBLS	10//99-12//99
	South Carolina	S	11.24 MW	11.93 AW	24820 AAW	SCBLS	10//99-12//99
	South Dakota	S	10.15 MW	10.93 AW	22740 AAW	SDBLS	10//99-12//99
	Tennessee	S	13.26 MW	13.45 AW	27980 AAW	TNBLS	10//99-12//99
	Texas	S	13.62 MW	14.03 AW	29170 AAW	TXBLS	10//99-12//99
	Utah	S	10.24 MW	11.29 AW	23490 AAW	UTBLS	10//99-12//99
	Vermont	S	13.07 MW	13.62 AW	28340 AAW	VTBLS	10//99-12//99
	Virginia	S	12.8 MW	13.13 AW	27310 AAW	VABLS	10//99-12//99
	Washington	S	17.3 MW	17.96 AW	37350 AAW	WABLS	10//99-12//99
	West Virginia	S	11.73 MW	11.08 AW	23040 AAW	WVBLS	10//99-12//99
	Wisconsin	S	13.28 MW	14.36 AW	29870 AAW	WIBLS	10//99-12//99
	Wyoming	S	10.74 MW	9.97 AW	20740 AAW	WYBLS	10//99-12//99
	Puerto Rico	S	9.98 MW	11.15 AW	23180 AAW	PRBLS	10//99-12//99
Preschool Teacher							
Except Special Education	Alabama	S	6.55 MW	7.28 AW	15140 AAW	ALBLS	10//99-12//99
Except Special Education	Alaska	S	9.76 MW	11.24 AW	23380 AAW	AKBLS	10//99-12//99
Except Special Education	Arizona	S	6.88 MW	7.89 AW	16420 AAW	AZBLS	10//99-12//99
Except Special Education	Arkansas	S	6.88 MW	7.98 AW	16600 AAW	ARBLS	10//99-12//99
Except Special Education	California	S	9.42 MW	10.16 AW	21130 AAW	CABLS	10//99-12//99
Except Special Education	Colorado	S	8.51 MW	9.03 AW	18780 AAW	COBLS	10//99-12//99
Except Special Education	Connecticut	S	9.9 MW	11.05 AW	22990 AAW	CTBLS	10//99-12//99
Except Special Education	Delaware	S	8.08 MW	8.77 AW	18230 AAW	DEBLS	10//99-12//99
Except Special Education	District of Columbia	S	11.21 MW	12.29 AW	25570 AAW	DCBLS	10//99-12//99
Except Special Education	Florida	S	7.69 MW	8.30 AW	17270 AAW	FLBLS	10//99-12//99
Except Special Education	Georgia	S	8.18 MW	9.64 AW	20060 AAW	GABLS	10//99-12//99
Except Special Education	Hawaii	S	10.54 MW	10.42 AW	21680 AAW	HIBLS	10//99-12//99
Except Special Education	Idaho	S	7.53 MW	7.90 AW	16430 AAW	IDBLS	10//99-12//99
Except Special Education	Illinois	S	8.68 MW	9.65 AW	20080 AAW	ILBLS	10//99-12//99
Except Special Education	Indiana	S	7.85 MW	8.54 AW	17760 AAW	INBLS	10//99-12//99
Except Special Education	Iowa	S	7.54 MW	8.17 AW	16980 AAW	IABLS	10//99-12//99
Except Special Education	Kansas	S	8.3 MW	9.09 AW	18920 AAW	KSBLS	10//99-12//99
Except Special Education	Kentucky	S	7.75 MW	8.88 AW	18470 AAW	KYBLS	10//99-12//99
Except Special Education	Louisiana	S	6.95 MW	8.60 AW	17880 AAW	LABLS	10//99-12//99
Except Special Education	Maine	S	8.68 MW	8.97 AW	18650 AAW	MEBLS	10//99-12//99
Except Special Education	Maryland	S	9.75 MW	11.30 AW	23500 AAW	MDBLS	10//99-12//99
Except Special Education	Massachusetts	S	10.84 MW	11.37 AW	23650 AAW	MABLS	10//99-12//99
Except Special Education	Michigan	S	10.12 MW	11.23 AW	23370 AAW	MIBLS	10//99-12//99
Except Special Education	Minnesota	S	10.08 MW	11.42 AW	23750 AAW	MNBLS	10//99-12//99
Except Special Education	Mississippi	S	7.49 MW	7.98 AW	16600 AAW	MSBLS	10//99-12//99
Except Special Education	Missouri	S	7.36 MW	8.53 AW	17740 AAW	MOBLS	10//99-12//99
Except Special Education	Montana	S	8.17 MW	9.21 AW	19150 AAW	MTBLS	10//99-12//99
Except Special Education	Nebraska	S	7.7 MW	8.33 AW	17330 AAW	NEBLS	10//99-12//99
Except Special Education	Nevada	S	8.04 MW	8.78 AW	18260 AAW	NVBLS	10//99-12//99
Except Special Education	New Hampshire	S	9.04 MW	9.34 AW	19420 AAW	NHBLS	10//99-12//99
Except Special Education	New Jersey	S	9.76 MW	10.62 AW	22080 AAW	NJBLS	10//99-12//99
Except Special Education	New Mexico	S	7.37 MW	8.02 AW	16680 AAW	NMBLS	10//99-12//99
Except Special Education	New York	S	9.74 MW	10.61 AW	22070 AAW	NYBLS	10//99-12//99
Except Special Education	North Carolina	S	7.76 MW	8.49 AW	17670 AAW	NCBLS	10//99-12//99
Except Special Education	North Dakota	S	7.53 MW	8.01 AW	16670 AAW	NDBLS	10//99-12//99
Except Special Education	Ohio	S	7.86 MW	8.89 AW	18500 AAW	OHBLS	10//99-12//99
Except Special Education	Oklahoma	S	6.85 MW	7.55 AW	15710 AAW	OKBLS	10//99-12//99
Except Special Education	Oregon	S	8.42 MW	9.13 AW	18990 AAW	ORBLS	10//99-12//99
Except Special Education	Pennsylvania	S	8.39 MW	9.18 AW	19090 AAW	PABLS	10//99-12//99
Except Special Education	Rhode Island	S	10.11 MW	10.92 AW	22720 AAW	RIBLS	10//99-12//99
Except Special Education	South Carolina	S	7.85 MW	9.31 AW	19360 AAW	SCBLS	10//99-12//99
Except Special Education	South Dakota	S	9.45 MW	9.68 AW	20140 AAW	SDBLS	10//99-12//99
Except Special Education	Tennessee	S	6.92 MW	7.39 AW	15380 AAW	TNBLS	10//99-12//99
Except Special Education	Texas	S	7.28 MW	8.42 AW	17520 AAW	TXBLS	10//99-12//99

AAW Average annual wage	AOH Average offered, high	ASH Average starting, high	H Hourly	M Monthly	S Special: hourly and annual
AE Average entry wage	AOL Average offered, low	ASL Average starting, low	HI Highest wage paid	MTC Median total compensation	TQ Third quartile wage
AEX Average experienced wage	APH Average pay, high range	AW Average wage paid	HR High end range	MW Median wage paid	W Weekly
AO Average offered	APL Average pay, low range	FQ First quartile wage	LR Low end range	SQ Second quartile wage	Y Yearly

Occupation/Type/Industry	Location	Per	Low	Mid	High	Source	Date
Preschool Teacher							
Except Special Education	Utah	S	7.73 MW	8.56 AW	17810 AAW	UTBLS	10//99-12//99
Except Special Education	Vermont	S	9.52 MW	10.70 AW	22260 AAW	VTBLS	10//99-12//99
Except Special Education	Virginia	S	8.07 MW	9.23 AW	19190 AAW	VABLS	10//99-12//99
Except Special Education	Washington	S	8.69 MW	9.79 AW	20370 AAW	WABLS	10//99-12//99
Except Special Education	West Virginia	S	7.79 MW	9.06 AW	18850 AAW	WVBLS	10//99-12//99
Except Special Education	Wisconsin	S	8 MW	9.06 AW	18840 AAW	WIBLS	10//99-12//99
Except Special Education	Wyoming	S	8.78 MW	9.26 AW	19270 AAW	WYBLS	10//99-12//99
Except Special Education	Puerto Rico	S	7.55 MW	7.65 AW	15910 AAW	PRBLS	10//99-12//99
Except Special Education	Guam	S	8.56 MW	9.67 AW	20110 AAW	GUBLS	10//99-12//99
President							
2-Year College	United States	Y		113176 AW		AS&U2	1999-2000
4-Year College	United States	Y		142253 AW		AS&U2	1999-2000
Construction Contractor	United States	Y		150000 MW		ENR2	1999
Foundry	United States	Y	120000 MW	140800 AW		MODCAS	1999
On-line Enterprise	United States	Y		234100 AW		WSJ1	2000
Public Relations/Communications	United States	Y		135000 AW		COMW	1999
President/CEO/Executive Vice President							
Real Estate	United States	Y		150555 AW		TRAVWK4	1999
Presser							
Textile, Garment, and Related Material	Alabama	S	7.24 MW	7.45 AW	15500 AAW	ALBLS	10//99-12//99
Textile, Garment, and Related Material	Arizona	S	7.51 MW	7.57 AW	15740 AAW	AZBLS	10//99-12//99
Textile, Garment, and Related Material	Arkansas	S	6.92 MW	7.15 AW	14860 AAW	ARBLS	10//99-12//99
Textile, Garment, and Related Material	California	S	7.31 MW	7.84 AW	16310 AAW	CABLS	10//99-12//99
Textile, Garment, and Related Material	Colorado	S	8.45 MW	8.13 AW	16910 AAW	COBLS	10//99-12//99
Textile, Garment, and Related Material	Connecticut	S	8.38 MW	8.73 AW	18160 AAW	CTBLS	10//99-12//99
Textile, Garment, and Related Material	Delaware	S	6.66 MW	7.36 AW	15320 AAW	DEBLS	10//99-12//99
Textile, Garment, and Related Material	District of Columbia	S	7.59 MW	7.64 AW	15880 AAW	DCBLS	10//99-12//99
Textile, Garment, and Related Material	Florida	S	7.73 MW	7.87 AW	16380 AAW	FLBLS	10//99-12//99
Textile, Garment, and Related Material	Georgia	S	7.34 MW	7.39 AW	15370 AAW	GABLS	10//99-12//99
Textile, Garment, and Related Material	Hawaii	S	7.58 MW	7.78 AW	16170 AAW	HIBLS	10//99-12//99
Textile, Garment, and Related Material	Idaho	S	7.07 MW	7.17 AW	14900 AAW	IDBLS	10//99-12//99
Textile, Garment, and Related Material	Illinois	S	7.98 MW	8.55 AW	17780 AAW	ILBLS	10//99-12//99
Textile, Garment, and Related Material	Indiana	S	7.96 MW	8.16 AW	16980 AAW	INBLS	10//99-12//99
Textile, Garment, and Related Material	Iowa	S	7.78 MW	7.99 AW	16630 AAW	IABLS	10//99-12//99
Textile, Garment, and Related Material	Kansas	S	7.37 MW	7.69 AW	15990 AAW	KSBLS	10//99-12//99
Textile, Garment, and Related Material	Kentucky	S	6.99 MW	7.35 AW	15290 AAW	KYBLS	10//99-12//99
Textile, Garment, and Related Material	Louisiana	S	6.37 MW	6.60 AW	13740 AAW	LABLS	10//99-12//99
Textile, Garment, and Related Material	Maine	S	7.63 MW	7.77 AW	16160 AAW	MEBLS	10//99-12//99
Textile, Garment, and Related Material	Maryland	S	7.68 MW	8.00 AW	16640 AAW	MDBLS	10//99-12//99
Textile, Garment, and Related Material	Massachusetts	S	8.65 MW	9.03 AW	18780 AAW	MABLS	10//99-12//99
Textile, Garment, and Related Material	Michigan	S	7.72 MW	7.74 AW	16100 AAW	MIBLS	10//99-12//99
Textile, Garment, and Related Material	Minnesota	S	9.12 MW	8.95 AW	18620 AAW	MNBLS	10//99-12//99
Textile, Garment, and Related Material	Mississippi	S	6.73 MW	6.91 AW	14380 AAW	MSBLS	10//99-12//99
Textile, Garment, and Related Material	Missouri	S	7.81 MW	7.86 AW	16350 AAW	MOBLS	10//99-12//99
Textile, Garment, and Related Material	Montana	S	7.09 MW	7.00 AW	14550 AAW	MTBLS	10//99-12//99
Textile, Garment, and Related Material	Nebraska	S	7.56 MW	7.53 AW	15660 AAW	NEBLS	10//99-12//99
Textile, Garment, and Related Material	Nevada	S	7.99 MW	8.03 AW	16700 AAW	NVBLS	10//99-12//99
Textile, Garment, and Related Material	New Hampshire	S	7.95 MW	8.03 AW	16690 AAW	NHBLS	10//99-12//99
Textile, Garment, and Related Material	New Jersey	S	8.69 MW	8.85 AW	18400 AAW	NJBLS	10//99-12//99
Textile, Garment, and Related Material	New Mexico	S	6.5 MW	6.94 AW	14430 AAW	NMBLS	10//99-12//99
Textile, Garment, and Related Material	New York	S	7.71 MW	8.24 AW	17130 AAW	NYBLS	10//99-12//99
Textile, Garment, and Related Material	North Carolina	S	7.65 MW	7.81 AW	16240 AAW	NCBLS	10//99-12//99
Textile, Garment, and Related Material	North Dakota	S	6.7 MW	7.01 AW	14580 AAW	NDBLS	10//99-12//99
Textile, Garment, and Related Material	Ohio	S	7.52 MW	7.65 AW	15900 AAW	OHBLS	10//99-12//99
Textile, Garment, and Related Material	Oklahoma	S	6.61 MW	6.88 AW	14310 AAW	OKBLS	10//99-12//99
Textile, Garment, and Related Material	Oregon	S	8.84 MW	8.95 AW	18610 AAW	ORBLS	10//99-12//99
Textile, Garment, and Related Material	Pennsylvania	S	7.64 MW	7.93 AW	16500 AAW	PABLS	10//99-12//99
Textile, Garment, and Related Material	Rhode Island	S	10.73 MW	12.41 AW	25800 AAW	RIBLS	10//99-12//99
Textile, Garment, and Related Material	South Carolina	S	7.42 MW	7.42 AW	15440 AAW	SCBLS	10//99-12//99
Textile, Garment, and Related Material	South Dakota	S	7.1 MW	7.18 AW	14940 AAW	SDBLS	10//99-12//99
Textile, Garment, and Related Material	Tennessee	S	6.98 MW	7.16 AW	14880 AAW	TNBLS	10//99-12//99
Textile, Garment, and Related Material	Texas	S	6.72 MW	6.99 AW	14540 AAW	TXBLS	10//99-12//99
Textile, Garment, and Related Material	Utah	S	7.58 MW	8.05 AW	16730 AAW	UTBLS	10//99-12//99
Textile, Garment, and Related Material	Vermont	S	6.85 MW	7.17 AW	14920 AAW	VTBLS	10//99-12//99
Textile, Garment, and Related Material	Virginia	S	7.33 MW	7.58 AW	15760 AAW	VABLS	10//99-12//99
Textile, Garment, and Related Material	Washington	S	8.84 MW	8.94 AW	18600 AAW	WABLS	10//99-12//99
Textile, Garment, and Related Material	West Virginia	S	6.3 MW	6.64 AW	13800 AAW	WVBLS	10//99-12//99

AAW Average annual wage	AOH Average offered, high	ASH Average starting, high	H Hourly	M Monthly	S Special: hourly and annual
AE Average entry wage	AOL Average offered, low	ASL Average starting, low	HI Highest wage paid	MTC Median total compensation	TQ Third quartile wage
AEX Average experienced wage	APH Average pay, high range	AW Average wage paid	HR High end range	MW Median wage paid	W Weekly
AO Average offered	APL Average pay, low range	FQ First quartile wage	LR Low end range	SQ Second quartile wage	Y Yearly

Occupation/Type/Industry	Location	Per	Low	Mid	High	Source	Date
Presser							
Textile, Garment, and Related Material	Wisconsin	S	7.72 MW	7.80 AW	16220 AAW	WIBLS	10//99-12//99
Textile, Garment, and Related Material	Wyoming	S	6.15 MW	6.61 AW	13740 AAW	WYBLS	10//99-12//99
Textile, Garment, and Related Material	Puerto Rico	S	6.07 MW	5.93 AW	12330 AAW	PRBLS	10//99-12//99
Textile, Garment, and Related Material	Virgin Islands	S	5.88 MW	5.77 AW	12000 AAW	VIBLS	10//99-12//99
Principal							
School	Cobb County, GA	Y		75399 AW		ATJOCO	1998
Printing Machine Operator	Alabama	S	11.55 MW	11.97 AW	24890 AAW	ALBLS	10//99-12//99
	Alaska	S	15.92 MW	18.68 AW	38860 AAW	AKBLS	10//99-12//99
	Arizona	S	11.56 MW	12.29 AW	25560 AAW	AZBLS	10//99-12//99
	Arkansas	S	11.28 MW	11.73 AW	24400 AAW	ARBLS	10//99-12//99
	California	S	12.78 MW	14.28 AW	29700 AAW	CABLS	10//99-12//99
	Colorado	S	13.38 MW	14.10 AW	29320 AAW	COBLS	10//99-12//99
	Connecticut	S	14.45 MW	15.04 AW	31270 AAW	CTBLS	10//99-12//99
	Delaware	S	15.54 MW	16.44 AW	34190 AAW	DEBLS	10//99-12//99
	Florida	S	11.74 MW	12.27 AW	25510 AAW	FLBLS	10//99-12//99
	Georgia	S	12.78 MW	13.92 AW	28950 AAW	GABLS	10//99-12//99
	Hawaii	S	12.21 MW	12.64 AW	26280 AAW	HIBLS	10//99-12//99
	Idaho	S	12.8 MW	13.00 AW	27050 AAW	IDBLS	10//99-12//99
	Illinois	S	13.76 MW	14.69 AW	30560 AAW	ILBLS	10//99-12//99
	Indiana	S	12.97 MW	13.26 AW	27590 AAW	INBLS	10//99-12//99
	Iowa	S	11.95 MW	12.64 AW	26290 AAW	IABLS	10//99-12//99
	Kansas	S	12.22 MW	12.90 AW	26840 AAW	KSBLS	10//99-12//99
	Kentucky	S	12.78 MW	13.10 AW	27240 AAW	KYBLS	10//99-12//99
	Louisiana	S	10.86 MW	11.33 AW	23570 AAW	LABLS	10//99-12//99
	Maine	S	11.35 MW	11.86 AW	24660 AAW	MEBLS	10//99-12//99
	Maryland	S	14.91 MW	15.56 AW	32360 AAW	MDBLS	10//99-12//99
	Massachusetts	S	14.25 MW	15.19 AW	31600 AAW	MABLS	10//99-12//99
	Michigan	S	13.33 MW	13.89 AW	28880 AAW	MIBLS	10//99-12//99
	Minnesota	S	14.81 MW	15.49 AW	32210 AAW	MNBLS	10//99-12//99
	Mississippi	S	11.55 MW	12.01 AW	24970 AAW	MSBLS	10//99-12//99
	Missouri	S	12.86 MW	13.74 AW	28590 AAW	MOBLS	10//99-12//99
	Montana	S	10.2 MW	10.82 AW	22500 AAW	MTBLS	10//99-12//99
	Nebraska	S	11.98 MW	12.93 AW	26890 AAW	NEBLS	10//99-12//99
	Nevada	S	12.18 MW	13.31 AW	27680 AAW	NVBLS	10//99-12//99
	New Hampshire	S	13.43 MW	13.86 AW	28820 AAW	NHBLS	10//99-12//99
	New Jersey	S	14.75 MW	15.81 AW	32890 AAW	NJBLS	10//99-12//99
	New Mexico	S	10.49 MW	10.72 AW	22290 AAW	NMBLS	10//99-12//99
	New York	S	13.61 MW	14.99 AW	31180 AAW	NYBLS	10//99-12//99
	North Carolina	S	12.14 MW	12.73 AW	26490 AAW	NCBLS	10//99-12//99
	North Dakota	S	11.92 MW	12.50 AW	26010 AAW	NDBLS	10//99-12//99
	Ohio	S	13.24 MW	13.79 AW	28680 AAW	OHBLS	10//99-12//99
	Oklahoma	S	10.96 MW	11.48 AW	23870 AAW	OKBLS	10//99-12//99
	Oregon	S	14.29 MW	14.63 AW	30430 AAW	ORBLS	10//99-12//99
	Pennsylvania	S	13.62 MW	14.13 AW	29390 AAW	PABLS	10//99-12//99
	Rhode Island	S	12.11 MW	12.87 AW	26760 AAW	RIBLS	10//99-12//99
	South Carolina	S	10.58 MW	11.22 AW	23340 AAW	SCBLS	10//99-12//99
	South Dakota	S	11.35 MW	11.75 AW	24450 AAW	SDBLS	10//99-12//99
	Tennessee	S	11.46 MW	12.24 AW	25460 AAW	TNBLS	10//99-12//99
	Texas	S	11.61 MW	12.69 AW	26390 AAW	TXBLS	10//99-12//99
	Utah	S	11.22 MW	12.06 AW	25090 AAW	UTBLS	10//99-12//99
	Vermont	S	13.5 MW	14.01 AW	29140 AAW	VTBLS	10//99-12//99
	Virginia	S	12.97 MW	13.63 AW	28350 AAW	VABLS	10//99-12//99
	Washington	S	14.24 MW	14.58 AW	30330 AAW	WABLS	10//99-12//99
	West Virginia	S	10.64 MW	11.35 AW	23600 AAW	WVBLS	10//99-12//99
	Wisconsin	S	13.39 MW	14.21 AW	29550 AAW	WIBLS	10//99-12//99
	Wyoming	S	10.95 MW	11.01 AW	22900 AAW	WYBLS	10//99-12//99
	Puerto Rico	S	7.42 MW	8.54 AW	17760 AAW	PRBLS	10//99-12//99
	Guam	S	10.79 MW	10.89 AW	22650 AAW	GUBLS	10//99-12//99
Private Detective and Investigator	Alabama	S	6.45 MW	8.79 AW	18270 AAW	ALBLS	10//99-12//99
	Mobile MSA, AL	S	10.15 MW	6.57 AW	21110 AAW	ALBLS	10//99-12//99
	Arizona	S	13.4 MW	15.18 AW	31580 AAW	AZBLS	10//99-12//99
	Phoenix-Mesa MSA, AZ	S	14.28 MW	13.17 AW	29700 AAW	AZBLS	10//99-12//99
	Tucson MSA, AZ	S	16.59 MW	17.68 AW	34510 AAW	AZBLS	10//99-12//99
	Arkansas	S	14.03 MW	16.62 AW	34560 AAW	ARBLS	10//99-12//99
	Little Rock-North Little Rock MSA, AR	S	12.99 MW	14.11 AW	27030 AAW	ARBLS	10//99-12//99
	California	S	15.31 MW	17.31 AW	36000 AAW	CABLS	10//99-12//99
	Los Angeles-Long Beach PMSA, CA	S	15.91 MW	13.20 AW	33090 AAW	CABLS	10//99-12//99

AAW Average annual wage	**AOH** Average offered, high	**ASH** Average starting, high	**H** Hourly	**M** Monthly	**S** Special: hourly and annual
AE Average entry wage	**AOL** Average offered, low	**ASL** Average starting, low	**HI** Highest wage paid	**MTC** Median total compensation	**TQ** Third quartile wage
AEX Average experienced wage	**APH** Average pay, high range	**AW** Average wage paid	**HR** High end range	**MW** Median wage paid	**W** Weekly
AO Average offered	**APL** Average pay, low range	**FQ** First quartile wage	**LR** Low end range	**SQ** Second quartile wage	**Y** Yearly

Occupation/Type/Industry	Location	Per	Low	Mid	High	Source	Date
Private Detective and Investigator	Oakland PMSA, CA	S	11.27 MW	9.74 AW	23450 AAW	CABLS	10//99-12//99
	Orange County PMSA, CA	S	12.55 MW	10.55 AW	26100 AAW	CABLS	10//99-12//99
	Riverside-San Bernardino PMSA, CA	S	17.10 MW	17.29 AW	35560 AAW	CABLS	10//99-12//99
	Sacramento PMSA, CA	S	14.01 MW	13.13 AW	29130 AAW	CABLS	10//99-12//99
	San Diego MSA, CA	S	17.41 MW	18.36 AW	36210 AAW	CABLS	10//99-12//99
	San Francisco PMSA, CA	S	24.48 MW	22.42 AW	50910 AAW	CABLS	10//99-12//99
	San Jose PMSA, CA	S	16.79 MW	15.38 AW	34910 AAW	CABLS	10//99-12//99
	Colorado	S	11.79 MW	13.05 AW	27150 AAW	COBLS	10//99-12//99
	Denver PMSA, CO	S	13.27 MW	11.91 AW	27600 AAW	COBLS	10//99-12//99
	Connecticut	S	10.69 MW	12.87 AW	26780 AAW	CTBLS	10//99-12//99
	Hartford MSA, CT	S	14.39 MW	11.70 AW	29930 AAW	CTBLS	10//99-12//99
	New Haven-Meriden PMSA, CT	S	10.94 MW	10.33 AW	22760 AAW	CTBLS	10//99-12//99
	Stamford-Norwalk PMSA, CT	S	15.79 MW	11.84 AW	32830 AAW	CTBLS	10//99-12//99
	Waterbury PMSA, CT	S	11.07 MW	10.26 AW	23020 AAW	CTBLS	10//99-12//99
	Delaware	S	14.38 MW	16.17 AW	33640 AAW	DEBLS	10//99-12//99
	Wilmington-Newark PMSA, DE-MD	S	19.15 MW	18.44 AW	39830 AAW	DEBLS	10//99-12//99
	Washington PMSA, DC-MD-VA-WV	S	12.57 MW	11.92 AW	26150 AAW	DCBLS	10//99-12//99
	Florida	S	12.58 MW	13.05 AW	27140 AAW	FLBLS	10//99-12//99
	Fort Lauderdale PMSA, FL	S	14.64 MW	14.23 AW	30440 AAW	FLBLS	10//99-12//99
	Jacksonville MSA, FL	S	13.06 MW	12.53 AW	27160 AAW	FLBLS	10//99-12//99
	Lakeland-Winter Haven MSA, FL	S	13.17 MW	13.38 AW	27390 AAW	FLBLS	10//99-12//99
	Miami PMSA, FL	S	14.41 MW	13.93 AW	29980 AAW	FLBLS	10//99-12//99
	Naples MSA, FL	S	11.24 MW	11.41 AW	23380 AAW	FLBLS	10//99-12//99
	Orlando MSA, FL	S	13.74 MW	13.59 AW	28580 AAW	FLBLS	10//99-12//99
	Pensacola MSA, FL	S	16.82 MW	17.56 AW	34990 AAW	FLBLS	10//99-12//99
	Sarasota-Bradenton MSA, FL	S	13.04 MW	12.72 AW	27130 AAW	FLBLS	10//99-12//99
	Tampa-St. Petersburg-Clearwater MSA, FL	S	12.17 MW	12.06 AW	25310 AAW	FLBLS	10//99-12//99
	West Palm Beach-Boca Raton MSA, FL	S	13.01 MW	12.48 AW	27060 AAW	FLBLS	10//99-12//99
	Georgia	S	15.2 MW	15.81 AW	32880 AAW	GABLS	10//99-12//99
	Atlanta MSA, GA	S	16.50 MW	16.40 AW	34320 AAW	GABLS	10//99-12//99
	Hawaii	S	10.47 MW	11.43 AW	23780 AAW	HIBLS	10//99-12//99
	Honolulu MSA, HI	S	11.44 MW	9.68 AW	23800 AAW	HIBLS	10//99-12//99
	Illinois	S	18.24 MW	17.23 AW	35850 AAW	ILBLS	10//99-12//99
	Chicago PMSA, IL	S	17.62 MW	18.48 AW	36640 AAW	ILBLS	10//99-12//99
	Indiana	S	10.5 MW	12.33 AW	25650 AAW	INBLS	10//99-12//99
	Indianapolis MSA, IN	S	14.82 MW	13.32 AW	30840 AAW	INBLS	10//99-12//99
	Terre Haute MSA, IN	S	7.98 MW	7.81 AW	16600 AAW	INBLS	10//99-12//99
	Iowa	S	15.23 MW	19.20 AW	39950 AAW	IABLS	10//99-12//99
	Cedar Rapids MSA, IA	S	16.16 MW	14.12 AW	33610 AAW	IABLS	10//99-12//99
	Des Moines MSA, IA	S	26.39 MW	29.91 AW	54900 AAW	IABLS	10//99-12//99
	Kansas	S	9.97 MW	11.51 AW	23940 AAW	KSBLS	10//99-12//99
	Wichita MSA, KS	S	9.61 MW	9.41 AW	20000 AAW	KSBLS	10//99-12//99
	Kentucky	S	10.42 MW	12.97 AW	26980 AAW	KYBLS	10//99-12//99
	Lexington MSA, KY	S	16.42 MW	11.90 AW	34150 AAW	KYBLS	10//99-12//99
	Louisville MSA, KY-IN	S	11.90 MW	10.41 AW	24760 AAW	KYBLS	10//99-12//99
	Louisiana	S	14.71 MW	14.50 AW	30150 AAW	LABLS	10//99-12//99
	New Orleans MSA, LA	S	15.90 MW	16.45 AW	33080 AAW	LABLS	10//99-12//99
	Maine	S	10.6 MW	12.53 AW	26060 AAW	MEBLS	10//99-12//99
	Maryland	S	11.62 MW	14.02 AW	29160 AAW	MDBLS	10//99-12//99
	Baltimore PMSA, MD	S	14.66 MW	11.81 AW	30490 AAW	MDBLS	10//99-12//99
	Massachusetts	S	17.9 MW	16.24 AW	33770 AAW	MABLS	10//99-12//99
	Boston PMSA, MA-NH	S	17.48 MW	18.56 AW	36350 AAW	MABLS	10//99-12//99
	Pittsfield MSA, MA	S	10.13 MW	9.83 AW	21080 AAW	MABLS	10//99-12//99
	Michigan	S	10.96 MW	11.63 AW	24180 AAW	MIBLS	10//99-12//99
	Ann Arbor PMSA, MI	S	11.01 MW	11.54 AW	22910 AAW	MIBLS	10//99-12//99
	Detroit PMSA, MI	S	12.99 MW	11.62 AW	27010 AAW	MIBLS	10//99-12//99
	Flint PMSA, MI	S	14.30 MW	12.03 AW	29750 AAW	MIBLS	10//99-12//99
	Grand Rapids-Muskegon-Holland MSA, MI	S	11.42 MW	11.56 AW	23740 AAW	MIBLS	10//99-12//99
	Lansing-East Lansing MSA, MI	S	12.29 MW	10.89 AW	25570 AAW	MIBLS	10//99-12//99
	Saginaw-Bay City-Midland MSA, MI	S	10.72 MW	11.01 AW	22300 AAW	MIBLS	10//99-12//99
	Minnesota	S	12.76 MW	15.84 AW	32950 AAW	MNBLS	10//99-12//99
	Minneapolis-St. Paul MSA, MN-WI	S	15.14 MW	12.89 AW	31480 AAW	MNBLS	10//99-12//99

AAW Average annual wage	**AOH** Average offered, high	**ASH** Average starting, high	**H** Hourly	**M** Monthly	**S** Special: hourly and annual
AE Average entry wage	**AOL** Average offered, low	**ASL** Average starting, low	**HI** Highest wage paid	**MTC** Median total compensation	**TQ** Third quartile wage
AEX Average experienced wage	**APH** Average pay, high range	**AW** Average wage paid	**HR** High end range	**MW** Median wage paid	**W** Weekly
AO Average offered	**APL** Average pay, low range	**FQ** First quartile wage	**LR** Low end range	**SQ** Second quartile wage	**Y** Yearly

Occupation/Type/Industry	Location	Per	Low	Mid	High	Source	Date
Private Detective and Investigator	Mississippi	S	10.22 MW	10.93 AW	22740 AAW	MSBLS	10//99-12//99
	Jackson MSA, MS	S	13.14 MW	10.46 AW	27330 AAW	MSBLS	10//99-12//99
	Missouri	S	13.78 MW	15.32 AW	31870 AAW	MOBLS	10//99-12//99
	Kansas City MSA, MO-KS	S	18.11 MW	21.11 AW	37670 AAW	MOBLS	10//99-12//99
	St. Louis MSA, MO-IL	S	12.66 MW	12.12 AW	26320 AAW	MOBLS	10//99-12//99
	Nebraska	S	9.56 MW	9.60 AW	19970 AAW	NEBLS	10//99-12//99
	Nevada	S	14.32 MW	14.30 AW	29740 AAW	NVBLS	10//99-12//99
	Las Vegas MSA, NV-AZ	S	17.41 MW	15.78 AW	36200 AAW	NVBLS	10//99-12//99
	New Hampshire	S	11.16 MW	12.92 AW	26860 AAW	NHBLS	10//99-12//99
	Atlantic-Cape May PMSA, NJ	S	16.10 MW	15.82 AW	33490 AAW	NJBLS	10//99-12//99
	Bergen-Passaic PMSA, NJ	S	23.47 MW	24.51 AW	48810 AAW	NJBLS	10//99-12//99
	Middlesex-Somerset- Hunterdon PMSA, NJ	S	11.82 MW	8.64 AW	24600 AAW	NJBLS	10//99-12//99
	Newark PMSA, NJ	S	22.49 MW	22.76 AW	46770 AAW	NJBLS	10//99-12//99
	New Mexico	S	7.74 MW	9.31 AW	19370 AAW	NMBLS	10//99-12//99
	Albuquerque MSA, NM	S	9.24 MW	8.92 AW	19220 AAW	NMBLS	10//99-12//99
	New York	S	11.07 MW	15.52 AW	32280 AAW	NYBLS	10//99-12//99
	Albany-Schenectady-Troy MSA, NY	S	14.60 MW	17.36 AW	30370 AAW	NYBLS	10//99-12//99
	Binghamton MSA, NY	S	11.36 MW	8.12 AW	23620 AAW	NYBLS	10//99-12//99
	Buffalo-Niagara Falls MSA, NY	S	16.65 MW	11.20 AW	34640 AAW	NYBLS	10//99-12//99
	Nassau-Suffolk PMSA, NY	S	17.69 MW	16.38 AW	36800 AAW	NYBLS	10//99-12//99
	New York PMSA, NY	S	17.26 MW	12.78 AW	35900 AAW	NYBLS	10//99-12//99
	Newburgh PMSA, NY-PA	S	12.10 MW	8.20 AW	25180 AAW	NYBLS	10//99-12//99
	Rochester MSA, NY	S	14.36 MW	10.12 AW	29870 AAW	NYBLS	10//99-12//99
	Syracuse MSA, NY	S	10.67 MW	9.70 AW	22190 AAW	NYBLS	10//99-12//99
	North Carolina	S	12.64 MW	14.62 AW	30400 AAW	NCBLS	10//99-12//99
	Charlotte-Gastonia-Rock Hill MSA, NC-SC	S	16.59 MW	17.62 AW	34510 AAW	NCBLS	10//99-12//99
	Greensboro--Winston-Salem-- High Point MSA, NC	S	15.61 MW	11.48 AW	32460 AAW	NCBLS	10//99-12//99
	Raleigh-Durham-Chapel Hill MSA, NC	S	13.51 MW	12.26 AW	28110 AAW	NCBLS	10//99-12//99
	Ohio	S	11.9 MW	12.27 AW	25530 AAW	OHBLS	10//99-12//99
	Cincinnati PMSA, OH-KY-IN	S	11.50 MW	9.75 AW	23910 AAW	OHBLS	10//99-12//99
	Cleveland-Lorain-Elyria PMSA, OH	S	12.58 MW	12.23 AW	26160 AAW	OHBLS	10//99-12//99
	Columbus MSA, OH	S	11.98 MW	11.54 AW	24930 AAW	OHBLS	10//99-12//99
	Dayton-Springfield MSA, OH	S	10.72 MW	10.35 AW	22300 AAW	OHBLS	10//99-12//99
	Toledo MSA, OH	S	10.92 MW	10.53 AW	22710 AAW	OHBLS	10//99-12//99
	Oklahoma	S	9.89 MW	11.28 AW	23470 AAW	OKBLS	10//99-12//99
	Oklahoma City MSA, OK	S	12.29 MW	10.26 AW	25570 AAW	OKBLS	10//99-12//99
	Tulsa MSA, OK	S	11.77 MW	10.07 AW	24470 AAW	OKBLS	10//99-12//99
	Oregon	S	11.42 MW	12.46 AW	25920 AAW	ORBLS	10//99-12//99
	Portland-Vancouver PMSA, OR-WA	S	12.46 MW	11.56 AW	25920 AAW	ORBLS	10//99-12//99
	Pennsylvania	S	17.22 MW	17.93 AW	37300 AAW	PABLS	10//99-12//99
	Harrisburg-Lebanon-Carlisle MSA, PA	S	20.78 MW	19.10 AW	43220 AAW	PABLS	10//99-12//99
	Pittsburgh MSA, PA	S	19.01 MW	18.15 AW	39530 AAW	PABLS	10//99-12//99
	Rhode Island	S	10.41 MW	11.16 AW	23220 AAW	RIBLS	10//99-12//99
	Providence-Fall River- Warwick MSA, RI-MA	S	11.89 MW	10.66 AW	24720 AAW	RIBLS	10//99-12//99
	South Carolina	S	12.31 MW	13.62 AW	28330 AAW	SCBLS	10//99-12//99
	Greenville-Spartanburg- Anderson MSA, SC	S	11.80 MW	10.04 AW	24550 AAW	SCBLS	10//99-12//99
	Myrtle Beach MSA, SC	S	13.32 MW	11.49 AW	27710 AAW	SCBLS	10//99-12//99
	Tennessee	S	12.24 MW	13.42 AW	27920 AAW	TNBLS	10//99-12//99
	Clarksville-Hopkinsville MSA, TN-KY	S	11.64 MW	10.56 AW	24220 AAW	TNBLS	10//99-12//99
	Knoxville MSA, TN	S	13.10 MW	11.84 AW	27240 AAW	TNBLS	10//99-12//99
	Memphis MSA, TN-AR-MS	S	12.10 MW	11.93 AW	25180 AAW	MSBLS	10//99-12//99
	Nashville MSA, TN	S	13.24 MW	12.82 AW	27530 AAW	TNBLS	10//99-12//99
	Texas	S	15.13 MW	16.07 AW	33430 AAW	TXBLS	10//99-12//99
	Amarillo MSA, TX	S	21.94 MW	19.80 AW	45630 AAW	TXBLS	10//99-12//99
	Beaumont-Port Arthur MSA, TX	S	10.37 MW	8.85 AW	21570 AAW	TXBLS	10//99-12//99
	Corpus Christi MSA, TX	S	15.26 MW	12.95 AW	31730 AAW	TXBLS	10//99-12//99
	Dallas PMSA, TX	S	19.93 MW	19.15 AW	41460 AAW	TXBLS	10//99-12//99
	El Paso MSA, TX	S	12.15 MW	11.74 AW	25280 AAW	TXBLS	10//99-12//99

AAW Average annual wage	**AOH** Average offered, high	**ASH** Average starting, high	**H** Hourly	**M** Monthly	**S** Special: hourly and annual
AE Average entry wage	**AOL** Average offered, low	**ASL** Average starting, low	**HI** Highest wage paid	**MTC** Median total compensation	**TQ** Third quartile wage
AEX Average experienced wage	**APH** Average pay, high range	**AW** Average wage paid	**HR** High end range	**MW** Median wage paid	**W** Weekly
AO Average offered	**APL** Average pay, low range	**FQ** First quartile wage	**LR** Low end range	**SQ** Second quartile wage	**Y** Yearly

Occupation/Type/Industry	Location	Per	Low	Mid	High	Source	Date
Private Detective and Investigator	Fort Worth-Arlington PMSA, TX	S	13.35 MW	11.52 AW	27760 AAW	TXBLS	10//99-12//99
	Galveston-Texas City PMSA, TX	S	15.34 MW	15.12 AW	31910 AAW	TXBLS	10//99-12//99
	Houston PMSA, TX	S	14.28 MW	14.06 AW	29700 AAW	TXBLS	10//99-12//99
	McAllen-Edinburg-Mission MSA, TX	S	13.91 MW	13.29 AW	28940 AAW	TXBLS	10//99-12//99
	San Antonio MSA, TX	S	13.60 MW	12.83 AW	28280 AAW	TXBLS	10//99-12//99
	Tyler MSA, TX	S	10.80 MW	9.92 AW	22460 AAW	TXBLS	10//99-12//99
	Utah	S	10.33 MW	13.54 AW	28160 AAW	UTBLS	10//99-12//99
	Salt Lake City-Ogden MSA, UT	S	10.90 MW	10.10 AW	22670 AAW	UTBLS	10//99-12//99
	Vermont	S	9.78 MW	10.73 AW	22330 AAW	VTBLS	10//99-12//99
	Burlington MSA, VT	S	9.51 MW	9.63 AW	19780 AAW	VTBLS	10//99-12//99
	Virginia	S	10.2 MW	10.85 AW	22560 AAW	VABLS	10//99-12//99
	Charlottesville MSA, VA	S	9.72 MW	9.64 AW	20220 AAW	VABLS	10//99-12//99
	Norfolk-Virginia Beach-Newport News MSA, VA-NC	S	11.81 MW	11.67 AW	24560 AAW	VABLS	10//99-12//99
	Washington	S	22.29 MW	19.82 AW	41220 AAW	WABLS	10//99-12//99
	Seattle-Bellevue-Everett PMSA, WA	S	20.04 MW	20.59 AW	41670 AAW	WABLS	10//99-12//99
	Yakima MSA, WA	S	23.30 MW	24.20 AW	48470 AAW	WABLS	10//99-12//99
	West Virginia	S	10.92 MW	11.60 AW	24130 AAW	WVBLS	10//99-12//99
	Wisconsin	S	10.74 MW	12.00 AW	24950 AAW	WIBLS	10//99-12//99
	Green Bay MSA, WI	S	9.45 MW	9.38 AW	19650 AAW	WIBLS	10//99-12//99
	Madison MSA, WI	S	15.44 MW	13.96 AW	32120 AAW	WIBLS	10//99-12//99
	Milwaukee-Waukesha PMSA, WI	S	12.03 MW	10.64 AW	25020 AAW	WIBLS	10//99-12//99
Probation Officer and Correctional Treatment Specialist	Alabama	S	17.77 MW	17.80 AW	37020 AAW	ALBLS	10//99-12//99
	Alaska	S	20.31 MW	20.91 AW	43490 AAW	AKBLS	10//99-12//99
	Arizona	S	15.84 MW	16.37 AW	34040 AAW	AZBLS	10//99-12//99
	Flagstaff MSA, AZ-UT	S	15.16 MW	15.25 AW	31530 AAW	AZBLS	10//99-12//99
	Arkansas	S	12.28 MW	12.78 AW	26590 AAW	ARBLS	10//99-12//99
	Fayetteville-Springdale-Rogers MSA, AR	S	12.00 MW	11.88 AW	24960 AAW	ARBLS	10//99-12//99
	Little Rock-North Little Rock MSA, AR	S	14.54 MW	13.63 AW	30240 AAW	ARBLS	10//99-12//99
	California	S	23.9 MW	23.96 AW	49840 AAW	CABLS	10//99-12//99
	Fresno MSA, CA	S	31.60 MW	31.55 AW	65730 AAW	CABLS	10//99-12//99
	Los Angeles-Long Beach PMSA, CA	S	24.34 MW	24.15 AW	50620 AAW	CABLS	10//99-12//99
	Riverside-San Bernardino PMSA, CA	S	23.44 MW	23.38 AW	48750 AAW	CABLS	10//99-12//99
	San Francisco PMSA, CA	S	30.54 MW	30.59 AW	63520 AAW	CABLS	10//99-12//99
	Denver PMSA, CO	S	20.01 MW	19.97 AW	41620 AAW	COBLS	10//99-12//99
	Florida	S	15.19 MW	15.49 AW	32210 AAW	FLBLS	10//99-12//99
	Georgia	S	14.4 MW	15.08 AW	31370 AAW	GABLS	10//99-12//99
	Atlanta MSA, GA	S	13.78 MW	13.14 AW	28660 AAW	GABLS	10//99-12//99
	Augusta-Aiken MSA, GA-SC	S	13.41 MW	12.60 AW	27880 AAW	GABLS	10//99-12//99
	Idaho	S	15.45 MW	15.55 AW	32340 AAW	IDBLS	10//99-12//99
	Illinois	S	18.7 MW	18.39 AW	38250 AAW	ILBLS	10//99-12//99
	Chicago PMSA, IL	S	18.43 MW	18.70 AW	38340 AAW	ILBLS	10//99-12//99
	Indiana	S	16.11 MW	15.96 AW	33190 AAW	INBLS	10//99-12//99
	Fort Wayne MSA, IN	S	18.12 MW	18.32 AW	37690 AAW	INBLS	10//99-12//99
	Indianapolis MSA, IN	S	14.56 MW	14.67 AW	30290 AAW	INBLS	10//99-12//99
	Iowa	S	11.76 MW	11.62 AW	24170 AAW	IABLS	10//99-12//99
	Lawrence PMSA, MA-NH	S	19.24 MW	19.70 AW	40020 AAW	MABLS	10//99-12//99
	Michigan	S	20.98 MW	21.44 AW	44600 AAW	MIBLS	10//99-12//99
	Detroit PMSA, MI	S	21.61 MW	20.99 AW	44950 AAW	MIBLS	10//99-12//99
	Kalamazoo-Battle Creek MSA, MI	S	21.42 MW	21.42 AW	44560 AAW	MIBLS	10//99-12//99
	Minnesota	S	23.26 MW	23.38 AW	48630 AAW	MNBLS	10//99-12//99
	Minneapolis-St. Paul MSA, MN-WI	S	23.80 MW	24.02 AW	49500 AAW	MNBLS	10//99-12//99
	Mississippi	S	10.68 MW	11.33 AW	23560 AAW	MSBLS	10//99-12//99
	Kansas City MSA, MO-KS	S	17.38 MW	16.17 AW	36150 AAW	MOBLS	10//99-12//99
	Billings MSA, MT	S	15.11 MW	15.20 AW	31430 AAW	MTBLS	10//99-12//99
	Nebraska	S	12.53 MW	12.17 AW	25320 AAW	NEBLS	10//99-12//99

AAW	Average annual wage	AOH	Average offered, high	ASH	Average starting, high	H	Hourly
AE	Average entry wage	AOL	Average offered, low	ASL	Average starting, low	HI	Highest wage paid
AEX	Average experienced wage	APH	Average pay, high range	AW	Average wage paid	HR	High end range
AO	Average offered	APL	Average pay, low range	FQ	First quartile wage	LR	Low end range

M	Monthly	S	Special: hourly and annual
MTC	Median total compensation	TQ	Third quartile wage
MW	Median wage paid	W	Weekly
SQ	Second quartile wage	Y	Yearly

Occupation/Type/Industry	Location	Per	Low	Mid	High	Source	Date
Probation Officer and Correctional Treatment Specialist	Omaha MSA, NE-IA	S	14.18 MW	14.10 AW	29480 AAW	NEBLS	10//99-12//99
	Nevada	S	20.87 MW	22.04 AW	45850 AAW	NVBLS	10//99-12//99
	New Jersey	S	20.38 MW	21.30 AW	44310 AAW	NJBLS	10//99-12//99
	New York	S	21.71 MW	21.79 AW	45310 AAW	NYBLS	10//99-12//99
	Albany-Schenectady-Troy MSA, NY	S	22.64 MW	21.49 AW	47090 AAW	NYBLS	10//99-12//99
	Buffalo-Niagara Falls MSA, NY	S	22.55 MW	23.46 AW	46910 AAW	NYBLS	10//99-12//99
	Nassau-Suffolk PMSA, NY	S	23.56 MW	23.62 AW	49010 AAW	NYBLS	10//99-12//99
	Rochester MSA, NY	S	18.80 MW	18.90 AW	39100 AAW	NYBLS	10//99-12//99
	North Carolina	S	14.05 MW	14.34 AW	29830 AAW	NCBLS	10//99-12//99
	Charlotte-Gastonia-Rock Hill MSA, NC-SC	S	13.51 MW	13.09 AW	28100 AAW	NCBLS	10//99-12//99
	Canton-Massillon MSA, OH	S	14.34 MW	13.27 AW	29820 AAW	OHBLS	10//99-12//99
	Cleveland-Lorain-Elyria PMSA, OH	S	15.32 MW	14.49 AW	31860 AAW	OHBLS	10//99-12//99
	Toledo MSA, OH	S	14.07 MW	13.18 AW	29270 AAW	OHBLS	10//99-12//99
	Oregon	S	19.08 MW	18.98 AW	39480 AAW	ORBLS	10//99-12//99
	Portland-Vancouver PMSA, OR-WA	S	18.79 MW	18.83 AW	39080 AAW	ORBLS	10//99-12//99
	Pennsylvania	S	14.97 MW	15.20 AW	31610 AAW	PABLS	10//99-12//99
	Philadelphia PMSA, PA-NJ	S	15.75 MW	15.41 AW	32760 AAW	PABLS	10//99-12//99
	South Carolina	S	12.94 MW	13.60 AW	28290 AAW	SCBLS	10//99-12//99
	Charleston-North Charleston MSA, SC	S	12.95 MW	11.94 AW	26930 AAW	SCBLS	10//99-12//99
	Texas	S	14.81 MW	14.84 AW	30880 AAW	TXBLS	10//99-12//99
	Dallas PMSA, TX	S	14.66 MW	14.42 AW	30500 AAW	TXBLS	10//99-12//99
	Longview-Marshall MSA, TX	S	15.41 MW	15.27 AW	32050 AAW	TXBLS	10//99-12//99
	Texarkana MSA, TX-Texarkana, AR	S	14.17 MW	14.06 AW	29470 AAW	TXBLS	10//99-12//99
	Virginia	S	17.62 MW	18.37 AW	38200 AAW	VABLS	10//99-12//99
	Washington	S	18.74 MW	18.64 AW	38770 AAW	WABLS	10//99-12//99
	Bremerton PMSA, WA	S	21.89 MW	22.39 AW	45520 AAW	WABLS	10//99-12//99
	West Virginia	S	10.24 MW	10.27 AW	21370 AAW	WVBLS	10//99-12//99
	Wyoming	S	10.85 MW	11.00 AW	22870 AAW	WYBLS	10//99-12//99
Procurement Clerk	Alabama	S	11.53 MW	11.82 AW	24590 AAW	ALBLS	10//99-12//99
	Alaska	S	14.83 MW	15.71 AW	32670 AAW	AKBLS	10//99-12//99
	Arizona	S	11.77 MW	12.03 AW	25010 AAW	AZBLS	10//99-12//99
	Arkansas	S	10.59 MW	11.01 AW	22890 AAW	ARBLS	10//99-12//99
	California	S	14.04 MW	14.25 AW	29650 AAW	CABLS	10//99-12//99
	Colorado	S	13.07 MW	12.95 AW	26940 AAW	COBLS	10//99-12//99
	Connecticut	S	13.21 MW	13.52 AW	28120 AAW	CTBLS	10//99-12//99
	Delaware	S	13.2 MW	13.84 AW	28780 AAW	DEBLS	10//99-12//99
	Florida	S	10.66 MW	11.01 AW	22910 AAW	FLBLS	10//99-12//99
	Georgia	S	11.74 MW	12.01 AW	24980 AAW	GABLS	10//99-12//99
	Idaho	S	11.46 MW	11.41 AW	23730 AAW	IDBLS	10//99-12//99
	Illinois	S	11.9 MW	12.35 AW	25690 AAW	ILBLS	10//99-12//99
	Indiana	S	10.67 MW	11.15 AW	23190 AAW	INBLS	10//99-12//99
	Iowa	S	10.44 MW	10.99 AW	22860 AAW	IABLS	10//99-12//99
	Kansas	S	11.74 MW	12.14 AW	25260 AAW	KSBLS	10//99-12//99
	Kentucky	S	10.45 MW	10.90 AW	22680 AAW	KYBLS	10//99-12//99
	Louisiana	S	11.09 MW	11.74 AW	24420 AAW	LABLS	10//99-12//99
	Maine	S	12.23 MW	12.50 AW	26000 AAW	MEBLS	10//99-12//99
	Maryland	S	12.91 MW	13.18 AW	27410 AAW	MDBLS	10//99-12//99
	Massachusetts	S	13.35 MW	13.64 AW	28370 AAW	MABLS	10//99-12//99
	Michigan	S	12.08 MW	13.46 AW	28000 AAW	MIBLS	10//99-12//99
	Minnesota	S	11.95 MW	12.31 AW	25610 AAW	MNBLS	10//99-12//99
	Mississippi	S	11.27 MW	11.43 AW	23770 AAW	MSBLS	10//99-12//99
	Missouri	S	10.79 MW	11.46 AW	23830 AAW	MOBLS	10//99-12//99
	Montana	S	10.4 MW	10.53 AW	21910 AAW	MTBLS	10//99-12//99
	Nebraska	S	10.78 MW	11.00 AW	22880 AAW	NEBLS	10//99-12//99
	Nevada	S	12.89 MW	12.73 AW	26490 AAW	NVBLS	10//99-12//99
	New Hampshire	S	11.52 MW	12.18 AW	25330 AAW	NHBLS	10//99-12//99
	New Jersey	S	13.48 MW	13.90 AW	28910 AAW	NJBLS	10//99-12//99
	New Mexico	S	12.56 MW	12.42 AW	25830 AAW	NMBLS	10//99-12//99
	New York	S	12.52 MW	12.92 AW	26870 AAW	NYBLS	10//99-12//99
	North Carolina	S	11.87 MW	12.17 AW	25310 AAW	NCBLS	10//99-12//99
	North Dakota	S	10.69 MW	10.72 AW	22310 AAW	NDBLS	10//99-12//99
	Ohio	S	11.98 MW	12.27 AW	25510 AAW	OHBLS	10//99-12//99

AAW Average annual wage	AOH Average offered, high	ASH Average starting, high	H Hourly	M Monthly	S Special: hourly and annual
AE Average entry wage	AOL Average offered, low	ASL Average starting, low	HI Highest wage paid	MTC Median total compensation	TQ Third quartile wage
AEX Average experienced wage	APH Average pay, high range	AW Average wage paid	HR High end range	MW Median wage paid	W Weekly
AO Average offered	APL Average pay, low range	FQ First quartile wage	LR Low end range	SQ Second quartile wage	Y Yearly

Occupation/Type/Industry	Location	Per	Low	Mid	High	Source	Date
Procurement Clerk	Oklahoma	S	11.96 MW	12.19 AW	25360 AAW	OKBLS	10//99-12//99
	Oregon	S	12.75 MW	13.06 AW	27170 AAW	ORBLS	10//99-12//99
	Pennsylvania	S	13.13 MW	12.96 AW	26960 AAW	PABLS	10//99-12//99
	Rhode Island	S	10.76 MW	11.17 AW	23240 AAW	RIBLS	10//99-12//99
	South Carolina	S	10.87 MW	11.73 AW	24390 AAW	SCBLS	10//99-12//99
	South Dakota	S	10.1 MW	10.64 AW	22120 AAW	SDBLS	10//99-12//99
	Tennessee	S	10.86 MW	11.30 AW	23500 AAW	TNBLS	10//99-12//99
	Texas	S	12.58 MW	12.75 AW	26520 AAW	TXBLS	10//99-12//99
	Utah	S	13.45 MW	13.16 AW	27370 AAW	UTBLS	10//99-12//99
	Vermont	S	10.36 MW	10.71 AW	22280 AAW	VTBLS	10//99-12//99
	Virginia	S	12.71 MW	12.67 AW	26350 AAW	VABLS	10//99-12//99
	Washington	S	13.75 MW	14.35 AW	29860 AAW	WABLS	10//99-12//99
	West Virginia	S	13 MW	13.07 AW	27180 AAW	WVBLS	10//99-12//99
	Wisconsin	S	11.73 MW	12.49 AW	25970 AAW	WIBLS	10//99-12//99
	Wyoming	S	11.87 MW	11.65 AW	24230 AAW	WYBLS	10//99-12//99
	Puerto Rico	S	8.69 MW	9.37 AW	19500 AAW	PRBLS	10//99-12//99
Producer and Director	Alabama	Y		40370 AAW		ALBLS	10//99-12//99
	Birmingham MSA, AL	Y		47200 AAW		ALBLS	10//99-12//99
	Mobile MSA, AL	Y		33190 AAW		ALBLS	10//99-12//99
	Montgomery MSA, AL	Y		28430 AAW		ALBLS	10//99-12//99
	Alaska	Y		35600 AAW		AKBLS	10//99-12//99
	Anchorage MSA, AK	Y		36960 AAW		AKBLS	10//99-12//99
	Arizona	Y		43550 AAW		AZBLS	10//99-12//99
	Phoenix-Mesa MSA, AZ	Y		47350 AAW		AZBLS	10//99-12//99
	Tucson MSA, AZ	Y		37960 AAW		AZBLS	10//99-12//99
	Arkansas	Y		26060 AAW		ARBLS	10//99-12//99
	Fayetteville-Springdale-Rogers MSA, AR	Y		22880 AAW		ARBLS	10//99-12//99
	Fort Smith MSA, AR-OK	Y		25040 AAW		ARBLS	10//99-12//99
	Little Rock-North Little Rock MSA, AR	Y		33510 AAW		ARBLS	10//99-12//99
	California	Y		83440 AAW		CABLS	10//99-12//99
	Los Angeles-Long Beach PMSA, CA	Y		97200 AAW		CABLS	10//99-12//99
	Oakland PMSA, CA	Y		59440 AAW		CABLS	10//99-12//99
	Orange County PMSA, CA	Y		40140 AAW		CABLS	10//99-12//99
	Riverside-San Bernardino PMSA, CA	Y		61090 AAW		CABLS	10//99-12//99
	Sacramento PMSA, CA	Y		59450 AAW		CABLS	10//99-12//99
	San Diego MSA, CA	Y		48360 AAW		CABLS	10//99-12//99
	San Francisco PMSA, CA	Y		79760 AAW		CABLS	10//99-12//99
	San Jose PMSA, CA	Y		36840 AAW		CABLS	10//99-12//99
	Santa Barbara-Santa Maria-Lompoc MSA, CA	Y		45710 AAW		CABLS	10//99-12//99
	Colorado	Y		41470 AAW		COBLS	10//99-12//99
	Denver PMSA, CO	Y		52830 AAW		COBLS	10//99-12//99
	Connecticut	Y		65800 AAW		CTBLS	10//99-12//99
	Danbury PMSA, CT	Y		59790 AAW		CTBLS	10//99-12//99
	Hartford MSA, CT	Y		49840 AAW		CTBLS	10//99-12//99
	District of Columbia	Y		49800 AAW		DCBLS	10//99-12//99
	Washington PMSA, DC-MD-VA-WV	Y		52180 AAW		DCBLS	10//99-12//99
	Florida	Y		39810 AAW		FLBLS	10//99-12//99
	Fort Lauderdale PMSA, FL	Y		33610 AAW		FLBLS	10//99-12//99
	Fort Myers-Cape Coral MSA, FL	Y		25430 AAW		FLBLS	10//99-12//99
	Gainesville MSA, FL	Y		26750 AAW		FLBLS	10//99-12//99
	Jacksonville MSA, FL	Y		30470 AAW		FLBLS	10//99-12//99
	Lakeland-Winter Haven MSA, FL	Y		37850 AAW		FLBLS	10//99-12//99
	Melbourne-Titusville-Palm Bay MSA, FL	Y		26140 AAW		FLBLS	10//99-12//99
	Miami PMSA, FL	Y		46580 AAW		FLBLS	10//99-12//99
	Orlando MSA, FL	Y		40780 AAW		FLBLS	10//99-12//99
	Pensacola MSA, FL	Y		32390 AAW		FLBLS	10//99-12//99
	Sarasota-Bradenton MSA, FL	Y		42410 AAW		FLBLS	10//99-12//99
	Tampa-St. Petersburg-Clearwater MSA, FL	Y		40500 AAW		FLBLS	10//99-12//99
	West Palm Beach-Boca Raton MSA, FL	Y		55450 AAW		FLBLS	10//99-12//99
	Georgia	Y		45750 AAW		GABLS	10//99-12//99
	Atlanta MSA, GA	Y		46530 AAW		GABLS	10//99-12//99

AAW Average annual wage	AOH Average offered, high	ASH Average starting, high	H Hourly	M Monthly	S Special: hourly and annual
AE Average entry wage	AOL Average offered, low	ASL Average starting, low	HI Highest wage paid	MTC Median total compensation	TQ Third quartile wage
AEX Average experienced wage	APH Average pay, high range	AW Average wage paid	HR High end range	MW Median wage paid	W Weekly
AO Average offered	APL Average pay, low range	FQ First quartile wage	LR Low end range	SQ Second quartile wage	Y Yearly

Occupation/Type/Industry	Location	Per	Low	Mid	High	Source	Date
Producer and Director	Macon MSA, GA	Y		36340 AAW		GABLS	10//99-12//99
	Hawaii	Y		48640 AAW		HIBLS	10//99-12//99
	Honolulu MSA, HI	Y		47880 AAW		HIBLS	10//99-12//99
	Illinois	Y		54250 AAW		ILBLS	10//99-12//99
	Chicago PMSA, IL	Y		56780 AAW		ILBLS	10//99-12//99
	Indiana	Y		39660 AAW		INBLS	10//99-12//99
	Bloomington MSA, IN	Y		27250 AAW		INBLS	10//99-12//99
	Fort Wayne MSA, IN	Y		31590 AAW		INBLS	10//99-12//99
	Iowa	Y		34610 AAW		IABLS	10//99-12//99
	Davenport-Moline-Rock Island MSA, IA-IL	Y		39250 AAW		IABLS	10//99-12//99
	Des Moines MSA, IA	Y		39400 AAW		IABLS	10//99-12//99
	Waterloo-Cedar Falls MSA, IA	Y		27990 AAW		IABLS	10//99-12//99
	Kansas	Y		33640 AAW		KSBLS	10//99-12//99
	Topeka MSA, KS	Y		28980 AAW		KSBLS	10//99-12//99
	Wichita MSA, KS	Y		35220 AAW		KSBLS	10//99-12//99
	Kentucky	Y		30000 AAW		KYBLS	10//99-12//99
	Lexington MSA, KY	Y		33060 AAW		KYBLS	10//99-12//99
	Louisville MSA, KY-IN	Y		33200 AAW		KYBLS	10//99-12//99
	Louisiana	Y		23690 AAW		LABLS	10//99-12//99
	Lafayette MSA, LA	Y		39300 AAW		LABLS	10//99-12//99
	New Orleans MSA, LA	Y		39340 AAW		LABLS	10//99-12//99
	Shreveport-Bossier City MSA, LA	Y		44360 AAW		LABLS	10//99-12//99
	Maine	Y		36930 AAW		MEBLS	10//99-12//99
	Portland MSA, ME	Y		40180 AAW		MEBLS	10//99-12//99
	Maryland	Y		45340 AAW		MDBLS	10//99-12//99
	Baltimore PMSA, MD	Y		44600 AAW		MDBLS	10//99-12//99
	Massachusetts	Y		43900 AAW		MABLS	10//99-12//99
	Boston PMSA, MA-NH	Y		45270 AAW		MABLS	10//99-12//99
	Detroit PMSA, MI	Y		52660 AAW		MIBLS	10//99-12//99
	Kalamazoo-Battle Creek MSA, MI	Y		35520 AAW		MIBLS	10//99-12//99
	Lansing-East Lansing MSA, MI	Y		38680 AAW		MIBLS	10//99-12//99
	Minnesota	Y		38750 AAW		MNBLS	10//99-12//99
	Minneapolis-St. Paul MSA, MN-WI	Y		42130 AAW		MNBLS	10//99-12//99
	Mississippi	Y		31940 AAW		MSBLS	10//99-12//99
	Biloxi-Gulfport-Pascagoula MSA, MS	Y		34490 AAW		MSBLS	10//99-12//99
	Missouri	Y		32160 AAW		MOBLS	10//99-12//99
	St. Louis MSA, MO-IL	Y		50080 AAW		MOBLS	10//99-12//99
	Montana	Y		38600 AAW		MTBLS	10//99-12//99
	Missoula MSA, MT	Y		35420 AAW		MTBLS	10//99-12//99
	Nebraska	Y		34000 AAW		NEBLS	10//99-12//99
	Lincoln MSA, NE	Y		39760 AAW		NEBLS	10//99-12//99
	Omaha MSA, NE-IA	Y		33770 AAW		NEBLS	10//99-12//99
	Nevada	Y		43370 AAW		NVBLS	10//99-12//99
	Las Vegas MSA, NV-AZ	Y		45760 AAW		NVBLS	10//99-12//99
	Reno MSA, NV	Y		27290 AAW		NVBLS	10//99-12//99
	New Hampshire	Y		31950 AAW		NHBLS	10//99-12//99
	New Jersey	Y		48720 AAW		NJBLS	10//99-12//99
	Bergen-Passaic PMSA, NJ	Y		47500 AAW		NJBLS	10//99-12//99
	Monmouth-Ocean PMSA, NJ	Y		59730 AAW		NJBLS	10//99-12//99
	Newark PMSA, NJ	Y		41950 AAW		NJBLS	10//99-12//99
	Trenton PMSA, NJ	Y		54600 AAW		NJBLS	10//99-12//99
	Albuquerque MSA, NM	Y		26850 AAW		NMBLS	10//99-12//99
	New York	Y		42580 AAW		NYBLS	10//99-12//99
	Albany-Schenectady-Troy MSA, NY	Y		43190 AAW		NYBLS	10//99-12//99
	Binghamton MSA, NY	Y		39820 AAW		NYBLS	10//99-12//99
	Buffalo-Niagara Falls MSA, NY	Y		37210 AAW		NYBLS	10//99-12//99
	Nassau-Suffolk PMSA, NY	Y		57090 AAW		NYBLS	10//99-12//99
	New York PMSA, NY	Y		41120 AAW		NYBLS	10//99-12//99
	Syracuse MSA, NY	Y		67730 AAW		NYBLS	10//99-12//99
	North Carolina	Y		36070 AAW		NCBLS	10//99-12//99
	Charlotte-Gastonia-Rock Hill MSA, NC-SC	Y		41870 AAW		NCBLS	10//99-12//99
	Greensboro--Winston-Salem--High Point MSA, NC	Y		35920 AAW		NCBLS	10//99-12//99
	Greenville MSA, NC	Y		21060 AAW		NCBLS	10//99-12//99

Occupation/Type/Industry	Location	Per	Low	Mid	High	Source	Date
Producer and Director	Raleigh-Durham-Chapel Hill MSA, NC	Y		38900 AAW		NCBLS	10//99-12//99
	Wilmington MSA, NC	Y		33650 AAW		NCBLS	10//99-12//99
	North Dakota	Y		32560 AAW		NDBLS	10//99-12//99
	Fargo-Moorhead MSA, ND-MN	Y		31680 AAW		NDBLS	10//99-12//99
	Ohio	Y		39140 AAW		OHBLS	10//99-12//99
	Canton-Massillon MSA, OH	Y		16430 AAW		OHBLS	10//99-12//99
	Cincinnati PMSA, OH-KY-IN	Y		36280 AAW		OHBLS	10//99-12//99
	Cleveland-Lorain-Elyria PMSA, OH	Y		47360 AAW		OHBLS	10//99-12//99
	Columbus MSA, OH	Y		38830 AAW		OHBLS	10//99-12//99
	Toledo MSA, OH	Y		28300 AAW		OHBLS	10//99-12//99
	Youngstown-Warren MSA, OH	Y		32400 AAW		OHBLS	10//99-12//99
	Tulsa MSA, OK	Y		23080 AAW		OKBLS	10//99-12//99
	Oregon	Y		37540 AAW		ORBLS	10//99-12//99
	Portland-Vancouver PMSA, OR-WA	Y		36690 AAW		ORBLS	10//99-12//99
	Pennsylvania	Y		38000 AAW		PABLS	10//99-12//99
	Allentown-Bethlehem-Easton MSA, PA	Y		43010 AAW		PABLS	10//99-12//99
	Erie MSA, PA	Y		20480 AAW		PABLS	10//99-12//99
	Harrisburg-Lebanon-Carlisle MSA, PA	Y		28300 AAW		PABLS	10//99-12//99
	Johnstown MSA, PA	Y		22380 AAW		PABLS	10//99-12//99
	Lancaster MSA, PA	Y		47930 AAW		PABLS	10//99-12//99
	Philadelphia PMSA, PA-NJ	Y		42310 AAW		PABLS	10//99-12//99
	Pittsburgh MSA, PA	Y		33030 AAW		PABLS	10//99-12//99
	Scranton--Wilkes-Barre--Hazleton MSA, PA	Y		23040 AAW		PABLS	10//99-12//99
	York MSA, PA	Y		26310 AAW		PABLS	10//99-12//99
	Rhode Island	Y		42950 AAW		RIBLS	10//99-12//99
	Providence-Fall River-Warwick MSA, RI-MA	Y		42220 AAW		RIBLS	10//99-12//99
	South Carolina	Y		36840 AAW		SCBLS	10//99-12//99
	Columbia MSA, SC	Y		33670 AAW		SCBLS	10//99-12//99
	Greenville-Spartanburg-Anderson MSA, SC	Y		35480 AAW		SCBLS	10//99-12//99
	South Dakota	Y		34480 AAW		SDBLS	10//99-12//99
	Sioux Falls MSA, SD	Y		36010 AAW		SDBLS	10//99-12//99
	Tennessee	Y		38920 AAW		TNBLS	10//99-12//99
	Chattanooga MSA, TN-GA	Y		26000 AAW		TNBLS	10//99-12//99
	Johnson City-Kingsport-Bristol MSA, TN-VA	Y		31690 AAW		TNBLS	10//99-12//99
	Knoxville MSA, TN	Y		47230 AAW		TNBLS	10//99-12//99
	Memphis MSA, TN-AR-MS	Y		33660 AAW		MSBLS	10//99-12//99
	Nashville MSA, TN	Y		37400 AAW		TNBLS	10//99-12//99
	Texas	Y		38630 AAW		TXBLS	10//99-12//99
	Austin-San Marcos MSA, TX	Y		26910 AAW		TXBLS	10//99-12//99
	Bryan-College Station MSA, TX	Y		55980 AAW		TXBLS	10//99-12//99
	Dallas PMSA, TX	Y		44950 AAW		TXBLS	10//99-12//99
	El Paso MSA, TX	Y		34360 AAW		TXBLS	10//99-12//99
	Fort Worth-Arlington PMSA, TX	Y		34500 AAW		TXBLS	10//99-12//99
	Houston PMSA, TX	Y		37460 AAW		TXBLS	10//99-12//99
	Lubbock MSA, TX	Y		30830 AAW		TXBLS	10//99-12//99
	San Antonio MSA, TX	Y		53470 AAW		TXBLS	10//99-12//99
	Waco MSA, TX	Y		33060 AAW		TXBLS	10//99-12//99
	Salt Lake City-Ogden MSA, UT	Y		34470 AAW		UTBLS	10//99-12//99
	Vermont	Y		27080 AAW		VTBLS	10//99-12//99
	Virginia	Y		41410 AAW		VABLS	10//99-12//99
	Charlottesville MSA, VA	Y		26790 AAW		VABLS	10//99-12//99
	Norfolk-Virginia Beach-Newport News MSA, VA-NC	Y		40420 AAW		VABLS	10//99-12//99
	Richmond-Petersburg MSA, VA	Y		32640 AAW		VABLS	10//99-12//99
	Roanoke MSA, VA	Y		35460 AAW		VABLS	10//99-12//99
	Washington	Y		37770 AAW		WABLS	10//99-12//99
	Bremerton PMSA, WA	Y		31390 AAW		WABLS	10//99-12//99

AAW	Average annual wage	AOH	Average offered, high	ASH	Average starting, high	H	Hourly	M	Monthly	S	Special: hourly and annual
AE	Average entry wage	AOL	Average offered, low	ASL	Average starting, low	HI	Highest wage paid	MTC	Median total compensation	TQ	Third quartile wage
AEX	Average experienced wage	APH	Average pay, high range	AW	Average wage paid	HR	High end range	MW	Median wage paid	W	Weekly
AO	Average offered	APL	Average pay, low range	FQ	First quartile wage	LR	Low end range	SQ	Second quartile wage	Y	Yearly

Occupation/Type/Industry	Location	Per	Low	Mid	High	Source	Date
Producer and Director	Seattle-Bellevue-Everett						
	PMSA, WA	Y		42690 AAW		WABLS	10//99-12//99
	Spokane MSA, WA	Y		34020 AAW		WABLS	10//99-12//99
	West Virginia	Y		36270 AAW		WVBLS	10//99-12//99
	Huntington-Ashland MSA,						
	WV-KY-OH	Y		40550 AAW		WVBLS	10//99-12//99
	Wheeling MSA, WV-OH	Y		15740 AAW		WVBLS	10//99-12//99
	Wisconsin	Y		36730 AAW		WIBLS	10//99-12//99
	Appleton-Oshkosh-Neenah						
	MSA, WI	Y		29700 AAW		WIBLS	10//99-12//99
	Eau Claire MSA, WI	Y		35340 AAW		WIBLS	10//99-12//99
	Green Bay MSA, WI	Y		34060 AAW		WIBLS	10//99-12//99
	La Crosse MSA, WI-MN	Y		40080 AAW		WIBLS	10//99-12//99
	Madison MSA, WI	Y		42640 AAW		WIBLS	10//99-12//99
	Milwaukee-Waukesha PMSA,						
	WI	Y		37060 AAW		WIBLS	10//99-12//99
	Puerto Rico	Y		34650 AAW		PRBLS	10//99-12//99
	San Juan-Bayamon PMSA, PR	Y		34710 AAW		PRBLS	10//99-12//99
Production Director							
Magazine	United States	Y		70600 AW		FOLIO	2000
Production Manager							
Foundry	United States	Y	51500 MW	63900 AW		MODCAS	1999
Magazine	United States	Y		48200 AW		FOLIO	2000
Production, Planning, and							
Expediting Clerk	Alabama	S	12.86 MW	13.72 AW	28540 AAW	ALBLS	10//99-12//99
	Alaska	S	18.27 MW	19.16 AW	39850 AAW	AKBLS	10//99-12//99
	Arizona	S	13.82 MW	14.68 AW	30530 AAW	AZBLS	10//99-12//99
	Arkansas	S	12.04 MW	13.12 AW	27280 AAW	ARBLS	10//99-12//99
	California	S	15.3 MW	16.14 AW	33570 AAW	CABLS	10//99-12//99
	Colorado	S	14.25 MW	14.86 AW	30900 AAW	COBLS	10//99-12//99
	Connecticut	S	15.55 MW	16.10 AW	33480 AAW	CTBLS	10//99-12//99
	Delaware	S	16.3 MW	17.79 AW	36990 AAW	DEBLS	10//99-12//99
	District of Columbia	S	16.99 MW	15.66 AW	32580 AAW	DCBLS	10//99-12//99
	Florida	S	12.59 MW	13.34 AW	27750 AAW	FLBLS	10//99-12//99
	Georgia	S	13.29 MW	14.26 AW	29660 AAW	GABLS	10//99-12//99
	Hawaii	S	14.74 MW	15.52 AW	32270 AAW	HIBLS	10//99-12//99
	Idaho	S	12.9 MW	14.07 AW	29270 AAW	IDBLS	10//99-12//99
	Illinois	S	14.34 MW	14.86 AW	30900 AAW	ILBLS	10//99-12//99
	Indiana	S	14.6 MW	15.12 AW	31450 AAW	INBLS	10//99-12//99
	Iowa	S	14.6 MW	14.39 AW	29940 AAW	IABLS	10//99-12//99
	Kansas	S	14.52 MW	15.37 AW	31970 AAW	KSBLS	10//99-12//99
	Kentucky	S	14.18 MW	15.21 AW	31640 AAW	KYBLS	10//99-12//99
	Louisiana	S	12.06 MW	13.48 AW	28030 AAW	LABLS	10//99-12//99
	Maine	S	17.16 MW	16.73 AW	34810 AAW	MEBLS	10//99-12//99
	Maryland	S	15.65 MW	15.80 AW	32860 AAW	MDBLS	10//99-12//99
	Massachusetts	S	16.87 MW	17.22 AW	35820 AAW	MABLS	10//99-12//99
	Michigan	S	16.77 MW	17.14 AW	35650 AAW	MIBLS	10//99-12//99
	Minnesota	S	14.85 MW	15.24 AW	31710 AAW	MNBLS	10//99-12//99
	Mississippi	S	12.11 MW	13.31 AW	27690 AAW	MSBLS	10//99-12//99
	Missouri	S	13.78 MW	14.75 AW	30680 AAW	MOBLS	10//99-12//99
	Montana	S	10.76 MW	12.05 AW	25060 AAW	MTBLS	10//99-12//99
	Nebraska	S	11.66 MW	12.46 AW	25910 AAW	NEBLS	10//99-12//99
	Nevada	S	12.53 MW	13.59 AW	28260 AAW	NVBLS	10//99-12//99
	New Hampshire	S	13.45 MW	14.12 AW	29380 AAW	NHBLS	10//99-12//99
	New Jersey	S	15.5 MW	16.07 AW	33420 AAW	NJBLS	10//99-12//99
	New Mexico	S	12.64 MW	13.57 AW	28240 AAW	NMBLS	10//99-12//99
	New York	S	16 MW	16.64 AW	34610 AAW	NYBLS	10//99-12//99
	North Carolina	S	12.59 MW	13.71 AW	28520 AAW	NCBLS	10//99-12//99
	North Dakota	S	12.2 MW	13.45 AW	27970 AAW	NDBLS	10//99-12//99
	Ohio	S	13.76 MW	14.89 AW	30960 AAW	OHBLS	10//99-12//99
	Oklahoma	S	13.44 MW	13.96 AW	29040 AAW	OKBLS	10//99-12//99
	Oregon	S	14.55 MW	14.87 AW	30930 AAW	ORBLS	10//99-12//99
	Pennsylvania	S	15.37 MW	15.72 AW	32700 AAW	PABLS	10//99-12//99
	Rhode Island	S	14.18 MW	14.79 AW	30770 AAW	RIBLS	10//99-12//99
	South Carolina	S	12.06 MW	13.03 AW	27100 AAW	SCBLS	10//99-12//99
	South Dakota	S	11.21 MW	12.02 AW	25000 AAW	SDBLS	10//99-12//99
	Tennessee	S	13.37 MW	14.30 AW	29740 AAW	TNBLS	10//99-12//99
	Texas	S	14.76 MW	15.45 AW	32130 AAW	TXBLS	10//99-12//99
	Utah	S	12.85 MW	13.51 AW	28090 AAW	UTBLS	10//99-12//99

AAW	Average annual wage	AOH	Average offered, high	ASH	Average starting, high	H	Hourly	M	Monthly	S	Special: hourly and annual
AE	Average entry wage	AOL	Average offered, low	ASL	Average starting, low	HI	Highest wage paid	MTC	Median total compensation	TQ	Third quartile wage
AEX	Average experienced wage	APH	Average pay, high range	AW	Average wage paid	HR	High end range	MW	Median wage paid	W	Weekly
AO	Average offered	APL	Average pay, low range	FQ	First quartile wage	LR	Low end range	SQ	Second quartile wage	Y	Yearly

Occupation/Type/Industry	Location	Per	Low	Mid	High	Source	Date
Production, Planning, and Expediting Clerk	Vermont	S	14.04 MW	14.32 AW	29790 AAW	VTBLS	10//99-12//99
	Virginia	S	13.97 MW	14.89 AW	30970 AAW	VABLS	10//99-12//99
	Washington	S	16.8 MW	17.25 AW	35870 AAW	WABLS	10//99-12//99
	West Virginia	S	13.49 MW	14.24 AW	29620 AAW	WVBLS	10//99-12//99
	Wisconsin	S	13.43 MW	14.46 AW	30080 AAW	WIBLS	10//99-12//99
	Wyoming	S	19.68 MW	18.37 AW	38210 AAW	WYBLS	10//99-12//99
	Puerto Rico	S	9.97 MW	11.03 AW	22950 AAW	PRBLS	10//99-12//99
	Guam	S	14.47 MW	15.47 AW	32170 AAW	GUBLS	10//99-12//99
Professional Services Chief							
Hospital	United States	Y		105400 MW		HHN	2000
Professor							
2-Year College	United States	Y		48929 AW		AS&U2	1999-2000
4-Year College	United States	Y		58214 AW		AS&U2	1999-2000
Agricultural Engineering	United States	Y	49319 APL	73397 AW	107325 APH	RESC	1998-1999
Assistant, Agricultural Engineering	United States	Y	34847 APL	49556 AW	75002 APH	RESC	1998-1999
Associate, Agricultural Engineering	United States	Y	22903 APL	56472 AW	92457 APH	RESC	1998-1999
Doctoral Level, Nursing Faculty	United States	Y		66132 AW		AWHONN	1998-1999
Medical Technology	United States	Y	55200 APL	80287 AW	122247 APH	LABMED	1999
Nondoctoral Level, Nursing Faculty	Unites States	Y		62959 AW		AWHONN	1998-1999
Project Manager							
Mechanical Contracting Firm	United States	Y		50900 AW		CONTR	1998
Proofreader and Copy Marker	Alabama	S	7.38 MW	8.03 AW	16710 AAW	ALBLS	10//99-12//99
	Birmingham MSA, AL	S	9.32 MW	9.15 AW	19380 AAW	ALBLS	10//99-12//99
	Arizona	S	9.89 MW	10.65 AW	22150 AAW	AZBLS	10//99-12//99
	Phoenix-Mesa MSA, AZ	S	11.14 MW	10.45 AW	23180 AAW	AZBLS	10//99-12//99
	Tucson MSA, AZ	S	9.45 MW	8.05 AW	19650 AAW	AZBLS	10//99-12//99
	Arkansas	S	7.46 MW	8.09 AW	16820 AAW	ARBLS	10//99-12//99
	California	S	9.12 MW	10.39 AW	21620 AAW	CABLS	10//99-12//99
	Los Angeles-Long Beach PMSA, CA	S	11.47 MW	10.06 AW	23870 AAW	CABLS	10//99-12//99
	Oakland PMSA, CA	S	11.22 MW	10.14 AW	23330 AAW	CABLS	10//99-12//99
	Orange County PMSA, CA	S	10.10 MW	9.17 AW	21010 AAW	CABLS	10//99-12//99
	Riverside-San Bernardino PMSA, CA	S	10.29 MW	9.63 AW	21410 AAW	CABLS	10//99-12//99
	Sacramento PMSA, CA	S	8.35 MW	7.98 AW	17380 AAW	CABLS	10//99-12//99
	Salinas MSA, CA	S	10.72 MW	10.74 AW	22310 AAW	CABLS	10//99-12//99
	San Diego MSA, CA	S	9.78 MW	9.61 AW	20330 AAW	CABLS	10//99-12//99
	San Francisco PMSA, CA	S	10.90 MW	9.96 AW	22660 AAW	CABLS	10//99-12//99
	Santa Barbara-Santa Maria-Lompoc MSA, CA	S	10.53 MW	9.93 AW	21910 AAW	CABLS	10//99-12//99
	Ventura PMSA, CA	S	9.72 MW	9.38 AW	20210 AAW	CABLS	10//99-12//99
	Colorado	S	10.96 MW	11.15 AW	23190 AAW	COBLS	10//99-12//99
	Colorado Springs MSA, CO	S	11.63 MW	11.50 AW	24200 AAW	COBLS	10//99-12//99
	Denver PMSA, CO	S	11.31 MW	11.04 AW	23530 AAW	COBLS	10//99-12//99
	Connecticut	S	10.23 MW	10.81 AW	22480 AAW	CTBLS	10//99-12//99
	Bridgeport PMSA, CT	S	12.10 MW	12.42 AW	25170 AAW	CTBLS	10//99-12//99
	New Haven-Meriden PMSA, CT	S	12.50 MW	13.01 AW	26000 AAW	CTBLS	10//99-12//99
	Waterbury PMSA, CT	S	9.66 MW	9.58 AW	20100 AAW	CTBLS	10//99-12//99
	Delaware	S	8.51 MW	9.33 AW	19410 AAW	DEBLS	10//99-12//99
	Wilmington-Newark PMSA, DE-MD	S	9.76 MW	8.62 AW	20310 AAW	DEBLS	10//99-12//99
	District of Columbia	S	11.49 MW	11.85 AW	24650 AAW	DCBLS	10//99-12//99
	Washington PMSA, DC-MD-VA-WV	S	12.55 MW	12.17 AW	26110 AAW	DCBLS	10//99-12//99
	Florida	S	8.41 MW	9.21 AW	19150 AAW	FLBLS	10//99-12//99
	Fort Lauderdale PMSA, FL	S	8.03 MW	7.80 AW	16690 AAW	FLBLS	10//99-12//99
	Jacksonville MSA, FL	S	10.57 MW	9.81 AW	21980 AAW	FLBLS	10//99-12//99
	Lakeland-Winter Haven MSA, FL	S	8.73 MW	8.62 AW	18160 AAW	FLBLS	10//99-12//99
	Miami PMSA, FL	S	9.81 MW	8.19 AW	20400 AAW	FLBLS	10//99-12//99
	Naples MSA, FL	S	9.93 MW	9.51 AW	20660 AAW	FLBLS	10//99-12//99
	Orlando MSA, FL	S	9.31 MW	8.80 AW	19370 AAW	FLBLS	10//99-12//99
	Tallahassee MSA, FL	S	8.32 MW	8.52 AW	17300 AAW	FLBLS	10//99-12//99
	Tampa-St. Petersburg-Clearwater MSA, FL	S	9.55 MW	8.63 AW	19860 AAW	FLBLS	10//99-12//99
	West Palm Beach-Boca Raton MSA, FL	S	11.29 MW	10.42 AW	23480 AAW	FLBLS	10//99-12//99

AAW Average annual wage	**AOH** Average offered, high	**ASH** Average starting, high	**H** Hourly	**M** Monthly	**S** Special: hourly and annual
AE Average entry wage	**AOL** Average offered, low	**ASL** Average starting, low	**HI** Highest wage paid	**MTC** Median total compensation	**TQ** Third quartile wage
AEX Average experienced wage	**APH** Average pay, high range	**AW** Average wage paid	**HR** High end range	**MW** Median wage paid	**W** Weekly
AO Average offered	**APL** Average pay, low range	**FQ** First quartile wage	**LR** Low end range	**SQ** Second quartile wage	**Y** Yearly

Occupation/Type/Industry	Location	Per	Low	Mid	High	Source	Date
Proofreader and Copy Marker	Georgia	S	9.35 MW	9.60 AW	19980 AAW	GABLS	10//99-12//99
	Atlanta MSA, GA	S	10.10 MW	9.98 AW	21010 AAW	GABLS	10//99-12//99
	Hawaii	S	10.22 MW	10.87 AW	22610 AAW	HIBLS	10//99-12//99
	Honolulu MSA, HI	S	10.69 MW	10.18 AW	22240 AAW	HIBLS	10//99-12//99
	Idaho	S	8.52 MW	10.42 AW	21670 AAW	IDBLS	10//99-12//99
	Illinois	S	8.39 MW	9.31 AW	19370 AAW	ILBLS	10//99-12//99
	Chicago PMSA, IL	S	9.25 MW	8.37 AW	19230 AAW	ILBLS	10//99-12//99
	Peoria-Pekin MSA, IL	S	11.09 MW	8.03 AW	23060 AAW	ILBLS	10//99-12//99
	Springfield MSA, IL	S	12.23 MW	11.13 AW	25430 AAW	ILBLS	10//99-12//99
	Indiana	S	10.31 MW	10.46 AW	21760 AAW	INBLS	10//99-12//99
	Indianapolis MSA, IN	S	11.51 MW	11.81 AW	23940 AAW	INBLS	10//99-12//99
	Iowa	S	8.28 MW	8.45 AW	17570 AAW	IABLS	10//99-12//99
	Dubuque MSA, IA	S	9.84 MW	9.61 AW	20460 AAW	IABLS	10//99-12//99
	Kansas	S	8.96 MW	9.80 AW	20380 AAW	KSBLS	10//99-12//99
	Kentucky	S	8.12 MW	8.61 AW	17900 AAW	KYBLS	10//99-12//99
	Lexington MSA, KY	S	8.60 MW	7.80 AW	17890 AAW	KYBLS	10//99-12//99
	Louisville MSA, KY-IN	S	10.23 MW	10.51 AW	21280 AAW	KYBLS	10//99-12//99
	Louisiana	S	7.9 MW	8.59 AW	17860 AAW	LABLS	10//99-12//99
	Baton Rouge MSA, LA	S	8.66 MW	7.89 AW	18010 AAW	LABLS	10//99-12//99
	New Orleans MSA, LA	S	9.12 MW	8.30 AW	18970 AAW	LABLS	10//99-12//99
	Maine	S	8.19 MW	8.59 AW	17880 AAW	MEBLS	10//99-12//99
	Maryland	S	10.27 MW	11.17 AW	23230 AAW	MDBLS	10//99-12//99
	Baltimore PMSA, MD	S	9.97 MW	9.31 AW	20740 AAW	MDBLS	10//99-12//99
	Massachusetts	S	13.32 MW	13.65 AW	28390 AAW	MABLS	10//99-12//99
	Boston PMSA, MA-NH	S	14.31 MW	14.26 AW	29760 AAW	MABLS	10//99-12//99
	Lowell PMSA, MA-NH	S	12.46 MW	12.46 AW	25910 AAW	MABLS	10//99-12//99
	Worcester PMSA, MA-CT	S	12.19 MW	11.86 AW	25350 AAW	MABLS	10//99-12//99
	Michigan	S	8.57 MW	9.28 AW	19300 AAW	MIBLS	10//99-12//99
	Ann Arbor PMSA, MI	S	10.04 MW	9.81 AW	20880 AAW	MIBLS	10//99-12//99
	Detroit PMSA, MI	S	9.67 MW	8.69 AW	20110 AAW	MIBLS	10//99-12//99
	Grand Rapids-Muskegon-Holland MSA, MI	S	8.52 MW	8.44 AW	17730 AAW	MIBLS	10//99-12//99
	Kalamazoo-Battle Creek MSA, MI	S	10.93 MW	10.11 AW	22740 AAW	MIBLS	10//99-12//99
	Saginaw-Bay City-Midland MSA, MI	S	8.32 MW	7.91 AW	17310 AAW	MIBLS	10//99-12//99
	Minnesota	S	10.38 MW	10.74 AW	22350 AAW	MNBLS	10//99-12//99
	Minneapolis-St. Paul MSA, MN-WI	S	12.03 MW	11.23 AW	25020 AAW	MNBLS	10//99-12//99
	St. Cloud MSA, MN	S	9.12 MW	8.29 AW	18980 AAW	MNBLS	10//99-12//99
	Mississippi	S	9.21 MW	9.33 AW	19410 AAW	MSBLS	10//99-12//99
	Missouri	S	9.38 MW	9.44 AW	19630 AAW	MOBLS	10//99-12//99
	Kansas City MSA, MO-KS	S	10.55 MW	10.00 AW	21940 AAW	MOBLS	10//99-12//99
	St. Louis MSA, MO-IL	S	9.33 MW	9.24 AW	19410 AAW	MOBLS	10//99-12//99
	Montana	S	7.91 MW	7.97 AW	16580 AAW	MTBLS	10//99-12//99
	Nebraska	S	9.55 MW	10.05 AW	20910 AAW	NEBLS	10//99-12//99
	Omaha MSA, NE-IA	S	10.53 MW	10.17 AW	21900 AAW	NEBLS	10//99-12//99
	Nevada	S	11.12 MW	12.18 AW	25330 AAW	NVBLS	10//99-12//99
	Las Vegas MSA, NV-AZ	S	13.04 MW	11.66 AW	27120 AAW	NVBLS	10//99-12//99
	New Hampshire	S	9.42 MW	9.81 AW	20400 AAW	NHBLS	10//99-12//99
	New Jersey	S	11.97 MW	12.54 AW	26080 AAW	NJBLS	10//99-12//99
	Bergen-Passaic PMSA, NJ	S	14.10 MW	12.83 AW	29320 AAW	NJBLS	10//99-12//99
	Middlesex-Somerset-Hunterdon PMSA, NJ	S	11.51 MW	10.65 AW	23930 AAW	NJBLS	10//99-12//99
	Monmouth-Ocean PMSA, NJ	S	11.04 MW	10.31 AW	22960 AAW	NJBLS	10//99-12//99
	Newark PMSA, NJ	S	12.59 MW	12.21 AW	26180 AAW	NJBLS	10//99-12//99
	Trenton PMSA, NJ	S	13.15 MW	12.22 AW	27360 AAW	NJBLS	10//99-12//99
	New Mexico	S	8.85 MW	9.90 AW	20590 AAW	NMBLS	10//99-12//99
	New York	S	12.82 MW	13.03 AW	27100 AAW	NYBLS	10//99-12//99
	Albany-Schenectady-Troy MSA, NY	S	9.92 MW	9.50 AW	20640 AAW	NYBLS	10//99-12//99
	Buffalo-Niagara Falls MSA, NY	S	9.83 MW	9.31 AW	20450 AAW	NYBLS	10//99-12//99
	Nassau-Suffolk PMSA, NY	S	11.78 MW	10.96 AW	24510 AAW	NYBLS	10//99-12//99
	New York PMSA, NY	S	14.17 MW	13.96 AW	29470 AAW	NYBLS	10//99-12//99
	Rochester MSA, NY	S	10.73 MW	10.13 AW	22310 AAW	NYBLS	10//99-12//99
	North Carolina	S	9.18 MW	9.71 AW	20190 AAW	NCBLS	10//99-12//99
	Charlotte-Gastonia-Rock Hill MSA, NC-SC	S	11.11 MW	10.27 AW	23110 AAW	NCBLS	10//99-12//99
	Greensboro--Winston-Salem--High Point MSA, NC	S	10.14 MW	9.96 AW	21090 AAW	NCBLS	10//99-12//99
	North Dakota	S	7.26 MW	7.21 AW	14990 AAW	NDBLS	10//99-12//99

AAW Average annual wage	**AOH** Average offered, high	**ASH** Average starting, high	**H** Hourly	**M** Monthly	**S** Special: hourly and annual
AE Average entry wage	**AOL** Average offered, low	**ASL** Average starting, low	**HI** Highest wage paid	**MTC** Median total compensation	**TQ** Third quartile wage
AEX Average experienced wage	**APH** Average pay, high range	**AW** Average wage paid	**HR** High end range	**MW** Median wage paid	**W** Weekly
AO Average offered	**APL** Average pay, low range	**FQ** First quartile wage	**LR** Low end range	**SQ** Second quartile wage	**Y** Yearly

Occupation/Type/Industry	Location	Per	Low	Mid	High	Source	Date
Proofreader and Copy Marker	Ohio	S	9.59 MW	10.41 AW	21660 AAW	OHBLS	10//99-12//99
	Akron PMSA, OH	S	9.84 MW	10.09 AW	20470 AAW	OHBLS	10//99-12//99
	Cincinnati PMSA, OH-KY-IN	S	10.54 MW	10.37 AW	21920 AAW	OHBLS	10//99-12//99
	Cleveland-Lorain-Elyria PMSA, OH	S	11.28 MW	9.68 AW	23470 AAW	OHBLS	10//99-12//99
	Columbus MSA, OH	S	9.90 MW	9.21 AW	20590 AAW	OHBLS	10//99-12//99
	Dayton-Springfield MSA, OH	S	10.87 MW	10.73 AW	22620 AAW	OHBLS	10//99-12//99
	Toledo MSA, OH	S	11.59 MW	10.78 AW	24100 AAW	OHBLS	10//99-12//99
	Youngstown-Warren MSA, OH	S	8.24 MW	6.57 AW	17130 AAW	OHBLS	10//99-12//99
	Oklahoma	S	8.98 MW	9.75 AW	20280 AAW	OKBLS	10//99-12//99
	Oklahoma City MSA, OK	S	9.54 MW	9.15 AW	19850 AAW	OKBLS	10//99-12//99
	Tulsa MSA, OK	S	9.16 MW	8.47 AW	19050 AAW	OKBLS	10//99-12//99
	Oregon	S	8.64 MW	9.42 AW	19590 AAW	ORBLS	10//99-12//99
	Pennsylvania	S	10.04 MW	11.76 AW	24460 AAW	PABLS	10//99-12//99
	Allentown-Bethlehem-Easton MSA, PA	S	12.93 MW	13.34 AW	26900 AAW	PABLS	10//99-12//99
	Harrisburg-Lebanon-Carlisle MSA, PA	S	9.19 MW	8.54 AW	19120 AAW	PABLS	10//99-12//99
	Lancaster MSA, PA	S	10.95 MW	10.17 AW	22780 AAW	PABLS	10//99-12//99
	Philadelphia PMSA, PA-NJ	S	13.95 MW	13.12 AW	29020 AAW	PABLS	10//99-12//99
	Pittsburgh MSA, PA	S	9.96 MW	8.47 AW	20730 AAW	PABLS	10//99-12//99
	York MSA, PA	S	9.18 MW	8.49 AW	19100 AAW	PABLS	10//99-12//99
	Rhode Island	S	12.49 MW	12.43 AW	25860 AAW	RIBLS	10//99-12//99
	Providence-Fall River-Warwick MSA, RI-MA	S	12.33 MW	12.39 AW	25650 AAW	RIBLS	10//99-12//99
	South Carolina	S	11.19 MW	10.55 AW	21940 AAW	SCBLS	10//99-12//99
	Columbia MSA, SC	S	11.01 MW	11.68 AW	22900 AAW	SCBLS	10//99-12//99
	Greenville-Spartanburg-Anderson MSA, SC	S	9.91 MW	10.09 AW	20600 AAW	SCBLS	10//99-12//99
	South Dakota	S	6.45 MW	6.64 AW	13800 AAW	SDBLS	10//99-12//99
	Tennessee	S	9.75 MW	10.33 AW	21500 AAW	TNBLS	10//99-12//99
	Memphis MSA, TN-AR-MS	S	10.01 MW	9.51 AW	20810 AAW	MSBLS	10//99-12//99
	Nashville MSA, TN	S	10.43 MW	10.31 AW	21700 AAW	TNBLS	10//99-12//99
	Texas	S	8.8 MW	9.30 AW	19340 AAW	TXBLS	10//99-12//99
	Austin-San Marcos MSA, TX	S	11.14 MW	10.23 AW	23170 AAW	TXBLS	10//99-12//99
	Beaumont-Port Arthur MSA, TX	S	8.62 MW	8.73 AW	17930 AAW	TXBLS	10//99-12//99
	Dallas PMSA, TX	S	10.11 MW	9.63 AW	21020 AAW	TXBLS	10//99-12//99
	El Paso MSA, TX	S	7.65 MW	7.43 AW	15920 AAW	TXBLS	10//99-12//99
	Fort Worth-Arlington PMSA, TX	S	10.69 MW	10.24 AW	22230 AAW	TXBLS	10//99-12//99
	Houston PMSA, TX	S	9.00 MW	8.28 AW	18720 AAW	TXBLS	10//99-12//99
	Killeen-Temple MSA, TX	S	8.86 MW	8.49 AW	18430 AAW	TXBLS	10//99-12//99
	San Antonio MSA, TX	S	9.14 MW	8.75 AW	19010 AAW	TXBLS	10//99-12//99
	Utah	S	8.71 MW	9.52 AW	19800 AAW	UTBLS	10//99-12//99
	Salt Lake City-Ogden MSA, UT	S	10.21 MW	8.80 AW	21240 AAW	UTBLS	10//99-12//99
	Vermont	S	11.17 MW	11.58 AW	24080 AAW	VTBLS	10//99-12//99
	Virginia	S	9.39 MW	10.00 AW	20810 AAW	VABLS	10//99-12//99
	Norfolk-Virginia Beach-Newport News MSA, VA-NC	S	9.95 MW	9.26 AW	20690 AAW	VABLS	10//99-12//99
	Richmond-Petersburg MSA, VA	S	8.91 MW	8.29 AW	18530 AAW	VABLS	10//99-12//99
	Washington	S	11.05 MW	12.15 AW	25260 AAW	WABLS	10//99-12//99
	Tacoma PMSA, WA	S	9.13 MW	9.13 AW	18990 AAW	WABLS	10//99-12//99
	West Virginia	S	6.57 MW	7.69 AW	16000 AAW	WVBLS	10//99-12//99
	Wisconsin	S	9.89 MW	10.30 AW	21420 AAW	WIBLS	10//99-12//99
	Madison MSA, WI	S	10.19 MW	8.91 AW	21200 AAW	WIBLS	10//99-12//99
	Milwaukee-Waukesha PMSA, WI	S	11.22 MW	11.17 AW	23340 AAW	WIBLS	10//99-12//99
	Wyoming	S	7.28 MW	7.31 AW	15210 AAW	WYBLS	10//99-12//99
	Puerto Rico	S	7.76 MW	8.58 AW	17840 AAW	PRBLS	10//99-12//99
	San Juan-Bayamon PMSA, PR	S	8.87 MW	8.10 AW	18450 AAW	PRBLS	10//99-12//99
Property Management Officer Real Estate	United States	Y		138666 AW		TRAVWK4	2000
Property Manager Office/Industrial, 500,000 to 1M square feet	United States	Y		60800 MW	70800 HI	URLAN	1998
Office/Industrial, Less than 500,000 square feet	United States	Y		48300 MW	57400 HI	URLAN	1998

AAW Average annual wage	**AOH** Average offered, high	**ASH** Average starting, high	**H** Hourly	**M** Monthly	**S** Special: hourly and annual
AE Average entry wage	**AOL** Average offered, low	**ASL** Average starting, low	**HI** Highest wage paid	**MTC** Median total compensation	**TQ** Third quartile wage
AEX Average experienced wage	**APH** Average pay, high range	**AW** Average wage paid	**HR** High end range	**MW** Median wage paid	**W** Weekly
AO Average offered	**APL** Average pay, low range	**FQ** First quartile wage	**LR** Low end range	**SQ** Second quartile wage	**Y** Yearly

Occupation/Type/Industry	Location	Per	Low	Mid	High	Source	Date
Property Manager							
Office/Industrial, More than 1 million square feet	United States	Y		78000 MW	91200 HI	URLAN	1998
Retail, 300,001 to 500,000 square feet	United States	Y		51000 MW	57000 HI	URLAN	1998
Retail, 500,001 to 750,000 square feet	United States	Y		60000 MW	71500 HI	URLAN	1998
Retail, Less than 300,000 square feet	United States	Y		45000 MW	53700 HI	URLAN	1998
Property, Real Estate, and Community Association Manager	Alabama	S	9.94 MW	13.67 AW	28430 AAW	ALBLS	10//99-12//99
	Birmingham MSA, AL	S	15.80 MW	10.50 AW	32850 AAW	ALBLS	10//99-12//99
	Florence MSA, AL	S	10.95 MW	10.86 AW	22770 AAW	ALBLS	10//99-12//99
	Huntsville MSA, AL	S	12.36 MW	9.87 AW	25700 AAW	ALBLS	10//99-12//99
	Alaska	S	18.65 MW	18.88 AW	39260 AAW	AKBLS	10//99-12//99
	Anchorage MSA, AK	S	18.38 MW	18.62 AW	38240 AAW	AKBLS	10//99-12//99
	Arizona	S	14.57 MW	17.32 AW	36030 AAW	AZBLS	10//99-12//99
	Flagstaff MSA, AZ-UT	S	13.13 MW	12.38 AW	27310 AAW	AZBLS	10//99-12//99
	Phoenix-Mesa MSA, AZ	S	19.66 MW	15.68 AW	40890 AAW	AZBLS	10//99-12//99
	Tucson MSA, AZ	S	13.22 MW	11.75 AW	27500 AAW	AZBLS	10//99-12//99
	Arkansas	S	9.77 MW	14.46 AW	30070 AAW	ARBLS	10//99-12//99
	Fayetteville-Springdale-Rogers MSA, AR	S	17.92 MW	11.25 AW	37280 AAW	ARBLS	10//99-12//99
	Fort Smith MSA, AR-OK	S	16.62 MW	8.28 AW	34570 AAW	ARBLS	10//99-12//99
	Jonesboro MSA, AR	S	10.84 MW	7.86 AW	22540 AAW	ARBLS	10//99-12//99
	Little Rock-North Little Rock MSA, AR	S	12.98 MW	9.44 AW	26990 AAW	ARBLS	10//99-12//99
	California	S	24.28 MW	26.42 AW	54950 AAW	CABLS	10//99-12//99
	Bakersfield MSA, CA	S	26.03 MW	20.63 AW	54140 AAW	CABLS	10//99-12//99
	Fresno MSA, CA	S	21.03 MW	20.06 AW	43750 AAW	CABLS	10//99-12//99
	Los Angeles-Long Beach PMSA, CA	S	26.88 MW	25.85 AW	55910 AAW	CABLS	10//99-12//99
	Modesto MSA, CA	S	26.05 MW	26.19 AW	54190 AAW	CABLS	10//99-12//99
	Oakland PMSA, CA	S	26.72 MW	20.73 AW	55580 AAW	CABLS	10//99-12//99
	Orange County PMSA, CA	S	25.84 MW	22.72 AW	53750 AAW	CABLS	10//99-12//99
	Riverside-San Bernardino PMSA, CA	S	25.05 MW	23.67 AW	52100 AAW	CABLS	10//99-12//99
	Sacramento PMSA, CA	S	29.24 MW	22.70 AW	60810 AAW	CABLS	10//99-12//99
	Salinas MSA, CA	S	16.27 MW	15.07 AW	33830 AAW	CABLS	10//99-12//99
	San Diego MSA, CA	S	25.36 MW	24.14 AW	52760 AAW	CABLS	10//99-12//99
	San Francisco PMSA, CA	S	31.61 MW	27.50 AW	65750 AAW	CABLS	10//99-12//99
	San Jose PMSA, CA	S	27.90 MW	28.60 AW	58040 AAW	CABLS	10//99-12//99
	San Luis Obispo-Atascadero-Paso Robles MSA, CA	S	28.09 MW	26.07 AW	58430 AAW	CABLS	10//99-12//99
	Santa Barbara-Santa Maria-Lompoc MSA, CA	S	34.40 MW	36.90 AW	71550 AAW	CABLS	10//99-12//99
	Santa Rosa PMSA, CA	S	14.05 MW	12.30 AW	29220 AAW	CABLS	10//99-12//99
	Stockton-Lodi MSA, CA	S	12.37 MW	10.77 AW	25720 AAW	CABLS	10//99-12//99
	Visalia-Tulare-Porterville MSA, CA	S	31.67 MW	29.80 AW	65880 AAW	CABLS	10//99-12//99
	Colorado	S	17.06 MW	18.99 AW	39510 AAW	COBLS	10//99-12//99
	Colorado Springs MSA, CO	S	19.49 MW	18.55 AW	40540 AAW	COBLS	10//99-12//99
	Denver PMSA, CO	S	20.01 MW	17.79 AW	41620 AAW	COBLS	10//99-12//99
	Connecticut	S	20.83 MW	25.65 AW	53360 AAW	CTBLS	10//99-12//99
	Bridgeport PMSA, CT	S	17.39 MW	15.86 AW	36170 AAW	CTBLS	10//99-12//99
	Danbury PMSA, CT	S	18.56 MW	14.83 AW	38600 AAW	CTBLS	10//99-12//99
	Hartford MSA, CT	S	23.25 MW	16.34 AW	48370 AAW	CTBLS	10//99-12//99
	New Haven-Meriden PMSA, CT	S	16.79 MW	16.01 AW	34930 AAW	CTBLS	10//99-12//99
	New London-Norwich MSA, CT-RI	S	25.41 MW	20.60 AW	52860 AAW	CTBLS	10//99-12//99
	Stamford-Norwalk PMSA, CT	S	42.97 MW	33.69 AW	89380 AAW	CTBLS	10//99-12//99
	Waterbury PMSA, CT	S	18.04 MW	16.09 AW	37530 AAW	CTBLS	10//99-12//99
	Delaware	S	15.59 MW	18.61 AW	38700 AAW	DEBLS	10//99-12//99
	Dover MSA, DE	S	14.16 MW	13.71 AW	29450 AAW	DEBLS	10//99-12//99
	Wilmington-Newark PMSA, DE-MD	S	17.42 MW	15.58 AW	36240 AAW	DEBLS	10//99-12//99
	District of Columbia	S	22.01 MW	24.17 AW	50280 AAW	DCBLS	10//99-12//99
	Washington PMSA, DC-MD-VA-WV	S	22.76 MW	21.45 AW	47350 AAW	DCBLS	10//99-12//99
	Florida	S	14.1 MW	16.85 AW	35050 AAW	FLBLS	10//99-12//99
	Daytona Beach MSA, FL	S	14.16 MW	13.63 AW	29450 AAW	FLBLS	10//99-12//99
	Fort Lauderdale PMSA, FL	S	21.30 MW	17.87 AW	44300 AAW	FLBLS	10//99-12//99

AAW Average annual wage	**AOH** Average offered, high	**ASH** Average starting, high	**H** Hourly	**M** Monthly	**S** Special: hourly and annual
AE Average entry wage	**AOL** Average offered, low	**ASL** Average starting, low	**HI** Highest wage paid	**MTC** Median total compensation	**TQ** Third quartile wage
AEX Average experienced wage	**APH** Average pay, high range	**AW** Average wage paid	**HR** High end range	**MW** Median wage paid	**W** Weekly
AO Average offered	**APL** Average pay, low range	**FQ** First quartile wage	**LR** Low end range	**SQ** Second quartile wage	**Y** Yearly

Occupation/Type/Industry	Location	Per	Low	Mid	High	Source	Date
Property, Real Estate, and Community Association Manager							
	Fort Myers-Cape Coral MSA, FL	S	15.83 MW	14.61 AW	32930 AAW	FLBLS	10//99-12//99
	Lakeland-Winter Haven MSA, FL	S	15.33 MW	10.32 AW	31890 AAW	FLBLS	10//99-12//99
	Melbourne-Titusville-Palm Bay MSA, FL	S	14.49 MW	10.25 AW	30150 AAW	FLBLS	10//99-12//99
	Miami PMSA, FL	S	15.48 MW	12.49 AW	32190 AAW	FLBLS	10//99-12//99
	Naples MSA, FL	S	16.44 MW	15.43 AW	34190 AAW	FLBLS	10//99-12//99
	Ocala MSA, FL	S	16.60 MW	15.71 AW	34530 AAW	FLBLS	10//99-12//99
	Pensacola MSA, FL	S	15.68 MW	15.49 AW	32610 AAW	FLBLS	10//99-12//99
	Punta Gorda MSA, FL	S	11.83 MW	11.98 AW	24600 AAW	FLBLS	10//99-12//99
	Sarasota-Bradenton MSA, FL	S	11.47 MW	6.74 AW	23860 AAW	FLBLS	10//99-12//99
	Tampa-St. Petersburg-Clearwater MSA, FL	S	19.20 MW	16.21 AW	39940 AAW	FLBLS	10//99-12//99
	West Palm Beach-Boca Raton MSA, FL	S	22.71 MW	20.73 AW	47240 AAW	FLBLS	10//99-12//99
	Georgia	S	17.85 MW	19.35 AW	40250 AAW	GABLS	10//99-12//99
	Albany MSA, GA	S	15.12 MW	14.70 AW	31450 AAW	GABLS	10//99-12//99
	Athens MSA, GA	S	14.39 MW	13.36 AW	29920 AAW	GABLS	10//99-12//99
	Atlanta MSA, GA	S	20.22 MW	18.40 AW	42060 AAW	GABLS	10//99-12//99
	Columbus MSA, GA-AL	S	19.40 MW	18.83 AW	40350 AAW	GABLS	10//99-12//99
	Macon MSA, GA	S	22.26 MW	23.08 AW	46310 AAW	GABLS	10//99-12//99
	Savannah MSA, GA	S	17.56 MW	16.93 AW	36510 AAW	GABLS	10//99-12//99
	Hawaii	S	18.87 MW	23.47 AW	48820 AAW	HIBLS	10//99-12//99
	Honolulu MSA, HI	S	23.61 MW	19.55 AW	49100 AAW	HIBLS	10//99-12//99
	Idaho	S	14.12 MW	15.48 AW	32210 AAW	IDBLS	10//99-12//99
	Illinois	S	19.66 MW	21.19 AW	44070 AAW	ILBLS	10//99-12//99
	Bloomington-Normal MSA, IL	S	23.36 MW	14.81 AW	48580 AAW	ILBLS	10//99-12//99
	Champaign-Urbana MSA, IL	S	21.75 MW	13.24 AW	45250 AAW	ILBLS	10//99-12//99
	Chicago PMSA, IL	S	21.45 MW	20.07 AW	44620 AAW	ILBLS	10//99-12//99
	Kankakee PMSA, IL	S	12.13 MW	13.99 AW	25240 AAW	ILBLS	10//99-12//99
	Peoria-Pekin MSA, IL	S	16.08 MW	14.82 AW	33440 AAW	ILBLS	10//99-12//99
	Indiana	S	15.72 MW	16.42 AW	34150 AAW	INBLS	10//99-12//99
	Elkhart-Goshen MSA, IN	S	15.18 MW	15.50 AW	31560 AAW	INBLS	10//99-12//99
	Evansville-Henderson MSA, IN-KY	S	14.01 MW	14.26 AW	29140 AAW	INBLS	10//99-12//99
	Fort Wayne MSA, IN	S	21.32 MW	20.03 AW	44350 AAW	INBLS	10//99-12//99
	Gary PMSA, IN	S	12.96 MW	14.29 AW	26960 AAW	INBLS	10//99-12//99
	Indianapolis MSA, IN	S	19.61 MW	18.15 AW	40790 AAW	INBLS	10//99-12//99
	Lafayette MSA, IN	S	13.10 MW	14.21 AW	27250 AAW	INBLS	10//99-12//99
	South Bend MSA, IN	S	10.05 MW	9.62 AW	20900 AAW	INBLS	10//99-12//99
	Iowa	S	12.25 MW	14.68 AW	30530 AAW	IABLS	10//99-12//99
	Cedar Rapids MSA, IA	S	16.20 MW	13.90 AW	33690 AAW	IABLS	10//99-12//99
	Davenport-Moline-Rock Island MSA, IA-IL	S	16.61 MW	15.93 AW	34540 AAW	IABLS	10//99-12//99
	Des Moines MSA, IA	S	14.30 MW	8.52 AW	29750 AAW	IABLS	10//99-12//99
	Iowa City MSA, IA	S	15.57 MW	14.78 AW	32390 AAW	IABLS	10//99-12//99
	Kansas	S	11.75 MW	13.96 AW	29040 AAW	KSBLS	10//99-12//99
	Lawrence MSA, KS	S	11.88 MW	10.98 AW	24720 AAW	KSBLS	10//99-12//99
	Topeka MSA, KS	S	12.02 MW	6.71 AW	25000 AAW	KSBLS	10//99-12//99
	Wichita MSA, KS	S	15.63 MW	14.73 AW	32500 AAW	KSBLS	10//99-12//99
	Kentucky	S	12.72 MW	15.88 AW	33020 AAW	KYBLS	10//99-12//99
	Lexington MSA, KY	S	10.62 MW	9.30 AW	22080 AAW	KYBLS	10//99-12//99
	Louisville MSA, KY-IN	S	19.32 MW	16.14 AW	40190 AAW	KYBLS	10//99-12//99
	Louisiana	S	12.1 MW	15.62 AW	32480 AAW	LABLS	10//99-12//99
	Baton Rouge MSA, LA	S	21.09 MW	15.02 AW	43870 AAW	LABLS	10//99-12//99
	Lake Charles MSA, LA	S	15.07 MW	12.46 AW	31350 AAW	LABLS	10//99-12//99
	Monroe MSA, LA	S	10.25 MW	6.35 AW	21330 AAW	LABLS	10//99-12//99
	New Orleans MSA, LA	S	19.44 MW	14.51 AW	40430 AAW	LABLS	10//99-12//99
	Shreveport-Bossier City MSA, LA	S	12.34 MW	12.05 AW	25670 AAW	LABLS	10//99-12//99
	Maine	S	11.86 MW	15.00 AW	31200 AAW	MEBLS	10//99-12//99
	Bangor MSA, ME	S	17.33 MW	16.59 AW	36040 AAW	MEBLS	10//99-12//99
	Lewiston-Auburn MSA, ME	S	13.79 MW	12.63 AW	28690 AAW	MEBLS	10//99-12//99
	Portland MSA, ME	S	16.29 MW	13.94 AW	33880 AAW	MEBLS	10//99-12//99
	Maryland	S	20.25 MW	21.26 AW	44220 AAW	MDBLS	10//99-12//99
	Baltimore PMSA, MD	S	22.16 MW	20.51 AW	46090 AAW	MDBLS	10//99-12//99
	Massachusetts	S	21.21 MW	24.39 AW	50730 AAW	MABLS	10//99-12//99
	Boston PMSA, MA-NH	S	24.78 MW	21.40 AW	51540 AAW	MABLS	10//99-12//99
	Lawrence PMSA, MA-NH	S	18.18 MW	18.30 AW	37810 AAW	MABLS	10//99-12//99

AAW Average annual wage	**AOH** Average offered, high	**ASH** Average starting, high	**H** Hourly	**M** Monthly	**S** Special: hourly and annual
AE Average entry wage	**AOL** Average offered, low	**ASL** Average starting, low	**HI** Highest wage paid	**MTC** Median total compensation	**TQ** Third quartile wage
AEX Average experienced wage	**APH** Average pay, high range	**AW** Average wage paid	**HR** High end range	**MW** Median wage paid	**W** Weekly
AO Average offered	**APL** Average pay, low range	**FQ** First quartile wage	**LR** Low end range	**SQ** Second quartile wage	**Y** Yearly

Occupation/Type/Industry	Location	Per	Low	Mid	High	Source	Date
Property, Real Estate, and Community Association Manager							
	Lowell PMSA, MA-NH	S	21.96 MW	19.37 AW	45680 AAW	MABLS	10//99-12//99
	Springfield MSA, MA	S	21.12 MW	20.36 AW	43930 AAW	MABLS	10//99-12//99
	Worcester PMSA, MA-CT	S	28.45 MW	24.90 AW	59170 AAW	MABLS	10//99-12//99
	Michigan	S	19.15 MW	21.06 AW	43800 AAW	MIBLS	10//99-12//99
	Ann Arbor PMSA, MI	S	24.60 MW	20.95 AW	51160 AAW	MIBLS	10//99-12//99
	Detroit PMSA, MI	S	22.50 MW	20.02 AW	46810 AAW	MIBLS	10//99-12//99
	Grand Rapids-Muskegon-Holland MSA, MI	S	15.43 MW	15.40 AW	32100 AAW	MIBLS	10//99-12//99
	Kalamazoo-Battle Creek MSA, MI	S	13.33 MW	11.88 AW	27730 AAW	MIBLS	10//99-12//99
	Lansing-East Lansing MSA, MI	S	20.93 MW	12.53 AW	43530 AAW	MIBLS	10//99-12//99
	Saginaw-Bay City-Midland MSA, MI	S	22.94 MW	22.18 AW	47720 AAW	MIBLS	10//99-12//99
	Minnesota	S	14 MW	16.33 AW	33960 AAW	MNBLS	10//99-12//99
	Minneapolis-St. Paul MSA, MN-WI	S	18.16 MW	16.49 AW	37770 AAW	MNBLS	10//99-12//99
	St. Cloud MSA, MN	S	16.60 MW	15.59 AW	34530 AAW	MNBLS	10//99-12//99
	Mississippi	S	14.51 MW	17.29 AW	35970 AAW	MSBLS	10//99-12//99
	Biloxi-Gulfport-Pascagoula MSA, MS	S	19.35 MW	14.89 AW	40240 AAW	MSBLS	10//99-12//99
	Hattiesburg MSA, MS	S	13.89 MW	12.87 AW	28890 AAW	MSBLS	10//99-12//99
	Jackson MSA, MS	S	21.08 MW	16.60 AW	43860 AAW	MSBLS	10//99-12//99
	Missouri	S	10.69 MW	14.29 AW	29720 AAW	MOBLS	10//99-12//99
	Columbia MSA, MO	S	11.84 MW	9.88 AW	24630 AAW	MOBLS	10//99-12//99
	Joplin MSA, MO	S	11.38 MW	10.18 AW	23680 AAW	MOBLS	10//99-12//99
	Kansas City MSA, MO-KS	S	20.39 MW	17.77 AW	42410 AAW	MOBLS	10//99-12//99
	St. Louis MSA, MO-IL	S	17.21 MW	16.25 AW	35790 AAW	MOBLS	10//99-12//99
	Montana	S	23.55 MW	23.54 AW	48970 AAW	MTBLS	10//99-12//99
	Billings MSA, MT	S	24.92 MW	25.62 AW	51840 AAW	MTBLS	10//99-12//99
	Nebraska	S	9.84 MW	13.17 AW	27390 AAW	NEBLS	10//99-12//99
	Lincoln MSA, NE	S	11.88 MW	8.39 AW	24720 AAW	NEBLS	10//99-12//99
	Omaha MSA, NE-IA	S	14.30 MW	11.43 AW	29750 AAW	NEBLS	10//99-12//99
	Nevada	S	10.57 MW	13.61 AW	28310 AAW	NVBLS	10//99-12//99
	Las Vegas MSA, NV-AZ	S	12.93 MW	9.84 AW	26890 AAW	NVBLS	10//99-12//99
	Reno MSA, NV	S	13.91 MW	11.45 AW	28930 AAW	NVBLS	10//99-12//99
	New Hampshire	S	13.81 MW	16.13 AW	33540 AAW	NHBLS	10//99-12//99
	Manchester PMSA, NH	S	16.88 MW	17.04 AW	35110 AAW	NHBLS	10//99-12//99
	Nashua PMSA, NH	S	16.87 MW	13.47 AW	35090 AAW	NHBLS	10//99-12//99
	Portsmouth-Rochester PMSA, NH-ME	S	24.60 MW	22.33 AW	51170 AAW	NHBLS	10//99-12//99
	New Jersey	S	26.32 MW	29.57 AW	61500 AAW	NJBLS	10//99-12//99
	Atlantic-Cape May PMSA, NJ	S	29.34 MW	29.63 AW	61030 AAW	NJBLS	10//99-12//99
	Bergen-Passaic PMSA, NJ	S	29.58 MW	26.64 AW	61540 AAW	NJBLS	10//99-12//99
	Jersey City PMSA, NJ	S	29.78 MW	25.36 AW	61940 AAW	NJBLS	10//99-12//99
	Middlesex-Somerset-Hunterdon PMSA, NJ	S	33.75 MW	26.53 AW	70190 AAW	NJBLS	10//99-12//99
	Monmouth-Ocean PMSA, NJ	S	34.82 MW	27.82 AW	72420 AAW	NJBLS	10//99-12//99
	Newark PMSA, NJ	S	23.76 MW	16.89 AW	49420 AAW	NJBLS	10//99-12//99
	Trenton PMSA, NJ	S	24.60 MW	21.10 AW	51170 AAW	NJBLS	10//99-12//99
	Vineland-Millville-Bridgeton PMSA, NJ	S	20.50 MW	19.27 AW	42650 AAW	NJBLS	10//99-12//99
	New Mexico	S	13.79 MW	16.31 AW	33910 AAW	NMBLS	10//99-12//99
	Albuquerque MSA, NM	S	15.77 MW	14.75 AW	32810 AAW	NMBLS	10//99-12//99
	Las Cruces MSA, NM	S	11.09 MW	10.30 AW	23060 AAW	NMBLS	10//99-12//99
	New York	S	21.43 MW	25.84 AW	53750 AAW	NYBLS	10//99-12//99
	Binghamton MSA, NY	S	17.68 MW	16.41 AW	36770 AAW	NYBLS	10//99-12//99
	Buffalo-Niagara Falls MSA, NY	S	28.48 MW	23.92 AW	59240 AAW	NYBLS	10//99-12//99
	Dutchess County PMSA, NY	S	16.61 MW	15.73 AW	34540 AAW	NYBLS	10//99-12//99
	Glens Falls MSA, NY	S	15.89 MW	15.63 AW	33050 AAW	NYBLS	10//99-12//99
	Nassau-Suffolk PMSA, NY	S	35.34 MW	34.99 AW	73500 AAW	NYBLS	10//99-12//99
	New York PMSA, NY	S	25.98 MW	22.69 AW	54040 AAW	NYBLS	10//99-12//99
	Newburgh PMSA, NY-PA	S	17.48 MW	13.25 AW	36350 AAW	NYBLS	10//99-12//99
	Syracuse MSA, NY	S	25.80 MW	28.03 AW	53660 AAW	NYBLS	10//99-12//99
	Utica-Rome MSA, NY	S	16.17 MW	13.39 AW	33630 AAW	NYBLS	10//99-12//99
	North Carolina	S	14.81 MW	18.43 AW	38330 AAW	NCBLS	10//99-12//99
	Charlotte-Gastonia-Rock Hill MSA, NC-SC	S	21.55 MW	16.62 AW	44820 AAW	NCBLS	10//99-12//99
	Fayetteville MSA, NC	S	15.76 MW	12.82 AW	32790 AAW	NCBLS	10//99-12//99

AAW Average annual wage	**AOH** Average offered, high	**ASH** Average starting, high	**H** Hourly	**M** Monthly	**S** Special: hourly and annual
AE Average entry wage	**AOL** Average offered, low	**ASL** Average starting, low	**HI** Highest wage paid	**MTC** Median total compensation	**TQ** Third quartile wage
AEX Average experienced wage	**APH** Average pay, high range	**AW** Average wage paid	**HR** High end range	**MW** Median wage paid	**W** Weekly
AO Average offered	**APL** Average pay, low range	**FQ** First quartile wage	**LR** Low end range	**SQ** Second quartile wage	**Y** Yearly

Occupation/Type/Industry	Location	Per	Low	Mid	High	Source	Date
Property, Real Estate, and Community Association Manager	Greensboro--Winston-Salem--High Point MSA, NC	S	12.89 MW	11.48 AW	26820 AAW	NCBLS	10//99-12//99
	Hickory-Morganton-Lenoir MSA, NC	S	30.30 MW	32.34 AW	63030 AAW	NCBLS	10//99-12//99
	Raleigh-Durham-Chapel Hill MSA, NC	S	18.69 MW	15.37 AW	38880 AAW	NCBLS	10//99-12//99
	Wilmington MSA, NC	S	18.29 MW	15.48 AW	38040 AAW	NCBLS	10//99-12//99
	North Dakota	S	9.29 MW	11.91 AW	24780 AAW	NDBLS	10//99-12//99
	Ohio	S	14.38 MW	16.55 AW	34430 AAW	OHBLS	10//99-12//99
	Akron PMSA, OH	S	15.01 MW	15.05 AW	31210 AAW	OHBLS	10//99-12//99
	Canton-Massillon MSA, OH	S	11.23 MW	10.06 AW	23350 AAW	OHBLS	10//99-12//99
	Cincinnati PMSA, OH-KY-IN	S	17.75 MW	14.80 AW	36920 AAW	OHBLS	10//99-12//99
	Cleveland-Lorain-Elyria PMSA, OH	S	18.86 MW	17.67 AW	39220 AAW	OHBLS	10//99-12//99
	Columbus MSA, OH	S	15.56 MW	14.20 AW	32370 AAW	OHBLS	10//99-12//99
	Dayton-Springfield MSA, OH	S	17.43 MW	15.89 AW	36250 AAW	OHBLS	10//99-12//99
	Hamilton-Middletown PMSA, OH	S	11.08 MW	9.74 AW	23040 AAW	OHBLS	10//99-12//99
	Lima MSA, OH	S	22.37 MW	27.95 AW	46540 AAW	OHBLS	10//99-12//99
	Steubenville-Weirton MSA, OH-WV	S	9.94 MW	11.20 AW	20680 AAW	OHBLS	10//99-12//99
	Toledo MSA, OH	S	30.40 MW	29.59 AW	63240 AAW	OHBLS	10//99-12//99
	Oklahoma	S	15.42 MW	15.99 AW	33270 AAW	OKBLS	10//99-12//99
	Lawton MSA, OK	S	19.40 MW	19.25 AW	40350 AAW	OKBLS	10//99-12//99
	Oklahoma City MSA, OK	S	16.12 MW	12.97 AW	33540 AAW	OKBLS	10//99-12//99
	Tulsa MSA, OK	S	15.50 MW	14.79 AW	32240 AAW	OKBLS	10//99-12//99
	Oregon	S	10.91 MW	16.81 AW	34960 AAW	ORBLS	10//99-12//99
	Corvallis MSA, OR	S	17.32 MW	18.79 AW	36020 AAW	ORBLS	10//99-12//99
	Eugene-Springfield MSA, OR	S	10.09 MW	8.53 AW	20980 AAW	ORBLS	10//99-12//99
	Medford-Ashland MSA, OR	S	12.60 MW	11.54 AW	26210 AAW	ORBLS	10//99-12//99
	Portland-Vancouver PMSA, OR-WA	S	18.69 MW	12.66 AW	38880 AAW	ORBLS	10//99-12//99
	Salem PMSA, OR	S	10.63 MW	9.43 AW	22110 AAW	ORBLS	10//99-12//99
	Pennsylvania	S	15.88 MW	19.27 AW	40070 AAW	PABLS	10//99-12//99
	Allentown-Bethlehem-Easton MSA, PA	S	16.01 MW	14.72 AW	33310 AAW	PABLS	10//99-12//99
	Altoona MSA, PA	S	13.04 MW	12.59 AW	27120 AAW	PABLS	10//99-12//99
	Harrisburg-Lebanon-Carlisle MSA, PA	S	23.25 MW	23.13 AW	48370 AAW	PABLS	10//99-12//99
	Lancaster MSA, PA	S	14.49 MW	13.57 AW	30140 AAW	PABLS	10//99-12//99
	Philadelphia PMSA, PA-NJ	S	22.76 MW	16.46 AW	47330 AAW	PABLS	10//99-12//99
	Pittsburgh MSA, PA	S	18.85 MW	16.50 AW	39210 AAW	PABLS	10//99-12//99
	Reading MSA, PA	S	21.49 MW	23.21 AW	44690 AAW	PABLS	10//99-12//99
	Williamsport MSA, PA	S	15.79 MW	15.41 AW	32850 AAW	PABLS	10//99-12//99
	York MSA, PA	S	14.77 MW	12.52 AW	30710 AAW	PABLS	10//99-12//99
	Rhode Island	S	30.31 MW	30.79 AW	64050 AAW	RIBLS	10//99-12//99
	Providence-Fall River-Warwick MSA, RI-MA	S	32.62 MW	34.89 AW	67840 AAW	RIBLS	10//99-12//99
	South Carolina	S	15.22 MW	16.96 AW	35270 AAW	SCBLS	10//99-12//99
	Charleston-North Charleston MSA, SC	S	17.79 MW	18.06 AW	37010 AAW	SCBLS	10//99-12//99
	Columbia MSA, SC	S	17.73 MW	13.15 AW	36870 AAW	SCBLS	10//99-12//99
	Florence MSA, SC	S	8.48 MW	8.88 AW	17640 AAW	SCBLS	10//99-12//99
	Greenville-Spartanburg-Anderson MSA, SC	S	16.27 MW	16.39 AW	33840 AAW	SCBLS	10//99-12//99
	Myrtle Beach MSA, SC	S	19.34 MW	17.79 AW	40220 AAW	SCBLS	10//99-12//99
	South Dakota	S	11.17 MW	14.01 AW	29140 AAW	SDBLS	10//99-12//99
	Rapid City MSA, SD	S	11.05 MW	9.87 AW	22990 AAW	SDBLS	10//99-12//99
	Sioux Falls MSA, SD	S	16.45 MW	13.44 AW	34220 AAW	SDBLS	10//99-12//99
	Tennessee	S	14.41 MW	17.53 AW	36470 AAW	TNBLS	10//99-12//99
	Chattanooga MSA, TN-GA	S	21.83 MW	18.20 AW	45410 AAW	TNBLS	10//99-12//99
	Knoxville MSA, TN	S	23.03 MW	24.06 AW	47900 AAW	TNBLS	10//99-12//99
	Memphis MSA, TN-AR-MS	S	20.03 MW	14.05 AW	41670 AAW	MSBLS	10//99-12//99
	Nashville MSA, TN	S	17.82 MW	17.13 AW	37060 AAW	TNBLS	10//99-12//99
	Texas	S	15.08 MW	18.49 AW	38460 AAW	TXBLS	10//99-12//99
	Abilene MSA, TX	S	13.45 MW	13.35 AW	27980 AAW	TXBLS	10//99-12//99
	Amarillo MSA, TX	S	13.15 MW	13.78 AW	27350 AAW	TXBLS	10//99-12//99
	Austin-San Marcos MSA, TX	S	14.20 MW	12.32 AW	29540 AAW	TXBLS	10//99-12//99
	Beaumont-Port Arthur MSA, TX	S	14.91 MW	10.92 AW	31010 AAW	TXBLS	10//99-12//99

AAW	Average annual wage	AOH	Average offered, high	ASH	Average starting, high
AE	Average entry wage	AOL	Average offered, low	ASL	Average starting, low
AEX	Average experienced wage	APH	Average pay, high range	AW	Average wage paid
AO	Average offered	APL	Average pay, low range	FQ	First quartile wage

H	Hourly	M	Monthly
HI	Highest wage paid	MTC	Median total compensation
HR	High end range	MW	Median wage paid
LR	Low end range	SQ	Second quartile wage

S	Special: hourly and annual
TQ	Third quartile wage
W	Weekly
Y	Yearly

Occupation/Type/Industry	Location	Per	Low	Mid	High	Source	Date
Property, Real Estate, and Community Association Manager	Brazoria PMSA, TX	S	23.74 MW	24.27 AW	49390 AAW	TXBLS	10//99-12//99
	Brownsville-Harlingen-San Benito MSA, TX	S	15.98 MW	15.15 AW	33240 AAW	TXBLS	10//99-12//99
	Bryan-College Station MSA, TX	S	9.53 MW	8.15 AW	19820 AAW	TXBLS	10//99-12//99
	Corpus Christi MSA, TX	S	14.74 MW	11.94 AW	30660 AAW	TXBLS	10//99-12//99
	Dallas PMSA, TX	S	25.36 MW	22.01 AW	52750 AAW	TXBLS	10//99-12//99
	El Paso MSA, TX	S	14.03 MW	11.87 AW	29180 AAW	TXBLS	10//99-12//99
	Fort Worth-Arlington PMSA, TX	S	16.56 MW	16.12 AW	34430 AAW	TXBLS	10//99-12//99
	Houston PMSA, TX	S	17.55 MW	11.72 AW	36510 AAW	TXBLS	10//99-12//99
	Killeen-Temple MSA, TX	S	16.48 MW	12.36 AW	34270 AAW	TXBLS	10//99-12//99
	Longview-Marshall MSA, TX	S	12.84 MW	11.89 AW	26700 AAW	TXBLS	10//99-12//99
	Lubbock MSA, TX	S	14.85 MW	11.91 AW	30880 AAW	TXBLS	10//99-12//99
	McAllen-Edinburg-Mission MSA, TX	S	11.26 MW	10.57 AW	23430 AAW	TXBLS	10//99-12//99
	Odessa-Midland MSA, TX	S	14.05 MW	7.51 AW	29220 AAW	TXBLS	10//99-12//99
	San Antonio MSA, TX	S	18.19 MW	14.32 AW	37830 AAW	TXBLS	10//99-12//99
	Sherman-Denison MSA, TX	S	16.92 MW	12.92 AW	35200 AAW	TXBLS	10//99-12//99
	Texarkana MSA, TX-Texarkana, AR	S	11.05 MW	11.67 AW	22990 AAW	TXBLS	10//99-12//99
	Tyler MSA, TX	S	12.50 MW	12.22 AW	25990 AAW	TXBLS	10//99-12//99
	Wichita Falls MSA, TX	S	11.50 MW	10.10 AW	23930 AAW	TXBLS	10//99-12//99
	Utah	S	15.72 MW	18.69 AW	38880 AAW	UTBLS	10//99-12//99
	Provo-Orem MSA, UT	S	23.67 MW	28.54 AW	49220 AAW	UTBLS	10//99-12//99
	Salt Lake City-Ogden MSA, UT	S	16.17 MW	14.89 AW	33640 AAW	UTBLS	10//99-12//99
	Vermont	S	21.37 MW	24.24 AW	50410 AAW	VTBLS	10//99-12//99
	Burlington MSA, VT	S	24.92 MW	22.68 AW	51840 AAW	VTBLS	10//99-12//99
	Virginia	S	18.95 MW	21.00 AW	43670 AAW	VABLS	10//99-12//99
	Norfolk-Virginia Beach-Newport News MSA, VA-NC	S	19.75 MW	18.44 AW	41090 AAW	VABLS	10//99-12//99
	Richmond-Petersburg MSA, VA	S	22.49 MW	19.54 AW	46780 AAW	VABLS	10//99-12//99
	Roanoke MSA, VA	S	16.37 MW	14.75 AW	34050 AAW	VABLS	10//99-12//99
	Washington	S	18.57 MW	21.46 AW	44630 AAW	WABLS	10//99-12//99
	Spokane MSA, WA	S	12.80 MW	12.17 AW	26620 AAW	WABLS	10//99-12//99
	Tacoma PMSA, WA	S	19.16 MW	18.35 AW	39840 AAW	WABLS	10//99-12//99
	West Virginia	S	12.31 MW	14.69 AW	30560 AAW	WVBLS	10//99-12//99
	Charleston MSA, WV	S	21.10 MW	16.00 AW	43890 AAW	WVBLS	10//99-12//99
	Huntington-Ashland MSA, WV-KY-OH	S	13.27 MW	12.19 AW	27600 AAW	WVBLS	10//99-12//99
	Parkersburg-Marietta MSA, WV-OH	S	11.20 MW	10.01 AW	23290 AAW	WVBLS	10//99-12//99
	Wheeling MSA, WV-OH	S	11.60 MW	11.72 AW	24120 AAW	WVBLS	10//99-12//99
	Appleton-Oshkosh-Neenah MSA, WI	S	19.94 MW	18.96 AW	41470 AAW	WIBLS	10//99-12//99
	Eau Claire MSA, WI	S	24.21 MW	17.99 AW	50350 AAW	WIBLS	10//99-12//99
	Green Bay MSA, WI	S	17.98 MW	15.85 AW	37390 AAW	WIBLS	10//99-12//99
	Kenosha PMSA, WI	S	16.18 MW	15.03 AW	33650 AAW	WIBLS	10//99-12//99
	Milwaukee-Waukesha PMSA, WI	S	16.04 MW	14.42 AW	33350 AAW	WIBLS	10//99-12//99
	Wyoming	S	11.45 MW	12.99 AW	27020 AAW	WYBLS	10//99-12//99
	Cheyenne MSA, WY	S	13.11 MW	11.29 AW	27270 AAW	WYBLS	10//99-12//99
	Puerto Rico	S	18.81 MW	23.63 AW	49150 AAW	PRBLS	10//99-12//99
	Virgin Islands	S	15.11 MW	15.68 AW	32620 AAW	VIBLS	10//99-12//99
	Guam	S	17.83 MW	18.18 AW	37820 AAW	GUBLS	10//99-12//99
Psychiatric Aide	Alabama	S	7.77 MW	8.14 AW	16940 AAW	ALBLS	10//99-12//99
	Arizona	S	9.07 MW	9.22 AW	19180 AAW	AZBLS	10//99-12//99
	Arkansas	S	8.3 MW	8.97 AW	18660 AAW	ARBLS	10//99-12//99
	California	S	9.51 MW	9.68 AW	20140 AAW	CABLS	10//99-12//99
	Colorado	S	11.88 MW	11.34 AW	23590 AAW	COBLS	10//99-12//99
	Connecticut	S	13.38 MW	14.52 AW	30210 AAW	CTBLS	10//99-12//99
	Florida	S	9.18 MW	9.70 AW	20170 AAW	FLBLS	10//99-12//99
	Georgia	S	9.48 MW	9.88 AW	20540 AAW	GABLS	10//99-12//99
	Idaho	S	8.78 MW	9.29 AW	19320 AAW	IDBLS	10//99-12//99
	Illinois	S	11.49 MW	11.11 AW	23110 AAW	ILBLS	10//99-12//99
	Indiana	S	9.31 MW	9.29 AW	19320 AAW	INBLS	10//99-12//99

Occupation/Type/Industry	Location	Per	Low	Mid	High	Source	Date
Psychiatric Aide	Iowa	S	11.03 MW	11.19 AW	23280 AAW	IABLS	10//99-12//99
	Kansas	S	7.93 MW	8.28 AW	17230 AAW	KSBLS	10//99-12//99
	Kentucky	S	7.71 MW	7.77 AW	16170 AAW	KYBLS	10//99-12//99
	Louisiana	S	7.48 MW	7.75 AW	16120 AAW	LABLS	10//99-12//99
	Maine	S	10.05 MW	10.10 AW	21010 AAW	MEBLS	10//99-12//99
	Maryland	S	10.87 MW	10.72 AW	22310 AAW	MDBLS	10//99-12//99
	Massachusetts	S	11.9 MW	12.04 AW	25050 AAW	MABLS	10//99-12//99
	Michigan	S	13.76 MW	12.94 AW	26920 AAW	MIBLS	10//99-12//99
	Minnesota	S	9.78 MW	9.92 AW	20640 AAW	MNBLS	10//99-12//99
	Mississippi	S	7.3 MW	7.70 AW	16020 AAW	MSBLS	10//99-12//99
	Montana	S	10.15 MW	10.72 AW	22300 AAW	MTBLS	10//99-12//99
	Nebraska	S	8.91 MW	8.83 AW	18360 AAW	NEBLS	10//99-12//99
	New Jersey	S	10.97 MW	10.82 AW	22500 AAW	NJBLS	10//99-12//99
	New York	S	14.15 MW	13.18 AW	27420 AAW	NYBLS	10//99-12//99
	North Carolina	S	8.91 MW	9.09 AW	18900 AAW	NCBLS	10//99-12//99
	Oklahoma	S	8.1 MW	8.26 AW	17170 AAW	OKBLS	10//99-12//99
	Oregon	S	11.89 MW	11.94 AW	24830 AAW	ORBLS	10//99-12//99
	Pennsylvania	S	12.32 MW	12.24 AW	25450 AAW	PABLS	10//99-12//99
	Rhode Island	S	10.13 MW	10.58 AW	22020 AAW	RIBLS	10//99-12//99
	Tennessee	S	9.27 MW	9.26 AW	19260 AAW	TNBLS	10//99-12//99
	Texas	S	8.12 MW	8.36 AW	17400 AAW	TXBLS	10//99-12//99
	Vermont	S	8.51 MW	9.00 AW	18730 AAW	VTBLS	10//99-12//99
	Virginia	S	9.52 MW	9.78 AW	20350 AAW	VABLS	10//99-12//99
	Washington	S	13.73 MW	13.25 AW	27560 AAW	WABLS	10//99-12//99
	West Virginia	S	7.63 MW	8.05 AW	16750 AAW	WVBLS	10//99-12//99
	Wisconsin	S	10.23 MW	10.47 AW	21780 AAW	WIBLS	10//99-12//99
Psychiatric Technician	Alabama	S	7.18 MW	7.53 AW	15660 AAW	ALBLS	10//99-12//99
	Arizona	S	9.4 MW	9.52 AW	19790 AAW	AZBLS	10//99-12//99
	Arkansas	S	8.64 MW	9.34 AW	19420 AAW	ARBLS	10//99-12//99
	California	S	15.83 MW	15.94 AW	33160 AAW	CABLS	10//99-12//99
	Colorado	S	10.74 MW	11.19 AW	23280 AAW	COBLS	10//99-12//99
	Connecticut	S	20.15 MW	19.81 AW	41200 AAW	CTBLS	10//99-12//99
	Delaware	S	10.44 MW	11.11 AW	23120 AAW	DEBLS	10//99-12//99
	District of Columbia	S	11.17 MW	12.28 AW	25540 AAW	DCBLS	10//99-12//99
	Florida	S	9.61 MW	9.86 AW	20520 AAW	FLBLS	10//99-12//99
	Georgia	S	9.13 MW	9.50 AW	19750 AAW	GABLS	10//99-12//99
	Idaho	S	7.56 MW	8.19 AW	17030 AAW	IDBLS	10//99-12//99
	Illinois	S	11.97 MW	11.52 AW	23960 AAW	ILBLS	10//99-12//99
	Indiana	S	9.19 MW	9.20 AW	19130 AAW	INBLS	10//99-12//99
	Iowa	S	9.66 MW	10.84 AW	22550 AAW	IABLS	10//99-12//99
	Kansas	S	11.15 MW	11.40 AW	23700 AAW	KSBLS	10//99-12//99
	Kentucky	S	8.58 MW	8.71 AW	18110 AAW	KYBLS	10//99-12//99
	Louisiana	S	8.14 MW	8.75 AW	18200 AAW	LABLS	10//99-12//99
	Maine	S	9.93 MW	9.91 AW	20620 AAW	MEBLS	10//99-12//99
	Maryland	S	10.85 MW	11.79 AW	24530 AAW	MDBLS	10//99-12//99
	Massachusetts	S	11.51 MW	12.08 AW	25120 AAW	MABLS	10//99-12//99
	Michigan	S	12.44 MW	11.99 AW	24950 AAW	MIBLS	10//99-12//99
	Minnesota	S	13.58 MW	13.91 AW	28930 AAW	MNBLS	10//99-12//99
	Mississippi	S	11.89 MW	12.04 AW	25040 AAW	MSBLS	10//99-12//99
	New Jersey	S	12.01 MW	13.11 AW	27270 AAW	NJBLS	10//99-12//99
	New Mexico	S	9 MW	9.02 AW	18770 AAW	NMBLS	10//99-12//99
	New York	S	11.19 MW	11.60 AW	24130 AAW	NYBLS	10//99-12//99
	North Carolina	S	9.81 MW	10.21 AW	21240 AAW	NCBLS	10//99-12//99
	Ohio	S	9.82 MW	10.25 AW	21330 AAW	OHBLS	10//99-12//99
	Oklahoma	S	9.58 MW	11.58 AW	24080 AAW	OKBLS	10//99-12//99
	Oregon	S	15.87 MW	15.71 AW	32670 AAW	ORBLS	10//99-12//99
	Pennsylvania	S	11.11 MW	11.87 AW	24700 AAW	PABLS	10//99-12//99
	Texas	S	7.99 MW	8.48 AW	17630 AAW	TXBLS	10//99-12//99
	Utah	S	8.95 MW	9.42 AW	19600 AAW	UTBLS	10//99-12//99
	Vermont	S	12.76 MW	13.74 AW	28580 AAW	VTBLS	10//99-12//99
	Virginia	S	10.09 MW	10.44 AW	21710 AAW	VABLS	10//99-12//99
	Washington	S	15.13 MW	14.94 AW	31080 AAW	WABLS	10//99-12//99
	West Virginia	S	8.43 MW	9.52 AW	19790 AAW	WVBLS	10//99-12//99
	Wisconsin	S	11.9 MW	12.33 AW	25660 AAW	WIBLS	10//99-12//99
Psychiatrist	Alabama	S	61.04 MW	56.01 AW	116500 AAW	ALBLS	10//99-12//99
	Arizona	S	47.61 MW	43.61 AW	90700 AAW	AZBLS	10//99-12//99
	Phoenix-Mesa MSA, AZ	S	54.67 MW	54.25 AW	113720 AAW	AZBLS	10//99-12//99
	Arkansas	S	26.4 MW	37.80 AW	78610 AAW	ARBLS	10//99-12//99
	Little Rock-North Little Rock MSA, AR	S	35.19 MW	26.03 AW	73190 AAW	ARBLS	10//99-12//99
	California	S	56.58 MW	52.96 AW	110160 AAW	CABLS	10//99-12//99

Occupation/Type/Industry	Location	Per	Low	Mid	High	Source	Date
Psychiatrist	Los Angeles-Long Beach						
	PMSA, CA	S	46.96 MW	50.48 AW	97680 AAW	CABLS	10//99-12//99
	Orange County PMSA, CA	S	58.92 MW	61.92 AW	122550 AAW	CABLS	10//99-12//99
	Riverside-San Bernardino						
	PMSA, CA	S	53.07 MW	56.73 AW	110390 AAW	CABLS	10//99-12//99
	Sacramento PMSA, CA	S	58.17 MW	60.57 AW	121000 AAW	CABLS	10//99-12//99
	San Diego MSA, CA	S	59.97 MW	63.82 AW	124740 AAW	CABLS	10//99-12//99
	San Francisco PMSA, CA	S	59.01 MW	62.05 AW	122730 AAW	CABLS	10//99-12//99
	San Jose PMSA, CA	S	55.73 MW	61.58 AW	115920 AAW	CABLS	10//99-12//99
	Vallejo-Fairfield-Napa PMSA,						
	CA	S	58.28 MW	61.50 AW	121220 AAW	CABLS	10//99-12//99
	Bridgeport PMSA, CT	S	53.76 MW	52.11 AW	111830 AAW	CTBLS	10//99-12//99
	Hartford MSA, CT	S	50.39 MW	51.41 AW	104810 AAW	CTBLS	10//99-12//99
	Washington PMSA, DC-MD-						
	VA-WV	S	52.65 MW	59.26 AW	109510 AAW	DCBLS	10//99-12//99
	Florida	S	67.91 MW	57.26 AW	119100 AAW	FLBLS	10//99-12//99
	Melbourne-Titusville-Palm						
	Bay MSA, FL	S	60.04 MW	62.75 AW	124890 AAW	FLBLS	10//99-12//99
	Miami PMSA, FL	S	48.51 MW	50.71 AW	100900 AAW	FLBLS	10//99-12//99
	Tampa-St. Petersburg-						
	Clearwater MSA, FL	S	56.49 MW		117510 AAW	FLBLS	10//99-12//99
	Georgia	S	60.13 MW	55.28 AW	114980 AAW	GABLS	10//99-12//99
	Atlanta MSA, GA	S	52.16 MW	56.94 AW	108500 AAW	GABLS	10//99-12//99
	Illinois	S	42.51 MW	45.51 AW	94650 AAW	ILBLS	10//99-12//99
	Chicago PMSA, IL	S	41.45 MW	40.38 AW	86210 AAW	ILBLS	10//99-12//99
	Indiana	S		61.61 AW	128140 AAW	INBLS	10//99-12//99
	Indianapolis MSA, IN	S	69.26 MW		144060 AAW	INBLS	10//99-12//99
	Kansas	S	63.23 MW	59.13 AW	122990 AAW	KSBLS	10//99-12//99
	Wichita MSA, KS	S	61.02 MW	63.54 AW	126920 AAW	KSBLS	10//99-12//99
	Kentucky	S		65.26 AW	135730 AAW	KYBLS	10//99-12//99
	Louisiana	S		66.31 AW	137930 AAW	LABLS	10//99-12//99
	Maine	S	64.35 MW	61.13 AW	127160 AAW	MEBLS	10//99-12//99
	Maryland	S	59.52 MW	53.18 AW	110610 AAW	MDBLS	10//99-12//99
	Baltimore PMSA, MD	S	54.80 MW	60.97 AW	113980 AAW	MDBLS	10//99-12//99
	Massachusetts	S	51.53 MW	49.34 AW	102630 AAW	MABLS	10//99-12//99
	Boston PMSA, MA-NH	S	48.29 MW	48.18 AW	100450 AAW	MABLS	10//99-12//99
	Michigan	S		61.08 AW	127040 AAW	MIBLS	10//99-12//99
	Detroit PMSA, MI	S	66.66 MW		138640 AAW	MIBLS	10//99-12//99
	Grand Rapids-Muskegon-						
	Holland MSA, MI	S	59.95 MW	68.86 AW	124710 AAW	MIBLS	10//99-12//99
	Minnesota	S	31.15 MW	37.80 AW	78630 AAW	MNBLS	10//99-12//99
	Missouri	S	62.69 MW	54.98 AW	114360 AAW	MOBLS	10//99-12//99
	St. Louis MSA, MO-IL	S	57.93 MW	62.47 AW	120500 AAW	MOBLS	10//99-12//99
	Nebraska	S	69.04 MW	59.25 AW	123240 AAW	NEBLS	10//99-12//99
	Nevada	S	62.34 MW	58.34 AW	121360 AAW	NVBLS	10//99-12//99
	Las Vegas MSA, NV-AZ	S	57.88 MW	62.38 AW	120390 AAW	NVBLS	10//99-12//99
	New Hampshire	S	64.73 MW	59.84 AW	124460 AAW	NHBLS	10//99-12//99
	New Jersey	S	54.86 MW	53.95 AW	112210 AAW	NJBLS	10//99-12//99
	Middlesex-Somerset-						
	Hunterdon PMSA, NJ	S	48.42 MW	49.21 AW	100720 AAW	NJBLS	10//99-12//99
	Newark PMSA, NJ	S	55.36 MW	55.24 AW	115140 AAW	NJBLS	10//99-12//99
	New Mexico	S	52.82 MW	52.24 AW	108650 AAW	NMBLS	10//99-12//99
	New York	S	53.21 MW	53.80 AW	111910 AAW	NYBLS	10//99-12//99
	Binghamton MSA, NY	S	55.28 MW	52.42 AW	114980 AAW	NYBLS	10//99-12//99
	Buffalo-Niagara Falls MSA,						
	NY	S	57.93 MW	54.80 AW	120490 AAW	NYBLS	10//99-12//99
	Nassau-Suffolk PMSA, NY	S	49.22 MW	49.81 AW	102370 AAW	NYBLS	10//99-12//99
	New York PMSA, NY	S	50.33 MW	51.29 AW	104690 AAW	NYBLS	10//99-12//99
	Rochester MSA, NY	S	58.49 MW	65.81 AW	121650 AAW	NYBLS	10//99-12//99
	Syracuse MSA, NY	S	50.98 MW	50.61 AW	106040 AAW	NYBLS	10//99-12//99
	North Carolina	S		58.29 AW	121240 AAW	NCBLS	10//99-12//99
	Cincinnati PMSA, OH-KY-IN	S	62.44 MW	69.46 AW	129870 AAW	OHBLS	10//99-12//99
	Cleveland-Lorain-Elyria						
	PMSA, OH	S	58.08 MW	64.07 AW	120800 AAW	OHBLS	10//99-12//99
	Columbus MSA, OH	S	57.87 MW	62.90 AW	120380 AAW	OHBLS	10//99-12//99
	Dayton-Springfield MSA, OH	S	59.00 MW		122710 AAW	OHBLS	10//99-12//99
	Toledo MSA, OH	S	52.67 MW	63.12 AW	109560 AAW	OHBLS	10//99-12//99
	Oklahoma	S	58.58 MW	50.22 AW	104460 AAW	OKBLS	10//99-12//99
	Tulsa MSA, OK	S	63.05 MW	69.61 AW	131140 AAW	OKBLS	10//99-12//99
	Pennsylvania	S	54.48 MW	52.89 AW	110020 AAW	PABLS	10//99-12//99
	Harrisburg-Lebanon-Carlisle						
	MSA, PA	S	55.92 MW	59.35 AW	116320 AAW	PABLS	10//99-12//99

Occupation/Type/Industry	Location	Per	Low	Mid	High	Source	Date
Psychiatrist	Philadelphia PMSA, PA-NJ	S	54.61 MW	55.85 AW	113590 AAW	PABLS	10//99-12//99
	Pittsburgh MSA, PA	S	47.94 MW	52.14 AW	99720 AAW	PABLS	10//99-12//99
	Reading MSA, PA	S	57.14 MW	55.17 AW	118850 AAW	PABLS	10//99-12//99
	Scranton--Wilkes-Barre--						
	Hazleton MSA, PA	S	54.60 MW	56.80 AW	113560 AAW	PABLS	10//99-12//99
	Rhode Island	S	57.72 MW	49.64 AW	103250 AAW	RIBLS	10//99-12//99
	Providence-Fall River-						
	Warwick MSA, RI-MA	S	50.07 MW	58.10 AW	104150 AAW	RIBLS	10//99-12//99
	South Carolina	S	45.36 MW	45.83 AW	95330 AAW	SCBLS	10//99-12//99
	Greenville-Spartanburg-						
	Anderson MSA, SC	S	54.11 MW	55.40 AW	112560 AAW	SCBLS	10//99-12//99
	Texas	S	56.7 MW	47.46 AW	98720 AAW	TXBLS	10//99-12//99
	Austin-San Marcos MSA, TX	S	57.02 MW	66.59 AW	118600 AAW	TXBLS	10//99-12//99
	Dallas PMSA, TX	S	41.67 MW	48.61 AW	86670 AAW	TXBLS	10//99-12//99
	Fort Worth-Arlington PMSA,						
	TX	S	50.01 MW	60.56 AW	104020 AAW	TXBLS	10//99-12//99
	San Antonio MSA, TX	S	47.11 MW	58.53 AW	97980 AAW	TXBLS	10//99-12//99
	Vermont	S	63.9 MW	58.49 AW	121660 AAW	VTBLS	10//99-12//99
	Virginia	S	69.6 MW	62.77 AW	130560 AAW	VABLS	10//99-12//99
	Washington	S	46.77 MW	41.56 AW	86450 AAW	WABLS	10//99-12//99
	Seattle-Bellevue-Everett						
	PMSA, WA	S	53.30 MW	57.51 AW	110870 AAW	WABLS	10//99-12//99
	Spokane MSA, WA	S	35.35 MW	43.80 AW	73530 AAW	WABLS	10//99-12//99
	Tacoma PMSA, WA	S	34.13 MW	21.50 AW	70990 AAW	WABLS	10//99-12//99
	West Virginia	S	62.71 MW	56.77 AW	118090 AAW	WVBLS	10//99-12//99
	Huntington-Ashland MSA,						
	WV-KY-OH	S	48.61 MW	52.99 AW	101100 AAW	WVBLS	10//99-12//99
	Puerto Rico	S	56.8 MW	50.94 AW	105950 AAW	PRBLS	10//99-12//99
	San Juan-Bayamon PMSA, PR	S	53.75 MW	59.50 AW	111810 AAW	PRBLS	10//99-12//99
Behavioral Health Organization	United States	Y	101440 APL	116965 AW	141471 APH	ADAW	2000
Psychologist	United States	H		24.19 AW		NCS98	1998
	Chicago, IL	Y	32182 AE			CARWO2	2000
	New York, NY	Y	30595 AE			CARWO2	2000
Psychology Teacher							
Postsecondary	Alabama	Y		38720 AAW		ALBLS	10//99-12//99
Postsecondary	Arizona	Y		48040 AAW		AZBLS	10//99-12//99
Postsecondary	Arkansas	Y		40900 AAW		ARBLS	10//99-12//99
Postsecondary	California	Y		59160 AAW		CABLS	10//99-12//99
Postsecondary	Fresno MSA, CA	Y		52880 AAW		CABLS	10//99-12//99
Postsecondary	Los Angeles-Long Beach						
	PMSA, CA	Y		53560 AAW		CABLS	10//99-12//99
Postsecondary	Orange County PMSA, CA	Y		65280 AAW		CABLS	10//99-12//99
Postsecondary	Riverside-San Bernardino						
	PMSA, CA	Y		56910 AAW		CABLS	10//99-12//99
Postsecondary	Sacramento PMSA, CA	Y		54920 AAW		CABLS	10//99-12//99
Postsecondary	San Diego MSA, CA	Y		62470 AAW		CABLS	10//99-12//99
Postsecondary	San Francisco PMSA, CA	Y		59480 AAW		CABLS	10//99-12//99
Postsecondary	Colorado	Y		49840 AAW		COBLS	10//99-12//99
Postsecondary	Denver PMSA, CO	Y		49960 AAW		COBLS	10//99-12//99
Postsecondary	Connecticut	Y		59690 AAW		CTBLS	10//99-12//99
Postsecondary	New Haven-Meriden PMSA,						
	CT	Y		56920 AAW		CTBLS	10//99-12//99
Postsecondary	District of Columbia	Y		52050 AAW		DCBLS	10//99-12//99
Postsecondary	Washington PMSA, DC-MD-						
	VA-WV	Y		53840 AAW		DCBLS	10//99-12//99
Postsecondary	Florida	Y		62530 AAW		FLBLS	10//99-12//99
Postsecondary	Gainesville MSA, FL	Y		73360 AAW		FLBLS	10//99-12//99
Postsecondary	Miami PMSA, FL	Y		62310 AAW		FLBLS	10//99-12//99
Postsecondary	Orlando MSA, FL	Y		51750 AAW		FLBLS	10//99-12//99
Postsecondary	Tampa-St. Petersburg-						
	Clearwater MSA, FL	Y		63520 AAW		FLBLS	10//99-12//99
Postsecondary	West Palm Beach-Boca Raton						
	MSA, FL	Y		60140 AAW		FLBLS	10//99-12//99
Postsecondary	Georgia	Y		49220 AAW		GABLS	10//99-12//99
Postsecondary	Atlanta MSA, GA	Y		51440 AAW		GABLS	10//99-12//99
Postsecondary	Savannah MSA, GA	Y		43670 AAW		GABLS	10//99-12//99
Postsecondary	Idaho	Y		45340 AAW		IDBLS	10//99-12//99
Postsecondary	Illinois	Y		51680 AAW		ILBLS	10//99-12//99
Postsecondary	Chicago PMSA, IL	Y		51750 AAW		ILBLS	10//99-12//99
Postsecondary	Indiana	Y		44100 AAW		INBLS	10//99-12//99
Postsecondary	Fort Wayne MSA, IN	Y		45280 AAW		INBLS	10//99-12//99

Psychology Teacher

Occupation/Type/Industry	Location	Per	Low	Mid	High	Source	Date
Postsecondary	Gary PMSA, IN	Y		41840 AAW		INBLS	10//99-12//99
Postsecondary	Indianapolis MSA, IN	Y		41520 AAW		INBLS	10//99-12//99
Postsecondary	South Bend MSA, IN	Y		45260 AAW		INBLS	10//99-12//99
Postsecondary	Iowa	Y		51940 AAW		IABLS	10//99-12//99
Postsecondary	Des Moines MSA, IA	Y		44420 AAW		IABLS	10//99-12//99
Postsecondary	Kansas	Y		34530 AAW		KSBLS	10//99-12//99
Postsecondary	Kentucky	Y		46570 AAW		KYBLS	10//99-12//99
Postsecondary	Louisiana	Y		47350 AAW		LABLS	10//99-12//99
Postsecondary	Maryland	Y		54500 AAW		MDBLS	10//99-12//99
Postsecondary	Baltimore PMSA, MD	Y		53080 AAW		MDBLS	10//99-12//99
Postsecondary	Massachusetts	Y		58220 AAW		MABLS	10//99-12//99
Postsecondary	Boston PMSA, MA-NH	Y		62490 AAW		MABLS	10//99-12//99
Postsecondary	Brockton PMSA, MA	Y		43860 AAW		MABLS	10//99-12//99
Postsecondary	Springfield MSA, MA	Y		54050 AAW		MABLS	10//99-12//99
Postsecondary	Worcester PMSA, MA-CT	Y		54250 AAW		MABLS	10//99-12//99
Postsecondary	Michigan	Y		54980 AAW		MIBLS	10//99-12//99
Postsecondary	Detroit PMSA, MI	Y		47570 AAW		MIBLS	10//99-12//99
Postsecondary	Minnesota	Y		56670 AAW		MNBLS	10//99-12//99
Postsecondary	Duluth-Superior MSA, MN-WI	Y		50320 AAW		MNBLS	10//99-12//99
Postsecondary	Minneapolis-St. Paul MSA, MN-WI	Y		59500 AAW		MNBLS	10//99-12//99
Postsecondary	Mississippi	Y		41520 AAW		MSBLS	10//99-12//99
Postsecondary	Jackson MSA, MS	Y		34180 AAW		MSBLS	10//99-12//99
Postsecondary	Missouri	Y		44170 AAW		MOBLS	10//99-12//99
Postsecondary	Kansas City MSA, MO-KS	Y		42640 AAW		MOBLS	10//99-12//99
Postsecondary	St. Louis MSA, MO-IL	Y		43660 AAW		MOBLS	10//99-12//99
Postsecondary	Montana	Y		61960 AAW		MTBLS	10//99-12//99
Postsecondary	Omaha MSA, NE-IA	Y		46600 AAW		NEBLS	10//99-12//99
Postsecondary	Nevada	Y		43690 AAW		NVBLS	10//99-12//99
Postsecondary	New Hampshire	Y		54010 AAW		NHBLS	10//99-12//99
Postsecondary	New Jersey	Y		64020 AAW		NJBLS	10//99-12//99
Postsecondary	Bergen-Passaic PMSA, NJ	Y		60250 AAW		NJBLS	10//99-12//99
Postsecondary	Monmouth-Ocean PMSA, NJ	Y		60870 AAW		NJBLS	10//99-12//99
Postsecondary	Newark PMSA, NJ	Y		61990 AAW		NJBLS	10//99-12//99
Postsecondary	New Mexico	Y		48970 AAW		NMBLS	10//99-12//99
Postsecondary	New York	Y		53740 AAW		NYBLS	10//99-12//99
Postsecondary	Albany-Schenectady-Troy MSA, NY	Y		46880 AAW		NYBLS	10//99-12//99
Postsecondary	Nassau-Suffolk PMSA, NY	Y		62810 AAW		NYBLS	10//99-12//99
Postsecondary	New York PMSA, NY	Y		56700 AAW		NYBLS	10//99-12//99
Postsecondary	Utica-Rome MSA, NY	Y		51640 AAW		NYBLS	10//99-12//99
Postsecondary	North Carolina	Y		45980 AAW		NCBLS	10//99-12//99
Postsecondary	Asheville MSA, NC	Y		47590 AAW		NCBLS	10//99-12//99
Postsecondary	Charlotte-Gastonia-Rock Hill MSA, NC-SC	Y		42930 AAW		NCBLS	10//99-12//99
Postsecondary	Greensboro--Winston-Salem--High Point MSA, NC	Y		45780 AAW		NCBLS	10//99-12//99
Postsecondary	Hickory-Morganton-Lenoir MSA, NC	Y		34970 AAW		NCBLS	10//99-12//99
Postsecondary	Raleigh-Durham-Chapel Hill MSA, NC	Y		47330 AAW		NCBLS	10//99-12//99
Postsecondary	North Dakota	Y		42370 AAW		NDBLS	10//99-12//99
Postsecondary	Grand Forks MSA, ND-MN	Y		43780 AAW		NDBLS	10//99-12//99
Postsecondary	Ohio	Y		46120 AAW		OHBLS	10//99-12//99
Postsecondary	Canton-Massillon MSA, OH	Y		41050 AAW		OHBLS	10//99-12//99
Postsecondary	Cincinnati PMSA, OH-KY-IN	Y		43030 AAW		OHBLS	10//99-12//99
Postsecondary	Cleveland-Lorain-Elyria PMSA, OH	Y		47640 AAW		OHBLS	10//99-12//99
Postsecondary	Columbus MSA, OH	Y		50040 AAW		OHBLS	10//99-12//99
Postsecondary	Dayton-Springfield MSA, OH	Y		36700 AAW		OHBLS	10//99-12//99
Postsecondary	Toledo MSA, OH	Y		41110 AAW		OHBLS	10//99-12//99
Postsecondary	Oklahoma	Y		44300 AAW		OKBLS	10//99-12//99
Postsecondary	Oklahoma City MSA, OK	Y		44780 AAW		OKBLS	10//99-12//99
Postsecondary	Tulsa MSA, OK	Y		48780 AAW		OKBLS	10//99-12//99
Postsecondary	Oregon	Y		51420 AAW		ORBLS	10//99-12//99
Postsecondary	Portland-Vancouver PMSA, OR-WA	Y		50620 AAW		ORBLS	10//99-12//99
Postsecondary	Pennsylvania	Y		55400 AAW		PABLS	10//99-12//99
Postsecondary	Allentown-Bethlehem-Easton MSA, PA	Y		48280 AAW		PABLS	10//99-12//99
Postsecondary	Erie MSA, PA	Y		59910 AAW		PABLS	10//99-12//99

AAW Average annual wage	AOH Average offered, high	ASH Average starting, high	H Hourly	M Monthly	S Special: hourly and annual
AE Average entry wage	AOL Average offered, low	ASL Average starting, low	HI Highest wage paid	MTC Median total compensation	TQ Third quartile wage
AEX Average experienced wage	APH Average pay, high range	AW Average wage paid	HR High end range	MW Median wage paid	W Weekly
AO Average offered	APL Average pay, low range	FQ First quartile wage	LR Low end range	SQ Second quartile wage	Y Yearly

Occupation/Type/Industry	Location	Per	Low	Mid	High	Source	Date
Psychology Teacher							
Postsecondary	Harrisburg-Lebanon-Carlisle MSA, PA	Y		58070 AAW		PABLS	10//99-12//99
Postsecondary	Philadelphia PMSA, PA-NJ	Y		58190 AAW		PABLS	10//99-12//99
Postsecondary	Pittsburgh MSA, PA	Y		57410 AAW		PABLS	10//99-12//99
Postsecondary	Reading MSA, PA	Y		50760 AAW		PABLS	10//99-12//99
Postsecondary	Scranton--Wilkes-Barre--Hazleton MSA, PA	Y		43640 AAW		PABLS	10//99-12//99
Postsecondary	Rhode Island	Y		71740 AAW		RIBLS	10//99-12//99
Postsecondary	Providence-Fall River-Warwick MSA, RI-MA	Y		71660 AAW		RIBLS	10//99-12//99
Postsecondary	South Carolina	Y		51350 AAW		SCBLS	10//99-12//99
Postsecondary	Greenville-Spartanburg-Anderson MSA, SC	Y		54960 AAW		SCBLS	10//99-12//99
Postsecondary	South Dakota	Y		41240 AAW		SDBLS	10//99-12//99
Postsecondary	Tennessee	Y		50820 AAW		TNBLS	10//99-12//99
Postsecondary	Johnson City-Kingsport-Bristol MSA, TN-VA	Y		57300 AAW		TNBLS	10//99-12//99
Postsecondary	Nashville MSA, TN	Y		51900 AAW		TNBLS	10//99-12//99
Postsecondary	Texas	Y		46500 AAW		TXBLS	10//99-12//99
Postsecondary	Dallas PMSA, TX	Y		46800 AAW		TXBLS	10//99-12//99
Postsecondary	El Paso MSA, TX	Y		37560 AAW		TXBLS	10//99-12//99
Postsecondary	Houston PMSA, TX	Y		55430 AAW		TXBLS	10//99-12//99
Postsecondary	Odessa-Midland MSA, TX	Y		40210 AAW		TXBLS	10//99-12//99
Postsecondary	San Antonio MSA, TX	Y		50190 AAW		TXBLS	10//99-12//99
Postsecondary	Vermont	Y		54720 AAW		VTBLS	10//99-12//99
Postsecondary	Burlington MSA, VT	Y		57270 AAW		VTBLS	10//99-12//99
Postsecondary	Virginia	Y		48330 AAW		VABLS	10//99-12//99
Postsecondary	Norfolk-Virginia Beach-Newport News MSA, VA-NC	Y		52900 AAW		VABLS	10//99-12//99
Postsecondary	Richmond-Petersburg MSA, VA	Y		49850 AAW		VABLS	10//99-12//99
Postsecondary	Washington	Y		46880 AAW		WABLS	10//99-12//99
Postsecondary	Seattle-Bellevue-Everett PMSA, WA	Y		54130 AAW		WABLS	10//99-12//99
Postsecondary	Spokane MSA, WA	Y		42990 AAW		WABLS	10//99-12//99
Postsecondary	Tacoma PMSA, WA	Y		43280 AAW		WABLS	10//99-12//99
Postsecondary	West Virginia	Y		53640 AAW		WVBLS	10//99-12//99
Postsecondary	Milwaukee-Waukesha PMSA, WI	Y		37680 AAW		WIBLS	10//99-12//99
Postsecondary	Wyoming	Y		48780 AAW		WYBLS	10//99-12//99
Postsecondary	Puerto Rico	Y		37870 AAW		PRBLS	10//99-12//99
Postsecondary	San Juan-Bayamon PMSA, PR	Y		39840 AAW		PRBLS	10//99-12//99
Public Relations Coordinator	United States	Y		37500 AW		COMW	1999
Public Relations Director	United States	Y		79000 AW		COMW	1999
Public Relations Executive	Washington, DC	Y		82547 AW		PRWEEK	1//99-2000
	Los Angeles/Orange County, NY	Y		78707 AW		PRWEEK	1//99-2000
	Atlanta, NY	Y		66108 AW		PRWEEK	1//99-2000
	Boston, NY	Y		67568 AW		PRWEEK	1//99-2000
	Chicago, NY	Y		64779 AW		PRWEEK	1//99-2000
	Dallas, NY	Y		64764 AW		PRWEEK	1//99-2000
	Denver, NY	Y		55794 AW		PRWEEK	1//99-2000
	Houston, NY	Y		71580 AW		PRWEEK	1//99-2000
	Minneapolis, NY	Y		53886 AW		PRWEEK	1//99-2000
	New York, NY	Y		84566 AW		PRWEEK	1//99-2000
	San Franciso, NY	Y		76842 AW		PRWEEK	1//99-2000
	Seattle, NY	Y		63473 AW		PRWEEK	1//99-2000
Public Relations Manager	United States	Y		56000 AW		COMW	1999
	Alabama	S	15.96 MW	17.71 AW	36830 AAW	ALBLS	10//99-12//99
	Birmingham MSA, AL	S	20.17 MW	17.89 AW	41960 AAW	ALBLS	10//99-12//99
	Huntsville MSA, AL	S	20.46 MW	20.01 AW	42550 AAW	ALBLS	10//99-12//99
	Mobile MSA, AL	S	15.46 MW	14.33 AW	32160 AAW	ALBLS	10//99-12//99
	Montgomery MSA, AL	S	19.97 MW	16.90 AW	41540 AAW	ALBLS	10//99-12//99
	Tuscaloosa MSA, AL	S	18.57 MW	18.76 AW	38630 AAW	ALBLS	10//99-12//99
	Alaska	S	26.52 MW	28.32 AW	58910 AAW	AKBLS	10//99-12//99
	Anchorage MSA, AK	S	25.38 MW	23.99 AW	52780 AAW	AKBLS	10//99-12//99
	Arizona	S	26.8 MW	29.71 AW	61800 AAW	AZBLS	10//99-12//99

AAW Average annual wage	**AOH** Average offered, high	**ASH** Average starting, high	**H** Hourly	**M** Monthly	**S** Special: hourly and annual
AE Average entry wage	**AOL** Average offered, low	**ASL** Average starting, low	**HI** Highest wage paid	**MTC** Median total compensation	**TQ** Third quartile wage
AEX Average experienced wage	**APH** Average pay, high range	**AW** Average wage paid	**HR** High end range	**MW** Median wage paid	**W** Weekly
AO Average offered	**APL** Average pay, low range	**FQ** First quartile wage	**LR** Low end range	**SQ** Second quartile wage	**Y** Yearly

Occupation/Type/Industry	Location	Per	Low	Mid	High	Source	Date
Public Relations Manager	Phoenix-Mesa MSA, AZ	S	31.95 MW	29.92 AW	66470 AAW	AZBLS	10//99-12//99
	Tucson MSA, AZ	S	22.84 MW	22.71 AW	47500 AAW	AZBLS	10//99-12//99
	Little Rock-North Little Rock MSA, AR	S	27.33 MW	23.60 AW	56840 AAW	ARBLS	10//99-12//99
	California	S	28.51 MW	30.23 AW	62870 AAW	CABLS	10//99-12//99
	Bakersfield MSA, CA	S	22.00 MW	22.68 AW	45760 AAW	CABLS	10//99-12//99
	Fresno MSA, CA	S	30.46 MW	29.70 AW	63360 AAW	CABLS	10//99-12//99
	Los Angeles-Long Beach PMSA, CA	S	29.07 MW	28.25 AW	60460 AAW	CABLS	10//99-12//99
	Modesto MSA, CA	S	21.11 MW	19.86 AW	43900 AAW	CABLS	10//99-12//99
	Orange County PMSA, CA	S	27.27 MW	26.27 AW	56720 AAW	CABLS	10//99-12//99
	Riverside-San Bernardino PMSA, CA	S	22.95 MW	20.55 AW	47740 AAW	CABLS	10//99-12//99
	Sacramento PMSA, CA	S	23.21 MW	16.91 AW	48280 AAW	CABLS	10//99-12//99
	Salinas MSA, CA	S	29.83 MW	32.92 AW	62050 AAW	CABLS	10//99-12//99
	San Diego MSA, CA	S	28.45 MW	28.23 AW	59170 AAW	CABLS	10//99-12//99
	San Francisco PMSA, CA	S	33.46 MW	29.97 AW	69600 AAW	CABLS	10//99-12//99
	San Jose PMSA, CA	S	33.90 MW	32.32 AW	70520 AAW	CABLS	10//99-12//99
	Santa Barbara-Santa Maria-Lompoc MSA, CA	S	20.68 MW	16.65 AW	43020 AAW	CABLS	10//99-12//99
	Santa Rosa PMSA, CA	S	35.67 MW	30.85 AW	74190 AAW	CABLS	10//99-12//99
	Stockton-Lodi MSA, CA	S	22.75 MW	19.87 AW	47320 AAW	CABLS	10//99-12//99
	Vallejo-Fairfield-Napa PMSA, CA	S	26.83 MW	28.92 AW	55800 AAW	CABLS	10//99-12//99
	Ventura PMSA, CA	S	22.18 MW	18.23 AW	46140 AAW	CABLS	10//99-12//99
	Yuba City MSA, CA	S	24.58 MW	21.27 AW	51130 AAW	CABLS	10//99-12//99
	Colorado	S	22.21 MW	26.19 AW	54480 AAW	COBLS	10//99-12//99
	Boulder-Longmont PMSA, CO	S	24.95 MW	21.15 AW	51900 AAW	COBLS	10//99-12//99
	Denver PMSA, CO	S	25.09 MW	22.22 AW	52180 AAW	COBLS	10//99-12//99
	Connecticut	S	26.72 MW	29.75 AW	61880 AAW	CTBLS	10//99-12//99
	Bridgeport PMSA, CT	S	33.09 MW	34.16 AW	68830 AAW	CTBLS	10//99-12//99
	Danbury PMSA, CT	S	23.63 MW	19.41 AW	49140 AAW	CTBLS	10//99-12//99
	Hartford MSA, CT	S	28.38 MW	25.03 AW	59030 AAW	CTBLS	10//99-12//99
	New Haven-Meriden PMSA, CT	S	33.22 MW	32.41 AW	69090 AAW	CTBLS	10//99-12//99
	New London-Norwich MSA, CT-RI	S	22.23 MW	22.85 AW	46250 AAW	CTBLS	10//99-12//99
	Stamford-Norwalk PMSA, CT	S	31.04 MW	26.28 AW	64560 AAW	CTBLS	10//99-12//99
	Waterbury PMSA, CT	S	31.15 MW	29.94 AW	64790 AAW	CTBLS	10//99-12//99
	Delaware	S	28.94 MW	31.83 AW	66210 AAW	DEBLS	10//99-12//99
	Wilmington-Newark PMSA, DE-MD	S	32.17 MW	29.07 AW	66900 AAW	DEBLS	10//99-12//99
	District of Columbia	S	31.67 MW	32.79 AW	68200 AAW	DCBLS	10//99-12//99
	Washington PMSA, DC-MD-VA-WV	S	33.67 MW	32.10 AW	70040 AAW	DCBLS	10//99-12//99
	Florida	S	25.99 MW	30.25 AW	62910 AAW	FLBLS	10//99-12//99
	Fort Lauderdale PMSA, FL	S	30.46 MW	28.31 AW	63350 AAW	FLBLS	10//99-12//99
	Fort Myers-Cape Coral MSA, FL	S	26.83 MW	25.36 AW	55810 AAW	FLBLS	10//99-12//99
	Fort Pierce-Port St. Lucie MSA, FL	S	23.87 MW	24.28 AW	49660 AAW	FLBLS	10//99-12//99
	Gainesville MSA, FL	S	27.64 MW	28.41 AW	57490 AAW	FLBLS	10//99-12//99
	Jacksonville MSA, FL	S	26.76 MW	22.15 AW	55670 AAW	FLBLS	10//99-12//99
	Lakeland-Winter Haven MSA, FL	S	20.87 MW	19.99 AW	43410 AAW	FLBLS	10//99-12//99
	Melbourne-Titusville-Palm Bay MSA, FL	S	20.77 MW	16.60 AW	43210 AAW	FLBLS	10//99-12//99
	Miami PMSA, FL	S	24.16 MW	20.55 AW	50260 AAW	FLBLS	10//99-12//99
	Naples MSA, FL	S	20.73 MW	19.59 AW	43120 AAW	FLBLS	10//99-12//99
	Ocala MSA, FL	S	22.97 MW	21.13 AW	47790 AAW	FLBLS	10//99-12//99
	Orlando MSA, FL	S	29.82 MW	25.20 AW	62020 AAW	FLBLS	10//99-12//99
	Pensacola MSA, FL	S	27.47 MW	24.50 AW	57130 AAW	FLBLS	10//99-12//99
	Sarasota-Bradenton MSA, FL	S	27.33 MW	27.71 AW	56840 AAW	FLBLS	10//99-12//99
	Tallahassee MSA, FL	S	44.77 MW	49.16 AW	93120 AAW	FLBLS	10//99-12//99
	Tampa-St. Petersburg-Clearwater MSA, FL	S	32.16 MW	29.33 AW	66880 AAW	FLBLS	10//99-12//99
	West Palm Beach-Boca Raton MSA, FL	S	30.79 MW	25.95 AW	64030 AAW	FLBLS	10//99-12//99
	Georgia	S	21.54 MW	25.74 AW	53530 AAW	GABLS	10//99-12//99
	Atlanta MSA, GA	S	29.22 MW	25.59 AW	60790 AAW	GABLS	10//99-12//99
	Augusta-Aiken MSA, GA-SC	S	26.28 MW	28.24 AW	54670 AAW	GABLS	10//99-12//99
	Macon MSA, GA	S	23.18 MW	21.16 AW	48210 AAW	GABLS	10//99-12//99

AAW Average annual wage	**AOH** Average offered, high	**ASH** Average starting, high	**H** Hourly	**M** Monthly	**S** Special: hourly and annual
AE Average entry wage	**AOL** Average offered, low	**ASL** Average starting, low	**HI** Highest wage paid	**MTC** Median total compensation	**TQ** Third quartile wage
AEX Average experienced wage	**APH** Average pay, high range	**AW** Average wage paid	**HR** High end range	**MW** Median wage paid	**W** Weekly
AO Average offered	**APL** Average pay, low range	**FQ** First quartile wage	**LR** Low end range	**SQ** Second quartile wage	**Y** Yearly

Occupation/Type/Industry	Location	Per	Low	Mid	High	Source	Date
Public Relations Manager	Hawaii	s	26.1 MW	27.23 AW	56640 AAW	HIBLS	10//99-12//99
	Honolulu MSA, HI	s	27.56 MW	26.60 AW	57320 AAW	HIBLS	10//99-12//99
	Idaho	s	24.12 MW	23.35 AW	48570 AAW	IDBLS	10//99-12//99
	Boise City MSA, ID	s	23.96 MW	24.39 AW	49840 AAW	IDBLS	10//99-12//99
	Illinois	s	25.28 MW	29.71 AW	61790 AAW	ILBLS	10//99-12//99
	Bloomington-Normal MSA, IL	s	27.00 MW	24.20 AW	56150 AAW	ILBLS	10//99-12//99
	Champaign-Urbana MSA, IL	s	19.43 MW	14.83 AW	40420 AAW	ILBLS	10//99-12//99
	Chicago PMSA, IL	s	33.17 MW	26.66 AW	69000 AAW	ILBLS	10//99-12//99
	Peoria-Pekin MSA, IL	s	26.05 MW	25.66 AW	54170 AAW	ILBLS	10//99-12//99
	Rockford MSA, IL	s	21.15 MW	16.63 AW	43990 AAW	ILBLS	10//99-12//99
	Springfield MSA, IL	s	24.44 MW	24.34 AW	50830 AAW	ILBLS	10//99-12//99
	Indiana	s	23.65 MW	24.79 AW	51550 AAW	INBLS	10//99-12//99
	Evansville-Henderson MSA, IN-KY	s	19.63 MW	16.94 AW	40830 AAW	INBLS	10//99-12//99
	Fort Wayne MSA, IN	s	24.01 MW	16.60 AW	49930 AAW	INBLS	10//99-12//99
	Gary PMSA, IN	s	30.74 MW	31.57 AW	63950 AAW	INBLS	10//99-12//99
	Indianapolis MSA, IN	s	28.38 MW	26.31 AW	59030 AAW	INBLS	10//99-12//99
	Lafayette MSA, IN	s	24.97 MW	20.54 AW	51930 AAW	INBLS	10//99-12//99
	Muncie MSA, IN	s	28.71 MW	30.31 AW	59710 AAW	INBLS	10//99-12//99
	South Bend MSA, IN	s	17.82 MW	17.58 AW	37070 AAW	INBLS	10//99-12//99
	Terre Haute MSA, IN	s	25.92 MW	24.62 AW	53910 AAW	INBLS	10//99-12//99
	Iowa	s	17.52 MW	20.69 AW	43040 AAW	IABLS	10//99-12//99
	Davenport-Moline-Rock Island MSA, IA-IL	s	21.77 MW	19.12 AW	45270 AAW	IABLS	10//99-12//99
	Des Moines MSA, IA	s	22.54 MW	19.91 AW	46890 AAW	IABLS	10//99-12//99
	Sioux City MSA, IA-NE	s	17.31 MW	15.61 AW	36000 AAW	IABLS	10//99-12//99
	Waterloo-Cedar Falls MSA, IA	s	20.51 MW	19.42 AW	42650 AAW	IABLS	10//99-12//99
	Kansas	s	20.66 MW	24.65 AW	51270 AAW	KSBLS	10//99-12//99
	Lawrence MSA, KS	s	18.44 MW	18.02 AW	38350 AAW	KSBLS	10//99-12//99
	Topeka MSA, KS	s	18.85 MW	15.70 AW	39210 AAW	KSBLS	10//99-12//99
	Wichita MSA, KS	s	23.48 MW	18.82 AW	48830 AAW	KSBLS	10//99-12//99
	Kentucky	s	20.79 MW	22.61 AW	47030 AAW	KYBLS	10//99-12//99
	Lexington MSA, KY	s	25.55 MW	22.88 AW	53140 AAW	KYBLS	10//99-12//99
	Louisville MSA, KY-IN	s	23.30 MW	20.73 AW	48470 AAW	KYBLS	10//99-12//99
	Louisiana	s	19.75 MW	22.17 AW	46110 AAW	LABLS	10//99-12//99
	Baton Rouge MSA, LA	s	19.69 MW	16.56 AW	40950 AAW	LABLS	10//99-12//99
	New Orleans MSA, LA	s	22.67 MW	19.96 AW	47160 AAW	LABLS	10//99-12//99
	Shreveport-Bossier City MSA, LA	s	23.56 MW	22.79 AW	48990 AAW	LABLS	10//99-12//99
	Maine	s	18.97 MW	20.46 AW	42550 AAW	MEBLS	10//99-12//99
	Bangor MSA, ME	s	19.84 MW	19.39 AW	41270 AAW	MEBLS	10//99-12//99
	Portland MSA, ME	s	25.14 MW	22.71 AW	52280 AAW	MEBLS	10//99-12//99
	Maryland	s	24.39 MW	26.44 AW	54990 AAW	MDBLS	10//99-12//99
	Baltimore PMSA, MD	s	26.58 MW	24.30 AW	55290 AAW	MDBLS	10//99-12//99
	Massachusetts	s	28.99 MW	30.50 AW	63440 AAW	MABLS	10//99-12//99
	Boston PMSA, MA-NH	s	32.04 MW	30.94 AW	66650 AAW	MABLS	10//99-12//99
	Lawrence PMSA, MA-NH	s	20.55 MW	17.25 AW	42750 AAW	MABLS	10//99-12//99
	Springfield MSA, MA	s	25.80 MW	20.92 AW	53660 AAW	MABLS	10//99-12//99
	Worcester PMSA, MA-CT	s	22.37 MW	18.02 AW	46530 AAW	MABLS	10//99-12//99
	Michigan	s	25.09 MW	27.39 AW	56970 AAW	MIBLS	10//99-12//99
	Ann Arbor PMSA, MI	s	25.36 MW	22.07 AW	52740 AAW	MIBLS	10//99-12//99
	Detroit PMSA, MI	s	28.61 MW	26.11 AW	59510 AAW	MIBLS	10//99-12//99
	Flint PMSA, MI	s	31.18 MW	31.21 AW	64850 AAW	MIBLS	10//99-12//99
	Grand Rapids-Muskegon-Holland MSA, MI	s	24.84 MW	20.24 AW	51670 AAW	MIBLS	10//99-12//99
	Kalamazoo-Battle Creek MSA, MI	s	28.80 MW	26.93 AW	59900 AAW	MIBLS	10//99-12//99
	Lansing-East Lansing MSA, MI	s	26.53 MW	21.05 AW	55180 AAW	MIBLS	10//99-12//99
	Minnesota	s	28.62 MW	29.84 AW	62060 AAW	MNBLS	10//99-12//99
	Duluth-Superior MSA, MN-WI	s	24.60 MW	27.64 AW	51160 AAW	MNBLS	10//99-12//99
	Minneapolis-St. Paul MSA, MN-WI	s	30.92 MW	29.47 AW	64320 AAW	MNBLS	10//99-12//99
	Mississippi	s	19.62 MW	20.88 AW	43440 AAW	MSBLS	10//99-12//99
	Biloxi-Gulfport-Pascagoula MSA, MS	s	19.87 MW	15.47 AW	41330 AAW	MSBLS	10//99-12//99
	Jackson MSA, MS	s	20.47 MW	16.32 AW	42570 AAW	MSBLS	10//99-12//99
	Missouri	s	25.17 MW	25.70 AW	53460 AAW	MOBLS	10//99-12//99
	Columbia MSA, MO	s	13.03 MW	14.53 AW	27090 AAW	MOBLS	10//99-12//99
	Joplin MSA, MO	s	25.07 MW	27.49 AW	52150 AAW	MOBLS	10//99-12//99
	Kansas City MSA, MO-KS	s	28.41 MW	28.24 AW	59090 AAW	MOBLS	10//99-12//99
	St. Joseph MSA, MO	s	20.65 MW	22.81 AW	42940 AAW	MOBLS	10//99-12//99
	St. Louis MSA, MO-IL	s	26.34 MW	25.81 AW	54780 AAW	MOBLS	10//99-12//99

AAW Average annual wage	**AOH** Average offered, high	**ASH** Average starting, high	**H** Hourly	**M** Monthly	**S** Special: hourly and annual
AE Average entry wage	**AOL** Average offered, low	**ASL** Average starting, low	**HI** Highest wage paid	**MTC** Median total compensation	**TQ** Third quartile wage
AEX Average experienced wage	**APH** Average pay, high range	**AW** Average wage paid	**HR** High end range	**MW** Median wage paid	**W** Weekly
AO Average offered	**APL** Average pay, low range	**FQ** First quartile wage	**LR** Low end range	**SQ** Second quartile wage	**Y** Yearly

Occupation/Type/Industry	Location	Per	Low	Mid	High	Source	Date
Public Relations Manager	Springfield MSA, MO	S	21.37 MW	19.80 AW	44460 AAW	MOBLS	10//99-12//99
	Montana	S	13.17 MW	17.62 AW	36650 AAW	MTBLS	10//99-12//99
	Billings MSA, MT	S	14.55 MW	12.50 AW	30270 AAW	MTBLS	10//99-12//99
	Nebraska	S	23.04 MW	22.51 AW	46830 AAW	NEBLS	10//99-12//99
	Lincoln MSA, NE	S	23.84 MW	24.56 AW	49580 AAW	NEBLS	10//99-12//99
	Omaha MSA, NE-IA	S	22.98 MW	22.98 AW	47800 AAW	NEBLS	10//99-12//99
	Nevada	S	21.5 MW	25.21 AW	52440 AAW	NVBLS	10//99-12//99
	Las Vegas MSA, NV-AZ	S	26.24 MW	22.73 AW	54580 AAW	NVBLS	10//99-12//99
	Reno MSA, NV	S	20.90 MW	18.35 AW	43460 AAW	NVBLS	10//99-12//99
	New Hampshire	S	23.35 MW	25.87 AW	53810 AAW	NHBLS	10//99-12//99
	Manchester PMSA, NH	S	27.62 MW	27.62 AW	57440 AAW	NHBLS	10//99-12//99
	Nashua PMSA, NH	S	31.94 MW	25.06 AW	66440 AAW	NHBLS	10//99-12//99
	Portsmouth-Rochester PMSA, NH-ME	S	27.62 MW	23.95 AW	57450 AAW	NHBLS	10//99-12//99
	New Jersey	S	33.82 MW	35.04 AW	72890 AAW	NJBLS	10//99-12//99
	Atlantic-Cape May PMSA, NJ	S	34.25 MW	36.35 AW	71230 AAW	NJBLS	10//99-12//99
	Bergen-Passaic PMSA, NJ	S	34.50 MW	34.60 AW	71750 AAW	NJBLS	10//99-12//99
	Jersey City PMSA, NJ	S	35.56 MW	32.76 AW	73970 AAW	NJBLS	10//99-12//99
	Middlesex-Somerset-Hunterdon PMSA, NJ	S	36.30 MW	34.03 AW	75490 AAW	NJBLS	10//99-12//99
	Monmouth-Ocean PMSA, NJ	S	34.21 MW	36.17 AW	71160 AAW	NJBLS	10//99-12//99
	Newark PMSA, NJ	S	34.86 MW	30.01 AW	72510 AAW	NJBLS	10//99-12//99
	Trenton PMSA, NJ	S	39.72 MW	39.41 AW	82620 AAW	NJBLS	10//99-12//99
	New Mexico	S	23.57 MW	24.90 AW	51800 AAW	NMBLS	10//99-12//99
	Albuquerque MSA, NM	S	24.86 MW	24.28 AW	51700 AAW	NMBLS	10//99-12//99
	Santa Fe MSA, NM	S	29.94 MW	32.27 AW	62270 AAW	NMBLS	10//99-12//99
	New York	S	31.37 MW	36.33 AW	75560 AAW	NYBLS	10//99-12//99
	Albany-Schenectady-Troy MSA, NY	S	32.08 MW	27.81 AW	66730 AAW	NYBLS	10//99-12//99
	Buffalo-Niagara Falls MSA, NY	S	24.56 MW	21.94 AW	51080 AAW	NYBLS	10//99-12//99
	Dutchess County PMSA, NY	S	21.54 MW	19.97 AW	44800 AAW	NYBLS	10//99-12//99
	Nassau-Suffolk PMSA, NY	S	42.02 MW	34.44 AW	87400 AAW	NYBLS	10//99-12//99
	New York PMSA, NY	S	37.70 MW	33.17 AW	78420 AAW	NYBLS	10//99-12//99
	Rochester MSA, NY	S	25.13 MW	24.26 AW	52280 AAW	NYBLS	10//99-12//99
	Syracuse MSA, NY	S	30.04 MW	26.43 AW	62480 AAW	NYBLS	10//99-12//99
	Utica-Rome MSA, NY	S	23.55 MW	21.19 AW	48980 AAW	NYBLS	10//99-12//99
	North Carolina	S	21.65 MW	22.99 AW	47820 AAW	NCBLS	10//99-12//99
	Asheville MSA, NC	S	20.27 MW	17.97 AW	42170 AAW	NCBLS	10//99-12//99
	Charlotte-Gastonia-Rock Hill MSA, NC-SC	S	27.14 MW	24.31 AW	56450 AAW	NCBLS	10//99-12//99
	Fayetteville MSA, NC	S	18.43 MW	15.54 AW	38340 AAW	NCBLS	10//99-12//99
	Greensboro--Winston-Salem--High Point MSA, NC	S	24.74 MW	25.10 AW	51450 AAW	NCBLS	10//99-12//99
	Hickory-Morganton-Lenoir MSA, NC	S	20.23 MW	18.82 AW	42080 AAW	NCBLS	10//99-12//99
	Raleigh-Durham-Chapel Hill MSA, NC	S	22.52 MW	22.06 AW	46830 AAW	NCBLS	10//99-12//99
	North Dakota	S	17 MW	19.35 AW	40250 AAW	NDBLS	10//99-12//99
	Bismarck MSA, ND	S	16.81 MW	14.75 AW	34960 AAW	NDBLS	10//99-12//99
	Fargo-Moorhead MSA, ND-MN	S	25.74 MW	24.06 AW	53530 AAW	NDBLS	10//99-12//99
	Ohio	S	21.08 MW	23.98 AW	49870 AAW	OHBLS	10//99-12//99
	Akron PMSA, OH	S	20.37 MW	17.61 AW	42380 AAW	OHBLS	10//99-12//99
	Canton-Massillon MSA, OH	S	16.75 MW	17.14 AW	34840 AAW	OHBLS	10//99-12//99
	Cincinnati PMSA, OH-KY-IN	S	23.44 MW	21.81 AW	48750 AAW	OHBLS	10//99-12//99
	Cleveland-Lorain-Elyria PMSA, OH	S	27.80 MW	23.45 AW	57820 AAW	OHBLS	10//99-12//99
	Columbus MSA, OH	S	22.69 MW	21.22 AW	47190 AAW	OHBLS	10//99-12//99
	Dayton-Springfield MSA, OH	S	20.15 MW	19.41 AW	41910 AAW	OHBLS	10//99-12//99
	Toledo MSA, OH	S	30.26 MW	21.67 AW	62950 AAW	OHBLS	10//99-12//99
	Youngstown-Warren MSA, OH	S	19.59 MW	18.80 AW	40740 AAW	OHBLS	10//99-12//99
	Oklahoma	S	17.11 MW	21.67 AW	45070 AAW	OKBLS	10//99-12//99
	Oklahoma City MSA, OK	S	23.13 MW	24.00 AW	48110 AAW	OKBLS	10//99-12//99
	Tulsa MSA, OK	S	18.94 MW	15.52 AW	39390 AAW	OKBLS	10//99-12//99
	Oregon	S	26.77 MW	27.16 AW	56490 AAW	ORBLS	10//99-12//99
	Eugene-Springfield MSA, OR	S	22.30 MW	18.83 AW	46390 AAW	ORBLS	10//99-12//99
	Portland-Vancouver PMSA, OR-WA	S	28.33 MW	26.97 AW	58920 AAW	ORBLS	10//99-12//99
	Salem PMSA, OR	S	24.89 MW	27.80 AW	51770 AAW	ORBLS	10//99-12//99
	Pennsylvania	S	22.42 MW	24.91 AW	51820 AAW	PABLS	10//99-12//99

AAW	Average annual wage	AOH	Average offered, high	ASH	Average starting, high
AE	Average entry wage	AOL	Average offered, low	ASL	Average starting, low
AEX	Average experienced wage	APH	Average pay, high range	AW	Average wage paid
AO	Average offered	APL	Average pay, low range	FQ	First quartile wage

H	Hourly	M	Monthly
HI	Highest wage paid	MTC	Median total compensation
HR	High end range	MW	Median wage paid
LR	Low end range	SQ	Second quartile wage

S	Special: hourly and annual
TQ	Third quartile wage
W	Weekly
Y	Yearly

Occupation/Type/Industry	Location	Per	Low	Mid	High	Source	Date
Public Relations Manager	Allentown-Bethlehem-Easton MSA, PA	S	21.45 MW	19.56 AW	44620 AAW	PABLS	10//99-12//99
	Erie MSA, PA	S	16.82 MW	14.84 AW	34990 AAW	PABLS	10//99-12//99
	Harrisburg-Lebanon-Carlisle MSA, PA	S	30.00 MW	29.20 AW	62410 AAW	PABLS	10//99-12//99
	Lancaster MSA, PA	S	20.28 MW	16.61 AW	42180 AAW	PABLS	10//99-12//99
	Philadelphia PMSA, PA-NJ	S	27.60 MW	24.53 AW	57410 AAW	PABLS	10//99-12//99
	Pittsburgh MSA, PA	S	25.23 MW	22.74 AW	52470 AAW	PABLS	10//99-12//99
	Reading MSA, PA	S	15.95 MW	12.78 AW	33170 AAW	PABLS	10//99-12//99
	Scranton--Wilkes-Barre--Hazleton MSA, PA	S	18.48 MW	16.61 AW	38440 AAW	PABLS	10//99-12//99
	Rhode Island	S	30.13 MW	36.92 AW	76780 AAW	RIBLS	10//99-12//99
	Providence-Fall River-Warwick MSA, RI-MA	S	37.53 MW	30.61 AW	78070 AAW	RIBLS	10//99-12//99
	South Carolina	S	16.67 MW	21.28 AW	44260 AAW	SCBLS	10//99-12//99
	Charleston-North Charleston MSA, SC	S	20.81 MW	18.21 AW	43280 AAW	SCBLS	10//99-12//99
	Columbia MSA, SC	S	17.61 MW	16.10 AW	36620 AAW	SCBLS	10//99-12//99
	Greenville-Spartanburg-Anderson MSA, SC	S	20.91 MW	15.79 AW	43490 AAW	SCBLS	10//99-12//99
	Myrtle Beach MSA, SC	S	20.34 MW	19.48 AW	42300 AAW	SCBLS	10//99-12//99
	South Dakota	S	26.71 MW	28.15 AW	58560 AAW	SDBLS	10//99-12//99
	Sioux Falls MSA, SD	S	26.76 MW	25.52 AW	55660 AAW	SDBLS	10//99-12//99
	Tennessee	S	19.97 MW	21.87 AW	45500 AAW	TNBLS	10//99-12//99
	Chattanooga MSA, TN-GA	S	18.63 MW	16.36 AW	38750 AAW	TNBLS	10//99-12//99
	Johnson City-Kingsport-Bristol MSA, TN-VA	S	12.73 MW	13.81 AW	26480 AAW	TNBLS	10//99-12//99
	Knoxville MSA, TN	S	23.31 MW	20.48 AW	48490 AAW	TNBLS	10//99-12//99
	Memphis MSA, TN-AR-MS	S	22.28 MW	19.57 AW	46350 AAW	MSBLS	10//99-12//99
	Nashville MSA, TN	S	23.01 MW	22.52 AW	47860 AAW	TNBLS	10//99-12//99
	Texas	S	22.16 MW	25.53 AW	53100 AAW	TXBLS	10//99-12//99
	Amarillo MSA, TX	S	18.90 MW	17.71 AW	39310 AAW	TXBLS	10//99-12//99
	Austin-San Marcos MSA, TX	S	25.35 MW	24.20 AW	52740 AAW	TXBLS	10//99-12//99
	Beaumont-Port Arthur MSA, TX	S	29.45 MW	24.36 AW	61250 AAW	TXBLS	10//99-12//99
	Brazoria PMSA, TX	S	18.92 MW	21.70 AW	39340 AAW	TXBLS	10//99-12//99
	Corpus Christi MSA, TX	S	25.91 MW	25.43 AW	53890 AAW	TXBLS	10//99-12//99
	Dallas PMSA, TX	S	30.00 MW	28.34 AW	62400 AAW	TXBLS	10//99-12//99
	Fort Worth-Arlington PMSA, TX	S	26.58 MW	24.05 AW	55280 AAW	TXBLS	10//99-12//99
	Houston PMSA, TX	S	23.42 MW	20.68 AW	48710 AAW	TXBLS	10//99-12//99
	Killeen-Temple MSA, TX	S	19.99 MW	16.40 AW	41590 AAW	TXBLS	10//99-12//99
	Laredo MSA, TX	S	16.75 MW	15.36 AW	34840 AAW	TXBLS	10//99-12//99
	Longview-Marshall MSA, TX	S	32.99 MW	38.00 AW	68630 AAW	TXBLS	10//99-12//99
	McAllen-Edinburg-Mission MSA, TX	S	17.18 MW	17.07 AW	35730 AAW	TXBLS	10//99-12//99
	Odessa-Midland MSA, TX	S	24.95 MW	23.97 AW	51910 AAW	TXBLS	10//99-12//99
	San Angelo MSA, TX	S	19.27 MW	16.34 AW	40070 AAW	TXBLS	10//99-12//99
	San Antonio MSA, TX	S	27.41 MW	25.14 AW	57000 AAW	TXBLS	10//99-12//99
	Tyler MSA, TX	S	22.94 MW	23.32 AW	47710 AAW	TXBLS	10//99-12//99
	Waco MSA, TX	S	16.77 MW	13.23 AW	34880 AAW	TXBLS	10//99-12//99
	Utah	S	26.3 MW	31.83 AW	66210 AAW	UTBLS	10//99-12//99
	Provo-Orem MSA, UT	S	29.54 MW	25.73 AW	61430 AAW	UTBLS	10//99-12//99
	Vermont	S	24.53 MW	24.72 AW	51420 AAW	VTBLS	10//99-12//99
	Virginia	S	33.54 MW	34.36 AW	71470 AAW	VABLS	10//99-12//99
	Norfolk-Virginia Beach-Newport News MSA, VA-NC	S	25.41 MW	23.14 AW	52850 AAW	VABLS	10//99-12//99
	Richmond-Petersburg MSA, VA	S	25.71 MW	21.03 AW	53480 AAW	VABLS	10//99-12//99
	Roanoke MSA, VA	S	23.98 MW	20.97 AW	49870 AAW	VABLS	10//99-12//99
	Washington	S	29.35 MW	30.15 AW	62720 AAW	WABLS	10//99-12//99
	Bellingham MSA, WA	S	22.27 MW	21.43 AW	46330 AAW	WABLS	10//99-12//99
	Olympia PMSA, WA	S	22.06 MW	23.24 AW	45880 AAW	WABLS	10//99-12//99
	Seattle-Bellevue-Everett PMSA, WA	S	32.62 MW	32.36 AW	67850 AAW	WABLS	10//99-12//99
	Tacoma PMSA, WA	S	26.69 MW	25.32 AW	55520 AAW	WABLS	10//99-12//99
	Yakima MSA, WA	S	27.91 MW	28.38 AW	58050 AAW	WABLS	10//99-12//99
	West Virginia	S	16.15 MW	17.90 AW	37230 AAW	WVBLS	10//99-12//99
	Charleston MSA, WV	S	19.83 MW	18.04 AW	41250 AAW	WVBLS	10//99-12//99
	Wisconsin	S	19.03 MW	23.05 AW	47940 AAW	WIBLS	10//99-12//99

AAW	Average annual wage	AOH	Average offered, high	ASH	Average starting, high
AE	Average entry wage	AOL	Average offered, low	ASL	Average starting, low
AEX	Average experienced wage	APH	Average pay, high range	AW	Average wage paid
AO	Average offered	APL	Average pay, low range	FQ	First quartile wage

H	Hourly	M	Monthly	S	Special: hourly and annual
HI	Highest wage paid	MTC	Median total compensation	TQ	Third quartile wage
HR	High end range	MW	Median wage paid	W	Weekly
LR	Low end range	SQ	Second quartile wage	Y	Yearly

Occupation/Type/Industry	Location	Per	Low	Mid	High	Source	Date
Public Relations Manager	Appleton-Oshkosh-Neenah						
	MSA, WI	S	19.12 MW	19.70 AW	39770 AAW	WIBLS	10//99-12//99
	Eau Claire MSA, WI	S	29.23 MW	25.01 AW	60790 AAW	WIBLS	10//99-12//99
	Green Bay MSA, WI	S	23.12 MW	21.25 AW	48080 AAW	WIBLS	10//99-12//99
	Kenosha PMSA, WI	S	22.38 MW	21.22 AW	46550 AAW	WIBLS	10//99-12//99
	Madison MSA, WI	S	20.64 MW	18.62 AW	42940 AAW	WIBLS	10//99-12//99
	Milwaukee-Waukesha PMSA,						
	WI	S	25.23 MW	18.83 AW	52470 AAW	WIBLS	10//99-12//99
	Wyoming	S	23.74 MW	24.94 AW	51870 AAW	WYBLS	10//99-12//99
	Cheyenne MSA, WY	S	26.20 MW	26.54 AW	54500 AAW	WYBLS	10//99-12//99
	Puerto Rico	S	16.25 MW	19.73 AW	41040 AAW	PRBLS	10//99-12//99
Public Relations Specialist	United States	H		20.63 AW		NCS98	1998
	United States	Y		41000 AW		COMW	1999
	Alabama	S	15.38 MW	16.94 AW	35230 AAW	ALBLS	10//99-12//99
	Birmingham MSA, AL	S	16.66 MW	14.48 AW	34650 AAW	ALBLS	10//99-12//99
	Huntsville MSA, AL	S	17.76 MW	17.04 AW	36950 AAW	ALBLS	10//99-12//99
	Mobile MSA, AL	S	16.47 MW	14.80 AW	34250 AAW	ALBLS	10//99-12//99
	Montgomery MSA, AL	S	17.88 MW	17.98 AW	37190 AAW	ALBLS	10//99-12//99
	Alaska	S	20.78 MW	21.26 AW	44210 AAW	AKBLS	10//99-12//99
	Anchorage MSA, AK	S	20.51 MW	19.55 AW	42670 AAW	AKBLS	10//99-12//99
	Arizona	S	17.32 MW	18.36 AW	38180 AAW	AZBLS	10//99-12//99
	Flagstaff MSA, AZ-UT	S	15.76 MW	15.28 AW	32790 AAW	AZBLS	10//99-12//99
	Phoenix-Mesa MSA, AZ	S	18.55 MW	17.48 AW	38580 AAW	AZBLS	10//99-12//99
	Tucson MSA, AZ	S	19.00 MW	17.85 AW	39520 AAW	AZBLS	10//99-12//99
	Arkansas	S	13.89 MW	14.87 AW	30930 AAW	ARBLS	10//99-12//99
	Fayetteville-Springdale-Rogers						
	MSA, AR	S	15.13 MW	14.77 AW	31460 AAW	ARBLS	10//99-12//99
	Fort Smith MSA, AR-OK	S	12.06 MW	11.49 AW	25090 AAW	ARBLS	10//99-12//99
	Jonesboro MSA, AR	S	13.34 MW	13.37 AW	27740 AAW	ARBLS	10//99-12//99
	Little Rock-North Little Rock						
	MSA, AR	S	15.81 MW	14.86 AW	32880 AAW	ARBLS	10//99-12//99
	California	S	20.07 MW	21.66 AW	45060 AAW	CABLS	10//99-12//99
	Bakersfield MSA, CA	S	19.99 MW	18.85 AW	41580 AAW	CABLS	10//99-12//99
	Fresno MSA, CA	S	15.72 MW	13.68 AW	32700 AAW	CABLS	10//99-12//99
	Los Angeles-Long Beach						
	PMSA, CA	S	22.02 MW	20.71 AW	45790 AAW	CABLS	10//99-12//99
	Merced MSA, CA	S	21.84 MW	21.70 AW	45430 AAW	CABLS	10//99-12//99
	Modesto MSA, CA	S	13.53 MW	11.93 AW	28140 AAW	CABLS	10//99-12//99
	Oakland PMSA, CA	S	23.53 MW	23.10 AW	48940 AAW	CABLS	10//99-12//99
	Orange County PMSA, CA	S	18.85 MW	17.19 AW	39200 AAW	CABLS	10//99-12//99
	Riverside-San Bernardino						
	PMSA, CA	S	18.75 MW	17.83 AW	39000 AAW	CABLS	10//99-12//99
	Sacramento PMSA, CA	S	26.73 MW	25.69 AW	55600 AAW	CABLS	10//99-12//99
	Salinas MSA, CA	S	16.24 MW	15.03 AW	33770 AAW	CABLS	10//99-12//99
	San Diego MSA, CA	S	20.23 MW	18.20 AW	42090 AAW	CABLS	10//99-12//99
	San Francisco PMSA, CA	S	22.80 MW	20.74 AW	47420 AAW	CABLS	10//99-12//99
	San Jose PMSA, CA	S	22.79 MW	20.31 AW	47410 AAW	CABLS	10//99-12//99
	San Luis Obispo-Atascadero-						
	Paso Robles MSA, CA	S	15.66 MW	15.47 AW	32570 AAW	CABLS	
	Santa Barbara-Santa Maria-						
	Lompoc MSA, CA	S	18.01 MW	17.69 AW	37460 AAW	CABLS	10//99-12//99
	Santa Rosa PMSA, CA	S	17.44 MW	17.30 AW	36280 AAW	CABLS	10//99-12//99
	Stockton-Lodi MSA, CA	S	17.41 MW	16.88 AW	36220 AAW	CABLS	10//99-12//99
	Vallejo-Fairfield-Napa PMSA,						
	CA	S	17.07 MW	15.68 AW	35500 AAW	CABLS	10//99-12//99
	Ventura PMSA, CA	S	21.49 MW	20.59 AW	44710 AAW	CABLS	10//99-12//99
	Visalia-Tulare-Porterville						
	MSA, CA	S	19.79 MW	18.43 AW	41160 AAW	CABLS	10//99-12//99
	Yolo PMSA, CA	S	18.13 MW	17.47 AW	37710 AAW	CABLS	10//99-12//99
	Colorado	S	17.83 MW	18.58 AW	38660 AAW	COBLS	10//99-12//99
	Boulder-Longmont PMSA, CO	S	19.09 MW	18.15 AW	39700 AAW	COBLS	10//99-12//99
	Colorado Springs MSA, CO	S	14.44 MW	12.66 AW	30030 AAW	COBLS	10//99-12//99
	Denver PMSA, CO	S	19.89 MW	18.94 AW	41370 AAW	COBLS	10//99-12//99
	Fort Collins-Loveland MSA,						
	CO	S	20.19 MW	18.73 AW	41990 AAW	COBLS	10//99-12//99
	Pueblo MSA, CO	S	17.46 MW	17.50 AW	36330 AAW	COBLS	10//99-12//99
	Connecticut	S	19.86 MW	21.49 AW	44690 AAW	CTBLS	10//99-12//99
	Bridgeport PMSA, CT	S	22.50 MW	20.28 AW	46810 AAW	CTBLS	10//99-12//99
	Hartford MSA, CT	S	22.68 MW	21.59 AW	47180 AAW	CTBLS	10//99-12//99
	New Haven-Meriden PMSA,						
	CT	S	22.58 MW	20.62 AW	46960 AAW	CTBLS	10//99-12//99

Occupation/Type/Industry	Location	Per	Low	Mid	High	Source	Date
Public Relations Specialist	New London-Norwich MSA, CT-RI	S	16.14 MW	15.74 AW	33570 AAW	CTBLS	10//99-12//99
	Stamford-Norwalk PMSA, CT	S	20.23 MW	17.25 AW	42070 AAW	CTBLS	10//99-12//99
	Delaware	S	16.91 MW	17.89 AW	37220 AAW	DEBLS	10//99-12//99
	Dover MSA, DE	S	17.06 MW	17.21 AW	35480 AAW	DEBLS	10//99-12//99
	Wilmington-Newark PMSA, DE-MD	S	17.80 MW	16.52 AW	37010 AAW	DEBLS	10//99-12//99
	District of Columbia	S	26.45 MW	29.08 AW	60480 AAW	DCBLS	10//99-12//99
	Washington PMSA, DC-MD-VA-WV	S	26.31 MW	23.33 AW	54720 AAW	DCBLS	10//99-12//99
	Florida	S	14.22 MW	16.25 AW	33790 AAW	FLBLS	10//99-12//99
	Daytona Beach MSA, FL	S	13.40 MW	12.88 AW	27870 AAW	FLBLS	10//99-12//99
	Fort Lauderdale PMSA, FL	S	13.70 MW	12.42 AW	28490 AAW	FLBLS	10//99-12//99
	Fort Myers-Cape Coral MSA, FL	S	13.88 MW	13.31 AW	28860 AAW	FLBLS	10//99-12//99
	Fort Pierce-Port St. Lucie MSA, FL	S	14.83 MW	13.43 AW	30840 AAW	FLBLS	10//99-12//99
	Fort Walton Beach MSA, FL	S	14.36 MW	13.22 AW	29860 AAW	FLBLS	10//99-12//99
	Gainesville MSA, FL	S	14.31 MW	13.77 AW	29760 AAW	FLBLS	10//99-12//99
	Jacksonville MSA, FL	S	15.91 MW	14.16 AW	33090 AAW	FLBLS	10//99-12//99
	Lakeland-Winter Haven MSA, FL	S	14.54 MW	13.36 AW	30250 AAW	FLBLS	10//99-12//99
	Melbourne-Titusville-Palm Bay MSA, FL	S	20.56 MW	16.45 AW	42770 AAW	FLBLS	10//99-12//99
	Miami PMSA, FL	S	17.24 MW	15.19 AW	35860 AAW	FLBLS	10//99-12//99
	Naples MSA, FL	S	15.47 MW	15.29 AW	32170 AAW	FLBLS	10//99-12//99
	Ocala MSA, FL	S	17.55 MW	17.13 AW	36500 AAW	FLBLS	10//99-12//99
	Orlando MSA, FL	S	15.20 MW	13.89 AW	31610 AAW	FLBLS	10//99-12//99
	Panama City MSA, FL	S	10.75 MW	9.59 AW	22360 AAW	FLBLS	10//99-12//99
	Pensacola MSA, FL	S	14.72 MW	12.96 AW	30630 AAW	FLBLS	10//99-12//99
	Punta Gorda MSA, FL	S	12.24 MW	10.16 AW	25460 AAW	FLBLS	10//99-12//99
	Sarasota-Bradenton MSA, FL	S	14.98 MW	13.70 AW	31160 AAW	FLBLS	10//99-12//99
	Tallahassee MSA, FL	S	18.18 MW	15.07 AW	37810 AAW	FLBLS	10//99-12//99
	Tampa-St. Petersburg-Clearwater MSA, FL	S	15.26 MW	14.40 AW	31740 AAW	FLBLS	10//99-12//99
	West Palm Beach-Boca Raton MSA, FL	S	16.77 MW	15.43 AW	34870 AAW	FLBLS	10//99-12//99
	Georgia	S	15.66 MW	17.01 AW	35390 AAW	GABLS	10//99-12//99
	Athens MSA, GA	S	16.31 MW	15.78 AW	33920 AAW	GABLS	10//99-12//99
	Atlanta MSA, GA	S	17.43 MW	16.02 AW	36260 AAW	GABLS	10//99-12//99
	Augusta-Aiken MSA, GA-SC	S	18.55 MW	13.56 AW	38590 AAW	GABLS	10//99-12//99
	Columbus MSA, GA-AL	S	17.96 MW	16.56 AW	37350 AAW	GABLS	10//99-12//99
	Macon MSA, GA	S	16.58 MW	15.68 AW	34500 AAW	GABLS	10//99-12//99
	Savannah MSA, GA	S	17.60 MW	15.59 AW	36610 AAW	GABLS	10//99-12//99
	Hawaii	S	17.79 MW	18.72 AW	38930 AAW	HIBLS	10//99-12//99
	Honolulu MSA, HI	S	18.93 MW	17.98 AW	39360 AAW	HIBLS	10//99-12//99
	Idaho	S	17.8 MW	19.57 AW	40700 AAW	IDBLS	10//99-12//99
	Boise City MSA, ID	S	18.63 MW	17.45 AW	38760 AAW	IDBLS	10//99-12//99
	Illinois	S	18.46 MW	19.71 AW	40990 AAW	ILBLS	10//99-12//99
	Bloomington-Normal MSA, IL	S	23.18 MW	20.95 AW	48210 AAW	ILBLS	10//99-12//99
	Champaign-Urbana MSA, IL	S	18.90 MW	18.20 AW	39310 AAW	ILBLS	10//99-12//99
	Chicago PMSA, IL	S	20.37 MW	19.20 AW	42380 AAW	ILBLS	10//99-12//99
	Kankakee PMSA, IL	S	18.44 MW	17.99 AW	38360 AAW	ILBLS	10//99-12//99
	Peoria-Pekin MSA, IL	S	16.02 MW	13.63 AW	33320 AAW	ILBLS	10//99-12//99
	Rockford MSA, IL	S	17.61 MW	18.68 AW	36640 AAW	ILBLS	10//99-12//99
	Springfield MSA, IL	S	16.39 MW	16.53 AW	34090 AAW	ILBLS	10//99-12//99
	Indiana	S	14.75 MW	15.99 AW	33260 AAW	INBLS	10//99-12//99
	Bloomington MSA, IN	S	15.46 MW	14.15 AW	32160 AAW	INBLS	10//99-12//99
	Evansville-Henderson MSA, IN-KY	S	17.35 MW	15.82 AW	36090 AAW	INBLS	10//99-12//99
	Fort Wayne MSA, IN	S	16.84 MW	15.07 AW	35020 AAW	INBLS	10//99-12//99
	Gary PMSA, IN	S	17.41 MW	18.47 AW	36210 AAW	INBLS	10//99-12//99
	Indianapolis MSA, IN	S	16.82 MW	15.27 AW	34990 AAW	INBLS	10//99-12//99
	Kokomo MSA, IN	S	10.90 MW	10.07 AW	22670 AAW	INBLS	10//99-12//99
	Lafayette MSA, IN	S	12.98 MW	11.68 AW	26990 AAW	INBLS	10//99-12//99
	Muncie MSA, IN	S	15.38 MW	14.87 AW	31980 AAW	INBLS	10//99-12//99
	South Bend MSA, IN	S	16.05 MW	15.78 AW	33380 AAW	INBLS	10//99-12//99
	Terre Haute MSA, IN	S	15.88 MW	15.61 AW	33030 AAW	INBLS	10//99-12//99
	Iowa	S	14.83 MW	15.86 AW	33000 AAW	IABLS	10//99-12//99
	Cedar Rapids MSA, IA	S	17.29 MW	15.27 AW	35970 AAW	IABLS	10//99-12//99
	Davenport-Moline-Rock Island MSA, IA-IL	S	18.72 MW	17.41 AW	38940 AAW	IABLS	10//99-12//99

AAW Average annual wage	**AOH** Average offered, high	**ASH** Average starting, high	**H** Hourly	**M** Monthly	**S** Special: hourly and annual
AE Average entry wage	**AOL** Average offered, low	**ASL** Average starting, low	**HI** Highest wage paid	**MTC** Median total compensation	**TQ** Third quartile wage
AEX Average experienced wage	**APH** Average pay, high range	**AW** Average wage paid	**HR** High end range	**MW** Median wage paid	**W** Weekly
AO Average offered	**APL** Average pay, low range	**FQ** First quartile wage	**LR** Low end range	**SQ** Second quartile wage	**Y** Yearly

Occupation/Type/Industry	Location	Per	Low	Mid	High	Source	Date
Public Relations Specialist	Des Moines MSA, IA	S	16.64 mw	15.27 aw	34610 aaw	IABLS	10//99-12//99
	Dubuque MSA, IA	S	12.48 mw	12.05 aw	25970 aaw	IABLS	10//99-12//99
	Waterloo-Cedar Falls MSA, IA	S	15.69 mw	16.55 aw	32640 aaw	IABLS	10//99-12//99
	Kansas	S	16.65 mw	17.17 aw	35710 aaw	KSBLS	10//99-12//99
	Lawrence MSA, KS	S	14.21 mw	14.55 aw	29560 aaw	KSBLS	10//99-12//99
	Topeka MSA, KS	S	18.50 mw	18.21 aw	38470 aaw	KSBLS	10//99-12//99
	Wichita MSA, KS	S	16.58 mw	15.69 aw	34490 aaw	KSBLS	10//99-12//99
	Kentucky	S	15.26 mw	16.68 aw	34690 aaw	KYBLS	10//99-12//99
	Lexington MSA, KY	S	15.68 mw	14.39 aw	32620 aaw	KYBLS	10//99-12//99
	Louisville MSA, KY-IN	S	15.87 mw	13.95 aw	33010 aaw	KYBLS	10//99-12//99
	Louisiana	S	14.36 mw	16.20 aw	33690 aaw	LABLS	10//99-12//99
	Baton Rouge MSA, LA	S	14.65 mw	13.74 aw	30470 aaw	LABLS	10//99-12//99
	Lafayette MSA, LA	S	15.34 mw	13.81 aw	31920 aaw	LABLS	10//99-12//99
	Lake Charles MSA, LA	S	14.38 mw	12.84 aw	29920 aaw	LABLS	10//99-12//99
	New Orleans MSA, LA	S	18.02 mw	16.02 aw	37470 aaw	LABLS	10//99-12//99
	Shreveport-Bossier City MSA, LA	S	15.26 mw	12.69 aw	31730 aaw	LABLS	10//99-12//99
	Maine	S	14.97 mw	16.07 aw	33420 aaw	MEBLS	10//99-12//99
	Portland MSA, ME	S	15.99 mw	14.42 aw	33250 aaw	MEBLS	10//99-12//99
	Baltimore PMSA, MD	S	18.73 mw	16.50 aw	38960 aaw	MDBLS	10//99-12//99
	Massachusetts	S	19.36 mw	21.43 aw	44560 aaw	MABLS	10//99-12//99
	Boston PMSA, MA-NH	S	21.85 mw	19.59 aw	45440 aaw	MABLS	10//99-12//99
	Lawrence PMSA, MA-NH	S	18.21 mw	16.28 aw	37890 aaw	MABLS	10//99-12//99
	Lowell PMSA, MA-NH	S	24.22 mw	22.52 aw	50380 aaw	MABLS	10//99-12//99
	Springfield MSA, MA	S	17.62 mw	16.96 aw	36640 aaw	MABLS	10//99-12//99
	Worcester PMSA, MA-CT	S	18.97 mw	16.78 aw	39450 aaw	MABLS	10//99-12//99
	Michigan	S	17.68 mw	18.95 aw	39410 aaw	MIBLS	10//99-12//99
	Ann Arbor PMSA, MI	S	16.39 mw	15.67 aw	34090 aaw	MIBLS	10//99-12//99
	Detroit PMSA, MI	S	19.74 mw	18.39 aw	41060 aaw	MIBLS	10//99-12//99
	Flint PMSA, MI	S	20.69 mw	17.47 aw	43030 aaw	MIBLS	10//99-12//99
	Grand Rapids-Muskegon-Holland MSA, MI	S	15.79 mw	15.35 aw	32830 aaw	MIBLS	10//99-12//99
	Kalamazoo-Battle Creek MSA, MI	S	18.62 mw	17.17 aw	38730 aaw	MIBLS	10//99-12//99
	Lansing-East Lansing MSA, MI	S	21.02 mw	20.37 aw	43720 aaw	MIBLS	10//99-12//99
	Saginaw-Bay City-Midland MSA, MI	S	17.14 mw	12.31 aw	35650 aaw	MIBLS	10//99-12//99
	Minnesota	S	18.39 mw	19.20 aw	39940 aaw	MNBLS	10//99-12//99
	Duluth-Superior MSA, MN-WI	S	17.00 mw	15.54 aw	35370 aaw	MNBLS	10//99-12//99
	Minneapolis-St. Paul MSA, MN-WI	S	19.59 mw	18.82 aw	40740 aaw	MNBLS	10//99-12//99
	St. Cloud MSA, MN	S	16.80 mw	16.43 aw	34950 aaw	MNBLS	10//99-12//99
	Mississippi	S	13.63 mw	14.90 aw	30990 aaw	MSBLS	10//99-12//99
	Biloxi-Gulfport-Pascagoula MSA, MS	S	16.34 mw	15.88 aw	33990 aaw	MSBLS	10//99-12//99
	Jackson MSA, MS	S	15.12 mw	13.33 aw	31460 aaw	MSBLS	10//99-12//99
	Missouri	S	15.29 mw	17.06 aw	35490 aaw	MOBLS	10//99-12//99
	Columbia MSA, MO	S	15.04 mw	13.89 aw	31290 aaw	MOBLS	10//99-12//99
	Kansas City MSA, MO-KS	S	18.41 mw	16.41 aw	38300 aaw	MOBLS	10//99-12//99
	St. Louis MSA, MO-IL	S	17.46 mw	15.90 aw	36310 aaw	MOBLS	10//99-12//99
	Springfield MSA, MO	S	15.18 mw	13.90 aw	31580 aaw	MOBLS	10//99-12//99
	Montana	S	13.21 mw	14.95 aw	31090 aaw	MTBLS	10//99-12//99
	Missoula MSA, MT	S	16.07 mw	14.80 aw	33420 aaw	MTBLS	10//99-12//99
	Nebraska	S	15.41 mw	16.70 aw	34740 aaw	NEBLS	10//99-12//99
	Lincoln MSA, NE	S	17.12 mw	15.83 aw	35610 aaw	NEBLS	10//99-12//99
	Omaha MSA, NE-IA	S	16.74 mw	14.93 aw	34830 aaw	NEBLS	10//99-12//99
	Nevada	S	17.95 mw	19.25 aw	40040 aaw	NVBLS	10//99-12//99
	Las Vegas MSA, NV-AZ	S	19.66 mw	18.24 aw	40900 aaw	NVBLS	10//99-12//99
	Reno MSA, NV	S	16.85 mw	15.59 aw	35050 aaw	NVBLS	10//99-12//99
	New Hampshire	S	17.37 mw	18.21 aw	37870 aaw	NHBLS	10//99-12//99
	Manchester PMSA, NH	S	17.84 mw	17.55 aw	37110 aaw	NHBLS	10//99-12//99
	Nashua PMSA, NH	S	19.69 mw	18.62 aw	40960 aaw	NHBLS	10//99-12//99
	New Jersey	S	17.99 mw	19.84 aw	41270 aaw	NJBLS	10//99-12//99
	Atlantic-Cape May PMSA, NJ	S	17.22 mw	16.06 aw	35820 aaw	NJBLS	10//99-12//99
	Bergen-Passaic PMSA, NJ	S	19.32 mw	17.49 aw	40180 aaw	NJBLS	10//99-12//99
	Jersey City PMSA, NJ	S	20.39 mw	17.64 aw	42410 aaw	NJBLS	10//99-12//99
	Middlesex-Somerset-Hunterdon PMSA, NJ	S	18.46 mw	17.62 aw	38390 aaw	NJBLS	10//99-12//99
	Monmouth-Ocean PMSA, NJ	S	18.17 mw	16.21 aw	37790 aaw	NJBLS	10//99-12//99
	Newark PMSA, NJ	S	22.11 mw	20.56 aw	46000 aaw	NJBLS	10//99-12//99
	Trenton PMSA, NJ	S	23.18 mw	21.47 aw	48220 aaw	NJBLS	10//99-12//99
	New Mexico	S	15.67 mw	17.00 aw	35370 aaw	NMBLS	10//99-12//99

AAW Average annual wage	AOH Average offered, high	ASH Average starting, high	H Hourly	M Monthly	S Special: hourly and annual
AE Average entry wage	AOL Average offered, low	ASL Average starting, low	HI Highest wage paid	MTC Median total compensation	TQ Third quartile wage
AEX Average experienced wage	APH Average pay, high range	AW Average wage paid	HR High end range	MW Median wage paid	W Weekly
AO Average offered	APL Average pay, low range	FQ First quartile wage	LR Low end range	SQ Second quartile wage	Y Yearly

Occupation/Type/Industry	Location	Per	Low	Mid	High	Source	Date
Public Relations Specialist	Albuquerque MSA, NM	S	17.03 MW	15.80 AW	35420 AAW	NMBLS	10//99-12//99
	Santa Fe MSA, NM	S	17.65 MW	16.20 AW	36720 AAW	NMBLS	10//99-12//99
	New York	S	21.41 MW	24.11 AW	50150 AAW	NYBLS	10//99-12//99
	Albany-Schenectady-Troy MSA, NY	S	19.78 MW	20.11 AW	41150 AAW	NYBLS	10//99-12//99
	Binghamton MSA, NY	S	15.18 MW	14.37 AW	31570 AAW	NYBLS	10//99-12//99
	Buffalo-Niagara Falls MSA, NY	S	15.11 MW	13.74 AW	31430 AAW	NYBLS	10//99-12//99
	Dutchess County PMSA, NY	S	20.10 MW	17.83 AW	41810 AAW	NYBLS	10//99-12//99
	Elmira MSA, NY	S	12.13 MW	10.89 AW	25230 AAW	NYBLS	10//99-12//99
	Glens Falls MSA, NY	S	15.19 MW	15.65 AW	31590 AAW	NYBLS	10//99-12//99
	Nassau-Suffolk PMSA, NY	S	23.79 MW	18.97 AW	49470 AAW	NYBLS	10//99-12//99
	New York PMSA, NY	S	26.45 MW	22.77 AW	55020 AAW	NYBLS	10//99-12//99
	Newburgh PMSA, NY-PA	S	16.58 MW	17.52 AW	34490 AAW	NYBLS	10//99-12//99
	Rochester MSA, NY	S	17.65 MW	15.64 AW	36710 AAW	NYBLS	10//99-12//99
	Syracuse MSA, NY	S	16.87 MW	15.53 AW	35100 AAW	NYBLS	10//99-12//99
	Utica-Rome MSA, NY	S	14.36 MW	12.93 AW	29880 AAW	NYBLS	10//99-12//99
	North Carolina	S	15.68 MW	16.30 AW	33910 AAW	NCBLS	10//99-12//99
	Asheville MSA, NC	S	15.89 MW	15.31 AW	33050 AAW	NCBLS	10//99-12//99
	Charlotte-Gastonia-Rock Hill MSA, NC-SC	S	16.69 MW	16.06 AW	34710 AAW	NCBLS	10//99-12//99
	Fayetteville MSA, NC	S	14.59 MW	13.53 AW	30340 AAW	NCBLS	10//99-12//99
	Greensboro--Winston-Salem--High Point MSA, NC	S	16.68 MW	15.62 AW	34680 AAW	NCBLS	10//99-12//99
	Hickory-Morganton-Lenoir MSA, NC	S	15.01 MW	14.38 AW	31220 AAW	NCBLS	10//99-12//99
	Raleigh-Durham-Chapel Hill MSA, NC	S	17.60 MW	16.67 AW	36600 AAW	NCBLS	10//99-12//99
	Wilmington MSA, NC	S	12.92 MW	12.24 AW	26870 AAW	NCBLS	10//99-12//99
	North Dakota	S	15.5 MW	17.28 AW	35950 AAW	NDBLS	10//99-12//99
	Bismarck MSA, ND	S	19.73 MW	18.66 AW	41040 AAW	NDBLS	10//99-12//99
	Fargo-Moorhead MSA, ND-MN	S	14.74 MW	13.32 AW	30660 AAW	NDBLS	10//99-12//99
	Grand Forks MSA, ND-MN	S	16.28 MW	15.06 AW	33860 AAW	NDBLS	10//99-12//99
	Ohio	S	16.09 MW	17.58 AW	36570 AAW	OHBLS	10//99-12//99
	Akron PMSA, OH	S	16.86 MW	15.70 AW	35060 AAW	OHBLS	10//99-12//99
	Canton-Massillon MSA, OH	S	16.48 MW	15.04 AW	34290 AAW	OHBLS	10//99-12//99
	Cincinnati PMSA, OH-KY-IN	S	17.74 MW	16.28 AW	36900 AAW	OHBLS	10//99-12//99
	Cleveland-Lorain-Elyria PMSA, OH	S	17.90 MW	15.82 AW	37240 AAW	OHBLS	10//99-12//99
	Columbus MSA, OH	S	18.59 MW	18.37 AW	38680 AAW	OHBLS	10//99-12//99
	Dayton-Springfield MSA, OH	S	17.40 MW	16.30 AW	36200 AAW	OHBLS	10//99-12//99
	Hamilton-Middletown PMSA, OH	S	13.50 MW	13.70 AW	28070 AAW	OHBLS	10//99-12//99
	Lima MSA, OH	S	14.37 MW	12.94 AW	29900 AAW	OHBLS	10//99-12//99
	Toledo MSA, OH	S	17.61 MW	16.56 AW	36630 AAW	OHBLS	10//99-12//99
	Oklahoma	S	13 MW	14.06 AW	29240 AAW	OKBLS	10//99-12//99
	Oklahoma City MSA, OK	S	14.98 MW	13.93 AW	31160 AAW	OKBLS	10//99-12//99
	Tulsa MSA, OK	S	13.60 MW	12.82 AW	28290 AAW	OKBLS	10//99-12//99
	Oregon	S	17.6 MW	19.19 AW	39910 AAW	ORBLS	10//99-12//99
	Eugene-Springfield MSA, OR	S	16.67 MW	15.71 AW	34680 AAW	ORBLS	10//99-12//99
	Portland-Vancouver PMSA, OR-WA	S	19.88 MW	18.43 AW	41350 AAW	ORBLS	10//99-12//99
	Salem PMSA, OR	S	20.22 MW	18.73 AW	42060 AAW	ORBLS	10//99-12//99
	Pennsylvania	S	16.4 MW	18.21 AW	37880 AAW	PABLS	10//99-12//99
	Allentown-Bethlehem-Easton MSA, PA	S	16.92 MW	15.17 AW	35190 AAW	PABLS	10//99-12//99
	Erie MSA, PA	S	14.27 MW	12.55 AW	29680 AAW	PABLS	10//99-12//99
	Harrisburg-Lebanon-Carlisle MSA, PA	S	19.70 MW	17.78 AW	40980 AAW	PABLS	10//99-12//99
	Lancaster MSA, PA	S	17.53 MW	15.28 AW	36470 AAW	PABLS	10//99-12//99
	Philadelphia PMSA, PA-NJ	S	19.18 MW	16.74 AW	39900 AAW	PABLS	10//99-12//99
	Pittsburgh MSA, PA	S	15.43 MW	14.38 AW	32100 AAW	PABLS	10//99-12//99
	Reading MSA, PA	S	19.35 MW	16.01 AW	40240 AAW	PABLS	10//99-12//99
	Scranton--Wilkes-Barre--Hazleton MSA, PA	S	14.62 MW	13.12 AW	30400 AAW	PABLS	10//99-12//99
	York MSA, PA	S	16.12 MW	15.07 AW	33530 AAW	PABLS	10//99-12//99
	Rhode Island	S	18.26 MW	18.86 AW	39220 AAW	RIBLS	10//99-12//99
	Providence-Fall River-Warwick MSA, RI-MA	S	18.84 MW	18.18 AW	39190 AAW	RIBLS	10//99-12//99
	South Carolina	S	13.08 MW	14.64 AW	30440 AAW	SCBLS	10//99-12//99

AAW Average annual wage	AOH Average offered, high	ASH Average starting, high	H Hourly	M Monthly	S Special: hourly and annual
AE Average entry wage	AOL Average offered, low	ASL Average starting, low	HI Highest wage paid	MTC Median total compensation	TQ Third quartile wage
AEX Average experienced wage	APH Average pay, high range	AW Average wage paid	HR High end range	MW Median wage paid	W Weekly
AO Average offered	APL Average pay, low range	FQ First quartile wage	LR Low end range	SQ Second quartile wage	Y Yearly

Occupation/Type/Industry	Location	Per	Low	Mid	High	Source	Date
Public Relations Specialist	Charleston-North Charleston MSA, SC	S	15.57 MW	14.25 AW	32380 AAW	SCBLS	10//99-12//99
	Columbia MSA, SC	S	16.64 MW	15.43 AW	34610 AAW	SCBLS	10//99-12//99
	Greenville-Spartanburg-Anderson MSA, SC	S	16.22 MW	14.95 AW	33740 AAW	SCBLS	10//99-12//99
	Myrtle Beach MSA, SC	S	13.34 MW	12.08 AW	27740 AAW	SCBLS	10//99-12//99
	South Dakota	S	12.95 MW	13.85 AW	28810 AAW	SDBLS	10//99-12//99
	Rapid City MSA, SD	S	14.82 MW	13.94 AW	30830 AAW	SDBLS	10//99-12//99
	Sioux Falls MSA, SD	S	14.19 MW	12.80 AW	29510 AAW	SDBLS	10//99-12//99
	Tennessee	S	16.82 MW	18.43 AW	38340 AAW	TNBLS	10//99-12//99
	Chattanooga MSA, TN-GA	S	16.75 MW	16.43 AW	34830 AAW	TNBLS	10//99-12//99
	Johnson City-Kingsport-Bristol MSA, TN-VA	S	14.85 MW	13.72 AW	30880 AAW	TNBLS	10//99-12//99
	Knoxville MSA, TN	S	16.33 MW	15.06 AW	33970 AAW	TNBLS	10//99-12//99
	Memphis MSA, TN-AR-MS	S	20.05 MW	19.15 AW	41700 AAW	MSBLS	10//99-12//99
	Nashville MSA, TN	S	19.21 MW	17.18 AW	39960 AAW	TNBLS	10//99-12//99
	Texas	S	17.01 MW	18.99 AW	39510 AAW	TXBLS	10//99-12//99
	Abilene MSA, TX	S	14.68 MW	13.10 AW	30530 AAW	TXBLS	10//99-12//99
	Austin-San Marcos MSA, TX	S	20.30 MW	18.93 AW	42220 AAW	TXBLS	10//99-12//99
	Bryan-College Station MSA, TX	S	18.33 MW	17.40 AW	38120 AAW	TXBLS	10//99-12//99
	Corpus Christi MSA, TX	S	18.18 MW	15.56 AW	37820 AAW	TXBLS	10//99-12//99
	Dallas PMSA, TX	S	20.25 MW	17.95 AW	42120 AAW	TXBLS	10//99-12//99
	El Paso MSA, TX	S	17.99 MW	16.73 AW	37420 AAW	TXBLS	10//99-12//99
	Fort Worth-Arlington PMSA, TX	S	19.36 MW	16.83 AW	40270 AAW	TXBLS	10//99-12//99
	Galveston-Texas City PMSA, TX	S	17.17 MW	16.33 AW	35720 AAW	TXBLS	10//99-12//99
	Houston PMSA, TX	S	20.41 MW	18.33 AW	42460 AAW	TXBLS	10//99-12//99
	Killeen-Temple MSA, TX	S	13.89 MW	13.53 AW	28890 AAW	TXBLS	10//99-12//99
	Lubbock MSA, TX	S	12.40 MW	12.33 AW	25780 AAW	TXBLS	10//99-12//99
	McAllen-Edinburg-Mission MSA, TX	S	14.13 MW	13.76 AW	29400 AAW	TXBLS	10//99-12//99
	Odessa-Midland MSA, TX	S	15.72 MW	14.83 AW	32710 AAW	TXBLS	10//99-12//99
	San Antonio MSA, TX	S	16.72 MW	16.00 AW	34780 AAW	TXBLS	10//99-12//99
	Tyler MSA, TX	S	14.31 MW	14.46 AW	29760 AAW	TXBLS	10//99-12//99
	Waco MSA, TX	S	17.09 MW	14.79 AW	35540 AAW	TXBLS	10//99-12//99
	Utah	S	15.59 MW	16.90 AW	35150 AAW	UTBLS	10//99-12//99
	Provo-Orem MSA, UT	S	16.95 MW	15.50 AW	35260 AAW	UTBLS	10//99-12//99
	Salt Lake City-Ogden MSA, UT	S	17.02 MW	15.80 AW	35400 AAW	UTBLS	10//99-12//99
	Vermont	S	16.04 MW	17.31 AW	36000 AAW	VTBLS	10//99-12//99
	Burlington MSA, VT	S	17.35 MW	15.82 AW	36080 AAW	VTBLS	10//99-12//99
	Virginia	S	17.85 MW	19.90 AW	41380 AAW	VABLS	10//99-12//99
	Norfolk-Virginia Beach-Newport News MSA, VA-NC	S	17.54 MW	17.28 AW	36490 AAW	VABLS	10//99-12//99
	Richmond-Petersburg MSA, VA	S	17.43 MW	16.61 AW	36260 AAW	VABLS	10//99-12//99
	Roanoke MSA, VA	S	15.04 MW	14.31 AW	31290 AAW	VABLS	10//99-12//99
	Washington	S	18.39 MW	20.04 AW	41680 AAW	WABLS	10//99-12//99
	Bellingham MSA, WA	S	16.23 MW	15.41 AW	33770 AAW	WABLS	10//99-12//99
	Bremerton PMSA, WA	S	18.81 MW	17.31 AW	39130 AAW	WABLS	10//99-12//99
	Olympia PMSA, WA	S	24.75 MW	23.14 AW	51470 AAW	WABLS	10//99-12//99
	Richland-Kennewick-Pasco MSA, WA	S	22.97 MW	21.42 AW	47780 AAW	WABLS	10//99-12//99
	Seattle-Bellevue-Everett PMSA, WA	S	20.92 MW	18.80 AW	43510 AAW	WABLS	10//99-12//99
	Spokane MSA, WA	S	17.64 MW	16.41 AW	36690 AAW	WABLS	10//99-12//99
	Tacoma PMSA, WA	S	15.52 MW	14.99 AW	32290 AAW	WABLS	10//99-12//99
	Yakima MSA, WA	S	17.09 MW	16.21 AW	35540 AAW	WABLS	10//99-12//99
	West Virginia	S	13.47 MW	15.23 AW	31680 AAW	WVBLS	10//99-12//99
	Charleston MSA, WV	S	15.38 MW	13.67 AW	31990 AAW	WVBLS	10//99-12//99
	Huntington-Ashland MSA, WV-KY-OH	S	16.88 MW	15.01 AW	35110 AAW	WVBLS	10//99-12//99
	Wisconsin	S	15.05 MW	15.87 AW	33010 AAW	WIBLS	10//99-12//99
	Appleton-Oshkosh-Neenah MSA, WI	S	11.83 MW	10.98 AW	24620 AAW	WIBLS	10//99-12//99
	Eau Claire MSA, WI	S	15.92 MW	14.40 AW	33110 AAW	WIBLS	10//99-12//99
	Green Bay MSA, WI	S	15.07 MW	13.84 AW	31340 AAW	WIBLS	10//99-12//99
	Janesville-Beloit MSA, WI	S	14.34 MW	13.69 AW	29830 AAW	WIBLS	10//99-12//99
	Kenosha PMSA, WI	S	12.75 MW	11.76 AW	26510 AAW	WIBLS	10//99-12//99

AAW	Average annual wage	AOH	Average offered, high	ASH	Average starting, high	H	Hourly	M	Monthly	S	Special: hourly and annual
AE	Average entry wage	AOL	Average offered, low	ASL	Average starting, low	HI	Highest wage paid	MTC	Median total compensation	TQ	Third quartile wage
AEX	Average experienced wage	APH	Average pay, high range	AW	Average wage paid	HR	High end range	MW	Median wage paid	W	Weekly
AO	Average offered	APL	Average pay, low range	FQ	First quartile wage	LR	Low end range	SQ	Second quartile wage	Y	Yearly

Occupation/Type/Industry	Location	Per	Low	Mid	High	Source	Date
Public Relations Specialist	La Crosse MSA, WI-MN	S	14.31 MW	11.33 AW	29750 AAW	WIBLS	10//99-12//99
	Madison MSA, WI	S	18.09 MW	17.54 AW	37620 AAW	WIBLS	10//99-12//99
	Milwaukee-Waukesha PMSA, WI	S	16.90 MW	15.22 AW	35150 AAW	WIBLS	10//99-12//99
	Wausau MSA, WI	S	14.53 MW	12.92 AW	30210 AAW	WIBLS	10//99-12//99
	Wyoming	S	15.56 MW	16.41 AW	34140 AAW	WYBLS	10//99-12//99
	Casper MSA, WY	S	16.45 MW	15.71 AW	34220 AAW	WYBLS	10//99-12//99
	Cheyenne MSA, WY	S	14.95 MW	14.84 AW	31090 AAW	WYBLS	10//99-12//99
	Puerto Rico	S	11.99 MW	13.74 AW	28580 AAW	PRBLS	10//99-12//99
	Caguas PMSA, PR	S	8.25 MW	7.23 AW	17170 AAW	PRBLS	10//99-12//99
	San Juan-Bayamon PMSA, PR	S	14.48 MW	12.72 AW	30120 AAW	PRBLS	10//99-12//99
Pump Operator							
Except Wellhead Pumper	Alabama	S	14.1 MW	13.93 AW	28980 AAW	ALBLS	10//99-12//99
Except Wellhead Pumper	Alaska	S	24.26 MW	24.90 AW	51790 AAW	AKBLS	10//99-12//99
Except Wellhead Pumper	Arizona	S	10.8 MW	11.46 AW	23840 AAW	AZBLS	10//99-12//99
Except Wellhead Pumper	Arkansas	S	11.35 MW	13.27 AW	27600 AAW	ARBLS	10//99-12//99
Except Wellhead Pumper	California	S	18.04 MW	18.19 AW	37830 AAW	CABLS	10//99-12//99
Except Wellhead Pumper	Colorado	S	12.9 MW	13.64 AW	28370 AAW	COBLS	10//99-12//99
Except Wellhead Pumper	Florida	S	13.5 MW	15.92 AW	33120 AAW	FLBLS	10//99-12//99
Except Wellhead Pumper	Georgia	S	12.36 MW	13.33 AW	27730 AAW	GABLS	10//99-12//99
Except Wellhead Pumper	Hawaii	S	8.46 MW	8.94 AW	18600 AAW	HIBLS	10//99-12//99
Except Wellhead Pumper	Idaho	S	10.6 MW	10.40 AW	21640 AAW	IDBLS	10//99-12//99
Except Wellhead Pumper	Illinois	S	18.03 MW	18.30 AW	38070 AAW	ILBLS	10//99-12//99
Except Wellhead Pumper	Indiana	S	14.62 MW	15.14 AW	31490 AAW	INBLS	10//99-12//99
Except Wellhead Pumper	Kansas	S	12.33 MW	13.01 AW	27060 AAW	KSBLS	10//99-12//99
Except Wellhead Pumper	Kentucky	S	16.6 MW	15.92 AW	33110 AAW	KYBLS	10//99-12//99
Except Wellhead Pumper	Louisiana	S	21.03 MW	18.49 AW	38460 AAW	LABLS	10//99-12//99
Except Wellhead Pumper	Maryland	S	15.99 MW	15.53 AW	32310 AAW	MDBLS	10//99-12//99
Except Wellhead Pumper	Massachusetts	S	18.8 MW	17.58 AW	36570 AAW	MABLS	10//99-12//99
Except Wellhead Pumper	Michigan	S	13.77 MW	14.70 AW	30570 AAW	MIBLS	10//99-12//99
Except Wellhead Pumper	Minnesota	S	17.29 MW	16.06 AW	33410 AAW	MNBLS	10//99-12//99
Except Wellhead Pumper	Mississippi	S	17.24 MW	16.57 AW	34460 AAW	MSBLS	10//99-12//99
Except Wellhead Pumper	Nebraska	S	11.49 MW	11.76 AW	24450 AAW	NEBLS	10//99-12//99
Except Wellhead Pumper	Nevada	S	8.27 MW	10.42 AW	21680 AAW	NVBLS	10//99-12//99
Except Wellhead Pumper	New Jersey	S	20.68 MW	17.88 AW	37200 AAW	NJBLS	10//99-12//99
Except Wellhead Pumper	New Mexico	S	18.62 MW	16.93 AW	35210 AAW	NMBLS	10//99-12//99
Except Wellhead Pumper	New York	S	13.62 MW	13.97 AW	29060 AAW	NYBLS	10//99-12//99
Except Wellhead Pumper	North Dakota	S	14.77 MW	16.24 AW	33780 AAW	NDBLS	10//99-12//99
Except Wellhead Pumper	Oklahoma	S	12.6 MW	14.19 AW	29520 AAW	OKBLS	10//99-12//99
Except Wellhead Pumper	Pennsylvania	S	14.05 MW	14.50 AW	30170 AAW	PABLS	10//99-12//99
Except Wellhead Pumper	South Carolina	S	8.21 MW	8.96 AW	18640 AAW	SCBLS	10//99-12//99
Except Wellhead Pumper	Tennessee	S	11.75 MW	12.39 AW	25770 AAW	TNBLS	10//99-12//99
Except Wellhead Pumper	Texas	S	17.13 MW	18.51 AW	38500 AAW	TXBLS	10//99-12//99
Except Wellhead Pumper	Utah	S	17.47 MW	19.53 AW	40630 AAW	UTBLS	10//99-12//99
Except Wellhead Pumper	Virginia	S	14.62 MW	14.64 AW	30450 AAW	VABLS	10//99-12//99
Except Wellhead Pumper	Washington	S	17.68 MW	18.19 AW	37840 AAW	WABLS	10//99-12//99
Except Wellhead Pumper	West Virginia	S	11.58 MW	13.11 AW	27260 AAW	WVBLS	10//99-12//99
Except Wellhead Pumper	Wisconsin	S	17.61 MW	17.20 AW	35770 AAW	WIBLS	10//99-12//99
Except Wellhead Pumper	Wyoming	S	17.25 MW	16.63 AW	34590 AAW	WYBLS	10//99-12//99
Except Wellhead Pumper	Puerto Rico	S	9.26 MW	11.16 AW	23220 AAW	PRBLS	10//99-12//99
Purchasing Agent							
Electronics	United States	Y		59900 AW		ELBUY	2000
Except Wholesale, Retail, and Farm Product	Alabama	S	19.1 MW	20.25 AW	42130 AAW	ALBLS	10//99-12//99
Except Wholesale, Retail, and Farm Product	Anniston MSA, AL	S	18.79 MW	18.50 AW	39090 AAW	ALBLS	10//99-12//99
Except Wholesale, Retail, and Farm Product	Birmingham MSA, AL	S	18.11 MW	17.09 AW	37660 AAW	ALBLS	10//99-12//99
Except Wholesale, Retail, and Farm Product	Decatur MSA, AL	S	19.76 MW	20.50 AW	41100 AAW	ALBLS	10//99-12//99
Except Wholesale, Retail, and Farm Product	Dothan MSA, AL	S	16.32 MW	15.13 AW	33940 AAW	ALBLS	10//99-12//99
Except Wholesale, Retail, and Farm Product	Florence MSA, AL	S	19.20 MW	19.26 AW	39930 AAW	ALBLS	10//99-12//99
Except Wholesale, Retail, and Farm Product	Gadsden MSA, AL	S	15.23 MW	14.93 AW	31690 AAW	ALBLS	10//99-12//99
Except Wholesale, Retail, and Farm Product	Mobile MSA, AL	S	17.93 MW	17.05 AW	37300 AAW	ALBLS	10//99-12//99
Except Wholesale, Retail, and Farm Product	Montgomery MSA, AL	S	19.35 MW	18.21 AW	40250 AAW	ALBLS	10//99-12//99

Occupation/Type/Industry	Location	Per	Low	Mid	High	Source	Date
Purchasing Agent							
Except Wholesale, Retail, and Farm Product	Tuscaloosa MSA, AL	S	17.71 MW	17.23 AW	36830 AAW	ALBLS	10//99-12//99
Except Wholesale, Retail, and Farm Product	Alaska	S	19.67 MW	21.00 AW	43680 AAW	AKBLS	10//99-12//99
Except Wholesale, Retail, and Farm Product	Anchorage MSA, AK	S	20.21 MW	19.39 AW	42040 AAW	AKBLS	10//99-12//99
Except Wholesale, Retail, and Farm Product	Arizona	S	17.96 MW	19.67 AW	40900 AAW	AZBLS	10//99-12//99
Except Wholesale, Retail, and Farm Product	Flagstaff MSA, AZ-UT	S	17.08 MW	15.89 AW	35520 AAW	AZBLS	10//99-12//99
Except Wholesale, Retail, and Farm Product	Phoenix-Mesa MSA, AZ	S	20.18 MW	18.39 AW	41980 AAW	AZBLS	10//99-12//99
Except Wholesale, Retail, and Farm Product	Tucson MSA, AZ	S	17.58 MW	15.64 AW	36570 AAW	AZBLS	10//99-12//99
Except Wholesale, Retail, and Farm Product	Yuma MSA, AZ	S	19.64 MW	17.78 AW	40840 AAW	AZBLS	10//99-12//99
Except Wholesale, Retail, and Farm Product	Arkansas	S	16.16 MW	17.95 AW	37330 AAW	ARBLS	10//99-12//99
Except Wholesale, Retail, and Farm Product	Fayetteville-Springdale-Rogers MSA, AR	S	16.24 MW	15.25 AW	33770 AAW	ARBLS	10//99-12//99
Except Wholesale, Retail, and Farm Product	Fort Smith MSA, AR-OK	S	19.65 MW	19.04 AW	40870 AAW	ARBLS	10//99-12//99
Except Wholesale, Retail, and Farm Product	Jonesboro MSA, AR	S	16.10 MW	15.51 AW	33490 AAW	ARBLS	10//99-12//99
Except Wholesale, Retail, and Farm Product	Little Rock-North Little Rock MSA, AR	S	15.94 MW	14.86 AW	33160 AAW	ARBLS	10//99-12//99
Except Wholesale, Retail, and Farm Product	Pine Bluff MSA, AR	S	19.82 MW	19.25 AW	41220 AAW	ARBLS	10//99-12//99
Except Wholesale, Retail, and Farm Product	California	S	20.67 MW	22.28 AW	46340 AAW	CABLS	10//99-12//99
Except Wholesale, Retail, and Farm Product	Bakersfield MSA, CA	S	25.54 MW	24.75 AW	53130 AAW	CABLS	10//99-12//99
Except Wholesale, Retail, and Farm Product	Chico-Paradise MSA, CA	S	16.87 MW	16.03 AW	35080 AAW	CABLS	10//99-12//99
Except Wholesale, Retail, and Farm Product	Fresno MSA, CA	S	16.18 MW	15.73 AW	33650 AAW	CABLS	10//99-12//99
Except Wholesale, Retail, and Farm Product	Los Angeles-Long Beach PMSA, CA	S	23.40 MW	21.49 AW	48670 AAW	CABLS	10//99-12//99
Except Wholesale, Retail, and Farm Product	Merced MSA, CA	S	19.37 MW	19.07 AW	40300 AAW	CABLS	10//99-12//99
Except Wholesale, Retail, and Farm Product	Modesto MSA, CA	S	17.45 MW	16.23 AW	36300 AAW	CABLS	10//99-12//99
Except Wholesale, Retail, and Farm Product	Oakland PMSA, CA	S	21.25 MW	20.55 AW	44210 AAW	CABLS	10//99-12//99
Except Wholesale, Retail, and Farm Product	Orange County PMSA, CA	S	20.68 MW	19.44 AW	43010 AAW	CABLS	10//99-12//99
Except Wholesale, Retail, and Farm Product	Redding MSA, CA	S	18.07 MW	17.46 AW	37590 AAW	CABLS	10//99-12//99
Except Wholesale, Retail, and Farm Product	Riverside-San Bernardino PMSA, CA	S	17.51 MW	16.14 AW	36410 AAW	CABLS	10//99-12//99
Except Wholesale, Retail, and Farm Product	Sacramento PMSA, CA	S	21.87 MW	20.80 AW	45490 AAW	CABLS	10//99-12//99
Except Wholesale, Retail, and Farm Product	Salinas MSA, CA	S	20.27 MW	19.05 AW	42150 AAW	CABLS	10//99-12//99
Except Wholesale, Retail, and Farm Product	San Diego MSA, CA	S	22.48 MW	20.40 AW	46750 AAW	CABLS	10//99-12//99
Except Wholesale, Retail, and Farm Product	San Francisco PMSA, CA	S	23.43 MW	22.53 AW	48730 AAW	CABLS	10//99-12//99
Except Wholesale, Retail, and Farm Product	San Jose PMSA, CA	S	24.31 MW	22.74 AW	50570 AAW	CABLS	10//99-12//99
Except Wholesale, Retail, and Farm Product	San Luis Obispo-Atascadero-Paso Robles MSA, CA	S	18.24 MW	17.96 AW	37930 AAW	CABLS	10//99-12//99
Except Wholesale, Retail, and Farm Product	Santa Barbara-Santa Maria-Lompoc MSA, CA	S	21.54 MW	19.57 AW	44810 AAW	CABLS	10//99-12//99

AAW Average annual wage	**AOH** Average offered, high	**ASH** Average starting, high	**H** Hourly	**M** Monthly	**S** Special: hourly and annual
AE Average entry wage	**AOL** Average offered, low	**ASL** Average starting, low	**HI** Highest wage paid	**MTC** Median total compensation	**TQ** Third quartile wage
AEX Average experienced wage	**APH** Average pay, high range	**AW** Average wage paid	**HR** High end range	**MW** Median wage paid	**W** Weekly
AO Average offered	**APL** Average pay, low range	**FQ** First quartile wage	**LR** Low end range	**SQ** Second quartile wage	**Y** Yearly

Purchasing Agent

Occupation/Type/Industry	Location	Per	Low	Mid	High	Source	Date
Purchasing Agent							
Except Wholesale, Retail, and Farm Product	Santa Cruz-Watsonville PMSA, CA	S	19.89 MW	19.71 AW	41380 AAW	CABLS	10//99-12//99
Except Wholesale, Retail, and Farm Product	Santa Rosa PMSA, CA	S	19.96 MW	18.96 AW	41530 AAW	CABLS	10//99-12//99
Except Wholesale, Retail, and Farm Product	Stockton-Lodi MSA, CA	S	21.10 MW	19.88 AW	43900 AAW	CABLS	10//99-12//99
Except Wholesale, Retail, and Farm Product	Vallejo-Fairfield-Napa PMSA, CA	S	20.62 MW	19.97 AW	42880 AW	CABLS	10//99-12//99
Except Wholesale, Retail, and Farm Product	Ventura PMSA, CA	S	21.47 MW	20.29 AW	44650 AAW	CABLS	10//99-12//99
Except Wholesale, Retail, and Farm Product	Visalia-Tulare-Porterville MSA, CA	S	16.49 MW	15.61 AW	34300 AAW	CABLS	10//99-12//99
Except Wholesale, Retail, and Farm Product	Yolo PMSA, CA	S	18.84 MW	17.80 AW	39180 AAW	CABLS	10//99-12//99
Except Wholesale, Retail, and Farm Product	Yuba City MSA, CA	S	16.80 MW	16.00 AW	34940 AAW	CABLS	10//99-12//99
Except Wholesale, Retail, and Farm Product	Colorado	S	18.74 MW	19.76 AW	41100 AAW	COBLS	10//99-12//99
Except Wholesale, Retail, and Farm Product	Boulder-Longmont PMSA, CO	S	21.42 MW	19.40 AW	44560 AAW	COBLS	10//99-12//99
Except Wholesale, Retail, and Farm Product	Colorado Springs MSA, CO	S	20.04 MW	19.23 AW	41680 AAW	COBLS	10//99-12//99
Except Wholesale, Retail, and Farm Product	Denver PMSA, CO	S	19.65 MW	18.66 AW	40870 AAW	COBLS	10//99-12//99
Except Wholesale, Retail, and Farm Product	Fort Collins-Loveland MSA, CO	S	18.74 MW	18.64 AW	38980 AAW	COBLS	10//99-12//99
Except Wholesale, Retail, and Farm Product	Grand Junction MSA, CO	S	18.78 MW	16.54 AW	39070 AAW	COBLS	10//99-12//99
Except Wholesale, Retail, and Farm Product	Greeley PMSA, CO	S	19.66 MW	19.74 AW	40890 AAW	COBLS	10//99-12//99
Except Wholesale, Retail, and Farm Product	Connecticut	S	21.21 MW	22.33 AW	46450 AAW	CTBLS	10//99-12//99
Except Wholesale, Retail, and Farm Product	Bridgeport PMSA, CT	S	22.53 MW	21.96 AW	46850 AAW	CTBLS	10//99-12//99
Except Wholesale, Retail, and Farm Product	Danbury PMSA, CT	S	20.32 MW	18.83 AW	42270 AAW	CTBLS	10//99-12//99
Except Wholesale, Retail, and Farm Product	Hartford MSA, CT	S	22.38 MW	21.27 AW	46560 AAW	CTBLS	10//99-12//99
Except Wholesale, Retail, and Farm Product	New Haven-Meriden PMSA, CT	S	19.71 MW	19.17 AW	40990 AAW	CTBLS	10//99-12//99
Except Wholesale, Retail, and Farm Product	New London-Norwich MSA, CT-RI	S	19.99 MW	18.68 AW	41570 AAW	CTBLS	10//99-12//99
Except Wholesale, Retail, and Farm Product	Stamford-Norwalk PMSA, CT	S	26.74 MW	24.68 AW	55610 AAW	CTBLS	10//99-12//99
Except Wholesale, Retail, and Farm Product	Waterbury PMSA, CT	S	21.86 MW	20.54 AW	45460 AAW	CTBLS	10//99-12//99
Except Wholesale, Retail, and Farm Product	Delaware	S	20.21 MW	22.97 AW	47770 AAW	DEBLS	10//99-12//99
Except Wholesale, Retail, and Farm Product	Dover MSA, DE	S	18.93 MW	18.03 AW	39370 AAW	DEBLS	10//99-12//99
Except Wholesale, Retail, and Farm Product	Wilmington-Newark PMSA, DE-MD	S	24.02 MW	21.12 AW	49960 AAW	DEBLS	10//99-12//99
Except Wholesale, Retail, and Farm Product	Washington PMSA, DC-MD-VA-WV	S	25.61 MW	25.25 AW	53260 AAW	DCBLS	10//99-12//99
Except Wholesale, Retail, and Farm Product	Florida	S	15.82 MW	17.24 AW	35860 AAW	FLBLS	10//99-12//99
Except Wholesale, Retail, and Farm Product	Daytona Beach MSA, FL	S	15.72 MW	15.15 AW	32690 AAW	FLBLS	10//99-12//99
Except Wholesale, Retail, and Farm Product	Fort Lauderdale PMSA, FL	S	17.67 MW	16.77 AW	36750 AAW	FLBLS	10//99-12//99

AAW	Average annual wage	AOH	Average offered, high	ASH	Average starting, high
AE	Average entry wage	AOL	Average offered, low	ASL	Average starting, low
AEX	Average experienced wage	APH	Average pay, high range	AW	Average wage paid
AO	Average offered	APL	Average pay, low range	FQ	First quartile wage

H	Hourly	M	Monthly	S	Special: hourly and annual
HI	Highest wage paid	MTC	Median total compensation	TQ	Third quartile wage
HR	High end range	MW	Median wage paid	W	Weekly
LR	Low end range	SQ	Second quartile wage	Y	Yearly

Occupation/Type/Industry	Location	Per	Low	Mid	High	Source	Date
Purchasing Agent							
Except Wholesale, Retail, and Farm Product	Fort Myers-Cape Coral MSA, FL	S	14.38 MW	13.21 AW	29900 AAW	FLBLS	10//99-12//99
Except Wholesale, Retail, and Farm Product	Fort Pierce-Port St. Lucie MSA, FL	S	16.26 MW	14.98 AW	33820 AAW	FLBLS	10//99-12//99
Except Wholesale, Retail, and Farm Product	Gainesville MSA, FL	S	17.56 MW	16.02 AW	36520 AAW	FLBLS	10//99-12//99
Except Wholesale, Retail, and Farm Product	Jacksonville MSA, FL	S	17.18 MW	15.88 AW	35740 AAW	FLBLS	10//99-12//99
Except Wholesale, Retail, and Farm Product	Lakeland-Winter Haven MSA, FL	S	16.24 MW	14.76 AW	33780 AAW	FLBLS	10//99-12//99
Except Wholesale, Retail, and Farm Product	Melbourne-Titusville-Palm Bay MSA, FL	S	21.81 MW	21.64 AW	45370 AAW	FLBLS	10//99-12//99
Except Wholesale, Retail, and Farm Product	Miami PMSA, FL	S	15.35 MW	14.56 AW	31920 AAW	FLBLS	10//99-12//99
Except Wholesale, Retail, and Farm Product	Naples MSA, FL	S	16.88 MW	16.47 AW	35110 AAW	FLBLS	10//99-12//99
Except Wholesale, Retail, and Farm Product	Ocala MSA, FL	S	13.46 MW	12.37 AW	27990 AAW	FLBLS	10//99-12//99
Except Wholesale, Retail, and Farm Product	Orlando MSA, FL	S	18.21 MW	16.80 AW	37880 AAW	FLBLS	10//99-12//99
Except Wholesale, Retail, and Farm Product	Panama City MSA, FL	S	18.73 MW	17.78 AW	38960 AAW	FLBLS	10//99-12//99
Except Wholesale, Retail, and Farm Product	Pensacola MSA, FL	S	18.03 MW	16.02 AW	37500 AAW	FLBLS	10//99-12//99
Except Wholesale, Retail, and Farm Product	Sarasota-Bradenton MSA, FL	S	16.89 MW	15.91 AW	35130 AAW	FLBLS	10//99-12//99
Except Wholesale, Retail, and Farm Product	Tampa-St. Petersburg-Clearwater MSA, FL	S	17.05 MW	15.58 AW	35460 AAW	FLBLS	10//99-12//99
Except Wholesale, Retail, and Farm Product	West Palm Beach-Boca Raton MSA, FL	S	17.18 MW	16.28 AW	35730 AAW	FLBLS	10//99-12//99
Except Wholesale, Retail, and Farm Product	Georgia	S	18.18 MW	19.33 AW	40210 AAW	GABLS	10//99-12//99
Except Wholesale, Retail, and Farm Product	Albany MSA, GA	S	17.97 MW	16.15 AW	37380 AAW	GABLS	10//99-12//99
Except Wholesale, Retail, and Farm Product	Athens MSA, GA	S	18.16 MW	16.80 AW	37770 AAW	GABLS	10//99-12//99
Except Wholesale, Retail, and Farm Product	Atlanta MSA, GA	S	20.23 MW	19.02 AW	42070 AAW	GABLS	10//99-12//99
Except Wholesale, Retail, and Farm Product	Augusta-Aiken MSA, GA-SC	S	25.21 MW	24.24 AW	52430 AAW	GABLS	10//99-12//99
Except Wholesale, Retail, and Farm Product	Columbus MSA, GA-AL	S	19.97 MW	18.32 AW	41540 AAW	GABLS	10//99-12//99
Except Wholesale, Retail, and Farm Product	Savannah MSA, GA	S	18.04 MW	17.62 AW	37530 AAW	GABLS	10//99-12//99
Except Wholesale, Retail, and Farm Product	Hawaii	S	19.29 MW	20.02 AW	41640 AAW	HIBLS	10//99-12//99
Except Wholesale, Retail, and Farm Product	Honolulu MSA, HI	S	20.22 MW	19.57 AW	42060 AAW	HIBLS	10//99-12//99
Except Wholesale, Retail, and Farm Product	Idaho	S	18.01 MW	19.24 AW	40030 AAW	IDBLS	10//99-12//99
Except Wholesale, Retail, and Farm Product	Boise City MSA, ID	S	19.20 MW	17.98 AW	39950 AAW	IDBLS	10//99-12//99
Except Wholesale, Retail, and Farm Product	Illinois	S	19.31 MW	20.57 AW	42780 AAW	ILBLS	10//99-12//99
Except Wholesale, Retail, and Farm Product	Bloomington-Normal MSA, IL	S	21.16 MW	19.66 AW	44010 AAW	ILBLS	10//99-12//99
Except Wholesale, Retail, and Farm Product	Champaign-Urbana MSA, IL	S	17.02 MW	15.81 AW	35400 AAW	ILBLS	10//99-12//99
Except Wholesale, Retail, and Farm Product	Chicago PMSA, IL	S	20.47 MW	19.21 AW	42580 AAW	ILBLS	10//99-12//99
Except Wholesale, Retail, and Farm Product	Decatur MSA, IL	S	25.15 MW	24.18 AW	52310 AAW	ILBLS	10//99-12//99
Except Wholesale, Retail, and Farm Product	Kankakee PMSA, IL	S	23.16 MW	21.00 AW	48170 AAW	ILBLS	10//99-12//99

AAW Average annual wage	AOH Average offered, high	ASH Average starting, high	H Hourly	M Monthly	S Special: hourly and annual
AE Average entry wage	AOL Average offered, low	ASL Average starting, low	HI Highest wage paid	MTC Median total compensation	TQ Third quartile wage
AEX Average experienced wage	APH Average pay, high range	AW Average wage paid	HR High end range	MW Median wage paid	W Weekly
AO Average offered	APL Average pay, low range	FQ First quartile wage	LR Low end range	SQ Second quartile wage	Y Yearly

Occupation/Type/Industry	Location	Per	Low	Mid	High	Source	Date
Purchasing Agent							
Except Wholesale, Retail, and Farm Product	Peoria-Pekin MSA, IL	S	21.50 MW	19.81 AW	44720 AAW	ILBLS	10//99-12//99
Except Wholesale, Retail, and Farm Product	Rockford MSA, IL	S	19.92 MW	18.90 AW	41440 AAW	ILBLS	10//99-12//99
Except Wholesale, Retail, and Farm Product	Springfield MSA, IL	S	18.78 MW	18.22 AW	39060 AAW	ILBLS	10//99-12//99
Except Wholesale, Retail, and Farm Product	Indiana	S	18.14 MW	19.62 AW	40810 AAW	INBLS	10//99-12//99
Except Wholesale, Retail, and Farm Product	Bloomington MSA, IN	S	20.22 MW	19.03 AW	42070 AAW	INBLS	10//99-12//99
Except Wholesale, Retail, and Farm Product	Elkhart-Goshen MSA, IN	S	19.26 MW	18.29 AW	40060 AAW	INBLS	10//99-12//99
Except Wholesale, Retail, and Farm Product	Evansville-Henderson MSA, IN-KY	S	18.41 MW	16.84 AW	38280 AAW	INBLS	10//99-12//99
Except Wholesale, Retail, and Farm Product	Fort Wayne MSA, IN	S	20.97 MW	18.82 AW	43610 AAW	INBLS	10//99-12//99
Except Wholesale, Retail, and Farm Product	Gary PMSA, IN	S	21.93 MW	20.93 AW	45620 AAW	INBLS	10//99-12//99
Except Wholesale, Retail, and Farm Product	Indianapolis MSA, IN	S	19.82 MW	18.27 AW	41220 AAW	INBLS	10//99-12//99
Except Wholesale, Retail, and Farm Product	Lafayette MSA, IN	S	17.29 MW	16.54 AW	35970 AAW	INBLS	10//99-12//99
Except Wholesale, Retail, and Farm Product	Muncie MSA, IN	S	18.87 MW	15.47 AW	39250 AAW	INBLS	10//99-12//99
Except Wholesale, Retail, and Farm Product	South Bend MSA, IN	S	18.65 MW	17.59 AW	38790 AAW	INBLS	10//99-12//99
Except Wholesale, Retail, and Farm Product	Terre Haute MSA, IN	S	17.53 MW	15.25 AW	36450 AAW	INBLS	10//99-12//99
Except Wholesale, Retail, and Farm Product	Iowa	S	16.54 MW	16.90 AW	35150 AAW	IABLS	10//99-12//99
Except Wholesale, Retail, and Farm Product	Cedar Rapids MSA, IA	S	21.33 MW	19.62 AW	44380 AAW	IABLS	10//99-12//99
Except Wholesale, Retail, and Farm Product	Des Moines MSA, IA	S	16.68 MW	16.21 AW	34700 AAW	IABLS	10//99-12//99
Except Wholesale, Retail, and Farm Product	Dubuque MSA, IA	S	12.67 MW	12.06 AW	26340 AAW	IABLS	10//99-12//99
Except Wholesale, Retail, and Farm Product	Iowa City MSA, IA	S	19.00 MW	17.59 AW	39520 AAW	IABLS	10//99-12//99
Except Wholesale, Retail, and Farm Product	Sioux City MSA, IA-NE	S	15.11 MW	14.94 AW	31430 AAW	IABLS	10//99-12//99
Except Wholesale, Retail, and Farm Product	Waterloo-Cedar Falls MSA, IA	S	17.20 MW	17.05 AW	35770 AAW	IABLS	10//99-12//99
Except Wholesale, Retail, and Farm Product	Kansas	S	17.88 MW	19.91 AW	41400 AAW	KSBLS	10//99-12//99
Except Wholesale, Retail, and Farm Product	Topeka MSA, KS	S	19.05 MW	18.10 AW	39610 AAW	KSBLS	10//99-12//99
Except Wholesale, Retail, and Farm Product	Wichita MSA, KS	S	21.75 MW	18.86 AW	45240 AAW	KSBLS	10//99-12//99
Except Wholesale, Retail, and Farm Product	Kentucky	S	17.52 MW	18.60 AW	38680 AAW	KYBLS	10//99-12//99
Except Wholesale, Retail, and Farm Product	Lexington MSA, KY	S	17.77 MW	17.67 AW	36970 AAW	KYBLS	10//99-12//99
Except Wholesale, Retail, and Farm Product	Louisville MSA, KY-IN	S	20.08 MW	17.39 AW	41770 AAW	KYBLS	10//99-12//99
Except Wholesale, Retail, and Farm Product	Owensboro MSA, KY	S	20.27 MW	19.06 AW	42160 AAW	KYBLS	10//99-12//99
Except Wholesale, Retail, and Farm Product	Louisiana	S	16.09 MW	17.49 AW	36370 AAW	LABLS	10//99-12//99
Except Wholesale, Retail, and Farm Product	Alexandria MSA, LA	S	17.23 MW	15.35 AW	35830 AAW	LABLS	10//99-12//99
Except Wholesale, Retail, and Farm Product	Baton Rouge MSA, LA	S	15.64 MW	14.47 AW	32530 AAW	LABLS	10//99-12//99
Except Wholesale, Retail, and Farm Product	Houma MSA, LA	S	15.34 MW	14.10 AW	31910 AAW	LABLS	10//99-12//99
Except Wholesale, Retail, and Farm Product	Lafayette MSA, LA	S	16.33 MW	14.86 AW	33970 AAW	LABLS	10//99-12//99
Except Wholesale, Retail, and Farm Product	Lake Charles MSA, LA	S	17.33 MW	16.94 AW	36050 AAW	LABLS	10//99-12//99

AAW	Average annual wage	AOH	Average offered, high	ASH	Average starting, high
AE	Average entry wage	AOL	Average offered, low	ASL	Average starting, low
AEX	Average experienced wage	APH	Average pay, high range	AW	Average wage paid
AO	Average offered	APL	Average pay, low range	FQ	First quartile wage

H	Hourly	M	Monthly	S	Special: hourly and annual
HI	Highest wage paid	MTC	Median total compensation	TQ	Third quartile wage
HR	High end range	MW	Median wage paid	W	Weekly
LR	Low end range	SQ	Second quartile wage	Y	Yearly

Occupation/Type/Industry	Location	Per	Low	Mid	High	Source	Date
Purchasing Agent							
Except Wholesale, Retail, and Farm Product	New Orleans MSA, LA	S	18.42 MW	16.96 AW	38310 AAW	LABLS	10//99-12//99
Except Wholesale, Retail, and Farm Product	Shreveport-Bossier City MSA, LA	S	17.11 MW	15.74 AW	35600 AAW	LABLS	10//99-12//99
Except Wholesale, Retail, and Farm Product	Maine	S	17.01 MW	17.82 AW	37070 AAW	MEBLS	10//99-12//99
Except Wholesale, Retail, and Farm Product	Bangor MSA, ME	S	15.75 MW	15.01 AW	32750 AAW	MEBLS	10//99-12//99
Except Wholesale, Retail, and Farm Product	Lewiston-Auburn MSA, ME	S	16.72 MW	15.51 AW	34780 AAW	MEBLS	10//99-12//99
Except Wholesale, Retail, and Farm Product	Portland MSA, ME	S	18.48 MW	17.06 AW	38450 AAW	MEBLS	10//99-12//99
Except Wholesale, Retail, and Farm Product	Maryland	S	21.13 MW	22.41 AW	46600 AAW	MDBLS	10//99-12//99
Except Wholesale, Retail, and Farm Product	Baltimore PMSA, MD	S	20.42 MW	19.12 AW	42470 AAW	MDBLS	10//99-12//99
Except Wholesale, Retail, and Farm Product	Hagerstown PMSA, MD	S	20.73 MW	19.62 AW	43120 AAW	MDBLS	10//99-12//99
Except Wholesale, Retail, and Farm Product	Massachusetts	S	20.11 MW	21.31 AW	44330 AAW	MABLS	10//99-12//99
Except Wholesale, Retail, and Farm Product	Boston PMSA, MA-NH	S	21.26 MW	20.08 AW	44220 AAW	MABLS	10//99-12//99
Except Wholesale, Retail, and Farm Product	Brockton PMSA, MA	S	18.27 MW	16.77 AW	38010 AAW	MABLS	10//99-12//99
Except Wholesale, Retail, and Farm Product	Fitchburg-Leominster PMSA, MA	S	21.42 MW	19.86 AW	44560 AAW	MABLS	10//99-12//99
Except Wholesale, Retail, and Farm Product	Lawrence PMSA, MA-NH	S	22.64 MW	20.72 AW	47090 AAW	MABLS	10//99-12//99
Except Wholesale, Retail, and Farm Product	Lowell PMSA, MA-NH	S	20.02 MW	19.60 AW	41640 AAW	MABLS	10//99-12//99
Except Wholesale, Retail, and Farm Product	New Bedford PMSA, MA	S	19.57 MW	18.54 AW	40710 AAW	MABLS	10//99-12//99
Except Wholesale, Retail, and Farm Product	Pittsfield MSA, MA	S	19.47 MW	16.13 AW	40500 AAW	MABLS	10//99-12//99
Except Wholesale, Retail, and Farm Product	Springfield MSA, MA	S	18.40 MW	17.42 AW	38260 AAW	MABLS	10//99-12//99
Except Wholesale, Retail, and Farm Product	Worcester PMSA, MA-CT	S	20.35 MW	19.42 AW	42320 AAW	MABLS	10//99-12//99
Except Wholesale, Retail, and Farm Product	Michigan	S	21.66 MW	23.31 AW	48490 AAW	MIBLS	10//99-12//99
Except Wholesale, Retail, and Farm Product	Ann Arbor PMSA, MI	S	21.67 MW	19.59 AW	45070 AAW	MIBLS	10//99-12//99
Except Wholesale, Retail, and Farm Product	Benton Harbor MSA, MI	S	17.21 MW	15.76 AW	35810 AAW	MIBLS	10//99-12//99
Except Wholesale, Retail, and Farm Product	Detroit PMSA, MI	S	25.70 MW	25.75 AW	53460 AAW	MIBLS	10//99-12//99
Except Wholesale, Retail, and Farm Product	Flint PMSA, MI	S	26.75 MW	27.67 AW	55630 AAW	MIBLS	10//99-12//99
Except Wholesale, Retail, and Farm Product	Grand Rapids-Muskegon-Holland MSA, MI	S	18.67 MW	18.17 AW	38830 AAW	MIBLS	10//99-12//99
Except Wholesale, Retail, and Farm Product	Jackson MSA, MI	S	21.58 MW	20.15 AW	44890 AAW	MIBLS	10//99-12//99
Except Wholesale, Retail, and Farm Product	Kalamazoo-Battle Creek MSA, MI	S	20.84 MW	19.94 AW	43350 AAW	MIBLS	10//99-12//99
Except Wholesale, Retail, and Farm Product	Lansing-East Lansing MSA, MI	S	20.05 MW	19.05 AW	41700 AAW	MIBLS	10//99-12//99
Except Wholesale, Retail, and Farm Product	Saginaw-Bay City-Midland MSA, MI	S	23.16 MW	20.95 AW	48170 AAW	MIBLS	10//99-12//99
Except Wholesale, Retail, and Farm Product	Minnesota	S	19.36 MW	20.16 AW	41940 AAW	MNBLS	10//99-12//99
Except Wholesale, Retail, and Farm Product	Duluth-Superior MSA, MN-WI	S	18.65 MW	18.00 AW	38790 AAW	MNBLS	10//99-12//99
Except Wholesale, Retail, and Farm Product	Minneapolis-St. Paul MSA, MN-WI	S	20.96 MW	20.16 AW	43600 AAW	MNBLS	10//99-12//99

AAW Average annual wage	**AOH** Average offered, high	**ASH** Average starting, high	**H** Hourly	**M** Monthly	**S** Special: hourly and annual
AE Average entry wage	**AOL** Average offered, low	**ASL** Average starting, low	**HI** Highest wage paid	**MTC** Median total compensation	**TQ** Third quartile wage
AEX Average experienced wage	**APH** Average pay, high range	**AW** Average wage paid	**HR** High end range	**MW** Median wage paid	**W** Weekly
AO Average offered	**APL** Average pay, low range	**FQ** First quartile wage	**LR** Low end range	**SQ** Second quartile wage	**Y** Yearly

Occupation/Type/Industry	Location	Per	Low	Mid	High	Source	Date
Purchasing Agent							
Except Wholesale, Retail, and Farm Product	Rochester MSA, MN	S	20.65 MW	19.23 AW	42950 AAW	MNBLS	10//99-12//99
Except Wholesale, Retail, and Farm Product	St. Cloud MSA, MN	S	16.72 MW	15.51 AW	34780 AAW	MNBLS	10//99-12//99
Except Wholesale, Retail, and Farm Product	Mississippi	S	15.1 MW	16.37 AW	34040 AAW	MSBLS	10//99-12//99
Except Wholesale, Retail, and Farm Product	Biloxi-Gulfport-Pascagoula MSA, MS	S	17.90 MW	16.08 AW	37230 AAW	MSBLS	10//99-12//99
Except Wholesale, Retail, and Farm Product	Hattiesburg MSA, MS	S	13.82 MW	13.92 AW	28740 AAW	MSBLS	10//99-12//99
Except Wholesale, Retail, and Farm Product	Jackson MSA, MS	S	15.99 MW	14.96 AW	33260 AAW	MSBLS	10//99-12//99
Except Wholesale, Retail, and Farm Product	Missouri	S	17.88 MW	19.01 AW	39540 AAW	MOBLS	10//99-12//99
Except Wholesale, Retail, and Farm Product	Columbia MSA, MO	S	18.23 MW	16.47 AW	37930 AAW	MOBLS	10//99-12//99
Except Wholesale, Retail, and Farm Product	Joplin MSA, MO	S	15.78 MW	14.74 AW	32830 AAW	MOBLS	10//99-12//99
Except Wholesale, Retail, and Farm Product	Kansas City MSA, MO-KS	S	20.06 MW	19.13 AW	41720 AAW	MOBLS	10//99-12//99
Except Wholesale, Retail, and Farm Product	St. Joseph MSA, MO	S	19.89 MW	18.95 AW	41370 AAW	MOBLS	10//99-12//99
Except Wholesale, Retail, and Farm Product	St. Louis MSA, MO-IL	S	20.26 MW	19.37 AW	42130 AAW	MOBLS	10//99-12//99
Except Wholesale, Retail, and Farm Product	Springfield MSA, MO	S	16.23 MW	14.37 AW	33750 AAW	MOBLS	10//99-12//99
Except Wholesale, Retail, and Farm Product	Montana	S	15.92 MW	16.93 AW	35210 AAW	MTBLS	10//99-12//99
Except Wholesale, Retail, and Farm Product	Billings MSA, MT	S	18.17 MW	16.85 AW	37790 AAW	MTBLS	10//99-12//99
Except Wholesale, Retail, and Farm Product	Great Falls MSA, MT	S	17.98 MW	17.79 AW	37400 AAW	MTBLS	10//99-12//99
Except Wholesale, Retail, and Farm Product	Missoula MSA, MT	S	18.67 MW	17.82 AW	38830 AAW	MTBLS	10//99-12//99
Except Wholesale, Retail, and Farm Product	Nebraska	S	17.15 MW	18.43 AW	38330 AAW	NEBLS	10//99-12//99
Except Wholesale, Retail, and Farm Product	Lincoln MSA, NE	S	19.30 MW	17.76 AW	40140 AAW	NEBLS	10//99-12//99
Except Wholesale, Retail, and Farm Product	Omaha MSA, NE-IA	S	18.65 MW	17.48 AW	38790 AAW	NEBLS	10//99-12//99
Except Wholesale, Retail, and Farm Product	Nevada	S	18.26 MW	19.22 AW	39970 AAW	NVBLS	10//99-12//99
Except Wholesale, Retail, and Farm Product	Las Vegas MSA, NV-AZ	S	19.68 MW	18.56 AW	40920 AAW	NVBLS	10//99-12//99
Except Wholesale, Retail, and Farm Product	Reno MSA, NV	S	17.97 MW	17.38 AW	37370 AAW	NVBLS	10//99-12//99
Except Wholesale, Retail, and Farm Product	New Hampshire	S	18.48 MW	19.06 AW	39640 AAW	NHBLS	10//99-12//99
Except Wholesale, Retail, and Farm Product	Manchester PMSA, NH	S	19.06 MW	18.79 AW	39650 AAW	NHBLS	10//99-12//99
Except Wholesale, Retail, and Farm Product	Nashua PMSA, NH	S	19.97 MW	19.17 AW	41540 AAW	NHBLS	10//99-12//99
Except Wholesale, Retail, and Farm Product	Portsmouth-Rochester PMSA, NH-ME	S	18.61 MW	18.27 AW	38720 AAW	NHBLS	10//99-12//99
Except Wholesale, Retail, and Farm Product	New Jersey	S	21.35 MW	22.69 AW	47190 AAW	NJBLS	10//99-12//99
Except Wholesale, Retail, and Farm Product	Atlantic-Cape May PMSA, NJ	S	19.46 MW	16.74 AW	40490 AAW	NJBLS	10//99-12//99
Except Wholesale, Retail, and Farm Product	Bergen-Passaic PMSA, NJ	S	21.88 MW	20.89 AW	45520 AAW	NJBLS	10//99-12//99
Except Wholesale, Retail, and Farm Product	Jersey City PMSA, NJ	S	22.78 MW	20.95 AW	47380 AAW	NJBLS	10//99-12//99
Except Wholesale, Retail, and Farm Product	Middlesex-Somerset-Hunterdon PMSA, NJ	S	23.03 MW	21.77 AW	47900 AAW	NJBLS	10//99-12//99
Except Wholesale, Retail, and Farm Product	Monmouth-Ocean PMSA, NJ	S	23.72 MW	22.88 AW	49330 AAW	NJBLS	10//99-12//99

AAW	Average annual wage	AOH	Average offered, high	ASH	Average starting, high	H	Hourly
AE	Average entry wage	AOL	Average offered, low	ASL	Average starting, low	HI	Highest wage paid
AEX	Average experienced wage	APH	Average pay, high range	AW	Average wage paid	HR	High end range
AO	Average offered	APL	Average pay, low range	FQ	First quartile wage	LR	Low end range

M	Monthly	S	Special: hourly and annual
MTC	Median total compensation	TQ	Third quartile wage
MW	Median wage paid	W	Weekly
SQ	Second quartile wage	Y	Yearly

Occupation/Type/Industry	Location	Per	Low	Mid	High	Source	Date
Purchasing Agent							
Except Wholesale, Retail, and Farm Product	Newark PMSA, NJ	S	23.29 MW	21.60 AW	48430 AAW	NJBLS	10//99-12//99
Except Wholesale, Retail, and Farm Product	Trenton PMSA, NJ	S	22.86 MW	21.35 AW	47550 AAW	NJBLS	10//99-12//99
Except Wholesale, Retail, and Farm Product	Vineland-Millville-Bridgeton PMSA, NJ	S	21.80 MW	21.14 AW	45340 AAW	NJBLS	10//99-12//99
Except Wholesale, Retail, and Farm Product	New Mexico	S	17.07 MW	19.03 AW	39570 AAW	NMBLS	10//99-12//99
Except Wholesale, Retail, and Farm Product	Albuquerque MSA, NM	S	20.02 MW	18.96 AW	41630 AAW	NMBLS	10//99-12//99
Except Wholesale, Retail, and Farm Product	Las Cruces MSA, NM	S	18.73 MW	16.55 AW	38960 AAW	NMBLS	10//99-12//99
Except Wholesale, Retail, and Farm Product	New York	S	19.26 MW	20.84 AW	43350 AAW	NYBLS	10//99-12//99
Except Wholesale, Retail, and Farm Product	Albany-Schenectady-Troy MSA, NY	S	20.20 MW	19.50 AW	42020 AAW	NYBLS	10//99-12//99
Except Wholesale, Retail, and Farm Product	Binghamton MSA, NY	S	18.87 MW	17.95 AW	39250 AAW	NYBLS	10//99-12//99
Except Wholesale, Retail, and Farm Product	Buffalo-Niagara Falls MSA, NY	S	19.09 MW	16.86 AW	39710 AAW	NYBLS	10//99-12//99
Except Wholesale, Retail, and Farm Product	Elmira MSA, NY	S	19.35 MW	20.40 AW	40240 AAW	NYBLS	10//99-12//99
Except Wholesale, Retail, and Farm Product	Glens Falls MSA, NY	S	18.03 MW	17.42 AW	37510 AAW	NYBLS	10//99-12//99
Except Wholesale, Retail, and Farm Product	Jamestown MSA, NY	S	16.95 MW	15.82 AW	35260 AAW	NYBLS	10//99-12//99
Except Wholesale, Retail, and Farm Product	Nassau-Suffolk PMSA, NY	S	21.79 MW	20.32 AW	45320 AAW	NYBLS	10//99-12//99
Except Wholesale, Retail, and Farm Product	New York PMSA, NY	S	21.62 MW	19.65 AW	44980 AAW	NYBLS	10//99-12//99
Except Wholesale, Retail, and Farm Product	Rochester MSA, NY	S	20.81 MW	19.38 AW	43290 AAW	NYBLS	10//99-12//99
Except Wholesale, Retail, and Farm Product	Syracuse MSA, NY	S	19.31 MW	18.60 AW	40160 AAW	NYBLS	10//99-12//99
Except Wholesale, Retail, and Farm Product	Utica-Rome MSA, NY	S	18.78 MW	17.97 AW	39070 AAW	NYBLS	10//99-12//99
Except Wholesale, Retail, and Farm Product	North Carolina	S	18.21 MW	19.62 AW	40810 AAW	NCBLS	10//99-12//99
Except Wholesale, Retail, and Farm Product	Asheville MSA, NC	S	18.04 MW	16.49 AW	37510 AAW	NCBLS	10//99-12//99
Except Wholesale, Retail, and Farm Product	Charlotte-Gastonia-Rock Hill MSA, NC-SC	S	20.30 MW	18.36 AW	42220 AAW	NCBLS	10//99-12//99
Except Wholesale, Retail, and Farm Product	Greensboro--Winston-Salem-- High Point MSA, NC	S	19.45 MW	18.38 AW	40460 AAW	NCBLS	10//99-12//99
Except Wholesale, Retail, and Farm Product	Greenville MSA, NC	S	15.16 MW	13.96 AW	31530 AAW	NCBLS	10//99-12//99
Except Wholesale, Retail, and Farm Product	Hickory-Morganton-Lenoir MSA, NC	S	19.40 MW	17.71 AW	40360 AAW	NCBLS	10//99-12//99
Except Wholesale, Retail, and Farm Product	Raleigh-Durham-Chapel Hill MSA, NC	S	21.31 MW	19.85 AW	44320 AAW	NCBLS	10//99-12//99
Except Wholesale, Retail, and Farm Product	Rocky Mount MSA, NC	S	18.45 MW	17.83 AW	38380 AAW	NCBLS	10//99-12//99
Except Wholesale, Retail, and Farm Product	Wilmington MSA, NC	S	17.21 MW	16.75 AW	35790 AAW	NCBLS	10//99-12//99
Except Wholesale, Retail, and Farm Product	North Dakota	S	15.21 MW	16.48 AW	34280 AAW	NDBLS	10//99-12//99
Except Wholesale, Retail, and Farm Product	Bismarck MSA, ND	S	17.89 MW	16.10 AW	37220 AAW	NDBLS	10//99-12//99
Except Wholesale, Retail, and Farm Product	Fargo-Moorhead MSA, ND-MN	S	16.02 MW	15.11 AW	33330 AAW	NDBLS	10//99-12//99
Except Wholesale, Retail, and Farm Product	Grand Forks MSA, ND-MN	S	17.41 MW	16.14 AW	36220 AAW	NDBLS	10//99-12//99

AAW Average annual wage	**AOH** Average offered, high	**ASH** Average starting, high	**H** Hourly	**M** Monthly	**S** Special: hourly and annual
AE Average entry wage	**AOL** Average offered, low	**ASL** Average starting, low	**HI** Highest wage paid	**MTC** Median total compensation	**TQ** Third quartile wage
AEX Average experienced wage	**APH** Average pay, high range	**AW** Average wage paid	**HR** High end range	**MW** Median wage paid	**W** Weekly
AO Average offered	**APL** Average pay, low range	**FQ** First quartile wage	**LR** Low end range	**SQ** Second quartile wage	**Y** Yearly

Occupation/Type/Industry	Location	Per	Low	Mid	High	Source	Date
Purchasing Agent							
Except Wholesale, Retail, and Farm Product	Ohio	S	18.56 MW	19.73 AW	41040 AAW	OHBLS	10//99-12//99
Except Wholesale, Retail, and Farm Product	Akron PMSA, OH	S	17.33 MW	16.93 AW	36050 AAW	OHBLS	10//99-12//99
Except Wholesale, Retail, and Farm Product	Canton-Massillon MSA, OH	S	18.50 MW	18.53 AW	38490 AAW	OHBLS	10//99-12//99
Except Wholesale, Retail, and Farm Product	Cincinnati PMSA, OH-KY-IN	S	20.50 MW	19.32 AW	42630 AAW	OHBLS	10//99-12//99
Except Wholesale, Retail, and Farm Product	Cleveland-Lorain-Elyria PMSA, OH	S	20.10 MW	18.69 AW	41810 AAW	OHBLS	10//99-12//99
Except Wholesale, Retail, and Farm Product	Columbus MSA, OH	S	19.55 MW	18.89 AW	40670 AAW	OHBLS	10//99-12//99
Except Wholesale, Retail, and Farm Product	Dayton-Springfield MSA, OH	S	22.73 MW	21.73 AW	47280 AAW	OHBLS	10//99-12//99
Except Wholesale, Retail, and Farm Product	Hamilton-Middletown PMSA, OH	S	18.48 MW	17.99 AW	38440 AAW	OHBLS	10//99-12//99
Except Wholesale, Retail, and Farm Product	Lima MSA, OH	S	18.54 MW	17.98 AW	38560 AAW	OHBLS	10//99-12//99
Except Wholesale, Retail, and Farm Product	Mansfield MSA, OH	S	20.64 MW	16.83 AW	42940 AAW	OHBLS	10//99-12//99
Except Wholesale, Retail, and Farm Product	Steubenville-Weirton MSA, OH-WV	S	19.59 MW	18.52 AW	40750 AAW	OHBLS	10//99-12//99
Except Wholesale, Retail, and Farm Product	Toledo MSA, OH	S	17.42 MW	16.07 AW	36230 AAW	OHBLS	10//99-12//99
Except Wholesale, Retail, and Farm Product	Youngstown-Warren MSA, OH	S	19.18 MW	17.52 AW	39890 AAW	OHBLS	10//99-12//99
Except Wholesale, Retail, and Farm Product	Oklahoma	S	16.4 MW	17.91 AW	37250 AAW	OKBLS	10//99-12//99
Except Wholesale, Retail, and Farm Product	Lawton MSA, OK	S	17.82 MW	17.82 AW	37060 AAW	OKBLS	10//99-12//99
Except Wholesale, Retail, and Farm Product	Oklahoma City MSA, OK	S	19.67 MW	18.98 AW	40910 AAW	OKBLS	10//99-12//99
Except Wholesale, Retail, and Farm Product	Tulsa MSA, OK	S	18.01 MW	15.91 AW	37460 AAW	OKBLS	10//99-12//99
Except Wholesale, Retail, and Farm Product	Oregon	S	17.61 MW	18.67 AW	38840 AAW	ORBLS	10//99-12//99
Except Wholesale, Retail, and Farm Product	Eugene-Springfield MSA, OR	S	16.86 MW	16.06 AW	35070 AAW	ORBLS	10//99-12//99
Except Wholesale, Retail, and Farm Product	Medford-Ashland MSA, OR	S	15.17 MW	14.81 AW	31560 AAW	ORBLS	10//99-12//99
Except Wholesale, Retail, and Farm Product	Portland-Vancouver PMSA, OR-WA	S	19.71 MW	18.68 AW	41000 AAW	ORBLS	10//99-12//99
Except Wholesale, Retail, and Farm Product	Salem PMSA, OR	S	17.79 MW	16.65 AW	37000 AAW	ORBLS	10//99-12//99
Except Wholesale, Retail, and Farm Product	Pennsylvania	S	18.97 MW	20.19 AW	41990 AAW	PABLS	10//99-12//99
Except Wholesale, Retail, and Farm Product	Allentown-Bethlehem-Easton MSA, PA	S	20.79 MW	19.47 AW	43240 AAW	PABLS	10//99-12//99
Except Wholesale, Retail, and Farm Product	Altoona MSA, PA	S	18.69 MW	17.01 AW	38880 AAW	PABLS	10//99-12//99
Except Wholesale, Retail, and Farm Product	Erie MSA, PA	S	17.45 MW	16.76 AW	36290 AAW	PABLS	10//99-12//99
Except Wholesale, Retail, and Farm Product	Harrisburg-Lebanon-Carlisle MSA, PA	S	20.12 MW	19.48 AW	41840 AAW	PABLS	10//99-12//99
Except Wholesale, Retail, and Farm Product	Johnstown MSA, PA	S	18.06 MW	16.68 AW	37570 AAW	PABLS	10//99-12//99
Except Wholesale, Retail, and Farm Product	Lancaster MSA, PA	S	19.44 MW	18.43 AW	40440 AAW	PABLS	10//99-12//99
Except Wholesale, Retail, and Farm Product	Philadelphia PMSA, PA-NJ	S	21.55 MW	20.11 AW	44820 AAW	PABLS	10//99-12//99
Except Wholesale, Retail, and Farm Product	Pittsburgh MSA, PA	S	20.35 MW	19.12 AW	42330 AAW	PABLS	10//99-12//99
Except Wholesale, Retail, and Farm Product	Reading MSA, PA	S	20.49 MW	19.22 AW	42620 AAW	PABLS	10//99-12//99

AAW Average annual wage	**AOH** Average offered, high	**ASH** Average starting, high	**H** Hourly	**M** Monthly	**S** Special: hourly and annual
AE Average entry wage	**AOL** Average offered, low	**ASL** Average starting, low	**HI** Highest wage paid	**MTC** Median total compensation	**TQ** Third quartile wage
AEX Average experienced wage	**APH** Average pay, high range	**AW** Average wage paid	**HR** High end range	**MW** Median wage paid	**W** Weekly
AO Average offered	**APL** Average pay, low range	**FQ** First quartile wage	**LR** Low end range	**SQ** Second quartile wage	**Y** Yearly

Purchasing Agent

Occupation/Type/Industry	Location	Per	Low	Mid	High	Source	Date
Except Wholesale, Retail, and Farm Product	Scranton--Wilkes-Barre--Hazleton MSA, PA	S	17.37 MW	16.75 AW	36120 AAW	PABLS	10//99-12//99
Except Wholesale, Retail, and Farm Product	Sharon MSA, PA	S	17.87 MW	17.41 AW	37160 AAW	PABLS	10//99-12//99
Except Wholesale, Retail, and Farm Product	State College MSA, PA	S	17.21 MW	16.79 AW	35800 AAW	PABLS	10//99-12//99
Except Wholesale, Retail, and Farm Product	Williamsport MSA, PA	S	16.60 MW	15.75 AW	34520 AAW	PABLS	10//99-12//99
Except Wholesale, Retail, and Farm Product	York MSA, PA	S	17.20 MW	17.04 AW	35770 AAW	PABLS	10//99-12//99
Except Wholesale, Retail, and Farm Product	Rhode Island	S	18.62 MW	19.64 AW	40850 AAW	RIBLS	10//99-12//99
Except Wholesale, Retail, and Farm Product	Providence-Fall River-Warwick MSA, RI-MA	S	19.17 MW	18.12 AW	39870 AAW	RIBLS	10//99-12//99
Except Wholesale, Retail, and Farm Product	South Carolina	S	18.2 MW	20.09 AW	41790 AAW	SCBLS	10//99-12//99
Except Wholesale, Retail, and Farm Product	Charleston-North Charleston MSA, SC	S	22.15 MW	19.96 AW	46060 AAW	SCBLS	10//99-12//99
Except Wholesale, Retail, and Farm Product	Columbia MSA, SC	S	16.54 MW	15.62 AW	34400 AAW	SCBLS	10//99-12//99
Except Wholesale, Retail, and Farm Product	Florence MSA, SC	S	17.26 MW	17.29 AW	35910 AAW	SCBLS	10//99-12//99
Except Wholesale, Retail, and Farm Product	Greenville-Spartanburg-Anderson MSA, SC	S	19.29 MW	18.09 AW	40130 AAW	SCBLS	10//99-12//99
Except Wholesale, Retail, and Farm Product	Myrtle Beach MSA, SC	S	16.41 MW	14.58 AW	34130 AAW	SCBLS	10//99-12//99
Except Wholesale, Retail, and Farm Product	Sumter MSA, SC	S	17.98 MW	18.38 AW	37410 AAW	SCBLS	10//99-12//99
Except Wholesale, Retail, and Farm Product	South Dakota	S	16.29 MW	17.24 AW	35860 AAW	SDBLS	10//99-12//99
Except Wholesale, Retail, and Farm Product	Rapid City MSA, SD	S	18.60 MW	17.65 AW	38680 AAW	SDBLS	10//99-12//99
Except Wholesale, Retail, and Farm Product	Sioux Falls MSA, SD	S	16.42 MW	15.77 AW	34160 AAW	SDBLS	10//99-12//99
Except Wholesale, Retail, and Farm Product	Tennessee	S	16.88 MW	18.22 AW	37890 AAW	TNBLS	10//99-12//99
Except Wholesale, Retail, and Farm Product	Chattanooga MSA, TN-GA	S	17.36 MW	16.68 AW	36110 AAW	TNBLS	10//99-12//99
Except Wholesale, Retail, and Farm Product	Clarksville-Hopkinsville MSA, TN-KY	S	17.28 MW	16.67 AW	35950 AAW	TNBLS	10//99-12//99
Except Wholesale, Retail, and Farm Product	Jackson MSA, TN	S	17.54 MW	16.85 AW	36470 AAW	TNBLS	10//99-12//99
Except Wholesale, Retail, and Farm Product	Johnson City-Kingsport-Bristol MSA, TN-VA	S	17.99 MW	16.69 AW	37420 AAW	TNBLS	10//99-12//99
Except Wholesale, Retail, and Farm Product	Knoxville MSA, TN	S	18.83 MW	17.81 AW	39160 AAW	TNBLS	10//99-12//99
Except Wholesale, Retail, and Farm Product	Memphis MSA, TN-AR-MS	S	20.17 MW	17.77 AW	41960 AAW	MSBLS	10//99-12//99
Except Wholesale, Retail, and Farm Product	Nashville MSA, TN	S	17.32 MW	16.61 AW	36010 AAW	TNBLS	10//99-12//99
Except Wholesale, Retail, and Farm Product	Texas	S	18.87 MW	20.59 AW	42830 AAW	TXBLS	10//99-12//99
Except Wholesale, Retail, and Farm Product	Abilene MSA, TX	S	15.32 MW	14.58 AW	31860 AAW	TXBLS	10//99-12//99
Except Wholesale, Retail, and Farm Product	Amarillo MSA, TX	S	16.69 MW	15.51 AW	34710 AAW	TXBLS	10//99-12//99
Except Wholesale, Retail, and Farm Product	Austin-San Marcos MSA, TX	S	18.97 MW	16.77 AW	39460 AAW	TXBLS	10//99-12//99
Except Wholesale, Retail, and Farm Product	Beaumont-Port Arthur MSA, TX	S	21.12 MW	18.96 AW	43940 AAW	TXBLS	10//99-12//99
Except Wholesale, Retail, and Farm Product	Brazoria PMSA, TX	S	25.87 MW	29.09 AW	53800 AAW	TXBLS	10//99-12//99

AAW	Average annual wage	AOH	Average offered, high	ASH	Average starting, high
AE	Average entry wage	AOL	Average offered, low	ASL	Average starting, low
AEX	Average experienced wage	APH	Average pay, high range	AW	Average wage paid
AO	Average offered	APL	Average pay, low range	FQ	First quartile wage

H	Hourly	M	Monthly	S	Special: hourly and annual
HI	Highest wage paid	MTC	Median total compensation	TQ	Third quartile wage
HR	High end range	MW	Median wage paid	W	Weekly
LR	Low end range	SQ	Second quartile wage	Y	Yearly

Purchasing Agent

Occupation/Type/Industry	Location	Per	Low	Mid	High	Source	Date
Purchasing Agent							
Except Wholesale, Retail, and Farm Product	Brownsville-Harlingen-San Benito MSA, TX	S	14.86 MW	14.37 AW	30900 AAW	TXBLS	10//99-12//99
Except Wholesale, Retail, and Farm Product	Bryan-College Station MSA, TX	S	14.80 MW	14.35 AW	30780 AAW	TXBLS	10//99-12//99
Except Wholesale, Retail, and Farm Product	Corpus Christi MSA, TX	S	18.74 MW	16.29 AW	38980 AAW	TXBLS	10//99-12//99
Except Wholesale, Retail, and Farm Product	Dallas PMSA, TX	S	21.11 MW	19.51 AW	43910 AAW	TXBLS	10//99-12//99
Except Wholesale, Retail, and Farm Product	El Paso MSA, TX	S	18.19 MW	16.34 AW	37830 AAW	TXBLS	10//99-12//99
Except Wholesale, Retail, and Farm Product	Fort Worth-Arlington PMSA, TX	S	20.11 MW	19.56 AW	41840 AAW	TXBLS	10//99-12//99
Except Wholesale, Retail, and Farm Product	Galveston-Texas City PMSA, TX	S	17.42 MW	15.29 AW	36230 AAW	TXBLS	10//99-12//99
Except Wholesale, Retail, and Farm Product	Houston PMSA, TX	S	23.20 MW	21.51 AW	48250 AAW	TXBLS	10//99-12//99
Except Wholesale, Retail, and Farm Product	Killeen-Temple MSA, TX	S	17.18 MW	15.47 AW	35730 AAW	TXBLS	10//99-12//99
Except Wholesale, Retail, and Farm Product	Laredo MSA, TX	S	12.83 MW	12.21 AW	26680 AAW	TXBLS	10//99-12//99
Except Wholesale, Retail, and Farm Product	Longview-Marshall MSA, TX	S	16.72 MW	15.76 AW	34780 AAW	TXBLS	10//99-12//99
Except Wholesale, Retail, and Farm Product	Lubbock MSA, TX	S	17.60 MW	16.11 AW	36610 AAW	TXBLS	10//99-12//99
Except Wholesale, Retail, and Farm Product	McAllen-Edinburg-Mission MSA, TX	S	16.10 MW	15.12 AW	33490 AAW	TXBLS	10//99-12//99
Except Wholesale, Retail, and Farm Product	Odessa-Midland MSA, TX	S	20.21 MW	18.26 AW	42030 AAW	TXBLS	10//99-12//99
Except Wholesale, Retail, and Farm Product	San Angelo MSA, TX	S	15.81 MW	14.53 AW	32890 AAW	TXBLS	10//99-12//99
Except Wholesale, Retail, and Farm Product	Texarkana MSA, TX-Texarkana, AR	S	18.62 MW	18.44 AW	38730 AAW	TXBLS	10//99-12//99
Except Wholesale, Retail, and Farm Product	Tyler MSA, TX	S	18.85 MW	17.43 AW	39220 AAW	TXBLS	10//99-12//99
Except Wholesale, Retail, and Farm Product	Waco MSA, TX	S	16.72 MW	15.62 AW	34780 AAW	TXBLS	10//99-12//99
Except Wholesale, Retail, and Farm Product	Wichita Falls MSA, TX	S	18.53 MW	17.09 AW	38540 AAW	TXBLS	10//99-12//99
Except Wholesale, Retail, and Farm Product	Utah	S	18.21 MW	19.18 AW	39890 AAW	UTBLS	10//99-12//99
Except Wholesale, Retail, and Farm Product	Provo-Orem MSA, UT	S	15.73 MW	15.29 AW	32720 AAW	UTBLS	10//99-12//99
Except Wholesale, Retail, and Farm Product	Salt Lake City-Ogden MSA, UT	S	19.66 MW	18.93 AW	40890 AAW	UTBLS	10//99-12//99
Except Wholesale, Retail, and Farm Product	Vermont	S	17.87 MW	19.90 AW	41390 AAW	VTBLS	10//99-12//99
Except Wholesale, Retail, and Farm Product	Burlington MSA, VT	S	20.75 MW	18.89 AW	43170 AAW	VTBLS	10//99-12//99
Except Wholesale, Retail, and Farm Product	Virginia	S	19.48 MW	20.66 AW	42980 AAW	VABLS	10//99-12//99
Except Wholesale, Retail, and Farm Product	Charlottesville MSA, VA	S	18.03 MW	17.63 AW	37500 AAW	VABLS	10//99-12//99
Except Wholesale, Retail, and Farm Product	Norfolk-Virginia Beach-Newport News MSA, VA-NC	S	16.00 MW	15.41 AW	33280 AAW	VABLS	10//99-12//99
Except Wholesale, Retail, and Farm Product	Richmond-Petersburg MSA, VA	S	19.77 MW	18.75 AW	41130 AAW	VABLS	10//99-12//99
Except Wholesale, Retail, and Farm Product	Roanoke MSA, VA	S	15.79 MW	14.69 AW	32850 AAW	VABLS	10//99-12//99
Except Wholesale, Retail, and Farm Product	Washington	S	19.87 MW	21.04 AW	43760 AAW	WABLS	10//99-12//99

AAW Average annual wage; AE Average entry wage; AEX Average experienced wage; AO Average offered; AOH Average offered, high; AOL Average offered, low; APH Average pay, high range; APL Average pay, low range; ASH Average starting, high; ASL Average starting, low; AW Average wage paid; FQ First quartile wage; H Hourly; HI Highest wage paid; HR High end range; LR Low end range; M Monthly; MTC Median total compensation; MW Median wage paid; SQ Second quartile wage; S Special: hourly and annual; TQ Third quartile wage; W Weekly; Y Yearly

Occupation/Type/Industry	Location	Per	Low	Mid	High	Source	Date
Purchasing Agent							
Except Wholesale, Retail, and Farm Product	Bellingham MSA, WA	S	20.09 MW	18.07 AW	41790 AAW	WABLS	10//99-12//99
Except Wholesale, Retail, and Farm Product	Richland-Kennewick-Pasco MSA, WA	S	28.67 MW	26.95 AW	59630 AAW	WABLS	10//99-12//99
Except Wholesale, Retail, and Farm Product	Spokane MSA, WA	S	16.76 MW	15.73 AW	34860 AAW	WABLS	10//99-12//99
Except Wholesale, Retail, and Farm Product	Tacoma PMSA, WA	S	20.07 MW	19.25 AW	41740 AAW	WABLS	10//99-12//99
Except Wholesale, Retail, and Farm Product	Yakima MSA, WA	S	15.37 MW	15.15 AW	31970 AAW	WABLS	10//99-12//99
Except Wholesale, Retail, and Farm Product	West Virginia	S	16.08 MW	17.68 AW	36770 AAW	WVBLS	10//99-12//99
Except Wholesale, Retail, and Farm Product	Charleston MSA, WV	S	18.79 MW	16.47 AW	39070 AAW	WVBLS	10//99-12//99
Except Wholesale, Retail, and Farm Product	Huntington-Ashland MSA, WV-KY-OH	S	17.57 MW	16.46 AW	36540 AAW	WVBLS	10//99-12//99
Except Wholesale, Retail, and Farm Product	Parkersburg-Marietta MSA, WV-OH	S	16.69 MW	16.00 AW	34710 AAW	WVBLS	10//99-12//99
Except Wholesale, Retail, and Farm Product	Wisconsin	S	17.56 MW	18.38 AW	38220 AAW	WIBLS	10//99-12//99
Except Wholesale, Retail, and Farm Product	Appleton-Oshkosh-Neenah MSA, WI	S	17.32 MW	17.08 AW	36020 AAW	WIBLS	10//99-12//99
Except Wholesale, Retail, and Farm Product	Eau Claire MSA, WI	S	17.69 MW	15.62 AW	36800 AAW	WIBLS	10//99-12//99
Except Wholesale, Retail, and Farm Product	Green Bay MSA, WI	S	18.63 MW	17.93 AW	38750 AAW	WIBLS	10//99-12//99
Except Wholesale, Retail, and Farm Product	Janesville-Beloit MSA, WI	S	17.22 MW	16.12 AW	35830 AAW	WIBLS	10//99-12//99
Except Wholesale, Retail, and Farm Product	Kenosha PMSA, WI	S	19.32 MW	18.09 AW	40170 AAW	WIBLS	10//99-12//99
Except Wholesale, Retail, and Farm Product	La Crosse MSA, WI-MN	S	19.11 MW	17.60 AW	39740 AAW	WIBLS	10//99-12//99
Except Wholesale, Retail, and Farm Product	Madison MSA, WI	S	18.19 MW	17.61 AW	37840 AAW	WIBLS	10//99-12//99
Except Wholesale, Retail, and Farm Product	Milwaukee-Waukesha PMSA, WI	S	19.56 MW	18.52 AW	40690 AAW	WIBLS	10//99-12//99
Except Wholesale, Retail, and Farm Product	Racine PMSA, WI	S	18.06 MW	16.56 AW	37560 AAW	WIBLS	10//99-12//99
Except Wholesale, Retail, and Farm Product	Sheboygan MSA, WI	S	17.90 MW	15.62 AW	37230 AAW	WIBLS	10//99-12//99
Except Wholesale, Retail, and Farm Product	Wausau MSA, WI	S	16.42 MW	15.42 AW	34150 AAW	WIBLS	10//99-12//99
Except Wholesale, Retail, and Farm Product	Wyoming	S	19.32 MW	19.89 AW	41360 AAW	WYBLS	10//99-12//99
Except Wholesale, Retail, and Farm Product	Casper MSA, WY	S	20.54 MW	19.15 AW	42720 AAW	WYBLS	10//99-12//99
Except Wholesale, Retail, and Farm Product	Puerto Rico	S	10.68 MW	12.64 AW	26290 AAW	PRBLS	10//99-12//99
Except Wholesale, Retail, and Farm Product	Aguadilla MSA, PR	S	18.28 MW	13.35 AW	38030 AAW	PRBLS	10//99-12//99
Except Wholesale, Retail, and Farm Product	Caguas PMSA, PR	S	14.74 MW	12.61 AW	30660 AAW	PRBLS	10//99-12//99
Except Wholesale, Retail, and Farm Product	Mayaguez MSA, PR	S	12.06 MW	10.45 AW	25090 AAW	PRBLS	10//99-12//99
Except Wholesale, Retail, and Farm Product	Ponce MSA, PR	S	11.41 MW	10.35 AW	23740 AAW	PRBLS	10//99-12//99
Except Wholesale, Retail, and Farm Product	San Juan-Bayamon PMSA, PR	S	11.97 MW	10.13 AW	24900 AAW	PRBLS	10//99-12//99
Except Wholesale, Retail, and Farm Product	Virgin Islands	S	11.67 MW	14.36 AW	29860 AAW	VIBLS	10//99-12//99
Except Wholesale, Retail, and Farm Product	Guam	S	13.7 MW	14.61 AW	30380 AAW	GUBLS	10//99-12//99
Purchasing Agent and Buyer							
Farm Product	Alabama	S	15.09 MW	16.32 AW	33950 AAW	ALBLS	10//99-12//99
Farm Product	Birmingham MSA, AL	S	24.09 MW	20.49 AW	50100 AAW	ALBLS	10//99-12//99
Farm Product	Mobile MSA, AL	S	14.55 MW	14.83 AW	30260 AAW	ALBLS	10//99-12//99

AAW	Average annual wage	AOH	Average offered, high	ASH	Average starting, high
AE	Average entry wage	AOL	Average offered, low	ASL	Average starting, low
AEX	Average experienced wage	APH	Average pay, high range	AW	Average wage paid
AO	Average offered	APL	Average pay, low range	FQ	First quartile wage

H	Hourly	M	Monthly
HI	Highest wage paid	MTC	Median total compensation
HR	High end range	MW	Median wage paid
LR	Low end range	SQ	Second quartile wage

S	Special: hourly and annual
TQ	Third quartile wage
W	Weekly
Y	Yearly

Occupation/Type/Industry	Location	Per	Low	Mid	High	Source	Date
Purchasing Agent and Buyer							
Farm Product	Arizona	S	16.74 MW	21.41 AW	44530 AAW	AZBLS	10//99-12//99
Farm Product	Phoenix-Mesa MSA, AZ	S	21.47 MW	18.19 AW	44660 AAW	AZBLS	10//99-12//99
Farm Product	Arkansas	S	15.33 MW	16.85 AW	35050 AAW	ARBLS	10//99-12//99
Farm Product	Little Rock-North Little Rock MSA, AR	S	15.40 MW	15.40 AW	32040 AAW	ARBLS	10//99-12//99
Farm Product	California	S	20.51 MW	23.27 AW	48410 AAW	CABLS	10//99-12//99
Farm Product	Fresno MSA, CA	S	21.87 MW	20.43 AW	45500 AAW	CABLS	10//99-12//99
Farm Product	Los Angeles-Long Beach PMSA, CA	S	21.39 MW	20.33 AW	44490 AAW	CABLS	10//99-12//99
Farm Product	Modesto MSA, CA	S	13.92 MW	10.74 AW	28960 AAW	CABLS	10//99-12//99
Farm Product	Oakland PMSA, CA	S	25.89 MW	25.51 AW	53840 AAW	CABLS	10//99-12//99
Farm Product	Orange County PMSA, CA	S	24.38 MW	21.55 AW	50700 AAW	CABLS	10//99-12//99
Farm Product	Riverside-San Bernardino PMSA, CA	S	24.39 MW	19.72 AW	50740 AAW	CABLS	10//99-12//99
Farm Product	Sacramento PMSA, CA	S	17.93 MW	18.31 AW	37300 AAW	CABLS	10//99-12//99
Farm Product	San Diego MSA, CA	S	26.95 MW	20.06 AW	56060 AAW	CABLS	10//99-12//99
Farm Product	San Francisco PMSA, CA	S	34.27 MW	37.23 AW	71290 AAW	CABLS	10//99-12//99
Farm Product	San Jose PMSA, CA	S	22.18 MW	16.57 AW	46140 AAW	CABLS	10//99-12//99
Farm Product	Stockton-Lodi MSA, CA	S	20.68 MW	21.28 AW	43020 AAW	CABLS	10//99-12//99
Farm Product	Vallejo-Fairfield-Napa PMSA, CA	S	17.49 MW	16.17 AW	36380 AAW	CABLS	10//99-12//99
Farm Product	Yolo PMSA, CA	S	30.29 MW	20.86 AW	63010 AAW	CABLS	10//99-12//99
Farm Product	Colorado	S	15.85 MW	16.97 AW	35300 AAW	COBLS	10//99-12//99
Farm Product	Boulder-Longmont PMSA, CO	S	18.09 MW	18.82 AW	37620 AAW	COBLS	10//99-12//99
Farm Product	Denver PMSA, CO	S	16.45 MW	13.69 AW	34210 AAW	COBLS	10//99-12//99
Farm Product	Connecticut	S	24.22 MW	29.75 AW	61880 AAW	CTBLS	10//99-12//99
Farm Product	Delaware	S	13.85 MW	17.11 AW	35590 AAW	DEBLS	10//99-12//99
Farm Product	Wilmington-Newark PMSA, DE-MD	S	18.52 MW	14.49 AW	38510 AAW	DEBLS	10//99-12//99
Farm Product	District of Columbia	S	45.63 MW	36.24 AW	75390 AAW	DCBLS	10//99-12//99
Farm Product	Florida	S	19.47 MW	23.34 AW	48540 AAW	FLBLS	10//99-12//99
Farm Product	Fort Lauderdale PMSA, FL	S	34.22 MW	37.79 AW	71190 AAW	FLBLS	10//99-12//99
Farm Product	Lakeland-Winter Haven MSA, FL	S	22.02 MW	19.16 AW	45800 AAW	FLBLS	10//99-12//99
Farm Product	Miami PMSA, FL	S	15.34 MW	10.35 AW	31910 AAW	FLBLS	10//99-12//99
Farm Product	Tampa-St. Petersburg-Clearwater MSA, FL	S	19.61 MW	12.09 AW	40790 AAW	FLBLS	10//99-12//99
Farm Product	West Palm Beach-Boca Raton MSA, FL	S	30.63 MW	36.87 AW	63710 AAW	FLBLS	10//99-12//99
Farm Product	Idaho	S	8.2 MW	12.18 AW	25340 AAW	IDBLS	10//99-12//99
Farm Product	Illinois	S	15.92 MW	17.39 AW	36170 AAW	ILBLS	10//99-12//99
Farm Product	Chicago PMSA, IL	S	17.12 MW	15.55 AW	35610 AAW	ILBLS	10//99-12//99
Farm Product	Indiana	S	17.59 MW	17.93 AW	37290 AAW	INBLS	10//99-12//99
Farm Product	Elkhart-Goshen MSA, IN	S	19.32 MW	17.76 AW	40180 AAW	INBLS	10//99-12//99
Farm Product	Evansville-Henderson MSA, IN-KY	S	14.93 MW	11.31 AW	31060 AAW	INBLS	10//99-12//99
Farm Product	Fort Wayne MSA, IN	S	16.73 MW	18.23 AW	34800 AAW	INBLS	10//99-12//99
Farm Product	Indianapolis MSA, IN	S	15.74 MW	13.45 AW	32730 AAW	INBLS	10//99-12//99
Farm Product	Iowa	S	17.09 MW	18.70 AW	38890 AAW	IABLS	10//99-12//99
Farm Product	Cedar Rapids MSA, IA	S	23.07 MW	23.10 AW	47990 AAW	IABLS	10//99-12//99
Farm Product	Davenport-Moline-Rock Island MSA, IA-IL	S	13.63 MW	13.83 AW	28350 AAW	IABLS	10//99-12//99
Farm Product	Des Moines MSA, IA	S	16.45 MW	15.35 AW	34210 AAW	IABLS	10//99-12//99
Farm Product	Kansas	S	19.32 MW	21.66 AW	45050 AAW	KSBLS	10//99-12//99
Farm Product	Kentucky	S	15.74 MW	16.73 AW	34810 AAW	KYBLS	10//99-12//99
Farm Product	Lexington MSA, KY	S	14.11 MW	14.85 AW	29350 AAW	KYBLS	10//99-12//99
Farm Product	Louisville MSA, KY-IN	S	16.58 MW	16.56 AW	34490 AAW	KYBLS	10//99-12//99
Farm Product	Louisiana	S	15.98 MW	16.66 AW	34650 AAW	LABLS	10//99-12//99
Farm Product	Baton Rouge MSA, LA	S	18.84 MW	18.99 AW	39180 AAW	LABLS	10//99-12//99
Farm Product	Lafayette MSA, LA	S	17.87 MW	17.89 AW	37180 AAW	LABLS	10//99-12//99
Farm Product	New Orleans MSA, LA	S	18.37 MW	15.74 AW	38210 AAW	LABLS	10//99-12//99
Farm Product	Maine	S	15.79 MW	15.71 AW	32670 AAW	MEBLS	10//99-12//99
Farm Product	Maryland	S	17.43 MW	21.02 AW	43710 AAW	MDBLS	10//99-12//99
Farm Product	Baltimore PMSA, MD	S	22.27 MW	20.78 AW	46320 AAW	MDBLS	10//99-12//99
Farm Product	Massachusetts	S	22.45 MW	22.79 AW	47410 AAW	MABLS	10//99-12//99
Farm Product	Boston PMSA, MA-NH	S	22.78 MW	22.71 AW	47380 AAW	MABLS	10//99-12//99
Farm Product	Michigan	S	18.98 MW	21.25 AW	44200 AAW	MIBLS	10//99-12//99
Farm Product	Ann Arbor PMSA, MI	S	15.58 MW	13.94 AW	32410 AAW	MIBLS	10//99-12//99
Farm Product	Detroit PMSA, MI	S	28.95 MW	26.45 AW	60220 AAW	MIBLS	10//99-12//99
Farm Product	Grand Rapids-Muskegon-Holland MSA, MI	S	19.57 MW	17.75 AW	40710 AAW	MIBLS	10//99-12//99

AAW Average annual wage	**AOH** Average offered, high	**ASH** Average starting, high	**H** Hourly	**M** Monthly	**S** Special: hourly and annual
AE Average entry wage	**AOL** Average offered, low	**ASL** Average starting, low	**HI** Highest wage paid	**MTC** Median total compensation	**TQ** Third quartile wage
AEX Average experienced wage	**APH** Average pay, high range	**AW** Average wage paid	**HR** High end range	**MW** Median wage paid	**W** Weekly
AO Average offered	**APL** Average pay, low range	**FQ** First quartile wage	**LR** Low end range	**SQ** Second quartile wage	**Y** Yearly

Purchasing Agent and Buyer

Occupation/Type/Industry	Location	Per	Low	Mid	High	Source	Date
Farm Product	Lansing-East Lansing MSA, MI	S	13.92 MW	12.49 AW	28960 AAW	MIBLS	10//99-12//99
Farm Product	Saginaw-Bay City-Midland MSA, MI	S	21.95 MW	23.21 AW	45650 AAW	MIBLS	10//99-12//99
Farm Product	Minnesota	S	19.39 MW	22.75 AW	47330 AAW	MNBLS	10//99-12//99
Farm Product	Duluth-Superior MSA, MN-WI	S	15.19 MW	14.76 AW	31590 AAW	MNBLS	10//99-12//99
Farm Product	Minneapolis-St. Paul MSA, MN-WI	S	24.88 MW	20.60 AW	51740 AAW	MNBLS	10//99-12//99
Farm Product	Mississippi	S	15.33 MW	15.94 AW	33150 AAW	MSBLS	10//99-12//99
Farm Product	Jackson MSA, MS	S	15.69 MW	15.26 AW	32630 AAW	MSBLS	10//99-12//99
Farm Product	Missouri	S	15.89 MW	19.48 AW	40520 AAW	MOBLS	10//99-12//99
Farm Product	Kansas City MSA, MO-KS	S	18.61 MW	17.66 AW	38700 AAW	MOBLS	10//99-12//99
Farm Product	Montana	S	12.3 MW	15.37 AW	31960 AAW	MTBLS	10//99-12//99
Farm Product	Nebraska	S	16.34 MW	20.94 AW	43550 AAW	NEBLS	10//99-12//99
Farm Product	Omaha MSA, NE-IA	S	27.23 MW	25.32 AW	56640 AAW	NEBLS	10//99-12//99
Farm Product	Nevada	S	14.76 MW	16.65 AW	34630 AAW	NVBLS	10//99-12//99
Farm Product	Las Vegas MSA, NV-AZ	S	16.35 MW	14.89 AW	34000 AAW	NVBLS	10//99-12//99
Farm Product	New Jersey	S	21.75 MW	26.46 AW	55030 AAW	NJBLS	10//99-12//99
Farm Product	Bergen-Passaic PMSA, NJ	S	38.92 MW	45.11 AW	80950 AAW	NJBLS	10//99-12//99
Farm Product	Newark PMSA, NJ	S	31.95 MW	25.02 AW	66450 AAW	NJBLS	10//99-12//99
Farm Product	New York	S	15.95 MW	20.21 AW	42030 AAW	NYBLS	10//99-12//99
Farm Product	New York PMSA, NY	S	19.03 MW	15.32 AW	39570 AAW	NYBLS	10//99-12//99
Farm Product	Syracuse MSA, NY	S	13.97 MW	13.13 AW	29050 AAW	NYBLS	10//99-12//99
Farm Product	North Carolina	S	17.9 MW	20.95 AW	43570 AAW	NCBLS	10//99-12//99
Farm Product	Charlotte-Gastonia-Rock Hill MSA, NC-SC	S	17.26 MW	15.77 AW	35900 AAW	NCBLS	10//99-12//99
Farm Product	Raleigh-Durham-Chapel Hill MSA, NC	S	21.89 MW	19.31 AW	45520 AAW	NCBLS	10//99-12//99
Farm Product	North Dakota	S	24.4 MW	28.42 AW	59100 AAW	NDBLS	10//99-12//99
Farm Product	Fargo-Moorhead MSA, ND-MN	S	21.75 MW	23.02 AW	45230 AAW	NDBLS	10//99-12//99
Farm Product	Ohio	S	19.47 MW	20.52 AW	42690 AAW	OHBLS	10//99-12//99
Farm Product	Cincinnati PMSA, OH-KY-IN	S	16.94 MW	17.67 AW	35240 AAW	OHBLS	10//99-12//99
Farm Product	Cleveland-Lorain-Elyria PMSA, OH	S	18.93 MW	17.44 AW	39370 AAW	OHBLS	10//99-12//99
Farm Product	Oklahoma	S	13.99 MW	14.18 AW	29490 AAW	OKBLS	10//99-12//99
Farm Product	Oklahoma City MSA, OK	S	14.82 MW	17.40 AW	30830 AAW	OKBLS	10//99-12//99
Farm Product	Tulsa MSA, OK	S	16.54 MW	15.52 AW	34410 AAW	OKBLS	10//99-12//99
Farm Product	Oregon	S	20.06 MW	25.00 AW	52010 AAW	ORBLS	10//99-12//99
Farm Product	Eugene-Springfield MSA, OR	S	17.24 MW	18.36 AW	35860 AAW	ORBLS	10//99-12//99
Farm Product	Portland-Vancouver PMSA, OR-WA	S	30.31 MW	24.51 AW	63050 AAW	ORBLS	10//99-12//99
Farm Product	Pennsylvania	S	17.81 MW	26.20 AW	54500 AAW	PABLS	10//99-12//99
Farm Product	Philadelphia PMSA, PA-NJ	S	26.36 MW	23.22 AW	54840 AAW	PABLS	10//99-12//99
Farm Product	Pittsburgh MSA, PA	S	34.03 MW	16.72 AW	70790 AAW	PABLS	10//99-12//99
Farm Product	Reading MSA, PA	S	16.72 MW	16.19 AW	34790 AAW	PABLS	10//99-12//99
Farm Product	Rhode Island	S	21.97 MW	24.98 AW	51950 AAW	RIBLS	10//99-12//99
Farm Product	Providence-Fall River-Warwick MSA, RI-MA	S	25.23 MW	22.18 AW	52470 AAW	RIBLS	10//99-12//99
Farm Product	South Carolina	S	15.96 MW	19.21 AW	39950 AAW	SCBLS	10//99-12//99
Farm Product	Columbia MSA, SC	S	21.72 MW	16.31 AW	45190 AAW	SCBLS	10//99-12//99
Farm Product	Greenville-Spartanburg-Anderson MSA, SC	S	23.50 MW	16.34 AW	48890 AAW	SCBLS	10//99-12//99
Farm Product	South Dakota	S	16.81 MW	18.41 AW	38300 AAW	SDBLS	10//99-12//99
Farm Product	Tennessee	S	15.17 MW	17.76 AW	36930 AAW	TNBLS	10//99-12//99
Farm Product	Chattanooga MSA, TN-GA	S	13.78 MW	12.65 AW	28660 AAW	TNBLS	10//99-12//99
Farm Product	Memphis MSA, TN-AR-MS	S	24.48 MW	28.18 AW	50930 AAW	MSBLS	10//99-12//99
Farm Product	Nashville MSA, TN	S	15.84 MW	14.25 AW	32940 AAW	TNBLS	10//99-12//99
Farm Product	Texas	S	12.47 MW	19.33 AW	40210 AAW	TXBLS	10//99-12//99
Farm Product	Dallas PMSA, TX	S	31.12 MW	27.40 AW	64720 AAW	TXBLS	10//99-12//99
Farm Product	Houston PMSA, TX	S	24.27 MW	19.25 AW	50480 AAW	TXBLS	10//99-12//99
Farm Product	Lubbock MSA, TX	S	32.79 MW	36.97 AW	68200 AAW	TXBLS	10//99-12//99
Farm Product	McAllen-Edinburg-Mission MSA, TX	S	14.11 MW	14.29 AW	29360 AAW	TXBLS	10//99-12//99
Farm Product	San Antonio MSA, TX	S	25.66 MW	23.08 AW	53380 AAW	TXBLS	10//99-12//99
Farm Product	Vermont	S	21.47 MW	25.70 AW	53450 AAW	VTBLS	10//99-12//99
Farm Product	Burlington MSA, VT	S	23.66 MW	19.90 AW	49210 AAW	VTBLS	10//99-12//99
Farm Product	Virginia	S	17.3 MW	24.13 AW	50190 AAW	VABLS	10//99-12//99
Farm Product	Norfolk-Virginia Beach-Newport News MSA, VA-NC	S	13.64 MW	13.14 AW	28360 AAW	VABLS	10//99-12//99

Occupation/Type/Industry	Location	Per	Low	Mid	High	Source	Date
Purchasing Agent and Buyer							
Farm Product	Richmond-Petersburg MSA, VA	S	16.99 MW	14.84 AW	35350 AAW	VABLS	10//99-12//99
Farm Product	Washington	S	15 MW	15.50 AW	32240 AAW	WABLS	10//99-12//99
Farm Product	Seattle-Bellevue-Everett PMSA, WA	S	16.21 MW	17.80 AW	33720 AAW	WABLS	10//99-12//99
Farm Product	Tacoma PMSA, WA	S	13.73 MW	12.10 AW	28560 AAW	WABLS	10//99-12//99
Farm Product	Yakima MSA, WA	S	20.83 MW	16.81 AW	43330 AAW	WABLS	10//99-12//99
Farm Product	West Virginia	S	15.28 MW	16.68 AW	34680 AAW	WVBLS	10//99-12//99
Farm Product	Wisconsin	S	16.34 MW	19.25 AW	40040 AAW	WIBLS	10//99-12//99
Farm Product	Milwaukee-Waukesha PMSA, WI	S	23.58 MW	16.49 AW	49050 AAW	WIBLS	10//99-12//99
Farm Product	Wyoming	S	16.47 MW	19.10 AW	39740 AAW	WYBLS	10//99-12//99
Farm Product	Puerto Rico	S	9.89 MW	10.83 AW	22530 AAW	PRBLS	10//99-12//99
Purchasing Executive							
Senior	United States	Y		116000 AW		AMSHIP	2000
Purchasing Manager							
	United States	Y		56014 AW		MATMAN	1999
	Alabama	S	17.35 MW	19.01 AW	39540 AAW	ALBLS	10//99-12//99
	Anniston MSA, AL	S	20.45 MW	20.27 AW	42530 AAW	ALBLS	10//99-12//99
	Birmingham MSA, AL	S	17.06 MW	14.35 AW	35490 AAW	ALBLS	10//99-12//99
	Decatur MSA, AL	S	17.59 MW	16.37 AW	36580 AAW	ALBLS	10//99-12//99
	Dothan MSA, AL	S	21.26 MW	19.33 AW	44220 AAW	ALBLS	10//99-12//99
	Gadsden MSA, AL	S	16.21 MW	13.44 AW	33720 AAW	ALBLS	10//99-12//99
	Huntsville MSA, AL	S	26.00 MW	24.91 AW	54080 AAW	ALBLS	10//99-12//99
	Mobile MSA, AL	S	19.59 MW	17.99 AW	40750 AAW	ALBLS	10//99-12//99
	Montgomery MSA, AL	S	19.58 MW	17.10 AW	40730 AAW	ALBLS	10//99-12//99
	Tuscaloosa MSA, AL	S	14.76 MW	11.75 AW	30700 AAW	ALBLS	10//99-12//99
	Alaska	S	20.92 MW	23.48 AW	48840 AAW	AKBLS	10//99-12//99
	Anchorage MSA, AK	S	24.12 MW	21.53 AW	50170 AAW	AKBLS	10//99-12//99
	Arizona	S	24.44 MW	25.73 AW	53510 AAW	AZBLS	10//99-12//99
	Flagstaff MSA, AZ-UT	S	23.99 MW	23.07 AW	49890 AAW	AZBLS	10//99-12//99
	Phoenix-Mesa MSA, AZ	S	26.80 MW	25.33 AW	55740 AAW	AZBLS	10//99-12//99
	Tucson MSA, AZ	S	23.71 MW	22.80 AW	49320 AAW	AZBLS	10//99-12//99
	Arkansas	S	20.14 MW	21.93 AW	45610 AAW	ARBLS	10//99-12//99
	Fayetteville-Springdale-Rogers MSA, AR	S	22.93 MW	22.02 AW	47690 AAW	ARBLS	10//99-12//99
	Fort Smith MSA, AR-OK	S	21.84 MW	21.55 AW	45420 AAW	ARBLS	10//99-12//99
	Jonesboro MSA, AR	S	20.76 MW	19.76 AW	43180 AAW	ARBLS	10//99-12//99
	Little Rock-North Little Rock MSA, AR	S	22.34 MW	20.42 AW	46470 AAW	ARBLS	10//99-12//99
	California	S	23.4 MW	25.79 AW	53640 AAW	CABLS	10//99-12//99
	Bakersfield MSA, CA	S	21.67 MW	20.66 AW	45070 AAW	CABLS	10//99-12//99
	Chico-Paradise MSA, CA	S	20.70 MW	19.40 AW	43050 AAW	CABLS	10//99-12//99
	Fresno MSA, CA	S	22.68 MW	20.55 AW	47170 AAW	CABLS	10//99-12//99
	Los Angeles-Long Beach PMSA, CA	S	26.31 MW	23.48 AW	54730 AAW	CABLS	10//99-12//99
	Merced MSA, CA	S	22.38 MW	19.83 AW	46540 AAW	CABLS	10//99-12//99
	Modesto MSA, CA	S	20.06 MW	16.81 AW	41720 AAW	CABLS	10//99-12//99
	Oakland PMSA, CA	S	28.33 MW	25.50 AW	58930 AAW	CABLS	10//99-12//99
	Orange County PMSA, CA	S	25.81 MW	23.64 AW	53680 AAW	CABLS	10//99-12//99
	Redding MSA, CA	S	22.78 MW	19.42 AW	47380 AAW	CABLS	10//99-12//99
	Riverside-San Bernardino PMSA, CA	S	23.21 MW	21.06 AW	48280 AAW	CABLS	10//99-12//99
	Sacramento PMSA, CA	S	23.03 MW	21.45 AW	47900 AAW	CABLS	10//99-12//99
	Salinas MSA, CA	S	25.45 MW	24.00 AW	52940 AAW	CABLS	10//99-12//99
	San Diego MSA, CA	S	24.80 MW	23.29 AW	51580 AAW	CABLS	10//99-12//99
	San Francisco PMSA, CA	S	26.42 MW	24.26 AW	54940 AAW	CABLS	10//99-12//99
	San Jose PMSA, CA	S	30.44 MW	28.90 AW	63320 AAW	CABLS	10//99-12//99
	San Luis Obispo-Atascadero-Paso Robles MSA, CA	S	22.68 MW	19.93 AW	47170 AAW	CABLS	10//99-12//99
	Santa Barbara-Santa Maria-Lompoc MSA, CA	S	19.54 MW	15.32 AW	40640 AAW	CABLS	10//99-12//99
	Santa Cruz-Watsonville PMSA, CA	S	27.61 MW	24.80 AW	57420 AAW	CABLS	10//99-12//99
	Santa Rosa PMSA, CA	S	23.15 MW	20.05 AW	48150 AAW	CABLS	10//99-12//99
	Stockton-Lodi MSA, CA	S	23.49 MW	21.85 AW	48860 AAW	CABLS	10//99-12//99
	Vallejo-Fairfield-Napa PMSA, CA	S	22.41 MW	20.91 AW	46610 AAW	CABLS	10//99-12//99
	Ventura PMSA, CA	S	26.08 MW	23.69 AW	54240 AAW	CABLS	10//99-12//99
	Visalia-Tulare-Porterville MSA, CA	S	21.64 MW	21.27 AW	45010 AAW	CABLS	10//99-12//99

AAW	Average annual wage	AOH	Average offered, high	ASH	Average starting, high	H	Hourly	M	Monthly	S	Special: hourly and annual
AE	Average entry wage	AOL	Average offered, low	ASL	Average starting, low	HI	Highest wage paid	MTC	Median total compensation	TQ	Third quartile wage
AEX	Average experienced wage	APH	Average pay, high range	AW	Average wage paid	HR	High end range	MW	Median wage paid	W	Weekly
AO	Average offered	APL	Average pay, low range	FQ	First quartile wage	LR	Low end range	SQ	Second quartile wage	Y	Yearly

Occupation/Type/Industry	Location	Per	Low	Mid	High	Source	Date
Purchasing Manager	Yolo PMSA, CA	S	23.81 MW	22.30 AW	49520 AAW	CABLS	10//99-12//99
	Colorado	S	23.18 MW	25.48 AW	53010 AAW	COBLS	10//99-12//99
	Boulder-Longmont PMSA, CO	S	24.98 MW	23.88 AW	51970 AAW	COBLS	10//99-12//99
	Colorado Springs MSA, CO	S	28.51 MW	26.91 AW	59300 AAW	COBLS	10//99-12//99
	Denver PMSA, CO	S	27.28 MW	25.53 AW	56740 AAW	COBLS	10//99-12//99
	Fort Collins-Loveland MSA, CO	S	21.36 MW	20.32 AW	44430 AAW	COBLS	10//99-12//99
	Grand Junction MSA, CO	S	22.68 MW	21.67 AW	47170 AAW	COBLS	10//99-12//99
	Greeley PMSA, CO	S	25.27 MW	22.35 AW	52560 AAW	COBLS	10//99-12//99
	Pueblo MSA, CO	S	25.36 MW	22.15 AW	52750 AAW	COBLS	10//99-12//99
	Connecticut	S	27.48 MW	29.19 AW	60720 AAW	CTBLS	10//99-12//99
	Bridgeport PMSA, CT	S	27.93 MW	24.23 AW	58090 AAW	CTBLS	10//99-12//99
	Danbury PMSA, CT	S	25.26 MW	19.91 AW	52530 AAW	CTBLS	10//99-12//99
	Hartford MSA, CT	S	31.17 MW	31.31 AW	64840 AAW	CTBLS	10//99-12//99
	New Haven-Meriden PMSA, CT	S	24.54 MW	22.73 AW	51030 AAW	CTBLS	10//99-12//99
	New London-Norwich MSA, CT-RI	S	27.93 MW	26.39 AW	58080 AAW	CTBLS	10//99-12//99
	Stamford-Norwalk PMSA, CT	S	34.66 MW	34.00 AW	72090 AAW	CTBLS	10//99-12//99
	Waterbury PMSA, CT	S	28.86 MW	26.86 AW	60020 AAW	CTBLS	10//99-12//99
	Delaware	S	24.62 MW	26.18 AW	54450 AAW	DEBLS	10//99-12//99
	Dover MSA, DE	S	25.76 MW	22.86 AW	53580 AAW	DEBLS	10//99-12//99
	Wilmington-Newark PMSA, DE-MD	S	25.59 MW	24.85 AW	53230 AAW	DEBLS	10//99-12//99
	Washington PMSA, DC-MD-VA-WV	S	29.07 MW	29.32 AW	60470 AAW	DCBLS	10//99-12//99
	Florida	S	19.07 MW	21.79 AW	45320 AAW	FLBLS	10//99-12//99
	Daytona Beach MSA, FL	S	20.56 MW	19.07 AW	42750 AAW	FLBLS	10//99-12//99
	Fort Lauderdale PMSA, FL	S	22.76 MW	20.15 AW	47330 AAW	FLBLS	10//99-12//99
	Fort Myers-Cape Coral MSA, FL	S	19.67 MW	18.20 AW	40910 AAW	FLBLS	10//99-12//99
	Fort Pierce-Port St. Lucie MSA, FL	S	16.54 MW	14.08 AW	34400 AAW	FLBLS	10//99-12//99
	Gainesville MSA, FL	S	19.87 MW	17.65 AW	41330 AAW	FLBLS	10//99-12//99
	Jacksonville MSA, FL	S	20.45 MW	17.71 AW	42530 AAW	FLBLS	10//99-12//99
	Lakeland-Winter Haven MSA, FL	S	22.36 MW	19.77 AW	46500 AAW	FLBLS	10//99-12//99
	Melbourne-Titusville-Palm Bay MSA, FL	S	21.94 MW	19.58 AW	45630 AAW	FLBLS	10//99-12//99
	Miami PMSA, FL	S	20.98 MW	17.96 AW	43640 AAW	FLBLS	10//99-12//99
	Naples MSA, FL	S	21.63 MW	21.89 AW	44990 AAW	FLBLS	10//99-12//99
	Ocala MSA, FL	S	16.55 MW	12.12 AW	34410 AAW	FLBLS	10//99-12//99
	Orlando MSA, FL	S	22.84 MW	19.62 AW	47510 AAW	FLBLS	10//99-12//99
	Panama City MSA, FL	S	22.09 MW	20.63 AW	45940 AAW	FLBLS	10//99-12//99
	Sarasota-Bradenton MSA, FL	S	21.31 MW	19.18 AW	44320 AAW	FLBLS	10//99-12//99
	Tallahassee MSA, FL	S	21.39 MW	19.39 AW	44500 AAW	FLBLS	10//99-12//99
	Tampa-St. Petersburg-Clearwater MSA, FL	Per	23.64 MW	20.99 AW	49170 AAW	FLBLS	10//99-12//99
	West Palm Beach-Boca Raton MSA, FL	S	22.90 MW	18.21 AW	47630 AAW	FLBLS	10//99-12//99
	Georgia	S	23.47 MW	26.84 AW	55830 AAW	GABLS	10//99-12//99
	Albany MSA, GA	S	24.64 MW	21.94 AW	51240 AAW	GABLS	10//99-12//99
	Athens MSA, GA	S	23.52 MW	22.73 AW	48920 AAW	GABLS	10//99-12//99
	Atlanta MSA, GA	S	28.42 MW	24.16 AW	59110 AAW	GABLS	10//99-12//99
	Augusta-Aiken MSA, GA-SC	S	26.98 MW	26.74 AW	56130 AAW	GABLS	10//99-12//99
	Columbus MSA, GA-AL	S	23.25 MW	20.37 AW	48370 AAW	GABLS	10//99-12//99
	Savannah MSA, GA	S	20.96 MW	19.43 AW	43590 AAW	GABLS	10//99-12//99
	Hawaii	S	23.58 MW	25.41 AW	52850 AAW	HIBLS	10//99-12//99
	Honolulu MSA, HI	S	26.61 MW	24.55 AW	55340 AAW	HIBLS	10//99-12//99
	Idaho	S	17.96 MW	21.03 AW	43750 AAW	IDBLS	10//99-12//99
	Boise City MSA, ID	S	24.21 MW	19.86 AW	50360 AAW	IDBLS	10//99-12//99
	Illinois	S	21.04 MW	23.75 AW	49400 AAW	ILBLS	10//99-12//99
	Bloomington-Normal MSA, IL	S	18.97 MW	14.67 AW	39460 AAW	ILBLS	10//99-12//99
	Champaign-Urbana MSA, IL	S	24.81 MW	21.77 AW	51600 AAW	ILBLS	10//99-12//99
	Chicago PMSA, IL	S	24.55 MW	21.83 AW	51070 AAW	ILBLS	10//99-12//99
	Decatur MSA, IL	S	20.93 MW	17.75 AW	43540 AAW	ILBLS	10//99-12//99
	Kankakee PMSA, IL	S	28.97 MW	28.59 AW	60260 AAW	ILBLS	10//99-12//99
	Peoria-Pekin MSA, IL	S	23.26 MW	19.69 AW	48380 AAW	ILBLS	10//99-12//99
	Rockford MSA, IL	S	21.05 MW	19.29 AW	43790 AAW	ILBLS	10//99-12//99
	Springfield MSA, IL	S	19.42 MW	17.05 AW	40390 AAW	ILBLS	10//99-12//99
	Indiana	S	22.7 MW	24.45 AW	50860 AAW	INBLS	10//99-12//99
	Elkhart-Goshen MSA, IN	S	25.57 MW	24.13 AW	53190 AAW	INBLS	10//99-12//99

AAW Average annual wage	**AOH** Average offered, high	**ASH** Average starting, high	**H** Hourly	**M** Monthly	**S** Special: hourly and annual
AE Average entry wage	**AOL** Average offered, low	**ASL** Average starting, low	**HI** Highest wage paid	**MTC** Median total compensation	**TQ** Third quartile wage
AEX Average experienced wage	**APH** Average pay, high range	**AW** Average wage paid	**HR** High end range	**MW** Median wage paid	**W** Weekly
AO Average offered	**APL** Average pay, low range	**FQ** First quartile wage	**LR** Low end range	**SQ** Second quartile wage	**Y** Yearly

Occupation/Type/Industry	Location	Per	Low	Mid	High	Source	Date
Purchasing Manager	Evansville-Henderson MSA, IN-KY	S	23.64 MW	20.80 AW	49160 AAW	INBLS	10//99-12//99
	Fort Wayne MSA, IN	S	26.30 MW	23.97 AW	54710 AAW	INBLS	10//99-12//99
	Gary PMSA, IN	S	25.87 MW	23.79 AW	53810 AAW	INBLS	10//99-12//99
	Indianapolis MSA, IN	S	23.69 MW	21.47 AW	49270 AAW	INBLS	10//99-12//99
	Kokomo MSA, IN	S	27.57 MW	25.11 AW	57350 AAW	INBLS	10//99-12//99
	Lafayette MSA, IN	S	25.50 MW	25.01 AW	53050 AAW	INBLS	10//99-12//99
	South Bend MSA, IN	S	22.28 MW	20.98 AW	46340 AAW	INBLS	10//99-12//99
	Terre Haute MSA, IN	S	23.61 MW	22.16 AW	49100 AAW	INBLS	10//99-12//99
	Iowa	S	18.5 MW	20.37 AW	42370 AAW	IABLS	10//99-12//99
	Cedar Rapids MSA, IA	S	23.03 MW	17.64 AW	47900 AAW	IABLS	10//99-12//99
	Davenport-Moline-Rock Island MSA, IA-IL	S	19.86 MW	17.58 AW	41320 AAW	IABLS	10//99-12//99
	Des Moines MSA, IA	S	20.51 MW	19.76 AW	42670 AAW	IABLS	10//99-12//99
	Dubuque MSA, IA	S	23.38 MW	22.95 AW	48640 AAW	IABLS	10//99-12//99
	Sioux City MSA, IA-NE	S	18.60 MW	17.03 AW	38690 AAW	IABLS	10//99-12//99
	Kansas	S	22.52 MW	24.90 AW	51790 AAW	KSBLS	10//99-12//99
	Topeka MSA, KS	S	22.35 MW	20.02 AW	46480 AAW	KSBLS	10//99-12//99
	Wichita MSA, KS	S	28.57 MW	25.93 AW	59420 AAW	KSBLS	10//99-12//99
	Kentucky	S	20.27 MW	21.90 AW	45550 AAW	KYBLS	10//99-12//99
	Lexington MSA, KY	S	23.16 MW	21.60 AW	48170 AAW	KYBLS	10//99-12//99
	Louisville MSA, KY-IN	S	22.02 MW	19.90 AW	45810 AAW	KYBLS	10//99-12//99
	Owensboro MSA, KY	S	20.95 MW	18.22 AW	43580 AAW	KYBLS	10//99-12//99
	Louisiana	S	18.4 MW	20.48 AW	42600 AAW	LABLS	10//99-12//99
	Alexandria MSA, LA	S	22.06 MW	20.39 AW	45880 AAW	LABLS	10//99-12//99
	Baton Rouge MSA, LA	S	21.19 MW	18.74 AW	44070 AAW	LABLS	10//99-12//99
	Houma MSA, LA	S	20.67 MW	18.76 AW	42990 AAW	LABLS	10//99-12//99
	Lafayette MSA, LA	S	17.36 MW	15.18 AW	36100 AAW	LABLS	10//99-12//99
	Lake Charles MSA, LA	S	20.53 MW	17.62 AW	42710 AAW	LABLS	10//99-12//99
	Monroe MSA, LA	S	18.89 MW	16.99 AW	39300 AAW	LABLS	10//99-12//99
	New Orleans MSA, LA	S	21.24 MW	18.95 AW	44180 AAW	LABLS	10//99-12//99
	Shreveport-Bossier City MSA, LA	S	21.38 MW	20.04 AW	44480 AAW	LABLS	10//99-12//99
	Maine	S	18.17 MW	20.29 AW	42190 AAW	MEBLS	10//99-12//99
	Bangor MSA, ME	S	18.63 MW	17.20 AW	38760 AAW	MEBLS	10//99-12//99
	Lewiston-Auburn MSA, ME	S	19.22 MW	18.03 AW	39980 AAW	MEBLS	10//99-12//99
	Portland MSA, ME	S	24.09 MW	21.02 AW	50110 AAW	MEBLS	10//99-12//99
	Maryland	S	20.69 MW	23.37 AW	48600 AAW	MDBLS	10//99-12//99
	Baltimore PMSA, MD	S	21.24 MW	18.60 AW	44170 AAW	MDBLS	10//99-12//99
	Hagerstown PMSA, MD	S	20.83 MW	17.85 AW	43330 AAW	MDBLS	10//99-12//99
	Massachusetts	S	27.46 MW	28.53 AW	59340 AAW	MABLS	10//99-12//99
	Barnstable-Yarmouth MSA, MA	S	28.72 MW	22.26 AW	59730 AAW	MABLS	10//99-12//99
	Boston PMSA, MA-NH	S	30.14 MW	30.30 AW	62690 AAW	MABLS	10//99-12//99
	Brockton PMSA, MA	S	27.61 MW	24.84 AW	57430 AAW	MABLS	10//99-12//99
	Fitchburg-Leominster PMSA, MA	S	23.76 MW	22.79 AW	49420 AAW	MABLS	10//99-12//99
	Lawrence PMSA, MA-NH	S	27.47 MW	27.82 AW	57150 AAW	MABLS	10//99-12//99
	Lowell PMSA, MA-NH	S	28.33 MW	28.63 AW	58920 AAW	MABLS	10//99-12//99
	New Bedford PMSA, MA	S	20.50 MW	18.49 AW	42640 AAW	MABLS	10//99-12//99
	Pittsfield MSA, MA	S	23.60 MW	21.26 AW	49090 AAW	MABLS	10//99-12//99
	Springfield MSA, MA	S	23.21 MW	21.97 AW	48270 AAW	MABLS	10//99-12//99
	Worcester PMSA, MA-CT	S	27.76 MW	25.69 AW	57740 AAW	MABLS	10//99-12//99
	Michigan	S	23.68 MW	26.48 AW	55070 AAW	MIBLS	10//99-12//99
	Ann Arbor PMSA, MI	S	25.10 MW	22.44 AW	52220 AAW	MIBLS	10//99-12//99
	Benton Harbor MSA, MI	S	24.90 MW	23.51 AW	51800 AAW	MIBLS	10//99-12//99
	Detroit PMSA, MI	S	29.02 MW	25.41 AW	60370 AAW	MIBLS	10//99-12//99
	Flint PMSA, MI	S	24.74 MW	21.70 AW	51460 AAW	MIBLS	10//99-12//99
	Grand Rapids-Muskegon-Holland MSA, MI	S	26.97 MW	25.10 AW	56110 AAW	MIBLS	10//99-12//99
	Jackson MSA, MI	S	30.83 MW	31.27 AW	64130 AAW	MIBLS	10//99-12//99
	Kalamazoo-Battle Creek MSA, MI	S	25.21 MW	23.24 AW	52440 AAW	MIBLS	10//99-12//99
	Lansing-East Lansing MSA, MI	S	23.40 MW	21.81 AW	48660 AAW	MIBLS	10//99-12//99
	Saginaw-Bay City-Midland MSA, MI	S	20.25 MW	18.14 AW	42110 AAW	MIBLS	10//99-12//99
	Minnesota	S	24.15 MW	25.97 AW	54020 AAW	MNBLS	10//99-12//99
	Duluth-Superior MSA, MN-WI	S	22.37 MW	19.93 AW	46530 AAW	MNBLS	10//99-12//99
	Minneapolis-St. Paul MSA, MN-WI	S	27.78 MW	25.90 AW	57780 AAW	MNBLS	10//99-12//99
	Rochester MSA, MN	S	24.55 MW	20.83 AW	51070 AAW	MNBLS	10//99-12//99
	St. Cloud MSA, MN	S	23.68 MW	20.68 AW	49260 AAW	MNBLS	10//99-12//99

AAW	Average annual wage	AOH	Average offered, high	ASH	Average starting, high	H	Hourly
AE	Average entry wage	AOL	Average offered, low	ASL	Average starting, low	HI	Highest wage paid
AEX	Average experienced wage	APH	Average pay, high range	AW	Average wage paid	HR	High end range
AO	Average offered	APL	Average pay, low range	FQ	First quartile wage	LR	Low end range

M	Monthly	S	Special: hourly and annual
MTC	Median total compensation	TQ	Third quartile wage
MW	Median wage paid	W	Weekly
SQ	Second quartile wage	Y	Yearly

Purchasing Manager

Occupation/Type/Industry	Location	Per	Low	Mid	High	Source	Date
Purchasing Manager	Mississippi	S	19.23 MW	20.99 AW	43660 AAW	MSBLS	10//99-12//99
	Biloxi-Gulfport-Pascagoula MSA, MS	S	24.23 MW	24.33 AW	50410 AAW	MSBLS	10//99-12//99
	Jackson MSA, MS	S	21.92 MW	21.16 AW	45600 AAW	MSBLS	10//99-12//99
	Missouri	S	20.65 MW	22.91 AW	47650 AAW	MOBLS	10//99-12//99
	Columbia MSA, MO	S	22.14 MW	20.80 AW	46060 AAW	MOBLS	10//99-12//99
	Joplin MSA, MO	S	17.98 MW	17.24 AW	37400 AAW	MOBLS	10//99-12//99
	Kansas City MSA, MO-KS	S	24.20 MW	21.33 AW	50340 AAW	MOBLS	10//99-12//99
	St. Louis MSA, MO-IL	S	23.94 MW	21.32 AW	49800 AAW	MOBLS	10//99-12//99
	Springfield MSA, MO	S	22.65 MW	21.11 AW	47110 AAW	MOBLS	10//99-12//99
	Montana	S	17.95 MW	18.81 AW	39130 AAW	MTBLS	10//99-12//99
	Billings MSA, MT	S	20.26 MW	20.04 AW	42140 AAW	MTBLS	10//99-12//99
	Great Falls MSA, MT	S	20.26 MW	18.50 AW	42140 AAW	MTBLS	10//99-12//99
	Missoula MSA, MT	S	22.12 MW	20.18 AW	46020 AAW	MTBLS	10//99-12//99
	Nebraska	S	18.72 MW	20.92 AW	43510 AAW	NEBLS	10//99-12//99
	Lincoln MSA, NE	S	20.43 MW	18.49 AW	42490 AAW	NEBLS	10//99-12//99
	Omaha MSA, NE-IA	S	22.28 MW	20.18 AW	46340 AAW	NEBLS	10//99-12//99
	Nevada	S	21.81 MW	25.11 AW	52240 AAW	NVBLS	10//99-12//99
	Las Vegas MSA, NV-AZ	S	25.53 MW	21.86 AW	53110 AAW	NVBLS	10//99-12//99
	Reno MSA, NV	S	22.57 MW	20.66 AW	46950 AAW	NVBLS	10//99-12//99
	New Hampshire	S	20.25 MW	22.35 AW	46490 AAW	NHBLS	10//99-12//99
	Manchester PMSA, NH	S	21.38 MW	19.69 AW	44480 AAW	NHBLS	10//99-12//99
	Nashua PMSA, NH	S	28.25 MW	29.24 AW	58760 AAW	NHBLS	10//99-12//99
	Portsmouth-Rochester PMSA, NH-ME	S	19.84 MW	16.54 AW	41260 AAW	NHBLS	10//99-12//99
	New Jersey	S	34.51 MW	34.77 AW	72310 AAW	NJBLS	10//99-12//99
	Atlantic-Cape May PMSA, NJ	S	29.90 MW	25.88 AW	62190 AAW	NJBLS	10//99-12//99
	Bergen-Passaic PMSA, NJ	S	37.45 MW	36.50 AW	77900 AAW	NJBLS	10//99-12//99
	Jersey City PMSA, NJ	S	33.32 MW	33.03 AW	69310 AAW	NJBLS	10//99-12//99
	Middlesex-Somerset-Hunterdon PMSA, NJ	S	34.71 MW	34.44 AW	72190 AAW	NJBLS	10//99-12//99
	Monmouth-Ocean PMSA, NJ	S	33.13 MW	34.48 AW	68920 AAW	NJBLS	10//99-12//99
	Newark PMSA, NJ	S	35.99 MW	36.74 AW	74850 AAW	NJBLS	10//99-12//99
	Trenton PMSA, NJ	S	29.84 MW	29.05 AW	62070 AAW	NJBLS	10//99-12//99
	Vineland-Millville-Bridgeton PMSA, NJ	S	27.84 MW	27.08 AW	57910 AAW	NJBLS	10//99-12//99
	New Mexico	S	17.34 MW	19.76 AW	41090 AAW	NMBLS	10//99-12//99
	Albuquerque MSA, NM	S	22.13 MW	18.99 AW	46020 AAW	NMBLS	10//99-12//99
	Santa Fe MSA, NM	S	14.02 MW	10.56 AW	29160 AAW	NMBLS	10//99-12//99
	New York	S	26.25 MW	29.09 AW	60520 AAW	NYBLS	10//99-12//99
	Albany-Schenectady-Troy MSA, NY	S	25.79 MW	25.26 AW	53640 AAW	NYBLS	10//99-12//99
	Binghamton MSA, NY	S	29.57 MW	25.10 AW	61510 AAW	NYBLS	10//99-12//99
	Buffalo-Niagara Falls MSA, NY	S	25.73 MW	23.54 AW	53530 AAW	NYBLS	10//99-12//99
	Dutchess County PMSA, NY	S	28.56 MW	24.53 AW	59410 AAW	NYBLS	10//99-12//99
	Glens Falls MSA, NY	S	27.36 MW	26.47 AW	56910 AAW	NYBLS	10//99-12//99
	Nassau-Suffolk PMSA, NY	S	29.26 MW	28.73 AW	60860 AAW	NYBLS	10//99-12//99
	New York PMSA, NY	S	31.05 MW	27.39 AW	64580 AAW	NYBLS	10//99-12//99
	Newburgh PMSA, NY-PA	S	27.58 MW	24.84 AW	57370 AAW	NYBLS	10//99-12//99
	Rochester MSA, NY	S	25.89 MW	24.70 AW	53860 AAW	NYBLS	10//99-12//99
	Syracuse MSA, NY	S	25.08 MW	23.11 AW	52170 AAW	NYBLS	10//99-12//99
	Utica-Rome MSA, NY	S	24.67 MW	23.16 AW	51310 AAW	NYBLS	10//99-12//99
	North Carolina	S	20.15 MW	22.69 AW	47190 AAW	NCBLS	10//99-12//99
	Asheville MSA, NC	S	20.10 MW	18.55 AW	41810 AAW	NCBLS	10//99-12//99
	Charlotte-Gastonia-Rock Hill MSA, NC-SC	S	25.22 MW	22.75 AW	52450 AAW	NCBLS	10//99-12//99
	Fayetteville MSA, NC	S	19.07 MW	17.12 AW	39670 AAW	NCBLS	10//99-12//99
	Goldsboro MSA, NC	S	19.10 MW	16.02 AW	39730 AAW	NCBLS	10//99-12//99
	Greensboro--Winston-Salem--High Point MSA, NC	S	21.82 MW	19.23 AW	45390 AAW	NCBLS	10//99-12//99
	Greenville MSA, NC	S	21.70 MW	18.77 AW	45140 AAW	NCBLS	10//99-12//99
	Hickory-Morganton-Lenoir MSA, NC	S	20.48 MW	17.66 AW	42600 AAW	NCBLS	10//99-12//99
	Jacksonville MSA, NC	S	16.89 MW	15.75 AW	35120 AAW	NCBLS	10//99-12//99
	Raleigh-Durham-Chapel Hill MSA, NC	S	24.80 MW	22.34 AW	51580 AAW	NCBLS	10//99-12//99
	Rocky Mount MSA, NC	S	20.54 MW	20.79 AW	42720 AAW	NCBLS	10//99-12//99
	Wilmington MSA, NC	S	20.82 MW	16.34 AW	43320 AAW	NCBLS	10//99-12//99
	North Dakota	S	16.37 MW	19.25 AW	40040 AAW	NDBLS	10//99-12//99
	Bismarck MSA, ND	S	18.11 MW	15.69 AW	37660 AAW	NDBLS	10//99-12//99

Purchasing Manager

Occupation/Type/Industry	Location	Per	Low	Mid	High	Source	Date
Purchasing Manager	Fargo-Moorhead MSA, ND-MN	S	21.99 MW	19.96 AW	45740 AAW	NDBLS	10//99-12//99
	Grand Forks MSA, ND-MN	S	22.54 MW	18.58 AW	46880 AAW	NDBLS	10//99-12//99
	Ohio	S	22.29 MW	24.02 AW	49950 AAW	OHBLS	10//99-12//99
	Akron PMSA, OH	S	23.54 MW	22.57 AW	48960 AAW	OHBLS	10//99-12//99
	Canton-Massillon MSA, OH	S	22.28 MW	20.42 AW	46350 AAW	OHBLS	10//99-12//99
	Cincinnati PMSA, OH-KY-IN	S	26.24 MW	24.54 AW	54570 AAW	OHBLS	10//99-12//99
	Cleveland-Lorain-Elyria PMSA, OH	S	24.65 MW	22.84 AW	51270 AAW	OHBLS	10//99-12//99
	Columbus MSA, OH	S	24.41 MW	22.79 AW	50780 AAW	OHBLS	10//99-12//99
	Dayton-Springfield MSA, OH	S	26.58 MW	26.11 AW	55290 AAW	OHBLS	10//99-12//99
	Hamilton-Middletown PMSA, OH	S	21.78 MW	19.98 AW	45300 AAW	OHBLS	10//99-12//99
	Lima MSA, OH	S	17.44 MW	16.88 AW	36270 AAW	OHBLS	10//99-12//99
	Mansfield MSA, OH	S	19.91 MW	19.16 AW	41410 AAW	OHBLS	10//99-12//99
	Steubenville-Weirton MSA, OH-WV	S	19.26 MW	15.68 AW	40070 AAW	OHBLS	10//99-12//99
	Toledo MSA, OH	S	21.89 MW	20.52 AW	45520 AAW	OHBLS	10//99-12//99
	Youngstown-Warren MSA, OH	S	28.67 MW	22.27 AW	59630 AAW	OHBLS	10//99-12//99
	Oklahoma	S	18.12 MW	20.51 AW	42660 AAW	OKBLS	10//99-12//99
	Lawton MSA, OK	S	17.74 MW	14.95 AW	36900 AAW	OKBLS	10//99-12//99
	Oklahoma City MSA, OK	S	21.74 MW	19.28 AW	45210 AAW	OKBLS	10//99-12//99
	Tulsa MSA, OK	S	23.70 MW	21.35 AW	49290 AAW	OKBLS	10//99-12//99
	Oregon	S	24.01 MW	26.71 AW	55550 AAW	ORBLS	10//99-12//99
	Eugene-Springfield MSA, OR	S	25.58 MW	22.12 AW	53200 AAW	ORBLS	10//99-12//99
	Portland-Vancouver PMSA, OR-WA	S	27.80 MW	25.52 AW	57820 AAW	ORBLS	10//99-12//99
	Salem PMSA, OR	S	21.12 MW	19.56 AW	43930 AAW	ORBLS	10//99-12//99
	Pennsylvania	S	21.54 MW	23.56 AW	49000 AAW	PABLS	10//99-12//99
	Allentown-Bethlehem-Easton MSA, PA	S	24.07 MW	22.75 AW	50070 AAW	PABLS	10//99-12//99
	Altoona MSA, PA	S	23.19 MW	21.03 AW	48240 AAW	PABLS	10//99-12//99
	Erie MSA, PA	S	21.73 MW	21.10 AW	45190 AAW	PABLS	10//99-12//99
	Harrisburg-Lebanon-Carlisle MSA, PA	S	24.17 MW	23.23 AW	50270 AAW	PABLS	10//99-12//99
	Johnstown MSA, PA	S	20.39 MW	17.68 AW	42410 AAW	PABLS	10//99-12//99
	Lancaster MSA, PA	S	20.72 MW	17.53 AW	43090 AAW	PABLS	10//99-12//99
	Philadelphia PMSA, PA-NJ	S	28.47 MW	26.79 AW	59230 AAW	PABLS	10//99-12//99
	Pittsburgh MSA, PA	S	22.50 MW	20.81 AW	46790 AAW	PABLS	10//99-12//99
	Reading MSA, PA	S	22.65 MW	19.93 AW	47110 AAW	PABLS	10//99-12//99
	Scranton--Wilkes-Barre--Hazleton MSA, PA	S	20.84 MW	18.72 AW	43360 AAW	PABLS	10//99-12//99
	Sharon MSA, PA	S	20.90 MW	18.94 AW	43470 AAW	PABLS	10//99-12//99
	Williamsport MSA, PA	S	23.87 MW	22.79 AW	49650 AAW	PABLS	10//99-12//99
	York MSA, PA	S	24.33 MW	21.88 AW	50600 AAW	PABLS	10//99-12//99
	Rhode Island	S	25.01 MW	26.75 AW	55640 AAW	RIBLS	10//99-12//99
	Providence-Fall River-Warwick MSA, RI-MA	S	25.96 MW	24.18 AW	54000 AAW	RIBLS	10//99-12//99
	South Carolina	S	19.39 MW	21.76 AW	45260 AAW	SCBLS	10//99-12//99
	Charleston-North Charleston MSA, SC	S	21.24 MW	18.85 AW	44170 AAW	SCBLS	10//99-12//99
	Columbia MSA, SC	S	20.01 MW	17.77 AW	41630 AAW	SCBLS	10//99-12//99
	Florence MSA, SC	S	21.44 MW	19.77 AW	44590 AAW	SCBLS	10//99-12//99
	Greenville-Spartanburg-Anderson MSA, SC	S	21.48 MW	20.07 AW	44670 AAW	SCBLS	10//99-12//99
	Myrtle Beach MSA, SC	S	17.45 MW	15.81 AW	36290 AAW	SCBLS	10//99-12//99
	South Dakota	S	24.55 MW	26.46 AW	55040 AAW	SDBLS	10//99-12//99
	Sioux Falls MSA, SD	S	25.98 MW	24.40 AW	54040 AAW	SDBLS	10//99-12//99
	Tennessee	S	19.56 MW	20.88 AW	43430 AAW	TNBLS	10//99-12//99
	Chattanooga MSA, TN-GA	S	20.83 MW	19.75 AW	43330 AAW	TNBLS	10//99-12//99
	Clarksville-Hopkinsville MSA, TN-KY	S	23.39 MW	24.03 AW	48650 AAW	TNBLS	10//99-12//99
	Jackson MSA, TN	S	22.79 MW	21.73 AW	47400 AAW	TNBLS	10//99-12//99
	Johnson City-Kingsport-Bristol MSA, TN-VA	S	19.76 MW	18.47 AW	41100 AAW	TNBLS	10//99-12//99
	Memphis MSA, TN-AR-MS	S	22.73 MW	20.96 AW	47280 AAW	MSBLS	10//99-12//99
	Nashville MSA, TN	S	23.26 MW	21.25 AW	48370 AAW	TNBLS	10//99-12//99
	Texas	S	22.33 MW	24.76 AW	51490 AAW	TXBLS	10//99-12//99
	Abilene MSA, TX	S	17.24 MW	14.97 AW	35850 AAW	TXBLS	10//99-12//99
	Amarillo MSA, TX	S	21.13 MW	21.63 AW	43950 AAW	TXBLS	10//99-12//99
	Austin-San Marcos MSA, TX	S	22.33 MW	20.06 AW	46440 AAW	TXBLS	10//99-12//99

AAW Average annual wage	AOH Average offered, high	ASH Average starting, high	H Hourly	M Monthly	S Special: hourly and annual
AE Average entry wage	AOL Average offered, low	ASL Average starting, low	HI Highest wage paid	MTC Median total compensation	TQ Third quartile wage
AEX Average experienced wage	APH Average pay, high range	AW Average wage paid	HR High end range	MW Median wage paid	W Weekly
AO Average offered	APL Average pay, low range	FQ First quartile wage	LR Low end range	SQ Second quartile wage	Y Yearly

Purchasing Manager

Occupation/Type/Industry	Location	Per	Low	Mid	High	Source	Date
Purchasing Manager	Beaumont-Port Arthur MSA, TX	S	27.66 MW	25.92 AW	57530 AAW	TXBLS	10//99-12//99
	Brazoria PMSA, TX	S	25.16 MW	23.29 AW	52340 AAW	TXBLS	10//99-12//99
	Brownsville-Harlingen-San Benito MSA, TX	S	18.22 MW	16.85 AW	37900 AAW	TXBLS	10//99-12//99
	Bryan-College Station MSA, TX	S	19.50 MW	17.83 AW	40570 AAW	TXBLS	10//99-12//99
	Corpus Christi MSA, TX	S	21.71 MW	18.98 AW	45160 AAW	TXBLS	10//99-12//99
	Dallas PMSA, TX	S	27.33 MW	24.65 AW	56850 AAW	TXBLS	10//99-12//99
	El Paso MSA, TX	S	19.81 MW	17.99 AW	41200 AAW	TXBLS	10//99-12//99
	Fort Worth-Arlington PMSA, TX	S	24.91 MW	23.46 AW	51800 AAW	TXBLS	10//99-12//99
	Galveston-Texas City PMSA, TX	S	20.52 MW	18.16 AW	42670 AAW	TXBLS	10//99-12//99
	Houston PMSA, TX	S	26.12 MW	23.78 AW	54330 AAW	TXBLS	10//99-12//99
	Killeen-Temple MSA, TX	S	17.54 MW	14.46 AW	36490 AAW	TXBLS	10//99-12//99
	Laredo MSA, TX	S	21.50 MW	20.01 AW	44720 AAW	TXBLS	10//99-12//99
	Longview-Marshall MSA, TX	S	23.13 MW	21.44 AW	48110 AAW	TXBLS	10//99-12//99
	Lubbock MSA, TX	S	18.82 MW	15.61 AW	39150 AAW	TXBLS	10//99-12//99
	McAllen-Edinburg-Mission MSA, TX	S	24.63 MW	22.31 AW	51220 AAW	TXBLS	10//99-12//99
	Odessa-Midland MSA, TX	S	23.05 MW	20.78 AW	47940 AAW	TXBLS	10//99-12//99
	San Angelo MSA, TX	S	20.10 MW	18.40 AW	41820 AAW	TXBLS	10//99-12//99
	San Antonio MSA, TX	S	25.56 MW	24.05 AW	53160 AAW	TXBLS	10//99-12//99
	Sherman-Denison MSA, TX	S	20.97 MW	18.99 AW	43620 AAW	TXBLS	10//99-12//99
	Texarkana MSA, TX-Texarkana, AR	S	19.98 MW	17.72 AW	41550 AAW	TXBLS	10//99-12//99
	Tyler MSA, TX	S	19.25 MW	17.56 AW	40030 AAW	TXBLS	10//99-12//99
	Victoria MSA, TX	S	18.18 MW	16.62 AW	37820 AAW	TXBLS	10//99-12//99
	Waco MSA, TX	S	20.21 MW	19.30 AW	42040 AAW	TXBLS	10//99-12//99
	Wichita Falls MSA, TX	S	20.80 MW	20.10 AW	43270 AAW	TXBLS	10//99-12//99
	Utah	S	17.98 MW	20.18 AW	41980 AAW	UTBLS	10//99-12//99
	Provo-Orem MSA, UT	S	17.81 MW	16.35 AW	37040 AAW	UTBLS	10//99-12//99
	Salt Lake City-Ogden MSA, UT	S	21.27 MW	19.04 AW	44250 AAW	UTBLS	10//99-12//99
	Vermont	S	23.33 MW	25.08 AW	52170 AAW	VTBLS	10//99-12//99
	Burlington MSA, VT	S	29.13 MW	30.18 AW	60600 AAW	VTBLS	10//99-12//99
	Virginia	S	24.42 MW	25.94 AW	53950 AAW	VABLS	10//99-12//99
	Charlottesville MSA, VA	S	23.91 MW	22.20 AW	49730 AAW	VABLS	10//99-12//99
	Lynchburg MSA, VA	S	19.78 MW	21.17 AW	41140 AAW	VABLS	10//99-12//99
	Norfolk-Virginia Beach-Newport News MSA, VA-NC	S	25.52 MW	25.55 AW	53070 AAW	VABLS	10//99-12//99
	Richmond-Petersburg MSA, VA	S	26.08 MW	24.26 AW	54250 AAW	VABLS	10//99-12//99
	Roanoke MSA, VA	S	22.68 MW	21.54 AW	47180 AAW	VABLS	10//99-12//99
	Washington	S	23.27 MW	25.47 AW	52970 AAW	WABLS	10//99-12//99
	Bellingham MSA, WA	S	19.84 MW	17.71 AW	41260 AAW	WABLS	10//99-12//99
	Bremerton PMSA, WA	S	20.85 MW	17.10 AW	43370 AAW	WABLS	10//99-12//99
	Olympia PMSA, WA	S	20.27 MW	16.81 AW	42170 AAW	WABLS	10//99-12//99
	Richland-Kennewick-Pasco MSA, WA	S	23.39 MW	22.38 AW	48640 AAW	WABLS	10//99-12//99
	Seattle-Bellevue-Everett PMSA, WA	S	27.72 MW	25.50 AW	57660 AAW	WABLS	10//99-12//99
	Spokane MSA, WA	S	21.22 MW	19.52 AW	44150 AAW	WABLS	10//99-12//99
	Tacoma PMSA, WA	S	24.79 MW	23.45 AW	51560 AAW	WABLS	10//99-12//99
	Yakima MSA, WA	S	28.77 MW	23.38 AW	59830 AAW	WABLS	10//99-12//99
	West Virginia	S	15.97 MW	18.34 AW	38150 AAW	WVBLS	10//99-12//99
	Charleston MSA, WV	S	19.33 MW	17.42 AW	40210 AAW	WVBLS	10//99-12//99
	Huntington-Ashland MSA, WV-KY-OH	S	20.15 MW	18.77 AW	41920 AAW	WVBLS	10//99-12//99
	Parkersburg-Marietta MSA, WV-OH	S	19.17 MW	14.81 AW	39870 AAW	WVBLS	10//99-12//99
	Wheeling MSA, WV-OH	S	19.21 MW	16.20 AW	39960 AAW	WVBLS	10//99-12//99
	Wisconsin	S	20.02 MW	21.70 AW	45130 AAW	WIBLS	10//99-12//99
	Appleton-Oshkosh-Neenah MSA, WI	S	23.20 MW	22.65 AW	48260 AAW	WIBLS	10//99-12//99
	Eau Claire MSA, WI	S	16.99 MW	13.37 AW	35330 AAW	WIBLS	10//99-12//99
	Green Bay MSA, WI	S	24.56 MW	23.07 AW	51080 AAW	WIBLS	10//99-12//99
	Janesville-Beloit MSA, WI	S	23.10 MW	21.42 AW	48050 AAW	WIBLS	10//99-12//99
	Kenosha PMSA, WI	S	21.93 MW	20.90 AW	45620 AAW	WIBLS	10//99-12//99
	La Crosse MSA, WI-MN	S	22.60 MW	21.00 AW	47010 AAW	WIBLS	10//99-12//99

AAW Average annual wage	AOH Average offered, high	ASH Average starting, high	H Hourly	M Monthly	S Special: hourly and annual
AE Average entry wage	AOL Average offered, low	ASL Average starting, low	HI Highest wage paid	MTC Median total compensation	TQ Third quartile wage
AEX Average experienced wage	APH Average pay, high range	AW Average wage paid	HR High end range	MW Median wage paid	W Weekly
AO Average offered	APL Average pay, low range	FQ First quartile wage	LR Low end range	SQ Second quartile wage	Y Yearly

Occupation/Type/Industry	Location	Per	Low	Mid	High	Source	Date
Purchasing Manager	Madison MSA, WI	S	21.61 MW	19.84 AW	44940 AAW	WIBLS	10//99-12//99
	Milwaukee-Waukesha PMSA, WI	S	24.40 MW	22.63 AW	50750 AAW	WIBLS	10//99-12//99
	Racine PMSA, WI	S	24.66 MW	24.01 AW	51300 AAW	WIBLS	10//99-12//99
	Sheboygan MSA, WI	S	20.63 MW	18.87 AW	42900 AAW	WIBLS	10//99-12//99
	Wausau MSA, WI	S	19.83 MW	18.13 AW	41240 AAW	WIBLS	10//99-12//99
	Wyoming	S	14.7 MW	15.97 AW	33210 AAW	WYBLS	10//99-12//99
	Cheyenne MSA, WY	S	18.92 MW	18.48 AW	39360 AAW	WYBLS	10//99-12//99
	Puerto Rico	S	18.87 MW	21.25 AW	44210 AAW	PRBLS	10//99-12//99
	Caguas PMSA, PR	S	24.57 MW	20.97 AW	51100 AAW	PRBLS	10//99-12//99
	San Juan-Bayamon PMSA, PR	S	20.88 MW	18.38 AW	43420 AAW	PRBLS	10//99-12//99
	Virgin Islands	S	19.09 MW	20.78 AW	43230 AAW	VIBLS	10//99-12//99
	Guam	S	16.17 MW	17.58 AW	36570 AAW	GUBLS	10//99-12//99
Manufacturing	United States	Y		52637 AW		WARD3	1998
Quality Assurance Manager							
Foundry	United States	Y	46000 MW	49100 AW		MODCAS	1999
Information Technology	Atlanta, GA	Y		80986 AW		ATBUS	3//00
Quality Control Executive							
Senior, Supply Chain Management	United States	Y		105000 AW		AMSHIP	2000
Radiation Therapist	Alabama	S	19.4 MW	19.45 AW	40450 AAW	ALBLS	10//99-12//99
	Arizona	S	17.97 MW	18.19 AW	37830 AAW	AZBLS	10//99-12//99
	California	S	24.33 MW	24.07 AW	50050 AAW	CABLS	10//99-12//99
	Colorado	S	18.12 MW	18.34 AW	38150 AAW	COBLS	10//99-12//99
	Connecticut	S	24.12 MW	24.91 AW	51800 AAW	CTBLS	10//99-12//99
	District of Columbia	S	19.43 MW	18.18 AW	37810 AAW	DCBLS	10//99-12//99
	Florida	S	19.96 MW	20.72 AW	43100 AAW	FLBLS	10//99-12//99
	Georgia	S	17.95 MW	17.48 AW	36350 AAW	GABLS	10//99-12//99
	Illinois	S	21.15 MW	21.27 AW	44250 AAW	ILBLS	10//99-12//99
	Indiana	S	17.26 MW	23.08 AW	48000 AAW	INBLS	10//99-12//99
	Iowa	S	14.26 MW	14.88 AW	30950 AAW	IABLS	10//99-12//99
	Kansas	S	18.85 MW	19.60 AW	40760 AAW	KSBLS	10//99-12//99
	Kentucky	S	16.29 MW	18.01 AW	37470 AAW	KYBLS	10//99-12//99
	Louisiana	S	18.19 MW	18.45 AW	38380 AAW	LABLS	10//99-12//99
	Maine	S	16.26 MW	17.54 AW	36490 AAW	MEBLS	10//99-12//99
	Maryland	S	18.94 MW	22.80 AW	47430 AAW	MDBLS	10//99-12//99
	Massachusetts	S	24.33 MW	25.16 AW	52330 AAW	MABLS	10//99-12//99
	Michigan	S	22.15 MW	22.93 AW	47700 AAW	MIBLS	10//99-12//99
	Minnesota	S	18.92 MW	19.06 AW	39640 AAW	MNBLS	10//99-12//99
	Mississippi	S	18.48 MW	18.30 AW	38070 AAW	MSBLS	10//99-12//99
	Missouri	S	20.58 MW	20.99 AW	43660 AAW	MOBLS	10//99-12//99
	Montana	S	21.31 MW	21.65 AW	45040 AAW	MTBLS	10//99-12//99
	New Jersey	S	21.07 MW	22.57 AW	46940 AAW	NJBLS	10//99-12//99
	New York	S	24.47 MW	25.09 AW	52190 AAW	NYBLS	10//99-12//99
	North Carolina	S	18.76 MW	19.15 AW	39830 AAW	NCBLS	10//99-12//99
	Ohio	S	18.38 MW	18.59 AW	38670 AAW	OHBLS	10//99-12//99
	Oklahoma	S	16.25 MW	16.32 AW	33950 AAW	OKBLS	10//99-12//99
	Oregon	S	20.19 MW	20.68 AW	43020 AAW	ORBLS	10//99-12//99
	Pennsylvania	S	19.07 MW	19.28 AW	40100 AAW	PABLS	10//99-12//99
	South Carolina	S	17.93 MW	19.04 AW	39600 AAW	SCBLS	10//99-12//99
	Tennessee	S	19.02 MW	19.72 AW	41010 AAW	TNBLS	10//99-12//99
	Texas	S	19.01 MW	19.26 AW	40060 AAW	TXBLS	10//99-12//99
	Virginia	S	21.67 MW	22.89 AW	47600 AAW	VABLS	10//99-12//99
	Washington	S	22.51 MW	23.82 AW	49540 AAW	WABLS	10//99-12//99
	West Virginia	S	18.64 MW	19.41 AW	40380 AAW	WVBLS	10//99-12//99
	Wisconsin	S	19.69 MW	20.14 AW	41880 AAW	WIBLS	10//99-12//99
	Wyoming	S	15.63 MW	15.61 AW	32460 AAW	WYBLS	10//99-12//99
	Puerto Rico	S	8.92 MW	12.97 AW	26980 AAW	PRBLS	10//99-12//99
Radio Mechanic	Alabama	S	12.41 MW	12.88 AW	26780 AAW	ALBLS	10//99-12//99
	California	S	20.1 MW	19.48 AW	40510 AAW	CABLS	10//99-12//99
	Colorado	S	18.16 MW	17.33 AW	36060 AAW	COBLS	10//99-12//99
	Connecticut	S	14.12 MW	15.08 AW	31380 AAW	CTBLS	10//99-12//99
	Florida	S	14.72 MW	14.76 AW	30690 AAW	FLBLS	10//99-12//99
	Georgia	S	10.99 MW	11.57 AW	24070 AAW	GABLS	10//99-12//99
	Illinois	S	14.21 MW	14.58 AW	30330 AAW	ILBLS	10//99-12//99
	Indiana	S	13.02 MW	13.38 AW	27840 AAW	INBLS	10//99-12//99
	Kentucky	S	16.04 MW	16.64 AW	34610 AAW	KYBLS	10//99-12//99
	Michigan	S	17.45 MW	16.97 AW	35310 AAW	MIBLS	10//99-12//99
	Minnesota	S	17.62 MW	17.88 AW	37190 AAW	MNBLS	10//99-12//99
	Missouri	S	15.95 MW	15.86 AW	32990 AAW	MOBLS	10//99-12//99

AAW	Average annual wage	AOH	Average offered, high	ASH	Average starting, high	H	Hourly	M	Monthly	S	Special: hourly and annual
AE	Average entry wage	AOL	Average offered, low	ASL	Average starting, low	HI	Highest wage paid	MTC	Median total compensation	TQ	Third quartile wage
AEX	Average experienced wage	APH	Average pay, high range	AW	Average wage paid	HR	High end range	MW	Median wage paid	W	Weekly
AO	Average offered	APL	Average pay, low range	FQ	First quartile wage	LR	Low end range	SQ	Second quartile wage	Y	Yearly

1199

Occupation/Type/Industry	Location	Per	Low	Mid	High	Source	Date
Radio Mechanic	Nevada	S	17.52 MW	15.38 AW	31990 AAW	NVBLS	10//99-12//99
	New Hampshire	S	14.59 MW	14.79 AW	30770 AAW	NHBLS	10//99-12//99
	New Jersey	S	12.19 MW	12.46 AW	25920 AAW	NJBLS	10//99-12//99
	New York	S	13.99 MW	15.65 AW	32560 AAW	NYBLS	10//99-12//99
	North Carolina	S	15.13 MW	15.36 AW	31950 AAW	NCBLS	10//99-12//99
	North Dakota	S	10.08 MW	12.00 AW	24960 AAW	NDBLS	10//99-12//99
	Ohio	S	12.59 MW	13.69 AW	28470 AAW	OHBLS	10//99-12//99
	Oklahoma	S	15.13 MW	15.01 AW	31220 AAW	OKBLS	10//99-12//99
	Oregon	S	13.18 MW	14.30 AW	29750 AAW	ORBLS	10//99-12//99
	Pennsylvania	S	14.23 MW	14.50 AW	30170 AAW	PABLS	10//99-12//99
	South Carolina	S	17.78 MW	17.18 AW	35740 AAW	SCBLS	10//99-12//99
	South Dakota	S	13.17 MW	13.34 AW	27740 AAW	SDBLS	10//99-12//99
	Tennessee	S	17.09 MW	17.06 AW	35480 AAW	TNBLS	10//99-12//99
	Texas	S	13.9 MW	14.51 AW	30180 AAW	TXBLS	10//99-12//99
	Virginia	S	14.51 MW	14.35 AW	29860 AAW	VABLS	10//99-12//99
	Washington	S	17.96 MW	17.41 AW	36210 AAW	WABLS	10//99-12//99
	West Virginia	S	15.23 MW	15.80 AW	32870 AAW	WVBLS	10//99-12//99
	Wyoming	S	12.56 MW	14.63 AW	30420 AAW	WYBLS	10//99-12//99
Radio Operator	Alabama	S	11.5 MW	11.53 AW	23980 AAW	ALBLS	10//99-12//99
	California	S	11.93 MW	14.82 AW	30830 AAW	CABLS	10//99-12//99
	Connecticut	S	10.91 MW	11.19 AW	23270 AAW	CTBLS	10//99-12//99
	Delaware	S	13.53 MW	13.75 AW	28600 AAW	DEBLS	10//99-12//99
	Florida	S	11.46 MW	12.22 AW	25410 AAW	FLBLS	10//99-12//99
	Georgia	S	11.11 MW	12.09 AW	25140 AAW	GABLS	10//99-12//99
	Illinois	S	11.4 MW	11.11 AW	23100 AAW	ILBLS	10//99-12//99
	Iowa	S	8.39 MW	10.14 AW	21100 AAW	IABLS	10//99-12//99
	Louisiana	S	8.66 MW	9.31 AW	19360 AAW	LABLS	10//99-12//99
	Maryland	S	13.25 MW	13.29 AW	27640 AAW	MDBLS	10//99-12//99
	Michigan	S	13.65 MW	13.87 AW	28840 AAW	MIBLS	10//99-12//99
	Mississippi	S	9.15 MW	10.23 AW	21270 AAW	MSBLS	10//99-12//99
	New York	S	11.44 MW	14.50 AW	30160 AAW	NYBLS	10//99-12//99
	North Carolina	S	14.36 MW	14.02 AW	29160 AAW	NCBLS	10//99-12//99
	Pennsylvania	S	11.78 MW	12.70 AW	26410 AAW	PABLS	10//99-12//99
	South Carolina	S	6.09 MW	7.64 AW	15880 AAW	SCBLS	10//99-12//99
	Tennessee	S	9.74 MW	9.88 AW	20560 AAW	TNBLS	10//99-12//99
	Texas	S	14.2 MW	13.37 AW	27800 AAW	TXBLS	10//99-12//99
	Washington	S	15.53 MW	16.04 AW	33370 AAW	WABLS	10//99-12//99
	Puerto Rico	S	6.01 MW	6.11 AW	12710 AAW	PRBLS	10//99-12//99
Radiologic Technologist and Technician	Alabama	S	14.56 MW	14.54 AW	30240 AAW	ALBLS	10//99-12//99
	Alaska	S	21.07 MW	20.99 AW	43650 AAW	AKBLS	10//99-12//99
	Arizona	S	14.97 MW	15.05 AW	31290 AAW	AZBLS	10//99-12//99
	Arkansas	S	13.9 MW	14.56 AW	30270 AAW	ARBLS	10//99-12//99
	California	S	20.17 MW	20.85 AW	43370 AAW	CABLS	10//99-12//99
	Colorado	S	15.7 MW	15.93 AW	33140 AAW	COBLS	10//99-12//99
	Connecticut	S	17.7 MW	18.10 AW	37640 AAW	CTBLS	10//99-12//99
	Delaware	S	18.13 MW	17.85 AW	37120 AAW	DEBLS	10//99-12//99
	District of Columbia	S	16.89 MW	16.99 AW	35330 AAW	DCBLS	10//99-12//99
	Florida	S	16.27 MW	16.60 AW	34540 AAW	FLBLS	10//99-12//99
	Georgia	S	15.16 MW	15.16 AW	31540 AAW	GABLS	10//99-12//99
	Hawaii	S	19.68 MW	20.51 AW	42650 AAW	HIBLS	10//99-12//99
	Idaho	S	15.09 MW	15.42 AW	32070 AAW	IDBLS	10//99-12//99
	Illinois	S	15.61 MW	16.13 AW	33540 AAW	ILBLS	10//99-12//99
	Indiana	S	15.55 MW	15.37 AW	31980 AAW	INBLS	10//99-12//99
	Iowa	S	13.2 MW	13.79 AW	28690 AAW	IABLS	10//99-12//99
	Kansas	S	14.28 MW	14.26 AW	29660 AAW	KSBLS	10//99-12//99
	Kentucky	S	15.71 MW	16.38 AW	34080 AAW	KYBLS	10//99-12//99
	Louisiana	S	13.39 MW	13.79 AW	28680 AAW	LABLS	10//99-12//99
	Maine	S	15.12 MW	15.39 AW	32000 AAW	MEBLS	10//99-12//99
	Maryland	S	19.5 MW	19.55 AW	40660 AAW	MDBLS	10//99-12//99
	Massachusetts	S	19.38 MW	19.78 AW	41130 AAW	MABLS	10//99-12//99
	Michigan	S	16.8 MW	16.89 AW	35120 AAW	MIBLS	10//99-12//99
	Minnesota	S	16.14 MW	16.78 AW	34910 AAW	MNBLS	10//99-12//99
	Mississippi	S	14.95 MW	15.94 AW	33160 AAW	MSBLS	10//99-12//99
	Missouri	S	15.2 MW	15.35 AW	31920 AAW	MOBLS	10//99-12//99
	Montana	S	14.16 MW	14.58 AW	30330 AAW	MTBLS	10//99-12//99
	Nebraska	S	14.35 MW	14.56 AW	30290 AAW	NEBLS	10//99-12//99
	Nevada	S	18.28 MW	18.56 AW	38610 AAW	NVBLS	10//99-12//99
	New Hampshire	S	15.93 MW	16.08 AW	33450 AAW	NHBLS	10//99-12//99
	New Jersey	S	20.28 MW	20.46 AW	42560 AAW	NJBLS	10//99-12//99

AAW	Average annual wage	AOH	Average offered, high	ASH	Average starting, high	H	Hourly	M	Monthly	S	Special: hourly and annual
AE	Average entry wage	AOL	Average offered, low	ASL	Average starting, low	HI	Highest wage paid	MTC	Median total compensation	TQ	Third quartile wage
AEX	Average experienced wage	APH	Average pay, high range	AW	Average wage paid	HR	High end range	MW	Median wage paid	W	Weekly
AO	Average offered	APL	Average pay, low range	FQ	First quartile wage	LR	Low end range	SQ	Second quartile wage	Y	Yearly

Occupation/Type/Industry	Location	Per	Low	Mid	High	Source	Date
Radiologic Technologist and Technician	New Mexico	S	14.88 MW	15.04 AW	31290 AAW	NMBLS	10//99-12//99
	New York	S	19.36 MW	19.59 AW	40740 AAW	NYBLS	10//99-12//99
	North Carolina	S	15.06 MW	15.30 AW	31830 AAW	NCBLS	10//99-12//99
	Ohio	S	15.15 MW	15.10 AW	31400 AAW	OHBLS	10//99-12//99
	Oklahoma	S	14.13 MW	14.74 AW	30660 AAW	OKBLS	10//99-12//99
	Oregon	S	17.57 MW	17.51 AW	36420 AAW	ORBLS	10//99-12//99
	Pennsylvania	S	14.88 MW	15.29 AW	31810 AAW	PABLS	10//99-12//99
	Rhode Island	S	16.41 MW	17.15 AW	35680 AAW	RIBLS	10//99-12//99
	South Carolina	S	15.25 MW	16.18 AW	33660 AAW	SCBLS	10//99-12//99
	South Dakota	S	14.56 MW	14.78 AW	30730 AAW	SDBLS	10//99-12//99
	Tennessee	S	15.47 MW	15.61 AW	32470 AAW	TNBLS	10//99-12//99
	Texas	S	15.28 MW	15.50 AW	32230 AAW	TXBLS	10//99-12//99
	Utah	S	15.69 MW	16.11 AW	33520 AAW	UTBLS	10//99-12//99
	Vermont	S	16.04 MW	16.19 AW	33670 AAW	VTBLS	10//99-12//99
	Virginia	S	16.26 MW	16.95 AW	35250 AAW	VABLS	10//99-12//99
	Washington	S	18.33 MW	18.38 AW	38230 AAW	WABLS	10//99-12//99
	West Virginia	S	12.93 MW	13.32 AW	27700 AAW	WVBLS	10//99-12//99
	Wisconsin	S	15.07 MW	15.37 AW	31960 AAW	WIBLS	10//99-12//99
	Wyoming	S	12.54 MW	12.74 AW	26500 AAW	WYBLS	10//99-12//99
	Puerto Rico	S	7.61 MW	7.86 AW	16350 AAW	PRBLS	10//99-12//99
	Guam	S	14.27 MW	15.42 AW	32070 AAW	GUBLS	10//99-12//99
Radiological Technician	United States	H		16.73 AW		NCS98	1998
Rail Car Repairer	Alabama	S	18.06 MW	17.59 AW	36590 AAW	ALBLS	10//99-12//99
	Arizona	S	18.12 MW	17.64 AW	36690 AAW	AZBLS	10//99-12//99
	Arkansas	S	17.44 MW	17.04 AW	35450 AAW	ARBLS	10//99-12//99
	California	S	18.35 MW	18.72 AW	38930 AAW	CABLS	10//99-12//99
	Colorado	S	18.4 MW	18.87 AW	39240 AAW	COBLS	10//99-12//99
	Florida	S	16.51 MW	15.71 AW	32680 AAW	FLBLS	10//99-12//99
	Illinois	S	18.34 MW	18.28 AW	38020 AAW	ILBLS	10//99-12//99
	Kansas	S	18.61 MW	18.57 AW	38630 AAW	KSBLS	10//99-12//99
	Kentucky	S	17.7 MW	17.58 AW	36570 AAW	KYBLS	10//99-12//99
	Louisiana	S	18.46 MW	18.68 AW	38860 AAW	LABLS	10//99-12//99
	Maryland	S	18.81 MW	18.82 AW	39150 AAW	MDBLS	10//99-12//99
	Minnesota	S	19.79 MW	20.26 AW	42150 AAW	MNBLS	10//99-12//99
	Mississippi	S	13.12 MW	13.41 AW	27890 AAW	MSBLS	10//99-12//99
	Nebraska	S	17.29 MW	16.09 AW	33460 AAW	NEBLS	10//99-12//99
	New Jersey	S	19.95 MW	20.64 AW	42940 AAW	NJBLS	10//99-12//99
	New York	S	18.33 MW	18.16 AW	37770 AAW	NYBLS	10//99-12//99
	North Carolina	S	11.69 MW	13.00 AW	27040 AAW	NCBLS	10//99-12//99
	Ohio	S	17.97 MW	17.51 AW	36410 AAW	OHBLS	10//99-12//99
	Tennessee	S	17.76 MW	17.03 AW	35420 AAW	TNBLS	10//99-12//99
	Texas	S	17.66 MW	17.23 AW	35830 AAW	TXBLS	10//99-12//99
	Utah	S	18.44 MW	18.48 AW	38440 AAW	UTBLS	10//99-12//99
	Virginia	S	17.61 MW	17.00 AW	35350 AAW	VABLS	10//99-12//99
	Wisconsin	S	17.89 MW	17.64 AW	36700 AAW	WIBLS	10//99-12//99
Rail-Track Laying and Maintenance Equipment Operator	Alabama	S	17.88 MW	17.86 AW	37150 AAW	ALBLS	10//99-12//99
	Arizona	S	15.17 MW	16.26 AW	33820 AAW	AZBLS	10//99-12//99
	Arkansas	S	16.39 MW	15.40 AW	32030 AAW	ARBLS	10//99-12//99
	Colorado	S	18.49 MW	19.43 AW	40410 AAW	COBLS	10//99-12//99
	Florida	S	13.6 MW	13.83 AW	28770 AAW	FLBLS	10//99-12//99
	Illinois	S	17.78 MW	18.67 AW	38840 AAW	ILBLS	10//99-12//99
	Indiana	S	16.25 MW	16.49 AW	34290 AAW	INBLS	10//99-12//99
	Kansas	S	15.52 MW	16.09 AW	33460 AAW	KSBLS	10//99-12//99
	Kentucky	S	17.01 MW	16.84 AW	35030 AAW	KYBLS	10//99-12//99
	Maryland	S	15.32 MW	15.38 AW	31990 AAW	MDBLS	10//99-12//99
	Minnesota	S	17.92 MW	18.86 AW	39230 AAW	MNBLS	10//99-12//99
	Missouri	S	17.46 MW	16.91 AW	35170 AAW	MOBLS	10//99-12//99
	Montana	S	17.66 MW	18.16 AW	37780 AAW	MTBLS	10//99-12//99
	Nebraska	S	14.25 MW	14.41 AW	29980 AAW	NEBLS	10//99-12//99
	New Hampshire	S	15.5 MW	14.96 AW	31110 AAW	NHBLS	10//99-12//99
	New Jersey	S	19.88 MW	19.45 AW	40460 AAW	NJBLS	10//99-12//99
	North Carolina	S	15.2 MW	15.06 AW	31330 AAW	NCBLS	10//99-12//99
	North Dakota	S	18.35 MW	18.73 AW	38950 AAW	NDBLS	10//99-12//99
	Oklahoma	S	12.91 MW	12.37 AW	25720 AAW	OKBLS	10//99-12//99
	Oregon	S	17.23 MW	17.52 AW	36440 AAW	ORBLS	10//99-12//99
	South Carolina	S	14.87 MW	14.79 AW	30770 AAW	SCBLS	10//99-12//99

AAW Average annual wage	AOH Average offered, high	ASH Average starting, high	H Hourly	M Monthly	S Special: hourly and annual
AE Average entry wage	AOL Average offered, low	ASL Average starting, low	HI Highest wage paid	MTC Median total compensation	TQ Third quartile wage
AEX Average experienced wage	APH Average pay, high range	AW Average wage paid	HR High end range	MW Median wage paid	W Weekly
AO Average offered	APL Average pay, low range	FQ First quartile wage	LR Low end range	SQ Second quartile wage	Y Yearly

Occupation/Type/Industry	Location	Per	Low	Mid	High	Source	Date
Rail-Track Laying and Maintenance Equipment Operator							
	Tennessee	S	16.87 MW	16.86 AW	35070 AAW	TNBLS	10//99-12//99
	Texas	S	16.13 MW	16.08 AW	33450 AAW	TXBLS	10//99-12//99
	West Virginia	S	18.23 MW	17.03 AW	35420 AAW	WVBLS	10//99-12//99
	Wisconsin	S	17.91 MW	17.68 AW	36770 AAW	WIBLS	10//99-12//99
	Wyoming	S	12.48 MW	13.59 AW	28270 AAW	WYBLS	10//99-12//99
Rail Yard Engineer, Dinkey Operator, and Hostler							
	Arkansas	S	15.81 MW	19.44 AW	40440 AAW	ARBLS	10//99-12//99
	California	S	15.86 MW	16.03 AW	33350 AAW	CABLS	10//99-12//99
	Colorado	S	16.25 MW	17.51 AW	36410 AAW	COBLS	10//99-12//99
	Georgia	S	14.28 MW	14.75 AW	30680 AAW	GABLS	10//99-12//99
	Illinois	S	18.12 MW	18.41 AW	38280 AAW	ILBLS	10//99-12//99
	Indiana	S	18.15 MW	17.21 AW	35800 AAW	INBLS	10//99-12//99
	Iowa	S	12.22 MW	12.53 AW	26060 AAW	IABLS	10//99-12//99
	Minnesota	S	17.53 MW	17.82 AW	37070 AAW	MNBLS	10//99-12//99
	Montana	S	17.33 MW	18.26 AW	37980 AAW	MTBLS	10//99-12//99
	New Jersey	S	15.32 MW	16.56 AW	34450 AAW	NJBLS	10//99-12//99
	New York	S	17.38 MW	17.12 AW	35610 AAW	NYBLS	10//99-12//99
	Ohio	S	18.04 MW	17.71 AW	36830 AAW	OHBLS	10//99-12//99
	Oklahoma	S	17.73 MW	16.97 AW	35290 AAW	OKBLS	10//99-12//99
	Pennsylvania	S	18.56 MW	18.25 AW	37960 AAW	PABLS	10//99-12//99
	Texas	S	16.76 MW	16.13 AW	33560 AAW	TXBLS	10//99-12//99
	Virginia	S	17.6 MW	17.85 AW	37120 AAW	VABLS	10//99-12//99
Railroad Brake, Signal, and Switch Operator							
	Alabama	S	19.5 MW	20.77 AW	43190 AAW	ALBLS	10//99-12//99
	Arizona	S	18.65 MW	18.91 AW	39320 AAW	AZBLS	10//99-12//99
	Arkansas	S	17.9 MW	18.65 AW	38800 AAW	ARBLS	10//99-12//99
	California	S	21.3 MW	21.72 AW	45180 AAW	CABLS	10//99-12//99
	Connecticut	S	18.6 MW	19.27 AW	40090 AAW	CTBLS	10//99-12//99
	Florida	S	17.69 MW	18.09 AW	37630 AAW	FLBLS	10//99-12//99
	Georgia	S	18.88 MW	19.36 AW	40270 AAW	GABLS	10//99-12//99
	Illinois	S	18.81 MW	20.02 AW	41640 AAW	ILBLS	10//99-12//99
	Iowa	S	16.67 MW	18.53 AW	38550 AAW	IABLS	10//99-12//99
	Kansas	S	18.75 MW	19.38 AW	40310 AAW	KSBLS	10//99-12//99
	Kentucky	S	18.31 MW	19.18 AW	39900 AAW	KYBLS	10//99-12//99
	Louisiana	S	18.2 MW	19.14 AW	39800 AAW	LABLS	10//99-12//99
	Mississippi	S	18.44 MW	18.80 AW	39100 AAW	MSBLS	10//99-12//99
	New Jersey	S	21.97 MW	21.79 AW	45330 AAW	NJBLS	10//99-12//99
	New York	S	18.24 MW	18.38 AW	38220 AAW	NYBLS	10//99-12//99
	North Carolina	S	10.85 MW	10.96 AW	22790 AAW	NCBLS	10//99-12//99
	North Dakota	S	19.57 MW	20.00 AW	41590 AAW	NDBLS	10//99-12//99
	Ohio	S	16.97 MW	16.60 AW	34540 AAW	OHBLS	10//99-12//99
	Oklahoma	S	10.51 MW	13.62 AW	28330 AAW	OKBLS	10//99-12//99
	South Carolina	S	19.06 MW	19.11 AW	39740 AAW	SCBLS	10//99-12//99
	Tennessee	S	13.1 MW	14.88 AW	30950 AAW	TNBLS	10//99-12//99
	Texas	S	18.96 MW	20.77 AW	43210 AAW	TXBLS	10//99-12//99
	Utah	S	17.47 MW	17.52 AW	36430 AAW	UTBLS	10//99-12//99
Railroad Conductor and Yardmaster							
	Alabama	S	21.75 MW	23.34 AW	48550 AAW	ALBLS	10//99-12//99
	Arizona	S	19.86 MW	21.10 AW	43880 AAW	AZBLS	10//99-12//99
	Arkansas	S	17.75 MW	18.30 AW	38050 AAW	ARBLS	10//99-12//99
	California	S	25.93 MW	27.09 AW	56350 AAW	CABLS	10//99-12//99
	Connecticut	S	19.73 MW	20.88 AW	43430 AAW	CTBLS	10//99-12//99
	Florida	S	18.64 MW	18.73 AW	38960 AAW	FLBLS	10//99-12//99
	Idaho	S	19.5 MW	20.53 AW	42710 AAW	IDBLS	10//99-12//99
	Illinois	S	19.83 MW	21.29 AW	44280 AAW	ILBLS	10//99-12//99
	Iowa	S	19.08 MW	19.84 AW	41270 AAW	IABLS	10//99-12//99
	Kansas	S	19.81 MW	21.25 AW	44210 AAW	KSBLS	10//99-12//99
	Kentucky	S	19.11 MW	21.21 AW	44110 AAW	KYBLS	10//99-12//99
	Louisiana	S	19.12 MW	21.01 AW	43700 AAW	LABLS	10//99-12//99
	Michigan	S	19.87 MW	21.03 AW	43740 AAW	MIBLS	10//99-12//99
	Minnesota	S	18.85 MW	20.61 AW	42870 AAW	MNBLS	10//99-12//99
	Mississippi	S	14.81 MW	16.27 AW	33840 AAW	MSBLS	10//99-12//99
	Montana	S	19.56 MW	22.21 AW	46200 AAW	MTBLS	10//99-12//99
	New Jersey	S	20.3 MW	21.39 AW	44490 AAW	NJBLS	10//99-12//99
	New York	S	16.92 MW	16.89 AW	35120 AAW	NYBLS	10//99-12//99
	North Carolina	S	17.33 MW	18.02 AW	37490 AAW	NCBLS	10//99-12//99

AAW Average annual wage	**AOH** Average offered, high	**ASH** Average starting, high	**H** Hourly	**M** Monthly	**S** Special: hourly and annual
AE Average entry wage	**AOL** Average offered, low	**ASL** Average starting, low	**HI** Highest wage paid	**MTC** Median total compensation	**TQ** Third quartile wage
AEX Average experienced wage	**APH** Average pay, high range	**AW** Average wage paid	**HR** High end range	**MW** Median wage paid	**W** Weekly
AO Average offered	**APL** Average pay, low range	**FQ** First quartile wage	**LR** Low end range	**SQ** Second quartile wage	**Y** Yearly

Occupation/Type/Industry	Location	Per	Low	Mid	High	Source	Date
Railroad Conductor and							
Yardmaster	North Dakota	S	21.16 MW	23.08 AW	48010 AAW	NDBLS	10//99-12//99
	Ohio	S	18.91 MW	19.91 AW	41410 AAW	OHBLS	10//99-12//99
	Oklahoma	S	19.74 MW	20.61 AW	42870 AAW	OKBLS	10//99-12//99
	Oregon	S	18.7 MW	20.10 AW	41810 AAW	ORBLS	10//99-12//99
	South Carolina	S	17.71 MW	17.59 AW	36580 AAW	SCBLS	10//99-12//99
	Tennessee	S	14.73 MW	15.48 AW	32190 AAW	TNBLS	10//99-12//99
	Texas	S	22.45 MW	24.95 AW	51890 AAW	TXBLS	10//99-12//99
	Utah	S	20.06 MW	21.97 AW	45690 AAW	UTBLS	10//99-12//99
	Vermont	S	16.63 MW	17.06 AW	35480 AAW	VTBLS	10//99-12//99
	Virginia	S	19.01 MW	19.57 AW	40710 AAW	VABLS	10//99-12//99
	Wisconsin	S	25.95 MW	25.62 AW	53300 AAW	WIBLS	10//99-12//99
Real Estate Agent	Los Angeles County, CA	Y		34147 AW		LABJ	1999
Real Estate Broker	Tucson MSA, AZ	S	17.80 MW	21.16 AW	37020 AAW	AZBLS	10//99-12//99
	Arkansas	S	9.74 MW	11.14 AW	23160 AAW	ARBLS	10//99-12//99
	California	S	24.17 MW	28.10 AW	58440 AAW	CABLS	10//99-12//99
	Los Angeles-Long Beach PMSA, CA	S	38.15 MW	39.46 AW	79350 AAW	CABLS	10//99-12//99
	Orange County PMSA, CA	S	32.70 MW	26.52 AW	68010 AAW	CABLS	10//99-12//99
	Sacramento PMSA, CA	S	30.31 MW	25.03 AW	63040 AAW	CABLS	10//99-12//99
	San Diego MSA, CA	S	25.02 MW	26.10 AW	52050 AAW	CABLS	10//99-12//99
	Connecticut	S		53.16 AW	110580 AAW	CTBLS	10//99-12//99
	Florida	S	31.55 MW	31.88 AW	66310 AAW	FLBLS	10//99-12//99
	Georgia	S	29.78 MW	28.76 AW	59820 AAW	GABLS	10//99-12//99
	Atlanta MSA, GA	S	27.40 MW	29.54 AW	57000 AAW	GABLS	10//99-12//99
	Illinois	S	35.86 MW	44.70 AW	92980 AAW	ILBLS	10//99-12//99
	Chicago PMSA, IL	S	53.52 MW		111320 AAW	ILBLS	10//99-12//99
	Rockford MSA, IL	S	30.51 MW	30.88 AW	63470 AAW	ILBLS	10//99-12//99
	Indiana	S	19.25 MW	23.85 AW	49600 AAW	INBLS	10//99-12//99
	Gary PMSA, IN	S	20.54 MW	19.52 AW	42720 AAW	INBLS	10//99-12//99
	Indianapolis MSA, IN	S	50.30 MW	56.80 AW	104620 AAW	INBLS	10//99-12//99
	Iowa	S	16.61 MW	25.47 AW	52990 AAW	IABLS	10//99-12//99
	Cedar Rapids MSA, IA	S	26.51 MW	17.21 AW	55140 AAW	IABLS	10//99-12//99
	Kansas	S	34.13 MW	36.32 AW	75550 AAW	KSBLS	10//99-12//99
	Wichita MSA, KS	S	38.65 MW	36.43 AW	80400 AAW	KSBLS	10//99-12//99
	Kentucky	S	21.81 MW	26.77 AW	55680 AAW	KYBLS	10//99-12//99
	Louisville MSA, KY-IN	S	27.02 MW	22.07 AW	56210 AAW	KYBLS	10//99-12//99
	Louisiana	S	19.98 MW	22.33 AW	46450 AAW	LABLS	10//99-12//99
	New Orleans MSA, LA	S	24.66 MW	20.45 AW	51300 AAW	LABLS	10//99-12//99
	Maryland	S	21.15 MW	25.29 AW	52600 AAW	MDBLS	10//99-12//99
	Massachusetts	S	29.4 MW	35.36 AW	73550 AAW	MABLS	10//99-12//99
	Boston PMSA, MA-NH	S	36.28 MW	29.13 AW	75470 AAW	MABLS	10//99-12//99
	Michigan	S	30.26 MW	31.06 AW	64600 AAW	MIBLS	10//99-12//99
	Minnesota	S	16.17 MW	17.14 AW	35650 AAW	MNBLS	10//99-12//99
	Minneapolis-St. Paul MSA, MN-WI	S	21.37 MW	18.54 AW	44440 AAW	MNBLS	10//99-12//99
	Missouri	S	46.22 MW	36.02 AW	74920 AAW	MOBLS	10//99-12//99
	Kansas City MSA, MO-KS	S	38.08 MW	35.36 AW	79200 AAW	MOBLS	10//99-12//99
	Springfield MSA, MO	S	8.69 MW	7.88 AW	18080 AAW	MOBLS	10//99-12//99
	Omaha MSA, NE-IA	S	23.38 MW	16.67 AW	48630 AAW	NEBLS	10//99-12//99
	Nevada	S	12.31 MW	14.13 AW	29380 AAW	NVBLS	10//99-12//99
	Las Vegas MSA, NV-AZ	S	14.13 MW	12.31 AW	29380 AAW	NVBLS	10//99-12//99
	Monmouth-Ocean PMSA, NJ	S	39.81 MW	39.36 AW	82810 AAW	NJBLS	10//99-12//99
	Newark PMSA, NJ	S	46.12 MW	41.15 AW	95940 AAW	NJBLS	10//99-12//99
	New Mexico	S	14.9 MW	17.33 AW	36040 AAW	NMBLS	10//99-12//99
	Albuquerque MSA, NM	S	17.89 MW	15.46 AW	37200 AAW	NMBLS	10//99-12//99
	Greensboro--Winston-Salem--High Point MSA, NC	S	24.71 MW	22.69 AW	51400 AAW	NCBLS	10//99-12//99
	Akron PMSA, OH	S	29.94 MW	29.07 AW	62270 AAW	OHBLS	10//99-12//99
	Cincinnati PMSA, OH-KY-IN	S	27.22 MW	18.43 AW	56620 AAW	OHBLS	10//99-12//99
	Cleveland-Lorain-Elyria PMSA, OH	S	31.27 MW	27.04 AW	65030 AAW	OHBLS	10//99-12//99
	Dayton-Springfield MSA, OH	S	17.72 MW	12.81 AW	36860 AAW	OHBLS	10//99-12//99
	Toledo MSA, OH	S	33.27 MW	24.38 AW	69200 AAW	OHBLS	10//99-12//99
	Oklahoma City MSA, OK	S	31.71 MW	36.48 AW	65960 AAW	OKBLS	10//99-12//99
	Oregon	S	29.21 MW	24.70 AW	51370 AAW	ORBLS	10//99-12//99
	Portland-Vancouver PMSA, OR-WA	S	30.79 MW	31.58 AW	64040 AAW	ORBLS	10//99-12//99
	Pennsylvania	S	19.96 MW	29.27 AW	60880 AAW	PABLS	10//99-12//99
	Pittsburgh MSA, PA	S	22.78 MW	19.40 AW	47380 AAW	PABLS	10//99-12//99

Occupation/Type/Industry	Location	Per	Low	Mid	High	Source	Date
Real Estate Broker	Rhode Island	S	24.7 MW	22.63 AW	47060 AAW	RIBLS	10//99-12//99
	Providence-Fall River-Warwick MSA, RI-MA	S	22.73 MW	25.05 AW	47280 AAW	RIBLS	10//99-12//99
	South Carolina	S	13.25 MW	17.52 AW	36440 AAW	SCBLS	10//99-12//99
	Greenville-Spartanburg-Anderson MSA, SC	S	8.58 MW	8.00 AW	17840 AAW	SCBLS	10//99-12//99
	Myrtle Beach MSA, SC	S	22.76 MW	23.28 AW	47340 AAW	SCBLS	10//99-12//99
	South Dakota	S	9.67 MW	10.02 AW	20850 AAW	SDBLS	10//99-12//99
	Tennessee	S	37.11 MW	39.14 AW	81410 AAW	TNBLS	10//99-12//99
	Johnson City-Kingsport-Bristol MSA, TN-VA	S	20.42 MW	12.10 AW	42480 AAW	TNBLS	10//99-12//99
	Knoxville MSA, TN	S	35.53 MW	36.84 AW	73890 AAW	TNBLS	10//99-12//99
	Memphis MSA, TN-AR-MS	S	61.50 MW		127910 AAW	MSBLS	10//99-12//99
	Nashville MSA, TN	S	43.57 MW	42.45 AW	90630 AAW	TNBLS	10//99-12//99
	Dallas PMSA, TX	S	23.72 MW	15.73 AW	49330 AAW	TXBLS	10//99-12//99
	Fort Worth-Arlington PMSA, TX	S	21.42 MW	22.02 AW	44550 AAW	TXBLS	10//99-12//99
	Utah	S	32.63 MW	33.34 AW	69350 AAW	UTBLS	10//99-12//99
	Salt Lake City-Ogden MSA, UT	S	30.44 MW	29.34 AW	63310 AAW	UTBLS	10//99-12//99
	Vermont	S	25.12 MW	33.49 AW	69660 AAW	VTBLS	10//99-12//99
	Virginia	S	24.06 MW	34.35 AW	71450 AAW	VABLS	10//99-12//99
	Richmond-Petersburg MSA, VA	S	28.30 MW	24.17 AW	58870 AAW	VABLS	10//99-12//99
	Washington	S	58.04 MW	47.91 AW	99640 AAW	WABLS	10//99-12//99
	Seattle-Bellevue-Everett PMSA, WA	S	50.62 MW	59.82 AW	105280 AAW	WABLS	10//99-12//99
	West Virginia	S	6.15 MW	7.54 AW	15680 AAW	WVBLS	10//99-12//99
	Wisconsin	S	26.34 MW	26.28 AW	54660 AAW	WIBLS	10//99-12//99
	Madison MSA, WI	S	18.22 MW	10.67 AW	37890 AAW	WIBLS	10//99-12//99
Real Estate Sales Agent	Alabama	S	10.59 MW	14.21 AW	29560 AAW	ALBLS	10//99-12//99
	Birmingham MSA, AL	S	15.97 MW	10.74 AW	33220 AAW	ALBLS	10//99-12//99
	Dothan MSA, AL	S	19.91 MW	22.18 AW	41410 AAW	ALBLS	10//99-12//99
	Mobile MSA, AL	S	14.85 MW	13.09 AW	30900 AAW	ALBLS	10//99-12//99
	Montgomery MSA, AL	S	13.42 MW	8.74 AW	27900 AAW	ALBLS	10//99-12//99
	Alaska	S	19.46 MW	19.40 AW	40350 AAW	AKBLS	10//99-12//99
	Arizona	S	14.65 MW	19.61 AW	40800 AAW	AZBLS	10//99-12//99
	Phoenix-Mesa MSA, AZ	S	21.56 MW	15.65 AW	44840 AAW	AZBLS	10//99-12//99
	Tucson MSA, AZ	S	14.54 MW	10.95 AW	30240 AAW	AZBLS	10//99-12//99
	Yuma MSA, AZ	S	11.91 MW	10.26 AW	24770 AAW	AZBLS	10//99-12//99
	Arkansas	S	7.03 MW	10.21 AW	21230 AAW	ARBLS	10//99-12//99
	Little Rock-North Little Rock MSA, AR	S	15.02 MW	13.23 AW	31230 AAW	ARBLS	10//99-12//99
	Pine Bluff MSA, AR	S	10.27 MW	9.71 AW	21360 AAW	ARBLS	10//99-12//99
	California	S	11.77 MW	16.07 AW	33420 AAW	CABLS	10//99-12//99
	Bakersfield MSA, CA	S	17.28 MW	11.53 AW	35930 AAW	CABLS	10//99-12//99
	Fresno MSA, CA	S	10.49 MW	8.05 AW	21810 AAW	CABLS	10//99-12//99
	Los Angeles-Long Beach PMSA, CA	S	14.53 MW	11.05 AW	30220 AAW	CABLS	10//99-12//99
	Merced MSA, CA	S	19.99 MW	23.38 AW	41580 AAW	CABLS	10//99-12//99
	Modesto MSA, CA	S	13.74 MW	11.66 AW	28570 AAW	CABLS	10//99-12//99
	Oakland PMSA, CA	S	18.33 MW	13.89 AW	38120 AAW	CABLS	10//99-12//99
	Orange County PMSA, CA	S	14.77 MW	11.25 AW	30720 AAW	CABLS	10//99-12//99
	Riverside-San Bernardino PMSA, CA	S	19.20 MW	13.99 AW	39940 AAW	CABLS	10//99-12//99
	Sacramento PMSA, CA	S	20.74 MW	8.64 AW	43130 AAW	CABLS	10//99-12//99
	San Diego MSA, CA	S	11.55 MW	10.15 AW	24020 AAW	CABLS	10//99-12//99
	San Francisco PMSA, CA	S	20.67 MW	17.56 AW	42980 AAW	CABLS	10//99-12//99
	San Jose PMSA, CA	S	15.67 MW	12.77 AW	32600 AAW	CABLS	10//99-12//99
	San Luis Obispo-Atascadero-Paso Robles MSA, CA	S	10.87 MW	6.49 AW	22610 AAW	CABLS	10//99-12//99
	Santa Barbara-Santa Maria-Lompoc MSA, CA	S	17.82 MW	20.64 AW	37060 AAW	CABLS	10//99-12//99
	Santa Cruz-Watsonville PMSA, CA	S	27.47 MW	19.78 AW	57130 AAW	CABLS	10//99-12//99
	Santa Rosa PMSA, CA	S	22.22 MW	15.56 AW	46220 AAW	CABLS	10//99-12//99
	Vallejo-Fairfield-Napa PMSA, CA	S	20.23 MW	17.17 AW	42080 AAW	CABLS	10//99-12//99
	Ventura PMSA, CA	S	16.57 MW	15.40 AW	34460 AAW	CABLS	10//99-12//99
	Yolo PMSA, CA	S	9.71 MW	9.54 AW	20210 AAW	CABLS	10//99-12//99
	Colorado	S	13.15 MW	17.27 AW	35930 AAW	COBLS	10//99-12//99
	Colorado Springs MSA, CO	S	16.42 MW	16.20 AW	34140 AAW	COBLS	10//99-12//99

AAW	Average annual wage	AOH	Average offered, high	ASH	Average starting, high	H	Hourly	M	Monthly	S	Special: hourly and annual
AE	Average entry wage	AOL	Average offered, low	ASL	Average starting, low	HI	Highest wage paid	MTC	Median total compensation	TQ	Third quartile wage
AEX	Average experienced wage	APH	Average pay, high range	AW	Average wage paid	HR	High end range	MW	Median wage paid	W	Weekly
AO	Average offered	APL	Average pay, low range	FQ	First quartile wage	LR	Low end range	SQ	Second quartile wage	Y	Yearly

Occupation/Type/Industry	Location	Per	Low	Mid	High	Source	Date
Real Estate Sales Agent	Denver PMSA, CO	S	16.10 MW	12.30 AW	33500 AAW	COBLS	10//99-12//99
	Connecticut	S	15.01 MW	18.55 AW	38590 AAW	CTBLS	10//99-12//99
	Bridgeport PMSA, CT	S	14.47 MW	14.08 AW	30100 AAW	CTBLS	10//99-12//99
	Hartford MSA, CT	S	20.10 MW	11.07 AW	41820 AAW	CTBLS	10//99-12//99
	Stamford-Norwalk PMSA, CT	S	29.41 MW	31.86 AW	61180 AAW	CTBLS	10//99-12//99
	Delaware	S	14.23 MW	17.45 AW	36300 AAW	DEBLS	10//99-12//99
	Wilmington-Newark PMSA, DE-MD	S	17.91 MW	14.24 AW	37260 AAW	DEBLS	10//99-12//99
	Washington PMSA, DC-MD-VA-WV	S	18.99 MW	16.30 AW	39510 AAW	DCBLS	10//99-12//99
	Florida	S	10.91 MW	16.09 AW	33460 AAW	FLBLS	10//99-12//99
	Daytona Beach MSA, FL	S	15.27 MW	12.54 AW	31760 AAW	FLBLS	10//99-12//99
	Fort Lauderdale PMSA, FL	S	20.15 MW	15.32 AW	41920 AAW	FLBLS	10//99-12//99
	Fort Myers-Cape Coral MSA, FL	S	14.46 MW	14.07 AW	30070 AAW	FLBLS	10//99-12//99
	Jacksonville MSA, FL	S	15.67 MW	12.65 AW	32590 AAW	FLBLS	10//99-12//99
	Lakeland-Winter Haven MSA, FL	S	17.83 MW	16.38 AW	37080 AAW	FLBLS	10//99-12//99
	Melbourne-Titusville-Palm Bay MSA, FL	S	14.88 MW	14.23 AW	30960 AAW	FLBLS	10//99-12//99
	Miami PMSA, FL	S	17.43 MW	11.18 AW	36250 AAW	FLBLS	10//99-12//99
	Ocala MSA, FL	S	9.66 MW	8.22 AW	20090 AAW	FLBLS	10//99-12//99
	Orlando MSA, FL	S	12.56 MW	9.87 AW	26130 AAW	FLBLS	10//99-12//99
	Panama City MSA, FL	S	11.01 MW	6.63 AW	22890 AAW	FLBLS	10//99-12//99
	Pensacola MSA, FL	S	16.28 MW	14.36 AW	33860 AAW	FLBLS	10//99-12//99
	Punta Gorda MSA, FL	S	25.08 MW	12.97 AW	52170 AAW	FLBLS	10//99-12//99
	Sarasota-Bradenton MSA, FL	S	19.26 MW	13.38 AW	40060 AAW	FLBLS	10//99-12//99
	Tallahassee MSA, FL	S	14.45 MW	8.57 AW	30060 AAW	FLBLS	10//99-12//99
	Tampa-St. Petersburg-Clearwater MSA, FL	S	18.37 MW	13.51 AW	38220 AAW	FLBLS	10//99-12//99
	West Palm Beach-Boca Raton MSA, FL	S	18.95 MW	16.48 AW	39420 AAW	FLBLS	10//99-12//99
	Georgia	S	15.21 MW	18.13 AW	37720 AAW	GABLS	10//99-12//99
	Athens MSA, GA	S	14.68 MW	14.91 AW	30540 AAW	GABLS	10//99-12//99
	Atlanta MSA, GA	S	19.09 MW	15.65 AW	39720 AAW	GABLS	10//99-12//99
	Columbus MSA, GA-AL	S	11.49 MW	10.11 AW	23900 AAW	GABLS	10//99-12//99
	Hawaii	S	15.8 MW	20.42 AW	42470 AAW	HIBLS	10//99-12//99
	Honolulu MSA, HI	S	23.86 MW	19.71 AW	49620 AAW	HIBLS	10//99-12//99
	Idaho	S	10.75 MW	17.37 AW	36140 AAW	IDBLS	10//99-12//99
	Boise City MSA, ID	S	18.28 MW	10.02 AW	38030 AAW	IDBLS	10//99-12//99
	Illinois	S	13.34 MW	15.71 AW	32670 AAW	ILBLS	10//99-12//99
	Champaign-Urbana MSA, IL	S	20.70 MW	16.99 AW	43060 AAW	ILBLS	10//99-12//99
	Chicago PMSA, IL	S	15.45 MW	13.22 AW	32130 AAW	ILBLS	10//99-12//99
	Kankakee PMSA, IL	S	19.91 MW	19.35 AW	41420 AAW	ILBLS	10//99-12//99
	Peoria-Pekin MSA, IL	S	13.19 MW	11.17 AW	27430 AAW	ILBLS	10//99-12//99
	Indiana	S	10.51 MW	13.86 AW	28820 AAW	INBLS	10//99-12//99
	Bloomington MSA, IN	S	8.51 MW	8.00 AW	17690 AAW	INBLS	10//99-12//99
	Evansville-Henderson MSA, IN-KY	S	17.20 MW	21.79 AW	35770 AAW	INBLS	10//99-12//99
	Fort Wayne MSA, IN	S	13.49 MW	11.44 AW	28070 AAW	INBLS	10//99-12//99
	Gary PMSA, IN	S	12.29 MW	9.66 AW	25560 AAW	INBLS	10//99-12//99
	Indianapolis MSA, IN	S	15.35 MW	11.56 AW	31930 AAW	INBLS	10//99-12//99
	Kokomo MSA, IN	S	13.90 MW	13.64 AW	28920 AAW	INBLS	10//99-12//99
	Lafayette MSA, IN	S	12.58 MW	12.49 AW	26170 AAW	INBLS	10//99-12//99
	South Bend MSA, IN	S	14.25 MW	11.95 AW	29640 AAW	INBLS	10//99-12//99
	Iowa	S	11.98 MW	14.38 AW	29900 AAW	IABLS	10//99-12//99
	Davenport-Moline-Rock Island MSA, IA-IL	S	17.54 MW	17.41 AW	36480 AAW	IABLS	10//99-12//99
	Des Moines MSA, IA	S	12.82 MW	11.90 AW	26680 AAW	IABLS	10//99-12//99
	Kansas	S	9.8 MW	12.53 AW	26060 AAW	KSBLS	10//99-12//99
	Topeka MSA, KS	S	13.93 MW	14.53 AW	28980 AAW	KSBLS	10//99-12//99
	Wichita MSA, KS	S	12.54 MW	11.76 AW	26090 AAW	KSBLS	10//99-12//99
	Kentucky	S	12.65 MW	15.28 AW	31780 AAW	KYBLS	10//99-12//99
	Lexington MSA, KY	S	11.37 MW	8.27 AW	23660 AAW	KYBLS	10//99-12//99
	Louisville MSA, KY-IN	S	16.28 MW	14.75 AW	33870 AAW	KYBLS	10//99-12//99
	Louisiana	S	10.55 MW	16.11 AW	33510 AAW	LABLS	10//99-12//99
	Baton Rouge MSA, LA	S	15.74 MW	11.92 AW	32740 AAW	LABLS	10//99-12//99
	Lake Charles MSA, LA	S	7.63 MW	7.44 AW	15870 AAW	LABLS	10//99-12//99
	New Orleans MSA, LA	S	23.51 MW	17.31 AW	48900 AAW	LABLS	10//99-12//99
	Shreveport-Bossier City MSA, LA	S	11.54 MW	10.32 AW	24000 AAW	LABLS	10//99-12//99
	Maine	S	12.04 MW	15.43 AW	32100 AAW	MEBLS	10//99-12//99

AAW	Average annual wage	AOH	Average offered, high	ASH	Average starting, high
AE	Average entry wage	AOL	Average offered, low	ASL	Average starting, low
AEX	Average experienced wage	APH	Average pay, high range	AW	Average wage paid
AO	Average offered	APL	Average pay, low range	FQ	First quartile wage

H	Hourly	M	Monthly
HI	Highest wage paid	MTC	Median total compensation
HR	High end range	MW	Median wage paid
LR	Low end range	SQ	Second quartile wage

S	Special: hourly and annual
TQ	Third quartile wage
W	Weekly
Y	Yearly

Occupation/Type/Industry	Location	Per	Low	Mid	High	Source	Date
Real Estate Sales Agent	Portland MSA, ME	S	18.51 MW	12.70 AW	38500 AAW	MEBLS	10//99-12//99
	Maryland	S	12.23 MW	14.52 AW	30190 AAW	MDBLS	10//99-12//99
	Baltimore PMSA, MD	S	14.35 MW	12.40 AW	29840 AAW	MDBLS	10//99-12//99
	Massachusetts	S	17.26 MW	20.04 AW	41680 AAW	MABLS	10//99-12//99
	Barnstable-Yarmouth MSA, MA	S	19.78 MW	15.53 AW	41130 AAW	MABLS	10//99-12//99
	Boston PMSA, MA-NH	S	21.66 MW	19.01 AW	45060 AAW	MABLS	10//99-12//99
	Brockton PMSA, MA	S	21.53 MW	14.49 AW	44790 AAW	MABLS	10//99-12//99
	Worcester PMSA, MA-CT	S	25.67 MW	20.81 AW	53390 AAW	MABLS	10//99-12//99
	Michigan	S	21.47 MW	28.82 AW	59950 AAW	MIBLS	10//99-12//99
	Ann Arbor PMSA, MI	S	23.18 MW	26.75 AW	48210 AAW	MIBLS	10//99-12//99
	Benton Harbor MSA, MI	S	29.11 MW	30.06 AW	60540 AAW	MIBLS	10//99-12//99
	Detroit PMSA, MI	S	34.65 MW	34.71 AW	72070 AAW	MIBLS	10//99-12//99
	Flint PMSA, MI	S	12.04 MW	11.24 AW	25040 AAW	MIBLS	10//99-12//99
	Grand Rapids-Muskegon-Holland MSA, MI	S	15.57 MW	14.09 AW	32380 AAW	MIBLS	10//99-12//99
	Kalamazoo-Battle Creek MSA, MI	S	22.70 MW	14.89 AW	47210 AAW	MIBLS	10//99-12//99
	Lansing-East Lansing MSA, MI	S	24.02 MW	18.39 AW	49970 AAW	MIBLS	10//99-12//99
	Saginaw-Bay City-Midland MSA, MI	S	16.88 MW	11.37 AW	35110 AAW	MIBLS	10//99-12//99
	Minnesota	S	19.72 MW	23.04 AW	47930 AAW	MNBLS	10//99-12//99
	Minneapolis-St. Paul MSA, MN-WI	S	23.21 MW	19.63 AW	48290 AAW	MNBLS	10//99-12//99
	Mississippi	S	10.93 MW	12.40 AW	25790 AAW	MSBLS	10//99-12//99
	Biloxi-Gulfport-Pascagoula MSA, MS	S	11.47 MW	10.58 AW	23860 AAW	MSBLS	10//99-12//99
	Jackson MSA, MS	S	15.38 MW	14.86 AW	31980 AAW	MSBLS	10//99-12//99
	Missouri	S	15.01 MW	16.98 AW	35310 AAW	MOBLS	10//99-12//99
	St. Louis MSA, MO-IL	S	14.24 MW	12.95 AW	29610 AAW	MOBLS	10//99-12//99
	Springfield MSA, MO	S	17.35 MW	13.15 AW	36080 AAW	MOBLS	10//99-12//99
	Montana	S	13.7 MW	18.18 AW	37800 AAW	MTBLS	10//99-12//99
	Billings MSA, MT	S	15.06 MW	11.89 AW	31320 AAW	MTBLS	10//99-12//99
	Missoula MSA, MT	S	13.97 MW	10.44 AW	29060 AAW	MTBLS	10//99-12//99
	Nebraska	S	12.6 MW	15.81 AW	32880 AAW	NEBLS	10//99-12//99
	Lincoln MSA, NE	S	14.46 MW	13.17 AW	30090 AAW	NEBLS	10//99-12//99
	Omaha MSA, NE-IA	S	17.82 MW	14.16 AW	37060 AAW	NEBLS	10//99-12//99
	Nevada	S	14.62 MW	18.93 AW	39370 AAW	NVBLS	10//99-12//99
	Las Vegas MSA, NV-AZ	S	20.52 MW	16.51 AW	42670 AAW	NVBLS	10//99-12//99
	Reno MSA, NV	S	15.36 MW	12.13 AW	31940 AAW	NVBLS	10//99-12//99
	New Hampshire	S	15.68 MW	20.33 AW	42290 AAW	NHBLS	10//99-12//99
	Manchester PMSA, NH	S	15.59 MW	12.96 AW	32420 AAW	NHBLS	10//99-12//99
	Nashua PMSA, NH	S	18.80 MW	18.37 AW	39100 AAW	NHBLS	10//99-12//99
	Portsmouth-Rochester PMSA, NH-ME	S	13.42 MW	14.30 AW	27920 AAW	NHBLS	10//99-12//99
	New Jersey	S	19.89 MW	23.45 AW	48780 AAW	NJBLS	10//99-12//99
	Bergen-Passaic PMSA, NJ	S	26.87 MW	23.00 AW	55890 AAW	NJBLS	10//99-12//99
	Jersey City PMSA, NJ	S	17.77 MW	12.59 AW	36970 AAW	NJBLS	10//99-12//99
	Middlesex-Somerset-Hunterdon PMSA, NJ	S	19.90 MW	19.76 AW	41390 AAW	NJBLS	10//99-12//99
	Monmouth-Ocean PMSA, NJ	S	33.19 MW	28.69 AW	69030 AAW	NJBLS	10//99-12//99
	Newark PMSA, NJ	S	19.23 MW	14.12 AW	40010 AAW	NJBLS	10//99-12//99
	New Mexico	S	16.53 MW	20.69 AW	43030 AAW	NMBLS	10//99-12//99
	Albuquerque MSA, NM	S	24.68 MW	19.25 AW	51340 AAW	NMBLS	10//99-12//99
	Santa Fe MSA, NM	S	11.57 MW	10.32 AW	24060 AAW	NMBLS	10//99-12//99
	New York	S	19.83 MW	20.94 AW	43560 AAW	NYBLS	10//99-12//99
	Albany-Schenectady-Troy MSA, NY	S	10.82 MW	9.50 AW	22500 AAW	NYBLS	10//99-12//99
	Buffalo-Niagara Falls MSA, NY	S	17.53 MW	17.06 AW	36460 AAW	NYBLS	10//99-12//99
	Dutchess County PMSA, NY	S	18.11 MW	12.82 AW	37660 AAW	NYBLS	10//99-12//99
	Jamestown MSA, NY	S	10.45 MW	9.70 AW	21740 AAW	NYBLS	10//99-12//99
	Nassau-Suffolk PMSA, NY	S	17.99 MW	20.24 AW	37410 AAW	NYBLS	10//99-12//99
	New York PMSA, NY	S	25.19 MW	23.01 AW	52400 AAW	NYBLS	10//99-12//99
	Rochester MSA, NY	S	20.60 MW	16.65 AW	42850 AAW	NYBLS	10//99-12//99
	Syracuse MSA, NY	S	16.93 MW	14.11 AW	35200 AAW	NYBLS	10//99-12//99
	North Carolina	S	12.69 MW	15.85 AW	32970 AAW	NCBLS	10//99-12//99
	Asheville MSA, NC	S	11.90 MW	11.12 AW	24750 AAW	NCBLS	10//99-12//99
	Charlotte-Gastonia-Rock Hill MSA, NC-SC	S	21.18 MW	19.36 AW	44060 AAW	NCBLS	10//99-12//99
	Fayetteville MSA, NC	S	14.18 MW	9.55 AW	29490 AAW	NCBLS	10//99-12//99

AAW	Average annual wage	**AOH**	Average offered, high	**ASH**	Average starting, high	**H**	Hourly	**M**	Monthly	**S** Special: hourly and annual
AE	Average entry wage	**AOL**	Average offered, low	**ASL**	Average starting, low	**HI**	Highest wage paid	**MTC**	Median total compensation	**TQ** Third quartile wage
AEX	Average experienced wage	**APH**	Average pay, high range	**AW**	Average wage paid	**HR**	High end range	**MW**	Median wage paid	**W** Weekly
AO	Average offered	**APL**	Average pay, low range	**FQ**	First quartile wage	**LR**	Low end range	**SQ**	Second quartile wage	**Y** Yearly

Occupation/Type/Industry	Location	Per	Low	Mid	High	Source	Date
Real Estate Sales Agent	Greensboro--Winston-Salem--						
	High Point MSA, NC	S	12.06 MW	7.94 AW	25090 AAW	NCBLS	10//99-12//99
	Raleigh-Durham-Chapel Hill MSA, NC	S	16.60 MW	13.42 AW	34540 AAW	NCBLS	10//99-12//99
	North Dakota	S	10.33 MW	11.31 AW	23530 AAW	NDBLS	10//99-12//99
	Bismarck MSA, ND	S	17.24 MW	17.82 AW	35860 AAW	NDBLS	10//99-12//99
	Ohio	S	11.37 MW	15.39 AW	32010 AAW	OHBLS	10//99-12//99
	Akron PMSA, OH	S	12.66 MW	10.08 AW	26340 AAW	OHBLS	10//99-12//99
	Cincinnati PMSA, OH-KY-IN	S	14.44 MW	12.09 AW	30030 AAW	OHBLS	10//99-12//99
	Cleveland-Lorain-Elyria PMSA, OH	S	14.55 MW	9.91 AW	30270 AAW	OHBLS	10//99-12//99
	Columbus MSA, OH	S	17.91 MW	13.56 AW	37250 AAW	OHBLS	10//99-12//99
	Dayton-Springfield MSA, OH	S	14.55 MW	11.36 AW	30260 AAW	OHBLS	10//99-12//99
	Toledo MSA, OH	S	13.77 MW	14.34 AW	28630 AAW	OHBLS	10//99-12//99
	Oklahoma	S	19.59 MW	20.22 AW	42070 AAW	OKBLS	10//99-12//99
	Oklahoma City MSA, OK	S	22.77 MW	27.01 AW	47350 AAW	OKBLS	10//99-12//99
	Tulsa MSA, OK	S	14.98 MW	14.97 AW	31160 AAW	OKBLS	10//99-12//99
	Oregon	S	12.01 MW	18.11 AW	37670 AAW	ORBLS	10//99-12//99
	Portland-Vancouver PMSA, OR-WA	S	18.42 MW	10.99 AW	38310 AAW	ORBLS	10//99-12//99
	Pennsylvania	S	12.33 MW	15.03 AW	31250 AAW	PABLS	10//99-12//99
	Allentown-Bethlehem-Easton MSA, PA	S	13.26 MW	10.02 AW	27590 AAW	PABLS	10//99-12//99
	Philadelphia PMSA, PA-NJ	S	17.67 MW	14.20 AW	36750 AAW	PABLS	10//99-12//99
	Pittsburgh MSA, PA	S	13.37 MW	11.92 AW	27810 AAW	PABLS	10//99-12//99
	Reading MSA, PA	S	10.67 MW	8.21 AW	22200 AAW	PABLS	10//99-12//99
	Scranton--Wilkes-Barre--Hazleton MSA, PA	S	16.00 MW	12.78 AW	33290 AAW	PABLS	10//99-12//99
	Williamsport MSA, PA	S	8.58 MW	8.02 AW	17850 AAW	PABLS	10//99-12//99
	York MSA, PA	S	8.56 MW	7.43 AW	17810 AAW	PABLS	10//99-12//99
	Rhode Island	S	9.23 MW	10.99 AW	22860 AAW	RIBLS	10//99-12//99
	Providence-Fall River-Warwick MSA, RI-MA	S	10.17 MW	9.29 AW	21150 AAW	RIBLS	10//99-12//99
	South Carolina	S	14.71 MW	20.37 AW	42360 AAW	SCBLS	10//99-12//99
	Charleston-North Charleston MSA, SC	S	27.19 MW	20.92 AW	56560 AAW	SCBLS	10//99-12//99
	Columbia MSA, SC	S	20.92 MW	13.85 AW	43510 AAW	SCBLS	10//99-12//99
	Greenville-Spartanburg-Anderson MSA, SC	S	21.94 MW	16.50 AW	45640 AAW	SCBLS	10//99-12//99
	Myrtle Beach MSA, SC	S	20.35 MW	13.10 AW	42320 AAW	SCBLS	10//99-12//99
	South Dakota	S	17.43 MW	18.14 AW	37740 AAW	SDBLS	10//99-12//99
	Rapid City MSA, SD	S	15.72 MW	16.99 AW	32700 AAW	SDBLS	10//99-12//99
	Tennessee	S	10.52 MW	16.05 AW	33380 AAW	TNBLS	10//99-12//99
	Chattanooga MSA, TN-GA	S	9.62 MW	8.27 AW	20010 AAW	TNBLS	10//99-12//99
	Johnson City-Kingsport-Bristol MSA, TN-VA	S	10.83 MW	9.26 AW	22530 AAW	TNBLS	10//99-12//99
	Memphis MSA, TN-AR-MS	S	18.66 MW	18.51 AW	38810 AAW	MSBLS	10//99-12//99
	Nashville MSA, TN	S	15.56 MW	10.21 AW	32370 AAW	TNBLS	10//99-12//99
	Texas	S	19.24 MW	23.84 AW	49580 AAW	TXBLS	10//99-12//99
	Austin-San Marcos MSA, TX	S	16.76 MW	14.02 AW	34870 AAW	TXBLS	10//99-12//99
	Fort Worth-Arlington PMSA, TX	S	18.52 MW	17.21 AW	38530 AAW	TXBLS	10//99-12//99
	Houston PMSA, TX	S	26.83 MW	19.43 AW	55810 AAW	TXBLS	10//99-12//99
	Laredo MSA, TX	S	18.65 MW	16.57 AW	38790 AAW	TXBLS	10//99-12//99
	Lubbock MSA, TX	S	9.56 MW	9.49 AW	19880 AAW	TXBLS	10//99-12//99
	San Antonio MSA, TX	S	15.00 MW	11.93 AW	31210 AAW	TXBLS	10//99-12//99
	Utah	S	15.83 MW	22.28 AW	46340 AAW	UTBLS	10//99-12//99
	Salt Lake City-Ogden MSA, UT	S	22.44 MW	15.03 AW	46670 AAW	UTBLS	10//99-12//99
	Vermont	S	22.47 MW	25.55 AW	53130 AAW	VTBLS	10//99-12//99
	Virginia	S	16.79 MW	20.13 AW	41870 AAW	VABLS	10//99-12//99
	Charlottesville MSA, VA	S	19.84 MW	20.21 AW	41280 AAW	VABLS	10//99-12//99
	Lynchburg MSA, VA	S	17.66 MW	17.03 AW	36730 AAW	VABLS	10//99-12//99
	Norfolk-Virginia Beach-Newport News MSA, VA-NC	S	23.05 MW	17.07 AW	47950 AAW	VABLS	10//99-12//99
	Richmond-Petersburg MSA, VA	S	16.56 MW	13.01 AW	34450 AAW	VABLS	10//99-12//99
	Roanoke MSA, VA	S	24.19 MW	23.63 AW	50310 AAW	VABLS	10//99-12//99
	Washington	S	12.73 MW	18.48 AW	38440 AAW	WABLS	10//99-12//99
	Seattle-Bellevue-Everett PMSA, WA	S	19.72 MW	12.62 AW	41020 AAW	WABLS	10//99-12//99

Occupation/Type/Industry	Location	Per	Low	Mid	High	Source	Date
Real Estate Sales Agent	Spokane MSA, WA	S	14.66 MW	10.58 AW	30500 AAW	WABLS	10//99-12//99
	Tacoma PMSA, WA	S	15.29 MW	9.82 AW	31800 AAW	WABLS	10//99-12//99
	West Virginia	S	8.35 MW	11.88 AW	24710 AAW	WVBLS	10//99-12//99
	Charleston MSA, WV	S	15.38 MW	10.99 AW	31990 AAW	WVBLS	10//99-12//99
	Huntington-Ashland MSA, WV-KY-OH	S	17.08 MW	17.28 AW	35530 AAW	WVBLS	10//99-12//99
	Wisconsin	S	18.05 MW	20.02 AW	41640 AAW	WIBLS	10//99-12//99
	Appleton-Oshkosh-Neenah MSA, WI	S	11.89 MW	9.94 AW	24730 AAW	WIBLS	10//99-12//99
	Eau Claire MSA, WI	S	16.73 MW	17.28 AW	34790 AAW	WIBLS	10//99-12//99
	Green Bay MSA, WI	S	19.05 MW	21.12 AW	39620 AAW	WIBLS	10//99-12//99
	Janesville-Beloit MSA, WI	S	19.41 MW	18.88 AW	40380 AAW	WIBLS	10//99-12//99
	Madison MSA, WI	S	24.94 MW	18.94 AW	51880 AAW	WIBLS	10//99-12//99
	Milwaukee-Waukesha PMSA, WI	S	24.19 MW	22.42 AW	50320 AAW	WIBLS	10//99-12//99
	Wyoming	S	17.73 MW	17.79 AW	37000 AAW	WYBLS	10//99-12//99
	Casper MSA, WY	S	20.23 MW	16.39 AW	42080 AAW	WYBLS	10//99-12//99
	Puerto Rico	S	13.74 MW	15.04 AW	31280 AAW	PRBLS	10//99-12//99
	San Juan-Bayamon PMSA, PR	S	15.05 MW	13.20 AW	31300 AAW	PRBLS	10//99-12//99
Receptionist							
Health Care Office, Family Practice	United States	Y		18368 AW		MEDEC1	1999
Health Care Office, Internal Medicine	United States	Y		19062 AW		MEDEC1	1999
Health Care Office, Obstetrics-gynecology	United States	Y		20393 AW		MEDEC1	1999
Health Care Office, Pediatrics	United States	Y		20713 AW		MEDEC1	1999
Receptionist and Information Clerk	Alabama	S	8.27 MW	8.43 AW	17540 AAW	ALBLS	10//99-12//99
	Anniston MSA, AL	S	7.99 MW	7.74 AW	16620 AAW	ALBLS	10//99-12//99
	Auburn-Opelika MSA, AL	S	8.46 MW	8.36 AW	17590 AAW	ALBLS	10//99-12//99
	Birmingham MSA, AL	S	8.76 MW	8.74 AW	18220 AAW	ALBLS	10//99-12//99
	Decatur MSA, AL	S	8.54 MW	8.96 AW	17760 AAW	ALBLS	10//99-12//99
	Dothan MSA, AL	S	8.25 MW	8.12 AW	17160 AAW	ALBLS	10//99-12//99
	Florence MSA, AL	S	7.66 MW	7.41 AW	15930 AAW	ALBLS	10//99-12//99
	Gadsden MSA, AL	S	7.91 MW	7.90 AW	16440 AAW	ALBLS	10//99-12//99
	Huntsville MSA, AL	S	8.27 MW	8.13 AW	17200 AAW	ALBLS	10//99-12//99
	Mobile MSA, AL	S	7.92 MW	7.81 AW	16470 AAW	ALBLS	10//99-12//99
	Montgomery MSA, AL	S	8.79 MW	8.74 AW	18280 AAW	ALBLS	10//99-12//99
	Tuscaloosa MSA, AL	S	8.56 MW	8.20 AW	17800 AAW	ALBLS	10//99-12//99
	Alaska	S	10.57 MW	11.01 AW	22900 AAW	AKBLS	10//99-12//99
	Anchorage MSA, AK	S	10.95 MW	10.65 AW	22780 AAW	AKBLS	10//99-12//99
	Arizona	S	8.82 MW	9.07 AW	18860 AAW	AZBLS	10//99-12//99
	Flagstaff MSA, AZ-UT	S	8.76 MW	8.23 AW	18220 AAW	AZBLS	10//99-12//99
	Phoenix-Mesa MSA, AZ	S	9.28 MW	9.14 AW	19310 AAW	AZBLS	10//99-12//99
	Tucson MSA, AZ	S	8.69 MW	8.28 AW	18080 AAW	AZBLS	10//99-12//99
	Yuma MSA, AZ	S	8.25 MW	7.88 AW	17160 AAW	AZBLS	10//99-12//99
	Arkansas	S	7.91 MW	8.08 AW	16810 AAW	ARBLS	10//99-12//99
	Fayetteville-Springdale-Rogers MSA, AR	S	8.00 MW	7.87 AW	16630 AAW	ARBLS	10//99-12//99
	Fort Smith MSA, AR-OK	S	7.87 MW	7.84 AW	16380 AAW	ARBLS	10//99-12//99
	Jonesboro MSA, AR	S	8.39 MW	8.14 AW	17460 AAW	ARBLS	10//99-12//99
	Little Rock-North Little Rock MSA, AR	S	8.42 MW	8.11 AW	17520 AAW	ARBLS	10//99-12//99
	Pine Bluff MSA, AR	S	7.71 MW	7.58 AW	16030 AAW	ARBLS	10//99-12//99
	California	S	10.11 MW	10.43 AW	21700 AAW	CABLS	10//99-12//99
	Bakersfield MSA, CA	S	9.12 MW	9.03 AW	18960 AAW	CABLS	10//99-12//99
	Chico-Paradise MSA, CA	S	9.34 MW	9.06 AW	19430 AAW	CABLS	10//99-12//99
	Fresno MSA, CA	S	9.18 MW	9.12 AW	19100 AAW	CABLS	10//99-12//99
	Los Angeles-Long Beach PMSA, CA	S	10.27 MW	9.92 AW	21350 AAW	CABLS	10//99-12//99
	Merced MSA, CA	S	8.03 MW	7.68 AW	16690 AAW	CABLS	10//99-12//99
	Modesto MSA, CA	S	8.81 MW	8.44 AW	18320 AAW	CABLS	10//99-12//99
	Oakland PMSA, CA	S	11.56 MW	11.15 AW	24050 AAW	CABLS	10//99-12//99
	Orange County PMSA, CA	S	10.52 MW	10.33 AW	21880 AAW	CABLS	10//99-12//99
	Redding MSA, CA	S	9.56 MW	9.04 AW	19890 AAW	CABLS	10//99-12//99
	Riverside-San Bernardino PMSA, CA	S	9.48 MW	9.26 AW	19720 AAW	CABLS	10//99-12//99
	Sacramento PMSA, CA	S	10.52 MW	10.10 AW	21880 AAW	CABLS	10//99-12//99
	Salinas MSA, CA	S	10.37 MW	9.81 AW	21560 AAW	CABLS	10//99-12//99
	San Diego MSA, CA	S	10.09 MW	9.86 AW	20980 AAW	CABLS	10//99-12//99
	San Francisco PMSA, CA	S	11.65 MW	11.50 AW	24240 AAW	CABLS	10//99-12//99
	San Jose PMSA, CA	S	11.70 MW	11.45 AW	24340 AAW	CABLS	10//99-12//99

AAW	Average annual wage	AOH	Average offered, high	ASH	Average starting, high	H	Hourly	M	Monthly	S	Special: hourly and annual
AE	Average entry wage	AOL	Average offered, low	ASL	Average starting, low	HI	Highest wage paid	MTC	Median total compensation	TQ	Third quartile wage
AEX	Average experienced wage	APH	Average pay, high range	AW	Average wage paid	HR	High end range	MW	Median wage paid	W	Weekly
AO	Average offered	APL	Average pay, low range	FQ	First quartile wage	LR	Low end range	SQ	Second quartile wage	Y	Yearly

Occupation/Type/Industry	Location	Per	Low	Mid	High	Source	Date
Receptionist and Information Clerk	San Luis Obispo-Atascadero-Paso Robles MSA, CA	S	8.98 MW	8.41 AW	18680 AAW	CABLS	10//99-12//99
	Santa Barbara-Santa Maria-Lompoc MSA, CA	S	10.33 MW	10.36 AW	21500 AAW	CABLS	10//99-12//99
	Santa Cruz-Watsonville PMSA, CA	S	9.96 MW	9.95 AW	20720 AAW	CABLS	10//99-12//99
	Santa Rosa PMSA, CA	S	11.05 MW	10.74 AW	22990 AAW	CABLS	10//99-12//99
	Stockton-Lodi MSA, CA	S	9.23 MW	8.65 AW	19190 AAW	CABLS	10//99-12//99
	Vallejo-Fairfield-Napa PMSA, CA	S	10.50 MW	10.09 AW	21830 AAW	CABLS	10//99-12//99
	Ventura PMSA, CA	S	9.66 MW	9.38 AW	20100 AAW	CABLS	10//99-12//99
	Visalia-Tulare-Porterville MSA, CA	S	8.38 MW	8.16 AW	17430 AAW	CABLS	10//99-12//99
	Yolo PMSA, CA	S	9.96 MW	9.94 AW	20710 AAW	CABLS	10//99-12//99
	Yuba City MSA, CA	S	9.07 MW	8.63 AW	18870 AAW	CABLS	10//99-12//99
	Colorado	S	9.66 MW	9.77 AW	20330 AAW	COBLS	10//99-12//99
	Boulder-Longmont PMSA, CO	S	10.36 MW	10.10 AW	21550 AAW	COBLS	10//99-12//99
	Colorado Springs MSA, CO	S	9.43 MW	9.24 AW	19610 AAW	COBLS	10//99-12//99
	Denver PMSA, CO	S	10.13 MW	10.13 AW	21070 AAW	COBLS	10//99-12//99
	Fort Collins-Loveland MSA, CO	S	9.01 MW	8.82 AW	18750 AAW	COBLS	10//99-12//99
	Grand Junction MSA, CO	S	8.99 MW	8.74 AW	18710 AAW	COBLS	10//99-12//99
	Greeley PMSA, CO	S	9.20 MW	9.14 AW	19130 AAW	COBLS	10//99-12//99
	Pueblo MSA, CO	S	8.26 MW	8.39 AW	17180 AAW	COBLS	10//99-12//99
	Connecticut	S	10.96 MW	11.16 AW	23210 AAW	CTBLS	10//99-12//99
	Bridgeport PMSA, CT	S	11.73 MW	11.43 AW	24410 AAW	CTBLS	10//99-12//99
	Danbury PMSA, CT	S	10.80 MW	10.68 AW	22450 AAW	CTBLS	10//99-12//99
	Hartford MSA, CT	S	10.73 MW	10.59 AW	22320 AAW	CTBLS	10//99-12//99
	New Haven-Meriden PMSA, CT	S	11.31 MW	10.97 AW	23530 AAW	CTBLS	10//99-12//99
	New London-Norwich MSA, CT-RI	S	10.17 MW	9.89 AW	21160 AAW	CTBLS	10//99-12//99
	Stamford-Norwalk PMSA, CT	S	12.45 MW	12.29 AW	25900 AAW	CTBLS	10//99-12//99
	Waterbury PMSA, CT	S	10.50 MW	10.81 AW	21830 AAW	CTBLS	10//99-12//99
	Delaware	S	9.49 MW	9.68 AW	20140 AAW	DEBLS	10//99-12//99
	Dover MSA, DE	S	8.92 MW	8.31 AW	18560 AAW	DEBLS	10//99-12//99
	Wilmington-Newark PMSA, DE-MD	S	10.01 MW	9.81 AW	20810 AAW	DEBLS	10//99-12//99
	District of Columbia	S	10.99 MW	11.20 AW	23300 AAW	DCBLS	10//99-12//99
	Washington PMSA, DC-MD-VA-WV	S	10.40 MW	10.25 AW	21640 AAW	DCBLS	10//99-12//99
	Florida	S	8.76 MW	9.11 AW	18950 AAW	FLBLS	10//99-12//99
	Daytona Beach MSA, FL	S	8.36 MW	8.10 AW	17390 AAW	FLBLS	10//99-12//99
	Fort Lauderdale PMSA, FL	S	9.45 MW	9.17 AW	19660 AAW	FLBLS	10//99-12//99
	Fort Myers-Cape Coral MSA, FL	S	9.11 MW	9.07 AW	18950 AAW	FLBLS	10//99-12//99
	Fort Pierce-Port St. Lucie MSA, FL	S	8.79 MW	8.66 AW	18280 AAW	FLBLS	10//99-12//99
	Fort Walton Beach MSA, FL	S	8.66 MW	8.24 AW	18020 AAW	FLBLS	10//99-12//99
	Gainesville MSA, FL	S	8.42 MW	8.28 AW	17510 AAW	FLBLS	10//99-12//99
	Jacksonville MSA, FL	S	9.01 MW	8.81 AW	18740 AAW	FLBLS	10//99-12//99
	Lakeland-Winter Haven MSA, FL	S	8.37 MW	8.04 AW	17410 AAW	FLBLS	10//99-12//99
	Melbourne-Titusville-Palm Bay MSA, FL	S	8.81 MW	8.64 AW	18320 AAW	FLBLS	10//99-12//99
	Miami PMSA, FL	S	9.43 MW	9.33 AW	19620 AAW	FLBLS	10//99-12//99
	Naples MSA, FL	S	10.52 MW	9.78 AW	21880 AAW	FLBLS	10//99-12//99
	Ocala MSA, FL	S	8.36 MW	8.10 AW	17390 AAW	FLBLS	10//99-12//99
	Orlando MSA, FL	S	8.77 MW	8.41 AW	18240 AAW	FLBLS	10//99-12//99
	Panama City MSA, FL	S	8.10 MW	7.88 AW	16850 AAW	FLBLS	10//99-12//99
	Pensacola MSA, FL	S	8.11 MW	7.76 AW	16870 AAW	FLBLS	10//99-12//99
	Punta Gorda MSA, FL	S	8.02 MW	7.92 AW	16690 AAW	FLBLS	10//99-12//99
	Sarasota-Bradenton MSA, FL	S	8.91 MW	8.80 AW	18530 AAW	FLBLS	10//99-12//99
	Tallahassee MSA, FL	S	8.38 MW	8.05 AW	17440 AAW	FLBLS	10//99-12//99
	Tampa-St. Petersburg-Clearwater MSA, FL	S	9.38 MW	8.98 AW	19510 AAW	FLBLS	10//99-12//99
	West Palm Beach-Boca Raton MSA, FL	S	10.23 MW	9.84 AW	21270 AAW	FLBLS	10//99-12//99
	Georgia	S	9.13 MW	9.53 AW	19820 AAW	GABLS	10//99-12//99
	Albany MSA, GA	S	7.79 MW	7.64 AW	16210 AAW	GABLS	10//99-12//99
	Athens MSA, GA	S	8.26 MW	8.18 AW	17180 AAW	GABLS	10//99-12//99

AAW Average annual wage	**AOH** Average offered, high	**ASH** Average starting, high	**H** Hourly	**M** Monthly	**S** Special: hourly and annual
AE Average entry wage	**AOL** Average offered, low	**ASL** Average starting, low	**HI** Highest wage paid	**MTC** Median total compensation	**TQ** Third quartile wage
AEX Average experienced wage	**APH** Average pay, high range	**AW** Average wage paid	**HR** High end range	**MW** Median wage paid	**W** Weekly
AO Average offered	**APL** Average pay, low range	**FQ** First quartile wage	**LR** Low end range	**SQ** Second quartile wage	**Y** Yearly

Occupation/Type/Industry	Location	Per	Low	Mid	High	Source	Date
Receptionist and Information Clerk	Atlanta MSA, GA	S	10.33 MW	9.94 AW	21490 AAW	GABLS	10//99-12//99
	Augusta-Aiken MSA, GA-SC	S	8.70 MW	8.16 AW	18090 AAW	GABLS	10//99-12//99
	Columbus MSA, GA-AL	S	8.04 MW	7.91 AW	16720 AAW	GABLS	10//99-12//99
	Macon MSA, GA	S	8.73 MW	8.19 AW	18160 AAW	GABLS	10//99-12//99
	Savannah MSA, GA	S	8.50 MW	8.27 AW	17670 AAW	GABLS	10//99-12//99
	Hawaii	S	10.21 MW	10.25 AW	21310 AAW	HIBLS	10//99-12//99
	Honolulu MSA, HI	S	10.15 MW	9.99 AW	21100 AAW	HIBLS	10//99-12//99
	Idaho	S	8.92 MW	9.00 AW	18730 AAW	IDBLS	10//99-12//99
	Boise City MSA, ID	S	9.19 MW	8.95 AW	19110 AAW	IDBLS	10//99-12//99
	Pocatello MSA, ID	S	8.40 MW	8.32 AW	17470 AAW	IDBLS	10//99-12//99
	Illinois	S	9.57 MW	9.73 AW	20250 AAW	ILBLS	10//99-12//99
	Bloomington-Normal MSA, IL	S	9.16 MW	9.09 AW	19050 AAW	ILBLS	10//99-12//99
	Champaign-Urbana MSA, IL	S	9.12 MW	8.95 AW	18970 AAW	ILBLS	10//99-12//99
	Chicago PMSA, IL	S	10.04 MW	9.97 AW	20880 AAW	ILBLS	10//99-12//99
	Decatur MSA, IL	S	8.69 MW	8.26 AW	18080 AAW	ILBLS	10//99-12//99
	Kankakee PMSA, IL	S	8.63 MW	8.36 AW	17950 AAW	ILBLS	10//99-12//99
	Peoria-Pekin MSA, IL	S	9.43 MW	9.14 AW	19620 AAW	ILBLS	10//99-12//99
	Rockford MSA, IL	S	9.44 MW	8.92 AW	19640 AAW	ILBLS	10//99-12//99
	Springfield MSA, IL	S	9.03 MW	8.82 AW	18770 AAW	ILBLS	10//99-12//99
	Indiana	S	8.63 MW	8.78 AW	18260 AAW	INBLS	10//99-12//99
	Bloomington MSA, IN	S	8.87 MW	8.98 AW	18460 AAW	INBLS	10//99-12//99
	Elkhart-Goshen MSA, IN	S	9.14 MW	9.16 AW	19000 AAW	INBLS	10//99-12//99
	Evansville-Henderson MSA, IN-KY	S	8.09 MW	7.92 AW	16820 AAW	INBLS	10//99-12//99
	Fort Wayne MSA, IN	S	8.77 MW	8.62 AW	18250 AAW	INBLS	10//99-12//99
	Gary PMSA, IN	S	8.34 MW	8.12 AW	17350 AAW	INBLS	10//99-12//99
	Indianapolis MSA, IN	S	9.43 MW	9.39 AW	19610 AAW	INBLS	10//99-12//99
	Kokomo MSA, IN	S	8.09 MW	8.09 AW	16830 AAW	INBLS	10//99-12//99
	Lafayette MSA, IN	S	8.22 MW	7.92 AW	17090 AAW	INBLS	10//99-12//99
	Muncie MSA, IN	S	7.73 MW	7.53 AW	16080 AAW	INBLS	10//99-12//99
	South Bend MSA, IN	S	9.08 MW	8.96 AW	18880 AAW	INBLS	10//99-12//99
	Terre Haute MSA, IN	S	7.89 MW	7.68 AW	16400 AAW	INBLS	10//99-12//99
	Iowa	S	8.32 MW	8.58 AW	17840 AAW	IABLS	10//99-12//99
	Cedar Rapids MSA, IA	S	9.11 MW	8.91 AW	18940 AAW	IABLS	10//99-12//99
	Davenport-Moline-Rock Island MSA, IA-IL	S	8.26 MW	8.05 AW	17180 AAW	IABLS	10//99-12//99
	Des Moines MSA, IA	S	9.37 MW	9.26 AW	19480 AAW	IABLS	10//99-12//99
	Dubuque MSA, IA	S	8.34 MW	8.10 AW	17350 AAW	IABLS	10//99-12//99
	Iowa City MSA, IA	S	9.10 MW	8.91 AW	18920 AAW	IABLS	10//99-12//99
	Sioux City MSA, IA-NE	S	8.27 MW	8.23 AW	17190 AAW	IABLS	10//99-12//99
	Waterloo-Cedar Falls MSA, IA	S	8.37 MW	8.21 AW	17400 AAW	IABLS	10//99-12//99
	Kansas	S	8.63 MW	8.85 AW	18410 AAW	KSBLS	10//99-12//99
	Lawrence MSA, KS	S	8.32 MW	8.11 AW	17300 AAW	KSBLS	10//99-12//99
	Topeka MSA, KS	S	8.58 MW	8.30 AW	17840 AAW	KSBLS	10//99-12//99
	Wichita MSA, KS	S	8.82 MW	8.42 AW	18340 AAW	KSBLS	10//99-12//99
	Kentucky	S	8.31 MW	8.48 AW	17640 AAW	KYBLS	10//99-12//99
	Lexington MSA, KY	S	8.69 MW	8.69 AW	18080 AAW	KYBLS	10//99-12//99
	Louisville MSA, KY-IN	S	9.00 MW	8.86 AW	18730 AAW	KYBLS	10//99-12//99
	Owensboro MSA, KY	S	8.23 MW	8.05 AW	17110 AAW	KYBLS	10//99-12//99
	Louisiana	S	7.85 MW	8.10 AW	16850 AAW	LABLS	10//99-12//99
	Alexandria MSA, LA	S	7.86 MW	7.84 AW	16340 AAW	LABLS	10//99-12//99
	Baton Rouge MSA, LA	S	7.79 MW	7.62 AW	16210 AAW	LABLS	10//99-12//99
	Houma MSA, LA	S	8.07 MW	8.02 AW	16780 AAW	LABLS	10//99-12//99
	Lafayette MSA, LA	S	8.04 MW	7.85 AW	16720 AAW	LABLS	10//99-12//99
	Lake Charles MSA, LA	S	8.52 MW	8.20 AW	17720 AAW	LABLS	10//99-12//99
	Monroe MSA, LA	S	7.82 MW	7.60 AW	16260 AAW	LABLS	10//99-12//99
	New Orleans MSA, LA	S	8.46 MW	8.16 AW	17600 AAW	LABLS	10//99-12//99
	Shreveport-Bossier City MSA, LA	S	8.29 MW	7.87 AW	17250 AAW	LABLS	10//99-12//99
	Maine	S	8.76 MW	8.86 AW	18440 AAW	MEBLS	10//99-12//99
	Bangor MSA, ME	S	8.07 MW	7.92 AW	16790 AAW	MEBLS	10//99-12//99
	Lewiston-Auburn MSA, ME	S	8.35 MW	8.21 AW	17370 AAW	MEBLS	10//99-12//99
	Portland MSA, ME	S	9.70 MW	9.92 AW	20170 AAW	MEBLS	10//99-12//99
	Maryland	S	9.69 MW	10.01 AW	20820 AAW	MDBLS	10//99-12//99
	Baltimore PMSA, MD	S	9.84 MW	9.58 AW	20470 AAW	MDBLS	10//99-12//99
	Cumberland MSA, MD-WV	S	8.32 MW	7.76 AW	17300 AAW	MDBLS	10//99-12//99
	Hagerstown PMSA, MD	S	8.81 MW	8.89 AW	18320 AAW	MDBLS	10//99-12//99
	Massachusetts	S	10.44 MW	10.47 AW	21770 AAW	MABLS	10//99-12//99
	Barnstable-Yarmouth MSA, MA	S	9.99 MW	9.86 AW	20770 AAW	MABLS	10//99-12//99
	Boston PMSA, MA-NH	S	10.83 MW	10.76 AW	22520 AAW	MABLS	10//99-12//99

Occupation/Type/Industry	Location	Per	Low	Mid	High	Source	Date
Receptionist and Information Clerk							
	Brockton PMSA, MA	S	9.60 MW	9.07 AW	19970 AAW	MABLS	10//99-12//99
	Fitchburg-Leominster PMSA, MA	S	10.13 MW	10.13 AW	21080 AAW	MABLS	10//99-12//99
	Lawrence PMSA, MA-NH	S	9.75 MW	9.48 AW	20280 AAW	MABLS	10//99-12//99
	Lowell PMSA, MA-NH	S	10.83 MW	10.73 AW	22520 AAW	MABLS	10//99-12//99
	New Bedford PMSA, MA	S	9.24 MW	9.03 AW	19230 AAW	MABLS	10//99-12//99
	Pittsfield MSA, MA	S	9.91 MW	9.81 AW	20600 AAW	MABLS	10//99-12//99
	Springfield MSA, MA	S	9.91 MW	9.63 AW	20600 AAW	MABLS	10//99-12//99
	Worcester PMSA, MA-CT	S	9.84 MW	9.98 AW	20470 AAW	MABLS	10//99-12//99
	Michigan	S	9.18 MW	9.37 AW	19490 AAW	MIBLS	10//99-12//99
	Ann Arbor PMSA, MI	S	9.55 MW	9.35 AW	19860 AAW	MIBLS	10//99-12//99
	Benton Harbor MSA, MI	S	8.68 MW	8.39 AW	18060 AAW	MIBLS	10//99-12//99
	Detroit PMSA, MI	S	9.70 MW	9.59 AW	20170 AAW	MIBLS	10//99-12//99
	Flint PMSA, MI	S	8.76 MW	8.59 AW	18220 AAW	MIBLS	10//99-12//99
	Grand Rapids-Muskegon-Holland MSA, MI	S	9.37 MW	9.30 AW	19480 AAW	MIBLS	10//99-12//99
	Jackson MSA, MI	S	8.96 MW	8.89 AW	18630 AAW	MIBLS	10//99-12//99
	Kalamazoo-Battle Creek MSA, MI	S	8.74 MW	8.42 AW	18180 AAW	MIBLS	10//99-12//99
	Lansing-East Lansing MSA, MI	S	9.01 MW	8.66 AW	18740 AAW	MIBLS	10//99-12//99
	Saginaw-Bay City-Midland MSA, MI	S	8.46 MW	8.13 AW	17600 AAW	MIBLS	10//99-12//99
	Minnesota	S	9.81 MW	9.91 AW	20620 AAW	MNBLS	10//99-12//99
	Duluth-Superior MSA, MN-WI	S	8.60 MW	8.31 AW	17880 AAW	MNBLS	10//99-12//99
	Minneapolis-St. Paul MSA, MN-WI	S	10.36 MW	10.27 AW	21540 AAW	MNBLS	10//99-12//99
	St. Cloud MSA, MN	S	8.84 MW	8.57 AW	18390 AAW	MNBLS	10//99-12//99
	Mississippi	S	7.96 MW	8.14 AW	16930 AAW	MSBLS	10//99-12//99
	Biloxi-Gulfport-Pascagoula MSA, MS	S	7.88 MW	7.68 AW	16380 AAW	MSBLS	10//99-12//99
	Hattiesburg MSA, MS	S	7.36 MW	7.22 AW	15320 AAW	MSBLS	10//99-12//99
	Jackson MSA, MS	S	8.66 MW	8.46 AW	18010 AAW	MSBLS	10//99-12//99
	Missouri	S	8.43 MW	8.68 AW	18060 AAW	MOBLS	10//99-12//99
	Columbia MSA, MO	S	8.60 MW	8.44 AW	17900 AAW	MOBLS	10//99-12//99
	Joplin MSA, MO	S	7.95 MW	7.81 AW	16540 AAW	MOBLS	10//99-12//99
	Kansas City MSA, MO-KS	S	9.63 MW	9.58 AW	20020 AAW	MOBLS	10//99-12//99
	St. Joseph MSA, MO	S	7.67 MW	7.55 AW	15950 AAW	MOBLS	10//99-12//99
	St. Louis MSA, MO-IL	S	8.72 MW	8.49 AW	18140 AAW	MOBLS	10//99-12//99
	Springfield MSA, MO	S	7.85 MW	7.73 AW	16320 AAW	MOBLS	10//99-12//99
	Montana	S	7.62 MW	7.87 AW	16370 AAW	MTBLS	10//99-12//99
	Billings MSA, MT	S	8.49 MW	8.23 AW	17670 AAW	MTBLS	10//99-12//99
	Great Falls MSA, MT	S	7.97 MW	7.72 AW	16570 AAW	MTBLS	10//99-12//99
	Missoula MSA, MT	S	8.26 MW	8.07 AW	17190 AAW	MTBLS	10//99-12//99
	Nebraska	S	8.41 MW	8.64 AW	17960 AAW	NEBLS	10//99-12//99
	Lincoln MSA, NE	S	8.67 MW	8.57 AW	18030 AAW	NEBLS	10//99-12//99
	Omaha MSA, NE-IA	S	9.23 MW	9.03 AW	19190 AAW	NEBLS	10//99-12//99
	Nevada	S	9.44 MW	9.65 AW	20070 AAW	NVBLS	10//99-12//99
	Las Vegas MSA, NV-AZ	S	9.42 MW	9.31 AW	19590 AAW	NVBLS	10//99-12//99
	Reno MSA, NV	S	10.45 MW	9.83 AW	21740 AAW	NVBLS	10//99-12//99
	New Hampshire	S	9.32 MW	9.37 AW	19490 AAW	NHBLS	10//99-12//99
	Manchester PMSA, NH	S	9.68 MW	9.62 AW	20130 AAW	NHBLS	10//99-12//99
	Nashua PMSA, NH	S	9.72 MW	9.62 AW	20210 AAW	NHBLS	10//99-12//99
	Portsmouth-Rochester PMSA, NH-ME	S	9.57 MW	9.46 AW	19900 AAW	NHBLS	10//99-12//99
	New Jersey	S	10.24 MW	10.47 AW	21780 AAW	NJBLS	10//99-12//99
	Atlantic-Cape May PMSA, NJ	S	9.18 MW	8.85 AW	19100 AAW	NJBLS	10//99-12//99
	Bergen-Passaic PMSA, NJ	S	10.67 MW	10.41 AW	22190 AAW	NJBLS	10//99-12//99
	Jersey City PMSA, NJ	S	10.00 MW	9.08 AW	20800 AAW	NJBLS	10//99-12//99
	Middlesex-Somerset-Hunterdon PMSA, NJ	S	10.40 MW	10.21 AW	21640 AAW	NJBLS	10//99-12//99
	Monmouth-Ocean PMSA, NJ	S	9.61 MW	9.55 AW	19980 AAW	NJBLS	10//99-12//99
	Newark PMSA, NJ	S	11.15 MW	10.85 AW	23190 AAW	NJBLS	10//99-12//99
	Trenton PMSA, NJ	S	10.77 MW	10.52 AW	22400 AAW	NJBLS	10//99-12//99
	Vineland-Millville-Bridgeton PMSA, NJ	S	9.05 MW	9.18 AW	18830 AAW	NJBLS	10//99-12//99
	New Mexico	S	8.05 MW	8.29 AW	17240 AAW	NMBLS	10//99-12//99
	Albuquerque MSA, NM	S	8.47 MW	8.21 AW	17620 AAW	NMBLS	10//99-12//99
	Las Cruces MSA, NM	S	7.76 MW	7.27 AW	16140 AAW	NMBLS	10//99-12//99
	Santa Fe MSA, NM	S	9.49 MW	9.46 AW	19750 AAW	NMBLS	10//99-12//99
	New York	S	10.26 MW	10.49 AW	21810 AAW	NYBLS	10//99-12//99

AAW Average annual wage	**AOH** Average offered, high	**ASH** Average starting, high	**H** Hourly	**M** Monthly	**S** Special: hourly and annual
AE Average entry wage	**AOL** Average offered, low	**ASL** Average starting, low	**HI** Highest wage paid	**MTC** Median total compensation	**TQ** Third quartile wage
AEX Average experienced wage	**APH** Average pay, high range	**AW** Average wage paid	**HR** High end range	**MW** Median wage paid	**W** Weekly
AO Average offered	**APL** Average pay, low range	**FQ** First quartile wage	**LR** Low end range	**SQ** Second quartile wage	**Y** Yearly

Occupation/Type/Industry	Location	Per	Low	Mid	High	Source	Date
Receptionist and Information Clerk							
	Albany-Schenectady-Troy MSA, NY	S	9.41 MW	9.40 AW	19570 AAW	NYBLS	10//99-12//99
	Binghamton MSA, NY	S	7.87 MW	7.34 AW	16360 AAW	NYBLS	10//99-12//99
	Buffalo-Niagara Falls MSA, NY	S	8.87 MW	8.61 AW	18450 AAW	NYBLS	10//99-12//99
	Dutchess County PMSA, NY	S	10.15 MW	9.71 AW	21110 AAW	NYBLS	10//99-12//99
	Elmira MSA, NY	S	8.33 MW	8.26 AW	17330 AAW	NYBLS	10//99-12//99
	Glens Falls MSA, NY	S	8.74 MW	8.39 AW	18180 AAW	NYBLS	10//99-12//99
	Jamestown MSA, NY	S	8.36 MW	8.07 AW	17380 AAW	NYBLS	10//99-12//99
	Nassau-Suffolk PMSA, NY	S	10.64 MW	10.56 AW	22130 AAW	NYBLS	10//99-12//99
	New York PMSA, NY	S	11.37 MW	11.18 AW	23650 AAW	NYBLS	10//99-12//99
	Newburgh PMSA, NY-PA	S	9.22 MW	8.73 AW	19180 AAW	NYBLS	10//99-12//99
	Rochester MSA, NY	S	9.17 MW	9.21 AW	19080 AAW	NYBLS	10//99-12//99
	Syracuse MSA, NY	S	9.40 MW	9.10 AW	19550 AAW	NYBLS	10//99-12//99
	Utica-Rome MSA, NY	S	9.07 MW	8.94 AW	18870 AAW	NYBLS	10//99-12//99
	North Carolina	S	9.16 MW	9.29 AW	19330 AAW	NCBLS	10//99-12//99
	Asheville MSA, NC	S	8.48 MW	8.13 AW	17640 AAW	NCBLS	10//99-12//99
	Charlotte-Gastonia-Rock Hill MSA, NC-SC	S	10.03 MW	9.90 AW	20860 AAW	NCBLS	10//99-12//99
	Fayetteville MSA, NC	S	7.68 MW	7.59 AW	15970 AAW	NCBLS	10//99-12//99
	Goldsboro MSA, NC	S	9.12 MW	8.91 AW	18970 AAW	NCBLS	10//99-12//99
	Greensboro--Winston-Salem-- High Point MSA, NC	S	9.49 MW	9.33 AW	19740 AAW	NCBLS	10//99-12//99
	Greenville MSA, NC	S	8.26 MW	8.02 AW	17180 AAW	NCBLS	10//99-12//99
	Hickory-Morganton-Lenoir MSA, NC	S	9.28 MW	9.17 AW	19300 AAW	NCBLS	10//99-12//99
	Jacksonville MSA, NC	S	7.12 MW	6.87 AW	14820 AAW	NCBLS	10//99-12//99
	Raleigh-Durham-Chapel Hill MSA, NC	S	9.89 MW	9.82 AW	20570 AAW	NCBLS	10//99-12//99
	Rocky Mount MSA, NC	S	9.05 MW	8.91 AW	18830 AAW	NCBLS	10//99-12//99
	Wilmington MSA, NC	S	8.68 MW	8.81 AW	18050 AAW	NCBLS	10//99-12//99
	North Dakota	S	7.82 MW	8.17 AW	16990 AAW	NDBLS	10//99-12//99
	Bismarck MSA, ND	S	7.97 MW	7.65 AW	16580 AAW	NDBLS	10//99-12//99
	Fargo-Moorhead MSA, ND-MN	S	8.84 MW	8.56 AW	18390 AAW	NDBLS	10//99-12//99
	Grand Forks MSA, ND-MN	S	7.97 MW	7.74 AW	16590 AAW	NDBLS	10//99-12//99
	Ohio	S	8.72 MW	8.95 AW	18610 AAW	OHBLS	10//99-12//99
	Akron PMSA, OH	S	8.92 MW	8.76 AW	18550 AAW	OHBLS	10//99-12//99
	Canton-Massillon MSA, OH	S	8.49 MW	8.49 AW	17660 AAW	OHBLS	10//99-12//99
	Cincinnati PMSA, OH-KY-IN	S	9.44 MW	9.29 AW	19640 AAW	OHBLS	10//99-12//99
	Cleveland-Lorain-Elyria PMSA, OH	S	9.33 MW	9.12 AW	19410 AAW	OHBLS	10//99-12//99
	Columbus MSA, OH	S	9.08 MW	8.97 AW	18890 AAW	OHBLS	10//99-12//99
	Dayton-Springfield MSA, OH	S	8.44 MW	8.21 AW	17560 AAW	OHBLS	10//99-12//99
	Hamilton-Middletown PMSA, OH	S	8.90 MW	8.75 AW	18510 AAW	OHBLS	10//99-12//99
	Lima MSA, OH	S	8.38 MW	7.88 AW	17440 AAW	OHBLS	10//99-12//99
	Mansfield MSA, OH	S	8.55 MW	8.44 AW	17790 AAW	OHBLS	10//99-12//99
	Steubenville-Weirton MSA, OH-WV	S	7.33 MW	6.99 AW	15240 AAW	OHBLS	10//99-12//99
	Toledo MSA, OH	S	8.93 MW	8.69 AW	18570 AAW	OHBLS	10//99-12//99
	Youngstown-Warren MSA, OH	S	8.24 MW	7.97 AW	17140 AAW	OHBLS	10//99-12//99
	Oklahoma	S	8.11 MW	8.49 AW	17650 AAW	OKBLS	10//99-12//99
	Enid MSA, OK	S	8.64 MW	8.23 AW	17960 AAW	OKBLS	10//99-12//99
	Lawton MSA, OK	S	6.87 MW	6.57 AW	14280 AAW	OKBLS	10//99-12//99
	Oklahoma City MSA, OK	S	8.87 MW	8.43 AW	18450 AAW	OKBLS	10//99-12//99
	Tulsa MSA, OK	S	8.85 MW	8.87 AW	18400 AAW	OKBLS	10//99-12//99
	Oregon	S	9.76 MW	10.25 AW	21330 AAW	ORBLS	10//99-12//99
	Corvallis MSA, OR	S	9.95 MW	9.48 AW	20700 AAW	ORBLS	10//99-12//99
	Eugene-Springfield MSA, OR	S	9.97 MW	9.78 AW	20750 AAW	ORBLS	10//99-12//99
	Medford-Ashland MSA, OR	S	9.34 MW	8.92 AW	19430 AAW	ORBLS	10//99-12//99
	Portland-Vancouver PMSA, OR-WA	S	10.79 MW	10.14 AW	22440 AAW	ORBLS	10//99-12//99
	Salem PMSA, OR	S	9.94 MW	9.79 AW	20680 AAW	ORBLS	10//99-12//99
	Pennsylvania	S	9.04 MW	9.23 AW	19200 AAW	PABLS	10//99-12//99
	Allentown-Bethlehem-Easton MSA, PA	S	9.28 MW	9.20 AW	19300 AAW	PABLS	10//99-12//99
	Altoona MSA, PA	S	8.50 MW	8.18 AW	17680 AAW	PABLS	10//99-12//99
	Erie MSA, PA	S	8.01 MW	7.78 AW	16660 AAW	PABLS	10//99-12//99
	Harrisburg-Lebanon-Carlisle MSA, PA	S	9.45 MW	9.19 AW	19650 AAW	PABLS	10//99-12//99

AAW	Average annual wage	AOH	Average offered, high	ASH	Average starting, high
AE	Average entry wage	AOL	Average offered, low	ASL	Average starting, low
AEX	Average experienced wage	APH	Average pay, high range	AW	Average wage paid
AO	Average offered	APL	Average pay, low range	FQ	First quartile wage

H	Hourly	M	Monthly	S	Special: hourly and annual
HI	Highest wage paid	MTC	Median total compensation	TQ	Third quartile wage
HR	High end range	MW	Median wage paid	W	Weekly
LR	Low end range	SQ	Second quartile wage	Y	Yearly

Occupation/Type/Industry	Location	Per	Low	Mid	High	Source	Date
Receptionist and Information Clerk							
	Johnstown MSA, PA	S	7.46 MW	7.27 AW	15520 AAW	PABLS	10//99-12//99
	Lancaster MSA, PA	S	9.15 MW	9.10 AW	19030 AAW	PABLS	10//99-12//99
	Philadelphia PMSA, PA-NJ	S	10.08 MW	10.03 AW	20980 AAW	PABLS	10//99-12//99
	Pittsburgh MSA, PA	S	8.56 MW	8.17 AW	17810 AAW	PABLS	10//99-12//99
	Reading MSA, PA	S	8.85 MW	8.83 AW	18420 AAW	PABLS	10//99-12//99
	Scranton--Wilkes-Barre-- Hazleton MSA, PA	S	8.45 MW	8.31 AW	17570 AAW	PABLS	10//99-12//99
	Sharon MSA, PA	S	8.12 MW	8.00 AW	16890 AAW	PABLS	10//99-12//99
	State College MSA, PA	S	8.76 MW	8.69 AW	18210 AAW	PABLS	10//99-12//99
	Williamsport MSA, PA	S	7.67 MW	7.49 AW	15960 AAW	PABLS	10//99-12//99
	York MSA, PA	S	8.72 MW	8.50 AW	18140 AAW	PABLS	10//99-12//99
	Rhode Island	S	10.07 MW	10.47 AW	21770 AAW	RIBLS	10//99-12//99
	Providence-Fall River- Warwick MSA, RI-MA	S	10.28 MW	9.95 AW	21380 AAW	RIBLS	10//99-12//99
	South Carolina	S	8.48 MW	8.73 AW	18160 AAW	SCBLS	10//99-12//99
	Charleston-North Charleston MSA, SC	S	8.64 MW	8.42 AW	17960 AAW	SCBLS	10//99-12//99
	Columbia MSA, SC	S	8.65 MW	8.36 AW	17990 AAW	SCBLS	10//99-12//99
	Florence MSA, SC	S	9.74 MW	9.36 AW	20250 AAW	SCBLS	10//99-12//99
	Greenville-Spartanburg- Anderson MSA, SC	S	9.07 MW	8.97 AW	18860 AAW	SCBLS	10//99-12//99
	Myrtle Beach MSA, SC	S	7.91 MW	7.68 AW	16450 AAW	SCBLS	10//99-12//99
	Sumter MSA, SC	S	8.34 MW	8.23 AW	17350 AAW	SCBLS	10//99-12//99
	South Dakota	S	7.96 MW	8.01 AW	16660 AAW	SDBLS	10//99-12//99
	Rapid City MSA, SD	S	7.90 MW	7.81 AW	16430 AAW	SDBLS	10//99-12//99
	Sioux Falls MSA, SD	S	8.42 MW	8.39 AW	17520 AAW	SDBLS	10//99-12//99
	Tennessee	S	8.94 MW	9.01 AW	18750 AAW	TNBLS	10//99-12//99
	Chattanooga MSA, TN-GA	S	8.77 MW	8.75 AW	18240 AAW	TNBLS	10//99-12//99
	Clarksville-Hopkinsville MSA, TN-KY	S	8.03 MW	7.97 AW	16710 AAW	TNBLS	10//99-12//99
	Jackson MSA, TN	S	8.67 MW	8.56 AW	18020 AAW	TNBLS	10//99-12//99
	Johnson City-Kingsport-Bristol MSA, TN-VA	S	8.52 MW	8.22 AW	17720 AAW	TNBLS	10//99-12//99
	Knoxville MSA, TN	S	9.10 MW	8.83 AW	18920 AAW	TNBLS	10//99-12//99
	Memphis MSA, TN-AR-MS	S	9.09 MW	9.03 AW	18900 AAW	MSBLS	10//99-12//99
	Nashville MSA, TN	S	9.53 MW	9.54 AW	19830 AAW	TNBLS	10//99-12//99
	Texas	S	8.76 MW	9.13 AW	19000 AAW	TXBLS	10//99-12//99
	Abilene MSA, TX	S	8.29 MW	7.58 AW	17240 AAW	TXBLS	10//99-12//99
	Amarillo MSA, TX	S	8.11 MW	7.65 AW	16870 AAW	TXBLS	10//99-12//99
	Austin-San Marcos MSA, TX	S	10.31 MW	9.88 AW	21440 AAW	TXBLS	10//99-12//99
	Beaumont-Port Arthur MSA, TX	S	8.18 MW	7.87 AW	17020 AAW	TXBLS	10//99-12//99
	Brazoria PMSA, TX	S	7.84 MW	7.41 AW	16300 AAW	TXBLS	10//99-12//99
	Brownsville-Harlingen-San Benito MSA, TX	S	7.95 MW	7.75 AW	16540 AAW	TXBLS	10//99-12//99
	Bryan-College Station MSA, TX	S	8.01 MW	7.88 AW	16670 AAW	TXBLS	10//99-12//99
	Corpus Christi MSA, TX	S	7.87 MW	7.59 AW	16380 AAW	TXBLS	10//99-12//99
	Dallas PMSA, TX	S	9.87 MW	9.67 AW	20520 AAW	TXBLS	10//99-12//99
	El Paso MSA, TX	S	7.84 MW	7.47 AW	16300 AAW	TXBLS	10//99-12//99
	Fort Worth-Arlington PMSA, TX	S	9.25 MW	8.89 AW	19250 AAW	TXBLS	10//99-12//99
	Galveston-Texas City PMSA, TX	S	8.68 MW	8.56 AW	18050 AAW	TXBLS	10//99-12//99
	Houston PMSA, TX	S	9.54 MW	9.44 AW	19850 AAW	TXBLS	10//99-12//99
	Killeen-Temple MSA, TX	S	7.38 MW	7.20 AW	15360 AAW	TXBLS	10//99-12//99
	Laredo MSA, TX	S	7.36 MW	6.87 AW	15300 AAW	TXBLS	10//99-12//99
	Longview-Marshall MSA, TX	S	8.08 MW	7.89 AW	16800 AAW	TXBLS	10//99-12//99
	Lubbock MSA, TX	S	7.80 MW	7.63 AW	16220 AAW	TXBLS	10//99-12//99
	McAllen-Edinburg-Mission MSA, TX	S	7.03 MW	6.70 AW	14620 AAW	TXBLS	10//99-12//99
	Odessa-Midland MSA, TX	S	8.16 MW	7.98 AW	16960 AAW	TXBLS	10//99-12//99
	San Angelo MSA, TX	S	7.82 MW	7.30 AW	16280 AAW	TXBLS	10//99-12//99
	San Antonio MSA, TX	S	8.70 MW	8.28 AW	18100 AAW	TXBLS	10//99-12//99
	Sherman-Denison MSA, TX	S	8.84 MW	8.26 AW	18380 AAW	TXBLS	10//99-12//99
	Texarkana MSA, TX- Texarkana, AR	S	7.69 MW	7.33 AW	16000 AAW	TXBLS	10//99-12//99
	Tyler MSA, TX	S	8.17 MW	7.93 AW	16980 AAW	TXBLS	10//99-12//99
	Victoria MSA, TX	S	8.51 MW	8.01 AW	17690 AAW	TXBLS	10//99-12//99
	Waco MSA, TX	S	8.74 MW	8.46 AW	18180 AAW	TXBLS	10//99-12//99
	Wichita Falls MSA, TX	S	7.80 MW	7.44 AW	16220 AAW	TXBLS	10//99-12//99

AAW Average annual wage	**AOH** Average offered, high	**ASH** Average starting, high	**H** Hourly	**M** Monthly	**S** Special: hourly and annual
AE Average entry wage	**AOL** Average offered, low	**ASL** Average starting, low	**HI** Highest wage paid	**MTC** Median total compensation	**TQ** Third quartile wage
AEX Average experienced wage	**APH** Average pay, high range	**AW** Average wage paid	**HR** High end range	**MW** Median wage paid	**W** Weekly
AO Average offered	**APL** Average pay, low range	**FQ** First quartile wage	**LR** Low end range	**SQ** Second quartile wage	**Y** Yearly

Occupation/Type/Industry	Location	Per	Low	Mid	High	Source	Date
Receptionist and Information Clerk	Utah	S	8.48 MW	8.72 AW	18130 AAW	UTBLS	10//99-12//99
	Provo-Orem MSA, UT	S	8.19 MW	8.07 AW	17030 AAW	UTBLS	10//99-12//99
	Salt Lake City-Ogden MSA, UT	S	8.97 MW	8.75 AW	18660 AAW	UTBLS	10//99-12//99
	Vermont	S	9.4 MW	9.58 AW	19940 AAW	VTBLS	10//99-12//99
	Burlington MSA, VT	S	10.24 MW	9.99 AW	21290 AAW	VTBLS	10//99-12//99
	Virginia	S	8.74 MW	9.10 AW	18920 AAW	VABLS	10//99-12//99
	Charlottesville MSA, VA	S	9.07 MW	8.87 AW	18860 AAW	VABLS	10//99-12//99
	Danville MSA, VA	S	8.26 MW	8.03 AW	17190 AAW	VABLS	10//99-12//99
	Lynchburg MSA, VA	S	8.05 MW	7.73 AW	16740 AAW	VABLS	10//99-12//99
	Norfolk-Virginia Beach-Newport News MSA, VA-NC	S	8.28 MW	8.05 AW	17220 AAW	VABLS	10//99-12//99
	Richmond-Petersburg MSA, VA	S	8.81 MW	8.67 AW	18320 AAW	VABLS	10//99-12//99
	Roanoke MSA, VA	S	8.36 MW	8.15 AW	17390 AAW	VABLS	10//99-12//99
	Washington	S	9.97 MW	10.37 AW	21560 AAW	WABLS	10//99-12//99
	Bellingham MSA, WA	S	9.65 MW	9.70 AW	20070 AAW	WABLS	10//99-12//99
	Bremerton PMSA, WA	S	10.21 MW	9.76 AW	21250 AAW	WABLS	10//99-12//99
	Olympia PMSA, WA	S	9.57 MW	8.88 AW	19900 AAW	WABLS	10//99-12//99
	Richland-Kennewick-Pasco MSA, WA	S	10.60 MW	9.90 AW	22040 AAW	WABLS	10//99-12//99
	Seattle-Bellevue-Everett PMSA, WA	S	10.81 MW	10.29 AW	22480 AAW	WABLS	10//99-12//99
	Spokane MSA, WA	S	8.92 MW	8.73 AW	18540 AAW	WABLS	10//99-12//99
	Tacoma PMSA, WA	S	10.37 MW	10.38 AW	21580 AAW	WABLS	10//99-12//99
	Yakima MSA, WA	S	9.84 MW	9.69 AW	20470 AAW	WABLS	10//99-12//99
	West Virginia	S	7.56 MW	7.83 AW	16280 AAW	WVBLS	10//99-12//99
	Charleston MSA, WV	S	7.92 MW	7.71 AW	16480 AAW	WVBLS	10//99-12//99
	Huntington-Ashland MSA, WV-KY-OH	S	8.15 MW	7.88 AW	16940 AAW	WVBLS	10//99-12//99
	Parkersburg-Marietta MSA, WV-OH	S	7.99 MW	7.85 AW	16610 AAW	WVBLS	10//99-12//99
	Wheeling MSA, WV-OH	S	7.56 MW	7.25 AW	15710 AAW	WVBLS	10//99-12//99
	Wisconsin	S	9.03 MW	9.12 AW	18970 AAW	WIBLS	10//99-12//99
	Appleton-Oshkosh-Neenah MSA, WI	S	8.92 MW	8.80 AW	18560 AAW	WIBLS	10//99-12//99
	Eau Claire MSA, WI	S	8.85 MW	8.59 AW	18420 AAW	WIBLS	10//99-12//99
	Green Bay MSA, WI	S	8.75 MW	8.73 AW	18200 AAW	WIBLS	10//99-12//99
	Janesville-Beloit MSA, WI	S	8.52 MW	8.34 AW	17720 AAW	WIBLS	10//99-12//99
	Kenosha PMSA, WI	S	10.15 MW	8.90 AW	21110 AAW	WIBLS	10//99-12//99
	La Crosse MSA, WI-MN	S	9.10 MW	9.02 AW	18920 AAW	WIBLS	10//99-12//99
	Madison MSA, WI	S	9.76 MW	9.65 AW	20310 AAW	WIBLS	10//99-12//99
	Milwaukee-Waukesha PMSA, WI	S	9.61 MW	9.52 AW	19980 AAW	WIBLS	10//99-12//99
	Racine PMSA, WI	S	9.17 MW	8.92 AW	19080 AAW	WIBLS	10//99-12//99
	Sheboygan MSA, WI	S	9.22 MW	9.02 AW	19180 AAW	WIBLS	10//99-12//99
	Wausau MSA, WI	S	8.97 MW	8.83 AW	18660 AAW	WIBLS	10//99-12//99
	Wyoming	S	7.94 MW	8.11 AW	16870 AAW	WYBLS	10//99-12//99
	Casper MSA, WY	S	8.30 MW	8.12 AW	17260 AAW	WYBLS	10//99-12//99
	Cheyenne MSA, WY	S	7.17 MW	6.97 AW	14920 AAW	WYBLS	10//99-12//99
	Puerto Rico	S	6.32 MW	6.73 AW	14000 AAW	PRBLS	10//99-12//99
	Aguadilla MSA, PR	S	6.48 MW	6.15 AW	13480 AAW	PRBLS	10//99-12//99
	Arecibo PMSA, PR	S	6.47 MW	6.30 AW	13460 AAW	PRBLS	10//99-12//99
	Caguas PMSA, PR	S	6.85 MW	6.37 AW	14240 AAW	PRBLS	10//99-12//99
	Mayaguez MSA, PR	S	6.16 MW	6.10 AW	12800 AAW	PRBLS	10//99-12//99
	Ponce MSA, PR	S	6.93 MW	6.50 AW	14400 AAW	PRBLS	10//99-12//99
	San Juan-Bayamon PMSA, PR	S	6.79 MW	6.37 AW	14110 AAW	PRBLS	10//99-12//99
	Virgin Islands	S	7.99 MW	8.31 AW	17280 AAW	VIBLS	10//99-12//99
	Guam	S	7.98 MW	8.52 AW	17730 AAW	GUBLS	10//99-12//99
Recreation and Fitness Studies Teacher							
Postsecondary	Alabama	Y		35150 AAW		ALBLS	10//99-12//99
Postsecondary	Arkansas	Y		29910 AAW		ARBLS	10//99-12//99
Postsecondary	California	Y		50970 AAW		CABLS	10//99-12//99
Postsecondary	Colorado	Y		36400 AAW		COBLS	10//99-12//99
Postsecondary	Florida	Y		51070 AAW		FLBLS	10//99-12//99
Postsecondary	Georgia	Y		43270 AAW		GABLS	10//99-12//99
Postsecondary	Illinois	Y		45080 AAW		ILBLS	10//99-12//99
Postsecondary	Indiana	Y		39390 AAW		INBLS	10//99-12//99

AAW Average annual wage	**AOH** Average offered, high	**ASH** Average starting, high	**H** Hourly	**M** Monthly	**S** Special: hourly and annual
AE Average entry wage	**AOL** Average offered, low	**ASL** Average starting, low	**HI** Highest wage paid	**MTC** Median total compensation	**TQ** Third quartile wage
AEX Average experienced wage	**APH** Average pay, high range	**AW** Average wage paid	**HR** High end range	**MW** Median wage paid	**W** Weekly
AO Average offered	**APL** Average pay, low range	**FQ** First quartile wage	**LR** Low end range	**SQ** Second quartile wage	**Y** Yearly

Occupation/Type/Industry	Location	Per	Low	Mid	High	Source	Date
Recreation and Fitness Studies							
Teacher							
Postsecondary	Iowa	Y		47010 AAW		IABLS	10//99-12//99
Postsecondary	Kansas	Y		34140 AAW		KSBLS	10//99-12//99
Postsecondary	Kentucky	Y		28160 AAW		KYBLS	10//99-12//99
Postsecondary	Louisiana	Y		43090 AAW		LABLS	10//99-12//99
Postsecondary	Maryland	Y		57450 AAW		MDBLS	10//99-12//99
Postsecondary	Massachusetts	Y		50400 AAW		MABLS	10//99-12//99
Postsecondary	Michigan	Y		48100 AAW		MIBLS	10//99-12//99
Postsecondary	Minnesota	Y		47570 AAW		MNBLS	10//99-12//99
Postsecondary	Mississippi	Y		40230 AAW		MSBLS	10//99-12//99
Postsecondary	Missouri	Y		42330 AAW		MOBLS	10//99-12//99
Postsecondary	Nebraska	Y		33940 AAW		NEBLS	10//99-12//99
Postsecondary	New Hampshire	Y		46070 AAW		NHBLS	10//99-12//99
Postsecondary	New Jersey	Y		55820 AAW		NJBLS	10//99-12//99
Postsecondary	New Mexico	Y		23840 AAW		NMBLS	10//99-12//99
Postsecondary	New York	Y		65460 AAW		NYBLS	10//99-12//99
Postsecondary	North Carolina	Y		44260 AAW		NCBLS	10//99-12//99
Postsecondary	North Dakota	Y		34760 AAW		NDBLS	10//99-12//99
Postsecondary	Oklahoma	Y		32930 AAW		OKBLS	10//99-12//99
Postsecondary	Oregon	Y		47540 AAW		ORBLS	10//99-12//99
Postsecondary	Pennsylvania	Y		53120 AAW		PABLS	10//99-12//99
Postsecondary	South Carolina	Y		42430 AAW		SCBLS	10//99-12//99
Postsecondary	South Dakota	Y		40800 AAW		SDBLS	10//99-12//99
Postsecondary	Tennessee	Y		39560 AAW		TNBLS	10//99-12//99
Postsecondary	Texas	Y		39540 AAW		TXBLS	10//99-12//99
Postsecondary	Virginia	Y		40480 AAW		VABLS	10//99-12//99
Postsecondary	Washington	Y		53360 AAW		WABLS	10//99-12//99
Postsecondary	West Virginia	Y		46820 AAW		WVBLS	10//99-12//99
Postsecondary	Wisconsin	Y		38220 AAW		WIBLS	10//99-12//99
Postsecondary	Puerto Rico	Y		44790 AAW		PRBLS	10//99-12//99
Recreation Worker	United States	H		13.39 AW		NCS98	1998
	Alabama	S	7.78 MW	8.43 AW	17530 AAW	ALBLS	10//99-12//99
	Birmingham MSA, AL	S	9.36 MW	9.31 AW	19470 AAW	ALBLS	10//99-12//99
	Decatur MSA, AL	S	6.92 MW	7.07 AW	14400 AAW	ALBLS	10//99-12//99
	Dothan MSA, AL	S	7.44 MW	6.55 AW	15470 AAW	ALBLS	10//99-12//99
	Florence MSA, AL	S	6.89 MW	6.34 AW	14330 AAW	ALBLS	10//99-12//99
	Gadsden MSA, AL	S	7.22 MW	7.37 AW	15010 AAW	ALBLS	10//99-12//99
	Huntsville MSA, AL	S	8.00 MW	6.92 AW	16640 AAW	ALBLS	10//99-12//99
	Mobile MSA, AL	S	8.84 MW	8.90 AW	18400 AAW	ALBLS	10//99-12//99
	Montgomery MSA, AL	S	7.38 MW	7.18 AW	15350 AAW	ALBLS	10//99-12//99
	Tuscaloosa MSA, AL	S	10.16 MW	9.93 AW	21140 AAW	ALBLS	10//99-12//99
	Alaska	S	8.84 MW	9.49 AW	19740 AAW	AKBLS	10//99-12//99
	Anchorage MSA, AK	S	8.87 MW	8.37 AW	18450 AAW	AKBLS	10//99-12//99
	Arizona	S	8.31 MW	9.27 AW	19290 AAW	AZBLS	10//99-12//99
	Flagstaff MSA, AZ-UT	S	8.63 MW	6.74 AW	17940 AAW	AZBLS	10//99-12//99
	Phoenix-Mesa MSA, AZ	S	11.67 MW	10.17 AW	24280 AAW	AZBLS	10//99-12//99
	Tucson MSA, AZ	S	7.78 MW	6.64 AW	16180 AAW	AZBLS	10//99-12//99
	Yuma MSA, AZ	S	11.39 MW	9.78 AW	23690 AAW	AZBLS	10//99-12//99
	Arkansas	S	6.45 MW	7.23 AW	15030 AAW	ARBLS	10//99-12//99
	Fayetteville-Springdale-Rogers MSA, AR	S	8.92 MW	9.28 AW	18560 AAW	ARBLS	10//99-12//99
	Fort Smith MSA, AR-OK	S	8.91 MW	8.91 AW	18530 AAW	ARBLS	10//99-12//99
	Little Rock-North Little Rock MSA, AR	S	8.20 MW	7.54 AW	17050 AAW	ARBLS	10//99-12//99
	Pine Bluff MSA, AR	S	8.12 MW	7.49 AW	16890 AAW	ARBLS	10//99-12//99
	California	S	8.09 MW	9.51 AW	19790 AAW	CABLS	10//99-12//99
	Bakersfield MSA, CA	S	7.60 MW	6.56 AW	15800 AAW	CABLS	10//99-12//99
	Chico-Paradise MSA, CA	S	8.21 MW	7.70 AW	17080 AAW	CABLS	10//99-12//99
	Los Angeles-Long Beach PMSA, CA	S	9.06 MW	8.07 AW	18840 AAW	CABLS	10//99-12//99
	Merced MSA, CA	S	6.34 MW	6.27 AW	13200 AAW	CABLS	10//99-12//99
	Modesto MSA, CA	S	8.28 MW	7.62 AW	17220 AAW	CABLS	10//99-12//99
	Oakland PMSA, CA	S	9.66 MW	8.74 AW	20090 AAW	CABLS	10//99-12//99
	Orange County PMSA, CA	S	9.43 MW	8.34 AW	19620 AAW	CABLS	10//99-12//99
	Redding MSA, CA	S	8.86 MW	8.14 AW	18440 AAW	CABLS	10//99-12//99
	Riverside-San Bernardino PMSA, CA	S	8.49 MW	7.95 AW	17650 AAW	CABLS	10//99-12//99
	Sacramento PMSA, CA	S	8.86 MW	7.94 AW	18420 AAW	CABLS	10//99-12//99
	Salinas MSA, CA	S	8.44 MW	7.96 AW	17550 AAW	CABLS	10//99-12//99
	San Diego MSA, CA	S	8.12 MW	7.68 AW	16890 AAW	CABLS	10//99-12//99

Recreation Worker

Occupation/Type/Industry	Location	Per	Low	Mid	High	Source	Date
Recreation Worker	San Francisco PMSA, CA	S	10.18 MW	9.35 AW	21160 AAW	CABLS	10//99-12//99
	San Jose PMSA, CA	S	16.63 MW	10.60 AW	34590 AAW	CABLS	10//99-12//99
	San Luis Obispo-Atascadero-Paso Robles MSA, CA	S	6.71 MW	6.36 AW	13950 AAW	CABLS	10//99-12//99
	Santa Barbara-Santa Maria-Lompoc MSA, CA	S	8.59 MW	7.73 AW	17870 AAW	CABLS	10//99-12//99
	Santa Cruz-Watsonville PMSA, CA	S	9.12 MW	8.13 AW	18960 AAW	CABLS	10//99-12//99
	Santa Rosa PMSA, CA	S	9.06 MW	8.20 AW	18830 AAW	CABLS	10//99-12//99
	Stockton-Lodi MSA, CA	S	9.74 MW	7.84 AW	20250 AAW	CABLS	10//99-12//99
	Vallejo-Fairfield-Napa PMSA, CA	S	9.12 MW	8.25 AW	18970 AAW	CABLS	10//99-12//99
	Ventura PMSA, CA	S	7.84 MW	6.63 AW	16300 AAW	CABLS	10//99-12//99
	Visalia-Tulare-Porterville MSA, CA	S	7.83 MW	6.85 AW	16290 AAW	CABLS	10//99-12//99
	Yolo PMSA, CA	S	8.50 MW	6.65 AW	17680 AAW	CABLS	10//99-12//99
	Yuba City MSA, CA	S	7.41 MW	7.24 AW	15410 AAW	CABLS	10//99-12//99
	Colorado	S	8.77 MW	9.30 AW	19330 AAW	COBLS	10//99-12//99
	Boulder-Longmont PMSA, CO	S	9.86 MW	8.23 AW	20510 AAW	COBLS	10//99-12//99
	Colorado Springs MSA, CO	S	9.31 MW	8.62 AW	19360 AAW	COBLS	10//99-12//99
	Denver PMSA, CO	S	9.39 MW	9.01 AW	19530 AAW	COBLS	10//99-12//99
	Fort Collins-Loveland MSA, CO	S	9.85 MW	8.22 AW	20500 AAW	COBLS	10//99-12//99
	Grand Junction MSA, CO	S	7.50 MW	7.22 AW	15600 AAW	COBLS	10//99-12//99
	Greeley PMSA, CO	S	8.19 MW	7.76 AW	17030 AAW	COBLS	10//99-12//99
	Pueblo MSA, CO	S	8.36 MW	8.31 AW	17400 AAW	COBLS	10//99-12//99
	Connecticut	S	8.45 MW	10.25 AW	21330 AAW	CTBLS	10//99-12//99
	Bridgeport PMSA, CT	S	11.67 MW	10.45 AW	24280 AAW	CTBLS	10//99-12//99
	Danbury PMSA, CT	S	8.84 MW	6.59 AW	18380 AAW	CTBLS	10//99-12//99
	Hartford MSA, CT	S	9.51 MW	8.32 AW	19780 AAW	CTBLS	10//99-12//99
	New Haven-Meriden PMSA, CT	S	12.86 MW	10.26 AW	26750 AAW	CTBLS	10//99-12//99
	New London-Norwich MSA, CT-RI	S	8.87 MW	7.98 AW	18460 AAW	CTBLS	10//99-12//99
	Stamford-Norwalk PMSA, CT	S	10.47 MW	8.05 AW	21790 AAW	CTBLS	10//99-12//99
	Waterbury PMSA, CT	S	11.11 MW	10.51 AW	23120 AAW	CTBLS	10//99-12//99
	Delaware	S	8.26 MW	9.44 AW	19650 AAW	DEBLS	10//99-12//99
	Wilmington-Newark PMSA, DE-MD	S	9.26 MW	8.16 AW	19250 AAW	DEBLS	10//99-12//99
	District of Columbia	S	12.15 MW	12.12 AW	25200 AAW	DCBLS	10//99-12//99
	Washington PMSA, DC-MD-VA-WV	S	8.65 MW	7.82 AW	17980 AAW	DCBLS	10//99-12//99
	Florida	S	8.54 MW	8.97 AW	18650 AAW	FLBLS	10//99-12//99
	Daytona Beach MSA, FL	S	8.42 MW	8.24 AW	17500 AAW	FLBLS	10//99-12//99
	Fort Lauderdale PMSA, FL	S	9.70 MW	9.24 AW	20170 AAW	FLBLS	10//99-12//99
	Fort Myers-Cape Coral MSA, FL	S	11.03 MW	10.38 AW	22950 AAW	FLBLS	10//99-12//99
	Fort Pierce-Port St. Lucie MSA, FL	S	8.88 MW	8.70 AW	18460 AAW	FLBLS	10//99-12//99
	Fort Walton Beach MSA, FL	S	8.08 MW	6.90 AW	16810 AAW	FLBLS	10//99-12//99
	Gainesville MSA, FL	S	8.73 MW	8.57 AW	18170 AAW	FLBLS	10//99-12//99
	Jacksonville MSA, FL	S	6.93 MW	6.25 AW	14410 AAW	FLBLS	10//99-12//99
	Lakeland-Winter Haven MSA, FL	S	8.76 MW	8.48 AW	18210 AAW	FLBLS	10//99-12//99
	Melbourne-Titusville-Palm Bay MSA, FL	S	8.06 MW	7.92 AW	16770 AAW	FLBLS	10//99-12//99
	Miami PMSA, FL	S	9.45 MW	8.62 AW	19650 AAW	FLBLS	10//99-12//99
	Naples MSA, FL	S	7.40 MW	6.69 AW	15400 AAW	FLBLS	10//99-12//99
	Ocala MSA, FL	S	8.24 MW	7.92 AW	17130 AAW	FLBLS	10//99-12//99
	Orlando MSA, FL	S	7.41 MW	6.51 AW	15420 AAW	FLBLS	10//99-12//99
	Panama City MSA, FL	S	9.65 MW	9.08 AW	20080 AAW	FLBLS	10//99-12//99
	Pensacola MSA, FL	S	7.87 MW	6.71 AW	16360 AAW	FLBLS	10//99-12//99
	Punta Gorda MSA, FL	S	8.85 MW	8.70 AW	18410 AAW	FLBLS	10//99-12//99
	Sarasota-Bradenton MSA, FL	S	8.12 MW	7.81 AW	16880 AAW	FLBLS	10//99-12//99
	Tallahassee MSA, FL	S	8.78 MW	8.73 AW	18270 AAW	FLBLS	10//99-12//99
	Tampa-St. Petersburg-Clearwater MSA, FL	S	9.73 MW	9.14 AW	20230 AAW	FLBLS	10//99-12//99
	West Palm Beach-Boca Raton MSA, FL	S	8.16 MW	7.98 AW	16970 AAW	FLBLS	10//99-12//99
	Georgia	S	7.69 MW	8.57 AW	17820 AAW	GABLS	10//99-12//99
	Albany MSA, GA	S	11.54 MW	11.80 AW	24000 AAW	GABLS	10//99-12//99
	Atlanta MSA, GA	S	8.33 MW	7.07 AW	17320 AAW	GABLS	10//99-12//99

AAW Average annual wage	AOH Average offered, high	ASH Average starting, high	H Hourly	M Monthly	S Special: hourly and annual
AE Average entry wage	AOL Average offered, low	ASL Average starting, low	HI Highest wage paid	MTC Median total compensation	TQ Third quartile wage
AEX Average experienced wage	APH Average pay, high range	AW Average wage paid	HR High end range	MW Median wage paid	W Weekly
AO Average offered	APL Average pay, low range	FQ First quartile wage	LR Low end range	SQ Second quartile wage	Y Yearly

Occupation/Type/Industry	Location	Per	Low	Mid	High	Source	Date
Recreation Worker	Augusta-Aiken MSA, GA-SC	S	10.84 MW	10.26 AW	22550 AAW	GABLS	10//99-12//99
	Macon MSA, GA	S	8.15 MW	7.46 AW	16960 AAW	GABLS	10//99-12//99
	Savannah MSA, GA	S	7.66 MW	7.35 AW	15940 AAW	GABLS	10//99-12//99
	Hawaii	S	8.41 MW	10.04 AW	20870 AAW	HIBLS	10//99-12//99
	Honolulu MSA, HI	S	9.68 MW	8.09 AW	20120 AAW	HIBLS	10//99-12//99
	Idaho	S	8.39 MW	8.81 AW	18330 AAW	IDBLS	10//99-12//99
	Boise City MSA, ID	S	10.01 MW	9.61 AW	20820 AAW	IDBLS	10//99-12//99
	Illinois	S	10.24 MW	10.74 AW	22330 AAW	ILBLS	10//99-12//99
	Bloomington-Normal MSA, IL	S	12.53 MW	9.79 AW	26060 AAW	ILBLS	10//99-12//99
	Chicago PMSA, IL	S	10.45 MW	9.53 AW	21740 AAW	ILBLS	10//99-12//99
	Decatur MSA, IL	S	9.92 MW	9.45 AW	20640 AAW	ILBLS	10//99-12//99
	Peoria-Pekin MSA, IL	S	7.66 MW	7.23 AW	15940 AAW	ILBLS	10//99-12//99
	Rockford MSA, IL	S	8.67 MW	6.55 AW	18030 AAW	ILBLS	10//99-12//99
	Springfield MSA, IL	S	12.39 MW	12.82 AW	25780 AAW	ILBLS	10//99-12//99
	Indiana	S	7 MW	7.89 AW	16420 AAW	INBLS	10//99-12//99
	Elkhart-Goshen MSA, IN	S	9.35 MW	8.00 AW	19450 AAW	INBLS	10//99-12//99
	Evansville-Henderson MSA, IN-KY	S	8.22 MW	8.54 AW	17100 AAW	INBLS	10//99-12//99
	Fort Wayne MSA, IN	S	7.56 MW	6.59 AW	15720 AAW	INBLS	10//99-12//99
	Gary PMSA, IN	S	6.86 MW	6.39 AW	14270 AAW	INBLS	10//99-12//99
	Indianapolis MSA, IN	S	9.57 MW	8.98 AW	19900 AAW	INBLS	10//99-12//99
	Kokomo MSA, IN	S	6.81 MW	6.56 AW	14160 AAW	INBLS	10//99-12//99
	Lafayette MSA, IN	S	6.97 MW	6.43 AW	14510 AAW	INBLS	10//99-12//99
	Muncie MSA, IN	S	6.20 MW	6.06 AW	12900 AAW	INBLS	10//99-12//99
	South Bend MSA, IN	S	7.00 MW	6.47 AW	14550 AAW	INBLS	10//99-12//99
	Terre Haute MSA, IN	S	6.67 MW	6.10 AW	13880 AAW	INBLS	10//99-12//99
	Iowa	S	6.53 MW	7.38 AW	15350 AAW	IABLS	10//99-12//99
	Cedar Rapids MSA, IA	S	6.95 MW	6.29 AW	14450 AAW	IABLS	10//99-12//99
	Davenport-Moline-Rock Island MSA, IA-IL	S	9.39 MW	7.95 AW	19540 AAW	IABLS	10//99-12//99
	Des Moines MSA, IA	S	7.77 MW	7.43 AW	16170 AAW	IABLS	10//99-12//99
	Dubuque MSA, IA	S	7.59 MW	7.59 AW	15790 AAW	IABLS	10//99-12//99
	Iowa City MSA, IA	S	8.49 MW	6.74 AW	17650 AAW	IABLS	10//99-12//99
	Sioux City MSA, IA-NE	S	6.74 MW	6.26 AW	14010 AAW	IABLS	10//99-12//99
	Kansas	S	8.26 MW	8.99 AW	18700 AAW	KSBLS	10//99-12//99
	Topeka MSA, KS	S	7.34 MW	7.17 AW	15260 AAW	KSBLS	10//99-12//99
	Wichita MSA, KS	S	9.52 MW	8.67 AW	19790 AAW	KSBLS	10//99-12//99
	Kentucky	S	7.52 MW	8.24 AW	17130 AAW	KYBLS	10//99-12//99
	Lexington MSA, KY	S	8.96 MW	8.07 AW	18640 AAW	KYBLS	10//99-12//99
	Louisville MSA, KY-IN	S	8.31 MW	7.88 AW	17280 AAW	KYBLS	10//99-12//99
	Owensboro MSA, KY	S	6.30 MW	6.21 AW	13110 AAW	KYBLS	10//99-12//99
	Louisiana	S	6.46 MW	7.04 AW	14640 AAW	LABLS	10//99-12//99
	Alexandria MSA, LA	S	7.78 MW	7.31 AW	16190 AAW	LABLS	10//99-12//99
	Baton Rouge MSA, LA	S	6.41 MW	6.33 AW	13330 AAW	LABLS	10//99-12//99
	Houma MSA, LA	S	5.90 MW	6.01 AW	12280 AAW	LABLS	10//99-12//99
	Lafayette MSA, LA	S	8.11 MW	7.08 AW	16870 AAW	LABLS	10//99-12//99
	Lake Charles MSA, LA	S	7.97 MW	7.26 AW	16580 AAW	LABLS	10//99-12//99
	New Orleans MSA, LA	S	7.21 MW	6.49 AW	15010 AAW	LABLS	10//99-12//99
	Shreveport-Bossier City MSA, LA	S	8.41 MW	7.97 AW	17500 AAW	LABLS	10//99-12//99
	Maine	S	8.35 MW	8.84 AW	18390 AAW	MEBLS	10//99-12//99
	Bangor MSA, ME	S	6.86 MW	6.38 AW	14260 AAW	MEBLS	10//99-12//99
	Lewiston-Auburn MSA, ME	S	8.14 MW	7.94 AW	16930 AAW	MEBLS	10//99-12//99
	Portland MSA, ME	S	11.32 MW	10.43 AW	23540 AAW	MEBLS	10//99-12//99
	Maryland	S	7.39 MW	7.74 AW	16100 AAW	MDBLS	10//99-12//99
	Baltimore PMSA, MD	S	7.74 MW	7.36 AW	16090 AAW	MDBLS	10//99-12//99
	Cumberland MSA, MD-WV	S	8.80 MW	7.96 AW	18310 AAW	MDBLS	10//99-12//99
	Hagerstown PMSA, MD	S	14.23 MW	17.41 AW	29600 AAW	MDBLS	10//99-12//99
	Massachusetts	S	7.97 MW	8.85 AW	18420 AAW	MABLS	10//99-12//99
	Barnstable-Yarmouth MSA, MA	S	9.58 MW	9.35 AW	19930 AAW	MABLS	10//99-12//99
	Boston PMSA, MA-NH	S	8.69 MW	7.93 AW	18070 AAW	MABLS	10//99-12//99
	Brockton PMSA, MA	S	9.99 MW	9.65 AW	20770 AAW	MABLS	10//99-12//99
	Fitchburg-Leominster PMSA, MA	S	8.82 MW	9.18 AW	18350 AAW	MABLS	10//99-12//99
	Lawrence PMSA, MA-NH	S	9.29 MW	8.90 AW	19310 AAW	MABLS	10//99-12//99
	New Bedford PMSA, MA	S	9.36 MW	9.40 AW	19460 AAW	MABLS	10//99-12//99
	Springfield MSA, MA	S	9.94 MW	9.03 AW	20680 AAW	MABLS	10//99-12//99
	Worcester PMSA, MA-CT	S	8.68 MW	7.51 AW	18050 AAW	MABLS	10//99-12//99
	Michigan	S	9.3 MW	9.64 AW	20040 AAW	MIBLS	10//99-12//99
	Ann Arbor PMSA, MI	S	9.13 MW	8.55 AW	18990 AAW	MIBLS	10//99-12//99
	Detroit PMSA, MI	S	10.55 MW	9.80 AW	21940 AAW	MIBLS	10//99-12//99

Occupation/Type/Industry	Location	Per	Low	Mid	High	Source	Date
Recreation Worker	Flint PMSA, MI	S	7.03 MW	6.45 AW	14620 AAW	MIBLS	10//99-12//99
	Grand Rapids-Muskegon-Holland MSA, MI	S	8.81 MW	8.67 AW	18330 AAW	MIBLS	10//99-12//99
	Jackson MSA, MI	S	10.63 MW	10.10 AW	22100 AAW	MIBLS	10//99-12//99
	Kalamazoo-Battle Creek MSA, MI	S	9.23 MW	9.19 AW	19200 AAW	MIBLS	10//99-12//99
	Saginaw-Bay City-Midland MSA, MI	S	7.42 MW	6.35 AW	15440 AAW	MIBLS	10//99-12//99
	Minnesota	S	9.11 MW	10.51 AW	21850 AAW	MNBLS	10//99-12//99
	Duluth-Superior MSA, MN-WI	S	10.20 MW	7.92 AW	21220 AAW	MNBLS	10//99-12//99
	Minneapolis-St. Paul MSA, MN-WI	S	12.67 MW	10.47 AW	26360 AAW	MNBLS	10//99-12//99
	Rochester MSA, MN	S	12.52 MW	11.29 AW	26040 AAW	MNBLS	10//99-12//99
	St. Cloud MSA, MN	S	6.64 MW	6.27 AW	13810 AAW	MNBLS	10//99-12//99
	Mississippi	S	8 MW	8.90 AW	18510 AAW	MSBLS	10//99-12//99
	Biloxi-Gulfport-Pascagoula MSA, MS	S	9.15 MW	7.85 AW	19030 AAW	MSBLS	10//99-12//99
	Hattiesburg MSA, MS	S	6.60 MW	6.64 AW	13730 AAW	MSBLS	10//99-12//99
	Jackson MSA, MS	S	9.64 MW	10.12 AW	20060 AAW	MSBLS	10//99-12//99
	Missouri	S	8.07 MW	8.83 AW	18360 AAW	MOBLS	10//99-12//99
	Columbia MSA, MO	S	7.92 MW	6.45 AW	16480 AAW	MOBLS	10//99-12//99
	Kansas City MSA, MO-KS	S	10.47 MW	9.96 AW	21770 AAW	MOBLS	10//99-12//99
	St. Joseph MSA, MO	S	9.29 MW	9.38 AW	19330 AAW	MOBLS	10//99-12//99
	St. Louis MSA, MO-IL	S	8.29 MW	7.56 AW	17230 AAW	MOBLS	10//99-12//99
	Montana	S	7.43 MW	7.97 AW	16580 AAW	MTBLS	10//99-12//99
	Billings MSA, MT	S	6.64 MW	6.34 AW	13800 AAW	MTBLS	10//99-12//99
	Missoula MSA, MT	S	10.33 MW	9.94 AW	21490 AAW	MTBLS	10//99-12//99
	Nebraska	S	6.69 MW	7.39 AW	15370 AAW	NEBLS	10//99-12//99
	Lincoln MSA, NE	S	8.12 MW	7.15 AW	16900 AAW	NEBLS	10//99-12//99
	Omaha MSA, NE-IA	S	7.66 MW	7.20 AW	15930 AAW	NEBLS	10//99-12//99
	Nevada	S	6.63 MW	7.49 AW	15570 AAW	NVBLS	10//99-12//99
	Las Vegas MSA, NV-AZ	S	7.18 MW	6.37 AW	14930 AAW	NVBLS	10//99-12//99
	New Hampshire	S	8.06 MW	8.89 AW	18500 AAW	NHBLS	10//99-12//99
	Manchester PMSA, NH	S	9.16 MW	7.75 AW	19040 AAW	NHBLS	10//99-12//99
	Portsmouth-Rochester PMSA, NH-ME	S	9.46 MW	8.68 AW	19670 AAW	NHBLS	10//99-12//99
	New Jersey	S	8.05 MW	9.26 AW	19260 AAW	NJBLS	10//99-12//99
	Atlantic-Cape May PMSA, NJ	S	9.21 MW	8.19 AW	19160 AAW	NJBLS	10//99-12//99
	Bergen-Passaic PMSA, NJ	S	8.70 MW	7.97 AW	18090 AAW	NJBLS	10//99-12//99
	Jersey City PMSA, NJ	S	7.91 MW	7.77 AW	16460 AAW	NJBLS	10//99-12//99
	Middlesex-Somerset-Hunterdon PMSA, NJ	S	8.04 MW	7.18 AW	16720 AAW	NJBLS	10//99-12//99
	Monmouth-Ocean PMSA, NJ	S	8.64 MW	7.67 AW	17970 AAW	NJBLS	10//99-12//99
	Newark PMSA, NJ	S	8.87 MW	7.96 AW	18460 AAW	NJBLS	10//99-12//99
	Trenton PMSA, NJ	S	8.92 MW	7.99 AW	18550 AAW	NJBLS	10//99-12//99
	New Mexico	S	7.62 MW	8.11 AW	16880 AAW	NMBLS	10//99-12//99
	Las Cruces MSA, NM	S	8.41 MW	7.78 AW	17500 AAW	NMBLS	10//99-12//99
	Santa Fe MSA, NM	S	9.65 MW	8.04 AW	20070 AAW	NMBLS	10//99-12//99
	New York	S	7.71 MW	8.97 AW	18650 AAW	NYBLS	10//99-12//99
	Albany-Schenectady-Troy MSA, NY	S	7.67 MW	7.10 AW	15960 AAW	NYBLS	10//99-12//99
	Binghamton MSA, NY	S	8.10 MW	7.88 AW	16850 AAW	NYBLS	10//99-12//99
	Buffalo-Niagara Falls MSA, NY	S	7.28 MW	6.56 AW	15150 AAW	NYBLS	10//99-12//99
	Dutchess County PMSA, NY	S	11.15 MW	9.76 AW	23200 AAW	NYBLS	10//99-12//99
	Elmira MSA, NY	S	15.66 MW	17.24 AW	32570 AAW	NYBLS	10//99-12//99
	Glens Falls MSA, NY	S	6.56 MW	6.26 AW	13650 AAW	NYBLS	10//99-12//99
	Jamestown MSA, NY	S	7.26 MW	6.41 AW	15100 AAW	NYBLS	10//99-12//99
	Nassau-Suffolk PMSA, NY	S	9.43 MW	8.47 AW	19620 AAW	NYBLS	10//99-12//99
	New York PMSA, NY	S	9.52 MW	7.90 AW	19800 AAW	NYBLS	10//99-12//99
	Newburgh PMSA, NY-PA	S	10.35 MW	8.88 AW	21530 AAW	NYBLS	10//99-12//99
	Rochester MSA, NY	S	9.32 MW	8.37 AW	19380 AAW	NYBLS	10//99-12//99
	Syracuse MSA, NY	S	10.23 MW	9.49 AW	21280 AAW	NYBLS	10//99-12//99
	Utica-Rome MSA, NY	S	10.68 MW	8.23 AW	22210 AAW	NYBLS	10//99-12//99
	North Carolina	S	6.97 MW	7.98 AW	16610 AAW	NCBLS	10//99-12//99
	Asheville MSA, NC	S	7.79 MW	7.13 AW	16200 AAW	NCBLS	10//99-12//99
	Charlotte-Gastonia-Rock Hill MSA, NC-SC	S	9.30 MW	8.26 AW	19340 AAW	NCBLS	10//99-12//99
	Fayetteville MSA, NC	S	6.72 MW	6.26 AW	13970 AAW	NCBLS	10//99-12//99
	Goldsboro MSA, NC	S	10.98 MW	10.50 AW	22840 AAW	NCBLS	10//99-12//99
	Greensboro--Winston-Salem--High Point MSA, NC	S	6.90 MW	6.42 AW	14350 AAW	NCBLS	10//99-12//99

AAW Average annual wage	**AOH** Average offered, high	**ASH** Average starting, high	**H** Hourly	**M** Monthly	**S** Special: hourly and annual
AE Average entry wage	**AOL** Average offered, low	**ASL** Average starting, low	**HI** Highest wage paid	**MTC** Median total compensation	**TQ** Third quartile wage
AEX Average experienced wage	**APH** Average pay, high range	**AW** Average wage paid	**HR** High end range	**MW** Median wage paid	**W** Weekly
AO Average offered	**APL** Average pay, low range	**FQ** First quartile wage	**LR** Low end range	**SQ** Second quartile wage	**Y** Yearly

Occupation/Type/Industry	Location	Per	Low	Mid	High	Source	Date
Recreation Worker	Greenville MSA, NC	S	7.19 MW	6.42 AW	14960 AAW	NCBLS	10//99-12//99
	Hickory-Morganton-Lenoir MSA, NC	S	9.47 MW	8.68 AW	19710 AAW	NCBLS	10//99-12//99
	Jacksonville MSA, NC	S	6.31 MW	6.04 AW	13120 AAW	NCBLS	10//99-12//99
	Rocky Mount MSA, NC	S	6.90 MW	6.41 AW	14360 AAW	NCBLS	10//99-12//99
	Wilmington MSA, NC	S	8.12 MW	6.96 AW	16880 AAW	NCBLS	10//99-12//99
	North Dakota	S	7.67 MW	7.88 AW	16390 AAW	NDBLS	10//99-12//99
	Fargo-Moorhead MSA, ND-MN	S	9.16 MW	8.10 AW	19050 AAW	NDBLS	10//99-12//99
	Grand Forks MSA, ND-MN	S	8.90 MW	8.59 AW	18510 AAW	NDBLS	10//99-12//99
	Ohio	S	7.49 MW	8.16 AW	16980 AAW	OHBLS	10//99-12//99
	Akron PMSA, OH	S	8.95 MW	8.37 AW	18610 AAW	OHBLS	10//99-12//99
	Canton-Massillon MSA, OH	S	6.87 MW	6.34 AW	14290 AAW	OHBLS	10//99-12//99
	Cincinnati PMSA, OH-KY-IN	S	7.32 MW	6.90 AW	15230 AAW	OHBLS	10//99-12//99
	Cleveland-Lorain-Elyria PMSA, OH	S	8.70 MW	7.85 AW	18090 AAW	OHBLS	10//99-12//99
	Columbus MSA, OH	S	9.66 MW	8.09 AW	20090 AAW	OHBLS	10//99-12//99
	Dayton-Springfield MSA, OH	S	8.40 MW	7.74 AW	17460 AAW	OHBLS	10//99-12//99
	Hamilton-Middletown PMSA, OH	S	8.71 MW	7.90 AW	18120 AAW	OHBLS	10//99-12//99
	Lima MSA, OH	S	8.61 MW	8.37 AW	17910 AAW	OHBLS	10//99-12//99
	Mansfield MSA, OH	S	8.10 MW	7.85 AW	16860 AAW	OHBLS	10//99-12//99
	Steubenville-Weirton MSA, OH-WV	S	6.20 MW	6.13 AW	12900 AAW	OHBLS	10//99-12//99
	Toledo MSA, OH	S	8.06 MW	7.55 AW	16770 AAW	OHBLS	10//99-12//99
	Youngstown-Warren MSA, OH	S	7.24 MW	6.56 AW	15070 AAW	OHBLS	10//99-12//99
	Oklahoma	S	6.56 MW	7.29 AW	15160 AAW	OKBLS	10//99-12//99
	Lawton MSA, OK	S	7.93 MW	7.56 AW	16500 AAW	OKBLS	10//99-12//99
	Oklahoma City MSA, OK	S	7.03 MW	6.35 AW	14620 AAW	OKBLS	10//99-12//99
	Tulsa MSA, OK	S	7.50 MW	6.74 AW	15600 AAW	OKBLS	10//99-12//99
	Oregon	S	9.27 MW	9.86 AW	20520 AAW	ORBLS	10//99-12//99
	Corvallis MSA, OR	S	7.25 MW	6.68 AW	15090 AAW	ORBLS	10//99-12//99
	Eugene-Springfield MSA, OR	S	8.74 MW	8.17 AW	18170 AAW	ORBLS	10//99-12//99
	Medford-Ashland MSA, OR	S	11.49 MW	11.95 AW	23900 AAW	ORBLS	10//99-12//99
	Portland-Vancouver PMSA, OR-WA	S	10.36 MW	10.27 AW	21540 AAW	ORBLS	10//99-12//99
	Salem PMSA, OR	S	10.67 MW	9.63 AW	22190 AAW	ORBLS	10//99-12//99
	Pennsylvania	S	7.64 MW	8.53 AW	17750 AAW	PABLS	10//99-12//99
	Allentown-Bethlehem-Easton MSA, PA	S	7.97 MW	6.55 AW	16570 AAW	PABLS	10//99-12//99
	Erie MSA, PA	S	8.49 MW	6.54 AW	17670 AAW	PABLS	10//99-12//99
	Harrisburg-Lebanon-Carlisle MSA, PA	S	9.29 MW	8.35 AW	19330 AAW	PABLS	10//99-12//99
	Johnstown MSA, PA	S	6.90 MW	6.15 AW	14350 AAW	PABLS	10//99-12//99
	Lancaster MSA, PA	S	9.34 MW	9.13 AW	19420 AAW	PABLS	10//99-12//99
	Philadelphia PMSA, PA-NJ	S	10.73 MW	9.69 AW	22320 AAW	PABLS	10//99-12//99
	Pittsburgh MSA, PA	S	7.25 MW	6.90 AW	15080 AAW	PABLS	10//99-12//99
	Reading MSA, PA	S	9.93 MW	9.64 AW	20660 AAW	PABLS	10//99-12//99
	Scranton--Wilkes-Barre--Hazleton MSA, PA	S	9.49 MW	9.18 AW	19730 AAW	PABLS	10//99-12//99
	State College MSA, PA	S	9.98 MW	8.46 AW	20770 AAW	PABLS	10//99-12//99
	Williamsport MSA, PA	S	7.83 MW	7.54 AW	16290 AAW	PABLS	10//99-12//99
	York MSA, PA	S	7.60 MW	6.65 AW	15810 AAW	PABLS	10//99-12//99
	Rhode Island	S	6.62 MW	7.85 AW	16330 AAW	RIBLS	10//99-12//99
	Providence-Fall River-Warwick MSA, RI-MA	S	7.76 MW	6.68 AW	16150 AAW	RIBLS	10//99-12//99
	South Carolina	S	7.54 MW	8.48 AW	17640 AAW	SCBLS	10//99-12//99
	Charleston-North Charleston MSA, SC	S	8.97 MW	7.75 AW	18670 AAW	SCBLS	10//99-12//99
	Columbia MSA, SC	S	9.43 MW	8.95 AW	19620 AAW	SCBLS	10//99-12//99
	Florence MSA, SC	S	8.96 MW	9.32 AW	18630 AAW	SCBLS	10//99-12//99
	Greenville-Spartanburg-Anderson MSA, SC	S	7.09 MW	6.37 AW	14740 AAW	SCBLS	10//99-12//99
	Myrtle Beach MSA, SC	S	9.53 MW	8.17 AW	19810 AAW	SCBLS	10//99-12//99
	Sumter MSA, SC	S	7.85 MW	7.08 AW	16340 AAW	SCBLS	10//99-12//99
	South Dakota	S	8.43 MW	9.11 AW	18950 AAW	SDBLS	10//99-12//99
	Rapid City MSA, SD	S	8.49 MW	8.38 AW	17660 AAW	SDBLS	10//99-12//99
	Sioux Falls MSA, SD	S	8.41 MW	8.01 AW	17490 AAW	SDBLS	10//99-12//99
	Tennessee	S	7.77 MW	8.52 AW	17730 AAW	TNBLS	10//99-12//99
	Chattanooga MSA, TN-GA	S	9.07 MW	9.02 AW	18870 AAW	TNBLS	10//99-12//99
	Clarksville-Hopkinsville MSA, TN-KY	S	8.07 MW	7.47 AW	16790 AAW	TNBLS	10//99-12//99

AAW	Average annual wage	AOH	Average offered, high	ASH	Average starting, high	H	Hourly	M	Monthly	S	Special: hourly and annual
AE	Average entry wage	AOL	Average offered, low	ASL	Average starting, low	HI	Highest wage paid	MTC	Median total compensation	TQ	Third quartile wage
AEX	Average experienced wage	APH	Average pay, high range	AW	Average wage paid	HR	High end range	MW	Median wage paid	W	Weekly
AO	Average offered	APL	Average pay, low range	FQ	First quartile wage	LR	Low end range	SQ	Second quartile wage	Y	Yearly

Occupation/Type/Industry	Location	Per	Low	Mid	High	Source	Date
Recreation Worker	Jackson MSA, TN	S	7.46 MW	6.54 AW	15520 AAW	TNBLS	10//99-12//99
	Johnson City-Kingsport-Bristol MSA, TN-VA	S	8.95 MW	7.48 AW	18620 AAW	TNBLS	10//99-12//99
	Knoxville MSA, TN	S	12.45 MW	12.40 AW	25900 AAW	TNBLS	10//99-12//99
	Memphis MSA, TN-AR-MS	S	8.40 MW	7.29 AW	17480 AAW	MSBLS	10//99-12//99
	Nashville MSA, TN	S	8.22 MW	7.71 AW	17100 AAW	TNBLS	10//99-12//99
	Texas	S	7.46 MW	8.51 AW	17700 AAW	TXBLS	10//99-12//99
	Abilene MSA, TX	S	9.30 MW	6.58 AW	19340 AAW	TXBLS	10//99-12//99
	Amarillo MSA, TX	S	8.83 MW	8.63 AW	18360 AAW	TXBLS	10//99-12//99
	Austin-San Marcos MSA, TX	S	8.79 MW	8.00 AW	18280 AAW	TXBLS	10//99-12//99
	Beaumont-Port Arthur MSA, TX	S	9.12 MW	7.86 AW	18980 AAW	TXBLS	10//99-12//99
	Brazoria PMSA, TX	S	9.07 MW	9.44 AW	18860 AAW	TXBLS	10//99-12//99
	Brownsville-Harlingen-San Benito MSA, TX	S	8.01 MW	7.24 AW	16670 AAW	TXBLS	10//99-12//99
	Bryan-College Station MSA, TX	S	7.51 MW	7.49 AW	15620 AAW	TXBLS	10//99-12//99
	Corpus Christi MSA, TX	S	6.75 MW	6.30 AW	14050 AAW	TXBLS	10//99-12//99
	Dallas PMSA, TX	S	8.23 MW	7.33 AW	17130 AAW	TXBLS	10//99-12//99
	El Paso MSA, TX	S	7.52 MW	6.45 AW	15650 AAW	TXBLS	10//99-12//99
	Fort Worth-Arlington PMSA, TX	S	13.45 MW	13.22 AW	27980 AAW	TXBLS	10//99-12//99
	Galveston-Texas City PMSA, TX	S	8.59 MW	8.27 AW	17860 AAW	TXBLS	10//99-12//99
	Houston PMSA, TX	S	7.93 MW	7.02 AW	16480 AAW	TXBLS	10//99-12//99
	Killeen-Temple MSA, TX	S	9.00 MW	9.34 AW	18710 AAW	TXBLS	10//99-12//99
	Longview-Marshall MSA, TX	S	6.99 MW	6.32 AW	14530 AAW	TXBLS	10//99-12//99
	Lubbock MSA, TX	S	7.85 MW	7.80 AW	16320 AAW	TXBLS	10//99-12//99
	McAllen-Edinburg-Mission MSA, TX	S	7.60 MW	6.59 AW	15810 AAW	TXBLS	10//99-12//99
	Odessa-Midland MSA, TX	S	7.79 MW	7.07 AW	16210 AAW	TXBLS	10//99-12//99
	San Antonio MSA, TX	S	7.79 MW	7.37 AW	16190 AAW	TXBLS	10//99-12//99
	Sherman-Denison MSA, TX	S	8.33 MW	6.46 AW	17320 AAW	TXBLS	10//99-12//99
	Texarkana MSA, TX- Texarkana, AR	S	9.74 MW	9.56 AW	20260 AAW	TXBLS	10//99-12//99
	Waco MSA, TX	S	11.36 MW	7.92 AW	23640 AAW	TXBLS	10//99-12//99
	Wichita Falls MSA, TX	S	6.73 MW	6.26 AW	13990 AAW	TXBLS	10//99-12//99
	Utah	S	8.08 MW	8.83 AW	18370 AAW	UTBLS	10//99-12//99
	Provo-Orem MSA, UT	S	7.78 MW	7.39 AW	16170 AAW	UTBLS	10//99-12//99
	Salt Lake City-Ogden MSA, UT	S	8.17 MW	7.34 AW	17000 AAW	UTBLS	10//99-12//99
	Vermont	S	7.94 MW	8.82 AW	18340 AAW	VTBLS	10//99-12//99
	Burlington MSA, VT	S	7.52 MW	6.70 AW	15630 AAW	VTBLS	10//99-12//99
	Virginia	S	8.35 MW	9.52 AW	19810 AAW	VABLS	10//99-12//99
	Charlottesville MSA, VA	S	9.12 MW	9.15 AW	18970 AAW	VABLS	10//99-12//99
	Danville MSA, VA	S	9.81 MW	8.28 AW	20410 AAW	VABLS	10//99-12//99
	Lynchburg MSA, VA	S	9.24 MW	8.07 AW	19210 AAW	VABLS	10//99-12//99
	Norfolk-Virginia Beach- Newport News MSA, VA- NC	S	8.36 MW	6.70 AW	17380 AAW	VABLS	10//99-12//99
	Richmond-Petersburg MSA, VA	S	8.11 MW	7.60 AW	16870 AAW	VABLS	10//99-12//99
	Roanoke MSA, VA	S	9.04 MW	7.63 AW	18810 AAW	VABLS	10//99-12//99
	Washington	S	8.53 MW	9.48 AW	19710 AAW	WABLS	10//99-12//99
	Bellingham MSA, WA	S	7.69 MW	7.47 AW	16000 AAW	WABLS	10//99-12//99
	Bremerton PMSA, WA	S	8.92 MW	7.98 AW	18550 AAW	WABLS	10//99-12//99
	Olympia PMSA, WA	S	14.68 MW	10.44 AW	30530 AAW	WABLS	10//99-12//99
	Seattle-Bellevue-Everett PMSA, WA	S	9.81 MW	9.38 AW	20400 AAW	WABLS	10//99-12//99
	Spokane MSA, WA	S	8.63 MW	7.51 AW	17960 AAW	WABLS	10//99-12//99
	Tacoma PMSA, WA	S	10.72 MW	8.21 AW	22300 AAW	WABLS	10//99-12//99
	Yakima MSA, WA	S	8.64 MW	8.27 AW	17980 AAW	WABLS	10//99-12//99
	West Virginia	S	7.02 MW	7.65 AW	15900 AAW	WVBLS	10//99-12//99
	Charleston MSA, WV	S	8.27 MW	8.68 AW	17190 AAW	WVBLS	10//99-12//99
	Huntington-Ashland MSA, WV-KY-OH	S	8.39 MW	7.93 AW	17460 AAW	WVBLS	10//99-12//99
	Parkersburg-Marietta MSA, WV-OH	S	8.14 MW	8.08 AW	16940 AAW	WVBLS	10//99-12//99
	Wheeling MSA, WV-OH	S	6.33 MW	6.29 AW	13170 AAW	WVBLS	10//99-12//99
	Wisconsin	S	7.48 MW	7.99 AW	16610 AAW	WIBLS	10//99-12//99
	Appleton-Oshkosh-Neenah MSA, WI	S	6.72 MW	6.11 AW	13980 AAW	WIBLS	10//99-12//99

AAW	Average annual wage	AOH	Average offered, high	ASH	Average starting, high	H	Hourly	M	Monthly	S	Special: hourly and annual
AE	Average entry wage	AOL	Average offered, low	ASL	Average starting, low	HI	Highest wage paid	MTC	Median total compensation	TQ	Third quartile wage
AEX	Average experienced wage	APH	Average pay, high range	AW	Average wage paid	HR	High end range	MW	Median wage paid	W	Weekly
AO	Average offered	APL	Average pay, low range	FQ	First quartile wage	LR	Low end range	SQ	Second quartile wage	Y	Yearly

Occupation/Type/Industry	Location	Per	Low	Mid	High	Source	Date
Recreation Worker	Eau Claire MSA, WI	S	9.08 MW	9.30 AW	18890 AAW	WIBLS	10//99-12//99
	Green Bay MSA, WI	S	8.44 MW	7.99 AW	17550 AAW	WIBLS	10//99-12//99
	Janesville-Beloit MSA, WI	S	7.80 MW	7.52 AW	16220 AAW	WIBLS	10//99-12//99
	Kenosha PMSA, WI	S	9.14 MW	8.04 AW	19000 AAW	WIBLS	10//99-12//99
	Madison MSA, WI	S	8.71 MW	8.83 AW	18120 AAW	WIBLS	10//99-12//99
	Milwaukee-Waukesha PMSA, WI	S	7.68 MW	7.35 AW	15980 AAW	WIBLS	10//99-12//99
	Racine PMSA, WI	S	7.75 MW	7.47 AW	16120 AAW	WIBLS	10//99-12//99
	Sheboygan MSA, WI	S	7.32 MW	7.41 AW	15220 AAW	WIBLS	10//99-12//99
	Wausau MSA, WI	S	9.38 MW	9.49 AW	19500 AAW	WIBLS	10//99-12//99
	Wyoming	S	8.48 MW	8.36 AW	17390 AAW	WYBLS	10//99-12//99
	Cheyenne MSA, WY	S	7.63 MW	7.46 AW	15860 AAW	WYBLS	10//99-12//99
	Puerto Rico	S	6.12 MW	6.18 AW	12860 AAW	PRBLS	10//99-12//99
	Caguas PMSA, PR	S	5.75 MW	5.95 AW	11960 AAW	PRBLS	10//99-12//99
	Ponce MSA, PR	S	6.00 MW	6.08 AW	12480 AAW	PRBLS	10//99-12//99
	San Juan-Bayamon PMSA, PR	S	6.18 MW	6.16 AW	12860 AAW	PRBLS	10//99-12//99
	Virgin Islands	S	8.25 MW	7.88 AW	16400 AAW	VIBLS	10//99-12//99
Recreational Therapist	Alabama	S	12.5 MW	12.77 AW	26560 AAW	ALBLS	10//99-12//99
	Arizona	S	10.33 MW	10.93 AW	22730 AAW	AZBLS	10//99-12//99
	Arkansas	S	10.37 MW	11.48 AW	23880 AAW	ARBLS	10//99-12//99
	California	S	16.74 MW	17.03 AW	35420 AAW	CABLS	10//99-12//99
	Colorado	S	13.19 MW	13.51 AW	28090 AAW	COBLS	10//99-12//99
	Connecticut	S	15.52 MW	16.77 AW	34880 AAW	CTBLS	10//99-12//99
	Delaware	S	13.44 MW	14.28 AW	29700 AAW	DEBLS	10//99-12//99
	District of Columbia	S	15.2 MW	15.39 AW	32000 AAW	DCBLS	10//99-12//99
	Florida	S	13.46 MW	14.49 AW	30140 AAW	FLBLS	10//99-12//99
	Georgia	S	13.34 MW	13.78 AW	28660 AAW	GABLS	10//99-12//99
	Hawaii	S	17.07 MW	16.37 AW	34050 AAW	HIBLS	10//99-12//99
	Idaho	S	14.32 MW	13.10 AW	27250 AAW	IDBLS	10//99-12//99
	Illinois	S	11.16 MW	12.44 AW	25880 AAW	ILBLS	10//99-12//99
	Indiana	S	11.66 MW	11.93 AW	24810 AAW	INBLS	10//99-12//99
	Iowa	S	10.38 MW	11.35 AW	23610 AAW	IABLS	10//99-12//99
	Kansas	S	13.8 MW	14.09 AW	29310 AAW	KSBLS	10//99-12//99
	Kentucky	S	11.7 MW	12.22 AW	25420 AAW	KYBLS	10//99-12//99
	Louisiana	S	13.05 MW	12.73 AW	26470 AAW	LABLS	10//99-12//99
	Maine	S	11.93 MW	11.95 AW	24850 AAW	MEBLS	10//99-12//99
	Maryland	S	13.13 MW	13.79 AW	28680 AAW	MDBLS	10//99-12//99
	Massachusetts	S	12.82 MW	14.18 AW	29490 AAW	MABLS	10//99-12//99
	Michigan	S	15.55 MW	15.20 AW	31610 AAW	MIBLS	10//99-12//99
	Minnesota	S	13.64 MW	13.91 AW	28940 AAW	MNBLS	10//99-12//99
	Mississippi	S	11.62 MW	11.71 AW	24350 AAW	MSBLS	10//99-12//99
	Missouri	S	11.12 MW	11.75 AW	24440 AAW	MOBLS	10//99-12//99
	Montana	S	10.46 MW	11.66 AW	24260 AAW	MTBLS	10//99-12//99
	Nebraska	S	11.34 MW	10.99 AW	22850 AAW	NEBLS	10//99-12//99
	Nevada	S	15.49 MW	15.44 AW	32110 AAW	NVBLS	10//99-12//99
	New Hampshire	S	13.11 MW	13.37 AW	27810 AAW	NHBLS	10//99-12//99
	New Jersey	S	14.72 MW	15.51 AW	32250 AAW	NJBLS	10//99-12//99
	New Mexico	S	13.44 MW	14.80 AW	30780 AAW	NMBLS	10//99-12//99
	New York	S	17.21 MW	16.44 AW	34180 AAW	NYBLS	10//99-12//99
	North Carolina	S	12.89 MW	13.41 AW	27900 AAW	NCBLS	10//99-12//99
	North Dakota	S	12.26 MW	11.63 AW	24190 AAW	NDBLS	10//99-12//99
	Ohio	S	14.38 MW	14.09 AW	29320 AAW	OHBLS	10//99-12//99
	Oklahoma	S	12.37 MW	12.30 AW	25590 AAW	OKBLS	10//99-12//99
	Oregon	S	16.16 MW	15.80 AW	32870 AAW	ORBLS	10//99-12//99
	Pennsylvania	S	13.32 MW	13.96 AW	29040 AAW	PABLS	10//99-12//99
	Rhode Island	S	17.41 MW	16.79 AW	34930 AAW	RIBLS	10//99-12//99
	South Carolina	S	8.39 MW	12.75 AW	26510 AAW	SCBLS	10//99-12//99
	South Dakota	S	13.36 MW	13.69 AW	28480 AAW	SDBLS	10//99-12//99
	Tennessee	S	11.42 MW	11.87 AW	24680 AAW	TNBLS	10//99-12//99
	Texas	S	11.97 MW	13.37 AW	27810 AAW	TXBLS	10//99-12//99
	Utah	S	13.93 MW	13.36 AW	27780 AAW	UTBLS	10//99-12//99
	Virginia	S	12.91 MW	13.20 AW	27460 AAW	VABLS	10//99-12//99
	Washington	S	16.3 MW	16.89 AW	35130 AAW	WABLS	10//99-12//99
	West Virginia	S	11.68 MW	11.96 AW	24880 AAW	WVBLS	10//99-12//99
	Wisconsin	S	12.24 MW	12.89 AW	26810 AAW	WIBLS	10//99-12//99
	Wyoming	S	11.8 MW	11.86 AW	24670 AAW	WYBLS	10//99-12//99
	Puerto Rico	S	14 MW	13.72 AW	28550 AAW	PRBLS	10//99-12//99
Recreational Vehicle Service Technician	Alaska	S	10.18 MW	11.31 AW	23530 AAW	AKBLS	10//99-12//99
	Arizona	S	12.64 MW	14.41 AW	29970 AAW	AZBLS	10//99-12//99

AAW Average annual wage	**AOH** Average offered, high	**ASH** Average starting, high	**H** Hourly	**M** Monthly	**S** Special: hourly and annual
AE Average entry wage	**AOL** Average offered, low	**ASL** Average starting, low	**HI** Highest wage paid	**MTC** Median total compensation	**TQ** Third quartile wage
AEX Average experienced wage	**APH** Average pay, high range	**AW** Average wage paid	**HR** High end range	**MW** Median wage paid	**W** Weekly
AO Average offered	**APL** Average pay, low range	**FQ** First quartile wage	**LR** Low end range	**SQ** Second quartile wage	**Y** Yearly

Occupation/Type/Industry	Location	Per	Low	Mid	High	Source	Date
Recreational Vehicle Service Technician	Arkansas	S	11.07 MW	10.84 AW	22540 AAW	ARBLS	10//99-12//99
	California	S	13.55 MW	15.58 AW	32410 AAW	CABLS	10//99-12//99
	Connecticut	S	11.63 MW	13.00 AW	27030 AAW	CTBLS	10//99-12//99
	Florida	S	10.22 MW	11.65 AW	24220 AAW	FLBLS	10//99-12//99
	Georgia	S	11.83 MW	12.45 AW	25900 AAW	GABLS	10//99-12//99
	Idaho	S	11.02 MW	11.39 AW	23690 AAW	IDBLS	10//99-12//99
	Illinois	S	9.71 MW	11.03 AW	22940 AAW	ILBLS	10//99-12//99
	Indiana	S	11.78 MW	11.72 AW	24380 AAW	INBLS	10//99-12//99
	Iowa	S	10.63 MW	10.78 AW	22410 AAW	IABLS	10//99-12//99
	Kansas	S	10.65 MW	10.52 AW	21880 AAW	KSBLS	10//99-12//99
	Louisiana	S	11.85 MW	11.83 AW	24610 AAW	LABLS	10//99-12//99
	Maine	S	13.63 MW	13.17 AW	27390 AAW	MEBLS	10//99-12//99
	Maryland	S	9.86 MW	10.02 AW	20840 AAW	MDBLS	10//99-12//99
	Massachusetts	S	11.88 MW	11.86 AW	24670 AAW	MABLS	10//99-12//99
	Michigan	S	12.1 MW	12.59 AW	26190 AAW	MIBLS	10//99-12//99
	Minnesota	S	12.29 MW	12.73 AW	26480 AAW	MNBLS	10//99-12//99
	Montana	S	11.73 MW	11.64 AW	24210 AAW	MTBLS	10//99-12//99
	Nebraska	S	6.7 MW	7.82 AW	16260 AAW	NEBLS	10//99-12//99
	Nevada	S	18.32 MW	17.47 AW	36340 AAW	NVBLS	10//99-12//99
	New Hampshire	S	14.01 MW	12.93 AW	26900 AAW	NHBLS	10//99-12//99
	New Mexico	S	12.01 MW	11.90 AW	24760 AAW	NMBLS	10//99-12//99
	New York	S	10.13 MW	10.51 AW	21870 AAW	NYBLS	10//99-12//99
	North Carolina	S	12.32 MW	12.06 AW	25080 AAW	NCBLS	10//99-12//99
	North Dakota	S	8.35 MW	8.94 AW	18600 AAW	NDBLS	10//99-12//99
	Oklahoma	S	9.77 MW	10.15 AW	21110 AAW	OKBLS	10//99-12//99
	Oregon	S	12.41 MW	13.01 AW	27060 AAW	ORBLS	10//99-12//99
	Pennsylvania	S	10.68 MW	10.51 AW	21850 AAW	PABLS	10//99-12//99
	South Carolina	S	9.17 MW	9.09 AW	18900 AAW	SCBLS	10//99-12//99
	Tennessee	S	11.49 MW	11.29 AW	23480 AAW	TNBLS	10//99-12//99
	Texas	S	13.34 MW	13.13 AW	27310 AAW	TXBLS	10//99-12//99
	Utah	S	14.08 MW	13.47 AW	28020 AAW	UTBLS	10//99-12//99
	Virginia	S	11.48 MW	12.25 AW	25490 AAW	VABLS	10//99-12//99
	Washington	S	14.04 MW	14.39 AW	29930 AAW	WABLS	10//99-12//99
	West Virginia	S	9.33 MW	8.93 AW	18580 AAW	WVBLS	10//99-12//99
	Wisconsin	S	10.68 MW	10.79 AW	22440 AAW	WIBLS	10//99-12//99
	Wyoming	S	8.89 MW	9.65 AW	20080 AAW	WYBLS	10//99-12//99
Refractory Materials Repairer							
Except Brickmason	Alabama	S	12.72 MW	14.20 AW	29540 AAW	ALBLS	10//99-12//99
Except Brickmason	California	S	18.34 MW	20.48 AW	42610 AAW	CABLS	10//99-12//99
Except Brickmason	Illinois	S	14.62 MW	15.92 AW	33120 AAW	ILBLS	10//99-12//99
Except Brickmason	Indiana	S	16.49 MW	16.61 AW	34540 AAW	INBLS	10//99-12//99
Except Brickmason	Kentucky	S	18.64 MW	20.18 AW	41970 AAW	KYBLS	10//99-12//99
Except Brickmason	Michigan	S	17.17 MW	17.39 AW	36170 AAW	MIBLS	10//99-12//99
Except Brickmason	Missouri	S	11.22 MW	12.92 AW	26870 AAW	MOBLS	10//99-12//99
Except Brickmason	New Jersey	S	19.84 MW	19.67 AW	40910 AAW	NJBLS	10//99-12//99
Except Brickmason	New York	S	16.27 MW	15.89 AW	33050 AAW	NYBLS	10//99-12//99
Except Brickmason	Ohio	S	13.62 MW	14.93 AW	31060 AAW	OHBLS	10//99-12//99
Except Brickmason	Pennsylvania	S	15.31 MW	15.76 AW	32780 AAW	PABLS	10//99-12//99
Except Brickmason	South Carolina	S	17.09 MW	15.84 AW	32950 AAW	SCBLS	10//99-12//99
Except Brickmason	Tennessee	S	13.28 MW	13.91 AW	28930 AAW	TNBLS	10//99-12//99
Except Brickmason	Texas	S	13.12 MW	13.65 AW	28390 AAW	TXBLS	10//99-12//99
Except Brickmason	West Virginia	S	16.32 MW	17.01 AW	35390 AAW	WVBLS	10//99-12//99
Except Brickmason	Wisconsin	S	12.21 MW	13.53 AW	28130 AAW	WIBLS	10//99-12//99
Refuse and Recyclable Material Collector							
	Alabama	S	8.21 MW	8.66 AW	18010 AAW	ALBLS	10//99-12//99
	Auburn-Opelika MSA, AL	S	8.76 MW	8.02 AW	18230 AAW	ALBLS	10//99-12//99
	Birmingham MSA, AL	S	8.58 MW	8.34 AW	17840 AAW	ALBLS	10//99-12//99
	Florence MSA, AL	S	8.69 MW	7.82 AW	18070 AAW	ALBLS	10//99-12//99
	Huntsville MSA, AL	S	9.48 MW	9.04 AW	19710 AAW	ALBLS	10//99-12//99
	Tuscaloosa MSA, AL	S	8.92 MW	8.93 AW	18550 AAW	ALBLS	10//99-12//99
	Alaska	S	15.4 MW	15.84 AW	32950 AAW	AKBLS	10//99-12//99
	Arizona	S	11.65 MW	12.40 AW	25800 AAW	AZBLS	10//99-12//99
	Phoenix-Mesa MSA, AZ	S	12.57 MW	11.89 AW	26140 AAW	AZBLS	10//99-12//99
	Tucson MSA, AZ	S	10.58 MW	9.61 AW	22000 AAW	AZBLS	10//99-12//99
	Arkansas	S	7.81 MW	8.19 AW	17030 AAW	ARBLS	10//99-12//99
	Fayetteville-Springdale-Rogers MSA, AR	S	9.41 MW	9.61 AW	19570 AAW	ARBLS	10//99-12//99
	Fort Smith MSA, AR-OK	S	8.72 MW	8.35 AW	18140 AAW	ARBLS	10//99-12//99

AAW Average annual wage	AOH Average offered, high	ASH Average starting, high	H Hourly	M Monthly	S Special: hourly and annual
AE Average entry wage	AOL Average offered, low	ASL Average starting, low	HI Highest wage paid	MTC Median total compensation	TQ Third quartile wage
AEX Average experienced wage	APH Average pay, high range	AW Average wage paid	HR High end range	MW Median wage paid	W Weekly
AO Average offered	APL Average pay, low range	FQ First quartile wage	LR Low end range	SQ Second quartile wage	Y Yearly

Occupation/Type/Industry	Location	Per	Low	Mid	High	Source	Date
Refuse and Recyclable Material Collector							
	Little Rock-North Little Rock MSA, AR	S	9.56 MW	8.99 AW	19890 AAW	ARBLS	10//99-12//99
	California	S	14.03 MW	14.87 AW	30920 AAW	CABLS	10//99-12//99
	Bakersfield MSA, CA	S	12.96 MW	12.90 AW	26960 AAW	CABLS	10//99-12//99
	Los Angeles-Long Beach PMSA, CA	S	12.94 MW	12.39 AW	26920 AAW	CABLS	10//99-12//99
	Merced MSA, CA	S	17.28 MW	17.79 AW	35940 AAW	CABLS	10//99-12//99
	Oakland PMSA, CA	S	16.36 MW	16.42 AW	34020 AAW	CABLS	10//99-12//99
	Orange County PMSA, CA	S	15.10 MW	13.72 AW	31420 AAW	CABLS	10//99-12//99
	Riverside-San Bernardino PMSA, CA	S	12.81 MW	11.93 AW	26650 AAW	CABLS	10//99-12//99
	Sacramento PMSA, CA	S	11.43 MW	11.06 AW	23770 AAW	CABLS	10//99-12//99
	San Diego MSA, CA	S	15.50 MW	15.97 AW	32230 AAW	CABLS	10//99-12//99
	San Francisco PMSA, CA	S	19.85 MW	20.03 AW	41280 AAW	CABLS	10//99-12//99
	San Jose PMSA, CA	S	15.93 MW	15.75 AW	33140 AAW	CABLS	10//99-12//99
	San Luis Obispo-Atascadero-Paso Robles MSA, CA	S	14.46 MW	14.66 AW	30070 AAW	CABLS	10//99-12//99
	Santa Barbara-Santa Maria-Lompoc MSA, CA	S	16.08 MW	15.32 AW	33450 AAW	CABLS	10//99-12//99
	Stockton-Lodi MSA, CA	S	14.21 MW	14.54 AW	29570 AAW	CABLS	10//99-12//99
	Vallejo-Fairfield-Napa PMSA, CA	S	15.76 MW	16.53 AW	32790 AAW	CABLS	10//99-12//99
	Ventura PMSA, CA	S	14.70 MW	13.70 AW	30570 AAW	CABLS	10//99-12//99
	Visalia-Tulare-Porterville MSA, CA	S	13.43 MW	14.05 AW	27930 AAW	CABLS	10//99-12//99
	Colorado	S	11.45 MW	11.96 AW	24880 AAW	COBLS	10//99-12//99
	Boulder-Longmont PMSA, CO	S	11.82 MW	11.70 AW	24580 AAW	COBLS	10//99-12//99
	Denver PMSA, CO	S	12.65 MW	12.08 AW	26310 AAW	COBLS	10//99-12//99
	Fort Collins-Loveland MSA, CO	S	10.57 MW	10.85 AW	21980 AAW	COBLS	10//99-12//99
	Grand Junction MSA, CO	S	13.32 MW	13.08 AW	27700 AAW	COBLS	10//99-12//99
	Greeley PMSA, CO	S	11.67 MW	12.33 AW	24280 AAW	COBLS	10//99-12//99
	Pueblo MSA, CO	S	10.07 MW	10.06 AW	20940 AAW	COBLS	10//99-12//99
	Connecticut	S	12.09 MW	11.98 AW	24920 AAW	CTBLS	10//99-12//99
	Bridgeport PMSA, CT	S	12.95 MW	13.38 AW	26940 AAW	CTBLS	10//99-12//99
	Danbury PMSA, CT	S	13.00 MW	14.45 AW	27040 AAW	CTBLS	10//99-12//99
	Hartford MSA, CT	S	9.56 MW	7.73 AW	19890 AAW	CTBLS	10//99-12//99
	New Haven-Meriden PMSA, CT	S	10.92 MW	10.09 AW	22710 AAW	CTBLS	10//99-12//99
	New London-Norwich MSA, CT-RI	S	12.43 MW	12.16 AW	25850 AAW	CTBLS	10//99-12//99
	Stamford-Norwalk PMSA, CT	S	15.96 MW	15.81 AW	33190 AAW	CTBLS	10//99-12//99
	Delaware	S	11.76 MW	11.40 AW	23720 AAW	DEBLS	10//99-12//99
	Wilmington-Newark PMSA, DE-MD	S	13.31 MW	13.19 AW	27680 AAW	DEBLS	10//99-12//99
	District of Columbia	S	7.57 MW	8.34 AW	17340 AAW	DCBLS	10//99-12//99
	Washington PMSA, DC-MD-VA-WV	S	10.08 MW	10.07 AW	20970 AAW	DCBLS	10//99-12//99
	Florida	S	11.12 MW	11.83 AW	24610 AAW	FLBLS	10//99-12//99
	Fort Lauderdale PMSA, FL	S	12.12 MW	11.44 AW	25210 AAW	FLBLS	10//99-12//99
	Fort Myers-Cape Coral MSA, FL	S	10.98 MW	10.01 AW	22850 AAW	FLBLS	10//99-12//99
	Fort Pierce-Port St. Lucie MSA, FL	S	14.19 MW	14.90 AW	29510 AAW	FLBLS	10//99-12//99
	Fort Walton Beach MSA, FL	S	8.02 MW	7.57 AW	16680 AAW	FLBLS	10//99-12//99
	Jacksonville MSA, FL	S	10.86 MW	11.19 AW	22600 AAW	FLBLS	10//99-12//99
	Lakeland-Winter Haven MSA, FL	S	9.50 MW	9.27 AW	19760 AAW	FLBLS	10//99-12//99
	Miami PMSA, FL	S	12.85 MW	12.69 AW	26730 AAW	FLBLS	10//99-12//99
	Orlando MSA, FL	S	13.05 MW	11.73 AW	27140 AAW	FLBLS	10//99-12//99
	Pensacola MSA, FL	S	10.39 MW	9.43 AW	21610 AAW	FLBLS	10//99-12//99
	Sarasota-Bradenton MSA, FL	S	11.24 MW	10.47 AW	23380 AAW	FLBLS	10//99-12//99
	Tampa-St. Petersburg-Clearwater MSA, FL	S	12.40 MW	11.87 AW	25790 AAW	FLBLS	10//99-12//99
	West Palm Beach-Boca Raton MSA, FL	S	12.15 MW	11.45 AW	25270 AAW	FLBLS	10//99-12//99
	Georgia	S	10.6 MW	10.71 AW	22270 AAW	GABLS	10//99-12//99
	Atlanta MSA, GA	S	11.87 MW	11.30 AW	24680 AAW	GABLS	10//99-12//99
	Augusta-Aiken MSA, GA-SC	S	9.16 MW	8.13 AW	19060 AAW	GABLS	10//99-12//99
	Columbus MSA, GA-AL	S	8.05 MW	6.73 AW	16750 AAW	GABLS	10//99-12//99
	Macon MSA, GA	S	8.79 MW	9.00 AW	18290 AAW	GABLS	10//99-12//99

AAW Average annual wage	**AOH** Average offered, high	**ASH** Average starting, high	**H** Hourly	**M** Monthly	**S** Special: hourly and annual
AE Average entry wage	**AOL** Average offered, low	**ASL** Average starting, low	**HI** Highest wage paid	**MTC** Median total compensation	**TQ** Third quartile wage
AEX Average experienced wage	**APH** Average pay, high range	**AW** Average wage paid	**HR** High end range	**MW** Median wage paid	**W** Weekly
AO Average offered	**APL** Average pay, low range	**FQ** First quartile wage	**LR** Low end range	**SQ** Second quartile wage	**Y** Yearly

Refuse and Recyclable Material Collector

Occupation/Type/Industry	Location	Per	Low	Mid	High	Source	Date
Refuse and Recyclable Material Collector	Savannah MSA, GA	S	8.45 MW	8.48 AW	17570 AAW	GABLS	10//99-12//99
	Hawaii	S	12.37 MW	12.39 AW	25760 AAW	HIBLS	10//99-12//99
	Idaho	S	10.72 MW	10.57 AW	21980 AAW	IDBLS	10//99-12//99
	Illinois	S	14.32 MW	14.24 AW	29620 AAW	ILBLS	10//99-12//99
	Champaign-Urbana MSA, IL	S	11.32 MW	9.86 AW	23550 AAW	ILBLS	10//99-12//99
	Chicago PMSA, IL	S	14.97 MW	15.21 AW	31130 AAW	ILBLS	10//99-12//99
	Rockford MSA, IL	S	13.72 MW	14.41 AW	28530 AAW	ILBLS	10//99-12//99
	Springfield MSA, IL	S	11.27 MW	10.12 AW	23430 AAW	ILBLS	10//99-12//99
	Indiana	S	11.67 MW	12.82 AW	26650 AAW	INBLS	10//99-12//99
	Evansville-Henderson MSA, IN-KY	S	11.93 MW	11.20 AW	24810 AAW	INBLS	10//99-12//99
	Fort Wayne MSA, IN	S	15.70 MW	14.01 AW	32660 AAW	INBLS	10//99-12//99
	Gary PMSA, IN	S	11.78 MW	11.89 AW	24510 AAW	INBLS	10//99-12//99
	Indianapolis MSA, IN	S	16.05 MW	14.07 AW	33380 AAW	INBLS	10//99-12//99
	Iowa	S	12.21 MW	12.21 AW	25390 AAW	IABLS	10//99-12//99
	Cedar Rapids MSA, IA	S	12.77 MW	13.17 AW	26570 AAW	IABLS	10//99-12//99
	Davenport-Moline-Rock Island MSA, IA-IL	S	12.32 MW	11.72 AW	25620 AAW	IABLS	10//99-12//99
	Des Moines MSA, IA	S	14.19 MW	13.82 AW	29520 AAW	IABLS	10//99-12//99
	Kansas	S	10.23 MW	11.61 AW	24150 AAW	KSBLS	10//99-12//99
	Kentucky	S	8.98 MW	9.00 AW	18720 AAW	KYBLS	10//99-12//99
	Lexington MSA, KY	S	8.38 MW	8.14 AW	17430 AAW	KYBLS	10//99-12//99
	Louisville MSA, KY-IN	S	10.32 MW	10.30 AW	21460 AAW	KYBLS	10//99-12//99
	Louisiana	S	7.88 MW	8.37 AW	17410 AAW	LABLS	10//99-12//99
	Alexandria MSA, LA	S	8.94 MW	8.42 AW	18590 AAW	LABLS	10//99-12//99
	Baton Rouge MSA, LA	S	7.55 MW	6.57 AW	15710 AAW	LABLS	10//99-12//99
	Lafayette MSA, LA	S	8.07 MW	6.90 AW	16790 AAW	LABLS	10//99-12//99
	New Orleans MSA, LA	S	7.78 MW	7.14 AW	16190 AAW	LABLS	10//99-12//99
	Shreveport-Bossier City MSA, LA	S	9.76 MW	9.68 AW	20310 AAW	LABLS	10//99-12//99
	Maine	S	8.4 MW	8.77 AW	18240 AAW	MEBLS	10//99-12//99
	Portland MSA, ME	S	10.66 MW	10.81 AW	22160 AAW	MEBLS	10//99-12//99
	Maryland	S	10.27 MW	10.68 AW	22210 AAW	MDBLS	10//99-12//99
	Baltimore PMSA, MD	S	10.75 MW	9.77 AW	22360 AAW	MDBLS	10//99-12//99
	Cumberland MSA, MD-WV	S	7.61 MW	7.11 AW	15820 AAW	MDBLS	10//99-12//99
	Massachusetts	S	14.25 MW	14.06 AW	29240 AAW	MABLS	10//99-12//99
	Boston PMSA, MA-NH	S	14.50 MW	14.61 AW	30160 AAW	MABLS	10//99-12//99
	Lawrence PMSA, MA-NH	S	15.96 MW	17.51 AW	33200 AAW	MABLS	10//99-12//99
	Springfield MSA, MA	S	15.21 MW	15.06 AW	31640 AAW	MABLS	10//99-12//99
	Michigan	S	12.56 MW	12.47 AW	25930 AAW	MIBLS	10//99-12//99
	Ann Arbor PMSA, MI	S	15.24 MW	13.82 AW	31700 AAW	MIBLS	10//99-12//99
	Detroit PMSA, MI	S	13.32 MW	13.43 AW	27690 AAW	MIBLS	10//99-12//99
	Kalamazoo-Battle Creek MSA, MI	S	12.45 MW	12.35 AW	25890 AAW	MIBLS	10//99-12//99
	Lansing-East Lansing MSA, MI	S	12.07 MW	11.89 AW	25100 AAW	MIBLS	10//99-12//99
	Minnesota	S	12.62 MW	13.50 AW	28070 AAW	MNBLS	10//99-12//99
	Duluth-Superior MSA, MN-WI	S	12.64 MW	13.17 AW	26290 AAW	MNBLS	10//99-12//99
	Minneapolis-St. Paul MSA, MN-WI	S	14.28 MW	13.90 AW	29690 AAW	MNBLS	10//99-12//99
	St. Cloud MSA, MN	S	11.93 MW	11.38 AW	24820 AAW	MNBLS	10//99-12//99
	Mississippi	S	8.08 MW	8.56 AW	17800 AAW	MSBLS	10//99-12//99
	Biloxi-Gulfport-Pascagoula MSA, MS	S	8.45 MW	8.69 AW	17570 AAW	MSBLS	10//99-12//99
	Missouri	S	10.75 MW	11.54 AW	24000 AAW	MOBLS	10//99-12//99
	St. Louis MSA, MO-IL	S	12.31 MW	11.72 AW	25610 AAW	MOBLS	10//99-12//99
	Montana	S	11.4 MW	10.57 AW	21980 AAW	MTBLS	10//99-12//99
	Billings MSA, MT	S	10.53 MW	12.44 AW	21910 AAW	MTBLS	10//99-12//99
	Nebraska	S	9.69 MW	9.74 AW	20260 AAW	NEBLS	10//99-12//99
	Lincoln MSA, NE	S	8.89 MW	9.27 AW	18480 AAW	NEBLS	10//99-12//99
	Omaha MSA, NE-IA	S	12.64 MW	12.74 AW	26300 AAW	NEBLS	10//99-12//99
	Nevada	S	11.37 MW	10.90 AW	22680 AAW	NVBLS	10//99-12//99
	Reno MSA, NV	S	11.91 MW	12.98 AW	24760 AAW	NVBLS	10//99-12//99
	New Hampshire	S	10.39 MW	11.00 AW	22890 AAW	NHBLS	10//99-12//99
	Manchester PMSA, NH	S	11.65 MW	11.54 AW	24230 AAW	NHBLS	10//99-12//99
	Portsmouth-Rochester PMSA, NH-ME	S	12.54 MW	10.53 AW	26090 AAW	NHBLS	10//99-12//99
	New Jersey	S	15.02 MW	15.04 AW	31290 AAW	NJBLS	10//99-12//99
	Atlantic-Cape May PMSA, NJ	S	12.98 MW	11.92 AW	26990 AAW	NJBLS	10//99-12//99
	Bergen-Passaic PMSA, NJ	S	15.22 MW	12.19 AW	31650 AAW	NJBLS	10//99-12//99
	Jersey City PMSA, NJ	S	14.91 MW	15.67 AW	31010 AAW	NJBLS	10//99-12//99

AAW Average annual wage	AOH Average offered, high	ASH Average starting, high	**H** Hourly	**M** Monthly	**S** Special: hourly and annual
AE Average entry wage	AOL Average offered, low	ASL Average starting, low	**HI** Highest wage paid	**MTC** Median total compensation	**TQ** Third quartile wage
AEX Average experienced wage	APH Average pay, high range	AW Average wage paid	**HR** High end range	**MW** Median wage paid	**W** Weekly
AO Average offered	APL Average pay, low range	FQ First quartile wage	**LR** Low end range	**SQ** Second quartile wage	**Y** Yearly

Occupation/Type/Industry	Location	Per	Low	Mid	High	Source	Date
Refuse and Recyclable Material Collector							
	Middlesex-Somerset-Hunterdon PMSA, NJ	S	16.04 MW	16.07 AW	33360 AAW	NJBLS	10//99-12//99
	Monmouth-Ocean PMSA, NJ	S	14.25 MW	14.64 AW	29640 AAW	NJBLS	10//99-12//99
	Newark PMSA, NJ	S	13.93 MW	13.15 AW	28980 AAW	NJBLS	10//99-12//99
	Vineland-Millville-Bridgeton PMSA, NJ	S	15.60 MW	16.87 AW	32450 AAW	NJBLS	10//99-12//99
	New Mexico	S	8.93 MW	9.20 AW	19130 AAW	NMBLS	10//99-12//99
	New York	S	18.26 MW	17.33 AW	36050 AAW	NYBLS	10//99-12//99
	Albany-Schenectady-Troy MSA, NY	S	10.28 MW	10.33 AW	21370 AAW	NYBLS	10//99-12//99
	Binghamton MSA, NY	S	10.01 MW	8.18 AW	20810 AAW	NYBLS	10//99-12//99
	Buffalo-Niagara Falls MSA, NY	S	13.70 MW	13.28 AW	28510 AAW	NYBLS	10//99-12//99
	Nassau-Suffolk PMSA, NY	S	15.97 MW	14.86 AW	33220 AAW	NYBLS	10//99-12//99
	Newburgh PMSA, NY-PA	S	13.90 MW	13.67 AW	28910 AAW	NYBLS	10//99-12//99
	Syracuse MSA, NY	S	12.40 MW	11.48 AW	25790 AAW	NYBLS	10//99-12//99
	North Carolina	S	8.68 MW	9.09 AW	18910 AAW	NCBLS	10//99-12//99
	Asheville MSA, NC	S	8.10 MW	7.97 AW	16850 AAW	NCBLS	10//99-12//99
	Charlotte-Gastonia-Rock Hill MSA, NC-SC	S	9.54 MW	9.81 AW	19850 AAW	NCBLS	10//99-12//99
	Fayetteville MSA, NC	S	8.23 MW	7.93 AW	17110 AAW	NCBLS	10//99-12//99
	Goldsboro MSA, NC	S	8.08 MW	8.01 AW	16800 AAW	NCBLS	10//99-12//99
	Greensboro--Winston-Salem--High Point MSA, NC	S	10.12 MW	10.34 AW	21040 AAW	NCBLS	10//99-12//99
	Hickory-Morganton-Lenoir MSA, NC	S	9.06 MW	8.51 AW	18840 AAW	NCBLS	10//99-12//99
	Raleigh-Durham-Chapel Hill MSA, NC	S	11.03 MW	10.69 AW	22950 AAW	NCBLS	10//99-12//99
	Rocky Mount MSA, NC	S	8.81 MW	9.14 AW	18330 AAW	NCBLS	10//99-12//99
	Wilmington MSA, NC	S	10.16 MW	9.96 AW	21140 AAW	NCBLS	10//99-12//99
	North Dakota	S	9.67 MW	9.46 AW	19670 AAW	NDBLS	10//99-12//99
	Fargo-Moorhead MSA, ND-MN	S	11.38 MW	11.31 AW	23670 AAW	NDBLS	10//99-12//99
	Ohio	S	12.27 MW	12.26 AW	25510 AAW	OHBLS	10//99-12//99
	Cincinnati PMSA, OH-KY-IN	S	12.64 MW	12.43 AW	26290 AAW	OHBLS	10//99-12//99
	Cleveland-Lorain-Elyria PMSA, OH	S	14.46 MW	14.62 AW	30070 AAW	OHBLS	10//99-12//99
	Columbus MSA, OH	S	13.32 MW	14.25 AW	27700 AAW	OHBLS	10//99-12//99
	Dayton-Springfield MSA, OH	S	11.46 MW	11.87 AW	23850 AAW	OHBLS	10//99-12//99
	Mansfield MSA, OH	S	11.01 MW	11.61 AW	22890 AAW	OHBLS	10//99-12//99
	Steubenville-Weirton MSA, OH-WV	S	10.24 MW	10.48 AW	21310 AAW	OHBLS	10//99-12//99
	Toledo MSA, OH	S	12.62 MW	12.63 AW	26240 AAW	OHBLS	10//99-12//99
	Oklahoma	S	6.39 MW	7.40 AW	15380 AAW	OKBLS	10//99-12//99
	Oklahoma City MSA, OK	S	7.08 MW	6.24 AW	14730 AAW	OKBLS	10//99-12//99
	Tulsa MSA, OK	S	9.98 MW	9.04 AW	20760 AAW	OKBLS	10//99-12//99
	Oregon	S	14.14 MW	14.02 AW	29160 AAW	ORBLS	10//99-12//99
	Portland-Vancouver PMSA, OR-WA	S	13.76 MW	14.02 AW	28610 AAW	ORBLS	10//99-12//99
	Salem PMSA, OR	S	14.47 MW	15.02 AW	30090 AAW	ORBLS	10//99-12//99
	Pennsylvania	S	10.75 MW	11.58 AW	24090 AAW	PABLS	10//99-12//99
	Erie MSA, PA	S	10.87 MW	10.17 AW	22600 AAW	PABLS	10//99-12//99
	Harrisburg-Lebanon-Carlisle MSA, PA	S	10.63 MW	10.58 AW	22110 AAW	PABLS	10//99-12//99
	Johnstown MSA, PA	S	9.03 MW	8.80 AW	18780 AAW	PABLS	10//99-12//99
	Philadelphia PMSA, PA-NJ	S	13.32 MW	13.40 AW	27710 AAW	PABLS	10//99-12//99
	Pittsburgh MSA, PA	S	13.65 MW	13.72 AW	28380 AAW	PABLS	10//99-12//99
	Reading MSA, PA	S	12.44 MW	11.91 AW	25880 AAW	PABLS	10//99-12//99
	Scranton--Wilkes-Barre--Hazleton MSA, PA	S	12.43 MW	12.59 AW	25860 AAW	PABLS	10//99-12//99
	Rhode Island	S	13.43 MW	12.88 AW	26800 AAW	RIBLS	10//99-12//99
	Providence-Fall River-Warwick MSA, RI-MA	S	12.89 MW	13.44 AW	26810 AAW	RIBLS	10//99-12//99
	South Carolina	S	7.64 MW	7.94 AW	16510 AAW	SCBLS	10//99-12//99
	Charleston-North Charleston MSA, SC	S	8.09 MW	7.90 AW	16820 AAW	SCBLS	10//99-12//99
	Columbia MSA, SC	S	7.87 MW	7.43 AW	16370 AAW	SCBLS	10//99-12//99
	Florence MSA, SC	S	7.38 MW	7.26 AW	15350 AAW	SCBLS	10//99-12//99
	Greenville-Spartanburg-Anderson MSA, SC	S	8.80 MW	8.52 AW	18300 AAW	SCBLS	10//99-12//99
	South Dakota	S	8.21 MW	8.45 AW	17570 AAW	SDBLS	10//99-12//99

AAW	Average annual wage	AOH	Average offered, high	ASH	Average starting, high
AE	Average entry wage	AOL	Average offered, low	ASL	Average starting, low
AEX	Average experienced wage	APH	Average pay, high range	AW	Average wage paid
AO	Average offered	APL	Average pay, low range	FQ	First quartile wage

H	Hourly	M	Monthly
HI	Highest wage paid	MTC	Median total compensation
HR	High end range	MW	Median wage paid
LR	Low end range	SQ	Second quartile wage

S	Special: hourly and annual
TQ	Third quartile wage
W	Weekly
Y	Yearly

Occupation/Type/Industry	Location	Per	Low	Mid	High	Source	Date
Refuse and Recyclable Material Collector	Tennessee	S	9.05 MW	9.23 AW	19190 AAW	TNBLS	10//99-12//99
	Chattanooga MSA, TN-GA	S	9.17 MW	9.06 AW	19080 AAW	TNBLS	10//99-12//99
	Johnson City-Kingsport-Bristol MSA, TN-VA	S	10.37 MW	10.39 AW	21570 AAW	TNBLS	10//99-12//99
	Knoxville MSA, TN	S	9.78 MW	10.23 AW	20350 AAW	TNBLS	10//99-12//99
	Memphis MSA, TN-AR-MS	S	9.01 MW	9.02 AW	18730 AAW	MSBLS	10//99-12//99
	Nashville MSA, TN	S	9.81 MW	10.07 AW	20400 AAW	TNBLS	10//99-12//99
	Texas	S	9.29 MW	9.48 AW	19710 AAW	TXBLS	10//99-12//99
	Austin-San Marcos MSA, TX	S	9.87 MW	9.64 AW	20530 AAW	TXBLS	10//99-12//99
	Beaumont-Port Arthur MSA, TX	S	12.37 MW	11.66 AW	25730 AAW	TXBLS	10//99-12//99
	Brazoria PMSA, TX	S	9.11 MW	9.44 AW	18950 AAW	TXBLS	10//99-12//99
	Brownsville-Harlingen-San Benito MSA, TX	S	7.56 MW	7.46 AW	15730 AAW	TXBLS	10//99-12//99
	Corpus Christi MSA, TX	S	6.52 MW	6.34 AW	13570 AAW	TXBLS	10//99-12//99
	Dallas PMSA, TX	S	10.02 MW	9.88 AW	20850 AAW	TXBLS	10//99-12//99
	Fort Worth-Arlington PMSA, TX	S	8.87 MW	8.48 AW	18460 AAW	TXBLS	10//99-12//99
	Houston PMSA, TX	S	9.45 MW	8.98 AW	19650 AAW	TXBLS	10//99-12//99
	Killeen-Temple MSA, TX	S	11.25 MW	11.20 AW	23410 AAW	TXBLS	10//99-12//99
	Lubbock MSA, TX	S	8.70 MW	8.69 AW	18090 AAW	TXBLS	10//99-12//99
	McAllen-Edinburg-Mission MSA, TX	S	9.17 MW	9.13 AW	19070 AAW	TXBLS	10//99-12//99
	Tyler MSA, TX	S	9.16 MW	9.25 AW	19050 AAW	TXBLS	10//99-12//99
	Utah	S	12.79 MW	12.81 AW	26640 AAW	UTBLS	10//99-12//99
	Salt Lake City-Ogden MSA, UT	S	13.30 MW	13.46 AW	27670 AAW	UTBLS	10//99-12//99
	Vermont	S	8.17 MW	8.59 AW	17860 AAW	VTBLS	10//99-12//99
	Virginia	S	9.65 MW	10.14 AW	21090 AAW	VABLS	10//99-12//99
	Charlottesville MSA, VA	S	10.32 MW	9.78 AW	21460 AAW	VABLS	10//99-12//99
	Lynchburg MSA, VA	S	9.96 MW	9.97 AW	20710 AAW	VABLS	10//99-12//99
	Norfolk-Virginia Beach-Newport News MSA, VA-NC	S	12.28 MW	12.40 AW	25540 AAW	VABLS	10//99-12//99
	Richmond-Petersburg MSA, VA	S	9.06 MW	8.64 AW	18840 AAW	VABLS	10//99-12//99
	Roanoke MSA, VA	S	9.05 MW	9.04 AW	18830 AAW	VABLS	10//99-12//99
	Washington	S	14.27 MW	13.77 AW	28640 AAW	WABLS	10//99-12//99
	Bremerton PMSA, WA	S	16.09 MW	16.68 AW	33460 AAW	WABLS	10//99-12//99
	Richland-Kennewick-Pasco MSA, WA	S	14.67 MW	14.77 AW	30500 AAW	WABLS	10//99-12//99
	Seattle-Bellevue-Everett PMSA, WA	S	13.35 MW	14.32 AW	27770 AAW	WABLS	10//99-12//99
	Tacoma PMSA, WA	S	17.48 MW	17.37 AW	36360 AAW	WABLS	10//99-12//99
	West Virginia	S	8.62 MW	8.39 AW	17450 AAW	WVBLS	10//99-12//99
	Charleston MSA, WV	S	8.47 MW	9.01 AW	17610 AAW	WVBLS	10//99-12//99
	Huntington-Ashland MSA, WV-KY-OH	S	8.45 MW	8.56 AW	17570 AAW	WVBLS	10//99-12//99
	Parkersburg-Marietta MSA, WV-OH	S	8.77 MW	8.92 AW	18240 AAW	WVBLS	10//99-12//99
	Wheeling MSA, WV-OH	S	9.01 MW	9.20 AW	18740 AAW	WVBLS	10//99-12//99
	Wisconsin	S	11.45 MW	11.47 AW	23860 AAW	WIBLS	10//99-12//99
	Appleton-Oshkosh-Neenah MSA, WI	S	12.49 MW	12.33 AW	25980 AAW	WIBLS	10//99-12//99
	Janesville-Beloit MSA, WI	S	15.39 MW	15.25 AW	32000 AAW	WIBLS	10//99-12//99
	La Crosse MSA, WI-MN	S	7.81 MW	6.42 AW	16240 AAW	WIBLS	10//99-12//99
	Milwaukee-Waukesha PMSA, WI	S	10.78 MW	9.76 AW	22430 AAW	WIBLS	10//99-12//99
	Wausau MSA, WI	S	8.87 MW	7.90 AW	18440 AAW	WIBLS	10//99-12//99
	Wyoming	S	8.7 MW	9.59 AW	19950 AAW	WYBLS	10//99-12//99
	Puerto Rico	S	5.94 MW	5.97 AW	12410 AAW	PRBLS	10//99-12//99
	San Juan-Bayamon PMSA, PR	S	5.82 MW	5.90 AW	12110 AAW	PRBLS	10//99-12//99
Regional Sales Manager Magazine	United States	Y		107000 AW		FOLIO	2000
Registered Nurse	United States	H		20.71 AW		NCS98	1998
	United States	Y	37440 AOL	40365 AO	49920 AOH	NURMAN3	1998
	United States	Y	28777 AE			CARWO1	2000
	Alabama	S	18.09 MW	18.65 AW	38790 AAW	ALBLS	10//99-12//99
	Auburn-Opelika MSA, AL	S	18.43 MW	17.61 AW	38340 AAW	ALBLS	10//99-12//99

AAW Average annual wage	**AOH** Average offered, high	**ASH** Average starting, high	**H** Hourly	**M** Monthly	**S** Special: hourly and annual
AE Average entry wage	**AOL** Average offered, low	**ASL** Average starting, low	**HI** Highest wage paid	**MTC** Median total compensation	**TQ** Third quartile wage
AEX Average experienced wage	**APH** Average pay, high range	**AW** Average wage paid	**HR** High end range	**MW** Median wage paid	**W** Weekly
AO Average offered	**APL** Average pay, low range	**FQ** First quartile wage	**LR** Low end range	**SQ** Second quartile wage	**Y** Yearly

Occupation/Type/Industry	Location	Per	Low	Mid	High	Source	Date
Registered Nurse	Birmingham MSA, AL	S	19.71 MW	19.17 AW	41000 AAW	ALBLS	10//99-12//99
	Decatur MSA, AL	S	16.60 MW	16.29 AW	34520 AAW	ALBLS	10//99-12//99
	Dothan MSA, AL	S	17.48 MW	16.86 AW	36360 AAW	ALBLS	10//99-12//99
	Florence MSA, AL	S	17.60 MW	16.98 AW	36620 AAW	ALBLS	10//99-12//99
	Huntsville MSA, AL	S	18.23 MW	17.40 AW	37920 AAW	ALBLS	10//99-12//99
	Mobile MSA, AL	S	18.66 MW	17.66 AW	38810 AAW	ALBLS	10//99-12//99
	Montgomery MSA, AL	S	18.47 MW	17.91 AW	38430 AAW	ALBLS	10//99-12//99
	Tuscaloosa MSA, AL	S	19.09 MW	18.53 AW	39700 AAW	ALBLS	10//99-12//99
	Alaska	S	23.02 MW	23.29 AW	48440 AAW	AKBLS	10//99-12//99
	Anchorage MSA, AK	S	23.19 MW	22.53 AW	48230 AAW	AKBLS	10//99-12//99
	Arizona	S	20.26 MW	20.84 AW	43340 AAW	AZBLS	10//99-12//99
	Flagstaff MSA, AZ-UT	S	20.29 MW	19.56 AW	42210 AAW	AZBLS	10//99-12//99
	Phoenix-Mesa MSA, AZ	S	21.43 MW	20.95 AW	44580 AAW	AZBLS	10//99-12//99
	Tucson MSA, AZ	S	20.38 MW	19.57 AW	42380 AAW	AZBLS	10//99-12//99
	Yuma MSA, AZ	S	18.34 MW	18.26 AW	38140 AAW	AZBLS	10//99-12//99
	Arkansas	S	17.18 MW	18.40 AW	38280 AAW	ARBLS	10//99-12//99
	Fayetteville-Springdale-Rogers MSA, AR	S	16.90 MW	16.31 AW	35140 AAW	ARBLS	10//99-12//99
	Fort Smith MSA, AR-OK	S	16.53 MW	15.88 AW	34390 AAW	ARBLS	10//99-12//99
	Little Rock-North Little Rock MSA, AR	S	20.65 MW	19.61 AW	42950 AAW	ARBLS	10//99-12//99
	Pine Bluff MSA, AR	S	20.74 MW	17.49 AW	43150 AAW	ARBLS	10//99-12//99
	California	S	25.12 MW	26.00 AW	54070 AAW	CABLS	10//99-12//99
	Bakersfield MSA, CA	S	23.26 MW	23.01 AW	48390 AAW	CABLS	10//99-12//99
	Chico-Paradise MSA, CA	S	20.29 MW	19.39 AW	42200 AAW	CABLS	10//99-12//99
	Fresno MSA, CA	S	25.63 MW	24.31 AW	53320 AAW	CABLS	10//99-12//99
	Los Angeles-Long Beach PMSA, CA	S	25.79 MW	24.94 AW	53640 AAW	CABLS	10//99-12//99
	Merced MSA, CA	S	24.81 MW	23.78 AW	51610 AAW	CABLS	10//99-12//99
	Modesto MSA, CA	S	24.82 MW	24.24 AW	51620 AAW	CABLS	10//99-12//99
	Oakland PMSA, CA	S	29.65 MW	31.14 AW	61680 AAW	CABLS	10//99-12//99
	Orange County PMSA, CA	S	25.23 MW	24.38 AW	52480 AAW	CABLS	10//99-12//99
	Redding MSA, CA	S	20.20 MW	19.89 AW	42030 AAW	CABLS	10//99-12//99
	Riverside-San Bernardino PMSA, CA	S	25.77 MW	24.36 AW	53600 AAW	CABLS	10//99-12//99
	Sacramento PMSA, CA	S	26.49 MW	25.51 AW	55090 AAW	CABLS	10//99-12//99
	Salinas MSA, CA	S	26.19 MW	25.99 AW	54470 AAW	CABLS	10//99-12//99
	San Diego County, CA	Y		43129 AW		ERDGE	1998
	San Diego MSA, CA	S	23.24 MW	22.64 AW	48330 AAW	CABLS	10//99-12//99
	San Francisco PMSA, CA	S	29.54 MW	31.12 AW	61440 AAW	CABLS	10//99-12//99
	San Jose PMSA, CA	S	29.37 MW	30.88 AW	61100 AAW	CABLS	10//99-12//99
	San Luis Obispo-Atascadero-Paso Robles MSA, CA	S	22.43 MW	23.07 AW	46650 AAW	CABLS	10//99-12//99
	Santa Barbara-Santa Maria-Lompoc MSA, CA	S	25.05 MW	24.04 AW	52100 AAW	CABLS	10//99-12//99
	Santa Cruz-Watsonville PMSA, CA	S	29.67 MW	32.61 AW	61710 AAW	CABLS	10//99-12//99
	Santa Rosa PMSA, CA	S	25.74 MW	25.66 AW	53530 AAW	CABLS	10//99-12//99
	Stockton-Lodi MSA, CA	S	26.32 MW	26.23 AW	54730 AAW	CABLS	10//99-12//99
	Vallejo-Fairfield-Napa PMSA, CA	S	26.52 MW	26.38 AW	55160 AAW	CABLS	10//99-12//99
	Ventura PMSA, CA	S	22.06 MW	21.93 AW	45890 AAW	CABLS	10//99-12//99
	Visalia-Tulare-Porterville MSA, CA	S	26.05 MW	25.19 AW	54190 AAW	CABLS	10//99-12//99
	Yolo PMSA, CA	S	20.20 MW	20.59 AW	42010 AAW	CABLS	10//99-12//99
	Yuba City MSA, CA	S	25.46 MW	24.88 AW	52950 AAW	CABLS	10//99-12//99
	Colorado	S	20.47 MW	21.01 AW	43700 AAW	COBLS	10//99-12//99
	Boulder-Longmont PMSA, CO	S	19.97 MW	19.45 AW	41530 AAW	COBLS	10//99-12//99
	Colorado Springs MSA, CO	S	19.78 MW	19.17 AW	41130 AAW	COBLS	10//99-12//99
	Denver PMSA, CO	S	22.13 MW	21.73 AW	46030 AAW	COBLS	10//99-12//99
	Fort Collins-Loveland MSA, CO	S	19.53 MW	19.30 AW	40630 AAW	COBLS	10//99-12//99
	Grand Junction MSA, CO	S	19.61 MW	18.88 AW	40780 AAW	COBLS	10//99-12//99
	Pueblo MSA, CO	S	20.56 MW	20.98 AW	42770 AAW	COBLS	10//99-12//99
	Connecticut	S	23.18 MW	23.79 AW	49480 AAW	CTBLS	10//99-12//99
	Bridgeport PMSA, CT	S	23.40 MW	23.06 AW	48680 AAW	CTBLS	10//99-12//99
	Danbury PMSA, CT	S	25.75 MW	25.63 AW	53560 AAW	CTBLS	10//99-12//99
	Hartford MSA, CT	S	23.82 MW	23.21 AW	49540 AAW	CTBLS	10//99-12//99
	New Haven-Meriden PMSA, CT	S	24.53 MW	23.73 AW	51030 AAW	CTBLS	10//99-12//99
	New London-Norwich MSA, CT-RI	S	23.16 MW	22.54 AW	48180 AAW	CTBLS	10//99-12//99

AAW Average annual wage	AOH Average offered, high	ASH Average starting, high	H Hourly	M Monthly	S Special: hourly and annual
AE Average entry salary	AOL Average offered, low	ASL Average starting, low	HI Highest wage paid	MTC Median total compensation	TQ Third quartile wage
AEX Average experienced wage	APH Average pay, high range	AW Average wage paid	HR High end range	MW Median wage paid	W Weekly
AO Average offered	APL Average pay, low range	FQ First quartile wage	LR Low end range	SQ Second quartile wage	Y Yearly

Occupation/Type/Industry	Location	Per	Low	Mid	High	Source	Date
Registered Nurse	Stamford-Norwalk PMSA, CT	S	24.47 MW	23.77 AW	50900 AAW	CTBLS	10//99-12//99
	Waterbury PMSA, CT	S	21.93 MW	22.26 AW	45620 AAW	CTBLS	10//99-12//99
	Delaware	S	20.28 MW	20.88 AW	43430 AAW	DEBLS	10//99-12//99
	Wilmington-Newark PMSA, DE-MD	S	21.42 MW	20.92 AW	44550 AAW	DEBLS	10//99-12//99
	District of Columbia	S	22.81 MW	22.82 AW	47460 AAW	DCBLS	10//99-12//99
	Washington PMSA, DC-MD-VA-WV	S	23.18 MW	22.81 AW	48200 AAW	DCBLS	10//99-12//99
	Florida	S	19.57 MW	20.36 AW	42350 AAW	FLBLS	10//99-12//99
	Daytona Beach MSA, FL	S	18.27 MW	18.07 AW	38010 AAW	FLBLS	10//99-12//99
	Fort Lauderdale PMSA, FL	S	21.72 MW	21.50 AW	45170 AAW	FLBLS	10//99-12//99
	Fort Myers-Cape Coral MSA, FL	S	18.88 MW	18.40 AW	39270 AAW	FLBLS	10//99-12//99
	Fort Pierce-Port St. Lucie MSA, FL	S	21.69 MW	20.39 AW	45110 AAW	FLBLS	10//99-12//99
	Fort Walton Beach MSA, FL	S	16.50 MW	16.01 AW	34330 AAW	FLBLS	10//99-12//99
	Gainesville MSA, FL	S	20.40 MW	19.33 AW	42420 AAW	FLBLS	10//99-12//99
	Jacksonville MSA, FL	S	19.20 MW	18.91 AW	39930 AAW	FLBLS	10//99-12//99
	Lakeland-Winter Haven MSA, FL	S	18.23 MW	17.93 AW	37920 AAW	FLBLS	10//99-12//99
	Melbourne-Titusville-Palm Bay MSA, FL	S	18.25 MW	17.55 AW	37960 AAW	FLBLS	10//99-12//99
	Miami PMSA, FL	S	22.47 MW	22.34 AW	46730 AAW	FLBLS	10//99-12//99
	Naples MSA, FL	S	20.86 MW	18.12 AW	43390 AAW	FLBLS	10//99-12//99
	Ocala MSA, FL	S	18.27 MW	17.94 AW	38010 AAW	FLBLS	10//99-12//99
	Orlando MSA, FL	S	19.24 MW	18.79 AW	40010 AAW	FLBLS	10//99-12//99
	Panama City MSA, FL	S	17.97 MW	17.65 AW	37380 AAW	FLBLS	10//99-12//99
	Pensacola MSA, FL	S	20.24 MW	17.86 AW	42090 AAW	FLBLS	10//99-12//99
	Punta Gorda MSA, FL	S	19.83 MW	19.29 AW	41240 AAW	FLBLS	10//99-12//99
	Sarasota-Bradenton MSA, FL	S	19.09 MW	17.73 AW	39710 AAW	FLBLS	10//99-12//99
	Tallahassee MSA, FL	S	23.09 MW	20.39 AW	48030 AAW	FLBLS	10//99-12//99
	Tampa-St. Petersburg-Clearwater MSA, FL	S	19.76 MW	19.02 AW	41100 AAW	FLBLS	10//99-12//99
	West Palm Beach-Boca Raton MSA, FL	S	21.63 MW	21.41 AW	44990 AAW	FLBLS	10//99-12//99
	Georgia	S	18.97 MW	19.56 AW	40670 AAW	GABLS	10//99-12//99
	Albany MSA, GA	S	17.52 MW	17.32 AW	36440 AAW	GABLS	10//99-12//99
	Athens MSA, GA	S	18.04 MW	17.15 AW	37520 AAW	GABLS	10//99-12//99
	Atlanta MSA, GA	S	20.23 MW	19.53 AW	42070 AAW	GABLS	10//99-12//99
	Augusta-Aiken MSA, GA-SC	S	19.60 MW	18.80 AW	40760 AAW	GABLS	10//99-12//99
	Columbus MSA, GA-AL	S	20.67 MW	19.52 AW	43000 AAW	GABLS	10//99-12//99
	Macon MSA, GA	S	18.53 MW	18.14 AW	38530 AAW	GABLS	10//99-12//99
	Savannah MSA, GA	S	19.78 MW	18.57 AW	41150 AAW	GABLS	10//99-12//99
	Hawaii	S	27.62 MW	27.37 AW	56930 AAW	HIBLS	10//99-12//99
	Honolulu MSA, HI	S	28.27 MW	29.37 AW	58790 AAW	HIBLS	10//99-12//99
	Idaho	S	19.2 MW	19.43 AW	40410 AAW	IDBLS	10//99-12//99
	Boise City MSA, ID	S	20.16 MW	19.63 AW	41930 AAW	IDBLS	10//99-12//99
	Pocatello MSA, ID	S	18.61 MW	18.20 AW	38720 AAW	IDBLS	10//99-12//99
	Illinois	S	19.53 MW	20.15 AW	41910 AAW	ILBLS	10//99-12//99
	Bloomington-Normal MSA, IL	S	17.56 MW	15.87 AW	36520 AAW	ILBLS	10//99-12//99
	Champaign-Urbana MSA, IL	S	18.50 MW	16.19 AW	38470 AAW	ILBLS	10//99-12//99
	Chicago PMSA, IL	S	21.45 MW	21.18 AW	44620 AAW	ILBLS	10//99-12//99
	Decatur MSA, IL	S	15.40 MW	15.11 AW	32020 AAW	ILBLS	10//99-12//99
	Kankakee PMSA, IL	S	19.84 MW	19.50 AW	41270 AAW	ILBLS	10//99-12//99
	Peoria-Pekin MSA, IL	S	17.48 MW	16.54 AW	36360 AAW	ILBLS	10//99-12//99
	Rockford MSA, IL	S	17.28 MW	16.36 AW	35950 AAW	ILBLS	10//99-12//99
	Springfield MSA, IL	S	19.11 MW	18.76 AW	39750 AAW	ILBLS	10//99-12//99
	Indiana	S	18.43 MW	18.98 AW	39480 AAW	INBLS	10//99-12//99
	Bloomington MSA, IN	S	16.52 MW	16.99 AW	34360 AAW	INBLS	10//99-12//99
	Elkhart-Goshen MSA, IN	S	19.26 MW	17.63 AW	40070 AAW	INBLS	10//99-12//99
	Evansville-Henderson MSA, IN-KY	S	16.95 MW	16.92 AW	35260 AAW	INBLS	10//99-12//99
	Fort Wayne MSA, IN	S	16.75 MW	16.11 AW	34840 AAW	INBLS	10//99-12//99
	Gary PMSA, IN	S	19.63 MW	20.01 AW	40830 AAW	INBLS	10//99-12//99
	Indianapolis MSA, IN	S	20.75 MW	20.22 AW	43160 AAW	INBLS	10//99-12//99
	Kokomo MSA, IN	S	18.09 MW	18.12 AW	37620 AAW	INBLS	10//99-12//99
	Lafayette MSA, IN	S	18.18 MW	16.98 AW	37820 AAW	INBLS	10//99-12//99
	Muncie MSA, IN	S	16.50 MW	16.07 AW	34320 AAW	INBLS	10//99-12//99
	South Bend MSA, IN	S	18.10 MW	18.14 AW	37650 AAW	INBLS	10//99-12//99
	Terre Haute MSA, IN	S	15.46 MW	15.28 AW	32170 AAW	INBLS	10//99-12//99
	Iowa	S	16.17 MW	16.76 AW	34860 AAW	IABLS	10//99-12//99
	Cedar Rapids MSA, IA	S	17.15 MW	17.55 AW	35660 AAW	IABLS	10//99-12//99

Occupation/Type/Industry	Location	Per	Low	Mid	High	Source	Date
Registered Nurse	Davenport-Moline-Rock Island MSA, IA-IL	S	15.40 MW	14.63 AW	32030 AAW	IABLS	10//99-12//99
	Dubuque MSA, IA	S	15.32 MW	15.24 AW	31860 AAW	IABLS	10//99-12//99
	Sioux City MSA, IA-NE	S	17.07 MW	16.78 AW	35500 AAW	IABLS	10//99-12//99
	Waterloo-Cedar Falls MSA, IA	S	16.35 MW	16.31 AW	34000 AAW	IABLS	10//99-12//99
	Kansas	S	17.69 MW	18.44 AW	38360 AAW	KSBLS	10//99-12//99
	Lawrence MSA, KS	S	19.09 MW	18.34 AW	39700 AAW	KSBLS	10//99-12//99
	Topeka MSA, KS	S	18.21 MW	17.80 AW	37880 AAW	KSBLS	10//99-12//99
	Wichita MSA, KS	S	18.31 MW	17.99 AW	38070 AAW	KSBLS	10//99-12//99
	Kentucky	S	18.38 MW	19.32 AW	40180 AAW	KYBLS	10//99-12//99
	Lexington MSA, KY	S	19.23 MW	18.38 AW	39990 AAW	KYBLS	10//99-12//99
	Louisville MSA, KY-IN	S	20.31 MW	19.45 AW	42250 AAW	KYBLS	10//99-12//99
	Owensboro MSA, KY	S	16.68 MW	16.20 AW	34700 AAW	KYBLS	10//99-12//99
	Louisiana	S	19.52 MW	20.27 AW	42150 AAW	LABLS	10//99-12//99
	Alexandria MSA, LA	S	20.49 MW	19.32 AW	42610 AAW	LABLS	10//99-12//99
	Baton Rouge MSA, LA	S	19.30 MW	18.74 AW	40140 AAW	LABLS	10//99-12//99
	Houma MSA, LA	S	18.92 MW	18.36 AW	39350 AAW	LABLS	10//99-12//99
	Lafayette MSA, LA	S	19.88 MW	19.36 AW	41350 AAW	LABLS	10//99-12//99
	Lake Charles MSA, LA	S	17.83 MW	18.26 AW	37080 AAW	LABLS	10//99-12//99
	Monroe MSA, LA	S	19.50 MW	18.11 AW	40560 AAW	LABLS	10//99-12//99
	New Orleans MSA, LA	S	21.91 MW	21.14 AW	45570 AAW	LABLS	10//99-12//99
	Shreveport-Bossier City MSA, LA	S	19.22 MW	18.02 AW	39970 AAW	LABLS	10//99-12//99
	Maine	S	18.72 MW	19.46 AW	40480 AAW	MEBLS	10//99-12//99
	Lewiston-Auburn MSA, ME	S	20.15 MW	19.52 AW	41910 AAW	MEBLS	10//99-12//99
	Portland MSA, ME	S	19.55 MW	18.72 AW	40660 AAW	MEBLS	10//99-12//99
	Maryland	S	22.78 MW	23.54 AW	48960 AAW	MDBLS	10//99-12//99
	Baltimore PMSA, MD	S	23.48 MW	22.79 AW	48850 AAW	MDBLS	10//99-12//99
	Cumberland MSA, MD-WV	S	19.32 MW	18.62 AW	40180 AAW	MDBLS	10//99-12//99
	Hagerstown PMSA, MD	S	21.02 MW	19.17 AW	43710 AAW	MDBLS	10//99-12//99
	Massachusetts	S	22.98 MW	23.66 AW	49200 AAW	MABLS	10//99-12//99
	Barnstable-Yarmouth MSA, MA	S	23.67 MW	22.57 AW	49230 AAW	MABLS	10//99-12//99
	Boston PMSA, MA-NH	S	24.82 MW	24.20 AW	51620 AAW	MABLS	10//99-12//99
	Brockton PMSA, MA	S	21.92 MW	22.65 AW	45590 AAW	MABLS	10//99-12//99
	Fitchburg-Leominster PMSA, MA	S	19.18 MW	18.73 AW	39900 AAW	MABLS	10//99-12//99
	Lawrence PMSA, MA-NH	S	20.97 MW	21.05 AW	43620 AAW	MABLS	10//99-12//99
	Lowell PMSA, MA-NH	S	22.43 MW	21.68 AW	46660 AAW	MABLS	10//99-12//99
	New Bedford PMSA, MA	S	20.26 MW	19.47 AW	42140 AAW	MABLS	10//99-12//99
	Pittsfield MSA, MA	S	21.36 MW	21.94 AW	44430 AAW	MABLS	10//99-12//99
	Springfield MSA, MA	S	21.29 MW	20.94 AW	44270 AAW	MABLS	10//99-12//99
	Worcester PMSA, MA-CT	S	22.52 MW	22.32 AW	46850 AAW	MABLS	10//99-12//99
	Michigan	S	21.42 MW	21.88 AW	45500 AAW	MIBLS	10//99-12//99
	Ann Arbor PMSA, MI	S	22.08 MW	20.87 AW	45920 AAW	MIBLS	10//99-12//99
	Benton Harbor MSA, MI	S	16.16 MW	15.96 AW	33610 AAW	MIBLS	10//99-12//99
	Detroit PMSA, MI	S	23.46 MW	22.82 AW	48800 AAW	MIBLS	10//99-12//99
	Flint PMSA, MI	S	22.45 MW	22.18 AW	46700 AAW	MIBLS	10//99-12//99
	Grand Rapids-Muskegon-Holland MSA, MI	S	20.79 MW	20.25 AW	43240 AAW	MIBLS	10//99-12//99
	Jackson MSA, MI	S	17.94 MW	17.78 AW	37320 AAW	MIBLS	10//99-12//99
	Kalamazoo-Battle Creek MSA, MI	S	20.80 MW	20.82 AW	43260 AAW	MIBLS	10//99-12//99
	Lansing-East Lansing MSA, MI	S	20.29 MW	20.27 AW	42200 AAW	MIBLS	10//99-12//99
	Saginaw-Bay City-Midland MSA, MI	S	20.67 MW	19.71 AW	42990 AAW	MIBLS	10//99-12//99
	Minnesota	S	22.47 MW	23.39 AW	48650 AAW	MNBLS	10//99-12//99
	Duluth-Superior MSA, MN-WI	S	24.59 MW	22.85 AW	51140 AAW	MNBLS	10//99-12//99
	Minneapolis-St. Paul MSA, MN-WI	S	24.48 MW	23.63 AW	50930 AAW	MNBLS	10//99-12//99
	Mississippi	S	18.16 MW	19.20 AW	39940 AAW	MSBLS	10//99-12//99
	Biloxi-Gulfport-Pascagoula MSA, MS	S	18.88 MW	18.53 AW	39280 AAW	MSBLS	10//99-12//99
	Jackson MSA, MS	S	20.00 MW	19.19 AW	41600 AAW	MSBLS	10//99-12//99
	Missouri	S	18.28 MW	18.92 AW	39360 AAW	MOBLS	10//99-12//99
	Columbia MSA, MO	S	18.30 MW	17.76 AW	38050 AAW	MOBLS	10//99-12//99
	Kansas City MSA, MO-KS	S	20.82 MW	20.09 AW	43310 AAW	MOBLS	10//99-12//99
	St. Joseph MSA, MO	S	17.50 MW	17.42 AW	36390 AAW	MOBLS	10//99-12//99
	St. Louis MSA, MO-IL	S	19.39 MW	18.82 AW	40340 AAW	MOBLS	10//99-12//99
	Springfield MSA, MO	S	17.78 MW	17.64 AW	36970 AAW	MOBLS	10//99-12//99
	Montana	S	17.28 MW	17.61 AW	36640 AAW	MTBLS	10//99-12//99
	Billings MSA, MT	S	16.68 MW	15.84 AW	34690 AAW	MTBLS	10//99-12//99

Registered Nurse

Occupation/Type/Industry	Location	Per	Low	Mid	High	Source	Date
Registered Nurse	Great Falls MSA, MT	S	18.53 MW	18.63 AW	38550 AAW	MTBLS	10//99-12//99
	Missoula MSA, MT	S	18.93 MW	18.84 AW	39380 AAW	MTBLS	10//99-12//99
	Nebraska	S	17.86 MW	18.07 AW	37590 AAW	NEBLS	10//99-12//99
	Lincoln MSA, NE	S	18.42 MW	17.68 AW	38310 AAW	NEBLS	10//99-12//99
	Omaha MSA, NE-IA	S	18.83 MW	18.58 AW	39160 AAW	NEBLS	10//99-12//99
	Nevada	S	22.58 MW	23.05 AW	47930 AAW	NVBLS	10//99-12//99
	Las Vegas MSA, NV-AZ	S	22.98 MW	22.66 AW	47800 AAW	NVBLS	10//99-12//99
	Reno MSA, NV	S	22.33 MW	22.04 AW	46450 AAW	NVBLS	10//99-12//99
	New Hampshire	S	18.37 MW	18.89 AW	39290 AAW	NHBLS	10//99-12//99
	Manchester PMSA, NH	S	20.28 MW	19.57 AW	42180 AAW	NHBLS	10//99-12//99
	Nashua PMSA, NH	S	19.18 MW	18.18 AW	39880 AAW	NHBLS	10//99-12//99
	Portsmouth-Rochester PMSA, NH-ME	S	19.17 MW	18.87 AW	39880 AAW	NHBLS	10//99-12//99
	New Jersey	S	23.74 MW	24.46 AW	50880 AAW	NJBLS	10//99-12//99
	Atlantic-Cape May PMSA, NJ	S	22.33 MW	22.47 AW	46440 AAW	NJBLS	10//99-12//99
	Bergen-Passaic PMSA, NJ	S	26.66 MW	26.22 AW	55450 AAW	NJBLS	10//99-12//99
	Jersey City PMSA, NJ	S	23.27 MW	22.78 AW	48400 AAW	NJBLS	10//99-12//99
	Middlesex-Somerset-Hunterdon PMSA, NJ	S	25.92 MW	25.19 AW	53920 AAW	NJBLS	10//99-12//99
	Monmouth-Ocean PMSA, NJ	S	23.05 MW	22.73 AW	47940 AAW	NJBLS	10//99-12//99
	Newark PMSA, NJ	S	24.75 MW	24.06 AW	51490 AAW	NJBLS	10//99-12//99
	Trenton PMSA, NJ	S	23.11 MW	22.51 AW	48060 AAW	NJBLS	10//99-12//99
	Vineland-Millville-Bridgeton PMSA, NJ	S	22.10 MW	21.07 AW	45970 AAW	NJBLS	10//99-12//99
	New Mexico	S	18.78 MW	19.34 AW	40220 AAW	NMBLS	10//99-12//99
	Albuquerque MSA, NM	S	20.14 MW	19.52 AW	41880 AAW	NMBLS	10//99-12//99
	Las Cruces MSA, NM	S	19.40 MW	18.95 AW	40360 AAW	NMBLS	10//99-12//99
	Santa Fe MSA, NM	S	20.94 MW	19.17 AW	43550 AAW	NMBLS	10//99-12//99
	New York	S	23.33 MW	24.27 AW	50470 AAW	NYBLS	10//99-12//99
	Albany-Schenectady-Troy MSA, NY	S	19.52 MW	18.67 AW	40610 AAW	NYBLS	10//99-12//99
	Binghamton MSA, NY	S	16.18 MW	15.63 AW	33660 AAW	NYBLS	10//99-12//99
	Buffalo-Niagara Falls MSA, NY	S	19.81 MW	19.35 AW	41210 AAW	NYBLS	10//99-12//99
	Dutchess County PMSA, NY	S	19.73 MW	19.06 AW	41030 AAW	NYBLS	10//99-12//99
	Elmira MSA, NY	S	16.37 MW	15.64 AW	34050 AAW	NYBLS	10//99-12//99
	Glens Falls MSA, NY	S	16.52 MW	14.49 AW	34360 AAW	NYBLS	10//99-12//99
	Jamestown MSA, NY	S	16.82 MW	16.94 AW	34990 AAW	NYBLS	10//99-12//99
	Nassau-Suffolk PMSA, NY	S	27.26 MW	26.62 AW	56710 AAW	NYBLS	10//99-12//99
	New York PMSA, NY	S	27.82 MW	27.03 AW	57870 AAW	NYBLS	10//99-12//99
	Newburgh PMSA, NY-PA	S	21.13 MW	20.84 AW	43940 AAW	NYBLS	10//99-12//99
	Rochester MSA, NY	S	18.92 MW	18.54 AW	39360 AAW	NYBLS	10//99-12//99
	Syracuse MSA, NY	S	18.97 MW	17.17 AW	39460 AAW	NYBLS	10//99-12//99
	Utica-Rome MSA, NY	S	17.86 MW	17.76 AW	37150 AAW	NYBLS	10//99-12//99
	North Carolina	S	18.92 MW	19.57 AW	40700 AAW	NCBLS	10//99-12//99
	Charlotte-Gastonia-Rock Hill MSA, NC-SC	S	20.10 MW	19.17 AW	41810 AAW	NCBLS	10//99-12//99
	Goldsboro MSA, NC	S	19.00 MW	18.00 AW	39520 AAW	NCBLS	10//99-12//99
	Greensboro--Winston-Salem--High Point MSA, NC	S	19.55 MW	18.88 AW	40660 AAW	NCBLS	10//99-12//99
	Hickory-Morganton-Lenoir MSA, NC	S	19.42 MW	18.74 AW	40390 AAW	NCBLS	10//99-12//99
	Jacksonville MSA, NC	S	17.96 MW	17.40 AW	37360 AAW	NCBLS	10//99-12//99
	Raleigh-Durham-Chapel Hill MSA, NC	S	20.65 MW	20.15 AW	42960 AAW	NCBLS	10//99-12//99
	Rocky Mount MSA, NC	S	19.27 MW	19.24 AW	40090 AAW	NCBLS	10//99-12//99
	North Dakota	S	17.72 MW	18.07 AW	37580 AAW	NDBLS	10//99-12//99
	Fargo-Moorhead MSA, ND-MN	S	19.59 MW	19.36 AW	40740 AAW	NDBLS	10//99-12//99
	Ohio	S	19.14 MW	19.69 AW	40950 AAW	OHBLS	10//99-12//99
	Akron PMSA, OH	S	20.36 MW	20.76 AW	42350 AAW	OHBLS	10//99-12//99
	Canton-Massillon MSA, OH	S	18.16 MW	18.23 AW	37780 AAW	OHBLS	10//99-12//99
	Cincinnati PMSA, OH-KY-IN	S	18.48 MW	18.32 AW	38430 AAW	OHBLS	10//99-12//99
	Cleveland-Lorain-Elyria PMSA, OH	S	21.66 MW	21.07 AW	45060 AAW	OHBLS	10//99-12//99
	Columbus MSA, OH	S	20.05 MW	19.08 AW	41700 AAW	OHBLS	10//99-12//99
	Dayton-Springfield MSA, OH	S	19.78 MW	19.10 AW	41140 AAW	OHBLS	10//99-12//99
	Hamilton-Middletown PMSA, OH	S	19.60 MW	19.13 AW	40770 AAW	OHBLS	10//99-12//99
	Lima MSA, OH	S	16.94 MW	17.02 AW	35240 AAW	OHBLS	10//99-12//99
	Mansfield MSA, OH	S	19.77 MW	18.41 AW	41120 AAW	OHBLS	10//99-12//99

AAW Average annual wage	AOH Average offered, high	ASH Average starting, high	H Hourly	M Monthly	S Special: hourly and annual
AE Average entry wage	AOL Average offered, low	ASL Average starting, low	HI Highest wage paid	MTC Median total compensation	TQ Third quartile wage
AEX Average experienced wage	APH Average pay, high range	AW Average wage paid	HR High end range	MW Median wage paid	W Weekly
AO Average offered	APL Average pay, low range	FQ First quartile wage	LR Low end range	SQ Second quartile wage	Y Yearly

Occupation/Type/Industry	Location	Per	Low	Mid	High	Source	Date
Registered Nurse	Steubenville-Weirton MSA, OH-WV	S	16.99 MW	15.20 AW	35330 AAW	OHBLS	10//99-12//99
	Toledo MSA, OH	S	18.79 MW	18.50 AW	39090 AAW	OHBLS	10//99-12//99
	Youngstown-Warren MSA, OH	S	19.97 MW	19.82 AW	41550 AAW	OHBLS	10//99-12//99
	Oklahoma	S	18.02 MW	18.76 AW	39020 AAW	OKBLS	10//99-12//99
	Enid MSA, OK	S	17.49 MW	17.22 AW	36380 AAW	OKBLS	10//99-12//99
	Lawton MSA, OK	S	18.44 MW	18.25 AW	38360 AAW	OKBLS	10//99-12//99
	Oklahoma City MSA, OK	S	18.40 MW	17.98 AW	38270 AAW	OKBLS	10//99-12//99
	Tulsa MSA, OK	S	20.33 MW	19.02 AW	42290 AAW	OKBLS	10//99-12//99
	Oregon	S	21.64 MW	22.45 AW	46690 AAW	ORBLS	10//99-12//99
	Medford-Ashland MSA, OR	S	22.54 MW	21.69 AW	46870 AAW	ORBLS	10//99-12//99
	Portland-Vancouver PMSA, OR-WA	S	23.24 MW	21.86 AW	48340 AAW	ORBLS	10//99-12//99
	Salem PMSA, OR	S	22.52 MW	22.77 AW	46850 AAW	ORBLS	10//99-12//99
	Pennsylvania	S	20.04 MW	20.92 AW	43510 AAW	PABLS	10//99-12//99
	Allentown-Bethlehem-Easton MSA, PA	S	21.21 MW	20.16 AW	44110 AAW	PABLS	10//99-12//99
	Altoona MSA, PA	S	17.09 MW	16.68 AW	35540 AAW	PABLS	10//99-12//99
	Erie MSA, PA	S	17.78 MW	16.80 AW	36980 AAW	PABLS	10//99-12//99
	Harrisburg-Lebanon-Carlisle MSA, PA	S	22.71 MW	22.38 AW	47240 AAW	PABLS	10//99-12//99
	Johnstown MSA, PA	S	15.90 MW	15.30 AW	33080 AAW	PABLS	10//99-12//99
	Lancaster MSA, PA	S	19.45 MW	18.74 AW	40460 AAW	PABLS	10//99-12//99
	Philadelphia PMSA, PA-NJ	S	22.79 MW	22.41 AW	47390 AAW	PABLS	10//99-12//99
	Pittsburgh MSA, PA	S	21.39 MW	19.99 AW	44490 AAW	PABLS	10//99-12//99
	Reading MSA, PA	S	20.11 MW	20.01 AW	41820 AAW	PABLS	10//99-12//99
	Scranton--Wilkes-Barre--Hazleton MSA, PA	S	17.74 MW	17.40 AW	36890 AAW	PABLS	10//99-12//99
	Sharon MSA, PA	S	19.63 MW	18.92 AW	40830 AAW	PABLS	10//99-12//99
	State College MSA, PA	S	19.49 MW	18.43 AW	40540 AAW	PABLS	10//99-12//99
	York MSA, PA	S	18.73 MW	18.18 AW	38960 AAW	PABLS	10//99-12//99
	Rhode Island	S	22.22 MW	23.10 AW	48040 AAW	RIBLS	10//99-12//99
	Providence-Fall River-Warwick MSA, RI-MA	S	22.83 MW	21.77 AW	47480 AAW	RIBLS	10//99-12//99
	South Carolina	S	19.32 MW	20.41 AW	42460 AAW	SCBLS	10//99-12//99
	Charleston-North Charleston MSA, SC	S	21.54 MW	21.46 AW	44810 AAW	SCBLS	10//99-12//99
	Columbia MSA, SC	S	20.39 MW	19.16 AW	42400 AAW	SCBLS	10//99-12//99
	Florence MSA, SC	S	18.79 MW	18.54 AW	39080 AAW	SCBLS	10//99-12//99
	Greenville-Spartanburg-Anderson MSA, SC	S	22.03 MW	20.45 AW	45820 AAW	SCBLS	10//99-12//99
	Myrtle Beach MSA, SC	S	17.56 MW	16.21 AW	36520 AAW	SCBLS	10//99-12//99
	South Dakota	S	17.26 MW	17.89 AW	37210 AAW	SDBLS	10//99-12//99
	Sioux Falls MSA, SD	S	19.11 MW	18.47 AW	39750 AAW	SDBLS	10//99-12//99
	Tennessee	S	18.05 MW	18.78 AW	39060 AAW	TNBLS	10//99-12//99
	Chattanooga MSA, TN-GA	S	18.99 MW	17.88 AW	39510 AAW	TNBLS	10//99-12//99
	Clarksville-Hopkinsville MSA, TN-KY	S	18.82 MW	17.96 AW	39150 AAW	TNBLS	10//99-12//99
	Jackson MSA, TN	S	18.36 MW	17.41 AW	38190 AAW	TNBLS	10//99-12//99
	Johnson City-Kingsport-Bristol MSA, TN-VA	S	18.91 MW	18.17 AW	39330 AAW	TNBLS	10//99-12//99
	Knoxville MSA, TN	S	17.89 MW	17.58 AW	37200 AAW	TNBLS	10//99-12//99
	Memphis MSA, TN-AR-MS	S	18.99 MW	17.42 AW	39510 AAW	MSBLS	10//99-12//99
	Nashville MSA, TN	S	19.74 MW	19.18 AW	41060 AAW	TNBLS	10//99-12//99
	Texas	S	19.48 MW	20.49 AW	42620 AAW	TXBLS	10//99-12//99
	Amarillo MSA, TX	S	18.07 MW	16.95 AW	37590 AAW	TXBLS	10//99-12//99
	Austin-San Marcos MSA, TX	S	20.37 MW	20.13 AW	42370 AAW	TXBLS	10//99-12//99
	Beaumont-Port Arthur MSA, TX	S	17.55 MW	18.03 AW	36500 AAW	TXBLS	10//99-12//99
	Brazoria PMSA, TX	S	18.97 MW	18.83 AW	39470 AAW	TXBLS	10//99-12//99
	Brownsville-Harlingen-San Benito MSA, TX	S	22.52 MW	21.14 AW	46840 AAW	TXBLS	10//99-12//99
	Bryan-College Station MSA, TX	S	20.92 MW	19.27 AW	43510 AAW	TXBLS	10//99-12//99
	Corpus Christi MSA, TX	S	18.92 MW	18.57 AW	39360 AAW	TXBLS	10//99-12//99
	Dallas PMSA, TX	S	20.26 MW	19.49 AW	42140 AAW	TXBLS	10//99-12//99
	El Paso MSA, TX	S	23.78 MW	22.51 AW	49460 AAW	TXBLS	10//99-12//99
	Fort Worth-Arlington PMSA, TX	S	20.46 MW	19.69 AW	42550 AAW	TXBLS	10//99-12//99
	Houston PMSA, TX	S	23.47 MW	22.15 AW	48820 AAW	TXBLS	10//99-12//99
	Killeen-Temple MSA, TX	S	20.15 MW	19.27 AW	41900 AAW	TXBLS	10//99-12//99
	Laredo MSA, TX	S	19.72 MW	18.61 AW	41010 AAW	TXBLS	10//99-12//99

AAW Average annual wage	AOH Average offered, high	ASH Average starting, high	H Hourly	M Monthly	S Special: hourly and annual
AE Average entry wage	AOL Average offered, low	ASL Average starting, low	HI Highest wage paid	MTC Median total compensation	TQ Third quartile wage
AEX Average experienced wage	APH Average pay, high range	AW Average wage paid	HR High end range	MW Median wage paid	W Weekly
AO Average offered	APL Average pay, low range	FQ First quartile wage	LR Low end range	SQ Second quartile wage	Y Yearly

Registered Nurse

Occupation/Type/Industry	Location	Per	Low	Mid	High	Source	Date
Registered Nurse	Longview-Marshall MSA, TX	S	19.08 MW	18.51 AW	39690 AAW	TXBLS	10//99-12//99
	Lubbock MSA, TX	S	17.34 MW	17.07 AW	36070 AAW	TXBLS	10//99-12//99
	McAllen-Edinburg-Mission MSA, TX	S	21.01 MW	19.98 AW	43690 AAW	TXBLS	10//99-12//99
	Odessa-Midland MSA, TX	S	17.88 MW	17.77 AW	37190 AAW	TXBLS	10//99-12//99
	San Angelo MSA, TX	S	16.45 MW	15.67 AW	34210 AAW	TXBLS	10//99-12//99
	San Antonio MSA, TX	S	19.20 MW	18.80 AW	39940 AAW	TXBLS	10//99-12//99
	Sherman-Denison MSA, TX	S	20.26 MW	19.61 AW	42140 AAW	TXBLS	10//99-12//99
	Texarkana MSA, TX-Texarkana, AR	S	18.38 MW	17.65 AW	38230 AAW	TXBLS	10//99-12//99
	Tyler MSA, TX	S	20.20 MW	19.87 AW	42010 AAW	TXBLS	10//99-12//99
	Victoria MSA, TX	S	17.95 MW	18.19 AW	37330 AAW	TXBLS	10//99-12//99
	Waco MSA, TX	S	17.58 MW	17.46 AW	36560 AAW	TXBLS	10//99-12//99
	Wichita Falls MSA, TX	S	18.65 MW	18.48 AW	38800 AAW	TXBLS	10//99-12//99
	Utah	S	19.87 MW	20.41 AW	42460 AAW	UTBLS	10//99-12//99
	Provo-Orem MSA, UT	S	18.86 MW	18.85 AW	39220 AAW	UTBLS	10//99-12//99
	Salt Lake City-Ogden MSA, UT	S	21.28 MW	20.76 AW	44260 AAW	UTBLS	10//99-12//99
	Vermont	S	18.96 MW	19.81 AW	41200 AAW	VTBLS	10//99-12//99
	Burlington MSA, VT	S	20.92 MW	20.01 AW	43500 AAW	VTBLS	10//99-12//99
	Virginia	S	19.1 MW	19.86 AW	41310 AAW	VABLS	10//99-12//99
	Danville MSA, VA	S	17.96 MW	16.96 AW	37350 AAW	VABLS	10//99-12//99
	Lynchburg MSA, VA	S	17.61 MW	17.02 AW	36630 AAW	VABLS	10//99-12//99
	Norfolk-Virginia Beach-Newport News MSA, VA-NC	S	19.12 MW	18.36 AW	39770 AAW	VABLS	10//99-12//99
	Richmond-Petersburg MSA, VA	S	20.42 MW	19.99 AW	42480 AAW	VABLS	10//99-12//99
	Roanoke MSA, VA	S	19.10 MW	18.18 AW	39720 AAW	VABLS	10//99-12//99
	Washington	S	22.67 MW	23.43 AW	48740 AAW	WABLS	10//99-12//99
	Bellingham MSA, WA	S	20.68 MW	20.00 AW	43010 AAW	WABLS	10//99-12//99
	Bremerton PMSA, WA	S	22.87 MW	21.90 AW	47580 AAW	WABLS	10//99-12//99
	Olympia PMSA, WA	S	22.01 MW	21.97 AW	45770 AAW	WABLS	10//99-12//99
	Richland-Kennewick-Pasco MSA, WA	S	23.39 MW	20.51 AW	48650 AAW	WABLS	10//99-12//99
	Seattle-Bellevue-Everett PMSA, WA	S	25.13 MW	24.37 AW	52280 AAW	WABLS	10//99-12//99
	Spokane MSA, WA	S	20.77 MW	20.26 AW	43200 AAW	WABLS	10//99-12//99
	Tacoma PMSA, WA	S	23.96 MW	23.40 AW	49840 AAW	WABLS	10//99-12//99
	Yakima MSA, WA	S	21.06 MW	20.08 AW	43810 AAW	WABLS	10//99-12//99
	West Virginia	S	16.86 MW	17.92 AW	37270 AAW	WVBLS	10//99-12//99
	Charleston MSA, WV	S	21.31 MW	19.33 AW	44330 AAW	WVBLS	10//99-12//99
	Huntington-Ashland MSA, WV-KY-OH	S	18.48 MW	18.31 AW	38450 AAW	WVBLS	10//99-12//99
	Parkersburg-Marietta MSA, WV-OH	S	16.74 MW	16.64 AW	34810 AAW	WVBLS	10//99-12//99
	Wheeling MSA, WV-OH	S	15.87 MW	14.53 AW	33000 AAW	WVBLS	10//99-12//99
	Wisconsin	S	19.03 MW	19.74 AW	41060 AAW	WIBLS	10//99-12//99
	Appleton-Oshkosh-Neenah MSA, WI	S	17.92 MW	18.08 AW	37270 AAW	WIBLS	10//99-12//99
	Eau Claire MSA, WI	S	18.82 MW	18.74 AW	39140 AAW	WIBLS	10//99-12//99
	Green Bay MSA, WI	S	19.86 MW	19.40 AW	41320 AAW	TXBLS	10//99-12//99
	Janesville-Beloit MSA, WI	S	18.40 MW	18.34 AW	38270 AAW	WIBLS	10//99-12//99
	Kenosha PMSA, WI	S	18.60 MW	18.69 AW	38690 AAW	WIBLS	10//99-12//99
	La Crosse MSA, WI-MN	S	18.45 MW	17.92 AW	38370 AAW	WIBLS	10//99-12//99
	Madison MSA, WI	S	20.41 MW	19.63 AW	42450 AAW	WIBLS	10//99-12//99
	Milwaukee-Waukesha PMSA, WI	S	21.09 MW	20.26 AW	43860 AAW	WIBLS	10//99-12//99
	Racine PMSA, WI	S	19.00 MW	18.88 AW	39510 AAW	WIBLS	10//99-12//99
	Sheboygan MSA, WI	S	18.86 MW	18.66 AW	39240 AAW	WIBLS	10//99-12//99
	Wyoming	S	16.93 MW	17.06 AW	35480 AAW	WYBLS	10//99-12//99
	Casper MSA, WY	S	17.70 MW	17.61 AW	36810 AAW	WYBLS	10//99-12//99
	Cheyenne MSA, WY	S	17.44 MW	17.31 AW	36270 AAW	WYBLS	10//99-12//99
	Puerto Rico	S	8.64 MW	9.35 AW	19450 AAW	PRBLS	10//99-12//99
	Arecibo PMSA, PR	S	8.19 MW	7.94 AW	17030 AAW	PRBLS	10//99-12//99
	Caguas PMSA, PR	S	7.68 MW	7.21 AW	15970 AAW	PRBLS	10//99-12//99
	Mayaguez MSA, PR	S	8.55 MW	8.16 AW	17780 AAW	PRBLS	10//99-12//99
	Ponce MSA, PR	S	8.60 MW	8.32 AW	17880 AAW	PRBLS	10//99-12//99
	San Juan-Bayamon PMSA, PR	S	9.16 MW	8.79 AW	19050 AAW	PRBLS	10//99-12//99
	Guam	S	17.76 MW	18.49 AW	38470 AAW	GUBLS	10//99-12//99
Acute Care	United States	Y		40150 AW		RN2	7//99
Ambulatory Care/HMO	United States	Y		36075 AW		RN2	7//99

AAW	Average annual wage	AOH	Average offered, high	ASH	Average starting, high
AE	Average entry wage	AOL	Average offered, low	ASL	Average starting, low
AEX	Average experienced wage	APH	Average pay, high range	AW	Average wage paid
AO	Average offered	APL	Average pay, low range	FQ	First quartile wage

H	Hourly	M	Monthly	S	Special: hourly and annual
HI	Highest wage paid	MTC	Median total compensation	TQ	Third quartile wage
HR	High end range	MW	Median wage paid	W	Weekly
LR	Low end range	SQ	Second quartile wage	Y	Yearly

Occupation/Type/Industry	Location	Per	Low	Mid	High	Source	Date
Registered Nurse							
Anesthesiology	United States	H		39.07 AW		RN1	1999
Cardiopulmonary Perfusionist	United States	H		33.13 AW		RN1	1999
Community/Home Health	United States	Y		38545 AW		RN2	7//99
Critical Care	Florida	H			22.74 HI	BJTAMP	2000
Emergency Room	United States	H		20.00 AW		RN1	1999
Extended Care/Psychiatric	United States	Y		39840 AW		RN2	7//99
Gerontology	United States	H		19.60 AW		RN1	1999
Health Care Office, Family Practice	United States	Y		30223 AW		MEDEC1	1999
Health Care Office, Internal Medicine	United States	Y		30202 AW		MEDEC1	1999
Health Care Office, Obstetrics-gynecology	United States	Y		30343 AW		MEDEC1	1999
Health Care Office, Pediatrics	United States	Y		33326 AW		MEDEC1	1999
Health Insurance Company	United States	Y		40065 AW		RN2	7//99
Hemodialysis	United States	H		21.62 AW		RN1	1999
Infection Control	United States	H		22.17 AW		RN1	1999
Medical Doctor's Office	United States	H		16.12 AEX		MEDEC	2000
Medical/Surgical	United States	H		19.16 AW		RN1	1999
Medical-surgical	Florida	H			21.87 HI	BJTAMP	2000
Neonatology/Perinatology	United States	H		20.44 AW		RN1	1999
OB/GYN	United States	H		19.53 AW		RN1	1999
Oncology	United States	H		19.69 AW		RN1	1999
Operating Room	United States	H		20.38 AW		RN1	1999
Operating Room	Central	Y		66194 AW		ORMAN	1999
Operating Room	East	Y		73483 AW		ORMAN	1999
Operating Room	South	Y		67084 AW		ORMAN	1999
Operating Room	West	Y		72520 AW		ORMAN	1999
Pediatric	United States	H		19.60 AW		RN1	1999
Physician's Offoce	United States	Y		35160 AW		RN2	7//99
Psychiatric	United States	H		19.99 AW		RN1	1999
Registered Nurse Anesthetist							
Certified	United States	Y	91000 AOL	104000 AO	153000 AOH	NURMAN3	1998
Rehabilitation Counselor	Alabama	S	9.78 MW	10.60 AW	22040 AAW	ALBLS	10//99-12//99
	Arizona	S	11.66 MW	12.88 AW	26790 AAW	AZBLS	10//99-12//99
	Arkansas	S	14.5 MW	15.31 AW	31850 AAW	ARBLS	10//99-12//99
	California	S	13.44 MW	15.29 AW	31790 AAW	CABLS	10//99-12//99
	Colorado	S	9.64 MW	10.92 AW	22710 AAW	COBLS	10//99-12//99
	Connecticut	S	15.18 MW	16.45 AW	34220 AAW	CTBLS	10//99-12//99
	Florida	S	12.58 MW	13.41 AW	27890 AAW	FLBLS	10//99-12//99
	Georgia	S	12.83 MW	13.53 AW	28150 AAW	GABLS	10//99-12//99
	Hawaii	S	11 MW	12.13 AW	25240 AAW	HIBLS	10//99-12//99
	Idaho	S	11.43 MW	11.75 AW	24440 AAW	IDBLS	10//99-12//99
	Illinois	S	10.07 MW	11.01 AW	22890 AAW	ILBLS	10//99-12//99
	Indiana	S	11.92 MW	13.39 AW	27860 AAW	INBLS	10//99-12//99
	Iowa	S	9.74 MW	10.50 AW	21840 AAW	IABLS	10//99-12//99
	Kansas	S	10.54 MW	10.99 AW	22870 AAW	KSBLS	10//99-12//99
	Kentucky	S	11.48 MW	12.87 AW	26780 AAW	KYBLS	10//99-12//99
	Louisiana	S	11.53 MW	12.04 AW	25040 AAW	LABLS	10//99-12//99
	Maine	S	9.57 MW	9.93 AW	20650 AAW	MEBLS	10//99-12//99
	Maryland	S	8.94 MW	9.85 AW	20490 AAW	MDBLS	10//99-12//99
	Michigan	S	15.8 MW	15.44 AW	32110 AAW	MIBLS	10//99-12//99
	Minnesota	S	12.43 MW	13.27 AW	27600 AAW	MNBLS	10//99-12//99
	Mississippi	S	20.46 MW	23.69 AW	49270 AAW	MSBLS	10//99-12//99
	Missouri	S	10.39 MW	11.55 AW	24020 AAW	MOBLS	10//99-12//99
	Montana	S	9.22 MW	9.75 AW	20270 AAW	MTBLS	10//99-12//99
	Nebraska	S	9.49 MW	11.84 AW	24630 AAW	NEBLS	10//99-12//99
	Nevada	S	12.34 MW	14.90 AW	30990 AAW	NVBLS	10//99-12//99
	New Hampshire	S	8.33 MW	9.26 AW	19270 AAW	NHBLS	10//99-12//99
	New Jersey	S	10.59 MW	13.08 AW	27200 AAW	NJBLS	10//99-12//99
	New Mexico	S	13.34 MW	14.45 AW	30060 AAW	NMBLS	10//99-12//99
	New York	S	11.05 MW	12.47 AW	25930 AAW	NYBLS	10//99-12//99
	North Carolina	S	9.57 MW	10.70 AW	22260 AAW	NCBLS	10//99-12//99
	North Dakota	S	12.71 MW	13.18 AW	27410 AAW	NDBLS	10//99-12//99
	Ohio	S	12.72 MW	13.88 AW	28870 AAW	OHBLS	10//99-12//99
	Oklahoma	S	8.16 MW	8.81 AW	18320 AAW	OKBLS	10//99-12//99
	Oregon	S	10.67 MW	12.55 AW	26090 AAW	ORBLS	10//99-12//99
	Pennsylvania	S	10.78 MW	11.80 AW	24550 AAW	PABLS	10//99-12//99
	Rhode Island	S	18.65 MW	19.31 AW	40160 AAW	RIBLS	10//99-12//99
	South Carolina	S	12.38 MW	13.07 AW	27180 AAW	SCBLS	10//99-12//99
	South Dakota	S	13.02 MW	15.88 AW	33030 AAW	SDBLS	10//99-12//99
	Tennessee	S	9.68 MW	10.35 AW	21530 AAW	TNBLS	10//99-12//99
	Texas	S	12.88 MW	12.97 AW	26980 AAW	TXBLS	10//99-12//99

AAW	Average annual wage	**AOH**	Average offered, high	**ASH**	Average starting, high	**H**	Hourly	
AE	Average entry wage	**AOL**	Average offered, low	**ASL**	Average starting, low	**HI**	Highest wage paid	
AEX	Average experienced wage	**APH**	Average pay, high range	**AW**	Average wage paid	**HR**	High end range	
AO	Average offered	**APL**	Average pay, low range	**FQ**	First quartile wage	**LR**	Low end range	

M	Monthly	**S**	Special: hourly and annual
MTC	Median total compensation	**TQ**	Third quartile wage
MW	Median wage paid	**W**	Weekly
SQ	Second quartile wage	**Y**	Yearly

Occupation/Type/Industry	Location	Per	Low	Mid	High	Source	Date
Rehabilitation Counselor	Virginia	S	10.13 MW	11.15 AW	23190 AAW	VABLS	10//99-12//99
	Washington	S	15.78 MW	15.76 AW	32780 AAW	WABLS	10//99-12//99
	West Virginia	S	11.96 MW	12.39 AW	25760 AAW	WVBLS	10//99-12//99
	Wisconsin	S	10.5 MW	12.24 AW	25460 AAW	WIBLS	10//99-12//99
	Wyoming	S	8.35 MW	9.78 AW	20330 AAW	WYBLS	10//99-12//99
	Puerto Rico	S	12.4 MW	13.88 AW	28860 AAW	PRBLS	10//99-12//99
Reinforcing Iron and Rebar Worker	Alabama	S	12.67 MW	12.92 AW	26870 AAW	ALBLS	10//99-12//99
	Arizona	S	12.05 MW	11.42 AW	23760 AAW	AZBLS	10//99-12//99
	Arkansas	S	12.88 MW	13.39 AW	27850 AAW	ARBLS	10//99-12//99
	California	S	21.8 MW	21.04 AW	43770 AAW	CABLS	10//99-12//99
	Colorado	S	13.33 MW	14.10 AW	29330 AAW	COBLS	10//99-12//99
	Connecticut	S	22.41 MW	20.48 AW	42590 AAW	CTBLS	10//99-12//99
	Delaware	S	14.89 MW	16.16 AW	33620 AAW	DEBLS	10//99-12//99
	Florida	S	13.79 MW	13.75 AW	28600 AAW	FLBLS	10//99-12//99
	Georgia	S	13.19 MW	13.64 AW	28370 AAW	GABLS	10//99-12//99
	Idaho	S	18.86 MW	18.86 AW	39220 AAW	IDBLS	10//99-12//99
	Illinois	S	31.92 MW	29.22 AW	60780 AAW	ILBLS	10//99-12//99
	Indiana	S	19.27 MW	18.06 AW	37560 AAW	INBLS	10//99-12//99
	Iowa	S	15.24 MW	16.68 AW	34700 AAW	IABLS	10//99-12//99
	Kansas	S	13.85 MW	14.87 AW	30940 AAW	KSBLS	10//99-12//99
	Kentucky	S	18.54 MW	18.54 AW	38550 AAW	KYBLS	10//99-12//99
	Louisiana	S	14.67 MW	14.57 AW	30300 AAW	LABLS	10//99-12//99
	Maryland	S	19.83 MW	19.31 AW	40160 AAW	MDBLS	10//99-12//99
	Massachusetts	S	25.09 MW	26.76 AW	55660 AAW	MABLS	10//99-12//99
	Michigan	S	21.48 MW	20.44 AW	42510 AAW	MIBLS	10//99-12//99
	Minnesota	S	21.79 MW	20.39 AW	42420 AAW	MNBLS	10//99-12//99
	Mississippi	S	11.54 MW	11.35 AW	23610 AAW	MSBLS	10//99-12//99
	Missouri	S	21.34 MW	19.60 AW	40780 AAW	MOBLS	10//99-12//99
	Montana	S	19.36 MW	19.48 AW	40520 AAW	MTBLS	10//99-12//99
	New Jersey	S	31.75 MW	29.05 AW	60420 AAW	NJBLS	10//99-12//99
	New Mexico	S	11.94 MW	14.53 AW	30220 AAW	NMBLS	10//99-12//99
	North Carolina	S	12.46 MW	13.13 AW	27310 AAW	NCBLS	10//99-12//99
	North Dakota	S	11.76 MW	12.27 AW	25520 AAW	NDBLS	10//99-12//99
	Ohio	S	23.36 MW	23.04 AW	47920 AAW	OHBLS	10//99-12//99
	Oklahoma	S	12.19 MW	14.54 AW	30250 AAW	OKBLS	10//99-12//99
	Oregon	S	23.38 MW	22.93 AW	47690 AAW	ORBLS	10//99-12//99
	Pennsylvania	S	16.33 MW	18.15 AW	37750 AAW	PABLS	10//99-12//99
	South Carolina	S	13.6 MW	13.63 AW	28360 AAW	SCBLS	10//99-12//99
	Tennessee	S	14.24 MW	14.42 AW	29990 AAW	TNBLS	10//99-12//99
	Texas	S	11.57 MW	11.91 AW	24770 AAW	TXBLS	10//99-12//99
	Vermont	S	12.75 MW	12.94 AW	26910 AAW	VTBLS	10//99-12//99
	Virginia	S	16.48 MW	16.03 AW	33350 AAW	VABLS	10//99-12//99
	Washington	S	22.17 MW	21.60 AW	44930 AAW	WABLS	10//99-12//99
	West Virginia	S	18.36 MW	18.51 AW	38490 AAW	WVBLS	10//99-12//99
	Wisconsin	S	22.01 MW	19.77 AW	41120 AAW	WIBLS	10//99-12//99
	Puerto Rico	S	6.36 MW	6.47 AW	13470 AAW	PRBLS	10//99-12//99
	Guam	S	10.06 MW	10.29 AW	21390 AAW	GUBLS	10//99-12//99
Reporter							
Newspaper, 17 Years Experienc	Long Island, NY	Y		72500 AW		CJR	1999
Newspaper, 20 Years Experience	Santa Fe, NM	Y		45000 AW		CJR	1999
Newspaper, 3-4 Years Experience	Cedar Rapids, IA	Y		29000 AW		CJR	1999
Newspaper, 5 Years Experienc	Carlsbad, CA	Y		23000 AW		CJR	1999
Newspaper, 5 Years Experienc	Peoria, IL	Y		37000 AW		CJR	1999
Newspaper, 5 Years Experienc	Chattanooga, TN	Y		32000 AW		CJR	1999
Research Technician							
R&D Lab	Midwest	Y		33290 AW		R&DM	1999
R&D Lab	Mountain	Y		34620 AW		R&DM	1999
R&D Lab	North Central	Y		33120 AW		R&DM	1999
R&D Lab	Northeast	Y		30830 AW		R&DM	1999
R&D Lab	Pacific	Y		36860 AW		R&DM	1998
R&D Lab	South	Y		41910 AW		R&DM	1999
R&D Lab	Southwest	Y		30310 AW		R&DM	1999
Researcher							
R&D Lab	Midwest	Y		51750 AW		R&DM	1999
R&D Lab	Mountain	Y		79460 AW		R&DM	1999
R&D Lab	North Central	Y		57600 AW		R&DM	1999
R&D Lab	Northeast	Y		67840 AW		R&DM	1999
R&D Lab	Pacific	Y		63140 AW		R&DM	1998

AAW Average annual wage	**AOH** Average offered, high	**ASH** Average starting, high	**H** Hourly	**M** Monthly	**S** Special: hourly and annual
AE Average entry wage	**AOL** Average offered, low	**ASL** Average starting, low	**HI** Highest wage paid	**MTC** Median total compensation	**TQ** Third quartile wage
AEX Average experienced wage	**APH** Average pay, high range	**AW** Average wage paid	**HR** High end range	**MW** Median wage paid	**W** Weekly
AO Average offered	**APL** Average pay, low range	**FQ** First quartile wage	**LR** Low end range	**SQ** Second quartile wage	**Y** Yearly

Occupation/Type/Industry	Location	Per	Low	Mid	High	Source	Date
Researcher							
R&D Lab	South	Y		58640 AW		R&DM	1999
R&D Lab	Southwest	Y		59470 AW		R&DM	1999
Reservation and Transportation Ticket Agent and Travel Clerk	Alabama	S	18.01 MW	16.47 AW	34250 AAW	ALBLS	10//99-12//99
	Alaska	S	12.29 MW	13.14 AW	27330 AAW	AKBLS	10//99-12//99
	Arizona	S	10.27 MW	10.64 AW	22140 AAW	AZBLS	10//99-12//99
	California	S	10.94 MW	13.17 AW	27400 AAW	CABLS	10//99-12//99
	Colorado	S	11.85 MW	11.92 AW	24790 AAW	COBLS	10//99-12//99
	Connecticut	S	10.97 MW	13.23 AW	27520 AAW	CTBLS	10//99-12//99
	Delaware	S	14.03 MW	13.54 AW	28150 AAW	DEBLS	10//99-12//99
	District of Columbia	S	12.44 MW	12.37 AW	25730 AAW	DCBLS	10//99-12//99
	Florida	S	10.29 MW	12.58 AW	26160 AAW	FLBLS	10//99-12//99
	Georgia	S	13.89 MW	14.36 AW	29870 AAW	GABLS	10//99-12//99
	Hawaii	S	11.77 MW	12.82 AW	26670 AAW	HIBLS	10//99-12//99
	Idaho	S	9.45 MW	10.46 AW	21750 AAW	IDBLS	10//99-12//99
	Illinois	S	10.37 MW	12.72 AW	26460 AAW	ILBLS	10//99-12//99
	Indiana	S	8.63 MW	9.83 AW	20450 AAW	INBLS	10//99-12//99
	Iowa	S	13.3 MW	14.58 AW	30330 AAW	IABLS	10//99-12//99
	Kansas	S	6.94 MW	7.30 AW	15190 AAW	KSBLS	10//99-12//99
	Kentucky	S	15.29 MW	14.50 AW	30160 AAW	KYBLS	10//99-12//99
	Louisiana	S	10.46 MW	12.62 AW	26250 AAW	LABLS	10//99-12//99
	Maine	S	8.58 MW	8.75 AW	18200 AAW	MEBLS	10//99-12//99
	Maryland	S	10.58 MW	10.72 AW	22300 AAW	MDBLS	10//99-12//99
	Massachusetts	S	10.63 MW	12.75 AW	26530 AAW	MABLS	10//99-12//99
	Michigan	S	16.91 MW	15.07 AW	31350 AAW	MIBLS	10//99-12//99
	Minnesota	S	9.63 MW	9.80 AW	20380 AAW	MNBLS	10//99-12//99
	Mississippi	S	8.4 MW	8.97 AW	18660 AAW	MSBLS	10//99-12//99
	Missouri	S	9.16 MW	10.00 AW	20790 AAW	MOBLS	10//99-12//99
	Montana	S	7.9 MW	8.35 AW	17360 AAW	MTBLS	10//99-12//99
	Nebraska	S	13.63 MW	12.67 AW	26360 AAW	NEBLS	10//99-12//99
	Nevada	S	10.59 MW	11.04 AW	22960 AAW	NVBLS	10//99-12//99
	New Hampshire	S	9.79 MW	11.78 AW	24490 AAW	NHBLS	10//99-12//99
	New Jersey	S	9.91 MW	11.53 AW	23990 AAW	NJBLS	10//99-12//99
	New Mexico	S	10.62 MW	11.28 AW	23460 AAW	NMBLS	10//99-12//99
	New York	S	13.76 MW	14.41 AW	29970 AAW	NYBLS	10//99-12//99
	North Carolina	S	17.5 MW	15.24 AW	31710 AAW	NCBLS	10//99-12//99
	Ohio	S	12.27 MW	13.22 AW	27500 AAW	OHBLS	10//99-12//99
	Oklahoma	S	7.27 MW	9.57 AW	19910 AAW	OKBLS	10//99-12//99
	Oregon	S	9.37 MW	9.96 AW	20710 AAW	ORBLS	10//99-12//99
	Pennsylvania	S	9.79 MW	11.80 AW	24540 AAW	PABLS	10//99-12//99
	Rhode Island	S	12.25 MW	14.50 AW	30160 AAW	RIBLS	10//99-12//99
	South Carolina	S	8.57 MW	8.93 AW	18570 AAW	SCBLS	10//99-12//99
	Tennessee	S	17.36 MW	14.76 AW	30710 AAW	TNBLS	10//99-12//99
	Texas	S	10.37 MW	11.61 AW	24150 AAW	TXBLS	10//99-12//99
	Vermont	S	17.04 MW	14.11 AW	29340 AAW	VTBLS	10//99-12//99
	Virginia	S	15.93 MW	14.75 AW	30670 AAW	VABLS	10//99-12//99
	Washington	S	11.9 MW	13.10 AW	27250 AAW	WABLS	10//99-12//99
	West Virginia	S	10.59 MW	12.37 AW	25720 AAW	WVBLS	10//99-12//99
	Wisconsin	S	12.51 MW	13.20 AW	27450 AAW	WIBLS	10//99-12//99
	Wyoming	S	7.8 MW	7.88 AW	16390 AAW	WYBLS	10//99-12//99
	Puerto Rico	S	11.27 MW	13.23 AW	27510 AAW	PRBLS	10//99-12//99
	Virgin Islands	S	9.52 MW	9.74 AW	20250 AAW	VIBLS	10//99-12//99
	Guam	S	11.57 MW	11.33 AW	23560 AAW	GUBLS	10//99-12//99
Residential Advisor	Alabama	S	8.45 MW	9.42 AW	19580 AAW	ALBLS	10//99-12//99
	Alaska	S	13.2 MW	15.33 AW	31890 AAW	AKBLS	10//99-12//99
	Arizona	S	9.64 MW	10.39 AW	21620 AAW	AZBLS	10//99-12//99
	Arkansas	S	7.74 MW	8.02 AW	16690 AAW	ARBLS	10//99-12//99
	California	S	8.69 MW	8.98 AW	18680 AAW	CABLS	10//99-12//99
	Colorado	S	10.01 MW	10.13 AW	21070 AAW	COBLS	10//99-12//99
	Connecticut	S	10.5 MW	10.88 AW	22620 AAW	CTBLS	10//99-12//99
	Delaware	S	9.8 MW	9.95 AW	20710 AAW	DEBLS	10//99-12//99
	District of Columbia	S	9.61 MW	9.59 AW	19940 AAW	DCBLS	10//99-12//99
	Florida	S	9.69 MW	9.99 AW	20780 AAW	FLBLS	10//99-12//99
	Georgia	S	8.08 MW	8.23 AW	17130 AAW	GABLS	10//99-12//99
	Hawaii	S	7.98 MW	9.72 AW	20210 AAW	HIBLS	10//99-12//99
	Idaho	S	9.65 MW	9.61 AW	19980 AAW	IDBLS	10//99-12//99
	Illinois	S	11.85 MW	12.04 AW	25050 AAW	ILBLS	10//99-12//99
	Indiana	S	9.27 MW	9.38 AW	19510 AAW	INBLS	10//99-12//99
	Iowa	S	9.55 MW	9.69 AW	20150 AAW	IABLS	10//99-12//99

AAW	Average annual wage	AOH	Average offered, high	ASH	Average starting, high	H	Hourly	M	Monthly	S	Special: hourly and annual
AE	Average entry wage	AOL	Average offered, low	ASL	Average starting, low	HI	Highest wage paid	MTC	Median total compensation	TQ	Third quartile wage
AEX	Average experienced wage	APH	Average pay, high range	AW	Average wage paid	HR	High end range	MW	Median wage paid	W	Weekly
AO	Average offered	APL	Average pay, low range	FQ	First quartile wage	LR	Low end range	SQ	Second quartile wage	Y	Yearly

Occupation/Type/Industry	Location	Per	Low	Mid	High	Source	Date
Residential Advisor	Kansas	S	6.66 MW	6.89 AW	14340 AAW	KSBLS	10//99-12//99
	Kentucky	S	7.07 MW	7.49 AW	15580 AAW	KYBLS	10//99-12//99
	Louisiana	S	6.6 MW	9.31 AW	19360 AAW	LABLS	10//99-12//99
	Maine	S	10.5 MW	12.39 AW	25780 AAW	MEBLS	10//99-12//99
	Maryland	S	10.51 MW	11.25 AW	23390 AAW	MDBLS	10//99-12//99
	Massachusetts	S	8.43 MW	9.37 AW	19490 AAW	MABLS	10//99-12//99
	Michigan	S	10.85 MW	11.78 AW	24510 AAW	MIBLS	10//99-12//99
	Minnesota	S	8.44 MW	9.49 AW	19740 AAW	MNBLS	10//99-12//99
	Mississippi	S	7.74 MW	7.93 AW	16500 AAW	MSBLS	10//99-12//99
	Missouri	S	9.36 MW	10.14 AW	21100 AAW	MOBLS	10//99-12//99
	Montana	S	8.07 MW	8.61 AW	17900 AAW	MTBLS	10//99-12//99
	Nebraska	S	11.19 MW	10.51 AW	21870 AAW	NEBLS	10//99-12//99
	New Hampshire	S	7.91 MW	8.29 AW	17230 AAW	NHBLS	10//99-12//99
	New Jersey	S	11.62 MW	12.32 AW	25620 AAW	NJBLS	10//99-12//99
	New Mexico	S	7.51 MW	7.87 AW	16360 AAW	NMBLS	10//99-12//99
	New York	S	11.79 MW	11.72 AW	24370 AAW	NYBLS	10//99-12//99
	North Carolina	S	8.13 MW	8.57 AW	17830 AAW	NCBLS	10//99-12//99
	North Dakota	S	10 MW	10.29 AW	21390 AAW	NDBLS	10//99-12//99
	Ohio	S	9.78 MW	10.42 AW	21680 AAW	OHBLS	10//99-12//99
	Oklahoma	S	7.81 MW	8.34 AW	17350 AAW	OKBLS	10//99-12//99
	Oregon	S	9.95 MW	10.76 AW	22370 AAW	ORBLS	10//99-12//99
	Pennsylvania	S	8.03 MW	9.11 AW	18950 AAW	PABLS	10//99-12//99
	Rhode Island	S	11.11 MW	12.45 AW	25890 AAW	RIBLS	10//99-12//99
	South Carolina	S	10.19 MW	10.78 AW	22430 AAW	SCBLS	10//99-12//99
	South Dakota	S	7.34 MW	7.48 AW	15560 AAW	SDBLS	10//99-12//99
	Tennessee	S	7.83 MW	8.18 AW	17010 AAW	TNBLS	10//99-12//99
	Texas	S	9.48 MW	9.59 AW	19950 AAW	TXBLS	10//99-12//99
	Virginia	S	9.92 MW	10.58 AW	22000 AAW	VABLS	10//99-12//99
	Washington	S	9.13 MW	10.25 AW	21310 AAW	WABLS	10//99-12//99
	West Virginia	S	9.1 MW	9.47 AW	19710 AAW	WVBLS	10//99-12//99
	Wisconsin	S	7.83 MW	8.93 AW	18580 AAW	WIBLS	10//99-12//99
Respiratory Therapist	United States	H		17.84 AW		NCS98	1998
	Alabama	S	15.2 MW	15.85 AW	32970 AAW	ALBLS	10//99-12//99
	Alaska	S	21.16 MW	21.16 AW	44020 AAW	AKBLS	10//99-12//99
	Arizona	S	14.8 MW	15.12 AW	31450 AAW	AZBLS	10//99-12//99
	Arkansas	S	14.84 MW	15.11 AW	31430 AAW	ARBLS	10//99-12//99
	California	S	19.47 MW	20.36 AW	42350 AAW	CABLS	10//99-12//99
	Colorado	S	16.94 MW	16.86 AW	35070 AAW	COBLS	10//99-12//99
	Connecticut	S	19.44 MW	20.05 AW	41690 AAW	CTBLS	10//99-12//99
	Delaware	S	19.43 MW	19.83 AW	41240 AAW	DEBLS	10//99-12//99
	District of Columbia	S	17.58 MW	17.70 AW	36820 AAW	DCBLS	10//99-12//99
	Florida	S	17.18 MW	17.51 AW	36420 AAW	FLBLS	10//99-12//99
	Georgia	S	17.67 MW	17.56 AW	36520 AAW	GABLS	10//99-12//99
	Hawaii	S	23.01 MW	23.23 AW	48330 AAW	HIBLS	10//99-12//99
	Idaho	S	15.95 MW	16.57 AW	34470 AAW	IDBLS	10//99-12//99
	Illinois	S	16.53 MW	16.93 AW	35220 AAW	ILBLS	10//99-12//99
	Indiana	S	16.61 MW	17.00 AW	35360 AAW	INBLS	10//99-12//99
	Iowa	S	15.47 MW	16.08 AW	33450 AAW	IABLS	10//99-12//99
	Kansas	S	15.57 MW	15.96 AW	33200 AAW	KSBLS	10//99-12//99
	Kentucky	S	14.08 MW	14.56 AW	30280 AAW	KYBLS	10//99-12//99
	Louisiana	S	16.22 MW	16.35 AW	34000 AAW	LABLS	10//99-12//99
	Maine	S	16.57 MW	16.83 AW	35010 AAW	MEBLS	10//99-12//99
	Maryland	S	19 MW	19.43 AW	40410 AAW	MDBLS	10//99-12//99
	Massachusetts	S	19.19 MW	19.55 AW	40660 AAW	MABLS	10//99-12//99
	Michigan	S	17.36 MW	17.29 AW	35960 AAW	MIBLS	10//99-12//99
	Minnesota	S	18.99 MW	19.47 AW	40490 AAW	MNBLS	10//99-12//99
	Mississippi	S	14.51 MW	15.00 AW	31200 AAW	MSBLS	10//99-12//99
	Missouri	S	15.99 MW	16.17 AW	33630 AAW	MOBLS	10//99-12//99
	Montana	S	13.74 MW	14.15 AW	29420 AAW	MTBLS	10//99-12//99
	Nebraska	S	17.03 MW	16.93 AW	35210 AAW	NEBLS	10//99-12//99
	Nevada	S	18.24 MW	18.30 AW	38060 AAW	NVBLS	10//99-12//99
	New Hampshire	S	18.13 MW	18.23 AW	37920 AAW	NHBLS	10//99-12//99
	New Jersey	S	20.55 MW	21.35 AW	44410 AAW	NJBLS	10//99-12//99
	New Mexico	S	16.8 MW	16.70 AW	34730 AAW	NMBLS	10//99-12//99
	New York	S	19.18 MW	19.71 AW	40990 AAW	NYBLS	10//99-12//99
	North Carolina	S	17.02 MW	18.51 AW	38500 AAW	NCBLS	10//99-12//99
	North Dakota	S	14.95 MW	14.93 AW	31060 AAW	NDBLS	10//99-12//99
	Ohio	S	17.5 MW	17.36 AW	36100 AAW	OHBLS	10//99-12//99
	Oklahoma	S	14.48 MW	14.05 AW	29220 AAW	OKBLS	10//99-12//99
	Oregon	S	17.23 MW	17.18 AW	35740 AAW	ORBLS	10//99-12//99
	Pennsylvania	S	17.46 MW	17.75 AW	36920 AAW	PABLS	10//99-12//99
	Rhode Island	S	18.86 MW	19.48 AW	40530 AAW	RIBLS	10//99-12//99

AAW Average annual wage	**AOH** Average offered, high	**ASH** Average starting, high	**H** Hourly	**M** Monthly	**S** Special: hourly and annual
AE Average entry wage	**AOL** Average offered, low	**ASL** Average starting, low	**HI** Highest wage paid	**MTC** Median total compensation	**TQ** Third quartile wage
AEX Average experienced wage	**APH** Average pay, high range	**AW** Average wage paid	**HR** High end range	**MW** Median wage paid	**W** Weekly
AO Average offered	**APL** Average pay, low range	**FQ** First quartile wage	**LR** Low end range	**SQ** Second quartile wage	**Y** Yearly

Occupation/Type/Industry	Location	Per	Low	Mid	High	Source	Date
Respiratory Therapist	South Carolina	S	17.25 MW	18.00 AW	37450 AAW	SCBLS	10//99-12//99
	South Dakota	S	16.01 MW	16.44 AW	34190 AAW	SDBLS	10//99-12//99
	Tennessee	S	16.28 MW	16.32 AW	33950 AAW	TNBLS	10//99-12//99
	Texas	S	16.02 MW	16.20 AW	33690 AAW	TXBLS	10//99-12//99
	Utah	S	16.52 MW	18.24 AW	37950 AAW	UTBLS	10//99-12//99
	Vermont	S	16.7 MW	17.19 AW	35760 AAW	VTBLS	10//99-12//99
	Virginia	S	17.52 MW	17.88 AW	37190 AAW	VABLS	10//99-12//99
	Washington	S	18.38 MW	18.47 AW	38410 AAW	WABLS	10//99-12//99
	West Virginia	S	15.13 MW	15.53 AW	32310 AAW	WVBLS	10//99-12//99
	Wisconsin	S	16.27 MW	16.45 AW	34220 AAW	WIBLS	10//99-12//99
	Wyoming	S	15.09 MW	15.07 AW	31350 AAW	WYBLS	10//99-12//99
	Puerto Rico	S	6.64 MW	7.11 AW	14780 AAW	PRBLS	10//99-12//99
Respiratory Therapy Technician	Alabama	S	12.29 MW	12.56 AW	26120 AAW	ALBLS	10//99-12//99
	Arizona	S	12.94 MW	14.35 AW	29840 AAW	AZBLS	10//99-12//99
	Arkansas	S	11.96 MW	11.69 AW	24320 AAW	ARBLS	10//99-12//99
	California	S	17.9 MW	17.70 AW	36820 AAW	CABLS	10//99-12//99
	Colorado	S	14.26 MW	13.58 AW	28240 AAW	COBLS	10//99-12//99
	Connecticut	S	16.98 MW	17.20 AW	35770 AAW	CTBLS	10//99-12//99
	Florida	S	14.78 MW	14.60 AW	30370 AAW	FLBLS	10//99-12//99
	Georgia	S	13.27 MW	13.50 AW	28070 AAW	GABLS	10//99-12//99
	Hawaii	S	18.69 MW	17.90 AW	37230 AAW	HIBLS	10//99-12//99
	Idaho	S	14.33 MW	14.07 AW	29260 AAW	IDBLS	10//99-12//99
	Illinois	S	12.65 MW	12.66 AW	26330 AAW	ILBLS	10//99-12//99
	Indiana	S	15.55 MW	15.63 AW	32520 AAW	INBLS	10//99-12//99
	Iowa	S	12.81 MW	12.72 AW	26460 AAW	IABLS	10//99-12//99
	Kansas	S	14.29 MW	13.59 AW	28260 AAW	KSBLS	10//99-12//99
	Kentucky	S	12.45 MW	12.43 AW	25850 AAW	KYBLS	10//99-12//99
	Louisiana	S	13.8 MW	14.14 AW	29420 AAW	LABLS	10//99-12//99
	Maine	S	13.17 MW	13.65 AW	28390 AAW	MEBLS	10//99-12//99
	Massachusetts	S	16.68 MW	16.36 AW	34030 AAW	MABLS	10//99-12//99
	Michigan	S	13.8 MW	13.62 AW	28320 AAW	MIBLS	10//99-12//99
	Minnesota	S	14.05 MW	14.03 AW	29180 AAW	MNBLS	10//99-12//99
	Mississippi	S	12.99 MW	13.72 AW	28540 AAW	MSBLS	10//99-12//99
	Missouri	S	11.89 MW	11.82 AW	24580 AAW	MOBLS	10//99-12//99
	Montana	S	14.77 MW	14.36 AW	29880 AAW	MTBLS	10//99-12//99
	Nebraska	S	14.34 MW	13.94 AW	28990 AAW	NEBLS	10//99-12//99
	Nevada	S	18.63 MW	18.56 AW	38610 AAW	NVBLS	10//99-12//99
	New Jersey	S	19.23 MW	19.42 AW	40400 AAW	NJBLS	10//99-12//99
	New Mexico	S	13.92 MW	13.97 AW	29060 AAW	NMBLS	10//99-12//99
	New York	S	15.11 MW	15.74 AW	32730 AAW	NYBLS	10//99-12//99
	North Carolina	S	15.78 MW	15.87 AW	33010 AAW	NCBLS	10//99-12//99
	Ohio	S	15.64 MW	15.63 AW	32520 AAW	OHBLS	10//99-12//99
	Oklahoma	S	10.9 MW	12.67 AW	26350 AAW	OKBLS	10//99-12//99
	Oregon	S	18.01 MW	17.62 AW	36650 AAW	ORBLS	10//99-12//99
	Pennsylvania	S	14.58 MW	14.84 AW	30870 AAW	PABLS	10//99-12//99
	South Carolina	S	14.41 MW	14.31 AW	29760 AAW	SCBLS	10//99-12//99
	Tennessee	S	13.87 MW	13.54 AW	28170 AAW	TNBLS	10//99-12//99
	Texas	S	14.1 MW	14.12 AW	29360 AAW	TXBLS	10//99-12//99
	Utah	S	14.06 MW	13.14 AW	27330 AAW	UTBLS	10//99-12//99
	Virginia	S	14.09 MW	14.90 AW	30990 AAW	VABLS	10//99-12//99
	Washington	S	16.24 MW	16.27 AW	33850 AAW	WABLS	10//99-12//99
	West Virginia	S	14.15 MW	15.42 AW	32080 AAW	WVBLS	10//99-12//99
	Wisconsin	S	16.08 MW	16.75 AW	34840 AAW	WIBLS	10//99-12//99
	Wyoming	S	10.51 MW	11.92 AW	24780 AAW	WYBLS	10//99-12//99
	Puerto Rico	S	6.04 MW	5.99 AW	12460 AAW	PRBLS	10//99-12//99
Retail Sales Clerk	Los Angeles County, CA	Y		19561 AW		LABJ	1999
Retail Salesperson	Alabama	S	7.09 MW	8.67 AW	18040 AAW	ALBLS	10//99-12//99
	Anniston MSA, AL	S	7.87 MW	6.54 AW	16360 AAW	ALBLS	10//99-12//99
	Auburn-Opelika MSA, AL	S	8.07 MW	6.63 AW	16790 AAW	ALBLS	10//99-12//99
	Birmingham MSA, AL	S	9.36 MW	7.65 AW	19470 AAW	ALBLS	10//99-12//99
	Decatur MSA, AL	S	8.20 MW	6.85 AW	17060 AAW	ALBLS	10//99-12//99
	Dothan MSA, AL	S	9.20 MW	7.31 AW	19140 AAW	ALBLS	10//99-12//99
	Florence MSA, AL	S	8.10 MW	6.65 AW	16850 AAW	ALBLS	10//99-12//99
	Gadsden MSA, AL	S	8.31 MW	6.76 AW	17280 AAW	ALBLS	10//99-12//99
	Huntsville MSA, AL	S	8.89 MW	7.23 AW	18500 AAW	ALBLS	10//99-12//99
	Mobile MSA, AL	S	8.72 MW	7.10 AW	18150 AAW	ALBLS	10//99-12//99
	Montgomery MSA, AL	S	9.03 MW	7.44 AW	18770 AAW	ALBLS	10//99-12//99
	Tuscaloosa MSA, AL	S	8.06 MW	6.57 AW	16770 AAW	ALBLS	10//99-12//99
	Alaska	S	9.27 MW	10.93 AW	22740 AAW	AKBLS	10//99-12//99
	Anchorage MSA, AK	S	11.01 MW	9.43 AW	22910 AAW	AKBLS	10//99-12//99

AAW	Average annual wage	AOH	Average offered, high	ASH	Average starting, high	H	Hourly
AE	Average entry wage	AOL	Average offered, low	ASL	Average starting, low	HI	Highest wage paid
AEX	Average experienced wage	APH	Average pay, high range	AW	Average wage paid	HR	High end range
AO	Average offered	APL	Average pay, low range	FQ	First quartile wage	LR	Low end range

M	Monthly	S	Special: hourly and annual
MTC	Median total compensation	TQ	Third quartile wage
MW	Median wage paid	W	Weekly
SQ	Second quartile wage	Y	Yearly

Occupation/Type/Industry	Location	Per	Low	Mid	High	Source	Date
Retail Salesperson	Arizona	S	8.15 MW	10.21 AW	21230 AAW	AZBLS	10//99-12//99
	Flagstaff MSA, AZ-UT	S	7.75 MW	6.95 AW	16130 AAW	AZBLS	10//99-12//99
	Phoenix-Mesa MSA, AZ	S	10.60 MW	8.41 AW	22060 AAW	AZBLS	10//99-12//99
	Tucson MSA, AZ	S	10.13 MW	7.94 AW	21070 AAW	AZBLS	10//99-12//99
	Yuma MSA, AZ	S	8.31 MW	6.66 AW	17290 AAW	AZBLS	10//99-12//99
	Arkansas	S	6.93 MW	8.15 AW	16950 AAW	ARBLS	10//99-12//99
	Fayetteville-Springdale-Rogers MSA, AR	S	7.82 MW	7.14 AW	16270 AAW	ARBLS	10//99-12//99
	Fort Smith MSA, AR-OK	S	8.26 MW	7.03 AW	17180 AAW	ARBLS	10//99-12//99
	Jonesboro MSA, AR	S	8.62 MW	7.17 AW	17920 AAW	ARBLS	10//99-12//99
	Little Rock-North Little Rock MSA, AR	S	8.67 MW	7.16 AW	18030 AAW	ARBLS	10//99-12//99
	Pine Bluff MSA, AR	S	7.79 MW	6.42 AW	16210 AAW	ARBLS	10//99-12//99
	California	S	7.88 MW	9.69 AW	20160 AAW	CABLS	10//99-12//99
	Bakersfield MSA, CA	S	10.11 MW	7.26 AW	21030 AAW	CABLS	10//99-12//99
	Chico-Paradise MSA, CA	S	8.38 MW	6.78 AW	17420 AAW	CABLS	10//99-12//99
	Fresno MSA, CA	S	8.76 MW	7.27 AW	18230 AAW	CABLS	10//99-12//99
	Los Angeles-Long Beach PMSA, CA	S	9.82 MW	7.98 AW	20420 AAW	CABLS	10//99-12//99
	Merced MSA, CA	S	8.58 MW	7.08 AW	17850 AAW	CABLS	10//99-12//99
	Modesto MSA, CA	S	9.21 MW	7.55 AW	19150 AAW	CABLS	10//99-12//99
	Oakland PMSA, CA	S	9.88 MW	8.05 AW	20550 AAW	CABLS	10//99-12//99
	Orange County PMSA, CA	S	10.20 MW	8.10 AW	21220 AAW	CABLS	10//99-12//99
	Redding MSA, CA	S	9.01 MW	7.70 AW	18730 AAW	CABLS	10//99-12//99
	Riverside-San Bernardino PMSA, CA	S	9.37 MW	7.69 AW	19500 AAW	CABLS	10//99-12//99
	Sacramento PMSA, CA	S	10.17 MW	7.98 AW	21160 AAW	CABLS	10//99-12//99
	Salinas MSA, CA	S	9.38 MW	8.24 AW	19510 AAW	CABLS	10//99-12//99
	San Diego MSA, CA	S	9.79 MW	7.64 AW	20370 AAW	CABLS	10//99-12//99
	San Francisco PMSA, CA	S	9.85 MW	8.42 AW	20480 AAW	CABLS	10//99-12//99
	San Jose PMSA, CA	S	9.75 MW	7.84 AW	20290 AAW	CABLS	10//99-12//99
	San Luis Obispo-Atascadero-Paso Robles MSA, CA	S	8.61 MW	7.41 AW	17910 AAW	CABLS	10//99-12//99
	Santa Barbara-Santa Maria-Lompoc MSA, CA	S	8.63 MW	7.76 AW	17960 AAW	CABLS	10//99-12//99
	Santa Cruz-Watsonville PMSA, CA	S	8.91 MW	7.78 AW	18530 AAW	CABLS	10//99-12//99
	Santa Rosa PMSA, CA	S	10.07 MW	8.15 AW	20960 AAW	CABLS	10//99-12//99
	Stockton-Lodi MSA, CA	S	9.48 MW	7.47 AW	19710 AAW	CABLS	10//99-12//99
	Vallejo-Fairfield-Napa PMSA, CA	S	9.33 MW	7.74 AW	19410 AAW	CABLS	10//99-12//99
	Ventura PMSA, CA	S	9.55 MW	7.89 AW	19860 AAW	CABLS	10//99-12//99
	Visalia-Tulare-Porterville MSA, CA	S	9.02 MW	7.37 AW	18760 AAW	CABLS	10//99-12//99
	Yolo PMSA, CA	S	8.39 MW	7.04 AW	17440 AAW	CABLS	10//99-12//99
	Yuba City MSA, CA	S	8.63 MW	7.46 AW	17960 AAW	CABLS	10//99-12//99
	Colorado	S	8.12 MW	9.75 AW	20290 AAW	COBLS	10//99-12//99
	Boulder-Longmont PMSA, CO	S	9.89 MW	8.27 AW	20570 AAW	COBLS	10//99-12//99
	Colorado Springs MSA, CO	S	9.61 MW	7.77 AW	19990 AAW	COBLS	10//99-12//99
	Denver PMSA, CO	S	10.02 MW	8.26 AW	20840 AAW	COBLS	10//99-12//99
	Fort Collins-Loveland MSA, CO	S	9.30 MW	7.72 AW	19350 AAW	COBLS	10//99-12//99
	Grand Junction MSA, CO	S	8.95 MW	7.45 AW	18610 AAW	COBLS	10//99-12//99
	Greeley PMSA, CO	S	9.79 MW	7.96 AW	20360 AAW	COBLS	10//99-12//99
	Pueblo MSA, CO	S	8.98 MW	7.60 AW	18680 AAW	COBLS	10//99-12//99
	Connecticut	S	8.23 MW	10.08 AW	20970 AAW	CTBLS	10//99-12//99
	Bridgeport PMSA, CT	S	10.44 MW	8.21 AW	21720 AAW	CTBLS	10//99-12//99
	Danbury PMSA, CT	S	9.80 MW	8.27 AW	20380 AAW	CTBLS	10//99-12//99
	Hartford MSA, CT	S	9.85 MW	8.18 AW	20480 AAW	CTBLS	10//99-12//99
	New Haven-Meriden PMSA, CT	S	9.75 MW	8.11 AW	20280 AAW	CTBLS	10//99-12//99
	New London-Norwich MSA, CT-RI	S	9.22 MW	7.84 AW	19180 AAW	CTBLS	10//99-12//99
	Stamford-Norwalk PMSA, CT	S	12.36 MW	9.76 AW	25720 AAW	CTBLS	10//99-12//99
	Waterbury PMSA, CT	S	9.18 MW	7.87 AW	19090 AAW	CTBLS	10//99-12//99
	Delaware	S	7.66 MW	9.30 AW	19330 AAW	DEBLS	10//99-12//99
	Dover MSA, DE	S	8.42 MW	6.94 AW	17520 AAW	DEBLS	10//99-12//99
	Wilmington-Newark PMSA, DE-MD	S	9.73 MW	7.98 AW	20250 AAW	DEBLS	10//99-12//99
	District of Columbia	S	9.26 MW	10.79 AW	22450 AAW	DCBLS	10//99-12//99
	Washington PMSA, DC-MD-VA-WV	S	9.53 MW	7.92 AW	19820 AAW	DCBLS	10//99-12//99

AAW Average annual wage	AOH Average offered, high	ASH Average starting, high	H Hourly	M Monthly	S Special: hourly and annual
AE Average entry wage	AOL Average offered, low	ASL Average starting, low	HI Highest wage paid	MTC Median total compensation	TQ Third quartile wage
AEX Average experienced wage	APH Average pay, high range	AW Average wage paid	HR High end range	MW Median wage paid	W Weekly
AO Average offered	APL Average pay, low range	FQ First quartile wage	LR Low end range	SQ Second quartile wage	Y Yearly

Occupation/Type/Industry	Location	Per	Low	Mid	High	Source	Date
Retail Salesperson	Florida	s	7.8 MW	9.20 AW	19130 AAW	FLBLS	10//99-12//99
	Daytona Beach MSA, FL	s	8.48 MW	7.59 AW	17640 AAW	FLBLS	10//99-12//99
	Fort Lauderdale PMSA, FL	s	10.07 MW	8.04 AW	20940 AAW	FLBLS	10//99-12//99
	Fort Myers-Cape Coral MSA, FL	s	10.20 MW	8.22 AW	21220 AAW	FLBLS	10//99-12//99
	Fort Pierce-Port St. Lucie MSA, FL	s	9.23 MW	7.99 AW	19190 AAW	FLBLS	10//99-12//99
	Fort Walton Beach MSA, FL	s	8.42 MW	7.39 AW	17500 AAW	FLBLS	10//99-12//99
	Gainesville MSA, FL	s	8.67 MW	7.42 AW	18030 AAW	FLBLS	10//99-12//99
	Jacksonville MSA, FL	s	9.02 MW	7.70 AW	18770 AAW	FLBLS	10//99-12//99
	Lakeland-Winter Haven MSA, FL	s	9.50 MW	7.85 AW	19760 AAW	FLBLS	10//99-12//99
	Melbourne-Titusville-Palm Bay MSA, FL	s	8.33 MW	7.32 AW	17320 AAW	FLBLS	10//99-12//99
	Miami PMSA, FL	s	8.90 MW	7.82 AW	18500 AAW	FLBLS	10//99-12//99
	Naples MSA, FL	s	10.04 MW	8.67 AW	20880 AAW	FLBLS	10//99-12//99
	Ocala MSA, FL	s	8.65 MW	7.50 AW	18000 AAW	FLBLS	10//99-12//99
	Orlando MSA, FL	s	9.17 MW	7.66 AW	19080 AAW	FLBLS	10//99-12//99
	Panama City MSA, FL	s	8.25 MW	7.52 AW	17150 AAW	FLBLS	10//99-12//99
	Pensacola MSA, FL	s	8.48 MW	7.27 AW	17650 AAW	FLBLS	10//99-12//99
	Punta Gorda MSA, FL	s	8.99 MW	7.70 AW	18700 AAW	FLBLS	10//99-12//99
	Sarasota-Bradenton MSA, FL	s	9.28 MW	7.89 AW	19310 AAW	FLBLS	10//99-12//99
	Tallahassee MSA, FL	s	8.61 MW	7.36 AW	17910 AAW	FLBLS	10//99-12//99
	Tampa-St. Petersburg-Clearwater MSA, FL	s	9.67 MW	7.98 AW	20110 AAW	FLBLS	10//99-12//99
	West Palm Beach-Boca Raton MSA, FL	s	9.93 MW	8.20 AW	20650 AAW	FLBLS	10//99-12//99
	Georgia	s	7.61 MW	9.02 AW	18770 AAW	GABLS	10//99-12//99
	Albany MSA, GA	s	8.18 MW	6.77 AW	17020 AAW	GABLS	10//99-12//99
	Athens MSA, GA	s	9.03 MW	7.19 AW	18790 AAW	GABLS	10//99-12//99
	Atlanta MSA, GA	s	9.55 MW	8.03 AW	19870 AAW	GABLS	10//99-12//99
	Augusta-Aiken MSA, GA-SC	s	8.83 MW	7.20 AW	18360 AAW	GABLS	10//99-12//99
	Columbus MSA, GA-AL	s	8.82 MW	7.19 AW	18330 AAW	GABLS	10//99-12//99
	Macon MSA, GA	s	9.02 MW	7.34 AW	18750 AAW	GABLS	10//99-12//99
	Savannah MSA, GA	s	8.14 MW	6.96 AW	16940 AAW	GABLS	10//99-12//99
	Hawaii	s	7.93 MW	8.99 AW	18700 AAW	HIBLS	10//99-12//99
	Honolulu MSA, HI	s	9.02 MW	7.94 AW	18770 AAW	HIBLS	10//99-12//99
	Idaho	s	7.72 MW	9.56 AW	19880 AAW	IDBLS	10//99-12//99
	Boise City MSA, ID	s	9.45 MW	7.78 AW	19650 AAW	IDBLS	10//99-12//99
	Pocatello MSA, ID	s	8.73 MW	7.26 AW	18160 AAW	IDBLS	10//99-12//99
	Illinois	s	7.92 MW	9.53 AW	19830 AAW	ILBLS	10//99-12//99
	Bloomington-Normal MSA, IL	s	8.62 MW	7.49 AW	17920 AAW	ILBLS	10//99-12//99
	Champaign-Urbana MSA, IL	s	8.69 MW	7.63 AW	18080 AAW	ILBLS	10//99-12//99
	Chicago PMSA, IL	s	9.79 MW	8.17 AW	20370 AAW	ILBLS	10//99-12//99
	Decatur MSA, IL	s	9.07 MW	7.40 AW	18870 AAW	ILBLS	10//99-12//99
	Kankakee PMSA, IL	s	10.77 MW	7.91 AW	22400 AAW	ILBLS	10//99-12//99
	Peoria-Pekin MSA, IL	s	9.51 MW	7.21 AW	19780 AAW	ILBLS	10//99-12//99
	Rockford MSA, IL	s	9.39 MW	7.50 AW	19530 AAW	ILBLS	10//99-12//99
	Springfield MSA, IL	s	8.84 MW	7.63 AW	18390 AAW	ILBLS	10//99-12//99
	Indiana	s	7.44 MW	9.02 AW	18760 AAW	INBLS	10//99-12//99
	Bloomington MSA, IN	s	7.81 MW	6.70 AW	16240 AAW	INBLS	10//99-12//99
	Elkhart-Goshen MSA, IN	s	11.38 MW	8.16 AW	23680 AAW	INBLS	10//99-12//99
	Evansville-Henderson MSA, IN-KY	s	9.05 MW	7.36 AW	18820 AAW	INBLS	10//99-12//99
	Fort Wayne MSA, IN	s	8.89 MW	7.58 AW	18490 AAW	INBLS	10//99-12//99
	Gary PMSA, IN	s	9.27 MW	7.10 AW	19280 AAW	INBLS	10//99-12//99
	Indianapolis MSA, IN	s	9.41 MW	7.77 AW	19570 AAW	INBLS	10//99-12//99
	Kokomo MSA, IN	s	8.63 MW	7.08 AW	17940 AAW	INBLS	10//99-12//99
	Lafayette MSA, IN	s	8.81 MW	7.32 AW	18330 AAW	INBLS	10//99-12//99
	Muncie MSA, IN	s	8.14 MW	7.30 AW	16930 AAW	INBLS	10//99-12//99
	South Bend MSA, IN	s	8.93 MW	7.49 AW	18580 AAW	INBLS	10//99-12//99
	Terre Haute MSA, IN	s	8.29 MW	6.66 AW	17250 AAW	INBLS	10//99-12//99
	Iowa	s	7.32 MW	8.90 AW	18510 AAW	IABLS	10//99-12//99
	Cedar Rapids MSA, IA	s	9.51 MW	7.63 AW	19790 AAW	IABLS	10//99-12//99
	Davenport-Moline-Rock Island MSA, IA-IL	s	9.22 MW	7.63 AW	19180 AAW	IABLS	10//99-12//99
	Des Moines MSA, IA	s	9.96 MW	7.98 AW	20710 AAW	IABLS	10//99-12//99
	Dubuque MSA, IA	s	7.91 MW	6.83 AW	16450 AAW	IABLS	10//99-12//99
	Iowa City MSA, IA	s	7.89 MW	7.06 AW	16410 AAW	IABLS	10//99-12//99
	Sioux City MSA, IA-NE	s	9.23 MW	7.69 AW	19200 AAW	IABLS	10//99-12//99
	Waterloo-Cedar Falls MSA, IA	s	8.23 MW	6.95 AW	17110 AAW	IABLS	10//99-12//99
	Kansas	s	7.06 MW	8.67 AW	18030 AAW	KSBLS	10//99-12//99

Occupation/Type/Industry	Location	Per	Low	Mid	High	Source	Date
Retail Salesperson	Lawrence MSA, KS	S	7.21 MW	6.43 AW	14990 AAW	KSBLS	10//99-12//99
	Topeka MSA, KS	S	8.69 MW	6.94 AW	18080 AAW	KSBLS	10//99-12//99
	Wichita MSA, KS	S	8.97 MW	7.23 AW	18660 AAW	KSBLS	10//99-12//99
	Kentucky	S	7.04 MW	8.37 AW	17410 AAW	KYBLS	10//99-12//99
	Lexington MSA, KY	S	8.88 MW	7.58 AW	18470 AAW	KYBLS	10//99-12//99
	Louisville MSA, KY-IN	S	8.94 MW	7.56 AW	18590 AAW	KYBLS	10//99-12//99
	Owensboro MSA, KY	S	8.80 MW	6.68 AW	18300 AAW	KYBLS	10//99-12//99
	Louisiana	S	6.93 MW	8.59 AW	17870 AAW	LABLS	10//99-12//99
	Alexandria MSA, LA	S	7.84 MW	6.64 AW	16310 AAW	LABLS	10//99-12//99
	Baton Rouge MSA, LA	S	8.87 MW	6.82 AW	18440 AAW	LABLS	10//99-12//99
	Houma MSA, LA	S	8.50 MW	6.64 AW	17680 AAW	LABLS	10//99-12//99
	Lafayette MSA, LA	S	8.68 MW	6.96 AW	18050 AAW	LABLS	10//99-12//99
	Lake Charles MSA, LA	S	8.63 MW	7.06 AW	17950 AAW	LABLS	10//99-12//99
	Monroe MSA, LA	S	8.27 MW	7.18 AW	17210 AAW	LABLS	10//99-12//99
	New Orleans MSA, LA	S	8.72 MW	7.18 AW	18150 AAW	LABLS	10//99-12//99
	Shreveport-Bossier City MSA, LA	S	8.77 MW	7.05 AW	18230 AAW	LABLS	10//99-12//99
	Maine	S	7.58 MW	8.55 AW	17780 AAW	MEBLS	10//99-12//99
	Bangor MSA, ME	S	8.71 MW	7.35 AW	18120 AAW	MEBLS	10//99-12//99
	Lewiston-Auburn MSA, ME	S	7.85 MW	6.76 AW	16320 AAW	MEBLS	10//99-12//99
	Portland MSA, ME	S	9.02 MW	8.08 AW	18770 AAW	MEBLS	10//99-12//99
	Maryland	S	7.8 MW	9.45 AW	19650 AAW	MDBLS	10//99-12//99
	Baltimore PMSA, MD	S	9.29 MW	7.78 AW	19320 AAW	MDBLS	10//99-12//99
	Cumberland MSA, MD-WV	S	7.17 MW	6.32 AW	14910 AAW	MDBLS	10//99-12//99
	Hagerstown PMSA, MD	S	8.55 MW	7.39 AW	17790 AAW	MDBLS	10//99-12//99
	Massachusetts	S	7.94 MW	9.55 AW	19860 AAW	MABLS	10//99-12//99
	Barnstable-Yarmouth MSA, MA	S	9.33 MW	7.91 AW	19410 AAW	MABLS	10//99-12//99
	Boston PMSA, MA-NH	S	9.79 MW	8.02 AW	20370 AAW	MABLS	10//99-12//99
	Brockton PMSA, MA	S	9.29 MW	8.12 AW	19330 AAW	MABLS	10//99-12//99
	Fitchburg-Leominster PMSA, MA	S	8.87 MW	7.48 AW	18450 AAW	MABLS	10//99-12//99
	Lawrence PMSA, MA-NH	S	8.67 MW	7.38 AW	18040 AAW	MABLS	10//99-12//99
	Lowell PMSA, MA-NH	S	9.97 MW	8.15 AW	20730 AAW	MABLS	10//99-12//99
	New Bedford PMSA, MA	S	8.78 MW	7.81 AW	18260 AAW	MABLS	10//99-12//99
	Pittsfield MSA, MA	S	8.09 MW	7.46 AW	16820 AAW	MABLS	10//99-12//99
	Springfield MSA, MA	S	8.75 MW	7.50 AW	18190 AAW	MABLS	10//99-12//99
	Worcester PMSA, MA-CT	S	9.95 MW	8.03 AW	20700 AAW	MABLS	10//99-12//99
	Michigan	S	7.71 MW	9.44 AW	19630 AAW	MIBLS	10//99-12//99
	Ann Arbor PMSA, MI	S	9.88 MW	7.74 AW	20550 AAW	MIBLS	10//99-12//99
	Benton Harbor MSA, MI	S	9.14 MW	7.59 AW	19020 AAW	MIBLS	10//99-12//99
	Detroit PMSA, MI	S	9.77 MW	7.85 AW	20310 AAW	MIBLS	10//99-12//99
	Flint PMSA, MI	S	9.29 MW	7.67 AW	19330 AAW	MIBLS	10//99-12//99
	Grand Rapids-Muskegon-Holland MSA, MI	S	9.55 MW	7.73 AW	19860 AAW	MIBLS	10//99-12//99
	Jackson MSA, MI	S	9.51 MW	7.48 AW	19790 AAW	MIBLS	10//99-12//99
	Kalamazoo-Battle Creek MSA, MI	S	8.57 MW	7.44 AW	17820 AAW	MIBLS	10//99-12//99
	Lansing-East Lansing MSA, MI	S	9.06 MW	7.43 AW	18850 AAW	MIBLS	10//99-12//99
	Saginaw-Bay City-Midland MSA, MI	S	8.09 MW	6.85 AW	16830 AAW	MIBLS	10//99-12//99
	Minnesota	S	7.79 MW	9.15 AW	19030 AAW	MNBLS	10//99-12//99
	Duluth-Superior MSA, MN-WI	S	8.57 MW	7.41 AW	17830 AAW	MNBLS	10//99-12//99
	Minneapolis-St. Paul MSA, MN-WI	S	9.61 MW	8.09 AW	19980 AAW	MNBLS	10//99-12//99
	Rochester MSA, MN	S	8.83 MW	7.73 AW	18360 AAW	MNBLS	10//99-12//99
	St. Cloud MSA, MN	S	8.92 MW	6.96 AW	18560 AAW	MNBLS	10//99-12//99
	Mississippi	S	6.87 MW	8.19 AW	17030 AAW	MSBLS	10//99-12//99
	Biloxi-Gulfport-Pascagoula MSA, MS	S	8.26 MW	7.25 AW	17190 AAW	MSBLS	10//99-12//99
	Hattiesburg MSA, MS	S	7.97 MW	7.01 AW	16570 AAW	MSBLS	10//99-12//99
	Jackson MSA, MS	S	9.03 MW	7.35 AW	18780 AAW	MSBLS	10//99-12//99
	Missouri	S	7.3 MW	9.04 AW	18790 AAW	MOBLS	10//99-12//99
	Columbia MSA, MO	S	8.03 MW	6.72 AW	16690 AAW	MOBLS	10//99-12//99
	Joplin MSA, MO	S	7.87 MW	6.48 AW	16370 AAW	MOBLS	10//99-12//99
	Kansas City MSA, MO-KS	S	9.57 MW	7.74 AW	19900 AAW	MOBLS	10//99-12//99
	St. Joseph MSA, MO	S	8.51 MW	6.94 AW	17710 AAW	MOBLS	10//99-12//99
	St. Louis MSA, MO-IL	S	9.21 MW	7.45 AW	19160 AAW	MOBLS	10//99-12//99
	Springfield MSA, MO	S	8.68 MW	6.97 AW	18050 AAW	MOBLS	10//99-12//99
	Montana	S	7.12 MW	8.60 AW	17880 AAW	MTBLS	10//99-12//99
	Billings MSA, MT	S	9.09 MW	7.40 AW	18900 AAW	MTBLS	10//99-12//99
	Great Falls MSA, MT	S	8.70 MW	7.42 AW	18090 AAW	MTBLS	10//99-12//99

AAW	Average annual wage	AOH	Average offered, high	ASH	Average starting, high	H	Hourly	M	Monthly	S	Special: hourly and annual
AE	Average entry wage	AOL	Average offered, low	ASL	Average starting, low	HI	Highest wage paid	MTC	Median total compensation	TQ	Third quartile wage
AEX	Average experienced wage	APH	Average pay, high range	AW	Average wage paid	HR	High end range	MW	Median wage paid	W	Weekly
AO	Average offered	APL	Average pay, low range	FQ	First quartile wage	LR	Low end range	SQ	Second quartile wage	Y	Yearly

Occupation/Type/Industry	Location	Per	Low	Mid	High	Source	Date
Retail Salesperson	Missoula MSA, MT	S	8.33 MW	6.85 AW	17330 AAW	MTBLS	10//99-12//99
	Nebraska	S	7.39 MW	8.61 AW	17910 AAW	NEBLS	10//99-12//99
	Lincoln MSA, NE	S	8.36 MW	7.31 AW	17380 AAW	NEBLS	10//99-12//99
	Omaha MSA, NE-IA	S	9.27 MW	7.81 AW	19270 AAW	NEBLS	10//99-12//99
	Nevada	S	8.02 MW	9.62 AW	20020 AAW	NVBLS	10//99-12//99
	Las Vegas MSA, NV-AZ	S	9.48 MW	7.91 AW	19710 AAW	NVBLS	10//99-12//99
	Reno MSA, NV	S	10.50 MW	8.50 AW	21840 AAW	NVBLS	10//99-12//99
	New Hampshire	S	7.55 MW	8.84 AW	18390 AAW	NHBLS	10//99-12//99
	Manchester PMSA, NH	S	9.36 MW	7.69 AW	19460 AAW	NHBLS	10//99-12//99
	Nashua PMSA, NH	S	9.35 MW	7.95 AW	19450 AAW	NHBLS	10//99-12//99
	Portsmouth-Rochester PMSA, NH-ME	S	8.76 MW	7.74 AW	18230 AAW	NHBLS	10//99-12//99
	New Jersey	S	8.11 MW	10.01 AW	20820 AAW	NJBLS	10//99-12//99
	Atlantic-Cape May PMSA, NJ	S	8.98 MW	7.66 AW	18680 AAW	NJBLS	10//99-12//99
	Bergen-Passaic PMSA, NJ	S	10.36 MW	8.61 AW	21550 AAW	NJBLS	10//99-12//99
	Jersey City PMSA, NJ	S	9.01 MW	7.63 AW	18740 AAW	NJBLS	10//99-12//99
	Middlesex-Somerset-Hunterdon PMSA, NJ	S	10.64 MW	8.05 AW	22120 AAW	NJBLS	10//99-12//99
	Monmouth-Ocean PMSA, NJ	S	10.23 MW	8.16 AW	21280 AAW	NJBLS	10//99-12//99
	Newark PMSA, NJ	S	10.22 MW	8.29 AW	21260 AAW	NJBLS	10//99-12//99
	Trenton PMSA, NJ	S	9.50 MW	8.09 AW	19770 AAW	NJBLS	10//99-12//99
	Vineland-Millville-Bridgeton PMSA, NJ	S	9.14 MW	7.34 AW	19010 AAW	NJBLS	10//99-12//99
	New Mexico	S	7.69 MW	9.21 AW	19160 AAW	NMBLS	10//99-12//99
	Albuquerque MSA, NM	S	9.53 MW	7.83 AW	19820 AAW	NMBLS	10//99-12//99
	Las Cruces MSA, NM	S	8.98 MW	7.26 AW	18680 AAW	NMBLS	10//99-12//99
	Santa Fe MSA, NM	S	9.67 MW	8.64 AW	20110 AAW	NMBLS	10//99-12//99
	New York	S	7.61 MW	9.26 AW	19270 AAW	NYBLS	10//99-12//99
	Albany-Schenectady-Troy MSA, NY	S	8.68 MW	7.36 AW	18050 AAW	NYBLS	10//99-12//99
	Binghamton MSA, NY	S	8.34 MW	7.17 AW	17350 AAW	NYBLS	10//99-12//99
	Buffalo-Niagara Falls MSA, NY	S	8.21 MW	6.75 AW	17080 AAW	NYBLS	10//99-12//99
	Dutchess County PMSA, NY	S	8.91 MW	7.64 AW	18540 AAW	NYBLS	10//99-12//99
	Elmira MSA, NY	S	7.93 MW	6.22 AW	16500 AAW	NYBLS	10//99-12//99
	Glens Falls MSA, NY	S	8.31 MW	7.38 AW	17280 AAW	NYBLS	10//99-12//99
	Jamestown MSA, NY	S	8.42 MW	6.68 AW	17520 AAW	NYBLS	10//99-12//99
	Nassau-Suffolk PMSA, NY	S	9.91 MW	8.01 AW	20610 AAW	NYBLS	10//99-12//99
	New York PMSA, NY	S	9.74 MW	7.87 AW	20260 AAW	NYBLS	10//99-12//99
	Newburgh PMSA, NY-PA	S	8.71 MW	7.71 AW	18110 AAW	NYBLS	10//99-12//99
	Rochester MSA, NY	S	8.74 MW	7.41 AW	18180 AAW	NYBLS	10//99-12//99
	Syracuse MSA, NY	S	8.16 MW	6.98 AW	16980 AAW	NYBLS	10//99-12//99
	Utica-Rome MSA, NY	S	8.18 MW	6.73 AW	17010 AAW	NYBLS	10//99-12//99
	North Carolina	S	7.65 MW	9.12 AW	18970 AAW	NCBLS	10//99-12//99
	Asheville MSA, NC	S	8.86 MW	7.52 AW	18440 AAW	NCBLS	10//99-12//99
	Charlotte-Gastonia-Rock Hill MSA, NC-SC	S	9.68 MW	8.10 AW	20120 AAW	NCBLS	10//99-12//99
	Fayetteville MSA, NC	S	8.45 MW	7.17 AW	17570 AAW	NCBLS	10//99-12//99
	Goldsboro MSA, NC	S	9.05 MW	7.19 AW	18830 AAW	NCBLS	10//99-12//99
	Greensboro--Winston-Salem--High Point MSA, NC	S	9.40 MW	7.78 AW	19540 AAW	NCBLS	10//99-12//99
	Greenville MSA, NC	S	8.19 MW	6.69 AW	17030 AAW	NCBLS	10//99-12//99
	Hickory-Morganton-Lenoir MSA, NC	S	9.35 MW	7.66 AW	19440 AAW	NCBLS	10//99-12//99
	Jacksonville MSA, NC	S	8.25 MW	6.85 AW	17170 AAW	NCBLS	10//99-12//99
	Raleigh-Durham-Chapel Hill MSA, NC	S	9.32 MW	7.99 AW	19380 AAW	NCBLS	10//99-12//99
	Rocky Mount MSA, NC	S	8.97 MW	7.52 AW	18660 AAW	NCBLS	10//99-12//99
	Wilmington MSA, NC	S	8.89 MW	7.53 AW	18480 AAW	NCBLS	10//99-12//99
	North Dakota	S	6.8 MW	8.54 AW	17760 AAW	NDBLS	10//99-12//99
	Bismarck MSA, ND	S	8.27 MW	6.70 AW	17200 AAW	NDBLS	10//99-12//99
	Fargo-Moorhead MSA, ND-MN	S	8.89 MW	7.37 AW	18490 AAW	NDBLS	10//99-12//99
	Grand Forks MSA, ND-MN	S	8.03 MW	6.28 AW	16690 AAW	NDBLS	10//99-12//99
	Ohio	S	7.27 MW	8.82 AW	18350 AAW	OHBLS	10//99-12//99
	Akron PMSA, OH	S	9.03 MW	7.35 AW	18780 AAW	OHBLS	10//99-12//99
	Canton-Massillon MSA, OH	S	8.12 MW	6.64 AW	16900 AAW	OHBLS	10//99-12//99
	Cincinnati PMSA, OH-KY-IN	S	9.28 MW	7.63 AW	19310 AAW	OHBLS	10//99-12//99
	Cleveland-Lorain-Elyria PMSA, OH	S	9.02 MW	7.45 AW	18760 AAW	OHBLS	10//99-12//99
	Columbus MSA, OH	S	9.25 MW	7.65 AW	19240 AAW	OHBLS	10//99-12//99
	Dayton-Springfield MSA, OH	S	8.49 MW	7.27 AW	17660 AAW	OHBLS	10//99-12//99

AAW Average annual wage	AOH Average offered, high	ASH Average starting, high	H Hourly	M Monthly	S Special: hourly and annual
AE Average entry wage	AOL Average offered, low	ASL Average starting, low	HI Highest wage paid	MTC Median total compensation	TQ Third quartile wage
AEX Average experienced wage	APH Average pay, high range	AW Average wage paid	HR High end range	MW Median wage paid	W Weekly
AO Average offered	APL Average pay, low range	FQ First quartile wage	LR Low end range	SQ Second quartile wage	Y Yearly

Retail Salesperson

Occupation/Type/Industry	Location	Per	Low	Mid	High	Source	Date
Retail Salesperson	Hamilton-Middletown PMSA, OH	S	8.50 MW	7.37 AW	17680 AAW	OHBLS	10//99-12//99
	Lima MSA, OH	S	8.59 MW	6.59 AW	17860 AAW	OHBLS	10//99-12//99
	Mansfield MSA, OH	S	8.68 MW	6.85 AW	18050 AAW	OHBLS	10//99-12//99
	Steubenville-Weirton MSA, OH-WV	S	7.50 MW	6.52 AW	15600 AAW	OHBLS	10//99-12//99
	Toledo MSA, OH	S	8.86 MW	7.31 AW	18430 AAW	OHBLS	10//99-12//99
	Youngstown-Warren MSA, OH	S	8.24 MW	6.56 AW	17150 AAW	OHBLS	10//99-12//99
	Oklahoma	S	7.48 MW	9.08 AW	18890 AAW	OKBLS	10//99-12//99
	Enid MSA, OK	S	8.65 MW	7.25 AW	17980 AAW	OKBLS	10//99-12//99
	Lawton MSA, OK	S	8.17 MW	7.33 AW	16990 AAW	OKBLS	10//99-12//99
	Oklahoma City MSA, OK	S	9.00 MW	7.47 AW	18720 AAW	OKBLS	10//99-12//99
	Tulsa MSA, OK	S	10.36 MW	8.07 AW	21550 AAW	OKBLS	10//99-12//99
	Oregon	S	8.32 MW	10.13 AW	21080 AAW	ORBLS	10//99-12//99
	Corvallis MSA, OR	S	9.35 MW	8.13 AW	19450 AAW	ORBLS	10//99-12//99
	Eugene-Springfield MSA, OR	S	9.79 MW	8.28 AW	20360 AAW	ORBLS	10//99-12//99
	Medford-Ashland MSA, OR	S	9.75 MW	8.32 AW	20280 AAW	ORBLS	10//99-12//99
	Portland-Vancouver PMSA, OR-WA	S	10.59 MW	8.47 AW	22020 AAW	ORBLS	10//99-12//99
	Salem PMSA, OR	S	10.05 MW	8.23 AW	20910 AAW	ORBLS	10//99-12//99
	Pennsylvania	S	7.34 MW	8.65 AW	18000 AAW	PABLS	10//99-12//99
	Allentown-Bethlehem-Easton MSA, PA	S	8.75 MW	7.62 AW	18210 AAW	PABLS	10//99-12//99
	Altoona MSA, PA	S	8.08 MW	7.01 AW	16810 AAW	PABLS	10//99-12//99
	Erie MSA, PA	S	8.07 MW	6.84 AW	16780 AAW	PABLS	10//99-12//99
	Harrisburg-Lebanon-Carlisle MSA, PA	S	8.57 MW	7.37 AW	17830 AAW	PABLS	10//99-12//99
	Johnstown MSA, PA	S	7.68 MW	6.74 AW	15970 AAW	PABLS	10//99-12//99
	Lancaster MSA, PA	S	8.89 MW	7.54 AW	18500 AAW	PABLS	10//99-12//99
	Philadelphia PMSA, PA-NJ	S	9.34 MW	7.79 AW	19430 AAW	PABLS	10//99-12//99
	Pittsburgh MSA, PA	S	8.30 MW	6.94 AW	17260 AAW	PABLS	10//99-12//99
	Reading MSA, PA	S	8.96 MW	7.75 AW	18630 AAW	PABLS	10//99-12//99
	Scranton--Wilkes-Barre--Hazleton MSA, PA	S	8.26 MW	6.83 AW	17180 AAW	PABLS	10//99-12//99
	Sharon MSA, PA	S	7.65 MW	6.61 AW	15900 AAW	PABLS	10//99-12//99
	State College MSA, PA	S	7.39 MW	6.48 AW	15360 AAW	PABLS	10//99-12//99
	Williamsport MSA, PA	S	8.15 MW	6.98 AW	16940 AAW	PABLS	10//99-12//99
	York MSA, PA	S	8.38 MW	7.29 AW	17440 AAW	PABLS	10//99-12//99
	Rhode Island	S	8.04 MW	9.63 AW	20030 AAW	RIBLS	10//99-12//99
	Providence-Fall River-Warwick MSA, RI-MA	S	9.46 MW	7.88 AW	19670 AAW	RIBLS	10//99-12//99
	South Carolina	S	7.58 MW	9.16 AW	19060 AAW	SCBLS	10//99-12//99
	Charleston-North Charleston MSA, SC	S	9.31 MW	7.88 AW	19360 AAW	SCBLS	10//99-12//99
	Columbia MSA, SC	S	9.55 MW	7.70 AW	19870 AAW	SCBLS	10//99-12//99
	Florence MSA, SC	S	9.02 MW	7.39 AW	18760 AAW	SCBLS	10//99-12//99
	Greenville-Spartanburg-Anderson MSA, SC	S	9.54 MW	7.77 AW	19830 AAW	SCBLS	10//99-12//99
	Myrtle Beach MSA, SC	S	8.46 MW	7.39 AW	17600 AAW	SCBLS	10//99-12//99
	Sumter MSA, SC	S	8.98 MW	7.06 AW	18670 AAW	SCBLS	10//99-12//99
	South Dakota	S	7.44 MW	8.59 AW	17870 AAW	SDBLS	10//99-12//99
	Rapid City MSA, SD	S	8.65 MW	7.75 AW	17990 AAW	SDBLS	10//99-12//99
	Sioux Falls MSA, SD	S	9.58 MW	8.01 AW	19920 AAW	SDBLS	10//99-12//99
	Tennessee	S	7.51 MW	9.17 AW	19070 AAW	TNBLS	10//99-12//99
	Chattanooga MSA, TN-GA	S	8.46 MW	6.84 AW	17600 AAW	TNBLS	10//99-12//99
	Clarksville-Hopkinsville MSA, TN-KY	S	8.61 MW	7.11 AW	17910 AAW	TNBLS	10//99-12//99
	Jackson MSA, TN	S	8.69 MW	7.05 AW	18080 AAW	TNBLS	10//99-12//99
	Johnson City-Kingsport-Bristol MSA, TN-VA	S	8.11 MW	6.60 AW	16860 AAW	TNBLS	10//99-12//99
	Knoxville MSA, TN	S	9.37 MW	7.65 AW	19490 AAW	TNBLS	10//99-12//99
	Memphis MSA, TN-AR-MS	S	9.53 MW	7.67 AW	19830 AAW	MSBLS	10//99-12//99
	Nashville MSA, TN	S	9.95 MW	8.11 AW	20700 AAW	TNBLS	10//99-12//99
	Texas	S	7.5 MW	9.26 AW	19250 AAW	TXBLS	10//99-12//99
	Abilene MSA, TX	S	9.63 MW	7.51 AW	20030 AAW	TXBLS	10//99-12//99
	Amarillo MSA, TX	S	9.34 MW	7.05 AW	19430 AAW	TXBLS	10//99-12//99
	Austin-San Marcos MSA, TX	S	10.16 MW	8.04 AW	21130 AAW	TXBLS	10//99-12//99
	Beaumont-Port Arthur MSA, TX	S	8.70 MW	7.00 AW	18090 AAW	TXBLS	10//99-12//99
	Brazoria PMSA, TX	S	9.26 MW	6.83 AW	19250 AAW	TXBLS	10//99-12//99
	Brownsville-Harlingen-San Benito MSA, TX	S	7.92 MW	6.57 AW	16480 AAW	TXBLS	10//99-12//99

AAW Average annual wage	**AOH** Average offered, high	**ASH** Average starting, high	**H** Hourly	**M** Monthly	**S** Special: hourly and annual
AE Average entry wage	**AOL** Average offered, low	**ASL** Average starting, low	**HI** Highest wage paid	**MTC** Median total compensation	**TQ** Third quartile wage
AEX Average experienced wage	**APH** Average pay, high range	**AW** Average wage paid	**HR** High end range	**MW** Median wage paid	**W** Weekly
AO Average offered	**APL** Average pay, low range	**FQ** First quartile wage	**LR** Low end range	**SQ** Second quartile wage	**Y** Yearly

Occupation/Type/Industry	Location	Per	Low	Mid	High	Source	Date
Retail Salesperson	Bryan-College Station MSA, TX	S	7.85 mw	6.51 aw	16320 aaw	TXBLS	10//99-12//99
	Corpus Christi MSA, TX	S	8.87 mw	7.00 aw	18450 aaw	TXBLS	10//99-12//99
	Dallas PMSA, TX	S	10.34 mw	8.24 aw	21510 aaw	TXBLS	10//99-12//99
	El Paso MSA, TX	S	7.73 mw	6.69 aw	16080 aaw	TXBLS	10//99-12//99
	Fort Worth-Arlington PMSA, TX	S	9.61 mw	7.92 aw	19990 aaw	TXBLS	10//99-12//99
	Galveston-Texas City PMSA, TX	S	8.26 mw	6.70 aw	17170 aaw	TXBLS	10//99-12//99
	Houston PMSA, TX	S	9.42 mw	7.68 aw	19600 aaw	TXBLS	10//99-12//99
	Killeen-Temple MSA, TX	S	7.96 mw	6.57 aw	16550 aaw	TXBLS	10//99-12//99
	Laredo MSA, TX	S	7.39 mw	6.41 aw	15380 aaw	TXBLS	10//99-12//99
	Longview-Marshall MSA, TX	S	8.38 mw	6.69 aw	17440 aaw	TXBLS	10//99-12//99
	Lubbock MSA, TX	S	9.03 mw	7.06 aw	18790 aaw	TXBLS	10//99-12//99
	McAllen-Edinburg-Mission MSA, TX	S	7.92 mw	6.48 aw	16470 aaw	TXBLS	10//99-12//99
	Odessa-Midland MSA, TX	S	8.37 mw	6.83 aw	17420 aaw	TXBLS	10//99-12//99
	San Angelo MSA, TX	S	8.21 mw	6.59 aw	17070 aaw	TXBLS	10//99-12//99
	San Antonio MSA, TX	S	9.02 mw	7.47 aw	18770 aaw	TXBLS	10//99-12//99
	Sherman-Denison MSA, TX	S	8.72 mw	7.27 aw	18130 aaw	TXBLS	10//99-12//99
	Texarkana MSA, TX-Texarkana, AR	S	8.43 mw	6.77 aw	17520 aaw	TXBLS	10//99-12//99
	Tyler MSA, TX	S	8.46 mw	6.88 aw	17600 aaw	TXBLS	10//99-12//99
	Victoria MSA, TX	S	8.37 mw	7.13 aw	17410 aaw	TXBLS	10//99-12//99
	Waco MSA, TX	S	8.42 mw	7.26 aw	17520 aaw	TXBLS	10//99-12//99
	Wichita Falls MSA, TX	S	8.40 mw	6.58 aw	17460 aaw	TXBLS	10//99-12//99
	Utah	S	7.43 mw	8.93 aw	18570 aaw	UTBLS	10//99-12//99
	Provo-Orem MSA, UT	S	9.08 mw	7.44 aw	18890 aaw	UTBLS	10//99-12//99
	Salt Lake City-Ogden MSA, UT	S	9.07 mw	7.56 aw	18870 aaw	UTBLS	10//99-12//99
	Vermont	S	7.79 mw	8.91 aw	18530 aaw	VTBLS	10//99-12//99
	Burlington MSA, VT	S	8.85 mw	7.66 aw	18400 aaw	VTBLS	10//99-12//99
	Virginia	S	7.36 mw	8.51 aw	17700 aaw	VABLS	10//99-12//99
	Charlottesville MSA, VA	S	8.02 mw	7.39 aw	16680 aaw	VABLS	10//99-12//99
	Danville MSA, VA	S	7.85 mw	6.67 aw	16330 aaw	VABLS	10//99-12//99
	Lynchburg MSA, VA	S	7.73 mw	6.69 aw	16080 aaw	VABLS	10//99-12//99
	Norfolk-Virginia Beach-Newport News MSA, VA-NC	S	8.21 mw	7.04 aw	17070 aaw	VABLS	10//99-12//99
	Richmond-Petersburg MSA, VA	S	8.73 mw	7.63 aw	18160 aaw	VABLS	10//99-12//99
	Roanoke MSA, VA	S	8.58 mw	7.35 aw	17850 aaw	VABLS	10//99-12//99
	Washington	S	8.8 mw	10.53 aw	21900 aaw	WABLS	10//99-12//99
	Bellingham MSA, WA	S	9.66 mw	8.02 aw	20100 aaw	WABLS	10//99-12//99
	Bremerton PMSA, WA	S	9.76 mw	8.46 aw	20290 aaw	WABLS	10//99-12//99
	Olympia PMSA, WA	S	9.83 mw	8.34 aw	20460 aaw	WABLS	10//99-12//99
	Richland-Kennewick-Pasco MSA, WA	S	8.99 mw	7.60 aw	18700 aaw	WABLS	10//99-12//99
	Seattle-Bellevue-Everett PMSA, WA	S	11.04 mw	9.32 aw	22960 aaw	WABLS	10//99-12//99
	Spokane MSA, WA	S	10.09 mw	8.28 aw	21000 aaw	WABLS	10//99-12//99
	Tacoma PMSA, WA	S	11.11 mw	9.43 aw	23120 aaw	WABLS	10//99-12//99
	Yakima MSA, WA	S	9.73 mw	8.31 aw	20230 aaw	WABLS	10//99-12//99
	West Virginia	S	6.45 mw	7.66 aw	15940 aaw	WVBLS	10//99-12//99
	Charleston MSA, WV	S	7.64 mw	6.33 aw	15880 aaw	WVBLS	10//99-12//99
	Huntington-Ashland MSA, WV-KY-OH	S	7.55 mw	6.39 aw	15710 aaw	WVBLS	10//99-12//99
	Parkersburg-Marietta MSA, WV-OH	S	7.96 mw	6.80 aw	16570 aaw	WVBLS	10//99-12//99
	Wheeling MSA, WV-OH	S	7.60 mw	6.53 aw	15800 aaw	WVBLS	10//99-12//99
	Wisconsin	S	7.45 mw	8.86 aw	18430 aaw	WIBLS	10//99-12//99
	Appleton-Oshkosh-Neenah MSA, WI	S	9.04 mw	7.46 aw	18800 aaw	WIBLS	10//99-12//99
	Eau Claire MSA, WI	S	8.51 mw	6.98 aw	17690 aaw	WIBLS	10//99-12//99
	Green Bay MSA, WI	S	9.45 mw	7.95 aw	19660 aaw	WIBLS	10//99-12//99
	Janesville-Beloit MSA, WI	S	8.40 mw	7.37 aw	17470 aaw	WIBLS	10//99-12//99
	Kenosha PMSA, WI	S	8.58 mw	7.46 aw	17850 aaw	WIBLS	10//99-12//99
	La Crosse MSA, WI-MN	S	9.19 mw	7.02 aw	19120 aaw	WIBLS	10//99-12//99
	Madison MSA, WI	S	9.30 mw	7.87 aw	19340 aaw	WIBLS	10//99-12//99
	Milwaukee-Waukesha PMSA, WI	S	8.96 mw	7.46 aw	18640 aaw	WIBLS	10//99-12//99
	Racine PMSA, WI	S	8.35 mw	7.18 aw	17360 aaw	WIBLS	10//99-12//99

AAW Average annual wage; AE Average entry wage; AEX Average experienced wage; AO Average offered; AOH Average offered, high; AOL Average offered, low; APH Average pay, high range; APL Average pay, low range; ASH Average starting, high; ASL Average starting, low; AW Average wage paid; FQ First quartile wage; H Hourly; HI Highest wage paid; HR High end range; LR Low end range; M Monthly; MTC Median total compensation; MW Median wage paid; SQ Second quartile wage; S Special: hourly and annual; TQ Third quartile wage; W Weekly; Y Yearly

Occupation/Type/Industry	Location	Per	Low	Mid	High	Source	Date
Retail Salesperson	Sheboygan MSA, WI	S	9.60 MW	7.86 AW	19970 AAW	WIBLS	10//99-12//99
	Wausau MSA, WI	S	9.41 MW	7.49 AW	19580 AAW	WIBLS	10//99-12//99
	Wyoming	S	6.67 MW	7.87 AW	16360 AAW	WYBLS	10//99-12//99
	Casper MSA, WY	S	8.38 MW	6.52 AW	17430 AAW	WYBLS	10//99-12//99
	Cheyenne MSA, WY	S	8.32 MW	6.91 AW	17310 AAW	WYBLS	10//99-12//99
	Puerto Rico	S	6.08 MW	6.64 AW	13820 AAW	PRBLS	10//99-12//99
	Aguadilla MSA, PR	S	6.32 MW	6.05 AW	13140 AAW	PRBLS	10//99-12//99
	Arecibo PMSA, PR	S	6.31 MW	6.05 AW	13120 AAW	PRBLS	10//99-12//99
	Caguas PMSA, PR	S	6.98 MW	6.08 AW	14520 AAW	PRBLS	10//99-12//99
	Mayaguez MSA, PR	S	6.32 MW	6.07 AW	13150 AAW	PRBLS	10//99-12//99
	Ponce MSA, PR	S	6.21 MW	6.05 AW	12920 AAW	PRBLS	10//99-12//99
	San Juan-Bayamon PMSA, PR	S	6.78 MW	6.09 AW	14100 AAW	PRBLS	10//99-12//99
	Virgin Islands	S	7.52 MW	8.18 AW	17020 AAW	VIBLS	10//99-12//99
	Guam	S	6.55 MW	7.61 AW	15830 AAW	GUBLS	10//99-12//99
Rigger	Alabama	S	16.65 MW	17.15 AW	35680 AAW	ALBLS	10//99-12//99
	Arkansas	S	10.39 MW	10.55 AW	21950 AAW	ARBLS	10//99-12//99
	California	S	18.62 MW	18.04 AW	37530 AAW	CABLS	10//99-12//99
	Connecticut	S	14.79 MW	14.69 AW	30560 AAW	CTBLS	10//99-12//99
	Florida	S	9.88 MW	10.83 AW	22530 AAW	FLBLS	10//99-12//99
	Georgia	S	16.61 MW	16.04 AW	33360 AAW	GABLS	10//99-12//99
	Idaho	S	11.97 MW	13.69 AW	28470 AAW	IDBLS	10//99-12//99
	Illinois	S	16.79 MW	17.31 AW	36010 AAW	ILBLS	10//99-12//99
	Indiana	S	12.41 MW	12.87 AW	26770 AAW	INBLS	10//99-12//99
	Kentucky	S	18.65 MW	20.24 AW	42110 AAW	KYBLS	10//99-12//99
	Louisiana	S	11.2 MW	12.95 AW	26930 AAW	LABLS	10//99-12//99
	Maryland	S	15.23 MW	15.47 AW	32170 AAW	MDBLS	10//99-12//99
	Massachusetts	S	16.98 MW	16.95 AW	35250 AAW	MABLS	10//99-12//99
	Michigan	S	18.61 MW	17.82 AW	37060 AAW	MIBLS	10//99-12//99
	Minnesota	S	16.28 MW	19.02 AW	39550 AAW	MNBLS	10//99-12//99
	Nevada	S	11.83 MW	12.81 AW	26640 AAW	NVBLS	10//99-12//99
	New Jersey	S	14.65 MW	15.76 AW	32780 AAW	NJBLS	10//99-12//99
	North Carolina	S	13.28 MW	13.85 AW	28820 AAW	NCBLS	10//99-12//99
	Oklahoma	S	17.52 MW	16.47 AW	34250 AAW	OKBLS	10//99-12//99
	Pennsylvania	S	14.72 MW	14.76 AW	30710 AAW	PABLS	10//99-12//99
	Rhode Island	S	15.31 MW	15.71 AW	32670 AAW	RIBLS	10//99-12//99
	South Carolina	S	16.04 MW	19.02 AW	39570 AAW	SCBLS	10//99-12//99
	Tennessee	S	15.04 MW	14.47 AW	30100 AAW	TNBLS	10//99-12//99
	Texas	S	14.81 MW	15.05 AW	31310 AAW	TXBLS	10//99-12//99
	Virginia	S	15.38 MW	15.30 AW	31830 AAW	VABLS	10//99-12//99
	Washington	S	18.65 MW	18.43 AW	38330 AAW	WABLS	10//99-12//99
	Wisconsin	S	16.45 MW	18.20 AW	37850 AAW	WIBLS	10//99-12//99
	Puerto Rico	S	6.73 MW	7.67 AW	15960 AAW	PRBLS	10//99-12//99
Risk Manager Safety, Health, and Environment	United States	Y		66000 AW		SAFHE	1999
Rock Splitter							
Quarry	Arizona	S	11.86 MW	11.44 AW	23790 AAW	AZBLS	10//99-12//99
Quarry	California	S	12.8 MW	12.17 AW	25310 AAW	CABLS	10//99-12//99
Quarry	Colorado	S	12.95 MW	14.26 AW	29650 AAW	COBLS	10//99-12//99
Quarry	Georgia	S	12.47 MW	13.90 AW	28900 AAW	GABLS	10//99-12//99
Quarry	Illinois	S	13.53 MW	12.18 AW	25330 AAW	ILBLS	10//99-12//99
Quarry	Iowa	S	12.08 MW	11.98 AW	24910 AAW	IABLS	10//99-12//99
Quarry	Kansas	S	11.53 MW	11.31 AW	23520 AAW	KSBLS	10//99-12//99
Quarry	New Mexico	S	11.65 MW	11.85 AW	24640 AAW	NMBLS	10//99-12//99
Quarry	Oklahoma	S	28.1 MW	22.70 AW	47210 AAW	OKBLS	10//99-12//99
Quarry	Pennsylvania	S	9.11 MW	8.43 AW	17540 AAW	PABLS	10//99-12//99
Quarry	Tennessee	S	10.27 MW	10.45 AW	21740 AAW	TNBLS	10//99-12//99
Quarry	Texas	S	7.87 MW	7.96 AW	16560 AAW	TXBLS	10//99-12//99
Quarry	Utah	S	12.62 MW	13.16 AW	27370 AAW	UTBLS	10//99-12//99
Quarry	Vermont	S	10.01 MW	10.55 AW	21940 AAW	VTBLS	10//99-12//99
Quarry	Virginia	S	11.27 MW	13.40 AW	27870 AAW	VABLS	10//99-12//99
Quarry	Wisconsin	S	10.64 MW	11.58 AW	24080 AAW	WIBLS	10//99-12//99
Quarry	Puerto Rico	S	6 MW	6.59 AW	13700 AAW	PRBLS	10//99-12//99
Rolling Machine Setter, Operator, and Tender							
Metals and Plastics	Alabama	S	16.16 MW	16.56 AW	34450 AAW	ALBLS	10//99-12//99
Metals and Plastics	Birmingham MSA, AL	S	17.30 MW	17.50 AW	35990 AAW	ALBLS	10//99-12//99
Metals and Plastics	Arizona	S	10.48 MW	11.08 AW	23050 AAW	AZBLS	10//99-12//99
Metals and Plastics	Phoenix-Mesa MSA, AZ	S	11.32 MW	10.63 AW	23540 AAW	AZBLS	10//99-12//99
Metals and Plastics	Tucson MSA, AZ	S	10.25 MW	9.64 AW	21320 AAW	AZBLS	10//99-12//99

AAW	Average annual wage	AOH	Average offered, high	ASH	Average starting, high	H	Hourly	M	Monthly	S	Special: hourly and annual
AE	Average entry wage	AOL	Average offered, low	ASL	Average starting, low	HI	Highest wage paid	MTC	Median total compensation	TQ	Third quartile wage
AEX	Average experienced wage	APH	Average pay, high range	AW	Average wage paid	HR	High end range	MW	Median wage paid	W	Weekly
AO	Average offered	APL	Average pay, low range	FQ	First quartile wage	LR	Low end range	SQ	Second quartile wage	Y	Yearly

Occupation/Type/Industry	Location	Per	Low	Mid	High	Source	Date
Rolling Machine Setter, Operator, and Tender							
Metals and Plastics	Arkansas	S	11.53 MW	13.13 AW	27310 AAW	ARBLS	10//99-12//99
Metals and Plastics	California	S	10.1 MW	11.15 AW	23180 AAW	CABLS	10//99-12//99
Metals and Plastics	Los Angeles-Long Beach PMSA, CA	S	11.35 MW	10.91 AW	23610 AAW	CABLS	10//99-12//99
Metals and Plastics	Oakland PMSA, CA	S	8.93 MW	8.17 AW	18570 AAW	CABLS	10//99-12//99
Metals and Plastics	Orange County PMSA, CA	S	9.16 MW	8.57 AW	19060 AAW	CABLS	10//99-12//99
Metals and Plastics	Riverside-San Bernardino PMSA, CA	S	17.24 MW	18.33 AW	35860 AAW	CABLS	10//99-12//99
Metals and Plastics	San Diego MSA, CA	S	9.87 MW	8.95 AW	20520 AAW	CABLS	10//99-12//99
Metals and Plastics	Colorado	S	13.7 MW	12.88 AW	26790 AAW	COBLS	10//99-12//99
Metals and Plastics	Denver PMSA, CO	S	12.79 MW	13.35 AW	26600 AAW	COBLS	10//99-12//99
Metals and Plastics	Connecticut	S	15.38 MW	16.55 AW	34420 AAW	CTBLS	10//99-12//99
Metals and Plastics	Bridgeport PMSA, CT	S	11.93 MW	12.18 AW	24820 AAW	CTBLS	10//99-12//99
Metals and Plastics	Hartford MSA, CT	S	18.22 MW	16.88 AW	37890 AAW	CTBLS	10//99-12//99
Metals and Plastics	Florida	S	9.14 MW	9.60 AW	19960 AAW	FLBLS	10//99-12//99
Metals and Plastics	Fort Lauderdale PMSA, FL	S	8.93 MW	9.04 AW	18570 AAW	FLBLS	10//99-12//99
Metals and Plastics	Jacksonville MSA, FL	S	9.60 MW	9.36 AW	19970 AAW	FLBLS	10//99-12//99
Metals and Plastics	Lakeland-Winter Haven MSA, FL	S	10.23 MW	8.60 AW	21290 AAW	FLBLS	10//99-12//99
Metals and Plastics	Miami PMSA, FL	S	10.16 MW	9.99 AW	21140 AAW	FLBLS	10//99-12//99
Metals and Plastics	Orlando MSA, FL	S	10.19 MW	9.84 AW	21190 AAW	FLBLS	10//99-12//99
Metals and Plastics	Tampa-St. Petersburg-Clearwater MSA, FL	S	11.15 MW	9.97 AW	23200 AAW	FLBLS	10//99-12//99
Metals and Plastics	Georgia	S	13.7 MW	12.74 AW	26500 AAW	GABLS	10//99-12//99
Metals and Plastics	Atlanta MSA, GA	S	9.74 MW	8.97 AW	20250 AAW	GABLS	10//99-12//99
Metals and Plastics	Illinois	S	13.02 MW	13.08 AW	27200 AAW	ILBLS	10//99-12//99
Metals and Plastics	Chicago PMSA, IL	S	13.03 MW	12.93 AW	27110 AAW	ILBLS	10//99-12//99
Metals and Plastics	Indiana	S	10.44 MW	11.17 AW	23230 AAW	INBLS	10//99-12//99
Metals and Plastics	Fort Wayne MSA, IN	S	9.54 MW	9.47 AW	19850 AAW	INBLS	10//99-12//99
Metals and Plastics	Indianapolis MSA, IN	S	12.10 MW	11.18 AW	25170 AAW	INBLS	10//99-12//99
Metals and Plastics	Iowa	S	12.88 MW	12.77 AW	26570 AAW	IABLS	10//99-12//99
Metals and Plastics	Kentucky	S	18.71 MW	17.94 AW	37320 AAW	KYBLS	10//99-12//99
Metals and Plastics	Louisville MSA, KY-IN	S	15.28 MW	15.91 AW	31770 AAW	KYBLS	10//99-12//99
Metals and Plastics	Louisiana	S	15.39 MW	14.01 AW	29140 AAW	LABLS	10//99-12//99
Metals and Plastics	New Orleans MSA, LA	S	17.69 MW	18.38 AW	36800 AAW	LABLS	10//99-12//99
Metals and Plastics	Maryland	S	11.14 MW	11.04 AW	22960 AAW	MDBLS	10//99-12//99
Metals and Plastics	Baltimore PMSA, MD	S	11.23 MW	11.36 AW	23360 AAW	MDBLS	10//99-12//99
Metals and Plastics	Massachusetts	S	13.51 MW	13.24 AW	27550 AAW	MABLS	10//99-12//99
Metals and Plastics	Boston PMSA, MA-NH	S	14.23 MW	14.20 AW	29600 AAW	MABLS	10//99-12//99
Metals and Plastics	New Bedford PMSA, MA	S	13.98 MW	14.49 AW	29080 AAW	MABLS	10//99-12//99
Metals and Plastics	Worcester PMSA, MA-CT	S	13.86 MW	13.82 AW	28830 AAW	MABLS	10//99-12//99
Metals and Plastics	Michigan	S	10.26 MW	11.53 AW	23980 AAW	MIBLS	10//99-12//99
Metals and Plastics	Ann Arbor PMSA, MI	S	11.39 MW	10.79 AW	23700 AAW	MIBLS	10//99-12//99
Metals and Plastics	Detroit PMSA, MI	S	10.54 MW	9.86 AW	21930 AAW	MIBLS	10//99-12//99
Metals and Plastics	Grand Rapids-Muskegon-Holland MSA, MI	S	14.97 MW	13.28 AW	31140 AAW	MIBLS	10//99-12//99
Metals and Plastics	Minnesota	S	12.74 MW	13.51 AW	28100 AAW	MNBLS	10//99-12//99
Metals and Plastics	Minneapolis-St. Paul MSA, MN-WI	S	13.61 MW	12.83 AW	28320 AAW	MNBLS	10//99-12//99
Metals and Plastics	Mississippi	S	11.48 MW	10.88 AW	22620 AAW	MSBLS	10//99-12//99
Metals and Plastics	Missouri	S	15.48 MW	15.27 AW	31760 AAW	MOBLS	10//99-12//99
Metals and Plastics	St. Louis MSA, MO-IL	S	13.10 MW	13.26 AW	27250 AAW	MOBLS	10//99-12//99
Metals and Plastics	Nebraska	S	11.83 MW	11.97 AW	24890 AAW	NEBLS	10//99-12//99
Metals and Plastics	Nevada	S	10.26 MW	10.79 AW	22450 AAW	NVBLS	10//99-12//99
Metals and Plastics	Las Vegas MSA, NV-AZ	S	10.77 MW	10.22 AW	22410 AAW	NVBLS	10//99-12//99
Metals and Plastics	New Hampshire	S	9.14 MW	9.51 AW	19790 AAW	NHBLS	10//99-12//99
Metals and Plastics	New Jersey	S	15.97 MW	15.94 AW	33150 AAW	NJBLS	10//99-12//99
Metals and Plastics	Bergen-Passaic PMSA, NJ	S	12.13 MW	10.62 AW	25220 AAW	NJBLS	10//99-12//99
Metals and Plastics	Middlesex-Somerset-Hunterdon PMSA, NJ	S	16.73 MW	16.73 AW	34790 AAW	NJBLS	10//99-12//99
Metals and Plastics	Newark PMSA, NJ	S	17.89 MW	18.33 AW	37210 AAW	NJBLS	10//99-12//99
Metals and Plastics	New York	S	14.04 MW	13.74 AW	28580 AAW	NYBLS	10//99-12//99
Metals and Plastics	Buffalo-Niagara Falls MSA, NY	S	13.00 MW	13.80 AW	27050 AAW	NYBLS	10//99-12//99
Metals and Plastics	Nassau-Suffolk PMSA, NY	S	13.45 MW	14.30 AW	27970 AAW	NYBLS	10//99-12//99
Metals and Plastics	New York PMSA, NY	S	10.49 MW	10.41 AW	21810 AAW	NYBLS	10//99-12//99
Metals and Plastics	Syracuse MSA, NY	S	18.00 MW	18.59 AW	37430 AAW	NYBLS	10//99-12//99
Metals and Plastics	North Carolina	S	11.59 MW	12.61 AW	26230 AAW	NCBLS	10//99-12//99
Metals and Plastics	Charlotte-Gastonia-Rock Hill MSA, NC-SC	S	12.43 MW	11.66 AW	25860 AAW	NCBLS	10//99-12//99

Occupation/Type/Industry	Location	Per	Low	Mid	High	Source	Date
Rolling Machine Setter, Operator,							
and Tender							
Metals and Plastics	Greensboro--Winston-Salem--						
	High Point MSA, NC	S	14.49 MW	12.01 AW	30150 AAW	NCBLS	10//99-12//99
Metals and Plastics	Ohio	S	12.85 MW	12.73 AW	26480 AAW	OHBLS	10//99-12//99
Metals and Plastics	Akron PMSA, OH	S	12.89 MW	12.86 AW	26810 AAW	OHBLS	10//99-12//99
Metals and Plastics	Canton-Massillon MSA, OH	S	12.29 MW	12.38 AW	25560 AAW	OHBLS	10//99-12//99
Metals and Plastics	Cincinnati PMSA, OH-KY-IN	S	15.73 MW	16.74 AW	32710 AAW	OHBLS	10//99-12//99
Metals and Plastics	Cleveland-Lorain-Elyria						
	PMSA, OH	S	10.25 MW	9.96 AW	21310 AAW	OHBLS	10//99-12//99
Metals and Plastics	Columbus MSA, OH	S	12.44 MW	12.76 AW	25880 AAW	OHBLS	10//99-12//99
Metals and Plastics	Toledo MSA, OH	S	11.83 MW	10.69 AW	24600 AAW	OHBLS	10//99-12//99
Metals and Plastics	Youngstown-Warren MSA, OH	S	13.68 MW	14.28 AW	28450 AAW	OHBLS	10//99-12//99
Metals and Plastics	Oklahoma	S	7.85 MW	8.50 AW	17680 AAW	OKBLS	10//99-12//99
Metals and Plastics	Tulsa MSA, OK	S	8.27 MW	7.74 AW	17200 AAW	OKBLS	10//99-12//99
Metals and Plastics	Oregon	S	10.46 MW	14.69 AW	30560 AAW	ORBLS	10//99-12//99
Metals and Plastics	Portland-Vancouver PMSA,						
	OR-WA	S	14.71 MW	10.34 AW	30590 AAW	ORBLS	10//99-12//99
Metals and Plastics	Pennsylvania	S	15.29 MW	15.46 AW	32150 AAW	PABLS	10//99-12//99
Metals and Plastics	Lancaster MSA, PA	S	17.12 MW	17.23 AW	35600 AAW	PABLS	10//99-12//99
Metals and Plastics	Philadelphia PMSA, PA-NJ	S	14.88 MW	14.87 AW	30940 AAW	PABLS	10//99-12//99
Metals and Plastics	Pittsburgh MSA, PA	S	15.67 MW	15.16 AW	32590 AAW	PABLS	10//99-12//99
Metals and Plastics	Reading MSA, PA	S	18.55 MW	18.82 AW	38570 AAW	PABLS	10//99-12//99
Metals and Plastics	York MSA, PA	S	12.37 MW	12.31 AW	25740 AAW	PABLS	10//99-12//99
Metals and Plastics	Rhode Island	S	11.47 MW	11.55 AW	24020 AAW	RIBLS	10//99-12//99
Metals and Plastics	Providence-Fall River-						
	Warwick MSA, RI-MA	S	10.74 MW	10.26 AW	22340 AAW	RIBLS	10//99-12//99
Metals and Plastics	South Carolina	S	21.54 MW	17.76 AW	36940 AAW	SCBLS	10//99-12//99
Metals and Plastics	Greenville-Spartanburg-						
	Anderson MSA, SC	S	20.59 MW	23.57 AW	42830 AAW	SCBLS	10//99-12//99
Metals and Plastics	South Dakota	S	9.13 MW	9.24 AW	19220 AAW	SDBLS	10//99-12//99
Metals and Plastics	Sioux Falls MSA, SD	S	8.05 MW	7.83 AW	16740 AAW	SDBLS	10//99-12//99
Metals and Plastics	Tennessee	S	15.21 MW	14.94 AW	31080 AAW	TNBLS	10//99-12//99
Metals and Plastics	Chattanooga MSA, TN-GA	S	11.32 MW	11.61 AW	23550 AAW	TNBLS	10//99-12//99
Metals and Plastics	Memphis MSA, TN-AR-MS	S	16.50 MW	17.20 AW	34320 AAW	MSBLS	10//99-12//99
Metals and Plastics	Nashville MSA, TN	S	14.99 MW	15.27 AW	31180 AAW	TNBLS	10//99-12//99
Metals and Plastics	Texas	S	9 MW	9.54 AW	19850 AAW	TXBLS	10//99-12//99
Metals and Plastics	Austin-San Marcos MSA, TX	S	8.89 MW	8.77 AW	18490 AAW	TXBLS	10//99-12//99
Metals and Plastics	Dallas PMSA, TX	S	9.93 MW	8.86 AW	20660 AAW	TXBLS	10//99-12//99
Metals and Plastics	El Paso MSA, TX	S	8.26 MW	7.72 AW	17190 AAW	TXBLS	10//99-12//99
Metals and Plastics	Houston PMSA, TX	S	11.67 MW	9.93 AW	24270 AAW	TXBLS	10//99-12//99
Metals and Plastics	Waco MSA, TX	S	6.72 MW	6.44 AW	13980 AAW	TXBLS	10//99-12//99
Metals and Plastics	Utah	S	9.05 MW	9.83 AW	20440 AAW	UTBLS	10//99-12//99
Metals and Plastics	Salt Lake City-Ogden MSA,						
	UT	S	9.71 MW	8.47 AW	20210 AAW	UTBLS	10//99-12//99
Metals and Plastics	Virginia	S	12.39 MW	12.35 AW	25690 AAW	VABLS	10//99-12//99
Metals and Plastics	Washington	S	22.36 MW	20.27 AW	42160 AAW	WABLS	10//99-12//99
Metals and Plastics	Seattle-Bellevue-Everett						
	PMSA, WA	S	20.21 MW	22.47 AW	42030 AAW	WABLS	10//99-12//99
Metals and Plastics	Spokane MSA, WA	S	20.01 MW	22.08 AW	41630 AAW	WABLS	10//99-12//99
Metals and Plastics	Wisconsin	S	12.99 MW	12.80 AW	26630 AAW	WIBLS	10//99-12//99
Metals and Plastics	Green Bay MSA, WI	S	17.54 MW	17.63 AW	36490 AAW	WIBLS	10//99-12//99
Metals and Plastics	Milwaukee-Waukesha PMSA,						
	WI	S	15.49 MW	15.40 AW	32210 AAW	WIBLS	10//99-12//99
Metals and Plastics	Puerto Rico	S	7.68 MW	9.48 AW	19720 AAW	PRBLS	10//99-12//99
Metals and Plastics	San Juan-Bayamon PMSA, PR	S	9.36 MW	7.49 AW	19470 AAW	PRBLS	10//99-12//99
Roof Bolter							
Mining	Alabama	S	17.37 MW	16.96 AW	35290 AAW	ALBLS	10//99-12//99
Mining	Colorado	S	18.31 MW	17.14 AW	35650 AAW	COBLS	10//99-12//99
Mining	Illinois	S	18.57 MW	18.57 AW	38620 AAW	ILBLS	10//99-12//99
Mining	Indiana	S	16.04 MW	16.97 AW	35300 AAW	INBLS	10//99-12//99
Mining	Kentucky	S	14.01 MW	14.70 AW	30580 AAW	KYBLS	10//99-12//99
Mining	Pennsylvania	S	18.73 MW	18.77 AW	39050 AAW	PABLS	10//99-12//99
Mining	Tennessee	S	14.06 MW	14.63 AW	30420 AAW	TNBLS	10//99-12//99
Mining	Virginia	S	15.87 MW	16.53 AW	34390 AAW	VABLS	10//99-12//99
Mining	West Virginia	S	18.3 MW	20.75 AW	43160 AAW	WVBLS	10//99-12//99
Roofer							
	Alabama	S	10.41 MW	10.66 AW	22180 AAW	ALBLS	10//99-12//99
	Birmingham MSA, AL	S	11.63 MW	11.28 AW	24190 AAW	ALBLS	10//99-12//99
	Dothan MSA, AL	S	10.83 MW	11.51 AW	22540 AAW	ALBLS	10//99-12//99
	Florence MSA, AL	S	8.73 MW	9.35 AW	18150 AAW	ALBLS	10//99-12//99

AAW	Average annual wage	**AOH**	Average offered, high	**ASH**	Average starting, high	**H**	Hourly	
AE	Average entry wage	**AOL**	Average offered, low	**ASL**	Average starting, low	**HI**	Highest wage paid	
AEX	Average experienced wage	**APH**	Average pay, high range	**AW**	Average wage paid	**HR**	High end range	
AO	Average offered	**APL**	Average pay, low range	**FQ**	First quartile wage	**LR**	Low end range	

M	Monthly	**S**	Special: hourly and annual
MTC	Median total compensation	**TQ**	Third quartile wage
MW	Median wage paid	**W**	Weekly
SQ	Second quartile wage	**Y**	Yearly

Roofer

Occupation/Type/Industry	Location	Per	Low	Mid	High	Source	Date
Roofer	Huntsville MSA, AL	S	9.96 MW	9.91 AW	20720 AAW	ALBLS	10//99-12//99
	Mobile MSA, AL	S	11.24 MW	11.40 AW	23370 AAW	ALBLS	10//99-12//99
	Montgomery MSA, AL	S	10.52 MW	10.26 AW	21890 AAW	ALBLS	10//99-12//99
	Tuscaloosa MSA, AL	S	10.86 MW	10.87 AW	22590 AAW	ALBLS	10//99-12//99
	Alaska	S	18.85 MW	19.41 AW	40360 AAW	AKBLS	10//99-12//99
	Anchorage MSA, AK	S	19.03 MW	18.29 AW	39580 AAW	AKBLS	10//99-12//99
	Arizona	S	10.74 MW	11.37 AW	23650 AAW	AZBLS	10//99-12//99
	Phoenix-Mesa MSA, AZ	S	11.17 MW	10.25 AW	23220 AAW	AZBLS	10//99-12//99
	Tucson MSA, AZ	S	12.60 MW	11.99 AW	26210 AAW	AZBLS	10//99-12//99
	Yuma MSA, AZ	S	9.52 MW	9.48 AW	19800 AAW	AZBLS	10//99-12//99
	Arkansas	S	11.1 MW	11.34 AW	23580 AAW	ARBLS	10//99-12//99
	Little Rock-North Little Rock MSA, AR	S	12.88 MW	12.62 AW	26800 AAW	ARBLS	10//99-12//99
	California	S	14.03 MW	15.20 AW	31620 AAW	CABLS	10//99-12//99
	Bakersfield MSA, CA	S	12.68 MW	12.39 AW	26370 AAW	CABLS	10//99-12//99
	Chico-Paradise MSA, CA	S	12.73 MW	12.95 AW	26480 AAW	CABLS	10//99-12//99
	Fresno MSA, CA	S	16.24 MW	17.59 AW	33780 AAW	CABLS	10//99-12//99
	Los Angeles-Long Beach PMSA, CA	S	15.19 MW	14.38 AW	31600 AAW	CABLS	10//99-12//99
	Merced MSA, CA	S	12.04 MW	10.61 AW	25040 AAW	CABLS	10//99-12//99
	Modesto MSA, CA	S	11.30 MW	10.37 AW	23500 AAW	CABLS	10//99-12//99
	Oakland PMSA, CA	S	16.88 MW	16.50 AW	35110 AAW	CABLS	10//99-12//99
	Orange County PMSA, CA	S	14.82 MW	13.57 AW	30820 AAW	CABLS	10//99-12//99
	Redding MSA, CA	S	12.95 MW	12.77 AW	26940 AAW	CABLS	10//99-12//99
	Riverside-San Bernardino PMSA, CA	S	14.83 MW	13.55 AW	30850 AAW	CABLS	10//99-12//99
	Sacramento PMSA, CA	S	16.39 MW	17.24 AW	34080 AAW	CABLS	10//99-12//99
	Salinas MSA, CA	S	17.34 MW	17.49 AW	36080 AAW	CABLS	10//99-12//99
	San Diego MSA, CA	S	14.33 MW	13.12 AW	29800 AAW	CABLS	10//99-12//99
	San Francisco PMSA, CA	S	16.54 MW	15.60 AW	34410 AAW	CABLS	10//99-12//99
	San Jose PMSA, CA	S	18.22 MW	18.16 AW	37900 AAW	CABLS	10//99-12//99
	San Luis Obispo-Atascadero-Paso Robles MSA, CA	S	12.27 MW	11.62 AW	25530 AAW	CABLS	10//99-12//99
	Santa Barbara-Santa Maria-Lompoc MSA, CA	S	11.33 MW	11.28 AW	23570 AAW	CABLS	10//99-12//99
	Santa Cruz-Watsonville PMSA, CA	S	14.09 MW	13.84 AW	29310 AAW	CABLS	10//99-12//99
	Santa Rosa PMSA, CA	S	15.01 MW	14.01 AW	31230 AAW	CABLS	10//99-12//99
	Stockton-Lodi MSA, CA	S	13.21 MW	10.62 AW	27470 AAW	CABLS	10//99-12//99
	Vallejo-Fairfield-Napa PMSA, CA	S	13.92 MW	12.25 AW	28960 AAW	CABLS	10//99-12//99
	Ventura PMSA, CA	S	13.63 MW	13.32 AW	28350 AAW	CABLS	10//99-12//99
	Visalia-Tulare-Porterville MSA, CA	S	11.35 MW	10.62 AW	23610 AAW	CABLS	10//99-12//99
	Yolo PMSA, CA	S	16.56 MW	17.21 AW	34440 AAW	CABLS	10//99-12//99
	Yuba City MSA, CA	S	11.59 MW	10.70 AW	24100 AAW	CABLS	10//99-12//99
	Colorado	S	12.1 MW	12.39 AW	25780 AAW	COBLS	10//99-12//99
	Boulder-Longmont PMSA, CO	S	12.86 MW	12.61 AW	26740 AAW	COBLS	10//99-12//99
	Colorado Springs MSA, CO	S	12.69 MW	11.93 AW	26400 AAW	COBLS	10//99-12//99
	Denver PMSA, CO	S	12.20 MW	12.24 AW	25370 AAW	COBLS	10//99-12//99
	Pueblo MSA, CO	S	10.87 MW	10.82 AW	22600 AAW	COBLS	10//99-12//99
	Connecticut	S	18.48 MW	18.49 AW	38470 AAW	CTBLS	10//99-12//99
	Danbury PMSA, CT	S	16.63 MW	15.68 AW	34590 AAW	CTBLS	10//99-12//99
	Hartford MSA, CT	S	19.65 MW	21.57 AW	40870 AAW	CTBLS	10//99-12//99
	New Haven-Meriden PMSA, CT	S	17.11 MW	17.07 AW	35590 AAW	CTBLS	10//99-12//99
	Stamford-Norwalk PMSA, CT	S	18.31 MW	18.05 AW	38090 AAW	CTBLS	10//99-12//99
	Delaware	S	12.61 MW	12.78 AW	26590 AAW	DEBLS	10//99-12//99
	Wilmington-Newark PMSA, DE-MD	S	13.41 MW	13.18 AW	27890 AAW	DEBLS	10//99-12//99
	Washington PMSA, DC-MD-VA-WV	S	14.79 MW	14.36 AW	30760 AAW	DCBLS	10//99-12//99
	Florida	S	11.09 MW	11.54 AW	24010 AAW	FLBLS	10//99-12//99
	Daytona Beach MSA, FL	S	12.11 MW	11.55 AW	25190 AAW	FLBLS	10//99-12//99
	Fort Lauderdale PMSA, FL	S	12.56 MW	11.55 AW	26130 AAW	FLBLS	10//99-12//99
	Fort Myers-Cape Coral MSA, FL	S	11.37 MW	10.97 AW	23640 AAW	FLBLS	10//99-12//99
	Fort Pierce-Port St. Lucie MSA, FL	S	12.13 MW	11.53 AW	25220 AAW	FLBLS	10//99-12//99
	Gainesville MSA, FL	S	11.13 MW	11.28 AW	23140 AAW	FLBLS	10//99-12//99
	Jacksonville MSA, FL	S	13.17 MW	12.08 AW	27390 AAW	FLBLS	10//99-12//99

AAW Average annual wage	AOH Average offered, high	ASH Average starting, high	H Hourly	M Monthly	S Special: hourly and annual
AE Average entry wage	AOL Average offered, low	ASL Average starting, low	HI Highest wage paid	MTC Median total compensation	TQ Third quartile wage
AEX Average experienced wage	APH Average pay, high range	AW Average wage paid	HR High end range	MW Median wage paid	W Weekly
AO Average offered	APL Average pay, low range	FQ First quartile wage	LR Low end range	SQ Second quartile wage	Y Yearly

Occupation/Type/Industry	Location	Per	Low	Mid	High	Source	Date
Roofer	Lakeland-Winter Haven MSA, FL	S	10.38 MW	10.19 AW	21580 AAW	FLBLS	10//99-12//99
	Melbourne-Titusville-Palm Bay MSA, FL	S	10.64 MW	9.99 AW	22120 AAW	FLBLS	10//99-12//99
	Miami PMSA, FL	S	11.97 MW	12.04 AW	24890 AAW	FLBLS	10//99-12//99
	Naples MSA, FL	S	12.19 MW	11.63 AW	25350 AAW	FLBLS	10//99-12//99
	Ocala MSA, FL	S	10.50 MW	10.52 AW	21850 AAW	FLBLS	10//99-12//99
	Orlando MSA, FL	S	12.14 MW	11.42 AW	25260 AAW	FLBLS	10//99-12//99
	Panama City MSA, FL	S	12.03 MW	10.87 AW	25030 AAW	FLBLS	10//99-12//99
	Sarasota-Bradenton MSA, FL	S	12.15 MW	10.46 AW	25260 AAW	FLBLS	10//99-12//99
	Tallahassee MSA, FL	S	10.95 MW	10.13 AW	22780 AAW	FLBLS	10//99-12//99
	Tampa-St. Petersburg-Clearwater MSA, FL	S	10.32 MW	10.46 AW	21470 AAW	FLBLS	10//99-12//99
	West Palm Beach-Boca Raton MSA, FL	S	11.33 MW	11.14 AW	23560 AAW	FLBLS	10//99-12//99
	Georgia	S	12.12 MW	12.06 AW	25090 AAW	GABLS	10//99-12//99
	Albany MSA, GA	S	10.72 MW	10.82 AW	22290 AAW	GABLS	10//99-12//99
	Atlanta MSA, GA	S	12.78 MW	12.67 AW	26580 AAW	GABLS	10//99-12//99
	Augusta-Aiken MSA, GA-SC	S	11.74 MW	11.84 AW	24430 AAW	GABLS	10//99-12//99
	Cobb County, GA	Y		28080 AW		ATJOCO	1998
	Savannah MSA, GA	S	10.69 MW	10.10 AW	22220 AAW	GABLS	10//99-12//99
	Hawaii	S	15.67 MW	16.36 AW	34020 AAW	HIBLS	10//99-12//99
	Honolulu MSA, HI	S	15.61 MW	14.40 AW	32470 AAW	HIBLS	10//99-12//99
	Idaho	S	11.45 MW	12.15 AW	25270 AAW	IDBLS	10//99-12//99
	Boise City MSA, ID	S	11.80 MW	11.27 AW	24540 AAW	IDBLS	10//99-12//99
	Illinois	S	17.07 MW	19.64 AW	40850 AAW	ILBLS	10//99-12//99
	Champaign-Urbana MSA, IL	S	19.55 MW	22.16 AW	40660 AAW	ILBLS	10//99-12//99
	Chicago PMSA, IL	S	20.58 MW	16.85 AW	42800 AAW	ILBLS	10//99-12//99
	Decatur MSA, IL	S	19.96 MW	18.75 AW	41510 AAW	ILBLS	10//99-12//99
	Peoria-Pekin MSA, IL	S	19.90 MW	19.12 AW	41400 AAW	ILBLS	10//99-12//99
	Rockford MSA, IL	S	16.95 MW	16.04 AW	35260 AAW	ILBLS	10//99-12//99
	Springfield MSA, IL	S	19.70 MW	19.30 AW	40990 AAW	ILBLS	10//99-12//99
	Indiana	S	13.9 MW	14.99 AW	31180 AAW	INBLS	10//99-12//99
	Bloomington MSA, IN	S	11.44 MW	11.25 AW	23790 AAW	INBLS	10//99-12//99
	Elkhart-Goshen MSA, IN	S	11.41 MW	10.18 AW	23740 AAW	INBLS	10//99-12//99
	Evansville-Henderson MSA, IN-KY	S	13.14 MW	12.21 AW	27340 AAW	INBLS	10//99-12//99
	Fort Wayne MSA, IN	S	14.29 MW	13.52 AW	29730 AAW	INBLS	10//99-12//99
	Gary PMSA, IN	S	20.34 MW	20.66 AW	42310 AAW	INBLS	10//99-12//99
	Indianapolis MSA, IN	S	14.18 MW	13.49 AW	29490 AAW	INBLS	10//99-12//99
	Kokomo MSA, IN	S	13.61 MW	12.55 AW	28320 AAW	INBLS	10//99-12//99
	Lafayette MSA, IN	S	14.37 MW	14.73 AW	29890 AAW	INBLS	10//99-12//99
	Terre Haute MSA, IN	S	14.68 MW	14.07 AW	30530 AAW	INBLS	10//99-12//99
	Iowa	S	11.47 MW	12.37 AW	25730 AAW	IABLS	10//99-12//99
	Cedar Rapids MSA, IA	S	12.83 MW	12.41 AW	26680 AAW	IABLS	10//99-12//99
	Davenport-Moline-Rock Island MSA, IA-IL	S	17.27 MW	18.05 AW	35920 AAW	IABLS	10//99-12//99
	Des Moines MSA, IA	S	12.80 MW	12.44 AW	26620 AAW	IABLS	10//99-12//99
	Dubuque MSA, IA	S	14.06 MW	14.32 AW	29240 AAW	IABLS	10//99-12//99
	Sioux City MSA, IA-NE	S	13.19 MW	13.45 AW	27430 AAW	IABLS	10//99-12//99
	Waterloo-Cedar Falls MSA, IA	S	10.91 MW	10.90 AW	22690 AAW	IABLS	10//99-12//99
	Kansas	S	11.35 MW	12.32 AW	25630 AAW	KSBLS	10//99-12//99
	Lawrence MSA, KS	S	11.94 MW	11.67 AW	24840 AAW	KSBLS	10//99-12//99
	Topeka MSA, KS	S	12.34 MW	11.17 AW	25670 AAW	KSBLS	10//99-12//99
	Wichita MSA, KS	S	12.87 MW	12.22 AW	26770 AAW	KSBLS	10//99-12//99
	Kentucky	S	12.24 MW	12.68 AW	26370 AAW	KYBLS	10//99-12//99
	Lexington MSA, KY	S	11.32 MW	11.64 AW	23540 AAW	KYBLS	10//99-12//99
	Louisville MSA, KY-IN	S	13.85 MW	13.63 AW	28810 AAW	KYBLS	10//99-12//99
	Louisiana	S	11.04 MW	11.54 AW	23990 AAW	LABLS	10//99-12//99
	Baton Rouge MSA, LA	S	13.73 MW	14.52 AW	28560 AAW	LABLS	10//99-12//99
	Lafayette MSA, LA	S	11.47 MW	11.25 AW	23860 AAW	LABLS	10//99-12//99
	Monroe MSA, LA	S	8.80 MW	8.84 AW	18310 AAW	LABLS	10//99-12//99
	New Orleans MSA, LA	S	11.41 MW	10.97 AW	23730 AAW	LABLS	10//99-12//99
	Shreveport-Bossier City MSA, LA	S	11.15 MW	11.22 AW	23200 AAW	LABLS	10//99-12//99
	Maine	S	9.65 MW	9.68 AW	20140 AAW	MEBLS	10//99-12//99
	Portland MSA, ME	S	11.40 MW	10.72 AW	23720 AAW	MEBLS	10//99-12//99
	Maryland	S	12.63 MW	12.86 AW	26750 AAW	MDBLS	10//99-12//99
	Baltimore PMSA, MD	S	12.69 MW	13.20 AW	26390 AAW	MDBLS	10//99-12//99
	Hagerstown PMSA, MD	S	10.40 MW	10.67 AW	21630 AAW	MDBLS	10//99-12//99
	Massachusetts	S	18.11 MW	17.81 AW	37040 AAW	MABLS	10//99-12//99
	Boston PMSA, MA-NH	S	19.52 MW	20.94 AW	40590 AAW	MABLS	10//99-12//99

AAW Average annual wage	**AOH** Average offered, high	**ASH** Average starting, high	**H** Hourly	**M** Monthly	**S** Special: hourly and annual
AE Average entry wage	**AOL** Average offered, low	**ASL** Average starting, low	**HI** Highest wage paid	**MTC** Median total compensation	**TQ** Third quartile wage
AEX Average experienced wage	**APH** Average pay, high range	**AW** Average wage paid	**HR** High end range	**MW** Median wage paid	**W** Weekly
AO Average offered	**APL** Average pay, low range	**FQ** First quartile wage	**LR** Low end range	**SQ** Second quartile wage	**Y** Yearly

Occupation/Type/Industry	Location	Per	Low	Mid	High	Source	Date
Roofer	Brockton PMSA, MA	S	15.48 MW	14.96 AW	32190 AAW	MABLS	10//99-12//99
	Lawrence PMSA, MA-NH	S	13.54 MW	13.12 AW	28170 AAW	MABLS	10//99-12//99
	Lowell PMSA, MA-NH	S	15.13 MW	15.43 AW	31480 AAW	MABLS	10//99-12//99
	Worcester PMSA, MA-CT	S	15.58 MW	15.30 AW	32400 AAW	MABLS	10//99-12//99
	Michigan	S	13.22 MW	14.87 AW	30920 AAW	MIBLS	10//99-12//99
	Ann Arbor PMSA, MI	S	17.34 MW	18.49 AW	36070 AAW	MIBLS	10//99-12//99
	Benton Harbor MSA, MI	S	11.87 MW	10.60 AW	24700 AAW	MIBLS	10//99-12//99
	Detroit PMSA, MI	S	17.44 MW	18.49 AW	36270 AAW	MIBLS	10//99-12//99
	Grand Rapids-Muskegon-Holland MSA, MI	S	13.02 MW	10.25 AW	27080 AAW	MIBLS	10//99-12//99
	Kalamazoo-Battle Creek MSA, MI	S	10.84 MW	10.28 AW	22550 AAW	MIBLS	10//99-12//99
	Lansing-East Lansing MSA, MI	S	11.83 MW	11.03 AW	24610 AAW	MIBLS	10//99-12//99
	Saginaw-Bay City-Midland MSA, MI	S	11.62 MW	9.96 AW	24160 AAW	MIBLS	10//99-12//99
	Minnesota	S	14.7 MW	16.46 AW	34240 AAW	MNBLS	10//99-12//99
	Duluth-Superior MSA, MN-WI	S	16.94 MW	17.65 AW	35230 AAW	MNBLS	10//99-12//99
	Minneapolis-St. Paul MSA, MN-WI	S	17.85 MW	16.51 AW	37120 AAW	MNBLS	10//99-12//99
	Rochester MSA, MN	S	15.09 MW	14.77 AW	31390 AAW	MNBLS	10//99-12//99
	St. Cloud MSA, MN	S	15.87 MW	14.91 AW	33000 AAW	MNBLS	10//99-12//99
	Mississippi	S	10.04 MW	10.45 AW	21730 AAW	MSBLS	10//99-12//99
	Hattiesburg MSA, MS	S	10.76 MW	10.60 AW	22380 AAW	MSBLS	10//99-12//99
	Jackson MSA, MS	S	11.15 MW	11.41 AW	23190 AAW	MSBLS	10//99-12//99
	Missouri	S	15.84 MW	15.78 AW	32820 AAW	MOBLS	10//99-12//99
	Joplin MSA, MO	S	11.81 MW	12.03 AW	24560 AAW	MOBLS	10//99-12//99
	Kansas City MSA, MO-KS	S	17.61 MW	18.49 AW	36640 AAW	MOBLS	10//99-12//99
	St. Louis MSA, MO-IL	S	17.18 MW	18.17 AW	35730 AAW	MOBLS	10//99-12//99
	Montana	S	11.36 MW	11.12 AW	23130 AAW	MTBLS	10//99-12//99
	Billings MSA, MT	S	12.16 MW	12.38 AW	25290 AAW	MTBLS	10//99-12//99
	Nebraska	S	10.67 MW	10.96 AW	22790 AAW	NEBLS	10//99-12//99
	Lincoln MSA, NE	S	11.33 MW	11.36 AW	23560 AAW	NEBLS	10//99-12//99
	Omaha MSA, NE-IA	S	11.49 MW	11.08 AW	23890 AAW	NEBLS	10//99-12//99
	Nevada	S	16.2 MW	17.45 AW	36300 AAW	NVBLS	10//99-12//99
	Las Vegas MSA, NV-AZ	S	17.37 MW	15.90 AW	36130 AAW	NVBLS	10//99-12//99
	Reno MSA, NV	S	16.61 MW	16.55 AW	34540 AAW	NVBLS	10//99-12//99
	New Hampshire	S	13.99 MW	14.26 AW	29650 AAW	NHBLS	10//99-12//99
	Portsmouth-Rochester PMSA, NH-ME	S	11.74 MW	12.14 AW	24410 AAW	NHBLS	10//99-12//99
	New Jersey	S	16.87 MW	18.66 AW	38810 AAW	NJBLS	10//99-12//99
	Atlantic-Cape May PMSA, NJ	S	20.26 MW	18.28 AW	42140 AAW	NJBLS	10//99-12//99
	Bergen-Passaic PMSA, NJ	S	18.70 MW	19.08 AW	38890 AAW	NJBLS	10//99-12//99
	Jersey City PMSA, NJ	S	23.54 MW	24.42 AW	48960 AAW	NJBLS	10//99-12//99
	Middlesex-Somerset-Hunterdon PMSA, NJ	S	18.11 MW	16.24 AW	37680 AAW	NJBLS	10//99-12//99
	Newark PMSA, NJ	S	16.70 MW	14.14 AW	34730 AAW	NJBLS	10//99-12//99
	New Mexico	S	10.26 MW	10.78 AW	22420 AAW	NMBLS	10//99-12//99
	Albuquerque MSA, NM	S	11.31 MW	10.73 AW	23530 AAW	NMBLS	10//99-12//99
	Las Cruces MSA, NM	S	9.70 MW	9.23 AW	20180 AAW	NMBLS	10//99-12//99
	Santa Fe MSA, NM	S	12.50 MW	11.63 AW	26000 AAW	NMBLS	10//99-12//99
	New York	S	17.72 MW	18.97 AW	39450 AAW	NYBLS	10//99-12//99
	Albany-Schenectady-Troy MSA, NY	S	14.53 MW	13.62 AW	30220 AAW	NYBLS	10//99-12//99
	Buffalo-Niagara Falls MSA, NY	S	16.65 MW	16.01 AW	34640 AAW	NYBLS	10//99-12//99
	Dutchess County PMSA, NY	S	13.77 MW	13.91 AW	28640 AAW	NYBLS	10//99-12//99
	Glens Falls MSA, NY	S	15.63 MW	16.89 AW	32500 AAW	NYBLS	10//99-12//99
	Nassau-Suffolk PMSA, NY	S	24.40 MW	26.00 AW	50740 AAW	NYBLS	10//99-12//99
	New York PMSA, NY	S	21.47 MW	21.68 AW	44670 AAW	NYBLS	10//99-12//99
	Rochester MSA, NY	S	15.35 MW	14.76 AW	31920 AAW	NYBLS	10//99-12//99
	Syracuse MSA, NY	S	16.72 MW	17.53 AW	34770 AAW	NYBLS	10//99-12//99
	Utica-Rome MSA, NY	S	13.82 MW	12.88 AW	28750 AAW	NYBLS	10//99-12//99
	North Carolina	S	9.98 MW	10.25 AW	21320 AAW	NCBLS	10//99-12//99
	Asheville MSA, NC	S	10.21 MW	10.24 AW	21230 AAW	NCBLS	10//99-12//99
	Charlotte-Gastonia-Rock Hill MSA, NC-SC	S	11.11 MW	10.94 AW	23100 AAW	NCBLS	10//99-12//99
	Fayetteville MSA, NC	S	12.12 MW	11.70 AW	25210 AAW	NCBLS	10//99-12//99
	Greensboro--Winston-Salem--High Point MSA, NC	S	11.11 MW	10.54 AW	23120 AAW	NCBLS	10//99-12//99
	Greenville MSA, NC	S	10.21 MW	10.02 AW	21230 AAW	NCBLS	10//99-12//99
	Hickory-Morganton-Lenoir MSA, NC	S	10.24 MW	9.97 AW	21300 AAW	NCBLS	10//99-12//99

Occupation/Type/Industry	Location	Per	Low	Mid	High	Source	Date
Roofer	Jacksonville MSA, NC	S	9.88 MW	9.48 AW	20560 AAW	NCBLS	10//99-12//99
	Raleigh-Durham-Chapel Hill MSA, NC	S	11.22 MW	11.23 AW	23330 AAW	NCBLS	10//99-12//99
	Wilmington MSA, NC	S	10.98 MW	10.47 AW	22840 AAW	NCBLS	10//99-12//99
	North Dakota	S	10.91 MW	11.53 AW	23970 AAW	NDBLS	10//99-12//99
	Bismarck MSA, ND	S	11.08 MW	11.41 AW	23040 AAW	NDBLS	10//99-12//99
	Fargo-Moorhead MSA, ND-MN	S	10.97 MW	10.21 AW	22810 AAW	NDBLS	10//99-12//99
	Ohio	S	13.42 MW	14.83 AW	30840 AAW	OHBLS	10//99-12//99
	Akron PMSA, OH	S	13.58 MW	12.52 AW	28260 AAW	OHBLS	10//99-12//99
	Canton-Massillon MSA, OH	S	17.22 MW	18.20 AW	35830 AAW	OHBLS	10//99-12//99
	Cincinnati PMSA, OH-KY-IN	S	16.12 MW	14.00 AW	33520 AAW	OHBLS	10//99-12//99
	Cleveland-Lorain-Elyria PMSA, OH	S	15.44 MW	13.83 AW	32120 AAW	OHBLS	10//99-12//99
	Columbus MSA, OH	S	12.73 MW	11.75 AW	26480 AAW	OHBLS	10//99-12//99
	Dayton-Springfield MSA, OH	S	14.42 MW	13.81 AW	29990 AAW	OHBLS	10//99-12//99
	Hamilton-Middletown PMSA, OH	S	17.41 MW	18.11 AW	36220 AAW	OHBLS	10//99-12//99
	Lima MSA, OH	S	13.36 MW	13.68 AW	27790 AAW	OHBLS	10//99-12//99
	Mansfield MSA, OH	S	13.05 MW	12.83 AW	27140 AAW	OHBLS	10//99-12//99
	Toledo MSA, OH	S	18.89 MW	20.99 AW	39290 AAW	OHBLS	10//99-12//99
	Youngstown-Warren MSA, OH	S	13.85 MW	12.57 AW	28800 AAW	OHBLS	10//99-12//99
	Oklahoma	S	11.37 MW	11.76 AW	24460 AAW	OKBLS	10//99-12//99
	Oklahoma City MSA, OK	S	12.35 MW	12.22 AW	25690 AAW	OKBLS	10//99-12//99
	Tulsa MSA, OK	S	11.28 MW	11.56 AW	23460 AAW	OKBLS	10//99-12//99
	Oregon	S	14.97 MW	16.20 AW	33700 AAW	ORBLS	10//99-12//99
	Eugene-Springfield MSA, OR	S	13.54 MW	12.42 AW	28160 AAW	ORBLS	10//99-12//99
	Medford-Ashland MSA, OR	S	12.15 MW	11.47 AW	25280 AAW	ORBLS	10//99-12//99
	Portland-Vancouver PMSA, OR-WA	S	18.19 MW	18.11 AW	37830 AAW	ORBLS	10//99-12//99
	Salem PMSA, OR	S	15.28 MW	13.50 AW	31780 AAW	ORBLS	10//99-12//99
	Pennsylvania	S	14.49 MW	15.07 AW	31340 AAW	PABLS	10//99-12//99
	Allentown-Bethlehem-Easton MSA, PA	S	11.57 MW	8.93 AW	24070 AAW	PABLS	10//99-12//99
	Altoona MSA, PA	S	12.65 MW	11.89 AW	26320 AAW	PABLS	10//99-12//99
	Erie MSA, PA	S	15.09 MW	15.80 AW	31390 AAW	PABLS	10//99-12//99
	Harrisburg-Lebanon-Carlisle MSA, PA	S	14.51 MW	14.07 AW	30180 AAW	PABLS	10//99-12//99
	Lancaster MSA, PA	S	14.01 MW	14.85 AW	29140 AAW	PABLS	10//99-12//99
	Philadelphia PMSA, PA-NJ	S	18.36 MW	17.83 AW	38190 AAW	PABLS	10//99-12//99
	Pittsburgh MSA, PA	S	16.34 MW	15.77 AW	33980 AAW	PABLS	10//99-12//99
	Reading MSA, PA	S	18.26 MW	16.69 AW	37990 AAW	PABLS	10//99-12//99
	Scranton--Wilkes-Barre--Hazleton MSA, PA	S	12.56 MW	11.24 AW	26120 AAW	PABLS	10//99-12//99
	Williamsport MSA, PA	S	13.09 MW	12.79 AW	27240 AAW	PABLS	10//99-12//99
	York MSA, PA	S	13.40 MW	12.59 AW	27870 AAW	PABLS	10//99-12//99
	Rhode Island	S	13.75 MW	13.54 AW	28170 AAW	RIBLS	10//99-12//99
	Providence-Fall River-Warwick MSA, RI-MA	S	14.00 MW	14.01 AW	29120 AAW	RIBLS	10//99-12//99
	South Carolina	S	10.39 MW	10.15 AW	21120 AAW	SCBLS	10//99-12//99
	Charleston-North Charleston MSA, SC	S	10.66 MW	10.80 AW	22170 AAW	SCBLS	10//99-12//99
	Columbia MSA, SC	S	10.91 MW	10.84 AW	22690 AAW	SCBLS	10//99-12//99
	Greenville-Spartanburg-Anderson MSA, SC	S	9.98 MW	10.57 AW	20750 AAW	SCBLS	10//99-12//99
	Myrtle Beach MSA, SC	S	10.13 MW	10.48 AW	21080 AAW	SCBLS	10//99-12//99
	South Dakota	S	9.88 MW	10.05 AW	20900 AAW	SDBLS	10//99-12//99
	Sioux Falls MSA, SD	S	10.97 MW	10.53 AW	22810 AAW	SDBLS	10//99-12//99
	Tennessee	S	11.9 MW	11.94 AW	24840 AAW	TNBLS	10//99-12//99
	Chattanooga MSA, TN-GA	S	13.16 MW	12.88 AW	27380 AAW	TNBLS	10//99-12//99
	Johnson City-Kingsport-Bristol MSA, TN-VA	S	11.03 MW	10.78 AW	22940 AAW	TNBLS	10//99-12//99
	Knoxville MSA, TN	S	11.80 MW	12.04 AW	24550 AAW	TNBLS	10//99-12//99
	Memphis MSA, TN-AR-MS	S	12.11 MW	12.58 AW	25180 AAW	MSBLS	10//99-12//99
	Nashville MSA, TN	S	12.76 MW	12.30 AW	26540 AAW	TNBLS	10//99-12//99
	Texas	S	11.01 MW	11.38 AW	23680 AAW	TXBLS	10//99-12//99
	Austin-San Marcos MSA, TX	S	12.36 MW	12.38 AW	25710 AAW	TXBLS	10//99-12//99
	Beaumont-Port Arthur MSA, TX	S	11.58 MW	11.54 AW	24090 AAW	TXBLS	10//99-12//99
	Brownsville-Harlingen-San Benito MSA, TX	S	8.39 MW	8.19 AW	17450 AAW	TXBLS	10//99-12//99
	Corpus Christi MSA, TX	S	9.28 MW	8.94 AW	19310 AAW	TXBLS	10//99-12//99

AAW Average annual wage	AOH Average offered, high	ASH Average starting, high	H Hourly	M Monthly	S Special: hourly and annual
AE Average entry wage	AOL Average offered, low	ASL Average starting, low	HI Highest wage paid	MTC Median total compensation	TQ Third quartile wage
AEX Average experienced wage APH Average pay, high range	AW Average wage paid	HR High end range	MW Median wage paid	W Weekly
AO Average offered	APL Average pay, low range	FQ First quartile wage	LR Low end range	SQ Second quartile wage	Y Yearly

Occupation/Type/Industry	Location	Per	Low	Mid	High	Source	Date
Roofer	Dallas PMSA, TX	S	13.46 MW	13.95 AW	28000 AAW	TXBLS	10//99-12//99
	El Paso MSA, TX	S	7.80 MW	7.79 AW	16220 AAW	TXBLS	10//99-12//99
	Fort Worth-Arlington PMSA, TX	S	11.14 MW	11.05 AW	23160 AAW	TXBLS	10//99-12//99
	Galveston-Texas City PMSA, TX	S	9.13 MW	9.00 AW	18990 AAW	TXBLS	10//99-12//99
	Houston PMSA, TX	S	12.89 MW	12.55 AW	26810 AAW	TXBLS	10//99-12//99
	Lubbock MSA, TX	S	11.17 MW	10.66 AW	23240 AAW	TXBLS	10//99-12//99
	McAllen-Edinburg-Mission MSA, TX	S	7.51 MW	7.49 AW	15620 AAW	TXBLS	10//99-12//99
	Odessa-Midland MSA, TX	S	8.40 MW	8.13 AW	17470 AAW	TXBLS	10//99-12//99
	San Antonio MSA, TX	S	9.92 MW	10.12 AW	20620 AAW	TXBLS	10//99-12//99
	Sherman-Denison MSA, TX	S	10.22 MW	8.32 AW	21270 AAW	TXBLS	10//99-12//99
	Tyler MSA, TX	S	10.06 MW	9.88 AW	20930 AAW	TXBLS	10//99-12//99
	Waco MSA, TX	S	11.01 MW	11.25 AW	22900 AAW	TXBLS	10//99-12//99
	Utah	S	12.67 MW	12.81 AW	26640 AAW	UTBLS	10//99-12//99
	Provo-Orem MSA, UT	S	12.70 MW	11.27 AW	26420 AAW	UTBLS	10//99-12//99
	Salt Lake City-Ogden MSA, UT	S	12.77 MW	12.71 AW	26560 AAW	UTBLS	10//99-12//99
	Vermont	S	10.51 MW	11.06 AW	23010 AAW	VTBLS	10//99-12//99
	Burlington MSA, VT	S	11.71 MW	11.28 AW	24350 AAW	VTBLS	10//99-12//99
	Virginia	S	12.22 MW	12.89 AW	26800 AAW	VABLS	10//99-12//99
	Charlottesville MSA, VA	S	11.84 MW	11.64 AW	24620 AAW	VABLS	10//99-12//99
	Danville MSA, VA	S	10.49 MW	10.19 AW	21830 AAW	VABLS	10//99-12//99
	Lynchburg MSA, VA	S	10.23 MW	9.99 AW	21270 AAW	VABLS	10//99-12//99
	Norfolk-Virginia Beach-Newport News MSA, VA-NC	S	13.18 MW	11.74 AW	27410 AAW	VABLS	10//99-12//99
	Richmond-Petersburg MSA, VA	S	12.61 MW	12.54 AW	26230 AAW	VABLS	10//99-12//99
	Roanoke MSA, VA	S	10.70 MW	10.72 AW	22260 AAW	VABLS	10//99-12//99
	Washington	S	16.61 MW	16.89 AW	35130 AAW	WABLS	10//99-12//99
	Bellingham MSA, WA	S	14.39 MW	13.71 AW	29940 AAW	WABLS	10//99-12//99
	Bremerton PMSA, WA	S	14.86 MW	15.06 AW	30910 AAW	WABLS	10//99-12//99
	Seattle-Bellevue-Everett PMSA, WA	S	17.50 MW	17.59 AW	36410 AAW	WABLS	10//99-12//99
	Spokane MSA, WA	S	17.49 MW	16.56 AW	36390 AAW	WABLS	10//99-12//99
	Tacoma PMSA, WA	S	17.18 MW	17.35 AW	35730 AAW	WABLS	10//99-12//99
	Yakima MSA, WA	S	15.20 MW	16.55 AW	31610 AAW	WABLS	10//99-12//99
	West Virginia	S	10.57 MW	11.90 AW	24750 AAW	WVBLS	10//99-12//99
	Charleston MSA, WV	S	13.74 MW	11.58 AW	28580 AAW	WVBLS	10//99-12//99
	Huntington-Ashland MSA, WV-KY-OH	S	12.16 MW	10.30 AW	25300 AAW	WVBLS	10//99-12//99
	Parkersburg-Marietta MSA, WV-OH	S	12.54 MW	11.19 AW	26070 AAW	WVBLS	10//99-12//99
	Wisconsin	S	13.57 MW	14.43 AW	30010 AAW	WIBLS	10//99-12//99
	Appleton-Oshkosh-Neenah MSA, WI	S	12.62 MW	11.94 AW	26250 AAW	WIBLS	10//99-12//99
	Eau Claire MSA, WI	S	11.68 MW	11.15 AW	24300 AAW	WIBLS	10//99-12//99
	Green Bay MSA, WI	S	12.18 MW	11.30 AW	25330 AAW	WIBLS	10//99-12//99
	Janesville-Beloit MSA, WI	S	11.38 MW	10.58 AW	23660 AAW	WIBLS	10//99-12//99
	Madison MSA, WI	S	12.90 MW	12.37 AW	26840 AAW	WIBLS	10//99-12//99
	Milwaukee-Waukesha PMSA, WI	S	17.19 MW	16.81 AW	35750 AAW	WIBLS	10//99-12//99
	Wausau MSA, WI	S	10.94 MW	10.97 AW	22750 AAW	WIBLS	10//99-12//99
	Wyoming	S	12.1 MW	12.61 AW	26240 AAW	WYBLS	10//99-12//99
	Cheyenne MSA, WY	S	13.78 MW	14.66 AW	28670 AAW	WYBLS	10//99-12//99
	Puerto Rico	S	8.02 MW	9.75 AW	20280 AAW	PRBLS	10//99-12//99
	Ponce MSA, PR	S	7.29 MW	6.23 AW	15160 AAW	PRBLS	10//99-12//99
	San Juan-Bayamon PMSA, PR	S	10.06 MW	8.31 AW	20920 AAW	PRBLS	10//99-12//99
	Virgin Islands	S	11.24 MW	11.19 AW	23280 AAW	VIBLS	10//99-12//99
Rotary Drill Operator							
Oil and Gas	Alabama	S	14.08 MW	15.31 AW	31840 AAW	ALBLS	10//99-12//99
Oil and Gas	Alaska	S	35.31 MW	31.46 AW	65440 AAW	AKBLS	10//99-12//99
Oil and Gas	Arizona	S	22.19 MW	20.52 AW	42680 AAW	AZBLS	10//99-12//99
Oil and Gas	Arkansas	S	12.26 MW	12.18 AW	25340 AAW	ARBLS	10//99-12//99
Oil and Gas	California	S	16.73 MW	16.91 AW	35170 AAW	CABLS	10//99-12//99
Oil and Gas	Colorado	S	15.77 MW	15.92 AW	33110 AAW	COBLS	10//99-12//99
Oil and Gas	Kansas	S	11.37 MW	11.76 AW	24460 AAW	KSBLS	10//99-12//99
Oil and Gas	Louisiana	S	20.34 MW	18.43 AW	38340 AAW	LABLS	10//99-12//99
Oil and Gas	Michigan	S	15.4 MW	15.84 AW	32940 AAW	MIBLS	10//99-12//99
Oil and Gas	Mississippi	S	15.97 MW	18.98 AW	39490 AAW	MSBLS	10//99-12//99

AAW Average annual wage	**AOH** Average offered, high	**ASH** Average starting, high	**H** Hourly	**M** Monthly	**S** Special: hourly and annual
AE Average entry wage	**AOL** Average offered, low	**ASL** Average starting, low	**HI** Highest wage paid	**MTC** Median total compensation	**TQ** Third quartile wage
AEX Average experienced wage	**APH** Average pay, high range	**AW** Average wage paid	**HR** High end range	**MW** Median wage paid	**W** Weekly
AO Average offered	**APL** Average pay, low range	**FQ** First quartile wage	**LR** Low end range	**SQ** Second quartile wage	**Y** Yearly

Occupation/Type/Industry	Location	Per	Low	Mid	High	Source	Date
Rotary Drill Operator							
Oil and Gas	Montana	S	17.8 MW	16.28 AW	33870 AAW	MTBLS	10//99-12//99
Oil and Gas	New Mexico	S	15.56 MW	15.90 AW	33080 AAW	NMBLS	10//99-12//99
Oil and Gas	Oklahoma	S	12.09 MW	14.20 AW	29540 AAW	OKBLS	10//99-12//99
Oil and Gas	Pennsylvania	S	13.57 MW	15.29 AW	31810 AAW	PABLS	10//99-12//99
Oil and Gas	Tennessee	S	14.09 MW	16.04 AW	33350 AAW	TNBLS	10//99-12//99
Oil and Gas	Texas	S	15.98 MW	18.38 AW	38240 AAW	TXBLS	10//99-12//99
Oil and Gas	Virginia	S	14.75 MW	15.75 AW	32770 AAW	VABLS	10//99-12//99
Oil and Gas	West Virginia	S	13.55 MW	15.13 AW	31470 AAW	WVBLS	10//99-12//99
Oil and Gas	Wyoming	S	21.29 MW	28.11 AW	58460 AAW	WYBLS	10//99-12//99
Roustabout							
Oil and Gas	Alabama	S	11.3 MW	11.56 AW	24050 AAW	ALBLS	10//99-12//99
Oil and Gas	Alaska	S	17.36 MW	16.79 AW	34920 AAW	AKBLS	10//99-12//99
Oil and Gas	Arkansas	S	11.22 MW	11.14 AW	23170 AAW	ARBLS	10//99-12//99
Oil and Gas	California	S	14.99 MW	18.51 AW	38490 AAW	CABLS	10//99-12//99
Oil and Gas	Colorado	S	11.1 MW	11.18 AW	23260 AAW	COBLS	10//99-12//99
Oil and Gas	Illinois	S	8.89 MW	9.35 AW	19450 AAW	ILBLS	10//99-12//99
Oil and Gas	Indiana	S	10.38 MW	10.76 AW	22380 AAW	INBLS	10//99-12//99
Oil and Gas	Kansas	S	9.56 MW	10.26 AW	21340 AAW	KSBLS	10//99-12//99
Oil and Gas	Kentucky	S	10.41 MW	10.79 AW	22440 AAW	KYBLS	10//99-12//99
Oil and Gas	Louisiana	S	9.65 MW	9.94 AW	20670 AAW	LABLS	10//99-12//99
Oil and Gas	Michigan	S	11.56 MW	11.82 AW	24580 AAW	MIBLS	10//99-12//99
Oil and Gas	Mississippi	S	10.23 MW	10.93 AW	22740 AAW	MSBLS	10//99-12//99
Oil and Gas	Montana	S	11.58 MW	11.91 AW	24770 AAW	MTBLS	10//99-12//99
Oil and Gas	New Mexico	S	11 MW	11.69 AW	24320 AAW	NMBLS	10//99-12//99
Oil and Gas	North Dakota	S	8.75 MW	9.47 AW	19700 AAW	NDBLS	10//99-12//99
Oil and Gas	Oklahoma	S	9.3 MW	9.36 AW	19480 AAW	OKBLS	10//99-12//99
Oil and Gas	Pennsylvania	S	9.84 MW	12.29 AW	25550 AAW	PABLS	10//99-12//99
Oil and Gas	Texas	S	10.02 MW	10.95 AW	22780 AAW	TXBLS	10//99-12//99
Oil and Gas	Utah	S	11.24 MW	11.10 AW	23090 AAW	UTBLS	10//99-12//99
Oil and Gas	Virginia	S	12.04 MW	11.89 AW	24740 AAW	VABLS	10//99-12//99
Oil and Gas	West Virginia	S	8.06 MW	8.42 AW	17520 AAW	WVBLS	10//99-12//99
Oil and Gas	Wyoming	S	11.84 MW	13.82 AW	28750 AAW	WYBLS	10//99-12//99
Safety, Health, and Environment Professional	United States	Y		62700 AW		SAFHE	1999
Sailor and Marine Oiler	Alaska	S	14.6 MW	15.00 AW	31200 AAW	AKBLS	10//99-12//99
	Arkansas	S	9.26 MW	11.17 AW	23240 AAW	ARBLS	10//99-12//99
	California	S	17.2 MW	16.20 AW	33690 AAW	CABLS	10//99-12//99
	Connecticut	S	10.74 MW	10.45 AW	21730 AAW	CTBLS	10//99-12//99
	Florida	S	14.21 MW	13.03 AW	27110 AAW	FLBLS	10//99-12//99
	Hawaii	S	11.93 MW	12.19 AW	25360 AAW	HIBLS	10//99-12//99
	Illinois	S	12.64 MW	12.84 AW	26700 AAW	ILBLS	10//99-12//99
	Indiana	S	14.13 MW	14.18 AW	29490 AAW	INBLS	10//99-12//99
	Kentucky	S	11.34 MW	11.42 AW	23750 AAW	KYBLS	10//99-12//99
	Louisiana	S	8.98 MW	9.45 AW	19650 AAW	LABLS	10//99-12//99
	Maine	S	9.69 MW	10.36 AW	21550 AAW	MEBLS	10//99-12//99
	Maryland	S	11.47 MW	11.22 AW	23330 AAW	MDBLS	10//99-12//99
	Massachusetts	S	7.51 MW	8.55 AW	17780 AAW	MABLS	10//99-12//99
	Michigan	S	17.02 MW	16.26 AW	33830 AAW	MIBLS	10//99-12//99
	Minnesota	S	13.55 MW	13.69 AW	28460 AAW	MNBLS	10//99-12//99
	New Jersey	S	12.96 MW	13.76 AW	28620 AAW	NJBLS	10//99-12//99
	New York	S	13.21 MW	13.97 AW	29050 AAW	NYBLS	10//99-12//99
	North Carolina	S	11.61 MW	11.48 AW	23870 AAW	NCBLS	10//99-12//99
	Ohio	S	14.6 MW	13.65 AW	28390 AAW	OHBLS	10//99-12//99
	Oregon	S	18.02 MW	17.52 AW	36430 AAW	ORBLS	10//99-12//99
	Pennsylvania	S	10.4 MW	12.06 AW	25080 AAW	PABLS	10//99-12//99
	Rhode Island	S	9.47 MW	10.09 AW	20990 AAW	RIBLS	10//99-12//99
	South Carolina	S	10.46 MW	11.18 AW	23250 AAW	SCBLS	10//99-12//99
	Tennessee	S	11.88 MW	12.01 AW	24970 AAW	TNBLS	10//99-12//99
	Texas	S	9.47 MW	10.59 AW	22030 AAW	TXBLS	10//99-12//99
	Washington	S	17.57 MW	16.01 AW	33300 AAW	WABLS	10//99-12//99
	West Virginia	S	14.32 MW	14.47 AW	30100 AAW	WVBLS	10//99-12//99
	Wisconsin	S	8.61 MW	9.08 AW	18880 AAW	WIBLS	10//99-12//99
	Virgin Islands	S	7.65 MW	7.78 AW	16190 AAW	VIBLS	10//99-12//99
Sales Engineer	Alabama	S	22.77 MW	25.52 AW	53080 AAW	ALBLS	10//99-12//99
	Arizona	S	27.82 MW	29.60 AW	61580 AAW	AZBLS	10//99-12//99
	Arkansas	S	20.93 MW	22.52 AW	46830 AAW	ARBLS	10//99-12//99
	California	S	29.93 MW	30.97 AW	64420 AAW	CABLS	10//99-12//99
	Colorado	S	30.39 MW	31.48 AW	65480 AAW	COBLS	10//99-12//99

AAW	Average annual wage	AOH	Average offered, high	ASH	Average starting, high
AE	Average entry wage	AOL	Average offered, low	ASL	Average starting, low
AEX	Average experienced wage	APH	Average pay, high range	AW	Average wage paid
AO	Average offered	APL	Average pay, low range	FQ	First quartile wage

H	Hourly	M	Monthly	S	Special: hourly and annual
HI	Highest wage paid	MTC	Median total compensation	TQ	Third quartile wage
HR	High end range	MW	Median wage paid	W	Weekly
LR	Low end range	SQ	Second quartile wage	Y	Yearly

Occupation/Type/Industry	Location	Per	Low	Mid	High	Source	Date
Sales Engineer	Connecticut	S	29.99 MW	29.43 AW	61210 AAW	CTBLS	10//99-12//99
	Delaware	S	23.63 MW	24.55 AW	51060 AAW	DEBLS	10//99-12//99
	District of Columbia	S	19.75 MW	20.03 AW	41670 AAW	DCBLS	10//99-12//99
	Florida	S	26.65 MW	29.09 AW	60500 AAW	FLBLS	10//99-12//99
	Georgia	S	28.22 MW	29.04 AW	60400 AAW	GABLS	10//99-12//99
	Hawaii	S	28.09 MW	28.32 AW	58900 AAW	HIBLS	10//99-12//99
	Idaho	S	21.75 MW	23.82 AW	49540 AAW	IDBLS	10//99-12//99
	Illinois	S	24.6 MW	26.54 AW	55190 AAW	ILBLS	10//99-12//99
	Indiana	S	25.76 MW	28.09 AW	58420 AAW	INBLS	10//99-12//99
	Iowa	S	22.21 MW	24.90 AW	51780 AAW	IABLS	10//99-12//99
	Kansas	S	29.01 MW	29.38 AW	61100 AAW	KSBLS	10//99-12//99
	Kentucky	S	25.68 MW	28.12 AW	58500 AAW	KYBLS	10//99-12//99
	Louisiana	S	22.16 MW	22.89 AW	47610 AAW	LABLS	10//99-12//99
	Maine	S	26.5 MW	28.97 AW	60260 AAW	MEBLS	10//99-12//99
	Maryland	S	24.87 MW	26.59 AW	55300 AAW	MDBLS	10//99-12//99
	Massachusetts	S	29.99 MW	31.45 AW	65410 AAW	MABLS	10//99-12//99
	Michigan	S	30.45 MW	30.94 AW	64360 AAW	MIBLS	10//99-12//99
	Minnesota	S	24.32 MW	27.79 AW	57800 AAW	MNBLS	10//99-12//99
	Mississippi	S	21.47 MW	25.09 AW	52190 AAW	MSBLS	10//99-12//99
	Missouri	S	25.75 MW	26.50 AW	55120 AAW	MOBLS	10//99-12//99
	Montana	S	27.2 MW	29.12 AW	60560 AAW	MTBLS	10//99-12//99
	Nebraska	S	23.78 MW	30.01 AW	62420 AAW	NEBLS	10//99-12//99
	Nevada	S	21.13 MW	22.20 AW	46170 AAW	NVBLS	10//99-12//99
	New Hampshire	S	26.44 MW	27.35 AW	56880 AAW	NHBLS	10//99-12//99
	New Jersey	S	28.36 MW	29.25 AW	60830 AAW	NJBLS	10//99-12//99
	New Mexico	S	21.77 MW	24.65 AW	51280 AAW	NMBLS	10//99-12//99
	New York	S	25.54 MW	27.61 AW	57440 AAW	NYBLS	10//99-12//99
	North Carolina	S	25.26 MW	26.82 AW	55790 AAW	NCBLS	10//99-12//99
	North Dakota	S	21.92 MW	23.18 AW	48210 AAW	NDBLS	10//99-12//99
	Ohio	S	24.93 MW	26.75 AW	55630 AAW	OHBLS	10//99-12//99
	Oklahoma	S	23.11 MW	25.43 AW	52900 AAW	OKBLS	10//99-12//99
	Oregon	S	35.84 MW	36.74 AW	76420 AAW	ORBLS	10//99-12//99
	Pennsylvania	S	24.77 MW	26.39 AW	54900 AAW	PABLS	10//99-12//99
	Rhode Island	S	24.34 MW	25.68 AW	53420 AAW	RIBLS	10//99-12//99
	South Carolina	S	21.41 MW	21.95 AW	45650 AAW	SCBLS	10//99-12//99
	South Dakota	S	25.18 MW	27.09 AW	56350 AAW	SDBLS	10//99-12//99
	Tennessee	S	23.14 MW	24.11 AW	50150 AAW	TNBLS	10//99-12//99
	Texas	S	25.93 MW	27.58 AW	57370 AAW	TXBLS	10//99-12//99
	Utah	S	25.98 MW	28.29 AW	58840 AAW	UTBLS	10//99-12//99
	Vermont	S	24.88 MW	26.06 AW	54200 AAW	VTBLS	10//99-12//99
	Virginia	S	17.44 MW	20.29 AW	42210 AAW	VABLS	10//99-12//99
	Washington	S	27.61 MW	28.43 AW	59130 AAW	WABLS	10//99-12//99
	West Virginia	S	22.28 MW	23.81 AW	49530 AAW	WVBLS	10//99-12//99
	Wisconsin	S	26.03 MW	26.81 AW	55770 AAW	WIBLS	10//99-12//99
	Puerto Rico	S	20.12 MW	21.83 AW	45400 AAW	PRBLS	10//99-12//99
Sales Executive							
Beer Wholesaling	United States	Y	80000 MW	92000 AW		BEVW	1999
Sales Manager	Alabama	S	20.4 MW	23.89 AW	49690 AAW	ALBLS	10//99-12//99
	Anniston MSA, AL	S	25.15 MW	27.39 AW	52310 AAW	ALBLS	10//99-12//99
	Auburn-Opelika MSA, AL	S	20.23 MW	15.54 AW	42070 AAW	ALBLS	10//99-12//99
	Birmingham MSA, AL	S	27.60 MW	27.37 AW	57410 AAW	ALBLS	10//99-12//99
	Decatur MSA, AL	S	22.70 MW	23.80 AW	47210 AAW	ALBLS	10//99-12//99
	Dothan MSA, AL	S	24.69 MW	23.50 AW	51350 AAW	ALBLS	10//99-12//99
	Florence MSA, AL	S	22.39 MW	18.67 AW	46570 AAW	ALBLS	10//99-12//99
	Gadsden MSA, AL	S	22.30 MW	14.76 AW	46390 AAW	ALBLS	10//99-12//99
	Huntsville MSA, AL	S	27.87 MW	24.41 AW	57970 AAW	ALBLS	10//99-12//99
	Mobile MSA, AL	S	24.09 MW	20.60 AW	50110 AAW	ALBLS	10//99-12//99
	Montgomery MSA, AL	S	26.99 MW	28.51 AW	56130 AAW	ALBLS	10//99-12//99
	Tuscaloosa MSA, AL	S	23.73 MW	21.43 AW	49350 AAW	ALBLS	10//99-12//99
	Alaska	S	21.02 MW	25.28 AW	52580 AAW	AKBLS	10//99-12//99
	Anchorage MSA, AK	S	24.27 MW	20.15 AW	50480 AAW	AKBLS	10//99-12//99
	Arizona	S	29.01 MW	30.73 AW	63910 AAW	AZBLS	10//99-12//99
	Flagstaff MSA, AZ-UT	S	28.16 MW	28.74 AW	58560 AAW	AZBLS	10//99-12//99
	Phoenix-Mesa MSA, AZ	S	31.23 MW	29.55 AW	64960 AAW	AZBLS	10//99-12//99
	Tucson MSA, AZ	S	31.02 MW	29.62 AW	64520 AAW	AZBLS	10//99-12//99
	Yuma MSA, AZ	S	22.30 MW	16.45 AW	46390 AAW	AZBLS	10//99-12//99
	Arkansas	S	26.39 MW	29.03 AW	60380 AAW	ARBLS	10//99-12//99
	Fayetteville-Springdale-Rogers MSA, AR	S	20.91 MW	18.78 AW	43500 AAW	ARBLS	10//99-12//99
	Fort Smith MSA, AR-OK	S	31.61 MW	25.75 AW	65750 AAW	ARBLS	10//99-12//99

Occupation/Type/Industry	Location	Per	Low	Mid	High	Source	Date
Sales Manager	Little Rock-North Little Rock						
	MSA, AR	S	28.60 MW	27.82 AW	59490 AAW	ARBLS	10//99-12//99
	California	S	34.97 MW	37.76 AW	78540 AAW	CABLS	10//99-12//99
	Bakersfield MSA, CA	S	29.85 MW	29.19 AW	62080 AAW	CABLS	10//99-12//99
	Chico-Paradise MSA, CA	S	29.83 MW	24.87 AW	62040 AAW	CABLS	10//99-12//99
	Fresno MSA, CA	S	29.69 MW	25.88 AW	61750 AAW	CABLS	10//99-12//99
	Los Angeles-Long Beach						
	PMSA, CA	S	36.81 MW	34.32 AW	76560 AAW	CABLS	10//99-12//99
	Merced MSA, CA	S	39.43 MW	36.71 AW	82020 AAW	CABLS	10//99-12//99
	Modesto MSA, CA	S	27.31 MW	23.32 AW	56800 AAW	CABLS	10//99-12//99
	Oakland PMSA, CA	S	45.17 MW	42.65 AW	93960 AAW	CABLS	10//99-12//99
	Orange County PMSA, CA	S	38.06 MW	34.21 AW	79160 AAW	CABLS	10//99-12//99
	Redding MSA, CA	S	35.48 MW	35.54 AW	73800 AAW	CABLS	10//99-12//99
	Riverside-San Bernardino						
	PMSA, CA	S	33.04 MW	30.06 AW	68720 AAW	CABLS	10//99-12//99
	Sacramento PMSA, CA	S	32.95 MW	31.70 AW	68530 AAW	CABLS	10//99-12//99
	Salinas MSA, CA	S	41.39 MW	38.79 AW	86100 AAW	CABLS	10//99-12//99
	San Diego MSA, CA	S	33.97 MW	29.04 AW	70650 AAW	CABLS	10//99-12//99
	San Francisco PMSA, CA	S	41.15 MW	39.67 AW	85580 AAW	CABLS	10//99-12//99
	San Jose PMSA, CA	S	45.41 MW	45.30 AW	94450 AAW	CABLS	10//99-12//99
	San Luis Obispo-Atascadero-						
	Paso Robles MSA, CA	S	29.56 MW	29.16 AW	61480 AAW	CABLS	10//99-12//99
	Santa Barbara-Santa Maria-						
	Lompoc MSA, CA	S	29.09 MW	23.15 AW	60500 AAW	CABLS	10//99-12//99
	Santa Cruz-Watsonville						
	PMSA, CA	S	33.85 MW	32.32 AW	70410 AAW	CABLS	10//99-12//99
	Santa Rosa PMSA, CA	S	34.90 MW	31.75 AW	72590 AAW	CABLS	10//99-12//99
	Stockton-Lodi MSA, CA	S	29.53 MW	26.06 AW	61420 AAW	CABLS	10//99-12//99
	Vallejo-Fairfield-Napa PMSA,						
	CA	S	31.53 MW	26.43 AW	65590 AAW	CABLS	10//99-12//99
	Ventura PMSA, CA	S	39.34 MW	34.51 AW	81830 AAW	CABLS	10//99-12//99
	Visalia-Tulare-Porterville						
	MSA, CA	S	28.60 MW	29.59 AW	59500 AAW	CABLS	10//99-12//99
	Yolo PMSA, CA	S	33.79 MW	27.94 AW	70280 AAW	CABLS	10//99-12//99
	Colorado	S	32.44 MW	35.80 AW	74470 AAW	COBLS	10//99-12//99
	Denver PMSA, CO	S	36.49 MW	32.91 AW	75890 AAW	COBLS	10//99-12//99
	Connecticut	S	34.4 MW	37.65 AW	78310 AAW	CTBLS	10//99-12//99
	Bridgeport PMSA, CT	S	35.16 MW	32.78 AW	73130 AAW	CTBLS	10//99-12//99
	Danbury PMSA, CT	S	38.09 MW	36.65 AW	79220 AAW	CTBLS	10//99-12//99
	Hartford MSA, CT	S	37.78 MW	35.35 AW	78580 AAW	CTBLS	10//99-12//99
	New Haven-Meriden PMSA,						
	CT	S	34.17 MW	31.39 AW	71080 AAW	CTBLS	10//99-12//99
	New London-Norwich MSA,						
	CT-RI	S	37.43 MW	36.08 AW	77860 AAW	CTBLS	10//99-12//99
	Stamford-Norwalk PMSA, CT	S	42.21 MW	40.21 AW	87810 AAW	CTBLS	10//99-12//99
	Waterbury PMSA, CT	S	32.57 MW	29.91 AW	67750 AAW	CTBLS	10//99-12//99
	Delaware	S	24.96 MW	29.70 AW	61780 AAW	DEBLS	10//99-12//99
	Dover MSA, DE	S	21.00 MW	16.61 AW	43690 AAW	DEBLS	10//99-12//99
	Wilmington-Newark PMSA,						
	DE-MD	S	32.59 MW	27.56 AW	67790 AAW	DEBLS	10//99-12//99
	District of Columbia	S	27.67 MW	31.74 AW	66010 AAW	DCBLS	10//99-12//99
	Washington PMSA, DC-MD-						
	VA-WV	S	32.89 MW	29.65 AW	68400 AAW	DCBLS	10//99-12//99
	Florida	S	27.54 MW	31.05 AW	64590 AAW	FLBLS	10//99-12//99
	Daytona Beach MSA, FL	S	22.18 MW	18.18 AW	46140 AAW	FLBLS	10//99-12//99
	Fort Lauderdale PMSA, FL	S	31.83 MW	26.88 AW	66200 AAW	FLBLS	10//99-12//99
	Fort Myers-Cape Coral MSA,						
	FL	S	31.67 MW	27.24 AW	65860 AAW	FLBLS	10//99-12//99
	Fort Pierce-Port St. Lucie						
	MSA, FL	S	22.70 MW	17.34 AW	47220 AAW	FLBLS	10//99-12//99
	Fort Walton Beach MSA, FL	S	24.07 MW	22.10 AW	50060 AAW	FLBLS	10//99-12//99
	Gainesville MSA, FL	S	25.70 MW	20.54 AW	53450 AAW	FLBLS	10//99-12//99
	Jacksonville MSA, FL	S	32.29 MW	29.11 AW	67160 AAW	FLBLS	10//99-12//99
	Lakeland-Winter Haven MSA,						
	FL	S	34.00 MW	37.21 AW	70720 AAW	FLBLS	10//99-12//99
	Melbourne-Titusville-Palm						
	Bay MSA, FL	S	28.77 MW	24.11 AW	59830 AAW	FLBLS	10//99-12//99
	Miami PMSA, FL	S	31.33 MW	27.29 AW	65160 AAW	FLBLS	10//99-12//99
	Naples MSA, FL	S	32.71 MW	26.35 AW	68030 AAW	FLBLS	10//99-12//99
	Ocala MSA, FL	S	26.26 MW	23.47 AW	54610 AAW	FLBLS	10//99-12//99
	Orlando MSA, FL	S	31.62 MW	27.34 AW	65770 AAW	FLBLS	10//99-12//99
	Panama City MSA, FL	S	28.80 MW	25.42 AW	59900 AAW	FLBLS	10//99-12//99

AAW Average annual wage	**AOH** Average offered, high	**ASH** Average starting, high	**H** Hourly	**M** Monthly	**S** Special: hourly and annual
AE Average entry wage	**AOL** Average offered, low	**ASL** Average starting, low	**HI** Highest wage paid	**MTC** Median total compensation	**TQ** Third quartile wage
AEX Average experienced wage	**APH** Average pay, high range	**AW** Average wage paid	**HR** High end range	**MW** Median wage paid	**W** Weekly
AO Average offered	**APL** Average pay, low range	**FQ** First quartile wage	**LR** Low end range	**SQ** Second quartile wage	**Y** Yearly

Sales Manager

Occupation/Type/Industry	Location	Per	Low	Mid	High	Source	Date
Sales Manager	Pensacola MSA, FL	S	28.89 MW	29.40 AW	60090 AAW	FLBLS	10//99-12//99
	Punta Gorda MSA, FL	S	27.33 MW	28.47 AW	56840 AAW	FLBLS	10//99-12//99
	Sarasota-Bradenton MSA, FL	S	29.91 MW	28.66 AW	62210 AAW	FLBLS	10//99-12//99
	Tallahassee MSA, FL	S	22.40 MW	21.70 AW	46590 AAW	FLBLS	10//99-12//99
	Tampa-St. Petersburg-Clearwater MSA, FL	S	29.76 MW	27.18 AW	61900 AAW	FLBLS	10//99-12//99
	West Palm Beach-Boca Raton MSA, FL	S	36.67 MW	34.54 AW	76280 AAW	FLBLS	10//99-12//99
	Georgia	S	32.73 MW	36.48 AW	75870 AAW	GABLS	10//99-12//99
	Albany MSA, GA	S	23.04 MW	21.38 AW	47920 AAW	GABLS	10//99-12//99
	Athens MSA, GA	S	30.14 MW	27.96 AW	62690 AAW	GABLS	10//99-12//99
	Atlanta MSA, GA	S	35.77 MW	32.89 AW	74400 AAW	GABLS	10//99-12//99
	Augusta-Aiken MSA, GA-SC	S	24.75 MW	23.44 AW	51480 AAW	GABLS	10//99-12//99
	Columbus MSA, GA-AL	S	31.69 MW	25.29 AW	65920 AAW	GABLS	10//99-12//99
	Macon MSA, GA	S	24.36 MW	20.51 AW	50670 AAW	GABLS	10//99-12//99
	Savannah MSA, GA	S	35.29 MW	36.58 AW	73410 AAW	GABLS	10//99-12//99
	Hawaii	S	25.08 MW	27.15 AW	56480 AAW	HIBLS	10//99-12//99
	Honolulu MSA, HI	S	28.08 MW	26.08 AW	58410 AAW	HIBLS	10//99-12//99
	Idaho	S	25.63 MW	28.04 AW	58330 AAW	IDBLS	10//99-12//99
	Boise City MSA, ID	S	28.06 MW	25.76 AW	58370 AAW	IDBLS	10//99-12//99
	Pocatello MSA, ID	S	28.75 MW	27.54 AW	59800 AAW	IDBLS	10//99-12//99
	Illinois	S	30.24 MW	32.88 AW	68380 AAW	ILBLS	10//99-12//99
	Bloomington-Normal MSA, IL	S	22.69 MW	20.74 AW	47190 AAW	ILBLS	10//99-12//99
	Champaign-Urbana MSA, IL	S	28.66 MW	29.45 AW	59610 AAW	ILBLS	10//99-12//99
	Chicago PMSA, IL	S	34.09 MW	30.90 AW	70900 AAW	ILBLS	10//99-12//99
	Decatur MSA, IL	S	27.40 MW	24.81 AW	56990 AAW	ILBLS	10//99-12//99
	Kankakee PMSA, IL	S	33.33 MW	24.66 AW	69320 AAW	ILBLS	10//99-12//99
	Peoria-Pekin MSA, IL	S	24.23 MW	23.60 AW	50400 AAW	ILBLS	10//99-12//99
	Rockford MSA, IL	S	26.49 MW	27.75 AW	55090 AAW	ILBLS	10//99-12//99
	Springfield MSA, IL	S	29.51 MW	25.13 AW	61390 AAW	ILBLS	10//99-12//99
	Indiana	S	30.4 MW	32.77 AW	68160 AAW	INBLS	10//99-12//99
	Bloomington MSA, IN	S	26.60 MW	27.56 AW	55320 AAW	INBLS	10//99-12//99
	Elkhart-Goshen MSA, IN	S	34.99 MW	31.21 AW	72790 AAW	INBLS	10//99-12//99
	Evansville-Henderson MSA, IN-KY	S	32.99 MW	29.73 AW	68610 AAW	INBLS	10//99-12//99
	Fort Wayne MSA, IN	S	31.21 MW	30.08 AW	64920 AAW	INBLS	10//99-12//99
	Gary PMSA, IN	S	31.17 MW	26.88 AW	64830 AAW	INBLS	10//99-12//99
	Indianapolis MSA, IN	S	35.99 MW	32.80 AW	74850 AAW	INBLS	10//99-12//99
	Kokomo MSA, IN	S	47.55 MW	48.31 AW	98900 AAW	INBLS	10//99-12//99
	Lafayette MSA, IN	S	36.24 MW	37.06 AW	75380 AAW	INBLS	10//99-12//99
	Muncie MSA, IN	S	27.37 MW	26.33 AW	56930 AAW	INBLS	10//99-12//99
	South Bend MSA, IN	S	34.25 MW	31.56 AW	71230 AAW	INBLS	10//99-12//99
	Terre Haute MSA, IN	S	22.91 MW	20.54 AW	47660 AAW	INBLS	10//99-12//99
	Iowa	S	21.37 MW	24.63 AW	51230 AAW	IABLS	10//99-12//99
	Cedar Rapids MSA, IA	S	27.80 MW	25.02 AW	57820 AAW	IABLS	10//99-12//99
	Davenport-Moline-Rock Island MSA, IA-IL	S	24.38 MW	20.99 AW	50710 AAW	IABLS	10//99-12//99
	Des Moines MSA, IA	S	25.17 MW	22.70 AW	52350 AAW	IABLS	10//99-12//99
	Dubuque MSA, IA	S	17.69 MW	16.20 AW	36790 AAW	IABLS	10//99-12//99
	Iowa City MSA, IA	S	17.77 MW	15.24 AW	36950 AAW	IABLS	10//99-12//99
	Sioux City MSA, IA-NE	S	22.36 MW	21.29 AW	46500 AAW	IABLS	10//99-12//99
	Waterloo-Cedar Falls MSA, IA	S	29.98 MW	28.84 AW	62360 AAW	IABLS	10//99-12//99
	Kansas	S	29.19 MW	30.69 AW	63840 AAW	KSBLS	10//99-12//99
	Topeka MSA, KS	S	29.88 MW	29.38 AW	62160 AAW	KSBLS	10//99-12//99
	Wichita MSA, KS	S	26.78 MW	25.28 AW	55710 AAW	KSBLS	10//99-12//99
	Kentucky	S	22.57 MW	25.75 AW	53570 AAW	KYBLS	10//99-12//99
	Lexington MSA, KY	S	28.35 MW	24.31 AW	58960 AAW	KYBLS	10//99-12//99
	Louisville MSA, KY-IN	S	28.12 MW	25.22 AW	58480 AAW	KYBLS	10//99-12//99
	Louisiana	S	24.97 MW	26.44 AW	54990 AAW	LABLS	10//99-12//99
	Alexandria MSA, LA	S	27.34 MW	26.98 AW	56880 AAW	LABLS	10//99-12//99
	Baton Rouge MSA, LA	S	24.73 MW	21.07 AW	51430 AAW	LABLS	10//99-12//99
	Houma MSA, LA	S	27.25 MW	24.54 AW	56690 AAW	LABLS	10//99-12//99
	Lafayette MSA, LA	S	29.34 MW	28.80 AW	61020 AAW	LABLS	10//99-12//99
	Lake Charles MSA, LA	S	25.79 MW	27.50 AW	53640 AAW	LABLS	10//99-12//99
	Monroe MSA, LA	S	31.97 MW	30.07 AW	66490 AAW	LABLS	10//99-12//99
	New Orleans MSA, LA	S	25.07 MW	24.07 AW	52150 AAW	LABLS	10//99-12//99
	Shreveport-Bossier City MSA, LA	S	26.53 MW	24.33 AW	55170 AAW	LABLS	10//99-12//99
	Maine	S	24.01 MW	27.49 AW	57180 AAW	MEBLS	10//99-12//99
	Bangor MSA, ME	S	23.07 MW	20.59 AW	47980 AAW	MEBLS	10//99-12//99
	Lewiston-Auburn MSA, ME	S	23.52 MW	22.46 AW	48920 AAW	MEBLS	10//99-12//99
	Portland MSA, ME	S	31.97 MW	26.85 AW	66490 AAW	MEBLS	10//99-12//99

AAW	Average annual wage	AOH	Average offered, high	ASH	Average starting, high	H	Hourly	M	Monthly	S	Special: hourly and annual
AE	Average entry wage	AOL	Average offered, low	ASL	Average starting, low	HI	Highest wage paid	MTC	Median total compensation	TQ	Third quartile wage
AEX	Average experienced wage	APH	Average pay, high range	AW	Average wage paid	HR	High end range	MW	Median wage paid	W	Weekly
AO	Average offered	APL	Average pay, low range	FQ	First quartile wage	LR	Low end range	SQ	Second quartile wage	Y	Yearly

Occupation/Type/Industry	Location	Per	Low	Mid	High	Source	Date
Sales Manager	Maryland	S	26.76 MW	30.46 AW	63350 AAW	MDBLS	10//99-12//99
	Baltimore PMSA, MD	S	30.49 MW	26.72 AW	63420 AAW	MDBLS	10//99-12//99
	Cumberland MSA, MD-WV	S	26.00 MW	27.95 AW	54090 AAW	MDBLS	10//99-12//99
	Hagerstown PMSA, MD	S	34.29 MW	29.31 AW	71330 AAW	MDBLS	10//99-12//99
	Massachusetts	S	37.67 MW	39.93 AW	83060 AAW	MABLS	10//99-12//99
	Barnstable-Yarmouth MSA, MA	S	28.83 MW	24.80 AW	59970 AAW	MABLS	10//99-12//99
	Boston PMSA, MA-NH	S	41.13 MW	38.64 AW	85560 AAW	MABLS	10//99-12//99
	Brockton PMSA, MA	S	44.01 MW	41.60 AW	91550 AAW	MABLS	10//99-12//99
	Lawrence PMSA, MA-NH	S	34.07 MW	32.38 AW	70870 AAW	MABLS	10//99-12//99
	Lowell PMSA, MA-NH	S	42.22 MW	41.93 AW	87810 AAW	MABLS	10//99-12//99
	New Bedford PMSA, MA	S	31.08 MW	26.82 AW	64640 AAW	MABLS	10//99-12//99
	Pittsfield MSA, MA	S	28.08 MW	21.55 AW	58410 AAW	MABLS	10//99-12//99
	Springfield MSA, MA	S	34.78 MW	34.50 AW	72340 AAW	MABLS	10//99-12//99
	Worcester PMSA, MA-CT	S	37.79 MW	37.82 AW	78610 AAW	MABLS	10//99-12//99
	Michigan	S	35.81 MW	37.98 AW	79000 AAW	MIBLS	10//99-12//99
	Ann Arbor PMSA, MI	S	38.31 MW	34.16 AW	79680 AAW	MIBLS	10//99-12//99
	Benton Harbor MSA, MI	S	34.54 MW	30.18 AW	71850 AAW	MIBLS	10//99-12//99
	Detroit PMSA, MI	S	40.11 MW	38.10 AW	83420 AAW	MIBLS	10//99-12//99
	Flint PMSA, MI	S	42.50 MW	43.08 AW	88410 AAW	MIBLS	10//99-12//99
	Grand Rapids-Muskegon-Holland MSA, MI	S	36.61 MW	33.50 AW	76140 AAW	MIBLS	10//99-12//99
	Jackson MSA, MI	S	31.20 MW	30.82 AW	64890 AAW	MIBLS	10//99-12//99
	Kalamazoo-Battle Creek MSA, MI	S	37.06 MW	33.12 AW	77080 AAW	MIBLS	10//99-12//99
	Lansing-East Lansing MSA, MI	S	26.87 MW	24.54 AW	55890 AAW	MIBLS	10//99-12//99
	Saginaw-Bay City-Midland MSA, MI	S	33.35 MW	32.80 AW	69380 AAW	MIBLS	10//99-12//99
	Minnesota	S	33.86 MW	36.38 AW	75660 AAW	MNBLS	10//99-12//99
	Duluth-Superior MSA, MN-WI	S	32.31 MW	29.84 AW	67200 AAW	MNBLS	10//99-12//99
	Minneapolis-St. Paul MSA, MN-WI	S	37.15 MW	34.41 AW	77280 AAW	MNBLS	10//99-12//99
	Rochester MSA, MN	S	32.79 MW	30.35 AW	68200 AAW	MNBLS	10//99-12//99
	St. Cloud MSA, MN	S	34.07 MW	29.51 AW	70870 AAW	MNBLS	10//99-12//99
	Mississippi	S	24.59 MW	27.42 AW	57040 AAW	MSBLS	10//99-12//99
	Biloxi-Gulfport-Pascagoula MSA, MS	S	21.89 MW	22.61 AW	45540 AAW	MSBLS	10//99-12//99
	Hattiesburg MSA, MS	S	26.73 MW	29.34 AW	55600 AAW	MSBLS	10//99-12//99
	Jackson MSA, MS	S	30.46 MW	28.55 AW	63350 AAW	MSBLS	10//99-12//99
	Missouri	S	31.59 MW	32.62 AW	67850 AAW	MOBLS	10//99-12//99
	Columbia MSA, MO	S	30.52 MW	26.79 AW	63470 AAW	MOBLS	10//99-12//99
	Joplin MSA, MO	S	25.87 MW	25.95 AW	53800 AAW	MOBLS	10//99-12//99
	Kansas City MSA, MO-KS	S	33.66 MW	33.15 AW	70020 AAW	MOBLS	10//99-12//99
	St. Joseph MSA, MO	S	30.74 MW	29.92 AW	63940 AAW	MOBLS	10//99-12//99
	St. Louis MSA, MO-IL	S	35.55 MW	35.46 AW	73940 AAW	MOBLS	10//99-12//99
	Springfield MSA, MO	S	28.53 MW	21.90 AW	59350 AAW	MOBLS	10//99-12//99
	Montana	S	18.98 MW	23.10 AW	48050 AAW	MTBLS	10//99-12//99
	Billings MSA, MT	S	20.14 MW	18.56 AW	41900 AAW	MTBLS	10//99-12//99
	Great Falls MSA, MT	S	19.26 MW	21.90 AW	40060 AAW	MTBLS	10//99-12//99
	Missoula MSA, MT	S	35.22 MW	36.40 AW	73260 AAW	MTBLS	10//99-12//99
	Nebraska	S	25.23 MW	26.83 AW	55810 AAW	NEBLS	10//99-12//99
	Lincoln MSA, NE	S	25.52 MW	25.39 AW	53070 AAW	NEBLS	10//99-12//99
	Omaha MSA, NE-IA	S	29.02 MW	28.26 AW	60350 AAW	NEBLS	10//99-12//99
	Nevada	S	27.35 MW	31.28 AW	65060 AAW	NVBLS	10//99-12//99
	Las Vegas MSA, NV-AZ	S	30.61 MW	26.11 AW	63670 AAW	NVBLS	10//99-12//99
	Reno MSA, NV	S	31.80 MW	28.40 AW	66130 AAW	NVBLS	10//99-12//99
	New Hampshire	S	31.14 MW	33.69 AW	70080 AAW	NHBLS	10//99-12//99
	Manchester PMSA, NH	S	36.80 MW	38.22 AW	76540 AAW	NHBLS	10//99-12//99
	Nashua PMSA, NH	S	32.77 MW	30.12 AW	68160 AAW	NHBLS	10//99-12//99
	Portsmouth-Rochester PMSA, NH-ME	S	32.06 MW	30.48 AW	66680 AAW	NHBLS	10//99-12//99
	New Jersey	S	41.25 MW	41.61 AW	86550 AAW	NJBLS	10//99-12//99
	Bergen-Passaic PMSA, NJ	S	40.89 MW	41.01 AW	85050 AAW	NJBLS	10//99-12//99
	Jersey City PMSA, NJ	S	36.25 MW	33.99 AW	75410 AAW	NJBLS	10//99-12//99
	Middlesex-Somerset-Hunterdon PMSA, NJ	S	40.02 MW	39.73 AW	83240 AAW	NJBLS	10//99-12//99
	Monmouth-Ocean PMSA, NJ	S	39.63 MW	38.11 AW	82430 AAW	NJBLS	10//99-12//99
	Trenton PMSA, NJ	S	33.10 MW	30.02 AW	68860 AAW	NJBLS	10//99-12//99
	New Mexico	S	21.44 MW	23.47 AW	48810 AAW	NMBLS	10//99-12//99
	Albuquerque MSA, NM	S	24.88 MW	22.97 AW	51760 AAW	NMBLS	10//99-12//99
	Las Cruces MSA, NM	S	24.41 MW	16.18 AW	50780 AAW	NMBLS	10//99-12//99
	Santa Fe MSA, NM	S	18.45 MW	12.66 AW	38380 AAW	NMBLS	10//99-12//99

Occupation/Type/Industry	Location	Per	Low	Mid	High	Source	Date
Sales Manager	New York	S	41.8 MW	43.20 AW	89850 AAW	NYBLS	10//99-12//99
	Albany-Schenectady-Troy MSA, NY	S	36.35 MW	37.05 AW	75600 AAW	NYBLS	10//99-12//99
	Binghamton MSA, NY	S	29.00 MW	25.51 AW	60320 AAW	NYBLS	10//99-12//99
	Buffalo-Niagara Falls MSA, NY	S	33.27 MW	30.79 AW	69200 AAW	NYBLS	10//99-12//99
	Dutchess County PMSA, NY	S	29.59 MW	27.19 AW	61540 AAW	NYBLS	10//99-12//99
	Jamestown MSA, NY	S	32.55 MW	30.28 AW	67710 AAW	NYBLS	10//99-12//99
	Nassau-Suffolk PMSA, NY	S	38.30 MW	37.24 AW	79660 AAW	NYBLS	10//99-12//99
	New York PMSA, NY	S	48.25 MW	51.12 AW	100370 AAW	NYBLS	10//99-12//99
	Rochester MSA, NY	S	39.61 MW	39.96 AW	82390 AAW	NYBLS	10//99-12//99
	Syracuse MSA, NY	S	36.59 MW	36.66 AW	76100 AAW	NYBLS	10//99-12//99
	Utica-Rome MSA, NY	S	38.24 MW	36.70 AW	79530 AAW	NYBLS	10//99-12//99
	North Carolina	S	29.35 MW	31.43 AW	65370 AAW	NCBLS	10//99-12//99
	Asheville MSA, NC	S	28.07 MW	25.12 AW	58380 AAW	NCBLS	10//99-12//99
	Charlotte-Gastonia-Rock Hill MSA, NC-SC	S	30.57 MW	27.13 AW	63590 AAW	NCBLS	10//99-12//99
	Fayetteville MSA, NC	S	28.09 MW	24.31 AW	58420 AAW	NCBLS	10//99-12//99
	Goldsboro MSA, NC	S	14.21 MW	12.08 AW	29560 AAW	NCBLS	10//99-12//99
	Greensboro--Winston-Salem-- High Point MSA, NC	S	31.52 MW	29.81 AW	65550 AAW	NCBLS	10//99-12//99
	Greenville MSA, NC	S	37.03 MW	39.99 AW	77030 AAW	NCBLS	10//99-12//99
	Hickory-Morganton-Lenoir MSA, NC	S	29.32 MW	25.57 AW	60980 AAW	NCBLS	10//99-12//99
	Raleigh-Durham-Chapel Hill MSA, NC	S	33.73 MW	32.84 AW	70150 AAW	NCBLS	10//99-12//99
	Rocky Mount MSA, NC	S	27.27 MW	25.01 AW	56720 AAW	NCBLS	10//99-12//99
	Wilmington MSA, NC	S	34.68 MW	26.45 AW	72140 AAW	NCBLS	10//99-12//99
	North Dakota	S	22.72 MW	24.70 AW	51370 AAW	NDBLS	10//99-12//99
	Bismarck MSA, ND	S	30.18 MW	24.50 AW	62780 AAW	NDBLS	10//99-12//99
	Fargo-Moorhead MSA, ND-MN	S	28.01 MW	27.70 AW	58260 AAW	NDBLS	10//99-12//99
	Grand Forks MSA, ND-MN	S	26.82 MW	23.49 AW	55780 AAW	NDBLS	10//99-12//99
	Ohio	S	27.68 MW	30.49 AW	63410 AAW	OHBLS	10//99-12//99
	Akron PMSA, OH	S	30.84 MW	30.04 AW	64140 AAW	OHBLS	10//99-12//99
	Canton-Massillon MSA, OH	S	24.80 MW	22.82 AW	51580 AAW	OHBLS	10//99-12//99
	Cincinnati PMSA, OH-KY-IN	S	30.97 MW	28.66 AW	64420 AAW	OHBLS	10//99-12//99
	Cleveland-Lorain-Elyria PMSA, OH	S	32.14 MW	29.33 AW	66860 AAW	OHBLS	10//99-12//99
	Columbus MSA, OH	S	30.18 MW	27.91 AW	62770 AAW	OHBLS	10//99-12//99
	Dayton-Springfield MSA, OH	S	28.38 MW	24.19 AW	59040 AAW	OHBLS	10//99-12//99
	Hamilton-Middletown PMSA, OH	S	30.82 MW	28.95 AW	64110 AAW	OHBLS	10//99-12//99
	Lima MSA, OH	S	24.85 MW	21.38 AW	51680 AAW	OHBLS	10//99-12//99
	Mansfield MSA, OH	S	27.98 MW	26.15 AW	58190 AAW	OHBLS	10//99-12//99
	Steubenville-Weirton MSA, OH-WV	S	26.34 MW	26.34 AW	54780 AAW	OHBLS	10//99-12//99
	Toledo MSA, OH	S	33.35 MW	31.82 AW	69370 AAW	OHBLS	10//99-12//99
	Youngstown-Warren MSA, OH	S	31.24 MW	27.42 AW	64980 AAW	OHBLS	10//99-12//99
	Oklahoma	S	23.67 MW	26.29 AW	54690 AAW	OKBLS	10//99-12//99
	Enid MSA, OK	S	11.97 MW	10.04 AW	24900 AAW	OKBLS	10//99-12//99
	Lawton MSA, OK	S	17.93 MW	16.48 AW	37290 AAW	OKBLS	10//99-12//99
	Oklahoma City MSA, OK	S	28.61 MW	25.06 AW	59500 AAW	OKBLS	10//99-12//99
	Tulsa MSA, OK	S	28.79 MW	28.03 AW	59880 AAW	OKBLS	10//99-12//99
	Oregon	S	37.38 MW	38.98 AW	81080 AAW	ORBLS	10//99-12//99
	Eugene-Springfield MSA, OR	S	35.89 MW	34.42 AW	74640 AAW	ORBLS	10//99-12//99
	Medford-Ashland MSA, OR	S	36.41 MW	32.54 AW	75720 AAW	ORBLS	10//99-12//99
	Portland-Vancouver PMSA, OR-WA	S	40.14 MW	38.58 AW	83490 AAW	ORBLS	10//99-12//99
	Salem PMSA, OR	S	32.48 MW	24.83 AW	67550 AAW	ORBLS	10//99-12//99
	Pennsylvania	S	31.85 MW	34.89 AW	72570 AAW	PABLS	10//99-12//99
	Allentown-Bethlehem-Easton MSA, PA	S	30.48 MW	27.78 AW	63390 AAW	PABLS	10//99-12//99
	Altoona MSA, PA	S	21.12 MW	15.80 AW	43920 AAW	PABLS	10//99-12//99
	Erie MSA, PA	S	28.62 MW	25.06 AW	59520 AAW	PABLS	10//99-12//99
	Harrisburg-Lebanon-Carlisle MSA, PA	S	33.18 MW	31.67 AW	69020 AAW	PABLS	10//99-12//99
	Johnstown MSA, PA	S	27.99 MW	25.54 AW	58220 AAW	PABLS	10//99-12//99
	Lancaster MSA, PA	S	35.11 MW	33.00 AW	73030 AAW	PABLS	10//99-12//99
	Philadelphia PMSA, PA-NJ	S	37.48 MW	33.99 AW	77950 AAW	PABLS	10//99-12//99
	Pittsburgh MSA, PA	S	36.94 MW	34.91 AW	76840 AAW	PABLS	10//99-12//99
	Reading MSA, PA	S	34.10 MW	32.03 AW	70930 AAW	PABLS	10//99-12//99

AAW Average annual wage	**AOH** Average offered, high	**ASH** Average starting, high	**H** Hourly	**M** Monthly	**S** Special: hourly and annual
AE Average entry wage	**AOL** Average offered, low	**ASL** Average starting, low	**HI** Highest wage paid	**MTC** Median total compensation	**TQ** Third quartile wage
AEX Average experienced wage	**APH** Average pay, high range	**AW** Average wage paid	**HR** High end range	**MW** Median wage paid	**W** Weekly
AO Average offered	**APL** Average pay, low range	**FQ** First quartile wage	**LR** Low end range	**SQ** Second quartile wage	**Y** Yearly

Occupation/Type/Industry	Location	Per	Low	Mid	High	Source	Date
Sales Manager	Scranton--Wilkes-Barre--						
	Hazleton MSA, PA	S	24.67 MW	21.89 AW	51310 AAW	PABLS	10//99-12//99
	Sharon MSA, PA	S	28.18 MW	25.75 AW	58620 AAW	PABLS	10//99-12//99
	State College MSA, PA	S	22.12 MW	17.25 AW	46010 AAW	PABLS	10//99-12//99
	Williamsport MSA, PA	S	23.16 MW	22.20 AW	48180 AAW	PABLS	10//99-12//99
	York MSA, PA	S	26.46 MW	25.02 AW	55030 AAW	PABLS	10//99-12//99
	Rhode Island	S	33.1 MW	38.62 AW	80320 AAW	RIBLS	10//99-12//99
	Providence-Fall River-						
	Warwick MSA, RI-MA	S	36.39 MW	31.10 AW	75690 AAW	RIBLS	10//99-12//99
	South Carolina	S	23.6 MW	26.53 AW	55180 AAW	SCBLS	10//99-12//99
	Charleston-North Charleston						
	MSA, SC	S	27.50 MW	23.84 AW	57210 AAW	SCBLS	10//99-12//99
	Columbia MSA, SC	S	32.44 MW	31.78 AW	67480 AAW	SCBLS	10//99-12//99
	Florence MSA, SC	S	30.11 MW	28.45 AW	62640 AAW	SCBLS	10//99-12//99
	Greenville-Spartanburg-						
	Anderson MSA, SC	S	27.54 MW	23.80 AW	57290 AAW	SCBLS	10//99-12//99
	Myrtle Beach MSA, SC	S	22.61 MW	22.32 AW	47040 AAW	SCBLS	10//99-12//99
	Sumter MSA, SC	S	16.64 MW	13.39 AW	34610 AAW	SCBLS	10//99-12//99
	South Dakota	S	32.59 MW	36.27 AW	75440 AAW	SDBLS	10//99-12//99
	Rapid City MSA, SD	S	36.96 MW	32.14 AW	76880 AAW	SDBLS	10//99-12//99
	Tennessee	S	26.09 MW	28.57 AW	59430 AAW	TNBLS	10//99-12//99
	Chattanooga MSA, TN-GA	S	25.05 MW	23.51 AW	52100 AAW	TNBLS	10//99-12//99
	Clarksville-Hopkinsville MSA,						
	TN-KY	S	26.89 MW	25.73 AW	55920 AAW	TNBLS	10//99-12//99
	Jackson MSA, TN	S	31.70 MW	28.53 AW	65940 AAW	TNBLS	10//99-12//99
	Johnson City-Kingsport-Bristol						
	MSA, TN-VA	S	17.77 MW	13.34 AW	36960 AAW	TNBLS	10//99-12//99
	Knoxville MSA, TN	S	29.13 MW	27.45 AW	60600 AAW	TNBLS	10//99-12//99
	Memphis MSA, TN-AR-MS	S	31.68 MW	29.08 AW	65890 AAW	MSBLS	10//99-12//99
	Nashville MSA, TN	S	31.61 MW	29.56 AW	65750 AAW	TNBLS	10//99-12//99
	Texas	S	29.56 MW	31.84 AW	66220 AAW	TXBLS	10//99-12//99
	Abilene MSA, TX	S	21.92 MW	20.74 AW	45600 AAW	TXBLS	10//99-12//99
	Amarillo MSA, TX	S	24.12 MW	19.86 AW	50180 AAW	TXBLS	10//99-12//99
	Austin-San Marcos MSA, TX	S	34.95 MW	35.40 AW	72700 AAW	TXBLS	10//99-12//99
	Brazoria PMSA, TX	S	28.28 MW	27.75 AW	58830 AAW	TXBLS	10//99-12//99
	Bryan-College Station MSA,						
	TX	S	27.50 MW	22.05 AW	57210 AAW	TXBLS	10//99-12//99
	Corpus Christi MSA, TX	S	25.36 MW	24.22 AW	52750 AAW	TXBLS	10//99-12//99
	Dallas PMSA, TX	S	36.15 MW	33.35 AW	75180 AAW	TXBLS	10//99-12//99
	El Paso MSA, TX	S	23.46 MW	16.35 AW	48790 AAW	TXBLS	10//99-12//99
	Fort Worth-Arlington PMSA,						
	TX	S	32.02 MW	31.21 AW	66600 AAW	TXBLS	10//99-12//99
	Galveston-Texas City PMSA,						
	TX	S	29.33 MW	28.31 AW	61010 AAW	TXBLS	10//99-12//99
	Houston PMSA, TX	S	30.61 MW	28.50 AW	63670 AAW	TXBLS	10//99-12//99
	Laredo MSA, TX	S	25.60 MW	23.95 AW	53250 AAW	TXBLS	10//99-12//99
	Longview-Marshall MSA, TX	S	25.28 MW	23.54 AW	52580 AAW	TXBLS	10//99-12//99
	Lubbock MSA, TX	S	31.92 MW	30.24 AW	66400 AAW	TXBLS	10//99-12//99
	McAllen-Edinburg-Mission						
	MSA, TX	S	35.58 MW	35.70 AW	74000 AAW	TXBLS	10//99-12//99
	Odessa-Midland MSA, TX	S	28.29 MW	25.74 AW	58840 AAW	TXBLS	10//99-12//99
	San Angelo MSA, TX	S	29.76 MW	25.23 AW	61890 AAW	TXBLS	10//99-12//99
	San Antonio MSA, TX	S	29.17 MW	27.05 AW	60680 AAW	TXBLS	10//99-12//99
	Sherman-Denison MSA, TX	S	28.52 MW	29.63 AW	59330 AAW	TXBLS	10//99-12//99
	Texarkana MSA, TX-						
	Texarkana, AR	S	22.24 MW	23.37 AW	46260 AAW	TXBLS	10//99-12//99
	Tyler MSA, TX	S	30.50 MW	27.51 AW	63440 AAW	TXBLS	10//99-12//99
	Victoria MSA, TX	S	23.14 MW	16.98 AW	48130 AAW	TXBLS	10//99-12//99
	Waco MSA, TX	S	22.51 MW	17.55 AW	46810 AAW	TXBLS	10//99-12//99
	Wichita Falls MSA, TX	S	26.43 MW	24.30 AW	54980 AAW	TXBLS	10//99-12//99
	Utah	S	23.64 MW	26.28 AW	54660 AAW	UTBLS	10//99-12//99
	Provo-Orem MSA, UT	S	24.84 MW	21.81 AW	51660 AAW	UTBLS	10//99-12//99
	Salt Lake City-Ogden MSA,						
	UT	S	26.91 MW	24.17 AW	55980 AAW	UTBLS	10//99-12//99
	Vermont	S	44.49 MW	40.83 AW	84920 AAW	VTBLS	10//99-12//99
	Burlington MSA, VT	S	42.23 MW	45.68 AW	87840 AAW	VTBLS	10//99-12//99
	Virginia	S	29.03 MW	32.75 AW	68120 AAW	VABLS	10//99-12//99
	Charlottesville MSA, VA	S	28.42 MW	22.89 AW	59110 AAW	VABLS	10//99-12//99
	Lynchburg MSA, VA	S	31.66 MW	35.19 AW	65840 AAW	VABLS	10//99-12//99
	Norfolk-Virginia Beach-						
	Newport News MSA, VA-						
	NC	S	33.65 MW	29.43 AW	70000 AAW	VABLS	10//99-12//99

AAW Average annual wage	AOH Average offered, high	ASH Average starting, high	H Hourly	M Monthly	S Special: hourly and annual
AE Average entry wage	AOL Average offered, low	ASL Average starting, low	HI Highest wage paid	MTC Median total compensation	TQ Third quartile wage
AEX Average experienced wage	APH Average pay, high range	AW Average wage paid	HR High end range	MW Median wage paid	W Weekly
AO Average offered	APL Average pay, low range	FQ First quartile wage	LR Low end range	SQ Second quartile wage	Y Yearly

Occupation/Type/Industry	Location	Per	Low	Mid	High	Source	Date
Sales Manager	Richmond-Petersburg MSA, VA	S	31.88 MW	27.33 AW	66320 AAW	VABLS	10//99-12//99
	Roanoke MSA, VA	S	34.21 MW	31.99 AW	71170 AAW	VABLS	10//99-12//99
	Washington	S	33.06 MW	35.63 AW	74110 AAW	WABLS	10//99-12//99
	Bellingham MSA, WA	S	24.85 MW	21.34 AW	51690 AAW	WABLS	10//99-12//99
	Bremerton PMSA, WA	S	28.93 MW	27.36 AW	60170 AAW	WABLS	10//99-12//99
	Richland-Kennewick-Pasco MSA, WA	S	36.13 MW	34.79 AW	75160 AAW	WABLS	10//99-12//99
	Seattle-Bellevue-Everett PMSA, WA	S	36.71 MW	34.13 AW	76360 AAW	WABLS	10//99-12//99
	Spokane MSA, WA	S	31.62 MW	27.97 AW	65770 AAW	WABLS	10//99-12//99
	Tacoma PMSA, WA	S	33.19 MW	30.16 AW	69040 AAW	WABLS	10//99-12//99
	Yakima MSA, WA	S	34.82 MW	32.27 AW	72430 AAW	WABLS	10//99-12//99
	West Virginia	S	21.57 MW	25.31 AW	52650 AAW	WVBLS	10//99-12//99
	Charleston MSA, WV	S	28.52 MW	27.11 AW	59320 AAW	WVBLS	10//99-12//99
	Huntington-Ashland MSA, WV-KY-OH	S	27.57 MW	20.73 AW	57340 AAW	WVBLS	10//99-12//99
	Parkersburg-Marietta MSA, WV-OH	S	30.82 MW	30.58 AW	64110 AAW	WVBLS	10//99-12//99
	Wheeling MSA, WV-OH	S	18.78 MW	16.53 AW	39060 AAW	WVBLS	10//99-12//99
	Wisconsin	S	27.35 MW	29.18 AW	60700 AAW	WIBLS	10//99-12//99
	Appleton-Oshkosh-Neenah MSA, WI	S	27.74 MW	26.39 AW	57690 AAW	WIBLS	10//99-12//99
	Eau Claire MSA, WI	S	22.46 MW	17.13 AW	46710 AAW	WIBLS	10//99-12//99
	Green Bay MSA, WI	S	32.50 MW	31.27 AW	67600 AAW	WIBLS	10//99-12//99
	Janesville-Beloit MSA, WI	S	24.74 MW	23.54 AW	51460 AAW	WIBLS	10//99-12//99
	Kenosha PMSA, WI	S	24.11 MW	20.45 AW	50160 AAW	WIBLS	10//99-12//99
	La Crosse MSA, WI-MN	S	24.61 MW	21.66 AW	51190 AAW	WIBLS	10//99-12//99
	Madison MSA, WI	S	30.05 MW	29.02 AW	62510 AAW	WIBLS	10//99-12//99
	Milwaukee-Waukesha PMSA, WI	S	31.95 MW	29.98 AW	66450 AAW	WIBLS	10//99-12//99
	Racine PMSA, WI	S	28.60 MW	29.01 AW	59480 AAW	WIBLS	10//99-12//99
	Sheboygan MSA, WI	S	25.58 MW	20.81 AW	53210 AAW	WIBLS	10//99-12//99
	Wausau MSA, WI	S	24.87 MW	21.32 AW	51730 AAW	WIBLS	10//99-12//99
	Wyoming	S	20.2 MW	22.47 AW	46730 AAW	WYBLS	10//99-12//99
	Casper MSA, WY	S	23.57 MW	22.41 AW	49030 AAW	WYBLS	10//99-12//99
	Cheyenne MSA, WY	S	25.40 MW	21.22 AW	52840 AAW	WYBLS	10//99-12//99
	Puerto Rico	S	24.43 MW	26.10 AW	54290 AAW	PRBLS	10//99-12//99
	Caguas PMSA, PR	S	25.31 MW	18.95 AW	52650 AAW	PRBLS	10//99-12//99
	Mayaguez MSA, PR	S	17.44 MW	17.98 AW	36270 AAW	PRBLS	10//99-12//99
	Ponce MSA, PR	S	22.33 MW	22.95 AW	46440 AAW	PRBLS	10//99-12//99
	San Juan-Bayamon PMSA, PR	S	27.25 MW	25.88 AW	56680 AAW	PRBLS	10//99-12//99
	Guam	S	16.42 MW	20.12 AW	41850 AAW	GUBLS	10//99-12//99
Beer Wholesaling	United States	Y	56180 MW	58834 AW		BEVW	1999
Computer Reseller	United States	Y		75000 AW		CORES3	2000
Foundry	United States	Y	63800 MW	61400 AW		MODCAS	1999
Sales Person							
Computer Reseller	United States	Y		54000 MW		CORES	1999
Female, Real Estate	United States	Y		30420 AW		TRAVWK4	2000
Male, Real Estate	United States	Y		39884 AW		TRAVWK4	2000
Sales Representative							
Wholesale and Manufacturing, Except Technical and Scientific Product	Alabama	S	16.99 MW	19.85 AW	41280 AAW	ALBLS	10//99-12//99
Wholesale and Manufacturing, Except Technical and Scientific Product	Anniston MSA, AL	S	14.13 MW	13.09 AW	29390 AAW	ALBLS	10//99-12//99
Wholesale and Manufacturing, Except Technical and Scientific Product	Auburn-Opelika MSA, AL	S	17.62 MW	15.18 AW	36650 AAW	ALBLS	10//99-12//99
Wholesale and Manufacturing, Except Technical and Scientific Product	Birmingham MSA, AL	S	20.49 MW	17.17 AW	42610 AAW	ALBLS	10//99-12//99
Wholesale and Manufacturing, Except Technical and Scientific Product	Decatur MSA, AL	S	16.87 MW	16.23 AW	35100 AAW	ALBLS	10//99-12//99
Wholesale and Manufacturing, Except Technical and Scientific Product	Dothan MSA, AL	S	15.26 MW	14.39 AW	31730 AAW	ALBLS	10//99-12//99
Wholesale and Manufacturing, Except Technical and Scientific Product	Florence MSA, AL	S	19.18 MW	15.59 AW	39900 AAW	ALBLS	10//99-12//99
Wholesale and Manufacturing, Except Technical and Scientific Product	Gadsden MSA, AL	S	16.00 MW	14.30 AW	33280 AAW	ALBLS	10//99-12//99
Wholesale and Manufacturing, Except Technical and Scientific Product	Huntsville MSA, AL	S	20.86 MW	19.16 AW	43380 AAW	ALBLS	10//99-12//99

AAW	Average annual wage	AOH	Average offered, high	ASH	Average starting, high	H	Hourly	M	Monthly	S	Special: hourly and annual
AE	Average entry wage	AOL	Average offered, low	ASL	Average starting, low	HI	Highest wage paid	MTC	Median total compensation	TQ	Third quartile wage
AEX	Average experienced wage	APH	Average pay, high range	AW	Average wage paid	HR	High end range	MW	Median wage paid	W	Weekly
AO	Average offered	APL	Average pay, low range	FQ	First quartile wage	LR	Low end range	SQ	Second quartile wage	Y	Yearly

Sales Representative

Occupation/Type/Industry	Location	Per	Low	Mid	High	Source	Date
Wholesale and Manufacturing, Except Technical and Scientific Product	Mobile MSA, AL	S	18.47 MW	16.15 AW	38420 AAW	ALBLS	10//99-12//99
Wholesale and Manufacturing, Except Technical and Scientific Product	Montgomery MSA, AL	S	18.75 MW	16.76 AW	39010 AAW	ALBLS	10//99-12//99
Wholesale and Manufacturing, Except Technical and Scientific Product	Tuscaloosa MSA, AL	S	16.94 MW	13.23 AW	35230 AAW	ALBLS	10//99-12//99
Wholesale and Manufacturing, Except Technical and Scientific Product	Alaska	S	17.08 MW	17.87 AW	37160 AAW	AKBLS	10//99-12//99
Wholesale and Manufacturing, Except Technical and Scientific Product	Anchorage MSA, AK	S	18.16 MW	16.85 AW	37780 AAW	AKBLS	10//99-12//99
Wholesale and Manufacturing, Except Technical and Scientific Product	Arizona	S	16.19 MW	18.78 AW	39050 AAW	AZBLS	10//99-12//99
Wholesale and Manufacturing, Except Technical and Scientific Product	Flagstaff MSA, AZ-UT	S	20.43 MW	14.86 AW	42500 AAW	AZBLS	10//99-12//99
Wholesale and Manufacturing, Except Technical and Scientific Product	Phoenix-Mesa MSA, AZ	S	19.52 MW	17.07 AW	40590 AAW	AZBLS	10//99-12//99
Wholesale and Manufacturing, Except Technical and Scientific Product	Tucson MSA, AZ	S	15.27 MW	12.98 AW	31750 AAW	AZBLS	10//99-12//99
Wholesale and Manufacturing, Except Technical and Scientific Product	Yuma MSA, AZ	S	15.35 MW	14.29 AW	31940 AAW	AZBLS	10//99-12//99
Wholesale and Manufacturing, Except Technical and Scientific Product	Arkansas	S	15.28 MW	17.67 AW	36740 AAW	ARBLS	10//99-12//99
Wholesale and Manufacturing, Except Technical and Scientific Product	Fayetteville-Springdale-Rogers MSA, AR	S	17.24 MW	15.22 AW	35860 AAW	ARBLS	10//99-12//99
Wholesale and Manufacturing, Except Technical and Scientific Product	Fort Smith MSA, AR-OK	S	16.15 MW	13.89 AW	33590 AAW	ARBLS	10//99-12//99
Wholesale and Manufacturing, Except Technical and Scientific Product	Jonesboro MSA, AR	S	21.91 MW	17.53 AW	45570 AAW	ARBLS	10//99-12//99
Wholesale and Manufacturing, Except Technical and Scientific Product	Little Rock-North Little Rock MSA, AR	S	18.66 MW	16.21 AW	38800 AAW	ARBLS	10//99-12//99
Wholesale and Manufacturing, Except Technical and Scientific Product	Pine Bluff MSA, AR	S	15.93 MW	14.21 AW	33130 AAW	ARBLS	10//99-12//99
Wholesale and Manufacturing, Except Technical and Scientific Product	California	S	19.07 MW	21.93 AW	45620 AAW	CABLS	10//99-12//99
Wholesale and Manufacturing, Except Technical and Scientific Product	Bakersfield MSA, CA	S	19.39 MW	17.89 AW	40330 AAW	CABLS	10//99-12//99
Wholesale and Manufacturing, Except Technical and Scientific Product	Chico-Paradise MSA, CA	S	17.30 MW	15.36 AW	35990 AAW	CABLS	10//99-12//99
Wholesale and Manufacturing, Except Technical and Scientific Product	Fresno MSA, CA	S	18.41 MW	16.77 AW	38290 AAW	CABLS	10//99-12//99
Wholesale and Manufacturing, Except Technical and Scientific Product	Los Angeles-Long Beach PMSA, CA	S	21.38 MW	18.58 AW	44470 AAW	CABLS	10//99-12//99
Wholesale and Manufacturing, Except Technical and Scientific Product	Merced MSA, CA	S	19.56 MW	17.66 AW	40690 AAW	CABLS	10//99-12//99
Wholesale and Manufacturing, Except Technical and Scientific Product	Modesto MSA, CA	S	18.52 MW	16.45 AW	38530 AAW	CABLS	10//99-12//99
Wholesale and Manufacturing, Except Technical and Scientific Product	Oakland PMSA, CA	S	23.56 MW	20.53 AW	49010 AAW	CABLS	10//99-12//99
Wholesale and Manufacturing, Except Technical and Scientific Product	Orange County PMSA, CA	S	22.73 MW	19.52 AW	47280 AAW	CABLS	10//99-12//99
Wholesale and Manufacturing, Except Technical and Scientific Product	Redding MSA, CA	S	15.30 MW	13.92 AW	31820 AAW	CABLS	10//99-12//99
Wholesale and Manufacturing, Except Technical and Scientific Product	Riverside-San Bernardino PMSA, CA	S	21.39 MW	20.09 AW	44480 AAW	CABLS	10//99-12//99
Wholesale and Manufacturing, Except Technical and Scientific Product	Sacramento PMSA, CA	S	19.44 MW	16.79 AW	40440 AAW	CABLS	10//99-12//99
Wholesale and Manufacturing, Except Technical and Scientific Product	Salinas MSA, CA	S	19.94 MW	17.12 AW	41470 AAW	CABLS	10//99-12//99
Wholesale and Manufacturing, Except Technical and Scientific Product	San Diego MSA, CA	S	20.12 MW	17.92 AW	41850 AAW	CABLS	10//99-12//99
Wholesale and Manufacturing, Except Technical and Scientific Product	San Francisco PMSA, CA	S	23.25 MW	20.29 AW	48360 AAW	CABLS	10//99-12//99
Wholesale and Manufacturing, Except Technical and Scientific Product	San Jose PMSA, CA	S	26.06 MW	22.12 AW	54210 AAW	CABLS	10//99-12//99

AAW Average annual wage	**AOH** Average offered, high	**ASH** Average starting, high	**H** Hourly
AE Average entry wage	**AOL** Average offered, low	**ASL** Average starting, low	**HI** Highest wage paid
AEX Average experienced wage	**APH** Average pay, high range	**AW** Average wage paid	**HR** High end range
AO Average offered	**APL** Average pay, low range	**FQ** First quartile wage	**LR** Low end range

M Monthly	**S** Special: hourly and annual	
MTC Median total compensation	**TQ** Third quartile wage	
MW Median wage paid	**W** Weekly	
SQ Second quartile wage	**Y** Yearly	

Occupation/Type/Industry	Location	Per	Low	Mid	High	Source	Date
Sales Representative							
Wholesale and Manufacturing, Except Technical and Scientific Product	San Luis Obispo-Atascadero-Paso Robles MSA, CA	S	17.40 MW	16.20 AW	36190 AAW	CABLS	10//99-12//99
Wholesale and Manufacturing, Except Technical and Scientific Product	Santa Barbara-Santa Maria-Lompoc MSA, CA	S	19.89 MW	17.72 AW	41370 AAW	CABLS	10//99-12//99
Wholesale and Manufacturing, Except Technical and Scientific Product	Santa Cruz-Watsonville PMSA, CA	S	21.68 MW	18.76 AW	45100 AAW	CABLS	10//99-12//99
Wholesale and Manufacturing, Except Technical and Scientific Product	Santa Rosa PMSA, CA	S	19.72 MW	17.08 AW	41010 AAW	CABLS	10//99-12//99
Wholesale and Manufacturing, Except Technical and Scientific Product	Stockton-Lodi MSA, CA	S	19.08 MW	16.97 AW	39690 AAW	CABLS	10//99-12//99
Wholesale and Manufacturing, Except Technical and Scientific Product	Vallejo-Fairfield-Napa PMSA, CA	S	19.88 MW	19.31 AW	41360 AAW	CABLS	10//99-12//99
Wholesale and Manufacturing, Except Technical and Scientific Product	Ventura PMSA, CA	S	19.63 MW	17.44 AW	40820 AAW	CABLS	10//99-12//99
Wholesale and Manufacturing, Except Technical and Scientific Product	Visalia-Tulare-Porterville MSA, CA	S	20.19 MW	18.45 AW	41990 AAW	CABLS	10//99-12//99
Wholesale and Manufacturing, Except Technical and Scientific Product	Yolo PMSA, CA	S	20.54 MW	18.12 AW	42710 AAW	CABLS	10//99-12//99
Wholesale and Manufacturing, Except Technical and Scientific Product	Yuba City MSA, CA	S	16.93 MW	14.69 AW	35210 AAW	CABLS	10//99-12//99
Wholesale and Manufacturing, Except Technical and Scientific Product	Colorado	S	17.88 MW	21.01 AW	43710 AAW	COBLS	10//99-12//99
Wholesale and Manufacturing, Except Technical and Scientific Product	Boulder-Longmont PMSA, CO	S	21.68 MW	18.29 AW	45090 AAW	COBLS	10//99-12//99
Wholesale and Manufacturing, Except Technical and Scientific Product	Colorado Springs MSA, CO	S	18.51 MW	16.06 AW	38500 AAW	COBLS	10//99-12//99
Wholesale and Manufacturing, Except Technical and Scientific Product	Denver PMSA, CO	S	21.40 MW	18.36 AW	44510 AAW	COBLS	10//99-12//99
Wholesale and Manufacturing, Except Technical and Scientific Product	Fort Collins-Loveland MSA, CO	S	19.73 MW	16.37 AW	41040 AAW	COBLS	10//99-12//99
Wholesale and Manufacturing, Except Technical and Scientific Product	Grand Junction MSA, CO	S	20.09 MW	18.30 AW	41790 AAW	COBLS	10//99-12//99
Wholesale and Manufacturing, Except Technical and Scientific Product	Greeley PMSA, CO	S	18.70 MW	16.04 AW	38910 AAW	COBLS	10//99-12//99
Wholesale and Manufacturing, Except Technical and Scientific Product	Pueblo MSA, CO	S	17.02 MW	14.72 AW	35400 AAW	COBLS	10//99-12//99
Wholesale and Manufacturing, Except Technical and Scientific Product	Connecticut	S	20.13 MW	23.21 AW	48280 AAW	CTBLS	10//99-12//99
Wholesale and Manufacturing, Except Technical and Scientific Product	Bridgeport PMSA, CT	S	23.08 MW	19.91 AW	48010 AAW	CTBLS	10//99-12//99
Wholesale and Manufacturing, Except Technical and Scientific Product	Danbury PMSA, CT	S	24.94 MW	21.71 AW	51870 AAW	CTBLS	10//99-12//99
Wholesale and Manufacturing, Except Technical and Scientific Product	Hartford MSA, CT	S	22.63 MW	19.96 AW	47080 AAW	CTBLS	10//99-12//99
Wholesale and Manufacturing, Except Technical and Scientific Product	New Haven-Meriden PMSA, CT	S	20.99 MW	17.45 AW	43660 AAW	CTBLS	10//99-12//99
Wholesale and Manufacturing, Except Technical and Scientific Product	New London-Norwich MSA, CT-RI	S	19.54 MW	17.97 AW	40650 AAW	CTBLS	10//99-12//99
Wholesale and Manufacturing, Except Technical and Scientific Product	Stamford-Norwalk PMSA, CT	S	25.68 MW	21.81 AW	53400 AAW	CTBLS	10//99-12//99
Wholesale and Manufacturing, Except Technical and Scientific Product	Waterbury PMSA, CT	S	21.88 MW	19.20 AW	45520 AAW	CTBLS	10//99-12//99
Wholesale and Manufacturing, Except Technical and Scientific Product	Delaware	S	13.19 MW	15.61 AW	32470 AAW	DEBLS	10//99-12//99
Wholesale and Manufacturing, Except Technical and Scientific Product	Dover MSA, DE	S	13.77 MW	11.14 AW	28640 AAW	DEBLS	10//99-12//99
Wholesale and Manufacturing, Except Technical and Scientific Product	Wilmington-Newark PMSA, DE-MD	S	15.03 MW	12.66 AW	31250 AAW	DEBLS	10//99-12//99
Wholesale and Manufacturing, Except Technical and Scientific Product	District of Columbia	S	17.45 MW	19.66 AW	40890 AAW	DCBLS	10//99-12//99

Occupation/Type/Industry	Location	Per	Low	Mid	High	Source	Date
Sales Representative							
Wholesale and Manufacturing, Except Technical and Scientific Product	Washington PMSA, DC-MD-VA-WV	S	22.44 MW	19.83 AW	46670 AAW	DCBLS	10//99-12//99
Wholesale and Manufacturing, Except Technical and Scientific Product	Florida	S	15.07 MW	17.67 AW	36750 AAW	FLBLS	10//99-12//99
Wholesale and Manufacturing, Except Technical and Scientific Product	Daytona Beach MSA, FL	S	14.63 MW	13.15 AW	30440 AAW	FLBLS	10//99-12//99
Wholesale and Manufacturing, Except Technical and Scientific Product	Fort Lauderdale PMSA, FL	S	19.26 MW	16.67 AW	40070 AAW	FLBLS	10//99-12//99
Wholesale and Manufacturing, Except Technical and Scientific Product	Fort Myers-Cape Coral MSA, FL	S	19.32 MW	16.70 AW	40190 AAW	FLBLS	10//99-12//99
Wholesale and Manufacturing, Except Technical and Scientific Product	Fort Pierce-Port St. Lucie MSA, FL	S	17.38 MW	14.80 AW	36150 AAW	FLBLS	10//99-12//99
Wholesale and Manufacturing, Except Technical and Scientific Product	Fort Walton Beach MSA, FL	S	14.58 MW	12.49 AW	30330 AAW	FLBLS	10//99-12//99
Wholesale and Manufacturing, Except Technical and Scientific Product	Gainesville MSA, FL	S	17.18 MW	15.37 AW	35740 AAW	FLBLS	10//99-12//99
Wholesale and Manufacturing, Except Technical and Scientific Product	Jacksonville MSA, FL	S	16.64 MW	14.41 AW	34620 AAW	FLBLS	10//99-12//99
Wholesale and Manufacturing, Except Technical and Scientific Product	Lakeland-Winter Haven MSA, FL	S	18.83 MW	15.98 AW	39160 AAW	FLBLS	10//99-12//99
Wholesale and Manufacturing, Except Technical and Scientific Product	Melbourne-Titusville-Palm Bay MSA, FL	S	15.53 MW	13.69 AW	32310 AAW	FLBLS	10//99-12//99
Wholesale and Manufacturing, Except Technical and Scientific Product	Miami PMSA, FL	S	16.57 MW	13.97 AW	34480 AAW	FLBLS	10//99-12//99
Wholesale and Manufacturing, Except Technical and Scientific Product	Naples MSA, FL	S	22.69 MW	17.08 AW	47190 AAW	FLBLS	10//99-12//99
Wholesale and Manufacturing, Except Technical and Scientific Product	Ocala MSA, FL	S	14.42 MW	12.51 AW	29990 AAW	FLBLS	10//99-12//99
Wholesale and Manufacturing, Except Technical and Scientific Product	Orlando MSA, FL	S	19.97 MW	16.81 AW	41550 AAW	FLBLS	10//99-12//99
Wholesale and Manufacturing, Except Technical and Scientific Product	Panama City MSA, FL	S	16.31 MW	14.31 AW	33920 AAW	FLBLS	10//99-12//99
Wholesale and Manufacturing, Except Technical and Scientific Product	Pensacola MSA, FL	S	16.55 MW	12.52 AW	34410 AAW	FLBLS	10//99-12//99
Wholesale and Manufacturing, Except Technical and Scientific Product	Punta Gorda MSA, FL	S	17.59 MW	12.91 AW	36600 AAW	FLBLS	10//99-12//99
Wholesale and Manufacturing, Except Technical and Scientific Product	Sarasota-Bradenton MSA, FL	S	15.21 MW	12.81 AW	31640 AAW	FLBLS	10//99-12//99
Wholesale and Manufacturing, Except Technical and Scientific Product	Tallahassee MSA, FL	S	20.03 MW	16.96 AW	41660 AAW	FLBLS	10//99-12//99
Wholesale and Manufacturing, Except Technical and Scientific Product	Tampa-St. Petersburg-Clearwater MSA, FL	S	17.36 MW	15.00 AW	36100 AAW	FLBLS	10//99-12//99
Wholesale and Manufacturing, Except Technical and Scientific Product	West Palm Beach-Boca Raton MSA, FL	S	19.50 MW	17.16 AW	40570 AAW	FLBLS	10//99-12//99
Wholesale and Manufacturing, Except Technical and Scientific Product	Georgia	S	17.78 MW	20.74 AW	43140 AAW	GABLS	10//99-12//99
Wholesale and Manufacturing, Except Technical and Scientific Product	Albany MSA, GA	S	17.89 MW	15.78 AW	37210 AAW	GABLS	10//99-12//99
Wholesale and Manufacturing, Except Technical and Scientific Product	Athens MSA, GA	S	18.54 MW	15.87 AW	38570 AAW	GABLS	10//99-12//99
Wholesale and Manufacturing, Except Technical and Scientific Product	Atlanta MSA, GA	S	21.54 MW	18.24 AW	44800 AAW	GABLS	10//99-12//99
Wholesale and Manufacturing, Except Technical and Scientific Product	Columbus MSA, GA-AL	S	19.00 MW	16.71 AW	39520 AAW	GABLS	10//99-12//99
Wholesale and Manufacturing, Except Technical and Scientific Product	Macon MSA, GA	S	20.69 MW	17.84 AW	43040 AAW	GABLS	10//99-12//99
Wholesale and Manufacturing, Except Technical and Scientific Product	Savannah MSA, GA	S	18.02 MW	16.24 AW	37490 AAW	GABLS	10//99-12//99
Wholesale and Manufacturing, Except Technical and Scientific Product	Hawaii	S	15.34 MW	16.72 AW	34780 AAW	HIBLS	10//99-12//99
Wholesale and Manufacturing, Except Technical and Scientific Product	Honolulu MSA, HI	S	17.11 MW	15.52 AW	35590 AAW	HIBLS	10//99-12//99

AAW Average annual wage | AOH Average offered, high | ASH Average starting, high | H Hourly | M Monthly | S Special: hourly and annual
AE Average entry wage | AOL Average offered, low | ASL Average starting, low | HI Highest wage paid | MTC Median total compensation | TQ Third quartile wage
AEX Average experienced wage | APH Average pay, high range | AW Average wage paid | HR High end range | MW Median wage paid | W Weekly
AO Average offered | APL Average pay, low range | FQ First quartile wage | LR Low end range | SQ Second quartile wage | Y Yearly

Sales Representative

Occupation/Type/Industry	Location	Per	Low	Mid	High	Source	Date
Wholesale and Manufacturing, Except Technical and Scientific Product	Idaho	S	15.96 MW	18.59 AW	38670 AAW	IDBLS	10//99-12//99
Wholesale and Manufacturing, Except Technical and Scientific Product	Boise City MSA, ID	S	20.64 MW	16.58 AW	42930 AAW	IDBLS	10//99-12//99
Wholesale and Manufacturing, Except Technical and Scientific Product	Pocatello MSA, ID	S	16.44 MW	15.90 AW	34200 AAW	IDBLS	10//99-12//99
Wholesale and Manufacturing, Except Technical and Scientific Product	Illinois	S	18.09 MW	20.62 AW	42890 AAW	ILBLS	10//99-12//99
Wholesale and Manufacturing, Except Technical and Scientific Product	Bloomington-Normal MSA, IL	S	18.24 MW	17.11 AW	37930 AAW	ILBLS	10//99-12//99
Wholesale and Manufacturing, Except Technical and Scientific Product	Champaign-Urbana MSA, IL	S	15.84 MW	13.93 AW	32940 AAW	ILBLS	10//99-12//99
Wholesale and Manufacturing, Except Technical and Scientific Product	Chicago PMSA, IL	S	21.09 MW	18.44 AW	43860 AAW	ILBLS	10//99-12//99
Wholesale and Manufacturing, Except Technical and Scientific Product	Decatur MSA, IL	S	21.18 MW	18.55 AW	44060 AAW	ILBLS	10//99-12//99
Wholesale and Manufacturing, Except Technical and Scientific Product	Kankakee PMSA, IL	S	19.77 MW	17.25 AW	41120 AAW	ILBLS	10//99-12//99
Wholesale and Manufacturing, Except Technical and Scientific Product	Peoria-Pekin MSA, IL	S	19.12 MW	16.83 AW	39780 AAW	ILBLS	10//99-12//99
Wholesale and Manufacturing, Except Technical and Scientific Product	Rockford MSA, IL	S	20.92 MW	19.23 AW	43520 AAW	ILBLS	10//99-12//99
Wholesale and Manufacturing, Except Technical and Scientific Product	Springfield MSA, IL	S	17.99 MW	15.61 AW	37430 AAW	ILBLS	10//99-12//99
Wholesale and Manufacturing, Except Technical and Scientific Product	Indiana	S	17.9 MW	20.68 AW	43020 AAW	INBLS	10//99-12//99
Wholesale and Manufacturing, Except Technical and Scientific Product	Bloomington MSA, IN	S	14.22 MW	12.37 AW	29570 AAW	INBLS	10//99-12//99
Wholesale and Manufacturing, Except Technical and Scientific Product	Elkhart-Goshen MSA, IN	S	22.41 MW	20.40 AW	46620 AAW	INBLS	10//99-12//99
Wholesale and Manufacturing, Except Technical and Scientific Product	Evansville-Henderson MSA, IN-KY	S	17.98 MW	15.98 AW	37400 AAW	INBLS	10//99-12//99
Wholesale and Manufacturing, Except Technical and Scientific Product	Fort Wayne MSA, IN	S	20.03 MW	16.91 AW	41660 AAW	INBLS	10//99-12//99
Wholesale and Manufacturing, Except Technical and Scientific Product	Gary PMSA, IN	S	19.88 MW	17.47 AW	41340 AAW	INBLS	10//99-12//99
Wholesale and Manufacturing, Except Technical and Scientific Product	Indianapolis MSA, IN	S	21.93 MW	18.68 AW	45620 AAW	INBLS	10//99-12//99
Wholesale and Manufacturing, Except Technical and Scientific Product	Kokomo MSA, IN	S	19.45 MW	16.88 AW	40450 AAW	INBLS	10//99-12//99
Wholesale and Manufacturing, Except Technical and Scientific Product	Lafayette MSA, IN	S	16.25 MW	13.32 AW	33790 AAW	INBLS	10//99-12//99
Wholesale and Manufacturing, Except Technical and Scientific Product	Muncie MSA, IN	S	20.89 MW	18.73 AW	43440 AAW	INBLS	10//99-12//99
Wholesale and Manufacturing, Except Technical and Scientific Product	South Bend MSA, IN	S	19.82 MW	18.22 AW	41220 AAW	INBLS	10//99-12//99
Wholesale and Manufacturing, Except Technical and Scientific Product	Terre Haute MSA, IN	S	16.91 MW	15.02 AW	35170 AAW	INBLS	10//99-12//99
Wholesale and Manufacturing, Except Technical and Scientific Product	Iowa	S	16.37 MW	18.75 AW	39010 AAW	IABLS	10//99-12//99
Wholesale and Manufacturing, Except Technical and Scientific Product	Cedar Rapids MSA, IA	S	17.33 MW	15.48 AW	36060 AAW	IABLS	10//99-12//99
Wholesale and Manufacturing, Except Technical and Scientific Product	Davenport-Moline-Rock Island MSA, IA-IL	S	17.21 MW	14.97 AW	35800 AAW	IABLS	10//99-12//99
Wholesale and Manufacturing, Except Technical and Scientific Product	Des Moines MSA, IA	S	20.52 MW	17.80 AW	42680 AAW	IABLS	10//99-12//99
Wholesale and Manufacturing, Except Technical and Scientific Product	Dubuque MSA, IA	S	18.57 MW	16.72 AW	38630 AAW	IABLS	10//99-12//99
Wholesale and Manufacturing, Except Technical and Scientific Product	Iowa City MSA, IA	S	18.82 MW	16.94 AW	39150 AAW	IABLS	10//99-12//99
Wholesale and Manufacturing, Except Technical and Scientific Product	Sioux City MSA, IA-NE	S	19.04 MW	16.49 AW	39610 AAW	IABLS	10//99-12//99
Wholesale and Manufacturing, Except Technical and Scientific Product	Waterloo-Cedar Falls MSA, IA	S	18.98 MW	16.99 AW	39470 AAW	IABLS	10//99-12//99
Wholesale and Manufacturing, Except Technical and Scientific Product	Kansas	S	17.5 MW	20.27 AW	42160 AAW	KSBLS	10//99-12//99
Wholesale and Manufacturing, Except Technical and Scientific Product	Lawrence MSA, KS	S	20.36 MW	16.45 AW	42340 AAW	KSBLS	10//99-12//99

AAW	Average annual wage	AOH	Average offered, high	ASH	Average starting, high	H	Hourly	M	Monthly	S	Special: hourly and annual
AE	Average entry wage	AOL	Average offered, low	ASL	Average starting, low	HI	Highest wage paid	MTC	Median total compensation	TQ	Third quartile wage
AEX	Average experienced wage	APH	Average pay, high range	AW	Average wage paid	HR	High end range	MW	Median wage paid	W	Weekly
AO	Average offered	APL	Average pay, low range	FQ	First quartile wage	LR	Low end range	SQ	Second quartile wage	Y	Yearly

1263

Occupation/Type/Industry	Location	Per	Low	Mid	High	Source	Date
Sales Representative							
Wholesale and Manufacturing, Except Technical and Scientific Product	Topeka MSA, KS	S	18.71 MW	17.30 AW	38910 AAW	KSBLS	10//99-12//99
Wholesale and Manufacturing, Except Technical and Scientific Product	Wichita MSA, KS	S	20.13 MW	16.89 AW	41860 AAW	KSBLS	10//99-12//99
Wholesale and Manufacturing, Except Technical and Scientific Product	Kentucky	S	16.17 MW	19.00 AW	39530 AAW	KYBLS	10//99-12//99
Wholesale and Manufacturing, Except Technical and Scientific Product	Lexington MSA, KY	S	19.09 MW	16.39 AW	39710 AAW	KYBLS	10//99-12//99
Wholesale and Manufacturing, Except Technical and Scientific Product	Louisville MSA, KY-IN	S	20.12 MW	17.29 AW	41850 AAW	KYBLS	10//99-12//99
Wholesale and Manufacturing, Except Technical and Scientific Product	Owensboro MSA, KY	S	17.54 MW	15.86 AW	36480 AAW	KYBLS	10//99-12//99
Wholesale and Manufacturing, Except Technical and Scientific Product	Louisiana	S	15.78 MW	17.93 AW	37300 AAW	LABLS	10//99-12//99
Wholesale and Manufacturing, Except Technical and Scientific Product	Alexandria MSA, LA	S	13.28 MW	11.85 AW	27610 AAW	LABLS	10//99-12//99
Wholesale and Manufacturing, Except Technical and Scientific Product	Baton Rouge MSA, LA	S	20.04 MW	18.25 AW	41690 AAW	LABLS	10//99-12//99
Wholesale and Manufacturing, Except Technical and Scientific Product	Houma MSA, LA	S	18.44 MW	17.24 AW	38350 AAW	LABLS	10//99-12//99
Wholesale and Manufacturing, Except Technical and Scientific Product	Lafayette MSA, LA	S	18.25 MW	15.72 AW	37960 AAW	LABLS	10//99-12//99
Wholesale and Manufacturing, Except Technical and Scientific Product	Lake Charles MSA, LA	S	16.44 MW	15.01 AW	34200 AAW	LABLS	10//99-12//99
Wholesale and Manufacturing, Except Technical and Scientific Product	Monroe MSA, LA	S	18.86 MW	15.68 AW	39220 AAW	LABLS	10//99-12//99
Wholesale and Manufacturing, Except Technical and Scientific Product	New Orleans MSA, LA	S	17.18 MW	14.92 AW	35740 AAW	LABLS	10//99-12//99
Wholesale and Manufacturing, Except Technical and Scientific Product	Shreveport-Bossier City MSA, LA	S	19.10 MW	16.64 AW	39730 AAW	LABLS	10//99-12//99
Wholesale and Manufacturing, Except Technical and Scientific Product	Maine	S	17.03 MW	19.67 AW	40920 AAW	MEBLS	10//99-12//99
Wholesale and Manufacturing, Except Technical and Scientific Product	Bangor MSA, ME	S	18.80 MW	16.43 AW	39100 AAW	MEBLS	10//99-12//99
Wholesale and Manufacturing, Except Technical and Scientific Product	Lewiston-Auburn MSA, ME	S	17.42 MW	16.23 AW	36230 AAW	MEBLS	10//99-12//99
Wholesale and Manufacturing, Except Technical and Scientific Product	Portland MSA, ME	S	19.41 MW	17.11 AW	40370 AAW	MEBLS	10//99-12//99
Wholesale and Manufacturing, Except Technical and Scientific Product	Maryland	S	19.09 MW	21.47 AW	44660 AAW	MDBLS	10//99-12//99
Wholesale and Manufacturing, Except Technical and Scientific Product	Baltimore PMSA, MD	S	20.88 MW	18.48 AW	43430 AAW	MDBLS	10//99-12//99
Wholesale and Manufacturing, Except Technical and Scientific Product	Cumberland MSA, MD-WV	S	16.24 MW	14.16 AW	33770 AAW	MDBLS	10//99-12//99
Wholesale and Manufacturing, Except Technical and Scientific Product	Hagerstown PMSA, MD	S	17.03 MW	13.78 AW	35430 AAW	MDBLS	10//99-12//99
Wholesale and Manufacturing, Except Technical and Scientific Product	Massachusetts	S	20.04 MW	23.13 AW	48100 AAW	MABLS	10//99-12//99
Wholesale and Manufacturing, Except Technical and Scientific Product	Barnstable-Yarmouth MSA, MA	S	18.31 MW	14.37 AW	38080 AAW	MABLS	10//99-12//99
Wholesale and Manufacturing, Except Technical and Scientific Product	Boston PMSA, MA-NH	S	23.44 MW	20.07 AW	48750 AAW	MABLS	10//99-12//99
Wholesale and Manufacturing, Except Technical and Scientific Product	Brockton PMSA, MA	S	24.81 MW	22.65 AW	51600 AAW	MABLS	10//99-12//99
Wholesale and Manufacturing, Except Technical and Scientific Product	Fitchburg-Leominster PMSA, MA	S	23.60 MW	20.50 AW	49080 AAW	MABLS	10//99-12//99
Wholesale and Manufacturing, Except Technical and Scientific Product	Lawrence PMSA, MA-NH	S	22.33 MW	19.14 AW	46450 AAW	MABLS	10//99-12//99
Wholesale and Manufacturing, Except Technical and Scientific Product	Lowell PMSA, MA-NH	S	27.93 MW	23.30 AW	58100 AAW	MABLS	10//99-12//99
Wholesale and Manufacturing, Except Technical and Scientific Product	New Bedford PMSA, MA	S	18.06 MW	15.54 AW	37570 AAW	MABLS	10//99-12//99
Wholesale and Manufacturing, Except Technical and Scientific Product	Pittsfield MSA, MA	S	20.68 MW	18.71 AW	43020 AAW	MABLS	10//99-12//99
Wholesale and Manufacturing, Except Technical and Scientific Product	Springfield MSA, MA	S	21.16 MW	19.31 AW	44020 AAW	MABLS	10//99-12//99

AAW	Average annual wage	AOH	Average offered, high	ASH	Average starting, high
AE	Average entry wage	AOL	Average offered, low	ASL	Average starting, low
AEX	Average experienced wage	APH	Average pay, high range	AW	Average wage paid
AO	Average offered	APL	Average pay, low range	FQ	First quartile wage

H	Hourly	M	Monthly	S	Special: hourly and annual
HI	Highest wage paid	MTC	Median total compensation	TQ	Third quartile wage
HR	High end range	MW	Median wage paid	W	Weekly
LR	Low end range	SQ	Second quartile wage	Y	Yearly

Occupation/Type/Industry	Location	Per	Low	Mid	High	Source	Date
Sales Representative							
Wholesale and Manufacturing, Except Technical and Scientific Product	Worcester PMSA, MA-CT	S	22.61 MW	19.83 AW	47030 AAW	MABLS	10//99-12//99
Wholesale and Manufacturing, Except Technical and Scientific Product	Michigan	S	18.63 MW	21.91 AW	45580 AAW	MIBLS	10//99-12//99
Wholesale and Manufacturing, Except Technical and Scientific Product	Ann Arbor PMSA, MI	S	19.66 MW	16.12 AW	40900 AAW	MIBLS	10//99-12//99
Wholesale and Manufacturing, Except Technical and Scientific Product	Benton Harbor MSA, MI	S	17.25 MW	15.15 AW	35890 AAW	MIBLS	10//99-12//99
Wholesale and Manufacturing, Except Technical and Scientific Product	Detroit PMSA, MI	S	23.51 MW	20.12 AW	48910 AAW	MIBLS	10//99-12//99
Wholesale and Manufacturing, Except Technical and Scientific Product	Flint PMSA, MI	S	19.37 MW	17.17 AW	40290 AAW	MIBLS	10//99-12//99
Wholesale and Manufacturing, Except Technical and Scientific Product	Grand Rapids-Muskegon-Holland MSA, MI	S	21.78 MW	19.06 AW	45300 AAW	MIBLS	10//99-12//99
Wholesale and Manufacturing, Except Technical and Scientific Product	Jackson MSA, MI	S	23.12 MW	19.76 AW	48100 AAW	MIBLS	10//99-12//99
Wholesale and Manufacturing, Except Technical and Scientific Product	Kalamazoo-Battle Creek MSA, MI	S	19.77 MW	16.67 AW	41120 AAW	MIBLS	10//99-12//99
Wholesale and Manufacturing, Except Technical and Scientific Product	Lansing-East Lansing MSA, MI	S	19.66 MW	17.66 AW	40900 AAW	MIBLS	10//99-12//99
Wholesale and Manufacturing, Except Technical and Scientific Product	Saginaw-Bay City-Midland MSA, MI	S	18.26 MW	16.68 AW	37980 AAW	MIBLS	10//99-12//99
Wholesale and Manufacturing, Except Technical and Scientific Product	Minnesota	S	19.99 MW	23.55 AW	48970 AAW	MNBLS	10//99-12//99
Wholesale and Manufacturing, Except Technical and Scientific Product	Duluth-Superior MSA, MN-WI	S	16.96 MW	15.58 AW	35280 AAW	MNBLS	10//99-12//99
Wholesale and Manufacturing, Except Technical and Scientific Product	Minneapolis-St. Paul MSA, MN-WI	S	24.29 MW	20.60 AW	50530 AAW	MNBLS	10//99-12//99
Wholesale and Manufacturing, Except Technical and Scientific Product	Rochester MSA, MN	S	18.26 MW	16.67 AW	37970 AAW	MNBLS	10//99-12//99
Wholesale and Manufacturing, Except Technical and Scientific Product	St. Cloud MSA, MN	S	25.29 MW	20.43 AW	52600 AAW	MNBLS	10//99-12//99
Wholesale and Manufacturing, Except Technical and Scientific Product	Mississippi	S	15.98 MW	17.98 AW	37400 AAW	MSBLS	10//99-12//99
Wholesale and Manufacturing, Except Technical and Scientific Product	Biloxi-Gulfport-Pascagoula MSA, MS	S	15.17 MW	14.31 AW	31550 AAW	MSBLS	10//99-12//99
Wholesale and Manufacturing, Except Technical and Scientific Product	Hattiesburg MSA, MS	S	16.39 MW	13.94 AW	34090 AAW	MSBLS	10//99-12//99
Wholesale and Manufacturing, Except Technical and Scientific Product	Jackson MSA, MS	S	18.18 MW	16.33 AW	37810 AAW	MSBLS	10//99-12//99
Wholesale and Manufacturing, Except Technical and Scientific Product	Missouri	S	16.88 MW	19.50 AW	40560 AAW	MOBLS	10//99-12//99
Wholesale and Manufacturing, Except Technical and Scientific Product	Columbia MSA, MO	S	15.00 MW	13.30 AW	31200 AAW	MOBLS	10//99-12//99
Wholesale and Manufacturing, Except Technical and Scientific Product	Joplin MSA, MO	S	15.23 MW	13.33 AW	31690 AAW	MOBLS	10//99-12//99
Wholesale and Manufacturing, Except Technical and Scientific Product	Kansas City MSA, MO-KS	S	22.13 MW	20.01 AW	46020 AAW	MOBLS	10//99-12//99
Wholesale and Manufacturing, Except Technical and Scientific Product	St. Joseph MSA, MO	S	16.26 MW	13.51 AW	33830 AAW	MOBLS	10//99-12//99
Wholesale and Manufacturing, Except Technical and Scientific Product	St. Louis MSA, MO-IL	S	19.91 MW	17.22 AW	41410 AAW	MOBLS	10//99-12//99
Wholesale and Manufacturing, Except Technical and Scientific Product	Springfield MSA, MO	S	17.33 MW	15.31 AW	36050 AAW	MOBLS	10//99-12//99
Wholesale and Manufacturing, Except Technical and Scientific Product	Montana	S	14.75 MW	16.84 AW	35030 AAW	MTBLS	10//99-12//99
Wholesale and Manufacturing, Except Technical and Scientific Product	Billings MSA, MT	S	16.91 MW	15.15 AW	35170 AAW	MTBLS	10//99-12//99
Wholesale and Manufacturing, Except Technical and Scientific Product	Great Falls MSA, MT	S	17.79 MW	15.14 AW	36990 AAW	MTBLS	10//99-12//99
Wholesale and Manufacturing, Except Technical and Scientific Product	Missoula MSA, MT	S	16.42 MW	15.78 AW	34140 AAW	MTBLS	10//99-12//99
Wholesale and Manufacturing, Except Technical and Scientific Product	Nebraska	S	16.67 MW	18.47 AW	38420 AAW	NEBLS	10//99-12//99

AAW	Average annual wage	AOH	Average offered, high	ASH	Average starting, high	H	Hourly	M	Monthly	S	Special: hourly and annual
AE	Average entry wage	AOL	Average offered, low	ASL	Average starting, low	HI	Highest wage paid	MTC	Median total compensation	TQ	Third quartile wage
AEX	Average experienced wage	APH	Average pay, high range	AW	Average wage paid	HR	High end range	MW	Median wage paid	W	Weekly
AO	Average offered	APL	Average pay, low range	FQ	First quartile wage	LR	Low end range	SQ	Second quartile wage	Y	Yearly

Sales Representative

Occupation/Type/Industry	Location	Per	Low	Mid	High	Source	Date
Wholesale and Manufacturing, Except Technical and Scientific Product	Lincoln MSA, NE	S	19.66 MW	17.20 AW	40900 AAW	NEBLS	10//99-12//99
Wholesale and Manufacturing, Except Technical and Scientific Product	Omaha MSA, NE-IA	S	18.75 MW	17.39 AW	39010 AAW	NEBLS	10//99-12//99
Wholesale and Manufacturing, Except Technical and Scientific Product	Nevada	S	17.42 MW	20.35 AW	42330 AAW	NVBLS	10//99-12//99
Wholesale and Manufacturing, Except Technical and Scientific Product	Las Vegas MSA, NV-AZ	S	19.78 MW	16.80 AW	41150 AAW	NVBLS	10//99-12//99
Wholesale and Manufacturing, Except Technical and Scientific Product	Reno MSA, NV	S	20.17 MW	17.62 AW	41940 AAW	NVBLS	10//99-12//99
Wholesale and Manufacturing, Except Technical and Scientific Product	New Hampshire	S	18.88 MW	21.51 AW	44740 AAW	NHBLS	10//99-12//99
Wholesale and Manufacturing, Except Technical and Scientific Product	Manchester PMSA, NH	S	21.90 MW	19.72 AW	45550 AAW	NHBLS	10//99-12//99
Wholesale and Manufacturing, Except Technical and Scientific Product	Nashua PMSA, NH	S	20.75 MW	17.62 AW	43170 AAW	NHBLS	10//99-12//99
Wholesale and Manufacturing, Except Technical and Scientific Product	Portsmouth-Rochester PMSA, NH-ME	S	22.03 MW	19.07 AW	45820 AAW	NHBLS	10//99-12//99
Wholesale and Manufacturing, Except Technical and Scientific Product	New Jersey	S	22.68 MW	25.82 AW	53710 AAW	NJBLS	10//99-12//99
Wholesale and Manufacturing, Except Technical and Scientific Product	Atlantic-Cape May PMSA, NJ	S	19.82 MW	16.67 AW	41230 AAW	NJBLS	10//99-12//99
Wholesale and Manufacturing, Except Technical and Scientific Product	Bergen-Passaic PMSA, NJ	S	25.55 MW	21.55 AW	53140 AAW	NJBLS	10//99-12//99
Wholesale and Manufacturing, Except Technical and Scientific Product	Jersey City PMSA, NJ	S	29.53 MW	26.24 AW	61420 AAW	NJBLS	10//99-12//99
Wholesale and Manufacturing, Except Technical and Scientific Product	Middlesex-Somerset-Hunterdon PMSA, NJ	S	26.13 MW	24.36 AW	54350 AAW	NJBLS	10//99-12//99
Wholesale and Manufacturing, Except Technical and Scientific Product	Monmouth-Ocean PMSA, NJ	S	22.01 MW	18.02 AW	45770 AAW	NJBLS	10//99-12//99
Wholesale and Manufacturing, Except Technical and Scientific Product	Newark PMSA, NJ	S	27.33 MW	23.88 AW	56860 AAW	NJBLS	10//99-12//99
Wholesale and Manufacturing, Except Technical and Scientific Product	Trenton PMSA, NJ	S	22.54 MW	20.37 AW	46890 AAW	NJBLS	10//99-12//99
Wholesale and Manufacturing, Except Technical and Scientific Product	Vineland-Millville-Bridgeton PMSA, NJ	S	19.82 MW	17.19 AW	41230 AAW	NJBLS	10//99-12//99
Wholesale and Manufacturing, Except Technical and Scientific Product	New Mexico	S	14.79 MW	16.28 AW	33850 AAW	NMBLS	10//99-12//99
Wholesale and Manufacturing, Except Technical and Scientific Product	Albuquerque MSA, NM	S	16.99 MW	15.20 AW	35340 AAW	NMBLS	10//99-12//99
Wholesale and Manufacturing, Except Technical and Scientific Product	Las Cruces MSA, NM	S	16.27 MW	12.64 AW	33840 AAW	NMBLS	10//99-12//99
Wholesale and Manufacturing, Except Technical and Scientific Product	Santa Fe MSA, NM	S	15.59 MW	13.35 AW	32420 AAW	NMBLS	10//99-12//99
Wholesale and Manufacturing, Except Technical and Scientific Product	New York	S	18.94 MW	22.64 AW	47080 AAW	NYBLS	10//99-12//99
Wholesale and Manufacturing, Except Technical and Scientific Product	Albany-Schenectady-Troy MSA, NY	S	19.87 MW	17.37 AW	41340 AAW	NYBLS	10//99-12//99
Wholesale and Manufacturing, Except Technical and Scientific Product	Binghamton MSA, NY	S	18.16 MW	15.55 AW	37780 AAW	NYBLS	10//99-12//99
Wholesale and Manufacturing, Except Technical and Scientific Product	Buffalo-Niagara Falls MSA, NY	S	18.64 MW	15.92 AW	38770 AAW	NYBLS	10//99-12//99
Wholesale and Manufacturing, Except Technical and Scientific Product	Dutchess County PMSA, NY	S	18.71 MW	17.83 AW	38930 AAW	NYBLS	10//99-12//99
Wholesale and Manufacturing, Except Technical and Scientific Product	Elmira MSA, NY	S	18.09 MW	15.70 AW	37630 AAW	NYBLS	10//99-12//99
Wholesale and Manufacturing, Except Technical and Scientific Product	Glens Falls MSA, NY	S	19.19 MW	17.47 AW	39910 AAW	NYBLS	10//99-12//99
Wholesale and Manufacturing, Except Technical and Scientific Product	Jamestown MSA, NY	S	22.51 MW	16.13 AW	46830 AAW	NYBLS	10//99-12//99
Wholesale and Manufacturing, Except Technical and Scientific Product	Nassau-Suffolk PMSA, NY	S	22.07 MW	18.80 AW	45910 AAW	NYBLS	10//99-12//99
Wholesale and Manufacturing, Except Technical and Scientific Product	New York PMSA, NY	S	24.17 MW	20.08 AW	50280 AAW	NYBLS	10//99-12//99

AAW	Average annual wage	AOH	Average offered, high	ASH	Average starting, high	H	Hourly	M	Monthly	S	Special: hourly and annual
AE	Average entry wage	AOL	Average offered, low	ASL	Average starting, low	HI	Highest wage paid	MTC	Median total compensation	TQ	Third quartile wage
AEX	Average experienced wage	APH	Average pay, high range	AW	Average wage paid	HR	High end range	MW	Median wage paid	W	Weekly
AO	Average offered	APL	Average pay, low range	FQ	First quartile wage	LR	Low end range	SQ	Second quartile wage	Y	Yearly

Sales Representative

Occupation/Type/Industry	Location	Per	Low	Mid	High	Source	Date
Wholesale and Manufacturing, Except Technical and Scientific Product	Newburgh PMSA, NY-PA	S	22.21 MW	19.67 AW	46190 AAW	NYBLS	10//99-12//99
Wholesale and Manufacturing, Except Technical and Scientific Product	Rochester MSA, NY	S	22.03 MW	19.19 AW	45830 AAW	NYBLS	10//99-12//99
Wholesale and Manufacturing, Except Technical and Scientific Product	Syracuse MSA, NY	S	19.25 MW	17.18 AW	40040 AAW	NYBLS	10//99-12//99
Wholesale and Manufacturing, Except Technical and Scientific Product	Utica-Rome MSA, NY	S	19.11 MW	17.93 AW	39740 AAW	NYBLS	10//99-12//99
Wholesale and Manufacturing, Except Technical and Scientific Product	North Carolina	S	17.14 MW	19.92 AW	41420 AAW	NCBLS	10//99-12//99
Wholesale and Manufacturing, Except Technical and Scientific Product	Asheville MSA, NC	S	14.87 MW	12.65 AW	30920 AAW	NCBLS	10//99-12//99
Wholesale and Manufacturing, Except Technical and Scientific Product	Charlotte-Gastonia-Rock Hill MSA, NC-SC	S	20.75 MW	17.82 AW	43150 AAW	NCBLS	10//99-12//99
Wholesale and Manufacturing, Except Technical and Scientific Product	Fayetteville MSA, NC	S	15.92 MW	14.44 AW	33120 AAW	NCBLS	10//99-12//99
Wholesale and Manufacturing, Except Technical and Scientific Product	Goldsboro MSA, NC	S	15.14 MW	13.72 AW	31480 AAW	NCBLS	10//99-12//99
Wholesale and Manufacturing, Except Technical and Scientific Product	Greensboro--Winston-Salem--High Point MSA, NC	S	23.07 MW	18.84 AW	47990 AAW	NCBLS	10//99-12//99
Wholesale and Manufacturing, Except Technical and Scientific Product	Greenville MSA, NC	S	17.84 MW	17.47 AW	37110 AAW	NCBLS	10//99-12//99
Wholesale and Manufacturing, Except Technical and Scientific Product	Hickory-Morganton-Lenoir MSA, NC	S	20.30 MW	16.65 AW	42220 AAW	NCBLS	10//99-12//99
Wholesale and Manufacturing, Except Technical and Scientific Product	Jacksonville MSA, NC	S	11.43 MW	10.28 AW	23770 AAW	NCBLS	10//99-12//99
Wholesale and Manufacturing, Except Technical and Scientific Product	Raleigh-Durham-Chapel Hill MSA, NC	S	20.39 MW	17.94 AW	42420 AAW	NCBLS	10//99-12//99
Wholesale and Manufacturing, Except Technical and Scientific Product	Rocky Mount MSA, NC	S	19.61 MW	16.56 AW	40800 AAW	NCBLS	10//99-12//99
Wholesale and Manufacturing, Except Technical and Scientific Product	Wilmington MSA, NC	S	15.96 MW	14.28 AW	33200 AAW	NCBLS	10//99-12//99
Wholesale and Manufacturing, Except Technical and Scientific Product	North Dakota	S	14.65 MW	16.00 AW	33280 AAW	NDBLS	10//99-12//99
Wholesale and Manufacturing, Except Technical and Scientific Product	Bismarck MSA, ND	S	15.20 MW	14.78 AW	31620 AAW	NDBLS	10//99-12//99
Wholesale and Manufacturing, Except Technical and Scientific Product	Fargo-Moorhead MSA, ND-MN	S	17.76 MW	16.22 AW	36950 AAW	NDBLS	10//99-12//99
Wholesale and Manufacturing, Except Technical and Scientific Product	Grand Forks MSA, ND-MN	S	16.45 MW	14.51 AW	34210 AAW	NDBLS	10//99-12//99
Wholesale and Manufacturing, Except Technical and Scientific Product	Ohio	S	18.25 MW	21.30 AW	44300 AAW	OHBLS	10//99-12//99
Wholesale and Manufacturing, Except Technical and Scientific Product	Akron PMSA, OH	S	19.14 MW	16.70 AW	39810 AAW	OHBLS	10//99-12//99
Wholesale and Manufacturing, Except Technical and Scientific Product	Canton-Massillon MSA, OH	S	20.73 MW	18.05 AW	43130 AAW	OHBLS	10//99-12//99
Wholesale and Manufacturing, Except Technical and Scientific Product	Cincinnati PMSA, OH-KY-IN	S	22.68 MW	19.39 AW	47170 AAW	OHBLS	10//99-12//99
Wholesale and Manufacturing, Except Technical and Scientific Product	Cleveland-Lorain-Elyria PMSA, OH	S	21.10 MW	18.08 AW	43880 AAW	OHBLS	10//99-12//99
Wholesale and Manufacturing, Except Technical and Scientific Product	Columbus MSA, OH	S	23.29 MW	19.19 AW	48450 AAW	OHBLS	10//99-12//99
Wholesale and Manufacturing, Except Technical and Scientific Product	Dayton-Springfield MSA, OH	S	21.99 MW	18.70 AW	45730 AAW	OHBLS	10//99-12//99
Wholesale and Manufacturing, Except Technical and Scientific Product	Hamilton-Middletown PMSA, OH	S	22.64 MW	19.57 AW	47090 AAW	OHBLS	10//99-12//99
Wholesale and Manufacturing, Except Technical and Scientific Product	Lima MSA, OH	S	17.10 MW	14.28 AW	35560 AAW	OHBLS	10//99-12//99
Wholesale and Manufacturing, Except Technical and Scientific Product	Mansfield MSA, OH	S	17.85 MW	15.80 AW	37130 AAW	OHBLS	10//99-12//99
Wholesale and Manufacturing, Except Technical and Scientific Product	Steubenville-Weirton MSA, OH-WV	S	18.29 MW	16.79 AW	38050 AAW	OHBLS	10//99-12//99

AAW	Average annual wage	AOH	Average offered, high	ASH	Average starting, high
AE	Average entry wage	AOL	Average offered, low	ASL	Average starting, low
AEX	Average experienced wage	APH	Average pay, high range	AW	Average wage paid
AO	Average offered	APL	Average pay, low range	FQ	First quartile wage

H	Hourly	M	Monthly	S	Special: hourly and annual
HI	Highest wage paid	MTC	Median total compensation	TQ	Third quartile wage
HR	High end range	MW	Median wage paid	W	Weekly
LR	Low end range	SQ	Second quartile wage	Y	Yearly

Occupation/Type/Industry	Location	Per	Low	Mid	High	Source	Date
Sales Representative							
Wholesale and Manufacturing, Except Technical and Scientific Product	Toledo MSA, OH	s	19.93 MW	17.88 AW	41460 AAW	OHBLS	10//99-12//99
Wholesale and Manufacturing, Except Technical and Scientific Product	Youngstown-Warren MSA, OH	s	16.52 MW	14.39 AW	34370 AAW	OHBLS	10//99-12//99
Wholesale and Manufacturing, Except Technical and Scientific Product	Oklahoma	s	15.04 MW	17.05 AW	35470 AAW	OKBLS	10//99-12//99
Wholesale and Manufacturing, Except Technical and Scientific Product	Enid MSA, OK	s	15.65 MW	12.90 AW	32550 AAW	OKBLS	10//99-12//99
Wholesale and Manufacturing, Except Technical and Scientific Product	Lawton MSA, OK	s	12.51 MW	12.35 AW	26020 AAW	OKBLS	10//99-12//99
Wholesale and Manufacturing, Except Technical and Scientific Product	Oklahoma City MSA, OK	s	16.96 MW	15.03 AW	35270 AAW	OKBLS	10//99-12//99
Wholesale and Manufacturing, Except Technical and Scientific Product	Tulsa MSA, OK	s	17.69 MW	15.61 AW	36790 AAW	OKBLS	10//99-12//99
Wholesale and Manufacturing, Except Technical and Scientific Product	Oregon	s	18.28 MW	20.69 AW	43030 AAW	ORBLS	10//99-12//99
Wholesale and Manufacturing, Except Technical and Scientific Product	Corvallis MSA, OR	s	16.10 MW	14.99 AW	33480 AAW	ORBLS	10//99-12//99
Wholesale and Manufacturing, Except Technical and Scientific Product	Eugene-Springfield MSA, OR	s	20.54 MW	17.16 AW	42720 AAW	ORBLS	10//99-12//99
Wholesale and Manufacturing, Except Technical and Scientific Product	Medford-Ashland MSA, OR	s	17.68 MW	15.33 AW	36780 AAW	ORBLS	10//99-12//99
Wholesale and Manufacturing, Except Technical and Scientific Product	Portland-Vancouver PMSA, OR-WA	s	21.12 MW	18.89 AW	43930 AAW	ORBLS	10//99-12//99
Wholesale and Manufacturing, Except Technical and Scientific Product	Salem PMSA, OR	s	19.09 MW	16.96 AW	39710 AAW	ORBLS	10//99-12//99
Wholesale and Manufacturing, Except Technical and Scientific Product	Pennsylvania	s	18.57 MW	20.93 AW	43520 AAW	PABLS	10//99-12//99
Wholesale and Manufacturing, Except Technical and Scientific Product	Allentown-Bethlehem-Easton MSA, PA	s	18.37 MW	16.64 AW	38210 AAW	PABLS	10//99-12//99
Wholesale and Manufacturing, Except Technical and Scientific Product	Altoona MSA, PA	s	18.55 MW	15.90 AW	38570 AAW	PABLS	10//99-12//99
Wholesale and Manufacturing, Except Technical and Scientific Product	Erie MSA, PA	s	18.28 MW	16.32 AW	38020 AAW	PABLS	10//99-12//99
Wholesale and Manufacturing, Except Technical and Scientific Product	Harrisburg-Lebanon-Carlisle MSA, PA	s	19.13 MW	17.41 AW	39780 AAW	PABLS	10//99-12//99
Wholesale and Manufacturing, Except Technical and Scientific Product	Johnstown MSA, PA	s	15.42 MW	13.99 AW	32070 AAW	PABLS	10//99-12//99
Wholesale and Manufacturing, Except Technical and Scientific Product	Lancaster MSA, PA	s	19.91 MW	17.19 AW	41420 AAW	PABLS	10//99-12//99
Wholesale and Manufacturing, Except Technical and Scientific Product	Philadelphia PMSA, PA-NJ	s	23.87 MW	20.98 AW	49650 AAW	PABLS	10//99-12//99
Wholesale and Manufacturing, Except Technical and Scientific Product	Pittsburgh MSA, PA	s	18.35 MW	16.66 AW	38170 AAW	PABLS	10//99-12//99
Wholesale and Manufacturing, Except Technical and Scientific Product	Reading MSA, PA	s	20.14 MW	18.06 AW	41890 AAW	PABLS	10//99-12//99
Wholesale and Manufacturing, Except Technical and Scientific Product	Scranton--Wilkes-Barre--Hazleton MSA, PA	s	18.70 MW	17.48 AW	38890 AAW	PABLS	10//99-12//99
Wholesale and Manufacturing, Except Technical and Scientific Product	Sharon MSA, PA	s	16.47 MW	14.70 AW	34250 AAW	PABLS	10//99-12//99
Wholesale and Manufacturing, Except Technical and Scientific Product	State College MSA, PA	s	15.89 MW	14.40 AW	33060 AAW	PABLS	10//99-12//99
Wholesale and Manufacturing, Except Technical and Scientific Product	Williamsport MSA, PA	s	18.05 MW	16.71 AW	37550 AAW	PABLS	10//99-12//99
Wholesale and Manufacturing, Except Technical and Scientific Product	York MSA, PA	s	22.02 MW	19.53 AW	45810 AAW	PABLS	10//99-12//99
Wholesale and Manufacturing, Except Technical and Scientific Product	Rhode Island	s	18.14 MW	20.44 AW	42520 AAW	RIBLS	10//99-12//99
Wholesale and Manufacturing, Except Technical and Scientific Product	Providence-Fall River-Warwick MSA, RI-MA	s	20.04 MW	17.95 AW	41680 AAW	RIBLS	10//99-12//99
Wholesale and Manufacturing, Except Technical and Scientific Product	South Carolina	s	16.17 MW	19.24 AW	40020 AAW	SCBLS	10//99-12//99
Wholesale and Manufacturing, Except Technical and Scientific Product	Charleston-North Charleston MSA, SC	s	17.82 MW	15.44 AW	37060 AAW	SCBLS	10//99-12//99

AAW	Average annual wage	AOH	Average offered, high	ASH	Average starting, high	H	Hourly	M	Monthly	S	Special: hourly and annual
AE	Average entry wage	AOL	Average offered, low	ASL	Average starting, low	HI	Highest wage paid	MTC	Median total compensation	TQ	Third quartile wage
AEX	Average experienced wage	APH	Average pay, high range	AW	Average wage paid	HR	High end range	MW	Median wage paid	W	Weekly
AO	Average offered	APL	Average pay, low range	FQ	First quartile wage	LR	Low end range	SQ	Second quartile wage	Y	Yearly

Occupation/Type/Industry	Location	Per	Low	Mid	High	Source	Date
Sales Representative							
Wholesale and Manufacturing, Except Technical and Scientific Product	Columbia MSA, SC	S	18.37 MW	14.94 AW	38200 AAW	SCBLS	10//99-12//99
Wholesale and Manufacturing, Except Technical and Scientific Product	Florence MSA, SC	S	17.67 MW	14.92 AW	36760 AAW	SCBLS	10//99-12//99
Wholesale and Manufacturing, Except Technical and Scientific Product	Greenville-Spartanburg-Anderson MSA, SC	S	20.34 MW	16.61 AW	42310 AAW	SCBLS	10//99-12//99
Wholesale and Manufacturing, Except Technical and Scientific Product	Myrtle Beach MSA, SC	S	15.92 MW	15.05 AW	33110 AAW	SCBLS	10//99-12//99
Wholesale and Manufacturing, Except Technical and Scientific Product	Sumter MSA, SC	S	16.49 MW	12.24 AW	34300 AAW	SCBLS	10//99-12//99
Wholesale and Manufacturing, Except Technical and Scientific Product	South Dakota	S	16.43 MW	17.65 AW	36720 AAW	SDBLS	10//99-12//99
Wholesale and Manufacturing, Except Technical and Scientific Product	Rapid City MSA, SD	S	16.85 MW	15.62 AW	35050 AAW	SDBLS	10//99-12//99
Wholesale and Manufacturing, Except Technical and Scientific Product	Sioux Falls MSA, SD	S	18.51 MW	17.30 AW	38510 AAW	SDBLS	10//99-12//99
Wholesale and Manufacturing, Except Technical and Scientific Product	Tennessee	S	17.67 MW	20.06 AW	41730 AAW	TNBLS	10//99-12//99
Wholesale and Manufacturing, Except Technical and Scientific Product	Chattanooga MSA, TN-GA	S	19.44 MW	17.86 AW	40440 AAW	TNBLS	10//99-12//99
Wholesale and Manufacturing, Except Technical and Scientific Product	Clarksville-Hopkinsville MSA, TN-KY	S	14.69 MW	12.17 AW	30560 AAW	TNBLS	10//99-12//99
Wholesale and Manufacturing, Except Technical and Scientific Product	Jackson MSA, TN	S	20.66 MW	18.06 AW	42980 AAW	TNBLS	10//99-12//99
Wholesale and Manufacturing, Except Technical and Scientific Product	Johnson City-Kingsport-Bristol MSA, TN-VA	S	16.29 MW	13.93 AW	33880 AAW	TNBLS	10//99-12//99
Wholesale and Manufacturing, Except Technical and Scientific Product	Knoxville MSA, TN	S	19.19 MW	16.14 AW	39910 AAW	TNBLS	10//99-12//99
Wholesale and Manufacturing, Except Technical and Scientific Product	Memphis MSA, TN-AR-MS	S	19.91 MW	17.24 AW	41410 AAW	MSBLS	10//99-12//99
Wholesale and Manufacturing, Except Technical and Scientific Product	Nashville MSA, TN	S	19.93 MW	18.28 AW	41460 AAW	TNBLS	10//99-12//99
Wholesale and Manufacturing, Except Technical and Scientific Product	Texas	S	17.4 MW	20.43 AW	42490 AAW	TXBLS	10//99-12//99
Wholesale and Manufacturing, Except Technical and Scientific Product	Abilene MSA, TX	S	13.43 MW	12.49 AW	27930 AAW	TXBLS	10//99-12//99
Wholesale and Manufacturing, Except Technical and Scientific Product	Amarillo MSA, TX	S	18.48 MW	16.10 AW	38430 AAW	TXBLS	10//99-12//99
Wholesale and Manufacturing, Except Technical and Scientific Product	Austin-San Marcos MSA, TX	S	20.48 MW	16.77 AW	42610 AAW	TXBLS	10//99-12//99
Wholesale and Manufacturing, Except Technical and Scientific Product	Beaumont-Port Arthur MSA, TX	S	18.00 MW	15.90 AW	37440 AAW	TXBLS	10//99-12//99
Wholesale and Manufacturing, Except Technical and Scientific Product	Brazoria PMSA, TX	S	22.55 MW	20.07 AW	46900 AAW	TXBLS	10//99-12//99
Wholesale and Manufacturing, Except Technical and Scientific Product	Brownsville-Harlingen-San Benito MSA, TX	S	13.05 MW	11.86 AW	27150 AAW	TXBLS	10//99-12//99
Wholesale and Manufacturing, Except Technical and Scientific Product	Bryan-College Station MSA, TX	S	15.12 MW	14.60 AW	31440 AAW	TXBLS	10//99-12//99
Wholesale and Manufacturing, Except Technical and Scientific Product	Corpus Christi MSA, TX	S	17.82 MW	16.10 AW	37070 AAW	TXBLS	10//99-12//99
Wholesale and Manufacturing, Except Technical and Scientific Product	Dallas PMSA, TX	S	23.01 MW	19.54 AW	47870 AAW	TXBLS	10//99-12//99
Wholesale and Manufacturing, Except Technical and Scientific Product	El Paso MSA, TX	S	15.92 MW	13.47 AW	33110 AAW	TXBLS	10//99-12//99
Wholesale and Manufacturing, Except Technical and Scientific Product	Fort Worth-Arlington PMSA, TX	S	21.66 MW	18.60 AW	45040 AAW	TXBLS	10//99-12//99
Wholesale and Manufacturing, Except Technical and Scientific Product	Galveston-Texas City PMSA, TX	S	15.12 MW	10.97 AW	31450 AAW	TXBLS	10//99-12//99
Wholesale and Manufacturing, Except Technical and Scientific Product	Houston PMSA, TX	S	20.55 MW	17.68 AW	42740 AAW	TXBLS	10//99-12//99
Wholesale and Manufacturing, Except Technical and Scientific Product	Killeen-Temple MSA, TX	S	16.13 MW	14.30 AW	33540 AAW	TXBLS	10//99-12//99

AAW	Average annual wage	AOH	Average offered, high	ASH	Average starting, high
AE	Average entry wage	AOL	Average offered, low	ASL	Average starting, low
AEX	Average experienced wage	APH	Average pay, high range	AW	Average wage paid
AO	Average offered	APL	Average pay, low range	FQ	First quartile wage

H	Hourly	M	Monthly
HI	Highest wage paid	MTC	Median total compensation
HR	High end range	MW	Median wage paid
LR	Low end range	SQ	Second quartile wage

S	Special: hourly and annual
TQ	Third quartile wage
W	Weekly
Y	Yearly

Occupation/Type/Industry	Location	Per	Low	Mid	High	Source	Date
Sales Representative							
Wholesale and Manufacturing, Except Technical and Scientific Product	Laredo MSA, TX	S	12.48 MW	11.20 AW	25970 AAW	TXBLS	10//99-12//99
Wholesale and Manufacturing, Except Technical and Scientific Product	Longview-Marshall MSA, TX	S	16.22 MW	14.35 AW	33740 AAW	TXBLS	10//99-12//99
Wholesale and Manufacturing, Except Technical and Scientific Product	Lubbock MSA, TX	S	21.07 MW	18.99 AW	43830 AAW	TXBLS	10//99-12//99
Wholesale and Manufacturing, Except Technical and Scientific Product	McAllen-Edinburg-Mission MSA, TX	S	15.56 MW	13.45 AW	32370 AAW	TXBLS	10//99-12//99
Wholesale and Manufacturing, Except Technical and Scientific Product	Odessa-Midland MSA, TX	S	19.58 MW	17.89 AW	40720 AAW	TXBLS	10//99-12//99
Wholesale and Manufacturing, Except Technical and Scientific Product	San Angelo MSA, TX	S	15.50 MW	13.80 AW	32230 AAW	TXBLS	10//99-12//99
Wholesale and Manufacturing, Except Technical and Scientific Product	San Antonio MSA, TX	S	18.07 MW	15.47 AW	37580 AAW	TXBLS	10//99-12//99
Wholesale and Manufacturing, Except Technical and Scientific Product	Sherman-Denison MSA, TX	S	16.55 MW	15.39 AW	34430 AAW	TXBLS	10//99-12//99
Wholesale and Manufacturing, Except Technical and Scientific Product	Texarkana MSA, TX-Texarkana, AR	S	15.91 MW	14.04 AW	33100 AAW	TXBLS	10//99-12//99
Wholesale and Manufacturing, Except Technical and Scientific Product	Tyler MSA, TX	S	21.29 MW	15.53 AW	44290 AAW	TXBLS	10//99-12//99
Wholesale and Manufacturing, Except Technical and Scientific Product	Victoria MSA, TX	S	15.18 MW	13.22 AW	31570 AAW	TXBLS	10//99-12//99
Wholesale and Manufacturing, Except Technical and Scientific Product	Waco MSA, TX	S	17.44 MW	15.03 AW	36280 AAW	TXBLS	10//99-12//99
Wholesale and Manufacturing, Except Technical and Scientific Product	Wichita Falls MSA, TX	S	15.18 MW	13.03 AW	31560 AAW	TXBLS	10//99-12//99
Wholesale and Manufacturing, Except Technical and Scientific Product	Utah	S	17.93 MW	20.00 AW	41610 AAW	UTBLS	10//99-12//99
Wholesale and Manufacturing, Except Technical and Scientific Product	Provo-Orem MSA, UT	S	19.56 MW	16.07 AW	40690 AAW	UTBLS	10//99-12//99
Wholesale and Manufacturing, Except Technical and Scientific Product	Salt Lake City-Ogden MSA, UT	S	20.55 MW	18.55 AW	42740 AAW	UTBLS	10//99-12//99
Wholesale and Manufacturing, Except Technical and Scientific Product	Vermont	S	17.17 MW	19.23 AW	39990 AAW	VTBLS	10//99-12//99
Wholesale and Manufacturing, Except Technical and Scientific Product	Burlington MSA, VT	S	19.56 MW	17.14 AW	40690 AAW	VTBLS	10//99-12//99
Wholesale and Manufacturing, Except Technical and Scientific Product	Virginia	S	17.38 MW	20.32 AW	42280 AAW	VABLS	10//99-12//99
Wholesale and Manufacturing, Except Technical and Scientific Product	Charlottesville MSA, VA	S	16.20 MW	14.08 AW	33700 AAW	VABLS	10//99-12//99
Wholesale and Manufacturing, Except Technical and Scientific Product	Danville MSA, VA	S	18.52 MW	15.60 AW	38520 AAW	VABLS	10//99-12//99
Wholesale and Manufacturing, Except Technical and Scientific Product	Lynchburg MSA, VA	S	18.89 MW	17.42 AW	39280 AAW	VABLS	10//99-12//99
Wholesale and Manufacturing, Except Technical and Scientific Product	Norfolk-Virginia Beach-Newport News MSA, VA-NC	S	19.36 MW	16.49 AW	40260 AAW	VABLS	10//99-12//99
Wholesale and Manufacturing, Except Technical and Scientific Product	Richmond-Petersburg MSA, VA	S	20.25 MW	18.26 AW	42120 AAW	VABLS	10//99-12//99
Wholesale and Manufacturing, Except Technical and Scientific Product	Roanoke MSA, VA	S	19.05 MW	16.52 AW	39620 AAW	VABLS	10//99-12//99
Wholesale and Manufacturing, Except Technical and Scientific Product	Washington	S	17.15 MW	19.71 AW	41000 AAW	WABLS	10//99-12//99
Wholesale and Manufacturing, Except Technical and Scientific Product	Bellingham MSA, WA	S	20.20 MW	16.53 AW	42010 AAW	WABLS	10//99-12//99
Wholesale and Manufacturing, Except Technical and Scientific Product	Bremerton PMSA, WA	S	15.61 MW	13.45 AW	32480 AAW	WABLS	10//99-12//99
Wholesale and Manufacturing, Except Technical and Scientific Product	Olympia PMSA, WA	S	17.91 MW	16.64 AW	37250 AAW	WABLS	10//99-12//99
Wholesale and Manufacturing, Except Technical and Scientific Product	Richland-Kennewick-Pasco MSA, WA	S	16.63 MW	14.91 AW	34580 AAW	WABLS	10//99-12//99
Wholesale and Manufacturing, Except Technical and Scientific Product	Seattle-Bellevue-Everett PMSA, WA	S	20.30 MW	17.71 AW	42220 AAW	WABLS	10//99-12//99

AAW	Average annual wage	**AOH**	Average offered, high	**ASH**	Average starting, high	**H**	Hourly	**M**	Monthly	**S**	Special: hourly and annual
AE	Average entry wage	**AOL**	Average offered, low	**ASL**	Average starting, low	**HI**	Highest wage paid	**MTC**	Median total compensation	**TQ**	Third quartile wage
AEX	Average experienced wage	**APH**	Average pay, high range	**AW**	Average wage paid	**HR**	High end range	**MW**	Median wage paid	**W**	Weekly
AO	Average offered	**APL**	Average pay, low range	**FQ**	First quartile wage	**LR**	Low end range	**SQ**	Second quartile wage	**Y**	Yearly

Sales Representative

Occupation/Type/Industry	Location	Per	Low	Mid	High	Source	Date
Wholesale and Manufacturing, Except Technical and Scientific Product	Spokane MSA, WA	S	18.23 MW	16.14 AW	37920 AAW	WABLS	10//99-12//99
Wholesale and Manufacturing, Except Technical and Scientific Product	Tacoma PMSA, WA	S	18.40 MW	16.28 AW	38280 AAW	WABLS	10//99-12//99
Wholesale and Manufacturing, Except Technical and Scientific Product	Yakima MSA, WA	S	22.63 MW	19.04 AW	47080 AAW	WABLS	10//99-12//99
Wholesale and Manufacturing, Except Technical and Scientific Product	West Virginia	S	14.76 MW	15.81 AW	32880 AAW	WVBLS	10//99-12//99
Wholesale and Manufacturing, Except Technical and Scientific Product	Charleston MSA, WV	S	16.13 MW	13.83 AW	33550 AAW	WVBLS	10//99-12//99
Wholesale and Manufacturing, Except Technical and Scientific Product	Huntington-Ashland MSA, WV-KY-OH	S	15.21 MW	13.44 AW	31630 AAW	WVBLS	10//99-12//99
Wholesale and Manufacturing, Except Technical and Scientific Product	Parkersburg-Marietta MSA, WV-OH	S	13.24 MW	12.64 AW	27540 AAW	WVBLS	10//99-12//99
Wholesale and Manufacturing, Except Technical and Scientific Product	Wheeling MSA, WV-OH	S	15.81 MW	14.03 AW	32880 AAW	WVBLS	10//99-12//99
Wholesale and Manufacturing, Except Technical and Scientific Product	Wisconsin	S	18.57 MW	21.06 AW	43810 AAW	WIBLS	10//99-12//99
Wholesale and Manufacturing, Except Technical and Scientific Product	Appleton-Oshkosh-Neenah MSA, WI	S	22.61 MW	19.39 AW	47020 AAW	WIBLS	10//99-12//99
Wholesale and Manufacturing, Except Technical and Scientific Product	Eau Claire MSA, WI	S	20.24 MW	18.52 AW	42110 AAW	WIBLS	10//99-12//99
Wholesale and Manufacturing, Except Technical and Scientific Product	Green Bay MSA, WI	S	21.65 MW	18.97 AW	45030 AAW	WIBLS	10//99-12//99
Wholesale and Manufacturing, Except Technical and Scientific Product	Janesville-Beloit MSA, WI	S	21.84 MW	22.12 AW	45440 AAW	WIBLS	10//99-12//99
Wholesale and Manufacturing, Except Technical and Scientific Product	Kenosha PMSA, WI	S	21.12 MW	18.22 AW	43920 AAW	WIBLS	10//99-12//99
Wholesale and Manufacturing, Except Technical and Scientific Product	La Crosse MSA, WI-MN	S	17.17 MW	15.52 AW	35720 AAW	WIBLS	10//99-12//99
Wholesale and Manufacturing, Except Technical and Scientific Product	Madison MSA, WI	S	19.42 MW	17.21 AW	40390 AAW	WIBLS	10//99-12//99
Wholesale and Manufacturing, Except Technical and Scientific Product	Milwaukee-Waukesha PMSA, WI	S	22.87 MW	20.23 AW	47570 AAW	WIBLS	10//99-12//99
Wholesale and Manufacturing, Except Technical and Scientific Product	Racine PMSA, WI	S	21.40 MW	16.55 AW	44510 AAW	WIBLS	10//99-12//99
Wholesale and Manufacturing, Except Technical and Scientific Product	Sheboygan MSA, WI	S	23.13 MW	22.59 AW	48110 AAW	WIBLS	10//99-12//99
Wholesale and Manufacturing, Except Technical and Scientific Product	Wausau MSA, WI	S	19.49 MW	17.37 AW	40540 AAW	WIBLS	10//99-12//99
Wholesale and Manufacturing, Except Technical and Scientific Product	Wyoming	S	15.98 MW	16.63 AW	34590 AAW	WYBLS	10//99-12//99
Wholesale and Manufacturing, Except Technical and Scientific Product	Casper MSA, WY	S	16.21 MW	15.86 AW	33720 AAW	WYBLS	10//99-12//99
Wholesale and Manufacturing, Except Technical and Scientific Product	Cheyenne MSA, WY	S	15.66 MW	14.06 AW	32570 AAW	WYBLS	10//99-12//99
Wholesale and Manufacturing, Except Technical and Scientific Product	Puerto Rico	S	10.43 MW	12.26 AW	25500 AAW	PRBLS	10//99-12//99
Wholesale and Manufacturing, Except Technical and Scientific Product	Arecibo PMSA, PR	S	12.58 MW	10.51 AW	26160 AAW	PRBLS	10//99-12//99
Wholesale and Manufacturing, Except Technical and Scientific Product	Caguas PMSA, PR	S	10.90 MW	8.73 AW	22670 AAW	PRBLS	10//99-12//99
Wholesale and Manufacturing, Except Technical and Scientific Product	Mayaguez MSA, PR	S	10.71 MW	9.90 AW	22280 AAW	PRBLS	10//99-12//99
Wholesale and Manufacturing, Except Technical and Scientific Product	Ponce MSA, PR	S	10.32 MW	8.81 AW	21460 AAW	PRBLS	10//99-12//99
Wholesale and Manufacturing, Except Technical and Scientific Product	San Juan-Bayamon PMSA, PR	S	12.47 MW	10.62 AW	25940 AAW	PRBLS	10//99-12//99
Wholesale and Manufacturing, Except Technical and Scientific Product	Virgin Islands	S	11.11 MW	12.62 AW	26240 AAW	VIBLS	10//99-12//99
Wholesale and Manufacturing, Except Technical and Scientific Product	Guam	S	10.3 MW	11.49 AW	23890 AAW	GUBLS	10//99-12//99
Wholesale and Manufacturing, Technical and Scientific Product	Alabama	S	20.47 MW	24.70 AW	51380 AAW	ALBLS	10//99-12//99
Wholesale and Manufacturing, Technical and Scientific Product	Birmingham MSA, AL	S	23.13 MW	19.92 AW	48120 AAW	ALBLS	10//99-12//99

AAW	Average annual wage	AOH	Average offered, high	ASH	Average starting, high	H	Hourly	M	Monthly	S	Special: hourly and annual
AE	Average entry wage	AOL	Average offered, low	ASL	Average starting, low	HI	Highest wage paid	MTC	Median total compensation	TQ	Third quartile wage
AEX	Average experienced wage	APH	Average pay, high range	AW	Average wage paid	HR	High end range	MW	Median wage paid	W	Weekly
AO	Average offered	APL	Average pay, low range	FQ	First quartile wage	LR	Low end range	SQ	Second quartile wage	Y	Yearly

Occupation/Type/Industry	Location	Per	Low	Mid	High	Source	Date
Sales Representative							
Wholesale and Manufacturing, Technical and Scientific Product	Decatur MSA, AL	S	18.33 mw	16.69 aw	38120 aaw	ALBLS	10//99-12//99
Wholesale and Manufacturing, Technical and Scientific Product	Dothan MSA, AL	S	22.76 mw	19.73 aw	47330 aaw	ALBLS	10//99-12//99
Wholesale and Manufacturing, Technical and Scientific Product	Florence MSA, AL	S	24.59 mw	23.26 aw	51140 aaw	ALBLS	10//99-12//99
Wholesale and Manufacturing, Technical and Scientific Product	Huntsville MSA, AL	S	20.84 mw	18.44 aw	43350 aaw	ALBLS	10//99-12//99
Wholesale and Manufacturing, Technical and Scientific Product	Mobile MSA, AL	S	18.46 mw	16.51 aw	38390 aaw	ALBLS	10//99-12//99
Wholesale and Manufacturing, Technical and Scientific Product	Montgomery MSA, AL	S	17.34 mw	17.69 aw	36070 aaw	ALBLS	10//99-12//99
Wholesale and Manufacturing, Technical and Scientific Product	Alaska	S	19.68 mw	21.59 aw	44910 aaw	AKBLS	10//99-12//99
Wholesale and Manufacturing, Technical and Scientific Product	Anchorage MSA, AK	S	21.60 mw	19.73 aw	44940 aaw	AKBLS	10//99-12//99
Wholesale and Manufacturing, Technical and Scientific Product	Arizona	S	19.92 mw	23.19 aw	48240 aaw	AZBLS	10//99-12//99
Wholesale and Manufacturing, Technical and Scientific Product	Phoenix-Mesa MSA, AZ	S	23.24 mw	19.96 aw	48340 aaw	AZBLS	10//99-12//99
Wholesale and Manufacturing, Technical and Scientific Product	Tucson MSA, AZ	S	24.12 mw	20.39 aw	50170 aaw	AZBLS	10//99-12//99
Wholesale and Manufacturing, Technical and Scientific Product	Yuma MSA, AZ	S	18.67 mw	17.78 aw	38840 aaw	AZBLS	10//99-12//99
Wholesale and Manufacturing, Technical and Scientific Product	Arkansas	S	19.03 mw	20.72 aw	43100 aaw	ARBLS	10//99-12//99
Wholesale and Manufacturing, Technical and Scientific Product	Fayetteville-Springdale-Rogers MSA, AR	S	18.99 mw	16.01 aw	39500 aaw	ARBLS	10//99-12//99
Wholesale and Manufacturing, Technical and Scientific Product	Fort Smith MSA, AR-OK	S	21.56 mw	15.28 aw	44830 aaw	ARBLS	10//99-12//99
Wholesale and Manufacturing, Technical and Scientific Product	Little Rock-North Little Rock MSA, AR	S	20.55 mw	19.05 aw	42750 aaw	ARBLS	10//99-12//99
Wholesale and Manufacturing, Technical and Scientific Product	California	S	24.16 mw	27.11 aw	56380 aaw	CABLS	10//99-12//99
Wholesale and Manufacturing, Technical and Scientific Product	Bakersfield MSA, CA	S	24.46 mw	21.95 aw	50870 aaw	CABLS	10//99-12//99
Wholesale and Manufacturing, Technical and Scientific Product	Fresno MSA, CA	S	22.79 mw	20.37 aw	47400 aaw	CABLS	10//99-12//99
Wholesale and Manufacturing, Technical and Scientific Product	Los Angeles-Long Beach PMSA, CA	S	25.40 mw	22.50 aw	52820 aaw	CABLS	10//99-12//99
Wholesale and Manufacturing, Technical and Scientific Product	Modesto MSA, CA	S	19.90 mw	19.59 aw	41390 aaw	CABLS	10//99-12//99
Wholesale and Manufacturing, Technical and Scientific Product	Oakland PMSA, CA	S	27.01 mw	24.75 aw	56190 aaw	CABLS	10//99-12//99
Wholesale and Manufacturing, Technical and Scientific Product	Orange County PMSA, CA	S	28.09 mw	26.35 aw	58420 aaw	CABLS	10//99-12//99
Wholesale and Manufacturing, Technical and Scientific Product	Redding MSA, CA	S	16.65 mw	14.27 aw	34630 aaw	CABLS	10//99-12//99
Wholesale and Manufacturing, Technical and Scientific Product	Riverside-San Bernardino PMSA, CA	S	22.77 mw	19.72 aw	47360 aaw	CABLS	10//99-12//99
Wholesale and Manufacturing, Technical and Scientific Product	Sacramento PMSA, CA	S	27.37 mw	22.51 aw	56920 aaw	CABLS	10//99-12//99
Wholesale and Manufacturing, Technical and Scientific Product	Salinas MSA, CA	S	21.79 mw	17.45 aw	45320 aaw	CABLS	10//99-12//99
Wholesale and Manufacturing, Technical and Scientific Product	San Diego MSA, CA	S	27.34 mw	23.38 aw	56870 aaw	CABLS	10//99-12//99
Wholesale and Manufacturing, Technical and Scientific Product	San Francisco PMSA, CA	S	26.55 mw	24.36 aw	55220 aaw	CABLS	10//99-12//99
Wholesale and Manufacturing, Technical and Scientific Product	San Jose PMSA, CA	S	32.02 mw	29.23 aw	66600 aaw	CABLS	10//99-12//99
Wholesale and Manufacturing, Technical and Scientific Product	San Luis Obispo-Atascadero-Paso Robles MSA, CA	S	23.28 mw	18.29 aw	48420 aaw	CABLS	10//99-12//99
Wholesale and Manufacturing, Technical and Scientific Product	Santa Barbara-Santa Maria-Lompoc MSA, CA	S	23.08 mw	21.36 aw	48010 aaw	CABLS	10//99-12//99

AAW Average annual wage	**AOH** Average offered, high	**ASH** Average starting, high	**H** Hourly	**M** Monthly	**S** Special: hourly and annual
AE Average entry wage	**AOL** Average offered, low	**ASL** Average starting, low	**HI** Highest wage paid	**MTC** Median total compensation	**TQ** Third quartile wage
AEX Average experienced wage	**APH** Average pay, high range	**AW** Average wage paid	**HR** High end range	**MW** Median wage paid	**W** Weekly
AO Average offered	**APL** Average pay, low range	**FQ** First quartile wage	**LR** Low end range	**SQ** Second quartile wage	**Y** Yearly

Occupation/Type/Industry	Location	Per	Low	Mid	High	Source	Date
Sales Representative							
Wholesale and Manufacturing, Technical and Scientific Product	Santa Cruz-Watsonville PMSA, CA	S	22.36 MW	20.26 AW	46500 AAW	CABLS	10//99-12//99
Wholesale and Manufacturing, Technical and Scientific Product	Santa Rosa PMSA, CA	S	29.10 MW	29.23 AW	60530 AAW	CABLS	10//99-12//99
Wholesale and Manufacturing, Technical and Scientific Product	Stockton-Lodi MSA, CA	S	23.22 MW	19.21 AW	48300 AAW	CABLS	10//99-12//99
Wholesale and Manufacturing, Technical and Scientific Product	Vallejo-Fairfield-Napa PMSA, CA	S	24.27 MW	21.00 AW	50480 AAW	CABLS	10//99-12//99
Wholesale and Manufacturing, Technical and Scientific Product	Ventura PMSA, CA	S	28.10 MW	24.15 AW	58460 AAW	CABLS	10//99-12//99
Wholesale and Manufacturing, Technical and Scientific Product	Visalia-Tulare-Porterville MSA, CA	S	25.75 MW	22.48 AW	53560 AAW	CABLS	10//99-12//99
Wholesale and Manufacturing, Technical and Scientific Product	Yolo PMSA, CA	S	23.50 MW	20.28 AW	48890 AAW	CABLS	10//99-12//99
Wholesale and Manufacturing, Technical and Scientific Product	Colorado	S	30.83 MW	32.59 AW	67780 AAW	COBLS	10//99-12//99
Wholesale and Manufacturing, Technical and Scientific Product	Boulder-Longmont PMSA, CO	S	26.27 MW	24.63 AW	54640 AAW	COBLS	10//99-12//99
Wholesale and Manufacturing, Technical and Scientific Product	Colorado Springs MSA, CO	S	31.44 MW	30.08 AW	65400 AAW	COBLS	10//99-12//99
Wholesale and Manufacturing, Technical and Scientific Product	Denver PMSA, CO	S	34.18 MW	33.38 AW	71090 AAW	COBLS	10//99-12//99
Wholesale and Manufacturing, Technical and Scientific Product	Fort Collins-Loveland MSA, CO	S	28.81 MW	30.33 AW	59930 AAW	COBLS	10//99-12//99
Wholesale and Manufacturing, Technical and Scientific Product	Grand Junction MSA, CO	S	26.59 MW	23.35 AW	55300 AAW	COBLS	10//99-12//99
Wholesale and Manufacturing, Technical and Scientific Product	Greeley PMSA, CO	S	21.47 MW	18.36 AW	44660 AAW	COBLS	10//99-12//99
Wholesale and Manufacturing, Technical and Scientific Product	Connecticut	S	25.07 MW	27.22 AW	56610 AAW	CTBLS	10//99-12//99
Wholesale and Manufacturing, Technical and Scientific Product	Bridgeport PMSA, CT	S	23.69 MW	21.53 AW	49270 AAW	CTBLS	10//99-12//99
Wholesale and Manufacturing, Technical and Scientific Product	Hartford MSA, CT	S	28.23 MW	25.70 AW	58710 AAW	CTBLS	10//99-12//99
Wholesale and Manufacturing, Technical and Scientific Product	New Haven-Meriden PMSA, CT	S	27.05 MW	26.56 AW	56270 AAW	CTBLS	10//99-12//99
Wholesale and Manufacturing, Technical and Scientific Product	New London-Norwich MSA, CT-RI	S	25.72 MW	23.79 AW	53490 AAW	CTBLS	10//99-12//99
Wholesale and Manufacturing, Technical and Scientific Product	Stamford-Norwalk PMSA, CT	S	27.64 MW	23.83 AW	57480 AAW	CTBLS	10//99-12//99
Wholesale and Manufacturing, Technical and Scientific Product	Waterbury PMSA, CT	S	33.60 MW	29.72 AW	69880 AAW	CTBLS	10//99-12//99
Wholesale and Manufacturing, Technical and Scientific Product	Delaware	S	22.08 MW	22.65 AW	47120 AAW	DEBLS	10//99-12//99
Wholesale and Manufacturing, Technical and Scientific Product	Dover MSA, DE	S	15.24 MW	11.76 AW	31690 AAW	DEBLS	10//99-12//99
Wholesale and Manufacturing, Technical and Scientific Product	Wilmington-Newark PMSA, DE-MD	S	23.64 MW	22.52 AW	49170 AAW	DEBLS	10//99-12//99
Wholesale and Manufacturing, Technical and Scientific Product	District of Columbia	S	24.03 MW	27.12 AW	56400 AAW	DCBLS	10//99-12//99
Wholesale and Manufacturing, Technical and Scientific Product	Washington PMSA, DC-MD-VA-WV	S	27.18 MW	26.04 AW	56530 AAW	DCBLS	10//99-12//99
Wholesale and Manufacturing, Technical and Scientific Product	Florida	S	18.71 MW	22.05 AW	45860 AAW	FLBLS	10//99-12//99
Wholesale and Manufacturing, Technical and Scientific Product	Daytona Beach MSA, FL	S	17.02 MW	14.86 AW	35410 AAW	FLBLS	10//99-12//99
Wholesale and Manufacturing, Technical and Scientific Product	Fort Lauderdale PMSA, FL	S	21.68 MW	18.27 AW	45090 AAW	FLBLS	10//99-12//99
Wholesale and Manufacturing, Technical and Scientific Product	Fort Myers-Cape Coral MSA, FL	S	20.85 MW	19.90 AW	43380 AAW	FLBLS	10//99-12//99

Occupation/Type/Industry	Location	Per	Low	Mid	High	Source	Date
Sales Representative							
Wholesale and Manufacturing, Technical and Scientific Product	Fort Walton Beach MSA, FL	S	17.03 MW	17.18 AW	35420 AAW	FLBLS	10//99-12//99
Wholesale and Manufacturing, Technical and Scientific Product	Gainesville MSA, FL	S	24.30 MW	23.09 AW	50550 AAW	FLBLS	10//99-12//99
Wholesale and Manufacturing, Technical and Scientific Product	Jacksonville MSA, FL	S	21.71 MW	19.55 AW	45160 AAW	FLBLS	10//99-12//99
Wholesale and Manufacturing, Technical and Scientific Product	Lakeland-Winter Haven MSA, FL	S	21.80 MW	19.73 AW	45350 AAW	FLBLS	10//99-12//99
Wholesale and Manufacturing, Technical and Scientific Product	Melbourne-Titusville-Palm Bay MSA, FL	S	22.91 MW	18.76 AW	47660 AAW	FLBLS	10//99-12//99
Wholesale and Manufacturing, Technical and Scientific Product	Miami PMSA, FL	S	21.97 MW	18.69 AW	45700 AAW	FLBLS	10//99-12//99
Wholesale and Manufacturing, Technical and Scientific Product	Naples MSA, FL	S	24.79 MW	19.49 AW	51560 AAW	FLBLS	10//99-12//99
Wholesale and Manufacturing, Technical and Scientific Product	Ocala MSA, FL	S	18.27 MW	14.92 AW	38010 AAW	FLBLS	10//99-12//99
Wholesale and Manufacturing, Technical and Scientific Product	Orlando MSA, FL	S	24.50 MW	22.62 AW	50950 AAW	FLBLS	10//99-12//99
Wholesale and Manufacturing, Technical and Scientific Product	Pensacola MSA, FL	S	17.55 MW	16.54 AW	36490 AAW	FLBLS	10//99-12//99
Wholesale and Manufacturing, Technical and Scientific Product	Sarasota-Bradenton MSA, FL	S	23.92 MW	21.41 AW	49760 AAW	FLBLS	10//99-12//99
Wholesale and Manufacturing, Technical and Scientific Product	Tallahassee MSA, FL	S	27.80 MW	21.35 AW	57820 AAW	FLBLS	10//99-12//99
Wholesale and Manufacturing, Technical and Scientific Product	Tampa-St. Petersburg-Clearwater MSA, FL	S	19.92 MW	15.22 AW	41440 AAW	FLBLS	10//99-12//99
Wholesale and Manufacturing, Technical and Scientific Product	West Palm Beach-Boca Raton MSA, FL	S	26.34 MW	19.61 AW	54790 AAW	FLBLS	10//99-12//99
Wholesale and Manufacturing, Technical and Scientific Product	Georgia	S	21.08 MW	23.63 AW	49140 AAW	GABLS	10//99-12//99
Wholesale and Manufacturing, Technical and Scientific Product	Albany MSA, GA	S	19.27 MW	18.43 AW	40070 AAW	GABLS	10//99-12//99
Wholesale and Manufacturing, Technical and Scientific Product	Atlanta MSA, GA	S	24.28 MW	21.33 AW	50510 AAW	GABLS	10//99-12//99
Wholesale and Manufacturing, Technical and Scientific Product	Augusta-Aiken MSA, GA-SC	S	19.33 MW	17.29 AW	40200 AAW	GABLS	10//99-12//99
Wholesale and Manufacturing, Technical and Scientific Product	Columbus MSA, GA-AL	S	25.90 MW	24.14 AW	53860 AAW	GABLS	10//99-12//99
Wholesale and Manufacturing, Technical and Scientific Product	Macon MSA, GA	S	22.34 MW	19.96 AW	46470 AAW	GABLS	10//99-12//99
Wholesale and Manufacturing, Technical and Scientific Product	Savannah MSA, GA	S	21.35 MW	19.42 AW	44400 AAW	GABLS	10//99-12//99
Wholesale and Manufacturing, Technical and Scientific Product	Hawaii	S	18.17 MW	19.83 AW	41240 AAW	HIBLS	10//99-12//99
Wholesale and Manufacturing, Technical and Scientific Product	Honolulu MSA, HI	S	20.91 MW	18.69 AW	43500 AAW	HIBLS	10//99-12//99
Wholesale and Manufacturing, Technical and Scientific Product	Idaho	S	15.29 MW	17.16 AW	35700 AAW	IDBLS	10//99-12//99
Wholesale and Manufacturing, Technical and Scientific Product	Boise City MSA, ID	S	18.96 MW	16.37 AW	39440 AAW	IDBLS	10//99-12//99
Wholesale and Manufacturing, Technical and Scientific Product	Pocatello MSA, ID	S	18.68 MW	16.85 AW	38860 AAW	IDBLS	10//99-12//99
Wholesale and Manufacturing, Technical and Scientific Product	Illinois	S	19.32 MW	21.71 AW	45160 AAW	ILBLS	10//99-12//99
Wholesale and Manufacturing, Technical and Scientific Product	Bloomington-Normal MSA, IL	S	28.00 MW	22.93 AW	58230 AAW	ILBLS	10//99-12//99
Wholesale and Manufacturing, Technical and Scientific Product	Champaign-Urbana MSA, IL	S	19.28 MW	17.26 AW	40110 AAW	ILBLS	10//99-12//99
Wholesale and Manufacturing, Technical and Scientific Product	Chicago PMSA, IL	S	21.58 MW	19.22 AW	44890 AAW	ILBLS	10//99-12//99
Wholesale and Manufacturing, Technical and Scientific Product	Decatur MSA, IL	S	23.00 MW	18.16 AW	47850 AAW	ILBLS	10//99-12//99
Wholesale and Manufacturing, Technical and Scientific Product	Kankakee PMSA, IL	S	25.81 MW	22.60 AW	53690 AAW	ILBLS	10//99-12//99
Wholesale and Manufacturing, Technical and Scientific Product	Peoria-Pekin MSA, IL	S	19.58 MW	16.73 AW	40730 AAW	ILBLS	10//99-12//99

AAW Average annual wage	**AOH** Average offered, high	**ASH** Average starting, high	**H** Hourly	**M** Monthly	**S** Special: hourly and annual
AE Average entry wage	**AOL** Average offered, low	**ASL** Average starting, low	**HI** Highest wage paid	**MTC** Median total compensation	**TQ** Third quartile wage
AEX Average experienced wage	**APH** Average pay, high range	**AW** Average wage paid	**HR** High end range	**MW** Median wage paid	**W** Weekly
AO Average offered	**APL** Average pay, low range	**FQ** First quartile wage	**LR** Low end range	**SQ** Second quartile wage	**Y** Yearly

Occupation/Type/Industry	Location	Per	Low	Mid	High	Source	Date
Sales Representative							
Wholesale and Manufacturing, Technical and Scientific Product	Rockford MSA, IL	S	22.52 MW	20.13 AW	46840 AAW	ILBLS	10//99-12//99
Wholesale and Manufacturing, Technical and Scientific Product	Springfield MSA, IL	S	15.32 MW	13.57 AW	31880 AAW	ILBLS	10//99-12//99
Wholesale and Manufacturing, Technical and Scientific Product	Indiana	S	22.25 MW	24.92 AW	51830 AAW	INBLS	10//99-12//99
Wholesale and Manufacturing, Technical and Scientific Product	Bloomington MSA, IN	S	25.58 MW	25.70 AW	53200 AAW	INBLS	10//99-12//99
Wholesale and Manufacturing, Technical and Scientific Product	Elkhart-Goshen MSA, IN	S	25.90 MW	22.46 AW	53860 AAW	INBLS	10//99-12//99
Wholesale and Manufacturing, Technical and Scientific Product	Evansville-Henderson MSA, IN-KY	S	22.70 MW	20.46 AW	47210 AAW	INBLS	10//99-12//99
Wholesale and Manufacturing, Technical and Scientific Product	Fort Wayne MSA, IN	S	21.43 MW	18.91 AW	44580 AAW	INBLS	10//99-12//99
Wholesale and Manufacturing, Technical and Scientific Product	Gary PMSA, IN	S	26.63 MW	19.72 AW	55390 AAW	INBLS	10//99-12//99
Wholesale and Manufacturing, Technical and Scientific Product	Indianapolis MSA, IN	S	24.18 MW	22.36 AW	50300 AAW	INBLS	10//99-12//99
Wholesale and Manufacturing, Technical and Scientific Product	Kokomo MSA, IN	S	26.68 MW	23.34 AW	55490 AAW	INBLS	10//99-12//99
Wholesale and Manufacturing, Technical and Scientific Product	Lafayette MSA, IN	S	27.75 MW	28.10 AW	57720 AAW	INBLS	10//99-12//99
Wholesale and Manufacturing, Technical and Scientific Product	Muncie MSA, IN	S	21.54 MW	20.67 AW	44790 AAW	INBLS	10//99-12//99
Wholesale and Manufacturing, Technical and Scientific Product	South Bend MSA, IN	S	21.14 MW	19.27 AW	43970 AAW	INBLS	10//99-12//99
Wholesale and Manufacturing, Technical and Scientific Product	Terre Haute MSA, IN	S	24.12 MW	24.67 AW	50170 AAW	INBLS	10//99-12//99
Wholesale and Manufacturing, Technical and Scientific Product	Iowa	S	18.29 MW	21.66 AW	45040 AAW	IABLS	10//99-12//99
Wholesale and Manufacturing, Technical and Scientific Product	Cedar Rapids MSA, IA	S	25.12 MW	23.05 AW	52250 AAW	IABLS	10//99-12//99
Wholesale and Manufacturing, Technical and Scientific Product	Davenport-Moline-Rock Island MSA, IA-IL	S	20.02 MW	18.75 AW	41640 AAW	IABLS	10//99-12//99
Wholesale and Manufacturing, Technical and Scientific Product	Des Moines MSA, IA	S	21.33 MW	18.30 AW	44370 AAW	IABLS	10//99-12//99
Wholesale and Manufacturing, Technical and Scientific Product	Dubuque MSA, IA	S	20.29 MW	17.13 AW	42210 AAW	IABLS	10//99-12//99
Wholesale and Manufacturing, Technical and Scientific Product	Iowa City MSA, IA	S	22.97 MW	18.69 AW	47780 AAW	IABLS	10//99-12//99
Wholesale and Manufacturing, Technical and Scientific Product	Sioux City MSA, IA-NE	S	17.33 MW	18.11 AW	36040 AAW	IABLS	10//99-12//99
Wholesale and Manufacturing, Technical and Scientific Product	Waterloo-Cedar Falls MSA, IA	S	16.32 MW	13.22 AW	33950 AAW	IABLS	10//99-12//99
Wholesale and Manufacturing, Technical and Scientific Product	Kansas	S	22.94 MW	25.84 AW	53740 AAW	KSBLS	10//99-12//99
Wholesale and Manufacturing, Technical and Scientific Product	Topeka MSA, KS	S	25.76 MW	23.05 AW	53580 AAW	KSBLS	10//99-12//99
Wholesale and Manufacturing, Technical and Scientific Product	Wichita MSA, KS	S	23.39 MW	21.90 AW	48650 AAW	KSBLS	10//99-12//99
Wholesale and Manufacturing, Technical and Scientific Product	Kentucky	S	19.75 MW	23.45 AW	48780 AAW	KYBLS	10//99-12//99
Wholesale and Manufacturing, Technical and Scientific Product	Lexington MSA, KY	S	23.63 MW	19.41 AW	49160 AAW	KYBLS	10//99-12//99
Wholesale and Manufacturing, Technical and Scientific Product	Louisville MSA, KY-IN	S	19.60 MW	16.06 AW	40780 AAW	KYBLS	10//99-12//99
Wholesale and Manufacturing, Technical and Scientific Product	Owensboro MSA, KY	S	25.69 MW	23.65 AW	53440 AAW	KYBLS	10//99-12//99
Wholesale and Manufacturing, Technical and Scientific Product	Louisiana	S	18.63 MW	21.07 AW	43820 AAW	LABLS	10//99-12//99
Wholesale and Manufacturing, Technical and Scientific Product	Baton Rouge MSA, LA	S	22.69 MW	19.29 AW	47200 AAW	LABLS	10//99-12//99
Wholesale and Manufacturing, Technical and Scientific Product	Houma MSA, LA	S	16.93 MW	16.55 AW	35220 AAW	LABLS	10//99-12//99
Wholesale and Manufacturing, Technical and Scientific Product	Lafayette MSA, LA	S	25.24 MW	23.40 AW	52500 AAW	LABLS	10//99-12//99
Wholesale and Manufacturing, Technical and Scientific Product	Lake Charles MSA, LA	S	19.11 MW	17.66 AW	39740 AAW	LABLS	10//99-12//99

AAW Average annual wage	**AOH** Average offered, high	**ASH** Average starting, high	**H** Hourly	**M** Monthly	**S** Special: hourly and annual
AE Average entry wage	**AOL** Average offered, low	**ASL** Average starting, low	**HI** Highest wage paid	**MTC** Median total compensation	**TQ** Third quartile wage
AEX Average experienced wage	**APH** Average pay, high range	**AW** Average wage paid	**HR** High end range	**MW** Median wage paid	**W** Weekly
AO Average offered	**APL** Average pay, low range	**FQ** First quartile wage	**LR** Low end range	**SQ** Second quartile wage	**Y** Yearly

Occupation/Type/Industry	Location	Per	Low	Mid	High	Source	Date
Sales Representative							
Wholesale and Manufacturing, Technical and Scientific Product	Monroe MSA, LA	S	16.37 MW	16.67 AW	34050 AAW	LABLS	10//99-12//99
Wholesale and Manufacturing, Technical and Scientific Product	New Orleans MSA, LA	S	23.71 MW	20.99 AW	49310 AAW	LABLS	10//99-12//99
Wholesale and Manufacturing, Technical and Scientific Product	Shreveport-Bossier City MSA, LA	S	19.73 MW	20.33 AW	41050 AAW	LABLS	10//99-12//99
Wholesale and Manufacturing, Technical and Scientific Product	Maine	S	23.49 MW	25.62 AW	53280 AAW	MEBLS	10//99-12//99
Wholesale and Manufacturing, Technical and Scientific Product	Bangor MSA, ME	S	22.58 MW	19.41 AW	46980 AAW	MEBLS	10//99-12//99
Wholesale and Manufacturing, Technical and Scientific Product	Lewiston-Auburn MSA, ME	S	22.83 MW	22.16 AW	47490 AAW	MEBLS	10//99-12//99
Wholesale and Manufacturing, Technical and Scientific Product	Portland MSA, ME	S	26.31 MW	24.32 AW	54720 AAW	MEBLS	10//99-12//99
Wholesale and Manufacturing, Technical and Scientific Product	Maryland	S	21.58 MW	24.65 AW	51270 AAW	MDBLS	10//99-12//99
Wholesale and Manufacturing, Technical and Scientific Product	Baltimore PMSA, MD	S	24.66 MW	22.32 AW	51290 AAW	MDBLS	10//99-12//99
Wholesale and Manufacturing, Technical and Scientific Product	Hagerstown PMSA, MD	S	24.95 MW	21.06 AW	51900 AAW	MDBLS	10//99-12//99
Wholesale and Manufacturing, Technical and Scientific Product	Massachusetts	S	25.1 MW	27.38 AW	56960 AAW	MABLS	10//99-12//99
Wholesale and Manufacturing, Technical and Scientific Product	Barnstable-Yarmouth MSA, MA	S	32.12 MW	26.76 AW	66820 AAW	MABLS	10//99-12//99
Wholesale and Manufacturing, Technical and Scientific Product	Boston PMSA, MA-NH	S	27.81 MW	25.19 AW	57850 AAW	MABLS	10//99-12//99
Wholesale and Manufacturing, Technical and Scientific Product	Brockton PMSA, MA	S	20.48 MW	15.95 AW	42600 AAW	MABLS	10//99-12//99
Wholesale and Manufacturing, Technical and Scientific Product	Fitchburg-Leominster PMSA, MA	S	26.41 MW	24.57 AW	54940 AAW	MABLS	10//99-12//99
Wholesale and Manufacturing, Technical and Scientific Product	Lawrence PMSA, MA-NH	S	31.24 MW	30.42 AW	64970 AAW	MABLS	10//99-12//99
Wholesale and Manufacturing, Technical and Scientific Product	Lowell PMSA, MA-NH	S	30.88 MW	32.12 AW	64220 AAW	MABLS	10//99-12//99
Wholesale and Manufacturing, Technical and Scientific Product	New Bedford PMSA, MA	S	20.17 MW	19.08 AW	41950 AAW	MABLS	10//99-12//99
Wholesale and Manufacturing, Technical and Scientific Product	Springfield MSA, MA	S	21.85 MW	20.28 AW	45460 AAW	MABLS	10//99-12//99
Wholesale and Manufacturing, Technical and Scientific Product	Worcester PMSA, MA-CT	S	23.89 MW	19.52 AW	49700 AAW	MABLS	10//99-12//99
Wholesale and Manufacturing, Technical and Scientific Product	Michigan	S	23.94 MW	26.75 AW	55630 AAW	MIBLS	10//99-12//99
Wholesale and Manufacturing, Technical and Scientific Product	Ann Arbor PMSA, MI	S	30.60 MW	29.00 AW	63650 AAW	MIBLS	10//99-12//99
Wholesale and Manufacturing, Technical and Scientific Product	Benton Harbor MSA, MI	S	19.64 MW	16.44 AW	40860 AAW	MIBLS	10//99-12//99
Wholesale and Manufacturing, Technical and Scientific Product	Detroit PMSA, MI	S	27.64 MW	24.65 AW	57490 AAW	MIBLS	10//99-12//99
Wholesale and Manufacturing, Technical and Scientific Product	Flint PMSA, MI	S	28.04 MW	28.70 AW	58330 AAW	MIBLS	10//99-12//99
Wholesale and Manufacturing, Technical and Scientific Product	Grand Rapids-Muskegon-Holland MSA, MI	S	25.62 MW	22.34 AW	53290 AAW	MIBLS	10//99-12//99
Wholesale and Manufacturing, Technical and Scientific Product	Jackson MSA, MI	S	23.66 MW	21.91 AW	49210 AAW	MIBLS	10//99-12//99
Wholesale and Manufacturing, Technical and Scientific Product	Kalamazoo-Battle Creek MSA, MI	S	32.64 MW	35.69 AW	67890 AAW	MIBLS	10//99-12//99
Wholesale and Manufacturing, Technical and Scientific Product	Lansing-East Lansing MSA, MI	S	21.85 MW	18.20 AW	45440 AAW	MIBLS	10//99-12//99
Wholesale and Manufacturing, Technical and Scientific Product	Saginaw-Bay City-Midland MSA, MI	S	25.06 MW	23.66 AW	52130 AAW	MIBLS	10//99-12//99
Wholesale and Manufacturing, Technical and Scientific Product	Minnesota	S	23.79 MW	26.82 AW	55780 AAW	MNBLS	10//99-12//99
Wholesale and Manufacturing, Technical and Scientific Product	Duluth-Superior MSA, MN-WI	S	18.89 MW	16.48 AW	39280 AAW	MNBLS	10//99-12//99

AAW Average annual wage	**AOH** Average offered, high	**ASH** Average starting, high	**H** Hourly	**M** Monthly	**S** Special: hourly and annual
AE Average entry wage	**AOL** Average offered, low	**ASL** Average starting, low	**HI** Highest wage paid	**MTC** Median total compensation	**TQ** Third quartile wage
AEX Average experienced wage	**APH** Average pay, high range	**AW** Average wage paid	**HR** High end range	**MW** Median wage paid	**W** Weekly
AO Average offered	**APL** Average pay, low range	**FQ** First quartile wage	**LR** Low end range	**SQ** Second quartile wage	**Y** Yearly

Sales Representative

Occupation/Type/Industry	Location	Per	Low	Mid	High	Source	Date
Wholesale and Manufacturing, Technical and Scientific Product	Minneapolis-St. Paul MSA, MN-WI	S	27.54 MW	23.96 AW	57290 AAW	MNBLS	10//99-12//99
Wholesale and Manufacturing, Technical and Scientific Product	Rochester MSA, MN	S	24.03 MW	20.83 AW	49980 AAW	MNBLS	10//99-12//99
Wholesale and Manufacturing, Technical and Scientific Product	St. Cloud MSA, MN	S	21.55 MW	19.18 AW	44830 AAW	MNBLS	10//99-12//99
Wholesale and Manufacturing, Technical and Scientific Product	Mississippi	S	22.09 MW	24.40 AW	50750 AAW	MSBLS	10//99-12//99
Wholesale and Manufacturing, Technical and Scientific Product	Biloxi-Gulfport-Pascagoula MSA, MS	S	21.63 MW	18.49 AW	44980 AAW	MSBLS	10//99-12//99
Wholesale and Manufacturing, Technical and Scientific Product	Jackson MSA, MS	S	23.04 MW	19.75 AW	47910 AAW	MSBLS	10//99-12//99
Wholesale and Manufacturing, Technical and Scientific Product	Missouri	S	20.01 MW	23.62 AW	49140 AAW	MOBLS	10//99-12//99
Wholesale and Manufacturing, Technical and Scientific Product	Kansas City MSA, MO-KS	S	25.63 MW	21.69 AW	53320 AAW	MOBLS	10//99-12//99
Wholesale and Manufacturing, Technical and Scientific Product	St. Joseph MSA, MO	S	21.57 MW	19.18 AW	44860 AAW	MOBLS	10//99-12//99
Wholesale and Manufacturing, Technical and Scientific Product	St. Louis MSA, MO-IL	S	22.17 MW	19.31 AW	46110 AAW	MOBLS	10//99-12//99
Wholesale and Manufacturing, Technical and Scientific Product	Springfield MSA, MO	S	25.09 MW	18.90 AW	52190 AAW	MOBLS	10//99-12//99
Wholesale and Manufacturing, Technical and Scientific Product	Montana	S	18.92 MW	20.29 AW	42210 AAW	MTBLS	10//99-12//99
Wholesale and Manufacturing, Technical and Scientific Product	Billings MSA, MT	S	18.73 MW	17.67 AW	38960 AAW	MTBLS	10//99-12//99
Wholesale and Manufacturing, Technical and Scientific Product	Great Falls MSA, MT	S	19.52 MW	16.44 AW	40590 AAW	MTBLS	10//99-12//99
Wholesale and Manufacturing, Technical and Scientific Product	Missoula MSA, MT	S	22.06 MW	19.55 AW	45890 AAW	MTBLS	10//99-12//99
Wholesale and Manufacturing, Technical and Scientific Product	Nebraska	S	21.55 MW	24.02 AW	49950 AAW	NEBLS	10//99-12//99
Wholesale and Manufacturing, Technical and Scientific Product	Lincoln MSA, NE	S	25.27 MW	22.60 AW	52560 AAW	NEBLS	10//99-12//99
Wholesale and Manufacturing, Technical and Scientific Product	Omaha MSA, NE-IA	S	25.11 MW	22.49 AW	52230 AAW	NEBLS	10//99-12//99
Wholesale and Manufacturing, Technical and Scientific Product	Nevada	S	20.05 MW	21.98 AW	45720 AAW	NVBLS	10//99-12//99
Wholesale and Manufacturing, Technical and Scientific Product	Las Vegas MSA, NV-AZ	S	22.38 MW	20.55 AW	46560 AAW	NVBLS	10//99-12//99
Wholesale and Manufacturing, Technical and Scientific Product	Reno MSA, NV	S	20.60 MW	17.94 AW	42850 AAW	NVBLS	10//99-12//99
Wholesale and Manufacturing, Technical and Scientific Product	New Hampshire	S	23.17 MW	26.98 AW	56130 AAW	NHBLS	10//99-12//99
Wholesale and Manufacturing, Technical and Scientific Product	Manchester PMSA, NH	S	31.85 MW	28.12 AW	66250 AAW	NHBLS	10//99-12//99
Wholesale and Manufacturing, Technical and Scientific Product	Nashua PMSA, NH	S	22.02 MW	15.71 AW	45790 AAW	NHBLS	10//99-12//99
Wholesale and Manufacturing, Technical and Scientific Product	Portsmouth-Rochester PMSA, NH-ME	S	22.99 MW	16.72 AW	47820 AAW	NHBLS	10//99-12//99
Wholesale and Manufacturing, Technical and Scientific Product	New Jersey	S	27.72 MW	28.85 AW	60000 AAW	NJBLS	10//99-12//99
Wholesale and Manufacturing, Technical and Scientific Product	Bergen-Passaic PMSA, NJ	S	31.73 MW	29.50 AW	66000 AAW	NJBLS	10//99-12//99
Wholesale and Manufacturing, Technical and Scientific Product	Jersey City PMSA, NJ	S	27.80 MW	24.95 AW	57820 AAW	NJBLS	10//99-12//99
Wholesale and Manufacturing, Technical and Scientific Product	Middlesex-Somerset-Hunterdon PMSA, NJ	S	28.14 MW	26.84 AW	58530 AAW	NJBLS	10//99-12//99
Wholesale and Manufacturing, Technical and Scientific Product	Monmouth-Ocean PMSA, NJ	S	35.00 MW	33.20 AW	72790 AAW	NJBLS	10//99-12//99
Wholesale and Manufacturing, Technical and Scientific Product	Newark PMSA, NJ	S	27.20 MW	27.53 AW	56570 AAW	NJBLS	10//99-12//99
Wholesale and Manufacturing, Technical and Scientific Product	Trenton PMSA, NJ	S	30.91 MW	29.56 AW	64290 AAW	NJBLS	10//99-12//99

AAW	Average annual wage	AOH	Average offered, high	ASH	Average starting, high	H	Hourly	M	Monthly	S	Special: hourly and annual
AE	Average entry wage	AOL	Average offered, low	ASL	Average starting, low	HI	Highest wage paid	MTC	Median total compensation	TQ	Third quartile wage
AEX	Average experienced wage	APH	Average pay, high range	AW	Average wage paid	HR	High end range	MW	Median wage paid	W	Weekly
AO	Average offered	APL	Average pay, low range	FQ	First quartile wage	LR	Low end range	SQ	Second quartile wage	Y	Yearly

Occupation/Type/Industry	Location	Per	Low	Mid	High	Source	Date
Sales Representative							
Wholesale and Manufacturing, Technical and Scientific Product	Vineland-Millville-Bridgeton PMSA, NJ	S	20.26 MW	16.23 AW	42140 AAW	NJBLS	10//99-12//99
Wholesale and Manufacturing, Technical and Scientific Product	New Mexico	S	18.94 MW	21.19 AW	44080 AAW	NMBLS	10//99-12//99
Wholesale and Manufacturing, Technical and Scientific Product	Albuquerque MSA, NM	S	20.13 MW	18.65 AW	41860 AAW	NMBLS	10//99-12//99
Wholesale and Manufacturing, Technical and Scientific Product	Las Cruces MSA, NM	S	14.98 MW	12.55 AW	31160 AAW	NMBLS	10//99-12//99
Wholesale and Manufacturing, Technical and Scientific Product	Santa Fe MSA, NM	S	20.97 MW	17.51 AW	43620 AAW	NMBLS	10//99-12//99
Wholesale and Manufacturing, Technical and Scientific Product	New York	S	22.83 MW	26.35 AW	54800 AAW	NYBLS	10//99-12//99
Wholesale and Manufacturing, Technical and Scientific Product	Albany-Schenectady-Troy MSA, NY	S	23.88 MW	21.92 AW	49670 AAW	NYBLS	10//99-12//99
Wholesale and Manufacturing, Technical and Scientific Product	Binghamton MSA, NY	S	24.15 MW	20.33 AW	50220 AAW	NYBLS	10//99-12//99
Wholesale and Manufacturing, Technical and Scientific Product	Buffalo-Niagara Falls MSA, NY	S	21.24 MW	18.79 AW	44180 AAW	NYBLS	10//99-12//99
Wholesale and Manufacturing, Technical and Scientific Product	Elmira MSA, NY	S	23.45 MW	22.20 AW	48770 AAW	NYBLS	10//99-12//99
Wholesale and Manufacturing, Technical and Scientific Product	Jamestown MSA, NY	S	21.68 MW	21.98 AW	45090 AAW	NYBLS	10//99-12//99
Wholesale and Manufacturing, Technical and Scientific Product	Nassau-Suffolk PMSA, NY	S	29.90 MW	26.26 AW	62190 AAW	NYBLS	10//99-12//99
Wholesale and Manufacturing, Technical and Scientific Product	New York PMSA, NY	S	27.47 MW	23.26 AW	57130 AAW	NYBLS	10//99-12//99
Wholesale and Manufacturing, Technical and Scientific Product	Newburgh PMSA, NY-PA	S	21.22 MW	19.13 AW	44140 AAW	NYBLS	10//99-12//99
Wholesale and Manufacturing, Technical and Scientific Product	Rochester MSA, NY	S	23.00 MW	21.32 AW	47840 AAW	NYBLS	10//99-12//99
Wholesale and Manufacturing, Technical and Scientific Product	Syracuse MSA, NY	S	26.17 MW	24.90 AW	54440 AAW	NYBLS	10//99-12//99
Wholesale and Manufacturing, Technical and Scientific Product	Utica-Rome MSA, NY	S	20.61 MW	18.06 AW	42870 AAW	NYBLS	10//99-12//99
Wholesale and Manufacturing, Technical and Scientific Product	North Carolina	S	18.75 MW	21.31 AW	44320 AAW	NCBLS	10//99-12//99
Wholesale and Manufacturing, Technical and Scientific Product	Asheville MSA, NC	S	17.05 MW	16.38 AW	35460 AAW	NCBLS	10//99-12//99
Wholesale and Manufacturing, Technical and Scientific Product	Charlotte-Gastonia-Rock Hill MSA, NC-SC	S	23.25 MW	19.83 AW	48350 AAW	NCBLS	10//99-12//99
Wholesale and Manufacturing, Technical and Scientific Product	Fayetteville MSA, NC	S	15.95 MW	14.25 AW	33170 AAW	NCBLS	10//99-12//99
Wholesale and Manufacturing, Technical and Scientific Product	Goldsboro MSA, NC	S	17.78 MW	15.11 AW	36980 AAW	NCBLS	10//99-12//99
Wholesale and Manufacturing, Technical and Scientific Product	Greensboro--Winston-Salem--High Point MSA, NC	S	27.24 MW	24.44 AW	56660 AAW	NCBLS	10//99-12//99
Wholesale and Manufacturing, Technical and Scientific Product	Greenville MSA, NC	S	13.79 MW	13.77 AW	28680 AAW	NCBLS	10//99-12//99
Wholesale and Manufacturing, Technical and Scientific Product	Hickory-Morganton-Lenoir MSA, NC	S	23.77 MW	22.09 AW	49430 AAW	NCBLS	10//99-12//99
Wholesale and Manufacturing, Technical and Scientific Product	Jacksonville MSA, NC	S	13.52 MW	13.17 AW	28130 AAW	NCBLS	10//99-12//99
Wholesale and Manufacturing, Technical and Scientific Product	Raleigh-Durham-Chapel Hill MSA, NC	S	16.52 MW	11.93 AW	34370 AAW	NCBLS	10//99-12//99
Wholesale and Manufacturing, Technical and Scientific Product	Wilmington MSA, NC	S	19.64 MW	18.78 AW	40860 AAW	NCBLS	10//99-12//99
Wholesale and Manufacturing, Technical and Scientific Product	North Dakota	S	20.54 MW	22.93 AW	47690 AAW	NDBLS	10//99-12//99
Wholesale and Manufacturing, Technical and Scientific Product	Bismarck MSA, ND	S	21.44 MW	19.88 AW	44600 AAW	NDBLS	10//99-12//99
Wholesale and Manufacturing, Technical and Scientific Product	Fargo-Moorhead MSA, ND-MN	S	23.86 MW	21.20 AW	49620 AAW	NDBLS	10//99-12//99

AAW Average annual wage	**AOH** Average offered, high	**ASH** Average starting, high	**H** Hourly	**M** Monthly	**S** Special: hourly and annual
AE Average entry wage	**AOL** Average offered, low	**ASL** Average starting, low	**HI** Highest wage paid	**MTC** Median total compensation	**TQ** Third quartile wage
AEX Average experienced wage	**APH** Average pay, high range	**AW** Average wage paid	**HR** High end range	**MW** Median wage paid	**W** Weekly
AO Average offered	**APL** Average pay, low range	**FQ** First quartile wage	**LR** Low end range	**SQ** Second quartile wage	**Y** Yearly

Sales Representative

Occupation/Type/Industry	Location	Per	Low	Mid	High	Source	Date
Sales Representative							
Wholesale and Manufacturing, Technical and Scientific Product	Ohio	S	22.03 MW	25.06 AW	52130 AAW	OHBLS	10//99-12//99
Wholesale and Manufacturing, Technical and Scientific Product	Akron PMSA, OH	S	24.13 MW	21.55 AW	50190 AAW	OHBLS	10//99-12//99
Wholesale and Manufacturing, Technical and Scientific Product	Canton-Massillon MSA, OH	S	21.41 MW	19.73 AW	44530 AAW	OHBLS	10//99-12//99
Wholesale and Manufacturing, Technical and Scientific Product	Cleveland-Lorain-Elyria PMSA, OH	S	23.86 MW	20.65 AW	49630 AAW	OHBLS	10//99-12//99
Wholesale and Manufacturing, Technical and Scientific Product	Columbus MSA, OH	S	26.93 MW	23.98 AW	56010 AAW	OHBLS	10//99-12//99
Wholesale and Manufacturing, Technical and Scientific Product	Hamilton-Middletown PMSA, OH	S	24.02 MW	20.82 AW	49970 AAW	OHBLS	10//99-12//99
Wholesale and Manufacturing, Technical and Scientific Product	Lima MSA, OH	S	19.79 MW	17.83 AW	41160 AAW	OHBLS	10//99-12//99
Wholesale and Manufacturing, Technical and Scientific Product	Mansfield MSA, OH	S	20.15 MW	19.11 AW	41900 AAW	OHBLS	10//99-12//99
Wholesale and Manufacturing, Technical and Scientific Product	Toledo MSA, OH	S	23.49 MW	20.81 AW	48850 AAW	OHBLS	10//99-12//99
Wholesale and Manufacturing, Technical and Scientific Product	Youngstown-Warren MSA, OH	S	21.76 MW	17.87 AW	45260 AAW	OHBLS	10//99-12//99
Wholesale and Manufacturing, Technical and Scientific Product	Oklahoma	S	18.82 MW	20.78 AW	43220 AAW	OKBLS	10//99-12//99
Wholesale and Manufacturing, Technical and Scientific Product	Oklahoma City MSA, OK	S	19.24 MW	17.72 AW	40020 AAW	OKBLS	10//99-12//99
Wholesale and Manufacturing, Technical and Scientific Product	Tulsa MSA, OK	S	22.83 MW	21.28 AW	47490 AAW	OKBLS	10//99-12//99
Wholesale and Manufacturing, Technical and Scientific Product	Oregon	S	24.23 MW	29.31 AW	60970 AAW	ORBLS	10//99-12//99
Wholesale and Manufacturing, Technical and Scientific Product	Corvallis MSA, OR	S	22.85 MW	20.12 AW	47530 AAW	ORBLS	10//99-12//99
Wholesale and Manufacturing, Technical and Scientific Product	Eugene-Springfield MSA, OR	S	25.69 MW	23.77 AW	53440 AAW	ORBLS	10//99-12//99
Wholesale and Manufacturing, Technical and Scientific Product	Medford-Ashland MSA, OR	S	18.09 MW	13.13 AW	37630 AAW	ORBLS	10//99-12//99
Wholesale and Manufacturing, Technical and Scientific Product	Portland-Vancouver PMSA, OR-WA	S	30.52 MW	24.99 AW	63490 AAW	ORBLS	10//99-12//99
Wholesale and Manufacturing, Technical and Scientific Product	Salem PMSA, OR	S	18.72 MW	18.60 AW	38950 AAW	ORBLS	10//99-12//99
Wholesale and Manufacturing, Technical and Scientific Product	Pennsylvania	S	23.62 MW	26.36 AW	54830 AAW	PABLS	10//99-12//99
Wholesale and Manufacturing, Technical and Scientific Product	Allentown-Bethlehem-Easton MSA, PA	S	23.65 MW	21.08 AW	49200 AAW	PABLS	10//99-12//99
Wholesale and Manufacturing, Technical and Scientific Product	Altoona MSA, PA	S	22.46 MW	20.92 AW	46720 AAW	PABLS	10//99-12//99
Wholesale and Manufacturing, Technical and Scientific Product	Erie MSA, PA	S	19.47 MW	19.27 AW	40510 AAW	PABLS	10//99-12//99
Wholesale and Manufacturing, Technical and Scientific Product	Harrisburg-Lebanon-Carlisle MSA, PA	S	22.91 MW	21.95 AW	47660 AAW	PABLS	10//99-12//99
Wholesale and Manufacturing, Technical and Scientific Product	Johnstown MSA, PA	S	20.03 MW	19.79 AW	41660 AAW	PABLS	10//99-12//99
Wholesale and Manufacturing, Technical and Scientific Product	Lancaster MSA, PA	S	20.23 MW	17.54 AW	42070 AAW	PABLS	10//99-12//99
Wholesale and Manufacturing, Technical and Scientific Product	Philadelphia PMSA, PA-NJ	S	27.72 MW	25.43 AW	57660 AAW	PABLS	10//99-12//99
Wholesale and Manufacturing, Technical and Scientific Product	Pittsburgh MSA, PA	S	22.02 MW	21.10 AW	45800 AAW	PABLS	10//99-12//99
Wholesale and Manufacturing, Technical and Scientific Product	Reading MSA, PA	S	24.42 MW	21.53 AW	50800 AAW	PABLS	10//99-12//99
Wholesale and Manufacturing, Technical and Scientific Product	Scranton--Wilkes-Barre--Hazleton MSA, PA	S	24.12 MW	20.19 AW	50180 AAW	PABLS	10//99-12//99
Wholesale and Manufacturing, Technical and Scientific Product	Sharon MSA, PA	S	24.37 MW	23.42 AW	50680 AAW	PABLS	10//99-12//99
Wholesale and Manufacturing, Technical and Scientific Product	Williamsport MSA, PA	S	23.41 MW	18.81 AW	48680 AAW	PABLS	10//99-12//99

AAW	Average annual wage	**AOH**	Average offered, high	**ASH**	Average starting, high	**H**	Hourly	**M**	Monthly	**S**	Special: hourly and annual
AE	Average entry wage	**AOL**	Average offered, low	**ASL**	Average starting, low	**HI**	Highest wage paid	**MTC**	Median total compensation	**TQ**	Third quartile wage
AEX	Average experienced wage	**APH**	Average pay, high range	**AW**	Average wage paid	**HR**	High end range	**MW**	Median wage paid	**W**	Weekly
AO	Average offered	**APL**	Average pay, low range	**FQ**	First quartile wage	**LR**	Low end range	**SQ**	Second quartile wage	**Y**	Yearly

Occupation/Type/Industry	Location	Per	Low	Mid	High	Source	Date
Sales Representative							
Wholesale and Manufacturing, Technical and Scientific Product	York MSA, PA	S	24.30 MW	23.21 AW	50540 AAW	PABLS	10//99-12//99
Wholesale and Manufacturing, Technical and Scientific Product	Rhode Island	S	23.27 MW	25.12 AW	52250 AAW	RIBLS	10//99-12//99
Wholesale and Manufacturing, Technical and Scientific Product	Providence-Fall River-Warwick MSA, RI-MA	S	24.27 MW	22.71 AW	50480 AAW	RIBLS	10//99-12//99
Wholesale and Manufacturing, Technical and Scientific Product	South Carolina	S	18.17 MW	20.97 AW	43620 AAW	SCBLS	10//99-12//99
Wholesale and Manufacturing, Technical and Scientific Product	Charleston-North Charleston MSA, SC	S	20.30 MW	18.56 AW	42220 AAW	SCBLS	10//99-12//99
Wholesale and Manufacturing, Technical and Scientific Product	Columbia MSA, SC	S	16.73 MW	13.26 AW	34810 AAW	SCBLS	10//99-12//99
Wholesale and Manufacturing, Technical and Scientific Product	Florence MSA, SC	S	19.82 MW	15.84 AW	41220 AAW	SCBLS	10//99-12//99
Wholesale and Manufacturing, Technical and Scientific Product	Greenville-Spartanburg-Anderson MSA, SC	S	22.69 MW	19.25 AW	47200 AAW	SCBLS	10//99-12//99
Wholesale and Manufacturing, Technical and Scientific Product	Myrtle Beach MSA, SC	S	14.75 MW	12.18 AW	30680 AAW	SCBLS	10//99-12//99
Wholesale and Manufacturing, Technical and Scientific Product	South Dakota	S	20.82 MW	22.35 AW	46500 AAW	SDBLS	10//99-12//99
Wholesale and Manufacturing, Technical and Scientific Product	Rapid City MSA, SD	S	20.40 MW	18.06 AW	42430 AAW	SDBLS	10//99-12//99
Wholesale and Manufacturing, Technical and Scientific Product	Sioux Falls MSA, SD	S	23.90 MW	21.99 AW	49720 AAW	SDBLS	10//99-12//99
Wholesale and Manufacturing, Technical and Scientific Product	Tennessee	S	20.86 MW	24.62 AW	51210 AAW	TNBLS	10//99-12//99
Wholesale and Manufacturing, Technical and Scientific Product	Chattanooga MSA, TN-GA	S	22.09 MW	19.31 AW	45950 AAW	TNBLS	10//99-12//99
Wholesale and Manufacturing, Technical and Scientific Product	Clarksville-Hopkinsville MSA, TN-KY	S	15.72 MW	13.57 AW	32700 AAW	TNBLS	10//99-12//99
Wholesale and Manufacturing, Technical and Scientific Product	Jackson MSA, TN	S	17.59 MW	14.98 AW	36590 AAW	TNBLS	10//99-12//99
Wholesale and Manufacturing, Technical and Scientific Product	Johnson City-Kingsport-Bristol MSA, TN-VA	S	20.82 MW	17.93 AW	43310 AAW	TNBLS	10//99-12//99
Wholesale and Manufacturing, Technical and Scientific Product	Knoxville MSA, TN	S	24.00 MW	22.99 AW	49910 AAW	TNBLS	10//99-12//99
Wholesale and Manufacturing, Technical and Scientific Product	Memphis MSA, TN-AR-MS	S	22.66 MW	19.77 AW	47130 AAW	MSBLS	10//99-12//99
Wholesale and Manufacturing, Technical and Scientific Product	Nashville MSA, TN	S	24.13 MW	19.65 AW	50190 AAW	TNBLS	10//99-12//99
Wholesale and Manufacturing, Technical and Scientific Product	Texas	S	23.22 MW	26.12 AW	54340 AAW	TXBLS	10//99-12//99
Wholesale and Manufacturing, Technical and Scientific Product	Abilene MSA, TX	S	17.45 MW	17.06 AW	36290 AAW	TXBLS	10//99-12//99
Wholesale and Manufacturing, Technical and Scientific Product	Amarillo MSA, TX	S	20.39 MW	19.20 AW	42420 AAW	TXBLS	10//99-12//99
Wholesale and Manufacturing, Technical and Scientific Product	Austin-San Marcos MSA, TX	S	23.81 MW	22.43 AW	49530 AAW	TXBLS	10//99-12//99
Wholesale and Manufacturing, Technical and Scientific Product	Beaumont-Port Arthur MSA, TX	S	22.37 MW	19.30 AW	46520 AAW	TXBLS	10//99-12//99
Wholesale and Manufacturing, Technical and Scientific Product	Brazoria PMSA, TX	S	20.55 MW	18.52 AW	42740 AAW	TXBLS	10//99-12//99
Wholesale and Manufacturing, Technical and Scientific Product	Brownsville-Harlingen-San Benito MSA, TX	S	16.93 MW	13.62 AW	35220 AAW	TXBLS	10//99-12//99
Wholesale and Manufacturing, Technical and Scientific Product	Corpus Christi MSA, TX	S	19.33 MW	17.26 AW	40210 AAW	TXBLS	10//99-12//99
Wholesale and Manufacturing, Technical and Scientific Product	Dallas PMSA, TX	S	27.62 MW	25.55 AW	57460 AAW	TXBLS	10//99-12//99
Wholesale and Manufacturing, Technical and Scientific Product	El Paso MSA, TX	S	24.06 MW	15.68 AW	50040 AAW	TXBLS	10//99-12//99
Wholesale and Manufacturing, Technical and Scientific Product	Fort Worth-Arlington PMSA, TX	S	22.45 MW	20.06 AW	46690 AAW	TXBLS	10//99-12//99

AAW Average annual wage	**AOH** Average offered, high	**ASH** Average starting, high	**H** Hourly	**M** Monthly	**S** Special: hourly and annual
AE Average entry wage	**AOL** Average offered, low	**ASL** Average starting, low	**HI** Highest wage paid	**MTC** Median total compensation	**TQ** Third quartile wage
AEX Average experienced wage	**APH** Average pay, high range	**AW** Average wage paid	**HR** High end range	**MW** Median wage paid	**W** Weekly
AO Average offered	**API** Average pay, low range	**FQ** First quartile wage	**LR** Low end range	**SQ** Second quartile wage	**Y** Yearly

Sales Representative

Occupation/Type/Industry	Location	Per	Low	Mid	High	Source	Date
Wholesale and Manufacturing, Technical and Scientific Product	Galveston-Texas City PMSA, TX	S	24.59 MW	18.86 AW	51150 AAW	TXBLS	10//99-12//99
Wholesale and Manufacturing, Technical and Scientific Product	Houston PMSA, TX	S	27.93 MW	24.20 AW	58090 AAW	TXBLS	10//99-12//99
Wholesale and Manufacturing, Technical and Scientific Product	Laredo MSA, TX	S	19.55 MW	17.82 AW	40660 AAW	TXBLS	10//99-12//99
Wholesale and Manufacturing, Technical and Scientific Product	Longview-Marshall MSA, TX	S	26.15 MW	23.29 AW	54390 AAW	TXBLS	10//99-12//99
Wholesale and Manufacturing, Technical and Scientific Product	Lubbock MSA, TX	S	21.79 MW	19.06 AW	45330 AAW	TXBLS	10//99-12//99
Wholesale and Manufacturing, Technical and Scientific Product	McAllen-Edinburg-Mission MSA, TX	S	24.15 MW	21.81 AW	50230 AAW	TXBLS	10//99-12//99
Wholesale and Manufacturing, Technical and Scientific Product	Odessa-Midland MSA, TX	S	23.39 MW	20.82 AW	48650 AAW	TXBLS	10//99-12//99
Wholesale and Manufacturing, Technical and Scientific Product	San Antonio MSA, TX	S	22.01 MW	19.34 AW	45780 AAW	TXBLS	10//99-12//99
Wholesale and Manufacturing, Technical and Scientific Product	Sherman-Denison MSA, TX	S	21.90 MW	18.97 AW	45550 AAW	TXBLS	10//99-12//99
Wholesale and Manufacturing, Technical and Scientific Product	Texarkana MSA, TX-Texarkana, AR	S	22.30 MW	20.94 AW	46380 AAW	TXBLS	10//99-12//99
Wholesale and Manufacturing, Technical and Scientific Product	Tyler MSA, TX	S	24.56 MW	23.16 AW	51080 AAW	TXBLS	10//99-12//99
Wholesale and Manufacturing, Technical and Scientific Product	Waco MSA, TX	S	22.06 MW	20.50 AW	45880 AAW	TXBLS	10//99-12//99
Wholesale and Manufacturing, Technical and Scientific Product	Wichita Falls MSA, TX	S	18.41 MW	16.25 AW	38300 AAW	TXBLS	10//99-12//99
Wholesale and Manufacturing, Technical and Scientific Product	Utah	S	22.63 MW	26.34 AW	54780 AAW	UTBLS	10//99-12//99
Wholesale and Manufacturing, Technical and Scientific Product	Provo-Orem MSA, UT	S	24.01 MW	18.14 AW	49940 AAW	UTBLS	10//99-12//99
Wholesale and Manufacturing, Technical and Scientific Product	Salt Lake City-Ogden MSA, UT	S	27.52 MW	23.18 AW	57240 AAW	UTBLS	10//99-12//99
Wholesale and Manufacturing, Technical and Scientific Product	Vermont	S	19.81 MW	22.39 AW	46570 AAW	VTBLS	10//99-12//99
Wholesale and Manufacturing, Technical and Scientific Product	Burlington MSA, VT	S	24.06 MW	23.15 AW	50050 AAW	VTBLS	10//99-12//99
Wholesale and Manufacturing, Technical and Scientific Product	Virginia	S	24.81 MW	26.12 AW	54330 AAW	VABLS	10//99-12//99
Wholesale and Manufacturing, Technical and Scientific Product	Lynchburg MSA, VA	S	25.51 MW	24.31 AW	53070 AAW	VABLS	10//99-12//99
Wholesale and Manufacturing, Technical and Scientific Product	Norfolk-Virginia Beach-Newport News MSA, VA-NC	S	22.44 MW	17.63 AW	46670 AAW	VABLS	10//99-12//99
Wholesale and Manufacturing, Technical and Scientific Product	Roanoke MSA, VA	S	23.96 MW	20.05 AW	49840 AAW	VABLS	10//99-12//99
Wholesale and Manufacturing, Technical and Scientific Product	Washington	S	21.64 MW	23.26 AW	48380 AAW	WABLS	10//99-12//99
Wholesale and Manufacturing, Technical and Scientific Product	Bellingham MSA, WA	S	23.67 MW	22.01 AW	49230 AAW	WABLS	10//99-12//99
Wholesale and Manufacturing, Technical and Scientific Product	Olympia PMSA, WA	S	20.59 MW	16.59 AW	42830 AAW	WABLS	10//99-12//99
Wholesale and Manufacturing, Technical and Scientific Product	Richland-Kennewick-Pasco MSA, WA	S	23.81 MW	20.56 AW	49530 AAW	WABLS	10//99-12//99
Wholesale and Manufacturing, Technical and Scientific Product	Seattle-Bellevue-Everett PMSA, WA	S	23.70 MW	22.76 AW	49310 AAW	WABLS	10//99-12//99
Wholesale and Manufacturing, Technical and Scientific Product	Spokane MSA, WA	S	20.73 MW	18.69 AW	43120 AAW	WABLS	10//99-12//99
Wholesale and Manufacturing, Technical and Scientific Product	Tacoma PMSA, WA	S	21.07 MW	15.69 AW	43830 AAW	WABLS	10//99-12//99
Wholesale and Manufacturing, Technical and Scientific Product	Yakima MSA, WA	S	17.71 MW	17.27 AW	36840 AAW	WABLS	10//99-12//99
Wholesale and Manufacturing, Technical and Scientific Product	West Virginia	S	19.47 MW	20.78 AW	43220 AAW	WVBLS	10//99-12//99

AAW Average annual wage	**AOH** Average offered, high	**ASH** Average starting, high	**H** Hourly	**M** Monthly	**S** Special: hourly and annual
AE Average entry wage	**AOL** Average offered, low	**ASL** Average starting, low	**HI** Highest wage paid	**MTC** Median total compensation	**TQ** Third quartile wage
AEX Average experienced wage	**APH** Average pay, high range	**AW** Average wage paid	**HR** High end range	**MW** Median wage paid	**W** Weekly
AO Average offered	**APL** Average pay, low range	**FQ** First quartile wage	**LR** Low end range	**SQ** Second quartile wage	**Y** Yearly

Occupation/Type/Industry	Location	Per	Low	Mid	High	Source	Date
Sales Representative							
Wholesale and Manufacturing, Technical and Scientific Product	Charleston MSA, WV	S	23.10 MW	23.08 AW	48040 AAW	WVBLS	10//99-12//99
Wholesale and Manufacturing, Technical and Scientific Product	Huntington-Ashland MSA, WV-KY-OH	S	17.24 MW	16.69 AW	35860 AAW	WVBLS	10//99-12//99
Wholesale and Manufacturing, Technical and Scientific Product	Parkersburg-Marietta MSA, WV-OH	S	18.05 MW	17.02 AW	37550 AAW	WVBLS	10//99-12//99
Wholesale and Manufacturing, Technical and Scientific Product	Wheeling MSA, WV-OH	S	19.40 MW	18.78 AW	40350 AAW	WVBLS	10//99-12//99
Wholesale and Manufacturing, Technical and Scientific Product	Wisconsin	S	22.55 MW	25.99 AW	54060 AAW	WIBLS	10//99-12//99
Wholesale and Manufacturing, Technical and Scientific Product	Appleton-Oshkosh-Neenah MSA, WI	S	23.42 MW	20.33 AW	48710 AAW	WIBLS	10//99-12//99
Wholesale and Manufacturing, Technical and Scientific Product	Eau Claire MSA, WI	S	20.85 MW	18.57 AW	43360 AAW	WIBLS	10//99-12//99
Wholesale and Manufacturing, Technical and Scientific Product	Green Bay MSA, WI	S	25.25 MW	23.20 AW	52530 AAW	WIBLS	10//99-12//99
Wholesale and Manufacturing, Technical and Scientific Product	Janesville-Beloit MSA, WI	S	22.34 MW	22.53 AW	46470 AAW	WIBLS	10//99-12//99
Wholesale and Manufacturing, Technical and Scientific Product	Kenosha PMSA, WI	S	24.70 MW	22.90 AW	51380 AAW	WIBLS	10//99-12//99
Wholesale and Manufacturing, Technical and Scientific Product	La Crosse MSA, WI-MN	S	19.70 MW	17.99 AW	40970 AAW	WIBLS	10//99-12//99
Wholesale and Manufacturing, Technical and Scientific Product	Madison MSA, WI	S	22.91 MW	20.49 AW	47650 AAW	WIBLS	10//99-12//99
Wholesale and Manufacturing, Technical and Scientific Product	Milwaukee-Waukesha PMSA, WI	S	29.59 MW	25.65 AW	61540 AAW	WIBLS	10//99-12//99
Wholesale and Manufacturing, Technical and Scientific Product	Racine PMSA, WI	S	21.52 MW	18.93 AW	44770 AAW	WIBLS	10//99-12//99
Wholesale and Manufacturing, Technical and Scientific Product	Sheboygan MSA, WI	S	23.57 MW	19.39 AW	49020 AAW	WIBLS	10//99-12//99
Wholesale and Manufacturing, Technical and Scientific Product	Wausau MSA, WI	S	20.62 MW	18.74 AW	42880 AAW	WIBLS	10//99-12//99
Wholesale and Manufacturing, Technical and Scientific Product	Wyoming	S	24.24 MW	24.99 AW	51980 AAW	WYBLS	10//99-12//99
Wholesale and Manufacturing, Technical and Scientific Product	Casper MSA, WY	S	26.02 MW	27.24 AW	54130 AAW	WYBLS	10//99-12//99
Wholesale and Manufacturing, Technical and Scientific Product	Cheyenne MSA, WY	S	26.30 MW	30.11 AW	54700 AAW	WYBLS	10//99-12//99
Wholesale and Manufacturing, Technical and Scientific Product	Puerto Rico	S	16.38 MW	17.42 AW	36230 AAW	PRBLS	10//99-12//99
Wholesale and Manufacturing, Technical and Scientific Product	Caguas PMSA, PR	S	19.33 MW	16.69 AW	40210 AAW	PRBLS	10//99-12//99
Wholesale and Manufacturing, Technical and Scientific Product	San Juan-Bayamon PMSA, PR	S	17.33 MW	16.55 AW	36040 AAW	PRBLS	10//99-12//99
Salesman							
New Cars, Auto Dealership	United States	Y		51976 AW		WARD1	1999
Used Cars, Auto Dealership	United States	Y		49731 AW		WARD1	1999
Salesperson							
Real Estate	United States	Y		33200 MW		REALM	4//99
Sample Maker							
Garment Company, $10-25 Million in Sales	Los Angeles, CA	H		9.80 AW		CAAPN	1998
Sawing Machine Setter, Operator, and Tender, Wood	Alabama	S	9.68 MW	10.08 AW	20970 AAW	ALBLS	10//99-12//99
	Birmingham MSA, AL	S	9.67 MW	9.38 AW	20100 AAW	ALBLS	10//99-12//99
	Decatur MSA, AL	S	8.33 MW	8.06 AW	17320 AAW	ALBLS	10//99-12//99
	Mobile MSA, AL	S	8.48 MW	8.52 AW	17640 AAW	ALBLS	10//99-12//99
	Montgomery MSA, AL	S	10.86 MW	9.47 AW	22600 AAW	ALBLS	10//99-12//99
	Tuscaloosa MSA, AL	S	11.15 MW	10.45 AW	23200 AAW	ALBLS	10//99-12//99
	Alaska	S	10.59 MW	12.11 AW	25190 AAW	AKBLS	10//99-12//99
	Arizona	S	9.83 MW	9.92 AW	20630 AAW	AZBLS	10//99-12//99
	Phoenix-Mesa MSA, AZ	S	10.05 MW	9.94 AW	20910 AAW	AZBLS	10//99-12//99
	Tucson MSA, AZ	S	8.57 MW	7.33 AW	17830 AAW	AZBLS	10//99-12//99
	Arkansas	S	8.41 MW	8.84 AW	18390 AAW	ARBLS	10//99-12//99
	Fort Smith MSA, AR-OK	S	8.32 MW	8.21 AW	17300 AAW	ARBLS	10//99-12//99

AAW	Average annual wage	**AOH**	Average offered, high	**ASH**	Average starting, high	**H**	Hourly	**M**	Monthly	**S**	Special: hourly and annual
AE	Average entry wage	**AOL**	Average offered, low	**ASL**	Average starting, low	**HI**	Highest wage paid	**MTC**	Median total compensation	**TQ**	Third quartile wage
AEX	Average experienced wage	**APH**	Average pay, high range	**AW**	Average wage paid	**HR**	High end range	**MW**	Median wage paid	**W**	Weekly
AO	Average offered	**APL**	Average pay, low range	**FQ**	First quartile wage	**LR**	Low end range	**SQ**	Second quartile wage	**Y**	Yearly

Occupation/Type/Industry	Location	Per	Low	Mid	High	Source	Date
Sawing Machine Setter, Operator, and Tender, Wood	Little Rock-North Little Rock MSA, AR	S	9.85 MW	10.54 AW	20490 AAW	ARBLS	10//99-12//99
	California	S	9.29 MW	10.39 AW	21600 AAW	CABLS	10//99-12//99
	Fresno MSA, CA	S	8.85 MW	8.68 AW	18400 AAW	CABLS	10//99-12//99
	Los Angeles-Long Beach PMSA, CA	S	8.75 MW	8.35 AW	18190 AAW	CABLS	10//99-12//99
	Modesto MSA, CA	S	8.53 MW	8.05 AW	17740 AAW	CABLS	10//99-12//99
	Orange County PMSA, CA	S	8.52 MW	7.81 AW	17730 AAW	CABLS	10//99-12//99
	Redding MSA, CA	S	13.28 MW	13.13 AW	27630 AAW	CABLS	10//99-12//99
	Riverside-San Bernardino PMSA, CA	S	9.08 MW	8.32 AW	18880 AAW	CABLS	10//99-12//99
	Sacramento PMSA, CA	S	10.79 MW	9.28 AW	22440 AAW	CABLS	10//99-12//99
	San Diego MSA, CA	S	9.25 MW	8.97 AW	19230 AAW	CABLS	10//99-12//99
	Santa Rosa PMSA, CA	S	10.82 MW	10.72 AW	22510 AAW	CABLS	10//99-12//99
	Stockton-Lodi MSA, CA	S	10.29 MW	9.56 AW	21410 AAW	CABLS	10//99-12//99
	Colorado	S	9.99 MW	10.20 AW	21210 AAW	COBLS	10//99-12//99
	Colorado Springs MSA, CO	S	10.30 MW	10.23 AW	21420 AAW	COBLS	10//99-12//99
	Denver PMSA, CO	S	10.17 MW	9.94 AW	21150 AAW	COBLS	10//99-12//99
	Fort Collins-Loveland MSA, CO	S	12.91 MW	11.71 AW	26860 AAW	COBLS	10//99-12//99
	Connecticut	S	11.15 MW	11.37 AW	23660 AAW	CTBLS	10//99-12//99
	Hartford MSA, CT	S	12.86 MW	12.72 AW	26740 AAW	CTBLS	10//99-12//99
	Washington PMSA, DC-MD-VA-WV	S	10.00 MW	9.28 AW	20810 AAW	DCBLS	10//99-12//99
	Florida	S	9.11 MW	9.40 AW	19550 AAW	FLBLS	10//99-12//99
	Daytona Beach MSA, FL	S	8.62 MW	8.59 AW	17940 AAW	FLBLS	10//99-12//99
	Fort Lauderdale PMSA, FL	S	10.15 MW	9.95 AW	21120 AAW	FLBLS	10//99-12//99
	Jacksonville MSA, FL	S	9.32 MW	9.26 AW	19390 AAW	FLBLS	10//99-12//99
	Lakeland-Winter Haven MSA, FL	S	8.75 MW	8.76 AW	18190 AAW	FLBLS	10//99-12//99
	Melbourne-Titusville-Palm Bay MSA, FL	S	8.98 MW	8.92 AW	18690 AAW	FLBLS	10//99-12//99
	Miami PMSA, FL	S	8.08 MW	7.84 AW	16810 AAW	FLBLS	10//99-12//99
	Ocala MSA, FL	S	10.24 MW	8.72 AW	21290 AAW	FLBLS	10//99-12//99
	Sarasota-Bradenton MSA, FL	S	9.45 MW	9.63 AW	19660 AAW	FLBLS	10//99-12//99
	Tampa-St. Petersburg-Clearwater MSA, FL	S	9.06 MW	8.57 AW	18840 AAW	FLBLS	10//99-12//99
	West Palm Beach-Boca Raton MSA, FL	S	9.63 MW	9.71 AW	20020 AAW	FLBLS	10//99-12//99
	Georgia	S	9.21 MW	9.65 AW	20070 AAW	GABLS	10//99-12//99
	Atlanta MSA, GA	S	10.33 MW	9.48 AW	21490 AAW	GABLS	10//99-12//99
	Macon MSA, GA	S	8.52 MW	8.32 AW	17720 AAW	GABLS	10//99-12//99
	Idaho	S	11.47 MW	12.30 AW	25580 AAW	IDBLS	10//99-12//99
	Boise City MSA, ID	S	8.63 MW	8.63 AW	17950 AAW	IDBLS	10//99-12//99
	Illinois	S	10.78 MW	10.82 AW	22520 AAW	ILBLS	10//99-12//99
	Chicago PMSA, IL	S	11.21 MW	11.24 AW	23320 AAW	ILBLS	10//99-12//99
	Indiana	S	9.64 MW	9.91 AW	20610 AAW	INBLS	10//99-12//99
	Elkhart-Goshen MSA, IN	S	9.38 MW	9.19 AW	19510 AAW	INBLS	10//99-12//99
	Evansville-Henderson MSA, IN-KY	S	9.10 MW	9.18 AW	18930 AAW	INBLS	10//99-12//99
	Fort Wayne MSA, IN	S	9.41 MW	9.64 AW	19570 AAW	INBLS	10//99-12//99
	Gary PMSA, IN	S	8.50 MW	8.09 AW	17670 AAW	INBLS	10//99-12//99
	Indianapolis MSA, IN	S	10.52 MW	10.18 AW	21890 AAW	INBLS	10//99-12//99
	Iowa	S	12.93 MW	12.21 AW	25390 AAW	IABLS	10//99-12//99
	Kansas	S	8.15 MW	8.47 AW	17620 AAW	KSBLS	10//99-12//99
	Kentucky	S	8.31 MW	8.64 AW	17960 AAW	KYBLS	10//99-12//99
	Louisville MSA, KY-IN	S	9.41 MW	9.14 AW	19570 AAW	KYBLS	10//99-12//99
	Louisiana	S	9.34 MW	9.56 AW	19890 AAW	LABLS	10//99-12//99
	Baton Rouge MSA, LA	S	10.70 MW	10.92 AW	22250 AAW	LABLS	10//99-12//99
	Monroe MSA, LA	S	7.95 MW	7.64 AW	16550 AAW	LABLS	10//99-12//99
	Maine	S	9.36 MW	9.93 AW	20660 AAW	MEBLS	10//99-12//99
	Bangor MSA, ME	S	10.79 MW	10.79 AW	22450 AAW	MEBLS	10//99-12//99
	Maryland	S	9.42 MW	10.02 AW	20840 AAW	MDBLS	10//99-12//99
	Baltimore PMSA, MD	S	10.49 MW	9.66 AW	21820 AAW	MDBLS	10//99-12//99
	Massachusetts	S	11.08 MW	11.91 AW	24770 AAW	MABLS	10//99-12//99
	Boston PMSA, MA-NH	S	14.25 MW	13.56 AW	29640 AAW	MABLS	10//99-12//99
	Springfield MSA, MA	S	11.89 MW	11.56 AW	24720 AAW	MABLS	10//99-12//99
	Worcester PMSA, MA-CT	S	9.57 MW	9.31 AW	19900 AAW	MABLS	10//99-12//99
	Michigan	S	9.81 MW	10.19 AW	21200 AAW	MIBLS	10//99-12//99
	Ann Arbor PMSA, MI	S	11.54 MW	10.24 AW	24010 AAW	MIBLS	10//99-12//99
	Benton Harbor MSA, MI	S	11.32 MW	11.75 AW	23550 AAW	MIBLS	10//99-12//99

Occupation/Type/Industry	Location	Per	Low	Mid	High	Source	Date
Sawing Machine Setter, Operator, and Tender, Wood	Detroit PMSA, MI	S	11.24 MW	10.16 AW	23380 AAW	MIBLS	10//99-12//99
	Grand Rapids-Muskegon-Holland MSA, MI	S	11.37 MW	11.31 AW	23660 AAW	MIBLS	10//99-12//99
	Minnesota	S	10.81 MW	11.09 AW	23060 AAW	MNBLS	10//99-12//99
	Duluth-Superior MSA, MN-WI	S	12.34 MW	11.79 AW	25670 AAW	MNBLS	10//99-12//99
	Minneapolis-St. Paul MSA, MN-WI	S	12.16 MW	12.19 AW	25290 AAW	MNBLS	10//99-12//99
	Mississippi	S	9.34 MW	9.51 AW	19780 AAW	MSBLS	10//99-12//99
	Jackson MSA, MS	S	8.69 MW	8.32 AW	18070 AAW	MSBLS	10//99-12//99
	Missouri	S	8.6 MW	9.00 AW	18710 AAW	MOBLS	10//99-12//99
	Joplin MSA, MO	S	8.64 MW	8.66 AW	17960 AAW	MOBLS	10//99-12//99
	Kansas City MSA, MO-KS	S	9.75 MW	9.18 AW	20280 AAW	MOBLS	10//99-12//99
	St. Louis MSA, MO-IL	S	10.10 MW	9.41 AW	21010 AAW	MOBLS	10//99-12//99
	Springfield MSA, MO	S	9.38 MW	9.46 AW	19520 AAW	MOBLS	10//99-12//99
	Montana	S	11.88 MW	11.40 AW	23720 AAW	MTBLS	10//99-12//99
	Missoula MSA, MT	S	12.78 MW	13.22 AW	26580 AAW	MTBLS	10//99-12//99
	Nebraska	S	8.73 MW	8.68 AW	18040 AAW	NEBLS	10//99-12//99
	Nevada	S	10.38 MW	11.03 AW	22950 AAW	NVBLS	10//99-12//99
	Las Vegas MSA, NV-AZ	S	10.86 MW	10.52 AW	22590 AAW	NVBLS	10//99-12//99
	New Hampshire	S	10.13 MW	10.55 AW	21930 AAW	NHBLS	10//99-12//99
	New Jersey	S	8.99 MW	9.75 AW	20280 AAW	NJBLS	10//99-12//99
	Newark PMSA, NJ	S	10.24 MW	9.45 AW	21300 AAW	NJBLS	10//99-12//99
	New York	S	9.82 MW	10.26 AW	21340 AAW	NYBLS	10//99-12//99
	Albany-Schenectady-Troy MSA, NY	S	9.60 MW	8.92 AW	19970 AAW	NYBLS	10//99-12//99
	Buffalo-Niagara Falls MSA, NY	S	10.14 MW	10.66 AW	21080 AAW	NYBLS	10//99-12//99
	Glens Falls MSA, NY	S	8.87 MW	8.98 AW	18450 AAW	NYBLS	10//99-12//99
	Jamestown MSA, NY	S	10.44 MW	10.12 AW	21720 AAW	NYBLS	10//99-12//99
	Nassau-Suffolk PMSA, NY	S	10.33 MW	9.30 AW	21490 AAW	NYBLS	10//99-12//99
	New York PMSA, NY	S	11.39 MW	10.72 AW	23700 AAW	NYBLS	10//99-12//99
	Rochester MSA, NY	S	9.68 MW	9.17 AW	20130 AAW	NYBLS	10//99-12//99
	Syracuse MSA, NY	S	11.76 MW	10.86 AW	24460 AAW	NYBLS	10//99-12//99
	Utica-Rome MSA, NY	S	8.71 MW	8.27 AW	18130 AAW	NYBLS	10//99-12//99
	North Carolina	S	10.02 MW	10.25 AW	21310 AAW	NCBLS	10//99-12//99
	Asheville MSA, NC	S	9.88 MW	9.91 AW	20560 AAW	NCBLS	10//99-12//99
	Charlotte-Gastonia-Rock Hill MSA, NC-SC	S	8.76 MW	8.31 AW	18230 AAW	NCBLS	10//99-12//99
	Greensboro--Winston-Salem--High Point MSA, NC	S	9.91 MW	9.77 AW	20620 AAW	NCBLS	10//99-12//99
	Hickory-Morganton-Lenoir MSA, NC	S	11.53 MW	11.29 AW	23970 AAW	NCBLS	10//99-12//99
	Raleigh-Durham-Chapel Hill MSA, NC	S	11.58 MW	11.44 AW	24080 AAW	NCBLS	10//99-12//99
	Rocky Mount MSA, NC	S	7.65 MW	7.54 AW	15910 AAW	NCBLS	10//99-12//99
	North Dakota	S	9.99 MW	9.93 AW	20650 AAW	NDBLS	10//99-12//99
	Fargo-Moorhead MSA, ND-MN	S	10.09 MW	10.35 AW	20980 AAW	NDBLS	10//99-12//99
	Ohio	S	9.91 MW	10.09 AW	20980 AAW	OHBLS	10//99-12//99
	Cincinnati PMSA, OH-KY-IN	S	11.33 MW	10.76 AW	23560 AAW	OHBLS	10//99-12//99
	Columbus MSA, OH	S	9.06 MW	8.94 AW	18850 AAW	OHBLS	10//99-12//99
	Dayton-Springfield MSA, OH	S	9.99 MW	10.45 AW	20770 AAW	OHBLS	10//99-12//99
	Toledo MSA, OH	S	10.65 MW	11.07 AW	22160 AAW	OHBLS	10//99-12//99
	Youngstown-Warren MSA, OH	S	9.25 MW	9.31 AW	19230 AAW	OHBLS	10//99-12//99
	Oklahoma	S	9.96 MW	11.90 AW	24760 AAW	OKBLS	10//99-12//99
	Tulsa MSA, OK	S	15.82 MW	14.53 AW	32910 AAW	OKBLS	10//99-12//99
	Oregon	S	12.4 MW	12.75 AW	26520 AAW	ORBLS	10//99-12//99
	Eugene-Springfield MSA, OR	S	12.11 MW	12.06 AW	25190 AAW	ORBLS	10//99-12//99
	Medford-Ashland MSA, OR	S	11.94 MW	12.19 AW	24830 AAW	ORBLS	10//99-12//99
	Portland-Vancouver PMSA, OR-WA	S	12.13 MW	11.35 AW	25240 AAW	ORBLS	10//99-12//99
	Pennsylvania	S	10.22 MW	10.43 AW	21690 AAW	PABLS	10//99-12//99
	Erie MSA, PA	S	11.69 MW	11.31 AW	24310 AAW	PABLS	10//99-12//99
	Harrisburg-Lebanon-Carlisle MSA, PA	S	9.97 MW	9.67 AW	20730 AAW	PABLS	10//99-12//99
	Lancaster MSA, PA	S	10.72 MW	11.05 AW	22300 AAW	PABLS	10//99-12//99
	Philadelphia PMSA, PA-NJ	S	9.49 MW	9.14 AW	19740 AAW	PABLS	10//99-12//99
	Pittsburgh MSA, PA	S	10.85 MW	9.90 AW	22560 AAW	PABLS	10//99-12//99
	Reading MSA, PA	S	11.79 MW	11.76 AW	24510 AAW	PABLS	10//99-12//99
	Scranton--Wilkes-Barre--Hazleton MSA, PA	S	10.32 MW	10.12 AW	21470 AAW	PABLS	10//99-12//99

AAW	Average annual wage	AOH	Average offered, high	ASH	Average starting, high	H	Hourly	M	Monthly	S	Special: hourly and annual
AE	Average entry wage	AOL	Average offered, low	ASL	Average starting, low	HI	Highest wage paid	MTC	Median total compensation	TQ	Third quartile wage
AEX	Average experienced wage	APH	Average pay, high range	AW	Average wage paid	HR	High end range	MW	Median wage paid	W	Weekly
AO	Average offered	APL	Average pay, low range	FQ	First quartile wage	LR	Low end range	SQ	Second quartile wage	Y	Yearly

Occupation/Type/Industry	Location	Per	Low	Mid	High	Source	Date
Sawing Machine Setter, Operator, and Tender, Wood	York MSA, PA	S	10.37 MW	10.44 AW	21560 AAW	PABLS	10//99-12//99
	Rhode Island	S	10.62 MW	10.91 AW	22700 AAW	RIBLS	10//99-12//99
	Providence-Fall River-Warwick MSA, RI-MA	S	10.81 MW	10.16 AW	22480 AAW	RIBLS	10//99-12//99
	South Carolina	S	9.22 MW	9.44 AW	19630 AAW	SCBLS	10//99-12//99
	Columbia MSA, SC	S	10.11 MW	10.03 AW	21020 AAW	SCBLS	10//99-12//99
	Greenville-Spartanburg-Anderson MSA, SC	S	10.12 MW	9.97 AW	21050 AAW	SCBLS	10//99-12//99
	South Dakota	S	9.83 MW	9.77 AW	20310 AAW	SDBLS	10//99-12//99
	Sioux Falls MSA, SD	S	10.16 MW	10.18 AW	21130 AAW	SDBLS	10//99-12//99
	Tennessee	S	8.8 MW	9.15 AW	19030 AAW	TNBLS	10//99-12//99
	Johnson City-Kingsport-Bristol MSA, TN-VA	S	9.33 MW	8.97 AW	19400 AAW	TNBLS	10//99-12//99
	Knoxville MSA, TN	S	9.34 MW	9.09 AW	19430 AAW	TNBLS	10//99-12//99
	Memphis MSA, TN-AR-MS	S	8.45 MW	8.42 AW	17580 AAW	MSBLS	10//99-12//99
	Nashville MSA, TN	S	10.82 MW	10.94 AW	22500 AAW	TNBLS	10//99-12//99
	Texas	S	8.11 MW	8.81 AW	18320 AAW	TXBLS	10//99-12//99
	Austin-San Marcos MSA, TX	S	7.98 MW	7.89 AW	16590 AAW	TXBLS	10//99-12//99
	Dallas PMSA, TX	S	8.71 MW	8.21 AW	18110 AAW	TXBLS	10//99-12//99
	Fort Worth-Arlington PMSA, TX	S	7.85 MW	7.64 AW	16320 AAW	TXBLS	10//99-12//99
	Houston PMSA, TX	S	8.38 MW	7.53 AW	17440 AAW	TXBLS	10//99-12//99
	Longview-Marshall MSA, TX	S	14.21 MW	14.06 AW	29560 AAW	TXBLS	10//99-12//99
	San Antonio MSA, TX	S	8.41 MW	8.06 AW	17500 AAW	TXBLS	10//99-12//99
	Utah	S	9.96 MW	10.16 AW	21140 AAW	UTBLS	10//99-12//99
	Salt Lake City-Ogden MSA, UT	S	10.21 MW	10.18 AW	21240 AAW	UTBLS	10//99-12//99
	Vermont	S	10.05 MW	10.50 AW	21840 AAW	VTBLS	10//99-12//99
	Virginia	S	9.23 MW	9.74 AW	20260 AAW	VABLS	10//99-12//99
	Danville MSA, VA	S	7.61 MW	6.77 AW	15830 AAW	VABLS	10//99-12//99
	Lynchburg MSA, VA	S	9.81 MW	9.27 AW	20400 AAW	VABLS	10//99-12//99
	Norfolk-Virginia Beach-Newport News MSA, VA-NC	S	12.14 MW	10.38 AW	25240 AAW	VABLS	10//99-12//99
	Richmond-Petersburg MSA, VA	S	10.62 MW	9.87 AW	22100 AAW	VABLS	10//99-12//99
	Washington	S	12.9 MW	13.61 AW	28310 AAW	WABLS	10//99-12//99
	Bellingham MSA, WA	S	12.20 MW	10.97 AW	25380 AAW	WABLS	10//99-12//99
	Seattle-Bellevue-Everett PMSA, WA	S	14.24 MW	13.62 AW	29620 AAW	WABLS	10//99-12//99
	Spokane MSA, WA	S	9.70 MW	9.74 AW	20170 AAW	WABLS	10//99-12//99
	Tacoma PMSA, WA	S	12.39 MW	11.89 AW	25770 AAW	WABLS	10//99-12//99
	West Virginia	S	8.81 MW	10.76 AW	22370 AAW	WVBLS	10//99-12//99
	Charleston MSA, WV	S	7.93 MW	6.31 AW	16500 AAW	WVBLS	10//99-12//99
	Huntington-Ashland MSA, WV-KY-OH	S	16.56 MW	6.35 AW	34450 AAW	WVBLS	10//99-12//99
	Wisconsin	S	9.88 MW	10.12 AW	21050 AAW	WIBLS	10//99-12//99
	Appleton-Oshkosh-Neenah MSA, WI	S	9.76 MW	9.56 AW	20300 AAW	WIBLS	10//99-12//99
	Eau Claire MSA, WI	S	10.39 MW	10.26 AW	21620 AAW	WIBLS	10//99-12//99
	Janesville-Beloit MSA, WI	S	9.12 MW	9.13 AW	18970 AAW	WIBLS	10//99-12//99
	La Crosse MSA, WI-MN	S	7.77 MW	7.63 AW	16150 AAW	WIBLS	10//99-12//99
	Milwaukee-Waukesha PMSA, WI	S	10.57 MW	10.82 AW	21980 AAW	WIBLS	10//99-12//99
	Sheboygan MSA, WI	S	11.06 MW	11.25 AW	23000 AAW	WIBLS	10//99-12//99
	Wausau MSA, WI	S	10.48 MW	9.95 AW	21810 AAW	WIBLS	10//99-12//99
	Wyoming	S	10.16 MW	10.60 AW	22040 AAW	WYBLS	10//99-12//99
	Puerto Rico	S	6.21 MW	6.25 AW	13000 AAW	PRBLS	10//99-12//99
Schoolbus Driver	Kansas City, MO	Y	10.71 AE		13.44 HI	KCSTAR	2000
Secondary School Teacher							
Except Special and Vocational Education	Alabama	Y		36790 AAW		ALBLS	10//99-12//99
Except Special and Vocational Education	Alaska	Y		46300 AAW		AKBLS	10//99-12//99
Except Special and Vocational Education	Arizona	Y		37910 AAW		AZBLS	10//99-12//99
Except Special and Vocational Education	Arkansas	Y		32960 AAW		ARBLS	10//99-12//99
Except Special and Vocational Education	California	Y		47580 AAW		CABLS	10//99-12//99
Except Special and Vocational Education	Colorado	Y		39340 AAW		COBLS	10//99-12//99
Except Special and Vocational Education	Connecticut	Y		47590 AAW		CTBLS	10//99-12//99
Except Special and Vocational Education	Delaware	Y		47010 AAW		DEBLS	10//99-12//99
Except Special and Vocational Education	Florida	Y		39180 AAW		FLBLS	10//99-12//99

AAW Average annual wage	AOH Average offered, high	ASH Average starting, high	H Hourly	-M Monthly	S Special: hourly and annual
AE Average entry wage	AOL Average offered, low	ASL Average starting, low	HI Highest wage paid	MTC Median total compensation	TQ Third quartile wage
AEX Average experienced wage	APH Average pay, high range	AW Average wage paid	HR High end range	MW Median wage paid	W Weekly
AO Average offered	APL Average pay, low range	FQ First quartile wage	LR Low end range	SQ Second quartile wage	Y Yearly

Occupation/Type/Industry	Location	Per	Low	Mid	High	Source	Date
Secondary School Teacher							
Except Special and Vocational Education	Georgia	Y		41160 AAW		GABLS	10//99-12//99
Except Special and Vocational Education	Hawaii	Y		43470 AAW		HIBLS	10//99-12//99
Except Special and Vocational Education	Idaho	Y		32590 AAW		IDBLS	10//99-12//99
Except Special and Vocational Education	Illinois	Y		48780 AAW		ILBLS	10//99-12//99
Except Special and Vocational Education	Indiana	Y		42170 AAW		INBLS	10//99-12//99
Except Special and Vocational Education	Iowa	Y		34190 AAW		IABLS	10//99-12//99
Except Special and Vocational Education	Kansas	Y		32590 AAW		KSBLS	10//99-12//99
Except Special and Vocational Education	Kentucky	Y		35640 AAW		KYBLS	10//99-12//99
Except Special and Vocational Education	Louisiana	Y		32190 AAW		LABLS	10//99-12//99
Except Special and Vocational Education	Maine	Y		35290 AAW		MEBLS	10//99-12//99
Except Special and Vocational Education	Maryland	Y		42350 AAW		MDBLS	10//99-12//99
Except Special and Vocational Education	Massachusetts	Y		44850 AAW		MABLS	10//99-12//99
Except Special and Vocational Education	Michigan	Y		43910 AAW		MIBLS	10//99-12//99
Except Special and Vocational Education	Minnesota	Y		40790 AAW		MNBLS	10//99-12//99
Except Special and Vocational Education	Mississippi	Y		30960 AAW		MSBLS	10//99-12//99
Except Special and Vocational Education	Missouri	Y		35820 AAW		MOBLS	10//99-12//99
Except Special and Vocational Education	Montana	Y		31000 AAW		MTBLS	10//99-12//99
Except Special and Vocational Education	Nebraska	Y		34540 AAW		NEBLS	10//99-12//99
Except Special and Vocational Education	Nevada	Y		43380 AAW		NVBLS	10//99-12//99
Except Special and Vocational Education	New Hampshire	Y		35090 AAW		NHBLS	10//99-12//99
Except Special and Vocational Education	New Jersey	Y		53350 AAW		NJBLS	10//99-12//99
Except Special and Vocational Education	New Mexico	Y		35770 AAW		NMBLS	10//99-12//99
Except Special and Vocational Education	New York	Y		49150 AAW		NYBLS	10//99-12//99
Except Special and Vocational Education	North Carolina	Y		35750 AAW		NCBLS	10//99-12//99
Except Special and Vocational Education	North Dakota	Y		31430 AAW		NDBLS	10//99-12//99
Except Special and Vocational Education	Ohio	Y		39990 AAW		OHBLS	10//99-12//99
Except Special and Vocational Education	Oklahoma	Y		32500 AAW		OKBLS	10//99-12//99
Except Special and Vocational Education	Oregon	Y		42690 AAW		ORBLS	10//99-12//99
Except Special and Vocational Education	Pennsylvania	Y		42570 AAW		PABLS	10//99-12//99
Except Special and Vocational Education	Rhode Island	Y		47020 AAW		RIBLS	10//99-12//99
Except Special and Vocational Education	South Carolina	Y		36050 AAW		SCBLS	10//99-12//99
Except Special and Vocational Education	South Dakota	Y		28450 AAW		SDBLS	10//99-12//99
Except Special and Vocational Education	Tennessee	Y		32240 AAW		TNBLS	10//99-12//99
Except Special and Vocational Education	Texas	Y		37920 AAW		TXBLS	10//99-12//99
Except Special and Vocational Education	Utah	Y		35290 AAW		UTBLS	10//99-12//99
Except Special and Vocational Education	Vermont	Y		37900 AAW		VTBLS	10//99-12//99
Except Special and Vocational Education	Virginia	Y		36070 AAW		VABLS	10//99-12//99
Except Special and Vocational Education	Washington	Y		40910 AAW		WABLS	10//99-12//99
Except Special and Vocational Education	West Virginia	Y		35460 AAW		WVBLS	10//99-12//99
Except Special and Vocational Education	Wisconsin	Y		40730 AAW		WIBLS	10//99-12//99
Except Special and Vocational Education	Wyoming	Y		30140 AAW		WYBLS	10//99-12//99
Except Special and Vocational Education	Puerto Rico	Y		19790 AAW		PRBLS	10//99-12//99
Except Special and Vocational Education	Virgin Islands	Y		41690 AAW		VIBLS	10//99-12//99
Except Special and Vocational Education	Guam	Y		34570 AAW		GUBLS	10//99-12//99
Secretary							
Bilingual	Los Angeles County, CA	Y		31945 AW		LABJ	1999
Except Legal, Medical, and Executive	Alabama	S	9.19 MW	9.76 AW	20290 AAW	ALBLS	10//99-12//99
Except Legal, Medical, and Executive	Anniston MSA, AL	S	10.07 MW	9.46 AW	20940 AAW	ALBLS	10//99-12//99
Except Legal, Medical, and Executive	Auburn-Opelika MSA, AL	S	9.33 MW	8.93 AW	19400 AAW	ALBLS	10//99-12//99
Except Legal, Medical, and Executive	Birmingham MSA, AL	S	10.14 MW	9.54 AW	21080 AAW	ALBLS	10//99-12//99
Except Legal, Medical, and Executive	Decatur MSA, AL	S	9.77 MW	9.25 AW	20320 AAW	ALBLS	10//99-12//99
Except Legal, Medical, and Executive	Dothan MSA, AL	S	9.31 MW	8.41 AW	19360 AAW	ALBLS	10//99-12//99
Except Legal, Medical, and Executive	Florence MSA, AL	S	8.67 MW	8.27 AW	18030 AAW	ALBLS	10//99-12//99
Except Legal, Medical, and Executive	Gadsden MSA, AL	S	8.62 MW	7.99 AW	17920 AAW	ALBLS	10//99-12//99
Except Legal, Medical, and Executive	Huntsville MSA, AL	S	11.75 MW	11.70 AW	24430 AAW	ALBLS	10//99-12//99
Except Legal, Medical, and Executive	Mobile MSA, AL	S	9.93 MW	9.57 AW	20650 AAW	ALBLS	10//99-12//99
Except Legal, Medical, and Executive	Montgomery MSA, AL	S	9.75 MW	9.01 AW	20280 AAW	ALBLS	10//99-12//99
Except Legal, Medical, and Executive	Tuscaloosa MSA, AL	S	8.72 MW	8.29 AW	18130 AAW	ALBLS	10//99-12//99
Except Legal, Medical, and Executive	Alaska	S	13.84 MW	14.05 AW	29230 AAW	AKBLS	10//99-12//99
Except Legal, Medical, and Executive	Anchorage MSA, AK	S	13.33 MW	12.75 AW	27720 AAW	AKBLS	10//99-12//99
Except Legal, Medical, and Executive	Arizona	S	10.65 MW	11.26 AW	23420 AAW	AZBLS	10//99-12//99
Except Legal, Medical, and Executive	Flagstaff MSA, AZ-UT	S	11.13 MW	10.82 AW	23150 AAW	AZBLS	10//99-12//99
Except Legal, Medical, and Executive	Phoenix-Mesa MSA, AZ	S	11.79 MW	11.16 AW	24510 AAW	AZBLS	10//99-12//99
Except Legal, Medical, and Executive	Tucson MSA, AZ	S	9.90 MW	9.29 AW	20590 AAW	AZBLS	10//99-12//99
Except Legal, Medical, and Executive	Yuma MSA, AZ	S	10.35 MW	10.37 AW	21530 AAW	AZBLS	10//99-12//99
Except Legal, Medical, and Executive	Arkansas	S	8.44 MW	8.68 AW	18060 AAW	ARBLS	10//99-12//99
Except Legal, Medical, and Executive	Fayetteville-Springdale-Rogers MSA, AR	S	8.38 MW	8.36 AW	17430 AAW	ARBLS	10//99-12//99
Except Legal, Medical, and Executive	Fort Smith MSA, AR-OK	S	8.81 MW	8.66 AW	18320 AAW	ARBLS	10//99-12//99
Except Legal, Medical, and Executive	Jonesboro MSA, AR	S	8.32 MW	8.08 AW	17310 AAW	ARBLS	10//99-12//99

Occupation/Type/Industry	Location	Per	Low	Mid	High	Source	Date
Secretary							
Except Legal, Medical, and Executive	Little Rock-North Little Rock MSA, AR	S	9.50 MW	9.41 AW	19760 AAW	ARBLS	10//99-12//99
Except Legal, Medical, and Executive	Pine Bluff MSA, AR	S	8.79 MW	8.26 AW	18270 AAW	ARBLS	10//99-12//99
Except Legal, Medical, and Executive	California	S	13.26 MW	13.45 AW	27980 AAW	CABLS	10//99-12//99
Except Legal, Medical, and Executive	Bakersfield MSA, CA	S	12.25 MW	12.04 AW	25480 AAW	CABLS	10//99-12//99
Except Legal, Medical, and Executive	Chico-Paradise MSA, CA	S	9.63 MW	9.40 AW	20040 AAW	CABLS	10//99-12//99
Except Legal, Medical, and Executive	Fresno MSA, CA	S	11.24 MW	10.89 AW	23380 AAW	CABLS	10//99-12//99
Except Legal, Medical, and Executive	Los Angeles-Long Beach PMSA, CA	S	13.90 MW	13.89 AW	28920 AAW	CABLS	10//99-12//99
Except Legal, Medical, and Executive	Merced MSA, CA	S	9.46 MW	8.51 AW	19670 AAW	CABLS	10//99-12//99
Except Legal, Medical, and Executive	Modesto MSA, CA	S	9.67 MW	8.69 AW	20110 AAW	CABLS	10//99-12//99
Except Legal, Medical, and Executive	Oakland PMSA, CA	S	14.03 MW	14.00 AW	29190 AAW	CABLS	10//99-12//99
Except Legal, Medical, and Executive	Orange County PMSA, CA	S	14.40 MW	14.37 AW	29960 AAW	CABLS	10//99-12//99
Except Legal, Medical, and Executive	Redding MSA, CA	S	11.00 MW	10.83 AW	22870 AAW	CABLS	10//99-12//99
Except Legal, Medical, and Executive	Riverside-San Bernardino PMSA, CA	S	12.25 MW	12.35 AW	25470 AAW	CABLS	10//99-12//99
Except Legal, Medical, and Executive	Sacramento PMSA, CA	S	12.39 MW	12.29 AW	25770 AAW	CABLS	10//99-12//99
Except Legal, Medical, and Executive	Salinas MSA, CA	S	12.06 MW	11.92 AW	25090 AAW	CABLS	10//99-12//99
Except Legal, Medical, and Executive	San Diego MSA, CA	S	13.38 MW	12.84 AW	27820 AAW	CABLS	10//99-12//99
Except Legal, Medical, and Executive	San Francisco PMSA, CA	S	15.54 MW	15.34 AW	32330 AAW	CABLS	10//99-12//99
Except Legal, Medical, and Executive	San Jose PMSA, CA	S	15.40 MW	15.68 AW	32020 AAW	CABLS	10//99-12//99
Except Legal, Medical, and Executive	San Luis Obispo-Atascadero-Paso Robles MSA, CA	S	9.68 MW	8.01 AW	20140 AAW	CABLS	10//99-12//99
Except Legal, Medical, and Executive	Santa Barbara-Santa Maria-Lompoc MSA, CA	S	13.58 MW	13.11 AW	28250 AAW	CABLS	10//99-12//99
Except Legal, Medical, and Executive	Santa Cruz-Watsonville PMSA, CA	S	12.57 MW	12.52 AW	26140 AAW	CABLS	10//99-12//99
Except Legal, Medical, and Executive	Santa Rosa PMSA, CA	S	12.68 MW	12.58 AW	26370 AAW	CABLS	10//99-12//99
Except Legal, Medical, and Executive	Stockton-Lodi MSA, CA	S	12.98 MW	13.12 AW	26990 AAW	CABLS	10//99-12//99
Except Legal, Medical, and Executive	Vallejo-Fairfield-Napa PMSA, CA	S	12.33 MW	12.23 AW	25650 AAW	CABLS	10//99-12//99
Except Legal, Medical, and Executive	Ventura PMSA, CA	S	12.50 MW	12.27 AW	26000 AAW	CABLS	10//99-12//99
Except Legal, Medical, and Executive	Visalia-Tulare-Porterville MSA, CA	S	10.49 MW	9.86 AW	21820 AAW	CABLS	10//99-12//99
Except Legal, Medical, and Executive	Yolo PMSA, CA	S	11.27 MW	10.88 AW	23440 AAW	CABLS	10//99-12//99
Except Legal, Medical, and Executive	Yuba City MSA, CA	S	11.70 MW	11.74 AW	24330 AAW	CABLS	10//99-12//99
Except Legal, Medical, and Executive	Colorado	S	11.7 MW	11.81 AW	24570 AAW	COBLS	10//99-12//99
Except Legal, Medical, and Executive	Boulder-Longmont PMSA, CO	S	12.43 MW	12.29 AW	25860 AAW	COBLS	10//99-12//99
Except Legal, Medical, and Executive	Colorado Springs MSA, CO	S	12.10 MW	11.73 AW	25160 AAW	COBLS	10//99-12//99
Except Legal, Medical, and Executive	Denver PMSA, CO	S	12.80 MW	12.76 AW	26620 AAW	COBLS	10//99-12//99
Except Legal, Medical, and Executive	Fort Collins-Loveland MSA, CO	S	10.17 MW	9.71 AW	21150 AAW	COBLS	10//99-12//99
Except Legal, Medical, and Executive	Grand Junction MSA, CO	S	11.09 MW	11.24 AW	23060 AAW	COBLS	10//99-12//99
Except Legal, Medical, and Executive	Greeley PMSA, CO	S	9.53 MW	9.37 AW	19830 AAW	COBLS	10//99-12//99
Except Legal, Medical, and Executive	Pueblo MSA, CO	S	8.61 MW	8.21 AW	17910 AAW	COBLS	10//99-12//99
Except Legal, Medical, and Executive	Connecticut	S	13.53 MW	13.60 AW	28290 AAW	CTBLS	10//99-12//99
Except Legal, Medical, and Executive	Bridgeport PMSA, CT	S	13.28 MW	13.29 AW	27630 AAW	CTBLS	10//99-12//99
Except Legal, Medical, and Executive	Danbury PMSA, CT	S	12.99 MW	12.92 AW	27020 AAW	CTBLS	10//99-12//99
Except Legal, Medical, and Executive	Hartford MSA, CT	S	14.22 MW	14.09 AW	29570 AAW	CTBLS	10//99-12//99
Except Legal, Medical, and Executive	New Haven-Meriden PMSA, CT	S	13.17 MW	13.15 AW	27390 AAW	CTBLS	10//99-12//99
Except Legal, Medical, and Executive	New London-Norwich MSA, CT-RI	S	12.55 MW	12.29 AW	26110 AAW	CTBLS	10//99-12//99
Except Legal, Medical, and Executive	Stamford-Norwalk PMSA, CT	S	14.63 MW	14.73 AW	30440 AAW	CTBLS	10//99-12//99
Except Legal, Medical, and Executive	Waterbury PMSA, CT	S	12.20 MW	11.95 AW	25380 AAW	CTBLS	10//99-12//99
Except Legal, Medical, and Executive	Delaware	S	11.85 MW	11.99 AW	24930 AAW	DEBLS	10//99-12//99
Except Legal, Medical, and Executive	Dover MSA, DE	S	11.07 MW	10.46 AW	23030 AAW	DEBLS	10//99-12//99
Except Legal, Medical, and Executive	Wilmington-Newark PMSA, DE-MD	S	12.21 MW	12.16 AW	25400 AAW	DEBLS	10//99-12//99
Except Legal, Medical, and Executive	District of Columbia	S	14.94 MW	15.44 AW	32110 AAW	DCBLS	10//99-12//99
Except Legal, Medical, and Executive	Washington PMSA, DC-MD-VA-WV	S	13.50 MW	13.02 AW	28080 AAW	DCBLS	10//99-12//99
Except Legal, Medical, and Executive	Florida	S	10.24 MW	10.64 AW	22130 AAW	FLBLS	10//99-12//99
Except Legal, Medical, and Executive	Daytona Beach MSA, FL	S	9.66 MW	9.26 AW	20090 AAW	FLBLS	10//99-12//99
Except Legal, Medical, and Executive	Fort Lauderdale PMSA, FL	S	11.39 MW	10.65 AW	23680 AAW	FLBLS	10//99-12//99
Except Legal, Medical, and Executive	Fort Myers-Cape Coral MSA, FL	S	10.11 MW	9.88 AW	21030 AAW	FLBLS	10//99-12//99
Except Legal, Medical, and Executive	Fort Pierce-Port St. Lucie MSA, FL	S	9.94 MW	9.86 AW	20670 AAW	FLBLS	10//99-12//99
Except Legal, Medical, and Executive	Fort Walton Beach MSA, FL	S	10.37 MW	9.89 AW	21580 AAW	FLBLS	10//99-12//99
Except Legal, Medical, and Executive	Gainesville MSA, FL	S	10.45 MW	10.04 AW	21730 AAW	FLBLS	10//99-12//99

AAW	Average annual wage	AOH	Average offered, high	ASH	Average starting, high	H	Hourly	M	Monthly	S	Special: hourly and annual
AE	Average entry wage	AOL	Average offered, low	ASL	Average starting, low	HI	Highest wage paid	MTC	Median total compensation	TQ	Third quartile wage
AEX	Average experienced wage	APH	Average pay, high range	AW	Average wage paid	HR	High end range	MW	Median wage paid	W	Weekly
AO	Average offered	APL	Average pay, low range	FQ	First quartile wage	LR	Low end range	SQ	Second quartile wage	Y	Yearly

Secretary

Occupation/Type/Industry	Location	Per	Low	Mid	High	Source	Date
Except Legal, Medical, and Executive	Jacksonville MSA, FL	S	10.80 MW	10.38 AW	22460 AAW	FLBLS	10//99-12//99
Except Legal, Medical, and Executive	Lakeland-Winter Haven MSA, FL	S	9.65 MW	9.32 AW	20070 AAW	FLBLS	10//99-12//99
Except Legal, Medical, and Executive	Melbourne-Titusville-Palm Bay MSA, FL	S	11.06 MW	10.91 AW	23010 AAW	FLBLS	10//99-12//99
Except Legal, Medical, and Executive	Miami PMSA, FL	S	11.64 MW	11.52 AW	24200 AAW	FLBLS	10//99-12//99
Except Legal, Medical, and Executive	Naples MSA, FL	S	11.29 MW	11.30 AW	23480 AAW	FLBLS	10//99-12//99
Except Legal, Medical, and Executive	Ocala MSA, FL	S	9.89 MW	9.76 AW	20580 AAW	FLBLS	10//99-12//99
Except Legal, Medical, and Executive	Orlando MSA, FL	S	10.60 MW	10.13 AW	22040 AAW	FLBLS	10//99-12//99
Except Legal, Medical, and Executive	Panama City MSA, FL	S	10.24 MW	9.67 AW	21290 AAW	FLBLS	10//99-12//99
Except Legal, Medical, and Executive	Pensacola MSA, FL	S	9.96 MW	8.96 AW	20710 AAW	FLBLS	10//99-12//99
Except Legal, Medical, and Executive	Punta Gorda MSA, FL	S	8.40 MW	8.10 AW	17470 AAW	FLBLS	10//99-12//99
Except Legal, Medical, and Executive	Sarasota-Bradenton MSA, FL	S	10.44 MW	10.29 AW	21720 AAW	FLBLS	10//99-12//99
Except Legal, Medical, and Executive	Tallahassee MSA, FL	S	10.32 MW	9.94 AW	21460 AAW	FLBLS	10//99-12//99
Except Legal, Medical, and Executive	Tampa-St. Petersburg-Clearwater MSA, FL	S	10.43 MW	9.97 AW	21690 AAW	FLBLS	10//99-12//99
Except Legal, Medical, and Executive	West Palm Beach-Boca Raton MSA, FL	S	11.45 MW	11.26 AW	23810 AAW	FLBLS	10//99-12//99
Except Legal, Medical, and Executive	Georgia	S	10.54 MW	10.93 AW	22740 AAW	GABLS	10//99-12//99
Except Legal, Medical, and Executive	Albany MSA, GA	S	10.02 MW	9.85 AW	20840 AAW	GABLS	10//99-12//99
Except Legal, Medical, and Executive	Atlanta MSA, GA	S	11.61 MW	11.27 AW	24160 AAW	GABLS	10//99-12//99
Except Legal, Medical, and Executive	Augusta-Aiken MSA, GA-SC	S	9.92 MW	9.68 AW	20630 AAW	GABLS	10//99-12//99
Except Legal, Medical, and Executive	Columbus MSA, GA-AL	S	9.18 MW	8.91 AW	19090 AAW	GABLS	10//99-12//99
Except Legal, Medical, and Executive	Macon MSA, GA	S	11.00 MW	10.43 AW	22870 AAW	GABLS	10//99-12//99
Except Legal, Medical, and Executive	Savannah MSA, GA	S	10.74 MW	10.70 AW	22350 AAW	GABLS	10//99-12//99
Except Legal, Medical, and Executive	Hawaii	S	13.74 MW	13.82 AW	28740 AAW	HIBLS	10//99-12//99
Except Legal, Medical, and Executive	Honolulu MSA, HI	S	13.91 MW	13.88 AW	28940 AAW	HIBLS	10//99-12//99
Except Legal, Medical, and Executive	Idaho	S	10.4 MW	10.62 AW	22090 AAW	IDBLS	10//99-12//99
Except Legal, Medical, and Executive	Boise City MSA, ID	S	11.21 MW	11.14 AW	23320 AAW	IDBLS	10//99-12//99
Except Legal, Medical, and Executive	Pocatello MSA, ID	S	8.96 MW	8.76 AW	18650 AAW	IDBLS	10//99-12//99
Except Legal, Medical, and Executive	Illinois	S	11.96 MW	12.06 AW	25090 AAW	ILBLS	10//99-12//99
Except Legal, Medical, and Executive	Bloomington-Normal MSA, IL	S	12.00 MW	10.79 AW	24950 AAW	ILBLS	10//99-12//99
Except Legal, Medical, and Executive	Chicago PMSA, IL	S	12.96 MW	12.67 AW	26970 AAW	ILBLS	10//99-12//99
Except Legal, Medical, and Executive	Decatur MSA, IL	S	9.54 MW	8.65 AW	19840 AAW	ILBLS	10//99-12//99
Except Legal, Medical, and Executive	Kankakee PMSA, IL	S	10.17 MW	10.54 AW	21150 AAW	ILBLS	10//99-12//99
Except Legal, Medical, and Executive	Peoria-Pekin MSA, IL	S	10.77 MW	10.21 AW	22390 AAW	ILBLS	10//99-12//99
Except Legal, Medical, and Executive	Rockford MSA, IL	S	10.22 MW	9.89 AW	21250 AAW	ILBLS	10//99-12//99
Except Legal, Medical, and Executive	Springfield MSA, IL	S	11.61 MW	11.35 AW	24140 AAW	ILBLS	10//99-12//99
Except Legal, Medical, and Executive	Indiana	S	10.29 MW	10.54 AW	21910 AAW	INBLS	10//99-12//99
Except Legal, Medical, and Executive	Bloomington MSA, IN	S	10.42 MW	9.93 AW	21670 AAW	INBLS	10//99-12//99
Except Legal, Medical, and Executive	Elkhart-Goshen MSA, IN	S	11.02 MW	11.28 AW	22930 AAW	INBLS	10//99-12//99
Except Legal, Medical, and Executive	Evansville-Henderson MSA, IN-KY	S	8.65 MW	8.12 AW	17980 AAW	INBLS	10//99-12//99
Except Legal, Medical, and Executive	Fort Wayne MSA, IN	S	11.27 MW	11.33 AW	23450 AAW	INBLS	10//99-12//99
Except Legal, Medical, and Executive	Gary PMSA, IN	S	10.76 MW	10.32 AW	22380 AAW	INBLS	10//99-12//99
Except Legal, Medical, and Executive	Indianapolis MSA, IN	S	11.22 MW	10.94 AW	23340 AAW	INBLS	10//99-12//99
Except Legal, Medical, and Executive	Kokomo MSA, IN	S	10.98 MW	10.41 AW	22830 AAW	INBLS	10//99-12//99
Except Legal, Medical, and Executive	Lafayette MSA, IN	S	11.78 MW	11.83 AW	24510 AAW	INBLS	10//99-12//99
Except Legal, Medical, and Executive	Muncie MSA, IN	S	9.80 MW	9.62 AW	20380 AAW	INBLS	10//99-12//99
Except Legal, Medical, and Executive	South Bend MSA, IN	S	10.52 MW	10.20 AW	21880 AAW	INBLS	10//99-12//99
Except Legal, Medical, and Executive	Terre Haute MSA, IN	S	10.56 MW	10.02 AW	21960 AAW	INBLS	10//99-12//99
Except Legal, Medical, and Executive	Iowa	S	9.96 MW	10.27 AW	21360 AAW	IABLS	10//99-12//99
Except Legal, Medical, and Executive	Cedar Rapids MSA, IA	S	8.93 MW	9.21 AW	18580 AAW	IABLS	10//99-12//99
Except Legal, Medical, and Executive	Davenport-Moline-Rock Island MSA, IA-IL	S	10.79 MW	10.74 AW	22450 AAW	IABLS	10//99-12//99
Except Legal, Medical, and Executive	Des Moines MSA, IA	S	11.47 MW	11.43 AW	23850 AAW	IABLS	10//99-12//99
Except Legal, Medical, and Executive	Dubuque MSA, IA	S	8.99 MW	9.10 AW	18690 AAW	IABLS	10//99-12//99
Except Legal, Medical, and Executive	Iowa City MSA, IA	S	11.73 MW	11.66 AW	24400 AAW	IABLS	10//99-12//99
Except Legal, Medical, and Executive	Sioux City MSA, IA-NE	S	8.86 MW	8.44 AW	18430 AAW	IABLS	10//99-12//99
Except Legal, Medical, and Executive	Waterloo-Cedar Falls MSA, IA	S	11.29 MW	11.12 AW	23490 AAW	IABLS	10//99-12//99
Except Legal, Medical, and Executive	Kansas	S	9.66 MW	9.90 AW	20600 AAW	KSBLS	10//99-12//99
Except Legal, Medical, and Executive	Lawrence MSA, KS	S	9.89 MW	9.91 AW	20570 AAW	KSBLS	10//99-12//99
Except Legal, Medical, and Executive	Topeka MSA, KS	S	9.80 MW	9.57 AW	20370 AAW	KSBLS	10//99-12//99
Except Legal, Medical, and Executive	Wichita MSA, KS	S	9.60 MW	9.38 AW	19970 AAW	KSBLS	10//99-12//99
Except Legal, Medical, and Executive	Kentucky	S	9.69 MW	9.95 AW	20700 AAW	KYBLS	10//99-12//99
Except Legal, Medical, and Executive	Lexington MSA, KY	S	10.50 MW	10.27 AW	21830 AAW	KYBLS	10//99-12//99
Except Legal, Medical, and Executive	Louisville MSA, KY-IN	S	10.81 MW	10.64 AW	22490 AAW	KYBLS	10//99-12//99
Except Legal, Medical, and Executive	Owensboro MSA, KY	S	9.33 MW	9.25 AW	19410 AAW	KYBLS	10//99-12//99
Except Legal, Medical, and Executive	Louisiana	S	9.25 MW	9.58 AW	19930 AAW	LABLS	10//99-12//99
Except Legal, Medical, and Executive	Alexandria MSA, LA	S	8.97 MW	8.46 AW	18660 AAW	LABLS	10//99-12//99
Except Legal, Medical, and Executive	Baton Rouge MSA, LA	S	10.20 MW	9.80 AW	21210 AAW	LABLS	10//99-12//99

AAW	Average annual wage	AOH	Average offered, high	ASH	Average starting, high	H	Hourly	M	Monthly	S	Special: hourly and annual
AE	Average entry wage	AOL	Average offered, low	ASL	Average starting, low	HI	Highest wage paid	MTC	Median total compensation	TQ	Third quartile wage
AEX	Average experienced wage	APH	Average pay, high range	AW	Average wage paid	HR	High end range	MW	Median wage paid	W	Weekly
AO	Average offered	APL	Average pay, low range	FQ	First quartile wage	LR	Low end range	SQ	Second quartile wage	Y	Yearly

Secretary

Occupation/Type/Industry	Location	Per	Low	Mid	High	Source	Date
Secretary							
Except Legal, Medical, and Executive	Houma MSA, LA	S	10.75 MW	11.15 AW	22350 AAW	LABLS	10//99-12//99
Except Legal, Medical, and Executive	Lafayette MSA, LA	S	8.45 MW	7.96 AW	17570 AAW	LABLS	10//99-12//99
Except Legal, Medical, and Executive	Lake Charles MSA, LA	S	8.57 MW	8.10 AW	17820 AAW	LABLS	10//99-12//99
Except Legal, Medical, and Executive	Monroe MSA, LA	S	8.43 MW	8.13 AW	17540 AAW	LABLS	10//99-12//99
Except Legal, Medical, and Executive	New Orleans MSA, LA	S	10.05 MW	9.76 AW	20910 AAW	LABLS	10//99-12//99
Except Legal, Medical, and Executive	Shreveport-Bossier City MSA, LA	S	9.95 MW	9.63 AW	20700 AAW	LABLS	10//99-12//99
Except Legal, Medical, and Executive	Maine	S	10.32 MW	10.50 AW	21850 AAW	MEBLS	10//99-12//99
Except Legal, Medical, and Executive	Bangor MSA, ME	S	9.49 MW	9.31 AW	19740 AAW	MEBLS	10//99-12//99
Except Legal, Medical, and Executive	Lewiston-Auburn MSA, ME	S	9.56 MW	9.58 AW	19890 AAW	MEBLS	10//99-12//99
Except Legal, Medical, and Executive	Portland MSA, ME	S	11.19 MW	11.14 AW	23270 AAW	MEBLS	10//99-12//99
Except Legal, Medical, and Executive	Maryland	S	11.58 MW	11.65 AW	24240 AAW	MDBLS	10//99-12//99
Except Legal, Medical, and Executive	Baltimore PMSA, MD	S	11.43 MW	11.41 AW	23770 AAW	MDBLS	10//99-12//99
Except Legal, Medical, and Executive	Cumberland MSA, MD-WV	S	8.87 MW	8.66 AW	18460 AAW	MDBLS	10//99-12//99
Except Legal, Medical, and Executive	Hagerstown PMSA, MD	S	10.71 MW	10.97 AW	22280 AAW	MDBLS	10//99-12//99
Except Legal, Medical, and Executive	Massachusetts	S	12.53 MW	12.69 AW	26400 AAW	MABLS	10//99-12//99
Except Legal, Medical, and Executive	Barnstable-Yarmouth MSA, MA	S	12.66 MW	12.56 AW	26330 AAW	MABLS	10//99-12//99
Except Legal, Medical, and Executive	Boston PMSA, MA-NH	S	13.44 MW	13.20 AW	27960 AAW	MABLS	10//99-12//99
Except Legal, Medical, and Executive	Fitchburg-Leominster PMSA, MA	S	11.30 MW	11.37 AW	23510 AAW	MABLS	10//99-12//99
Except Legal, Medical, and Executive	Lawrence PMSA, MA-NH	S	11.53 MW	11.39 AW	23980 AAW	MABLS	10//99-12//99
Except Legal, Medical, and Executive	Lowell PMSA, MA-NH	S	12.52 MW	12.29 AW	26030 AAW	MABLS	10//99-12//99
Except Legal, Medical, and Executive	New Bedford PMSA, MA	S	10.53 MW	10.16 AW	21900 AAW	MABLS	10//99-12//99
Except Legal, Medical, and Executive	Pittsfield MSA, MA	S	10.81 MW	10.59 AW	22490 AAW	MABLS	10//99-12//99
Except Legal, Medical, and Executive	Springfield MSA, MA	S	11.92 MW	11.48 AW	24800 AAW	MABLS	10//99-12//99
Except Legal, Medical, and Executive	Worcester PMSA, MA-CT	S	11.49 MW	11.48 AW	23910 AAW	MABLS	10//99-12//99
Except Legal, Medical, and Executive	Michigan	S	11.69 MW	11.97 AW	24900 AAW	MIBLS	10//99-12//99
Except Legal, Medical, and Executive	Ann Arbor PMSA, MI	S	12.09 MW	11.75 AW	25150 AAW	MIBLS	10//99-12//99
Except Legal, Medical, and Executive	Benton Harbor MSA, MI	S	10.64 MW	10.31 AW	22130 AAW	MIBLS	10//99-12//99
Except Legal, Medical, and Executive	Detroit PMSA, MI	S	12.93 MW	12.71 AW	26890 AAW	MIBLS	10//99-12//99
Except Legal, Medical, and Executive	Flint PMSA, MI	S	10.25 MW	10.00 AW	21320 AAW	MIBLS	10//99-12//99
Except Legal, Medical, and Executive	Grand Rapids-Muskegon-Holland MSA, MI	S	11.74 MW	11.75 AW	24410 AAW	MIBLS	10//99-12//99
Except Legal, Medical, and Executive	Jackson MSA, MI	S	11.03 MW	10.58 AW	22940 AAW	MIBLS	10//99-12//99
Except Legal, Medical, and Executive	Kalamazoo-Battle Creek MSA, MI	S	11.42 MW	11.38 AW	23750 AAW	MIBLS	10//99-12//99
Except Legal, Medical, and Executive	Lansing-East Lansing MSA, MI	S	12.36 MW	11.88 AW	25710 AAW	MIBLS	10//99-12//99
Except Legal, Medical, and Executive	Saginaw-Bay City-Midland MSA, MI	S	10.48 MW	10.77 AW	21790 AAW	MIBLS	10//99-12//99
Except Legal, Medical, and Executive	Minnesota	S	12.38 MW	12.52 AW	26050 AAW	MNBLS	10//99-12//99
Except Legal, Medical, and Executive	Duluth-Superior MSA, MN-WI	S	11.69 MW	11.50 AW	24310 AAW	MNBLS	10//99-12//99
Except Legal, Medical, and Executive	Minneapolis-St. Paul MSA, MN-WI	S	13.30 MW	13.03 AW	27670 AAW	MNBLS	10//99-12//99
Except Legal, Medical, and Executive	St. Cloud MSA, MN	S	10.27 MW	10.18 AW	21350 AAW	MNBLS	10//99-12//99
Except Legal, Medical, and Executive	Mississippi	S	9.25 MW	9.56 AW	19880 AAW	MSBLS	10//99-12//99
Except Legal, Medical, and Executive	Biloxi-Gulfport-Pascagoula MSA, MS	S	10.15 MW	9.64 AW	21110 AAW	MSBLS	10//99-12//99
Except Legal, Medical, and Executive	Hattiesburg MSA, MS	S	8.44 MW	7.79 AW	17560 AAW	MSBLS	10//99-12//99
Except Legal, Medical, and Executive	Jackson MSA, MS	S	10.26 MW	10.32 AW	21330 AAW	MSBLS	10//99-12//99
Except Legal, Medical, and Executive	Missouri	S	10.01 MW	10.47 AW	21780 AAW	MOBLS	10//99-12//99
Except Legal, Medical, and Executive	Columbia MSA, MO	S	9.28 MW	8.83 AW	19300 AAW	MOBLS	10//99-12//99
Except Legal, Medical, and Executive	Joplin MSA, MO	S	8.59 MW	8.30 AW	17870 AAW	MOBLS	10//99-12//99
Except Legal, Medical, and Executive	Kansas City MSA, MO-KS	S	11.58 MW	11.31 AW	24090 AAW	MOBLS	10//99-12//99
Except Legal, Medical, and Executive	St. Joseph MSA, MO	S	8.32 MW	7.13 AW	17300 AAW	MOBLS	10//99-12//99
Except Legal, Medical, and Executive	St. Louis MSA, MO-IL	S	11.44 MW	10.96 AW	23790 AAW	MOBLS	10//99-12//99
Except Legal, Medical, and Executive	Springfield MSA, MO	S	9.41 MW	9.19 AW	19580 AAW	MOBLS	10//99-12//99
Except Legal, Medical, and Executive	Montana	S	9 MW	9.17 AW	19070 AAW	MTBLS	10//99-12//99
Except Legal, Medical, and Executive	Billings MSA, MT	S	9.26 MW	9.24 AW	19250 AAW	MTBLS	10//99-12//99
Except Legal, Medical, and Executive	Great Falls MSA, MT	S	9.25 MW	9.35 AW	19250 AAW	MTBLS	10//99-12//99
Except Legal, Medical, and Executive	Missoula MSA, MT	S	8.36 MW	8.24 AW	17390 AAW	MTBLS	10//99-12//99
Except Legal, Medical, and Executive	Nebraska	S	9.13 MW	9.45 AW	19650 AAW	NEBLS	10//99-12//99
Except Legal, Medical, and Executive	Lincoln MSA, NE	S	10.05 MW	9.45 AW	20900 AAW	NEBLS	10//99-12//99
Except Legal, Medical, and Executive	Omaha MSA, NE-IA	S	10.74 MW	10.28 AW	22350 AAW	NEBLS	10//99-12//99
Except Legal, Medical, and Executive	Nevada	S	11.75 MW	11.98 AW	24920 AAW	NVBLS	10//99-12//99
Except Legal, Medical, and Executive	Las Vegas MSA, NV-AZ	S	11.79 MW	11.73 AW	24520 AAW	NVBLS	10//99-12//99
Except Legal, Medical, and Executive	Reno MSA, NV	S	11.09 MW	10.61 AW	23080 AAW	NVBLS	10//99-12//99
Except Legal, Medical, and Executive	New Hampshire	S	10.38 MW	10.86 AW	22600 AAW	NHBLS	10//99-12//99
Except Legal, Medical, and Executive	Manchester PMSA, NH	S	11.49 MW	11.00 AW	23900 AAW	NHBLS	10//99-12//99
Except Legal, Medical, and Executive	Nashua PMSA, NH	S	11.02 MW	10.26 AW	22910 AAW	NHBLS	10//99-12//99

AAW	Average annual wage	AOH	Average offered, high	ASH	Average starting, high	H	Hourly	M	Monthly	S	Special: hourly and annual
AE	Average entry wage	AOL	Average offered, low	ASL	Average starting, low	HI	Highest wage paid	MTC	Median total compensation	TQ	Third quartile wage
AEX	Average experienced wage	APH	Average pay, high range	AW	Average wage paid	HR	High end range	MW	Median wage paid	W	Weekly
AO	Average offered	APL	Average pay, low range	FQ	First quartile wage	LR	Low end range	SQ	Second quartile wage	Y	Yearly

Occupation/Type/Industry	Location	Per	Low	Mid	High	Source	Date
Secretary							
Except Legal, Medical, and Executive	Portsmouth-Rochester PMSA, NH-ME	S	11.44 MW	11.36 AW	23790 AAW	NHBLS	10//99-12//99
Except Legal, Medical, and Executive	New Jersey	S	14.15 MW	14.51 AW	30190 AAW	NJBLS	10//99-12//99
Except Legal, Medical, and Executive	Atlantic-Cape May PMSA, NJ	S	13.12 MW	12.43 AW	27290 AAW	NJBLS	10//99-12//99
Except Legal, Medical, and Executive	Bergen-Passaic PMSA, NJ	S	14.70 MW	14.36 AW	30570 AAW	NJBLS	10//99-12//99
Except Legal, Medical, and Executive	Jersey City PMSA, NJ	S	15.24 MW	15.39 AW	31700 AAW	NJBLS	10//99-12//99
Except Legal, Medical, and Executive	Middlesex-Somerset-Hunterdon PMSA, NJ	S	15.34 MW	15.17 AW	31900 AAW	NJBLS	10//99-12//99
Except Legal, Medical, and Executive	Monmouth-Ocean PMSA, NJ	S	13.33 MW	12.69 AW	27720 AAW	NJBLS	10//99-12//99
Except Legal, Medical, and Executive	Newark PMSA, NJ	S	14.84 MW	14.29 AW	30860 AAW	NJBLS	10//99-12//99
Except Legal, Medical, and Executive	Trenton PMSA, NJ	S	16.03 MW	16.19 AW	33350 AAW	NJBLS	10//99-12//99
Except Legal, Medical, and Executive	Vineland-Millville-Bridgeton PMSA, NJ	S	13.03 MW	12.58 AW	27100 AAW	NJBLS	10//99-12//99
Except Legal, Medical, and Executive	New Mexico	S	9.49 MW	9.90 AW	20600 AAW	NMBLS	10//99-12//99
Except Legal, Medical, and Executive	Albuquerque MSA, NM	S	10.64 MW	10.25 AW	22140 AAW	NMBLS	10//99-12//99
Except Legal, Medical, and Executive	Las Cruces MSA, NM	S	8.23 MW	7.19 AW	17110 AAW	NMBLS	10//99-12//99
Except Legal, Medical, and Executive	Santa Fe MSA, NM	S	10.68 MW	9.98 AW	22200 AAW	NMBLS	10//99-12//99
Except Legal, Medical, and Executive	New York	S	13.41 MW	13.69 AW	28470 AAW	NYBLS	10//99-12//99
Except Legal, Medical, and Executive	Albany-Schenectady-Troy MSA, NY	S	14.04 MW	13.92 AW	29210 AAW	NYBLS	10//99-12//99
Except Legal, Medical, and Executive	Binghamton MSA, NY	S	10.94 MW	10.52 AW	22750 AAW	NYBLS	10//99-12//99
Except Legal, Medical, and Executive	Buffalo-Niagara Falls MSA, NY	S	11.23 MW	10.66 AW	23360 AAW	NYBLS	10//99-12//99
Except Legal, Medical, and Executive	Dutchess County PMSA, NY	S	11.88 MW	11.66 AW	24710 AAW	NYBLS	10//99-12//99
Except Legal, Medical, and Executive	Elmira MSA, NY	S	11.65 MW	11.09 AW	24240 AAW	NYBLS	10//99-12//99
Except Legal, Medical, and Executive	Glens Falls MSA, NY	S	9.23 MW	9.00 AW	19200 AAW	NYBLS	10//99-12//99
Except Legal, Medical, and Executive	Jamestown MSA, NY	S	8.81 MW	8.24 AW	18330 AAW	NYBLS	10//99-12//99
Except Legal, Medical, and Executive	Nassau-Suffolk PMSA, NY	S	14.50 MW	14.49 AW	30160 AAW	NYBLS	10//99-12//99
Except Legal, Medical, and Executive	New York PMSA, NY	S	15.22 MW	14.80 AW	31650 AAW	NYBLS	10//99-12//99
Except Legal, Medical, and Executive	Newburgh PMSA, NY-PA	S	11.31 MW	11.43 AW	23530 AAW	NYBLS	10//99-12//99
Except Legal, Medical, and Executive	Rochester MSA, NY	S	11.36 MW	10.65 AW	23640 AAW	NYBLS	10//99-12//99
Except Legal, Medical, and Executive	Syracuse MSA, NY	S	11.44 MW	10.44 AW	23790 AAW	NYBLS	10//99-12//99
Except Legal, Medical, and Executive	Utica-Rome MSA, NY	S	10.92 MW	10.65 AW	22700 AAW	NYBLS	10//99-12//99
Except Legal, Medical, and Executive	North Carolina	S	10.62 MW	10.93 AW	22740 AAW	NCBLS	10//99-12//99
Except Legal, Medical, and Executive	Asheville MSA, NC	S	10.32 MW	9.89 AW	21460 AAW	NCBLS	10//99-12//99
Except Legal, Medical, and Executive	Charlotte-Gastonia-Rock Hill MSA, NC-SC	S	11.23 MW	10.68 AW	23350 AAW	NCBLS	10//99-12//99
Except Legal, Medical, and Executive	Fayetteville MSA, NC	S	10.35 MW	9.94 AW	21530 AAW	NCBLS	10//99-12//99
Except Legal, Medical, and Executive	Goldsboro MSA, NC	S	9.33 MW	9.24 AW	19410 AAW	NCBLS	10//99-12//99
Except Legal, Medical, and Executive	Greensboro--Winston-Salem--High Point MSA, NC	S	11.37 MW	11.27 AW	23650 AAW	NCBLS	10//99-12//99
Except Legal, Medical, and Executive	Hickory-Morganton-Lenoir MSA, NC	S	9.72 MW	9.74 AW	20210 AAW	NCBLS	10//99-12//99
Except Legal, Medical, and Executive	Jacksonville MSA, NC	S	8.87 MW	8.05 AW	18450 AAW	NCBLS	10//99-12//99
Except Legal, Medical, and Executive	Raleigh-Durham-Chapel Hill MSA, NC	S	12.42 MW	12.24 AW	25840 AAW	NCBLS	10//99-12//99
Except Legal, Medical, and Executive	Rocky Mount MSA, NC	S	9.63 MW	9.46 AW	20030 AAW	NCBLS	10//99-12//99
Except Legal, Medical, and Executive	Wilmington MSA, NC	S	10.70 MW	10.58 AW	22250 AAW	NCBLS	10//99-12//99
Except Legal, Medical, and Executive	North Dakota	S	8.94 MW	9.20 AW	19130 AAW	NDBLS	10//99-12//99
Except Legal, Medical, and Executive	Bismarck MSA, ND	S	9.65 MW	9.53 AW	20070 AAW	NDBLS	10//99-12//99
Except Legal, Medical, and Executive	Fargo-Moorhead MSA, ND-MN	S	9.81 MW	9.54 AW	20400 AAW	NDBLS	10//99-12//99
Except Legal, Medical, and Executive	Grand Forks MSA, ND-MN	S	9.37 MW	8.81 AW	19490 AAW	NDBLS	10//99-12//99
Except Legal, Medical, and Executive	Ohio	S	10.94 MW	11.22 AW	23330 AAW	OHBLS	10//99-12//99
Except Legal, Medical, and Executive	Akron PMSA, OH	S	10.75 MW	10.35 AW	22360 AAW	OHBLS	10//99-12//99
Except Legal, Medical, and Executive	Canton-Massillon MSA, OH	S	10.53 MW	10.06 AW	21890 AAW	OHBLS	10//99-12//99
Except Legal, Medical, and Executive	Cincinnati PMSA, OH-KY-IN	S	11.16 MW	10.68 AW	23220 AAW	OHBLS	10//99-12//99
Except Legal, Medical, and Executive	Cleveland-Lorain-Elyria PMSA, OH	S	12.37 MW	12.19 AW	25720 AAW	OHBLS	10//99-12//99
Except Legal, Medical, and Executive	Columbus MSA, OH	S	12.32 MW	12.37 AW	25620 AAW	OHBLS	10//99-12//99
Except Legal, Medical, and Executive	Dayton-Springfield MSA, OH	S	11.37 MW	10.98 AW	23640 AAW	OHBLS	10//99-12//99
Except Legal, Medical, and Executive	Hamilton-Middletown PMSA, OH	S	10.34 MW	9.96 AW	21510 AAW	OHBLS	10//99-12//99
Except Legal, Medical, and Executive	Lima MSA, OH	S	8.79 MW	8.64 AW	18270 AAW	OHBLS	10//99-12//99
Except Legal, Medical, and Executive	Mansfield MSA, OH	S	9.84 MW	9.79 AW	20470 AAW	OHBLS	10//99-12//99
Except Legal, Medical, and Executive	Steubenville-Weirton MSA, OH-WV	S	8.63 MW	8.12 AW	17960 AAW	OHBLS	10//99-12//99
Except Legal, Medical, and Executive	Toledo MSA, OH	S	11.15 MW	11.08 AW	23190 AAW	OHBLS	10//99-12//99
Except Legal, Medical, and Executive	Youngstown-Warren MSA, OH	S	9.70 MW	9.27 AW	20180 AAW	OHBLS	10//99-12//99
Except Legal, Medical, and Executive	Oklahoma	S	9.44 MW	9.80 AW	20380 AAW	OKBLS	10//99-12//99
Except Legal, Medical, and Executive	Enid MSA, OK	S	8.96 MW	9.03 AW	18640 AAW	OKBLS	10//99-12//99

AAW Average annual wage	**AOH** Average offered, high	**ASH** Average starting, high	**H** Hourly	**M** Monthly	**S** Special: hourly and annual
AE Average entry wage	**AOL** Average offered, low	**ASL** Average starting, low	**HI** Highest wage paid	**MTC** Median total compensation	**TQ** Third quartile wage
AEX Average experienced wage	**APH** Average pay, high range	**AW** Average wage paid	**HR** High end range	**MW** Median wage paid	**W** Weekly
AO Average offered	**APL** Average pay, low range	**FQ** First quartile wage	**LR** Low end range	**SQ** Second quartile wage	**Y** Yearly

Occupation/Type/Industry	Location	Per	Low	Mid	High	Source	Date
Secretary							
Except Legal, Medical, and Executive	Lawton MSA, OK	S	10.34 MW	9.83 AW	21510 AAW	OKBLS	10//99-12//99
Except Legal, Medical, and Executive	Oklahoma City MSA, OK	S	10.38 MW	10.01 AW	21590 AAW	OKBLS	10//99-12//99
Except Legal, Medical, and Executive	Tulsa MSA, OK	S	10.62 MW	10.14 AW	22090 AAW	OKBLS	10//99-12//99
Except Legal, Medical, and Executive	Oregon	S	11.74 MW	11.93 AW	24810 AAW	ORBLS	10//99-12//99
Except Legal, Medical, and Executive	Corvallis MSA, OR	S	10.40 MW	9.79 AW	21630 AAW	ORBLS	10//99-12//99
Except Legal, Medical, and Executive	Eugene-Springfield MSA, OR	S	10.15 MW	9.35 AW	21100 AAW	ORBLS	10//99-12//99
Except Legal, Medical, and Executive	Medford-Ashland MSA, OR	S	9.78 MW	9.56 AW	20340 AAW	ORBLS	10//99-12//99
Except Legal, Medical, and Executive	Portland-Vancouver PMSA, OR-WA	S	12.66 MW	12.44 AW	26340 AAW	ORBLS	10//99-12//99
Except Legal, Medical, and Executive	Salem PMSA, OR	S	11.24 MW	10.56 AW	23370 AAW	ORBLS	10//99-12//99
Except Legal, Medical, and Executive	Pennsylvania	S	10.71 MW	11.16 AW	23220 AAW	PABLS	10//99-12//99
Except Legal, Medical, and Executive	Allentown-Bethlehem-Easton MSA, PA	S	10.78 MW	10.32 AW	22430 AAW	PABLS	10//99-12//99
Except Legal, Medical, and Executive	Altoona MSA, PA	S	8.21 MW	7.75 AW	17080 AAW	PABLS	10//99-12//99
Except Legal, Medical, and Executive	Erie MSA, PA	S	10.14 MW	9.98 AW	21100 AAW	PABLS	10//99-12//99
Except Legal, Medical, and Executive	Harrisburg-Lebanon-Carlisle MSA, PA	S	11.57 MW	11.04 AW	24070 AAW	PABLS	10//99-12//99
Except Legal, Medical, and Executive	Johnstown MSA, PA	S	8.98 MW	8.52 AW	18670 AAW	PABLS	10//99-12//99
Except Legal, Medical, and Executive	Lancaster MSA, PA	S	10.80 MW	10.21 AW	22460 AAW	PABLS	10//99-12//99
Except Legal, Medical, and Executive	Philadelphia PMSA, PA-NJ	S	12.66 MW	12.43 AW	26330 AAW	PABLS	10//99-12//99
Except Legal, Medical, and Executive	Pittsburgh MSA, PA	S	10.89 MW	10.52 AW	22650 AAW	PABLS	10//99-12//99
Except Legal, Medical, and Executive	Reading MSA, PA	S	10.44 MW	10.17 AW	21720 AAW	PABLS	10//99-12//99
Except Legal, Medical, and Executive	Scranton--Wilkes-Barre--Hazleton MSA, PA	S	9.93 MW	9.59 AW	20660 AAW	PABLS	10//99-12//99
Except Legal, Medical, and Executive	Sharon MSA, PA	S	8.67 MW	8.54 AW	18030 AAW	PABLS	10//99-12//99
Except Legal, Medical, and Executive	State College MSA, PA	S	10.29 MW	9.87 AW	21400 AAW	PABLS	10//99-12//99
Except Legal, Medical, and Executive	Williamsport MSA, PA	S	9.65 MW	9.65 AW	20060 AAW	PABLS	10//99-12//99
Except Legal, Medical, and Executive	York MSA, PA	S	10.33 MW	10.30 AW	21490 AAW	PABLS	10//99-12//99
Except Legal, Medical, and Executive	Rhode Island	S	11.58 MW	11.65 AW	24220 AAW	RIBLS	10//99-12//99
Except Legal, Medical, and Executive	Providence-Fall River-Warwick MSA, RI-MA	S	11.31 MW	10.91 AW	23520 AAW	RIBLS	10//99-12//99
Except Legal, Medical, and Executive	South Carolina	S	9.77 MW	10.16 AW	21140 AAW	SCBLS	10//99-12//99
Except Legal, Medical, and Executive	Charleston-North Charleston MSA, SC	S	10.32 MW	9.79 AW	21470 AAW	SCBLS	10//99-12//99
Except Legal, Medical, and Executive	Columbia MSA, SC	S	10.27 MW	9.84 AW	21360 AAW	SCBLS	10//99-12//99
Except Legal, Medical, and Executive	Florence MSA, SC	S	9.95 MW	9.67 AW	20690 AAW	SCBLS	10//99-12//99
Except Legal, Medical, and Executive	Greenville-Spartanburg-Anderson MSA, SC	S	10.36 MW	10.01 AW	21550 AAW	SCBLS	10//99-12//99
Except Legal, Medical, and Executive	Myrtle Beach MSA, SC	S	9.87 MW	9.43 AW	20540 AAW	SCBLS	10//99-12//99
Except Legal, Medical, and Executive	Sumter MSA, SC	S	9.25 MW	8.68 AW	19240 AAW	SCBLS	10//99-12//99
Except Legal, Medical, and Executive	South Dakota	S	9.17 MW	9.19 AW	19110 AAW	SDBLS	10//99-12//99
Except Legal, Medical, and Executive	Rapid City MSA, SD	S	9.45 MW	9.25 AW	19650 AAW	SDBLS	10//99-12//99
Except Legal, Medical, and Executive	Sioux Falls MSA, SD	S	10.04 MW	9.87 AW	20880 AAW	SDBLS	10//99-12//99
Except Legal, Medical, and Executive	Tennessee	S	9.63 MW	9.99 AW	20770 AAW	TNBLS	10//99-12//99
Except Legal, Medical, and Executive	Chattanooga MSA, TN-GA	S	10.58 MW	10.29 AW	22010 AAW	TNBLS	10//99-12//99
Except Legal, Medical, and Executive	Clarksville-Hopkinsville MSA, TN-KY	S	9.37 MW	9.02 AW	19480 AAW	TNBLS	10//99-12//99
Except Legal, Medical, and Executive	Jackson MSA, TN	S	8.39 MW	8.03 AW	17460 AAW	TNBLS	10//99-12//99
Except Legal, Medical, and Executive	Johnson City-Kingsport-Bristol MSA, TN-VA	S	9.13 MW	8.79 AW	18980 AAW	TNBLS	10//99-12//99
Except Legal, Medical, and Executive	Knoxville MSA, TN	S	10.04 MW	9.60 AW	20880 AAW	TNBLS	10//99-12//99
Except Legal, Medical, and Executive	Memphis MSA, TN-AR-MS	S	10.39 MW	9.95 AW	21610 AAW	MSBLS	10//99-12//99
Except Legal, Medical, and Executive	Nashville MSA, TN	S	11.15 MW	10.75 AW	23180 AAW	TNBLS	10//99-12//99
Except Legal, Medical, and Executive	Texas	S	10.47 MW	10.90 AW	22680 AAW	TXBLS	10//99-12//99
Except Legal, Medical, and Executive	Abilene MSA, TX	S	9.21 MW	8.84 AW	19160 AAW	TXBLS	10//99-12//99
Except Legal, Medical, and Executive	Amarillo MSA, TX	S	10.19 MW	9.43 AW	21190 AAW	TXBLS	10//99-12//99
Except Legal, Medical, and Executive	Austin-San Marcos MSA, TX	S	11.20 MW	11.00 AW	23290 AAW	TXBLS	10//99-12//99
Except Legal, Medical, and Executive	Beaumont-Port Arthur MSA, TX	S	11.01 MW	10.35 AW	22900 AAW	TXBLS	10//99-12//99
Except Legal, Medical, and Executive	Brazoria PMSA, TX	S	9.80 MW	9.80 AW	20370 AAW	TXBLS	10//99-12//99
Except Legal, Medical, and Executive	Brownsville-Harlingen-San Benito MSA, TX	S	8.50 MW	8.09 AW	17680 AAW	TXBLS	10//99-12//99
Except Legal, Medical, and Executive	Bryan-College Station MSA, TX	S	9.46 MW	9.41 AW	19690 AAW	TXBLS	10//99-12//99
Except Legal, Medical, and Executive	Corpus Christi MSA, TX	S	10.57 MW	9.91 AW	21990 AAW	TXBLS	10//99-12//99
Except Legal, Medical, and Executive	Dallas PMSA, TX	S	12.28 MW	12.20 AW	25530 AAW	TXBLS	10//99-12//99
Except Legal, Medical, and Executive	El Paso MSA, TX	S	9.22 MW	9.06 AW	19190 AAW	TXBLS	10//99-12//99
Except Legal, Medical, and Executive	Fort Worth-Arlington PMSA, TX	S	11.43 MW	11.14 AW	23780 AAW	TXBLS	10//99-12//99
Except Legal, Medical, and Executive	Galveston-Texas City PMSA, TX	S	10.34 MW	10.17 AW	21500 AAW	TXBLS	10//99-12//99

AAW	Average annual wage	AOH	Average offered, high	ASH	Average starting, high	H	Hourly	M	Monthly	S	Special: hourly and annual
AE	Average entry wage	AOL	Average offered, low	ASL	Average starting, low	HI	Highest wage paid	MTC	Median total compensation	TQ	Third quartile wage
AEX	Average experienced wage	APH	Average pay, high range	AW	Average wage paid	HR	High end range	MW	Median wage paid	W	Weekly
AO	Average offered	APL	Average pay, low range	FQ	First quartile wage	LR	Low end range	SQ	Second quartile wage	Y	Yearly

Occupation/Type/Industry	Location	Per	Low	Mid	High	Source	Date
Secretary							
Except Legal, Medical, and Executive	Houston PMSA, TX	S	12.30 MW	12.17 AW	25590 AAW	TXBLS	10//99-12//99
Except Legal, Medical, and Executive	Killeen-Temple MSA, TX	S	9.47 MW	9.08 AW	19700 AAW	TXBLS	10//99-12//99
Except Legal, Medical, and Executive	Laredo MSA, TX	S	8.52 MW	7.90 AW	17730 AAW	TXBLS	10//99-12//99
Except Legal, Medical, and Executive	Longview-Marshall MSA, TX	S	8.65 MW	8.24 AW	17990 AAW	TXBLS	10//99-12//99
Except Legal, Medical, and Executive	Lubbock MSA, TX	S	8.52 MW	7.94 AW	17720 AAW	TXBLS	10//99-12//99
Except Legal, Medical, and Executive	McAllen-Edinburg-Mission MSA, TX	S	8.78 MW	8.87 AW	18270 AAW	TXBLS	10//99-12//99
Except Legal, Medical, and Executive	Odessa-Midland MSA, TX	S	11.80 MW	10.12 AW	24540 AAW	TXBLS	10//99-12//99
Except Legal, Medical, and Executive	San Angelo MSA, TX	S	9.59 MW	9.04 AW	19950 AAW	TXBLS	10//99-12//99
Except Legal, Medical, and Executive	San Antonio MSA, TX	S	10.33 MW	9.91 AW	21480 AAW	TXBLS	10//99-12//99
Except Legal, Medical, and Executive	Sherman-Denison MSA, TX	S	9.59 MW	9.06 AW	19960 AAW	TXBLS	10//99-12//99
Except Legal, Medical, and Executive	Texarkana MSA, TX-Texarkana, AR	S	10.15 MW	8.80 AW	21110 AAW	TXBLS	10//99-12//99
Except Legal, Medical, and Executive	Tyler MSA, TX	S	9.93 MW	9.65 AW	20660 AAW	TXBLS	10//99-12//99
Except Legal, Medical, and Executive	Victoria MSA, TX	S	9.70 MW	10.04 AW	20180 AAW	TXBLS	10//99-12//99
Except Legal, Medical, and Executive	Waco MSA, TX	S	9.27 MW	8.42 AW	19290 AAW	TXBLS	10//99-12//99
Except Legal, Medical, and Executive	Wichita Falls MSA, TX	S	10.34 MW	9.92 AW	21500 AAW	TXBLS	10//99-12//99
Except Legal, Medical, and Executive	Utah	S	10.2 MW	10.49 AW	21820 AAW	UTBLS	10//99-12//99
Except Legal, Medical, and Executive	Provo-Orem MSA, UT	S	10.47 MW	10.11 AW	21770 AAW	UTBLS	10//99-12//99
Except Legal, Medical, and Executive	Salt Lake City-Ogden MSA, UT	S	11.01 MW	10.63 AW	22900 AAW	UTBLS	10//99-12//99
Except Legal, Medical, and Executive	Vermont	S	10.77 MW	11.06 AW	23000 AAW	VTBLS	10//99-12//99
Except Legal, Medical, and Executive	Burlington MSA, VT	S	11.80 MW	10.64 AW	24540 AAW	VTBLS	10//99-12//99
Except Legal, Medical, and Executive	Virginia	S	10.74 MW	11.30 AW	23500 AAW	VABLS	10//99-12//99
Except Legal, Medical, and Executive	Charlottesville MSA, VA	S	10.43 MW	10.03 AW	21700 AAW	VABLS	10//99-12//99
Except Legal, Medical, and Executive	Danville MSA, VA	S	9.47 MW	9.44 AW	19710 AAW	VABLS	10//99-12//99
Except Legal, Medical, and Executive	Lynchburg MSA, VA	S	9.51 MW	9.35 AW	19780 AAW	VABLS	10//99-12//99
Except Legal, Medical, and Executive	Norfolk-Virginia Beach-Newport News MSA, VA-NC	S	10.84 MW	10.39 AW	22550 AAW	VABLS	10//99-12//99
Except Legal, Medical, and Executive	Richmond-Petersburg MSA, VA	S	11.50 MW	11.26 AW	23920 AAW	VABLS	10//99-12//99
Except Legal, Medical, and Executive	Roanoke MSA, VA	S	10.28 MW	9.72 AW	21380 AAW	VABLS	10//99-12//99
Except Legal, Medical, and Executive	Washington	S	12.18 MW	12.29 AW	25570 AAW	WABLS	10//99-12//99
Except Legal, Medical, and Executive	Bellingham MSA, WA	S	10.79 MW	10.37 AW	22440 AAW	WABLS	10//99-12//99
Except Legal, Medical, and Executive	Bremerton PMSA, WA	S	12.80 MW	12.58 AW	26620 AAW	WABLS	10//99-12//99
Except Legal, Medical, and Executive	Olympia PMSA, WA	S	12.73 MW	12.64 AW	26480 AAW	WABLS	10//99-12//99
Except Legal, Medical, and Executive	Richland-Kennewick-Pasco MSA, WA	S	11.14 MW	11.31 AW	23160 AAW	WABLS	10//99-12//99
Except Legal, Medical, and Executive	Seattle-Bellevue-Everett PMSA, WA	S	13.03 MW	12.78 AW	27100 AAW	WABLS	10//99-12//99
Except Legal, Medical, and Executive	Spokane MSA, WA	S	10.08 MW	9.82 AW	20970 AAW	WABLS	10//99-12//99
Except Legal, Medical, and Executive	Tacoma PMSA, WA	S	12.13 MW	12.04 AW	25230 AAW	WABLS	10//99-12//99
Except Legal, Medical, and Executive	Yakima MSA, WA	S	11.43 MW	11.77 AW	23780 AAW	WABLS	10//99-12//99
Except Legal, Medical, and Executive	West Virginia	S	9.04 MW	9.31 AW	19370 AAW	WVBLS	10//99-12//99
Except Legal, Medical, and Executive	Charleston MSA, WV	S	9.68 MW	9.47 AW	20140 AAW	WVBLS	10//99-12//99
Except Legal, Medical, and Executive	Huntington-Ashland MSA, WV-KY-OH	S	8.80 MW	8.13 AW	18310 AAW	WVBLS	10//99-12//99
Except Legal, Medical, and Executive	Parkersburg-Marietta MSA, WV-OH	S	8.57 MW	8.03 AW	17820 AAW	WVBLS	10//99-12//99
Except Legal, Medical, and Executive	Wheeling MSA, WV-OH	S	8.47 MW	8.24 AW	17610 AAW	WVBLS	10//99-12//99
Except Legal, Medical, and Executive	Wisconsin	S	11.32 MW	11.39 AW	23690 AAW	WIBLS	10//99-12//99
Except Legal, Medical, and Executive	Appleton-Oshkosh-Neenah MSA, WI	S	11.16 MW	11.42 AW	23210 AAW	WIBLS	10//99-12//99
Except Legal, Medical, and Executive	Eau Claire MSA, WI	S	11.46 MW	11.70 AW	23840 AAW	WIBLS	10//99-12//99
Except Legal, Medical, and Executive	Green Bay MSA, WI	S	11.23 MW	10.44 AW	23350 AAW	WIBLS	10//99-12//99
Except Legal, Medical, and Executive	Janesville-Beloit MSA, WI	S	10.92 MW	10.98 AW	22700 AAW	WIBLS	10//99-12//99
Except Legal, Medical, and Executive	Kenosha PMSA, WI	S	11.64 MW	11.57 AW	24210 AAW	WIBLS	10//99-12//99
Except Legal, Medical, and Executive	La Crosse MSA, WI-MN	S	9.35 MW	9.62 AW	19460 AAW	WIBLS	10//99-12//99
Except Legal, Medical, and Executive	Madison MSA, WI	S	12.14 MW	12.08 AW	25250 AAW	WIBLS	10//99-12//99
Except Legal, Medical, and Executive	Milwaukee-Waukesha PMSA, WI	S	12.16 MW	11.95 AW	25290 AAW	WIBLS	10//99-12//99
Except Legal, Medical, and Executive	Racine PMSA, WI	S	11.13 MW	11.25 AW	23160 AAW	WIBLS	10//99-12//99
Except Legal, Medical, and Executive	Sheboygan MSA, WI	S	10.78 MW	10.48 AW	22430 AAW	WIBLS	10//99-12//99
Except Legal, Medical, and Executive	Wausau MSA, WI	S	10.72 MW	10.47 AW	22290 AAW	WIBLS	10//99-12//99
Except Legal, Medical, and Executive	Wyoming	S	9.46 MW	9.52 AW	19800 AAW	WYBLS	10//99-12//99
Except Legal, Medical, and Executive	Casper MSA, WY	S	9.38 MW	9.49 AW	19510 AAW	WYBLS	10//99-12//99
Except Legal, Medical, and Executive	Cheyenne MSA, WY	S	10.22 MW	10.26 AW	21250 AAW	WYBLS	10//99-12//99
Except Legal, Medical, and Executive	Puerto Rico	S	6.67 MW	7.35 AW	15290 AAW	PRBLS	10//99-12//99
Except Legal, Medical, and Executive	Aguadilla MSA, PR	S	6.12 MW	6.15 AW	12740 AAW	PRBLS	10//99-12//99
Except Legal, Medical, and Executive	Arecibo PMSA, PR	S	6.08 MW	6.08 AW	12640 AAW	PRBLS	10//99-12//99

AAW Average annual wage	AOH Average offered, high	ASH Average starting, high	H Hourly	M Monthly	S Special: hourly and annual
AE Average entry wage	AOL Average offered, low	ASL Average starting, low	HI Highest wage paid	MTC Median total compensation	TQ Third quartile wage
AEX Average experienced wage	APH Average pay, high range	AW Average wage paid	HR High end range	MW Median wage paid	W Weekly
AO Average offered	APL Average pay, low range	FQ First quartile wage	LR Low end range	SQ Second quartile wage	Y Yearly

Occupation/Type/Industry	Location	Per	Low	Mid	High	Source	Date
Secretary							
Except Legal, Medical, and Executive	Caguas PMSA, PR	S	6.66 MW	6.21 AW	13860 AAW	PRBLS	10//99-12//99
Except Legal, Medical, and Executive	Mayaguez MSA, PR	S	6.87 MW	6.41 AW	14290 AAW	PRBLS	10//99-12//99
Except Legal, Medical, and Executive	Ponce MSA, PR	S	6.34 MW	6.23 AW	13190 AAW	PRBLS	10//99-12//99
Except Legal, Medical, and Executive	San Juan-Bayamon PMSA, PR	S	7.95 MW	7.49 AW	16530 AAW	PRBLS	10//99-12//99
Except Legal, Medical, and Executive	Virgin Islands	S	9.83 MW	9.96 AW	20710 AAW	VIBLS	10//99-12//99
Except Legal, Medical, and Executive	Guam	S	9.65 MW	9.97 AW	20730 AAW	GUBLS	10//99-12//99
Securities, Commodities, and Financial Services Sales Agent	Alabama	S	24.24 MW	32.83 AW	68280 AAW	ALBLS	10//99-12//99
	Birmingham MSA, AL	S	33.16 MW	23.72 AW	68970 AAW	ALBLS	10//99-12//99
	Huntsville MSA, AL	S	44.64 MW	45.25 AW	92860 AAW	ALBLS	10//99-12//99
	Montgomery MSA, AL	S	32.09 MW	20.85 AW	66760 AAW	ALBLS	10//99-12//99
	Arizona	S	26.34 MW	32.91 AW	68450 AAW	AZBLS	10//99-12//99
	Phoenix-Mesa MSA, AZ	S	33.00 MW	24.93 AW	68630 AAW	AZBLS	10//99-12//99
	Tucson MSA, AZ	S	31.89 MW	34.16 AW	66340 AAW	AZBLS	10//99-12//99
	Arkansas	S	20.81 MW	29.87 AW	62130 AAW	ARBLS	10//99-12//99
	Fayetteville-Springdale-Rogers MSA, AR	S	29.91 MW	26.62 AW	62200 AAW	ARBLS	10//99-12//99
	Little Rock-North Little Rock MSA, AR	S	33.77 MW	21.90 AW	70240 AAW	ARBLS	10//99-12//99
	California	S	24.92 MW	33.07 AW	68790 AAW	CABLS	10//99-12//99
	Bakersfield MSA, CA	S	16.11 MW	14.89 AW	33510 AAW	CABLS	10//99-12//99
	Fresno MSA, CA	S	38.09 MW	34.57 AW	79220 AAW	CABLS	10//99-12//99
	Los Angeles-Long Beach PMSA, CA	S	25.13 MW	20.42 AW	52270 AAW	CABLS	10//99-12//99
	Modesto MSA, CA	S	31.24 MW	31.69 AW	64980 AAW	CABLS	10//99-12//99
	Oakland PMSA, CA	S	24.06 MW	16.68 AW	50040 AAW	CABLS	10//99-12//99
	Orange County PMSA, CA	S	32.50 MW	25.05 AW	67590 AAW	CABLS	10//99-12//99
	Riverside-San Bernardino PMSA, CA	S	36.75 MW	36.60 AW	76450 AAW	CABLS	10//99-12//99
	Sacramento PMSA, CA	S	20.28 MW	18.36 AW	42170 AAW	CABLS	10//99-12//99
	Salinas MSA, CA	S	21.73 MW	20.58 AW	45200 AAW	CABLS	10//99-12//99
	San Diego MSA, CA	S	27.71 MW	19.17 AW	57640 AAW	CABLS	10//99-12//99
	San Francisco PMSA, CA	S	42.43 MW	43.99 AW	88250 AAW	CABLS	10//99-12//99
	San Jose PMSA, CA	S	36.28 MW	37.25 AW	75470 AAW	CABLS	10//99-12//99
	Santa Barbara-Santa Maria-Lompoc MSA, CA	S	28.77 MW	20.76 AW	59840 AAW	CABLS	10//99-12//99
	Santa Cruz-Watsonville PMSA, CA	S	25.16 MW	20.65 AW	52330 AAW	CABLS	10//99-12//99
	Stockton-Lodi MSA, CA	S	24.17 MW	21.41 AW	50270 AAW	CABLS	10//99-12//99
	Ventura PMSA, CA	S	54.58 MW		113530 AAW	CABLS	10//99-12//99
	Connecticut	S	43.03 MW	42.16 AW	87700 AAW	CTBLS	10//99-12//99
	Bridgeport PMSA, CT	S	21.90 MW	21.82 AW	45540 AAW	CTBLS	10//99-12//99
	Danbury PMSA, CT	S	38.71 MW	29.19 AW	80510 AAW	CTBLS	10//99-12//99
	Hartford MSA, CT	S	26.94 MW	15.23 AW	56030 AAW	CTBLS	10//99-12//99
	New Haven-Meriden PMSA, CT	S	49.87 MW	53.68 AW	103730 AAW	CTBLS	10//99-12//99
	Stamford-Norwalk PMSA, CT	S	49.65 MW	51.67 AW	103260 AAW	CTBLS	10//99-12//99
	Waterbury PMSA, CT	S	29.18 MW	24.76 AW	60680 AAW	CTBLS	10//99-12//99
	Delaware	S	24.22 MW	31.21 AW	64910 AAW	DEBLS	10//99-12//99
	Wilmington-Newark PMSA, DE-MD	S	31.30 MW	24.39 AW	65100 AAW	DEBLS	10//99-12//99
	Washington PMSA, DC-MD-VA-WV	S	24.95 MW	21.66 AW	51900 AAW	DCBLS	10//99-12//99
	Florida	S	29.47 MW	35.06 AW	72920 AAW	FLBLS	10//99-12//99
	Fort Myers-Cape Coral MSA, FL	S	27.88 MW	22.45 AW	57980 AAW	FLBLS	10//99-12//99
	Gainesville MSA, FL	S	30.55 MW	30.45 AW	63540 AAW	FLBLS	10//99-12//99
	Melbourne-Titusville-Palm Bay MSA, FL	S	22.23 MW	17.10 AW	46240 AAW	FLBLS	10//99-12//99
	Naples MSA, FL	S	30.45 MW	30.52 AW	63340 AAW	FLBLS	10//99-12//99
	Ocala MSA, FL	S	34.99 MW	35.06 AW	72770 AAW	FLBLS	10//99-12//99
	Punta Gorda MSA, FL	S	34.56 MW	30.91 AW	71870 AAW	FLBLS	10//99-12//99
	Sarasota-Bradenton MSA, FL	S	26.57 MW	24.38 AW	55270 AAW	FLBLS	10//99-12//99
	Georgia	S	19.66 MW	27.19 AW	56550 AAW	GABLS	10//99-12//99
	Atlanta MSA, GA	S	28.02 MW	20.03 AW	58290 AAW	GABLS	10//99-12//99
	Augusta-Aiken MSA, GA-SC	S	28.22 MW	18.45 AW	58700 AAW	GABLS	10//99-12//99
	Macon MSA, GA	S	29.49 MW	19.86 AW	61340 AAW	GABLS	10//99-12//99
	Idaho	S	36.89 MW	36.04 AW	74950 AAW	IDBLS	10//99-12//99
	Boise City MSA, ID	S	34.13 MW	36.42 AW	70980 AAW	IDBLS	10//99-12//99
	Illinois	S	32.38 MW	38.77 AW	80650 AAW	ILBLS	10//99-12//99

AAW Average annual wage	AOH Average offered, high	ASH Average starting, high	H Hourly	M Monthly	S Special: hourly and annual
AE Average entry wage	AOL Average offered, low	ASL Average starting, low	HI Highest wage paid	MTC Median total compensation	TQ Third quartile wage
AEX Average experienced wage	APH Average pay, high range	AW Average wage paid	HR High end range	MW Median wage paid	W Weekly
AO Average offered	APL Average pay, low range	FQ First quartile wage	LR Low end range	SQ Second quartile wage	Y Yearly

Occupation/Type/Industry	Location	Per	Low	Mid	High	Source	Date
Securities, Commodities, and Financial Services Sales Agent	Chicago PMSA, IL	S	39.52 MW	34.07 AW	82210 AAW	ILBLS	10//99-12//99
	Indiana	S	19.12 MW	24.11 AW	50140 AAW	INBLS	10//99-12//99
	Fort Wayne MSA, IN	S	22.12 MW	16.42 AW	46010 AAW	INBLS	10//99-12//99
	Gary PMSA, IN	S	17.60 MW	16.51 AW	36610 AAW	INBLS	10//99-12//99
	Indianapolis MSA, IN	S	25.91 MW	20.89 AW	53890 AAW	INBLS	10//99-12//99
	Lafayette MSA, IN	S	35.42 MW	24.38 AW	73680 AAW	INBLS	10//99-12//99
	Muncie MSA, IN	S	37.65 MW	45.68 AW	78320 AAW	INBLS	10//99-12//99
	South Bend MSA, IN	S	21.07 MW	15.11 AW	43820 AAW	INBLS	10//99-12//99
	Iowa	S	13.49 MW	20.87 AW	43410 AAW	IABLS	10//99-12//99
	Cedar Rapids MSA, IA	S	21.37 MW	13.20 AW	44450 AAW	IABLS	10//99-12//99
	Kansas	S	13.44 MW	15.94 AW	33150 AAW	KSBLS	10//99-12//99
	Wichita MSA, KS	S	16.01 MW	13.28 AW	33290 AAW	KSBLS	10//99-12//99
	Kentucky	S	23.4 MW	31.26 AW	65030 AAW	KYBLS	10//99-12//99
	Louisville MSA, KY-IN	S	22.09 MW	16.46 AW	45940 AAW	KYBLS	10//99-12//99
	Owensboro MSA, KY	S	26.58 MW	19.75 AW	55290 AAW	KYBLS	10//99-12//99
	Louisiana	S	27.19 MW	33.37 AW	69410 AAW	LABLS	10//99-12//99
	Baton Rouge MSA, LA	S	47.37 MW		98540 AAW	LABLS	10//99-12//99
	New Orleans MSA, LA	S	29.23 MW	25.52 AW	60800 AAW	LABLS	10//99-12//99
	Maine	S	25.95 MW	28.90 AW	60100 AAW	MEBLS	10//99-12//99
	Bangor MSA, ME	S	32.31 MW	25.36 AW	67200 AAW	MEBLS	10//99-12//99
	Portland MSA, ME	S	30.13 MW	24.02 AW	62670 AAW	MEBLS	10//99-12//99
	Hagerstown PMSA, MD	S	65.93 MW		137130 AAW	MDBLS	10//99-12//99
	Massachusetts	S	34.07 MW	35.98 AW	74840 AAW	MABLS	10//99-12//99
	Boston PMSA, MA-NH	S	36.66 MW	35.29 AW	76250 AAW	MABLS	10//99-12//99
	Springfield MSA, MA	S	26.98 MW	25.46 AW	56110 AAW	MABLS	10//99-12//99
	Michigan	S	22.27 MW	28.50 AW	59290 AAW	MIBLS	10//99-12//99
	Detroit PMSA, MI	S	28.69 MW	20.79 AW	59680 AAW	MIBLS	10//99-12//99
	Flint PMSA, MI	S	31.76 MW	21.17 AW	66050 AAW	MIBLS	10//99-12//99
	Grand Rapids-Muskegon-Holland MSA, MI	S	31.36 MW	25.59 AW	65230 AAW	MIBLS	10//99-12//99
	Saginaw-Bay City-Midland MSA, MI	S	18.39 MW	15.00 AW	38240 AAW	MIBLS	10//99-12//99
	Minnesota	S	28.36 MW	34.64 AW	72040 AAW	MNBLS	10//99-12//99
	Duluth-Superior MSA, MN-WI	S	38.60 MW	40.67 AW	80290 AAW	MNBLS	10//99-12//99
	Minneapolis-St. Paul MSA, MN-WI	S	35.70 MW	31.71 AW	74270 AAW	MNBLS	10//99-12//99
	Rochester MSA, MN	S	41.83 MW	47.49 AW	87000 AAW	MNBLS	10//99-12//99
	Mississippi	S	39.08 MW	40.55 AW	84340 AAW	MSBLS	10//99-12//99
	Jackson MSA, MS	S	44.58 MW	44.43 AW	92720 AAW	MSBLS	10//99-12//99
	Kansas City MSA, MO-KS	S	25.77 MW	17.98 AW	53610 AAW	MOBLS	10//99-12//99
	Montana	S	34.37 MW	39.58 AW	82320 AAW	MTBLS	10//99-12//99
	Billings MSA, MT	S	30.21 MW	24.58 AW	62850 AAW	MTBLS	10//99-12//99
	Nebraska	S	32.83 MW	31.96 AW	66470 AAW	NEBLS	10//99-12//99
	Nevada	S	30.7 MW	35.45 AW	73730 AAW	NVBLS	10//99-12//99
	Las Vegas MSA, NV-AZ	S	32.41 MW	28.39 AW	67420 AAW	NVBLS	10//99-12//99
	Reno MSA, NV	S	46.34 MW	50.06 AW	96380 AAW	NVBLS	10//99-12//99
	New Hampshire	S	14.76 MW	21.86 AW	45460 AAW	NHBLS	10//99-12//99
	New Jersey	S	30.41 MW	35.15 AW	73120 AAW	NJBLS	10//99-12//99
	Atlantic-Cape May PMSA, NJ	S	23.03 MW	18.81 AW	47890 AAW	NJBLS	10//99-12//99
	Bergen-Passaic PMSA, NJ	S	31.77 MW	31.48 AW	66080 AAW	NJBLS	10//99-12//99
	Jersey City PMSA, NJ	S	38.17 MW	33.56 AW	79390 AAW	NJBLS	10//99-12//99
	Middlesex-Somerset-Hunterdon PMSA, NJ	S	30.71 MW	29.53 AW	63870 AAW	NJBLS	10//99-12//99
	Monmouth-Ocean PMSA, NJ	S	30.30 MW	24.53 AW	63020 AAW	NJBLS	10//99-12//99
	Newark PMSA, NJ	S	39.86 MW	36.23 AW	82910 AAW	NJBLS	10//99-12//99
	Trenton PMSA, NJ	S	37.52 MW	32.97 AW	78040 AAW	NJBLS	10//99-12//99
	New Mexico	S	17.82 MW	24.80 AW	51580 AAW	NMBLS	10//99-12//99
	Albuquerque MSA, NM	S	24.72 MW	16.33 AW	51420 AAW	NMBLS	10//99-12//99
	New York	S	49.89 MW	46.05 AW	95790 AAW	NYBLS	10//99-12//99
	Albany-Schenectady-Troy MSA, NY	S	32.33 MW	35.47 AW	67250 AAW	NYBLS	10//99-12//99
	Buffalo-Niagara Falls MSA, NY	S	39.71 MW	39.24 AW	82600 AAW	NYBLS	10//99-12//99
	Jamestown MSA, NY	S	10.15 MW	6.34 AW	21110 AAW	NYBLS	10//99-12//99
	New York PMSA, NY	S	48.08 MW	50.99 AW	100010 AAW	NYBLS	10//99-12//99
	Rochester MSA, NY	S	35.01 MW	30.29 AW	72820 AAW	NYBLS	10//99-12//99
	Syracuse MSA, NY	S	24.81 MW	20.60 AW	51600 AAW	NYBLS	10//99-12//99
	North Carolina	S	19.9 MW	29.29 AW	60920 AAW	NCBLS	10//99-12//99
	Charlotte-Gastonia-Rock Hill MSA, NC-SC	S	30.12 MW	19.77 AW	62650 AAW	NCBLS	10//99-12//99
	Goldsboro MSA, NC	S	16.10 MW	14.57 AW	33480 AAW	NCBLS	10//99-12//99

Occupation/Type/Industry	Location	Per	Low	Mid	High	Source	Date
Securities, Commodities, and Financial Services Sales Agent	Raleigh-Durham-Chapel Hill MSA, NC	S	27.82 MW	20.86 AW	57860 AAW	NCBLS	10//99-12//99
	Wilmington MSA, NC	S	33.08 MW	26.87 AW	68800 AAW	NCBLS	10//99-12//99
	North Dakota	S	22.24 MW	33.97 AW	70650 AAW	NDBLS	10//99-12//99
	Bismarck MSA, ND	S	40.40 MW	27.18 AW	84020 AAW	NDBLS	10//99-12//99
	Ohio	S	30.32 MW	37.75 AW	78520 AAW	OHBLS	10//99-12//99
	Akron PMSA, OH	S	20.79 MW	19.62 AW	43250 AAW	OHBLS	10//99-12//99
	Cleveland-Lorain-Elyria PMSA, OH	S	41.89 MW	38.26 AW	87120 AAW	OHBLS	10//99-12//99
	Columbus MSA, OH	S	40.19 MW	32.06 AW	83590 AAW	OHBLS	10//99-12//99
	Dayton-Springfield MSA, OH	S	33.11 MW	26.53 AW	68870 AAW	OHBLS	10//99-12//99
	Toledo MSA, OH	S	34.18 MW	29.17 AW	71100 AAW	OHBLS	10//99-12//99
	Youngstown-Warren MSA, OH	S	33.95 MW	33.77 AW	70620 AAW	OHBLS	10//99-12//99
	Oklahoma	S	18.7 MW	25.73 AW	53530 AAW	OKBLS	10//99-12//99
	Oklahoma City MSA, OK	S	24.55 MW	19.58 AW	51060 AAW	OKBLS	10//99-12//99
	Tulsa MSA, OK	S	22.81 MW	16.51 AW	47430 AAW	OKBLS	10//99-12//99
	Pennsylvania	S	14.66 MW	20.49 AW	42610 AAW	PABLS	10//99-12//99
	Allentown-Bethlehem-Easton MSA, PA	S	37.05 MW	26.03 AW	77070 AAW	PABLS	10//99-12//99
	Harrisburg-Lebanon-Carlisle MSA, PA	S	33.13 MW	20.44 AW	68910 AAW	PABLS	10//99-12//99
	Lancaster MSA, PA	S	23.41 MW	17.21 AW	48690 AAW	PABLS	10//99-12//99
	Philadelphia PMSA, PA-NJ	S	21.91 MW	14.32 AW	45580 AAW	PABLS	10//99-12//99
	Pittsburgh MSA, PA	S	20.35 MW	17.58 AW	42320 AAW	PABLS	10//99-12//99
	Reading MSA, PA	S	27.02 MW	14.46 AW	56200 AAW	PABLS	10//99-12//99
	Rhode Island	S	24.03 MW	29.86 AW	62100 AAW	RIBLS	10//99-12//99
	Providence-Fall River-Warwick MSA, RI-MA	S	30.06 MW	24.29 AW	62520 AAW	RIBLS	10//99-12//99
	South Carolina	S	15.7 MW	19.68 AW	40930 AAW	SCBLS	10//99-12//99
	Charleston-North Charleston MSA, SC	S	24.04 MW	16.23 AW	50000 AAW	SCBLS	10//99-12//99
	Columbia MSA, SC	S	20.12 MW	19.48 AW	41860 AAW	SCBLS	10//99-12//99
	Greenville-Spartanburg-Anderson MSA, SC	S	22.29 MW	15.12 AW	46360 AAW	SCBLS	10//99-12//99
	Myrtle Beach MSA, SC	S	16.40 MW	15.40 AW	34110 AAW	SCBLS	10//99-12//99
	Sumter MSA, SC	S	17.90 MW	15.14 AW	37230 AAW	SCBLS	10//99-12//99
	Tennessee	S	38.38 MW	40.51 AW	84250 AAW	TNBLS	10//99-12//99
	Chattanooga MSA, TN-GA	S	51.45 MW	60.44 AW	107030 AAW	TNBLS	10//99-12//99
	Jackson MSA, TN	S	34.90 MW	27.49 AW	72590 AAW	TNBLS	10//99-12//99
	Johnson City-Kingsport-Bristol MSA, TN-VA	S	35.59 MW	22.75 AW	74030 AAW	TNBLS	10//99-12//99
	Knoxville MSA, TN	S	35.97 MW	27.28 AW	74820 AAW	TNBLS	10//99-12//99
	Memphis MSA, TN-AR-MS	S	40.71 MW	38.15 AW	84670 AAW	MSBLS	10//99-12//99
	Nashville MSA, TN	S	39.20 MW	38.07 AW	81530 AAW	TNBLS	10//99-12//99
	Texas	S	20.67 MW	31.67 AW	65880 AAW	TXBLS	10//99-12//99
	Brownsville-Harlingen-San Benito MSA, TX	S	30.36 MW	24.00 AW	63140 AAW	TXBLS	10//99-12//99
	Corpus Christi MSA, TX	S	23.87 MW	16.88 AW	49650 AAW	TXBLS	10//99-12//99
	El Paso MSA, TX	S	37.55 MW	34.62 AW	78110 AAW	TXBLS	10//99-12//99
	Fort Worth-Arlington PMSA, TX	S	28.64 MW	16.78 AW	59570 AAW	TXBLS	10//99-12//99
	Houston PMSA, TX	S	40.73 MW	39.06 AW	84710 AAW	TXBLS	10//99-12//99
	Lubbock MSA, TX	S	30.37 MW	28.89 AW	63180 AAW	TXBLS	10//99-12//99
	McAllen-Edinburg-Mission MSA, TX	S	20.20 MW	19.45 AW	42020 AAW	TXBLS	10//99-12//99
	San Angelo MSA, TX	S	20.55 MW	17.07 AW	42750 AAW	TXBLS	10//99-12//99
	San Antonio MSA, TX	S	18.53 MW	14.35 AW	38550 AAW	TXBLS	10//99-12//99
	Utah	S	18.54 MW	19.55 AW	40670 AAW	UTBLS	10//99-12//99
	Salt Lake City-Ogden MSA, UT	S	20.34 MW	17.63 AW	42300 AAW	UTBLS	10//99-12//99
	Vermont	S	19.67 MW	26.60 AW	55330 AAW	VTBLS	10//99-12//99
	Burlington MSA, VT	S	40.95 MW	27.73 AW	85170 AAW	VTBLS	10//99-12//99
	Virginia	S	26.73 MW	32.71 AW	68040 AAW	VABLS	10//99-12//99
	Lynchburg MSA, VA	S	27.94 MW	19.75 AW	58110 AAW	VABLS	10//99-12//99
	Norfolk-Virginia Beach-Newport News MSA, VA-NC	S	35.49 MW	35.91 AW	73830 AAW	VABLS	10//99-12//99
	Richmond-Petersburg MSA, VA	S	34.40 MW	26.43 AW	71550 AAW	VABLS	10//99-12//99
	Roanoke MSA, VA	S	49.43 MW	47.72 AW	102820 AAW	VABLS	10//99-12//99
	Washington	S	35.8 MW	37.76 AW	78550 AAW	WABLS	10//99-12//99

AAW Average annual wage	**AOH** Average offered, high	**ASH** Average starting, high	**H** Hourly	**M** Monthly	**S** Special: hourly and annual
AE Average entry wage	**AOL** Average offered, low	**ASL** Average starting, low	**HI** Highest wage paid	**MTC** Median total compensation	**TQ** Third quartile wage
AEX Average experienced wage	**APH** Average pay, high range	**AW** Average wage paid	**HR** High end range	**MW** Median wage paid	**W** Weekly
AO Average offered	**APL** Average pay, low range	**FQ** First quartile wage	**LR** Low end range	**SQ** Second quartile wage	**Y** Yearly

Occupation/Type/Industry	Location	Per	Low	Mid	High	Source	Date
Securities, Commodities, and Financial Services Sales Agent	Bellingham MSA, WA	S	26.91 MW	13.32 AW	55980 AAW	WABLS	10//99-12//99
	Olympia PMSA, WA	S	27.29 MW	21.17 AW	56760 AAW	WABLS	10//99-12//99
	Seattle-Bellevue-Everett PMSA, WA	S	39.93 MW	38.97 AW	83060 AAW	WABLS	10//99-12//99
	Spokane MSA, WA	S	39.83 MW	37.08 AW	82840 AAW	WABLS	10//99-12//99
	Tacoma PMSA, WA	S	27.73 MW	25.02 AW	57680 AAW	WABLS	10//99-12//99
	Yakima MSA, WA	S	40.39 MW	39.01 AW	84000 AAW	WABLS	10//99-12//99
	West Virginia	S	26.93 MW	31.11 AW	64700 AAW	WVBLS	10//99-12//99
	Charleston MSA, WV	S	44.66 MW	46.20 AW	92900 AAW	WVBLS	10//99-12//99
	Huntington-Ashland MSA, WV-KY-OH	S	24.19 MW	19.01 AW	50320 AAW	WVBLS	10//99-12//99
	Wheeling MSA, WV-OH	S	36.43 MW	27.04 AW	75770 AAW	WVBLS	10//99-12//99
	Wisconsin	S	30.85 MW	32.75 AW	68130 AAW	WIBLS	10//99-12//99
	Green Bay MSA, WI	S	37.43 MW	28.10 AW	77860 AAW	WIBLS	10//99-12//99
	Madison MSA, WI	S	34.76 MW	26.85 AW	72300 AAW	WIBLS	10//99-12//99
	Milwaukee-Waukesha PMSA, WI	S	31.48 MW	31.46 AW	65480 AAW	WIBLS	10//99-12//99
	Wyoming	S	37.64 MW	38.09 AW	79230 AAW	WYBLS	10//99-12//99
	Casper MSA, WY	S	22.00 MW	15.04 AW	45750 AAW	WYBLS	10//99-12//99
	Puerto Rico	S	28.61 MW	33.68 AW	70040 AAW	PRBLS	10//99-12//99
	San Juan-Bayamon PMSA, PR	S	36.00 MW	32.14 AW	74880 AAW	PRBLS	10//99-12//99
Security and Fire Alarm Systems Installer	Alabama	S	12.18 MW	13.32 AW	27710 AAW	ALBLS	10//99-12//99
	Alaska	S	15.4 MW	13.78 AW	28660 AAW	AKBLS	10//99-12//99
	Arizona	S	14.11 MW	14.41 AW	29960 AAW	AZBLS	10//99-12//99
	California	S	16.04 MW	17.71 AW	36830 AAW	CABLS	10//99-12//99
	Colorado	S	17.64 MW	16.89 AW	35140 AAW	COBLS	10//99-12//99
	Connecticut	S	19.14 MW	19.88 AW	41360 AAW	CTBLS	10//99-12//99
	Delaware	S	16.64 MW	17.25 AW	35870 AAW	DEBLS	10//99-12//99
	Florida	S	11.95 MW	12.41 AW	25820 AAW	FLBLS	10//99-12//99
	Georgia	S	12.55 MW	14.93 AW	31050 AAW	GABLS	10//99-12//99
	Idaho	S	11.67 MW	11.65 AW	24230 AAW	IDBLS	10//99-12//99
	Illinois	S	17.93 MW	20.69 AW	43040 AAW	ILBLS	10//99-12//99
	Indiana	S	21.87 MW	21.59 AW	44910 AAW	INBLS	10//99-12//99
	Iowa	S	12.85 MW	14.29 AW	29720 AAW	IABLS	10//99-12//99
	Louisiana	S	11.23 MW	11.84 AW	24630 AAW	LABLS	10//99-12//99
	Maine	S	14.53 MW	13.94 AW	29000 AAW	MEBLS	10//99-12//99
	Maryland	S	15.76 MW	15.78 AW	32820 AAW	MDBLS	10//99-12//99
	Michigan	S	14.49 MW	14.79 AW	30770 AAW	MIBLS	10//99-12//99
	Minnesota	S	11.46 MW	13.01 AW	27060 AAW	MNBLS	10//99-12//99
	Mississippi	S	12.87 MW	13.08 AW	27210 AAW	MSBLS	10//99-12//99
	Nevada	S	16.01 MW	16.61 AW	34540 AAW	NVBLS	10//99-12//99
	New Hampshire	S	13.56 MW	13.66 AW	28410 AAW	NHBLS	10//99-12//99
	New Jersey	S	19.32 MW	18.93 AW	39360 AAW	NJBLS	10//99-12//99
	New Mexico	S	13.92 MW	14.45 AW	30060 AAW	NMBLS	10//99-12//99
	New York	S	12.1 MW	12.43 AW	25850 AAW	NYBLS	10//99-12//99
	North Carolina	S	15.56 MW	16.16 AW	33610 AAW	NCBLS	10//99-12//99
	Ohio	S	16.63 MW	17.58 AW	36570 AAW	OHBLS	10//99-12//99
	Oklahoma	S	9.54 MW	11.30 AW	23500 AAW	OKBLS	10//99-12//99
	Oregon	S	15.84 MW	15.98 AW	33230 AAW	ORBLS	10//99-12//99
	Pennsylvania	S	15.75 MW	16.47 AW	34270 AAW	PABLS	10//99-12//99
	South Carolina	S	13.1 MW	19.73 AW	41040 AAW	SCBLS	10//99-12//99
	Tennessee	S	8.64 MW	9.61 AW	19990 AAW	TNBLS	10//99-12//99
	Texas	S	10.35 MW	11.32 AW	23550 AAW	TXBLS	10//99-12//99
	Virginia	S	12.81 MW	13.73 AW	28550 AAW	VABLS	10//99-12//99
	Washington	S	15.56 MW	16.08 AW	33440 AAW	WABLS	10//99-12//99
	West Virginia	S	20.73 MW	20.58 AW	42800 AAW	WVBLS	10//99-12//99
	Wisconsin	S	15.59 MW	16.26 AW	33820 AAW	WIBLS	10//99-12//99
	Puerto Rico	S	13.17 MW	13.44 AW	27950 AAW	PRBLS	10//99-12//99
Security Guard	Alabama	S	7.14 MW	7.86 AW	16340 AAW	ALBLS	10//99-12//99
	Anniston MSA, AL	S	10.25 MW	10.29 AW	21330 AAW	ALBLS	10//99-12//99
	Auburn-Opelika MSA, AL	S	8.60 MW	6.58 AW	17880 AAW	ALBLS	10//99-12//99
	Birmingham MSA, AL	S	7.95 MW	7.46 AW	16530 AAW	ALBLS	10//99-12//99
	Decatur MSA, AL	S	10.20 MW	8.17 AW	21220 AAW	ALBLS	10//99-12//99
	Dothan MSA, AL	S	6.60 MW	6.11 AW	13720 AAW	ALBLS	10//99-12//99
	Gadsden MSA, AL	S	7.83 MW	6.94 AW	16290 AAW	ALBLS	10//99-12//99
	Huntsville MSA, AL	S	7.59 MW	6.81 AW	15790 AAW	ALBLS	10//99-12//99
	Mobile MSA, AL	S	6.89 MW	6.38 AW	14330 AAW	ALBLS	10//99-12//99
	Montgomery MSA, AL	S	7.93 MW	6.59 AW	16480 AAW	ALBLS	10//99-12//99

Occupation/Type/Industry	Location	Per	Low	Mid	High	Source	Date
Security Guard	Tuscaloosa MSA, AL	S	9.54 MW	8.68 AW	19840 AAW	ALBLS	10//99-12//99
	Alaska	S	10.09 MW	11.57 AW	24060 AAW	AKBLS	10//99-12//99
	Anchorage MSA, AK	S	10.76 MW	9.70 AW	22380 AAW	AKBLS	10//99-12//99
	Arizona	S	7.95 MW	8.65 AW	18000 AAW	AZBLS	10//99-12//99
	Flagstaff MSA, AZ-UT	S	8.71 MW	8.79 AW	18120 AAW	AZBLS	10//99-12//99
	Phoenix-Mesa MSA, AZ	S	8.65 MW	7.97 AW	17990 AAW	AZBLS	10//99-12//99
	Tucson MSA, AZ	S	8.66 MW	7.58 AW	18020 AAW	AZBLS	10//99-12//99
	Yuma MSA, AZ	S	7.59 MW	6.74 AW	15780 AAW	AZBLS	10//99-12//99
	Arkansas	S	7.38 MW	8.12 AW	16900 AAW	ARBLS	10//99-12//99
	Fayetteville-Springdale-Rogers MSA, AR	S	8.78 MW	7.97 AW	18260 AAW	ARBLS	10//99-12//99
	Fort Smith MSA, AR-OK	S	7.37 MW	6.70 AW	15330 AAW	ARBLS	10//99-12//99
	Little Rock-North Little Rock MSA, AR	S	7.95 MW	7.22 AW	16530 AAW	ARBLS	10//99-12//99
	Pine Bluff MSA, AR	S	10.54 MW	10.98 AW	21930 AAW	ARBLS	10//99-12//99
	California	S	7.88 MW	8.68 AW	18050 AAW	CABLS	10//99-12//99
	Bakersfield MSA, CA	S	7.75 MW	7.05 AW	16120 AAW	CABLS	10//99-12//99
	Chico-Paradise MSA, CA	S	7.94 MW	7.30 AW	16520 AAW	CABLS	10//99-12//99
	Fresno MSA, CA	S	7.38 MW	6.66 AW	15360 AAW	CABLS	10//99-12//99
	Los Angeles-Long Beach PMSA, CA	S	8.45 MW	7.77 AW	17570 AAW	CABLS	10//99-12//99
	Merced MSA, CA	S	8.53 MW	6.86 AW	17730 AAW	CABLS	10//99-12//99
	Modesto MSA, CA	S	7.59 MW	6.55 AW	15790 AAW	CABLS	10//99-12//99
	Oakland PMSA, CA	S	9.39 MW	8.44 AW	19530 AAW	CABLS	10//99-12//99
	Orange County PMSA, CA	S	9.20 MW	8.07 AW	19140 AAW	CABLS	10//99-12//99
	Redding MSA, CA	S	7.11 MW	6.56 AW	14780 AAW	CABLS	10//99-12//99
	Riverside-San Bernardino PMSA, CA	S	7.97 MW	7.41 AW	16580 AAW	CABLS	10//99-12//99
	Sacramento PMSA, CA	S	8.08 MW	7.76 AW	16810 AAW	CABLS	10//99-12//99
	Salinas MSA, CA	S	7.31 MW	6.82 AW	15200 AAW	CABLS	10//99-12//99
	San Diego MSA, CA	S	8.64 MW	7.58 AW	17970 AAW	CABLS	10//99-12//99
	San Francisco PMSA, CA	S	10.19 MW	9.34 AW	21200 AAW	CABLS	10//99-12//99
	San Jose PMSA, CA	S	9.72 MW	9.35 AW	20210 AAW	CABLS	10//99-12//99
	San Luis Obispo-Atascadero-Paso Robles MSA, CA	S	12.39 MW	8.99 AW	25780 AAW	CABLS	10//99-12//99
	Santa Barbara-Santa Maria-Lompoc MSA, CA	S	7.82 MW	7.38 AW	16260 AAW	CABLS	10//99-12//99
	Santa Cruz-Watsonville PMSA, CA	S	8.34 MW	7.93 AW	17340 AAW	CABLS	10//99-12//99
	Santa Rosa PMSA, CA	S	9.57 MW	8.94 AW	19910 AAW	CABLS	10//99-12//99
	Stockton-Lodi MSA, CA	S	7.86 MW	7.36 AW	16350 AAW	CABLS	10//99-12//99
	Vallejo-Fairfield-Napa PMSA, CA	S	10.33 MW	8.73 AW	21490 AAW	CABLS	10//99-12//99
	Ventura PMSA, CA	S	8.20 MW	7.73 AW	17050 AAW	CABLS	10//99-12//99
	Visalia-Tulare-Porterville MSA, CA	S	7.63 MW	6.78 AW	15880 AAW	CABLS	10//99-12//99
	Yolo PMSA, CA	S	11.04 MW	11.25 AW	22970 AAW	CABLS	10//99-12//99
	Yuba City MSA, CA	S	9.28 MW	9.22 AW	19300 AAW	CABLS	10//99-12//99
	Colorado	S	9.38 MW	10.36 AW	21540 AAW	COBLS	10//99-12//99
	Boulder-Longmont PMSA, CO	S	9.73 MW	9.28 AW	20240 AAW	COBLS	10//99-12//99
	Colorado Springs MSA, CO	S	8.89 MW	8.16 AW	18490 AAW	COBLS	10//99-12//99
	Denver PMSA, CO	S	10.81 MW	9.66 AW	22480 AAW	COBLS	10//99-12//99
	Fort Collins-Loveland MSA, CO	S	9.44 MW	8.66 AW	19630 AAW	COBLS	10//99-12//99
	Pueblo MSA, CO	S	9.48 MW	8.30 AW	19720 AAW	COBLS	10//99-12//99
	Connecticut	S	8.36 MW	9.29 AW	19320 AAW	CTBLS	10//99-12//99
	Bridgeport PMSA, CT	S	9.13 MW	8.30 AW	18990 AAW	CTBLS	10//99-12//99
	Danbury PMSA, CT	S	10.21 MW	9.15 AW	21240 AAW	CTBLS	10//99-12//99
	Hartford MSA, CT	S	9.45 MW	8.38 AW	19660 AAW	CTBLS	10//99-12//99
	New London-Norwich MSA, CT-RI	S	9.17 MW	8.47 AW	19060 AAW	CTBLS	10//99-12//99
	Stamford-Norwalk PMSA, CT	S	9.12 MW	8.34 AW	18960 AAW	CTBLS	10//99-12//99
	Waterbury PMSA, CT	S	9.42 MW	9.27 AW	19600 AAW	CTBLS	10//99-12//99
	Delaware	S	8.12 MW	8.72 AW	18130 AAW	DEBLS	10//99-12//99
	Dover MSA, DE	S	9.45 MW	9.27 AW	19650 AAW	DEBLS	10//99-12//99
	Wilmington-Newark PMSA, DE-MD	S	8.66 MW	8.04 AW	18010 AAW	DEBLS	10//99-12//99
	District of Columbia	S	10.49 MW	10.59 AW	22040 AAW	DCBLS	10//99-12//99
	Washington PMSA, DC-MD-VA-WV	S	10.14 MW	9.60 AW	21090 AAW	DCBLS	10//99-12//99
	Florida	S	7.62 MW	7.92 AW	16460 AAW	FLBLS	10//99-12//99
	Daytona Beach MSA, FL	S	7.29 MW	7.08 AW	15170 AAW	FLBLS	10//99-12//99

AAW	Average annual wage	AOH	Average offered, high	ASH	Average starting, high	H	Hourly		M	Monthly		S	Special: hourly and annual
AE	Average entry wage	AOL	Average offered, low	ASL	Average starting, low	HI	Highest wage paid		MTC	Median total compensation		TQ	Third quartile wage
AEX	Average experienced wage	APH	Average pay, high range	AW	Average wage paid	HR	High end range		MW	Median wage paid		W	Weekly
AO	Average offered	APL	Average pay, low range	FQ	First quartile wage	LR	Low end range		SQ	Second quartile wage		Y	Yearly

Occupation/Type/Industry	Location	Per	Low	Mid	High	Source	Date
Security Guard	Fort Lauderdale PMSA, FL	S	7.84 MW	7.60 AW	16300 AAW	FLBLS	10//99-12//99
	Fort Myers-Cape Coral MSA, FL	S	7.35 MW	7.14 AW	15300 AAW	FLBLS	10//99-12//99
	Fort Pierce-Port St. Lucie MSA, FL	S	7.59 MW	7.50 AW	15780 AAW	FLBLS	10//99-12//99
	Fort Walton Beach MSA, FL	S	7.48 MW	7.23 AW	15560 AAW	FLBLS	10//99-12//99
	Gainesville MSA, FL	S	7.77 MW	6.90 AW	16150 AAW	FLBLS	10//99-12//99
	Jacksonville MSA, FL	S	8.34 MW	7.78 AW	17350 AAW	FLBLS	10//99-12//99
	Lakeland-Winter Haven MSA, FL	S	7.38 MW	7.12 AW	15350 AAW	FLBLS	10//99-12//99
	Melbourne-Titusville-Palm Bay MSA, FL	S	7.29 MW	6.37 AW	15160 AAW	FLBLS	10//99-12//99
	Miami PMSA, FL	S	7.93 MW	7.43 AW	16490 AAW	FLBLS	10//99-12//99
	Naples MSA, FL	S	9.32 MW	8.18 AW	19380 AAW	FLBLS	10//99-12//99
	Ocala MSA, FL	S	6.47 MW	6.26 AW	13460 AAW	FLBLS	10//99-12//99
	Orlando MSA, FL	S	8.17 MW	7.86 AW	16980 AAW	FLBLS	10//99-12//99
	Panama City MSA, FL	S	7.31 MW	6.56 AW	15200 AAW	FLBLS	10//99-12//99
	Pensacola MSA, FL	S	7.69 MW	7.30 AW	15990 AAW	FLBLS	10//99-12//99
	Punta Gorda MSA, FL	S	7.01 MW	6.99 AW	14580 AAW	FLBLS	10//99-12//99
	Sarasota-Bradenton MSA, FL	S	7.66 MW	7.18 AW	15920 AAW	FLBLS	10//99-12//99
	Tallahassee MSA, FL	S	8.82 MW	6.51 AW	18340 AAW	FLBLS	10//99-12//99
	Tampa-St. Petersburg-Clearwater MSA, FL	S	7.50 MW	7.29 AW	15590 AAW	FLBLS	10//99-12//99
	West Palm Beach-Boca Raton MSA, FL	S	8.28 MW	8.16 AW	17210 AAW	FLBLS	10//99-12//99
	Georgia	S	7.74 MW	8.26 AW	17170 AAW	GABLS	10//99-12//99
	Albany MSA, GA	S	7.45 MW	7.16 AW	15500 AAW	GABLS	10//99-12//99
	Athens MSA, GA	S	8.60 MW	7.71 AW	17890 AAW	GABLS	10//99-12//99
	Atlanta MSA, GA	S	8.30 MW	7.82 AW	17260 AAW	GABLS	10//99-12//99
	Augusta-Aiken MSA, GA-SC	S	10.24 MW	8.02 AW	21300 AAW	GABLS	10//99-12//99
	Columbus MSA, GA-AL	S	8.05 MW	7.95 AW	16750 AAW	GABLS	10//99-12//99
	Macon MSA, GA	S	7.84 MW	7.16 AW	16310 AAW	GABLS	10//99-12//99
	Savannah MSA, GA	S	8.61 MW	7.52 AW	17910 AAW	GABLS	10//99-12//99
	Hawaii	S	8.43 MW	9.09 AW	18910 AAW	HIBLS	10//99-12//99
	Honolulu MSA, HI	S	8.67 MW	8.13 AW	18040 AAW	HIBLS	10//99-12//99
	Idaho	S	8.44 MW	9.58 AW	19930 AAW	IDBLS	10//99-12//99
	Boise City MSA, ID	S	8.84 MW	8.34 AW	18380 AAW	IDBLS	10//99-12//99
	Pocatello MSA, ID	S	6.90 MW	5.96 AW	14350 AAW	IDBLS	10//99-12//99
	Illinois	S	8.43 MW	9.15 AW	19030 AAW	ILBLS	10//99-12//99
	Champaign-Urbana MSA, IL	S	9.22 MW	9.15 AW	19170 AAW	ILBLS	10//99-12//99
	Chicago PMSA, IL	S	9.26 MW	8.53 AW	19250 AAW	ILBLS	10//99-12//99
	Decatur MSA, IL	S	8.02 MW	7.50 AW	16690 AAW	ILBLS	10//99-12//99
	Kankakee PMSA, IL	S	12.81 MW	13.78 AW	26640 AAW	ILBLS	10//99-12//99
	Peoria-Pekin MSA, IL	S	10.13 MW	8.38 AW	21070 AAW	ILBLS	10//99-12//99
	Rockford MSA, IL	S	8.22 MW	7.86 AW	17100 AAW	ILBLS	10//99-12//99
	Springfield MSA, IL	S	8.28 MW	7.59 AW	17220 AAW	ILBLS	10//99-12//99
	Indiana	S	8.15 MW	8.89 AW	18500 AAW	INBLS	10//99-12//99
	Bloomington MSA, IN	S	8.41 MW	7.68 AW	17500 AAW	INBLS	10//99-12//99
	Elkhart-Goshen MSA, IN	S	8.13 MW	7.72 AW	16910 AAW	INBLS	10//99-12//99
	Evansville-Henderson MSA, IN-KY	S	8.77 MW	7.31 AW	18240 AAW	INBLS	10//99-12//99
	Fort Wayne MSA, IN	S	9.64 MW	9.15 AW	20040 AAW	INBLS	10//99-12//99
	Gary PMSA, IN	S	8.69 MW	7.74 AW	18070 AAW	INBLS	10//99-12//99
	Indianapolis MSA, IN	S	8.44 MW	7.91 AW	17550 AAW	INBLS	10//99-12//99
	Kokomo MSA, IN	S	7.24 MW	6.30 AW	15050 AAW	INBLS	10//99-12//99
	Lafayette MSA, IN	S	9.87 MW	8.97 AW	20530 AAW	INBLS	10//99-12//99
	Muncie MSA, IN	S	11.43 MW	13.50 AW	23780 AAW	INBLS	10//99-12//99
	South Bend MSA, IN	S	9.47 MW	8.25 AW	19690 AAW	INBLS	10//99-12//99
	Terre Haute MSA, IN	S	9.01 MW	7.63 AW	18730 AAW	INBLS	10//99-12//99
	Iowa	S	7.85 MW	8.45 AW	17570 AAW	IABLS	10//99-12//99
	Cedar Rapids MSA, IA	S	7.50 MW	7.32 AW	15600 AAW	IABLS	10//99-12//99
	Davenport-Moline-Rock Island MSA, IA-IL	S	8.29 MW	7.79 AW	17240 AAW	IABLS	10//99-12//99
	Des Moines MSA, IA	S	8.60 MW	7.85 AW	17900 AAW	IABLS	10//99-12//99
	Dubuque MSA, IA	S	9.08 MW	8.81 AW	18890 AAW	IABLS	10//99-12//99
	Iowa City MSA, IA	S	9.76 MW	9.91 AW	20300 AAW	IABLS	10//99-12//99
	Sioux City MSA, IA-NE	S	8.53 MW	8.30 AW	17740 AAW	IABLS	10//99-12//99
	Waterloo-Cedar Falls MSA, IA	S	10.45 MW	8.72 AW	21740 AAW	IABLS	10//99-12//99
	Kansas	S	8.43 MW	9.53 AW	19810 AAW	KSBLS	10//99-12//99
	Lawrence MSA, KS	S	8.91 MW	8.18 AW	18530 AAW	KSBLS	10//99-12//99
	Topeka MSA, KS	S	9.05 MW	8.31 AW	18820 AAW	KSBLS	10//99-12//99
	Wichita MSA, KS	S	10.72 MW	9.09 AW	22300 AAW	KSBLS	10//99-12//99

AAW	Average annual wage	**AOH**	Average offered, high	**ASH**	Average starting, high	**H**	Hourly	**M**	Monthly	**S**	Special: hourly and annual
AE	Average entry wage	**AOL**	Average offered, low	**ASL**	Average starting, low	**HI**	Highest wage paid	**MTC**	Median total compensation	**TQ**	Third quartile wage
AEX	Average experienced wage	**APH**	Average pay, high range	**AW**	Average wage paid	**HR**	High end range	**MW**	Median wage paid	**W**	Weekly
AO	Average offered	**APL**	Average pay, low range	**FQ**	First quartile wage	**LR**	Low end range	**SQ**	Second quartile wage	**Y**	Yearly

Occupation/Type/Industry	Location	Per	Low	Mid	High	Source	Date
Security Guard	Kentucky	S	7.16 MW	7.74 AW	16100 AAW	KYBLS	10//99-12//99
	Lexington MSA, KY	S	7.81 MW	7.53 AW	16250 AAW	KYBLS	10//99-12//99
	Louisville MSA, KY-IN	S	8.61 MW	7.75 AW	17920 AAW	KYBLS	10//99-12//99
	Owensboro MSA, KY	S	7.05 MW	6.00 AW	14660 AAW	KYBLS	10//99-12//99
	Louisiana	S	6.69 MW	7.82 AW	16270 AAW	LABLS	10//99-12//99
	Alexandria MSA, LA	S	7.61 MW	6.33 AW	15830 AAW	LABLS	10//99-12//99
	Baton Rouge MSA, LA	S	8.33 MW	7.13 AW	17330 AAW	LABLS	10//99-12//99
	Houma MSA, LA	S	7.75 MW	6.94 AW	16110 AAW	LABLS	10//99-12//99
	Lafayette MSA, LA	S	6.68 MW	5.96 AW	13890 AAW	LABLS	10//99-12//99
	Lake Charles MSA, LA	S	7.78 MW	6.92 AW	16190 AAW	LABLS	10//99-12//99
	Monroe MSA, LA	S	7.89 MW	6.78 AW	16400 AAW	LABLS	10//99-12//99
	New Orleans MSA, LA	S	7.61 MW	6.51 AW	15830 AAW	LABLS	10//99-12//99
	Shreveport-Bossier City MSA, LA	S	8.05 MW	6.82 AW	16750 AAW	LABLS	10//99-12//99
	Maine	S	7.77 MW	8.39 AW	17460 AAW	MEBLS	10//99-12//99
	Bangor MSA, ME	S	7.94 MW	6.87 AW	16510 AAW	MEBLS	10//99-12//99
	Lewiston-Auburn MSA, ME	S	7.17 MW	6.73 AW	14910 AAW	MEBLS	10//99-12//99
	Portland MSA, ME	S	8.50 MW	8.43 AW	17670 AAW	MEBLS	10//99-12//99
	Maryland	S	8.51 MW	9.72 AW	20220 AAW	MDBLS	10//99-12//99
	Baltimore PMSA, MD	S	8.95 MW	8.10 AW	18620 AAW	MDBLS	10//99-12//99
	Cumberland MSA, MD-WV	S	8.54 MW	6.70 AW	17770 AAW	MDBLS	10//99-12//99
	Hagerstown PMSA, MD	S	8.37 MW	7.77 AW	17420 AAW	MDBLS	10//99-12//99
	Massachusetts	S	8.38 MW	9.08 AW	18890 AAW	MABLS	10//99-12//99
	Barnstable-Yarmouth MSA, MA	S	9.87 MW	9.70 AW	20530 AAW	MABLS	10//99-12//99
	Boston PMSA, MA-NH	S	9.05 MW	8.40 AW	18820 AAW	MABLS	10//99-12//99
	Brockton PMSA, MA	S	9.54 MW	8.59 AW	19840 AAW	MABLS	10//99-12//99
	Fitchburg-Leominster PMSA, MA	S	9.02 MW	8.34 AW	18760 AAW	MABLS	10//99-12//99
	Lawrence PMSA, MA-NH	S	9.71 MW	8.89 AW	20200 AAW	MABLS	10//99-12//99
	New Bedford PMSA, MA	S	8.65 MW	7.82 AW	18000 AAW	MABLS	10//99-12//99
	Pittsfield MSA, MA	S	8.71 MW	7.95 AW	18120 AAW	MABLS	10//99-12//99
	Springfield MSA, MA	S	8.24 MW	7.71 AW	17140 AAW	MABLS	10//99-12//99
	Worcester PMSA, MA-CT	S	8.87 MW	8.38 AW	18450 AAW	MABLS	10//99-12//99
	Michigan	S	8.35 MW	9.12 AW	18980 AAW	MIBLS	10//99-12//99
	Ann Arbor PMSA, MI	S	9.68 MW	9.41 AW	20140 AAW	MIBLS	10//99-12//99
	Benton Harbor MSA, MI	S	7.06 MW	6.08 AW	14690 AAW	MIBLS	10//99-12//99
	Detroit PMSA, MI	S	9.22 MW	8.45 AW	19170 AAW	MIBLS	10//99-12//99
	Grand Rapids-Muskegon-Holland MSA, MI	S	9.22 MW	8.33 AW	19170 AAW	MIBLS	10//99-12//99
	Kalamazoo-Battle Creek MSA, MI	S	10.19 MW	9.60 AW	21190 AAW	MIBLS	10//99-12//99
	Lansing-East Lansing MSA, MI	S	8.54 MW	7.57 AW	17770 AAW	MIBLS	10//99-12//99
	Saginaw-Bay City-Midland MSA, MI	S	9.92 MW	7.49 AW	20630 AAW	MIBLS	10//99-12//99
	Minnesota	S	9.43 MW	9.88 AW	20560 AAW	MNBLS	10//99-12//99
	Duluth-Superior MSA, MN-WI	S	7.48 MW	7.31 AW	15560 AAW	MNBLS	10//99-12//99
	Minneapolis-St. Paul MSA, MN-WI	S	9.83 MW	9.46 AW	20450 AAW	MNBLS	10//99-12//99
	Rochester MSA, MN	S	11.80 MW	11.05 AW	24540 AAW	MNBLS	10//99-12//99
	St. Cloud MSA, MN	S	10.09 MW	8.46 AW	21000 AAW	MNBLS	10//99-12//99
	Mississippi	S	7.43 MW	7.68 AW	15970 AAW	MSBLS	10//99-12//99
	Biloxi-Gulfport-Pascagoula MSA, MS	S	8.26 MW	8.02 AW	17170 AAW	MSBLS	10//99-12//99
	Hattiesburg MSA, MS	S	7.57 MW	7.14 AW	15750 AAW	MSBLS	10//99-12//99
	Jackson MSA, MS	S	7.49 MW	7.45 AW	15570 AAW	MSBLS	10//99-12//99
	Missouri	S	8.33 MW	9.29 AW	19310 AAW	MOBLS	10//99-12//99
	Joplin MSA, MO	S	7.40 MW	6.51 AW	15400 AAW	MOBLS	10//99-12//99
	Kansas City MSA, MO-KS	S	10.54 MW	9.58 AW	21930 AAW	MOBLS	10//99-12//99
	St. Louis MSA, MO-IL	S	8.89 MW	7.88 AW	18480 AAW	MOBLS	10//99-12//99
	Springfield MSA, MO	S	8.98 MW	7.79 AW	18680 AAW	MOBLS	10//99-12//99
	Montana	S	7.24 MW	7.90 AW	16430 AAW	MTBLS	10//99-12//99
	Billings MSA, MT	S	7.17 MW	6.80 AW	14910 AAW	MTBLS	10//99-12//99
	Great Falls MSA, MT	S	7.45 MW	6.72 AW	15490 AAW	MTBLS	10//99-12//99
	Missoula MSA, MT	S	9.89 MW	8.77 AW	20560 AAW	MTBLS	10//99-12//99
	Nebraska	S	8.27 MW	9.20 AW	19150 AAW	NEBLS	10//99-12//99
	Lincoln MSA, NE	S	8.95 MW	8.12 AW	18610 AAW	NEBLS	10//99-12//99
	Omaha MSA, NE-IA	S	9.44 MW	8.38 AW	19630 AAW	NEBLS	10//99-12//99
	Nevada	S	8.92 MW	9.41 AW	19580 AAW	NVBLS	10//99-12//99
	Las Vegas MSA, NV-AZ	S	9.55 MW	9.06 AW	19850 AAW	NVBLS	10//99-12//99
	Reno MSA, NV	S	8.52 MW	8.34 AW	17720 AAW	NVBLS	10//99-12//99
	New Hampshire	S	8.83 MW	9.45 AW	19650 AAW	NHBLS	10//99-12//99

AAW Average annual wage	**AOH** Average offered, high	**ASH** Average starting, high	**H** Hourly	**M** Monthly	**S** Special: hourly and annual
AE Average entry wage	**AOL** Average offered, low	**ASL** Average starting, low	**HI** Highest wage paid	**MTC** Median total compensation	**TQ** Third quartile wage
AEX Average experienced wage	**APH** Average pay, high range	**AW** Average wage paid	**HR** High end range	**MW** Median wage paid	**W** Weekly
AO Average offered	**APL** Average pay, low range	**FQ** First quartile wage	**LR** Low end range	**SQ** Second quartile wage	**Y** Yearly

Occupation/Type/Industry	Location	Per	Low	Mid	High	Source	Date
Security Guard	Manchester PMSA, NH	S	8.21 MW	7.99 AW	17080 AAW	NHBLS	10//99-12//99
	Nashua PMSA, NH	S	9.97 MW	9.57 AW	20740 AAW	NHBLS	10//99-12//99
	Portsmouth-Rochester PMSA, NH-ME	S	8.40 MW	8.29 AW	17460 AAW	NHBLS	10//99-12//99
	New Jersey	S	8.79 MW	9.85 AW	20490 AAW	NJBLS	10//99-12//99
	Atlantic-Cape May PMSA, NJ	S	9.12 MW	8.78 AW	18970 AAW	NJBLS	10//99-12//99
	Bergen-Passaic PMSA, NJ	S	9.86 MW	8.72 AW	20510 AAW	NJBLS	10//99-12//99
	Jersey City PMSA, NJ	S	10.42 MW	9.55 AW	21670 AAW	NJBLS	10//99-12//99
	Middlesex-Somerset-Hunterdon PMSA, NJ	S	9.66 MW	8.84 AW	20090 AAW	NJBLS	10//99-12//99
	Monmouth-Ocean PMSA, NJ	S	9.36 MW	8.55 AW	19460 AAW	NJBLS	10//99-12//99
	Newark PMSA, NJ	S	9.90 MW	8.62 AW	20600 AAW	NJBLS	10//99-12//99
	Trenton PMSA, NJ	S	11.54 MW	10.45 AW	24010 AAW	NJBLS	10//99-12//99
	Vineland-Millville-Bridgeton PMSA, NJ	S	7.59 MW	7.20 AW	15790 AAW	NJBLS	10//99-12//99
	New Mexico	S	7.79 MW	8.26 AW	17180 AAW	NMBLS	10//99-12//99
	Albuquerque MSA, NM	S	8.38 MW	7.90 AW	17440 AAW	NMBLS	10//99-12//99
	Las Cruces MSA, NM	S	8.21 MW	6.58 AW	17080 AAW	NMBLS	10//99-12//99
	Santa Fe MSA, NM	S	8.33 MW	7.87 AW	17330 AAW	NMBLS	10//99-12//99
	New York	S	8.66 MW	9.95 AW	20700 AAW	NYBLS	10//99-12//99
	Albany-Schenectady-Troy MSA, NY	S	10.11 MW	9.40 AW	21040 AAW	NYBLS	10//99-12//99
	Binghamton MSA, NY	S	9.98 MW	8.02 AW	20770 AAW	NYBLS	10//99-12//99
	Buffalo-Niagara Falls MSA, NY	S	8.02 MW	6.75 AW	16680 AAW	NYBLS	10//99-12//99
	Dutchess County PMSA, NY	S	9.57 MW	9.24 AW	19900 AAW	NYBLS	10//99-12//99
	Elmira MSA, NY	S	11.15 MW	9.16 AW	23200 AAW	NYBLS	10//99-12//99
	Glens Falls MSA, NY	S	7.11 MW	6.68 AW	14780 AAW	NYBLS	10//99-12//99
	Jamestown MSA, NY	S	8.76 MW	7.21 AW	18220 AAW	NYBLS	10//99-12//99
	Nassau-Suffolk PMSA, NY	S	9.97 MW	9.21 AW	20740 AAW	NYBLS	10//99-12//99
	New York PMSA, NY	S	10.10 MW	8.67 AW	21000 AAW	NYBLS	10//99-12//99
	Rochester MSA, NY	S	9.46 MW	9.10 AW	19670 AAW	NYBLS	10//99-12//99
	Syracuse MSA, NY	S	8.70 MW	8.07 AW	18090 AAW	NYBLS	10//99-12//99
	Utica-Rome MSA, NY	S	12.19 MW	10.60 AW	25360 AAW	NYBLS	10//99-12//99
	North Carolina	S	7.9 MW	8.50 AW	17680 AAW	NCBLS	10//99-12//99
	Asheville MSA, NC	S	7.83 MW	6.98 AW	16290 AAW	NCBLS	10//99-12//99
	Charlotte-Gastonia-Rock Hill MSA, NC-SC	S	8.86 MW	7.94 AW	18420 AAW	NCBLS	10//99-12//99
	Fayetteville MSA, NC	S	8.55 MW	8.07 AW	17780 AAW	NCBLS	10//99-12//99
	Goldsboro MSA, NC	S	8.75 MW	8.97 AW	18200 AAW	NCBLS	10//99-12//99
	Greensboro--Winston-Salem--High Point MSA, NC	S	8.62 MW	7.94 AW	17930 AAW	NCBLS	10//99-12//99
	Greenville MSA, NC	S	6.64 MW	6.39 AW	13820 AAW	NCBLS	10//99-12//99
	Jacksonville MSA, NC	S	6.41 MW	6.22 AW	13340 AAW	NCBLS	10//99-12//99
	Raleigh-Durham-Chapel Hill MSA, NC	S	9.20 MW	8.70 AW	19130 AAW	NCBLS	10//99-12//99
	Wilmington MSA, NC	S	8.03 MW	7.75 AW	16690 AAW	NCBLS	10//99-12//99
	North Dakota	S	7.95 MW	8.40 AW	17470 AAW	NDBLS	10//99-12//99
	Bismarck MSA, ND	S	7.65 MW	7.53 AW	15920 AAW	NDBLS	10//99-12//99
	Fargo-Moorhead MSA, ND-MN	S	7.86 MW	7.53 AW	16350 AAW	NDBLS	10//99-12//99
	Grand Forks MSA, ND-MN	S	8.59 MW	7.74 AW	17870 AAW	NDBLS	10//99-12//99
	Ohio	S	7.8 MW	9.15 AW	19040 AAW	OHBLS	10//99-12//99
	Akron PMSA, OH	S	8.05 MW	7.07 AW	16740 AAW	OHBLS	10//99-12//99
	Canton-Massillon MSA, OH	S	7.68 MW	6.72 AW	15980 AAW	OHBLS	10//99-12//99
	Cincinnati PMSA, OH-KY-IN	S	9.30 MW	8.03 AW	19340 AAW	OHBLS	10//99-12//99
	Cleveland-Lorain-Elyria PMSA, OH	S	9.56 MW	7.93 AW	19880 AAW	OHBLS	10//99-12//99
	Columbus MSA, OH	S	9.60 MW	8.08 AW	19980 AAW	OHBLS	10//99-12//99
	Dayton-Springfield MSA, OH	S	8.37 MW	7.92 AW	17400 AAW	OHBLS	10//99-12//99
	Lima MSA, OH	S	8.10 MW	7.36 AW	16840 AAW	OHBLS	10//99-12//99
	Steubenville-Weirton MSA, OH-WV	S	7.96 MW	6.99 AW	16560 AAW	OHBLS	10//99-12//99
	Toledo MSA, OH	S	7.49 MW	6.68 AW	15580 AAW	OHBLS	10//99-12//99
	Youngstown-Warren MSA, OH	S	8.92 MW	7.36 AW	18550 AAW	OHBLS	10//99-12//99
	Oklahoma	S	7.79 MW	8.23 AW	17110 AAW	OKBLS	10//99-12//99
	Enid MSA, OK	S	10.90 MW	11.03 AW	22670 AAW	OKBLS	10//99-12//99
	Lawton MSA, OK	S	7.15 MW	6.43 AW	14880 AAW	OKBLS	10//99-12//99
	Oklahoma City MSA, OK	S	8.32 MW	7.85 AW	17300 AAW	OKBLS	10//99-12//99
	Tulsa MSA, OK	S	8.27 MW	7.84 AW	17200 AAW	OKBLS	10//99-12//99
	Oregon	S	8.44 MW	9.40 AW	19550 AAW	ORBLS	10//99-12//99
	Eugene-Springfield MSA, OR	S	8.38 MW	7.86 AW	17420 AAW	ORBLS	10//99-12//99

AAW Average annual wage	**AOH** Average offered, high	**ASH** Average starting, high	**H** Hourly	**M** Monthly	**S** Special: hourly and annual
AE Average entry wage	**AOL** Average offered, low	**ASL** Average starting, low	**HI** Highest wage paid	**MTC** Median total compensation	**TQ** Third quartile wage
AEX Average experienced wage	**APH** Average pay, high range	**AW** Average wage paid	**HR** High end range	**MW** Median wage paid	**W** Weekly
AO Average offered	**APL** Average pay, low range	**FQ** First quartile wage	**LR** Low end range	**SQ** Second quartile wage	**Y** Yearly

Occupation/Type/Industry	Location	Per	Low	Mid	High	Source	Date
Security Guard	Portland-Vancouver PMSA, OR-WA	S	9.46 MW	8.66 AW	19670 AAW	ORBLS	10//99-12//99
	Salem PMSA, OR	S	9.77 MW	8.69 AW	20310 AAW	ORBLS	10//99-12//99
	Pennsylvania	S	8.05 MW	8.63 AW	17940 AAW	PABLS	10//99-12//99
	Allentown-Bethlehem-Easton MSA, PA	S	8.17 MW	7.66 AW	17000 AAW	PABLS	10//99-12//99
	Altoona MSA, PA	S	6.88 MW	6.37 AW	14310 AAW	PABLS	10//99-12//99
	Erie MSA, PA	S	7.38 MW	6.66 AW	15360 AAW	PABLS	10//99-12//99
	Harrisburg-Lebanon-Carlisle MSA, PA	S	9.00 MW	8.53 AW	18720 AAW	PABLS	10//99-12//99
	Johnstown MSA, PA	S	8.26 MW	7.45 AW	17190 AAW	PABLS	10//99-12//99
	Lancaster MSA, PA	S	9.14 MW	8.62 AW	19010 AAW	PABLS	10//99-12//99
	Philadelphia PMSA, PA-NJ	S	9.12 MW	8.53 AW	18980 AAW	PABLS	10//99-12//99
	Pittsburgh MSA, PA	S	8.40 MW	7.69 AW	17480 AAW	PABLS	10//99-12//99
	Reading MSA, PA	S	8.63 MW	8.01 AW	17940 AAW	PABLS	10//99-12//99
	Scranton--Wilkes-Barre--Hazleton MSA, PA	S	8.46 MW	7.78 AW	17590 AAW	PABLS	10//99-12//99
	Sharon MSA, PA	S	8.95 MW	8.45 AW	18610 AAW	PABLS	10//99-12//99
	State College MSA, PA	S	8.61 MW	6.35 AW	17910 AAW	PABLS	10//99-12//99
	Williamsport MSA, PA	S	8.05 MW	8.02 AW	16750 AAW	PABLS	10//99-12//99
	Rhode Island	S	7.76 MW	8.78 AW	18270	RIBLS	10//99-12//99
	Providence-Fall River-Warwick MSA, RI-MA	S	8.77 MW	7.78 AW	18240 AAW	RIBLS	10//99-12//99
	South Carolina	S	7.98 MW	9.02 AW	18760 AAW	SCBLS	10//99-12//99
	Charleston-North Charleston MSA, SC	S	7.64 MW	7.34 AW	15890 AAW	SCBLS	10//99-12//99
	Columbia MSA, SC	S	8.62 MW	7.85 AW	17930 AAW	SCBLS	10//99-12//99
	Greenville-Spartanburg-Anderson MSA, SC	S	9.18 MW	7.87 AW	19090 AAW	SCBLS	10//99-12//99
	Myrtle Beach MSA, SC	S	8.38 MW	8.16 AW	17440 AAW	SCBLS	10//99-12//99
	South Dakota	S	8.57 MW	8.86 AW	18430 AAW	SDBLS	10//99-12//99
	Rapid City MSA, SD	S	8.49 MW	8.61 AW	17660 AAW	SDBLS	10//99-12//99
	Sioux Falls MSA, SD	S	9.49 MW	9.43 AW	19750 AAW	SDBLS	10//99-12//99
	Tennessee	S	7.79 MW	8.65 AW	18000 AAW	TNBLS	10//99-12//99
	Chattanooga MSA, TN-GA	S	8.30 MW	7.66 AW	17260 AAW	TNBLS	10//99-12//99
	Clarksville-Hopkinsville MSA, TN-KY	S	6.84 MW	6.22 AW	14220 AAW	TNBLS	10//99-12//99
	Johnson City-Kingsport-Bristol MSA, TN-VA	S	7.75 MW	7.23 AW	16110 AAW	TNBLS	10//99-12//99
	Knoxville MSA, TN	S	11.19 MW	9.31 AW	23270 AAW	TNBLS	10//99-12//99
	Memphis MSA, TN-AR-MS	S	7.99 MW	7.65 AW	16610 AAW	MSBLS	10//99-12//99
	Nashville MSA, TN	S	9.31 MW	7.97 AW	19370 AAW	TNBLS	10//99-12//99
	Texas	S	7.65 MW	8.90 AW	18510 AAW	TXBLS	10//99-12//99
	Abilene MSA, TX	S	7.40 MW	6.36 AW	15400 AAW	TXBLS	10//99-12//99
	Amarillo MSA, TX	S	8.96 MW	8.05 AW	18630 AAW	TXBLS	10//99-12//99
	Austin-San Marcos MSA, TX	S	8.59 MW	7.79 AW	17880 AAW	TXBLS	10//99-12//99
	Beaumont-Port Arthur MSA, TX	S	9.42 MW	7.84 AW	19580 AAW	TXBLS	10//99-12//99
	Brazoria PMSA, TX	S	10.83 MW	9.48 AW	22520 AAW	TXBLS	10//99-12//99
	Brownsville-Harlingen-San Benito MSA, TX	S	8.00 MW	6.80 AW	16640 AAW	TXBLS	10//99-12//99
	Bryan-College Station MSA, TX	S	7.50 MW	7.20 AW	15610 AAW	TXBLS	10//99-12//99
	Corpus Christi MSA, TX	S	7.40 MW	6.56 AW	15400 AAW	TXBLS	10//99-12//99
	Dallas PMSA, TX	S	8.64 MW	7.94 AW	17970 AAW	TXBLS	10//99-12//99
	El Paso MSA, TX	S	8.58 MW	7.71 AW	17850 AAW	TXBLS	10//99-12//99
	Fort Worth-Arlington PMSA, TX	S	11.79 MW	8.06 AW	24530 AAW	TXBLS	10//99-12//99
	Galveston-Texas City PMSA, TX	S	9.56 MW	8.22 AW	19880 AAW	TXBLS	10//99-12//99
	Houston PMSA, TX	S	8.97 MW	7.88 AW	18650 AAW	TXBLS	10//99-12//99
	Killeen-Temple MSA, TX	S	7.72 MW	6.50 AW	16060 AAW	TXBLS	10//99-12//99
	Laredo MSA, TX	S	6.35 MW	6.08 AW	13210 AAW	TXBLS	10//99-12//99
	Longview-Marshall MSA, TX	S	7.07 MW	6.30 AW	14700 AAW	TXBLS	10//99-12//99
	Lubbock MSA, TX	S	8.68 MW	6.94 AW	18060 AAW	TXBLS	10//99-12//99
	McAllen-Edinburg-Mission MSA, TX	S	7.21 MW	6.43 AW	14990 AAW	TXBLS	10//99-12//99
	Odessa-Midland MSA, TX	S	9.13 MW	7.19 AW	19000 AAW	TXBLS	10//99-12//99
	San Angelo MSA, TX	S	10.95 MW	9.68 AW	22770 AAW	TXBLS	10//99-12//99
	San Antonio MSA, TX	S	7.36 MW	6.57 AW	15310 AAW	TXBLS	10//99-12//99
	Sherman-Denison MSA, TX	S	7.86 MW	7.63 AW	16350 AAW	TXBLS	10//99-12//99

AAW	Average annual wage	AOH	Average offered, high	ASH	Average starting, high	H	Hourly	M	Monthly	S	Special: hourly and annual
AE	Average entry wage	AOL	Average offered, low	ASL	Average starting, low	HI	Highest wage paid	MTC	Median total compensation	TQ	Third quartile wage
AEX	Average experienced wage	APH	Average pay, high range	AW	Average wage paid	HR	High end range	MW	Median wage paid	W	Weekly
AO	Average offered	APL	Average pay, low range	FQ	First quartile wage	LR	Low end range	SQ	Second quartile wage	Y	Yearly

Occupation/Type/Industry	Location	Per	Low	Mid	High	Source	Date
Security Guard	Texarkana MSA, TX-Texarkana, AR	S	8.61 MW	7.83 AW	17910 AAW	TXBLS	10//99-12//99
	Tyler MSA, TX	S	7.84 MW	6.50 AW	16300 AAW	TXBLS	10//99-12//99
	Victoria MSA, TX	S	7.73 MW	7.02 AW	16080 AAW	TXBLS	10//99-12//99
	Waco MSA, TX	S	7.56 MW	6.58 AW	15720 AAW	TXBLS	10//99-12//99
	Wichita Falls MSA, TX	S	8.72 MW	6.68 AW	18140 AAW	TXBLS	10//99-12//99
	Utah	S	8.43 MW	9.27 AW	19290 AAW	UTBLS	10//99-12//99
	Provo-Orem MSA, UT	S	8.78 MW	8.28 AW	18260 AAW	UTBLS	10//99-12//99
	Salt Lake City-Ogden MSA, UT	S	9.03 MW	8.32 AW	18780 AAW	UTBLS	10//99-12//99
	Vermont	S	8.83 MW	9.70 AW	20180 AAW	VTBLS	10//99-12//99
	Burlington MSA, VT	S	9.30 MW	8.71 AW	19350 AAW	VTBLS	10//99-12//99
	Virginia	S	7.84 MW	8.59 AW	17860 AAW	VABLS	10//99-12//99
	Charlottesville MSA, VA	S	8.47 MW	8.01 AW	17610 AAW	VABLS	10//99-12//99
	Danville MSA, VA	S	7.64 MW	6.87 AW	15890 AAW	VABLS	10//99-12//99
	Lynchburg MSA, VA	S	9.73 MW	6.84 AW	20250 AAW	VABLS	10//99-12//99
	Norfolk-Virginia Beach-Newport News MSA, VA-NC	S	7.77 MW	6.94 AW	16170 AAW	VABLS	10//99-12//99
	Richmond-Petersburg MSA, VA	S	8.99 MW	7.87 AW	18710 AAW	VABLS	10//99-12//99
	Roanoke MSA, VA	S	7.56 MW	7.14 AW	15720 AAW	VABLS	10//99-12//99
	Washington	S	8.97 MW	10.19 AW	21190 AAW	WABLS	10//99-12//99
	Bellingham MSA, WA	S	9.72 MW	8.40 AW	20210 AAW	WABLS	10//99-12//99
	Bremerton PMSA, WA	S	11.11 MW	11.19 AW	23120 AAW	WABLS	10//99-12//99
	Olympia PMSA, WA	S	9.59 MW	8.78 AW	19940 AAW	WABLS	10//99-12//99
	Richland-Kennewick-Pasco MSA, WA	S	18.49 MW	19.77 AW	38450 AAW	WABLS	10//99-12//99
	Seattle-Bellevue-Everett PMSA, WA	S	10.21 MW	8.80 AW	21230 AAW	WABLS	10//99-12//99
	Spokane MSA, WA	S	9.17 MW	8.32 AW	19060 AAW	WABLS	10//99-12//99
	Tacoma PMSA, WA	S	10.28 MW	9.74 AW	21380 AAW	WABLS	10//99-12//99
	Yakima MSA, WA	S	8.74 MW	7.83 AW	18190 AAW	WABLS	10//99-12//99
	West Virginia	S	6.42 MW	7.16 AW	14880 AAW	WVBLS	10//99-12//99
	Charleston MSA, WV	S	6.90 MW	6.46 AW	14350 AAW	WVBLS	10//99-12//99
	Huntington-Ashland MSA, WV-KY-OH	S	6.72 MW	5.97 AW	13980 AAW	WVBLS	10//99-12//99
	Parkersburg-Marietta MSA, WV-OH	S	7.42 MW	6.46 AW	15430 AAW	WVBLS	10//99-12//99
	Wheeling MSA, WV-OH	S	6.90 MW	6.31 AW	14350 AAW	WVBLS	10//99-12//99
	Wisconsin	S	8.19 MW	8.74 AW	18180 AAW	WIBLS	10//99-12//99
	Appleton-Oshkosh-Neenah MSA, WI	S	8.27 MW	7.83 AW	17200 AAW	WIBLS	10//99-12//99
	Eau Claire MSA, WI	S	8.51 MW	8.16 AW	17700 AAW	WIBLS	10//99-12//99
	Green Bay MSA, WI	S	8.40 MW	7.87 AW	17480 AAW	WIBLS	10//99-12//99
	Kenosha PMSA, WI	S	8.53 MW	8.07 AW	17730 AAW	WIBLS	10//99-12//99
	La Crosse MSA, WI-MN	S	9.26 MW	8.92 AW	19270 AAW	WIBLS	10//99-12//99
	Madison MSA, WI	S	9.00 MW	8.40 AW	18720 AAW	WIBLS	10//99-12//99
	Milwaukee-Waukesha PMSA, WI	S	8.43 MW	8.13 AW	17540 AAW	WIBLS	10//99-12//99
	Racine PMSA, WI	S	10.45 MW	9.08 AW	21740 AAW	WIBLS	10//99-12//99
	Wausau MSA, WI	S	7.72 MW	7.56 AW	16060 AAW	WIBLS	10//99-12//99
	Wyoming	S	7.59 MW	8.02 AW	16680 AAW	WYBLS	10//99-12//99
	Cheyenne MSA, WY	S	7.37 MW	7.28 AW	15340 AAW	WYBLS	10//99-12//99
	Puerto Rico	S	5.95 MW	6.01 AW	12510 AAW	PRBLS	10//99-12//99
	Aguadilla MSA, PR	S	6.50 MW	6.06 AW	13510 AAW	PRBLS	10//99-12//99
	Arecibo PMSA, PR	S	5.97 MW	5.85 AW	12420 AAW	PRBLS	10//99-12//99
	Caguas PMSA, PR	S	6.19 MW	5.98 AW	12870 AAW	PRBLS	10//99-12//99
	Mayaguez MSA, PR	S	6.37 MW	5.99 AW	13250 AAW	PRBLS	10//99-12//99
	Ponce MSA, PR	S	5.85 MW	5.98 AW	12170 AAW	PRBLS	10//99-12//99
	San Juan-Bayamon PMSA, PR	S	5.99 MW	5.94 AW	12460 AAW	PRBLS	10//99-12//99
	Virgin Islands	S	6.52 MW	7.44 AW	15480 AAW	VIBLS	10//99-12//99
	Guam	S	6.23 MW	6.28 AW	13070 AAW	GUBLS	10//99-12//99
Segmental Paver	California	S	16.34 MW	16.56 AW	34440 AAW	CABLS	10//99-12//99
	Connecticut	S	10.05 MW	11.92 AW	24800 AAW	CTBLS	10//99-12//99
	Georgia	S	11.4 MW	11.52 AW	23960 AAW	GABLS	10//99-12//99
	Minnesota	S	20.44 MW	19.46 AW	40470 AAW	MNBLS	10//99-12//99
	New York	S	10.41 MW	12.34 AW	25660 AAW	NYBLS	10//99-12//99
	Pennsylvania	S	10.32 MW	11.63 AW	24180 AAW	PABLS	10//99-12//99
	South Carolina	S	9.55 MW	10.07 AW	20950 AAW	SCBLS	10//99-12//99
	Tennessee	S	8.39 MW	8.73 AW	18170 AAW	TNBLS	10//99-12//99

AAW Average annual wage	AOH Average offered, high	ASH Average starting, high	H Hourly	M Monthly	S Special: hourly and annual
AE Average entry wage	AOL Average offered, low	ASL Average starting, low	HI Highest wage paid	MTC Median total compensation	TQ Third quartile wage
AEX Average experienced wage	APH Average pay, high range	AW Average wage paid	HR High end range	MW Median wage paid	W Weekly
AO Average offered	APL Average pay, low range	FQ First quartile wage	LR Low end range	SQ Second quartile wage	Y Yearly

Occupation/Type/Industry	Location	Per	Low	Mid	High	Source	Date
Self-Enrichment Education Teacher							
	Alabama	S	10.17 MW	12.33 AW	25640 AAW	ALBLS	10//99-12//99
	Alaska	S	16.6 MW	18.94 AW	39390 AAW	AKBLS	10//99-12//99
	Arizona	S	10.97 MW	11.07 AW	23030 AAW	AZBLS	10//99-12//99
	Arkansas	S	7.83 MW	8.75 AW	18190 AAW	ARBLS	10//99-12//99
	California	S	13.91 MW	16.51 AW	34340 AAW	CABLS	10//99-12//99
	Colorado	S	13.54 MW	13.20 AW	27450 AAW	COBLS	10//99-12//99
	Connecticut	S	13.96 MW	16.99 AW	35350 AAW	CTBLS	10//99-12//99
	Delaware	S	17.72 MW	18.31 AW	38090 AAW	DEBLS	10//99-12//99
	District of Columbia	S	12.44 MW	14.56 AW	30280 AAW	DCBLS	10//99-12//99
	Florida	S	10.02 MW	11.25 AW	23400 AAW	FLBLS	10//99-12//99
	Georgia	S	12.27 MW	13.69 AW	28470 AAW	GABLS	10//99-12//99
	Idaho	S	13.01 MW	12.72 AW	26460 AAW	IDBLS	10//99-12//99
	Illinois	S	11.12 MW	12.24 AW	25460 AAW	ILBLS	10//99-12//99
	Indiana	S	6.7 MW	8.80 AW	18310 AAW	INBLS	10//99-12//99
	Iowa	S	9.74 MW	10.98 AW	22840 AAW	IABLS	10//99-12//99
	Kansas	S	15.8 MW	16.62 AW	34570 AAW	KSBLS	10//99-12//99
	Kentucky	S	9.55 MW	12.72 AW	26460 AAW	KYBLS	10//99-12//99
	Louisiana	S	13.85 MW	13.99 AW	29100 AAW	LABLS	10//99-12//99
	Maine	S	10.4 MW	11.51 AW	23950 AAW	MEBLS	10//99-12//99
	Maryland	S	10.45 MW	14.00 AW	29130 AAW	MDBLS	10//99-12//99
	Massachusetts	S	16.86 MW	18.88 AW	39280 AAW	MABLS	10//99-12//99
	Michigan	S	12.39 MW	13.79 AW	28680 AAW	MIBLS	10//99-12//99
	Minnesota	S	12.16 MW	13.18 AW	27410 AAW	MNBLS	10//99-12//99
	Mississippi	S	7.92 MW	9.91 AW	20610 AAW	MSBLS	10//99-12//99
	Missouri	S	8.41 MW	10.07 AW	20940 AAW	MOBLS	10//99-12//99
	Montana	S	10.75 MW	11.95 AW	24850 AAW	MTBLS	10//99-12//99
	Nebraska	S	9.93 MW	11.93 AW	24810 AAW	NEBLS	10//99-12//99
	Nevada	S	18.9 MW	17.93 AW	37290 AAW	NVBLS	10//99-12//99
	New Hampshire	S	17.72 MW	17.53 AW	36460 AAW	NHBLS	10//99-12//99
	New Jersey	S	15.77 MW	18.15 AW	37760 AAW	NJBLS	10//99-12//99
	New Mexico	S	9.64 MW	10.94 AW	22760 AAW	NMBLS	10//99-12//99
	New York	S	13.75 MW	15.12 AW	31440 AAW	NYBLS	10//99-12//99
	North Carolina	S	12.36 MW	12.58 AW	26160 AAW	NCBLS	10//99-12//99
	North Dakota	S	14.39 MW	15.15 AW	31510 AAW	NDBLS	10//99-12//99
	Ohio	S	10.09 MW	12.10 AW	25160 AAW	OHBLS	10//99-12//99
	Oklahoma	S	9.13 MW	11.74 AW	24420 AAW	OKBLS	10//99-12//99
	Oregon	S	11.54 MW	12.49 AW	25990 AAW	ORBLS	10//99-12//99
	Pennsylvania	S	10.56 MW	12.49 AW	25990 AAW	PABLS	10//99-12//99
	Rhode Island	S	21.8 MW	20.39 AW	42400 AAW	RIBLS	10//99-12//99
	South Carolina	S	11.27 MW	13.52 AW	28120 AAW	SCBLS	10//99-12//99
	South Dakota	S	8.34 MW	8.96 AW	18640 AAW	SDBLS	10//99-12//99
	Tennessee	S	9.87 MW	10.85 AW	22570 AAW	TNBLS	10//99-12//99
	Texas	S	13.34 MW	15.10 AW	31400 AAW	TXBLS	10//99-12//99
	Utah	S	11.41 MW	11.74 AW	24430 AAW	UTBLS	10//99-12//99
	Vermont	S	14.88 MW	14.80 AW	30790 AAW	VTBLS	10//99-12//99
	Virginia	S	15.16 MW	15.50 AW	32240 AAW	VABLS	10//99-12//99
	Washington	S	18.76 MW	18.52 AW	38520 AAW	WABLS	10//99-12//99
	West Virginia	S	9.6 MW	10.06 AW	20920 AAW	WVBLS	10//99-12//99
	Wisconsin	S	10.18 MW	11.95 AW	24850 AAW	WIBLS	10//99-12//99
	Wyoming	S	10.43 MW	12.80 AW	26610 AAW	WYBLS	10//99-12//99
	Puerto Rico	S	7.47 MW	7.98 AW	16600 AAW	PRBLS	10//99-12//99
Semiconductor Processor	California	S	12.38 MW	13.04 AW	27130 AAW	CABLS	10//99-12//99
	Los Angeles-Long Beach PMSA, CA	S	13.41 MW	12.45 AW	27890 AAW	CABLS	10//99-12//99
	Oakland PMSA, CA	S	15.56 MW	14.39 AW	32370 AAW	CABLS	10//99-12//99
	Orange County PMSA, CA	S	10.92 MW	10.94 AW	22710 AAW	CABLS	10//99-12//99
	San Diego MSA, CA	S	14.45 MW	13.95 AW	30050 AAW	CABLS	10//99-12//99
	San Jose PMSA, CA	S	12.97 MW	12.35 AW	26990 AAW	CABLS	10//99-12//99
	Colorado	S	9.99 MW	10.84 AW	22540 AAW	COBLS	10//99-12//99
	Boulder-Longmont PMSA, CO	S	12.82 MW	12.15 AW	26670 AAW	COBLS	10//99-12//99
	Connecticut	S	12.79 MW	12.85 AW	26730 AAW	CTBLS	10//99-12//99
	Florida	S	7.92 MW	8.17 AW	16990 AAW	FLBLS	10//99-12//99
	Boise City MSA, ID	S	10.40 MW	10.97 AW	21620 AAW	IDBLS	10//99-12//99
	Illinois	S	12.03 MW	12.87 AW	26770 AAW	ILBLS	10//99-12//99
	Massachusetts	S	12.87 MW	13.42 AW	27920 AAW	MABLS	10//99-12//99
	Boston PMSA, MA-NH	S	12.76 MW	11.52 AW	26550 AAW	MABLS	10//99-12//99
	New Hampshire	S	13.19 MW	13.72 AW	28530 AAW	NHBLS	10//99-12//99
	New Jersey	S	10.44 MW	12.03 AW	25020 AAW	NJBLS	10//99-12//99
	New York	S	14.97 MW	15.84 AW	32950 AAW	NYBLS	10//99-12//99

Occupation/Type/Industry	Location	Per	Low	Mid	High	Source	Date
Semiconductor Processor	Cleveland-Lorain-Elyria						
	PMSA, OH	S	13.69 MW	12.66 AW	28480 AAW	OHBLS	10//99-12//99
	Pennsylvania	S	12.22 MW	11.61 AW	24150 AAW	PABLS	10//99-12//99
	Philadelphia PMSA, PA-NJ	S	11.46 MW	11.39 AW	23850 AAW	PABLS	10//99-12//99
	Texas	S	12.19 MW	13.62 AW	28320 AAW	TXBLS	10//99-12//99
	Austin-San Marcos MSA, TX	S	12.65 MW	10.97 AW	26310 AAW	TXBLS	10//99-12//99
	Dallas PMSA, TX	S	14.50 MW	13.02 AW	30150 AAW	TXBLS	10//99-12//99
	Virginia	S	12.64 MW	13.61 AW	28300 AAW	VABLS	10//99-12//99
Senior Consultant							
Consulting	United States	Y		58630 MW		TRAVWK5	2000
Separating, Filtering, Clarifying,							
Precipitating, and Still Machine							
Setter, Operator, and Tender	Alabama	S	15.11 MW	14.76 AW	30690 AAW	ALBLS	10//99-12//99
	Birmingham MSA, AL	S	10.90 MW	10.04 AW	22670 AAW	ALBLS	10//99-12//99
	Mobile MSA, AL	S	17.09 MW	17.64 AW	35540 AAW	ALBLS	10//99-12//99
	Arkansas	S	10.06 MW	10.37 AW	21570 AAW	ARBLS	10//99-12//99
	California	S	12.6 MW	12.89 AW	26820 AAW	CABLS	10//99-12//99
	Fresno MSA, CA	S	13.37 MW	12.84 AW	27810 AAW	CABLS	10//99-12//99
	Los Angeles-Long Beach						
	PMSA, CA	S	12.35 MW	12.66 AW	25700 AAW	CABLS	10//99-12//99
	Merced MSA, CA	S	13.35 MW	14.15 AW	27780 AAW	CABLS	10//99-12//99
	Oakland PMSA, CA	S	17.02 MW	17.89 AW	35400 AAW	CABLS	10//99-12//99
	Orange County PMSA, CA	S	12.00 MW	11.05 AW	24970 AAW	CABLS	10//99-12//99
	Riverside-San Bernardino						
	PMSA, CA	S	10.93 MW	10.19 AW	22730 AAW	CABLS	10//99-12//99
	Sacramento PMSA, CA	S	15.22 MW	15.68 AW	31660 AAW	CABLS	10//99-12//99
	San Jose PMSA, CA	S	14.05 MW	12.87 AW	29210 AAW	CABLS	10//99-12//99
	San Luis Obispo-Atascadero-						
	Paso Robles MSA, CA	S	9.58 MW	9.48 AW	19930 AAW	CABLS	10//99-12//99
	Santa Rosa PMSA, CA	S	12.38 MW	11.68 AW	25750 AAW	CABLS	10//99-12//99
	Stockton-Lodi MSA, CA	S	12.92 MW	12.81 AW	26880 AAW	CABLS	10//99-12//99
	Vallejo-Fairfield-Napa PMSA,						
	CA	S	14.73 MW	13.13 AW	30640 AAW	CABLS	10//99-12//99
	Visalia-Tulare-Porterville						
	MSA, CA	S	15.53 MW	15.74 AW	32300 AAW	CABLS	10//99-12//99
	Colorado	S	12.09 MW	11.76 AW	24460 AAW	COBLS	10//99-12//99
	Denver PMSA, CO	S	9.83 MW	8.54 AW	20450 AAW	COBLS	10//99-12//99
	Connecticut	S	12.49 MW	13.94 AW	28990 AAW	CTBLS	10//99-12//99
	Delaware	S	17.31 MW	16.12 AW	33520 AAW	DEBLS	10//99-12//99
	Wilmington-Newark PMSA,						
	DE-MD	S	17.54 MW	18.31 AW	36480 AAW	DEBLS	10//99-12//99
	Washington PMSA, DC-MD-						
	VA-WV	S	14.26 MW	15.00 AW	29660 AAW	DCBLS	10//99-12//99
	Florida	S	11.68 MW	11.94 AW	24840 AAW	FLBLS	10//99-12//99
	Lakeland-Winter Haven MSA,						
	FL	S	11.67 MW	11.11 AW	24270 AAW	FLBLS	10//99-12//99
	Pensacola MSA, FL	S	9.16 MW	8.67 AW	19060 AAW	FLBLS	10//99-12//99
	Georgia	S	10.67 MW	11.96 AW	24880 AAW	GABLS	10//99-12//99
	Atlanta MSA, GA	S	10.22 MW	8.89 AW	21250 AAW	GABLS	10//99-12//99
	Augusta-Aiken MSA, GA-SC	S	18.20 MW	15.97 AW	37850 AAW	GABLS	10//99-12//99
	Savannah MSA, GA	S	14.32 MW	14.33 AW	29780 AAW	GABLS	10//99-12//99
	Idaho	S	11.3 MW	11.11 AW	23100 AAW	IDBLS	10//99-12//99
	Illinois	S	13.72 MW	13.89 AW	28890 AAW	ILBLS	10//99-12//99
	Chicago PMSA, IL	S	14.77 MW	14.57 AW	30720 AAW	ILBLS	10//99-12//99
	Peoria-Pekin MSA, IL	S	12.77 MW	12.52 AW	26560 AAW	ILBLS	10//99-12//99
	Indiana	S	15.26 MW	15.42 AW	32060 AAW	INBLS	10//99-12//99
	Evansville-Henderson MSA,						
	IN-KY	S	8.79 MW	7.98 AW	18280 AAW	INBLS	10//99-12//99
	Lafayette MSA, IN	S	16.20 MW	16.03 AW	33690 AAW	INBLS	10//99-12//99
	Iowa	S	14.6 MW	14.57 AW	30300 AAW	IABLS	10//99-12//99
	Sioux City MSA, IA-NE	S	10.53 MW	9.87 AW	21900 AAW	IABLS	10//99-12//99
	Kansas	S	11.8 MW	11.67 AW	24270 AAW	KSBLS	10//99-12//99
	Wichita MSA, KS	S	13.20 MW	12.47 AW	27450 AAW	KSBLS	10//99-12//99
	Kentucky	S	13 MW	13.12 AW	27290 AAW	KYBLS	10//99-12//99
	Louisville MSA, KY-IN	S	13.23 MW	12.71 AW	27520 AAW	KYBLS	10//99-12//99
	Louisiana	S	16.06 MW	17.41 AW	36220 AAW	LABLS	10//99-12//99
	Maine	S	14.85 MW	14.76 AW	30710 AAW	MEBLS	10//99-12//99
	Portland MSA, ME	S	11.40 MW	12.04 AW	23710 AAW	MEBLS	10//99-12//99
	Maryland	S	12.77 MW	12.39 AW	25760 AAW	MDBLS	10//99-12//99
	Baltimore PMSA, MD	S	12.63 MW	13.03 AW	26270 AAW	MDBLS	10//99-12//99

AAW	Average annual wage	AOH	Average offered, high	ASH	Average starting, high	H	Hourly	M	Monthly	S	Special: hourly and annual
AE	Average entry wage	AOL	Average offered, low	ASL	Average starting, low	HI	Highest wage paid	MTC	Median total compensation	TQ	Third quartile wage
AEX	Average experienced wage	APH	Average pay, high range	AW	Average wage paid	HR	High end range	MW	Median wage paid	W	Weekly
AO	Average offered	APL	Average pay, low range	FQ	First quartile wage	LR	Low end range	SQ	Second quartile wage	Y	Yearly

Occupation/Type/Industry	Location	Per	Low	Mid	High	Source	Date
Separating, Filtering, Clarifying, Precipitating, and Still Machine Setter, Operator, and Tender	Massachusetts	S	14.93 MW	14.73 AW	30640 AAW	MABLS	10//99-12//99
	Boston PMSA, MA-NH	S	15.39 MW	15.31 AW	32020 AAW	MABLS	10//99-12//99
	Springfield MSA, MA	S	13.34 MW	14.34 AW	27760 AAW	MABLS	10//99-12//99
	Michigan	S	14.1 MW	13.54 AW	28160 AAW	MIBLS	10//99-12//99
	Detroit PMSA, MI	S	13.99 MW	13.64 AW	29100 AAW	MIBLS	10//99-12//99
	Saginaw-Bay City-Midland MSA, MI	S	11.52 MW	10.41 AW	23970 AAW	MIBLS	10//99-12//99
	Minnesota	S	12.67 MW	12.63 AW	26270 AAW	MNBLS	10//99-12//99
	Minneapolis-St. Paul MSA, MN-WI	S	15.01 MW	14.94 AW	31210 AAW	MNBLS	10//99-12//99
	Mississippi	S	10.26 MW	10.38 AW	21590 AAW	MSBLS	10//99-12//99
	Missouri	S	13.37 MW	13.13 AW	27310 AAW	MOBLS	10//99-12//99
	Kansas City MSA, MO-KS	S	13.34 MW	13.88 AW	27740 AAW	MOBLS	10//99-12//99
	Montana	S	12.66 MW	12.62 AW	26250 AAW	MTBLS	10//99-12//99
	Nebraska	S	11.85 MW	11.87 AW	24690 AAW	NEBLS	10//99-12//99
	Nevada	S	17.08 MW	16.63 AW	34590 AAW	NVBLS	10//99-12//99
	Las Vegas MSA, NV-AZ	S	16.29 MW	16.96 AW	33870 AAW	NVBLS	10//99-12//99
	New Hampshire	S	11.6 MW	11.79 AW	24510 AAW	NHBLS	10//99-12//99
	New Jersey	S	13.57 MW	14.24 AW	29610 AAW	NJBLS	10//99-12//99
	Middlesex-Somerset-Hunterdon PMSA, NJ	S	12.28 MW	10.68 AW	25530 AAW	NJBLS	10//99-12//99
	Newark PMSA, NJ	S	14.71 MW	15.15 AW	30590 AAW	NJBLS	10//99-12//99
	New Mexico	S	9.51 MW	10.33 AW	21500 AAW	NMBLS	10//99-12//99
	New York	S	12.43 MW	12.50 AW	25990 AAW	NYBLS	10//99-12//99
	Albany-Schenectady-Troy MSA, NY	S	11.06 MW	11.99 AW	23010 AAW	NYBLS	10//99-12//99
	Nassau-Suffolk PMSA, NY	S	10.64 MW	9.75 AW	22130 AAW	NYBLS	10//99-12//99
	New York PMSA, NY	S	13.51 MW	13.04 AW	28100 AAW	NYBLS	10//99-12//99
	Rochester MSA, NY	S	11.01 MW	10.12 AW	22900 AAW	NYBLS	10//99-12//99
	Syracuse MSA, NY	S	13.55 MW	10.45 AW	28170 AAW	NYBLS	10//99-12//99
	North Carolina	S	14.05 MW	14.64 AW	30460 AAW	NCBLS	10//99-12//99
	Charlotte-Gastonia-Rock Hill MSA, NC-SC	S	14.79 MW	13.22 AW	30760 AAW	NCBLS	10//99-12//99
	Greensboro--Winston-Salem--High Point MSA, NC	S	16.89 MW	14.96 AW	35120 AAW	NCBLS	10//99-12//99
	North Dakota	S	11.96 MW	11.58 AW	24090 AAW	NDBLS	10//99-12//99
	Ohio	S	14.21 MW	13.79 AW	28690 AAW	OHBLS	10//99-12//99
	Cincinnati PMSA, OH-KY-IN	S	14.69 MW	14.88 AW	30550 AAW	OHBLS	10//99-12//99
	Columbus MSA, OH	S	13.56 MW	14.32 AW	28210 AAW	OHBLS	10//99-12//99
	Oklahoma	S	15.84 MW	16.75 AW	34830 AAW	OKBLS	10//99-12//99
	Oregon	S	12.43 MW	12.68 AW	26370 AAW	ORBLS	10//99-12//99
	Portland-Vancouver PMSA, OR-WA	S	13.72 MW	14.12 AW	28530 AAW	ORBLS	10//99-12//99
	Salem PMSA, OR	S	10.22 MW	9.83 AW	21260 AAW	ORBLS	10//99-12//99
	Pennsylvania	S	14.34 MW	14.43 AW	30020 AAW	PABLS	10//99-12//99
	Harrisburg-Lebanon-Carlisle MSA, PA	S	13.32 MW	12.94 AW	27700 AAW	PABLS	10//99-12//99
	Johnstown MSA, PA	S	11.17 MW	11.27 AW	23230 AAW	PABLS	10//99-12//99
	Lancaster MSA, PA	S	12.71 MW	12.66 AW	26440 AAW	PABLS	10//99-12//99
	Philadelphia PMSA, PA-NJ	S	16.23 MW	15.56 AW	33760 AAW	PABLS	10//99-12//99
	Pittsburgh MSA, PA	S	17.23 MW	16.53 AW	35840 AAW	PABLS	10//99-12//99
	York MSA, PA	S	14.72 MW	14.94 AW	30620 AAW	PABLS	10//99-12//99
	Rhode Island	S	14.12 MW	14.38 AW	29900 AAW	RIBLS	10//99-12//99
	Providence-Fall River-Warwick MSA, RI-MA	S	14.46 MW	14.02 AW	30080 AAW	RIBLS	10//99-12//99
	South Carolina	S	12.58 MW	13.68 AW	28450 AAW	SCBLS	10//99-12//99
	Greenville-Spartanburg-Anderson MSA, SC	S	14.30 MW	13.52 AW	29730 AAW	SCBLS	10//99-12//99
	South Dakota	S	10.71 MW	11.16 AW	23210 AAW	SDBLS	10//99-12//99
	Tennessee	S	12.37 MW	12.70 AW	26420 AAW	TNBLS	10//99-12//99
	Chattanooga MSA, TN-GA	S	11.60 MW	11.65 AW	24120 AAW	TNBLS	10//99-12//99
	Johnson City-Kingsport-Bristol MSA, TN-VA	S	13.84 MW	14.06 AW	28790 AAW	TNBLS	10//99-12//99
	Memphis MSA, TN-AR-MS	S	11.89 MW	11.49 AW	24730 AAW	MSBLS	10//99-12//99
	Nashville MSA, TN	S	11.55 MW	11.56 AW	24030 AAW	TNBLS	10//99-12//99
	Texas	S	12.36 MW	14.61 AW	30390 AAW	TXBLS	10//99-12//99
	Austin-San Marcos MSA, TX	S	8.31 MW	7.94 AW	17280 AAW	TXBLS	10//99-12//99
	Dallas PMSA, TX	S	13.37 MW	12.01 AW	27820 AAW	TXBLS	10//99-12//99
	Fort Worth-Arlington PMSA, TX	S	14.50 MW	14.00 AW	30160 AAW	TXBLS	10//99-12//99

AAW Average annual wage	**AOH** Average offered, high	**ASH** Average starting, high	**H** Hourly	**M** Monthly	**S** Special: hourly and annual
AE Average entry wage	**AOL** Average offered, low	**ASL** Average starting, low	**HI** Highest wage paid	**MTC** Median total compensation	**TQ** Third quartile wage
AEX Average experienced wage	**APH** Average pay, high range	**AW** Average wage paid	**HR** High end range	**MW** Median wage paid	**W** Weekly
AO Average offered	**APL** Average pay, low range	**FQ** First quartile wage	**LR** Low end range	**SQ** Second quartile wage	**Y** Yearly

Occupation/Type/Industry	Location	Per	Low	Mid	High	Source	Date
Separating, Filtering, Clarifying, Precipitating, and Still Machine Setter, Operator, and Tender	Houston PMSA, TX	S	14.96 MW	11.94 AW	31110 AAW	TXBLS	10//99-12//99
	Utah	S	13.66 MW	13.94 AW	28990 AAW	UTBLS	10//99-12//99
	Salt Lake City-Ogden MSA, UT	S	14.75 MW	14.07 AW	30690 AAW	UTBLS	10//99-12//99
	Vermont	S	10.98 MW	11.45 AW	23810 AAW	VTBLS	10//99-12//99
	Virginia	S	16.26 MW	15.25 AW	31710 AAW	VABLS	10//99-12//99
	Norfolk-Virginia Beach-Newport News MSA, VA-NC	S	13.51 MW	11.08 AW	28100 AAW	VABLS	10//99-12//99
	Richmond-Petersburg MSA, VA	S	14.39 MW	16.09 AW	29930 AAW	VABLS	10//99-12//99
	Washington	S	14.33 MW	14.71 AW	30590 AAW	WABLS	10//99-12//99
	Richland-Kennewick-Pasco MSA, WA	S	13.87 MW	14.24 AW	28850 AAW	WABLS	10//99-12//99
	Seattle-Bellevue-Everett PMSA, WA	S	16.19 MW	17.19 AW	33680 AAW	WABLS	10//99-12//99
	Spokane MSA, WA	S	15.31 MW	16.71 AW	31850 AAW	WABLS	10//99-12//99
	Tacoma PMSA, WA	S	18.37 MW	18.65 AW	38210 AAW	WABLS	10//99-12//99
	Yakima MSA, WA	S	12.31 MW	12.44 AW	25610 AAW	WABLS	10//99-12//99
	Wisconsin	S	12.76 MW	13.23 AW	27510 AAW	WIBLS	10//99-12//99
	Appleton-Oshkosh-Neenah MSA, WI	S	13.13 MW	12.77 AW	27300 AAW	WIBLS	10//99-12//99
	Green Bay MSA, WI	S	12.01 MW	11.71 AW	24980 AAW	WIBLS	10//99-12//99
	Madison MSA, WI	S	12.08 MW	12.20 AW	25130 AAW	WIBLS	10//99-12//99
	Milwaukee-Waukesha PMSA, WI	S	15.52 MW	14.59 AW	32270 AAW	WIBLS	10//99-12//99
	Wausau MSA, WI	S	14.56 MW	13.43 AW	30280 AAW	WIBLS	10//99-12//99
	Wyoming	S	10.95 MW	14.77 AW	30720 AAW	WYBLS	10//99-12//99
	Puerto Rico	S	8.49 MW	8.56 AW	17800 AAW	PRBLS	10//99-12//99
	Virgin Islands	S	8.93 MW	8.48 AW	17650 AAW	VIBLS	10//99-12//99
Septic Tank Service' and Sewer Pipe Cleaner	Arizona	S	13.55 MW	14.35 AW	29850 AAW	AZBLS	10//99-12//99
	Phoenix-Mesa MSA, AZ	S	17.53 MW	19.60 AW	36450 AAW	AZBLS	10//99-12//99
	California	S	15.25 MW	15.67 AW	32600 AAW	CABLS	10//99-12//99
	Riverside-San Bernardino PMSA, CA	S	15.40 MW	14.87 AW	32040 AAW	CABLS	10//99-12//99
	Salinas MSA, CA	S	17.96 MW	17.81 AW	37360 AAW	CABLS	10//99-12//99
	Yuba City MSA, CA	S	11.69 MW	11.93 AW	24320 AAW	CABLS	10//99-12//99
	Colorado	S	14.87 MW	14.26 AW	29650 AAW	COBLS	10//99-12//99
	Denver PMSA, CO	S	13.21 MW	11.88 AW	27470 AAW	COBLS	10//99-12//99
	Connecticut	S	12.36 MW	13.22 AW	27490 AAW	CTBLS	10//99-12//99
	New London-Norwich MSA, CT-RI	S	14.07 MW	13.88 AW	29260 AAW	CTBLS	10//99-12//99
	Washington PMSA, DC-MD-VA-WV	S	12.84 MW	13.11 AW	26710 AAW	DCBLS	10//99-12//99
	Florida	S	11.67 MW	12.09 AW	25160 AAW	FLBLS	10//99-12//99
	Orlando MSA, FL	S	12.14 MW	11.72 AW	25250 AAW	FLBLS	10//99-12//99
	Georgia	S	15.32 MW	15.68 AW	32610 AAW	GABLS	10//99-12//99
	Illinois	S	12.05 MW	12.89 AW	26810 AAW	ILBLS	10//99-12//99
	Indiana	S	9.74 MW	10.42 AW	21670 AAW	INBLS	10//99-12//99
	Gary PMSA, IN	S	9.83 MW	9.75 AW	20450 AAW	INBLS	10//99-12//99
	Indianapolis MSA, IN	S	13.15 MW	11.52 AW	27350 AAW	INBLS	10//99-12//99
	Kansas	S	13.26 MW	14.76 AW	30710 AAW	KSBLS	10//99-12//99
	Louisiana	S	13.87 MW	13.30 AW	27670 AAW	LABLS	10//99-12//99
	Maine	S	13.16 MW	13.36 AW	27780 AAW	MEBLS	10//99-12//99
	Portland MSA, ME	S	9.14 MW	9.25 AW	19020 AAW	MEBLS	10//99-12//99
	Maryland	S	14.33 MW	13.72 AW	28540 AAW	MDBLS	10//99-12//99
	Massachusetts	S	13.1 MW	12.64 AW	26280 AAW	MABLS	10//99-12//99
	Boston PMSA, MA-NH	S	12.47 MW	13.06 AW	25940 AAW	MABLS	10//99-12//99
	Michigan	S	14.31 MW	14.89 AW	30970 AAW	MIBLS	10//99-12//99
	Detroit PMSA, MI	S	19.19 MW	17.08 AW	39900 AAW	MIBLS	10//99-12//99
	Grand Rapids-Muskegon-Holland MSA, MI	S	12.74 MW	14.15 AW	26510 AAW	MIBLS	10//99-12//99
	Minnesota	S	11.8 MW	11.82 AW	24590 AAW	MNBLS	10//99-12//99
	Minneapolis-St. Paul MSA, MN-WI	S	13.02 MW	12.79 AW	27090 AAW	MNBLS	10//99-12//99
	Mississippi	S	7.59 MW	7.50 AW	15590 AAW	MSBLS	10//99-12//99
	Missouri	S	12.86 MW	13.65 AW	28400 AAW	MOBLS	10//99-12//99

Occupation/Type/Industry	Location	Per	Low	Mid	High	Source	Date
Septic Tank Service' and Sewer Pipe Cleaner	Nebraska	S	11.51 MW	12.24 AW	25460 AAW	NEBLS	10//99-12//99
	Nevada	S	14.42 MW	15.09 AW	31380 AAW	NVBLS	10//99-12//99
	Reno MSA, NV	S	13.62 MW	12.66 AW	28330 AAW	NVBLS	10//99-12//99
	New Hampshire	S	11.23 MW	12.22 AW	25420 AAW	NHBLS	10//99-12//99
	Portsmouth-Rochester PMSA, NH-ME	S	16.71 MW	15.20 AW	34760 AAW	NHBLS	10//99-12//99
	New Jersey	S	15.35 MW	15.45 AW	32130 AAW	NJBLS	10//99-12//99
	Middlesex-Somerset-Hunterdon PMSA, NJ	S	16.42 MW	16.49 AW	34160 AAW	NJBLS	10//99-12//99
	New Mexico	S	10.69 MW	10.86 AW	22600 AAW	NMBLS	10//99-12//99
	Albuquerque MSA, NM	S	11.05 MW	10.71 AW	22980 AAW	NMBLS	10//99-12//99
	Santa Fe MSA, NM	S	11.51 MW	11.50 AW	23930 AAW	NMBLS	10//99-12//99
	New York	S	14.74 MW	17.57 AW	36550 AAW	NYBLS	10//99-12//99
	Nassau-Suffolk PMSA, NY	S	19.87 MW	17.54 AW	41320 AAW	NYBLS	10//99-12//99
	New York PMSA, NY	S	16.49 MW	11.97 AW	34300 AAW	NYBLS	10//99-12//99
	North Carolina	S	11.87 MW	11.81 AW	24570 AAW	NCBLS	10//99-12//99
	Ohio	S	14.68 MW	14.90 AW	30990 AAW	OHBLS	10//99-12//99
	Cincinnati PMSA, OH-KY-IN	S	13.58 MW	12.82 AW	28240 AAW	OHBLS	10//99-12//99
	Toledo MSA, OH	S	11.17 MW	11.03 AW	23230 AAW	OHBLS	10//99-12//99
	Oklahoma	S	12.75 MW	13.56 AW	28200 AAW	OKBLS	10//99-12//99
	Oregon	S	13.13 MW	14.46 AW	30070 AAW	ORBLS	10//99-12//99
	Portland-Vancouver PMSA, OR-WA	S	14.95 MW	13.44 AW	31100 AAW	ORBLS	10//99-12//99
	Pennsylvania	S	11.83 MW	12.76 AW	26550 AAW	PABLS	10//99-12//99
	Philadelphia PMSA, PA-NJ	S	16.23 MW	16.62 AW	33760 AAW	PABLS	10//99-12//99
	Rhode Island	S	19.17 MW	19.07 AW	39660 AAW	RIBLS	10//99-12//99
	South Carolina	S	13.73 MW	13.03 AW	27100 AAW	SCBLS	10//99-12//99
	South Dakota	S	9.07 MW	9.24 AW	19220 AAW	SDBLS	10//99-12//99
	Tennessee	S	13.06 MW	14.89 AW	30980 AAW	TNBLS	10//99-12//99
	Texas	S	11.12 MW	11.16 AW	23210 AAW	TXBLS	10//99-12//99
	Virginia	S	10.87 MW	11.47 AW	23850 AAW	VABLS	10//99-12//99
	Norfolk-Virginia Beach-Newport News MSA, VA-NC	S	11.98 MW	11.98 AW	24910 AAW	VABLS	10//99-12//99
	Washington	S	13.31 MW	13.51 AW	28100 AAW	WABLS	10//99-12//99
	West Virginia	S	6.99 MW	8.14 AW	16930 AAW	WVBLS	10//99-12//99
	Wisconsin	S	13.65 MW	13.71 AW	28510 AAW	WIBLS	10//99-12//99
	Green Bay MSA, WI	S	18.80 MW	22.35 AW	39110 AAW	WIBLS	10//99-12//99
	Wyoming	S	12.11 MW	11.78 AW	24490 AAW	WYBLS	10//99-12//99
Service Manager Auto Dealership	United States	Y		56071 MW		WARD2	1999
Service Station Attendant	Alabama	S	7.35 MW	7.70 AW	16020 AAW	ALBLS	10//99-12//99
	Alaska	S	7.92 MW	8.49 AW	17650 AAW	AKBLS	10//99-12//99
	Arizona	S	6.87 MW	7.50 AW	15600 AAW	AZBLS	10//99-12//99
	Arkansas	S	7.68 MW	7.61 AW	15830 AAW	ARBLS	10//99-12//99
	California	S	6.91 MW	7.67 AW	15960 AAW	CABLS	10//99-12//99
	Colorado	S	7.82 MW	7.96 AW	16570 AAW	COBLS	10//99-12//99
	Connecticut	S	7.45 MW	7.84 AW	16300 AAW	CTBLS	10//99-12//99
	Delaware	S	7.75 MW	8.39 AW	17460 AAW	DEBLS	10//99-12//99
	Florida	S	7.31 MW	7.95 AW	16540 AAW	FLBLS	10//99-12//99
	Georgia	S	8.05 MW	8.93 AW	18570 AAW	GABLS	10//99-12//99
	Hawaii	S	6.69 MW	7.61 AW	15830 AAW	HIBLS	10//99-12//99
	Idaho	S	7.92 MW	8.53 AW	17740 AAW	IDBLS	10//99-12//99
	Illinois	S	7.29 MW	7.97 AW	16570 AAW	ILBLS	10//99-12//99
	Indiana	S	7.54 MW	7.74 AW	16090 AAW	INBLS	10//99-12//99
	Iowa	S	6.62 MW	7.07 AW	14710 AAW	IABLS	10//99-12//99
	Kansas	S	7.54 MW	7.77 AW	16160 AAW	KSBLS	10//99-12//99
	Kentucky	S	6.59 MW	6.96 AW	14470 AAW	KYBLS	10//99-12//99
	Louisiana	S	6.95 MW	7.68 AW	15970 AAW	LABLS	10//99-12//99
	Maine	S	6.29 MW	6.75 AW	14030 AAW	MEBLS	10//99-12//99
	Maryland	S	7.35 MW	7.75 AW	16120 AAW	MDBLS	10//99-12//99
	Massachusetts	S	7.6 MW	7.87 AW	16370 AAW	MABLS	10//99-12//99
	Michigan	S	7.28 MW	7.62 AW	15860 AAW	MIBLS	10//99-12//99
	Minnesota	S	7.34 MW	7.82 AW	16270 AAW	MNBLS	10//99-12//99
	Mississippi	S	7.43 MW	7.58 AW	15770 AAW	MSBLS	10//99-12//99
	Missouri	S	7.28 MW	7.66 AW	15930 AAW	MOBLS	10//99-12//99
	Montana	S	7.16 MW	7.41 AW	15420 AAW	MTBLS	10//99-12//99
	Nebraska	S	7.92 MW	8.48 AW	17630 AAW	NEBLS	10//99-12//99
	Nevada	S	7.5 MW	8.04 AW	16710 AAW	NVBLS	10//99-12//99

AAW	Average annual wage	AOH	Average offered, high	ASH	Average starting, high	H	Hourly	M	Monthly	S	Special: hourly and annual
AE	Average entry wage	AOL	Average offered, low	ASL	Average starting, low	HI	Highest wage paid	MTC	Median total compensation	TQ	Third quartile wage
AEX	Average experienced wage	APH	Average pay, high range	AW	Average wage paid	HR	High end range	MW	Median wage paid	W	Weekly
AO	Average offered	APL	Average pay, low range	FQ	First quartile wage	LR	Low end range	SQ	Second quartile wage	Y	Yearly

Occupation/Type/Industry	Location	Per	Low	Mid	High	Source	Date
Service Station Attendant	New Hampshire	S	7.38 MW	7.41 AW	15420 AAW	NHBLS	10//99-12//99
	New Jersey	S	6.96 MW	7.35 AW	15290 AAW	NJBLS	10//99-12//99
	New Mexico	S	6.97 MW	7.43 AW	15450 AAW	NMBLS	10//99-12//99
	New York	S	6.13 MW	6.82 AW	14180 AAW	NYBLS	10//99-12//99
	North Carolina	S	7.58 MW	7.93 AW	16500 AAW	NCBLS	10//99-12//99
	North Dakota	S	6.79 MW	7.28 AW	15140 AAW	NDBLS	10//99-12//99
	Ohio	S	6.85 MW	7.27 AW	15130 AAW	OHBLS	10//99-12//99
	Oklahoma	S	6.4 MW	6.61 AW	13750 AAW	OKBLS	10//99-12//99
	Oregon	S	7.1 MW	7.68 AW	15980 AAW	ORBLS	10//99-12//99
	Pennsylvania	S	6.29 MW	6.73 AW	13990 AAW	PABLS	10//99-12//99
	Rhode Island	S	7.45 MW	7.52 AW	15650 AAW	RIBLS	10//99-12//99
	South Carolina	S	7.02 MW	7.34 AW	15260 AAW	SCBLS	10//99-12//99
	South Dakota	S	6.82 MW	7.01 AW	14590 AAW	SDBLS	10//99-12//99
	Tennessee	S	7.53 MW	8.19 AW	17030 AAW	TNBLS	10//99-12//99
	Texas	S	7.39 MW	7.65 AW	15910 AAW	TXBLS	10//99-12//99
	Vermont	S	7.28 MW	7.45 AW	15490 AAW	VTBLS	10//99-12//99
	Virginia	S	7.86 MW	8.05 AW	16740 AAW	VABLS	10//99-12//99
	Washington	S	7.68 MW	8.36 AW	17380 AAW	WABLS	10//99-12//99
	West Virginia	S	6.1 MW	6.33 AW	13180 AAW	WVBLS	10//99-12//99
	Wisconsin	S	7.3 MW	7.87 AW	16360 AAW	WIBLS	10//99-12//99
	Wyoming	S	6.15 MW	6.70 AW	13930 AAW	WYBLS	10//99-12//99
	Puerto Rico	S	5.94 MW	5.96 AW	12400 AAW	PRBLS	10//99-12//99
	Virgin Islands	S	6.07 MW	6.17 AW	12840 AAW	VIBLS	10//99-12//99
	Guam	S	6.14 MW	6.17 AW	12830 AAW	GUBLS	10//99-12//99
Service Technician							
Auto Dealership	United States	Y		42429 MW		WARD2	1999
Service Unit Operator							
Oil, Gas, and Mining	Alabama	S	11.17 MW	11.88 AW	24710 AAW	ALBLS	10//99-12//99
Oil, Gas, and Mining	Arkansas	S	11.68 MW	11.18 AW	23260 AAW	ARBLS	10//99-12//99
Oil, Gas, and Mining	California	S	13.44 MW	14.64 AW	30460 AAW	CABLS	10//99-12//99
Oil, Gas, and Mining	Colorado	S	13.99 MW	15.97 AW	33210 AAW	COBLS	10//99-12//99
Oil, Gas, and Mining	Illinois	S	11.24 MW	12.33 AW	25640 AAW	ILBLS	10//99-12//99
Oil, Gas, and Mining	Kansas	S	11.02 MW	12.45 AW	25890 AAW	KSBLS	10//99-12//99
Oil, Gas, and Mining	Kentucky	S	9.43 MW	9.37 AW	19490 AAW	KYBLS	10//99-12//99
Oil, Gas, and Mining	Louisiana	S	11.64 MW	12.49 AW	25970 AAW	LABLS	10//99-12//99
Oil, Gas, and Mining	Michigan	S	12.32 MW	12.43 AW	25840 AAW	MIBLS	10//99-12//99
Oil, Gas, and Mining	Mississippi	S	13.06 MW	14.80 AW	30780 AAW	MSBLS	10//99-12//99
Oil, Gas, and Mining	Montana	S	13.55 MW	13.79 AW	28680 AAW	MTBLS	10//99-12//99
Oil, Gas, and Mining	Nebraska	S	12.47 MW	15.01 AW	31220 AAW	NEBLS	10//99-12//99
Oil, Gas, and Mining	New Mexico	S	12.46 MW	14.01 AW	29140 AAW	NMBLS	10//99-12//99
Oil, Gas, and Mining	New York	S	13.56 MW	13.29 AW	27650 AAW	NYBLS	10//99-12//99
Oil, Gas, and Mining	North Dakota	S	11.08 MW	11.77 AW	24480 AAW	NDBLS	10//99-12//99
Oil, Gas, and Mining	Ohio	S	9.92 MW	10.56 AW	21960 AAW	OHBLS	10//99-12//99
Oil, Gas, and Mining	Oklahoma	S	10.9 MW	11.20 AW	23290 AAW	OKBLS	10//99-12//99
Oil, Gas, and Mining	Pennsylvania	S	11.28 MW	11.79 AW	24520 AAW	PABLS	10//99-12//99
Oil, Gas, and Mining	Texas	S	10.81 MW	12.06 AW	25070 AAW	TXBLS	10//99-12//99
Oil, Gas, and Mining	West Virginia	S	10.08 MW	11.43 AW	23780 AAW	WVBLS	10//99-12//99
Oil, Gas, and Mining	Wyoming	S	13.31 MW	14.11 AW	29340 AAW	WYBLS	10//99-12//99
Set and Exhibit Designer	Arizona	S	12.26 MW	13.21 AW	27470 AAW	AZBLS	10//99-12//99
	California	S	17.14 MW	17.61 AW	36640 AAW	CABLS	10//99-12//99
	Colorado	S	14.41 MW	15.60 AW	32440 AAW	COBLS	10//99-12//99
	Connecticut	S	20.48 MW	19.83 AW	41250 AAW	CTBLS	10//99-12//99
	Florida	S	10.46 MW	11.72 AW	24370 AAW	FLBLS	10//99-12//99
	Georgia	S	11.12 MW	11.86 AW	24660 AAW	GABLS	10//99-12//99
	Iowa	S	9.33 MW	9.60 AW	19970 AAW	IABLS	10//99-12//99
	Kansas	S	9.95 MW	10.04 AW	20870 AAW	KSBLS	10//99-12//99
	Kentucky	S	7.21 MW	7.76 AW	16140 AAW	KYBLS	10//99-12//99
	Louisiana	S	14.1 MW	14.35 AW	29860 AAW	LABLS	10//99-12//99
	Maryland	S	19.52 MW	19.44 AW	40430 AAW	MDBLS	10//99-12//99
	Massachusetts	S	17.35 MW	17.80 AW	37020 AAW	MABLS	10//99-12//99
	Minnesota	S	20.37 MW	21.13 AW	43950 AAW	MNBLS	10//99-12//99
	Montana	S	9.04 MW	9.50 AW	19770 AAW	MTBLS	10//99-12//99
	New Jersey	S	26.52 MW	24.25 AW	50450 AAW	NJBLS	10//99-12//99
	New Mexico	S	10.43 MW	10.99 AW	22850 AAW	NMBLS	10//99-12//99
	North Carolina	S	10.95 MW	13.22 AW	27500 AAW	NCBLS	10//99-12//99
	Ohio	S	18.3 MW	17.99 AW	37410 AAW	OHBLS	10//99-12//99
	Pennsylvania	S	19.04 MW	19.16 AW	39850 AAW	PABLS	10//99-12//99
	Tennessee	S	13.03 MW	13.69 AW	28470 AAW	TNBLS	10//99-12//99
	Texas	S	14.66 MW	15.09 AW	31400 AAW	TXBLS	10//99-12//99
	Utah	S	7.83 MW	8.47 AW	17620 AAW	UTBLS	10//99-12//99

AAW Average annual wage	**AOH** Average offered, high	**ASH** Average starting, high	**H** Hourly	**M** Monthly	**S** Special: hourly and annual
AE Average entry wage	**AOL** Average offered, low	**ASL** Average starting, low	**HI** Highest wage paid	**MTC** Median total compensation	**TQ** Third quartile wage
AEX Average experienced wage	**APH** Average pay, high range	**AW** Average wage paid	**HR** High end range	**MW** Median wage paid	**W** Weekly
AO Average offered	**APL** Average pay, low range	**FQ** First quartile wage	**LR** Low end range	**SQ** Second quartile wage	**Y** Yearly

Occupation/Type/Industry	Location	Per	Low	Mid	High	Source	Date
Set and Exhibit Designer	Virginia	S	14.91 MW	14.96 AW	31110 AAW	VABLS	10//99-12//99
Sewer, Hand	Alabama	S	9.38 MW	9.02 AW	18760 AAW	ALBLS	10//99-12//99
	Arizona	S	6.3 MW	6.36 AW	13220 AAW	AZBLS	10//99-12//99
	Arkansas	S	8.74 MW	8.48 AW	17640 AAW	ARBLS	10//99-12//99
	California	S	7.51 MW	8.66 AW	18010 AAW	CABLS	10//99-12//99
	Colorado	S	7.82 MW	8.10 AW	16840 AAW	COBLS	10//99-12//99
	Connecticut	S	7.96 MW	8.46 AW	17590 AAW	CTBLS	10//99-12//99
	Florida	S	7.52 MW	7.54 AW	15680 AAW	FLBLS	10//99-12//99
	Georgia	S	8.7 MW	8.87 AW	18450 AAW	GABLS	10//99-12//99
	Illinois	S	9.16 MW	9.43 AW	19610 AAW	ILBLS	10//99-12//99
	Indiana	S	8.41 MW	8.51 AW	17700 AAW	INBLS	10//99-12//99
	Iowa	S	7.65 MW	7.58 AW	15770 AAW	IABLS	10//99-12//99
	Kansas	S	6.59 MW	7.66 AW	15920 AAW	KSBLS	10//99-12//99
	Kentucky	S	8.29 MW	7.95 AW	16530 AAW	KYBLS	10//99-12//99
	Louisiana	S	7.19 MW	7.61 AW	15840 AAW	LABLS	10//99-12//99
	Maine	S	10.14 MW	10.54 AW	21920 AAW	MEBLS	10//99-12//99
	Maryland	S	8.13 MW	8.24 AW	17150 AAW	MDBLS	10//99-12//99
	Massachusetts	S	8.91 MW	9.41 AW	19580 AAW	MABLS	10//99-12//99
	Michigan	S	8.68 MW	8.79 AW	18290 AAW	MIBLS	10//99-12//99
	Mississippi	S	7.49 MW	7.30 AW	15180 AAW	MSBLS	10//99-12//99
	Missouri	S	6.76 MW	7.18 AW	14930 AAW	MOBLS	10//99-12//99
	Nevada	S	8.73 MW	9.12 AW	18970 AAW	NVBLS	10//99-12//99
	New Jersey	S	7.35 MW	8.14 AW	16920 AAW	NJBLS	10//99-12//99
	New Mexico	S	6.32 MW	6.88 AW	14320 AAW	NMBLS	10//99-12//99
	New York	S	10.59 MW	15.34 AW	31900 AAW	NYBLS	10//99-12//99
	North Carolina	S	8.13 MW	8.30 AW	17270 AAW	NCBLS	10//99-12//99
	Ohio	S	8.37 MW	8.72 AW	18130 AAW	OHBLS	10//99-12//99
	Oregon	S	9.85 MW	10.65 AW	22150 AAW	ORBLS	10//99-12//99
	Pennsylvania	S	7.76 MW	7.84 AW	16300 AAW	PABLS	10//99-12//99
	Rhode Island	S	7.9 MW	8.60 AW	17890 AAW	RIBLS	10//99-12//99
	South Carolina	S	7.08 MW	7.63 AW	15860 AAW	SCBLS	10//99-12//99
	Tennessee	S	8.28 MW	8.09 AW	16830 AAW	TNBLS	10//99-12//99
	Texas	S	7.23 MW	7.24 AW	15060 AAW	TXBLS	10//99-12//99
	Utah	S	7.26 MW	7.05 AW	14670 AAW	UTBLS	10//99-12//99
	Vermont	S	6.66 MW	7.28 AW	15150 AAW	VTBLS	10//99-12//99
	Virginia	S	7.78 MW	7.92 AW	16470 AAW	VABLS	10//99-12//99
	Washington	S	9.8 MW	10.84 AW	22540 AAW	WABLS	10//99-12//99
	West Virginia	S	6.17 MW	6.41 AW	13340 AAW	WVBLS	10//99-12//99
	Wisconsin	S	7.75 MW	7.85 AW	16320 AAW	WIBLS	10//99-12//99
	Puerto Rico	S	5.97 MW	5.82 AW	12100 AAW	PRBLS	10//99-12//99
Sewer-pipe Cleaner	United States	Y		26780 AW		MENHEL	1999
Sewing Machine Operator	Alabama	S	7.79 MW	7.97 AW	16580 AAW	ALBLS	10//99-12//99
	Anniston MSA, AL	S	8.37 MW	8.11 AW	17420 AAW	ALBLS	10//99-12//99
	Auburn-Opelika MSA, AL	S	7.66 MW	6.97 AW	15930 AAW	ALBLS	10//99-12//99
	Birmingham MSA, AL	S	8.06 MW	8.03 AW	16760 AAW	ALBLS	10//99-12//99
	Decatur MSA, AL	S	7.19 MW	6.95 AW	14960 AAW	ALBLS	10//99-12//99
	Dothan MSA, AL	S	7.37 MW	7.40 AW	15330 AAW	ALBLS	10//99-12//99
	Florence MSA, AL	S	9.56 MW	9.57 AW	19880 AAW	ALBLS	10//99-12//99
	Huntsville MSA, AL	S	7.25 MW	6.48 AW	15090 AAW	ALBLS	10//99-12//99
	Tuscaloosa MSA, AL	S	7.43 MW	7.09 AW	15460 AAW	ALBLS	10//99-12//99
	Arizona	S	8.07 MW	8.32 AW	17310 AAW	AZBLS	10//99-12//99
	Phoenix-Mesa MSA, AZ	S	8.40 MW	8.18 AW	17480 AAW	AZBLS	10//99-12//99
	Tucson MSA, AZ	S	8.48 MW	8.10 AW	17640 AAW	AZBLS	10//99-12//99
	Yuma MSA, AZ	S	7.52 MW	7.41 AW	15640 AAW	AZBLS	10//99-12//99
	Arkansas	S	7.47 MW	7.55 AW	15700 AAW	ARBLS	10//99-12//99
	Fort Smith MSA, AR-OK	S	8.69 MW	8.61 AW	18080 AAW	ARBLS	10//99-12//99
	Little Rock-North Little Rock MSA, AR	S	8.19 MW	7.84 AW	17040 AAW	ARBLS	10//99-12//99
	California	S	6.7 MW	7.32 AW	15220 AAW	CABLS	10//99-12//99
	Chico-Paradise MSA, CA	S	7.73 MW	7.47 AW	16070 AAW	CABLS	10//99-12//99
	Fresno MSA, CA	S	7.04 MW	6.52 AW	14650 AAW	CABLS	10//99-12//99
	Los Angeles-Long Beach PMSA, CA	S	7.21 MW	6.65 AW	14990 AAW	CABLS	10//99-12//99
	Modesto MSA, CA	S	8.88 MW	8.44 AW	18470 AAW	CABLS	10//99-12//99
	Oakland PMSA, CA	S	7.68 MW	6.68 AW	15980 AAW	CABLS	10//99-12//99
	Orange County PMSA, CA	S	7.37 MW	6.74 AW	15330 AAW	CABLS	10//99-12//99
	Riverside-San Bernardino PMSA, CA	S	8.00 MW	7.22 AW	16640 AAW	CABLS	10//99-12//99
	Sacramento PMSA, CA	S	8.04 MW	7.40 AW	16730 AAW	CABLS	10//99-12//99
	San Diego MSA, CA	S	7.65 MW	7.25 AW	15920 AAW	CABLS	10//99-12//99

AAW	Average annual wage	AOH	Average offered, high	ASH	Average starting, high	H	Hourly	M	Monthly	S	Special: hourly and annual
AE	Average entry wage	AOL	Average offered, low	ASL	Average starting, low	HI	Highest wage paid	MTC	Median total compensation	TQ	Third quartile wage
AEX	Average experienced wage	APH	Average pay, high range	AW	Average wage paid	HR	High end range	MW	Median wage paid	W	Weekly
AO	Average offered	APL	Average pay, low range	FQ	First quartile wage	LR	Low end range	SQ	Second quartile wage	Y	Yearly

Occupation/Type/Industry	Location	Per	Low	Mid	High	Source	Date
Sewing Machine Operator	San Francisco PMSA, CA	S	7.39 MW	6.69 AW	15370 AAW	CABLS	10//99-12//99
	San Jose PMSA, CA	S	9.15 MW	9.04 AW	19030 AAW	CABLS	10//99-12//99
	San Luis Obispo-Atascadero- Paso Robles MSA, CA	S	8.78 MW	8.39 AW	18260 AAW	CABLS	10//99-12//99
	Santa Barbara-Santa Maria- Lompoc MSA, CA	S	8.45 MW	7.91 AW	17580 AAW	CABLS	10//99-12//99
	Santa Cruz-Watsonville PMSA, CA	S	8.32 MW	7.71 AW	17310 AAW	CABLS	10//99-12//99
	Santa Rosa PMSA, CA	S	7.72 MW	7.31 AW	16060 AAW	CABLS	10//99-12//99
	Ventura PMSA, CA	S	7.29 MW	6.62 AW	15170 AAW	CABLS	10//99-12//99
	Colorado	S	7.87 MW	8.14 AW	16920 AAW	COBLS	10//99-12//99
	Boulder-Longmont PMSA, CO	S	7.78 MW	7.72 AW	16190 AAW	COBLS	10//99-12//99
	Colorado Springs MSA, CO	S	8.94 MW	8.71 AW	18600 AAW	COBLS	10//99-12//99
	Denver PMSA, CO	S	8.33 MW	7.96 AW	17330 AAW	COBLS	10//99-12//99
	Fort Collins-Loveland MSA, CO	S	9.19 MW	9.41 AW	19110 AAW	COBLS	10//99-12//99
	Grand Junction MSA, CO	S	7.62 MW	7.49 AW	15840 AAW	COBLS	10//99-12//99
	Connecticut	S	8.48 MW	8.67 AW	18030 AAW	CTBLS	10//99-12//99
	Bridgeport PMSA, CT	S	7.97 MW	7.67 AW	16580 AAW	CTBLS	10//99-12//99
	Hartford MSA, CT	S	8.99 MW	8.55 AW	18700 AAW	CTBLS	10//99-12//99
	New Haven-Meriden PMSA, CT	S	9.28 MW	9.18 AW	19310 AAW	CTBLS	10//99-12//99
	New London-Norwich MSA, CT-RI	S	9.24 MW	9.15 AW	19210 AAW	CTBLS	10//99-12//99
	Stamford-Norwalk PMSA, CT	S	9.29 MW	9.07 AW	19330 AAW	CTBLS	10//99-12//99
	Delaware	S	7.91 MW	8.59 AW	17880 AAW	DEBLS	10//99-12//99
	Dover MSA, DE	S	8.11 MW	7.63 AW	16870 AAW	DEBLS	10//99-12//99
	Wilmington-Newark PMSA, DE-MD	S	9.39 MW	8.52 AW	19530 AAW	DEBLS	10//99-12//99
	District of Columbia	S	11.67 MW	11.82 AW	24590 AAW	DCBLS	10//99-12//99
	Washington PMSA, DC-MD- VA-WV	S	9.09 MW	8.78 AW	18910 AAW	DCBLS	10//99-12//99
	Florida	S	7.21 MW	7.56 AW	15720 AAW	FLBLS	10//99-12//99
	Daytona Beach MSA, FL	S	7.92 MW	7.61 AW	16470 AAW	FLBLS	10//99-12//99
	Fort Lauderdale PMSA, FL	S	8.92 MW	8.45 AW	18560 AAW	FLBLS	10//99-12//99
	Fort Myers-Cape Coral MSA, FL	S	7.87 MW	7.73 AW	16370 AAW	FLBLS	10//99-12//99
	Fort Pierce-Port St. Lucie MSA, FL	S	7.90 MW	6.94 AW	16440 AAW	FLBLS	10//99-12//99
	Jacksonville MSA, FL	S	8.62 MW	8.25 AW	17940 AAW	FLBLS	10//99-12//99
	Lakeland-Winter Haven MSA, FL	S	8.04 MW	7.74 AW	16720 AAW	FLBLS	10//99-12//99
	Melbourne-Titusville-Palm Bay MSA, FL	S	8.09 MW	7.96 AW	16830 AAW	FLBLS	10//99-12//99
	Miami PMSA, FL	S	6.83 MW	6.43 AW	14200 AAW	FLBLS	10//99-12//99
	Naples MSA, FL	S	8.56 MW	8.41 AW	17800 AAW	FLBLS	10//99-12//99
	Ocala MSA, FL	S	7.63 MW	7.52 AW	15880 AAW	FLBLS	10//99-12//99
	Orlando MSA, FL	S	7.87 MW	7.76 AW	16370 AAW	FLBLS	10//99-12//99
	Pensacola MSA, FL	S	7.15 MW	6.65 AW	14880 AAW	FLBLS	10//99-12//99
	Sarasota-Bradenton MSA, FL	S	9.20 MW	8.82 AW	19140 AAW	FLBLS	10//99-12//99
	Tallahassee MSA, FL	S	10.06 MW	9.99 AW	20930 AAW	FLBLS	10//99-12//99
	Tampa-St. Petersburg- Clearwater MSA, FL	S	7.29 MW	7.14 AW	15170 AAW	FLBLS	10//99-12//99
	West Palm Beach-Boca Raton MSA, FL	S	8.21 MW	7.90 AW	17080 AAW	FLBLS	10//99-12//99
	Georgia	S	7.86 MW	7.99 AW	16620 AAW	GABLS	10//99-12//99
	Atlanta MSA, GA	S	8.11 MW	7.92 AW	16860 AAW	GABLS	10//99-12//99
	Augusta-Aiken MSA, GA-SC	S	7.50 MW	7.45 AW	15600 AAW	GABLS	10//99-12//99
	Columbus MSA, GA-AL	S	8.67 MW	9.28 AW	18040 AAW	GABLS	10//99-12//99
	Hawaii	S	6.49 MW	7.39 AW	15370 AAW	HIBLS	10//99-12//99
	Honolulu MSA, HI	S	7.27 MW	6.44 AW	15110 AAW	HIBLS	10//99-12//99
	Idaho	S	7.88 MW	7.92 AW	16480 AAW	IDBLS	10//99-12//99
	Boise City MSA, ID	S	8.45 MW	8.88 AW	17570 AAW	IDBLS	10//99-12//99
	Illinois	S	8.02 MW	8.28 AW	17220 AAW	ILBLS	10//99-12//99
	Chicago PMSA, IL	S	8.36 MW	8.12 AW	17390 AAW	ILBLS	10//99-12//99
	Rockford MSA, IL	S	7.66 MW	7.64 AW	15940 AAW	ILBLS	10//99-12//99
	Indiana	S	8.46 MW	8.60 AW	17890 AAW	INBLS	10//99-12//99
	Elkhart-Goshen MSA, IN	S	9.09 MW	9.23 AW	18910 AAW	INBLS	10//99-12//99
	Fort Wayne MSA, IN	S	8.78 MW	8.53 AW	18270 AAW	INBLS	10//99-12//99
	Gary PMSA, IN	S	8.06 MW	8.23 AW	16760 AAW	INBLS	10//99-12//99
	Indianapolis MSA, IN	S	9.05 MW	8.41 AW	18830 AAW	INBLS	10//99-12//99
	South Bend MSA, IN	S	7.73 MW	7.73 AW	16080 AAW	INBLS	10//99-12//99

AAW Average annual wage	**AOH** Average offered, high	**ASH** Average starting, high	**H** Hourly	**M** Monthly	**S** Special: hourly and annual
AE Average entry wage	**AOL** Average offered, low	**ASL** Average starting, low	**HI** Highest wage paid	**MTC** Median total compensation	**TQ** Third quartile wage
AEX Average experienced wage	**APH** Average pay, high range	**AW** Average wage paid	**HR** High end range	**MW** Median wage paid	**W** Weekly
AO Average offered	**APL** Average pay, low range	**FQ** First quartile wage	**LR** Low end range	**SQ** Second quartile wage	**Y** Yearly

Occupation/Type/Industry	Location	Per	Low	Mid	High	Source	Date
Sewing Machine Operator	Terre Haute MSA, IN	S	8.69 MW	9.24 AW	18080 AAW	INBLS	10//99-12//99
	Iowa	S	7.97 MW	8.18 AW	17010 AAW	IABLS	10//99-12//99
	Cedar Rapids MSA, IA	S	8.32 MW	8.13 AW	17300 AAW	IABLS	10//99-12//99
	Davenport-Moline-Rock Island MSA, IA-IL	S	8.28 MW	8.08 AW	17220 AAW	IABLS	10//99-12//99
	Des Moines MSA, IA	S	7.71 MW	7.74 AW	16040 AAW	IABLS	10//99-12//99
	Waterloo-Cedar Falls MSA, IA	S	6.42 MW	6.17 AW	13340 AAW	IABLS	10//99-12//99
	Kansas	S	7.8 MW	8.15 AW	16950 AAW	KSBLS	10//99-12//99
	Topeka MSA, KS	S	9.41 MW	9.18 AW	19570 AAW	KSBLS	10//99-12//99
	Wichita MSA, KS	S	7.72 MW	7.41 AW	16050 AAW	KSBLS	10//99-12//99
	Kentucky	S	8.41 MW	8.40 AW	17470 AAW	KYBLS	10//99-12//99
	Lexington MSA, KY	S	9.27 MW	9.27 AW	19280 AAW	KYBLS	10//99-12//99
	Louisville MSA, KY-IN	S	8.52 MW	8.78 AW	17720 AAW	KYBLS	10//99-12//99
	Owensboro MSA, KY	S	8.41 MW	8.39 AW	17500 AAW	KYBLS	10//99-12//99
	Louisiana	S	6.12 MW	6.92 AW	14390 AAW	LABLS	10//99-12//99
	Alexandria MSA, LA	S	6.47 MW	6.04 AW	13470 AAW	LABLS	10//99-12//99
	Baton Rouge MSA, LA	S	7.87 MW	7.63 AW	16370 AAW	LABLS	10//99-12//99
	Lafayette MSA, LA	S	7.52 MW	6.31 AW	15640 AAW	LABLS	10//99-12//99
	New Orleans MSA, LA	S	7.22 MW	6.66 AW	15020 AAW	LABLS	10//99-12//99
	Shreveport-Bossier City MSA, LA	S	9.08 MW	8.40 AW	18890 AAW	LABLS	10//99-12//99
	Maine	S	7.57 MW	7.75 AW	16120 AAW	MEBLS	10//99-12//99
	Bangor MSA, ME	S	8.70 MW	7.61 AW	18090 AAW	MEBLS	10//99-12//99
	Lewiston-Auburn MSA, ME	S	8.30 MW	8.10 AW	17260 AAW	MEBLS	10//99-12//99
	Portland MSA, ME	S	7.59 MW	7.47 AW	15790 AAW	MEBLS	10//99-12//99
	Maryland	S	8.35 MW	8.60 AW	17900 AAW	MDBLS	10//99-12//99
	Baltimore PMSA, MD	S	8.62 MW	8.50 AW	17920 AAW	MDBLS	10//99-12//99
	Hagerstown PMSA, MD	S	8.83 MW	7.87 AW	18370 AAW	MDBLS	10//99-12//99
	Massachusetts	S	9.19 MW	9.67 AW	20110 AAW	MABLS	10//99-12//99
	Boston PMSA, MA-NH	S	10.31 MW	9.44 AW	21450 AAW	MABLS	10//99-12//99
	Brockton PMSA, MA	S	9.25 MW	8.37 AW	19250 AAW	MABLS	10//99-12//99
	Lowell PMSA, MA-NH	S	8.85 MW	8.27 AW	18410 AAW	MABLS	10//99-12//99
	New Bedford PMSA, MA	S	8.91 MW	8.99 AW	18530 AAW	MABLS	10//99-12//99
	Springfield MSA, MA	S	8.11 MW	7.92 AW	16860 AAW	MABLS	10//99-12//99
	Worcester PMSA, MA-CT	S	9.47 MW	8.68 AW	19690 AAW	MABLS	10//99-12//99
	Michigan	S	10.24 MW	12.60 AW	26210 AAW	MIBLS	10//99-12//99
	Ann Arbor PMSA, MI	S	9.83 MW	10.18 AW	20440 AAW	MIBLS	10//99-12//99
	Detroit PMSA, MI	S	14.78 MW	10.54 AW	30740 AAW	MIBLS	10//99-12//99
	Grand Rapids-Muskegon-Holland MSA, MI	S	12.51 MW	10.92 AW	26030 AAW	MIBLS	10//99-12//99
	Lansing-East Lansing MSA, MI	S	10.47 MW	8.07 AW	21780 AAW	MIBLS	10//99-12//99
	Saginaw-Bay City-Midland MSA, MI	S	7.89 MW	7.32 AW	16400 AAW	MIBLS	10//99-12//99
	Minnesota	S	8.77 MW	9.11 AW	18950 AAW	MNBLS	10//99-12//99
	Duluth-Superior MSA, MN-WI	S	7.80 MW	7.71 AW	16220 AAW	MNBLS	10//99-12//99
	Minneapolis-St. Paul MSA, MN-WI	S	9.88 MW	9.59 AW	20550 AAW	MNBLS	10//99-12//99
	Mississippi	S	8.1 MW	8.36 AW	17390 AAW	MSBLS	10//99-12//99
	Jackson MSA, MS	S	8.60 MW	7.96 AW	17890 AAW	MSBLS	10//99-12//99
	Missouri	S	7.46 MW	7.70 AW	16010 AAW	MOBLS	10//99-12//99
	Joplin MSA, MO	S	9.75 MW	9.68 AW	20280 AAW	MOBLS	10//99-12//99
	Kansas City MSA, MO-KS	S	8.14 MW	7.92 AW	16930 AAW	MOBLS	10//99-12//99
	St. Louis MSA, MO-IL	S	7.33 MW	6.86 AW	15250 AAW	MOBLS	10//99-12//99
	Springfield MSA, MO	S	6.95 MW	6.13 AW	14450 AAW	MOBLS	10//99-12//99
	Montana	S	7.31 MW	7.62 AW	15860 AAW	MTBLS	10//99-12//99
	Nebraska	S	7.96 MW	8.14 AW	16930 AAW	NEBLS	10//99-12//99
	Lincoln MSA, NE	S	8.37 MW	8.10 AW	17400 AAW	NEBLS	10//99-12//99
	Omaha MSA, NE-IA	S	8.22 MW	8.06 AW	17100 AAW	NEBLS	10//99-12//99
	Nevada	S	8.61 MW	8.53 AW	17750 AAW	NVBLS	10//99-12//99
	Las Vegas MSA, NV-AZ	S	8.58 MW	8.77 AW	17840 AAW	NVBLS	10//99-12//99
	Reno MSA, NV	S	8.11 MW	8.08 AW	16860 AAW	NVBLS	10//99-12//99
	New Hampshire	S	8.41 MW	8.74 AW	18180 AAW	NHBLS	10//99-12//99
	Manchester PMSA, NH	S	9.40 MW	9.27 AW	19550 AAW	NHBLS	10//99-12//99
	Nashua PMSA, NH	S	9.34 MW	8.74 AW	19420 AAW	NHBLS	10//99-12//99
	Portsmouth-Rochester PMSA, NH-ME	S	10.05 MW	9.99 AW	20900 AAW	NHBLS	10//99-12//99
	New Jersey	S	7.68 MW	8.03 AW	16710 AAW	NJBLS	10//99-12//99
	Atlantic-Cape May PMSA, NJ	S	8.97 MW	8.23 AW	18660 AAW	NJBLS	10//99-12//99
	Bergen-Passaic PMSA, NJ	S	8.00 MW	7.57 AW	16650 AAW	NJBLS	10//99-12//99
	Jersey City PMSA, NJ	S	7.49 MW	7.26 AW	15570 AAW	NJBLS	10//99-12//99
	Middlesex-Somerset-Hunterdon PMSA, NJ	S	7.82 MW	7.35 AW	16270 AAW	NJBLS	10//99-12//99

AAW Average annual wage	AOH Average offered, high	ASH Average starting, high	H Hourly	M Monthly	S Special: hourly and annual
AE Average entry wage	AOL Average offered, low	ASL Average starting, low	HI Highest wage paid	MTC Median total compensation	TQ Third quartile wage
AEX Average experienced wage	APH Average pay, high range	AW Average wage paid	HR High end range	MW Median wage paid	W Weekly
AO Average offered	APL Average pay, low range	FQ First quartile wage	LR Low end range	SQ Second quartile wage	Y Yearly

Occupation/Type/Industry	Location	Per	Low	Mid	High	Source	Date
Sewing Machine Operator	Monmouth-Ocean PMSA, NJ	S	9.31 MW	9.40 AW	19370 AAW	NJBLS	10//99-12//99
	Newark PMSA, NJ	S	8.29 MW	7.96 AW	17240 AAW	NJBLS	10//99-12//99
	Trenton PMSA, NJ	S	8.93 MW	8.42 AW	18580 AAW	NJBLS	10//99-12//99
	Vineland-Millville-Bridgeton PMSA, NJ	S	8.40 MW	8.22 AW	17470 AAW	NJBLS	10//99-12//99
	New Mexico	S	7.9 MW	8.04 AW	16710 AAW	NMBLS	10//99-12//99
	Albuquerque MSA, NM	S	7.60 MW	7.74 AW	15800 AAW	NMBLS	10//99-12//99
	New York	S	7.13 MW	8.25 AW	17160 AAW	NYBLS	10//99-12//99
	Albany-Schenectady-Troy MSA, NY	S	9.08 MW	8.32 AW	18900 AAW	NYBLS	10//99-12//99
	Binghamton MSA, NY	S	8.37 MW	7.97 AW	17400 AAW	NYBLS	10//99-12//99
	Buffalo-Niagara Falls MSA, NY	S	9.89 MW	9.63 AW	20570 AAW	NYBLS	10//99-12//99
	Dutchess County PMSA, NY	S	9.18 MW	9.29 AW	19090 AAW	NYBLS	10//99-12//99
	Jamestown MSA, NY	S	7.76 MW	7.04 AW	16150 AAW	NYBLS	10//99-12//99
	Nassau-Suffolk PMSA, NY	S	9.38 MW	8.43 AW	19520 AAW	NYBLS	10//99-12//99
	New York PMSA, NY	S	8.13 MW	6.88 AW	16910 AAW	NYBLS	10//99-12//99
	Newburgh PMSA, NY-PA	S	8.68 MW	8.12 AW	18060 AAW	NYBLS	10//99-12//99
	Rochester MSA, NY	S	8.47 MW	8.01 AW	17620 AAW	NYBLS	10//99-12//99
	Syracuse MSA, NY	S	8.69 MW	9.11 AW	18070 AAW	NYBLS	10//99-12//99
	Utica-Rome MSA, NY	S	7.26 MW	7.09 AW	15110 AAW	NYBLS	10//99-12//99
	North Carolina	S	8.26 MW	8.65 AW	17990 AAW	NCBLS	10//99-12//99
	Asheville MSA, NC	S	7.81 MW	7.73 AW	16240 AAW	NCBLS	10//99-12//99
	Charlotte-Gastonia-Rock Hill MSA, NC-SC	S	8.91 MW	9.05 AW	18540 AAW	NCBLS	10//99-12//99
	Goldsboro MSA, NC	S	8.12 MW	8.09 AW	16890 AAW	NCBLS	10//99-12//99
	Greensboro--Winston-Salem--High Point MSA, NC	S	9.07 MW	8.59 AW	18860 AAW	NCBLS	10//99-12//99
	Greenville MSA, NC	S	7.32 MW	7.11 AW	15230 AAW	NCBLS	10//99-12//99
	Hickory-Morganton-Lenoir MSA, NC	S	10.93 MW	10.23 AW	22740 AAW	NCBLS	10//99-12//99
	Raleigh-Durham-Chapel Hill MSA, NC	S	7.89 MW	7.71 AW	16400 AAW	NCBLS	10//99-12//99
	Rocky Mount MSA, NC	S	7.62 MW	7.47 AW	15840 AAW	NCBLS	10//99-12//99
	Wilmington MSA, NC	S	6.78 MW	6.63 AW	14100 AAW	NCBLS	10//99-12//99
	Fargo-Moorhead MSA, ND-MN	S	8.38 MW	8.43 AW	17440 AAW	NDBLS	10//99-12//99
	Ohio	S	8.58 MW	8.94 AW	18590 AAW	OHBLS	10//99-12//99
	Akron PMSA, OH	S	8.80 MW	9.17 AW	18300 AAW	OHBLS	10//99-12//99
	Canton-Massillon MSA, OH	S	8.12 MW	8.21 AW	16880 AAW	OHBLS	10//99-12//99
	Cincinnati PMSA, OH-KY-IN	S	9.34 MW	8.80 AW	19420 AAW	OHBLS	10//99-12//99
	Cleveland-Lorain-Elyria PMSA, OH	S	8.11 MW	7.90 AW	16860 AAW	OHBLS	10//99-12//99
	Columbus MSA, OH	S	10.11 MW	9.22 AW	21030 AAW	OHBLS	10//99-12//99
	Dayton-Springfield MSA, OH	S	9.10 MW	8.55 AW	18930 AAW	OHBLS	10//99-12//99
	Hamilton-Middletown PMSA, OH	S	9.96 MW	10.51 AW	20710 AAW	OHBLS	10//99-12//99
	Mansfield MSA, OH	S	8.24 MW	8.27 AW	17140 AAW	OHBLS	10//99-12//99
	Toledo MSA, OH	S	9.70 MW	9.43 AW	20180 AAW	OHBLS	10//99-12//99
	Youngstown-Warren MSA, OH	S	8.16 MW	7.94 AW	16980 AAW	OHBLS	10//99-12//99
	Oklahoma	S	7.23 MW	7.43 AW	15460 AAW	OKBLS	10//99-12//99
	Lawton MSA, OK	S	7.28 MW	7.29 AW	15140 AAW	OKBLS	10//99-12//99
	Oklahoma City MSA, OK	S	7.48 MW	7.25 AW	15550 AAW	OKBLS	10//99-12//99
	Tulsa MSA, OK	S	8.12 MW	7.75 AW	16880 AAW	OKBLS	10//99-12//99
	Oregon	S	8.08 MW	8.52 AW	17710 AAW	ORBLS	10//99-12//99
	Eugene-Springfield MSA, OR	S	8.01 MW	7.89 AW	16670 AAW	ORBLS	10//99-12//99
	Medford-Ashland MSA, OR	S	8.38 MW	8.31 AW	17440 AAW	ORBLS	10//99-12//99
	Portland-Vancouver PMSA, OR-WA	S	8.60 MW	8.07 AW	17890 AAW	ORBLS	10//99-12//99
	Salem PMSA, OR	S	8.18 MW	7.93 AW	17010 AAW	ORBLS	10//99-12//99
	Pennsylvania	S	7.71 MW	7.98 AW	16610 AAW	PABLS	10//99-12//99
	Allentown-Bethlehem-Easton MSA, PA	S	8.02 MW	7.87 AW	16680 AAW	PABLS	10//99-12//99
	Altoona MSA, PA	S	8.17 MW	7.82 AW	16990 AAW	PABLS	10//99-12//99
	Erie MSA, PA	S	10.58 MW	10.10 AW	22010 AAW	PABLS	10//99-12//99
	Harrisburg-Lebanon-Carlisle MSA, PA	S	7.70 MW	7.55 AW	16020 AAW	PABLS	10//99-12//99
	Johnstown MSA, PA	S	7.87 MW	7.74 AW	16360 AAW	PABLS	10//99-12//99
	Lancaster MSA, PA	S	8.11 MW	7.64 AW	16870 AAW	PABLS	10//99-12//99
	Philadelphia PMSA, PA-NJ	S	8.27 MW	7.86 AW	17200 AAW	PABLS	10//99-12//99
	Pittsburgh MSA, PA	S	8.01 MW	7.63 AW	16670 AAW	PABLS	10//99-12//99
	Reading MSA, PA	S	8.16 MW	7.85 AW	16970 AAW	PABLS	10//99-12//99

AAW Average annual wage	**AOH** Average offered, high	**ASH** Average starting, high	**H** Hourly	**M** Monthly	**S** Special: hourly and annual
AE Average entry wage	**AOL** Average offered, low	**ASL** Average starting, low	**HI** Highest wage paid	**MTC** Median total compensation	**TQ** Third quartile wage
AEX Average experienced wage	**APH** Average pay, high range	**AW** Average wage paid	**HR** High end range	**MW** Median wage paid	**W** Weekly
AO Average offered	**APL** Average pay, low range	**FQ** First quartile wage	**LR** Low end range	**SQ** Second quartile wage	**Y** Yearly

Occupation/Type/Industry	Location	Per	Low	Mid	High	Source	Date
Sewing Machine Operator	Scranton--Wilkes-Barre--Hazleton MSA, PA	S	7.89 MW	7.19 AW	16400 AAW	PABLS	10//99-12//99
	State College MSA, PA	S	7.98 MW	7.66 AW	16590 AAW	PABLS	10//99-12//99
	Williamsport MSA, PA	S	7.28 MW	7.33 AW	15140 AAW	PABLS	10//99-12//99
	York MSA, PA	S	8.20 MW	8.04 AW	17050 AAW	PABLS	10//99-12//99
	Rhode Island	S	7.96 MW	8.32 AW	17300 AAW	RIBLS	10//99-12//99
	Providence-Fall River-Warwick MSA, RI-MA	S	9.26 MW	9.01 AW	19250 AAW	RIBLS	10//99-12//99
	South Carolina	S	7.38 MW	7.60 AW	15800 AAW	SCBLS	10//99-12//99
	Charleston-North Charleston MSA, SC	S	6.99 MW	6.65 AW	14530 AAW	SCBLS	10//99-12//99
	Columbia MSA, SC	S	7.17 MW	6.91 AW	14900 AAW	SCBLS	10//99-12//99
	Florence MSA, SC	S	6.93 MW	6.91 AW	14410 AAW	SCBLS	10//99-12//99
	Greenville-Spartanburg-Anderson MSA, SC	S	7.58 MW	7.09 AW	15780 AAW	SCBLS	10//99-12//99
	Myrtle Beach MSA, SC	S	6.99 MW	6.81 AW	14540 AAW	SCBLS	10//99-12//99
	Sumter MSA, SC	S	6.92 MW	6.58 AW	14390 AAW	SCBLS	10//99-12//99
	South Dakota	S	7.85 MW	7.89 AW	16410 AAW	SDBLS	10//99-12//99
	Tennessee	S	7.89 MW	8.05 AW	16740 AAW	TNBLS	10//99-12//99
	Chattanooga MSA, TN-GA	S	7.61 MW	7.53 AW	15830 AAW	TNBLS	10//99-12//99
	Johnson City-Kingsport-Bristol MSA, TN-VA	S	7.41 MW	7.39 AW	15410 AAW	TNBLS	10//99-12//99
	Knoxville MSA, TN	S	7.80 MW	7.84 AW	16220 AAW	TNBLS	10//99-12//99
	Memphis MSA, TN-AR-MS	S	8.45 MW	8.28 AW	17580 AAW	MSBLS	10//99-12//99
	Nashville MSA, TN	S	8.88 MW	9.12 AW	18470 AAW	TNBLS	10//99-12//99
	Texas	S	7.52 MW	7.69 AW	15990 AAW	TXBLS	10//99-12//99
	Amarillo MSA, TX	S	6.72 MW	6.54 AW	13970 AAW	TXBLS	10//99-12//99
	Austin-San Marcos MSA, TX	S	7.90 MW	7.71 AW	16440 AAW	TXBLS	10//99-12//99
	Beaumont-Port Arthur MSA, TX	S	6.61 MW	6.48 AW	13740 AAW	TXBLS	10//99-12//99
	Brownsville-Harlingen-San Benito MSA, TX	S	8.48 MW	9.21 AW	17640 AAW	TXBLS	10//99-12//99
	Dallas PMSA, TX	S	7.84 MW	7.72 AW	16310 AAW	TXBLS	10//99-12//99
	El Paso MSA, TX	S	7.63 MW	7.53 AW	15880 AAW	TXBLS	10//99-12//99
	Fort Worth-Arlington PMSA, TX	S	7.43 MW	7.29 AW	15450 AAW	TXBLS	10//99-12//99
	Houston PMSA, TX	S	8.03 MW	7.73 AW	16700 AAW	TXBLS	10//99-12//99
	Killeen-Temple MSA, TX	S	7.76 MW	7.64 AW	16130 AAW	TXBLS	10//99-12//99
	Laredo MSA, TX	S	6.27 MW	6.30 AW	13030 AAW	TXBLS	10//99-12//99
	Longview-Marshall MSA, TX	S	7.38 MW	6.95 AW	15340 AAW	TXBLS	10//99-12//99
	Lubbock MSA, TX	S	8.56 MW	7.76 AW	17800 AAW	TXBLS	10//99-12//99
	McAllen-Edinburg-Mission MSA, TX	S	7.68 MW	7.71 AW	15970 AAW	TXBLS	10//99-12//99
	Odessa-Midland MSA, TX	S	7.31 MW	6.90 AW	15200 AAW	TXBLS	10//99-12//99
	San Angelo MSA, TX	S	6.53 MW	6.21 AW	13580 AAW	TXBLS	10//99-12//99
	San Antonio MSA, TX	S	8.52 MW	7.78 AW	17730 AAW	TXBLS	10//99-12//99
	Sherman-Denison MSA, TX	S	6.83 MW	6.70 AW	14210 AAW	TXBLS	10//99-12//99
	Tyler MSA, TX	S	8.73 MW	9.40 AW	18150 AAW	TXBLS	10//99-12//99
	Waco MSA, TX	S	6.83 MW	6.19 AW	14210 AAW	TXBLS	10//99-12//99
	Utah	S	7.94 MW	8.23 AW	17120 AAW	UTBLS	10//99-12//99
	Provo-Orem MSA, UT	S	6.90 MW	6.53 AW	14360 AAW	UTBLS	10//99-12//99
	Salt Lake City-Ogden MSA, UT	S	8.55 MW	8.05 AW	17780 AAW	UTBLS	10//99-12//99
	Vermont	S	8.08 MW	8.49 AW	17670 AAW	VTBLS	10//99-12//99
	Burlington MSA, VT	S	8.27 MW	8.15 AW	17200 AAW	VTBLS	10//99-12//99
	Virginia	S	7.39 MW	7.58 AW	15760 AAW	VABLS	10//99-12//99
	Norfolk-Virginia Beach-Newport News MSA, VA-NC	S	7.97 MW	7.46 AW	16590 AAW	VABLS	10//99-12//99
	Richmond-Petersburg MSA, VA	S	7.80 MW	7.56 AW	16220 AAW	VABLS	10//99-12//99
	Roanoke MSA, VA	S	6.94 MW	6.57 AW	14430 AAW	VABLS	10//99-12//99
	Washington	S	7.97 MW	8.40 AW	17470 AAW	WABLS	10//99-12//99
	Seattle-Bellevue-Everett PMSA, WA	S	8.36 MW	8.02 AW	17390 AAW	WABLS	10//99-12//99
	Spokane MSA, WA	S	7.35 MW	6.68 AW	15280 AAW	WABLS	10//99-12//99
	Tacoma PMSA, WA	S	8.42 MW	8.00 AW	17520 AAW	WABLS	10//99-12//99
	Yakima MSA, WA	S	9.97 MW	9.91 AW	20740 AAW	WABLS	10//99-12//99
	West Virginia	S	7.13 MW	7.82 AW	16260 AAW	WVBLS	10//99-12//99
	Parkersburg-Marietta MSA, WV-OH	S	11.74 MW	12.19 AW	24420 AAW	WVBLS	10//99-12//99
	Wisconsin	S	8.43 MW	8.81 AW	18320 AAW	WIBLS	10//99-12//99

AAW Average annual wage	**AOH** Average offered, high	**ASH** Average starting, high	**H** Hourly	**M** Monthly	**S** Special: hourly and annual
AE Average entry wage	**AOL** Average offered, low	**ASL** Average starting, low	**HI** Highest wage paid	**MTC** Median total compensation	**TQ** Third quartile wage
AEX Average experienced wage	**APH** Average pay, high range	**AW** Average wage paid	**HR** High end range	**MW** Median wage paid	**W** Weekly
AO Average offered	**APL** Average pay, low range	**FQ** First quartile wage	**LR** Low end range	**SQ** Second quartile wage	**Y** Yearly

Occupation/Type/Industry	Location	Per	Low	Mid	High	Source	Date
Sewing Machine Operator	Appleton-Oshkosh-Neenah MSA, WI	S	8.45 MW	7.96 AW	17580 AAW	WIBLS	10//99-12//99
	Green Bay MSA, WI	S	8.44 MW	8.20 AW	17550 AAW	WIBLS	10//99-12//99
	Kenosha PMSA, WI	S	8.35 MW	8.34 AW	17360 AAW	WIBLS	10//99-12//99
	Madison MSA, WI	S	10.24 MW	10.49 AW	21300 AAW	WIBLS	10//99-12//99
	Milwaukee-Waukesha PMSA, WI	S	9.23 MW	9.10 AW	19190 AAW	WIBLS	10//99-12//99
	Racine PMSA, WI	S	8.93 MW	8.16 AW	18570 AAW	WIBLS	10//99-12//99
	Wausau MSA, WI	S	8.60 MW	8.06 AW	17890 AAW	WIBLS	10//99-12//99
	Wyoming	S	7.27 MW	7.31 AW	15200 AAW	WYBLS	10//99-12//99
	Puerto Rico	S	5.98 MW	5.79 AW	12040 AAW	PRBLS	10//99-12//99
	Aguadilla MSA, PR	S	5.74 MW	5.92 AW	11930 AAW	PRBLS	10//99-12//99
	Caguas PMSA, PR	S	5.78 MW	5.94 AW	12020 AAW	PRBLS	10//99-12//99
	Mayaguez MSA, PR	S	5.78 MW	5.98 AW	12020 AAW	PRBLS	10//99-12//99
	Ponce MSA, PR	S	6.00 MW	6.10 AW	12480 AAW	PRBLS	10//99-12//99
	San Juan-Bayamon PMSA, PR	S	5.76 MW	5.92 AW	11970 AAW	PRBLS	10//99-12//99
	Virgin Islands	S	8.59 MW	8.39 AW	17450 AAW	VIBLS	10//99-12//99
Shampooer	Alabama	S	5.95 MW	6.22 AW	12930 AAW	ALBLS	10//99-12//99
	Arizona	S	6.66 MW	6.96 AW	14480 AAW	AZBLS	10//99-12//99
	California	S	6.39 MW	6.56 AW	13650 AAW	CABLS	10//99-12//99
	Connecticut	S	7.46 MW	7.67 AW	15940 AAW	CTBLS	10//99-12//99
	Delaware	S	6.27 MW	6.61 AW	13750 AAW	DEBLS	10//99-12//99
	District of Columbia	S	8.78 MW	9.09 AW	18910 AAW	DCBLS	10//99-12//99
	Florida	S	6.16 MW	6.62 AW	13770 AAW	FLBLS	10//99-12//99
	Georgia	S	6.04 MW	6.43 AW	13370 AAW	GABLS	10//99-12//99
	Illinois	S	6.04 MW	6.25 AW	12990 AAW	ILBLS	10//99-12//99
	Kansas	S	6.15 MW	6.32 AW	13150 AAW	KSBLS	10//99-12//99
	Kentucky	S	7.24 MW	7.74 AW	16110 AAW	KYBLS	10//99-12//99
	Louisiana	S	6.05 MW	6.41 AW	13330 AAW	LABLS	10//99-12//99
	Maryland	S	6.11 MW	6.38 AW	13260 AAW	MDBLS	10//99-12//99
	Massachusetts	S	7.51 MW	7.79 AW	16200 AAW	MABLS	10//99-12//99
	Michigan	S	6.24 MW	7.26 AW	15110 AAW	MIBLS	10//99-12//99
	Missouri	S	6.51 MW	6.62 AW	13780 AAW	MOBLS	10//99-12//99
	New Jersey	S	6 MW	6.25 AW	13000 AAW	NJBLS	10//99-12//99
	New York	S	6.62 MW	6.77 AW	14090 AAW	NYBLS	10//99-12//99
	North Carolina	S	6.37 MW	6.56 AW	13650 AAW	NCBLS	10//99-12//99
	Ohio	S	5.93 MW	5.96 AW	12400 AAW	OHBLS	10//99-12//99
	Pennsylvania	S	6.11 MW	6.53 AW	13590 AAW	PABLS	10//99-12//99
	Tennessee	S	7.64 MW	7.56 AW	15730 AAW	TNBLS	10//99-12//99
	Texas	S	6.97 MW	7.14 AW	14850 AAW	TXBLS	10//99-12//99
	Virginia	S	6.5 MW	7.20 AW	14990 AAW	VABLS	10//99-12//99
	Wisconsin	S	9.92 MW	9.79 AW	20370 AAW	WIBLS	10//99-12//99
	Puerto Rico	S	5.88 MW	5.86 AW	12180 AAW	PRBLS	10//99-12//99
Sheet Metal Worker	Alabama	S	11.65 MW	11.93 AW	24810 AAW	ALBLS	10//99-12//99
	Anniston MSA, AL	S	11.91 MW	10.89 AW	24770 AAW	ALBLS	10//99-12//99
	Auburn-Opelika MSA, AL	S	11.75 MW	11.86 AW	24450 AAW	ALBLS	10//99-12//99
	Birmingham MSA, AL	S	12.30 MW	12.45 AW	25590 AAW	ALBLS	10//99-12//99
	Decatur MSA, AL	S	11.54 MW	11.09 AW	23990 AAW	ALBLS	10//99-12//99
	Dothan MSA, AL	S	11.09 MW	10.98 AW	23070 AAW	ALBLS	10//99-12//99
	Florence MSA, AL	S	14.42 MW	13.51 AW	29990 AAW	ALBLS	10//99-12//99
	Gadsden MSA, AL	S	13.06 MW	11.91 AW	27170 AAW	ALBLS	10//99-12//99
	Huntsville MSA, AL	S	10.43 MW	9.54 AW	21700 AAW	ALBLS	10//99-12//99
	Mobile MSA, AL	S	12.26 MW	11.95 AW	25490 AAW	ALBLS	10//99-12//99
	Montgomery MSA, AL	S	11.31 MW	11.67 AW	23530 AAW	ALBLS	10//99-12//99
	Tuscaloosa MSA, AL	S	11.07 MW	10.83 AW	23030 AAW	ALBLS	10//99-12//99
	Alaska	S	22.8 MW	22.59 AW	46990 AAW	AKBLS	10//99-12//99
	Anchorage MSA, AK	S	20.21 MW	19.76 AW	42030 AAW	AKBLS	10//99-12//99
	Arizona	S	11.34 MW	13.33 AW	27730 AAW	AZBLS	10//99-12//99
	Phoenix-Mesa MSA, AZ	S	13.54 MW	11.48 AW	28170 AAW	AZBLS	10//99-12//99
	Tucson MSA, AZ	S	13.05 MW	11.27 AW	27150 AAW	AZBLS	10//99-12//99
	Arkansas	S	11.48 MW	11.79 AW	24510 AAW	ARBLS	10//99-12//99
	Fayetteville-Springdale-Rogers MSA, AR	S	11.15 MW	10.99 AW	23200 AAW	ARBLS	10//99-12//99
	Fort Smith MSA, AR-OK	S	11.19 MW	10.88 AW	23280 AAW	ARBLS	10//99-12//99
	Little Rock-North Little Rock MSA, AR	S	12.23 MW	12.46 AW	25440 AAW	ARBLS	10//99-12//99
	California	S	14.32 MW	16.98 AW	35310 AAW	CABLS	10//99-12//99
	Bakersfield MSA, CA	S	14.18 MW	14.14 AW	29490 AAW	CABLS	10//99-12//99
	Fresno MSA, CA	S	14.86 MW	12.58 AW	30900 AAW	CABLS	10//99-12//99
	Los Angeles-Long Beach PMSA, CA	S	14.12 MW	11.67 AW	29370 AAW	CABLS	10//99-12//99

Sheet Metal Worker

Occupation/Type/Industry	Location	Per	Low	Mid	High	Source	Date
Sheet Metal Worker	Modesto MSA, CA	S	15.12 MW	12.50 AW	31450 AAW	CABLS	10//99-12//99
	Oakland PMSA, CA	S	18.98 MW	16.77 AW	39480 AAW	CABLS	10//99-12//99
	Orange County PMSA, CA	S	16.48 MW	14.24 AW	34280 AAW	CABLS	10//99-12//99
	Redding MSA, CA	S	12.86 MW	12.67 AW	26750 AAW	CABLS	10//99-12//99
	Riverside-San Bernardino PMSA, CA	S	12.89 MW	11.34 AW	26820 AAW	CABLS	10//99-12//99
	Sacramento PMSA, CA	S	19.41 MW	17.14 AW	40370 AAW	CABLS	10//99-12//99
	Salinas MSA, CA	S	19.42 MW	17.48 AW	40390 AAW	CABLS	10//99-12//99
	San Diego MSA, CA	S	16.56 MW	16.63 AW	34450 AAW	CABLS	10//99-12//99
	San Francisco PMSA, CA	S	23.03 MW	21.95 AW	47900 AAW	CABLS	10//99-12//99
	San Jose PMSA, CA	S	24.51 MW	27.15 AW	50990 AAW	CABLS	10//99-12//99
	San Luis Obispo-Atascadero-Paso Robles MSA, CA	S	14.58 MW	13.88 AW	30320 AAW	CABLS	10//99-12//99
	Santa Cruz-Watsonville PMSA, CA	S	17.83 MW	15.52 AW	37080 AAW	CABLS	10//99-12//99
	Stockton-Lodi MSA, CA	S	19.21 MW	18.08 AW	39960 AAW	CABLS	10//99-12//99
	Vallejo-Fairfield-Napa PMSA, CA	S	14.60 MW	12.72 AW	30360 AAW	CABLS	10//99-12//99
	Ventura PMSA, CA	S	11.81 MW	9.46 AW	24570 AAW	CABLS	10//99-12//99
	Visalia-Tulare-Porterville MSA, CA	S	14.11 MW	13.64 AW	29340 AAW	CABLS	10//99-12//99
	Yuba City MSA, CA	S	24.27 MW	26.07 AW	50470 AAW	CABLS	10//99-12//99
	Colorado	S	15.1 MW	15.49 AW	32210 AAW	COBLS	10//99-12//99
	Colorado Springs MSA, CO	S	17.10 MW	17.79 AW	35560 AAW	COBLS	10//99-12//99
	Denver PMSA, CO	S	16.05 MW	15.38 AW	33380 AAW	COBLS	10//99-12//99
	Fort Collins-Loveland MSA, CO	S	16.01 MW	15.32 AW	33290 AAW	COBLS	10//99-12//99
	Grand Junction MSA, CO	S	15.48 MW	15.55 AW	32200 AAW	COBLS	10//99-12//99
	Greeley PMSA, CO	S	16.25 MW	15.31 AW	33810 AAW	COBLS	10//99-12//99
	Connecticut	S	15.19 MW	15.88 AW	33030 AAW	CTBLS	10//99-12//99
	Bridgeport PMSA, CT	S	16.26 MW	16.31 AW	33830 AAW	CTBLS	10//99-12//99
	Danbury PMSA, CT	S	14.76 MW	14.22 AW	30690 AAW	CTBLS	10//99-12//99
	Hartford MSA, CT	S	14.78 MW	13.53 AW	30740 AAW	CTBLS	10//99-12//99
	New Haven-Meriden PMSA, CT	S	17.13 MW	17.29 AW	35630 AAW	CTBLS	10//99-12//99
	New London-Norwich MSA, CT-RI	S	17.40 MW	17.98 AW	36190 AAW	CTBLS	10//99-12//99
	Stamford-Norwalk PMSA, CT	S	19.31 MW	17.06 AW	40170 AAW	CTBLS	10//99-12//99
	Waterbury PMSA, CT	S	14.44 MW	13.76 AW	30040 AAW	CTBLS	10//99-12//99
	Delaware	S	13.89 MW	14.71 AW	30600 AAW	DEBLS	10//99-12//99
	Dover MSA, DE	S	13.50 MW	12.36 AW	28080 AAW	DEBLS	10//99-12//99
	Wilmington-Newark PMSA, DE-MD	S	14.91 MW	14.48 AW	31000 AAW	DEBLS	10//99-12//99
	District of Columbia	S	19.76 MW	19.77 AW	41120 AAW	DCBLS	10//99-12//99
	Washington PMSA, DC-MD-VA-WV	S	16.56 MW	15.79 AW	34440 AAW	DCBLS	10//99-12//99
	Florida	S	12.57 MW	13.03 AW	27090 AAW	FLBLS	10//99-12//99
	Daytona Beach MSA, FL	S	11.95 MW	11.96 AW	24860 AAW	FLBLS	10//99-12//99
	Fort Lauderdale PMSA, FL	S	12.74 MW	12.94 AW	26500 AAW	FLBLS	10//99-12//99
	Fort Myers-Cape Coral MSA, FL	S	12.46 MW	12.06 AW	25910 AAW	FLBLS	10//99-12//99
	Fort Pierce-Port St. Lucie MSA, FL	S	12.47 MW	12.94 AW	25940 AAW	FLBLS	10//99-12//99
	Fort Walton Beach MSA, FL	S	11.23 MW	10.46 AW	23350 AAW	FLBLS	10//99-12//99
	Gainesville MSA, FL	S	11.30 MW	10.53 AW	23490 AAW	FLBLS	10//99-12//99
	Lakeland-Winter Haven MSA, FL	S	12.02 MW	12.08 AW	25010 AAW	FLBLS	10//99-12//99
	Melbourne-Titusville-Palm Bay MSA, FL	S	12.36 MW	11.15 AW	25700 AAW	FLBLS	10//99-12//99
	Miami PMSA, FL	S	11.52 MW	11.05 AW	23970 AAW	FLBLS	10//99-12//99
	Naples MSA, FL	S	14.05 MW	13.97 AW	29230 AAW	FLBLS	10//99-12//99
	Ocala MSA, FL	S	12.25 MW	11.40 AW	25470 AAW	FLBLS	10//99-12//99
	Orlando MSA, FL	S	14.28 MW	13.42 AW	29700 AAW	FLBLS	10//99-12//99
	Panama City MSA, FL	S	11.46 MW	11.09 AW	23840 AAW	FLBLS	10//99-12//99
	Pensacola MSA, FL	S	11.76 MW	11.27 AW	24470 AAW	FLBLS	10//99-12//99
	Punta Gorda MSA, FL	S	11.08 MW	10.32 AW	23050 AAW	FLBLS	10//99-12//99
	Sarasota-Bradenton MSA, FL	S	14.02 MW	13.13 AW	29170 AAW	FLBLS	10//99-12//99
	Tallahassee MSA, FL	S	10.18 MW	9.38 AW	21180 AAW	FLBLS	10//99-12//99
	Tampa-St. Petersburg-Clearwater MSA, FL	S	13.12 MW	12.36 AW	27290 AAW	FLBLS	10//99-12//99
	West Palm Beach-Boca Raton MSA, FL	S	14.51 MW	14.23 AW	30190 AAW	FLBLS	10//99-12//99

AAW	Average annual wage	AOH	Average offered, high	ASH	Average starting, high	H	Hourly	M	Monthly	S	Special: hourly and annual
AE	Average entry wage	AOL	Average offered, low	ASL	Average starting, low	HI	Highest wage paid	MTC	Median total compensation	TQ	Third quartile wage
AEX	Average experienced wage	APH	Average pay, high range	AW	Average wage paid	HR	High end range	MW	Median wage paid	W	Weekly
AO	Average offered	APL	Average pay, low range	FQ	First quartile wage	LR	Low end range	SQ	Second quartile wage	Y	Yearly

Sheet Metal Worker

Occupation/Type/Industry	Location	Per	Low	Mid	High	Source	Date
Sheet Metal Worker	Georgia	S	14.13 MW	15.13 AW	31460 AAW	GABLS	10//99-12//99
	Albany MSA, GA	S	12.69 MW	11.84 AW	26380 AAW	GABLS	10//99-12//99
	Athens MSA, GA	S	12.28 MW	11.90 AW	25540 AAW	GABLS	10//99-12//99
	Atlanta MSA, GA	S	17.23 MW	17.87 AW	35850 AAW	GABLS	10//99-12//99
	Augusta-Aiken MSA, GA-SC	S	13.07 MW	12.21 AW	27190 AAW	GABLS	10//99-12//99
	Columbus MSA, GA-AL	S	11.85 MW	11.42 AW	24650 AAW	GABLS	10//99-12//99
	Savannah MSA, GA	S	11.46 MW	10.14 AW	23840 AAW	GABLS	10//99-12//99
	Hawaii	S	24.56 MW	24.41 AW	50770 AAW	HIBLS	10//99-12//99
	Honolulu MSA, HI	S	24.65 MW	24.67 AW	51280 AAW	HIBLS	10//99-12//99
	Idaho	S	13.4 MW	13.73 AW	28560 AAW	IDBLS	10//99-12//99
	Boise City MSA, ID	S	13.89 MW	13.45 AW	28900 AAW	IDBLS	10//99-12//99
	Pocatello MSA, ID	S	12.44 MW	12.12 AW	25870 AAW	IDBLS	10//99-12//99
	Illinois	S	21.4 MW	21.21 AW	44120 AAW	ILBLS	10//99-12//99
	Champaign-Urbana MSA, IL	S	20.08 MW	21.16 AW	41760 AAW	ILBLS	10//99-12//99
	Chicago PMSA, IL	S	22.63 MW	23.23 AW	47060 AAW	ILBLS	10//99-12//99
	Decatur MSA, IL	S	13.78 MW	12.80 AW	28660 AAW	ILBLS	10//99-12//99
	Kankakee PMSA, IL	S	22.24 MW	22.72 AW	46250 AAW	ILBLS	10//99-12//99
	Peoria-Pekin MSA, IL	S	21.40 MW	22.15 AW	44510 AAW	ILBLS	10//99-12//99
	Rockford MSA, IL	S	19.00 MW	17.63 AW	39530 AAW	ILBLS	10//99-12//99
	Springfield MSA, IL	S	20.68 MW	22.55 AW	43020 AAW	ILBLS	10//99-12//99
	Indiana	S	14.43 MW	16.65 AW	34630 AAW	INBLS	10//99-12//99
	Bloomington MSA, IN	S	19.38 MW	15.83 AW	40310 AAW	INBLS	10//99-12//99
	Elkhart-Goshen MSA, IN	S	15.65 MW	12.84 AW	32540 AAW	INBLS	10//99-12//99
	Evansville-Henderson MSA, IN-KY	S	17.22 MW	17.58 AW	35820 AAW	INBLS	10//99-12//99
	Fort Wayne MSA, IN	S	18.16 MW	16.69 AW	37760 AAW	INBLS	10//99-12//99
	Gary PMSA, IN	S	23.14 MW	24.53 AW	48120 AAW	INBLS	10//99-12//99
	Indianapolis MSA, IN	S	15.43 MW	13.04 AW	32090 AAW	INBLS	10//99-12//99
	Kokomo MSA, IN	S	19.54 MW	22.33 AW	40650 AAW	INBLS	10//99-12//99
	Muncie MSA, IN	S	16.01 MW	12.48 AW	33300 AAW	INBLS	10//99-12//99
	South Bend MSA, IN	S	20.71 MW	21.91 AW	43070 AAW	INBLS	10//99-12//99
	Terre Haute MSA, IN	S	14.56 MW	12.97 AW	30280 AAW	INBLS	10//99-12//99
	Iowa	S	13.35 MW	14.93 AW	31060 AAW	IABLS	10//99-12//99
	Cedar Rapids MSA, IA	S	16.96 MW	15.00 AW	35270 AAW	IABLS	10//99-12//99
	Davenport-Moline-Rock Island MSA, IA-IL	S	14.73 MW	13.44 AW	30640 AAW	IABLS	10//99-12//99
	Des Moines MSA, IA	S	15.89 MW	14.47 AW	33050 AAW	IABLS	10//99-12//99
	Dubuque MSA, IA	S	16.44 MW	16.12 AW	34190 AAW	IABLS	10//99-12//99
	Sioux City MSA, IA-NE	S	14.59 MW	14.42 AW	30340 AAW	IABLS	10//99-12//99
	Waterloo-Cedar Falls MSA, IA	S	15.62 MW	13.47 AW	32480 AAW	IABLS	10//99-12//99
	Kansas	S	14.64 MW	15.98 AW	33240 AAW	KSBLS	10//99-12//99
	Topeka MSA, KS	S	17.82 MW	18.06 AW	37070 AAW	KSBLS	10//99-12//99
	Wichita MSA, KS	S	15.00 MW	14.34 AW	31190 AAW	KSBLS	10//99-12//99
	Kentucky	S	13.03 MW	14.49 AW	30130 AAW	KYBLS	10//99-12//99
	Lexington MSA, KY	S	12.81 MW	12.33 AW	26640 AAW	KYBLS	10//99-12//99
	Louisville MSA, KY-IN	S	14.09 MW	13.10 AW	29310 AAW	KYBLS	10//99-12//99
	Louisiana	S	11.74 MW	12.21 AW	25400 AAW	LABLS	10//99-12//99
	Alexandria MSA, LA	S	9.40 MW	8.25 AW	19550 AAW	LABLS	10//99-12//99
	Baton Rouge MSA, LA	S	14.38 MW	14.99 AW	29910 AAW	LABLS	10//99-12//99
	Lafayette MSA, LA	S	11.39 MW	10.65 AW	23690 AAW	LABLS	10//99-12//99
	New Orleans MSA, LA	S	12.02 MW	11.85 AW	25000 AAW	LABLS	10//99-12//99
	Shreveport-Bossier City MSA, LA	S	12.25 MW	11.29 AW	25490 AAW	LABLS	10//99-12//99
	Maine	S	14.2 MW	13.56 AW	28210 AAW	MEBLS	10//99-12//99
	Lewiston-Auburn MSA, ME	S	14.76 MW	15.41 AW	30700 AAW	MEBLS	10//99-12//99
	Maryland	S	14.64 MW	15.61 AW	32470 AAW	MDBLS	10//99-12//99
	Baltimore PMSA, MD	S	14.69 MW	14.26 AW	30560 AAW	MDBLS	10//99-12//99
	Cumberland MSA, MD-WV	S	15.55 MW	15.88 AW	32350 AAW	MDBLS	10//99-12//99
	Hagerstown PMSA, MD	S	12.91 MW	12.42 AW	26850 AAW	MDBLS	10//99-12//99
	Massachusetts	S	18.11 MW	20.16 AW	41940 AAW	MABLS	10//99-12//99
	Barnstable-Yarmouth MSA, MA	S	15.23 MW	15.44 AW	31680 AAW	MABLS	10//99-12//99
	Boston PMSA, MA-NH	S	22.37 MW	20.22 AW	46530 AAW	MABLS	10//99-12//99
	Brockton PMSA, MA	S	21.11 MW	17.75 AW	43910 AAW	MABLS	10//99-12//99
	Fitchburg-Leominster PMSA, MA	S	18.42 MW	18.30 AW	38310 AAW	MABLS	10//99-12//99
	Lawrence PMSA, MA-NH	S	16.09 MW	15.55 AW	33480 AAW	MABLS	10//99-12//99
	Lowell PMSA, MA-NH	S	17.58 MW	15.31 AW	36560 AAW	MABLS	10//99-12//99
	Springfield MSA, MA	S	18.68 MW	16.19 AW	38850 AAW	MABLS	10//99-12//99
	Worcester PMSA, MA-CT	S	18.12 MW	18.36 AW	37680 AAW	MABLS	10//99-12//99
	Michigan	S	17.95 MW	18.14 AW	37730 AAW	MIBLS	10//99-12//99
	Ann Arbor PMSA, MI	S	19.87 MW	21.82 AW	41330 AAW	MIBLS	10//99-12//99

AAW Average annual wage	**AOH** Average offered, high	**ASH** Average starting, high	**H** Hourly	**M** Monthly	**S** Special: hourly and annual
AE Average entry wage	**AOL** Average offered, low	**ASL** Average starting, low	**HI** Highest wage paid	**MTC** Median total compensation	**TQ** Third quartile wage
AEX Average experienced wage	**APH** Average pay, high range	**AW** Average wage paid	**HR** High end range	**MW** Median wage paid	**W** Weekly
AO Average offered	**APL** Average pay, low range	**FQ** First quartile wage	**LR** Low end range	**SQ** Second quartile wage	**Y** Yearly

Sheet Metal Worker

Occupation/Type/Industry	Location	Per	Low	Mid	High	Source	Date
Sheet Metal Worker	Benton Harbor MSA, MI	S	17.54 MW	20.30 AW	36490 AAW	MIBLS	10//99-12//99
	Detroit PMSA, MI	S	18.76 MW	19.87 AW	39030 AAW	MIBLS	10//99-12//99
	Flint PMSA, MI	S	22.78 MW	23.88 AW	47380 AAW	MIBLS	10//99-12//99
	Grand Rapids-Muskegon-Holland MSA, MI	S	15.51 MW	14.50 AW	32250 AAW	MIBLS	10//99-12//99
	Jackson MSA, MI	S	15.26 MW	15.03 AW	31740 AAW	MIBLS	10//99-12//99
	Kalamazoo-Battle Creek MSA, MI	S	20.93 MW	22.18 AW	43540 AAW	MIBLS	10//99-12//99
	Lansing-East Lansing MSA, MI	S	22.75 MW	23.42 AW	47320 AAW	MIBLS	10//99-12//99
	Saginaw-Bay City-Midland MSA, MI	S	17.23 MW	18.99 AW	35840 AAW	MIBLS	10//99-12//99
	Minnesota	S	15.77 MW	17.48 AW	36350 AAW	MNBLS	10//99-12//99
	Duluth-Superior MSA, MN-WI	S	18.42 MW	20.02 AW	38320 AAW	MNBLS	10//99-12//99
	Minneapolis-St. Paul MSA, MN-WI	S	18.21 MW	16.40 AW	37880 AAW	MNBLS	10//99-12//99
	St. Cloud MSA, MN	S	15.88 MW	14.26 AW	33030 AAW	MNBLS	10//99-12//99
	Mississippi	S	11.09 MW	11.55 AW	24020 AAW	MSBLS	10//99-12//99
	Biloxi-Gulfport-Pascagoula MSA, MS	S	14.51 MW	14.96 AW	30180 AAW	MSBLS	10//99-12//99
	Hattiesburg MSA, MS	S	11.38 MW	11.06 AW	23670 AAW	MSBLS	10//99-12//99
	Jackson MSA, MS	S	12.42 MW	11.94 AW	25820 AAW	MSBLS	10//99-12//99
	Missouri	S	19.48 MW	19.66 AW	40890 AAW	MOBLS	10//99-12//99
	Columbia MSA, MO	S	18.01 MW	18.25 AW	37470 AAW	MOBLS	10//99-12//99
	Joplin MSA, MO	S	11.04 MW	10.71 AW	22970 AAW	MOBLS	10//99-12//99
	Kansas City MSA, MO-KS	S	21.97 MW	22.79 AW	45710 AAW	MOBLS	10//99-12//99
	St. Louis MSA, MO-IL	S	21.56 MW	22.10 AW	44840 AAW	MOBLS	10//99-12//99
	Springfield MSA, MO	S	15.13 MW	12.80 AW	31470 AAW	MOBLS	10//99-12//99
	Montana	S	18.11 MW	16.76 AW	34860 AAW	MTBLS	10//99-12//99
	Billings MSA, MT	S	16.34 MW	18.03 AW	33980 AAW	MTBLS	10//99-12//99
	Great Falls MSA, MT	S	17.31 MW	18.56 AW	36000 AAW	MTBLS	10//99-12//99
	Missoula MSA, MT	S	18.58 MW	20.33 AW	38640 AAW	MTBLS	10//99-12//99
	Nebraska	S	12.5 MW	13.90 AW	28900 AAW	NEBLS	10//99-12//99
	Lincoln MSA, NE	S	12.83 MW	12.46 AW	26680 AAW	NEBLS	10//99-12//99
	Omaha MSA, NE-IA	S	16.19 MW	15.11 AW	33670 AAW	NEBLS	10//99-12//99
	Nevada	S	15.79 MW	18.08 AW	37600 AAW	NVBLS	10//99-12//99
	Las Vegas MSA, NV-AZ	S	19.48 MW	16.05 AW	40520 AAW	NVBLS	10//99-12//99
	Reno MSA, NV	S	15.80 MW	15.56 AW	32860 AAW	NVBLS	10//99-12//99
	New Hampshire	S	12.98 MW	14.08 AW	29280 AAW	NHBLS	10//99-12//99
	Manchester PMSA, NH	S	17.94 MW	18.59 AW	37310 AAW	NHBLS	10//99-12//99
	Nashua PMSA, NH	S	12.23 MW	11.75 AW	25430 AAW	NHBLS	10//99-12//99
	Portsmouth-Rochester PMSA, NH-ME	S	13.36 MW	12.96 AW	27800 AAW	NHBLS	10//99-12//99
	New Jersey	S	19.33 MW	21.27 AW	44230 AAW	NJBLS	10//99-12//99
	Jersey City PMSA, NJ	S	22.73 MW	25.14 AW	47270 AAW	NJBLS	10//99-12//99
	Middlesex-Somerset-Hunterdon PMSA, NJ	S	18.52 MW	16.79 AW	38520 AAW	NJBLS	10//99-12//99
	Monmouth-Ocean PMSA, NJ	S	24.33 MW	25.54 AW	50600 AAW	NJBLS	10//99-12//99
	Newark PMSA, NJ	S	16.53 MW	12.53 AW	34380 AAW	NJBLS	10//99-12//99
	Vineland-Millville-Bridgeton PMSA, NJ	S	16.73 MW	16.27 AW	34810 AAW	NJBLS	10//99-12//99
	New Mexico	S	12.58 MW	13.69 AW	28470 AAW	NMBLS	10//99-12//99
	Albuquerque MSA, NM	S	14.18 MW	13.19 AW	29500 AAW	NMBLS	10//99-12//99
	Las Cruces MSA, NM	S	13.18 MW	11.37 AW	27410 AAW	NMBLS	10//99-12//99
	New York	S	17.58 MW	19.50 AW	40560 AAW	NYBLS	10//99-12//99
	Albany-Schenectady-Troy MSA, NY	S	15.70 MW	14.78 AW	32650 AAW	NYBLS	10//99-12//99
	Binghamton MSA, NY	S	13.52 MW	12.67 AW	28120 AAW	NYBLS	10//99-12//99
	Buffalo-Niagara Falls MSA, NY	S	17.36 MW	17.66 AW	36120 AAW	NYBLS	10//99-12//99
	Elmira MSA, NY	S	17.23 MW	15.75 AW	35830 AAW	NYBLS	10//99-12//99
	Glens Falls MSA, NY	S	19.60 MW	20.88 AW	40760 AAW	NYBLS	10//99-12//99
	Jamestown MSA, NY	S	14.36 MW	12.25 AW	29860 AAW	NYBLS	10//99-12//99
	Nassau-Suffolk PMSA, NY	S	18.47 MW	15.81 AW	38410 AAW	NYBLS	10//99-12//99
	New York PMSA, NY	S	24.45 MW	26.87 AW	50860 AAW	NYBLS	10//99-12//99
	Newburgh PMSA, NY-PA	S	19.39 MW	20.10 AW	40340 AAW	NYBLS	10//99-12//99
	Rochester MSA, NY	S	16.40 MW	15.54 AW	34120 AAW	NYBLS	10//99-12//99
	Syracuse MSA, NY	S	14.87 MW	14.29 AW	30930 AAW	NYBLS	10//99-12//99
	Utica-Rome MSA, NY	S	11.00 MW	9.92 AW	22880 AAW	NYBLS	10//99-12//99
	North Carolina	S	11.36 MW	11.79 AW	24520 AAW	NCBLS	10//99-12//99
	Asheville MSA, NC	S	12.38 MW	12.02 AW	25750 AAW	NCBLS	10//99-12//99
	Charlotte-Gastonia-Rock Hill MSA, NC-SC	S	11.68 MW	11.51 AW	24290 AAW	NCBLS	10//99-12//99

AAW Average annual wage	AOH Average offered, high	ASH Average starting, high	H Hourly	M Monthly	S Special: hourly and annual
AE Average entry wage	AOL Average offered, low	ASL Average starting, low	HI Highest wage paid	MTC Median total compensation	TQ Third quartile wage
AEX Average experienced wage	APH Average pay, high range	AW Average wage paid	HR High end range	MW Median wage paid	W Weekly
AO Average offered	APL Average pay, low range	FQ First quartile wage	LR Low end range	SQ Second quartile wage	Y Yearly

Occupation/Type/Industry	Location	Per	Low	Mid	High	Source	Date
Sheet Metal Worker	Fayetteville MSA, NC	S	10.36 MW	11.34 AW	21560 AAW	NCBLS	10//99-12//99
	Goldsboro MSA, NC	S	10.34 MW	10.69 AW	21500 AAW	NCBLS	10//99-12//99
	Greensboro--Winston-Salem--						
	High Point MSA, NC	S	12.70 MW	12.02 AW	26410 AAW	NCBLS	10//99-12//99
	Hickory-Morganton-Lenoir						
	MSA, NC	S	11.71 MW	11.46 AW	24370 AAW	NCBLS	10//99-12//99
	Jacksonville MSA, NC	S	10.10 MW	8.43 AW	21010 AAW	NCBLS	10//99-12//99
	Raleigh-Durham-Chapel Hill						
	MSA, NC	S	11.74 MW	11.37 AW	24420 AAW	NCBLS	10//99-12//99
	Rocky Mount MSA, NC	S	12.08 MW	11.87 AW	25130 AAW	NCBLS	10//99-12//99
	Wilmington MSA, NC	S	11.82 MW	11.33 AW	24590 AAW	NCBLS	10//99-12//99
	North Dakota	S	12.96 MW	13.64 AW	28370 AAW	NDBLS	10//99-12//99
	Bismarck MSA, ND	S	12.65 MW	12.31 AW	26320 AAW	NDBLS	10//99-12//99
	Fargo-Moorhead MSA, ND-MN	S	14.63 MW	13.93 AW	30420 AAW	NDBLS	10//99-12//99
	Grand Forks MSA, ND-MN	S	13.09 MW	11.61 AW	27230 AAW	NDBLS	10//99-12//99
	Ohio	S	14.77 MW	16.64 AW	34610 AAW	OHBLS	10//99-12//99
	Akron PMSA, OH	S	16.06 MW	14.88 AW	33400 AAW	OHBLS	10//99-12//99
	Canton-Massillon MSA, OH	S	18.37 MW	21.21 AW	38210 AAW	OHBLS	10//99-12//99
	Cincinnati PMSA, OH-KY-IN	S	13.93 MW	12.70 AW	28970 AAW	OHBLS	10//99-12//99
	Cleveland-Lorain-Elyria						
	PMSA, OH	S	19.65 MW	20.32 AW	40870 AAW	OHBLS	10//99-12//99
	Columbus MSA, OH	S	14.42 MW	13.47 AW	29980 AAW	OHBLS	10//99-12//99
	Dayton-Springfield MSA, OH	S	17.74 MW	18.69 AW	36900 AAW	OHBLS	10//99-12//99
	Hamilton-Middletown PMSA,						
	OH	S	24.37 MW	26.82 AW	50700 AAW	OHBLS	10//99-12//99
	Lima MSA, OH	S	16.52 MW	15.24 AW	34360 AAW	OHBLS	10//99-12//99
	Mansfield MSA, OH	S	16.32 MW	15.80 AW	33940 AAW	OHBLS	10//99-12//99
	Steubenville-Weirton MSA,						
	OH-WV	S	12.11 MW	9.54 AW	25180 AAW	OHBLS	10//99-12//99
	Toledo MSA, OH	S	17.75 MW	17.92 AW	36920 AAW	OHBLS	10//99-12//99
	Youngstown-Warren MSA, OH	S	18.98 MW	20.16 AW	39480 AAW	OHBLS	10//99-12//99
	Oklahoma	S	12.29 MW	13.42 AW	27900 AAW	OKBLS	10//99-12//99
	Oklahoma City MSA, OK	S	14.89 MW	16.84 AW	30970 AAW	OKBLS	10//99-12//99
	Tulsa MSA, OK	S	12.94 MW	12.32 AW	26910 AAW	OKBLS	10//99-12//99
	Oregon	S	15.55 MW	16.20 AW	33690 AAW	ORBLS	10//99-12//99
	Corvallis MSA, OR	S	12.46 MW	12.94 AW	25920 AAW	ORBLS	10//99-12//99
	Eugene-Springfield MSA, OR	S	16.74 MW	16.47 AW	34820 AAW	ORBLS	10//99-12//99
	Medford-Ashland MSA, OR	S	14.38 MW	15.12 AW	29900 AAW	ORBLS	10//99-12//99
	Portland-Vancouver PMSA,						
	OR-WA	S	17.79 MW	16.98 AW	37010 AAW	ORBLS	10//99-12//99
	Salem PMSA, OR	S	17.67 MW	16.14 AW	36750 AAW	ORBLS	10//99-12//99
	Pennsylvania	S	16.54 MW	16.74 AW	34830 AAW	PABLS	10//99-12//99
	Allentown-Bethlehem-Easton						
	MSA, PA	S	17.63 MW	19.72 AW	36680 AAW	PABLS	10//99-12//99
	Altoona MSA, PA	S	10.61 MW	10.22 AW	22080 AAW	PABLS	10//99-12//99
	Erie MSA, PA	S	15.92 MW	16.71 AW	33120 AAW	PABLS	10//99-12//99
	Harrisburg-Lebanon-Carlisle						
	MSA, PA	S	17.52 MW	16.45 AW	36450 AAW	PABLS	10//99-12//99
	Johnstown MSA, PA	S	13.66 MW	11.69 AW	28410 AAW	PABLS	10//99-12//99
	Lancaster MSA, PA	S	15.63 MW	15.17 AW	32500 AAW	PABLS	10//99-12//99
	Philadelphia PMSA, PA-NJ	S	18.99 MW	17.64 AW	39500 AAW	PABLS	10//99-12//99
	Pittsburgh MSA, PA	S	17.79 MW	19.44 AW	37010 AAW	PABLS	10//99-12//99
	Reading MSA, PA	S	16.81 MW	15.72 AW	34960 AAW	PABLS	10//99-12//99
	Scranton--Wilkes-Barre--						
	Hazleton MSA, PA	S	15.13 MW	16.95 AW	31480 AAW	PABLS	10//99-12//99
	Williamsport MSA, PA	S	14.60 MW	15.01 AW	30360 AAW	PABLS	10//99-12//99
	York MSA, PA	S	14.64 MW	13.93 AW	30440 AAW	PABLS	10//99-12//99
	Rhode Island	S	15.51 MW	16.26 AW	33810 AAW	RIBLS	10//99-12//99
	Providence-Fall River-						
	Warwick MSA, RI-MA	S	15.80 MW	15.07 AW	32850 AAW	RIBLS	10//99-12//99
	South Carolina	S	11.68 MW	12.18 AW	25340 AAW	SCBLS	10//99-12//99
	Charleston-North Charleston						
	MSA, SC	S	11.68 MW	11.25 AW	24290 AAW	SCBLS	10//99-12//99
	Columbia MSA, SC	S	11.57 MW	11.31 AW	24060 AAW	SCBLS	10//99-12//99
	Florence MSA, SC	S	11.42 MW	11.12 AW	23750 AAW	SCBLS	10//99-12//99
	Greenville-Spartanburg-						
	Anderson MSA, SC	S	13.05 MW	12.62 AW	27150 AAW	SCBLS	10//99-12//99
	Myrtle Beach MSA, SC	S	13.37 MW	12.20 AW	27810 AAW	SCBLS	10//99-12//99
	South Dakota	S	10.58 MW	11.19 AW	23270 AAW	SDBLS	10//99-12//99
	Rapid City MSA, SD	S	11.07 MW	11.04 AW	23030 AAW	SDBLS	10//99-12//99
	Tennessee	S	12.4 MW	13.06 AW	27160 AAW	TNBLS	10//99-12//99

AAW Average annual wage	AOH Average offered, high	ASH Average starting, high	H Hourly	M Monthly	S Special: hourly and annual
AE Average entry wage	AOL Average offered, low	ASL Average starting, low	HI Highest wage paid	MTC Median total compensation	TQ Third quartile wage
AEX Average experienced wage	APH Average pay, high range	AW Average wage paid	HR High end range	MW Median wage paid	W Weekly
AO Average offered	APL Average pay, low range	FQ First quartile wage	LR Low end range	SQ Second quartile wage	Y Yearly

Occupation/Type/Industry	Location	Per	Low	Mid	High	Source	Date
Sheet Metal Worker	Chattanooga MSA, TN-GA	S	12.73 MW	12.63 AW	26470 AAW	TNBLS	10//99-12//99
	Jackson MSA, TN	S	13.00 MW	12.59 AW	27030 AAW	TNBLS	10//99-12//99
	Johnson City-Kingsport-Bristol MSA, TN-VA	S	9.98 MW	9.82 AW	20770 AAW	TNBLS	10//99-12//99
	Knoxville MSA, TN	S	12.90 MW	11.88 AW	26830 AAW	TNBLS	10//99-12//99
	Memphis MSA, TN-AR-MS	S	13.38 MW	12.50 AW	27830 AAW	MSBLS	10//99-12//99
	Nashville MSA, TN	S	13.82 MW	12.88 AW	28740 AAW	TNBLS	10//99-12//99
	Texas	S	11.13 MW	12.13 AW	25230 AAW	TXBLS	10//99-12//99
	Abilene MSA, TX	S	10.94 MW	10.30 AW	22760 AAW	TXBLS	10//99-12//99
	Amarillo MSA, TX	S	13.65 MW	13.54 AW	28390 AAW	TXBLS	10//99-12//99
	Austin-San Marcos MSA, TX	S	13.75 MW	13.79 AW	28610 AAW	TXBLS	10//99-12//99
	Beaumont-Port Arthur MSA, TX	S	13.65 MW	13.08 AW	28390 AAW	TXBLS	10//99-12//99
	Brazoria PMSA, TX	S	11.29 MW	9.99 AW	23490 AAW	TXBLS	10//99-12//99
	Brownsville-Harlingen-San Benito MSA, TX	S	9.02 MW	8.28 AW	18770 AAW	TXBLS	10//99-12//99
	Bryan-College Station MSA, TX	S	9.84 MW	9.61 AW	20460 AAW	TXBLS	10//99-12//99
	Corpus Christi MSA, TX	S	15.43 MW	17.36 AW	32090 AAW	TXBLS	10//99-12//99
	Dallas PMSA, TX	S	11.70 MW	10.71 AW	24330 AAW	TXBLS	10//99-12//99
	El Paso MSA, TX	S	9.34 MW	8.87 AW	19430 AAW	TXBLS	10//99-12//99
	Fort Worth-Arlington PMSA, TX	S	12.37 MW	11.60 AW	25740 AAW	TXBLS	10//99-12//99
	Galveston-Texas City PMSA, TX	S	12.81 MW	13.60 AW	26640 AAW	TXBLS	10//99-12//99
	Houston PMSA, TX	S	13.25 MW	12.55 AW	27570 AAW	TXBLS	10//99-12//99
	Killeen-Temple MSA, TX	S	11.72 MW	10.76 AW	24370 AAW	TXBLS	10//99-12//99
	Laredo MSA, TX	S	9.87 MW	9.68 AW	20520 AAW	TXBLS	10//99-12//99
	Longview-Marshall MSA, TX	S	11.05 MW	10.50 AW	22980 AAW	TXBLS	10//99-12//99
	Lubbock MSA, TX	S	12.92 MW	11.72 AW	26880 AAW	TXBLS	10//99-12//99
	McAllen-Edinburg-Mission MSA, TX	S	8.29 MW	8.16 AW	17250 AAW	TXBLS	10//99-12//99
	Odessa-Midland MSA, TX	S	10.81 MW	11.10 AW	22490 AAW	TXBLS	10//99-12//99
	San Angelo MSA, TX	S	10.48 MW	10.91 AW	21800 AAW	TXBLS	10//99-12//99
	San Antonio MSA, TX	S	11.23 MW	10.35 AW	23370 AAW	TXBLS	10//99-12//99
	Texarkana MSA, TX-Texarkana, AR	S	12.42 MW	11.97 AW	25840 AAW	TXBLS	10//99-12//99
	Tyler MSA, TX	S	11.79 MW	11.38 AW	24530 AAW	TXBLS	10//99-12//99
	Victoria MSA, TX	S	9.32 MW	8.89 AW	19380 AAW	TXBLS	10//99-12//99
	Waco MSA, TX	S	11.27 MW	10.42 AW	23430 AAW	TXBLS	10//99-12//99
	Wichita Falls MSA, TX	S	11.54 MW	10.97 AW	23990 AAW	TXBLS	10//99-12//99
	Utah	S	14.43 MW	14.64 AW	30450 AAW	UTBLS	10//99-12//99
	Salt Lake City-Ogden MSA, UT	S	14.92 MW	14.91 AW	31040 AAW	UTBLS	10//99-12//99
	Vermont	S	13.37 MW	13.52 AW	28120 AAW	VTBLS	10//99-12//99
	Burlington MSA, VT	S	13.48 MW	12.95 AW	28050 AAW	VTBLS	10//99-12//99
	Virginia	S	13.53 MW	13.36 AW	27790 AAW	VABLS	10//99-12//99
	Charlottesville MSA, VA	S	11.96 MW	12.16 AW	24870 AAW	VABLS	10//99-12//99
	Lynchburg MSA, VA	S	12.25 MW	12.44 AW	25490 AAW	VABLS	10//99-12//99
	Norfolk-Virginia Beach-Newport News MSA, VA-NC	S	13.76 MW	14.59 AW	28630 AAW	VABLS	10//99-12//99
	Richmond-Petersburg MSA, VA	S	13.14 MW	12.62 AW	27320 AAW	VABLS	10//99-12//99
	Roanoke MSA, VA	S	12.20 MW	11.12 AW	25380 AAW	VABLS	10//99-12//99
	Washington	S	19.25 MW	19.89 AW	41380 AAW	WABLS	10//99-12//99
	Bellingham MSA, WA	S	19.64 MW	18.17 AW	40840 AAW	WABLS	10//99-12//99
	Richland-Kennewick-Pasco MSA, WA	S	20.73 MW	22.48 AW	43110 AAW	WABLS	10//99-12//99
	Seattle-Bellevue-Everett PMSA, WA	S	21.50 MW	20.37 AW	44720 AAW	WABLS	10//99-12//99
	Spokane MSA, WA	S	15.15 MW	13.61 AW	31510 AAW	WABLS	10//99-12//99
	Tacoma PMSA, WA	S	17.99 MW	16.65 AW	37420 AAW	WABLS	10//99-12//99
	Yakima MSA, WA	S	15.95 MW	15.35 AW	33180 AAW	WABLS	10//99-12//99
	West Virginia	S	18.62 MW	17.50 AW	36400 AAW	WVBLS	10//99-12//99
	Charleston MSA, WV	S	15.66 MW	17.96 AW	32560 AAW	WVBLS	10//99-12//99
	Huntington-Ashland MSA, WV-KY-OH	S	17.27 MW	17.96 AW	35930 AAW	WVBLS	10//99-12//99
	Parkersburg-Marietta MSA, WV-OH	S	14.41 MW	11.91 AW	29980 AAW	WVBLS	10//99-12//99
	Wisconsin	S	15.69 MW	16.74 AW	34810 AAW	WIBLS	10//99-12//99

AAW Average annual wage	AOH Average offered, high	ASH Average starting, high	H Hourly	M Monthly	S Special: hourly and annual
AE Average entry wage	AOL Average offered, low	ASL Average starting, low	HI Highest wage paid	MTC Median total compensation	TQ Third quartile wage
AEX Average experienced wage	APH Average pay, high range	AW Average wage paid	HR High end range	MW Median wage paid	W Weekly
AO Average offered	APL Average pay, low range	FQ First quartile wage	LR Low end range	SQ Second quartile wage	Y Yearly

Occupation/Type/Industry	Location	Per	Low	Mid	High	Source	Date
Sheet Metal Worker	Appleton-Oshkosh-Neenah MSA, WI	S	15.42 MW	14.66 AW	32080 AAW	WIBLS	10//99-12//99
	Eau Claire MSA, WI	S	14.35 MW	13.72 AW	29840 AAW	WIBLS	10//99-12//99
	Green Bay MSA, WI	S	16.56 MW	15.61 AW	34450 AAW	WIBLS	10//99-12//99
	Janesville-Beloit MSA, WI	S	18.45 MW	18.07 AW	38370 AAW	WIBLS	10//99-12//99
	Kenosha PMSA, WI	S	19.58 MW	20.01 AW	40720 AAW	WIBLS	10//99-12//99
	La Crosse MSA, WI-MN	S	13.82 MW	12.77 AW	28740 AAW	WIBLS	10//99-12//99
	Madison MSA, WI	S	16.39 MW	15.13 AW	34090 AAW	WIBLS	10//99-12//99
	Milwaukee-Waukesha PMSA, WI	S	18.85 MW	18.37 AW	39210 AAW	WIBLS	10//99-12//99
	Racine PMSA, WI	S	18.53 MW	15.27 AW	38540 AAW	WIBLS	10//99-12//99
	Wausau MSA, WI	S	16.80 MW	15.05 AW	34930 AAW	WIBLS	10//99-12//99
	Wyoming	S	12.57 MW	12.81 AW	26650 AAW	WYBLS	10//99-12//99
	Casper MSA, WY	S	14.28 MW	13.71 AW	29700 AAW	WYBLS	10//99-12//99
	Cheyenne MSA, WY	S	13.02 MW	13.80 AW	27070 AAW	WYBLS	10//99-12//99
	Puerto Rico	S	6.38 MW	7.39 AW	15370 AAW	PRBLS	10//99-12//99
	Mayaguez MSA, PR	S	8.95 MW	7.77 AW	18610 AAW	PRBLS	10//99-12//99
	San Juan-Bayamon PMSA, PR	S	7.12 MW	6.17 AW	14810 AAW	PRBLS	10//99-12//99
	Guam	S	13.86 MW	14.22 AW	29590 AAW	GUBLS	10//99-12//99
Sheriff, Bailiff	United States	H		16.02 AW		NCS98	1998
Ship Engineer	California	S	23.46 MW	23.35 AW	48570 AAW	CABLS	10//99-12//99
	Florida	S	18.87 MW	20.07 AW	41750 AAW	FLBLS	10//99-12//99
	Hawaii	S	19.31 MW	20.17 AW	41950 AAW	HIBLS	10//99-12//99
	Illinois	S	21.22 MW	22.45 AW	46700 AAW	ILBLS	10//99-12//99
	Kentucky	S	18.39 MW	17.76 AW	36950 AAW	KYBLS	10//99-12//99
	Louisiana	S	16.43 MW	16.88 AW	35110 AAW	LABLS	10//99-12//99
	Maryland	S	24.2 MW	24.28 AW	50500 AAW	MDBLS	10//99-12//99
	Massachusetts	S	15.62 MW	17.56 AW	36530 AAW	MABLS	10//99-12//99
	Michigan	S	26.95 MW	25.37 AW	52760 AAW	MIBLS	10//99-12//99
	New Jersey	S	24.11 MW	26.48 AW	55080 AAW	NJBLS	10//99-12//99
	New York	S	22.92 MW	24.73 AW	51430 AAW	NYBLS	10//99-12//99
	Pennsylvania	S	23.63 MW	26.35 AW	54820 AAW	PABLS	10//99-12//99
	Tennessee	S	21.31 MW	20.36 AW	42350 AAW	TNBLS	10//99-12//99
	Texas	S	22.59 MW	23.71 AW	49320 AAW	TXBLS	10//99-12//99
	Washington	S	23.99 MW	24.08 AW	50080 AAW	WABLS	10//99-12//99
	West Virginia	S	20.67 MW	20.76 AW	43170 AAW	WVBLS	10//99-12//99
Shipping, Receiving, and Traffic Clerk	Alabama	S	8.73 MW	9.48 AW	19710 AAW	ALBLS	10//99-12//99
	Alaska	S	11.85 MW	12.84 AW	26710 AAW	AKBLS	10//99-12//99
	Arizona	S	8.81 MW	9.66 AW	20100 AAW	AZBLS	10//99-12//99
	Arkansas	S	8.95 MW	9.60 AW	19960 AAW	ARBLS	10//99-12//99
	California	S	9.96 MW	10.72 AW	22290 AAW	CABLS	10//99-12//99
	Colorado	S	9.95 MW	10.43 AW	21700 AAW	COBLS	10//99-12//99
	Connecticut	S	11.41 MW	11.86 AW	24670 AAW	CTBLS	10//99-12//99
	Delaware	S	9.59 MW	10.40 AW	21640 AAW	DEBLS	10//99-12//99
	District of Columbia	S	12.58 MW	13.04 AW	27130 AAW	DCBLS	10//99-12//99
	Florida	S	9 MW	9.62 AW	20010 AAW	FLBLS	10//99-12//99
	Georgia	S	10.11 MW	10.43 AW	21700 AAW	GABLS	10//99-12//99
	Hawaii	S	10.68 MW	12.18 AW	25340 AAW	HIBLS	10//99-12//99
	Idaho	S	8.94 MW	9.71 AW	20190 AAW	IDBLS	10//99-12//99
	Illinois	S	10.4 MW	10.96 AW	22790 AAW	ILBLS	10//99-12//99
	Indiana	S	10.16 MW	10.55 AW	21950 AAW	INBLS	10//99-12//99
	Iowa	S	9.86 MW	10.31 AW	21450 AAW	IABLS	10//99-12//99
	Kansas	S	9.63 MW	10.36 AW	21550 AAW	KSBLS	10//99-12//99
	Kentucky	S	10.04 MW	10.42 AW	21670 AAW	KYBLS	10//99-12//99
	Louisiana	S	9 MW	9.74 AW	20250 AAW	LABLS	10//99-12//99
	Maine	S	10.03 MW	10.15 AW	21100 AAW	MEBLS	10//99-12//99
	Maryland	S	10.2 MW	10.73 AW	22320 AAW	MDBLS	10//99-12//99
	Massachusetts	S	11.15 MW	11.67 AW	24270 AAW	MABLS	10//99-12//99
	Michigan	S	10.96 MW	11.87 AW	24690 AAW	MIBLS	10//99-12//99
	Minnesota	S	11.07 MW	11.51 AW	23950 AAW	MNBLS	10//99-12//99
	Mississippi	S	8.98 MW	9.37 AW	19480 AAW	MSBLS	10//99-12//99
	Missouri	S	9.77 MW	10.43 AW	21700 AAW	MOBLS	10//99-12//99
	Montana	S	8.08 MW	8.65 AW	18000 AAW	MTBLS	10//99-12//99
	Nebraska	S	9.54 MW	9.86 AW	20500 AAW	NEBLS	10//99-12//99
	Nevada	S	9.95 MW	10.43 AW	21700 AAW	NVBLS	10//99-12//99
	New Hampshire	S	10.63 MW	10.77 AW	22400 AAW	NHBLS	10//99-12//99
	New Jersey	S	11.24 MW	11.91 AW	24780 AAW	NJBLS	10//99-12//99
	New Mexico	S	8.57 MW	9.16 AW	19050 AAW	NMBLS	10//99-12//99

AAW Average annual wage	**AOH** Average offered, high	**ASH** Average starting, high	**H** Hourly	**M** Monthly	**S** Special: hourly and annual
AE Average entry wage	**AOL** Average offered, low	**ASL** Average starting, low	**HI** Highest wage paid	**MTC** Median total compensation	**TQ** Third quartile wage
AEX Average experienced wage	**APH** Average pay, high range	**AW** Average wage paid	**HR** High end range	**MW** Median wage paid	**W** Weekly
AO Average offered	**APL** Average pay, low range	**FQ** First quartile wage	**LR** Low end range	**SQ** Second quartile wage	**Y** Yearly

Occupation/Type/Industry	Location	Per	Low	Mid	High	Source	Date
Shipping, Receiving, and Traffic Clerk	New York	S	10.02 MW	10.89 AW	22640 AAW	NYBLS	10//99-12//99
	North Carolina	S	9.8 MW	10.15 AW	21120 AAW	NCBLS	10//99-12//99
	North Dakota	S	8.86 MW	9.36 AW	19460 AAW	NDBLS	10//99-12//99
	Ohio	S	10.31 MW	10.81 AW	22490 AAW	OHBLS	10//99-12//99
	Oklahoma	S	9.07 MW	9.72 AW	20220 AAW	OKBLS	10//99-12//99
	Oregon	S	10.27 MW	10.88 AW	22630 AAW	ORBLS	10//99-12//99
	Pennsylvania	S	10.35 MW	10.87 AW	22620 AAW	PABLS	10//99-12//99
	Rhode Island	S	10.08 MW	10.71 AW	22280 AAW	RIBLS	10//99-12//99
	South Carolina	S	9.64 MW	10.10 AW	21000 AAW	SCBLS	10//99-12//99
	South Dakota	S	9.41 MW	9.42 AW	19590 AAW	SDBLS	10//99-12//99
	Tennessee	S	9.66 MW	10.05 AW	20910 AAW	TNBLS	10//99-12//99
	Texas	S	9.27 MW	9.94 AW	20660 AAW	TXBLS	10//99-12//99
	Utah	S	9.97 MW	10.44 AW	21720 AAW	UTBLS	10//99-12//99
	Vermont	S	10.22 MW	10.49 AW	21820 AAW	VTBLS	10//99-12//99
	Virginia	S	9.69 MW	10.21 AW	21230 AAW	VABLS	10//99-12//99
	Washington	S	11.2 MW	12.08 AW	25140 AAW	WABLS	10//99-12//99
	West Virginia	S	8.32 MW	9.16 AW	19060 AAW	WVBLS	10//99-12//99
	Wisconsin	S	10 MW	10.41 AW	21660 AAW	WIBLS	10//99-12//99
	Wyoming	S	9.24 MW	10.23 AW	21270 AAW	WYBLS	10//99-12//99
	Puerto Rico	S	6.72 MW	7.69 AW	15980 AAW	PRBLS	10//99-12//99
	Virgin Islands	S	8.91 MW	9.96 AW	20720 AAW	VIBLS	10//99-12//99
	Guam	S	12.33 MW	11.91 AW	24780 AAW	GUBLS	10//99-12//99
Shoe and Leather Worker and Repairer	Alabama	S	7.78 MW	7.87 AW	16380 AAW	ALBLS	10//99-12//99
	Arizona	S	7.07 MW	7.55 AW	15700 AAW	AZBLS	10//99-12//99
	Arkansas	S	6.85 MW	7.58 AW	15770 AAW	ARBLS	10//99-12//99
	California	S	6.63 MW	7.34 AW	15260 AAW	CABLS	10//99-12//99
	Florida	S.	7.45 MW	8.24 AW	17130 AAW	FLBLS	10//99-12//99
	Georgia	S	6.74 MW	7.55 AW	15700 AAW	GABLS	10//99-12//99
	Illinois	S	9.59 MW	9.47 AW	19700 AAW	ILBLS	10//99-12//99
	Indiana	S	10.91 MW	11.29 AW	23470 AAW	INBLS	10//99-12//99
	Kansas	S	8.08 MW	8.27 AW	17210 AAW	KSBLS	10//99-12//99
	Kentucky	S	7.12 MW	7.67 AW	15940 AAW	KYBLS	10//99-12//99
	Maine	S	7.92 MW	8.04 AW	16730 AAW	MEBLS	10//99-12//99
	Maryland	S	9.52 MW	9.55 AW	19860 AAW	MDBLS	10//99-12//99
	Massachusetts	S	12.08 MW	11.97 AW	24890 AAW	MABLS	10//99-12//99
	Michigan	S	14.59 MW	14.48 AW	30120 AAW	MIBLS	10//99-12//99
	Minnesota	S	8.7 MW	8.79 AW	18280 AAW	MNBLS	10//99-12//99
	Nevada	S	7.93 MW	7.78 AW	16180 AAW	NVBLS	10//99-12//99
	New Hampshire	S	6.14 MW	6.27 AW	13030 AAW	NHBLS	10//99-12//99
	New Jersey	S	7.86 MW	8.79 AW	18270 AAW	NJBLS	10//99-12//99
	New York	S	7.75 MW	8.91 AW	18530 AAW	NYBLS	10//99-12//99
	North Carolina	S	8.01 MW	8.42 AW	17510 AAW	NCBLS	10//99-12//99
	Ohio	S	9.89 MW	10.77 AW	22390 AAW	OHBLS	10//99-12//99
	Oklahoma	S	6 MW	6.00 AW	12490 AAW	OKBLS	10//99-12//99
	Oregon	S	9.83 MW	10.31 AW	21440 AAW	ORBLS	10//99-12//99
	Pennsylvania	S	12.18 MW	11.85 AW	24640 AAW	PABLS	10//99-12//99
	South Carolina	S	10.95 MW	10.25 AW	21310 AAW	SCBLS	10//99-12//99
	South Dakota	S	8.88 MW	8.24 AW	17150 AAW	SDBLS	10//99-12//99
	Tennessee	S	8.22 MW	8.55 AW	17790 AAW	TNBLS	10//99-12//99
	Texas	S	7.3 MW	7.53 AW	15660 AAW	TXBLS	10//99-12//99
	Virginia	S	9.81 MW	9.85 AW	20480 AAW	VABLS	10//99-12//99
	Washington	S	11.51 MW	11.26 AW	23430 AAW	WABLS	10//99-12//99
	Puerto Rico	S	6.22 MW	6.20 AW	12890 AAW	PRBLS	10//99-12//99
Shoe Machine Operator and Tender	California	S	7.35 MW	7.45 AW	15500 AAW	CABLS	10//99-12//99
	Los Angeles-Long Beach PMSA, CA	S	7.52 MW	7.39 AW	15650 AAW	CABLS	10//99-12//99
	Florida	S	7.14 MW	7.82 AW	16270 AAW	FLBLS	10//99-12//99
	Georgia	S	8.86 MW	8.36 AW	17380 AAW	GABLS	10//99-12//99
	Atlanta MSA, GA	S	8.39 MW	8.94 AW	17450 AAW	GABLS	10//99-12//99
	Illinois	S	9.36 MW	8.89 AW	18480 AAW	ILBLS	10//99-12//99
	Chicago PMSA, IL	S	8.89 MW	9.36 AW	18480 AAW	ILBLS	10//99-12//99
	Maine	S	7.98 MW	8.03 AW	16710 AAW	MEBLS	10//99-12//99
	Massachusetts	S	9.7 MW	9.99 AW	20780 AAW	MABLS	10//99-12//99
	Missouri	S	9.45 MW	9.22 AW	19170 AAW	MOBLS	10//99-12//99
	New York	S	7.49 MW	7.63 AW	15880 AAW	NYBLS	10//99-12//99
	Ohio	S	7.6 MW	8.03 AW	16710 AAW	OHBLS	10//99-12//99
	Oregon	S	11.8 MW	11.53 AW	23990 AAW	ORBLS	10//99-12//99

AAW Average annual wage	AOH Average offered, high	ASH Average starting, high	H Hourly	M Monthly	S Special: hourly and annual
AE Average entry wage	AOL Average offered, low	ASL Average starting, low	HI Highest wage paid	MTC Median total compensation	TQ Third quartile wage
AEX Average experienced wage	APH Average pay, high range	AW Average wage paid	HR High end range	MW Median wage paid	W Weekly
AO Average offered	APL Average pay, low range	FQ First quartile wage	LR Low end range	SQ Second quartile wage	Y Yearly

Occupation/Type/Industry	Location	Per	Low	Mid	High	Source	Date
Shoe Machine Operator and							
Tender	Pennsylvania	S	8.28 MW	8.61 AW	17910 AAW	PABLS	10//99-12//99
	Texas	S	7.71 MW	7.86 AW	16350 AAW	TXBLS	10//99-12//99
	Wisconsin	S	9.99 MW	9.76 AW	20290 AAW	WIBLS	10//99-12//99
	Milwaukee-Waukesha PMSA, WI	S	10.23 MW	11.36 AW	21270 AAW	WIBLS	10//99-12//99
	Puerto Rico	S	5.96 MW	5.79 AW	12040 AAW	PRBLS	10//99-12//99
	Aguadilla MSA, PR	S	5.99 MW	6.03 AW	12450 AAW	PRBLS	10//99-12//99
Shuttle Car Operator	Illinois	S	18.57 MW	18.63 AW	38740 AAW	ILBLS	10//99-12//99
	Kentucky	S	13.99 MW	14.53 AW	30230 AAW	KYBLS	10//99-12//99
	Pennsylvania	S	18.4 MW	18.23 AW	37920 AAW	PABLS	10//99-12//99
	Virginia	S	15.67 MW	15.85 AW	32970 AAW	VABLS	10//99-12//99
	West Virginia	S	17.83 MW	17.15 AW	35680 AAW	WVBLS	10//99-12//99
Signal and Track Switch Repairer	Alabama	S	19.37 MW	20.77 AW	43210 AAW	ALBLS	10//99-12//99
	Arkansas	S	19.36 MW	19.43 AW	40410 AAW	ARBLS	10//99-12//99
	Delaware	S	13.99 MW	15.11 AW	31430 AAW	DEBLS	10//99-12//99
	Florida	S	13.56 MW	12.57 AW	26150 AAW	FLBLS	10//99-12//99
	Illinois	S	19.31 MW	21.11 AW	43920 AAW	ILBLS	10//99-12//99
	Louisiana	S	19.42 MW	20.50 AW	42640 AAW	LABLS	10//99-12//99
	Minnesota	S	23.9 MW	24.52 AW	51000 AAW	MNBLS	10//99-12//99
	Mississippi	S	19.74 MW	19.85 AW	41280 AAW	MSBLS	10//99-12//99
	New York	S	13.18 MW	14.44 AW	30030 AAW	NYBLS	10//99-12//99
	North Carolina	S	17.68 MW	17.15 AW	35660 AAW	NCBLS	10//99-12//99
	Ohio	S	17.78 MW	17.95 AW	37340 AAW	OHBLS	10//99-12//99
	South Carolina	S	15.41 MW	15.66 AW	32580 AAW	SCBLS	10//99-12//99
	Tennessee	S	18.47 MW	19.20 AW	39930 AAW	TNBLS	10//99-12//99
Skin Care Specialist	Alabama	S	7.72 MW	8.10 AW	16850 AAW	ALBLS	10//99-12//99
	Arizona	S	7.86 MW	9.88 AW	20550 AAW	AZBLS	10//99-12//99
	California	S	12.54 MW	12.78 AW	26580 AAW	CABLS	10//99-12//99
	Connecticut	S	9.91 MW	10.93 AW	22740 AAW	CTBLS	10//99-12//99
	Florida	S	9 MW	10.10 AW	21000 AAW	FLBLS	10//99-12//99
	Georgia	S	8.04 MW	9.17 AW	19080 AAW	GABLS	10//99-12//99
	Hawaii	S	9.63 MW	14.37 AW	29880 AAW	HIBLS	10//99-12//99
	Illinois	S	9.6 MW	10.11 AW	21030 AAW	ILBLS	10//99-12//99
	Indiana	S	7.55 MW	7.56 AW	15720 AAW	INBLS	10//99-12//99
	Kansas	S	11.93 MW	11.66 AW	24260 AAW	KSBLS	10//99-12//99
	Kentucky	S	8.33 MW	8.78 AW	18260 AAW	KYBLS	10//99-12//99
	Louisiana	S	8.06 MW	9.54 AW	19850 AAW	LABLS	10//99-12//99
	Maryland	S	8.31 MW	8.41 AW	17480 AAW	MDBLS	10//99-12//99
	Massachusetts	S	9.01 MW	9.45 AW	19660 AAW	MABLS	10//99-12//99
	Michigan	S	9.2 MW	9.02 AW	18760 AAW	MIBLS	10//99-12//99
	Minnesota	S	11.82 MW	12.45 AW	25900 AAW	MNBLS	10//99-12//99
	Mississippi	S	7.22 MW	7.02 AW	14610 AAW	MSBLS	10//99-12//99
	Missouri	S	9.85 MW	11.59 AW	24110 AAW	MOBLS	10//99-12//99
	Nebraska	S	6.43 MW	8.45 AW	17590 AAW	NEBLS	10//99-12//99
	New Hampshire	S	8.21 MW	9.68 AW	20130 AAW	NHBLS	10//99-12//99
	New Jersey	S	10.06 MW	11.52 AW	23970 AAW	NJBLS	10//99-12//99
	New Mexico	S	8.19 MW	9.97 AW	20740 AAW	NMBLS	10//99-12//99
	New York	S	8.11 MW	9.44 AW	19630 AAW	NYBLS	10//99-12//99
	North Carolina	S	10.54 MW	12.07 AW	25100 AAW	NCBLS	10//99-12//99
	Ohio	S	9.73 MW	10.32 AW	21470 AAW	OHBLS	10//99-12//99
	Oklahoma	S	6.48 MW	6.68 AW	13890 AAW	OKBLS	10//99-12//99
	Oregon	S	10.69 MW	12.63 AW	26260 AAW	ORBLS	10//99-12//99
	Pennsylvania	S	8.57 MW	8.92 AW	18560 AAW	PABLS	10//99-12//99
	Tennessee	S	8.81 MW	11.48 AW	23880 AAW	TNBLS	10//99-12//99
	Texas	S	6.72 MW	8.20 AW	17050 AAW	TXBLS	10//99-12//99
	Utah	S	7.58 MW	7.55 AW	15710 AAW	UTBLS	10//99-12//99
	Virginia	S	9.77 MW	11.21 AW	23320 AAW	VABLS	10//99-12//99
	Washington	S	9.68 MW	13.07 AW	27180 AAW	WABLS	10//99-12//99
	West Virginia	S	7.34 MW	7.36 AW	15310 AAW	WVBLS	10//99-12//99
	Wisconsin	S	6.12 MW	6.73 AW	14000 AAW	WIBLS	10//99-12//99
	Puerto Rico	S	8.86 MW	8.41 AW	17490 AAW	PRBLS	10//99-12//99
Slaughterer and Meat Packer	Alabama	S	6.74 MW	6.88 AW	14300 AAW	ALBLS	10//99-12//99
	Arizona	S	8.67 MW	8.45 AW	17570 AAW	AZBLS	10//99-12//99
	Arkansas	S	9.07 MW	8.85 AW	18420 AAW	ARBLS	10//99-12//99
	California	S	7.53 MW	7.74 AW	16100 AAW	CABLS	10//99-12//99
	Los Angeles-Long Beach PMSA, CA	S	7.39 MW	7.28 AW	15370 AAW	CABLS	10//99-12//99
	Colorado	S	9.52 MW	9.37 AW	19500 AAW	COBLS	10//99-12//99

AAW Average annual wage	**AOH** Average offered, high	**ASH** Average starting, high	**H** Hourly	**M** Monthly	**S** Special: hourly and annual
AE Average entry wage	**AOL** Average offered, low	**ASL** Average starting, low	**HI** Highest wage paid	**MTC** Median total compensation	**TQ** Third quartile wage
AEX Average experienced wage	**APH** Average pay, high range	**AW** Average wage paid	**HR** High end range	**MW** Median wage paid	**W** Weekly
AO Average offered	**APL** Average pay, low range	**FQ** First quartile wage	**LR** Low end range	**SQ** Second quartile wage	**Y** Yearly

Occupation/Type/Industry	Location	Per	Low	Mid	High	Source	Date
Slaughterer and Meat Packer	Denver PMSA, CO	S	7.79 MW	7.48 AW	16200 AAW	COBLS	10//99-12//99
	Florida	S	8.94 MW	9.17 AW	19080 AAW	FLBLS	10//99-12//99
	Georgia	S	7.67 MW	7.62 AW	15850 AAW	GABLS	10//99-12//99
	Atlanta MSA, GA	S	7.66 MW	7.69 AW	15930 AAW	GABLS	10//99-12//99
	Augusta-Aiken MSA, GA-SC	S	7.43 MW	7.56 AW	15460 AAW	GABLS	10//99-12//99
	Idaho	S	9.75 MW	9.85 AW	20490 AAW	IDBLS	10//99-12//99
	Boise City MSA, ID	S	9.91 MW	9.79 AW	20610 AAW	IDBLS	10//99-12//99
	Illinois	S	11.38 MW	10.74 AW	22350 AAW	ILBLS	10//99-12//99
	Chicago PMSA, IL	S	10.88 MW	11.53 AW	22630 AAW	ILBLS	10//99-12//99
	Indiana	S	9.89 MW	9.91 AW	20610 AAW	INBLS	10//99-12//99
	Iowa	S	9.82 MW	9.93 AW	20650 AAW	IABLS	10//99-12//99
	Kansas	S	8.58 MW	8.99 AW	18710 AAW	KSBLS	10//99-12//99
	Kentucky	S	9.57 MW	9.48 AW	19710 AAW	KYBLS	10//99-12//99
	Louisiana	S	8.37 MW	8.54 AW	17770 AAW	LABLS	10//99-12//99
	New Orleans MSA, LA	S	10.67 MW	10.48 AW	22190 AAW	LABLS	10//99-12//99
	Massachusetts	S	10.27 MW	10.30 AW	21420 AAW	MABLS	10//99-12//99
	Boston PMSA, MA-NH	S	10.25 MW	10.19 AW	21320 AAW	MABLS	10//99-12//99
	Michigan	S	9.51 MW	9.78 AW	20330 AAW	MIBLS	10//99-12//99
	Minnesota	S	9.25 MW	9.18 AW	19090 AAW	MNBLS	10//99-12//99
	Minneapolis-St. Paul MSA, MN-WI	S	8.56 MW	8.58 AW	17800 AAW	MNBLS	10//99-12//99
	Mississippi	S	9.2 MW	8.95 AW	18620 AAW	MSBLS	10//99-12//99
	Biloxi-Gulfport-Pascagoula MSA, MS	S	5.75 MW	5.95 AW	11960 AAW	MSBLS	10//99-12//99
	Missouri	S	8.06 MW	8.21 AW	17090 AAW	MOBLS	10//99-12//99
	Montana	S	9.61 MW	9.63 AW	20020 AAW	MTBLS	10//99-12//99
	Nebraska	S	9.53 MW	9.42 AW	19600 AAW	NEBLS	10//99-12//99
	Omaha MSA, NE-IA	S	9.44 MW	9.60 AW	19640 AAW	NEBLS	10//99-12//99
	New Jersey	S	7.82 MW	7.94 AW	16510 AAW	NJBLS	10//99-12//99
	Newark PMSA, NJ	S	8.26 MW	7.81 AW	17180 AAW	NJBLS	10//99-12//99
	New York	S	8.51 MW	8.77 AW	18240 AAW	NYBLS	10//99-12//99
	New York PMSA, NY	S	8.27 MW	8.08 AW	17210 AAW	NYBLS	10//99-12//99
	North Carolina	S	7.97 MW	8.12 AW	16900 AAW	NCBLS	10//99-12//99
	Ohio	S	9.27 MW	9.14 AW	19010 AAW	OHBLS	10//99-12//99
	Youngstown-Warren MSA, OH	S	10.34 MW	10.83 AW	21520 AAW	OHBLS	10//99-12//99
	Oklahoma	S	8.83 MW	8.21 AW	17070 AAW	OKBLS	10//99-12//99
	Pennsylvania	S	10.13 MW	10.32 AW	21460 AAW	PABLS	10//99-12//99
	Philadelphia PMSA, PA-NJ	S	10.04 MW	9.87 AW	20890 AAW	PABLS	10//99-12//99
	South Carolina	S	7.98 MW	8.28 AW	17230 AAW	SCBLS	10//99-12//99
	Columbia MSA, SC	S	8.02 MW	8.09 AW	16690 AAW	SCBLS	10//99-12//99
	South Dakota	S	9.41 MW	9.45 AW	19660 AAW	SDBLS	10//99-12//99
	Tennessee	S	7.39 MW	7.40 AW	15400 AAW	TNBLS	10//99-12//99
	Nashville MSA, TN	S	7.39 MW	7.48 AW	15370 AAW	TNBLS	10//99-12//99
	Texas	S	9.39 MW	9.05 AW	18820 AAW	TXBLS	10//99-12//99
	Dallas PMSA, TX	S	7.48 MW	7.25 AW	15550 AAW	TXBLS	10//99-12//99
	San Antonio MSA, TX	S	8.26 MW	8.19 AW	17190 AAW	TXBLS	10//99-12//99
	Virginia	S	9.04 MW	8.83 AW	18360 AAW	VABLS	10//99-12//99
	Washington	S	8.05 MW	8.25 AW	17170 AAW	WABLS	10//99-12//99
	Wisconsin	S	9.5 MW	9.51 AW	19780 AAW	WIBLS	10//99-12//99
	Madison MSA, WI	S	10.60 MW	9.75 AW	22060 AAW	WIBLS	10//99-12//99
	Racine PMSA, WI	S	9.12 MW	9.22 AW	18960 AAW	WIBLS	10//99-12//99
Slot Key Person	Arizona	S	13.67 MW	13.61 AW	28310 AAW	AZBLS	10//99-12//99
	California	S	7.55 MW	10.22 AW	21270 AAW	CABLS	10//99-12//99
	Florida	S	11.29 MW	12.24 AW	25460 AAW	FLBLS	10//99-12//99
	Georgia	S	9.47 MW	10.25 AW	21320 AAW	GABLS	10//99-12//99
	Iowa	S	9.13 MW	9.37 AW	19480 AAW	IABLS	10//99-12//99
	Louisiana	S	8.54 MW	8.83 AW	18360 AAW	LABLS	10//99-12//99
	Minnesota	S	10.4 MW	10.50 AW	21850 AAW	MNBLS	10//99-12//99
	Mississippi	S	10.47 MW	10.93 AW	22740 AAW	MSBLS	10//99-12//99
	Missouri	S	12.13 MW	12.25 AW	25480 AAW	MOBLS	10//99-12//99
	Nevada	S	11.34 MW	12.30 AW	25570 AAW	NVBLS	10//99-12//99
	New York	S	11.13 MW	12.04 AW	25050 AAW	NYBLS	10//99-12//99
	Oklahoma	S	7.82 MW	7.97 AW	16570 AAW	OKBLS	10//99-12//99
	South Dakota	S	9.25 MW	9.01 AW	18750 AAW	SDBLS	10//99-12//99
	Washington	S	10.46 MW	12.50 AW	26010 AAW	WABLS	10//99-12//99
	Wisconsin	S	9.45 MW	10.53 AW	21890 AAW	WIBLS	10//99-12//99
	Puerto Rico	S	8.36 MW	8.82 AW	18340 AAW	PRBLS	10//99-12//99
Soccer Player Indoor	United States	Y	40000 LR		50000 HR	WSJ3	2000

AAW	Average annual wage	AOH	Average offered, high	ASH	Average starting, high	H	Hourly	M	Monthly	S	Special: hourly and annual
AE	Average entry wage	AOL	Average offered, low	ASL	Average starting, low	HI	Highest wage paid	MTC	Median total compensation	TQ	Third quartile wage
AEX	Average experienced wage	APH	Average pay, high range	AW	Average wage paid	HR	High end range	MW	Median wage paid	W	Weekly
AO	Average offered	APL	Average pay, low range	FQ	First quartile wage	LR	Low end range	SQ	Second quartile wage	Y	Yearly

Occupation/Type/Industry	Location	Per	Low	Mid	High	Source	Date
Social and Community Service Manager	Alabama	S	13.05 MW	14.86 AW	30910 AAW	ALBLS	10//99-12//99
	Alaska	S	20.38 MW	21.34 AW	44390 AAW	AKBLS	10//99-12//99
	Arizona	S	16.74 MW	19.12 AW	39770 AAW	AZBLS	10//99-12//99
	Arkansas	S	18.74 MW	18.39 AW	38250 AAW	ARBLS	10//99-12//99
	California	S	19.13 MW	21.23 AW	44150 AAW	CABLS	10//99-12//99
	Colorado	S	17.75 MW	18.60 AW	38690 AAW	COBLS	10//99-12//99
	Connecticut	S	22.52 MW	23.29 AW	48440 AAW	CTBLS	10//99-12//99
	District of Columbia	S	23.93 MW	23.05 AW	47950 AAW	DCBLS	10//99-12//99
	Florida	S	17 MW	19.00 AW	39530 AAW	FLBLS	10//99-12//99
	Georgia	S	23.51 MW	23.83 AW	49560 AAW	GABLS	10//99-12//99
	Hawaii	S	18.95 MW	19.76 AW	41110 AAW	HIBLS	10//99-12//99
	Idaho	S	13.39 MW	16.83 AW	35010 AAW	IDBLS	10//99-12//99
	Illinois	S	15.89 MW	17.24 AW	35850 AAW	ILBLS	10//99-12//99
	Indiana	S	15.27 MW	16.53 AW	34390 AAW	INBLS	10//99-12//99
	Iowa	S	15.79 MW	16.81 AW	34970 AAW	IABLS	10//99-12//99
	Kansas	S	13.98 MW	15.46 AW	32150 AAW	KSBLS	10//99-12//99
	Kentucky	S	17.13 MW	18.70 AW	38910 AAW	KYBLS	10//99-12//99
	Louisiana	S	16.28 MW	17.63 AW	36660 AAW	LABLS	10//99-12//99
	Maine	S	16.2 MW	17.44 AW	36280 AAW	MEBLS	10//99-12//99
	Maryland	S	21.29 MW	23.20 AW	48260 AAW	MDBLS	10//99-12//99
	Massachusetts	S	17.78 MW	18.94 AW	39390 AAW	MABLS	10//99-12//99
	Michigan	S	19.41 MW	21.58 AW	44890 AAW	MIBLS	10//99-12//99
	Minnesota	S	19.86 MW	22.37 AW	46530 AAW	MNBLS	10//99-12//99
	Mississippi	S	17.9 MW	17.66 AW	36730 AAW	MSBLS	10//99-12//99
	Missouri	S	14.61 MW	15.36 AW	31940 AAW	MOBLS	10//99-12//99
	Montana	S	10.66 MW	12.22 AW	25410 AAW	MTBLS	10//99-12//99
	Nebraska	S	18.56 MW	18.97 AW	39450 AAW	NEBLS	10//99-12//99
	Nevada	S	28.04 MW	26.80 AW	55750 AAW	NVBLS	10//99-12//99
	New Hampshire	S	18.61 MW	19.38 AW	40300 AAW	NHBLS	10//99-12//99
	New Jersey	S	21.14 MW	23.26 AW	48380 AAW	NJBLS	10//99-12//99
	New Mexico	S	16.64 MW	17.42 AW	36230 AAW	NMBLS	10//99-12//99
	New York	S	21.79 MW	23.35 AW	48560 AAW	NYBLS	10//99-12//99
	North Carolina	S	16.7 MW	19.00 AW	39520 AAW	NCBLS	10//99-12//99
	North Dakota	S	15.26 MW	15.21 AW	31640 AAW	NDBLS	10//99-12//99
	Ohio	S	16.68 MW	18.07 AW	37580 AAW	OHBLS	10//99-12//99
	Oklahoma	S	13.02 MW	14.38 AW	29920 AAW	OKBLS	10//99-12//99
	Oregon	S	17.9 MW	18.86 AW	39230 AAW	ORBLS	10//99-12//99
	Pennsylvania	S	16.58 MW	18.46 AW	38400 AAW	PABLS	10//99-12//99
	Rhode Island	S	16.5 MW	19.50 AW	40570 AAW	RIBLS	10//99-12//99
	South Carolina	S	17.85 MW	19.92 AW	41440 AAW	SCBLS	10//99-12//99
	South Dakota	S	20.93 MW	21.16 AW	44000 AAW	SDBLS	10//99-12//99
	Tennessee	S	15.06 MW	15.78 AW	32830 AAW	TNBLS	10//99-12//99
	Texas	S	16.32 MW	17.63 AW	36670 AAW	TXBLS	10//99-12//99
	Utah	S	19.13 MW	20.18 AW	41980 AAW	UTBLS	10//99-12//99
	Vermont	S	19.37 MW	22.43 AW	46650 AAW	VTBLS	10//99-12//99
	Virginia	S	19.81 MW	21.96 AW	45670 AAW	VABLS	10//99-12//99
	Washington	S	20.85 MW	22.74 AW	47300 AAW	WABLS	10//99-12//99
	West Virginia	S	14.17 MW	14.90 AW	31000 AAW	WVBLS	10//99-12//99
	Wisconsin	S	16.1 MW	17.37 AW	36130 AAW	WIBLS	10//99-12//99
	Wyoming	S	13.25 MW	15.98 AW	33230 AAW	WYBLS	10//99-12//99
	Puerto Rico	S	12.85 MW	14.35 AW	29850 AAW	PRBLS	10//99-12//99
Social and Human Service Assistant	Alabama	S	10.55 MW	11.09 AW	23060 AAW	ALBLS	10//99-12//99
	Birmingham MSA, AL	S	11.65 MW	11.44 AW	24220 AAW	ALBLS	10//99-12//99
	Decatur MSA, AL	S	7.77 MW	6.34 AW	16170 AAW	ALBLS	10//99-12//99
	Dothan MSA, AL	S	10.92 MW	10.07 AW	22710 AAW	ALBLS	10//99-12//99
	Florence MSA, AL	S	9.89 MW	8.32 AW	20580 AAW	ALBLS	10//99-12//99
	Huntsville MSA, AL	S	9.03 MW	8.06 AW	18780 AAW	ALBLS	10//99-12//99
	Mobile MSA, AL	S	10.17 MW	9.55 AW	21150 AAW	ALBLS	10//99-12//99
	Montgomery MSA, AL	S	11.39 MW	10.74 AW	23680 AAW	ALBLS	10//99-12//99
	Tuscaloosa MSA, AL	S	10.64 MW	10.91 AW	22130 AAW	ALBLS	10//99-12//99
	Alaska	S	12.48 MW	13.59 AW	28260 AAW	AKBLS	10//99-12//99
	Anchorage MSA, AK	S	11.13 MW	10.55 AW	23140 AAW	AKBLS	10//99-12//99
	Arizona	S	9.76 MW	10.46 AW	21750 AAW	AZBLS	10//99-12//99
	Flagstaff MSA, AZ-UT	S	11.24 MW	11.17 AW	23380 AAW	AZBLS	10//99-12//99
	Phoenix-Mesa MSA, AZ	S	10.73 MW	10.00 AW	22320 AAW	AZBLS	10//99-12//99
	Tucson MSA, AZ	S	9.01 MW	8.33 AW	18740 AAW	AZBLS	10//99-12//99
	Arkansas	S	9.16 MW	9.66 AW	20100 AAW	ARBLS	10//99-12//99
	Fort Smith MSA, AR-OK	S	9.18 MW	7.93 AW	19090 AAW	ARBLS	10//99-12//99

AAW	Average annual wage	**AOH**	Average offered, high	**ASH**	Average starting, high	**H**	Hourly	**M**	Monthly	**S**	Special: hourly and annual
AE	Average entry wage	**AOL**	Average offered, low	**ASL**	Average starting, low	**HI**	Highest wage paid	**MTC**	Median total compensation	**TQ**	Third quartile wage
AEX	Average experienced wage	**APH**	Average pay, high range	**AW**	Average wage paid	**HR**	High end range	**MW**	Median wage paid	**W**	Weekly
AO	Average offered	**APL**	Average pay, low range	**FQ**	First quartile wage	**LR**	Low end range	**SQ**	Second quartile wage	**Y**	Yearly

Occupation/Type/Industry	Location	Per	Low	Mid	High	Source	Date
Social and Human Service Assistant	Little Rock-North Little Rock MSA, AR	S	9.11 MW	8.47 AW	18940 AAW	ARBLS	10//99-12//99
	California	S	11.75 MW	12.64 AW	26300 AAW	CABLS	10//99-12//99
	Bakersfield MSA, CA	S	10.14 MW	7.92 AW	21090 AAW	CABLS	10//99-12//99
	Fresno MSA, CA	S	13.82 MW	11.82 AW	28750 AAW	CABLS	10//99-12//99
	Los Angeles-Long Beach PMSA, CA	S	12.01 MW	11.77 AW	24980 AAW	CABLS	10//99-12//99
	Modesto MSA, CA	S	9.91 MW	9.66 AW	20620 AAW	CABLS	10//99-12//99
	Oakland PMSA, CA	S	16.32 MW	16.26 AW	33950 AAW	CABLS	10//99-12//99
	Orange County PMSA, CA	S	13.25 MW	12.99 AW	27550 AAW	CABLS	10//99-12//99
	Redding MSA, CA	S	15.36 MW	16.63 AW	31950 AAW	CABLS	10//99-12//99
	Riverside-San Bernardino PMSA, CA	S	12.81 MW	10.36 AW	26640 AAW	CABLS	10//99-12//99
	Sacramento PMSA, CA	S	14.26 MW	11.68 AW	29660 AAW	CABLS	10//99-12//99
	Salinas MSA, CA	S	9.74 MW	9.47 AW	20260 AAW	CABLS	10//99-12//99
	San Diego MSA, CA	S	10.70 MW	10.33 AW	22260 AAW	CABLS	10//99-12//99
	San Francisco PMSA, CA	S	13.28 MW	12.13 AW	27620 AAW	CABLS	10//99-12//99
	San Jose PMSA, CA	S	15.80 MW	15.06 AW	32860 AAW	CABLS	10//99-12//99
	Santa Barbara-Santa Maria-Lompoc MSA, CA	S	12.03 MW	10.68 AW	25010 AAW	CABLS	10//99-12//99
	Santa Cruz-Watsonville PMSA, CA	S	11.58 MW	10.70 AW	24080 AAW	CABLS	10//99-12//99
	Santa Rosa PMSA, CA	S	12.87 MW	12.39 AW	26770 AAW	CABLS	10//99-12//99
	Stockton-Lodi MSA, CA	S	12.77 MW	11.66 AW	26550 AAW	CABLS	10//99-12//99
	Vallejo-Fairfield-Napa PMSA, CA	S	11.34 MW	10.76 AW	23580 AAW	CABLS	10//99-12//99
	Ventura PMSA, CA	S	9.76 MW	9.30 AW	20300 AAW	CABLS	10//99-12//99
	Visalia-Tulare-Porterville MSA, CA	S	16.08 MW	15.85 AW	33440 AAW	CABLS	10//99-12//99
	Yolo PMSA, CA	S	10.37 MW	10.69 AW	21580 AAW	CABLS	10//99-12//99
	Yuba City MSA, CA	S	13.15 MW	12.27 AW	27350 AAW	CABLS	10//99-12//99
	Colorado	S	10.62 MW	10.88 AW	22630 AAW	COBLS	10//99-12//99
	Boulder-Longmont PMSA, CO	S	12.32 MW	12.05 AW	25610 AAW	COBLS	10//99-12//99
	Colorado Springs MSA, CO	S	11.45 MW	11.04 AW	23810 AAW	COBLS	10//99-12//99
	Denver PMSA, CO	S	11.20 MW	11.23 AW	23300 AAW	COBLS	10//99-12//99
	Grand Junction MSA, CO	S	8.96 MW	8.25 AW	18630 AAW	COBLS	10//99-12//99
	Greeley PMSA, CO	S	9.35 MW	9.46 AW	19460 AAW	COBLS	10//99-12//99
	Connecticut	S	12.62 MW	13.68 AW	28450 AAW	CTBLS	10//99-12//99
	Bridgeport PMSA, CT	S	15.13 MW	14.82 AW	31480 AAW	CTBLS	10//99-12//99
	Danbury PMSA, CT	S	17.37 MW	17.10 AW	36140 AAW	CTBLS	10//99-12//99
	Hartford MSA, CT	S	14.50 MW	13.54 AW	30150 AAW	CTBLS	10//99-12//99
	New Haven-Meriden PMSA, CT	S	13.25 MW	12.04 AW	27550 AAW	CTBLS	10//99-12//99
	New London-Norwich MSA, CT-RI	S	11.87 MW	11.57 AW	24690 AAW	CTBLS	10//99-12//99
	Stamford-Norwalk PMSA, CT	S	12.74 MW	11.88 AW	26490 AAW	CTBLS	10//99-12//99
	Waterbury PMSA, CT	S	13.46 MW	12.40 AW	28000 AAW	CTBLS	10//99-12//99
	Delaware	S	8.35 MW	9.61 AW	19980 AAW	DEBLS	10//99-12//99
	Wilmington-Newark PMSA, DE-MD	S	10.22 MW	9.91 AW	21260 AAW	DEBLS	10//99-12//99
	District of Columbia	S	15.25 MW	15.04 AW	31290 AAW	DCBLS	10//99-12//99
	Washington PMSA, DC-MD-VA-WV	S	12.65 MW	12.23 AW	26310 AAW	DCBLS	10//99-12//99
	Florida	S	9.58 MW	9.99 AW	20790 AAW	FLBLS	10//99-12//99
	Daytona Beach MSA, FL	S	8.93 MW	8.71 AW	18570 AAW	FLBLS	10//99-12//99
	Fort Lauderdale PMSA, FL	S	11.39 MW	10.16 AW	23700 AAW	FLBLS	10//99-12//99
	Fort Myers-Cape Coral MSA, FL	S	14.16 MW	13.34 AW	29450 AAW	FLBLS	10//99-12//99
	Fort Pierce-Port St. Lucie MSA, FL	S	8.62 MW	8.96 AW	17920 AAW	FLBLS	10//99-12//99
	Fort Walton Beach MSA, FL	S	7.41 MW	6.80 AW	15410 AAW	FLBLS	10//99-12//99
	Gainesville MSA, FL	S	10.29 MW	10.11 AW	21400 AAW	FLBLS	10//99-12//99
	Jacksonville MSA, FL	S	9.04 MW	8.83 AW	18810 AAW	FLBLS	10//99-12//99
	Lakeland-Winter Haven MSA, FL	S	11.69 MW	10.62 AW	24320 AAW	FLBLS	10//99-12//99
	Melbourne-Titusville-Palm Bay MSA, FL	S	11.23 MW	10.20 AW	23370 AAW	FLBLS	10//99-12//99
	Miami PMSA, FL	S	9.95 MW	9.30 AW	20690 AAW	FLBLS	10//99-12//99
	Naples MSA, FL	S	8.24 MW	7.97 AW	17130 AAW	FLBLS	10//99-12//99
	Ocala MSA, FL	S	10.80 MW	9.46 AW	22460 AAW	FLBLS	10//99-12//99
	Orlando MSA, FL	S	9.87 MW	9.64 AW	20540 AAW	FLBLS	10//99-12//99

AAW Average annual wage	**AOH** Average offered, high	**ASH** Average starting, high	**H** Hourly
AE Average entry wage	**AOL** Average offered, low	**ASL** Average starting, low	**HI** Highest wage paid
AEX Average experienced wage	**APH** Average pay, high range	**AW** Average wage paid	**HR** High end range
AO Average offered	**APL** Average pay, low range	**FQ** First quartile wage	**LR** Low end range

M Monthly	**S** Special: hourly and annual
MTC Median total compensation	**TQ** Third quartile wage
MW Median wage paid	**W** Weekly
SQ Second quartile wage	**Y** Yearly

Occupation/Type/Industry	Location	Per	Low	Mid	High	Source	Date
Social and Human Service Assistant	Panama City MSA, FL	S	6.24 MW	6.12 AW	12980 AAW	FLBLS	10//99-12//99
	Pensacola MSA, FL	S	10.39 MW	10.43 AW	21610 AAW	FLBLS	10//99-12//99
	Sarasota-Bradenton MSA, FL	S	8.18 MW	7.69 AW	17010 AAW	FLBLS	10//99-12//99
	Tallahassee MSA, FL	S	8.59 MW	8.31 AW	17870 AAW	FLBLS	10//99-12//99
	Tampa-St. Petersburg-Clearwater MSA, FL	S	10.56 MW	10.56 AW	21960 AAW	FLBLS	
	West Palm Beach-Boca Raton MSA, FL	S	13.18 MW	12.29 AW	27410 AAW	FLBLS	10//99-12//99
	Georgia	S	10.09 MW	10.45 AW	21740 AAW	GABLS	10//99-12//99
	Albany MSA, GA	S	8.74 MW	8.12 AW	18190 AAW	GABLS	10//99-12//99
	Atlanta MSA, GA	S	10.94 MW	10.81 AW	22760 AAW	GABLS	10//99-12//99
	Augusta-Aiken MSA, GA-SC	S	11.01 MW	11.14 AW	22910 AAW	GABLS	10//99-12//99
	Columbus MSA, GA-AL	S	9.78 MW	9.39 AW	20350 AAW	GABLS	10//99-12//99
	Macon MSA, GA	S	7.66 MW	7.59 AW	15940 AAW	GABLS	10//99-12//99
	Hawaii	S	10.31 MW	10.92 AW	22710 AAW	HIBLS	10//99-12//99
	Honolulu MSA, HI	S	11.32 MW	10.52 AW	23550 AAW	HIBLS	10//99-12//99
	Idaho	S	8.17 MW	9.37 AW	19480 AAW	IDBLS	10//99-12//99
	Boise City MSA, ID	S	13.19 MW	12.57 AW	27430 AAW	IDBLS	10//99-12//99
	Pocatello MSA, ID	S	10.27 MW	7.94 AW	21370 AAW	IDBLS	10//99-12//99
	Illinois	S	9.44 MW	9.73 AW	20240 AAW	ILBLS	10//99-12//99
	Bloomington-Normal MSA, IL	S	9.48 MW	8.28 AW	19720 AAW	ILBLS	10//99-12//99
	Champaign-Urbana MSA, IL	S	9.98 MW	9.65 AW	20750 AAW	ILBLS	10//99-12//99
	Chicago PMSA, IL	S	9.78 MW	9.49 AW	20350 AAW	ILBLS	10//99-12//99
	Decatur MSA, IL	S	10.09 MW	9.66 AW	20990 AAW	ILBLS	10//99-12//99
	Kankakee PMSA, IL	S	7.37 MW	6.59 AW	15320 AAW	ILBLS	10//99-12//99
	Peoria-Pekin MSA, IL	S	10.17 MW	10.41 AW	21160 AAW	ILBLS	10//99-12//99
	Rockford MSA, IL	S	9.51 MW	8.86 AW	19790 AAW	ILBLS	10//99-12//99
	Springfield MSA, IL	S	11.89 MW	11.60 AW	24740 AAW	ILBLS	10//99-12//99
	Indiana	S	10.22 MW	10.52 AW	21890 AAW	INBLS	10//99-12//99
	Bloomington MSA, IN	S	7.24 MW	7.24 AW	15050 AAW	INBLS	10//99-12//99
	Elkhart-Goshen MSA, IN	S	9.78 MW	9.21 AW	20330 AAW	INBLS	10//99-12//99
	Evansville-Henderson MSA, IN-KY	S	8.72 MW	8.57 AW	18150 AAW	INBLS	10//99-12//99
	Fort Wayne MSA, IN	S	10.77 MW	10.86 AW	22400 AAW	INBLS	10//99-12//99
	Gary PMSA, IN	S	10.61 MW	11.16 AW	22070 AAW	INBLS	10//99-12//99
	Indianapolis MSA, IN	S	12.26 MW	11.99 AW	25490 AAW	INBLS	10//99-12//99
	Lafayette MSA, IN	S	8.99 MW	9.37 AW	18690 AAW	INBLS	10//99-12//99
	Muncie MSA, IN	S	10.06 MW	9.59 AW	20930 AAW	INBLS	10//99-12//99
	South Bend MSA, IN	S	10.64 MW	10.84 AW	22140 AAW	INBLS	10//99-12//99
	Iowa	S	10.46 MW	10.87 AW	22610 AAW	IABLS	10//99-12//99
	Cedar Rapids MSA, IA	S	8.19 MW	7.68 AW	17040 AAW	IABLS	10//99-12//99
	Davenport-Moline-Rock Island MSA, IA-IL	S	8.37 MW	7.62 AW	17410 AAW	IABLS	10//99-12//99
	Des Moines MSA, IA	S	10.93 MW	10.08 AW	22730 AAW	IABLS	10//99-12//99
	Iowa City MSA, IA	S	9.26 MW	8.65 AW	19260 AAW	IABLS	10//99-12//99
	Sioux City MSA, IA-NE	S	12.75 MW	10.15 AW	26520 AAW	IABLS	10//99-12//99
	Kansas	S	10.81 MW	10.59 AW	22020 AAW	KSBLS	10//99-12//99
	Lawrence MSA, KS	S	11.14 MW	11.22 AW	23180 AAW	KSBLS	10//99-12//99
	Topeka MSA, KS	S	11.68 MW	11.90 AW	24290 AAW	KSBLS	10//99-12//99
	Wichita MSA, KS	S	11.54 MW	11.37 AW	24010 AAW	KSBLS	10//99-12//99
	Kentucky	S	8.84 MW	9.41 AW	19580 AAW	KYBLS	10//99-12//99
	Lexington MSA, KY	S	8.86 MW	7.81 AW	18430 AAW	KYBLS	10//99-12//99
	Louisville MSA, KY-IN	S	12.01 MW	11.73 AW	24980 AAW	KYBLS	10//99-12//99
	Owensboro MSA, KY	S	9.19 MW	8.85 AW	19110 AAW	KYBLS	10//99-12//99
	Louisiana	S	7.74 MW	8.25 AW	17150 AAW	LABLS	10//99-12//99
	Baton Rouge MSA, LA	S	7.99 MW	7.67 AW	16610 AAW	LABLS	10//99-12//99
	Houma MSA, LA	S	8.90 MW	8.69 AW	18510 AAW	LABLS	10//99-12//99
	Lafayette MSA, LA	S	10.67 MW	9.32 AW	22200 AAW	LABLS	10//99-12//99
	Lake Charles MSA, LA	S	8.74 MW	8.66 AW	18180 AAW	LABLS	10//99-12//99
	Monroe MSA, LA	S	7.91 MW	6.95 AW	16460 AAW	LABLS	10//99-12//99
	New Orleans MSA, LA	S	9.02 MW	9.00 AW	18760 AAW	LABLS	10//99-12//99
	Shreveport-Bossier City MSA, LA	S	8.25 MW	8.06 AW	17160 AAW	LABLS	10//99-12//99
	Maine	S	10.33 MW	10.37 AW	21570 AAW	MEBLS	10//99-12//99
	Bangor MSA, ME	S	11.07 MW	11.08 AW	23020 AAW	MEBLS	10//99-12//99
	Lewiston-Auburn MSA, ME	S	9.63 MW	9.55 AW	20040 AAW	MEBLS	10//99-12//99
	Portland MSA, ME	S	11.36 MW	11.36 AW	23620 AAW	MEBLS	10//99-12//99
	Maryland	S	11.81 MW	12.40 AW	25800 AAW	MDBLS	10//99-12//99
	Baltimore PMSA, MD	S	12.61 MW	12.02 AW	26230 AAW	MDBLS	10//99-12//99
	Hagerstown PMSA, MD	S	11.18 MW	11.45 AW	23250 AAW	MDBLS	10//99-12//99
	Massachusetts	S	10.73 MW	11.73 AW	24410 AAW	MABLS	10//99-12//99

AAW Average annual wage	AOH Average offered, high	ASH Average starting, high	H Hourly	M Monthly	S Special: hourly and annual
AE Average entry wage	AOL Average offered, low	ASL Average starting, low	HI Highest wage paid	MTC Median total compensation	TQ Third quartile wage
AEX Average experienced wage	APH Average pay, high range	AW Average wage paid	HR High end range	MW Median wage paid	W Weekly
AO Average offered	APL Average pay, low range	FQ First quartile wage	LR Low end range	SQ Second quartile wage	Y Yearly

Occupation/Type/Industry	Location	Per	Low	Mid	High	Source	Date
Social and Human Service Assistant	Barnstable-Yarmouth MSA, MA	S	13.78 mw	13.88 aw	28670 aaw	MABLS	10//99-12//99
	Boston PMSA, MA-NH	S	12.05 mw	11.69 aw	25060 aaw	MABLS	10//99-12//99
	Brockton PMSA, MA	S	11.66 mw	10.37 aw	24250 aaw	MABLS	10//99-12//99
	Fitchburg-Leominster PMSA, MA	S	13.46 mw	10.43 aw	28010 aaw	MABLS	10//99-12//99
	Lawrence PMSA, MA-NH	S	12.63 mw	12.35 aw	26270 aaw	MABLS	10//99-12//99
	Lowell PMSA, MA-NH	S	9.46 mw	8.69 aw	19690 aaw	MABLS	10//99-12//99
	New Bedford PMSA, MA	S	11.74 mw	10.53 aw	24420 aaw	MABLS	10//99-12//99
	Pittsfield MSA, MA	S	8.88 mw	7.49 aw	18460 aaw	MABLS	10//99-12//99
	Springfield MSA, MA	S	11.94 mw	10.18 aw	24830 aaw	MABLS	10//99-12//99
	Worcester PMSA, MA-CT	S	11.63 mw	10.09 aw	24200 aaw	MABLS	10//99-12//99
	Michigan	S	11.04 mw	11.20 aw	23300 aaw	MIBLS	10//99-12//99
	Ann Arbor PMSA, MI	S	12.44 mw	11.79 aw	25870 aaw	MIBLS	10//99-12//99
	Detroit PMSA, MI	S	10.48 mw	10.26 aw	21800 aaw	MIBLS	10//99-12//99
	Flint PMSA, MI	S	10.67 mw	10.88 aw	22190 aaw	MIBLS	10//99-12//99
	Grand Rapids-Muskegon-Holland MSA, MI	S	13.32 mw	13.61 aw	27700 aaw	MIBLS	10//99-12//99
	Kalamazoo-Battle Creek MSA, MI	S	11.99 mw	11.15 aw	24950 aaw	MIBLS	10//99-12//99
	Lansing-East Lansing MSA, MI	S	13.72 mw	12.82 aw	28540 aaw	MIBLS	10//99-12//99
	Saginaw-Bay City-Midland MSA, MI	S	11.00 mw	11.25 aw	22870 aaw	MIBLS	10//99-12//99
	Minnesota	S	10.72 mw	11.30 aw	23500 aaw	MNBLS	10//99-12//99
	Duluth-Superior MSA, MN-WI	S	8.87 mw	8.05 aw	18450 aaw	MNBLS	10//99-12//99
	Minneapolis-St. Paul MSA, MN-WI	S	12.01 mw	11.44 aw	24970 aaw	MNBLS	10//99-12//99
	Rochester MSA, MN	S	12.83 mw	12.59 aw	26690 aaw	MNBLS	10//99-12//99
	Mississippi	S	8.14 mw	8.71 aw	18120 aaw	MSBLS	10//99-12//99
	Biloxi-Gulfport-Pascagoula MSA, MS	S	8.65 mw	8.12 aw	17980 aaw	MSBLS	10//99-12//99
	Jackson MSA, MS	S	7.94 mw	6.69 aw	16520 aaw	MSBLS	10//99-12//99
	Missouri	S	9.47 mw	10.14 aw	21080 aaw	MOBLS	10//99-12//99
	Columbia MSA, MO	S	9.71 mw	8.59 aw	20200 aaw	MOBLS	10//99-12//99
	Joplin MSA, MO	S	10.14 mw	9.65 aw	21090 aaw	MOBLS	10//99-12//99
	Kansas City MSA, MO-KS	S	10.80 mw	11.27 aw	22460 aaw	MOBLS	10//99-12//99
	St. Joseph MSA, MO	S	11.62 mw	11.28 aw	24170 aaw	MOBLS	10//99-12//99
	St. Louis MSA, MO-IL	S	9.68 mw	8.88 aw	20120 aaw	MOBLS	10//99-12//99
	Springfield MSA, MO	S	8.70 mw	8.22 aw	18100 aaw	MOBLS	10//99-12//99
	Montana	S	8.38 mw	8.68 aw	18060 aaw	MTBLS	10//99-12//99
	Billings MSA, MT	S	7.63 mw	6.85 aw	15880 aaw	MTBLS	10//99-12//99
	Great Falls MSA, MT	S	9.52 mw	8.78 aw	19800 aaw	MTBLS	10//99-12//99
	Missoula MSA, MT	S	10.03 mw	9.75 aw	20870 aaw	MTBLS	10//99-12//99
	Nebraska	S	11.36 mw	11.59 aw	24100 aaw	NEBLS	10//99-12//99
	Lincoln MSA, NE	S	10.42 mw	10.21 aw	21670 aaw	NEBLS	10//99-12//99
	Omaha MSA, NE-IA	S	10.49 mw	10.06 aw	21830 aaw	NEBLS	10//99-12//99
	Nevada	S	10.25 mw	10.79 aw	22440 aaw	NVBLS	10//99-12//99
	Las Vegas MSA, NV-AZ	S	10.33 mw	9.73 aw	21490 aaw	NVBLS	10//99-12//99
	New Hampshire	S	9 mw	9.25 aw	19240 aaw	NHBLS	10//99-12//99
	Manchester PMSA, NH	S	9.50 mw	9.30 aw	19760 aaw	NHBLS	10//99-12//99
	Nashua PMSA, NH	S	8.43 mw	8.10 aw	17540 aaw	NHBLS	10//99-12//99
	Portsmouth-Rochester PMSA, NH-ME	S	10.52 mw	10.16 aw	21890 aaw	NHBLS	10//99-12//99
	New Jersey	S	10.12 mw	11.15 aw	23180 aaw	NJBLS	10//99-12//99
	Atlantic-Cape May PMSA, NJ	S	11.26 mw	11.58 aw	23430 aaw	NJBLS	10//99-12//99
	Bergen-Passaic PMSA, NJ	S	10.20 mw	9.72 aw	21220 aaw	NJBLS	10//99-12//99
	Middlesex-Somerset-Hunterdon PMSA, NJ	S	11.23 mw	10.17 aw	23370 aaw	NJBLS	10//99-12//99
	Monmouth-Ocean PMSA, NJ	S	12.88 mw	13.85 aw	26800 aaw	NJBLS	10//99-12//99
	Newark PMSA, NJ	S	11.45 mw	10.22 aw	23820 aaw	NJBLS	10//99-12//99
	Trenton PMSA, NJ	S	10.87 mw	8.72 aw	22620 aaw	NJBLS	10//99-12//99
	Vineland-Millville-Bridgeton PMSA, NJ	S	11.73 mw	9.94 aw	24390 aaw	NJBLS	10//99-12//99
	New Mexico	S	9.17 mw	9.38 aw	19510 aaw	NMBLS	10//99-12//99
	Albuquerque MSA, NM	S	10.67 mw	10.44 aw	22190 aaw	NMBLS	10//99-12//99
	Las Cruces MSA, NM	S	8.70 mw	8.78 aw	18090 aaw	NMBLS	10//99-12//99
	New York	S	11.9 mw	12.27 aw	25530 aaw	NYBLS	10//99-12//99
	Albany-Schenectady-Troy MSA, NY	S	12.26 mw	11.22 aw	25500 aaw	NYBLS	10//99-12//99
	Binghamton MSA, NY	S	8.26 mw	7.39 aw	17180 aaw	NYBLS	10//99-12//99

AAW Average annual wage	**AOH** Average offered, high	**ASH** Average starting, high	**H** Hourly	**M** Monthly	**S** Special: hourly and annual
AE Average entry wage	**AOL** Average offered, low	**ASL** Average starting, low	**HI** Highest wage paid	**MTC** Median total compensation	**TQ** Third quartile wage
AEX Average experienced wage	**APH** Average pay, high range	**AW** Average wage paid	**HR** High end range	**MW** Median wage paid	**W** Weekly
AO Average offered	**APL** Average pay, low range	**FQ** First quartile wage	**LR** Low end range	**SQ** Second quartile wage	**Y** Yearly

Occupation/Type/Industry	Location	Per	Low	Mid	High	Source	Date
Social and Human Service Assistant							
	Buffalo-Niagara Falls MSA, NY	S	13.03 MW	13.57 AW	27100 AAW	NYBLS	10//99-12//99
	Dutchess County PMSA, NY	S	15.34 MW	15.40 AW	31910 AAW	NYBLS	10//99-12//99
	Elmira MSA, NY	S	11.73 MW	10.40 AW	24390 AAW	NYBLS	10//99-12//99
	Jamestown MSA, NY	S	11.86 MW	11.78 AW	24670 AAW	NYBLS	10//99-12//99
	Nassau-Suffolk PMSA, NY	S	12.86 MW	12.72 AW	26740 AAW	NYBLS	10//99-12//99
	New York PMSA, NY	S	12.26 MW	12.07 AW	25490 AAW	NYBLS	10//99-12//99
	Newburgh PMSA, NY-PA	S	12.82 MW	11.39 AW	26660 AAW	NYBLS	10//99-12//99
	Rochester MSA, NY	S	12.75 MW	12.41 AW	26530 AAW	NYBLS	10//99-12//99
	Syracuse MSA, NY	S	10.07 MW	9.50 AW	20940 AAW	NYBLS	10//99-12//99
	Utica-Rome MSA, NY	S	10.54 MW	10.10 AW	21930 AAW	NYBLS	10//99-12//99
	North Carolina	S	9.8 MW	10.24 AW	21300 AAW	NCBLS	10//99-12//99
	Asheville MSA, NC	S	9.22 MW	9.58 AW	19170 AAW	NCBLS	10//99-12//99
	Charlotte-Gastonia-Rock Hill MSA, NC-SC	S	10.50 MW	10.12 AW	21850 AAW	NCBLS	10//99-12//99
	Fayetteville MSA, NC	S	12.51 MW	11.94 AW	26020 AAW	NCBLS	10//99-12//99
	Goldsboro MSA, NC	S	8.69 MW	8.10 AW	18070 AAW	NCBLS	10//99-12//99
	Greensboro--Winston-Salem--High Point MSA, NC	S	9.82 MW	8.71 AW	20430 AAW	NCBLS	10//99-12//99
	Greenville MSA, NC	S	7.80 MW	6.44 AW	16220 AAW	NCBLS	10//99-12//99
	Hickory-Morganton-Lenoir MSA, NC	S	14.90 MW	13.98 AW	30980 AAW	NCBLS	10//99-12//99
	Raleigh-Durham-Chapel Hill MSA, NC	S	9.71 MW	9.32 AW	20190 AAW	NCBLS	10//99-12//99
	Rocky Mount MSA, NC	S	11.95 MW	12.04 AW	24860 AAW	NCBLS	10//99-12//99
	Wilmington MSA, NC	S	10.83 MW	10.68 AW	22530 AAW	NCBLS	10//99-12//99
	North Dakota	S	9.53 MW	9.87 AW	20520 AAW	NDBLS	10//99-12//99
	Bismarck MSA, ND	S	9.69 MW	9.64 AW	20150 AAW	NDBLS	10//99-12//99
	Fargo-Moorhead MSA, ND-MN	S	11.38 MW	11.87 AW	23670 AAW	NDBLS	10//99-12//99
	Grand Forks MSA, ND-MN	S	11.41 MW	11.39 AW	23740 AAW	NDBLS	10//99-12//99
	Ohio	S	10.48 MW	10.80 AW	22460 AAW	OHBLS	10//99-12//99
	Akron PMSA, OH	S	10.45 MW	10.31 AW	21740 AAW	OHBLS	10//99-12//99
	Canton-Massillon MSA, OH	S	12.12 MW	11.69 AW	25220 AAW	OHBLS	10//99-12//99
	Cincinnati PMSA, OH-KY-IN	S	10.85 MW	10.58 AW	22560 AAW	OHBLS	10//99-12//99
	Cleveland-Lorain-Elyria PMSA, OH	S	10.31 MW	10.04 AW	21440 AAW	OHBLS	10//99-12//99
	Columbus MSA, OH	S	12.25 MW	12.35 AW	25470 AAW	OHBLS	10//99-12//99
	Dayton-Springfield MSA, OH	S	10.53 MW	10.09 AW	21900 AAW	OHBLS	10//99-12//99
	Lima MSA, OH	S	10.85 MW	10.52 AW	22570 AAW	OHBLS	10//99-12//99
	Mansfield MSA, OH	S	9.54 MW	9.30 AW	19830 AAW	OHBLS	10//99-12//99
	Toledo MSA, OH	S	11.93 MW	11.73 AW	24810 AAW	OHBLS	10//99-12//99
	Youngstown-Warren MSA, OH	S	10.36 MW	10.14 AW	21540 AAW	OHBLS	10//99-12//99
	Oklahoma	S	9.68 MW	10.12 AW	21050 AAW	OKBLS	10//99-12//99
	Lawton MSA, OK	S	9.91 MW	9.69 AW	20610 AAW	OKBLS	10//99-12//99
	Oklahoma City MSA, OK	S	9.66 MW	9.19 AW	20090 AAW	OKBLS	10//99-12//99
	Tulsa MSA, OK	S	11.94 MW	11.23 AW	24830 AAW	OKBLS	10//99-12//99
	Oregon	S	9.12 MW	9.78 AW	20350 AAW	ORBLS	10//99-12//99
	Corvallis MSA, OR	S	8.22 MW	7.85 AW	17100 AAW	ORBLS	10//99-12//99
	Eugene-Springfield MSA, OR	S	8.41 MW	8.01 AW	17490 AAW	ORBLS	10//99-12//99
	Medford-Ashland MSA, OR	S	10.60 MW	10.29 AW	22040 AAW	ORBLS	10//99-12//99
	Portland-Vancouver PMSA, OR-WA	S	9.44 MW	9.19 AW	19640 AAW	ORBLS	10//99-12//99
	Salem PMSA, OR	S	11.84 MW	10.31 AW	24620 AAW	ORBLS	10//99-12//99
	Pennsylvania	S	9.78 MW	10.30 AW	21430 AAW	PABLS	10//99-12//99
	Allentown-Bethlehem-Easton MSA, PA	S	10.80 MW	10.13 AW	22450 AAW	PABLS	10//99-12//99
	Erie MSA, PA	S	7.97 MW	7.83 AW	16570 AAW	PABLS	10//99-12//99
	Harrisburg-Lebanon-Carlisle MSA, PA	S	10.41 MW	9.60 AW	21640 AAW	PABLS	10//99-12//99
	Lancaster MSA, PA	S	11.30 MW	11.01 AW	23500 AAW	PABLS	10//99-12//99
	Philadelphia PMSA, PA-NJ	S	11.24 MW	10.67 AW	23370 AAW	PABLS	10//99-12//99
	Pittsburgh MSA, PA	S	8.93 MW	8.91 AW	18570 AAW	PABLS	10//99-12//99
	Reading MSA, PA	S	9.45 MW	9.22 AW	19660 AAW	PABLS	10//99-12//99
	Scranton--Wilkes-Barre--Hazleton MSA, PA	S	9.86 MW	9.66 AW	20500 AAW	PABLS	10//99-12//99
	State College MSA, PA	S	12.73 MW	11.84 AW	26470 AAW	PABLS	10//99-12//99
	York MSA, PA	S	8.33 MW	8.13 AW	17330 AAW	PABLS	10//99-12//99
	Rhode Island	S	9.2 MW	9.71 AW	20200 AAW	RIBLS	10//99-12//99
	Providence-Fall River-Warwick MSA, RI-MA	S	9.79 MW	9.19 AW	20370 AAW	RIBLS	10//99-12//99

AAW	Average annual wage	AOH	Average offered, high	ASH	Average starting, high
AE	Average entry wage	AOL	Average offered, low	ASL	Average starting, low
AEX	Average experienced wage	APH	Average pay, high range	AW	Average wage paid
AO	Average offered	APL	Average pay, low range	FQ	First quartile wage

H	Hourly	M	Monthly	S	Special: hourly and annual
HI	Highest wage paid	MTC	Median total compensation	TQ	Third quartile wage
HR	High end range	MW	Median wage paid	W	Weekly
LR	Low end range	SQ	Second quartile wage	Y	Yearly

Occupation/Type/Industry	Location	Per	Low	Mid	High	Source	Date
Social and Human Service Assistant	South Carolina	S	8.06 MW	8.90 AW	18510 AAW	SCBLS	10//99-12//99
	Greenville-Spartanburg-Anderson MSA, SC	S	8.56 MW	8.16 AW	17810 AAW	SCBLS	10//99-12//99
	Sumter MSA, SC	S	7.67 MW	7.62 AW	15960 AAW	SCBLS	10//99-12//99
	South Dakota	S	9.17 MW	9.21 AW	19150 AAW	SDBLS	10//99-12//99
	Rapid City MSA, SD	S	9.31 MW	9.22 AW	19370 AAW	SDBLS	10//99-12//99
	Tennessee	S	11.93 MW	12.02 AW	25000 AAW	TNBLS	10//99-12//99
	Chattanooga MSA, TN-GA	S	12.40 MW	11.35 AW	25800 AAW	TNBLS	10//99-12//99
	Clarksville-Hopkinsville MSA, TN-KY	S	8.75 MW	6.74 AW	18200 AAW	TNBLS	10//99-12//99
	Johnson City-Kingsport-Bristol MSA, TN-VA	S	7.52 MW	6.37 AW	15640 AAW	TNBLS	10//99-12//99
	Knoxville MSA, TN	S	11.79 MW	10.67 AW	24520 AAW	TNBLS	10//99-12//99
	Memphis MSA, TN-AR-MS	S	12.06 MW	11.92 AW	25090 AAW	MSBLS	10//99-12//99
	Nashville MSA, TN	S	12.96 MW	12.67 AW	26950 AAW	TNBLS	10//99-12//99
	Texas	S	9.97 MW	10.55 AW	21940 AAW	TXBLS	10//99-12//99
	Amarillo MSA, TX	S	9.98 MW	9.47 AW	20750 AAW	TXBLS	10//99-12//99
	Austin-San Marcos MSA, TX	S	10.45 MW	9.90 AW	21730 AAW	TXBLS	10//99-12//99
	Beaumont-Port Arthur MSA, TX	S	11.79 MW	10.32 AW	24510 AAW	TXBLS	10//99-12//99
	Corpus Christi MSA, TX	S	9.70 MW	9.53 AW	20170 AAW	TXBLS	10//99-12//99
	Dallas PMSA, TX	S	13.55 MW	12.60 AW	28180 AAW	TXBLS	10//99-12//99
	El Paso MSA, TX	S	10.80 MW	10.86 AW	22460 AAW	TXBLS	10//99-12//99
	Fort Worth-Arlington PMSA, TX	S	9.66 MW	8.97 AW	20100 AAW	TXBLS	10//99-12//99
	Galveston-Texas City PMSA, TX	S	10.10 MW	9.95 AW	21010 AAW	TXBLS	10//99-12//99
	Houston PMSA, TX	S	9.90 MW	9.88 AW	20600 AAW	TXBLS	10//99-12//99
	Killeen-Temple MSA, TX	S	8.82 MW	7.84 AW	18340 AAW	TXBLS	10//99-12//99
	Laredo MSA, TX	S	9.93 MW	8.13 AW	20660 AAW	TXBLS	10//99-12//99
	Longview-Marshall MSA, TX	S	8.19 MW	7.92 AW	17040 AAW	TXBLS	10//99-12//99
	McAllen-Edinburg-Mission MSA, TX	S	9.74 MW	11.07 AW	20260 AAW	TXBLS	10//99-12//99
	Odessa-Midland MSA, TX	S	8.72 MW	9.25 AW	18130 AAW	TXBLS	10//99-12//99
	San Angelo MSA, TX	S	12.14 MW	11.50 AW	25250 AAW	TXBLS	10//99-12//99
	San Antonio MSA, TX	S	13.22 MW	13.15 AW	27510 AAW	TXBLS	10//99-12//99
	Texarkana MSA, TX-Texarkana, AR	S	10.91 MW	10.99 AW	22700 AAW	TXBLS	10//99-12//99
	Wichita Falls MSA, TX	S	8.14 MW	7.70 AW	16940 AAW	TXBLS	10//99-12//99
	Utah	S	9.13 MW	10.04 AW	20890 AAW	UTBLS	10//99-12//99
	Provo-Orem MSA, UT	S	9.83 MW	8.87 AW	20450 AAW	UTBLS	10//99-12//99
	Salt Lake City-Ogden MSA, UT	S	10.51 MW	9.88 AW	21850 AAW	UTBLS	10//99-12//99
	Vermont	S	11.98 MW	11.90 AW	24750 AAW	VTBLS	10//99-12//99
	Burlington MSA, VT	S	13.07 MW	12.65 AW	27180 AAW	VTBLS	10//99-12//99
	Virginia	S	10.86 MW	11.04 AW	22950 AAW	VABLS	10//99-12//99
	Lynchburg MSA, VA	S	8.13 MW	7.68 AW	16910 AAW	VABLS	10//99-12//99
	Norfolk-Virginia Beach-Newport News MSA, VA-NC	S	9.80 MW	9.78 AW	20380 AAW	VABLS	10//99-12//99
	Richmond-Petersburg MSA, VA	S	10.32 MW	10.36 AW	21470 AAW	VABLS	10//99-12//99
	Roanoke MSA, VA	S	10.04 MW	9.77 AW	20880 AAW	VABLS	10//99-12//99
	Washington	S	10.63 MW	11.63 AW	24200 AAW	WABLS	10//99-12//99
	Bellingham MSA, WA	S	13.28 MW	14.29 AW	27610 AAW	WABLS	10//99-12//99
	Bremerton PMSA, WA	S	9.44 MW	8.79 AW	19630 AAW	WABLS	10//99-12//99
	Olympia PMSA, WA	S	9.47 MW	9.48 AW	19690 AAW	WABLS	10//99-12//99
	Richland-Kennewick-Pasco MSA, WA	S	12.12 MW	13.78 AW	25210 AAW	WABLS	10//99-12//99
	Seattle-Bellevue-Everett PMSA, WA	S	12.69 MW	12.21 AW	26400 AAW	WABLS	10//99-12//99
	Spokane MSA, WA	S	10.39 MW	9.00 AW	21620 AAW	WABLS	10//99-12//99
	Tacoma PMSA, WA	S	11.40 MW	10.17 AW	23710 AAW	WABLS	10//99-12//99
	Yakima MSA, WA	S	10.89 MW	10.97 AW	22650 AAW	WABLS	10//99-12//99
	West Virginia	S	6.59 MW	7.21 AW	14990 AAW	WVBLS	10//99-12//99
	Charleston MSA, WV	S	7.44 MW	6.12 AW	15470 AAW	WVBLS	10//99-12//99
	Huntington-Ashland MSA, WV-KY-OH	S	9.66 MW	8.06 AW	20080 AAW	WVBLS	10//99-12//99
	Parkersburg-Marietta MSA, WV-OH	S	6.80 MW	6.55 AW	14140 AAW	WVBLS	10//99-12//99
	Wisconsin	S	9.83 MW	10.58 AW	22000 AAW	WIBLS	10//99-12//99

AAW	Average annual wage	AOH	Average offered, high	ASH	Average starting, high
AE	Average entry wage	AOL	Average offered, low	ASL	Average starting, low
AEX	Average experienced wage	APH	Average pay, high range	AW	Average wage paid
AO	Average offered	APL	Average pay, low range	FQ	First quartile wage

H	Hourly	M	Monthly	S	Special: hourly and annual
HI	Highest wage paid	MTC	Median total compensation	TQ	Third quartile wage
HR	High end range	MW	Median wage paid	W	Weekly
LR	Low end range	SQ	Second quartile wage	Y	Yearly

Occupation/Type/Industry	Location	Per	Low	Mid	High	Source	Date
Social and Human Service Assistant	Appleton-Oshkosh-Neenah MSA, WI	S	10.42 MW	10.28 AW	21670 AAW	WIBLS	10//99-12//99
	Eau Claire MSA, WI	S	11.77 MW	11.55 AW	24470 AAW	WIBLS	10//99-12//99
	Green Bay MSA, WI	S	13.05 MW	12.27 AW	27140 AAW	WIBLS	·10//99-12//99
	Janesville-Beloit MSA, WI	S	11.25 MW	11.54 AW	23410 AAW	WIBLS	10//99-12//99
	La Crosse MSA, WI-MN	S	9.35 MW	9.24 AW	19450 AAW	WIBLS	10//99-12//99
	Madison MSA, WI	S	11.75 MW	10.22 AW	24440 AAW	WIBLS	10//99-12//99
	Milwaukee-Waukesha PMSA, WI	S	9.42 MW	8.94 AW	19590 AAW	WIBLS	10//99-12//99
	Racine PMSA, WI	S	8.77 MW	8.48 AW	18250 AAW	WIBLS	10//99-12//99
	Sheboygan MSA, WI	S	10.36 MW	9.73 AW	21540 AAW	WIBLS	10//99-12//99
	Wyoming	S	9.09 MW	9.23 AW	19210 AAW	WYBLS	10//99-12//99
	Cheyenne MSA, WY	S	10.55 MW	10.27 AW	21940 AAW	WYBLS	10//99-12//99
	Caguas PMSA, PR	S	8.24 MW	7.80 AW	17140 AAW	PRBLS	10//99-12//99
	Mayaguez MSA, PR	S	6.25 MW	6.26 AW	12990 AAW	PRBLS	10//99-12//99
Social Work Teacher							
Postsecondary	Alabama	Y		43170 AAW		ALBLS	10//99-12//99
Postsecondary	California	Y		38770 AAW		CABLS	10//99-12//99
Postsecondary	Colorado	Y		54950 AAW		COBLS	10//99-12//99
Postsecondary	Connecticut	Y		63910 AAW		CTBLS	10//99-12//99
Postsecondary	Idaho	Y		47540 AAW		IDBLS	10//99-12//99
Postsecondary	Illinois	Y		51640 AAW		ILBLS	10//99-12//99
Postsecondary	Indiana	Y		44230 AAW		INBLS	10//99-12//99
Postsecondary	Iowa	Y		43410 AAW		IABLS	10//99-12//99
Postsecondary	Kansas	Y		41790 AAW		KSBLS	10//99-12//99
Postsecondary	Kentucky	Y		37020 AAW		KYBLS	10//99-12//99
Postsecondary	Louisiana	Y		42170 AAW		LABLS	10//99-12//99
Postsecondary	Maryland	Y		49470 AAW		MDBLS	10//99-12//99
Postsecondary	Massachusetts	Y		45170 AAW		MABLS	10//99-12//99
Postsecondary	Michigan	Y		51220 AAW		MIBLS	10//99-12//99
Postsecondary	Minnesota	Y		49600 AAW		MNBLS	10//99-12//99
Postsecondary	Mississippi	Y		38680 AAW		MSBLS	10//99-12//99
Postsecondary	Missouri	Y		47060 AAW		MOBLS	10//99-12//99
Postsecondary	New Hampshire	Y		33930 AAW		NHBLS	10//99-12//99
Postsecondary	New Jersey	Y		52540 AAW		NJBLS	10//99-12//99
Postsecondary	New York	Y		45480 AAW		NYBLS	10//99-12//99
Postsecondary	North Carolina	Y		49120 AAW		NCBLS	10//99-12//99
Postsecondary	Ohio	·Y		36880 AAW		OHBLS	10//99-12//99
Postsecondary	Oklahoma	Y		41340 AAW		OKBLS	10//99-12//99
Postsecondary	Pennsylvania	Y		42080 AAW		PABLS	10//99-12//99
Postsecondary	Rhode Island	Y		44980 AAW		RIBLS	10//99-12//99
Postsecondary	South Carolina	Y		46790 AAW		SCBLS	10//99-12//99
Postsecondary	Tennessee	Y		43770 AAW		TNBLS	10//99-12//99
Postsecondary	Texas	Y		40510 AAW		TXBLS	10//99-12//99
Postsecondary	Vermont	Y		48460 AAW		VTBLS	10//99-12//99
Postsecondary	Virginia	Y		40370 AAW		VABLS	10//99-12//99
Postsecondary	Washington	Y		48870 AAW		WABLS	10//99-12//99
Postsecondary	West Virginia	Y		51200 AAW		WVBLS	10//99-12//99
Postsecondary	Wisconsin	Y		40770 AAW		WIBLS	10//99-12//99
Postsecondary	Puerto Rico	Y		34650 AAW		PRBLS	10//99-12//99
Social Worker	United States	H		16.08 AW		NCS98	.1998
Female	United States	Y		29536 MW		WOWO2	1998
Female	United States	Y		30108 MW		WOWO2	1999
Male	United States	Y		34372 MW		WOWO1	1999
Male	United States	Y		31668 MW		WOWO2	1998
Masters, Licensed, Behavioral Health Organization	United States	Y	28847 APL	34642 AW	41900 APH	ADAW	2000
Sociologist	United States	H		17.54 AW		NCS98	1998
	California	S	18.55 MW	16.92 AW	35190 AAW	CABLS	10//99-12//99
	District of Columbia	S	31.33 MW	32.06 AW	66680 AAW	DCBLS	10//99-12//99
	Washington PMSA, DC-MD-VA-WV	S	31.37 MW	30.08 AW	65250 AAW	DCBLS	10//99-12//99
	New Jersey	S	15.42 MW	16.65 AW	34640 AAW	NJBLS	10//99-12//99
	Pennsylvania	S	19.71 MW	22.94 AW	47710 AAW	PABLS	10//99-12//99
	Philadelphia PMSA, PA-NJ	S	22.13 MW	19.40 AW	46030 AAW	PABLS	10//99-12//99
	Washington	S	30.71 MW	33.34 AW	69350 AAW	WABLS	10//99-12//99
	Seattle-Bellevue-Everett PMSA, WA	S	33.47 MW	30.85 AW	69630 AAW	WABLS	10//99-12//99

AAW Average annual wage	AOH Average offered, high	ASH Average starting, high	H Hourly	M Monthly	S Special: hourly and annual
AE Average entry wage	AOL Average offered, low	ASL Average starting, low	HI Highest wage paid	MTC Median total compensation	TQ Third quartile wage
AEX Average experienced wage	APH Average pay, high range	AW Average wage paid	HR High end range	MW Median wage paid	W Weekly
AO Average offered	APL Average pay, low range	FQ First quartile wage	LR Low end range	SQ Second quartile wage	Y Yearly

Sociology Teacher

Occupation/Type/Industry	Location	Per	Low	Mid	High	Source	Date
Sociology Teacher							
Postsecondary	Alabama	Y		28310 AAW		ALBLS	10//99-12//99
Postsecondary	Arkansas	Y		49060 AAW		ARBLS	10//99-12//99
Postsecondary	California	Y		59370 AAW		CABLS	10//99-12//99
Postsecondary	Colorado	Y		53680 AAW		COBLS	10//99-12//99
Postsecondary	Washington PMSA, DC-MD-VA-WV	Y		55760 AAW		DCBLS	10//99-12//99
Postsecondary	Florida	Y		52300 AAW		FLBLS	10//99-12//99
Postsecondary	Miami PMSA, FL	Y		79100 AAW		FLBLS	10//99-12//99
Postsecondary	Tampa-St. Petersburg-Clearwater MSA, FL	Y		35190 AAW		FLBLS	10//99-12//99
Postsecondary	Georgia	Y		43650 AAW		GABLS	10//99-12//99
Postsecondary	Illinois	Y		56900 AAW		ILBLS	10//99-12//99
Postsecondary	Chicago PMSA, IL	Y		54780 AAW		ILBLS	10//99-12//99
Postsecondary	Indiana	Y		45170 AAW		INBLS	10//99-12//99
Postsecondary	Iowa	Y		61510 AAW		IABLS	10//99-12//99
Postsecondary	Kansas	Y		32600 AAW		KSBLS	10//99-12//99
Postsecondary	Kentucky	Y		33820 AAW		KYBLS	10//99-12//99
Postsecondary	Louisiana	Y		50700 AAW		LABLS	10//99-12//99
Postsecondary	Maryland	Y		49140 AAW		MDBLS	10//99-12//99
Postsecondary	Baltimore PMSA, MD	Y		47270 AAW		MDBLS	10//99-12//99
Postsecondary	Massachusetts	Y		50290 AAW		MABLS	10//99-12//99
Postsecondary	Boston PMSA, MA-NH	Y		49450 AAW		MABLS	10//99-12//99
Postsecondary	Michigan	Y		55290 AAW		MIBLS	10//99-12//99
Postsecondary	Detroit PMSA, MI	Y		56200 AAW		MIBLS	10//99-12//99
Postsecondary	Minnesota	Y		57950 AAW		MNBLS	10//99-12//99
Postsecondary	Minneapolis-St. Paul MSA, MN-WI	Y		71160 AAW		MNBLS	10//99-12//99
Postsecondary	Mississippi	Y		37800 AAW		MSBLS	10//99-12//99
Postsecondary	Montana	Y		60730 AAW		MTBLS	10//99-12//99
Postsecondary	Nebraska	Y		46540 AAW		NEBLS	10//99-12//99
Postsecondary	Nevada	Y		46910 AAW		NVBLS	10//99-12//99
Postsecondary	New Hampshire	Y		41130 AAW		NHBLS	10//99-12//99
Postsecondary	New Jersey	Y		60360 AAW		NJBLS	10//99-12//99
Postsecondary	Newark PMSA, NJ	Y		58200 AAW		NJBLS	10//99-12//99
Postsecondary	New York	Y		70040 AAW		NYBLS	10//99-12//99
Postsecondary	New York PMSA, NY	Y		68430 AAW		NYBLS	10//99-12//99
Postsecondary	North Carolina	Y		44450 AAW		NCBLS	10//99-12//99
Postsecondary	Asheville MSA, NC	Y		43100 AAW		NCBLS	10//99-12//99
Postsecondary	Greensboro--Winston-Salem--High Point MSA, NC	Y		47260 AAW		NCBLS	10//99-12//99
Postsecondary	North Dakota	Y		37510 AAW		NDBLS	10//99-12//99
Postsecondary	Ohio	Y		41430 AAW		OHBLS	10//99-12//99
Postsecondary	Cleveland-Lorain-Elyria PMSA, OH	Y		49680 AAW		OHBLS	10//99-12//99
Postsecondary	Columbus MSA, OH	Y		40270 AAW		OHBLS	10//99-12//99
Postsecondary	Dayton-Springfield MSA, OH	Y		38640 AAW		OHBLS	10//99-12//99
Postsecondary	Oklahoma	Y		39780 AAW		OKBLS	10//99-12//99
Postsecondary	Oklahoma City MSA, OK	Y		39430 AAW		OKBLS	10//99-12//99
Postsecondary	Oregon	Y		45610 AAW		ORBLS	10//99-12//99
Postsecondary	Portland-Vancouver PMSA, OR-WA	Y		45540 AAW		ORBLS	10//99-12//99
Postsecondary	Pennsylvania	Y		53830 AAW		PABLS	10//99-12//99
Postsecondary	Allentown-Bethlehem-Easton MSA, PA	Y		42300 AAW		PABLS	10//99-12//99
Postsecondary	Philadelphia PMSA, PA-NJ	Y		55370 AAW		PABLS	10//99-12//99
Postsecondary	Pittsburgh MSA, PA	Y		52370 AAW		PABLS	10//99-12//99
Postsecondary	Scranton--Wilkes-Barre--Hazleton MSA, PA	Y		53280 AAW		PABLS	10//99-12//99
Postsecondary	South Carolina	Y		39010 AAW		SCBLS	10//99-12//99
Postsecondary	Greenville-Spartanburg-Anderson MSA, SC	Y		41000 AAW		SCBLS	10//99-12//99
Postsecondary	South Dakota	Y		47700 AAW		SDBLS	10//99-12//99
Postsecondary	Tennessee	Y		56480 AAW		TNBLS	10//99-12//99
Postsecondary	Texas	Y		51080 AAW		TXBLS	10//99-12//99
Postsecondary	Houston PMSA, TX	Y		52710 AAW		TXBLS	10//99-12//99
Postsecondary	Virginia	Y		51420 AAW		VABLS	10//99-12//99
Postsecondary	Washington	Y		38210 AAW		WABLS	10//99-12//99
Postsecondary	Seattle-Bellevue-Everett PMSA, WA	Y		39960 AAW		WABLS	10//99-12//99
Postsecondary	Tacoma PMSA, WA	Y		57050 AAW		WABLS	10//99-12//99
Postsecondary	West Virginia	Y		54930 AAW		WVBLS	10//99-12//99

AAW	Average annual wage	AOH	Average offered, high	ASH	Average starting, high	H	Hourly
AE	Average entry wage	AOL	Average offered, low	ASL	Average starting, low	HI	Highest wage paid
AEX	Average experienced wage	APH	Average pay, high range	AW	Average wage paid	HR	High end range
AO	Average offered	APL	Average pay, low range	FQ	First quartile wage	LR	Low end range

M	Monthly	S	Special: hourly and annual
MTC	Median total compensation	TQ	Third quartile wage
MW	Median wage paid	W	Weekly
SQ	Second quartile wage	Y	Yearly

Occupation/Type/Industry	Location	Per	Low	Mid	High	Source	Date
Sociology Teacher							
Postsecondary	Wisconsin	Y		43230 AAW		WIBLS	10//99-12//99
Postsecondary	Milwaukee-Waukesha PMSA, WI	Y		44010 AAW		WIBLS	10//99-12//99
Postsecondary	Puerto Rico	Y		43110 AAW		PRBLS	10//99-12//99
Software Design Manager	Los Angeles County, CA	Y		97055 AW		LABJ	1999
Software Engineer	Phoenix, AZ	Y		75017 AW		PBJI	2000
Software Programmer/Developer							
Internet	United States	Y		64501 MW		BUS2	2000
Sound Engineering Technician	Arizona	S	12.31 MW	15.75 AW	32760 AAW	AZBLS	10//99-12//99
	Arkansas	S	6.69 MW	8.03 AW	16700 AAW	ARBLS	10//99-12//99
	California	S	19.41 MW	19.36 AW	40260 AAW	CABLS	10//99-12//99
	Colorado	S	13.99 MW	13.73 AW	28560 AAW	COBLS	10//99-12//99
	Connecticut	S	11.84 MW	13.14 AW	27330 AAW	CTBLS	10//99-12//99
	Florida	S	10.1 MW	11.65 AW	24230 AAW	FLBLS	10//99-12//99
	Georgia	S	13.78 MW	13.57 AW	28230 AAW	GABLS	10//99-12//99
	Illinois	S	20.03 MW	23.90 AW	49720 AAW	ILBLS	10//99-12//99
	Indiana	S	14.21 MW	13.06 AW	27150 AAW	INBLS	10//99-12//99
	Iowa	S	11.92 MW	12.65 AW	26310 AAW	IABLS	10//99-12//99
	Maryland	S	19.86 MW	22.83 AW	47490 AAW	MDBLS	10//99-12//99
	Massachusetts	S	12.27 MW	13.56 AW	28200 AAW	MABLS	10//99-12//99
	Michigan	S	25 MW	25.85 AW	53760 AAW	MIBLS	10//99-12//99
	Minnesota	S	10.49 MW	10.74 AW	22350 AAW	MNBLS	10//99-12//99
	Missouri	S	17.15 MW	16.12 AW	33520 AAW	MOBLS	10//99-12//99
	Nebraska	S	15.15 MW	17.66 AW	36740 AAW	NEBLS	10//99-12//99
	Nevada	S	24.13 MW	23.19 AW	48230 AAW	NVBLS	10//99-12//99
	New Jersey	S	21.77 MW	22.14 AW	46060 AAW	NJBLS	10//99-12//99
	New Mexico	S	13.28 MW	13.23 AW	27530 AAW	NMBLS	10//99-12//99
	New York	S	20.58 MW	20.97 AW	43610 AAW	NYBLS	10//99-12//99
	North Carolina	S	10.38 MW	11.03 AW	22940 AAW	NCBLS	10//99-12//99
	Oklahoma	S	12.44 MW	14.64 AW	30460 AAW	OKBLS	10//99-12//99
	Oregon	S	14.24 MW	15.42 AW	32080 AAW	ORBLS	10//99-12//99
	Pennsylvania	S	9.15 MW	10.91 AW	22700 AAW	PABLS	10//99-12//99
	South Carolina	S	12.12 MW	17.72 AW	36850 AAW	SCBLS	10//99-12//99
	Tennessee	S	14.73 MW	16.74 AW	34830 AAW	TNBLS	10//99-12//99
	Texas	S	10.15 MW	11.96 AW	24870 AAW	TXBLS	10//99-12//99
	Virginia	S	15.51 MW	16.86 AW	35080 AAW	VABLS	10//99-12//99
	Washington	S	19.44 MW	19.24 AW	40010 AAW	WABLS	10//99-12//99
Special Education Teacher							
Middle School	Alabama	Y		37680 AAW		ALBLS	10//99-12//99
Middle School	Birmingham MSA, AL	Y		38170 AAW		ALBLS	10//99-12//99
Middle School	Decatur MSA, AL	Y		36470 AAW		ALBLS	10//99-12//99
Middle School	Florence MSA, AL	Y		40100 AAW		ALBLS	10//99-12//99
Middle School	Alaska	Y		45720 AAW		AKBLS	10//99-12//99
Middle School	Arizona	Y		28330 AAW		AZBLS	10//99-12//99
Middle School	Phoenix-Mesa MSA, AZ	Y		29470 AAW		AZBLS	10//99-12//99
Middle School	Tucson MSA, AZ	Y		34970 AAW		AZBLS	10//99-12//99
Middle School	Arkansas	Y		30630 AAW		ARBLS	10//99-12//99
Middle School	Fayetteville-Springdale-Rogers MSA, AR	Y		30560 AAW		ARBLS	10//99-12//99
Middle School	Fort Smith MSA, AR-OK	Y		32670 AAW		ARBLS	10//99-12//99
Middle School	Little Rock-North Little Rock MSA, AR	Y		29640 AAW		ARBLS	10//99-12//99
Middle School	California	Y		46940 AAW		CABLS	10//99-12//99
Middle School	Bakersfield MSA, CA	Y		44750 AAW		CABLS	10//99-12//99
Middle School	Fresno MSA, CA	Y		45420 AAW		CABLS	10//99-12//99
Middle School	Los Angeles-Long Beach PMSA, CA	Y		48030 AAW		CABLS	10//99-12//99
Middle School	Oakland PMSA, CA	Y		48470 AAW		CABLS	10//99-12//99
Middle School	Redding MSA, CA	Y		36700 AAW		CABLS	10//99-12//99
Middle School	Riverside-San Bernardino PMSA, CA	Y		47100 AAW		CABLS	10//99-12//99
Middle School	Salinas MSA, CA	Y		46230 AAW		CABLS	10//99-12//99
Middle School	San Francisco PMSA, CA	Y		46570 AAW		CABLS	10//99-12//99
Middle School	San Jose PMSA, CA	Y		46720 AAW		CABLS	10//99-12//99
Middle School	San Luis Obispo-Atascadero-Paso Robles MSA, CA	Y		44170 AAW		CABLS	10//99-12//99
Middle School	Santa Rosa PMSA, CA	Y		43610 AAW		CABLS	10//99-12//99

AAW Average annual wage	**AOH** Average offered, high	**ASH** Average starting, high	**H** Hourly	**M** Monthly	**S** Special: hourly and annual
AE Average entry wage	**AOL** Average offered, low	**ASL** Average starting, low	**HI** Highest wage paid	**MTC** Median total compensation	**TQ** Third quartile wage
AEX Average experienced wage	**APH** Average pay, high range	**AW** Average wage paid	**HR** High end range	**MW** Median wage paid	**W** Weekly
AO Average offered	**APL** Average pay, low range	**FQ** First quartile wage	**LR** Low end range	**SQ** Second quartile wage	**Y** Yearly

Special Education Teacher

Occupation/Type/Industry	Location	Per	Low	Mid	High	Source	Date
Special Education Teacher							
Middle School	Visalia-Tulare-Porterville MSA, CA	Y		44690 AAW		CABLS	10//99-12//99
Middle School	Yolo PMSA, CA	Y		39770 AAW		CABLS	10//99-12//99
Middle School	Yuba City MSA, CA	Y		37640 AAW		CABLS	10//99-12//99
Middle School	Colorado	Y		43840 AAW		COBLS	10//99-12//99
Middle School	Denver PMSA, CO	Y		41920 AAW		COBLS	10//99-12//99
Middle School	Greeley PMSA, CO	Y		36340 AAW		COBLS	10//99-12//99
Middle School	Connecticut	Y		48680 AAW		CTBLS	10//99-12//99
Middle School	Bridgeport PMSA, CT	Y		45940 AAW		CTBLS	10//99-12//99
Middle School	Hartford MSA, CT	Y		50050 AAW		CTBLS	10//99-12//99
Middle School	New Haven-Meriden PMSA, CT	Y		47510 AAW		CTBLS	10//99-12//99
Middle School	New London-Norwich MSA, CT-RI	Y		45450 AAW		CTBLS	10//99-12//99
Middle School	Stamford-Norwalk PMSA, CT	Y		51710 AAW		CTBLS	10//99-12//99
Middle School	Waterbury PMSA, CT	Y		52420 AAW		CTBLS	10//99-12//99
Middle School	Washington PMSA, DC-MD-VA-WV	Y		37750 AAW		DCBLS	10//99-12//99
Middle School	Florida	Y		36960 AAW		FLBLS	10//99-12//99
Middle School	Georgia	Y		40870 AAW		GABLS	10//99-12//99
Middle School	Athens MSA, GA	Y		52540 AAW		GABLS	10//99-12//99
Middle School	Atlanta MSA, GA	Y		41300 AAW		GABLS	10//99-12//99
Middle School	Illinois	Y		38220 AAW		ILBLS	10//99-12//99
Middle School	Chicago PMSA, IL	Y		40460 AAW		ILBLS	10//99-12//99
Middle School	Peoria-Pekin MSA, IL	Y		34090 AAW		ILBLS	10//99-12//99
Middle School	Rockford MSA, IL	Y		36350 AAW		ILBLS	10//99-12//99
Middle School	Indiana	Y		42170 AAW		INBLS	10//99-12//99
Middle School	Indianapolis MSA, IN	Y		47970 AAW		INBLS	10//99-12//99
Middle School	Iowa	Y		33460 AAW		IABLS	10//99-12//99
Middle School	Cedar Rapids MSA, IA	Y		38550 AAW		IABLS	10//99-12//99
Middle School	Davenport-Moline-Rock Island MSA, IA-IL	Y		42330 AAW		IABLS	10//99-12//99
Middle School	Kansas	Y		34020 AAW		KSBLS	10//99-12//99
Middle School	Kentucky	Y		33470 AAW		KYBLS	10//99-12//99
Middle School	Louisiana	Y		28320 AAW		LABLS	10//99-12//99
Middle School	New Orleans MSA, LA	Y		27890 AAW		LABLS	10//99-12//99
Middle School	Maine	Y		33660 AAW		MEBLS	10//99-12//99
Middle School	Bangor MSA, ME	Y		37170 AAW		MEBLS	10//99-12//99
Middle School	Lewiston-Auburn MSA, ME	Y		27720 AAW		MEBLS	10//99-12//99
Middle School	Portland MSA, ME	Y		34290 AAW		MEBLS	10//99-12//99
Middle School	Massachusetts	Y		39810 AAW		MABLS	10//99-12//99
Middle School	Barnstable-Yarmouth MSA, MA	Y		32530 AAW		MABLS	10//99-12//99
Middle School	Boston PMSA, MA-NH	Y		37410 AAW		MABLS	10//99-12//99
Middle School	Brockton PMSA, MA	Y		42840 AAW		MABLS	10//99-12//99
Middle School	Lawrence PMSA, MA-NH	Y		40180 AAW		MABLS	10//99-12//99
Middle School	Lowell PMSA, MA-NH	Y		43250 AAW		MABLS	10//99-12//99
Middle School	Springfield MSA, MA	Y		52480 AAW		MABLS	10//99-12//99
Middle School	Worcester PMSA, MA-CT	Y		42820 AAW		MABLS	10//99-12//99
Middle School	Michigan	Y		47270 AAW		MIBLS	10//99-12//99
Middle School	Ann Arbor PMSA, MI	Y		50270 AAW		MIBLS	10//99-12//99
Middle School	Detroit PMSA, MI	Y		47390 AAW		MIBLS	10//99-12//99
Middle School	Grand Rapids-Muskegon-Holland MSA, MI	Y		47420 AAW		MIBLS	10//99-12//99
Middle School	Kalamazoo-Battle Creek MSA, MI	Y		43410 AAW		MIBLS	10//99-12//99
Middle School	Minnesota	Y		37570 AAW		MNBLS	10//99-12//99
Middle School	Minneapolis-St. Paul MSA, MN-WI	Y		39500 AAW		MNBLS	10//99-12//99
Middle School	Mississippi	Y		31150 AAW		MSBLS	10//99-12//99
Middle School	Biloxi-Gulfport-Pascagoula MSA, MS	Y		28840 AAW		MSBLS	10//99-12//99
Middle School	Missouri	Y		30110 AAW		MOBLS	10//99-12//99
Middle School	Kansas City MSA, MO-KS	Y		36550 AAW		MOBLS	10//99-12//99
Middle School	St. Louis MSA, MO-IL	Y		32510 AAW		MOBLS	10//99-12//99
Middle School	Montana	Y		31460 AAW		MTBLS	10//99-12//99
Middle School	Nebraska	Y		35590 AAW		NEBLS	10//99-12//99
Middle School	Omaha MSA, NE-IA	Y		32110 AAW		NEBLS	10//99-12//99
Middle School	Nevada	Y		45510 AAW		NVBLS	10//99-12//99
Middle School	New Hampshire	Y		33450 AAW		NHBLS	10//99-12//99
Middle School	Nashua PMSA, NH	Y		32820 AAW		NHBLS	10//99-12//99

AAW	Average annual wage	AOH	Average offered, high	ASH	Average starting, high	H	Hourly	M	Monthly	S	Special: hourly and annual
AE	Average entry wage	AOL	Average offered, low	ASL	Average starting, low	HI	Highest wage paid	MTC	Median total compensation	TQ	Third quartile wage
AEX	Average experienced wage	APH	Average pay, high range	AW	Average wage paid	HR	High end range	MW	Median wage paid	W	Weekly
AO	Average offered	APL	Average pay, low range	FQ	First quartile wage	LR	Low end range	SQ	Second quartile wage	Y	Yearly

Occupation/Type/Industry	Location	Per	Low	Mid	High	Source	Date
Special Education Teacher							
Middle School	Portsmouth-Rochester PMSA, NH-ME	Y		32730 AAW		NHBLS	10//99-12//99
Middle School	New Jersey	Y		49130 AAW		NJBLS	10//99-12//99
Middle School	Atlantic-Cape May PMSA, NJ	Y		47250 AAW		NJBLS	10//99-12//99
Middle School	Bergen-Passaic PMSA, NJ	Y		50090 AAW		NJBLS	10//99-12//99
Middle School	Middlesex-Somerset-Hunterdon PMSA, NJ	Y		44180 AAW		NJBLS	10//99-12//99
Middle School	Monmouth-Ocean PMSA, NJ	Y		45480 AAW		NJBLS	10//99-12//99
Middle School	Newark PMSA, NJ	Y		57290 AAW		NJBLS	10//99-12//99
Middle School	Vineland-Millville-Bridgeton PMSA, NJ	Y		48930 AAW		NJBLS	10//99-12//99
Middle School	New Mexico	Y		31370 AAW		NMBLS	10//99-12//99
Middle School	New York	Y		44770 AAW		NYBLS	10//99-12//99
Middle School	Albany-Schenectady-Troy MSA, NY	Y		43560 AAW		NYBLS	10//99-12//99
Middle School	Binghamton MSA, NY	Y		35750 AAW		NYBLS	10//99-12//99
Middle School	Buffalo-Niagara Falls MSA, NY	Y		44490 AAW		NYBLS	10//99-12//99
Middle School	Dutchess County PMSA, NY	Y		42370 AAW		NYBLS	10//99-12//99
Middle School	Glens Falls MSA, NY	Y		42530 AAW		NYBLS	10//99-12//99
Middle School	Jamestown MSA, NY	Y		36190 AAW		NYBLS	10//99-12//99
Middle School	Nassau-Suffolk PMSA, NY	Y		48480 AAW		NYBLS	10//99-12//99
Middle School	New York PMSA, NY	Y		62810 AAW		NYBLS	10//99-12//99
Middle School	Newburgh PMSA, NY-PA	Y		47490 AAW		NYBLS	10//99-12//99
Middle School	Syracuse MSA, NY	Y		40250 AAW		NYBLS	10//99-12//99
Middle School	Utica-Rome MSA, NY	Y		37130 AAW		NYBLS	10//99-12//99
Middle School	North Carolina	Y		33670 AAW		NCBLS	10//99-12//99
Middle School	Charlotte-Gastonia-Rock Hill MSA, NC-SC	Y		35030 AAW		NCBLS	10//99-12//99
Middle School	Greensboro--Winston-Salem--High Point MSA, NC	Y		35560 AAW		NCBLS	10//99-12//99
Middle School	Hickory-Morganton-Lenoir MSA, NC	Y		25500 AAW		NCBLS	10//99-12//99
Middle School	Raleigh-Durham-Chapel Hill MSA, NC	Y		38760 AAW		NCBLS	10//99-12//99
Middle School	Ohio	Y		40360 AAW		OHBLS	10//99-12//99
Middle School	Akron PMSA, OH	Y		40310 AAW		OHBLS	10//99-12//99
Middle School	Canton-Massillon MSA, OH	Y		41090 AAW		OHBLS	10//99-12//99
Middle School	Cincinnati PMSA, OH-KY-IN	Y		38260 AAW		OHBLS	10//99-12//99
Middle School	Cleveland-Lorain-Elyria PMSA, OH	Y		46990 AAW		OHBLS	10//99-12//99
Middle School	Columbus MSA, OH	Y		43540 AAW		OHBLS	10//99-12//99
Middle School	Dayton-Springfield MSA, OH	Y		39380 AAW		OHBLS	10//99-12//99
Middle School	Hamilton-Middletown PMSA, OH	Y		39300 AAW		OHBLS	10//99-12//99
Middle School	Lima MSA, OH	Y		36680 AAW		OHBLS	10//99-12//99
Middle School	Mansfield MSA, OH	Y		38920 AAW		OHBLS	10//99-12//99
Middle School	Steubenville-Weirton MSA, OH-WV	Y		39190 AAW		OHBLS	10//99-12//99
Middle School	Toledo MSA, OH	Y		42790 AAW		OHBLS	10//99-12//99
Middle School	Youngstown-Warren MSA, OH	Y		33180 AAW		OHBLS	10//99-12//99
Middle School	Oklahoma	Y		31960 AAW		OKBLS	10//99-12//99
Middle School	Oklahoma City MSA, OK	Y		34540 AAW		OKBLS	10//99-12//99
Middle School	Oregon	Y		40770 AAW		ORBLS	10//99-12//99
Middle School	Medford-Ashland MSA, OR	Y		34180 AAW		ORBLS	10//99-12//99
Middle School	Portland-Vancouver PMSA, OR-WA	Y		45540 AAW		ORBLS	10//99-12//99
Middle School	Pennsylvania	Y		46310 AAW		PABLS	10//99-12//99
Middle School	Erie MSA, PA	Y		43370 AAW		PABLS	10//99-12//99
Middle School	Harrisburg-Lebanon-Carlisle MSA, PA	Y		38170 AAW		PABLS	10//99-12//99
Middle School	Johnstown MSA, PA	Y		42290 AAW		PABLS	10//99-12//99
Middle School	Lancaster MSA, PA	Y		41600 AAW		PABLS	10//99-12//99
Middle School	Philadelphia PMSA, PA-NJ	Y		45490 AAW		PABLS	10//99-12//99
Middle School	Pittsburgh MSA, PA	Y		55840 AAW		PABLS	10//99-12//99
Middle School	Reading MSA, PA	Y		42360 AAW		PABLS	10//99-12//99
Middle School	Scranton--Wilkes-Barre--Hazleton MSA, PA	Y		49060 AAW		PABLS	10//99-12//99
Middle School	York MSA, PA	Y		40680 AAW		PABLS	10//99-12//99
Middle School	Rhode Island	Y		42820 AAW		RIBLS	10//99-12//99

Occupation/Type/Industry	Location	Per	Low	Mid	High	Source	Date
Special Education Teacher							
Middle School	Providence-Fall River-Warwick MSA, RI-MA	Y		42870 AAW		RIBLS	10//99-12//99
Middle School	South Carolina	Y		35910 AAW		SCBLS	10//99-12//99
Middle School	Greenville-Spartanburg-Anderson MSA, SC	Y		33450 AAW		SCBLS	10//99-12//99
Middle School	South Dakota	Y		27780 AAW		SDBLS	10//99-12//99
Middle School	Tennessee	Y		30420 AAW		TNBLS	10//99-12//99
Middle School	Chattanooga MSA, TN-GA	Y		37380 AAW		TNBLS	10//99-12//99
Middle School	Knoxville MSA, TN	Y		30510 AAW		TNBLS	10//99-12//99
Middle School	Nashville MSA, TN	Y		30230 AAW		TNBLS	10//99-12//99
Middle School	Texas	Y		37000 AAW		TXBLS	10//99-12//99
Middle School	Austin-San Marcos MSA, TX	Y		36980 AAW		TXBLS	10//99-12//99
Middle School	Beaumont-Port Arthur MSA, TX	Y		35240 AAW		TXBLS	10//99-12//99
Middle School	Corpus Christi MSA, TX	Y		37870 AAW		TXBLS	10//99-12//99
Middle School	Dallas PMSA, TX	Y		34610 AAW		TXBLS	10//99-12//99
Middle School	Fort Worth-Arlington PMSA, TX	Y		38130 AAW		TXBLS	10//99-12//99
Middle School	Galveston-Texas City PMSA, TX	Y		36730 AAW		TXBLS	10//99-12//99
Middle School	Houston PMSA, TX	Y		37330 AAW		TXBLS	10//99-12//99
Middle School	Killeen-Temple MSA, TX	Y		28540 AAW		TXBLS	10//99-12//99
Middle School	Longview-Marshall MSA, TX	Y		37520 AAW		TXBLS	10//99-12//99
Middle School	McAllen-Edinburg-Mission MSA, TX	Y		38330 AAW		TXBLS	10//99-12//99
Middle School	San Antonio MSA, TX	Y		38190 AAW		TXBLS	10//99-12//99
Middle School	Sherman-Denison MSA, TX	Y		36690 AAW		TXBLS	10//99-12//99
Middle School	Texarkana MSA, TX-Texarkana, AR	Y		34200 AAW		TXBLS	10//99-12//99
Middle School	Waco MSA, TX	Y		32050 AAW		TXBLS	10//99-12//99
Middle School	Utah	Y		34040 AAW		UTBLS	10//99-12//99
Middle School	Salt Lake City-Ogden MSA, UT	Y		36560 AAW		UTBLS	10//99-12//99
Middle School	Vermont	Y		36210 AAW		VTBLS	10//99-12//99
Middle School	Burlington MSA, VT	Y		43980 AAW		VTBLS	10//99-12//99
Middle School	Virginia	Y		32830 AAW		VABLS	10//99-12//99
Middle School	Washington	Y		39710 AAW		WABLS	10//99-12//99
Middle School	Bellingham MSA, WA	Y		35420 AAW		WABLS	10//99-12//99
Middle School	Richland-Kennewick-Pasco MSA, WA	Y		40240 AAW		WABLS	10//99-12//99
Middle School	Seattle-Bellevue-Everett PMSA, WA	Y		37880 AAW		WABLS	10//99-12//99
Middle School	Spokane MSA, WA	Y		35560 AAW		WABLS	10//99-12//99
Middle School	Tacoma PMSA, WA	Y		40590 AAW		WABLS	10//99-12//99
Middle School	West Virginia	Y		34460 AAW		WVBLS	10//99-12//99
Middle School	Huntington-Ashland MSA, WV-KY-OH	Y		35340 AAW		WVBLS	10//99-12//99
Middle School	Wheeling MSA, WV-OH	Y		34610 AAW		WVBLS	10//99-12//99
Middle School	Wisconsin	Y		36980 AAW		WIBLS	10//99-12//99
Middle School	Appleton-Oshkosh-Neenah MSA, WI	Y		27480 AAW		WIBLS	10//99-12//99
Middle School	Madison MSA, WI	Y		38870 AAW		WIBLS	10//99-12//99
Middle School	Wyoming	Y		30400 AAW		WYBLS	10//99-12//99
Preschool, Kindergarten, and Elementary School	Alabama	Y		31040 AAW		ALBLS	10//99-12//99
Preschool, Kindergarten, and Elementary School	Birmingham MSA, AL	Y		25250 AAW		ALBLS	10//99-12//99
Preschool, Kindergarten, and Elementary School	Decatur MSA, AL	Y		34360 AAW		ALBLS	10//99-12//99
Preschool, Kindergarten, and Elementary School	Dothan MSA, AL	Y		35550 AAW		ALBLS	10//99-12//99
Preschool, Kindergarten, and Elementary School	Florence MSA, AL	Y		36920 AAW		ALBLS	10//99-12//99
Preschool, Kindergarten, and Elementary School	Huntsville MSA, AL	Y		36850 AAW		ALBLS	10//99-12//99
Preschool, Kindergarten, and Elementary School	Montgomery MSA, AL	Y		28590 AAW		ALBLS	10//99-12//99
Preschool, Kindergarten, and Elementary School	Alaska	Y		46140 AAW		AKBLS	10//99-12//99

AAW Average annual wage	**AOH** Average offered, high	**ASH** Average starting, high	**H** Hourly	**M** Monthly	**S** Special: hourly and annual
AE Average entry wage	**AOL** Average offered, low	**ASL** Average starting, low	**HI** Highest wage paid	**MTC** Median total compensation	**TQ** Third quartile wage
AEX Average experienced wage	**APH** Average pay, high range	**AW** Average wage paid	**HR** High end range	**MW** Median wage paid	**W** Weekly
AO Average offered	**APL** Average pay, low range	**FQ** First quartile wage	**LR** Low end range	**SQ** Second quartile wage	**Y** Yearly

Occupation/Type/Industry	Location	Per	Low	Mid	High	Source	Date
Special Education Teacher							
Preschool, Kindergarten, and Elementary School	Arizona	Y		29830 AAW		AZBLS	10//99-12//99
Preschool, Kindergarten, and Elementary School	Phoenix-Mesa MSA, AZ	Y		28440 AAW		AZBLS	10//99-12//99
Preschool, Kindergarten, and Elementary School	Tucson MSA, AZ	Y		40130 AAW		AZBLS	10//99-12//99
Preschool, Kindergarten, and Elementary School	Arkansas	Y		31090 AAW		ARBLS	10//99-12//99
Preschool, Kindergarten, and Elementary School	Fayetteville-Springdale-Rogers MSA, AR	Y		29110 AAW		ARBLS	10//99-12//99
Preschool, Kindergarten, and Elementary School	Fort Smith MSA, AR-OK	Y		32960 AAW		ARBLS	10//99-12//99
Preschool, Kindergarten, and Elementary School	Little Rock-North Little Rock MSA, AR	Y		33180 AAW		ARBLS	10//99-12//99
Preschool, Kindergarten, and Elementary School	California	Y		47420 AAW		CABLS	10//99-12//99
Preschool, Kindergarten, and Elementary School	Bakersfield MSA, CA	Y		49390 AAW		CABLS	10//99-12//99
Preschool, Kindergarten, and Elementary School	Fresno MSA, CA	Y		30760 AAW		CABLS	10//99-12//99
Preschool, Kindergarten, and Elementary School	Los Angeles-Long Beach PMSA, CA	Y		49090 AAW		CABLS	10//99-12//99
Preschool, Kindergarten, and Elementary School	Oakland PMSA, CA	Y		42130 AAW		CABLS	10//99-12//99
Preschool, Kindergarten, and Elementary School	Orange County PMSA, CA	Y		53590 AAW		CABLS	10//99-12//99
Preschool, Kindergarten, and Elementary School	Redding MSA, CA	Y		42960 AAW		CABLS	10//99-12//99
Preschool, Kindergarten, and Elementary School	Riverside-San Bernardino PMSA, CA	Y		47890 AAW		CABLS	10//99-12//99
Preschool, Kindergarten, and Elementary School	Sacramento PMSA, CA	Y		48300 AAW		CABLS	10//99-12//99
Preschool, Kindergarten, and Elementary School	Salinas MSA, CA	Y		47280 AAW		CABLS	10//99-12//99
Preschool, Kindergarten, and Elementary School	San Diego MSA, CA	Y		47870 AAW		CABLS	10//99-12//99
Preschool, Kindergarten, and Elementary School	San Francisco PMSA, CA	Y		50910 AAW		CABLS	10//99-12//99
Preschool, Kindergarten, and Elementary School	San Jose PMSA, CA	Y		36470 AAW		CABLS	10//99-12//99
Preschool, Kindergarten, and Elementary School	Santa Barbara-Santa Maria-Lompoc MSA, CA	Y		58180 AAW		CABLS	10//99-12//99
Preschool, Kindergarten, and Elementary School	Santa Rosa PMSA, CA	Y		44450 AAW		CABLS	10//99-12//99
Preschool, Kindergarten, and Elementary School	Stockton-Lodi MSA, CA	Y		46330 AAW		CABLS	10//99-12//99
Preschool, Kindergarten, and Elementary School	Vallejo-Fairfield-Napa PMSA, CA	Y		54300 AAW		CABLS	10//99-12//99
Preschool, Kindergarten, and Elementary School	Ventura PMSA, CA	Y		52900 AAW		CABLS	10//99-12//99
Preschool, Kindergarten, and Elementary School	Yolo PMSA, CA	Y		41920 AAW		CABLS	10//99-12//99
Preschool, Kindergarten, and Elementary School	Yuba City MSA, CA	Y		37590 AAW		CABLS	10//99-12//99
Preschool, Kindergarten, and Elementary School	Colorado	Y		38380 AAW		COBLS	10//99-12//99
Preschool, Kindergarten, and Elementary School	Boulder-Longmont PMSA, CO	Y		32280 AAW		COBLS	10//99-12//99
Preschool, Kindergarten, and Elementary School	Denver PMSA, CO	Y		36980 AAW		COBLS	10//99-12//99
Preschool, Kindergarten, and Elementary School	Greeley PMSA, CO	Y		32650 AAW		COBLS	10//99-12//99
Preschool, Kindergarten, and Elementary School	Connecticut	Y		50590 AAW		CTBLS	10//99-12//99

AAW	Average annual wage	AOH	Average offered, high	ASH	Average starting, high	H	Hourly	M	Monthly	S	Special: hourly and annual
AE	Average entry wage	AOL	Average offered, low	ASL	Average starting, low	HI	Highest wage paid	MTC	Median total compensation	TQ	Third quartile wage
AEX	Average experienced wage	APH	Average pay, high range	AW	Average wage paid	HR	High end range	MW	Median wage paid	W	Weekly
AO	Average offered	APL	Average pay, low range	FQ	First quartile wage	LR	Low end range	SQ	Second quartile wage	Y	Yearly

Special Education Teacher

Occupation/Type/Industry	Location	Per	Low	Mid	High	Source	Date
Preschool, Kindergarten, and Elementary School	Bridgeport PMSA, CT	Y		47460 AAW		CTBLS	10//99-12//99
Preschool, Kindergarten, and Elementary School	Danbury PMSA, CT	Y		53430 AAW		CTBLS	10//99-12//99
Preschool, Kindergarten, and Elementary School	Hartford MSA, CT	Y		50070 AAW		CTBLS	10//99-12//99
Preschool, Kindergarten, and Elementary School	New Haven-Meriden PMSA, CT	Y		48890 AAW		CTBLS	10//99-12//99
Preschool, Kindergarten, and Elementary School	New London-Norwich MSA, CT-RI	Y		55140 AAW		CTBLS	10//99-12//99
Preschool, Kindergarten, and Elementary School	Stamford-Norwalk PMSA, CT	Y		55510 AAW		CTBLS	10//99-12//99
Preschool, Kindergarten, and Elementary School	Waterbury PMSA, CT	Y		53420 AAW		CTBLS	10//99-12//99
Preschool, Kindergarten, and Elementary School	Delaware	Y		45200 AAW		DEBLS	10//99-12//99
Preschool, Kindergarten, and Elementary School	Wilmington-Newark PMSA, DE-MD	Y		45910 AAW		DEBLS	10//99-12//99
Preschool, Kindergarten, and Elementary School	District of Columbia	Y		63040 AAW		DCBLS	10//99-12//99
Preschool, Kindergarten, and Elementary School	Washington PMSA, DC-MD-VA-WV	Y		44590 AAW		DCBLS	10//99-12//99
Preschool, Kindergarten, and Elementary School	Florida	Y		37660 AAW		FLBLS	10//99-12//99
Preschool, Kindergarten, and Elementary School	Jacksonville MSA, FL	Y		45410 AAW		FLBLS	10//99-12//99
Preschool, Kindergarten, and Elementary School	Orlando MSA, FL	Y		34590 AAW		FLBLS	10//99-12//99
Preschool, Kindergarten, and Elementary School	Georgia	Y		41490 AAW		GABLS	10//99-12//99
Preschool, Kindergarten, and Elementary School	Atlanta MSA, GA	Y		42850 AAW		GABLS	10//99-12//99
Preschool, Kindergarten, and Elementary School	Columbus MSA, GA-AL	Y		42510 AAW		GABLS	10//99-12//99
Preschool, Kindergarten, and Elementary School	Macon MSA, GA	Y		39440 AAW		GABLS	10//99-12//99
Preschool, Kindergarten, and Elementary School	Savannah MSA, GA	Y		39990 AAW		GABLS	10//99-12//99
Preschool, Kindergarten, and Elementary School	Hawaii	Y		36170 AAW		HIBLS	10//99-12//99
Preschool, Kindergarten, and Elementary School	Illinois	Y		38430 AAW		ILBLS	10//99-12//99
Preschool, Kindergarten, and Elementary School	Champaign-Urbana MSA, IL	Y		41280 AAW		ILBLS	10//99-12//99
Preschool, Kindergarten, and Elementary School	Chicago PMSA, IL	Y		40360 AAW		ILBLS	10//99-12//99
Preschool, Kindergarten, and Elementary School	Decatur MSA, IL	Y		49730 AAW		ILBLS	10//99-12//99
Preschool, Kindergarten, and Elementary School	Peoria-Pekin MSA, IL	Y		37750 AAW		ILBLS	10//99-12//99
Preschool, Kindergarten, and Elementary School	Rockford MSA, IL	Y		37330 AAW		ILBLS	10//99-12//99
Preschool, Kindergarten, and Elementary School	Springfield MSA, IL	Y		34640 AAW		ILBLS	10//99-12//99
Preschool, Kindergarten, and Elementary School	Indiana	Y		41730 AAW		INBLS	10//99-12//99
Preschool, Kindergarten, and Elementary School	Fort Wayne MSA, IN	Y		37800 AAW		INBLS	10//99-12//99
Preschool, Kindergarten, and Elementary School	Gary PMSA, IN	Y		43640 AAW		INBLS	10//99-12//99
Preschool, Kindergarten, and Elementary School	Indianapolis MSA, IN	Y		45910 AAW		INBLS	10//99-12//99
Preschool, Kindergarten, and Elementary School	Kokomo MSA, IN	Y		40730 AAW		INBLS	10//99-12//99
Preschool, Kindergarten, and Elementary School	Terre Haute MSA, IN	Y		41860 AAW		INBLS	10//99-12//99

AAW	Average annual wage	AOH	Average offered, high	ASH	Average starting, high	H	Hourly	M	Monthly	S	Special: hourly and annual
AE	Average entry wage	AOL	Average offered, low	ASL	Average starting, low	HI	Highest wage paid	MTC	Median total compensation	TQ	Third quartile wage
AEX	Average experienced wage	APH	Average pay, high range	AW	Average wage paid	HR	High end range	MW	Median wage paid	W	Weekly
AO	Average offered	APL	Average pay, low range	FQ	First quartile wage	LR	Low end range	SQ	Second quartile wage	Y	Yearly

Occupation/Type/Industry	Location	Per	Low	Mid	High	Source	Date
Special Education Teacher							
Preschool, Kindergarten, and Elementary School	Iowa	Y		32600 AAW		IABLS	10//99-12//99
Preschool, Kindergarten, and Elementary School	Cedar Rapids MSA, IA	Y		36240 AAW		IABLS	10//99-12//99
Preschool, Kindergarten, and Elementary School	Davenport-Moline-Rock Island MSA, IA-IL	Y		44490 AAW		IABLS	10//99-12//99
Preschool, Kindergarten, and Elementary School	Des Moines MSA, IA	Y		30050 AAW		IABLS	10//99-12//99
Preschool, Kindergarten, and Elementary School	Sioux City MSA, IA-NE	Y		29660 AAW		IABLS	10//99-12//99
Preschool, Kindergarten, and Elementary School	Kansas	Y		37370 AAW		KSBLS	10//99-12//99
Preschool, Kindergarten, and Elementary School	Wichita MSA, KS	Y		36370 AAW		KSBLS	10//99-12//99
Preschool, Kindergarten, and Elementary School	Kentucky	Y		33630 AAW		KYBLS	10//99-12//99
Preschool, Kindergarten, and Elementary School	Lexington MSA, KY	Y		32600 AAW		KYBLS	10//99-12//99
Preschool, Kindergarten, and Elementary School	Louisiana	Y		16750 AAW		LABLS	10//99-12//99
Preschool, Kindergarten, and Elementary School	New Orleans MSA, LA	Y		21890 AAW		LABLS	10//99-12//99
Preschool, Kindergarten, and Elementary School	Maine	Y		34940 AAW		MEBLS	10//99-12//99
Preschool, Kindergarten, and Elementary School	Lewiston-Auburn MSA, ME	Y		34750 AAW		MEBLS	10//99-12//99
Preschool, Kindergarten, and Elementary School	Portland MSA, ME	Y		36910 AAW		MEBLS	10//99-12//99
Preschool, Kindergarten, and Elementary School	Maryland	Y		45700 AAW		MDBLS	10//99-12//99
Preschool, Kindergarten, and Elementary School	Baltimore PMSA, MD	Y		45570 AAW		MDBLS	10//99-12//99
Preschool, Kindergarten, and Elementary School	Massachusetts	Y		38790 AAW		MABLS	10//99-12//99
Preschool, Kindergarten, and Elementary School	Barnstable-Yarmouth MSA, MA	Y		40590 AAW		MABLS	10//99-12//99
Preschool, Kindergarten, and Elementary School	Boston PMSA, MA-NH	Y		36960 AAW		MABLS	10//99-12//99
Preschool, Kindergarten, and Elementary School	Brockton PMSA, MA	Y		44910 AAW		MABLS	10//99-12//99
Preschool, Kindergarten, and Elementary School	Lawrence PMSA, MA-NH	Y		41980 AAW		MABLS	10//99-12//99
Preschool, Kindergarten, and Elementary School	Lowell PMSA, MA-NH	Y		43060 AAW		MABLS	10//99-12//99
Preschool, Kindergarten, and Elementary School	New Bedford PMSA, MA	Y		38540 AAW		MABLS	10//99-12//99
Preschool, Kindergarten, and Elementary School	Pittsfield MSA, MA	Y		43630 AAW		MABLS	10//99-12//99
Preschool, Kindergarten, and Elementary School	Springfield MSA, MA	Y		44200 AAW		MABLS	10//99-12//99
Preschool, Kindergarten, and Elementary School	Worcester PMSA, MA-CT	Y		43930 AAW		MABLS	10//99-12//99
Preschool, Kindergarten, and Elementary School	Michigan	Y		46000 AAW		MIBLS	10//99-12//99
Preschool, Kindergarten, and Elementary School	Ann Arbor PMSA, MI	Y		55290 AAW		MIBLS	10//99-12//99
Preschool, Kindergarten, and Elementary School	Benton Harbor MSA, MI	Y		44730 AAW		MIBLS	10//99-12//99
Preschool, Kindergarten, and Elementary School	Detroit PMSA, MI	Y		48390 AAW		MIBLS	10//99-12//99
Preschool, Kindergarten, and Elementary School	Grand Rapids-Muskegon-Holland MSA, MI	Y		44370 AAW		MIBLS	10//99-12//99
Preschool, Kindergarten, and Elementary School	Kalamazoo-Battle Creek MSA, MI	Y		38040 AAW		MIBLS	10//99-12//99
Preschool, Kindergarten, and Elementary School	Lansing-East Lansing MSA, MI	Y		48110 AAW		MIBLS	10//99-12//99

AAW Average annual wage	**AOH** Average offered, high	**ASH** Average starting, high	**H** Hourly	**M** Monthly	**S** Special: hourly and annual
AE Average entry wage	**AOL** Average offered, low	**ASL** Average starting, low	**HI** Highest wage paid	**MTC** Median total compensation	**TQ** Third quartile wage
AEX Average experienced wage	**APH** Average pay, high range	**AW** Average wage paid	**HR** High end range	**MW** Median wage paid	**W** Weekly
AO Average offered	**APL** Average pay, low range	**FQ** First quartile wage	**LR** Low end range	**SQ** Second quartile wage	**Y** Yearly

Occupation/Type/Industry	Location	Per	Low	Mid	High	Source	Date
Special Education Teacher							
Preschool, Kindergarten, and Elementary School	Minnesota	Y		40560 AAW		MNBLS	10//99-12//99
Preschool, Kindergarten, and Elementary School	Duluth-Superior MSA, MN-WI	Y		32530 AAW		MNBLS	10//99-12//99
Preschool, Kindergarten, and Elementary School	Minneapolis-St. Paul MSA, MN-WI	Y		43020 AAW		MNBLS	10//99-12//99
Preschool, Kindergarten, and Elementary School	St. Cloud MSA, MN	Y		44250 AAW		MNBLS	10//99-12//99
Preschool, Kindergarten, and Elementary School	Mississippi	Y		31400 AAW		MSBLS	10//99-12//99
Preschool, Kindergarten, and Elementary School	Biloxi-Gulfport-Pascagoula MSA, MS	Y		29600 AAW		MSBLS	10//99-12//99
Preschool, Kindergarten, and Elementary School	Hattiesburg MSA, MS	Y		26150 AAW		MSBLS	10//99-12//99
Preschool, Kindergarten, and Elementary School	Jackson MSA, MS	Y		27230 AAW		MSBLS	10//99-12//99
Preschool, Kindergarten, and Elementary School	Missouri	Y		32270 AAW		MOBLS	10//99-12//99
Preschool, Kindergarten, and Elementary School	Joplin MSA, MO	Y		26560 AAW		MOBLS	10//99-12//99
Preschool, Kindergarten, and Elementary School	Kansas City MSA, MO-KS	Y		34450 AAW		MOBLS	10//99-12//99
Preschool, Kindergarten, and Elementary School	St. Louis MSA, MO-IL	Y		36390 AAW		MOBLS	10//99-12//99
Preschool, Kindergarten, and Elementary School	Springfield MSA, MO	Y		28360 AAW		MOBLS	10//99-12//99
Preschool, Kindergarten, and Elementary School	Montana	Y		29560 AAW		MTBLS	10//99-12//99
Preschool, Kindergarten, and Elementary School	Nebraska	Y		29980 AAW		NEBLS	10//99-12//99
Preschool, Kindergarten, and Elementary School	Omaha MSA, NE-IA	Y		29630 AAW		NEBLS	10//99-12//99
Preschool, Kindergarten, and Elementary School	Nevada	Y		38570 AAW		NVBLS	10//99-12//99
Preschool, Kindergarten, and Elementary School	New Hampshire	Y		34430 AAW		NHBLS	10//99-12//99
Preschool, Kindergarten, and Elementary School	Nashua PMSA, NH	Y		34020 AAW		NHBLS	10//99-12//99
Preschool, Kindergarten, and Elementary School	Portsmouth-Rochester PMSA, NH-ME	Y		35510 AAW		NHBLS	10//99-12//99
Preschool, Kindergarten, and Elementary School	New Jersey	Y		46240 AAW		NJBLS	10//99-12//99
Preschool, Kindergarten, and Elementary School	Atlantic-Cape May PMSA, NJ	Y		43590 AAW		NJBLS	10//99-12//99
Preschool, Kindergarten, and Elementary School	Bergen-Passaic PMSA, NJ	Y		45870 AAW		NJBLS	10//99-12//99
Preschool, Kindergarten, and Elementary School	Jersey City PMSA, NJ	Y		41600 AAW		NJBLS	10//99-12//99
Preschool, Kindergarten, and Elementary School	Middlesex-Somerset-Hunterdon PMSA, NJ	Y		44270 AAW		NJBLS	10//99-12//99
Preschool, Kindergarten, and Elementary School	Monmouth-Ocean PMSA, NJ	Y		40400 AAW		NJBLS	10//99-12//99
Preschool, Kindergarten, and Elementary School	Newark PMSA, NJ	Y		51830 AAW		NJBLS	10//99-12//99
Preschool, Kindergarten, and Elementary School	Trenton PMSA, NJ	Y		45740 AAW		NJBLS	10//99-12//99
Preschool, Kindergarten, and Elementary School	Vineland-Millville-Bridgeton PMSA, NJ	Y		52000 AAW		NJBLS	10//99-12//99
Preschool, Kindergarten, and Elementary School	New Mexico	Y		31050 AAW		NMBLS	10//99-12//99
Preschool, Kindergarten, and Elementary School	New York	Y		50810 AAW		NYBLS	10//99-12//99
Preschool, Kindergarten, and Elementary School	Albany-Schenectady-Troy MSA, NY	Y		39070 AAW		NYBLS	10//99-12//99

AAW Average annual wage	**AOH** Average offered, high	**ASH** Average starting, high	**H** Hourly	**M** Monthly	**S** Special: hourly and annual
AE Average entry wage	**AOL** Average offered, low	**ASL** Average starting, low	**HI** Highest wage paid	**MTC** Median total compensation	**TQ** Third quartile wage
AEX Average experienced wage	**APH** Average pay, high range	**AW** Average wage paid	**HR** High end range	**MW** Median wage paid	**W** Weekly
AO Average offered	**APL** Average pay, low range	**FQ** First quartile wage	**LR** Low end range	**SQ** Second quartile wage	**Y** Yearly

Occupation/Type/Industry	Location	Per	Low	Mid	High	Source	Date
Special Education Teacher							
Preschool, Kindergarten, and Elementary School	Binghamton MSA, NY	Y		38500 AAW		NYBLS	10//99-12//99
Preschool, Kindergarten, and Elementary School	Buffalo-Niagara Falls MSA, NY	Y		47680 AAW		NYBLS	10//99-12//99
Preschool, Kindergarten, and Elementary School	Dutchess County PMSA, NY	Y		47380 AAW		NYBLS	10//99-12//99
Preschool, Kindergarten, and Elementary School	Glens Falls MSA, NY	Y		36750 AAW		NYBLS	10//99-12//99
Preschool, Kindergarten, and Elementary School	Jamestown MSA, NY	Y		37000 AAW		NYBLS	10//99-12//99
Preschool, Kindergarten, and Elementary School	Nassau-Suffolk PMSA, NY	Y		60910 AAW		NYBLS	10//99-12//99
Preschool, Kindergarten, and Elementary School	New York PMSA, NY	Y		63070 AAW		NYBLS	10//99-12//99
Preschool, Kindergarten, and Elementary School	Newburgh PMSA, NY-PA	Y		45120 AAW		NYBLS	10//99-12//99
Preschool, Kindergarten, and Elementary School	Rochester MSA, NY	Y		42650 AAW		NYBLS	10//99-12//99
Preschool, Kindergarten, and Elementary School	Syracuse MSA, NY	Y		38500 AAW		NYBLS	10//99-12//99
Preschool, Kindergarten, and Elementary School	Utica-Rome MSA, NY	Y		39030 AAW		NYBLS	10//99-12//99
Preschool, Kindergarten, and Elementary School	North Carolina	Y		34500 AAW		NCBLS	10//99-12//99
Preschool, Kindergarten, and Elementary School	Asheville MSA, NC	Y		33460 AAW		NCBLS	10//99-12//99
Preschool, Kindergarten, and Elementary School	Charlotte-Gastonia-Rock Hill MSA, NC-SC	Y		35560 AAW		NCBLS	10//99-12//99
Preschool, Kindergarten, and Elementary School	Greensboro--Winston-Salem--High Point MSA, NC	Y		36430 AAW		NCBLS	10//99-12//99
Preschool, Kindergarten, and Elementary School	Hickory-Morganton-Lenoir MSA, NC	Y		34970 AAW		NCBLS	10//99-12//99
Preschool, Kindergarten, and Elementary School	Raleigh-Durham-Chapel Hill MSA, NC	Y		37520 AAW		NCBLS	10//99-12//99
Preschool, Kindergarten, and Elementary School	North Dakota	Y		32850 AAW		NDBLS	10//99-12//99
Preschool, Kindergarten, and Elementary School	Fargo-Moorhead MSA, ND-MN	Y		34470 AAW		NDBLS	10//99-12//99
Preschool, Kindergarten, and Elementary School	Ohio	Y		39100 AAW		OHBLS	10//99-12//99
Preschool, Kindergarten, and Elementary School	Akron PMSA, OH	Y		40990 AAW		OHBLS	10//99-12//99
Preschool, Kindergarten, and Elementary School	Canton-Massillon MSA, OH	Y		38380 AAW		OHBLS	10//99-12//99
Preschool, Kindergarten, and Elementary School	Cincinnati PMSA, OH-KY-IN	Y		39100 AAW		OHBLS	10//99-12//99
Preschool, Kindergarten, and Elementary School	Cleveland-Lorain-Elyria PMSA, OH	Y		48220 AAW		OHBLS	10//99-12//99
Preschool, Kindergarten, and Elementary School	Columbus MSA, OH	Y		37440 AAW		OHBLS	10//99-12//99
Preschool, Kindergarten, and Elementary School	Dayton-Springfield MSA, OH	Y		33080 AAW		OHBLS	10//99-12//99
Preschool, Kindergarten, and Elementary School	Hamilton-Middletown PMSA, OH	Y		39020 AAW		OHBLS	10//99-12//99
Preschool, Kindergarten, and Elementary School	Lima MSA, OH	Y		34880 AAW		OHBLS	10//99-12//99
Preschool, Kindergarten, and Elementary School	Mansfield MSA, OH	Y		37900 AAW		OHBLS	10//99-12//99
Preschool, Kindergarten, and Elementary School	Steubenville-Weirton MSA, OH-WV	Y		37500 AAW		OHBLS	10//99-12//99

AAW	Average annual wage	AOH	Average offered, high	ASH	Average starting, high	H	Hourly	M	Monthly	S	Special: hourly and annual
AE	Average entry wage	AOL	Average offered, low	ASL	Average starting, low	HI	Highest wage paid	MTC	Median total compensation	TQ	Third quartile wage
AEX	Average experienced wage	APH	Average pay, high range	AW	Average wage paid	HR	High end range	MW	Median wage paid	W	Weekly
AO	Average offered	APL	Average pay, low range	FQ	First quartile wage	LR	Low end range	SQ	Second quartile wage	Y	Yearly

Occupation/Type/Industry	Location	Per	Low	Mid	High	Source	Date
Special Education Teacher							
Preschool, Kindergarten, and Elementary School	Toledo MSA, OH	Y		42130 AAW		OHBLS	10//99-12//99
Preschool, Kindergarten, and Elementary School	Youngstown-Warren MSA, OH	Y		33860 AAW		OHBLS	10//99-12//99
Preschool, Kindergarten, and Elementary School	Oklahoma	Y		31340 AAW		OKBLS	10//99-12//99
Preschool, Kindergarten, and Elementary School	Oklahoma City MSA, OK	Y		29300 AAW		OKBLS	10//99-12//99
Preschool, Kindergarten, and Elementary School	Tulsa MSA, OK	Y		33500 AAW		OKBLS	10//99-12//99
Preschool, Kindergarten, and Elementary School	Oregon	Y		41020 AAW		ORBLS	10//99-12//99
Preschool, Kindergarten, and Elementary School	Eugene-Springfield MSA, OR	Y		38190 AAW		ORBLS	10//99-12//99
Preschool, Kindergarten, and Elementary School	Portland-Vancouver PMSA, OR-WA	Y		47080 AAW		ORBLS	10//99-12//99
Preschool, Kindergarten, and Elementary School	Salem PMSA, OR	Y		43430 AAW		ORBLS	10//99-12//99
Preschool, Kindergarten, and Elementary School	Pennsylvania	Y		45740 AAW		PABLS	10//99-12//99
Preschool, Kindergarten, and Elementary School	Altoona MSA, PA	Y		40660 AAW		PABLS	10//99-12//99
Preschool, Kindergarten, and Elementary School	Erie MSA, PA	Y		42850 AAW		PABLS	10//99-12//99
Preschool, Kindergarten, and Elementary School	Harrisburg-Lebanon-Carlisle MSA, PA	Y		44040 AAW		PABLS	10//99-12//99
Preschool, Kindergarten, and Elementary School	Johnstown MSA, PA	Y		47570 AAW		PABLS	10//99-12//99
Preschool, Kindergarten, and Elementary School	Lancaster MSA, PA	Y		45110 AAW		PABLS	10//99-12//99
Preschool, Kindergarten, and Elementary School	Philadelphia PMSA, PA-NJ	Y		51690 AAW		PABLS	10//99-12//99
Preschool, Kindergarten, and Elementary School	Pittsburgh MSA, PA	Y		46690 AAW		PABLS	10//99-12//99
Preschool, Kindergarten, and Elementary School	Reading MSA, PA	Y		43080 AAW		PABLS	10//99-12//99
Preschool, Kindergarten, and Elementary School	Scranton--Wilkes-Barre--Hazleton MSA, PA	Y		45350 AAW		PABLS	10//99-12//99
Preschool, Kindergarten, and Elementary School	Sharon MSA, PA	Y		41980 AAW		PABLS	10//99-12//99
Preschool, Kindergarten, and Elementary School	State College MSA, PA	Y		45860 AAW		PABLS	10//99-12//99
Preschool, Kindergarten, and Elementary School	York MSA, PA	Y		40470 AAW		PABLS	10//99-12//99
Preschool, Kindergarten, and Elementary School	Rhode Island	Y		41260 AAW		RIBLS	10//99-12//99
Preschool, Kindergarten, and Elementary School	Providence-Fall River-Warwick MSA, RI-MA	Y		40620 AAW		RIBLS	10//99-12//99
Preschool, Kindergarten, and Elementary School	South Carolina	Y		36370 AAW		SCBLS	10//99-12//99
Preschool, Kindergarten, and Elementary School	Charleston-North Charleston MSA, SC	Y		37940 AAW		SCBLS	10//99-12//99
Preschool, Kindergarten, and Elementary School	Columbia MSA, SC	Y		42340 AAW		SCBLS	10//99-12//99
Preschool, Kindergarten, and Elementary School	Florence MSA, SC	Y		32010 AAW		SCBLS	10//99-12//99
Preschool, Kindergarten, and Elementary School	Greenville-Spartanburg-Anderson MSA, SC	Y		34950 AAW		SCBLS	10//99-12//99
Preschool, Kindergarten, and Elementary School	Sumter MSA, SC	Y		25090 AAW		SCBLS	10//99-12//99
Preschool, Kindergarten, and Elementary School	South Dakota	Y		28130 AAW		SDBLS	10//99-12//99
Preschool, Kindergarten, and Elementary School	Tennessee	Y		30610 AAW		TNBLS	10//99-12//99

AAW	Average annual wage	AOH	Average offered, high	ASH	Average starting, high
AE	Average entry wage	AOL	Average offered, low	ASL	Average starting, low
AEX	Average experienced wage	APH	Average pay, high range	AW	Average wage paid
AO	Average offered	APL	Average pay, low range	FQ	First quartile wage

H	Hourly	M	Monthly	S	Special: hourly and annual
HI	Highest wage paid	MTC	Median total compensation	TQ	Third quartile wage
HR	High end range	MW	Median wage paid	W	Weekly
LR	Low end range	SQ	Second quartile wage	Y	Yearly

Special Education Teacher

Occupation/Type/Industry	Location	Per	Low	Mid	High	Source	Date
Preschool, Kindergarten, and Elementary School	Chattanooga MSA, TN-GA	Y		31680 AAW		TNBLS	10//99-12//99
Preschool, Kindergarten, and Elementary School	Johnson City-Kingsport-Bristol MSA, TN-VA	Y		25900 AAW		TNBLS	10//99-12//99
Preschool, Kindergarten, and Elementary School	Knoxville MSA, TN	Y		30890 AAW		TNBLS	10//99-12//99
Preschool, Kindergarten, and Elementary School	Nashville MSA, TN	Y		33740 AAW		TNBLS	10//99-12//99
Preschool, Kindergarten, and Elementary School	Texas	Y		36670 AAW		TXBLS	10//99-12//99
Preschool, Kindergarten, and Elementary School	Austin-San Marcos MSA, TX	Y		36860 AAW		TXBLS	10//99-12//99
Preschool, Kindergarten, and Elementary School	Beaumont-Port Arthur MSA, TX	Y		35800 AAW		TXBLS	10//99-12//99
Preschool, Kindergarten, and Elementary School	Corpus Christi MSA, TX	Y		37960 AAW		TXBLS	10//99-12//99
Preschool, Kindergarten, and Elementary School	Dallas PMSA, TX	Y		34670 AAW		TXBLS	10//99-12//99
Preschool, Kindergarten, and Elementary School	Fort Worth-Arlington PMSA, TX	Y		38200 AAW		TXBLS	10//99-12//99
Preschool, Kindergarten, and Elementary School	Galveston-Texas City PMSA, TX	Y		35730 AAW		TXBLS	10//99-12//99
Preschool, Kindergarten, and Elementary School	Houston PMSA, TX	Y		38020 AAW		TXBLS	10//99-12//99
Preschool, Kindergarten, and Elementary School	Killeen-Temple MSA, TX	Y		33270 AAW		TXBLS	10//99-12//99
Preschool, Kindergarten, and Elementary School	Longview-Marshall MSA, TX	Y		33290 AAW		TXBLS	10//99-12//99
Preschool, Kindergarten, and Elementary School	McAllen-Edinburg-Mission MSA, TX	Y		37930 AAW		TXBLS	10//99-12//99
Preschool, Kindergarten, and Elementary School	San Antonio MSA, TX	Y		39350 AAW		TXBLS	10//99-12//99
Preschool, Kindergarten, and Elementary School	Sherman-Denison MSA, TX	Y		26830 AAW		TXBLS	10//99-12//99
Preschool, Kindergarten, and Elementary School	Texarkana MSA, TX-Texarkana, AR	Y		32410 AAW		TXBLS	10//99-12//99
Preschool, Kindergarten, and Elementary School	Waco MSA, TX	Y		33680 AAW		TXBLS	10//99-12//99
Preschool, Kindergarten, and Elementary School	Utah	Y		33960 AAW		UTBLS	10//99-12//99
Preschool, Kindergarten, and Elementary School	Salt Lake City-Ogden MSA, UT	Y		31340 AAW		UTBLS	10//99-12//99
Preschool, Kindergarten, and Elementary School	Vermont	Y		37390 AAW		VTBLS	10//99-12//99
Preschool, Kindergarten, and Elementary School	Burlington MSA, VT	Y		45480 AAW		VTBLS	10//99-12//99
Preschool, Kindergarten, and Elementary School	Virginia	Y		32750 AAW		VABLS	10//99-12//99
Preschool, Kindergarten, and Elementary School	Norfolk-Virginia Beach-Newport News MSA, VA-NC	Y		31330 AAW		VABLS	10//99-12//99
Preschool, Kindergarten, and Elementary School	Washington	Y		41550 AAW		WABLS	10//99-12//99
Preschool, Kindergarten, and Elementary School	Bellingham MSA, WA	Y		40290 AAW		WABLS	10//99-12//99
Preschool, Kindergarten, and Elementary School	Richland-Kennewick-Pasco MSA, WA	Y		38220 AAW		WABLS	10//99-12//99
Preschool, Kindergarten, and Elementary School	Seattle-Bellevue-Everett PMSA, WA	Y		40710 AAW		WABLS	10//99-12//99

AAW Average annual wage	**AOH** Average offered, high	**ASH** Average starting, high	**H** Hourly	**M** Monthly	**S** Special: hourly and annual
AE Average entry wage	**AOL** Average offered, low	**ASL** Average starting, low	**HI** Highest wage paid	**MTC** Median total compensation	**TQ** Third quartile wage
AEX Average experienced wage	**APH** Average pay, high range	**AW** Average wage paid	**HR** High end range	**MW** Median wage paid	**W** Weekly
AO Average offered	**APL** Average pay, low range	**FQ** First quartile wage	**LR** Low end range	**SQ** Second quartile wage	**Y** Yearly

Occupation/Type/Industry	Location	Per	Low	Mid	High	Source	Date
Special Education Teacher							
Preschool, Kindergarten, and Elementary School	Spokane MSA, WA	Y		35740 AAW		WABLS	10//99-12//99
Preschool, Kindergarten, and Elementary School	Tacoma PMSA, WA	Y		39430 AAW		WABLS	10//99-12//99
Preschool, Kindergarten, and Elementary School	Yakima MSA, WA	Y		40630 AAW		WABLS	10//99-12//99
Preschool, Kindergarten, and Elementary School	West Virginia	Y		34450 AAW		WVBLS	10//99-12//99
Preschool, Kindergarten, and Elementary School	Huntington-Ashland MSA, WV-KY-OH	Y		34300 AAW		WVBLS	10//99-12//99
Preschool, Kindergarten, and Elementary School	Wheeling MSA, WV-OH	Y		34180 AAW		WVBLS	10//99-12//99
Preschool, Kindergarten, and Elementary School	Wisconsin	Y		37530 AAW		WIBLS	10//99-12//99
Preschool, Kindergarten, and Elementary School	Appleton-Oshkosh-Neenah MSA, WI	Y		36610 AAW		WIBLS	10//99-12//99
Preschool, Kindergarten, and Elementary School	Eau Claire MSA, WI	Y		39880 AAW		WIBLS	10//99-12//99
Preschool, Kindergarten, and Elementary School	Janesville-Beloit MSA, WI	Y		37910 AAW		WIBLS	10//99-12//99
Preschool, Kindergarten, and Elementary School	Kenosha PMSA, WI	Y		37270 AAW		WIBLS	10//99-12//99
Preschool, Kindergarten, and Elementary School	La Crosse MSA, WI-MN	Y		36680 AAW		WIBLS	10//99-12//99
Preschool, Kindergarten, and Elementary School	Madison MSA, WI	Y		37830 AAW		WIBLS	10//99-12//99
Preschool, Kindergarten, and Elementary School	Milwaukee-Waukesha PMSA, WI	Y		41110 AAW		WIBLS	10//99-12//99
Preschool, Kindergarten, and Elementary School	Racine PMSA, WI	Y		39540 AAW		WIBLS	10//99-12//99
Preschool, Kindergarten, and Elementary School	Sheboygan MSA, WI	Y		36800 AAW		WIBLS	10//99-12//99
Preschool, Kindergarten, and Elementary School	Wyoming	Y		31200 AAW		WYBLS	10//99-12//99
Preschool, Kindergarten, and Elementary School	Puerto Rico	Y		19770 AAW		PRBLS	10//99-12//99
Preschool, Kindergarten, and Elementary School	San Juan-Bayamon PMSA, PR	Y		19780 AAW		PRBLS	10//99-12//99
Secondary School	Alabama	Y		36220 AAW		ALBLS	10//99-12//99
Secondary School	Anniston MSA, AL	Y		35570 AAW		ALBLS	10//99-12//99
Secondary School	Birmingham MSA, AL	Y		36040 AAW		ALBLS	10//99-12//99
Secondary School	Decatur MSA, AL	Y		32960 AAW		ALBLS	10//99-12//99
Secondary School	Dothan MSA, AL	Y		37400 AAW		ALBLS	10//99-12//99
Secondary School	Florence MSA, AL	Y		39430 AAW		ALBLS	10//99-12//99
Secondary School	Montgomery MSA, AL	Y		36380 AAW		ALBLS	10//99-12//99
Secondary School	Alaska	Y		46540 AAW		AKBLS	10//99-12//99
Secondary School	Arizona	Y		33970 AAW		AZBLS	10//99-12//99
Secondary School	Phoenix-Mesa MSA, AZ	Y		34180 AAW		AZBLS	10//99-12//99
Secondary School	Tucson MSA, AZ	Y		34540 AAW		AZBLS	10//99-12//99
Secondary School	Arkansas	Y		32110 AAW		ARBLS	10//99-12//99
Secondary School	Fayetteville-Springdale-Rogers MSA, AR	Y		36820 AAW		ARBLS	10//99-12//99
Secondary School	Fort Smith MSA, AR-OK	Y		30400 AAW		ARBLS	10//99-12//99
Secondary School	Little Rock-North Little Rock MSA, AR	Y		31730 AAW		ARBLS	10//99-12//99
Secondary School	California	Y		51070 AAW		CABLS	10//99-12//99
Secondary School	Fresno MSA, CA	Y		48340 AAW		CABLS	10//99-12//99
Secondary School	Los Angeles-Long Beach PMSA, CA	Y		54510 AAW		CABLS	10//99-12//99
Secondary School	Oakland PMSA, CA	Y		47020 AAW		CABLS	10//99-12//99
Secondary School	Riverside-San Bernardino PMSA, CA	Y		43410 AAW		CABLS	10//99-12//99
Secondary School	Sacramento PMSA, CA	Y		48990 AAW		CABLS	10//99-12//99
Secondary School	San Diego MSA, CA	Y		51400 AAW		CABLS	10//99-12//99
Secondary School	San Jose PMSA, CA	Y		53370 AAW		CABLS	10//99-12//99
Secondary School	San Luis Obispo-Atascadero-Paso Robles MSA, CA	Y		47620 AAW		CABLS	10//99-12//99

AAW	Average annual wage	AOH	Average offered, high	ASH	Average starting, high
AE	Average entry wage	AOL	Average offered, low	ASL	Average starting, low
AEX	Average experienced wage	APH	Average pay, high range	AW	Average wage paid
AO	Average offered	APL	Average pay, low range	FQ	First quartile wage

H	Hourly	M	Monthly	S	Special: hourly and annual
HI	Highest wage paid	MTC	Median total compensation	TQ	Third quartile wage
HR	High end range	MW	Median wage paid	W	Weekly
LR	Low end range	SQ	Second quartile wage	Y	Yearly

Special Education Teacher

Occupation/Type/Industry	Location	Per	Low	Mid	High	Source	Date
Special Education Teacher							
Secondary School	Santa Barbara-Santa Maria-Lompoc MSA, CA	Y		46060 AAW		CABLS	10//99-12//99
Secondary School	Santa Rosa PMSA, CA	Y		48770 AAW		CABLS	10//99-12//99
Secondary School	Stockton-Lodi MSA, CA	Y		47250 AAW		CABLS	10//99-12//99
Secondary School	Ventura PMSA, CA	Y		49540 AAW		CABLS	10//99-12//99
Secondary School	Visalia-Tulare-Porterville MSA, CA	Y		47160 AAW		CABLS	10//99-12//99
Secondary School	Yolo PMSA, CA	Y		36030 AAW		CABLS	10//99-12//99
Secondary School	Colorado	Y		38260 AAW		COBLS	10//99-12//99
Secondary School	Denver PMSA, CO	Y		36710 AAW		COBLS	10//99-12//99
Secondary School	Connecticut	Y		54140 AAW		CTBLS	10//99-12//99
Secondary School	Bridgeport PMSA, CT	Y		56570 AAW		CTBLS	10//99-12//99
Secondary School	Danbury PMSA, CT	Y		45500 AAW		CTBLS	10//99-12//99
Secondary School	Hartford MSA, CT	Y		52380 AAW		CTBLS	10//99-12//99
Secondary School	New Haven-Meriden PMSA, CT	Y		54140 AAW		CTBLS	10//99-12//99
Secondary School	New London-Norwich MSA, CT-RI	Y		49350 AAW		CTBLS	10//99-12//99
Secondary School	Stamford-Norwalk PMSA, CT	Y		61740 AAW		CTBLS	10//99-12//99
Secondary School	Waterbury PMSA, CT	Y		58570 AAW		CTBLS	10//99-12//99
Secondary School	Washington PMSA, DC-MD-VA-WV	Y		40200 AAW		DCBLS	10//99-12//99
Secondary School	Florida	Y		40520 AAW		FLBLS	10//99-12//99
Secondary School	Jacksonville MSA, FL	Y		39420 AAW		FLBLS	10//99-12//99
Secondary School	Orlando MSA, FL	Y		39170 AAW		FLBLS	10//99-12//99
Secondary School	Georgia	Y		39870 AAW		GABLS	10//99-12//99
Secondary School	Atlanta MSA, GA	Y		42830 AAW		GABLS	10//99-12//99
Secondary School	Columbus MSA, GA-AL	Y		43130 AAW		GABLS	10//99-12//99
Secondary School	Macon MSA, GA	Y		42500 AAW		GABLS	10//99-12//99
Secondary School	Illinois	Y		49960 AAW		ILBLS	10//99-12//99
Secondary School	Champaign-Urbana MSA, IL	Y		47430 AAW		ILBLS	10//99-12//99
Secondary School	Chicago PMSA, IL	Y		59250 AAW		ILBLS	10//99-12//99
Secondary School	Peoria-Pekin MSA, IL	Y		37020 AAW		ILBLS	10//99-12//99
Secondary School	Rockford MSA, IL	Y		40380 AAW		ILBLS	10//99-12//99
Secondary School	Indiana	Y		45930 AAW		INBLS	10//99-12//99
Secondary School	Elkhart-Goshen MSA, IN	Y		40030 AAW		INBLS	10//99-12//99
Secondary School	Fort Wayne MSA, IN	Y		41700 AAW		INBLS	10//99-12//99
Secondary School	Gary PMSA, IN	Y		43180 AAW		INBLS	10//99-12//99
Secondary School	Indianapolis MSA, IN	Y		49660 AAW		INBLS	10//99-12//99
Secondary School	Iowa	Y		34060 AAW		IABLS	10//99-12//99
Secondary School	Cedar Rapids MSA, IA	Y		41700 AAW		IABLS	10//99-12//99
Secondary School	Davenport-Moline-Rock Island MSA, IA-IL	Y		42400 AAW		IABLS	10//99-12//99
Secondary School	Des Moines MSA, IA	Y		36560 AAW		IABLS	10//99-12//99
Secondary School	Sioux City MSA, IA-NE	Y		27750 AAW		IABLS	10//99-12//99
Secondary School	Kansas	Y		36980 AAW		KSBLS	10//99-12//99
Secondary School	Wichita MSA, KS	Y		35600 AAW		KSBLS	10//99-12//99
Secondary School	Kentucky	Y		34980 AAW		KYBLS	10//99-12//99
Secondary School	Lexington MSA, KY	Y		30850 AAW		KYBLS	10//99-12//99
Secondary School	Louisiana	Y		40310 AAW		LABLS	10//99-12//99
Secondary School	New Orleans MSA, LA	Y		40130 AAW		LABLS	10//99-12//99
Secondary School	Maine	Y		34280 AAW		MEBLS	10//99-12//99
Secondary School	Portland MSA, ME	Y		37010 AAW		MEBLS	10//99-12//99
Secondary School	Massachusetts	Y		46010 AAW		MABLS	10//99-12//99
Secondary School	Barnstable-Yarmouth MSA, MA	Y		38220 AAW		MABLS	10//99-12//99
Secondary School	Boston PMSA, MA-NH	Y		45890 AAW		MABLS	10//99-12//99
Secondary School	Brockton PMSA, MA	Y		47400 AAW		MABLS	10//99-12//99
Secondary School	Lawrence PMSA, MA-NH	Y		44070 AAW		MABLS	10//99-12//99
Secondary School	Lowell PMSA, MA-NH	Y		49700 AAW		MABLS	10//99-12//99
Secondary School	New Bedford PMSA, MA	Y		43750 AAW		MABLS	10//99-12//99
Secondary School	Springfield MSA, MA	Y		49050 AAW		MABLS	10//99-12//99
Secondary School	Worcester PMSA, MA-CT	Y		44940 AAW		MABLS	10//99-12//99
Secondary School	Michigan	Y		48470 AAW		MIBLS	10//99-12//99
Secondary School	Ann Arbor PMSA, MI	Y		55870 AAW		MIBLS	10//99-12//99
Secondary School	Benton Harbor MSA, MI	Y		47020 AAW		MIBLS	10//99-12//99
Secondary School	Detroit PMSA, MI	Y		51240 AAW		MIBLS	10//99-12//99
Secondary School	Grand Rapids-Muskegon-Holland MSA, MI	Y		47200 AAW		MIBLS	10//99-12//99
Secondary School	Kalamazoo-Battle Creek MSA, MI	Y		43530 AAW		MIBLS	10//99-12//99

AAW Average annual wage	**AOH** Average offered, high	**ASH** Average starting, high	**H** Hourly	**M** Monthly	**S** Special: hourly and annual
AE Average entry wage	**AOL** Average offered, low	**ASL** Average starting, low	**HI** Highest wage paid	**MTC** Median total compensation	**TQ** Third quartile wage
AEX Average experienced wage	**APH** Average pay, high range	**AW** Average wage paid	**HR** High end range	**MW** Median wage paid	**W** Weekly
AO Average offered	**APL** Average pay, low range	**FQ** First quartile wage	**LR** Low end range	**SQ** Second quartile wage	**Y** Yearly

Occupation/Type/Industry	Location	Per	Low	Mid	High	Source	Date
Special Education Teacher							
Secondary School	Lansing-East Lansing MSA, MI	Y		47570 AAW		MIBLS	10//99-12//99
Secondary School	Minnesota	Y		39840 AAW		MNBLS	10//99-12//99
Secondary School	Duluth-Superior MSA, MN-WI	Y		46460 AAW		MNBLS	10//99-12//99
Secondary School	Minneapolis-St. Paul MSA, MN-WI	Y		42690 AAW		MNBLS	10//99-12//99
Secondary School	Mississippi	Y		30690 AAW		MSBLS	10//99-12//99
Secondary School	Biloxi-Gulfport-Pascagoula MSA, MS	Y		28260 AAW		MSBLS	10//99-12//99
Secondary School	Hattiesburg MSA, MS	Y		28750 AAW		MSBLS	10//99-12//99
Secondary School	Jackson MSA, MS	Y		29220 AAW		MSBLS	10//99-12//99
Secondary School	Missouri	Y		31440 AAW		MOBLS	10//99-12//99
Secondary School	Joplin MSA, MO	Y		30720 AAW		MOBLS	10//99-12//99
Secondary School	Kansas City MSA, MO-KS	Y		35320 AAW		MOBLS	10//99-12//99
Secondary School	St. Louis MSA, MO-IL	Y		34860 AAW		MOBLS	10//99-12//99
Secondary School	Springfield MSA, MO	Y		30140 AAW		MOBLS	10//99-12//99
Secondary School	Montana	Y		31960 AAW		MTBLS	10//99-12//99
Secondary School	Billings MSA, MT	Y		30770 AAW		MTBLS	10//99-12//99
Secondary School	Great Falls MSA, MT	Y		32640 AAW		MTBLS	10//99-12//99
Secondary School	Nebraska	Y		32350 AAW		NEBLS	10//99-12//99
Secondary School	Omaha MSA, NE-IA	Y		31830 AAW		NEBLS	10//99-12//99
Secondary School	Nevada	Y		40270 AAW		NVBLS	10//99-12//99
Secondary School	New Hampshire	Y		29880 AAW		NHBLS	10//99-12//99
Secondary School	Nashua PMSA, NH	Y		35430 AAW		NHBLS	10//99-12//99
Secondary School	Portsmouth-Rochester PMSA, NH-ME	Y		31870 AAW		NHBLS	10//99-12//99
Secondary School	New Jersey	Y		49920 AAW		NJBLS	10//99-12//99
Secondary School	Atlantic-Cape May PMSA, NJ	Y		48310 AAW		NJBLS	10//99-12//99
Secondary School	Bergen-Passaic PMSA, NJ	Y		54210 AAW		NJBLS	10//99-12//99
Secondary School	Jersey City PMSA, NJ	Y		47860 AAW		NJBLS	10//99-12//99
Secondary School	Middlesex-Somerset-Hunterdon PMSA, NJ	Y		52420 AAW		NJBLS	10//99-12//99
Secondary School	Monmouth-Ocean PMSA, NJ	Y		46040 AAW		NJBLS	10//99-12//99
Secondary School	Newark PMSA, NJ	Y		52330 AAW		NJBLS	10//99-12//99
Secondary School	Trenton PMSA, NJ	Y		47250 AAW		NJBLS	10//99-12//99
Secondary School	Vineland-Millville-Bridgeton PMSA, NJ	Y		46060 AAW		NJBLS	10//99-12//99
Secondary School	New Mexico	Y		30540 AAW		NMBLS	10//99-12//99
Secondary School	New York	Y		50950 AAW		NYBLS	10//99-12//99
Secondary School	Albany-Schenectady-Troy MSA, NY	Y		42840 AAW		NYBLS	10//99-12//99
Secondary School	Binghamton MSA, NY	Y		39300 AAW		NYBLS	10//99-12//99
Secondary School	Buffalo-Niagara Falls MSA, NY	Y		51990 AAW		NYBLS	10//99-12//99
Secondary School	Glens Falls MSA, NY	Y		41800 AAW		NYBLS	10//99-12//99
Secondary School	Jamestown MSA, NY	Y		42750 AAW		NYBLS	10//99-12//99
Secondary School	Nassau-Suffolk PMSA, NY	Y		62810 AAW		NYBLS	10//99-12//99
Secondary School	New York PMSA, NY	Y		60710 AAW		NYBLS	10//99-12//99
Secondary School	Newburgh PMSA, NY-PA	Y		50750 AAW		NYBLS	10//99-12//99
Secondary School	Rochester MSA, NY	Y		42130 AAW		NYBLS	10//99-12//99
Secondary School	Syracuse MSA, NY	Y		38820 AAW		NYBLS	10//99-12//99
Secondary School	Utica-Rome MSA, NY	Y		36510 AAW		NYBLS	10//99-12//99
Secondary School	North Carolina	Y		34490 AAW		NCBLS	10//99-12//99
Secondary School	Charlotte-Gastonia-Rock Hill MSA, NC-SC	Y		36410 AAW		NCBLS	10//99-12//99
Secondary School	Greensboro--Winston-Salem--High Point MSA, NC	Y		32850 AAW		NCBLS	10//99-12//99
Secondary School	North Dakota	Y		32070 AAW		NDBLS	10//99-12//99
Secondary School	Fargo-Moorhead MSA, ND-MN	Y		32960 AAW		NDBLS	10//99-12//99
Secondary School	Grand Forks MSA, ND-MN	Y		35030 AAW		NDBLS	10//99-12//99
Secondary School	Ohio	Y		38790 AAW		OHBLS	10//99-12//99
Secondary School	Akron PMSA, OH	Y		43710 AAW		OHBLS	10//99-12//99
Secondary School	Canton-Massillon MSA, OH	Y		38700 AAW		OHBLS	10//99-12//99
Secondary School	Cincinnati PMSA, OH-KY-IN	Y		32480 AAW		OHBLS	10//99-12//99
Secondary School	Cleveland-Lorain-Elyria PMSA, OH	Y		41210 AAW		OHBLS	10//99-12//99
Secondary School	Columbus MSA, OH	Y		43000 AAW		OHBLS	10//99-12//99
Secondary School	Dayton-Springfield MSA, OH	Y		42170 AAW		OHBLS	10//99-12//99
Secondary School	Hamilton-Middletown PMSA, OH	Y		41870 AAW		OHBLS	10//99-12//99
Secondary School	Lima MSA, OH	Y		38390 AAW		OHBLS	10//99-12//99

AAW	Average annual wage	AOH	Average offered, high	ASH	Average starting, high	H	Hourly	M	Monthly	S	Special: hourly and annual
AE	Average entry wage	AOL	Average offered, low	ASL	Average starting, low	HI	Highest wage paid	MTC	Median total compensation	TQ	Third quartile wage
AEX	Average experienced wage	APH	Average pay, high range	AW	Average wage paid	HR	High end range	MW	Median wage paid	W	Weekly
AO	Average offered	APL	Average pay, low range	FQ	First quartile wage	LR	Low end range	SQ	Second quartile wage	Y	Yearly

Occupation/Type/Industry	Location	Per	Low	Mid	High	Source	Date
Special Education Teacher							
Secondary School	Mansfield MSA, OH	Y		38780 AAW		OHBLS	10//99-12//99
Secondary School	Toledo MSA, OH	Y		39650 AAW		OHBLS	10//99-12//99
Secondary School	Youngstown-Warren MSA, OH	Y		35010 AAW		OHBLS	10//99-12//99
Secondary School	Oklahoma	Y		31650 AAW		OKBLS	10//99-12//99
Secondary School	Oklahoma City MSA, OK	Y		29010 AAW		OKBLS	10//99-12//99
Secondary School	Tulsa MSA, OK	Y		32990 AAW		OKBLS	10//99-12//99
Secondary School	Oregon	Y		41390 AAW		ORBLS	10//99-12//99
Secondary School	Portland-Vancouver PMSA, OR-WA	Y		43730 AAW		ORBLS	10//99-12//99
Secondary School	Pennsylvania	Y		41790 AAW		PABLS	10//99-12//99
Secondary School	Altoona MSA, PA	Y		34940 AAW		PABLS	10//99-12//99
Secondary School	Erie MSA, PA	Y		42130 AAW		PABLS	10//99-12//99
Secondary School	Harrisburg-Lebanon-Carlisle MSA, PA	Y		43150 AAW		PABLS	10//99-12//99
Secondary School	Johnstown MSA, PA	Y		40670 AAW		PABLS	10//99-12//99
Secondary School	Lancaster MSA, PA	Y		47110 AAW		PABLS	10//99-12//99
Secondary School	Philadelphia PMSA, PA-NJ	Y		44390 AAW		PABLS	10//99-12//99
Secondary School	Pittsburgh MSA, PA	Y		39740 AAW		PABLS	10//99-12//99
Secondary School	Reading MSA, PA	Y		42390 AAW		PABLS	10//99-12//99
Secondary School	Scranton--Wilkes-Barre--Hazleton MSA, PA	Y		42360 AAW		PABLS	10//99-12//99
Secondary School	Sharon MSA, PA	Y		40410 AAW		PABLS	10//99-12//99
Secondary School	State College MSA, PA	Y		44280 AAW		PABLS	10//99-12//99
Secondary School	York MSA, PA	Y		41910 AAW		PABLS	10//99-12//99
Secondary School	Rhode Island	Y		51270 AAW		RIBLS	10//99-12//99
Secondary School	Providence-Fall River-Warwick MSA, RI-MA	Y		49750 AAW		RIBLS	10//99-12//99
Secondary School	South Carolina	Y		36230 AAW		SCBLS	10//99-12//99
Secondary School	Greenville-Spartanburg-Anderson MSA, SC	Y		31000 AAW		SCBLS	10//99-12//99
Secondary School	South Dakota	Y		29200 AAW		SDBLS	10//99-12//99
Secondary School	Tennessee	Y		32620 AAW		TNBLS	10//99-12//99
Secondary School	Chattanooga MSA, TN-GA	Y		31850 AAW		TNBLS	10//99-12//99
Secondary School	Johnson City-Kingsport-Bristol MSA, TN-VA	Y		30730 AAW		TNBLS	10//99-12//99
Secondary School	Knoxville MSA, TN	Y		35520 AAW		TNBLS	10//99-12//99
Secondary School	Memphis MSA, TN-AR-MS	Y		43290 AAW		MSBLS	10//99-12//99
Secondary School	Nashville MSA, TN	Y		30730 AAW		TNBLS	10//99-12//99
Secondary School	Texas	Y		36820 AAW		TXBLS	10//99-12//99
Secondary School	Austin-San Marcos MSA, TX	Y		37600 AAW		TXBLS	10//99-12//99
Secondary School	Beaumont-Port Arthur MSA, TX	Y		34100 AAW		TXBLS	10//99-12//99
Secondary School	Dallas PMSA, TX	Y		31350 AAW		TXBLS	10//99-12//99
Secondary School	Fort Worth-Arlington PMSA, TX	Y		40750 AAW		TXBLS	10//99-12//99
Secondary School	Galveston-Texas City PMSA, TX	Y		36730 AAW		TXBLS	10//99-12//99
Secondary School	Houston PMSA, TX	Y		41200 AAW		TXBLS	10//99-12//99
Secondary School	Killeen-Temple MSA, TX	Y		33750 AAW		TXBLS	10//99-12//99
Secondary School	Longview-Marshall MSA, TX	Y		35600 AAW		TXBLS	10//99-12//99
Secondary School	McAllen-Edinburg-Mission MSA, TX	Y		38230 AAW		TXBLS	10//99-12//99
Secondary School	San Antonio MSA, TX	Y		38440 AAW		TXBLS	10//99-12//99
Secondary School	Sherman-Denison MSA, TX	Y		37790 AAW		TXBLS	10//99-12//99
Secondary School	Texarkana MSA, TX-Texarkana, AR	Y		31310 AAW		TXBLS	10//99-12//99
Secondary School	Waco MSA, TX	Y		34650 AAW		TXBLS	10//99-12//99
Secondary School	Vermont	Y		36750 AAW		VTBLS	10//99-12//99
Secondary School	Burlington MSA, VT	Y		41720 AAW		VTBLS	10//99-12//99
Secondary School	Virginia	Y		32920 AAW		VABLS	10//99-12//99
Secondary School	Norfolk-Virginia Beach-Newport News MSA, VA-NC	Y		33200 AAW		VABLS	10//99-12//99
Secondary School	Washington	Y		41330 AAW		WABLS	10//99-12//99
Secondary School	Bellingham MSA, WA	Y		39380 AAW		WABLS	10//99-12//99
Secondary School	Richland-Kennewick-Pasco MSA, WA	Y		41490 AAW		WABLS	10//99-12//99
Secondary School	Seattle-Bellevue-Everett PMSA, WA	Y		39770 AAW		WABLS	10//99-12//99
Secondary School	Spokane MSA, WA	Y		44790 AAW		WABLS	10//99-12//99
Secondary School	Tacoma PMSA, WA	Y		42880 AAW		WABLS	10//99-12//99

AAW	Average annual wage	AOH	Average offered, high	ASH	Average starting, high	H	Hourly
AE	Average entry wage	AOL	Average offered, low	ASL	Average starting, low	HI	Highest wage paid
AEX	Average experienced wage	APH	Average pay, high range	AW	Average wage paid	HR	High end range
AO	Average offered	APL	Average pay, low range	FQ	First quartile wage	LR	Low end range

M	Monthly	S	Special: hourly and annual
MTC	Median total compensation	TQ	Third quartile wage
MW	Median wage paid	W	Weekly
SQ	Second quartile wage	Y	Yearly

Occupation/Type/Industry	Location	Per	Low	Mid	High	Source	Date
Special Education Teacher							
Secondary School	Yakima MSA, WA	Y		37390 AAW		WABLS	10//99-12//99
Secondary School	West Virginia	Y		34580 AAW		WVBLS	10//99-12//99
Secondary School	Huntington-Ashland MSA, WV-KY-OH	Y		36300 AAW		WVBLS	10//99-12//99
Secondary School	Wheeling MSA, WV-OH	Y		32540 AAW		WVBLS	10//99-12//99
Secondary School	Wisconsin	Y		40490 AAW		WIBLS	10//99-12//99
Secondary School	Appleton-Oshkosh-Neenah MSA, WI	Y		44120 AAW		WIBLS	10//99-12//99
Secondary School	La Crosse MSA, WI-MN	Y		36490 AAW		WIBLS	10//99-12//99
Secondary School	Madison MSA, WI	Y		41220 AAW		WIBLS	10//99-12//99
Secondary School	Milwaukee-Waukesha PMSA, WI	Y		41460 AAW		WIBLS	10//99-12//99
Secondary School	Wyoming	Y		32490 AAW		WYBLS	10//99-12//99
Speech-Language Pathologist	Alabama	S	17.96 MW	18.98 AW	39480 AAW	ALBLS	10//99-12//99
	Alaska	S	24.37 MW	24.97 AW	51940 AAW	AKBLS	10//99-12//99
	Arizona	S	17.44 MW	20.46 AW	42560 AAW	AZBLS	10//99-12//99
	Arkansas	S	18.84 MW	19.34 AW	40220 AAW	ARBLS	10//99-12//99
	California	S	26.87 MW	26.40 AW	54910 AAW	CABLS	10//99-12//99
	Colorado	S	20.32 MW	21.41 AW	44530 AAW	COBLS	10//99-12//99
	Connecticut	S	28.04 MW	27.77 AW	57770 AAW	CTBLS	10//99-12//99
	Delaware	S	25.05 MW	25.29 AW	52600 AAW	DEBLS	10//99-12//99
	District of Columbia	S	23.09 MW	23.82 AW	49550 AAW	DCBLS	10//99-12//99
	Florida	S	22.66 MW	23.51 AW	48900 AAW	FLBLS	10//99-12//99
	Georgia	S	22.01 MW	22.47 AW	46740 AAW	GABLS	10//99-12//99
	Hawaii	S	22.56 MW	21.71 AW	45160 AAW	HIBLS	10//99-12//99
	Idaho	S	19.53 MW	19.17 AW	39860 AAW	IDBLS	10//99-12//99
	Illinois	S	24.35 MW	25.07 AW	52140 AAW	ILBLS	10//99-12//99
	Indiana	S	21.06 MW	21.48 AW	44680 AAW	INBLS	10//99-12//99
	Iowa	S	20.51 MW	21.35 AW	44410 AAW	IABLS	10//99-12//99
	Kansas	S	19.36 MW	19.91 AW	41410 AAW	KSBLS	10//99-12//99
	Kentucky	S	18.81 MW	19.42 AW	40400 AAW	KYBLS	10//99-12//99
	Louisiana	S	20.12 MW	21.96 AW	45680 AAW	LABLS	10//99-12//99
	Maine	S	18.58 MW	19.25 AW	40050 AAW	MEBLS	10//99-12//99
	Maryland	S	22.31 MW	23.41 AW	48680 AAW	MDBLS	10//99-12//99
	Massachusetts	S	24.19 MW	25.35 AW	52740 AAW	MABLS	10//99-12//99
	Michigan	S	23.54 MW	23.98 AW	49880 AAW	MIBLS	10//99-12//99
	Minnesota	S	19.86 MW	20.46 AW	42570 AAW	MNBLS	10//99-12//99
	Mississippi	S	17.9 MW	19.44 AW	40440 AAW	MSBLS	10//99-12//99
	Missouri	S	19.98 MW	20.52 AW	42670 AAW	MOBLS	10//99-12//99
	Montana	S	19.51 MW	20.09 AW	41790 AAW	MTBLS	10//99-12//99
	Nebraska	S	16.29 MW	16.78 AW	34900 AAW	NEBLS	10//99-12//99
	Nevada	S	24.57 MW	25.55 AW	53140 AAW	NVBLS	10//99-12//99
	New Hampshire	S	22.94 MW	23.38 AW	48630 AAW	NHBLS	10//99-12//99
	New Jersey	S	25.89 MW	26.74 AW	55620 AAW	NJBLS	10//99-12//99
	New Mexico	S	18.11 MW	19.68 AW	40930 AAW	NMBLS	10//99-12//99
	New York	S	22.29 MW	23.86 AW	49620 AAW	NYBLS	10//99-12//99
	North Carolina	S	20.65 MW	22.40 AW	46580 AAW	NCBLS	10//99-12//99
	North Dakota	S	17.16 MW	17.39 AW	36170 AAW	NDBLS	10//99-12//99
	Ohio	S	22.16 MW	22.45 AW	46690 AAW	OHBLS	10//99-12//99
	Oklahoma	S	17.04 MW	18.24 AW	37930 AAW	OKBLS	10//99-12//99
	Oregon	S	22.25 MW	21.47 AW	44650 AAW	ORBLS	10//99-12//99
	Pennsylvania	S	23.96 MW	25.03 AW	52060 AAW	PABLS	10//99-12//99
	Rhode Island	S	23.33 MW	23.84 AW	49590 AAW	RIBLS	10//99-12//99
	South Dakota	S	16.08 MW	17.04 AW	35450 AAW	SDBLS	10//99-12//99
	Tennessee	S	19.65 MW	20.51 AW	42660 AAW	TNBLS	10//99-12//99
	Texas	S	19.89 MW	20.43 AW	42490 AAW	TXBLS	10//99-12//99
	Utah	S	21.19 MW	21.09 AW	43870 AAW	UTBLS	10//99-12//99
	Vermont	S	19.97 MW	21.52 AW	44750 AAW	VTBLS	10//99-12//99
	Virginia	S	20.37 MW	20.79 AW	43250 AAW	VABLS	10//99-12//99
	Washington	S	21.87 MW	21.69 AW	45110 AAW	WABLS	10//99-12//99
	West Virginia	S	20.33 MW	21.47 AW	44660 AAW	WVBLS	10//99-12//99
	Wisconsin	S	20.99 MW	20.82 AW	43300 AAW	WIBLS	10//99-12//99
	Wyoming	S	18.98 MW	19.33 AW	40210 AAW	WYBLS	10//99-12//99
	Puerto Rico	S	10.3 MW	12.36 AW	25710 AAW	PRBLS	10//99-12//99
Speech Pathologist	United States	Y		44000 AW		PETENG	1999
Speech Therapist	United States	H		23.26 AW		NCS98	1998
Staffing Specialist							
Human Resources	United States	Y		52000 AW		HRMAG	1999

AAW	Average annual wage	AOH	Average offered, high	ASH	Average starting, high	H	Hourly
AE	Average entry wage	AOL	Average offered, low	ASL	Average starting, low	HI	Highest wage paid
AEX	Average experienced wage	APH	Average pay, high range	AW	Average wage paid	HR	High end range
AO	Average offered	APL	Average pay, low range	FQ	First quartile wage	LR	Low end range

M	Monthly	S	Special: hourly and annual
MTC	Median total compensation	TQ	Third quartile wage
MW	Median wage paid	W	Weekly
SQ	Second quartile wage	Y	Yearly

Occupation/Type/Industry	Location	Per	Low	Mid	High	Source	Date
Stationary Engineer and Boiler Operator	Alabama	S	18.95 MW	18.17 AW	37800 AAW	ALBLS	10//99-12//99
	Alaska	S	24.43 MW	24.31 AW	50560 AAW	AKBLS	10//99-12//99
	Arizona	S	21.86 MW	20.59 AW	42830 AAW	AZBLS	10//99-12//99
	Arkansas	S	13.16 MW	14.82 AW	30830 AAW	ARBLS	10//99-12//99
	California	S	22.5 MW	22.13 AW	46030 AAW	CABLS	10//99-12//99
	Colorado	S	19.23 MW	19.26 AW	40070 AAW	COBLS	10//99-12//99
	Connecticut	S	19.17 MW	19.77 AW	41130 AAW	CTBLS	10//99-12//99
	Delaware	S	19.96 MW	21.99 AW	45740 AAW	DEBLS	10//99-12//99
	District of Columbia	S	19.28 MW	18.84 AW	39190 AAW	DCBLS	10//99-12//99
	Florida	S	14.58 MW	15.63 AW	32520 AAW	FLBLS	10//99-12//99
	Georgia	S	18.79 MW	18.10 AW	37650 AAW	GABLS	10//99-12//99
	Idaho	S	14.11 MW	14.31 AW	29760 AAW	IDBLS	10//99-12//99
	Illinois	S	19.04 MW	18.52 AW	38520 AAW	ILBLS	10//99-12//99
	Indiana	S	18.38 MW	18.49 AW	38470 AAW	INBLS	10//99-12//99
	Iowa	S	16.11 MW	16.89 AW	35130 AAW	IABLS	10//99-12//99
	Kansas	S	16.76 MW	17.02 AW	35390 AAW	KSBLS	10//99-12//99
	Kentucky	S	19.88 MW	18.28 AW	38020 AAW	KYBLS	10//99-12//99
	Louisiana	S	15.51 MW	16.54 AW	34390 AAW	LABLS	10//99-12//99
	Maine	S	17.72 MW	17.53 AW	36460 AAW	MEBLS	10//99-12//99
	Maryland	S	20.56 MW	20.28 AW	42180 AAW	MDBLS	10//99-12//99
	Massachusetts	S	17.99 MW	18.49 AW	38460 AAW	MABLS	10//99-12//99
	Michigan	S	22.57 MW	22.08 AW	45930 AAW	MIBLS	10//99-12//99
	Minnesota	S	16.7 MW	17.51 AW	36420 AAW	MNBLS	10//99-12//99
	Mississippi	S	18.3 MW	18.14 AW	37740 AAW	MSBLS	10//99-12//99
	Missouri	S	16.49 MW	16.94 AW	35240 AAW	MOBLS	10//99-12//99
	Montana	S	14.68 MW	15.45 AW	32140 AAW	MTBLS	10//99-12//99
	Nebraska	S	14.74 MW	15.55 AW	32340 AAW	NEBLS	10//99-12//99
	Nevada	S	18.75 MW	17.44 AW	36270 AAW	NVBLS	10//99-12//99
	New Hampshire	S	16.39 MW	15.44 AW	32120 AAW	NHBLS	10//99-12//99
	New Jersey	S	18.78 MW	19.33 AW	40200 AAW	NJBLS	10//99-12//99
	New Mexico	S	11.92 MW	11.83 AW	24610 AAW	NMBLS	10//99-12//99
	New York	S	19.47 MW	20.67 AW	42990 AAW	NYBLS	10//99-12//99
	North Carolina	S	13.26 MW	15.15 AW	31510 AAW	NCBLS	10//99-12//99
	North Dakota	S	13.38 MW	14.26 AW	29670 AAW	NDBLS	10//99-12//99
	Ohio	S	18.9 MW	19.45 AW	40460 AAW	OHBLS	10//99-12//99
	Oklahoma	S	17.66 MW	17.22 AW	35830 AAW	OKBLS	10//99-12//99
	Oregon	S	18.34 MW	18.47 AW	38410 AAW	ORBLS	10//99-12//99
	Pennsylvania	S	17.62 MW	17.25 AW	35890 AAW	PABLS	10//99-12//99
	Rhode Island	S	16.8 MW	17.01 AW	35380 AAW	RIBLS	10//99-12//99
	South Carolina	S	18.34 MW	19.75 AW	41070 AAW	SCBLS	10//99-12//99
	South Dakota	S	11.71 MW	11.97 AW	24900 AAW	SDBLS	10//99-12//99
	Tennessee	S	16.93 MW	16.46 AW	34240 AAW	TNBLS	10//99-12//99
	Texas	S	15.47 MW	16.75 AW	34840 AAW	TXBLS	10//99-12//99
	Utah	S	17.65 MW	18.49 AW	38470 AAW	UTBLS	10//99-12//99
	Vermont	S	14.03 MW	14.02 AW	29160 AAW	VTBLS	10//99-12//99
	Virginia	S	17.31 MW	17.57 AW	36550 AAW	VABLS	10//99-12//99
	Washington	S	18.04 MW	18.80 AW	39100 AAW	WABLS	10//99-12//99
	West Virginia	S	18.35 MW	17.01 AW	35380 AAW	WVBLS	10//99-12//99
	Wisconsin	S	16.47 MW	17.71 AW	36850 AAW	WIBLS	10//99-12//99
	Wyoming	S	22.88 MW	21.59 AW	44910 AAW	WYBLS	10//99-12//99
	Puerto Rico	S	12.66 MW	13.44 AW	27960 AAW	PRBLS	10//99-12//99
	Virgin Islands	S	14.92 MW	14.71 AW	30610 AAW	VIBLS	10//99-12//99
	Guam	S	13.58 MW	13.28 AW	27620 AAW	GUBLS	10//99-12//99
Statistical Assistant	Alabama	S	9.09 MW	10.37 AW	21570 AAW	ALBLS	10//99-12//99
	Alaska	S	16.43 MW	17.80 AW	37020 AAW	AKBLS	10//99-12//99
	Arizona	S	10.77 MW	11.84 AW	24640 AAW	AZBLS	10//99-12//99
	Arkansas	S	8.06 MW	8.52 AW	17710 AAW	ARBLS	10//99-12//99
	California	S	14.5 MW	14.85 AW	30880 AAW	CABLS	10//99-12//99
	Colorado	S	11.19 MW	12.13 AW	25230 AAW	COBLS	10//99-12//99
	Connecticut	S	15.24 MW	15.95 AW	33180 AAW	CTBLS	10//99-12//99
	District of Columbia	S	13.6 MW	14.14 AW	29420 AAW	DCBLS	10//99-12//99
	Florida	S	11.06 MW	11.84 AW	24630 AAW	FLBLS	10//99-12//99
	Georgia	S	11.6 MW	12.30 AW	25590 AAW	GABLS	10//99-12//99
	Hawaii	S	13.28 MW	14.63 AW	30420 AAW	HIBLS	10//99-12//99
	Idaho	S	14 MW	14.61 AW	30380 AAW	IDBLS	10//99-12//99
	Illinois	S	14.95 MW	14.85 AW	30880 AAW	ILBLS	10//99-12//99
	Iowa	S	10.89 MW	11.34 AW	23580 AAW	IABLS	10//99-12//99
	Kansas	S	9.17 MW	10.77 AW	22400 AAW	KSBLS	10//99-12//99
	Kentucky	S	9.11 MW	9.39 AW	19530 AAW	KYBLS	10//99-12//99
	Louisiana	S	8.14 MW	9.40 AW	19550 AAW	LABLS	10//99-12//99

AAW Average annual wage	**AOH** Average offered, high	**ASH** Average starting, high	**H** Hourly	**M** Monthly	**S** Special: hourly and annual
AE Average entry wage	**AOL** Average offered, low	**ASL** Average starting, low	**HI** Highest wage paid	**MTC** Median total compensation	**TQ** Third quartile wage
AEX Average experienced wage	**APH** Average pay, high range	**AW** Average wage paid	**HR** High end range	**MW** Median wage paid	**W** Weekly
AO Average offered	**APL** Average pay, low range	**FQ** First quartile wage	**LR** Low end range	**SQ** Second quartile wage	**Y** Yearly

Occupation/Type/Industry	Location	Per	Low	Mid	High	Source	Date
Statistical Assistant	Maryland	S	12.69 MW	13.23 AW	27530 AAW	MDBLS	10//99-12//99
	Massachusetts	S	11.21 MW	12.32 AW	25620 AAW	MABLS	10//99-12//99
	Michigan	S	11.05 MW	11.56 AW	24040 AAW	MIBLS	10//99-12//99
	Minnesota	S	10.68 MW	11.75 AW	24440 AAW	MNBLS	10//99-12//99
	Mississippi	S	9.58 MW	10.29 AW	21410 AAW	MSBLS	10//99-12//99
	Missouri	S	9.7 MW	11.24 AW	23380 AAW	MOBLS	10//99-12//99
	Montana	S	11.46 MW	11.58 AW	24080 AAW	MTBLS	10//99-12//99
	Nebraska	S	9.25 MW	10.26 AW	21330 AAW	NEBLS	10//99-12//99
	Nevada	S	10.47 MW	11.03 AW	22950 AAW	NVBLS	10//99-12//99
	New Hampshire	S	12.04 MW	12.30 AW	25580 AAW	NHBLS	10//99-12//99
	New Jersey	S	16.67 MW	15.32 AW	31860 AAW	NJBLS	10//99-12//99
	New Mexico	S	10.82 MW	11.25 AW	23410 AAW	NMBLS	10//99-12//99
	New York	S	13.58 MW	14.20 AW	29540 AAW	NYBLS	10//99-12//99
	North Carolina	S	12.03 MW	12.41 AW	25810 AAW	NCBLS	10//99-12//99
	North Dakota	S	8.06 MW	8.64 AW	17970 AAW	NDBLS	10//99-12//99
	Ohio	S	10.47 MW	11.28 AW	23470 AAW	OHBLS	10//99-12//99
	Oklahoma	S	10.46 MW	11.47 AW	23860 AAW	OKBLS	10//99-12//99
	Oregon	S	9.87 MW	10.85 AW	22570 AAW	ORBLS	10//99-12//99
	Pennsylvania	S	12.14 MW	13.07 AW	27180 AAW	PABLS	10//99-12//99
	Rhode Island	S	14.78 MW	14.74 AW	30670 AAW	RIBLS	10//99-12//99
	South Carolina	S	12.07 MW	13.97 AW	29060 AAW	SCBLS	10//99-12//99
	South Dakota	S	10.32 MW	11.44 AW	23780 AAW	SDBLS	10//99-12//99
	Tennessee	S	10.83 MW	11.88 AW	24720 AAW	TNBLS	10//99-12//99
	Texas	S	10.56 MW	11.92 AW	24800 AAW	TXBLS	10//99-12//99
	Utah	S	10.68 MW	11.71 AW	24360 AAW	UTBLS	10//99-12//99
	Vermont	S	10.41 MW	11.36 AW	23630 AAW	VTBLS	10//99-12//99
	Virginia	S	12.81 MW	13.35 AW	27760 AAW	VABLS	10//99-12//99
	Washington	S	12.93 MW	13.37 AW	27810 AAW	WABLS	10//99-12//99
	West Virginia	S	9.94 MW	10.77 AW	22400 AAW	WVBLS	10//99-12//99
	Wisconsin	S	10.95 MW	11.75 AW	24440 AAW	WIBLS	10//99-12//99
	Puerto Rico	S	6.08 MW	6.60 AW	13720 AAW	PRBLS	10//99-12//99
Statistician	United States	H		23.83 AW		NCS98	1998
	Alabama	S	20.55 MW	21.69 AW	45120 AAW	ALBLS	10//99-12//99
	Arizona	S	20.15 MW	21.33 AW	44360 AAW	AZBLS	10//99-12//99
	Phoenix-Mesa MSA, AZ	S	21.42 MW	20.37 AW	44550 AAW	AZBLS	10//99-12//99
	Arkansas	S	16.34 MW	17.03 AW	35430 AAW	ARBLS	10//99-12//99
	California	S	19.47 MW	23.08 AW	48000 AAW	CABLS	10//99-12//99
	Los Angeles-Long Beach PMSA, CA	S	32.54 MW	27.77 AW	67680 AAW	CABLS	10//99-12//99
	Riverside-San Bernardino PMSA, CA	S	26.32 MW	27.32 AW	54740 AAW	CABLS	10//99-12//99
	Sacramento PMSA, CA	S	24.93 MW	24.20 AW	51860 AAW	CABLS	10//99-12//99
	San Diego MSA, CA	S	26.64 MW	23.91 AW	55410 AAW	CABLS	10//99-12//99
	San Francisco PMSA, CA	S	30.03 MW	28.73 AW	62460 AAW	CABLS	10//99-12//99
	San Jose PMSA, CA	S	30.74 MW	28.44 AW	63940 AAW	CABLS	10//99-12//99
	Colorado	S	25.31 MW	26.50 AW	55120 AAW	COBLS	10//99-12//99
	Denver PMSA, CO	S	25.83 MW	24.96 AW	53730 AAW	COBLS	10//99-12//99
	Connecticut	S	24.96 MW	28.12 AW	58500 AAW	CTBLS	10//99-12//99
	Hartford MSA, CT	S	23.65 MW	21.15 AW	49190 AAW	CTBLS	10//99-12//99
	Delaware	S	29.85 MW	27.95 AW	58130 AAW	DEBLS	10//99-12//99
	Wilmington-Newark PMSA, DE-MD	S	30.07 MW	31.48 AW	62550 AAW	DEBLS	10//99-12//99
	Washington PMSA, DC-MD-VA-WV	S	28.59 MW	29.32 AW	59470 AAW	DCBLS	10//99-12//99
	Florida	S	15.33 MW	16.77 AW	34880 AAW	FLBLS	10//99-12//99
	Gainesville MSA, FL	S	17.39 MW	16.39 AW	36180 AAW	FLBLS	10//99-12//99
	Jacksonville MSA, FL	S	18.61 MW	19.11 AW	38710 AAW	FLBLS	10//99-12//99
	Miami PMSA, FL	S	18.54 MW	15.96 AW	38570 AAW	FLBLS	10//99-12//99
	Orlando MSA, FL	S	19.59 MW	18.25 AW	40760 AAW	FLBLS	10//99-12//99
	Tallahassee MSA, FL	S	15.16 MW	13.77 AW	31540 AAW	FLBLS	10//99-12//99
	Tampa-St. Petersburg-Clearwater MSA, FL	S	12.82 MW	11.16 AW	26670 AAW	FLBLS	10//99-12//99
	Georgia	S	22.35 MW	24.04 AW	49990 AAW	GABLS	10//99-12//99
	Atlanta MSA, GA	S	23.87 MW	21.53 AW	49640 AAW	GABLS	10//99-12//99
	Illinois	S	20.88 MW	24.64 AW	51250 AAW	ILBLS	10//99-12//99
	Bloomington-Normal MSA, IL	S	22.83 MW	20.00 AW	47480 AAW	ILBLS	10//99-12//99
	Chicago PMSA, IL	S	24.64 MW	20.81 AW	51250 AAW	ILBLS	10//99-12//99
	Indiana	S	18.59 MW	19.53 AW	40610 AAW	INBLS	10//99-12//99
	Indianapolis MSA, IN	S	17.31 MW	15.85 AW	36010 AAW	INBLS	10//99-12//99
	Kansas	S	21.23 MW	26.08 AW	54240 AAW	KSBLS	10//99-12//99
	Kentucky	S	18.22 MW	19.35 AW	40240 AAW	KYBLS	10//99-12//99
	Louisiana	S	19.46 MW	22.67 AW	47140 AAW	LABLS	10//99-12//99

AAW	Average annual wage	AOH	Average offered, high	ASH	Average starting, high	H	Hourly	M	Monthly	S	Special: hourly and annual
AE	Average entry wage	AOL	Average offered, low	ASL	Average starting, low	HI	Highest wage paid	MTC	Median total compensation	TQ	Third quartile wage
AEX	Average experienced wage	APH	Average pay, high range	AW	Average wage paid	HR	High end range	MW	Median wage paid	W	Weekly
AO	Average offered	APL	Average pay, low range	FQ	First quartile wage	LR	Low end range	SQ	Second quartile wage	Y	Yearly

1349

Occupation/Type/Industry	Location	Per	Low	Mid	High	Source	Date
Statistician	Baton Rouge MSA, LA	S	26.55 mw	26.61 aw	55230 aaw	LABLS	10//99-12//99
	Baltimore PMSA, MD	S	24.91 mw	23.46 aw	51800 aaw	MDBLS	10//99-12//99
	Massachusetts	S	23.19 mw	25.32 aw	52670 aaw	MABLS	10//99-12//99
	Boston PMSA, MA-NH	S	24.95 mw	21.74 aw	51900 aaw	MABLS	10//99-12//99
	Michigan	S	24.56 mw	25.17 aw	52360 aaw	MIBLS	10//99-12//99
	Detroit PMSA, MI	S	25.35 mw	24.23 aw	52720 aaw	MIBLS	10//99-12//99
	Minnesota	S	28.12 mw	27.95 aw	58130 aaw	MNBLS	10//99-12//99
	Minneapolis-St. Paul MSA, MN-WI	S	25.95 mw	25.09 aw	53970 aaw	MNBLS	10//99-12//99
	Mississippi	S	17.22 mw	19.29 aw	40130 aaw	MSBLS	10//99-12//99
	Missouri	S	23.23 mw	24.65 aw	51270 aaw	MOBLS	10//99-12//99
	Kansas City MSA, MO-KS	S	24.35 mw	22.79 aw	50650 aaw	MOBLS	10//99-12//99
	St. Louis MSA, MO-IL	S	23.25 mw	22.28 aw	48350 aaw	MOBLS	10//99-12//99
	Montana	S	15.86 mw	17.37 aw	36130 aaw	MTBLS	10//99-12//99
	Nebraska	S	20.82 mw	25.34 aw	52700 aaw	NEBLS	10//99-12//99
	Nevada	S	16.8 mw	20.19 aw	42000 aaw	NVBLS	10//99-12//99
	New Hampshire	S	18.92 mw	20.47 aw	42570 aaw	NHBLS	10//99-12//99
	New Jersey	S	25.43 mw	28.56 aw	59410 aaw	NJBLS	10//99-12//99
	Bergen-Passaic PMSA, NJ	S	30.29 mw	25.69 aw	63000 aaw	NJBLS	10//99-12//99
	Newark PMSA, NJ	S	30.59 mw	30.28 aw	63620 aaw	NJBLS	10//99-12//99
	Trenton PMSA, NJ	S	30.37 mw	26.97 aw	63170 aaw	NJBLS	10//99-12//99
	New Mexico	S	29.61 mw	27.98 aw	58200 aaw	NMBLS	10//99-12//99
	Albuquerque MSA, NM	S	27.50 mw	28.05 aw	57210 aaw	NMBLS	10//99-12//99
	New York	S	21.33 mw	22.33 aw	46450 aaw	NYBLS	10//99-12//99
	New York PMSA, NY	S	21.34 mw	20.29 aw	44390 aaw	NYBLS	10//99-12//99
	North Carolina	S	23.72 mw	25.13 aw	52260 aaw	NCBLS	10//99-12//99
	Charlotte-Gastonia-Rock Hill MSA, NC-SC	S	25.89 mw	21.35 aw	53850 aaw	NCBLS	10//99-12//99
	Raleigh-Durham-Chapel Hill MSA, NC	S	25.55 mw	24.34 aw	53150 aaw	NCBLS	10//99-12//99
	Wilmington MSA, NC	S	28.82 mw	29.02 aw	59940 aaw	NCBLS	10//99-12//99
	Ohio	S	23.17 mw	23.32 aw	48510 aaw	OHBLS	10//99-12//99
	Cincinnati PMSA, OH-KY-IN	S	22.98 mw	22.54 aw	47800 aaw	OHBLS	10//99-12//99
	Cleveland-Lorain-Elyria PMSA, OH	S	25.02 mw	24.89 aw	52050 aaw	OHBLS	10//99-12//99
	Columbus MSA, OH	S	21.29 mw	21.52 aw	44280 aaw	OHBLS	10//99-12//99
	Toledo MSA, OH	S	22.40 mw	23.15 aw	46580 aaw	OHBLS	10//99-12//99
	Oklahoma	S	12.99 mw	14.23 aw	29610 aaw	OKBLS	10//99-12//99
	Oklahoma City MSA, OK	S	14.12 mw	12.81 aw	29370 aaw	OKBLS	10//99-12//99
	Oregon	S	20.43 mw	21.31 aw	44320 aaw	ORBLS	10//99-12//99
	Portland-Vancouver PMSA, OR-WA	S	22.94 mw	22.26 aw	47710 aaw	ORBLS	10//99-12//99
	Pennsylvania	S	23.75 mw	26.60 aw	55330 aaw	PABLS	10//99-12//99
	Harrisburg-Lebanon-Carlisle MSA, PA	S	18.24 mw	18.34 aw	37940 aaw	PABLS	10//99-12//99
	Philadelphia PMSA, PA-NJ	S	27.41 mw	24.99 aw	57000 aaw	PABLS	10//99-12//99
	Pittsburgh MSA, PA	S	21.07 mw	19.12 aw	43830 aaw	PABLS	10//99-12//99
	Greenville-Spartanburg-Anderson MSA, SC	S	17.11 mw	15.30 aw	35590 aaw	SCBLS	10//99-12//99
	Texas	S	18.29 mw	20.94 aw	43550 aaw	TXBLS	10//99-12//99
	Dallas PMSA, TX	S	24.49 mw	23.87 aw	50930 aaw	TXBLS	10//99-12//99
	Houston PMSA, TX	S	22.65 mw	20.44 aw	47120 aaw	TXBLS	10//99-12//99
	San Antonio MSA, TX	S	19.23 mw	15.77 aw	40000 aaw	TXBLS	10//99-12//99
	Utah	S	22.42 mw	22.85 aw	47530 aaw	UTBLS	10//99-12//99
	Salt Lake City-Ogden MSA, UT	S	21.70 mw	21.47 aw	45140 aaw	UTBLS	10//99-12//99
	Virginia	S	24.97 mw	24.55 aw	51070 aaw	VABLS	10//99-12//99
	Roanoke MSA, VA	S	27.75 mw	29.39 aw	57710 aaw	VABLS	10//99-12//99
	Washington	S	23.57 mw	25.22 aw	52450 aaw	WABLS	10//99-12//99
	Seattle-Bellevue-Everett PMSA, WA	S	27.46 mw	26.80 aw	57110 aaw	WABLS	10//99-12//99
	West Virginia	S	23.79 mw	23.40 aw	48660 aaw	WVBLS	10//99-12//99
	Wisconsin	S	24.43 mw	25.03 aw	52070 aaw	WIBLS	10//99-12//99
	Madison MSA, WI	S	27.03 mw	27.24 aw	56220 aaw	WIBLS	10//99-12//99
	Milwaukee-Waukesha PMSA, WI	S	21.18 mw	19.13 aw	44050 aaw	WIBLS	10//99-12//99
	Puerto Rico	S	8.31 mw	9.78 aw	20350 aaw	PRBLS	10//99-12//99
	San Juan-Bayamon PMSA, PR	S	9.79 mw	8.26 aw	20360 aaw	PRBLS	10//99-12//99
Stilt-walker	Louisville, KY	H		75.00 aw		LOUMAG	1999-2000
Stock Clerk and Order Filler	Alabama	S	7.71 mw	8.54 aw	17760 aaw	ALBLS	10//99-12//99
	Alaska	S	10.92 mw	11.93 aw	24810 aaw	AKBLS	10//99-12//99

Occupation/Type/Industry	Location	Per	Low	Mid	High	Source	Date
Stock Clerk and Order Filler	Arizona	S	8.35 MW	9.43 AW	19610 AAW	AZBLS	10//99-12//99
	Arkansas	S	7.54 MW	8.31 AW	17280 AAW	ARBLS	10//99-12//99
	California	S	8.87 MW	10.30 AW	21420 AAW	CABLS	10//99-12//99
	Colorado	S	9.57 MW	10.62 AW	22090 AAW	COBLS	10//99-12//99
	Connecticut	S	9.2 MW	10.56 AW	21970 AAW	CTBLS	10//99-12//99
	Delaware	S	8.79 MW	10.43 AW	21700 AAW	DEBLS	10//99-12//99
	District of Columbia	S	9.98 MW	11.63 AW	24200 AAW	DCBLS	10//99-12//99
	Florida	S	8.11 MW	8.75 AW	18190 AAW	FLBLS	10//99-12//99
	Georgia	S	8.47 MW	9.05 AW	18830 AAW	GABLS	10//99-12//99
	Hawaii	S	9.58 MW	10.25 AW	21310 AAW	HIBLS	10//99-12//99
	Idaho	S	7.99 MW	8.91 AW	18540 AAW	IDBLS	10//99-12//99
	Illinois	S	8.4 MW	9.47 AW	19700 AAW	ILBLS	10//99-12//99
	Indiana	S	7.87 MW	8.80 AW	18310 AAW	INBLS	10//99-12//99
	Iowa	S	7.57 MW	8.72 AW	18150 AAW	IABLS	10//99-12//99
	Kansas	S	8.17 MW	9.36 AW	19470 AAW	KSBLS	10//99-12//99
	Kentucky	S	7.82 MW	8.60 AW	17900 AAW	KYBLS	10//99-12//99
	Louisiana	S	7.02 MW	8.08 AW	16800 AAW	LABLS	10//99-12//99
	Maine	S	8.67 MW	9.10 AW	18930 AAW	MEBLS	10//99-12//99
	Maryland	S	8.76 MW	9.87 AW	20520 AAW	MDBLS	10//99-12//99
	Massachusetts	S	9.2 MW	10.45 AW	21740 AAW	MABLS	10//99-12//99
	Michigan	S	8.5 MW	9.94 AW	20680 AAW	MIBLS	10//99-12//99
	Minnesota	S	8.88 MW	10.00 AW	20810 AAW	MNBLS	10//99-12//99
	Mississippi	S	7.44 MW	8.09 AW	16830 AAW	MSBLS	10//99-12//99
	Missouri	S	8.01 MW	9.22 AW	19170 AAW	MOBLS	10//99-12//99
	Montana	S	7.74 MW	9.00 AW	18720 AAW	MTBLS	10//99-12//99
	Nebraska	S	8.18 MW	8.94 AW	18590 AAW	NEBLS	10//99-12//99
	Nevada	S	9.18 MW	10.11 AW	21020 AAW	NVBLS	10//99-12//99
	New Hampshire	S	8.8 MW	9.53 AW	19830 AAW	NHBLS	10//99-12//99
	New Jersey	S	9.11 MW	10.41 AW	21660 AAW	NJBLS	10//99-12//99
	New Mexico	S	7.98 MW	8.92 AW	18550 AAW	NMBLS	10//99-12//99
	New York	S	8.3 MW	9.87 AW	20540 AAW	NYBLS	10//99-12//99
	North Carolina	S	8.36 MW	8.92 AW	18550 AAW	NCBLS	10//99-12//99
	North Dakota	S	7.5 MW	8.43 AW	17540 AAW	NDBLS	10//99-12//99
	Ohio	S	8.09 MW	9.08 AW	18890 AAW	OHBLS	10//99-12//99
	Oklahoma	S	7.52 MW	8.47 AW	17610 AAW	OKBLS	10//99-12//99
	Oregon	S	9.6 MW	10.50 AW	21840 AAW	ORBLS	10//99-12//99
	Pennsylvania	S	7.95 MW	9.05 AW	18820 AAW	PABLS	10//99-12//99
	Rhode Island	S	8.66 MW	9.87 AW	20540 AAW	RIBLS	10//99-12//99
	South Carolina	S	8.15 MW	8.79 AW	18290 AAW	SCBLS	10//99-12//99
	South Dakota	S	6.95 MW	7.95 AW	16530 AAW	SDBLS	10//99-12//99
	Tennessee	S	8.14 MW	8.83 AW	18360 AAW	TNBLS	10//99-12//99
	Texas	S	8.22 MW	9.26 AW	19250 AAW	TXBLS	10//99-12//99
	Utah	S	8.58 MW	9.30 AW	19350 AAW	UTBLS	10//99-12//99
	Vermont	S	7.79 MW	8.83 AW	18380 AAW	VTBLS	10//99-12//99
	Virginia	S	8.17 MW	9.04 AW	18810 AAW	VABLS	10//99-12//99
	Washington	S	10.11 MW	10.87 AW	22610 AAW	WABLS	10//99-12//99
	West Virginia	S	7.34 MW	8.84 AW	18380 AAW	WVBLS	10//99-12//99
	Wisconsin	S	7.99 MW	8.95 AW	18610 AAW	WIBLS	10//99-12//99
	Wyoming	S	7.74 MW	8.99 AW	18700 AAW	WYBLS	10//99-12//99
	Puerto Rico	S	6.08 MW	6.74 AW	14010 AAW	PRBLS	10//99-12//99
	Virgin Islands	S	6.91 MW	7.84 AW	16300 AAW	VIBLS	10//99-12//99
	Guam	S	7.1 MW	8.16 AW	16970 AAW	GUBLS	10//99-12//99
Stonemason	Alabama	S	15.65 MW	15.09 AW	31380 AAW	ALBLS	10//99-12//99
	Arizona	S	11.61 MW	11.86 AW	24670 AAW	AZBLS	10//99-12//99
	California	S	18.7 MW	19.29 AW	40120 AAW	CABLS	10//99-12//99
	Orange County PMSA, CA	S	20.35 MW	21.95 AW	42340 AAW	CABLS	10//99-12//99
	Riverside-San Bernardino PMSA, CA	S	18.05 MW	17.65 AW	37550 AAW	CABLS	10//99-12//99
	San Francisco PMSA, CA	S	15.20 MW	13.33 AW	31620 AAW	CABLS	10//99-12//99
	Colorado	S	16 MW	16.13 AW	33550 AAW	COBLS	10//99-12//99
	Denver PMSA, CO	S	17.56 MW	17.30 AW	36530 AAW	COBLS	10//99-12//99
	Connecticut	S	16.68 MW	18.37 AW	38210 AAW	CTBLS	10//99-12//99
	District of Columbia	S	16.81 MW	17.90 AW	37220 AAW	DCBLS	10//99-12//99
	Washington PMSA, DC-MD-VA-WV	S	13.92 MW	14.44 AW	28960 AAW	DCBLS	10//99-12//99
	Florida	S	11.44 MW	12.85 AW	26720 AAW	FLBLS	10//99-12//99
	Georgia	S	12.3 MW	11.65 AW	24230 AAW	GABLS	10//99-12//99
	Atlanta MSA, GA	S	13.73 MW	13.61 AW	28550 AAW	GABLS	10//99-12//99
	Indiana	S	20.95 MW	19.31 AW	40170 AAW	INBLS	10//99-12//99
	Iowa	S	11.71 MW	12.29 AW	25570 AAW	IABLS	10//99-12//99
	Kentucky	S	12.81 MW	13.47 AW	28020 AAW	KYBLS	10//99-12//99
	Lexington MSA, KY	S	17.64 MW	18.37 AW	36700 AAW	KYBLS	10//99-12//99

AAW	Average annual wage	AOH	Average offered, high	ASH	Average starting, high	H	Hourly	M	Monthly	S	Special: hourly and annual
AE	Average entry wage	AOL	Average offered, low	ASL	Average starting, low	HI	Highest wage paid	MTC	Median total compensation	TQ	Third quartile wage
AEX	Average experienced wage	APH	Average pay, high range	AW	Average wage paid	HR	High end range	MW	Median wage paid	W	Weekly
AO	Average offered	APL	Average pay, low range	FQ	First quartile wage	LR	Low end range	SQ	Second quartile wage	Y	Yearly

Occupation/Type/Industry	Location	Per	Low	Mid	High	Source	Date
Stonemason	Maryland	S	15.54 MW	15.36 AW	31960 AAW	MDBLS	10//99-12//99
	Baltimore PMSA, MD	S	14.77 MW	14.76 AW	30710 AAW	MDBLS	10//99-12//99
	Massachusetts	S	17.97 MW	16.91 AW	35170 AAW	MABLS	10//99-12//99
	Minnesota	S	16.58 MW	19.11 AW	39750 AAW	MNBLS	10//99-12//99
	Montana	S	18.84 MW	18.08 AW	37600 AAW	MTBLS	10//99-12//99
	New Hampshire	S	16.27 MW	16.51 AW	34350 AAW	NHBLS	10//99-12//99
	New Jersey	S	19.01 MW	20.91 AW	43490 AAW	NJBLS	10//99-12//99
	Bergen-Passaic PMSA, NJ	S	20.09 MW	19.57 AW	41790 AAW	NJBLS	10//99-12//99
	New York	S	18.29 MW	17.83 AW	37090 AAW	NYBLS	10//99-12//99
	New York PMSA, NY	S	19.40 MW	18.91 AW	40340 AAW	NYBLS	10//99-12//99
	North Carolina	S	12.44 MW	12.84 AW	26710 AAW	NCBLS	10//99-12//99
	Charlotte-Gastonia-Rock Hill MSA, NC-SC	S	14.25 MW	10.54 AW	29630 AAW	NCBLS	10//99-12//99
	Ohio	S	19.53 MW	18.37 AW	38210 AAW	OHBLS	10//99-12//99
	Cleveland-Lorain-Elyria PMSA, OH	S	17.73 MW	16.36 AW	36880 AAW	OHBLS	10//99-12//99
	Columbus MSA, OH	S	18.30 MW	20.59 AW	38060 AAW	OHBLS	10//99-12//99
	Oklahoma	S	11.17 MW	12.15 AW	25260 AAW	OKBLS	10//99-12//99
	Oregon	S	15.95 MW	18.82 AW	39140 AAW	ORBLS	10//99-12//99
	Portland-Vancouver PMSA, OR-WA	S	24.79 MW	27.09 AW	51570 AAW	ORBLS	10//99-12//99
	Pennsylvania	S	18.73 MW	19.16 AW	39840 AAW	PABLS	10//99-12//99
	Lancaster MSA, PA	S	17.76 MW	13.73 AW	36940 AAW	PABLS	10//99-12//99
	Philadelphia PMSA, PA-NJ	S	23.93 MW	22.46 AW	49780 AAW	PABLS	10//99-12//99
	Rhode Island	S	18.27 MW	17.09 AW	35540 AAW	RIBLS	10//99-12//99
	Providence-Fall River-Warwick MSA, RI-MA	S	18.12 MW	18.67 AW	37690 AAW	RIBLS	10//99-12//99
	South Carolina	S	24.75 MW	21.72 AW	45180 AAW	SCBLS	10//99-12//99
	Tennessee	S	14.76 MW	14.58 AW	30320 AAW	TNBLS	10//99-12//99
	Texas	S	12.05 MW	11.57 AW	24060 AAW	TXBLS	10//99-12//99
	Virginia	S	13.21 MW	13.31 AW	27680 AAW	VABLS	10//99-12//99
	Norfolk-Virginia Beach-Newport News MSA, VA-NC	S	16.06 MW	17.39 AW	33410 AAW	VABLS	10//99-12//99
	Washington	S	13.42 MW	15.44 AW	32110 AAW	WABLS	10//99-12//99
	Seattle-Bellevue-Everett PMSA, WA	S	15.25 MW	13.54 AW	31720 AAW	WABLS	10//99-12//99
	Wisconsin	S	17.99 MW	19.62 AW	40820 AAW	WIBLS	10//99-12//99
	Milwaukee-Waukesha PMSA, WI	S	21.58 MW	20.04 AW	44890 AAW	WIBLS	10//99-12//99
	Puerto Rico	S	7.98 MW	7.84 AW	16310 AAW	PRBLS	10//99-12//99
	Ponce MSA, PR	S	6.75 MW	6.61 AW	14050 AAW	PRBLS	10//99-12//99
	San Juan-Bayamon PMSA, PR	S	8.02 MW	8.21 AW	16690 AAW	PRBLS	10//99-12//99
	Virgin Islands	S	15.1 MW	15.08 AW	31360 AAW	VIBLS	10//99-12//99
Store Manager							
Apparel & Accessories Retailer	United States	Y		35000 MW		STORES	2000
Gas/Convenience Store	United States	Y		29500 MW		STORES	2000
Restaurant	United States	Y		35600 MW		STORES	2000
Specialty Store	United States	Y		29600 MW		STORES	2000
Supermarket	United States	Y		57200 MW		STORES	2000
Structural Iron and Steel Worker	Alabama	S	13.81 MW	15.51 AW	32260 AAW	ALBLS	10//99-12//99
	Birmingham MSA, AL	S	14.35 MW	12.89 AW	29840 AAW	ALBLS	10//99-12//99
	Mobile MSA, AL	S	14.17 MW	14.20 AW	29470 AAW	ALBLS	10//99-12//99
	Montgomery MSA, AL	S	17.45 MW	18.09 AW	36300 AAW	ALBLS	10//99-12//99
	Alaska	S	19.89 MW	20.47 AW	42580 AAW	AKBLS	10//99-12//99
	Anchorage MSA, AK	S	19.34 MW	18.94 AW	40220 AAW	AKBLS	10//99-12//99
	Arizona	S	16.08 MW	16.54 AW	34410 AAW	AZBLS	10//99-12//99
	Phoenix-Mesa MSA, AZ	S	17.78 MW	17.22 AW	36990 AAW	AZBLS	10//99-12//99
	Tucson MSA, AZ	S	13.48 MW	12.58 AW	28040 AAW	AZBLS	10//99-12//99
	Arkansas	S	11.57 MW	11.98 AW	24930 AAW	ARBLS	10//99-12//99
	Little Rock-North Little Rock MSA, AR	S	12.32 MW	12.43 AW	25630 AAW	ARBLS	10//99-12//99
	California	S	19.92 MW	20.34 AW	42310 AAW	CABLS	10//99-12//99
	Los Angeles-Long Beach PMSA, CA	S	19.91 MW	19.02 AW	41410 AAW	CABLS	10//99-12//99
	Modesto MSA, CA	S	12.63 MW	10.99 AW	26270 AAW	CABLS	10//99-12//99
	Oakland PMSA, CA	S	23.89 MW	24.79 AW	49690 AAW	CABLS	10//99-12//99
	Orange County PMSA, CA	S	24.21 MW	24.74 AW	50360 AAW	CABLS	10//99-12//99
	Riverside-San Bernardino PMSA, CA	S	21.34 MW	22.81 AW	44390 AAW	CABLS	10//99-12//99
	Sacramento PMSA, CA	S	15.87 MW	14.92 AW	33010 AAW	CABLS	10//99-12//99

AAW Average annual wage	**AOH** Average offered, high	**ASH** Average starting, high	**H** Hourly	**M** Monthly	**S** Special: hourly and annual
AE Average entry wage	**AOL** Average offered, low	**ASL** Average starting, low	**HI** Highest wage paid	**MTC** Median total compensation	**TQ** Third quartile wage
AEX Average experienced wage	**APH** Average pay, high range	**AW** Average wage paid	**HR** High end range	**MW** Median wage paid	**W** Weekly
AO Average offered	**APL** Average pay, low range	**FQ** First quartile wage	**LR** Low end range	**SQ** Second quartile wage	**Y** Yearly

Occupation/Type/Industry	Location	Per	Low	Mid	High	Source	Date
Structural Iron and Steel Worker	San Diego MSA, CA	S	18.03 MW	15.70 AW	37500 AAW	CABLS	10//99-12//99
	San Jose PMSA, CA	S	26.79 MW	29.01 AW	55720 AAW	CABLS	10//99-12//99
	San Luis Obispo-Atascadero-Paso Robles MSA, CA	S	19.74 MW	20.39 AW	41060 AAW	CABLS	10//99-12//99
	Stockton-Lodi MSA, CA	S	21.21 MW	23.33 AW	44110 AAW	CABLS	10//99-12//99
	Vallejo-Fairfield-Napa PMSA, CA	S	28.28 MW	31.20 AW	58820 AAW	CABLS	10//99-12//99
	Visalia-Tulare-Porterville MSA, CA	S	15.27 MW	14.82 AW	31760 AAW	CABLS	10//99-12//99
	Colorado	S	16.47 MW	16.39 AW	34090 AAW	COBLS	10//99-12//99
	Colorado Springs MSA, CO	S	13.56 MW	13.46 AW	28210 AAW	COBLS	10//99-12//99
	Denver PMSA, CO	S	18.46 MW	18.70 AW	38390 AAW	COBLS	10//99-12//99
	Grand Junction MSA, CO	S	13.46 MW	13.40 AW	28000 AAW	COBLS	10//99-12//99
	Greeley PMSA, CO	S	17.33 MW	18.46 AW	36040 AAW	COBLS	10//99-12//99
	Connecticut	S	19.43 MW	18.97 AW	39470 AAW	CTBLS	10//99-12//99
	Bridgeport PMSA, CT	S	22.35 MW	22.84 AW	46490 AAW	CTBLS	10//99-12//99
	Hartford MSA, CT	S	17.62 MW	17.68 AW	36650 AAW	CTBLS	10//99-12//99
	Delaware	S	17.96 MW	17.52 AW	36440 AAW	DEBLS	10//99-12//99
	Wilmington-Newark PMSA, DE-MD	S	18.47 MW	18.67 AW	38420 AAW	DEBLS	10//99-12//99
	Washington PMSA, DC-MD-VA-WV	S	15.24 MW	14.76 AW	31700 AAW	DCBLS	10//99-12//99
	Florida	S	14.68 MW	14.57 AW	30320 AAW	FLBLS	10//99-12//99
	Fort Lauderdale PMSA, FL	S	14.39 MW	14.01 AW	29930 AAW	FLBLS	10//99-12//99
	Fort Myers-Cape Coral MSA, FL	S	11.53 MW	11.14 AW	23980 AAW	FLBLS	10//99-12//99
	Jacksonville MSA, FL	S	15.53 MW	15.65 AW	32290 AAW	FLBLS	10//99-12//99
	Lakeland-Winter Haven MSA, FL	S	14.67 MW	14.92 AW	30520 AAW	FLBLS	10//99-12//99
	Melbourne-Titusville-Palm Bay MSA, FL	S	16.84 MW	17.03 AW	35020 AAW	FLBLS	10//99-12//99
	Miami PMSA, FL	S	12.53 MW	12.01 AW	26070 AAW	FLBLS	10//99-12//99
	Orlando MSA, FL	S	17.91 MW	18.39 AW	37250 AAW	FLBLS	10//99-12//99
	Sarasota-Bradenton MSA, FL	S	12.79 MW	13.19 AW	26590 AAW	FLBLS	10//99-12//99
	Tampa-St. Petersburg-Clearwater MSA, FL	S	15.46 MW	16.11 AW	32160 AAW	FLBLS	10//99-12//99
	Georgia	S	14.4 MW	15.11 AW	31430 AAW	GABLS	10//99-12//99
	Atlanta MSA, GA	S	15.68 MW	14.66 AW	32620 AAW	GABLS	10//99-12//99
	Augusta-Aiken MSA, GA-SC	S	15.57 MW	14.80 AW	32390 AAW	GABLS	10//99-12//99
	Macon MSA, GA	S	12.54 MW	11.41 AW	26070 AAW	GABLS	10//99-12//99
	Hawaii	S	23.63 MW	23.21 AW	48290 AAW	HIBLS	10//99-12//99
	Honolulu MSA, HI	S	22.90 MW	23.64 AW	47620 AAW	HIBLS	10//99-12//99
	Idaho	S	10.1 MW	12.18 AW	25340 AAW	IDBLS	10//99-12//99
	Boise City MSA, ID	S	13.83 MW	12.82 AW	28770 AAW	IDBLS	10//99-12//99
	Illinois	S	21.98 MW	21.23 AW	44170 AAW	ILBLS	10//99-12//99
	Chicago PMSA, IL	S	22.39 MW	23.39 AW	46570 AAW	ILBLS	10//99-12//99
	Peoria-Pekin MSA, IL	S	17.09 MW	16.12 AW	35540 AAW	ILBLS	10//99-12//99
	Indiana	S	19.66 MW	18.38 AW	38240 AAW	INBLS	10//99-12//99
	Evansville-Henderson MSA, IN-KY	S	20.06 MW	20.81 AW	41720 AAW	INBLS	10//99-12//99
	Fort Wayne MSA, IN	S	17.19 MW	15.73 AW	35750 AAW	INBLS	10//99-12//99
	Gary PMSA, IN	S	19.89 MW	21.41 AW	41360 AAW	INBLS	10//99-12//99
	Indianapolis MSA, IN	S	20.63 MW	19.57 AW	42920 AAW	INBLS	10//99-12//99
	South Bend MSA, IN	S	17.38 MW	18.01 AW	36140 AAW	INBLS	10//99-12//99
	Terre Haute MSA, IN	S	17.49 MW	18.72 AW	36390 AAW	INBLS	10//99-12//99
	Iowa	S	17.6 MW	16.19 AW	33680 AAW	IABLS	10//99-12//99
	Cedar Rapids MSA, IA	S	19.76 MW	19.80 AW	41100 AAW	IABLS	10//99-12//99
	Davenport-Moline-Rock Island MSA, IA-IL	S	19.25 MW	19.02 AW	40030 AAW	IABLS	10//99-12//99
	Dubuque MSA, IA	S	17.21 MW	19.07 AW	35790 AAW	IABLS	10//99-12//99
	Kansas	S	17.57 MW	15.96 AW	33200 AAW	KSBLS	10//99-12//99
	Kentucky	S	17.06 MW	16.57 AW	34470 AAW	KYBLS	10//99-12//99
	Lexington MSA, KY	S	14.25 MW	12.98 AW	29650 AAW	KYBLS	10//99-12//99
	Louisville MSA, KY-IN	S	16.95 MW	16.86 AW	35250 AAW	KYBLS	10//99-12//99
	Owensboro MSA, KY	S	20.64 MW	22.17 AW	42930 AAW	KYBLS	10//99-12//99
	Louisiana	S	14.43 MW	14.09 AW	29320 AAW	LABLS	10//99-12//99
	Baton Rouge MSA, LA	S	15.27 MW	15.40 AW	31750 AAW	LABLS	10//99-12//99
	Houma MSA, LA	S	14.46 MW	14.72 AW	30070 AAW	LABLS	10//99-12//99
	Lafayette MSA, LA	S	13.73 MW	10.59 AW	28550 AAW	LABLS	10//99-12//99
	Lake Charles MSA, LA	S	14.72 MW	15.09 AW	30610 AAW	LABLS	10//99-12//99
	Monroe MSA, LA	S	13.03 MW	13.59 AW	27090 AAW	LABLS	10//99-12//99
	New Orleans MSA, LA	S	13.51 MW	14.26 AW	28100 AAW	LABLS	10//99-12//99

AAW	Average annual wage	AOH	Average offered, high	ASH	Average starting, high	H	Hourly
AE	Average entry wage	AOL	Average offered, low	ASL	Average starting, low	HI	Highest wage paid
AEX	Average experienced wage	APH	Average pay, high range	AW	Average wage paid	HR	High end range
AO	Average offered	APL	Average pay, low range	FQ	First quartile wage	LR	Low end range

M	Monthly	S	Special: hourly and annual
MTC	Median total compensation	TQ	Third quartile wage
MW	Median wage paid	W	Weekly
SQ	Second quartile wage	Y	Yearly

Occupation/Type/Industry	Location	Per	Low	Mid	High	Source	Date
Structural Iron and Steel Worker	Maine	S	13.46 MW	14.07 AW	29270 AAW	MEBLS	10//99-12//99
	Maryland	S	13.51 MW	14.37 AW	29890 AAW	MDBLS	10//99-12//99
	Baltimore PMSA, MD	S	14.60 MW	13.32 AW	30370 AAW	MDBLS	10//99-12//99
	Hagerstown PMSA, MD	S	14.56 MW	14.75 AW	30280 AAW	MDBLS	10//99-12//99
	Massachusetts	S	23.35 MW	23.61 AW	49100 AAW	MABLS	10//99-12//99
	Boston PMSA, MA-NH	S	23.50 MW	23.96 AW	48890 AAW	MABLS	10//99-12//99
	Michigan	S	21.74 MW	20.44 AW	42520 AAW	MIBLS	10//99-12//99
	Detroit PMSA, MI	S	21.50 MW	22.59 AW	44710 AAW	MIBLS	10//99-12//99
	Grand Rapids-Muskegon-Holland MSA, MI	S	12.28 MW	11.28 AW	25550 AAW	MIBLS	10//99-12//99
	Lansing-East Lansing MSA, MI	S	19.60 MW	19.37 AW	40760 AAW	MIBLS	10//99-12//99
	Minnesota	S	24.65 MW	24.83 AW	51640 AAW	MNBLS	10//99-12//99
	Minneapolis-St. Paul MSA, MN-WI	S	26.33 MW	26.35 AW	54760 AAW	MNBLS	10//99-12//99
	Mississippi	S	12.65 MW	12.64 AW	26300 AAW	MSBLS	10//99-12//99
	Biloxi-Gulfport-Pascagoula MSA, MS	S	13.49 MW	13.90 AW	28070 AAW	MSBLS	10//99-12//99
	Jackson MSA, MS	S	14.98 MW	14.89 AW	31150 AAW	MSBLS	10//99-12//99
	Missouri	S	19.3 MW	18.45 AW	38380 AAW	MOBLS	10//99-12//99
	Kansas City MSA, MO-KS	S	19.87 MW	20.37 AW	41330 AAW	MOBLS	10//99-12//99
	Nebraska	S	15.53 MW	16.14 AW	33580 AAW	NEBLS	10//99-12//99
	Omaha MSA, NE-IA	S	19.90 MW	19.26 AW	41390 AAW	NEBLS	10//99-12//99
	Nevada	S	22.07 MW	21.05 AW	43780 AAW	NVBLS	10//99-12//99
	Las Vegas MSA, NV-AZ	S	20.90 MW	21.93 AW	43460 AAW	NVBLS	10//99-12//99
	Reno MSA, NV	S	22.49 MW	23.05 AW	46790 AAW	NVBLS	10//99-12//99
	New Hampshire	S	15.52 MW	15.83 AW	32930 AAW	NHBLS	10//99-12//99
	New Jersey	S	29.88 MW	29.09 AW	60500 AAW	NJBLS	10//99-12//99
	Atlantic-Cape May PMSA, NJ	S	27.82 MW	28.38 AW	57870 AAW	NJBLS	10//99-12//99
	Bergen-Passaic PMSA, NJ	S	31.51 MW	33.67 AW	65550 AAW	NJBLS	10//99-12//99
	Monmouth-Ocean PMSA, NJ	S	29.15 MW	29.90 AW	60630 AAW	NJBLS	10//99-12//99
	Newark PMSA, NJ	S	23.48 MW	21.79 AW	48840 AAW	NJBLS	10//99-12//99
	New Mexico	S	16.51 MW	16.45 AW	34220 AAW	NMBLS	10//99-12//99
	Albuquerque MSA, NM	S	17.36 MW	17.62 AW	36110 AAW	NMBLS	10//99-12//99
	New York	S	28.49 MW	26.86 AW	55860 AAW	NYBLS	10//99-12//99
	Albany-Schenectady-Troy MSA, NY	S	25.17 MW	24.37 AW	52340 AAW	NYBLS	10//99-12//99
	Nassau-Suffolk PMSA, NY	S	26.80 MW	28.29 AW	55750 AAW	NYBLS	10//99-12//99
	New York PMSA, NY	S	29.72 MW	30.47 AW	61810 AAW	NYBLS	10//99-12//99
	Newburgh PMSA, NY-PA	S	24.19 MW	23.74 AW	50320 AAW	NYBLS	10//99-12//99
	Rochester MSA, NY	S	21.43 MW	22.34 AW	44580 AAW	NYBLS	10//99-12//99
	Syracuse MSA, NY	S	21.96 MW	21.32 AW	45690 AAW	NYBLS	10//99-12//99
	Utica-Rome MSA, NY	S	17.88 MW	17.92 AW	37190 AAW	NYBLS	10//99-12//99
	North Carolina	S	13.56 MW	13.83 AW	28770 AAW	NCBLS	10//99-12//99
	Charlotte-Gastonia-Rock Hill MSA, NC-SC	S	14.37 MW	14.00 AW	29890 AAW	NCBLS	10//99-12//99
	Fayetteville MSA, NC	S	13.15 MW	13.15 AW	27350 AAW	NCBLS	10//99-12//99
	Greensboro--Winston-Salem--High Point MSA, NC	S	15.29 MW	14.02 AW	31810 AAW	NCBLS	10//99-12//99
	Greenville MSA, NC	S	12.58 MW	13.83 AW	26160 AAW	NCBLS	10//99-12//99
	Hickory-Morganton-Lenoir MSA, NC	S	12.47 MW	12.46 AW	25930 AAW	NCBLS	10//99-12//99
	North Dakota	S	14.56 MW	14.46 AW	30090 AAW	NDBLS	10//99-12//99
	Ohio	S	21.39 MW	20.24 AW	42110 AAW	OHBLS	10//99-12//99
	Akron PMSA, OH	S	19.58 MW	18.68 AW	40730 AAW	OHBLS	10//99-12//99
	Canton-Massillon MSA, OH	S	17.90 MW	19.93 AW	37240 AAW	OHBLS	10//99-12//99
	Cincinnati PMSA, OH-KY-IN	S	20.34 MW	21.83 AW	42300 AAW	OHBLS	10//99-12//99
	Cleveland-Lorain-Elyria PMSA, OH	S	23.40 MW	23.17 AW	48670 AAW	OHBLS	10//99-12//99
	Columbus MSA, OH	S	19.52 MW	21.11 AW	40600 AAW	OHBLS	10//99-12//99
	Dayton-Springfield MSA, OH	S	18.60 MW	20.66 AW	38700 AAW	OHBLS	10//99-12//99
	Hamilton-Middletown PMSA, OH	S	17.53 MW	18.30 AW	36460 AAW	OHBLS	10//99-12//99
	Toledo MSA, OH	S	20.93 MW	21.38 AW	43540 AAW	OHBLS	10//99-12//99
	Youngstown-Warren MSA, OH	S	22.53 MW	22.64 AW	46850 AAW	OHBLS	10//99-12//99
	Oklahoma	S	15.33 MW	15.46 AW	32170 AAW	OKBLS	10//99-12//99
	Oklahoma City MSA, OK	S	13.02 MW	13.04 AW	27090 AAW	OKBLS	10//99-12//99
	Oregon	S	21.48 MW	19.98 AW	41550 AAW	ORBLS	10//99-12//99
	Portland-Vancouver PMSA, OR-WA	S	22.39 MW	22.81 AW	46580 AAW	ORBLS	10//99-12//99
	Salem PMSA, OR	S	18.50 MW	18.75 AW	38470 AAW	ORBLS	10//99-12//99
	Pennsylvania	S	22.67 MW	22.42 AW	46630 AAW	PABLS	10//99-12//99
	Johnstown MSA, PA	S	16.86 MW	18.00 AW	35070 AAW	PABLS	10//99-12//99

AAW Average annual wage	AOH Average offered, high	ASH Average starting, high	H Hourly	M Monthly	S Special: hourly and annual
AE Average entry wage	AOL Average offered, low	ASL Average starting, low	HI Highest wage paid	MTC Median total compensation	TQ Third quartile wage
AEX Average experienced wage	APH Average pay, high range	AW Average wage paid	HR High end range	MW Median wage paid	W Weekly
AO Average offered	APL Average pay, low range	FQ First quartile wage	LR Low end range	SQ Second quartile wage	Y Yearly

Occupation/Type/Industry	Location	Per	Low	Mid	High	Source	Date
Structural Iron and Steel Worker	Lancaster MSA, PA	S	14.51 MW	14.54 AW	30190 AAW	PABLS	10//99-12//99
	Philadelphia PMSA, PA-NJ	S	33.54 MW	32.58 AW	69760 AAW	PABLS	10//99-12//99
	Pittsburgh MSA, PA	S	22.82 MW	23.49 AW	47460 AAW	PABLS	10//99-12//99
	Scranton--Wilkes-Barre-- Hazleton MSA, PA	S	15.66 MW	14.70 AW	32580 AAW	PABLS	10//99-12//99
	York MSA, PA	S	14.72 MW	14.19 AW	30610 AAW	PABLS	10//99-12//99
	Rhode Island	S	20.99 MW	20.27 AW	42150 AAW	RIBLS	10//99-12//99
	Providence-Fall River- Warwick MSA, RI-MA	S	18.95 MW	19.26 AW	39420 AAW	RIBLS	10//99-12//99
	South Carolina	S	12.59 MW	13.52 AW	28120 AAW	SCBLS	10//99-12//99
	Charleston-North Charleston MSA, SC	S	13.46 MW	12.75 AW	28000 AAW	SCBLS	10//99-12//99
	Columbia MSA, SC	S	11.56 MW	11.38 AW	24040 AAW	SCBLS	10//99-12//99
	Greenville-Spartanburg- Anderson MSA, SC	S	14.01 MW	12.79 AW	29130 AAW	SCBLS	10//99-12//99
	Sumter MSA, SC	S	16.38 MW	14.12 AW	34080 AAW	SCBLS	10//99-12//99
	South Dakota	S	11.61 MW	12.51 AW	26030 AAW	SDBLS	10//99-12//99
	Sioux Falls MSA, SD	S	12.29 MW	11.31 AW	25560 AAW	SDBLS	10//99-12//99
	Tennessee	S	14.46 MW	14.40 AW	29960 AAW	TNBLS	10//99-12//99
	Chattanooga MSA, TN-GA	S	13.99 MW	13.73 AW	29110 AAW	TNBLS	10//99-12//99
	Jackson MSA, TN	S	15.76 MW	16.77 AW	32780 AAW	TNBLS	10//99-12//99
	Knoxville MSA, TN	S	13.98 MW	13.40 AW	29080 AAW	TNBLS	10//99-12//99
	Memphis MSA, TN-AR-MS	S	14.53 MW	14.06 AW	30220 AAW	MSBLS	10//99-12//99
	Nashville MSA, TN	S	15.08 MW	15.08 AW	31370 AAW	TNBLS	10//99-12//99
	Texas	S	11.91 MW	12.25 AW	25470 AAW	TXBLS	10//99-12//99
	Abilene MSA, TX	S	10.10 MW	9.99 AW	21000 AAW	TXBLS	10//99-12//99
	Austin-San Marcos MSA, TX	S	15.32 MW	15.37 AW	31860 AAW	TXBLS	10//99-12//99
	Beaumont-Port Arthur MSA, TX	S	12.69 MW	11.15 AW	26400 AAW	TXBLS	10//99-12//99
	Corpus Christi MSA, TX	S	13.07 MW	13.87 AW	27190 AAW	TXBLS	10//99-12//99
	Dallas PMSA, TX	S	12.34 MW	12.92 AW	25680 AAW	TXBLS	10//99-12//99
	El Paso MSA, TX	S	9.23 MW	9.15 AW	19210 AAW	TXBLS	10//99-12//99
	Fort Worth-Arlington PMSA, TX	S	11.11 MW	8.75 AW	23100 AAW	TXBLS	10//99-12//99
	Houston PMSA, TX	S	12.27 MW	11.94 AW	25510 AAW	TXBLS	10//99-12//99
	Longview-Marshall MSA, TX	S	11.50 MW	11.37 AW	23930 AAW	TXBLS	10//99-12//99
	Odessa-Midland MSA, TX	S	17.36 MW	15.20 AW	36120 AAW	TXBLS	10//99-12//99
	San Antonio MSA, TX	S	13.24 MW	14.02 AW	27530 AAW	TXBLS	10//99-12//99
	Utah	S	15.75 MW	16.29 AW	33880 AAW	UTBLS	10//99-12//99
	Provo-Orem MSA, UT	S	17.26 MW	17.91 AW	35900 AAW	UTBLS	10//99-12//99
	Virginia	S	14.74 MW	14.81 AW	30800 AAW	VABLS	10//99-12//99
	Norfolk-Virginia Beach- Newport News MSA, VA- NC	S	13.65 MW	13.68 AW	28400 AAW	VABLS	10//99-12//99
	Richmond-Petersburg MSA, VA	S	16.92 MW	16.74 AW	35180 AAW	VABLS	10//99-12//99
	Washington	S	21.86 MW	21.16 AW	44010 AAW	WABLS	10//99-12//99
	Bellingham MSA, WA	S	17.80 MW	17.73 AW	37030 AAW	WABLS	10//99-12//99
	Richland-Kennewick-Pasco MSA, WA	S	20.86 MW	21.78 AW	43390 AAW	WABLS	10//99-12//99
	Seattle-Bellevue-Everett PMSA, WA	S	22.04 MW	22.35 AW	45840 AAW	WABLS	10//99-12//99
	Spokane MSA, WA	S	20.30 MW	21.90 AW	42230 AAW	WABLS	10//99-12//99
	Tacoma PMSA, WA	S	20.70 MW	22.74 AW	43050 AAW	WABLS	10//99-12//99
	West Virginia	S	18.94 MW	18.14 AW	37740 AAW	WVBLS	10//99-12//99
	Charleston MSA, WV	S	17.47 MW	18.67 AW	36330 AAW	WVBLS	10//99-12//99
	Huntington-Ashland MSA, WV-KY-OH	S	14.60 MW	14.61 AW	30360 AAW	WVBLS	10//99-12//99
	Parkersburg-Marietta MSA, WV-OH	S	20.72 MW	21.19 AW	43090 AAW	WVBLS	10//99-12//99
	Wheeling MSA, WV-OH	S	20.30 MW	20.47 AW	42220 AAW	WVBLS	10//99-12//99
	Wisconsin	S	15.66 MW	17.95 AW	37330 AAW	WIBLS	10//99-12//99
	Green Bay MSA, WI	S	15.91 MW	16.55 AW	33100 AAW	WIBLS	10//99-12//99
	Madison MSA, WI	S	19.28 MW	17.61 AW	40100 AAW	WIBLS	10//99-12//99
	Milwaukee-Waukesha PMSA, WI	S	23.57 MW	26.44 AW	49020 AAW	WIBLS	10//99-12//99
	Wausau MSA, WI	S	16.65 MW	17.16 AW	34630 AAW	WIBLS	10//99-12//99
	Wyoming	S	16.05 MW	16.43 AW	34180 AAW	WYBLS	10//99-12//99
	Puerto Rico	S	6.2 MW	6.12 AW	12730 AAW	PRBLS	10//99-12//99
	Ponce MSA, PR	S	6.05 MW	6.19 AW	12580 AAW	PRBLS	10//99-12//99
	San Juan-Bayamon PMSA, PR	S	6.12 MW	6.22 AW	12740 AAW	PRBLS	10//99-12//99
	Guam	S	9.76 MW	9.94 AW	20680 AAW	GUBLS	10//99-12//99

AAW	Average annual wage	AOH	Average offered, high	ASH	Average starting, high	H	Hourly	M	Monthly	S	Special: hourly and annual
AE	Average entry wage	AOL	Average offered, low	ASL	Average starting, low	HI	Highest wage paid	MTC	Median total compensation	TQ	Third quartile wage
AEX	Average experienced wage	APH	Average pay, high range	AW	Average wage paid	HR	High end range	MW	Median wage paid	W	Weekly
AO	Average offered	APL	Average pay, low range	FQ	First quartile wage	LR	Low end range	SQ	Second quartile wage	Y	Yearly

Occupation/Type/Industry	Location	Per	Low	Mid	High	Source	Date
Structural Metal Fabricator and Fitter							
	Alabama	S	13.95 MW	13.92 AW	28940 AAW	ALBLS	10//99-12//99
	Anniston MSA, AL	S	11.98 MW	12.08 AW	24910 AAW	ALBLS	10//99-12//99
	Auburn-Opelika MSA, AL	S	9.77 MW	8.58 AW	20310 AAW	ALBLS	10//99-12//99
	Birmingham MSA, AL	S	13.26 MW	13.85 AW	27570 AAW	ALBLS	10//99-12//99
	Huntsville MSA, AL	S	9.11 MW	9.38 AW	18950 AAW	ALBLS	10//99-12//99
	Mobile MSA, AL	S	17.68 MW	18.46 AW	36770 AAW	ALBLS	10//99-12//99
	Montgomery MSA, AL	S	11.02 MW	11.03 AW	22920 AAW	ALBLS	10//99-12//99
	Arizona	S	12.43 MW	12.67 AW	26350 AAW	AZBLS	10//99-12//99
	Phoenix-Mesa MSA, AZ	S	13.73 MW	13.51 AW	28560 AAW	AZBLS	10//99-12//99
	Tucson MSA, AZ	S	12.06 MW	11.79 AW	25080 AAW	AZBLS	10//99-12//99
	Arkansas	S	10.54 MW	11.31 AW	23530 AAW	ARBLS	10//99-12//99
	California	S	14.18 MW	13.66 AW	28420 AAW	CABLS	10//99-12//99
	Fresno MSA, CA	S	13.19 MW	14.07 AW	27430 AAW	CABLS	10//99-12//99
	Los Angeles-Long Beach PMSA, CA	S	13.53 MW	13.01 AW	28150 AAW	CABLS	10//99-12//99
	Modesto MSA, CA	S	14.49 MW	14.77 AW	30150 AAW	CABLS	10//99-12//99
	Oakland PMSA, CA	S	14.95 MW	14.97 AW	31090 AAW	CABLS	10//99-12//99
	Orange County PMSA, CA	S	10.86 MW	9.10 AW	22580 AAW	CABLS	10//99-12//99
	Riverside-San Bernardino PMSA, CA	S	13.62 MW	14.45 AW	28320 AAW	CABLS	10//99-12//99
	Sacramento PMSA, CA	S	11.11 MW	10.99 AW	23120 AAW	CABLS	10//99-12//99
	San Diego MSA, CA	S	11.04 MW	9.49 AW	22960 AAW	CABLS	10//99-12//99
	San Francisco PMSA, CA	S	14.36 MW	14.67 AW	29860 AAW	CABLS	10//99-12//99
	San Jose PMSA, CA	S	13.94 MW	14.35 AW	29000 AAW	CABLS	10//99-12//99
	Vallejo-Fairfield-Napa PMSA, CA	S	15.54 MW	15.40 AW	32310 AAW	CABLS	10//99-12//99
	Visalia-Tulare-Porterville MSA, CA	S	10.54 MW	9.99 AW	21920 AAW	CABLS	10//99-12//99
	Colorado	S	12.58 MW	12.92 AW	26870 AAW	COBLS	10//99-12//99
	Colorado Springs MSA, CO	S	14.44 MW	12.72 AW	30030 AAW	COBLS	10//99-12//99
	Denver PMSA, CO	S	13.81 MW	13.31 AW	28710 AAW	COBLS	10//99-12//99
	Connecticut	S	16.61 MW	16.35 AW	34020 AAW	CTBLS	10//99-12//99
	Bridgeport PMSA, CT	S	15.33 MW	16.88 AW	31880 AAW	CTBLS	10//99-12//99
	Hartford MSA, CT	S	17.30 MW	17.35 AW	35990 AAW	CTBLS	10//99-12//99
	New Haven-Meriden PMSA, CT	S	14.37 MW	14.54 AW	29880 AAW	CTBLS	10//99-12//99
	Delaware	S	12.56 MW	12.93 AW	26900 AAW	DEBLS	10//99-12//99
	Wilmington-Newark PMSA, DE-MD	S	13.47 MW	13.30 AW	28020 AAW	DEBLS	10//99-12//99
	Washington PMSA, DC-MD-VA-WV	S	13.11 MW	12.45 AW	27270 AAW	DCBLS	10//99-12//99
	Florida	S	11.31 MW	11.30 AW	23510 AAW	FLBLS	10//99-12//99
	Daytona Beach MSA, FL	S	12.41 MW	13.36 AW	25820 AAW	FLBLS	10//99-12//99
	Fort Lauderdale PMSA, FL	S	14.87 MW	13.93 AW	30940 AAW	FLBLS	10//99-12//99
	Fort Myers-Cape Coral MSA, FL	S	10.98 MW	11.25 AW	22840 AAW	FLBLS	10//99-12//99
	Gainesville MSA, FL	S	12.37 MW	11.39 AW	25730 AAW	FLBLS	10//99-12//99
	Jacksonville MSA, FL	S	11.98 MW	12.01 AW	24910 AAW	FLBLS	10//99-12//99
	Lakeland-Winter Haven MSA, FL	S	12.65 MW	12.76 AW	26310 AAW	FLBLS	10//99-12//99
	Melbourne-Titusville-Palm Bay MSA, FL	S	12.57 MW	13.53 AW	26150 AAW	FLBLS	10//99-12//99
	Miami PMSA, FL	S	10.01 MW	10.54 AW	20830 AAW	FLBLS	10//99-12//99
	Orlando MSA, FL	S	10.56 MW	10.06 AW	21970 AAW	FLBLS	10//99-12//99
	Panama City MSA, FL	S	11.14 MW	11.80 AW	23180 AAW	FLBLS	10//99-12//99
	Pensacola MSA, FL	S	12.03 MW	12.20 AW	25030 AAW	FLBLS	10//99-12//99
	Sarasota-Bradenton MSA, FL	S	10.58 MW	10.22 AW	22010 AAW	FLBLS	10//99-12//99
	Tampa-St. Petersburg-Clearwater MSA, FL	S	10.97 MW	11.35 AW	22810 AAW	FLBLS	10//99-12//99
	West Palm Beach-Boca Raton MSA, FL	S	11.61 MW	11.79 AW	24140 AAW	FLBLS	10//99-12//99
	Georgia	S	12.73 MW	12.91 AW	26860 AAW	GABLS	10//99-12//99
	Atlanta MSA, GA	S	12.89 MW	12.81 AW	26810 AAW	GABLS	10//99-12//99
	Columbus MSA, GA-AL	S	11.65 MW	11.43 AW	24220 AAW	GABLS	10//99-12//99
	Macon MSA, GA	S	15.70 MW	17.57 AW	32650 AAW	GABLS	10//99-12//99
	Idaho	S	11.75 MW	11.53 AW	23980 AAW	IDBLS	10//99-12//99
	Boise City MSA, ID	S	11.66 MW	11.77 AW	24250 AAW	IDBLS	10//99-12//99
	Illinois	S	10.47 MW	11.45 AW	23810 AAW	ILBLS	10//99-12//99
	Chicago PMSA, IL	S	11.57 MW	10.54 AW	24060 AAW	ILBLS	10//99-12//99
	Peoria-Pekin MSA, IL	S	12.71 MW	12.85 AW	26430 AAW	ILBLS	10//99-12//99
	Rockford MSA, IL	S	12.41 MW	10.21 AW	25820 AAW	ILBLS	10//99-12//99

AAW Average annual wage	AOH Average offered, high	ASH Average starting, high	H Hourly	M Monthly	S Special: hourly and annual
AE Average entry wage	AOL Average offered, low	ASL Average starting, low	HI Highest wage paid	MTC Median total compensation	TQ Third quartile wage
AEX Average experienced wage	APH Average pay, high range	AW Average wage paid	HR High end range	MW Median wage paid	W Weekly
AO Average offered	APL Average pay, low range	FQ First quartile wage	LR Low end range	SQ Second quartile wage	Y Yearly

Occupation/Type/Industry	Location	Per	Low	Mid	High	Source	Date
Structural Metal Fabricator and Fitter	Indiana	S	12.25 MW	12.83 AW	26680 AAW	INBLS	10//99-12//99
	Elkhart-Goshen MSA, IN	S	9.64 MW	9.02 AW	20050 AAW	INBLS	10//99-12//99
	Evansville-Henderson MSA, IN-KY	S	13.72 MW	14.18 AW	28530 AAW	INBLS	10//99-12//99
	Fort Wayne MSA, IN	S	15.63 MW	14.71 AW	32510 AAW	INBLS	10//99-12//99
	Gary PMSA, IN	S	12.30 MW	12.21 AW	25590 AAW	INBLS	10//99-12//99
	Indianapolis MSA, IN	S	14.27 MW	13.35 AW	29690 AAW	INBLS	10//99-12//99
	Terre Haute MSA, IN	S	10.24 MW	9.56 AW	21300 AAW	INBLS	10//99-12//99
	Iowa	S	10.26 MW	11.35 AW	23620 AAW	IABLS	10//99-12//99
	Des Moines MSA, IA	S	14.20 MW	14.43 AW	29540 AAW	IABLS	10//99-12//99
	Dubuque MSA, IA	S	15.20 MW	15.25 AW	31620 AAW	IABLS	10//99-12//99
	Sioux City MSA, IA-NE	S	10.15 MW	8.34 AW	21120 AAW	IABLS	10//99-12//99
	Waterloo-Cedar Falls MSA, IA	S	14.39 MW	14.19 AW	29930 AAW	IABLS	10//99-12//99
	Kansas	S	11.42 MW	11.27 AW	23430 AAW	KSBLS	10//99-12//99
	Wichita MSA, KS	S	11.74 MW	11.29 AW	24420 AAW	KSBLS	10//99-12//99
	Kentucky	S	10.12 MW	10.11 AW	21030 AAW	KYBLS	10//99-12//99
	Louisville MSA, KY-IN	S	12.00 MW	12.03 AW	24960 AAW	KYBLS	10//99-12//99
	Louisiana	S	12.41 MW	12.62 AW	26260 AAW	LABLS	10//99-12//99
	Baton Rouge MSA, LA	S	16.62 MW	13.08 AW	34560 AAW	LABLS	10//99-12//99
	Houma MSA, LA	S	13.71 MW	13.97 AW	28520 AAW	LABLS	10//99-12//99
	Lafayette MSA, LA	S	10.17 MW	9.79 AW	21150 AAW	LABLS	10//99-12//99
	New Orleans MSA, LA	S	12.28 MW	12.22 AW	25530 AAW	LABLS	10//99-12//99
	Shreveport-Bossier City MSA, LA	S	11.78 MW	11.81 AW	24500 AAW	LABLS	10//99-12//99
	Portland MSA, ME	S	13.13 MW	13.70 AW	27310 AAW	MEBLS	10//99-12//99
	Maryland	S	14.13 MW	14.96 AW	31110 AAW	MDBLS	10//99-12//99
	Baltimore PMSA, MD	S	15.11 MW	15.32 AW	31420 AAW	MDBLS	10//99-12//99
	Massachusetts	S	16.11 MW	16.20 AW	33690 AAW	MABLS	10//99-12//99
	Boston PMSA, MA-NH	S	15.32 MW	15.26 AW	31860 AAW	MABLS	10//99-12//99
	Lawrence PMSA, MA-NH	S	17.46 MW	17.90 AW	36310 AAW	MABLS	10//99-12//99
	Lowell PMSA, MA-NH	S	18.95 MW	19.06 AW	39410 AAW	MABLS	10//99-12//99
	Springfield MSA, MA	S	13.94 MW	14.80 AW	29000 AAW	MABLS	10//99-12//99
	Worcester PMSA, MA-CT	S	19.12 MW	19.17 AW	39770 AAW	MABLS	10//99-12//99
	Michigan	S	19.41 MW	20.65 AW	42950 AAW	MIBLS	10//99-12//99
	Detroit PMSA, MI	S	23.20 MW	23.50 AW	48260 AAW	MIBLS	10//99-12//99
	Grand Rapids-Muskegon-Holland MSA, MI	S	15.16 MW	14.81 AW	31530 AAW	MIBLS	10//99-12//99
	Minnesota	S	13.53 MW	13.91 AW	28930 AAW	MNBLS	10//99-12//99
	Duluth-Superior MSA, MN-WI	S	19.92 MW	22.31 AW	41440 AAW	MNBLS	10//99-12//99
	Minneapolis-St. Paul MSA, MN-WI	S	14.23 MW	14.41 AW	29610 AAW	MNBLS	10//99-12//99
	Mississippi	S	9.99 MW	10.17 AW	21150 AAW	MSBLS	10//99-12//99
	Biloxi-Gulfport-Pascagoula MSA, MS	S	13.40 MW	13.20 AW	27870 AAW	MSBLS	10//99-12//99
	Missouri	S	12.94 MW	12.93 AW	26890 AAW	MOBLS	10//99-12//99
	Kansas City MSA, MO-KS	S	12.05 MW	12.56 AW	25060 AAW	MOBLS	10//99-12//99
	St. Louis MSA, MO-IL	S	12.55 MW	13.91 AW	26110 AAW	MOBLS	10//99-12//99
	Montana	S	11.69 MW	11.57 AW	24060 AAW	MTBLS	10//99-12//99
	Nebraska	S	10.52 MW	10.72 AW	22290 AAW	NEBLS	10//99-12//99
	Lincoln MSA, NE	S	11.75 MW	11.67 AW	24450 AAW	NEBLS	10//99-12//99
	Omaha MSA, NE-IA	S	11.04 MW	10.74 AW	22960 AAW	NEBLS	10//99-12//99
	Nevada	S	18.58 MW	17.82 AW	37060 AAW	NVBLS	10//99-12//99
	Las Vegas MSA, NV-AZ	S	18.28 MW	19.61 AW	38030 AAW	NVBLS	10//99-12//99
	New Hampshire	S	11.91 MW	12.26 AW	25490 AAW	NHBLS	10//99-12//99
	New Jersey	S	13.22 MW	14.22 AW	29580 AAW	NJBLS	10//99-12//99
	Bergen-Passaic PMSA, NJ	S	14.62 MW	15.46 AW	30420 AAW	NJBLS	10//99-12//99
	Middlesex-Somerset-Hunterdon PMSA, NJ	S	13.63 MW	13.85 AW	28350 AAW	NJBLS	10//99-12//99
	Monmouth-Ocean PMSA, NJ	S	11.63 MW	10.77 AW	24180 AAW	NJBLS	10//99-12//99
	Newark PMSA, NJ	S	14.60 MW	13.38 AW	30370 AAW	NJBLS	10//99-12//99
	New Mexico	S	10.48 MW	11.67 AW	24270 AAW	NMBLS	10//99-12//99
	New York	S	13.29 MW	16.20 AW	33690 AAW	NYBLS	10//99-12//99
	Albany-Schenectady-Troy MSA, NY	S	20.05 MW	19.82 AW	41710 AAW	NYBLS	10//99-12//99
	Buffalo-Niagara Falls MSA, NY	S	12.36 MW	13.53 AW	25710 AAW	NYBLS	10//99-12//99
	Elmira MSA, NY	S	14.53 MW	14.64 AW	30220 AAW	NYBLS	10//99-12//99
	Nassau-Suffolk PMSA, NY	S	13.83 MW	13.16 AW	28770 AAW	NYBLS	10//99-12//99
	New York PMSA, NY	S	18.45 MW	16.33 AW	38380 AAW	NYBLS	10//99-12//99
	Newburgh PMSA, NY-PA	S	14.94 MW	14.58 AW	31070 AAW	NYBLS	10//99-12//99
	Rochester MSA, NY	S	10.49 MW	10.36 AW	21820 AAW	NYBLS	10//99-12//99

AAW Average annual wage	**AOH** Average offered, high	**ASH** Average starting, high	**H** Hourly	**M** Monthly	**S** Special: hourly and annual
AE Average entry wage	**AOL** Average offered, low	**ASL** Average starting, low	**HI** Highest wage paid	**MTC** Median total compensation	**TQ** Third quartile wage
AEX Average experienced wage	**APH** Average pay, high range	**AW** Average wage paid	**HR** High end range	**MW** Median wage paid	**W** Weekly
AO Average offered	**APL** Average pay, low range	**FQ** First quartile wage	**LR** Low end range	**SQ** Second quartile wage	**Y** Yearly

Structural Metal Fabricator and Fitter

Occupation/Type/Industry	Location	Per	Low	Mid	High	Source	Date
Structural Metal Fabricator and Fitter	Syracuse MSA, NY	S	15.83 MW	15.83 AW	32940 AAW	NYBLS	10//99-12//99
	Utica-Rome MSA, NY	S	11.14 MW	11.54 AW	23170 AAW	NYBLS	10//99-12//99
	North Carolina	S	10.79 MW	11.68 AW	24290 AAW	NCBLS	10//99-12//99
	Asheville MSA, NC	S	11.44 MW	10.13 AW	23790 AAW	NCBLS	10//99-12//99
	Charlotte-Gastonia-Rock Hill MSA, NC-SC	S	12.06 MW	11.78 AW	25090 AAW	NCBLS	10//99-12//99
	Greensboro--Winston-Salem--High Point MSA, NC	S	12.78 MW	12.56 AW	26580 AAW	NCBLS	10//99-12//99
	Hickory-Morganton-Lenoir MSA, NC	S	19.07 MW	21.12 AW	39670 AAW	NCBLS	10//99-12//99
	Raleigh-Durham-Chapel Hill MSA, NC	S	12.64 MW	12.45 AW	26300 AAW	NCBLS	10//99-12//99
	Rocky Mount MSA, NC	S	12.76 MW	12.46 AW	26550 AAW	NCBLS	10//99-12//99
	Wilmington MSA, NC	S	12.05 MW	12.03 AW	25070 AAW	NCBLS	10//99-12//99
	North Dakota	S	10.53 MW	11.00 AW	22870 AAW	NDBLS	10//99-12//99
	Fargo-Moorhead MSA, ND-MN	S	11.92 MW	12.12 AW	24800 AAW	NDBLS	10//99-12//99
	Ohio	S	14.02 MW	13.61 AW	28320 AAW	OHBLS	10//99-12//99
	Akron PMSA, OH	S	14.50 MW	14.89 AW	30160 AAW	OHBLS	10//99-12//99
	Canton-Massillon MSA, OH	S	10.90 MW	10.08 AW	22660 AAW	OHBLS	10//99-12//99
	Cincinnati PMSA, OH-KY-IN	S	13.16 MW	13.83 AW	27380 AAW	OHBLS	10//99-12//99
	Cleveland-Lorain-Elyria PMSA, OH	S	12.95 MW	12.41 AW	26940 AAW	OHBLS	10//99-12//99
	Columbus MSA, OH	S	13.51 MW	13.67 AW	28100 AAW	OHBLS	10//99-12//99
	Dayton-Springfield MSA, OH	S	11.87 MW	11.66 AW	24690 AAW	OHBLS	10//99-12//99
	Hamilton-Middletown PMSA, OH	S	15.51 MW	15.49 AW	32270 AAW	OHBLS	10//99-12//99
	Lima MSA, OH	S	14.06 MW	14.15 AW	29240 AAW	OHBLS	10//99-12//99
	Mansfield MSA, OH	S	9.40 MW	9.56 AW	19550 AAW	OHBLS	10//99-12//99
	Toledo MSA, OH	S	15.47 MW	15.57 AW	32180 AAW	OHBLS	10//99-12//99
	Youngstown-Warren MSA, OH	S	11.37 MW	10.26 AW	23660 AAW	OHBLS	10//99-12//99
	Oklahoma	S	12.04 MW	12.38 AW	25750 AAW	OKBLS	10//99-12//99
	Oklahoma City MSA, OK	S	11.99 MW	12.11 AW	24930 AAW	OKBLS	10//99-12//99
	Tulsa MSA, OK	S	13.67 MW	12.52 AW	28420 AAW	OKBLS	10//99-12//99
	Oregon	S	17.34 MW	17.49 AW	36390 AAW	ORBLS	10//99-12//99
	Eugene-Springfield MSA, OR	S	13.24 MW	12.42 AW	27540 AAW	ORBLS	10//99-12//99
	Medford-Ashland MSA, OR	S	14.05 MW	13.18 AW	29230 AAW	ORBLS	10//99-12//99
	Portland-Vancouver PMSA, OR-WA	S	18.48 MW	19.24 AW	38430 AAW	ORBLS	10//99-12//99
	Salem PMSA, OR	S	18.46 MW	16.72 AW	38400 AAW	ORBLS	10//99-12//99
	Pennsylvania	S	12.84 MW	13.11 AW	27260 AAW	PABLS	10//99-12//99
	Allentown-Bethlehem-Easton MSA, PA	S	14.48 MW	15.57 AW	30110 AAW	PABLS	10//99-12//99
	Erie MSA, PA	S	11.92 MW	12.10 AW	24800 AAW	PABLS	10//99-12//99
	Harrisburg-Lebanon-Carlisle MSA, PA	S	13.39 MW	13.62 AW	27860 AAW	PABLS	10//99-12//99
	Johnstown MSA, PA	S	12.27 MW	11.54 AW	25520 AAW	PABLS	10//99-12//99
	Lancaster MSA, PA	S	11.58 MW	11.63 AW	24090 AAW	PABLS	10//99-12//99
	Philadelphia PMSA, PA-NJ	S	15.01 MW	13.47 AW	31210 AAW	PABLS	10//99-12//99
	Pittsburgh MSA, PA	S	12.96 MW	13.01 AW	26960 AAW	PABLS	10//99-12//99
	Reading MSA, PA	S	12.74 MW	12.65 AW	26490 AAW	PABLS	10//99-12//99
	Scranton--Wilkes-Barre--Hazleton MSA, PA	S	12.40 MW	12.36 AW	25790 AAW	PABLS	10//99-12//99
	Sharon MSA, PA	S	14.66 MW	15.13 AW	30490 AAW	PABLS	10//99-12//99
	York MSA, PA	S	13.95 MW	14.39 AW	29020 AAW	PABLS	10//99-12//99
	Rhode Island	S	12.93 MW	13.74 AW	28580 AAW	RIBLS	10//99-12//99
	Providence-Fall River-Warwick MSA, RI-MA	S	13.61 MW	12.84 AW	28320 AAW	RIBLS	10//99-12//99
	South Carolina	S	10.81 MW	11.34 AW	23590 AAW	SCBLS	10//99-12//99
	Charleston-North Charleston MSA, SC	S	10.65 MW	10.05 AW	22150 AAW	SCBLS	10//99-12//99
	Columbia MSA, SC	S	8.91 MW	8.57 AW	18540 AAW	SCBLS	10//99-12//99
	Greenville-Spartanburg-Anderson MSA, SC	S	11.83 MW	11.75 AW	24610 AAW	SCBLS	10//99-12//99
	Sumter MSA, SC	S	11.66 MW	12.09 AW	24260 AAW	SCBLS	10//99-12//99
	South Dakota	S	9.9 MW	10.00 AW	20810 AAW	SDBLS	10//99-12//99
	Sioux Falls MSA, SD	S	10.92 MW	11.08 AW	22710 AAW	SDBLS	10//99-12//99
	Tennessee	S	11.87 MW	11.55 AW	24020 AAW	TNBLS	10//99-12//99
	Chattanooga MSA, TN-GA	S	12.25 MW	12.33 AW	25480 AAW	TNBLS	10//99-12//99
	Johnson City-Kingsport-Bristol MSA, TN-VA	S	11.98 MW	12.10 AW	24910 AAW	TNBLS	10//99-12//99

AAW Average annual wage	AOH Average offered, high	ASH Average starting, high	H Hourly	M Monthly	S Special: hourly and annual
AE Average entry wage	AOL Average offered, low	ASL Average starting, low	HI Highest wage paid	MTC Median total compensation	TQ Third quartile wage
AEX Average experienced wage	APH Average pay, high range	AW Average wage paid	HR High end range	MW Median wage paid	W Weekly
AO Average offered	APL Average pay, low range	FQ First quartile wage	LR Low end range	SQ Second quartile wage	Y Yearly

Occupation/Type/Industry	Location	Per	Low	Mid	High	Source	Date
Structural Metal Fabricator and Fitter							
	Knoxville MSA, TN	S	10.77 MW	11.31 AW	22410 AAW	TNBLS	10//99-12//99
	Memphis MSA, TN-AR-MS	S	14.03 MW	14.66 AW	29190 AAW	MSBLS	10//99-12//99
	Nashville MSA, TN	S	13.53 MW	13.34 AW	28140 AAW	TNBLS	10//99-12//99
	Texas	S	10.59 MW	11.03 AW	22940 AAW	TXBLS	10//99-12//99
	Austin-San Marcos MSA, TX	S	10.46 MW	10.36 AW	21770 AAW	TXBLS	10//99-12//99
	Beaumont-Port Arthur MSA, TX	S	14.09 MW	14.04 AW	29310 AAW	TXBLS	10//99-12//99
	Brazoria PMSA, TX	S	17.08 MW	17.35 AW	35520 AAW	TXBLS	10//99-12//99
	Brownsville-Harlingen-San Benito MSA, TX	S	8.48 MW	8.19 AW	17640 AAW	TXBLS	10//99-12//99
	Dallas PMSA, TX	S	11.34 MW	10.73 AW	23590 AAW	TXBLS	10//99-12//99
	El Paso MSA, TX	S	7.32 MW	6.50 AW	15220 AAW	TXBLS	10//99-12//99
	Fort Worth-Arlington PMSA, TX	S	10.22 MW	7.70 AW	21260 AAW	TXBLS	10//99-12//99
	Galveston-Texas City PMSA, TX	S	11.15 MW	11.67 AW	23190 AAW	TXBLS	10//99-12//99
	Houston PMSA, TX	S	11.65 MW	11.53 AW	24230 AAW	TXBLS	10//99-12//99
	Longview-Marshall MSA, TX	S	11.22 MW	11.49 AW	23340 AAW	TXBLS	10//99-12//99
	Odessa-Midland MSA, TX	S	8.76 MW	9.14 AW	18220 AAW	TXBLS	10//99-12//99
	San Antonio MSA, TX	S	9.47 MW	9.31 AW	19710 AAW	TXBLS	10//99-12//99
	Wichita Falls MSA, TX	S	14.60 MW	14.58 AW	30370 AAW	TXBLS	10//99-12//99
	Utah	S	12.77 MW	13.05 AW	27140 AAW	UTBLS	10//99-12//99
	Provo-Orem MSA, UT	S	11.15 MW	11.37 AW	23190 AAW	UTBLS	10//99-12//99
	Salt Lake City-Ogden MSA, UT	S	13.39 MW	13.29 AW	27840 AAW	UTBLS	10//99-12//99
	Virginia	S	13.17 MW	12.86 AW	26740 AAW	VABLS	10//99-12//99
	Lynchburg MSA, VA	S	12.05 MW	11.82 AW	25060 AAW	VABLS	10//99-12//99
	Norfolk-Virginia Beach-Newport News MSA, VA-NC	S	14.85 MW	15.12 AW	30890 AAW	VABLS	10//99-12//99
	Richmond-Petersburg MSA, VA	S	13.44 MW	12.04 AW	27960 AAW	VABLS	10//99-12//99
	Roanoke MSA, VA	S	9.69 MW	9.40 AW	20150 AAW	VABLS	10//99-12//99
	Washington	S	14.7 MW	15.43 AW	32100 AAW	WABLS	10//99-12//99
	Bellingham MSA, WA	S	16.36 MW	16.22 AW	34020 AAW	WABLS	10//99-12//99
	Seattle-Bellevue-Everett PMSA, WA	S	14.66 MW	12.96 AW	30500 AAW	WABLS	10//99-12//99
	Spokane MSA, WA	S	12.35 MW	12.27 AW	25690 AAW	WABLS	10//99-12//99
	West Virginia	S	11.91 MW	12.23 AW	25440 AAW	WVBLS	10//99-12//99
	Huntington-Ashland MSA, WV-KY-OH	S	10.80 MW	10.91 AW	22470 AAW	WVBLS	10//99-12//99
	Wisconsin	S	13.55 MW	13.33 AW	27720 AAW	WIBLS	10//99-12//99
	Green Bay MSA, WI	S	16.75 MW	16.36 AW	34830 AAW	WIBLS	10//99-12//99
	La Crosse MSA, WI-MN	S	9.68 MW	9.47 AW	20140 AAW	WIBLS	10//99-12//99
	Milwaukee-Waukesha PMSA, WI	S	15.08 MW	14.64 AW	31360 AAW	WIBLS	10//99-12//99
	Wausau MSA, WI	S	12.64 MW	12.63 AW	26290 AAW	WIBLS	10//99-12//99
	Puerto Rico	S	10.28 MW	11.23 AW	23350 AAW	PRBLS	10//99-12//99
Substance Abuse and Behavioral Disorder Counselor							
	Alabama	S	13.34 MW	12.97 AW	26980 AAW	ALBLS	10//99-12//99
	Alaska	S	12.75 MW	14.43 AW	30020 AAW	AKBLS	10//99-12//99
	Arizona	S	10.34 MW	12.26 AW	25500 AAW	AZBLS	10//99-12//99
	Arkansas	S	8.25 MW	9.04 AW	18810 AAW	ARBLS	10//99-12//99
	California	S	11.75 MW	12.38 AW	25750 AAW	CABLS	10//99-12//99
	Colorado	S	12.41 MW	13.04 AW	27110 AAW	COBLS	10//99-12//99
	Connecticut	S	15.48 MW	16.33 AW	33960 AAW	CTBLS	10//99-12//99
	Delaware	S	14.23 MW	16.54 AW	34410 AAW	DEBLS	10//99-12//99
	District of Columbia	S	15.69 MW	17.57 AW	36540 AAW	DCBLS	10//99-12//99
	Florida	S	11.04 MW	11.57 AW	24060 AAW	FLBLS	10//99-12//99
	Georgia	S	12.61 MW	12.91 AW	26840 AAW	GABLS	10//99-12//99
	Hawaii	S	19.15 MW	21.17 AW	44030 AAW	HIBLS	10//99-12//99
	Idaho	S	13.76 MW	14.07 AW	29270 AAW	IDBLS	10//99-12//99
	Illinois	S	10.85 MW	12.38 AW	25750 AAW	ILBLS	10//99-12//99
	Indiana	S	13.34 MW	13.51 AW	28100 AAW	INBLS	10//99-12//99
	Iowa	S	12.32 MW	12.52 AW	26040 AAW	IABLS	10//99-12//99
	Kansas	S	14.07 MW	13.86 AW	28820 AAW	KSBLS	10//99-12//99
	Kentucky	S	11.07 MW	12.11 AW	25180 AAW	KYBLS	10//99-12//99
	Louisiana	S	12.06 MW	12.70 AW	26420 AAW	LABLS	10//99-12//99
	Maine	S	13.73 MW	13.95 AW	29020 AAW	MEBLS	10//99-12//99
	Maryland	S	15.12 MW	15.31 AW	31850 AAW	MDBLS	10//99-12//99

Occupation/Type/Industry	Location	Per	Low	Mid	High	Source	Date
Substance Abuse and Behavioral Disorder Counselor	Massachusetts	S	12.9 MW	13.99 AW	29110 AAW	MABLS	10//99-12//99
	Michigan	S	12.09 MW	13.65 AW	28380 AAW	MIBLS	10//99-12//99
	Minnesota	S	14.01 MW	14.76 AW	30700 AAW	MNBLS	10//99-12//99
	Mississippi	S	10.19 MW	10.90 AW	22670 AAW	MSBLS	10//99-12//99
	Missouri	S	11.81 MW	12.62 AW	26260 AAW	MOBLS	10//99-12//99
	Montana	S	11.97 MW	11.40 AW	23710 AAW	MTBLS	10//99-12//99
	Nebraska	S	10.75 MW	11.68 AW	24300 AAW	NEBLS	10//99-12//99
	Nevada	S	10.33 MW	11.24 AW	23380 AAW	NVBLS	10//99-12//99
	New Hampshire	S	11.86 MW	11.29 AW	23490 AAW	NHBLS	10//99-12//99
	New Jersey	S	13.53 MW	15.59 AW	32440 AAW	NJBLS	10//99-12//99
	New Mexico	S	11.21 MW	11.52 AW	23960 AAW	NMBLS	10//99-12//99
	New York	S	15.95 MW	17.87 AW	37170 AAW	NYBLS	10//99-12//99
	North Carolina	S	12.47 MW	12.81 AW	26640 AAW	NCBLS	10//99-12//99
	North Dakota	S	15.5 MW	15.37 AW	31960 AAW	NDBLS	10//99-12//99
	Ohio	S	12.94 MW	13.41 AW	27880 AAW	OHBLS	10//99-12//99
	Oklahoma	S	7.93 MW	8.88 AW	18460 AAW	OKBLS	10//99-12//99
	Oregon	S	13.15 MW	14.66 AW	30490 AAW	ORBLS	10//99-12//99
	Pennsylvania	S	12.32 MW	12.82 AW	26660 AAW	PABLS	10//99-12//99
	Rhode Island	S	13.12 MW	15.05 AW	31310 AAW	RIBLS	10//99-12//99
	South Carolina	S	14.5 MW	15.89 AW	33050 AAW	SCBLS	10//99-12//99
	South Dakota	S	12.9 MW	13.75 AW	28600 AAW	SDBLS	10//99-12//99
	Tennessee	S	12.14 MW	13.07 AW	27190 AAW	TNBLS	10//99-12//99
	Texas	S	11.72 MW	11.93 AW	24810 AAW	TXBLS	10//99-12//99
	Utah	S	14.13 MW	14.81 AW	30800 AAW	UTBLS	10//99-12//99
	Virginia	S	17.62 MW	17.34 AW	36060 AAW	VABLS	10//99-12//99
	Washington	S	14.22 MW	13.87 AW	28850 AAW	WABLS	10//99-12//99
	West Virginia	S	13.02 MW	14.52 AW	30210 AAW	WVBLS	10//99-12//99
	Wisconsin	S	20.31 MW	24.70 AW	51370 AAW	WIBLS	10//99-12//99
	Wyoming	S	9.7 MW	10.10 AW	21010 AAW	WYBLS	10//99-12//99
Subway and Streetcar Operator	California	S	18.32 MW	18.00 AW	37430 AAW	CABLS	10//99-12//99
	Florida	S	6.67 MW	6.71 AW	13960 AAW	FLBLS	10//99-12//99
	Texas	S	10.79 MW	13.40 AW	27870 AAW	TXBLS	10//99-12//99
Superintendent							
Population 10,000 to 24,999, Water Wastewater Plant	United States	Y		50043 AW		AC&C2	6//99
Population 100,000 or more, Water Wastewater Plant	United States	Y		69351 AW		AC&C2	6//99
Population 25,000 to 49,999, Water Wastewater Plant	United States	Y		52272 AW		AC&C2	6//99
Population 50,000 to 99,999, Water Wastewater Plant	United States	Y		56759 AW		AC&C2	6//99
Population Less than 10,000, Water Wastewater Plant	United States	Y		34121 AW		AC&C2	6//99
Public School	United States	Y		86149 AW		AS&U	1999-2000
Supervisor							
Female, Logistics	United States	Y	46500 FQ	59000 SQ	73000 TQ	TRAFWD	2000
Surgeon	Alabama	S		69.43 AW	144400 AAW	ALBLS	10//99-12//99
	Auburn-Opelika MSA, AL	S	67.85 MW		141140 AAW	ALBLS	10//99-12//99
	Arizona	S	65.21 MW	61.30 AW	127510 AAW	AZBLS	10//99-12//99
	Phoenix-Mesa MSA, AZ	S	58.55 MW	62.23 AW	121790 AAW	AZBLS	10//99-12//99
	California	S	68.59 MW	58.25 AW	121170 AAW	CABLS	10//99-12//99
	Riverside-San Bernardino PMSA, CA	S	54.77 MW	56.85 AW	113920 AAW	CABLS	10//99-12//99
	San Diego MSA, CA	S	54.67 MW	57.79 AW	113720 AAW	CABLS	10//99-12//99
	Vallejo-Fairfield-Napa PMSA, CA	S	53.41 MW	53.65 AW	111090 AAW	CABLS	10//99-12//99
	Connecticut	S		64.14 AW	133420 AAW	CTBLS	10//99-12//99
	Hartford MSA, CT	S	64.98 MW		135150 AAW	CTBLS	10//99-12//99
	New London-Norwich MSA, CT-RI	S	68.54 MW		142560 AAW	CTBLS	10//99-12//99
	Florida	S		68.90 AW	143310 AAW	FLBLS	10//99-12//99
	Augusta-Aiken MSA, GA-SC	S	68.40 MW		142270 AAW	GABLS	10//99-12//99
	Illinois	S	50.83 MW	51.39 AW	106890 AAW	ILBLS	10//99-12//99
	Chicago PMSA, IL	S	57.21 MW	60.73 AW	119000 AAW	ILBLS	10//99-12//99
	Indiana	S		69.90 AW	145400 AAW	INBLS	10//99-12//99
	Indianapolis MSA, IN	S	70.00 MW		145600 AAW	INBLS	10//99-12//99
	Kansas	S		69.96 AW	145520 AAW	KSBLS	10//99-12//99
	Topeka MSA, KS	S	69.55 MW		144660 AAW	KSBLS	10//99-12//99

AAW Average annual wage	**AOH** Average offered, high	**ASH** Average starting, high	**H** Hourly	**M** Monthly	**S** Special: hourly and annual
AE Average entry wage	**AOL** Average offered, low	**ASL** Average starting, low	**HI** Highest wage paid	**MTC** Median total compensation	**TQ** Third quartile wage
AEX Average experienced wage	**APH** Average pay, high range	**AW** Average wage paid	**HR** High end range	**MW** Median wage paid	**W** Weekly
AO Average offered	**APL** Average pay, low range	**FQ** First quartile wage	**LR** Low end range	**SQ** Second quartile wage	**Y** Yearly

Occupation/Type/Industry	Location	Per	Low	Mid	High	Source	Date
Surgeon	Kentucky	s		67.34 AW	140080 AAW	KYBLS	10//99-12//99
	Louisville MSA, KY-IN	s	68.56 MW		142610 AAW	KYBLS	10//99-12//99
	Louisiana	s		67.82 AW	141060 AAW	LABLS	10//99-12//99
	Maryland	s		69.54 AW	144640 AAW	MDBLS	10//99-12//99
	Massachusetts	s		67.65 AW	140710 AAW	MABLS	10//99-12//99
	Lawrence PMSA, MA-NH	s	70.00 MW		145600 AAW	MABLS	10//99-12//99
	Michigan	s		67.90 AW	141230 AAW	MIBLS	10//99-12//99
	Detroit PMSA, MI	s	67.70 MW		140830 AAW	MIBLS	10//99-12//99
	Minnesota	s		65.49 AW	136210 AAW	MNBLS	10//99-12//99
	Minneapolis-St. Paul MSA, MN-WI	s	64.60 MW		134370 AAW	MNBLS	10//99-12//99
	Mississippi	s		64.74 AW	134650 AAW	MSBLS	10//99-12//99
	Missouri	s		69.09 AW	143700 AAW	MOBLS	10//99-12//99
	Montana	s		67.84 AW	141110 AAW	MTBLS	10//99-12//99
	Nebraska	s		68.27 AW	142000	NEBLS	10//99-12//99
	Lincoln MSA, NE	s	68.45 MW		142380 AAW	NEBLS	10//99-12//99
	New Hampshire	s		68.53 AW	142540 AAW	NHBLS	10//99-12//99
	New Jersey	s		66.02 AW	137320 AAW	NJBLS	10//99-12//99
	New York	s		62.81 AW	130650 AAW	NYBLS	10//99-12//99
	Dutchess County PMSA, NY	s	60.48 MW	67.00 AW	125790 AAW	NYBLS	10//99-12//99
	New York PMSA, NY	s	55.87 MW	63.29 AW	116220 AAW	NYBLS	10//99-12//99
	Syracuse MSA, NY	s	70.00 MW		145600 AAW	NYBLS	10//99-12//99
	North Carolina	s		67.64 AW	140700 AAW	NCBLS	10//99-12//99
	Asheville MSA, NC	s	65.31 MW		135850 AAW	NCBLS	10//99-12//99
	Charlotte-Gastonia-Rock Hill MSA, NC-SC	s	69.60 MW		144770 AAW	NCBLS	10//99-12//99
	North Dakota	s		70.00 AW	145600 AAW	NDBLS	10//99-12//99
	Ohio	s		63.70 AW	132500 AAW	OHBLS	10//99-12//99
	Canton-Massillon MSA, OH	s	70.00 MW		145600 AAW	OHBLS	10//99-12//99
	Cincinnati PMSA, OH-KY-IN	s	64.44 MW		134040 AAW	OHBLS	10//99-12//99
	Cleveland-Lorain-Elyria PMSA, OH	s	47.56 MW	44.49 AW	98920 AAW	OHBLS	10//99-12//99
	Columbus MSA, OH	s	70.00 MW		145600 AAW	OHBLS	10//99-12//99
	Dayton-Springfield MSA, OH	s	58.01 MW	60.93 AW	120660 AAW	OHBLS	10//99-12//99
	Oklahoma	s		69.94 AW	145480 AAW	OKBLS	10//99-12//99
	Pennsylvania	s		66.90 AW	139140 AAW	PABLS	10//99-12//99
	Philadelphia PMSA, PA-NJ	s	63.40 MW		131880 AAW	PABLS	10//99-12//99
	Pittsburgh MSA, PA	s	68.97 MW		143460 AAW	PABLS	10//99-12//99
	Rhode Island	s		66.77 AW	138870 AAW	RIBLS	10//99-12//99
	Providence-Fall River-Warwick MSA, RI-MA	s	66.06 MW		137410 AAW	RIBLS	10//99-12//99
	South Carolina	s		66.74 AW	138830 AAW	SCBLS	10//99-12//99
	Tennessee	s		69.06 AW	143640 AAW	TNBLS	10//99-12//99
	Jackson MSA, TN	s	68.04 MW		141520 AAW	TNBLS	10//99-12//99
	Johnson City-Kingsport-Bristol MSA, TN-VA	s	66.53 MW		138390 AAW	TNBLS	10//99-12//99
	Memphis MSA, TN-AR-MS	s	69.77 MW		145120 AAW	MSBLS	10//99-12//99
	Texas	s		68.63 AW	142750 AAW	TXBLS	10//99-12//99
	Fort Worth-Arlington PMSA, TX	s	67.56 MW		140530 AAW	TXBLS	10//99-12//99
	Utah	s		59.66 AW	124090 AAW	UTBLS	10//99-12//99
	Virginia	s		66.22 AW	137740 AAW	VABLS	10//99-12//99
	Washington	s		66.55 AW	138420 AAW	WABLS	10//99-12//99
	West Virginia	s		67.23 AW	139840 AAW	WVBLS	10//99-12//99
	Wisconsin	s		67.43 AW	140250 AAW	WIBLS	10//99-12//99
	Wyoming	s		67.28 AW	139950 AAW	WYBLS	10//99-12//99
	Puerto Rico	s	37.8 MW	37.08 AW	77120 AAW	PRBLS	10//99-12//99
	San Juan-Bayamon PMSA, PR	s	32.13 MW	32.86 AW	66830 AAW	PRBLS	10//99-12//99
Surgical Technologist	Alabama	s	10.18 MW	10.58 AW	22010 AAW	ALBLS	10//99-12//99
	Birmingham MSA, AL	s	10.04 MW	9.77 AW	20890 AAW	ALBLS	10//99-12//99
	Dothan MSA, AL	s	9.94 MW	9.79 AW	20670 AAW	ALBLS	10//99-12//99
	Mobile MSA, AL	s	9.86 MW	9.85 AW	20500 AAW	ALBLS	10//99-12//99
	Montgomery MSA, AL	s	13.88 MW	12.59 AW	28870 AAW	ALBLS	10//99-12//99
	Tuscaloosa MSA, AL	s	11.25 MW	11.73 AW	23390 AAW	ALBLS	10//99-12//99
	Alaska	s	14.49 MW	14.43 AW	30020 AAW	AKBLS	10//99-12//99
	Arizona	s	12.63 MW	12.64 AW	26300 AAW	AZBLS	10//99-12//99
	Phoenix-Mesa MSA, AZ	s	13.02 MW	12.85 AW	27070 AAW	AZBLS	10//99-12//99
	Tucson MSA, AZ	s	12.25 MW	12.45 AW	25490 AAW	AZBLS	10//99-12//99
	Arkansas	s	11.44 MW	11.34 AW	23590 AAW	ARBLS	10//99-12//99
	California	s	15.19 MW	15.37 AW	31960 AAW	CABLS	10//99-12//99
	Bakersfield MSA, CA	s	14.60 MW	14.61 AW	30370 AAW	CABLS	10//99-12//99
	Chico-Paradise MSA, CA	s	15.01 MW	14.73 AW	31220 AAW	CABLS	10//99-12//99

AAW	Average annual wage	AOH	Average offered, high	ASH	Average starting, high	H	Hourly	M	Monthly	S	Special: hourly and annual
AE	Average entry wage	AOL	Average offered, low	ASL	Average starting, low	HI	Highest wage paid	MTC	Median total compensation	TQ	Third quartile wage
AEX	Average experienced wage	APH	Average pay, high range	AW	Average wage paid	HR	High end range	MW	Median wage paid	W	Weekly
AO	Average offered	APL	Average pay, low range	FQ	First quartile wage	LR	Low end range	SQ	Second quartile wage	Y	Yearly

Occupation/Type/Industry	Location	Per	Low	Mid	High	Source	Date
Surgical Technologist	Fresno MSA, CA	S	14.60 MW	14.17 AW	30370 AAW	CABLS	10//99-12//99
	Los Angeles-Long Beach PMSA, CA	S	15.07 MW	14.88 AW	31340 AAW	CABLS	10//99-12//99
	Modesto MSA, CA	S	14.34 MW	13.91 AW	29820 AAW	CABLS	10//99-12//99
	Oakland PMSA, CA	S	17.50 MW	17.93 AW	36400 AAW	CABLS	10//99-12//99
	Orange County PMSA, CA	S	15.27 MW	15.11 AW	31760 AAW	CABLS	10//99-12//99
	Redding MSA, CA	S	11.17 MW	9.92 AW	23230 AAW	CABLS	10//99-12//99
	Riverside-San Bernardino PMSA, CA	S	14.42 MW	14.07 AW	30000 AAW	CABLS	10//99-12//99
	Sacramento PMSA, CA	S	15.43 MW	15.52 AW	32100 AAW	CABLS	10//99-12//99
	San Diego MSA, CA	S	15.41 MW	15.24 AW	32050 AAW	CABLS	10//99-12//99
	San Francisco PMSA, CA	S	16.49 MW	16.83 AW	34300 AAW	CABLS	10//99-12//99
	San Jose PMSA, CA	S	17.08 MW	17.59 AW	35530 AAW	CABLS	10//99-12//99
	Santa Barbara-Santa Maria-Lompoc MSA, CA	S	16.52 MW	15.89 AW	34370 AAW	CABLS	10//99-12//99
	Santa Rosa PMSA, CA	S	13.74 MW	14.30 AW	28580 AAW	CABLS	10//99-12//99
	Stockton-Lodi MSA, CA	S	14.49 MW	14.37 AW	30140 AAW	CABLS	10//99-12//99
	Visalia-Tulare-Porterville MSA, CA	S	15.97 MW	15.79 AW	33210 AAW	CABLS	10//99-12//99
	Colorado	S	12.6 MW	13.12 AW	27290 AAW	COBLS	10//99-12//99
	Colorado Springs MSA, CO	S	13.42 MW	13.19 AW	27920 AAW	COBLS	10//99-12//99
	Denver PMSA, CO	S	13.34 MW	12.62 AW	27750 AAW	COBLS	10//99-12//99
	Connecticut	S	16.21 MW	16.00 AW	33280 AAW	CTBLS	10//99-12//99
	Bridgeport PMSA, CT	S	16.72 MW	16.73 AW	34780 AAW	CTBLS	10//99-12//99
	Hartford MSA, CT	S	16.23 MW	16.32 AW	33760 AAW	CTBLS	10//99-12//99
	Stamford-Norwalk PMSA, CT	S	16.57 MW	17.09 AW	34470 AAW	CTBLS	10//99-12//99
	Delaware	S	11.65 MW	12.33 AW	25650 AAW	DEBLS	10//99-12//99
	District of Columbia	S	11.27 MW	11.60 AW	24140 AAW	DCBLS	10//99-12//99
	Washington PMSA, DC-MD-VA-WV	S	13.69 MW	13.23 AW	28470 AAW	DCBLS	10//99-12//99
	Florida	S	12.4 MW	12.82 AW	26660 AAW	FLBLS	10//99-12//99
	Fort Lauderdale PMSA, FL	S	13.78 MW	13.75 AW	28660 AAW	FLBLS	10//99-12//99
	Fort Myers-Cape Coral MSA, FL	S	12.97 MW	12.52 AW	26980 AAW	FLBLS	10//99-12//99
	Fort Pierce-Port St. Lucie MSA, FL	S	14.23 MW	14.46 AW	29590 AAW	FLBLS	10//99-12//99
	Fort Walton Beach MSA, FL	S	12.00 MW	12.08 AW	24950 AAW	FLBLS	10//99-12//99
	Jacksonville MSA, FL	S	12.17 MW	11.80 AW	25320 AAW	FLBLS	10//99-12//99
	Lakeland-Winter Haven MSA, FL	S	15.28 MW	12.64 AW	31780 AAW	FLBLS	10//99-12//99
	Melbourne-Titusville-Palm Bay MSA, FL	S	12.88 MW	12.91 AW	26780 AAW	FLBLS	10//99-12//99
	Miami PMSA, FL	S	12.60 MW	12.39 AW	26210 AAW	FLBLS	10//99-12//99
	Orlando MSA, FL	S	12.44 MW	12.34 AW	25880 AAW	FLBLS	10//99-12//99
	Pensacola MSA, FL	S	12.82 MW	12.23 AW	26670 AAW	FLBLS	10//99-12//99
	Punta Gorda MSA, FL	S	14.87 MW	14.66 AW	30920 AAW	FLBLS	10//99-12//99
	Sarasota-Bradenton MSA, FL	S	11.84 MW	11.50 AW	24620 AAW	FLBLS	10//99-12//99
	Tallahassee MSA, FL	S	13.09 MW	12.72 AW	27230 AAW	FLBLS	10//99-12//99
	Tampa-St. Petersburg-Clearwater MSA, FL	S	12.23 MW	12.10 AW	25440 AAW	FLBLS	10//99-12//99
	West Palm Beach-Boca Raton MSA, FL	S	14.05 MW	13.79 AW	29220 AAW	FLBLS	10//99-12//99
	Georgia	S	11.51 MW	11.64 AW	24200 AAW	GABLS	10//99-12//99
	Athens MSA, GA	S	9.63 MW	9.74 AW	20030 AAW	GABLS	10//99-12//99
	Atlanta MSA, GA	S	12.11 MW	12.05 AW	25180 AAW	GABLS	10//99-12//99
	Macon MSA, GA	S	10.14 MW	9.61 AW	21080 AAW	GABLS	10//99-12//99
	Savannah MSA, GA	S	11.15 MW	11.02 AW	23200 AAW	GABLS	10//99-12//99
	Hawaii	S	15.19 MW	15.47 AW	32190 AAW	HIBLS	10//99-12//99
	Honolulu MSA, HI	S	15.49 MW	15.21 AW	32220 AAW	HIBLS	10//99-12//99
	Idaho	S	14.19 MW	14.19 AW	29510 AAW	IDBLS	10//99-12//99
	Illinois	S	13.17 MW	13.80 AW	28700 AAW	ILBLS	10//99-12//99
	Champaign-Urbana MSA, IL	S	14.42 MW	13.66 AW	29990 AAW	ILBLS	10//99-12//99
	Chicago PMSA, IL	S	14.21 MW	13.60 AW	29560 AAW	ILBLS	10//99-12//99
	Indiana	S	13.17 MW	13.72 AW	28530 AAW	INBLS	10//99-12//99
	Elkhart-Goshen MSA, IN	S	14.38 MW	13.00 AW	29900 AAW	INBLS	10//99-12//99
	Evansville-Henderson MSA, IN-KY	S	12.25 MW	12.23 AW	25480 AAW	INBLS	10//99-12//99
	Fort Wayne MSA, IN	S	13.12 MW	13.11 AW	27300 AAW	INBLS	10//99-12//99
	Gary PMSA, IN	S	13.01 MW	12.89 AW	27050 AAW	INBLS	10//99-12//99
	Indianapolis MSA, IN	S	15.37 MW	14.22 AW	31970 AAW	INBLS	10//99-12//99
	Terre Haute MSA, IN	S	12.74 MW	12.45 AW	26500 AAW	INBLS	10//99-12//99
	Iowa	S	11.91 MW	12.41 AW	25810 AAW	IABLS	10//99-12//99

AAW Average annual wage	**AOH** Average offered, high	**ASH** Average starting, high	**H** Hourly	**M** Monthly	**S** Special: hourly and annual
AE Average entry wage	**AOL** Average offered, low	**ASL** Average starting, low	**HI** Highest wage paid	**MTC** Median total compensation	**TQ** Third quartile wage
AEX Average experienced wage	**APH** Average pay, high range	**AW** Average wage paid	**HR** High end range	**MW** Median wage paid	**W** Weekly
AO Average offered	**APL** Average pay, low range	**FQ** First quartile wage	**LR** Low end range	**SQ** Second quartile wage	**Y** Yearly

Occupation/Type/Industry	Location	Per	Low	Mid	High	Source	Date
Surgical Technologist	Davenport-Moline-Rock Island MSA, IA-IL	S	14.00 MW	13.31 AW	29120 AAW	IABLS	10//99-12//99
	Kansas	S	11.81 MW	11.82 AW	24590 AAW	KSBLS	10//99-12//99
	Topeka MSA, KS	S	12.14 MW	11.95 AW	25240 AAW	KSBLS	10//99-12//99
	Wichita MSA, KS	S	11.98 MW	11.98 AW	24920 AAW	KSBLS	10//99-12//99
	Kentucky	S	11.85 MW	12.18 AW	25330 AAW	KYBLS	10//99-12//99
	Lexington MSA, KY	S	12.07 MW	11.54 AW	25110 AAW	KYBLS	10//99-12//99
	Louisville MSA, KY-IN	S	12.49 MW	12.23 AW	25970 AAW	KYBLS	10//99-12//99
	Louisiana	S	11.41 MW	11.55 AW	24030 AAW	LABLS	10//99-12//99
	Baton Rouge MSA, LA	S	11.15 MW	10.58 AW	23190 AAW	LABLS	10//99-12//99
	Lafayette MSA, LA	S	10.44 MW	10.71 AW	21710 AAW	LABLS	10//99-12//99
	New Orleans MSA, LA	S	12.38 MW	12.18 AW	25750 AAW	LABLS	10//99-12//99
	Shreveport-Bossier City MSA, LA	S	11.67 MW	11.67 AW	24270 AAW	LABLS	10//99-12//99
	Maine	S	12.29 MW	12.39 AW	25780 AAW	MEBLS	10//99-12//99
	Maryland	S	13.91 MW	14.54 AW	30230 AAW	MDBLS	10//99-12//99
	Baltimore PMSA, MD	S	13.38 MW	13.38 AW	27820 AAW	MDBLS	10//99-12//99
	Cumberland MSA, MD-WV	S	13.77 MW	13.61 AW	28650 AAW	MDBLS	10//99-12//99
	Massachusetts	S	14.78 MW	15.87 AW	33020 AAW	MABLS	10//99-12//99
	Boston PMSA, MA-NH	S	16.49 MW	14.88 AW	34290 AAW	MABLS	10//99-12//99
	Lowell PMSA, MA-NH	S	13.66 MW	13.50 AW	28420 AAW	MABLS	10//99-12//99
	Springfield MSA, MA	S	15.36 MW	14.85 AW	31960 AAW	MABLS	10//99-12//99
	Worcester PMSA, MA-CT	S	14.22 MW	14.12 AW	29580 AAW	MABLS	10//99-12//99
	Michigan	S	13.82 MW	14.00 AW	29120 AAW	MIBLS	10//99-12//99
	Detroit PMSA, MI	S	14.41 MW	14.26 AW	29970 AAW	MIBLS	10//99-12//99
	Grand Rapids-Muskegon-Holland MSA, MI	S	14.32 MW	13.90 AW	29780 AAW	MIBLS	10//99-12//99
	Kalamazoo-Battle Creek MSA, MI	S	14.42 MW	13.83 AW	30000 AAW	MIBLS	10//99-12//99
	Lansing-East Lansing MSA, MI	S	14.44 MW	14.15 AW	30030 AAW	MIBLS	10//99-12//99
	Minnesota	S	14.84 MW	14.83 AW	30860 AAW	MNBLS	10//99-12//99
	Duluth-Superior MSA, MN-WI	S	14.63 MW	14.32 AW	30420 AAW	MNBLS	10//99-12//99
	Minneapolis-St. Paul MSA, MN-WI	S	15.27 MW	15.37 AW	31760 AAW	MNBLS	10//99-12//99
	Mississippi	S	10.01 MW	10.32 AW	21470 AAW	MSBLS	10//99-12//99
	Biloxi-Gulfport-Pascagoula MSA, MS	S	10.74 MW	10.44 AW	22330 AAW	MSBLS	10//99-12//99
	Jackson MSA, MS	S	10.57 MW	10.23 AW	21980 AAW	MSBLS	10//99-12//99
	Missouri	S	11.79 MW	13.10 AW	27250 AAW	MOBLS	10//99-12//99
	Kansas City MSA, MO-KS	S	16.29 MW	14.81 AW	33880 AAW	MOBLS	10//99-12//99
	St. Louis MSA, MO-IL	S	11.80 MW	11.38 AW	24530 AAW	MOBLS	10//99-12//99
	Montana	S	11.99 MW	12.02 AW	25000 AAW	MTBLS	10//99-12//99
	Great Falls MSA, MT	S	11.51 MW	11.55 AW	23950 AAW	MTBLS	10//99-12//99
	Missoula MSA, MT	S	12.62 MW	12.82 AW	26260 AAW	MTBLS	10//99-12//99
	Nebraska	S	12.62 MW	13.12 AW	27280 AAW	NEBLS	10//99-12//99
	Omaha MSA, NE-IA	S	13.71 MW	13.21 AW	28520 AAW	NEBLS	10//99-12//99
	Nevada	S	14.7 MW	15.58 AW	32410 AAW	NVBLS	10//99-12//99
	Las Vegas MSA, NV-AZ	S	15.09 MW	13.83 AW	31390 AAW	NVBLS	10//99-12//99
	Reno MSA, NV	S	15.57 MW	15.38 AW	32380 AAW	NVBLS	10//99-12//99
	New Hampshire	S	13.66 MW	13.42 AW	27920 AAW	NHBLS	10//99-12//99
	Portsmouth-Rochester PMSA, NH-ME	S	12.88 MW	13.08 AW	26800 AAW	NHBLS	10//99-12//99
	New Jersey	S	14.55 MW	15.12 AW	31440 AAW	NJBLS	10//99-12//99
	Bergen-Passaic PMSA, NJ	S	16.51 MW	15.54 AW	34340 AAW	NJBLS	10//99-12//99
	Middlesex-Somerset-Hunterdon PMSA, NJ	S	13.59 MW	13.81 AW	28280 AAW	NJBLS	10//99-12//99
	Monmouth-Ocean PMSA, NJ	S	14.92 MW	14.19 AW	31030 AAW	NJBLS	10//99-12//99
	Newark PMSA, NJ	S	15.19 MW	14.55 AW	31590 AAW	NJBLS	10//99-12//99
	New Mexico	S	10.97 MW	11.05 AW	22970 AAW	NMBLS	10//99-12//99
	New York	S	12.68 MW	13.31 AW	27670 AAW	NYBLS	10//99-12//99
	Albany-Schenectady-Troy MSA, NY	S	13.42 MW	12.57 AW	27900 AAW	NYBLS	10//99-12//99
	Buffalo-Niagara Falls MSA, NY	S	13.04 MW	12.56 AW	27120 AAW	NYBLS	10//99-12//99
	Nassau-Suffolk PMSA, NY	S	15.02 MW	14.65 AW	31240 AAW	NYBLS	10//99-12//99
	New York PMSA, NY	S	13.38 MW	12.72 AW	27830 AAW	NYBLS	10//99-12//99
	Newburgh PMSA, NY-PA	S	13.27 MW	13.03 AW	27600 AAW	NYBLS	10//99-12//99
	Rochester MSA, NY	S	11.75 MW	11.87 AW	24430 AAW	NYBLS	10//99-12//99
	Syracuse MSA, NY	S	12.03 MW	11.49 AW	25020 AAW	NYBLS	10//99-12//99
	Utica-Rome MSA, NY	S	11.50 MW	11.23 AW	23920 AAW	NYBLS	10//99-12//99
	North Carolina	S	12.6 MW	13.37 AW	27800 AAW	NCBLS	10//99-12//99

AAW   Average annual wage
AE   Average entry wage
AEX   Average experienced wage
AO   Average offered

AOH   Average offered, high
AOL   Average offered, low
APH   Average pay, high range
APL   Average pay, low range

ASH   Average starting, high
ASL   Average starting, low
AW   Average wage paid
FQ   First quartile wage

H   Hourly
HI   Highest wage paid
HR   High end range
LR   Low end range

M   Monthly
MTC   Median total compensation
MW   Median wage paid
SQ   Second quartile wage

S   Special: hourly and annual
TQ   Third quartile wage
W   Weekly
Y   Yearly

Occupation/Type/Industry	Location	Per	Low	Mid	High	Source	Date
Surgical Technologist	Charlotte-Gastonia-Rock Hill MSA, NC-SC	s	14.35 MW	13.88 AW	29850 AAW	NCBLS	10//99-12//99
	Greensboro--Winston-Salem--High Point MSA, NC	s	15.96 MW	13.57 AW	33190 AAW	NCBLS	10//99-12//99
	Hickory-Morganton-Lenoir MSA, NC	s	13.21 MW	13.48 AW	27470 AAW	NCBLS	10//99-12//99
	Raleigh-Durham-Chapel Hill MSA, NC	s	12.87 MW	12.77 AW	26780 AAW	NCBLS	10//99-12//99
	Wilmington MSA, NC	s	11.75 MW	11.73 AW	24440 AAW	NCBLS	10//99-12//99
	North Dakota	s	11.33 MW	11.30 AW	23490 AAW	NDBLS	10//99-12//99
	Fargo-Moorhead MSA, ND-MN	s	11.76 MW	11.59 AW	24460 AAW	NDBLS	10//99-12//99
	Ohio	s	13.31 MW	13.62 AW	28330 AAW	OHBLS	10//99-12//99
	Akron PMSA, OH	s	13.16 MW	12.66 AW	27370 AAW	OHBLS	10//99-12//99
	Cincinnati PMSA, OH-KY-IN	s	13.59 MW	13.37 AW	28260 AAW	OHBLS	10//99-12//99
	Cleveland-Lorain-Elyria PMSA, OH	s	14.47 MW	14.48 AW	30100 AAW	OHBLS	10//99-12//99
	Columbus MSA, OH	s	13.42 MW	13.09 AW	27920 AAW	OHBLS	10//99-12//99
	Dayton-Springfield MSA, OH	s	13.15 MW	12.91 AW	27360 AAW	OHBLS	10//99-12//99
	Hamilton-Middletown PMSA, OH	s	13.47 MW	13.16 AW	28010 AAW	OHBLS	10//99-12//99
	Toledo MSA, OH	s	14.60 MW	14.15 AW	30370 AAW	OHBLS	10//99-12//99
	Youngstown-Warren MSA, OH	s	13.30 MW	13.20 AW	27670 AAW	OHBLS	10//99-12//99
	Oklahoma	s	11.48 MW	11.88 AW	24710 AAW	OKBLS	10//99-12//99
	Oklahoma City MSA, OK	s	12.05 MW	11.67 AW	25070 AAW	OKBLS	10//99-12//99
	Tulsa MSA, OK	s	12.33 MW	12.14 AW	25650 AAW	OKBLS	10//99-12//99
	Oregon	s	13.54 MW	13.51 AW	28090 AAW	ORBLS	10//99-12//99
	Portland-Vancouver PMSA, OR-WA	s	13.16 MW	13.21 AW	27370 AAW	ORBLS	10//99-12//99
	Salem PMSA, OR	s	14.71 MW	14.95 AW	30590 AAW	ORBLS	10//99-12//99
	Pennsylvania	s	12.72 MW	12.97 AW	26970 AAW	PABLS	10//99-12//99
	Allentown-Bethlehem-Easton MSA, PA	s	12.60 MW	13.00 AW	26200 AAW	PABLS	10//99-12//99
	Erie MSA, PA	s	13.07 MW	12.62 AW	27180 AAW	PABLS	10//99-12//99
	Harrisburg-Lebanon-Carlisle MSA, PA	s	13.59 MW	13.60 AW	28270 AAW	PABLS	10//99-12//99
	Johnstown MSA, PA	s	11.54 MW	11.31 AW	24010 AAW	PABLS	10//99-12//99
	Lancaster MSA, PA	s	13.17 MW	12.88 AW	27400 AAW	PABLS	10//99-12//99
	Philadelphia PMSA, PA-NJ	s	13.67 MW	13.49 AW	28430 AAW	PABLS	10//99-12//99
	Pittsburgh MSA, PA	s	13.35 MW	13.21 AW	27770 AAW	PABLS	10//99-12//99
	Reading MSA, PA	s	12.49 MW	12.57 AW	25980 AAW	PABLS	10//99-12//99
	Scranton--Wilkes-Barre--Hazleton MSA, PA	s	12.04 MW	11.34 AW	25050 AAW	PABLS	10//99-12//99
	Rhode Island	s	15.81 MW	15.75 AW	32750 AAW	RIBLS	10//99-12//99
	Providence-Fall River-Warwick MSA, RI-MA	s	15.53 MW	15.63 AW	32300 AAW	RIBLS	10//99-12//99
	South Carolina	s	11.88 MW	11.97 AW	24910 AAW	SCBLS	10//99-12//99
	Charleston-North Charleston MSA, SC	s	12.85 MW	12.96 AW	26740 AAW	SCBLS	10//99-12//99
	Columbia MSA, SC	s	12.20 MW	11.88 AW	25380 AAW	SCBLS	10//99-12//99
	Greenville-Spartanburg-Anderson MSA, SC	s	11.54 MW	11.23 AW	24010 AAW	SCBLS	10//99-12//99
	South Dakota	s	12.08 MW	12.45 AW	25900 AAW	SDBLS	10//99-12//99
	Tennessee	s	12.19 MW	12.29 AW	25560 AAW	TNBLS	10//99-12//99
	Johnson City-Kingsport-Bristol MSA, TN-VA	s	11.78 MW	11.94 AW	24500 AAW	TNBLS	10//99-12//99
	Knoxville MSA, TN	s	11.00 MW	11.26 AW	22870 AAW	TNBLS	10//99-12//99
	Memphis MSA, TN-AR-MS	s	12.93 MW	13.75 AW	26890 AAW	MSBLS	10//99-12//99
	Nashville MSA, TN	s	13.42 MW	12.99 AW	27910 AAW	TNBLS	10//99-12//99
	Texas	s	11.67 MW	11.75 AW	24450 AAW	TXBLS	10//99-12//99
	Austin-San Marcos MSA, TX	s	13.40 MW	13.93 AW	27880 AAW	TXBLS	10//99-12//99
	Beaumont-Port Arthur MSA, TX	s	12.13 MW	12.17 AW	25240 AAW	TXBLS	10//99-12//99
	Corpus Christi MSA, TX	s	12.01 MW	11.96 AW	24980 AAW	TXBLS	10//99-12//99
	Dallas PMSA, TX	s	12.04 MW	12.13 AW	25040 AAW	TXBLS	10//99-12//99
	El Paso MSA, TX	s	11.80 MW	11.62 AW	24550 AAW	TXBLS	10//99-12//99
	Fort Worth-Arlington PMSA, TX	s	10.76 MW	10.15 AW	22390 AAW	TXBLS	10//99-12//99
	Houston PMSA, TX	s	12.18 MW	12.33 AW	25330 AAW	TXBLS	10//99-12//99
	Killeen-Temple MSA, TX	s	11.20 MW	10.69 AW	23290 AAW	TXBLS	10//99-12//99
	Longview-Marshall MSA, TX	s	11.60 MW	11.42 AW	24120 AAW	TXBLS	10//99-12//99
	Lubbock MSA, TX	s	10.07 MW	9.69 AW	20950 AAW	TXBLS	10//99-12//99

AAW Average annual wage	**AOH** Average offered, high	**ASH** Average starting, high	**H** Hourly	**M** Monthly	**S** Special: hourly and annual
AE Average entry wage	**AOL** Average offered, low	**ASL** Average starting, low	**HI** Highest wage paid	**MTC** Median total compensation	**TQ** Third quartile wage
AEX Average experienced wage	**APH** Average pay, high range	**AW** Average wage paid	**HR** High end range	**MW** Median wage paid	**W** Weekly
AO Average offered	**APL** Average pay, low range	**FQ** First quartile wage	**LR** Low end range	**SQ** Second quartile wage	**Y** Yearly

Occupation/Type/Industry	Location	Per	Low	Mid	High	Source	Date
Surgical Technologist	McAllen-Edinburg-Mission MSA, TX	S	10.40 MW	9.50 AW	21630 AAW	TXBLS	10//99-12//99
	San Antonio MSA, TX	S	11.32 MW	11.24 AW	23540 AAW	TXBLS	10//99-12//99
	Tyler MSA, TX	S	11.55 MW	11.57 AW	24030 AAW	TXBLS	10//99-12//99
	Utah	S	11.92 MW	12.35 AW	25680 AAW	UTBLS	10//99-12//99
	Salt Lake City-Ogden MSA, UT	S	12.61 MW	12.23 AW	26240 AAW	UTBLS	10//99-12//99
	Virginia	S	12.52 MW	12.89 AW	26810 AAW	VABLS	10//99-12//99
	Norfolk-Virginia Beach-Newport News MSA, VA-NC	S	12.47 MW	11.94 AW	25950 AAW	VABLS	10//99-12//99
	Richmond-Petersburg MSA, VA	S	13.00 MW	12.85 AW	27040 AAW	VABLS	10//99-12//99
	Washington	S	14.39 MW	14.71 AW	30600 AAW	WABLS	10//99-12//99
	Bellingham MSA, WA	S	13.94 MW	13.79 AW	28990 AAW	WABLS	10//99-12//99
	Olympia PMSA, WA	S	13.68 MW	13.52 AW	28460 AAW	WABLS	10//99-12//99
	Seattle-Bellevue-Everett PMSA, WA	S	15.45 MW	14.89 AW	32130 AAW	WABLS	10//99-12//99
	Spokane MSA, WA	S	14.78 MW	14.73 AW	30750 AAW	WABLS	10//99-12//99
	Yakima MSA, WA	S	14.47 MW	14.64 AW	30100 AAW	WABLS	10//99-12//99
	West Virginia	S	11.63 MW	12.06 AW	25080 AAW	WVBLS	10//99-12//99
	Charleston MSA, WV	S	12.34 MW	11.65 AW	25660 AAW	WVBLS	10//99-12//99
	Huntington-Ashland MSA, WV-KY-OH	S	12.17 MW	11.81 AW	25310 AAW	WVBLS	10//99-12//99
	Wheeling MSA, WV-OH	S	12.24 MW	11.85 AW	25460 AAW	WVBLS	10//99-12//99
	Wisconsin	S	13.07 MW	13.42 AW	27910 AAW	WIBLS	10//99-12//99
	Appleton-Oshkosh-Neenah MSA, WI	S	12.92 MW	12.81 AW	26880 AAW	WIBLS	10//99-12//99
	Green Bay MSA, WI	S	13.28 MW	12.88 AW	27610 AAW	WIBLS	10//99-12//99
	Janesville-Beloit MSA, WI	S	14.36 MW	13.40 AW	29860 AAW	WIBLS	10//99-12//99
	Madison MSA, WI	S	13.47 MW	13.26 AW	28010 AAW	WIBLS	10//99-12//99
	Milwaukee-Waukesha PMSA, WI	S	13.59 MW	13.26 AW	28270 AAW	WIBLS	10//99-12//99
	Wyoming	S	11.49 MW	11.60 AW	24120 AAW	WYBLS	10//99-12//99
	Puerto Rico	S	6.27 MW	6.59 AW	13700 AAW	PRBLS	10//99-12//99
	San Juan-Bayamon PMSA, PR	S	6.58 MW	6.23 AW	13690 AAW	PRBLS	10//99-12//99
Survey Researcher	Alabama	S	12.69 MW	12.59 AW	26180 AAW	ALBLS	10//99-12//99
	Alaska	S	12.46 MW	14.27 AW	29680 AAW	AKBLS	10//99-12//99
	Arizona	S	15.96 MW	16.17 AW	33630 AAW	AZBLS	10//99-12//99
	California	S	8.14 MW	10.22 AW	21270 AAW	CABLS	10//99-12//99
	Colorado	S	8.2 MW	9.63 AW	20030 AAW	COBLS	10//99-12//99
	Connecticut	S	21.57 MW	22.07 AW	45900 AAW	CTBLS	10//99-12//99
	District of Columbia	S	19.24 MW	22.95 AW	47740 AAW	DCBLS	10//99-12//99
	Florida	S	10.94 MW	11.56 AW	24050 AAW	FLBLS	10//99-12//99
	Georgia	S	9.69 MW	9.85 AW	20480 AAW	GABLS	10//99-12//99
	Hawaii	S	12.51 MW	12.77 AW	26560 AAW	HIBLS	10//99-12//99
	Illinois	S	7.93 MW	11.06 AW	23010 AAW	ILBLS	10//99-12//99
	Indiana	S	8.13 MW	9.17 AW	19070 AAW	INBLS	10//99-12//99
	Maine	S	12.84 MW	12.86 AW	26750 AAW	MEBLS	10//99-12//99
	Maryland	S	13.38 MW	14.15 AW	29440 AAW	MDBLS	10//99-12//99
	Michigan	S	7.85 MW	8.51 AW	17700 AAW	MIBLS	10//99-12//99
	Minnesota	S	14.81 MW	17.38 AW	36140 AAW	MNBLS	10//99-12//99
	Missouri	S	14.25 MW	13.83 AW	28780 AAW	MOBLS	10//99-12//99
	Montana	S	7.95 MW	8.38 AW	17430 AAW	MTBLS	10//99-12//99
	Nevada	S	7.64 MW	7.57 AW	15750 AAW	NVBLS	10//99-12//99
	New Jersey	S	16.32 MW	18.92 AW	39350 AAW	NJBLS	10//99-12//99
	North Carolina	S	9.34 MW	10.25 AW	21320 AAW	NCBLS	10//99-12//99
	Oklahoma	S	15.22 MW	15.10 AW	31400 AAW	OKBLS	10//99-12//99
	Oregon	S	19.62 MW	22.10 AW	45960 AAW	ORBLS	10//99-12//99
	Pennsylvania	S	17.47 MW	19.67 AW	40910 AAW	PABLS	10//99-12//99
	South Carolina	S	8.41 MW	10.04 AW	20880 AAW	SCBLS	10//99-12//99
	Utah	S	8.42 MW	9.35 AW	19450 AAW	UTBLS	10//99-12//99
	Virginia	S	12.89 MW	15.93 AW	33130 AAW	VABLS	10//99-12//99
	Washington	S	9.24 MW	10.82 AW	22500 AAW	WABLS	10//99-12//99
	Wisconsin	S	7.4 MW	7.61 AW	15830 AAW	WIBLS	10//99-12//99
Survey Technician	United States	H		16.04 AW		NCS98	1998
Surveying and Mapping Technician	Alabama	S	10.26 MW	11.18 AW	23250 AAW	ALBLS	10//99-12//99
	Alaska	S	18.33 MW	19.00 AW	39530 AAW	AKBLS	10//99-12//99

Occupation/Type/Industry	Location	Per	Low	Mid	High	Source	Date
Surveying and Mapping Technician	Arizona	S	16.08 MW	16.93 AW	35220 AAW	AZBLS	10//99-12//99
	Arkansas	S	10.61 MW	10.93 AW	22730 AAW	ARBLS	10//99-12//99
	California	S	21.4 MW	21.81 AW	45370 AAW	CABLS	10//99-12//99
	Colorado	S	14.75 MW	15.25 AW	31710 AAW	COBLS	10//99-12//99
	Connecticut	S	13.9 MW	14.72 AW	30620 AAW	CTBLS	10//99-12//99
	Delaware	S	12.4 MW	13.16 AW	27370 AAW	DEBLS	10//99-12//99
	District of Columbia	S	15.5 MW	15.47 AW	32170 AAW	DCBLS	10//99-12//99
	Florida	S	10.73 MW	11.78 AW	24500 AAW	FLBLS	10//99-12//99
	Georgia	S	12.04 MW	12.63 AW	26270 AAW	GABLS	10//99-12//99
	Hawaii	S	15.58 MW	16.46 AW	34230 AAW	HIBLS	10//99-12//99
	Idaho	S	12.39 MW	12.47 AW	25930 AAW	IDBLS	10//99-12//99
	Illinois	S	12.71 MW	13.49 AW	28070 AAW	ILBLS	10//99-12//99
	Indiana	S	12.35 MW	13.03 AW	27110 AAW	INBLS	10//99-12//99
	Iowa	S	14.99 MW	15.65 AW	32560 AAW	IABLS	10//99-12//99
	Kansas	S	11.93 MW	13.16 AW	27370 AAW	KSBLS	10//99-12//99
	Kentucky	S	10.61 MW	11.84 AW	24630 AAW	KYBLS	10//99-12//99
	Louisiana	S	11.1 MW	12.90 AW	26820 AAW	LABLS	10//99-12//99
	Maine	S	15.31 MW	14.82 AW	30820 AAW	MEBLS	10//99-12//99
	Maryland	S	15.35 MW	14.79 AW	30760 AAW	MDBLS	10//99-12//99
	Massachusetts	S	16.72 MW	16.76 AW	34850 AAW	MABLS	10//99-12//99
	Michigan	S	14.04 MW	13.99 AW	29100 AAW	MIBLS	10//99-12//99
	Minnesota	S	14.89 MW	15.27 AW	31770 AAW	MNBLS	10//99-12//99
	Mississippi	S	10.02 MW	10.98 AW	22840 AAW	MSBLS	10//99-12//99
	Missouri	S	13.93 MW	14.94 AW	31070 AAW	MOBLS	10//99-12//99
	Montana	S	12.89 MW	14.12 AW	29370 AAW	MTBLS	10//99-12//99
	Nebraska	S	11.27 MW	12.54 AW	26090 AAW	NEBLS	10//99-12//99
	Nevada	S	17.98 MW	18.89 AW	39290 AAW	NVBLS	10//99-12//99
	New Hampshire	S	13.04 MW	14.28 AW	29700 AAW	NHBLS	10//99-12//99
	New Jersey	S	14.38 MW	15.90 AW	33070 AAW	NJBLS	10//99-12//99
	New Mexico	S	12.46 MW	14.49 AW	30130 AAW	NMBLS	10//99-12//99
	New York	S	12.7 MW	14.53 AW	30220 AAW	NYBLS	10//99-12//99
	North Carolina	S	11.41 MW	12.11 AW	25180 AAW	NCBLS	10//99-12//99
	North Dakota	S	11.04 MW	12.94 AW	26910 AAW	NDBLS	10//99-12//99
	Ohio	S	12.57 MW	13.35 AW	27760 AAW	OHBLS	10//99-12//99
	Oklahoma	S	13.73 MW	14.16 AW	29460 AAW	OKBLS	10//99-12//99
	Oregon	S	15.22 MW	15.47 AW	32180 AAW	ORBLS	10//99-12//99
	Pennsylvania	S	13.25 MW	14.01 AW	29150 AAW	PABLS	10//99-12//99
	South Carolina	S	12.01 MW	12.10 AW	25170 AAW	SCBLS	10//99-12//99
	South Dakota	S	10.11 MW	10.71 AW	22270 AAW	SDBLS	10//99-12//99
	Tennessee	S	11.7 MW	12.55 AW	26100 AAW	TNBLS	10//99-12//99
	Texas	S	11.07 MW	12.74 AW	26500 AAW	TXBLS	10//99-12//99
	Utah	S	13.25 MW	13.91 AW	28940 AAW	UTBLS	10//99-12//99
	Vermont	S	11.54 MW	12.55 AW	26110 AAW	VTBLS	10//99-12//99
	Virginia	S	13.03 MW	13.28 AW	27620 AAW	VABLS	10//99-12//99
	Washington	S	17.97 MW	18.32 AW	38110 AAW	WABLS	10//99-12//99
	West Virginia	S	10.71 MW	12.13 AW	25230 AAW	WVBLS	10//99-12//99
	Wisconsin	S	12.19 MW	12.80 AW	26630 AAW	WIBLS	10//99-12//99
	Wyoming	S	11.41 MW	12.64 AW	26300 AAW	WYBLS	10//99-12//99
	Puerto Rico	S	6.7 MW	7.83 AW	16290 AAW	PRBLS	10//99-12//99
Surveyor	Alabama	S	8 MW	11.21 AW	23320 AAW	ALBLS	10//99-12//99
	Dothan MSA, AL	S	10.95 MW	9.43 AW	22780 AAW	ALBLS	10//99-12//99
	Mobile MSA, AL	S	8.07 MW	7.68 AW	16780 AAW	ALBLS	10//99-12//99
	Tuscaloosa MSA, AL	S	13.79 MW	10.97 AW	28680 AAW	ALBLS	10//99-12//99
	Alaska	S	22.7 MW	22.97 AW	47790 AAW	AKBLS	10//99-12//99
	Anchorage MSA, AK	S	22.74 MW	22.43 AW	47310 AAW	AKBLS	10//99-12//99
	Arizona	S	15.19 MW	16.38 AW	34060 AAW	AZBLS	10//99-12//99
	Flagstaff MSA, AZ-UT	S	18.30 MW	15.61 AW	38060 AAW	AZBLS	10//99-12//99
	Phoenix-Mesa MSA, AZ	S	18.14 MW	17.48 AW	37730 AAW	AZBLS	10//99-12//99
	Tucson MSA, AZ	S	11.91 MW	10.61 AW	24780 AAW	AZBLS	10//99-12//99
	Yuma MSA, AZ	S	24.05 MW	24.38 AW	50030 AAW	AZBLS	10//99-12//99
	Arkansas	S	16.38 MW	15.17 AW	31550 AAW	ARBLS	10//99-12//99
	Little Rock-North Little Rock MSA, AR	S	16.80 MW	18.09 AW	34950 AAW	ARBLS	10//99-12//99
	California	S	26.54 MW	25.66 AW	53380 AAW	CABLS	10//99-12//99
	Bakersfield MSA, CA	S	18.75 MW	16.98 AW	38990 AAW	CABLS	10//99-12//99
	Fresno MSA, CA	S	18.91 MW	17.21 AW	39320 AAW	CABLS	10//99-12//99
	Los Angeles-Long Beach PMSA, CA	S	28.36 MW	28.62 AW	58990 AAW	CABLS	10//99-12//99
	Oakland PMSA, CA	S	29.26 MW	29.83 AW	60850 AAW	CABLS	10//99-12//99
	Orange County PMSA, CA	S	27.44 MW	28.16 AW	57080 AAW	CABLS	10//99-12//99

AAW	Average annual wage	AOH	Average offered, high	ASH	Average starting, high	H	Hourly	M	Monthly	S	Special: hourly and annual
AE	Average entry wage	AOL	Average offered, low	ASL	Average starting, low	HI	Highest wage paid	MTC	Median total compensation	TQ	Third quartile wage
AEX	Average experienced wage	APH	Average pay, high range	AW	Average wage paid	HR	High end range	MW	Median wage paid	W	Weekly
AO	Average offered	APL	Average pay, low range	FQ	First quartile wage	LR	Low end range	SQ	Second quartile wage	Y	Yearly

Occupation/Type/Industry	Location	Per	Low	Mid	High	Source	Date
Surveyor	Riverside-San Bernardino PMSA, CA	S	21.91 MW	22.77 AW	45570 AAW	CABLS	10//99-12//99
	Sacramento PMSA, CA	S	33.66 MW	33.98 AW	70020 AAW	CABLS	10//99-12//99
	San Diego MSA, CA	S	26.18 MW	27.44 AW	54460 AAW	CABLS	10//99-12//99
	San Francisco PMSA, CA	S	26.09 MW	26.00 AW	54260 AAW	CABLS	10//99-12//99
	San Luis Obispo-Atascadero-Paso Robles MSA, CA	S	21.64 MW	20.44 AW	45020 AAW	CABLS	10//99-12//99
	Stockton-Lodi MSA, CA	S	16.12 MW	13.65 AW	33530 AAW	CABLS	10//99-12//99
	Vallejo-Fairfield-Napa PMSA, CA	S	24.17 MW	23.35 AW	50270 AAW	CABLS	10//99-12//99
	Ventura PMSA, CA	S	22.15 MW	20.52 AW	46070 AAW	CABLS	10//99-12//99
	Colorado	S	16.37 MW	17.35 AW	36090 AAW	COBLS	10//99-12//99
	Boulder-Longmont PMSA, CO	S	17.59 MW	18.57 AW	36580 AAW	COBLS	10//99-12//99
	Denver PMSA, CO	S	17.98 MW	16.82 AW	37410 AAW	COBLS	10//99-12//99
	Greeley PMSA, CO	S	16.60 MW	15.68 AW	34530 AAW	COBLS	10//99-12//99
	Connecticut	S	18.09 MW	19.33 AW	40210 AAW	CTBLS	10//99-12//99
	Bridgeport PMSA, CT	S	21.41 MW	17.95 AW	44540 AAW	CTBLS	10//99-12//99
	Hartford MSA, CT	S	22.95 MW	21.46 AW	47740 AAW	CTBLS	10//99-12//99
	New Haven-Meriden PMSA, CT	S	17.15 MW	17.62 AW	35680 AAW	CTBLS	10//99-12//99
	Waterbury PMSA, CT	S	16.72 MW	16.33 AW	34780 AAW	CTBLS	10//99-12//99
	Delaware	S	16.06 MW	17.57 AW	36560 AAW	DEBLS	10//99-12//99
	Dover MSA, DE	S	14.50 MW	14.76 AW	30160 AAW	DEBLS	10//99-12//99
	Wilmington-Newark PMSA, DE-MD	S	19.11 MW	17.55 AW	39760 AAW	DEBLS	10//99-12//99
	District of Columbia	S	19.39 MW	20.63 AW	42910 AAW	DCBLS	10//99-12//99
	Washington PMSA, DC-MD-VA-WV	S	16.94 MW	16.64 AW	35230 AAW	DCBLS	10//99-12//99
	Florida	S	19.03 MW	19.57 AW	40710 AAW	FLBLS	10//99-12//99
	Fort Lauderdale PMSA, FL	S	23.36 MW	21.34 AW	48580 AAW	FLBLS	10//99-12//99
	Fort Myers-Cape Coral MSA, FL	S	23.08 MW	22.57 AW	48010 AAW	FLBLS	10//99-12//99
	Fort Pierce-Port St. Lucie MSA, FL	S	18.19 MW	18.42 AW	37840 AAW	FLBLS	10//99-12//99
	Fort Walton Beach MSA, FL	S	15.11 MW	15.16 AW	31420 AAW	FLBLS	10//99-12//99
	Gainesville MSA, FL	S	22.36 MW	28.14 AW	46500 AAW	FLBLS	10//99-12//99
	Jacksonville MSA, FL	S	14.80 MW	13.99 AW	30780 AAW	FLBLS	10//99-12//99
	Lakeland-Winter Haven MSA, FL	S	13.72 MW	13.27 AW	28530 AAW	FLBLS	10//99-12//99
	Melbourne-Titusville-Palm Bay MSA, FL	S	16.27 MW	13.00 AW	33840 AAW	FLBLS	10//99-12//99
	Miami PMSA, FL	S	23.89 MW	23.69 AW	49700 AAW	FLBLS	10//99-12//99
	Ocala MSA, FL	S	13.00 MW	10.42 AW	27050 AAW	FLBLS	10//99-12//99
	Orlando MSA, FL	S	17.56 MW	17.69 AW	36530 AAW	FLBLS	10//99-12//99
	Panama City MSA, FL	S	17.58 MW	18.52 AW	36560 AAW	FLBLS	10//99-12//99
	Pensacola MSA, FL	S	12.57 MW	12.36 AW	26150 AAW	FLBLS	10//99-12//99
	Punta Gorda MSA, FL	S	16.71 MW	15.98 AW	34750 AAW	FLBLS	10//99-12//99
	Sarasota-Bradenton MSA, FL	S	20.51 MW	21.73 AW	42650 AAW	FLBLS	10//99-12//99
	Tallahassee MSA, FL	S	19.23 MW	18.90 AW	40010 AAW	FLBLS	10//99-12//99
	Tampa-St. Petersburg-Clearwater MSA, FL	S	20.83 MW	19.86 AW	43330 AAW	FLBLS	10//99-12//99
	West Palm Beach-Boca Raton MSA, FL	S	18.85 MW	18.14 AW	39210 AAW	FLBLS	10//99-12//99
	Georgia	S	20.83 MW	20.79 AW	43240 AAW	GABLS	10//99-12//99
	Atlanta MSA, GA	S	20.85 MW	21.08 AW	43380 AAW	GABLS	10//99-12//99
	Augusta-Aiken MSA, GA-SC	S	24.15 MW	25.02 AW	50240 AAW	GABLS	10//99-12//99
	Hawaii	S	19.72 MW	20.34 AW	42300 AAW	HIBLS	10//99-12//99
	Honolulu MSA, HI	S	21.83 MW	20.60 AW	45400 AAW	HIBLS	10//99-12//99
	Idaho	S	20.5 MW	20.82 AW	43310 AAW	IDBLS	10//99-12//99
	Boise City MSA, ID	S	20.92 MW	20.47 AW	43510 AAW	IDBLS	10//99-12//99
	Illinois	S	18.41 MW	18.37 AW	38220 AAW	ILBLS	10//99-12//99
	Champaign-Urbana MSA, IL	S	14.41 MW	12.47 AW	29970 AAW	ILBLS	10//99-12//99
	Chicago PMSA, IL	S	18.95 MW	18.84 AW	39420 AAW	ILBLS	10//99-12//99
	Indiana	S	13.76 MW	15.11 AW	31420 AAW	INBLS	10//99-12//99
	Evansville-Henderson MSA, IN-KY	S	14.14 MW	11.93 AW	29410 AAW	INBLS	10//99-12//99
	Fort Wayne MSA, IN	S	18.03 MW	16.39 AW	37510 AAW	INBLS	10//99-12//99
	Indianapolis MSA, IN	S	15.10 MW	13.46 AW	31410 AAW	INBLS	10//99-12//99
	Iowa	S	19.6 MW	21.25 AW	44200 AAW	IABLS	10//99-12//99
	Cedar Rapids MSA, IA	S	19.71 MW	18.84 AW	40990 AAW	IABLS	10//99-12//99
	Kansas	S	15.81 MW	16.22 AW	33740 AAW	KSBLS	10//99-12//99
	Wichita MSA, KS	S	17.63 MW	18.18 AW	36670 AAW	KSBLS	10//99-12//99

AAW	Average annual wage	AOH	Average offered, high	ASH	Average starting, high	H	Hourly	M	Monthly	S	Special: hourly and annual
AE	Average entry wage	AOL	Average offered, low	ASL	Average starting, low	HI	Highest wage paid	MTC	Median total compensation	TQ	Third quartile wage
AEX	Average experienced wage	APH	Average pay, high range	AW	Average wage paid	HR	High end range	MW	Median wage paid	W	Weekly
AO	Average offered	APL	Average pay, low range	FQ	First quartile wage	LR	Low end range	SQ	Second quartile wage	Y	Yearly

Occupation/Type/Industry	Location	Per	Low	Mid	High	Source	Date
Surveyor	Kentucky	S	14.97 MW	16.43 AW	34170 AAW	KYBLS	10//99-12//99
	Lexington MSA, KY	S	14.46 MW	13.23 AW	30070 AAW	KYBLS	10//99-12//99
	Louisville MSA, KY-IN	S	24.01 MW	21.64 AW	49930 AAW	KYBLS	10//99-12//99
	Louisiana	S	17.64 MW	18.25 AW	37960 AAW	LABLS	10//99-12//99
	Baton Rouge MSA, LA	S	18.50 MW	18.36 AW	38490 AAW	LABLS	10//99-12//99
	Lafayette MSA, LA	S	15.12 MW	12.80 AW	31460 AAW	LABLS	10//99-12//99
	New Orleans MSA, LA	S	20.41 MW	21.92 AW	42440 AAW	LABLS	10//99-12//99
	Maine	S	18.52 MW	17.25 AW	35880 AAW	MEBLS	10//99-12//99
	Maryland	S	16.96 MW	17.49 AW	36370 AAW	MDBLS	10//99-12//99
	Baltimore PMSA, MD	S	17.50 MW	17.29 AW	36400 AAW	MDBLS	10//99-12//99
	Hagerstown PMSA, MD	S	11.51 MW	9.58 AW	23950 AAW	MDBLS	10//99-12//99
	Massachusetts	S	18.61 MW	19.62 AW	40800 AAW	MABLS	10//99-12//99
	Boston PMSA, MA-NH	S	21.15 MW	20.06 AW	44000 AAW	MABLS	10//99-12//99
	Brockton PMSA, MA	S	23.05 MW	21.50 AW	47950 AAW	MABLS	10//99-12//99
	Fitchburg-Leominster PMSA, MA	S	15.72 MW	17.01 AW	32700 AAW	MABLS	10//99-12//99
	Lawrence PMSA, MA-NH	S	14.43 MW	14.95 AW	30010 AAW	MABLS	10//99-12//99
	Worcester PMSA, MA-CT	S	19.56 MW	18.52 AW	40690 AAW	MABLS	10//99-12//99
	Michigan	S	16.14 MW	16.58 AW	34490 AAW	MIBLS	10//99-12//99
	Ann Arbor PMSA, MI	S	14.78 MW	13.03 AW	30750 AAW	MIBLS	10//99-12//99
	Benton Harbor MSA, MI	S	13.94 MW	13.34 AW	29000 AAW	MIBLS	10//99-12//99
	Detroit PMSA, MI	S	16.13 MW	16.35 AW	33550 AAW	MIBLS	10//99-12//99
	Grand Rapids-Muskegon-Holland MSA, MI	S	17.83 MW	17.07 AW	37080 AAW	MIBLS	10//99-12//99
	Lansing-East Lansing MSA, MI	S	19.24 MW	18.55 AW	40020 AAW	MIBLS	10//99-12//99
	Saginaw-Bay City-Midland MSA, MI	S	16.37 MW	15.36 AW	34040 AAW	MIBLS	10//99-12//99
	Minnesota	S	19.87 MW	20.77 AW	43200 AAW	MNBLS	10//99-12//99
	Minneapolis-St. Paul MSA, MN-WI	S	20.68 MW	19.66 AW	43020 AAW	MNBLS	10//99-12//99
	Mississippi	S	14.63 MW	14.03 AW	29180 AAW	MSBLS	10//99-12//99
	Biloxi-Gulfport-Pascagoula MSA, MS	S	11.69 MW	9.85 AW	24320 AAW	MSBLS	10//99-12//99
	Jackson MSA, MS	S	15.13 MW	14.67 AW	31480 AAW	MSBLS	10//99-12//99
	Missouri	S	15.03 MW	16.33 AW	33960 AAW	MOBLS	10//99-12//99
	St. Louis MSA, MO-IL	S	18.30 MW	16.75 AW	38070 AAW	MOBLS	10//99-12//99
	Springfield MSA, MO	S	12.80 MW	11.92 AW	26610 AAW	MOBLS	10//99-12//99
	Montana	S	16.62 MW	18.00 AW	37440 AAW	MTBLS	10//99-12//99
	Billings MSA, MT	S	15.90 MW	15.31 AW	33060 AAW	MTBLS	10//99-12//99
	Nebraska	S	14.56 MW	14.59 AW	30350 AAW	NEBLS	10//99-12//99
	Lincoln MSA, NE	S	13.92 MW	13.88 AW	28960 AAW	NEBLS	10//99-12//99
	Omaha MSA, NE-IA	S	14.99 MW	14.88 AW	31170 AAW	NEBLS	10//99-12//99
	Nevada	S	25.77 MW	27.09 AW	56350 AAW	NVBLS	10//99-12//99
	Las Vegas MSA, NV-AZ	S	29.35 MW	26.73 AW	61060 AAW	NVBLS	10//99-12//99
	Reno MSA, NV	S	25.78 MW	25.27 AW	53630 AAW	NVBLS	10//99-12//99
	New Hampshire	S	18.01 MW	17.36 AW	36110 AAW	NHBLS	10//99-12//99
	New Jersey	S	20.37 MW	21.76 AW	45260 AAW	NJBLS	10//99-12//99
	Bergen-Passaic PMSA, NJ	S	23.78 MW	22.29 AW	49450 AAW	NJBLS	10//99-12//99
	Middlesex-Somerset-Hunterdon PMSA, NJ	S	21.49 MW	19.63 AW	44710 AAW	NJBLS	10//99-12//99
	Monmouth-Ocean PMSA, NJ	S	19.68 MW	19.92 AW	40930 AAW	NJBLS	10//99-12//99
	Newark PMSA, NJ	S	23.36 MW	20.47 AW	48580 AAW	NJBLS	10//99-12//99
	New Mexico	S	12.6 MW	13.04 AW	27130 AAW	NMBLS	10//99-12//99
	Albuquerque MSA, NM	S	14.76 MW	14.83 AW	30710 AAW	NMBLS	10//99-12//99
	Las Cruces MSA, NM	S	9.96 MW	8.49 AW	20710 AAW	NMBLS	10//99-12//99
	Santa Fe MSA, NM	S	16.43 MW	15.35 AW	34170 AAW	NMBLS	10//99-12//99
	New York	S	18.64 MW	19.70 AW	40970 AAW	NYBLS	10//99-12//99
	Albany-Schenectady-Troy MSA, NY	S	20.02 MW	19.88 AW	41640 AAW	NYBLS	10//99-12//99
	Buffalo-Niagara Falls MSA, NY	S	24.47 MW	24.89 AW	50910 AAW	NYBLS	10//99-12//99
	Nassau-Suffolk PMSA, NY	S	25.14 MW	24.80 AW	52290 AAW	NYBLS	10//99-12//99
	New York PMSA, NY	S	17.27 MW	14.97 AW	35920 AAW	NYBLS	10//99-12//99
	Rochester MSA, NY	S	19.06 MW	18.35 AW	39640 AAW	NYBLS	10//99-12//99
	North Carolina	S	13.42 MW	15.61 AW	32480 AAW	NCBLS	10//99-12//99
	Charlotte-Gastonia-Rock Hill MSA, NC-SC	S	14.23 MW	11.72 AW	29600 AAW	NCBLS	10//99-12//99
	Fayetteville MSA, NC	S	19.23 MW	19.00 AW	39990 AAW	NCBLS	10//99-12//99
	Greensboro--Winston-Salem--High Point MSA, NC	S	14.71 MW	14.02 AW	30590 AAW	NCBLS	10//99-12//99
	Greenville MSA, NC	S	13.16 MW	11.56 AW	27360 AAW	NCBLS	10//99-12//99

AAW	Average annual wage	AOH	Average offered, high	ASH	Average starting, high
AE	Average entry wage	AOL	Average offered, low	ASL	Average starting, low
AEX	Average experienced wage	APH	Average pay, high range	AW	Average wage paid
AO	Average offered	APL	Average pay, low range	FQ	First quartile wage

H	Hourly	M	Monthly
HI	Highest wage paid	MTC	Median total compensation
HR	High end range	MW	Median wage paid
LR	Low end range	SQ	Second quartile wage

S	Special: hourly and annual
TQ	Third quartile wage
W	Weekly
Y	Yearly

Occupation/Type/Industry	Location	Per	Low	Mid	High	Source	Date
Surveyor	Raleigh-Durham-Chapel Hill						
	MSA, NC	S	20.65 MW	20.14 AW	42960 AAW	NCBLS	10//99-12//99
	Wilmington MSA, NC	S	10.58 MW	11.01 AW	22000 AAW	NCBLS	10//99-12//99
	North Dakota	S	15.63 MW	16.41 AW	34120 AAW	NDBLS	10//99-12//99
	Grand Forks MSA, ND-MN	S	16.52 MW	13.45 AW	34360 AAW	NDBLS	10//99-12//99
	Ohio	S	14.92 MW	16.46 AW	34240 AAW	OHBLS	10//99-12//99
	Akron PMSA, OH	S	12.89 MW	11.87 AW	26820 AAW	OHBLS	10//99-12//99
	Canton-Massillon MSA, OH	S	12.42 MW	11.05 AW	25830 AAW	OHBLS	10//99-12//99
	Cleveland-Lorain-Elyria						
	PMSA, OH	S	16.10 MW	14.07 AW	33490 AAW	OHBLS	10//99-12//99
	Columbus MSA, OH	S	15.84 MW	16.03 AW	32950 AAW	OHBLS	10//99-12//99
	Dayton-Springfield MSA, OH	S	17.08 MW	17.21 AW	35530 AAW	OHBLS	10//99-12//99
	Youngstown-Warren MSA, OH	S	17.22 MW	15.82 AW	35820 AAW	OHBLS	10//99-12//99
	Oklahoma	S	11.99 MW	13.24 AW	27550 AAW	OKBLS	10//99-12//99
	Oklahoma City MSA, OK	S	13.33 MW	11.98 AW	27720 AAW	OKBLS	10//99-12//99
	Oregon	S	19.37 MW	19.54 AW	40640 AAW	ORBLS	10//99-12//99
	Corvallis MSA, OR	S	17.20 MW	15.35 AW	35770 AAW	ORBLS	10//99-12//99
	Eugene-Springfield MSA, OR	S	22.19 MW	23.01 AW	46150 AAW	ORBLS	10//99-12//99
	Medford-Ashland MSA, OR	S	16.14 MW	16.88 AW	33570 AAW	ORBLS	10//99-12//99
	Portland-Vancouver PMSA,						
	OR-WA	S	18.94 MW	18.70 AW	39390 AAW	ORBLS	10//99-12//99
	Salem PMSA, OR	S	22.99 MW	23.19 AW	47820 AAW	ORBLS	10//99-12//99
	Pennsylvania	S	16.37 MW	16.70 AW	34730 AAW	PABLS	10//99-12//99
	Allentown-Bethlehem-Easton						
	MSA, PA	S	18.21 MW	16.85 AW	37870 AAW	PABLS	10//99-12//99
	Harrisburg-Lebanon-Carlisle						
	MSA, PA	S	17.77 MW	17.83 AW	36960 AAW	PABLS	10//99-12//99
	Johnstown MSA, PA	S	9.98 MW	9.89 AW	20750 AAW	PABLS	10//99-12//99
	Lancaster MSA, PA	S	16.83 MW	16.06 AW	35000 AAW	PABLS	10//99-12//99
	Philadelphia PMSA, PA-NJ	S	18.56 MW	18.43 AW	38600 AAW	PABLS	10//99-12//99
	Pittsburgh MSA, PA	S	14.74 MW	13.93 AW	30670 AAW	PABLS	10//99-12//99
	Scranton--Wilkes-Barre--						
	Hazleton MSA, PA	S	15.98 MW	15.33 AW	33230 AAW	PABLS	10//99-12//99
	York MSA, PA	S	16.70 MW	15.68 AW	34730 AAW	PABLS	10//99-12//99
	Rhode Island	S	16.69 MW	17.86 AW	37150 AAW	RIBLS	10//99-12//99
	Providence-Fall River-						
	Warwick MSA, RI-MA	S	18.23 MW	17.44 AW	37920 AAW	RIBLS	10//99-12//99
	South Carolina	S	14.43 MW	15.24 AW	31700 AAW	SCBLS	10//99-12//99
	Charleston-North Charleston						
	MSA, SC	S	16.40 MW	15.85 AW	34120 AAW	SCBLS	10//99-12//99
	Myrtle Beach MSA, SC	S	13.85 MW	11.98 AW	28820 AAW	SCBLS	10//99-12//99
	Sumter MSA, SC	S	18.27 MW	22.00 AW	38000 AAW	SCBLS	10//99-12//99
	South Dakota	S	13.33 MW	14.07 AW	29260 AAW	SDBLS	10//99-12//99
	Tennessee	S	12.28 MW	13.21 AW	27470 AAW	TNBLS	10//99-12//99
	Chattanooga MSA, TN-GA	S	13.89 MW	12.45 AW	28900 AAW	TNBLS	10//99-12//99
	Johnson City-Kingsport-Bristol						
	MSA, TN-VA	S	10.70 MW	10.29 AW	22250 AAW	TNBLS	10//99-12//99
	Knoxville MSA, TN	S	13.88 MW	13.27 AW	28860 AAW	TNBLS	10//99-12//99
	Memphis MSA, TN-AR-MS	S	14.86 MW	14.92 AW	30900 AAW	MSBLS	10//99-12//99
	Nashville MSA, TN	S	19.13 MW	19.73 AW	39790 AAW	TNBLS	10//99-12//99
	Texas	S	11.67 MW	13.99 AW	29110 AAW	TXBLS	10//99-12//99
	Abilene MSA, TX	S	10.55 MW	9.23 AW	21940 AAW	TXBLS	10//99-12//99
	Amarillo MSA, TX	S	15.49 MW	17.57 AW	32210 AAW	TXBLS	10//99-12//99
	Austin-San Marcos MSA, TX	S	14.30 MW	12.01 AW	29730 AAW	TXBLS	10//99-12//99
	Brazoria PMSA, TX	S	17.41 MW	18.78 AW	36210 AAW	TXBLS	10//99-12//99
	Dallas PMSA, TX	S	17.13 MW	15.34 AW	35620 AAW	TXBLS	10//99-12//99
	Fort Worth-Arlington PMSA,						
	TX	S	19.87 MW	17.01 AW	41340 AAW	TXBLS	10//99-12//99
	Houston PMSA, TX	S	13.41 MW	11.14 AW	27900 AAW	TXBLS	10//99-12//99
	Killeen-Temple MSA, TX	S	12.30 MW	12.05 AW	25580 AAW	TXBLS	10//99-12//99
	Longview-Marshall MSA, TX	S	19.14 MW	18.02 AW	39810 AAW	TXBLS	10//99-12//99
	McAllen-Edinburg-Mission						
	MSA, TX	S	8.90 MW	8.49 AW	18520 AAW	TXBLS	10//99-12//99
	San Antonio MSA, TX	S	12.92 MW	10.26 AW	26870 AAW	TXBLS	10//99-12//99
	Wichita Falls MSA, TX	S	13.15 MW	12.35 AW	27350 AAW	TXBLS	10//99-12//99
	Utah	S	15.48 MW	15.34 AW	31910 AAW	UTBLS	10//99-12//99
	Salt Lake City-Ogden MSA,						
	UT	S	17.72 MW	18.22 AW	36860 AAW	UTBLS	10//99-12//99
	Vermont	S	18.45 MW	18.36 AW	38180 AAW	VTBLS	10//99-12//99
	Burlington MSA, VT	S	17.21 MW	17.70 AW	35800 AAW	VTBLS	10//99-12//99
	Virginia	S	15.55 MW	15.80 AW	32860 AAW	VABLS	10//99-12//99

AAW	Average annual wage	AOH	Average offered, high	ASH	Average starting, high
AE	Average entry wage	AOL	Average offered, low	ASL	Average starting, low
AEX	Average experienced wage	APH	Average pay, high range	AW	Average wage paid
AO	Average offered	APL	Average pay, low range	FQ	First quartile wage

H	Hourly	M	Monthly	S	Special: hourly and annual
HI	Highest wage paid	MTC	Median total compensation	TQ	Third quartile wage
HR	High end range	MW	Median wage paid	W	Weekly
LR	Low end range	SQ	Second quartile wage	Y	Yearly

Occupation/Type/Industry	Location	Per	Low	Mid	High	Source	Date
Surveyor	Norfolk-Virginia Beach-Newport News MSA, VA-NC	S	18.64 MW	18.41 AW	38760 AAW	VABLS	10//99-12//99
	Richmond-Petersburg MSA, VA	S	15.23 MW	14.88 AW	31680 AAW	VABLS	10//99-12//99
	Roanoke MSA, VA	S	18.29 MW	18.49 AW	38040 AAW	VABLS	10//99-12//99
	Washington	S	20.33 MW	24.95 AW	51890 AAW	WABLS	10//99-12//99
	Olympia PMSA, WA	S	23.23 MW	21.51 AW	48310 AAW	WABLS	10//99-12//99
	Seattle-Bellevue-Everett PMSA, WA	S	29.47 MW	22.56 AW	61300 AAW	WABLS	10//99-12//99
	Tacoma PMSA, WA	S	21.21 MW	20.04 AW	44120 AAW	WABLS	10//99-12//99
	Yakima MSA, WA	S	19.02 MW	19.05 AW	39570 AAW	WABLS	10//99-12//99
	West Virginia	S	10.28 MW	11.43 AW	23770 AAW	WVBLS	10//99-12//99
	Huntington-Ashland MSA, WV-KY-OH	S	14.76 MW	15.41 AW	30690 AAW	WVBLS	10//99-12//99
	Wisconsin	S	17.91 MW	17.39 AW	36160 AAW	WIBLS	10//99-12//99
	Milwaukee-Waukesha PMSA, WI	S	16.14 MW	16.67 AW	33570 AAW	WIBLS	10//99-12//99
	Wausau MSA, WI	S	16.24 MW	17.89 AW	33770 AAW	WIBLS	10//99-12//99
	Wyoming	S	20.5 MW	19.76 AW	41090 AAW	WYBLS	10//99-12//99
	Puerto Rico	S	10.38 MW	10.90 AW	22660 AAW	PRBLS	10//99-12//99
	Caguas PMSA, PR	S	8.30 MW	8.04 AW	17270 AAW	PRBLS	10//99-12//99
	Ponce MSA, PR	S	8.37 MW	7.83 AW	17410 AAW	PRBLS	10//99-12//99
	San Juan-Bayamon PMSA, PR	S	11.41 MW	10.93 AW	23720 AAW	PRBLS	10//99-12//99
Surveyor and Mapping Scientist	United States	H		21.23 AW		NCS98	1998
Switchboard Operator							
Including Answering Service	Alabama	S	8.12 MW	8.36 AW	17390 AAW	ALBLS	10//99-12//99
Including Answering Service	Alaska	S	10.98 MW	11.30 AW	23500 AAW	AKBLS	10//99-12//99
Including Answering Service	Arizona	S	9.44 MW	9.61 AW	19980 AAW	AZBLS	10//99-12//99
Including Answering Service	Arkansas	S	7.71 MW	8.75 AW	18200 AAW	ARBLS	10//99-12//99
Including Answering Service	California	S	9.76 MW	10.21 AW	21230 AAW	CABLS	10//99-12//99
Including Answering Service	Colorado	S	9.12 MW	9.34 AW	19420 AAW	COBLS	10//99-12//99
Including Answering Service	Connecticut	S	10.22 MW	10.52 AW	21880 AAW	CTBLS	10//99-12//99
Including Answering Service	Delaware	S	9.53 MW	9.67 AW	20100 AAW	DEBLS	10//99-12//99
Including Answering Service	District of Columbia	S	11.27 MW	11.30 AW	23500 AAW	DCBLS	10//99-12//99
Including Answering Service	Florida	S	7.98 MW	8.22 AW	17100 AAW	FLBLS	10//99-12//99
Including Answering Service	Georgia	S	8.78 MW	9.04 AW	18800 AAW	GABLS	10//99-12//99
Including Answering Service	Hawaii	S	11.82 MW	11.54 AW	24010 AAW	HIBLS	10//99-12//99
Including Answering Service	Idaho	S	7.82 MW	8.06 AW	16770 AAW	IDBLS	10//99-12//99
Including Answering Service	Illinois	S	9.34 MW	9.49 AW	19750 AAW	ILBLS	10//99-12//99
Including Answering Service	Indiana	S	8.49 MW	8.67 AW	18030 AAW	INBLS	10//99-12//99
Including Answering Service	Iowa	S	8.95 MW	9.65 AW	20080 AAW	IABLS	10//99-12//99
Including Answering Service	Kansas	S	8.56 MW	9.44 AW	19630 AAW	KSBLS	10//99-12//99
Including Answering Service	Kentucky	S	8.42 MW	8.74 AW	18190 AAW	KYBLS	10//99-12//99
Including Answering Service	Louisiana	S	7.52 MW	7.69 AW	15990 AAW	LABLS	10//99-12//99
Including Answering Service	Maine	S	8.76 MW	8.91 AW	18540 AAW	MEBLS	10//99-12//99
Including Answering Service	Maryland	S	9.36 MW	9.54 AW	19850 AAW	MDBLS	10//99-12//99
Including Answering Service	Massachusetts	S	10.73 MW	11.38 AW	23670 AAW	MABLS	10//99-12//99
Including Answering Service	Michigan	S	9.68 MW	9.92 AW	20630 AAW	MIBLS	10//99-12//99
Including Answering Service	Minnesota	S	10.1 MW	10.16 AW	21140 AAW	MNBLS	10//99-12//99
Including Answering Service	Mississippi	S	7.99 MW	8.20 AW	17050 AAW	MSBLS	10//99-12//99
Including Answering Service	Missouri	S	8.56 MW	9.23 AW	19200 AAW	MOBLS	10//99-12//99
Including Answering Service	Montana	S	7.71 MW	8.00 AW	16640 AAW	MTBLS	10//99-12//99
Including Answering Service	Nebraska	S	8.9 MW	9.31 AW	19370 AAW	NEBLS	10//99-12//99
Including Answering Service	Nevada	S	10.21 MW	9.99 AW	20780 AAW	NVBLS	10//99-12//99
Including Answering Service	New Hampshire	S	8.99 MW	9.27 AW	19280 AAW	NHBLS	10//99-12//99
Including Answering Service	New Jersey	S	10.6 MW	10.55 AW	21930 AAW	NJBLS	10//99-12//99
Including Answering Service	New Mexico	S	8.24 MW	8.46 AW	17590 AAW	NMBLS	10//99-12//99
Including Answering Service	New York	S	10.17 MW	10.76 AW	22370 AAW	NYBLS	10//99-12//99
Including Answering Service	North Carolina	S	9.21 MW	9.43 AW	19620 AAW	NCBLS	10//99-12//99
Including Answering Service	North Dakota	S	7.76 MW	7.83 AW	16280 AAW	NDBLS	10//99-12//99
Including Answering Service	Ohio	S	9.25 MW	9.36 AW	19470 AAW	OHBLS	10//99-12//99
Including Answering Service	Oklahoma	S	8.14 MW	9.04 AW	18800 AAW	OKBLS	10//99-12//99
Including Answering Service	Oregon	S	9.33 MW	9.47 AW	19690 AAW	ORBLS	10//99-12//99
Including Answering Service	Pennsylvania	S	9.24 MW	9.47 AW	19700 AAW	PABLS	10//99-12//99
Including Answering Service	Rhode Island	S	9.63 MW	9.93 AW	20660 AAW	RIBLS	10//99-12//99
Including Answering Service	South Carolina	S	8.16 MW	8.25 AW	17160 AAW	SCBLS	10//99-12//99
Including Answering Service	South Dakota	S	8.73 MW	9.39 AW	19530 AAW	SDBLS	10//99-12//99
Including Answering Service	Tennessee	S	8.76 MW	9.05 AW	18810 AAW	TNBLS	10//99-12//99
Including Answering Service	Texas	S	8.6 MW	9.16 AW	19060 AAW	TXBLS	10//99-12//99
Including Answering Service	Utah	S	8.83 MW	9.34 AW	19420 AAW	UTBLS	10//99-12//99

AAW	Average annual wage	AOH	Average offered, high	ASH	Average starting, high	H	Hourly	M	Monthly	S	Special: hourly and annual
AE	Average entry wage	AOL	Average offered, low	ASL	Average starting, low	HI	Highest wage paid	MTC	Median total compensation	TQ	Third quartile wage
AEX	Average experienced wage	APH	Average pay, high range	AW	Average wage paid	HR	High end range	MW	Median wage paid	W	Weekly
AO	Average offered	APL	Average pay, low range	FQ	First quartile wage	LR	Low end range	SQ	Second quartile wage	Y	Yearly

Occupation/Type/Industry	Location	Per	Low	Mid	High	Source	Date
Switchboard Operator							
Including Answering Service	Vermont	S	8.46 MW	9.06 AW	18840 AAW	VTBLS	10//99-12//99
Including Answering Service	Virginia	S	8.62 MW	8.72 AW	18140 AAW	VABLS	10//99-12//99
Including Answering Service	Washington	S	10.24 MW	10.34 AW	21500 AAW	WABLS	10//99-12//99
Including Answering Service	West Virginia	S	7.22 MW	7.57 AW	15750 AAW	WVBLS	10//99-12//99
Including Answering Service	Wisconsin	S	9.17 MW	9.26 AW	19260 AAW	WIBLS	10//99-12//99
Including Answering Service	Wyoming	S	7.82 MW	7.98 AW	16600 AAW	WYBLS	10//99-12//99
Including Answering Service	Puerto Rico	S	6.28 MW	6.73 AW	13990 AAW	PRBLS	10//99-12//99
Including Answering Service	Virgin Islands	S	8.09 MW	8.21 AW	17070 AAW	VIBLS	10//99-12//99
Including Answering Service	Guam	S	7.79 MW	8.29 AW	17240 AAW	GUBLS	10//99-12//99
Systems Administrator							
Internet	United States	Y		50501 MW		BUS2	2000
Tailor, Dressmaker, and Custom Sewer							
	Alabama	S	8.34 MW	9.18 AW	19100 AAW	ALBLS	10//99-12//99
	Birmingham MSA, AL	S	8.85 MW	9.09 AW	18410 AAW	ALBLS	10//99-12//99
	Dothan MSA, AL	S	7.86 MW	7.72 AW	16340 AAW	ALBLS	10//99-12//99
	Mobile MSA, AL	S	8.41 MW	9.12 AW	17490 AAW	ALBLS	10//99-12//99
	Montgomery MSA, AL	S	11.05 MW	8.30 AW	22990 AAW	ALBLS	10//99-12//99
	Alaska	S	13.59 MW	13.84 AW	28780 AAW	AKBLS	10//99-12//99
	Anchorage MSA, AK	S	13.72 MW	13.58 AW	28530 AAW	AKBLS	10//99-12//99
	Arizona	S	9.9 MW	10.52 AW	21890 AAW	AZBLS	10//99-12//99
	Phoenix-Mesa MSA, AZ	S	11.11 MW	10.67 AW	23120 AAW	AZBLS	10//99-12//99
	Tucson MSA, AZ	S	8.73 MW	8.12 AW	18150 AAW	AZBLS	10//99-12//99
	Arkansas	S	6.98 MW	7.23 AW	15040 AAW	ARBLS	10//99-12//99
	Little Rock-North Little Rock MSA, AR	S	8.28 MW	8.01 AW	17220 AAW	ARBLS	10//99-12//99
	California	S	10.11 MW	11.27 AW	23430 AAW	CABLS	10//99-12//99
	Los Angeles-Long Beach PMSA, CA	S	11.94 MW	10.60 AW	24840 AAW	CABLS	10//99-12//99
	Oakland PMSA, CA	S	12.33 MW	11.62 AW	25650 AAW	CABLS	10//99-12//99
	Orange County PMSA, CA	S	11.18 MW	10.11 AW	23250 AAW	CABLS	10//99-12//99
	Riverside-San Bernardino PMSA, CA	S	11.77 MW	11.47 AW	24490 AAW	CABLS	10//99-12//99
	Sacramento PMSA, CA	S	11.68 MW	12.20 AW	24300 AAW	CABLS	10//99-12//99
	San Diego MSA, CA	S	10.34 MW	9.66 AW	21500 AAW	CABLS	10//99-12//99
	San Francisco PMSA, CA	S	14.94 MW	12.80 AW	31080 AAW	CABLS	10//99-12//99
	San Jose PMSA, CA	S	10.70 MW	10.71 AW	22260 AAW	CABLS	10//99-12//99
	Santa Barbara-Santa Maria-Lompoc MSA, CA	S	12.75 MW	12.92 AW	26520 AAW	CABLS	10//99-12//99
	Vallejo-Fairfield-Napa PMSA, CA	S	7.52 MW	7.54 AW	15640 AAW	CABLS	10//99-12//99
	Visalia-Tulare-Porterville MSA, CA	S	8.13 MW	7.65 AW	16900 AAW	CABLS	10//99-12//99
	Yolo PMSA, CA	S	10.36 MW	10.60 AW	21550 AAW	CABLS	10//99-12//99
	Colorado	S	10.73 MW	11.88 AW	24710 AAW	COBLS	10//99-12//99
	Colorado Springs MSA, CO	S	10.52 MW	11.26 AW	21880 AAW	COBLS	10//99-12//99
	Denver PMSA, CO	S	13.49 MW	13.20 AW	28050 AAW	COBLS	10//99-12//99
	Fort Collins-Loveland MSA, CO	S	12.88 MW	10.85 AW	26780 AAW	COBLS	10//99-12//99
	Connecticut	S	11.1 MW	11.47 AW	23850 AAW	CTBLS	10//99-12//99
	Bridgeport PMSA, CT	S	11.48 MW	10.95 AW	23870 AAW	CTBLS	10//99-12//99
	Danbury PMSA, CT	S	11.96 MW	11.95 AW	24870 AAW	CTBLS	10//99-12//99
	Hartford MSA, CT	S	12.06 MW	11.46 AW	25080 AAW	CTBLS	10//99-12//99
	New Haven-Meriden PMSA, CT	S	9.46 MW	8.37 AW	19680 AAW	CTBLS	10//99-12//99
	New London-Norwich MSA, CT-RI	S	11.61 MW	10.35 AW	24140 AAW	CTBLS	10//99-12//99
	Stamford-Norwalk PMSA, CT	S	13.76 MW	12.41 AW	28620 AAW	CTBLS	10//99-12//99
	Washington PMSA, DC-MD-VA-WV	S	11.67 MW	11.39 AW	24280 AAW	DCBLS	10//99-12//99
	Florida	S	9.43 MW	10.07 AW	20950 AAW	FLBLS	10//99-12//99
	Fort Lauderdale PMSA, FL	S	9.39 MW	8.54 AW	19540 AAW	FLBLS	10//99-12//99
	Fort Myers-Cape Coral MSA, FL	S	8.72 MW	9.04 AW	18140 AAW	FLBLS	10//99-12//99
	Fort Walton Beach MSA, FL	S	10.59 MW	9.43 AW	22020 AAW	FLBLS	10//99-12//99
	Jacksonville MSA, FL	S	8.57 MW	8.16 AW	17830 AAW	FLBLS	10//99-12//99
	Miami PMSA, FL	S	9.84 MW	8.86 AW	20470 AAW	FLBLS	10//99-12//99
	Naples MSA, FL	S	12.65 MW	12.18 AW	26300 AAW	FLBLS	10//99-12//99
	Sarasota-Bradenton MSA, FL	S	10.28 MW	10.40 AW	21380 AAW	FLBLS	10//99-12//99

AAW	Average annual wage	AOH	Average offered, high	ASH	Average starting, high
AE	Average entry wage	AOL	Average offered, low	ASL	Average starting, low
AEX	Average experienced wage	APH	Average pay, high range	AW	Average wage paid
AO	Average offered	APL	Average pay, low range	FQ	First quartile wage

H	Hourly	M	Monthly
HI	Highest wage paid	MTC	Median total compensation
HR	High end range	MW	Median wage paid
LR	Low end range	SQ	Second quartile wage

S	Special: hourly and annual
TQ	Third quartile wage
W	Weekly
Y	Yearly

Occupation/Type/Industry	Location	Per	Low	Mid	High	Source	Date
Tailor, Dressmaker, and Custom Sewer							
	Tampa-St. Petersburg-Clearwater MSA, FL	S	9.23 MW	8.32 AW	19190 AAW	FLBLS	10//99-12//99
	West Palm Beach-Boca Raton MSA, FL	S	13.00 MW	12.81 AW	27030 AAW	FLBLS	10//99-12//99
	Georgia	S	9.5 MW	9.65 AW	20060 AAW	GABLS	10//99-12//99
	Athens MSA, GA	S	8.79 MW	8.81 AW	18290 AAW	GABLS	10//99-12//99
	Atlanta MSA, GA	S	11.12 MW	10.36 AW	23120 AAW	GABLS	10//99-12//99
	Augusta-Aiken MSA, GA-SC	S	7.97 MW	7.60 AW	16580 AAW	GABLS	10//99-12//99
	Macon MSA, GA	S	9.41 MW	9.73 AW	19580 AAW	GABLS	10//99-12//99
	Savannah MSA, GA	S	9.20 MW	9.37 AW	19140 AAW	GABLS	10//99-12//99
	Hawaii	S	6.81 MW	7.96 AW	16550 AAW	HIBLS	10//99-12//99
	Honolulu MSA, HI	S	7.79 MW	6.61 AW	16210 AAW	HIBLS	10//99-12//99
	Illinois	S	10.33 MW	10.00 AW	20800 AAW	ILBLS	10//99-12//99
	Champaign-Urbana MSA, IL	S	7.10 MW	6.88 AW	14770 AAW	ILBLS	10//99-12//99
	Chicago PMSA, IL	S	10.28 MW	10.66 AW	21390 AAW	ILBLS	10//99-12//99
	Indiana	S	8.99 MW	9.06 AW	18850 AAW	INBLS	10//99-12//99
	Evansville-Henderson MSA, IN-KY	S	8.92 MW	8.49 AW	18540 AAW	INBLS	10//99-12//99
	Gary PMSA, IN	S	9.27 MW	9.41 AW	19290 AAW	INBLS	10//99-12//99
	Indianapolis MSA, IN	S	9.05 MW	8.57 AW	18830 AAW	INBLS	10//99-12//99
	Lafayette MSA, IN	S	10.34 MW	10.33 AW	21510 AAW	INBLS	10//99-12//99
	South Bend MSA, IN	S	9.58 MW	9.36 AW	19930 AAW	INBLS	10//99-12//99
	Iowa	S	7.66 MW	7.88 AW	16380 AAW	IABLS	10//99-12//99
	Cedar Rapids MSA, IA	S	8.79 MW	9.04 AW	18290 AAW	IABLS	10//99-12//99
	Davenport-Moline-Rock Island MSA, IA-IL	S	7.17 MW	6.94 AW	14910 AAW	IABLS	10//99-12//99
	Des Moines MSA, IA	S	9.29 MW	8.93 AW	19330 AAW	IABLS	10//99-12//99
	Kansas	S	8.66 MW	9.44 AW	19640 AAW	KSBLS	10//99-12//99
	Wichita MSA, KS	S	9.55 MW	8.93 AW	19860 AAW	KSBLS	10//99-12//99
	Kentucky	S	7.62 MW	8.04 AW	16730 AAW	KYBLS	10//99-12//99
	Louisville MSA, KY-IN	S	9.02 MW	8.65 AW	18770 AAW	KYBLS	10//99-12//99
	Louisiana	S	6.63 MW	7.20 AW	14980 AAW	LABLS	10//99-12//99
	Baton Rouge MSA, LA	S	7.02 MW	6.49 AW	14590 AAW	LABLS	10//99-12//99
	Lafayette MSA, LA	S	7.53 MW	7.46 AW	15660 AAW	LABLS	10//99-12//99
	New Orleans MSA, LA	S	7.42 MW	6.72 AW	15440 AAW	LABLS	10//99-12//99
	Shreveport-Bossier City MSA, LA	S	6.84 MW	6.13 AW	14230 AAW	LABLS	10//99-12//99
	Maryland	S	10.78 MW	10.59 AW	22020 AAW	MDBLS	10//99-12//99
	Baltimore PMSA, MD	S	10.28 MW	10.18 AW	21380 AAW	MDBLS	10//99-12//99
	Massachusetts	S	15.44 MW	15.47 AW	32170 AAW	MABLS	10//99-12//99
	Boston PMSA, MA-NH	S	17.93 MW	20.20 AW	37300 AAW	MABLS	10//99-12//99
	Worcester PMSA, MA-CT	S	12.96 MW	12.34 AW	26970 AAW	MABLS	10//99-12//99
	Michigan	S	9.85 MW	10.22 AW	21260 AAW	MIBLS	10//99-12//99
	Detroit PMSA, MI	S	10.91 MW	10.52 AW	22690 AAW	MIBLS	10//99-12//99
	Flint PMSA, MI	S	9.91 MW	9.63 AW	20610 AAW	MIBLS	10//99-12//99
	Grand Rapids-Muskegon-Holland MSA, MI	S	12.36 MW	10.58 AW	25700 AAW	MIBLS	10//99-12//99
	Saginaw-Bay City-Midland MSA, MI	S	6.79 MW	6.50 AW	14120 AAW	MIBLS	10//99-12//99
	Minnesota	S	9.68 MW	10.49 AW	21820 AAW	MNBLS	10//99-12//99
	Minneapolis-St. Paul MSA, MN-WI	S	10.87 MW	10.29 AW	22610 AAW	MNBLS	10//99-12//99
	Mississippi	S	8.39 MW	8.57 AW	17820 AAW	MSBLS	10//99-12//99
	Biloxi-Gulfport-Pascagoula MSA, MS	S	8.11 MW	8.06 AW	16860 AAW	MSBLS	10//99-12//99
	Jackson MSA, MS	S	9.55 MW	8.85 AW	19860 AAW	MSBLS	10//99-12//99
	Missouri	S	8.49 MW	9.65 AW	20060 AAW	MOBLS	10//99-12//99
	Kansas City MSA, MO-KS	S	10.81 MW	10.32 AW	22480 AAW	MOBLS	10//99-12//99
	St. Louis MSA, MO-IL	S	9.53 MW	8.46 AW	19830 AAW	MOBLS	10//99-12//99
	Montana	S	7.23 MW	7.11 AW	14790 AAW	MTBLS	10//99-12//99
	Nebraska	S	6.87 MW	7.60 AW	15800 AAW	NEBLS	10//99-12//99
	Omaha MSA, NE-IA	S	9.44 MW	9.25 AW	19640 AAW	NEBLS	10//99-12//99
	Nevada	S	9.74 MW	10.54 AW	21930 AAW	NVBLS	10//99-12//99
	Las Vegas MSA, NV-AZ	S	10.64 MW	9.77 AW	22130 AAW	NVBLS	10//99-12//99
	Reno MSA, NV	S	9.39 MW	9.32 AW	19520 AAW	NVBLS	10//99-12//99
	New Hampshire	S	10.99 MW	10.92 AW	22720 AAW	NHBLS	10//99-12//99
	Nashua PMSA, NH	S	12.46 MW	12.33 AW	25910 AAW	NHBLS	10//99-12//99
	New Jersey	S	11.05 MW	11.75 AW	24440 AAW	NJBLS	10//99-12//99
	Bergen-Passaic PMSA, NJ	S	10.99 MW	10.27 AW	22860 AAW	NJBLS	10//99-12//99
	Jersey City PMSA, NJ	S	13.61 MW	13.49 AW	28320 AAW	NJBLS	10//99-12//99

AAW Average annual wage	**AOH** Average offered, high	**ASH** Average starting, high	**H** Hourly	**M** Monthly	**S** Special: hourly and annual
AE Average entry wage	**AOL** Average offered, low	**ASL** Average starting, low	**HI** Highest wage paid	**MTC** Median total compensation	**TQ** Third quartile wage
AEX Average experienced wage	**APH** Average pay, high range	**AW** Average wage paid	**HR** High end range	**MW** Median wage paid	**W** Weekly
AO Average offered	**APL** Average pay, low range	**FQ** First quartile wage	**LR** Low end range	**SQ** Second quartile wage	**Y** Yearly

Occupation/Type/Industry	Location	Per	Low	Mid	High	Source	Date
Tailor, Dressmaker, and Custom Sewer							
	Middlesex-Somerset-Hunterdon PMSA, NJ	S	12.13 MW	12.19 AW	25220 AAW	NJBLS	10//99-12//99
	Monmouth-Ocean PMSA, NJ	S	14.83 MW	12.61 AW	30850 AAW	NJBLS	10//99-12//99
	Newark PMSA, NJ	S	11.05 MW	10.71 AW	22980 AAW	NJBLS	10//99-12//99
	New Mexico	S	6.56 MW	7.30 AW	15180 AAW	NMBLS	10//99-12//99
	New York	S	10.71 MW	12.38 AW	25740 AAW	NYBLS	10//99-12//99
	Albany-Schenectady-Troy MSA, NY	S	10.42 MW	10.58 AW	21670 AAW	NYBLS	10//99-12//99
	Buffalo-Niagara Falls MSA, NY	S	9.00 MW	8.37 AW	18720 AAW	NYBLS	10//99-12//99
	Nassau-Suffolk PMSA, NY	S	10.11 MW	8.29 AW	21030 AAW	NYBLS	10//99-12//99
	New York PMSA, NY	S	14.07 MW	12.55 AW	29260 AAW	NYBLS	10//99-12//99
	Newburgh PMSA, NY-PA	S	13.14 MW	11.34 AW	27330 AAW	NYBLS	10//99-12//99
	Rochester MSA, NY	S	9.83 MW	9.09 AW	20450 AAW	NYBLS	10//99-12//99
	Syracuse MSA, NY	S	8.92 MW	7.95 AW	18560 AAW	NYBLS	10//99-12//99
	Utica-Rome MSA, NY	S	9.44 MW	9.75 AW	19640 AAW	NYBLS	10//99-12//99
	North Carolina	S	8.68 MW	8.86 AW	18430 AAW	NCBLS	10//99-12//99
	Charlotte-Gastonia-Rock Hill MSA, NC-SC	S	10.30 MW	10.70 AW	21410 AAW	NCBLS	10//99-12//99
	Greensboro--Winston-Salem--High Point MSA, NC	S	8.97 MW	9.41 AW	18660 AAW	NCBLS	10//99-12//99
	Hickory-Morganton-Lenoir MSA, NC	S	7.41 MW	7.55 AW	15410 AAW	NCBLS	10//99-12//99
	Raleigh-Durham-Chapel Hill MSA, NC	S	9.88 MW	9.39 AW	20560 AAW	NCBLS	10//99-12//99
	Wilmington MSA, NC	S	9.19 MW	9.04 AW	19120 AAW	NCBLS	10//99-12//99
	North Dakota	S	7.79 MW	8.74 AW	18180 AAW	NDBLS	10//99-12//99
	Ohio	S	9.59 MW	10.31 AW	21440 AAW	OHBLS	10//99-12//99
	Akron PMSA, OH	S	10.50 MW	9.73 AW	21840 AAW	OHBLS	10//99-12//99
	Canton-Massillon MSA, OH	S	7.20 MW	6.54 AW	14970 AAW	OHBLS	10//99-12//99
	Cincinnati PMSA, OH-KY-IN	S	10.53 MW	10.17 AW	21910 AAW	OHBLS	10//99-12//99
	Cleveland-Lorain-Elyria PMSA, OH	S	10.48 MW	9.96 AW	21800 AAW	OHBLS	10//99-12//99
	Columbus MSA, OH	S	12.18 MW	10.96 AW	25340 AAW	OHBLS	10//99-12//99
	Dayton-Springfield MSA, OH	S	9.98 MW	9.76 AW	20760 AAW	OHBLS	10//99-12//99
	Toledo MSA, OH	S	12.54 MW	9.78 AW	26090 AAW	OHBLS	10//99-12//99
	Youngstown-Warren MSA, OH	S	9.11 MW	8.67 AW	18950 AAW	OHBLS	10//99-12//99
	Oklahoma	S	7.35 MW	8.30 AW	17250 AAW	OKBLS	10//99-12//99
	Oklahoma City MSA, OK	S	7.37 MW	6.11 AW	15330 AAW	OKBLS	10//99-12//99
	Oregon	S	10.35 MW	11.25 AW	23390 AAW	ORBLS	10//99-12//99
	Eugene-Springfield MSA, OR	S	9.99 MW	9.54 AW	20780 AAW	ORBLS	10//99-12//99
	Portland-Vancouver PMSA, OR-WA	S	11.93 MW	11.32 AW	24810 AAW	ORBLS	10//99-12//99
	Salem PMSA, OR	S	10.52 MW	10.26 AW	21890 AAW	ORBLS	10//99-12//99
	Pennsylvania	S	9.68 MW	10.70 AW	22250 AAW	PABLS	10//99-12//99
	Allentown-Bethlehem-Easton MSA, PA	S	9.94 MW	9.00 AW	20670 AAW	PABLS	10//99-12//99
	Harrisburg-Lebanon-Carlisle MSA, PA	S	11.04 MW	10.14 AW	22950 AAW	PABLS	10//99-12//99
	Lancaster MSA, PA	S	10.57 MW	9.77 AW	21990 AAW	PABLS	10//99-12//99
	Philadelphia PMSA, PA-NJ	S	12.40 MW	11.61 AW	25780 AAW	PABLS	10//99-12//99
	Pittsburgh MSA, PA	S	9.22 MW	8.76 AW	19170 AAW	PABLS	10//99-12//99
	Scranton--Wilkes-Barre--Hazleton MSA, PA	S	8.52 MW	7.89 AW	17730 AAW	PABLS	10//99-12//99
	Sharon MSA, PA	S	10.26 MW	10.22 AW	21340 AAW	PABLS	10//99-12//99
	Rhode Island	S	11.22 MW	11.33 AW	23570 AAW	RIBLS	10//99-12//99
	Providence-Fall River-Warwick MSA, RI-MA	S	11.07 MW	11.09 AW	23020 AAW	RIBLS	10//99-12//99
	South Carolina	S	6.82 MW	7.22 AW	15020 AAW	SCBLS	10//99-12//99
	Charleston-North Charleston MSA, SC	S	9.50 MW	9.11 AW	19760 AAW	SCBLS	10//99-12//99
	Columbia MSA, SC	S	9.10 MW	9.16 AW	18930 AAW	SCBLS	10//99-12//99
	Greenville-Spartanburg-Anderson MSA, SC	S	7.73 MW	7.24 AW	16070 AAW	SCBLS	10//99-12//99
	Tennessee	S	7.54 MW	8.07 AW	16790 AAW	TNBLS	10//99-12//99
	Knoxville MSA, TN	S	10.29 MW	10.78 AW	21400 AAW	TNBLS	10//99-12//99
	Nashville MSA, TN	S	9.03 MW	8.85 AW	18780 AAW	TNBLS	10//99-12//99
	Texas	S	7.89 MW	8.87 AW	18460 AAW	TXBLS	10//99-12//99
	Austin-San Marcos MSA, TX	S	9.61 MW	9.12 AW	20000 AAW	TXBLS	10//99-12//99
	Brownsville-Harlingen-San Benito MSA, TX	S	7.54 MW	7.36 AW	15690 AAW	TXBLS	10//99-12//99

AAW	Average annual wage	AOH	Average offered, high	ASH	Average starting, high
AE	Average entry wage	AOL	Average offered, low	ASL	Average starting, low
AEX	Average experienced wage	APH	Average pay, high range	AW	Average wage paid
AO	Average offered	APL	Average pay, low range	FQ	First quartile wage

H	Hourly	M	Monthly
HI	Highest wage paid	MTC	Median total compensation
HR	High end range	MW	Median wage paid
LR	Low end range	SQ	Second quartile wage

S	Special: hourly and annual
TQ	Third quartile wage
W	Weekly
Y	Yearly

Occupation/Type/Industry	Location	Per	Low	Mid	High	Source	Date
Tailor, Dressmaker, and Custom Sewer	Dallas PMSA, TX	S	11.40 MW	9.82 AW	23710 AAW	TXBLS	10//99-12//99
	Fort Worth-Arlington PMSA, TX	S	8.67 MW	8.19 AW	18030 AAW	TXBLS	10//99-12//99
	Houston PMSA, TX	S	8.23 MW	6.85 AW	17120 AAW	TXBLS	10//99-12//99
	Laredo MSA, TX	S	6.55 MW	6.40 AW	13630 AAW	TXBLS	10//99-12//99
	McAllen-Edinburg-Mission MSA, TX	S	6.28 MW	6.08 AW	13070 AAW	TXBLS	10//99-12//99
	San Antonio MSA, TX	S	8.88 MW	8.22 AW	18470 AAW	TXBLS	10//99-12//99
	Tyler MSA, TX	S	10.68 MW	9.95 AW	22210 AAW	TXBLS	10//99-12//99
	Waco MSA, TX	S	7.65 MW	7.70 AW	15920 AAW	TXBLS	10//99-12//99
	Utah	S	8.78 MW	9.46 AW	19680 AAW	UTBLS	10//99-12//99
	Provo-Orem MSA, UT	S	7.57 MW	7.39 AW	15750 AAW	UTBLS	10//99-12//99
	Virginia	S	9.8 MW	10.57 AW	21990 AAW	VABLS	10//99-12//99
	Norfolk-Virginia Beach-Newport News MSA, VA-NC	S	9.87 MW	9.50 AW	20530 AAW	VABLS	10//99-12//99
	Richmond-Petersburg MSA, VA	S	10.86 MW	9.95 AW	22590 AAW	VABLS	10//99-12//99
	Roanoke MSA, VA	S	7.07 MW	6.83 AW	14700 AAW	VABLS	10//99-12//99
	Washington	S	11.59 MW	11.55 AW	24030 AAW	WABLS	10//99-12//99
	Seattle-Bellevue-Everett PMSA, WA	S	12.22 MW	12.20 AW	25420 AAW	WABLS	10//99-12//99
	West Virginia	S	7.45 MW	7.72 AW	16050 AAW	WVBLS	10//99-12//99
	Charleston MSA, WV	S	8.71 MW	8.39 AW	18120 AAW	WVBLS	10//99-12//99
	Huntington-Ashland MSA, WV-KY-OH	S	7.82 MW	7.37 AW	16260 AAW	WVBLS	10//99-12//99
	Wisconsin	S	9.05 MW	9.50 AW	19760 AAW	WIBLS	10//99-12//99
	Appleton-Oshkosh-Neenah MSA, WI	S	9.59 MW	9.43 AW	19950 AAW	WIBLS	10//99-12//99
	Eau Claire MSA, WI	S	8.50 MW	7.82 AW	17680 AAW	WIBLS	10//99-12//99
	Milwaukee-Waukesha PMSA, WI	S	11.29 MW	10.68 AW	23490 AAW	WIBLS	10//99-12//99
	Puerto Rico	S	6 MW	6.18 AW	12860 AAW	PRBLS	10//99-12//99
	Guam	S	6.6 MW	7.51 AW	15620 AAW	GUBLS	10//99-12//99
Tank Car, Truck, and Ship Loader	Alabama	S	14.24 MW	13.33 AW	27720 AAW	ALBLS	10//99-12//99
	Arizona	S	10 MW	10.93 AW	22730 AAW	AZBLS	10//99-12//99
	Arkansas	S	11.23 MW	12.36 AW	25710 AAW	ARBLS	10//99-12//99
	California	S	11.44 MW	12.57 AW	26150 AAW	CABLS	10//99-12//99
	Los Angeles-Long Beach PMSA, CA	S	12.74 MW	11.62 AW	26500 AAW	CABLS	10//99-12//99
	Modesto MSA, CA	S	12.02 MW	12.11 AW	25000 AAW	CABLS	10//99-12//99
	Orange County PMSA, CA	S	15.16 MW	15.15 AW	31530 AAW	CABLS	10//99-12//99
	Riverside-San Bernardino PMSA, CA	S	11.95 MW	11.52 AW	24850 AAW	CABLS	10//99-12//99
	Stockton-Lodi MSA, CA	S	11.19 MW	10.43 AW	23280 AAW	CABLS	10//99-12//99
	Colorado	S	13.09 MW	14.34 AW	29830 AAW	COBLS	10//99-12//99
	Denver PMSA, CO	S	15.10 MW	13.60 AW	31400 AAW	COBLS	10//99-12//99
	Delaware	S	12.04 MW	13.00 AW	27040 AAW	DEBLS	10//99-12//99
	Florida	S	22.99 MW	19.87 AW	41330 AAW	FLBLS	10//99-12//99
	Jacksonville MSA, FL	S	23.13 MW	24.03 AW	48110 AAW	FLBLS	10//99-12//99
	Lakeland-Winter Haven MSA, FL	S	9.76 MW	10.76 AW	20310 AAW	FLBLS	10//99-12//99
	Orlando MSA, FL	S	11.55 MW	10.29 AW	24020 AAW	FLBLS	10//99-12//99
	Tampa-St. Petersburg-Clearwater MSA, FL	S	10.66 MW	10.91 AW	22180 AAW	FLBLS	10//99-12//99
	Georgia	S	16.45 MW	16.98 AW	35310 AAW	GABLS	10//99-12//99
	Atlanta MSA, GA	S	13.84 MW	14.75 AW	28790 AAW	GABLS	10//99-12//99
	Idaho	S	11.9 MW	11.35 AW	23600 AAW	IDBLS	10//99-12//99
	Illinois	S	18.24 MW	17.62 AW	36640 AAW	ILBLS	10//99-12//99
	Chicago PMSA, IL	S	17.76 MW	18.39 AW	36950 AAW	ILBLS	10//99-12//99
	Indiana	S	13.74 MW	14.37 AW	29880 AAW	INBLS	10//99-12//99
	Evansville-Henderson MSA, IN-KY	S	15.65 MW	15.54 AW	32560 AAW	INBLS	10//99-12//99
	Fort Wayne MSA, IN	S	16.94 MW	14.87 AW	35230 AAW	INBLS	10//99-12//99
	Iowa	S	11.46 MW	11.44 AW	23790 AAW	IABLS	10//99-12//99
	Kansas	S	11.2 MW	10.76 AW	22390 AAW	KSBLS	10//99-12//99
	Kentucky	S	13.5 MW	12.73 AW	26490 AAW	KYBLS	10//99-12//99
	Louisville MSA, KY-IN	S	14.67 MW	15.22 AW	30520 AAW	KYBLS	10//99-12//99
	Louisiana	S	9.97 MW	10.60 AW	22050 AAW	LABLS	10//99-12//99

AAW Average annual wage	**AOH** Average offered, high	**ASH** Average starting, high	**H** Hourly	**M** Monthly	**S** Special: hourly and annual
AE Average entry wage	**AOL** Average offered, low	**ASL** Average starting, low	**HI** Highest wage paid	**MTC** Median total compensation	**TQ** Third quartile wage
AEX Average experienced wage	**APH** Average pay, high range	**AW** Average wage paid	**HR** High end range	**MW** Median wage paid	**W** Weekly
AO Average offered	**APL** Average pay, low range	**FQ** First quartile wage	**LR** Low end range	**SQ** Second quartile wage	**Y** Yearly

Occupation/Type/Industry	Location	Per	Low	Mid	High	Source	Date
Tank Car, Truck, and Ship Loader	Baton Rouge MSA, LA	S	10.92 MW	10.82 AW	22720 AAW	LABLS	10//99-12//99
	New Orleans MSA, LA	S	10.66 MW	9.99 AW	22170 AAW	LABLS	10//99-12//99
	Maine	S	14.77 MW	13.83 AW	28760 AAW	MEBLS	10//99-12//99
	Maryland	S	10.09 MW	11.44 AW	23790 AAW	MDBLS	10//99-12//99
	Minnesota	S	14.39 MW	14.37 AW	29890 AAW	MNBLS	10//99-12//99
	Duluth-Superior MSA, MN-WI	S	11.99 MW	11.95 AW	24940 AAW	MNBLS	10//99-12//99
	Mississippi	S	12.14 MW	13.07 AW	27190 AAW	MSBLS	10//99-12//99
	Missouri	S	12.05 MW	13.19 AW	27430 AAW	MOBLS	10//99-12//99
	Nebraska	S	11.11 MW	10.66 AW	22170 AAW	NEBLS	10//99-12//99
	New Hampshire	S	14.93 MW	14.60 AW	30360 AAW	NHBLS	10//99-12//99
	New Jersey	S	13.38 MW	14.77 AW	30720 AAW	NJBLS	10//99-12//99
	Middlesex-Somerset-Hunterdon PMSA, NJ	S	16.30 MW	17.54 AW	33900 AAW	NJBLS	10//99-12//99
	Newark PMSA, NJ	S	14.42 MW	12.96 AW	29990 AAW	NJBLS	10//99-12//99
	New York	S	17.38 MW	17.18 AW	35740 AAW	NYBLS	10//99-12//99
	New York PMSA, NY	S	16.08 MW	17.87 AW	33440 AAW	NYBLS	10//99-12//99
	North Carolina	S	9.05 MW	9.71 AW	20190 AAW	NCBLS	10//99-12//99
	Charlotte-Gastonia-Rock Hill MSA, NC-SC	S	8.00 MW	7.84 AW	16650 AAW	NCBLS	10//99-12//99
	Greensboro--Winston-Salem--High Point MSA, NC	S	10.84 MW	10.44 AW	22550 AAW	NCBLS	10//99-12//99
	Ohio	S	14.56 MW	14.92 AW	31030 AAW	OHBLS	10//99-12//99
	Cleveland-Lorain-Elyria PMSA, OH	S	17.41 MW	17.82 AW	36210 AAW	OHBLS	10//99-12//99
	Oklahoma	S	9.68 MW	9.84 AW	20460 AAW	OKBLS	10//99-12//99
	Pennsylvania	S	15.12 MW	16.45 AW	34210 AAW	PABLS	10//99-12//99
	Philadelphia PMSA, PA-NJ	S	16.79 MW	15.26 AW	34920 AAW	PABLS	10//99-12//99
	Pittsburgh MSA, PA	S	13.57 MW	13.49 AW	28230 AAW	PABLS	10//99-12//99
	Tennessee	S	10.13 MW	11.86 AW	24660 AAW	TNBLS	10//99-12//99
	Texas	S	11.99 MW	13.48 AW	28030 AAW	TXBLS	10//99-12//99
	Beaumont-Port Arthur MSA, TX	S	16.24 MW	17.13 AW	33770 AAW	TXBLS	10//99-12//99
	Dallas PMSA, TX	S	12.74 MW	9.90 AW	26510 AAW	TXBLS	10//99-12//99
	Galveston-Texas City PMSA, TX	S	17.63 MW	18.92 AW	36680 AAW	TXBLS	10//99-12//99
	Houston PMSA, TX	S	16.33 MW	18.84 AW	33960 AAW	TXBLS	10//99-12//99
	San Antonio MSA, TX	S	7.70 MW	7.71 AW	16010 AAW	TXBLS	10//99-12//99
	Virginia	S	18.04 MW	16.90 AW	35160 AAW	VABLS	10//99-12//99
	Washington	S	26.59 MW	24.64 AW	51250 AAW	WABLS	10//99-12//99
	West Virginia	S	15.6 MW	14.84 AW	30870 AAW	WVBLS	10//99-12//99
	Wisconsin	S	10.99 MW	10.63 AW	22110 AAW	WIBLS	10//99-12//99
	Wyoming	S	10.49 MW	12.08 AW	25140 AAW	WYBLS	10//99-12//99
Taper	Alabama	S	11.82 MW	12.26 AW	25500 AAW	ALBLS	10//99-12//99
	Alaska	S	23.53 MW	23.59 AW	49070 AAW	AKBLS	10//99-12//99
	Arizona	S	12.51 MW	12.18 AW	25330 AAW	AZBLS	10//99-12//99
	California	S	18.92 MW	18.71 AW	38920 AAW	CABLS	10//99-12//99
	Colorado	S	13.82 MW	13.51 AW	28100 AAW	COBLS	10//99-12//99
	Delaware	S	13.2 MW	15.55 AW	32340 AAW	DEBLS	10//99-12//99
	Florida	S	13.79 MW	13.81 AW	28730 AAW	FLBLS	10//99-12//99
	Georgia	S	12.64 MW	12.90 AW	26840 AAW	GABLS	10//99-12//99
	Hawaii	S	31.88 MW	29.66 AW	61700 AAW	HIBLS	10//99-12//99
	Idaho	S	12.35 MW	12.65 AW	26310 AAW	IDBLS	10//99-12//99
	Illinois	S	23.22 MW	22.57 AW	46940 AAW	ILBLS	10//99-12//99
	Indiana	S	15.07 MW	14.79 AW	30750 AAW	INBLS	10//99-12//99
	Iowa	S	16.68 MW	16.47 AW	34260 AAW	IABLS	10//99-12//99
	Kansas	S	13.51 MW	15.29 AW	31800 AAW	KSBLS	10//99-12//99
	Kentucky	S	13.42 MW	13.13 AW	27310 AAW	KYBLS	10//99-12//99
	Louisiana	S	12.09 MW	12.49 AW	25970 AAW	LABLS	10//99-12//99
	Maine	S	14.43 MW	13.83 AW	28770 AAW	MEBLS	10//99-12//99
	Maryland	S	15.22 MW	15.24 AW	31690 AAW	MDBLS	10//99-12//99
	Massachusetts	S	28.11 MW	25.36 AW	52750 AAW	MABLS	10//99-12//99
	Michigan	S	16.62 MW	16.62 AW	34580 AAW	MIBLS	10//99-12//99
	Minnesota	S	20.01 MW	18.68 AW	38860 AAW	MNBLS	10//99-12//99
	Nebraska	S	14.25 MW	14.31 AW	29760 AAW	NEBLS	10//99-12//99
	Nevada	S	19.15 MW	18.87 AW	39240 AAW	NVBLS	10//99-12//99
	New Jersey	S	19.86 MW	21.40 AW	44510 AAW	NJBLS	10//99-12//99
	New Mexico	S	11.56 MW	12.72 AW	26460 AAW	NMBLS	10//99-12//99
	New York	S	18.17 MW	19.91 AW	41410 AAW	NYBLS	10//99-12//99
	North Carolina	S	12.79 MW	13.88 AW	28860 AAW	NCBLS	10//99-12//99
	Ohio	S	16.33 MW	17.18 AW	35740 AAW	OHBLS	10//99-12//99

AAW Average annual wage	**AOH** Average offered, high	**ASH** Average starting, high	**H** Hourly	**M** Monthly	**S** Special: hourly and annual
AE Average entry wage	**AOL** Average offered, low	**ASL** Average starting, low	**HI** Highest wage paid	**MTC** Median total compensation	**TQ** Third quartile wage
AEX Average experienced wage	**APH** Average pay, high range	**AW** Average wage paid	**HR** High end range	**MW** Median wage paid	**W** Weekly
AO Average offered	**APL** Average pay, low range	**FQ** First quartile wage	**LR** Low end range	**SQ** Second quartile wage	**Y** Yearly

Occupation/Type/Industry	Location	Per	Low	Mid	High	Source	Date
Taper	Oklahoma	S	14.98 MW	14.23 AW	29590 AAW	OKBLS	10//99-12//99
	Oregon	S	17.03 MW	17.42 AW	36230 AAW	ORBLS	10//99-12//99
	Pennsylvania	S	17.09 MW	18.13 AW	37710 AAW	PABLS	10//99-12//99
	Rhode Island	S	18.46 MW	18.92 AW	39340 AAW	RIBLS	10//99-12//99
	South Carolina	S	10.78 MW	12.47 AW	25930 AAW	SCBLS	10//99-12//99
	Tennessee	S	13.3 MW	13.34 AW	27740 AAW	TNBLS	10//99-12//99
	Texas	S	11.86 MW	11.07 AW	23030 AAW	TXBLS	10//99-12//99
	Utah	S	15.73 MW	15.78 AW	32820 AAW	UTBLS	10//99-12//99
	Vermont	S	17.49 MW	17.16 AW	35700 AAW	VTBLS	10//99-12//99
	Virginia	S	12.7 MW	12.56 AW	26120 AAW	VABLS	10//99-12//99
	Washington	S	20.95 MW	21.03 AW	43730 AAW	WABLS	10//99-12//99
	Wisconsin	S	16.5 MW	16.26 AW	33820 AAW	WIBLS	10//99-12//99
Tasting Room Worker Winery/Vineyard, Over 150K Cases/Year	United States	Y	21700 MW	22969 AW		PWV	1999
Tax Examiner, Collector, and Revenue Agent	Alabama	S	20.19 MW	20.01 AW	41620 AAW	ALBLS	10//99-12//99
	Arkansas	S	12.33 MW	14.37 AW	29880 AAW	ARBLS	10//99-12//99
	California	S	19.92 MW	21.48 AW	44680 AAW	CABLS	10//99-12//99
	Colorado	S	22.02 MW	22.79 AW	47410 AAW	COBLS	10//99-12//99
	Connecticut	S	24.44 MW	24.31 AW	50570 AAW	CTBLS	10//99-12//99
	Delaware	S	22.05 MW	23.38 AW	48640 AAW	DEBLS	10//99-12//99
	Florida	S	13.22 MW	16.40 AW	34120 AAW	FLBLS	10//99-12//99
	Idaho	S	16.16 MW	17.38 AW	36150 AAW	IDBLS	10//99-12//99
	Illinois	S	20.49 MW	22.24 AW	46260 AAW	ILBLS	10//99-12//99
	Indiana	S	15.19 MW	18.18 AW	37820 AAW	INBLS	10//99-12//99
	Iowa	S	18.97 MW	20.05 AW	41710 AAW	IABLS	10//99-12//99
	Kentucky	S	15.53 MW	16.78 AW	34910 AAW	KYBLS	10//99-12//99
	Louisiana	S	18.42 MW	19.13 AW	39800 AAW	LABLS	10//99-12//99
	Maine	S	15.71 MW	17.29 AW	35970 AAW	MEBLS	10//99-12//99
	Massachusetts	S	18.48 MW	20.24 AW	42090 AAW	MABLS	10//99-12//99
	Michigan	S	21.01 MW	21.73 AW	45200 AAW	MIBLS	10//99-12//99
	Minnesota	S	25.22 MW	24.93 AW	51850 AAW	MNBLS	10//99-12//99
	Mississippi	S	13.05 MW	14.76 AW	30700 AAW	MSBLS	10//99-12//99
	Missouri	S	14.75 MW	16.76 AW	34860 AAW	MOBLS	10//99-12//99
	Montana	S	17.23 MW	17.86 AW	37140 AAW	MTBLS	10//99-12//99
	Nebraska	S	20.79 MW	21.37 AW	44450 AAW	NEBLS	10//99-12//99
	Nevada	S	20.66 MW	21.99 AW	45730 AAW	NVBLS	10//99-12//99
	New Hampshire	S	16.73 MW	18.16 AW	37780 AAW	NHBLS	10//99-12//99
	New Jersey	S	23.23 MW	23.98 AW	49880 AAW	NJBLS	10//99-12//99
	New Mexico	S	13.59 MW	15.29 AW	31810 AAW	NMBLS	10//99-12//99
	New York	S	20.59 MW	21.61 AW	44940 AAW	NYBLS	10//99-12//99
	North Carolina	S	15.54 MW	17.12 AW	35610 AAW	NCBLS	10//99-12//99
	North Dakota	S	21.2 MW	20.10 AW	41800 AAW	NDBLS	10//99-12//99
	Ohio	S	19.48 MW	20.32 AW	42260 AAW	OHBLS	10//99-12//99
	Oklahoma	S	12.99 MW	16.86 AW	35070 AAW	OKBLS	10//99-12//99
	Oregon	S	17.38 MW	19.07 AW	39660 AAW	ORBLS	10//99-12//99
	Pennsylvania	S	14.3 MW	15.38 AW	31990 AAW	PABLS	10//99-12//99
	Rhode Island	S	21.99 MW	22.15 AW	46060 AAW	RIBLS	10//99-12//99
	South Carolina	S	18.54 MW	19.49 AW	40550 AAW	SCBLS	10//99-12//99
	South Dakota	S	14.15 MW	16.03 AW	33350 AAW	SDBLS	10//99-12//99
	Tennessee	S	15.6 MW	17.27 AW	35910 AAW	TNBLS	10//99-12//99
	Texas	S	17.52 MW	19.23 AW	40000 AAW	TXBLS	10//99-12//99
	Vermont	S	16.03 MW	17.61 AW	36630 AAW	VTBLS	10//99-12//99
	Virginia	S	18.48 MW	19.37 AW	40290 AAW	VABLS	10//99-12//99
	Washington	S	19.66 MW	20.70 AW	43050 AAW	WABLS	10//99-12//99
	West Virginia	S	10.72 MW	14.51 AW	30180 AAW	WVBLS	10//99-12//99
	Wisconsin	S	17.16 MW	17.93 AW	37290 AAW	WIBLS	10//99-12//99
	Wyoming	S	19.27 MW	20.12 AW	41850 AAW	WYBLS	10//99-12//99
Tax Preparer	Alabama	S	15.24 MW	13.86 AW	28820 AAW	ALBLS	10//99-12//99
	Anniston MSA, AL	S	12.25 MW	9.62 AW	25470 AAW	ALBLS	10//99-12//99
	Birmingham MSA, AL	S	19.43 MW	18.70 AW	40420 AAW	ALBLS	10//99-12//99
	Montgomery MSA, AL	S	12.54 MW	14.66 AW	26080 AAW	ALBLS	10//99-12//99
	Alaska	S	17.76 MW	16.66 AW	34650 AAW	AKBLS	10//99-12//99
	Arizona	S	9.87 MW	13.21 AW	27470 AAW	AZBLS	10//99-12//99
	Phoenix-Mesa MSA, AZ	S	15.35 MW	11.74 AW	31920 AAW	AZBLS	10//99-12//99
	Tucson MSA, AZ	S	9.85 MW	8.88 AW	20480 AAW	AZBLS	10//99-12//99
	Arkansas	S	8.36 MW	11.78 AW	24510 AAW	ARBLS	10//99-12//99
	California	S	12.04 MW	14.37 AW	29890 AAW	CABLS	10//99-12//99
	Bakersfield MSA, CA	S	19.08 MW	18.72 AW	39680 AAW	CABLS	10//99-12//99

AAW Average annual wage	**AOH** Average offered, high	**ASH** Average starting, high	**H** Hourly	**M** Monthly	**S** Special: hourly and annual
AE Average entry wage	**AOL** Average offered, low	**ASL** Average starting, low	**HI** Highest wage paid	**MTC** Median total compensation	**TQ** Third quartile wage
AEX Average experienced wage	**APH** Average pay, high range	**AW** Average wage paid	**HR** High end range	**MW** Median wage paid	**W** Weekly
AO Average offered	**APL** Average pay, low range	**FQ** First quartile wage	**LR** Low end range	**SQ** Second quartile wage	**Y** Yearly

Occupation/Type/Industry	Location	Per	Low	Mid	High	Source	Date
Tax Preparer	Los Angeles-Long Beach						
	PMSA, CA	S	16.22 MW	15.02 AW	33740 AAW	CABLS	10//99-12//99
	Orange County PMSA, CA	S	24.85 MW	27.78 AW	51680 AAW	CABLS	10//99-12//99
	San Diego MSA, CA	S	12.19 MW	10.52 AW	25360 AAW	CABLS	10//99-12//99
	San Jose PMSA, CA	S	29.07 MW	23.82 AW	60470 AAW	CABLS	10//99-12//99
	Santa Barbara-Santa Maria-						
	Lompoc MSA, CA	S	21.67 MW	19.47 AW	45080 AAW	CABLS	10//99-12//99
	Colorado	S	13.51 MW	14.57 AW	30300 AAW	COBLS	10//99-12//99
	Boulder-Longmont PMSA, CO	S	16.55 MW	16.57 AW	34420 AAW	COBLS	10//99-12//99
	Denver PMSA, CO	S	14.76 MW	14.47 AW	30700 AAW	COBLS	10//99-12//99
	Grand Junction MSA, CO	S	14.82 MW	14.62 AW	30810 AAW	COBLS	10//99-12//99
	Connecticut	S	17.55 MW	18.48 AW	38450 AAW	CTBLS	10//99-12//99
	Stamford-Norwalk PMSA, CT	S	21.52 MW	18.88 AW	44760 AAW	CTBLS	10//99-12//99
	District of Columbia	S	21.72 MW	23.22 AW	48300 AAW	DCBLS	10//99-12//99
	Washington PMSA, DC-MD-						
	VA-WV	S	20.25 MW	17.72 AW	42130 AAW	DCBLS	10//99-12//99
	Florida	S	9.24 MW	11.69 AW	24310 AAW	FLBLS	10//99-12//99
	Fort Lauderdale PMSA, FL	S	16.32 MW	16.74 AW	33940 AAW	FLBLS	10//99-12//99
	Fort Myers-Cape Coral MSA,						
	FL	S	16.01 MW	16.03 AW	33300 AAW	FLBLS	10//99-12//99
	Fort Pierce-Port St. Lucie						
	MSA, FL	S	9.70 MW	7.46 AW	20180 AAW	FLBLS	10//99-12//99
	Jacksonville MSA, FL	S	13.08 MW	10.35 AW	27210 AAW	FLBLS	10//99-12//99
	Lakeland-Winter Haven MSA,						
	FL	S	10.21 MW	8.21 AW	21230 AAW	FLBLS	10//99-12//99
	Melbourne-Titusville-Palm						
	Bay MSA, FL	S	13.14 MW	11.26 AW	27320 AAW	FLBLS	10//99-12//99
	Miami PMSA, FL	S	14.25 MW	12.74 AW	29630 AAW	FLBLS	10//99-12//99
	Orlando MSA, FL	S	18.48 MW	16.65 AW	38430 AAW	FLBLS	10//99-12//99
	Panama City MSA, FL	S	8.53 MW	7.77 AW	17730 AAW	FLBLS	10//99-12//99
	Pensacola MSA, FL	S	8.32 MW	7.91 AW	17310 AAW	FLBLS	10//99-12//99
	Sarasota-Bradenton MSA, FL	S	10.99 MW	12.04 AW	22850 AAW	FLBLS	10//99-12//99
	Tampa-St. Petersburg-						
	Clearwater MSA, FL	S	12.78 MW	10.07 AW	26580 AAW	FLBLS	10//99-12//99
	West Palm Beach-Boca Raton						
	MSA, FL	S	8.38 MW	7.78 AW	17430 AAW	FLBLS	10//99-12//99
	Georgia	S	16.65 MW	15.43 AW	32100 AAW	GABLS	10//99-12//99
	Atlanta MSA, GA	S	15.92 MW	17.32 AW	33100 AAW	GABLS	10//99-12//99
	Idaho	S	7.75 MW	9.49 AW	19750 AAW	IDBLS	10//99-12//99
	Illinois	S	14.57 MW	16.83 AW	35000 AAW	ILBLS	10//99-12//99
	Bloomington-Normal MSA, IL	S	9.53 MW	8.62 AW	19830 AAW	ILBLS	10//99-12//99
	Chicago PMSA, IL	S	17.14 MW	14.72 AW	35650 AAW	ILBLS	10//99-12//99
	Peoria-Pekin MSA, IL	S	11.19 MW	10.20 AW	23280 AAW	ILBLS	10//99-12//99
	Indiana	S	11.63 MW	13.44 AW	27950 AAW	INBLS	10//99-12//99
	Evansville-Henderson MSA,						
	IN-KY	S	13.05 MW	12.38 AW	27140 AAW	INBLS	10//99-12//99
	Fort Wayne MSA, IN	S	19.09 MW	19.67 AW	39720 AAW	INBLS	10//99-12//99
	Gary PMSA, IN	S	13.93 MW	12.13 AW	28980 AAW	INBLS	10//99-12//99
	Indianapolis MSA, IN	S	16.51 MW	15.57 AW	34340 AAW	INBLS	10//99-12//99
	South Bend MSA, IN	S	9.09 MW	9.26 AW	18900 AAW	INBLS	10//99-12//99
	Iowa	S	12.82 MW	13.80 AW	28700 AAW	IABLS	10//99-12//99
	Davenport-Moline-Rock Island						
	MSA, IA-IL	S	17.06 MW	14.48 AW	35480 AAW	IABLS	10//99-12//99
	Dubuque MSA, IA	S	19.31 MW	18.32 AW	40160 AAW	IABLS	10//99-12//99
	Kansas	S	8.48 MW	12.31 AW	25600 AAW	KSBLS	10//99-12//99
	Topeka MSA, KS	S	10.62 MW	8.14 AW	22100 AAW	KSBLS	10//99-12//99
	Wichita MSA, KS	S	19.49 MW	18.39 AW	40530 AAW	KSBLS	10//99-12//99
	Kentucky	S	9.87 MW	12.58 AW	26160 AAW	KYBLS	10//99-12//99
	Lexington MSA, KY	S	25.92 MW	20.52 AW	53920 AAW	KYBLS	10//99-12//99
	Louisville MSA, KY-IN	S	13.65 MW	13.58 AW	28400 AAW	KYBLS	10//99-12//99
	Louisiana	S	7.83 MW	10.42 AW	21680 AAW	LABLS	10//99-12//99
	Lake Charles MSA, LA	S	7.03 MW	6.16 AW	14610 AAW	LABLS	10//99-12//99
	Baltimore PMSA, MD	S	12.05 MW	9.16 AW	25060 AAW	MDBLS	10//99-12//99
	Massachusetts	S	19.01 MW	21.72 AW	45170 AAW	MABLS	10//99-12//99
	Boston PMSA, MA-NH	S	24.98 MW	22.70 AW	51960 AAW	MABLS	10//99-12//99
	Springfield MSA, MA	S	14.16 MW	12.57 AW	29460 AAW	MABLS	10//99-12//99
	Worcester PMSA, MA-CT	S	17.61 MW	16.96 AW	36630 AAW	MABLS	10//99-12//99
	Michigan	S	15.15 MW	16.39 AW	34090 AAW	MIBLS	10//99-12//99
	Detroit PMSA, MI	S	18.26 MW	18.28 AW	37970 AAW	MIBLS	10//99-12//99
	Flint PMSA, MI	S	12.54 MW	12.39 AW	26090 AAW	MIBLS	10//99-12//99
	Grand Rapids-Muskegon-						
	Holland MSA, MI	S	17.28 MW	17.42 AW	35950 AAW	MIBLS	10//99-12//99

AAW	Average annual wage	AOH	Average offered, high	ASH	Average starting, high
AE	Average entry wage	AOL	Average offered, low	ASL	Average starting, low
AEX	Average experienced wage	APH	Average pay, high range	AW	Average wage paid
AO	Average offered	APL	Average pay, low range	FQ	First quartile wage

H	Hourly	M	Monthly
HI	Highest wage paid	MTC	Median total compensation
HR	High end range	MW	Median wage paid
LR	Low end range	SQ	Second quartile wage

S	Special: hourly and annual
TQ	Third quartile wage
W	Weekly
Y	Yearly

Occupation/Type/Industry	Location	Per	Low	Mid	High	Source	Date
Tax Preparer	Minnesota	S	17.44 MW	19.16 AW	39860 AAW	MNBLS	10//99-12//99
	Duluth-Superior MSA, MN-WI	S	9.70 MW	8.70 AW	20180 AAW	MNBLS	10//99-12//99
	Minneapolis-St. Paul MSA, MN-WI	S	23.28 MW	22.15 AW	48430 AAW	MNBLS	10//99-12//99
	St. Cloud MSA, MN	S	9.88 MW	9.29 AW	20560 AAW	MNBLS	10//99-12//99
	Mississippi	S	8.89 MW	12.52 AW	26040 AAW	MSBLS	10//99-12//99
	Jackson MSA, MS	S	20.38 MW	21.68 AW	42400 AAW	MSBLS	10//99-12//99
	Missouri	S	11.67 MW	14.13 AW	29380 AAW	MOBLS	10//99-12//99
	Montana	S	12.14 MW	12.14 AW	25250 AAW	MTBLS	10//99-12//99
	Nebraska	S	11.28 MW	12.89 AW	26820 AAW	NEBLS	10//99-12//99
	Omaha MSA, NE-IA	S	15.29 MW	15.92 AW	31810 AAW	NEBLS	10//99-12//99
	Nevada	S	14.46 MW	15.65 AW	32550 AAW	NVBLS	10//99-12//99
	Reno MSA, NV	S	17.27 MW	16.99 AW	35920 AAW	NVBLS	10//99-12//99
	New Hampshire	S	14.52 MW	15.56 AW	32370 AAW	NHBLS	10//99-12//99
	New Jersey	S	16 MW	17.73 AW	36880 AAW	NJBLS	10//99-12//99
	Bergen-Passaic PMSA, NJ	S	13.41 MW	13.57 AW	27880 AAW	NJBLS	10//99-12//99
	Middlesex-Somerset-Hunterdon PMSA, NJ	S	19.84 MW	16.87 AW	41270 AAW	NJBLS	10//99-12//99
	Newark PMSA, NJ	S	17.90 MW	16.17 AW	37220 AAW	NJBLS	10//99-12//99
	Trenton PMSA, NJ	S	15.51 MW	13.97 AW	32250 AAW	NJBLS	10//99-12//99
	New Mexico	S	10.32 MW	12.20 AW	25370 AAW	NMBLS	10//99-12//99
	New York	S	12.3 MW	17.60 AW	36600 AAW	NYBLS	10//99-12//99
	Dutchess County PMSA, NY	S	15.68 MW	12.50 AW	32610 AAW	NYBLS	10//99-12//99
	New York PMSA, NY	S	20.37 MW	14.63 AW	42370 AAW	NYBLS	10//99-12//99
	Rochester MSA, NY	S	12.37 MW	9.12 AW	25720 AAW	NYBLS	10//99-12//99
	Syracuse MSA, NY	S	15.42 MW	12.71 AW	32080 AAW	NYBLS	10//99-12//99
	North Carolina	S	13.56 MW	14.40 AW	29940 AAW	NCBLS	10//99-12//99
	Charlotte-Gastonia-Rock Hill MSA, NC-SC	S	15.26 MW	14.09 AW	31740 AAW	NCBLS	10//99-12//99
	Rocky Mount MSA, NC	S	14.90 MW	14.61 AW	30980 AAW	NCBLS	10//99-12//99
	Wilmington MSA, NC	S	7.42 MW	6.09 AW	15430 AAW	NCBLS	10//99-12//99
	North Dakota	S	13.67 MW	14.83 AW	30840 AAW	NDBLS	10//99-12//99
	Ohio	S	11.95 MW	14.69 AW	30560 AAW	OHBLS	10//99-12//99
	Cincinnati PMSA, OH-KY-IN	S	17.83 MW	18.61 AW	37090 AAW	OHBLS	10//99-12//99
	Cleveland-Lorain-Elyria PMSA, OH	S	20.79 MW	16.77 AW	43240 AAW	OHBLS	10//99-12//99
	Dayton-Springfield MSA, OH	S	13.43 MW	11.44 AW	27930 AAW	OHBLS	10//99-12//99
	Toledo MSA, OH	S	10.80 MW	8.54 AW	22460 AAW	OHBLS	10//99-12//99
	Oklahoma	S	21.81 MW	21.73 AW	45210 AAW	OKBLS	10//99-12//99
	Oklahoma City MSA, OK	S	26.81 MW	27.36 AW	55760 AAW	OKBLS	10//99-12//99
	Oregon	S	11.06 MW	13.25 AW	27570 AAW	ORBLS	10//99-12//99
	Eugene-Springfield MSA, OR	S	11.02 MW	10.16 AW	22910 AAW	ORBLS	10//99-12//99
	Salem PMSA, OR	S	12.43 MW	11.86 AW	25850 AAW	ORBLS	10//99-12//99
	Pennsylvania	S	16.87 MW	21.25 AW	44210 AAW	PABLS	10//99-12//99
	Allentown-Bethlehem-Easton MSA, PA	S	17.82 MW	16.02 AW	37060 AAW	PABLS	10//99-12//99
	Harrisburg-Lebanon-Carlisle MSA, PA	S	16.49 MW	15.59 AW	34300 AAW	PABLS	10//99-12//99
	Lancaster MSA, PA	S	24.28 MW	18.26 AW	50500 AAW	PABLS	10//99-12//99
	Philadelphia PMSA, PA-NJ	S	22.07 MW	17.30 AW	45900 AAW	PABLS	10//99-12//99
	Pittsburgh MSA, PA	S	22.62 MW	17.37 AW	47040 AAW	PABLS	10//99-12//99
	Rhode Island	S	13.72 MW	13.97 AW	29070 AAW	RIBLS	10//99-12//99
	Providence-Fall River-Warwick MSA, RI-MA	S	13.93 MW	13.74 AW	28970 AAW	RIBLS	10//99-12//99
	South Carolina	S	10.99 MW	12.75 AW	26520 AAW	SCBLS	10//99-12//99
	Charleston-North Charleston MSA, SC	S	11.80 MW	9.94 AW	24540 AAW	SCBLS	10//99-12//99
	Columbia MSA, SC	S	10.81 MW	11.08 AW	22480 AAW	SCBLS	10//99-12//99
	Greenville-Spartanburg-Anderson MSA, SC	S	15.84 MW	13.68 AW	32960 AAW	SCBLS	10//99-12//99
	South Dakota	S	14.64 MW	15.05 AW	31300 AAW	SDBLS	10//99-12//99
	Sioux Falls MSA, SD	S	19.17 MW	16.04 AW	39880 AAW	SDBLS	10//99-12//99
	Tennessee	S	11.22 MW	12.57 AW	26140 AAW	TNBLS	10//99-12//99
	Johnson City-Kingsport-Bristol MSA, TN-VA	S	16.50 MW	10.38 AW	34320 AAW	TNBLS	10//99-12//99
	Knoxville MSA, TN	S	11.02 MW	11.13 AW	22910 AAW	TNBLS	10//99-12//99
	Memphis MSA, TN-AR-MS	S	13.21 MW	10.99 AW	27470 AAW	MSBLS	10//99-12//99
	Nashville MSA, TN	S	10.37 MW	6.99 AW	21580 AAW	TNBLS	10//99-12//99
	Texas	S	12.46 MW	14.87 AW	30920 AAW	TXBLS	10//99-12//99
	Austin-San Marcos MSA, TX	S	13.63 MW	12.01 AW	28340 AAW	TXBLS	10//99-12//99
	Brownsville-Harlingen-San Benito MSA, TX	S	11.18 MW	9.46 AW	23250 AAW	TXBLS	10//99-12//99

AAW	Average annual wage	AOH	Average offered, high	ASH	Average starting, high	H	Hourly	M	Monthly	S	Special: hourly and annual
AE	Average entry wage	AOL	Average offered, low	ASL	Average starting, low	HI	Highest wage paid	MTC	Median total compensation	TQ	Third quartile wage
AEX	Average experienced wage	APH	Average pay, high range	AW	Average wage paid	HR	High end range	MW	Median wage paid	W	Weekly
AO	Average offered	APL	Average pay, low range	FQ	First quartile wage	LR	Low end range	SQ	Second quartile wage	Y	Yearly

Occupation/Type/Industry	Location	Per	Low	Mid	High	Source	Date
Tax Preparer	Dallas PMSA, TX	S	18.55 MW	17.08 AW	38580 AAW	TXBLS	10//99-12//99
	El Paso MSA, TX	S	13.80 MW	8.40 AW	28690 AAW	TXBLS	10//99-12//99
	Fort Worth-Arlington PMSA, TX	S	14.09 MW	13.91 AW	29300 AAW	TXBLS	10//99-12//99
	Houston PMSA, TX	S	15.92 MW	13.31 AW	33120 AAW	TXBLS	10//99-12//99
	Lubbock MSA, TX	S	9.75 MW	9.42 AW	20280 AAW	TXBLS	10//99-12//99
	McAllen-Edinburg-Mission MSA, TX	S	11.06 MW	6.52 AW	23010 AAW	TXBLS	10//99-12//99
	San Antonio MSA, TX	S	14.97 MW	14.26 AW	31140 AAW	TXBLS	10//99-12//99
	Sherman-Denison MSA, TX	S	9.05 MW	8.35 AW	18820 AAW	TXBLS	10//99-12//99
	Waco MSA, TX	S	10.95 MW	10.00 AW	22790 AAW	TXBLS	10//99-12//99
	Virginia	S	12.34 MW	17.14 AW	35660 AAW	VABLS	10//99-12//99
	Norfolk-Virginia Beach-Newport News MSA, VA-NC	S	10.49 MW	10.54 AW	21820 AAW	VABLS	10//99-12//99
	Richmond-Petersburg MSA, VA	S	19.43 MW	17.73 AW	40420 AAW	VABLS	10//99-12//99
	Washington	S	14.78 MW	15.95 AW	33180 AAW	WABLS	10//99-12//99
	Seattle-Bellevue-Everett PMSA, WA	S	16.25 MW	10.46 AW	33790 AAW	WABLS	10//99-12//99
	Spokane MSA, WA	S	12.08 MW	8.94 AW	25120 AAW	WABLS	10//99-12//99
	West Virginia	S	9.94 MW	10.43 AW	21690 AAW	WVBLS	10//99-12//99
	Charleston MSA, WV	S	9.67 MW	6.96 AW	20110 AAW	WVBLS	10//99-12//99
	Wisconsin	S	13.42 MW	14.02 AW	29150 AAW	WIBLS	10//99-12//99
	Milwaukee-Waukesha PMSA, WI	S	15.40 MW	17.35 AW	32030 AAW	WIBLS	10//99-12//99
	Puerto Rico	S	19.54 MW	19.81 AW	41210 AAW	PRBLS	10//99-12//99
	San Juan-Bayamon PMSA, PR	S	20.02 MW	19.55 AW	41650 AAW	PRBLS	10//99-12//99
Taxi Driver and Chauffeur	Alabama	S	7.88 MW	8.26 AW	17180 AAW	ALBLS	10//99-12//99
	Birmingham MSA, AL	S	7.58 MW	7.43 AW	15760 AAW	ALBLS	10//99-12//99
	Mobile MSA, AL	S	6.94 MW	7.12 AW	14440 AAW	ALBLS	10//99-12//99
	Montgomery MSA, AL	S	9.47 MW	9.02 AW	19700 AAW	ALBLS	10//99-12//99
	Alaska	S	8.05 MW	9.41 AW	19570 AAW	AKBLS	10//99-12//99
	Anchorage MSA, AK	S	10.19 MW	8.63 AW	21200 AAW	AKBLS	10//99-12//99
	Arizona	S	7.61 MW	7.80 AW	16210 AAW	AZBLS	10//99-12//99
	Phoenix-Mesa MSA, AZ	S	7.83 MW	7.68 AW	16300 AAW	AZBLS	10//99-12//99
	Tucson MSA, AZ	S	8.42 MW	8.35 AW	17520 AAW	AZBLS	10//99-12//99
	Arkansas	S	6.46 MW	6.91 AW	14370 AAW	ARBLS	10//99-12//99
	Little Rock-North Little Rock MSA, AR	S	7.92 MW	6.99 AW	16470 AAW	ARBLS	10//99-12//99
	California	S	7.89 MW	9.08 AW	18880 AAW	CABLS	10//99-12//99
	Bakersfield MSA, CA	S	7.75 MW	7.62 AW	16120 AAW	CABLS	10//99-12//99
	Chico-Paradise MSA, CA	S	10.40 MW	10.00 AW	21630 AAW	CABLS	10//99-12//99
	Fresno MSA, CA	S	9.63 MW	9.76 AW	20020 AAW	CABLS	10//99-12//99
	Los Angeles-Long Beach PMSA, CA	S	9.98 MW	9.16 AW	20750 AAW	CABLS	10//99-12//99
	Oakland PMSA, CA	S	8.41 MW	7.33 AW	17490 AAW	CABLS	10//99-12//99
	Orange County PMSA, CA	S	9.02 MW	8.05 AW	18760 AAW	CABLS	10//99-12//99
	Riverside-San Bernardino PMSA, CA	S	7.16 MW	6.68 AW	14900 AAW	CABLS	10//99-12//99
	Sacramento PMSA, CA	S	7.81 MW	7.46 AW	16250 AAW	CABLS	10//99-12//99
	San Diego MSA, CA	S	8.54 MW	6.71 AW	17770 AAW	CABLS	10//99-12//99
	San Francisco PMSA, CA	S	10.17 MW	8.85 AW	21150 AAW	CABLS	10//99-12//99
	San Jose PMSA, CA	S	7.99 MW	6.89 AW	16610 AAW	CABLS	10//99-12//99
	San Luis Obispo-Atascadero-Paso Robles MSA, CA	S	12.20 MW	8.97 AW	25380 AAW	CABLS	10//99-12//99
	Santa Barbara-Santa Maria-Lompoc MSA, CA	S	7.54 MW	6.72 AW	15690 AAW	CABLS	10//99-12//99
	Santa Rosa PMSA, CA	S	9.05 MW	8.14 AW	18830 AAW	CABLS	10//99-12//99
	Ventura PMSA, CA	S	9.77 MW	8.95 AW	20310 AAW	CABLS	10//99-12//99
	Yuba City MSA, CA	S	8.48 MW	6.81 AW	17640 AAW	CABLS	10//99-12//99
	Colorado	S	8.33 MW	8.57 AW	17820 AAW	COBLS	10//99-12//99
	Boulder-Longmont PMSA, CO	S	9.02 MW	7.61 AW	18760 AAW	COBLS	10//99-12//99
	Colorado Springs MSA, CO	S	6.70 MW	6.03 AW	13930 AAW	COBLS	10//99-12//99
	Denver PMSA, CO	S	8.75 MW	8.46 AW	18190 AAW	COBLS	10//99-12//99
	Grand Junction MSA, CO	S	6.45 MW	6.20 AW	13410 AAW	COBLS	10//99-12//99
	Pueblo MSA, CO	S	8.78 MW	8.10 AW	18270 AAW	COBLS	10//99-12//99
	Connecticut	S	9.64 MW	10.47 AW	21770 AAW	CTBLS	10//99-12//99
	Bridgeport PMSA, CT	S	9.49 MW	7.92 AW	19750 AAW	CTBLS	10//99-12//99
	Danbury PMSA, CT	S	11.32 MW	11.04 AW	23550 AAW	CTBLS	10//99-12//99
	Hartford MSA, CT	S	9.19 MW	9.24 AW	19110 AAW	CTBLS	10//99-12//99

Occupation/Type/Industry	Location	Per	Low	Mid	High	Source	Date
Taxi Driver and Chauffeur	New Haven-Meriden PMSA, CT	S	8.60 MW	8.09 AW	17880 AAW	CTBLS	10//99-12//99
	New London-Norwich MSA, CT-RI	S	8.32 MW	8.00 AW	17300 AAW	CTBLS	10//99-12//99
	Stamford-Norwalk PMSA, CT	S	14.34 MW	13.36 AW	29820 AAW	CTBLS	10//99-12//99
	Waterbury PMSA, CT	S	10.63 MW	10.84 AW	22110 AAW	CTBLS	10//99-12//99
	Delaware	S	8.51 MW	9.99 AW	20780 AAW	DEBLS	10//99-12//99
	Dover MSA, DE	S	8.97 MW	7.87 AW	18670 AAW	DEBLS	10//99-12//99
	Wilmington-Newark PMSA, DE-MD	S	10.56 MW	9.07 AW	21960 AAW	DEBLS	10//99-12//99
	District of Columbia	S	9.71 MW	10.41 AW	21660 AAW	DCBLS	10//99-12//99
	Washington PMSA, DC-MD-VA-WV	S	9.36 MW	8.98 AW	19470 AAW	DCBLS	10//99-12//99
	Florida	S	7.8 MW	8.59 AW	17870 AAW	FLBLS	10//99-12//99
	Daytona Beach MSA, FL	S	7.49 MW	7.50 AW	15570 AAW	FLBLS	10//99-12//99
	Fort Lauderdale PMSA, FL	S	8.86 MW	8.34 AW	18430 AAW	FLBLS	10//99-12//99
	Fort Myers-Cape Coral MSA, FL	S	7.90 MW	7.76 AW	16430 AAW	FLBLS	10//99-12//99
	Fort Pierce-Port St. Lucie MSA, FL	S	7.56 MW	7.27 AW	15730 AAW	FLBLS	10//99-12//99
	Gainesville MSA, FL	S	8.17 MW	7.42 AW	17000 AAW	FLBLS	10//99-12//99
	Jacksonville MSA, FL	S	7.92 MW	7.61 AW	16480 AAW	FLBLS	10//99-12//99
	Melbourne-Titusville-Palm Bay MSA, FL	S	6.73 MW	6.34 AW	13990 AAW	FLBLS	10//99-12//99
	Miami PMSA, FL	S	9.11 MW	8.64 AW	18950 AAW	FLBLS	10//99-12//99
	Orlando MSA, FL	S	10.18 MW	7.08 AW	21180 AAW	FLBLS	10//99-12//99
	Pensacola MSA, FL	S	7.18 MW	7.13 AW	14930 AAW	FLBLS	10//99-12//99
	Sarasota-Bradenton MSA, FL	S	7.73 MW	7.74 AW	16080 AAW	FLBLS	10//99-12//99
	Tallahassee MSA, FL	S	7.91 MW	7.85 AW	16460 AAW	FLBLS	10//99-12//99
	Tampa-St. Petersburg-Clearwater MSA, FL	S	7.90 MW	7.79 AW	16440 AAW	FLBLS	10//99-12//99
	West Palm Beach-Boca Raton MSA, FL	S	9.08 MW	8.34 AW	18880 AAW	FLBLS	10//99-12//99
	Georgia	S	7.2 MW	7.87 AW	16370 AAW	GABLS	10//99-12//99
	Albany MSA, GA	S	7.76 MW	6.61 AW	16150 AAW	GABLS	10//99-12//99
	Athens MSA, GA	S	8.04 MW	7.80 AW	16730 AAW	GABLS	10//99-12//99
	Atlanta MSA, GA	S	8.24 MW	8.04 AW	17140 AAW	GABLS	10//99-12//99
	Augusta-Aiken MSA, GA-SC	S	7.11 MW	6.61 AW	14790 AAW	GABLS	10//99-12//99
	Columbus MSA, GA-AL	S	6.56 MW	6.39 AW	13640 AAW	GABLS	10//99-12//99
	Macon MSA, GA	S	8.15 MW	7.72 AW	16950 AAW	GABLS	10//99-12//99
	Savannah MSA, GA	S	6.60 MW	6.49 AW	13720 AAW	GABLS	10//99-12//99
	Hawaii	S	11.06 MW	10.78 AW	22410 AAW	HIBLS	10//99-12//99
	Honolulu MSA, HI	S	10.90 MW	11.13 AW	22660 AAW	HIBLS	10//99-12//99
	Idaho	S	7.3 MW	8.71 AW	18120 AAW	IDBLS	10//99-12//99
	Boise City MSA, ID	S	9.14 MW	7.14 AW	19000 AAW	IDBLS	10//99-12//99
	Illinois	S	8.7 MW	9.74 AW	20270 AAW	ILBLS	10//99-12//99
	Chicago PMSA, IL	S	10.68 MW	9.71 AW	22210 AAW	ILBLS	10//99-12//99
	Decatur MSA, IL	S	9.60 MW	8.18 AW	19960 AAW	ILBLS	10//99-12//99
	Peoria-Pekin MSA, IL	S	9.69 MW	8.16 AW	20150 AAW	ILBLS	10//99-12//99
	Rockford MSA, IL	S	9.31 MW	8.82 AW	19370 AAW	ILBLS	10//99-12//99
	Springfield MSA, IL	S	7.26 MW	6.86 AW	15100 AAW	ILBLS	10//99-12//99
	Indiana	S	6.89 MW	7.42 AW	15440 AAW	INBLS	10//99-12//99
	Evansville-Henderson MSA, IN-KY	S	7.39 MW	7.15 AW	15370 AAW	INBLS	10//99-12//99
	Fort Wayne MSA, IN	S	7.42 MW	7.47 AW	15440 AAW	INBLS	10//99-12//99
	Gary PMSA, IN	S	7.17 MW	6.64 AW	14920 AAW	INBLS	10//99-12//99
	Indianapolis MSA, IN	S	7.39 MW	6.72 AW	15360 AAW	INBLS	10//99-12//99
	Lafayette MSA, IN	S	6.84 MW	6.46 AW	14220 AAW	INBLS	10//99-12//99
	South Bend MSA, IN	S	8.56 MW	7.20 AW	17800 AAW	INBLS	10//99-12//99
	Iowa	S	6.79 MW	7.52 AW	15650 AAW	IABLS	10//99-12//99
	Davenport-Moline-Rock Island MSA, IA-IL	S	8.01 MW	7.32 AW	16650 AAW	IABLS	10//99-12//99
	Des Moines MSA, IA	S	9.60 MW	7.13 AW	19970 AAW	IABLS	10//99-12//99
	Iowa City MSA, IA	S	7.96 MW	7.40 AW	16550 AAW	IABLS	10//99-12//99
	Sioux City MSA, IA-NE	S	7.10 MW	7.07 AW	14780 AAW	IABLS	10//99-12//99
	Kansas	S	7.21 MW	7.98 AW	16600 AAW	KSBLS	10//99-12//99
	Topeka MSA, KS	S	7.53 MW	6.98 AW	15650 AAW	KSBLS	10//99-12//99
	Wichita MSA, KS	S	6.48 MW	6.50 AW	13470 AAW	KSBLS	10//99-12//99
	Kentucky	S	6.85 MW	7.27 AW	15130 AAW	KYBLS	10//99-12//99
	Lexington MSA, KY	S	8.62 MW	7.31 AW	17930 AAW	KYBLS	10//99-12//99
	Louisville MSA, KY-IN	S	7.54 MW	7.28 AW	15680 AAW	KYBLS	10//99-12//99
	Louisiana	S	7.4 MW	8.28 AW	17220 AAW	LABLS	10//99-12//99

AAW Average annual wage	**AOH** Average offered, high	**ASH** Average starting, high	**H** Hourly	**M** Monthly	**S** Special: hourly and annual
AE Average entry wage	**AOL** Average offered, low	**ASL** Average starting, low	**HI** Highest wage paid	**MTC** Median total compensation	**TQ** Third quartile wage
AEX Average experienced wage	**APH** Average pay, high range	**AW** Average wage paid	**HR** High end range	**MW** Median wage paid	**W** Weekly
AO Average offered	**APL** Average pay, low range	**FQ** First quartile wage	**LR** Low end range	**SQ** Second quartile wage	**Y** Yearly

Occupation/Type/Industry	Location	Per	Low	Mid	High	Source	Date
Taxi Driver and Chauffeur	Alexandria MSA, LA	S	7.25 MW	6.54 AW	15080 AAW	LABLS	10//99-12//99
	Baton Rouge MSA, LA	S	7.52 MW	7.24 AW	15650 AAW	LABLS	10//99-12//99
	Houma MSA, LA	S	6.49 MW	6.24 AW	13500 AAW	LABLS	10//99-12//99
	Lafayette MSA, LA	S	7.93 MW	7.07 AW	16500 AAW	LABLS	10//99-12//99
	Lake Charles MSA, LA	S	7.18 MW	6.63 AW	14930 AAW	LABLS	10//99-12//99
	Monroe MSA, LA	S	8.92 MW	7.90 AW	18550 AAW	LABLS	10//99-12//99
	New Orleans MSA, LA	S	8.57 MW	7.56 AW	17830 AAW	LABLS	10//99-12//99
	Shreveport-Bossier City MSA, LA	S	9.20 MW	8.13 AW	19140 AAW	LABLS	10//99-12//99
	Maine	S	7.84 MW	8.07 AW	16790 AAW	MEBLS	10//99-12//99
	Bangor MSA, ME	S	8.09 MW	7.43 AW	16830 AAW	MEBLS	10//99-12//99
	Lewiston-Auburn MSA, ME	S	8.53 MW	8.14 AW	17730 AAW	MEBLS	10//99-12//99
	Portland MSA, ME	S	8.30 MW	7.97 AW	17260 AAW	MEBLS	10//99-12//99
	Maryland	S	8.21 MW	8.79 AW	18290 AAW	MDBLS	10//99-12//99
	Baltimore PMSA, MD	S	8.57 MW	8.01 AW	17830 AAW	MDBLS	10//99-12//99
	Hagerstown PMSA, MD	S	6.30 MW	6.24 AW	13100 AAW	MDBLS	10//99-12//99
	Massachusetts	S	8.35 MW	9.01 AW	18730 AAW	MABLS	10//99-12//99
	Barnstable-Yarmouth MSA, MA	S	8.92 MW	8.43 AW	18560 AAW	MABLS	10//99-12//99
	Boston PMSA, MA-NH	S	9.12 MW	8.76 AW	18980 AAW	MABLS	10//99-12//99
	Brockton PMSA, MA	S	9.29 MW	8.93 AW	19330 AAW	MABLS	10//99-12//99
	Fitchburg-Leominster PMSA, MA	S	8.10 MW	7.71 AW	16850 AAW	MABLS	10//99-12//99
	Lawrence PMSA, MA-NH	S	8.11 MW	7.75 AW	16880 AAW	MABLS	10//99-12//99
	Lowell PMSA, MA-NH	S	11.31 MW	11.54 AW	23530 AAW	MABLS	10//99-12//99
	New Bedford PMSA, MA	S	8.23 MW	7.89 AW	17130 AAW	MABLS	10//99-12//99
	Pittsfield MSA, MA	S	9.10 MW	8.62 AW	18930 AAW	MABLS	10//99-12//99
	Springfield MSA, MA	S	9.26 MW	8.35 AW	19260 AAW	MABLS	10//99-12//99
	Worcester PMSA, MA-CT	S	7.93 MW	7.06 AW	16490 AAW	MABLS	10//99-12//99
	Michigan	S	8.19 MW	9.84 AW	20470 AAW	MIBLS	10//99-12//99
	Ann Arbor PMSA, MI	S	11.16 MW	9.57 AW	23210 AAW	MIBLS	10//99-12//99
	Benton Harbor MSA, MI	S	6.77 MW	6.30 AW	14090 AAW	MIBLS	10//99-12//99
	Detroit PMSA, MI	S	10.65 MW	8.85 AW	22150 AAW	MIBLS	10//99-12//99
	Flint PMSA, MI	S	11.41 MW	9.16 AW	23720 AAW	MIBLS	10//99-12//99
	Grand Rapids-Muskegon-Holland MSA, MI	S	7.34 MW	6.95 AW	15270 AAW	MIBLS	
	Saginaw-Bay City-Midland MSA, MI	S	7.06 MW	7.04 AW	14680 AAW	MIBLS	10//99-12//99
	Minnesota	S	8.62 MW	8.68 AW	18060 AAW	MNBLS	10//99-12//99
	Minneapolis-St. Paul MSA, MN-WI	S	8.54 MW	8.43 AW	17750 AAW	MNBLS	10//99-12//99
	Rochester MSA, MN	S	10.28 MW	10.44 AW	21390 AAW	MNBLS	10//99-12//99
	Mississippi	S	6.52 MW	6.68 AW	13880 AAW	MSBLS	10//99-12//99
	Biloxi-Gulfport-Pascagoula MSA, MS	S	6.33 MW	6.23 AW	13170 AAW	MSBLS	10//99-12//99
	Missouri	S	7.26 MW	7.80 AW	16220 AAW	MOBLS	10//99-12//99
	Joplin MSA, MO	S	9.29 MW	7.43 AW	19320 AAW	MOBLS	10//99-12//99
	Kansas City MSA, MO-KS	S	7.68 MW	7.15 AW	15980 AAW	MOBLS	10//99-12//99
	St. Louis MSA, MO-IL	S	8.36 MW	7.61 AW	17380 AAW	MOBLS	10//99-12//99
	Springfield MSA, MO	S	6.72 MW	6.62 AW	13970 AAW	MOBLS	10//99-12//99
	Montana	S	6.84 MW	7.03 AW	14620 AAW	MTBLS	10//99-12//99
	Billings MSA, MT	S	6.86 MW	6.56 AW	14260 AAW	MTBLS	10//99-12//99
	Missoula MSA, MT	S	7.41 MW	7.39 AW	15420 AAW	MTBLS	10//99-12//99
	Nebraska	S	7.21 MW	7.22 AW	15020 AAW	NEBLS	10//99-12//99
	Lincoln MSA, NE	S	7.34 MW	7.42 AW	15260 AAW	NEBLS	10//99-12//99
	Omaha MSA, NE-IA	S	7.01 MW	6.76 AW	14570 AAW	NEBLS	10//99-12//99
	Nevada	S	12.12 MW	11.74 AW	24420 AAW	NVBLS	10//99-12//99
	Las Vegas MSA, NV-AZ	S	11.85 MW	12.19 AW	24650 AAW	NVBLS	10//99-12//99
	Reno MSA, NV	S	10.73 MW	11.36 AW	22310 AAW	NVBLS	10//99-12//99
	New Hampshire	S	7.76 MW	7.89 AW	16410 AAW	NHBLS	10//99-12//99
	Manchester PMSA, NH	S	8.99 MW	9.00 AW	18710 AAW	NHBLS	10//99-12//99
	Nashua PMSA, NH	S	8.72 MW	9.14 AW	18130 AAW	NHBLS	10//99-12//99
	Portsmouth-Rochester PMSA, NH-ME	S	6.90 MW	6.51 AW	14350 AAW	NHBLS	10//99-12//99
	New Jersey	S	8.63 MW	9.31 AW	19360 AAW	NJBLS	10//99-12//99
	Atlantic-Cape May PMSA, NJ	S	7.14 MW	6.61 AW	14860 AAW	NJBLS	10//99-12//99
	Bergen-Passaic PMSA, NJ	S	9.64 MW	9.32 AW	20050 AAW	NJBLS	10//99-12//99
	Jersey City PMSA, NJ	S	11.18 MW	10.95 AW	23260 AAW	NJBLS	10//99-12//99
	Middlesex-Somerset-Hunterdon PMSA, NJ	S	8.91 MW	8.68 AW	18540 AAW	NJBLS	10//99-12//99
	Monmouth-Ocean PMSA, NJ	S	8.96 MW	7.75 AW	18650 AAW	NJBLS	10//99-12//99
	Newark PMSA, NJ	S	10.31 MW	9.90 AW	21450 AAW	NJBLS	10//99-12//99

AAW Average annual wage	**AOH** Average offered, high	**ASH** Average starting, high	**H** Hourly	**M** Monthly	**S** Special: hourly and annual
AE Average entry wage	**AOL** Average offered, low	**ASL** Average starting, low	**HI** Highest wage paid	**MTC** Median total compensation	**TQ** Third quartile wage
AEX Average experienced wage	**APH** Average pay, high range	**AW** Average wage paid	**HR** High end range	**MW** Median wage paid	**W** Weekly
AO Average offered	**APL** Average pay, low range	**FQ** First quartile wage	**LR** Low end range	**SQ** Second quartile wage	**Y** Yearly

Occupation/Type/Industry	Location	Per	Low	Mid	High	Source	Date
Taxi Driver and Chauffeur	Vineland-Millville-Bridgeton						
	PMSA, NJ	S	7.72 mw	7.62 aw	16050 aaw	NJBLS	10//99-12//99
	New Mexico	S	7.69 mw	8.11 aw	16870 aaw	NMBLS	10//99-12//99
	Albuquerque MSA, NM	S	8.16 mw	7.88 aw	16970 aaw	NMBLS	10//99-12//99
	Las Cruces MSA, NM	S	7.14 mw	7.32 aw	14850 aaw	NMBLS	10//99-12//99
	Santa Fe MSA, NM	S	7.07 mw	7.31 aw	14710 aaw	NMBLS	10//99-12//99
	New York	S	8.27 mw	9.42 aw	19600 aaw	NYBLS	10//99-12//99
	Albany-Schenectady-Troy						
	MSA, NY	S	7.74 mw	6.94 aw	16090 aaw	NYBLS	10//99-12//99
	Binghamton MSA, NY	S	6.93 mw	6.72 aw	14410 aaw	NYBLS	10//99-12//99
	Buffalo-Niagara Falls MSA,						
	NY	S	8.02 mw	7.34 aw	16670 aaw	NYBLS	10//99-12//99
	Dutchess County PMSA, NY	S	8.42 mw	8.27 aw	17510 aaw	NYBLS	10//99-12//99
	Jamestown MSA, NY	S	7.01 mw	6.80 aw	14570 aaw	NYBLS	10//99-12//99
	Nassau-Suffolk PMSA, NY	S	9.77 mw	9.81 aw	20330 aaw	NYBLS	10//99-12//99
	New York PMSA, NY	S	10.26 mw	8.58 aw	21350 aaw	NYBLS	10//99-12//99
	Newburgh PMSA, NY-PA	S	8.24 mw	6.71 aw	17140 aaw	NYBLS	10//99-12//99
	Rochester MSA, NY	S	8.78 mw	7.97 aw	18260 aaw	NYBLS	10//99-12//99
	Syracuse MSA, NY	S	6.17 mw	5.97 aw	12830 aaw	NYBLS	10//99-12//99
	Utica-Rome MSA, NY	S	6.97 mw	6.72 aw	14500 aaw	NYBLS	10//99-12//99
	North Carolina	S	7 mw	7.60 aw	15810 aaw	NCBLS	10//99-12//99
	Asheville MSA, NC	S	6.83 mw	6.65 aw	14200 aaw	NCBLS	10//99-12//99
	Charlotte-Gastonia-Rock Hill						
	MSA, NC-SC	S	8.80 mw	7.99 aw	18300 aaw	NCBLS	10//99-12//99
	Greensboro--Winston-Salem--						
	High Point MSA, NC	S	7.34 mw	6.86 aw	15280 aaw	NCBLS	10//99-12//99
	Greenville MSA, NC	S	8.82 mw	8.70 aw	18350 aaw	NCBLS	10//99-12//99
	Raleigh-Durham-Chapel Hill						
	MSA, NC	S	7.45 mw	6.86 aw	15500 aaw	NCBLS	10//99-12//99
	Wilmington MSA, NC	S	7.95 mw	7.04 aw	16530 aaw	NCBLS	10//99-12//99
	North Dakota	S	6.84 mw	6.85 aw	14250 aaw	NDBLS	10//99-12//99
	Bismarck MSA, ND	S	6.83 mw	6.99 aw	14210 aaw	NDBLS	10//99-12//99
	Ohio	S	6.88 mw	7.59 aw	15780 aaw	OHBLS	10//99-12//99
	Akron PMSA, OH	S	8.22 mw	8.00 aw	17090 aaw	OHBLS	10//99-12//99
	Canton-Massillon MSA, OH	S	8.39 mw	8.02 aw	17450 aaw	OHBLS	10//99-12//99
	Cincinnati PMSA, OH-KY-IN	S	6.89 mw	6.62 aw	14340 aaw	OHBLS	10//99-12//99
	Cleveland-Lorain-Elyria						
	PMSA, OH	S	8.27 mw	7.92 aw	17190 aaw	OHBLS	10//99-12//99
	Columbus MSA, OH	S	7.13 mw	6.43 aw	14830 aaw	OHBLS	10//99-12//99
	Dayton-Springfield MSA, OH	S	9.55 mw	7.45 aw	19860 aaw	OHBLS	10//99-12//99
	Lima MSA, OH	S	6.86 mw	6.18 aw	14270 aaw	OHBLS	10//99-12//99
	Toledo MSA, OH	S	8.61 mw	7.41 aw	17910 aaw	OHBLS	10//99-12//99
	Youngstown-Warren MSA, OH	S	6.93 mw	6.47 aw	14420 aaw	OHBLS	10//99-12//99
	Oklahoma	S	6.43 mw	7.04 aw	14630 aaw	OKBLS	10//99-12//99
	Oklahoma City MSA, OK	S	7.45 mw	6.62 aw	15490 aaw	OKBLS	10//99-12//99
	Tulsa MSA, OK	S	6.15 mw	5.95 aw	12780 aaw	OKBLS	10//99-12//99
	Oregon	S	7.99 mw	8.38 aw	17430 aaw	ORBLS	10//99-12//99
	Eugene-Springfield MSA, OR	S	7.85 mw	7.56 aw	16330 aaw	ORBLS	10//99-12//99
	Salem PMSA, OR	S	9.40 mw	8.35 aw	19550 aaw	ORBLS	10//99-12//99
	Pennsylvania	S	7.28 mw	7.97 aw	16580 aaw	PABLS	10//99-12//99
	Allentown-Bethlehem-Easton						
	MSA, PA	S	8.49 mw	8.05 aw	17650 aaw	PABLS	10//99-12//99
	Altoona MSA, PA	S	6.10 mw	6.18 aw	12680 aaw	PABLS	10//99-12//99
	Erie MSA, PA	S	7.47 mw	7.18 aw	15530 aaw	PABLS	10//99-12//99
	Harrisburg-Lebanon-Carlisle						
	MSA, PA	S	7.40 mw	6.85 aw	15390 aaw	PABLS	10//99-12//99
	Johnstown MSA, PA	S	6.98 mw	6.68 aw	14530 aaw	PABLS	10//99-12//99
	Philadelphia PMSA, PA-NJ	S	8.20 mw	7.62 aw	17060 aaw	PABLS	10//99-12//99
	Pittsburgh MSA, PA	S	7.56 mw	6.65 aw	15710 aaw	PABLS	10//99-12//99
	Reading MSA, PA	S	7.75 mw	7.27 aw	16120 aaw	PABLS	10//99-12//99
	Scranton--Wilkes-Barre--						
	Hazleton MSA, PA	S	6.92 mw	6.52 aw	14390 aaw	PABLS	10//99-12//99
	Williamsport MSA, PA	S	8.71 mw	6.97 aw	18120 aaw	PABLS	10//99-12//99
	York MSA, PA	S	7.10 mw	6.57 aw	14770 aaw	PABLS	10//99-12//99
	Rhode Island	S	7.76 mw	8.37 aw	17410 aaw	RIBLS	10//99-12//99
	Providence-Fall River-						
	Warwick MSA, RI-MA	S	8.21 mw	7.58 aw	17080 aaw	RIBLS	10//99 12//99
	South Carolina	S	7.37 mw	7.81 aw	16240 aaw	SCBLS	10//99-12//99
	Charleston-North Charleston						
	MSA, SC	S	7.06 mw	6.87 aw	14690 aaw	SCBLS	10//99-12//99
	Columbia MSA, SC	S	8.27 mw	8.35 aw	17200 aaw	SCBLS	10//99-12//99

Occupation/Type/Industry	Location	Per	Low	Mid	High	Source	Date
Taxi Driver and Chauffeur	Greenville-Spartanburg-Anderson MSA, SC	S	6.97 MW	6.49 AW	14500 AAW	SCBLS	10//99-12//99
	South Dakota	S	7.83 MW	7.91 AW	16450 AAW	SDBLS	10//99-12//99
	Tennessee	S	6.66 MW	7.31 AW	15210 AAW	TNBLS	10//99-12//99
	Chattanooga MSA, TN-GA	S	6.88 MW	7.07 AW	14320 AAW	TNBLS	10//99-12//99
	Johnson City-Kingsport-Bristol MSA, TN-VA	S	6.79 MW	6.80 AW	14130 AAW	TNBLS	10//99-12//99
	Knoxville MSA, TN	S	6.85 MW	6.74 AW	14240 AAW	TNBLS	10//99-12//99
	Memphis MSA, TN-AR-MS	S	7.18 MW	7.16 AW	14940 AAW	MSBLS	10//99-12//99
	Nashville MSA, TN	S	7.67 MW	6.40 AW	15960 AAW	TNBLS	10//99-12//99
	Texas	S	7.23 MW	7.93 AW	16500 AAW	TXBLS	10//99-12//99
	Abilene MSA, TX	S	6.22 MW	6.15 AW	12940 AAW	TXBLS	10//99-12//99
	Amarillo MSA, TX	S	7.87 MW	6.94 AW	16370 AAW	TXBLS	10//99-12//99
	Austin-San Marcos MSA, TX	S	10.19 MW	9.64 AW	21200 AAW	TXBLS	10//99-12//99
	Beaumont-Port Arthur MSA, TX	S	6.81 MW	6.74 AW	14160 AAW	TXBLS	10//99-12//99
	Brownsville-Harlingen-San Benito MSA, TX	S	6.32 MW	6.32 AW	13140 AAW	TXBLS	10//99-12//99
	Corpus Christi MSA, TX	S	7.63 MW	6.73 AW	15870 AAW	TXBLS	10//99-12//99
	Dallas PMSA, TX	S	9.23 MW	8.18 AW	19200 AAW	TXBLS	10//99-12//99
	El Paso MSA, TX	S	6.24 MW	6.12 AW	12990 AAW	TXBLS	10//99-12//99
	Fort Worth-Arlington PMSA, TX	S	7.63 MW	7.56 AW	15880 AAW	TXBLS	10//99-12//99
	Galveston-Texas City PMSA, TX	S	6.95 MW	6.57 AW	14450 AAW	TXBLS	10//99-12//99
	Houston PMSA, TX	S	7.68 MW	6.87 AW	15980 AAW	TXBLS	10//99-12//99
	Laredo MSA, TX	S	5.83 MW	5.95 AW	12130 AAW	TXBLS	10//99-12//99
	Lubbock MSA, TX	S	7.37 MW	6.58 AW	15340 AAW	TXBLS	10//99-12//99
	McAllen-Edinburg-Mission MSA, TX	S	6.14 MW	6.23 AW	12770 AAW	TXBLS	10//99-12//99
	San Angelo MSA, TX	S	6.51 MW	6.08 AW	13550 AAW	TXBLS	10//99-12//99
	San Antonio MSA, TX	S	7.47 MW	7.14 AW	15530 AAW	TXBLS	10//99-12//99
	Sherman-Denison MSA, TX	S	6.08 MW	6.01 AW	12640 AAW	TXBLS	10//99-12//99
	Tyler MSA, TX	S	9.41 MW	9.51 AW	19580 AAW	TXBLS	10//99-12//99
	Waco MSA, TX	S	7.13 MW	6.50 AW	14820 AAW	TXBLS	10//99-12//99
	Utah	S	8.46 MW	10.83 AW	22520 AAW	UTBLS	10//99-12//99
	Salt Lake City-Ogden MSA, UT	S	12.26 MW	8.75 AW	25490 AAW	UTBLS	10//99-12//99
	Vermont	S	6.67 MW	7.13 AW	14840 AAW	VTBLS	10//99-12//99
	Burlington MSA, VT	S	6.86 MW	6.21 AW	14270 AAW	VTBLS	10//99-12//99
	Virginia	S	7.94 MW	8.34 AW	17350 AAW	VABLS	10//99-12//99
	Charlottesville MSA, VA	S	9.27 MW	9.02 AW	19270 AAW	VABLS	10//99-12//99
	Norfolk-Virginia Beach-Newport News MSA, VA-NC	S	8.50 MW	8.22 AW	17680 AAW	VABLS	10//99-12//99
	Richmond-Petersburg MSA, VA	S	9.25 MW	8.45 AW	19230 AAW	VABLS	10//99-12//99
	Roanoke MSA, VA	S	6.51 MW	6.31 AW	13530 AAW	VABLS	10//99-12//99
	Washington	S	7.71 MW	8.44 AW	17550 AAW	WABLS	10//99-12//99
	Richland-Kennewick-Pasco MSA, WA	S	7.47 MW	7.51 AW	15530 AAW	WABLS	10//99-12//99
	Seattle-Bellevue-Everett PMSA, WA	S	7.98 MW	7.50 AW	16600 AAW	WABLS	10//99-12//99
	West Virginia	S	6.24 MW	7.06 AW	14690 AAW	WVBLS	10//99-12//99
	Charleston MSA, WV	S	9.19 MW	10.57 AW	19120 AAW	WVBLS	10//99-12//99
	Huntington-Ashland MSA, WV-KY-OH	S	6.79 MW	6.72 AW	14130 AAW	WVBLS	10//99-12//99
	Wheeling MSA, WV-OH	S	6.09 MW	5.96 AW	12670 AAW	WVBLS	10//99-12//99
	Wisconsin	S	7.22 MW	7.49 AW	15580 AAW	WIBLS	10//99-12//99
	Appleton-Oshkosh-Neenah MSA, WI	S	7.12 MW	6.86 AW	14810 AAW	WIBLS	10//99-12//99
	Green Bay MSA, WI	S	7.38 MW	7.16 AW	15340 AAW	WIBLS	10//99-12//99
	Janesville-Beloit MSA, WI	S	7.21 MW	7.21 AW	15000 AAW	WIBLS	10//99-12//99
	Madison MSA, WI	S	9.12 MW	8.21 AW	18980 AAW	WIBLS	10//99-12//99
	Milwaukee-Waukesha PMSA, WI	S	7.71 MW	7.31 AW	16030 AAW	WIBLS	10//99-12//99
	Wausau MSA, WI	S	7.08 MW	7.05 AW	14730 AAW	WIBLS	10//99-12//99
	Wyoming	S	7.42 MW	8.29 AW	17240 AAW	WYBLS	10//99-12//99
	Cheyenne MSA, WY	S	6.45 MW	6.30 AW	13410 AAW	WYBLS	10//99-12//99
	Puerto Rico	S	6.49 MW	7.16 AW	14890 AAW	PRBLS	10//99-12//99
	Arecibo PMSA, PR	S	5.78 MW	5.93 AW	12030 AAW	PRBLS	10//99-12//99
	Caguas PMSA, PR	S	7.97 MW	6.85 AW	16580 AAW	PRBLS	10//99-12//99

AAW Average annual wage	**AOH** Average offered, high	**ASH** Average starting, high	**H** Hourly	**M** Monthly	**S** Special: hourly and annual
AE Average entry wage	**AOL** Average offered, low	**ASL** Average starting, low	**HI** Highest wage paid	**MTC** Median total compensation	**TQ** Third quartile wage
AEX Average experienced wage	**APH** Average pay, high range	**AW** Average wage paid	**HR** High end range	**MW** Median wage paid	**W** Weekly
AO Average offered	**APL** Average pay, low range	**FQ** First quartile wage	**LR** Low end range	**SQ** Second quartile wage	**Y** Yearly

Occupation/Type/Industry	Location	Per	Low	Mid	High	Source	Date
Taxi Driver and Chauffeur	San Juan-Bayamon PMSA, PR	S	7.33 MW	6.68 AW	15250 AAW	PRBLS	10//99-12//99
	Guam	S	7.43 MW	7.46 AW	15520 AAW	GUBLS	10//99-12//99
Teacher	Sarasota County, FL	Y		40551 AW		SARHT	1999
	Sarasota County, FL	Y		40551 AW		SHTR	2000
	Chatham County	Y		35580 AW		TRIBUS	1999-2000
	Durham County	Y		37452 AW		TRIBUS	1999-2000
	Franklin County	Y		33935 AW		TRIBUS	1999-2000
	Johnston County	Y		36093 AW		TRIBUS	1999-2000
	Orange County	Y		35845 AW		TRIBUS	1999-2000
	Wake County	Y		35700 AW		TRIBUS	1999-2000
	Arlington, TX	Y	33500 AE			FWST	2000
	Fort Worth, TX	Y	35000 AE			FWST	2000
	Mansfield, TX	Y	34507 AE			FWST	2000
Catholic School	United States	Y		19993 AW		NATCAT	3//00
Elementary	United States	H		27.75 AW		NCS98	1998
Prekindergarten and Kindergarten	United States	H		21.43 AW		NCS98	1998
Public School	United States	Y		37667 AW		AS&U	1999-2000
Public School	Cuyahoga County, OH	Y		43535 AW		CRCLEV	2000
School	Cobb County, GA	Y		34938 AW		ATJOCO	1998
Secondary	United States	H		27.84 AW		NCS98	1998
Special Education	United States	H		28.26 AW		NCS98	1998
Substitute	United States	H		10.90 AW		NCS98	1998
Teacher Assistant	Alabama	Y		13920 AAW		ALBLS	10//99-12//99
	Alaska	Y		27660 AAW		AKBLS	10//99-12//99
	Arizona	Y		16190 AAW		AZBLS	10//99-12//99
	Arkansas	Y		13240 AAW		ARBLS	10//99-12//99
	California	Y		20490 AAW		CABLS	10//99-12//99
	Colorado	Y		16660 AAW		COBLS	10//99-12//99
	Connecticut	Y		20520 AAW		CTBLS	10//99-12//99
	District of Columbia	Y		24840 AAW		DCBLS	10//99-12//99
	Florida	Y		15340 AAW		FLBLS	10//99-12//99
	Georgia	Y		14700 AAW		GABLS	10//99-12//99
	Hawaii	Y		17810 AAW		HIBLS	10//99-12//99
	Idaho	Y		16510 AAW		IDBLS	10//99-12//99
	Illinois	Y		17440 AAW		ILBLS	10//99-12//99
	Indiana	Y		16980 AAW		INBLS	10//99-12//99
	Iowa	Y		15390 AAW		IABLS	10//99-12//99
	Kansas	Y		16300 AAW		KSBLS	10//99-12//99
	Kentucky	Y		16140 AAW		KYBLS	10//99-12//99
	Louisiana	Y		14400 AAW		LABLS	10//99-12//99
	Maine	Y		18050 AAW		MEBLS	10//99-12//99
	Maryland	Y		18000 AAW		MDBLS	10//99-12//99
	Massachusetts	Y		19280 AAW		MABLS	10//99-12//99
	Michigan	Y		19150 AAW		MIBLS	10//99-12//99
	Minnesota	Y		20620 AAW		MNBLS	10//99-12//99
	Mississippi	Y		12800 AAW		MSBLS	10//99-12//99
	Missouri	Y		14510 AAW		MOBLS	10//99-12//99
	Montana	Y		16070 AAW		MTBLS	10//99-12//99
	Nebraska	Y		14310 AAW		NEBLS	10//99-12//99
	Nevada	Y		22640 AAW		NVBLS	10//99-12//99
	New Hampshire	Y		17080 AAW		NHBLS	10//99-12//99
	New Jersey	Y		17490 AAW		NJBLS	10//99-12//99
	New Mexico	Y		14840 AAW		NMBLS	10//99-12//99
	New York	Y		18950 AAW		NYBLS	10//99-12//99
	North Carolina	Y		16130 AAW		NCBLS	10//99-12//99
	North Dakota	Y		17180 AAW		NDBLS	10//99-12//99
	Ohio	Y		17810 AAW		OHBLS	10//99-12//99
	Oklahoma	Y		14140 AAW		OKBLS	10//99-12//99
	Oregon	Y		20030 AAW		ORBLS	10//99-12//99
	Pennsylvania	Y		16550 AAW		PABLS	10//99-12//99
	Rhode Island	Y		19770 AAW		RIBLS	10//99-12//99
	South Carolina	Y		14840 AAW		SCBLS	10//99-12//99
	South Dakota	Y		17300 AAW		SDBLS	10//99-12//99
	Tennessee	Y		14370 AAW		TNBLS	10//99-12//99
	Texas	Y		14220 AAW		TXBLS	10//99-12//99
	Utah	Y		17380 AAW		UTBLS	10//99-12//99
	Vermont	Y		17230 AAW		VTBLS	10//99-12//99
	Virginia	Y		15410 AAW		VABLS	10//99-12//99
	Washington	Y		20710 AAW		WABLS	10//99-12//99
	West Virginia	Y		17630 AAW		WVBLS	10//99-12//99
	Wisconsin	Y		17800 AAW		WIBLS	10//99-12//99

AAW	Average annual wage	**AOH**	Average offered, high	**ASH**	Average starting, high	**H**	Hourly	**M**	Monthly	**S**	Special: hourly and annual
AE	Average entry wage	**AOL**	Average offered, low	**ASL**	Average starting, low	**HI**	Highest wage paid	**MTC**	Median total compensation	**TQ**	Third quartile wage
AEX	Average experienced wage	**APH**	Average pay, high range	**AW**	Average wage paid	**HR**	High end range	**MW**	Median wage paid	**W**	Weekly
AO	Average offered	**APL**	Average pay, low range	**FQ**	First quartile wage	**LR**	Low end range	**SQ**	Second quartile wage	**Y**	Yearly

Occupation/Type/Industry	Location	Per	Low	Mid	High	Source	Date
Teacher Assistant	Wyoming	Y		14980 AAW		WYBLS	10//99-12//99
	Puerto Rico	Y		13480 AAW		PRBLS	10//99-12//99
Team Assembler	Alabama	S	9.99 MW	10.45 AW	21740 AAW	ALBLS	10//99-12//99
	Alaska	S	10.14 MW	11.12 AW	23130 AAW	AKBLS	10//99-12//99
	Arizona	S	9.35 MW	9.85 AW	20480 AAW	AZBLS	10//99-12//99
	Arkansas	S	8.79 MW	8.98 AW	18680 AAW	ARBLS	10//99-12//99
	California	S	8.98 MW	10.18 AW	21170 AAW	CABLS	10//99-12//99
	Colorado	S	9.27 MW	9.67 AW	20110 AAW	COBLS	10//99-12//99
	Connecticut	S	12.3 MW	12.36 AW	25710 AAW	CTBLS	10//99-12//99
	Delaware	S	8.6 MW	9.37 AW	19480 AAW	DEBLS	10//99-12//99
	Florida	S	8.22 MW	8.82 AW	18350 AAW	FLBLS	10//99-12//99
	Georgia	S	9.61 MW	10.03 AW	20850 AAW	GABLS	10//99-12//99
	Hawaii	S	10 MW	9.94 AW	20670 AAW	HIBLS	10//99-12//99
	Idaho	S	9.56 MW	9.61 AW	19990 AAW	IDBLS	10//99-12//99
	Illinois	S	11.15 MW	12.64 AW	26300 AAW	ILBLS	10//99-12//99
	Indiana	S	10.24 MW	11.06 AW	23010 AAW	INBLS	10//99-12//99
	Iowa	S	10.86 MW	11.71 AW	24350 AAW	IABLS	10//99-12//99
	Kansas	S	9.86 MW	10.51 AW	21870 AAW	KSBLS	10//99-12//99
	Kentucky	S	10.41 MW	11.40 AW	23710 AAW	KYBLS	10//99-12//99
	Louisiana	S	9.44 MW	10.40 AW	21640 AAW	LABLS	10//99-12//99
	Maine	S	9.19 MW	9.43 AW	19620 AAW	MEBLS	10//99-12//99
	Maryland	S	10.38 MW	11.60 AW	24120 AAW	MDBLS	10//99-12//99
	Massachusetts	S	10.46 MW	11.13 AW	23150 AAW	MABLS	10//99-12//99
	Michigan	S	11.39 MW	12.43 AW	25860 AAW	MIBLS	10//99-12//99
	Minnesota	S	11.09 MW	11.21 AW	23310 AAW	MNBLS	10//99-12//99
	Mississippi	S	8.75 MW	9.20 AW	19140 AAW	MSBLS	10//99-12//99
	Missouri	S	9.99 MW	12.08 AW	25140 AAW	MOBLS	10//99-12//99
	Montana	S	10.56 MW	10.18 AW	21170 AAW	MTBLS	10//99-12//99
	Nebraska	S	9.75 MW	10.24 AW	21310 AAW	NEBLS	10//99-12//99
	Nevada	S	9.29 MW	10.07 AW	20950 AAW	NVBLS	10//99-12//99
	New Hampshire	S	9.86 MW	10.43 AW	21680 AAW	NHBLS	10//99-12//99
	New Jersey	S	10.3 MW	11.17 AW	23230 AAW	NJBLS	10//99-12//99
	New Mexico	S	9.34 MW	9.57 AW	19900 AAW	NMBLS	10//99-12//99
	New York	S	9.47 MW	10.26 AW	21340 AAW	NYBLS	10//99-12//99
	North Carolina	S	10.12 MW	10.45 AW	21730 AAW	NCBLS	10//99-12//99
	North Dakota	S	8.9 MW	9.38 AW	19500 AAW	NDBLS	10//99-12//99
	Ohio	S	10.62 MW	11.11 AW	23100 AAW	OHBLS	10//99-12//99
	Oklahoma	S	9.73 MW	11.91 AW	24770 AAW	OKBLS	10//99-12//99
	Oregon	S	9.81 MW	10.44 AW	21710 AAW	ORBLS	10//99-12//99
	Pennsylvania	S	10.24 MW	10.82 AW	22500 AAW	PABLS	10//99-12//99
	Rhode Island	S	7.92 MW	8.78 AW	18270 AAW	RIBLS	10//99-12//99
	South Carolina	S	10.73 MW	11.66 AW	24260 AAW	SCBLS	10//99-12//99
	South Dakota	S	8.79 MW	8.74 AW	18170 AAW	SDBLS	10//99-12//99
	Tennessee	S	10.11 MW	10.18 AW	21180 AAW	TNBLS	10//99-12//99
	Texas	S	8.61 MW	9.19 AW	19110 AAW	TXBLS	10//99-12//99
	Utah	S	8.8 MW	9.11 AW	18950 AAW	UTBLS	10//99-12//99
	Vermont	S	9.65 MW	10.24 AW	21310 AAW	VTBLS	10//99-12//99
	Virginia	S	9.79 MW	10.19 AW	21200 AAW	VABLS	10//99-12//99
	Washington	S	10.73 MW	11.13 AW	23150 AAW	WABLS	10//99-12//99
	West Virginia	S	7.99 MW	8.60 AW	17890 AAW	WVBLS	10//99-12//99
	Wisconsin	S	10.1 MW	10.56 AW	21960 AAW	WIBLS	10//99-12//99
	Wyoming	S	7.92 MW	8.95 AW	18610 AAW	WYBLS	10//99-12//99
	Puerto Rico	S	7.07 MW	7.21 AW	14990 AAW	PRBLS	10//99-12//99
	Guam	S	8.21 MW	9.07 AW	18870 AAW	GUBLS	10//99-12//99
Technical Manager Computer Reseller	United States	Y		64000 AW		CORES3	2000
Technical Writer	United States	H		21.66 AW		NCS98	1998
	Alabama	S	17.91 MW	17.64 AW	36690 AAW	ALBLS	10//99-12//99
	Birmingham MSA, AL	S	15.66 MW	15.19 AW	32570 AAW	ALBLS	10//99-12//99
	Huntsville MSA, AL	S	20.66 MW	20.49 AW	42980 AAW	ALBLS	10//99-12//99
	Mobile MSA, AL	S	14.86 MW	14.16 AW	30910 AAW	ALBLS	10//99-12//99
	Montgomery MSA, AL	S	16.42 MW	16.02 AW	34140 AAW	ALBLS	10//99-12//99
	Alaska	S	20.81 MW	20.79 AW	43240 AAW	AKBLS	10//99-12//99
	Arizona	S	22.37 MW	22.36 AW	46510 AAW	AZBLS	10//99-12//99
	Phoenix-Mesa MSA, AZ	S	23.03 MW	23.10 AW	47910 AAW	AZBLS	10//99-12//99
	Tucson MSA, AZ	S	18.25 MW	16.48 AW	37960 AAW	AZBLS	10//99-12//99
	Arkansas	S	15.18 MW	20.46 AW	42560 AAW	ARBLS	10//99-12//99
	Little Rock-North Little Rock MSA, AR	S	19.40 MW	13.33 AW	40340 AAW	ARBLS	10//99-12//99
	California	S	25.93 MW	27.88 AW	57980 AAW	CABLS	10//99-12//99

AAW	Average annual wage	AOH	Average offered, high	ASH	Average starting, high	H	Hourly	M	Monthly	S	Special: hourly and annual
AE	Average entry wage	AOL	Average offered, low	ASL	Average starting, low	HI	Highest wage paid	MTC	Median total compensation	TQ	Third quartile wage
AEX	Average experienced wage	APH	Average pay, high range	AW	Average wage paid	HR	High end range	MW	Median wage paid	W	Weekly
AO	Average offered	APL	Average pay, low range	FQ	First quartile wage	LR	Low end range	SQ	Second quartile wage	Y	Yearly

Occupation/Type/Industry	Location	Per	Low	Mid	High	Source	Date
Technical Writer	Los Angeles-Long Beach						
	PMSA, CA	S	28.35 MW	25.78 AW	58960 AAW	CABLS	10//99-12//99
	Oakland PMSA, CA	S	25.15 MW	23.98 AW	52310 AAW	CABLS	10//99-12//99
	Orange County PMSA, CA	S	23.26 MW	22.40 AW	48390 AAW	CABLS	10//99-12//99
	Riverside-San Bernardino						
	PMSA, CA	S	16.73 MW	12.88 AW	34790 AAW	CABLS	10//99-12//99
	Sacramento PMSA, CA	S	26.24 MW	26.08 AW	54580 AAW	CABLS	10//99-12//99
	San Diego MSA, CA	S	23.35 MW	22.00 AW	48560 AAW	CABLS	10//99-12//99
	San Francisco PMSA, CA	S	37.02 MW	34.87 AW	77000 AAW	CABLS	10//99-12//99
	San Jose PMSA, CA	S	28.95 MW	28.41 AW	60210 AAW	CABLS	10//99-12//99
	Santa Barbara-Santa Maria-						
	Lompoc MSA, CA	S	22.71 MW	22.53 AW	47230 AAW	CABLS	10//99-12//99
	Santa Cruz-Watsonville						
	PMSA, CA	S	32.91 MW	30.55 AW	68440 AAW	CABLS	10//99-12//99
	Ventura PMSA, CA	S	21.73 MW	19.84 AW	45200 AAW	CABLS	10//99-12//99
	Colorado	S	21.39 MW	21.90 AW	45550 AAW	COBLS	10//99-12//99
	Boulder-Longmont PMSA, CO	S	22.74 MW	22.01 AW	47300 AAW	COBLS	10//99-12//99
	Colorado Springs MSA, CO	S	17.90 MW	16.82 AW	37230 AAW	COBLS	10//99-12//99
	Denver PMSA, CO	S	23.32 MW	23.21 AW	48510 AAW	COBLS	10//99-12//99
	Fort Collins-Loveland MSA,						
	CO	S	22.25 MW	20.35 AW	46290 AAW	COBLS	10//99-12//99
	Connecticut	S	24.74 MW	25.06 AW	52130 AAW	CTBLS	10//99-12//99
	Bridgeport PMSA, CT	S	23.86 MW	23.41 AW	49630 AAW	CTBLS	10//99-12//99
	Hartford MSA, CT	S	25.31 MW	25.11 AW	52640 AAW	CTBLS	10//99-12//99
	New Haven-Meriden PMSA,						
	CT	S	21.31 MW	19.99 AW	44330 AAW	CTBLS	10//99-12//99
	Stamford-Norwalk PMSA, CT	S	26.92 MW	26.85 AW	55990 AAW	CTBLS	10//99-12//99
	Delaware	S	18.73 MW	21.02 AW	43720 AAW	DEBLS	10//99-12//99
	Wilmington-Newark PMSA,						
	DE-MD	S	21.55 MW	20.37 AW	44820 AAW	DEBLS	10//99-12//99
	District of Columbia	S	23.95 MW	24.38 AW	50720 AAW	DCBLS	10//99-12//99
	Washington PMSA, DC-MD-						
	VA-WV	S	22.95 MW	22.65 AW	47740 AAW	DCBLS	10//99-12//99
	Florida	S	18.29 MW	18.98 AW	39470 AAW	FLBLS	10//99-12//99
	Fort Lauderdale PMSA, FL	S	20.33 MW	19.03 AW	42290 AAW	FLBLS	10//99-12//99
	Gainesville MSA, FL	S	16.18 MW	15.72 AW	33650 AAW	FLBLS	10//99-12//99
	Jacksonville MSA, FL	S	17.27 MW	16.29 AW	35920 AAW	FLBLS	10//99-12//99
	Melbourne-Titusville-Palm						
	Bay MSA, FL	S	21.72 MW	22.01 AW	45180 AAW	FLBLS	10//99-12//99
	Miami PMSA, FL	S	16.65 MW	15.92 AW	34630 AAW	FLBLS	10//99-12//99
	Orlando MSA, FL	S	19.78 MW	19.55 AW	41140 AAW	FLBLS	10//99-12//99
	Pensacola MSA, FL	S	18.02 MW	17.79 AW	37480 AAW	FLBLS	10//99-12//99
	Sarasota-Bradenton MSA, FL	S	20.04 MW	19.54 AW	41690 AAW	FLBLS	10//99-12//99
	Tampa-St. Petersburg-						
	Clearwater MSA, FL	S	18.29 MW	17.70 AW	38030 AAW	FLBLS	10//99-12//99
	West Palm Beach-Boca Raton						
	MSA, FL	S	21.76 MW	22.69 AW	45260 AAW	FLBLS	10//99-12//99
	Georgia	S	21.23 MW	22.32 AW	46440 AAW	GABLS	10//99-12//99
	Atlanta MSA, GA	S	23.18 MW	21.87 AW	48220 AAW	GABLS	10//99-12//99
	Augusta-Aiken MSA, GA-SC	S	18.30 MW	16.03 AW	38050 AAW	GABLS	10//99-12//99
	Columbus MSA, GA-AL	S	17.93 MW	17.73 AW	37280 AAW	GABLS	10//99-12//99
	Savannah MSA, GA	S	16.84 MW	15.99 AW	35020 AAW	GABLS	10//99-12//99
	Idaho	S	16.81 MW	17.51 AW	36420 AAW	IDBLS	10//99-12//99
	Boise City MSA, ID	S	15.77 MW	16.15 AW	32790 AAW	IDBLS	10//99-12//99
	Illinois	S	17.71 MW	18.89 AW	39300 AAW	ILBLS	10//99-12//99
	Chicago PMSA, IL	S	18.85 MW	17.20 AW	39210 AAW	ILBLS	10//99-12//99
	Peoria-Pekin MSA, IL	S	15.56 MW	13.14 AW	32360 AAW	ILBLS	10//99-12//99
	Rockford MSA, IL	S	20.21 MW	20.07 AW	42040 AAW	ILBLS	10//99-12//99
	Indiana	S	17.88 MW	19.16 AW	39860 AAW	INBLS	10//99-12//99
	Fort Wayne MSA, IN	S	19.81 MW	16.93 AW	41200 AAW	INBLS	10//99-12//99
	Indianapolis MSA, IN	S	19.47 MW	17.10 AW	40500 AAW	INBLS	10//99-12//99
	South Bend MSA, IN	S	17.65 MW	16.60 AW	36710 AAW	INBLS	10//99-12//99
	Iowa	S	16.2 MW	17.13 AW	35630 AAW	IABLS	10//99-12//99
	Davenport-Moline-Rock Island						
	MSA, IA-IL	S	20.74 MW	20.78 AW	43130 AAW	IABLS	10//99-12//99
	Des Moines MSA, IA	S	20.91 MW	18.78 AW	43480 AAW	IABLS	10//99-12//99
	Waterloo-Cedar Falls MSA, IA	S	17.00 MW	16.07 AW	35370 AAW	IABLS	10//99-12//99
	Kansas	S	18.97 MW	19.72 AW	41020 AAW	KSBLS	10//99-12//99
	Kentucky	S	21.18 MW	20.61 AW	42880 AAW	KYBLS	10//99-12//99
	Louisville MSA, KY-IN	S	20.30 MW	19.91 AW	42230 AAW	KYBLS	10//99-12//99
	Louisiana	S	16.94 MW	17.65 AW	36720 AAW	LABLS	10//99-12//99
	Baton Rouge MSA, LA	S	19.69 MW	18.63 AW	40950 AAW	LABLS	10//99-12//99

AAW Average annual wage	AOH Average offered, high	ASH Average starting, high	H Hourly	M Monthly	S Special: hourly and annual
AE Average entry wage	AOL Average offered, low	ASL Average starting, low	HI Highest wage paid	MTC Median total compensation	TQ Third quartile wage
AEX Average experienced wage	APH Average pay, high range	AW Average wage paid	HR High end range	MW Median wage paid	W Weekly
AO Average offered	APL Average pay, low range	FQ First quartile wage	LR Low end range	SQ Second quartile wage	Y Yearly

Occupation/Type/Industry	Location	Per	Low	Mid	High	Source	Date
Technical Writer	New Orleans MSA, LA	S	17.28 MW	16.43 AW	35930 AAW	LABLS	10//99-12//99
	Maine	S	20.54 MW	25.46 AW	52960 AAW	MEBLS	10//99-12//99
	Maryland	S	23.34 MW	23.49 AW	48860 AAW	MDBLS	10//99-12//99
	Baltimore PMSA, MD	S	22.65 MW	22.68 AW	47110 AAW	MDBLS	10//99-12//99
	Massachusetts	S	24.39 MW	25.01 AW	52020 AAW	MABLS	10//99-12//99
	Boston PMSA, MA-NH	S	24.67 MW	24.10 AW	51310 AAW	MABLS	10//99-12//99
	Lawrence PMSA, MA-NH	S	24.08 MW	21.31 AW	50090 AAW	MABLS	10//99-12//99
	Lowell PMSA, MA-NH	S	27.71 MW	27.35 AW	57640 AAW	MABLS	10//99-12//99
	Michigan	S	21.17 MW	22.02 AW	45810 AAW	MIBLS	10//99-12//99
	Ann Arbor PMSA, MI	S	21.71 MW	23.24 AW	45160 AAW	MIBLS	10//99-12//99
	Benton Harbor MSA, MI	S	21.01 MW	19.96 AW	43710 AAW	MIBLS	10//99-12//99
	Detroit PMSA, MI	S	23.60 MW	22.68 AW	49080 AAW	MIBLS	10//99-12//99
	Flint PMSA, MI	S	18.01 MW	18.57 AW	37460 AAW	MIBLS	10//99-12//99
	Grand Rapids-Muskegon-Holland MSA, MI	S	20.75 MW	20.08 AW	43160 AAW	MIBLS	10//99-12//99
	Kalamazoo-Battle Creek MSA, MI	S	18.91 MW	18.22 AW	39330 AAW	MIBLS	10//99-12//99
	Saginaw-Bay City-Midland MSA, MI	S	18.41 MW	16.38 AW	38280 AAW	MIBLS	10//99-12//99
	Minnesota	S	22.3 MW	21.95 AW	45660 AAW	MNBLS	10//99-12//99
	Duluth-Superior MSA, MN-WI	S	15.30 MW	13.10 AW	31830 AAW	MNBLS	10//99-12//99
	Minneapolis-St. Paul MSA, MN-WI	S	22.42 MW	22.72 AW	46640 AAW	MNBLS	10//99-12//99
	Rochester MSA, MN	S	21.01 MW	20.39 AW	43700 AAW	MNBLS	10//99-12//99
	Mississippi	S	16.81 MW	16.58 AW	34480 AAW	MSBLS	10//99-12//99
	Missouri	S	16.11 MW	16.75 AW	34830 AAW	MOBLS	10//99-12//99
	Kansas City MSA, MO-KS	S	20.56 MW	19.39 AW	42760 AAW	MOBLS	10//99-12//99
	St. Louis MSA, MO-IL	S	16.90 MW	16.18 AW	35150 AAW	MOBLS	10//99-12//99
	Montana	S	17.48 MW	18.32 AW	38110 AAW	MTBLS	10//99-12//99
	Nebraska	S	18.75 MW	19.82 AW	41230 AAW	NEBLS	10//99-12//99
	Lincoln MSA, NE	S	17.73 MW	17.67 AW	36880 AAW	NEBLS	10//99-12//99
	Omaha MSA, NE-IA	S	20.59 MW	19.58 AW	42820 AAW	NEBLS	10//99-12//99
	Nevada	S	20.2 MW	19.92 AW	41420 AAW	NVBLS	10//99-12//99
	Las Vegas MSA, NV-AZ	S	20.87 MW	20.77 AW	43410 AAW	NVBLS	10//99-12//99
	Reno MSA, NV	S	22.61 MW	20.53 AW	47030 AAW	NVBLS	10//99-12//99
	New Hampshire	S	21.48 MW	26.35 AW	54810 AAW	NHBLS	10//99-12//99
	Manchester PMSA, NH	S	30.00 MW	31.64 AW	62410 AAW	NHBLS	10//99-12//99
	Nashua PMSA, NH	S	22.71 MW	21.19 AW	47250 AAW	NHBLS	10//99-12//99
	New Jersey	S	23 MW	24.03 AW	49970 AAW	NJBLS	10//99-12//99
	Atlantic-Cape May PMSA, NJ	S	23.42 MW	22.21 AW	48720 AAW	NJBLS	10//99-12//99
	Bergen-Passaic PMSA, NJ	S	24.60 MW	23.48 AW	51170 AAW	NJBLS	10//99-12//99
	Jersey City PMSA, NJ	S	22.94 MW	21.29 AW	47710 AAW	NJBLS	10//99-12//99
	Middlesex-Somerset-Hunterdon PMSA, NJ	S	26.75 MW	24.67 AW	55640 AAW	NJBLS	10//99-12//99
	Monmouth-Ocean PMSA, NJ	S	23.62 MW	24.21 AW	49120 AAW	NJBLS	10//99-12//99
	Newark PMSA, NJ	S	20.54 MW	19.15 AW	42720 AAW	NJBLS	10//99-12//99
	Trenton PMSA, NJ	S	25.43 MW	24.17 AW	52890 AAW	NJBLS	10//99-12//99
	New Mexico	S	20.72 MW	20.20 AW	42010 AAW	NMBLS	10//99-12//99
	Albuquerque MSA, NM	S	20.27 MW	21.07 AW	42170 AAW	NMBLS	10//99-12//99
	New York	S	23.25 MW	24.82 AW	51630 AAW	NYBLS	10//99-12//99
	Albany-Schenectady-Troy MSA, NY	S	20.00 MW	19.01 AW	41600 AAW	NYBLS	10//99-12//99
	Buffalo-Niagara Falls MSA, NY	S	14.75 MW	11.90 AW	30690 AAW	NYBLS	10//99-12//99
	Dutchess County PMSA, NY	S	24.05 MW	24.47 AW	50020 AAW	NYBLS	10//99-12//99
	Nassau-Suffolk PMSA, NY	S	24.05 MW	24.34 AW	50030 AAW	NYBLS	10//99-12//99
	New York PMSA, NY	S	27.81 MW	24.64 AW	57850 AAW	NYBLS	10//99-12//99
	Rochester MSA, NY	S	22.71 MW	23.35 AW	47230 AAW	NYBLS	10//99-12//99
	Syracuse MSA, NY	S	19.37 MW	18.53 AW	40290 AAW	NYBLS	10//99-12//99
	North Carolina	S	23.03 MW	23.16 AW	48180 AAW	NCBLS	10//99-12//99
	Charlotte-Gastonia-Rock Hill MSA, NC-SC	S	22.33 MW	22.08 AW	46450 AAW	NCBLS	10//99-12//99
	Greensboro--Winston-Salem--High Point MSA, NC	S	25.39 MW	25.44 AW	52810 AAW	NCBLS	10//99-12//99
	Raleigh-Durham-Chapel Hill MSA, NC	S	24.02 MW	23.84 AW	49960 AAW	NCBLS	10//99-12//99
	Wilmington MSA, NC	S	22.81 MW	21.23 AW	47440 AAW	NCBLS	10//99-12//99
	North Dakota	S	17.84 MW	18.42 AW	38310 AAW	NDBLS	10//99-12//99
	Bismarck MSA, ND	S	18.57 MW	17.44 AW	38630 AAW	NDBLS	10//99-12//99
	Ohio	S	19.19 MW	19.74 AW	41050 AAW	OHBLS	10//99-12//99
	Cincinnati PMSA, OH-KY-IN	S	18.21 MW	18.01 AW	37880 AAW	OHBLS	10//99-12//99

AAW	Average annual wage	AOH	Average offered, high	ASH	Average starting, high
AE	Average entry wage	AOL	Average offered, low	ASL	Average starting, low
AEX	Average experienced wage	APH	Average pay, high range	AW	Average wage paid
AO	Average offered	APL	Average pay, low range	FQ	First quartile wage

H	Hourly	M	Monthly
HI	Highest wage paid	MTC	Median total compensation
HR	High end range	MW	Median wage paid
LR	Low end range	SQ	Second quartile wage

S	Special: hourly and annual
TQ	Third quartile wage
W	Weekly
Y	Yearly

Occupation/Type/Industry	Location	Per	Low	Mid	High	Source	Date
Technical Writer	Cleveland-Lorain-Elyria						
	PMSA, OH	S	16.53 MW	15.66 AW	34390 AAW	OHBLS	10//99-12//99
	Columbus MSA, OH	S	23.03 MW	23.56 AW	47890 AAW	OHBLS	10//99-12//99
	Dayton-Springfield MSA, OH	S	18.14 MW	17.17 AW	37740 AAW	OHBLS	10//99-12//99
	Youngstown-Warren MSA, OH	S	18.59 MW	16.55 AW	38660 AAW	OHBLS	10//99-12//99
	Oklahoma	S	17.93 MW	17.47 AW	36330 AAW	OKBLS	10//99-12//99
	Oklahoma City MSA, OK	S	17.25 MW	17.72 AW	35870 AAW	OKBLS	10//99-12//99
	Tulsa MSA, OK	S	20.60 MW	20.41 AW	42850 AAW	OKBLS	10//99-12//99
	Oregon	S	22.56 MW	23.51 AW	48910 AAW	ORBLS	10//99-12//99
	Portland-Vancouver PMSA, OR-WA	S	24.29 MW	23.48 AW	50530 AAW	ORBLS	10//99-12//99
	Pennsylvania	S	19.65 MW	20.98 AW	43630 AAW	PABLS	10//99-12//99
	Allentown-Bethlehem-Easton MSA, PA	S	20.59 MW	20.37 AW	42820 AAW	PABLS	10//99-12//99
	Harrisburg-Lebanon-Carlisle MSA, PA	S	16.82 MW	16.00 AW	34990 AAW	PABLS	10//99-12//99
	Philadelphia PMSA, PA-NJ	S	23.30 MW	22.92 AW	48460 AAW	PABLS	10//99-12//99
	Pittsburgh MSA, PA	S	17.59 MW	16.30 AW	36590 AAW	PABLS	10//99-12//99
	Reading MSA, PA	S	16.22 MW	15.92 AW	33740 AAW	PABLS	10//99-12//99
	Scranton--Wilkes-Barre--Hazleton MSA, PA	S	21.55 MW	20.36 AW	44820 AAW	PABLS	10//99-12//99
	York MSA, PA	S	15.68 MW	17.06 AW	32620 AAW	PABLS	10//99-12//99
	Rhode Island	S	18.86 MW	20.62 AW	42900 AAW	RIBLS	10//99-12//99
	Providence-Fall River-Warwick MSA, RI-MA	S	22.11 MW	19.85 AW	46000 AAW	RIBLS	10//99-12//99
	South Carolina	S	23.38 MW	25.39 AW	52810 AAW	SCBLS	10//99-12//99
	Charleston-North Charleston MSA, SC	S	21.30 MW	20.55 AW	44300 AAW	SCBLS	10//99-12//99
	Columbia MSA, SC	S	21.56 MW	20.04 AW	44840 AAW	SCBLS	10//99-12//99
	Greenville-Spartanburg-Anderson MSA, SC	S	21.07 MW	20.80 AW	43820 AAW	SCBLS	10//99-12//99
	South Dakota	S	14.44 MW	14.42 AW	29990 AAW	SDBLS	10//99-12//99
	Tennessee	S	21.43 MW	22.09 AW	45950 AAW	TNBLS	10//99-12//99
	Chattanooga MSA, TN-GA	S	27.23 MW	27.75 AW	56650 AAW	TNBLS	10//99-12//99
	Knoxville MSA, TN	S	26.00 MW	26.14 AW	54080 AAW	TNBLS	10//99-12//99
	Memphis MSA, TN-AR-MS	S	21.88 MW	20.57 AW	45500 AAW	MSBLS	10//99-12//99
	Nashville MSA, TN	S	21.20 MW	21.05 AW	44100 AAW	TNBLS	10//99-12//99
	Texas	S	20.6 MW	22.40 AW	46600 AAW	TXBLS	10//99-12//99
	Austin-San Marcos MSA, TX	S	23.82 MW	23.48 AW	49540 AAW	TXBLS	10//99-12//99
	Dallas PMSA, TX	S	24.87 MW	22.41 AW	51720 AAW	TXBLS	10//99-12//99
	Fort Worth-Arlington PMSA, TX	S	23.02 MW	22.52 AW	47880 AAW	TXBLS	10//99-12//99
	Houston PMSA, TX	S	20.66 MW	19.25 AW	42970 AAW	TXBLS	10//99-12//99
	San Antonio MSA, TX	S	17.51 MW	16.34 AW	36410 AAW	TXBLS	10//99-12//99
	Waco MSA, TX	S	14.92 MW	15.00 AW	31030 AAW	TXBLS	10//99-12//99
	Utah	S	20.67 MW	21.87 AW	45490 AAW	UTBLS	10//99-12//99
	Provo-Orem MSA, UT	S	20.68 MW	20.17 AW	43020 AAW	UTBLS	10//99-12//99
	Vermont	S	23.96 MW	24.73 AW	51430 AAW	VTBLS	10//99-12//99
	Virginia	S	21.46 MW	21.50 AW	44710 AAW	VABLS	10//99-12//99
	Norfolk-Virginia Beach-Newport News MSA, VA-NC	S	21.07 MW	21.28 AW	43820 AAW	VABLS	10//99-12//99
	Richmond-Petersburg MSA, VA	S	20.64 MW	20.80 AW	42930 AAW	VABLS	10//99-12//99
	Roanoke MSA, VA	S	20.76 MW	21.11 AW	43170 AAW	VABLS	10//99-12//99
	Washington	S	23.02 MW	23.50 AW	48870 AAW	WABLS	10//99-12//99
	Seattle-Bellevue-Everett PMSA, WA	S	24.02 MW	23.85 AW	49970 AAW	WABLS	10//99-12//99
	Spokane MSA, WA	S	14.84 MW	14.33 AW	30860 AAW	WABLS	10//99-12//99
	Wisconsin	S	20.95 MW	21.61 AW	44950 AAW	WIBLS	10//99-12//99
	Appleton-Oshkosh-Neenah MSA, WI	S	21.56 MW	21.99 AW	44840 AAW	WIBLS	10//99-12//99
	Madison MSA, WI	S	19.77 MW	16.52 AW	41120 AAW	WIBLS	10//99-12//99
	Milwaukee-Waukesha PMSA, WI	S	23.85 MW	23.48 AW	49610 AAW	WIBLS	10//99-12//99
Technician							
Computer-aided Design, Apparel Industry	United States	Y		29900 AW		BOBBIN	1999
Computer Reseller	United States	Y		58000 MW		CORES	1999
Computer Reseller Organization	United States	Y		58000 MW		CORES2	1999
Technician, Senior							
Transportation, Fleet with 25-99 vehicles	United States	H		15.12 AW		TFM	1999

AAW	Average annual wage	AOH	Average offered, high	ASH	Average starting, high	H	Hourly	M	Monthly	S	Special: hourly and annual
AE	Average entry wage	AOL	Average offered, low	ASL	Average starting, low	HI	Highest wage paid	MTC	Median total compensation	TQ	Third quartile wage
AEX	Average experienced wage	APH	Average pay, high range	AW	Average wage paid	HR	High end range	MW	Median wage paid	W	Weekly
AO	Average offered	APL	Average pay, low range	FQ	First quartile wage	LR	Low end range	SQ	Second quartile wage	Y	Yearly

Occupation/Type/Industry	Location	Per	Low	Mid	High	Source	Date
Technician, Senior							
Transportation, Fleet with 500+ vehicles	United States	H		20.05 AW		TFM	1999
Telecom Manager							
Information Technology	Atlanta, GA	Y		73844 AW		ATBUS	3//00
Telecommunications Equipment							
Installer and Repairer							
Except Line Installer	Alabama	S	18.78 MW	18.40 AW	38270 AAW	ALBLS	10//99-12//99
Except Line Installer	Alaska	S	28.96 MW	27.03 AW	56220 AAW	AKBLS	10//99-12//99
Except Line Installer	Arizona	S	22.65 MW	21.24 AW	44180 AAW	AZBLS	10//99-12//99
Except Line Installer	Arkansas	S	19.34 MW	19.04 AW	39610 AAW	ARBLS	10//99-12//99
Except Line Installer	California	S	22.07 MW	20.77 AW	43200 AAW	CABLS	10//99-12//99
Except Line Installer	Colorado	S	23.09 MW	21.61 AW	44940 AAW	COBLS	10//99-12//99
Except Line Installer	Connecticut	S	17.31 MW	17.59 AW	36580 AAW	CTBLS	10//99-12//99
Except Line Installer	Delaware	S	15.13 MW	15.18 AW	31570 AAW	DEBLS	10//99-12//99
Except Line Installer	District of Columbia	S	21.57 MW	19.97 AW	41540 AAW	DCBLS	10//99-12//99
Except Line Installer	Florida	S	17.83 MW	17.83 AW	37080 AAW	FLBLS	10//99-12//99
Except Line Installer	Georgia	S	16.17 MW	16.25 AW	33810 AAW	GABLS	10//99-12//99
Except Line Installer	Hawaii	S	21.1 MW	20.77 AW	43190 AAW	HIBLS	10//99-12//99
Except Line Installer	Idaho	S	22.96 MW	20.82 AW	43310 AAW	IDBLS	10//99-12//99
Except Line Installer	Illinois	S	17.15 MW	17.14 AW	35660 AAW	ILBLS	10//99-12//99
Except Line Installer	Indiana	S	15.48 MW	16.02 AW	33320 AAW	INBLS	10//99-12//99
Except Line Installer	Iowa	S	15.99 MW	16.79 AW	34920 AAW	IABLS	10//99-12//99
Except Line Installer	Kansas	S	20.85 MW	19.35 AW	40250 AAW	KSBLS	10//99-12//99
Except Line Installer	Kentucky	S	18.36 MW	17.62 AW	36640 AAW	KYBLS	10//99-12//99
Except Line Installer	Louisiana	S	14.43 MW	14.88 AW	30960 AAW	LABLS	10//99-12//99
Except Line Installer	Maine	S	21.12 MW	20.62 AW	42880 AAW	MEBLS	10//99-12//99
Except Line Installer	Maryland	S	23.43 MW	22.33 AW	46450 AAW	MDBLS	10//99-12//99
Except Line Installer	Massachusetts	S	28.08 MW	27.73 AW	57680 AAW	MABLS	10//99-12//99
Except Line Installer	Michigan	S	15.57 MW	15.57 AW	32380 AAW	MIBLS	10//99-12//99
Except Line Installer	Minnesota	S	23.65 MW	22.37 AW	46530 AAW	MNBLS	10//99-12//99
Except Line Installer	Mississippi	S	16.3 MW	16.18 AW	33650 AAW	MSBLS	10//99-12//99
Except Line Installer	Missouri	S	16.55 MW	17.07 AW	35500 AAW	MOBLS	10//99-12//99
Except Line Installer	Montana	S	17.35 MW	16.34 AW	33990 AAW	MTBLS	10//99-12//99
Except Line Installer	Nebraska	S	18.5 MW	17.84 AW	37110 AAW	NEBLS	10//99-12//99
Except Line Installer	Nevada	S	13.15 MW	14.94 AW	31080 AAW	NVBLS	10//99-12//99
Except Line Installer	New Hampshire	S	22.15 MW	19.74 AW	41060 AAW	NHBLS	10//99-12//99
Except Line Installer	New Jersey	S	23.4 MW	21.87 AW	45490 AAW	NJBLS	10//99-12//99
Except Line Installer	New Mexico	S	28.4 MW	25.43 AW	52890 AAW	NMBLS	10//99-12//99
Except Line Installer	New York	S	24.38 MW	24.48 AW	50910 AAW	NYBLS	10//99-12//99
Except Line Installer	North Carolina	S	20.31 MW	20.61 AW	42880 AAW	NCBLS	10//99-12//99
Except Line Installer	North Dakota	S	19.2 MW	19.07 AW	39660 AAW	NDBLS	10//99-12//99
Except Line Installer	Ohio	S	17.6 MW	16.90 AW	35160 AAW	OHBLS	10//99-12//99
Except Line Installer	Oklahoma	S	21.96 MW	20.86 AW	43380 AAW	OKBLS	10//99-12//99
Except Line Installer	Oregon	S	22.98 MW	21.66 AW	45050 AAW	ORBLS	10//99-12//99
Except Line Installer	Pennsylvania	S	18.42 MW	18.86 AW	39230 AAW	PABLS	10//99-12//99
Except Line Installer	Rhode Island	S	22.15 MW	21.03 AW	43750 AAW	RIBLS	10//99-12//99
Except Line Installer	South Carolina	S	17.45 MW	17.62 AW	36640 AAW	SCBLS	10//99-12//99
Except Line Installer	South Dakota	S	17.48 MW	17.90 AW	37220 AAW	SDBLS	10//99-12//99
Except Line Installer	Tennessee	S	17.98 MW	17.49 AW	36390 AAW	TNBLS	10//99-12//99
Except Line Installer	Texas	S	18.9 MW	17.98 AW	37390 AAW	TXBLS	10//99-12//99
Except Line Installer	Utah	S	22.46 MW	20.43 AW	42490 AAW	UTBLS	10//99-12//99
Except Line Installer	Vermont	S	21.73 MW	20.86 AW	43390 AAW	VTBLS	10//99-12//99
Except Line Installer	Virginia	S	19.23 MW	18.99 AW	39500 AAW	VABLS	10//99-12//99
Except Line Installer	Washington	S	21.85 MW	19.89 AW	41380 AAW	WABLS	10//99-12//99
Except Line Installer	West Virginia	S	23.47 MW	21.93 AW	45610 AAW	WVBLS	10//99-12//99
Except Line Installer	Wisconsin	S	15.52 MW	15.93 AW	33140 AAW	WIBLS	10//99-12//99
Except Line Installer	Wyoming	S	18.74 MW	18.09 AW	37630 AAW	WYBLS	10//99-12//99
Except Line Installer	Puerto Rico	S	11.39 MW	11.11 AW	23110 AAW	PRBLS	10//99-12//99
Except Line Installer	Virgin Islands	S	15.08 MW	14.88 AW	30940 AAW	VIBLS	10//99-12//99
Telecommunications Line							
Installer and Repairer	Alabama	S	15.19 MW	15.51 AW	32270 AAW	ALBLS	10//99-12//99
	Anniston MSA, AL	S	16.53 MW	17.73 AW	34380 AAW	ALBLS	10//99-12//99
	Birmingham MSA, AL	S	15.83 MW	15.99 AW	32930 AAW	ALBLS	10//99-12//99
	Decatur MSA, AL	S	11.49 MW	11.21 AW	23890 AAW	ALBLS	10//99-12//99
	Dothan MSA, AL	S	10.41 MW	10.04 AW	21650 AAW	ALBLS	10//99-12//99
	Gadsden MSA, AL	S	18.93 MW	19.46 AW	39370 AAW	ALBLS	10//99-12//99
	Huntsville MSA, AL	S	17.15 MW	18.11 AW	35670 AAW	ALBLS	10//99-12//99
	Mobile MSA, AL	S	14.86 MW	15.17 AW	30920 AAW	ALBLS	10//99-12//99
	Montgomery MSA, AL	S	14.55 MW	14.30 AW	30270 AAW	ALBLS	10//99-12//99

AAW	Average annual wage	AOH	Average offered, high	ASH	Average starting, high	H	Hourly
AE	Average entry wage	AOL	Average offered, low	ASL	Average starting, low	HI	Highest wage paid
AEX	Average experienced wage	APH	Average pay, high range	AW	Average wage paid	HR	High end range
AO	Average offered	APL	Average pay, low range	FQ	First quartile wage	LR	Low end range

M	Monthly	S	Special: hourly and annual
MTC	Median total compensation	TQ	Third quartile wage
MW	Median wage paid	W	Weekly
SQ	Second quartile wage	Y	Yearly

Occupation/Type/Industry	Location	Per	Low	Mid	High	Source	Date
Telecommunications Line Installer and Repairer	Alaska	S	19.48 MW	19.94 AW	41470 AAW	AKBLS	10//99-12//99
	Anchorage MSA, AK	S	19.19 MW	19.64 AW	39900 AAW	AKBLS	10//99-12//99
	Arizona	S	11.88 MW	13.71 AW	28510 AAW	AZBLS	10//99-12//99
	Phoenix-Mesa MSA, AZ	S	13.79 MW	11.97 AW	28680 AAW	AZBLS	10//99-12//99
	Arkansas	S	12.92 MW	14.76 AW	30710 AAW	ARBLS	10//99-12//99
	Fayetteville-Springdale-Rogers MSA, AR	S	15.01 MW	12.72 AW	31220 AAW	ARBLS	10//99-12//99
	Little Rock-North Little Rock MSA, AR	S	15.48 MW	14.32 AW	32200 AAW	ARBLS	10//99-12//99
	California	S	17.58 MW	17.60 AW	36610 AAW	CABLS	10//99-12//99
	Bakersfield MSA, CA	S	21.80 MW	22.43 AW	45350 AAW	CABLS	10//99-12//99
	Chico-Paradise MSA, CA	S	20.88 MW	21.95 AW	43430 AAW	CABLS	10//99-12//99
	Fresno MSA, CA	S	17.41 MW	16.80 AW	36210 AAW	CABLS	10//99-12//99
	Los Angeles-Long Beach PMSA, CA	S	17.25 MW	17.53 AW	35870 AAW	CABLS	10//99-12//99
	Oakland PMSA, CA	S	18.05 MW	18.46 AW	37540 AAW	CABLS	10//99-12//99
	Orange County PMSA, CA	S	16.20 MW	15.46 AW	33690 AAW	CABLS	10//99-12//99
	Riverside-San Bernardino PMSA, CA	S	18.10 MW	18.60 AW	37640 AAW	CABLS	10//99-12//99
	Sacramento PMSA, CA	S	17.84 MW	18.49 AW	37110 AAW	CABLS	10//99-12//99
	Salinas MSA, CA	S	16.81 MW	16.34 AW	34970 AAW	CABLS	10//99-12//99
	San Diego MSA, CA	S	16.63 MW	16.87 AW	34590 AAW	CABLS	10//99-12//99
	San Francisco PMSA, CA	S	17.79 MW	17.42 AW	36990 AAW	CABLS	10//99-12//99
	San Jose PMSA, CA	S	20.23 MW	20.33 AW	42070 AAW	CABLS	10//99-12//99
	San Luis Obispo-Atascadero-Paso Robles MSA, CA	S	15.37 MW	13.77 AW	31960 AAW	CABLS	10//99-12//99
	Santa Rosa PMSA, CA	S	17.91 MW	18.00 AW	37250 AAW	CABLS	10//99-12//99
	Stockton-Lodi MSA, CA	S	18.94 MW	20.04 AW	39400 AAW	CABLS	10//99-12//99
	Vallejo-Fairfield-Napa PMSA, CA	S	20.54 MW	20.07 AW	42720 AAW	CABLS	10//99-12//99
	Ventura PMSA, CA	S	17.57 MW	17.22 AW	36540 AAW	CABLS	10//99-12//99
	Visalia-Tulare-Porterville MSA, CA	S	15.81 MW	15.41 AW	32880 AAW	CABLS	10//99-12//99
	Yuba City MSA, CA	S	21.66 MW	23.28 AW	45060 AAW	CABLS	10//99-12//99
	Colorado	S	11.75 MW	13.46 AW	28000 AAW	COBLS	10//99-12//99
	Colorado Springs MSA, CO	S	16.61 MW	17.00 AW	34540 AAW	COBLS	10//99-12//99
	Denver PMSA, CO	S	13.18 MW	11.62 AW	27410 AAW	COBLS	10//99-12//99
	Pueblo MSA, CO	S	14.67 MW	13.96 AW	30500 AAW	COBLS	10//99-12//99
	Connecticut	S	19.32 MW	18.50 AW	38490 AAW	CTBLS	10//99-12//99
	Bridgeport PMSA, CT	S	17.01 MW	15.76 AW	35370 AAW	CTBLS	10//99-12//99
	Hartford MSA, CT	S	19.31 MW	21.01 AW	40160 AAW	CTBLS	10//99-12//99
	New Haven-Meriden PMSA, CT	S	15.51 MW	13.80 AW	32260 AAW	CTBLS	10//99-12//99
	Waterbury PMSA, CT	S	21.55 MW	22.30 AW	44820 AAW	CTBLS	10//99-12//99
	Delaware	S	12.15 MW	12.79 AW	26590 AAW	DEBLS	10//99-12//99
	Washington PMSA, DC-MD-VA-WV	S	17.25 MW	14.85 AW	35880 AAW	DCBLS	10//99-12//99
	Florida	S	12.49 MW	14.76 AW	30690 AAW	FLBLS	10//99-12//99
	Fort Lauderdale PMSA, FL	S	14.04 MW	11.91 AW	29200 AAW	FLBLS	10//99-12//99
	Jacksonville MSA, FL	S	14.13 MW	12.17 AW	29400 AAW	FLBLS	10//99-12//99
	Melbourne-Titusville-Palm Bay MSA, FL	S	12.64 MW	11.31 AW	26300 AAW	FLBLS	10//99-12//99
	Miami PMSA, FL	S	15.73 MW	16.72 AW	32730 AAW	FLBLS	10//99-12//99
	Ocala MSA, FL	S	16.33 MW	15.02 AW	33960 AAW	FLBLS	10//99-12//99
	Orlando MSA, FL	S	12.35 MW	10.87 AW	25700 AAW	FLBLS	10//99-12//99
	Pensacola MSA, FL	S	12.12 MW	11.02 AW	25210 AAW	FLBLS	10//99-12//99
	Sarasota-Bradenton MSA, FL	S	11.38 MW	10.62 AW	23680 AAW	FLBLS	10//99-12//99
	Tallahassee MSA, FL	S	14.99 MW	14.60 AW	31190 AAW	FLBLS	10//99-12//99
	Georgia	S	14.93 MW	14.94 AW	31060 AAW	GABLS	10//99-12//99
	Albany MSA, GA	S	14.73 MW	14.33 AW	30630 AAW	GABLS	10//99-12//99
	Athens MSA, GA	S	15.68 MW	15.20 AW	32620 AAW	GABLS	10//99-12//99
	Atlanta MSA, GA	S	15.49 MW	15.25 AW	32210 AAW	GABLS	10//99-12//99
	Augusta-Aiken MSA, GA-SC	S	13.13 MW	12.75 AW	27310 AAW	GABLS	10//99-12//99
	Columbus MSA, GA-AL	S	15.95 MW	16.73 AW	33170 AAW	GABLS	10//99-12//99
	Macon MSA, GA	S	13.90 MW	13.11 AW	28900 AAW	GABLS	10//99-12//99
	Savannah MSA, GA	S	14.16 MW	13.96 AW	29440 AAW	GABLS	10//99-12//99
	Hawaii	S	21.95 MW	21.31 AW	44330 AAW	HIBLS	10//99-12//99
	Honolulu MSA, HI	S	21.73 MW	22.23 AW	45200 AAW	HIBLS	10//99-12//99
	Idaho	S	15.26 MW	15.92 AW	33120 AAW	IDBLS	10//99-12//99
	Boise City MSA, ID	S	14.86 MW	14.56 AW	30910 AAW	IDBLS	10//99-12//99
	Illinois	S	19.12 MW	17.95 AW	37330 AAW	ILBLS	10//99-12//99

AAW Average annual wage	**AOH** Average offered, high	**ASH** Average starting, high	**H** Hourly	**M** Monthly	**S** Special: hourly and annual
AE Average entry wage	**AOL** Average offered, low	**ASL** Average starting, low	**HI** Highest wage paid	**MTC** Median total compensation	**TQ** Third quartile wage
AEX Average experienced wage	**APH** Average pay, high range	**AW** Average wage paid	**HR** High end range	**MW** Median wage paid	**W** Weekly
AO Average offered	**APL** Average pay, low range	**FQ** First quartile wage	**LR** Low end range	**SQ** Second quartile wage	**Y** Yearly

Occupation/Type/Industry	Location	Per	Low	Mid	High	Source	Date
Telecommunications Line Installer and Repairer	Bloomington-Normal MSA, IL	S	21.91 MW	22.26 AW	45580 AAW	ILBLS	10//99-12//99
	Chicago PMSA, IL	S	18.95 MW	20.41 AW	39420 AAW	ILBLS	10//99-12//99
	Peoria-Pekin MSA, IL	S	18.15 MW	18.77 AW	37750 AAW	ILBLS	10//99-12//99
	Springfield MSA, IL	S	13.97 MW	13.75 AW	29070 AAW	ILBLS	10//99-12//99
	Indiana	S	13.06 MW	14.65 AW	30470 AAW	INBLS	10//99-12//99
	Evansville-Henderson MSA, IN-KY	S	14.38 MW	11.40 AW	29920 AAW	INBLS	10//99-12//99
	Fort Wayne MSA, IN	S	12.41 MW	11.91 AW	25820 AAW	INBLS	10//99-12//99
	Gary PMSA, IN	S	15.39 MW	13.64 AW	32010 AAW	INBLS	10//99-12//99
	Indianapolis MSA, IN	S	15.70 MW	13.37 AW	32660 AAW	INBLS	10//99-12//99
	Terre Haute MSA, IN	S	12.62 MW	12.42 AW	26250 AAW	INBLS	10//99-12//99
	Iowa	S	14.61 MW	14.67 AW	30520 AAW	IABLS	10//99-12//99
	Davenport-Moline-Rock Island MSA, IA-IL	S	18.08 MW	19.39 AW	37600 AAW	IABLS	10//99-12//99
	Waterloo-Cedar Falls MSA, IA	S	14.90 MW	14.12 AW	31000 AAW	IABLS	10//99-12//99
	Kansas	S	21.5 MW	18.89 AW	39300 AAW	KSBLS	10//99-12//99
	Lawrence MSA, KS	S	18.98 MW	22.46 AW	39470 AAW	KSBLS	10//99-12//99
	Topeka MSA, KS	S	18.19 MW	21.63 AW	37840 AAW	KSBLS	10//99-12//99
	Wichita MSA, KS	S	19.78 MW	22.05 AW	41150 AAW	KSBLS	10//99-12//99
	Kentucky	S	14.33 MW	15.17 AW	31540 AAW	KYBLS	10//99-12//99
	Lexington MSA, KY	S	14.34 MW	13.16 AW	29820 AAW	KYBLS	10//99-12//99
	Louisville MSA, KY-IN	S	17.57 MW	18.67 AW	36550 AAW	KYBLS	10//99-12//99
	Owensboro MSA, KY	S	14.98 MW	16.19 AW	31160 AAW	KYBLS	10//99-12//99
	Louisiana	S	18.21 MW	17.45 AW	36300 AAW	LABLS	10//99-12//99
	Alexandria MSA, LA	S	17.35 MW	18.76 AW	36100 AAW	LABLS	10//99-12//99
	Baton Rouge MSA, LA	S	14.30 MW	14.03 AW	29740 AAW	LABLS	10//99-12//99
	Houma MSA, LA	S	17.23 MW	18.40 AW	35840 AAW	LABLS	10//99-12//99
	Lake Charles MSA, LA	S	13.17 MW	11.89 AW	27400 AAW	LABLS	10//99-12//99
	Monroe MSA, LA	S	19.43 MW	20.66 AW	40410 AAW	LABLS	10//99-12//99
	New Orleans MSA, LA	S	20.06 MW	21.68 AW	41710 AAW	LABLS	10//99-12//99
	Shreveport-Bossier City MSA, LA	S	15.39 MW	17.03 AW	32000 AAW	LABLS	10//99-12//99
	Maine	S	13.17 MW	16.00 AW	33290 AAW	MEBLS	10//99-12//99
	Portland MSA, ME	S	20.87 MW	19.68 AW	43400 AAW	MEBLS	10//99-12//99
	Maryland	S	14.76 MW	15.92 AW	33120 AAW	MDBLS	10//99-12//99
	Baltimore PMSA, MD	S	13.30 MW	12.57 AW	27660 AAW	MDBLS	10//99-12//99
	Massachusetts	S	21.78 MW	21.14 AW	43970 AAW	MABLS	10//99-12//99
	Boston PMSA, MA-NH	S	21.39 MW	22.07 AW	44490 AAW	MABLS	10//99-12//99
	Brockton PMSA, MA	S	22.43 MW	19.79 AW	46660 AAW	MABLS	10//99-12//99
	Lawrence PMSA, MA-NH	S	18.60 MW	20.48 AW	38700 AAW	MABLS	10//99-12//99
	Lowell PMSA, MA-NH	S	15.00 MW	14.60 AW	31200 AAW	MABLS	10//99-12//99
	Springfield MSA, MA	S	25.08 MW	25.57 AW	52160 AAW	MABLS	10//99-12//99
	Worcester PMSA, MA-CT	S	22.79 MW	23.92 AW	47400 AAW	MABLS	10//99-12//99
	Michigan	S	15.31 MW	15.90 AW	33070 AAW	MIBLS	10//99-12//99
	Detroit PMSA, MI	S	17.20 MW	17.41 AW	35770 AAW	MIBLS	10//99-12//99
	Grand Rapids-Muskegon-Holland MSA, MI	S	14.53 MW	14.15 AW	30220 AAW	MIBLS	10//99-12//99
	Kalamazoo-Battle Creek MSA, MI	S	17.59 MW	18.72 AW	36590 AAW	MIBLS	10//99-12//99
	Minnesota	S	14.86 MW	15.48 AW	32190 AAW	MNBLS	10//99-12//99
	Duluth-Superior MSA, MN-WI	S	14.65 MW	14.32 AW	30460 AAW	MNBLS	10//99-12//99
	Minneapolis-St. Paul MSA, MN-WI	S	16.20 MW	15.61 AW	33700 AAW	MNBLS	10//99-12//99
	Mississippi	S	15.9 MW	16.12 AW	33520 AAW	MSBLS	10//99-12//99
	Biloxi-Gulfport-Pascagoula MSA, MS	S	18.31 MW	19.41 AW	38080 AAW	MSBLS	10//99-12//99
	Jackson MSA, MS	S	17.94 MW	19.07 AW	37310 AAW	MSBLS	10//99-12//99
	Missouri	S	20.18 MW	17.93 AW	37290 AAW	MOBLS	10//99-12//99
	Kansas City MSA, MO-KS	S	19.31 MW	21.42 AW	40160 AAW	MOBLS	10//99-12//99
	St. Louis MSA, MO-IL	S	18.33 MW	20.66 AW	38120 AAW	MOBLS	10//99-12//99
	Montana	S	20.14 MW	17.79 AW	36990 AAW	MTBLS	10//99-12//99
	Nebraska	S	15.23 MW	16.05 AW	33390 AAW	NEBLS	10//99-12//99
	Omaha MSA, NE-IA	S	17.44 MW	17.90 AW	36280 AAW	NEBLS	10//99-12//99
	Nevada	S	20.92 MW	19.70 AW	40970 AAW	NVBLS	10//99-12//99
	Las Vegas MSA, NV-AZ	S	20.63 MW	21.78 AW	42910 AAW	NVBLS	10//99-12//99
	Reno MSA, NV	S	17.72 MW	16.09 AW	36860 AAW	NVBLS	10//99-12//99
	New Hampshire	S	20.09 MW	19.31 AW	40160 AAW	NHBLS	10//99-12//99
	Manchester PMSA, NH	S	23.06 MW	22.94 AW	47960 AAW	NHBLS	10//99-12//99
	Nashua PMSA, NH	S	19.37 MW	21.19 AW	40280 AAW	NHBLS	10//99-12//99
	New Jersey	S	19.33 MW	18.49 AW	38460 AAW	NJBLS	10//99-12//99
	Bergen-Passaic PMSA, NJ	S	16.45 MW	15.90 AW	34220 AAW	NJBLS	10//99-12//99

AAW	Average annual wage	AOH	Average offered, high	ASH	Average starting, high	H	Hourly	M	Monthly	S	Special: hourly and annual
AE	Average entry wage	AOL	Average offered, low	ASL	Average starting, low	HI	Highest wage paid	MTC	Median total compensation	TQ	Third quartile wage
AEX	Average experienced wage	APH	Average pay, high range	AW	Average wage paid	HR	High end range	MW	Median wage paid	W	Weekly
AO	Average offered	APL	Average pay, low range	FQ	First quartile wage	LR	Low end range	SQ	Second quartile wage	Y	Yearly

Occupation/Type/Industry	Location	Per	Low	Mid	High	Source	Date
Telecommunications Line Installer and Repairer	Jersey City PMSA, NJ	S	15.03 MW	13.21 AW	31260 AAW	NJBLS	10//99-12//99
	Middlesex-Somerset-Hunterdon PMSA, NJ	S	20.13 MW	20.55 AW	41880 AAW	NJBLS	10//99-12//99
	Newark PMSA, NJ	S	21.14 MW	22.54 AW	43970 AAW	NJBLS	10//99-12//99
	New Mexico	S	12.89 MW	14.80 AW	30780 AAW	NMBLS	10//99-12//99
	Albuquerque MSA, NM	S	14.73 MW	13.36 AW	30640 AAW	NMBLS	10//99-12//99
	Santa Fe MSA, NM	S	11.63 MW	10.37 AW	24190 AAW	NMBLS	10//99-12//99
	New York	S	23.97 MW	23.45 AW	48770 AAW	NYBLS	10//99-12//99
	Albany-Schenectady-Troy MSA, NY	S	20.69 MW	19.55 AW	43030 AAW	NYBLS	10//99-12//99
	Binghamton MSA, NY	S	16.82 MW	17.89 AW	34980 AAW	NYBLS	10//99-12//99
	Buffalo-Niagara Falls MSA, NY	S	21.44 MW	22.96 AW	44590 AAW	NYBLS	10//99-12//99
	Nassau-Suffolk PMSA, NY	S	22.62 MW	23.70 AW	47040 AAW	NYBLS	10//99-12//99
	New York PMSA, NY	S	24.32 MW	24.53 AW	50580 AAW	NYBLS	10//99-12//99
	Newburgh PMSA, NY-PA	S	21.68 MW	22.81 AW	45100 AAW	NYBLS	10//99-12//99
	Rochester MSA, NY	S	22.87 MW	23.16 AW	47570 AAW	NYBLS	10//99-12//99
	Syracuse MSA, NY	S	22.17 MW	22.49 AW	46120 AAW	NYBLS	10//99-12//99
	Utica-Rome MSA, NY	S	19.52 MW	21.96 AW	40610 AAW	NYBLS	10//99-12//99
	North Carolina	S	14.75 MW	14.93 AW	31060 AAW	NCBLS	10//99-12//99
	Asheville MSA, NC	S	13.28 MW	12.39 AW	27630 AAW	NCBLS	10//99-12//99
	Charlotte-Gastonia-Rock Hill MSA, NC-SC	S	14.60 MW	14.62 AW	30370 AAW	NCBLS	10//99-12//99
	Goldsboro MSA, NC	S	14.32 MW	13.30 AW	29800 AAW	NCBLS	10//99-12//99
	Greensboro--Winston-Salem--High Point MSA, NC	S	16.93 MW	15.96 AW	35210 AAW	NCBLS	10//99-12//99
	Hickory-Morganton-Lenoir MSA, NC	S	13.51 MW	14.10 AW	28100 AAW	NCBLS	10//99-12//99
	Raleigh-Durham-Chapel Hill MSA, NC	S	13.87 MW	13.08 AW	28850 AAW	NCBLS	10//99-12//99
	Wilmington MSA, NC	S	14.22 MW	13.65 AW	29580 AAW	NCBLS	10//99-12//99
	North Dakota	S	16.5 MW	15.70 AW	32660 AAW	NDBLS	10//99-12//99
	Grand Forks MSA, ND-MN	S	18.24 MW	18.62 AW	37940 AAW	NDBLS	10//99-12//99
	Ohio	S	16.35 MW	16.68 AW	34700 AAW	OHBLS	10//99-12//99
	Akron PMSA, OH	S	18.68 MW	19.65 AW	38840 AAW	OHBLS	10//99-12//99
	Cincinnati PMSA, OH-KY-IN	S	16.16 MW	16.37 AW	33610 AAW	OHBLS	10//99-12//99
	Cleveland-Lorain-Elyria PMSA, OH	S	17.20 MW	18.21 AW	35770 AAW	OHBLS	10//99-12//99
	Columbus MSA, OH	S	16.12 MW	15.13 AW	33540 AAW	OHBLS	10//99-12//99
	Dayton-Springfield MSA, OH	S	15.66 MW	15.22 AW	32580 AAW	OHBLS	10//99-12//99
	Hamilton-Middletown PMSA, OH	S	20.12 MW	21.70 AW	41850 AAW	OHBLS	10//99-12//99
	Toledo MSA, OH	S	18.27 MW	19.17 AW	38000 AAW	OHBLS	10//99-12//99
	Youngstown-Warren MSA, OH	S	13.82 MW	14.43 AW	28750 AAW	OHBLS	10//99-12//99
	Oklahoma	S	18.36 MW	17.09 AW	35540 AAW	OKBLS	10//99-12//99
	Oklahoma City MSA, OK	S	19.01 MW	21.58 AW	39530 AAW	OKBLS	10//99-12//99
	Tulsa MSA, OK	S	15.29 MW	13.43 AW	31810 AAW	OKBLS	10//99-12//99
	Oregon	S	16.91 MW	16.55 AW	34420 AAW	ORBLS	10//99-12//99
	Eugene-Springfield MSA, OR	S	12.82 MW	12.03 AW	26670 AAW	ORBLS	10//99-12//99
	Portland-Vancouver PMSA, OR-WA	S	17.08 MW	17.41 AW	35530 AAW	ORBLS	10//99-12//99
	Salem PMSA, OR	S	17.08 MW	15.93 AW	35530 AAW	ORBLS	10//99-12//99
	Pennsylvania	S	15.78 MW	15.88 AW	33040 AAW	PABLS	10//99-12//99
	Allentown-Bethlehem-Easton MSA, PA	S	15.48 MW	14.22 AW	32190 AAW	PABLS	10//99-12//99
	Harrisburg-Lebanon-Carlisle MSA, PA	S	16.17 MW	16.34 AW	33640 AAW	PABLS	10//99-12//99
	Johnstown MSA, PA	S	12.92 MW	11.45 AW	26880 AAW	PABLS	10//99-12//99
	Lancaster MSA, PA	S	15.17 MW	15.06 AW	31550 AAW	PABLS	10//99-12//99
	Philadelphia PMSA, PA-NJ	S	16.98 MW	16.79 AW	35310 AAW	PABLS	10//99-12//99
	Pittsburgh MSA, PA	S	14.69 MW	14.61 AW	30560 AAW	PABLS	10//99-12//99
	Reading MSA, PA	S	17.81 MW	18.45 AW	37050 AAW	PABLS	10//99-12//99
	Scranton--Wilkes-Barre--Hazleton MSA, PA	S	15.36 MW	15.61 AW	31950 AAW	PABLS	10//99-12//99
	York MSA, PA	S	16.30 MW	17.60 AW	33890 AAW	PABLS	10//99-12//99
	South Carolina	S	16.33 MW	15.40 AW	32040 AAW	SCBLS	10//99-12//99
	Charleston-North Charleston MSA, SC	S	13.66 MW	14.38 AW	28420 AAW	SCBLS	10//99-12//99
	Columbia MSA, SC	S	15.61 MW	16.99 AW	32460 AAW	SCBLS	10//99-12//99
	Florence MSA, SC	S	14.79 MW	16.89 AW	30770 AAW	SCBLS	10//99-12//99

AAW	Average annual wage	AOH	Average offered, high	ASH	Average starting, high	H	Hourly	M	Monthly	S	Special: hourly and annual
AE	Average entry wage	AOL	Average offered, low	ASL	Average starting, low	HI	Highest wage paid	MTC	Median total compensation	TQ	Third quartile wage
AEX	Average experienced wage	APH	Average pay, high range	AW	Average wage paid	HR	High end range	MW	Median wage paid	W	Weekly
AO	Average offered	APL	Average pay, low range	FQ	First quartile wage	LR	Low end range	SQ	Second quartile wage	Y	Yearly

Occupation/Type/Industry	Location	Per	Low	Mid	High	Source	Date
Telecommunications Line Installer and Repairer	Greenville-Spartanburg-Anderson MSA, SC	S	14.92 MW	15.95 AW	31020 AAW	SCBLS	10//99-12//99
	Myrtle Beach MSA, SC	S	17.37 MW	17.53 AW	36140 AAW	SCBLS	10//99-12//99
	South Dakota	S	14.58 MW	15.37 AW	31980 AAW	SDBLS	10//99-12//99
	Sioux Falls MSA, SD	S	16.70 MW	17.41 AW	34730 AAW	SDBLS	10//99-12//99
	Tennessee	S	16.07 MW	16.17 AW	33630 AAW	TNBLS	10//99-12//99
	Chattanooga MSA, TN-GA	S	14.60 MW	14.27 AW	30370 AAW	TNBLS	10//99-12//99
	Clarksville-Hopkinsville MSA, TN-KY	S	14.91 MW	13.42 AW	31010 AAW	TNBLS	10//99-12//99
	Johnson City-Kingsport-Bristol MSA, TN-VA	S	15.14 MW	13.60 AW	31500 AAW	TNBLS	10//99-12//99
	Knoxville MSA, TN	S	16.15 MW	17.54 AW	33580 AAW	TNBLS	10//99-12//99
	Memphis MSA, TN-AR-MS	S	17.24 MW	17.15 AW	35860 AAW	MSBLS	10//99-12//99
	Nashville MSA, TN	S	16.67 MW	17.06 AW	34680 AAW	TNBLS	10//99-12//99
	Texas	S	15.87 MW	16.87 AW	35090 AAW	TXBLS	10//99-12//99
	Abilene MSA, TX	S	17.07 MW	17.93 AW	35500 AAW	TXBLS	10//99-12//99
	Amarillo MSA, TX	S	18.91 MW	22.03 AW	39330 AAW	TXBLS	10//99-12//99
	Austin-San Marcos MSA, TX	S	14.47 MW	14.15 AW	30090 AAW	TXBLS	10//99-12//99
	Bryan-College Station MSA, TX	S	11.74 MW	10.13 AW	24430 AAW	TXBLS	10//99-12//99
	Corpus Christi MSA, TX	S	14.04 MW	11.81 AW	29200 AAW	TXBLS	10//99-12//99
	Dallas PMSA, TX	S	18.53 MW	16.65 AW	38530 AAW	TXBLS	10//99-12//99
	Fort Worth-Arlington PMSA, TX	S	15.24 MW	13.06 AW	31710 AAW	TXBLS	10//99-12//99
	Houston PMSA, TX	S	17.34 MW	17.81 AW	36070 AAW	TXBLS	10//99-12//99
	San Antonio MSA, TX	S	17.07 MW	18.01 AW	35500 AAW	TXBLS	10//99-12//99
	Sherman-Denison MSA, TX	S	14.36 MW	12.63 AW	29870 AAW	TXBLS	10//99-12//99
	Texarkana MSA, TX-Texarkana, AR	S	15.51 MW	16.35 AW	32260 AAW	TXBLS	10//99-12//99
	Tyler MSA, TX	S	17.00 MW	17.39 AW	35360 AAW	TXBLS	10//99-12//99
	Waco MSA, TX	S	15.48 MW	13.83 AW	32200 AAW	TXBLS	10//99-12//99
	Utah	S	14 MW	14.77 AW	30720 AAW	UTBLS	10//99-12//99
	Vermont	S	12.92 MW	14.55 AW	30260 AAW	VTBLS	10//99-12//99
	Burlington MSA, VT	S	13.60 MW	12.52 AW	28290 AAW	VTBLS	10//99-12//99
	Virginia	S	12.61 MW	15.51 AW	32270 AAW	VABLS	10//99-12//99
	Lynchburg MSA, VA	S	17.41 MW	19.61 AW	36210 AAW	VABLS	10//99-12//99
	Norfolk-Virginia Beach-Newport News MSA, VA-NC	S	13.23 MW	11.79 AW	27520 AAW	VABLS	10//99-12//99
	Richmond-Petersburg MSA, VA	S	11.51 MW	10.69 AW	23940 AAW	VABLS	10//99-12//99
	Roanoke MSA, VA	S	11.11 MW	10.17 AW	23110 AAW	VABLS	10//99-12//99
	Washington	S	16.5 MW	16.68 AW	34700 AAW	WABLS	10//99-12//99
	Bremerton PMSA, WA	S	14.49 MW	12.07 AW	30140 AAW	WABLS	10//99-12//99
	Olympia PMSA, WA	S	11.45 MW	10.68 AW	23810 AAW	WABLS	10//99-12//99
	Seattle-Bellevue-Everett PMSA, WA	S	17.57 MW	17.58 AW	36550 AAW	WABLS	10//99-12//99
	Spokane MSA, WA	S	14.25 MW	13.29 AW	29640 AAW	WABLS	10//99-12//99
	Tacoma PMSA, WA	S	15.75 MW	14.99 AW	32770 AAW	WABLS	10//99-12//99
	Yakima MSA, WA	S	16.58 MW	17.04 AW	34490 AAW	WABLS	10//99-12//99
	West Virginia	S	11.17 MW	12.52 AW	26050 AAW	WVBLS	10//99-12//99
	Huntington-Ashland MSA, WV-KY-OH	S	12.35 MW	10.89 AW	25690 AAW	WVBLS	10//99-12//99
	Wisconsin	S	15.34 MW	15.29 AW	31800 AAW	WIBLS	10//99-12//99
	Eau Claire MSA, WI	S	14.57 MW	16.52 AW	30300 AAW	WIBLS	10//99-12//99
	Green Bay MSA, WI	S	13.89 MW	13.71 AW	28890 AAW	WIBLS	10//99-12//99
	Madison MSA, WI	S	16.55 MW	16.75 AW	34410 AAW	WIBLS	10//99-12//99
	Milwaukee-Waukesha PMSA, WI	S	15.89 MW	15.89 AW	33060 AAW	WIBLS	10//99-12//99
	Racine PMSA, WI	S	20.72 MW	22.34 AW	43090 AAW	WIBLS	10//99-12//99
	Wyoming	S	12.72 MW	13.78 AW	28660 AAW	WYBLS	10//99-12//99
	Puerto Rico	S	10.05 MW	10.07 AW	20940 AAW	PRBLS	10//99-12//99
	Caguas PMSA, PR	S	11.35 MW	10.83 AW	23610 AAW	PRBLS	10//99-12//99
	Ponce MSA, PR	S	7.76 MW	5.96 AW	16150 AAW	PRBLS	10//99-12//99
	San Juan-Bayamon PMSA, PR	S	9.84 MW	9.76 AW	20460 AAW	PRBLS	10//99-12//99
Telemarketer	Alabama	S	7.62 MW	8.12 AW	16880 AAW	ALBLS	10//99-12//99
	Birmingham MSA, AL	S	8.29 MW	7.59 AW	17240 AAW	ALBLS	10//99-12//99
	Montgomery MSA, AL	S	7.73 MW	7.62 AW	16070 AAW	ALBLS	10//99-12//99
	Arizona	S	7.71 MW	8.42 AW	17510 AAW	AZBLS	10//99-12//99
	Flagstaff MSA, AZ-UT	S	8.86 MW	8.06 AW	18430 AAW	AZBLS	10//99-12//99

AAW Average annual wage	AOH Average offered, high	ASH Average starting, high	H Hourly	M Monthly	S Special: hourly and annual
AE Average entry wage	AOL Average offered, low	ASL Average starting, low	HI Highest wage paid	MTC Median total compensation	TQ Third quartile wage
AEX Average experienced wage	APH Average pay, high range	AW Average wage paid	HR High end range	MW Median wage paid	W Weekly
AO Average offered	APL Average pay, low range	FQ First quartile wage	LR Low end range	SQ Second quartile wage	Y Yearly

Occupation/Type/Industry	Location	Per	Low	Mid	High	Source	Date
Telemarketer	Phoenix-Mesa MSA, AZ	S	8.36 MW	7.63 AW	17380 AAW	AZBLS	10//99-12//99
	Tucson MSA, AZ	S	8.29 MW	7.40 AW	17240 AAW	AZBLS	10//99-12//99
	Arkansas	S	7.01 MW	8.10 AW	16850 AAW	ARBLS	10//99-12//99
	Fayetteville-Springdale-Rogers MSA, AR	S	6.00 MW	6.03 AW	12470 AAW	ARBLS	10//99-12//99
	Fort Smith MSA, AR-OK	S	6.33 MW	6.04 AW	13160 AAW	ARBLS	10//99-12//99
	Little Rock-North Little Rock MSA, AR	S	9.19 MW	7.96 AW	19110 AAW	ARBLS	10//99-12//99
	California	S	9.62 MW	11.04 AW	22970 AAW	CABLS	10//99-12//99
	Bakersfield MSA, CA	S	7.55 MW	7.46 AW	15710 AAW	CABLS	10//99-12//99
	Chico-Paradise MSA, CA	S	10.45 MW	8.70 AW	21740 AAW	CABLS	10//99-12//99
	Fresno MSA, CA	S	10.01 MW	8.30 AW	20810 AAW	CABLS	10//99-12//99
	Los Angeles County, CA	Y		32304 AW		LABJ	1999
	Los Angeles-Long Beach PMSA, CA	S	9.54 MW	8.05 AW	19850 AAW	CABLS	10//99-12//99
	Modesto MSA, CA	S	9.92 MW	10.29 AW	20630 AAW	CABLS	10//99-12//99
	Oakland PMSA, CA	S	13.89 MW	12.59 AW	28900 AAW	CABLS	10//99-12//99
	Orange County PMSA, CA	S	11.61 MW	9.33 AW	24140 AAW	CABLS	10//99-12//99
	Redding MSA, CA	S	9.43 MW	8.73 AW	19610 AAW	CABLS	10//99-12//99
	Riverside-San Bernardino PMSA, CA	S	10.82 MW	8.45 AW	22510 AAW	CABLS	10//99-12//99
	Sacramento PMSA, CA	S	9.97 MW	7.58 AW	20740 AAW	CABLS	10//99-12//99
	San Diego MSA, CA	S	10.63 MW	11.13 AW	22100 AAW	CABLS	10//99-12//99
	San Francisco PMSA, CA	S	12.32 MW	9.66 AW	25630 AAW	CABLS	10//99-12//99
	San Jose PMSA, CA	S	10.26 MW	8.55 AW	21330 AAW	CABLS	10//99-12//99
	San Luis Obispo-Atascadero-Paso Robles MSA, CA	S	10.19 MW	8.76 AW	21190 AAW	CABLS	10//99-12//99
	Santa Barbara-Santa Maria-Lompoc MSA, CA	S	9.84 MW	9.37 AW	20470 AAW	CABLS	10//99-12//99
	Santa Cruz-Watsonville PMSA, CA	S	8.11 MW	7.86 AW	16870 AAW	CABLS	10//99-12//99
	Santa Rosa PMSA, CA	S	9.55 MW	8.16 AW	19860 AAW	CABLS	10//99-12//99
	Stockton-Lodi MSA, CA	S	12.93 MW	13.55 AW	26900 AAW	CABLS	10//99-12//99
	Vallejo-Fairfield-Napa PMSA, CA	S	9.23 MW	9.19 AW	19200 AAW	CABLS	10//99-12//99
	Ventura PMSA, CA	S	10.68 MW	9.72 AW	22220 AAW	CABLS	10//99-12//99
	Visalia-Tulare-Porterville MSA, CA	S	8.89 MW	8.01 AW	18500 AAW	CABLS	10//99-12//99
	Yolo PMSA, CA	S	13.15 MW	13.82 AW	27350 AAW	CABLS	10//99-12//99
	Colorado	S	7.9 MW	8.45 AW	17570 AAW	COBLS	10//99-12//99
	Denver PMSA, CO	S	8.53 MW	7.96 AW	17750 AAW	COBLS	10//99-12//99
	Fort Collins-Loveland MSA, CO	S	7.81 MW	7.68 AW	16250 AAW	COBLS	10//99-12//99
	Connecticut	S	10.18 MW	11.06 AW	23010 AAW	CTBLS	10//99-12//99
	Bridgeport PMSA, CT	S	11.12 MW	10.21 AW	23130 AAW	CTBLS	10//99-12//99
	Danbury PMSA, CT	S	11.21 MW	10.17 AW	23320 AAW	CTBLS	10//99-12//99
	Hartford MSA, CT	S	11.13 MW	10.25 AW	23160 AAW	CTBLS	10//99-12//99
	New Haven-Meriden PMSA, CT	S	11.04 MW	10.20 AW	22970 AAW	CTBLS	10//99-12//99
	New London-Norwich MSA, CT-RI	S	9.35 MW	8.12 AW	19440 AAW	CTBLS	10//99-12//99
	Stamford-Norwalk PMSA, CT	S	12.01 MW	13.17 AW	24980 AAW	CTBLS	10//99-12//99
	Waterbury PMSA, CT	S	12.74 MW	12.00 AW	26500 AAW	CTBLS	10//99-12//99
	Delaware	S	8.97 MW	9.04 AW	18800 AAW	DEBLS	10//99-12//99
	Dover MSA, DE	S	8.24 MW	7.63 AW	17140 AAW	DEBLS	10//99-12//99
	Wilmington-Newark PMSA, DE-MD	S	9.85 MW	9.86 AW	20500 AAW	DEBLS	10//99-12//99
	District of Columbia	S	9.81 MW	11.02 AW	22920 AAW	DCBLS	10//99-12//99
	Washington PMSA, DC-MD-VA-WV	S	11.08 MW	9.65 AW	23050 AAW	DCBLS	10//99-12//99
	Florida	S	9.55 MW	10.67 AW	22200 AAW	FLBLS	10//99-12//99
	Daytona Beach MSA, FL	S	6.76 MW	6.51 AW	14070 AAW	FLBLS	10//99-12//99
	Fort Lauderdale PMSA, FL	S	9.97 MW	8.27 AW	20740 AAW	FLBLS	10//99-12//99
	Fort Myers-Cape Coral MSA, FL	S	10.70 MW	10.99 AW	22260 AAW	FLBLS	10//99-12//99
	Fort Pierce-Port St. Lucie MSA, FL	S	7.82 MW	7.62 AW	16270 AAW	FLBLS	10//99-12//99
	Fort Walton Beach MSA, FL	S	8.14 MW	7.81 AW	16930 AAW	FLBLS	10//99-12//99
	Jacksonville MSA, FL	S	11.15 MW	10.80 AW	23190 AAW	FLBLS	10//99-12//99
	Lakeland-Winter Haven MSA, FL	S	10.39 MW	9.56 AW	21600 AAW	FLBLS	10//99-12//99
	Miami PMSA, FL	S	10.17 MW	9.45 AW	21160 AAW	FLBLS	10//99-12//99

AAW Average annual wage	**AOH** Average offered, high	**ASH** Average starting, high	**H** Hourly	**M** Monthly	**S** Special: hourly and annual
AE Average entry wage	**AOL** Average offered, low	**ASL** Average starting, low	**HI** Highest wage paid	**MTC** Median total compensation	**TQ** Third quartile wage
AEX Average experienced wage	**APH** Average pay, high range	**AW** Average wage paid	**HR** High end range	**MW** Median wage paid	**W** Weekly
AO Average offered	**APL** Average pay, low range	**FQ** First quartile wage	**LR** Low end range	**SQ** Second quartile wage	**Y** Yearly

Occupation/Type/Industry	Location	Per	Low	Mid	High	Source	Date
Telemarketer	Naples MSA, FL	S	8.16 MW	7.83 AW	16970 AAW	FLBLS	10//99-12//99
	Ocala MSA, FL	S	7.18 MW	7.13 AW	14930 AAW	FLBLS	10//99-12//99
	Orlando MSA, FL	S	10.85 MW	9.68 AW	22570 AAW	FLBLS	10//99-12//99
	Pensacola MSA, FL	S	7.56 MW	7.62 AW	15730 AAW	FLBLS	10//99-12//99
	Punta Gorda MSA, FL	S	7.25 MW	6.22 AW	15070 AAW	FLBLS	10//99-12//99
	Sarasota-Bradenton MSA, FL	S	9.82 MW	7.72 AW	20430 AAW	FLBLS	10//99-12//99
	Tallahassee MSA, FL	S	6.14 MW	6.05 AW	12760 AAW	FLBLS	10//99-12//99
	Tampa-St. Petersburg-Clearwater MSA, FL	S	11.59 MW	10.15 AW	24100 AAW	FLBLS	10//99-12//99
	West Palm Beach-Boca Raton MSA, FL	S	10.43 MW	9.73 AW	21690 AAW	FLBLS	10//99-12//99
	Georgia	S	9.19 MW	9.67 AW	20100 AAW	GABLS	10//99-12//99
	Athens MSA, GA	S	7.80 MW	7.79 AW	16230 AAW	GABLS	10//99-12//99
	Atlanta MSA, GA	S	10.14 MW	9.14 AW	21100 AAW	GABLS	10//99-12//99
	Augusta-Aiken MSA, GA-SC	S	8.85 MW	8.96 AW	18400 AAW	GABLS	10//99-12//99
	Columbus MSA, GA-AL	S	6.73 MW	6.56 AW	14000 AAW	GABLS	10//99-12//99
	Macon MSA, GA	S	8.41 MW	8.06 AW	17490 AAW	GABLS	10//99-12//99
	Savannah MSA, GA	S	9.16 MW	9.21 AW	19050 AAW	GABLS	10//99-12//99
	Hawaii	S	8.7 MW	9.11 AW	18960 AAW	HIBLS	10//99-12//99
	Honolulu MSA, HI	S	9.31 MW	9.06 AW	19360 AAW	HIBLS	10//99-12//99
	Idaho	S	7.7 MW	7.94 AW	16510 AAW	IDBLS	10//99-12//99
	Boise City MSA, ID	S	10.10 MW	8.77 AW	21020 AAW	IDBLS	10//99-12//99
	Illinois	S	8.99 MW	9.24 AW	19220 AAW	ILBLS	10//99-12//99
	Bloomington-Normal MSA, IL	S	11.30 MW	13.02 AW	23510 AAW	ILBLS	10//99-12//99
	Champaign-Urbana MSA, IL	S	8.60 MW	8.72 AW	17880 AAW	ILBLS	10//99-12//99
	Chicago PMSA, IL	S	9.47 MW	9.27 AW	19700 AAW	ILBLS	10//99-12//99
	Peoria-Pekin MSA, IL	S	7.34 MW	6.84 AW	15260 AAW	ILBLS	10//99-12//99
	Rockford MSA, IL	S	7.35 MW	7.40 AW	15290 AAW	ILBLS	10//99-12//99
	Springfield MSA, IL	S	7.88 MW	7.47 AW	16390 AAW	ILBLS	10//99-12//99
	Indiana	S	9.51 MW	9.72 AW	20220 AAW	INBLS	10//99-12//99
	Bloomington MSA, IN	S	9.68 MW	9.68 AW	20140 AAW	INBLS	10//99-12//99
	Elkhart-Goshen MSA, IN	S	7.87 MW	6.67 AW	16370 AAW	INBLS	10//99-12//99
	Evansville-Henderson MSA, IN-KY	S	8.98 MW	9.10 AW	18670 AAW	INBLS	10//99-12//99
	Fort Wayne MSA, IN	S	13.44 MW	12.53 AW	27950 AAW	INBLS	10//99-12//99
	Gary PMSA, IN	S	7.30 MW	7.40 AW	15190 AAW	INBLS	10//99-12//99
	Indianapolis MSA, IN	S	9.51 MW	9.59 AW	19780 AAW	INBLS	10//99-12//99
	Lafayette MSA, IN	S	7.76 MW	6.46 AW	16140 AAW	INBLS	10//99-12//99
	South Bend MSA, IN	S	8.17 MW	7.94 AW	16990 AAW	INBLS	10//99-12//99
	Iowa	S	7.65 MW	7.85 AW	16340 AAW	IABLS	10//99-12//99
	Cedar Rapids MSA, IA	S	9.27 MW	9.47 AW	19290 AAW	IABLS	10//99-12//99
	Davenport-Moline-Rock Island MSA, IA-IL	S	8.44 MW	7.93 AW	17550 AAW	IABLS	10//99-12//99
	Des Moines MSA, IA	S	9.71 MW	9.60 AW	20200 AAW	IABLS	10//99-12//99
	Dubuque MSA, IA	S	9.25 MW	9.52 AW	19240 AAW	IABLS	10//99-12//99
	Iowa City MSA, IA	S	6.68 MW	6.49 AW	13900 AAW	IABLS	10//99-12//99
	Waterloo-Cedar Falls MSA, IA	S	7.08 MW	6.70 AW	14730 AAW	IABLS	10//99-12//99
	Kansas	S	10.24 MW	11.19 AW	23260 AAW	KSBLS	10//99-12//99
	Topeka MSA, KS	S	11.82 MW	11.08 AW	24590 AAW	KSBLS	10//99-12//99
	Wichita MSA, KS	S	8.72 MW	9.21 AW	18140 AAW	KSBLS	10//99-12//99
	Kentucky	S	8 MW	8.43 AW	17520 AAW	KYBLS	10//99-12//99
	Lexington MSA, KY	S	7.65 MW	6.92 AW	15920 AAW	KYBLS	10//99-12//99
	Louisville MSA, KY-IN	S	8.30 MW	7.98 AW	17270 AAW	KYBLS	10//99-12//99
	Louisiana	S	14.59 MW	25.02 AW	52050 AAW	LABLS	10//99-12//99
	Baton Rouge MSA, LA	S	7.66 MW	7.55 AW	15930 AAW	LABLS	10//99-12//99
	Lafayette MSA, LA	S	9.18 MW	7.72 AW	19100 AAW	LABLS	10//99-12//99
	New Orleans MSA, LA	S	31.49 MW	20.46 AW	65490 AAW	LABLS	10//99-12//99
	Shreveport-Bossier City MSA, LA	S	7.60 MW	7.66 AW	15800 AAW	LABLS	10//99-12//99
	Maine	S	8.41 MW	9.32 AW	19380 AAW	MEBLS	10//99-12//99
	Lewiston-Auburn MSA, ME	S	9.78 MW	9.68 AW	20350 AAW	MEBLS	10//99-12//99
	Portland MSA, ME	S	11.38 MW	10.24 AW	23670 AAW	MEBLS	10//99-12//99
	Maryland	S	8.83 MW	9.85 AW	20490 AAW	MDBLS	10//99-12//99
	Baltimore PMSA, MD	S	9.83 MW	8.96 AW	20440 AAW	MDBLS	10//99-12//99
	Hagerstown PMSA, MD	S	8.19 MW	8.08 AW	17030 AAW	MDBLS	10//99-12//99
	Massachusetts	S	12.61 MW	13.61 AW	28320 AAW	MABLS	10//99-12//99
	Boston PMSA, MA-NH	S	13.91 MW	12.91 AW	28930 AAW	MABLS	10//99-12//99
	Brockton PMSA, MA	S	8.75 MW	8.88 AW	18210 AAW	MABLS	10//99-12//99
	Lawrence PMSA, MA-NH	S	11.23 MW	10.36 AW	23360 AAW	MABLS	10//99-12//99
	Lowell PMSA, MA-NH	S	14.81 MW	12.84 AW	30810 AAW	MABLS	10//99-12//99
	Springfield MSA, MA	S	12.63 MW	14.17 AW	26260 AAW	MABLS	10//99-12//99
	Worcester PMSA, MA-CT	S	12.43 MW	9.00 AW	25840 AAW	MABLS	10//99-12//99

AAW	Average annual wage	**AOH**	Average offered, high	**ASH**	Average starting, high	**H**	Hourly	**M**	Monthly	**S**	Special: hourly and annual
AE	Average entry wage	**AOL**	Average offered, low	**ASL**	Average starting, low	**HI**	Highest wage paid	**MTC**	Median total compensation	**TQ**	Third quartile wage
AEX	Average experienced wage	**APH**	Average pay, high range	**AW**	Average wage paid	**HR**	High end range	**MW**	Median wage paid	**W**	Weekly
AO	Average offered	**APL**	Average pay, low range	**FQ**	First quartile wage	**LR**	Low end range	**SQ**	Second quartile wage	**Y**	Yearly

Occupation/Type/Industry	Location	Per	Low	Mid	High	Source	Date
Telemarketer	Michigan	S	9.48 MW	10.29 AW	21410 AAW	MIBLS	10//99-12//99
	Ann Arbor PMSA, MI	S	7.94 MW	7.57 AW	16510 AAW	MIBLS	10//99-12//99
	Detroit PMSA, MI	S	11.00 MW	10.79 AW	22870 AAW	MIBLS	10//99-12//99
	Grand Rapids-Muskegon-Holland MSA, MI	S	10.24 MW	9.78 AW	21310 AAW	MIBLS	10//99-12//99
	Jackson MSA, MI	S	11.72 MW	11.57 AW	24380 AAW	MIBLS	10//99-12//99
	Kalamazoo-Battle Creek MSA, MI	S	17.33 MW	15.92 AW	36050 AAW	MIBLS	10//99-12//99
	Lansing-East Lansing MSA, MI	S	8.89 MW	7.55 AW	18490 AAW	MIBLS	10//99-12//99
	Saginaw-Bay City-Midland MSA, MI	S	11.33 MW	9.96 AW	23560 AAW	MIBLS	10//99-12//99
	Minnesota	S	9.81 MW	11.68 AW	24300 AAW	MNBLS	10//99-12//99
	Duluth-Superior MSA, MN-WI	S	8.00 MW	7.84 AW	16640 AAW	MNBLS	10//99-12//99
	Minneapolis-St. Paul MSA, MN-WI	S	14.29 MW	12.92 AW	29710 AAW	MNBLS	10//99-12//99
	Mississippi	S	7.17 MW	8.24 AW	17140 AAW	MSBLS	10//99-12//99
	Biloxi-Gulfport-Pascagoula MSA, MS	S	7.40 MW	6.36 AW	15390 AAW	MSBLS	10//99-12//99
	Jackson MSA, MS	S	7.63 MW	6.59 AW	15870 AAW	MSBLS	10//99-12//99
	Missouri	S	7.88 MW	9.01 AW	18740 AAW	MOBLS	10//99-12//99
	Columbia MSA, MO	S	7.77 MW	7.66 AW	16150 AAW	MOBLS	10//99-12//99
	St. Louis MSA, MO-IL	S	9.72 MW	8.88 AW	20210 AAW	MOBLS	10//99-12//99
	Montana	S	7.5 MW	7.52 AW	15640 AAW	MTBLS	10//99-12//99
	Billings MSA, MT	S	7.27 MW	7.48 AW	15120 AAW	MTBLS	10//99-12//99
	Nebraska	S	7.32 MW	7.53 AW	15660 AAW	NEBLS	10//99-12//99
	Lincoln MSA, NE	S	7.63 MW	7.66 AW	15870 AAW	NEBLS	10//99-12//99
	Omaha MSA, NE-IA	S	8.03 MW	7.57 AW	16710 AAW	NEBLS	10//99-12//99
	Nevada	S	10.11 MW	12.45 AW	25890 AAW	NVBLS	10//99-12//99
	Las Vegas MSA, NV-AZ	S	12.34 MW	10.20 AW	25660 AAW	NVBLS	10//99-12//99
	Reno MSA, NV	S	10.85 MW	9.72 AW	22570 AAW	NVBLS	10//99-12//99
	New Hampshire	S	9.49 MW	11.20 AW	23290 AAW	NHBLS	10//99-12//99
	Manchester PMSA, NH	S	14.02 MW	12.16 AW	29160 AAW	NHBLS	10//99-12//99
	Nashua PMSA, NH	S	14.51 MW	10.63 AW	30180 AAW	NHBLS	10//99-12//99
	Portsmouth-Rochester PMSA, NH-ME	S	13.66 MW	13.75 AW	28410 AAW	NHBLS	10//99-12//99
	New Jersey	S	11.72 MW	12.32 AW	25620 AAW	NJBLS	10//99-12//99
	Atlantic-Cape May PMSA, NJ	S	11.78 MW	11.94 AW	24500 AAW	NJBLS	10//99-12//99
	Bergen-Passaic PMSA, NJ	S	11.33 MW	9.69 AW	23560 AAW	NJBLS	10//99-12//99
	Jersey City PMSA, NJ	S	11.65 MW	10.63 AW	24240 AAW	NJBLS	10//99-12//99
	Middlesex-Somerset-Hunterdon PMSA, NJ	S	11.36 MW	11.74 AW	23640 AAW	NJBLS	10//99-12//99
	Monmouth-Ocean PMSA, NJ	S	15.32 MW	11.51 AW	31860 AAW	NJBLS	10//99-12//99
	Newark PMSA, NJ	S	13.53 MW	13.41 AW	28150 AAW	NJBLS	10//99-12//99
	Trenton PMSA, NJ	S	11.78 MW	10.11 AW	24500 AAW	NJBLS	10//99-12//99
	New Mexico	S	10.28 MW	10.53 AW	21900 AAW	NMBLS	10//99-12//99
	Albuquerque MSA, NM	S	10.43 MW	10.28 AW	21690 AAW	NMBLS	10//99-12//99
	Santa Fe MSA, NM	S	7.33 MW	6.67 AW	15250 AAW	NMBLS	10//99-12//99
	New York	S	10.99 MW	11.02 AW	22920 AAW	NYBLS	10//99-12//99
	Albany-Schenectady-Troy MSA, NY	S	9.97 MW	9.54 AW	20730 AAW	NYBLS	10//99-12//99
	Binghamton MSA, NY	S	10.38 MW	7.85 AW	21590 AAW	NYBLS	10//99-12//99
	Buffalo-Niagara Falls MSA, NY	S	8.63 MW	8.11 AW	17960 AAW	NYBLS	10//99-12//99
	Dutchess County PMSA, NY	S	7.49 MW	6.39 AW	15580 AAW	NYBLS	10//99-12//99
	Nassau-Suffolk PMSA, NY	S	12.05 MW	11.96 AW	25060 AAW	NYBLS	10//99-12//99
	New York PMSA, NY	S	10.75 MW	10.09 AW	22370 AAW	NYBLS	10//99-12//99
	Newburgh PMSA, NY-PA	S	8.49 MW	7.62 AW	17660 AAW	NYBLS	10//99-12//99
	Rochester MSA, NY	S	9.36 MW	9.03 AW	19480 AAW	NYBLS	10//99-12//99
	Syracuse MSA, NY	S	8.80 MW	7.77 AW	18300 AAW	NYBLS	10//99-12//99
	Utica-Rome MSA, NY	S	9.06 MW	9.44 AW	18850 AAW	NYBLS	10//99-12//99
	North Carolina	S	8.12 MW	8.73 AW	18150 AAW	NCBLS	10//99-12//99
	Asheville MSA, NC	S	8.15 MW	7.80 AW	16960 AAW	NCBLS	10//99-12//99
	Charlotte-Gastonia-Rock Hill MSA, NC-SC	S	8.74 MW	8.44 AW	18180 AAW	NCBLS	10//99-12//99
	Fayetteville MSA, NC	S	7.61 MW	7.63 AW	15820 AAW	NCBLS	10//99-12//99
	Greensboro--Winston-Salem--High Point MSA, NC	S	9.77 MW	9.34 AW	20330 AAW	NCBLS	10//99-12//99
	Hickory-Morganton-Lenoir MSA, NC	S	8.11 MW	7.96 AW	16860 AAW	NCBLS	10//99-12//99
	Raleigh-Durham-Chapel Hill MSA, NC	S	11.43 MW	11.00 AW	23760 AAW	NCBLS	10//99-12//99
	Wilmington MSA, NC	S	7.32 MW	7.50 AW	15220 AAW	NCBLS	10//99-12//99

AAW Average annual wage	**AOH** Average offered, high	**ASH** Average starting, high	**H** Hourly	**M** Monthly	**S** Special: hourly and annual
AE Average entry wage	**AOL** Average offered, low	**ASL** Average starting, low	**HI** Highest wage paid	**MTC** Median total compensation	**TQ** Third quartile wage
AEX Average experienced wage	**APH** Average pay, high range	**AW** Average wage paid	**HR** High end range	**MW** Median wage paid	**W** Weekly
AO Average offered	**APL** Average pay, low range	**FQ** First quartile wage	**LR** Low end range	**SQ** Second quartile wage	**Y** Yearly

Occupation/Type/Industry	Location	Per	Low	Mid	High	Source	Date
Telemarketer	North Dakota	S	7.68 MW	7.75 AW	16120 AAW	NDBLS	10//99-12//99
	Fargo-Moorhead MSA, ND-MN	S	7.13 MW	6.65 AW	14830 AAW	NDBLS	10//99-12//99
	Ohio	S	8.01 MW	8.90 AW	18510 AAW	OHBLS	10//99-12//99
	Akron PMSA, OH	S	9.32 MW	7.83 AW	19390 AAW	OHBLS	10//99-12//99
	Cincinnati PMSA, OH-KY-IN	S	9.58 MW	8.18 AW	19920 AAW	OHBLS	10//99-12//99
	Cleveland-Lorain-Elyria PMSA, OH	S	8.75 MW	8.12 AW	18200 AAW	OHBLS	10//99-12//99
	Columbus MSA, OH	S	9.03 MW	8.73 AW	18770 AAW	OHBLS	10//99-12//99
	Dayton-Springfield MSA, OH	S	8.33 MW	7.82 AW	17330 AAW	OHBLS	10//99-12//99
	Hamilton-Middletown PMSA, OH	S	6.28 MW	6.17 AW	13060 AAW	OHBLS	10//99-12//99
	Lima MSA, OH	S	9.22 MW	8.49 AW	19180 AAW	OHBLS	10//99-12//99
	Steubenville-Weirton MSA, OH-WV	S	8.17 MW	7.96 AW	16990 AAW	OHBLS	10//99-12//99
	Toledo MSA, OH	S	10.00 MW	7.92 AW	20800 AAW	OHBLS	10//99-12//99
	Oklahoma	S	7.28 MW	7.24 AW	15050 AAW	OKBLS	10//99-12//99
	Oklahoma City MSA, OK	S	7.70 MW	7.71 AW	16020 AAW	OKBLS	10//99-12//99
	Tulsa MSA, OK	S	6.96 MW	6.82 AW	14480 AAW	OKBLS	10//99-12//99
	Oregon	S	8.39 MW	9.82 AW	20430 AAW	ORBLS	10//99-12//99
	Eugene-Springfield MSA, OR	S	11.05 MW	9.52 AW	22990 AAW	ORBLS	10//99-12//99
	Pennsylvania	S	7.97 MW	9.00 AW	18720 AAW	PABLS	10//99-12//99
	Allentown-Bethlehem-Easton MSA, PA	S	8.67 MW	8.43 AW	18030 AAW	PABLS	10//99-12//99
	Erie MSA, PA	S	7.78 MW	7.05 AW	16180 AAW	PABLS	10//99-12//99
	Harrisburg-Lebanon-Carlisle MSA, PA	S	7.53 MW	7.01 AW	15660 AAW	PABLS	10//99-12//99
	Johnstown MSA, PA	S	7.92 MW	7.89 AW	16480 AAW	PABLS	10//99-12//99
	Lancaster MSA, PA	S	9.76 MW	8.95 AW	20300 AAW	PABLS	10//99-12//99
	Philadelphia PMSA, PA-NJ	S	9.74 MW	8.35 AW	20270 AAW	PABLS	10//99-12//99
	Pittsburgh MSA, PA	S	9.43 MW	8.07 AW	19620 AAW	PABLS	10//99-12//99
	Reading MSA, PA	S	10.62 MW	9.44 AW	22090 AAW	PABLS	10//99-12//99
	Scranton--Wilkes-Barre--Hazleton MSA, PA	S	7.64 MW	7.63 AW	15890 AAW	PABLS	10//99-12//99
	State College MSA, PA	S	7.51 MW	7.59 AW	15630 AAW	PABLS	10//99-12//99
	York MSA, PA	S	7.48 MW	6.56 AW	15560 AAW	PABLS	10//99-12//99
	Rhode Island	S	9.67 MW	10.66 AW	22170 AAW	RIBLS	10//99-12//99
	Providence-Fall River-Warwick MSA, RI-MA	S	10.76 MW	9.68 AW	22390 AAW	RIBLS	10//99-12//99
	South Carolina	S	7.51 MW	7.91 AW	16450 AAW	SCBLS	10//99-12//99
	Charleston-North Charleston MSA, SC	S	6.69 MW	6.63 AW	13920 AAW	SCBLS	10//99-12//99
	Columbia MSA, SC	S	8.44 MW	7.65 AW	17550 AAW	SCBLS	10//99-12//99
	Greenville-Spartanburg-Anderson MSA, SC	S	7.72 MW	7.57 AW	16050 AAW	SCBLS	10//99-12//99
	South Dakota	S	8.17 MW	8.67 AW	18030 AAW	SDBLS	10//99-12//99
	Sioux Falls MSA, SD	S	8.57 MW	8.29 AW	17830 AAW	SDBLS	10//99-12//99
	Tennessee	S	10.9 MW	11.79 AW	24530 AAW	TNBLS	10//99-12//99
	Chattanooga MSA, TN-GA	S	9.36 MW	8.48 AW	19460 AAW	TNBLS	10//99-12//99
	Clarksville-Hopkinsville MSA, TN-KY	S	7.38 MW	7.55 AW	15350 AAW	TNBLS	10//99-12//99
	Johnson City-Kingsport-Bristol MSA, TN-VA	S	8.92 MW	8.04 AW	18560 AAW	TNBLS	10//99-12//99
	Knoxville MSA, TN	S	10.60 MW	9.16 AW	22050 AAW	TNBLS	10//99-12//99
	Memphis MSA, TN-AR-MS	S	10.41 MW	8.26 AW	21650 AAW	MSBLS	10//99-12//99
	Nashville MSA, TN	S	11.91 MW	11.42 AW	24770 AAW	TNBLS	10//99-12//99
	Texas	S	9.14 MW	11.03 AW	22940 AAW	TXBLS	10//99-12//99
	Abilene MSA, TX	S	6.26 MW	6.15 AW	13030 AAW	TXBLS	10//99-12//99
	Amarillo MSA, TX	S	6.81 MW	6.80 AW	14170 AAW	TXBLS	10//99-12//99
	Austin-San Marcos MSA, TX	S	10.67 MW	8.20 AW	22190 AAW	TXBLS	10//99-12//99
	Brownsville-Harlingen-San Benito MSA, TX	S	7.30 MW	7.32 AW	15170 AAW	TXBLS	10//99-12//99
	Dallas PMSA, TX	S	15.76 MW	15.34 AW	32790 AAW	TXBLS	10//99-12//99
	Fort Worth-Arlington PMSA, TX	S	8.81 MW	8.06 AW	18330 AAW	TXBLS	10//99-12//99
	Galveston-Texas City PMSA, TX	S	8.94 MW	8.12 AW	18590 AAW	TXBLS	10//99-12//99
	Houston PMSA, TX	S	10.45 MW	9.69 AW	21730 AAW	TXBLS	10//99-12//99
	Killeen-Temple MSA, TX	S	7.51 MW	7.52 AW	15620 AAW	TXBLS	10//99-12//99
	Longview-Marshall MSA, TX	S	7.79 MW	7.61 AW	16200 AAW	TXBLS	10//99-12//99
	McAllen-Edinburg-Mission MSA, TX	S	10.38 MW	11.22 AW	21600 AAW	TXBLS	10//99-12//99

AAW	Average annual wage	AOH	Average offered, high	ASH	Average starting, high
AE	Average entry wage	AOL	Average offered, low	ASL	Average starting, low
AEX	Average experienced wage	APH	Average pay, high range	AW	Average wage paid
AO	Average offered	APL	Average pay, low range	FQ	First quartile wage

H	Hourly	M	Monthly
HI	Highest wage paid	MTC	Median total compensation
HR	High end range	MW	Median wage paid
LR	Low end range	SQ	Second quartile wage

S	Special: hourly and annual
TQ	Third quartile wage
W	Weekly
Y	Yearly

Occupation/Type/Industry	Location	Per	Low	Mid	High	Source	Date
Telemarketer	San Antonio MSA, TX	S	7.72 MW	6.34 AW	16060 AAW	TXBLS	10//99-12//99
	Tyler MSA, TX	S	9.61 MW	7.87 AW	19990 AAW	TXBLS	10//99-12//99
	Waco MSA, TX	S	8.39 MW	7.90 AW	17450 AAW	TXBLS	10//99-12//99
	Utah	S	9.24 MW	12.83 AW	26690 AAW	UTBLS	10//99-12//99
	Salt Lake City-Ogden MSA, UT	S	12.98 MW	9.21 AW	27000 AAW	UTBLS	10//99-12//99
	Vermont	S	9.97 MW	11.68 AW	24290 AAW	VTBLS	10//99-12//99
	Burlington MSA, VT	S	12.49 MW	10.87 AW	25980 AAW	VTBLS	10//99-12//99
	Virginia	S	10.61 MW	11.30 AW	23500 AAW	VABLS	10//99-12//99
	Charlottesville MSA, VA	S	8.61 MW	7.81 AW	17900 AAW	VABLS	10//99-12//99
	Norfolk-Virginia Beach-Newport News MSA, VA-NC	S	9.72 MW	9.32 AW	20230 AAW	VABLS	10//99-12//99
	Richmond-Petersburg MSA, VA	S	12.50 MW	12.86 AW	25990 AAW	VABLS	10//99-12//99
	Roanoke MSA, VA	S	10.48 MW	10.14 AW	21800 AAW	VABLS	10//99-12//99
	Washington	S	8.37 MW	11.85 AW	24650 AAW	WABLS	10//99-12//99
	Bellingham MSA, WA	S	11.44 MW	9.52 AW	23800 AAW	WABLS	10//99-12//99
	Olympia PMSA, WA	S	11.21 MW	9.50 AW	23320 AAW	WABLS	10//99-12//99
	Seattle-Bellevue-Everett PMSA, WA	S	13.87 MW	12.04 AW	28850 AAW	WABLS	10//99-12//99
	Spokane MSA, WA	S	10.00 MW	7.75 AW	20790 AAW	WABLS	10//99-12//99
	Tacoma PMSA, WA	S	6.70 MW	6.36 AW	13930 AAW	WABLS	10//99-12//99
	West Virginia	S	6.51 MW	6.95 AW	14450 AAW	WVBLS	10//99-12//99
	Charleston MSA, WV	S	11.25 MW	10.23 AW	23390 AAW	WVBLS	10//99-12//99
	Huntington-Ashland MSA, WV-KY-OH	S	6.50 MW	6.47 AW	13510 AAW	WVBLS	10//99-12//99
	Parkersburg-Marietta MSA, WV-OH	S	8.99 MW	8.97 AW	18690 AAW	WVBLS	10//99-12//99
	Wheeling MSA, WV-OH	S	6.40 MW	6.12 AW	13300 AAW	WVBLS	10//99-12//99
	Wisconsin	S	7.85 MW	8.95 AW	18620 AAW	WIBLS	10//99-12//99
	Appleton-Oshkosh-Neenah MSA, WI	S	8.81 MW	7.91 AW	18330 AAW	WIBLS	10//99-12//99
	Eau Claire MSA, WI	S	9.39 MW	8.33 AW	19530 AAW	WIBLS	10//99-12//99
	Madison MSA, WI	S	6.71 MW	6.29 AW	13960 AAW	WIBLS	10//99-12//99
	Milwaukee-Waukesha PMSA, WI	S	10.89 MW	9.56 AW	22640 AAW	WIBLS	10//99-12//99
	Racine PMSA, WI	S	10.50 MW	10.30 AW	21830 AAW	WIBLS	10//99-12//99
	Wyoming	S	6.3 MW	7.86 AW	16340 AAW	WYBLS	10//99-12//99
	Puerto Rico	S	7.4 MW	8.01 AW	16660 AAW	PRBLS	10//99-12//99
	Caguas PMSA, PR	S	6.02 MW	6.04 AW	12520 AAW	PRBLS	10//99-12//99
	San Juan-Bayamon PMSA, PR	S	8.41 MW	7.60 AW	17490 AAW	PRBLS	10//99-12//99
Telephone Operator	Arizona	S	13.83 MW	13.33 AW	27730 AAW	AZBLS	10//99-12//99
	California	S	14.89 MW	13.97 AW	29070 AAW	CABLS	10//99-12//99
	Los Angeles-Long Beach PMSA, CA	S	14.48 MW	15.49 AW	30120 AAW	CABLS	10//99-12//99
	Oakland PMSA, CA	S	13.90 MW	14.11 AW	28920 AAW	CABLS	10//99-12//99
	Riverside-San Bernardino PMSA, CA	S	14.94 MW	16.93 AW	31080 AAW	CABLS	10//99-12//99
	San Diego MSA, CA	S	14.31 MW	15.23 AW	29760 AAW	CABLS	10//99-12//99
	San Francisco PMSA, CA	S	13.70 MW	15.09 AW	28500 AAW	CABLS	10//99-12//99
	Colorado	S	8.46 MW	9.48 AW	19720 AAW	COBLS	10//99-12//99
	Denver PMSA, CO	S	9.08 MW	8.29 AW	18890 AAW	COBLS	10//99-12//99
	District of Columbia	S	11.45 MW	12.12 AW	25210 AAW	DCBLS	10//99-12//99
	Washington PMSA, DC-MD-VA-WV	S	10.66 MW	11.00 AW	22160 AAW	DCBLS	10//99-12//99
	Florida	S	9.1 MW	10.13 AW	21060 AAW	FLBLS	10//99-12//99
	Tampa-St. Petersburg-Clearwater MSA, FL	S	10.17 MW	8.37 AW	21160 AAW	FLBLS	10//99-12//99
	Georgia	S	14.47 MW	13.64 AW	28380 AAW	GABLS	10//99-12//99
	Atlanta MSA, GA	S	13.83 MW	14.73 AW	28770 AAW	GABLS	10//99-12//99
	Hawaii	S	12.28 MW	11.92 AW	24780 AAW	HIBLS	10//99-12//99
	Idaho	S	13.54 MW	12.41 AW	25820 AAW	IDBLS	10//99-12//99
	Illinois	S	14.21 MW	13.22 AW	27490 AAW	ILBLS	10//99-12//99
	Chicago PMSA, IL	S	13.08 MW	13.90 AW	27200 AAW	ILBLS	10//99-12//99
	Iowa	S	10.25 MW	11.74 AW	24420 AAW	IABLS	10//99-12//99
	Cedar Rapids MSA, IA	S	10.55 MW	9.69 AW	21950 AAW	IABLS	10//99-12//99
	Kansas	S	17.11 MW	15.77 AW	32800 AAW	KSBLS	10//99-12//99
	Alexandria MSA, LA	S	10.48 MW	10.11 AW	21810 AAW	LABLS	10//99-12//99
	Baton Rouge MSA, LA	S	9.07 MW	8.16 AW	18870 AAW	LABLS	10//99-12//99
	Maryland	S	15.7 MW	14.91 AW	31010 AAW	MDBLS	10//99-12//99
	Boston PMSA, MA-NH	S	15.09 MW	14.53 AW	31400 AAW	MABLS	10//99-12//99

AAW	Average annual wage	AOH	Average offered, high	ASH	Average starting, high	H	Hourly	M	Monthly	S	Special: hourly and annual
AE	Average entry wage	AOL	Average offered, low	ASL	Average starting, low	HI	Highest wage paid	MTC	Median total compensation	TQ	Third quartile wage
AEX	Average experienced wage	APH	Average pay, high range	AW	Average wage paid	HR	High end range	MW	Median wage paid	W	Weekly
AO	Average offered	APL	Average pay, low range	FQ	First quartile wage	LR	Low end range	SQ	Second quartile wage	Y	Yearly

Occupation/Type/Industry	Location	Per	Low	Mid	High	Source	Date
Telephone Operator	Minnesota	S	14.45 MW	12.95 AW	26940 AAW	MNBLS	10//99-12//99
	Missouri	S	11.89 MW	11.67 AW	24280 AAW	MOBLS	10//99-12//99
	St. Louis MSA, MO-IL	S	11.82 MW	12.03 AW	24590 AAW	MOBLS	10//99-12//99
	Nebraska	S	8.31 MW	8.92 AW	18540 AAW	NEBLS	10//99-12//99
	New Jersey	S	16.86 MW	14.89 AW	30970 AAW	NJBLS	10//99-12//99
	New York PMSA, NY	S	15.15 MW	17.69 AW	31510 AAW	NYBLS	10//99-12//99
	North Carolina	S	13.66 MW	13.42 AW	27920 AAW	NCBLS	10//99-12//99
	Charlotte-Gastonia-Rock Hill MSA, NC-SC	S	13.88 MW	14.53 AW	28880 AAW	NCBLS	10//99-12//99
	Raleigh-Durham-Chapel Hill MSA, NC	S	14.31 MW	14.82 AW	29760 AAW	NCBLS	10//99-12//99
	Ohio	S	14.11 MW	13.64 AW	28380 AAW	OHBLS	10//99-12//99
	Cincinnati PMSA, OH-KY-IN	S	12.46 MW	12.85 AW	25920 AAW	OHBLS	10//99-12//99
	Oklahoma	S	14.22 MW	12.67 AW	26350 AAW	OKBLS	10//99-12//99
	Oklahoma City MSA, OK	S	9.76 MW	6.60 AW	20300 AAW	OKBLS	10//99-12//99
	Tulsa MSA, OK	S	14.17 MW	14.96 AW	29470 AAW	OKBLS	10//99-12//99
	Pennsylvania	S	13.62 MW	13.50 AW	28080 AAW	PABLS	10//99-12//99
	Philadelphia PMSA, PA-NJ	S	14.16 MW	15.06 AW	29440 AAW	PABLS	10//99-12//99
	South Carolina	S	14.97 MW	14.32 AW	29790 AAW	SCBLS	10//99-12//99
	Tennessee	S	15.18 MW	14.55 AW	30260 AAW	TNBLS	10//99-12//99
	Johnson City-Kingsport-Bristol MSA, TN-VA	S	9.07 MW	6.39 AW	18860 AAW	TNBLS	10//99-12//99
	Texas	S	13.36 MW	12.61 AW	26240 AAW	TXBLS	10//99-12//99
	Dallas PMSA, TX	S	11.75 MW	12.12 AW	24430 AAW	TXBLS	10//99-12//99
	Houston PMSA, TX	S	11.08 MW	11.52 AW	23060 AAW	TXBLS	10//99-12//99
	Utah	S	14.42 MW	12.73 AW	26480 AAW	UTBLS	10//99-12//99
	Salt Lake City-Ogden MSA, UT	S	14.05 MW	14.86 AW	29230 AAW	UTBLS	10//99-12//99
	Virginia	S	12.11 MW	11.59 AW	24100 AAW	VABLS	10//99-12//99
	West Virginia	S	15.38 MW	14.61 AW	30380 AAW	WVBLS	10//99-12//99
	Milwaukee-Waukesha PMSA, WI	S	14.19 MW	14.41 AW	29520 AAW	WIBLS	10//99-12//99
Telephone Sales Representative Sales Organization	United States	Y	3600 APL	23256 MW	48000 APH	SMR	1999
Teller	Alabama	S	7.65 MW	7.75 AW	16130 AAW	ALBLS	10//99-12//99
	Anniston MSA, AL	S	7.23 MW	7.33 AW	15030 AAW	ALBLS	10//99-12//99
	Auburn-Opelika MSA, AL	S	7.25 MW	7.12 AW	15090 AAW	ALBLS	10//99-12//99
	Birmingham MSA, AL	S	8.11 MW	7.95 AW	16880 AAW	ALBLS	10//99-12//99
	Decatur MSA, AL	S	7.55 MW	7.54 AW	15700 AAW	ALBLS	10//99-12//99
	Dothan MSA, AL	S	7.57 MW	7.59 AW	15740 AAW	ALBLS	10//99-12//99
	Florence MSA, AL	S	8.46 MW	8.01 AW	17600 AAW	ALBLS	10//99-12//99
	Gadsden MSA, AL	S	8.30 MW	7.83 AW	17270 AAW	ALBLS	10//99-12//99
	Huntsville MSA, AL	S	7.78 MW	7.70 AW	16180 AAW	ALBLS	10//99-12//99
	Mobile MSA, AL	S	7.55 MW	7.54 AW	15700 AAW	ALBLS	10//99-12//99
	Montgomery MSA, AL	S	7.71 MW	7.65 AW	16030 AAW	ALBLS	10//99-12//99
	Tuscaloosa MSA, AL	S	7.88 MW	7.75 AW	16380 AAW	ALBLS	10//99-12//99
	Alaska	S	9.88 MW	9.94 AW	20680 AAW	AKBLS	10//99-12//99
	Anchorage MSA, AK	S	9.55 MW	9.61 AW	19860 AAW	AKBLS	10//99-12//99
	Arizona	S	9.68 MW	9.48 AW	19710 AAW	AZBLS	10//99-12//99
	Flagstaff MSA, AZ-UT	S	9.27 MW	9.57 AW	19280 AAW	AZBLS	10//99-12//99
	Phoenix-Mesa MSA, AZ	S	9.60 MW	9.73 AW	19980 AAW	AZBLS	10//99-12//99
	Tucson MSA, AZ	S	9.07 MW	9.40 AW	18860 AAW	AZBLS	10//99-12//99
	Yuma MSA, AZ	S	9.21 MW	9.48 AW	19160 AAW	AZBLS	10//99-12//99
	Arkansas	S	8.06 MW	8.27 AW	17200 AAW	ARBLS	10//99-12//99
	Fayetteville-Springdale-Rogers MSA, AR	S	8.45 MW	8.38 AW	17570 AAW	ARBLS	10//99-12//99
	Fort Smith MSA, AR-OK	S	8.03 MW	7.95 AW	16710 AAW	ARBLS	10//99-12//99
	Jonesboro MSA, AR	S	8.34 MW	8.09 AW	17340 AAW	ARBLS	10//99-12//99
	Little Rock-North Little Rock MSA, AR	S	8.63 MW	8.30 AW	17950 AAW	ARBLS	10//99-12//99
	Pine Bluff MSA, AR	S	9.27 MW	8.84 AW	19270 AAW	ARBLS	10//99-12//99
	California	S	9.39 MW	9.54 AW	19830 AAW	CABLS	10//99-12//99
	Bakersfield MSA, CA	S	8.95 MW	8.91 AW	18610 AAW	CABLS	10//99-12//99
	Chico-Paradise MSA, CA	S	8.87 MW	8.58 AW	18450 AAW	CABLS	10//99-12//99
	Fresno MSA, CA	S	8.97 MW	8.57 AW	18660 AAW	CABLS	10//99-12//99
	Los Angeles-Long Beach PMSA, CA	S	9.47 MW	9.28 AW	19700 AAW	CABLS	10//99-12//99
	Merced MSA, CA	S	8.63 MW	8.24 AW	17940 AAW	CABLS	10//99-12//99
	Modesto MSA, CA	S	9.04 MW	8.85 AW	18790 AAW	CABLS	10//99-12//99
	Oakland PMSA, CA	S	9.78 MW	9.65 AW	20340 AAW	CABLS	10//99-12//99
	Orange County PMSA, CA	S	9.74 MW	9.61 AW	20250 AAW	CABLS	10//99-12//99

AAW Average annual wage	AOH Average offered, high	ASH Average starting, high	H Hourly	M Monthly	S Special: hourly and annual
AE Average entry wage	AOL Average offered, low	ASL Average starting, low	HI Highest wage paid	MTC Median total compensation	TQ Third quartile wage
AEX Average experienced wage	APH Average pay, high range	AW Average wage paid	HR High end range	MW Median wage paid	W Weekly
AO Average offered	APL Average pay, low range	FQ First quartile wage	LR Low end range	SQ Second quartile wage	Y Yearly

Occupation/Type/Industry	Location	Per	Low	Mid	High	Source	Date
Teller	Redding MSA, CA	S	9.28 MW	9.20 AW	19310 AAW	CABLS	10//99-12//99
	Riverside-San Bernardino PMSA, CA	S	8.99 MW	8.93 AW	18700 AAW	CABLS	10//99-12//99
	Sacramento PMSA, CA	S	9.45 MW	9.36 AW	19650 AAW	CABLS	10//99-12//99
	Salinas MSA, CA	S	9.59 MW	9.32 AW	19940 AAW	CABLS	10//99-12//99
	San Diego MSA, CA	S	9.21 MW	9.22 AW	19150 AAW	CABLS	10//99-12//99
	San Francisco PMSA, CA	S	10.10 MW	9.86 AW	21000 AAW	CABLS	10//99-12//99
	San Jose PMSA, CA	S	10.61 MW	10.07 AW	22070 AAW	CABLS	10//99-12//99
	San Luis Obispo-Atascadero-Paso Robles MSA, CA	S	9.36 MW	9.27 AW	19470 AAW	CABLS	10//99-12//99
	Santa Barbara-Santa Maria-Lompoc MSA, CA	S	8.91 MW	8.83 AW	18530 AAW	CABLS	10//99-12//99
	Santa Cruz-Watsonville PMSA, CA	S	9.80 MW	9.65 AW	20390 AAW	CABLS	10//99-12//99
	Santa Rosa PMSA, CA	S	10.06 MW	9.82 AW	20930 AAW	CABLS	10//99-12//99
	Stockton-Lodi MSA, CA	S	9.11 MW	8.68 AW	18940 AAW	CABLS	10//99-12//99
	Vallejo-Fairfield-Napa PMSA, CA	S	9.13 MW	8.98 AW	18990 AAW	CABLS	10//99-12//99
	Ventura PMSA, CA	S	9.90 MW	9.74 AW	20600 AAW	CABLS	10//99-12//99
	Visalia-Tulare-Porterville MSA, CA	S	9.37 MW	9.26 AW	19490 AAW	CABLS	10//99-12//99
	Yuba City MSA, CA	S	9.27 MW	8.97 AW	19270 AAW	CABLS	10//99-12//99
	Colorado	S	9.34 MW	9.27 AW	19270 AAW	COBLS	10//99-12//99
	Boulder-Longmont PMSA, CO	S	9.42 MW	9.54 AW	19590 AAW	COBLS	10//99-12//99
	Colorado Springs MSA, CO	S	8.66 MW	8.39 AW	18020 AAW	COBLS	10//99-12//99
	Denver PMSA, CO	S	9.72 MW	9.69 AW	20220 AAW	COBLS	10//99-12//99
	Fort Collins-Loveland MSA, CO	S	8.25 MW	8.18 AW	17150 AAW	COBLS	10//99-12//99
	Grand Junction MSA, CO	S	8.43 MW	8.25 AW	17530 AAW	COBLS	10//99-12//99
	Greeley PMSA, CO	S	9.40 MW	8.95 AW	19550 AAW	COBLS	10//99-12//99
	Pueblo MSA, CO	S	8.25 MW	8.09 AW	17150 AAW	COBLS	10//99-12//99
	Connecticut	S	9.96 MW	9.98 AW	20770 AAW	CTBLS	10//99-12//99
	Bridgeport PMSA, CT	S	9.95 MW	10.21 AW	20690 AAW	CTBLS	10//99-12//99
	Danbury PMSA, CT	S	10.62 MW	10.25 AW	22080 AAW	CTBLS	10//99-12//99
	Hartford MSA, CT	S	10.13 MW	9.98 AW	21080 AAW	CTBLS	10//99-12//99
	New Haven-Meriden PMSA, CT	S	9.78 MW	10.28 AW	20340 AAW	CTBLS	10//99-12//99
	New London-Norwich MSA, CT-RI	S	8.90 MW	8.38 AW	18510 AAW	CTBLS	10//99-12//99
	Stamford-Norwalk PMSA, CT	S	10.66 MW	10.55 AW	22170 AAW	CTBLS	10//99-12//99
	Waterbury PMSA, CT	S	9.33 MW	9.10 AW	19410 AAW	CTBLS	10//99-12//99
	Delaware	S	9.26 MW	9.10 AW	18920 AAW	DEBLS	10//99-12//99
	Dover MSA, DE	S	8.52 MW	8.29 AW	17730 AAW	DEBLS	10//99-12//99
	Wilmington-Newark PMSA, DE-MD	S	9.18 MW	9.37 AW	19090 AAW	DEBLS	10//99-12//99
	District of Columbia	S	9.63 MW	9.46 AW	19680 AAW	DCBLS	10//99-12//99
	Washington PMSA, DC-MD-VA-WV	S	9.54 MW	9.54 AW	19830 AAW	DCBLS	10//99-12//99
	Florida	S	8.82 MW	8.96 AW	18640 AAW	FLBLS	10//99-12//99
	Daytona Beach MSA, FL	S	8.26 MW	8.18 AW	17180 AAW	FLBLS	10//99-12//99
	Fort Lauderdale PMSA, FL	S	9.81 MW	9.89 AW	20410 AAW	FLBLS	10//99-12//99
	Fort Myers-Cape Coral MSA, FL	S	8.86 MW	8.73 AW	18430 AAW	FLBLS	10//99-12//99
	Fort Pierce-Port St. Lucie MSA, FL	S	8.52 MW	8.15 AW	17720 AAW	FLBLS	10//99-12//99
	Fort Walton Beach MSA, FL	S	8.26 MW	8.18 AW	17180 AAW	FLBLS	10//99-12//99
	Gainesville MSA, FL	S	8.22 MW	8.26 AW	17100 AAW	FLBLS	10//99-12//99
	Jacksonville MSA, FL	S	9.08 MW	8.94 AW	18880 AAW	FLBLS	10//99-12//99
	Lakeland-Winter Haven MSA, FL	S	8.48 MW	8.39 AW	17630 AAW	FLBLS	10//99-12//99
	Melbourne-Titusville-Palm Bay MSA, FL	S	8.74 MW	9.01 AW	18180 AAW	FLBLS	10//99-12//99
	Miami PMSA, FL	S	9.14 MW	9.13 AW	19010 AAW	FLBLS	10//99-12//99
	Naples MSA, FL	S	9.66 MW	9.65 AW	20090 AAW	FLBLS	10//99-12//99
	Ocala MSA, FL	S	8.81 MW	8.87 AW	18320 AAW	FLBLS	10//99-12//99
	Orlando MSA, FL	S	8.57 MW	8.49 AW	17830 AAW	FLBLS	10//99-12//99
	Panama City MSA, FL	S	7.85 MW	7.83 AW	16320 AAW	FLBLS	10//99-12//99
	Pensacola MSA, FL	S	8.15 MW	8.13 AW	16960 AAW	FLBLS	10//99-12//99
	Punta Gorda MSA, FL	S	8.94 MW	8.82 AW	18600 AAW	FLBLS	10//99-12//99
	Sarasota-Bradenton MSA, FL	S	8.86 MW	8.68 AW	18420 AAW	FLBLS	10//99-12//99
	Tallahassee MSA, FL	S	8.18 MW	8.13 AW	17020 AAW	FLBLS	10//99-12//99

AAW Average annual wage	**AOH** Average offered, high	**ASH** Average starting, high	**H** Hourly	**M** Monthly	**S** Special: hourly and annual
AE Average entry wage	**AOL** Average offered, low	**ASL** Average starting, low	**HI** Highest wage paid	**MTC** Median total compensation	**TQ** Third quartile wage
AEX Average experienced wage	**APH** Average pay, high range	**AW** Average wage paid	**HR** High end range	**MW** Median wage paid	**W** Weekly
AO Average offered	**APL** Average pay, low range	**FQ** First quartile wage	**LR** Low end range	**SQ** Second quartile wage	**Y** Yearly

Occupation/Type/Industry	Location	Per	Low	Mid	High	Source	Date
Teller	Tampa-St. Petersburg-Clearwater MSA, FL	S	9.31 MW	9.01 AW	19360 AAW	FLBLS	10//99-12//99
	West Palm Beach-Boca Raton MSA, FL	S	9.44 MW	9.51 AW	19630 AAW	FLBLS	10//99-12//99
	Georgia	S	8.58 MW	8.60 AW	17890 AAW	GABLS	10//99-12//99
	Albany MSA, GA	S	7.81 MW	7.69 AW	16250 AAW	GABLS	10//99-12//99
	Athens MSA, GA	S	8.06 MW	7.97 AW	16760 AAW	GABLS	10//99-12//99
	Atlanta MSA, GA	S	9.05 MW	9.15 AW	18820 AAW	GABLS	10//99-12//99
	Augusta-Aiken MSA, GA-SC	S	8.83 MW	8.64 AW	18360 AAW	GABLS	10//99-12//99
	Columbus MSA, GA-AL	S	8.24 MW	8.14 AW	17140 AAW	GABLS	10//99-12//99
	Macon MSA, GA	S	8.36 MW	8.32 AW	17390 AAW	GABLS	10//99-12//99
	Savannah MSA, GA	S	8.27 MW	8.27 AW	17200 AAW	GABLS	10//99-12//99
	Hawaii	S	10.06 MW	10.20 AW	21220 AAW	HIBLS	10//99-12//99
	Honolulu MSA, HI	S	10.27 MW	10.07 AW	21360 AAW	HIBLS	10//99-12//99
	Idaho	S	8.02 MW	8.22 AW	17100 AAW	IDBLS	10//99-12//99
	Boise City MSA, ID	S	8.27 MW	7.96 AW	17200 AAW	IDBLS	10//99-12//99
	Pocatello MSA, ID	S	8.19 MW	8.16 AW	17040 AAW	IDBLS	10//99-12//99
	Illinois	S	8.34 MW	8.62 AW	17930 AAW	ILBLS	10//99-12//99
	Bloomington-Normal MSA, IL	S	7.92 MW	7.82 AW	16470 AAW	ILBLS	10//99-12//99
	Champaign-Urbana MSA, IL	S	7.85 MW	7.68 AW	16330 AAW	ILBLS	10//99-12//99
	Chicago PMSA, IL	S	9.04 MW	8.83 AW	18800 AAW	ILBLS	10//99-12//99
	Decatur MSA, IL	S	7.78 MW	7.76 AW	16180 AAW	ILBLS	10//99-12//99
	Kankakee PMSA, IL	S	7.81 MW	7.74 AW	16250 AAW	ILBLS	10//99-12//99
	Peoria-Pekin MSA, IL	S	7.78 MW	7.78 AW	16190 AAW	ILBLS	10//99-12//99
	Rockford MSA, IL	S	8.91 MW	8.54 AW	18530 AAW	ILBLS	10//99-12//99
	Springfield MSA, IL	S	7.98 MW	7.81 AW	16600 AAW	ILBLS	10//99-12//99
	Indiana	S	8.04 MW	8.21 AW	17070 AAW	INBLS	10//99-12//99
	Bloomington MSA, IN	S	7.94 MW	7.91 AW	16520 AAW	INBLS	10//99-12//99
	Elkhart-Goshen MSA, IN	S	8.40 MW	8.24 AW	17480 AAW	INBLS	10//99-12//99
	Evansville-Henderson MSA, IN-KY	S	8.34 MW	8.23 AW	17350 AAW	INBLS	10//99-12//99
	Fort Wayne MSA, IN	S	8.01 MW	7.93 AW	16660 AAW	INBLS	10//99-12//99
	Gary PMSA, IN	S	8.14 MW	7.93 AW	16920 AAW	INBLS	10//99-12//99
	Indianapolis MSA, IN	S	8.27 MW	8.07 AW	17200 AAW	INBLS	10//99-12//99
	Kokomo MSA, IN	S	8.72 MW	8.36 AW	18130 AAW	INBLS	10//99-12//99
	Lafayette MSA, IN	S	8.15 MW	8.04 AW	16950 AAW	INBLS	10//99-12//99
	Muncie MSA, IN	S	8.05 MW	7.98 AW	16750 AAW	INBLS	10//99-12//99
	South Bend MSA, IN	S	9.04 MW	8.71 AW	18800 AAW	INBLS	10//99-12//99
	Terre Haute MSA, IN	S	7.87 MW	7.82 AW	16370 AAW	INBLS	10//99-12//99
	Iowa	S	8.15 MW	8.29 AW	17250 AAW	IABLS	10//99-12//99
	Cedar Rapids MSA, IA	S	9.45 MW	9.53 AW	19650 AAW	IABLS	10//99-12//99
	Davenport-Moline-Rock Island MSA, IA-IL	S	8.75 MW	8.45 AW	18200 AAW	IABLS	10//99-12//99
	Des Moines MSA, IA	S	8.38 MW	8.36 AW	17430 AAW	IABLS	10//99-12//99
	Dubuque MSA, IA	S	8.39 MW	8.29 AW	17460 AAW	IABLS	10//99-12//99
	Iowa City MSA, IA	S	8.14 MW	8.06 AW	16930 AAW	IABLS	10//99-12//99
	Sioux City MSA, IA-NE	S	8.36 MW	8.33 AW	17390 AAW	IABLS	10//99-12//99
	Waterloo-Cedar Falls MSA, IA	S	8.06 MW	7.95 AW	16760 AAW	IABLS	10//99-12//99
	Kansas	S	7.93 MW	7.99 AW	16610 AAW	KSBLS	10//99-12//99
	Lawrence MSA, KS	S	8.54 MW	8.40 AW	17770 AAW	KSBLS	10//99-12//99
	Topeka MSA, KS	S	8.11 MW	8.00 AW	16880 AAW	KSBLS	10//99-12//99
	Wichita MSA, KS	S	7.40 MW	7.43 AW	15400 AAW	KSBLS	10//99-12//99
	Kentucky	S	7.9 MW	8.14 AW	16930 AAW	KYBLS	10//99-12//99
	Lexington MSA, KY	S	8.36 MW	8.09 AW	17380 AAW	KYBLS	10//99-12//99
	Louisville MSA, KY-IN	S	8.69 MW	8.37 AW	18080 AAW	KYBLS	10//99-12//99
	Owensboro MSA, KY	S	7.91 MW	7.83 AW	16450 AAW	KYBLS	10//99-12//99
	Louisiana	S	8.05 MW	8.23 AW	17120 AAW	LABLS	10//99-12//99
	Alexandria MSA, LA	S	7.62 MW	7.70 AW	15840 AAW	LABLS	10//99-12//99
	Baton Rouge MSA, LA	S	8.05 MW	7.91 AW	16750 AAW	LABLS	10//99-12//99
	Houma MSA, LA	S	6.79 MW	6.60 AW	14130 AAW	LABLS	10//99-12//99
	Lafayette MSA, LA	S	7.74 MW	7.61 AW	16100 AAW	LABLS	10//99-12//99
	Lake Charles MSA, LA	S	7.91 MW	7.67 AW	16450 AAW	LABLS	10//99-12//99
	Monroe MSA, LA	S	7.90 MW	7.71 AW	16420 AAW	LABLS	10//99-12//99
	New Orleans MSA, LA	S	8.73 MW	8.51 AW	18160 AAW	LABLS	10//99-12//99
	Shreveport-Bossier City MSA, LA	S	8.87 MW	8.36 AW	18460 AAW	LABLS	10//99-12//99
	Maine	S	8.08 MW	8.29 AW	17240 AAW	MEBLS	10//99-12//99
	Bangor MSA, ME	S	8.30 MW	8.02 AW	17260 AAW	MEBLS	10//99-12//99
	Lewiston-Auburn MSA, ME	S	8.29 MW	8.15 AW	17250 AAW	MEBLS	10//99-12//99
	Portland MSA, ME	S	8.40 MW	8.17 AW	17480 AAW	MEBLS	10//99-12//99
	Maryland	S	9.51 MW	9.57 AW	19900 AAW	MDBLS	10//99-12//99
	Baltimore PMSA, MD	S	9.33 MW	9.27 AW	19400 AAW	MDBLS	10//99-12//99

AAW Average annual wage	**AOH** Average offered, high	**ASH** Average starting, high	**H** Hourly	**M** Monthly	**S** Special: hourly and annual
AE Average entry wage	**AOL** Average offered, low	**ASL** Average starting, low	**HI** Highest wage paid	**MTC** Median total compensation	**TQ** Third quartile wage
AEX Average experienced wage	**APH** Average pay, high range	**AW** Average wage paid	**HR** High end range	**MW** Median wage paid	**W** Weekly
AO Average offered	**APL** Average pay, low range	**FQ** First quartile wage	**LR** Low end range	**SQ** Second quartile wage	**Y** Yearly

Occupation/Type/Industry	Location	Per	Low	Mid	High	Source	Date
Teller	Cumberland MSA, MD-WV	S	8.44 MW	8.29 AW	17550 AAW	MDBLS	10//99-12//99
	Massachusetts	S	10.03 MW	10.22 AW	21260 AAW	MABLS	10//99-12//99
	Barnstable-Yarmouth MSA, MA	S	10.29 MW	10.07 AW	21400 AAW	MABLS	10//99-12//99
	Boston PMSA, MA-NH	S	10.65 MW	10.42 AW	22150 AAW	MABLS	10//99-12//99
	Brockton PMSA, MA	S	9.92 MW	9.71 AW	20620 AAW	MABLS	10//99-12//99
	Fitchburg-Leominster PMSA, MA	S	9.12 MW	8.81 AW	18970 AAW	MABLS	10//99-12//99
	Lawrence PMSA, MA-NH	S	9.74 MW	9.69 AW	20270 AAW	MABLS	10//99-12//99
	Lowell PMSA, MA-NH	S	9.09 MW	8.96 AW	18900 AAW	MABLS	10//99-12//99
	New Bedford PMSA, MA	S	8.94 MW	8.92 AW	18600 AAW	MABLS	10//99-12//99
	Pittsfield MSA, MA	S	9.86 MW	9.82 AW	20510 AAW	MABLS	10//99-12//99
	Springfield MSA, MA	S	10.02 MW	9.72 AW	20840 AAW	MABLS	10//99-12//99
	Worcester PMSA, MA-CT	S	9.32 MW	9.36 AW	19390 AAW	MABLS	10//99-12//99
	Michigan	S	8.69 MW	8.90 AW	18520 AAW	MIBLS	10//99-12//99
	Ann Arbor PMSA, MI	S	8.96 MW	8.79 AW	18640 AAW	MIBLS	10//99-12//99
	Benton Harbor MSA, MI	S	8.64 MW	8.42 AW	17980 AAW	MIBLS	10//99-12//99
	Detroit PMSA, MI	S	9.44 MW	9.55 AW	19640 AAW	MIBLS	10//99-12//99
	Flint PMSA, MI	S	9.49 MW	8.92 AW	19730 AAW	MIBLS	10//99-12//99
	Grand Rapids-Muskegon-Holland MSA, MI	S	8.91 MW	8.71 AW	18530 AAW	MIBLS	10//99-12//99
	Jackson MSA, MI	S	8.46 MW	8.20 AW	17600 AAW	MIBLS	10//99-12//99
	Kalamazoo-Battle Creek MSA, MI	S	8.79 MW	8.58 AW	18280 AAW	MIBLS	10//99-12//99
	Lansing-East Lansing MSA, MI	S	8.85 MW	8.17 AW	18400 AAW	MIBLS	10//99-12//99
	Saginaw-Bay City-Midland MSA, MI	S	8.01 MW	7.57 AW	16670 AAW	MIBLS	10//99-12//99
	Minnesota	S	8.5 MW	8.59 AW	17870 AAW	MNBLS	10//99-12//99
	Duluth-Superior MSA, MN-WI	S	7.93 MW	7.90 AW	16500 AAW	MNBLS	10//99-12//99
	Minneapolis-St. Paul MSA, MN-WI	S	8.95 MW	8.90 AW	18620 AAW	MNBLS	10//99-12//99
	Rochester MSA, MN	S	9.36 MW	8.83 AW	19470 AAW	MNBLS	10//99-12//99
	St. Cloud MSA, MN	S	8.04 MW	8.00 AW	16720 AAW	MNBLS	10//99-12//99
	Mississippi	S	7.89 MW	8.01 AW	16660 AAW	MSBLS	10//99-12//99
	Biloxi-Gulfport-Pascagoula MSA, MS	S	7.70 MW	7.66 AW	16030 AAW	MSBLS	10//99-12//99
	Hattiesburg MSA, MS	S	8.39 MW	8.21 AW	17460 AAW	MSBLS	10//99-12//99
	Jackson MSA, MS	S	8.22 MW	8.10 AW	17100 AAW	MSBLS	10//99-12//99
	Missouri	S	7.8	7.94 AW	16510 AAW	MOBLS	10//99-12//99
	Kansas City MSA, MO-KS	S	8.57 MW	8.46 AW	17830 AAW	MOBLS	10//99-12//99
	St. Joseph MSA, MO	S	6.68 MW	6.17 AW	13900 AAW	MOBLS	10//99-12//99
	St. Louis MSA, MO-IL	S	8.08 MW	7.98 AW	16800 AAW	MOBLS	10//99-12//99
	Springfield MSA, MO	S	7.57 MW	7.58 AW	15750 AAW	MOBLS	10//99-12//99
	Montana	S	7.6	7.70 AW	16010 AAW	MTBLS	10//99-12//99
	Billings MSA, MT	S	7.87 MW	7.79 AW	16360 AAW	MTBLS	10//99-12//99
	Great Falls MSA, MT	S	8.21 MW	7.55 AW	17070 AAW	MTBLS	10//99-12//99
	Missoula MSA, MT	S	7.75 MW	7.67 AW	16130 AAW	MTBLS	10//99-12//99
	Nebraska	S	8.2 MW	8.38 AW	17440 AAW	NEBLS	10//99-12//99
	Lincoln MSA, NE	S	9.45 MW	9.43 AW	19670 AAW	NEBLS	10//99-12//99
	Omaha MSA, NE-IA	S	8.73 MW	8.63 AW	18170 AAW	NEBLS	10//99-12//99
	Nevada	S	10.07 MW	10.03 AW	20870 AAW	NVBLS	10//99-12//99
	Las Vegas MSA, NV-AZ	S	10.04 MW	10.06 AW	20890 AAW	NVBLS	10//99-12//99
	Reno MSA, NV	S	9.95 MW	10.16 AW	20690 AAW	NVBLS	10//99-12//99
	New Hampshire	S	8.61 MW	9.00 AW	18720 AAW	NHBLS	10//99-12//99
	Manchester PMSA, NH	S	10.17 MW	9.22 AW	21160 AAW	NHBLS	10//99-12//99
	Nashua PMSA, NH	S	9.69 MW	9.72 AW	20150 AAW	NHBLS	10//99-12//99
	Portsmouth-Rochester PMSA, NH-ME	S	8.55 MW	8.37 AW	17790 AAW	NHBLS	10//99-12//99
	New Jersey	S	9.33 MW	9.22 AW	19170 AAW	NJBLS	10//99-12//99
	Atlantic-Cape May PMSA, NJ	S	9.25 MW	9.38 AW	19230 AAW	NJBLS	10//99-12//99
	Bergen-Passaic PMSA, NJ	S	9.38 MW	9.61 AW	19520 AAW	NJBLS	10//99-12//99
	Jersey City PMSA, NJ	S	8.65 MW	8.44 AW	18000 AAW	NJBLS	10//99-12//99
	Middlesex-Somerset-Hunterdon PMSA, NJ	S	8.81 MW	8.58 AW	18330 AAW	NJBLS	10//99-12//99
	Monmouth-Ocean PMSA, NJ	S	8.99 MW	8.96 AW	18700 AAW	NJBLS	10//99-12//99
	Newark PMSA, NJ	S	9.54 MW	9.54 AW	19840 AAW	NJBLS	10//99-12//99
	Trenton PMSA, NJ	S	9.18 MW	9.22 AW	19090 AAW	NJBLS	10//99-12//99
	New Mexico	S	8.07 MW	8.28 AW	17230 AAW	NMBLS	10//99-12//99
	Albuquerque MSA, NM	S	8.54 MW	8.23 AW	17770 AAW	NMBLS	10//99-12//99
	Las Cruces MSA, NM	S	7.46 MW	7.45 AW	15520 AAW	NMBLS	10//99-12//99
	Santa Fe MSA, NM	S	9.17 MW	8.89 AW	19080 AAW	NMBLS	10//99-12//99
	New York	S	9.28 MW	9.51 AW	19770 AAW	NYBLS	10//99-12//99

AAW Average annual wage	AOH Average offered, high	ASH Average starting, high	H Hourly	M Monthly	S Special: hourly and annual
AE Average entry wage	AOL Average offered, low	ASL Average starting, low	HI Highest wage paid	MTC Median total compensation	TQ Third quartile wage
AEX Average experienced wage	APH Average pay, high range	AW Average wage paid	HR High end range	MW Median wage paid	W Weekly
AO Average offered	APL Average pay, low range	FQ First quartile wage	LR Low end range	SQ Second quartile wage	Y Yearly

Occupation/Type/Industry	Location	Per	Low	Mid	High	Source	Date
Teller	Albany-Schenectady-Troy						
	MSA, NY	S	8.21 MW	8.06 AW	17080 AAW	NYBLS	10//99-12//99
	Binghamton MSA, NY	S	7.78 MW	7.72 AW	16190 AAW	NYBLS	10//99-12//99
	Buffalo-Niagara Falls MSA,						
	NY	S	9.36 MW	8.46 AW	19480 AAW	NYBLS	10//99-12//99
	Dutchess County PMSA, NY	S	8.85 MW	8.69 AW	18400 AAW	NYBLS	10//99-12//99
	Elmira MSA, NY	S	8.35 MW	8.29 AW	17370 AAW	NYBLS	10//99-12//99
	Glens Falls MSA, NY	S	8.26 MW	7.96 AW	17170 AAW	NYBLS	10//99-12//99
	Jamestown MSA, NY	S	8.36 MW	8.34 AW	17390 AAW	NYBLS	10//99-12//99
	Nassau-Suffolk PMSA, NY	S	9.72 MW	9.56 AW	20230 AAW	NYBLS	10//99-12//99
	New York PMSA, NY	S	10.04 MW	9.91 AW	20880 AAW	NYBLS	10//99-12//99
	Newburgh PMSA, NY-PA	S	8.39 MW	8.18 AW	17460 AAW	NYBLS	10//99-12//99
	Rochester MSA, NY	S	8.46 MW	8.16 AW	17590 AAW	NYBLS	10//99-12//99
	Syracuse MSA, NY	S	8.14 MW	8.09 AW	16930 AAW	NYBLS	10//99-12//99
	Utica-Rome MSA, NY	S	9.17 MW	9.47 AW	19060 AAW	NYBLS	10//99-12//99
	North Carolina	S	8.62 MW	8.71 AW	18120 AAW	NCBLS	10//99-12//99
	Asheville MSA, NC	S	8.82 MW	8.58 AW	18350 AAW	NCBLS	10//99-12//99
	Charlotte-Gastonia-Rock Hill						
	MSA, NC-SC	S	8.97 MW	8.74 AW	18650 AAW	NCBLS	10//99-12//99
	Fayetteville MSA, NC	S	8.72 MW	8.49 AW	18130 AAW	NCBLS	10//99-12//99
	Goldsboro MSA, NC	S	8.01 MW	7.90 AW	16660 AAW	NCBLS	10//99-12//99
	Greensboro--Winston-Salem--						
	High Point MSA, NC	S	8.75 MW	9.00 AW	18200 AAW	NCBLS	10//99-12//99
	Greenville MSA, NC	S	7.40 MW	6.84 AW	15400 AAW	NCBLS	10//99-12//99
	Hickory-Morganton-Lenoir						
	MSA, NC	S	9.11 MW	8.72 AW	18950 AAW	NCBLS	10//99-12//99
	Jacksonville MSA, NC	S	8.58 MW	8.46 AW	17850 AAW	NCBLS	10//99-12//99
	Raleigh-Durham-Chapel Hill						
	MSA, NC	S	9.32 MW	9.42 AW	19380 AAW	NCBLS	10//99-12//99
	Rocky Mount MSA, NC	S	8.67 MW	8.69 AW	18040 AAW	NCBLS	10//99-12//99
	Wilmington MSA, NC	S	8.11 MW	8.00 AW	16870 AAW	NCBLS	10//99-12//99
	North Dakota	S	7.8 MW	7.83 AW	16290 AAW	NDBLS	10//99-12//99
	Bismarck MSA, ND	S	7.88 MW	7.81 AW	16400 AAW	NDBLS	10//99-12//99
	Fargo-Moorhead MSA, ND-						
	MN	S	7.74 MW	7.76 AW	16090 AAW	NDBLS	10//99-12//99
	Grand Forks MSA, ND-MN	S	7.86 MW	7.84 AW	16350 AAW	NDBLS	10//99-12//99
	Ohio	S	8.15 MW	8.40 AW	17470 AAW	OHBLS	10//99-12//99
	Akron PMSA, OH	S	8.38 MW	8.31 AW	17420 AAW	OHBLS	10//99-12//99
	Canton-Massillon MSA, OH	S	8.07 MW	8.00 AW	16790 AAW	OHBLS	10//99-12//99
	Cincinnati PMSA, OH-KY-IN	S	8.54 MW	8.36 AW	17760 AAW	OHBLS	10//99-12//99
	Cleveland-Lorain-Elyria						
	PMSA, OH	S	8.81 MW	8.32 AW	18330 AAW	OHBLS	10//99-12//99
	Columbus MSA, OH	S	8.94 MW	8.91 AW	18590 AAW	OHBLS	10//99-12//99
	Dayton-Springfield MSA, OH	S	8.41 MW	8.12 AW	17490 AAW	OHBLS	10//99-12//99
	Hamilton-Middletown PMSA,						
	OH	S	8.49 MW	8.42 AW	17660 AAW	OHBLS	10//99-12//99
	Lima MSA, OH	S	8.18 MW	7.98 AW	17010 AAW	OHBLS	10//99-12//99
	Mansfield MSA, OH	S	7.98 MW	7.78 AW	16600 AAW	OHBLS	10//99-12//99
	Steubenville-Weirton MSA,						
	OH-WV	S	7.25 MW	7.16 AW	15080 AAW	OHBLS	10//99-12//99
	Toledo MSA, OH	S	9.02 MW	8.74 AW	18760 AAW	OHBLS	10//99-12//99
	Youngstown-Warren MSA, OH	S	7.69 MW	7.34 AW	16000 AAW	OHBLS	10//99-12//99
	Oklahoma	S	7.78 MW	7.87 AW	16370 AAW	OKBLS	10//99-12//99
	Enid MSA, OK	S	7.70 MW	7.62 AW	16020 AAW	OKBLS	10//99-12//99
	Lawton MSA, OK	S	6.81 MW	6.39 AW	14170 AAW	OKBLS	10//99-12//99
	Oklahoma City MSA, OK	S	8.14 MW	7.98 AW	16920 AAW	OKBLS	10//99-12//99
	Tulsa MSA, OK	S	8.24 MW	8.16 AW	17130 AAW	OKBLS	10//99-12//99
	Oregon	S	8.71 MW	8.84 AW	18390 AAW	ORBLS	10//99-12//99
	Corvallis MSA, OR	S	8.80 MW	8.58 AW	18300 AAW	ORBLS	10//99-12//99
	Eugene-Springfield MSA, OR	S	8.72 MW	8.60 AW	18140 AAW	ORBLS	10//99-12//99
	Medford-Ashland MSA, OR	S	8.67 MW	8.82 AW	18030 AAW	ORBLS	10//99-12//99
	Portland-Vancouver PMSA,						
	OR-WA	S	9.13 MW	8.99 AW	19000 AAW	ORBLS	10//99-12//99
	Salem PMSA, OR	S	8.70 MW	8.61 AW	18100 AAW	ORBLS	10//99-12//99
	Pennsylvania	S	7.93 MW	8.34 AW	17340 AAW	PABLS	10//99-12//99
	Allentown-Bethlehem-Easton						
	MSA, PA	S	9.14 MW	9.01 AW	19010 AAW	PABLS	10//99-12//99
	Altoona MSA, PA	S	7.78 MW	7.70 AW	16170 AAW	PABLS	10//99-12//99
	Erie MSA, PA	S	8.24 MW	8.15 AW	17150 AAW	PABLS	10//99-12//99
	Harrisburg-Lebanon-Carlisle						
	MSA, PA	S	8.29 MW	8.12 AW	17240 AAW	PABLS	10//99-12//99
	Johnstown MSA, PA	S	8.45 MW	8.32 AW	17580 AAW	PABLS	10//99-12//99

AAW	Average annual wage	AOH	Average offered, high	ASH	Average starting, high
AE	Average entry wage	AOL	Average offered, low	ASL	Average starting, low
AEX	Average experienced wage	APH	Average pay, high range	AW	Average wage paid
AO	Average offered	APL	Average pay, low range	FQ	First quartile wage

H	Hourly	M	Monthly	S	Special: hourly and annual
HI	Highest wage paid	MTC	Median total compensation	TQ	Third quartile wage
HR	High end range	MW	Median wage paid	W	Weekly
LR	Low end range	SQ	Second quartile wage	Y	Yearly

Occupation/Type/Industry	Location	Per	Low	Mid	High	Source	Date
Teller	Lancaster MSA, PA	s	9.25 MW	8.96 AW	19230 AAW	PABLS	10//99-12//99
	Philadelphia PMSA, PA-NJ	s	9.51 MW	9.39 AW	19770 AAW	PABLS	10//99-12//99
	Pittsburgh MSA, PA	s	9.00 MW	8.57 AW	18710 AAW	PABLS	10//99-12//99
	Reading MSA, PA	s	8.76 MW	8.56 AW	18230 AAW	PABLS	10//99-12//99
	Scranton--Wilkes-Barre-- Hazleton MSA, PA	s	8.52 MW	8.59 AW	17730 AAW	PABLS	10//99-12//99
	Sharon MSA, PA	s	7.97 MW	7.75 AW	16580 AAW	PABLS	10//99-12//99
	Williamsport MSA, PA	s	9.09 MW	9.08 AW	18910 AAW	PABLS	10//99-12//99
	Rhode Island	s	9.51 MW	9.72 AW	20210 AAW	RIBLS	10//99-12//99
	Providence-Fall River- Warwick MSA, RI-MA	s	9.27 MW	8.88 AW	19280 AAW	RIBLS	10//99-12//99
	South Carolina	s	8.6 MW	8.78 AW	18250 AAW	SCBLS	10//99-12//99
	Charleston-North Charleston MSA, SC	s	8.81 MW	8.69 AW	18330 AAW	SCBLS	10//99-12//99
	Columbia MSA, SC	s	8.74 MW	8.82 AW	18170 AAW	SCBLS	10//99-12//99
	Florence MSA, SC	s	8.30 MW	8.05 AW	17270 AAW	SCBLS	10//99-12//99
	Greenville-Spartanburg- Anderson MSA, SC	s	8.98 MW	8.66 AW	18680 AAW	SCBLS	10//99-12//99
	Myrtle Beach MSA, SC	s	8.75 MW	8.61 AW	18200 AAW	SCBLS	10//99-12//99
	Sumter MSA, SC	s	9.28 MW	9.40 AW	19290 AAW	SCBLS	10//99-12//99
	South Dakota	s	7.93 MW	8.07 AW	16780 AAW	SDBLS	10//99-12//99
	Rapid City MSA, SD	s	7.83 MW	7.77 AW	16280 AAW	SDBLS	10//99-12//99
	Sioux Falls MSA, SD	s	8.49 MW	8.09 AW	17650 AAW	SDBLS	10//99-12//99
	Tennessee	s	7.96 MW	8.06 AW	16760 AAW	TNBLS	10//99-12//99
	Chattanooga MSA, TN-GA	s	8.84 MW	8.41 AW	18380 AAW	TNBLS	10//99-12//99
	Clarksville-Hopkinsville MSA, TN-KY	s	8.23 MW	8.05 AW	17110 AAW	TNBLS	10//99-12//99
	Jackson MSA, TN	s	8.72 MW	8.29 AW	18150 AAW	TNBLS	10//99-12//99
	Johnson City-Kingsport-Bristol MSA, TN-VA	s	7.68 MW	7.56 AW	15970 AAW	TNBLS	10//99-12//99
	Knoxville MSA, TN	s	8.18 MW	8.01 AW	17010 AAW	TNBLS	10//99-12//99
	Memphis MSA, TN-AR-MS	s	8.66 MW	8.60 AW	18000 AAW	MSBLS	10//99-12//99
	Nashville MSA, TN	s	8.14 MW	8.11 AW	16930 AAW	TNBLS	10//99-12//99
	Texas	s	8.65 MW	8.73 AW	18170 AAW	TXBLS	10//99-12//99
	Abilene MSA, TX	s	8.39 MW	8.05 AW	17460 AAW	TXBLS	10//99-12//99
	Amarillo MSA, TX	s	8.40 MW	8.24 AW	17480 AAW	TXBLS	10//99-12//99
	Austin-San Marcos MSA, TX	s	8.60 MW	8.68 AW	17880 AAW	TXBLS	10//99-12//99
	Beaumont-Port Arthur MSA, TX	s	9.20 MW	8.82 AW	19140 AAW	TXBLS	10//99-12//99
	Brazoria PMSA, TX	s	8.61 MW	8.65 AW	17910 AAW	TXBLS	10//99-12//99
	Brownsville-Harlingen-San Benito MSA, TX	s	7.49 MW	7.42 AW	15580 AAW	TXBLS	10//99-12//99
	Bryan-College Station MSA, TX	s	8.98 MW	8.95 AW	18670 AAW	TXBLS	10//99-12//99
	Corpus Christi MSA, TX	s	8.70 MW	8.40 AW	18090 AAW	TXBLS	10//99-12//99
	Dallas PMSA, TX	s	9.71 MW	9.66 AW	20200 AAW	TXBLS	10//99-12//99
	El Paso MSA, TX	s	7.60 MW	7.51 AW	15800 AAW	TXBLS	10//99-12//99
	Fort Worth-Arlington PMSA, TX	s	9.73 MW	9.68 AW	20240 AAW	TXBLS	10//99-12//99
	Galveston-Texas City PMSA, TX	s	8.32 MW	8.14 AW	17300 AAW	TXBLS	10//99-12//99
	Houston PMSA, TX	s	9.06 MW	9.08 AW	18830 AAW	TXBLS	10//99-12//99
	Killeen-Temple MSA, TX	s	7.60 MW	7.33 AW	15800 AAW	TXBLS	10//99-12//99
	Laredo MSA, TX	s	7.95 MW	7.86 AW	16540 AAW	TXBLS	10//99-12//99
	Longview-Marshall MSA, TX	s	8.05 MW	7.95 AW	16750 AAW	TXBLS	10//99-12//99
	Lubbock MSA, TX	s	8.19 MW	7.81 AW	17040 AAW	TXBLS	10//99-12//99
	McAllen-Edinburg-Mission MSA, TX	s	8.34 MW	8.20 AW	17360 AAW	TXBLS	10//99-12//99
	Odessa-Midland MSA, TX	s	8.07 MW	7.99 AW	16790 AAW	TXBLS	10//99-12//99
	San Angelo MSA, TX	s	7.75 MW	7.66 AW	16110 AAW	TXBLS	10//99-12//99
	San Antonio MSA, TX	s	8.72 MW	8.40 AW	18140 AAW	TXBLS	10//99-12//99
	Sherman-Denison MSA, TX	s	8.07 MW	7.94 AW	16780 AAW	TXBLS	10//99-12//99
	Texarkana MSA, TX- Texarkana, AR	s	7.74 MW	7.68 AW	16090 AAW	TXBLS	10//99-12//99
	Tyler MSA, TX	s	8.47 MW	8.25 AW	17610 AAW	TXBLS	10//99-12//99
	Victoria MSA, TX	s	8.76 MW	8.36 AW	18220 AAW	TXBLS	10//99-12//99
	Waco MSA, TX	s	8.15 MW	7.94 AW	16940 AAW	TXBLS	10//99-12//99
	Wichita Falls MSA, TX	s	7.90 MW	7.75 AW	16420 AAW	TXBLS	10//99-12//99
	Utah	s	8.23 MW	8.47 AW	17610 AAW	UTBLS	10//99-12//99
	Provo-Orem MSA, UT	s	7.86 MW	7.80 AW	16340 AAW	UTBLS	10//99-12//99
	Salt Lake City-Ogden MSA, UT	s	8.46 MW	8.29 AW	17590 AAW	UTBLS	10//99-12//99

Occupation/Type/Industry	Location	Per	Low	Mid	High	Source	Date
Teller	Vermont	S	8.13 MW	8.47 AW	17620 AAW	VTBLS	10//99-12//99
	Burlington MSA, VT	S	8.48 MW	7.84 AW	17630 AAW	VTBLS	10//99-12//99
	Virginia	S	8.64 MW	8.90 AW	18510 AAW	VABLS	10//99-12//99
	Charlottesville MSA, VA	S	7.86 MW	7.74 AW	16360 AAW	VABLS	10//99-12//99
	Danville MSA, VA	S	8.63 MW	8.27 AW	17950 AAW	VABLS	10//99-12//99
	Lynchburg MSA, VA	S	8.97 MW	8.99 AW	18660 AAW	VABLS	10//99-12//99
	Norfolk-Virginia Beach-Newport News MSA, VA-NC	S	8.68 MW	8.28 AW	18050 AAW	VABLS	10//99-12//99
	Richmond-Petersburg MSA, VA	S	9.02 MW	8.66 AW	18760 AAW	VABLS	10//99-12//99
	Roanoke MSA, VA	S	8.72 MW	8.43 AW	18130 AAW	VABLS	10//99-12//99
	Washington	S	9.88 MW	9.93 AW	20660 AAW	WABLS	10//99-12//99
	Bremerton PMSA, WA	S	9.86 MW	9.77 AW	20500 AAW	WABLS	10//99-12//99
	Olympia PMSA, WA	S	9.74 MW	9.68 AW	20260 AAW	WABLS	10//99-12//99
	Richland-Kennewick-Pasco MSA, WA	S	9.19 MW	8.73 AW	19110 AAW	WABLS	10//99-12//99
	Seattle-Bellevue-Everett PMSA, WA	S	10.33 MW	10.30 AW	21490 AAW	WABLS	10//99-12//99
	Spokane MSA, WA	S	8.68 MW	8.26 AW	18060 AAW	WABLS	10//99-12//99
	Tacoma PMSA, WA	S	9.51 MW	9.63 AW	19780 AAW	WABLS	10//99-12//99
	Yakima MSA, WA	S	9.81 MW	9.85 AW	20400 AAW	WABLS	10//99-12//99
	West Virginia	S	7.49 MW	7.60 AW	15800 AAW	WVBLS	10//99-12//99
	Charleston MSA, WV	S	8.14 MW	8.02 AW	16930 AAW	WVBLS	10//99-12//99
	Huntington-Ashland MSA, WV-KY-OH	S	7.48 MW	7.31 AW	15550 AAW	WVBLS	10//99-12//99
	Parkersburg-Marietta MSA, WV-OH	S	7.43 MW	7.36 AW	15460 AAW	WVBLS	10//99-12//99
	Wheeling MSA, WV-OH	S	7.32 MW	7.14 AW	15220 AAW	WVBLS	10//99-12//99
	Wisconsin	S	8.16 MW	8.31 AW	17290 AAW	WIBLS	10//99-12//99
	Appleton-Oshkosh-Neenah MSA, WI	S	8.17 MW	8.01 AW	16980 AAW	WIBLS	10//99-12//99
	Eau Claire MSA, WI	S	7.47 MW	7.40 AW	15540 AAW	WIBLS	10//99-12//99
	Green Bay MSA, WI	S	8.45 MW	8.31 AW	17570 AAW	WIBLS	10//99-12//99
	Janesville-Beloit MSA, WI	S	8.66 MW	8.34 AW	18020 AAW	WIBLS	10//99-12//99
	Kenosha PMSA, WI	S	8.51 MW	8.42 AW	17690 AAW	WIBLS	10//99-12//99
	La Crosse MSA, WI-MN	S	7.86 MW	7.82 AW	16340 AAW	WIBLS	10//99-12//99
	Madison MSA, WI	S	8.95 MW	8.98 AW	18610 AAW	WIBLS	10//99-12//99
	Milwaukee-Waukesha PMSA, WI	S	8.44 MW	8.30 AW	17550 AAW	WIBLS	10//99-12//99
	Racine PMSA, WI	S	7.97 MW	7.90 AW	16580 AAW	WIBLS	10//99-12//99
	Sheboygan MSA, WI	S	8.11 MW	8.05 AW	16860 AAW	WIBLS	10//99-12//99
	Wausau MSA, WI	S	8.00 MW	7.93 AW	16630 AAW	WIBLS	10//99-12//99
	Wyoming	S	7.44 MW	7.55 AW	15700 AAW	WYBLS	10//99-12//99
	Casper MSA, WY	S	8.16 MW	8.10 AW	16980 AAW	WYBLS	10//99-12//99
	Cheyenne MSA, WY	S	7.93 MW	7.94 AW	16490 AAW	WYBLS	10//99-12//99
	Puerto Rico	S	6.24 MW	6.50 AW	13520 AAW	PRBLS	10//99-12//99
	Aguadilla MSA, PR	S	6.55 MW	6.38 AW	13620 AAW	PRBLS	10//99-12//99
	Arecibo PMSA, PR	S	6.35 MW	6.25 AW	13200 AAW	PRBLS	10//99-12//99
	Caguas PMSA, PR	S	6.51 MW	6.16 AW	13540 AAW	PRBLS	10//99-12//99
	Mayaguez MSA, PR	S	6.46 MW	6.17 AW	13440 AAW	PRBLS	10//99-12//99
	Ponce MSA, PR	S	6.65 MW	6.14 AW	13830 AAW	PRBLS	10//99-12//99
	San Juan-Bayamon PMSA, PR	S	6.49 MW	6.25 AW	13500 AAW	PRBLS	10//99-12//99
	Virgin Islands	S	8.03 MW	8.18 AW	17020 AAW	VIBLS	10//99-12//99
	Guam	S	8.28 MW	8.57 AW	17820 AAW	GUBLS	10//99-12//99
Terrazzo Worker and Finisher	California	S	14.29 MW	15.00 AW	31200 AAW	CABLS	10//99-12//99
	Florida	S	9.64 MW	9.89 AW	20580 AAW	FLBLS	10//99-12//99
	Illinois	S	19.29 MW	19.37 AW	40290 AAW	ILBLS	10//99-12//99
	Minnesota	S	21.72 MW	19.81 AW	41200 AAW	MNBLS	10//99-12//99
	Mississippi	S	10.61 MW	14.86 AW	30900 AAW	MSBLS	10//99-12//99
	Texas	S	10.47 MW	12.66 AW	26330 AAW	TXBLS	10//99-12//99
	Virginia	S	13.31 MW	15.24 AW	31700 AAW	VABLS	10//99-12//99
	Puerto Rico	S	6.7 MW	6.61 AW	13740 AAW	PRBLS	10//99-12//99
Textile Bleaching and Dyeing Machine Operator and Tender	Alabama	S	9.12 MW	9.07 AW	18860 AAW	ALBLS	10//99-12//99
	California	S	7.93 MW	8.24 AW	17140 AAW	CABLS	10//99-12//99
	Los Angeles-Long Beach PMSA, CA	S	7.58 MW	6.64 AW	15770 AAW	CABLS	10//99-12//99
	Orange County PMSA, CA	S	9.46 MW	9.63 AW	19680 AAW	CABLS	10//99-12//99
	San Diego MSA, CA	S	9.16 MW	6.64 AW	19040 AAW	CABLS	10//99-12//99

AAW	Average annual wage	AOH	Average offered, high	ASH	Average starting, high	H	Hourly	M	Monthly	S	Special: hourly and annual
AE	American entry wage	AOL	Average offered, low	ASL	Average starting, low	HI	Highest wage paid	MTC	Median total compensation	TQ	Third quartile wage
AEX	Average experienced wage	APH	Average pay, high range	AW	Average wage paid	HR	High end range	MW	Median wage paid	W	Weekly
AO	Average offered	APL	Average pay, low range	FQ	First quartile wage	LR	Low end range	SQ	Second quartile wage	Y	Yearly

Occupation/Type/Industry	Location	Per	Low	Mid	High	Source	Date
Textile Bleaching and Dyeing Machine Operator and Tender	Florida	S	7.85 MW	8.04 AW	16710 AAW	FLBLS	10//99-12//99
	Miami PMSA, FL	S	9.07 MW	9.23 AW	18860 AAW	FLBLS	10//99-12//99
	Georgia	S	8.47 MW	9.11 AW	18950 AAW	GABLS	10//99-12//99
	Atlanta MSA, GA	S	8.43 MW	8.04 AW	17530 AAW	GABLS	10//99-12//99
	Columbus MSA, GA-AL	S	10.89 MW	11.27 AW	22660 AAW	GABLS	10//99-12//99
	Illinois	S	7.7 MW	8.06 AW	16760 AAW	ILBLS	10//99-12//99
	Chicago PMSA, IL	S	8.00 MW	7.69 AW	16630 AAW	ILBLS	10//99-12//99
	Indiana	S	9.75 MW	9.76 AW	20300 AAW	INBLS	10//99-12//99
	Kentucky	S	7.7 MW	7.77 AW	16150 AAW	KYBLS	10//99-12//99
	Massachusetts	S	11.6 MW	10.93 AW	22740 AAW	MABLS	10//99-12//99
	Worcester PMSA, MA-CT	S	11.13 MW	11.39 AW	23150 AAW	MABLS	10//99-12//99
	Mississippi	S	9.03 MW	8.73 AW	18160 AAW	MSBLS	10//99-12//99
	Missouri	S	9.24 MW	8.82 AW	18340 AAW	MOBLS	10//99-12//99
	St. Louis MSA, MO-IL	S	9.12 MW	9.47 AW	18970 AAW	MOBLS	10//99-12//99
	New Hampshire	S	9.67 MW	9.55 AW	19860 AAW	NHBLS	10//99-12//99
	New Jersey	S	11.81 MW	11.47 AW	23850 AAW	NJBLS	10//99-12//99
	Bergen-Passaic PMSA, NJ	S	11.92 MW	12.01 AW	24790 AAW	NJBLS	10//99-12//99
	New York	S	8.96 MW	9.08 AW	18890 AAW	NYBLS	10//99-12//99
	New York PMSA, NY	S	8.59 MW	8.06 AW	17870 AAW	NYBLS	10//99-12//99
	North Carolina	S	9.27 MW	9.09 AW	18920 AAW	NCBLS	10//99-12//99
	Charlotte-Gastonia-Rock Hill MSA, NC-SC	S	10.07 MW	9.86 AW	20940 AAW	NCBLS	10//99-12//99
	Greensboro--Winston-Salem-- High Point MSA, NC	S	9.26 MW	9.16 AW	19250 AAW	NCBLS	10//99-12//99
	Hickory-Morganton-Lenoir MSA, NC	S	8.28 MW	8.83 AW	17230 AAW	NCBLS	10//99-12//99
	Raleigh-Durham-Chapel Hill MSA, NC	S	9.52 MW	10.78 AW	19800 AAW	NCBLS	10//99-12//99
	Rocky Mount MSA, NC	S	8.77 MW	8.63 AW	18240 AAW	NCBLS	10//99-12//99
	Pennsylvania	S	9.73 MW	9.93 AW	20650 AAW	PABLS	10//99-12//99
	Philadelphia PMSA, PA-NJ	S	11.20 MW	11.68 AW	23300 AAW	PABLS	10//99-12//99
	Reading MSA, PA	S	7.31 MW	7.28 AW	15190 AAW	PABLS	10//99-12//99
	Rhode Island	S	10.39 MW	10.42 AW	21670 AAW	RIBLS	10//99-12//99
	Providence-Fall River- Warwick MSA, RI-MA	S	11.25 MW	11.73 AW	23410 AAW	RIBLS	10//99-12//99
	South Carolina	S	10.35 MW	10.62 AW	22090 AAW	SCBLS	10//99-12//99
	Greenville-Spartanburg- Anderson MSA, SC	S	11.19 MW	10.34 AW	23270 AAW	SCBLS	10//99-12//99
	Sumter MSA, SC	S	7.06 MW	7.19 AW	14690 AAW	SCBLS	10//99-12//99
	Tennessee	S	9.29 MW	8.98 AW	18680 AAW	TNBLS	10//99-12//99
	Chattanooga MSA, TN-GA	S	9.30 MW	8.64 AW	19350 AAW	TNBLS	10//99-12//99
	Knoxville MSA, TN	S	9.10 MW	9.34 AW	18930 AAW	TNBLS	10//99-12//99
	Texas	S	7.23 MW	7.74 AW	16090 AAW	TXBLS	10//99-12//99
	Virginia	S	9.98 MW	9.86 AW	20520 AAW	VABLS	10//99-12//99
	Wisconsin	S	8.03 MW	8.10 AW	16840 AAW	WIBLS	10//99-12//99
	Puerto Rico	S	6.06 MW	5.96 AW	12400 AAW	PRBLS	10//99-12//99
Textile Cutting Machine Setter, Operator, and Tender	Alabama	S	8.51 MW	8.52 AW	17720 AAW	ALBLS	10//99-12//99
	Arizona	S	7.75 MW	7.85 AW	16340 AAW	AZBLS	10//99-12//99
	Phoenix-Mesa MSA, AZ	S	8.12 MW	7.98 AW	16900 AAW	AZBLS	10//99-12//99
	Arkansas	S	8.61 MW	8.18 AW	17010 AAW	ARBLS	10//99-12//99
	California	S	8.48 MW	9.11 AW	18940 AAW	CABLS	10//99-12//99
	Los Angeles-Long Beach PMSA, CA	S	8.76 MW	8.39 AW	18220 AAW	CABLS	10//99-12//99
	Oakland PMSA, CA	S	12.13 MW	11.91 AW	25220 AAW	CABLS	10//99-12//99
	Orange County PMSA, CA	S	7.74 MW	6.85 AW	16100 AAW	CABLS	10//99-12//99
	Riverside-San Bernardino PMSA, CA	S	13.00 MW	14.43 AW	27040 AAW	CABLS	10//99-12//99
	San Diego MSA, CA	S	8.80 MW	8.92 AW	18290 AAW	CABLS	10//99-12//99
	San Francisco PMSA, CA	S	9.52 MW	9.05 AW	19810 AAW	CABLS	10//99-12//99
	San Jose PMSA, CA	S	10.26 MW	9.17 AW	21350 AAW	CABLS	10//99-12//99
	Colorado	S	8.83 MW	9.64 AW	20050 AAW	COBLS	10//99-12//99
	Connecticut	S	8.83 MW	8.70 AW	18100 AAW	CTBLS	10//99-12//99
	Hartford MSA, CT	S	7.90 MW	7.88 AW	16440 AAW	CTBLS	10//99-12//99
	Florida	S	7.2 MW	7.84 AW	16310 AAW	FLBLS	10//99-12//99
	Fort Lauderdale PMSA, FL	S	12.08 MW	12.22 AW	25120 AAW	FLBLS	10//99-12//99
	Jacksonville MSA, FL	S	8.93 MW	8.27 AW	18580 AAW	FLBLS	10//99-12//99
	Miami PMSA, FL	S	7.43 MW	6.66 AW	15460 AAW	FLBLS	10//99-12//99
	West Palm Beach-Boca Raton MSA, FL	S	8.76 MW	8.93 AW	18230 AAW	FLBLS	10//99-12//99

AAW	Average annual wage	AOH	Average offered, high	ASH	Average starting, high	H	Hourly	M	Monthly	S	Special: hourly and annual
AE	Average entry wage	AOL	Average offered, low	ASL	Average starting, low	HI	Highest wage paid	MTC	Median total compensation	TQ	Third quartile wage
AEX	Average experienced wage	APH	Average pay, high range	AW	Average wage paid	HR	High end range	MW	Median wage paid	W	Weekly
AO	Average offered	APL	Average pay, low range	FQ	First quartile wage	LR	Low end range	SQ	Second quartile wage	Y	Yearly

Occupation/Type/Industry	Location	Per	Low	Mid	High	Source	Date
Textile Cutting Machine Setter, Operator, and Tender	Georgia	S	8.65 MW	9.08 AW	18890 AAW	GABLS	10//99-12//99
	Atlanta MSA, GA	S	8.68 MW	8.25 AW	18060 AAW	GABLS	10//99-12//99
	Illinois	S	9.76 MW	9.70 AW	20180 AAW	ILBLS	10//99-12//99
	Chicago PMSA, IL	S	9.98 MW	10.88 AW	20750 AAW	ILBLS	10//99-12//99
	Indiana	S	9.36 MW	9.62 AW	20020 AAW	INBLS	10//99-12//99
	Fort Wayne MSA, IN	S	12.04 MW	12.13 AW	25040 AAW	INBLS	10//99-12//99
	Indianapolis MSA, IN	S	10.60 MW	10.54 AW	22050 AAW	INBLS	10//99-12//99
	Iowa	S	7.65 MW	8.08 AW	16800 AAW	IABLS	10//99-12//99
	Kansas	S	10 MW	10.30 AW	21420 AAW	KSBLS	10//99-12//99
	Kentucky	S	11.04 MW	10.38 AW	21600 AAW	KYBLS	10//99-12//99
	Louisville MSA, KY-IN	S	9.66 MW	9.26 AW	20090 AAW	KYBLS	10//99-12//99
	Louisiana	S	6.32 MW	6.76 AW	14060 AAW	LABLS	10//99-12//99
	New Orleans MSA, LA	S	9.31 MW	9.40 AW	19370 AAW	LABLS	10//99-12//99
	Maine	S	8.62 MW	9.04 AW	18800 AAW	MEBLS	10//99-12//99
	Maryland	S	9.4 MW	10.00 AW	20790 AAW	MDBLS	10//99-12//99
	Baltimore PMSA, MD	S	9.90 MW	9.31 AW	20600 AAW	MDBLS	10//99-12//99
	Massachusetts	S	10.36 MW	10.84 AW	22550 AAW	MABLS	10//99-12//99
	Boston PMSA, MA-NH	S	10.52 MW	10.21 AW	21890 AAW	MABLS	10//99-12//99
	New Bedford PMSA, MA	S	8.98 MW	9.10 AW	18670 AAW	MABLS	10//99-12//99
	Michigan	S	9.14 MW	9.04 AW	18800 AAW	MIBLS	10//99-12//99
	Detroit PMSA, MI	S	8.92 MW	9.07 AW	18560 AAW	MIBLS	10//99-12//99
	Grand Rapids-Muskegon-Holland MSA, MI	S	9.58 MW	9.58 AW	19920 AAW	MIBLS	10//99-12//99
	Minnesota	S	8.6 MW	9.36 AW	19460 AAW	MNBLS	10//99-12//99
	Minneapolis-St. Paul MSA, MN-WI	S	9.35 MW	8.48 AW	19450 AAW	MNBLS	10//99-12//99
	Mississippi	S	9.59 MW	10.04 AW	20880 AAW	MSBLS	10//99-12//99
	Jackson MSA, MS	S	11.54 MW	11.73 AW	23990 AAW	MSBLS	10//99-12//99
	Missouri	S	8.03 MW	8.81 AW	18320 AAW	MOBLS	10//99-12//99
	Nebraska	S	9.45 MW	9.68 AW	20130 AAW	NEBLS	10//99-12//99
	Omaha MSA, NE-IA	S	9.53 MW	9.64 AW	19830 AAW	NEBLS	10//99-12//99
	New Hampshire	S	9.86 MW	10.10 AW	21010 AAW	NHBLS	10//99-12//99
	New Jersey	S	9.93 MW	11.36 AW	23620 AAW	NJBLS	10//99-12//99
	Bergen-Passaic PMSA, NJ	S	10.41 MW	9.73 AW	21660 AAW	NJBLS	10//99-12//99
	Jersey City PMSA, NJ	S	13.29 MW	14.98 AW	27650 AAW	NJBLS	10//99-12//99
	Middlesex-Somerset-Hunterdon PMSA, NJ	S	9.55 MW	9.35 AW	19860 AAW	NJBLS	10//99-12//99
	Monmouth-Ocean PMSA, NJ	S	8.97 MW	9.03 AW	18660 AAW	NJBLS	10//99-12//99
	New York	S	9.33 MW	10.39 AW	21620 AAW	NYBLS	10//99-12//99
	Albany-Schenectady-Troy MSA, NY	S	8.33 MW	8.10 AW	17320 AAW	NYBLS	10//99-12//99
	Buffalo-Niagara Falls MSA, NY	S	10.42 MW	8.40 AW	21680 AAW	NYBLS	10//99-12//99
	Nassau-Suffolk PMSA, NY	S	9.55 MW	9.28 AW	19850 AAW	NYBLS	10//99-12//99
	New York PMSA, NY	S	10.67 MW	9.47 AW	22200 AAW	NYBLS	10//99-12//99
	Syracuse MSA, NY	S	9.51 MW	9.63 AW	19780 AAW	NYBLS	10//99-12//99
	North Carolina	S	9.02 MW	9.40 AW	19550 AAW	NCBLS	10//99-12//99
	Charlotte-Gastonia-Rock Hill MSA, NC-SC	S	8.26 MW	7.87 AW	17180 AAW	NCBLS	10//99-12//99
	Greensboro--Winston-Salem--High Point MSA, NC	S	9.99 MW	9.61 AW	20780 AAW	NCBLS	10//99-12//99
	Hickory-Morganton-Lenoir MSA, NC	S	12.17 MW	11.91 AW	25300 AAW	NCBLS	10//99-12//99
	Raleigh-Durham-Chapel Hill MSA, NC	S	9.75 MW	8.45 AW	20290 AAW	NCBLS	10//99-12//99
	Rocky Mount MSA, NC	S	8.24 MW	7.56 AW	17140 AAW	NCBLS	10//99-12//99
	Ohio	S	9.89 MW	10.29 AW	21400 AAW	OHBLS	10//99-12//99
	Cincinnati PMSA, OH-KY-IN	S	10.33 MW	10.60 AW	21490 AAW	OHBLS	10//99-12//99
	Oklahoma	S	6.78 MW	6.96 AW	14480 AAW	OKBLS	10//99-12//99
	Tulsa MSA, OK	S	6.43 MW	6.28 AW	13380 AAW	OKBLS	10//99-12//99
	Oregon	S	9.45 MW	9.28 AW	19310 AAW	ORBLS	10//99-12//99
	Portland-Vancouver PMSA, OR-WA	S	9.41 MW	9.52 AW	19560 AAW	ORBLS	10//99-12//99
	Pennsylvania	S	9.74 MW	10.15 AW	21110 AAW	PABLS	10//99-12//99
	Allentown-Bethlehem-Easton MSA, PA	S	9.08 MW	8.10 AW	18880 AAW	PABLS	10//99-12//99
	Lancaster MSA, PA	S	10.73 MW	9.96 AW	22310 AAW	PABLS	10//99-12//99
	Philadelphia PMSA, PA-NJ	S	11.49 MW	11.28 AW	23900 AAW	PABLS	10//99-12//99
	Pittsburgh MSA, PA	S	10.55 MW	10.10 AW	21950 AAW	PABLS	10//99-12//99
	Reading MSA, PA	S	8.14 MW	7.73 AW	16930 AAW	PABLS	10//99-12//99

AAW	Average annual wage	AOH	Average offered, high	ASH	Average starting, high	H	Hourly	M	Monthly	S	Special: hourly and annual
AE	Average entry wage	AOL	Average offered, low	ASL	Average starting, low	HI	Highest wage paid	MTC	Median total compensation	TQ	Third quartile wage
AEX	Average experienced wage	APH	Average pay, high range	AW	Average wage paid	HR	High end range	MW	Median wage paid	W	Weekly
AO	Average offered	APL	Average pay, low range	FQ	First quartile wage	LR	Low end range	SQ	Second quartile wage	Y	Yearly

Occupation/Type/Industry	Location	Per	Low	Mid	High	Source	Date
Textile Cutting Machine Setter, Operator, and Tender	Scranton--Wilkes-Barre--Hazleton MSA, PA	S	9.77 MW	9.47 AW	20320 AAW	PABLS	10//99-12//99
	Rhode Island	S	9.58 MW	9.58 AW	19920 AAW	RIBLS	10//99-12//99
	Providence-Fall River-Warwick MSA, RI-MA	S	11.09 MW	11.04 AW	23060 AAW	RIBLS	10//99-12//99
	South Carolina	S	10.76 MW	10.97 AW	22810 AAW	SCBLS	10//99-12//99
	Greenville-Spartanburg-Anderson MSA, SC	S	11.27 MW	11.26 AW	23450 AAW	SCBLS	10//99-12//99
	South Dakota	S	9.63 MW	9.51 AW	19780 AAW	SDBLS	10//99-12//99
	Tennessee	S	8.14 MW	8.64 AW	17970 AAW	TNBLS	10//99-12//99
	Chattanooga MSA, TN-GA	S	7.55 MW	7.53 AW	15690 AAW	TNBLS	10//99-12//99
	Johnson City-Kingsport-Bristol MSA, TN-VA	S	8.73 MW	7.97 AW	18150 AAW	TNBLS	10//99-12//99
	Knoxville MSA, TN	S	9.80 MW	9.79 AW	20390 AAW	TNBLS	10//99-12//99
	Nashville MSA, TN	S	9.80 MW	9.87 AW	20390 AAW	TNBLS	10//99-12//99
	Texas	S	7.9 MW	8.12 AW	16890 AAW	TXBLS	10//99-12//99
	Dallas PMSA, TX	S	10.26 MW	10.23 AW	21350 AAW	TXBLS	10//99-12//99
	El Paso MSA, TX	S	7.40 MW	7.36 AW	15400 AAW	TXBLS	10//99-12//99
	Houston PMSA, TX	S	8.55 MW	7.94 AW	17790 AAW	TXBLS	10//99-12//99
	San Antonio MSA, TX	S	7.87 MW	7.85 AW	16360 AAW	TXBLS	10//99-12//99
	Virginia	S	8.7 MW	9.00 AW	18720 AAW	VABLS	10//99-12//99
	Norfolk-Virginia Beach-Newport News MSA, VA-NC	S	7.12 MW	7.31 AW	14810 AAW	VABLS	10//99-12//99
	Washington	S	9.55 MW	9.42 AW	19590 AAW	WABLS	10//99-12//99
	Seattle-Bellevue-Everett PMSA, WA	S	9.87 MW	9.81 AW	20530 AAW	WABLS	10//99-12//99
	West Virginia	S	11.75 MW	11.33 AW	23570 AAW	WVBLS	10//99-12//99
	Wisconsin	S	9.4 MW	9.35 AW	19450 AAW	WIBLS	10//99-12//99
	Milwaukee-Waukesha PMSA, WI	S	10.18 MW	10.38 AW	21180 AAW	WIBLS	10//99-12//99
	Puerto Rico	S	6.02 MW	5.90 AW	12270 AAW	PRBLS	10//99-12//99
	Caguas PMSA, PR	S	6.53 MW	6.58 AW	13570 AAW	PRBLS	10//99-12//99
	San Juan-Bayamon PMSA, PR	S	5.81 MW	5.96 AW	12080 AAW	PRBLS	10//99-12//99
Textile Knitting and Weaving Machine Setter, Operator, and Tender	Alabama	S	9.1 MW	9.21 AW	19150 AAW	ALBLS	10//99-12//99
	Arizona	S	11.09 MW	11.05 AW	22980 AAW	AZBLS	10//99-12//99
	California	S	6.72 MW	7.46 AW	15510 AAW	CABLS	10//99-12//99
	Los Angeles-Long Beach PMSA, CA	S	7.12 MW	6.56 AW	14810 AAW	CABLS	10//99-12//99
	Oakland PMSA, CA	S	8.35 MW	7.66 AW	17360 AAW	CABLS	10//99-12//99
	Orange County PMSA, CA	S	8.94 MW	9.17 AW	18590 AAW	CABLS	10//99-12//99
	Connecticut	S	8.05 MW	8.71 AW	18110 AAW	CTBLS	10//99-12//99
	Florida	S	9.11 MW	9.64 AW	20050 AAW	FLBLS	10//99-12//99
	Miami PMSA, FL	S	8.05 MW	7.98 AW	16750 AAW	FLBLS	10//99-12//99
	Georgia	S	11.19 MW	11.41 AW	23730 AAW	GABLS	10//99-12//99
	Atlanta MSA, GA	S	11.12 MW	10.47 AW	23120 AAW	GABLS	10//99-12//99
	Illinois	S	9.43 MW	10.34 AW	21510 AAW	ILBLS	10//99-12//99
	Chicago PMSA, IL	S	10.34 MW	9.43 AW	21510 AAW	ILBLS	10//99-12//99
	Indiana	S	12.09 MW	12.26 AW	25490 AAW	INBLS	10//99-12//99
	Iowa	S	10.5 MW	13.08 AW	27200 AAW	IABLS	10//99-12//99
	Kentucky	S	12.01 MW	11.72 AW	24380 AAW	KYBLS	10//99-12//99
	Maine	S	10.39 MW	10.69 AW	22230 AAW	MEBLS	10//99-12//99
	Maryland	S	7.63 MW	9.32 AW	19380 AAW	MDBLS	10//99-12//99
	Massachusetts	S	11.4 MW	11.01 AW	22910 AAW	MABLS	10//99-12//99
	Boston PMSA, MA-NH	S	9.51 MW	9.63 AW	19780 AAW	MABLS	10//99-12//99
	New Bedford PMSA, MA	S	11.17 MW	11.58 AW	23240 AAW	MABLS	10//99-12//99
	Worcester PMSA, MA-CT	S	12.60 MW	12.39 AW	26210 AAW	MABLS	10//99-12//99
	Michigan	S	12.36 MW	16.06 AW	33400 AAW	MIBLS	10//99-12//99
	Minnesota	S	7.65 MW	7.67 AW	15960 AAW	MNBLS	10//99-12//99
	Mississippi	S	8.23 MW	9.62 AW	20010 AAW	MSBLS	10//99-12//99
	New Hampshire	S	10.7 MW	10.94 AW	22750 AAW	NHBLS	10//99-12//99
	New Jersey	S	9.28 MW	9.59 AW	19940 AAW	NJBLS	10//99-12//99
	Bergen-Passaic PMSA, NJ	S	9.89 MW	9.82 AW	20570 AAW	NJBLS	10//99-12//99
	Jersey City PMSA, NJ	S	10.39 MW	9.25 AW	21610 AAW	NJBLS	10//99-12//99
	Newark PMSA, NJ	S	8.69 MW	9.10 AW	18080 AAW	NJBLS	10//99-12//99
	New York	S	7.86 MW	8.65 AW	17990 AAW	NYBLS	10//99-12//99

AAW Average annual wage	AOH Average offered, high	ASH Average starting, high	H Hourly	M Monthly	S Special: hourly and annual
AE Average entry wage	AOL Average offered, low	ASL Average starting, low	HI Highest wage paid	MTC Median total compensation	TQ Third quartile wage
AEX Average experienced wage	APH Average pay, high range	AW Average wage paid	HR High end range	MW Median wage paid	W Weekly
AO Average offered	APL Average pay, low range	FQ First quartile wage	LR Low end range	SQ Second quartile wage	Y Yearly

Occupation/Type/Industry	Location	Per	Low	Mid	High	Source	Date
Textile Knitting and Weaving Machine Setter, Operator, and Tender	Buffalo-Niagara Falls MSA, NY	S	8.22 MW	7.75 AW	17090 AAW	NYBLS	10//99-12//99
	New York PMSA, NY	S	8.51 MW	7.78 AW	17700 AAW	NYBLS	10//99-12//99
	North Carolina	S	9.82 MW	9.90 AW	20600 AAW	NCBLS	10//99-12//99
	Asheville MSA, NC	S	12.24 MW	14.01 AW	25470 AAW	NCBLS	10//99-12//99
	Charlotte-Gastonia-Rock Hill MSA, NC-SC	S	9.33 MW	9.29 AW	19400 AAW	NCBLS	10//99-12//99
	Greensboro--Winston-Salem--High Point MSA, NC	S	10.07 MW	9.91 AW	20940 AAW	NCBLS	10//99-12//99
	Hickory-Morganton-Lenoir MSA, NC	S	8.94 MW	9.00 AW	18590 AAW	NCBLS	10//99-12//99
	Raleigh-Durham-Chapel Hill MSA, NC	S	10.63 MW	9.75 AW	22100 AAW	NCBLS	10//99-12//99
	Rocky Mount MSA, NC	S	8.77 MW	8.45 AW	18250 AAW	NCBLS	10//99-12//99
	Ohio	S	10.08 MW	11.13 AW	23140 AAW	OHBLS	10//99-12//99
	Oklahoma	S	6.88 MW	6.74 AW	14010 AAW	OKBLS	10//99-12//99
	Oklahoma City MSA, OK	S	6.74 MW	6.88 AW	14010 AAW	OKBLS	10//99-12//99
	Pennsylvania	S	11.96 MW	11.86 AW	24660 AAW	PABLS	10//99-12//99
	Philadelphia PMSA, PA-NJ	S	11.85 MW	11.96 AW	24650 AAW	PABLS	10//99-12//99
	Reading MSA, PA	S	12.42 MW	13.59 AW	25840 AAW	PABLS	10//99-12//99
	Scranton--Wilkes-Barre--Hazleton MSA, PA	S	10.68 MW	10.13 AW	22220 AAW	PABLS	10//99-12//99
	York MSA, PA	S	10.10 MW	10.32 AW	21010 AAW	PABLS	10//99-12//99
	Rhode Island	S	6.57 MW	7.34 AW	15270 AAW	RIBLS	10//99-12//99
	Providence-Fall River-Warwick MSA, RI-MA	S	9.32 MW	9.82 AW	19380 AAW	RIBLS	10//99-12//99
	South Carolina	S	11.3 MW	11.31 AW	23530 AAW	SCBLS	10//99-12//99
	Greenville-Spartanburg-Anderson MSA, SC	S	11.61 MW	11.57 AW	24140 AAW	SCBLS	10//99-12//99
	Tennessee	S	9.57 MW	9.59 AW	19950 AAW	TNBLS	10//99-12//99
	Chattanooga MSA, TN-GA	S	10.40 MW	10.26 AW	21640 AAW	TNBLS	10//99-12//99
	Johnson City-Kingsport-Bristol MSA, TN-VA	S	8.79 MW	8.31 AW	18270 AAW	TNBLS	10//99-12//99
	Texas	S	8.81 MW	8.55 AW	17790 AAW	TXBLS	10//99-12//99
	Dallas PMSA, TX	S	8.02 MW	7.71 AW	16670 AAW	TXBLS	10//99-12//99
	Virginia	S	9.65 MW	9.78 AW	20340 AAW	VABLS	10//99-12//99
	Washington	S	10.03 MW	10.18 AW	21170 AAW	WABLS	10//99-12//99
	West Virginia	S	11.65 MW	11.20 AW	23300 AAW	WVBLS	10//99-12//99
	Wisconsin	S	11.55 MW	13.51 AW	28110 AAW	WIBLS	10//99-12//99
	Milwaukee-Waukesha PMSA, WI	S	9.31 MW	9.50 AW	19360 AAW	WIBLS	10//99-12//99
Textile Winding, Twisting, and Drawing Out Machine Setter, Operator, and Tender	Alabama	S	9.74 MW	9.74 AW	20250 AAW	ALBLS	10//99-12//99
	California	S	9.03 MW	8.93 AW	18580 AAW	CABLS	10//99-12//99
	Los Angeles-Long Beach PMSA, CA	S	8.95 MW	9.04 AW	18610 AAW	CABLS	10//99-12//99
	Orange County PMSA, CA	S	6.87 MW	6.45 AW	14290 AAW	CABLS	10//99-12//99
	Connecticut	S	7.52 MW	7.38 AW	15350 AAW	CTBLS	10//99-12//99
	Delaware	S	15.4 MW	15.49 AW	32210 AAW	DEBLS	10//99-12//99
	Florida	S	9.98 MW	10.85 AW	22570 AAW	FLBLS	10//99-12//99
	Miami PMSA, FL	S	9.17 MW	9.33 AW	19080 AAW	FLBLS	10//99-12//99
	Georgia	S	9.72 MW	9.72 AW	20220 AAW	GABLS	10//99-12//99
	Atlanta MSA, GA	S	10.26 MW	11.23 AW	21350 AAW	GABLS	10//99-12//99
	Kentucky	S	9.6 MW	9.49 AW	19740 AAW	KYBLS	10//99-12//99
	Maine	S	10.1 MW	10.21 AW	21230 AAW	MEBLS	10//99-12//99
	Massachusetts	S	9.24 MW	9.38 AW	19500 AAW	MABLS	10//99-12//99
	Boston PMSA, MA-NH	S	8.36 MW	7.69 AW	17380 AAW	MABLS	10//99-12//99
	New Bedford PMSA, MA	S	9.68 MW	9.70 AW	20140 AAW	MABLS	10//99-12//99
	Springfield MSA, MA	S	9.55 MW	9.36 AW	19860 AAW	MABLS	10//99-12//99
	Worcester PMSA, MA-CT	S	9.61 MW	9.61 AW	20000 AAW	MABLS	10//99-12//99
	Michigan	S	8.66 MW	8.82 AW	18350 AAW	MIBLS	10//99-12//99
	Mississippi	S	10.6 MW	10.29 AW	21400 AAW	MSBLS	10//99-12//99
	Missouri	S	12.08 MW	11.78 AW	24500 AAW	MOBLS	10//99-12//99
	New Hampshire	S	9.63 MW	9.57 AW	19910 AAW	NHBLS	10//99-12//99
	New Jersey	S	11.01 MW	10.57 AW	21990 AAW	NJBLS	10//99-12//99
	Bergen-Passaic PMSA, NJ	S	11.15 MW	11.71 AW	23180 AAW	NJBLS	10//99-12//99
	New York	S	8.44 MW	8.58 AW	17840 AAW	NYBLS	10//99-12//99

AAW	Average annual wage	AOH	Average offered, high	ASH	Average starting, high
AE	Average entry wage	AOL	Average offered, low	ASL	Average starting, low
AEX	Average experienced wage	APH	Average pay, high range	AW	Average wage paid
AO	Average offered	APL	Average pay, low range	FQ	First quartile wage

H	Hourly	M	Monthly
HI	Highest wage paid	MTC	Median total compensation
HR	High end range	MW	Median wage paid
LR	Low end range	SQ	Second quartile wage

S	Special: hourly and annual
TQ	Third quartile wage
W	Weekly
Y	Yearly

Occupation/Type/Industry	Location	Per	Low	Mid	High	Source	Date
Textile Winding, Twisting, and Drawing Out Machine Setter, Operator, and Tender	New York PMSA, NY	S	8.63 MW	8.31 AW	17940 AAW	NYBLS	10//99-12//99
	North Carolina	S	10.07 MW	10.48 AW	21800 AAW	NCBLS	10//99-12//99
	Charlotte-Gastonia-Rock Hill MSA, NC-SC	S	9.04 MW	9.11 AW	18800 AAW	NCBLS	10//99-12//99
	Greensboro--Winston-Salem--High Point MSA, NC	S	10.25 MW	10.28 AW	21320 AAW	NCBLS	10//99-12//99
	Hickory-Morganton-Lenoir MSA, NC	S	9.98 MW	9.56 AW	20760 AAW	NCBLS	10//99-12//99
	Raleigh-Durham-Chapel Hill MSA, NC	S	12.32 MW	12.47 AW	25630 AAW	NCBLS	10//99-12//99
	Rocky Mount MSA, NC	S	8.30 MW	8.19 AW	17260 AAW	NCBLS	10//99-12//99
	Ohio	S	9.42 MW	9.21 AW	19150 AAW	OHBLS	10//99-12//99
	Pennsylvania	S	7.57 MW	7.96 AW	16550 AAW	PABLS	10//99-12//99
	Philadelphia PMSA, PA-NJ	S	7.48 MW	6.50 AW	15550 AAW	PABLS	10//99-12//99
	Scranton--Wilkes-Barre--Hazleton MSA, PA	S	7.58 MW	7.65 AW	15770 AAW	PABLS	10//99-12//99
	Rhode Island	S	8.17 MW	8.24 AW	17140 AAW	RIBLS	10//99-12//99
	Providence-Fall River-Warwick MSA, RI-MA	S	8.91 MW	9.15 AW	18530 AAW	RIBLS	10//99-12//99
	South Carolina	S	10.18 MW	10.56 AW	21970 AAW	SCBLS	10//99-12//99
	Greenville-Spartanburg-Anderson MSA, SC	S	10.62 MW	10.17 AW	22090 AAW	SCBLS	10//99-12//99
	Tennessee	S	9.69 MW	9.75 AW	20290 AAW	TNBLS	10//99-12//99
	Chattanooga MSA, TN-GA	S	8.98 MW	9.20 AW	18680 AAW	TNBLS	10//99-12//99
	Texas	S	8.91 MW	8.86 AW	18430 AAW	TXBLS	10//99-12//99
	Virginia	S	10.24 MW	10.86 AW	22590 AAW	VABLS	10//99-12//99
	Washington	S	9.9 MW	9.96 AW	20710 AAW	WABLS	10//99-12//99
	Bellingham MSA, WA	S	10.11 MW	10.08 AW	21020 AAW	WABLS	10//99-12//99
	Wisconsin	S	12.34 MW	13.73 AW	28560 AAW	WIBLS	10//99-12//99
	Milwaukee-Waukesha PMSA, WI	S	10.79 MW	10.47 AW	22440 AAW	WIBLS	10//99-12//99
Tile and Marble Setter	Alabama	S	14.53 MW	14.70 AW	30570 AAW	ALBLS	10//99-12//99
	Arizona	S	12.48 MW	12.52 AW	26050 AAW	AZBLS	10//99-12//99
	Tucson MSA, AZ	S	12.19 MW	12.01 AW	25360 AAW	AZBLS	10//99-12//99
	Arkansas	S	9.47 MW	9.14 AW	19000 AAW	ARBLS	10//99-12//99
	California	S	21.89 MW	21.14 AW	43960 AAW	CABLS	10//99-12//99
	Los Angeles-Long Beach PMSA, CA	S	16.68 MW	15.91 AW	34690 AAW	CABLS	10//99-12//99
	Orange County PMSA, CA	S	20.10 MW	21.88 AW	41810 AAW	CABLS	10//99-12//99
	Riverside-San Bernardino PMSA, CA	S	19.97 MW	18.48 AW	41550 AAW	CABLS	10//99-12//99
	San Diego MSA, CA	S	22.99 MW	23.60 AW	47810 AAW	CABLS	10//99-12//99
	San Jose PMSA, CA	S	20.43 MW	21.67 AW	42490 AAW	CABLS	10//99-12//99
	Vallejo-Fairfield-Napa PMSA, CA	S	26.71 MW	26.22 AW	55570 AAW	CABLS	10//99-12//99
	Denver PMSA, CO	S	18.12 MW	18.93 AW	37680 AAW	COBLS	10//99-12//99
	Connecticut	S	20.3 MW	20.50 AW	42630 AAW	CTBLS	10//99-12//99
	Washington PMSA, DC-MD-VA-WV	S	14.74 MW	14.96 AW	30650 AAW	DCBLS	10//99-12//99
	Florida	S	12.59 MW	12.46 AW	25930 AAW	FLBLS	10//99-12//99
	Fort Myers-Cape Coral MSA, FL	S	13.13 MW	12.69 AW	27320 AAW	FLBLS	10//99-12//99
	Jacksonville MSA, FL	S	11.78 MW	12.34 AW	24490 AAW	FLBLS	10//99-12//99
	Tampa-St. Petersburg-Clearwater MSA, FL	S	11.17 MW	10.61 AW	23240 AAW	FLBLS	10//99-12//99
	West Palm Beach-Boca Raton MSA, FL	S	13.91 MW	13.83 AW	28940 AAW	FLBLS	10//99-12//99
	Georgia	S	19.14 MW	19.21 AW	39950 AAW	GABLS	10//99-12//99
	Hawaii	S	33.23 MW	30.56 AW	63570 AAW	HIBLS	10//99-12//99
	Honolulu MSA, HI	S	31.53 MW	35.46 AW	65590 AAW	HIBLS	10//99-12//99
	Illinois	S	22.01 MW	19.35 AW	40240 AAW	ILBLS	10//99-12//99
	Chicago PMSA, IL	S	18.98 MW	21.21 AW	39480 AAW	ILBLS	10//99-12//99
	Indiana	S	17.63 MW	16.22 AW	33740 AAW	INBLS	10//99-12//99
	Kansas	S	15.83 MW	16.08 AW	33450 AAW	KSBLS	10//99-12//99
	Kentucky	S	18.96 MW	18.37 AW	38220 AAW	KYBLS	10//99-12//99
	Louisville MSA, KY-IN	S	16.73 MW	18.46 AW	34800 AAW	KYBLS	10//99-12//99
	Louisiana	S	14.86 MW	14.38 AW	29910 AAW	LABLS	10//99-12//99
	New Orleans MSA, LA	S	16.02 MW	15.94 AW	33320 AAW	LABLS	10//99-12//99
	Maryland	S	15.51 MW	15.33 AW	31890 AAW	MDBLS	10//99-12//99

AAW	Average annual wage	AOH	Average offered, high	ASH	Average starting, high
AE	Average entry wage	AOL	Average offered, low	ASL	Average starting, low
AEX	Average experienced wage	APH	Average pay, high range	AW	Average wage paid
AO	Average offered	APL	Average pay, low range	FQ	First quartile wage

H	Hourly	M	Monthly
HI	Highest wage paid	MTC	Median total compensation
HR	High end range	MW	Median wage paid
LR	Low end range	SQ	Second quartile wage

S	Special: hourly and annual
TQ	Third quartile wage
W	Weekly
Y	Yearly

Occupation/Type/Industry	Location	Per	Low	Mid	High	Source	Date
Tile and Marble Setter	Massachusetts	S	23.89 MW	21.93 AW	45610 AAW	MABLS	10//99-12//99
	Michigan	S	23.09 MW	21.31 AW	44330 AAW	MIBLS	10//99-12//99
	Kalamazoo-Battle Creek MSA, MI	S	19.69 MW	19.89 AW	40950 AAW	MIBLS	10//99-12//99
	Minnesota	S	21.41 MW	20.75 AW	43160 AAW	MNBLS	10//99-12//99
	Minneapolis-St. Paul MSA, MN-WI	S	20.51 MW	21.36 AW	42650 AAW	MNBLS	10//99-12//99
	Mississippi	S	10.62 MW	11.19 AW	23270 AAW	MSBLS	10//99-12//99
	Missouri	S	18.88 MW	18.57 AW	38630 AAW	MOBLS	10//99-12//99
	St. Louis MSA, MO-IL	S	18.05 MW	18.51 AW	37550 AAW	MOBLS	10//99-12//99
	Montana	S	12.92 MW	14.55 AW	30260 AAW	MTBLS	10//99-12//99
	Nebraska	S	18.66 MW	17.87 AW	37180 AAW	NEBLS	10//99-12//99
	Omaha MSA, NE-IA	S	18.28 MW	18.82 AW	38020 AAW	NEBLS	10//99-12//99
	Nevada	S	15.41 MW	16.74 AW	34810 AAW	NVBLS	10//99-12//99
	Las Vegas MSA, NV-AZ	S	16.43 MW	15.16 AW	34170 AAW	NVBLS	10//99-12//99
	Reno MSA, NV	S	16.31 MW	15.42 AW	33930 AAW	NVBLS	10//99-12//99
	New Jersey	S	28.42 MW	27.20 AW	56580 AAW	NJBLS	10//99-12//99
	New York	S	17.37 MW	20.01 AW	41610 AAW	NYBLS	10//99-12//99
	Binghamton MSA, NY	S	19.26 MW	19.25 AW	40060 AAW	NYBLS	10//99-12//99
	Nassau-Suffolk PMSA, NY	S	27.86 MW	29.77 AW	57940 AAW	NYBLS	10//99-12//99
	New York PMSA, NY	S	15.31 MW	15.50 AW	31840 AAW	NYBLS	10//99-12//99
	North Carolina	S	13.86 MW	15.39 AW	32020 AAW	NCBLS	10//99-12//99
	Charlotte-Gastonia-Rock Hill MSA, NC-SC	S	18.61 MW	14.56 AW	38720 AAW	NCBLS	10//99-12//99
	Ohio	S	18.58 MW	17.79 AW	37010 AAW	OHBLS	10//99-12//99
	Cleveland-Lorain-Elyria PMSA, OH	S	16.11 MW	14.92 AW	33520 AAW	OHBLS	10//99-12//99
	Oklahoma	S	16.36 MW	15.23 AW	31680 AAW	OKBLS	10//99-12//99
	Oklahoma City MSA, OK	S	14.42 MW	14.95 AW	29990 AAW	OKBLS	10//99-12//99
	Oregon	S	14.1 MW	16.58 AW	34490 AAW	ORBLS	10//99-12//99
	Portland-Vancouver PMSA, OR-WA	S	20.07 MW	16.60 AW	41750 AAW	ORBLS	10//99-12//99
	Pennsylvania	S	21.91 MW	19.71 AW	40990 AAW	PABLS	10//99-12//99
	Philadelphia PMSA, PA-NJ	S	22.68 MW	24.01 AW	47170 AAW	PABLS	10//99-12//99
	South Carolina	S	12.81 MW	13.76 AW	28620 AAW	SCBLS	10//99-12//99
	Tennessee	S	12.51 MW	12.68 AW	26370 AAW	TNBLS	10//99-12//99
	Texas	S	10.58 MW	11.49 AW	23910 AAW	TXBLS	10//99-12//99
	Beaumont-Port Arthur MSA, TX	S	8.91 MW	8.09 AW	18530 AAW	TXBLS	10//99-12//99
	Dallas PMSA, TX	S	16.43 MW	16.06 AW	34170 AAW	TXBLS	10//99-12//99
	Houston PMSA, TX	S	10.33 MW	9.33 AW	21480 AAW	TXBLS	10//99-12//99
	Virginia	S	16.07 MW	16.62 AW	34570 AAW	VABLS	10//99-12//99
	Norfolk-Virginia Beach-Newport News MSA, VA-NC	S	18.45 MW	16.30 AW	38380 AAW	VABLS	10//99-12//99
	Washington	S	20.5 MW	20.68 AW	43020 AAW	WABLS	10//99-12//99
	Seattle-Bellevue-Everett PMSA, WA	S	20.93 MW	21.21 AW	43530 AAW	WABLS	10//99-12//99
	West Virginia	S	18.67 MW	21.02 AW	43710 AAW	WVBLS	10//99-12//99
	Wisconsin	S	18.33 MW	18.96 AW	39440 AAW	WIBLS	10//99-12//99
	Puerto Rico	S	9.51 MW	11.05 AW	22990 AAW	PRBLS	10//99-12//99
Timing Device Assembler, Adjuster, and Calibrator	California	S	9.25 MW	10.84 AW	22540 AAW	CABLS	10//99-12//99
	Connecticut	S	15.39 MW	15.24 AW	31690 AAW	CTBLS	10//99-12//99
	Florida	S	7.89 MW	8.09 AW	16830 AAW	FLBLS	10//99-12//99
	Indiana	S	13.63 MW	12.84 AW	26710 AAW	INBLS	10//99-12//99
	Iowa	S	10.68 MW	10.47 AW	21790 AAW	IABLS	10//99-12//99
	Massachusetts	S	8.26 MW	9.53 AW	19810 AAW	MABLS	10//99-12//99
	Michigan	S	9.76 MW	10.06 AW	20920 AAW	MIBLS	10//99-12//99
	Minnesota	S	12.16 MW	12.15 AW	25260 AAW	MNBLS	10//99-12//99
	Nebraska	S	18.55 MW	17.17 AW	35720 AAW	NEBLS	10//99-12//99
	New York	S	9.9 MW	11.35 AW	23600 AAW	NYBLS	10//99-12//99
	North Carolina	S	11.76 MW	11.42 AW	23750 AAW	NCBLS	10//99-12//99
	Oklahoma	S	9.25 MW	9.20 AW	19150 AAW	OKBLS	10//99-12//99
	Pennsylvania	S	7.71 MW	8.79 AW	18270 AAW	PABLS	10//99-12//99
	Texas	S	12 MW	12.26 AW	25500 AAW	TXBLS	10//99-12//99
	Virginia	S	12.71 MW	12.94 AW	26920 AAW	VABLS	10//99-12//99
	Washington	S	10.62 MW	12.44 AW	25870 AAW	WABLS	10//99-12//99
Tire Builder	Alabama	S	19.14 MW	19.83 AW	41250 AAW	ALBLS	10//99-12//99
	Arkansas	S	16.09 MW	17.23 AW	35840 AAW	ARBLS	10//99-12//99

AAW	Average annual wage	AOH	Average offered, high	ASH	Average starting, high	H	Hourly	M	Monthly	S	Special: hourly and annual
AE	Average entry salaries	AOL	Average offered, low	ASL	Average starting, low	HI	Highest wage paid	MTC	Median total compensation	TQ	Third quartile wage
AEX	Average experienced wage	APH	Average pay, high range	AW	Average wage paid	HR	High end range	MW	Median wage paid	W	Weekly
AO	Average offered	APL	Average pay, low range	FQ	First quartile wage	LR	Low end range	SQ	Second quartile wage	Y	Yearly

Occupation/Type/Industry	Location	Per	Low	Mid	High	Source	Date
Tire Builder	Georgia	S	14.07 mw	14.09 aw	29310 aaw	GABLS	10//99-12//99
	North Carolina	S	17.52 mw	16.66 aw	34650 aaw	NCBLS	10//99-12//99
	Tennessee	S	17.01 mw	16.73 aw	34790 aaw	TNBLS	10//99-12//99
	Virginia	S	19.37 mw	19.72 aw	41010 aaw	VABLS	10//99-12//99
Tire Repairer and Changer	Alabama	S	7.64 mw	8.04 aw	16730 aaw	ALBLS	10//99-12//99
	Auburn-Opelika MSA, AL	S	8.92 mw	9.11 aw	18550 aaw	ALBLS	10//99-12//99
	Birmingham MSA, AL	S	8.81 mw	8.06 aw	18330 aaw	ALBLS	10//99-12//99
	Dothan MSA, AL	S	8.81 mw	8.75 aw	18320 aaw	ALBLS	10//99-12//99
	Florence MSA, AL	S	9.09 mw	9.29 aw	18910 aaw	ALBLS	10//99-12//99
	Huntsville MSA, AL	S	7.61 mw	7.37 aw	15820 aaw	ALBLS	10//99-12//99
	Mobile MSA, AL	S	6.66 mw	6.33 aw	13840 aaw	ALBLS	10//99-12//99
	Montgomery MSA, AL	S	9.73 mw	8.22 aw	20240 aaw	ALBLS	10//99-12//99
	Tuscaloosa MSA, AL	S	8.36 mw	8.75 aw	17390 aaw	ALBLS	10//99-12//99
	Alaska	S	9.52 mw	9.86 aw	20500 aaw	AKBLS	10//99-12//99
	Anchorage MSA, AK	S	8.94 mw	8.67 aw	18590 aaw	AKBLS	10//99-12//99
	Arizona	S	7.82 mw	8.00 aw	16650 aaw	AZBLS	10//99-12//99
	Flagstaff MSA, AZ-UT	S	8.35 mw	7.82 aw	17380 aaw	AZBLS	10//99-12//99
	Phoenix-Mesa MSA, AZ	S	8.03 mw	7.88 aw	16700 aaw	AZBLS	10//99-12//99
	Tucson MSA, AZ	S	8.31 mw	8.08 aw	17280 aaw	AZBLS	10//99-12//99
	Yuma MSA, AZ	S	6.96 mw	7.14 aw	14480 aaw	AZBLS	10//99-12//99
	Arkansas	S	7.92 mw	8.11 aw	16860 aaw	ARBLS	10//99-12//99
	Fayetteville-Springdale-Rogers MSA, AR	S	8.93 mw	8.39 aw	18570 aaw	ARBLS	10//99-12//99
	Fort Smith MSA, AR-OK	S	7.87 mw	7.82 aw	16360 aaw	ARBLS	10//99-12//99
	Little Rock-North Little Rock MSA, AR		8.27 mw	8.14 aw	17190 aaw	ARBLS	10//99-12//99
	Pine Bluff MSA, AR	S	7.78 mw	7.62 aw	16170 aaw	ARBLS	10//99-12//99
	California	S	8.4 mw	9.18 aw	19100 aaw	CABLS	10//99-12//99
	Bakersfield MSA, CA	S	9.08 mw	8.13 aw	18890 aaw	CABLS	10//99-12//99
	Fresno MSA, CA	S	8.17 mw	6.86 aw	17000 aaw	CABLS	10//99-12//99
	Los Angeles-Long Beach PMSA, CA	S	9.14 mw	8.30 aw	19010 aaw	CABLS	10//99-12//99
	Modesto MSA, CA	S	9.61 mw	8.45 aw	19980 aaw	CABLS	10//99-12//99
	Oakland PMSA, CA	S	10.39 mw	10.05 aw	21600 aaw	CABLS	10//99-12//99
	Orange County PMSA, CA	S	9.74 mw	8.72 aw	20260 aaw	CABLS	10//99-12//99
	Riverside-San Bernardino PMSA, CA	S	9.73 mw	8.90 aw	20230 aaw	CABLS	10//99-12//99
	Sacramento PMSA, CA	S	7.71 mw	7.27 aw	16040 aaw	CABLS	10//99-12//99
	Salinas MSA, CA	S	9.84 mw	9.89 aw	20470 aaw	CABLS	10//99-12//99
	San Diego MSA, CA	S	8.48 mw	7.32 aw	17650 aaw	CABLS	10//99-12//99
	San Francisco PMSA, CA	S	10.41 mw	9.66 aw	21660 aaw	CABLS	10//99-12//99
	San Jose PMSA, CA	S	9.82 mw	9.24 aw	20420 aaw	CABLS	10//99-12//99
	Santa Barbara-Santa Maria-Lompoc MSA, CA	S	9.35 mw	8.25 aw	19460 aaw	CABLS	10//99-12//99
	Santa Cruz-Watsonville PMSA, CA	S	8.94 mw	7.99 aw	18600 aaw	CABLS	10//99-12//99
	Santa Rosa PMSA, CA	S	10.95 mw	11.13 aw	22770 aaw	CABLS	10//99-12//99
	Stockton-Lodi MSA, CA	S	8.22 mw	7.71 aw	17090 aaw	CABLS	10//99-12//99
	Vallejo-Fairfield-Napa PMSA, CA	S	8.97 mw	8.32 aw	18650 aaw	CABLS	10//99-12//99
	Ventura PMSA, CA	S	9.75 mw	9.48 aw	20270 aaw	CABLS	10//99-12//99
	Visalia-Tulare-Porterville MSA, CA	S	8.34 mw	8.14 aw	17340 aaw	CABLS	10//99-12//99
	Yolo PMSA, CA	S	10.23 mw	10.29 aw	21280 aaw	CABLS	10//99-12//99
	Colorado	S	8.65 mw	9.12 aw	18980 aaw	COBLS	10//99-12/
	Colorado Springs MSA, CO	S	9.79 mw	8.37 aw	20360 aaw	COBLS	10//99-12/
	Denver PMSA, CO	S	9.32 mw	9.17 aw	19380 aaw	COBLS	10//99-12/
	Grand Junction MSA, CO	S	8.95 mw	8.46 aw	18620 aaw	COBLS	10//99-12/
	Greeley PMSA, CO	S	9.27 mw	9.25 aw	19280 aaw	COBLS	10//99-12/
	Pueblo MSA, CO	S	8.01 mw	7.79 aw	16670 aaw	COBLS	10//99-12/
	Connecticut	S	7.72 mw	8.29 aw	17240 aaw	CTBLS	10//99-12/
	Bridgeport PMSA, CT	S	9.51 mw	8.22 aw	19790 aaw	CTBLS	10//99-12/
	Danbury PMSA, CT	S	8.17 mw	7.91 aw	17000 aaw	CTBLS	10//99-12/
	Hartford MSA, CT	S	7.41 mw	7.04 aw	15400 aaw	CTBLS	10//99-12/
	New Haven-Meriden PMSA, CT	S	8.08 mw	7.73 aw	16800 aaw	CTBLS	10//99-12//99
	Delaware	S	7.86 mw	8.22 aw	17100 aaw	DEBLS	10//99-12//99
	Dover MSA, DE	S	7.89 mw	7.84 aw	16420 aaw	DEBLS	10//99-12//99
	Wilmington-Newark PMSA, DE-MD	S	8.39 mw	7.94 aw	17440 aaw	DEBLS	10//99-12//99
	Washington PMSA, DC-MD-VA-WV	S	11.51 mw	9.24 aw	23930 aaw	DCBLS	10//99-12//99

AAW Average annual wage	**AOH** Average offered, high	**ASH** Average starting, high	**H** Hourly	**M** Monthly	**S** Special: hourly and annual
AE Average entry wage	**AOL** Average offered, low	**ASL** Average starting, low	**HI** Highest wage paid	**MTC** Median total compensation	**TQ** Third quartile wage
AEX Average experienced wage	**APH** Average pay, high range	**AW** Average wage paid	**HR** High end range	**MW** Median wage paid	**W** Weekly
AO Average offered	**APL** Average pay, low range	**FQ** First quartile wage	**LR** Low end range	**SQ** Second quartile wage	**Y** Yearly

Occupation/Type/Industry	Location	Per	Low	Mid	High	Source	Date
Tire Repairer and Changer	Florida	S	8.18 MW	8.44 AW	17550 AAW	FLBLS	10//99-12//99
	Daytona Beach MSA, FL	S	7.75 MW	7.68 AW	16120 AAW	FLBLS	10//99-12//99
	Fort Lauderdale PMSA, FL	S	9.06 MW	8.49 AW	18840 AAW	FLBLS	10//99-12//99
	Fort Myers-Cape Coral MSA, FL	S	8.20 MW	7.80 AW	17060 AAW	FLBLS	10//99-12//99
	Jacksonville MSA, FL	S	8.41 MW	8.16 AW	17490 AAW	FLBLS	10//99-12//99
	Lakeland-Winter Haven MSA, FL	S	8.53 MW	8.21 AW	17750 AAW	FLBLS	10//99-12//99
	Melbourne-Titusville-Palm Bay MSA, FL	S	8.21 MW	7.85 AW	17090 AAW	FLBLS	10//99-12//99
	Miami PMSA, FL	S	9.32 MW	9.87 AW	19380 AAW	FLBLS	10//99-12//99
	Ocala MSA, FL	S	9.17 MW	9.15 AW	19060 AAW	FLBLS	10//99-12//99
	Orlando MSA, FL	S	8.23 MW	7.92 AW	17110 AAW	FLBLS	10//99-12//99
	Panama City MSA, FL	S	6.47 MW	6.40 AW	13460 AAW	FLBLS	10//99-12//99
	Pensacola MSA, FL	S	6.65 MW	6.03 AW	13830 AAW	FLBLS	10//99-12//99
	Punta Gorda MSA, FL	S	9.77 MW	9.47 AW	20320 AAW	FLBLS	10//99-12//99
	Sarasota-Bradenton MSA, FL	S	8.47 MW	8.29 AW	17630 AAW	FLBLS	10//99-12//99
	Tallahassee MSA, FL	S	8.20 MW	7.90 AW	17050 AAW	FLBLS	10//99-12//99
	Tampa-St. Petersburg-Clearwater MSA, FL	S	8.41 MW	8.26 AW	17490 AAW	FLBLS	10//99-12//99
	West Palm Beach-Boca Raton MSA, FL	S	9.07 MW	8.84 AW	18870 AAW	FLBLS	10//99-12//99
	Georgia	S	9.05 MW	9.12 AW	18970 AAW	GABLS	10//99-12//99
	Albany MSA, GA	S	7.69 MW	7.55 AW	16000 AAW	GABLS	10//99-12//99
	Atlanta MSA, GA	S	9.71 MW	9.58 AW	20200 AAW	GABLS	10//99-12//99
	Augusta-Aiken MSA, GA-SC	S	8.84 MW	9.00 AW	18380 AAW	GABLS	10//99-12//99
	Columbus MSA, GA-AL	S	8.27 MW	8.21 AW	17190 AAW	GABLS	10//99-12//99
	Macon MSA, GA	S	8.56 MW	8.46 AW	17800 AAW	GABLS	10//99-12//99
	Hawaii	S	10.84 MW	10.82 AW	22510 AAW	HIBLS	10//99-12//99
	Honolulu MSA, HI	S	11.39 MW	11.24 AW	23700 AAW	HIBLS	10//99-12//99
	Idaho	S	8.77 MW	9.16 AW	19050 AAW	IDBLS	10//99-12//99
	Boise City MSA, ID	S	10.07 MW	9.91 AW	20950 AAW	IDBLS	10//99-12//99
	Pocatello MSA, ID	S	8.85 MW	8.58 AW	18400 AAW	IDBLS	10//99-12//99
	Illinois	S	9.11 MW	9.55 AW	19870 AAW	ILBLS	10//99-12//99
	Bloomington-Normal MSA, IL	S	8.49 MW	7.92 AW	17650 AAW	ILBLS	10//99-12//99
	Chicago PMSA, IL	S	9.52 MW	9.12 AW	19810 AAW	ILBLS	10//99-12//99
	Peoria-Pekin MSA, IL	S	10.18 MW	9.32 AW	21180 AAW	ILBLS	10//99-12//99
	Rockford MSA, IL	S	10.31 MW	10.62 AW	21440 AAW	ILBLS	10//99-12//99
	Indiana	S	8.84 MW	9.53 AW	19820 AAW	INBLS	10//99-12//99
	Bloomington MSA, IN	S	8.27 MW	8.04 AW	17200 AAW	INBLS	10//99-12//99
	Elkhart-Goshen MSA, IN	S	12.22 MW	13.55 AW	25410 AAW	INBLS	10//99-12//99
	Evansville-Henderson MSA, IN-KY	S	7.27 MW	6.96 AW	15120 AAW	INBLS	10//99-12//99
	Fort Wayne MSA, IN	S	8.75 MW	8.29 AW	18200 AAW	INBLS	10//99-12//99
	Gary PMSA, IN	S	9.41 MW	8.35 AW	19560 AAW	INBLS	10//99-12//99
	Indianapolis MSA, IN	S	11.16 MW	10.75 AW	23220 AAW	INBLS	10//99-12//99
	Kokomo MSA, IN	S	8.05 MW	7.80 AW	16730 AAW	INBLS	10//99-12//99
	Lafayette MSA, IN	S	8.28 MW	8.02 AW	17230 AAW	INBLS	10//99-12//99
	Muncie MSA, IN	S	8.75 MW	8.13 AW	18200 AAW	INBLS	10//99-12//99
	South Bend MSA, IN	S	9.04 MW	8.66 AW	18800 AAW	INBLS	10//99-12//99
	Terre Haute MSA, IN	S	8.61 MW	8.24 AW	17900 AAW	INBLS	10//99-12//99
	Iowa	S	7.87 MW	8.39 AW	17460 AAW	IABLS	10//99-12//99
	Cedar Rapids MSA, IA	S	10.18 MW	10.11 AW	21180 AAW	IABLS	10//99-12//99
	Davenport-Moline-Rock Island MSA, IA-IL	S	9.99 MW	9.17 AW	20780 AAW	IABLS	10//99-12//99
	Des Moines MSA, IA	S	7.30 MW	6.82 AW	15190 AAW	IABLS	10//99-12//99
	Sioux City MSA, IA-NE	S	8.75 MW	7.96 AW	18210 AAW	IABLS	10//99-12//99
	Kansas	S	8.16 MW	8.39 AW	17450 AAW	KSBLS	10//99-12//99
	Lawrence MSA, KS	S	8.49 MW	8.16 AW	17650 AAW	KSBLS	10//99-12//99
	Topeka MSA, KS	S	9.26 MW	9.36 AW	19270 AAW	KSBLS	10//99-12//99
	Wichita MSA, KS	S	8.78 MW	8.82 AW	18260 AAW	KSBLS	10//99-12//99
	Kentucky	S	8.61 MW	9.32 AW	19390 AAW	KYBLS	10//99-12//99
	Lexington MSA, KY	S	8.97 MW	8.87 AW	18660 AAW	KYBLS	10//99-12//99
	Louisville MSA, KY-IN	S	10.31 MW	9.54 AW	21440 AAW	KYBLS	10//99-12//99
	Owensboro MSA, KY	S	8.08 MW	7.83 AW	16810 AAW	KYBLS	10//99-12//99
	Louisiana	S	7.63 MW	7.98 AW	16600 AAW	LABLS	10//99-12//99
	Alexandria MSA, LA	S	7.00 MW	6.77 AW	14560 AAW	LABLS	10//99-12//99
	Baton Rouge MSA, LA	S	7.94 MW	7.32 AW	16520 AAW	LABLS	10//99-12//99
	Houma MSA, LA	S	7.66 MW	7.64 AW	15930 AAW	LABLS	10//99-12//99
	Lafayette MSA, LA	S	7.92 MW	6.85 AW	16470 AAW	LABLS	10//99-12//99
	Lake Charles MSA, LA	S	9.02 MW	9.06 AW	18760 AAW	LABLS	10//99-12//99
	Monroe MSA, LA	S	8.11 MW	8.00 AW	16870 AAW	LABLS	10//99-12//99

AAW Average annual wage	**AOH** Average offered, high	**ASH** Average starting, high	**H** Hourly	**M** Monthly	**S** Special: hourly and annual
AE Average entry wage	**AOL** Average offered, low	**ASL** Average starting, low	**HI** Highest wage paid	**MTC** Median total compensation	**TQ** Third quartile wage
AEX Average experienced wage	**APH** Average pay, high range	**AW** Average wage paid	**HR** High end range	**MW** Median wage paid	**W** Weekly
AO Average offered	**APL** Average pay, low range	**FQ** First quartile wage	**LR** Low end range	**SQ** Second quartile wage	**Y** Yearly

Tire Repairer and Changer

Occupation/Type/Industry	Location	Per	Low	Mid	High	Source	Date
Tire Repairer and Changer	New Orleans MSA, LA	S	8.09 MW	8.03 AW	16830 AAW	LABLS	10//99-12//99
	Shreveport-Bossier City MSA, LA	S	8.56 MW	8.87 AW	17810 AAW	LABLS	10//99-12//99
	Maine	S	8.18 MW	8.82 AW	18350 AAW	MEBLS	10//99-12//99
	Bangor MSA, ME	S	8.74 MW	8.67 AW	18180 AAW	MEBLS	10//99-12//99
	Portland MSA, ME	S	8.38 MW	8.08 AW	17430 AAW	MEBLS	10//99-12//99
	Maryland	S	8.76 MW	9.67 AW	20110 AAW	MDBLS	10//99-12//99
	Baltimore PMSA, MD	S	8.76 MW	8.42 AW	18230 AAW	MDBLS	10//99-12//99
	Cumberland MSA, MD-WV	S	8.30 MW	7.65 AW	17270 AAW	MDBLS	10//99-12//99
	Massachusetts	S	9.85 MW	9.69 AW	20140 AAW	MABLS	10//99-12//99
	Boston PMSA, MA-NH	S	10.19 MW	10.48 AW	21190 AAW	MABLS	10//99-12//99
	Lawrence PMSA, MA-NH	S	8.89 MW	8.40 AW	18490 AAW	MABLS	10//99-12//99
	New Bedford PMSA, MA	S	8.65 MW	7.89 AW	17980 AAW	MABLS	10//99-12//99
	Worcester PMSA, MA-CT	S	8.59 MW	8.06 AW	17860 AAW	MABLS	10//99-12//99
	Michigan	S	8.31 MW	8.88 AW	18470 AAW	MIBLS	10//99-12//99
	Ann Arbor PMSA, MI	S	9.21 MW	9.00 AW	19160 AAW	MIBLS	10//99-12//99
	Benton Harbor MSA, MI	S	8.70 MW	8.41 AW	18110 AAW	MIBLS	10//99-12//99
	Detroit PMSA, MI	S	8.89 MW	8.01 AW	18490 AAW	MIBLS	10//99-12//99
	Flint PMSA, MI	S	7.59 MW	7.67 AW	15790 AAW	MIBLS	10//99-12//99
	Grand Rapids-Muskegon-Holland MSA, MI	S	9.05 MW	8.71 AW	18820 AAW	MIBLS	10//99-12//99
	Lansing-East Lansing MSA, MI	S	8.41 MW	8.12 AW	17490 AAW	MIBLS	10//99-12//99
	Saginaw-Bay City-Midland MSA, MI	S	8.32 MW	8.06 AW	17310 AAW	MIBLS	10//99-12//99
	Minnesota	S	8.32 MW	8.92 AW	18540 AAW	MNBLS	10//99-12//99
	Duluth-Superior MSA, MN-WI	S	8.81 MW	8.20 AW	18320 AAW	MNBLS	10//99-12//99
	Minneapolis-St. Paul MSA, MN-WI	S	8.91 MW	8.50 AW	18540 AAW	MNBLS	10//99-12//99
	St. Cloud MSA, MN	S	10.83 MW	9.19 AW	22520 AAW	MNBLS	10//99-12//99
	Mississippi	S	7.35 MW	7.58 AW	15760 AAW	MSBLS	10//99-12//99
	Jackson MSA, MS	S	7.33 MW	6.73 AW	15240 AAW	MSBLS	10//99-12//99
	Missouri	S	8.2 MW	8.71 AW	18120 AAW	MOBLS	10//99-12//99
	Joplin MSA, MO	S	8.43 MW	7.94 AW	17530 AAW	MOBLS	10//99-12//99
	Kansas City MSA, MO-KS	S	8.88 MW	8.35 AW	18460 AAW	MOBLS	10//99-12//99
	St. Joseph MSA, MO	S	7.84 MW	7.70 AW	16300 AAW	MOBLS	10//99-12//99
	St. Louis MSA, MO-IL	S	10.04 MW	9.86 AW	20880 AAW	MOBLS	10//99-12//99
	Springfield MSA, MO	S	8.29 MW	7.91 AW	17250 AAW	MOBLS	10//99-12//99
	Montana	S	8.54 MW	9.05 AW	18830 AAW	MTBLS	10//99-12//99
	Billings MSA, MT	S	8.94 MW	9.26 AW	18590 AAW	MTBLS	10//99-12//99
	Nebraska	S	8.34 MW	8.70 AW	18100 AAW	NEBLS	10//99-12//99
	Omaha MSA, NE-IA	S	8.89 MW	8.54 AW	18480 AAW	NEBLS	10//99-12//99
	Nevada	S	7.82 MW	8.86 AW	18430 AAW	NVBLS	10//99-12//99
	Las Vegas MSA, NV-AZ	S	8.33 MW	6.98 AW	17320 AAW	NVBLS	10//99-12//99
	Reno MSA, NV	S	9.95 MW	9.30 AW	20690 AAW	NVBLS	10//99-12//99
	New Hampshire	S	8.09 MW	8.40 AW	17480 AAW	NHBLS	10//99-12//99
	Nashua PMSA, NH	S	8.19 MW	8.20 AW	17040 AAW	NHBLS	10//99-12//99
	Portsmouth-Rochester PMSA, NH-ME	S	7.90 MW	7.65 AW	16440 AAW	NHBLS	10//99-12//99
	New Jersey	S	9.83 MW	10.43 AW	21700 AAW	NJBLS	10//99-12//99
	Atlantic-Cape May PMSA, NJ	S	10.53 MW	11.21 AW	21890 AAW	NJBLS	10//99-12//99
	Bergen-Passaic PMSA, NJ	S	9.52 MW	10.07 AW	19790 AAW	NJBLS	10//99-12//99
	Jersey City PMSA, NJ	S	10.19 MW	10.08 AW	21200 AAW	NJBLS	10//99-12//99
	Middlesex-Somerset-Hunterdon PMSA, NJ	S	9.45 MW	8.96 AW	19660 AAW	NJBLS	10//99-12//99
	Monmouth-Ocean PMSA, NJ	S	10.56 MW	10.55 AW	21950 AAW	NJBLS	10//99-12//99
	Newark PMSA, NJ	S	11.77 MW	10.49 AW	24490 AAW	NJBLS	10//99-12//99
	New Mexico	S	7.82 MW	8.02 AW	16690 AAW	NMBLS	10//99-12//99
	Albuquerque MSA, NM	S	8.56 MW	8.23 AW	17800 AAW	NMBLS	10//99-12//99
	Las Cruces MSA, NM	S	7.76 MW	7.69 AW	16130 AAW	NMBLS	10//99-12//99
	Santa Fe MSA, NM	S	8.14 MW	8.03 AW	16930 AAW	NMBLS	10//99-12//99
	New York	S	8.45 MW	8.96 AW	18650 AAW	NYBLS	10//99-12//99
	Albany-Schenectady-Troy MSA, NY	S	8.44 MW	8.18 AW	17560 AAW	NYBLS	10//99-12//99
	Binghamton MSA, NY	S	9.50 MW	9.30 AW	19760 AAW	NYBLS	10//99-12//99
	Buffalo-Niagara Falls MSA, NY	S	9.04 MW	8.69 AW	18810 AAW	NYBLS	10//99-12//99
	Dutchess County PMSA, NY	S	10.01 MW	7.97 AW	20810 AAW	NYBLS	10//99-12//99
	Nassau-Suffolk PMSA, NY	S	9.96 MW	10.11 AW	20710 AAW	NYBLS	10//99-12//99
	New York PMSA, NY	S	8.62 MW	7.97 AW	17940 AAW	NYBLS	10//99-12//99
	Newburgh PMSA, NY-PA	S	9.66 MW	9.47 AW	20080 AAW	NYBLS	10//99-12//99
	Rochester MSA, NY	S	8.87 MW	8.54 AW	18450 AAW	NYBLS	10//99-12//99
	Syracuse MSA, NY	S	9.20 MW	8.53 AW	19140 AAW	NYBLS	10//99-12//99

AAW Average annual wage	**AOH** Average offered, high	**ASH** Average starting, high	**H** Hourly	**M** Monthly	**S** Special: hourly and annual
AE Average entry wage	**AOL** Average offered, low	**ASL** Average starting, low	**HI** Highest wage paid	**MTC** Median total compensation	**TQ** Third quartile wage
AEX Average experienced wage	**APH** Average pay, high range	**AW** Average wage paid	**HR** High end range	**MW** Median wage paid	**W** Weekly
AO Average offered	**APL** Average pay, low range	**FQ** First quartile wage	**LR** Low end range	**SQ** Second quartile wage	**Y** Yearly

Occupation/Type/Industry	Location	Per	Low	Mid	High	Source	Date
Tire Repairer and Changer	Utica-Rome MSA, NY	S	9.21 MW	8.39 AW	19150 AAW	NYBLS	10//99-12//99
	North Carolina	S	8.19 MW	8.58 AW	17840 AAW	NCBLS	10//99-12//99
	Asheville MSA, NC	S	8.92 MW	8.82 AW	18550 AAW	NCBLS	10//99-12//99
	Charlotte-Gastonia-Rock Hill MSA, NC-SC	S	9.95 MW	8.81 AW	20690 AAW	NCBLS	10//99-12//99
	Fayetteville MSA, NC	S	7.26 MW	6.86 AW	15110 AAW	NCBLS	10//99-12//99
	Goldsboro MSA, NC	S	7.34 MW	6.86 AW	15270 AAW	NCBLS	10//99-12//99
	Greensboro--Winston-Salem--High Point MSA, NC	S	9.04 MW	8.77 AW	18800 AAW	NCBLS	10//99-12//99
	Greenville MSA, NC	S	7.68 MW	6.75 AW	15980 AAW	NCBLS	10//99-12//99
	Hickory-Morganton-Lenoir MSA, NC	S	8.73 MW	8.33 AW	18160 AAW	NCBLS	10//99-12//99
	Jacksonville MSA, NC	S	7.43 MW	6.46 AW	15460 AAW	NCBLS	10//99-12//99
	Raleigh-Durham-Chapel Hill MSA, NC	S	8.45 MW	8.41 AW	17580 AAW	NCBLS	10//99-12//99
	Rocky Mount MSA, NC	S	7.35 MW	7.38 AW	15280 AAW	NCBLS	10//99-12//99
	North Dakota	S	8.93 MW	9.05 AW	18830 AAW	NDBLS	10//99-12//99
	Bismarck MSA, ND	S	9.28 MW	8.53 AW	19290 AAW	NDBLS	10//99-12//99
	Fargo-Moorhead MSA, ND-MN	S	8.97 MW	8.76 AW	18670 AAW	NDBLS	10//99-12//99
	Grand Forks MSA, ND-MN	S	8.94 MW	8.71 AW	18590 AAW	NDBLS	10//99-12//99
	Ohio	S	8.28 MW	8.92 AW	18560 AAW	OHBLS	10//99-12//99
	Akron PMSA, OH	S	8.22 MW	8.03 AW	17100 AAW	OHBLS	10//99-12//99
	Canton-Massillon MSA, OH	S	10.09 MW	9.76 AW	20990 AAW	OHBLS	10//99-12//99
	Cincinnati PMSA, OH-KY-IN	S	9.17 MW	8.30 AW	19060 AAW	OHBLS	10//99-12//99
	Cleveland-Lorain-Elyria PMSA, OH	S	10.36 MW	8.56 AW	21560 AAW	OHBLS	10//99-12//99
	Columbus MSA, OH	S	9.45 MW	8.60 AW	19650 AAW	OHBLS	10//99-12//99
	Dayton-Springfield MSA, OH	S	9.34 MW	8.51 AW	19440 AAW	OHBLS	10//99-12//99
	Hamilton-Middletown PMSA, OH	S	10.23 MW	10.92 AW	21280 AAW	OHBLS	10//99-12//99
	Toledo MSA, OH	S	8.65 MW	7.67 AW	18000 AAW	OHBLS	10//99-12//99
	Youngstown-Warren MSA, OH	S	7.83 MW	7.08 AW	16290 AAW	OHBLS	10//99-12//99
	Oklahoma	S	7.85 MW	8.00 AW	16640 AAW	OKBLS	10//99-12//99
	Enid MSA, OK	S	8.24 MW	7.70 AW	17130 AAW	OKBLS	10//99-12//99
	Oklahoma City MSA, OK	S	8.24 MW	8.03 AW	17130 AAW	OKBLS	10//99-12//99
	Tulsa MSA, OK	S	8.08 MW	7.95 AW	16810 AAW	OKBLS	10//99-12//99
	Oregon	S	11.02 MW	11.15 AW	23200 AAW	ORBLS	10//99-12//99
	Eugene-Springfield MSA, OR	S	12.35 MW	12.76 AW	25690 AAW	ORBLS	10//99-12//99
	Medford-Ashland MSA, OR	S	11.89 MW	11.95 AW	24740 AAW	ORBLS	10//99-12//99
	Portland-Vancouver PMSA, OR-WA	S	11.14 MW	11.16 AW	23180 AAW	ORBLS	10//99-12//99
	Salem PMSA, OR	S	11.25 MW	11.07 AW	23400 AAW	ORBLS	10//99-12//99
	Pennsylvania	S	8.47 MW	9.33 AW	19420 AAW	PABLS	10//99-12//99
	Allentown-Bethlehem-Easton MSA, PA	S	8.97 MW	8.96 AW	18660 AAW	PABLS	10//99-12//99
	Altoona MSA, PA	S	7.69 MW	7.48 AW	16000 AAW	PABLS	10//99-12//99
	Erie MSA, PA	S	7.26 MW	6.35 AW	15090 AAW	PABLS	10//99-12//99
	Harrisburg-Lebanon-Carlisle MSA, PA	S	10.15 MW	8.76 AW	21120 AAW	PABLS	10//99-12//99
	Johnstown MSA, PA	S	8.88 MW	9.12 AW	18480 AAW	PABLS	10//99-12//99
	Lancaster MSA, PA	S	10.21 MW	10.63 AW	21240 AAW	PABLS	10//99-12//99
	Philadelphia PMSA, PA-NJ	S	10.28 MW	8.67 AW	21390 AAW	PABLS	10//99-12//99
	Pittsburgh MSA, PA	S	8.41 MW	8.16 AW	17490 AAW	PABLS	10//99-12//99
	Reading MSA, PA	S	9.51 MW	9.37 AW	19790 AAW	PABLS	10//99-12//99
	Scranton--Wilkes-Barre--Hazleton MSA, PA	S	10.02 MW	9.53 AW	20850 AAW	PABLS	10//99-12//99
	York MSA, PA	S	9.59 MW	9.66 AW	19950 AAW	PABLS	10//99-12//99
	Rhode Island	S	7.36 MW	8.33 AW	17330 AAW	RIBLS	10//99-12//99
	Providence-Fall River-Warwick MSA, RI-MA	S	8.25 MW	7.63 AW	17160 AAW	RIBLS	10//99-12//99
	South Carolina	S	7.75 MW	8.01 AW	16650 AAW	SCBLS	10//99-12//99
	Charleston-North Charleston MSA, SC	S	7.95 MW	7.77 AW	16530 AAW	SCBLS	10//99-12//99
	Columbia MSA, SC	S	7.75 MW	7.63 AW	16120 AAW	SCBLS	10//99-12//99
	Greenville-Spartanburg-Anderson MSA, SC	S	8.23 MW	8.04 AW	17120 AAW	SCBLS	10//99-12//99
	Myrtle Beach MSA, SC	S	8.18 MW	8.02 AW	17020 AAW	SCBLS	10//99-12//99
	South Dakota	S	8.11 MW	8.26 AW	17170 AAW	SDBLS	10//99-12//99
	Rapid City MSA, SD	S	8.22 MW	8.22 AW	17090 AAW	SDBLS	10//99-12//99
	Sioux Falls MSA, SD	S	8.67 MW	8.33 AW	18040 AAW	SDBLS	10//99-12//99
	Tennessee	S	8.86 MW	9.08 AW	18890 AAW	TNBLS	10//99-12//99

AAW	Average annual wage	AOH	Average offered, high	ASH	Average starting, high
AE	Average entry wage	AOL	Average offered, low	ASL	Average starting, low
AEX	Average experienced wage	APH	Average pay, high range	AW	Average wage paid
AO	Average offered	APL	Average pay, low range	FQ	First quartile wage

H	Hourly	M	Monthly	S	Special: hourly and annual
HI	Highest wage paid	MTC	Median total compensation	TQ	Third quartile wage
HR	High end range	MW	Median wage paid	W	Weekly
LR	Low end range	SQ	Second quartile wage	Y	Yearly

Occupation/Type/Industry	Location	Per	Low	Mid	High	Source	Date
Tire Repairer and Changer	Chattanooga MSA, TN-GA	S	8.29 MW	8.18 AW	17240 AAW	TNBLS	10//99-12//99
	Jackson MSA, TN	S	7.53 MW	7.04 AW	15670 AAW	TNBLS	10//99-12//99
	Johnson City-Kingsport-Bristol MSA, TN-VA	S	7.82 MW	7.72 AW	16260 AAW	TNBLS	10//99-12//99
	Knoxville MSA, TN	S	8.40 MW	8.58 AW	17460 AAW	TNBLS	10//99-12//99
	Memphis MSA, TN-AR-MS	S	8.50 MW	8.26 AW	17680 AAW	MSBLS	10//99-12//99
	Nashville MSA, TN	S	10.15 MW	10.02 AW	21110 AAW	TNBLS	10//99-12//99
	Texas	S	8.1 MW	8.51 AW	17710 AAW	TXBLS	10//99-12//99
	Amarillo MSA, TX	S	7.74 MW	7.74 AW	16090 AAW	TXBLS	10//99-12//99
	Austin-San Marcos MSA, TX	S	9.30 MW	9.29 AW	19350 AAW	TXBLS	10//99-12//99
	Beaumont-Port Arthur MSA, TX	S	9.09 MW	8.33 AW	18910 AAW	TXBLS	10//99-12//99
	Brazoria PMSA, TX	S	8.08 MW	7.87 AW	16800 AAW	TXBLS	10//99-12//99
	Brownsville-Harlingen-San Benito MSA, TX	S	7.51 MW	7.01 AW	15620 AAW	TXBLS	10//99-12//99
	Bryan-College Station MSA, TX	S	7.57 MW	7.58 AW	15750 AAW	TXBLS	10//99-12//99
	Corpus Christi MSA, TX	S	8.69 MW	8.17 AW	18070 AAW	TXBLS	10//99-12//99
	Dallas PMSA, TX	S	9.07 MW	8.62 AW	18850 AAW	TXBLS	10//99-12//99
	El Paso MSA, TX	S	10.00 MW	9.40 AW	20800 AAW	TXBLS	10//99-12//99
	Fort Worth-Arlington PMSA, TX	S	7.79 MW	7.66 AW	16210 AAW	TXBLS	10//99-12//99
	Galveston-Texas City PMSA, TX	S	8.35 MW	8.15 AW	17380 AAW	TXBLS	10//99-12//99
	Houston PMSA, TX	S	8.53 MW	7.95 AW	17740 AAW	TXBLS	10//99-12//99
	Killeen-Temple MSA, TX	S	7.30 MW	6.88 AW	15180 AAW	TXBLS	10//99-12//99
	Laredo MSA, TX	S	8.61 MW	8.50 AW	17920 AAW	TXBLS	10//99-12//99
	Longview-Marshall MSA, TX	S	11.19 MW	12.31 AW	23280 AAW	TXBLS	10//99-12//99
	Lubbock MSA, TX	S	8.39 MW	8.25 AW	17460 AAW	TXBLS	10//99-12//99
	McAllen-Edinburg-Mission MSA, TX	S	8.17 MW	7.94 AW	16980 AAW	TXBLS	10//99-12//99
	Odessa-Midland MSA, TX	S	9.68 MW	10.57 AW	20130 AAW	TXBLS	10//99-12//99
	San Angelo MSA, TX	S	7.30 MW	6.83 AW	15180 AAW	TXBLS	10//99-12//99
	San Antonio MSA, TX	S	7.87 MW	7.70 AW	16370 AAW	TXBLS	10//99-12//99
	Texarkana MSA, TX-Texarkana, AR	S	8.05 MW	7.97 AW	16730 AAW	TXBLS	10//99-12//99
	Tyler MSA, TX	S	7.38 MW	7.37 AW	15360 AAW	TXBLS	10//99-12//99
	Victoria MSA, TX	S	11.02 MW	9.79 AW	22920 AAW	TXBLS	10//99-12//99
	Waco MSA, TX	S	9.08 MW	8.35 AW	18880 AAW	TXBLS	10//99-12//99
	Utah	S	7.78 MW	7.96 AW	16570 AAW	UTBLS	10//99-12//99
	Provo-Orem MSA, UT	S	7.53 MW	7.57 AW	15670 AAW	UTBLS	10//99-12//99
	Salt Lake City-Ogden MSA, UT	S	7.93 MW	7.76 AW	16490 AAW	UTBLS	10//99-12//99
	Vermont	S	8.81 MW	9.38 AW	19510 AAW	VTBLS	10//99-12//99
	Burlington MSA, VT	S	8.57 MW	8.24 AW	17820 AAW	VTBLS	10//99-12//99
	Virginia	S	7.89 MW	9.23 AW	19210 AAW	VABLS	10//99-12//99
	Charlottesville MSA, VA	S	9.73 MW	9.79 AW	20240 AAW	VABLS	10//99-12//99
	Danville MSA, VA	S	9.61 MW	9.22 AW	19980 AAW	VABLS	10//99-12//99
	Lynchburg MSA, VA	S	9.28 MW	8.48 AW	19310 AAW	VABLS	10//99-12//99
	Norfolk-Virginia Beach-Newport News MSA, VA-NC	S	7.86 MW	6.77 AW	16360 AAW	VABLS	10//99-12//99
	Richmond-Petersburg MSA, VA	S	8.85 MW	8.26 AW	18420 AAW	VABLS	10//99-12//99
	Roanoke MSA, VA	S	8.69 MW	8.15 AW	18080 AAW	VABLS	10//99-12//99
	Washington	S	10.14 MW	10.39 AW	21600 AAW	WABLS	10//99-12//99
	Bellingham MSA, WA	S	8.67 MW	8.42 AW	18040 AAW	WABLS	10//99-12//99
	Bremerton PMSA, WA	S	9.25 MW	8.30 AW	19240 AAW	WABLS	10//99-12//99
	Richland-Kennewick-Pasco MSA, WA	S	8.88 MW	8.69 AW	18480 AAW	WABLS	10//99-12//99
	Seattle-Bellevue-Everett PMSA, WA	S	11.14 MW	11.71 AW	23170 AAW	WABLS	10//99-12//99
	Spokane MSA, WA	S	10.45 MW	10.66 AW	21740 AAW	WABLS	10//99-12//99
	Tacoma PMSA, WA	S	10.86 MW	10.45 AW	22580 AAW	WABLS	10//99-12//99
	Yakima MSA, WA	S	8.93 MW	8.54 AW	18580 AAW	WABLS	10//99-12//99
	West Virginia	S	7.83 MW	7.99 AW	16630 AAW	WVBLS	10//99-12//99
	Charleston MSA, WV	S	7.32 MW	6.80 AW	15230 AAW	WVBLS	10//99-12//99
	Huntington-Ashland MSA, WV-KY-OH	S	7.04 MW	6.84 AW	14640 AAW	WVBLS	10//99-12//99
	Parkersburg-Marietta MSA, WV-OH	S	6.89 MW	6.75 AW	14320 AAW	WVBLS	10//99-12//99
	Wheeling MSA, WV-OH	S	7.81 MW	7.88 AW	16240 AAW	WVBLS	10//99-12//99

AAW Average annual wage	AOH Average offered, high	ASH Average starting, high	H Hourly	M Monthly	S Special: hourly and annual
AE Average entry wage	AOL Average offered, low	ASL Average starting, low	HI Highest wage paid	MTC Median total compensation	TQ Third quartile wage
AEX Average experienced wage	APH Average pay, high range	AW Average wage paid	HR High end range	MW Median wage paid	W Weekly
AO Average offered	APL Average pay, low range	FQ First quartile wage	LR Low end range	SQ Second quartile wage	Y Yearly

Occupation/Type/Industry	Location	Per	Low	Mid	High	Source	Date
Tire Repairer and Changer	Wisconsin	S	9.07 MW	9.13 AW	19000 AAW	WIBLS	10//99-12//99
	Appleton-Oshkosh-Neenah MSA, WI	S	8.22 MW	8.23 AW	17110 AAW	WIBLS	10//99-12//99
	Green Bay MSA, WI	S	9.14 MW	8.71 AW	19000 AAW	WIBLS	10//99-12//99
	Janesville-Beloit MSA, WI	S	9.39 MW	9.44 AW	19530 AAW	WIBLS	10//99-12//99
	La Crosse MSA, WI-MN	S	8.55 MW	8.56 AW	17780 AAW	WIBLS	10//99-12//99
	Madison MSA, WI	S	9.53 MW	9.58 AW	19820 AAW	WIBLS	10//99-12//99
	Milwaukee-Waukesha PMSA, WI	S	9.17 MW	8.66 AW	19070 AAW	WIBLS	10//99-12//99
	Wausau MSA, WI	S	9.38 MW	9.41 AW	19510 AAW	WIBLS	10//99-12//99
	Wyoming	S	8.26 MW	8.55 AW	17790 AAW	WYBLS	10//99-12//99
	Casper MSA, WY	S	8.94 MW	7.91 AW	18600 AAW	WYBLS	10//99-12//99
	Cheyenne MSA, WY	S	8.11 MW	6.97 AW	16860 AAW	WYBLS	10//99-12//99
	Puerto Rico	S	6.06 MW	6.03 AW	12540 AAW	PRBLS	10//99-12//99
	Caguas PMSA, PR	S	6.27 MW	6.22 AW	13040 AAW	PRBLS	10//99-12//99
	Ponce MSA, PR	S	6.10 MW	6.08 AW	12690 AAW	PRBLS	10//99-12//99
	San Juan-Bayamon PMSA, PR	S	6.02 MW	6.08 AW	12520 AAW	PRBLS	10//99-12//99
	Virgin Islands	S	7.57 MW	7.68 AW	15970 AAW	VIBLS	10//99-12//99
	Guam	S	6.5 MW	6.83 AW	14220 AAW	GUBLS	10//99-12//99
Title Examiner, Abstractor, and Searcher	Alabama	S	10.11 MW	10.30 AW	21420 AAW	ALBLS	10//99-12//99
	Birmingham MSA, AL	S	10.88 MW	11.23 AW	22620 AAW	ALBLS	10//99-12//99
	Mobile MSA, AL	S	11.62 MW	11.02 AW	24160 AAW	ALBLS	10//99-12//99
	Alaska	S	18.72 MW	19.41 AW	40370 AAW	AKBLS	10//99-12//99
	Anchorage MSA, AK	S	19.42 MW	19.00 AW	40390 AAW	AKBLS	10//99-12//99
	Arizona	S	13.16 MW	14.01 AW	29140 AAW	AZBLS	10//99-12//99
	Phoenix-Mesa MSA, AZ	S	13.84 MW	13.01 AW	28790 AAW	AZBLS	10//99-12//99
	Arkansas	S	9.92 MW	10.69 AW	22240 AAW	ARBLS	10//99-12//99
	Fayetteville-Springdale-Rogers MSA, AR	S	10.65 MW	9.78 AW	22150 AAW	ARBLS	10//99-12//99
	Fort Smith MSA, AR-OK	S	11.67 MW	10.87 AW	24260 AAW	ARBLS	10//99-12//99
	Little Rock-North Little Rock MSA, AR	S	12.19 MW	11.80 AW	25360 AAW	ARBLS	10//99-12//99
	California	S	17.33 MW	18.09 AW	37620 AAW	CABLS	10//99-12//99
	Fresno MSA, CA	S	18.72 MW	18.19 AW	38940 AAW	CABLS	10//99-12//99
	Los Angeles-Long Beach PMSA, CA	S	18.41 MW	17.36 AW	38290 AAW	CABLS	10//99-12//99
	Modesto MSA, CA	S	16.11 MW	16.05 AW	33520 AAW	CABLS	10//99-12//99
	Oakland PMSA, CA	S	17.00 MW	16.23 AW	35350 AAW	CABLS	10//99-12//99
	Orange County PMSA, CA	S	19.78 MW	18.71 AW	41140 AAW	CABLS	10//99-12//99
	Redding MSA, CA	S	14.39 MW	14.10 AW	29920 AAW	CABLS	10//99-12//99
	Riverside-San Bernardino PMSA, CA	S	16.99 MW	16.18 AW	35340 AAW	CABLS	10//99-12//99
	Sacramento PMSA, CA	S	18.17 MW	17.76 AW	37800 AAW	CABLS	10//99-12//99
	Salinas MSA, CA	S	15.75 MW	15.18 AW	32770 AAW	CABLS	10//99-12//99
	San Diego MSA, CA	S	18.13 MW	17.52 AW	37700 AAW	CABLS	10//99-12//99
	San Francisco PMSA, CA	S	18.70 MW	17.85 AW	38890 AAW	CABLS	10//99-12//99
	San Jose PMSA, CA	S	18.35 MW	17.97 AW	38170 AAW	CABLS	10//99-12//99
	Santa Barbara-Santa Maria-Lompoc MSA, CA	S	19.48 MW	18.90 AW	40520 AAW	CABLS	10//99-12//99
	Santa Rosa PMSA, CA	S	18.71 MW	18.34 AW	38910 AAW	CABLS	10//99-12//99
	Stockton-Lodi MSA, CA	S	17.85 MW	17.75 AW	37130 AAW	CABLS	10//99-12//99
	Vallejo-Fairfield-Napa PMSA, CA	S	18.13 MW	18.16 AW	37710 AAW	CABLS	10//99-12//99
	Ventura PMSA, CA	S	18.17 MW	16.47 AW	37790 AAW	CABLS	10//99-12//99
	Yolo PMSA, CA	S	18.08 MW	17.32 AW	37610 AAW	CABLS	10//99-12//99
	Colorado	S	12.72 MW	13.84 AW	28780 AAW	COBLS	10//99-12//99
	Boulder-Longmont PMSA, CO	S	13.28 MW	12.48 AW	27620 AAW	COBLS	10//99-12//99
	Colorado Springs MSA, CO	S	13.57 MW	12.90 AW	28230 AAW	COBLS	10//99-12//99
	Denver PMSA, CO	S	14.59 MW	13.31 AW	30340 AAW	COBLS	10//99-12//99
	Fort Collins-Loveland MSA, CO	S	13.32 MW	12.76 AW	27710 AAW	COBLS	10//99-12//99
	Grand Junction MSA, CO	S	12.35 MW	11.49 AW	25690 AAW	COBLS	10//99-12//99
	Connecticut	S	14.6 MW	14.69 AW	30560 AAW	CTBLS	10//99-12//99
	Hartford MSA, CT	S	15.48 MW	15.56 AW	32200 AAW	CTBLS	10//99-12//99
	Delaware	S	13.58 MW	14.28 AW	29700 AAW	DEBLS	10//99-12//99
	Wilmington-Newark PMSA, DE-MD	S	15.21 MW	14.42 AW	31640 AAW	DEBLS	10//99-12//99
	District of Columbia	S	13.66 MW	15.35 AW	31930 AAW	DCBLS	10//99-12//99
	Washington PMSA, DC-MD-VA-WV	S	16.97 MW	14.00 AW	35290 AAW	DCBLS	10//99-12//99

AAW Average annual wage	**AOH** Average offered, high	**ASH** Average starting, high	**H** Hourly	**M** Monthly	**S** Special: hourly and annual
AE Average entry wage	**AOL** Average offered, low	**ASL** Average starting, low	**HI** Highest wage paid	**MTC** Median total compensation	**TQ** Third quartile wage
AEX Average experienced wage	**APH** Average pay, high range	**AW** Average wage paid	**HR** High end range	**MW** Median wage paid	**W** Weekly
AO Average offered	**APL** Average pay, low range	**FQ** First quartile wage	**LR** Low end range	**SQ** Second quartile wage	**Y** Yearly

Occupation/Type/Industry	Location	Per	Low	Mid	High	Source	Date
Title Examiner, Abstractor, and Searcher							
	Florida	S	12.92 MW	13.92 AW	28950 AAW	FLBLS	10//99-12//99
	Daytona Beach MSA, FL	S	12.60 MW	13.16 AW	26210 AAW	FLBLS	10//99-12//99
	Fort Lauderdale PMSA, FL	S	15.88 MW	15.18 AW	33030 AAW	FLBLS	10//99-12//99
	Fort Myers-Cape Coral MSA, FL	S	11.84 MW	11.83 AW	24620 AAW	FLBLS	10//99-12//99
	Fort Pierce-Port St. Lucie MSA, FL	S	14.62 MW	14.78 AW	30410 AAW	FLBLS	10//99-12//99
	Fort Walton Beach MSA, FL	S	12.66 MW	13.17 AW	26340 AAW	FLBLS	10//99-12//99
	Gainesville MSA, FL	S	15.28 MW	15.17 AW	31780 AAW	FLBLS	10//99-12//99
	Jacksonville MSA, FL	S	13.57 MW	13.10 AW	28230 AAW	FLBLS	10//99-12//99
	Miami PMSA, FL	S	14.08 MW	12.01 AW	29280 AAW	FLBLS	10//99-12//99
	Naples MSA, FL	S	14.94 MW	15.21 AW	31070 AAW	FLBLS	10//99-12//99
	Ocala MSA, FL	S	13.32 MW	12.85 AW	27710 AAW	FLBLS	10//99-12//99
	Orlando MSA, FL	S	11.74 MW	11.56 AW	24420 AAW	FLBLS	10//99-12//99
	Panama City MSA, FL	S	13.44 MW	13.14 AW	27960 AAW	FLBLS	10//99-12//99
	Sarasota-Bradenton MSA, FL	S	18.96 MW	15.54 AW	39430 AAW	FLBLS	10//99-12//99
	Tallahassee MSA, FL	S	13.81 MW	11.96 AW	28730 AAW	FLBLS	10//99-12//99
	Tampa-St. Petersburg-Clearwater MSA, FL	S	14.30 MW	12.97 AW	29740 AAW	FLBLS	10//99-12//99
	Georgia	S	18.84 MW	20.17 AW	41950 AAW	GABLS	10//99-12//99
	Atlanta MSA, GA	S	21.34 MW	20.17 AW	44390 AAW	GABLS	10//99-12//99
	Augusta-Aiken MSA, GA-SC	S	16.73 MW	13.01 AW	34800 AAW	GABLS	10//99-12//99
	Macon MSA, GA	S	18.91 MW	15.88 AW	39320 AAW	GABLS	10//99-12//99
	Hawaii	S	15.23 MW	15.47 AW	32190 AAW	HIBLS	10//99-12//99
	Honolulu MSA, HI	S	15.46 MW	15.17 AW	32150 AAW	HIBLS	10//99-12//99
	Idaho	S	12.71 MW	14.17 AW	29470 AAW	IDBLS	10//99-12//99
	Boise City MSA, ID	S	15.48 MW	14.02 AW	32190 AAW	IDBLS	10//99-12//99
	Illinois	S	14.64 MW	14.48 AW	30120 AAW	ILBLS	10//99-12//99
	Chicago PMSA, IL	S	15.50 MW	16.41 AW	32240 AAW	ILBLS	10//99-12//99
	Peoria-Pekin MSA, IL	S	10.94 MW	10.30 AW	22760 AAW	ILBLS	10//99-12//99
	Rockford MSA, IL	S	13.71 MW	12.43 AW	28520 AAW	ILBLS	10//99-12//99
	Springfield MSA, IL	S	14.29 MW	14.40 AW	29720 AAW	ILBLS	10//99-12//99
	Indiana	S	11.27 MW	12.80 AW	26620 AAW	INBLS	10//99-12//99
	Evansville-Henderson MSA, IN-KY	S	11.25 MW	10.09 AW	23400 AAW	INBLS	10//99-12//99
	Fort Wayne MSA, IN	S	11.67 MW	10.63 AW	24270 AAW	INBLS	10//99-12//99
	Gary PMSA, IN	S	13.79 MW	11.99 AW	28690 AAW	INBLS	10//99-12//99
	Indianapolis MSA, IN	S	12.42 MW	12.30 AW	25840 AAW	INBLS	10//99-12//99
	Terre Haute MSA, IN	S	9.00 MW	8.95 AW	18720 AAW	INBLS	10//99-12//99
	Iowa	S	8.71 MW	10.21 AW	21230 AAW	IABLS	10//99-12//99
	Des Moines MSA, IA	S	13.01 MW	12.08 AW	27060 AAW	IABLS	10//99-12//99
	Kansas	S	11.23 MW	12.99 AW	27020 AAW	KSBLS	10//99-12//99
	Topeka MSA, KS	S	9.55 MW	8.66 AW	19860 AAW	KSBLS	10//99-12//99
	Wichita MSA, KS	S	13.49 MW	11.64 AW	28060 AAW	KSBLS	10//99-12//99
	Kentucky	S	11.69 MW	12.06 AW	25090 AAW	KYBLS	10//99-12//99
	Lexington MSA, KY	S	11.43 MW	10.76 AW	23780 AAW	KYBLS	10//99-12//99
	Louisville MSA, KY-IN	S	13.20 MW	12.89 AW	27460 AAW	KYBLS	10//99-12//99
	Louisiana	S	10.74 MW	13.20 AW	27460 AAW	LABLS	10//99-12//99
	Baton Rouge MSA, LA	S	17.41 MW	14.14 AW	36210 AAW	LABLS	10//99-12//99
	Monroe MSA, LA	S	8.69 MW	8.71 AW	18080 AAW	LABLS	10//99-12//99
	Shreveport-Bossier City MSA, LA	S	11.82 MW	10.39 AW	24590 AAW	LABLS	10//99-12//99
	Maine	S	13.66 MW	14.06 AW	29250 AAW	MEBLS	10//99-12//99
	Portland MSA, ME	S	14.36 MW	14.09 AW	29860 AAW	MEBLS	10//99-12//99
	Maryland	S	12.7 MW	13.83 AW	28770 AAW	MDBLS	10//99-12//99
	Baltimore PMSA, MD	S	13.22 MW	12.47 AW	27490 AAW	MDBLS	10//99-12//99
	Massachusetts	S	14.11 MW	15.61 AW	32460 AAW	MABLS	10//99-12//99
	Boston PMSA, MA-NH	S	18.02 MW	16.84 AW	37480 AAW	MABLS	10//99-12//99
	Worcester PMSA, MA-CT	S	17.82 MW	17.10 AW	37060 AAW	MABLS	10//99-12//99
	Michigan	S	12.47 MW	13.19 AW	27440 AAW	MIBLS	10//99-12//99
	Ann Arbor PMSA, MI	S	13.57 MW	12.74 AW	28230 AAW	MIBLS	10//99-12//99
	Detroit PMSA, MI	S	14.47 MW	14.07 AW	30090 AAW	MIBLS	10//99-12//99
	Grand Rapids-Muskegon-Holland MSA, MI	S	15.11 MW	14.03 AW	31420 AAW	MIBLS	10//99-12//99
	Kalamazoo-Battle Creek MSA, MI	S	10.26 MW	9.97 AW	21340 AAW	MIBLS	10//99-12//99
	Saginaw-Bay City-Midland MSA, MI	S	13.59 MW	12.63 AW	28260 AAW	MIBLS	10//99-12//99
	Minnesota	S	13.21 MW	14.50 AW	30160 AAW	MNBLS	10//99-12//99
	Minneapolis-St. Paul MSA, MN-WI	S	15.04 MW	13.75 AW	31290 AAW	MNBLS	10//99-12//99

Occupation/Type/Industry	Location	Per	Low	Mid	High	Source	Date
Title Examiner, Abstractor, and Searcher							
	St. Cloud MSA, MN	S	18.57 MW	15.29 AW	38610 AAW	MNBLS	10//99-12//99
	Mississippi	S	13.01 MW	13.83 AW	28780 AAW	MSBLS	10//99-12//99
	Jackson MSA, MS	S	13.90 MW	12.70 AW	28910 AAW	MSBLS	10//99-12//99
	Missouri	S	9.99 MW	10.84 AW	22550 AAW	MOBLS	10//99-12//99
	Kansas City MSA, MO-KS	S	13.95 MW	12.45 AW	29030 AAW	MOBLS	10//99-12//99
	St. Louis MSA, MO-IL	S	11.50 MW	10.54 AW	23920 AAW	MOBLS	10//99-12//99
	Montana	S	12.08 MW	12.23 AW	25440 AAW	MTBLS	10//99-12//99
	Nebraska	S	10.89 MW	11.17 AW	23220 AAW	NEBLS	10//99-12//99
	Omaha MSA, NE-IA	S	11.01 MW	10.79 AW	22910 AAW	NEBLS	10//99-12//99
	Nevada	S	12.46 MW	13.72 AW	28550 AAW	NVBLS	10//99-12//99
	Las Vegas MSA, NV-AZ	S	13.97 MW	12.90 AW	29060 AAW	NVBLS	10//99-12//99
	New Hampshire	S	13.99 MW	13.94 AW	28990 AAW	NHBLS	10//99-12//99
	Manchester PMSA, NH	S	13.86 MW	14.05 AW	28830 AAW	NHBLS	10//99-12//99
	New Jersey	S	16.49 MW	19.28 AW	40110 AAW	NJBLS	10//99-12//99
	Atlantic-Cape May PMSA, NJ	S	14.83 MW	12.79 AW	30850 AAW	NJBLS	10//99-12//99
	Middlesex-Somerset-Hunterdon PMSA, NJ	S	17.30 MW	15.64 AW	35980 AAW	NJBLS	10//99-12//99
	Monmouth-Ocean PMSA, NJ	S	24.43 MW	21.15 AW	50820 AAW	NJBLS	10//99-12//99
	Newark PMSA, NJ	S	20.01 MW	18.61 AW	41610 AAW	NJBLS	10//99-12//99
	Trenton PMSA, NJ	S	20.39 MW	15.98 AW	42410 AAW	NJBLS	10//99-12//99
	New Mexico	S	10.55 MW	11.27 AW	23430 AAW	NMBLS	10//99-12//99
	Albuquerque MSA, NM	S	12.49 MW	12.45 AW	25980 AAW	NMBLS	10//99-12//99
	Las Cruces MSA, NM	S	10.56 MW	9.55 AW	21960 AAW	NMBLS	10//99-12//99
	Santa Fe MSA, NM	S	13.07 MW	12.98 AW	27190 AAW	NMBLS	10//99-12//99
	New York	S	14.57 MW	17.46 AW	36310 AAW	NYBLS	10//99-12//99
	Albany-Schenectady-Troy MSA, NY	S	15.01 MW	14.30 AW	31230 AAW	NYBLS	10//99-12//99
	Buffalo-Niagara Falls MSA, NY	S	12.82 MW	11.93 AW	26670 AAW	NYBLS	10//99-12//99
	Nassau-Suffolk PMSA, NY	S	18.73 MW	14.92 AW	38960 AAW	NYBLS	10//99-12//99
	New York PMSA, NY	S	22.94 MW	19.46 AW	47720 AAW	NYBLS	10//99-12//99
	Rochester MSA, NY	S	13.01 MW	12.86 AW	27060 AAW	NYBLS	10//99-12//99
	Syracuse MSA, NY	S	12.52 MW	11.98 AW	26040 AAW	NYBLS	10//99-12//99
	North Carolina	S	14.7 MW	14.29 AW	29730 AAW	NCBLS	10//99-12//99
	Charlotte-Gastonia-Rock Hill MSA, NC-SC	S	12.94 MW	12.43 AW	26920 AAW	NCBLS	10//99-12//99
	Raleigh-Durham-Chapel Hill MSA, NC	S	16.25 MW	15.66 AW	33800 AAW	NCBLS	10//99-12//99
	North Dakota	S	12.37 MW	15.26 AW	31740 AAW	NDBLS	10//99-12//99
	Ohio	S	12.85 MW	13.42 AW	27920 AAW	OHBLS	10//99-12//99
	Akron PMSA, OH	S	13.76 MW	12.95 AW	28620 AAW	OHBLS	10//99-12//99
	Canton-Massillon MSA, OH	S	13.25 MW	13.12 AW	27550 AAW	OHBLS	10//99-12//99
	Cincinnati PMSA, OH-KY-IN	S	13.26 MW	11.55 AW	27590 AAW	OHBLS	10//99-12//99
	Cleveland-Lorain-Elyria PMSA, OH	S	13.44 MW	12.84 AW	27950 AAW	OHBLS	10//99-12//99
	Columbus MSA, OH	S	12.99 MW	12.36 AW	27010 AAW	OHBLS	10//99-12//99
	Dayton-Springfield MSA, OH	S	14.36 MW	13.69 AW	29870 AAW	OHBLS	10//99-12//99
	Toledo MSA, OH	S	14.31 MW	14.13 AW	29760 AAW	OHBLS	10//99-12//99
	Youngstown-Warren MSA, OH	S	12.04 MW	12.21 AW	25040 AAW	OHBLS	10//99-12//99
	Oklahoma	S	12.78 MW	15.24 AW	31700 AAW	OKBLS	10//99-12//99
	Oklahoma City MSA, OK	S	17.29 MW	17.04 AW	35970 AAW	OKBLS	10//99-12//99
	Tulsa MSA, OK	S	18.23 MW	16.64 AW	37910 AAW	OKBLS	10//99-12//99
	Oregon	S	15.28 MW	15.87 AW	33000 AAW	ORBLS	10//99-12//99
	Eugene-Springfield MSA, OR	S	15.71 MW	15.26 AW	32670 AAW	ORBLS	10//99-12//99
	Portland-Vancouver PMSA, OR-WA	S	15.29 MW	14.59 AW	31800 AAW	ORBLS	10//99-12//99
	Pennsylvania	S	12.59 MW	12.78 AW	26580 AAW	PABLS	10//99-12//99
	Allentown-Bethlehem-Easton MSA, PA	S	14.40 MW	14.32 AW	29950 AAW	PABLS	10//99-12//99
	Harrisburg-Lebanon-Carlisle MSA, PA	S	12.94 MW	12.90 AW	26910 AAW	PABLS	10//99-12//99
	Lancaster MSA, PA	S	15.23 MW	13.11 AW	31680 AAW	PABLS	10//99-12//99
	Philadelphia PMSA, PA-NJ	S	13.97 MW	13.34 AW	29050 AAW	PABLS	10//99-12//99
	Pittsburgh MSA, PA	S	12.98 MW	13.37 AW	27000 AAW	PABLS	10//99-12//99
	Scranton--Wilkes-Barre--Hazleton MSA, PA	S	10.64 MW	10.59 AW	22130 AAW	PABLS	10//99-12//99
	Rhode Island	S	15.64 MW	15.60 AW	32440 AAW	RIBLS	10//99-12//99
	Providence-Fall River-Warwick MSA, RI-MA	S	16.37 MW	16.61 AW	34060 AAW	RIBLS	10//99-12//99
	South Carolina	S	15.34 MW	14.65 AW	30470 AAW	SCBLS	10//99-12//99
	Columbia MSA, SC	S	13.33 MW	13.15 AW	27730 AAW	SCBLS	10//99 12//99

AAW Average annual wage	**AOH** Average offered, high	**ASH** Average starting, high	**H** Hourly	**M** Monthly	**S** Special: hourly and annual
AE Average entry wage	**AOL** Average offered, low	**ASL** Average starting, low	**HI** Highest wage paid	**MTC** Median total compensation	**TQ** Third quartile wage
AEX Average experienced wage	**APH** Average pay, high range	**AW** Average wage paid	**HR** High end range	**MW** Median wage paid	**W** Weekly
AO Average offered	**APL** Average pay, low range	**FQ** First quartile wage	**LR** Low end range	**SQ** Second quartile wage	**Y** Yearly

Occupation/Type/Industry	Location	Per	Low	Mid	High	Source	Date
Title Examiner, Abstractor, and Searcher	Myrtle Beach MSA, SC	S	9.28 MW	9.21 AW	19290 AAW	SCBLS	10//99-12//99
	South Dakota	S	10.21 MW	10.86 AW	22590 AAW	SDBLS	10//99-12//99
	Tennessee	S	12.65 MW	13.76 AW	28620 AAW	TNBLS	10//99-12//99
	Chattanooga MSA, TN-GA	S	14.55 MW	14.69 AW	30260 AAW	TNBLS	10//99-12//99
	Knoxville MSA, TN	S	15.86 MW	14.10 AW	32990 AAW	TNBLS	10//99-12//99
	Memphis MSA, TN-AR-MS	S	11.84 MW	11.11 AW	24620 AAW	MSBLS	10//99-12//99
	Nashville MSA, TN	S	15.70 MW	15.30 AW	32650 AAW	TNBLS	10//99-12//99
	Texas	S	13.8 MW	16.04 AW	33360 AAW	TXBLS	10//99-12//99
	Amarillo MSA, TX	S	12.51 MW	10.68 AW	26020 AAW	TXBLS	10//99-12//99
	Austin-San Marcos MSA, TX	S	15.00 MW	14.35 AW	31210 AAW	TXBLS	10//99-12//99
	Beaumont-Port Arthur MSA, TX	S	16.19 MW	13.00 AW	33680 AAW	TXBLS	10//99-12//99
	Dallas PMSA, TX	S	19.92 MW	18.74 AW	41420 AAW	TXBLS	10//99-12//99
	Fort Worth-Arlington PMSA, TX	S	14.35 MW	12.26 AW	29840 AAW	TXBLS	10//99-12//99
	Houston PMSA, TX	S	15.49 MW	12.83 AW	32230 AAW	TXBLS	10//99-12//99
	Killeen-Temple MSA, TX	S	8.41 MW	7.58 AW	17480 AAW	TXBLS	10//99-12//99
	McAllen-Edinburg-Mission MSA, TX	S	12.52 MW	11.04 AW	26040 AAW	TXBLS	10//99-12//99
	Odessa-Midland MSA, TX	S	12.06 MW	12.04 AW	25080 AAW	TXBLS	10//99-12//99
	San Antonio MSA, TX	S	15.54 MW	13.88 AW	32320 AAW	TXBLS	10//99-12//99
	Texarkana MSA, TX-Texarkana, AR	S	9.95 MW	9.10 AW	20700 AAW	TXBLS	10//99-12//99
	Waco MSA, TX	S	11.16 MW	9.99 AW	23220 AAW	TXBLS	10//99-12//99
	Utah	S	14.59 MW	17.83 AW	37090 AAW	UTBLS	10//99-12//99
	Virginia	S	12.28 MW	15.01 AW	31220 AAW	VABLS	10//99-12//99
	Norfolk-Virginia Beach-Newport News MSA, VA-NC	S	10.24 MW	10.03 AW	21300 AAW	VABLS	10//99-12//99
	Richmond-Petersburg MSA, VA	S	12.83 MW	12.16 AW	26680 AAW	VABLS	10//99-12//99
	Roanoke MSA, VA	S	15.90 MW	13.88 AW	33060 AAW	VABLS	10//99-12//99
	Washington	S	15.44 MW	16.33 AW	33960 AAW	WABLS	10//99-12//99
	Olympia PMSA, WA	S	18.72 MW	18.76 AW	38940 AAW	WABLS	10//99-12//99
	Seattle-Bellevue-Everett PMSA, WA	S	17.90 MW	16.58 AW	37230 AAW	WABLS	10//99-12//99
	Tacoma PMSA, WA	S	13.37 MW	12.96 AW	27810 AAW	WABLS	10//99-12//99
	Yakima MSA, WA	S	12.72 MW	11.22 AW	26450 AAW	WABLS	10//99-12//99
	West Virginia	S	12.41 MW	11.64 AW	24210 AAW	WVBLS	10//99-12//99
	Wisconsin	S	12.83 MW	13.09 AW	27220 AAW	WIBLS	10//99-12//99
	Appleton-Oshkosh-Neenah MSA, WI	S	13.27 MW	13.97 AW	27600 AAW	WIBLS	10//99-12//99
	Green Bay MSA, WI	S	12.27 MW	12.41 AW	25520 AAW	WIBLS	10//99-12//99
	Janesville-Beloit MSA, WI	S	10.44 MW	11.17 AW	21720 AAW	WIBLS	10//99-12//99
	Madison MSA, WI	S	16.01 MW	15.17 AW	33310 AAW	WIBLS	10//99-12//99
	Milwaukee-Waukesha PMSA, WI	S	12.96 MW	11.96 AW	26960 AAW	WIBLS	10//99-12//99
	Racine PMSA, WI	S	12.54 MW	12.36 AW	26080 AAW	WIBLS	10//99-12//99
	Wyoming	S	10.47 MW	11.02 AW	22920 AAW	WYBLS	10//99-12//99
	Casper MSA, WY	S	12.83 MW	12.63 AW	26680 AAW	WYBLS	10//99-12//99
Tool and Die Maker	Alabama	S	16.35 MW	17.46 AW	36310 AAW	ALBLS	10//99-12//99
	Anniston MSA, AL	S	16.29 MW	17.17 AW	33880 AAW	ALBLS	10//99-12//99
	Birmingham MSA, AL	S	15.72 MW	15.47 AW	32700 AAW	ALBLS	10//99-12//99
	Decatur MSA, AL	S	15.77 MW	14.79 AW	32800 AAW	ALBLS	10//99-12//99
	Dothan MSA, AL	S	25.05 MW	28.72 AW	52110 AAW	ALBLS	10//99-12//99
	Florence MSA, AL	S	13.39 MW	13.53 AW	27840 AAW	ALBLS	10//99-12//99
	Gadsden MSA, AL	S	14.03 MW	14.53 AW	29180 AAW	ALBLS	10//99-12//99
	Huntsville MSA, AL	S	22.27 MW	22.09 AW	46320 AAW	ALBLS	10//99-12//99
	Mobile MSA, AL	S	15.65 MW	17.21 AW	32560 AAW	ALBLS	10//99-12//99
	Arizona	S	18.67 MW	18.04 AW	37530 AAW	AZBLS	10//99-12//99
	Flagstaff MSA, AZ-UT	S	10.51 MW	7.96 AW	21860 AAW	AZBLS	10//99-12//99
	Phoenix-Mesa MSA, AZ	S	18.74 MW	19.15 AW	38980 AAW	AZBLS	10//99-12//99
	Tucson MSA, AZ	S	16.65 MW	17.20 AW	34630 AAW	AZBLS	10//99-12//99
	Yuma MSA, AZ	S	11.68 MW	10.44 AW	24300 AAW	AZBLS	10//99-12//99
	Arkansas	S	14.7 MW	14.75 AW	30670 AAW	ARBLS	10//99-12//99
	Fayetteville-Springdale-Rogers MSA, AR	S	13.62 MW	13.81 AW	28320 AAW	ARBLS	10//99-12//99
	Fort Smith MSA, AR-OK	S	13.33 MW	14.42 AW	27740 AAW	ARBLS	10//99-12//99
	Jonesboro MSA, AR	S	15.99 MW	15.38 AW	33260 AAW	ARBLS	10//99-12//99

AAW Average annual wage	AOH Average offered, high	ASH Average starting, high	H Hourly	M Monthly	S Special: hourly and annual
AE Average entry wage	AOL Average offered, low	ASL Average starting, low	HI Highest wage paid	MTC Median total compensation	TQ Third quartile wage
AEX Average experienced wage	APH Average pay, high range	AW Average wage paid	HR High end range	MW Median wage paid	W Weekly
AO Average offered	APL Average pay, low range	FQ First quartile wage	LR Low end range	SQ Second quartile wage	Y Yearly

Occupation/Type/Industry	Location	Per	Low	Mid	High	Source	Date
Tool and Die Maker	Little Rock-North Little Rock MSA, AR	S	16.59 MW	16.85 AW	34510 AAW	ARBLS	10//99-12//99
	California	S	20.09 MW	20.01 AW	41620 AAW	CABLS	10//99-12//99
	Los Angeles-Long Beach PMSA, CA	S	19.30 MW	19.31 AW	40130 AAW	CABLS	10//99-12//99
	Modesto MSA, CA	S	17.90 MW	18.38 AW	37220 AAW	CABLS	10//99-12//99
	Oakland PMSA, CA	S	26.29 MW	25.54 AW	54690 AAW	CABLS	10//99-12//99
	Orange County PMSA, CA	S	20.25 MW	20.65 AW	42130 AAW	CABLS	10//99-12//99
	Riverside-San Bernardino PMSA, CA	S	19.11 MW	19.21 AW	39740 AAW	CABLS	10//99-12//99
	Sacramento PMSA, CA	S	18.97 MW	19.03 AW	39460 AAW	CABLS	10//99-12//99
	San Diego MSA, CA	S	19.58 MW	20.30 AW	40730 AAW	CABLS	10//99-12//99
	San Francisco PMSA, CA	S	16.04 MW	13.14 AW	33360 AAW	CABLS	10//99-12//99
	San José PMSA, CA	S	22.95 MW	22.97 AW	47730 AAW	CABLS	10//99-12//99
	Ventura PMSA, CA	S	18.18 MW	18.47 AW	37820 AAW	CABLS	10//99-12//99
	Colorado	S	18.92 MW	19.15 AW	39840 AAW	COBLS	10//99-12//99
	Boulder-Longmont PMSA, CO	S	19.75 MW	20.04 AW	41080 AAW	COBLS	10//99-12//99
	Denver PMSA, CO	S	18.25 MW	18.34 AW	37950 AAW	COBLS	10//99-12//99
	Greeley PMSA, CO	S	20.79 MW	21.38 AW	43250 AAW	COBLS	10//99-12//99
	Connecticut	S	19.53 MW	19.81 AW	41210 AAW	CTBLS	10//99-12//99
	Bridgeport PMSA, CT	S	20.03 MW	19.96 AW	41650 AAW	CTBLS	10//99-12//99
	Danbury PMSA, CT	S	21.12 MW	21.17 AW	43930 AAW	CTBLS	10//99-12//99
	Hartford MSA, CT	S	19.69 MW	19.31 AW	40960 AAW	CTBLS	10//99-12//99
	New Haven-Meriden PMSA, CT	S	19.47 MW	19.69 AW	40500 AAW	CTBLS	10//99-12//99
	New London-Norwich MSA, CT-RI	S	18.12 MW	18.20 AW	37690 AAW	CTBLS	10//99-12//99
	Stamford-Norwalk PMSA, CT	S	21.47 MW	22.49 AW	44650 AAW	CTBLS	10//99-12//99
	Waterbury PMSA, CT	S	20.25 MW	19.69 AW	42130 AAW	CTBLS	10//99-12//99
	Washington PMSA, DC-MD-VA-WV	S	17.69 MW	15.04 AW	36800 AAW	DCBLS	10//99-12//99
	Florida	S	16.66 MW	16.56 AW	34450 AAW	FLBLS	10//99-12//99
	Daytona Beach MSA, FL	S	16.36 MW	17.41 AW	34030 AAW	FLBLS	10//99-12//99
	Fort Lauderdale PMSA, FL	S	18.58 MW	18.32 AW	38650 AAW	FLBLS	10//99-12//99
	Jacksonville MSA, FL	S	15.72 MW	15.72 AW	32700 AAW	FLBLS	10//99-12//99
	Melbourne-Titusville-Palm Bay MSA, FL	S	15.66 MW	16.82 AW	32570 AAW	FLBLS	10//99-12//99
	Miami PMSA, FL	S	15.47 MW	14.89 AW	32170 AAW	FLBLS	10//99-12//99
	Orlando MSA, FL	S	17.47 MW	17.19 AW	36340 AAW	FLBLS	10//99-12//99
	Sarasota-Bradenton MSA, FL	S	16.60 MW	15.64 AW	34530 AAW	FLBLS	10//99-12//99
	Tampa-St. Petersburg-Clearwater MSA, FL	S	15.84 MW	15.76 AW	32950 AAW	FLBLS	10//99-12//99
	West Palm Beach-Boca Raton MSA, FL	S	18.46 MW	18.55 AW	38390 AAW	FLBLS	10//99-12//99
	Georgia	S	16.57 MW	16.94 AW	35230 AAW	GABLS	10//99-12//99
	Athens MSA, GA	S	19.82 MW	19.23 AW	41220 AAW	GABLS	10//99-12//99
	Atlanta MSA, GA	S	17.60 MW	17.26 AW	36600 AAW	GABLS	10//99-12//99
	Columbus MSA, GA-AL	S	14.84 MW	14.76 AW	30860 AAW	GABLS	10//99-12//99
	Macon MSA, GA	S	18.96 MW	19.65 AW	39450 AAW	GABLS	10//99-12//99
	Idaho	S	16.81 MW	16.21 AW	33710 AAW	IDBLS	10//99-12//99
	Boise City MSA, ID	S	15.49 MW	16.11 AW	32220 AAW	IDBLS	10//99-12//99
	Illinois	S	18.81 MW	19.41 AW	40370 AAW	ILBLS	10//99-12//99
	Bloomington-Normal MSA, IL	S	23.41 MW	24.57 AW	48690 AAW	ILBLS	10//99-12//99
	Chicago PMSA, IL	S	19.66 MW	19.11 AW	40900 AAW	ILBLS	10//99-12//99
	Peoria-Pekin MSA, IL	S	21.58 MW	22.87 AW	44880 AAW	ILBLS	10//99-12//99
	Rockford MSA, IL	S	19.95 MW	19.51 AW	41490 AAW	ILBLS	10//99-12//99
	Indiana	S	18.81 MW	19.77 AW	41120 AAW	INBLS	10//99-12//99
	Elkhart-Goshen MSA, IN	S	16.05 MW	16.03 AW	33380 AAW	INBLS	10//99-12//99
	Evansville-Henderson MSA, IN-KY	S	17.01 MW	16.51 AW	35380 AAW	INBLS	10//99-12//99
	Fort Wayne MSA, IN	S	18.01 MW	17.70 AW	37470 AAW	INBLS	10//99-12//99
	Gary PMSA, IN	S	18.76 MW	18.70 AW	39010 AAW	INBLS	10//99-12//99
	Indianapolis MSA, IN	S	25.18 MW	24.73 AW	52380 AAW	INBLS	10//99-12//99
	Kokomo MSA, IN	S	24.47 MW	24.35 AW	50900 AAW	INBLS	10//99-12//99
	Lafayette MSA, IN	S	18.49 MW	16.80 AW	38460 AAW	INBLS	10//99-12//99
	Muncie MSA, IN	S	17.63 MW	18.57 AW	36680 AAW	INBLS	10//99-12//99
	South Bend MSA, IN	S	18.82 MW	18.25 AW	39140 AAW	INBLS	10//99-12//99
	Iowa	S	17.11 MW	17.42 AW	36220 AAW	IABLS	10//99-12//99
	Cedar Rapids MSA, IA	S	18.13 MW	18.58 AW	37700 AAW	IABLS	10//99-12//99
	Davenport-Moline-Rock Island MSA, IA-IL	S	17.90 MW	18.31 AW	37240 AAW	IABLS	10//99-12//99
	Des Moines MSA, IA	S	17.49 MW	16.86 AW	36380 AAW	IABLS	10//99-12//99

AAW Average annual wage	AOH Average offered, high	ASH Average starting, high	H Hourly	M Monthly	S Special: hourly and annual
AE Average entry wage	AOL Average offered, low	ASL Average starting, low	HI Highest wage paid	MTC Median total compensation	TQ Third quartile wage
AEX Average experienced wage	APH Average pay, high range	AW Average wage paid	HR High end range	MW Median wage paid	W Weekly
AO Average offered	APL Average pay, low range	FQ First quartile wage	LR Low end range	SQ Second quartile wage	Y Yearly

Occupation/Type/Industry	Location	Per	Low	Mid	High	Source	Date
Tool and Die Maker	Dubuque MSA, IA	S	19.02 MW	19.70 AW	39560 AAW	IABLS	10//99-12//99
	Waterloo-Cedar Falls MSA, IA	S	19.16 MW	19.64 AW	39850 AAW	IABLS	10//99-12//99
	Kansas	S	17.7 MW	19.81 AW	41210 AAW	KSBLS	10//99-12//99
	Wichita MSA, KS	S	21.23 MW	18.96 AW	44150 AAW	KSBLS	10//99-12//99
	Kentucky	S	16.7 MW	16.81 AW	34960 AAW	KYBLS	10//99-12//99
	Lexington MSA, KY	S	15.91 MW	16.66 AW	33090 AAW	KYBLS	10//99-12//99
	Louisville MSA, KY-IN	S	17.77 MW	18.51 AW	36950 AAW	KYBLS	10//99-12//99
	Louisiana	S	16.28 MW	18.29 AW	38040 AAW	LABLS	10//99-12//99
	Shreveport-Bossier City MSA, LA	S	22.86 MW	21.84 AW	47550 AAW	LABLS	10//99-12//99
	Maine	S	17.99 MW	17.41 AW	36210 AAW	MEBLS	10//99-12//99
	Portland MSA, ME	S	15.38 MW	15.53 AW	31990 AAW	MEBLS	10//99-12//99
	Maryland	S	15.16 MW	17.36 AW	36110 AAW	MDBLS	10//99-12//99
	Baltimore PMSA, MD	S	17.37 MW	11.98 AW	36120 AAW	MDBLS	10//99-12//99
	Massachusetts	S	18.06 MW	18.13 AW	37720 AAW	MABLS	10//99-12//99
	Boston PMSA, MA-NH	S	18.28 MW	18.28 AW	38010 AAW	MABLS	10//99-12//99
	Brockton PMSA, MA	S	17.26 MW	17.68 AW	35910 AAW	MABLS	10//99-12//99
	Fitchburg-Leominster PMSA, MA	S	19.05 MW	20.59 AW	39620 AAW	MABLS	10//99-12//99
	Lawrence PMSA, MA-NH	S	22.60 MW	23.29 AW	47010 AAW	MABLS	10//99-12//99
	Lowell PMSA, MA-NH	S	16.15 MW	17.04 AW	33590 AAW	MABLS	10//99-12//99
	Pittsfield MSA, MA	S	17.89 MW	18.47 AW	37210 AAW	MABLS	10//99-12//99
	Springfield MSA, MA	S	17.52 MW	16.24 AW	36440 AAW	MABLS	10//99-12//99
	Worcester PMSA, MA-CT	S	18.33 MW	18.16 AW	38120 AAW	MABLS	10//99-12//99
	Michigan	S	21.41 MW	21.39 AW	44490 AAW	MIBLS	10//99-12//99
	Ann Arbor PMSA, MI	S	21.56 MW	22.34 AW	44840 AAW	MIBLS	10//99-12//99
	Benton Harbor MSA, MI	S	16.08 MW	16.71 AW	33440 AAW	MIBLS	10//99-12//99
	Detroit PMSA, MI	S	21.78 MW	21.95 AW	45300 AAW	MIBLS	10//99-12//99
	Grand Rapids-Muskegon-Holland MSA, MI	S	21.31 MW	21.43 AW	44320 AAW	MIBLS	10//99-12//99
	Jackson MSA, MI	S	18.38 MW	18.70 AW	38230 AAW	MIBLS	10//99-12//99
	Kalamazoo-Battle Creek MSA, MI	S	21.51 MW	21.93 AW	44750 AAW	MIBLS	10//99-12//99
	Lansing-East Lansing MSA, MI	S	23.81 MW	23.26 AW	49530 AAW	MIBLS	10//99-12//99
	Minnesota	S	19.3 MW	19.27 AW	40090 AAW	MNBLS	10//99-12//99
	Minneapolis-St. Paul MSA, MN-WI	S	20.26 MW	20.54 AW	42150 AAW	MNBLS	10//99-12//99
	Rochester MSA, MN	S	19.83 MW	19.82 AW	41240 AAW	MNBLS	10//99-12//99
	Mississippi	S	15.16 MW	17.06 AW	35490 AAW	MSBLS	10//99-12//99
	Biloxi-Gulfport-Pascagoula MSA, MS	S	14.16 MW	14.54 AW	29450 AAW	MSBLS	10//99-12//99
	Missouri	S	18.32 MW	18.66 AW	38800 AAW	MOBLS	10//99-12//99
	Joplin MSA, MO	S	14.35 MW	14.50 AW	29850 AAW	MOBLS	10//99-12//99
	Kansas City MSA, MO-KS	S	20.68 MW	19.66 AW	43010 AAW	MOBLS	10//99-12//99
	St. Joseph MSA, MO	S	14.74 MW	14.80 AW	30660 AAW	MOBLS	10//99-12//99
	St. Louis MSA, MO-IL	S	20.86 MW	20.88 AW	43400 AAW	MOBLS	10//99-12//99
	Springfield MSA, MO	S	14.12 MW	14.00 AW	29370 AAW	MOBLS	10//99-12//99
	Nebraska	S	16.19 MW	16.84 AW	35020 AAW	NEBLS	10//99-12//99
	Omaha MSA, NE-IA	S	19.33 MW	20.23 AW	40200 AAW	NEBLS	10//99-12//99
	Nevada	S	18.34 MW	18.66 AW	38810 AAW	NVBLS	10//99-12//99
	Las Vegas MSA, NV-AZ	S	16.76 MW	17.18 AW	34860 AAW	NVBLS	10//99-12//99
	Reno MSA, NV	S	18.84 MW	18.94 AW	39190 AAW	NVBLS	10//99-12//99
	New Hampshire	S	14.82 MW	15.47 AW	32170 AAW	NHBLS	10//99-12//99
	Manchester PMSA, NH	S	16.37 MW	16.36 AW	34040 AAW	NHBLS	10//99-12//99
	Nashua PMSA, NH	S	19.46 MW	19.44 AW	40470 AAW	NHBLS	10//99-12//99
	Portsmouth-Rochester PMSA, NH-ME	S	18.42 MW	18.35 AW	38310 AAW	NHBLS	10//99-12//99
	New Jersey	S	20.01 MW	20.80 AW	43270 AAW	NJBLS	10//99-12//99
	Bergen-Passaic PMSA, NJ	S	19.82 MW	19.07 AW	41230 AAW	NJBLS	10//99-12//99
	Jersey City PMSA, NJ	S	18.78 MW	17.51 AW	39050 AAW	NJBLS	10//99-12//99
	Middlesex-Somerset-Hunterdon PMSA, NJ	S	20.82 MW	21.23 AW	43300 AAW	NJBLS	10//99-12//99
	Monmouth-Ocean PMSA, NJ	S	21.12 MW	20.67 AW	43930 AAW	NJBLS	10//99-12//99
	Newark PMSA, NJ	S	21.93 MW	20.94 AW	45620 AAW	NJBLS	10//99-12//99
	Trenton PMSA, NJ	S	26.33 MW	28.49 AW	54780 AAW	NJBLS	10//99-12//99
	New Mexico	S	15.03 MW	16.92 AW	35200 AAW	NMBLS	10//99-12//99
	New York	S	18.8 MW	18.98 AW	39480 AAW	NYBLS	10//99-12//99
	Albany-Schenectady-Troy MSA, NY	S	16.81 MW	16.49 AW	34960 AAW	NYBLS	10//99-12//99
	Binghamton MSA, NY	S	16.87 MW	16.04 AW	35090 AAW	NYBLS	10//99-12//99
	Buffalo-Niagara Falls MSA, NY	S	22.01 MW	22.92 AW	45780 AAW	NYBLS	10//99-12//99

AAW Average annual wage	AOH Average offered, high	ASH Average starting, high	H Hourly	M Monthly	S Special: hourly and annual
AE Average entry wage	AOL Average offered, low	ASL Average starting, low	HI Highest wage paid	MTC Median total compensation	TQ Third quartile wage
AEX Average experienced wage	APH Average pay, high range	AW Average wage paid	HR High end range	MW Median wage paid	W Weekly
AO Average offered	APL Average pay, low range	FQ First quartile wage	LR Low end range	SQ Second quartile wage	Y Yearly

Occupation/Type/Industry	Location	Per	Low	Mid	High	Source	Date
Tool and Die Maker	Elmira MSA, NY	S	15.09 MW	15.56 AW	31390 AAW	NYBLS	10//99-12//99
	Jamestown MSA, NY	S	16.14 MW	16.63 AW	33580 AAW	NYBLS	10//99-12//99
	Nassau-Suffolk PMSA, NY	S	21.11 MW	21.03 AW	43910 AAW	NYBLS	10//99-12//99
	New York PMSA, NY	S	19.57 MW	19.13 AW	40710 AAW	NYBLS	10//99-12//99
	Rochester MSA, NY	S	18.06 MW	17.85 AW	37570 AAW	NYBLS	10//99-12//99
	Syracuse MSA, NY	S	19.34 MW	19.38 AW	40220 AAW	NYBLS	10//99-12//99
	Utica-Rome MSA, NY	S	16.15 MW	15.69 AW	33590 AAW	NYBLS	10//99-12//99
	North Carolina	S	17.19 MW	17.26 AW	35890 AAW	NCBLS	10//99-12//99
	Asheville MSA, NC	S	18.26 MW	17.82 AW	37970 AAW	NCBLS	10//99-12//99
	Charlotte-Gastonia-Rock Hill MSA, NC-SC	S	18.26 MW	17.44 AW	37980 AAW	NCBLS	10//99-12//99
	Fayetteville MSA, NC	S	19.02 MW	18.88 AW	39550 AAW	NCBLS	10//99-12//99
	Greensboro--Winston-Salem--High Point MSA, NC	S	17.12 MW	17.57 AW	35610 AAW	NCBLS	10//99-12//99
	Hickory-Morganton-Lenoir MSA, NC	S	17.27 MW	15.88 AW	35920 AAW	NCBLS	10//99-12//99
	Raleigh-Durham-Chapel Hill MSA, NC	S	17.85 MW	18.31 AW	37120 AAW	NCBLS	10//99-12//99
	North Dakota	S	15.12 MW	15.48 AW	32200 AAW	NDBLS	10//99-12//99
	Fargo-Moorhead MSA, ND-MN	S	15.17 MW	14.45 AW	31550 AAW	NDBLS	10//99-12//99
	Ohio	S	18.47 MW	18.94 AW	39400 AAW	OHBLS	10//99-12//99
	Akron PMSA, OH	S	19.54 MW	19.94 AW	40650 AAW	OHBLS	10//99-12//99
	Canton-Massillon MSA, OH	S	16.46 MW	16.45 AW	34230 AAW	OHBLS	10//99-12//99
	Cincinnati PMSA, OH-KY-IN	S	18.59 MW	18.39 AW	38670 AAW	OHBLS	10//99-12//99
	Cleveland-Lorain-Elyria PMSA, OH	S	18.80 MW	18.47 AW	39110 AAW	OHBLS	10//99-12//99
	Columbus MSA, OH	S	19.11 MW	19.21 AW	39760 AAW	OHBLS	10//99-12//99
	Dayton-Springfield MSA, OH	S	19.61 MW	18.98 AW	40790 AAW	OHBLS	10//99-12//99
	Hamilton-Middletown PMSA, OH	S	16.53 MW	17.38 AW	34390 AAW	OHBLS	10//99-12//99
	Lima MSA, OH	S	16.71 MW	16.32 AW	34750 AAW	OHBLS	10//99-12//99
	Mansfield MSA, OH	S	22.35 MW	22.99 AW	46490 AAW	OHBLS	10//99-12//99
	Toledo MSA, OH	S	20.58 MW	20.48 AW	42810 AAW	OHBLS	10//99-12//99
	Youngstown-Warren MSA, OH	S	21.54 MW	21.83 AW	44800 AAW	OHBLS	10//99-12//99
	Oklahoma	S	18.81 MW	19.50 AW	40550 AAW	OKBLS	10//99-12//99
	Oklahoma City MSA, OK	S	19.97 MW	18.76 AW	41530 AAW	OKBLS	10//99-12//99
	Tulsa MSA, OK	S	19.63 MW	19.58 AW	40830 AAW	OKBLS	10//99-12//99
	Oregon	S	18.63 MW	19.77 AW	41120 AAW	ORBLS	10//99-12//99
	Eugene-Springfield MSA, OR	S	16.07 MW	15.50 AW	33410 AAW	ORBLS	10//99-12//99
	Portland-Vancouver PMSA, OR-WA	S	20.81 MW	19.66 AW	43280 AAW	ORBLS	10//99-12//99
	Salem PMSA, OR	S	14.95 MW	15.44 AW	31100 AAW	ORBLS	10//99-12//99
	Pennsylvania	S	17.66 MW	18.11 AW	37670 AAW	PABLS	10//99-12//99
	Allentown-Bethlehem-Easton MSA, PA	S	19.90 MW	18.39 AW	41400 AAW	PABLS	10//99-12//99
	Erie MSA, PA	S	18.29 MW	18.85 AW	38040 AAW	PABLS	10//99-12//99
	Harrisburg-Lebanon-Carlisle MSA, PA	S	16.09 MW	15.60 AW	33460 AAW	PABLS	10//99-12//99
	Johnstown MSA, PA	S	17.00 MW	16.37 AW	35350 AAW	PABLS	10//99-12//99
	Lancaster MSA, PA	S	18.92 MW	18.75 AW	39360 AAW	PABLS	10//99-12//99
	Philadelphia PMSA, PA-NJ	S	19.03 MW	18.72 AW	39580 AAW	PABLS	10//99-12//99
	Pittsburgh MSA, PA	S	19.99 MW	18.18 AW	41570 AAW	PABLS	10//99-12//99
	Reading MSA, PA	S	22.00 MW	19.65 AW	45760 AAW	PABLS	10//99-12//99
	Scranton--Wilkes-Barre--Hazleton MSA, PA	S	14.03 MW	14.19 AW	29180 AAW	PABLS	10//99-12//99
	Sharon MSA, PA	S	13.52 MW	12.79 AW	28120 AAW	PABLS	10//99-12//99
	Williamsport MSA, PA	S	14.90 MW	15.07 AW	31000 AAW	PABLS	10//99-12//99
	York MSA, PA	S	15.72 MW	15.58 AW	32700 AAW	PABLS	10//99-12//99
	Rhode Island	S	18.46 MW	18.58 AW	38640 AAW	RIBLS	10//99-12//99
	Providence-Fall River-Warwick MSA, RI-MA	S	18.33 MW	18.33 AW	38130 AAW	RIBLS	10//99-12//99
	South Carolina	S	16.32 MW	16.58 AW	34480 AAW	SCBLS	10//99-12//99
	Charleston-North Charleston MSA, SC	S	19.22 MW	20.45 AW	39980 AAW	SCBLS	10//99-12//99
	Florence MSA, SC	S	17.41 MW	16.69 AW	36220 AAW	SCBLS	10//99-12//99
	Greenville-Spartanburg-Anderson MSA, SC	S	16.47 MW	16.06 AW	34260 AAW	SCBLS	10//99-12//99
	South Dakota	S	14.38 MW	14.49 AW	30130 AAW	SDBLS	10//99-12//99
	Tennessee	S	16.57 MW	17.06 AW	35480 AAW	TNBLS	10//99-12//99
	Chattanooga MSA, TN-GA	S	16.67 MW	15.37 AW	34680 AAW	TNBLS	10//99-12//99

AAW	Average annual wage	AOH	Average offered, high	ASH	Average starting, high	H	Hourly	M	Monthly	S	Special: hourly and annual
AE	Average entry wage	AOL	Average offered, low	ASL	Average starting, low	HI	Highest wage paid	MTC	Median total compensation	TQ	Third quartile wage
AEX	Average experienced wage	APH	Average pay, high range	AW	Average wage paid	HR	High end range	MW	Median wage paid	W	Weekly
AO	Average offered	APL	Average pay, low range	FQ	First quartile wage	LR	Low end range	SQ	Second quartile wage	Y	Yearly

Occupation/Type/Industry	Location	Per	Low	Mid	High	Source	Date
Tool and Die Maker	Clarksville-Hopkinsville MSA, TN-KY	S	17.88 MW	17.83 AW	37190 AAW	TNBLS	10//99-12//99
	Jackson MSA, TN	S	16.51 MW	16.73 AW	34330 AAW	TNBLS	10//99-12//99
	Johnson City-Kingsport-Bristol MSA, TN-VA	S	14.65 MW	14.90 AW	30480 AAW	TNBLS	10//99-12//99
	Knoxville MSA, TN	S	15.95 MW	16.87 AW	33170 AAW	TNBLS	10//99-12//99
	Memphis MSA, TN-AR-MS	S	17.03 MW	16.97 AW	35420 AAW	MSBLS	10//99-12//99
	Nashville MSA, TN	S	16.97 MW	17.12 AW	35300 AAW	TNBLS	10//99-12//99
	Texas	S	17.44 MW	17.08 AW	35520 AAW	TXBLS	10//99-12//99
	Austin-San Marcos MSA, TX	S	18.34 MW	18.75 AW	38150 AAW	TXBLS	10//99-12//99
	Brownsville-Harlingen-San Benito MSA, TX	S	12.60 MW	12.24 AW	26200 AAW	TXBLS	10//99-12//99
	Dallas PMSA, TX	S	17.27 MW	17.75 AW	35920 AAW	TXBLS	10//99-12//99
	El Paso MSA, TX	S	13.58 MW	13.71 AW	28240 AAW	TXBLS	10//99-12//99
	Fort Worth-Arlington PMSA, TX	S	20.58 MW	20.84 AW	42800 AAW	TXBLS	10//99-12//99
	Houston PMSA, TX	S	18.22 MW	18.38 AW	.37900 AAW	TXBLS	10//99-12//99
	Killeen-Temple MSA, TX	S	15.81 MW	16.62 AW	32890 AAW	TXBLS	10//99-12//99
	Longview-Marshall MSA, TX	S	17.48 MW	17.48 AW	36350 AAW	TXBLS	10//99-12//99
	Sherman-Denison MSA, TX	S	16.73 MW	16.92 AW	34790 AAW	TXBLS	10//99-12//99
	Utah	S	19.16 MW	18.54 AW	38570 AAW	UTBLS	10//99-12//99
	Salt Lake City-Ogden MSA, UT	S	18.82 MW	19.12 AW	39150 AAW	UTBLS	10//99-12//99
	Vermont	S	15.76 MW	16.43 AW	34160 AAW	VTBLS	10//99-12//99
	Virginia	S	16.4 MW	16.43 AW	34170 AAW	VABLS	10//99-12//99
	Lynchburg MSA, VA	S	17.22 MW	17.88 AW	35810 AAW	VABLS	10//99-12//99
	Norfolk-Virginia Beach-Newport News MSA, VA-NC	S	16.66 MW	16.54 AW	34640 AAW	VABLS	10//99-12//99
	Richmond-Petersburg MSA, VA	S	16.56 MW	16.43 AW	34450 AAW	VABLS	10//99-12//99
	Roanoke MSA, VA	S	16.44 MW	15.59 AW	34200 AAW	VABLS	10//99-12//99
	Washington	S	22.15 MW	22.39 AW	46560 AAW	WABLS	10//99-12//99
	Seattle-Bellevue-Everett PMSA, WA	S	23.57 MW	23.15 AW	49030 AAW	WABLS	10//99-12//99
	Spokane MSA, WA	S	16.75 MW	16.93 AW	34830 AAW	WABLS	10//99-12//99
	Tacoma PMSA, WA	S	20.27 MW	20.91 AW	42170 AAW	WABLS	10//99-12//99
	West Virginia	S	13.45 MW	14.98 AW	31160 AAW	WVBLS	10//99-12//99
	Huntington-Ashland MSA, WV-KY-OH	S	12.91 MW	13.34 AW	26850 AAW	WVBLS	10//99-12//99
	Wisconsin	S	18.58 MW	18.83 AW	39170 AAW	WIBLS	10//99-12//99
	Appleton-Oshkosh-Neenah MSA, WI	S	19.29 MW	18.91 AW	40120 AAW	WIBLS	10//99-12//99
	Eau Claire MSA, WI	S	16.76 MW	16.49 AW	34860 AAW	WIBLS	10//99-12//99
	Green Bay MSA, WI	S	17.74 MW	17.49 AW	36890 AAW	WIBLS	10//99-12//99
	Janesville-Beloit MSA, WI	S	22.90 MW	19.93 AW	47640 AAW	WIBLS	10//99-12//99
	Kenosha PMSA, WI	S	17.41 MW	17.16 AW	36220 AAW	WIBLS	10//99-12//99
	La Crosse MSA, WI-MN	S	16.94 MW	17.03 AW	35230 AAW	WIBLS	10//99-12//99
	Madison MSA, WI	S	18.09 MW	17.95 AW	37630 AAW	WIBLS	10//99-12//99
	Milwaukee-Waukesha PMSA, WI	S	20.15 MW	19.75 AW	41920 AAW	WIBLS	10//99-12//99
	Racine PMSA, WI	S	18.55 MW	18.56 AW	38580 AAW	WIBLS	10//99-12//99
	Wausau MSA, WI	S	17.03 MW	17.61 AW	35420 AAW	WIBLS	10//99-12//99
	Puerto Rico	S	10.61 MW	10.74 AW	22350 AAW	PRBLS	10//99-12//99
	San Juan-Bayamon PMSA, PR	S	10.29 MW	10.09 AW	21400 AAW	PRBLS	10//99-12//99
Tool Grinder, Filer, and Sharpener	Alabama	S	12.57 MW	12.44 AW	25870 AAW	ALBLS	10//99-12//99
	Birmingham MSA, AL	S	14.12 MW	13.34 AW	29370 AAW	ALBLS	10//99-12//99
	Florence MSA, AL	S	10.04 MW	10.17 AW	20890 AAW	ALBLS	10//99-12//99
	Arizona	S	11.47 MW	11.76 AW	24450 AAW	AZBLS	10//99-12//99
	Phoenix-Mesa MSA, AZ	S	11.67 MW	11.40 AW	24260 AAW	AZBLS	10//99-12//99
	Tucson MSA, AZ	S	12.42 MW	11.85 AW	25830 AAW	AZBLS	10//99-12//99
	Arkansas	S	10.95 MW	10.79 AW	22450 AAW	ARBLS	10//99-12//99
	California	S	10.23 MW	11.47 AW	23860 AAW	CABLS	10//99-12//99
	Los Angeles-Long Beach PMSA, CA	S	10.58 MW	9.40 AW	22010 AAW	CABLS	10//99-12//99
	Modesto MSA, CA	S	10.93 MW	10.01 AW	22740 AAW	CABLS	10//99-12//99
	Orange County PMSA, CA	S	13.67 MW	12.22 AW	28430 AAW	CABLS	10//99-12//99
	Riverside-San Bernardino PMSA, CA	S	11.75 MW	10.90 AW	24430 AAW	CABLS	10//99-12//99
	San Diego MSA, CA	S	11.06 MW	9.28 AW	23000 AAW	CABLS	10//99-12//99

AAW Average annual wage	AOH Average offered, high	ASH Average starting, high	H Hourly	M Monthly	S Special: hourly and annual
AE Average entry wage	AOL Average offered, low	ASL Average starting, low	HI Highest wage paid	MTC Median total compensation	TQ Third quartile wage
AEX Average experienced wage	APH Average pay, high range	AW Average wage paid	HR High end range	MW Median wage paid	W Weekly
AO Average offered	APL Average pay, low range	FQ First quartile wage	LR Low end range	SQ Second quartile wage	Y Yearly

Occupation/Type/Industry	Location	Per	Low	Mid	High	Source	Date
Tool Grinder, Filer, and Sharpener	San Jose PMSA, CA	S	15.05 MW	13.42 AW	31310 AAW	CABLS	10//99-12//99
	Santa Cruz-Watsonville PMSA, CA	S	11.20 MW	10.52 AW	23290 AAW	CABLS	10//99-12//99
	Ventura PMSA, CA	S	11.89 MW	11.31 AW	24730 AAW	CABLS	10//99-12//99
	Colorado	S	16.38 MW	15.88 AW	33040 AAW	COBLS	10//99-12//99
	Denver PMSA, CO	S	17.51 MW	17.62 AW	36420 AAW	COBLS	10//99-12//99
	Grand Junction MSA, CO	S	10.96 MW	10.35 AW	22800 AAW	COBLS	10//99-12//99
	Connecticut	S	14.66 MW	14.92 AW	31040 AAW	CTBLS	10//99-12//99
	Bridgeport PMSA, CT	S	15.59 MW	15.57 AW	32420 AAW	CTBLS	10//99-12//99
	Hartford MSA, CT	S	15.18 MW	15.25 AW	31570 AAW	CTBLS	10//99-12//99
	New Haven-Meriden PMSA, CT	S	15.20 MW	14.81 AW	31620 AAW	CTBLS	10//99-12//99
	Waterbury PMSA, CT	S	12.66 MW	12.82 AW	26320 AAW	CTBLS	10//99-12//99
	Florida	S	10.88 MW	11.64 AW	24210 AAW	FLBLS	10//99-12//99
	Melbourne-Titusville-Palm Bay MSA, FL	S	14.35 MW	14.25 AW	29840 AAW	FLBLS	10//99-12//99
	Miami PMSA, FL	S	11.49 MW	11.63 AW	23890 AAW	FLBLS	10//99-12//99
	Orlando MSA, FL	S	13.55 MW	13.16 AW	28190 AAW	FLBLS	10//99-12//99
	Sarasota-Bradenton MSA, FL	S	12.69 MW	12.34 AW	26390 AAW	FLBLS	10//99-12//99
	Tampa-St. Petersburg-Clearwater MSA, FL	S	9.91 MW	9.58 AW	20620 AAW	FLBLS	10//99-12//99
	Georgia	S	11.67 MW	11.92 AW	24800 AAW	GABLS	10//99-12//99
	Atlanta MSA, GA	S	11.25 MW	10.24 AW	23400 AAW	GABLS	10//99-12//99
	Idaho	S	14.21 MW	14.08 AW	29280 AAW	IDBLS	10//99-12//99
	Boise City MSA, ID	S	11.25 MW	12.27 AW	23410 AAW	IDBLS	10//99-12//99
	Illinois	S	13.97 MW	14.31 AW	29760 AAW	ILBLS	10//99-12//99
	Chicago PMSA, IL	S	13.89 MW	13.84 AW	28880 AAW	ILBLS	10//99-12//99
	Peoria-Pekin MSA, IL	S	19.97 MW	22.59 AW	41540 AAW	ILBLS	10//99-12//99
	Rockford MSA, IL	S	14.28 MW	14.19 AW	29700 AAW	ILBLS	10//99-12//99
	Indiana	S	15.34 MW	16.75 AW	34850 AAW	INBLS	10//99-12//99
	Fort Wayne MSA, IN	S	13.16 MW	11.58 AW	27370 AAW	INBLS	10//99-12//99
	Indianapolis MSA, IN	S	21.44 MW	20.87 AW	44590 AAW	INBLS	10//99-12//99
	Iowa	S	13.53 MW	14.02 AW	29160 AAW	IABLS	10//99-12//99
	Davenport-Moline-Rock Island MSA, IA-IL	S	12.54 MW	10.56 AW	26090 AAW	IABLS	10//99-12//99
	Kansas	S	13.45 MW	17.92 AW	37280 AAW	KSBLS	10//99-12//99
	Wichita MSA, KS	S	20.38 MW	13.85 AW	42400 AAW	KSBLS	10//99-12//99
	Kentucky	S	12.19 MW	12.54 AW	26080 AAW	KYBLS	10//99-12//99
	Lexington MSA, KY	S	11.40 MW	11.89 AW	23710 AAW	KYBLS	10//99-12//99
	Louisiana	S	14.12 MW	14.29 AW	29720 AAW	LABLS	10//99-12//99
	Baton Rouge MSA, LA	S	12.74 MW	12.39 AW	26500 AAW	LABLS	10//99-12//99
	Maine	S	11.65 MW	11.98 AW	24930 AAW	MEBLS	10//99-12//99
	Maryland	S	11.92 MW	13.31 AW	27680 AAW	MDBLS	10//99-12//99
	Baltimore PMSA, MD	S	12.56 MW	11.89 AW	26130 AAW	MDBLS	10//99-12//99
	Massachusetts	S	14.34 MW	14.88 AW	30950 AAW	MABLS	10//99-12//99
	Boston PMSA, MA-NH	S	17.24 MW	17.20 AW	35870 AAW	MABLS	10//99-12//99
	Lawrence PMSA, MA-NH	S	12.56 MW	10.91 AW	26120 AAW	MABLS	10//99-12//99
	Springfield MSA, MA	S	12.98 MW	12.91 AW	26990 AAW	MABLS	10//99-12//99
	Worcester PMSA, MA-CT	S	12.47 MW	11.99 AW	25930 AAW	MABLS	10//99-12//99
	Michigan	S	16.29 MW	17.22 AW	35820 AAW	MIBLS	10//99-12//99
	Ann Arbor PMSA, MI	S	12.07 MW	10.20 AW	25100 AAW	MIBLS	10//99-12//99
	Detroit PMSA, MI	S	18.74 MW	18.30 AW	38990 AAW	MIBLS	10//99-12//99
	Flint PMSA, MI	S	15.95 MW	17.33 AW	33170 AAW	MIBLS	10//99-12//99
	Grand Rapids-Muskegon-Holland MSA, MI	S	14.11 MW	13.11 AW	29350 AAW	MIBLS	10//99-12//99
	Jackson MSA, MI	S	16.30 MW	17.24 AW	33910 AAW	MIBLS	10//99-12//99
	Kalamazoo-Battle Creek MSA, MI	S	21.22 MW	22.90 AW	44130 AAW	MIBLS	10//99-12//99
	Lansing-East Lansing MSA, MI	S	15.36 MW	13.55 AW	31950 AAW	MIBLS	10//99-12//99
	Saginaw-Bay City-Midland MSA, MI	S	12.89 MW	13.80 AW	26810 AAW	MIBLS	10//99-12//99
	Minnesota	S	13.97 MW	14.73 AW	30640 AAW	MNBLS	10//99-12//99
	Minneapolis-St. Paul MSA, MN-WI	S	15.51 MW	14.79 AW	32260 AAW	MNBLS	10//99-12//99
	Mississippi	S	12.72 MW	12.44 AW	25880 AAW	MSBLS	10//99-12//99
	Missouri	S	13.43 MW	13.43 AW	27930 AAW	MOBLS	10//99-12//99
	Kansas City MSA, MO-KS	S	12.21 MW	12.43 AW	25400 AAW	MOBLS	10//99-12//99
	St. Louis MSA, MO-IL	S	13.94 MW	13.73 AW	28990 AAW	MOBLS	10//99-12//99
	Montana	S	11.93 MW	11.54 AW	24010 AAW	MTBLS	10//99-12//99
	Nebraska	S	12.47 MW	12.28 AW	25550 AAW	NEBLS	10//99-12//99
	Omaha MSA, NE-IA	S	12.95 MW	12.36 AW	26940 AAW	NEBLS	10//99-12//99

AAW	Average annual wage	AOH	Average offered, high	ASH	Average starting, high	H	Hourly	M	Monthly	S	Special: hourly and annual
AE	Average entry wage	AOL	Average offered, low	ASL	Average starting, low	HI	Highest wage paid	MTC	Median total compensation	TQ	Third quartile wage
AEX	Average experienced wage	APH	Average pay, high range	AW	Average wage paid	HR	High end range	MW	Median wage paid	W	Weekly
AO	Average offered	APL	Average pay, low range	FQ	First quartile wage	LR	Low end range	SQ	Second quartile wage	Y	Yearly

Occupation/Type/Industry	Location	Per	Low	Mid	High	Source	Date
Tool Grinder, Filer, and Sharpener	New Hampshire	S	11.31 MW	11.87 AW	24690 AAW	NHBLS	10//99-12//99
	Manchester PMSA, NH	S	11.25 MW	10.85 AW	23390 AAW	NHBLS	10//99-12//99
	New Jersey	S	12.42 MW	12.83 AW	26690 AAW	NJBLS	10//99-12//99
	Bergen-Passaic PMSA, NJ	S	13.35 MW	12.62 AW	27780 AAW	NJBLS	10//99-12//99
	Middlesex-Somerset-Hunterdon PMSA, NJ	S	12.24 MW	11.58 AW	25470 AAW	NJBLS	10//99-12//99
	Newark PMSA, NJ	S	11.32 MW	10.98 AW	23550 AAW	NJBLS	10//99-12//99
	New Mexico	S	10.98 MW	10.73 AW	22330 AAW	NMBLS	10//99-12//99
	New York	S	12.57 MW	13.27 AW	27600 AAW	NYBLS	10//99-12//99
	Albany-Schenectady-Troy MSA, NY	S	13.00 MW	13.09 AW	27040 AAW	NYBLS	10//99-12//99
	Buffalo-Niagara Falls MSA, NY	S	13.83 MW	14.13 AW	28760 AAW	NYBLS	10//99-12//99
	Jamestown MSA, NY	S	12.45 MW	12.60 AW	25900 AAW	NYBLS	10//99-12//99
	Nassau-Suffolk PMSA, NY	S	14.11 MW	14.06 AW	29340 AAW	NYBLS	10//99-12//99
	New York PMSA, NY	S	13.25 MW	11.71 AW	27550 AAW	NYBLS	10//99-12//99
	Syracuse MSA, NY	S	14.25 MW	13.31 AW	29640 AAW	NYBLS	10//99-12//99
	North Carolina	S	12.41 MW	12.74 AW	26490 AAW	NCBLS	10//99-12//99
	Asheville MSA, NC	S	13.39 MW	13.78 AW	27850 AAW	NCBLS	10//99-12//99
	Charlotte-Gastonia-Rock Hill MSA, NC-SC	S	13.58 MW	12.92 AW	28250 AAW	NCBLS	10//99-12//99
	Greensboro--Winston-Salem--High Point MSA, NC	S	11.49 MW	10.97 AW	23900 AAW	NCBLS	10//99-12//99
	Hickory-Morganton-Lenoir MSA, NC	S	11.38 MW	11.35 AW	23670 AAW	NCBLS	10//99-12//99
	Raleigh-Durham-Chapel Hill MSA, NC	S	11.67 MW	11.16 AW	24280 AAW	NCBLS	10//99-12//99
	Ohio	S	14.42 MW	14.57 AW	30300 AAW	OHBLS	10//99-12//99
	Akron PMSA, OH	S	13.53 MW	13.86 AW	28130 AAW	OHBLS	10//99-12//99
	Canton-Massillon MSA, OH	S	13.32 MW	13.47 AW	27700 AAW	OHBLS	10//99-12//99
	Cincinnati PMSA, OH-KY-IN	S	14.92 MW	15.28 AW	31030 AAW	OHBLS	10//99-12//99
	Cleveland-Lorain-Elyria PMSA, OH	S	15.07 MW	14.80 AW	31340 AAW	OHBLS	10//99-12//99
	Dayton-Springfield MSA, OH	S	18.12 MW	17.87 AW	37690 AAW	OHBLS	10//99-12//99
	Mansfield MSA, OH	S	13.49 MW	13.52 AW	28060 AAW	OHBLS	10//99-12//99
	Youngstown-Warren MSA, OH	S	13.61 MW	13.78 AW	28300 AAW	OHBLS	10//99-12//99
	Oklahoma	S	13.94 MW	13.27 AW	27610 AAW	OKBLS	10//99-12//99
	Oklahoma City MSA, OK	S	16.51 MW	16.81 AW	34340 AAW	OKBLS	10//99-12//99
	Tulsa MSA, OK	S	13.99 MW	14.19 AW	29110 AAW	OKBLS	10//99-12//99
	Oregon	S	14.57 MW	15.01 AW	31230 AAW	ORBLS	10//99-12//99
	Eugene-Springfield MSA, OR	S	14.15 MW	13.86 AW	29420 AAW	ORBLS	10//99-12//99
	Medford-Ashland MSA, OR	S	13.57 MW	13.05 AW	28220 AAW	ORBLS	10//99-12//99
	Portland-Vancouver PMSA, OR-WA	S	15.43 MW	14.53 AW	32100 AAW	ORBLS	10//99-12//99
	Pennsylvania	S	13.91 MW	14.24 AW	29620 AAW	PABLS	10//99-12//99
	Erie MSA, PA	S	13.44 MW	13.57 AW	27960 AAW	PABLS	10//99-12//99
	Lancaster MSA, PA	S	11.11 MW	10.34 AW	23110 AAW	PABLS	10//99-12//99
	Philadelphia PMSA, PA-NJ	S	16.83 MW	16.11 AW	35000 AAW	PABLS	10//99-12//99
	Pittsburgh MSA, PA	S	14.67 MW	14.53 AW	30510 AAW	PABLS	10//99-12//99
	York MSA, PA	S	15.34 MW	15.54 AW	31910 AAW	PABLS	10//99-12//99
	Rhode Island	S	14.27 MW	14.47 AW	30100 AAW	RIBLS	10//99-12//99
	Providence-Fall River-Warwick MSA, RI-MA	S	14.46 MW	14.14 AW	30080 AAW	RIBLS	10//99-12//99
	South Carolina	S	12.32 MW	12.95 AW	26930 AAW	SCBLS	10//99-12//99
	Columbia MSA, SC	S	11.93 MW	10.47 AW	24820 AAW	SCBLS	10//99-12//99
	Greenville-Spartanburg-Anderson MSA, SC	S	12.86 MW	11.99 AW	26760 AAW	SCBLS	10//99-12//99
	South Dakota	S	11.84 MW	11.63 AW	24180 AAW	SDBLS	10//99-12//99
	Tennessee	S	12 MW	12.40 AW	25800 AAW	TNBLS	10//99-12//99
	Chattanooga MSA, TN-GA	S	11.70 MW	10.70 AW	24340 AAW	TNBLS	10//99-12//99
	Johnson City-Kingsport-Bristol MSA, TN-VA	S	10.66 MW	10.07 AW	22180 AAW	TNBLS	10//99-12//99
	Knoxville MSA, TN	S	12.35 MW	13.61 AW	25700 AAW	TNBLS	10//99-12//99
	Texas	S	13.35 MW	13.38 AW	27840 AAW	TXBLS	10//99-12//99
	Dallas PMSA, TX	S	13.25 MW	14.25 AW	27560 AAW	TXBLS	10//99-12//99
	Fort Worth-Arlington PMSA, TX	S	16.34 MW	17.87 AW	33990 AAW	TXBLS	10//99-12//99
	Houston PMSA, TX	S	12.67 MW	11.56 AW	26350 AAW	TXBLS	10//99-12//99
	Utah	S	11.09 MW	12.18 AW	25340 AAW	UTBLS	10//99-12//99
	Virginia	S	10.33 MW	10.68 AW	22220 AAW	VABLS	10//99-12//99
	Lynchburg MSA, VA	S	12.85 MW	12.86 AW	26720 AAW	VABLS	10//99-12//99

AAW Average annual wage	AOH Average offered, high	ASH Average starting, high	H Hourly	M Monthly	S Special: hourly and annual
AE Average entry wage	AOL Average offered, low	ASL Average starting, low	HI Highest wage paid	MTC Median total compensation	TQ Third quartile wage
AEX Average experienced wage	APH Average pay, high range	AW Average wage paid	HR High end range	MW Median wage paid	W Weekly
AO Average offered	APL Average pay, low range	FQ First quartile wage	LR Low end range	SQ Second quartile wage	Y Yearly

Occupation/Type/Industry	Location	Per	Low	Mid	High	Source	Date
Tool Grinder, Filer, and Sharpener	Norfolk-Virginia Beach-Newport News MSA, VA-NC	S	12.08 MW	10.44 AW	25120 AAW	VABLS	10//99-12//99
	Washington	S	16.46 MW	17.08 AW	35530 AAW	WABLS	10//99-12//99
	Spokane MSA, WA	S	12.36 MW	12.19 AW	25720 AAW	WABLS	10//99-12//99
	Tacoma PMSA, WA	S	13.55 MW	12.40 AW	28190 AAW	WABLS	10//99-12//99
	West Virginia	S	12.58 MW	12.74 AW	26500 AAW	WVBLS	10//99-12//99
	Wisconsin	S	13.08 MW	14.15 AW	29430 AAW	WIBLS	10//99-12//99
	Milwaukee-Waukesha PMSA, WI	S	16.61 MW	16.74 AW	34550 AAW	WIBLS	10//99-12//99
	Racine PMSA, WI	S	11.45 MW	11.07 AW	23830 AAW	WIBLS	10//99-12//99
Top Facilities Manager Real Estate	United States	Y		138666 AW		TRAVWK4	2000
Top Officer Real Estate	United States	Y		236666 AW		TRAVWK4	1999
Tour Guide and Escort	Alabama	S	6.08 MW	6.96 AW	14480 AAW	ALBLS	10//99-12//99
	Alaska	S	6.97 MW	8.25 AW	17150 AAW	AKBLS	10//99-12//99
	Arizona	S	10.25 MW	10.63 AW	22100 AAW	AZBLS	10//99-12//99
	Arkansas	S	7.79 MW	8.05 AW	16740 AAW	ARBLS	10//99-12//99
	California	S	10.07 MW	11.11 AW	23110 AAW	CABLS	10//99-12//99
	Colorado	S	11.66 MW	11.36 AW	23630 AAW	COBLS	10//99-12//99
	Connecticut	S	8.34 MW	8.56 AW	17810 AAW	CTBLS	10//99-12//99
	Delaware	S	11.74 MW	11.32 AW	23550 AAW	DEBLS	10//99-12//99
	District of Columbia	S	16.45 MW	16.94 AW	35240 AAW	DCBLS	10//99-12//99
	Florida	S	8.88 MW	8.62 AW	17920 AAW	FLBLS	10//99-12//99
	Georgia	S	8.54 MW	8.17 AW	16990 AAW	GABLS	10//99-12//99
	Idaho	S	9.15 MW	9.60 AW	19980 AAW	IDBLS	10//99-12//99
	Illinois	S	8.04 MW	9.10 AW	18930 AAW	ILBLS	10//99-12//99
	Indiana	S	6.32 MW	7.62 AW	15860 AAW	INBLS	10//99-12//99
	Iowa	S	7.13 MW	7.17 AW	14910 AAW	IABLS	10//99-12//99
	Kansas	S	7.48 MW	7.48 AW	15550 AAW	KSBLS	10//99-12//99
	Kentucky	S	7.28 MW	7.36 AW	15320 AAW	KYBLS	10//99-12//99
	Louisiana	S	6.26 MW	6.77 AW	14070 AAW	LABLS	10//99-12//99
	Maine	S	6.89 MW	7.36 AW	15310 AAW	MEBLS	10//99-12//99
	Maryland	S	13.43 MW	13.20 AW	27460 AAW	MDBLS	10//99-12//99
	Massachusetts	S	9.01 MW	9.73 AW	20240 AAW	MABLS	10//99-12//99
	Minnesota	S	8.49 MW	11.04 AW	22960 AAW	MNBLS	10//99-12//99
	Mississippi	S	7.76 MW	8.00 AW	16650 AAW	MSBLS	10//99-12//99
	Missouri	S	6.46 MW	7.47 AW	15550 AAW	MOBLS	10//99-12//99
	Montana	S	6.03 MW	5.97 AW	12420 AAW	MTBLS	10//99-12//99
	Nebraska	S	6.59 MW	7.05 AW	14660 AAW	NEBLS	10//99-12//99
	Nevada	S	11.16 MW	11.40 AW	23710 AAW	NVBLS	10//99-12//99
	New Hampshire	S	7.12 MW	7.29 AW	15170 AAW	NHBLS	10//99-12//99
	New Jersey	S	8.35 MW	8.83 AW	18370 AAW	NJBLS	10//99-12//99
	New Mexico	S	7.58 MW	7.62 AW	15840 AAW	NMBLS	10//99-12//99
	New York	S	8.23 MW	9.37 AW	19480 AAW	NYBLS	10//99-12//99
	North Carolina	S	7.52 MW	7.64 AW	15900 AAW	NCBLS	10//99-12//99
	Ohio	S	6.22 MW	6.58 AW	13680 AAW	OHBLS	10//99-12//99
	Oklahoma	S	11.44 MW	10.52 AW	21880 AAW	OKBLS	10//99-12//99
	Oregon	S	9.22 MW	10.10 AW	21010 AAW	ORBLS	10//99-12//99
	Pennsylvania	S	6.21 MW	6.80 AW	14140 AAW	PABLS	10//99-12//99
	Rhode Island	S	7.65 MW	7.56 AW	15730 AAW	RIBLS	10//99-12//99
	South Carolina	S	7.94 MW	8.98 AW	18670 AAW	SCBLS	10//99-12//99
	South Dakota	S	7.48 MW	7.31 AW	15190 AAW	SDBLS	10//99-12//99
	Tennessee	S	6.13 MW	6.79 AW	14130 AAW	TNBLS	10//99-12//99
	Texas	S	8.61 MW	9.05 AW	18830 AAW	TXBLS	10//99-12//99
	Utah	S	7.85 MW	7.96 AW	16560 AAW	UTBLS	10//99-12//99
	Virginia	S	6.49 MW	6.95 AW	14460 AAW	VABLS	10//99-12//99
	Washington	S	11.78 MW	11.32 AW	23540 AAW	WABLS	10//99-12//99
	West Virginia	S	6.07 MW	6.27 AW	13040 AAW	WVBLS	10//99-12//99
	Wisconsin	S	6.07 MW	6.04 AW	12560 AAW	WIBLS	10//99-12//99
	Wyoming	S	9.63 MW	9.57 AW	19900 AAW	WYBLS	10//99-12//99
	Puerto Rico	S	7.78 MW	9.28 AW	19300 AAW	PRBLS	10//99-12//99
	Virgin Islands	S	8.27 MW	8.61 AW	17900 AAW	VIBLS	10//99-12//99
Traffic Technician	Alabama	S	16.35 MW	16.20 AW	33700 AAW	ALBLS	10//99-12//99
	Birmingham MSA, AL	S	19.86 MW	19.73 AW	41310 AAW	ALBLS	10//99-12//99
	Arizona	S	19.37 MW	20.42 AW	42470 AAW	AZBLS	10//99-12//99
	Phoenix-Mesa MSA, AZ	S	20.39 MW	19.38 AW	42410 AAW	AZBLS	10//99-12//99

AAW	Average annual wage	AOH	Average offered, high	ASH	Average starting, high	H	Hourly	M	Monthly	S	Special: hourly and annual
AE	Average entry wage	AOL	Average offered, low	ASL	Average starting, low	HI	Highest wage paid	MTC	Median total compensation	TQ	Third quartile wage
AEX	Average experienced wage	APH	Average pay, high range	AW	Average wage paid	HR	High end range	MW	Median wage paid	W	Weekly
AO	Average offered	APL	Average pay, low range	FQ	First quartile wage	LR	Low end range	SQ	Second quartile wage	Y	Yearly

Occupation/Type/Industry	Location	Per	Low	Mid	High	Source	Date
Traffic Technician	California	S	20.62 MW	21.53 AW	44790 AAW	CABLS	10//99-12//99
	Los Angeles-Long Beach PMSA, CA	S	20.40 MW	19.54 AW	42440 AAW	CABLS	10//99-12//99
	Oakland PMSA, CA	S	22.28 MW	21.07 AW	46330 AAW	CABLS	10//99-12//99
	Colorado	S	17.89 MW	18.67 AW	38830 AAW	COBLS	10//99-12//99
	Denver PMSA, CO	S	19.43 MW	19.70 AW	40420 AAW	COBLS	10//99-12//99
	Connecticut	S	16.29 MW	16.61 AW	34540 AAW	CTBLS	10//99-12//99
	Washington PMSA, DC-MD-VA-WV	S	19.70 MW	19.99 AW	40980 AAW	DCBLS	10//99-12//99
	Florida	S	13.29 MW	13.60 AW	28290 AAW	FLBLS	10//99-12//99
	Tampa-St. Petersburg-Clearwater MSA, FL	S	17.06 MW	15.00 AW	35480 AAW	FLBLS	10//99-12//99
	Georgia	S	12.73 MW	13.48 AW	28030 AAW	GABLS	10//99-12//99
	Atlanta MSA, GA	S	14.10 MW	13.18 AW	29330 AAW	GABLS	10//99-12//99
	Idaho	S	10.6 MW	11.12 AW	23130 AAW	IDBLS	10//99-12//99
	Illinois	S	15.86 MW	16.80 AW	34950 AAW	ILBLS	10//99-12//99
	Indiana	S	13.62 MW	13.98 AW	29070 AAW	INBLS	10//99-12//99
	Indianapolis MSA, IN	S	13.85 MW	13.28 AW	28800 AAW	INBLS	10//99-12//99
	Iowa	S	14.65 MW	13.79 AW	28690 AAW	IABLS	10//99-12//99
	Kentucky	S	10.5 MW	11.20 AW	23290 AAW	KYBLS	10//99-12//99
	Louisiana	S	12.42 MW	14.05 AW	29220 AAW	LABLS	10//99-12//99
	Maryland	S	17.06 MW	17.67 AW	36750 AAW	MDBLS	10//99-12//99
	Massachusetts	S	23.85 MW	25.14 AW	52300 AAW	MABLS	10//99-12//99
	Boston PMSA, MA-NH	S	24.84 MW	23.18 AW	51660 AAW	MABLS	10//99-12//99
	Michigan	S	15.81 MW	16.97 AW	35290 AAW	MIBLS	10//99-12//99
	Mississippi	S	10.37 MW	12.38 AW	25760 AAW	MSBLS	10//99-12//99
	Nevada	S	21.46 MW	18.92 AW	39360 AAW	NVBLS	10//99-12//99
	New Jersey	S	19.41 MW	18.80 AW	39100 AAW	NJBLS	10//99-12//99
	New Mexico	S	13.05 MW	12.78 AW	26580 AAW	NMBLS	10//99-12//99
	New York	S	23.69 MW	23.67 AW	49230 AAW	NYBLS	10//99-12//99
	Nassau-Suffolk PMSA, NY	S	23.16 MW	22.90 AW	48170 AAW	NYBLS	10//99-12//99
	New York PMSA, NY	S	22.12 MW	22.15 AW	46020 AAW	NYBLS	10//99-12//99
	North Carolina	S	15.25 MW	16.14 AW	33570 AAW	NCBLS	10//99-12//99
	Raleigh-Durham-Chapel Hill MSA, NC	S	17.86 MW	16.38 AW	37140 AAW	NCBLS	10//99-12//99
	Ohio	S	15.81 MW	15.85 AW	32970 AAW	OHBLS	10//99-12//99
	Cleveland-Lorain-Elyria PMSA, OH	S	13.86 MW	13.28 AW	28830 AAW	OHBLS	10//99-12//99
	Oklahoma	S	10.56 MW	12.03 AW	25010 AAW	OKBLS	10//99-12//99
	Oklahoma City MSA, OK	S	11.14 MW	9.15 AW	23170 AAW	OKBLS	10//99-12//99
	Pennsylvania	S	22.06 MW	22.23 AW	46240 AAW	PABLS	10//99-12//99
	Philadelphia PMSA, PA-NJ	S	20.12 MW	22.10 AW	41840 AAW	PABLS	10//99-12//99
	South Carolina	S	12.87 MW	12.60 AW	26200 AAW	SCBLS	10//99-12//99
	Texas	S	12.02 MW	12.07 AW	25110 AAW	TXBLS	10//99-12//99
	Dallas PMSA, TX	S	13.00 MW	13.06 AW	27040 AAW	TXBLS	10//99-12//99
	Houston PMSA, TX	S	15.60 MW	15.25 AW	32440 AAW	TXBLS	10//99-12//99
	Utah	S	15.93 MW	16.08 AW	33450 AAW	UTBLS	10//99-12//99
	Salt Lake City-Ogden MSA, UT	S	16.11 MW	15.99 AW	33500 AAW	UTBLS	10//99-12//99
	Virginia	S	15.29 MW	15.87 AW	33000 AAW	VABLS	10//99-12//99
	Washington	S	20.52 MW	19.65 AW	40860 AAW	WABLS	10//99-12//99
	Seattle-Bellevue-Everett PMSA, WA	S	23.82 MW	24.23 AW	49550 AAW	WABLS	10//99-12//99
Training Administrator Company/Organization	United States	Y		35900 AW		TRDEV	1999
Training and Development Specialist	Alabama	S	16.9 MW	17.54 AW	36480 AAW	ALBLS	10//99-12//99
	Alaska	S	19.5 MW	20.77 AW	43200 AAW	AKBLS	10//99-12//99
	Arizona	S	16.17 MW	17.50 AW	36400 AAW	AZBLS	10//99-12//99
	Arkansas	S	13.63 MW	16.57 AW	34470 AAW	ARBLS	10//99-12//99
	California	S	21.95 MW	22.26 AW	46310 AAW	CABLS	10//99-12//99
	Colorado	S	17.74 MW	18.85 AW	39200 AAW	COBLS	10//99-12//99
	Connecticut	S	23.23 MW	23.93 AW	49770 AAW	CTBLS	10//99-12//99
	District of Columbia	S	24.31 MW	23.32 AW	48500 AAW	DCBLS	10//99-12//99
	Florida	S	16.5 MW	17.87 AW	37170 AAW	FLBLS	10//99-12//99
	Georgia	S	18.54 MW	19.40 AW	40340 AAW	GABLS	10//99-12//99
	Hawaii	S	17.67 MW	19.77 AW	41120 AAW	HIBLS	10//99-12//99
	Idaho	S	18.72 MW	18.83 AW	39160 AAW	IDBLS	10//99-12//99
	Illinois	S	23.14 MW	23.77 AW	49440 AAW	ILBLS	10//99-12//99
	Indiana	S	16.48 MW	17.64 AW	36690 AAW	INBLS	10//99-12//99

AAW Average annual wage	AOH Average offered, high	ASH Average starting, high	H Hourly	M Monthly	S Special: hourly and annual
AE Average entry wage	AOL Average offered, low	ASL Average starting, low	HI Highest wage paid	MTC Median total compensation	TQ Third quartile wage
AEX Average experienced wage	APH Average pay, high range	AW Average wage paid	HR High end range	MW Median wage paid	W Weekly
AO Average offered	APL Average pay, low range	FQ First quartile wage	LR Low end range	SQ Second quartile wage	Y Yearly

Occupation/Type/Industry	Location	Per	Low	Mid	High	Source	Date
Training and Development Specialist							
	Iowa	S	14.57 MW	16.16 AW	33620 AAW	IABLS	10//99-12//99
	Kansas	S	17.09 MW	18.75 AW	39010 AAW	KSBLS	10//99-12//99
	Kentucky	S	17.44 MW	19.40 AW	40360 AAW	KYBLS	10//99-12//99
	Louisiana	S	15.58 MW	16.73 AW	34810 AAW	LABLS	10//99-12//99
	Maine	S	15.55 MW	16.82 AW	34990 AAW	MEBLS	10//99-12//99
	Maryland	S	20.6 MW	21.27 AW	44230 AAW	MDBLS	10//99-12//99
	Massachusetts	S	20.81 MW	22.36 AW	46520 AAW	MABLS	10//99-12//99
	Michigan	S	21.69 MW	23.26 AW	48390 AAW	MIBLS	10//99-12//99
	Minnesota	S	18.41 MW	19.04 AW	39610 AAW	MNBLS	10//99-12//99
	Mississippi	S	14.87 MW	16.00 AW	33280 AAW	MSBLS	10//99-12//99
	Missouri	S	16.85 MW	17.91 AW	37250 AAW	MOBLS	10//99-12//99
	Montana	S	15.03 MW	15.16 AW	31530 AAW	MTBLS	10//99-12//99
	Nebraska	S	14.78 MW	16.41 AW	34140 AAW	NEBLS	10//99-12//99
	Nevada	S	18.93 MW	19.58 AW	40720 AAW	NVBLS	10//99-12//99
	New Hampshire	S	21.82 MW	22.41 AW	46600 AAW	NHBLS	10//99-12//99
	New Jersey	S	21.75 MW	22.96 AW	47760 AAW	NJBLS	10//99-12//99
	New Mexico	S	18.42 MW	19.50 AW	40550 AAW	NMBLS	10//99-12//99
	New York	S	21.78 MW	22.05 AW	45870 AAW	NYBLS	10//99-12//99
	North Carolina	S	17.14 MW	18.38 AW	38230 AAW	NCBLS	10//99-12//99
	North Dakota	S	16 MW	16.64 AW	34610 AAW	NDBLS	10//99-12//99
	Ohio	S	16.76 MW	18.05 AW	37540 AAW	OHBLS	10//99-12//99
	Oklahoma	S	16.38 MW	17.11 AW	35590 AAW	OKBLS	10//99-12//99
	Oregon	S	19.13 MW	19.65 AW	40860 AAW	ORBLS	10//99-12//99
	Pennsylvania	S	16.03 MW	18.49 AW	38460 AAW	PABLS	10//99-12//99
	Rhode Island	S	21.38 MW	22.82 AW	47460 AAW	RIBLS	10//99-12//99
	South Carolina	S	16.81 MW	17.72 AW	36850 AAW	SCBLS	10//99-12//99
	South Dakota	S	13.65 MW	14.57 AW	30300 AAW	SDBLS	10//99-12//99
	Tennessee	S	16.22 MW	17.61 AW	36630 AAW	TNBLS	10//99-12//99
	Texas	S	19.69 MW	20.95 AW	43580 AAW	TXBLS	10//99-12//99
	Utah	S	15.72 MW	16.68 AW	34690 AAW	UTBLS	10//99-12//99
	Vermont	S	18.35 MW	18.07 AW	37590 AAW	VTBLS	10//99-12//99
	Virginia	S	18.06 MW	19.32 AW	40190 AAW	VABLS	10//99-12//99
	Washington	S	21.37 MW	23.48 AW	48840 AAW	WABLS	10//99-12//99
	West Virginia	S	12.16 MW	13.76 AW	28620 AAW	WVBLS	10//99-12//99
	Wisconsin	S	16.06 MW	17.06 AW	35490 AAW	WIBLS	10//99-12//99
	Wyoming	S	14.3 MW	16.64 AW	34600 AAW	WYBLS	10//99-12//99
	Puerto Rico	S	11.56 MW	12.82 AW	26670 AAW	PRBLS	10//99-12//99
	Guam	S	9.87 MW	10.26 AW	21330 AAW	GUBLS	10//99-12//99
Training Executive							
Human Resources	United States	Y		82448 AW		TRAIN	1999
Human Resources	Central	Y		81356 AW		TRAIN2	2000
Human Resources	Great Lakes	Y		81278 AW		TRAIN2	2000
Human Resources	Northeast	Y		88155 AW		TRAIN2	2000
Human Resources	Pacific	Y		91026 AW		TRAIN2	2000
Human Resources	Southeast	Y		82100 AW		TRAIN2	2000
Human Resources	West Central	Y		65443 AW		TRAIN2	2000
Human Resources, Five or more direct reports	Central	Y		61843 AW		TRAIN2	2000
Human Resources, Five or more direct reports	Great Lakes	Y		68892 AW		TRAIN2	2000
Human Resources, Five or more direct reports	Northeast	Y		68042 AW		TRAIN2	2000
Human Resources, Five or more direct reports	West Central	Y		60378 AW		TRAIN2	2000
Human Resources, One-person department	Central	Y		43504 AW		TRAIN2	2000
Human Resources, One-person department	Great Lakes	Y		47016 AW		TRAIN2	2000
Human Resources, One-person department	Northeast	Y		56001 AW		TRAIN2	2000
Human Resources, One-person department	Southeast	Y		49104 AW		TRAIN2	2000
Human Resources, One-person department	West Central	Y		45538 AW		TRAIN2	2000
Human Resources, One to four direct reports	Central	Y		56743 AW		TRAIN2	2000
Human Resources, One to four direct reports	Great Lakes	Y		60167 AW		TRAIN2	2000
Human Resources, One to four direct reports	Northeast	Y		65964 AW		TRAIN2	2000
Human Resources, One to four direct reports	Southeast	Y		67757 AW		TRAIN2	2000
Human Resources, One to four direct reports	Southeast	Y		57809 AW		TRAIN2	2000

AAW	Average annual wage	AOH	Average offered, high	ASH	Average starting, high	H	Hourly	
AE	Average entry wage	AOL	Average offered, low	ASL	Average starting, low	HI	Highest wage paid	
AEX	Average experienced wage	APH	Average pay, high range	AW	Average wage paid	HR	High end range	
AO	Average offered	APL	Average pay, low range	FQ	First quartile wage	LR	Low end range	

M	Monthly	S	Special: hourly and annual	
MTC	Median total compensation	TQ	Third quartile wage	
MW	Median wage paid	W	Weekly	
SQ	Second quartile wage	Y.	Yearly	

Occupation/Type/Industry	Location	Per	Low	Mid	High	Source	Date
Training Executive							
Human Resources, One to four direct reports	West Central	Y		54586 AW		TRAIN2	2000
Training Manager							
Human Resources, Five or more direct reports	United States	Y		62722 AW		TRAIN	1999
Human Resources, Five or more direct reports	Pacific	Y		74369 AW		TRAIN2	2000
Human Resources, One-person department	Pacific	Y		55190 AW		TRAIN2	2000
Human Resources, One to four direct reports	United States	Y		58128 AW		TRAIN	1999
Human Resources, One to four direct reports	Pacific	Y		68447 AW		TRAIN2	2000
Training Officer							
Human Resources, One-person department	United States	Y		47115 AW		TRAIN	1999
Training Specialist							
Associate	United States	Y		39900 AW		TRDEV	1999
Senior	United States	Y		51600 AW		TRDEV	1999
Transit and Railroad Police	California	S	22.79 MW	22.90 AW	47630 AAW	CABLS	10//99-12//99
	Georgia	S	16.57 MW	17.56 AW	36530 AAW	GABLS	10//99-12//99
	Illinois	S	20.24 MW	21.25 AW	44190 AAW	ILBLS	10//99-12//99
	Louisiana	S	19.88 MW	21.05 AW	43790 AAW	LABLS	10//99-12//99
	Minnesota	S	21.97 MW	20.72 AW	43100 AAW	MNBLS	10//99-12//99
	New York	S	19.16 MW	19.89 AW	41370 AAW	NYBLS	10//99-12//99
	Tennessee	S	17.65 MW	17.60 AW	36600 AAW	TNBLS	10//99-12//99
	Texas	S	18.46 MW	19.02 AW	39560 AAW	TXBLS	10//99-12//99
	Virginia	S	21.2 MW	21.43 AW	44570 AAW	VABLS	10//99-12//99
	Wisconsin	S	17.61 MW	18.96 AW	39440 AAW	WIBLS	10//99-12//99
	Puerto Rico	S	6.68 MW	11.43 AW	23780 AAW	PRBLS	10//99-12//99
Transportation Attendant							
Except Flight Attendant and Baggage Porter	Arizona	S	7.33 MW	7.34 AW	15270 AAW	AZBLS	10//99-12//99
Except Flight Attendant and Baggage Porter	Arkansas	S	7.21 MW	7.33 AW	15250 AAW	ARBLS	10//99-12//99
Except Flight Attendant and Baggage Porter	California	S	7.92 MW	9.54 AW	19850 AAW	CABLS	10//99-12//99
Except Flight Attendant and Baggage Porter	Colorado	S	8.3 MW	8.49 AW	17650 AAW	COBLS	10//99-12//99
Except Flight Attendant and Baggage Porter	Connecticut	S	8 MW	8.25 AW	17160 AAW	CTBLS	10//99-12//99
Except Flight Attendant and Baggage Porter	Florida	S	8.05 MW	8.86 AW	18420 AAW	FLBLS	10//99-12//99
Except Flight Attendant and Baggage Porter	Georgia	S	8.56 MW	10.19 AW	21190 AAW	GABLS	10//99-12//99
Except Flight Attendant and Baggage Porter	Hawaii	S	9.28 MW	9.26 AW	19250 AAW	HIBLS	10//99-12//99
Except Flight Attendant and Baggage Porter	Illinois	S	7.32 MW	8.18 AW	17020 AAW	ILBLS	10//99-12//99
Except Flight Attendant and Baggage Porter	Indiana	S	14.25 MW	13.14 AW	27330 AAW	INBLS	10//99-12//99
Except Flight Attendant and Baggage Porter	Louisiana	S	6.16 MW	6.59 AW	13700 AAW	LABLS	10//99-12//99
Except Flight Attendant and Baggage Porter	Maryland	S	9.35 MW	10.85 AW	22560 AAW	MDBLS	10//99-12//99
Except Flight Attendant and Baggage Porter	Massachusetts	S	7.48 MW	7.61 AW	15820 AAW	MABLS	10//99-12//99
Except Flight Attendant and Baggage Porter	Minnesota	S	7.88 MW	8.18 AW	17020 AAW	MNBLS	10//99-12//99
Except Flight Attendant and Baggage Porter	Missouri	S	7.68 MW	8.58 AW	17840 AAW	MOBLS	10//99-12//99
Except Flight Attendant and Baggage Porter	Nevada	S	7.24 MW	8.17 AW	16990 AAW	NVBLS	10//99-12//99
Except Flight Attendant and Baggage Porter	New Hampshire	S	6.41 MW	7.12 AW	14820 AAW	NHBLS	10//99-12//99
Except Flight Attendant and Baggage Porter	New Jersey	S	7.62 MW	7.96 AW	16560 AAW	NJBLS	10//99-12//99

Occupation/Type/Industry	Location	Per	Low	Mid	High	Source	Date
Transportation Attendant							
Except Flight Attendant and Baggage Porter	New Mexico	S	8.71 MW	8.43 AW	17530 AAW	NMBLS	10//99-12//99
Except Flight Attendant and Baggage Porter	Ohio	S	6.39 MW	7.28 AW	15140 AAW	OHBLS	10//99-12//99
Except Flight Attendant and Baggage Porter	Oklahoma	S	6.92 MW	7.24 AW	15060 AAW	OKBLS	10//99-12//99
Except Flight Attendant and Baggage Porter	Pennsylvania	S	7.47 MW	7.87 AW	16370 AAW	PABLS	10//99-12//99
Except Flight Attendant and Baggage Porter	South Carolina	S	8.74 MW	11.96 AW	24890 AAW	SCBLS	10//99-12//99
Except Flight Attendant and Baggage Porter	Tennessee	S	6.26 MW	7.85 AW	16320 AAW	TNBLS	10//99-12//99
Except Flight Attendant and Baggage Porter	Texas	S	6.69 MW	7.24 AW	15060 AAW	TXBLS	10//99-12//99
Except Flight Attendant and Baggage Porter	Virginia	S	12.02 MW	11.25 AW	23410 AAW	VABLS	10//99-12//99
Except Flight Attendant and Baggage Porter	Wisconsin	S	7.8 MW	8.58 AW	17860 AAW	WIBLS	10//99-12//99
Transportation Inspector	Alabama	S	19.63 MW	20.98 AW	43640 AAW	ALBLS	10//99-12//99
	Arizona	S	18.04 MW	20.20 AW	42010 AAW	AZBLS	10//99-12//99
	Arkansas	S	18.23 MW	18.09 AW	37620 AAW	ARBLS	10//99-12//99
	California	S	24.12 MW	24.62 AW	51220 AAW	CABLS	10//99-12//99
	Colorado	S	19.63 MW	21.44 AW	44600 AAW	COBLS	10//99-12//99
	Connecticut	S	26.3 MW	24.78 AW	51540 AAW	CTBLS	10//99-12//99
	Florida	S	19.11 MW	20.79 AW	43250 AAW	FLBLS	10//99-12//99
	Georgia	S	21.14 MW	23.14 AW	48120 AAW	GABLS	10//99-12//99
	Illinois	S	18.94 MW	21.42 AW	44550 AAW	ILBLS	10//99-12//99
	Indiana	S	21.72 MW	20.18 AW	41980 AAW	INBLS	10//99-12//99
	Iowa	S	20.65 MW	22.12 AW	46010 AAW	IABLS	10//99-12//99
	Kansas	S	19.26 MW	20.18 AW	41980 AAW	KSBLS	10//99-12//99
	Kentucky	S	18.23 MW	17.83 AW	37080 AAW	KYBLS	10//99-12//99
	Louisiana	S	16.91 MW	17.37 AW	36120 AAW	LABLS	10//99-12//99
	Maryland	S	17.02 MW	19.79 AW	41170 AAW	MDBLS	10//99-12//99
	Massachusetts	S	28.49 MW	27.06 AW	56290 AAW	MABLS	10//99-12//99
	Michigan	S	20.42 MW	21.13 AW	43940 AAW	MIBLS	10//99-12//99
	Minnesota	S	24.18 MW	25.09 AW	52180 AAW	MNBLS	10//99-12//99
	Mississippi	S	17.67 MW	17.51 AW	36420 AAW	MSBLS	10//99-12//99
	Missouri	S	21.58 MW	22.03 AW	45810 AAW	MOBLS	10//99-12//99
	Montana	S	23.85 MW	24.86 AW	51710 AAW	MTBLS	10//99-12//99
	Nebraska	S	19.52 MW	20.89 AW	43450 AAW	NEBLS	10//99-12//99
	Nevada	S	21.3 MW	23.91 AW	49720 AAW	NVBLS	10//99-12//99
	New Jersey	S	22.94 MW	22.85 AW	47540 AAW	NJBLS	10//99-12//99
	New Mexico	S	14.99 MW	17.16 AW	35700 AAW	NMBLS	10//99-12//99
	Oklahoma	S	16.89 MW	18.43 AW	38330 AAW	OKBLS	10//99-12//99
	Oregon	S	20.63 MW	20.58 AW	42820 AAW	ORBLS	10//99-12//99
	Pennsylvania	S	23.8 MW	22.58 AW	46970 AAW	PABLS	10//99-12//99
	Rhode Island	S	18.02 MW	16.06 AW	33410 AAW	RIBLS	10//99-12//99
	South Carolina	S	13.04 MW	15.86 AW	32980 AAW	SCBLS	10//99-12//99
	South Dakota	S	12.67 MW	15.51 AW	32260 AAW	SDBLS	10//99-12//99
	Tennessee	S	10.86 MW	14.78 AW	30750 AAW	TNBLS	10//99-12//99
	Texas	S	16 MW	16.82 AW	34980 AAW	TXBLS	10//99-12//99
	Utah	S	17.25 MW	19.26 AW	40070 AAW	UTBLS	10//99-12//99
	Virginia	S	19.33 MW	21.69 AW	45120 AAW	VABLS	10//99-12//99
	Washington	S	23.18 MW	23.39 AW	48650 AAW	WABLS	10//99-12//99
	West Virginia	S	17.77 MW	17.83 AW	37090 AAW	WVBLS	10//99-12//99
	Wisconsin	S	18.8 MW	19.38 AW	40310 AAW	WIBLS	10//99-12//99
	Wyoming	S	18.19 MW	18.25 AW	37960 AAW	WYBLS	10//99-12//99
	Puerto Rico	S	6.27 MW	8.08 AW	16810 AAW	PRBLS	10//99-12//99
	Virgin Islands	S	12.17 MW	12.54 AW	26080 AAW	VIBLS	10//99-12//99
Transportation Manager							
Supply Chain Management	United States	Y		70900 AW		AMSHIP	2000
Transportation, Storage, and Distribution Manager	Alabama	S	18.95 MW	20.43 AW	42500 AAW	ALBLS	10//99-12//99
	Anniston MSA, AL	S	22.71 MW	24.05 AW	47240 AAW	ALBLS	10//99-12//99
	Birmingham MSA, AL	S	20.00 MW	17.79 AW	41610 AAW	ALBLS	10//99-12//99
	Decatur MSA, AL	S	21.26 MW	19.22 AW	44220 AAW	ALBLS	10//99-12//99
	Dothan MSA, AL	S	20.04 MW	20.42 AW	41670 AAW	ALBLS	10//99-12//99
	Florence MSA, AL	S	22.93 MW	20.92 AW	47690 AAW	ALBLS	10//99-12//99

Occupation/Type/Industry	Location	Per	Low	Mid	High	Source	Date
Transportation, Storage, and Distribution Manager	Huntsville MSA, AL	S	19.19 MW	17.65 AW	39910 AAW	ALBLS	10//99-12//99
	Mobile MSA, AL	S	21.58 MW	19.64 AW	44880 AAW	ALBLS	10//99-12//99
	Montgomery MSA, AL	S	20.16 MW	18.62 AW	41940 AAW	ALBLS	10//99-12//99
	Tuscaloosa MSA, AL	S	21.21 MW	21.85 AW	44130 AAW	ALBLS	10//99-12//99
	Alaska	S	26.6 MW	27.91 AW	58050 AAW	AKBLS	10//99-12//99
	Anchorage MSA, AK	S	23.87 MW	22.70 AW	49660 AAW	AKBLS	10//99-12//99
	Arizona	S	23.6 MW	24.23 AW	50400 AAW	AZBLS	10//99-12//99
	Phoenix-Mesa MSA, AZ	S	24.00 MW	23.46 AW	49920 AAW	AZBLS	10//99-12//99
	Tucson MSA, AZ	S	25.32 MW	24.53 AW	52670 AAW	AZBLS	10//99-12//99
	Arkansas	S	25.75 MW	26.37 AW	54850 AAW	ARBLS	10//99-12//99
	Fayetteville-Springdale-Rogers MSA, AR	S	25.39 MW	24.69 AW	52810 AAW	ARBLS	10//99-12//99
	Fort Smith MSA, AR-OK	S	23.04 MW	22.92 AW	47920 AAW	ARBLS	10//99-12//99
	Little Rock-North Little Rock MSA, AR	S	30.32 MW	29.21 AW	63070 AAW	ARBLS	10//99-12//99
	California	S	26.02 MW	27.29 AW	56770 AAW	CABLS	10//99-12//99
	Bakersfield MSA, CA	S	26.75 MW	26.71 AW	55640 AAW	CABLS	10//99-12//99
	Chico-Paradise MSA, CA	S	24.32 MW	24.81 AW	50580 AAW	CABLS	10//99-12//99
	Fresno MSA, CA	S	28.81 MW	32.37 AW	59930 AAW	CABLS	10//99-12//99
	Los Angeles-Long Beach PMSA, CA	S	27.37 MW	26.22 AW	56920 AAW	CABLS	10//99-12//99
	Merced MSA, CA	S	29.01 MW	26.64 AW	60330 AAW	CABLS	10//99-12//99
	Modesto MSA, CA	S	25.98 MW	25.02 AW	54040 AAW	CABLS	10//99-12//99
	Oakland PMSA, CA	S	28.75 MW	27.85 AW	59800 AAW	CABLS	10//99-12//99
	Orange County PMSA, CA	S	26.84 MW	25.95 AW	55840 AAW	CABLS	10//99-12//99
	Redding MSA, CA	S	28.37 MW	29.84 AW	59000 AAW	CABLS	10//99-12//99
	Riverside-San Bernardino PMSA, CA	S	25.52 MW	24.24 AW	53080 AAW	CABLS	10//99-12//99
	Sacramento PMSA, CA	S	25.65 MW	24.45 AW	53360 AAW	CABLS	10//99-12//99
	Salinas MSA, CA	S	26.28 MW	26.25 AW	54670 AAW	CABLS	10//99-12//99
	San Diego MSA, CA	S	26.29 MW	25.20 AW	54690 AAW	CABLS	10//99-12//99
	San Francisco PMSA, CA	S	27.12 MW	27.00 AW	56410 AAW	CABLS	10//99-12//99
	San Jose PMSA, CA	S	32.35 MW	30.19 AW	67280 AAW	CABLS	10//99-12//99
	San Luis Obispo-Atascadero-Paso Robles MSA, CA	S	23.99 MW	20.50 AW	49900 AAW	CABLS	10//99-12//99
	Santa Barbara-Santa Maria-Lompoc MSA, CA	S	23.97 MW	23.81 AW	49860 AAW	CABLS	10//99-12//99
	Santa Cruz-Watsonville PMSA, CA	S	24.84 MW	23.86 AW	51670 AAW	CABLS	10//99-12//99
	Santa Rosa PMSA, CA	S	29.25 MW	27.55 AW	60840 AAW	CABLS	10//99-12//99
	Stockton-Lodi MSA, CA	S	26.76 MW	25.93 AW	55650 AAW	CABLS	10//99-12//99
	Vallejo-Fairfield-Napa PMSA, CA	S	24.83 MW	24.30 AW	51650 AAW	CABLS	10//99-12//99
	Ventura PMSA, CA	S	31.04 MW	26.51 AW	64560 AAW	CABLS	10//99-12//99
	Visalia-Tulare-Porterville MSA, CA	S	18.83 MW	18.54 AW	39160 AAW	CABLS	10//99-12//99
	Yolo PMSA, CA	S	20.54 MW	18.92 AW	42720 AAW	CABLS	10//99-12//99
	Colorado	S	24.65 MW	25.99 AW	54060 AAW	COBLS	10//99-12//99
	Boulder-Longmont PMSA, CO	S	27.79 MW	27.08 AW	57790 AAW	COBLS	10//99-12//99
	Denver PMSA, CO	S	27.48 MW	25.49 AW	57160 AAW	COBLS	10//99-12//99
	Fort Collins-Loveland MSA, CO	S	24.70 MW	23.56 AW	51380 AAW	COBLS	10//99-12//99
	Connecticut	S	28.85 MW	30.86 AW	64190 AAW	CTBLS	10//99-12//99
	Bridgeport PMSA, CT	S	30.85 MW	31.03 AW	64170 AAW	CTBLS	10//99-12//99
	Danbury PMSA, CT	S	27.30 MW	24.20 AW	56780 AAW	CTBLS	10//99-12//99
	Hartford MSA, CT	S	32.84 MW	30.48 AW	68320 AAW	CTBLS	10//99-12//99
	New Haven-Meriden PMSA, CT	S	28.03 MW	26.34 AW	58300 AAW	CTBLS	10//99-12//99
	New London-Norwich MSA, CT-RI	S	26.56 MW	26.20 AW	55250 AAW	CTBLS	10//99-12//99
	Stamford-Norwalk PMSA, CT	S	33.43 MW	30.47 AW	69530 AAW	CTBLS	10//99-12//99
	Waterbury PMSA, CT	S	29.54 MW	28.80 AW	61440 AAW	CTBLS	10//99-12//99
	Delaware	S	25.43 MW	26.97 AW	56110 AAW	DEBLS	10//99-12//99
	Dover MSA, DE	S	24.46 MW	23.82 AW	50880 AAW	DEBLS	10//99-12//99
	Wilmington-Newark PMSA, DE-MD	S	28.29 MW	26.35 AW	58850 AAW	DEBLS	10//99-12//99
	Washington PMSA, DC-MD-VA-WV	S	29.34 MW	28.46 AW	61040 AAW	DCBLS	10//99-12//99
	Florida	S	21.5 MW	23.78 AW	49460 AAW	FLBLS	10//99-12//99
	Daytona Beach MSA, FL	S	19.73 MW	17.04 AW	41050 AAW	FLBLS	10//99-12//99
	Fort Lauderdale PMSA, FL	S	23.48 MW	22.87 AW	48840 AAW	FLBLS	10//99-12//99

AAW Average annual wage	**AOH** Average offered, high	**ASH** Average starting, high	**H** Hourly	**M** Monthly	**S** Special: hourly and annual
AE Average entry wage	**AOL** Average offered, low	**ASL** Average starting, low	**HI** Highest wage paid	**MTC** Median total compensation	**TQ** Third quartile wage
AEX Average experienced wage	**APH** Average pay, high range	**AW** Average wage paid	**HR** High end range	**MW** Median wage paid	**W** Weekly
AO Average offered	**APL** Average pay, low range	**FQ** First quartile wage	**LR** Low end range	**SQ** Second quartile wage	**Y** Yearly

Occupation/Type/Industry	Location	Per	Low	Mid	High	Source	Date
Transportation, Storage, and Distribution Manager	Fort Myers-Cape Coral MSA, FL	S	21.31 MW	19.18 AW	44330 AAW	FLBLS	10//99-12//99
	Fort Pierce-Port St. Lucie MSA, FL	S	15.88 MW	14.79 AW	33020 AAW	FLBLS	10//99-12//99
	Fort Walton Beach MSA, FL	S	19.38 MW	19.35 AW	40300 AAW	FLBLS	10//99-12//99
	Gainesville MSA, FL	S	23.60 MW	20.84 AW	49090 AAW	FLBLS	10//99-12//99
	Jacksonville MSA, FL	S	22.45 MW	20.37 AW	46690 AAW	FLBLS	10//99-12//99
	Lakeland-Winter Haven MSA, FL	S	23.11 MW	21.16 AW	48070 AAW	FLBLS	10//99-12//99
	Melbourne-Titusville-Palm Bay MSA, FL	S	23.92 MW	24.59 AW	49740 AAW	FLBLS	10//99-12//99
	Miami PMSΛ, FL	S	24.10 MW	23.21 AW	50140 AAW	FLBLS	10//99-12//99
	Naples MSA, FL	S	30.45 MW	22.97 AW	63330 AAW	FLBLS	10//99-12//99
	Ocala MSA, FL	S	25.56 MW	23.79 AW	53170 AAW	FLBLS	10//99-12//99
	Orlando MSA, FL	S	25.76 MW	20.95 AW	53590 AAW	FLBLS	10//99-12//99
	Panama City MSA, FL	S	22.62 MW	20.29 AW	47040 AAW	FLBLS	10//99-12//99
	Pensacola MSA, FL	S	24.39 MW	25.26 AW	50740 AAW	FLBLS	10//99-12//99
	Sarasota-Bradenton MSA, FL	S	23.22 MW	20.92 AW	48300 AAW	FLBLS	10//99-12//99
	Tallahassee MSA, FL	S	25.20 MW	24.89 AW	52410 AAW	FLBLS	10//99-12//99
	Tampa-St. Petersburg-Clearwater MSA, FL	S	25.68 MW	23.28 AW	53420 AAW	FLBLS	10//99-12//99
	West Palm Beach-Boca Raton MSA, FL	S	22.63 MW	19.86 AW	47060 AAW	FLBLS	10//99-12//99
	Georgia	S	24.08 MW	25.36 AW	52750 AAW	GABLS	10//99-12//99
	Albany MSA, GA	S	20.35 MW	19.36 AW	42320 AAW	GABLS	10//99-12//99
	Athens MSA, GA	S	23.49 MW	20.82 AW	48850 AAW	GABLS	10//99-12//99
	Atlanta MSA, GA	S	28.27 MW	27.31 AW	58800 AAW	GABLS	10//99-12//99
	Columbus MSA, GA-AL	S	20.14 MW	20.03 AW	41890 AAW	GABLS	10//99-12//99
	Macon MSA, GA	S	24.46 MW	22.32 AW	50880 AAW	GABLS	10//99-12//99
	Savannah MSA, GA	S	23.19 MW	23.63 AW	48240 AAW	GABLS	10//99-12//99
	Hawaii	S	23.33 MW	24.82 AW	51630 AAW	HIBLS	10//99-12//99
	Honolulu MSA, HI	S	25.45 MW	23.82 AW	52930 AAW	HIBLS	10//99-12//99
	Idaho	S	18.51 MW	21.53 AW	44780 AAW	IDBLS	10//99-12//99
	Boise City MSA, ID	S	25.93 MW	23.76 AW	53940 AAW	IDBLS	10//99-12//99
	Illinois	S	22.95 MW	24.60 AW	51170 AAW	ILBLS	10//99-12//99
	Bloomington-Normal MSA, IL	S	35.27 MW	32.59 AW	73360 AAW	ILBLS	10//99-12//99
	Champaign-Urbana MSA, IL	S	23.45 MW	21.35 AW	48770 AAW	ILBLS	10//99-12//99
	Chicago PMSA, IL	S	24.15 MW	22.36 AW	50240 AAW	ILBLS	10//99-12//99
	Decatur MSA, IL	S	27.89 MW	25.18 AW	58010 AAW	ILBLS	10//99-12//99
	Peoria-Pekin MSA, IL	S	21.02 MW	19.93 AW	43730 AAW	ILBLS	10//99-12//99
	Rockford MSA, IL	S	23.83 MW	22.14 AW	49560 AAW	ILBLS	10//99-12//99
	Springfield MSA, IL	S	28.02 MW	28.85 AW	58280 AAW	ILBLS	10//99-12//99
	Indiana	S	24.05 MW	25.55 AW	53140 AAW	INBLS	10//99-12//99
	Elkhart-Goshen MSA, IN	S	22.88 MW	21.01 AW	47590 AAW	INBLS	10//99-12//99
	Evansville-Henderson MSA, IN-KY	S	23.22 MW	23.71 AW	48300 AAW	INBLS	10//99-12//99
	Fort Wayne MSA, IN	S	24.14 MW	23.26 AW	50210 AAW	INBLS	10//99-12//99
	Gary PMSA, IN	S	21.81 MW	21.21 AW	45360 AAW	INBLS	10//99-12//99
	Indianapolis MSA, IN	S	28.74 MW	26.06 AW	59770 AAW	INBLS	10//99-12//99
	Kokomo MSA, IN	S	27.10 MW	28.58 AW	56370 AAW	INBLS	10//99-12//99
	Lafayette MSA, IN	S	29.42 MW	28.92 AW	61180 AAW	INBLS	10//99-12//99
	South Bend MSA, IN	S	23.93 MW	21.27 AW	49770 AAW	INBLS	10//99-12//99
	Terre Haute MSA, IN	S	26.04 MW	22.60 AW	54170 AAW	INBLS	10//99-12//99
	Iowa	S	22.89 MW	23.92 AW	49760 AAW	IABLS	10//99-12//99
	Cedar Rapids MSA, IA	S	26.73 MW	24.65 AW	55600 AAW	IABLS	10//99-12//99
	Davenport-Moline-Rock Island MSA, IA-IL	S	26.66 MW	24.84 AW	55460 AAW	IABLS	10//99-12//99
	Des Moines MSA, IA	S	22.91 MW	21.65 AW	47650 AAW	IABLS	10//99-12//99
	Dubuque MSA, IA	S	22.83 MW	22.16 AW	47480 AAW	IABLS	10//99-12//99
	Iowa City MSA, IA	S	28.19 MW	26.96 AW	58640 AAW	IABLS	10//99-12//99
	Sioux City MSA, IA-NE	S	25.51 MW	25.85 AW	53060 AAW	IABLS	10//99-12//99
	Kansas	S	23.56 MW	24.18 AW	50280 AAW	KSBLS	10//99-12//99
	Topeka MSA, KS	S	24.63 MW	23.08 AW	51230 AAW	KSBLS	10//99-12//99
	Wichita MSA, KS	S	24.64 MW	25.64 AW	51260 AAW	KSBLS	10//99-12//99
	Kentucky	S	24.18 MW	24.27 AW	50480 AAW	KYBLS	10//99-12//99
	Lexington MSA, KY	S	24.37 MW	23.91 AW	50680 AAW	KYBLS	10//99-12//99
	Louisville MSA, KY-IN	S	23.67 MW	22.50 AW	49240 AAW	KYBLS	10//99-12//99
	Owensboro MSA, KY	S	22.30 MW	22.61 AW	46390 AAW	KYBLS	10//99-12//99
	Louisiana	S	21.66 MW	23.40 AW	48660 AAW	LABLS	10//99-12//99
	Alexandria MSA, LA	S	29.80 MW	31.63 AW	61970 AAW	LABLS	10//99-12//99
	Baton Rouge MSA, LA	S	24.06 MW	23.94 AW	50050 AAW	LABLS	10//99-12//99

AAW Average annual wage	**AOH** Average offered, high	**ASH** Average starting, high	**H** Hourly	**M** Monthly	**S** Special: hourly and annual
AE Average entry wage	**AOL** Average offered, low	**ASL** Average starting, low	**HI** Highest wage paid	**MTC** Median total compensation	**TQ** Third quartile wage
AEX Average experienced wage	**APH** Average pay, high range	**AW** Average wage paid	**HR** High end range	**MW** Median wage paid	**W** Weekly
AO Average offered	**APL** Average pay, low range	**FQ** First quartile wage	**LR** Low end range	**SQ** Second quartile wage	**Y** Yearly

Occupation/Type/Industry	Location	Per	Low	Mid	High	Source	Date
Transportation, Storage, and Distribution Manager	Houma MSA, LA	S	18.72 MW	18.63 AW	38930 AAW	LABLS	10//99-12//99
	Lafayette MSA, LA	S	25.10 MW	24.13 AW	52220 AAW	LABLS	10//99-12//99
	Lake Charles MSA, LA	S	21.14 MW	19.77 AW	43970 AAW	LABLS	10//99-12//99
	Monroe MSA, LA	S	19.65 MW	19.48 AW	40870 AAW	LABLS	10//99-12//99
	New Orleans MSA, LA	S	23.91 MW	21.42 AW	49730 AAW	LABLS	10//99-12//99
	Shreveport-Bossier City MSA, LA	S	27.03 MW	20.86 AW	56210 AAW	LABLS	10//99-12//99
	Maine	S	17.36 MW	19.10 AW	39730 AAW	MEBLS	10//99-12//99
	Lewiston-Auburn MSA, ME	S	17.62 MW	16.57 AW	36650 AAW	MEBLS	10//99-12//99
	Portland MSA, ME	S	21.78 MW	20.63 AW	45310 AAW	MEBLS	10//99-12//99
	Maryland	S	26.32 MW	28.03 AW	58290 AAW	MDBLS	10//99-12//99
	Baltimore PMSA, MD	S	25.91 MW	24.67 AW	53890 AAW	MDBLS	10//99-12//99
	Hagerstown PMSA, MD	S	28.76 MW	26.55 AW	59820 AAW	MDBLS	10//99-12//99
	Massachusetts	S	26.17 MW	27.49 AW	57190 AAW	MABLS	10//99-12//99
	Boston PMSA, MA-NH	S	27.93 MW	26.54 AW	58100 AAW	MABLS	10//99-12//99
	Brockton PMSA, MA	S	23.51 MW	23.25 AW	48900 AAW	MABLS	10//99-12//99
	Fitchburg-Leominster PMSA, MA	S	21.24 MW	19.52 AW	44170 AAW	MABLS	10//99-12//99
	Lawrence PMSA, MA-NH	S	27.58 MW	25.51 AW	57370 AAW	MABLS	10//99-12//99
	Lowell PMSA, MA-NH	S	25.63 MW	23.91 AW	53310 AAW	MABLS	10//99-12//99
	New Bedford PMSA, MA	S	25.93 MW	25.91 AW	53920 AAW	MABLS	10//99-12//99
	Springfield MSA, MA	S	28.54 MW	26.99 AW	59360 AAW	MABLS	10//99-12//99
	Worcester PMSA, MA-CT	S	31.24 MW	29.13 AW	64970 AAW	MABLS	10//99-12//99
	Michigan	S	29.36 MW	30.06 AW	62520 AAW	MIBLS	10//99-12//99
	Ann Arbor PMSA, MI	S	28.03 MW	28.02 AW	58310 AAW	MIBLS	10//99-12//99
	Detroit PMSA, MI	S	32.03 MW	30.83 AW	66610 AAW	MIBLS	10//99-12//99
	Flint PMSA, MI	S	37.24 MW	33.14 AW	77450 AAW	MIBLS	10//99-12//99
	Grand Rapids-Muskegon-Holland MSA, MI	S	26.11 MW	26.66 AW	54310 AAW	MIBLS	10//99-12//99
	Kalamazoo-Battle Creek MSA, MI	S	29.61 MW	28.89 AW	61600 AAW	MIBLS	10//99-12//99
	Lansing-East Lansing MSA, MI	S	26.57 MW	26.57 AW	55260 AAW	MIBLS	10//99-12//99
	Saginaw-Bay City-Midland MSA, MI	S	35.26 MW	28.65 AW	73350 AAW	MIBLS	10//99-12//99
	Minnesota	S	25.91 MW	27.63 AW	57470 AAW	MNBLS	10//99-12//99
	Duluth-Superior MSA, MN-WI	S	30.10 MW	25.22 AW	62600 AAW	MNBLS	10//99-12//99
	Minneapolis-St. Paul MSA, MN-WI	S	27.24 MW	25.13 AW	56650 AAW	MNBLS	10//99-12//99
	Rochester MSA, MN	S	21.41 MW	23.83 AW	44530 AAW	MNBLS	10//99-12//99
	Mississippi	S	15.69 MW	17.53 AW	36460 AAW	MSBLS	10//99-12//99
	Biloxi-Gulfport-Pascagoula MSA, MS	S	19.15 MW	18.92 AW	39820 AAW	MSBLS	10//99-12//99
	Jackson MSA, MS	S	20.69 MW	20.00 AW	43040 AAW	MSBLS	10//99-12//99
	Missouri	S	24.83 MW	26.19 AW	54470 AAW	MOBLS	10//99-12//99
	Columbia MSA, MO	S	29.62 MW	31.04 AW	61610 AAW	MOBLS	10//99-12//99
	Kansas City MSA, MO-KS	S	25.89 MW	24.16 AW	53850 AAW	MOBLS	10//99-12//99
	St. Joseph MSA, MO	S	25.47 MW	25.85 AW	52970 AAW	MOBLS	10//99-12//99
	St. Louis MSA, MO-IL	S	27.84 MW	26.15 AW	57900 AAW	MOBLS	10//99-12//99
	Springfield MSA, MO	S	31.66 MW	32.69 AW	65850 AAW	MOBLS	10//99-12//99
	Montana	S	22.95 MW	25.08 AW	52160 AAW	MTBLS	10//99-12//99
	Billings MSA, MT	S	18.08 MW	14.72 AW	37600 AAW	MTBLS	10//99-12//99
	Nebraska	S	17.03 MW	18.36 AW	38190 AAW	NEBLS	10//99-12//99
	Lincoln MSA, NE	S	19.56 MW	19.30 AW	40680 AAW	NEBLS	10//99-12//99
	Omaha MSA, NE-IA	S	22.21 MW	19.83 AW	46200 AAW	NEBLS	10//99-12//99
	Nevada	S	20.07 MW	22.34 AW	46460 AAW	NVBLS	10//99-12//99
	Las Vegas MSA, NV-AZ	S	22.36 MW	19.96 AW	46500 AAW	NVBLS	10//99-12//99
	Reno MSA, NV	S	22.03 MW	20.94 AW	45830 AAW	NVBLS	10//99-12//99
	New Hampshire	S	24.94 MW	25.99 AW	54060 AAW	NHBLS	10//99-12//99
	Manchester PMSA, NH	S	24.65 MW	22.72 AW	51270 AAW	NHBLS	10//99-12//99
	Nashua PMSA, NH	S	24.72 MW	24.80 AW	51410 AAW	NHBLS	10//99-12//99
	Portsmouth-Rochester PMSA, NH-ME	S	27.37 MW	25.97 AW	56930 AAW	NHBLS	10//99-12//99
	New Jersey	S	31.64 MW	33.45 AW	69580 AAW	NJBLS	10//99-12//99
	Atlantic-Cape May PMSA, NJ	S	28.09 MW	27.05 AW	58430 AAW	NJBLS	10//99-12//99
	Bergen-Passaic PMSA, NJ	S	35.24 MW	31.75 AW	73300 AAW	NJBLS	10//99-12//99
	Jersey City PMSA, NJ	S	34.96 MW	35.15 AW	72710 AAW	NJBLS	10//99-12//99
	Middlesex-Somerset-Hunterdon PMSA, NJ	S	35.28 MW	35.52 AW	73380 AAW	NJBLS	10//99-12//99
	Monmouth-Ocean PMSA, NJ	S	31.48 MW	26.94 AW	65490 AAW	NJBLS	10//99-12//99
	Newark PMSA, NJ	S	31.84 MW	30.21 AW	66230 AAW	NJBLS	10//99-12//99
	Trenton PMSA, NJ	S	32.00 MW	32.10 AW	66570 AAW	NJBLS	10//99-12//99

AAW Average annual wage	**AOH** Average offered, high	**ASH** Average starting, high	**H** Hourly	**M** Monthly	**S** Special: hourly and annual
AE Average entry wage	**AOL** Average offered, low	**ASL** Average starting, low	**HI** Highest wage paid	**MTC** Median total compensation	**TQ** Third quartile wage
AEX Average experienced wage	**APH** Average pay, high range	**AW** Average wage paid	**HR** High end range	**MW** Median wage paid	**W** Weekly
AO Average offered	**APL** Average pay, low range	**FQ** First quartile wage	**LR** Low end range	**SQ** Second quartile wage	**Y** Yearly

Occupation/Type/Industry	Location	Per	Low	Mid	High	Source	Date
Transportation, Storage, and Distribution Manager	New Mexico	S	16.82 MW	18.95 AW	39410 AAW	NMBLS	10//99-12//99
	Albuquerque MSA, NM	S	24.41 MW	24.04 AW	50780 AAW	NMBLS	10//99-12//99
	Santa Fe MSA, NM	S	19.65 MW	19.38 AW	40870 AAW	NMBLS	10//99-12//99
	New York	S	30.12 MW	33.26 AW	69190 AAW	NYBLS	10//99-12//99
	Albany-Schenectady-Troy MSA, NY	S	29.41 MW	28.43 AW	61170 AAW	NYBLS	10//99-12//99
	Binghamton MSA, NY	S	29.06 MW	27.88 AW	60450 AAW	NYBLS	10//99-12//99
	Buffalo-Niagara Falls MSA, NY	S	30.21 MW	29.12 AW	62840 AAW	NYBLS	10//99-12//99
	Dutchess County PMSA, NY	S	24.66 MW	21.14 AW	51300 AAW	NYBLS	10//99-12//99
	Glens Falls MSA, NY	S	27.47 MW	23.95 AW	57130 AAW	NYBLS	10//99-12//99
	Nassau-Suffolk PMSA, NY	S	34.18 MW	32.85 AW	71090 AAW	NYBLS	10//99-12//99
	New York PMSA, NY	S	35.53 MW	31.25 AW	73900 AAW	NYBLS	10//99-12//99
	Newburgh PMSA, NY-PA	S	33.87 MW	31.99 AW	70450 AAW	NYBLS	10//99-12//99
	Rochester MSA, NY	S	26.52 MW	26.56 AW	55160 AAW	NYBLS	10//99-12//99
	Syracuse MSA, NY	S	30.46 MW	29.93 AW	63360 AAW	NYBLS	10//99-12//99
	Utica-Rome MSA, NY	S	33.57 MW	30.18 AW	69830 AAW	NYBLS	10//99-12//99
	North Carolina	S	22.4 MW	24.53 AW	51020 AAW	NCBLS	10//99-12//99
	Asheville MSA, NC	S	20.56 MW	19.19 AW	42760 AAW	NCBLS	10//99-12//99
	Charlotte-Gastonia-Rock Hill MSA, NC-SC	S	25.33 MW	23.02 AW	52680 AAW	NCBLS	10//99-12//99
	Fayetteville MSA, NC	S	17.26 MW	14.19 AW	35890 AAW	NCBLS	10//99-12//99
	Greensboro--Winston-Salem--High Point MSA, NC	S	26.42 MW	24.39 AW	54950 AAW	NCBLS	10//99-12//99
	Greenville MSA, NC	S	21.37 MW	19.68 AW	44440 AAW	NCBLS	10//99-12//99
	Hickory-Morganton-Lenoir MSA, NC	S	22.30 MW	19.05 AW	46370 AAW	NCBLS	10//99-12//99
	Raleigh-Durham-Chapel Hill MSA, NC	S	27.65 MW	25.53 AW	57520 AAW	NCBLS	10//99-12//99
	Rocky Mount MSA, NC	S	23.87 MW	22.82 AW	49650 AAW	NCBLS	10//99-12//99
	Wilmington MSA, NC	S	22.88 MW	19.99 AW	47600 AAW	NCBLS	10//99-12//99
	North Dakota	S	19.95 MW	20.08 AW	41770 AAW	NDBLS	10//99-12//99
	Bismarck MSA, ND	S	21.06 MW	19.62 AW	43810 AAW	NDBLS	10//99-12//99
	Fargo-Moorhead MSA, ND-MN	S	20.20 MW	17.68 AW	42020 AAW	NDBLS	10//99-12//99
	Ohio	S	22.39 MW	23.56 AW	49000 AAW	OHBLS	10//99-12//99
	Akron PMSA, OH	S	24.80 MW	24.15 AW	51570 AAW	OHBLS	10//99-12//99
	Canton-Massillon MSA, OH	S	25.12 MW	23.99 AW	52250 AAW	OHBLS	10//99-12//99
	Cincinnati PMSA, OH-KY-IN	S	23.97 MW	23.32 AW	49850 AAW	OHBLS	10//99-12//99
	Cleveland-Lorain-Elyria PMSA, OH	S	24.84 MW	23.80 AW	51670 AAW	OHBLS	10//99-12//99
	Columbus MSA, OH	S	25.70 MW	24.29 AW	53460 AAW	OHBLS	10//99-12//99
	Dayton-Springfield MSA, OH	S	23.78 MW	21.61 AW	49470 AAW	OHBLS	10//99-12//99
	Hamilton-Middletown PMSA, OH	S	24.74 MW	22.04 AW	51470 AAW	OHBLS	10//99-12//99
	Lima MSA, OH	S	24.69 MW	24.16 AW	51350 AAW	OHBLS	10//99-12//99
	Mansfield MSA, OH	S	25.74 MW	25.45 AW	53530 AAW	OHBLS	10//99-12//99
	Toledo MSA, OH	S	23.92 MW	22.90 AW	49760 AAW	OHBLS	10//99-12//99
	Youngstown-Warren MSA, OH	S	23.60 MW	23.35 AW	49090 AAW	OHBLS	10//99-12//99
	Oklahoma	S	21.18 MW	21.76 AW	45270 AAW	OKBLS	10//99-12//99
	Oklahoma City MSA, OK	S	21.38 MW	20.33 AW	44460 AAW	OKBLS	10//99-12//99
	Tulsa MSA, OK	S	24.80 MW	26.56 AW	51570 AAW	OKBLS	10//99-12//99
	Oregon	S	26.58 MW	27.94 AW	58110 AAW	ORBLS	10//99-12//99
	Eugene-Springfield MSA, OR	S	25.46 MW	22.83 AW	52960 AAW	ORBLS	10//99-12//99
	Medford-Ashland MSA, OR	S	29.47 MW	29.67 AW	61300 AAW	ORBLS	10//99-12//99
	Portland-Vancouver PMSA, OR-WA	S	28.80 MW	27.03 AW	59910 AAW	ORBLS	10//99-12//99
	Salem PMSA, OR	S	27.43 MW	26.22 AW	57050 AAW	ORBLS	10//99-12//99
	Pennsylvania	S	24.6 MW	26.16 AW	54420 AAW	PABLS	10//99-12//99
	Allentown-Bethlehem-Easton MSA, PA	S	25.82 MW	21.26 AW	53710 AAW	PABLS	10//99-12//99
	Altoona MSA, PA	S	17.68 MW	15.69 AW	36780 AAW	PABLS	10//99-12//99
	Erie MSA, PA	S	24.77 MW	23.85 AW	51520 AAW	PABLS	10//99-12//99
	Harrisburg-Lebanon-Carlisle MSA, PA	S	30.51 MW	29.71 AW	63460 AAW	PABLS	10//99-12//99
	Johnstown MSA, PA	S	21.73 MW	20.18 AW	45190 AAW	PABLS	10//99-12//99
	Lancaster MSA, PA	S	23.44 MW	22.23 AW	48750 AAW	PABLS	10//99-12//99
	Philadelphia PMSA, PA-NJ	S	29.14 MW	27.97 AW	60600 AAW	PABLS	10//99-12//99
	Pittsburgh MSA, PA	S	23.94 MW	22.51 AW	49800 AAW	PABLS	10//99-12//99
	Reading MSA, PA	S	24.79 MW	23.32 AW	51560 AAW	PABLS	10//99-12//99

AAW	Average annual wage	AOH	Average offered, high	ASH	Average starting, high	H	Hourly	M	Monthly	S	Special: hourly and annual
AE	Average entry wage	AOL	Average offered, low	ASL	Average starting, low	HI	Highest wage paid	MTC	Median total compensation	TQ	Third quartile wage
AEX	Average experienced wage	APH	Average pay, high range	AW	Average wage paid	HR	High end range	MW	Median wage paid	W	Weekly
AO	Average offered	APL	Average pay, low range	FQ	First quartile wage	LR	Low end range	SQ	Second quartile wage	Y	Yearly

Occupation/Type/Industry	Location	Per	Low	Mid	High	Source	Date
Transportation, Storage, and Distribution Manager	Scranton--Wilkes-Barre--						
	Hazleton MSA, PA	S	28.85 MW	29.27 AW	60000 AAW	PABLS	10//99-12//99
	Sharon MSA, PA	S	22.62 MW	19.28 AW	47050 AAW	PABLS	10//99-12//99
	Williamsport MSA, PA	S	23.29 MW	20.39 AW	48430 AAW	PABLS	10//99-12//99
	York MSA, PA	S	22.77 MW	21.94 AW	47370 AAW	PABLS	10//99-12//99
	Rhode Island	S	32.34 MW	32.70 AW	68020 AAW	RIBLS	10//99-12//99
	Providence-Fall River-						
	Warwick MSA, RI-MA	S	32.40 MW	31.99 AW	67380 AAW	RIBLS	10//99-12//99
	South Carolina	S	24.36 MW	25.75 AW	53560 AAW	SCBLS	10//99-12//99
	Charleston-North Charleston						
	MSA, SC	S	21.95 MW	22.40 AW	45650 AAW	SCBLS	10//99-12//99
	Columbia MSA, SC	S	30.39 MW	34.85 AW	63220 AAW	SCBLS	10//99-12//99
	Greenville-Spartanburg-						
	Anderson MSA, SC	S	20.69 MW	19.22 AW	43040 AAW	SCBLS	10//99-12//99
	Myrtle Beach MSA, SC	S	17.97 MW	17.56 AW	37380 AAW	SCBLS	10//99-12//99
	South Dakota	S	25.61 MW	29.25 AW	60840 AAW	SDBLS	10//99-12//99
	Sioux Falls MSA, SD	S	29.17 MW	25.21 AW	60680 AAW	SDBLS	10//99-12//99
	Tennessee	S	23.06 MW	23.80 AW	49510 AAW	TNBLS	10//99-12//99
	Chattanooga MSA, TN-GA	S	20.85 MW	20.01 AW	43360 AAW	TNBLS	10//99-12//99
	Clarksville-Hopkinsville MSA,						
	TN-KY	S	20.19 MW	18.80 AW	41990 AAW	TNBLS	10//99-12//99
	Jackson MSA, TN	S	22.94 MW	24.24 AW	47710 AAW	TNBLS	10//99-12//99
	Johnson City-Kingsport-Bristol						
	MSA, TN-VA	S	24.05 MW	24.66 AW	50030 AAW	TNBLS	10//99-12//99
	Knoxville MSA, TN	S	21.33 MW	19.82 AW	44370 AAW	TNBLS	10//99-12//99
	Memphis MSA, TN-AR-MS	S	25.33 MW	23.67 AW	52680 AAW	MSBLS	10//99-12//99
	Nashville MSA, TN	S	24.86 MW	23.98 AW	51710 AAW	TNBLS	10//99-12//99
	Texas	S	23.3 MW	25.15 AW	52320 AAW	TXBLS	10//99-12//99
	Abilene MSA, TX	S	27.78 MW	29.22 AW	57770 AAW	TXBLS	10//99-12//99
	Amarillo MSA, TX	S	24.25 MW	20.39 AW	50440 AAW	TXBLS	10//99-12//99
	Austin-San Marcos MSA, TX	S	24.70 MW	22.13 AW	51380 AAW	TXBLS	10//99-12//99
	Beaumont-Port Arthur MSA,						
	TX	S	28.93 MW	27.55 AW	60170 AAW	TXBLS	10//99-12//99
	Brazoria PMSA, TX	S	31.92 MW	32.95 AW	66390 AAW	TXBLS	10//99-12//99
	Brownsville-Harlingen-San						
	Benito MSA, TX	S	19.61 MW	20.10 AW	40790 AAW	TXBLS	10//99-12//99
	Bryan-College Station MSA,						
	TX	S	28.20 MW	25.61 AW	58650 AAW	TXBLS	10//99-12//99
	Corpus Christi MSA, TX	S	21.32 MW	19.33 AW	44340 AAW	TXBLS	10//99-12//99
	Dallas PMSA, TX	S	25.75 MW	23.36 AW	53560 AAW	TXBLS	10//99-12//99
	El Paso MSA, TX	S	22.76 MW	20.79 AW	47350 AAW	TXBLS	10//99-12//99
	Fort Worth-Arlington PMSA,						
	TX	S	31.17 MW	30.20 AW	64840 AAW	TXBLS	10//99-12//99
	Galveston-Texas City PMSA,						
	TX	S	21.32 MW	20.29 AW	44340 AAW	TXBLS	10//99-12//99
	Houston PMSA, TX	S	26.92 MW	25.83 AW	55990 AAW	TXBLS	10//99-12//99
	Killeen-Temple MSA, TX	S	24.03 MW	23.27 AW	49990 AAW	TXBLS	10//99-12//99
	Longview-Marshall MSA, TX	S	19.59 MW	19.23 AW	40750 AAW	TXBLS	10//99-12//99
	Lubbock MSA, TX	S	24.28 MW	25.79 AW	50500 AAW	TXBLS	10//99-12//99
	McAllen-Edinburg-Mission						
	MSA, TX	S	16.99 MW	14.87 AW	35330 AAW	TXBLS	10//99-12//99
	Odessa-Midland MSA, TX	S	22.05 MW	20.65 AW	45860 AAW	TXBLS	10//99-12//99
	San Antonio MSA, TX	S	21.10 MW	19.64 AW	43890 AAW	TXBLS	10//99-12//99
	Sherman-Denison MSA, TX	S	25.05 MW	23.28 AW	52100 AAW	TXBLS	10//99-12//99
	Texarkana MSA, TX-						
	Texarkana, AR	S	24.89 MW	24.40 AW	51770 AAW	TXBLS	10//99-12//99
	Tyler MSA, TX	S	21.57 MW	20.48 AW	44860 AAW	TXBLS	10//99-12//99
	Victoria MSA, TX	S	19.89 MW	19.93 AW	41370 AAW	TXBLS	10//99-12//99
	Waco MSA, TX	S	19.16 MW	19.20 AW	39850 AAW	TXBLS	10//99-12//99
	Wichita Falls MSA, TX	S	17.59 MW	15.42 AW	36580 AAW	TXBLS	10//99-12//99
	Utah	S	24.95 MW	25.59 AW	53230 AAW	UTBLS	10//99-12//99
	Provo-Orem MSA, UT	S	23.28 MW	24.25 AW	48420 AAW	UTBLS	10//99-12//99
	Salt Lake City-Ogden MSA,						
	UT	S	25.63 MW	25.01 AW	53300 AAW	UTBLS	10//99-12//99
	Vermont	S	28.01 MW	31.24 AW	64970 AAW	VTBLS	10//99-12//99
	Burlington MSA, VT	S	25.73 MW	25.22 AW	53510 AAW	VTBLS	10//99-12//99
	Virginia	S	24.63 MW	25.81 AW	53670 AAW	VABLS	10//99-12//99
	Charlottesville MSA, VA	S	25.50 MW	24.81 AW	53030 AAW	VABLS	10//99-12//99
	Lynchburg MSA, VA	S	19.75 MW	19.53 AW	41080 AAW	VABLS	10//99-12//99

AAW	Average annual wage	AOH	Average offered, high	ASH	Average starting, high
AE	Average entry wage	AOL	Average offered, low	ASL	Average starting, low
AEX	Average experienced wage	APH	Average pay, high range	AW	Average wage paid
AO	Average offered	APL	Average pay, low range	FQ	First quartile wage

H	Hourly	M	Monthly
HI	Highest wage paid	MTC	Median total compensation
HR	High end range	MW	Median wage paid
LR	Low end range	SQ	Second quartile wage

S	Special: hourly and annual
TQ	Third quartile wage
W	Weekly
Y	Yearly

Occupation/Type/Industry	Location	Per	Low	Mid	High	Source	Date
Transportation, Storage, and Distribution Manager	Norfolk-Virginia Beach-Newport News MSA, VA-NC	S	22.77 MW	22.12 AW	47350 AAW	VABLS	10//99-12//99
	Richmond-Petersburg MSA, VA	S	24.88 MW	23.79 AW	51750 AAW	VABLS	10//99-12//99
	Roanoke MSA, VA	S	21.00 MW	20.10 AW	43690 AAW	VABLS	10//99-12//99
	Washington	S	25.65 MW	27.59 AW	57380 AAW	WABLS	10//99-12//99
	Bellingham MSA, WA	S	22.35 MW	23.25 AW	46490 AAW	WABLS	10//99-12//99
	Bremerton PMSA, WA	S	27.11 MW	25.81 AW	56400 AAW	WABLS	10//99-12//99
	Olympia PMSA, WA	S	28.17 MW	29.79 AW	58600 AAW	WABLS	10//99-12//99
	Richland-Kennewick-Pasco MSA, WA	S	31.39 MW	31.00 AW	65280 AAW	WABLS	10//99-12//99
	Seattle-Bellevue-Everett PMSA, WA	S	26.07 MW	24.30 AW	54230 AAW	WABLS	10//99-12//99
	Spokane MSA, WA	S	28.63 MW	28.16 AW	59560 AAW	WABLS	10//99-12//99
	Tacoma PMSA, WA	S	29.77 MW	27.39 AW	61920 AAW	WABLS	10//99-12//99
	Yakima MSA, WA	S	21.35 MW	22.21 AW	44410 AAW	WABLS	10//99-12//99
	West Virginia	S	22.02 MW	23.75 AW	49400 AAW	WVBLS	10//99-12//99
	Charleston MSA, WV	S	25.05 MW	24.78 AW	52100 AAW	WVBLS	10//99-12//99
	Huntington-Ashland MSA, WV-KY-OH	S	19.79 MW	21.89 AW	41160 AAW	WVBLS	10//99-12//99
	Parkersburg-Marietta MSA, WV-OH	S	26.35 MW	25.98 AW	54810 AAW	WVBLS	10//99-12//99
	Wheeling MSA, WV-OH	S	22.51 MW	23.42 AW	46830 AAW	WVBLS	10//99-12//99
	Wisconsin	S	23.4 MW	24.28 AW	50500 AAW	WIBLS	10//99-12//99
	Appleton-Oshkosh-Neenah MSA, WI	S	28.24 MW	27.60 AW	58740 AAW	WIBLS	10//99-12//99
	Eau Claire MSA, WI	S	21.58 MW	18.96 AW	44890 AAW	WIBLS	10//99-12//99
	Green Bay MSA, WI	S	23.85 MW	22.18 AW	49610 AAW	WIBLS	10//99-12//99
	Kenosha PMSA, WI	S	26.38 MW	29.26 AW	54860 AAW	WIBLS	10//99-12//99
	La Crosse MSA, WI-MN	S	21.94 MW	22.76 AW	45630 AAW	WIBLS	10//99-12//99
	Madison MSA, WI	S	25.41 MW	24.63 AW	52850 AAW	WIBLS	10//99-12//99
	Milwaukee-Waukesha PMSA, WI	S	25.31 MW	24.95 AW	52650 AAW	WIBLS	10//99-12//99
	Racine PMSA, WI	S	29.98 MW	28.71 AW	62350 AAW	WIBLS	10//99-12//99
	Sheboygan MSA, WI	S	24.97 MW	24.85 AW	51940 AAW	WIBLS	10//99-12//99
	Wausau MSA, WI	S	18.38 MW	16.48 AW	38240 AAW	WIBLS	10//99-12//99
	Wyoming	S	21.58 MW	20.22 AW	42050 AAW	WYBLS	10//99-12//99
	Puerto Rico	S	20.33 MW	23.11 AW	48080 AAW	PRBLS	10//99-12//99
	Caguas PMSA, PR	S	20.48 MW	16.67 AW	42600 AAW	PRBLS	10//99-12//99
	San Juan-Bayamon PMSA, PR	S	23.21 MW	20.42 AW	48270 AAW	PRBLS	10//99-12//99
	Guam	S	16.11 MW	19.14 AW	39820 AAW	GUBLS	10//99-12//99
Travel Agent	Alabama	S	9.33 MW	9.80 AW	20370 AAW	ALBLS	10//99-12//99
	Birmingham MSA, AL	S	9.74 MW	9.22 AW	20260 AAW	ALBLS	10//99-12//99
	Huntsville MSA, AL	S	10.59 MW	10.57 AW	22030 AAW	ALBLS	10//99-12//99
	Mobile MSA, AL	S	11.00 MW	10.53 AW	22890 AAW	ALBLS	10//99-12//99
	Montgomery MSA, AL	S	9.86 MW	8.53 AW	20520 AAW	ALBLS	10//99-12//99
	Alaska	S	11.81 MW	12.07 AW	25110 AAW	AKBLS	10//99-12//99
	Anchorage MSA, AK	S	12.35 MW	12.30 AW	25690 AAW	AKBLS	10//99-12//99
	Arizona	S	9.91 MW	9.88 AW	20550 AAW	AZBLS	10//99-12//99
	Phoenix-Mesa MSA, AZ	S	9.78 MW	10.01 AW	20340 AAW	AZBLS	10//99-12//99
	Tucson MSA, AZ	S	10.35 MW	10.06 AW	21530 AAW	AZBLS	10//99-12//99
	Arkansas	S	9.28 MW	9.67 AW	20120 AAW	ARBLS	10//99-12//99
	Fayetteville-Springdale-Rogers MSA, AR	S	10.24 MW	10.29 AW	21290 AAW	ARBLS	10//99-12//99
	Fort Smith MSA, AR-OK	S	10.47 MW	10.42 AW	21780 AAW	ARBLS	10//99-12//99
	Little Rock-North Little Rock MSA, AR	S	10.08 MW	9.67 AW	20970 AAW	ARBLS	10//99-12//99
	California	S	12.47 MW	13.42 AW	27910 AAW	CABLS	10//99-12//99
	Bakersfield MSA, CA	S	11.20 MW	12.38 AW	23300 AAW	CABLS	10//99-12//99
	Fresno MSA, CA	S	10.85 MW	10.31 AW	22560 AAW	CABLS	10//99-12//99
	Los Angeles-Long Beach PMSA, CA	S	13.83 MW	12.49 AW	28760 AAW	CABLS	10//99-12//99
	Merced MSA, CA	S	8.22 MW	7.96 AW	17110 AAW	CABLS	10//99-12//99
	Modesto MSA, CA	S	13.34 MW	14.03 AW	27750 AAW	CABLS	10//99-12//99
	Oakland PMSA, CA	S	14.09 MW	14.09 AW	29310 AAW	CABLS	10//99-12//99
	Orange County PMSA, CA	S	13.23 MW	13.28 AW	27510 AAW	CABLS	10//99-12//99
	Riverside-San Bernardino PMSA, CA	S	11.95 MW	11.69 AW	24850 AAW	CABLS	10//99-12//99
	Sacramento PMSA, CA	S	12.07 MW	11.94 AW	25100 AAW	CABLS	10//99-12//99

AAW Average annual wage	AOH Average offered, high	ASH Average starting, high	H Hourly	M Monthly	S Special: hourly and annual
AE Average entry wage	AOL Average offered, low	ASL Average starting, low	HI Highest wage paid	MTC Median total compensation	TQ Third quartile wage
AEX Average experienced wage	APH Average pay, high range	AW Average wage paid	HR High end range	MW Median wage paid	W Weekly
AO Average offered	APL Average pay, low range	FQ First quartile wage	LR Low end range	SQ Second quartile wage	Y Yearly

Occupation/Type/Industry	Location	Per	Low	Mid	High	Source	Date
Travel Agent	Salinas MSA, CA	S	10.06 MW	8.58 AW	20920 AAW	CABLS	10//99-12//99
	San Diego MSA, CA	S	11.48 MW	10.83 AW	23880 AAW	CABLS	10//99-12//99
	San Francisco PMSA, CA	S	17.01 MW	15.12 AW	35380 AAW	CABLS	10//99-12//99
	San Jose PMSA, CA	S	13.52 MW	12.09 AW	28120 AAW	CABLS	10//99-12//99
	San Luis Obispo-Atascadero- Paso Robles MSA, CA	S	10.92 MW	10.72 AW	22710 AAW	CABLS	10//99-12//99
	Santa Barbara-Santa Maria- Lompoc MSA, CA	S	11.35 MW	11.75 AW	23600 AAW	CABLS	10//99-12//99
	Santa Cruz-Watsonville PMSA, CA	S	11.65 MW	11.68 AW	24240 AAW	CABLS	10//99-12//99
	Santa Rosa PMSA, CA	S	12.07 MW	12.07 AW	25090 AAW	CABLS	10//99-12//99
	Stockton-Lodi MSA, CA	S	12.79 MW	11.51 AW	26610 AAW	CABLS	10//99-12//99
	Vallejo-Fairfield-Napa PMSA, CA	S	12.44 MW	13.91 AW	25870 AAW	CABLS	10//99-12//99
	Ventura PMSA, CA	S	12.28 MW	12.44 AW	25540 AAW	CABLS	10//99-12//99
	Visalia-Tulare-Porterville MSA, CA	S	10.03 MW	8.37 AW	20870 AAW	CABLS	10//99-12//99
	Yolo PMSA, CA	S	12.31 MW	12.59 AW	25610 AAW	CABLS	10//99-12//99
	Colorado	S	10.72 MW	11.07 AW	23030 AAW	COBLS	10//99-12//99
	Boulder-Longmont PMSA, CO	S	10.92 MW	10.06 AW	22710 AAW	COBLS	10//99-12//99
	Colorado Springs MSA, CO	S	10.59 MW	10.21 AW	22020 AAW	COBLS	10//99-12//99
	Denver PMSA, CO	S	11.32 MW	11.18 AW	23550 AAW	COBLS	10//99-12//99
	Fort Collins-Loveland MSA, CO	S	10.20 MW	9.80 AW	21210 AAW	COBLS	10//99-12//99
	Greeley PMSA, CO	S	9.66 MW	8.90 AW	20100 AAW	COBLS	10//99-12//99
	Pueblo MSA, CO	S	10.17 MW	8.96 AW	21150 AAW	COBLS	10//99-12//99
	Connecticut	S	13.66 MW	13.75 AW	28590 AAW	CTBLS	10//99-12//99
	Bridgeport PMSA, CT	S	12.90 MW	11.75 AW	26840 AAW	CTBLS	10//99-12//99
	Danbury PMSA, CT	S	12.08 MW	12.00 AW	25130 AAW	CTBLS	10//99-12//99
	Hartford MSA, CT	S	14.49 MW	14.74 AW	30140 AAW	CTBLS	10//99-12//99
	New London-Norwich MSA, CT-RI	S	11.09 MW	10.91 AW	23060 AAW	CTBLS	10//99-12//99
	Stamford-Norwalk PMSA, CT	S	14.54 MW	14.47 AW	30250 AAW	CTBLS	10//99-12//99
	Waterbury PMSA, CT	S	12.39 MW	12.29 AW	25760 AAW	CTBLS	10//99-12//99
	Delaware	S	10.31 MW	10.67 AW	22190 AAW	DEBLS	10//99-12//99
	Wilmington-Newark PMSA, DE-MD	S	10.35 MW	10.09 AW	21520 AAW	DEBLS	10//99-12//99
	District of Columbia	S	13.34 MW	14.04 AW	29200 AAW	DCBLS	10//99-12//99
	Washington PMSA, DC-MD- VA-WV	S	13.17 MW	12.75 AW	27390 AAW	DCBLS	10//99-12//99
	Florida	S	10.8 MW	10.94 AW	22760 AAW	FLBLS	10//99-12//99
	Daytona Beach MSA, FL	S	9.81 MW	10.30 AW	20410 AAW	FLBLS	10//99-12//99
	Fort Lauderdale PMSA, FL	S	10.99 MW	10.01 AW	22860 AAW	FLBLS	10//99-12//99
	Fort Myers-Cape Coral MSA, FL	S	10.11 MW	9.20 AW	21020 AAW	FLBLS	10//99-12//99
	Fort Pierce-Port St. Lucie MSA, FL	S	11.17 MW	10.54 AW	23240 AAW	FLBLS	10//99-12//99
	Fort Walton Beach MSA, FL	S	9.75 MW	8.03 AW	20270 AAW	FLBLS	10//99-12//99
	Gainesville MSA, FL	S	9.30 MW	8.49 AW	19330 AAW	FLBLS	10//99-12//99
	Jacksonville MSA, FL	S	12.53 MW	12.31 AW	26070 AAW	FLBLS	10//99-12//99
	Lakeland-Winter Haven MSA, FL	S	8.84 MW	8.03 AW	18390 AAW	FLBLS	10//99-12//99
	Melbourne-Titusville-Palm Bay MSA, FL	S	10.08 MW	10.02 AW	20970 AAW	FLBLS	10//99-12//99
	Miami PMSA, FL	S	10.64 MW	9.76 AW	22140 AAW	FLBLS	10//99-12//99
	Ocala MSA, FL	S	8.63 MW	8.69 AW	17960 AAW	FLBLS	10//99-12//99
	Orlando MSA, FL	S	10.95 MW	11.90 AW	22770 AAW	FLBLS	10//99-12//99
	Panama City MSA, FL	S	9.52 MW	9.46 AW	19800 AAW	FLBLS	10//99-12//99
	Pensacola MSA, FL	S	10.68 MW	10.00 AW	22210 AAW	FLBLS	10//99-12//99
	Punta Gorda MSA, FL	S	9.84 MW	9.90 AW	20460 AAW	FLBLS	10//99-12//99
	Sarasota-Bradenton MSA, FL	S	8.95 MW	9.35 AW	18620 AAW	FLBLS	10//99-12//99
	Tallahassee MSA, FL	S	12.05 MW	12.04 AW	25070 AAW	FLBLS	10//99-12//99
	Tampa-St. Petersburg- Clearwater MSA, FL	S	11.55 MW	11.61 AW	24020 AAW	FLBLS	10//99-12//99
	West Palm Beach-Boca Raton MSA, FL	S	13.32 MW	13.20 AW	27710 AAW	FLBLS	10//99-12//99
	Georgia	S	12.27 MW	12.36 AW	25710 AAW	GABLS	10//99-12//99
	Atlanta MSA, GA	S	12.73 MW	12.45 AW	26490 AAW	GABLS	10//99-12//99
	Augusta-Aiken MSA, GA-SC	S	10.38 MW	10.18 AW	21600 AAW	GABLS	10//99-12//99
	Macon MSA, GA	S	12.47 MW	11.15 AW	25930 AAW	GABLS	10//99-12//99
	Hawaii	S	11.74 MW	12.42 AW	25820 AAW	HIBLS	10//99-12//99
	Honolulu MSA, HI	S	12.37 MW	11.29 AW	25740 AAW	HIBLS	10//99-12//99

AAW Average annual wage	**AOH** Average offered, high	**ASH** Average starting, high	**H** Hourly	**M** Monthly	**S** Special: hourly and annual
AE Average entry wage	**AOL** Average offered, low	**ASL** Average starting, low	**HI** Highest wage paid	**MTC** Median total compensation	**TQ** Third quartile wage
AEX Average experienced wage	**APH** Average pay, high range	**AW** Average wage paid	**HR** High end range	**MW** Median wage paid	**W** Weekly
AO Average offered	**APL** Average pay, low range	**FQ** First quartile wage	**LR** Low end range	**SQ** Second quartile wage	**Y** Yearly

Occupation/Type/Industry	Location	Per	Low	Mid	High	Source	Date
Travel Agent	Idaho	s	10.64 MW	11.13 AW	23140 AAW	IDBLS	10//99-12//99
	Boise City MSA, ID	s	11.86 MW	11.18 AW	24670 AAW	IDBLS	10//99-12//99
	Pocatello MSA, ID	s	7.92 MW	7.59 AW	16460 AAW	IDBLS	10//99-12//99
	Illinois	s	9.3 MW	10.36 AW	21550 AAW	ILBLS	10//99-12//99
	Champaign-Urbana MSA, IL	s	10.08 MW	10.22 AW	20960 AAW	ILBLS	10//99-12//99
	Chicago PMSA, IL	s	10.39 MW	9.31 AW	21600 AAW	ILBLS	10//99-12//99
	Decatur MSA, IL	s	8.70 MW	8.19 AW	18090 AAW	ILBLS	10//99-12//99
	Peoria-Pekin MSA, IL	s	10.17 MW	10.30 AW	21150 AAW	ILBLS	10//99-12//99
	Rockford MSA, IL	s	9.59 MW	9.13 AW	19950 AAW	ILBLS	10//99-12//99
	Springfield MSA, IL	s	11.14 MW	10.52 AW	23180 AAW	ILBLS	10//99-12//99
	Indiana	s	10.34 MW	10.93 AW	22740 AAW	INBLS	10//99-12//99
	Bloomington MSA, IN	s	9.76 MW	9.83 AW	20300 AAW	INBLS	10//99-12//99
	Evansville-Henderson MSA, IN-KY	s	10.35 MW	10.23 AW	21540 AAW	INBLS	10//99-12//99
	Fort Wayne MSA, IN	s	9.56 MW	8.97 AW	19890 AAW	INBLS	10//99-12//99
	Gary PMSA, IN	s	7.32 MW	6.65 AW	15230 AAW	INBLS	10//99-12//99
	Indianapolis MSA, IN	s	12.65 MW	11.21 AW	26320 AAW	INBLS	10//99-12//99
	Lafayette MSA, IN	s	9.24 MW	9.21 AW	19220 AAW	INBLS	10//99-12//99
	Muncie MSA, IN	s	7.65 MW	6.67 AW	15910 AAW	INBLS	10//99-12//99
	South Bend MSA, IN	s	11.37 MW	11.57 AW	23640 AAW	INBLS	10//99-12//99
	Iowa	s	8.52 MW	8.84 AW	18390 AAW	IABLS	10//99-12//99
	Cedar Rapids MSA, IA	s	8.84 MW	8.34 AW	18390 AAW	IABLS	10//99-12//99
	Davenport-Moline-Rock Island MSA, IA-IL	s	9.25 MW	9.04 AW	19250 AAW	IABLS	10//99-12//99
	Des Moines MSA, IA	s	9.39 MW	9.04 AW	19530 AAW	IABLS	10//99-12//99
	Kansas	s	10.77 MW	11.33 AW	23570 AAW	KSBLS	10//99-12//99
	Lawrence MSA, KS	s	10.04 MW	9.67 AW	20880 AAW	KSBLS	10//99-12//99
	Topeka MSA, KS	s	10.18 MW	10.24 AW	21170 AAW	KSBLS	10//99-12//99
	Wichita MSA, KS	s	11.58 MW	9.67 AW	24090 AAW	KSBLS	10//99-12//99
	Kentucky	s	9.44 MW	9.64 AW	20050 AAW	KYBLS	10//99-12//99
	Lexington MSA, KY	s	10.65 MW	10.13 AW	22160 AAW	KYBLS	10//99-12//99
	Louisville MSA, KY-IN	s	10.28 MW	10.27 AW	21380 AAW	KYBLS	10//99-12//99
	Louisiana	s	8.71 MW	9.42 AW	19590 AAW	LABLS	10//99-12//99
	Baton Rouge MSA, LA	s	9.41 MW	8.33 AW	19570 AAW	LABLS	10//99-12//99
	Houma MSA, LA	s	8.36 MW	8.91 AW	17400 AAW	LABLS	10//99-12//99
	Lafayette MSA, LA	s	8.98 MW	8.31 AW	18680 AAW	LABLS	10//99-12//99
	New Orleans MSA, LA	s	9.57 MW	8.81 AW	19900 AAW	LABLS	10//99-12//99
	Shreveport-Bossier City MSA, LA	s	9.16 MW	8.63 AW	19050 AAW	LABLS	10//99-12//99
	Maine	s	10.02 MW	10.18 AW	21180 AAW	MEBLS	10//99-12//99
	Lewiston-Auburn MSA, ME	s	10.36 MW	10.26 AW	21540 AAW	MEBLS	10//99-12//99
	Portland MSA, ME	s	11.74 MW	11.64 AW	24410 AAW	MEBLS	10//99-12//99
	Maryland	s	11.34 MW	11.84 AW	24620 AAW	MDBLS	10//99-12//99
	Baltimore PMSA, MD	s	10.82 MW	9.67 AW	22500 AAW	MDBLS	10//99-12//99
	Massachusetts	s	12.45 MW	13.30 AW	27670 AAW	MABLS	10//99-12//99
	Barnstable-Yarmouth MSA, MA	s	12.45 MW	11.99 AW	25890 AAW	MABLS	10//99-12//99
	Boston PMSA, MA-NH	s	13.92 MW	13.24 AW	28950 AAW	MABLS	10//99-12//99
	Brockton PMSA, MA	s	11.37 MW	11.28 AW	23640 AAW	MABLS	10//99-12//99
	Fitchburg-Leominster PMSA, MA	s	11.90 MW	11.26 AW	24750 AAW	MABLS	10//99-12//99
	Lawrence PMSA, MA-NH	s	11.47 MW	10.87 AW	23860 AAW	MABLS	10//99-12//99
	Lowell PMSA, MA-NH	s	12.47 MW	12.60 AW	25930 AAW	MABLS	10//99-12//99
	New Bedford PMSA, MA	s	10.63 MW	10.66 AW	22110 AAW	MABLS	10//99-12//99
	Pittsfield MSA, MA	s	10.52 MW	10.60 AW	21870 AAW	MABLS	10//99-12//99
	Springfield MSA, MA	s	8.97 MW	8.41 AW	18660 AAW	MABLS	10//99-12//99
	Worcester PMSA, MA-CT	s	11.86 MW	11.52 AW	24680 AAW	MABLS	10//99-12//99
	Michigan	s	11.02 MW	11.60 AW	24130 AAW	MIBLS	10//99-12//99
	Ann Arbor PMSA, MI	s	10.46 MW	9.99 AW	21750 AAW	MIBLS	10//99-12//99
	Detroit PMSA, MI	s	12.32 MW	11.87 AW	25630 AAW	MIBLS	10//99-12//99
	Flint PMSA, MI	s	9.49 MW	9.46 AW	19730 AAW	MIBLS	10//99-12//99
	Grand Rapids-Muskegon-Holland MSA, MI	s	12.39 MW	11.40 AW	25770 AAW	MIBLS	10//99-12//99
	Jackson MSA, MI	s	8.62 MW	8.80 AW	17930 AAW	MIBLS	10//99-12//99
	Kalamazoo-Battle Creek MSA, MI	s	10.65 MW	9.92 AW	22140 AAW	MIBLS	10//99-12//99
	Lansing-East Lansing MSA, MI	s	11.81 MW	11.43 AW	24560 AAW	MIBLS	10//99-12//99
	Saginaw-Bay City-Midland MSA, MI	s	10.31 MW	10.23 AW	21450 AAW	MIBLS	10//99-12//99
	Minnesota	s	11.44 MW	12.10 AW	25170 AAW	MNBLS	10//99-12//99
	Duluth-Superior MSA, MN-WI	s	8.15 MW	8.16 AW	16950 AAW	MNBLS	10//99-12//99

AAW Average annual wage	**AOH** Average offered, high	**ASH** Average starting, high	**H** Hourly	**M** Monthly	**S** Special: hourly and annual
AE Average entry wage	**AOL** Average offered, low	**ASL** Average starting, low	**HI** Highest wage paid	**MTC** Median total compensation	**TQ** Third quartile wage
AEX Average experienced wage	**APH** Average pay, high range	**AW** Average wage paid	**HR** High end range	**MW** Median wage paid	**W** Weekly
AO Average offered	**APL** Average pay, low range	**FQ** First quartile wage	**LR** Low end range	**SQ** Second quartile wage	**Y** Yearly

Occupation/Type/Industry	Location	Per	Low	Mid	High	Source	Date
Travel Agent	Minneapolis-St. Paul MSA, MN-WI	S	12.47 MW	11.92 AW	25930 AAW	MNBLS	10//99-12//99
	Rochester MSA, MN	S	10.92 MW	10.48 AW	22710 AAW	MNBLS	10//99-12//99
	St. Cloud MSA, MN	S	10.70 MW	10.10 AW	22250 AAW	MNBLS	10//99-12//99
	Mississippi	S	9.77 MW	9.81 AW	20400 AAW	MSBLS	10//99-12//99
	Biloxi-Gulfport-Pascagoula MSA, MS	S	9.73 MW	9.71 AW	20230 AAW	MSBLS	10//99-12//99
	Missouri	S	11.06 MW	11.80 AW	24550 AAW	MOBLS	10//99-12//99
	Columbia MSA, MO	S	10.68 MW	10.53 AW	22220 AAW	MOBLS	10//99-12//99
	Kansas City MSA, MO-KS	S	11.36 MW	10.95 AW	23620 AAW	MOBLS	10//99-12//99
	Montana	S	9.75 MW	9.62 AW	20010 AAW	MTBLS	10//99-12//99
	Billings MSA, MT	S	7.84 MW	7.83 AW	16310 AAW	MTBLS	10//99-12//99
	Nebraska	S	9.88 MW	10.69 AW	22240 AAW	NEBLS	10//99-12//99
	Lincoln MSA, NE	S	10.67 MW	10.18 AW	22200 AAW	NEBLS	10//99-12//99
	Omaha MSA, NE-IA	S	10.43 MW	9.70 AW	21700 AAW	NEBLS	10//99-12//99
	Nevada	S	10.87 MW	11.09 AW	23060 AAW	NVBLS	10//99-12//99
	Las Vegas MSA, NV-AZ	S	11.03 MW	10.84 AW	22950 AAW	NVBLS	10//99-12//99
	Reno MSA, NV	S	10.71 MW	11.06 AW	22270 AAW	NVBLS	10//99-12//99
	New Hampshire	S	11.63 MW	12.14 AW	25250 AAW	NHBLS	10//99-12//99
	Manchester PMSA, NH	S	11.96 MW	11.37 AW	24880 AAW	NHBLS	10//99-12//99
	Nashua PMSA, NH	S	14.65 MW	14.53 AW	30460 AAW	NHBLS	10//99-12//99
	Portsmouth-Rochester PMSA, NH-ME	S	12.07 MW	12.42 AW	25100 AAW	NHBLS	10//99-12//99
	New Jersey	S	12.78 MW	13.51 AW	28110 AAW	NJBLS	10//99-12//99
	Atlantic-Cape May PMSA, NJ	S	11.05 MW	11.08 AW	22990 AAW	NJBLS	10//99-12//99
	Bergen-Passaic PMSA, NJ	S	15.24 MW	14.36 AW	31710 AAW	NJBLS	10//99-12//99
	Jersey City PMSA, NJ	S	10.80 MW	11.47 AW	22470 AAW	NJBLS	10//99-12//99
	Middlesex-Somerset-Hunterdon PMSA, NJ	S	13.49 MW	13.10 AW	28050 AAW	NJBLS	10//99-12//99
	Monmouth-Ocean PMSA, NJ	S	12.27 MW	11.50 AW	25520 AAW	NJBLS	10//99-12//99
	Newark PMSA, NJ	S	12.78 MW	11.78 AW	26580 AAW	NJBLS	10//99-12//99
	Trenton PMSA, NJ	S	14.22 MW	14.32 AW	29590 AAW	NJBLS	10//99-12//99
	Vineland-Millville-Bridgeton PMSA, NJ	S	13.05 MW	13.68 AW	27130 AAW	NJBLS	10//99-12//99
	New Mexico	S	8.61 MW	9.74 AW	20270 AAW	NMBLS	10//99-12//99
	Albuquerque MSA, NM	S	9.69 MW	8.48 AW	20160 AAW	NMBLS	10//99-12//99
	Santa Fe MSA, NM	S	12.63 MW	12.46 AW	26280 AAW	NMBLS	10//99-12//99
	New York	S	12.01 MW	12.99 AW	27030 AAW	NYBLS	10//99-12//99
	Albany-Schenectady-Troy MSA, NY	S	11.54 MW	11.39 AW	24010 AAW	NYBLS	10//99-12//99
	Binghamton MSA, NY	S	11.05 MW	11.11 AW	22990 AAW	NYBLS	10//99-12//99
	Buffalo-Niagara Falls MSA, NY	S	11.18 MW	10.92 AW	23250 AAW	NYBLS	10//99-12//99
	Dutchess County PMSA, NY	S	8.44 MW	8.40 AW	17550 AAW	NYBLS	10//99-12//99
	Jamestown MSA, NY	S	7.18 MW	6.53 AW	14930 AAW	NYBLS	10//99-12//99
	Nassau-Suffolk PMSA, NY	S	11.97 MW	11.69 AW	24900 AAW	NYBLS	10//99-12//99
	New York PMSA, NY	S	14.10 MW	13.13 AW	29320 AAW	NYBLS	10//99-12//99
	Newburgh PMSA, NY-PA	S	10.92 MW	11.38 AW	22710 AAW	NYBLS	10//99-12//99
	Rochester MSA, NY	S	11.36 MW	11.60 AW	23630 AAW	NYBLS	10//99-12//99
	Syracuse MSA, NY	S	12.60 MW	11.74 AW	26220 AAW	NYBLS	10//99-12//99
	Utica-Rome MSA, NY	S	8.82 MW	8.97 AW	18340 AAW	NYBLS	10//99-12//99
	North Carolina	S	11.18 MW	11.49 AW	23900 AAW	NCBLS	10//99-12//99
	Asheville MSA, NC	S	9.17 MW	8.23 AW	19070 AAW	NCBLS	10//99-12//99
	Charlotte-Gastonia-Rock Hill MSA, NC-SC	S	13.22 MW	12.71 AW	27500 AAW	NCBLS	10//99-12//99
	Fayetteville MSA, NC	S	9.49 MW	8.87 AW	19740 AAW	NCBLS	10//99-12//99
	Greensboro--Winston-Salem--High Point MSA, NC	S	10.59 MW	10.11 AW	22020 AAW	NCBLS	10//99-12//99
	Hickory-Morganton-Lenoir MSA, NC	S	11.53 MW	11.44 AW	23990 AAW	NCBLS	10//99-12//99
	Raleigh-Durham-Chapel Hill MSA, NC	S	11.44 MW	11.30 AW	23800 AAW	NCBLS	10//99-12//99
	Wilmington MSA, NC	S	11.81 MW	11.14 AW	24560 AAW	NCBLS	10//99-12//99
	North Dakota	S	10.5 MW	10.05 AW	20910 AAW	NDBLS	10//99-12//99
	Bismarck MSA, ND	S	10.45 MW	11.40 AW	21730 AAW	NDBLS	10//99-12//99
	Fargo-Moorhead MSA, ND-MN	S	9.37 MW	9.34 AW	19480 AAW	NDBLS	10//99-12//99
	Grand Forks MSA, ND-MN	S	8.63 MW	8.27 AW	17950 AAW	NDBLS	10//99-12//99
	Ohio	S	10.41 MW	10.55 AW	21940 AAW	OHBLS	10//99-12//99
	Akron PMSA, OH	S	11.06 MW	10.73 AW	23000 AAW	OHBLS	10//99-12//99
	Canton-Massillon MSA, OH	S	9.17 MW	9.28 AW	19070 AAW	OHBLS	10//99-12//99
	Cincinnati PMSA, OH-KY-IN	S	10.98 MW	10.51 AW	22850 AAW	OHBLS	10//99-12//99

Travel Agent

Occupation/Type/Industry	Location	Per	Low	Mid	High	Source	Date
Travel Agent	Cleveland-Lorain-Elyria PMSA, OH	S	10.51 MW	10.82 AW	21860 AAW	OHBLS	10//99-12//99
	Columbus MSA, OH	S	11.19 MW	11.16 AW	23260 AAW	OHBLS	10//99-12//99
	Dayton-Springfield MSA, OH	S	10.32 MW	10.13 AW	21460 AAW	OHBLS	10//99-12//99
	Hamilton-Middletown PMSA, OH	S	10.54 MW	10.75 AW	21920 AAW	OHBLS	10//99-12//99
	Lima MSA, OH	S	9.03 MW	8.28 AW	18770 AAW	OHBLS	10//99-12//99
	Toledo MSA, OH	S	9.69 MW	9.06 AW	20160 AAW	OHBLS	10//99-12//99
	Youngstown-Warren MSA, OH	S	8.79 MW	9.05 AW	18290 AAW	OHBLS	10//99-12//99
	Oklahoma	S	10.37 MW	10.79 AW	22450 AAW	OKBLS	10//99-12//99
	Oklahoma City MSA, OK	S	9.88 MW	10.02 AW	20550 AAW	OKBLS	10//99-12//99
	Tulsa MSA, OK	S	13.82 MW	13.24 AW	28750 AAW	OKBLS	10//99-12//99
	Oregon	S	11.17 MW	11.30 AW	23500 AAW	ORBLS	10//99-12//99
	Corvallis MSA, OR	S	10.79 MW	9.78 AW	22430 AAW	ORBLS	10//99-12//99
	Eugene-Springfield MSA, OR	S	11.61 MW	10.90 AW	24160 AAW	ORBLS	10//99-12//99
	Medford-Ashland MSA, OR	S	11.97 MW	9.99 AW	24900 AAW	ORBLS	10//99-12//99
	Portland-Vancouver PMSA, OR-WA	S	11.57 MW	11.71 AW	24060 AAW	ORBLS	10//99-12//99
	Salem PMSA, OR	S	11.18 MW	11.25 AW	23260 AAW	ORBLS	10//99-12//99
	Pennsylvania	S	10.97 MW	11.27 AW	23450 AAW	PABLS	10//99-12//99
	Allentown-Bethlehem-Easton MSA, PA	S	13.34 MW	13.26 AW	27750 AAW	PABLS	10//99-12//99
	Erie MSA, PA	S	10.34 MW	10.13 AW	21510 AAW	PABLS	10//99-12//99
	Harrisburg-Lebanon-Carlisle MSA, PA	S	10.72 MW	10.42 AW	22300 AAW	PABLS	10//99-12//99
	Lancaster MSA, PA	S	12.22 MW	12.67 AW	25420 AAW	PABLS	10//99-12//99
	Philadelphia PMSA, PA-NJ	S	12.21 MW	11.48 AW	25390 AAW	PABLS	10//99-12//99
	Pittsburgh MSA, PA	S	9.43 MW	9.28 AW	19620 AAW	PABLS	10//99-12//99
	Reading MSA, PA	S	12.76 MW	12.76 AW	26550 AAW	PABLS	10//99-12//99
	Scranton--Wilkes-Barre--Hazleton MSA, PA	S	10.53 MW	9.93 AW	21910 AAW	PABLS	10//99-12//99
	State College MSA, PA	S	10.54 MW	10.33 AW	21930 AAW	PABLS	10//99-12//99
	York MSA, PA	S	10.23 MW	9.94 AW	21280 AAW	PABLS	10//99-12//99
	Rhode Island	S	10.07 MW	10.71 AW	22280 AAW	RIBLS	10//99-12//99
	Providence-Fall River-Warwick MSA, RI-MA	S	10.71 MW	10.19 AW	22280 AAW	RIBLS	10//99-12//99
	South Carolina	S	10.11 MW	10.76 AW	22390 AAW	SCBLS	10//99-12//99
	Charleston-North Charleston MSA, SC	S	10.64 MW	10.17 AW	22120 AAW	SCBLS	10//99-12//99
	Columbia MSA, SC	S	10.70 MW	9.61 AW	22250 AAW	SCBLS	10//99-12//99
	Greenville-Spartanburg-Anderson MSA, SC	S	11.64 MW	11.34 AW	24200 AAW	SCBLS	10//99-12//99
	Myrtle Beach MSA, SC	S	9.68 MW	8.94 AW	20140 AAW	SCBLS	10//99-12//99
	South Dakota	S	8.52 MW	9.07 AW	18870 AAW	SDBLS	10//99-12//99
	Rapid City MSA, SD	S	8.59 MW	8.24 AW	17870 AAW	SDBLS	10//99-12//99
	Sioux Falls MSA, SD	S	9.92 MW	9.36 AW	20640 AAW	SDBLS	10//99-12//99
	Tennessee	S	11.34 MW	11.54 AW	24000 AAW	TNBLS	10//99-12//99
	Johnson City-Kingsport-Bristol MSA, TN-VA	S	9.41 MW	8.83 AW	19580 AAW	TNBLS	10//99-12//99
	Knoxville MSA, TN	S	9.52 MW	9.08 AW	19810 AAW	TNBLS	10//99-12//99
	Memphis MSA, TN-AR-MS	S	12.02 MW	11.86 AW	25000 AAW	MSBLS	10//99-12//99
	Nashville MSA, TN	S	12.14 MW	12.06 AW	25260 AAW	TNBLS	10//99-12//99
	Texas	S	12.06 MW	12.60 AW	26200 AAW	TXBLS	10//99-12//99
	Austin-San Marcos MSA, TX	S	11.80 MW	11.83 AW	24540 AAW	TXBLS	10//99-12//99
	Brownsville-Harlingen-San Benito MSA, TX	S	8.51 MW	9.08 AW	17690 AAW	TXBLS	10//99-12//99
	Bryan-College Station MSA, TX	S	10.43 MW	10.52 AW	21680 AAW	TXBLS	10//99-12//99
	Corpus Christi MSA, TX	S	12.16 MW	10.95 AW	25300 AAW	TXBLS	10//99-12//99
	Dallas PMSA, TX	S	14.20 MW	14.13 AW	29540 AAW	TXBLS	10//99-12//99
	El Paso MSA, TX	S	8.98 MW	9.08 AW	18670 AAW	TXBLS	10//99-12//99
	Fort Worth-Arlington PMSA, TX	S	13.59 MW	11.42 AW	28260 AAW	TXBLS	10//99-12//99
	Galveston-Texas City PMSA, TX	S	10.33 MW	10.10 AW	21480 AAW	TXBLS	10//99-12//99
	Houston PMSA, TX	S	12.72 MW	11.24 AW	26450 AAW	TXBLS	10//99-12//99
	Killeen-Temple MSA, TX	S	9.24 MW	9.07 AW	19230 AAW	TXBLS	10//99-12//99
	McAllen-Edinburg-Mission MSA, TX	S	9.40 MW	9.88 AW	19540 AAW	TXBLS	10//99-12//99
	Odessa-Midland MSA, TX	S	9.14 MW	9.44 AW	19000 AAW	TXBLS	10//99-12//99
	San Antonio MSA, TX	S	10.63 MW	10.11 AW	22110 AAW	TXBLS	10//99-12//99
	Tyler MSA, TX	S	11.49 MW	11.53 AW	23900 AAW	TXBLS	10//99-12//99

AAW Average annual wage	AOH Average offered, high	ASH Average starting, high	H Hourly	M Monthly	S Special: hourly and annual
AE Average entry wage	AOL Average offered, low	ASL Average starting, low	HI Highest wage paid	MTC Median total compensation	TQ Third quartile wage
AEX Average experienced wage	APH Average pay, high range	AW Average wage paid	HR High end range	MW Median wage paid	W Weekly
AO Average offered	APL Average pay, low range	FQ First quartile wage	LR Low end range	SQ Second quartile wage	Y Yearly

Occupation/Type/Industry	Location	Per	Low	Mid	High	Source	Date
Travel Agent	Wichita Falls MSA, TX	S	11.38 MW	10.88 AW	23670 AAW	TXBLS	10//99-12//99
	Utah	S	10.72 MW	11.13 AW	23150 AAW	UTBLS	10//99-12//99
	Provo-Orem MSA, UT	S	11.55 MW	11.16 AW	24020 AAW	UTBLS	10//99-12//99
	Vermont	S	11.33 MW	11.95 AW	24850 AAW	VTBLS	10//99-12//99
	Burlington MSA, VT	S	12.79 MW	12.12 AW	26600 AAW	VTBLS	10//99-12//99
	Virginia	S	11.55 MW	12.15 AW	25270 AAW	VABLS	10//99-12//99
	Lynchburg MSA, VA	S	10.82 MW	10.99 AW	22500 AAW	VABLS	10//99-12//99
	Norfolk-Virginia Beach-Newport News MSA, VA-NC	S	9.53 MW	8.80 AW	19820 AAW	VABLS	10//99-12//99
	Richmond-Petersburg MSA, VA	S	11.16 MW	10.83 AW	23200 AAW	VABLS	10//99-12//99
	Washington	S	10.84 MW	10.96 AW	22800 AAW	WABLS	10//99-12//99
	Bellingham MSA, WA	S	9.22 MW	8.94 AW	19170 AAW	WABLS	10//99-12//99
	Bremerton PMSA, WA	S	13.03 MW	11.75 AW	27100 AAW	WABLS	10//99-12//99
	Olympia PMSA, WA	S	11.64 MW	10.44 AW	24210 AAW	WABLS	10//99-12//99
	Richland-Kennewick-Pasco MSA, WA	S	11.69 MW	12.15 AW	24310 AAW	WABLS	10//99-12//99
	Seattle-Bellevue-Everett PMSA, WA	S	11.21 MW	11.48 AW	23310 AAW	WABLS	10//99-12//99
	Tacoma PMSA, WA	S	10.55 MW	10.93 AW	21940 AAW	WABLS	10//99-12//99
	Yakima MSA, WA	S	11.61 MW	11.25 AW	24140 AAW	WABLS	10//99-12//99
	West Virginia	S	8.75 MW	8.89 AW	18490 AAW	WVBLS	10//99-12//99
	Parkersburg-Marietta MSA, WV-OH	S	9.38 MW	9.23 AW	19510 AAW	WVBLS	10//99-12//99
	Wheeling MSA, WV-OH	S	7.29 MW	6.38 AW	15160 AAW	WVBLS	10//99-12//99
	Wisconsin	S	10.13 MW	10.24 AW	21290 AAW	WIBLS	10//99-12//99
	Green Bay MSA, WI	S	11.71 MW	11.65 AW	24350 AAW	WIBLS	10//99-12//99
	Janesville-Beloit MSA, WI	S	9.61 MW	9.67 AW	19980 AAW	WIBLS	10//99-12//99
	Madison MSA, WI	S	9.59 MW	9.35 AW	19950 AAW	WIBLS	10//99-12//99
	Milwaukee-Waukesha PMSA, WI	S	10.49 MW	10.93 AW	21810 AAW	WIBLS	10//99-12//99
	Racine PMSA, WI	S	11.56 MW	10.88 AW	24050 AAW	WIBLS	10//99-12//99
	Wausau MSA, WI	S	8.54 MW	8.21 AW	17750 AAW	WIBLS	10//99-12//99
	Puerto Rico	S	6.4 MW	7.37 AW	15340 AAW	PRBLS	10//99-12//99
	San Juan-Bayamon PMSA, PR	S	7.64 MW	6.46 AW	15900 AAW	PRBLS	10//99-12//99
	Virgin Islands	S	8.18 MW	8.98 AW	18680 AAW	VIBLS	10//99-12//99
	Guam	S	11.53 MW	11.54 AW	24000 AAW	GUBLS	10//99-12//99
Female Executive	United States	Y		34200 AW		TRAVWK1	1999
Female Frontliner	United States	Y		28200 AW		TRAVWK1	1999
Female Manager	United States	Y		32000 AW		TRAVWK1	1999
Male Executive	United States	Y		40400 AW		TRAVWK1	1999
Male Frontliner	United States	Y		29300 AW		TRAVWK1	1999
Male Manager	United States	Y		37100 AW		TRAVWK1	1999
Travel Guide	Arizona	S	7.86 MW	9.71 AW	20190 AAW	AZBLS	10//99-12//99
	California	S	27.84 MW	22.51 AW	46820 AAW	CABLS	10//99-12//99
	Oakland PMSA, CA	S	28.07 MW	30.22 AW	58390 AAW	CABLS	10//99-12//99
	Colorado	S	9.06 MW	9.44 AW	19650 AAW	COBLS	10//99-12//99
	Washington PMSA, DC-MD-VA-WV	S	13.94 MW	14.17 AW	28990 AAW	DCBLS	10//99-12//99
	Hawaii	S	11.52 MW	11.15 AW	23190 AAW	HIBLS	10//99-12//99
	Honolulu MSA, HI	S	12.96 MW	12.46 AW	26960 AAW	HIBLS	10//99-12//99
	Illinois	S	17.1 MW	17.36 AW	36100 AAW	ILBLS	10//99-12//99
	Chicago PMSA, IL	S	17.47 MW	17.19 AW	36330 AAW	ILBLS	10//99-12//99
	Indiana	S	9.71 MW	10.14 AW	21100 AAW	INBLS	10//99-12//99
	Iowa	S	10.73 MW	10.15 AW	21120 AAW	IABLS	10//99-12//99
	Maine	S	14.77 MW	14.48 AW	30120 AAW	MEBLS	10//99-12//99
	Boston PMSA, MA-NH	S	16.95 MW	17.04 AW	35250 AAW	MABLS	10//99-12//99
	Michigan	S	12.33 MW	12.35 AW	25690 AAW	MIBLS	10//99-12//99
	Detroit PMSA, MI	S	11.19 MW	10.75 AW	23270 AAW	MIBLS	10//99-12//99
	Missouri	S	10.31 MW	11.42 AW	23760 AAW	MOBLS	10//99-12//99
	Montana	S	18.36 MW	17.22 AW	35830 AAW	MTBLS	10//99-12//99
	Nevada	S	12.39 MW	12.37 AW	25740 AAW	NVBLS	10//99-12//99
	North Carolina	S	11.79 MW	11.71 AW	24370 AAW	NCBLS	10//99-12//99
	Charlotte-Gastonia-Rock Hill MSA, NC-SC	S	12.59 MW	13.02 AW	26190 AAW	NCBLS	10//99-12//99
	Oklahoma	S	10.11 MW	11.35 AW	23610 AAW	OKBLS	10//99-12//99
	Pennsylvania	S	13.88 MW	12.03 AW	25020 AAW	PABLS	10//99-12//99
	South Carolina	S	8.73 MW	9.61 AW	19990 AAW	SCBLS	10//99-12//99
	Virginia	S	13.83 MW	13.35 AW	27760 AAW	VABLS	10//99-12//99
	Washington	S	13.85 MW	15.05 AW	31310 AAW	WABLS	10//99-12//99
	Wisconsin	S	12.73 MW	13.09 AW	27220 AAW	WIBLS	10//99-12//99

AAW	Average annual wage	**AOH**	Average offered, high	**ASH**	Average starting, high	**H**	Hourly
AE	Average entry wage	**AOL**	Average offered, low	**ASL**	Average starting, low	**HI**	Highest wage paid
AEX	Average experienced wage	**APH**	Average pay, high range	**AW**	Average wage paid	**HR**	High end range
AO	Average offered	**APL**	Average pay, low range	**FQ**	First quartile wage	**LR**	Low end range

M	Monthly	**S**	Special: hourly and annual
MTC	Median total compensation	**TQ**	Third quartile wage
MW	Median wage paid	**W**	Weekly
SQ	Second quartile wage	**Y**	Yearly

Occupation/Type/Industry	Location	Per	Low	Mid	High	Source	Date
Tree Trimmer and Pruner	Alabama	S	9.64 MW	9.68 AW	20130 AAW	ALBLS	10//99-12//99
	Arizona	S	7.86 MW	8.35 AW	17380 AAW	AZBLS	10//99-12//99
	Arkansas	S	9.26 MW	10.38 AW	21590 AAW	ARBLS	10//99-12//99
	California	S	12.53 MW	12.43 AW	25860 AAW	CABLS	10//99-12//99
	Colorado	S	13.63 MW	13.59 AW	28270 AAW	COBLS	10//99-12//99
	Connecticut	S	13.14 MW	13.39 AW	27860 AAW	CTBLS	10//99-12//99
	Delaware	S	11.23 MW	12.23 AW	25430 AAW	DEBLS	10//99-12//99
	Florida	S	8.24 MW	8.85 AW	18410 AAW	FLBLS	10//99-12//99
	Georgia	S	9.47 MW	9.99 AW	20770 AAW	GABLS	10//99-12//99
	Hawaii	S	11.81 MW	11.83 AW	24620 AAW	HIBLS	10//99-12//99
	Idaho	S	11.24 MW	12.64 AW	26280 AAW	IDBLS	10//99-12//99
	Illinois	S	12.86 MW	12.62 AW	26250 AAW	ILBLS	10//99-12//99
	Indiana	S	10.9 MW	11.20 AW	23300 AAW	INBLS	10//99-12//99
	Kansas	S	13.6 MW	14.37 AW	29890 AAW	KSBLS	10//99-12//99
	Kentucky	S	7.98 MW	8.40 AW	17480 AAW	KYBLS	10//99-12//99
	Louisiana	S	7.76 MW	8.61 AW	17900 AAW	LABLS	10//99-12//99
	Maine	S	10.89 MW	11.35 AW	23620 AAW	MEBLS	10//99-12//99
	Maryland	S	12.65 MW	13.45 AW	27980 AAW	MDBLS	10//99-12//99
	Massachusetts	S	13.28 MW	13.51 AW	28110 AAW	MABLS	10//99-12//99
	Michigan	S	13.53 MW	13.78 AW	28660 AAW	MIBLS	10//99-12//99
	Minnesota	S	12.19 MW	12.07 AW	25110 AAW	MNBLS	10//99-12//99
	Mississippi	S	10.06 MW	9.85 AW	20480 AAW	MSBLS	10//99-12//99
	Missouri	S	9.21 MW	9.74 AW	20250 AAW	MOBLS	10//99-12//99
	Nebraska	S	10 MW	10.32 AW	21470 AAW	NEBLS	10//99-12//99
	Nevada	S	10.77 MW	11.31 AW	23520 AAW	NVBLS	10//99-12//99
	New Jersey	S	14.24 MW	15.05 AW	31300 AAW	NJBLS	10//99-12//99
	New Mexico	S	8.37 MW	9.90 AW	20580 AAW	NMBLS	10//99-12//99
	New York	S	12.99 MW	14.20 AW	29540 AAW	NYBLS	10//99-12//99
	North Carolina	S	10.48 MW	10.53 AW	21910 AAW	NCBLS	10//99-12//99
	Ohio	S	11.21 MW	11.53 AW	23980 AAW	OHBLS	10//99-12//99
	Oklahoma	S	9.37 MW	9.46 AW	19670 AAW	OKBLS	10//99-12//99
	Oregon	S	15.29 MW	15.62 AW	32490 AAW	ORBLS	10//99-12//99
	Pennsylvania	S	12.33 MW	13.64 AW	28360 AAW	PABLS	10//99-12//99
	South Carolina	S	11.29 MW	11.03 AW	22950 AAW	SCBLS	10//99-12//99
	South Dakota	S	9.97 MW	10.07 AW	20950 AAW	SDBLS	10//99-12//99
	Tennessee	S	9.78 MW	9.51 AW	19780 AAW	TNBLS	10//99-12//99
	Texas	S	7.76 MW	8.16 AW	16980 AAW	TXBLS	10//99-12//99
	Vermont	S	10.76 MW	11.08 AW	23050 AAW	VTBLS	10//99-12//99
	Virginia	S	9.51 MW	10.20 AW	21210 AAW	VABLS	10//99-12//99
	Washington	S	11.62 MW	12.96 AW	26950 AAW	WABLS	10//99-12//99
	West Virginia	S	11.49 MW	11.02 AW	22930 AAW	WVBLS	10//99-12//99
	Wisconsin	S	13.57 MW	13.65 AW	28400 AAW	WIBLS	10//99-12//99
	Wyoming	S	7.52 MW	7.63 AW	15860 AAW	WYBLS	10//99-12//99
Truck Driver							
Heavy and Tractor-Trailer	Alabama	S	13.09 MW	14.13 AW	29400 AAW	ALBLS	10//99-12//99
Heavy and Tractor-Trailer	Anniston MSA, AL	S	13.74 MW	13.18 AW	28580 AAW	ALBLS	10//99-12//99
Heavy and Tractor-Trailer	Auburn-Opelika MSA, AL	S	10.97 MW	10.20 AW	22810 AAW	ALBLS	10//99-12//99
Heavy and Tractor-Trailer	Birmingham MSA, AL	S	15.46 MW	15.30 AW	32150 AAW	ALBLS	10//99-12//99
Heavy and Tractor-Trailer	Decatur MSA, AL	S	14.79 MW	15.12 AW	30760 AAW	ALBLS	10//99-12//99
Heavy and Tractor-Trailer	Dothan MSA, AL	S	17.47 MW	18.71 AW	36330 AAW	ALBLS	10//99-12//99
Heavy and Tractor-Trailer	Florence MSA, AL	S	16.69 MW	13.98 AW	34720 AAW	ALBLS	10//99-12//99
Heavy and Tractor-Trailer	Gadsden MSA, AL	S	17.01 MW	17.26 AW	35390 AAW	ALBLS	10//99-12//99
Heavy and Tractor-Trailer	Huntsville MSA, AL	S	14.93 MW	13.29 AW	31050 AAW	ALBLS	10//99-12//99
Heavy and Tractor-Trailer	Mobile MSA, AL	S	13.90 MW	13.45 AW	28910 AAW	ALBLS	10//99-12//99
Heavy and Tractor-Trailer	Montgomery MSA, AL	S	13.17 MW	12.63 AW	27390 AAW	ALBLS	10//99-12//99
Heavy and Tractor-Trailer	Tuscaloosa MSA, AL	S	15.55 MW	15.80 AW	32350 AAW	ALBLS	10//99-12//99
Heavy and Tractor-Trailer	Alaska	S	19.41 MW	20.37 AW	42380 AAW	AKBLS	10//99-12//99
Heavy and Tractor-Trailer	Anchorage MSA, AK	S	18.71 MW	16.84 AW	38910 AAW	AKBLS	10//99-12//99
Heavy and Tractor-Trailer	Arizona	S	14.05 MW	14.84 AW	30880 AAW	AZBLS	10//99-12//99
Heavy and Tractor-Trailer	Flagstaff MSA, AZ-UT	S	14.08 MW	14.03 AW	29280 AAW	AZBLS	10//99-12//99
Heavy and Tractor-Trailer	Phoenix-Mesa MSA, AZ	S	15.21 MW	14.19 AW	31630 AAW	AZBLS	10//99-12//99
Heavy and Tractor-Trailer	Tucson MSA, AZ	S	14.13 MW	12.86 AW	29400 AAW	AZBLS	10//99-12//99
Heavy and Tractor-Trailer	Yuma MSA, AZ	S	10.22 MW	10.07 AW	21250 AAW	AZBLS	10//99-12//99
Heavy and Tractor-Trailer	Arkansas	S	13.48 MW	14.05 AW	29230 AAW	ARBLS	10//99-12//99
Heavy and Tractor-Trailer	Fayetteville-Springdale-Rogers MSA, AR	S	15.39 MW	13.34 AW	32000 AAW	ARBLS	10//99-12//99
Heavy and Tractor-Trailer	Fort Smith MSA, AR-OK	S	13.11 MW	14.30 AW	27260 AAW	ARBLS	10//99-12//99
Heavy and Tractor-Trailer	Jonesboro MSA, AR	S	13.58 MW	11.44 AW	28250 AAW	ARBLS	10//99-12//99
Heavy and Tractor-Trailer	Little Rock-North Little Rock MSA, AR	S	16.42 MW	15.72 AW	34160 AAW	ARBLS	10//99-12//99
Heavy and Tractor-Trailer	Pine Bluff MSA, AR	S	14.22 MW	10.42 AW	29570 AAW	ARBLS	10//99-12//99
Heavy and Tractor-Trailer	California	S	15.44 MW	15.83 AW	32930 AAW	CABLS	10//99-12//99

AAW	Average annual wage	AOH	Average offered, high	ASH	Average starting, high	H	Hourly	M	Monthly	S	Special: hourly and annual
AE	Average entry wage	AOL	Average offered, low	ASL	Average starting, low	HI	Highest wage paid	MTC	Median total compensation	TQ	Third quartile wage
AEX	Average experienced wage	APH	Average pay, high range	AW	Average wage paid	HR	High end range	MW	Median wage paid	W	Weekly
AO	Average offered	APL	Average pay, low range	FQ	First quartile wage	LR	Low end range	SQ	Second quartile wage	Y	Yearly

Occupation/Type/Industry	Location	Per	Low	Mid	High	Source	Date
Truck Driver							
Heavy and Tractor-Trailer	Bakersfield MSA, CA	S	15.12 MW	14.51 AW	31440 AAW	CABLS	10//99-12//99
Heavy and Tractor-Trailer	Chico-Paradise MSA, CA	S	14.45 MW	14.04 AW	30060 AAW	CABLS	10//99-12//99
Heavy and Tractor-Trailer	Fresno MSA, CA	S	14.19 MW	13.38 AW	29520 AAW	CABLS	10//99-12//99
Heavy and Tractor-Trailer	Los Angeles-Long Beach PMSA, CA	S	15.75 MW	15.71 AW	32760 AAW	CABLS	10//99-12//99
Heavy and Tractor-Trailer	Merced MSA, CA	S	13.50 MW	12.86 AW	28070 AAW	CABLS	10//99-12//99
Heavy and Tractor-Trailer	Modesto MSA, CA	S	13.01 MW	12.21 AW	27070 AAW	CABLS	10//99-12//99
Heavy and Tractor-Trailer	Oakland PMSA, CA	S	17.24 MW	16.29 AW	35860 AAW	CABLS	10//99-12//99
Heavy and Tractor-Trailer	Orange County PMSA, CA	S	15.22 MW	15.02 AW	31660 AAW	CABLS	10//99-12//99
Heavy and Tractor-Trailer	Redding MSA, CA	S	12.96 MW	12.46 AW	26950 AAW	CABLS	10//99-12//99
Heavy and Tractor-Trailer	Riverside-San Bernardino PMSA, CA	S	17.11 MW	16.49 AW	35590 AAW	CABLS	10//99-12//99
Heavy and Tractor-Trailer	Sacramento PMSA, CA	S	15.18 MW	14.94 AW	31570 AAW	CABLS	10//99-12//99
Heavy and Tractor-Trailer	Salinas MSA, CA	S	17.09 MW	16.79 AW	35550 AAW	CABLS	10//99-12//99
Heavy and Tractor-Trailer	San Diego MSA, CA	S	15.68 MW	15.14 AW	32620 AAW	CABLS	10//99-12//99
Heavy and Tractor-Trailer	San Francisco PMSA, CA	S	16.42 MW	16.94 AW	34140 AAW	CABLS	10//99-12//99
Heavy and Tractor-Trailer	San Jose PMSA, CA	S	16.40 MW	16.07 AW	34120 AAW	CABLS	10//99-12//99
Heavy and Tractor-Trailer	San Luis Obispo-Atascadero-Paso Robles MSA, CA	S	15.10 MW	14.67 AW	31400 AAW	CABLS	10//99-12//99
Heavy and Tractor-Trailer	Santa Barbara-Santa Maria-Lompoc MSA, CA	S	14.58 MW	14.54 AW	30330 AAW	CABLS	10//99-12//99
Heavy and Tractor-Trailer	Santa Cruz-Watsonville PMSA, CA	S	16.57 MW	17.68 AW	34480 AAW	CABLS	10//99-12//99
Heavy and Tractor-Trailer	Santa Rosa PMSA, CA	S	16.65 MW	16.33 AW	34630 AAW	CABLS	10//99-12//99
Heavy and Tractor-Trailer	Stockton-Lodi MSA, CA	S	15.47 MW	14.01 AW	32180 AAW	CABLS	10//99-12//99
Heavy and Tractor-Trailer	Vallejo-Fairfield-Napa PMSA, CA	S	15.60 MW	16.19 AW	32450 AAW	CABLS	10//99-12//99
Heavy and Tractor-Trailer	Ventura PMSA, CA	S	14.16 MW	14.21 AW	29450 AAW	CABLS	10//99-12//99
Heavy and Tractor-Trailer	Visalia-Tulare-Porterville MSA, CA	S	15.74 MW	15.73 AW	32730 AAW	CABLS	10//99-12//99
Heavy and Tractor-Trailer	Yolo PMSA, CA	S	16.05 MW	15.89 AW	33390 AAW	CABLS	10//99-12//99
Heavy and Tractor-Trailer	Yuba City MSA, CA	S	12.49 MW	12.26 AW	25980 AAW	CABLS	10//99-12//99
Heavy and Tractor-Trailer	Colorado	S	14.25 MW	14.92 AW	31030 AAW	COBLS	10//99-12//99
Heavy and Tractor-Trailer	Boulder-Longmont PMSA, CO	S	12.99 MW	12.74 AW	27030 AAW	COBLS	10//99-12//99
Heavy and Tractor-Trailer	Colorado Springs MSA, CO	S	13.97 MW	13.28 AW	29060 AAW	COBLS	10//99-12//99
Heavy and Tractor-Trailer	Denver PMSA, CO	S	15.63 MW	14.71 AW	32520 AAW	COBLS	10//99-12//99
Heavy and Tractor-Trailer	Fort Collins-Loveland MSA, CO	S	13.20 MW	13.00 AW	27450 AAW	COBLS	10//99-12//99
Heavy and Tractor-Trailer	Grand Junction MSA, CO	S	14.42 MW	14.75 AW	29990 AAW	COBLS	10//99-12//99
Heavy and Tractor-Trailer	Greeley PMSA, CO	S	13.48 MW	13.87 AW	28030 AAW	COBLS	10//99-12//99
Heavy and Tractor-Trailer	Pueblo MSA, CO	S	12.06 MW	11.71 AW	25080 AAW	COBLS	10//99-12//99
Heavy and Tractor-Trailer	Connecticut	S	15.41 MW	15.67 AW	32590 AAW	CTBLS	10//99-12//99
Heavy and Tractor-Trailer	Bridgeport PMSA, CT	S	16.37 MW	17.26 AW	34050 AAW	CTBLS	10//99-12//99
Heavy and Tractor-Trailer	Danbury PMSA, CT	S	15.56 MW	15.52 AW	32360 AAW	CTBLS	10//99-12//99
Heavy and Tractor-Trailer	Hartford MSA, CT	S	15.72 MW	15.18 AW	32700 AAW	CTBLS	10//99-12//99
Heavy and Tractor-Trailer	New Haven-Meriden PMSA, CT	S	15.80 MW	15.59 AW	32870 AAW	CTBLS	10//99-12//99
Heavy and Tractor-Trailer	New London-Norwich MSA, CT-RI	S	14.12 MW	14.16 AW	29370 AAW	CTBLS	10//99-12//99
Heavy and Tractor-Trailer	Stamford-Norwalk PMSA, CT	S	15.98 MW	15.81 AW	33240 AAW	CTBLS	10//99-12//99
Heavy and Tractor-Trailer	Waterbury PMSA, CT	S	15.34 MW	14.94 AW	31920 AAW	CTBLS	10//99-12//99
Heavy and Tractor-Trailer	Delaware	S	13.69 MW	14.43 AW	30020 AAW	DEBLS	10//99-12//99
Heavy and Tractor-Trailer	Dover MSA, DE	S	13.58 MW	13.12 AW	28240 AAW	DEBLS	10//99-12//99
Heavy and Tractor-Trailer	Wilmington-Newark PMSA, DE-MD	S	15.96 MW	15.46 AW	33200 AAW	DEBLS	10//99-12//99
Heavy and Tractor-Trailer	District of Columbia	S	16.62 MW	16.53 AW	34380 AAW	DCBLS	10//99-12//99
Heavy and Tractor-Trailer	Washington PMSA, DC-MD-VA-WV	S	16.33 MW	15.46 AW	33960 AAW	DCBLS	10//99-12//99
Heavy and Tractor-Trailer	Florida	S	13.25 MW	14.42 AW	29980 AAW	FLBLS	10//99-12//99
Heavy and Tractor-Trailer	Daytona Beach MSA, FL	S	15.37 MW	12.50 AW	31970 AAW	FLBLS	10//99-12//99
Heavy and Tractor-Trailer	Fort Lauderdale PMSA, FL	S	13.86 MW	13.08 AW	28830 AAW	FLBLS	10//99-12//99
Heavy and Tractor-Trailer	Fort Walton Beach MSA, FL	S	9.22 MW	9.37 AW	19170 AAW	FLBLS	10//99-12//99
Heavy and Tractor-Trailer	Jacksonville MSA, FL	S	14.69 MW	13.97 AW	30560 AAW	FLBLS	10//99-12//99
Heavy and Tractor-Trailer	Lakeland-Winter Haven MSA, FL	S	13.70 MW	13.35 AW	28500 AAW	FLBLS	10//99-12//99
Heavy and Tractor-Trailer	Melbourne-Titusville-Palm Bay MSA, FL	S	12.73 MW	13.74 AW	26480 AAW	FLBLS	10//99-12//99
Heavy and Tractor-Trailer	Miami PMSA, FL	S	14.43 MW	13.09 AW	30020 AAW	FLBLS	10//99-12//99
Heavy and Tractor-Trailer	Naples MSA, FL	S	14.49 MW	14.28 AW	30140 AAW	FLBLS	10//99-12//99
Heavy and Tractor-Trailer	Ocala MSA, FL	S	13.55 MW	10.68 AW	28180 AAW	FLBLS	10//99-12//99
Heavy and Tractor-Trailer	Orlando MSA, FL	S	15.51 MW	14.33 AW	32260 AAW	FLBLS	10//99-12//99

AAW Average annual wage	**AOH** Average offered, high	**ASH** Average starting, high	**H** Hourly	**M** Monthly	**S** Special: hourly and annual
AE Average entry wage	**AOL** Average offered, low	**ASL** Average starting, low	**HI** Highest wage paid	**MTC** Median total compensation	**TQ** Third quartile wage
AEX Average experienced wage	**APH** Average pay, high range	**AW** Average wage paid	**HR** High end range	**MW** Median wage paid	**W** Weekly
AO Average offered	**APL** Average pay, low range	**FQ** First quartile wage	**LR** Low end range	**SQ** Second quartile wage	**Y** Yearly

Occupation/Type/Industry	Location	Per	Low	Mid	High	Source	Date
Truck Driver							
Heavy and Tractor-Trailer	Pensacola MSA, FL	S	12.61 MW	10.49 AW	26220 AAW	FLBLS	10//99-12//99
Heavy and Tractor-Trailer	Punta Gorda MSA, FL	S	10.66 MW	10.97 AW	22180 AAW	FLBLS	10//99-12//99
Heavy and Tractor-Trailer	Sarasota-Bradenton MSA, FL	S	13.21 MW	11.59 AW	27470 AAW	FLBLS	10//99-12//99
Heavy and Tractor-Trailer	Tallahassee MSA, FL	S	10.97 MW	9.97 AW	22820 AAW	FLBLS	10//99-12//99
Heavy and Tractor-Trailer	Tampa-St. Petersburg-Clearwater MSA, FL	S	13.59 MW	13.28 AW	28260 AAW	FLBLS	10//99-12//99
Heavy and Tractor-Trailer	Georgia	S	15.2 MW	15.77 AW	32790 AAW	GABLS	10//99-12//99
Heavy and Tractor-Trailer	Albany MSA, GA	S	15.75 MW	15.04 AW	32750 AAW	GABLS	10//99-12//99
Heavy and Tractor-Trailer	Athens MSA, GA	S	18.07 MW	15.88 AW	37580 AAW	GABLS	10//99-12//99
Heavy and Tractor-Trailer	Atlanta MSA, GA	S	16.89 MW	16.45 AW	35140 AAW	GABLS	10//99-12//99
Heavy and Tractor-Trailer	Columbus MSA, GA-AL	S	13.01 MW	12.16 AW	27060 AAW	GABLS	10//99-12//99
Heavy and Tractor-Trailer	Macon MSA, GA	S	13.59 MW	12.35 AW	28260 AAW	GABLS	10//99-12//99
Heavy and Tractor-Trailer	Savannah MSA, GA	S	16.01 MW	15.21 AW	33310 AAW	GABLS	10//99-12//99
Heavy and Tractor-Trailer	Hawaii	S	13.13 MW	15.24 AW	31700 AAW	HIBLS	10//99-12//99
Heavy and Tractor-Trailer	Honolulu MSA, HI	S	16.02 MW	13.40 AW	33310 AAW	HIBLS	10//99-12//99
Heavy and Tractor-Trailer	Idaho	S	13.09 MW	13.12 AW	27280 AAW	IDBLS	10//99-12//99
Heavy and Tractor-Trailer	Boise City MSA, ID	S	13.49 MW	13.34 AW	28050 AAW	IDBLS	10//99-12//99
Heavy and Tractor-Trailer	Pocatello MSA, ID	S	19.73 MW	19.21 AW	41040 AAW	IDBLS	10//99-12//99
Heavy and Tractor-Trailer	Illinois	S	15.77 MW	17.00 AW	35360 AAW	ILBLS	10//99-12//99
Heavy and Tractor-Trailer	Bloomington-Normal MSA, IL	S	15.29 MW	15.53 AW	31810 AAW	ILBLS	10//99-12//99
Heavy and Tractor-Trailer	Champaign-Urbana MSA, IL	S	20.65 MW	21.31 AW	42950 AAW	ILBLS	10//99-12//99
Heavy and Tractor-Trailer	Chicago PMSA, IL	S	18.52 MW	16.96 AW	38520 AAW	ILBLS	10//99-12//99
Heavy and Tractor-Trailer	Decatur MSA, IL	S	12.90 MW	12.69 AW	26840 AAW	ILBLS	10//99-12//99
Heavy and Tractor-Trailer	Kankakee PMSA, IL	S	16.13 MW	15.23 AW	33540 AAW	ILBLS	10//99-12//99
Heavy and Tractor-Trailer	Peoria-Pekin MSA, IL	S	16.30 MW	16.34 AW	33910 AAW	ILBLS	10//99-12//99
Heavy and Tractor-Trailer	Rockford MSA, IL	S	16.64 MW	16.48 AW	34620 AAW	ILBLS	10//99-12//99
Heavy and Tractor-Trailer	Springfield MSA, IL	S	13.30 MW	14.00 AW	27650 AAW	ILBLS	10//99-12//99
Heavy and Tractor-Trailer	Indiana	S	14.89 MW	15.65 AW	32550 AAW	INBLS	10//99-12//99
Heavy and Tractor-Trailer	Bloomington MSA, IN	S	21.56 MW	19.94 AW	44840 AAW	INBLS	10//99-12//99
Heavy and Tractor-Trailer	Elkhart-Goshen MSA, IN	S	14.34 MW	13.86 AW	29830 AAW	INBLS	10//99-12//99
Heavy and Tractor-Trailer	Evansville-Henderson MSA, IN-KY	S	13.48 MW	12.77 AW	28030 AAW	INBLS	10//99-12//99
Heavy and Tractor-Trailer	Fort Wayne MSA, IN	S	17.88 MW	18.23 AW	37180 AAW	INBLS	10//99-12//99
Heavy and Tractor-Trailer	Gary PMSA, IN	S	17.20 MW	16.58 AW	35770 AAW	INBLS	10//99-12//99
Heavy and Tractor-Trailer	Indianapolis MSA, IN	S	16.24 MW	15.42 AW	33770 AAW	INBLS	10//99-12//99
Heavy and Tractor-Trailer	Kokomo MSA, IN	S	16.01 MW	15.62 AW	33290 AAW	INBLS	10//99-12//99
Heavy and Tractor-Trailer	Lafayette MSA, IN	S	15.26 MW	15.32 AW	31740 AAW	INBLS	10//99-12//99
Heavy and Tractor-Trailer	South Bend MSA, IN	S	14.49 MW	12.62 AW	30150 AAW	INBLS	10//99-12//99
Heavy and Tractor-Trailer	Terre Haute MSA, IN	S	12.25 MW	11.94 AW	25480 AAW	INBLS	10//99-12//99
Heavy and Tractor-Trailer	Iowa	S	15.94 MW	15.58 AW	32400 AAW	IABLS	10//99-12//99
Heavy and Tractor-Trailer	Cedar Rapids MSA, IA	S	16.38 MW	16.12 AW	34070 AAW	IABLS	10//99-12//99
Heavy and Tractor-Trailer	Davenport-Moline-Rock Island MSA, IA-IL	S	16.02 MW	15.71 AW	33320 AAW	IABLS	10//99-12//99
Heavy and Tractor-Trailer	Des Moines MSA, IA	S	17.64 MW	18.44 AW	36690 AAW	IABLS	10//99-12//99
Heavy and Tractor-Trailer	Dubuque MSA, IA	S	18.59 MW	18.67 AW	38660 AAW	IABLS	10//99-12//99
Heavy and Tractor-Trailer	Iowa City MSA, IA	S	12.51 MW	12.13 AW	26010 AAW	IABLS	10//99-12//99
Heavy and Tractor-Trailer	Sioux City MSA, IA-NE	S	14.39 MW	14.03 AW	29930 AAW	IABLS	10//99-12//99
Heavy and Tractor-Trailer	Waterloo-Cedar Falls MSA, IA	S	11.10 MW	10.50 AW	23090 AAW	IABLS	10//99-12//99
Heavy and Tractor-Trailer	Kansas	S	13.59 MW	13.78 AW	28650 AAW	KSBLS	10//99-12//99
Heavy and Tractor-Trailer	Lawrence MSA, KS	S	15.03 MW	15.17 AW	31250 AAW	KSBLS	10//99-12//99
Heavy and Tractor-Trailer	Topeka MSA, KS	S	12.60 MW	12.51 AW	26210 AAW	KSBLS	10//99-12//99
Heavy and Tractor-Trailer	Wichita MSA, KS	S	13.77 MW	14.14 AW	28640 AAW	KSBLS	10//99-12//99
Heavy and Tractor-Trailer	Kentucky	S	12.35 MW	13.58 AW	28240 AAW	KYBLS	10//99-12//99
Heavy and Tractor-Trailer	Lexington MSA, KY	S	16.86 MW	16.65 AW	35060 AAW	KYBLS	10//99-12//99
Heavy and Tractor-Trailer	Louisville MSA, KY-IN	S	14.78 MW	14.53 AW	30750 AAW	KYBLS	10//99-12//99
Heavy and Tractor-Trailer	Owensboro MSA, KY	S	12.32 MW	11.95 AW	25630 AAW	KYBLS	10//99-12//99
Heavy and Tractor-Trailer	Louisiana	S	13.58 MW	13.62 AW	28330 AAW	LABLS	10//99-12//99
Heavy and Tractor-Trailer	Alexandria MSA, LA	S	13.51 MW	13.54 AW	28100 AAW	LABLS	10//99-12//99
Heavy and Tractor-Trailer	Baton Rouge MSA, LA	S	14.21 MW	14.70 AW	29550 AAW	LABLS	10//99-12//99
Heavy and Tractor-Trailer	Houma MSA, LA	S	9.36 MW	8.47 AW	19470 AAW	LABLS	10//99-12//99
Heavy and Tractor-Trailer	Lafayette MSA, LA	S	13.42 MW	12.30 AW	27910 AAW	LABLS	10//99-12//99
Heavy and Tractor-Trailer	Lake Charles MSA, LA	S	13.28 MW	12.59 AW	27620 AAW	LABLS	10//99-12//99
Heavy and Tractor-Trailer	Monroe MSA, LA	S	14.25 MW	13.82 AW	29640 AAW	LABLS	10//99-12//99
Heavy and Tractor-Trailer	New Orleans MSA, LA	S	13.42 MW	13.30 AW	27910 AAW	LABLS	10//99-12//99
Heavy and Tractor-Trailer	Shreveport-Bossier City MSA, LA	S	15.39 MW	15.71 AW	32010 AAW	LABLS	10//99-12//99
Heavy and Tractor-Trailer	Maine	S	12.54 MW	13.70 AW	28500 AAW	MEBLS	10//99-12//99
Heavy and Tractor-Trailer	Lewiston-Auburn MSA, ME	S	14.00 MW	12.73 AW	29110 AAW	MEBLS	10//99-12//99
Heavy and Tractor-Trailer	Portland MSA, ME	S	13.80 MW	13.00 AW	28700 AAW	MEBLS	10//99-12//99
Heavy and Tractor-Trailer	Maryland	S	14.89 MW	15.56 AW	32360 AAW	MDBLS	10//99-12//99
Heavy and Tractor-Trailer	Baltimore PMSA, MD	S	15.68 MW	15.08 AW	32610 AAW	MDBLS	10//99-12//99

AAW	Average annual wage	AOH	Average offered, high	ASH	Average starting, high
AE	Average entry wage	AOL	Average offered, low	ASL	Average starting, low
AEX	Average experienced wage	APH	Average pay, high range	AW	Average wage paid
AO	Average offered	APL	Average pay, low range	FQ	First quartile wage

H	Hourly
HI	Highest wage paid
HR	High end range
LR	Low end range

M	Monthly
MTC	Median total compensation
MW	Median wage paid
SQ	Second quartile wage

S	Special: hourly and annual
TQ	Third quartile wage
W	Weekly
Y	Yearly

Occupation/Type/Industry	Location	Per	Low	Mid	High	Source	Date
Truck Driver							
Heavy and Tractor-Trailer	Cumberland MSA, MD-WV	S	11.56 MW	10.40 AW	24040 AAW	MDBLS	10//99-12//99
Heavy and Tractor-Trailer	Hagerstown PMSA, MD	S	12.79 MW	10.75 AW	26600 AAW	MDBLS	10//99-12//99
Heavy and Tractor-Trailer	Massachusetts	S	16.18 MW	16.95 AW	35250 AAW	MABLS	10//99-12//99
Heavy and Tractor-Trailer	Barnstable-Yarmouth MSA, MA	S	13.67 MW	13.50 AW	28440 AAW	MABLS	10//99-12//99
Heavy and Tractor-Trailer	Boston PMSA, MA-NH	S	18.24 MW	17.56 AW	37940 AAW	MABLS	10//99-12//99
Heavy and Tractor-Trailer	Brockton PMSA, MA	S	16.15 MW	15.20 AW	33590 AAW	MABLS	10//99-12//99
Heavy and Tractor-Trailer	Fitchburg-Leominster PMSA, MA	S	16.42 MW	16.85 AW	34160 AAW	MABLS	10//99-12//99
Heavy and Tractor-Trailer	Lawrence PMSA, MA-NH	S	14.71 MW	13.15 AW	30590 AAW	MABLS	10//99-12//99
Heavy and Tractor-Trailer	Lowell PMSA, MA-NH	S	16.62 MW	17.45 AW	34570 AAW	MABLS	10//99-12//99
Heavy and Tractor-Trailer	New Bedford PMSA, MA	S	12.88 MW	12.90 AW	26790 AAW	MABLS	10//99-12//99
Heavy and Tractor-Trailer	Pittsfield MSA, MA	S	14.43 MW	13.95 AW	30020 AAW	MABLS	10//99-12//99
Heavy and Tractor-Trailer	Springfield MSA, MA	S	14.56 MW	14.50 AW	30270 AAW	MABLS	10//99-12//99
Heavy and Tractor-Trailer	Worcester PMSA, MA-CT	S	17.07 MW	16.11 AW	35500 AAW	MABLS	10//99-12//99
Heavy and Tractor-Trailer	Michigan	S	15.07 MW	15.50 AW	32240 AAW	MIBLS	10//99-12//99
Heavy and Tractor-Trailer	Ann Arbor PMSA, MI	S	17.55 MW	17.95 AW	36510 AAW	MIBLS	10//99-12//99
Heavy and Tractor-Trailer	Benton Harbor MSA, MI	S	13.40 MW	12.74 AW	27870 AAW	MIBLS	10//99-12//99
Heavy and Tractor-Trailer	Detroit PMSA, MI	S	16.52 MW	15.81 AW	34370 AAW	MIBLS	10//99-12//99
Heavy and Tractor-Trailer	Flint PMSA, MI	S	16.49 MW	17.04 AW	34290 AAW	MIBLS	10//99-12//99
Heavy and Tractor-Trailer	Grand Rapids-Muskegon-Holland MSA, MI	S	15.44 MW	14.81 AW	32120 AAW	MIBLS	10//99-12//99
Heavy and Tractor-Trailer	Jackson MSA, MI	S	18.10 MW	16.99 AW	37650 AAW	MIBLS	10//99-12//99
Heavy and Tractor-Trailer	Kalamazoo-Battle Creek MSA, MI	S	14.37 MW	13.55 AW	29890 AAW	MIBLS	10//99-12//99
Heavy and Tractor-Trailer	Lansing-East Lansing MSA, MI	S	16.23 MW	16.13 AW	33750 AAW	MIBLS	10//99-12//99
Heavy and Tractor-Trailer	Saginaw-Bay City-Midland MSA, MI	S	13.39 MW	13.73 AW	27850 AAW	MIBLS	10//99-12//99
Heavy and Tractor-Trailer	Minnesota	S	15.73 MW	15.99 AW	33250 AAW	MNBLS	10//99-12//99
Heavy and Tractor-Trailer	Duluth-Superior MSA, MN-WI	S	12.33 MW	11.56 AW	25650 AAW	MNBLS	10//99-12//99
Heavy and Tractor-Trailer	Minneapolis-St. Paul MSA, MN-WI	S	17.92 MW	17.50 AW	37270 AAW	MNBLS	10//99-12//99
Heavy and Tractor-Trailer	Rochester MSA, MN	S	12.96 MW	12.65 AW	26950 AAW	MNBLS	10//99-12//99
Heavy and Tractor-Trailer	St. Cloud MSA, MN	S	15.31 MW	15.14 AW	31840 AAW	MNBLS	10//99-12//99
Heavy and Tractor-Trailer	Mississippi	S	13.26 MW	14.18 AW	29490 AAW	MSBLS	10//99-12//99
Heavy and Tractor-Trailer	Biloxi-Gulfport-Pascagoula MSA, MS	S	13.31 MW	12.20 AW	27680 AAW	MSBLS	10//99-12//99
Heavy and Tractor-Trailer	Hattiesburg MSA, MS	S	10.19 MW	10.10 AW	21200 AAW	MSBLS	10//99-12//99
Heavy and Tractor-Trailer	Jackson MSA, MS	S	12.44 MW	11.19 AW	25880 AAW	MSBLS	10//99-12//99
Heavy and Tractor-Trailer	Missouri	S	15.58 MW	15.95 AW	33180 AAW	MOBLS	10//99-12//99
Heavy and Tractor-Trailer	Columbia MSA, MO	S	15.25 MW	14.61 AW	31720 AAW	MOBLS	10//99-12//99
Heavy and Tractor-Trailer	Joplin MSA, MO	S	16.57 MW	17.22 AW	34460 AAW	MOBLS	10//99-12//99
Heavy and Tractor-Trailer	Kansas City MSA, MO-KS	S	14.80 MW	14.83 AW	30770 AAW	MOBLS	10//99-12//99
Heavy and Tractor-Trailer	St. Joseph MSA, MO	S	17.48 MW	16.85 AW	36360 AAW	MOBLS	10//99-12//99
Heavy and Tractor-Trailer	St. Louis MSA, MO-IL	S	16.83 MW	15.70 AW	35000 AAW	MOBLS	10//99-12//99
Heavy and Tractor-Trailer	Springfield MSA, MO	S	16.86 MW	17.80 AW	35080 AAW	MOBLS	10//99-12//99
Heavy and Tractor-Trailer	Montana	S	12.49 MW	13.51 AW	28110 AAW	MTBLS	10//99-12//99
Heavy and Tractor-Trailer	Billings MSA, MT	S	11.68 MW	8.32 AW	24290 AAW	MTBLS	10//99-12//99
Heavy and Tractor-Trailer	Great Falls MSA, MT	S	11.23 MW	11.48 AW	23360 AAW	MTBLS	10//99-12//99
Heavy and Tractor-Trailer	Missoula MSA, MT	S	13.59 MW	13.22 AW	28270 AAW	MTBLS	10//99-12//99
Heavy and Tractor-Trailer	Nebraska	S	14.48 MW	14.88 AW	30960 AAW	NEBLS	10//99-12//99
Heavy and Tractor-Trailer	Lincoln MSA, NE	S	11.96 MW	11.20 AW	24880 AAW	NEBLS	10//99-12//99
Heavy and Tractor-Trailer	Omaha MSA, NE-IA	S	16.26 MW	15.75 AW	33810 AAW	NEBLS	10//99-12//99
Heavy and Tractor-Trailer	Nevada	S	16.23 MW	16.01 AW	33300 AAW	NVBLS	10//99-12//99
Heavy and Tractor-Trailer	Las Vegas MSA, NV-AZ	S	15.68 MW	15.75 AW	32610 AAW	NVBLS	10//99-12//99
Heavy and Tractor-Trailer	Reno MSA, NV	S	16.89 MW	16.85 AW	35120 AAW	NVBLS	10//99-12//99
Heavy and Tractor-Trailer	New Hampshire	S	12.92 MW	14.14 AW	29400 AAW	NHBLS	10//99-12//99
Heavy and Tractor-Trailer	Manchester PMSA, NH	S	13.68 MW	13.64 AW	28460 AAW	NHBLS	10//99-12//99
Heavy and Tractor-Trailer	Nashua PMSA, NH	S	14.01 MW	13.35 AW	29150 AAW	NHBLS	10//99-12//99
Heavy and Tractor-Trailer	Portsmouth-Rochester PMSA, NH-ME	S	14.74 MW	13.42 AW	30650 AAW	NHBLS	10//99-12//99
Heavy and Tractor-Trailer	New Jersey	S	16.13 MW	16.55 AW	34420 AAW	NJBLS	10//99-12//99
Heavy and Tractor-Trailer	Atlantic-Cape May PMSA, NJ	S	14.89 MW	14.87 AW	30970 AAW	NJBLS	10//99-12//99
Heavy and Tractor-Trailer	Bergen-Passaic PMSA, NJ	S	16.90 MW	16.86 AW	35150 AAW	NJBLS	10//99-12//99
Heavy and Tractor-Trailer	Jersey City PMSA, NJ	S	17.48 MW	16.46 AW	36350 AAW	NJBLS	10//99-12//99
Heavy and Tractor-Trailer	Middlesex-Somerset-Hunterdon PMSA, NJ	S	18.09 MW	18.26 AW	37620 AAW	NJBLS	10//99-12//99
Heavy and Tractor-Trailer	Monmouth-Ocean PMSA, NJ	S	15.20 MW	14.79 AW	31620 AAW	NJBLS	10//99-12//99
Heavy and Tractor-Trailer	Newark PMSA, NJ	S	16.53 MW	16.24 AW	34380 AAW	NJBLS	10//99-12//99
Heavy and Tractor-Trailer	Trenton PMSA, NJ	S	14.07 MW	14.20 AW	29260 AAW	NJBLS	10//99-12//99

AAW	Average annual wage	AOH	Average offered, high	ASH	Average starting, high	H	Hourly		M	Monthly	S	Special: hourly and annual
AE	Average entry wage	AOL	Average offered, low	ASL	Average starting, low	HI	Highest wage paid		MTC	Median total compensation	TQ	Third quartile wage
AEX	Average experienced wage	APH	Average pay, high range	AW	Average wage paid	HR	High end range		MW	Median wage paid	W	Weekly
AO	Average offered	APL	Average pay, low range	FQ	First quartile wage	LR	Low end range		SQ	Second quartile wage	Y	Yearly

Occupation/Type/Industry	Location	Per	Low	Mid	High	Source	Date
Truck Driver							
Heavy and Tractor-Trailer	Vineland-Millville-Bridgeton PMSA, NJ	S	14.72 MW	13.45 AW	30630 AAW	NJBLS	10//99-12//99
Heavy and Tractor-Trailer	New Mexico	S	11.79 MW	12.59 AW	26190 AAW	NMBLS	10//99-12//99
Heavy and Tractor-Trailer	Albuquerque MSA, NM	S	13.65 MW	13.41 AW	28390 AAW	NMBLS	10//99-12//99
Heavy and Tractor-Trailer	Las Cruces MSA, NM	S	11.85 MW	10.77 AW	24640 AAW	NMBLS	10//99-12//99
Heavy and Tractor-Trailer	Santa Fe MSA, NM	S	13.07 MW	12.24 AW	27190 AAW	NMBLS	10//99-12//99
Heavy and Tractor-Trailer	New York	S	15.55 MW	16.46 AW	34240 AAW	NYBLS	10//99-12//99
Heavy and Tractor-Trailer	Albany-Schenectady-Troy MSA, NY	S	17.07 MW	16.27 AW	35500 AAW	NYBLS	10//99-12//99
Heavy and Tractor-Trailer	Binghamton MSA, NY	S	15.30 MW	14.26 AW	31830 AAW	NYBLS	10//99-12//99
Heavy and Tractor-Trailer	Buffalo-Niagara Falls MSA, NY	S	16.78 MW	15.87 AW	34890 AAW	NYBLS	10//99-12//99
Heavy and Tractor-Trailer	Glens Falls MSA, NY	S	14.50 MW	14.54 AW	30170 AAW	NYBLS	10//99-12//99
Heavy and Tractor-Trailer	Jamestown MSA, NY	S	15.80 MW	15.70 AW	32860 AAW	NYBLS	10//99-12//99
Heavy and Tractor-Trailer	Nassau-Suffolk PMSA, NY	S	18.61 MW	17.30 AW	38710 AAW	NYBLS	10//99-12//99
Heavy and Tractor-Trailer	New York PMSA, NY	S	16.92 MW	16.01 AW	35200 AAW	NYBLS	10//99-12//99
Heavy and Tractor-Trailer	Newburgh PMSA, NY-PA	S	18.98 MW	18.94 AW	39480 AAW	NYBLS	10//99-12//99
Heavy and Tractor-Trailer	Rochester MSA, NY	S	12.81 MW	11.80 AW	26640 AAW	NYBLS	10//99-12//99
Heavy and Tractor-Trailer	Syracuse MSA, NY	S	16.02 MW	15.34 AW	33320 AAW	NYBLS	10//99-12//99
Heavy and Tractor-Trailer	Utica-Rome MSA, NY	S	13.77 MW	12.43 AW	28640 AAW	NYBLS	10//99-12//99
Heavy and Tractor-Trailer	North Carolina	S	14 MW	14.63 AW	30440 AAW	NCBLS	10//99-12//99
Heavy and Tractor-Trailer	Asheville MSA, NC	S	14.46 MW	14.68 AW	30090 AAW	NCBLS	10//99-12//99
Heavy and Tractor-Trailer	Charlotte-Gastonia-Rock Hill MSA, NC-SC	S	16.34 MW	15.96 AW	33980 AAW	NCBLS	10//99-12//99
Heavy and Tractor-Trailer	Fayetteville MSA, NC	S	13.18 MW	11.58 AW	27410 AAW	NCBLS	10//99-12//99
Heavy and Tractor-Trailer	Goldsboro MSA, NC	S	11.46 MW	10.43 AW	23850 AAW	NCBLS	10//99-12//99
Heavy and Tractor-Trailer	Greensboro--Winston-Salem--High Point MSA, NC	S	15.12 MW	14.89 AW	31450 AAW	NCBLS	10//99-12//99
Heavy and Tractor-Trailer	Greenville MSA, NC	S	11.35 MW	10.91 AW	23620 AAW	NCBLS	10//99-12//99
Heavy and Tractor-Trailer	Hickory-Morganton-Lenoir MSA, NC	S	16.15 MW	14.96 AW	33580 AAW	NCBLS	10//99-12//99
Heavy and Tractor-Trailer	Jacksonville MSA, NC	S	10.60 MW	10.36 AW	22050 AAW	NCBLS	10//99-12//99
Heavy and Tractor-Trailer	Raleigh-Durham-Chapel Hill MSA, NC	S	11.24 MW	11.48 AW	23380 AAW	NCBLS	10//99-12//99
Heavy and Tractor-Trailer	Rocky Mount MSA, NC	S	13.26 MW	12.74 AW	27580 AAW	NCBLS	10//99-12//99
Heavy and Tractor-Trailer	Wilmington MSA, NC	S	14.97 MW	15.06 AW	31140 AAW	NCBLS	10//99-12//99
Heavy and Tractor-Trailer	North Dakota	S	12.75 MW	13.57 AW	28230 AAW	NDBLS	10//99-12//99
Heavy and Tractor-Trailer	Bismarck MSA, ND	S	13.11 MW	12.41 AW	27260 AAW	NDBLS	10//99-12//99
Heavy and Tractor-Trailer	Fargo-Moorhead MSA, ND-MN	S	15.96 MW	15.89 AW	33190 AAW	NDBLS	10//99-12//99
Heavy and Tractor-Trailer	Grand Forks MSA, ND-MN	S	11.85 MW	11.79 AW	24650 AAW	NDBLS	10//99-12//99
Heavy and Tractor-Trailer	Ohio	S	15.5 MW	15.90 AW	33060 AAW	OHBLS	10//99-12//99
Heavy and Tractor-Trailer	Akron PMSA, OH	S	16.27 MW	15.97 AW	33840 AAW	OHBLS	10//99-12//99
Heavy and Tractor-Trailer	Canton-Massillon MSA, OH	S	15.09 MW	14.66 AW	31400 AAW	OHBLS	10//99-12//99
Heavy and Tractor-Trailer	Cincinnati PMSA, OH-KY-IN	S	16.34 MW	15.73 AW	33990 AAW	OHBLS	10//99-12//99
Heavy and Tractor-Trailer	Cleveland-Lorain-Elyria PMSA, OH	S	18.30 MW	18.51 AW	38070 AAW	OHBLS	10//99-12//99
Heavy and Tractor-Trailer	Columbus MSA, OH	S	16.19 MW	15.82 AW	33680 AAW	OHBLS	10//99-12//99
Heavy and Tractor-Trailer	Dayton-Springfield MSA, OH	S	14.98 MW	15.06 AW	31150 AAW	OHBLS	10//99-12//99
Heavy and Tractor-Trailer	Hamilton-Middletown PMSA, OH	S	13.79 MW	13.33 AW	28680 AAW	OHBLS	10//99-12//99
Heavy and Tractor-Trailer	Lima MSA, OH	S	14.20 MW	13.14 AW	29530 AAW	OHBLS	10//99-12//99
Heavy and Tractor-Trailer	Mansfield MSA, OH	S	11.60 MW	10.98 AW	24120 AAW	OHBLS	10//99-12//99
Heavy and Tractor-Trailer	Steubenville-Weirton MSA, OH-WV	S	12.70 MW	12.64 AW	26420 AAW	OHBLS	10//99-12//99
Heavy and Tractor-Trailer	Toledo MSA, OH	S	15.48 MW	14.79 AW	32190 AAW	OHBLS	10//99-12//99
Heavy and Tractor-Trailer	Youngstown-Warren MSA, OH	S	14.15 MW	14.36 AW	29430 AAW	OHBLS	10//99-12//99
Heavy and Tractor-Trailer	Oklahoma	S	12.66 MW	14.26 AW	29670 AAW	OKBLS	10//99-12//99
Heavy and Tractor-Trailer	Enid MSA, OK	S	12.24 MW	10.22 AW	25450 AAW	OKBLS	10//99-12//99
Heavy and Tractor-Trailer	Lawton MSA, OK	S	11.60 MW	11.89 AW	24120 AAW	OKBLS	10//99-12//99
Heavy and Tractor-Trailer	Oklahoma City MSA, OK	S	14.00 MW	12.92 AW	29130 AAW	OKBLS	10//99-12//99
Heavy and Tractor-Trailer	Tulsa MSA, OK	S	16.92 MW	13.37 AW	35190 AAW	OKBLS	10//99-12//99
Heavy and Tractor-Trailer	Oregon	S	14.78 MW	15.04 AW	31290 AAW	ORBLS	10//99-12//99
Heavy and Tractor-Trailer	Corvallis MSA, OR	S	12.88 MW	12.77 AW	26790 AAW	ORBLS	10//99-12//99
Heavy and Tractor-Trailer	Eugene-Springfield MSA, OR	S	14.37 MW	13.26 AW	29890 AAW	ORBLS	10//99-12//99
Heavy and Tractor-Trailer	Medford-Ashland MSA, OR	S	12.30 MW	12.16 AW	25580 AAW	ORBLS	10//99-12//99
Heavy and Tractor-Trailer	Portland-Vancouver PMSA, OR-WA	S	16.12 MW	16.16 AW	33540 AAW	ORBLS	10//99-12//99
Heavy and Tractor-Trailer	Salem PMSA, OR	S	14.18 MW	13.66 AW	29500 AAW	ORBLS	10//99-12//99
Heavy and Tractor-Trailer	Pennsylvania	S	14.76 MW	15.27 AW	31760 AAW	PABLS	10//99-12//99

AAW	Average annual wage	AOH	Average offered, high	ASH	Average starting, high
AE	Average entry wage	AOL	Average offered, low	ASL	Average starting, low
AEX	Average experienced wage	APH	Average pay, high range	AW	Average wage paid
AO	Average offered	APL	Average pay, low range	FQ	First quartile wage

H	Hourly	M	Monthly
HI	Highest wage paid	MTC	Median total compensation
HR	High end range	MW	Median wage paid
LR	Low end range	SQ	Second quartile wage

S	Special: hourly and annual
TQ	Third quartile wage
W	Weekly
Y	Yearly

Truck Driver

Occupation/Type/Industry	Location	Per	Low	Mid	High	Source	Date
Truck Driver							
Heavy and Tractor-Trailer	Allentown-Bethlehem-Easton MSA, PA	S	14.55 MW	14.06 AW	30260 AAW	PABLS	10//99-12//99
Heavy and Tractor-Trailer	Altoona MSA, PA	S	15.30 MW	14.98 AW	31820 AAW	PABLS	10//99-12//99
Heavy and Tractor-Trailer	Erie MSA, PA	S	15.01 MW	15.00 AW	31220 AAW	PABLS	10//99-12//99
Heavy and Tractor-Trailer	Harrisburg-Lebanon-Carlisle MSA, PA	S	16.96 MW	17.72 AW	35280 AAW	PABLS	10//99-12//99
Heavy and Tractor-Trailer	Johnstown MSA, PA	S	11.41 MW	10.71 AW	23740 AAW	PABLS	10//99-12//99
Heavy and Tractor-Trailer	Lancaster MSA, PA	S	14.52 MW	13.35 AW	30210 AAW	PABLS	10//99-12//99
Heavy and Tractor-Trailer	Philadelphia PMSA, PA-NJ	S	15.70 MW	15.06 AW	32670 AAW	PABLS	10//99-12//99
Heavy and Tractor-Trailer	Pittsburgh MSA, PA	S	15.91 MW	15.08 AW	33090 AAW	PABLS	10//99-12//99
Heavy and Tractor-Trailer	Reading MSA, PA	S	13.91 MW	13.19 AW	28930 AAW	PABLS	10//99-12//99
Heavy and Tractor-Trailer	Scranton--Wilkes-Barre--Hazleton MSA, PA	S	16.70 MW	17.20 AW	34730 AAW	PABLS	10//99-12//99
Heavy and Tractor-Trailer	Sharon MSA, PA	S	13.79 MW	13.03 AW	28680 AAW	PABLS	10//99-12//99
Heavy and Tractor-Trailer	State College MSA, PA	S	13.20 MW	12.78 AW	27450 AAW	PABLS	10//99-12//99
Heavy and Tractor-Trailer	Williamsport MSA, PA	S	15.04 MW	15.68 AW	31290 AAW	PABLS	10//99-12//99
Heavy and Tractor-Trailer	York MSA, PA	S	13.54 MW	12.68 AW	28150 AAW	PABLS	10//99-12//99
Heavy and Tractor-Trailer	Rhode Island	S	14.5 MW	14.87 AW	30930 AAW	RIBLS	10//99-12//99
Heavy and Tractor-Trailer	Providence-Fall River-Warwick MSA, RI-MA	S	14.95 MW	14.59 AW	31090 AAW	RIBLS	10//99-12//99
Heavy and Tractor-Trailer	South Carolina	S	15.03 MW	15.64 AW	32540 AAW	SCBLS	10//99-12//99
Heavy and Tractor-Trailer	Charleston-North Charleston MSA, SC	S	13.39 MW	12.23 AW	27860 AAW	SCBLS	10//99-12//99
Heavy and Tractor-Trailer	Columbia MSA, SC	S	15.54 MW	14.74 AW	32310 AAW	SCBLS	10//99-12//99
Heavy and Tractor-Trailer	Florence MSA, SC	S	14.00 MW	13.11 AW	29130 AAW	SCBLS	10//99-12//99
Heavy and Tractor-Trailer	Greenville-Spartanburg-Anderson MSA, SC	S	17.16 MW	16.23 AW	35680 AAW	SCBLS	10//99-12//99
Heavy and Tractor-Trailer	Myrtle Beach MSA, SC	S	14.23 MW	13.04 AW	29590 AAW	SCBLS	10//99-12//99
Heavy and Tractor-Trailer	Sumter MSA, SC	S	11.49 MW	10.30 AW	23900 AAW	SCBLS	10//99-12//99
Heavy and Tractor-Trailer	South Dakota	S	13.45 MW	14.74 AW	30650 AAW	SDBLS	10//99-12//99
Heavy and Tractor-Trailer	Rapid City MSA, SD	S	13.87 MW	12.52 AW	28850 AAW	SDBLS	10//99-12//99
Heavy and Tractor-Trailer	Sioux Falls MSA, SD	S	16.62 MW	17.38 AW	34580 AAW	SDBLS	10//99-12//99
Heavy and Tractor-Trailer	Tennessee	S	15.92 MW	15.79 AW	32840 AAW	TNBLS	10//99-12//99
Heavy and Tractor-Trailer	Chattanooga MSA, TN-GA	S	16.47 MW	16.00 AW	34260 AAW	TNBLS	10//99-12//99
Heavy and Tractor-Trailer	Clarksville-Hopkinsville MSA, TN-KY	S	13.82 MW	12.86 AW	28740 AAW	TNBLS	10//99-12//99
Heavy and Tractor-Trailer	Jackson MSA, TN	S	15.11 MW	15.06 AW	31430 AAW	TNBLS	10//99-12//99
Heavy and Tractor-Trailer	Johnson City-Kingsport-Bristol MSA, TN-VA	S	14.84 MW	13.80 AW	30870 AAW	TNBLS	10//99-12//99
Heavy and Tractor-Trailer	Knoxville MSA, TN	S	14.85 MW	14.53 AW	30890 AAW	TNBLS	10//99-12//99
Heavy and Tractor-Trailer	Memphis MSA, TN-AR-MS	S	16.67 MW	17.53 AW	34670 AAW	MSBLS	10//99-12//99
Heavy and Tractor-Trailer	Nashville MSA, TN	S	16.29 MW	15.93 AW	33880 AAW	TNBLS	10//99-12//99
Heavy and Tractor-Trailer	Texas	S	13.86 MW	15.13 AW	31460 AAW	TXBLS	10//99-12//99
Heavy and Tractor-Trailer	Abilene MSA, TX	S	11.49 MW	11.42 AW	23890 AAW	TXBLS	10//99-12//99
Heavy and Tractor-Trailer	Amarillo MSA, TX	S	13.47 MW	13.36 AW	28020 AAW	TXBLS	10//99-12//99
Heavy and Tractor-Trailer	Austin-San Marcos MSA, TX	S	13.78 MW	13.22 AW	28660 AAW	TXBLS	10//99-12//99
Heavy and Tractor-Trailer	Beaumont-Port Arthur MSA, TX	S	11.76 MW	11.50 AW	24450 AAW	TXBLS	10//99-12//99
Heavy and Tractor-Trailer	Brazoria PMSA, TX	S	13.98 MW	13.83 AW	29080 AAW	TXBLS	10//99-12//99
Heavy and Tractor-Trailer	Brownsville-Harlingen-San Benito MSA, TX	S	13.32 MW	14.57 AW	27700 AAW	TXBLS	10//99-12//99
Heavy and Tractor-Trailer	Bryan-College Station MSA, TX	S	9.95 MW	9.56 AW	20700 AAW	TXBLS	10//99-12//99
Heavy and Tractor-Trailer	Corpus Christi MSA, TX	S	10.01 MW	9.64 AW	20810 AAW	TXBLS	10//99-12//99
Heavy and Tractor-Trailer	Dallas PMSA, TX	S	17.41 MW	15.32 AW	36210 AAW	TXBLS	10//99-12//99
Heavy and Tractor-Trailer	El Paso MSA, TX	S	13.79 MW	14.30 AW	28690 AAW	TXBLS	10//99-12//99
Heavy and Tractor-Trailer	Fort Worth-Arlington PMSA, TX	S	14.31 MW	13.22 AW	29760 AAW	TXBLS	10//99-12//99
Heavy and Tractor-Trailer	Galveston-Texas City PMSA, TX	S	12.94 MW	12.40 AW	26920 AAW	TXBLS	10//99-12//99
Heavy and Tractor-Trailer	Houston PMSA, TX	S	14.85 MW	13.02 AW	30890 AAW	TXBLS	10//99-12//99
Heavy and Tractor-Trailer	Laredo MSA, TX	S	14.74 MW	14.80 AW	30660 AAW	TXBLS	10//99-12//99
Heavy and Tractor-Trailer	Longview-Marshall MSA, TX	S	10.83 MW	9.83 AW	22520 AAW	TXBLS	10//99-12//99
Heavy and Tractor-Trailer	Lubbock MSA, TX	S	13.62 MW	13.09 AW	28330 AAW	TXBLS	10//99-12//99
Heavy and Tractor-Trailer	McAllen-Edinburg-Mission MSA, TX	S	15.70 MW	17.36 AW	32660 AAW	TXBLS	10//99-12//99
Heavy and Tractor-Trailer	Odessa-Midland MSA, TX	S	12.66 MW	13.83 AW	26330 AAW	TXBLS	10//99-12//99
Heavy and Tractor-Trailer	San Angelo MSA, TX	S	9.70 MW	9.42 AW	20170 AAW	TXBLS	10//99-12//99
Heavy and Tractor-Trailer	San Antonio MSA, TX	S	14.38 MW	13.16 AW	29900 AAW	TXBLS	10//99-12//99
Heavy and Tractor-Trailer	Sherman-Denison MSA, TX	S	15.38 MW	14.86 AW	32000 AAW	TXBLS	10//99-12//99

AAW Average annual wage	AOH Average offered, high	ASH Average starting, high	H Hourly	M Monthly	S Special: hourly and annual
AE Average entry wage	AOL Average offered, low	ASL Average starting, low	HI Highest wage paid	MTC Median total compensation	TQ Third quartile wage
AEX Average experienced wage	APH Average pay, high range	AW Average wage paid	HR High end range	MW Median wage paid	W Weekly
AO Average offered	APL Average pay, low range	FQ First quartile wage	LR Low end range	SQ Second quartile wage	Y Yearly

Truck Driver

Occupation/Type/Industry	Location	Per	Low	Mid	High	Source	Date
Heavy and Tractor-Trailer	Texarkana MSA, TX-Texarkana, AR	S	13.93 MW	14.77 AW	28970 AAW	TXBLS	10//99-12//99
Heavy and Tractor-Trailer	Tyler MSA, TX	S	13.24 MW	10.69 AW	27540 AAW	TXBLS	10//99-12//99
Heavy and Tractor-Trailer	Victoria MSA, TX	S	10.91 MW	10.11 AW	22690 AAW	TXBLS	10//99-12//99
Heavy and Tractor-Trailer	Waco MSA, TX	S	14.33 MW	12.38 AW	29810 AAW	TXBLS	10//99-12//99
Heavy and Tractor-Trailer	Wichita Falls MSA, TX	S	11.75 MW	10.33 AW	24440 AAW	TXBLS	10//99-12//99
Heavy and Tractor-Trailer	Utah	S	14.14 MW	16.00 AW	33270 AAW	UTBLS	10//99-12//99
Heavy and Tractor-Trailer	Provo-Orem MSA, UT	S	17.70 MW	16.65 AW	36810 AAW	UTBLS	10//99-12//99
Heavy and Tractor-Trailer	Salt Lake City-Ogden MSA, UT	S	15.55 MW	13.60 AW	32330 AAW	UTBLS	10//99-12//99
Heavy and Tractor-Trailer	Vermont	S	11.9 MW	12.72 AW	26460 AAW	VTBLS	10//99-12//99
Heavy and Tractor-Trailer	Burlington MSA, VT	S	13.97 MW	12.66 AW	29060 AAW	VTBLS	10//99-12//99
Heavy and Tractor-Trailer	Virginia	S	14.07 MW	14.65 AW	30460 AAW	VABLS	10//99-12//99
Heavy and Tractor-Trailer	Charlottesville MSA, VA	S	13.77 MW	13.73 AW	28630 AAW	VABLS	10//99-12//99
Heavy and Tractor-Trailer	Danville MSA, VA	S	12.34 MW	12.19 AW	25660 AAW	VABLS	10//99-12//99
Heavy and Tractor-Trailer	Lynchburg MSA, VA	S	12.64 MW	12.15 AW	26300 AAW	VABLS	10//99-12//99
Heavy and Tractor-Trailer	Norfolk-Virginia Beach-Newport News MSA, VA-NC	S	14.28 MW	13.32 AW	29700 AAW	VABLS	10//99-12//99
Heavy and Tractor-Trailer	Richmond-Petersburg MSA, VA	S	15.65 MW	14.58 AW	32540 AAW	VABLS	10//99-12//99
Heavy and Tractor-Trailer	Roanoke MSA, VA	S	14.23 MW	13.56 AW	29610 AAW	VABLS	10//99-12//99
Heavy and Tractor-Trailer	Washington	S	15.47 MW	15.98 AW	33230 AAW	WABLS	10//99-12//99
Heavy and Tractor-Trailer	Bellingham MSA, WA	S	14.46 MW	14.18 AW	30070 AAW	WABLS	10//99-12//99
Heavy and Tractor-Trailer	Bremerton PMSA, WA	S	15.84 MW	15.95 AW	32950 AAW	WABLS	10//99-12//99
Heavy and Tractor-Trailer	Olympia PMSA, WA	S	13.82 MW	14.29 AW	28760 AAW	WABLS	10//99-12//99
Heavy and Tractor-Trailer	Richland-Kennewick-Pasco MSA, WA	S	14.80 MW	14.82 AW	30790 AAW	WABLS	10//99-12//99
Heavy and Tractor-Trailer	Seattle-Bellevue-Everett PMSA, WA	S	17.28 MW	16.50 AW	35940 AAW	WABLS	10//99-12//99
Heavy and Tractor-Trailer	Spokane MSA, WA	S	16.24 MW	16.74 AW	33780 AAW	WABLS	10//99-12//99
Heavy and Tractor-Trailer	Tacoma PMSA, WA	S	16.92 MW	16.32 AW	35190 AAW	WABLS	10//99-12//99
Heavy and Tractor-Trailer	Yakima MSA, WA	S	13.85 MW	13.67 AW	28800 AAW	WABLS	10//99-12//99
Heavy and Tractor-Trailer	West Virginia	S	12.65 MW	13.38 AW	27830 AAW	WVBLS	10//99-12//99
Heavy and Tractor-Trailer	Charleston MSA, WV	S	13.42 MW	13.89 AW	27910 AAW	WVBLS	10//99-12//99
Heavy and Tractor-Trailer	Huntington-Ashland MSA, WV-KY-OH	S	12.60 MW	12.02 AW	26210 AAW	WVBLS	10//99-12//99
Heavy and Tractor-Trailer	Parkersburg-Marietta MSA, WV-OH	S	12.65 MW	11.95 AW	26300 AAW	WVBLS	10//99-12//99
Heavy and Tractor-Trailer	Wheeling MSA, WV-OH	S	11.40 MW	10.45 AW	23720 AAW	WVBLS	10//99-12//99
Heavy and Tractor-Trailer	Wisconsin	S	15.22 MW	15.88 AW	33020 AAW	WIBLS	10//99-12//99
Heavy and Tractor-Trailer	Appleton-Oshkosh-Neenah MSA, WI	S	16.18 MW	16.88 AW	33650 AAW	WIBLS	10//99-12//99
Heavy and Tractor-Trailer	Eau Claire MSA, WI	S	13.87 MW	13.03 AW	28850 AAW	WIBLS	10//99-12//99
Heavy and Tractor-Trailer	Green Bay MSA, WI	S	15.94 MW	15.08 AW	33150 AAW	WIBLS	10//99-12//99
Heavy and Tractor-Trailer	Janesville-Beloit MSA, WI	S	15.91 MW	15.28 AW	33090 AAW	WIBLS	10//99-12//99
Heavy and Tractor-Trailer	Kenosha PMSA, WI	S	16.11 MW	15.70 AW	33510 AAW	WIBLS	10//99-12//99
Heavy and Tractor-Trailer	La Crosse MSA, WI-MN	S	15.47 MW	13.05 AW	32180 AAW	WIBLS	10//99-12//99
Heavy and Tractor-Trailer	Madison MSA, WI	S	17.24 MW	16.06 AW	35870 AAW	WIBLS	10//99-12//99
Heavy and Tractor-Trailer	Milwaukee-Waukesha PMSA, WI	S	17.38 MW	17.47 AW	36150 AAW	WIBLS	10//99-12//99
Heavy and Tractor-Trailer	Racine PMSA, WI	S	15.16 MW	14.54 AW	31540 AAW	WIBLS	10//99-12//99
Heavy and Tractor-Trailer	Sheboygan MSA, WI	S	15.97 MW	15.43 AW	33220 AAW	WIBLS	10//99-12//99
Heavy and Tractor-Trailer	Wausau MSA, WI	S	17.64 MW	16.63 AW	36690 AAW	WIBLS	10//99-12//99
Heavy and Tractor-Trailer	Wyoming	S	12.64 MW	13.10 AW	27240 AAW	WYBLS	10//99-12//99
Heavy and Tractor-Trailer	Casper MSA, WY	S	15.63 MW	15.14 AW	32510 AAW	WYBLS	10//99-12//99
Heavy and Tractor-Trailer	Cheyenne MSA, WY	S	12.87 MW	12.29 AW	26760 AAW	WYBLS	10//99-12//99
Heavy and Tractor-Trailer	Puerto Rico	S	6.37 MW	7.06 AW	14690 AAW	PRBLS	10//99-12//99
Heavy and Tractor-Trailer	Aguadilla MSA, PR	S	5.75 MW	5.95 AW	11960 AAW	PRBLS	10//99-12//99
Heavy and Tractor-Trailer	Arecibo PMSA, PR	S	6.02 MW	6.07 AW	12520 AAW	PRBLS	10//99-12//99
Heavy and Tractor-Trailer	Caguas PMSA, PR	S	6.80 MW	6.56 AW	14140 AAW	PRBLS	10//99-12//99
Heavy and Tractor-Trailer	Mayaguez MSA, PR	S	6.03 MW	6.04 AW	12550 AAW	PRBLS	10//99-12//99
Heavy and Tractor-Trailer	Ponce MSA, PR	S	6.84 MW	6.28 AW	14230 AAW	PRBLS	10//99-12//99
Heavy and Tractor-Trailer	San Juan-Bayamon PMSA, PR	S	7.40 MW	6.51 AW	15380 AAW	PRBLS	10//99-12//99
Heavy and Tractor-Trailer	Virgin Islands	S	10.61 MW	11.60 AW	24120 AAW	VIBLS	10//99-12//99
Heavy and Tractor-Trailer	Guam	S	9.94 MW	10.46 AW	21770 AAW	GUBLS	10//99-12//99
Light or Delivery Service	Alabama	S	9.58 MW	11.22 AW	23340 AAW	ALBLS	10//99-12//99
Light or Delivery Service	Anniston MSA, AL	S	13.52 MW	10.47 AW	28110 AAW	ALBLS	10//99-12//99
Light or Delivery Service	Auburn-Opelika MSA, AL	S	9.83 MW	9.31 AW	20450 AAW	ALBLS	10//99-12//99
Light or Delivery Service	Birmingham MSA, AL	S	12.07 MW	10.53 AW	25100 AAW	ALBLS	10//99-12//99
Light or Delivery Service	Decatur MSA, AL	S	11.84 MW	9.03 AW	24630 AAW	ALBLS	10//99-12//99

Truck Driver

Occupation/Type/Industry	Location	Per	Low	Mid	High	Source	Date
Light or Delivery Service	Dothan MSA, AL	S	10.36 MW	7.83 AW	21560 AAW	ALBLS	10//99-12//99
Light or Delivery Service	Florence MSA, AL	S	7.90 MW	7.47 AW	16420 AAW	ALBLS	10//99-12//99
Light or Delivery Service	Gadsden MSA, AL	S	13.21 MW	9.04 AW	27470 AAW	ALBLS	10//99-12//99
Light or Delivery Service	Huntsville MSA, AL	S	13.06 MW	11.26 AW	27160 AAW	ALBLS	10//99-12//99
Light or Delivery Service	Mobile MSA, AL	S	8.49 MW	7.60 AW	17660 AAW	ALBLS	10//99-12//99
Light or Delivery Service	Montgomery MSA, AL	S	12.28 MW	10.14 AW	25550 AAW	ALBLS	10//99-12//99
Light or Delivery Service	Tuscaloosa MSA, AL	S	11.20 MW	8.43 AW	23300 AAW	ALBLS	10//99-12//99
Light or Delivery Service	Alaska	S	10.67 MW	11.30 AW	23500 AAW	AKBLS	10//99-12//99
Light or Delivery Service	Anchorage MSA, AK	S	11.38 MW	11.36 AW	23660 AAW	AKBLS	10//99-12//99
Light or Delivery Service	Arizona	S	9.85 MW	10.69 AW	22230 AAW	AZBLS	10//99-12//99
Light or Delivery Service	Flagstaff MSA, AZ-UT	S	10.06 MW	8.38 AW	20920 AAW	AZBLS	10//99-12//99
Light or Delivery Service	Phoenix-Mesa MSA, AZ	S	11.30 MW	10.42 AW	23510 AAW	AZBLS	10//99-12//99
Light or Delivery Service	Tucson MSA, AZ	S	8.13 MW	7.63 AW	16900 AAW	AZBLS	10//99-12//99
Light or Delivery Service	Yuma MSA, AZ	S	12.24 MW	12.17 AW	25450 AAW	AZBLS	10//99-12//99
Light or Delivery Service	Arkansas	S	8.38 MW	9.80 AW	20380 AAW	ARBLS	10//99-12//99
Light or Delivery Service	Fayetteville-Springdale-Rogers MSA, AR	S	10.35 MW	9.96 AW	21520 AAW	ARBLS	10//99-12//99
Light or Delivery Service	Fort Smith MSA, AR-OK	S	8.24 MW	8.01 AW	17150 AAW	ARBLS	10//99-12//99
Light or Delivery Service	Jonesboro MSA, AR	S	7.98 MW	7.82 AW	16600 AAW	ARBLS	10//99-12//99
Light or Delivery Service	Little Rock-North Little Rock MSA, AR	S	11.36 MW	9.29 AW	23630 AAW	ARBLS	10//99-12//99
Light or Delivery Service	Pine Bluff MSA, AR	S	10.32 MW	8.00 AW	21470 AAW	ARBLS	10//99-12//99
Light or Delivery Service	California	S	10.76 MW	11.54 AW	24000 AAW	CABLS	10//99-12//99
Light or Delivery Service	Bakersfield MSA, CA	S	10.10 MW	8.55 AW	21010 AAW	CABLS	10//99-12//99
Light or Delivery Service	Chico-Paradise MSA, CA	S	10.78 MW	10.84 AW	22430 AAW	CABLS	10//99-12//99
Light or Delivery Service	Fresno MSA, CA	S	10.25 MW	9.19 AW	21320 AAW	CABLS	10//99-12//99
Light or Delivery Service	Los Angeles-Long Beach PMSA, CA	S	11.61 MW	10.63 AW	24140 AAW	CABLS	10//99-12//99
Light or Delivery Service	Merced MSA, CA	S	10.36 MW	10.59 AW	21560 AAW	CABLS	10//99-12//99
Light or Delivery Service	Modesto MSA, CA	S	11.60 MW	11.12 AW	24120 AAW	CABLS	10//99-12//99
Light or Delivery Service	Oakland PMSA, CA	S	11.13 MW	9.89 AW	23150 AAW	CABLS	10//99-12//99
Light or Delivery Service	Orange County PMSA, CA	S	12.06 MW	11.06 AW	25090 AAW	CABLS	10//99-12//99
Light or Delivery Service	Redding MSA, CA	S	10.49 MW	8.64 AW	21810 AAW	CABLS	10//99-12//99
Light or Delivery Service	Riverside-San Bernardino PMSA, CA	S	13.07 MW	12.67 AW	27190 AAW	CABLS	10//99-12//99
Light or Delivery Service	Sacramento PMSA, CA	S	10.55 MW	9.83 AW	21950 AAW	CABLS	10//99-12//99
Light or Delivery Service	Salinas MSA, CA	S	12.95 MW	12.69 AW	26930 AAW	CABLS	10//99-12//99
Light or Delivery Service	San Diego MSA, CA	S	10.52 MW	9.62 AW	21880 AAW	CABLS	10//99-12//99
Light or Delivery Service	San Francisco PMSA, CA	S	12.31 MW	12.09 AW	25600 AAW	CABLS	10//99-12//99
Light or Delivery Service	San Jose PMSA, CA	S	13.02 MW	12.54 AW	27080 AAW	CABLS	10//99-12//99
Light or Delivery Service	San Luis Obispo-Atascadero-Paso Robles MSA, CA	S	9.26 MW	8.56 AW	19250 AAW	CABLS	10//99-12//99
Light or Delivery Service	Santa Barbara-Santa Maria-Lompoc MSA, CA	S	9.48 MW	8.93 AW	19730 AAW	CABLS	10//99-12//99
Light or Delivery Service	Santa Cruz-Watsonville PMSA, CA	S	11.46 MW	11.83 AW	23840 AAW	CABLS	10//99-12//99
Light or Delivery Service	Santa Rosa PMSA, CA	S	9.89 MW	9.00 AW	20570 AAW	CABLS	10//99-12//99
Light or Delivery Service	Stockton-Lodi MSA, CA	S	12.06 MW	11.95 AW	25090 AAW	CABLS	10//99-12//99
Light or Delivery Service	Vallejo-Fairfield-Napa PMSA, CA	S	11.05 MW	10.42 AW	22980 AAW	CABLS	10//99-12//99
Light or Delivery Service	Ventura PMSA, CA	S	10.51 MW	9.85 AW	21850 AAW	CABLS	10//99-12//99
Light or Delivery Service	Visalia-Tulare-Porterville MSA, CA	S	11.21 MW	10.20 AW	23320 AAW	CABLS	10//99-12//99
Light or Delivery Service	Yolo PMSA, CA	S	10.14 MW	8.51 AW	21090 AAW	CABLS	10//99-12//99
Light or Delivery Service	Yuba City MSA, CA	S	8.34 MW	6.70 AW	17340 AAW	CABLS	10//99-12//99
Light or Delivery Service	Colorado	S	10.71 MW	11.18 AW	23250 AAW	COBLS	10//99-12//99
Light or Delivery Service	Boulder-Longmont PMSA, CO	S	10.71 MW	10.50 AW	22270 AAW	COBLS	10//99-12//99
Light or Delivery Service	Colorado Springs MSA, CO	S	10.01 MW	9.79 AW	20830 AAW	COBLS	10//99-12//99
Light or Delivery Service	Denver PMSA, CO	S	11.58 MW	11.26 AW	24090 AAW	COBLS	10//99-12//99
Light or Delivery Service	Fort Collins-Loveland MSA, CO	S	9.48 MW	9.05 AW	19720 AAW	COBLS	10//99-12//99
Light or Delivery Service	Grand Junction MSA, CO	S	10.42 MW	9.81 AW	21670 AAW	COBLS	10//99-12//99
Light or Delivery Service	Greeley PMSA, CO	S	9.92 MW	9.60 AW	20630 AAW	COBLS	10//99-12//99
Light or Delivery Service	Pueblo MSA, CO	S	12.46 MW	10.98 AW	25910 AAW	COBLS	10//99-12//99
Light or Delivery Service	Connecticut	S	11.58 MW	12.01 AW	24980 AAW	CTBLS	10//99-12//99
Light or Delivery Service	Bridgeport PMSA, CT	S	12.22 MW	12.02 AW	25410 AAW	CTBLS	10//99-12//99
Light or Delivery Service	Danbury PMSA, CT	S	12.98 MW	12.18 AW	26990 AAW	CTBLS	10//99-12//99
Light or Delivery Service	Hartford MSA, CT	S	12.36 MW	11.75 AW	25710 AAW	CTBLS	10//99-12//99
Light or Delivery Service	New Haven-Meriden PMSA, CT	S	12.40 MW	11.78 AW	25780 AAW	CTBLS	10//99-12//99

AAW	Average annual wage	AOH	Average offered, high	ASH	Average starting, high	H	Hourly
AE	Average entry wage	AOL	Average offered, low	ASL	Average starting, low	HI	Highest wage paid
AEX	Average experienced wage	APH	Average pay, high range	AW	Average wage paid	HR	High end range
AO	Average offered	APL	Average pay, low range	FQ	First quartile wage	LR	Low end range

M	Monthly	S	Special: hourly and annual
MTC	Median total compensation	TQ	Third quartile wage
MW	Median wage paid	W	Weekly
SQ	Second quartile wage	Y	Yearly

Occupation/Type/Industry	Location	Per	Low	Mid	High	Source	Date
Truck Driver							
Light or Delivery Service	New London-Norwich MSA, CT-RI	S	12.91 MW	12.10 AW	26850 AAW	CTBLS	10//99-12//99
Light or Delivery Service	Stamford-Norwalk PMSA, CT	S	10.78 MW	10.80 AW	22430 AAW	CTBLS	10//99-12//99
Light or Delivery Service	Waterbury PMSA, CT	S	11.72 MW	11.39 AW	24370 AAW	CTBLS	10//99-12//99
Light or Delivery Service	Delaware	S	13.71 MW	13.57 AW	28220 AAW	DEBLS	10//99-12//99
Light or Delivery Service	Dover MSA, DE	S	9.77 MW	8.95 AW	20310 AAW	DEBLS	10//99-12//99
Light or Delivery Service	Wilmington-Newark PMSA, DE-MD	S	14.43 MW	15.16 AW	30000 AAW	DEBLS	10//99-12//99
Light or Delivery Service	District of Columbia	S	9.36 MW	11.69 AW	24310 AAW	DCBLS	10//99-12//99
Light or Delivery Service	Washington PMSA, DC-MD-VA-WV	S	11.47 MW	10.13 AW	23850 AAW	DCBLS	10//99-12//99
Light or Delivery Service	Florida	S	9.79 MW	10.93 AW	22730 AAW	FLBLS	10//99-12//99
Light or Delivery Service	Daytona Beach MSA, FL	S	8.31 MW	8.15 AW	17290 AAW	FLBLS	10//99-12//99
Light or Delivery Service	Fort Lauderdale PMSA, FL	S	11.12 MW	10.92 AW	23120 AAW	FLBLS	10//99-12//99
Light or Delivery Service	Fort Myers-Cape Coral MSA, FL	S	10.73 MW	9.79 AW	22320 AAW	FLBLS	10//99-12//99
Light or Delivery Service	Fort Pierce-Port St. Lucie MSA, FL	S	12.25 MW	9.26 AW	25480 AAW	FLBLS	10//99-12//99
Light or Delivery Service	Fort Walton Beach MSA, FL	S	9.91 MW	8.66 AW	20620 AAW	FLBLS	10//99-12//99
Light or Delivery Service	Gainesville MSA, FL	S	11.06 MW	8.56 AW	22990 AAW	FLBLS	10//99-12//99
Light or Delivery Service	Jacksonville MSA, FL	S	11.93 MW	10.54 AW	24820 AAW	FLBLS	10//99-12//99
Light or Delivery Service	Lakeland-Winter Haven MSA, FL	S	9.27 MW	8.99 AW	19270 AAW	FLBLS	10//99-12//99
Light or Delivery Service	Melbourne-Titusville-Palm Bay MSA, FL	S	9.21 MW	8.78 AW	19160 AAW	FLBLS	10//99-12//99
Light or Delivery Service	Miami PMSA, FL	S	10.93 MW	9.16 AW	22730 AAW	FLBLS	10//99-12//99
Light or Delivery Service	Naples MSA, FL	S	10.78 MW	10.31 AW	22410 AAW	FLBLS	10//99-12//99
Light or Delivery Service	Ocala MSA, FL	S	8.73 MW	8.32 AW	18160 AAW	FLBLS	10//99-12//99
Light or Delivery Service	Orlando MSA, FL	S	11.49 MW	10.41 AW	23900 AAW	FLBLS	10//99-12//99
Light or Delivery Service	Panama City MSA, FL	S	8.19 MW	7.77 AW	17040 AAW	FLBLS	10//99-12//99
Light or Delivery Service	Pensacola MSA, FL	S	8.68 MW	7.49 AW	18060 AAW	FLBLS	10//99-12//99
Light or Delivery Service	Punta Gorda MSA, FL	S	7.78 MW	7.54 AW	16190 AAW	FLBLS	10//99-12//99
Light or Delivery Service	Sarasota-Bradenton MSA, FL	S	10.19 MW	9.69 AW	21190 AAW	FLBLS	10//99-12//99
Light or Delivery Service	Tampa-St. Petersburg-Clearwater MSA, FL	S	11.81 MW	10.69 AW	24560 AAW	FLBLS	10//99-12//99
Light or Delivery Service	West Palm Beach-Boca Raton MSA, FL	S	9.85 MW	9.65 AW	20490 AAW	FLBLS	10//99-12//99
Light or Delivery Service	Georgia	S	10.23 MW	10.93 AW	22730 AAW	GABLS	10//99-12//99
Light or Delivery Service	Albany MSA, GA	S	9.17 MW	8.85 AW	19070 AAW	GABLS	10//99-12//99
Light or Delivery Service	Athens MSA, GA	S	9.45 MW	8.21 AW	19660 AAW	GABLS	10//99-12//99
Light or Delivery Service	Atlanta MSA, GA	S	12.32 MW	11.94 AW	25630 AAW	GABLS	10//99-12//99
Light or Delivery Service	Augusta-Aiken MSA, GA-SC	S	9.55 MW	8.70 AW	19870 AAW	GABLS	10//99-12//99
Light or Delivery Service	Columbus MSA, GA-AL	S	10.18 MW	9.14 AW	21180 AAW	GABLS	10//99-12//99
Light or Delivery Service	Macon MSA, GA	S	8.77 MW	8.56 AW	18250 AAW	GABLS	10//99-12//99
Light or Delivery Service	Savannah MSA, GA	S	9.26 MW	8.29 AW	19260 AAW	GABLS	10//99-12//99
Light or Delivery Service	Hawaii	S	9.61 MW	10.80 AW	22470 AAW	HIBLS	10//99-12//99
Light or Delivery Service	Honolulu MSA, HI	S	10.81 MW	10.07 AW	22480 AAW	HIBLS	10//99-12//99
Light or Delivery Service	Idaho	S	9.72 MW	10.65 AW	22160 AAW	IDBLS	10//99-12//99
Light or Delivery Service	Boise City MSA, ID	S	11.03 MW	10.01 AW	22940 AAW	IDBLS	10//99-12//99
Light or Delivery Service	Pocatello MSA, ID	S	9.64 MW	9.27 AW	20040 AAW	IDBLS	10//99-12//99
Light or Delivery Service	Illinois	S	11.7 MW	12.27 AW	25520 AAW	ILBLS	10//99-12//99
Light or Delivery Service	Bloomington-Normal MSA, IL	S	11.89 MW	11.22 AW	24740 AAW	ILBLS	10//99-12//99
Light or Delivery Service	Champaign-Urbana MSA, IL	S	12.77 MW	11.97 AW	26560 AAW	ILBLS	10//99-12//99
Light or Delivery Service	Chicago PMSA, IL	S	12.72 MW	12.04 AW	26460 AAW	ILBLS	10//99-12//99
Light or Delivery Service	Decatur MSA, IL	S	12.56 MW	12.12 AW	26110 AAW	ILBLS	10//99-12//99
Light or Delivery Service	Kankakee PMSA, IL	S	11.10 MW	11.51 AW	23090 AAW	ILBLS	10//99-12//99
Light or Delivery Service	Peoria-Pekin MSA, IL	S	10.88 MW	11.19 AW	22640 AAW	ILBLS	10//99-12//99
Light or Delivery Service	Rockford MSA, IL	S	11.23 MW	11.24 AW	23350 AAW	ILBLS	10//99-12//99
Light or Delivery Service	Springfield MSA, IL	S	14.63 MW	12.38 AW	30420 AAW	ILBLS	10//99-12//99
Light or Delivery Service	Indiana	S	10.57 MW	12.17 AW	25320 AAW	INBLS	10//99-12//99
Light or Delivery Service	Bloomington MSA, IN	S	9.83 MW	10.10 AW	20450 AAW	INBLS	10//99-12//99
Light or Delivery Service	Elkhart-Goshen MSA, IN	S	9.64 MW	9.73 AW	20060 AAW	INBLS	10//99-12//99
Light or Delivery Service	Evansville-Henderson MSA, IN-KY	S	8.24 MW	7.93 AW	17140 AAW	INBLS	10//99-12//99
Light or Delivery Service	Fort Wayne MSA, IN	S	9.64 MW	9.58 AW	20050 AAW	INBLS	10//99-12//99
Light or Delivery Service	Gary PMSA, IN	S	12.16 MW	11.72 AW	25280 AAW	INBLS	10//99-12//99
Light or Delivery Service	Indianapolis MSA, IN	S	14.14 MW	12.59 AW	29400 AAW	INBLS	10//99-12//99
Light or Delivery Service	Kokomo MSA, IN	S	7.92 MW	7.95 AW	16460 AAW	INBLS	10//99-12//99
Light or Delivery Service	Lafayette MSA, IN	S	8.71 MW	8.16 AW	18110 AAW	INBLS	10//99-12//99
Light or Delivery Service	Muncie MSA, IN	S	11.75 MW	10.42 AW	24440 AAW	INBLS	10//99-12//99
Light or Delivery Service	South Bend MSA, IN	S	13.14 MW	10.84 AW	27330 AAW	INBLS	10//99-12//99

AAW	Average annual wage	AOH	Average offered, high	ASH	Average starting, high
AE	Average entry wage	AOL	Average offered, low	ASL	Average starting, low
AEX	Average experienced wage	APH	Average pay, high range	AW	Average wage paid
AO	Average offered	APL	Average pay, low range	FQ	First quartile wage

H	Hourly	M	Monthly
HI	Highest wage paid	MTC	Median total compensation
HR	High end range	MW	Median wage paid
LR	Low end range	SQ	Second quartile wage

S	Special: hourly and annual
TQ	Third quartile wage
W	Weekly
Y	Yearly

Occupation/Type/Industry	Location	Per	Low	Mid	High	Source	Date
Truck Driver							
Light or Delivery Service	Terre Haute MSA, IN	S	8.22 MW	8.30 AW	17100 AAW	INBLS	10//99-12//99
Light or Delivery Service	Iowa	S	10.64 MW	11.93 AW	24810 AAW	IABLS	10//99-12//99
Light or Delivery Service	Cedar Rapids MSA, IA	S	10.31 MW	10.42 AW	21450 AAW	IABLS	10//99-12//99
Light or Delivery Service	Davenport-Moline-Rock Island MSA, IA-IL	S	12.77 MW	12.25 AW	26560 AAW	IABLS	10//99-12//99
Light or Delivery Service	Des Moines MSA, IA	S	11.69 MW	11.49 AW	24310 AAW	IABLS	10//99-12//99
Light or Delivery Service	Dubuque MSA, IA	S	11.12 MW	11.31 AW	23120 AAW	IABLS	10//99-12//99
Light or Delivery Service	Iowa City MSA, IA	S	17.23 MW	21.51 AW	35840 AAW	IABLS	10//99-12//99
Light or Delivery Service	Sioux City MSA, IA-NE	S	11.64 MW	10.30 AW	24220 AAW	IABLS	10//99-12//99
Light or Delivery Service	Waterloo-Cedar Falls MSA, IA	S	12.06 MW	10.12 AW	25090 AAW	IABLS	10//99-12//99
Light or Delivery Service	Kansas	S	8.32 MW	10.08 AW	20980 AAW	KSBLS	10//99-12//99
Light or Delivery Service	Lawrence MSA, KS	S	6.62 MW	6.20 AW	13760 AAW	KSBLS	10//99-12//99
Light or Delivery Service	Topeka MSA, KS	S	8.52 MW	6.37 AW	17710 AAW	KSBLS	10//99-12//99
Light or Delivery Service	Wichita MSA, KS	S	10.55 MW	7.18 AW	21940 AAW	KSBLS	10//99-12//99
Light or Delivery Service	Kentucky	S	8.85 MW	9.58 AW	19920 AAW	KYBLS	10//99-12//99
Light or Delivery Service	Lexington MSA, KY	S	10.19 MW	9.65 AW	21190 AAW	KYBLS	10//99-12//99
Light or Delivery Service	Louisville MSA, KY-IN	S	10.45 MW	9.94 AW	21740 AAW	KYBLS	10//99-12//99
Light or Delivery Service	Owensboro MSA, KY	S	7.98 MW	7.22 AW	16600 AAW	KYBLS	10//99-12//99
Light or Delivery Service	Louisiana	S	9.71 MW	10.69 AW	22240 AAW	LABLS	10//99-12//99
Light or Delivery Service	Alexandria MSA, LA	S	9.32 MW	8.91 AW	19390 AAW	LABLS	10//99-12//99
Light or Delivery Service	Baton Rouge MSA, LA	S	11.61 MW	9.79 AW	24150 AAW	LABLS	10//99-12//99
Light or Delivery Service	Houma MSA, LA	S	9.90 MW	8.29 AW	20590 AAW	LABLS	10//99-12//99
Light or Delivery Service	Lafayette MSA, LA	S	9.14 MW	8.88 AW	19020 AAW	LABLS	10//99-12//99
Light or Delivery Service	Lake Charles MSA, LA	S	9.71 MW	9.07 AW	20190 AAW	LABLS	10//99-12//99
Light or Delivery Service	Monroe MSA, LA	S	10.33 MW	9.98 AW	21480 AAW	LABLS	10//99-12//99
Light or Delivery Service	New Orleans MSA, LA	S	11.63 MW	11.03 AW	24200 AAW	LABLS	10//99-12//99
Light or Delivery Service	Shreveport-Bossier City MSA, LA	S	10.66 MW	10.51 AW	22180 AAW	LABLS	10//99-12//99
Light or Delivery Service	Maine	S	9.3 MW	9.86 AW	20510 AAW	MEBLS	10//99-12//99
Light or Delivery Service	Bangor MSA, ME	S	8.73 MW	8.51 AW	18160 AAW	MEBLS	10//99-12//99
Light or Delivery Service	Lewiston-Auburn MSA, ME	S	9.12 MW	9.24 AW	18960 AAW	MEBLS	10//99-12//99
Light or Delivery Service	Portland MSA, ME	S	11.28 MW	11.12 AW	23460 AAW	MEBLS	10//99-12//99
Light or Delivery Service	Maryland	S	11.08 MW	12.52 AW	26040 AAW	MDBLS	10//99-12//99
Light or Delivery Service	Baltimore PMSA, MD	S	12.28 MW	10.62 AW	25540 AAW	MDBLS	10//99-12//99
Light or Delivery Service	Cumberland MSA, MD-WV	S	9.62 MW	8.55 AW	20010 AAW	MDBLS	10//99-12//99
Light or Delivery Service	Hagerstown PMSA, MD	S	9.79 MW	9.71 AW	20370 AAW	MDBLS	10//99-12//99
Light or Delivery Service	Massachusetts	S	12.19 MW	12.82 AW	26670 AAW	MABLS	10//99-12//99
Light or Delivery Service	Barnstable-Yarmouth MSA, MA	S	11.32 MW	10.11 AW	23550 AAW	MABLS	10//99-12//99
Light or Delivery Service	Boston PMSA, MA-NH	S	13.82 MW	13.09 AW	28740 AAW	MABLS	10//99-12//99
Light or Delivery Service	Brockton PMSA, MA	S	11.57 MW	11.65 AW	24070 AAW	MABLS	10//99-12//99
Light or Delivery Service	Fitchburg-Leominster PMSA, MA	S	13.22 MW	11.60 AW	27500 AAW	MABLS	10//99-12//99
Light or Delivery Service	Lawrence PMSA, MA-NH	S	9.43 MW	8.96 AW	19620 AAW	MABLS	10//99-12//99
Light or Delivery Service	Lowell PMSA, MA-NH	S	10.60 MW	10.21 AW	22050 AAW	MABLS	10//99-12//99
Light or Delivery Service	New Bedford PMSA, MA	S	10.99 MW	11.32 AW	22850 AAW	MABLS	10//99-12//99
Light or Delivery Service	Pittsfield MSA, MA	S	9.20 MW	8.13 AW	19140 AAW	MABLS	10//99-12//99
Light or Delivery Service	Springfield MSA, MA	S	10.64 MW	10.23 AW	22130 AAW	MABLS	10//99-12//99
Light or Delivery Service	Worcester PMSA, MA-CT	S	12.12 MW	11.35 AW	25210 AAW	MABLS	10//99-12//99
Light or Delivery Service	Michigan	S	10.52 MW	11.86 AW	24680 AAW	MIBLS	10//99-12//99
Light or Delivery Service	Ann Arbor PMSA, MI	S	12.40 MW	11.64 AW	25790 AAW	MIBLS	10//99-12//99
Light or Delivery Service	Benton Harbor MSA, MI	S	9.59 MW	9.62 AW	19960 AAW	MIBLS	10//99-12//99
Light or Delivery Service	Detroit PMSA, MI	S	12.16 MW	10.51 AW	25290 AAW	MIBLS	10//99-12//99
Light or Delivery Service	Flint PMSA, MI	S	10.88 MW	9.00 AW	22620 AAW	MIBLS	10//99-12//99
Light or Delivery Service	Grand Rapids-Muskegon-Holland MSA, MI	S	12.15 MW	11.44 AW	25280 AAW	MIBLS	10//99-12//99
Light or Delivery Service	Jackson MSA, MI	S	10.62 MW	11.08 AW	22090 AAW	MIBLS	10//99-12//99
Light or Delivery Service	Kalamazoo-Battle Creek MSA, MI	S	10.76 MW	9.73 AW	22370 AAW	MIBLS	10//99-12//99
Light or Delivery Service	Lansing-East Lansing MSA, MI	S	13.29 MW	13.08 AW	27650 AAW	MIBLS	10//99-12//99
Light or Delivery Service	Saginaw-Bay City-Midland MSA, MI	S	12.20 MW	10.45 AW	25380 AAW	MIBLS	10//99-12//99
Light or Delivery Service	Minnesota	S	11.74 MW	12.99 AW	27020 AAW	MNBLS	10//99-12//99
Light or Delivery Service	Duluth-Superior MSA, MN-WI	S	9.37 MW	8.83 AW	19480 AAW	MNBLS	10//99-12//99
Light or Delivery Service	Minneapolis-St. Paul MSA, MN-WI	S	13.23 MW	12.13 AW	27530 AAW	MNBLS	10//99-12//99
Light or Delivery Service	Rochester MSA, MN	S	10.37 MW	10.31 AW	21560 AAW	MNBLS	10//99-12//99
Light or Delivery Service	St. Cloud MSA, MN	S	10.28 MW	9.49 AW	21380 AAW	MNBLS	10//99-12//99
Light or Delivery Service	Mississippi	S	9.58 MW	12.43 AW	25850 AAW	MSBLS	10//99-12//99
Light or Delivery Service	Biloxi-Gulfport-Pascagoula MSA, MS	S	9.98 MW	7.98 AW	20750 AAW	MSBLS	10//99-12//99

AAW Average annual wage	**AOH** Average offered, high	**ASH** Average starting, high	**H** Hourly	**M** Monthly	**S** Special: hourly and annual
AE Average entry wage	**AOL** Average offered, low	**ASL** Average starting, low	**HI** Highest wage paid	**MTC** Median total compensation	**TQ** Third quartile wage
AEX Average experienced wage	**APH** Average pay, high range	**AW** Average wage paid	**HR** High end range	**MW** Median wage paid	**W** Weekly
AO Average offered	**APL** Average pay, low range	**FQ** First quartile wage	**LR** Low end range	**SQ** Second quartile wage	**Y** Yearly

Truck Driver

Occupation/Type/Industry	Location	Per	Low	Mid	High	Source	Date
Truck Driver							
Light or Delivery Service	Hattiesburg MSA, MS	S	11.00 MW	10.42 AW	22890 AAW	MSBLS	10//99-12//99
Light or Delivery Service	Jackson MSA, MS	S	9.47 MW	9.48 AW	19700 AAW	MSBLS	10//99-12//99
Light or Delivery Service	Missouri	S	11.04 MW	12.57 AW	26150 AAW	MOBLS	10//99-12//99
Light or Delivery Service	Columbia MSA, MO	S	11.16 MW	8.23 AW	23220 AAW	MOBLS	10//99-12//99
Light or Delivery Service	Joplin MSA, MO	S	9.88 MW	8.89 AW	20540 AAW	MOBLS	10//99-12//99
Light or Delivery Service	Kansas City MSA, MO-KS	S	11.48 MW	11.47 AW	23890 AAW	MOBLS	10//99-12//99
Light or Delivery Service	St. Joseph MSA, MO	S	9.52 MW	9.32 AW	19810 AAW	MOBLS	10//99-12//99
Light or Delivery Service	St. Louis MSA, MO-IL	S	13.58 MW	12.36 AW	28260 AAW	MOBLS	10//99-12//99
Light or Delivery Service	Springfield MSA, MO	S	14.17 MW	11.84 AW	29480 AAW	MOBLS	10//99-12//99
Light or Delivery Service	Montana	S	8.21 MW	8.87 AW	18450 AAW	MTBLS	10//99-12//99
Light or Delivery Service	Billings MSA, MT	S	7.27 MW	7.30 AW	15110 AAW	MTBLS	10//99-12//99
Light or Delivery Service	Great Falls MSA, MT	S	10.54 MW	10.86 AW	21930 AAW	MTBLS	10//99-12//99
Light or Delivery Service	Missoula MSA, MT	S	9.23 MW	8.57 AW	19200 AAW	MTBLS	10//99-12//99
Light or Delivery Service	Nebraska	S	9.21 MW	10.32 AW	21470 AAW	NEBLS	10//99-12//99
Light or Delivery Service	Lincoln MSA, NE	S	13.16 MW	10.35 AW	27370 AAW	NEBLS	10//99-12//99
Light or Delivery Service	Omaha MSA, NE-IA	S	10.85 MW	10.85 AW	22580 AAW	NEBLS	10//99-12//99
Light or Delivery Service	Nevada	S	9.06 MW	9.73 AW	20230 AAW	NVBLS	10//99-12//99
Light or Delivery Service	Las Vegas MSA, NV-AZ	S	9.21 MW	8.20 AW	19160 AAW	NVBLS	10//99-12//99
Light or Delivery Service	Reno MSA, NV	S	12.35 MW	11.34 AW	25700 AAW	NVBLS	10//99-12//99
Light or Delivery Service	New Hampshire	S	10.04 MW	11.52 AW	23960 AAW	NHBLS	10//99-12//99
Light or Delivery Service	Manchester PMSA, NH	S	14.07 MW	10.80 AW	29260 AAW	NHBLS	10//99-12//99
Light or Delivery Service	Nashua PMSA, NH	S	9.50 MW	9.37 AW	19760 AAW	NHBLS	10//99-12//99
Light or Delivery Service	Portsmouth-Rochester PMSA, NH-ME	S	11.33 MW	10.72 AW	23560 AAW	NHBLS	10//99-12//99
Light or Delivery Service	New Jersey	S	11.17 MW	11.93 AW	24820 AAW	NJBLS	10//99-12//99
Light or Delivery Service	Atlantic-Cape May PMSA, NJ	S	11.28 MW	11.13 AW	23460 AAW	NJBLS	10//99-12//99
Light or Delivery Service	Bergen-Passaic PMSA, NJ	S	11.85 MW	10.66 AW	24650 AAW	NJBLS	10//99-12//99
Light or Delivery Service	Jersey City PMSA, NJ	S	11.57 MW	10.40 AW	24080 AAW	NJBLS	10//99-12//99
Light or Delivery Service	Middlesex-Somerset-Hunterdon PMSA, NJ	S	11.46 MW	10.91 AW	23840 AAW	NJBLS	10//99-12//99
Light or Delivery Service	Monmouth-Ocean PMSA, NJ	S	11.27 MW	11.18 AW	23430 AAW	NJBLS	10//99-12//99
Light or Delivery Service	Newark PMSA, NJ	S	12.11 MW	10.93 AW	25180 AAW	NJBLS	10//99-12//99
Light or Delivery Service	Trenton PMSA, NJ	S	10.94 MW	11.10 AW	22760 AAW	NJBLS	10//99-12//99
Light or Delivery Service	Vineland-Millville-Bridgeton PMSA, NJ	S	9.75 MW	9.34 AW	20280 AAW	NJBLS	10//99-12//99
Light or Delivery Service	New Mexico	S	8.9 MW	9.34 AW	19430 AAW	NMBLS	10//99-12//99
Light or Delivery Service	Albuquerque MSA, NM	S	9.53 MW	9.07 AW	19820 AAW	NMBLS	10//99-12//99
Light or Delivery Service	Las Cruces MSA, NM	S	10.88 MW	8.46 AW	22630 AAW	NMBLS	10//99-12//99
Light or Delivery Service	Santa Fe MSA, NM	S	9.98 MW	9.72 AW	20760 AAW	NMBLS	10//99-12//99
Light or Delivery Service	New York	S	11.51 MW	12.27 AW	25520 AAW	NYBLS	10//99-12//99
Light or Delivery Service	Albany-Schenectady-Troy MSA, NY	S	12.26 MW	12.05 AW	25490 AAW	NYBLS	10//99-12//99
Light or Delivery Service	Binghamton MSA, NY	S	9.08 MW	8.08 AW	18890 AAW	NYBLS	10//99-12//99
Light or Delivery Service	Buffalo-Niagara Falls MSA, NY	S	10.29 MW	9.70 AW	21400 AAW	NYBLS	10//99-12//99
Light or Delivery Service	Elmira MSA, NY	S	11.86 MW	13.68 AW	24660 AAW	NYBLS	10//99-12//99
Light or Delivery Service	Glens Falls MSA, NY	S	9.40 MW	8.29 AW	19540 AAW	NYBLS	10//99-12//99
Light or Delivery Service	Jamestown MSA, NY	S	9.42 MW	8.93 AW	19600 AAW	NYBLS	10//99-12//99
Light or Delivery Service	Nassau-Suffolk PMSA, NY	S	14.84 MW	13.37 AW	30870 AAW	NYBLS	10//99-12//99
Light or Delivery Service	New York PMSA, NY	S	13.73 MW	13.23 AW	28560 AAW	NYBLS	10//99-12//99
Light or Delivery Service	Newburgh PMSA, NY-PA	S	11.87 MW	10.68 AW	24690 AAW	NYBLS	10//99-12//99
Light or Delivery Service	Rochester MSA, NY	S	7.54 MW	6.37 AW	15690 AAW	NYBLS	10//99-12//99
Light or Delivery Service	Syracuse MSA, NY	S	12.70 MW	12.35 AW	26410 AAW	NYBLS	10//99-12//99
Light or Delivery Service	Utica-Rome MSA, NY	S	8.04 MW	7.39 AW	16720 AAW	NYBLS	10//99-12//99
Light or Delivery Service	North Carolina	S	11.51 MW	12.32 AW	25630 AAW	NCBLS	10//99-12//99
Light or Delivery Service	Asheville MSA, NC	S	11.55 MW	11.67 AW	24020 AAW	NCBLS	10//99-12//99
Light or Delivery Service	Charlotte-Gastonia-Rock Hill MSA, NC-SC	S	13.66 MW	13.00 AW	28420 AAW	NCBLS	10//99-12//99
Light or Delivery Service	Greensboro--Winston-Salem--High Point MSA, NC	S	11.83 MW	11.86 AW	24600 AAW	NCBLS	10//99-12//99
Light or Delivery Service	Greenville MSA, NC	S	11.24 MW	9.07 AW	23390 AAW	NCBLS	10//99-12//99
Light or Delivery Service	Hickory-Morganton-Lenoir MSA, NC	S	13.00 MW	11.86 AW	27030 AAW	NCBLS	10//99-12//99
Light or Delivery Service	Jacksonville MSA, NC	S	7.44 MW	7.24 AW	15460 AAW	NCBLS	10//99-12//99
Light or Delivery Service	Raleigh-Durham-Chapel Hill MSA, NC	S	12.65 MW	10.89 AW	26320 AAW	NCBLS	10//99-12//99
Light or Delivery Service	Rocky Mount MSA, NC	S	11.15 MW	10.36 AW	23200 AAW	NCBLS	10//99-12//99
Light or Delivery Service	Wilmington MSA, NC	S	11.76 MW	11.74 AW	24450 AAW	NCBLS	10//99-12//99
Light or Delivery Service	North Dakota	S	10.47 MW	12.26 AW	25490 AAW	NDBLS	10//99-12//99
Light or Delivery Service	Grand Forks MSA, ND-MN	S	11.88 MW	9.41 AW	24700 AAW	NDBLS	10//99-12//99
Light or Delivery Service	Ohio	S	10.33 MW	11.51 AW	23940 AAW	OHBLS	10//99-12//99

AAW Average annual wage	**AOH** Average offered, high	**ASH** Average starting, high	**H** Hourly	**M** Monthly	**S** Special: hourly and annual
AE Average entry wage	**AOL** Average offered, low	**ASL** Average starting, low	**HI** Highest wage paid	**MTC** Median total compensation	**TQ** Third quartile wage
AEX Average experienced wage	**APH** Average pay, high range	**AW** Average wage paid	**HR** High end range	**MW** Median wage paid	**W** Weekly
AO Average offered	**APL** Average pay, low range	**FQ** First quartile wage	**LR** Low end range	**SQ** Second quartile wage	**Y** Yearly

Occupation/Type/Industry	Location	Per	Low	Mid	High	Source	Date
Truck Driver							
Light or Delivery Service	Akron PMSA, OH	S	13.57 MW	12.35 AW	28230 AAW	OHBLS	10//99-12//99
Light or Delivery Service	Canton-Massillon MSA, OH	S	10.74 MW	9.64 AW	22340 AAW	OHBLS	10//99-12//99
Light or Delivery Service	Cincinnati PMSA, OH-KY-IN	S	12.23 MW	11.84 AW	25430 AAW	OHBLS	10//99-12//99
Light or Delivery Service	Cleveland-Lorain-Elyria PMSA, OH	S	12.77 MW	11.72 AW	26550 AAW	OHBLS	10//99-12//99
Light or Delivery Service	Columbus MSA, OH	S	11.58 MW	11.32 AW	24080 AAW	OHBLS	10//99-12//99
Light or Delivery Service	Dayton-Springfield MSA, OH	S	8.74 MW	6.86 AW	18170 AAW	OHBLS	10//99-12//99
Light or Delivery Service	Hamilton-Middletown PMSA, OH	S	12.94 MW	11.19 AW	26920 AAW	OHBLS	10//99-12//99
Light or Delivery Service	Lima MSA, OH	S	8.97 MW	8.38 AW	18650 AAW	OHBLS	10//99-12//99
Light or Delivery Service	Mansfield MSA, OH	S	9.66 MW	9.41 AW	20090 AAW	OHBLS	10//99-12//99
Light or Delivery Service	Steubenville-Weirton MSA, OH-WV	S	9.92 MW	8.40 AW	20630 AAW	OHBLS	10//99-12//99
Light or Delivery Service	Toledo MSA, OH	S	9.71 MW	9.53 AW	20190 AAW	OHBLS	10//99-12//99
Light or Delivery Service	Youngstown-Warren MSA, OH	S	10.38 MW	8.92 AW	21590 AAW	OHBLS	10//99-12//99
Light or Delivery Service	Oklahoma	S	8.15 MW	9.13 AW	18990 AAW	OKBLS	10//99-12//99
Light or Delivery Service	Enid MSA, OK	S	8.70 MW	8.12 AW	18090 AAW	OKBLS	10//99-12//99
Light or Delivery Service	Lawton MSA, OK	S	8.87 MW	7.54 AW	18450 AAW	OKBLS	10//99-12//99
Light or Delivery Service	Oklahoma City MSA, OK	S	9.04 MW	7.50 AW	18810 AAW	OKBLS	10//99-12//99
Light or Delivery Service	Tulsa MSA, OK	S	9.91 MW	9.52 AW	20610 AAW	OKBLS	10//99-12//99
Light or Delivery Service	Oregon	S	10.26 MW	10.77 AW	22400 AAW	ORBLS	10//99-12//99
Light or Delivery Service	Corvallis MSA, OR	S	9.80 MW	8.52 AW	20390 AAW	ORBLS	10//99-12//99
Light or Delivery Service	Eugene-Springfield MSA, OR	S	9.40 MW	8.94 AW	19540 AAW	ORBLS	10//99-12//99
Light or Delivery Service	Medford-Ashland MSA, OR	S	11.10 MW	9.62 AW	23080 AAW	ORBLS	10//99-12//99
Light or Delivery Service	Portland-Vancouver PMSA, OR-WA	S	11.05 MW	10.52 AW	22990 AAW	ORBLS	10//99-12//99
Light or Delivery Service	Salem PMSA, OR	S	8.47 MW	8.17 AW	17610 AAW	ORBLS	10//99-12//99
Light or Delivery Service	Pennsylvania	S	9.87 MW	11.46 AW	23840 AAW	PABLS	10//99-12//99
Light or Delivery Service	Allentown-Bethlehem-Easton MSA, PA	S	11.81 MW	10.52 AW	24560 AAW	PABLS	10//99-12//99
Light or Delivery Service	Altoona MSA, PA	S	9.43 MW	9.11 AW	19620 AAW	PABLS	10//99-12//99
Light or Delivery Service	Erie MSA, PA	S	9.33 MW	6.84 AW	19400 AAW	PABLS	10//99-12//99
Light or Delivery Service	Harrisburg-Lebanon-Carlisle MSA, PA	S	10.82 MW	9.72 AW	22500 AAW	PABLS	10//99-12//99
Light or Delivery Service	Johnstown MSA, PA	S	7.79 MW	7.15 AW	16190 AAW	PABLS	10//99-12//99
Light or Delivery Service	Lancaster MSA, PA	S	10.96 MW	10.29 AW	22800 AAW	PABLS	10//99-12//99
Light or Delivery Service	Philadelphia PMSA, PA-NJ	S	12.53 MW	11.22 AW	26060 AAW	PABLS	10//99-12//99
Light or Delivery Service	Pittsburgh MSA, PA	S	13.37 MW	10.68 AW	27810 AAW	PABLS	10//99-12//99
Light or Delivery Service	Reading MSA, PA	S	9.12 MW	8.47 AW	18960 AAW	PABLS	10//99-12//99
Light or Delivery Service	Scranton--Wilkes-Barre--Hazleton MSA, PA	S	9.36 MW	8.46 AW	19470 AAW	PABLS	10//99-12//99
Light or Delivery Service	Sharon MSA, PA	S	10.25 MW	9.80 AW	21320 AAW	PABLS	10//99-12//99
Light or Delivery Service	State College MSA, PA	S	8.83 MW	8.60 AW	18360 AAW	PABLS	10//99-12//99
Light or Delivery Service	Williamsport MSA, PA	S	10.94 MW	9.03 AW	22760 AAW	PABLS	10//99-12//99
Light or Delivery Service	York MSA, PA	S	9.46 MW	9.21 AW	19670 AAW	PABLS	10//99-12//99
Light or Delivery Service	Rhode Island	S	10.06 MW	11.00 AW	22880 AAW	RIBLS	10//99-12//99
Light or Delivery Service	Providence-Fall River-Warwick MSA, RI-MA	S	11.26 MW	10.40 AW	23420 AAW	RIBLS	10//99-12//99
Light or Delivery Service	South Carolina	S	9.81 MW	10.78 AW	22410 AAW	SCBLS	10//99-12//99
Light or Delivery Service	Charleston-North Charleston MSA, SC	S	10.49 MW	10.27 AW	21820 AAW	SCBLS	10//99-12//99
Light or Delivery Service	Columbia MSA, SC	S	12.06 MW	10.44 AW	25090 AAW	SCBLS	10//99-12//99
Light or Delivery Service	Florence MSA, SC	S	11.60 MW	11.64 AW	24130 AAW	SCBLS	10//99-12//99
Light or Delivery Service	Greenville-Spartanburg-Anderson MSA, SC	S	11.28 MW	10.37 AW	23470 AAW	SCBLS	10//99-12//99
Light or Delivery Service	Myrtle Beach MSA, SC	S	10.64 MW	10.01 AW	22130 AAW	SCBLS	10//99-12//99
Light or Delivery Service	Sumter MSA, SC	S	8.71 MW	8.28 AW	18120 AAW	SCBLS	10//99-12//99
Light or Delivery Service	South Dakota	S	9.48 MW	11.25 AW	23390 AAW	SDBLS	10//99-12//99
Light or Delivery Service	Sioux Falls MSA, SD	S	9.38 MW	8.77 AW	19500 AAW	SDBLS	10//99-12//99
Light or Delivery Service	Tennessee	S	9.98 MW	11.21 AW	23320 AAW	TNBLS	10//99-12//99
Light or Delivery Service	Chattanooga MSA, TN-GA	S	9.62 MW	9.70 AW	20000 AAW	TNBLS	10//99-12//99
Light or Delivery Service	Clarksville-Hopkinsville MSA, TN-KY	S	7.66 MW	7.20 AW	15930 AAW	TNBLS	10//99-12//99
Light or Delivery Service	Jackson MSA, TN	S	8.91 MW	9.00 AW	18530 AAW	TNBLS	10//99-12//99
Light or Delivery Service	Johnson City-Kingsport-Bristol MSA, TN-VA	S	10.16 MW	8.06 AW	21130 AAW	TNBLS	10//99-12//99
Light or Delivery Service	Knoxville MSA, TN	S	12.11 MW	11.41 AW	25200 AAW	TNBLS	10//99-12//99
Light or Delivery Service	Memphis MSA, TN-AR-MS	S	10.45 MW	9.32 AW	21740 AAW	MSBLS	10//99-12//99
Light or Delivery Service	Nashville MSA, TN	S	12.49 MW	10.44 AW	25990 AAW	TNBLS	10//99-12//99
Light or Delivery Service	Texas	S	9.47 MW	10.23 AW	21280 AAW	TXBLS	10//99-12//99
Light or Delivery Service	Abilene MSA, TX	S	12.15 MW	10.48 AW	25260 AAW	TXBLS	10//99-12//99

Occupation/Type/Industry	Location	Per	Low	Mid	High	Source	Date
Truck Driver							
Light or Delivery Service	Amarillo MSA, TX	s	10.63 MW	11.02 AW	22110 AAW	TXBLS	10//99-12//99
Light or Delivery Service	Austin-San Marcos MSA, TX	s	9.54 MW	9.27 AW	19840 AAW	TXBLS	10//99-12//99
Light or Delivery Service	Beaumont-Port Arthur MSA, TX	s	10.43 MW	8.04 AW	21690 AAW	TXBLS	10//99-12//99
Light or Delivery Service	Brazoria PMSA, TX	s	9.04 MW	8.68 AW	18790 AAW	TXBLS	10//99-12//99
Light or Delivery Service	Brownsville-Harlingen-San Benito MSA, TX	s	8.00 MW	7.40 AW	16640 AAW	TXBLS	10//99-12//99
Light or Delivery Service	Bryan-College Station MSA, TX	s	10.96 MW	11.26 AW	22800 AAW	TXBLS	10//99-12//99
Light or Delivery Service	Corpus Christi MSA, TX	s	8.61 MW	7.80 AW	17920 AAW	TXBLS	10//99-12//99
Light or Delivery Service	Dallas PMSA, TX	s	11.29 MW	10.99 AW	23480 AAW	TXBLS	10//99-12//99
Light or Delivery Service	El Paso MSA, TX	s	8.92 MW	7.76 AW	18540 AAW	TXBLS	10//99-12//99
Light or Delivery Service	Fort Worth-Arlington PMSA, TX	s	10.03 MW	9.81 AW	20860 AAW	TXBLS	10//99-12//99
Light or Delivery Service	Galveston-Texas City PMSA, TX	s	8.44 MW	8.09 AW	17560 AAW	TXBLS	10//99-12//99
Light or Delivery Service	Houston PMSA, TX	s	9.96 MW	9.34 AW	20720 AAW	TXBLS	10//99-12//99
Light or Delivery Service	Killeen-Temple MSA, TX	s	9.25 MW	8.66 AW	19230 AAW	TXBLS	10//99-12//99
Light or Delivery Service	Laredo MSA, TX	s	9.10 MW	8.76 AW	18940 AAW	TXBLS	10//99-12//99
Light or Delivery Service	Longview-Marshall MSA, TX	s	8.76 MW	8.22 AW	18210 AAW	TXBLS	10//99-12//99
Light or Delivery Service	Lubbock MSA, TX	s	8.98 MW	8.28 AW	18680 AAW	TXBLS	10//99-12//99
Light or Delivery Service	McAllen-Edinburg-Mission MSA, TX	s	8.81 MW	7.66 AW	18320 AAW	TXBLS	10//99-12//99
Light or Delivery Service	Odessa-Midland MSA, TX	s	9.99 MW	9.43 AW	20770 AAW	TXBLS	10//99-12//99
Light or Delivery Service	San Angelo MSA, TX	s	7.78 MW	7.42 AW	16170 AAW	TXBLS	10//99-12//99
Light or Delivery Service	San Antonio MSA, TX	s	9.68 MW	9.25 AW	20120 AAW	TXBLS	10//99-12//99
Light or Delivery Service	Sherman-Denison MSA, TX	s	8.07 MW	8.67 AW	16780 AAW	TXBLS	10//99-12//99
Light or Delivery Service	Texarkana MSA, TX-Texarkana, AR	s	9.17 MW	7.97 AW	19080 AAW	TXBLS	10//99-12//99
Light or Delivery Service	Tyler MSA, TX	s	12.15 MW	9.14 AW	25270 AAW	TXBLS	10//99-12//99
Light or Delivery Service	Victoria MSA, TX	s	8.32 MW	7.72 AW	17310 AAW	TXBLS	10//99-12//99
Light or Delivery Service	Waco MSA, TX	s	10.46 MW	9.15 AW	21760 AAW	TXBLS	10//99-12//99
Light or Delivery Service	Wichita Falls MSA, TX	s	11.08 MW	11.64 AW	23040 AAW	TXBLS	10//99-12//99
Light or Delivery Service	Utah	s	11.3 MW	11.57 AW	24060 AAW	UTBLS	10//99-12//99
Light or Delivery Service	Provo-Orem MSA, UT	s	9.71 MW	9.58 AW	20190 AAW	UTBLS	10//99-12//99
Light or Delivery Service	Salt Lake City-Ogden MSA, UT	s	12.05 MW	11.78 AW	25060 AAW	UTBLS	10//99-12//99
Light or Delivery Service	Vermont	s	8.74 MW	9.38 AW	19510 AAW	VTBLS	10//99-12//99
Light or Delivery Service	Burlington MSA, VT	s	9.22 MW	8.15 AW	19190 AAW	VTBLS	10//99-12//99
Light or Delivery Service	Virginia	s	9.44 MW	9.87 AW	20540 AAW	VABLS	10//99-12//99
Light or Delivery Service	Charlottesville MSA, VA	s	10.78 MW	10.32 AW	22420 AAW	VABLS	10//99-12//99
Light or Delivery Service	Danville MSA, VA	s	8.05 MW	7.71 AW	16740 AAW	VABLS	10//99-12//99
Light or Delivery Service	Lynchburg MSA, VA	s	11.07 MW	10.83 AW	23020 AAW	VABLS	10//99-12//99
Light or Delivery Service	Norfolk-Virginia Beach-Newport News MSA, VA-NC	s	9.14 MW	8.71 AW	19000 AAW	VABLS	10//99-12//99
Light or Delivery Service	Richmond-Petersburg MSA, VA	s	11.91 MW	11.79 AW	24770 AAW	VABLS	10//99-12//99
Light or Delivery Service	Roanoke MSA, VA	s	8.08 MW	6.44 AW	16810 AAW	VABLS	10//99-12//99
Light or Delivery Service	Washington	s	11.68 MW	12.01 AW	24980 AAW	WABLS	10//99-12//99
Light or Delivery Service	Bellingham MSA, WA	s	11.98 MW	11.90 AW	24910 AAW	WABLS	10//99-12//99
Light or Delivery Service	Bremerton PMSA, WA	s	12.20 MW	12.12 AW	25380 AAW	WABLS	10//99-12//99
Light or Delivery Service	Olympia PMSA, WA	s	10.48 MW	9.95 AW	21790 AAW	WABLS	10//99-12//99
Light or Delivery Service	Richland-Kennewick-Pasco MSA, WA	s	9.30 MW	8.85 AW	19350 AAW	WABLS	10//99-12//99
Light or Delivery Service	Seattle-Bellevue-Everett PMSA, WA	s	12.84 MW	12.50 AW	26710 AAW	WABLS	10//99-12//99
Light or Delivery Service	Spokane MSA, WA	s	9.40 MW	8.74 AW	19560 AAW	WABLS	10//99-12//99
Light or Delivery Service	Tacoma PMSA, WA	s	12.44 MW	12.07 AW	25880 AAW	WABLS	10//99-12//99
Light or Delivery Service	Yakima MSA, WA	s	11.00 MW	11.35 AW	22880 AAW	WABLS	10//99-12//99
Light or Delivery Service	West Virginia	s	8.2 MW	9.58 AW	19920 AAW	WVBLS	10//99-12//99
Light or Delivery Service	Charleston MSA, WV	s	9.15 MW	7.73 AW	19030 AAW	WVBLS	10//99-12//99
Light or Delivery Service	Huntington-Ashland MSA, WV-KY-OH	s	8.09 MW	7.42 AW	16830 AAW	WVBLS	10//99-12//99
Light or Delivery Service	Parkersburg-Marietta MSA, WV-OH	s	10.52 MW	8.50 AW	21870 AAW	WVBLS	10//99-12//99
Light or Delivery Service	Wheeling MSA, WV-OH	s	10.46 MW	8.39 AW	21750 AAW	WVBLS	10//99-12//99
Light or Delivery Service	Wisconsin	s	9.45 MW	9.87 AW	20530 AAW	WIBLS	10//99-12//99
Light or Delivery Service	Appleton-Oshkosh-Neenah MSA, WI	s	9.23 MW	9.17 AW	19200 AAW	WIBLS	10//99-12//99
Light or Delivery Service	Eau Claire MSA, WI	s	11.31 MW	11.07 AW	23530 AAW	WIBLS	10//99-12//99

AAW Average annual wage	**AOH** Average offered, high	**ASH** Average starting, high	**H** Hourly	**M** Monthly	**S** Special: hourly and annual
AE Average entry wage	**AOL** Average offered, low	**ASL** Average starting, low	**HI** Highest wage paid	**MTC** Median total compensation	**TQ** Third quartile wage
AEX Average experienced wage	**APH** Average pay, high range	**AW** Average wage paid	**HR** High end range	**MW** Median wage paid	**W** Weekly
AO Average offered	**APL** Average pay, low range	**FQ** First quartile wage	**LR** Low end range	**SQ** Second quartile wage	**Y** Yearly

Occupation/Type/Industry	Location	Per	Low	Mid	High	Source	Date
Truck Driver							
Light or Delivery Service	Green Bay MSA, WI	S	7.67 MW	6.30 AW	15950 AAW	WIBLS	10//99-12//99
Light or Delivery Service	Janesville-Beloit MSA, WI	S	9.70 MW	9.02 AW	20170 AAW	WIBLS	10//99-12//99
Light or Delivery Service	Kenosha PMSA, WI	S	9.75 MW	9.62 AW	20280 AAW	WIBLS	10//99-12//99
Light or Delivery Service	La Crosse MSA, WI-MN	S	10.32 MW	9.89 AW	21470 AAW	WIBLS	10//99-12//99
Light or Delivery Service	Madison MSA, WI	S	10.45 MW	10.39 AW	21740 AAW	WIBLS	10//99-12//99
Light or Delivery Service	Milwaukee-Waukesha PMSA, WI	S	10.51 MW	9.89 AW	21860 AAW	WIBLS	10//99-12//99
Light or Delivery Service	Racine PMSA, WI	S	8.95 MW	8.20 AW	18610 AAW	WIBLS	10//99-12//99
Light or Delivery Service	Sheboygan MSA, WI	S	9.98 MW	9.81 AW	20760 AAW	WIBLS	10//99-12//99
Light or Delivery Service	Wausau MSA, WI	S	9.09 MW	8.33 AW	18900 AAW	WIBLS	10//99-12//99
Light or Delivery Service	Wyoming	S	8.15 MW	9.41 AW	19580 AAW	WYBLS	10//99-12//99
Light or Delivery Service	Casper MSA, WY	S	8.56 MW	8.61 AW	17810 AAW	WYBLS	10//99-12//99
Light or Delivery Service	Cheyenne MSA, WY	S	7.17 MW	6.42 AW	14910 AAW	WYBLS	10//99-12//99
Light or Delivery Service	Puerto Rico	S	6.36 MW	7.90 AW	16440 AAW	PRBLS	10//99-12//99
Light or Delivery Service	Aguadilla MSA, PR	S	5.86 MW	6.00 AW	12190 AAW	PRBLS	10//99-12//99
Light or Delivery Service	Arecibo PMSA, PR	S	5.95 MW	6.05 AW	12370 AAW	PRBLS	10//99-12//99
Light or Delivery Service	Caguas PMSA, PR	S	7.82 MW	6.18 AW	16270 AAW	PRBLS	10//99-12//99
Light or Delivery Service	Mayaguez MSA, PR	S	11.55 MW	6.45 AW	24030 AAW	PRBLS	10//99-12//99
Light or Delivery Service	Ponce MSA, PR	S	6.07 MW	6.10 AW	12630 AAW	PRBLS	10//99-12//99
Light or Delivery Service	San Juan-Bayamon PMSA, PR	S	8.17 MW	6.46 AW	16990 AAW	PRBLS	10//99-12//99
Light or Delivery Service	Virgin Islands	S	9.18 MW	9.16 AW	19050 AAW	VIBLS	10//99-12//99
Light or Delivery Service	Guam	S	7.55 MW	8.06 AW	16750 AAW	GUBLS	10//99-12//99
Tractor Trailer	Los Angeles County, CA	Y		33502 AW		LABJ	1999
TV News Anchor	United States	Y	9000 APL	44000 MW	800000 APH	AMJOUR	10//98-12//98
TV News Reporter	United States	Y	14000 APL	24000 MW	130000 APH	AMJOUR	10//98-12//98
TV Sports Anchor	United States	Y	15000 APL	33000 MW	260000 APH	AMJOUR	10//98-12//98
TV Sports Reporter	United States	Y	7000 APL	22000 MW	153000 APH	AMJOUR	10//98-12//98
Ultrasound Technician							
Hospital	Florida	H			21.54 HI	BJTAMP	2000
Medical Doctor's Office	United States	H		19.84 AEX		MEDEC	2000
Umpire, Referee, and Other Sports Official	California	Y		25610 AAW		CABLS	10//99-12//99
	Colorado	Y		19890 AAW		COBLS	10//99-12//99
	Denver PMSA, CO	Y		19010 AAW		COBLS	10//99-12//99
	Connecticut	Y		22820 AAW		CTBLS	10//99-12//99
	Hartford MSA, CT	Y		22820 AAW		CTBLS	10//99-12//99
	Washington PMSA, DC-MD-VA-WV	Y		22060 AAW		DCBLS	10//99-12//99
	Florida	Y		19850 AAW		FLBLS	10//99-12//99
	Orlando MSA, FL	Y		19040 AAW		FLBLS	10//99-12//99
	Indiana	Y		16110 AAW		INBLS	10//99-12//99
	Kansas	Y		15550 AAW		KSBLS	10//99-12//99
	Kentucky	Y		28520 AAW		KYBLS	10//99-12//99
	Maryland	Y		22260 AAW		MDBLS	10//99-12//99
	Minnesota	Y		17060 AAW		MNBLS	10//99-12//99
	Missouri	Y		25260 AAW		MOBLS	10//99-12//99
	Kansas City MSA, MO-KS	Y		18800 AAW		MOBLS	10//99-12//99
	Montana	Y		12140 AAW		MTBLS	10//99-12//99
	New York	Y		25320 AAW		NYBLS	10//99-12//99
	New York PMSA, NY	Y		42050 AAW		NYBLS	10//99-12//99
	Ohio	Y		20140 AAW		OHBLS	10//99-12//99
	Philadelphia PMSA, PA-NJ	Y		15730 AAW		PABLS	10//99-12//99
	South Carolina	Y		19680 AAW		SCBLS	10//99-12//99
	Texas	Y		26070 AAW		TXBLS	10//99-12//99
	Virginia	Y		21280 AAW		VABLS	10//99-12//99
	Washington	Y		29050 AAW		WABLS	10//99-12//99
	West Virginia	Y		23450 AAW		WVBLS	10//99-12//99
	Wisconsin	Y		25280 AAW		WIBLS	10//99-12//99
UNIX System Administrator	Phoenix, AZ	Y		77571 AW		PBJI	2000
Information Technology	Atlanta, GA	Y		75851 AW		ATBUS	3//00
Upholsterer	Alabama	S	9.49 MW	9.56 AW	19890 AAW	ALBLS	10//99-12//99
	Birmingham MSA, AL	S	11.76 MW	11.89 AW	24460 AAW	ALBLS	10//99-12//99
	Mobile MSA, AL	S	8.11 MW	6.52 AW	16870 AAW	ALBLS	10//99-12//99
	Arizona	S	10.52 MW	10.61 AW	22060 AAW	AZBLS	10//99-12//99

AAW	Average annual wage	**AOH**	Average offered, high	**ASH**	Average starting, high	**H**	Hourly	**M** Monthly
AE	Average entry wage	**AOL**	Average offered, low	**ASL**	Average starting, low	**HI**	Highest wage paid	**MTC** Median total compensation
AEX	Average experienced wage	**APH**	Average pay, high range	**AW**	Average wage paid	**HR**	High end range	**MW** Median wage paid
AO	Average offered	**APL**	Average pay, low range	**FQ**	First quartile wage	**LR**	Low end range	**SQ** Second quartile wage

S	Special: hourly and annual
TQ	Third quartile wage
W	Weekly
Y	Yearly

Occupation/Type/Industry	Location	Per	Low	Mid	High	Source	Date
Upholsterer	Phoenix-Mesa MSA, AZ	S	10.23 MW	10.82 AW	21290 AAW	AZBLS	10//99-12//99
	Tucson MSA, AZ	S	15.03 MW	13.08 AW	31270 AAW	AZBLS	10//99-12//99
	Arkansas	S	8.8 MW	9.33 AW	19410 AAW	ARBLS	10//99-12//99
	Little Rock-North Little Rock MSA, AR	S	9.14 MW	8.25 AW	19010 AAW	ARBLS	10//99-12//99
	California	S	10.38 MW	10.92 AW	22710 AAW	CABLS	10//99-12//99
	Los Angeles-Long Beach PMSA, CA	S	10.45 MW	10.37 AW	21740 AAW	CABLS	10//99-12//99
	Modesto MSA, CA	S	8.07 MW	7.61 AW	16780 AAW	CABLS	10//99-12//99
	Oakland PMSA, CA	S	12.47 MW	11.39 AW	25950 AAW	CABLS	10//99-12//99
	Orange County PMSA, CA	S	11.25 MW	9.89 AW	23410 AAW	CABLS	10//99-12//99
	Riverside-San Bernardino PMSA, CA	S	10.57 MW	10.05 AW	21980 AAW	CABLS	10//99-12//99
	Sacramento PMSA, CA	S	9.69 MW	8.54 AW	20150 AAW	CABLS	10//99-12//99
	San Diego MSA, CA	S	10.05 MW	8.99 AW	20910 AAW	CABLS	10//99-12//99
	San Francisco PMSA, CA	S	12.94 MW	12.54 AW	26910 AAW	CABLS	10//99-12//99
	San Jose PMSA, CA	S	12.70 MW	11.16 AW	26420 AAW	CABLS	10//99-12//99
	Santa Rosa PMSA, CA	S	16.40 MW	18.17 AW	34110 AAW	CABLS	10//99-12//99
	Colorado	S	12.46 MW	12.78 AW	26590 AAW	COBLS	10//99-12//99
	Denver PMSA, CO	S	12.90 MW	12.77 AW	26840 AAW	COBLS	10//99-12//99
	Connecticut	S	11.23 MW	12.37 AW	25740 AAW	CTBLS	10//99-12//99
	Bridgeport PMSA, CT	S	15.82 MW	14.92 AW	32900 AAW	CTBLS	10//99-12//99
	Hartford MSA, CT	S	11.76 MW	11.51 AW	24470 AAW	CTBLS	10//99-12//99
	New Haven-Meriden PMSA, CT	S	9.06 MW	9.00 AW	18840 AAW	CTBLS	10//99-12//99
	Stamford-Norwalk PMSA, CT	S	11.97 MW	11.14 AW	24900 AAW	CTBLS	10//99-12//99
	Washington PMSA, DC-MD-VA-WV	S	12.81 MW	13.09 AW	26640 AAW	DCBLS	10//99-12//99
	Florida	S	9.65 MW	10.29 AW	21410 AAW	FLBLS	10//99-12//99
	Fort Lauderdale PMSA, FL	S	11.11 MW	11.27 AW	23100 AAW	FLBLS	10//99-12//99
	Fort Myers-Cape Coral MSA, FL	S	9.46 MW	9.49 AW	19670 AAW	FLBLS	10//99-12//99
	Jacksonville MSA, FL	S	9.30 MW	7.90 AW	19340 AAW	FLBLS	10//99-12//99
	Lakeland-Winter Haven MSA, FL	S	9.08 MW	8.61 AW	18880 AAW	FLBLS	10//99-12//99
	Melbourne-Titusville-Palm Bay MSA, FL	S	9.97 MW	9.87 AW	20740 AAW	FLBLS	10//99-12//99
	Miami PMSA, FL	S	11.28 MW	11.05 AW	23460 AAW	FLBLS	10//99-12//99
	Orlando MSA, FL	S	10.39 MW	10.48 AW	21620 AAW	FLBLS	10//99-12//99
	Sarasota-Bradenton MSA, FL	S	10.81 MW	10.59 AW	22480 AAW	FLBLS	10//99-12//99
	Tampa-St. Petersburg-Clearwater MSA, FL	S	8.95 MW	8.38 AW	18620 AAW	FLBLS	10//99-12//99
	West Palm Beach-Boca Raton MSA, FL	S	16.19 MW	17.70 AW	33670 AAW	FLBLS	10//99-12//99
	Georgia	S	10.11 MW	10.36 AW	21550 AAW	GABLS	10//99-12//99
	Atlanta MSA, GA	S	10.82 MW	10.60 AW	22510 AAW	GABLS	10//99-12//99
	Macon MSA, GA	S	9.69 MW	10.41 AW	20160 AAW	GABLS	10//99-12//99
	Idaho	S	11.78 MW	11.98 AW	24910 AAW	IDBLS	10//99-12//99
	Boise City MSA, ID	S	12.32 MW	11.24 AW	25620 AAW	IDBLS	10//99-12//99
	Illinois	S	9.93 MW	10.87 AW	22610 AAW	ILBLS	10//99-12//99
	Chicago PMSA, IL	S	10.90 MW	9.42 AW	22670 AAW	ILBLS	10//99-12//99
	Peoria-Pekin MSA, IL	S	11.67 MW	10.89 AW	24270 AAW	ILBLS	10//99-12//99
	Indiana	S	10.47 MW	10.63 AW	22100 AAW	INBLS	10//99-12//99
	Elkhart-Goshen MSA, IN	S	10.47 MW	10.42 AW	21770 AAW	INBLS	10//99-12//99
	Fort Wayne MSA, IN	S	10.56 MW	9.90 AW	21970 AAW	INBLS	10//99-12//99
	Indianapolis MSA, IN	S	12.22 MW	11.89 AW	25410 AAW	INBLS	10//99-12//99
	Iowa	S	11.52 MW	11.92 AW	24790 AAW	IABLS	10//99-12//99
	Waterloo-Cedar Falls MSA, IA	S	12.65 MW	14.20 AW	26310 AAW	IABLS	10//99-12//99
	Kansas	S	10.47 MW	10.97 AW	22810 AAW	KSBLS	10//99-12//99
	Wichita MSA, KS	S	11.54 MW	10.72 AW	24010 AAW	KSBLS	10//99-12//99
	Kentucky	S	10.33 MW	11.12 AW	23120 AAW	KYBLS	10//99-12//99
	Lexington MSA, KY	S	8.98 MW	8.44 AW	18680 AAW	KYBLS	10//99-12//99
	Louisville MSA, KY-IN	S	10.79 MW	10.86 AW	22440 AAW	KYBLS	10//99-12//99
	Louisiana	S	9.16 MW	9.09 AW	18910 AAW	LABLS	10//99-12//99
	Lafayette MSA, LA	S	8.67 MW	6.25 AW	18030 AAW	LABLS	10//99-12//99
	New Orleans MSA, LA	S	9.73 MW	9.87 AW	20250 AAW	LABLS	10//99-12//99
	Shreveport-Bossier City MSA, LA	S	6.37 MW	6.14 AW	13250 AAW	LABLS	10//99-12//99
	Maine	S	12.23 MW	11.09 AW	23070 AAW	MEBLS	10//99-12//99
	Maryland	S	11.47 MW	11.70 AW	24340 AAW	MDBLS	10//99-12//99
	Baltimore PMSA, MD	S	9.33 MW	7.42 AW	19420 AAW	MDBLS	10//99-12//99
	Massachusetts	S	11.45 MW	12.04 AW	25050 AAW	MABLS	10//99-12//99

AAW Average annual wage	**AOH** Average offered, high	**ASH** Average starting, high	**H** Hourly	**M** Monthly	**S** Special: hourly and annual
AE Average entry wage	**AOL** Average offered, low	**ASL** Average starting, low	**HI** Highest wage paid	**MTC** Median total compensation	**TQ** Third quartile wage
AEX Average experienced wage	**APH** Average pay, high range	**AW** Average wage paid	**HR** High end range	**MW** Median wage paid	**W** Weekly
AO Average offered	**APL** Average pay, low range	**FQ** First quartile wage	**LR** Low end range	**SQ** Second quartile wage	**Y** Yearly

Occupation/Type/Industry	Location	Per	Low	Mid	High	Source	Date
Upholsterer	Boston PMSA, MA-NH	S	11.65 MW	11.60 AW	24230 AAW	MABLS	10//99-12//99
	Michigan	S	11.03 MW	11.49 AW	23900 AAW	MIBLS	10//99-12//99
	Detroit PMSA, MI	S	12.27 MW	12.14 AW	25530 AAW	MIBLS	10//99-12//99
	Grand Rapids-Muskegon- Holland MSA, MI	S	11.52 MW	11.64 AW	23950 AAW	MIBLS	10//99-12//99
	Minnesota	S	11.53 MW	12.35 AW	25690 AAW	MNBLS	10//99-12//99
	Minneapolis-St. Paul MSA, MN-WI	S	12.43 MW	11.52 AW	25850 AAW	MNBLS	10//99-12//99
	Mississippi	S	10.64 MW	10.72 AW	22300 AAW	MSBLS	10//99-12//99
	Missouri	S	11.22 MW	11.54 AW	24000 AAW	MOBLS	10//99-12//99
	Montana	S	8.73 MW	9.72 AW	20210 AAW	MTBLS	10//99-12//99
	Billings MSA, MT	S	8.37 MW	7.86 AW	17400 AAW	MTBLS	10//99-12//99
	Nebraska	S	9.45 MW	10.09 AW	20990 AAW	NEBLS	10//99-12//99
	Omaha MSA, NE-IA	S	9.04 MW	8.22 AW	18800 AAW	NEBLS	10//99-12//99
	Nevada	S	11.15 MW	12.08 AW	25130 AAW	NVBLS	10//99-12//99
	Las Vegas MSA, NV-AZ	S	11.93 MW	11.13 AW	24820 AAW	NVBLS	10//99-12//99
	Reno MSA, NV	S	12.11 MW	10.66 AW	25180 AAW	NVBLS	10//99-12//99
	New Hampshire	S	10.12 MW	10.10 AW	21000 AAW	NHBLS	10//99-12//99
	New Jersey	S	11.73 MW	12.12 AW	25220 AAW	NJBLS	10//99-12//99
	Bergen-Passaic PMSA, NJ	S	12.96 MW	12.50 AW	26970 AAW	NJBLS	10//99-12//99
	Middlesex-Somerset- Hunterdon PMSA, NJ	S	12.76 MW	11.80 AW	26550 AAW	NJBLS	10//99-12//99
	Newark PMSA, NJ	S	13.33 MW	13.54 AW	27720 AAW	NJBLS	10//99-12//99
	Trenton PMSA, NJ	S	10.67 MW	10.93 AW	22190 AAW	NJBLS	10//99-12//99
	New York	S	12.14 MW	12.96 AW	26950 AAW	NYBLS	10//99-12//99
	Nassau-Suffolk PMSA, NY	S	12.74 MW	13.22 AW	26500 AAW	NYBLS	10//99-12//99
	New York PMSA, NY	S	13.97 MW	13.91 AW	29050 AAW	NYBLS	10//99-12//99
	Rochester MSA, NY	S	11.69 MW	11.28 AW	24310 AAW	NYBLS	10//99-12//99
	North Carolina	S	13.63 MW	14.14 AW	29410 AAW	NCBLS	10//99-12//99
	Charlotte-Gastonia-Rock Hill MSA, NC-SC	S	11.76 MW	11.61 AW	24460 AAW	NCBLS	10//99-12//99
	Greensboro--Winston-Salem-- High Point MSA, NC	S	13.41 MW	12.92 AW	27890 AAW	NCBLS	10//99-12//99
	Hickory-Morganton-Lenoir MSA, NC	S	15.57 MW	15.07 AW	32390 AAW	NCBLS	10//99-12//99
	Raleigh-Durham-Chapel Hill MSA, NC	S	10.50 MW	10.24 AW	21840 AAW	NCBLS	10//99-12//99
	Ohio	S	8.44 MW	10.09 AW	20990 AAW	OHBLS	10//99-12//99
	Akron PMSA, OH	S	8.28 MW	7.96 AW	17230 AAW	OHBLS	10//99-12//99
	Canton-Massillon MSA, OH	S	7.39 MW	6.53 AW	15370 AAW	OHBLS	10//99-12//99
	Cincinnati PMSA, OH-KY-IN	S	10.15 MW	10.79 AW	21100 AAW	OHBLS	10//99-12//99
	Youngstown-Warren MSA, OH	S	11.48 MW	11.12 AW	23870 AAW	OHBLS	10//99-12//99
	Oklahoma	S	10.92 MW	11.34 AW	23590 AAW	OKBLS	10//99-12//99
	Oklahoma City MSA, OK	S	11.01 MW	11.15 AW	22900 AAW	OKBLS	10//99-12//99
	Tulsa MSA, OK	S	10.76 MW	10.53 AW	22380 AAW	OKBLS	10//99-12//99
	Oregon	S	11.25 MW	12.01 AW	24980 AAW	ORBLS	10//99-12//99
	Eugene-Springfield MSA, OR	S	11.20 MW	10.10 AW	23290 AAW	ORBLS	10//99-12//99
	Portland-Vancouver PMSA, OR-WA	S	12.20 MW	11.54 AW	25370 AAW	ORBLS	10//99-12//99
	Salem PMSA, OR	S	10.75 MW	11.31 AW	22370 AAW	ORBLS	10//99-12//99
	Pennsylvania	S	11.28 MW	11.66 AW	24250 AAW	PABLS	10//99-12//99
	Allentown-Bethlehem-Easton MSA, PA	S	11.41 MW	11.15 AW	23730 AAW	PABLS	10//99-12//99
	Erie MSA, PA	S	11.98 MW	11.75 AW	24910 AAW	PABLS	10//99-12//99
	Philadelphia PMSA, PA-NJ	S	11.30 MW	10.58 AW	23500 AAW	PABLS	10//99-12//99
	Pittsburgh MSA, PA	S	11.34 MW	11.57 AW	23580 AAW	PABLS	10//99-12//99
	Reading MSA, PA	S	10.18 MW	8.00 AW	21170 AAW	PABLS	10//99-12//99
	Scranton--Wilkes-Barre-- Hazleton MSA, PA	S	11.08 MW	10.84 AW	23050 AAW	PABLS	10//99-12//99
	Rhode Island	S	12.85 MW	12.59 AW	26190 AAW	RIBLS	10//99-12//99
	Providence-Fall River- Warwick MSA, RI-MA	S	12.64 MW	12.96 AW	26290 AAW	RIBLS	10//99-12//99
	South Carolina	S	8.24 MW	8.76 AW	18220 AAW	SCBLS	10//99-12//99
	Columbia MSA, SC	S	9.25 MW	8.91 AW	19240 AAW	SCBLS	10//99-12//99
	Greenville-Spartanburg- Anderson MSA, SC	S	11.06 MW	10.25 AW	23000 AAW	SCBLS	10//99-12//99
	Myrtle Beach MSA, SC	S	10.72 MW	11.35 AW	22290 AAW	SCBLS	10//99-12//99
	South Dakota	S	8.16 MW	9.28 AW	19300 AAW	SDBLS	10//99-12//99
	Rapid City MSA, SD	S	9.31 MW	8.29 AW	19360 AAW	SDBLS	10//99-12//99
	Tennessee	S	12.11 MW	11.38 AW	23660 AAW	TNBLS	10//99-12//99
	Chattanooga MSA, TN-GA	S	10.93 MW	11.43 AW	22730 AAW	TNBLS	10//99-12//99
	Knoxville MSA, TN	S	9.31 MW	9.06 AW	19360 AAW	TNBLS	10//99-12//99

AAW Average annual wage	**AOH** Average offered, high	**ASH** Average starting, high	**H** Hourly	**M** Monthly	**S** Special: hourly and annual
AE Average entry wage	**AOL** Average offered, low	**ASL** Average starting, low	**HI** Highest wage paid	**MTC** Median total compensation	**TQ** Third quartile wage
AEX Average experienced wage	**APH** Average pay, high range	**AW** Average wage paid	**HR** High end range	**MW** Median wage paid	**W** Weekly
AO Average offered	**APL** Average pay, low range	**FQ** First quartile wage	**LR** Low end range	**SQ** Second quartile wage	**Y** Yearly

Occupation/Type/Industry	Location	Per	Low	Mid	High	Source	Date
Upholsterer	Memphis MSA, TN-AR-MS	S	12.05 MW	12.09 AW	25070 AAW	MSBLS	10//99-12//99
	Texas	S	10.15 MW	10.60 AW	22050 AAW	TXBLS	10//99-12//99
	Austin-San Marcos MSA, TX	S	10.50 MW	10.29 AW	21850 AAW	TXBLS	10//99-12//99
	Corpus Christi MSA, TX	S	13.08 MW	12.44 AW	27200 AAW	TXBLS	10//99-12//99
	Dallas PMSA, TX	S	10.47 MW	9.89 AW	21790 AAW	TXBLS	10//99-12//99
	El Paso MSA, TX	S	7.70 MW	7.70 AW	16020 AAW	TXBLS	10//99-12//99
	Houston PMSA, TX	S	12.14 MW	12.68 AW	25250 AAW	TXBLS	10//99-12//99
	San Antonio MSA, TX	S	9.63 MW	9.51 AW	20030 AAW	TXBLS	10//99-12//99
	Waco MSA, TX	S	10.57 MW	10.50 AW	21980 AAW	TXBLS	10//99-12//99
	Utah	S	13.18 MW	12.84 AW	26700 AAW	UTBLS	10//99-12//99
	Salt Lake City-Ogden MSA, UT	S	11.50 MW	10.35 AW	23930 AAW	UTBLS	10//99-12//99
	Virginia	S	9.33 MW	9.79 AW	20360 AAW	VABLS	10//99-12//99
	Norfolk-Virginia Beach-Newport News MSA, VA-NC	S	8.83 MW	7.72 AW	18360 AAW	VABLS	10//99-12//99
	Richmond-Petersburg MSA, VA	S	10.58 MW	10.88 AW	22000 AAW	VABLS	10//99-12//99
	Washington	S	11.05 MW	11.15 AW	23200 AAW	WABLS	10//99-12//99
	Seattle-Bellevue-Everett PMSA, WA	S	10.83 MW	10.81 AW	22520 AAW	WABLS	10//99-12//99
	Tacoma PMSA, WA	S	13.13 MW	12.66 AW	27310 AAW	WABLS	10//99-12//99
	Wisconsin	S	11.28 MW	12.65 AW	26300 AAW	WIBLS	10//99-12//99
	Appleton-Oshkosh-Neenah MSA, WI	S	11.94 MW	11.61 AW	24830 AAW	WIBLS	10//99-12//99
	Madison MSA, WI	S	11.64 MW	9.90 AW	24210 AAW	WIBLS	10//99-12//99
	Milwaukee-Waukesha PMSA, WI	S	13.08 MW	11.33 AW	27210 AAW	WIBLS	10//99-12//99
	Puerto Rico	S	6.26 MW	6.73 AW	13990 AAW	PRBLS	10//99-12//99
	San Juan-Bayamon PMSA, PR	S	6.89 MW	6.33 AW	14330 AAW	PRBLS	10//99-12//99
UPS Package Handler	Louisville, KY	H		8.50 AW		LOUMAG	1999-2000
UPS Pilot							
Second Year	Louisville, KY	Y		55500 AW		LOUMAG	1999-2000
Urban and Regional Planner	Alabama	S	19.49 MW	20.22 AW	42060 AAW	ALBLS	10//99-12//99
	Birmingham MSA, AL	S	21.87 MW	20.79 AW	45490 AAW	ALBLS	10//99-12//99
	Alaska	S	23.74 MW	24.84 AW	51660 AAW	AKBLS	10//99-12//99
	Arizona	S	20.98 MW	22.94 AW	47710 AAW	AZBLS	10//99-12//99
	Flagstaff MSA, AZ-UT	S	23.08 MW	21.55 AW	48000 AAW	AZBLS	10//99-12//99
	Phoenix-Mesa MSA, AZ	S	25.76 MW	23.51 AW	53590 AAW	AZBLS	10//99-12//99
	Tucson MSA, AZ	S	17.82 MW	16.45 AW	37060 AAW	AZBLS	10//99-12//99
	Arkansas	S	15.01 MW	15.26 AW	31750 AAW	ARBLS	10//99-12//99
	California	S	25.23 MW	26.13 AW	54340 AAW	CABLS	10//99-12//99
	Bakersfield MSA, CA	S	26.08 MW	24.77 AW	54240 AAW	CABLS	10//99-12//99
	Fresno MSA, CA	S	21.75 MW	22.45 AW	45240 AAW	CABLS	10//99-12//99
	Los Angeles-Long Beach PMSA, CA	S	24.44 MW	24.16 AW	50830 AAW	CABLS	10//99-12//99
	Oakland PMSA, CA	S	31.07 MW	30.06 AW	64630 AAW	CABLS	10//99-12//99
	Orange County PMSA, CA	S	26.65 MW	26.90 AW	55430 AAW	CABLS	10//99-12//99
	Riverside-San Bernardino PMSA, CA	S	27.24 MW	25.43 AW	56650 AAW	CABLS	10//99-12//99
	San Diego MSA, CA	S	24.92 MW	24.92 AW	51840 AAW	CABLS	10//99-12//99
	San Francisco PMSA, CA	S	28.15 MW	26.58 AW	58540 AAW	CABLS	10//99-12//99
	San Jose PMSA, CA	S	23.39 MW	22.78 AW	48650 AAW	CABLS	10//99-12//99
	San Luis Obispo-Atascadero-Paso Robles MSA, CA	S	23.97 MW	24.14 AW	49850 AAW	CABLS	10//99-12//99
	Santa Barbara-Santa Maria-Lompoc MSA, CA	S	25.08 MW	24.55 AW	52160 AAW	CABLS	10//99-12//99
	Santa Rosa PMSA, CA	S	26.99 MW	25.95 AW	56150 AAW	CABLS	10//99-12//99
	Stockton-Lodi MSA, CA	S	22.27 MW	22.49 AW	46330 AAW	CABLS	10//99-12//99
	Vallejo-Fairfield-Napa PMSA, CA	S	29.08 MW	30.15 AW	60490 AAW	CABLS	10//99-12//99
	Ventura PMSA, CA	S	23.87 MW	22.68 AW	49640 AAW	CABLS	10//99-12//99
	Visalia-Tulare-Porterville MSA, CA	S	25.33 MW	24.44 AW	52700 AAW	CABLS	10//99-12//99
	Yolo PMSA, CA	S	23.07 MW	23.65 AW	47980 AAW	CABLS	10//99-12//99
	Colorado	S	22.13 MW	23.18 AW	48210 AAW	COBLS	10//99-12//99
	Boulder-Longmont PMSA, CO	S	23.47 MW	22.94 AW	48820 AAW	COBLS	10//99-12//99
	Colorado Springs MSA, CO	S	25.84 MW	22.67 AW	53750 AAW	COBLS	10//99-12//99
	Denver PMSA, CO	S	24.17 MW	23.46 AW	50270 AAW	COBLS	10//99-12//99

AAW Average annual wage	**AOH** Average offered, high	**ASH** Average starting, high	**H** Hourly	**M** Monthly	**S** Special: hourly and annual
AE Average entry wage	**AOL** Average offered, low	**ASL** Average starting, low	**HI** Highest wage paid	**MTC** Median total compensation	**TQ** Third quartile wage
AEX Average experienced wage	**APH** Average pay, high range	**AW** Average wage paid	**HR** High end range	**MW** Median wage paid	**W** Weekly
AO Average offered	**APL** Average pay, low range	**FQ** First quartile wage	**LR** Low end range	**SQ** Second quartile wage	**Y** Yearly

Occupation/Type/Industry	Location	Per	Low	Mid	High	Source	Date
Urban and Regional Planner	Fort Collins-Loveland MSA, CO	S	22.88 MW	20.52 AW	47580 AAW	COBLS	10//99-12//99
	Greeley PMSA, CO	S	21.35 MW	20.42 AW	44400 AAW	COBLS	10//99-12//99
	Connecticut	S	26.38 MW	26.47 AW	55050 AAW	CTBLS	10//99-12//99
	Delaware	S	21.69 MW	23.63 AW	49140 AAW	DEBLS	10//99-12//99
	Wilmington-Newark PMSA, DE-MD	S	25.80 MW	22.57 AW	53670 AAW	DEBLS	10//99-12//99
	District of Columbia	S	26.79 MW	28.02 AW	58290 AAW	DCBLS	10//99-12//99
	Washington PMSA, DC-MD-VA-WV	S	27.45 MW	26.45 AW	57100 AAW	DCBLS	10//99-12//99
	Florida	S	19.97 MW	21.12 AW	43940 AAW	FLBLS	10//99-12//99
	Daytona Beach MSA, FL	S	19.23 MW	18.52 AW	39990 AAW	FLBLS	10//99-12//99
	Fort Lauderdale PMSA, FL	S	21.99 MW	20.07 AW	45730 AAW	FLBLS	10//99-12//99
	Fort Myers-Cape Coral MSA, FL	S	18.46 MW	17.19 AW	38400 AAW	FLBLS	10//99-12//99
	Fort Pierce-Port St. Lucie MSA, FL	S	19.98 MW	20.77 AW	41560 AAW	FLBLS	10//99-12//99
	Gainesville MSA, FL	S	14.71 MW	13.65 AW	30600 AAW	FLBLS	10//99-12//99
	Jacksonville MSA, FL	S	18.70 MW	16.55 AW	38900 AAW	FLBLS	10//99-12//99
	Miami PMSA, FL	S	25.02 MW	23.49 AW	52040 AAW	FLBLS	10//99-12//99
	Naples MSA, FL	S	27.48 MW	24.64 AW	57150 AAW	FLBLS	10//99-12//99
	Orlando MSA, FL	S	21.59 MW	20.98 AW	44910 AAW	FLBLS	10//99-12//99
	Pensacola MSA, FL	S	15.12 MW	13.75 AW	31460 AAW	FLBLS	10//99-12//99
	Tallahassee MSA, FL	S	21.51 MW	20.49 AW	44740 AAW	FLBLS	10//99-12//99
	Tampa-St. Petersburg-Clearwater MSA, FL	S	23.62 MW	21.37 AW	49120 AAW	FLBLS	10//99-12//99
	West Palm Beach-Boca Raton MSA, FL	S	20.93 MW	21.20 AW	43540 AAW	FLBLS	10//99-12//99
	Georgia	S	17.84 MW	19.30 AW	40140 AAW	GABLS	10//99-12//99
	Atlanta MSA, GA	S	19.63 MW	18.42 AW	40820 AAW	GABLS	10//99-12//99
	Macon MSA, GA	S	22.36 MW	22.95 AW	46510 AAW	GABLS	10//99-12//99
	Savannah MSA, GA	S	17.82 MW	16.53 AW	37070 AAW	GABLS	10//99-12//99
	Hawaii	S	22.45 MW	22.85 AW	47520 AAW	HIBLS	10//99-12//99
	Idaho	S	17.98 MW	18.42 AW	38310 AAW	IDBLS	10//99-12//99
	Boise City MSA, ID	S	19.21 MW	18.55 AW	39950 AAW	IDBLS	10//99-12//99
	Illinois	S	21.23 MW	22.08 AW	45930 AAW	ILBLS	10//99-12//99
	Chicago PMSA, IL	S	23.07 MW	21.98 AW	47990 AAW	ILBLS	10//99-12//99
	Rockford MSA, IL	S	20.51 MW	19.80 AW	42650 AAW	ILBLS	10//99-12//99
	Indiana	S	14.19 MW	14.81 AW	30800 AAW	INBLS	10//99-12//99
	Fort Wayne MSA, IN	S	17.02 MW	18.28 AW	35400 AAW	INBLS	10//99-12//99
	Indianapolis MSA, IN	S	16.02 MW	15.17 AW	33320 AAW	INBLS	10//99-12//99
	Iowa	S	17.24 MW	17.28 AW	35940 AAW	IABLS	10//99-12//99
	Davenport-Moline-Rock Island MSA, IA-IL	S	17.78 MW	16.94 AW	36980 AAW	IABLS	10//99-12//99
	Kansas	S	15.83 MW	18.91 AW	39330 AAW	KSBLS	10//99-12//99
	Kentucky	S	14.8 MW	16.10 AW	33490 AAW	KYBLS	10//99-12//99
	Louisville MSA, KY-IN	S	17.64 MW	16.72 AW	36700 AAW	KYBLS	10//99-12//99
	Louisiana	S	16.78 MW	17.23 AW	35830 AAW	LABLS	10//99-12//99
	Baton Rouge MSA, LA	S	18.60 MW	16.95 AW	38690 AAW	LABLS	10//99-12//99
	New Orleans MSA, LA	S	18.71 MW	17.71 AW	38920 AAW	LABLS	10//99-12//99
	Shreveport-Bossier City MSA, LA	S	14.84 MW	14.41 AW	30860 AAW	LABLS	10//99-12//99
	Maine	S	18.88 MW	19.29 AW	40110 AAW	MEBLS	10//99-12//99
	Lewiston-Auburn MSA, ME	S	18.63 MW	17.79 AW	38750 AAW	MEBLS	10//99-12//99
	Portland MSA, ME	S	22.01 MW	20.26 AW	45770 AAW	MEBLS	10//99-12//99
	Maryland	S	20.92 MW	21.73 AW	45210 AAW	MDBLS	10//99-12//99
	Baltimore PMSA, MD	S	21.20 MW	20.58 AW	44100 AAW	MDBLS	10//99-12//99
	Massachusetts	S	22.42 MW	25.20 AW	52410 AAW	MABLS	10//99-12//99
	Brockton PMSA, MA	S	17.28 MW	17.26 AW	35940 AAW	MABLS	10//99-12//99
	Worcester PMSA, MA-CT	S	18.92 MW	18.38 AW	39360 AAW	MABLS	10//99-12//99
	Michigan	S	24.63 MW	26.97 AW	56100 AAW	MIBLS	10//99-12//99
	Ann Arbor PMSA, MI	S	24.92 MW	23.40 AW	51830 AAW	MIBLS	10//99-12//99
	Benton Harbor MSA, MI	S	29.49 MW	26.83 AW	61350 AAW	MIBLS	10//99-12//99
	Detroit PMSA, MI	S	28.28 MW	26.36 AW	58810 AAW	MIBLS	10//99-12//99
	Grand Rapids-Muskegon-Holland MSA, MI	S	22.32 MW	21.81 AW	46440 AAW	MIBLS	10//99-12//99
	Kalamazoo-Battle Creek MSA, MI	S	21.78 MW	20.13 AW	45300 AAW	MIBLS	10//99-12//99
	Minnesota	S	22.74 MW	23.71 AW	49310 AAW	MNBLS	10//99-12//99
	Duluth-Superior MSA, MN-WI	S	22.58 MW	21.22 AW	46960 AAW	MNBLS	10//99-12//99
	Minneapolis-St. Paul MSA, MN-WI	S	24.52 MW	23.45 AW	50990 AAW	MNBLS	10//99-12//99

AAW	Average annual wage	AOH	Average offered, high	ASH	Average starting, high	H	Hourly	M	Monthly	S	Special: hourly and annual
AE	Average entry wage	AOL	Average offered, low	ASL	Average starting, low	HI	Highest wage paid	MTC	Median total compensation	TQ	Third quartile wage
AEX	Average experienced wage	APH	Average pay, high range	AW	Average wage paid	HR	High end range	MW	Median wage paid	W	Weekly
AO	Average offered	APL	Average pay, low range	FQ	First quartile wage	LR	Low end range	SQ	Second quartile wage	Y	Yearly

Occupation/Type/Industry	Location	Per	Low	Mid	High	Source	Date
Urban and Regional Planner	Rochester MSA, MN	S	20.57 MW	19.93 AW	42790 AAW	MNBLS	10//99-12//99
	Mississippi	S	18.12 MW	18.44 AW	38340 AAW	MSBLS	10//99-12//99
	Biloxi-Gulfport-Pascagoula						
	MSA, MS	S	17.11 MW	16.71 AW	35590 AAW	MSBLS	10//99-12//99
	Missouri	S	18.49 MW	19.03 AW	39580 AAW	MOBLS	10//99-12//99
	Montana	S	14.51 MW	14.61 AW	30390 AAW	MTBLS	10//99-12//99
	Nebraska	S	21.76 MW	20.43 AW	42490 AAW	NEBLS	10//99-12//99
	Nevada	S	25.16 MW	25.36 AW	52750 AAW	NVBLS	10//99-12//99
	Las Vegas MSA, NV-AZ	S	25.26 MW	25.42 AW	52550 AAW	NVBLS	10//99-12//99
	Reno MSA, NV	S	24.82 MW	23.77 AW	51620 AAW	NVBLS	10//99-12//99
	New Hampshire	S	18.96 MW	19.64 AW	40850 AAW	NHBLS	10//99-12//99
	Portsmouth-Rochester PMSA,						
	NH-ME	S	19.36 MW	18.20 AW	40280 AAW	NHBLS	10//99-12//99
	New Jersey	S	21.46 MW	23.09 AW	48030 AAW	NJBLS	10//99-12//99
	Atlantic-Cape May PMSA, NJ	S	19.40 MW	18.69 AW	40340 AAW	NJBLS	10//99-12//99
	Bergen-Passaic PMSA, NJ	S	22.27 MW	19.66 AW	46320 AAW	NJBLS	10//99-12//99
	Middlesex-Somerset-						
	Hunterdon PMSA, NJ	S	21.80 MW	19.54 AW	45350 AAW	NJBLS	10//99-12//99
	Monmouth-Ocean PMSA, NJ	S	22.95 MW	21.03 AW	47740 AAW	NJBLS	10//99-12//99
	Newark PMSA, NJ	S	24.35 MW	22.83 AW	50650 AAW	NJBLS	10//99-12//99
	New Mexico	S	17.35 MW	18.34 AW	38160 AAW	NMBLS	10//99-12//99
	Albuquerque MSA, NM	S	21.12 MW	19.26 AW	43940 AAW	NMBLS	10//99-12//99
	New York	S	22.61 MW	22.42 AW	46640 AAW	NYBLS	10//99-12//99
	Albany-Schenectady-Troy						
	MSA, NY	S	21.92 MW	22.77 AW	45590 AAW	NYBLS	10//99-12//99
	Buffalo-Niagara Falls MSA,						
	NY	S	20.12 MW	18.45 AW	41840 AAW	NYBLS	10//99-12//99
	Nassau-Suffolk PMSA, NY	S	23.99 MW	25.00 AW	49900 AAW	NYBLS	10//99-12//99
	North Carolina	S	19.37 MW	20.90 AW	43470 AAW	NCBLS	10//99-12//99
	Charlotte-Gastonia-Rock Hill						
	MSA, NC-SC	S	20.75 MW	20.51 AW	43150 AAW	NCBLS	10//99-12//99
	Greensboro--Winston-Salem--						
	High Point MSA, NC	S	21.08 MW	20.10 AW	43850 AAW	NCBLS	10//99-12//99
	Raleigh-Durham-Chapel Hill						
	MSA, NC	S	22.20 MW	20.72 AW	46170 AAW	NCBLS	10//99-12//99
	North Dakota	S	15.82 MW	16.02 AW	33330 AAW	NDBLS	10//99-12//99
	Ohio	S	18.98 MW	20.32 AW	42270 AAW	OHBLS	10//99-12//99
	Akron PMSA, OH	S	20.61 MW	20.12 AW	42860 AAW	OHBLS	10//99-12//99
	Cleveland-Lorain-Elyria						
	PMSA, OH	S	20.23 MW	19.86 AW	42070 AAW	OHBLS	10//99-12//99
	Columbus MSA, OH	S	20.21 MW	19.66 AW	42040 AAW	OHBLS	10//99-12//99
	Dayton-Springfield MSA, OH	S	18.59 MW	17.60 AW	38670 AAW	OHBLS	10//99-12//99
	Toledo MSA, OH	S	18.48 MW	16.72 AW	38430 AAW	OHBLS	10//99-12//99
	Oklahoma	S	15.05 MW	17.36 AW	36100 AAW	OKBLS	10//99-12//99
	Oklahoma City MSA, OK	S	23.64 MW	23.83 AW	49180 AAW	OKBLS	10//99-12//99
	Oregon	S	21.86 MW	22.34 AW	46460 AAW	ORBLS	10//99-12//99
	Eugene-Springfield MSA, OR	S	23.48 MW	22.60 AW	48830 AAW	ORBLS	10//99-12//99
	Medford-Ashland MSA, OR	S	19.48 MW	18.66 AW	40530 AAW	ORBLS	10//99-12//99
	Portland-Vancouver PMSA,						
	OR-WA	S	23.27 MW	22.67 AW	48400 AAW	ORBLS	10//99-12//99
	Salem PMSA, OR	S	22.76 MW	23.12 AW	47340 AAW	ORBLS	10//99-12//99
	Pennsylvania	S	19.21 MW	20.40 AW	42430 AAW	PABLS	10//99-12//99
	Philadelphia PMSA, PA-NJ	S	22.18 MW	23.04 AW	46130 AAW	PABLS	10//99-12//99
	Pittsburgh MSA, PA	S	21.51 MW	20.80 AW	44750 AAW	PABLS	10//99-12//99
	Scranton--Wilkes-Barre--						
	Hazleton MSA, PA	S	18.07 MW	17.68 AW	37590 AAW	PABLS	10//99-12//99
	Rhode Island	S	23.4 MW	24.10 AW	50120 AAW	RIBLS	10//99-12//99
	Providence-Fall River-						
	Warwick MSA, RI-MA	S	22.96 MW	22.34 AW	47760 AAW	RIBLS	10//99-12//99
	South Carolina	S	17.85 MW	19.96 AW	41520 AAW	SCBLS	10//99-12//99
	Charleston-North Charleston						
	MSA, SC	S	19.36 MW	18.19 AW	40270 AAW	SCBLS	10//99-12//99
	Greenville-Spartanburg-						
	Anderson MSA, SC	S	17.04 MW	16.03 AW	35450 AAW	SCBLS	10//99-12//99
	South Dakota	S	10.23 MW	13.11 AW	27260 AAW	SDBLS	10//99-12//99
	Tennessee	S	16.67 MW	17.57 AW	36540 AAW	TNBLS	10//99-12//99
	Knoxville MSA, TN	S	16.74 MW	16.49 AW	34810 AAW	TNBLS	10//99-12//99
	Memphis MSA, TN-AR-MS	S	19.51 MW	18.78 AW	40590 AAW	MSBLS	10//99-12//99
	Nashville MSA, TN	S	17.39 MW	16.32 AW	36170 AAW	TNBLS	10//99-12//99
	Texas	S	17.98 MW	20.02 AW	41630 AAW	TXBLS	10//99-12//99
	Dallas PMSA, TX	S	21.79 MW	20.82 AW	45320 AAW	TXBLS	10//99-12//99
	El Paso MSA, TX	S	19.06 MW	16.94 AW	39640 AAW	TXBLS	10//99-12//99

AAW	Average annual wage	AOH	Average offered, high	ASH	Average starting, high
AE	Average entry wage	AOL	Average offered, low	ASL	Average starting, low
AEX	Average experienced wage	APH	Average pay, high range	AW	Average wage paid
AO	Average offered	APL	Average pay, low range	FQ	First quartile wage

H	Hourly	M	Monthly	S	Special: hourly and annual
HI	Highest wage paid	MTC	Median total compensation	TQ	Third quartile wage
HR	High end range	MW	Median wage paid	W	Weekly
LR	Low end range	SQ	Second quartile wage	Y	Yearly

Occupation/Type/Industry	Location	Per	Low	Mid	High	Source	Date
Urban and Regional Planner	Fort Worth-Arlington PMSA, TX	S	24.56 MW	21.16 AW	51090 AAW	TXBLS	10//99-12//99
	Houston PMSA, TX	S	17.92 MW	13.78 AW	37270 AAW	TXBLS	10//99-12//99
	San Antonio MSA, TX	S	27.65 MW	30.14 AW	57510 AAW	TXBLS	10//99-12//99
	Utah	S	19.26 MW	20.15 AW	41910 AAW	UTBLS	10//99-12//99
	Provo-Orem MSA, UT	S	23.25 MW	20.52 AW	48360 AAW	UTBLS	10//99-12//99
	Salt Lake City-Ogden MSA, UT	S	19.32 MW	18.94 AW	40180 AAW	UTBLS	10//99-12//99
	Vermont	S	18.75 MW	20.43 AW	42500 AAW	VTBLS	10//99-12//99
	Burlington MSA, VT	S	20.16 MW	19.76 AW	41920 AAW	VTBLS	10//99-12//99
	Virginia	S	23.27 MW	25.09 AW	52200 AAW	VABLS	10//99-12//99
	Charlottesville MSA, VA	S	19.60 MW	18.24 AW	40770 AAW	VABLS	10//99-12//99
	Norfolk-Virginia Beach-Newport News MSA, VA-NC	S	23.22 MW	22.37 AW	48290 AAW	VABLS	10//99-12//99
	Richmond-Petersburg MSA, VA	S	21.62 MW	20.53 AW	44970 AAW	VABLS	10//99-12//99
	Washington	S	23.93 MW	24.39 AW	50730 AAW	WABLS	10//99-12//99
	Richland-Kennewick-Pasco MSA, WA	S	24.26 MW	24.27 AW	50450 AAW	WABLS	10//99-12//99
	Seattle-Bellevue-Everett PMSA, WA	S	25.11 MW	24.55 AW	52230 AAW	WABLS	10//99-12//99
	Spokane MSA, WA	S	24.45 MW	23.63 AW	50850 AAW	WABLS	10//99-12//99
	Tacoma PMSA, WA	S	25.17 MW	23.97 AW	52350 AAW	WABLS	10//99-12//99
	Yakima MSA, WA	S	21.69 MW	20.15 AW	45110 AAW	WABLS	10//99-12//99
	West Virginia	S	16.12 MW	16.56 AW	34440 AAW	WVBLS	10//99-12//99
	Wheeling MSA, WV-OH	S	16.15 MW	16.62 AW	33590 AAW	WVBLS	10//99-12//99
	Wisconsin	S	19.3 MW	19.08 AW	39690 AAW	WIBLS	10//99-12//99
	Appleton-Oshkosh-Neenah MSA, WI	S	23.59 MW	23.16 AW	49070 AAW	WIBLS	10//99-12//99
	Janesville-Beloit MSA, WI	S	20.54 MW	19.14 AW	42730 AAW	WIBLS	10//99-12//99
	Madison MSA, WI	S	25.11 MW	23.93 AW	52220 AAW	WIBLS	10//99-12//99
	Milwaukee-Waukesha PMSA, WI	S	16.10 MW	16.30 AW	33490 AAW	WIBLS	10//99-12//99
	Puerto Rico	S	13.02 MW	13.57 AW	28230 AAW	PRBLS	10//99-12//99
	San Juan-Bayamon PMSA, PR	S	13.99 MW	13.30 AW	29110 AAW	PRBLS	10//99-12//99
Urban Planner	United States	H		22.12 AW		NCS98	1998
Used Car Manager Auto Dealership	United States	Y		75714 MW		WARD2	1999
Used Car Salesperson Auto Dealership	United States	Y		45000 MW		WARD2	1999
Usher, Lobby Attendant, and Ticket Taker	Alabama	S	5.99 MW	5.87 AW	12210 AAW	ALBLS	10//99-12//99
	Arizona	S	6.11 MW	6.37 AW	13240 AAW	AZBLS	10//99-12//99
	Arkansas	S	6.02 MW	6.20 AW	12910 AAW	ARBLS	10//99-12//99
	California	S	6.57 MW	7.74 AW	16100 AAW	CABLS	10//99-12//99
	Colorado	S	6.03 MW	6.17 AW	12840 AAW	COBLS	10//99-12//99
	Connecticut	S	6.17 MW	6.74 AW	14020 AAW	CTBLS	10//99-12//99
	Delaware	S	6.53 MW	7.64 AW	15900 AAW	DEBLS	10//99-12//99
	District of Columbia	S	6.57 MW	7.53 AW	15660 AAW	DCBLS	10//99-12//99
	Florida	S	6.16 MW	6.35 AW	13210 AAW	FLBLS	10//99-12//99
	Georgia	S	6.01 MW	5.98 AW	12440 AAW	GABLS	10//99-12//99
	Idaho	S	5.89 MW	5.79 AW	12040 AAW	IDBLS	10//99-12//99
	Illinois	S	6.06 MW	6.27 AW	13040 AAW	ILBLS	10//99-12//99
	Indiana	S	6.08 MW	6.32 AW	13140 AAW	INBLS	10//99-12//99
	Iowa	S	6.06 MW	6.06 AW	12600 AAW	IABLS	10//99-12//99
	Kansas	S	5.94 MW	6.17 AW	12830 AAW	KSBLS	10//99-12//99
	Kentucky	S	6.07 MW	6.19 AW	12870 AAW	KYBLS	10//99-12//99
	Louisiana	S	6.08 MW	6.17 AW	12840 AAW	LABLS	10//99-12//99
	Maine	S	6.05 MW	6.02 AW	12520 AAW	MEBLS	10//99-12//99
	Maryland	S	6.07 MW	6.32 AW	13150 AAW	MDBLS	10//99-12//99
	Massachusetts	S	6.58 MW	6.95 AW	14450 AAW	MABLS	10//99-12//99
	Michigan	S	6.26 MW	6.68 AW	13900 AAW	MIBLS	10//99-12//99
	Minnesota	S	6.15 MW	6.25 AW	13000 AAW	MNBLS	10//99-12//99
	Mississippi	S	6 MW	6.17 AW	12840 AAW	MSBLS	10//99-12//99
	Missouri	S	6.24 MW	6.80 AW	14130 AAW	MOBLS	10//99-12//99
	Montana	S	5.97 MW	6.40 AW	13300 AAW	MTBLS	10//99-12//99
	Nebraska	S	6.44 MW	6.51 AW	13540 AAW	NEBLS	10//99-12//99
	Nevada	S	6.11 MW	6.98 AW	14530 AAW	NVBLS	10//99-12//99

AAW Average annual wage	**AOH** Average offered, high	**ASH** Average starting, high	**H** Hourly	**M** Monthly	**S** Special: hourly and annual
AE Average entry wage	**AOL** Average offered, low	**ASL** Average starting, low	**HI** Highest wage paid	**MTC** Median total compensation	**TQ** Third quartile wage
AEX Average experienced wage	**APH** Average pay, high range	**AW** Average wage paid	**HR** High end range	**MW** Median wage paid	**W** Weekly
AO Average offered	**APL** Average pay, low range	**FQ** First quartile wage	**LR** Low end range	**SQ** Second quartile wage	**Y** Yearly

Occupation/Type/Industry	Location	Per	Low	Mid	High	Source	Date
Usher, Lobby Attendant, and Ticket Taker	New Hampshire	S	6.21 MW	6.32 AW	13140 AAW	NHBLS	10//99-12//99
	New Jersey	S	6.25 MW	6.44 AW	13390 AAW	NJBLS	10//99-12//99
	New Mexico	S	5.98 MW	5.96 AW	12400 AAW	NMBLS	10//99-12//99
	New York	S	6.37 MW	7.88 AW	16390 AAW	NYBLS	10//99-12//99
	North Carolina	S	6.01 MW	5.96 AW	12400 AAW	NCBLS	10//99-12//99
	Ohio	S	6.18 MW	6.84 AW	14240 AAW	OHBLS	10//99-12//99
	Oklahoma	S	5.92 MW	5.95 AW	12380 AAW	OKBLS	10//99-12//99
	Oregon	S	6.78 MW	7.09 AW	14750 AAW	ORBLS	10//99-12//99
	Pennsylvania	S	6.25 MW	6.61 AW	13740 AAW	PABLS	10//99-12//99
	Rhode Island	S	6.6 MW	6.84 AW	14240 AAW	RIBLS	10//99-12//99
	South Carolina	S	6.11 MW	6.11 AW	12710 AAW	SCBLS	10//99-12//99
	South Dakota	S	5.88 MW	5.84 AW	12140 AAW	SDBLS	10//99-12//99
	Tennessee	S	6.3 MW	6.44 AW	13400 AAW	TNBLS	10//99-12//99
	Texas	S	6.1 MW	6.18 AW	12850 AAW	TXBLS	10//99-12//99
	Utah	S	6.03 MW	6.18 AW	12850 AAW	UTBLS	10//99-12//99
	Vermont	S	6.19 MW	6.34 AW	13190 AAW	VTBLS	10//99-12//99
	Virginia	S	6.3 MW	6.40 AW	13310 AAW	VABLS	10//99-12//99
	Washington	S	6.49 MW	7.08 AW	14720 AAW	WABLS	10//99-12//99
	West Virginia	S	6.28 MW	6.50 AW	13520 AAW	WVBLS	10//99-12//99
	Wisconsin	S	6.05 MW	6.46 AW	13430 AAW	WIBLS	10//99-12//99
	Wyoming	S	5.95 MW	5.94 AW	12360 AAW	WYBLS	10//99-12//99
	Puerto Rico	S	5.97 MW	5.91 AW	12300 AAW	PRBLS	10//99-12//99
Veterinarian	Alabama	S	24.82 MW	26.74 AW	55610 AAW	ALBLS	10//99-12//99
	Birmingham MSA, AL	S	24.87 MW	24.63 AW	51720 AAW	ALBLS	10//99-12//99
	Florence MSA, AL	S	23.57 MW	24.23 AW	49020 AAW	ALBLS	10//99-12//99
	Huntsville MSA, AL	S	21.28 MW	19.25 AW	44270 AAW	ALBLS	10//99-12//99
	Mobile MSA, AL	S	28.30 MW	28.98 AW	58860 AAW	ALBLS	10//99-12//99
	Alaska	S	31.48 MW	34.38 AW	71520 AAW	AKBLS	10//99-12//99
	Anchorage MSA, AK	S	35.94 MW	32.25 AW	74750 AAW	AKBLS	10//99-12//99
	Arizona	S	29.56 MW	29.65 AW	61670 AAW	AZBLS	10//99-12//99
	Phoenix-Mesa MSA, AZ	S	30.26 MW	30.30 AW	62940 AAW	AZBLS	10//99-12//99
	Tucson MSA, AZ	S	26.39 MW	25.70 AW	54890 AAW	AZBLS	10//99-12//99
	Arkansas	S	19.29 MW	21.71 AW	45160 AAW	ARBLS	10//99-12//99
	Fayetteville-Springdale-Rogers MSA, AR	S	30.85 MW	30.66 AW	64170 AAW	ARBLS	10//99-12//99
	Little Rock-North Little Rock MSA, AR	S	17.83 MW	17.18 AW	37080 AAW	ARBLS	10//99-12//99
	California	S	37.42 MW	39.87 AW	82930 AAW	CABLS	10//99-12//99
	Bakersfield MSA, CA	S	33.60 MW	27.89 AW	69900 AAW	CABLS	10//99-12//99
	Fresno MSA, CA	S	30.87 MW	25.40 AW	64210 AAW	CABLS	10//99-12//99
	Los Angeles-Long Beach PMSA, CA	S	45.77 MW	42.72 AW	95210 AAW	CABLS	10//99-12//99
	Modesto MSA, CA	S	27.31 MW	25.27 AW	56800 AAW	CABLS	10//99-12//99
	Orange County PMSA, CA	S	36.44 MW	36.29 AW	75790 AAW	CABLS	10//99-12//99
	Riverside-San Bernardino PMSA, CA	S	38.08 MW	33.95 AW	79210 AAW	CABLS	10//99-12//99
	Sacramento PMSA, CA	S	43.88 MW	38.91 AW	91280 AAW	CABLS	10//99-12//99
	San Diego MSA, CA	S	36.09 MW	37.17 AW	75060 AAW	CABLS	10//99-12//99
	San Francisco PMSA, CA	S	44.95 MW	42.67 AW	93500 AAW	CABLS	10//99-12//99
	San Jose PMSA, CA	S	29.27 MW	28.50 AW	60890 AAW	CABLS	10//99-12//99
	Santa Barbara-Santa Maria-Lompoc MSA, CA	S	40.97 MW	44.72 AW	85220 AAW	CABLS	10//99-12//99
	Santa Cruz-Watsonville PMSA, CA	S	48.17 MW	54.78 AW	100190 AAW	CABLS	10//99-12//99
	Vallejo-Fairfield-Napa PMSA, CA	S	27.78 MW	30.88 AW	57790 AAW	CABLS	10//99-12//99
	Ventura PMSA, CA	S	38.68 MW	37.46 AW	80460 AAW	CABLS	10//99-12//99
	Visalia-Tulare-Porterville MSA, CA	S	31.59 MW	26.23 AW	65700 AAW	CABLS	10//99-12//99
	Colorado	S	28.72 MW	30.48 AW	63390 AAW	COBLS	10//99-12//99
	Denver PMSA, CO	S	34.56 MW	35.13 AW	71890 AAW	COBLS	10//99-12//99
	Fort Collins-Loveland MSA, CO	S	27.52 MW	22.17 AW	57250 AAW	COBLS	10//99-12//99
	Connecticut	S	29.6 MW	34.13 AW	70980 AAW	CTBLS	10//99-12//99
	Bridgeport PMSA, CT	S	43.14 MW	37.68 AW	89730 AAW	CTBLS	10//99-12//99
	Hartford MSA, CT	S	34.04 MW	30.88 AW	70790 AAW	CTBLS	10//99-12//99
	New Haven-Meriden PMSA, CT	S	27.39 MW	26.11 AW	56970 AAW	CTBLS	10//99-12//99
	Delaware	S	29.36 MW	31.45 AW	65420 AAW	DEBLS	10//99-12//99
	Dover MSA, DE	S	35.62 MW	37.16 AW	74090 AAW	DEBLS	10//99-12//99

AAW	Average annual wage	AOH	Average offered, high	ASH	Average starting, high	H	Hourly	M	Monthly	S	Special: hourly and annual
AE	Average entry wage	AOL	Average offered, low	ASL	Average starting, low	HI	Highest wage paid	MTC	Median total compensation	TQ	Third quartile wage
AEX	Average experienced wage	APH	Average pay, high range	AW	Average wage paid	HR	High end range	MW	Median wage paid	W	Weekly
AO	Average offered	APL	Average pay, low range	FQ	First quartile wage	LR	Low end range	SQ	Second quartile wage	Y	Yearly

Occupation/Type/Industry	Location	Per	Low	Mid	High	Source	Date
Veterinarian	Wilmington-Newark PMSA, DE-MD	S	29.91 MW	26.76 AW	62210 AAW	DEBLS	10//99-12//99
	District of Columbia	S	25.52 MW	27.83 AW	57890 AAW	DCBLS	10//99-12//99
	Washington PMSA, DC-MD-VA-WV	S	34.01 MW	31.23 AW	70750 AAW	DCBLS	10//99-12//99
	Florida	S	32.08 MW	36.57 AW	76060 AAW	FLBLS	10//99-12//99
	Fort Lauderdale PMSA, FL	S	32.97 MW	33.25 AW	68580 AAW	FLBLS	10//99-12//99
	Fort Pierce-Port St. Lucie MSA, FL	S	30.40 MW	26.64 AW	63240 AAW	FLBLS	10//99-12//99
	Gainesville MSA, FL	S	24.20 MW	24.44 AW	50330 AAW	FLBLS	10//99-12//99
	Jacksonville MSA, FL	S	33.90 MW	30.59 AW	70520 AAW	FLBLS	10//99-12//99
	Miami PMSA, FL	S	32.71 MW	35.83 AW	68030 AAW	FLBLS	10//99-12//99
	Ocala MSA, FL	S	29.84 MW	21.91 AW	62060 AAW	FLBLS	10//99-12//99
	Orlando MSA, FL	S	40.98 MW	35.21 AW	85240 AAW	FLBLS	10//99-12//99
	Georgia	S	26.87 MW	30.04 AW	62480 AAW	GABLS	10//99-12//99
	Atlanta MSA, GA	S	27.40 MW	25.75 AW	56990 AAW	GABLS	10//99-12//99
	Augusta-Aiken MSA, GA-SC	S	40.22 MW	33.49 AW	83650 AAW	GABLS	10//99-12//99
	Hawaii	S	31.83 MW	34.36 AW	71460 AAW	HIBLS	10//99-12//99
	Honolulu MSA, HI	S	34.80 MW	32.28 AW	72370 AAW	HIBLS	10//99-12//99
	Idaho	S	19.72 MW	20.94 AW	43560 AAW	IDBLS	10//99-12//99
	Boise City MSA, ID	S	20.69 MW	16.68 AW	43040 AAW	IDBLS	10//99-12//99
	Illinois	S	30.65 MW	31.86 AW	66270 AAW	ILBLS	10//99-12//99
	Chicago PMSA, IL	S	31.61 MW	31.72 AW	65750 AAW	ILBLS	10//99-12//99
	Peoria-Pekin MSA, IL	S	36.97 MW	44.25 AW	76900 AAW	ILBLS	10//99-12//99
	Indiana	S	28.45 MW	29.99 AW	62380 AAW	INBLS	10//99-12//99
	Elkhart-Goshen MSA, IN	S	28.76 MW	24.54 AW	59810 AAW	INBLS	10//99-12//99
	Evansville-Henderson MSA, IN-KY	S	27.32 MW	25.64 AW	56830 AAW	INBLS	10//99-12//99
	Fort Wayne MSA, IN	S	40.77 MW	30.88 AW	84810 AAW	INBLS	10//99-12//99
	Gary PMSA, IN	S	27.33 MW	25.99 AW	56840 AAW	INBLS	10//99-12//99
	Indianapolis MSA, IN	S	28.52 MW	28.56 AW	59310 AAW	INBLS	10//99-12//99
	South Bend MSA, IN	S	31.16 MW	34.50 AW	64810 AAW	INBLS	10//99-12//99
	Iowa	S	26.05 MW	28.37 AW	59020 AAW	IABLS	10//99-12//99
	Davenport-Moline-Rock Island MSA, IA-IL	S	24.69 MW	23.70 AW	51360 AAW	IABLS	10//99-12//99
	Des Moines MSA, IA	S	24.58 MW	20.32 AW	51140 AAW	IABLS	10//99-12//99
	Iowa City MSA, IA	S	43.34 MW	43.24 AW	90140 AAW	IABLS	10//99-12//99
	Kansas	S	24.98 MW	27.24 AW	56650 AAW	KSBLS	10//99-12//99
	Wichita MSA, KS	S	34.18 MW	26.18 AW	71090 AAW	KSBLS	10//99-12//99
	Kentucky	S	29.05 MW	36.48 AW	75880 AAW	KYBLS	10//99-12//99
	Lexington MSA, KY	S	47.37 MW	58.90 AW	98520 AAW	KYBLS	10//99-12//99
	Louisville MSA, KY-IN	S	33.24 MW	29.42 AW	69150 AAW	KYBLS	10//99-12//99
	Louisiana	S	22.73 MW	23.65 AW	49190 AAW	LABLS	10//99-12//99
	Baton Rouge MSA, LA	S	21.24 MW	16.72 AW	44190 AAW	LABLS	10//99-12//99
	Lake Charles MSA, LA	S	24.88 MW	19.25 AW	51760 AAW	LABLS	10//99-12//99
	New Orleans MSA, LA	S	25.88 MW	24.75 AW	53830 AAW	LABLS	10//99-12//99
	Maine	S	23.07 MW	25.12 AW	52240 AAW	MEBLS	10//99-12//99
	Maryland	S	31.28 MW	33.70 AW	70090 AAW	MDBLS	10//99-12//99
	Baltimore PMSA, MD	S	33.66 MW	30.26 AW	70020 AAW	MDBLS	10//99-12//99
	Massachusetts	S	25.18 MW	27.68 AW	57580 AAW	MABLS	10//99-12//99
	Springfield MSA, MA	S	36.00 MW	38.18 AW	74870 AAW	MABLS	10//99-12//99
	Michigan	S	28.02 MW	33.28 AW	69210 AAW	MIBLS	10//99-12//99
	Detroit PMSA, MI	S	32.12 MW	28.10 AW	66800 AAW	MIBLS	10//99-12//99
	Flint PMSA, MI	S	37.33 MW	30.73 AW	77650 AAW	MIBLS	10//99-12//99
	Grand Rapids-Muskegon-Holland MSA, MI	S	35.22 MW	26.93 AW	73250 AAW	MIBLS	10//99-12//99
	Kalamazoo-Battle Creek MSA, MI	S	23.28 MW	20.68 AW	48410 AAW	MIBLS	10//99-12//99
	Lansing-East Lansing MSA, MI	S	27.56 MW	28.63 AW	57320 AAW	MIBLS	10//99-12//99
	Minnesota	S	27.78 MW	29.42 AW	61190 AAW	MNBLS	10//99-12//99
	Minneapolis-St. Paul MSA, MN-WI	S	26.92 MW	25.61 AW	56000 AAW	MNBLS	10//99-12//99
	St. Cloud MSA, MN	S	33.65 MW	34.14 AW	70000 AAW	MNBLS	10//99-12//99
	Mississippi	S	32.17 MW	34.03 AW	70770 AAW	MSBLS	10//99-12//99
	Jackson MSA, MS	S	32.89 MW	25.35 AW	68410 AAW	MSBLS	10//99-12//99
	Missouri	S	23.27 MW	25.39 AW	52810 AAW	MOBLS	10//99-12//99
	Columbia MSA, MO	S	17.61 MW	18.13 AW	36630 AAW	MOBLS	10//99-12//99
	Kansas City MSA, MO-KS	S	28.45 MW	25.83 AW	59170 AAW	MOBLS	10//99-12//99
	St. Louis MSA, MO-IL	S	26.57 MW	25.31 AW	55270 AAW	MOBLS	10//99-12//99
	Springfield MSA, MO	S	23.02 MW	21.33 AW	47890 AAW	MOBLS	10//99-12//99
	Montana	S	21.23 MW	23.31 AW	48480 AAW	MTBLS	10//99-12//99
	Billings MSA, MT	S	23.06 MW	21.80 AW	47960 AAW	MTBLS	10//99-12//99

AAW	Average annual wage	AOH	Average offered, high	ASH	Average starting, high	H	Hourly	M	Monthly	S	Special: hourly and annual
AE	Average entry wage	AOL	Average offered, low	ASL	Average starting, low	HI	Highest wage paid	MTC	Median total compensation	TQ	Third quartile wage
AEX	Average experienced wage	APH	Average pay, high range	AW	Average wage paid	HR	High end range	MW	Median wage paid	W	Weekly
AO	Average offered	APL	Average pay, low range	FQ	First quartile wage	LR	Low end range	SQ	Second quartile wage	Y	Yearly

Occupation/Type/Industry	Location	Per	Low	Mid	High	Source	Date
Veterinarian	Nebraska	S	21.74 MW	20.86 AW	43390 AAW	NEBLS	10//99-12//99
	Nevada	S	30.76 MW	33.49 AW	69650 AAW	NVBLS	10//99-12//99
	Las Vegas MSA, NV-AZ	S	32.74 MW	29.97 AW	68100 AAW	NVBLS	10//99-12//99
	Reno MSA, NV	S	29.15 MW	30.33 AW	60630 AAW	NVBLS	10//99-12//99
	New Hampshire	S	33.36 MW	31.49 AW	65490 AAW	NHBLS	10//99-12//99
	Portsmouth-Rochester PMSA, NH-ME	S	21.51 MW	19.50 AW	44730 AAW	NHBLS	10//99-12//99
	New Jersey	S	33.95 MW	40.44 AW	84110 AAW	NJBLS	10//99-12//99
	Bergen-Passaic PMSA, NJ	S	40.07 MW	35.19 AW	83350 AAW	NJBLS	10//99-12//99
	Monmouth-Ocean PMSA, NJ	S	39.56 MW	32.55 AW	82280 AAW	NJBLS	10//99-12//99
	New Mexico	S	17.98 MW	18.39 AW	38240 AAW	NMBLS	10//99-12//99
	Albuquerque MSA, NM	S	16.52 MW	15.98 AW	34360 AAW	NMBLS	10//99-12//99
	Santa Fe MSA, NM	S	20.55 MW	19.34 AW	42740 AAW	NMBLS	10//99-12//99
	New York	S	30.57 MW	33.34 AW	69340 AAW	NYBLS	10//99-12//99
	Albany-Schenectady-Troy MSA, NY	S	30.98 MW	26.36 AW	64450 AAW	NYBLS	10//99-12//99
	Buffalo-Niagara Falls MSA, NY	S	34.02 MW	31.78 AW	70760 AAW	NYBLS	10//99-12//99
	Nassau-Suffolk PMSA, NY	S	40.47 MW	38.62 AW	84170 AAW	NYBLS	10//99-12//99
	New York PMSA, NY	S	30.89 MW	27.07 AW	64260 AAW	NYBLS	10//99-12//99
	Rochester MSA, NY	S	30.99 MW	29.27 AW	64450 AAW	NYBLS	10//99-12//99
	Syracuse MSA, NY	S	35.28 MW	32.06 AW	73390 AAW	NYBLS	10//99-12//99
	Utica-Rome MSA, NY	S	26.00 MW	23.98 AW	54080 AAW	NYBLS	10//99-12//99
	North Carolina	S	25.63 MW	29.26 AW	60860 AAW	NCBLS	10//99-12//99
	Charlotte-Gastonia-Rock Hill MSA, NC-SC	S	28.19 MW	24.98 AW	58640 AAW	NCBLS	10//99-12//99
	Hickory-Morganton-Lenoir MSA, NC	S	34.86 MW	30.88 AW	72510 AAW	NCBLS	10//99-12//99
	Raleigh-Durham-Chapel Hill MSA, NC	S	29.78 MW	27.58 AW	61950 AAW	NCBLS	10//99-12//99
	Wilmington MSA, NC	S	26.06 MW	26.93 AW	54200 AAW	NCBLS	10//99-12//99
	North Dakota	S	30.72 MW	30.19 AW	62800 AAW	NDBLS	10//99-12//99
	Ohio	S	30.02 MW	31.92 AW	66400 AAW	OHBLS	10//99-12//99
	Akron PMSA, OH	S	28.31 MW	28.07 AW	58890 AAW	OHBLS	10//99-12//99
	Cincinnati PMSA, OH-KY-IN	S	24.38 MW	25.21 AW	50720 AAW	OHBLS	10//99-12//99
	Cleveland-Lorain-Elyria PMSA, OH	S	30.78 MW	30.71 AW	64030 AAW	OHBLS	10//99-12//99
	Oklahoma	S	32.12 MW	29.72 AW	61820 AAW	OKBLS	10//99-12//99
	Oklahoma City MSA, OK	S	33.34 MW	34.98 AW	69350 AAW	OKBLS	10//99-12//99
	Tulsa MSA, OK	S	19.43 MW	15.34 AW	40410 AAW	OKBLS	10//99-12//99
	Oregon	S	23.97 MW	25.12 AW	52240 AAW	ORBLS	10//99-12//99
	Portland-Vancouver PMSA, OR-WA	S	24.50 MW	24.52 AW	50960 AAW	ORBLS	10//99-12//99
	Salem PMSA, OR	S	21.41 MW	20.09 AW	44530 AAW	ORBLS	10//99-12//99
	Pennsylvania	S	29.36 MW	32.71 AW	68050 AAW	PABLS	10//99-12//99
	Harrisburg-Lebanon-Carlisle MSA, PA	S	26.69 MW	24.45 AW	55510 AAW	PABLS	10//99-12//99
	Lancaster MSA, PA	S	30.59 MW	34.32 AW	63630 AAW	PABLS	10//99-12//99
	Philadelphia PMSA, PA-NJ	S	38.08 MW	35.31 AW	79220 AAW	PABLS	10//99-12//99
	Pittsburgh MSA, PA	S	31.85 MW	30.16 AW	66250 AAW	PABLS	10//99-12//99
	State College MSA, PA	S	25.16 MW	25.05 AW	52320 AAW	PABLS	10//99-12//99
	Rhode Island	S	36.75 MW	37.60 AW	78210 AAW	RIBLS	10//99-12//99
	Providence-Fall River-Warwick MSA, RI-MA	S	37.60 MW	36.75 AW	78210 AAW	RIBLS	10//99-12//99
	South Carolina	S	31.6 MW	34.24 AW	71210 AAW	SCBLS	10//99-12//99
	Charleston-North Charleston MSA, SC	S	31.42 MW	30.12 AW	65360 AAW	SCBLS	10//99-12//99
	Greenville-Spartanburg-Anderson MSA, SC	S	39.58 MW	39.06 AW	82320 AAW	SCBLS	10//99-12//99
	South Dakota	S	21.05 MW	23.96 AW	49840 AAW	SDBLS	10//99-12//99
	Sioux Falls MSA, SD	S	19.68 MW	19.47 AW	40940 AAW	SDBLS	10//99-12//99
	Tennessee	S	25.86 MW	28.43 AW	59140 AAW	TNBLS	10//99-12//99
	Johnson City-Kingsport-Bristol MSA, TN-VA	S	27.40 MW	27.51 AW	57000 AAW	TNBLS	10//99-12//99
	Memphis MSA, TN-AR-MS	S	33.41 MW	26.69 AW	69500 AAW	MSBLS	10//99-12//99
	Nashville MSA, TN	S	32.45 MW	30.69 AW	67490 AAW	TNBLS	10//99-12//99
	Texas	S	24.55 MW	30.12 AW	62640 AAW	TXBLS	10//99-12//99
	Austin-San Marcos MSA, TX	S	29.36 MW	26.29 AW	61070 AAW	TXBLS	10//99-12//99
	Brazoria PMSA, TX	S	38.59 MW	33.13 AW	80270 AAW	TXBLS	10//99-12//99
	Bryan-College Station MSA, TX	S	23.70 MW	21.56 AW	49300 AAW	TXBLS	10//99-12//99
	Corpus Christi MSA, TX	S	30.52 MW	32.04 AW	63480 AAW	TXBLS	10//99-12//99

AAW	Average annual wage	AOH	Average offered, high	ASH	Average starting, high	H	Hourly	M	Monthly	S	Special: hourly and annual
AE	Average entry wage	AOL	Average offered, low	ASL	Average starting, low	HI	Highest wage paid	MTC	Median total compensation	TQ	Third quartile wage
AEX	Average experienced wage	APH	Average pay, high range	AW	Average wage paid	HR	High end range	MW	Median wage paid	W	Weekly
AO	Average offered	APL	Average pay, low range	FQ	First quartile wage	LR	Low end range	SQ	Second quartile wage	Y	Yearly

Occupation/Type/Industry	Location	Per	Low	Mid	High	Source	Date
Veterinarian	Dallas PMSA, TX	S	26.82 MW	19.48 AW	55790 AAW	TXBLS	10//99-12//99
	Galveston-Texas City PMSA, TX	S	29.78 MW	28.86 AW	61940 AAW	TXBLS	10//99-12//99
	Houston PMSA, TX	S	36.59 MW	34.15 AW	76110 AAW	TXBLS	10//99-12//99
	Longview-Marshall MSA, TX	S	24.13 MW	20.63 AW	50200 AAW	TXBLS	10//99-12//99
	San Antonio MSA, TX	S	36.04 MW	34.51 AW	74970 AAW	TXBLS	10//99-12//99
	Utah	S	25.33 MW	27.68 AW	57570 AAW	UTBLS	10//99-12//99
	Salt Lake City-Ogden MSA, UT	S	28.25 MW	25.38 AW	58760 AAW	UTBLS	10//99-12//99
	Vermont	S	23.78 MW	26.15 AW	54400 AAW	VTBLS	10//99-12//99
	Virginia	S	26.6 MW	29.13 AW	60600 AAW	VABLS	10//99-12//99
	Charlottesville MSA, VA	S	33.44 MW	28.46 AW	69550 AAW	VABLS	10//99-12//99
	Norfolk-Virginia Beach-Newport News MSA, VA-NC	S	26.30 MW	24.38 AW	54690 AAW	VABLS	10//99-12//99
	Richmond-Petersburg MSA, VA	S	22.52 MW	23.45 AW	46830 AAW	VABLS	10//99-12//99
	Roanoke MSA, VA	S	34.50 MW	28.39 AW	71750 AAW	VABLS	10//99-12//99
	Washington	S	26.71 MW	27.43 AW	57050 AAW	WABLS	10//99-12//99
	Olympia PMSA, WA	S	19.44 MW	19.34 AW	40440 AAW	WABLS	10//99-12//99
	Richland-Kennewick-Pasco MSA, WA	S	36.18 MW	44.96 AW	75260 AAW	WABLS	10//99-12//99
	Seattle-Bellevue-Everett PMSA, WA	S	25.77 MW	25.04 AW	53600 AAW	WABLS	10//99-12//99
	Tacoma PMSA, WA	S	28.03 MW	26.05 AW	58310 AAW	WABLS	10//99-12//99
	West Virginia	S	35.5 MW	35.59 AW	74020 AAW	WVBLS	10//99-12//99
	Charleston MSA, WV	S	24.66 MW	25.11 AW	51300 AAW	WVBLS	10//99-12//99
	Wheeling MSA, WV-OH	S	29.53 MW	27.78 AW	61430 AAW	WVBLS	10//99-12//99
	Wisconsin	S	33.38 MW	38.54 AW	80160 AAW	WIBLS	10//99-12//99
	Appleton-Oshkosh-Neenah MSA, WI	S	30.48 MW	30.89 AW	63400 AAW	WIBLS	10//99-12//99
	Eau Claire MSA, WI	S	28.13 MW	27.62 AW	58510 AAW	WIBLS	10//99-12//99
	Green Bay MSA, WI	S	26.91 MW	26.03 AW	55980 AAW	WIBLS	10//99-12//99
	Janesville-Beloit MSA, WI	S	35.26 MW	36.82 AW	73330 AAW	WIBLS	10//99-12//99
	Kenosha PMSA, WI	S	37.99 MW	26.02 AW	79010 AAW	WIBLS	10//99-12//99
	Madison MSA, WI	S	30.21 MW	26.57 AW	62830 AAW	WIBLS	10//99-12//99
	Milwaukee-Waukesha PMSA, WI	S	23.03 MW	20.42 AW	47890 AAW	WIBLS	10//99-12//99
	Wyoming	S	19.9 MW	22.66 AW	47130 AAW	WYBLS	10//99-12//99
	Puerto Rico	S	16.54 MW	18.94 AW	39390 AAW	PRBLS	10//99-12//99
	San Juan-Bayamon PMSA, PR	S	18.64 MW	16.37 AW	38760 AAW	PRBLS	10//99-12//99
College or University	United States	Y		76984 AW		DVMAG	1997
Equine Practice	United States	Y		76089 AW		DVMAG	1997
Federal Government	United States	Y		68153 AW		DVMAG	1997
Industrial	United States	Y		109941 AW		DVMAG	1997
Large Animals Exclusively	United States	Y		76360 AW		DVMAG	1997
Large Animals Predominantly	United States	Y		61087 AW		DVMAG	1997
Mixed Animal Practice	United States	Y		59076 AW		DVMAG	1997
Small Animal Practice	United States	Y		67562 AW		DVMAG	1997
Small Animals Predominantly	United States	Y		61856 AW		DVMAG	1997
State or Local Government	United States	Y		65294 AW		DVMAG	1997
Uniformed Services	United States	Y		60097 AW		DVMAG	1997
Veterinary Assistant and Laboratory Animal Caretaker	Alabama	S	6.54 MW	7.30 AW	15190 AAW	ALBLS	10//99-12//99
	Alaska	S	8.7 MW	8.42 AW	17510 AAW	AKBLS	10//99-12//99
	Arizona	S	7.66 MW	7.68 AW	15980 AAW	AZBLS	10//99-12//99
	Arkansas	S	7.86 MW	8.21 AW	17080 AAW	ARBLS	10//99-12//99
	California	S	7.38 MW	8.02 AW	16680 AAW	CABLS	10//99-12//99
	Colorado	S	7.91 MW	8.23 AW	17120 AAW	COBLS	10//99-12//99
	Connecticut	S	8.81 MW	8.99 AW	18710 AAW	CTBLS	10//99-12//99
	Delaware	S	7.82 MW	8.21 AW	17090 AAW	DEBLS	10//99-12//99
	Florida	S	7.48 MW	7.78 AW	16180 AAW	FLBLS	10//99-12//99
	Georgia	S	9.3 MW	9.33 AW	19400 AAW	GABLS	10//99-12//99
	Idaho	S	6.06 MW	5.96 AW	12390 AAW	IDBLS	10//99-12//99
	Illinois	S	6.52 MW	6.56 AW	13640 AAW	ILBLS	10//99-12//99
	Indiana	S	6.62 MW	6.96 AW	14480 AAW	INBLS	10//99-12//99
	Iowa	S	7.29 MW	8.09 AW	16830 AAW	IABLS	10//99-12//99
	Kansas	S	7.18 MW	7.51 AW	15630 AAW	KSBLS	10//99-12//99
	Kentucky	S	8.02 MW	8.06 AW	16760 AAW	KYBLS	10//99-12//99
	Louisiana	S	6.22 MW	6.29 AW	13090 AAW	LABLS	10//99-12//99
	Massachusetts	S	9.66 MW	10.44 AW	21720 AAW	MABLS	10//99-12//99

Occupation/Type/Industry	Location	Per	Low	Mid	High	Source	Date
Veterinary Assistant and							
Laboratory Animal Caretaker	Michigan	S	7.43 MW	7.36 AW	15310 AAW	MIBLS	10//99-12//99
	Minnesota	S	8.08 MW	8.35 AW	17380 AAW	MNBLS	10//99-12//99
	Mississippi	S	6.69 MW	6.70 AW	13940 AAW	MSBLS	10//99-12//99
	Missouri	S	6.72 MW	7.23 AW	15040 AAW	MOBLS	10//99-12//99
	Montana	S	6.18 MW	6.25 AW	12990 AAW	MTBLS	10//99-12//99
	Nebraska	S	6.4 MW	6.45 AW	13420 AAW	NEBLS	10//99-12//99
	Nevada	S	7.39 MW	7.74 AW	16100 AAW	NVBLS	10//99-12//99
	New Hampshire	S	6.71 MW	6.74 AW	14010 AAW	NHBLS	10//99-12//99
	New Jersey	S	9.27 MW	9.81 AW	20410 AAW	NJBLS	10//99-12//99
	New Mexico	S	6.25 MW	6.42 AW	13340 AAW	NMBLS	10//99-12//99
	New York	S	8.63 MW	8.96 AW	18640 AAW	NYBLS	10//99-12//99
	North Carolina	S	7.55 MW	7.64 AW	15890 AAW	NCBLS	10//99-12//99
	Ohio	S	7.39 MW	7.49 AW	15580 AAW	OHBLS	10//99-12//99
	Oklahoma	S	6.38 MW	6.81 AW	14170 AAW	OKBLS	10//99-12//99
	Oregon	S	7.59 MW	7.78 AW	16180 AAW	ORBLS	10//99-12//99
	Pennsylvania	S	8 MW	8.15 AW	16960 AAW	PABLS	10//99-12//99
	Rhode Island	S	8.01 MW	8.89 AW	18500 AAW	RIBLS	10//99-12//99
	South Carolina	S	6.19 MW	7.50 AW	15600 AAW	SCBLS	10//99-12//99
	South Dakota	S	6.23 MW	6.42 AW	13350 AAW	SDBLS	10//99-12//99
	Tennessee	S	6.87 MW	6.97 AW	14490 AAW	TNBLS	10//99-12//99
	Texas	S	8.52 MW	8.72 AW	18140 AAW	TXBLS	10//99-12//99
	Utah	S	7.49 MW	7.44 AW	15470 AAW	UTBLS	10//99-12//99
	Vermont	S	7.8 MW	8.54 AW	17770 AAW	VTBLS	10//99-12//99
	Virginia	S	7.35 MW	7.64 AW	15880 AAW	VABLS	10//99-12//99
	Washington	S	7.54 MW	7.57 AW	15740 AAW	WABLS	10//99-12//99
	West Virginia	S	6.18 MW	6.18 AW	12850 AAW	WVBLS	10//99-12//99
	Wisconsin	S	7.33 MW	7.58 AW	15770 AAW	WIBLS	10//99-12//99
	Wyoming	S	7.56 MW	8.34 AW	17350 AAW	WYBLS	10//99-12//99
	Puerto Rico	S	6.38 MW	6.52 AW	13560 AAW	PRBLS	10//99-12//99
Veterinary Technician							
Biomedical Research	United States	Y		34486 AW		VETTECH	1999
Companion Animal	United States	Y		24197 AW		VETTECH	1999
County/City Government	United States	Y		29166 AW		VETTECH	1999
Emergency	United States	Y		25477 AW		VETTECH	1999
Federal/State Government	United States	Y		27813 AW		VETTECH	1999
Industry/Sales	United States	Y		34417 AW		VETTECH	1999
Mixed Animal	United States	Y		21965 AW		VETTECH	1999
Nonprofit Agency	United States	Y		25857 AW		VETTECH	1999
Specialty	United States	Y		26168 AW		VETTECH	1999
University/College	United States	Y		27292 AW		VETTECH	1999
Veterinary Technology Education	United States	Y		33254 AW		VETTECH	1999
Veterinary Technologist and							
Technician	Alabama	S	7.97 MW	8.22 AW	17100 AAW	ALBLS	10//99-12//99
	Alaska	S	12.42 MW	12.80 AW	26630 AAW	AKBLS	10//99-12//99
	Arizona	S	8.27 MW	8.76 AW	18220 AAW	AZBLS	10//99-12//99
	Arkansas	S	7.9 MW	8.09 AW	16830 AAW	ARBLS	10//99-12//99
	California	S	10.52 MW	10.89 AW	22650 AAW	CABLS	10//99-12//99
	Colorado	S	11.36 MW	12.04 AW	25050 AAW	COBLS	10//99-12//99
	Connecticut	S	12.4 MW	12.67 AW	26360 AAW	CTBLS	10//99-12//99
	Delaware	S	11.36 MW	14.78 AW	30740 AAW	DEBLS	10//99-12//99
	Florida	S	8.79 MW	9.00 AW	18710 AAW	FLBLS	10//99-12//99
	Georgia	S	9.82 MW	10.36 AW	21550 AAW	GABLS	10//99-12//99
	Hawaii	S	8.88 MW	9.05 AW	18820 AAW	HIBLS	10//99-12//99
	Idaho	S	9.59 MW	9.94 AW	20680 AAW	IDBLS	10//99-12//99
	Illinois	S	10.71 MW	11.86 AW	24660 AAW	ILBLS	10//99-12//99
	Indiana	S	9.53 MW	10.02 AW	20850 AAW	INBLS	10//99-12//99
	Iowa	S	10.25 MW	10.47 AW	21790 AAW	IABLS	10//99-12//99
	Kansas	S	9.59 MW	9.73 AW	20230 AAW	KSBLS	10//99-12//99
	Kentucky	S	9.6 MW	9.62 AW	20020 AAW	KYBLS	10//99-12//99
	Louisiana	S	6.12 MW	6.19 AW	12880 AAW	LABLS	10//99-12//99
	Maine	S	10.3 MW	10.49 AW	21810 AAW	MEBLS	10//99-12//99
	Maryland	S	9.68 MW	9.86 AW	20510 AAW	MDBLS	10//99-12//99
	Massachusetts	S	12.31 MW	12.40 AW	25790 AAW	MABLS	10//99-12//99
	Michigan	S	9.98 MW	10.29 AW	21400 AAW	MIBLS	10//99-12//99
	Minnesota	S	11.85 MW	11.85 AW	24650 AAW	MNBLS	10//99-12//99
	Mississippi	S	9.88 MW	11.44 AW	23790 AAW	MSBLS	10//99-12//99
	Missouri	S	10.43 MW	10.32 AW	21470 AAW	MOBLS	10//99-12//99
	Montana	S	8.61 MW	9.25 AW	19250 AAW	MTBLS	10//99-12//99
	Nebraska	S	9.3 MW	9.27 AW	19290 AAW	NEBLS	10//99-12//99

AAW	Average annual wage	**AOH**	Average offered, high	**ASH**	Average starting, high	**H**	Hourly	**M**	Monthly	**S**	Special: hourly and annual
AE	Average entry wage	**AOL**	Average offered, low	**ASL**	Average starting, low	**HI**	Highest wage paid	**MTC**	Median total compensation	**TQ**	Third quartile wage
AEX	Average experienced wage	**APH**	Average pay, high range	**AW**	Average wage paid	**HR**	High end range	**MW**	Median wage paid	**W**	Weekly
AO	Average offered	**APL**	Average pay, low range	**FQ**	First quartile wage	**LR**	Low end range	**SQ**	Second quartile wage	**Y**	Yearly

Occupation/Type/Industry	Location	Per	Low	Mid	High	Source	Date
Veterinary Technologist and Technician	Nevada	S	9.53 MW	9.68 AW	20130 AAW	NVBLS	10//99-12//99
	New Hampshire	S	10.9 MW	11.17 AW	23220 AAW	NHBLS	10//99-12//99
	New Jersey	S	12.05 MW	13.00 AW	27040 AAW	NJBLS	10//99-12//99
	New Mexico	S	9.64 MW	9.77 AW	20330 AAW	NMBLS	10//99-12//99
	New York	S	11.95 MW	11.98 AW	24920 AAW	NYBLS	10//99-12//99
	North Carolina	S	9.39 MW	9.60 AW	19960 AAW	NCBLS	10//99-12//99
	Ohio	S	9.87 MW	10.36 AW	21560 AAW	OHBLS	10//99-12//99
	Oklahoma	S	8.55 MW	8.63 AW	17940 AAW	OKBLS	10//99-12//99
	Oregon	S	11.06 MW	11.05 AW	22970 AAW	ORBLS	10//99-12//99
	Pennsylvania	S	10.34 MW	10.65 AW	22150 AAW	PABLS	10//99-12//99
	Rhode Island	S	13.65 MW	12.46 AW	25910 AAW	RIBLS	10//99-12//99
	South Carolina	S	8.85 MW	8.63 AW	17950 AAW	SCBLS	10//99-12//99
	South Dakota	S	9.59 MW	9.50 AW	19760 AAW	SDBLS	10//99-12//99
	Tennessee	S	9.19 MW	9.34 AW	19420 AAW	TNBLS	10//99-12//99
	Texas	S	8.94 MW	9.88 AW	20550 AAW	TXBLS	10//99-12//99
	Utah	S	8.94 MW	8.68 AW	18050 AAW	UTBLS	10//99-12//99
	Vermont	S	9.38 MW	9.50 AW	19760 AAW	VTBLS	10//99-12//99
	Virginia	S	8.4 MW	9.68 AW	20140 AAW	VABLS	10//99-12//99
	Washington	S	10.16 MW	10.42 AW	21680 AAW	WABLS	10//99-12//99
	West Virginia	S	8.02 MW	8.11 AW	16870 AAW	WVBLS	10//99-12//99
	Wisconsin	S	9.62 MW	9.74 AW	20260 AAW	WIBLS	10//99-12//99
	Wyoming	S	10.55 MW	10.73 AW	22320 AAW	WYBLS	10//99-12//99
	Puerto Rico	S	9.38 MW	10.34 AW	21510 AAW	PRBLS	10//99-12//99
Vice President							
Business Development, Construction Contractor	United States	Y		97450 MW		ENR2	1999
Computer-aided Design, Apparel Industry	United States	Y		230000 AW		BOBBIN	1999
Consulting	United States	Y		93001 MW		TRAVWK5	2000
Estimating, Construction Contractor	United States	Y		96236 MW		ENR2	1999
Female, Logistics	United States	Y	100000 FQ	150000 SQ	200000 TQ	TRAFWD	2000
Finance	United States	Y		175047 AW		PENINV	2000
Financial Planning Firm	United States	Y		116500 AW		INVNEWS	2000
On-line Enterprise	United States	Y		152100 AW		WSJ1	2000
Operations, Construction Contractor	United States	Y		96495 MW		ENR2	1999
Video Store Clerk	Louisville, KY	H		5.75 AW		LOUMAG	1999-2000
Vineyard Worker							
Vineyard, Over 150K Cases/Year	United States	Y	23920 MW	24298 AW		PWV	1999
Vocational Counselor	United States	H		24.90 AW		NCS98	1998
Vocational Education Teacher							
Middle School	Alabama	Y		41970 AAW		ALBLS	10//99-12//99
Middle School	Alaska	Y		43730 AAW		AKBLS	10//99-12//99
Middle School	Arizona	Y		35200 AAW		AZBLS	10//99-12//99
Middle School	Arkansas	Y		33600 AAW		ARBLS	10//99-12//99
Middle School	Fort Smith MSA, AR-OK	Y		37030 AAW		ARBLS	10//99-12//99
Middle School	California	Y		39990 AAW		CABLS	10//99-12//99
Middle School	Connecticut	Y		48680 AAW		CTBLS	10//99-12//99
Middle School	Hartford MSA, CT	Y		51460 AAW		CTBLS	10//99-12//99
Middle School	New London-Norwich MSA, CT-RI	Y		44770 AAW		CTBLS	10//99-12//99
Middle School	Washington PMSA, DC-MD-VA-WV	Y		39490 AAW		DCBLS	10//99-12//99
Middle School	Florida	Y		36860 AAW		FLBLS	10//99-12//99
Middle School	Georgia	Y		42930 AAW		GABLS	10//99-12//99
Middle School	Atlanta MSA, GA	Y		42400 AAW		GABLS	10//99-12//99
Middle School	Macon MSA, GA	Y		40770 AAW		GABLS	10//99-12//99
Middle School	Illinois	Y		37950 AAW		ILBLS	10//99-12//99
Middle School	Chicago PMSA, IL	Y		39900 AAW		ILBLS	10//99-12//99
Middle School	Indiana	Y		42530 AAW		INBLS	10//99-12//99
Middle School	Kokomo MSA, IN	Y		39470 AAW		INBLS	10//99-12//99
Middle School	Iowa	Y		33720 AAW		IABLS	10//99-12//99
Middle School	Kentucky	Y		35960 AAW		KYBLS	10//99-12//99
Middle School	Maine	Y		37630 AAW		MEBLS	10//99-12//99
Middle School	Portland MSA, ME	Y		41350 AAW		MEBLS	10//99-12//99
Middle School	Massachusetts	Y		45610 AAW		MABLS	10//99-12//99
Middle School	Boston PMSA, MA-NH	Y		44950 AAW		MABLS	10//99-12//99
Middle School	Michigan	Y		50570 AAW		MIBLS	10//99-12//99
Middle School	Minnesota	Y		39810 AAW		MNBLS	10//99-12//99

Occupation/Type/Industry	Location	Per	Low	Mid	High	Source	Date
Vocational Education Teacher							
Middle School	Minneapolis-St. Paul MSA, MN-WI	Y		36950 AAW		MNBLS	10//99-12//99
Middle School	Mississippi	Y		31820 AAW		MSBLS	10//99-12//99
Middle School	St. Louis MSA, MO-IL	Y		43600 AAW		MOBLS	10//99-12//99
Middle School	Nebraska	Y		39370 AAW		NEBLS	10//99-12//99
Middle School	New Hampshire	Y		32110 AAW		NHBLS	10//99-12//99
Middle School	New Jersey	Y		51380 AAW		NJBLS	10//99-12//99
Middle School	Bergen-Passaic PMSA, NJ	Y		54880 AAW		NJBLS	10//99-12//99
Middle School	New Mexico	Y		30350 AAW		NMBLS	10//99-12//99
Middle School	New York	Y		56220 AAW		NYBLS	10//99-12//99
Middle School	Nassau-Suffolk PMSA, NY	Y		73100 AAW		NYBLS	10//99-12//99
Middle School	Rochester MSA, NY	Y		57790 AAW		NYBLS	10//99-12//99
Middle School	Syracuse MSA, NY	Y		27790 AAW		NYBLS	10//99-12//99
Middle School	North Carolina	Y		36570 AAW		NCBLS	10//99-12//99
Middle School	Charlotte-Gastonia-Rock Hill MSA, NC-SC	Y		39590 AAW		NCBLS	10//99-12//99
Middle School	Greensboro--Winston-Salem-- High Point MSA, NC	Y		36060 AAW		NCBLS	10//99-12//99
Middle School	Hickory-Morganton-Lenoir MSA, NC	Y		39990 AAW		NCBLS	10//99-12//99
Middle School	Ohio	Y		40420 AAW		OHBLS	10//99-12//99
Middle School	Akron PMSA, OH	Y		45650 AAW		OHBLS	10//99-12//99
Middle School	Canton-Massillon MSA, OH	Y		42000 AAW		OHBLS	10//99-12//99
Middle School	Cincinnati PMSA, OH-KY-IN	Y		39960 AAW		OHBLS	10//99-12//99
Middle School	Cleveland-Lorain-Elyria PMSA, OH	Y		44760 AAW		OHBLS	10//99-12//99
Middle School	Columbus MSA, OH	Y		40580 AAW		OHBLS	10//99-12//99
Middle School	Hamilton-Middletown PMSA, OH	Y		44470 AAW		OHBLS	10//99-12//99
Middle School	Toledo MSA, OH	Y		46260 AAW		OHBLS	10//99-12//99
Middle School	Youngstown-Warren MSA, OH	Y		41640 AAW		OHBLS	10//99-12//99
Middle School	Oklahoma	Y		38850 AAW		OKBLS	10//99-12//99
Middle School	Oklahoma City MSA, OK	Y		42140 AAW		OKBLS	10//99-12//99
Middle School	Oregon	Y		44040 AAW		ORBLS	10//99-12//99
Middle School	Portland-Vancouver PMSA, OR-WA	Y		46630 AAW		ORBLS	10//99-12//99
Middle School	Pennsylvania	Y		65640 AAW		PABLS	10//99-12//99
Middle School	Philadelphia PMSA, PA-NJ	Y		55620 AAW		PABLS	10//99-12//99
Middle School	Rhode Island	Y		44400 AAW		RIBLS	10//99-12//99
Middle School	Providence-Fall River- Warwick MSA, RI-MA	Y		44400 AAW		RIBLS	10//99-12//99
Middle School	South Carolina	Y		34110 AAW		SCBLS	10//99-12//99
Middle School	Tennessee	Y		30960 AAW		TNBLS	10//99-12//99
Middle School	Texas	Y		38940 AAW		TXBLS	10//99-12//99
Middle School	Austin-San Marcos MSA, TX	Y		34770 AAW		TXBLS	10//99-12//99
Middle School	Fort Worth-Arlington PMSA, TX	Y		47440 AAW		TXBLS	10//99-12//99
Middle School	Houston PMSA, TX	Y		38550 AAW		TXBLS	10//99-12//99
Middle School	McAllen-Edinburg-Mission MSA, TX	Y		43460 AAW		TXBLS	10//99-12//99
Middle School	San Antonio MSA, TX	Y		37000 AAW		TXBLS	10//99-12//99
Middle School	Virginia	Y		35510 AAW		VABLS	10//99-12//99
Middle School	Washington	Y		39170 AAW		WABLS	10//99-12//99
Middle School	Wisconsin	Y		43750 AAW		WIBLS	10//99-12//99
Middle School	Appleton-Oshkosh-Neenah MSA, WI	Y		45760 AAW		WIBLS	10//99-12//99
Middle School	Madison MSA, WI	Y		41780 AAW		WIBLS	10//99-12//99
Middle School	Wyoming	Y		30500 AAW		WYBLS	10//99-12//99
Postsecondary	Alabama	S	18.01 MW	16.83 AW	35000 AAW	ALBLS	10//99-12//99
Postsecondary	Mobile MSA, AL	S	14.81 MW	15.03 AW	30800 AAW	ALBLS	10//99-12//99
Postsecondary	Arizona	S	16.86 MW	16.57 AW	34460 AAW	AZBLS	10//99-12//99
Postsecondary	Phoenix-Mesa MSA, AZ	S	15.17 MW	14.94 AW	31560 AAW	AZBLS	10//99-12//99
Postsecondary	Arkansas	S	14.35 MW	15.36 AW	31940 AAW	ARBLS	10//99-12//99
Postsecondary	Little Rock-North Little Rock MSA, AR	S	16.31 MW	13.24 AW	33910 AAW	ARBLS	10//99-12//99
Postsecondary	California	S	17.97 MW	20.34 AW	42300 AAW	CABLS	10//99-12//99
Postsecondary	Bakersfield MSA, CA	S	18.29 MW	16.39 AW	38030 AAW	CABLS	10//99-12//99
Postsecondary	Fresno MSA, CA	S	21.68 MW	19.93 AW	45090 AAW	CABLS	10//99-12//99
Postsecondary	Los Angeles-Long Beach PMSA, CA	S	17.13 MW	16.00 AW	35620 AAW	CABLS	10//99-12//99
Postsecondary	Modesto MSA, CA	S	18.47 MW	15.69 AW	38410 AAW	CABLS	10//99-12//99

AAW Average annual wage	**AOH** Average offered, high	**ASH** Average starting, high	**H** Hourly	**M** Monthly	**S** Special: hourly and annual
AE Average entry wage	**AOL** Average offered, low	**ASL** Average starting, low	**HI** Highest wage paid	**MTC** Median total compensation	**TQ** Third quartile wage
AEX Average experienced wage	**APH** Average pay, high range	**AW** Average wage paid	**HR** High end range	**MW** Median wage paid	**W** Weekly
AO Average offered	**APL** Average pay, low range	**FQ** First quartile wage	**LR** Low end range	**SQ** Second quartile wage	**Y** Yearly

Occupation/Type/Industry	Location	Per	Low	Mid	High	Source	Date
Vocational Education Teacher							
Postsecondary	Oakland PMSA, CA	S	19.95 MW	18.96 AW	41510 AAW	CABLS	10//99-12//99
Postsecondary	Orange County PMSA, CA	S	25.22 MW	25.86 AW	52460 AAW	CABLS	10//99-12//99
Postsecondary	Riverside-San Bernardino PMSA, CA	S	19.25 MW	18.59 AW	40030 AAW	CABLS	10//99-12//99
Postsecondary	Sacramento PMSA, CA	S	14.62 MW	12.93 AW	30400 AAW	CABLS	10//99-12//99
Postsecondary	San Diego MSA, CA	S	21.44 MW	18.46 AW	44590 AAW	CABLS	10//99-12//99
Postsecondary	San Francisco PMSA, CA	S	26.19 MW	20.00 AW	54470 AAW	CABLS	10//99-12//99
Postsecondary	San Jose PMSA, CA	S	21.48 MW	17.96 AW	44690 AAW	CABLS	10//99-12//99
Postsecondary	Santa Barbara-Santa Maria-Lompoc MSA, CA	S	13.13 MW	9.96 AW	27300 AAW	CABLS	10//99-12//99
Postsecondary	Santa Rosa PMSA, CA	S	20.26 MW	19.56 AW	42130 AAW	CABLS	10//99-12//99
Postsecondary	Stockton-Lodi MSA, CA	S	17.19 MW	17.77 AW	35760 AAW	CABLS	10//99-12//99
Postsecondary	Vallejo-Fairfield-Napa PMSA, CA	S	22.10 MW	22.11 AW	45960 AAW	CABLS	10//99-12//99
Postsecondary	Ventura PMSA, CA	S	24.70 MW	21.14 AW	51370 AAW	CABLS	10//99-12//99
Postsecondary	Visalia-Tulare-Porterville MSA, CA	S	12.00 MW	10.95 AW	24950 AAW	CABLS	10//99-12//99
Postsecondary	Colorado	S	20.49 MW	19.87 AW	41320 AAW	COBLS	10//99-12//99
Postsecondary	Boulder-Longmont PMSA, CO	S	20.08 MW	16.67 AW	41770 AAW	COBLS	10//99-12//99
Postsecondary	Colorado Springs MSA, CO	S	17.72 MW	16.60 AW	36860 AAW	COBLS	10//99-12//99
Postsecondary	Denver PMSA, CO	S	18.52 MW	17.75 AW	38520 AAW	COBLS	10//99-12//99
Postsecondary	Fort Collins-Loveland MSA, CO	S	16.30 MW	15.49 AW	33910 AAW	COBLS	10//99-12//99
Postsecondary	Grand Junction MSA, CO	S	17.58 MW	18.43 AW	36570 AAW	COBLS	10//99-12//99
Postsecondary	Pueblo MSA, CO	S	18.65 MW	18.69 AW	38800 AAW	COBLS	10//99-12//99
Postsecondary	Connecticut	S	21.13 MW	22.02 AW	45790 AAW	CTBLS	10//99-12//99
Postsecondary	Hartford MSA, CT	S	21.54 MW	19.41 AW	44810 AAW	CTBLS	10//99-12//99
Postsecondary	New Haven-Meriden PMSA, CT	S	22.18 MW	23.66 AW	46130 AAW	CTBLS	10//99-12//99
Postsecondary	New London-Norwich MSA, CT-RI	S	18.32 MW	16.20 AW	38110 AAW	CTBLS	10//99-12//99
Postsecondary	Delaware	S	15.12 MW	15.35 AW	31920 AAW	DEBLS	10//99-12//99
Postsecondary	Washington PMSA, DC-MD-VA-WV	S	21.34 MW	20.56 AW	44390 AAW	DCBLS	10//99-12//99
Postsecondary	Florida	S	13.39 MW	15.54 AW	32330 AAW	FLBLS	10//99-12//99
Postsecondary	Daytona Beach MSA, FL	S	23.04 MW	23.30 AW	47930 AAW	FLBLS	10//99-12//99
Postsecondary	Fort Lauderdale PMSA, FL	S	13.91 MW	12.70 AW	28940 AAW	FLBLS	10//99-12//99
Postsecondary	Gainesville MSA, FL	S	15.73 MW	12.85 AW	32720 AAW	FLBLS	10//99-12//99
Postsecondary	Jacksonville MSA, FL	S	13.70 MW	14.63 AW	28490 AAW	FLBLS	10//99-12//99
Postsecondary	Lakeland-Winter Haven MSA, FL	S	14.23 MW	12.75 AW	29610 AAW	FLBLS	10//99-12//99
Postsecondary	Melbourne-Titusville-Palm Bay MSA, FL	S	16.47 MW	13.38 AW	34250 AAW	FLBLS	10//99-12//99
Postsecondary	Miami PMSA, FL	S	14.80 MW	12.71 AW	30790 AAW	FLBLS	10//99-12//99
Postsecondary	Orlando MSA, FL	S	15.73 MW	13.88 AW	32720 AAW	FLBLS	10//99-12//99
Postsecondary	Tampa-St. Petersburg-Clearwater MSA, FL	S	15.42 MW	14.85 AW	32070 AAW	FLBLS	10//99-12//99
Postsecondary	West Palm Beach-Boca Raton MSA, FL	S	15.99 MW	15.80 AW	33270 AAW	FLBLS	10//99-12//99
Postsecondary	Georgia	S	15.17 MW	16.37 AW	34060 AAW	GABLS	10//99-12//99
Postsecondary	Macon MSA, GA	S	19.43 MW	18.93 AW	40410 AAW	GABLS	10//99-12//99
Postsecondary	Savannah MSA, GA	S	20.68 MW	19.36 AW	43010 AAW	GABLS	10//99-12//99
Postsecondary	Hawaii	S	21.83 MW	23.77 AW	49450 AAW	HIBLS	10//99-12//99
Postsecondary	Honolulu MSA, HI	S	22.09 MW	19.85 AW	45940 AAW	HIBLS	10//99-12//99
Postsecondary	Idaho	S	19.42 MW	19.55 AW	40660 AAW	IDBLS	10//99-12//99
Postsecondary	Boise City MSA, ID	S	18.77 MW	18.70 AW	39050 AAW	IDBLS	10//99-12//99
Postsecondary	Illinois	S	18.08 MW	18.03 AW	37500 AAW	ILBLS	10//99-12//99
Postsecondary	Chicago PMSA, IL	S	18.91 MW	18.71 AW	39340 AAW	ILBLS	10//99-12//99
Postsecondary	Springfield MSA, IL	S	10.53 MW	9.78 AW	21890 AAW	ILBLS	10//99-12//99
Postsecondary	Indiana	S	17.7 MW	16.63 AW	34600 AAW	INBLS	10//99-12//99
Postsecondary	Evansville-Henderson MSA, IN-KY	S	17.13 MW	17.41 AW	35630 AAW	INBLS	10//99-12//99
Postsecondary	Fort Wayne MSA, IN	S	19.29 MW	19.31 AW	40120 AAW	INBLS	10//99-12//99
Postsecondary	Gary PMSA, IN	S	12.45 MW	11.70 AW	25890 AAW	INBLS	10//99-12//99
Postsecondary	Indianapolis MSA, IN	S	16.75 MW	17.76 AW	34840 AAW	INBLS	10//99-12//99
Postsecondary	Iowa	S	19.32 MW	19.39 AW	40320 AAW	IABLS	10//99-12//99
Postsecondary	Des Moines MSA, IA	S	21.13 MW	21.53 AW	43950 AAW	IABLS	10//99-12//99
Postsecondary	Kansas	S	15.18 MW	15.35 AW	31920 AAW	KSBLS	10//99-12//99
Postsecondary	Wichita MSA, KS	S	17.19 MW	17.44 AW	35760 AAW	KSBLS	10//99-12//99
Postsecondary	Kentucky	S	18.12 MW	18.63 AW	38760 AAW	KYBLS	10//99-12//99
Postsecondary	Lexington MSA, KY	S	17.16 MW	16.81 AW	35690 AAW	KYBLS	10//99-12//99

AAW	Average annual wage	AOH	Average offered, high	ASH	Average starting, high	H	Hourly	M	Monthly	S	Special: hourly and annual
AE	Average entry wage	AOL	Average offered, low	ASL	Average starting, low	HI	Highest wage paid	MTC	Median total compensation	TQ	Third quartile wage
AEX	Average experienced wage	APH	Average pay, high range	AW	Average wage paid	HR	High end range	MW	Median wage paid	W	Weekly
AO	Average offered	APL	Average pay, low range	FQ	First quartile wage	LR	Low end range	SQ	Second quartile wage	Y	Yearly

Occupation/Type/Industry	Location	Per	Low	Mid	High	Source	Date
Vocational Education Teacher							
Postsecondary	Louisville MSA, KY-IN	S	17.12 MW	16.62 AW	35600 AAW	KYBLS	10//99-12//99
Postsecondary	Louisiana	S	19.17 MW	19.62 AW	40810 AAW	LABLS	10//99-12//99
Postsecondary	Baton Rouge MSA, LA	S	15.74 MW	17.78 AW	32730 AAW	LABLS	10//99-12//99
Postsecondary	Lafayette MSA, LA	S	19.69 MW	19.48 AW	40950 AAW	LABLS	10//99-12//99
Postsecondary	New Orleans MSA, LA	S	23.22 MW	20.14 AW	48300 AAW	LABLS	10//99-12//99
Postsecondary	Shreveport-Bossier City MSA, LA	S	19.47 MW	19.35 AW	40500 AAW	LABLS	10//99-12//99
Postsecondary	Maine	S	18.96 MW	18.44 AW	38350 AAW	MEBLS	10//99-12//99
Postsecondary	Bangor MSA, ME	S	17.97 MW	18.69 AW	37380 AAW	MEBLS	10//99-12//99
Postsecondary	Portland MSA, ME	S	19.91 MW	20.02 AW	41400 AAW	MEBLS	10//99-12//99
Postsecondary	Maryland	S	18.88 MW	22.59 AW	46990 AAW	MDBLS	10//99-12//99
Postsecondary	Baltimore PMSA, MD	S	23.44 MW	18.91 AW	48750 AAW	MDBLS	10//99-12//99
Postsecondary	Massachusetts	S	14.2 MW	15.46 AW	32160 AAW	MABLS	10//99-12//99
Postsecondary	Boston PMSA, MA-NH	S	14.49 MW	13.69 AW	30140 AAW	MABLS	10//99-12//99
Postsecondary	Springfield MSA, MA	S	19.79 MW	22.53 AW	41170 AAW	MABLS	10//99-12//99
Postsecondary	Michigan	S	16.29 MW	17.79 AW	37010 AAW	MIBLS	10//99-12//99
Postsecondary	Ann Arbor PMSA, MI	S	14.46 MW	14.88 AW	30080 AAW	MIBLS	10//99-12//99
Postsecondary	Detroit PMSA, MI	S	19.43 MW	17.09 AW	40420 AAW	MIBLS	10//99-12//99
Postsecondary	Kalamazoo-Battle Creek MSA, MI	S	17.12 MW	15.78 AW	35610 AAW	MIBLS	10//99-12//99
Postsecondary	Minnesota	S	17.49 MW	18.21 AW	37880 AAW	MNBLS	10//99-12//99
Postsecondary	Duluth-Superior MSA, MN-WI	S	24.25 MW	24.81 AW	50430 AAW	MNBLS	10//99-12//99
Postsecondary	Minneapolis-St. Paul MSA, MN-WI	S	17.47 MW	13.86 AW	36340 AAW	MNBLS	10//99-12//99
Postsecondary	Mississippi	S	18.41 MW	18.19 AW	37830 AAW	MSBLS	10//99-12//99
Postsecondary	Jackson MSA, MS	S	10.33 MW	7.86 AW	21500 AAW	MSBLS	10//99-12//99
Postsecondary	Missouri	:S	17.29 MW	17.26 AW	35890 AAW	MOBLS	10//99-12//99
Postsecondary	Kansas City MSA, MO-KS	S	19.83 MW	20.46 AW	41250 AAW	MOBLS	10//99-12//99
Postsecondary	Montana	S	21.44 MW	21.00 AW	43680 AAW	MTBLS	10//99-12//99
Postsecondary	Nebraska	S	20.03 MW	20.98 AW	43650 AAW	NEBLS	10//99-12//99
Postsecondary	Omaha MSA, NE-IA	S	16.94 MW	17.79 AW	35240 AAW	NEBLS	10//99-12//99
Postsecondary	Nevada	S	15.73 MW	19.30 AW	40150 AAW	NVBLS	10//99-12//99
Postsecondary	Reno MSA, NV	S	10.24 MW	10.14 AW	21300 AAW	NVBLS	10//99-12//99
Postsecondary	New Hampshire	S	19.22 MW	19.50 AW	40550 AAW	NHBLS	10//99-12//99
Postsecondary	Nashua PMSA, NH	S	18.95 MW	17.89 AW	39420 AAW	NHBLS	10//99-12//99
Postsecondary	New Jersey	S	18.85 MW	20.54 AW	42710 AAW	NJBLS	10//99-12//99
Postsecondary	Middlesex-Somerset-Hunterdon PMSA, NJ	S	19.17 MW	18.50 AW	39870 AAW	NJBLS	10//99-12//99
Postsecondary	Monmouth-Ocean PMSA, NJ	S	21.90 MW	18.60 AW	45560 AAW	NJBLS	10//99-12//99
Postsecondary	Newark PMSA, NJ	S	20.10 MW	20.27 AW	41820 AAW	NJBLS	10//99-12//99
Postsecondary	Trenton PMSA, NJ	S	18.36 MW	18.73 AW	38200 AAW	NJBLS	10//99-12//99
Postsecondary	New Mexico	S	16.77 MW	16.91 AW	35170 AAW	NMBLS	10//99-12//99
Postsecondary	Albuquerque MSA, NM	S	17.80 MW	18.67 AW	37030 AAW	NMBLS	10//99-12//99
Postsecondary	New York	S	19.18 MW	20.95 AW	43570 AAW	NYBLS	10//99-12//99
Postsecondary	Albany-Schenectady-Troy MSA, NY	S	19.33 MW	19.27 AW	40210 AAW	NYBLS	10//99-12//99
Postsecondary	Buffalo-Niagara Falls MSA, NY	S	14.33 MW	10.54 AW	29810 AAW	NYBLS	10//99-12//99
Postsecondary	Dutchess County PMSA, NY	S	19.34 MW	19.05 AW	40220 AAW	NYBLS	10//99-12//99
Postsecondary	Elmira MSA, NY	S	14.78 MW	14.60 AW	30730 AAW	NYBLS	10//99-12//99
Postsecondary	Nassau-Suffolk PMSA, NY	S	23.62 MW	21.11 AW	49140 AAW	NYBLS	10//99-12//99
Postsecondary	New York PMSA, NY	S	26.47 MW	21.99 AW	55060 AAW	NYBLS	10//99-12//99
Postsecondary	Newburgh PMSA, NY-PA	S	18.67 MW	18.07 AW	38820 AAW	NYBLS	10//99-12//99
Postsecondary	Rochester MSA, NY	S	20.30 MW	21.11 AW	42210 AAW	NYBLS	10//99-12//99
Postsecondary	North Carolina	S	17.26 MW	17.82 AW	37060 AAW	NCBLS	10//99-12//99
Postsecondary	Charlotte-Gastonia-Rock Hill MSA, NC-SC	S	17.80 MW	17.13 AW	37030 AAW	NCBLS	10//99-12//99
Postsecondary	Greensboro--Winston-Salem--High Point MSA, NC	S	18.58 MW	17.31 AW	38650 AAW	NCBLS	10//99-12//99
Postsecondary	Raleigh-Durham-Chapel Hill MSA, NC	S	18.65 MW	18.36 AW	38790 AAW	NCBLS	10//99-12//99
Postsecondary	Ohio	S	15.77 MW	16.24 AW	33780 AAW	OHBLS	10//99-12//99
Postsecondary	Akron PMSA, OH	S	19.17 MW	19.41 AW	39880 AAW	OHBLS	10//99-12//99
Postsecondary	Cincinnati PMSA, OH-KY-IN	S	17.44 MW	16.61 AW	36270 AAW	OHBLS	10//99-12//99
Postsecondary	Cleveland-Lorain-Elyria PMSA, OH	S	14.73 MW	14.93 AW	30630 AAW	OHBLS	10//99-12//99
Postsecondary	Columbus MSA, OH	S	17.51 MW	16.77 AW	36410 AAW	OHBLS	10//99-12//99
Postsecondary	Dayton-Springfield MSA, OH	S	10.73 MW	9.53 AW	22320 AAW	OHBLS	10//99-12//99
Postsecondary	Hamilton-Middletown PMSA, OH	S	15.08 MW	15.14 AW	31360 AAW	OHBLS	10//99-12//99
Postsecondary	Toledo MSA, OH	S	20.51 MW	16.07 AW	42660 AAW	OHBLS	10//99-12//99

AAW	Average annual wage	AOH	Average offered, high	ASH	Average starting, high	H	Hourly	M	Monthly	S	Special: hourly and annual
AE	Average entry wage	AOL	Average offered, low	ASL	Average starting, low	HI	Highest wage paid	MTC	Median total compensation	TQ	Third quartile wage
AEX	Average experienced wage	APH	Average pay, high range	AW	Average wage paid	HR	High end range	MW	Median wage paid	W	Weekly
AO	Average offered	APL	Average pay, low range	FQ	First quartile wage	LR	Low end range	SQ	Second quartile wage	Y	Yearly

Occupation/Type/Industry	Location	Per	Low	Mid	High	Source	Date
Vocational Education Teacher							
Postsecondary	Youngstown-Warren MSA, OH	S	14.82 MW	16.32 AW	30830 AAW	OHBLS	10//99-12//99
Postsecondary	Oklahoma	S	17.16 MW	17.41 AW	36200 AAW	OKBLS	10//99-12//99
Postsecondary	Oklahoma City MSA, OK	S	22.75 MW	23.09 AW	47320 AAW	OKBLS	10//99-12//99
Postsecondary	Tulsa, OK	S	16.44 MW	13.11 AW	34200 AAW	OKBLS	10//99-12//99
Postsecondary	Oregon	S	25.41 MW	24.58 AW	51130 AAW	ORBLS	10//99-12//99
Postsecondary	Portland-Vancouver PMSA, OR-WA	S	23.65 MW	24.79 AW	49190 AAW	ORBLS	10//99-12//99
Postsecondary	Pennsylvania	S	15.16 MW	17.90 AW	37230 AAW	PABLS	10//99-12//99
Postsecondary	Harrisburg-Lebanon-Carlisle MSA, PA	S	19.71 MW	17.76 AW	40990 AAW	PABLS	10//99-12//99
Postsecondary	Lancaster MSA, PA	S	18.10 MW	15.78 AW	37640 AAW	PABLS	10//99-12//99
Postsecondary	Philadelphia PMSA, PA-NJ	S	23.82 MW	21.05 AW	49550 AAW	PABLS	10//99-12//99
Postsecondary	Pittsburgh MSA, PA	S	13.33 MW	12.34 AW	27720 AAW	PABLS	10//99-12//99
Postsecondary	Scranton--Wilkes-Barre--Hazleton MSA, PA	S	12.92 MW	12.00 AW	26870 AAW	PABLS	10//99-12//99
Postsecondary	York MSA, PA	S	14.10 MW	14.22 AW	29320 AAW	PABLS	10//99-12//99
Postsecondary	Rhode Island	S	19.49 MW	21.45 AW	44610 AAW	RIBLS	10//99-12//99
Postsecondary	Providence-Fall River-Warwick MSA, RI-MA	S	18.78 MW	17.79 AW	39060 AAW	RIBLS	10//99-12//99
Postsecondary	South Carolina	S	16.46 MW	18.59 AW	38660 AAW	SCBLS	10//99-12//99
Postsecondary	Columbia MSA, SC	S	23.84 MW	24.00 AW	49580 AAW	SCBLS	10//99-12//99
Postsecondary	Greenville-Spartanburg-Anderson MSA, SC	S	15.14 MW	15.10 AW	31490 AAW	SCBLS	10//99-12//99
Postsecondary	Sumter MSA, SC	S	7.85 MW	7.70 AW	16330 AAW	SCBLS	10//99-12//99
Postsecondary	South Dakota	S	18.99 MW	19.06 AW	39650 AAW	SDBLS	10//99-12//99
Postsecondary	Tennessee	S	16.04 MW	17.08 AW	35530 AAW	TNBLS	10//99-12//99
Postsecondary	Chattanooga MSA, TN-GA	S	14.06 MW	13.06 AW	29250 AAW	TNBLS	10//99-12//99
Postsecondary	Johnson City-Kingsport-Bristol MSA, TN-VA	S	14.39 MW	14.65 AW	29930 AAW	TNBLS	10//99-12//99
Postsecondary	Knoxville MSA, TN	S	14.78 MW	14.89 AW	30740 AAW	TNBLS	10//99-12//99
Postsecondary	Memphis MSA, TN-AR-MS	S	19.05 MW	19.35 AW	39620 AAW	MSBLS	10//99-12//99
Postsecondary	Nashville MSA, TN	S	19.76 MW	18.43 AW	41090 AAW	TNBLS	10//99-12//99
Postsecondary	Texas	S	15.55 MW	16.16 AW	33620 AAW	TXBLS	10//99-12//99
Postsecondary	Austin-San Marcos MSA, TX	S	13.97 MW	13.71 AW	29050 AAW	TXBLS	10//99-12//99
Postsecondary	Dallas PMSA, TX	S	16.77 MW	15.99 AW	34880 AAW	TXBLS	10//99-12//99
Postsecondary	El Paso MSA, TX	S	11.68 MW	9.71 AW	24290 AAW	TXBLS	10//99-12//99
Postsecondary	Fort Worth-Arlington PMSA, TX	S	17.45 MW	14.91 AW	36290 AAW	TXBLS	10//99-12//99
Postsecondary	Houston PMSA, TX	S	18.24 MW	16.64 AW	37950 AAW	TXBLS	10//99-12//99
Postsecondary	Killeen-Temple MSA, TX	S	17.30 MW	17.93 AW	35990 AAW	TXBLS	10//99-12//99
Postsecondary	San Antonio MSA, TX	S	15.62 MW	15.88 AW	32490 AAW	TXBLS	10//99-12//99
Postsecondary	Tyler MSA, TX	S	11.62 MW	7.92 AW	24170 AAW	TXBLS	10//99-12//99
Postsecondary	Utah	S	16.18 MW	18.05 AW	37540 AAW	UTBLS	10//99-12//99
Postsecondary	Vermont	S	15.85 MW	16.22 AW	33750 AAW	VTBLS	10//99-12//99
Postsecondary	Virginia	S	18.58 MW	18.78 AW	39070 AAW	VABLS	10//99-12//99
Postsecondary	Charlottesville MSA, VA	S	18.22 MW	18.72 AW	37900 AAW	VABLS	10//99-12//99
Postsecondary	Danville MSA, VA	S	14.72 MW	13.00 AW	30610 AAW	VABLS	10//99-12//99
Postsecondary	Norfolk-Virginia Beach-Newport News MSA, VA-NC	S	18.73 MW	18.44 AW	38960 AAW	VABLS	10//99-12//99
Postsecondary	Richmond-Petersburg MSA, VA	S	16.81 MW	17.07 AW	34970 AAW	VABLS	10//99-12//99
Postsecondary	Washington	S	13.5 MW	15.18 AW	31560 AAW	WABLS	10//99-12//99
Postsecondary	Bremerton PMSA, WA	S	15.32 MW	17.56 AW	31870 AAW	WABLS	10//99-12//99
Postsecondary	Richland-Kennewick-Pasco MSA, WA	S	25.32 MW	26.61 AW	52660 AAW	WABLS	10//99-12//99
Postsecondary	Seattle-Bellevue-Everett PMSA, WA	S	13.41 MW	12.56 AW	27880 AAW	WABLS	10//99-12//99
Postsecondary	Spokane MSA, WA	S	14.79 MW	14.42 AW	30760 AAW	WABLS	10//99-12//99
Postsecondary	Tacoma PMSA, WA	S	15.71 MW	13.42 AW	32680 AAW	WABLS	10//99-12//99
Postsecondary	Yakima MSA, WA	S	19.27 MW	19.77 AW	40090 AAW	WABLS	10//99-12//99
Postsecondary	Charleston MSA, WV	S	13.38 MW	12.47 AW	27830 AAW	WVBLS	10//99-12//99
Postsecondary	Parkersburg-Marietta MSA, WV-OH	S	11.28 MW	10.59 AW	23470 AAW	WVBLS	10//99-12//99
Postsecondary	Wheeling MSA, WV-OH	S	13.81 MW	12.60 AW	28730 AAW	WVBLS	10//99-12//99
Postsecondary	Milwaukee-Waukesha PMSA, WI	S	21.40 MW	22.19 AW	44520 AAW	WIBLS	10//99-12//99
Postsecondary	Wyoming	S	16.42 MW	19.35 AW	40240 AAW	WYBLS	10//99-12//99
Postsecondary	Puerto Rico	S	12.17 MW	14.01 AW	29140 AAW	PRBLS	10//99-12//99
Postsecondary	San Juan-Bayamon PMSA, PR	S	11.37 MW	11.51 AW	23660 AAW	PRBLS	10//99-12//99
Secondary School	Alabama	Y		42850 AAW		ALBLS	10//99-12//99

AAW	Average annual wage	AOH	Average offered, high	ASH	Average starting, high	H	Hourly	M	Monthly	S	Special: hourly and annual
AE	Average entry wage	AOL	Average offered, low	ASL	Average starting, low	HI	Highest wage paid	MTC	Median total compensation	TQ	Third quartile wage
AEX	Average experienced wage	APH	Average pay, high range	AW	Average wage paid	HR	High end range	MW	Median wage paid	W	Weekly
AO	Average offered	APL	Average pay, low range	FQ	First quartile wage	LR	Low end range	SQ	Second quartile wage	Y	Yearly

Occupation/Type/Industry	Location	Per	Low	Mid	High	Source	Date
Vocational Education Teacher							
Secondary School	Decatur MSA, AL	Y		41470 AAW		ALBLS	10//99-12//99
Secondary School	Dothan MSA, AL	Y		45410 AAW		ALBLS	10//99-12//99
Secondary School	Florence MSA, AL	Y		43020 AAW		ALBLS	10//99-12//99
Secondary School	Alaska	Y		51230 AAW		AKBLS	10//99-12//99
Secondary School	Arizona	Y		32250 AAW		AZBLS	10//99-12//99
Secondary School	Arkansas	Y		34550 AAW		ARBLS	10//99-12//99
Secondary School	Fayetteville-Springdale-Rogers MSA, AR	Y		35880 AAW		ARBLS	10//99-12//99
Secondary School	Fort Smith MSA, AR-OK	Y		33780 AAW		ARBLS	10//99-12//99
Secondary School	Little Rock-North Little Rock MSA, AR	Y		35640 AAW		ARBLS	10//99-12//99
Secondary School	California	Y		50410 AAW		CABLS	10//99-12//99
Secondary School	Fresno MSA, CA	Y		47140 AAW		CABLS	10//99-12//99
Secondary School	Los Angeles-Long Beach PMSA, CA	Y		56900 AAW		CABLS	10//99-12//99
Secondary School	Oakland PMSA, CA	Y		42140 AAW		CABLS	10//99-12//99
Secondary School	Riverside-San Bernardino PMSA, CA	Y		46690 AAW		CABLS	10//99-12//99
Secondary School	Sacramento PMSA, CA	Y		46140 AAW		CABLS	10//99-12//99
Secondary School	San Diego MSA, CA	Y		46580 AAW		CABLS	10//99-12//99
Secondary School	San Francisco PMSA, CA	Y		42720 AAW		CABLS	10//99-12//99
Secondary School	San Luis Obispo-Atascadero-Paso Robles MSA, CA	Y		47580 AAW		CABLS	10//99-12//99
Secondary School	Santa Rosa PMSA, CA	Y		47270 AAW		CABLS	10//99-12//99
Secondary School	Stockton-Lodi MSA, CA	Y		45400 AAW		CABLS	10//99-12//99
Secondary School	Ventura PMSA, CA	Y		46810 AAW		CABLS	10//99-12//99
Secondary School	Visalia-Tulare-Porterville MSA, CA	Y		47490 AAW		CABLS	10//99-12//99
Secondary School	Colorado	Y		37580 AAW		COBLS	10//99-12//99
Secondary School	Denver PMSA, CO	Y		40810 AAW		COBLS	10//99-12//99
Secondary School	Connecticut	Y		45410 AAW		CTBLS	10//99-12//99
Secondary School	Danbury PMSA, CT	Y		49400 AAW		CTBLS	10//99-12//99
Secondary School	Hartford MSA, CT	Y		54680 AAW		CTBLS	10//99-12//99
Secondary School	New Haven-Meriden PMSA, CT	Y		47670 AAW		CTBLS	10//99-12//99
Secondary School	New London-Norwich MSA, CT-RI	Y		52810 AAW		CTBLS	10//99-12//99
Secondary School	Washington PMSA, DC-MD-VA-WV	Y		41200 AAW		DCBLS	10//99-12//99
Secondary School	Florida	Y		40500 AAW		FLBLS	10//99-12//99
Secondary School	Fort Lauderdale PMSA, FL	Y		40980 AAW		FLBLS	10//99-12//99
Secondary School	Fort Pierce-Port St. Lucie MSA, FL	Y		51320 AAW		FLBLS	10//99-12//99
Secondary School	Jacksonville MSA, FL	Y		43140 AAW		FLBLS	10//99-12//99
Secondary School	Orlando MSA, FL	Y		39600 AAW		FLBLS	10//99-12//99
Secondary School	Pensacola MSA, FL	Y		41280 AAW		FLBLS	10//99-12//99
Secondary School	Tallahassee MSA, FL	Y		49260 AAW		FLBLS	10//99-12//99
Secondary School	Tampa-St. Petersburg-Clearwater MSA, FL	Y		36400 AAW		FLBLS	10//99-12//99
Secondary School	Georgia	Y		44530 AAW		GABLS	10//99-12//99
Secondary School	Atlanta MSA, GA	Y		45390 AAW		GABLS	10//99-12//99
Secondary School	Columbus MSA, GA-AL	Y		43350 AAW		GABLS	10//99-12//99
Secondary School	Macon MSA, GA	Y		42960 AAW		GABLS	10//99-12//99
Secondary School	Illinois	Y		45800 AAW		ILBLS	10//99-12//99
Secondary School	Chicago PMSA, IL	Y		54900 AAW		ILBLS	10//99-12//99
Secondary School	Peoria-Pekin MSA, IL	Y		39470 AAW		ILBLS	10//99-12//99
Secondary School	Rockford MSA, IL	Y		41500 AAW		ILBLS	10//99-12//99
Secondary School	Indiana	Y		44680 AAW		INBLS	10//99-12//99
Secondary School	Fort Wayne MSA, IN	Y		44760 AAW		INBLS	10//99-12//99
Secondary School	Gary PMSA, IN	Y		46810 AAW		INBLS	10//99-12//99
Secondary School	Indianapolis MSA, IN	Y		47620 AAW		INBLS	10//99-12//99
Secondary School	Lafayette MSA, IN	Y		49150 AAW		INBLS	10//99-12//99
Secondary School	Iowa	Y		35150 AAW		IABLS	10//99-12//99
Secondary School	Cedar Rapids MSA, IA	Y		31030 AAW		IABLS	10//99-12//99
Secondary School	Davenport-Moline-Rock Island MSA, IA-IL	Y		48100 AAW		IABLS	10//99-12//99
Secondary School	Kansas	Y		33820 AAW		KSBLS	10//99-12//99
Secondary School	Kentucky	Y		37870 AAW		KYBLS	10//99-12//99
Secondary School	Louisiana	Y		34650 AAW		LABLS	10//99-12//99
Secondary School	New Orleans MSA, LA	Y		36870 AAW		LABLS	10//99-12//99
Secondary School	Maine	Y		38740 AAW		MEBLS	10//99-12//99

AAW	Average annual wage	AOH	Average offered, high	ASH	Average starting, high	H	Hourly	M	Monthly	S	Special: hourly and annual
AE	Average entry wage	AOL	Average offered, low	ASL	Average starting, low	HI	Highest wage paid	MTC	Median total compensation	TQ	Third quartile wage
AEX	Average experienced wage	APH	Average pay, high range	AW	Average wage paid	HR	High end range	MW	Median wage paid	W	Weekly
AO	Average offered	APL	Average pay, low range	FQ	First quartile wage	LR	Low end range	SQ	Second quartile wage	Y	Yearly

Occupation/Type/Industry	Location	Per	Low	Mid	High	Source	Date
Vocational Education Teacher							
Secondary School	Maryland	Y		40120 AAW		MDBLS	10//99-12//99
Secondary School	Massachusetts	Y		47070 AAW		MABLS	10//99-12//99
Secondary School	Boston PMSA, MA-NH	Y		46940 AAW		MABLS	10//99-12//99
Secondary School	Springfield MSA, MA	Y		50010 AAW		MABLS	10//99-12//99
Secondary School	Michigan	Y		46840 AAW		MIBLS	10//99-12//99
Secondary School	Benton Harbor MSA, MI	Y		45030 AAW		MIBLS	10//99-12//99
Secondary School	Detroit PMSA, MI	Y		47310 AAW		MIBLS	10//99-12//99
Secondary School	Grand Rapids-Muskegon-Holland MSA, MI	Y		53050 AAW		MIBLS	10//99-12//99
Secondary School	Kalamazoo-Battle Creek MSA, MI	Y		45580 AAW		MIBLS	10//99-12//99
Secondary School	Minnesota	Y		40580 AAW		MNBLS	10//99-12//99
Secondary School	Duluth-Superior MSA, MN-WI	Y		42870 AAW		MNBLS	10//99-12//99
Secondary School	Minneapolis-St. Paul MSA, MN-WI	Y		44380 AAW		MNBLS	10//99-12//99
Secondary School	Mississippi	Y		33870 AAW		MSBLS	10//99-12//99
Secondary School	Biloxi-Gulfport-Pascagoula MSA, MS	Y		31010 AAW		MSBLS	10//99-12//99
Secondary School	Hattiesburg MSA, MS	Y		31310 AAW		MSBLS	10//99-12//99
Secondary School	Jackson MSA, MS	Y		38480 AAW		MSBLS	10//99-12//99
Secondary School	Missouri	Y		34270 AAW		MOBLS	10//99-12//99
Secondary School	Joplin MSA, MO	Y		28490 AAW		MOBLS	10//99-12//99
Secondary School	Kansas City MSA, MO-KS	Y		34810 AAW		MOBLS	10//99-12//99
Secondary School	St. Louis MSA, MO-IL	Y		42430 AAW		MOBLS	10//99-12//99
Secondary School	Springfield MSA, MO	Y		33230 AAW		MOBLS	10//99-12//99
Secondary School	Montana	Y		30730 AAW		MTBLS	10//99-12//99
Secondary School	Nebraska	Y		37250 AAW		NEBLS	10//99-12//99
Secondary School	Omaha MSA, NE-IA	Y		32440 AAW		NEBLS	10//99-12//99
Secondary School	Nevada	Y		40970 AAW		NVBLS	10//99-12//99
Secondary School	New Hampshire	Y		31870 AAW		NHBLS	10//99-12//99
Secondary School	Manchester PMSA, NH	Y		47620 AAW		NHBLS	10//99-12//99
Secondary School	New Jersey	Y		52610 AAW		NJBLS	10//99-12//99
Secondary School	Monmouth-Ocean PMSA, NJ	Y		54480 AAW		NJBLS	10//99-12//99
Secondary School	Newark PMSA, NJ	Y		52890 AAW		NJBLS	10//99-12//99
Secondary School	New Mexico	Y		34510 AAW		NMBLS	10//99-12//99
Secondary School	New York	Y		45700 AAW		NYBLS	10//99-12//99
Secondary School	Albany-Schenectady-Troy MSA, NY	Y		47910 AAW		NYBLS	10//99-12//99
Secondary School	Binghamton MSA, NY	Y		41770 AAW		NYBLS	10//99-12//99
Secondary School	Buffalo-Niagara Falls MSA, NY	Y		45560 AAW		NYBLS	10//99-12//99
Secondary School	Jamestown MSA, NY	Y		47220 AAW		NYBLS	10//99-12//99
Secondary School	Nassau-Suffolk PMSA, NY	Y		53300 AAW		NYBLS	10//99-12//99
Secondary School	New York PMSA, NY	Y		49230 AAW		NYBLS	10//99-12//99
Secondary School	Newburgh PMSA, NY-PA	Y		41160 AAW		NYBLS	10//99-12//99
Secondary School	Rochester MSA, NY	Y		43760 AAW		NYBLS	10//99-12//99
Secondary School	Syracuse MSA, NY	Y		38890 AAW		NYBLS	10//99-12//99
Secondary School	Utica-Rome MSA, NY	Y		44720 AAW		NYBLS	10//99-12//99
Secondary School	North Carolina	Y		37680 AAW		NCBLS	10//99-12//99
Secondary School	Asheville MSA, NC	Y		37660 AAW		NCBLS	10//99-12//99
Secondary School	Charlotte-Gastonia-Rock Hill MSA, NC-SC	Y		39910 AAW		NCBLS	10//99-12//99
Secondary School	Greensboro--Winston-Salem--High Point MSA, NC	Y		34870 AAW		NCBLS	10//99-12//99
Secondary School	Hickory-Morganton-Lenoir MSA, NC	Y		35680 AAW		NCBLS	10//99-12//99
Secondary School	North Dakota	Y		32360 AAW		NDBLS	10//99-12//99
Secondary School	Fargo-Moorhead MSA, ND-MN	Y		36670 AAW		NDBLS	10//99-12//99
Secondary School	Ohio	Y		44100 AAW		OHBLS	10//99-12//99
Secondary School	Akron PMSA, OH	Y		42730 AAW		OHBLS	10//99-12//99
Secondary School	Canton-Massillon MSA, OH	Y		45410 AAW		OHBLS	10//99-12//99
Secondary School	Cincinnati PMSA, OH-KY-IN	Y		41920 AAW		OHBLS	10//99-12//99
Secondary School	Cleveland-Lorain-Elyria PMSA, OH	Y		52490 AAW		OHBLS	10//99-12//99
Secondary School	Columbus MSA, OH	Y		48890 AAW		OHBLS	10//99-12//99
Secondary School	Dayton-Springfield MSA, OH	Y		46650 AAW		OHBLS	10//99-12//99
Secondary School	Hamilton-Middletown PMSA, OH	Y		44550 AAW		OHBLS	10//99-12//99
Secondary School	Lima MSA, OH	Y		48080 AAW		OHBLS	10//99-12//99
Secondary School	Mansfield MSA, OH	Y		44440 AAW		OHBLS	10//99-12//99

AAW	Average annual wage	AOH	Average offered, high	ASH	Average starting, high	H	Hourly
AE	Average entry wage	AOL	Average offered, low	ASL	Average starting, low	HI	Highest wage paid
AEX	Average experienced wage	APH	Average pay, high range	AW	Average wage paid	HR	High end range
AO	Average offered	APL	Average pay, low range	FQ	First quartile wage	LR	Low end range

M	Monthly	S	Special: hourly and annual
MTC	Median total compensation	TQ	Third quartile wage
MW	Median wage paid	W	Weekly
SQ	Second quartile wage	Y	Yearly

Occupation/Type/Industry	Location	Per	Low	Mid	High	Source	Date
Vocational Education Teacher							
Secondary School	Toledo MSA, OH	Y		45700 AAW		OHBLS	10//99-12//99
Secondary School	Youngstown-Warren MSA, OH	Y		39630 AAW		OHBLS	10//99-12//99
Secondary School	Oklahoma	Y		40440 AAW		OKBLS	10//99-12//99
Secondary School	Lawton MSA, OK	Y		31290 AAW		OKBLS	10//99-12//99
Secondary School	Oklahoma City MSA, OK	Y		43530 AAW		OKBLS	10//99-12//99
Secondary School	Tulsa MSA, OK	Y		41420 AAW		OKBLS	10//99-12//99
Secondary School	Oregon	Y		42670 AAW		ORBLS	10//99-12//99
Secondary School	Medford-Ashland MSA, OR	Y		41790 AAW		ORBLS	10//99-12//99
Secondary School	Portland-Vancouver PMSA, OR-WA	Y		41140 AAW		ORBLS	10//99-12//99
Secondary School	Pennsylvania	Y		45150 AAW		PABLS	10//99-12//99
Secondary School	Allentown-Bethlehem-Easton MSA, PA	Y		45630 AAW		PABLS	10//99-12//99
Secondary School	Altoona MSA, PA	Y		37310 AAW		PABLS	10//99-12//99
Secondary School	Erie MSA, PA	Y		45080 AAW		PABLS	10//99-12//99
Secondary School	Harrisburg-Lebanon-Carlisle MSA, PA	Y		36440 AAW		PABLS	10//99-12//99
Secondary School	Lancaster MSA, PA	Y		44750 AAW		PABLS	10//99-12//99
Secondary School	Philadelphia PMSA, PA-NJ	Y		46860 AAW		PABLS	10//99-12//99
Secondary School	Pittsburgh MSA, PA	Y		45820 AAW		PABLS	10//99-12//99
Secondary School	Reading MSA, PA	Y		45870 AAW		PABLS	10//99-12//99
Secondary School	Scranton--Wilkes-Barre--Hazleton MSA, PA	Y		43880 AAW		PABLS	10//99-12//99
Secondary School	Sharon MSA, PA	Y		42200 AAW		PABLS	10//99-12//99
Secondary School	York MSA, PA	Y		49220 AAW		PABLS	10//99-12//99
Secondary School	Rhode Island	Y		48350 AAW		RIBLS	10//99-12//99
Secondary School	Providence-Fall River-Warwick MSA, RI-MA	Y		47220 AAW		RIBLS	10//99-12//99
Secondary School	South Carolina	Y		37630 AAW		SCBLS	10//99-12//99
Secondary School	Columbia MSA, SC	Y		31400 AAW		SCBLS	10//99-12//99
Secondary School	Greenville-Spartanburg-Anderson MSA, SC	Y		39070 AAW		SCBLS	10//99-12//99
Secondary School	South Dakota	Y		28660 AAW		SDBLS	10//99-12//99
Secondary School	Tennessee	Y		34550 AAW		TNBLS	10//99-12//99
Secondary School	Chattanooga MSA, TN-GA	Y		37380 AAW		TNBLS	10//99-12//99
Secondary School	Johnson City-Kingsport-Bristol MSA, TN-VA	Y		32200 AAW		TNBLS	10//99-12//99
Secondary School	Knoxville MSA, TN	Y		34040 AAW		TNBLS	10//99-12//99
Secondary School	Memphis MSA, TN-AR-MS	Y		40890 AAW		MSBLS	10//99-12//99
Secondary School	Nashville MSA, TN	Y		33320 AAW		TNBLS	10//99-12//99
Secondary School	Texas	Y		40520 AAW		TXBLS	10//99-12//99
Secondary School	Austin-San Marcos MSA, TX	Y		38880 AAW		TXBLS	10//99-12//99
Secondary School	Beaumont-Port Arthur MSA, TX	Y		30920 AAW		TXBLS	10//99-12//99
Secondary School	Dallas PMSA, TX	Y		39230 AAW		TXBLS	10//99-12//99
Secondary School	Fort Worth-Arlington PMSA, TX	Y		42550 AAW		TXBLS	10//99-12//99
Secondary School	Galveston-Texas City PMSA, TX	Y		41820 AAW		TXBLS	10//99-12//99
Secondary School	Houston PMSA, TX	Y		42630 AAW		TXBLS	10//99-12//99
Secondary School	Killeen-Temple MSA, TX	Y		38120 AAW		TXBLS	10//99-12//99
Secondary School	Longview-Marshall MSA, TX	Y		38610 AAW		TXBLS	10//99-12//99
Secondary School	McAllen-Edinburg-Mission MSA, TX	Y		41740 AAW		TXBLS	10//99-12//99
Secondary School	San Antonio MSA, TX	Y		43680 AAW		TXBLS	10//99-12//99
Secondary School	Sherman-Denison MSA, TX	Y		41950 AAW		TXBLS	10//99-12//99
Secondary School	Texarkana MSA, TX-Texarkana, AR	Y		38860 AAW		TXBLS	10//99-12//99
Secondary School	Waco MSA, TX	Y		38910 AAW		TXBLS	10//99-12//99
Secondary School	Utah	Y		35590 AAW		UTBLS	10//99-12//99
Secondary School	Salt Lake City-Ogden MSA, UT	Y		37200 AAW		UTBLS	10//99-12//99
Secondary School	Vermont	Y		42070 AAW		VTBLS	10//99-12//99
Secondary School	Burlington MSA, VT	Y		45650 AAW		VTBLS	10//99-12//99
Secondary School	Virginia	Y		36070 AAW		VABLS	10//99-12//99
Secondary School	Norfolk-Virginia Beach-Newport News MSA, VA-NC	Y		32890 AAW		VABLS	10//99-12//99
Secondary School	Washington	Y		40920 AAW		WABLS	10//99-12//99
Secondary School	Bellingham MSA, WA	Y		39500 AAW		WABLS	10//99-12//99

AAW	Average annual wage	AOH	Average offered, high	ASH	Average starting, high	H	Hourly	M	Monthly	S	Special: hourly and annual
AE	Average entry wage	AOL	Average offered, low	ASL	Average starting, low	HI	Highest wage paid	MTC	Median total compensation	TQ	Third quartile wage
AEX	Average experienced wage	APH	Average pay, high range	AW	Average wage paid	HR	High end range	MW	Median wage paid	W	Weekly
AO	Average offered	APL	Average pay, low range	FQ	First quartile wage	LR	Low end range	SQ	Second quartile wage	Y	Yearly

Occupation/Type/Industry	Location	Per	Low	Mid	High	Source	Date
Vocational Education Teacher							
Secondary School	Richland-Kennewick-Pasco MSA, WA	Y		38810 AAW		WABLS	10//99-12//99
Secondary School	Seattle-Bellevue-Everett PMSA, WA	Y		40840 AAW		WABLS	10//99-12//99
Secondary School	Spokane MSA, WA	Y		43470 AAW		WABLS	10//99-12//99
Secondary School	Yakima MSA, WA	Y		38960 AAW		WABLS	10//99-12//99
Secondary School	West Virginia	Y		36390 AAW		WVBLS	10//99-12//99
Secondary School	Wisconsin	Y		42450 AAW		WIBLS	10//99-12//99
Secondary School	Appleton-Oshkosh-Neenah MSA, WI	Y		39260 AAW		WIBLS	10//99-12//99
Secondary School	Eau Claire MSA, WI	Y		43760 AAW		WIBLS	10//99-12//99
Secondary School	La Crosse MSA, WI-MN	Y		34790 AAW		WIBLS	10//99-12//99
Secondary School	Madison MSA, WI	Y		40270 AAW		WIBLS	10//99-12//99
Secondary School	Milwaukee-Waukesha PMSA, WI	Y		44390 AAW		WIBLS	10//99-12//99
Secondary School	Wyoming	Y		34770 AAW		WYBLS	10//99-12//99
Voting-Machine Technician	New York City, NY	Y	21190 AE			TIME	2000
Waiter and Waitress	Alabama	S	5.96 MW	6.02 AW	12510 AAW	ALBLS	10//99-12//99
	Anniston MSA, AL	S	5.82 MW	5.99 AW	12100 AAW	ALBLS	10//99-12//99
	Auburn-Opelika MSA, AL	S	6.03 MW	5.98 AW	12540 AAW	ALBLS	10//99-12//99
	Birmingham MSA, AL	S	6.13 MW	5.96 AW	12760 AAW	ALBLS	10//99-12//99
	Decatur MSA, AL	S	5.73 MW	5.89 AW	11920 AAW	ALBLS	10//99-12//99
	Dothan MSA, AL	S	5.89 MW	5.94 AW	12260 AAW	ALBLS	10//99-12//99
	Florence MSA, AL	S	6.29 MW	6.04 AW	13070 AAW	ALBLS	10//99-12//99
	Gadsden MSA, AL	S	5.94 MW	5.93 AW	12340 AAW	ALBLS	10//99-12//99
	Huntsville MSA, AL	S	6.02 MW	5.99 AW	12510 AAW	ALBLS	10//99-12//99
	Mobile MSA, AL	S	6.06 MW	5.94 AW	12610 AAW	ALBLS	10//99-12//99
	Montgomery MSA, AL	S	5.98 MW	5.98 AW	12430 AAW	ALBLS	10//99-12//99
	Tuscaloosa MSA, AL	S	6.25 MW	6.04 AW	13000 AAW	ALBLS	10//99-12//99
	Alaska	S	6.63 MW	7.09 AW	14740 AAW	AKBLS	10//99-12//99
	Anchorage MSA, AK	S	7.11 MW	6.55 AW	14780 AAW	AKBLS	10//99-12//99
	Arizona	S	5.96 MW	6.00 AW	12480 AAW	AZBLS	10//99-12//99
	Flagstaff MSA, AZ-UT	S	6.05 MW	6.00 AW	12580 AAW	AZBLS	10//99-12//99
	Phoenix-Mesa MSA, AZ	S	5.96 MW	5.96 AW	12390 AAW	AZBLS	10//99-12//99
	Tucson MSA, AZ	S	6.26 MW	5.97 AW	13030 AAW	AZBLS	10//99-12//99
	Yuma MSA, AZ	S	6.10 MW	6.07 AW	12690 AAW	AZBLS	10//99-12//99
	Arkansas	S	5.94 MW	5.96 AW	12400 AAW	ARBLS	10//99-12//99
	Fayetteville-Springdale-Rogers MSA, AR	S	5.94 MW	5.96 AW	12360 AAW	ARBLS	10//99-12//99
	Fort Smith MSA, AR-OK	S	6.23 MW	6.02 AW	12970 AAW	ARBLS	10//99-12//99
	Jonesboro MSA, AR	S	6.13 MW	5.92 AW	12750 AAW	ARBLS	10//99-12//99
	Little Rock-North Little Rock MSA, AR	S	6.24 MW	5.97 AW	12970 AAW	ARBLS	10//99-12//99
	Pine Bluff MSA, AR	S	5.74 MW	5.84 AW	11930 AAW	ARBLS	10//99-12//99
	California	S	6.3 MW	6.90 AW	14350 AAW	CABLS	10//99-12//99
	Bakersfield MSA, CA	S	6.38 MW	6.09 AW	13270 AAW	CABLS	10//99-12//99
	Chico-Paradise MSA, CA	S	6.62 MW	6.44 AW	13770 AAW	CABLS	10//99-12//99
	Fresno MSA, CA	S	6.42 MW	6.22 AW	13350 AAW	CABLS	10//99-12//99
	Los Angeles-Long Beach PMSA, CA	S	6.79 MW	6.23 AW	14130 AAW	CABLS	10//99-12//99
	Merced MSA, CA	S	6.56 MW	6.10 AW	13650 AAW	CABLS	10//99-12//99
	Modesto MSA, CA	S	7.07 MW	6.45 AW	14700 AAW	CABLS	10//99-12//99
	Oakland PMSA, CA	S	7.15 MW	6.51 AW	14880 AAW	CABLS	10//99-12//99
	Orange County PMSA, CA	S	6.54 MW	6.17 AW	13600 AAW	CABLS	10//99-12//99
	Redding MSA, CA	S	6.65 MW	6.43 AW	13830 AAW	CABLS	10//99-12//99
	Riverside-San Bernardino PMSA, CA	S	6.66 MW	6.13 AW	13850 AAW	CABLS	10//99-12//99
	Sacramento PMSA, CA	S	6.93 MW	6.43 AW	14410 AAW	CABLS	10//99-12//99
	Salinas MSA, CA	S	6.76 MW	6.11 AW	14060 AAW	CABLS	10//99-12//99
	San Diego MSA, CA	S	6.80 MW	6.32 AW	14140 AAW	CABLS	10//99-12//99
	San Francisco PMSA, CA	S	7.53 MW	6.61 AW	15660 AAW	CABLS	10//99-12//99
	San Jose PMSA, CA	S	7.09 MW	6.39 AW	14750 AAW	CABLS	10//99-12//99
	San Luis Obispo-Atascadero-Paso Robles MSA, CA	S	8.51 MW	6.67 AW	17700 AAW	CABLS	10//99-12//99
	Santa Barbara-Santa Maria-Lompoc MSA, CA	S	7.39 MW	6.29 AW	15380 AAW	CABLS	10//99-12//99
	Santa Cruz-Watsonville PMSA, CA	S	7.45 MW	6.27 AW	15500 AAW	CABLS	10//99-12//99
	Santa Rosa PMSA, CA	S	6.87 MW	6.34 AW	14300 AAW	CABLS	10//99-12//99
	Stockton-Lodi MSA, CA	S	6.43 MW	6.12 AW	13380 AAW	CABLS	10//99-12//99

AAW	Average annual wage	AOH	Average offered, high	ASH	Average starting, high	H	Hourly	M	Monthly	S	Special: hourly and annual
AE	Average entry wage	AOL	Average offered, low	ASL	Average starting, low	HI	Highest wage paid	MTC	Median total compensation	TQ	Third quartile wage
AEX	Average experienced wage	APH	Average pay, high range	AW	Average wage paid	HR	High end range	MW	Median wage paid	W	Weekly
AO	Average offered	APL	Average pay, low range	FQ	First quartile wage	LR	Low end range	SQ	Second quartile wage	Y	Yearly

Occupation/Type/Industry	Location	Per	Low	Mid	High	Source	Date
Waiter and Waitress	Vallejo-Fairfield-Napa PMSA, CA	S	6.67 MW	6.11 AW	13880 AAW	CABLS	10//99-12//99
	Ventura PMSA, CA	S	7.89 MW	6.36 AW	16400 AAW	CABLS	10//99-12//99
	Visalia-Tulare-Porterville MSA, CA	S	6.41 MW	6.12 AW	13330 AAW	CABLS	10//99-12//99
	Yolo PMSA, CA	S	6.49 MW	6.29 AW	13500 AAW	CABLS	10//99-12//99
	Yuba City MSA, CA	S	6.82 MW	6.41 AW	14190 AAW	CABLS	10//99-12//99
	Colorado	S	6.04 MW	7.01 AW	14590 AAW	COBLS	10//99-12//99
	Boulder-Longmont PMSA, CO	S	6.82 MW	6.07 AW	14190 AAW	COBLS	10//99-12//99
	Colorado Springs MSA, CO	S	7.15 MW	5.99 AW	14880 AAW	COBLS	10//99-12//99
	Denver PMSA, CO	S	7.37 MW	6.10 AW	15320 AAW	COBLS	10//99-12//99
	Fort Collins-Loveland MSA, CO	S	7.60 MW	6.11 AW	15800 AAW	COBLS	10//99-12//99
	Grand Junction MSA, CO	S	6.43 MW	6.11 AW	13360 AAW	COBLS	10//99-12//99
	Greeley PMSA, CO	S	5.77 MW	5.93 AW	11990 AAW	COBLS	10//99-12//99
	Pueblo MSA, CO	S	5.99 MW	5.97 AW	12460 AAW	COBLS	10//99-12//99
	Connecticut	S	6.12 MW	6.81 AW	14170 AAW	CTBLS	10//99-12//99
	Bridgeport PMSA, CT	S	7.13 MW	6.40 AW	14830 AAW	CTBLS	10//99-12//99
	Danbury PMSA, CT	S	6.26 MW	6.09 AW	13020 AAW	CTBLS	10//99-12//99
	Hartford MSA, CT	S	6.71 MW	6.07 AW	13950 AAW	CTBLS	10//99-12//99
	New Haven-Meriden PMSA, CT	S	6.83 MW	6.22 AW	14210 AAW	CTBLS	10//99-12//99
	New London-Norwich MSA, CT-RI	S	6.60 MW	6.11 AW	13720 AAW	CTBLS	10//99-12//99
	Stamford-Norwalk PMSA, CT	S	8.00 MW	6.59 AW	16640 AAW	CTBLS	10//99-12//99
	Waterbury PMSA, CT	S	6.38 MW	6.12 AW	13270 AAW	CTBLS	10//99-12//99
	Delaware	S	6.12 MW	6.74 AW	14010 AAW	DEBLS	10//99-12//99
	Dover MSA, DE	S	6.97 MW	6.37 AW	14500 AAW	DEBLS	10//99-12//99
	Wilmington-Newark PMSA, DE-MD	S	6.70 MW	6.12 AW	13940 AAW	DEBLS	10//99-12//99
	District of Columbia	S	6.74 MW	7.28 AW	15150 AAW	DCBLS	
	Washington PMSA, DC-MD-VA-WV	S	6.69 MW	6.35 AW	13920 AAW	DCBLS	10//99-12//99
	Florida	S	6.03 MW	6.36 AW	13240 AAW	FLBLS	10//99-12//99
	Daytona Beach MSA, FL	S	6.08 MW	5.97 AW	12640 AAW	FLBLS	10//99-12//99
	Fort Lauderdale PMSA, FL	S	6.18 MW	5.99 AW	12860 AAW	FLBLS	10//99-12//99
	Fort Myers-Cape Coral MSA, FL	S	6.40 MW	6.09 AW	13310 AAW	FLBLS	10//99-12//99
	Fort Pierce-Port St. Lucie MSA, FL	S	6.55 MW	5.99 AW	13630 AAW	FLBLS	10//99-12//99
	Fort Walton Beach MSA, FL	S	6.79 MW	5.97 AW	14120 AAW	FLBLS	10//99-12//99
	Gainesville MSA, FL	S	7.10 MW	6.06 AW	14770 AAW	FLBLS	10//99-12//99
	Jacksonville MSA, FL	S	6.43 MW	6.01 AW	13370 AAW	FLBLS	10//99-12//99
	Lakeland-Winter Haven MSA, FL	S	5.93 MW	5.93 AW	12320 AAW	FLBLS	10//99-12//99
	Melbourne-Titusville-Palm Bay MSA, FL	S	6.00 MW	5.95 AW	12480 AAW	FLBLS	10//99-12//99
	Miami PMSA, FL	S	6.82 MW	6.23 AW	14190 AAW	FLBLS	10//99-12//99
	Naples MSA, FL	S	7.22 MW	6.44 AW	15020 AAW	FLBLS	10//99-12//99
	Ocala MSA, FL	S	5.96 MW	6.00 AW	12400 AAW	FLBLS	10//99-12//99
	Orlando MSA, FL	S	6.23 MW	5.99 AW	12950 AAW	FLBLS	10//99-12//99
	Panama City MSA, FL	S	6.08 MW	5.90 AW	12650 AAW	FLBLS	10//99-12//99
	Pensacola MSA, FL	S	6.10 MW	6.01 AW	12680 AAW	FLBLS	10//99-12//99
	Punta Gorda MSA, FL	S	6.23 MW	5.97 AW	12950 AAW	FLBLS	10//99-12//99
	Sarasota-Bradenton MSA, FL	S	6.38 MW	6.09 AW	13270 AAW	FLBLS	10//99-12//99
	Tallahassee MSA, FL	S	6.44 MW	6.03 AW	13390 AAW	FLBLS	10//99-12//99
	Tampa-St. Petersburg-Clearwater MSA, FL	S	6.43 MW	6.07 AW	13370 AAW	FLBLS	10//99-12//99
	West Palm Beach-Boca Raton MSA, FL	S	6.41 MW	6.06 AW	13330 AAW	FLBLS	10//99-12//99
	Georgia	S	6 MW	6.29 AW	13090 AAW	GABLS	10//99-12//99
	Albany MSA, GA	S	6.07 MW	6.00 AW	12620 AAW	GABLS	10//99-12//99
	Athens MSA, GA	S	6.18 MW	6.05 AW	12850 AAW	GABLS	10//99-12//99
	Atlanta MSA, GA	S	6.34 MW	5.98 AW	13200 AAW	GABLS	10//99-12//99
	Augusta-Aiken MSA, GA-SC	S	6.21 MW	6.04 AW	12910 AAW	GABLS	10//99-12//99
	Columbus MSA, GA-AL	S	5.87 MW	5.90 AW	12210 AAW	GABLS	10//99-12//99
	Macon MSA, GA	S	5.87 MW	6.00 AW	12220 AAW	GABLS	10//99-12//99
	Savannah MSA, GA	S	6.18 MW	6.03 AW	12860 AAW	GABLS	10//99-12//99
	Hawaii	S	6.12 MW	7.08 AW	14720 AAW	HIBLS	10//99-12//99
	Honolulu MSA, HI	S	6.98 MW	6.07 AW	14520 AAW	HIBLS	10//99-12//99
	Idaho	S	5.94 MW	5.93 AW	12330 AAW	IDBLS	10//99-12//99
	Boise City MSA, ID	S	5.98 MW	5.94 AW	12440 AAW	IDBLS	10//99-12//99

AAW Average annual wage	**AOH** Average offered, high	**ASH** Average starting, high	**H** Hourly	**M** Monthly	**S** Special: hourly and annual
AE Average entry wage	**AOL** Average offered, low	**ASL** Average starting, low	**HI** Highest wage paid	**MTC** Median total compensation	**TQ** Third quartile wage
AEX Average experienced wage	**APH** Average pay, high range	**AW** Average wage paid	**HR** High end range	**MW** Median wage paid	**W** Weekly
AO Average offered	**APL** Average pay, low range	**FQ** First quartile wage	**LR** Low end range	**SQ** Second quartile wage	**Y** Yearly

Occupation/Type/Industry	Location	Per	Low	Mid	High	Source	Date
Waiter and Waitress	Pocatello MSA, ID	S	6.03 MW	5.94 AW	12550 AAW	IDBLS	10//99-12//99
	Illinois	S	6.1 MW	6.54 AW	13600 AAW	ILBLS	10//99-12//99
	Bloomington-Normal MSA, IL	S	5.81 MW	5.92 AW	12090 AAW	ILBLS	10//99-12//99
	Champaign-Urbana MSA, IL	S	6.26 MW	6.01 AW	13010 AAW	ILBLS	10//99-12//99
	Chicago PMSA, IL	S	6.70 MW	6.16 AW	13930 AAW	ILBLS	10//99-12//99
	Decatur MSA, IL	S	6.48 MW	6.30 AW	13490 AAW	ILBLS	10//99-12//99
	Kankakee PMSA, IL	S	5.91 MW	5.95 AW	12300 AAW	ILBLS	10//99-12//99
	Peoria-Pekin MSA, IL	S	6.15 MW	6.09 AW	12790 AAW	ILBLS	10//99-12//99
	Rockford MSA, IL	S	5.96 MW	5.94 AW	12390 AAW	ILBLS	10//99-12//99
	Springfield MSA, IL	S	6.48 MW	6.06 AW	13490 AAW	ILBLS	10//99-12//99
	Indiana	S	6.02 MW	6.21 AW	12920 AAW	INBLS	10//99-12//99
	Bloomington MSA, IN	S	6.11 MW	5.99 AW	12710 AAW	INBLS	10//99-12//99
	Elkhart-Goshen MSA, IN	S	6.74 MW	6.09 AW	14030 AAW	INBLS	10//99-12//99
	Evansville-Henderson MSA, IN-KY	S	6.74 MW	6.09 AW	14020 AAW	INBLS	10//99-12//99
	Fort Wayne MSA, IN	S	6.24 MW	6.01 AW	12970 AAW	INBLS	10//99-12//99
	Gary PMSA, IN	S	6.05 MW	5.96 AW	12570 AAW	INBLS	10//99-12//99
	Indianapolis MSA, IN	S	6.24 MW	6.06 AW	12970 AAW	INBLS	10//99-12//99
	Kokomo MSA, IN	S	6.05 MW	6.05 AW	12580 AAW	INBLS	10//99-12//99
	Lafayette MSA, IN	S	5.91 MW	5.95 AW	12300 AAW	INBLS	10//99-12//99
	Muncie MSA, IN	S	5.91 MW	6.03 AW	12290 AAW	INBLS	10//99-12//99
	South Bend MSA, IN	S	6.47 MW	6.05 AW	13460 AAW	INBLS	10//99-12//99
	Terre Haute MSA, IN	S	6.23 MW	6.02 AW	12960 AAW	INBLS	10//99-12//99
	Iowa	S	5.98 MW	6.08 AW	12650 AAW	IABLS	10//99-12//99
	Cedar Rapids MSA, IA	S	6.11 MW	6.02 AW	12700 AAW	IABLS	10//99-12//99
	Davenport-Moline-Rock Island MSA, IA-IL	S	6.35 MW	6.04 AW	13210 AAW	IABLS	10//99-12//99
	Des Moines MSA, IA	S	6.12 MW	5.99 AW	12720 AAW	IABLS	10//99-12//99
	Dubuque MSA, IA	S	6.52 MW	6.06 AW	13560 AAW	IABLS	10//99-12//99
	Iowa City MSA, IA	S	6.20 MW	6.00 AW	12900 AAW	IABLS	10//99-12//99
	Sioux City MSA, IA-NE	S	6.07 MW	6.03 AW	12630 AAW	IABLS	10//99-12//99
	Waterloo-Cedar Falls MSA, IA	S	6.12 MW	6.00 AW	12720 AAW	IABLS	10//99-12//99
	Kansas	S	5.97 MW	6.10 AW	12680 AAW	KSBLS	10//99-12//99
	Lawrence MSA, KS	S	6.36 MW	6.06 AW	13230 AAW	KSBLS	10//99-12//99
	Topeka MSA, KS	S	6.17 MW	6.04 AW	12820 AAW	KSBLS	10//99-12//99
	Wichita MSA, KS	S	6.03 MW	5.93 AW	12550 AAW	KSBLS	10//99-12//99
	Kentucky	S	5.98 MW	6.11 AW	12700 AAW	KYBLS	10//99-12//99
	Lexington MSA, KY	S	5.98 MW	5.96 AW	12440 AAW	KYBLS	10//99-12//99
	Louisville MSA, KY-IN	S	6.25 MW	6.03 AW	12990 AAW	KYBLS	10//99-12//99
	Owensboro MSA, KY	S	6.29 MW	5.99 AW	13090 AAW	KYBLS	10//99-12//99
	Louisiana	S	6.01 MW	6.39 AW	13300 AAW	LABLS	10//99-12//99
	Alexandria MSA, LA	S	6.08 MW	6.00 AW	12650 AAW	LABLS	10//99-12//99
	Baton Rouge MSA, LA	S	6.13 MW	5.97 AW	12740 AAW	LABLS	10//99-12//99
	Houma MSA, LA	S	6.14 MW	5.97 AW	12780 AAW	LABLS	10//99-12//99
	Lafayette MSA, LA	S	5.95 MW	5.96 AW	12370 AAW	LABLS	10//99-12//99
	Lake Charles MSA, LA	S	5.78 MW	5.88 AW	12030 AAW	LABLS	10//99-12//99
	Monroe MSA, LA	S	6.63 MW	6.12 AW	13790 AAW	LABLS	10//99-12//99
	New Orleans MSA, LA	S	6.74 MW	6.05 AW	14020 AAW	LABLS	10//99-12//99
	Shreveport-Bossier City MSA, LA	S	6.13 MW	5.95 AW	12750 AAW	LABLS	10//99-12//99
	Maine	S	5.97 MW	6.26 AW	13020 AAW	MEBLS	10//99-12//99
	Bangor MSA, ME	S	6.66 MW	5.99 AW	13840 AAW	MEBLS	10//99-12//99
	Lewiston-Auburn MSA, ME	S	5.73 MW	5.87 AW	11910 AAW	MEBLS	10//99-12//99
	Portland MSA, ME	S	6.25 MW	5.95 AW	13000 AAW	MEBLS	10//99-12//99
	Maryland	S	6 MW	6.22 AW	12940 AAW	MDBLS	10//99-12//99
	Baltimore PMSA, MD	S	6.18 MW	5.99 AW	12860 AAW	MDBLS	10//99-12//99
	Cumberland MSA, MD-WV	S	5.88 MW	5.96 AW	12220 AAW	MDBLS	10//99-12//99
	Hagerstown PMSA, MD	S	6.35 MW	5.99 AW	13200 AAW	MDBLS	10//99-12//99
	Massachusetts	S	6.12 MW	7.14 AW	14850 AAW	MABLS	10//99-12//99
	Barnstable-Yarmouth MSA, MA	S	6.32 MW	5.99 AW	13140 AAW	MABLS	10//99-12//99
	Boston PMSA, MA-NH	S	7.49 MW	6.23 AW	15570 AAW	MABLS	10//99-12//99
	Brockton PMSA, MA	S	6.91 MW	6.22 AW	14380 AAW	MABLS	10//99-12//99
	Fitchburg-Leominster PMSA, MA	S	6.17 MW	5.99 AW	12840 AAW	MABLS	10//99-12//99
	Lawrence PMSA, MA-NH	S	6.58 MW	6.07 AW	13680 AAW	MABLS	10//99-12//99
	Lowell PMSA, MA-NH	S	7.28 MW	6.30 AW	15140 AAW	MABLS	10//99-12//99
	New Bedford PMSA, MA	S	6.65 MW	6.07 AW	13830 AAW	MABLS	10//99-12//99
	Pittsfield MSA, MA	S	6.71 MW	6.05 AW	13950 AAW	MABLS	10//99-12//99
	Springfield MSA, MA	S	6.59 MW	6.06 AW	13710 AAW	MABLS	10//99-12//99
	Worcester PMSA, MA-CT	S	6.88 MW	6.14 AW	14320 AAW	MABLS	10//99-12//99
	Michigan	S	6 MW	6.16 AW	12820 AAW	MIBLS	10//99-12//99

Occupation/Type/Industry	Location	Per	Low	Mid	High	Source	Date
Waiter and Waitress	Ann Arbor PMSA, MI	S	6.10 MW	6.00 AW	12690 AAW	MIBLS	10//99-12//99
	Benton Harbor MSA, MI	S	6.21 MW	6.04 AW	12910 AAW	MIBLS	10//99-12//99
	Detroit PMSA, MI	S	6.27 MW	6.02 AW	13050 AAW	MIBLS	10//99-12//99
	Flint PMSA, MI	S	6.07 MW	5.94 AW	12620 AAW	MIBLS	10//99-12//99
	Grand Rapids-Muskegon-Holland MSA, MI	S	6.15 MW	5.99 AW	12790 AAW	MIBLS	10//99-12//99
	Jackson MSA, MI	S	6.07 MW	6.00 AW	12630 AAW	MIBLS	10//99-12//99
	Kalamazoo-Battle Creek MSA, MI	S	5.83 MW	5.97 AW	12130 AAW	MIBLS	10//99-12//99
	Lansing-East Lansing MSA, MI	S	6.16 MW	5.97 AW	12810 AAW	MIBLS	10//99-12//99
	Saginaw-Bay City-Midland MSA, MI	S	6.07 MW	5.97 AW	12620 AAW	MIBLS	10//99-12//99
	Minnesota	S	5.99 MW	6.12 AW	12730 AAW	MNBLS	10//99-12//99
	Duluth-Superior MSA, MN-WI	S	6.05 MW	5.98 AW	12580 AAW	MNBLS	10//99-12//99
	Minneapolis-St. Paul MSA, MN-WI	S	6.19 MW	5.99 AW	12870 AAW	MNBLS	10//99-12//99
	Rochester MSA, MN	S	6.11 MW	5.97 AW	12700 AAW	MNBLS	10//99-12//99
	St. Cloud MSA, MN	S	5.85 MW	5.95 AW	12170 AAW	MNBLS	10//99-12//99
	Mississippi	S	5.94 MW	5.90 AW	12260 AAW	MSBLS	10//99-12//99
	Biloxi-Gulfport-Pascagoula MSA, MS	S	5.83 MW	5.92 AW	12120 AAW	MSBLS	10//99-12//99
	Hattiesburg MSA, MS	S	6.56 MW	6.14 AW	13640 AAW	MSBLS	10//99-12//99
	Jackson MSA, MS	S	5.96 MW	5.94 AW	12400 AAW	MSBLS	10//99-12//99
	Missouri	S	6.03 MW	6.31 AW	13130 AAW	MOBLS	10//99-12//99
	Columbia MSA, MO	S	6.72 MW	6.29 AW	13980 AAW	MOBLS	10//99-12//99
	Joplin MSA, MO	S	5.86 MW	5.93 AW	12190 AAW	MOBLS	10//99-12//99
	Kansas City MSA, MO-KS	S	6.35 MW	6.04 AW	13200 AAW	MOBLS	10//99-12//99
	St. Joseph MSA, MO	S	5.85 MW	5.96 AW	12180 AAW	MOBLS	10//99-12//99
	St. Louis MSA, MO-IL	S	6.42 MW	6.06 AW	13350 AAW	MOBLS	10//99-12//99
	Springfield MSA, MO	S	6.49 MW	6.09 AW	13490 AAW	MOBLS	10//99-12//99
	Montana	S	5.96 MW	5.93 AW	12330 AAW	MTBLS	10//99-12//99
	Billings MSA, MT	S	5.96 MW	5.96 AW	12390 AAW	MTBLS	10//99-12//99
	Great Falls MSA, MT	S	6.16 MW	6.09 AW	12820 AAW	MTBLS	10//99-12//99
	Missoula MSA, MT	S	5.89 MW	5.94 AW	12240 AAW	MTBLS	10//99-12//99
	Nebraska	S	5.97 MW	6.07 AW	12630 AAW	NEBLS	10//99-12//99
	Lincoln MSA, NE	S	5.91 MW	5.89 AW	12280 AAW	NEBLS	10//99-12//99
	Omaha MSA, NE-IA	S	6.19 MW	6.01 AW	12880 AAW	NEBLS	10//99-12//99
	Nevada	S	6.6 MW	6.97 AW	14490 AAW	NVBLS	10//99-12//99
	Las Vegas MSA, NV-AZ	S	7.19 MW	6.93 AW	14960 AAW	NVBLS	10//99-12//99
	Reno MSA, NV	S	6.00 MW	6.00 AW	12480 AAW	NVBLS	10//99-12//99
	New Hampshire	S	6.06 MW	6.55 AW	13630 AAW	NHBLS	10//99-12//99
	Manchester PMSA, NH	S	6.77 MW	6.10 AW	14080 AAW	NHBLS	10//99-12//99
	Nashua PMSA, NH	S	6.74 MW	6.14 AW	14010 AAW	NHBLS	10//99-12//99
	Portsmouth-Rochester PMSA, NH-ME	S	6.53 MW	6.06 AW	13580 AAW	NHBLS	10//99-12//99
	New Jersey	S	6.08 MW	6.69 AW	13920 AAW	NJBLS	10//99-12//99
	Atlantic-Cape May PMSA, NJ	S	6.37 MW	6.11 AW	13250 AAW	NJBLS	10//99-12//99
	Bergen-Passaic PMSA, NJ	S	7.13 MW	6.09 AW	14830 AAW	NJBLS	10//99-12//99
	Jersey City PMSA, NJ	S	6.63 MW	6.05 AW	13800 AAW	NJBLS	10//99-12//99
	Middlesex-Somerset-Hunterdon PMSA, NJ	S	6.68 MW	6.02 AW	13890 AAW	NJBLS	10//99-12//99
	Monmouth-Ocean PMSA, NJ	S	6.78 MW	6.12 AW	14100 AAW	NJBLS	10//99-12//99
	Newark PMSA, NJ	S	7.10 MW	6.16 AW	14770 AAW	NJBLS	10//99-12//99
	Trenton PMSA, NJ	S	6.36 MW	6.07 AW	13220 AAW	NJBLS	10//99-12//99
	Vineland-Millville-Bridgeton PMSA, NJ	S	6.67 MW	6.28 AW	13880 AAW	NJBLS	10//99-12//99
	New Mexico	S	6.02 MW	6.14 AW	12770 AAW	NMBLS	10//99-12//99
	Albuquerque MSA, NM	S	6.23 MW	6.05 AW	12960 AAW	NMBLS	10//99-12//99
	Las Cruces MSA, NM	S	5.91 MW	5.96 AW	12300 AAW	NMBLS	10//99-12//99
	Santa Fe MSA, NM	S	6.57 MW	6.10 AW	13670 AAW	NMBLS	10//99-12//99
	New York	S	6.08 MW	7.04 AW	14650 AAW	NYBLS	10//99-12//99
	Albany-Schenectady-Troy MSA, NY	S	7.64 MW	6.12 AW	15880 AAW	NYBLS	10//99-12//99
	Binghamton MSA, NY	S	5.82 MW	5.89 AW	12110 AAW	NYBLS	10//99-12//99
	Buffalo-Niagara Falls MSA, NY	S	6.14 MW	5.95 AW	12760 AAW	NYBLS	10//99-12//99
	Dutchess County PMSA, NY	S	6.41 MW	6.00 AW	13320 AAW	NYBLS	10//99-12//99
	Elmira MSA, NY	S	6.40 MW	6.14 AW	13310 AAW	NYBLS	10//99-12//99
	Glens Falls MSA, NY	S	5.98 MW	6.01 AW	12430 AAW	NYBLS	10//99-12//99
	Jamestown MSA, NY	S	6.44 MW	6.04 AW	13400 AAW	NYBLS	10//99-12//99
	Nassau-Suffolk PMSA, NY	S	7.55 MW	6.49 AW	15710 AAW	NYBLS	10//99-12//99
	New York PMSA, NY	S	7.61 MW	6.18 AW	15830 AAW	NYBLS	10//99-12//99

AAW	Average annual wage	AOH	Average offered, high	ASH	Average starting, high	H	Hourly	M	Monthly	S	Special: hourly and annual
AE	Average entry wage	AOL	Average offered, low	ASL	Average starting, low	HI	Highest wage paid	MTC	Median total compensation	TQ	Third quartile wage
AEX	Average experienced wage	APH	Average pay, high range	AW	Average wage paid	HR	High end range	MW	Median wage paid	W	Weekly
AO	Average offered	APL	Average pay, low range	FQ	First quartile wage	LR	Low end range	SQ	Second quartile wage	Y	Yearly

Occupation/Type/Industry	Location	Per	Low	Mid	High	Source	Date
Waiter and Waitress	Newburgh PMSA, NY-PA	S	6.64 MW	6.16 AW	13810 AAW	NYBLS	10//99-12//99
	Rochester MSA, NY	S	6.06 MW	5.94 AW	12610 AAW	NYBLS	10//99-12//99
	Syracuse MSA, NY	S	6.26 MW	6.03 AW	13010 AAW	NYBLS	10//99-12//99
	Utica-Rome MSA, NY	S	6.22 MW	6.08 AW	12940 AAW	NYBLS	10//99-12//99
	North Carolina	S	6 MW	6.24 AW	12990 AAW	NCBLS	10//99-12//99
	Asheville MSA, NC	S	5.96 MW	5.93 AW	12400 AAW	NCBLS	10//99-12//99
	Charlotte-Gastonia-Rock Hill MSA, NC-SC	S	6.19 MW	6.01 AW	12870 AAW	NCBLS	10//99-12//99
	Fayetteville MSA, NC	S	6.23 MW	6.01 AW	12960 AAW	NCBLS	10//99-12//99
	Goldsboro MSA, NC	S	6.00 MW	5.97 AW	12480 AAW	NCBLS	10//99-12//99
	Greensboro--Winston-Salem--High Point MSA, NC	S	6.29 MW	6.06 AW	13070 AAW	NCBLS	10//99-12//99
	Greenville MSA, NC	S	5.81 MW	5.90 AW	12090 AAW	NCBLS	10//99-12//99
	Hickory-Morganton-Lenoir MSA, NC	S	6.74 MW	6.06 AW	14030 AAW	NCBLS	10//99-12//99
	Jacksonville MSA, NC	S	5.77 MW	5.89 AW	11990 AAW	NCBLS	10//99-12//99
	Raleigh-Durham-Chapel Hill MSA, NC	S	6.79 MW	6.03 AW	14130 AAW	NCBLS	10//99-12//99
	Rocky Mount MSA, NC	S	5.89 MW	5.96 AW	12250 AAW	NCBLS	10//99-12//99
	Wilmington MSA, NC	S	6.00 MW	5.97 AW	12470 AAW	NCBLS	10//99-12//99
	North Dakota	S	5.95 MW	5.93 AW	12340 AAW	NDBLS	10//99-12//99
	Bismarck MSA, ND	S	5.84 MW	5.95 AW	12150 AAW	NDBLS	10//99-12//99
	Fargo-Moorhead MSA, ND-MN	S	6.12 MW	5.97 AW	12730 AAW	NDBLS	10//99-12//99
	Grand Forks MSA, ND-MN	S	6.02 MW	5.99 AW	12520 AAW	NDBLS	10//99-12//99
	Ohio	S	6 MW	6.21 AW	12920 AAW	OHBLS	10//99-12//99
	Akron PMSA, OH	S	6.10 MW	5.99 AW	12690 AAW	OHBLS	10//99-12//99
	Canton-Massillon MSA, OH	S	6.04 MW	5.99 AW	12560 AAW	OHBLS	10//99-12//99
	Cincinnati PMSA, OH-KY-IN	S	6.57 MW	6.01 AW	13660 AAW	OHBLS	10//99-12//99
	Cleveland-Lorain-Elyria PMSA, OH	S	6.41 MW	6.03 AW	13330 AAW	OHBLS	10//99-12//99
	Columbus MSA, OH	S	6.22 MW	6.04 AW	12940 AAW	OHBLS	10//99-12//99
	Dayton-Springfield MSA, OH	S	6.09 MW	6.03 AW	12660 AAW	OHBLS	10//99-12//99
	Hamilton-Middletown PMSA, OH	S	5.98 MW	5.97 AW	12440 AAW	OHBLS	10//99-12//99
	Lima MSA, OH	S	6.04 MW	5.99 AW	12560 AAW	OHBLS	10//99-12//99
	Mansfield MSA, OH	S	5.94 MW	5.97 AW	12360 AAW	OHBLS	10//99-12//99
	Steubenville-Weirton MSA, OH-WV	S	5.94 MW	6.00 AW	12360 AAW	OHBLS	10//99-12//99
	Toledo MSA, OH	S	6.18 MW	5.98 AW	12860 AAW	OHBLS	10//99-12//99
	Youngstown-Warren MSA, OH	S	5.94 MW	5.96 AW	12360 AAW	OHBLS	10//99-12//99
	Oklahoma	S	5.97 MW	5.99 AW	12460 AAW	OKBLS	10//99-12//99
	Enid MSA, OK	S	5.79 MW	5.95 AW	12050 AAW	OKBLS	10//99-12//99
	Lawton MSA, OK	S	5.74 MW	5.91 AW	11930 AAW	OKBLS	10//99-12//99
	Oklahoma City MSA, OK	S	6.21 MW	6.03 AW	12920 AAW	OKBLS	10//99-12//99
	Tulsa MSA, OK	S	5.82 MW	5.92 AW	12100 AAW	OKBLS	10//99-12//99
	Oregon	S	6.84 MW	7.21 AW	14990 AAW	ORBLS	10//99-12//99
	Corvallis MSA, OR	S	7.36 MW	7.22 AW	15320 AAW	ORBLS	10//99-12//99
	Eugene-Springfield MSA, OR	S	7.33 MW	6.84 AW	15240 AAW	ORBLS	10//99-12//99
	Medford-Ashland MSA, OR	S	6.99 MW	6.78 AW	14550 AAW	ORBLS	10//99-12//99
	Portland-Vancouver PMSA, OR-WA	S	7.15 MW	6.81 AW	14880 AAW	ORBLS	10//99-12//99
	Salem PMSA, OR	S	7.08 MW	6.78 AW	14730 AAW	ORBLS	10//99-12//99
	Pennsylvania	S	6.02 MW	6.25 AW	13010 AAW	PABLS	10//99-12//99
	Allentown-Bethlehem-Easton MSA, PA	S	6.51 MW	6.10 AW	13540 AAW	PABLS	10//99-12//99
	Altoona MSA, PA	S	6.06 MW	5.98 AW	12610 AAW	PABLS	10//99-12//99
	Erie MSA, PA	S	6.09 MW	6.06 AW	12660 AAW	PABLS	10//99-12//99
	Harrisburg-Lebanon-Carlisle MSA, PA	S	6.15 MW	6.05 AW	12780 AAW	PABLS	10//99-12//99
	Johnstown MSA, PA	S	6.00 MW	5.95 AW	12470 AAW	PABLS	10//99-12//99
	Lancaster MSA, PA	S	6.55 MW	6.06 AW	13620 AAW	PABLS	10//99-12//99
	Philadelphia PMSA, PA-NJ	S	6.43 MW	6.05 AW	13370 AAW	PABLS	10//99-12//99
	Pittsburgh MSA, PA	S	6.06 MW	5.98 AW	12600 AAW	PABLS	10//99-12//99
	Reading MSA, PA	S	6.14 MW	6.03 AW	12770 AAW	PABLS	10//99-12//99
	Scranton--Wilkes-Barre--Hazleton MSA, PA	S	6.09 MW	5.97 AW	12670 AAW	PABLS	10//99-12//99
	Sharon MSA, PA	S	6.09 MW	6.04 AW	12660 AAW	PABLS	10//99-12//99
	State College MSA, PA	S	6.02 MW	5.98 AW	12530 AAW	PABLS	10//99-12//99
	Williamsport MSA, PA	S	6.13 MW	5.96 AW	12740 AAW	PABLS	10//99-12//99
	York MSA, PA	S	6.17 MW	5.99 AW	12840 AAW	PABLS	10//99-12//99
	Rhode Island	S	6.2 MW	6.69 AW	13910 AAW	RIBLS	10//99-12//99

AAW Average annual wage	AOH Average offered, high	ASH Average starting, high	H Hourly	M Monthly	S Special: hourly and annual
AE Average entry wage	AOL Average offered, low	ASL Average starting, low	HI Highest wage paid	MTC Median total compensation	TQ Third quartile wage
AEX Average experienced wage	APH Average pay, high range	AW Average wage paid	HR High end range	MW Median wage paid	W Weekly
AO Average offered	APL Average pay, low range	FQ First quartile wage	LR Low end range	SQ Second quartile wage	Y Yearly

Occupation/Type/Industry	Location	Per	Low	Mid	High	Source	Date
Waiter and Waitress	Providence-Fall River- Warwick MSA, RI-MA	S	6.68 MW	6.13 AW	13900 AAW	RIBLS	10//99-12//99
	South Carolina	S	6.03 MW	6.25 AW	13000 AAW	SCBLS	10//99-12//99
	Charleston-North Charleston MSA, SC	S	6.22 MW	6.03 AW	12940 AAW	SCBLS	10//99-12//99
	Columbia MSA, SC	S	6.13 MW	6.01 AW	12740 AAW	SCBLS	10//99-12//99
	Florence MSA, SC	S	6.10 MW	6.04 AW	12690 AAW	SCBLS	10//99-12//99
	Greenville-Spartanburg- Anderson MSA, SC	S	6.37 MW	6.05 AW	13260 AAW	SCBLS	10//99-12//99
	Myrtle Beach MSA, SC	S	6.43 MW	6.09 AW	13370 AAW	SCBLS	10//99-12//99
	Sumter MSA, SC	S	6.09 MW	5.98 AW	12670 AAW	SCBLS	10//99-12//99
	South Dakota	S	5.94 MW	5.82 AW	12100 AAW	SDBLS	10//99-12//99
	Rapid City MSA, SD	S	5.86 MW	5.96 AW	12180 AAW	SDBLS	10//99-12//99
	Sioux Falls MSA, SD	S	5.84 MW	5.94 AW	12140 AAW	SDBLS	10//99-12//99
	Tennessee	S	5.99 MW	6.22 AW	12940 AAW	TNBLS	10//99-12//99
	Chattanooga MSA, TN-GA	S	6.79 MW	6.03 AW	14130 AAW	TNBLS	10//99-12//99
	Clarksville-Hopkinsville MSA, TN-KY	S	6.26 MW	6.03 AW	13030 AAW	TNBLS	10//99-12//99
	Jackson MSA, TN	S	6.17 MW	6.05 AW	12820 AAW	TNBLS	10//99-12//99
	Johnson City-Kingsport-Bristol MSA, TN-VA	S	6.01 MW	5.97 AW	12510 AAW	TNBLS	10//99-12//99
	Knoxville MSA, TN	S	6.09 MW	5.97 AW	12670 AAW	TNBLS	10//99-12//99
	Memphis MSA, TN-AR-MS	S	6.56 MW	6.04 AW	13650 AAW	MSBLS	10//99-12//99
	Nashville MSA, TN	S	6.23 MW	5.98 AW	12970 AAW	TNBLS	10//99-12//99
	Texas	S	6.01 MW	6.26 AW	13010 AAW	TXBLS	10//99-12//99
	Abilene MSA, TX	S	5.90 MW	5.95 AW	12280 AAW	TXBLS	10//99-12//99
	Amarillo MSA, TX	S	6.66 MW	6.12 AW	13860 AAW	TXBLS	10//99-12//99
	Austin-San Marcos MSA, TX	S	6.63 MW	6.09 AW	13790 AAW	TXBLS	10//99-12//99
	Beaumont-Port Arthur MSA, TX	S	6.13 MW	5.95 AW	12750 AAW	TXBLS	10//99-12//99
	Brazoria PMSA, TX	S	5.83 MW	5.93 AW	12130 AAW	TXBLS	10//99-12//99
	Brownsville-Harlingen-San Benito MSA, TX	S	5.96 MW	5.95 AW	12400 AAW	TXBLS	10//99-12//99
	Bryan-College Station MSA, TX	S	6.36 MW	6.11 AW	13230 AAW	TXBLS	10//99-12//99
	Corpus Christi MSA, TX	S	6.04 MW	6.02 AW	12570 AAW	TXBLS	10//99-12//99
	Dallas PMSA, TX	S	6.33 MW	6.06 AW	13160 AAW	TXBLS	10//99-12//99
	El Paso MSA, TX	S	6.12 MW	5.99 AW	12720 AAW	TXBLS	10//99-12//99
	Fort Worth-Arlington PMSA, TX	S	6.25 MW	5.98 AW	13000 AAW	TXBLS	10//99-12//99
	Galveston-Texas City PMSA, TX	S	6.01 MW	6.07 AW	12510 AAW	TXBLS	10//99-12//99
	Houston PMSA, TX	S	6.21 MW	5.98 AW	12920 AAW	TXBLS	10//99-12//99
	Killeen-Temple MSA, TX	S	6.33 MW	6.12 AW	13170 AAW	TXBLS	10//99-12//99
	Laredo MSA, TX	S	6.24 MW	5.99 AW	12990 AAW	TXBLS	10//99-12//99
	Longview-Marshall MSA, TX	S	6.28 MW	6.22 AW	13070 AAW	TXBLS	10//99-12//99
	Lubbock MSA, TX	S	6.05 MW	5.94 AW	12580 AAW	TXBLS	10//99-12//99
	McAllen-Edinburg-Mission MSA, TX	S	5.98 MW	6.00 AW	12430 AAW	TXBLS	10//99-12//99
	Odessa-Midland MSA, TX	S	6.27 MW	5.95 AW	13040 AAW	TXBLS	10//99-12//99
	San Angelo MSA, TX	S	6.26 MW	6.08 AW	13010 AAW	TXBLS	10//99-12//99
	San Antonio MSA, TX	S	6.51 MW	6.04 AW	13530 AAW	TXBLS	10//99-12//99
	Sherman-Denison MSA, TX	S	6.31 MW	6.07 AW	13130 AAW	TXBLS	10//99-12//99
	Texarkana, MSA, TX- Texarkana, AR	S	6.03 MW	5.94 AW	12540 AAW	TXBLS	10//99-12//99
	Tyler MSA, TX	S	6.34 MW	6.04 AW	13200 AAW	TXBLS	10//99-12//99
	Victoria MSA, TX	S	5.94 MW	5.90 AW	12360 AAW	TXBLS	10//99-12//99
	Waco MSA, TX	S	6.33 MW	6.05 AW	13160 AAW	TXBLS	10//99-12//99
	Wichita Falls MSA, TX	S	6.20 MW	6.04 AW	12900 AAW	TXBLS	10//99-12//99
	Utah	S	6.06 MW	6.39 AW	13300 AAW	UTBLS	10//99-12//99
	Provo-Orem MSA, UT	S	6.31 MW	6.07 AW	13120 AAW	UTBLS	10//99-12//99
	Salt Lake City-Ogden MSA, UT	S	6.68 MW	6.19 AW	13900 AAW	UTBLS	10//99-12//99
	Vermont	S	6.18 MW	6.70 AW	13930 AAW	VTBLS	10//99-12//99
	Burlington MSA, VT	S	7.23 MW	6.18 AW	15040 AAW	VTBLS	10//99-12//99
	Virginia	S	6.03 MW	6.35 AW	13200 AAW	VABLS	10//99-12//99
	Charlottesville MSA, VA	S	6.38 MW	6.10 AW	13270 AAW	VABLS	10//99-12//99
	Danville MSA, VA	S	5.94 MW	5.96 AW	12350 AAW	VABLS	10//99-12//99
	Lynchburg MSA, VA	S	6.10 MW	5.98 AW	12690 AAW	VABLS	10//99-12//99
	Norfolk-Virginia Beach- Newport News MSA, VA- NC	S	6.27 MW	6.02 AW	13050 AAW	VABLS	10//99-12//99

AAW	Average annual wage	**AOH**	Average offered, high	**ASH**	Average starting, high	**H**	Hourly	**M**	Monthly
AE	Average entry wage	**AOL**	Average offered, low	**ASL**	Average starting, low	**HI**	Highest wage paid	**MTC**	Median total compensation
AEX	Average experienced wage	**APH**	Average pay, high range	**AW**	Average wage paid	**HR**	High end range	**MW**	Median wage paid
AO	Average offered	**APL**	Average pay, low range	**FQ**	First quartile wage	**LR**	Low end range	**SQ**	Second quartile wage

S	Special: hourly and annual	
TQ	Third quartile wage	
W	Weekly	
Y	Yearly	

Occupation/Type/Industry	Location	Per	Low	Mid	High	Source	Date
Waiter and Waitress	Richmond-Petersburg MSA, VA	S	6.28 MW	6.05 AW	13060 AAW	VABLS	10//99-12//99
	Roanoke MSA, VA	S	6.20 MW	6.03 AW	12890 AAW	VABLS	10//99-12//99
	Washington	S	6.09 MW	6.72 AW	13980 AAW	WABLS	10//99-12//99
	Bellingham MSA, WA	S	6.39 MW	6.06 AW	13280 AAW	WABLS	10//99-12//99
	Bremerton PMSA, WA	S	6.36 MW	6.06 AW	13230 AAW	WABLS	10//99-12//99
	Olympia PMSA, WA	S	6.72 MW	6.28 AW	13980 AAW	WABLS	10//99-12//99
	Richland-Kennewick-Pasco MSA, WA	S	6.73 MW	6.10 AW	14000 AAW	WABLS	10//99-12//99
	Seattle-Bellevue-Everett PMSA, WA	S	6.92 MW	6.09 AW	14390 AAW	WABLS	10//99-12//99
	Spokane MSA, WA	S	6.69 MW	6.12 AW	13910 AAW	WABLS	10//99-12//99
	Tacoma PMSA, WA	S	6.68 MW	6.12 AW	13890 AAW	WABLS	10//99-12//99
	Yakima MSA, WA	S	6.26 MW	6.06 AW	13010 AAW	WABLS	10//99-12//99
	West Virginia	S	5.94 MW	5.89 AW	12250 AAW	WVBLS	10//99-12//99
	Charleston MSA, WV	S	5.88 MW	5.97 AW	12240 AAW	WVBLS	10//99-12//99
	Huntington-Ashland MSA, WV-KY-OH	S	6.08 MW	6.01 AW	12640 AAW	WVBLS	10//99-12//99
	Parkersburg-Marietta MSA, WV-OH	S	6.03 MW	5.97 AW	12550 AAW	WVBLS	10//99-12//99
	Wheeling MSA, WV-OH	S	5.78 MW	5.90 AW	12020 AAW	WVBLS	10//99-12//99
	Wisconsin	S	5.98 MW	6.17 AW	12830 AAW	WIBLS	10//99-12//99
	Appleton-Oshkosh-Neenah MSA, WI	S	6.27 MW	6.03 AW	13050 AAW	WIBLS	10//99-12//99
	Eau Claire MSA, WI	S	6.63 MW	6.05 AW	13780 AAW	WIBLS	10//99-12//99
	Green Bay MSA, WI	S	6.29 MW	6.03 AW	13090 AAW	WIBLS	10//99-12//99
	Janesville-Beloit MSA, WI	S	5.96 MW	5.92 AW	12390 AAW	WIBLS	10//99-12//99
	Kenosha PMSA, WI	S	5.98 MW	5.97 AW	12440 AAW	WIBLS	10//99-12//99
	La Crosse MSA, WI-MN	S	6.42 MW	6.06 AW	13340 AAW	WIBLS	10//99-12//99
	Madison MSA, WI	S	6.23 MW	5.98 AW	12970 AAW	WIBLS	10//99-12//99
	Milwaukee-Waukesha PMSA, WI	S	6.24 MW	5.97 AW	12970 AAW	WIBLS	10//99-12//99
	Racine PMSA, WI	S	5.97 MW	5.97 AW	12410 AAW	WIBLS	10//99-12//99
	Sheboygan MSA, WI	S	5.96 MW	5.98 AW	12390 AAW	WIBLS	10//99-12//99
	Wausau MSA, WI	S	6.45 MW	6.07 AW	13410 AAW	WIBLS	10//99-12//99
	Wyoming	S	5.98 MW	5.95 AW	12370 AAW	WYBLS	10//99-12//99
	Casper MSA, WY	S	5.84 MW	5.99 AW	12150 AAW	WYBLS	10//99-12//99
	Cheyenne MSA, WY	S	6.21 MW	6.04 AW	12920 AAW	WYBLS	10//99-12//99
	Puerto Rico	S	5.96 MW	6.08 AW	12640 AAW	PRBLS	10//99-12//99
	Aguadilla MSA, PR	S	5.69 MW	5.85 AW	11840 AAW	PRBLS	10//99-12//99
	Arecibo PMSA, PR	S	5.93 MW	5.98 AW	12330 AAW	PRBLS	10//99-12//99
	Caguas PMSA, PR	S	5.87 MW	5.91 AW	12200 AAW	PRBLS	10//99-12//99
	Mayaguez MSA, PR	S	5.81 MW	6.00 AW	12090 AAW	PRBLS	10//99-12//99
	Ponce MSA, PR	S	5.75 MW	5.93 AW	11960 AAW	PRBLS	10//99-12//99
	San Juan-Bayamon PMSA, PR	S	6.14 MW	5.97 AW	12770 AAW	PRBLS	10//99-12//99
	Virgin Islands	S	6.03 MW	5.84 AW	12160 AAW	VIBLS	10//99-12//99
	Guam	S	6.18 MW	6.57 AW	13660 AAW	GUBLS	10//99-12//99
Warehouse Manager	United States	Y		53500 AW		MATMAN	1999
Watch Repairer	Alabama	S	12.13 MW	11.91 AW	24770 AAW	ALBLS	10//99-12//99
	Arizona	S	13.08 MW	13.37 AW	27810 AAW	AZBLS	10//99-12//99
	Phoenix-Mesa MSA, AZ	S	13.43 MW	13.39 AW	27930 AAW	AZBLS	10//99-12//99
	California	S	11.11 MW	12.28 AW	25540 AAW	CABLS	10//99-12//99
	Los Angeles-Long Beach PMSA, CA	S	14.27 MW	14.73 AW	29690 AAW	CABLS	10//99-12//99
	San Francisco PMSA, CA	S	8.63 MW	8.09 AW	17940 AAW	CABLS	10//99-12//99
	Connecticut	S	13.36 MW	13.76 AW	28620 AAW	CTBLS	10//99-12//99
	Florida	S	12.09 MW	12.90 AW	26820 AAW	FLBLS	10//99-12//99
	Fort Lauderdale PMSA, FL	S	13.39 MW	12.92 AW	27850 AAW	FLBLS	10//99-12//99
	Miami PMSA, FL	S	15.44 MW	15.17 AW	32120 AAW	FLBLS	10//99-12//99
	Orlando MSA, FL	S	7.50 MW	6.30 AW	15590 AAW	FLBLS	10//99-12//99
	Illinois	S	11.56 MW	11.60 AW	24130 AAW	ILBLS	10//99-12//99
	Chicago PMSA, IL	S	11.46 MW	11.60 AW	23840 AAW	ILBLS	10//99-12//99
	Kansas	S	12.21 MW	10.73 AW	22320 AAW	KSBLS	10//99-12//99
	Maryland	S	7.99 MW	9.39 AW	19520 AAW	MDBLS	10//99-12//99
	Baltimore PMSA, MD	S	9.32 MW	7.87 AW	19390 AAW	MDBLS	10//99-12//99
	Massachusetts	S	17.63 MW	17.27 AW	35930 AAW	MABLS	10//99-12//99
	Boston PMSA, MA-NH	S	17.52 MW	17.73 AW	36440 AAW	MABLS	10//99-12//99
	Michigan	S	14.6 MW	15.10 AW	31410 AAW	MIBLS	10//99-12//99
	Detroit PMSA, MI	S	13.92 MW	13.61 AW	28940 AAW	MIBLS	10//99-12//99
	Minnesota	S	9.71 MW	10.29 AW	21410 AAW	MNBLS	10//99-12//99
	Missouri	S	11.71 MW	11.74 AW	24410 AAW	MOBLS	10//99-12//99

Occupation/Type/Industry	Location	Per	Low	Mid	High	Source	Date
Watch Repairer	New Hampshire	S	6.81 MW	8.68 AW	18040 AAW	NHBLS	10//99-12//99
	New Jersey	S	12.69 MW	13.56 AW	28210 AAW	NJBLS	10//99-12//99
	Bergen-Passaic PMSA, NJ	S	13.86 MW	12.96 AW	28830 AAW	NJBLS	10//99-12//99
	New York	S	14.59 MW	15.57 AW	32380 AAW	NYBLS	10//99-12//99
	Nassau-Suffolk PMSA, NY	S	15.45 MW	15.32 AW	32130 AAW	NYBLS	10//99-12//99
	New York PMSA, NY	S	16.60 MW	15.23 AW	34540 AAW	NYBLS	10//99-12//99
	North Carolina	S	11.75 MW	12.71 AW	26440 AAW	NCBLS	10//99-12//99
	Ohio	S	11.15 MW	11.68 AW	24300 AAW	OHBLS	10//99-12//99
	Columbus MSA, OH	S	8.58 MW	8.86 AW	17840 AAW	OHBLS	10//99-12//99
	Dayton-Springfield MSA, OH	S	11.15 MW	9.92 AW	23190 AAW	OHBLS	10//99-12//99
	Oklahoma	S	10.82 MW	9.90 AW	20580 AAW	OKBLS	10//99-12//99
	Tulsa MSA, OK	S	12.00 MW	12.31 AW	24970 AAW	OKBLS	10//99-12//99
	South Carolina	S	12.81 MW	12.18 AW	25340 AAW	SCBLS	10//99-12//99
	Texas	S	9.75 MW	10.48 AW	21800 AAW	TXBLS	10//99-12//99
	Dallas PMSA, TX	S	10.60 MW	8.50 AW	22050 AAW	TXBLS	10//99-12//99
	Houston PMSA, TX	S	9.93 MW	9.80 AW	20660 AAW	TXBLS	10//99-12//99
	Virginia	S	14.97 MW	14.57 AW	30310 AAW	VABLS	10//99-12//99
	Richmond-Petersburg MSA, VA	S	11.32 MW	11.22 AW	23550 AAW	VABLS	10//99-12//99
	Washington	S	13.45 MW	14.10 AW	29330 AAW	WABLS	10//99-12//99
	Puerto Rico	S	5.84 MW	5.68 AW	11810 AAW	PRBLS	10//99-12//99
	San Juan-Bayamon PMSA, PR	S	5.68 MW	5.84 AW	11810 AAW	PRBLS	10//99-12//99
Water and Liquid Waste Treatment Plant and System Operator	Alabama	S	13.93 MW	13.72 AW	28550 AAW	ALBLS	10//99-12//99
	Anniston MSA, AL	S	14.06 MW	14.11 AW	29250 AAW	ALBLS	10//99-12//99
	Auburn-Opelika MSA, AL	S	13.45 MW	13.85 AW	27970 AAW	ALBLS	10//99-12//99
	Decatur MSA, AL	S	15.73 MW	16.17 AW	32720 AAW	ALBLS	10//99-12//99
	Florence MSA, AL	S	14.10 MW	13.64 AW	29320 AAW	ALBLS	10//99-12//99
	Huntsville MSA, AL	S	14.16 MW	13.51 AW	29460 AAW	ALBLS	10//99-12//99
	Tuscaloosa MSA, AL	S	14.08 MW	14.24 AW	29290 AAW	ALBLS	10//99-12//99
	Alaska	S	19.58 MW	19.02 AW	39570 AAW	AKBLS	10//99-12//99
	Arizona	S	16.09 MW	16.91 AW	35170 AAW	AZBLS	10//99-12//99
	Flagstaff MSA, AZ-UT	S	15.44 MW	15.64 AW	32110 AAW	AZBLS	10//99-12//99
	Phoenix-Mesa MSA, AZ	S	18.61 MW	18.31 AW	38710 AAW	AZBLS	10//99-12//99
	Tucson MSA, AZ	S	15.86 MW	15.96 AW	32980 AAW	AZBLS	10//99-12//99
	Yuma MSA, AZ	S	12.53 MW	13.08 AW	26050 AAW	AZBLS	10//99-12//99
	Arkansas	S	10.29 MW	11.14 AW	23170 AAW	ARBLS	10//99-12//99
	Fayetteville-Springdale-Rogers MSA, AR	S	10.60 MW	10.33 AW	22040 AAW	ARBLS	10//99-12//99
	Fort Smith MSA, AR-OK	S	11.39 MW	10.55 AW	23680 AAW	ARBLS	10//99-12//99
	Little Rock-North Little Rock MSA, AR	S	11.56 MW	11.07 AW	24050 AAW	ARBLS	10//99-12//99
	Pine Bluff MSA, AR	S	12.99 MW	12.09 AW	27010 AAW	ARBLS	10//99-12//99
	California	S	20.24 MW	20.71 AW	43080 AAW	CABLS	10//99-12//99
	Bakersfield MSA, CA	S	17.66 MW	16.09 AW	36730 AAW	CABLS	10//99-12//99
	Fresno MSA, CA	S	16.99 MW	16.05 AW	35340 AAW	CABLS	10//99-12//99
	Los Angeles-Long Beach PMSA, CA	S	20.66 MW	20.11 AW	42970 AAW	CABLS	10//99-12//99
	Merced MSA, CA	S	22.41 MW	22.74 AW	46610 AAW	CABLS	10//99-12//99
	Modesto MSA, CA	S	16.36 MW	16.33 AW	34040 AAW	CABLS	10//99-12//99
	Oakland PMSA, CA	S	26.87 MW	27.67 AW	55890 AAW	CABLS	10//99-12//99
	Orange County PMSA, CA	S	21.02 MW	20.25 AW	43710 AAW	CABLS	10//99-12//99
	Riverside-San Bernardino PMSA, CA	S	20.18 MW	19.50 AW	41970 AAW	CABLS	10//99-12//99
	Sacramento PMSA, CA	S	20.08 MW	19.49 AW	41760 AAW	CABLS	10//99-12//99
	Salinas MSA, CA	S	24.15 MW	24.00 AW	50230 AAW	CABLS	10//99-12//99
	San Diego MSA, CA	S	22.18 MW	22.48 AW	46140 AAW	CABLS	10//99-12//99
	San Francisco PMSA, CA	S	23.34 MW	23.01 AW	48550 AAW	CABLS	10//99-12//99
	San Jose PMSA, CA	S	21.22 MW	21.08 AW	44130 AAW	CABLS	10//99-12//99
	San Luis Obispo-Atascadero-Paso Robles MSA, CA	S	18.47 MW	17.93 AW	38420 AAW	CABLS	10//99-12//99
	Santa Barbara-Santa Maria-Lompoc MSA, CA	S	19.25 MW	18.93 AW	40040 AAW	CABLS	10//99-12//99
	Santa Rosa PMSA, CA	S	20.62 MW	19.39 AW	42890 AAW	CABLS	10//99-12//99
	Vallejo-Fairfield-Napa PMSA, CA	S	24.11 MW	23.12 AW	50150 AAW	CABLS	10//99-12//99
	Ventura PMSA, CA	S	17.86 MW	18.39 AW	37140 AAW	CABLS	10//99-12//99
	Visalia-Tulare-Porterville MSA, CA	S	14.93 MW	15.04 AW	31050 AAW	CABLS	10//99-12//99
	Yolo PMSA, CA	S	17.93 MW	18.54 AW	37300 AAW	CABLS	10//99-12//99

Occupation/Type/Industry	Location	Per	Low	Mid	High	Source	Date
Water and Liquid Waste Treatment Plant and System Operator	Colorado	S	15.56 MW	15.90 AW	33070 AAW	COBLS	10//99-12//99
	Boulder-Longmont PMSA, CO	S	16.84 MW	16.31 AW	35030 AAW	COBLS	10//99-12//99
	Colorado Springs MSA, CO	S	15.51 MW	15.30 AW	32270 AAW	COBLS	10//99-12//99
	Denver PMSA, CO	S	16.59 MW	15.80 AW	34510 AAW	COBLS	10//99-12//99
	Fort Collins-Loveland MSA, CO	S	18.52 MW	18.13 AW	38520 AAW	COBLS	10//99-12//99
	Connecticut	S	18.43 MW	18.45 AW	38380 AAW	CTBLS	10//99-12//99
	Bridgeport PMSA, CT	S	19.41 MW	19.76 AW	40380 AAW	CTBLS	10//99-12//99
	Hartford MSA, CT	S	18.25 MW	18.08 AW	37960 AAW	CTBLS	10//99-12//99
	New Haven-Meriden PMSA, CT	S	16.84 MW	17.58 AW	35020 AAW	CTBLS	10//99-12//99
	New London-Norwich MSA, CT-RI	S	17.29 MW	17.70 AW	35950 AAW	CTBLS	10//99-12//99
	Waterbury PMSA, CT	S	18.60 MW	18.63 AW	38700 AAW	CTBLS	10//99-12//99
	Delaware	S	15.4 MW	15.08 AW	31370 AAW	DEBLS	10//99-12//99
	Wilmington-Newark PMSA, DE-MD	S	16.14 MW	16.88 AW	33560 AAW	DEBLS	10//99-12//99
	Washington PMSA, DC-MD-VA-WV	S	16.35 MW	16.44 AW	34010 AAW	DCBLS	10//99-12//99
	Florida	S	13.52 MW	14.06 AW	29240 AAW	FLBLS	10//99-12//99
	Daytona Beach MSA, FL	S	13.23 MW	12.95 AW	27530 AAW	FLBLS	10//99-12//99
	Fort Lauderdale PMSA, FL	S	16.40 MW	16.05 AW	34120 AAW	FLBLS	10//99-12//99
	Fort Myers-Cape Coral MSA, FL	S	14.00 MW	13.50 AW	29120 AAW	FLBLS	10//99-12//99
	Fort Pierce-Port St. Lucie MSA, FL	S	14.30 MW	13.67 AW	29740 AAW	FLBLS	10//99-12//99
	Fort Walton Beach MSA, FL	S	10.76 MW	10.09 AW	22380 AAW	FLBLS	10//99-12//99
	Gainesville MSA, FL	S	11.43 MW	11.35 AW	23780 AAW	FLBLS	10//99-12//99
	Jacksonville MSA, FL	S	13.14 MW	12.64 AW	27340 AAW	FLBLS	10//99-12//99
	Lakeland-Winter Haven MSA, FL	S	12.76 MW	12.79 AW	26550 AAW	FLBLS	10//99-12//99
	Melbourne-Titusville-Palm Bay MSA, FL	S	13.11 MW	12.94 AW	27270 AAW	FLBLS	10//99-12//99
	Miami PMSA, FL	S	14.44 MW	14.50 AW	30030 AAW	FLBLS	10//99-12//99
	Naples MSA, FL	S	14.47 MW	14.35 AW	30090 AAW	FLBLS	10//99-12//99
	Orlando MSA, FL	S	12.99 MW	12.64 AW	27020 AAW	FLBLS	10//99-12//99
	Sarasota-Bradenton MSA, FL	S	12.93 MW	13.02 AW	26900 AAW	FLBLS	10//99-12//99
	Tampa-St. Petersburg-Clearwater MSA, FL	S	15.12 MW	14.50 AW	31440 AAW	FLBLS	10//99-12//99
	West Palm Beach-Boca Raton MSA, FL	S	16.15 MW	16.09 AW	33600 AAW	FLBLS	10//99-12//99
	Georgia	S	11.97 MW	12.40 AW	25800 AAW	GABLS	10//99-12//99
	Atlanta MSA, GA	S	13.58 MW	13.36 AW	28240 AAW	GABLS	10//99-12//99
	Augusta-Aiken MSA, GA-SC	S	14.82 MW	12.58 AW	30830 AAW	GABLS	10//99-12//99
	Columbus MSA, GA-AL	S	11.94 MW	11.41 AW	24840 AAW	GABLS	10//99-12//99
	Macon MSA, GA	S	13.01 MW	13.66 AW	27060 AAW	GABLS	10//99-12//99
	Savannah MSA, GA	S	13.41 MW	12.92 AW	27890 AAW	GABLS	10//99-12//99
	Hawaii	S	15.52 MW	15.81 AW	32890 AAW	HIBLS	10//99-12//99
	Idaho	S	12.86 MW	12.97 AW	26980 AAW	IDBLS	10//99-12//99
	Boise City MSA, ID	S	13.92 MW	13.98 AW	28960 AAW	IDBLS	10//99-12//99
	Illinois	S	15.1 MW	15.37 AW	31970 AAW	ILBLS	10//99-12//99
	Champaign-Urbana MSA, IL	S	12.51 MW	12.73 AW	26020 AAW	ILBLS	10//99-12//99
	Chicago PMSA, IL	S	16.70 MW	16.03 AW	34730 AAW	ILBLS	10//99-12//99
	Rockford MSA, IL	S	16.00 MW	15.96 AW	33280 AAW	ILBLS	10//99-12//99
	Springfield MSA, IL	S	15.35 MW	14.49 AW	31920 AAW	ILBLS	10//99-12//99
	Indiana	S	13.44 MW	14.00 AW	29110 AAW	INBLS	10//99-12//99
	Elkhart-Goshen MSA, IN	S	15.23 MW	15.03 AW	31670 AAW	INBLS	10//99-12//99
	Evansville-Henderson MSA, IN-KY	S	12.96 MW	12.01 AW	26960 AAW	INBLS	10//99-12//99
	Fort Wayne MSA, IN	S	13.53 MW	11.98 AW	28140 AAW	INBLS	10//99-12//99
	Gary PMSA, IN	S	14.59 MW	14.66 AW	30350 AAW	INBLS	10//99-12//99
	Indianapolis MSA, IN	S	16.36 MW	15.41 AW	34040 AAW	INBLS	10//99-12//99
	Lafayette MSA, IN	S	15.84 MW	15.60 AW	32950 AAW	INBLS	10//99-12//99
	Iowa	S	13.43 MW	13.79 AW	28690 AAW	IABLS	10//99-12//99
	Davenport-Moline-Rock Island MSA, IA-IL	S	15.05 MW	14.50 AW	31300 AAW	IABLS	10//99-12//99
	Des Moines MSA, IA	S	15.26 MW	15.23 AW	31750 AAW	IABLS	10//99-12//99
	Sioux City MSA, IA-NE	S	14.31 MW	14.09 AW	29770 AAW	IABLS	10//99-12//99
	Kansas	S	10.5 MW	10.69 AW	22230 AAW	KSBLS	10//99-12//99
	Wichita MSA, KS	S	8.05 MW	6.56 AW	16740 AAW	KSBLS	10//99-12//99

AAW	Average annual wage	AOH	Average offered, high	ASH	Average starting, high	H	Hourly	M	Monthly	S	Special: hourly and annual
AE	Average entry wage	AOL	Average offered, low	ASL	Average starting, low	HI	Highest wage paid	MTC	Median total compensation	TQ	Third quartile wage
AEX	Average experienced wage	APH	Average pay, high range	AW	Average wage paid	HR	High end range	MW	Median wage paid	W	Weekly
AO	Average offered	APL	Average pay, low range	FQ	First quartile wage	LR	Low end range	SQ	Second quartile wage	Y	Yearly

1484

Occupation/Type/Industry	Location	Per	Low	Mid	High	Source	Date
Water and Liquid Waste Treatment Plant and System Operator	Kentucky	S	11.64 MW	11.97 AW	24890 AAW	KYBLS	10//99-12//99
	Lexington MSA, KY	S	14.02 MW	13.75 AW	29150 AAW	KYBLS	10//99-12//99
	Louisville MSA, KY-IN	S	13.44 MW	13.53 AW	27960 AAW	KYBLS	10//99-12//99
	Louisiana	S	10.03 MW	10.89 AW	22660 AAW	LABLS	10//99-12//99
	Baton Rouge MSA, LA	S	11.12 MW	10.26 AW	23130 AAW	LABLS	10//99-12//99
	Houma MSA, LA	S	10.21 MW	10.31 AW	21230 AAW	LABLS	10//99-12//99
	Lafayette MSA, LA	S	10.72 MW	10.78 AW	22300 AAW	LABLS	10//99-12//99
	Lake Charles MSA, LA	S	11.19 MW	11.09 AW	23270 AAW	LABLS	10//99-12//99
	Monroe MSA, LA	S	10.15 MW	9.68 AW	21110 AAW	LABLS	10//99-12//99
	New Orleans MSA, LA	S	10.21 MW	9.71 AW	21240 AAW	LABLS	10//99-12//99
	Shreveport-Bossier City MSA, LA	S	11.30 MW	9.85 AW	23490 AAW	LABLS	10//99-12//99
	Maine	S	13.26 MW	13.62 AW	28320 AAW	MEBLS	10//99-12//99
	Lewiston-Auburn MSA, ME	S	17.29 MW	17.56 AW	35970 AAW	MEBLS	10//99-12//99
	Portland MSA, ME	S	15.56 MW	15.37 AW	32370 AAW	MEBLS	10//99-12//99
	Maryland	S	16.15 MW	16.72 AW	34770 AAW	MDBLS	10//99-12//99
	Baltimore PMSA, MD	S	17.27 MW	17.05 AW	35920 AAW	MDBLS	10//99-12//99
	Cumberland MSA, MD-WV	S	13.65 MW	13.40 AW	28400 AAW	MDBLS	10//99-12//99
	Massachusetts	S	16.52 MW	16.95 AW	35260 AAW	MABLS	10//99-12//99
	Barnstable-Yarmouth MSA, MA	S	19.17 MW	18.71 AW	39870 AAW	MABLS	10//99-12//99
	Boston PMSA, MA-NH	S	17.03 MW	16.70 AW	35410 AAW	MABLS	10//99-12//99
	Brockton PMSA, MA	S	18.02 MW	17.56 AW	37480 AAW	MABLS	10//99-12//99
	Fitchburg-Leominster PMSA, MA	S	15.48 MW	14.58 AW	32190 AAW	MABLS	10//99-12//99
	Lawrence PMSA, MA-NH	S	16.02 MW	17.07 AW	33320 AAW	MABLS	10//99-12//99
	Lowell PMSA, MA-NH	S	17.91 MW	17.23 AW	37250 AAW	MABLS	10//99-12//99
	New Bedford PMSA, MA	S	15.88 MW	15.56 AW	33030 AAW	MABLS	10//99-12//99
	Pittsfield MSA, MA	S	15.92 MW	16.05 AW	33100 AAW	MABLS	10//99-12//99
	Springfield MSA, MA	S	15.59 MW	15.28 AW	32420 AAW	MABLS	10//99-12//99
	Worcester PMSA, MA-CT	S	18.45 MW	18.35 AW	38380 AAW	MABLS	10//99-12//99
	Michigan	S	15.62 MW	16.19 AW	33670 AAW	MIBLS	10//99-12//99
	Ann Arbor PMSA, MI	S	18.01 MW	17.57 AW	37460 AAW	MIBLS	10//99-12//99
	Benton Harbor MSA, MI	S	15.55 MW	15.51 AW	32340 AAW	MIBLS	10//99-12//99
	Detroit PMSA, MI	S	16.94 MW	16.27 AW	35240 AAW	MIBLS	10//99-12//99
	Grand Rapids-Muskegon-Holland MSA, MI	S	17.36 MW	16.98 AW	36100 AAW	MIBLS	10//99-12//99
	Kalamazoo-Battle Creek MSA, MI	S	16.41 MW	15.67 AW	34140 AAW	MIBLS	10//99-12//99
	Lansing-East Lansing MSA, MI	S	18.46 MW	17.22 AW	38400 AAW	MIBLS	10//99-12//99
	Saginaw-Bay City-Midland MSA, MI	S	14.75 MW	14.03 AW	30680 AAW	MIBLS	10//99-12//99
	Minnesota	S	15.39 MW	15.31 AW	31840 AAW	MNBLS	10//99-12//99
	Duluth-Superior MSA, MN-WI	S	17.07 MW	17.32 AW	35510 AAW	MNBLS	10//99-12//99
	Minneapolis-St. Paul MSA, MN-WI	S	17.65 MW	17.77 AW	36720 AAW	MNBLS	10//99-12//99
	Mississippi	S	10.67 MW	11.08 AW	23050 AAW	MSBLS	10//99-12//99
	Biloxi-Gulfport-Pascagoula MSA, MS	S	10.63 MW	10.14 AW	22110 AAW	MSBLS	10//99-12//99
	Hattiesburg MSA, MS	S	8.67 MW	7.96 AW	18040 AAW	MSBLS	10//99-12//99
	Jackson MSA, MS	S	12.50 MW	11.62 AW	26000 AAW	MSBLS	10//99-12//99
	Missouri	S	12.36 MW	13.55 AW	28180 AAW	MOBLS	10//99-12//99
	Kansas City MSA, MO-KS	S	13.70 MW	12.26 AW	28490 AAW	MOBLS	10//99-12//99
	St. Louis MSA, MO-IL	S	15.13 MW	14.88 AW	31480 AAW	MOBLS	10//99-12//99
	Montana	S	13.18 MW	12.95 AW	26940 AAW	MTBLS	10//99-12//99
	Great Falls MSA, MT	S	13.34 MW	13.56 AW	27750 AAW	MTBLS	10//99-12//99
	Nebraska	S	11.91 MW	12.70 AW	26420 AAW	NEBLS	10//99-12//99
	Omaha MSA, NE-IA	S	16.16 MW	16.04 AW	33600 AAW	NEBLS	10//99-12//99
	Nevada	S	20.47 MW	20.60 AW	42840 AAW	NVBLS	10//99-12//99
	Las Vegas MSA, NV-AZ	S	20.92 MW	20.32 AW	43500 AAW	NVBLS	10//99-12//99
	Reno MSA, NV	S	20.37 MW	20.30 AW	42370 AAW	NVBLS	10//99-12//99
	New Hampshire	S	14.95 MW	14.86 AW	30910 AAW	NHBLS	10//99-12//99
	Nashua PMSA, NH	S	16.38 MW	16.72 AW	34070 AAW	NHBLS	10//99-12//99
	Portsmouth-Rochester PMSA, NH-ME	S	16.92 MW	15.90 AW	35200 AAW	NHBLS	10//99-12//99
	New Jersey	S	18.32 MW	19.35 AW	40240 AAW	NJBLS	10//99-12//99
	Bergen-Passaic PMSA, NJ	S	19.98 MW	19.56 AW	41550 AAW	NJBLS	10//99-12//99
	Jersey City PMSA, NJ	S	17.12 MW	16.41 AW	35610 AAW	NJBLS	10//99-12//99
	Middlesex-Somerset-Hunterdon PMSA, NJ	S	20.98 MW	19.27 AW	43630 AAW	NJBLS	10//99-12//99

AAW Average annual wage	**AOH** Average offered, high	**ASH** Average starting, high	**H** Hourly	**M** Monthly	**S** Special: hourly and annual
AE Average entry wage	**AOL** Average offered, low	**ASL** Average starting, low	**HI** Highest wage paid	**MTC** Median total compensation	**TQ** Third quartile wage
AEX Average experienced wage	**APH** Average pay, high range	**AW** Average wage paid	**HR** High end range	**MW** Median wage paid	**W** Weekly
AO Average offered	**APL** Average pay, low range	**FQ** First quartile wage	**LR** Low end range	**SQ** Second quartile wage	**Y** Yearly

Occupation/Type/Industry	Location	Per	Low	Mid	High	Source	Date
Water and Liquid Waste Treatment Plant and System Operator	Monmouth-Ocean PMSA, NJ	S	18.28 MW	18.26 AW	38030 AAW	NJBLS	10//99-12//99
	Newark PMSA, NJ	S	19.69 MW	18.41 AW	40950 AAW	NJBLS	10//99-12//99
	Trenton PMSA, NJ	S	20.06 MW	19.09 AW	41730 AAW	NJBLS	10//99-12//99
	New Mexico	S	12.6 MW	13.30 AW	27670 AAW	NMBLS	10//99-12//99
	Las Cruces MSA, NM	S	10.20 MW	9.58 AW	21210 AAW	NMBLS	10//99-12//99
	Santa Fe MSA, NM	S	17.13 MW	17.78 AW	35630 AAW	NMBLS	10//99-12//99
	New York	S	17.19 MW	17.49 AW	36370 AAW	NYBLS	10//99-12//99
	Albany-Schenectady-Troy MSA, NY	S	15.68 MW	15.33 AW	32610 AAW	NYBLS	10//99-12//99
	Buffalo-Niagara Falls MSA, NY	S	17.19 MW	16.72 AW	35750 AAW	NYBLS	10//99-12//99
	Glens Falls MSA, NY	S	13.48 MW	13.01 AW	28040 AAW	NYBLS	10//99-12//99
	Nassau-Suffolk PMSA, NY	S	19.74 MW	19.17 AW	41060 AAW	NYBLS	10//99-12//99
	Newburgh PMSA, NY-PA	S	17.13 MW	16.86 AW	35640 AAW	NYBLS	10//99-12//99
	Rochester MSA, NY	S	16.91 MW	16.15 AW	35170 AAW	NYBLS	10//99-12//99
	Syracuse MSA, NY	S	16.67 MW	16.19 AW	34670 AAW	NYBLS	10//99-12//99
	Utica-Rome MSA, NY	S	12.08 MW	11.73 AW	25140 AAW	NYBLS	10//99-12//99
	North Carolina	S	12.42 MW	12.81 AW	26640 AAW	NCBLS	10//99-12//99
	Asheville MSA, NC	S	14.99 MW	14.95 AW	31190 AAW	NCBLS	10//99-12//99
	Charlotte-Gastonia-Rock Hill MSA, NC-SC	S	12.99 MW	12.65 AW	27010 AAW	NCBLS	10//99-12//99
	Fayetteville MSA, NC	S	13.42 MW	13.61 AW	27910 AAW	NCBLS	10//99-12//99
	Goldsboro MSA, NC	S	11.88 MW	11.53 AW	24710 AAW	NCBLS	10//99-12//99
	Greensboro--Winston-Salem--High Point MSA, NC	S	12.97 MW	12.60 AW	26980 AAW	NCBLS	10//99-12//99
	Hickory-Morganton-Lenoir MSA, NC	S	12.38 MW	11.90 AW	25760 AAW	NCBLS	10//99-12//99
	Raleigh-Durham-Chapel Hill MSA, NC	S	13.05 MW	12.67 AW	27150 AAW	NCBLS	10//99-12//99
	Wilmington MSA, NC	S	13.69 MW	13.20 AW	28470 AAW	NCBLS	10//99-12//99
	North Dakota	S	12.4 MW	12.99 AW	27020 AAW	NDBLS	10//99-12//99
	Fargo-Moorhead MSA, ND-MN	S	13.86 MW	13.17 AW	28830 AAW	NDBLS	10//99-12//99
	Ohio	S	15.36 MW	15.60 AW	32460 AAW	OHBLS	10//99-12//99
	Akron PMSA, OH	S	16.27 MW	15.61 AW	33830 AAW	OHBLS	10//99-12//99
	Canton-Massillon MSA, OH	S	14.57 MW	14.56 AW	30320 AAW	OHBLS	10//99-12//99
	Cincinnati PMSA, OH-KY-IN	S	14.98 MW	14.81 AW	31150 AAW	OHBLS	10//99-12//99
	Cleveland-Lorain-Elyria PMSA, OH	S	17.18 MW	16.99 AW	35730 AAW	OHBLS	10//99-12//99
	Columbus MSA, OH	S	15.60 MW	15.20 AW	32440 AAW	OHBLS	10//99-12//99
	Dayton-Springfield MSA, OH	S	15.00 MW	14.84 AW	31210 AAW	OHBLS	10//99-12//99
	Hamilton-Middletown PMSA, OH	S	17.63 MW	17.60 AW	36670 AAW	OHBLS	10//99-12//99
	Mansfield MSA, OH	S	15.04 MW	14.51 AW	31290 AAW	OHBLS	10//99-12//99
	Steubenville-Weirton MSA, OH-WV	S	11.23 MW	11.18 AW	23350 AAW	OHBLS	10//99-12//99
	Toledo MSA, OH	S	16.51 MW	16.70 AW	34340 AAW	OHBLS	10//99-12//99
	Youngstown-Warren MSA, OH	S	15.51 MW	15.19 AW	32260 AAW	OHBLS	10//99-12//99
	Oklahoma	S	10.05 MW	10.34 AW	21500 AAW	OKBLS	10//99-12//99
	Enid MSA, OK	S	9.81 MW	9.73 AW	20400 AAW	OKBLS	10//99-12//99
	Lawton MSA, OK	S	9.35 MW	9.66 AW	19460 AAW	OKBLS	10//99-12//99
	Oklahoma City MSA, OK	S	11.26 MW	10.62 AW	23430 AAW	OKBLS	10//99-12//99
	Tulsa MSA, OK	S	11.29 MW	11.08 AW	23480 AAW	OKBLS	10//99-12//99
	Oregon	S	15.81 MW	16.18 AW	33660 AAW	ORBLS	10//99-12//99
	Eugene-Springfield MSA, OR	S	18.73 MW	18.38 AW	38950 AAW	ORBLS	10//99-12//99
	Portland-Vancouver PMSA, OR-WA	S	17.51 MW	16.73 AW	36420 AAW	ORBLS	10//99-12//99
	Pennsylvania	S	15.16 MW	15.19 AW	31600 AAW	PABLS	10//99-12//99
	Allentown-Bethlehem-Easton MSA, PA	S	16.13 MW	15.59 AW	33560 AAW	PABLS	10//99-12//99
	Altoona MSA, PA	S	14.77 MW	14.28 AW	30710 AAW	PABLS	10//99-12//99
	Harrisburg-Lebanon-Carlisle MSA, PA	S	14.30 MW	14.17 AW	29730 AAW	PABLS	10//99-12//99
	Johnstown MSA, PA	S	15.90 MW	15.36 AW	33080 AAW	PABLS	10//99-12//99
	Lancaster MSA, PA	S	14.68 MW	14.82 AW	30520 AAW	PABLS	10//99-12//99
	Philadelphia PMSA, PA-NJ	S	17.79 MW	17.49 AW	37010 AAW	PABLS	10//99-12//99
	Pittsburgh MSA, PA	S	16.22 MW	16.05 AW	33730 AAW	PABLS	10//99-12//99
	Reading MSA, PA	S	16.05 MW	15.70 AW	33380 AAW	PABLS	10//99-12//99
	Scranton--Wilkes-Barre--Hazleton MSA, PA	S	14.77 MW	14.87 AW	30720 AAW	PABLS	10//99-12//99

AAW Average annual wage	**AOH** Average offered, high	**ASH** Average starting, high	**H** Hourly	**M** Monthly	**S** Special: hourly and annual
AE Average entry wage	**AOL** Average offered, low	**ASL** Average starting, low	**HI** Highest wage paid	**MTC** Median total compensation	**TQ** Third quartile wage
AEX Average experienced wage	**APH** Average pay, high range	**AW** Average wage paid	**HR** High end range	**MW** Median wage paid	**W** Weekly
AO Average offered	**APL** Average pay, low range	**FQ** First quartile wage	**LR** Low end range	**SQ** Second quartile wage	**Y** Yearly

Occupation/Type/Industry	Location	Per	Low	Mid	High	Source	Date
Water and Liquid Waste Treatment Plant and System Operator							
	Sharon MSA, PA	S	14.93 MW	14.98 AW	31050 AAW	PABLS	10//99-12//99
	State College MSA, PA	S	10.03 MW	6.83 AW	20870 AAW	PABLS	10//99-12//99
	Williamsport MSA, PA	S	14.21 MW	14.53 AW	29550 AAW	PABLS	10//99-12//99
	York MSA, PA	S	14.61 MW	14.81 AW	30390 AAW	PABLS	10//99-12//99
	Rhode Island	S	15.1 MW	15.34 AW	31910 AAW	RIBLS	10//99-12//99
	Providence-Fall River- Warwick MSA, RI-MA	S	15.46 MW	15.19 AW	32150 AAW	RIBLS	10//99-12//99
	South Carolina	S	13.3 MW	15.10 AW	31410 AAW	SCBLS	10//99-12//99
	Charleston-North Charleston MSA, SC	S	14.82 MW	13.51 AW	30840 AAW	SCBLS	10//99-12//99
	Columbia MSA, SC	S	21.62 MW	17.41 AW	44960 AAW	SCBLS	10//99-12//99
	Florence MSA, SC	S	17.41 MW	12.15 AW	36220 AAW	SCBLS	10//99-12//99
	Greenville-Spartanburg- Anderson MSA, SC	S	15.55 MW	14.80 AW	32340 AAW	SCBLS	10//99-12//99
	Myrtle Beach MSA, SC	S	11.68 MW	11.62 AW	24290 AAW	SCBLS	10//99-12//99
	South Dakota	S	12.67 MW	13.31 AW	27690 AAW	SDBLS	10//99-12//99
	Tennessee	S	13.2 MW	13.80 AW	28700 AAW	TNBLS	10//99-12//99
	Chattanooga MSA, TN-GA	S	14.03 MW	12.56 AW	29180 AAW	TNBLS	10//99-12//99
	Johnson City-Kingsport-Bristol MSA, TN-VA	S	11.78 MW	11.65 AW	24510 AAW	TNBLS	10//99-12//99
	Knoxville MSA, TN	S	15.93 MW	15.97 AW	33130 AAW	TNBLS	10//99-12//99
	Memphis MSA, TN-AR-MS	S	14.44 MW	14.61 AW	30040 AAW	MSBLS	10//99-12//99
	Nashville MSA, TN	S	13.79 MW	12.99 AW	28690 AAW	TNBLS	10//99-12//99
	Texas	S	11.62 MW	12.28 AW	25550 AAW	TXBLS	10//99-12//99
	Abilene MSA, TX	S	12.97 MW	12.01 AW	26970 AAW	TXBLS	10//99-12//99
	Amarillo MSA, TX	S	14.34 MW	12.49 AW	29820 AAW	TXBLS	10//99-12//99
	Austin-San Marcos MSA, TX	S	12.21 MW	11.98 AW	25390 AAW	TXBLS	10//99-12//99
	Beaumont-Port Arthur MSA, TX	S	16.45 MW	16.49 AW	34220 AAW	TXBLS	10//99-12//99
	Brazoria PMSA, TX	S	14.60 MW	14.03 AW	30370 AAW	TXBLS	10//99-12//99
	Brownsville-Harlingen-San Benito MSA, TX	S	9.10 MW	8.57 AW	18930 AAW	TXBLS	10//99-12//99
	Bryan-College Station MSA, TX	S	11.87 MW	11.17 AW	24690 AAW	TXBLS	10//99-12//99
	Corpus Christi MSA, TX	S	12.53 MW	12.58 AW	26060 AAW	TXBLS	10//99-12//99
	Dallas PMSA, TX	S	14.20 MW	13.38 AW	29530 AAW	TXBLS	10//99-12//99
	El Paso MSA, TX	S	10.63 MW	10.93 AW	22100 AAW	TXBLS	10//99-12//99
	Fort Worth-Arlington PMSA, TX	S	13.36 MW	12.87 AW	27780 AAW	TXBLS	10//99-12//99
	Galveston-Texas City PMSA, TX	S	11.74 MW	12.19 AW	24420 AAW	TXBLS	10//99-12//99
	Houston PMSA, TX	S	13.35 MW	13.46 AW	27760 AAW	TXBLS	10//99-12//99
	Killeen-Temple MSA, TX	S	13.21 MW	13.89 AW	27480 AAW	TXBLS	10//99-12//99
	Longview-Marshall MSA, TX	S	14.18 MW	12.36 AW	29500 AAW	TXBLS	10//99-12//99
	McAllen-Edinburg-Mission MSA, TX	S	8.23 MW	8.31 AW	17120 AAW	TXBLS	10//99-12//99
	Odessa-Midland MSA, TX	S	11.09 MW	11.00 AW	23070 AAW	TXBLS	10//99-12//99
	San Antonio MSA, TX	S	13.22 MW	12.33 AW	27500 AAW	TXBLS	10//99-12//99
	Sherman-Denison MSA, TX	S	11.33 MW	11.30 AW	23560 AAW	TXBLS	10//99-12//99
	Texarkana MSA, TX- Texarkana, AR	S	10.97 MW	10.38 AW	22820 AAW	TXBLS	10//99-12//99
	Tyler MSA, TX	S	12.67 MW	12.24 AW	26360 AAW	TXBLS	10//99-12//99
	Waco MSA, TX	S	11.52 MW	11.01 AW	23970 AAW	TXBLS	10//99-12//99
	Wichita Falls MSA, TX	S	10.04 MW	9.87 AW	20880 AAW	TXBLS	10//99-12//99
	Utah	S	15.32 MW	15.60 AW	32460 AAW	UTBLS	10//99-12//99
	Salt Lake City-Ogden MSA, UT	S	16.34 MW	16.13 AW	33980 AAW	UTBLS	10//99-12//99
	Vermont	S	13.71 MW	13.62 AW	28320 AAW	VTBLS	10//99-12//99
	Burlington MSA, VT	S	16.27 MW	15.93 AW	33850 AAW	VTBLS	10//99-12//99
	Virginia	S	13.88 MW	14.38 AW	29910 AAW	VABLS	10//99-12//99
	Charlottesville MSA, VA	S	13.68 MW	13.27 AW	28440 AAW	VABLS	10//99-12//99
	Danville MSA, VA	S	13.27 MW	12.70 AW	27600 AAW	VABLS	10//99-12//99
	Lynchburg MSA, VA	S	13.59 MW	12.46 AW	28260 AAW	VABLS	10//99-12//99
	Norfolk-Virginia Beach- Newport News MSA, VA- NC	S	17.29 MW	17.62 AW	35970 AAW	VABLS	10//99-12//99
	Richmond-Petersburg MSA, VA	S	13.60 MW	13.86 AW	28280 AAW	VABLS	10//99-12//99
	Roanoke MSA, VA	S	12.73 MW	12.28 AW	26480 AAW	VABLS	10//99-12//99
	Washington	S	18.82 MW	19.08 AW	39700 AAW	WABLS	10//99-12//99

AAW	Average annual wage	AOH	Average offered, high	ASH	Average starting, high	H	Hourly	M	Monthly	S	Special: hourly and annual
AE	Average entry wage	AOL	Average offered, low	ASL	Average starting, low	HI	Highest wage paid	MTC	Median total compensation	TQ	Third quartile wage
AEX	Average experienced wage	APH	Average pay, high range	AW	Average wage paid	HR	High end range	MW	Median wage paid	W	Weekly
AO	Average offered	APL	Average pay, low range	FQ	First quartile wage	LR	Low end range	SQ	Second quartile wage	Y	Yearly

1487

Occupation/Type/Industry	Location	Per	Low	Mid	High	Source	Date
Water and Liquid Waste Treatment Plant and System Operator	Bellingham MSA, WA	S	24.82 mw	20.88 aw	51630 aaw	WABLS	10//99-12//99
	Bremerton PMSA, WA	S	18.41 mw	18.61 aw	38290 aaw	WABLS	10//99-12//99
	Richland-Kennewick-Pasco MSA, WA	S	20.87 mw	20.59 aw	43410 aaw	WABLS	10//99-12//99
	Seattle-Bellevue-Everett PMSA, WA	S	20.65 mw	21.01 aw	42950 aaw	WABLS	10//99-12//99
	Spokane MSA, WA	S	18.88 mw	17.64 aw	39280 aaw	WABLS	10//99-12//99
	Tacoma PMSA, WA	S	20.37 mw	19.92 aw	42360 aaw	WABLS	10//99-12//99
	Yakima MSA, WA	S	18.55 mw	17.42 aw	38580 aaw	WABLS	10//99-12//99
	West Virginia	S	10.23 mw	10.74 aw	22330 aaw	WVBLS	10//99-12//99
	Charleston MSA, WV	S	12.13 mw	9.97 aw	25230 aaw	WVBLS	10//99-12//99
	Huntington-Ashland MSA, WV-KY-OH	S	12.18 mw	11.04 aw	25340 aaw	WVBLS	10//99-12//99
	Parkersburg-Marietta MSA, WV-OH	S	11.96 mw	11.97 aw	24870 aaw	WVBLS	10//99-12//99
	Wheeling MSA, WV-OH	S	11.59 mw	11.40 aw	24110 aaw	WVBLS	10//99-12//99
	Wisconsin	S	16.16 mw	16.32 aw	33940 aaw	WIBLS	10//99-12//99
	Appleton-Oshkosh-Neenah MSA, WI	S	16.61 mw	16.97 aw	34560 aaw	WIBLS	10//99-12//99
	Janesville-Beloit MSA, WI	S	17.40 mw	17.33 aw	36200 aaw	WIBLS	10//99-12//99
	Madison MSA, WI	S	16.58 mw	17.39 aw	34490 aaw	WIBLS	10//99-12//99
	Milwaukee-Waukesha PMSA, WI	S	18.71 mw	18.58 aw	38910 aaw	WIBLS	10//99-12//99
	Racine PMSA, WI	S	19.41 mw	21.11 aw	40380 aaw	WIBLS	10//99-12//99
	Sheboygan MSA, WI	S	17.45 mw	17.38 aw	36290 aaw	WIBLS	10//99-12//99
	Wausau MSA, WI	S	13.35 mw	14.05 aw	27770 aaw	WIBLS	10//99-12//99
	Wyoming	S	15.11 mw	15.62 aw	32490 aaw	WYBLS	10//99-12//99
Weatherman							
Television	United States	Y	25000 lr		100000 hr	SCWO	1999
Web Content Developer	United States	Y		50986 aw		NEMED	1999
Web Designer	United States	Y		46734 aw		COUSE	2000
	United States	Y		46734 aw		NEMED	1999
	United States	Y		46734 aw		NEMED	1999
Internet	United States	Y		42501 mw		BUS2	2000
Web Media Producer							
Graphics, Audio, Video	United States	Y		48909 aw		NEMED	1999
Web Security Manager	United States	Y	65198 apl	82235 aw	96811 aph	PCWK	1999
	San Francisco, CA	Y	71288 apl	89916 aw	105854 aph	PCWK	1999
	Indianapolis/Fort Wayne, IN	Y	47627 apl	60072 aw	70719 aph	PCWK	1999
	Louisville, KY	Y	60671 apl	75525 aw	90088 aph	PCWK	1999
	New York, NY	Y	92017 apl	116062 aw	136634 aph	PCWK	1999
Web Writer/Editor	United States	Y		50000 aw		COUSE	2000
Webmaster	United States	Y		65343 aw		CRDET	1999
	Los Angeles, CA	Y		72712 aw		CRDET	1999
	San Francisco, CA	Y		75518 aw		CRDET	1999
	Washington, DC	Y		69309 aw		CRDET	1999
	Chicago, IL	Y		71254 aw		CRDET	1999
	Baltimore, MD	Y		65817 aw		CRDET	1999
	Detroit, MI	Y		71666 aw		CRDET	1999
	Minneapolis, MN	Y		68308 aw		CRDET	1999
	New York City, NY	Y		75228 aw		CRDET	1999
	Dallas, TX	Y		66993 aw		CRDET	1999
	Seattle, WA	Y		70226 aw		CRDET	1999
Weigher, Measurer, Checker, and Sampler, Recordkeeping	Alabama	S	8.8 mw	9.86 aw	20500 aaw	ALBLS	10//99-12//99
	Alaska	S	11.08 mw	11.32 aw	23550 aaw	AKBLS	10//99-12//99
	Arizona	S	10.03 mw	11.16 aw	23210 aaw	AZBLS	10//99-12//99
	Arkansas	S	8.34 mw	8.98 aw	18670 aaw	ARBLS	10//99-12//99
	California	S	10.73 mw	12.43 aw	25860 aaw	CABLS	10//99-12//99
	Colorado	S	10.27 mw	10.34 aw	21520 aaw	COBLS	10//99-12//99
	Connecticut	S	11.45 mw	12.31 aw	25610 aaw	CTBLS	10//99-12//99
	Delaware	S	13.07 mw	13.75 aw	28590 aaw	DEBLS	10//99-12//99
	District of Columbia	S	12.96 mw	13.90 aw	28910 aaw	DCBLS	10//99-12//99

AAW	Average annual wage	AOH	Average offered, high	ASH	Average starting, high	H	Hourly	M	Monthly	S	Special: hourly and annual
AE	Average entry wage	AOL	Average offered, low	ASL	Average starting, low	HI	Highest wage paid	MTC	Median total compensation	TQ	Third quartile wage
AEX	Average experienced wage	APH	Average pay, high range	AW	Average wage paid	HR	High end range	MW	Median wage paid	W	Weekly
AO	Average offered	APL	Average pay, low range	FQ	First quartile wage	LR	Low end range	SQ	Second quartile wage	Y	Yearly

1488

Occupation/Type/Industry	Location	Per	Low	Mid	High	Source	Date
Weigher, Measurer, Checker, and Sampler, Recordkeeping	Florida	S	10.58 MW	11.69 AW	24320 AAW	FLBLS	10//99-12//99
	Georgia	S	9.7 MW	10.29 AW	21400 AAW	GABLS	10//99-12//99
	Hawaii	S	15.6 MW	14.69 AW	30540 AAW	HIBLS	10//99-12//99
	Idaho	S	8.66 MW	8.72 AW	18140 AAW	IDBLS	10//99-12//99
	Illinois	S	9.89 MW	10.51 AW	21860 AAW	ILBLS	10//99-12//99
	Indiana	S	13.32 MW	14.76 AW	30710 AAW	INBLS	10//99-12//99
	Iowa	S	10.19 MW	11.24 AW	23370 AAW	IABLS	10//99-12//99
	Kansas	S	10.9 MW	11.45 AW	23810 AAW	KSBLS	10//99-12//99
	Kentucky	S	10.05 MW	11.18 AW	23260 AAW	KYBLS	10//99-12//99
	Louisiana	S	10.02 MW	10.12 AW	21050 AAW	LABLS	10//99-12//99
	Maine	S	9.92 MW	10.53 AW	21900 AAW	MEBLS	10//99-12//99
	Maryland	S	8.13 MW	9.24 AW	19230 AAW	MDBLS	10//99-12//99
	Massachusetts	S	13.86 MW	14.24 AW	29610 AAW	MABLS	10//99-12//99
	Michigan	S	20.36 MW	18.29 AW	38040 AAW	MIBLS	10//99-12//99
	Minnesota	S	10.14 MW	10.97 AW	22820 AAW	MNBLS	10//99-12//99
	Mississippi	S	7.89 MW	8.40 AW	17470 AAW	MSBLS	10//99-12//99
	Missouri	S	11.26 MW	12.28 AW	25530 AAW	MOBLS	10//99-12//99
	Montana	S	8.61 MW	9.18 AW	19100 AAW	MTBLS	10//99-12//99
	Nebraska	S	10.85 MW	10.77 AW	22400 AAW	NEBLS	10//99-12//99
	Nevada	S	11.17 MW	11.22 AW	23340 AAW	NVBLS	10//99-12//99
	New Hampshire	S	12.61 MW	13.62 AW	28330 AAW	NHBLS	10//99-12//99
	New Jersey	S	11.57 MW	11.98 AW	24910 AAW	NJBLS	10//99-12//99
	New Mexico	S	8.55 MW	9.17 AW	19080 AAW	NMBLS	10//99-12//99
	New York	S	11.85 MW	13.05 AW	27140 AAW	NYBLS	10//99-12//99
	North Carolina	S	9.9 MW	10.35 AW	21520 AAW	NCBLS	10//99-12//99
	North Dakota	S	8.07 MW	8.76 AW	18230 AAW	NDBLS	10//99-12//99
	Ohio	S	11.22 MW	12.11 AW	25180 AAW	OHBLS	10//99-12//99
	Oklahoma	S	10.6 MW	10.76 AW	22370 AAW	OKBLS	10//99-12//99
	Oregon	S	11.95 MW	12.75 AW	26530 AAW	ORBLS	10//99-12//99
	Pennsylvania	S	11.67 MW	11.64 AW	24220 AAW	PABLS	10//99-12//99
	Rhode Island	S	9.95 MW	10.82 AW	22510 AAW	RIBLS	10//99-12//99
	South Carolina	S	10.5 MW	10.56 AW	21960 AAW	SCBLS	10//99-12//99
	South Dakota	S	10.68 MW	10.08 AW	20970 AAW	SDBLS	10//99-12//99
	Tennessee	S	10.37 MW	10.62 AW	22080 AAW	TNBLS	10//99-12//99
	Texas	S	13.32 MW	14.12 AW	29370 AAW	TXBLS	10//99-12//99
	Vermont	S	9.85 MW	10.20 AW	21210 AAW	VTBLS	10//99-12//99
	Virginia	S	10.07 MW	11.49 AW	23900 AAW	VABLS	10//99-12//99
	Washington	S	9.55 MW	11.24 AW	23370 AAW	WABLS	10//99-12//99
	West Virginia	S	10.41 MW	10.65 AW	22140 AAW	WVBLS	10//99-12//99
	Wisconsin	S	15.02 MW	15.95 AW	33170 AAW	WIBLS	10//99-12//99
	Wyoming	S	10.04 MW	10.69 AW	22240 AAW	WYBLS	10//99-12//99
Welder, Cutter, Solderer, and Brazer	Alabama	S	11.64 MW	12.31 AW	25610 AAW	ALBLS	10//99-12//99
	Anniston MSA, AL	S	13.78 MW	13.73 AW	28650 AAW	ALBLS	10//99-12//99
	Auburn-Opelika MSA, AL	Per	11.45 MW	11.28 AW	23810 AAW	ALBLS	10//99-12//99
	Birmingham MSA, AL	S	12.93 MW	12.28 AW	26890 AAW	ALBLS	10//99-12//99
	Decatur MSA, AL	S	12.25 MW	11.33 AW	25490 AAW	ALBLS	10//99-12//99
	Dothan MSA, AL	S	11.11 MW	10.11 AW	23100 AAW	ALBLS	10//99-12//99
	Florence MSA, AL	S	10.95 MW	10.61 AW	22780 AAW	ALBLS	10//99-12//99
	Gadsden MSA, AL	S	12.74 MW	11.41 AW	26510 AAW	ALBLS	10//99-12//99
	Huntsville MSA, AL	S	14.37 MW	12.54 AW	29900 AAW	ALBLS	10//99-12//99
	Mobile MSA, AL	S	12.72 MW	12.52 AW	26450 AAW	ALBLS	10//99-12//99
	Montgomery MSA, AL	S	11.38 MW	11.16 AW	23670 AAW	ALBLS	10//99-12//99
	Tuscaloosa MSA, AL	S	13.60 MW	12.98 AW	28280 AAW	ALBLS	10//99-12//99
	Alaska	S	19.92 MW	20.44 AW	42520 AAW	AKBLS	10//99-12//99
	Anchorage MSA, AK	S	20.07 MW	18.96 AW	41750 AAW	AKBLS	10//99-12//99
	Arizona	S	11.55 MW	12.28 AW	25540 AAW	AZBLS	10//99-12//99
	Phoenix-Mesa MSA, AZ	S	12.30 MW	11.68 AW	25590 AAW	AZBLS	10//99-12//99
	Tucson MSA, AZ	S	11.14 MW	10.11 AW	23170 AAW	AZBLS	10//99-12//99
	Yuma MSA, AZ	S	10.58 MW	9.55 AW	22000 AAW	AZBLS	10//99-12//99
	Arkansas	S	10.9 MW	11.58 AW	24080 AAW	ARBLS	
	Fayetteville-Springdale-Rogers MSA, AR	S	10.35 MW	9.97 AW	21530 AAW	ARBLS	10//99-12//99
	Fort Smith MSA, AR-OK	S	11.50 MW	11.23 AW	23910 AAW	ARBLS	10//99-12//99
	Jonesboro MSA, AR	S	11.45 MW	11.43 AW	23810 AAW	ARBLS	10//99-12//99
	Little Rock-North Little Rock MSA, AR	S	12.87 MW	11.77 AW	26770 AAW	ARBLS	10//99-12//99
	Pine Bluff MSA, AR	S	15.12 MW	16.36 AW	31460 AAW	ARBLS	10//99-12//99
	California	S	12.24 MW	13.25 AW	27560 AAW	CABLS	10//99-12//99
	Bakersfield MSA, CA	S	13.80 MW	13.15 AW	28700 AAW	CABLS	10//99-12//99

AAW Average annual wage	**AOH** Average offered, high	**ASH** Average starting, high	**H** Hourly	**M** Monthly	**S** Special: hourly and annual
AE Average entry wage	**AOL** Average offered, low	**ASL** Average starting, low	**HI** Highest wage paid	**MTC** Median total compensation	**TQ** Third quartile wage
AEX Average experienced wage	**APH** Average pay, high range	**AW** Average wage paid	**HR** High end range	**MW** Median wage paid	**W** Weekly
AO Average offered	**APL** Average pay, low range	**FQ** First quartile wage	**LR** Low end range	**SQ** Second quartile wage	**Y** Yearly

Occupation/Type/Industry	Location	Per	Low	Mid	High	Source	Date
Welder, Cutter, Solderer, and Brazer							
	Chico-Paradise MSA, CA	S	12.55 mw	12.30 aw	26110 aaw	CABLS	10//99-12//99
	Fresno MSA, CA	S	11.96 mw	11.05 aw	24870 aaw	CABLS	10//99-12//99
	Los Angeles-Long Beach PMSA, CA	S	12.39 mw	11.32 aw	25770 aaw	CABLS	10//99-12//99
	Merced MSA, CA	S	10.06 mw	9.57 aw	20920 aaw	CABLS	10//99-12//99
	Modesto MSA, CA	S	13.47 mw	13.30 aw	28030 aaw	CABLS	10//99-12//99
	Oakland PMSA, CA	S	16.23 mw	15.67 aw	33760 aaw	CABLS	10//99-12//99
	Orange County PMSA, CA	S	13.76 mw	12.96 aw	28610 aaw	CABLS	10//99-12//99
	Redding MSA, CA	S	10.59 mw	10.46 aw	22030 aaw	CABLS	10//99-12//99
	Riverside-San Bernardino PMSA, CA	S	12.22 mw	11.37 aw	25420 aaw	CABLS	10//99-12//99
	Sacramento PMSA, CA	S	11.70 mw	10.95 aw	24340 aaw	CABLS	10//99-12//99
	Salinas MSA, CA	S	13.27 mw	13.06 aw	27600 aaw	CABLS	10//99-12//99
	San Diego MSA, CA	S	13.21 mw	12.41 aw	27470 aaw	CABLS	10//99-12//99
	San Francisco PMSA, CA	S	15.66 mw	14.37 aw	32580 aaw	CABLS	10//99-12//99
	San Jose PMSA, CA	S	13.55 mw	13.62 aw	28180 aaw	CABLS	10//99-12//99
	San Luis Obispo-Atascadero-Paso Robles MSA, CA	S	13.76 mw	12.60 aw	28620 aaw	CABLS	10//99-12//99
	Santa Barbara-Santa Maria-Lompoc MSA, CA	S	12.74 mw	12.36 aw	26490 aaw	CABLS	10//99-12//99
	Santa Cruz-Watsonville PMSA, CA	S	12.81 mw	11.68 aw	26640 aaw	CABLS	10//99-12//99
	Santa Rosa PMSA, CA	S	14.35 mw	13.15 aw	29860 aaw	CABLS	10//99-12//99
	Stockton-Lodi MSA, CA	S	14.00 mw	13.11 aw	29120 aaw	CABLS	10//99-12//99
	Vallejo-Fairfield-Napa PMSA, CA	S	14.34 mw	14.94 aw	29830 aaw	CABLS	10//99-12//99
	Ventura PMSA, CA	S	12.60 mw	11.10 aw	26210 aaw	CABLS	10//99-12//99
	Visalia-Tulare-Porterville MSA, CA	S	13.59 mw	12.17 aw	28280 aaw	CABLS	10//99-12//99
	Yolo PMSA, CA	S	11.38 mw	10.17 aw	23670 aaw	CABLS	10//99-12//99
	Yuba City MSA, CA	S	13.06 mw	12.41 aw	27170 aaw	CABLS	10//99-12//99
	Colorado	S	12.43 mw	13.41 aw	27890 aaw	CODLS	10//99 12//99
	Boulder-Longmont PMSA, CO	S	13.90 mw	14.46 aw	28910 aaw	CODLS	10//99-12//99
	Denver PMSA, CO	S	13.75 mw	13.13 aw	28600 aaw	CODLS	10//99-12//99
	Fort Collins-Loveland MSA, CO	S	11.75 mw	11.52 aw	24440 aaw	CODLS	10//99-12//99
	Grand Junction MSA, CO	S	12.84 mw	12.45 aw	26710 aaw	CODLS	10//99-12//99
	Greeley PMSA, CO	S	14.03 mw	11.99 aw	29190 aaw	CODLS	10//99-12//99
	Pueblo MSA, CO	S	12.62 mw	12.02 aw	26240 aaw	CODLS	10//99-12//99
	Connecticut	S	13.78 mw	14.21 aw	29550 aaw	CTBLS	10//99-12//99
	Bridgeport PMSA, CT	S	15.29 mw	14.91 aw	31800 aaw	CTBLS	10//99-12//99
	Danbury PMSA, CT	S	15.17 mw	15.16 aw	31560 aaw	CTBLS	10//99-12//99
	Hartford MSA, CT	S	14.80 mw	14.66 aw	30790 aaw	CTBLS	10//99-12//99
	New Haven-Meriden PMSA, CT	S	12.55 mw	12.17 aw	26100 aaw	CTBLS	10//99-12//99
	New London-Norwich MSA, CT-RI	S	13.77 mw	12.86 aw	28650 aaw	CTBLS	10//99-12//99
	Stamford-Norwalk PMSA, CT	S	15.91 mw	15.56 aw	33080 aaw	CTBLS	10//99-12//99
	Waterbury PMSA, CT	S	11.32 mw	11.17 aw	23540 aaw	CTBLS	10//99-12//99
	Delaware	S	16.12 mw	17.39 aw	36180 aaw	DEBLS	10//99-12//99
	Wilmington-Newark PMSA, DE-MD	S	18.25 mw	17.55 aw	37970 aaw	DEBLS	10//99-12//99
	District of Columbia	S	13.52 mw	14.53 aw	30220 aaw	DCBLS	10//99-12//99
	Washington PMSA, DC-MD-VA-WV	S	14.35 mw	14.06 aw	29860 aaw	DCBLS	10//99-12//99
	Florida	S	11.09 mw	11.52 aw	23970 aaw	FLBLS	10//99-12//99
	Daytona Beach MSA, FL	S	10.61 mw	10.48 aw	22070 aaw	FLBLS	10//99-12//99
	Fort Lauderdale PMSA, FL	S	13.12 mw	12.95 aw	27280 aaw	FLBLS	10//99-12//99
	Fort Myers-Cape Coral MSA, FL	S	11.76 mw	11.47 aw	24460 aaw	FLBLS	10//99-12//99
	Fort Pierce-Port St. Lucie MSA, FL	S	12.48 mw	12.18 aw	25950 aaw	FLBLS	10//99-12//99
	Fort Walton Beach MSA, FL	S	11.79 mw	11.14 aw	24520 aaw	FLBLS	10//99-12//99
	Gainesville MSA, FL	S	10.76 mw	10.73 aw	22380 aaw	FLBLS	10//99-12//99
	Jacksonville MSA, FL	S	12.42 mw	11.90 aw	25840 aaw	FLBLS	10//99-12//99
	Lakeland-Winter Haven MSA, FL	S	11.11 mw	10.92 aw	23110 aaw	FLBLS	10//99-12//99
	Melbourne-Titusville-Palm Bay MSA, FL	S	11.66 mw	11.60 aw	24250 aaw	FLBLS	10//99-12//99
	Miami PMSA, FL	S	10.92 mw	10.40 aw	22700 aaw	FLBLS	10//99-12//99
	Naples MSA, FL	S	12.08 mw	11.78 aw	25120 aaw	FLBLS	10//99-12//99

AAW Average annual wage	**AOH** Average offered, high	**ASH** Average starting, high	**H** Hourly	**M** Monthly	**S** Special: hourly and annual
AE Average entry wage	**AOL** Average offered, low	**ASL** Average starting, low	**HI** Highest wage paid	**MTC** Median total compensation	**TQ** Third quartile wage
AEX Average experienced wage	**APH** Average pay, high range	**AW** Average wage paid	**HR** High end range	**MW** Median wage paid	**W** Weekly
AO Average offered	**APL** Average pay, low range	**FQ** First quartile wage	**LR** Low end range	**SQ** Second quartile wage	**Y** Yearly

Occupation/Type/Industry	Location	Per	Low	Mid	High	Source	Date
Welder, Cutter, Solderer, and Brazer							
	Ocala MSA, FL	S	10.87 MW	10.72 AW	22600 AAW	FLBLS	10//99-12//99
	Orlando MSA, FL	S	11.10 MW	10.56 AW	23090 AAW	FLBLS	10//99-12//99
	Panama City MSA, FL	S	14.51 MW	14.12 AW	30180 AAW	FLBLS	10//99-12//99
	Pensacola MSA, FL	S	11.74 MW	11.17 AW	24410 AAW	FLBLS	10//99-12//99
	Sarasota-Bradenton MSA, FL	S	11.40 MW	11.26 AW	23710 AAW	FLBLS	10//99-12//99
	Tampa-St. Petersburg-Clearwater MSA, FL	S	11.27 MW	10.77 AW	23430 AAW	FLBLS	10//99-12//99
	West Palm Beach-Boca Raton MSA, FL	S	12.52 MW	11.76 AW	26040 AAW	FLBLS	10//99-12//99
	Georgia	S	12.05 MW	12.40 AW	25800 AAW	GABLS	10//99-12//99
	Albany MSA, GA	S	13.75 MW	14.14 AW	28590 AAW	GABLS	10//99-12//99
	Athens MSA, GA	S	12.76 MW	12.69 AW	26530 AAW	GABLS	10//99-12//99
	Atlanta MSA, GA	S	13.04 MW	12.98 AW	27110 AAW	GABLS	10//99-12//99
	Augusta-Aiken MSA, GA-SC	S	13.97 MW	13.06 AW	29060 AAW	GABLS	10//99-12//99
	Columbus MSA, GA-AL	S	11.39 MW	10.97 AW	23700 AAW	GABLS	10//99-12//99
	Macon MSA, GA	S	13.22 MW	12.97 AW	27500 AAW	GABLS	10//99-12//99
	Savannah MSA, GA	S	13.08 MW	12.12 AW	27200 AAW	GABLS	10//99-12//99
	Hawaii	S	21.57 MW	20.29 AW	42210 AAW	HIBLS	10//99-12//99
	Honolulu MSA, HI	S	21.27 MW	22.41 AW	44250 AAW	HIBLS	10//99-12//99
	Idaho	S	11.85 MW	12.51 AW	26020 AAW	IDBLS	10//99-12//99
	Boise City MSA, ID	S	12.51 MW	11.61 AW	26030 AAW	IDBLS	10//99-12//99
	Pocatello MSA, ID	S	11.39 MW	10.27 AW	23690 AAW	IDBLS	10//99-12//99
	Illinois	S	12.86 MW	13.51 AW	28090 AAW	ILBLS	10//99-12//99
	Bloomington-Normal MSA, IL	S	17.55 MW	16.60 AW	36500 AAW	ILBLS	10//99-12//99
	Champaign-Urbana MSA, IL	S	13.71 MW	14.33 AW	28520 AAW	ILBLS	10//99-12//99
	Chicago PMSA, IL	S	13.21 MW	12.19 AW	27480 AAW	ILBLS	10//99-12//99
	Decatur MSA, IL	S	13.49 MW	13.25 AW	28060 AAW	ILBLS	10//99-12//99
	Kankakee PMSA, IL	S	13.93 MW	13.81 AW	28980 AAW	ILBLS	10//99-12//99
	Peoria-Pekin MSA, IL	S	12.27 MW	11.59 AW	25520 AAW	ILBLS	10//99-12//99
	Rockford MSA, IL	S	14.82 MW	14.16 AW	30830 AAW	ILBLS	10//99-12//99
	Springfield MSA, IL	S	12.66 MW	13.53 AW	26330 AAW	ILBLS	10//99-12//99
	Indiana	S	12.17 MW	13.53 AW	28150 AAW	INBLS	10//99-12//99
	Elkhart-Goshen MSA, IN	S	12.36 MW	11.44 AW	25710 AAW	INBLS	10//99-12//99
	Evansville-Henderson MSA, IN-KY	S	11.55 MW	11.22 AW	24030 AAW	INBLS	10//99-12//99
	Fort Wayne MSA, IN	S	13.22 MW	11.81 AW	27490 AAW	INBLS	10//99-12//99
	Gary PMSA, IN	S	15.57 MW	15.86 AW	32390 AAW	INBLS	10//99-12//99
	Indianapolis MSA, IN	S	14.09 MW	12.61 AW	29310 AAW	INBLS	10//99-12//99
	Lafayette MSA, IN	S	11.76 MW	12.09 AW	24460 AAW	INBLS	10//99-12//99
	Muncie MSA, IN	S	12.64 MW	11.27 AW	26290 AAW	INBLS	10//99-12//99
	South Bend MSA, IN	S	12.33 MW	11.91 AW	25640 AAW	INBLS	10//99-12//99
	Terre Haute MSA, IN	S	11.64 MW	11.36 AW	24200 AAW	INBLS	10//99-12//99
	Iowa	S	12.24 MW	12.61 AW	26220 AAW	IABLS	10//99-12//99
	Cedar Rapids MSA, IA	S	13.96 MW	13.26 AW	29040 AAW	IABLS	10//99-12//99
	Davenport-Moline-Rock Island MSA, IA-IL	S	14.88 MW	14.55 AW	30950 AAW	IABLS	10//99-12//99
	Des Moines MSA, IA	S	13.62 MW	13.06 AW	28320 AAW	IABLS	10//99-12//99
	Dubuque MSA, IA	S	12.11 MW	11.13 AW	25180 AAW	IABLS	10//99-12//99
	Iowa City MSA, IA	S	20.10 MW	13.56 AW	41810 AAW	IABLS	10//99-12//99
	Sioux City MSA, IA-NE	S	12.52 MW	12.26 AW	26040 AAW	IABLS	10//99-12//99
	Waterloo-Cedar Falls MSA, IA	S	14.61 MW	14.97 AW	30380 AAW	IABLS	10//99-12//99
	Kansas	S	11.71 MW	12.67 AW	26360 AAW	KSBLS	10//99-12//99
	Topeka MSA, KS	S	11.33 MW	10.76 AW	23570 AAW	KSBLS	10//99-12//99
	Wichita MSA, KS	S	14.56 MW	14.27 AW	30270 AAW	KSBLS	10//99-12//99
	Kentucky	S	11.44 MW	12.04 AW	25030 AAW	KYBLS	10//99-12//99
	Lexington MSA, KY	S	12.14 MW	12.45 AW	25260 AAW	KYBLS	10//99-12//99
	Louisville MSA, KY-IN	S	13.10 MW	11.97 AW	27240 AAW	KYBLS	10//99-12//99
	Owensboro MSA, KY	S	11.07 MW	10.51 AW	23020 AAW	KYBLS	10//99-12//99
	Louisiana	S	14.47 MW	14.53 AW	30220 AAW	LABLS	10//99-12//99
	Alexandria MSA, LA	S	10.28 MW	9.46 AW	21370 AAW	LABLS	10//99-12//99
	Baton Rouge MSA, LA	S	15.59 MW	15.71 AW	32430 AAW	LABLS	10//99-12//99
	Houma MSA, LA	S	14.17 MW	14.23 AW	29470 AAW	LABLS	10//99-12//99
	Lafayette MSA, LA	S	12.67 MW	12.22 AW	26360 AAW	LABLS	10//99-12//99
	Lake Charles MSA, LA	S	14.74 MW	14.76 AW	30660 AAW	LABLS	10//99-12//99
	Monroe MSA, LA	S	12.08 MW	12.22 AW	25130 AAW	LABLS	10//99-12//99
	New Orleans MSA, LA	S	14.52 MW	14.18 AW	30200 AAW	LABLS	10//99-12//99
	Shreveport-Bossier City MSA, LA	S	15.55 MW	13.95 AW	32350 AAW	LABLS	10//99-12//99
	Maine	S	13.96 MW	13.41 AW	27890 AAW	MEBLS	10//99-12//99
	Lewiston-Auburn MSA, ME	S	11.59 MW	11.29 AW	24110 AAW	MEBLS	10//99-12//99
	Portland MSA, ME	S	12.21 MW	11.83 AW	25390 AAW	MEBLS	10//99-12//99

AAW	Average annual wage	AOH	Average offered, high	ASH	Average starting, high	H	Hourly	M	Monthly	S	Special: hourly and annual
AE	Average entry wage	AOL	Average offered, low	ASL	Average starting, low	HI	Highest wage paid	MTC	Median total compensation	TQ	Third quartile wage
AEX	Average experienced wage	APH	Average pay, high range	AW	Average wage paid	HR	High end range	MW	Median wage paid	W	Weekly
AO	Average offered	APL	Average pay, low range	FQ	First quartile wage	LR	Low end range	SQ	Second quartile wage	Y	Yearly

Occupation/Type/Industry	Location	Per	Low	Mid	High	Source	Date
Welder, Cutter, Solderer, and Brazer							
	Maryland	S	13.31 MW	14.10 AW	29330 AAW	MDBLS	10//99-12//99
	Baltimore PMSA, MD	S	13.98 MW	13.53 AW	29070 AAW	MDBLS	10//99-12//99
	Hagerstown PMSA, MD	S	12.05 MW	12.11 AW	25060 AAW	MDBLS	10//99-12//99
	Massachusetts	S	14.37 MW	14.72 AW	30610 AAW	MABLS	10//99-12//99
	Barnstable-Yarmouth MSA, MA	S	17.08 MW	16.02 AW	35520 AAW	MABLS	10//99-12//99
	Boston PMSA, MA-NH	S	15.12 MW	14.95 AW	31450 AAW	MABLS	10//99-12//99
	Brockton PMSA, MA	S	14.11 MW	13.10 AW	29360 AAW	MABLS	10//99-12//99
	Fitchburg-Leominster PMSA, MA	S	16.87 MW	17.68 AW	35080 AAW	MABLS	10//99-12//99
	Lawrence PMSA, MA-NH	S	14.91 MW	15.09 AW	31020 AAW	MABLS	10//99-12//99
	Lowell PMSA, MA-NH	S	14.63 MW	14.45 AW	30430 AAW	MABLS	10//99-12//99
	New Bedford PMSA, MA	S	13.36 MW	13.28 AW	27800 AAW	MABLS	10//99-12//99
	Springfield MSA, MA	S	14.79 MW	14.08 AW	30750 AAW	MABLS	10//99-12//99
	Worcester PMSA, MA-CT	S	13.59 MW	12.18 AW	28270 AAW	MABLS	10//99-12//99
	Michigan	S	14.22 MW	16.16 AW	33610 AAW	MIBLS	10//99-12//99
	Ann Arbor PMSA, MI	S	16.68 MW	14.47 AW	34700 AAW	MIBLS	10//99-12//99
	Benton Harbor MSA, MI	S	12.97 MW	11.51 AW	26980 AAW	MIBLS	10//99-12//99
	Detroit PMSA, MI	S	18.27 MW	19.76 AW	38000 AAW	MIBLS	10//99-12//99
	Grand Rapids-Muskegon-Holland MSA, MI	S	14.20 MW	13.36 AW	29530 AAW	MIBLS	10//99-12//99
	Jackson MSA, MI	S	12.26 MW	11.91 AW	25500 AAW	MIBLS	10//99-12//99
	Kalamazoo-Battle Creek MSA, MI	S	12.93 MW	12.48 AW	26900 AAW	MIBLS	10//99-12//99
	Lansing-East Lansing MSA, MI	S	17.72 MW	13.99 AW	36860 AAW	MIBLS	10//99-12//99
	Saginaw-Bay City-Midland MSA, MI	S	17.67 MW	20.59 AW	36750 AAW	MIBLS	10//99-12//99
	Minnesota	S	13.45 MW	14.20 AW	29530 AAW	MNBLS	10//99-12//99
	Duluth-Superior MSA, MN-WI	S	14.83 MW	13.97 AW	30850 AAW	MNBLS	10//99-12//99
	Minneapolis-St. Paul MSA, MN-WI	S	15.29 MW	15.07 AW	31790 AAW	MNBLS	10//99-12//99
	Rochester MSA, MN	S	12.19 MW	11.71 AW	25360 AAW	MNBLS	10//99-12//99
	St. Cloud MSA, MN	S	12.87 MW	12.93 AW	26760 AAW	MNBLS	10//99-12//99
	Mississippi	S	13.48 MW	13.50 AW	28070 AAW	MSBLS	10//99-12//99
	Biloxi-Gulfport-Pascagoula MSA, MS	S	15.37 MW	15.23 AW	31980 AAW	MSBLS	10//99-12//99
	Hattiesburg MSA, MS	S	11.74 MW	11.71 AW	24420 AAW	MSBLS	10//99-12//99
	Jackson MSA, MS	S	12.17 MW	12.11 AW	25310 AAW	MSBLS	10//99-12//99
	Missouri	S	11.21 MW	12.33 AW	25640 AAW	MOBLS	10//99-12//99
	Columbia MSA, MO	S	11.27 MW	11.10 AW	23440 AAW	MOBLS	10//99-12//99
	Joplin MSA, MO	S	11.33 MW	10.98 AW	23560 AAW	MOBLS	10//99-12//99
	Kansas City MSA, MO-KS	S	14.79 MW	13.03 AW	30760 AAW	MOBLS	10//99-12//99
	St. Louis MSA, MO-IL	S	13.50 MW	12.82 AW	28080 AAW	MOBLS	10//99-12//99
	Springfield MSA, MO	S	11.11 MW	11.16 AW	23110 AAW	MOBLS	10//99-12//99
	Montana	S	12.88 MW	13.72 AW	28540 AAW	MTBLS	10//99-12//99
	Nebraska	S	11.07 MW	11.46 AW	23830 AAW	NEBLS	10//99-12//99
	Lincoln MSA, NE	S	11.40 MW	10.62 AW	23710 AAW	NEBLS	10//99-12//99
	Omaha MSA, NE-IA	S	12.59 MW	12.55 AW	26180 AAW	NEBLS	10//99-12//99
	Nevada	S	13.85 MW	15.10 AW	31410 AAW	NVBLS	10//99-12//99
	Las Vegas MSA, NV-AZ	S	15.33 MW	13.91 AW	31880 AAW	NVBLS	10//99-12//99
	Reno MSA, NV	S	13.02 MW	12.70 AW	27090 AAW	NVBLS	10//99-12//99
	New Hampshire	S	13.19 MW	13.49 AW	28050 AAW	NHBLS	10//99-12//99
	Manchester PMSA, NH	S	12.97 MW	12.12 AW	26970 AAW	NHBLS	10//99-12//99
	Nashua PMSA, NH	S	13.00 MW	12.36 AW	27050 AAW	NHBLS	10//99-12//99
	Portsmouth-Rochester PMSA, NH-ME	S	14.42 MW	14.68 AW	29990 AAW	NHBLS	10//99-12//99
	New Jersey	S	15.3 MW	16.13 AW	33550 AAW	NJBLS	10//99-12//99
	Atlantic-Cape May PMSA, NJ	S	14.26 MW	13.26 AW	29660 AAW	NJBLS	10//99-12//99
	Bergen-Passaic PMSA, NJ	S	14.56 MW	14.71 AW	30280 AAW	NJBLS	10//99-12//99
	Jersey City PMSA, NJ	S	15.84 MW	14.49 AW	32940 AAW	NJBLS	10//99-12//99
	Middlesex-Somerset-Hunterdon PMSA, NJ	S	16.25 MW	15.06 AW	33790 AAW	NJBLS	10//99-12//99
	Monmouth-Ocean PMSA, NJ	S	15.47 MW	15.03 AW	32170 AAW	NJBLS	10//99-12//99
	Newark PMSA, NJ	S	17.40 MW	16.64 AW	36190 AAW	NJBLS	10//99-12//99
	Trenton PMSA, NJ	S	15.06 MW	14.91 AW	31330 AAW	NJBLS	10//99-12//99
	New Mexico	S	11.56 MW	12.61 AW	26230 AAW	NMBLS	10//99-12//99
	Albuquerque MSA, NM	S	11.42 MW	10.25 AW	23760 AAW	NMBLS	10//99-12//99
	Las Cruces MSA, NM	S	10.98 MW	10.23 AW	22830 AAW	NMBLS	10//99-12//99
	Santa Fe MSA, NM	S	14.84 MW	16.95 AW	30870 AAW	NMBLS	10//99-12//99
	New York	S	13.1 MW	14.02 AW	29160 AAW	NYBLS	10//99-12//99

AAW Average annual wage	**AOH** Average offered, high	**ASH** Average starting, high	**H** Hourly	**M** Monthly	**S** Special: hourly and annual
AE Average entry wage	**AOL** Average offered, low	**ASL** Average starting, low	**HI** Highest wage paid	**MTC** Median total compensation	**TQ** Third quartile wage
AEX Average experienced wage	**APH** Average pay, high range	**AW** Average wage paid	**HR** High end range	**MW** Median wage paid	**W** Weekly
AO Average offered	**APL** Average pay, low range	**FQ** First quartile wage	**LR** Low end range	**SQ** Second quartile wage	**Y** Yearly

Occupation/Type/Industry	Location	Per	Low	Mid	High	Source	Date
Welder, Cutter, Solderer, and Brazer							
	Albany-Schenectady-Troy MSA, NY	S	13.71 MW	13.98 AW	28510 AAW	NYBLS	10//99-12//99
	Binghamton MSA, NY	S	10.60 MW	9.63 AW	22050 AAW	NYBLS	10//99-12//99
	Buffalo-Niagara Falls MSA, NY	S	17.27 MW	16.68 AW	35910 AAW	NYBLS	10//99-12//99
	Dutchess County PMSA, NY	S	14.74 MW	14.92 AW	30650 AAW	NYBLS	10//99-12//99
	Elmira MSA, NY	S	13.77 MW	11.58 AW	28640 AAW	NYBLS	10//99-12//99
	Glens Falls MSA, NY	S	12.92 MW	11.73 AW	26860 AAW	NYBLS	10//99-12//99
	Jamestown MSA, NY	S	10.09 MW	10.73 AW	20990 AAW	NYBLS	10//99-12//99
	Nassau-Suffolk PMSA, NY	S	12.97 MW	12.52 AW	26970 AAW	NYBLS	10//99-12//99
	New York PMSA, NY	S	14.82 MW	12.56 AW	30820 AAW	NYBLS	10//99-12//99
	Newburgh PMSA, NY-PA	S	11.95 MW	12.05 AW	24860 AAW	NYBLS	10//99-12//99
	Rochester MSA, NY	S	12.49 MW	11.79 AW	25990 AAW	NYBLS	10//99-12//99
	Syracuse MSA, NY	S	12.86 MW	12.88 AW	26750 AAW	NYBLS	10//99-12//99
	Utica-Rome MSA, NY	S	11.89 MW	11.56 AW	24720 AAW	NYBLS	10//99-12//99
	North Carolina	S	12.78 MW	12.95 AW	26950 AAW	NCBLS	10//99-12//99
	Asheville MSA, NC	S	12.95 MW	13.26 AW	26940 AAW	NCBLS	10//99-12//99
	Charlotte-Gastonia-Rock Hill MSA, NC-SC	S	13.62 MW	13.28 AW	28330 AAW	NCBLS	10//99-12//99
	Fayetteville MSA, NC	S	13.83 MW	13.24 AW	28760 AAW	NCBLS	10//99-12//99
	Goldsboro MSA, NC	S	11.30 MW	11.39 AW	23500 AAW	NCBLS	10//99-12//99
	Greensboro--Winston-Salem--High Point MSA, NC	S	13.20 MW	13.30 AW	27460 AAW	NCBLS	10//99-12//99
	Greenville MSA, NC	S	13.07 MW	14.13 AW	27190 AAW	NCBLS	10//99-12//99
	Hickory-Morganton-Lenoir MSA, NC	S	10.72 MW	10.07 AW	22310 AAW	NCBLS	10//99-12//99
	Raleigh-Durham-Chapel Hill MSA, NC	S	13.09 MW	13.23 AW	27230 AAW	NCBLS	10//99-12//99
	Rocky Mount MSA, NC	S	12.95 MW	12.81 AW	26940 AAW	NCBLS	10//99-12//99
	Wilmington MSA, NC	S	13.49 MW	12.57 AW	28050 AAW	NCBLS	10//99-12//99
	North Dakota	S	12.76 MW	13.10 AW	27260 AAW	NDBLS	10//99-12//99
	Fargo-Moorhead MSA, ND-MN	S	13.01 MW	12.70 AW	27070 AAW	NDBLS	10//99-12//99
	Grand Forks MSA, ND-MN	S	9.85 MW	9.25 AW	20480 AAW	NDBLS	10//99-12//99
	Ohio	S	12.81 MW	14.09 AW	29300 AAW	OHBLS	10//99-12//99
	Akron PMSA, OH	S	11.92 MW	11.82 AW	24790 AAW	OHBLS	10//99-12//99
	Canton-Massillon MSA, OH	S	12.50 MW	12.58 AW	26000 AAW	OHBLS	10//99-12//99
	Cincinnati PMSA, OH-KY-IN	S	14.49 MW	13.27 AW	30130 AAW	OHBLS	10//99-12//99
	Cleveland-Lorain-Elyria PMSA, OH	S	14.66 MW	13.17 AW	30480 AAW	OHBLS	10//99-12//99
	Columbus MSA, OH	S	13.03 MW	12.21 AW	27110 AAW	OHBLS	10//99-12//99
	Dayton-Springfield MSA, OH	S	17.80 MW	17.71 AW	37020 AAW	OHBLS	10//99-12//99
	Hamilton-Middletown PMSA, OH	S	14.25 MW	13.58 AW	29630 AAW	OHBLS	10//99-12//99
	Lima MSA, OH	S	12.56 MW	11.63 AW	26130 AAW	OHBLS	10//99-12//99
	Mansfield MSA, OH	S	12.78 MW	11.57 AW	26590 AAW	OHBLS	10//99-12//99
	Steubenville-Weirton MSA, OH-WV	S	15.29 MW	16.12 AW	31800 AAW	OHBLS	10//99-12//99
	Toledo MSA, OH	S	16.43 MW	15.62 AW	34180 AAW	OHBLS	10//99-12//99
	Youngstown-Warren MSA, OH	S	12.64 MW	11.92 AW	26280 AAW	OHBLS	10//99-12//99
	Oklahoma	S	11.56 MW	12.57 AW	26150 AAW	OKBLS	10//99-12//99
	Enid MSA, OK	S	11.79 MW	11.16 AW	24530 AAW	OKBLS	10//99-12//99
	Oklahoma City MSA, OK	S	12.37 MW	11.21 AW	25740 AAW	OKBLS	10//99-12//99
	Tulsa MSA, OK	S	13.54 MW	12.85 AW	28170 AAW	OKBLS	10//99-12//99
	Oregon	S	13.23 MW	13.74 AW	28570 AAW	ORBLS	10//99-12//99
	Eugene-Springfield MSA, OR	S	12.58 MW	12.56 AW	26180 AAW	ORBLS	10//99-12//99
	Medford-Ashland MSA, OR	S	12.70 MW	11.60 AW	26420 AAW	ORBLS	10//99-12//99
	Portland-Vancouver PMSA, OR-WA	S	14.11 MW	13.87 AW	29360 AAW	ORBLS	10//99-12//99
	Pennsylvania	S	12.6 MW	13.06 AW	27170 AAW	PABLS	10//99-12//99
	Allentown-Bethlehem-Easton MSA, PA	S	14.81 MW	14.50 AW	30810 AAW	PABLS	10//99-12//99
	Altoona MSA, PA	S	12.20 MW	11.99 AW	25370 AAW	PABLS	10//99-12//99
	Erie MSA, PA	S	14.69 MW	16.37 AW	30550 AAW	PABLS	10//99-12//99
	Harrisburg-Lebanon-Carlisle MSA, PA	S	12.98 MW	12.72 AW	26990 AAW	PABLS	10//99-12//99
	Johnstown MSA, PA	S	10.28 MW	10.16 AW	21380 AAW	PABLS	10//99-12//99
	Lancaster MSA, PA	S	13.84 MW	13.64 AW	28780 AAW	PABLS	10//99-12//99
	Philadelphia PMSA, PA-NJ	S	13.95 MW	13.50 AW	29010 AAW	PABLS	10//99-12//99
	Pittsburgh MSA, PA	S	12.90 MW	12.14 AW	26840 AAW	PABLS	10//99-12//99
	Reading MSA, PA	S	14.05 MW	13.86 AW	29220 AAW	PABLS	10//99-12//99

AAW Average annual wage	**AOH** Average offered, high	**ASH** Average starting, high	**H** Hourly	**M** Monthly	**S** Special: hourly and annual
AE Average entry wage	**AOL** Average offered, low	**ASL** Average starting, low	**HI** Highest wage paid	**MTC** Median total compensation	**TQ** Third quartile wage
AEX Average experienced wage	**APH** Average pay, high range	**AW** Average wage paid	**HR** High end range	**MW** Median wage paid	**W** Weekly
AO Average offered	**APL** Average pay, low range	**FQ** First quartile wage	**LR** Low end range	**SQ** Second quartile wage	**Y** Yearly

Occupation/Type/Industry	Location	Per	Low	Mid	High	Source	Date
Welder, Cutter, Solderer, and Brazer	Scranton--Wilkes-Barre--						
	Hazleton MSA, PA	S	13.05 MW	12.67 AW	27140 AAW	PABLS	10//99-12//99
	Sharon MSA, PA	S	13.64 MW	13.94 AW	28370 AAW	PABLS	10//99-12//99
	Williamsport MSA, PA	S	12.01 MW	11.14 AW	24990 AAW	PABLS	10//99-12//99
	York MSA, PA	S	13.01 MW	12.93 AW	27060 AAW	PABLS	10//99-12//99
	Rhode Island	S	9.71 MW	10.94 AW	22760 AAW	RIBLS	10//99-12//99
	Providence-Fall River-						
	Warwick MSA, RI-MA	S	11.13 MW	10.28 AW	23150 AAW	RIBLS	10//99-12//99
	South Carolina	S	12.44 MW	13.25 AW	27570 AAW	SCBLS	10//99-12//99
	Charleston-North Charleston						
	MSA, SC	S	12.56 MW	12.42 AW	26130 AAW	SCBLS	10//99-12//99
	Columbia MSA, SC	S	11.94 MW	11.28 AW	24840 AAW	SCBLS	10//99-12//99
	Florence MSA, SC	S	15.27 MW	13.85 AW	31770 AAW	SCBLS	10//99-12//99
	Greenville-Spartanburg-						
	Anderson MSA, SC	S	14.00 MW	13.45 AW	29120 AAW	SCBLS	10//99-12//99
	Myrtle Beach MSA, SC	S	10.47 MW	10.43 AW	21770 AAW	SCBLS	10//99-12//99
	Sumter MSA, SC	S	11.78 MW	10.61 AW	24500 AAW	SCBLS	10//99-12//99
	South Dakota	S	10.69 MW	10.78 AW	22420 AAW	SDBLS	10//99-12//99
	Rapid City MSA, SD	S	10.04 MW	9.58 AW	20880 AAW	SDBLS	10//99-12//99
	Sioux Falls MSA, SD	S	11.72 MW	11.59 AW	24370 AAW	SDBLS	10//99-12//99
	Tennessee	S	11.6 MW	12.11 AW	25190 AAW	TNBLS	10//99-12//99
	Chattanooga MSA, TN-GA	S	11.83 MW	11.58 AW	24600 AAW	TNBLS	10//99-12//99
	Clarksville-Hopkinsville MSA,						
	TN-KY	S	13.27 MW	14.10 AW	27590 AAW	TNBLS	10//99-12//99
	Johnson City-Kingsport-Bristol						
	MSA, TN-VA	S	11.19 MW	10.66 AW	23280 AAW	TNBLS	10//99-12//99
	Knoxville MSA, TN	S	12.78 MW	12.73 AW	26590 AAW	TNBLS	10//99-12//99
	Memphis MSA, TN-AR-MS	S	13.15 MW	12.63 AW	27350 AAW	MSBLS	10//99-12//99
	Nashville MSA, TN	S	12.72 MW	12.14 AW	26460 AAW	TNBLS	10//99-12//99
	Texas	S	11.95 MW	12.61 AW	26220 AAW	TXBLS	10//99-12//99
	Abilene MSA, TX	S	8.96 MW	8.78 AW	18630 AAW	TXBLS	10//99-12//99
	Amarillo MSA, TX	S	12.20 MW	12.14 AW	25370 AAW	TXBLS	10//99-12//99
	Austin-San Marcos MSA, TX	S	11.72 MW	11.49 AW	24390 AAW	TXBLS	10//99-12//99
	Beaumont-Port Arthur MSA,						
	TX	S	15.42 MW	13.98 AW	32070 AAW	TXBLS	10//99-12//99
	Brazoria PMSA, TX	S	12.90 MW	11.61 AW	26830 AAW	TXBLS	10//99-12//99
	Brownsville-Harlingen-San						
	Benito MSA, TX	S	11.60 MW	12.36 AW	24130 AAW	TXBLS	10//99-12//99
	Bryan-College Station MSA,						
	TX	S	12.15 MW	12.44 AW	25270 AAW	TXBLS	10//99-12//99
	Corpus Christi MSA, TX	S	12.85 MW	12.41 AW	26730 AAW	TXBLS	10//99-12//99
	Dallas PMSA, TX	S	11.32 MW	11.02 AW	23550 AAW	TXBLS	10//99-12//99
	El Paso MSA, TX	S	9.54 MW	8.60 AW	19850 AAW	TXBLS	10//99-12//99
	Fort Worth-Arlington PMSA,						
	TX	S	13.33 MW	12.11 AW	27730 AAW	TXBLS	10//99-12//99
	Galveston-Texas City PMSA,						
	TX	S	13.21 MW	13.03 AW	27470 AAW	TXBLS	10//99-12//99
	Houston PMSA, TX	S	13.56 MW	13.12 AW	28210 AAW	TXBLS	10//99-12//99
	Killeen-Temple MSA, TX	S	10.59 MW	10.14 AW	22020 AAW	TXBLS	10//99-12//99
	Laredo MSA, TX	S	8.46 MW	8.09 AW	17590 AAW	TXBLS	10//99-12//99
	Longview-Marshall MSA, TX	S	12.13 MW	12.01 AW	25220 AAW	TXBLS	10//99-12//99
	Lubbock MSA, TX	S	10.34 MW	9.91 AW	21520 AAW	TXBLS	10//99-12//99
	McAllen-Edinburg-Mission						
	MSA, TX	S	9.44 MW	9.14 AW	19640 AAW	TXBLS	10//99-12//99
	Odessa-Midland MSA, TX	S	14.63 MW	12.93 AW	30430 AAW	TXBLS	10//99-12//99
	San Angelo MSA, TX	S	11.97 MW	11.64 AW	24900 AAW	TXBLS	10//99-12//99
	San Antonio MSA, TX	S	11.77 MW	10.53 AW	24470 AAW	TXBLS	10//99-12//99
	Sherman-Denison MSA, TX	S	9.71 MW	9.45 AW	20200 AAW	TXBLS	10//99-12//99
	Texarkana MSA, TX-						
	Texarkana, AR	S	13.08 MW	12.24 AW	27200 AAW	TXBLS	10//99-12//99
	Tyler MSA, TX	S	11.76 MW	11.78 AW	24470 AAW	TXBLS	10//99-12//99
	Victoria MSA, TX	S	13.03 MW	12.53 AW	27110 AAW	TXBLS	10//99-12//99
	Waco MSA, TX	S	9.76 MW	9.88 AW	20290 AAW	TXBLS	10//99-12//99
	Wichita Falls MSA, TX	S	11.78 MW	11.36 AW	24500 AAW	TXBLS	10//99-12//99
	Utah	S	12.54 MW	13.26 AW	27580 AAW	UTBLS	10//99-12//99
	Provo-Orem MSA, UT	S	11.76 MW	11.62 AW	24470 AAW	UTBLS	10//99-12//99
	Salt Lake City-Ogden MSA,						
	UT	S	13.15 MW	12.83 AW	27350 AAW	UTBLS	10//99-12//99
	Vermont	S	12.12 MW	12.80 AW	26630 AAW	VTBLS	10//99-12//99
	Burlington MSA, VT	S	14.82 MW	13.99 AW	30830 AAW	VTBLS	10//99-12//99
	Virginia	S	13.95 MW	13.98 AW	29090 AAW	VABLS	10//99-12//99

Occupation/Type/Industry	Location	Per	Low	Mid	High	Source	Date
Welder, Cutter, Solderer, and Brazer							
	Danville MSA, VA	S	10.99 MW	10.23 AW	22860 AAW	VABLS	10//99-12//99
	Lynchburg MSA, VA	S	12.05 MW	11.86 AW	25060 AAW	VABLS	10//99-12//99
	Norfolk-Virginia Beach-Newport News MSA, VA-NC	S	14.82 MW	14.88 AW	30820 AAW	VABLS	10//99-12//99
	Richmond-Petersburg MSA, VA	S	15.61 MW	14.45 AW	32470 AAW	VABLS	10//99-12//99
	Roanoke MSA, VA	S	10.86 MW	10.66 AW	22580 AAW	VABLS	10//99-12//99
	Washington	S	15.62 MW	15.84 AW	32940 AAW	WABLS	10//99-12//99
	Bellingham MSA, WA	S	15.65 MW	15.52 AW	32560 AAW	WABLS	10//99-12//99
	Olympia PMSA, WA	S	11.09 MW	10.90 AW	23060 AAW	WABLS	10//99-12//99
	Richland-Kennewick-Pasco MSA, WA	S	15.84 MW	15.53 AW	32950 AAW	WABLS	10//99-12//99
	Seattle-Bellevue-Everett PMSA, WA	S	16.17 MW	16.17 AW	33630 AAW	WABLS	10//99-12//99
	Spokane MSA, WA	S	13.78 MW	13.60 AW	28660 AAW	WABLS	10//99-12//99
	Tacoma PMSA, WA	S	14.63 MW	14.60 AW	30430 AAW	WABLS	10//99-12//99
	Yakima MSA, WA	S	13.70 MW	13.04 AW	28490 AAW	WABLS	10//99-12//99
	West Virginia	S	12.01 MW	13.06 AW	27160 AAW	WVBLS	10//99-12//99
	Charleston MSA, WV	S	14.12 MW	13.34 AW	29370 AAW	WVBLS	10//99-12//99
	Huntington-Ashland MSA, WV-KY-OH	S	13.01 MW	13.32 AW	27060 AAW	WVBLS	10//99-12//99
	Parkersburg-Marietta MSA, WV-OH	S	11.70 MW	10.67 AW	24340 AAW	WVBLS	10//99-12//99
	Wheeling MSA, WV-OH	S	14.41 MW	12.80 AW	29970 AAW	WVBLS	10//99-12//99
	Wisconsin	S	13.22 MW	13.55 AW	28170 AAW	WIBLS	10//99-12//99
	Appleton-Oshkosh-Neenah MSA, WI	S	15.69 MW	13.56 AW	32630 AAW	WIBLS	10//99-12//99
	Eau Claire MSA, WI	S	13.00 MW	12.78 AW	27040 AAW	WIBLS	10//99-12//99
	Green Bay MSA, WI	S	13.04 MW	12.64 AW	27130 AAW	WIBLS	10//99-12//99
	Janesville-Beloit MSA, WI	S	12.95 MW	12.72 AW	26940 AAW	WIBLS	10//99-12//99
	Kenosha PMSA, WI	S	13.74 MW	13.92 AW	28570 AAW	WIBLS	10//99-12//99
	Madison MSA, WI	S	13.18 MW	12.88 AW	27400 AAW	WIBLS	10//99-12//99
	Milwaukee-Waukesha PMSA, WI	S	14.11 MW	13.88 AW	29350 AAW	WIBLS	10//99-12//99
	Racine PMSA, WI	S	13.36 MW	13.17 AW	27790 AAW	WIBLS	10//99-12//99
	Sheboygan MSA, WI	S	12.61 MW	12.81 AW	26220 AAW	WIBLS	10//99-12//99
	Wausau MSA, WI	S	14.02 MW	13.98 AW	29160 AAW	WIBLS	10//99-12//99
	Wyoming	S	13.41 MW	14.64 AW	30460 AAW	WYBLS	10//99-12//99
	Casper MSA, WY	S	12.59 MW	11.95 AW	26190 AAW	WYBLS	10//99-12//99
	Cheyenne MSA, WY	S	11.03 MW	10.20 AW	22930 AAW	WYBLS	10//99-12//99
	Puerto Rico	S	7.43 MW	8.13 AW	16900 AAW	PRBLS	10//99-12//99
	Caguas PMSA, PR	S	7.26 MW	7.26 AW	15090 AAW	PRBLS	10//99-12//99
	Mayaguez MSA, PR	S	7.08 MW	6.97 AW	14720 AAW	PRBLS	10//99-12//99
	Ponce MSA, PR	S	7.27 MW	7.11 AW	15120 AAW	PRBLS	10//99-12//99
	San Juan-Bayamon PMSA, PR	S	8.58 MW	7.62 AW	17850 AAW	PRBLS	10//99-12//99
	Virgin Islands	S	15.33 MW	14.96 AW	31120 AAW	VIBLS	10//99-12//99
	Guam	S	12.78 MW	13.13 AW	27300 AAW	GUBLS	10//99-12//99
Welding, Soldering, and Brazing Machine Setter, Operator, and Tender							
	Alabama	S	11.52 MW	11.63 AW	24190 AAW	ALBLS	10//99-12//99
	Alaska	S	17.53 MW	18.50 AW	38480 AAW	AKBLS	10//99-12//99
	Arizona	S	11.04 MW	11.63 AW	24180 AAW	AZBLS	10//99-12//99
	Arkansas	S	11.42 MW	11.89 AW	24730 AAW	ARBLS	10//99-12//99
	California	S	11.37 MW	12.65 AW	26300 AAW	CABLS	10//99-12//99
	Colorado	S	11.07 MW	11.23 AW	23370 AAW	COBLS	10//99-12//99
	Connecticut	S	14.2 MW	15.99 AW	33250 AAW	CTBLS	10//99-12//99
	Florida	S	10.16 MW	10.85 AW	22560 AAW	FLBLS	10//99-12//99
	Georgia	S	11.24 MW	11.59 AW	24110 AAW	GABLS	10//99-12//99
	Idaho	S	12.18 MW	13.18 AW	27400 AAW	IDBLS	10//99-12//99
	Illinois	S	12.48 MW	13.49 AW	28060 AAW	ILBLS	10//99-12//99
	Indiana	S	12.65 MW	13.79 AW	28670 AAW	INBLS	10//99-12//99
	Iowa	S	12.18 MW	13.18 AW	27410 AAW	IABLS	10//99-12//99
	Kansas	S	11.81 MW	13.19 AW	27430 AAW	KSBLS	10//99-12//99
	Kentucky	S	11.47 MW	11.53 AW	23980 AAW	KYBLS	10//99-12//99
	Louisiana	S	13.08 MW	13.49 AW	28070 AAW	LABLS	10//99-12//99
	Maine	S	11.56 MW	12.41 AW	25820 AAW	MEBLS	10//99-12//99
	Maryland	S	13.15 MW	13.01 AW	27060 AAW	MDBLS	10//99-12//99
	Massachusetts	S	13.45 MW	13.69 AW	28470 AAW	MABLS	10//99-12//99

AAW Average annual wage	AOH Average offered, high	ASH Average starting, high	H Hourly	M Monthly	S Special: hourly and annual
AE Average entry wage	AOL Average offered, low	ASL Average starting, low	HI Highest wage paid	MTC Median total compensation	TQ Third quartile wage
AEX Average experienced wage	APH Average pay, high range	AW Average wage paid	HR High end range	MW Median wage paid	W Weekly
AO Average offered	APL Average pay, low range	FQ First quartile wage	LR Low end range	SQ Second quartile wage	Y Yearly

Occupation/Type/Industry	Location	Per	Low	Mid	High	Source	Date
Welding, Soldering, and Brazing Machine Setter, Operator, and Tender	Michigan	S	17.44 MW	17.29 AW	35960 AAW	MIBLS	10//99-12//99
	Minnesota	S	12.52 MW	12.87 AW	26770 AAW	MNBLS	10//99-12//99
	Mississippi	S	10.61 MW	11.02 AW	22920 AAW	MSBLS	10//99-12//99
	Missouri	S	10.56 MW	10.99 AW	22870 AAW	MOBLS	10//99-12//99
	Nebraska	S	12.18 MW	12.72 AW	26470 AAW	NEBLS	10//99-12//99
	Nevada	S	11.88 MW	12.46 AW	25910 AAW	NVBLS	10//99-12//99
	New Hampshire	S	11.94 MW	12.05 AW	25070 AAW	NHBLS	10//99-12//99
	New Jersey	S	13.74 MW	13.78 AW	28670 AAW	NJBLS	10//99-12//99
	New Mexico	S	11.03 MW	11.05 AW	22970 AAW	NMBLS	10//99-12//99
	New York	S	11.96 MW	12.90 AW	26840 AAW	NYBLS	10//99-12//99
	North Carolina	S	11.8 MW	12.12 AW	25210 AAW	NCBLS	10//99-12//99
	North Dakota	S	13.05 MW	13.09 AW	27240 AAW	NDBLS	10//99-12//99
	Ohio	S	13.2 MW	13.80 AW	28710 AAW	OHBLS	10//99-12//99
	Oklahoma	S	11.65 MW	12.04 AW	25040 AAW	OKBLS	10//99-12//99
	Pennsylvania	S	12.75 MW	13.28 AW	27620 AAW	PABLS	10//99-12//99
	Rhode Island	S	10.71 MW	11.49 AW	23900 AAW	RIBLS	10//99-12//99
	South Carolina	S	12.95 MW	12.95 AW	26940 AAW	SCBLS	10//99-12//99
	South Dakota	S	11.4 MW	12.13 AW	25240 AAW	SDBLS	10//99-12//99
	Tennessee	S	11.64 MW	11.93 AW	24800 AAW	TNBLS	10//99-12//99
	Texas	S	11.39 MW	11.70 AW	24330 AAW	TXBLS	10//99-12//99
	Utah	S	9.42 MW	9.87 AW	20530 AAW	UTBLS	10//99-12//99
	Vermont	S	10.15 MW	10.69 AW	22230 AAW	VTBLS	10//99-12//99
	Virginia	S	13.02 MW	13.02 AW	27080 AAW	VABLS	10//99-12//99
	Washington	S	15.94 MW	16.11 AW	33510 AAW	WABLS	10//99-12//99
	West Virginia	S	12.19 MW	12.22 AW	25410 AAW	WVBLS	10//99-12//99
	Wisconsin	S	12.94 MW	13.32 AW	27700 AAW	WIBLS	10//99-12//99
	Wyoming	S	22.02 MW	19.52 AW	40590 AAW	WYBLS	10//99-12//99
	Puerto Rico	S	7.6 MW	7.59 AW	15780 AAW	PRBLS	10//99-12//99
Wellhead Pumper	Arkansas	S	11.91 MW	16.99 AW	35330 AAW	ARBLS	10//99-12//99
	California	S	17.47 MW	16.71 AW	34750 AAW	CABLS	10//99-12//99
	Colorado	S	14.32 MW	15.45 AW	32140 AAW	COBLS	10//99-12//99
	Illinois	S	9.93 MW	10.38 AW	21590 AAW	ILBLS	10//99-12//99
	Kansas	S	19.52 MW	18.04 AW	37520 AAW	KSBLS	10//99-12//99
	Kentucky	S	9.82 MW	11.06 AW	23000 AAW	KYBLS	10//99-12//99
	Louisiana	S	17.08 MW	17.53 AW	36460 AAW	LABLS	10//99-12//99
	Michigan	S	15.41 MW	16.05 AW	33380 AAW	MIBLS	10//99-12//99
	Mississippi	S	20.56 MW	19.99 AW	41580 AAW	MSBLS	10//99-12//99
	Montana	S	17.91 MW	17.04 AW	35430 AAW	MTBLS	10//99-12//99
	New Mexico	S	17.72 MW	16.56 AW	34450 AAW	NMBLS	10//99-12//99
	New York	S	12.6 MW	13.69 AW	28480 AAW	NYBLS	10//99-12//99
	Oklahoma	S	16.57 MW	15.48 AW	32200 AAW	OKBLS	10//99-12//99
	Pennsylvania	S	12.55 MW	12.21 AW	25390 AAW	PABLS	10//99-12//99
	Texas	S	17.7 MW	17.07 AW	35510 AAW	TXBLS	10//99-12//99
	West Virginia	S	11.09 MW	11.50 AW	23920 AAW	WVBLS	10//99-12//99
	Wyoming	S	20.48 MW	20.11 AW	41820 AAW	WYBLS	10//99-12//99
Whitewater Rafting Guide	United States	D		125 AW		MENHEL	1999
Wholesale and Retail Buyer							
Except Farm Product	Alabama	S	15.37 MW	18.92 AW	39360 AAW	ALBLS	10//99-12//99
Except Farm Product	Birmingham MSA, AL	S	19.54 MW	15.83 AW	40630 AAW	ALBLS	10//99-12//99
Except Farm Product	Dothan MSA, AL	S	15.56 MW	14.60 AW	32370 AAW	ALBLS	10//99-12//99
Except Farm Product	Huntsville MSA, AL	S	17.24 MW	15.87 AW	35870 AAW	ALBLS	10//99-12//99
Except Farm Product	Mobile MSA, AL	S	13.13 MW	12.68 AW	27310 AAW	ALBLS	10//99-12//99
Except Farm Product	Montgomery MSA, AL	S	25.90 MW	31.24 AW	53880 AAW	ALBLS	10//99-12//99
Except Farm Product	Tuscaloosa MSA, AL	S	16.35 MW	15.29 AW	34010 AAW	ALBLS	10//99-12//99
Except Farm Product	Alaska	S	15.84 MW	17.38 AW	36160 AAW	AKBLS	10//99-12//99
Except Farm Product	Anchorage MSA, AK	S	17.60 MW	15.87 AW	36620 AAW	AKBLS	10//99-12//99
Except Farm Product	Arizona	S	15.79 MW	16.82 AW	34980 AAW	AZBLS	10//99-12//99
Except Farm Product	Phoenix-Mesa MSA, AZ	S	17.37 MW	16.56 AW	36140 AAW	AZBLS	10//99-12//99
Except Farm Product	Tucson MSA, AZ	S	15.84 MW	14.61 AW	32950 AAW	AZBLS	10//99-12//99
Except Farm Product	Arkansas	S	15.03 MW	17.82 AW	37070 AAW	ARBLS	10//99-12//99
Except Farm Product	Fort Smith MSA, AR-OK	S	14.56 MW	12.74 AW	30280 AAW	ARBLS	10//99-12//99
Except Farm Product	Little Rock-North Little Rock MSA, AR	S	17.31 MW	16.56 AW	36010 AAW	ARBLS	10//99-12//99
Except Farm Product	California	S	17.51 MW	19.61 AW	40780 AAW	CABLS	10//99-12//99
Except Farm Product	Bakersfield MSA, CA	S	15.00 MW	12.93 AW	31190 AAW	CABLS	10//99-12//99
Except Farm Product	Chico-Paradise MSA, CA	S	14.52 MW	11.45 AW	30200 AAW	CABLS	10//99-12//99
Except Farm Product	Fresno MSA, CA	S	16.28 MW	17.24 AW	33860 AAW	CABLS	10//99-12//99

AAW	Average annual wage	AOH	Average offered, high	ASH	Average starting, high	H	Hourly	M	Monthly	S	Special: hourly and annual
AE	Average entry wage	AOL	Average offered, low	ASL	Average starting, low	HI	Highest wage paid	MTC	Median total compensation	TQ	Third quartile wage
AEX	Average experienced wage	APH	Average pay, high range	AW	Average wage paid	HR	High end range	MW	Median wage paid	W	Weekly
AO	Average offered	APL	Average pay, low range	FQ	First quartile wage	LR	Low end range	SQ	Second quartile wage	Y	Yearly

Occupation/Type/Industry	Location	Per	Low	Mid	High	Source	Date
Wholesale and Retail Buyer							
Except Farm Product	Los Angeles-Long Beach PMSA, CA	S	20.52 MW	17.76 AW	42680 AAW	CABLS	10//99-12//99
Except Farm Product	Modesto MSA, CA	S	15.50 MW	13.87 AW	32240 AAW	CABLS	10//99-12//99
Except Farm Product	Oakland PMSA, CA	S	18.42 MW	17.76 AW	38310 AAW	CABLS	10//99-12//99
Except Farm Product	Orange County PMSA, CA	S	21.72 MW	20.12 AW	45170 AAW	CABLS	10//99-12//99
Except Farm Product	Redding MSA, CA	S	14.41 MW	13.89 AW	29980 AAW	CABLS	10//99-12//99
Except Farm Product	Riverside-San Bernardino PMSA, CA	S	18.34 MW	17.28 AW	38160 AAW	CABLS	10//99-12//99
Except Farm Product	Sacramento PMSA, CA	S	21.31 MW	17.67 AW	44320 AAW	CABLS	10//99-12//99
Except Farm Product	Salinas MSA, CA	S	34.17 MW	32.79 AW	71070 AAW	CABLS	10//99-12//99
Except Farm Product	San Diego MSA, CA	S	18.40 MW	16.32 AW	38270 AAW	CABLS	10//99-12//99
Except Farm Product	San Francisco PMSA, CA	S	21.92 MW	19.55 AW	45580 AAW	CABLS	10//99-12//99
Except Farm Product	San Jose PMSA, CA	S	18.15 MW	17.31 AW	37760 AAW	CABLS	10//99-12//99
Except Farm Product	San Luis Obispo-Atascadero-Paso Robles MSA, CA	S	12.86 MW	12.15 AW	26740 AAW	CABLS	10//99-12//99
Except Farm Product	Santa Barbara-Santa Maria-Lompoc MSA, CA	S	16.13 MW	13.48 AW	33540 AAW	CABLS	10//99-12//99
Except Farm Product	Santa Cruz-Watsonville PMSA, CA	S	15.82 MW	13.06 AW	32900 AAW	CABLS	10//99-12//99
Except Farm Product	Santa Rosa PMSA, CA	S	17.18 MW	14.78 AW	35740 AAW	CABLS	10//99-12//99
Except Farm Product	Stockton-Lodi MSA, CA	S	16.92 MW	14.94 AW	35180 AAW	CABLS	10//99-12//99
Except Farm Product	Vallejo-Fairfield-Napa PMSA, CA	S	13.03 MW	9.52 AW	27100 AAW	CABLS	10//99-12//99
Except Farm Product	Ventura PMSA, CA	S	18.52 MW	17.49 AW	38520 AAW	CABLS	10//99-12//99
Except Farm Product	Yolo PMSA, CA	S	21.30 MW	19.18 AW	44300 AAW	CABLS	10//99-12//99
Except Farm Product	Colorado	S	15.08 MW	18.73 AW	38960 AAW	COBLS	10//99-12//99
Except Farm Product	Boulder-Longmont PMSA, CO	S	18.84 MW	14.06 AW	39180 AAW	COBLS	10//99-12//99
Except Farm Product	Colorado Springs MSA, CO	S	13.33 MW	12.67 AW	27730 AAW	COBLS	10//99-12//99
Except Farm Product	Denver PMSA, CO	S	20.98 MW	16.61 AW	43640 AAW	COBLS	10//99-12//99
Except Farm Product	Connecticut	S	19.79 MW	22.46 AW	46710 AAW	CTBLS	10//99-12//99
Except Farm Product	Bridgeport PMSA, CT	S	20.62 MW	17.96 AW	42900 AAW	CTBLS	10//99-12//99
Except Farm Product	Danbury PMSA, CT	S	21.07 MW	19.11 AW	43820 AAW	CTBLS	10//99-12//99
Except Farm Product	Hartford MSA, CT	S	21.48 MW	19.77 AW	44670 AAW	CTBLS	10//99-12//99
Except Farm Product	New Haven-Meriden PMSA, CT	S	21.02 MW	21.84 AW	43730 AAW	CTBLS	10//99-12//99
Except Farm Product	New London-Norwich MSA, CT-RI	S	16.66 MW	15.55 AW	34650 AAW	CTBLS	10//99-12//99
Except Farm Product	Stamford-Norwalk PMSA, CT	S	27.64 MW	22.52 AW	57500 AAW	CTBLS	10//99-12//99
Except Farm Product	Waterbury PMSA, CT	S	17.29 MW	11.49 AW	35960 AAW	CTBLS	10//99-12//99
Except Farm Product	Delaware	S	16.69 MW	17.79 AW	37000 AAW	DEBLS	10//99-12//99
Except Farm Product	Wilmington-Newark PMSA, DE-MD	S	18.01 MW	16.56 AW	37470 AAW	DEBLS	10//99-12//99
Except Farm Product	District of Columbia	S	14.79 MW	16.44 AW	34200 AAW	DCBLS	10//99-12//99
Except Farm Product	Washington PMSA, DC-MD-VA-WV	S	17.91 MW	16.14 AW	37260 AAW	DCBLS	10//99-12//99
Except Farm Product	Florida	S	14.84 MW	17.32 AW	36020 AAW	FLBLS	10//99-12//99
Except Farm Product	Daytona Beach MSA, FL	S	18.72 MW	15.37 AW	38940 AAW	FLBLS	10//99-12//99
Except Farm Product	Fort Lauderdale PMSA, FL	S	20.68 MW	16.78 AW	43020 AAW	FLBLS	10//99-12//99
Except Farm Product	Fort Pierce-Port St. Lucie MSA, FL	S	15.68 MW	13.35 AW	32620 AAW	FLBLS	10//99-12//99
Except Farm Product	Fort Walton Beach MSA, FL	S	12.55 MW	10.69 AW	26090 AAW	FLBLS	10//99-12//99
Except Farm Product	Gainesville MSA, FL	S	12.83 MW	11.58 AW	26690 AAW	FLBLS	10//99-12//99
Except Farm Product	Jacksonville MSA, FL	S	14.48 MW	12.46 AW	30110 AAW	FLBLS	10//99-12//99
Except Farm Product	Lakeland-Winter Haven MSA, FL	S	20.05 MW	16.18 AW	41710 AAW	FLBLS	10//99-12//99
Except Farm Product	Miami PMSA, FL	S	16.68 MW	14.91 AW	34680 AAW	FLBLS	10//99-12//99
Except Farm Product	Naples MSA, FL	S	16.75 MW	13.42 AW	34840 AAW	FLBLS	10//99-12//99
Except Farm Product	Orlando MSA, FL	S	16.87 MW	14.88 AW	35090 AAW	FLBLS	10//99-12//99
Except Farm Product	Pensacola MSA, FL	S	13.87 MW	12.30 AW	28860 AAW	FLBLS	10//99-12//99
Except Farm Product	Sarasota-Bradenton MSA, FL	S	12.78 MW	11.46 AW	26590 AAW	FLBLS	10//99-12//99
Except Farm Product	Tallahassee MSA, FL	S	13.94 MW	12.16 AW	29000 AAW	FLBLS	10//99-12//99
Except Farm Product	Tampa-St. Petersburg-Clearwater MSA, FL	S	18.83 MW	15.20 AW	39170 AAW	FLBLS	10//99-12//99
Except Farm Product	West Palm Beach-Boca Raton MSA, FL	S	18.81 MW	16.25 AW	39120 AAW	FLBLS	10//99-12//99
Except Farm Product	Georgia	S	18.22 MW	19.82 AW	41220 AAW	GABLS	10//99-12//99
Except Farm Product	Athens MSA, GA	S	14.68 MW	14.34 AW	30530 AAW	GABLS	10//99-12//99
Except Farm Product	Atlanta MSA, GA	S	21.03 MW	20.63 AW	43740 AAW	GABLS	10//99-12//99
Except Farm Product	Augusta-Aiken MSA, GA-SC	S	19.36 MW	16.58 AW	40260 AAW	GABLS	10//99-12//99
Except Farm Product	Columbus MSA, GA-AL	S	24.00 MW	23.24 AW	49920 AAW	GABLS	10//99-12//99
Except Farm Product	Macon MSA, GA	S	18.22 MW	15.12 AW	37900 AAW	GABLS	10//99-12//99

AAW Average annual wage	**AOH** Average offered, high	**ASH** Average starting, high	**H** Hourly	**M** Monthly	**S** Special: hourly and annual
AE Average entry wage	**AOL** Average offered, low	**ASL** Average starting, low	**HI** Highest wage paid	**MTC** Median total compensation	**TQ** Third quartile wage
AEX Average experienced wage	**APH** Average pay, high range	**AW** Average wage paid	**HR** High end range	**MW** Median wage paid	**W** Weekly
AO Average offered	**APL** Average pay, low range	**FQ** First quartile wage	**LR** Low end range	**SQ** Second quartile wage	**Y** Yearly

Occupation/Type/Industry	Location	Per	Low	Mid	High	Source	Date
Wholesale and Retail Buyer							
Except Farm Product	Savannah MSA, GA	S	18.96 MW	14.78 AW	39430 AAW	GABLS	10//99-12//99
Except Farm Product	Hawaii	S	16.19 MW	18.44 AW	38360 AAW	HIBLS	10//99-12//99
Except Farm Product	Honolulu MSA, HI	S	19.14 MW	16.61 AW	39810 AAW	HIBLS	10//99-12//99
Except Farm Product	Idaho	S	16.48 MW	21.01 AW	43700 AAW	IDBLS	10//99-12//99
Except Farm Product	Boise City MSA, ID	S	20.52 MW	19.02 AW	42670 AAW	IDBLS	10//99-12//99
Except Farm Product	Illinois	S	19.03 MW	21.97 AW	45700 AAW	ILBLS	10//99-12//99
Except Farm Product	Bloomington-Normal MSA, IL	S	16.68 MW	15.16 AW	34700 AAW	ILBLS	10//99-12//99
Except Farm Product	Champaign-Urbana MSA, IL	S	13.84 MW	11.37 AW	28790 AAW	ILBLS	10//99-12//99
Except Farm Product	Chicago PMSA, IL	S	23.90 MW	20.21 AW	49710 AAW	ILBLS	10//99-12//99
Except Farm Product	Decatur MSA, IL	S	15.18 MW	12.15 AW	31580 AAW	ILBLS	10//99-12//99
Except Farm Product	Peoria-Pekin MSA, IL	S	15.24 MW	13.15 AW	31700 AAW	ILBLS	10//99-12//99
Except Farm Product	Rockford MSA, IL	S	17.45 MW	16.69 AW	36300 AAW	ILBLS	10//99-12//99
Except Farm Product	Springfield MSA, IL	S	13.48 MW	13.72 AW	28050 AAW	ILBLS	10//99-12//99
Except Farm Product	Indiana	S	13.96 MW	16.89 AW	35120 AAW	INBLS	10//99-12//99
Except Farm Product	Elkhart-Goshen MSA, IN	S	15.48 MW	13.65 AW	32210 AAW	INBLS	10//99-12//99
Except Farm Product	Evansville-Henderson MSA, IN-KY	S	14.40 MW	14.16 AW	29950 AAW	INBLS	10//99-12//99
Except Farm Product	Fort Wayne MSA, IN	S	20.09 MW	15.02 AW	41780 AAW	INBLS	10//99-12//99
Except Farm Product	Gary PMSA, IN	S	15.73 MW	12.12 AW	32720 AAW	INBLS	10//99-12//99
Except Farm Product	Indianapolis MSA, IN	S	19.21 MW	16.28 AW	39960 AAW	INBLS	10//99-12//99
Except Farm Product	Kokomo MSA, IN	S	13.52 MW	12.88 AW	28120 AAW	INBLS	10//99-12//99
Except Farm Product	Lafayette MSA, IN	S	18.95 MW	14.30 AW	39430 AAW	INBLS	10//99-12//99
Except Farm Product	South Bend MSA, IN	S	15.70 MW	12.60 AW	32660 AAW	INBLS	10//99-12//99
Except Farm Product	Terre Haute MSA, IN	S	12.37 MW	12.15 AW	25730 AAW	INBLS	10//99-12//99
Except Farm Product	Iowa	S	17.23 MW	19.90 AW	41390 AAW	IABLS	10//99-12//99
Except Farm Product	Cedar Rapids MSA, IA	S	17.91 MW	16.72 AW	37250 AAW	IABLS	10//99-12//99
Except Farm Product	Davenport-Moline-Rock Island MSA, IA-IL	S	16.95 MW	15.57 AW	35250 AAW	IABLS	10//99-12//99
Except Farm Product	Des Moines MSA, IA	S	19.10 MW	18.25 AW	39730 AAW	IABLS	10//99-12//99
Except Farm Product	Waterloo-Cedar Falls MSA, IA	S	15.56 MW	14.42 AW	32370 AAW	IABLS	10//99-12//99
Except Farm Product	Kansas	S	15.46 MW	16.67 AW	34680 AAW	KSBLS	10//99-12//99
Except Farm Product	Topeka MSA, KS	S	14.61 MW	13.22 AW	30380 AAW	KSBLS	10//99-12//99
Except Farm Product	Wichita MSA, KS	S	16.96 MW	16.68 AW	35280 AAW	KSBLS	10//99-12//99
Except Farm Product	Kentucky	S	13.35 MW	15.19 AW	31590 AAW	KYBLS	10//99-12//99
Except Farm Product	Lexington MSA, KY	S	14.99 MW	13.18 AW	31180 AAW	KYBLS	10//99-12//99
Except Farm Product	Louisville MSA, KY-IN	S	16.16 MW	14.74 AW	33610 AAW	KYBLS	10//99-12//99
Except Farm Product	Owensboro MSA, KY	S	16.49 MW	16.05 AW	34300 AAW	KYBLS	10//99-12//99
Except Farm Product	Louisiana	S	13.12 MW	15.25 AW	31720 AAW	LABLS	10//99-12//99
Except Farm Product	Baton Rouge MSA, LA	S	14.93 MW	14.49 AW	31040 AAW	LABLS	10//99-12//99
Except Farm Product	Houma MSA, LA	S	14.47 MW	13.61 AW	30100 AAW	LABLS	10//99-12//99
Except Farm Product	Lafayette MSA, LA	S	16.48 MW	15.22 AW	34290 AAW	LABLS	10//99-12//99
Except Farm Product	Lake Charles MSA, LA	S	12.85 MW	12.77 AW	26720 AAW	LABLS	10//99-12//99
Except Farm Product	Monroe MSA, LA	S	28.80 MW	28.38 AW	59910 AAW	LABLS	10//99-12//99
Except Farm Product	New Orleans MSA, LA	S	13.83 MW	11.94 AW	28770 AAW	LABLS	10//99-12//99
Except Farm Product	Shreveport-Bossier City MSA, LA	S	17.01 MW	15.27 AW	35380 AAW	LABLS	10//99-12//99
Except Farm Product	Maine	S	13.69 MW	14.67 AW	30520 AAW	MEBLS	10//99-12//99
Except Farm Product	Bangor MSA, ME	S	14.72 MW	12.72 AW	30620 AAW	MEBLS	10//99-12//99
Except Farm Product	Portland MSA, ME	S	16.82 MW	16.12 AW	34990 AAW	MEBLS	10//99-12//99
Except Farm Product	Maryland	S	15.53 MW	17.04 AW	35450 AAW	MDBLS	10//99-12//99
Except Farm Product	Baltimore PMSA, MD	S	16.58 MW	15.18 AW	34480 AAW	MDBLS	10//99-12//99
Except Farm Product	Massachusetts	S	18.32 MW	20.32 AW	42270 AAW	MABLS	10//99-12//99
Except Farm Product	Barnstable-Yarmouth MSA, MA	S	19.88 MW	17.29 AW	41340 AAW	MABLS	10//99-12//99
Except Farm Product	Boston PMSA, MA-NH	S	21.33 MW	19.45 AW	44370 AAW	MABLS	10//99-12//99
Except Farm Product	Brockton PMSA, MA	S	17.93 MW	16.08 AW	37290 AAW	MABLS	10//99-12//99
Except Farm Product	Fitchburg-Leominster PMSA, MA	S	14.43 MW	13.69 AW	30010 AAW	MABLS	10//99-12//99
Except Farm Product	Lawrence PMSA, MA-NH	S	24.67 MW	19.58 AW	51310 AAW	MABLS	10//99-12//99
Except Farm Product	Lowell PMSA, MA-NH	S	24.17 MW	19.51 AW	50280 AAW	MABLS	10//99-12//99
Except Farm Product	Springfield MSA, MA	S	14.72 MW	13.45 AW	30620 AAW	MABLS	10//99-12//99
Except Farm Product	Worcester PMSA, MA-CT	S	20.95 MW	18.77 AW	43580 AAW	MABLS	10//99-12//99
Except Farm Product	Michigan	S	17 MW	21.39 AW	44490 AAW	MIBLS	10//99-12//99
Except Farm Product	Ann Arbor PMSA, MI	S	21.48 MW	13.04 AW	44690 AAW	MIBLS	10//99-12//99
Except Farm Product	Benton Harbor MSA, MI	S	13.69 MW	12.30 AW	28470 AAW	MIBLS	10//99-12//99
Except Farm Product	Detroit PMSA, MI	S	24.65 MW	19.88 AW	51270 AAW	MIBLS	10//99-12//99
Except Farm Product	Flint PMSA, MI	S	18.00 MW	14.21 AW	37440 AAW	MIBLS	10//99-12//99
Except Farm Product	Grand Rapids-Muskegon-Holland MSA, MI	S	20.59 MW	17.91 AW	42830 AAW	MIBLS	10//99-12//99
Except Farm Product	Jackson MSA, MI	S	18.47 MW	18.34 AW	38420 AAW	MIBLS	10//99-12//99

AAW	Average annual wage	AOH	Average offered, high	ASH	Average starting, high	H	Hourly	M	Monthly	S	Special: hourly and annual
AE	Average entry wage	AOL	Average offered, low	ASL	Average starting, low	HI	Highest wage paid	MTC	Median total compensation	TQ	Third quartile wage
AEX	Average experienced wage	APH	Average pay, high range	AW	Average wage paid	HR	High end range	MW	Median wage paid	W	Weekly
AO	Average offered	APL	Average pay, low range	FQ	First quartile wage	LR	Low end range	SQ	Second quartile wage	Y	Yearly

Occupation/Type/Industry	Location	Per	Low	Mid	High	Source	Date
Wholesale and Retail Buyer							
Except Farm Product	Kalamazoo-Battle Creek MSA, MI	S	16.75 MW	15.68 AW	34850 AAW	MIBLS	10//99-12//99
Except Farm Product	Lansing-East Lansing MSA, MI	S	22.27 MW	19.31 AW	46310 AAW	MIBLS	10//99-12//99
Except Farm Product	Saginaw-Bay City-Midland MSA, MI	S	15.52 MW	12.50 AW	32280 AAW	MIBLS	10//99-12//99
Except Farm Product	Minnesota	S	17.33 MW	18.47 AW	38420 AAW	MNBLS	10//99-12//99
Except Farm Product	Duluth-Superior MSA, MN-WI	S	13.58 MW	12.64 AW	28240 AAW	MNBLS	10//99-12//99
Except Farm Product	Minneapolis-St. Paul MSA, MN-WI	S	19.63 MW	18.25 AW	40840 AAW	MNBLS	10//99-12//99
Except Farm Product	St. Cloud MSA, MN	S	16.49 MW	16.95 AW	34310 AAW	MNBLS	10//99-12//99
Except Farm Product	Mississippi	S	16.91 MW	19.24 AW	40020 AAW	MSBLS	10//99-12//99
Except Farm Product	Biloxi-Gulfport-Pascagoula MSA, MS	S	13.76 MW	13.50 AW	28620 AAW	MSBLS	10//99-12//99
Except Farm Product	Jackson MSA, MS	S	20.57 MW	20.08 AW	42780 AAW	MSBLS	10//99-12//99
Except Farm Product	Missouri	S	15.48 MW	17.12 AW	35600 AAW	MOBLS	10//99-12//99
Except Farm Product	Joplin MSA, MO	S	10.83 MW	9.34 AW	22520 AAW	MOBLS	10//99-12//99
Except Farm Product	Kansas City MSA, MO-KS	S	17.95 MW	16.52 AW	37340 AAW	MOBLS	10//99-12//99
Except Farm Product	St. Louis MSA, MO-IL	S	18.29 MW	16.67 AW	38040 AAW	MOBLS	10//99-12//99
Except Farm Product	Springfield MSA, MO	S	13.63 MW	12.98 AW	28350 AAW	MOBLS	10//99-12//99
Except Farm Product	Montana	S	10.74 MW	12.63 AW	26270 AAW	MTBLS	10//99-12//99
Except Farm Product	Billings MSA, MT	S	13.16 MW	12.41 AW	27370 AAW	MTBLS	10//99-12//99
Except Farm Product	Missoula MSA, MT	S	13.04 MW	10.42 AW	27120 AAW	MTBLS	10//99-12//99
Except Farm Product	Nebraska	S	14.08 MW	15.66 AW	32570 AAW	NEBLS	10//99-12//99
Except Farm Product	Lincoln MSA, NE	S	16.86 MW	15.69 AW	35060 AAW	NEBLS	10//99-12//99
Except Farm Product	Omaha MSA, NE-IA	S	15.13 MW	13.84 AW	31480 AAW	NEBLS	10//99-12//99
Except Farm Product	Nevada	S	15.69 MW	17.90 AW	37220 AAW	NVBLS	10//99-12//99
Except Farm Product	Las Vegas MSA, NV-AZ	S	18.66 MW	15.87 AW	38800 AAW	NVBLS	10//99-12//99
Except Farm Product	Reno MSA, NV	S	16.19 MW	14.56 AW	33660 AAW	NVBLS	10//99-12//99
Except Farm Product	New Hampshire	S	15.96 MW	18.79 AW	39070 AAW	NHBLS	10//99-12//99
Except Farm Product	Manchester PMSA, NH	S	17.26 MW	16.18 AW	35900 AAW	NHBLS	10//99-12//99
Except Farm Product	Nashua PMSA, NH	S	20.28 MW	17.71 AW	42180 AAW	NHBLS	10//99-12//99
Except Farm Product	Portsmouth-Rochester PMSA, NH-ME	S	17.17 MW	13.56 AW	35700 AAW	NHBLS	10//99-12//99
Except Farm Product	New Jersey	S	19.24 MW	22.18 AW	46130 AAW	NJBLS	10//99-12//99
Except Farm Product	Atlantic-Cape May PMSA, NJ	S	20.58 MW	18.10 AW	42810 AAW	NJBLS	10//99-12//99
Except Farm Product	Bergen-Passaic PMSA, NJ	S	22.19 MW	19.20 AW	46160 AAW	NJBLS	10//99-12//99
Except Farm Product	Jersey City PMSA, NJ	S	27.23 MW	23.93 AW	56640 AAW	NJBLS	10//99-12//99
Except Farm Product	Middlesex-Somerset-Hunterdon PMSA, NJ	S	22.40 MW	19.24 AW	46590 AAW	NJBLS	10//99-12//99
Except Farm Product	Monmouth-Ocean PMSA, NJ	S	17.80 MW	15.98 AW	37020 AAW	NJBLS	10//99-12//99
Except Farm Product	Newark PMSA, NJ	S	25.12 MW	21.63 AW	52250 AAW	NJBLS	10//99-12//99
Except Farm Product	Trenton PMSA, NJ	S	24.54 MW	19.74 AW	51040 AAW	NJBLS	10//99-12//99
Except Farm Product	Vineland-Millville-Bridgeton PMSA, NJ	S	18.26 MW	15.13 AW	37990 AAW	NJBLS	10//99-12//99
Except Farm Product	New Mexico	S	11.81 MW	12.93 AW	26900 AAW	NMBLS	10//99-12//99
Except Farm Product	Albuquerque MSA, NM	S	13.42 MW	11.83 AW	27920 AAW	NMBLS	10//99-12//99
Except Farm Product	Santa Fe MSA, NM	S	13.49 MW	13.87 AW	28050 AAW	NMBLS	10//99-12//99
Except Farm Product	New York	S	19 MW	22.85 AW	47520 AAW	NYBLS	10//99-12//99
Except Farm Product	Albany-Schenectady-Troy MSA, NY	S	18.27 MW	16.79 AW	38010 AAW	NYBLS	10//99-12//99
Except Farm Product	Binghamton MSA, NY	S	17.40 MW	15.35 AW	36180 AAW	NYBLS	10//99-12//99
Except Farm Product	Buffalo-Niagara Falls MSA, NY	S	17.50 MW	16.00 AW	36400 AAW	NYBLS	10//99-12//99
Except Farm Product	Nassau-Suffolk PMSA, NY	S	22.02 MW	19.20 AW	45800 AAW	NYBLS	10//99-12//99
Except Farm Product	New York PMSA, NY	S	25.95 MW	21.18 AW	53980 AAW	NYBLS	10//99-12//99
Except Farm Product	Rochester MSA, NY	S	19.51 MW	17.48 AW	40580 AAW	NYBLS	10//99-12//99
Except Farm Product	Syracuse MSA, NY	S	17.86 MW	15.76 AW	37150 AAW	NYBLS	10//99-12//99
Except Farm Product	Utica-Rome MSA, NY	S	17.98 MW	15.40 AW	37400 AAW	NYBLS	10//99-12//99
Except Farm Product	North Carolina	S	15.9 MW	18.17 AW	37790 AAW	NCBLS	10//99-12//99
Except Farm Product	Charlotte-Gastonia-Rock Hill MSA, NC-SC	S	21.89 MW	18.38 AW	45540 AAW	NCBLS	10//99-12//99
Except Farm Product	Fayetteville MSA, NC	S	15.61 MW	13.71 AW	32460 AAW	NCBLS	10//99-12//99
Except Farm Product	Greensboro--Winston-Salem--High Point MSA, NC	S	14.50 MW	13.68 AW	30160 AAW	NCBLS	10//99-12//99
Except Farm Product	Hickory-Morganton-Lenoir MSA, NC	S	18.86 MW	14.20 AW	39230 AAW	NCBLS	10//99-12//99
Except Farm Product	Jacksonville MSA, NC	S	12.85 MW	10.80 AW	26740 AAW	NCBLS	10//99-12//99
Except Farm Product	Raleigh-Durham-Chapel Hill MSA, NC	S	17.65 MW	16.46 AW	36720 AAW	NCBLS	10//99-12//99
Except Farm Product	Rocky Mount MSA, NC	S	17.09 MW	15.85 AW	35550 AAW	NCBLS	10//99-12//99
Except Farm Product	North Dakota	S	13.62 MW	15.15 AW	31510 AAW	NDBLS	10//99-12//99

AAW	Average annual wage	AOH	Average offered, high	ASH	Average starting, high	H	Hourly	M	Monthly	S	Special: hourly and annual
AE	Average entry wage	AOL	Average offered, low	ASL	Average starting, low	HI	Highest wage paid	MTC	Median total compensation	TQ	Third quartile wage
AEX	Average experienced wage	APH	Average pay, high range	AW	Average wage paid	HR	High end range	MW	Median wage paid	W	Weekly
AO	Average offered	APL	Average pay, low range	FQ	First quartile wage	LR	Low end range	SQ	Second quartile wage	Y	Yearly

Occupation/Type/Industry	Location	Per	Low	Mid	High	Source	Date
Wholesale and Retail Buyer							
Except Farm Product	Bismarck MSA, ND	S	13.40 MW	13.56 AW	27870 AAW	NDBLS	10//99-12//99
Except Farm Product	Fargo-Moorhead MSA, ND-MN	S	17.09 MW	15.77 AW	35550 AAW	NDBLS	10//99-12//99
Except Farm Product	Ohio	S	14.97 MW	17.74 AW	36900 AAW	OHBLS	10//99-12//99
Except Farm Product	Akron PMSA, OH	S	13.21 MW	11.92 AW	27470 AAW	OHBLS	10//99-12//99
Except Farm Product	Canton-Massillon MSA, OH	S	15.62 MW	15.28 AW	32500 AAW	OHBLS	10//99-12//99
Except Farm Product	Cincinnati PMSA, OH-KY-IN	S	18.79 MW	15.56 AW	39090 AAW	OHBLS	10//99-12//99
Except Farm Product	Cleveland-Lorain-Elyria PMSA, OH	S	17.31 MW	15.44 AW	36010 AAW	OHBLS	10//99-12//99
Except Farm Product	Columbus MSA, OH	S	22.06 MW	17.82 AW	45890 AAW	OHBLS	10//99-12//99
Except Farm Product	Dayton-Springfield MSA, OH	S	17.84 MW	15.29 AW	37100 AAW	OHBLS	10//99-12//99
Except Farm Product	Hamilton-Middletown PMSA, OH	S	13.30 MW	12.28 AW	27660 AAW	OHBLS	10//99-12//99
Except Farm Product	Lima MSA, OH	S	13.72 MW	14.14 AW	28540 AAW	OHBLS	10//99-12//99
Except Farm Product	Mansfield MSA, OH	S	16.43 MW	14.61 AW	34170 AAW	OHBLS	10//99-12//99
Except Farm Product	Toledo MSA, OH	S	16.15 MW	15.47 AW	33580 AAW	OHBLS	10//99-12//99
Except Farm Product	Youngstown-Warren MSA, OH	S	16.34 MW	12.18 AW	33980 AAW	OHBLS	10//99-12//99
Except Farm Product	Oklahoma	S	14.5 MW	16.03 AW	33340 AAW	OKBLS	10//99-12//99
Except Farm Product	Enid MSA, OK	S	13.92 MW	11.93 AW	28960 AAW	OKBLS	10//99-12//99
Except Farm Product	Oklahoma City MSA, OK	S	17.62 MW	16.96 AW	36660 AAW	OKBLS	10//99-12//99
Except Farm Product	Tulsa MSA, OK	S	16.38 MW	15.54 AW	34070 AAW	OKBLS	10//99-12//99
Except Farm Product	Oregon	S	16.32 MW	19.35 AW	40250 AAW	ORBLS	10//99-12//99
Except Farm Product	Eugene-Springfield MSA, OR	S	16.87 MW	15.91 AW	35100 AAW	ORBLS	10//99-12//99
Except Farm Product	Medford-Ashland MSA, OR	S	18.70 MW	14.22 AW	38900 AAW	ORBLS	10//99-12//99
Except Farm Product	Portland-Vancouver PMSA, OR-WA	S	20.87 MW	16.91 AW	43400 AAW	ORBLS	10//99-12//99
Except Farm Product	Salem PMSA, OR	S	15.04 MW	12.95 AW	31290 AAW	ORBLS	10//99-12//99
Except Farm Product	Pennsylvania	S	17 MW	19.72 AW	41010 AAW	PABLS	10//99-12//99
Except Farm Product	Allentown-Bethlehem-Easton MSA, PA	S	15.49 MW	13.84 AW	32220 AAW	PABLS	10//99-12//99
Except Farm Product	Altoona MSA, PA	S	25.74 MW	22.25 AW	53540 AAW	PABLS	10//99-12//99
Except Farm Product	Erie MSA, PA	S	14.20 MW	12.32 AW	29540 AAW	PABLS	10//99-12//99
Except Farm Product	Harrisburg-Lebanon-Carlisle MSA, PA	S	19.21 MW	16.38 AW	39960 AAW	PABLS	10//99-12//99
Except Farm Product	Lancaster MSA, PA	S	18.98 MW	15.72 AW	39480 AAW	PABLS	10//99-12//99
Except Farm Product	Philadelphia PMSA, PA-NJ	S	21.05 MW	19.30 AW	43790 AAW	PABLS	10//99-12//99
Except Farm Product	Pittsburgh MSA, PA	S	20.00 MW	17.60 AW	41600 AAW	PABLS	10//99-12//99
Except Farm Product	Reading MSA, PA	S	17.03 MW	14.97 AW	35430 AAW	PABLS	10//99-12//99
Except Farm Product	Scranton--Wilkes-Barre--Hazleton MSA, PA	S	16.55 MW	14.23 AW	34430 AAW	PABLS	10//99-12//99
Except Farm Product	Sharon MSA, PA	S	17.10 MW	15.82 AW	35570 AAW	PABLS	10//99-12//99
Except Farm Product	Williamsport MSA, PA	S	12.52 MW	11.96 AW	26040 AAW	PABLS	10//99-12//99
Except Farm Product	York MSA, PA	S	12.92 MW	12.16 AW	26880 AAW	PABLS	10//99-12//99
Except Farm Product	Rhode Island	S	18.6 MW	20.25 AW	42130 AAW	RIBLS	10//99-12//99
Except Farm Product	Providence-Fall River-Warwick MSA, RI-MA	S	20.62 MW	19.24 AW	42880 AAW	RIBLS	10//99-12//99
Except Farm Product	South Carolina	S	13.62 MW	16.29 AW	33890 AAW	SCBLS	10//99-12//99
Except Farm Product	Charleston-North Charleston MSA, SC	S	14.79 MW	12.69 AW	30770 AAW	SCBLS	10//99-12//99
Except Farm Product	Columbia MSA, SC	S	21.65 MW	14.50 AW	45030 AAW	SCBLS	10//99-12//99
Except Farm Product	Florence MSA, SC	S	15.41 MW	15.58 AW	32050 AAW	SCBLS	10//99-12//99
Except Farm Product	Greenville-Spartanburg-Anderson MSA, SC	S	15.16 MW	13.07 AW	31540 AAW	SCBLS	10//99-12//99
Except Farm Product	Myrtle Beach MSA, SC	S	19.33 MW	18.00 AW	40200 AAW	SCBLS	10//99-12//99
Except Farm Product	South Dakota	S	14.1 MW	14.77 AW	30720 AAW	SDBLS	10//99-12//99
Except Farm Product	Rapid City MSA, SD	S	14.13 MW	13.23 AW	29390 AAW	SDBLS	10//99-12//99
Except Farm Product	Sioux Falls MSA, SD	S	14.29 MW	13.63 AW	29730 AAW	SDBLS	10//99-12//99
Except Farm Product	Tennessee	S	15 MW	17.24 AW	35870 AAW	TNBLS	10//99-12//99
Except Farm Product	Chattanooga MSA, TN-GA	S	20.48 MW	15.34 AW	42590 AAW	TNBLS	10//99-12//99
Except Farm Product	Johnson City-Kingsport-Bristol MSA, TN-VA	S	12.37 MW	10.76 AW	25730 AAW	TNBLS	10//99-12//99
Except Farm Product	Knoxville MSA, TN	S	16.81 MW	14.21 AW	34960 AAW	TNBLS	10//99-12//99
Except Farm Product	Memphis MSA, TN-AR-MS	S	16.85 MW	14.94 AW	35050 AAW	MSBLS	10//99-12//99
Except Farm Product	Nashville MSA, TN	S	19.10 MW	17.02 AW	39730 AAW	TNBLS	10//99-12//99
Except Farm Product	Texas	S	17.74 MW	20.51 AW	42660 AAW	TXBLS	10//99-12//99
Except Farm Product	Amarillo MSA, TX	S	17.84 MW	14.91 AW	37120 AAW	TXBLS	10//99-12//99
Except Farm Product	Austin-San Marcos MSA, TX	S	16.64 MW	14.40 AW	34610 AAW	TXBLS	10//99-12//99
Except Farm Product	Brazoria PMSA, TX	S	15.89 MW	12.68 AW	33040 AAW	TXBLS	10//99-12//99
Except Farm Product	Brownsville-Harlingen-San Benito MSA, TX	S	17.73 MW	16.40 AW	36870 AAW	TXBLS	10//99-12//99

AAW	Average annual wage	AOH	Average offered, high	ASH	Average starting, high	H	Hourly
AE	Average entry wage	AOL	Average offered, low	ASL	Average starting, low	HI	Highest wage paid
AEX	Average experienced wage	APH	Average pay, high range	AW	Average wage paid	HR	High end range
AO	Average offered	APL	Average pay, low range	FQ	First quartile wage	LR	Low end range

M	Monthly	S	Special: hourly and annual
MTC	Median total compensation	TQ	Third quartile wage
MW	Median wage paid	W	Weekly
SQ	Second quartile wage	Y	Yearly

Occupation/Type/Industry	Location	Per	Low	Mid	High	Source	Date
Wholesale and Retail Buyer							
Except Farm Product	Bryan-College Station MSA, TX	S	15.45 MW	12.06 AW	32140 AAW	TXBLS	10//99-12//99
Except Farm Product	Corpus Christi MSA, TX	S	21.41 MW	20.25 AW	44530 AAW	TXBLS	10//99-12//99
Except Farm Product	Dallas PMSA, TX	S	23.81 MW	21.87 AW	49530 AAW	TXBLS	10//99-12//99
Except Farm Product	El Paso MSA, TX	S	16.25 MW	13.57 AW	33800 AAW	TXBLS	10//99-12//99
Except Farm Product	Fort Worth-Arlington PMSA, TX	S	19.63 MW	16.16 AW	40830 AAW	TXBLS	10//99-12//99
Except Farm Product	Houston PMSA, TX	S	22.68 MW	20.01 AW	47180 AAW	TXBLS	10//99-12//99
Except Farm Product	Lubbock MSA, TX	S	15.91 MW	14.33 AW	33100 AAW	TXBLS	10//99-12//99
Except Farm Product	McAllen-Edinburg-Mission MSA, TX	S	12.97 MW	10.48 AW	26980 AAW	TXBLS	10//99-12//99
Except Farm Product	Odessa-Midland MSA, TX	S	16.48 MW	13.41 AW	34280 AAW	TXBLS	10//99-12//99
Except Farm Product	San Antonio MSA, TX	S	20.83 MW	17.79 AW	43320 AAW	TXBLS	10//99-12//99
Except Farm Product	Tyler MSA, TX	S	16.80 MW	14.73 AW	34950 AAW	TXBLS	10//99-12//99
Except Farm Product	Waco MSA, TX	S	18.52 MW	16.89 AW	38530 AAW	TXBLS	10//99-12//99
Except Farm Product	Utah	S	15.17 MW	16.71 AW	34750 AAW	UTBLS	10//99-12//99
Except Farm Product	Salt Lake City-Ogden MSA, UT	S	17.70 MW	16.05 AW	36810 AAW	UTBLS	10//99-12//99
Except Farm Product	Vermont	S	14.52 MW	15.90 AW	33060 AAW	VTBLS	10//99-12//99
Except Farm Product	Burlington MSA, VT	S	17.16 MW	14.97 AW	35700 AAW	VTBLS	10//99-12//99
Except Farm Product	Virginia	S	15.95 MW	17.47 AW	36340 AAW	VABLS	10//99-12//99
Except Farm Product	Charlottesville MSA, VA	S	13.93 MW	12.84 AW	28980 AAW	VABLS	10//99-12//99
Except Farm Product	Lynchburg MSA, VA	S	15.38 MW	13.70 AW	31980 AAW	VABLS	10//99-12//99
Except Farm Product	Norfolk-Virginia Beach-Newport News MSA, VA-NC	S	17.54 MW	15.56 AW	36490 AAW	VABLS	10//99-12//99
Except Farm Product	Richmond-Petersburg MSA, VA	S	17.97 MW	16.72 AW	37380 AAW	VABLS	10//99-12//99
Except Farm Product	Roanoke MSA, VA	S	16.58 MW	15.65 AW	34490 AAW	VABLS	10//99-12//99
Except Farm Product	Washington	S	15.28 MW	17.74 AW	36910 AAW	WABLS	10//99-12//99
Except Farm Product	Bellingham MSA, WA	S	12.64 MW	11.96 AW	26290 AAW	WABLS	10//99-12//99
Except Farm Product	Bremerton PMSA, WA	S	13.66 MW	13.03 AW	28420 AAW	WABLS	10//99-12//99
Except Farm Product	Olympia PMSA, WA	S	14.47 MW	12.48 AW	30090 AAW	WABLS	10//99-12//99
Except Farm Product	Richland-Kennewick-Pasco MSA, WA	S	13.66 MW	13.44 AW	28410 AAW	WABLS	10//99-12//99
Except Farm Product	Seattle-Bellevue-Everett PMSA, WA	S	18.90 MW	16.36 AW	39310 AAW	WABLS	10//99-12//99
Except Farm Product	Spokane MSA, WA	S	16.63 MW	14.30 AW	34580 AAW	WABLS	10//99-12//99
Except Farm Product	Tacoma PMSA, WA	S	17.45 MW	14.40 AW	36290 AAW	WABLS	10//99-12//99
Except Farm Product	Yakima MSA, WA	S	12.38 MW	11.69 AW	25760 AAW	WABLS	10//99-12//99
Except Farm Product	West Virginia	S	12.76 MW	13.84 AW	28790 AAW	WVBLS	10//99-12//99
Except Farm Product	Charleston MSA, WV	S	13.04 MW	12.92 AW	27120 AAW	WVBLS	10//99-12//99
Except Farm Product	Huntington-Ashland MSA, WV-KY-OH	S	18.80 MW	16.31 AW	39110 AAW	WVBLS	10//99-12//99
Except Farm Product	Parkersburg-Marietta MSA, WV-OH	S	15.05 MW	15.20 AW	31300 AAW	WVBLS	10//99-12//99
Except Farm Product	Wheeling MSA, WV-OH	S	16.49 MW	11.87 AW	34300 AAW	WVBLS	10//99-12//99
Except Farm Product	Wisconsin	S	14.31 MW	15.70 AW	32660 AAW	WIBLS	10//99-12//99
Except Farm Product	Appleton-Oshkosh-Neenah MSA, WI	S	13.86 MW	13.56 AW	28820 AAW	WIBLS	10//99-12//99
Except Farm Product	Eau Claire MSA, WI	S	15.82 MW	15.37 AW	32900 AAW	WIBLS	10//99-12//99
Except Farm Product	Green Bay MSA, WI	S	16.92 MW	15.64 AW	35180 AAW	WIBLS	10//99-12//99
Except Farm Product	Kenosha PMSA, WI	S	18.17 MW	19.11 AW	37800 AAW	WIBLS	10//99-12//99
Except Farm Product	La Crosse MSA, WI-MN	S	16.32 MW	13.61 AW	33940 AAW	WIBLS	10//99-12//99
Except Farm Product	Madison MSA, WI	S	16.38 MW	14.92 AW	34060 AAW	WIBLS	10//99-12//99
Except Farm Product	Milwaukee-Waukesha PMSA, WI	S	16.37 MW	14.66 AW	34050 AAW	WIBLS	10//99-12//99
Except Farm Product	Racine PMSA, WI	S	17.89 MW	14.55 AW	37210 AAW	WIBLS	10//99-12//99
Except Farm Product	Wausau MSA, WI	S	15.84 MW	14.92 AW	32940 AAW	WIBLS	10//99-12//99
Except Farm Product	Wyoming	S	11.4 MW	13.38 AW	27820 AAW	WYBLS	10//99-12//99
Except Farm Product	Cheyenne MSA, WY	S	23.84 MW	14.24 AW	49600 AAW	WYBLS	10//99-12//99
Except Farm Product	Puerto Rico	S	8.75 MW	10.48 AW	21800 AAW	PRBLS	10//99-12//99
Except Farm Product	Caguas PMSA, PR	S	10.12 MW	7.41 AW	21040 AAW	PRBLS	10//99-12//99
Except Farm Product	Mayaguez MSA, PR	S	9.99 MW	8.51 AW	20780 AAW	PRBLS	10//99-12//99
Except Farm Product	Ponce MSA, PR	S	7.72 MW	7.20 AW	16060 AAW	PRBLS	10//99-12//99
Except Farm Product	San Juan-Bayamon PMSA, PR	S	10.86 MW	9.05 AW	22580 AAW	PRBLS	10//99-12//99
Except Farm Product	Guam	S	14.9 MW	18.00 AW	37440 AAW	GUBLS	10//99-12//99
Winemaker							
Winery/Vineyard, Over 150K Cases/Year	United States	Y	103000 MW	111847 AW		PWV	1999

AAW Average annual wage	**AOH** Average offered, high	**ASH** Average starting, high	**H** Hourly	**M** Monthly	**S** Special: hourly and annual
AE Average entry wage	**AOL** Average offered, low	**ASL** Average starting, low	**HI** Highest wage paid	**MTC** Median total compensation	**TQ** Third quartile wage
AEX Average experienced wage	**APH** Average pay, high range	**AW** Average wage paid	**HR** High end range	**MW** Median wage paid	**W** Weekly
AO Average offered	**APL** Average pay, low range	**FQ** First quartile wage	**LR** Low end range	**SQ** Second quartile wage	**Y** Yearly

Occupation/Type/Industry	Location	Per	Low	Mid	High	Source	Date

Woodworking Machine Setter, Operator, and Tender

Occupation/Type/Industry	Location	Per	Low	Mid	High	Source	Date
Except Sawing	Alabama	S	7.96 mw	7.91 aw	16450 aaw	ALBLS	10//99-12//99
Except Sawing	Birmingham MSA, AL	S	8.72 mw	8.88 aw	18130 aaw	ALBLS	10//99-12//99
Except Sawing	Decatur MSA, AL	S	9.11 mw	9.49 aw	18960 aaw	ALBLS	10//99-12//99
Except Sawing	Mobile MSA, AL	S	8.06 mw	7.91 aw	16770 aaw	ALBLS	10//99-12//99
Except Sawing	Montgomery MSA, AL	S	7.75 mw	6.66 aw	16110 aaw	ALBLS	10//99-12//99
Except Sawing	Arizona	S	7.75 mw	8.13 aw	16910 aaw	AZBLS	10//99-12//99
Except Sawing	Phoenix-Mesa MSA, AZ	S	8.17 mw	7.74 aw	16980 aaw	AZBLS	10//99-12//99
Except Sawing	Tucson MSA, AZ	S	7.44 mw	7.49 aw	15480 aaw	AZBLS	10//99-12//99
Except Sawing	Arkansas	S	8.14 mw	8.51 aw	17710 aaw	ARBLS	10//99-12//99
Except Sawing	Fort Smith MSA, AR-OK	S	8.04 mw	7.94 aw	16730 aaw	ARBLS	10//99-12//99
Except Sawing	Little Rock-North Little Rock MSA, AR	S	7.83 mw	7.77 aw	16290 aaw	ARBLS	10//99-12//99
Except Sawing	California	S	8.27 mw	9.30 aw	19350 aaw	CABLS	10//99-12//99
Except Sawing	Bakersfield MSA, CA	S	9.32 mw	8.83 aw	19380 aaw	CABLS	10//99-12//99
Except Sawing	Fresno MSA, CA	S	9.29 mw	9.58 aw	19320 aaw	CABLS	10//99-12//99
Except Sawing	Los Angeles-Long Beach PMSA, CA	S	8.86 mw	8.04 aw	18420 aaw	CABLS	10//99-12//99
Except Sawing	Modesto MSA, CA	S	8.59 mw	7.90 aw	17880 aaw	CABLS	10//99-12//99
Except Sawing	Oakland PMSA, CA	S	14.93 mw	14.31 aw	31050 aaw	CABLS	10//99-12//99
Except Sawing	Orange County PMSA, CA	S	8.55 mw	8.08 aw	17780 aaw	CABLS	10//99-12//99
Except Sawing	Riverside-San Bernardino PMSA, CA	S	7.43 mw	6.89 aw	15450 aaw	CABLS	10//99-12//99
Except Sawing	Sacramento PMSA, CA	S	10.99 mw	10.79 aw	22860 aaw	CABLS	10//99-12//99
Except Sawing	San Diego MSA, CA	S	8.21 mw	7.92 aw	17070 aaw	CABLS	10//99-12//99
Except Sawing	San Francisco PMSA, CA	S	12.17 mw	11.96 aw	25320 aaw	CABLS	10//99-12//99
Except Sawing	San Jose PMSA, CA	S	10.47 mw	9.23 aw	21770 aaw	CABLS	10//99-12//99
Except Sawing	Santa Cruz-Watsonville PMSA, CA	S	11.00 mw	9.74 aw	22880 aaw	CABLS	10//99-12//99
Except Sawing	Santa Rosa PMSA, CA	S	9.14 mw	8.29 aw	19000 aaw	CABLS	10//99-12//99
Except Sawing	Visalia-Tulare-Porterville MSA, CA	S	8.79 mw	8.99 aw	18280 aaw	CABLS	10//99-12//99
Except Sawing	Yuba City MSA, CA	S	10.25 mw	10.10 aw	21310 aaw	CABLS	10//99-12//99
Except Sawing	Colorado	S	9.87 mw	10.27 aw	21370 aaw	COBLS	10//99-12//99
Except Sawing	Boulder-Longmont PMSA, CO	S	10.09 mw	9.62 aw	20980 aaw	COBLS	10//99-12//99
Except Sawing	Denver PMSA, CO	S	10.54 mw	9.96 aw	21920 aaw	COBLS	10//99-12//99
Except Sawing	Grand Junction MSA, CO	S	10.49 mw	10.54 aw	21810 aaw	COBLS	10//99-12//99
Except Sawing	Connecticut	S	11.85 mw	11.79 aw	24530 aaw	CTBLS	10//99-12//99
Except Sawing	Hartford MSA, CT	S	11.92 mw	10.55 aw	24790 aaw	CTBLS	10//99-12//99
Except Sawing	New Haven-Meriden PMSA, CT	S	10.23 mw	11.05 aw	21280 aaw	CTBLS	10//99-12//99
Except Sawing	Washington PMSA, DC-MD-VA-WV	S	11.96 mw	11.66 aw	24880 aaw	DCBLS	10//99-12//99
Except Sawing	Florida	S	9.45 mw	9.53 aw	19810 aaw	FLBLS	10//99-12//99
Except Sawing	Fort Lauderdale PMSA, FL	S	10.47 mw	10.70 aw	21770 aaw	FLBLS	10//99-12//99
Except Sawing	Jacksonville MSA, FL	S	10.73 mw	11.47 aw	22320 aaw	FLBLS	10//99-12//99
Except Sawing	Miami PMSA, FL	S	9.81 mw	9.32 aw	20400 aaw	FLBLS	10//99-12//99
Except Sawing	Orlando MSA, FL	S	10.18 mw	9.91 aw	21170 aaw	FLBLS	10//99-12//99
Except Sawing	Sarasota-Bradenton MSA, FL	S	8.77 mw	8.88 aw	18240 aaw	FLBLS	10//99-12//99
Except Sawing	Tampa-St. Petersburg-Clearwater MSA, FL	S	8.93 mw	9.18 aw	18580 aaw	FLBLS	10//99-12//99
Except Sawing	Georgia	S	8.86 mw	9.09 aw	18900 aaw	GABLS	10//99-12//99
Except Sawing	Athens MSA, GA	S	8.08 mw	7.99 aw	16800 aaw	GABLS	10//99-12//99
Except Sawing	Atlanta MSA, GA	S	8.97 mw	8.01 aw	18660 aaw	GABLS	10//99-12//99
Except Sawing	Idaho	S	11.8 mw	11.62 aw	24170 aaw	IDBLS	10//99-12//99
Except Sawing	Boise City MSA, ID	S	9.47 mw	9.71 aw	19700 aaw	IDBLS	10//99-12//99
Except Sawing	Illinois	S	9.3 mw	9.64 aw	20060 aaw	ILBLS	10//99-12//99
Except Sawing	Chicago PMSA, IL	S	10.90 mw	9.79 aw	22660 aaw	ILBLS	10//99-12//99
Except Sawing	Peoria-Pekin MSA, IL	S	10.56 mw	10.76 aw	21960 aaw	ILBLS	10//99-12//99
Except Sawing	Indiana	S	10.39 mw	10.58 aw	22000 aaw	INBLS	10//99-12//99
Except Sawing	Elkhart-Goshen MSA, IN	S	10.58 mw	10.01 aw	22020 aaw	INBLS	10//99-12//99
Except Sawing	Fort Wayne MSA, IN	S	9.03 mw	9.31 aw	18790 aaw	INBLS	10//99-12//99
Except Sawing	Gary PMSA, IN	S	10.90 mw	11.16 aw	22670 aaw	INBLS	10//99-12//99
Except Sawing	Indianapolis MSA, IN	S	11.63 mw	11.46 aw	24200 aaw	INBLS	10//99-12//99
Except Sawing	Iowa	S	9.64 mw	9.56 aw	19890 aaw	IABLS	10//99-12//99
Except Sawing	Kansas	S	8.26 mw	8.60 aw	17880 aaw	KSBLS	10//99-12//99
Except Sawing	Wichita MSA, KS	S	8.26 mw	7.99 aw	17190 aaw	KSBLS	10//99-12//99
Except Sawing	Kentucky	S	8.8 mw	8.79 aw	18280 aaw	KYBLS	10//99-12//99
Except Sawing	Louisville MSA, KY-IN	S	10.30 mw	10.07 aw	21410 aaw	KYBLS	10//99-12//99
Except Sawing	Louisiana	S	11.89 mw	11.62 aw	24160 aaw	LABLS	10//99-12//99
Except Sawing	Baton Rouge MSA, LA	S	12.27 mw	12.23 aw	25520 aaw	LABLS	10//99-12//99

AAW	Average annual wage	AOH	Average offered, high	ASH	Average starting, high	H	Hourly	M	Monthly	S	Special: hourly and annual
AE	Average entry wage	AOL	Average offered, low	ASL	Average starting, low	HI	Highest wage paid	MTC	Median total compensation	TQ	Third quartile wage
AEX	Average experienced wage	APH	Average pay, high range	AW	Average wage paid	HR	High end range	MW	Median wage paid	W	Weekly
AO	Average offered	APL	Average pay, low range	FQ	First quartile wage	LR	Low end range	SQ	Second quartile wage	Y	Yearly

Occupation/Type/Industry	Location	Per	Low	Mid	High	Source	Date
Woodworking Machine Setter, Operator, and Tender							
Except Sawing	Shreveport-Bossier City MSA, LA	S	7.29 MW	7.31 AW	15160 AAW	LABLS	10//99-12//99
Except Sawing	Maine	S	8.31 MW	8.62 AW	17940 AAW	MEBLS	10//99-12//99
Except Sawing	Bangor MSA, ME	S	9.61 MW	9.58 AW	19990 AAW	MEBLS	10//99-12//99
Except Sawing	Portland MSA, ME	S	7.89 MW	7.71 AW	16410 AAW	MEBLS	10//99-12//99
Except Sawing	Maryland	S	10.87 MW	11.23 AW	23360 AAW	MDBLS	10//99-12//99
Except Sawing	Baltimore PMSA, MD	S	9.98 MW	8.33 AW	20750 AAW	MDBLS	10//99-12//99
Except Sawing	Cumberland MSA, MD-WV	S	7.29 MW	6.27 AW	15170 AAW	MDBLS	10//99-12//99
Except Sawing	Massachusetts	S	10.36 MW	10.81 AW	22480 AAW	MABLS	10//99-12//99
Except Sawing	Barnstable-Yarmouth MSA, MA	S	12.54 MW	11.39 AW	26080 AAW	MABLS	10//99-12//99
Except Sawing	Boston PMSA, MA-NH	S	10.62 MW	10.27 AW	22100 AAW	MABLS	10//99-12//99
Except Sawing	Fitchburg-Leominster PMSA, MA	S	11.93 MW	11.41 AW	24820 AAW	MABLS	10//99-12//99
Except Sawing	New Bedford PMSA, MA	S	8.33 MW	7.47 AW	17330 AAW	MABLS	10//99-12//99
Except Sawing	Worcester PMSA, MA-CT	S	8.78 MW	8.98 AW	18270 AAW	MABLS	10//99-12//99
Except Sawing	Michigan	S	11.55 MW	12.05 AW	25050 AAW	MIBLS	10//99-12//99
Except Sawing	Benton Harbor MSA, MI	S	10.42 MW	10.97 AW	21680 AAW	MIBLS	10//99-12//99
Except Sawing	Detroit PMSA, MI	S	17.66 MW	16.36 AW	36720 AAW	MIBLS	10//99-12//99
Except Sawing	Grand Rapids-Muskegon-Holland MSA, MI	S	12.09 MW	12.06 AW	25150 AAW	MIBLS	10//99-12//99
Except Sawing	Lansing-East Lansing MSA, MI	S	10.07 MW	9.90 AW	20950 AAW	MIBLS	10//99-12//99
Except Sawing	Minnesota	S	11.3 MW	11.25 AW	23400 AAW	MNBLS	10//99-12//99
Except Sawing	Duluth-Superior MSA, MN-WI	S	14.01 MW	14.82 AW	29130 AAW	MNBLS	10//99-12//99
Except Sawing	Minneapolis-St. Paul MSA, MN-WI	S	11.85 MW	11.84 AW	24640 AAW	MNBLS	10//99-12//99
Except Sawing	St. Cloud MSA, MN	S	10.04 MW	9.65 AW	20890 AAW	MNBLS	10//99-12//99
Except Sawing	Mississippi	S	8.69 MW	8.83 AW	18360 AAW	MSBLS	10//99-12//99
Except Sawing	Biloxi-Gulfport-Pascagoula MSA, MS	S	7.61 MW	7.67 AW	15830 AAW	MSBLS	10//99-12//99
Except Sawing	Jackson MSA, MS	S	8.90 MW	8.03 AW	18510 AAW	MSBLS	10//99-12//99
Except Sawing	Missouri	S	9.35 MW	11.12 AW	23130 AAW	MOBLS	10//99-12//99
Except Sawing	Joplin MSA, MO	S	15.33 MW	18.06 AW	31880 AAW	MOBLS	10//99-12//99
Except Sawing	Kansas City MSA, MO-KS	S	14.67 MW	12.71 AW	30510 AAW	MOBLS	10//99-12//99
Except Sawing	Springfield MSA, MO	S	8.58 MW	8.58 AW	17850 AAW	MOBLS	10//99-12//99
Except Sawing	Montana	S	10.59 MW	11.22 AW	23330 AAW	MTBLS	10//99-12//99
Except Sawing	Nebraska	S	9.76 MW	10.08 AW	20960 AAW	NEBLS	10//99-12//99
Except Sawing	Nevada	S	9.79 MW	9.89 AW	20580 AAW	NVBLS	10//99-12//99
Except Sawing	Las Vegas MSA, NV-AZ	S	9.76 MW	9.63 AW	20310 AAW	NVBLS	10//99-12//99
Except Sawing	New Hampshire	S	8.81 MW	9.78 AW	20330 AAW	NHBLS	10//99-12//99
Except Sawing	New Jersey	S	11.93 MW	13.27 AW	27590 AAW	NJBLS	10//99-12//99
Except Sawing	Newark PMSA, NJ	S	13.28 MW	13.81 AW	27610 AAW	NJBLS	10//99-12//99
Except Sawing	New Mexico	S	10.35 MW	12.13 AW	25230 AAW	NMBLS	10//99-12//99
Except Sawing	New York	S	9.13 MW	9.48 AW	19710 AAW	NYBLS	10//99-12//99
Except Sawing	Albany-Schenectady-Troy MSA, NY	S	10.02 MW	10.03 AW	20840 AAW	NYBLS	10//99-12//99
Except Sawing	Buffalo-Niagara Falls MSA, NY	S	9.72 MW	9.58 AW	20210 AAW	NYBLS	10//99-12//99
Except Sawing	Jamestown MSA, NY	S	9.63 MW	9.49 AW	20040 AAW	NYBLS	10//99-12//99
Except Sawing	Nassau-Suffolk PMSA, NY	S	7.73 MW	7.03 AW	16080 AAW	NYBLS	10//99-12//99
Except Sawing	New York PMSA, NY	S	10.51 MW	9.84 AW	21870 AAW	NYBLS	10//99-12//99
Except Sawing	Rochester MSA, NY	S	9.12 MW	9.04 AW	18960 AAW	NYBLS	10//99-12//99
Except Sawing	Syracuse MSA, NY	S	9.71 MW	8.85 AW	20200 AAW	NYBLS	10//99-12//99
Except Sawing	Utica-Rome MSA, NY	S	9.27 MW	9.32 AW	19290 AAW	NYBLS	10//99-12//99
Except Sawing	North Carolina	S	9.99 MW	10.21 AW	21240 AAW	NCBLS	10//99-12//99
Except Sawing	Charlotte-Gastonia-Rock Hill MSA, NC-SC	S	9.04 MW	8.19 AW	18800 AAW	NCBLS	10//99-12//99
Except Sawing	Greensboro--Winston-Salem--High Point MSA, NC	S	10.68 MW	10.38 AW	22210 AAW	NCBLS	10//99-12//99
Except Sawing	Hickory-Morganton-Lenoir MSA, NC	S	10.68 MW	10.61 AW	22210 AAW	NCBLS	10//99-12//99
Except Sawing	Raleigh-Durham-Chapel Hill MSA, NC	S	9.55 MW	9.60 AW	19860 AAW	NCBLS	10//99-12//99
Except Sawing	Rocky Mount MSA, NC	S	8.49 MW	8.38 AW	17670 AAW	NCBLS	10//99-12//99
Except Sawing	North Dakota	S	9.43 MW	9.38 AW	19500 AAW	NDBLS	10//99-12//99
Except Sawing	Ohio	S	9.99 MW	10.41 AW	21650 AAW	OHBLS	10//99-12//99
Except Sawing	Canton-Massillon MSA, OH	S	8.21 MW	7.50 AW	17080 AAW	OHBLS	10//99-12//99
Except Sawing	Cincinnati PMSA, OH-KY-IN	S	11.12 MW	10.42 AW	23140 AAW	OHBLS	10//99-12//99
Except Sawing	Cleveland-Lorain-Elyria PMSA, OH	S	11.49 MW	10.34 AW	23890 AAW	OHBLS	10//99-12//99

AAW	Average annual wage	AOH	Average offered, high	ASH	Average starting, high	H	Hourly	M	Monthly	S	Special: hourly and annual
AE	Average entry wage	AOL	Average offered, low	ASL	Average starting, low	HI	Highest wage paid	MTC	Median total compensation	TQ	Third quartile wage
AEX	Average experienced wage	APH	Average pay, high range	AW	Average wage paid	HR	High end range	MW	Median wage paid	W	Weekly
AO	Average offered	APL	Average pay, low range	FQ	First quartile wage	LR	Low end range	SQ	Second quartile wage	Y	Yearly

Occupation/Type/Industry	Location	Per	Low	Mid	High	Source	Date
Woodworking Machine Setter, Operator, and Tender							
Except Sawing	Columbus MSA, OH	S	11.00 MW	11.01 AW	22880 AAW	OHBLS	10//99-12//99
Except Sawing	Dayton-Springfield MSA, OH	S	9.92 MW	9.77 AW	20630 AAW	OHBLS	10//99-12//99
Except Sawing	Hamilton-Middletown PMSA, OH	S	10.11 MW	10.22 AW	21040 AAW	OHBLS	10//99-12//99
Except Sawing	Lima MSA, OH	S	9.21 MW	8.87 AW	19160 AAW	OHBLS	10//99-12//99
Except Sawing	Youngstown-Warren MSA, OH	S	10.60 MW	10.36 AW	22050 AAW	OHBLS	10//99-12//99
Except Sawing	Oklahoma	S	9.25 MW	9.61 AW	19980 AAW	OKBLS	10//99-12//99
Except Sawing	Oklahoma City MSA, OK	S	9.14 MW	9.09 AW	19010 AAW	OKBLS	10//99-12//99
Except Sawing	Tulsa MSA, OK	S	10.67 MW	9.69 AW	22190 AAW	OKBLS	10//99-12//99
Except Sawing	Oregon	S	12.6 MW	12.58 AW	26170 AAW	ORBLS	10//99-12//99
Except Sawing	Corvallis MSA, OR	S	14.17 MW	13.37 AW	29470 AAW	ORBLS	10//99-12//99
Except Sawing	Eugene-Springfield MSA, OR	S	12.80 MW	12.94 AW	26630 AAW	ORBLS	10//99-12//99
Except Sawing	Medford-Ashland MSA, OR	S	11.64 MW	11.75 AW	24220 AAW	ORBLS	10//99-12//99
Except Sawing	Portland-Vancouver PMSA, OR-WA	S	12.09 MW	12.76 AW	25140 AAW	ORBLS	10//99-12//99
Except Sawing	Pennsylvania	S	10.31 MW	10.39 AW	21610 AAW	PABLS	10//99-12//99
Except Sawing	Allentown-Bethlehem-Easton MSA, PA	S	12.67 MW	12.71 AW	26350 AAW	PABLS	10//99-12//99
Except Sawing	Erie MSA, PA	S	12.53 MW	12.08 AW	26070 AAW	PABLS	10//99-12//99
Except Sawing	Harrisburg-Lebanon-Carlisle MSA, PA	S	10.26 MW	10.51 AW	21330 AAW	PABLS	10//99-12//99
Except Sawing	Lancaster MSA, PA	S	10.81 MW	11.15 AW	22490 AAW	PABLS	10//99-12//99
Except Sawing	Philadelphia PMSA, PA-NJ	S	10.33 MW	9.85 AW	21480 AAW	PABLS	10//99-12//99
Except Sawing	Pittsburgh MSA, PA	S	10.38 MW	10.04 AW	21600 AAW	PABLS	10//99-12//99
Except Sawing	Scranton--Wilkes-Barre--Hazleton MSA, PA	S	11.26 MW	11.55 AW	23430 AAW	PABLS	10//99-12//99
Except Sawing	York MSA, PA	S	10.33 MW	9.82 AW	21480 AAW	PABLS	10//99-12//99
Except Sawing	Rhode Island	S	12.43 MW	12.24 AW	25470 AAW	RIBLS	10//99-12//99
Except Sawing	Providence-Fall River-Warwick MSA, RI-MA	S	11.17 MW	11.77 AW	23240 AAW	RIBLS	10//99-12//99
Except Sawing	South Carolina	S	10 MW	10.20 AW	21220 AAW	SCBLS	10//99-12//99
Except Sawing	Columbia MSA, SC	S	10.22 MW	10.31 AW	21260 AAW	SCBLS	10//99-12//99
Except Sawing	Greenville-Spartanburg-Anderson MSA, SC	S	8.87 MW	8.50 AW	18440 AAW	SCBLS	10//99-12//99
Except Sawing	Sumter MSA, SC	S	9.49 MW	9.55 AW	19740 AAW	SCBLS	10//99-12//99
Except Sawing	South Dakota	S	9.01 MW	9.52 AW	19810 AAW	SDBLS	10//99-12//99
Except Sawing	Sioux Falls MSA, SD	S	9.77 MW	9.63 AW	20310 AAW	SDBLS	10//99-12//99
Except Sawing	Tennessee	S	9.34 MW	9.34 AW	19430 AAW	TNBLS	10//99-12//99
Except Sawing	Jackson MSA, TN	S	10.08 MW	9.60 AW	20970 AAW	TNBLS	10//99-12//99
Except Sawing	Johnson City-Kingsport-Bristol MSA, TN-VA	S	9.94 MW	9.71 AW	20680 AAW	TNBLS	10//99-12//99
Except Sawing	Knoxville MSA, TN	S	9.77 MW	9.77 AW	20330 AAW	TNBLS	10//99-12//99
Except Sawing	Memphis MSA, TN-AR-MS	S	10.42 MW	10.20 AW	21680 AAW	MSBLS	10//99-12//99
Except Sawing	Nashville MSA, TN	S	10.23 MW	9.92 AW	21270 AAW	TNBLS	10//99-12//99
Except Sawing	Texas	S	7.95 MW	8.54 AW	17770 AAW	TXBLS	10//99-12//99
Except Sawing	Austin-San Marcos MSA, TX	S	8.87 MW	8.87 AW	18440 AAW	TXBLS	10//99-12//99
Except Sawing	Beaumont-Port Arthur MSA, TX	S	7.11 MW	7.15 AW	14800 AAW	TXBLS	10//99-12//99
Except Sawing	Dallas PMSA, TX	S	9.45 MW	8.47 AW	19660 AAW	TXBLS	10//99-12//99
Except Sawing	Fort Worth-Arlington PMSA, TX	S	8.80 MW	8.81 AW	18300 AAW	TXBLS	10//99-12//99
Except Sawing	Houston PMSA, TX	S	8.62 MW	8.09 AW	17930 AAW	TXBLS	10//99-12//99
Except Sawing	Longview-Marshall MSA, TX	S	8.34 MW	8.00 AW	17340 AAW	TXBLS	10//99-12//99
Except Sawing	San Antonio MSA, TX	S	8.50 MW	7.74 AW	17670 AAW	TXBLS	10//99-12//99
Except Sawing	Utah	S	11.28 MW	11.56 AW	24050 AAW	UTBLS	10//99-12//99
Except Sawing	Salt Lake City-Ogden MSA, UT	S	11.56 MW	11.31 AW	24050 AAW	UTBLS	10//99-12//99
Except Sawing	Vermont	S	9.97 MW	10.26 AW	21350 AAW	VTBLS	10//99-12//99
Except Sawing	Virginia	S	10.08 MW	9.92 AW	20630 AAW	VABLS	10//99-12//99
Except Sawing	Lynchburg MSA, VA	S	9.14 MW	8.39 AW	19000 AAW	VABLS	10//99-12//99
Except Sawing	Norfolk-Virginia Beach-Newport News MSA, VA-NC	S	9.91 MW	9.78 AW	20610 AAW	VABLS	10//99-12//99
Except Sawing	Richmond-Petersburg MSA, VA	S	9.77 MW	9.71 AW	20320 AAW	VABLS	10//99-12//99
Except Sawing	Washington	S	10.16 MW	10.81 AW	22490 AAW	WABLS	10//99-12//99
Except Sawing	Bellingham MSA, WA	S	14.17 MW	13.89 AW	29470 AAW	WABLS	10//99-12//99
Except Sawing	Bremerton PMSA, WA	S	9.88 MW	9.70 AW	20550 AAW	WABLS	10//99-12//99
Except Sawing	Seattle-Bellevue-Everett PMSA, WA	S	9.57 MW	9.33 AW	19890 AAW	WABLS	10//99-12//99

AAW	Average annual wage	**AOH**	Average offered, high	**ASH**	Average starting, high	**H**	Hourly	**M**	Monthly	**S** Special: hourly and annual
AE	Average entry wage	**AOL**	Average offered, low	**ASL**	Average starting, low	**HI**	Highest wage paid	**MTC**	Median total compensation	**TQ** Third quartile wage
AEX	Average experienced wage	**APH**	Average pay, high range	**AW**	Average wage paid	**HR**	High end range	**MW**	Median wage paid	**W** Weekly
AO	Average offered	**APL**	Average pay, low range	**FQ**	First quartile wage	**LR**	Low end range	**SQ**	Second quartile wage	**Y** Yearly

Occupation/Type/Industry	Location	Per	Low	Mid	High	Source	Date
Woodworking Machine Setter, Operator, and Tender							
Except Sawing	Tacoma PMSA, WA	S	13.97 MW	13.73 AW	29050 AAW	WABLS	10//99-12//99
Except Sawing	West Virginia	S	9.63 MW	9.98 AW	20760 AAW	WVBLS	10//99-12//99
Except Sawing	Huntington-Ashland MSA, WV-KY-OH	S	6.12 MW	6.17 AW	12740 AAW	WVBLS	10//99-12//99
Except Sawing	Wisconsin	S	9.75 MW	9.96 AW	20720 AAW	WIBLS	10//99-12//99
Except Sawing	Appleton-Oshkosh-Neenah MSA, WI	S	9.56 MW	9.62 AW	19880 AAW	WIBLS	10//99-12//99
Except Sawing	Eau Claire MSA, WI	S	10.73 MW	9.96 AW	22310 AAW	WIBLS	10//99-12//99
Except Sawing	Green Bay MSA, WI	S	9.13 MW	9.21 AW	18980 AAW	WIBLS	10//99-12//99
Except Sawing	Madison MSA, WI	S	10.68 MW	10.31 AW	22210 AAW	WIBLS	10//99-12//99
Except Sawing	Milwaukee-Waukesha PMSA, WI	S	10.20 MW	9.79 AW	21210 AAW	WIBLS	10//99-12//99
Except Sawing	Wausau MSA, WI	S	9.67 MW	9.70 AW	20120 AAW	WIBLS	10//99-12//99
Except Sawing	Puerto Rico	S	5.95 MW	5.75 AW	11960 AAW	PRBLS	10//99-12//99
Except Sawing	San Juan-Bayamon PMSA, PR	S	5.75 MW	5.95 AW	11960 AAW	PRBLS	10//99-12//99
Word Processor and Typist	Alabama	S	9.75 MW	9.92 AW	20640 AAW	ALBLS	10//99-12//99
	Birmingham MSA, AL	S	10.59 MW	10.26 AW	22020 AAW	ALBLS	10//99-12//99
	Dothan MSA, AL	S	9.55 MW	9.41 AW	19850 AAW	ALBLS	10//99-12//99
	Florence MSA, AL	S	10.02 MW	9.77 AW	20840 AAW	ALBLS	10//99-12//99
	Huntsville MSA, AL	S	11.32 MW	11.15 AW	23550 AAW	ALBLS	10//99-12//99
	Mobile MSA, AL	S	9.74 MW	9.69 AW	20250 AAW	ALBLS	10//99-12//99
	Montgomery MSA, AL	S	9.35 MW	9.39 AW	19450 AAW	ALBLS	10//99-12//99
	Tuscaloosa MSA, AL	S	9.94 MW	9.77 AW	20680 AAW	ALBLS	10//99-12//99
	Alaska	S	12.86 MW	13.06 AW	27160 AAW	AKBLS	10//99-12//99
	Anchorage MSA, AK	S	13.07 MW	13.32 AW	27190 AAW	AKBLS	10//99-12//99
	Arizona	S	9.87 MW	10.35 AW	21530 AAW	AZBLS	10//99-12//99
	Flagstaff MSA, AZ-UT	S	9.12 MW	8.57 AW	18980 AAW	AZBLS	10//99-12//99
	Phoenix-Mesa MSA, AZ	S	10.64 MW	10.02 AW	22130 AAW	AZBLS	10//99-12//99
	Tucson MSA, AZ	S	9.56 MW	9.44 AW	19890 AAW	AZBLS	10//99-12//99
	Yuma MSA, AZ	S	9.92 MW	9.62 AW	20620 AAW	AZBLS	10//99-12//99
	Arkansas	S	8.72 MW	9.27 AW	19270 AAW	ARBLS	10//99-12//99
	Fayetteville-Springdale-Rogers MSA, AR	S	8.92 MW	8.60 AW	18560 AAW	ARBLS	10//99-12//99
	Fort Smith MSA, AR-OK	S	9.19 MW	8.37 AW	19120 AAW	ARBLS	10//99-12//99
	Little Rock-North Little Rock MSA, AR	S	10.12 MW	10.01 AW	21050 AAW	ARBLS	10//99-12//99
	California	S	12.74 MW	13.16 AW	27360 AAW	CABLS	10//99-12//99
	Bakersfield MSA, CA	S	11.53 MW	11.80 AW	23980 AAW	CABLS	10//99-12//99
	Chico-Paradise MSA, CA	S	13.23 MW	12.62 AW	27520 AAW	CABLS	10//99-12//99
	Fresno MSA, CA	S	12.66 MW	12.29 AW	26340 AAW	CABLS	10//99-12//99
	Los Angeles-Long Beach PMSA, CA	S	13.01 MW	12.56 AW	27070 AAW	CABLS	10//99-12//99
	Merced MSA, CA	S	13.43 MW	12.80 AW	27940 AAW	CABLS	10//99-12//99
	Modesto MSA, CA	S	11.82 MW	11.39 AW	24580 AAW	CABLS	10//99-12//99
	Oakland PMSA, CA	S	13.79 MW	13.31 AW	28680 AAW	CABLS	10//99-12//99
	Orange County PMSA, CA	S	13.44 MW	13.21 AW	27950 AAW	CABLS	10//99-12//99
	Redding MSA, CA	S	12.01 MW	11.78 AW	24980 AAW	CABLS	10//99-12//99
	Riverside-San Bernardino PMSA, CA	S	11.88 MW	12.02 AW	24700 AAW	CABLS	10//99-12//99
	Salinas MSA, CA	S	13.20 MW	12.96 AW	27460 AAW	CABLS	10//99-12//99
	San Diego MSA, CA	S	11.77 MW	11.75 AW	24480 AAW	CABLS	10//99-12//99
	San Francisco PMSA, CA	S	16.34 MW	15.80 AW	33990 AAW	CABLS	10//99-12//99
	San Jose PMSA, CA	S	15.99 MW	15.31 AW	33250 AAW	CABLS	10//99-12//99
	San Luis Obispo-Atascadero-Paso Robles MSA, CA	S	12.86 MW	12.96 AW	26750 AAW	CABLS	10//99-12//99
	Santa Barbara-Santa Maria-Lompoc MSA, CA	S	12.91 MW	12.63 AW	26860 AAW	CABLS	10//99-12//99
	Santa Cruz-Watsonville PMSA, CA	S	12.27 MW	12.03 AW	25520 AAW	CABLS	10//99-12//99
	Santa Rosa PMSA, CA	S	13.32 MW	13.45 AW	27710 AAW	CABLS	10//99-12//99
	Stockton-Lodi MSA, CA	S	12.84 MW	12.45 AW	26710 AAW	CABLS	10//99-12//99
	Vallejo-Fairfield-Napa PMSA, CA	S	12.80 MW	12.69 AW	26630 AAW	CABLS	10//99-12//99
	Ventura PMSA, CA	S	12.06 MW	11.84 AW	25080 AAW	CABLS	10//99-12//99
	Visalia-Tulare-Porterville MSA, CA	S	12.25 MW	12.65 AW	25470 AAW	CABLS	10//99-12//99
	Yolo PMSA, CA	S	12.05 MW	12.25 AW	25050 AAW	CABLS	10//99-12//99
	Yuba City MSA, CA	S	12.63 MW	13.09 AW	26270 AAW	CABLS	10//99-12//99
	Colorado	S	10.46 MW	10.50 AW	21850 AAW	COBLS	10//99-12//99

AAW	Average annual wage	AOH	Average offered, high	ASH	Average starting, high	H	Hourly	M	Monthly	S	Special: hourly and annual
AE	Average entry wage	AOL	Average offered, low	ASL	Average starting, low	HI	Highest wage paid	MTC	Median total compensation	TQ	Third quartile wage
AEX	Average experienced wage	APH	Average pay, high range	AW	Average wage paid	HR	High end range	MW	Median wage paid	W	Weekly
AO	Average offered	APL	Average pay, low range	FQ	First quartile wage	LR	Low end range	SQ	Second quartile wage	Y	Yearly

Word Processor and Typist

Occupation/Type/Industry	Location	Per	Low	Mid	High	Source	Date
Word Processor and Typist	Boulder-Longmont PMSA, CO	S	11.24 MW	11.33 AW	23370 AAW	COBLS	10//99-12//99
	Colorado Springs MSA, CO	S	10.03 MW	9.90 AW	20860 AAW	COBLS	10//99-12//99
	Denver PMSA, CO	S	11.44 MW	11.21 AW	23790 AAW	COBLS	10//99-12//99
	Fort Collins-Loveland MSA, CO	S	11.05 MW	11.03 AW	22980 AAW	COBLS	10//99-12//99
	Grand Junction MSA, CO	S	10.95 MW	10.69 AW	22780 AAW	COBLS	10//99-12//99
	Pueblo MSA, CO	S	8.83 MW	9.04 AW	18380 AAW	COBLS	10//99-12//99
	Connecticut	S	11.82 MW	11.95 AW	24850 AAW	CTBLS	10//99-12//99
	Bridgeport PMSA, CT	S	13.13 MW	13.30 AW	27320 AAW	CTBLS	10//99-12//99
	Danbury PMSA, CT	S	12.82 MW	12.93 AW	26670 AAW	CTBLS	10//99-12//99
	Hartford MSA, CT	S	11.23 MW	11.32 AW	23370 AAW	CTBLS	10//99-12//99
	New Haven-Meriden PMSA, CT	S	13.96 MW	14.33 AW	29040 AAW	CTBLS	10//99-12//99
	New London-Norwich MSA, CT-RI	S	8.83 MW	8.88 AW	18370 AAW	CTBLS	10//99-12//99
	Stamford-Norwalk PMSA, CT	S	14.12 MW	13.85 AW	29370 AAW	CTBLS	10//99-12//99
	Waterbury PMSA, CT	S	10.62 MW	10.38 AW	22080 AAW	CTBLS	10//99-12//99
	Delaware	S	11.15 MW	11.39 AW	23680 AAW	DEBLS	10//99-12//99
	Dover MSA, DE	S	9.89 MW	10.08 AW	20570 AAW	DEBLS	10//99-12//99
	Wilmington-Newark PMSA, DE-MD	S	12.04 MW	11.72 AW	25040 AAW	DEBLS	10//99-12//99
	District of Columbia	S	11.53 MW	12.03 AW	25030 AAW	DCBLS	10//99-12//99
	Washington PMSA, DC-MD-VA-WV	S	12.00 MW	11.32 AW	24950 AAW	DCBLS	10//99-12//99
	Florida	S	9.95 MW	10.50 AW	21830 AAW	FLBLQ	10//99-12//99
	Daytona Beach MSA, FL	S	10.01 MW	9.96 AW	20820 AAW	FLBLS	10//99-12//99
	Fort Lauderdale PMSA, FL	S	10.37 MW	9.96 AW	21580 AAW	FLBLS	10//99-12//99
	Fort Myers-Cape Coral MSA, FL	S	10.30 MW	10.18 AW	21420 AAW	FLBLS	10//99-12//99
	Fort Pierce-Port St. Lucie MSA, FL	S	9.73 MW	9.38 AW	20240 AAW	FLBLS	10//99-12//99
	Fort Walton Beach MSA, FL	S	10.13 MW	10.16 AW	21080 AAW	FLBLS	10//99-12//99
	Gainesville MSA, FL	S	10.12 MW	10.09 AW	21050 AAW	FLBLS	10//99-12//99
	Jacksonville MSA, FL	S	10.72 MW	10.22 AW	22300 AAW	FLBLS	10//99-12//99
	Lakeland-Winter Haven MSA, FL	S	8.96 MW	8.61 AW	18640 AAW	FLBLS	10//99-12//99
	Melbourne-Titusville-Palm Bay MSA, FL	S	10.87 MW	10.36 AW	22610 AAW	FLBLS	10//99-12//99
	Miami PMSA, FL	S	12.37 MW	11.33 AW	25730 AAW	FLBLS	10//99-12//99
	Naples MSA, FL	S	10.62 MW	10.44 AW	22090 AAW	FLBLS	10//99-12//99
	Ocala MSA, FL	S	9.05 MW	9.46 AW	18830 AAW	FLBLS	10//99-12//99
	Orlando MSA, FL	S	10.10 MW	9.90 AW	21010 AAW	FLBLS	10//99-12//99
	Panama City MSA, FL	S	9.16 MW	9.22 AW	19040 AAW	FLBLS	10//99-12//99
	Pensacola MSA, FL	S	9.23 MW	8.96 AW	19200 AAW	FLBLS	10//99-12//99
	Punta Gorda MSA, FL	S	9.00 MW	8.57 AW	18710 AAW	FLBLS	10//99-12//99
	Sarasota-Bradenton MSA, FL	S	9.68 MW	9.57 AW	20130 AAW	FLBLS	10//99-12//99
	Tallahassee MSA, FL	S	9.53 MW	9.51 AW	19830 AAW	FLBLS	10//99-12//99
	Tampa-St. Petersburg-Clearwater MSA, FL	S	9.90 MW	9.66 AW	20580 AAW	FLBLS	10//99-12//99
	West Palm Beach-Boca Raton MSA, FL	S	11.23 MW	10.99 AW	23350 AAW	FLBLS	10//99-12//99
	Georgia	S	11.09 MW	11.60 AW	24140 AAW	GABLS	10//99-12//99
	Albany MSA, GA	S	10.93 MW	10.80 AW	22730 AAW	GABLS	10//99-12//99
	Athens MSA, GA	S	12.29 MW	11.76 AW	25560 AAW	GABLS	10//99-12//99
	Atlanta MSA, GA	S	12.47 MW	11.88 AW	25940 AAW	GABLS	10//99-12//99
	Macon MSA, GA	S	8.77 MW	8.30 AW	18230 AAW	GABLS	10//99-12//99
	Savannah MSA, GA	S	10.58 MW	10.27 AW	22010 AAW	GABLS	10//99-12//99
	Hawaii	S	10.68 MW	10.97 AW	22820 AAW	HIBLS	10//99-12//99
	Honolulu MSA, HI	S	10.95 MW	10.71 AW	22780 AAW	HIBLS	10//99-12//99
	Idaho	S	9.97 MW	9.99 AW	20780 AAW	IDBLS	10//99-12//99
	Boise City MSA, ID	S	10.52 MW	10.10 AW	21880 AAW	IDBLS	10//99-12//99
	Illinois	S	11.26 MW	11.24 AW	23370 AAW	ILBLS	10//99-12//99
	Bloomington-Normal MSA, IL	S	10.75 MW	10.41 AW	22350 AAW	ILBLS	10//99-12//99
	Champaign-Urbana MSA, IL	S	10.54 MW	10.39 AW	21930 AAW	ILBLS	10//99-12//99
	Chicago PMSA, IL	S	11.57 MW	11.62 AW	24060 AAW	ILBLS	10//99-12//99
	Decatur MSA, IL	S	7.44 MW	6.70 AW	15480 AAW	ILBLS	10//99-12//99
	Kankakee PMSA, IL	S	8.52 MW	8.02 AW	17720 AAW	ILBLS	10//99-12//99
	Peoria-Pekin MSA, IL	S	10.68 MW	10.23 AW	22210 AAW	ILBLS	10//99-12//99
	Rockford MSA, IL	S	10.53 MW	9.98 AW	21910 AAW	ILBLS	10//99-12//99
	Springfield MSA, IL	S	10.55 MW	10.90 AW	21950 AAW	ILBLS	10//99-12//99
	Indiana	S	9.56 MW	9.87 AW	20540 AAW	INBLS	10//99-12//99
	Elkhart-Goshen MSA, IN	S	10.50 MW	10.10 AW	21840 AAW	INBLS	10//99-12//99

AAW Average annual wage	**AOH** Average offered, high	**ASH** Average starting, high	**H** Hourly	**M** Monthly	**S** Special: hourly and annual
AE Average entry wage	**AOL** Average offered, low	**ASL** Average starting, low	**HI** Highest wage paid	**MTC** Median total compensation	**TQ** Third quartile wage
AEX Average experienced wage	**APH** Average pay, high range	**AW** Average wage paid	**HR** High end range	**MW** Median wage paid	**W** Weekly
AO Average offered	**APL** Average pay, low range	**FQ** First quartile wage	**LR** Low end range	**SQ** Second quartile wage	**Y** Yearly

Occupation/Type/Industry	Location	Per	Low	Mid	High	Source	Date
Word Processor and Typist	Evansville-Henderson MSA, IN-KY	S	8.65 MW	8.64 AW	17990 AAW	INBLS	10//99-12//99
	Fort Wayne MSA, IN	S	10.67 MW	10.11 AW	22190 AAW	INBLS	10//99-12//99
	Gary PMSA, IN	S	9.34 MW	8.84 AW	19440 AAW	INBLS	10//99-12//99
	Indianapolis MSA, IN	S	10.40 MW	9.99 AW	21630 AAW	INBLS	10//99-12//99
	Lafayette MSA, IN	S	9.47 MW	8.82 AW	19700 AAW	INBLS	10//99-12//99
	Muncie MSA, IN	S	9.51 MW	9.62 AW	19780 AAW	INBLS	10//99-12//99
	South Bend MSA, IN	S	10.40 MW	10.17 AW	21630 AAW	INBLS	10//99-12//99
	Terre Haute MSA, IN	S	9.75 MW	9.39 AW	20290 AAW	INBLS	10//99-12//99
	Iowa	S	10.4 MW	10.47 AW	21780 AAW	IABLS	10//99-12//99
	Cedar Rapids MSA, IA	S	9.80 MW	9.60 AW	20380 AAW	IABLS	10//99-12//99
	Davenport-Moline-Rock Island MSA, IA-IL	S	9.84 MW	9.76 AW	20470 AAW	IABLS	10//99-12//99
	Des Moines MSA, IA	S	10.61 MW	10.49 AW	22080 AAW	IABLS	10//99-12//99
	Dubuque MSA, IA	S	10.34 MW	10.38 AW	21510 AAW	IABLS	10//99-12//99
	Sioux City MSA, IA-NE	S	11.00 MW	11.15 AW	22870 AAW	IABLS	10//99-12//99
	Waterloo-Cedar Falls MSA, IA	S	10.07 MW	10.00 AW	20950 AAW	IABLS	10//99-12//99
	Kansas	S	9.34 MW	9.74 AW	20270 AAW	KSBLS	10//99-12//99
	Lawrence MSA, KS	S	11.05 MW	10.39 AW	22990 AAW	KSBLS	10//99-12//99
	Topeka MSA, KS	S	10.93 MW	10.62 AW	22730 AAW	KSBLS	10//99-12//99
	Wichita MSA, KS	S	8.87 MW	8.40 AW	18450 AAW	KSBLS	10//99-12//99
	Kentucky	S	9.69 MW	9.83 AW	20460 AAW	KYBLS	10//99-12//99
	Lexington MSA, KY	S	9.37 MW	9.00 AW	19480 AAW	KYBLS	10//99-12//99
	Louisville MSA, KY-IN	S	10.61 MW	10.39 AW	22070 AAW	KYBLS	10//99-12//99
	Louisiana	S	8.5 MW	8.71 AW	18120 AAW	LABLS	10//99-12//99
	Alexandria MSA, LA	S	8.79 MW	8.53 AW	18270 AAW	LABLS	10//99-12//99
	Baton Rouge MSA, LA	S	9.52 MW	9.00 AW	19800 AAW	LABLS	10//99-12//99
	Houma MSA, LA	S	7.87 MW	7.27 AW	16370 AAW	LABLS	10//99-12//99
	Lafayette MSA, LA	S	9.36 MW	9.04 AW	19470 AAW	LABLS	10//99-12//99
	Lake Charles MSA, LA	S	8.16 MW	8.04 AW	16960 AAW	LABLS	10//99-12//99
	Monroe MSA, LA	S	7.33 MW	7.27 AW	15250 AAW	LABLS	10//99-12//99
	New Orleans MSA, LA	S	8.93 MW	9.03 AW	18580 AAW	LABLS	10//99-12//99
	Shreveport-Bossier City MSA, LA	S	8.90 MW	8.61 AW	18510 AAW	LABLS	10//99-12//99
	Maine	S	10.06 MW	10.16 AW	21130 AAW	MEBLS	10//99-12//99
	Bangor MSA, ME	S	10.41 MW	10.00 AW	21650 AAW	MEBLS	10//99-12//99
	Lewiston-Auburn MSA, ME	S	9.76 MW	9.67 AW	20300 AAW	MEBLS	10//99-12//99
	Portland MSA, ME	S	10.21 MW	10.12 AW	21230 AAW	MEBLS	10//99-12//99
	Maryland	S	10.48 MW	10.73 AW	22320 AAW	MDBLS	10//99-12//99
	Baltimore PMSA, MD	S	10.29 MW	10.30 AW	21400 AAW	MDBLS	10//99-12//99
	Cumberland MSA, MD-WV	S	9.95 MW	9.47 AW	20700 AAW	MDBLS	10//99-12//99
	Hagerstown PMSA, MD	S	9.51 MW	8.92 AW	19780 AAW	MDBLS	10//99-12//99
	Massachusetts	S	12.43 MW	13.05 AW	27150 AAW	MABLS	10//99-12//99
	Barnstable-Yarmouth MSA, MA	S	12.22 MW	12.51 AW	25410 AAW	MABLS	10//99-12//99
	Boston PMSA, MA-NH	S	13.41 MW	12.67 AW	27900 AAW	MABLS	10//99-12//99
	Brockton PMSA, MA	S	12.32 MW	12.00 AW	25620 AAW	MABLS	10//99-12//99
	Fitchburg-Leominster PMSA, MA	S	11.85 MW	11.38 AW	24650 AAW	MABLS	10//99-12//99
	Lawrence PMSA, MA-NH	S	11.86 MW	11.79 AW	24660 AAW	MABLS	10//99-12//99
	Lowell PMSA, MA-NH	S	13.66 MW	12.08 AW	28410 AAW	MABLS	10//99-12//99
	Pittsfield MSA, MA	S	10.54 MW	10.31 AW	21920 AAW	MABLS	10//99-12//99
	Springfield MSA, MA	S	11.79 MW	11.86 AW	24530 AAW	MABLS	10//99-12//99
	Worcester PMSA, MA-CT	S	12.22 MW	11.72 AW	25420 AAW	MABLS	10//99-12//99
	Michigan	S	11.44 MW	11.68 AW	24300 AAW	MIBLS	10//99-12//99
	Ann Arbor PMSA, MI	S	11.85 MW	11.65 AW	24640 AAW	MIBLS	10//99-12//99
	Benton Harbor MSA, MI	S	11.52 MW	11.17 AW	23970 AAW	MIBLS	10//99-12//99
	Detroit PMSA, MI	S	11.89 MW	11.58 AW	24740 AAW	MIBLS	10//99-12//99
	Flint PMSA, MI	S	11.37 MW	11.25 AW	23640 AAW	MIBLS	10//99-12//99
	Grand Rapids-Muskegon-Holland MSA, MI	S	11.77 MW	11.58 AW	24480 AAW	MIBLS	10//99-12//99
	Jackson MSA, MI	S	11.02 MW	10.80 AW	22930 AAW	MIBLS	10//99-12//99
	Kalamazoo-Battle Creek MSA, MI	S	10.97 MW	10.46 AW	22830 AAW	MIBLS	10//99-12//99
	Lansing-East Lansing MSA, MI	S	12.85 MW	13.40 AW	26720 AAW	MIBLS	10//99-12//99
	Saginaw-Bay City-Midland MSA, MI	S	11.09 MW	10.96 AW	23070 AAW	MIBLS	10//99-12//99
	Minnesota	S	11.72 MW	12.01 AW	24970 AAW	MNBLS	10//99-12//99
	Duluth-Superior MSA, MN-WI	S	10.71 MW	10.78 AW	22280 AAW	MNBLS	10//99-12//99
	Minneapolis-St. Paul MSA, MN-WI	S	12.68 MW	12.24 AW	26370 AAW	MNBLS	10//99-12//99
	Rochester MSA, MN	S	11.88 MW	11.78 AW	24710 AAW	MNBLS	10//99-12//99

AAW Average annual wage	**AOH** Average offered, high	**ASH** Average starting, high	**H** Hourly	**M** Monthly	**S** Special: hourly and annual
AE Average entry wage	**AOL** Average offered, low	**ASL** Average starting, low	**HI** Highest wage paid	**MTC** Median total compensation	**TQ** Third quartile wage
AEX Average experienced wage	**APH** Average pay, high range	**AW** Average wage paid	**HR** High end range	**MW** Median wage paid	**W** Weekly
AO Average offered	**APL** Average pay, low range	**FQ** First quartile wage	**LR** Low end range	**SQ** Second quartile wage	**Y** Yearly

Occupation/Type/Industry	Location	Per	Low	Mid	High	Source	Date
Word Processor and Typist	St. Cloud MSA, MN	S	10.56 MW	10.93 AW	21960 AAW	MNBLS	10//99-12//99
	Mississippi	S	8.47 MW	8.89 AW	18490 AAW	MSBLS	10//99-12//99
	Biloxi-Gulfport-Pascagoula MSA, MS	S	9.49 MW	9.39 AW	19740 AAW	MSBLS	10//99-12//99
	Hattiesburg MSA, MS	S	7.95 MW	7.84 AW	16540 AAW	MSBLS	10//99-12//99
	Jackson MSA, MS	S	9.26 MW	8.74 AW	19250 AAW	MSBLS	10//99-12//99
	Missouri	S	9.35 MW	9.69 AW	20160 AAW	MOBLS	10//99-12//99
	Joplin MSA, MO	S	9.08 MW	8.47 AW	18880 AAW	MOBLS	10//99-12//99
	Kansas City MSA, MO-KS	S	11.33 MW	11.13 AW	23570 AAW	MOBLS	10//99-12//99
	St. Louis MSA, MO-IL	S	10.02 MW	9.86 AW	20840 AAW	MOBLS	10//99-12//99
	Springfield MSA, MO	S	8.13 MW	7.72 AW	16910 AAW	MOBLS	10//99-12//99
	Montana	S	9.34 MW	9.68 AW	20130 AAW	MTBLS	10//99-12//99
	Billings MSA, MT	S	9.72 MW	9.60 AW	20220 AAW	MTBLS	10//99-12//99
	Great Falls MSA, MT	S	9.67 MW	9.47 AW	20100 AAW	MTBLS	10//99-12//99
	Nebraska	S	9.76 MW	9.87 AW	20530 AAW	NEBLS	10//99-12//99
	Lincoln MSA, NE	S	10.10 MW	9.61 AW	21010 AAW	NEBLS	10//99-12//99
	Omaha MSA, NE-IA	S	10.50 MW	10.49 AW	21830 AAW	NEBLS	10//99-12//99
	Nevada	S	12.36 MW	12.57 AW	26140 AAW	NVBLS	10//99-12//99
	Las Vegas MSA, NV-AZ	S	12.43 MW	12.17 AW	25850 AAW	NVBLS	10//99-12//99
	Reno MSA, NV	S	12.69 MW	12.88 AW	26380 AAW	NVBLS	10//99-12//99
	New Hampshire	S	10.77 MW	11.05 AW	22980 AAW	NHBLS	10//99-12//99
	Portsmouth-Rochester PMSA, NH-ME	S	10.99 MW	11.00 AW	22850 AAW	NHBLS	10//99-12//99
	New Jersey	S	12.03 MW	12.23 AW	25440 AAW	NJBLS	10//99-12//99
	Atlantic-Cape May PMSA, NJ	S	12.22 MW	11.77 AW	25430 AAW	NJBLS	10//99-12//99
	Bergen-Passaic PMSA, NJ	S	12.80 MW	12.82 AW	26620 AAW	NJBLS	10//99-12//99
	Jersey City PMSA, NJ	S	12.56 MW	12.50 AW	26130 AAW	NJBLS	10//99-12//99
	Middlesex-Somerset-Hunterdon PMSA, NJ	S	12.88 MW	12.00 AW	26790 AAW	NJBLS	10//99-12//99
	Monmouth-Ocean PMSA, NJ	S	11.92 MW	11.44 AW	24800 AAW	NJBLS	10//99-12//99
	Newark PMSA, NJ	S	12.08 MW	12.09 AW	25120 AAW	NJBLS	10//99-12//99
	New Mexico	S	9.29 MW	9.78 AW	20350 AAW	NMBLS	10//99-12//99
	Albuquerque MSA, NM	S	9.58 MW	8.93 AW	19930 AAW	NMBLS	10//99-12//99
	Las Cruces MSA, NM	S	9.30 MW	8.21 AW	19350 AAW	NMBLS	10//99-12//99
	Santa Fe MSA, NM	S	11.38 MW	10.87 AW	23680 AAW	NMBLS	10//99-12//99
	New York	S	12.51 MW	13.38 AW	27840 AAW	NYBLS	10//99-12//99
	Albany-Schenectady-Troy MSA, NY	S	11.93 MW	11.83 AW	24820 AAW	NYBLS	10//99-12//99
	Binghamton MSA, NY	S	10.77 MW	10.51 AW	22390 AAW	NYBLS	10//99-12//99
	Buffalo-Niagara Falls MSA, NY	S	11.14 MW	11.28 AW	23160 AAW	NYBLS	10//99-12//99
	Elmira MSA, NY	S	10.29 MW	10.15 AW	21400 AAW	NYBLS	10//99-12//99
	Glens Falls MSA, NY	S	9.39 MW	9.39 AW	19530 AAW	NYBLS	10//99-12//99
	Jamestown MSA, NY	S	11.38 MW	11.28 AW	23670 AAW	NYBLS	10//99-12//99
	Nassau-Suffolk PMSA, NY	S	14.17 MW	13.35 AW	29460 AAW	NYBLS	10//99-12//99
	New York PMSA, NY	S	14.85 MW	13.94 AW	30890 AAW	NYBLS	10//99-12//99
	Newburgh PMSA, NY-PA	S	12.16 MW	11.96 AW	25290 AAW	NYBLS	10//99-12//99
	Rochester MSA, NY	S	11.57 MW	11.31 AW	24060 AAW	NYBLS	10//99-12//99
	Syracuse MSA, NY	S	10.80 MW	11.01 AW	22470 AAW	NYBLS	10//99-12//99
	Utica-Rome MSA, NY	S	10.38 MW	10.41 AW	21590 AAW	NYBLS	10//99-12//99
	North Carolina	S	10.25 MW	10.28 AW	21380 AAW	NCBLS	10//99-12//99
	Asheville MSA, NC	S	9.92 MW	9.84 AW	20640 AAW	NCBLS	10//99-12//99
	Charlotte-Gastonia-Rock Hill MSA, NC-SC	S	11.25 MW	11.28 AW	23400 AAW	NCBLS	10//99-12//99
	Fayetteville MSA, NC	S	9.74 MW	9.79 AW	20270 AAW	NCBLS	10//99-12//99
	Greensboro--Winston-Salem--High Point MSA, NC	S	9.62 MW	9.94 AW	20010 AAW	NCBLS	10//99-12//99
	Greenville MSA, NC	S	10.53 MW	10.51 AW	21900 AAW	NCBLS	10//99-12//99
	Hickory-Morganton-Lenoir MSA, NC	S	9.56 MW	9.66 AW	19890 AAW	NCBLS	10//99-12//99
	Raleigh-Durham-Chapel Hill MSA, NC	S	11.55 MW	11.56 AW	24030 AAW	NCBLS	10//99-12//99
	Wilmington MSA, NC	S	9.64 MW	8.59 AW	20050 AAW	NCBLS	10//99-12//99
	North Dakota	S	8.65 MW	8.59 AW	17870 AAW	NDBLS	10//99-12//99
	Bismarck MSA, ND	S	8.86 MW	9.18 AW	18420 AAW	NDBLS	10//99-12//99
	Fargo-Moorhead MSA, ND-MN	S	9.82 MW	9.69 AW	20430 AAW	NDBLS	10//99-12//99
	Ohio	S	10.77 MW	10.93 AW	22730 AAW	OHBLS	10//99-12//99
	Akron PMSA, OH	S	11.02 MW	10.83 AW	22920 AAW	OHBLS	10//99-12//99
	Canton-Massillon MSA, OH	S	9.82 MW	10.04 AW	20420 AAW	OHBLS	10//99-12//99
	Cincinnati PMSA, OH-KY-IN	S	11.56 MW	11.21 AW	24040 AAW	OHBLS	10//99-12//99

Occupation/Type/Industry	Location	Per	Low	Mid	High	Source	Date
Word Processor and Typist	Cleveland-Lorain-Elyria						
	PMSA, OH	S	11.24 MW	10.67 AW	23380 AAW	OHBLS	10//99-12//99
	Columbus MSA, OH	S	11.40 MW	11.37 AW	23720 AAW	OHBLS	10//99-12//99
	Dayton-Springfield MSA, OH	S	10.00 MW	9.76 AW	20790 AAW	OHBLS	10//99-12//99
	Hamilton-Middletown PMSA,						
	OH	S	11.54 MW	11.23 AW	24010 AAW	OHBLS	10//99-12//99
	Lima MSA, OH	S	10.93 MW	10.59 AW	22740 AAW	OHBLS	10//99-12//99
	Mansfield MSA, OH	S	8.15 MW	8.14 AW	16940 AAW	OHBLS	10//99-12//99
	Steubenville-Weirton MSA,						
	OH-WV	S	8.56 MW	7.96 AW	17810 AAW	OHBLS	10//99-12//99
	Toledo MSA, OH	S	10.78 MW	10.62 AW	22420 AAW	OHBLS	10//99-12//99
	Youngstown-Warren MSA, OH	S	9.77 MW	10.02 AW	20320 AAW	OHBLS	10//99-12//99
	Oklahoma	S	9.24 MW	9.45 AW	19660 AAW	OKBLS	10//99-12//99
	Enid MSA, OK	S	7.94 MW	7.46 AW	16500 AAW	OKBLS	10//99-12//99
	Oklahoma City MSA, OK	S	9.70 MW	9.58 AW	20180 AAW	OKBLS	10//99-12//99
	Tulsa MSA, OK	S	10.15 MW	10.00 AW	21110 AAW	OKBLS	10//99-12//99
	Oregon	S	11.99 MW	12.09 AW	25150 AAW	ORBLS	10//99-12//99
	Eugene-Springfield MSA, OR	S	12.40 MW	11.86 AW	25780 AAW	ORBLS	10//99-12//99
	Medford-Ashland MSA, OR	S	11.35 MW	12.08 AW	23610 AAW	ORBLS	10//99-12//99
	Portland-Vancouver PMSA,						
	OR-WA	S	12.42 MW	12.30 AW	25820 AAW	ORBLS	10//99-12//99
	Salem PMSA, OR	S	11.99 MW	11.83 AW	24950 AAW	ORBLS	10//99-12//99
	Pennsylvania	S	11.85 MW	12.02 AW	25000 AAW	PABLS	10//99-12//99
	Allentown-Bethlehem-Easton						
	MSA, PA	S	11.51 MW	11.43 AW	23930 AAW	PABLS	10//99-12//99
	Altoona MSA, PA	S	11.10 MW	11.16 AW	23100 AAW	PABLS	10//99-12//99
	Erie MSA, PA	S	10.27 MW	10.27 AW	21350 AAW	PABLS	10//99-12//99
	Johnstown MSA, PA	S	9.42 MW	8.56 AW	19600 AAW	PABLS	10//99-12//99
	Lancaster MSA, PA	S	11.12 MW	10.77 AW	23130 AAW	PABLS	10//99-12//99
	Philadelphia PMSA, PA-NJ	S	12.30 MW	12.07 AW	25580 AAW	PABLS	10//99-12//99
	Pittsburgh MSA, PA	S	12.15 MW	12.23 AW	25270 AAW	PABLS	10//99-12//99
	Reading MSA, PA	S	10.99 MW	10.59 AW	22860 AAW	PABLS	10//99-12//99
	Scranton--Wilkes-Barre--						
	Hazleton MSA, PA	S	11.47 MW	11.36 AW	23850 AAW	PABLS	10//99-12//99
	Sharon MSA, PA	S	12.03 MW	12.06 AW	25010 AAW	PABLS	10//99-12//99
	State College MSA, PA	S	12.18 MW	11.97 AW	25330 AAW	PABLS	10//99-12//99
	York MSA, PA	S	11.55 MW	11.24 AW	24030 AAW	PABLS	10//99-12//99
	Rhode Island	S	12.69 MW	13.03 AW	27110 AAW	RIBLS	10//99-12//99
	Providence-Fall River-						
	Warwick MSA, RI-MA	S	13.06 MW	12.70 AW	27170 AAW	RIBLS	10//99-12//99
	South Carolina	S	9.77 MW	10.23 AW	21280 AAW	SCBLS	10//99-12//99
	Charleston-North Charleston						
	MSA, SC	S	9.52 MW	9.11 AW	19790 AAW	SCBLS	10//99-12//99
	Columbia MSA, SC	S	9.65 MW	9.52 AW	20070 AAW	SCBLS	10//99-12//99
	Greenville-Spartanburg-						
	Anderson MSA, SC	S	10.02 MW	9.58 AW	20840 AAW	SCBLS	10//99-12//99
	Tennessee	S	9.95 MW	10.44 AW	21710 AAW	TNBLS	10//99-12//99
	Chattanooga MSA, TN-GA	S	9.95 MW	9.71 AW	20700 AAW	TNBLS	10//99-12//99
	Clarksville-Hopkinsville MSA,						
	TN-KY	S	10.30 MW	10.23 AW	21420 AAW	TNBLS	10//99-12//99
	Jackson MSA, TN	S	9.27 MW	9.36 AW	19290 AAW	TNBLS	10//99-12//99
	Johnson City-Kingsport-Bristol						
	MSA, TN-VA	S	9.38 MW	9.47 AW	19510 AAW	TNBLS	10//99-12//99
	Knoxville MSA, TN	S	10.42 MW	10.07 AW	21670 AAW	TNBLS	10//99-12//99
	Memphis MSA, TN-AR-MS	S	10.86 MW	10.75 AW	22590 AAW	MSBLS	10//99-12//99
	Nashville MSA, TN	S	10.93 MW	9.95 AW	22740 AAW	TNBLS	10//99-12//99
	Texas	S	10.73 MW	10.90 AW	22670 AAW	TXBLS	10//99-12//99
	Amarillo MSA, TX	S	8.50 MW	7.29 AW	17680 AAW	TXBLS	10//99-12//99
	Austin-San Marcos MSA, TX	S	11.51 MW	11.18 AW	23940 AAW	TXBLS	10//99-12//99
	Beaumont-Port Arthur MSA,						
	TX	S	10.19 MW	11.07 AW	21200 AAW	TXBLS	10//99-12//99
	Brazoria PMSA, TX	S	9.13 MW	8.54 AW	18980 AAW	TXBLS	10//99-12//99
	Brownsville-Harlingen-San						
	Benito MSA, TX	S	7.48 MW	6.78 AW	15560 AAW	TXBLS	10//99-12//99
	Corpus Christi MSA, TX	S	9.26 MW	9.48 AW	19260 AAW	TXBLS	10//99-12//99
	Dallas PMSA, TX	S	12.15 MW	11.84 AW	25270 AAW	TXBLS	10//99-12//99
	El Paso MSA, TX	S	9.19 MW	9.26 AW	19110 AAW	TXBLS	10//99-12//99
	Fort Worth-Arlington PMSA,						
	TX	S	11.09 MW	10.60 AW	23070 AAW	TXBLS	10//99-12//99
	Houston PMSA, TX	S	11.86 MW	11.61 AW	24680 AAW	TXBLS	10//99-12//99
	Killeen-Temple MSA, TX	S	11.20 MW	11.36 AW	23290 AAW	TXBLS	10//99-12//99
	Laredo MSA, TX	S	8.24 MW	7.98 AW	17130 AAW	TXBLS	10//99-12//99

AAW Average annual wage	**AOH** Average offered, high	**ASH** Average starting, high	**H** Hourly	**M** Monthly	**S** Special: hourly and annual
AE Average entry wage	**AOL** Average offered, low	**ASL** Average starting, low	**HI** Highest wage paid	**MTC** Median total compensation	**TQ** Third quartile wage
AEX Average experienced wage	**APH** Average pay, high range	**AW** Average wage paid	**HR** High end range	**MW** Median wage paid	**W** Weekly
AO Average offered	**APL** Average pay, low range	**FQ** First quartile wage	**LR** Low end range	**SQ** Second quartile wage	**Y** Yearly

Occupation/Type/Industry	Location	Per	Low	Mid	High	Source	Date
Word Processor and Typist	Longview-Marshall MSA, TX	S	9.49 mw	8.99 aw	19730 aaw	TXBLS	10//99-12//99
	Lubbock MSA, TX	S	9.85 mw	10.15 aw	20490 aaw	TXBLS	10//99-12//99
	McAllen-Edinburg-Mission MSA, TX	S	9.24 mw	8.99 aw	19220 aaw	TXBLS	10//99-12//99
	Odessa-Midland MSA, TX	S	11.04 mw	9.70 aw	22960 aaw	TXBLS	10//99-12//99
	San Angelo MSA, TX	S	8.93 mw	8.36 aw	18570 aaw	TXBLS	10//99-12//99
	San Antonio MSA, TX	S	10.16 mw	10.22 aw	21130 aaw	TXBLS	10//99-12//99
	Texarkana MSA, TX-Texarkana, AR	S	9.05 mw	8.04 aw	18820 aaw	TXBLS	10//99-12//99
	Tyler MSA, TX	S	10.27 mw	10.83 aw	21360 aaw	TXBLS	10//99-12//99
	Waco MSA, TX	S	10.06 mw	9.86 aw	20920 aaw	TXBLS	10//99-12//99
	Wichita Falls MSA, TX	S	9.18 mw	9.00 aw	19090 aaw	TXBLS	10//99-12//99
	Utah	S	9.82 mw	10.15 aw	21110 aaw	UTBLS	10//99-12//99
	Salt Lake City-Ogden MSA, UT	S	10.41 mw	10.33 aw	21650 aaw	UTBLS	10//99-12//99
	Vermont	S	10.29 mw	10.52 aw	21890 aaw	VTBLS	10//99-12//99
	Burlington MSA, VT	S	11.27 mw	11.22 aw	23430 aaw	VTBLS	10//99-12//99
	Virginia	S	10.53 mw	11.11 aw	23120 aaw	VABLS	10//99-12//99
	Charlottesville MSA, VA	S	10.17 mw	10.71 aw	21150 aaw	VABLS	10//99-12//99
	Lynchburg MSA, VA	S	9.34 mw	9.49 aw	19430 aaw	VABLS	10//99-12//99
	Norfolk-Virginia Beach-Newport News MSA, VA-NC	S	10.70 mw	10.76 aw	22260 aaw	VABLS	10//99-12//99
	Richmond-Petersburg MSA, VA	S	9.97 mw	10.05 aw	20740 aaw	VABLS	10//99-12//99
	Roanoke MSA, VA	S	9.12 mw	8.46 aw	18980 aaw	VABLS	10//99-12//99
	Washington	S	12.1 mw	12.59 aw	26180 aaw	WABLS	10//99-12//99
	Bellingham MSA, WA	S	11.28 mw	11.48 aw	23470 aaw	WABLS	10//99-12//99
	Bremerton PMSA, WA	S	12.06 mw	11.83 aw	25090 aaw	WABLS	10//99-12//99
	Olympia PMSA, WA	S	11.82 mw	11.56 aw	24580 aaw	WABLS	10//99-12//99
	Richland-Kennewick-Pasco MSA, WA	S	11.10 mw	11.05 aw	23080 aaw	WABLS	10//99-12//99
	Seattle-Bellevue-Everett PMSA, WA	S	13.83 mw	13.30 aw	28770 aaw	WABLS	10//99-12//99
	Spokane MSA, WA	S	11.69 mw	11.57 aw	24310 aaw	WABLS	10//99-12//99
	Tacoma PMSA, WA	S	11.63 mw	11.61 aw	24200 aaw	WABLS	10//99-12//99
	Yakima MSA, WA	S	10.98 mw	10.77 aw	22840 aaw	WABLS	10//99-12//99
	West Virginia	S	8.3 mw	9.01 aw	18740 aaw	WVBLS	10//99-12//99
	Charleston MSA, WV	S	9.59 mw	8.78 aw	19940 aaw	WVBLS	10//99-12//99
	Huntington-Ashland MSA, WV-KY-OH	S	8.35 mw	7.78 aw	17360 aaw	WVBLS	10//99-12//99
	Parkersburg-Marietta MSA, WV-OH	S	10.85 mw	10.79 aw	22570 aaw	WVBLS	10//99-12//99
	Wheeling MSA, WV-OH	S	9.39 mw	8.52 aw	19530 aaw	WVBLS	10//99-12//99
	Wisconsin	S	11.01 mw	10.91 aw	22700 aaw	WIBLS	10//99-12//99
	Appleton-Oshkosh-Neenah MSA, WI	S	10.52 mw	10.43 aw	21870 aaw	WIBLS	10//99-12//99
	Eau Claire MSA, WI	S	9.68 mw	9.28 aw	20130 aaw	WIBLS	10//99-12//99
	Green Bay MSA, WI	S	10.27 mw	10.28 aw	21350 aaw	WIBLS	10//99-12//99
	La Crosse MSA, WI-MN	S	9.97 mw	10.43 aw	20740 aaw	WIBLS	10//99-12//99
	Madison MSA, WI	S	11.40 mw	11.20 aw	23710 aaw	WIBLS	10//99-12//99
	Milwaukee-Waukesha PMSA, WI	S	11.35 mw	11.51 aw	23600 aaw	WIBLS	10//99-12//99
	Racine PMSA, WI	S	9.20 mw	8.83 aw	19140 aaw	WIBLS	10//99-12//99
	Sheboygan MSA, WI	S	10.83 mw	11.01 aw	22530 aaw	WIBLS	10//99-12//99
	Wausau MSA, WI	S	10.48 mw	10.71 aw	21810 aaw	WIBLS	10//99-12//99
	Wyoming	S	8.28 mw	8.57 aw	17820 aaw	WYBLS	10//99-12//99
	Puerto Rico	S	6.15 mw	6.53 aw	13580 aaw	PRBLS	10//99-12//99
	Arecibo PMSA, PR	S	6.45 mw	6.15 aw	13420 aaw	PRBLS	10//99-12//99
	Caguas PMSA, PR	S	6.39 mw	6.10 aw	13290 aaw	PRBLS	10//99-12//99
	Mayaguez MSA, PR	S	6.80 mw	6.06 aw	14150 aaw	PRBLS	10//99-12//99
	Ponce MSA, PR	S	6.61 mw	6.17 aw	13750 aaw	PRBLS	10//99-12//99
	San Juan-Bayamon PMSA, PR	S	6.54 mw	6.16 aw	13600 aaw	PRBLS	10//99-12//99
	Guam	S	10.95 mw	10.73 aw	22310 aaw	GUBLS	10//99-12//99
Work and Family Manager	United States	Y		75200 aw		TRAVWK2	1999
Wrestler Professional	United States	Y		160000 aw		DENE	1999
Writer Public Relations/Communications	United States	Y		50000 aw		COMW	1999

AAW	Average annual wage	**AOH**	Average offered, high	**ASH**	Average starting, high	**H** Hourly
AE	Average entry wage	**AOL**	Average offered, low	**ASL**	Average starting, low	**HI** Highest wage paid
AEX	Average experienced wage	**APH**	Average pay, high range	**AW**	Average wage paid	**HR** High end range
AO	Average offered	**APL**	Average pay, low range	**FQ**	First quartile wage	**LR** Low end range

M	Monthly	**S**	Special: hourly and annual
MTC	Median total compensation	**TQ**	Third quartile wage
MW	Median wage paid	**W**	Weekly
SQ	Second quartile wage	**Y**	Yearly

Occupation/Type/Industry	Location	Per	Low	Mid	High	Source	Date
Writer and Author	Alabama	S	12.88 MW	14.40 AW	29950 AAW	ALBLS	10//99-12//99
	Montgomery MSA, AL	S	15.14 MW	13.29 AW	31490 AAW	ALBLS	10//99-12//99
	Alaska	S	18.05 MW	18.03 AW	37510 AAW	AKBLS	10//99-12//99
	Anchorage MSA, AK	S	20.92 MW	20.41 AW	43510 AAW	AKBLS	10//99-12//99
	Arizona	S	17.76 MW	23.93 AW	49780 AAW	AZBLS	10//99-12//99
	Flagstaff MSA, AZ-UT	S	17.52 MW	15.48 AW	36440 AAW	AZBLS	10//99-12//99
	Tucson MSA, AZ	S	18.33 MW	15.49 AW	38130 AAW	AZBLS	10//99-12//99
	Arkansas	S	12.53 MW	13.55 AW	28180 AAW	ARBLS	10//99-12//99
	Fayetteville-Springdale-Rogers MSA, AR	S	11.94 MW	12.09 AW	24830 AAW	ARBLS	10//99-12//99
	Little Rock-North Little Rock MSA, AR	S	15.23 MW	14.32 AW	31680 AAW	ARBLS	10//99-12//99
	California	S	24.19 MW	27.35 AW	56890 AAW	CABLS	10//99-12//99
	Fresno MSA, CA	S	20.12 MW	20.13 AW	41850 AAW	CABLS	10//99-12//99
	Los Angeles-Long Beach PMSA, CA	S	27.30 MW	24.29 AW	56790 AAW	CABLS	10//99-12//99
	Oakland PMSA, CA	S	38.11 MW	36.06 AW	79270 AAW	CABLS	10//99-12//99
	Orange County PMSA, CA	S	23.31 MW	20.09 AW	48490 AAW	CABLS	10//99-12//99
	Riverside-San Bernardino PMSA, CA	S	13.55 MW	11.76 AW	28190 AAW	CABLS	10//99-12//99
	San Diego MSA, CA	S	15.56 MW	12.30 AW	32360 AAW	CABLS	10//99-12//99
	San Francisco PMSA, CA	S	31.89 MW	26.56 AW	66320 AAW	CABLS	10//99-12//99
	San Jose PMSA, CA	S	20.36 MW	15.96 AW	42360 AAW	CABLS	10//99-12//99
	Santa Barbara-Santa Maria-Lompoc MSA, CA	S	34.87 MW	21.74 AW	72530 AAW	CABLS	10//99-12//99
	Stockton-Lodi MSA, CA	S	13.47 MW	8.46 AW	28020 AAW	CABLS	10//99-12//99
	Ventura PMSA, CA	S	39.53 MW	26.99 AW	82230 AAW	CABLS	10//99-12//99
	Colorado	S	19.31 MW	19.71 AW	41000 AAW	COBLS	10//99-12//99
	Boulder-Longmont PMSA, CO	S	20.48 MW	20.25 AW	42590 AAW	COBLS	10//99-12//99
	Colorado Springs MSA, CO	S	17.04 MW	17.41 AW	35440 AAW	COBLS	10//99-12//99
	Denver PMSA, CO	S	19.90 MW	19.60 AW	41390 AAW	COBLS	10//99-12//99
	Fort Collins-Loveland MSA, CO	S	20.35 MW	17.53 AW	42320 AAW	COBLS	10//99-12//99
	Connecticut	S	23.62 MW	26.40 AW	54900 AAW	CTBLS	10//99-12//99
	Hartford MSA, CT	S	24.36 MW	21.38 AW	50660 AAW	CTBLS	10//99-12//99
	Stamford-Norwalk PMSA, CT	S	27.71 MW	24.09 AW	57630 AAW	CTBLS	10//99-12//99
	Delaware	S	16.06 MW	16.82 AW	34980 AAW	DEBLS	10//99-12//99
	Wilmington-Newark PMSA, DE-MD	S	16.19 MW	15.72 AW	33680 AAW	DEBLS	10//99-12//99
	District of Columbia	S	24.15 MW	25.45 AW	52940 AAW	DCBLS	10//99-12//99
	Washington PMSA, DC-MD-VA-WV	S	27.22 MW	24.60 AW	56620 AAW	DCBLS	10//99-12//99
	Florida	S	16.25 MW	20.30 AW	42230 AAW	FLBLS	10//99-12//99
	Fort Lauderdale PMSA, FL	S	30.60 MW	19.86 AW	63640 AAW	FLBLS	10//99-12//99
	Jacksonville MSA, FL	S	14.90 MW	13.39 AW	30990 AAW	FLBLS	10//99-12//99
	Miami PMSA, FL	S	22.86 MW	21.17 AW	47550 AAW	FLBLS	10//99-12//99
	Orlando MSA, FL	S	21.83 MW	15.25 AW	45410 AAW	FLBLS	10//99-12//99
	Pensacola MSA, FL	S	9.73 MW	9.04 AW	20240 AAW	FLBLS	10//99-12//99
	Sarasota-Bradenton MSA, FL	S	18.52 MW	15.27 AW	38530 AAW	FLBLS	10//99-12//99
	Tampa-St. Petersburg-Clearwater MSA, FL	S	21.92 MW	15.74 AW	45590 AAW	FLBLS	10//99-12//99
	West Palm Beach-Boca Raton MSA, FL	S	22.34 MW	18.43 AW	46460 AAW	FLBLS	10//99-12//99
	Georgia	S	24.27 MW	25.57 AW	53180 AAW	GABLS	10//99-12//99
	Atlanta MSA, GA	S	27.17 MW	26.70 AW	56520 AAW	GABLS	10//99-12//99
	Columbus MSA, GA-AL	S	18.32 MW	19.04 AW	38100 AAW	GABLS	10//99-12//99
	Hawaii	S	14.32 MW	14.47 AW	30090 AAW	HIBLS	10//99-12//99
	Idaho	S	12.61 MW	14.50 AW	30170 AAW	IDBLS	10//99-12//99
	Illinois	S	20.19 MW	21.53 AW	44790 AAW	ILBLS	10//99-12//99
	Chicago PMSA, IL	S	22.07 MW	20.40 AW	45900 AAW	ILBLS	10//99-12//99
	Springfield MSA, IL	S	16.53 MW	16.13 AW	34380 AAW	ILBLS	10//99-12//99
	Indiana	S	15.73 MW	16.03 AW	33340 AAW	INBLS	10//99-12//99
	Indianapolis MSA, IN	S	18.24 MW	17.65 AW	37940 AAW	INBLS	10//99-12//99
	Iowa	S	13.32 MW	13.44 AW	27950 AAW	IABLS	10//99-12//99
	Cedar Rapids MSA, IA	S	15.56 MW	15.11 AW	32370 AAW	IABLS	10//99-12//99
	Davenport-Moline-Rock Island MSA, IA-IL	S	18.20 MW	17.39 AW	37860 AAW	IABLS	10//99-12//99
	Waterloo-Cedar Falls MSA, IA	S	15.03 MW	15.03 AW	31270 AAW	IABLS	10//99-12//99
	Kansas	S	7.19 MW	8.85 AW	18410 AAW	KSBLS	10//99-12//99
	Wichita MSA, KS	S	14.72 MW	12.95 AW	30620 AAW	KSBLS	10//99-12//99
	Kentucky	S	13.7 MW	14.08 AW	29300 AAW	KYBLS	10//99-12//99
	Lexington MSA, KY	S	11.96 MW	11.62 AW	24880 AAW	KYBLS	10//99-12//99

AAW	Average annual wage	AOH	Average offered, high	ASH	Average starting, high	H	Hourly
AE	Average entry wage	AOL	Average offered, low	ASL	Average starting, low	HI	Highest wage paid
AEX	Average experienced wage	APH	Average pay, high range	AW	Average wage paid	HR	High end range
AO	Average offered	APL	Average pay, low range	FQ	First quartile wage	LR	Low end range

M   Monthly
MTC Median total compensation
MW Median wage paid
SQ Second quartile wage

S   Special: hourly and annual
TQ Third quartile wage
W   Weekly
Y   Yearly

Writer and Author

Occupation/Type/Industry	Location	Per	Low	Mid	High	Source	Date
Writer and Author	Louisville MSA, KY-IN	S	16.73 MW	15.46 AW	34790 AAW	KYBLS	10//99-12//99
	Louisiana	S	10.74 MW	11.37 AW	23650 AAW	LABLS	10//99-12//99
	Baton Rouge MSA, LA	S	13.42 MW	12.36 AW	27920 AAW	LABLS	10//99-12//99
	New Orleans MSA, LA	S	11.04 MW	10.91 AW	22960 AAW	LABLS	10//99-12//99
	Shreveport-Bossier City MSA, LA	S	15.75 MW	12.06 AW	32760 AAW	LABLS	10//99-12//99
	Maine	S	17.11 MW	16.72 AW	34780 AAW	MEBLS	10//99-12//99
	Maryland	S	28.26 MW	31.08 AW	64660 AAW	MDBLS	10//99-12//99
	Baltimore PMSA, MD	S	26.51 MW	25.53 AW	55150 AAW	MDBLS	10//99-12//99
	Massachusetts	S	20.97 MW	24.72 AW	51420 AAW	MABLS	10//99-12//99
	Boston PMSA, MA-NH	S	22.96 MW	21.06 AW	47760 AAW	MABLS	10//99-12//99
	Worcester PMSA, MA-CT	S	18.72 MW	15.57 AW	38930 AAW	MABLS	10//99-12//99
	Michigan	S	18.86 MW	20.98 AW	43630 AAW	MIBLS	10//99-12//99
	Ann Arbor PMSA, MI	S	21.63 MW	21.47 AW	45000 AAW	MIBLS	10//99-12//99
	Detroit PMSA, MI	S	22.05 MW	18.96 AW	45860 AAW	MIBLS	10//99-12//99
	Grand Rapids-Muskegon-Holland MSA, MI	S	21.38 MW	19.67 AW	44460 AAW	MIBLS	10//99-12//99
	Lansing-East Lansing MSA, MI	S	17.45 MW	18.02 AW	36290 AAW	MIBLS	10//99-12//99
	Minnesota	S	22.81 MW	21.95 AW	45650 AAW	MNBLS	10//99-12//99
	Minneapolis-St. Paul MSA, MN-WI	S	22.91 MW	23.24 AW	47660 AAW	MNBLS	10//99-12//99
	St. Cloud MSA, MN	S	13.10 MW	14.70 AW	27240 AAW	MNBLS	10//99-12//99
	Mississippi	S	14.44 MW	16.05 AW	33370 AAW	MSBLS	10//99-12//99
	Jackson MSA, MS	S	17.67 MW	17.52 AW	36760 AAW	MSBLS	10//99-12//99
	Missouri	S	15.18 MW	17.11 AW	35590 AAW	MOBLS	10//99-12//99
	Kansas City MSA, MO-KS	S	12.92 MW	13.05 AW	26870 AAW	MOBLS	10//99-12//99
	St. Louis MSA, MO-IL	S	20.64 MW	20.47 AW	42920 AAW	MOBLS	10//99-12//99
	Springfield MSA, MO	S	12.10 MW	12.19 AW	25160 AAW	MOBLS	10//99-12//99
	Montana	S	13.02 MW	13.36 AW	27780 AAW	MTBLS	10//99-12//99
	Nebraska	S	15.1 MW	16.55 AW	34430 AAW	NEBLS	10//99-12//99
	Lincoln MSA, NE	S	18.38 MW	15.16 AW	38240 AAW	NEBLS	10//99-12//99
	Omaha MSA, NE-IA	S	17.73 MW	16.45 AW	36880 AAW	NEBLS	10//99-12//99
	Nevada	S	21.09 MW	28.10 AW	58440 AAW	NVBLS	10//99-12//99
	New Hampshire	S	13.24 MW	16.14 AW	33570 AAW	NHBLS	10//99-12//99
	Portsmouth-Rochester PMSA, NH-ME	S	24.05 MW	24.38 AW	50030 AAW	NHBLS	10//99-12//99
	New Jersey	S	20.61 MW	23.36 AW	48600 AAW	NJBLS	10//99-12//99
	Atlantic-Cape May PMSA, NJ	S	17.46 MW	15.55 AW	36320 AAW	NJBLS	10//99-12//99
	Bergen-Passaic PMSA, NJ	S	25.46 MW	28.54 AW	52950 AAW	NJBLS	10//99-12//99
	Jersey City PMSA, NJ	S	25.77 MW	22.66 AW	53610 AAW	NJBLS	10//99-12//99
	Monmouth-Ocean PMSA, NJ	S	24.00 MW	20.65 AW	49930 AAW	NJBLS	10//99-12//99
	Newark PMSA, NJ	S	20.70 MW	19.19 AW	43050 AAW	NJBLS	10//99-12//99
	Trenton PMSA, NJ	S	18.12 MW	15.75 AW	37690 AAW	NJBLS	10//99-12//99
	New Mexico	S	15.56 MW	16.15 AW	33600 AAW	NMBLS	10//99-12//99
	Albuquerque MSA, NM	S	15.89 MW	15.57 AW	33060 AAW	NMBLS	10//99-12//99
	New York	S	20.23 MW	23.57 AW	49030 AAW	NYBLS	10//99-12//99
	Albany-Schenectady-Troy MSA, NY	S	23.64 MW	24.70 AW	49170 AAW	NYBLS	10//99-12//99
	Buffalo-Niagara Falls MSA, NY	S	11.95 MW	10.27 AW	24860 AAW	NYBLS	10//99-12//99
	Nassau-Suffolk PMSA, NY	S	19.62 MW	16.04 AW	40820 AAW	NYBLS	10//99-12//99
	New York PMSA, NY	S	24.32 MW	20.74 AW	50590 AAW	NYBLS	10//99-12//99
	Syracuse MSA, NY	S	18.27 MW	17.93 AW	38000 AAW	NYBLS	10//99-12//99
	North Carolina	S	15.21 MW	18.70 AW	38890 AAW	NCBLS	10//99-12//99
	Charlotte-Gastonia-Rock Hill MSA, NC-SC	S	19.55 MW	16.10 AW	40650 AAW	NCBLS	10//99-12//99
	Greensboro--Winston-Salem--High Point MSA, NC	S	22.84 MW	23.47 AW	47510 AAW	NCBLS	10//99-12//99
	North Dakota	S	19 MW	18.86 AW	39230 AAW	NDBLS	10//99-12//99
	Fargo-Moorhead MSA, ND-MN	S	19.11 MW	19.29 AW	39760 AAW	NDBLS	10//99-12//99
	Ohio	S	17.28 MW	17.84 AW	37100 AAW	OHBLS	10//99-12//99
	Cincinnati PMSA, OH-KY-IN	S	20.68 MW	19.54 AW	43020 AAW	OHBLS	10//99-12//99
	Cleveland-Lorain-Elyria PMSA, OH	S	17.06 MW	16.40 AW	35480 AAW	OHBLS	10//99-12//99
	Columbus MSA, OH	S	17.51 MW	16.14 AW	36420 AAW	OHBLS	10//99-12//99
	Dayton-Springfield MSA, OH	S	22.91 MW	20.42 AW	47650 AAW	OHBLS,	10//99-12//99
	Oklahoma	S	17.57 MW	16.88 AW	35120 AAW	OKBLS	10//99-12//99
	Oklahoma City MSA, OK	S	20.00 MW	19.20 AW	41610 AAW	OKBLS	10//99-12//99
	Tulsa MSA, OK	S	15.10 MW	15.59 AW	31400 AAW	OKBLS	10//99-12//99
	Oregon	S	14.66 MW	15.56 AW	32370 AAW	ORBLS	10//99-12//99
	Medford-Ashland MSA, OR	S	19.50 MW	18.86 AW	40570 AAW	ORBLS	10//99-12//99

AAW Average annual wage	**AOH** Average offered, high	**ASH** Average starting, high	**H** Hourly	**M** Monthly	**S** Special: hourly and annual
AE Average entry wage	**AOL** Average offered, low	**ASL** Average starting, low	**HI** Highest wage paid	**MTC** Median total compensation	**TQ** Third quartile wage
AEX Average experienced wage	**APH** Average pay, high range	**AW** Average wage paid	**HR** High end range	**MW** Median wage paid	**W** Weekly
AO Average offered	**APL** Average pay, low range	**FQ** First quartile wage	**LR** Low end range	**SQ** Second quartile wage	**Y** Yearly

Occupation/Type/Industry	Location	Per	Low	Mid	High	Source	Date
Writer and Author	Portland-Vancouver PMSA, OR-WA	S	15.85 MW	14.33 AW	32960 AAW	ORBLS	10//99-12//99
	Pennsylvania	S	16.38 MW	18.22 AW	37910 AAW	PABLS	10//99-12//99
	Allentown-Bethlehem-Easton MSA, PA	S	14.30 MW	9.82 AW	29740 AAW	PABLS	10//99-12//99
	Harrisburg-Lebanon-Carlisle MSA, PA	S	22.04 MW	22.28 AW	45840 AAW	PABLS	10//99-12//99
	Philadelphia PMSA, PA-NJ	S	22.74 MW	22.65 AW	47290 AAW	PABLS	10//99-12//99
	Pittsburgh MSA, PA	S	20.33 MW	15.50 AW	42280 AAW	PABLS	10//99-12//99
	Rhode Island	S	15.77 MW	17.11 AW	35600 AAW	RIBLS	10//99-12//99
	Providence-Fall River-Warwick MSA, RI-MA	S	17.69 MW	17.78 AW	36790 AAW	RIBLS	10//99-12//99
	South Carolina	S	23.26 MW	21.26 AW	44220 AAW	SCBLS	10//99-12//99
	Greenville-Spartanburg-Anderson MSA, SC	S	17.92 MW	15.29 AW	37270 AAW	SCBLS	10//99-12//99
	South Dakota	S	12.42 MW	12.72 AW	26450 AAW	SDBLS	10//99-12//99
	Sioux Falls MSA, SD	S	12.60 MW	12.56 AW	26220 AAW	SDBLS	10//99-12//99
	Tennessee	S	14.57 MW	15.34 AW	31900 AAW	TNBLS	10//99-12//99
	Chattanooga MSA, TN-GA	S	13.51 MW	10.13 AW	28090 AAW	TNBLS	10//99-12//99
	Memphis MSA, TN-AR-MS	S	16.09 MW	15.55 AW	33460 AAW	MSBLS	10//99-12//99
	Nashville MSA, TN	S	16.13 MW	13.10 AW	33550 AAW	TNBLS	10//99-12//99
	Texas	S	16.52 MW	18.15 AW	37760 AAW	TXBLS	10//99-12//99
	Austin-San Marcos MSA, TX	S	17.56 MW	14.14 AW	36530 AAW	TXBLS	10//99-12//99
	Bryan-College Station MSA, TX	S	16.50 MW	16.40 AW	34320 AAW	TXBLS	10//99-12//99
	Dallas PMSA, TX	S	19.88 MW	18.88 AW	41340 AAW	TXBLS	10//99-12//99
	Fort Worth-Arlington PMSA, TX	S	19.38 MW	16.40 AW	40300 AAW	TXBLS	10//99-12//99
	Houston PMSA, TX	S	18.06 MW	16.15 AW	37570 AAW	TXBLS	10//99-12//99
	San Antonio MSA, TX	S	23.76 MW	20.90 AW	49420 AAW	TXBLS	10//99-12//99
	Utah	S	9.69 MW	12.36 AW	25710 AAW	UTBLS	10//99-12//99
	Vermont	S	14.58 MW	15.39 AW	32010 AAW	VTBLS	10//99-12//99
	Burlington MSA, VT	S	13.58 MW	12.47 AW	28240 AAW	VTBLS	10//99-12//99
	Virginia	S	20.41 MW	20.41 AW	42440 AAW	VABLS	10//99-12//99
	Norfolk-Virginia Beach-Newport News MSA, VA-NC	S	16.32 MW	17.48 AW	33940 AAW	VABLS	10//99-12//99
	Richmond-Petersburg MSA, VA	S	20.78 MW	19.51 AW	43230 AAW	VABLS	10//99-12//99
	Washington	S	19.36 MW	20.02 AW	41650 AAW	WABLS	10//99-12//99
	Seattle-Bellevue-Everett PMSA, WA	S	20.60 MW	20.00 AW	42840 AAW	WABLS	10//99-12//99
	West Virginia	S	13.15 MW	16.54 AW	34410 AAW	WVBLS	10//99-12//99
	Wisconsin	S	15.05 MW	16.93 AW	35220 AAW	WIBLS	10//99-12//99
	Appleton-Oshkosh-Neenah MSA, WI	S	17.40 MW	17.17 AW	36190 AAW	WIBLS	10//99-12//99
	Eau Claire MSA, WI	S	10.52 MW	8.99 AW	21890 AAW	WIBLS	10//99-12//99
	Green Bay MSA, WI	S	12.17 MW	12.06 AW	25300 AAW	WIBLS	10//99-12//99
	Madison MSA, WI	S	22.86 MW	16.21 AW	47550 AAW	WIBLS	10//99-12//99
	Milwaukee-Waukesha PMSA, WI	S	16.29 MW	15.72 AW	33880 AAW	WIBLS	10//99-12//99
	Puerto Rico	S	19 MW	20.65 AW	42940 AAW	PRBLS	10//99-12//99
	San Juan-Bayamon PMSA, PR	S	20.82 MW	19.31 AW	43310 AAW	PRBLS	10//99-12//99
Zoo Worker Cage Cleaning	United States	Y		15950 AW		MENHEL	1999
Zoologist and Wildlife Biologist	Alabama	S	21.33 MW	22.91 AW	47660 AAW	ALBLS	10//99-12//99
	Alaska	S	19.78 MW	19.79 AW	41160 AAW	AKBLS	10//99-12//99
	Arizona	S	17.2 MW	17.94 AW	37310 AAW	AZBLS	10//99-12//99
	Arkansas	S	19.51 MW	19.66 AW	40890 AAW	ARBLS	10//99-12//99
	California	S	21.04 MW	21.43 AW	44570 AAW	CABLS	10//99-12//99
	Colorado	S	23.6 MW	24.07 AW	50060 AAW	COBLS	10//99-12//99
	Florida	S	17.74 MW	18.36 AW	38190 AAW	FLBLS	10//99-12//99
	Georgia	S	21.34 MW	22.01 AW	45780 AAW	GABLS	10//99-12//99
	Hawaii	S	19.79 MW	20.59 AW	42830 AAW	HIBLS	10//99-12//99
	Idaho	S	19.61 MW	19.78 AW	41140 AAW	IDBLS	10//99-12//99
	Illinois	S	27.26 MW	26.37 AW	54840 AAW	ILBLS	10//99-12//99
	Indiana	S	19.8 MW	21.36 AW	44420 AAW	INBLS	10//99-12//99
	Iowa	S	14.74 MW	17.42 AW	36230 AAW	IABLS	10//99-12//99
	Kentucky	S	18.89 MW	19.17 AW	39870 AAW	KYBLS	10//99-12//99
	Louisiana	S	23.37 MW	22.95 AW	47730 AAW	LABLS	10//99-12//99
	Massachusetts	S	21.41 MW	22.79 AW	47400 AAW	MABLS	10//99-12//99

AAW	Average annual wage	AOH	Average offered, high	ASH	Average starting, high	H	Hourly	M	Monthly	S	Special: hourly and annual
AE	Average entry wage	AOL	Average offered, low	ASL	Average starting, low	HI	Highest wage paid	MTC	Median total compensation	TQ	Third quartile wage
AEX	Average experienced wage	APH	Average pay, high range	AW	Average wage paid	HR	High end range	MW	Median wage paid	W	Weekly
AO	Average offered	APL	Average pay, low range	FQ	First quartile wage	LR	Low end range	SQ	Second quartile wage	Y	Yearly

Occupation/Type/Industry	Location	Per	Low	Mid	High	Source	Date
Zoologist and Wildlife Biologist	Michigan	S	24.59 MW	24.84 AW	51660 AAW	MIBLS	10//99-12//99
	Minnesota	S	23.49 MW	24.19 AW	50310 AAW	MNBLS	10//99-12//99
	Mississippi	S	19.86 MW	21.49 AW	44700 AAW	MSBLS	10//99-12//99
	Montana	S	19.19 MW	19.87 AW	41340 AAW	MTBLS	10//99-12//99
	New Hampshire	S	21.07 MW	22.67 AW	47140 AAW	NHBLS	10//99-12//99
	New Jersey	S	28.59 MW	27.14 AW	56440 AAW	NJBLS	10//99-12//99
	New Mexico	S	21.49 MW	21.38 AW	44470 AAW	NMBLS	10//99-12//99
	North Carolina	S	20.69 MW	21.99 AW	45740 AAW	NCBLS	10//99-12//99
	Ohio	S	15.38 MW	16.54 AW	34410 AAW	OHBLS	10//99-12//99
	Oregon	S	21.4 MW	22.40 AW	46600 AAW	ORBLS	10//99-12//99
	Pennsylvania	S	23.53 MW	23.89 AW	49700 AAW	PABLS	10//99-12//99
	South Carolina	S	21.18 MW	22.45 AW	46690 AAW	SCBLS	10//99-12//99
	South Dakota	S	18.32 MW	18.82 AW	39140 AAW	SDBLS	10//99-12//99
	Tennessee	S	12.08 MW	13.00 AW	27040 AAW	TNBLS	10//99-12//99
	Texas	S	21.47 MW	22.47 AW	46740 AAW	TXBLS	10//99-12//99
	Utah	S	19.34 MW	20.31 AW	42250 AAW	UTBLS	10//99-12//99
	Virginia	S	21.97 MW	23.43 AW	48740 AAW	VABLS	10//99-12//99
	Washington	S	23.18 MW	23.75 AW	49400 AAW	WABLS	10//99-12//99
	Wisconsin	S	18.5 MW	17.80 AW	37030 AAW	WIBLS	10//99-12//99
	Wyoming	S	23.2 MW	23.38 AW	48620 AAW	WYBLS	10//99-12//99

Appendix I

SOURCES

AC&C

"1999 Salary Survey," *American City & County*, August 1999, pp. SS3-SS10.

Survey Period: 1999

Note: Data are from a survey of information services directors conducted on behalf of *American City & County* by Intertec Marketing Research. Surveys were mailed to 468 information systems directors; a 25 percent return rate was achieved.

AC&C2

"Water/Wastewater Superintendents," *American City & County*, August 1999.

Survey Period: 1999

Note: Data are from a 1999 survey of water/wastewater superintendents. Data were provided by 267 individuals. The survey was conducted by Intertec Marketing Research.

ADAGE1

Craig Endicott, "Salaries Expected to Grow 6%" *Advertising Age*, December 4, 2000, p. S4.

Survey Period: 2000

Note: Data are from the Ninth Annual Advertising Age Salary Survey.

ADAW

"Salary survey offers look at range of community-based titles," *Alcoholism & Drug Abuse Weekly*, May 8, 2000, p. 5.

Survey Period: 2000

Note: Information for salaries shown is from the 2000 Behavioral Health *Salary Survey*.

AKBLS

1999 Occupational Employment and Wage Estimates, 1999.

Alaska Department of Labor
Research and Analysis
P.O. Box 25501
Juneau, AK 99802-5501
Telephone: (907) 465-4500
Online: http://www.labor.state.ak.us
Survey Period: October 1999 - December 1999

Note: All data are provided by the State Employment Security Administration to the Occupational Employment Statistics (OES) survey conducted by the U.S. Department of Labor, Bureau of Labor Statistics.

ALA

Mary Jo Lynch, "Librarians' Salaries Up 4.3%, Reflecting National Mean," *American Libraries*, October 2000, p. 62.

Survey Period: 2000

Note: Data are from the American Library Association 2000 salary survey.

ALBLS

1999 Occupational Employment and Wage Estimates, 1999.

Alabama Department of Industrial Relations
Labor Market Information
649 Monroe St., Room 422
Montgomery, AL 36130
Telephone: (334) 242-8800
Online: http://www.dir.state.al.us/lmi
Survey Period: October 1999 - December 1999

Note: All data are provided by the State Employment Security Administration to the Occupational Employment Statistics (OES) survey conducted by the U.S. Department of Labor, Bureau of Labor Statistics.

AMJOUR

Chris Tuohey, "The Olbermann Factor," *American Journalism Review*, May 1999, p. 42.

Survey Period: October 1998 - December 1998

Note: Data are from a survey conducted by RNTDA/Ball State University. Data were compiled from valid responses received from 793 television stations.

AMSHIP

"Logistics salaries on a roll," *American Shipper*, May 2000, p. 74.

Survey Period: 1999

Note: Data quoted from the *1999 Logistics and Supply Chain Management Compensation Survey*, William M. Mercer Inc.

ARBLS

1999 Occupational Employment and Wage Estimates, 1999.

Arkansas Employment Security Department
Labor Market Information
P.O. Box 2981
Little Rock, AR 72203-2981
Telephone: (501) 682-3159
Online: http://www.state.ar.us/esd
Survey Period: October 1999 - December 1999

Note: All data are provided by the State Employment Security Administration to the Occupational Employment Statistics (OES) survey conducted by the U.S. Department of Labor, Bureau of Labor Statistics.

AS&U

Joe Agron, "Getting Their Due," *American School & University*, January 1999, pp. 28-34.

Survey Period: 1999 - 2000

Note: Data are from AS&U's *14th Compensation Survey*. The survey was mailed to the nation's K-12 public school districts. Usable returns were received from 12 percent of respondents.

AS&U2

Joe Agron, "Small Rewards," *American School & University*, January 2000, p. 32.

Survey Period: 1999 - 2000

Note: Data are from AS&U's *14th Compensation Survey*. The survey was mailed 1,000 chief business officials at 4-year colleges and to 1,000 chief business officials at 2-year institutions.

ASMA

Tracy Casteuble, "Market Forces Push Up," *Association Management*, April 1999, p. 30.

Survey Period: 1998

Note: Data are from the 11th edition of Association Executive Compensation and Benefits Survey (AECBS). AECBS is an element of the American Society of Association Executives (ASAE).

ASSEMB

Austin Weber, "Trapped in a Time Warp," *2000 Assembly*, July 2000, p. 13.

Survey Period: 2000

Note: Data are from a 2000 salary survey of professionals in assembly operations in manufacturing, including engineers and managers.

ATBUS

Tonya Layman, "Salary Hikes Slowing, But Techies in Demand," *Atlanta Business Chronicle*, June 16, 2000, p. 37C.

Survey Period: 1999

Note: Data are from Matrix Resources.

ATJOCO

Clint Williams, "Costly Cobb home prices, income at odds for many," *The Atlanta Journal-Constitution*, April 1, 2000, p. H1.

Survey Period: 1998

Note: Data shown are from a 1998 survey by the Cobb Chamber of Commerce.

AVWEEK

Edward Phillips, "Mechanic Shortage Raises Growth, Safety Concerns," *Aviation Week & Space Technology*, April 17, 2000, p. 83.

Survey Period: 2000

AVWEEK2

"Despite Consolidation, Aerospace Offers Attractive Employment Opportunities and Salaries," *Aviation Week & Space Technology*, February 9, 1999, p. S3.

Survey Period: 1998

Note: Data are from the *Aviation Week*/ORC Careers Survey. The survey covers more than 700 aerospace or aerospace-related companies across the country.

AWHONN

"Nursing Faculty Salaries on the Increase," *AWHONN Lifelines*, August/September 1999, p. 17.

Survey Period: 1998 - 1999

Note: Data were compiled by the American Association of Colleges of Nursing.

AZBLS

1999 Occupational Employment and Wage Estimates, 1999.

Arizona Department of Economic Security
Research Administration
P.O. Box 6123, Site Code 733A
Phoenix, AZ 85005
Telephone: (602) 542-3871
Online: http://www.de.state.az.us/links/economic/
webpage/page6.html
Survey Period: October 1999 - December 1999

Note: All data are provided by the State Employment Security Administration to the Occupational Employment Statistics (OES) survey conducted by the U.S. Department of Labor, Bureau of Labor Statistics.

BEVW

Hank Behar, "Getting the pay you deserve," *Beverage World*, October 2000, p. 78.

Survey Period: 1999

Note: Data are from the *Beverage World* salary survey.

BICRET

"Bike Retail vs. McDonald's," *Bicycle Retailer*, June 1, 2000, p. 1.

Survey Period: 2000

Note: Data were compiled in interviews by *Bicycle Retailer* or obtained from McDonald's restaurants in selected states.

BJTAMP

Gary Shepherd, "Health Care Workers Paid Premium Wages," *Business Journal: Serving Greater Tampa Bay*, May 2, 2000, p. 4.

Survey Period: 2000

Note: Data from Report 2000, a salary survey, conducted by the Florida Hospital Association, covering 148,000 workers.

BOBBIN

"Average Annual CAD Salaries by Job Title," *Bobbin*, January 2000, p. 11.

Survey Period: 1999

Note: Data collected by FabriCAD as part of its 1999 CAD Salary and Job Satisfaction Survey. The survey covers computer-aided design professionals active in the apparel business.

BOM

"Average Pay For Facility Executives Jumps 18% In The Last Four Years," *Building Operating Management*, April 1999, p. 14.

Survey Period: 1999

Note: Data are based on the International Facility Management Association's 1998 Salary Survey.

BOSBU1

Chris Mahoney, "Study: Law Associates' Pay Up by Nearly 30 Percent," *Boston Business Journal*, September 8, 2000, p. 20.

Survey Period: 2000

Note: Data from National Association for Law Placement.

BOSBU2

Keath Regan, "As lawyers' pay skyrockets, support staff see modest gains," *Boston Business Journal*, June 30, 2000, p. 35.

Survey Period: 2000

Note: Data are from the the 2000 salary survey of the National Association of Legal Assistants. Values are "total compensation," including bonus and/or overtime.

BUS1BUF

Joe Iannarelli, "Rural charm, work force are keys to Wyoming County strategy," *Business First of Buffalo*, June 19, 2000, p. 38.

Survey Period: 2000

Note: Data based on a study conducted by PF Resources for the Wyoming County Chamber of Commerce.

BUS1COL

Jeff Bell, "Leagl salaries rising to compete with large firms, tech companies," *Business First-Columbus*, June 16, 2000, p. 7A.

Survey Period: 2000

Note: Data from National Association for Law Placement.

BUSI2

Jim Clark, "The Equity Equation," *Business 2.0*, March 2000, p. 171.

Survey Period: 2000

Note: Data obtained from "2000 Internet Industry Compensation & Benefits Survey Report."

BW

Emily Thornton and Heather Timmons, "The Street's Punishing Pay Stubs," *Business Week*, November 20, 2000, p. 154.

Survey Period: 2000

Note: Data are from Johnson Associates Inc.

C&EN1

Michael Heylin, "ChemCensus 2000," *C&EN*, August 14, 2000, p. 46.

Survey Period: 2000

Note: Data were collected as part of the American Chemical Society's "Salaries 2000" survey. A full copy of the study is available for $150 by writing to ACS, Office of Society Services, 115 - 16th Street N.W., Washington, DC 20036.

C&EN2

Michael Heylin, "No Big Changes in Pay or Jobs for Chemistry Graduates," *C&EN*, March 13, 2000, p. 13.

Survey Period: 1999

Note: Data are from the American Chemical Society's starting salary survey.

CAAPN

"Survey: Industry Wages Outstrip Old Assumptions," *California Apparel News*, March 11, 1999, p. 12.

Survey Period: 1998

Note: Data were collected by the Manufacturing Networks Initiative.

CABLS

1999 Occupational Employment and Wage Estimates, 1999.

California Employment Development Department
Labor Market Information Division
P.O. Box 826880, MIC 57
Sacramento, CA 94280-0001
Telephone: (916) 262-2160
Online: http://www.calmis.cahwnet.gov
Survey Period: October 1999 - December 1999

Note: All data are provided by the State Employment Security Administration to the Occupational Employment Statistics (OES) survey conducted by the U.S. Department of Labor, Bureau of Labor Statistics.

CARWO1

"Shortcut to a great job: The associate degree," *Career World*, January 2000, p. 2.

Survey Period: 2000

Note: Source for the data shown is American Association Community Colleges Hot Programs Survey.

CARWO2

"Entry level salaries depend on location," *Career World*, January 2000, p. 2.

Survey Period: September 1999

Note: Source of data is the National Association of Colleges and Employers Salary Survey.

CCA

Julie Crawshaw, "Critical Care Compensation: Will it Continue to Rise?" *Critical Care Alert*, October 2000, p. 81.

Survey Period: 1999

Note: Data are from a 2000 study by the American Medical Group Association (AMGA).

CHW1

"Salaries Increase For Continuing Care CEOs," *Catholic Health World*, July 15, 1999, p. 2.

Survey Period: October 1997 - October 1998

Note: Data are from the first American Association of Homes and Services for the Aging (AAHSA) Assisted Living Salary and Benefits Report.

CHW1

"Median Salaries For Nursing Home Administrators Rise Again," *Catholic Health World*, November 1, 1998, p. 2.

Survey Period: October 1997 - October 1998

Note: Data are from the first American Association of Homes and Services for the Aging (AAHSA) Assisted Living Salary and Benefits Report.

CHW1

"Survey Reports Median Salaries for Assisted Living Administrators," *Catholic Health World*, April 15, 1999, p. 2.

Survey Period: October 1997 - October 1998

Note: Data are from the first American Association of Homes and Services for the Aging (AAHSA) Assisted Living Salary and Benefits Report.

CIVENG

"Civils' Starting Pay Is Lowest Of Engineering Disciplines," *Civil Engineering*, March 2000, p. 25.

Survey Period: 1999

Note: Data obtained from Jobtrac.com.

CJR

Anne Colamosca, "Pay For Journalists Is Going Up," *Columbia Journalism Review*, July/August 1999, pp. 24-28.

Survey Period: 1999

Note: Data were obtained by interviews.

COBLS

1999 Occupational Employment and Wage Estimates, 1999.

Colorado Department of Labor and Employment
Labor Market Information
1515 Arapahoe St., Tower 2, Suite 400
Denver, CO 80202-2117
Telephone: (303) 620-4977
Online: http://lmi.cdle.state.co.us
Survey Period: October 1999 - December 1999

Note: All data are provided by the State Employment Security Administration to the Occupational Employment Statistics (OES) survey conducted by the U.S. Department of Labor, Bureau of Labor Statistics.

COLBIZ

Eliza Castaneda, "Sterling silver," *Coloradobiz*, April 2000, p. 64.

Survey Period: 2000

Note: Data were obtained from Starkey International Institute for Household Management.

COMW

"Profile 2000," *Communications World*, August-September 2000, p. A3.

Survey Period: 1999

Note: Data are from a 1999 study conducted by the International Association of Business Communicators (IABC) and the Public Relations Society of America (PRSA).

COMWO

Steve Alexander, "No Cure in Sight," *Computerworld*, March 29, 1999, p. 56.

Survey Period: January 1999 - February 1999

Note: *Computerworld* 1998 Annual Hiring Survey and IT Hiring Managers Survey. The IT Hiring Managers Survey included 537 individuals.

CONTR

Rob Heslebarth, "1999 Management Salary and Benefits Survey," *Contractor*, July 1999, p. 1.

Survey Period: 1998

Note: Data are from Kahner's Research and *Contractor* magazine.

CORES

Eric Hausman, "Exec, Employee Pay: The Numbers Are Numbing," *Computer Reseller News*, May 22, 2000, p. 48.

Survey Period: 1999

Note: Data were collected as part of *Computer Reseller News*'s annual survey of 130 publicly held companies in the Spring of 2000.

CORES2

"Research Insights," *Computer Reseller News*, May 8, 2000, p. 19.

Survey Period: 1998

Note: Data are from the *Computer Reseller News* 2000 Salary Survey.

CORES3

John Roberts and Scott Campbell, "New Economy Means New Rules," *Computer Reseller News*, May 22, 2000, p. 47.

Survey Period: 2000

Note: Data are from the *2000 CRN Salary Survey. CRN* interviewed 1,014 individuals working for "solution providers," computer consulting and service firms with average revenues of $10-15 million.

CORES4

John Robers and Mike Cruz, "Certification Makes Big Difference in Pay," *Computer Reseller News*, May 22, 2000, p. 57.

Survey Period: 2000

Note: Data are from the *2000 CRN Salary Survey. CRN* interviewed 562 technical people for this portion of its survey.

COUSE

Molly W. Joss, "Write your own job ticket." *Computer User*, November 2000, p. 77.

Survey Period: 2000

CRCLEV

Gayle Horowith, "Teachers, schools trying to resolve budget disputes," *Crain's Cleveland Business*, July 17, 2000, p. 3.

Survey Period: 2000

Note: Information cited is from the Ohio Department of Education.

CRDET

Jeffrey Kosseff, "Webmaster Salaries," *Crain's Detroit Business*, January 17, 2000, p. 12.

Survey Period: 1999

Note: Data reported are from Economic Research Institute Inc.

CSM1

"Where white-collar, entry-level jobs are," *The Christian Science Monitor*, August 14, 2000, p. 12.

Survey Period: 2000

Note: Data supplied by Jobtrac.com.

CTBLS

1999 Occupational Employment and Wage Estimates, 1999.

Connecticut Labor Department
Office of Research and Information
200 Folly Brook Blvd
Wethersfield, CT 06109-1114
Telephone: (860) 263-6255
Online: http://www.ctdol.state.ct.us/lmi/index.htm
Survey Period: October 1999 - December 1999

Note: All data are provided by the State Employment Security Administration to the Occupational Employment Statistics (OES) survey conducted by the U.S. Department of Labor, Bureau of Labor Statistics.

DANCE

Linda Hamilton, "Studying? Hedge Your Bets," *Dance Magazine*, December 2000, p. 74.

Survey Period: 2000

DCBLS

1999 Occupational Employment and Wage Estimates, 1999.

District of Columbia Department of Employment Services
Labor Market Information
500 C St. NW., Room 201
Washington, DC 20001
Telephone: (202) 724-7214
Survey Period: October 1999 - December 1999

Note: All data are provided by the State Employment Security Administration to the Occupational Employment Statistics (OES) survey conducted by the U.S. Department of Labor, Bureau of Labor Statistics.

DEBLS

1999 Occupational Employment and Wage Estimates, 1999.

Delaware Department of Labor
Labor Market Information
4425 N. Market St
Wilmington, DE 19802
Telephone: (302) 761-8060
Online: http://www.oolmi.net
Survey Period: October 1999 - December 1999

Note: All data are provided by the State Employment Security Administration to the Occupational Employment Statistics (OES) survey conducted by the U.S. Department of Labor, Bureau of Labor Statistics.

DENBUS

Lyn Berry, "IT workers in demand, attracting larger salaries," *Denver Business Journal*, August 25, 2000, p. 4A.

Survey Period: 2000

Note: Data shown were gathered by Hewitt Associates LLC, an Illinois-based global management consulting firm, as part of its 2000 U.S. Hot Technologies Survey. The survey obtained information from 215 large companies representing 38,465 information technology (IT) employees.

DENE

Benjamin Ames, "We're in the money," *Design News*, July 3, 2000, p. 60.

Survey Period: 2000

Note: Data are from *Occupational Outlook Handbook, 2000-01*. Information on professional wrestler is from the March 22, 1999 issue of *Forbes* magazine.

DHMAN

Rhonda Plourd, "A guide for employee pay," *Dairy Herd Management*, June 2000, p. 76.

Survey Period: 1999

Note: Data based on a 1999 Cornell University study focused on 93 members of the Northeast Dairy Producers Association.

DRTOP

Carol Ukens, "The Big Lure," *Drug Topics*, March 15, 1999, p. 4.

Survey Period: 1998

Note: Data are from the magazine's salary survey of retail pharmacists.

DVMNEW

James Furman, "Demand for DVMs in agriculture still strong," *DVM Newsmagazine*, March 2000, p. 3F.

Survey Period: 1997

Note: Data supplied by the American Veterinary Medical Association.

ELBUY

Corinne Bernstein, "Refashioning supply-chain management's role," *Electronic Buyer's News*, October 2, 2000, p. E4.

Survey Period: 2000

Note: Data are from the publication's annual Salary and Opinion Survey.

ELENTI

Terry Costlow, "Fresh Strategy for Reeling in the New Hires: Internships," *Electronic Engineering Times*, May 22, 2000, p. 186.

Survey Period: 2000

Note: Data are from National Association of Colleges and Employers.

ENR1

"The Dilemma of Good Times: More Work, Fewer Workers," *ENR*, October 30, 2000, pp. 14-16.

Survey Period: 2000

Note: Data are from the Construction Labor Research Council and show average hourly union compensation, including fringe benefits.

ENR2

"Contractor Executive Salaries Soar as Demand Reaches Frenzy," *ENR*, January 24, 2000, p. 19.

Survey Period: 1999

Note: Data based on a survey of 300 contracting organizations conducted by PAS Inc.

ENR3

"Labor: Costs May Be Hidden in Hiring," *ENR*, June 26, 2000, p. 96.

Survey Period: 2000

Note: Data were developed by PAS Inc.

ENT1

Joseph McKendrick, "ENT's 2000 Salary Survey," *ENT*, August 16, 2000, pp. 14-18.

Survey Period: 2000

Note: Data are from a salary survey conducted by *ENT*.

ERDGE

"1998-99 San Diego Salary Survey for Health-Care Professionals," , October 14, 1998, pp. 1-2.

The Eastridge Group
Survey Period: 1998

Note: Data are from a survey of Medical Resources Staffing, a division of The Eastridge Group.

FAJO

Dan Anderson, "Requiem For The Hired Man?" *Farm Journal*, March 1999, p. 47.

Survey Period: 1998

Note: Data are from a 1998 survey conducted by AgriCareers.

FLBLS

1999 Occupational Employment and Wage Estimates, 1999.

Florida Department of Labor and Employment Security
Bureau of Labor Market and Performance Information
2012 Capitol Circle SE Hartman Bldg., Suite 200
Tallahassee, FL 32399-2151
Telephone: (850) 488-1048
Online: http://lmi.floridajobs.org$
Survey Period: October 1999 - December 1999

Note: All data are provided by the State Employment Security Administration to the Occupational Employment Statistics (OES) survey conducted by the U.S. Department of Labor, Bureau of Labor Statistics.

FOLIO

Debra Judge Silber, "Summing Up Salaries," *Folio*, November 2000, p. 11.

Survey Period: 2000

Note: Data are from the magazine's annual salary survey.

FOODT

Neil H. Mermelstein, "1999 IFT Membership Employment & Salary Survey," *Food Technology*, April 2000, p. 75.

Survey Period: November 1999

Note: Data are based on a questionnaire mailed to members of the Institute of Food Technology in the United states in November 1999. The total sample was 19,348, of which 4,950 individuals returned responses.

FWST

L. Lamor Williams, "Officials see cuts if tax cap rejected," *Fort Worth Star-Telegram*, December 31, 2000, p. 1.

Survey Period: 2000

Note: Data are from the school districts cited.

GABLS

1999 Occupational Employment and Wage Estimates, 1999.

> Georgia Department of Labor
> Labor Market Information
> 148 International Boulevard NE
> Atlanta, GA 30303-1751
> **Telephone:** (404) 656-3177
> **Online:** http://www.dol.state.ga.us/lmi
> **Survey Period:** October 1999 - December 1999

Note: All data are provided by the State Employment Security Administration to the Occupational Employment Statistics (OES) survey conducted by the U.S. Department of Labor, Bureau of Labor Statistics.

GUBLS

1999 Occupational Employment and Wage Estimates, 1999.

> Department of Labor
> Guam Employment Services
> P.O. Box 9970
> Tamuning, Guam 96931
> **Telephone:** (671) 475-0111
> **Online:** http://gu.jobsearch.org
> **Survey Period:** October 1999 - December 1999

Note: All data are provided by the State Employment Security Administration to the Occupational Employment Statistics (OES) survey conducted by the U.S. Department of Labor, Bureau of Labor Statistics.

HEMAT

Betsy Hersher, "At the Millennium, How Happy are CIOs?" *Health Management Technology*, December 1999, p. 11.

Survey Period: 1999

Note: Data are from *The Year 2000 CIO Job Satisfaction and Benefits Survey* conducted by Jersher Associates, Ltd. Data were collected in September and October 1999 and covered 212 chief information officers in the health sector.

HFM

"Healthcare CFO Compensation: Salaries Grow, but Gains Unequal," *Healthcare Financial Management*, August 1999, pp. 61-63.

Survey Period: 1999

Note: Data are from a survey conducted by the magazine.

HFM2

"Jingle all the way?" *Health Facilities Management*, December 1998, p. 18.

Survey Period: 1998

Note: Data are from a survey by Hay Management Consultants sponsored by the American Society for Health Care Human Resource Administration. The survey covered 1,214 health care organizations in 1998.

HFM3

"Executives at Teaching Hospitals Highest Paid," *Healthcare Financial Management*, August 2000, p. 23.

Survey Period: 1999

Note: Data are from a study by Witt/Kieffer conducted in 1999.

HHN

Gordon W. Hawthorne and C. I. Bolster, "10th Annual Compensation & Salary Guide," *H&HN*, September 2000, p. 40.

Survey Period: 2000

Note: Data are from the 2000 Hay Hospital Compensation Survey.

HIBLS

1999 Occupational Employment and Wage Estimates, 1999.

Hawaii Department of Labor and Industrial Relations
Research and Statistics Office
830 Punchbowl St., Room 304
Honolulu, HI 96813
Telephone: (808) 586-8999
Online: http://dlir.state.hi.us
Survey Period: October 1999 - December 1999

Note: All data are provided by the State Employment Security Administration to the Occupational Employment Statistics (OES) survey conducted by the U.S. Department of Labor, Bureau of Labor Statistics.

HOTEL

Keith Kefgen and Rosemary Mahoney-Browning, "Hotel Management Salaries on the Rise," *Hotel Online*, November 1998, p. 3.

Survey Period: 1998

Note: Data are from the 1998 HCE Hospitality Compensation Exchange survey.

HRMAG

Mark Avery, "HR Pay Levels Continue to Grow," *HR Magazine*, October 1999, pp. 71-73.

Survey Period: 1999

Note: Data are taken from the annual SHRM/William M. Mercer Inc. compensation survey for 1999.

IABLS

1999 Occupational Employment and Wage Estimates, 1999.

Iowa Workforce Development
Research and Information Services
1000 East Grand Ave
Des Moines, IA 50319-0209
Telephone: (515) 281-6647
Online: http://www.state.ia.us/iwd
Survey Period: October 1999 - December 1999

Note: All data are provided by the State Employment Security Administration to the Occupational Employment Statistics (OES) survey conducted by the U.S. Department of Labor, Bureau of Labor Statistics.

IDBLS

1999 Occupational Employment and Wage Estimates, 1999.

Idaho Department of Labor
Bureau of Research and Analysis
317 Main St
Boise, ID 83735-0001
Telephone: (208) 334-6170
Online: http://www.sde.state.id.us/cis
Survey Period: October 1999 - December 1999

Note: All data are provided by the State Employment Security Administration to the Occupational Employment Statistics (OES) survey conducted by the U.S. Department of Labor, Bureau of Labor Statistics.

IIES

Steven Langer, "An IE's Worth," *IIES Solutions*, February 1999, p. 32.

Survey Period: 1998

Note: Data are from a 1998 income survey by the Institute of Industrial Engineers.

IIESOL

Erin O'Briant, "IIE's 2000 salary survey reveals steadily growing salaries," *IIE Solutions*, October 2000, p. 26.

Survey Period: 2000

Note: Data are based on a survey of members of the Institute of Industrial Engineers.

ILBLS

1999 Occupational Employment and Wage Estimates, 1999.

Illinois Department of Employment Security
Economic Information and Analysis
401 South State St., Suite 743
Chicago, IL 60605
Telephone: (312) 793-2316
Online: http://lmi.ides.state.il.us
Survey Period: October 1999 - December 1999

Note: All data are provided by the State Employment Security Administration to the Occupational Employment Statistics (OES) survey conducted by the U.S. Department of Labor, Bureau of Labor Statistics.

INBLS

1999 Occupational Employment and Wage Estimates, 1999.

Indiana Department of Workforce Development
Labor Market Information
Indiana Government Center, South , E211 10 North
Senate Ave
Indianapolis, IN 46204-2277
Telephone: (317) 232-7460
Online: http://www.dwd.state.in.us
Survey Period: October 1999 - December 1999

Note: All data are provided by the State Employment Security Administration to the Occupational Employment Statistics (OES) survey conducted by the U.S. Department of Labor, Bureau of Labor Statistics.

INFOWD

Loretta W. Prencipe, "Industry Outlook: Real estate," *InfoWorld*, August 7, 2000, p. 87.

Survey Period: 2000

Note: Data presented were drawn from the U.S. Bureau of Labor Statistics, National Association of Realtors, and the 2000 InfoWorld Compensation Survey.

INFOWD2

Jim Battey, "Job Titles: Help desk manager," *InfoWorld*, July 3, 2000, p. 61.

Survey Period: 2000

Note: Data are from the Information Technology Association of America.

INTECH

Gregory Hale, "Engineers see hike in incomes," *InTech*, August 2000, p. 59.

Survey Period: 2000

Note: Data are from the 2000 Income and Salary Survey conducted by the National Society of Professional Engineers (NSPE).

INVNEWS

Sarah O'Brian, "Planners average $$$ix-figure pay," *Investment News*, September 11, 2000, p. 1.

JEMS

Ty Mayfield, "Wages & benefits continue to decline," *JEMS*, May 1999, p. 46.

Survey Period: 1998

Note: Data are from the *JEMS* 1998 Salary Survey.

JOM

Tammy Beazley, "U.S. Engineering Salaries Remain Constant in 1999," *JOM - Journal of the Minerals, Metals, and Materials Society*, April 2000, p. 10.

Survey Period: January 1999

Note: Data from *Engineers' Salaries: Special Report 1999*, Engineering Workforce Commission of the American Association of Engineering Societies. Results reflect the base salaries of 45,377 engineers as of January 1999.

JOM2

Tammy Beazley, "Educators Lead Increases in 1998 U.S. Engineering Salaries," *JOM - Journal of the Minerals, Metals, and Materials Society*, March 1999, p. 10.

Survey Period: 1998

Note: Data are from *Salaries of Engineers in Education 1998*, a survey conducted by the Engineering Workforce Commission of the American Association of Engineering Societies and from *Engineers Salaries: Special Industry Report 1998* from the same source.

KCSTAR

Su Bacon, "Dependable school bus drivers in demand: Job ideal for those who like children, want split shifts," *Kansas City Star*, November 5, 2000, p. D2.

Survey Period: 2000

Note: Data from North Kansas City School District Transportation Department.

KRTBN

Knight-Ridder/Tribune Business News, October 9, 2000.

Survey Period: 2000

Note: Data based on an interview with Jane Williams, a Dallas-based writer who prepared a guide on pharmaceutical sales.

KSBLS

1999 Occupational Employment and Wage Estimates, 1999.

Kansas Department of Human Resources
401 SW Topeka Blvd
Topeka, KS 66603-3182
Telephone: (785) 296-5058
Online: http://entkdhr.ink.org/cgi-dir/newjob.cgi
Survey Period: October 1999 - December 1999

Note: All data are provided by the State Employment Security Administration to the Occupational Employment Statistics (OES) survey conducted by the U.S. Department of Labor, Bureau of Labor Statistics.

KYBLS

1999 Occupational Employment and Wage Estimates, 1999.

Kentucky Department of Employment Services
Division of Administration/Financial Management
275 East Main St., Suite 2-C
Frankfort, KY 40621
Telephone: (502) 564-7976
Online: http://www.des.state.ky.us/agencies/wforce/des/lmi/lmi.htm
Survey Period: October 1999 - December 1999

Note: All data are provided by the State Employment Security Administration to the Occupational Employment Statistics (OES) survey conducted by the U.S. Department of Labor, Bureau of Labor Statistics.

LABJ

Howard Fine, "Many L.A. Salaries See Hefty Boost," *Los Angeles Business Journal*, September 6, 1999, pp. 1-2.

Survey Period: 1999

Note: Data reported were supplied by Economic Research Institute.

LABLS

1999 Occupational Employment and Wage Estimates, 1999.

Louisiana Department of Labor
Research and Statistics Division
P.O. Box 94094, Baton Rouge, LA 70804-9094
Telephone: (225) 342-3140
Online: http://www.ldol.state.la.us/LMIQM.asp
Survey Period: October 1999 - December 1999

Note: All data are provided by the State Employment Security Administration to the Occupational Employment Statistics (OES) survey conducted by the U.S. Department of Labor, Bureau of Labor Statistics.

LABMED

Mary Koenn and Jean Holter, "Salaries Increase for Medical Technology and Clinical Laboratory Science Faculty," *Laboratory Medicine*, March 2000, p. 153.

Survey Period: 1999

Note: Data are based on a 1999 faculty-compensation survey.

LABMED2

Barbara M. Castleberry and Laurie L. Wargelin, "1998 Wage and Vacancy Survey of Medical Laboratories," *Laboratory Medicine*, March 1999, p. 176.

Survey Period: 1998

Note: Data are from a survey conducted by the Board of Registry of the American Society of Clinical Pathologists.

LOUMAG

Mary Alan Woodward, "Who is making what," *Louisville Magazine*, May 2000, p. 32.

Survey Period: 1999 - 2000

Note: Date based on the publication's own research using a variety of sources, including telephone calls.

MABLS

1999 Occupational Employment and Wage Estimates, 1999.

> Massachusetts Division of Employment and Training
> Labor Market Information and Research
> 19 Staniford St., 5th Floor
> Boston, MA 02114
> **Telephone:** (617) 626-6560
> **Online:** http://www.detma.org/lmiinfo.htm
> **Survey Period:** October 1999 - December 1999

Note: All data are provided by the State Employment Security Administration to the Occupational Employment Statistics (OES) survey conducted by the U.S. Department of Labor, Bureau of Labor Statistics.

MATMAN

Allen Jones, "Pay Day Bliss," *Materials Management & Distribution*, October 1999, p. 28.

> **Survey Period:** 1999

Note: Data are from the 12th annual Salary Survey conduted by *Materials Management & Distribution*.

MATPER

Jeff Littleton, "1999 U.S. Corrosion Career Survey," *Materials Performance*, January 2000, p. 17.

> **Survey Period:** 2000

Note: Data are from the magazine's survey of professionals in the corrosion specialization.

MDBLS

1999 Occupational Employment and Wage Estimates, 1999.

> Maryland Department of Labor
> Office of Labor Market Analysis and Information
> 1100 North Eutaw St., Room 601
> Baltimore, MD 21201
> **Telephone:** (410) 767-2250
> **Online:** http://www.dllr.state.md.us/lmi/index.htm
> **Survey Period:** October 1999 - December 1999

Note: All data are provided by the State Employment Security Administration to the Occupational Employment Statistics (OES) survey conducted by the U.S. Department of Labor, Bureau of Labor Statistics.

MEBLS

1999 Occupational Employment and Wage Estimates, 1999.

> Maine Department of Labor
> Labor Market Information Services
> 20 Union St
> Augusta, ME 04330
> **Telephone:** (207) 287-2271
> **Online:** http://www.state.me.us/labor/lmis/frdef.htm
> **Survey Period:** October 1999 - December 1999

Note: All data are provided by the State Employment Security Administration to the Occupational Employment Statistics (OES) survey conducted by the U.S. Department of Labor, Bureau of Labor Statistics.

MEDEC

"The purse strings won't be any looser this year," *Medical Economics*, April 10, 2000, p. 40.

> **Survey Period:** 2000

Note: Data are from *The Health Care Group Staff Salary Syrvey, Year 2000*. Figures are for individuals with 2 to 5 years of experience.

MEDEC1

"Clerical workers are getting much more expensive," *Medical Economics*, December 20, 1999, p. 3.

Survey Period: 1999

MEDEC2

"Specialists find the warmest welcome in years," *Medical Economics*, December 6, 1999, p. 36.

Survey Period: 1998 - 1999

Note: Data represent average salaries offered and are from Merrit, Hawkins Associates, a national physician recruiting firm.

MEDEC3

Anita J. Slomski, "How much are groups paying their doctors?" *Medical Economics*, January 10, 2000, p. 120.

Survey Period: 1998

Note: Data are from the Medical Group Management Association's annual survey of 1,609 group practices.

MENHEL

Brian Good, "Good Job?" *Men's Health*, September 1999, p. 83.

Survey Period: 1999

MIBLS

1999 Occupational Employment and Wage Estimates, 1999.

Michigan Jobs Commission, Employment Service Agency
Office of Labor Market Information
7310 Woodward Ave., Room 520
Detroit, MI 48202
Telephone: (313) 872-5904
Online: http://www.michlmi.org
Survey Period: October 1999 - December 1999

Note: All data are provided by the State Employment Security Administration to the Occupational Employment Statistics (OES) survey conducted by the U.S. Department of Labor, Bureau of Labor Statistics.

MLTC

"Administrators' pay jumps to $68,940," *McKnight's Long-Term Care News*, December 14, 1999, p. 32.

Survey Period: 1999

Note: Data are from the ninth annual *McKinght's Long-Term Care News* salary survey.

MNBLS

1999 Occupational Employment and Wage Estimates, 1999.

Minnesota Department of Economic Security
BLS Programs, Research and Statistical Office
390 North Robert St
St. Paul, MN 55104
Telephone: (612) 296-4087
Online: http://www.des.state.mn.us/lmi/careers
Survey Period: October 1999 - December 1999

Note: All data are provided by the State Employment Security Administration to the Occupational Employment Statistics (OES) survey conducted by the U.S. Department of Labor, Bureau of Labor Statistics.

MOBLS

1999 Occupational Employment and Wage Estimates, 1999.

Missouri Department of Labor and Industrial Relations
Research and Analysis 421 East Dunkin St
P.O. Box 59
Jefferson City, MO 65104-0059
Telephone: (573) 751-3637
Online: http://www.works.state.mo.us/lmi
Survey Period: October 1999 - December 1999

Note: All data are provided by the State Employment Security Administration to the Occupational Employment Statistics (OES) survey conducted by the U.S. Department of Labor, Bureau of Labor Statistics.

MODCAS

"Foundry Salaries Increased 2.6% in '99," *Modern Casting*, October 2000, p. 56.

Survey Period: 1999

Note: Data are from the American Foundry Society 2000 Confidential Salary Survey.

MODHE

J. Duncan Moore Jr., "Holding the line (for you down there)," *Modern Healthcare*, July 12, 1999, p. 43.

Survey Period: 1999

Note: Data are from surveys returned by 219 health care organizations; the sample included 417 hospitals.

MSBLS

1999 Occupational Employment and Wage Estimates, 1999.

Mississippi Employment Security Commission
Labor Market Information
P.O. Box 1699
Jackson, MS 39215-1699
Telephone: (601) 961-7424
Online: http://208.137.131.31/lmi/index.html
Survey Period: October 1999 - December 1999

Note: All data are provided by the State Employment Security Administration to the Occupational Employment Statistics (OES) survey conducted by the U.S. Department of Labor, Bureau of Labor Statistics.

MTBLS

1999 Occupational Employment and Wage Estimates, 1999.

Montana Department of Labor and Industry
Office of Research and Analysis
P.O. Box 1728
Helena, MT 59624-1728
Telephone: (406) 444-2430
Online: http://rad.dli.state.mt.us
Survey Period: October 1999 - December 1999

Note: All data are provided by the State Employment Security Administration to the Occupational Employment Statistics (OES) survey conducted by the U.S. Department of Labor, Bureau of Labor Statistics.

NATCAT

Teresa Malcolm, "Nation," *National Catholic Reporter*, October 27, 2000, p. 6.

Survey Period: March 2000

Note: Data are from the National Association of Catholic School Teachers.

NCBLS

1999 Occupational Employment and Wage Estimates, 1999.

North Carolina Employment Security Commission
Labor Market Information
P.O. Box 25903
Raleigh, NC 27611
Telephone: (919) 733-2936
Online: http://www.esc.state.nc.us
Survey Period: October 1999 - December 1999

Note: All data are provided by the State Employment Security Administration to the Occupational Employment Statistics (OES) survey conducted by the U.S. Department of Labor, Bureau of Labor Statistics.

NCS98

"National Compensation Survey: Occupational Wages in the United States, 1998, , December 1999.

U.S. Department of Labor
Bureau of Labor Statistics
2 Massachusetts Ave, N.E.
Washington, DC 20212
Telephone: (202) 691-6199
Online: OCLTINFO@bls.gov
Survey Period: 1998

NDBLS

1999 Occupational Employment and Wage Estimates, 1999.

North Dakota Job Service
Program Support
1000 East Divide Ave P.O. Box 5507
Bismarck, ND 58506-5507
Telephone: (701) 328-2868
Online: http://www.state.nd.us/jsnd/lmi.htm
Survey Period: October 1999 - December 1999

Note: All data are provided by the State Employment Security Administration to the Occupational Employment Statistics (OES) survey conducted by the U.S. Department of Labor, Bureau of Labor Statistics.

NEBLS

1999 Occupational Employment and Wage Estimates, 1999.

Nebraska Department of Labor
Labor Market Information
550 South 16th St
Lincoln, NE 68509-4600
Telephone: (402) 471-9964
Online: http://www.dol.state.ne.us/nelmi.htm
Survey Period: October 1999 - December 1999

Note: All data are provided by the State Employment Security Administration to the Occupational Employment Statistics (OES) survey conducted by the U.S. Department of Labor, Bureau of Labor Statistics.

NEMED

"Who's Top Rung," *newmedia.com*, May 1999, p. 18.

Survey Period: 1999

Note: Data provided by 1999 Association of Internet Professionals, Compensation and Benefits Survey.

NHBLS

1999 Occupational Employment and Wage Estimates, 1999.

New Hampshire Department of Employment Security
Economic and Labor Market Information Bureau
32 South Main St
Concord, NH 03301
Telephone: (603) 228-4123
Online: http://www.nhworks.state.nh.us/lmipage.htm
Survey Period: October 1999 - December 1999

Note: All data are provided by the State Employment Security Administration to the Occupational Employment Statistics (OES) survey conducted by the U.S. Department of Labor, Bureau of Labor Statistics.

NJBLS

1999 Occupational Employment and Wage Estimates, 1999.

New Jersey Department of Labor
Labor Planning and Analysis
P.O. Box 56, 5th Floor
Trenton, NJ 08625-0056
Telephone: (609) 292-2643
Online: http://www.state.nj.us/labor/lra/
Survey Period: October 1999 - December 1999

Note: All data are provided by the State Employment Security Administration to the Occupational Employment Statistics (OES) survey conducted by the U.S. Department of Labor, Bureau of Labor Statistics.

NMBLS

1999 Occupational Employment and Wage Estimates, 1999.

New Mexico Department of Labor
Economic Research and Analysis Bureau
401 Broadway Blvd. NE P.O. Box 1928
Albuquerque, NM 87103
Telephone: (505) 841-8645
Online: http://www3.state.nm.us/dol/dol_lmif.html
Survey Period: October 1999 - December 1999

Note: All data are provided by the State Employment Security Administration to the Occupational Employment Statistics (OES) survey conducted by the U.S. Department of Labor, Bureau of Labor Statistics.

NUR2

Cheryl Mee and Katherine Carey, "Nursing2000 salary survey," *Nursing2000*, April 2000, p. 58.

Survey Period: October 1999

Note: Data are from a survey conducted by the publication.

NURMAN

Melissa Fitzpatrick, Cheryl Mee, and Theresa Steltzer, "$alary Survey 2000," *Nursing Management*, August 2000, p. 31.

Survey Period: 2000

Note: Data are from the publication's 2nd Annual Nurse Manager/Executive Salary Survey. 1,200 individuals responded.

NURMAN2

"Exclusive Nurse Manager/Executive Salary Review," *Nursing Management*, July 1999, p. 21.

Survey Period: April 1999 - May 1999

Note: Data are from a survey conducted by *Nursing Management* based on a mailing to 800 readers and a posting on the magazine's web site.

NURMAN3

"Finders, Keepers," *Nursing Management*, August 1999, p. 34.

Survey Period: 1998

Note: Data supplied by Allied Consulting, Inc.

NV&A

"Summer 1999 AS/400 Managers Salary Survey," November 1, 1999.

Nate Viall & Associates
Survey Period: 1999

NVBLS

1999 Occupational Employment and Wage Estimates, 1999.

Department of Employment and Training
Information Development and Processing Division
500 East Third St
Carson City, NV 89713-0001
Telephone: (775) 687-4550
Online: http://www.state.nv.us/detr/lmi/index.htm
Survey Period: October 1999 - December 1999

Note: All data are provided by the State Employment Security Administration to the Occupational Employment Statistics (OES) survey conducted by the U.S. Department of Labor, Bureau of Labor Statistics.

NYBLS

1999 Occupational Employment and Wage Estimates, 1999.

New York Department of Labor
Division of Research and Statistics
State Office Building Campus, Room 400
Albany, NY 12240
Telephone: (518) 457-6369
Online: http://www.labor.state.ny.us/html/atool/lmiatool.htm
Survey Period: October 1999 - December 1999

Note: All data are provided by the State Employment Security Administration to the Occupational Employment Statistics (OES) survey conducted by the U.S. Department of Labor, Bureau of Labor Statistics.

NYT1

"Funeral Business's New Look," *The New York Times*, November 10, 2000, p. C7.

Survey Period: 2000

Note: Data supplied by the National Funeral Directors Association.

OHBLS

1999 Occupational Employment and Wage Estimates, 1999.

Labor Market Information Division, 145 South Front St
Ohio Bureau of Employment Services
P.O. Box 1618
Columbus, OH 43216-1618
Telephone: (614) 752-9494
Online: http://lmi.state.oh.us
Survey Period: October 1999 - December 1999

Note: All data are provided by the State Employment Security Administration to the Occupational Employment Statistics (OES) survey conducted by the U.S. Department of Labor, Bureau of Labor Statistics.

OILL

"Current Salary Results," *Oil-Link*, June 16, 1999, p. 1.

Survey Period: May 28, 1998 - September 3, 1998

Note: Data are from an on-line survey.

OKBLS

1999 Occupational Employment and Wage Estimates, 1999.

Oklahoma Employment Security Commission
Labor Market Information
2401 North Lincoln Will Rogers Memorial Office Bldg
Oklahoma City, OK 73105
Telephone: (405) 525-7265
Online: http://www.oesc.state.ok.us/lmi/default.htm
Survey Period: October 1999 - December 1999

Note: All data are provided by the State Employment Security Administration to the Occupational Employment Statistics (OES) survey conducted by the U.S. Department of Labor, Bureau of Labor Statistics.

ORBLS

1999 Occupational Employment and Wage Estimates, 1999.

Oregon Employment Department
Labor Market Information
875 Union St. NE
Salem, OR 97311
Telephone: (503) 947-1212
Online: http://olmis.emp.state.or.us
Survey Period: October 1999 - December 1999

Note: All data are provided by the State Employment Security Administration to the Occupational Employment Statistics (OES) survey conducted by the U.S. Department of Labor, Bureau of Labor Statistics.

ORMAN

"ORs are busy, but salary gains remain modest," *OR Manager*, October 1999, p. 11.

Survey Period: 1999

Note: Data are from *OR Manager*'s ninth annual salary/career survey of hospitals and ambulatory surgery centers.

ORMAN2

"In ASCs, two thirds earn raises," *OR Manager*, October 1999, p. 27.

Survey Period: 1999

Note: Data are from the ninth annual salary/career survey conducted by *OR Manager*. The survey polled 234 ambulatory surgery center managers; 33 percent of those contacted responded.

PABLS

1999 Occupational Employment and Wage Estimates, 1999.

Pennsylvania Department of Labor and Industry
Bureau of Research and Statistics
7th and Forester Streets, Room 101
Harrisburg, PA 17120-0001
Telephone: (717) 787-3266
Online: http://www.lmi.state.pa.us
Survey Period: October 1999 - December 1999

Note: All data are provided by the State Employment Security Administration to the Occupational Employment Statistics (OES) survey conducted by the U.S. Department of Labor, Bureau of Labor Statistics.

PBJI

Phoenix Business Journal, November 10, 2000.

Survey Period: 2000

Note: Data based on a survey conducted by Matrix Resources Inc., an information-technology staffing firm.

PCWK

"Web security manager," *PC Week*, April 26, 1999, p. 73.

Survey Period: June 1999

Note: Data are from Cromwell Foote Partners LLC.

PENINV

Christine Williamson, "At the Top: Finance industry well-compensated for work last year," *Pensions & Investments*, August 7, 2000, p. 8.

Survey Period: 1999

Note: Data shown were from a survey conducted by the Association for Financial Professionals, Bethesda, Md. The survey population was 11,800 corporate finance officials and bankers.

PETENG

"Hot-Track Salaries," *Petroleum Engineer International*, June 1999, p. 28.

   Survey Period: 1999

Note: Data cited were reported by *U.S. News Online*.

PRBLS

1999 Occupational Employment and Wage Estimates, 1999.

   Puerto Rico Bureau of Employment Security
   Research and Statistics Division
   505 Munoz Rivera Ave., 20th Floor
   Hato Rey, PR 00918
   Telephone: (787) 754-5385
   Survey Period: October 1999 - December 1999

Note: All data are provided by the State Employment Security Administration to the Occupational Employment Statistics (OES) survey conducted by the U.S. Department of Labor, Bureau of Labor Statistics.

PRISM

"Top Dollar," *Prism*, February 2000, p. 14.

   Survey Period: 1998 - 1999

Note: Basic data acquired from College and University Personnel Association.

PRWEEK

"PRWeek salary survey report 2000," *PRWeek*, March 27, 2000, p. 24.

   Survey Period: January 2000 - February 2000

Note: Data are from a survey conducted by *PRWeek* and tabulated by Impulse Research. 3,611 PR executives responded to a mailing to 30,000 individuals.

PUBMAN

"1998 Manager Salaries," *Public Management*, April 1999, p. 25.

   Survey Period: 1998

Note: Data are from a 1998 survey of city managers and chief administrative officers.

PUBWK

Jim Milliot, "Salary Survey," *Publishers Weekly*, July 3, 2000, p. 35.

   Survey Period: 1999

Note: Data are from *Publishers Weekly*'s annual salary survey.

PWV

Patrick F. Fetzer, "Wine industry employees benefit from economic boom," *Practical Winery & Vineyard*, November/December 1999, pp. 7-8.

   Survey Period: August 1999

Note: Data based on a salary survey conducted by the publication in August 1999.

QPRO

Miles Maguire, "Quality Progress' 1999 Salary Survey," *Quality Progress*, November 1999, p. 53.

   Survey Period: April 1999 - May 1999

Note: Data are based on a mailing to 9,000 quality professionals, with a useable return of 47.6 percent.

QPRO2

Miles Maguire, "Inspectors See Big Increases' Ahead of Technicians," *Quality Progress*, November 2000, p. 35.

Note: Data are from the 2000 *Quality Progress* salary survey.

R&DM

Tim Studt, "Researcher Contentment Hides Basic Issues," *R&D Magazine*, September 1999, p. 8SE.

Survey Period: 1998

Note: Data developed by Abbot Langer & Associates and *R&D Magazine*.

REALM

Robert Freedman, "How do you measure up?" *Realtor's Magazine*, September 1999, p. 32.

Survey Period: April 1999

Note: Data are from a survey conducted by *Realtor's Magazine*.

RESC

"Career dreams can come true in agriculture," *Resource*, December 1999, p. 15.

Survey Period: 1998 - 1999

Note: Data are from *Faculty Salary Survey by Discipline*, Oklahoma State University.

RIBLS

1999 Occupational Employment and Wage Estimates, 1999.

Rhode Island Department of Employment and Training
Labor Market Information
101 Friendship St
Providence, RI 02903-3740
Telephone: (401) 222-3730
Online: http://www.det.state.ri.us/webdev/lmi/ rioicchm.html
Survey Period: October 1999 - December 1999

Note: All data are provided by the State Employment Security Administration to the Occupational Employment Statistics (OES) survey conducted by the U.S. Department of Labor, Bureau of Labor Statistics.

RN1

"Which Specialty Pays Best," *RN*, June 2000, p. 14.

Survey Period: 1999

Note: Data are based on a 1999 national study. The study represented 409 hospitals and 140,000 nurses and nursing aides.

RN2

Marissa J. Ventura, "Bedside care is paying off," *RN*, October 1999, p. 55.

Survey Period: July 1999

Note: Data are from the 1999 *RN* Salary Survey. The survey was conducted by Medical Economics Research Services.

SAFHE

Lisa Finnegan, "What lies ahead for safety and health professionals," *Safety+Health*, December 1999, p. 45.

Survey Period: 1999

Note: Date are from a survey conducted by *Safety+Health*. Questionnaires were mailed to 2,000 readers; 601 responses were tabulated.

SARHT

Sarasota Herald-Tribune, October 7, 2000.

Survey Period: 1999

Note: Information based on a story about salary negotiations between the Sarasota School Board and teachers.

SCBLS

1999 Occupational Employment and Wage Estimates, 1999.

South Carolina Employment Security Commission
Labor Market Information
610 Hampton St P.O. Box 995
Columbia, SC 29202
Telephone: (803) 737-2660
Online: http://www.sces.org/lmi/index.htm
Survey Period: October 1999 - December 1999

Note: All data are provided by the State Employment Security Administration to the Occupational Employment Statistics (OES) survey conducted by the U.S. Department of Labor, Bureau of Labor Statistics.

SCW

Carl Bruno and Beth A. Richardson, "How Does Your Compensation Measure Up?" *Shopping Center World*, June 1999, p. 30.

Survey Period: 1999

Note: Data are from a 1999 salary survey conducted by FPL Associates.

SCW2

Carl Bruno and Beth A. Richardson, "Money Talks," *Shopping Center World*, p. 59.

Note: Data are from a compensation report provided to *Shopping Center World* by FPL Associates.

SCWO

"Wild Weatherman," *Science World*, December 13, 1999, p. 6.

Survey Period: 1999

SDBLS

1999 Occupational Employment and Wage Estimates, 1999.

South Dakota Department of Labor
Labor Market Center
P.O. Box 4730
Aberdeen, SD 57402-4730
Telephone: (605) 626-2314
Online: http://www.state.sd.us/dol/lmic/index.htm
Survey Period: October 1999 - December 1999

Note: All data are provided by the State Employment Security Administration to the Occupational Employment Statistics (OES) survey conducted by the U.S. Department of Labor, Bureau of Labor Statistics.

SDBUSJ

Brad Graves, "Survey Reveals Salaries in San Diego and Beyond," *San Diego Business Journal*, September 25, 2000, p. 46.

Survey Period: 2000

Note: Data from National Association for Law Placement.

SFIN

Karl E. Reichardt and David L. Schroeder, "IMA 99 Salary Guide," *Strategic Finance*, June 2000, p. 37.

Survey Period: 1999

Note: Data were obtained in a survey of Institute of Management Accountants (IMA) to a random sample of 5000 IMA members. 1,913 useable questionnaires were returned, representing 38 percent of persons suveyed.

SHTR

Patty Allen-Jones, "Board approves raises of 4.5%," *Satasota Herld Tribune*, November 9, 2000, p. BS1.

Survey Period: 2000

Note: Data are from the Sarasota School Board.

SITSEL

Lauri Joan Aron, "Auto-related Salary Comparisons," *Site Selection*, January 2000, p. 140.

Survey Period: 2000

Note: Data are from Ontario Investment Service.

SMR

"Compensation in the Call Center," *Sales Marketing Reporter*, August 1999, p. 75.

Survey Period: 1999

Note: Data are from a surveu conducted by the American Teleservices Association.

SPORTS

John Lombardo, "Pro payroll payoff: Peace and parity," *Street & Smith's Sportsbusiness Journal*, January 31-February 6, 2000, p. 29.

Survey Period: 1999

Note: Data are from the magazine's research, the players associations, *USA Today*, and Professional Association of Basketball Research.

STLA

"Barber and Beauty Shop Survey".

State of Louisiana

Note: Data were collected by the State of Louisiana in August 1998.

STORES

"Apparel Retailers Top Salary Survey," *Stores*, October 2000, p. 20.

Survey Period: 2000

Note: Data are from William Mercer.

TECHD

Tom Nguyen, "Collision Repair: Smart Training for Smart People for a Smarter Career," January 2000, p. 26.

Survey Period: 1998

Note: Data are from I-CAR Education Foundation 1998 Snapshot of the Industry Survey.

TFM

"Fleet Compensation Report," *Truck Fleet Management*, June 1999, pp. 31-34.

Survey Period: 1999

Note: Data obtained by questionnaires mailed by the magazine.

TIME

"Numbers," *Time*, December 25, 2000, p. 53.

Survey Period: 2000

Note: Data are from the New York City Board of Elections.

TNBLS

1999 Occupational Employment and Wage Estimates, 1999.

Tennessee Department of Employment Security
Research and Statistics Division
500 James Robertson Pkwy Davy Crockett Tower, 11th
Floor
Nashville, TN 37245-1000
Telephone: (615) 741-2284
Online: http://www.state.tn.us/empsec/lmi.htm
Survey Period: October 1999 - December 1999

Note: All data are provided by the State Employment Security Administration to the Occupational Employment Statistics (OES) survey conducted by the U.S. Department of Labor, Bureau of Labor Statistics.

TQUES

"Kids Today," *Techniques: Connecting Education & Careers*, January 2000, p. 2.

Survey Period: 1999

Note: Data cited were reprinted from U.S. Department of Labor; 13th Annual Salary Survey, September 1999, Computerworld Inc., and FFA Agricultural Career Center.

TRAFWD

Kathleen Hickey, "Right Place, Right Time," *Traffic World*, October 23, 2000, p. 19.

Survey Period: 3, 2000

Note: Data are from "2000 Career Patterns of Women in Logistics," a survey sponsored by the Council of Logistics Management. 344 women responded to the survey, which ended in the Spring of 2000.

TRAIN

Kevin Dobbs, "Trainers' Salaries 1999," *Training*, November 1999, pp. 29-33.

Survey Period: June 1999

Note: Data are based on a survey of *Training* subscribers by Lakewood Research.

TRAIN2

Donna Goldwasser, "Salary Survey," *Training*, November 2000, p. 90.

Survey Period: 2000

Note: Data are based on a survey of *Training* subscribers.

TRAVWK1

Travel Weekly, September 18, 2000.

Survey Period: 1999

Note: Information shown is from Runzheimer International.

TRAVWK2

Travel Weekly, September 18, 2000.

Survey Period: 1999

Note: Information is from William Mercer and Bureau of Labor Statistics.

TRAVWK3

Travel Weekly, September 18, 2000.

Survey Period: 1999

Note: Data are from Price Waterhouse Coopers.

TRAVWK4

Travel Weekly, September 18, 2000.

Survey Period: 2000

Note: Data presented were supplied by NACOR International.

TRAVWK5

Travel Weekly, September 18, 2000.

Survey Period: 2000

Note: Information from Abbot, Langer & Associates.

TRDEV

"HR Salary Survey," *Training & Development*, November 1999, p. 58.

Survey Period: 1999

Note: Data are from the *1999 SHRM/Mercer Human Resources Management Compensation Survey*. The survey reported data from nearly 1,000 companies on 86 different human resources positions.

TRIBUS

"Average teacher salary," *Triangle Business Journal (Raleigh, NC)*, June 9, 2000, p. 38.

Survey Period: 1999 - 2000

Note: Data are from the school districts of the counties included.

TXBLS

1999 Occupational Employment and Wage Estimates, 1999.

Texas Workforce Commission
Labor Market Information
9001 North IH-35, Suite 103A
Austin, TX 78778
Telephone: (512) 491-4802
Online: http://www.twc.state.tx.us/lmi/lmi.html
Survey Period: October 1999 - December 1999

Note: All data are provided by the State Employment Security Administration to the Occupational Employment Statistics (OES) survey conducted by the U.S. Department of Labor, Bureau of Labor Statistics.

TXMO

Gary Chapman, "Texas Needs Nerds," *Texas Monthly*, December 2000, p. 62.

Survey Period: 1999

Note: Data were reported by the Texas Advisory Council on the Digital Economy.

URLAN

Christopher E. Lee, "Compensation Cafeteria-Style," *Urban Land*, August 1999, p. 29.

Survey Period: December 1998

Note: Data provided by CEL & Associates from a survey completed December 1998.

USBANK

"Techies Can Be Tough to Find," *U.S. Banker*, January 2000, p. 38.

Survey Period: 2000

Note: Data reported by Robert Half International.

USCAT

"From the Book of Numbers," *U.S. Catholic*, February 2000, p. 10.

Survey Period: 1999

Note: Data are from the 1999 edition of the National Federation of Priests' Councils; report, *The Laborer Is Worthy of His Hire*.

UTBLS

1999 Occupational Employment and Wage Estimates, 1999.

Utah Department of Workforce Services
Labor Market Information
140 East 300 South P.O. Box 45249
Salt Lake City, UT 84145-0249
Telephone: (801) 526-9401
Online: http://www.dws.state.ut.us
Survey Period: October 1999 - December 1999

Note: All data are provided by the State Employment Security Administration to the Occupational Employment Statistics (OES) survey conducted by the U.S. Department of Labor, Bureau of Labor Statistics.

VABLS

1999 Occupational Employment and Wage Estimates, 1999.

Virginia Employment Commission
Economic Information and Services Division
703 East Main St P.O. Box 1358
Richmond, VA 23218-1358
Telephone: (804) 786-7496
Online: http://www.vec.state.va.us/lbrmkt/lmi.htm
Survey Period: October 1999 - December 1999

Note: All data are provided by the State Employment Security Administration to the Occupational Employment Statistics (OES) survey conducted by the U.S. Department of Labor, Bureau of Labor Statistics.

VETTECH

Carlene A. Decker and A. Patrick Navarre, "Survey Results - Salaries and Benefits," *Veterinary Technician*, July 2000, p. 388.

Survey Period: 1999

Note: Data are from The Statistical Research Group of the American Medical Association's Division of Membership and Field Services.

VIBLS

1999 Occupational Employment and Wage Estimates, 1999.

Virgin Islands Department of Labor
Bureau of Labor Statistics
53A and 54B Kronprindsens Gade
Charlotte Amalie, St. Thomas, VI 00820
Telephone: (340) 776-3700
Survey Period: October 1999 - December 1999

Note: All data are provided by the State Employment Security Administration to the Occupational Employment Statistics (OES) survey conducted by the U.S. Department of Labor, Bureau of Labor Statistics.

VTBLS

1999 Occupational Employment and Wage Estimates, 1999.

Vermont Department of Employment and Training
Research and Analysis
5 Green Mountain Dr P.O. Box 488
Montpelier, VT 05601-0488
Telephone: (802) 828-4153
Online: http://www.det.state.vt.us
Survey Period: October 1999 - December 1999

Note: All data are provided by the State Employment Security Administration to the Occupational Employment Statistics (OES) survey conducted by the U.S. Department of Labor, Bureau of Labor Statistics.

WABLS

1999 Occupational Employment and Wage Estimates, 1999.

    Employment Security Division
    Labor Market and Economic Analysis
    Mail Stop 6000; P.O. Box 9046
    Olympia, WA 98507-9046
    Telephone: (360) 438-4804
    Online: http://www.wa.gov/esd/lmea
    Survey Period: October 1999 - December 1999

Note: All data are provided by the State Employment Security Administration to the Occupational Employment Statistics (OES) survey conducted by the U.S. Department of Labor, Bureau of Labor Statistics.

WARD1

Tim Keenan, "The way dealers pay," *Ward's Dealer Business*, July 2000, p. 23.

    Survey Period: 1999

Note: Data are from the 2000 *Ward's Dealer Business* auto dealership compensation survey.

WARD2

Tim Keenan, "Dealers pay more to keep people," *Ward's Dealer Business*, July 1999, p. 22.

    Survey Period: 1999

Note: Data are from the *Ward's Dealer Business* compensation survey for 1999.

WARD3

"Manufacturing Salaries," *Ward's Auto World*, October 1998, p. 30.

    Survey Period: 1998

Note: Data are taken from *Compensation in Manufacturing, 18th Edition.*

WIBLS

1999 Occupational Employment and Wage Estimates, 1999.

    Wisconsin Department of Workforce Development
    LMI Data Development
    201 East Washington Ave., Room 2214
    Madison, WI 53702
    Telephone: (608) 266-2930
    Online: http://www.dwd.state.wi.us/dwelmi
    Survey Period: October 1999 - December 1999

Note: All data are provided by the State Employment Security Administration to the Occupational Employment Statistics (OES) survey conducted by the U.S. Department of Labor, Bureau of Labor Statistics.

WOODT

Katherine Haddox, "Survey indicates maturing industry, regional shifts," *Wood Technology*, January/February 1999, p. 28.

    Survey Period: June 1998

Note: Data are based on the magazine's reader's survey conducted in June of 1998.

WOWO1

Elizabeth Wasserman, "The new pay paradigm," *Working Woman*, July/August 2000, pp. 60-64.

    Survey Period: 1999

Note: Data on Clergy from Bureau of Labor Statistics (BLS), on Librarians from Special Libraries Association, on Pharmacist and Social worker from BLS.

WOWO2

Joanna L. Krotz, "Getting Even," *Working Woman*, July/August 1999, pp. 42-56.

    Survey Period: 1998

Note: Data from Bureau of Labor Statistics with the exception of data from Pharmacist, taken from *Drug Topics*.

WSJ1

"Raking it In," *The Wall Street Journal*, September 5, 2000, p. B16.

Survey Period: 2000

Note: Data are from a survey of 244 web site development companies compiled by Buck Consultants Inc., New York.

WSJ2

Margaret A. Jacobs, "Stenographers Fight for Their Day (Jobs) in Court," *The Wall Street Journal*, April 30, 1999, p. B1.

Survey Period: 1999

Note: Data are reported by the National Court Reporters Association.

WSJ3

"Indoor Soccer," *The Wall Street Journal*, January 9, 2001, p. A1.

Survey Period: 2000

WVBLS

1999 Occupational Employment and Wage Estimates, 1999.

West Virginia Bureau of Employment Programs
Research, Information and Analysis
112 California Ave
Charleston, WV 25305-0112
Telephone: (304) 558-2660
Online: http://www.state.wv.us/bep/lmi/default.htm
Survey Period: October 1999 - December 1999

Note: All data are provided by the State Employment Security Administration to the Occupational Employment Statistics (OES) survey conducted by the U.S. Department of Labor, Bureau of Labor Statistics.

WYBLS

1999 Occupational Employment and Wage Estimates, 1999.

Wyoming Department of Employment
Division of Administration
P.O. Box 2760
Casper, WY 82602-2760
Telephone: (307) 473-3801
Online: http://wydoe.state.wy.us
Survey Period: October 1999 - December 1999

Note: All data are provided by the State Employment Security Administration to the Occupational Employment Statistics (OES) survey conducted by the U.S. Department of Labor, Bureau of Labor Statistics.

Appendix II

SALARY CONVERSION TABLE

Hour	Week	Month	Year	Hour	Week	Month	Year	Hour	Week	Month	Year	Hour	Week	Month	Year
2.00	80	346	4,157	4.10	164	710	8,521	6.20	248	1,074	12,886	8.30	332	1,438	17,251
2.05	82	355	4,261	4.15	166	719	8,625	6.25	250	1,083	12,990	8.35	334	1,446	17,355
2.10	84	364	4,365	4.20	168	727	8,729	6.30	252	1,091	13,094	8.40	336	1,455	17,459
2.15	86	372	4,469	4.25	170	736	8,833	6.35	254	1,100	13,198	8.45	338	1,464	17,562
2.20	88	381	4,572	4.30	172	745	8,937	6.40	256	1,108	13,302	8.50	340	1,472	17,666
2.25	90	390	4,676	4.35	174	753	9,041	6.45	258	1,117	13,406	8.55	342	1,481	17,770
2.30	92	398	4,780	4.40	176	762	9,145	6.50	260	1,126	13,510	8.60	344	1,490	17,874
2.35	94	407	4,884	4.45	178	771	9,249	6.55	262	1,134	13,614	8.65	346	1,498	17,978
2.40	96	416	4,988	4.50	180	779	9,353	6.60	264	1,143	13,717	8.70	348	1,507	18,082
2.45	98	424	5,092	4.55	182	788	9,457	6.65	266	1,152	13,821	8.75	350	1,516	18,186
2.50	100	433	5,196	4.60	184	797	9,561	6.70	268	1,160	13,925	8.80	352	1,524	18,290
2.55	102	442	5,300	4.65	186	805	9,665	6.75	270	1,169	14,029	8.85	354	1,533	18,394
2.60	104	450	5,404	4.70	188	814	9,768	6.80	272	1,178	14,133	8.90	356	1,541	18,498
2.65	106	459	5,508	4.75	190	823	9,872	6.85	274	1,186	14,237	8.95	358	1,550	18,602
2.70	108	468	5,612	4.80	192	831	9,976	6.90	276	1,195	14,341	9.00	360	1,559	18,706
2.75	110	476	5,716	4.85	194	840	10,080	6.95	278	1,204	14,445	9.05	362	1,567	18,810
2.80	112	485	5,820	4.90	196	849	10,184	7.00	280	1,212	14,549	9.10	364	1,576	18,913
2.85	114	494	5,923	4.95	198	857	10,288	7.05	282	1,221	14,653	9.15	366	1,585	19,017
2.90	116	502	6,027	5.00	200	866	10,392	7.10	284	1,230	14,757	9.20	368	1,593	19,121
2.95	118	511	6,131	5.05	202	875	10,496	7.15	286	1,238	14,861	9.25	370	1,602	19,225
3.00	120	520	6,235	5.10	204	883	10,600	7.20	288	1,247	14,964	9.30	372	1,611	19,329
3.05	122	528	6,339	5.15	206	892	10,704	7.25	290	1,256	15,068	9.35	374	1,619	19,433
3.10	124	537	6,443	5.20	208	901	10,808	7.30	292	1,264	15,172	9.40	376	1,628	19,537
3.15	126	546	6,547	5.25	210	909	10,912	7.35	294	1,273	15,276	9.45	378	1,637	19,641
3.20	128	554	6,651	5.30	212	918	11,016	7.40	296	1,282	15,380	9.50	380	1,645	19,745
3.25	130	563	6,755	5.35	214	927	11,119	7.45	298	1,290	15,484	9.55	382	1,654	19,849
3.30	132	572	6,859	5.40	216	935	11,223	7.50	300	1,299	15,588	9.60	384	1,663	19,953
3.35	134	580	6,963	5.45	218	944	11,327	7.55	302	1,308	15,692	9.65	386	1,671	20,057
3.40	136	589	7,067	5.50	220	953	11,431	7.60	304	1,316	15,796	9.70	388	1,680	20,160
3.45	138	598	7,170	5.55	222	961	11,535	7.65	306	1,325	15,900	9.75	390	1,689	20,264
3.50	140	606	7,274	5.60	224	970	11,639	7.70	308	1,334	16,004	9.80	392	1,697	20,368
3.55	142	615	7,378	5.65	226	979	11,743	7.75	310	1,342	16,108	9.85	394	1,706	20,472
3.60	144	624	7,482	5.70	228	987	11,847	7.80	312	1,351	16,212	9.90	396	1,715	20,576
3.65	146	632	7,586	5.75	230	996	11,951	7.85	314	1,360	16,315	9.95	398	1,723	20,680
3.70	148	641	7,690	5.80	232	1,005	12,055	7.90	316	1,368	16,419	10.00	400	1,732	20,784
3.75	150	649	7,794	5.85	234	1,013	12,159	7.95	318	1,377	16,523	10.05	402	1,741	20,888
3.80	152	658	7,898	5.90	236	1,022	12,263	8.00	320	1,386	16,627	10.10	404	1,749	20,992
3.85	154	667	8,002	5.95	238	1,031	12,366	8.05	322	1,394	16,731	10.15	406	1,758	21,096
3.90	156	675	8,106	6.00	240	1,039	12,470	8.10	324	1,403	16,835	10.20	408	1,767	21,200
3.95	158	684	8,210	6.05	242	1,048	12,574	8.15	326	1,412	16,939	10.25	410	1,775	21,304
4.00	160	693	8,314	6.10	244	1,057	12,678	8.20	328	1,420	17,043	10.30	412	1,784	21,408
4.05	162	701	8,418	6.15	246	1,065	12,782	8.25	330	1,429	17,147	10.35	414	1,793	21,511

Hour	Week	Month	Year	Hour	Week	Month	Year	Hour	Week	Month	Year	Hour	Week	Month	Year
10.40	416	1,801	21,615	13.15	526	2,278	27,331	15.90	636	2,754	33,047	18.65	746	3,230	38,762
10.45	418	1,810	21,719	13.20	528	2,286	27,435	15.95	638	2,763	33,150	18.70	748	3,239	38,866
10.50	420	1,819	21,823	13.25	530	2,295	27,539	16.00	640	2,771	33,254	18.75	750	3,248	38,970
10.55	422	1,827	21,927	13.30	532	2,304	27,643	16.05	642	2,780	33,358	18.80	752	3,256	39,074
10.60	424	1,836	22,031	13.35	534	2,312	27,747	16.10	644	2,789	33,462	18.85	754	3,265	39,178
10.65	426	1,845	22,135	13.40	536	2,321	27,851	16.15	646	2,797	33,566	18.90	756	3,273	39,282
10.70	428	1,853	22,239	13.45	538	2,330	27,954	16.20	648	2,806	33,670	18.95	758	3,282	39,386
10.75	430	1,862	22,343	13.50	540	2,338	28,058	16.25	650	2,815	33,774	19.00	760	3,291	39,490
10.80	432	1,871	22,447	13.55	542	2,347	28,162	16.30	652	2,823	33,878	19.05	762	3,299	39,594
10.85	434	1,879	22,551	13.60	544	2,356	28,266	16.35	654	2,832	33,982	19.10	764	3,308	39,697
10.90	436	1,888	22,655	13.65	546	2,364	28,370	16.40	656	2,840	34,086	19.15	766	3,317	39,801
10.95	438	1,897	22,758	13.70	548	2,373	28,474	16.45	658	2,849	34,190	19.20	768	3,325	39,905
11.00	440	1,905	22,862	13.75	550	2,382	28,578	16.50	660	2,858	34,294	19.25	770	3,334	40,009
11.05	442	1,914	22,966	13.80	552	2,390	28,682	16.55	662	2,866	34,398	19.30	772	3,343	40,113
11.10	444	1,923	23,070	13.85	554	2,399	28,786	16.60	664	2,875	34,501	19.35	774	3,351	40,217
11.15	446	1,931	23,174	13.90	556	2,407	28,890	16.65	666	2,884	34,605	19.40	776	3,360	40,321
11.20	448	1,940	23,278	13.95	558	2,416	28,994	16.70	668	2,892	34,709	19.45	778	3,369	40,425
11.25	450	1,949	23,382	14.00	560	2,425	29,098	16.75	670	2,901	34,813	19.50	780	3,377	40,529
11.30	452	1,957	23,486	14.05	562	2,433	29,202	16.80	672	2,910	34,917	19.55	782	3,386	40,633
11.35	454	1,966	23,590	14.10	564	2,442	29,305	16.85	674	2,918	35,021	19.60	784	3,395	40,737
11.40	456	1,974	23,694	14.15	566	2,451	29,409	16.90	676	2,927	35,125	19.65	786	3,403	40,841
11.45	458	1,983	23,798	14.20	568	2,459	29,513	16.95	678	2,936	35,229	19.70	788	3,412	40,944
11.50	460	1,992	23,902	14.25	570	2,468	29,617	17.00	680	2,944	35,333	19.75	790	3,421	41,048
11.55	462	2,000	24,006	14.30	572	2,477	29,721	17.05	682	2,953	35,437	19.80	792	3,429	41,152
11.60	464	2,009	24,109	14.35	574	2,485	29,825	17.10	684	2,962	35,541	19.85	794	3,438	41,256
11.65	466	2,018	24,213	14.40	576	2,494	29,929	17.15	686	2,970	35,645	19.90	796	3,447	41,360
11.70	468	2,026	24,317	14.45	578	2,503	30,033	17.20	688	2,979	35,748	19.95	798	3,455	41,464
11.75	470	2,035	24,421	14.50	580	2,511	30,137	17.25	690	2,988	35,852	20.00	800	3,464	41,568
11.80	472	2,044	24,525	14.55	582	2,520	30,241	17.30	692	2,996	35,956	20.05	802	3,473	41,672
11.85	474	2,052	24,629	14.60	584	2,529	30,345	17.35	694	3,005	36,060	20.10	804	3,481	41,776
11.90	476	2,061	24,733	14.65	586	2,537	30,449	17.40	696	3,014	36,164	20.15	806	3,490	41,880
11.95	478	2,070	24,837	14.70	588	2,546	30,552	17.45	698	3,022	36,268	20.20	808	3,499	41,984
12.00	480	2,078	24,941	14.75	590	2,555	30,656	17.50	700	3,031	36,372	20.25	810	3,507	42,088
12.05	482	2,087	25,045	14.80	592	2,563	30,760	17.55	702	3,040	36,476	20.30	812	3,516	42,192
12.10	484	2,096	25,149	14.85	594	2,572	30,864	17.60	704	3,048	36,580	20.35	814	3,525	42,295
12.15	486	2,104	25,253	14.90	596	2,581	30,968	17.65	706	3,057	36,684	20.40	816	3,533	42,399
12.20	488	2,113	25,356	14.95	598	2,589	31,072	17.70	708	3,066	36,788	20.45	818	3,542	42,503
12.25	490	2,122	25,460	15.00	600	2,598	31,176	17.75	710	3,074	36,892	20.50	820	3,551	42,607
12.30	492	2,130	25,564	15.05	602	2,607	31,280	17.80	712	3,083	36,996	20.55	822	3,559	42,711
12.35	494	2,139	25,668	15.10	604	2,615	31,384	17.85	714	3,092	37,099	20.60	824	3,568	42,815
12.40	496	2,148	25,772	15.15	606	2,624	31,488	17.90	716	3,100	37,203	20.65	826	3,577	42,919
12.45	498	2,156	25,876	15.20	608	2,633	31,592	17.95	718	3,109	37,307	20.70	828	3,585	43,023
12.50	500	2,165	25,980	15.25	610	2,641	31,696	18.00	720	3,118	37,411	20.75	830	3,594	43,127
12.55	502	2,174	26,084	15.30	612	2,650	31,800	18.05	722	3,126	37,515	20.80	832	3,603	43,231
12.60	504	2,182	26,188	15.35	614	2,659	31,903	18.10	724	3,135	37,619	20.85	834	3,611	43,335
12.65	506	2,191	26,292	15.40	616	2,667	32,007	18.15	726	3,144	37,723	20.90	836	3,620	43,439
12.70	508	2,200	26,396	15.45	618	2,676	32,111	18.20	728	3,152	37,827	20.95	838	3,629	43,542
12.75	510	2,208	26,500	15.50	620	2,685	32,215	18.25	730	3,161	37,931	21.00	840	3,637	43,646
12.80	512	2,217	26,604	15.55	622	2,693	32,319	18.30	732	3,170	38,035	21.05	842	3,646	43,750
12.85	514	2,226	26,707	15.60	624	2,702	32,423	18.35	734	3,178	38,139	21.10	844	3,655	43,854
12.90	516	2,234	26,811	15.65	626	2,711	32,527	18.40	736	3,187	38,243	21.15	846	3,663	43,958
12.95	518	2,243	26,915	15.70	628	2,719	32,631	18.45	738	3,196	38,346	21.20	848	3,672	44,062
13.00	520	2,252	27,019	15.75	630	2,728	32,735	18.50	740	3,204	38,450	21.25	850	3,680	44,166
13.05	522	2,260	27,123	15.80	632	2,737	32,839	18.55	742	3,213	38,554	21.30	852	3,689	44,270
13.10	524	2,269	27,227	15.85	634	2,745	32,943	18.60	744	3,222	38,658	21.35	854	3,698	44,374

Hour	Week	Month	Year	Hour	Week	Month	Year	Hour	Week	Month	Year	Hour	Week	Month	Year
21.40	856	3,706	44,478	24.15	966	4,183	50,193	26.90	1,076	4,659	55,909	29.65	1,186	5,135	61,625
21.45	858	3,715	44,582	24.20	968	4,191	50,297	26.95	1,078	4,668	56,013	29.70	1,188	5,144	61,728
21.50	860	3,724	44,686	24.25	970	4,200	50,401	27.00	1,080	4,676	56,117	29.75	1,190	5,153	61,832
21.55	862	3,732	44,790	24.30	972	4,209	50,505	27.05	1,082	4,685	56,221	29.80	1,192	5,161	61,936
21.60	864	3,741	44,893	24.35	974	4,217	50,609	27.10	1,084	4,694	56,325	29.85	1,194	5,170	62,040
21.65	866	3,750	44,997	24.40	976	4,226	50,713	27.15	1,086	4,702	56,429	29.90	1,196	5,179	62,144
21.70	868	3,758	45,101	24.45	978	4,235	50,817	27.20	1,088	4,711	56,532	29.95	1,198	5,187	62,248
21.75	870	3,767	45,205	24.50	980	4,243	50,921	27.25	1,090	4,720	56,636	30.00	1,200	5,196	62,352
21.80	872	3,776	45,309	24.55	982	4,252	51,025	27.30	1,092	4,728	56,740	30.05	1,202	5,205	62,456
21.85	874	3,784	45,413	24.60	984	4,261	51,129	27.35	1,094	4,737	56,844	30.10	1,204	5,213	62,560
21.90	876	3,793	45,517	24.65	986	4,269	51,233	27.40	1,096	4,746	56,948	30.15	1,206	5,222	62,664
21.95	878	3,802	45,621	24.70	988	4,278	51,336	27.45	1,098	4,754	57,052	30.20	1,208	5,231	62,768
22.00	880	3,810	45,725	24.75	990	4,287	51,440	27.50	1,100	4,763	57,156	30.25	1,210	5,239	62,872
22.05	882	3,819	45,829	24.80	992	4,295	51,544	27.55	1,102	4,772	57,260	30.30	1,212	5,248	62,976
22.10	884	3,828	45,933	24.85	994	4,304	51,648	27.60	1,104	4,780	57,364	30.35	1,214	5,257	63,079
22.15	886	3,836	46,037	24.90	996	4,313	51,752	27.65	1,106	4,789	57,468	30.40	1,216	5,265	63,183
22.20	888	3,845	46,140	24.95	998	4,321	51,856	27.70	1,108	4,798	57,572	30.45	1,218	5,274	63,287
22.25	890	3,854	46,244	25.00	1,000	4,330	51,960	27.75	1,110	4,806	57,676	30.50	1,220	5,283	63,391
22.30	892	3,862	46,348	25.05	1,002	4,339	52,064	27.80	1,112	4,815	57,780	30.55	1,222	5,291	63,495
22.35	894	3,871	46,452	25.10	1,004	4,347	52,168	27.85	1,114	4,824	57,883	30.60	1,224	5,300	63,599
22.40	896	3,880	46,556	25.15	1,006	4,356	52,272	27.90	1,116	4,832	57,987	30.65	1,226	5,309	63,703
22.45	898	3,888	46,660	25.20	1,008	4,365	52,376	27.95	1,118	4,841	58,091	30.70	1,228	5,317	63,807
22.50	900	3,897	46,764	25.25	1,010	4,373	52,480	28.00	1,120	4,850	58,195	30.75	1,230	5,326	63,911
22.55	902	3,906	46,868	25.30	1,012	4,382	52,584	28.05	1,122	4,858	58,299	30.80	1,232	5,335	64,015
22.60	904	3,914	46,972	25.35	1,014	4,391	52,687	28.10	1,124	4,867	58,403	30.85	1,234	5,343	64,119
22.65	906	3,923	47,076	25.40	1,016	4,399	52,791	28.15	1,126	4,876	58,507	30.90	1,236	5,352	64,223
22.70	908	3,932	47,180	25.45	1,018	4,408	52,895	28.20	1,128	4,884	58,611	30.95	1,238	5,361	64,326
22.75	910	3,940	47,284	25.50	1,020	4,417	52,999	28.25	1,130	4,893	58,715	31.00	1,240	5,369	64,430
22.80	912	3,949	47,388	25.55	1,022	4,425	53,103	28.30	1,132	4,902	58,819	31.05	1,242	5,378	64,534
22.85	914	3,958	47,491	25.60	1,024	4,434	53,207	28.35	1,134	4,910	58,923	31.10	1,244	5,387	64,638
22.90	916	3,966	47,595	25.65	1,026	4,443	53,311	28.40	1,136	4,919	59,027	31.15	1,246	5,395	64,742
22.95	918	3,975	47,699	25.70	1,028	4,451	53,415	28.45	1,138	4,928	59,130	31.20	1,248	5,404	64,846
23.00	920	3,984	47,803	25.75	1,030	4,460	53,519	28.50	1,140	4,936	59,234	31.25	1,250	5,412	64,950
23.05	922	3,992	47,907	25.80	1,032	4,469	53,623	28.55	1,142	4,945	59,338	31.30	1,252	5,421	65,054
23.10	924	4,001	48,011	25.85	1,034	4,477	53,727	28.60	1,144	4,954	59,442	31.35	1,254	5,430	65,158
23.15	926	4,010	48,115	25.90	1,036	4,486	53,831	28.65	1,146	4,962	59,546	31.40	1,256	5,438	65,262
23.20	928	4,018	48,219	25.95	1,038	4,495	53,934	28.70	1,148	4,971	59,650	31.45	1,258	5,447	65,366
23.25	930	4,027	48,323	26.00	1,040	4,503	54,038	28.75	1,150	4,979	59,754	31.50	1,260	5,456	65,470
23.30	932	4,036	48,427	26.05	1,042	4,512	54,142	28.80	1,152	4,988	59,858	31.55	1,262	5,464	65,574
23.35	934	4,044	48,531	26.10	1,044	4,521	54,246	28.85	1,154	4,997	59,962	31.60	1,264	5,473	65,677
23.40	936	4,053	48,635	26.15	1,046	4,529	54,350	28.90	1,156	5,005	60,066	31.65	1,266	5,482	65,781
23.45	938	4,062	48,738	26.20	1,048	4,538	54,454	28.95	1,158	5,014	60,170	31.70	1,268	5,490	65,885
23.50	940	4,070	48,842	26.25	1,050	4,546	54,558	29.00	1,160	5,023	60,274	31.75	1,270	5,499	65,989
23.55	942	4,079	48,946	26.30	1,052	4,555	54,662	29.05	1,162	5,031	60,378	31.80	1,272	5,508	66,093
23.60	944	4,088	49,050	26.35	1,054	4,564	54,766	29.10	1,164	5,040	60,481	31.85	1,274	5,516	66,197
23.65	946	4,096	49,154	26.40	1,056	4,572	54,870	29.15	1,166	5,049	60,585	31.90	1,276	5,525	66,301
23.70	948	4,105	49,258	26.45	1,058	4,581	54,974	29.20	1,168	5,057	60,689	31.95	1,278	5,534	66,405
23.75	950	4,113	49,362	26.50	1,060	4,590	55,078	29.25	1,170	5,066	60,793	32.00	1,280	5,542	66,509
23.80	952	4,122	49,466	26.55	1,062	4,598	55,182	29.30	1,172	5,075	60,897	32.05	1,282	5,551	66,613
23.85	954	4,131	49,570	26.60	1,064	4,607	55,285	29.35	1,174	5,083	61,001	32.10	1,284	5,560	66,717
23.90	956	4,139	49,674	26.65	1,066	4,616	55,389	29.40	1,176	5,092	61,105	32.15	1,286	5,568	66,821
23.95	958	4,148	49,778	26.70	1,068	4,624	55,493	29.45	1,178	5,101	61,209	32.20	1,288	5,577	66,924
24.00	960	4,157	49,882	26.75	1,070	4,633	55,597	29.50	1,180	5,109	61,313	32.25	1,290	5,586	67,028
24.05	962	4,165	49,986	26.80	1,072	4,642	55,701	29.55	1,182	5,118	61,417	32.30	1,292	5,594	67,132
24.10	964	4,174	50,089	26.85	1,074	4,650	55,805	29.60	1,184	5,127	61,521	32.35	1,294	5,603	67,236

Hour	Week	Month	Year	Hour	Week	Month	Year	Hour	Week	Month	Year	Hour	Week	Month	Year
32.40	1,296	5,612	67,340	35.15	1,406	6,088	73,056	37.90	1,516	6,564	78,771	40.65	1,626	7,041	84,487
32.45	1,298	5,620	67,444	35.20	1,408	6,097	73,160	37.95	1,518	6,573	78,875	40.70	1,628	7,049	84,591
32.50	1,300	5,629	67,548	35.25	1,410	6,105	73,264	38.00	1,520	6,582	78,979	40.75	1,630	7,058	84,695
32.55	1,302	5,638	67,652	35.30	1,412	6,114	73,368	38.05	1,522	6,590	79,083	40.80	1,632	7,067	84,799
32.60	1,304	5,646	67,756	35.35	1,414	6,123	73,471	38.10	1,524	6,599	79,187	40.85	1,634	7,075	84,903
32.65	1,306	5,655	67,860	35.40	1,416	6,131	73,575	38.15	1,526	6,608	79,291	40.90	1,636	7,084	85,007
32.70	1,308	5,664	67,964	35.45	1,418	6,140	73,679	38.20	1,528	6,616	79,395	40.95	1,638	7,093	85,110
32.75	1,310	5,672	68,068	35.50	1,420	6,149	73,783	38.25	1,530	6,625	79,499	41.00	1,640	7,101	85,214
32.80	1,312	5,681	68,172	35.55	1,422	6,157	73,887	38.30	1,532	6,634	79,603	41.05	1,642	7,110	85,318
32.85	1,314	5,690	68,275	35.60	1,424	6,166	73,991	38.35	1,534	6,642	79,707	41.10	1,644	7,119	85,422
32.90	1,316	5,698	68,379	35.65	1,426	6,175	74,095	38.40	1,536	6,651	79,811	41.15	1,646	7,127	85,526
32.95	1,318	5,707	68,483	35.70	1,428	6,183	74,199	38.45	1,538	6,660	79,914	41.20	1,648	7,136	85,630
33.00	1,320	5,716	68,587	35.75	1,430	6,192	74,303	38.50	1,540	6,668	80,018	41.25	1,650	7,144	85,734
33.05	1,322	5,724	68,691	35.80	1,432	6,201	74,407	38.55	1,542	6,677	80,122	41.30	1,652	7,153	85,838
33.10	1,324	5,733	68,795	35.85	1,434	6,209	74,511	38.60	1,544	6,686	80,226	41.35	1,654	7,162	85,942
33.15	1,326	5,742	68,899	35.90	1,436	6,218	74,615	38.65	1,546	6,694	80,330	41.40	1,656	7,170	86,046
33.20	1,328	5,750	69,003	35.95	1,438	6,227	74,718	38.70	1,548	6,703	80,434	41.45	1,658	7,179	86,150
33.25	1,330	5,759	69,107	36.00	1,440	6,235	74,822	38.75	1,550	6,711	80,538	41.50	1,660	7,188	86,254
33.30	1,332	5,768	69,211	36.05	1,442	6,244	74,926	38.80	1,552	6,720	80,642	41.55	1,662	7,196	86,358
33.35	1,334	5,776	69,315	36.10	1,444	6,253	75,030	38.85	1,554	6,729	80,746	41.60	1,664	7,205	86,461
33.40	1,336	5,785	69,419	36.15	1,446	6,261	75,134	38.90	1,556	6,737	80,850	41.65	1,666	7,214	86,565
33.45	1,338	5,794	69,522	36.20	1,448	6,270	75,238	38.95	1,558	6,746	80,954	41.70	1,668	7,222	86,669
33.50	1,340	5,802	69,626	36.25	1,450	6,278	75,342	39.00	1,560	6,755	81,058	41.75	1,670	7,231	86,773
33.55	1,342	5,811	69,730	36.30	1,452	6,287	75,446	39.05	1,562	6,763	81,162	41.80	1,672	7,240	86,877
33.60	1,344	5,820	69,834	36.35	1,454	6,296	75,550	39.10	1,564	6,772	81,265	41.85	1,674	7,248	86,981
33.65	1,346	5,828	69,938	36.40	1,456	6,304	75,654	39.15	1,566	6,781	81,369	41.90	1,676	7,257	87,085
33.70	1,348	5,837	70,042	36.45	1,458	6,313	75,758	39.20	1,568	6,789	81,473	41.95	1,678	7,266	87,189
33.75	1,350	5,845	70,146	36.50	1,460	6,322	75,862	39.25	1,570	6,798	81,577	42.00	1,680	7,274	87,293
33.80	1,352	5,854	70,250	36.55	1,462	6,330	75,966	39.30	1,572	6,807	81,681	42.05	1,682	7,283	87,397
33.85	1,354	5,863	70,354	36.60	1,464	6,339	76,069	39.35	1,574	6,815	81,785	42.10	1,684	7,292	87,501
33.90	1,356	5,871	70,458	36.65	1,466	6,348	76,173	39.40	1,576	6,824	81,889	42.15	1,686	7,300	87,605
33.95	1,358	5,880	70,562	36.70	1,468	6,356	76,277	39.45	1,578	6,833	81,993	42.20	1,688	7,309	87,708
34.00	1,360	5,889	70,666	36.75	1,470	6,365	76,381	39.50	1,580	6,841	82,097	42.25	1,690	7,318	87,812
34.05	1,362	5,897	70,770	36.80	1,472	6,374	76,485	39.55	1,582	6,850	82,201	42.30	1,692	7,326	87,916
34.10	1,364	5,906	70,873	36.85	1,474	6,382	76,589	39.60	1,584	6,859	82,305	42.35	1,694	7,335	88,020
34.15	1,366	5,915	70,977	36.90	1,476	6,391	76,693	39.65	1,586	6,867	82,409	42.40	1,696	7,344	88,124
34.20	1,368	5,923	71,081	36.95	1,478	6,400	76,797	39.70	1,588	6,876	82,512	42.45	1,698	7,352	88,228
34.25	1,370	5,932	71,185	37.00	1,480	6,408	76,901	39.75	1,590	6,885	82,616	42.50	1,700	7,361	88,332
34.30	1,372	5,941	71,289	37.05	1,482	6,417	77,005	39.80	1,592	6,893	82,720	42.55	1,702	7,370	88,436
34.35	1,374	5,949	71,393	37.10	1,484	6,426	77,109	39.85	1,594	6,902	82,824	42.60	1,704	7,378	88,540
34.40	1,376	5,958	71,497	37.15	1,486	6,434	77,213	39.90	1,596	6,911	82,928	42.65	1,706	7,387	88,644
34.45	1,378	5,967	71,601	37.20	1,488	6,443	77,316	39.95	1,598	6,919	83,032	42.70	1,708	7,396	88,748
34.50	1,380	5,975	71,705	37.25	1,490	6,452	77,420	40.00	1,600	6,928	83,136	42.75	1,710	7,404	88,852
34.55	1,382	5,984	71,809	37.30	1,492	6,460	77,524	40.05	1,602	6,937	83,240	42.80	1,712	7,413	88,956
34.60	1,384	5,993	71,913	37.35	1,494	6,469	77,628	40.10	1,604	6,945	83,344	42.85	1,714	7,422	89,059
34.65	1,386	6,001	72,017	37.40	1,496	6,478	77,732	40.15	1,606	6,954	83,448	42.90	1,716	7,430	89,163
34.70	1,388	6,010	72,120	37.45	1,498	6,486	77,836	40.20	1,608	6,963	83,552	42.95	1,718	7,439	89,267
34.75	1,390	6,019	72,224	37.50	1,500	6,495	77,940	40.25	1,610	6,971	83,656	43.00	1,720	7,448	89,371
34.80	1,392	6,027	72,328	37.55	1,502	6,504	78,044	40.30	1,612	6,980	83,760	43.05	1,722	7,456	89,475
34.85	1,394	6,036	72,432	37.60	1,504	6,512	78,148	40.35	1,614	6,989	83,863	43.10	1,724	7,465	89,579
34.90	1,396	6,045	72,536	37.65	1,506	6,521	78,252	40.40	1,616	6,997	83,967	43.15	1,726	7,474	89,683
34.95	1,398	6,053	72,640	37.70	1,508	6,530	78,356	40.45	1,618	7,006	84,071	43.20	1,728	7,482	89,787
35.00	1,400	6,062	72,744	37.75	1,510	6,538	78,460	40.50	1,620	7,015	84,175	43.25	1,730	7,491	89,891
35.05	1,402	6,071	72,848	37.80	1,512	6,547	78,564	40.55	1,622	7,023	84,279	43.30	1,732	7,500	89,995
35.10	1,404	6,079	72,952	37.85	1,514	6,556	78,667	40.60	1,624	7,032	84,383	43.35	1,734	7,508	90,099

Hour	Week	Month	Year	Hour	Week	Month	Year	Hour	Week	Month	Year	Hour	Week	Month	Year
43.40	1,736	7,517	90,203	46.15	1,846	7,993	95,918	48.90	1,956	8,469	101,634	51.65	2,066	8,946	107,349
43.45	1,738	7,526	90,306	46.20	1,848	8,002	96,022	48.95	1,958	8,478	101,738	51.70	2,068	8,954	107,453
43.50	1,740	7,534	90,410	46.25	1,850	8,010	96,126	49.00	1,960	8,487	101,842	51.75	2,070	8,963	107,557
43.55	1,742	7,543	90,514	46.30	1,852	8,019	96,230	49.05	1,962	8,495	101,946	51.80	2,072	8,972	107,661
43.60	1,744	7,552	90,618	46.35	1,854	8,028	96,334	49.10	1,964	8,504	102,049	51.85	2,074	8,980	107,765
43.65	1,746	7,560	90,722	46.40	1,856	8,036	96,438	49.15	1,966	8,513	102,153	51.90	2,076	8,989	107,869
43.70	1,748	7,569	90,826	46.45	1,858	8,045	96,542	49.20	1,968	8,521	102,257	51.95	2,078	8,998	107,973
43.75	1,750	7,577	90,930	46.50	1,860	8,054	96,646	49.25	1,970	8,530	102,361	52.00	2,080	9,006	108,077
43.80	1,752	7,586	91,034	46.55	1,862	8,062	96,750	49.30	1,972	8,539	102,465	52.05	2,082	9,015	108,181
43.85	1,754	7,595	91,138	46.60	1,864	8,071	96,853	49.35	1,974	8,547	102,569	52.10	2,084	9,024	108,285
43.90	1,756	7,603	91,242	46.65	1,866	8,080	96,957	49.40	1,976	8,556	102,673	52.15	2,086	9,032	108,389
43.95	1,758	7,612	91,346	46.70	1,868	8,088	97,061	49.45	1,978	8,565	102,777	52.20	2,088	9,041	108,492
44.00	1,760	7,621	91,450	46.75	1,870	8,097	97,165	49.50	1,980	8,573	102,881	52.25	2,090	9,050	108,596
44.05	1,762	7,629	91,554	46.80	1,872	8,106	97,269	49.55	1,982	8,582	102,985	52.30	2,092	9,058	108,700
44.10	1,764	7,638	91,657	46.85	1,874	8,114	97,373	49.60	1,984	8,591	103,089	52.35	2,094	9,067	108,804
44.15	1,766	7,647	91,761	46.90	1,876	8,123	97,477	49.65	1,986	8,599	103,193	52.40	2,096	9,076	108,908
44.20	1,768	7,655	91,865	46.95	1,878	8,132	97,581	49.70	1,988	8,608	103,296	52.45	2,098	9,084	109,012
44.25	1,770	7,664	91,969	47.00	1,880	8,140	97,685	49.75	1,990	8,617	103,400	52.50	2,100	9,093	109,116
44.30	1,772	7,673	92,073	47.05	1,882	8,149	97,789	49.80	1,992	8,625	103,504	52.55	2,102	9,102	109,220
44.35	1,774	7,681	92,177	47.10	1,884	8,158	97,893	49.85	1,994	8,634	103,608	52.60	2,104	9,110	109,324
44.40	1,776	7,690	92,281	47.15	1,886	8,166	97,997	49.90	1,996	8,643	103,712	52.65	2,106	9,119	109,428
44.45	1,778	7,699	92,385	47.20	1,888	8,175	98,100	49.95	1,998	8,651	103,816	52.70	2,108	9,128	109,532
44.50	1,780	7,707	92,489	47.25	1,890	8,184	98,204	50.00	2,000	8,660	103,920	52.75	2,110	9,136	109,636
44.55	1,782	7,716	92,593	47.30	1,892	8,192	98,308	50.05	2,002	8,669	104,024	52.80	2,112	9,145	109,740
44.60	1,784	7,725	92,697	47.35	1,894	8,201	98,412	50.10	2,004	8,677	104,128	52.85	2,114	9,154	109,843
44.65	1,786	7,733	92,801	47.40	1,896	8,210	98,516	50.15	2,006	8,686	104,232	52.90	2,116	9,162	109,947
44.70	1,788	7,742	92,904	47.45	1,898	8,218	98,620	50.20	2,008	8,695	104,336	52.95	2,118	9,171	110,051
44.75	1,790	7,751	93,008	47.50	1,900	8,227	98,724	50.25	2,010	8,703	104,440	53.00	2,120	9,180	110,155
44.80	1,792	7,759	93,112	47.55	1,902	8,236	98,828	50.30	2,012	8,712	104,544	53.05	2,122	9,188	110,259
44.85	1,794	7,768	93,216	47.60	1,904	8,244	98,932	50.35	2,014	8,721	104,647	53.10	2,124	9,197	110,363
44.90	1,796	7,777	93,320	47.65	1,906	8,253	99,036	50.40	2,016	8,729	104,751	53.15	2,126	9,206	110,467
44.95	1,798	7,785	93,424	47.70	1,908	8,262	99,140	50.45	2,018	8,738	104,855	53.20	2,128	9,214	110,571
45.00	1,800	7,794	93,528	47.75	1,910	8,270	99,244	50.50	2,020	8,747	104,959	53.25	2,130	9,223	110,675
45.05	1,802	7,803	93,632	47.80	1,912	8,279	99,348	50.55	2,022	8,755	105,063	53.30	2,132	9,232	110,779
45.10	1,804	7,811	93,736	47.85	1,914	8,288	99,451	50.60	2,024	8,764	105,167	53.35	2,134	9,240	110,883
45.15	1,806	7,820	93,840	47.90	1,916	8,296	99,555	50.65	2,026	8,773	105,271	53.40	2,136	9,249	110,987
45.20	1,808	7,829	93,944	47.95	1,918	8,305	99,659	50.70	2,028	8,781	105,375	53.45	2,138	9,258	111,090
45.25	1,810	7,837	94,048	48.00	1,920	8,314	99,763	50.75	2,030	8,790	105,479	53.50	2,140	9,266	111,194
45.30	1,812	7,846	94,152	48.05	1,922	8,322	99,867	50.80	2,032	8,799	105,583	53.55	2,142	9,275	111,298
45.35	1,814	7,855	94,255	48.10	1,924	8,331	99,971	50.85	2,034	8,807	105,687	53.60	2,144	9,284	111,402
45.40	1,816	7,863	94,359	48.15	1,926	8,340	100,075	50.90	2,036	8,816	105,791	53.65	2,146	9,292	111,506
45.45	1,818	7,872	94,463	48.20	1,928	8,348	100,179	50.95	2,038	8,825	105,894	53.70	2,148	9,301	111,610
45.50	1,820	7,881	94,567	48.25	1,930	8,357	100,283	51.00	2,040	8,833	105,998	53.75	2,150	9,309	111,714
45.55	1,822	7,889	94,671	48.30	1,932	8,366	100,387	51.05	2,042	8,842	106,102	53.80	2,152	9,318	111,818
45.60	1,824	7,898	94,775	48.35	1,934	8,374	100,491	51.10	2,044	8,851	106,206	53.85	2,154	9,327	111,922
45.65	1,826	7,907	94,879	48.40	1,936	8,383	100,595	51.15	2,046	8,859	106,310	53.90	2,156	9,335	112,026
45.70	1,828	7,915	94,983	48.45	1,938	8,392	100,698	51.20	2,048	8,868	106,414	53.95	2,158	9,344	112,130
45.75	1,830	7,924	95,087	48.50	1,940	8,400	100,802	51.25	2,050	8,876	106,518	54.00	2,160	9,353	112,234
45.80	1,832	7,933	95,191	48.55	1,942	8,409	100,906	51.30	2,052	8,885	106,622	54.05	2,162	9,361	112,338
45.85	1,834	7,941	95,295	48.60	1,944	8,418	101,010	51.35	2,054	8,894	106,726	54.10	2,164	9,370	112,441
45.90	1,836	7,950	95,399	48.65	1,946	8,426	101,114	51.40	2,056	8,902	106,830	54.15	2,166	9,379	112,545
45.95	1,838	7,959	95,502	48.70	1,948	8,435	101,218	51.45	2,058	8,911	106,934	54.20	2,168	9,387	112,649
46.00	1,840	7,967	95,606	48.75	1,950	8,443	101,322	51.50	2,060	8,920	107,038	54.25	2,170	9,396	112,753
46.05	1,842	7,976	95,710	48.80	1,952	8,452	101,426	51.55	2,062	8,928	107,142	54.30	2,172	9,405	112,857
46.10	1,844	7,985	95,814	48.85	1,954	8,461	101,530	51.60	2,064	8,937	107,245	54.35	2,174	9,413	112,961

Appendix III

ABBREVIATIONS

Acronyms used to abbreviate data sources may be found in Appendix I.

3YF	Wage after three years with firm	ERP	Enterprise Resource Planning
A+	CompTIA PC Technician Certification	FQ	First quartile wage
AAW	Average annual wage	H	Hourly
AE	Average entry wage paid	HI	Highest wage paid
AEX	Average experienced wage	HIO	Highest wage offered
AHW	Average hourly wage	HR	High end of range
AO	Average Offered	HTML	Hypertext Markup Language
AOH	Average Offered, high	IR	Intermediate range
AOL	Average Offered, low	LAN	Local Area Network
APH	Average pay, high range	LO	Lowest wage paid
APL	Average pay, low range	LOO	Lowest wage offered
ASL	Average starting salary, low range	LR	Low end of range
ASH	Average starting salary, high range	M	Monthly
ASW	Average senior wage	MCP	Microsoft Certified Proffessional rating
AW	Average wage paid	MCSE	Microsoft Certified Systems Engineer rating
AWO	Average wage offered	MDO	Median wage offered
AWR	Average wage range	MRI	Magnetic Resonance Imaging
BOR	Beginning of range	MW	Median wage paid
BR	Beginning range	p	Publication date
CAD	Computer-Aided Design	PBX	Private Branch Exchange
CAT	Computerized Axial Tomography	PC	Personal Computer
CD-ROM	Compact Disk Read-Only Memory	S	Special: hourly and annual
CNC	Computerized Numerical Control	SCM	Supply Chain Management
CNE	Novell Engineer rating	SFA	Sales Force Automation
CRM	Customer Relations Management	SQ	Second quartile wage
CT	Computerized Axial Tomography	SR	Senior range
D	Daily	TMC	Total Median Compensation
EEG	Electroencephalograph	TQ	Third quartile wage
EKG	Electrocardiograph	WAN	Wide Area Network
EMT	Emergency Medical Technician	W	Weekly
ENF	Experienced; new to firm	XML	Extensible Markup Language
EOR	End of range	Y	Yearly

Appendix IV

EMPLOYMENT BY OCCUPATION - 1998 AND 2008

This appendix displays data from the *National Industry-Occupational Matrix* prepared by the Department of Labor (DOL) from time to time. The data show employment by occuption for 1998 with DOL projections to 2008. The appendix is divided into three parts. The first part shows the occupations in alphabetical order using occupation titles as defined by DOL. The only exceptions are cases where the DOL refers to "All other" followed by an occupation. These have been rendered by the name of the occupation, followed by the abbreviation 'nec' to indicate 'not elsewhere classified.' The second arrangement shows occupations by 1998 employment, largest category first. The third sort is by rate of growth, 1998 to 2008, the fastest growing occupation shown first. Data were released in November 1999 and are referred to as *National OES Matrices*.

Alphabetical Order

Total Employment 1998	2008	% Change	Occupation	Total Employment 1998	2008	% Change	Occupation
22,749	23,914	5.1	Able seamen, ordinary seamen, and marine oilers				operators
				342,278	392,132	14.6	Billing, cost, and rate clerks
1,079,726	1,201,630	11.3	Accountants and auditors	89,554	99,893	11.5	Bindery machine operators and set-up
160,024	198,129	23.8	Actors, directors, and producers				operators
16,160	17,299	7.0	Actuaries	80,950	109,275	35.0	Biological scientists
479,015	641,644	34.0	Adjustment clerks	2,197,772	2,394,074	8.9	Blue-collar worker supervisors
364,259	430,246	18.1	Administrative services managers	16,005	14,240	-11.0	Boiler operators and tenders, low pressure
13,578	14,169	4.4	Advertising clerks	18,298	18,587	1.6	Boilermakers
485,214	596,768	23.0	Advertising, marketing, promotions, public relations, and sales managers	6,627	5,621	-15.2	Bookbinders
				2,077,615	1,996,596	-3.9	Bookkeeping, accounting, and auditing clerks
53,035	57,680	8.8	Aerospace engineers	156,986	176,299	12.3	Bricklayers, blockmasons, and stonemasons
21,468	23,816	10.9	Agricultural and food scientists	36,607	38,792	6.0	Broadcast and sound technicians
373,194	379,396	1.7	Agricultural, forestry, fishing, and related workers nec	76,512	98,231	28.4	Brokerage clerks
				62,745	71,187	13.5	Brokers, real estate
29,739	30,425	2.3	Air traffic controllers	59,173	67,291	13.7	Budget analysts
16,631	19,840	19.3	Aircraft assemblers, precision	254,820	279,790	9.8	Bus and truck mechanics and diesel engine specialists
132,880	146,716	10.4	Aircraft mechanics and service technicians				
93,585	99,092	5.9	Aircraft pilots and flight engineers	434,753	511,118	17.6	Bus drivers, school
19,294	26,054	35.0	Ambulance drivers and attendants, except EMTs	203,323	235,444	15.8	Bus drivers, transit and intercity
				216,156	200,796	-7.1	Butchers and meatcutters
337,273	439,060	30.2	Amusement and recreation attendants	122,957	129,391	5.2	Cabinetmakers and bench carpenters
136,754	166,341	21.6	Animal caretakers, except farm	9,029	9,770	8.2	Camera and photographic equipment repairers
60,182	57,576	-4.3	Announcers	9,248	6,347	-31.4	Camera operators
99,162	117,885	18.9	Architects, except landscape and naval	49,541	43,581	-12.0	Cannery workers
23,202	26,134	12.6	Archivists, curators, museum technicians, and conservators	11,370	9,257	-18.6	Captains and other officers, fishing vessels
				18,552	19,109	3.0	Captains and pilots, water vessels
308,496	387,813	25.7	Artists and commercial artists	20,803	28,997	39.4	Cardiovascular technologists and technicians
1,976,184	2,174,526	10.0	Assemblers, fabricators, and hand workers nec	1,070,759	1,145,033	6.9	Carpenters
22,397	25,044	11.8	Assessors	84,524	87,560	3.6	Carpet installers
51,922	66,405	27.9	Athletes, coaches, umpires, and related workers	25,070	27,836	11.0	Carpet, floor, and tile installers and finishers
8,419	9,649	14.6	Atmospheric scientists	3,197,813	3,754,023	17.4	Cashiers
226,956	262,922	15.8	Automotive body and related repairers	15,580	16,971	8.9	Ceiling tile installers and acoustical carpenters
789,566	921,511	16.7	Automotive mechanics and service technicians	32,144	27,139	-15.6	Cement and gluing machine operators and tenders
39,814	45,257	13.7	Baggage porters and bellhops				
171,191	199,655	16.6	Bakers, bread and pastry	44,437	58,783	32.3	Central office and PBX installers and repairers
54,956	59,613	8.5	Bakers, manufacturing	23,023	19,195	-16.6	Central office operators
559,778	529,122	-5.5	Bank tellers	48,363	52,967	9.5	Chemical engineers
54,288	50,300	-7.3	Barbers	100,025	111,412	11.4	Chemical equipment controllers, operators and tenders
403,828	411,504	1.9	Bartenders				
10,817	13,257	22.6	Bicycle repairers	42,959	47,696	11.0	Chemical plant and system operators
310,774	420,454	35.3	Bill and account collectors	96,372	109,732	13.9	Chemists
106,559	103,835	-2.6	Billing and posting clerks and machine	904,542	1,140,588	26.1	Child care workers

Total Employment 1998	2008	% Change	Occupation	Total Employment 1998	2008	% Change	Occupation
306,377	209,157	-31.7	Child care workers, private household				and tenders
46,256	56,799	22.8	Chiropractors	14,931	11,881	-20.4	Dairy processing equipment operators, including setters
195,028	235,858	20.9	Civil engineers				
48,746	54,828	12.5	Claims examiners, property and casualty insurance	28,651	32,554	13.6	Dancers and choreographers
				434,803	473,991	9.0	Data entry keyers
600,311	529,618	-11.8	Cleaners and servants, private household	79,337	116,649	47.0	Data processing equipment repairers
287,607	359,556	25.0	Cleaners of vehicles and equipment	87,421	154,885	77.2	Database administrators
300,136	320,252	6.7	Cleaning and building service workers	228,877	325,429	42.2	Dental assistants
149,179	169,101	13.4	Clergy	143,342	201,449	40.5	Dental hygienists
953,300	1,115,534	17.0	Clerical and administrative support workers	43,840	44,272	1.0	Dental laboratory technicians, precision
313,040	366,377	17.0	Clinical laboratory technologists and technicians	160,139	165,115	3.1	Dentists
				335,260	425,952	27.1	Designers, except interior designers
129,051	140,261	8.7	Coating, painting, and spraying machine operators, tenders, setters, and set-up operators	25,607	44,200	72.6	Desktop publishing specialists
				79,167	95,802	21.0	Detectives and criminal investigators
				53,972	64,291	19.1	Dietitians and nutritionists
21,679	22,224	2.5	Coil winders, tapers, and finishers	405,469	421,509	4.0	Dining room and cafeteria attendants and bar helpers
27,015	31,216	15.6	Coin, vending, and amusement machine servicers and repairers				
				111,599	139,612	25.1	Directors, religious activities and education
865,356	1,060,502	22.6	College and university faculty	23,413	16,136	-31.1	Directory assistance operators
107,020	121,832	13.8	Combination machine tool setters, set-up operators, operators, and tenders, metal and plastic	162,561	185,935	14.4	Dispatchers, except police, fire, and ambulance
				85,438	92,236	8.0	Dispatchers, police, fire, and ambulance
				283,191	301,199	6.4	Drafters
195,951	233,723	19.3	Communication, transportation, and utilities operations managers	41,930	34,240	-18.3	Drilling and boring machine tool setters and set-up operators, metal and plastic
36,488	31,522	-13.6	Communications equipment operators	304,768	319,127	4.7	Driver/sales workers
13,649	11,064	-18.9	Compositors and typesetters, precision	163,021	175,234	7.5	Drywall installers and finishers
299,308	622,113	107.9	Computer engineers	197,036	200,731	1.9	Duplicating, mail, and other office machine operators
223,893	169,983	-24.1	Computer operators, except peripheral equipment				
				70,032	82,949	18.4	Economists and marketing research analysts
647,783	838,902	29.5	Computer programmers	447,158	505,456	13.0	Education administrators
97,493	212,093	117.5	Computer scientists	12,497	9,608	-23.1	EKG technicians
429,316	868,674	102.3	Computer support specialists	246,070	265,001	7.7	Electrical and electronic assemblers
139,194	147,703	6.1	Concrete finishers, cement masons, and terrazzo workers	200,922	213,037	6.0	Electrical and electronic equipment assemblers, precision
38,949	45,918	17.9	Conservation scientists and foresters	334,810	391,111	16.8	Electrical and electronic technicians and technologists
68,104	78,779	15.7	Construction and building inspectors				
270,041	307,817	14.0	Construction managers	356,954	449,582	25.9	Electrical and electronics engineers
146,393	154,760	5.7	Construction trades workers	98,758	99,847	1.1	Electrical powerline installers and repairers
30,516	27,929	-8.5	Cooking and roasting machine operators and tenders, food and tobacco	656,151	723,743	10.3	Electricians
				45,050	49,367	9.6	Electrolytic plating machine setters, set-up operators, operators, and tenders, metal and plastic
418,355	430,509	2.9	Cooks, institution or cafeteria				
4,511	2,196	-51.3	Cooks, private household	49,541	52,365	5.7	Electromechanical equipment assemblers, precision
783,180	929,469	18.7	Cooks, restaurant				
676,576	800,994	18.4	Cooks, short order and fast food	5,417	5,738	5.9	Electroneurodiagnostic technologists
383,408	531,756	38.7	Correctional officers	35,713	31,461	-11.9	Electronic home entertainment equipment repairers
24,877	27,912	12.2	Correspondence clerks				
151,687	171,394	13.0	Cost estimators	63,367	91,979	45.2	Electronic semiconductor processors
182,260	227,806	25.0	Counselors	71,558	80,623	12.7	Electronics repairers, commercial and industrial equipment
468,686	577,022	23.1	Counter and rental clerks				
119,729	130,284	8.8	Couriers and messengers	29,608	33,230	12.2	Elevator installers and repairers
51,209	56,750	10.8	Court clerks	149,961	197,353	31.6	Emergency medical technicians and paramedics
109,953	120,605	9.7	Court reporters, medical transciptionists, and stenographers				
48,564	48,789	0.5	Crane and tower operators	65,830	74,328	12.9	Employment interviewers, private or public employment service
41,971	50,317	19.9	Credit analysts				
16,906	15,092	-10.7	Credit authorizers	436,530	506,115	15.9	Engineering technicians and technologists
40,955	41,552	1.5	Credit checkers	326,229	467,983	43.5	Engineering, natural science, and computer and information systems managers
54,341	56,533	4.0	Crossing guards				
149,526	153,658	2.8	Crushing, grinding, mixing, and blending machine operators and tenders	414,611	508,512	22.6	Engineers
				105,966	122,160	15.3	Excavation and loading machine operators
73,641	67,459	-8.4	Custom tailors and sewers	151,998	173,468	14.1	Extraction and related workers
42,145	38,626	-8.3	Cutters and trimmers, hand	32,815	35,411	7.9	Extruding and forming machine operators and tenders, synthetic or glass fibers
95,988	102,158	6.4	Cutting and slicing machine setters, operators				

Total Employment 1998	2008	% Change	Occupation
125,555	131,829	5.0	Extruding and forming machine setters, operators and tenders
18,415	16,297	-11.5	Fallers and buckers
9,977	9,753	-2.2	Farm and home management advisors
49,408	46,846	-5.2	Farm equipment mechanics
175,026	173,686	-0.8	Farm managers
850,533	793,989	-6.6	Farm workers
1,307,712	1,135,018	-13.2	Farmers
272,113	298,344	9.6	File clerks
22,724	15,215	-33.0	Film strippers, printing
693,291	790,646	14.0	Financial managers
59,934	66,325	10.7	Fire fighting and prevention supervisors
14,516	17,010	17.2	Fire inspection occupations
239,320	250,608	4.7	Firefighters
39,726	30,715	-22.7	Fishers
16,713	14,539	-13.0	Fitters, structural metal, precision
99,053	128,881	30.1	Flight attendants
2,024,626	2,271,838	12.2	Food counter, fountain, and related workers
279,765	306,133	9.4	Food preparation and service workers
1,256,251	1,386,903	10.4	Food preparation workers
594,642	691,364	16.3	Food service and lodging managers
32,667	32,884	0.7	Forest and conservation workers
9,295	9,524	2.5	Foundry mold assembly and shake out workers
822,119	834,178	1.5	Freight, stock, and material movers, hand
27,527	31,953	16.1	Funeral directors and morticians
23,073	21,915	-5.0	Furnace operators and tenders
24,909	23,518	-5.6	Furnace, kiln, oven, drier, or kettle operators and tenders
38,486	38,096	-1.0	Furniture finishers
37,526	32,806	-12.6	Gas and petroleum plant and system occupations
3,362,395	3,913,196	16.4	General managers and top executives
43,880	50,690	15.5	Geologists, geophysicists, and oceanographers
44,266	45,994	3.9	Glaziers
79,793	82,042	2.8	Government chief executives and legislators
121,788	128,778	5.7	Grader, bulldozer, and scraper operators
80,628	84,066	4.3	Grinders and polishers, hand
74,996	67,763	-9.6	Grinding, lapping, and buffing machine tool setters and set-up operators, metal and plastic
1,026,723	1,320,797	28.6	Guards
605,165	666,969	10.2	Hairdressers, hairstylists, and cosmetologists
984,044	1,197,207	21.7	Hand packers and packagers
28,660	31,162	8.7	Hard tile setters
37,725	45,003	19.3	Hazardous materials removal workers
64,451	60,797	-5.7	Head sawyers and sawing machine operators and tenders, setters and set-up operators
509,525	687,761	35.0	Health professionals and paraprofessionals
184,924	226,211	22.3	Health service workers
23,344	22,376	-4.1	Heat treating, annealing, and tempering machine operators and tenders, metal and plastic
285,922	334,332	16.9	Heating, air conditioning, and refrigeration mechanics and installers
575,959	618,241	7.3	Helpers, construction trades
1,933,840	2,193,758	13.4	Helpers, laborers, and material movers, hand
155,284	172,510	11.1	Highway maintenance workers
10,627	11,263	6.0	Hoist and winch operators
50,894	53,722	5.6	Home appliance and power tool repairers
297,190	351,149	18.2	Hosts and hostesses, restaurant, lounge, or coffee shop
158,662	180,080	13.5	Hotel, motel, and resort desk clerks
17,160	9,883	-42.4	Housekeepers and butlers
141,775	144,666	2.0	Human resources assistants, except payroll and timekeeping
229,594	274,226	19.4	Human resources managers
367,370	432,966	17.9	Human resources, training, and labor relations specialists
126,303	142,427	12.8	Industrial engineers, except safety engineers
535,469	559,204	4.4	Industrial machinery mechanics
208,345	206,508	-0.9	Industrial production managers
415,443	453,769	9.2	Industrial truck and tractor operators
176,175	194,711	10.5	Inspectors and compliance officers, except construction
688,730	666,896	-3.2	Inspectors, testers, and graders, precision
87,412	96,549	10.5	Institutional cleaning supervisors
358,512	460,429	28.4	Instructors and coaches, sports and physical training
168,046	203,141	20.9	Instructors, adult (nonvocational) education
66,614	71,579	7.5	Insulation workers
180,112	216,881	20.4	Insurance adjusters, examiners, and investigators
10,452	12,122	16.0	Insurance appraisers, auto damage
159,506	182,583	14.5	Insurance claims clerks
9,532	11,184	17.3	Insurance examining clerks
169,806	183,286	7.9	Insurance policy processing clerks
387,295	395,811	2.2	Insurance sales agents
96,949	99,539	2.7	Insurance underwriters
53,291	67,799	27.2	Interior designers
128,057	157,845	23.3	Interviewing clerks, except personnel and social welfare
3,183,804	3,549,015	11.5	Janitors and cleaners, including maids and housekeeping cleaners
29,653	27,865	-6.0	Jewelers and precious stone and metal workers
17,049	17,777	4.3	Job printers
70,807	72,857	2.9	Judges, magistrates, and other judicial workers
1,129,934	1,364,383	20.7	Laborers, landscaping and groundskeeping
22,060	25,265	14.5	Landscape architects
72,226	66,150	-8.4	Lathe and turning machine tool setters and set-up operators, metal and plastic
167,423	183,753	9.8	Laundry and dry-cleaning machine operators and tenders, except pressing
86,354	103,606	20.0	Lawn service managers
680,955	798,039	17.2	Lawyers
85,959	95,922	11.6	Legal assistants, including law clerks
285,120	322,047	13.0	Legal secretaries
10,139	8,293	-18.2	Letterpress operators
152,094	159,401	4.8	Librarians
126,691	147,568	16.5	Library assistants and bookmobile drivers
72,254	85,418	18.2	Library technicians
24,103	27,259	13.1	License clerks
691,953	828,397	19.7	Licensed practical and licensed vocational nurses
965	1,125	16.6	Life scientists
179,306	200,389	11.8	Loan and credit clerks
227,410	275,572	21.2	Loan counselors and officers
16,379	13,598	-17.0	Loan interviewers
27,146	29,849	10.0	Locksmiths and safe repairers
33,179	34,788	4.8	Locomotive engineers
55,862	54,768	-2.0	Logging equipment operators
67,388	71,100	5.5	Machine assemblers
74,418	75,683	1.7	Machine builders and other precision machine assemblers
212,822	210,840	-0.9	Machine feeders and offbearers
162,881	156,579	-3.9	Machine forming operators and tenders, metal and plastic
634,971	731,515	15.2	Machine operators, tenders, setters, and set-up

Total Employment 1998	2008	% Change	Occupation	Total Employment 1998	2008	% Change	Occupation
			operators				and managers
109,331	87,579	-19.9	Machine tool cutting operators and tenders, metal and plastic	3,020,975	3,484,090	15.3	Office clerks, general
				58,383	67,492	15.6	Office machine and cash register servicers
217,821	234,526	7.7	Machine tool setters, set-up operators, metal and plastic nec	62,734	53,539	-14.7	Offset lithographic press operators
				39,598	39,603	0.0	Oil and gas extraction occupations nec
426,028	452,425	6.2	Machinists	125,500	135,370	7.9	Operating engineers
127,581	139,745	9.5	Mail clerks, except mail machine operators and postal service	76,320	82,984	8.7	Operations research analysts
				22,714	23,774	4.7	Ophthalmic laboratory technicians
1,232,476	1,327,288	7.7	Maintenance repairers, general utility	71,467	81,300	13.8	Opticians, dispensing
344,494	442,182	28.4	Management analysts	37,889	41,891	10.6	Optometrists
1,129,760	1,366,140	20.9	Management support workers nec	361,879	378,490	4.6	Order clerks
2,114,359	2,419,824	14.4	Managers and administrators nec	36,855	40,337	9.4	Other law enforcement occupations
48,851	61,530	26.0	Manicurists	376,592	425,240	12.9	Packaging and filling machine operators and tenders
2,583,772	2,846,839	10.2	Marketing and sales worker supervisors				
227,556	246,539	8.3	Material moving equipment operators nec	475,937	516,671	8.6	Painters and paperhangers
196,179	209,520	6.8	Material recording, scheduling, and distribution workers nec	41,864	45,634	9.0	Painters, transportation equipment
				39,129	46,071	17.7	Painting, coating, and decorating workers, hand
19,654	21,414	9.0	Materials engineers	61,894	59,332	-4.1	Paper goods machine setters and set-up operators
8,054	8,689	7.9	Mates, ship, boat, and barge				
14,036	13,271	-5.5	Mathematicians and all other mathematical scientists	136,045	220,448	62.0	Paralegals and legal assistants
				86,006	112,848	31.2	Parking lot attendants
142,983	177,653	24.2	Meat, poultry, and fish cutters and trimmers, hand	299,688	303,226	1.2	Parts salespersons
				9,037	4,413	-51.2	Paste-up workers
219,654	255,744	16.4	Mechanical engineers	15,968	15,363	-3.8	Patternmakers and layout workers, fabric and apparel
455,281	520,175	14.3	Mechanics, installers, and repairers nec				
222,441	296,569	33.3	Medical and health services managers	73,980	81,848	10.6	Paving, surfacing, and tamping equipment operators
252,246	397,955	57.8	Medical assistants				
10,715	12,160	13.5	Medical equipment repairers	171,512	160,921	-6.2	Payroll and timekeeping clerks
92,366	132,948	43.9	Medical records and health information technicians	27,209	16,965	-37.6	Peripheral equipment operators
				745,671	1,179,084	58.1	Personal care and home health aides
31,139	38,804	24.6	Medical scientists	51,865	65,021	25.4	Pest control workers
219,309	245,697	12.0	Medical secretaries	12,061	11,625	-3.6	Petroleum engineers
34,056	38,372	12.7	Merchandise displayers and window dressers	185,324	198,868	7.3	Pharmacists
148,078	165,732	11.9	Metal and plastic machine setters, operators, and related workers nec	61,301	71,020	15.9	Pharmacy aides
				108,690	125,790	15.7	Pharmacy technicians
45,790	49,210	7.5	Metal fabricators, structural metal products	2,747	1,332	-51.5	Photoengravers
57,606	62,766	9.0	Metal molding machine setters, set-up operators, operators, and tenders	6,769	5,752	-15.0	Photoengraving and lithographic machine operators and tenders
50,382	50,565	0.4	Meter readers, utilities	149,378	160,921	7.7	Photographers
82,331	80,805	-1.9	Millwrights	17,751	18,990	7.0	Photographic process workers, precision
4,444	3,883	-12.6	Mining engineers, including mine safety engineers	45,741	40,512	-11.4	Photographic processing machine operators and tenders
22,794	18,443	-19.1	Mining, quarrying, and tunneling occupations	33,178	40,716	22.7	Physical scientists nec
105,921	115,805	9.3	Mobile heavy equipment mechanics	119,999	160,754	34.0	Physical therapists
91,566	121,169	32.3	Models, demonstrators, and product promoters	82,147	118,043	43.7	Physical therapy assistants and aides
9,323	7,292	-21.8	Motion picture projectionists	66,263	98,102	48.0	Physician assistants
39,962	36,572	-8.5	Motor vehicle operators nec	576,870	698,946	21.2	Physicians
13,933	14,470	3.9	Motorcycle mechanics	17,932	18,328	2.2	Physicists and astronomers
24,795	27,751	11.9	Municipal clerks	57,355	60,187	4.9	Pipelayers and pipelaying fitters
12,591	13,407	6.5	Musical instrument repairers and tuners	147,739	164,092	11.1	Plant and system operators nec
273,327	313,909	14.8	Musicians, singers, and related workers	40,316	47,194	17.1	Plasterers and stucco masons
111,041	127,321	14.7	New accounts clerks, banking	171,082	196,185	14.7	Plastic molding machine setters, set-up operators, operators, and tenders
66,560	68,449	2.8	News analysts, reporters, and correspondents				
11,694	12,367	5.8	Nuclear engineers	14,537	13,779	-5.2	Platemakers
13,967	15,592	11.6	Nuclear medicine technologists	426,325	448,752	5.3	Plumbers, pipefitters, and steamfitters
87,978	107,844	22.6	Numerical control machine tool operators and tenders, metal and plastic	13,904	15,370	10.5	Podiatrists
				110,812	124,093	12.0	Police and detective supervisors
8,471	8,991	6.1	Numerical control machine tool programmers	445,632	586,423	31.6	Police patrol officers
5,154	5,931	15.1	Nursery and greenhouse managers	331,981	356,689	7.4	Postal mail carriers
1,366,632	1,691,547	23.8	Nursing aides, orderlies, and attendants	72,812	77,742	6.8	Postal service clerks
73,123	98,152	34.2	Occupational therapists	26,362	27,162	3.0	Postmasters and mail superintendents
18,619	26,025	39.8	Occupational therapy assistants and aides	13,702	12,033	-12.2	Power distributors and dispatchers
1,610,814	1,923,572	19.4	Office and administrative support supervisors	31,435	32,398	3.1	Power generating and reactor plant operators

Total Employment 1998	2008	% Change	Occupation	Total Employment 1998	2008	% Change	Occupation
63,860	66,219	3.7	Precision assemblers nec	303,053	427,386	41.0	Securities, commodities, and financial services sales agents
39,016	42,348	8.5	Precision food and tobacco workers nec				
33,310	31,970	-4.0	Precision instrument repairers	28,492	26,436	-7.2	Separating, filtering, clarifying, precipitating, and still machine operators and tenders
96,740	100,624	4.0	Precision metal workers nec				
55,187	57,639	4.4	Precision textile, apparel, and furnishings workers nec	140,679	138,987	-1.2	Service station attendants
				1,249,444	1,490,057	19.3	Service workers nec
27,460	26,760	-2.5	Precision woodworkers nec	9,790	8,337	-14.8	Sewers, hand
157,217	179,176	14.0	Precision workers nec	368,701	256,885	-30.3	Sewing machine operators, garment
13,467	11,931	-11.4	Pressers, hand	136,689	140,154	2.5	Sewing machine operators, non-garment
68,791	66,024	-4.0	Pressing machine operators and tenders, textile, garment, and related materials	14,788	16,933	14.5	Shampooers
				229,700	262,017	14.1	Sheet metal workers and duct installers
142,242	154,056	8.3	Printing press machine setters, operators and tenders	91,479	122,758	34.2	Sheriffs and deputy sheriffs
				6,236	6,505	4.3	Ship engineers
9,500	9,074	-4.5	Printing press setters and set-up operators	8,673	8,286	-4.5	Shipfitters
16,844	16,878	0.2	Printing workers, precision nec	999,864	1,031,146	3.1	Shipping, receiving, and traffic clerks
43,260	45,021	4.1	Printing, binding, and related workers nec	22,803	18,798	-17.6	Shoe and leather workers and repairers, precision
60,771	75,551	24.3	Private detectives and investigators				
58,103	49,498	-14.8	Procurement clerks	6,506	4,175	-35.8	Shoe sewing machine operators and tenders
248,148	249,156	0.4	Production, planning, and expediting clerks	38,063	39,981	5.0	Small engine mechanics
785,407	951,577	21.2	Professional workers nec	268,444	409,872	52.7	Social and human service assistants
41,401	34,323	-17.1	Proofreaders and copy markers	50,108	56,495	12.7	Social scientists nec
315,461	358,698	13.7	Property, real estate, and community association managers	604,102	822,148	36.1	Social workers
				35,281	40,349	14.4	Solderers and brazers
166,335	197,946	19.0	Protective service workers nec	12,087	13,079	8.2	Soldering and brazing machine operators and tenders
45,058	50,495	12.1	Pruners				
94,709	102,003	7.7	Psychiatric aides	105,024	145,424	38.5	Speech-language pathologists and audiologists
66,045	73,257	10.9	Psychiatric technicians	18,771	23,206	23.6	Sprayers/applicators
165,827	184,655	11.4	Psychologists	15,647	12,151	-22.3	Statement clerks
122,329	152,413	24.6	Public relations specialists	24,467	16,208	-33.8	Station installers and repairers, telephone
47,025	43,517	-7.5	Punching machine setters and set-up operators, metal and plastic	31,258	29,471	-5.7	Stationary engineers
				72,143	68,925	-4.5	Statistical clerks
28,980	30,428	5.0	Purchasing agents and buyers, farm	16,529	16,910	2.3	Statisticians
224,149	248,339	10.8	Purchasing agents, except wholesale, retail, and farm products	2,331,436	2,462,429	5.6	Stock clerks and order fillers
				80,842	87,307	8.0	Structural and reinforcing metal workers
175,977	188,483	7.1	Purchasing managers	3,329	3,565	7.1	Subway and streetcar operators
12,366	14,427	16.7	Radiation therapists	91,546	97,250	6.2	Supervisors, farming, forestry, and agricutural related occupations
7,030	6,930	-1.4	Radio mechanics				
161,662	194,076	20.1	Radiologic technologists and technicians	54,038	76,636	41.8	Surgical technologists
8,431	5,431	-35.6	Rail transportation workers nec	68,674	83,664	21.8	Surveying and mapping technicians
14,164	7,391	-47.8	Railroad brake, signal, and switch operators	41,333	41,913	1.4	Surveyors, cartographers, and photogrammetrists
25,421	23,710	-6.7	Railroad conductors and yardmasters				
47,896	53,241	11.2	Real estate appraisers	214,464	184,739	-13.9	Switchboard operators
1,293,450	1,598,873	23.6	Receptionists and information clerks	616,915	1,194,234	93.6	Systems analysts
240,651	286,938	19.2	Recreation workers	62,246	65,599	5.4	Tax examiners, collectors, and revenue agents
38,737	43,914	13.4	Recreational therapists	79,378	94,707	19.3	Tax preparers
98,801	102,637	3.9	Refuse and recyclable material collectors	131,576	157,887	20.0	Taxi drivers and chauffeurs
2,078,810	2,529,674	21.7	Registered nurses	1,191,790	1,566,888	31.5	Teacher assistants
42,996	47,591	10.7	Religious workers nec	643,658	738,577	14.7	Teachers and instructors nec
218,759	231,791	6.0	Reservation and transportation ticket agents and travel clerks	419,625	465,614	11.0	Teachers and instructors, vocational education and training
189,875	277,787	46.3	Residential counselors	1,754,475	1,959,221	11.7	Teachers, elementary school
86,449	123,238	42.6	Respiratory therapists	183,560	208,148	13.4	Teachers, kindergarten
4,056,472	4,619,676	13.9	Retail salespersons	345,575	437,223	26.5	Teachers, preschool
11,287	11,346	0.5	Riggers	1,426,213	1,748,529	22.6	Teachers, secondary school
157,774	176,638	12.0	Roofers	406,036	543,465	33.8	Teachers, special education
29,562	23,325	-21.1	Roustabouts, oil and gas	20,351	21,194	4.1	Technicians nec
284,627	310,352	9.0	Sales agents, real estate	49,361	55,927	13.3	Telecommunications equipment mechanics, installers, and repairers nec
3,387,590	3,945,308	16.5	Sales and related workers nec				
79,437	91,927	15.7	Sales engineers	180,224	234,747	30.3	Telephone and cable TV line installers and repairers
227,444	243,270	7.0	Science and mathematics technicians				
28,341	29,183	3.0	Screen printing machine setters and set-up operators	24,487	22,291	-9.0	Textile bleaching and dyeing machine operators and tenders
2,690,424	2,690,512	0.0	Secretaries, except legal and medical	191,588	141,129	-26.3	Textile draw-out and winding machine

Total Employment 1998	2008	% Change	Occupation	Total Employment 1998	2008	% Change	Occupation
			operators and tenders	1,426,213	1,748,529	22.6	Teachers, secondary school
28,220	25,522	-9.6	Textile machine setters and set-up operators	1,366,632	1,691,547	23.8	Nursing aides, orderlies, and attendants
39,973	54,242	35.7	Therapists nec	1,307,712	1,135,018	-13.2	Farmers
12,823	12,059	-6.0	Timber cutting and related logging workers nec	1,293,450	1,598,873	23.6	Receptionists and information clerks
17,648	17,397	-1.4	Tire building machine operators	1,256,251	1,386,903	10.4	Food preparation workers
83,140	91,827	10.4	Tire repairers and changers	1,249,444	1,490,057	19.3	Service workers nec
29,664	29,481	-0.6	Title examiners, abstractors, and searchers	1,232,476	1,327,288	7.7	Maintenance repairers, general utility
137,802	135,714	-1.5	Tool and die makers	1,191,790	1,566,888	31.5	Teacher assistants
182,679	221,985	21.5	Transportation and material moving equipment operators nec	1,129,934	1,364,383	20.7	Laborers, landscaping and groundskeeping
				1,129,760	1,366,140	20.9	Management support workers nec
137,897	163,241	18.4	Travel agents	1,079,726	1,201,630	11.3	Accountants and auditors
2,969,641	3,462,638	16.6	Truck drivers light and heavy	1,070,759	1,145,033	6.9	Carpenters
13,366	5,379	-59.8	Typesetting and composing machine operators and tenders	1,026,723	1,320,797	28.6	Guards
				999,864	1,031,146	3.1	Shipping, receiving, and traffic clerks
66,375	66,954	0.9	Upholsterers	984,044	1,197,207	21.7	Hand packers and packagers
34,702	40,755	17.4	Urban and regional planners	953,300	1,115,534	17.0	Clerical and administrative support workers
84,337	99,202	17.6	Ushers, lobby attendants, and ticket takers	904,542	1,140,588	26.1	Child care workers
57,038	71,126	24.7	Veterinarians	865,356	1,060,502	22.6	College and university faculty
44,598	57,086	28.0	Veterinary assistants	850,533	793,989	-6.6	Farm workers
32,035	37,224	16.2	Veterinary technologists and technicians	822,119	834,178	1.5	Freight, stock, and material movers, hand
2,018,569	2,321,822	15.0	Waiters and waitresses	789,566	921,511	16.7	Automotive mechanics and service technicians
8,449	8,097	-4.2	Watch repairers	785,407	951,577	21.2	Professional workers nec
98,267	112,184	14.2	Water and liquid waste treatment plant and system operators	783,180	929,469	18.7	Cooks, restaurant
				745,671	1,179,084	58.1	Personal care and home health aides
50,591	51,357	1.5	Weighers, measurers, checkers, and samplers, recordkeeping	693,291	790,646	14.0	Financial managers
				691,953	828,397	19.7	Licensed practical and licensed vocational nurses
367,708	398,362	8.3	Welders and cutters				
109,604	115,507	5.4	Welding machine setters, operators, and tenders	688,730	666,896	-3.2	Inspectors, testers, and graders, precision
				680,955	798,039	17.2	Lawyers
108,675	100,425	-7.6	Welfare eligibility workers and interviewers	676,576	800,994	18.4	Cooks, short order and fast food
118,201	117,731	-0.4	Wholesale and retail buyers, except farm products	656,151	723,743	10.3	Electricians
				647,783	838,902	29.5	Computer programmers
40,024	41,288	3.2	Wood machinists	643,658	738,577	14.7	Teachers and instructors nec
78,792	68,918	-12.5	Woodworking machine operators and tenders, setters and set-up operators	634,971	731,515	15.2	Machine operators, tenders, setters, and set-up operators
458,910	365,474	-20.4	Word processors and typists	616,915	1,194,234	93.6	Systems analysts
340,805	423,872	24.4	Writers and editors, including technical writers	605,165	666,969	10.2	Hairdressers, hairstylists, and cosmetologists
				604,102	822,148	36.1	Social workers
				600,311	529,618	-11.8	Cleaners and servants, private household
				594,642	691,364	16.3	Food service and lodging managers
				576,870	698,946	21.2	Physicians

Employment Order - 1998

4,056,472	4,619,676	13.9	Retail salespersons	575,959	618,241	7.3	Helpers, construction trades
3,387,590	3,945,308	16.5	Sales and related workers nec	559,778	529,122	-5.5	Bank tellers
3,362,395	3,913,196	16.4	General managers and top executives	535,469	559,204	4.4	Industrial machinery mechanics
3,197,813	3,754,023	17.4	Cashiers	509,525	687,761	35.0	Health professionals and paraprofessionals
3,183,804	3,549,015	11.5	Janitors and cleaners, including maids and housekeeping cleaners	485,214	596,768	23.0	Advertising, marketing, promotions, public relations, and sales managers
3,020,975	3,484,090	15.3	Office clerks, general				
2,969,641	3,462,638	16.6	Truck drivers light and heavy	479,015	641,644	34.0	Adjustment clerks
2,690,424	2,690,512	0.0	Secretaries, except legal and medical	475,937	516,671	8.6	Painters and paperhangers
2,583,772	2,846,839	10.2	Marketing and sales worker supervisors	468,686	577,022	23.1	Counter and rental clerks
2,331,436	2,462,429	5.6	Stock clerks and order fillers	458,910	365,474	-20.4	Word processors and typists
2,197,772	2,394,074	8.9	Blue-collar worker supervisors	455,281	520,175	14.3	Mechanics, installers, and repairers nec
2,114,359	2,419,824	14.4	Managers and administrators nec	447,158	505,456	13.0	Education administrators
2,078,810	2,529,674	21.7	Registered nurses	445,632	586,423	31.6	Police patrol officers
2,077,615	1,996,596	-3.9	Bookkeeping, accounting, and auditing clerks	436,530	506,115	15.9	Engineering technicians and technologists
2,024,626	2,271,838	12.2	Food counter, fountain, and related workers	434,803	473,991	9.0	Data entry keyers
2,018,569	2,321,822	15.0	Waiters and waitresses	434,753	511,118	17.6	Bus drivers, school
1,976,184	2,174,526	10.0	Assemblers, fabricators, and hand workers nec	429,316	868,674	102.3	Computer support specialists
1,933,840	2,193,758	13.4	Helpers, laborers, and material movers, hand	426,325	448,752	5.3	Plumbers, pipefitters, and steamfitters
1,754,475	1,959,221	11.7	Teachers, elementary school	426,028	452,425	6.2	Machinists
1,610,814	1,923,572	19.4	Office and administrative support supervisors and managers	419,625	465,614	11.0	Teachers and instructors, vocational education and training
				418,355	430,509	2.9	Cooks, institution or cafeteria

Total Employment		%	
1998	2008	Change	Occupation
415,443	453,769	9.2	Industrial truck and tractor operators
414,611	508,512	22.6	Engineers
406,036	543,465	33.8	Teachers, special education
405,469	421,509	4.0	Dining room and cafeteria attendants and bar helpers
403,828	411,504	1.9	Bartenders
387,295	395,811	2.2	Insurance sales agents
383,408	531,756	38.7	Correctional officers
376,592	425,240	12.9	Packaging and filling machine operators and tenders
373,194	379,396	1.7	Agricultural, forestry, fishing, and related workers nec
368,701	256,885	-30.3	Sewing machine operators, garment
367,708	398,362	8.3	Welders and cutters
367,370	432,966	17.9	Human resources, training, and labor relations specialists
364,259	430,246	18.1	Administrative services managers
361,879	378,490	4.6	Order clerks
358,512	460,429	28.4	Instructors and coaches, sports and physical training
356,954	449,582	25.9	Electrical and electronics engineers
345,575	437,223	26.5	Teachers, preschool
344,494	442,182	28.4	Management analysts
342,278	392,132	14.6	Billing, cost, and rate clerks
340,805	423,872	24.4	Writers and editors, including technical writers
337,273	439,060	30.2	Amusement and recreation attendants
335,260	425,952	27.1	Designers, except interior designers
334,810	391,111	16.8	Electrical and electronic technicians and technologists
331,981	356,689	7.4	Postal mail carriers
326,229	467,983	43.5	Engineering, natural science, and computer and information systems managers
315,461	358,698	13.7	Property, real estate, and community association managers
313,040	366,377	17.0	Clinical laboratory technologists and technicians
310,774	420,454	35.3	Bill and account collectors
308,496	387,813	25.7	Artists and commercial artists
306,377	209,157	-31.7	Child care workers, private household
304,768	319,127	4.7	Driver/sales workers
303,053	427,386	41.0	Securities, commodities, and financial services sales agents
300,136	320,252	6.7	Cleaning and building service workers
299,688	303,226	1.2	Parts salespersons
299,308	622,113	107.9	Computer engineers
297,190	351,149	18.2	Hosts and hostesses, restaurant, lounge, or coffee shop
287,607	359,556	25.0	Cleaners of vehicles and equipment
285,922	334,332	16.9	Heating, air conditioning, and refrigeration mechanics and installers
285,120	322,047	13.0	Legal secretaries
284,627	310,352	9.0	Sales agents, real estate
283,191	301,199	6.4	Drafters
279,765	306,133	9.4	Food preparation and service workers
273,327	313,909	14.8	Musicians, singers, and related workers
272,113	298,344	9.6	File clerks
270,041	307,817	14.0	Construction managers
268,444	409,872	52.7	Social and human service assistants
254,820	279,790	9.8	Bus and truck mechanics and diesel engine specialists
252,246	397,955	57.8	Medical assistants
248,148	249,156	0.4	Production, planning, and expediting clerks
246,070	265,001	7.7	Electrical and electronic assemblers

Total Employment		%	
1998	2008	Change	Occupation
240,651	286,938	19.2	Recreation workers
239,320	250,608	4.7	Firefighters
229,700	262,017	14.1	Sheet metal workers and duct installers
229,594	274,226	19.4	Human resources managers
228,877	325,429	42.2	Dental assistants
227,556	246,539	8.3	Material moving equipment operators nec
227,444	243,270	7.0	Science and mathematics technicians
227,410	275,572	21.2	Loan counselors and officers
226,956	262,922	15.8	Automotive body and related repairers
224,149	248,339	10.8	Purchasing agents, except wholesale, retail, and farm products
223,893	169,983	-24.1	Computer operators, except peripheral equipment
222,441	296,569	33.3	Medical and health services managers
219,654	255,744	16.4	Mechanical engineers
219,309	245,697	12.0	Medical secretaries
218,759	231,791	6.0	Reservation and transportation ticket agents and travel clerks
217,821	234,526	7.7	Machine tool setters, set-up operators, metal and plastic nec
216,156	200,796	-7.1	Butchers and meatcutters
214,464	184,739	-13.9	Switchboard operators
212,822	210,840	-0.9	Machine feeders and offbearers
208,345	206,508	-0.9	Industrial production managers
203,323	235,444	15.8	Bus drivers, transit and intercity
200,922	213,037	6.0	Electrical and electronic equipment assemblers, precision
197,036	200,731	1.9	Duplicating, mail, and other office machine operators
196,179	209,520	6.8	Material recording, scheduling, and distribution workers nec
195,951	233,723	19.3	Communication, transportation, and utilities operations managers
195,028	235,858	20.9	Civil engineers
191,588	141,129	-26.3	Textile draw-out and winding machine operators and tenders
189,875	277,787	46.3	Residential counselors
185,324	198,868	7.3	Pharmacists
184,924	226,211	22.3	Health service workers
183,560	208,148	13.4	Teachers, kindergarten
182,679	221,985	21.5	Transportation and material moving equipment operators nec
182,260	227,806	25.0	Counselors
180,224	234,747	30.3	Telephone and cable TV line installers and repairers
180,112	216,881	20.4	Insurance adjusters, examiners, and investigators
179,306	200,389	11.8	Loan and credit clerks
176,175	194,711	10.5	Inspectors and compliance officers, except construction
175,977	188,483	7.1	Purchasing managers
175,026	173,686	-0.8	Farm managers
171,512	160,921	-6.2	Payroll and timekeeping clerks
171,191	199,655	16.6	Bakers, bread and pastry
171,082	196,185	14.7	Plastic molding machine setters, set-up operators, operators, and tenders
169,806	183,286	7.9	Insurance policy processing clerks
168,046	203,141	20.9	Instructors, adult (nonvocational) education
167,423	183,753	9.8	Laundry and dry-cleaning machine operators and tenders, except pressing
166,335	197,946	19.0	Protective service workers nec
165,827	184,655	11.4	Psychologists
163,021	175,234	7.5	Drywall installers and finishers

Total Employment 1998	2008	% Change	Occupation
162,881	156,579	-3.9	Machine forming operators and tenders, metal and plastic
162,561	185,935	14.4	Dispatchers, except police, fire, and ambulance
161,662	194,076	20.1	Radiologic technologists and technicians
160,139	165,115	3.1	Dentists
160,024	198,129	23.8	Actors, directors, and producers
159,506	182,583	14.5	Insurance claims clerks
158,662	180,080	13.5	Hotel, motel, and resort desk clerks
157,774	176,638	12.0	Roofers
157,217	179,176	14.0	Precision workers nec
156,986	176,299	12.3	Bricklayers, blockmasons, and stonemasons
155,284	172,510	11.1	Highway maintenance workers
152,094	159,401	4.8	Librarians
151,998	173,468	14.1	Extraction and related workers
151,687	171,394	13.0	Cost estimators
149,961	197,353	31.6	Emergency medical technicians and paramedics
149,526	153,658	2.8	Crushing, grinding, mixing, and blending machine operators and tenders
149,378	160,921	7.7	Photographers
149,179	169,101	13.4	Clergy
148,078	165,732	11.9	Metal and plastic machine setters, operators, and related workers nec
147,739	164,092	11.1	Plant and system operators nec
146,393	154,760	5.7	Construction trades workers
143,342	201,449	40.5	Dental hygienists
142,983	177,653	24.2	Meat, poultry, and fish cutters and trimmers, hand
142,242	154,056	8.3	Printing press machine setters, operators and tenders
141,775	144,666	2.0	Human resources assistants, except payroll and timekeeping
140,679	138,987	-1.2	Service station attendants
139,194	147,703	6.1	Concrete finishers, cement masons, and terrazzo workers
137,897	163,241	18.4	Travel agents
137,802	135,714	-1.5	Tool and die makers
136,754	166,341	21.6	Animal caretakers, except farm
136,689	140,154	2.5	Sewing machine operators, non-garment
136,045	220,448	62.0	Paralegals and legal assistants
132,880	146,716	10.4	Aircraft mechanics and service technicians
131,576	157,887	20.0	Taxi drivers and chauffeurs
129,051	140,261	8.7	Coating, painting, and spraying machine operators, tenders, setters, and set-up operators
128,057	157,845	23.3	Interviewing clerks, except personnel and social welfare
127,581	139,745	9.5	Mail clerks, except mail machine operators and postal service
126,691	147,568	16.5	Library assistants and bookmobile drivers
126,303	142,427	12.8	Industrial engineers, except safety engineers
125,555	131,829	5.0	Extruding and forming machine setters, operators and tenders
125,500	135,370	7.9	Operating engineers
122,957	129,391	5.2	Cabinetmakers and bench carpenters
122,329	152,413	24.6	Public relations specialists
121,788	128,778	5.7	Grader, bulldozer, and scraper operators
119,999	160,754	34.0	Physical therapists
119,729	130,284	8.8	Couriers and messengers
118,201	117,731	-0.4	Wholesale and retail buyers, except farm products
111,599	139,612	25.1	Directors, religious activities and education
111,041	127,321	14.7	New accounts clerks, banking

Total Employment 1998	2008	% Change	Occupation
110,812	124,093	12.0	Police and detective supervisors
109,953	120,605	9.7	Court reporters, medical transciptionists, and stenographers
109,604	115,507	5.4	Welding machine setters, operators, and tenders
109,331	87,579	-19.9	Machine tool cutting operators and tenders, metal and plastic
108,690	125,790	15.7	Pharmacy technicians
108,675	100,425	-7.6	Welfare eligibility workers and interviewers
107,020	121,832	13.8	Combination machine tool setters, set-up operators, operators, and tenders, metal and plastic
106,559	103,835	-2.6	Billing and posting clerks and machine operators
105,966	122,160	15.3	Excavation and loading machine operators
105,921	115,805	9.3	Mobile heavy equipment mechanics
105,024	145,424	38.5	Speech-language pathologists and audiologists
100,025	111,412	11.4	Chemical equipment controllers, operators and tenders
99,162	117,885	18.9	Architects, except landscape and naval
99,053	128,881	30.1	Flight attendants
98,801	102,637	3.9	Refuse and recyclable material collectors
98,758	99,847	1.1	Electrical powerline installers and repairers
98,267	112,184	14.2	Water and liquid waste treatment plant and system operators
97,493	212,093	117.5	Computer scientists
96,949	99,539	2.7	Insurance underwriters
96,740	100,624	4.0	Precision metal workers nec
96,372	109,732	13.9	Chemists
95,988	102,158	6.4	Cutting and slicing machine setters, operators and tenders
94,709	102,003	7.7	Psychiatric aides
93,585	99,092	5.9	Aircraft pilots and flight engineers
92,366	132,948	43.9	Medical records and health information technicians
91,566	121,169	32.3	Models, demonstrators, and product promoters
91,546	97,250	6.2	Supervisors, farming, forestry, and agricultural related occupations
91,479	122,758	34.2	Sheriffs and deputy sheriffs
89,554	99,893	11.5	Bindery machine operators and set-up operators
87,978	107,844	22.6	Numerical control machine tool operators and tenders, metal and plastic
87,421	154,885	77.2	Database administrators
87,412	96,549	10.5	Institutional cleaning supervisors
86,449	123,238	42.6	Respiratory therapists
86,354	103,606	20.0	Lawn service managers
86,006	112,848	31.2	Parking lot attendants
85,959	95,922	11.6	Legal assistants, including law clerks
85,438	92,236	8.0	Dispatchers, police, fire, and ambulance
84,524	87,560	3.6	Carpet installers
84,337	99,202	17.6	Ushers, lobby attendants, and ticket takers
83,140	91,827	10.4	Tire repairers and changers
82,331	80,805	-1.9	Millwrights
82,147	118,043	43.7	Physical therapy assistants and aides
80,950	109,275	35.0	Biological scientists
80,842	87,307	8.0	Structural and reinforcing metal workers
80,628	84,066	4.3	Grinders and polishers, hand
79,793	82,042	2.8	Government chief executives and legislators
79,437	91,927	15.7	Sales engineers
79,378	94,707	19.3	Tax preparers
79,337	116,649	47.0	Data processing equipment repairers
79,167	95,802	21.0	Detectives and criminal investigators

Total Employment 1998	2008	% Change	Occupation	Total Employment 1998	2008	% Change	Occupation
78,792	68,918	-12.5	Woodworking machine operators and tenders, setters and set-up operators	53,035	57,680	8.8	Aerospace engineers
76,512	98,231	28.4	Brokerage clerks	51,922	66,405	27.9	Athletes, coaches, umpires, and related workers
76,320	82,984	8.7	Operations research analysts	51,865	65,021	25.4	Pest control workers
74,996	67,763	-9.6	Grinding, lapping, and buffing machine tool setters and set-up operators, metal and plastic	51,209	56,750	10.8	Court clerks
				50,894	53,722	5.6	Home appliance and power tool repairers
74,418	75,683	1.7	Machine builders and other precision machine assemblers	50,591	51,357	1.5	Weighers, measurers, checkers, and samplers, recordkeeping
73,980	81,848	10.6	Paving, surfacing, and tamping equipment operators	50,382	50,565	0.4	Meter readers, utilities
				50,108	56,495	12.7	Social scientists nec
73,641	67,459	-8.4	Custom tailors and sewers	49,541	43,581	-12.0	Cannery workers
73,123	98,152	34.2	Occupational therapists	49,541	52,365	5.7	Electromechanical equipment assemblers, precision
72,812	77,742	6.8	Postal service clerks				
72,254	85,418	18.2	Library technicians	49,408	46,846	-5.2	Farm equipment mechanics
72,226	66,150	-8.4	Lathe and turning machine tool setters and set-up operators, metal and plastic	49,361	55,927	13.3	Telecommunications equipment mechanics, installers, and repairers nec
72,143	68,925	-4.5	Statistical clerks	48,851	61,530	26.0	Manicurists
71,558	80,623	12.7	Electronics repairers, commercial and industrial equipment	48,746	54,828	12.5	Claims examiners, property and casualty insurance
71,467	81,300	13.8	Opticians, dispensing	48,564	48,789	0.5	Crane and tower operators
70,807	72,857	2.9	Judges, magistrates, and other judicial workers	48,363	52,967	9.5	Chemical engineers
70,032	82,949	18.4	Economists and marketing research analysts	47,896	53,241	11.2	Real estate appraisers
68,791	66,024	-4.0	Pressing machine operators and tenders, textile, garment, and related materials	47,025	43,517	-7.5	Punching machine setters and set-up operators, metal and plastic
68,674	83,664	21.8	Surveying and mapping technicians	46,256	56,799	22.8	Chiropractors
68,104	78,779	15.7	Construction and building inspectors	45,790	49,210	7.5	Metal fabricators, structural metal products
67,388	71,100	5.5	Machine assemblers	45,741	40,512	-11.4	Photographic processing machine operators and tenders
66,614	71,579	7.5	Insulation workers				
66,560	68,449	2.8	News analysts, reporters, and correspondents	45,058	50,495	12.1	Pruners
66,375	66,954	0.9	Upholsterers	45,050	49,367	9.6	Electrolytic plating machine setters, set-up operators, operators, and tenders, metal and plastic
66,263	98,102	48.0	Physician assistants				
66,045	73,257	10.9	Psychiatric technicians	44,598	57,086	28.0	Veterinary assistants
65,830	74,328	12.9	Employment interviewers, private or public employment service	44,437	58,783	32.3	Central office and PBX installers and repairers
				44,266	45,994	3.9	Glaziers
64,451	60,797	-5.7	Head sawyers and sawing machine operators and tenders, setters and set-up operators	43,880	50,690	15.5	Geologists, geophysicists, and oceanographers
				43,840	44,272	1.0	Dental laboratory technicians, precision
63,860	66,219	3.7	Precision assemblers nec	43,260	45,021	4.1	Printing, binding, and related workers nec
63,367	91,979	45.2	Electronic semiconductor processors	42,996	47,591	10.7	Religious workers nec
62,745	71,187	13.5	Brokers, real estate	42,959	47,696	11.0	Chemical plant and system operators
62,734	53,539	-14.7	Offset lithographic press operators	42,145	38,626	-8.3	Cutters and trimmers, hand
62,246	65,599	5.4	Tax examiners, collectors, and revenue agents	41,971	50,317	19.9	Credit analysts
61,894	59,332	-4.1	Paper goods machine setters and set-up operators	41,930	34,240	-18.3	Drilling and boring machine tool setters and set-up operators, metal and plastic
61,301	71,020	15.9	Pharmacy aides	41,864	45,634	9.0	Painters, transportation equipment
60,771	75,551	24.3	Private detectives and investigators	41,401	34,323	-17.1	Proofreaders and copy markers
60,182	57,576	-4.3	Announcers	41,333	41,913	1.4	Surveyors, cartographers, and photogrammetrists
59,934	66,325	10.7	Fire fighting and prevention supervisors				
59,173	67,291	13.7	Budget analysts	40,955	41,552	1.5	Credit checkers
58,383	67,492	15.6	Office machine and cash register servicers	40,316	47,194	17.1	Plasterers and stucco masons
58,103	49,498	-14.8	Procurement clerks	40,024	41,288	3.2	Wood machinists
57,606	62,766	9.0	Metal molding machine setters, set-up operators, operators, and tenders	39,973	54,242	35.7	Therapists nec
				39,962	36,572	-8.5	Motor vehicle operators nec
57,355	60,187	4.9	Pipelayers and pipelaying fitters	39,814	45,257	13.7	Baggage porters and bellhops
57,038	71,126	24.7	Veterinarians	39,726	30,715	-22.7	Fishers
55,862	54,768	-2.0	Logging equipment operators	39,598	39,603	0.0	Oil and gas extraction occupations nec
55,187	57,639	4.4	Precision textile, apparel, and furnishings workers nec	39,129	46,071	17.7	Painting, coating, and decorating workers, hand
				39,016	42,348	8.5	Precision food and tobacco workers nec
54,956	59,613	8.5	Bakers, manufacturing	38,949	45,918	17.9	Conservation scientists and foresters
54,341	56,533	4.0	Crossing guards	38,737	43,914	13.4	Recreational therapists
54,288	50,300	-7.3	Barbers	38,486	38,096	-1.0	Furniture finishers
54,038	76,636	41.8	Surgical technologists	38,063	39,981	5.0	Small engine mechanics
53,972	64,291	19.1	Dietitians and nutritionists	37,889	41,891	10.6	Optometrists
53,291	67,799	27.2	Interior designers	37,725	45,003	19.3	Hazardous materials removal workers

Total Employment 1998	2008	% Change	Occupation	Total Employment 1998	2008	% Change	Occupation
37,526	32,806	-12.6	Gas and petroleum plant and system occupations	22,803	18,798	-17.6	Shoe and leather workers and repairers, precision
36,855	40,337	9.4	Other law enforcement occupations	22,794	18,443	-19.1	Mining, quarrying, and tunneling occupations
36,607	38,792	6.0	Broadcast and sound technicians	22,749	23,914	5.1	Able seamen, ordinary seamen, and marine oilers
36,488	31,522	-13.6	Communications equipment operators	22,724	15,215	-33.0	Film strippers, printing
35,713	31,461	-11.9	Electronic home entertainment equipment repairers	22,714	23,774	4.7	Ophthalmic laboratory technicians
35,281	40,349	14.4	Solderers and brazers	22,397	25,044	11.8	Assessors
34,702	40,755	17.4	Urban and regional planners	22,060	25,265	14.5	Landscape architects
34,056	38,372	12.7	Merchandise displayers and window dressers	21,679	22,224	2.5	Coil winders, tapers, and finishers
33,310	31,970	-4.0	Precision instrument repairers	21,468	23,816	10.9	Agricultural and food scientists
33,179	34,788	4.8	Locomotive engineers	20,803	28,997	39.4	Cardiovascular technologists and technicians
33,178	40,716	22.7	Physical scientists nec	20,351	21,194	4.1	Technicians nec
32,815	35,411	7.9	Extruding and forming machine operators and tenders, synthetic or glass fibers	19,654	21,414	9.0	Materials engineers
				19,294	26,054	35.0	Ambulance drivers and attendants, except EMTs
32,667	32,884	0.7	Forest and conservation workers	18,771	23,206	23.6	Sprayers/applicators
32,144	27,139	-15.6	Cement and gluing machine operators and tenders	18,619	26,025	39.8	Occupational therapy assistants and aides
32,035	37,224	16.2	Veterinary technologists and technicians	18,552	19,109	3.0	Captains and pilots, water vessels
31,435	32,398	3.1	Power generating and reactor plant operators	18,415	16,297	-11.5	Fallers and buckers
31,258	29,471	-5.7	Stationary engineers	18,298	18,587	1.6	Boilermakers
31,139	38,804	24.6	Medical scientists	17,932	18,328	2.2	Physicists and astronomers
30,516	27,929	-8.5	Cooking and roasting machine operators and tenders, food and tobacco	17,751	18,990	7.0	Photographic process workers, precision
				17,648	17,397	-1.4	Tire building machine operators
29,739	30,425	2.3	Air traffic controllers	17,160	9,883	-42.4	Housekeepers and butlers
29,664	29,481	-0.6	Title examiners, abstractors, and searchers	17,049	17,777	4.3	Job printers
29,653	27,865	-6.0	Jewelers and precious stone and metal workers	16,906	15,092	-10.7	Credit authorizers
29,608	33,230	12.2	Elevator installers and repairers	16,844	16,878	0.2	Printing workers, precision nec
29,562	23,325	-21.1	Roustabouts, oil and gas	16,713	14,539	-13.0	Fitters, structural metal, precision
28,980	30,428	5.0	Purchasing agents and buyers, farm	16,631	19,840	19.3	Aircraft assemblers, precision
28,660	31,162	8.7	Hard tile setters	16,529	16,910	2.3	Statisticians
28,651	32,554	13.6	Dancers and choreographers	16,379	13,598	-17.0	Loan interviewers
28,492	26,436	-7.2	Separating, filtering, clarifying, precipitating, and still machine operators and tenders	16,160	17,299	7.0	Actuaries
				16,005	14,240	-11.0	Boiler operators and tenders, low pressure
28,341	29,183	3.0	Screen printing machine setters and set-up operators	15,968	15,363	-3.8	Patternmakers and layout workers, fabric and apparel
28,220	25,522	-9.6	Textile machine setters and set-up operators	15,647	12,151	-22.3	Statement clerks
27,527	31,953	16.1	Funeral directors and morticians	15,580	16,971	8.9	Ceiling tile installers and acoustical carpenters
27,460	26,760	-2.5	Precision woodworkers nec	14,931	11,881	-20.4	Dairy processing equipment operators, including setters
27,209	16,965	-37.6	Peripheral equipment operators				
27,146	29,849	10.0	Locksmiths and safe repairers	14,788	16,933	14.5	Shampooers
27,015	31,216	15.6	Coin, vending, and amusement machine servicers and repairers	14,537	13,779	-5.2	Platemakers
				14,516	17,010	17.2	Fire inspection occupations
26,362	27,162	3.0	Postmasters and mail superintendents	14,164	7,391	-47.8	Railroad brake, signal, and switch operators
25,607	44,200	72.6	Desktop publishing specialists	14,036	13,271	-5.5	Mathematicians and all other mathematical scientists
25,421	23,710	-6.7	Railroad conductors and yardmasters				
25,070	27,836	11.0	Carpet, floor, and tile installers and finishers	13,967	15,592	11.6	Nuclear medicine technologists
24,909	23,518	-5.6	Furnace, kiln, oven, drier, or kettle operators and tenders	13,933	14,470	3.9	Motorcycle mechanics
				13,904	15,370	10.5	Podiatrists
24,877	27,912	12.2	Correspondence clerks	13,702	12,033	-12.2	Power distributors and dispatchers
24,795	27,751	11.9	Municipal clerks	13,649	11,064	-18.9	Compositors and typesetters, precision
24,487	22,291	-9.0	Textile bleaching and dyeing machine operators and tenders	13,578	14,169	4.4	Advertising clerks
				13,467	11,931	-11.4	Pressers, hand
24,467	16,208	-33.8	Station installers and repairers, telephone	13,366	5,379	-59.8	Typesetting and composing machine operators and tenders
24,103	27,259	13.1	License clerks				
23,413	16,136	-31.1	Directory assistance operators	12,823	12,059	-6.0	Timber cutting and related logging workers nec
23,344	22,376	-4.1	Heat treating, annealing, and tempering machine operators and tenders, metal and plastic	12,591	13,407	6.5	Musical instrument repairers and tuners
				12,497	9,608	-23.1	EKG technicians
				12,366	14,427	16.7	Radiation therapists
23,202	26,134	12.6	Archivists, curators, museum technicians, and conservators	12,087	13,079	8.2	Soldering and brazing machine operators and tenders
23,073	21,915	-5.0	Furnace operators and tenders	12,061	11,625	-3.6	Petroleum engineers
23,023	19,195	-16.6	Central office operators	11,694	12,367	5.8	Nuclear engineers

Total Employment 1998	2008	% Change	Occupation
11,370	9,257	-18.6	Captains and other officers, fishing vessels
11,287	11,346	0.5	Riggers
10,817	13,257	22.6	Bicycle repairers
10,715	12,160	13.5	Medical equipment repairers
10,627	11,263	6.0	Hoist and winch operators
10,452	12,122	16.0	Insurance appraisers, auto damage
10,139	8,293	-18.2	Letterpress operators
9,977	9,753	-2.2	Farm and home management advisors
9,790	8,337	-14.8	Sewers, hand
9,532	11,184	17.3	Insurance examining clerks
9,500	9,074	-4.5	Printing press setters and set-up operators
9,323	7,292	-21.8	Motion picture projectionists
9,295	9,524	2.5	Foundry mold assembly and shake out workers
9,248	6,347	-31.4	Camera operators
9,037	4,413	-51.2	Paste-up workers
9,029	9,770	8.2	Camera and photographic equipment repairers
8,673	8,286	-4.5	Shipfitters
8,471	8,991	6.1	Numerical control machine tool programmers
8,449	8,097	-4.2	Watch repairers
8,431	5,431	-35.6	Rail transportation workers nec
8,419	9,649	14.6	Atmospheric scientists
8,054	8,689	7.9	Mates, ship, boat, and barge
7,030	6,930	-1.4	Radio mechanics
6,769	5,752	-15.0	Photoengraving and lithographic machine operators and tenders
6,627	5,621	-15.2	Bookbinders
6,506	4,175	-35.8	Shoe sewing machine operators and tenders
6,236	6,505	4.3	Ship engineers
5,417	5,738	5.9	Electroneurodiagnostic technologists
5,154	5,931	15.1	Nursery and greenhouse managers
4,511	2,196	-51.3	Cooks, private household
4,444	3,883	-12.6	Mining engineers, including mine safety engineers
3,329	3,565	7.1	Subway and streetcar operators
2,747	1,332	-51.5	Photoengravers
965	1,125	16.6	Life scientists

Growth/Decline Order - 1998 to 2008

Total Employment 1998	2008	% Change	Occupation
97,493	212,093	117.5	Computer scientists
299,308	622,113	107.9	Computer engineers
429,316	868,674	102.3	Computer support specialists
616,915	1,194,234	93.6	Systems analysts
87,421	154,885	77.2	Database administrators
25,607	44,200	72.6	Desktop publishing specialists
136,045	220,448	62.0	Paralegals and legal assistants
745,671	1,179,084	58.1	Personal care and home health aides
252,246	397,955	57.8	Medical assistants
268,444	409,872	52.7	Social and human service assistants
66,263	98,102	48.0	Physician assistants
79,337	116,649	47.0	Data processing equipment repairers
189,875	277,787	46.3	Residential counselors
63,367	91,979	45.2	Electronic semiconductor processors
92,366	132,948	43.9	Medical records and health information technicians
82,147	118,043	43.7	Physical therapy assistants and aides
326,229	467,983	43.5	Engineering, natural science, and computer and information systems managers
86,449	123,238	42.6	Respiratory therapists
228,877	325,429	42.2	Dental assistants
54,038	76,636	41.8	Surgical technologists
303,053	427,386	41.0	Securities, commodities, and financial services

Total Employment 1998	2008	% Change	Occupation
			sales agents
143,342	201,449	40.5	Dental hygienists
18,619	26,025	39.8	Occupational therapy assistants and aides
20,803	28,997	39.4	Cardiovascular technologists and technicians
383,408	531,756	38.7	Correctional officers
105,024	145,424	38.5	Speech-language pathologists and audiologists
604,102	822,148	36.1	Social workers
39,973	54,242	35.7	Therapists nec
310,774	420,454	35.3	Bill and account collectors
19,294	26,054	35.0	Ambulance drivers and attendants, except EMTs
80,950	109,275	35.0	Biological scientists
509,525	687,761	35.0	Health professionals and paraprofessionals
73,123	98,152	34.2	Occupational therapists
91,479	122,758	34.2	Sheriffs and deputy sheriffs
479,015	641,644	34.0	Adjustment clerks
119,999	160,754	34.0	Physical therapists
406,036	543,465	33.8	Teachers, special education
222,441	296,569	33.3	Medical and health services managers
44,437	58,783	32.3	Central office and PBX installers and repairers
91,566	121,169	32.3	Models, demonstrators, and product promoters
149,961	197,353	31.6	Emergency medical technicians and paramedics
445,632	586,423	31.6	Police patrol officers
1,191,790	1,566,888	31.5	Teacher assistants
86,006	112,848	31.2	Parking lot attendants
180,224	234,747	30.3	Telephone and cable TV line installers and repairers
337,273	439,060	30.2	Amusement and recreation attendants
99,053	128,881	30.1	Flight attendants
647,783	838,902	29.5	Computer programmers
1,026,723	1,320,797	28.6	Guards
76,512	98,231	28.4	Brokerage clerks
358,512	460,429	28.4	Instructors and coaches, sports and physical training
344,494	442,182	28.4	Management analysts
44,598	57,086	28.0	Veterinary assistants
51,922	66,405	27.9	Athletes, coaches, umpires, and related workers
53,291	67,799	27.2	Interior designers
335,260	425,952	27.1	Designers, except interior designers
345,575	437,223	26.5	Teachers, preschool
904,542	1,140,588	26.1	Child care workers
48,851	61,530	26.0	Manicurists
356,954	449,582	25.9	Electrical and electronics engineers
308,496	387,813	25.7	Artists and commercial artists
51,865	65,021	25.4	Pest control workers
111,599	139,612	25.1	Directors, religious activities and education
287,607	359,556	25.0	Cleaners of vehicles and equipment
182,260	227,806	25.0	Counselors
57,038	71,126	24.7	Veterinarians
31,139	38,804	24.6	Medical scientists
122,329	152,413	24.6	Public relations specialists
340,805	423,872	24.4	Writers and editors, including technical writers
60,771	75,551	24.3	Private detectives and investigators
142,983	177,653	24.2	Meat, poultry, and fish cutters and trimmers, hand
160,024	198,129	23.8	Actors, directors, and producers
1,366,632	1,691,547	23.8	Nursing aides, orderlies, and attendants
1,293,450	1,598,873	23.6	Receptionists and information clerks
18,771	23,206	23.6	Sprayers/applicators
128,057	157,845	23.3	Interviewing clerks, except personnel and social welfare
468,686	577,022	23.1	Counter and rental clerks

Total Employment 1998	2008	% Change	Occupation
485,214	596,768	23.0	Advertising, marketing, promotions, public relations, and sales managers
46,256	56,799	22.8	Chiropractors
33,178	40,716	22.7	Physical scientists nec
10,817	13,257	22.6	Bicycle repairers
865,356	1,060,502	22.6	College and university faculty
414,611	508,512	22.6	Engineers
87,978	107,844	22.6	Numerical control machine tool operators and tenders, metal and plastic
1,426,213	1,748,529	22.6	Teachers, secondary school
184,924	226,211	22.3	Health service workers
68,674	83,664	21.8	Surveying and mapping technicians
984,044	1,197,207	21.7	Hand packers and packagers
2,078,810	2,529,674	21.7	Registered nurses
136,754	166,341	21.6	Animal caretakers, except farm
182,679	221,985	21.5	Transportation and material moving equipment operators nec
227,410	275,572	21.2	Loan counselors and officers
576,870	698,946	21.2	Physicians
785,407	951,577	21.2	Professional workers nec
79,167	95,802	21.0	Detectives and criminal investigators
195,028	235,858	20.9	Civil engineers
168,046	203,141	20.9	Instructors, adult (nonvocational) education
1,129,760	1,366,140	20.9	Management support workers nec
1,129,934	1,364,383	20.7	Laborers, landscaping and groundskeeping
180,112	216,881	20.4	Insurance adjusters, examiners, and investigators
161,662	194,076	20.1	Radiologic technologists and technicians
86,354	103,606	20.0	Lawn service managers
131,576	157,887	20.0	Taxi drivers and chauffeurs
41,971	50,317	19.9	Credit analysts
691,953	828,397	19.7	Licensed practical and licensed vocational nurses
229,594	274,226	19.4	Human resources managers
1,610,814	1,923,572	19.4	Office and administrative support supervisors and managers
16,631	19,840	19.3	Aircraft assemblers, precision
195,951	233,723	19.3	Communication, transportation, and utilities operations managers
37,725	45,003	19.3	Hazardous materials removal workers
1,249,444	1,490,057	19.3	Service workers nec
79,378	94,707	19.3	Tax preparers
240,651	286,938	19.2	Recreation workers
53,972	64,291	19.1	Dietitians and nutritionists
166,335	197,946	19.0	Protective service workers nec
99,162	117,885	18.9	Architects, except landscape and naval
783,180	929,469	18.7	Cooks, restaurant
676,576	800,994	18.4	Cooks, short order and fast food
70,032	82,949	18.4	Economists and marketing research analysts
137,897	163,241	18.4	Travel agents
297,190	351,149	18.2	Hosts and hostesses, restaurant, lounge, or coffee shop
72,254	85,418	18.2	Library technicians
364,259	430,246	18.1	Administrative services managers
38,949	45,918	17.9	Conservation scientists and foresters
367,370	432,966	17.9	Human resources, training, and labor relations specialists
39,129	46,071	17.7	Painting, coating, and decorating workers, hand
434,753	511,118	17.6	Bus drivers, school
84,337	99,202	17.6	Ushers, lobby attendants, and ticket takers
3,197,813	3,754,023	17.4	Cashiers
34,702	40,755	17.4	Urban and regional planners
9,532	11,184	17.3	Insurance examining clerks

Total Employment 1998	2008	% Change	Occupation
14,516	17,010	17.2	Fire inspection occupations
680,955	798,039	17.2	Lawyers
40,316	47,194	17.1	Plasterers and stucco masons
953,300	1,115,534	17.0	Clerical and administrative support workers
313,040	366,377	17.0	Clinical laboratory technologists and technicians
285,922	334,332	16.9	Heating, air conditioning, and refrigeration mechanics and installers
334,810	391,111	16.8	Electrical and electronic technicians and technologists
789,566	921,511	16.7	Automotive mechanics and service technicians
12,366	14,427	16.7	Radiation therapists
171,191	199,655	16.6	Bakers, bread and pastry
965	1,125	16.6	Life scientists
2,969,641	3,462,638	16.6	Truck drivers light and heavy
126,691	147,568	16.5	Library assistants and bookmobile drivers
3,387,590	3,945,308	16.5	Sales and related workers nec
3,362,395	3,913,196	16.4	General managers and top executives
219,654	255,744	16.4	Mechanical engineers
594,642	691,364	16.3	Food service and lodging managers
32,035	37,224	16.2	Veterinary technologists and technicians
27,527	31,953	16.1	Funeral directors and morticians
10,452	12,122	16.0	Insurance appraisers, auto damage
436,530	506,115	15.9	Engineering technicians and technologists
61,301	71,020	15.9	Pharmacy aides
226,956	262,922	15.8	Automotive body and related repairers
203,323	235,444	15.8	Bus drivers, transit and intercity
68,104	78,779	15.7	Construction and building inspectors
108,690	125,790	15.7	Pharmacy technicians
79,437	91,927	15.7	Sales engineers
27,015	31,216	15.6	Coin, vending, and amusement machine servicers and repairers
58,383	67,492	15.6	Office machine and cash register servicers
43,880	50,690	15.5	Geologists, geophysicists, and oceanographers
105,966	122,160	15.3	Excavation and loading machine operators
3,020,975	3,484,090	15.3	Office clerks, general
634,971	731,515	15.2	Machine operators, tenders, setters, and set-up operators
5,154	5,931	15.1	Nursery and greenhouse managers
2,018,569	2,321,822	15.0	Waiters and waitresses
273,327	313,909	14.8	Musicians, singers, and related workers
111,041	127,321	14.7	New accounts clerks, banking
171,082	196,185	14.7	Plastic molding machine setters, set-up operators, operators, and tenders
643,658	738,577	14.7	Teachers and instructors nec
8,419	9,649	14.6	Atmospheric scientists
342,278	392,132	14.6	Billing, cost, and rate clerks
159,506	182,583	14.5	Insurance claims clerks
22,060	25,265	14.5	Landscape architects
14,788	16,933	14.5	Shampooers
162,561	185,935	14.4	Dispatchers, except police, fire, and ambulance
2,114,359	2,419,824	14.4	Managers and administrators nec
35,281	40,349	14.4	Solderers and brazers
455,281	520,175	14.3	Mechanics, installers, and repairers nec
98,267	112,184	14.2	Water and liquid waste treatment plant and system operators
151,998	173,468	14.1	Extraction and related workers
229,700	262,017	14.1	Sheet metal workers and duct installers
270,041	307,817	14.0	Construction managers
693,291	790,646	14.0	Financial managers
157,217	179,176	14.0	Precision workers nec
96,372	109,732	13.9	Chemists
4,056,472	4,619,676	13.9	Retail salespersons

Total Employment 1998	2008	% Change	Occupation
107,020	121,832	13.8	Combination machine tool setters, set-up operators, operators, and tenders, metal and plastic
71,467	81,300	13.8	Opticians, dispensing
39,814	45,257	13.7	Baggage porters and bellhops
59,173	67,291	13.7	Budget analysts
315,461	358,698	13.7	Property, real estate, and community association managers
28,651	32,554	13.6	Dancers and choreographers
62,745	71,187	13.5	Brokers, real estate
158,662	180,080	13.5	Hotel, motel, and resort desk clerks
10,715	12,160	13.5	Medical equipment repairers
149,179	169,101	13.4	Clergy
1,933,840	2,193,758	13.4	Helpers, laborers, and material movers, hand
38,737	43,914	13.4	Recreational therapists
183,560	208,148	13.4	Teachers, kindergarten
49,361	55,927	13.3	Telecommunications equipment mechanics, installers, and repairers nec
24,103	27,259	13.1	License clerks
151,687	171,394	13.0	Cost estimators
447,158	505,456	13.0	Education administrators
285,120	322,047	13.0	Legal secretaries
65,830	74,328	12.9	Employment interviewers, private or public employment service
376,592	425,240	12.9	Packaging and filling machine operators and tenders
126,303	142,427	12.8	Industrial engineers, except safety engineers
71,558	80,623	12.7	Electronics repairers, commercial and industrial equipment
34,056	38,372	12.7	Merchandise displayers and window dressers
50,108	56,495	12.7	Social scientists nec
23,202	26,134	12.6	Archivists, curators, museum technicians, and conservators
48,746	54,828	12.5	Claims examiners, property and casualty insurance
156,986	176,299	12.3	Bricklayers, blockmasons, and stonemasons
24,877	27,912	12.2	Correspondence clerks
29,608	33,230	12.2	Elevator installers and repairers
2,024,626	2,271,838	12.2	Food counter, fountain, and related workers
45,058	50,495	12.1	Pruners
219,309	245,697	12.0	Medical secretaries
110,812	124,093	12.0	Police and detective supervisors
157,774	176,638	12.0	Roofers
148,078	165,732	11.9	Metal and plastic machine setters, operators, and related workers nec
24,795	27,751	11.9	Municipal clerks
22,397	25,044	11.8	Assessors
179,306	200,389	11.8	Loan and credit clerks
1,754,475	1,959,221	11.7	Teachers, elementary school
85,959	95,922	11.6	Legal assistants, including law clerks
13,967	15,592	11.6	Nuclear medicine technologists
89,554	99,893	11.5	Bindery machine operators and set-up operators
3,183,804	3,549,015	11.5	Janitors and cleaners, including maids and housekeeping cleaners
100,025	111,412	11.4	Chemical equipment controllers, operators and tenders
165,827	184,655	11.4	Psychologists
1,079,726	1,201,630	11.3	Accountants and auditors
47,896	53,241	11.2	Real estate appraisers
155,284	172,510	11.1	Highway maintenance workers
147,739	164,092	11.1	Plant and system operators nec
25,070	27,836	11.0	Carpet, floor, and tile installers and finishers
42,959	47,696	11.0	Chemical plant and system operators
419,625	465,614	11.0	Teachers and instructors, vocational education and training
21,468	23,816	10.9	Agricultural and food scientists
66,045	73,257	10.9	Psychiatric technicians
51,209	56,750	10.8	Court clerks
224,149	248,339	10.8	Purchasing agents, except wholesale, retail, and farm products
59,934	66,325	10.7	Fire fighting and prevention supervisors
42,996	47,591	10.7	Religious workers nec
37,889	41,891	10.6	Optometrists
73,980	81,848	10.6	Paving, surfacing, and tamping equipment operators
176,175	194,711	10.5	Inspectors and compliance officers, except construction
87,412	96,549	10.5	Institutional cleaning supervisors
13,904	15,370	10.5	Podiatrists
132,880	146,716	10.4	Aircraft mechanics and service technicians
1,256,251	1,386,903	10.4	Food preparation workers
83,140	91,827	10.4	Tire repairers and changers
656,151	723,743	10.3	Electricians
605,165	666,969	10.2	Hairdressers, hairstylists, and cosmetologists
2,583,772	2,846,839	10.2	Marketing and sales worker supervisors
1,976,184	2,174,526	10.0	Assemblers, fabricators, and hand workers nec
27,146	29,849	10.0	Locksmiths and safe repairers
254,820	279,790	9.8	Bus and truck mechanics and diesel engine specialists
167,423	183,753	9.8	Laundry and dry-cleaning machine operators and tenders, except pressing
109,953	120,605	9.7	Court reporters, medical transciptionists, and stenographers
45,050	49,367	9.6	Electrolytic plating machine setters, set-up operators, operators, and tenders, metal and plastic
272,113	298,344	9.6	File clerks
48,363	52,967	9.5	Chemical engineers
127,581	139,745	9.5	Mail clerks, except mail machine operators and postal service
279,765	306,133	9.4	Food preparation and service workers
36,855	40,337	9.4	Other law enforcement occupations
105,921	115,805	9.3	Mobile heavy equipment mechanics
415,443	453,769	9.2	Industrial truck and tractor operators
434,803	473,991	9.0	Data entry keyers
19,654	21,414	9.0	Materials engineers
57,606	62,766	9.0	Metal molding machine setters, set-up operators, operators, and tenders
41,864	45,634	9.0	Painters, transportation equipment
284,627	310,352	9.0	Sales agents, real estate
2,197,772	2,394,074	8.9	Blue-collar worker supervisors
15,580	16,971	8.9	Ceiling tile installers and acoustical carpenters
53,035	57,680	8.8	Aerospace engineers
119,729	130,284	8.8	Couriers and messengers
129,051	140,261	8.7	Coating, painting, and spraying machine operators, tenders, setters, and set-up operators
28,660	31,162	8.7	Hard tile setters
76,320	82,984	8.7	Operations research analysts
475,937	516,671	8.6	Painters and paperhangers
54,956	59,613	8.5	Bakers, manufacturing
39,016	42,348	8.5	Precision food and tobacco workers nec
227,556	246,539	8.3	Material moving equipment operators nec
142,242	154,056	8.3	Printing press machine setters, operators and tenders

Total Employment 1998	2008	% Change	Occupation	Total Employment 1998	2008	% Change	Occupation
367,708	398,362	8.3	Welders and cutters	122,957	129,391	5.2	Cabinetmakers and bench carpenters
9,029	9,770	8.2	Camera and photographic equipment repairers	22,749	23,914	5.1	Able seamen, ordinary seamen, and marine oilers
12,087	13,079	8.2	Soldering and brazing machine operators and tenders	125,555	131,829	5.0	Extruding and forming machine setters, operators and tenders
85,438	92,236	8.0	Dispatchers, police, fire, and ambulance	28,980	30,428	5.0	Purchasing agents and buyers, farm
80,842	87,307	8.0	Structural and reinforcing metal workers	38,063	39,981	5.0	Small engine mechanics
32,815	35,411	7.9	Extruding and forming machine operators and tenders, synthetic or glass fibers	57,355	60,187	4.9	Pipelayers and pipelaying fitters
169,806	183,286	7.9	Insurance policy processing clerks	152,094	159,401	4.8	Librarians
8,054	8,689	7.9	Mates, ship, boat, and barge	33,179	34,788	4.8	Locomotive engineers
125,500	135,370	7.9	Operating engineers	304,768	319,127	4.7	Driver/sales workers
246,070	265,001	7.7	Electrical and electronic assemblers	239,320	250,608	4.7	Firefighters
217,821	234,526	7.7	Machine tool setters, set-up operators, metal and plastic nec	22,714	23,774	4.7	Ophthalmic laboratory technicians
				361,879	378,490	4.6	Order clerks
1,232,476	1,327,288	7.7	Maintenance repairers, general utility	13,578	14,169	4.4	Advertising clerks
149,378	160,921	7.7	Photographers	535,469	559,204	4.4	Industrial machinery mechanics
94,709	102,003	7.7	Psychiatric aides	55,187	57,639	4.4	Precision textile, apparel, and furnishings workers nec
163,021	175,234	7.5	Drywall installers and finishers				
66,614	71,579	7.5	Insulation workers	80,628	84,066	4.3	Grinders and polishers, hand
45,790	49,210	7.5	Metal fabricators, structural metal products	17,049	17,777	4.3	Job printers
331,981	356,689	7.4	Postal mail carriers	6,236	6,505	4.3	Ship engineers
575,959	618,241	7.3	Helpers, construction trades	43,260	45,021	4.1	Printing, binding, and related workers nec
185,324	198,868	7.3	Pharmacists	20,351	21,194	4.1	Technicians nec
175,977	188,483	7.1	Purchasing managers	54,341	56,533	4.0	Crossing guards
3,329	3,565	7.1	Subway and streetcar operators	405,469	421,509	4.0	Dining room and cafeteria attendants and bar helpers
16,160	17,299	7.0	Actuaries				
17,751	18,990	7.0	Photographic process workers, precision	96,740	100,624	4.0	Precision metal workers nec
227,444	243,270	7.0	Science and mathematics technicians	44,266	45,994	3.9	Glaziers
1,070,759	1,145,033	6.9	Carpenters	13,933	14,470	3.9	Motorcycle mechanics
196,179	209,520	6.8	Material recording, scheduling, and distribution workers nec	98,801	102,637	3.9	Refuse and recyclable material collectors
				63,860	66,219	3.7	Precision assemblers nec
72,812	77,742	6.8	Postal service clerks	84,524	87,560	3.6	Carpet installers
300,136	320,252	6.7	Cleaning and building service workers	40,024	41,288	3.2	Wood machinists
12,591	13,407	6.5	Musical instrument repairers and tuners	160,139	165,115	3.1	Dentists
95,988	102,158	6.4	Cutting and slicing machine setters, operators and tenders	31,435	32,398	3.1	Power generating and reactor plant operators
				999,864	1,031,146	3.1	Shipping, receiving, and traffic clerks
283,191	301,199	6.4	Drafters	18,552	19,109	3.0	Captains and pilots, water vessels
426,028	452,425	6.2	Machinists	26,362	27,162	3.0	Postmasters and mail superintendents
91,546	97,250	6.2	Supervisors, farming, forestry, and agricultural related occupations	28,341	29,183	3.0	Screen printing machine setters and set-up operators
139,194	147,703	6.1	Concrete finishers, cement masons, and terrazzo workers	418,355	430,509	2.9	Cooks, institution or cafeteria
				70,807	72,857	2.9	Judges, magistrates, and other judicial workers
8,471	8,991	6.1	Numerical control machine tool programmers	149,526	153,658	2.8	Crushing, grinding, mixing, and blending machine operators and tenders
36,607	38,792	6.0	Broadcast and sound technicians				
200,922	213,037	6.0	Electrical and electronic equipment assemblers, precision	79,793	82,042	2.8	Government chief executives and legislators
				66,560	68,449	2.8	News analysts, reporters, and correspondents
10,627	11,263	6.0	Hoist and winch operators	96,949	99,539	2.7	Insurance underwriters
218,759	231,791	6.0	Reservation and transportation ticket agents and travel clerks	21,679	22,224	2.5	Coil winders, tapers, and finishers
				9,295	9,524	2.5	Foundry mold assembly and shake out workers
93,585	99,092	5.9	Aircraft pilots and flight engineers	136,689	140,154	2.5	Sewing machine operators, non-garment
5,417	5,738	5.9	Electroneurodiagnostic technologists	29,739	30,425	2.3	Air traffic controllers
11,694	12,367	5.8	Nuclear engineers	16,529	16,910	2.3	Statisticians
146,393	154,760	5.7	Construction trades workers	387,295	395,811	2.2	Insurance sales agents
49,541	52,365	5.7	Electromechanical equipment assemblers, precision	17,932	18,328	2.2	Physicists and astronomers
				141,775	144,666	2.0	Human resources assistants, except payroll and timekeeping
121,788	128,778	5.7	Grader, bulldozer, and scraper operators				
50,894	53,722	5.6	Home appliance and power tool repairers	403,828	411,504	1.9	Bartenders
2,331,436	2,462,429	5.6	Stock clerks and order fillers	197,036	200,731	1.9	Duplicating, mail, and other office machine operators
67,388	71,100	5.5	Machine assemblers				
62,246	65,599	5.4	Tax examiners, collectors, and revenue agents	373,194	379,396	1.7	Agricultural, forestry, fishing, and related workers nec
109,604	115,507	5.4	Welding machine setters, operators, and tenders				
				74,418	75,683	1.7	Machine builders and other precision machine assemblers
426,325	448,752	5.3	Plumbers, pipefitters, and steamfitters				

Total Employment		%		Total Employment		%	
1998	2008	Change	Occupation	1998	2008	Change	Occupation
18,298	18,587	1.6	Boilermakers				and tenders
40,955	41,552	1.5	Credit checkers	64,451	60,797	-5.7	Head sawyers and sawing machine operators
822,119	834,178	1.5	Freight, stock, and material movers, hand				and tenders, setters and set-up operators
50,591	51,357	1.5	Weighers, measurers, checkers, and samplers,	31,258	29,471	-5.7	Stationary engineers
			recordkeeping	29,653	27,865	-6.0	Jewelers and precious stone and metal workers
41,333	41,913	1.4	Surveyors, cartographers, and	12,823	12,059	-6.0	Timber cutting and related logging workers nec
			photogrammetrists	171,512	160,921	-6.2	Payroll and timekeeping clerks
299,688	303,226	1.2	Parts salespersons	850,533	793,989	-6.6	Farm workers
98,758	99,847	1.1	Electrical powerline installers and repairers	25,421	23,710	-6.7	Railroad conductors and yardmasters
43,840	44,272	1.0	Dental laboratory technicians, precision	216,156	200,796	-7.1	Butchers and meatcutters
66,375	66,954	0.9	Upholsterers	28,492	26,436	-7.2	Separating, filtering, clarifying, precipitating,
32,667	32,884	0.7	Forest and conservation workers				and still machine operators and tenders
48,564	48,789	0.5	Crane and tower operators	54,288	50,300	-7.3	Barbers
11,287	11,346	0.5	Riggers	47,025	43,517	-7.5	Punching machine setters and set-up operators,
50,382	50,565	0.4	Meter readers, utilities				metal and plastic
248,148	249,156	0.4	Production, planning, and expediting clerks	108,675	100,425	-7.6	Welfare eligibility workers and interviewers
16,844	16,878	0.2	Printing workers, precision nec	42,145	38,626	-8.3	Cutters and trimmers, hand
39,598	39,603	0.0	Oil and gas extraction occupations nec	73,641	67,459	-8.4	Custom tailors and sewers
2,690,424	2,690,512	0.0	Secretaries, except legal and medical	72,226	66,150	-8.4	Lathe and turning machine tool setters and
118,201	117,731	-0.4	Wholesale and retail buyers, except farm				set-up operators, metal and plastic
			products	30,516	27,929	-8.5	Cooking and roasting machine operators and
29,664	29,481	-0.6	Title examiners, abstractors, and searchers				tenders, food and tobacco
175,026	173,686	-0.8	Farm managers	39,962	36,572	-8.5	Motor vehicle operators nec
208,345	206,508	-0.9	Industrial production managers	24,487	22,291	-9.0	Textile bleaching and dyeing machine
212,822	210,840	-0.9	Machine feeders and offbearers				operators and tenders
38,486	38,096	-1.0	Furniture finishers	74,996	67,763	-9.6	Grinding, lapping, and buffing machine tool
140,679	138,987	-1.2	Service station attendants				setters and set-up operators, metal and plastic
7,030	6,930	-1.4	Radio mechanics	28,220	25,522	-9.6	Textile machine setters and set-up operators
17,648	17,397	-1.4	Tire building machine operators	16,906	15,092	-10.7	Credit authorizers
137,802	135,714	-1.5	Tool and die makers	16,005	14,240	-11.0	Boiler operators and tenders, low pressure
82,331	80,805	-1.9	Millwrights	45,741	40,512	-11.4	Photographic processing machine operators
55,862	54,768	-2.0	Logging equipment operators				and tenders
9,977	9,753	-2.2	Farm and home management advisors	13,467	11,931	-11.4	Pressers, hand
27,460	26,760	-2.5	Precision woodworkers nec	18,415	16,297	-11.5	Fallers and buckers
106,559	103,835	-2.6	Billing and posting clerks and machine	600,311	529,618	-11.8	Cleaners and servants, private household
			operators	35,713	31,461	-11.9	Electronic home entertainment equipment
688,730	666,896	-3.2	Inspectors, testers, and graders, precision				repairers
12,061	11,625	-3.6	Petroleum engineers	49,541	43,581	-12.0	Cannery workers
15,968	15,363	-3.8	Patternmakers and layout workers, fabric and	13,702	12,033	-12.2	Power distributors and dispatchers
			apparel	78,792	68,918	-12.5	Woodworking machine operators and tenders,
2,077,615	1,996,596	-3.9	Bookkeeping, accounting, and auditing clerks				setters and set-up operators
162,881	156,579	-3.9	Machine forming operators and tenders, metal	37,526	32,806	-12.6	Gas and petroleum plant and system
			and plastic				occupations
33,310	31,970	-4.0	Precision instrument repairers	4,444	3,883	-12.6	Mining engineers, including mine safety
68,791	66,024	-4.0	Pressing machine operators and tenders, textile,				engineers
			garment, and related materials	16,713	14,539	-13.0	Fitters, structural metal, precision
23,344	22,376	-4.1	Heat treating, annealing, and tempering	1,307,712	1,135,018	-13.2	Farmers
			machine operators and tenders, metal and	36,488	31,522	-13.6	Communications equipment operators
			plastic	214,464	184,739	-13.9	Switchboard operators
61,894	59,332	-4.1	Paper goods machine setters and set-up	62,734	53,539	-14.7	Offset lithographic press operators
			operators	58,103	49,498	-14.8	Procurement clerks
8,449	8,097	-4.2	Watch repairers	9,790	8,337	-14.8	Sewers, hand
60,182	57,576	-4.3	Announcers	6,769	5,752	-15.0	Photoengraving and lithographic machine
9,500	9,074	-4.5	Printing press setters and set-up operators				operators and tenders
8,673	8,286	-4.5	Shipfitters	6,627	5,621	-15.2	Bookbinders
72,143	68,925	-4.5	Statistical clerks	32,144	27,139	-15.6	Cement and gluing machine operators and
23,073	21,915	-5.0	Furnace operators and tenders				tenders
49,408	46,846	-5.2	Farm equipment mechanics	23,023	19,195	-16.6	Central office operators
14,537	13,779	-5.2	Platemakers	16,379	13,598	-17.0	Loan interviewers
559,778	529,122	-5.5	Bank tellers	41,401	34,323	-17.1	Proofreaders and copy markers
14,036	13,271	-5.5	Mathematicians and all other mathematical	22,803	18,798	-17.6	Shoe and leather workers and repairers,
			scientists				precision
24,909	23,518	-5.6	Furnace, kiln, oven, drier, or kettle operators	10,139	8,293	-18.2	Letterpress operators

| Total Employment | | % | |
1998	2008	Change	Occupation
41,930	34,240	-18.3	Drilling and boring machine tool setters and set-up operators, metal and plastic
11,370	9,257	-18.6	Captains and other officers, fishing vessels
13,649	11,064	-18.9	Compositors and typesetters, precision
22,794	18,443	-19.1	Mining, quarrying, and tunneling occupations
109,331	87,579	-19.9	Machine tool cutting operators and tenders, metal and plastic
14,931	11,881	-20.4	Dairy processing equipment operators, including setters
458,910	365,474	-20.4	Word processors and typists
29,562	23,325	-21.1	Roustabouts, oil and gas
9,323	7,292	-21.8	Motion picture projectionists
15,647	12,151	-22.3	Statement clerks
39,726	30,715	-22.7	Fishers
12,497	9,608	-23.1	EKG technicians
223,893	169,983	-24.1	Computer operators, except peripheral equipment
191,588	141,129	-26.3	Textile draw-out and winding machine operators and tenders
368,701	256,885	-30.3	Sewing machine operators, garment
23,413	16,136	-31.1	Directory assistance operators
9,248	6,347	-31.4	Camera operators
306,377	209,157	-31.7	Child care workers, private household
22,724	15,215	-33.0	Film strippers, printing
24,467	16,208	-33.8	Station installers and repairers, telephone
8,431	5,431	-35.6	Rail transportation workers nec
6,506	4,175	-35.8	Shoe sewing machine operators and tenders
27,209	16,965	-37.6	Peripheral equipment operators
17,160	9,883	-42.4	Housekeepers and butlers
14,164	7,391	-47.8	Railroad brake, signal, and switch operators
9,037	4,413	-51.2	Paste-up workers
4,511	2,196	-51.3	Cooks, private household
2,747	1,332	-51.5	Photoengravers
13,366	5,379	-59.8	Typesetting and composing machine operators and tenders